1/1/13

To Hannah + her wonderful little family:

May it grow and grow. - Just a little gift to you for having been as wonderful as you were during my trying days. I, personally, know Sam enjoyed your visits, which were many and had he known all others that you did silently, he would have been extremely happy with a friend like you. I, selfishly hope our friendship never ends -

Lovingly

Lee

THE EARTH AND MAN

A RAND McNALLY WORLD ATLAS

THE EARTH AND MAN

A RAND McNALLY WORLD ATLAS

With a foreword by
Sir Julian Huxley, FRS

RAND McNALLY AND COMPANY
New York Chicago San Francisco
In association with Mitchell Beazley Ltd. London

Mitchell Beazley Ltd.
Editor: Tony Loftas
Deputy Editor: Martyn Bramwell
Text Editor: Bill Gunston
Assistant Text Editor: Max Monsarrat
Art Editor: Michael Ricketts

Design Director: Peter Kindersley
Editorial Director: Christopher Dorling

Rand McNally & Company
Cartographic & Design Director: Chris Arvetis
Geographer: Bruce Ogilvie
Senior Editor: Paul T. Tiddens

Library of Congress number: **70-654432**
ISBN 528-83050-3
Printed in the United States of America

Chief Editorial Consultants and Advisers

B. W. Atkinson, Ph.D., B.Sc.,
Dept. of Geography, Queen Mary College, University of London
C. F. Barnaby, Ph.D., M.Sc.,
Director, Stockholm International Peace Research Institute
W. J. Beecher, Ph.D.,
Director, Chicago Academy of Sciences
Prof. K. F. Bowden, D.Sc., S.Inst.P.,
Professor of Oceanography, University of Liverpool
D. Brothwell, M.A., B.Sc.,
Head, Dept. of Anthropology, Natural History Museum, London
Prof. A. J. Cain, D.Phil., M.A.,
Professor of Zoology, University of Liverpool
Graham Chedd, B.A.,
Life Science Editor, *New Scientist*
Prof. R. B. Clarke, Ph.D., D.Sc.,
Professor of Zoology, University of Newcastle-upon-Tyne
Miss A. Coleman, M.A.,
Reader in Geography, King's College, University of London
Prof. H. C. Darby, O.B.E., Lit.D., F.B.A.,
Professor of Geography, University of Cambridge
R. Dearnley, Ph.D., B.Sc., F.G.S.,
Principal Geologist, Institute of Geological Sciences, London
Prof. A. N. Duckham, C.B.E., F.I.Biol.,
Professor Emeritus, Dept. of Agriculture, University of Reading
F. W. Dunning, B.Sc., F.G.S.,
Curator, Geological Museum, London
Peter Fenwick, M.B., D.P.M.,
Institute of Psychiatry, University of London
George Fenton, M.B., M.R.C.P., D.P.M.,
Senior Lecturer, Institute of Psychiatry, University of London
David Fishlock,
Science Editor, *Financial Times*
Ken Gatland, F.R.A.S., F.B.I.S.,
Aerospace Consultant, Vice President, British Interplanetary Society
Arch C. Gerlach, Ph.D.,
Chief Geographer, U.S. Geological Survey
Prof. G. Melvyn Howe, Ph.D., M.Sc., F.R.G.S., F.R.Met.Soc.
Professor of Geography, University of Strathclyde
Prof. Emrys Jones, Ph.D., M.Sc., F.R.G.S.,
Professor of Geography, London School of Economics
Joe Lucas, B.Sc., F.R.G.S., M.I.Biol.,
International Union for the Conservation of Nature and Natural Resources
Ian MacPhail,
Former Director-General, The World Wildlife Fund
Kenneth Mellanby, C.B.E., Sc.D., F.I.Biol.,
Monks Wood Experimental Station (NERC), Hertfordshire
Patrick Moore, O.B.E., F.R.A.S.
A. Mountjoy, M.C., M.A., F.R.G.S.,
Reader in Geography, Bedford College, University of London
National Aeronautics and Space Administration
Laurence Nobles, Ph.D.,
Dean, Northwestern University
Prof. Sir Alan S. Parkes, C.B.E., Ph.D., D.Sc., Sc.D., F.R.S.
Chairman, The Galton Foundation, London
Brian Stafford,
Industrial Consultant
Jon Tinker, B.A.,
Environmental Consultant
Russell L. Voisin, M.A.,
formerly Chief Cartographer, now Vice President, Rand McNally and Company
Margaret Walters, Ph.D., B.Sc.,
formerly of Chester Beatty Research Institute, London
James Wray, Ph.D.,
Professor, Northwestern University

A further list of advisers is given on page 358

Contents

THE GOOD EARTH

THE EARTH IN SPACE

The Sun in the Galaxy 10–11
The Life and Death of the Earth 12–13
The Solar System 14–15
The Sun's Influence on Earth 16–17
Earth's Companion: The Moon 18–19
Earth from Space 20–23

THE STRUCTURE OF THE EARTH

The Atmosphere 26–27
The Structure of Weather Systems 28–29
Extremes of Weather 30–31
The Active Oceans 32–33
The Earth under the Sea 34–35
The Evolution of Land and Sea 36–37
The Active Earth 38–39
Anatomy of the Earth 40–41
Forces that Shape the Land 42–43
The Record in the Rocks 44–45
The Treasures of the Earth 46–47

LIFE ON EARTH

Life Begins 50–51
The Ocean Cradle 52–53
Advance to the Land 54–55
The Age of Mammals 56–57
The Evolution of Man 58–59
Digging for Man's History 60–61
The Origin of Species 62–63
Species and Variety 64–65
Earth's Diverse Environments 66–67
The Polar Caps 68–69
The Cold Lands 70–71
The Temperate Forests 72–73
The Tropical Forests 74–75
The Grasslands 76–77
The Deserts 78–79
The Mountains 80–81
The Lakes and the Rivers 82–83
The Oceans 84–85
The Endangered Animals 86–87

THE RESOURCES OF THE EARTH

From Landscape to Townscape 90–91
Battles for the Land 92–93
Patterns of Land Use 94–95
Prospecting for Minerals 96–97
Minerals under the Land 98–99
Earth's Energy Resources 100–101
Earth's Water Resources 102–103
The Oceans' Mineral Resources 104–105
The Oceans' Living Resources 106–107
The Food Resource 108–111

MAN ON EARTH

The Body of Man 114–115
The Mind of Man 116–117
The Family of Man 118–121
The Settled World 122–123
Religion and Language 124–125
The Health of Man 126–127
Human Nutrition 128–129
Man's Food Supplies 130–131
The Population Problem 132–133
The Abuse of the Earth 134–135
Pathways of Pollution 136–137
Controlling Pollution 138–139
Man the Aggressor 140–141
Promises to Keep 142–143

MAPS

LOCATOR MAP AND LEGEND 146-147

THE PHYSICAL WORLD 148-149

THE OCEAN WORLD 150-157

EUROPE AND THE SOVIET UNION

Europe 158-159
Northern Europe 160-161
British Isles 162-163
Central Europe 164-165
France and the Alps 166-167
Spain and Portugal 168-169
Italy 170-171
Southeastern Europe 172-173
London–Birmingham–Cardiff 174-175
Paris–London–Bruxelles 176-177
Amsterdam–Düsseldorf–Hamburg 178-179
Zürich–Genève–Strasbourg 180-181
Lyon–Marseille–Milano 182-183
Roma–Firenze–Napoli (Rome–Florence–Naples) 184-185
Soviet Union 186-187-188

ASIA

China, Japan and Korea 190-191
Japan 192-193
Northeast China and Korea 194-195
East and Southeast China 196-197
Southeast Asia 198-199
Burma, Thailand and Indochina 200-201
Philippines 202-203
India, Pakistan and Southwest Asia 204-205
Northern India and Pakistan 206-207
The Middle East 208-209
Yerushalayim–Dimashq (Jerusalem–Damascus) 210-211
Turkey and Cyprus 212-213

AFRICA

Northern Africa 214-215-216
Southern Africa 218-219
Egypt and Sudan 220-221
West Africa 222-223
Southern Africa and Madagascar 224-225

AUSTRALIA and NEW ZEALAND

Australia 226-227
Eastern Australia 228-229
New Zealand 230-231

ANGLO AMERICA

Canada 232-233
United States 234-235
Alaska and Yukon 236-237
Southwestern Canada 238-239
Southeastern Canada 240-241
Northeastern United States 242-243
Great Lakes Region 244-245
Southeastern United States 246-247
Mississippi Valley 248-249
Southern Great Plains 250-251
Northern Great Plains 252-253
Southern Rocky Mountains 254-255
Northwestern United States 256-257
California and Nevada 258-259
Montréal–Québec 260
Boston–New York–Albany 261
New York–Philadelphia–Washington–Norfolk 262-263
Toronto–Ottawa 264-265
Pittsburgh–Cleveland–Detroit 266-267
Chicago–Detroit–Milwaukee 268-269
Vancouver–Seattle–Portland 270-271
San Francisco–Reno–Bakersfield 272-273
Los Angeles–San Diego 274
Hawaii 275

LATIN AMERICA

Middle America 276-277
Mexico 278-279
Central America 280-281
Caribbean Region 282-283
Islands of the West Indies 284-285
Northern South America 286-287
Southern South America 288-289
Columbia, Ecuador, Venezuela and Guyana 290-291
Peru, Bolivia and Western Brazil 292-293
Central Argentina and Chile 294-295
Southeastern Brazil 296

WORLD AND U.S. FACTS AND FIGURES

Introduction 297
World Political Information Table 298-302
Largest Metropolitan Areas and Cities of the World 303
Population of Foreign Cities and Towns, Countries and Important Political Divisions 304-320
Population of U.S. Cities and Towns, Counties and States 321-352
Largest Metro Areas of the U.S. 353

INDEXES

SUBJECT INDEX 354-357
ACKNOWLEDGMENTS 358
GEOGRAPHIC INDEX 359-440

Foreword by Sir Julian Huxley, FRS

The Earth and Man is not merely a collection of maps, but an Encyclopaedia, dealing with the formation of the Earth and its oceans, the environment they provide for the vast and varied assemblage of their animal and plant inhabitants; the origin of life, and its history during the huge span of evolutionary time.

Sir Julian Huxley, F.R.S.
One of this century's most distinguished zoologists, Sir Julian Huxley, grandson of T. H. Huxley, was born in 1887. In the course of an outstanding academic career he has received honors from universities throughout the world, and has also become famous as a scientific writer for popular audiences. Recently, he has dedicated himself in particular to wildlife conservation.

It also deals with the origin of our own species, with the history of its achievements and with some of the problems now besetting it—violence and pollution, disunity and over-population.

As a scientific naturalist interested in human affairs as well as biology and geology, I welcome this splendid work, for only by understanding and knowledge shall we be able to cope with our enormous responsibility—for avoiding disaster to this planet and its inhabitants and for guiding its future towards greater sanity and greater achievement.

The mass of facts and ideas assembled in this *Atlas* was not handed to us on a plate: it needed millennia of thought and experiment, of intellectual and moral striving.

Let me attempt a brief history of this great adventure. Although some Greek philosophers concluded that the Earth was spherical, almost everyone in early times thought it was flat, and it was not until the great voyagers of the 16th and 17th centuries proved the Earth's sphericity by sailing round it that the theory was accepted. These bold adventurers made possible accurate maps and also discovered new animals and plants, new tribes and new nations with their own customs and legends.

But this was just one part of the struggle for knowledge. Early in this century, the German geologist Wegener propounded the theory of continental drift—the idea that all the Earth's land was originally one single mass, and that about 180 million years ago it started to split up, forming the separate continents we know today. We have also now discovered that the Earth's axis has shifted, so that different parts of the world have been exposed to Arctic and Antarctic cold at different periods—a fact brought home to me personally by seeing coal-mines in Spitzbergen.

The drifting is made possible by huge cracks or rifts, some in the ocean bed, others on land, such as the Great Rift of Africa and Palestine, and all, especially those in the oceans, constantly enlarging their diameter. We now know that Europe and North America are drifting further apart by nearly an inch every year.

When large chunks of crust drift against each other, as happened when India moved against Central Asia, the belt of contact is squashed up into great mountains—here the Karakoram and Himalayas. There are also interesting consequences of drift—animal and plant forms originally inhabiting part of the mass are now found in its separated regions—thus the beautiful Protea plants grown in South Africa and Australia, and the southern beech in Australia and the northern part of South America.

In addition to rocks upwelling in molten form below the surface, others are sedimentary, deposited by fresh water, such as clays, or on the ocean bed, such as chalk, made of shells of microscopic floating organisms. The sedimentary rocks are laid down in bands or strata, and often contain fossilized organisms—for example, ammonites, mammoth skeletons or petrified wood.

It was soon found that fossils in later deposited strata were more like existing species than those of earlier date, and that fossil types change gradually during geological time. In other words, life evolves.
But what brings evolution about? There were many suggestions. At the beginning of the 19th century,

Jean Lamarck (1744-1829)

Georges Cuvier (1769-1832)

Charles Darwin (1808-1882)

Gregor Mendel (1822-1884)

Alfred Wallace (1823-1913)

T. H. Huxley (1825-1895)

Cuvier, the great French zoologist, believed that each major epoch was brought to a close by some world-wide catastrophe and then the Almighty created a set of new types. This was soon found to be impossible. Meanwhile Lamarck, his contemporary, thought that structure was changed by individual effort—for instance that, when the ancestral giraffe stretched its neck to reach higher foliage, some of the extra height was inherited by the next generation. This too wouldn't work—characteristics acquired by the individual are not, and cannot be, inherited by its descendants. Finally, in 1858, two Englishmen, Charles Darwin and Alfred Russel Wallace, provided the answer: 'Natural selection', operating through the slight advantage enjoyed by those individuals best able to survive and reproduce themselves in a given environment.

Darwin and his adherents, like my grandfather T. H. Huxley, soon converted the majority of scientists, and eventually laymen, to this new view, which dispensed with cataclysms and divine intervention and worked automatically, producing delicate adaptations to the conditions of life, and also the sexual adornments, such as the peacock's tail, which promote success in mating. Here clearly was the key to evolution. But it worked through inheritance, and the mechanism of inheritance was still a puzzle.

I am old enough to remember how the puzzle was solved—by the rediscovery of the Abbé Mendel's work, showing that inheritance of given characteristics was due to a particular unit or set of units in the hereditary mechanism; and the later proof by T. H. Morgan that these units were parts of the visible chromosomes in the body's organs and reproductive cells that we call genes. Then the discovery that mutation-changes in the properties and effects of genes were taking place all the time, and H. J. Muller's demonstration that external agencies, such as X-rays and certain chemicals, could cause new mutations to occur.

Darwin also studied the development of 'mind', including instinct. This led on to modern psychology with its various types—extraverts and introverts, gifted and less gifted; and also to social anthropology and sociology—the study of human societies, their variety, their central systems of ideas, their change or evolution during historic times.

This *Atlas* also deals with the most important factors in man's present existence—his religion, his technology, the spread of pollution and its counter-measure, conservation. It also discusses population-increase, that most urgent of human problems.
I commend it to every intelligent human being—especially to the younger generation, for it is they who will have to continue man's efforts to cope with the ever-increasing challenge of the future—to keep our world fit to live in.

There are people who maintain that the evolution of man and his societies has reached an impasse. I do not believe this. Faith, goodwill and purposeful intelligence can overcome our problems, and knowledge helps us to understand them. This *Atlas* contributes both to our knowledge and understanding, and spurs us to action.

Julian Huxley

The Earth in Space

Our home the Earth is a small planet revolving round the Sun. The Sun is a star, but only one of the hundred thousand million which exist in the local system of stars, or galaxy, of which we are a part. Our own galaxy, we now know, is just one of millions of other galaxies in the universe, all almost unbelievably remote. The light now reaching us from the most distant observable star-systems began its journey towards us even before the Earth came into existence more than 4500 million years ago.

It is inconceivable that other stars in the universe do not have planetary systems like our own Sun. Although our neighbors in the Sun's family seem barren of life, some of those planets in other systems must support life in some form. Yet, barring some revolutionary new insight into the problems of time and space travel, it is difficult to realize that man will some day be able to explore the depths of the universe to find such life. For the present we on this Earth are alone.

Nebula in Sagittarius
The Trifid nebula in the constellation Sagittarius is so called because dark dust clouds appear to divide the glowing gas into three segments. The Trifid, which forms a typical emission nebula, contains hot early-type stars. Its distance from us is 2300 light-years.

The Sun in the Galaxy

Less than 2500 years ago the Greeks thought of the Earth as the center of all creation, and of the Sun as a bright body not more than 2 ft (0.6 m) across. Today we know that the Sun, although it is 864,950 mi (1,392,000 km) across, is merely one star among 100,000 million in a spiral organization of stars known as the Milky Way Galaxy; and this in turn is merely one among thousands of millions of other galaxies which make up the entire visible universe. The diagrams on these pages afford at least an indication of the relative sizes of stars, galaxies and the known universe. What nobody can yet answer is just how big the universe is, or what lies beyond it. The search for solutions to such problems is increasingly extending the mind of man. Complete answers will probably never be known. At present the universe is regarded as a three-dimensional space which seems to be swiftly expanding.

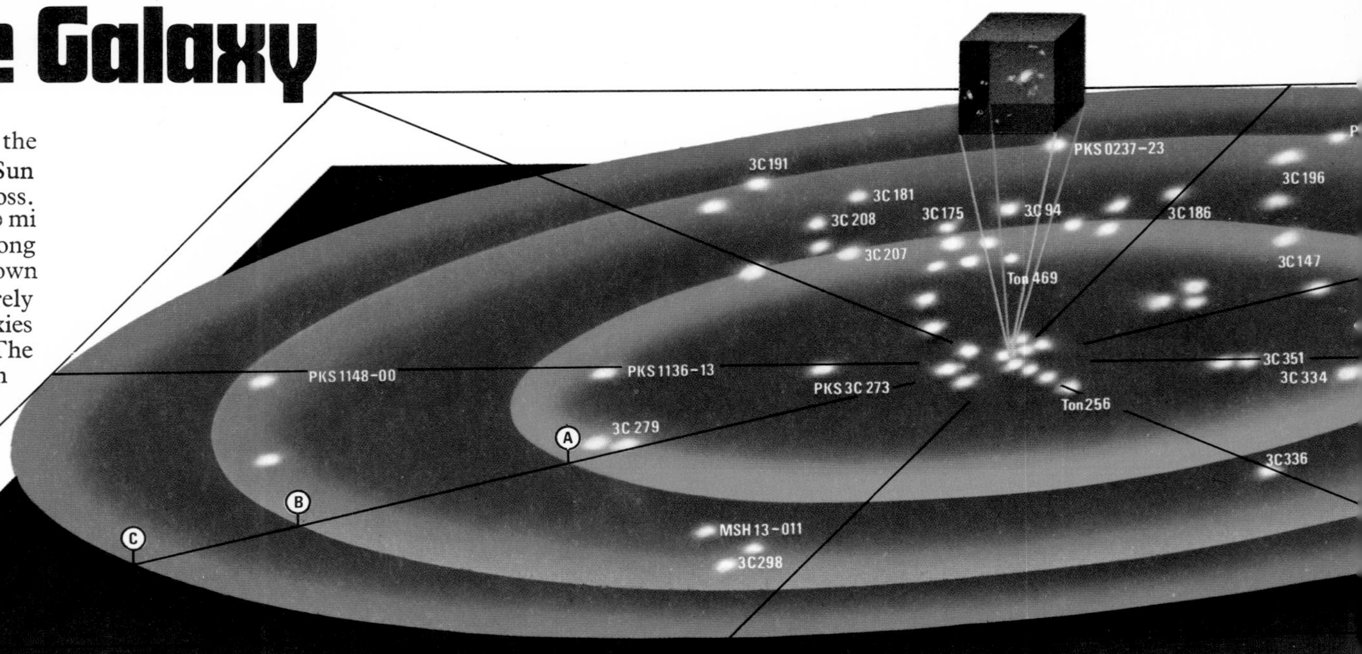

3C 191
PKS 0237-23
3C 196
3C 181
3C 208
3C 175
3C 94
3C 186
3C 207
3C 147
Ton 469
PKS 1148-00
PKS 1136-13
3C 351
3C 334
PKS 3C 273
Ton256
A
3C 279
3C 336
B
C
MSH 13-011
3C298

Leo II
Leo I
NGC 6822
SMC
LMC
NGC 147
NGC 185
Sculptor
Fornax
M31
NGC 205
M32
M33
Wolf-Lundmark
IC 1613

Scale of the universe *right*
On a cosmological scale, man's knowledge is extremely limited and fragmentary. So large is the observable universe that it is geometrically impossible to link it by diagrams with a familiar object except by introducing separate and increasing exaggerations of scale. The large box depicts symbolically our local group of galaxies, with our own Milky Way Galaxy at the center. Each galaxy, whether a spiral, a barred spiral or irregular in form, contains thousands of millions of stars. Some idea of the scale of this box is given by the fact that even with the fastest Moon rocket it would take more than 60000 million years to cross from our own galaxy to a similar one, M31 in the constellation of Andromeda, seen in the left of the box. Even the nearest objects known to lie outside our galaxy, the small and large Magellanic Clouds (SMC and LMC), which are really small galaxies of irregular shape, are so far away that no man is ever likely to visit them. But our local group is only one amongst millions that go to make up the universe that has been observed by successive generations of increasingly powerful telescopes and other analytical instruments. We now know that even what can be seen is far from being a static situation: the most distant objects that we can see appear to be receding from us; and, the farther away they are, the faster this 'speed of recession' becomes. In fact, the universe appears to be an expanding sphere, as if the whole of creation had once exploded from a central point. Nevertheless we can, by taking a tremendous leap in scale, portray our visible universe, as shown in the chart above the large box, although at this point our local galaxies (see small box projected into the center)have become no more than a pin-prick. On the chart, the innermost colored ring, A, marks the limit of objects that astronomers can see with optical telescopes; ring B contains the furthest objects detected by radio telescopes; and, finally, ring C is the radius at which objects appear to be moving from the Earth at a speed equal to that of light. This represents the limit to our observations; nothing can ever be seen from the Earth beyond C. The distance to this point, is 10000 million light years, or 120,000,000,000,000,000,000,000 mi (193 x 10^{21} km).

The Sun in the galaxy *below*
The Sun, though it dominates life here on the Earth, fades into total obscurity in the scale of the universe (top left) and even in the local group of galaxies (box, left). Just to locate our star a small segment has to be taken from one of the arms which curve out from the center of our spiral galaxy and be enlarged almost 40 times (chart below). Even then the Sun and the solar system is no more than a microscopic speck lost among great clusters of stars, vast dark clouds of an obscuring matter known as 'interstellar dust' and two forms of hydrogen, known as 'bright' and 'neutral', distinguished by their energy levels. These gas clouds can be mapped by plotting the distribution of their radiation. This section is 20000 light-years across (the scale is given in the prominent concentric rings) and its focal point, the Sun, is approximately 30000 light-years from the center of the galaxy. Still the Sun is invisible. To see it, much greater magnification of the surrounding areas is needed. With a further enlargement of 625 times the Sun at last becomes visible along with other stars in its neighborhood (lower chart). The radius chosen for this chart is 16 light-years, or some 10^{13}mi (1.6×10^{13}km). The most remarkable fact is that this distance is not sufficient to capture a single giant star. Indeed, of all the stars included, only three—Sirius, Procyon and the brighter member of the double star Proxima Centauri—are more luminous than the Sun; and even Sirius, with 26 times the luminosity of the Sun, is classified by astronomers as a dwarf star. Most of the other near neighbors are faint red dwarfs much less powerful than the Sun. One, Munich 15040, more commonly known as Barnard's star, is thought to be accompanied by two planets each about the size of Jupiter, which cause disturbances in its motion sufficiently large to be measured by astronomers. Even where such changes in motion have not been observed this does not necessarily mean that other neighboring stars do not also have planetary systems similar to our own. At present, no way exists of finding out. It would take the fastest present day Moon rocket about 120,000 years to reach the nearest star, Proxima Centauri. If we return now to the large box, itself a minute part of the entire observable universe, we can realize something of the vastness of space and the place of the Sun and therefore the planet Earth within it.

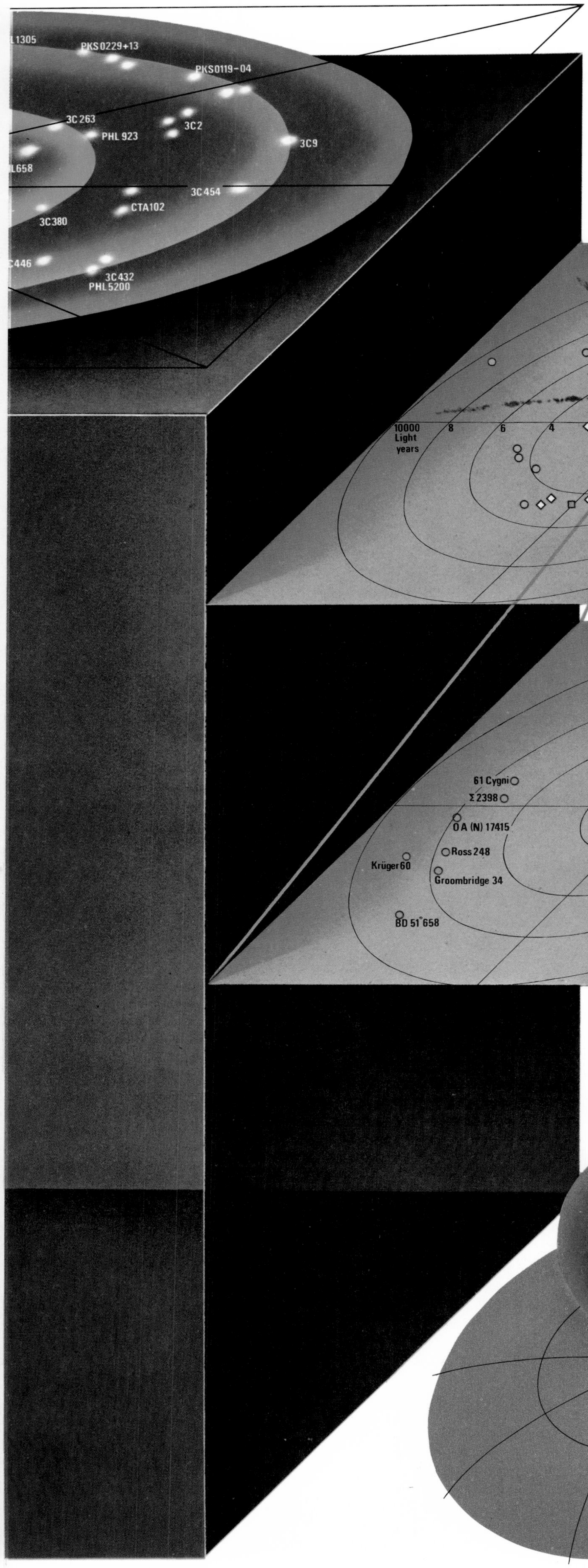

1305
PKS0229+13
PKS0119-04
3C263
3C2
PHL923
3C9
658
3C454
CTA102
3C380
446
3C432
PHL5200

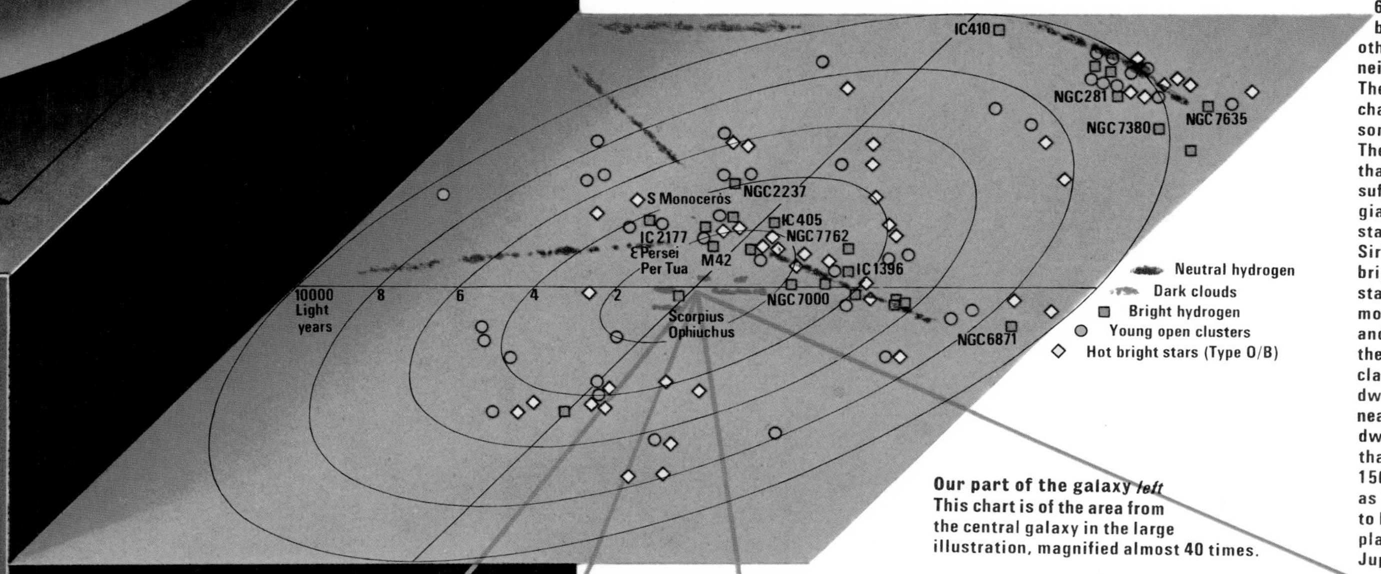

IC410
NGC281
NGC7380
NGC7635
S Monoceros
NGC2237
IC405
IC2177
NGC7762
ε Persei
Per Tua
M42
IC1396
10000 Light years
8
6
4
2
NGC7000
Scorpius Ophiuchus
NGC6871
Neutral hydrogen
Dark clouds
Bright hydrogen
Young open clusters
Hot bright stars (Type O/B)

Our part of the galaxy *left*
This chart is of the area from the central galaxy in the large illustration, magnified almost 40 times.

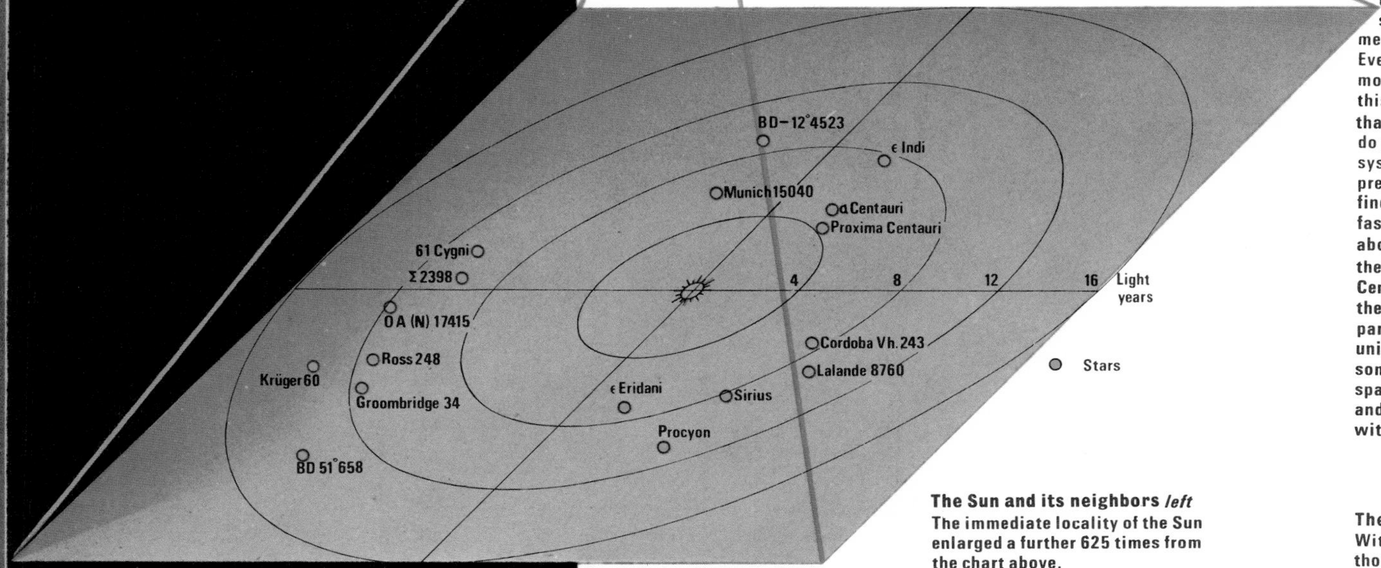

BD-12°4523
ε Indi
Munich15040
α Centauri
Proxima Centauri
61 Cygni
Σ2398
4
8
12
16
Light years
OA (N) 17415
Cordoba Vh.243
Ross248
Lalande 8760
Stars
Krüger60
Groombridge 34
ε Eridani
Sirius
Procyon
BD 51°658

The Sun and its neighbors *left*
The immediate locality of the Sun enlarged a further 625 times from the chart above.

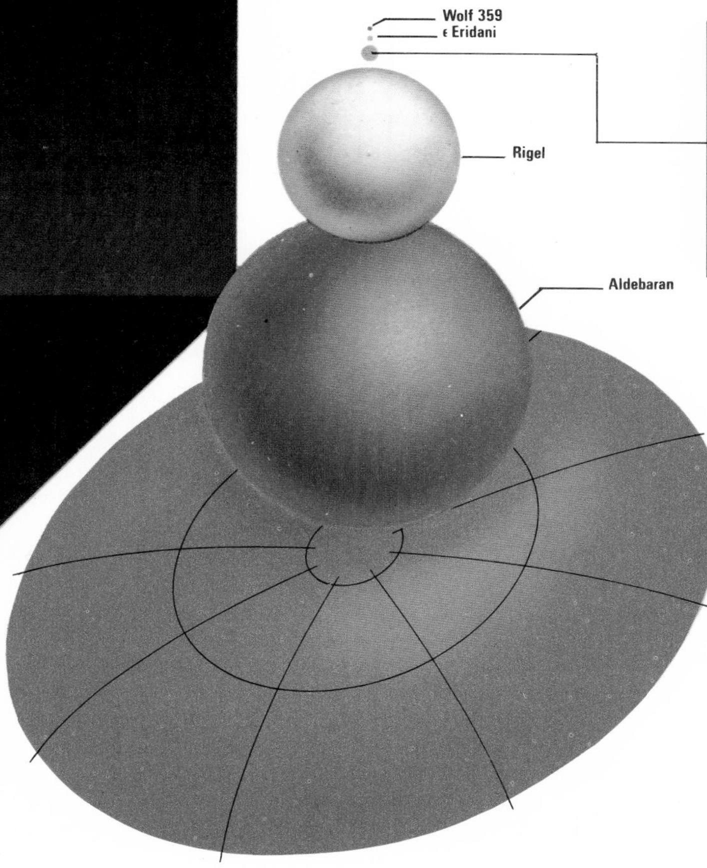

Wolf 359
ε Eridani
Rigel
Aldebaran
Antares
(small section shown)

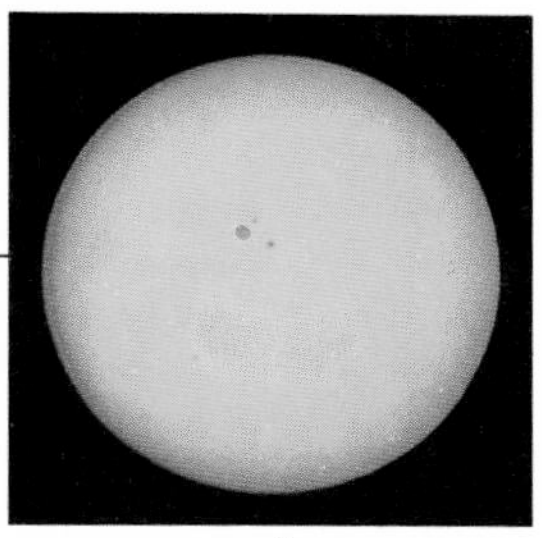

The size of our Sun *left*
With distances as immense as those in the universe, it seems natural that the sizes of its stars should also be immense. The diameter of our Sun, for example, is equal to 109 Earths placed side by side. However, we know from observations of other stars that its size is not fixed and will change with time. A star follows an evolutionary sequence, in the course of which it changes dramatically in size, surface temperature and luminosity. The star is probably formed in a nebula as a result of coalescing interstellar material. After about 100,000 years the young star joins the 'main sequence' as a very bright body with a surface temperature of some 40000°C. It grows in size and luminosity, sending out energy at a very high rate from its internal conversion of hydrogen to helium. Gradually it swells to a size 100 or more times larger than the Sun, cooling and becoming dulled. It finishes as a reddish dwarf and ultimately probably loses all luminosity. Wolf 359 is a faint red dwarf. Epsilon (ε) Eridani, a near neighbor of the Sun, is smaller and cooler than the Sun and may have a planetary system. Rigel is at the peak of its career. Aldebaran is a moderate example of a red giant. Antares, the largest red giant known, is so vast (250 million miles across) that only a very small segment of it can be shown at this scale.

The Life and Death of the Earth

1

1 According to the most widely accepted theory, (the 'accretion' theory) the solar system originally consisted only of a mass of tenuous gas, and dust. There was no true Sun, and there was no production of nuclear energy. The gas was made up chiefly of hydrogen, with occasional random condensations.

2 Gravitational forces now cause the cloud to shrink and assume a more regular shape. Its density and mass near the center increase, but there are still no nuclear processes.

3 The gas cloud begins to assume the form of a regular disk. The infant Sun begins to shine - by the energy from gravitational shrinkage.

4 Material is thrown off from the Sun to join that already in the solar cloud, whose condensations have become more noticeable.

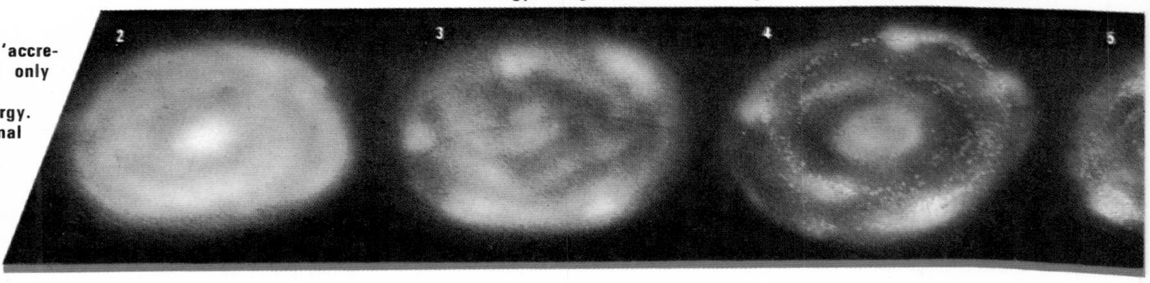

2
3
4
5

How did the Earth come into existence? This question has intrigued mankind for centuries but it was not until the start of true science that plausible theories were advanced. Although some theories held sway for many years, they were eventually deposed by the discovery of some fatal flaw. Even today, it is impossible to be sure that the main problem has been solved, but at least some concrete facts exist as a guide. It is now reasonably certain that the age of the Earth is of the order of 4550-4700 million years. The other planets are presumably about the same age, since they were probably formed by the same process in the same epoch.

Several centuries ago Archbishop Ussher of Armagh maintained that the world had come into being at a definite moment in the year 4004 BC. This estimate was made on purely religious grounds, and it soon became clear that the Earth is much older. In 1796 the French astronomer Laplace put forward the famous Nebular Hypothesis, according to which the Sun and the planets were formed from a rotating cloud of gas which shrank under the influence of gravitation. As it shrank, the cloud shed gaseous rings, each of which condensed into a planet. This would mean that the outer planets were older than those closer to the Sun which itself would represent the remaining part of the gas cloud.

The Nebular Hypothesis was accepted for many years, but eventually serious mathematical weaknesses were found in it. Next came a number of tidal theories according to which the Earth and other planets were formed from a cigar-shaped tongue of matter torn from the Sun by the gravitational pull of a passing star. The first plausible theory of this kind came from the English astronomer Sir James Jeans, but this too was found to be mathematically untenable and the idea had to be given up.

Most modern theories assume that the planets were formed by accretion from a rotating solar cloud of gas and finely-dispersed dust. If the Sun were originally attended by such a cloud, this cloud would, over a sufficiently long period of time, become a flat disk. If random concentration had become sufficiently massive, it would draw in extra material by virtue of its gravitational attraction, forming 'proto-planets'. When the Sun began to radiate strongly, part of the mass of each proto-planet would be driven off due to the high temperatures, leaving a solar system of the kind that exists today.

The fact that such an evolutionary sequence can be traced emphasizes that in talking about the origin of the Earth we are considering only a small part of a continuous story. What will become of the Earth in the far future? The Sun is radiating energy because of the nuclear process within it: hydrogen is being converted into helium causing mass to be lost with a resulting release of energy. However, when the supply of hydrogen begins to run low, the Sun must change radically. It will move towards a red giant stage swelling and engulfing the Earth. Fortunately, this will not happen for at least another 6000 million years, but eventually the Sun which sustains our planet will finally destroy it.

Alternative theories

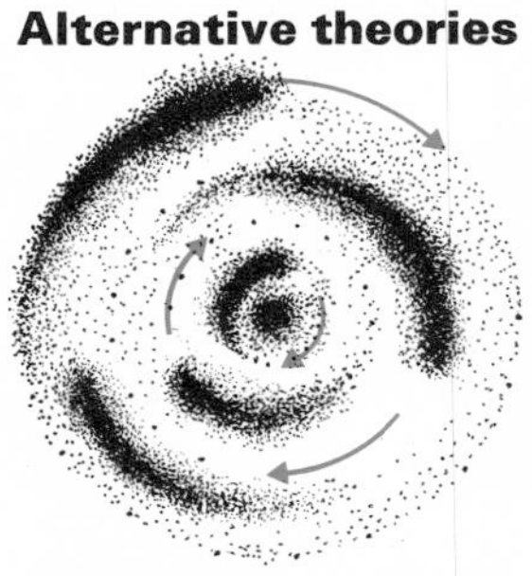

Contracting nebula *above* Laplace suggested that a contracting nebula might shed gas which then condensed.

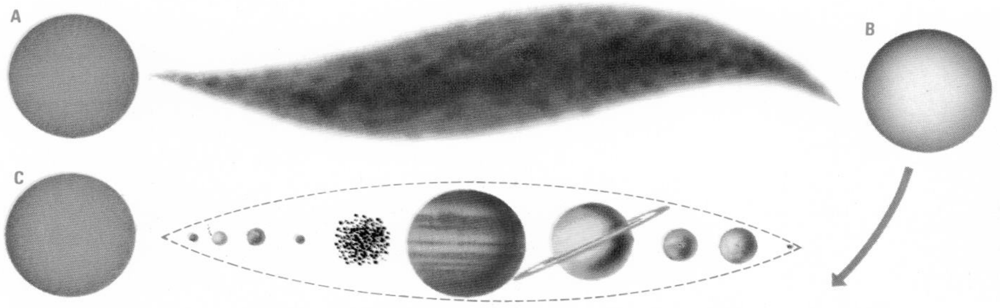

A
B
C

Tidal theories *above* In 1901 Sir James Jeans postulated that Sun A was attracted to another star B which passed at close range. A cloud of matter was drawn off by their gravitational attraction. Star B moved on while the cloud condensed to form planets circling our Sun at C.

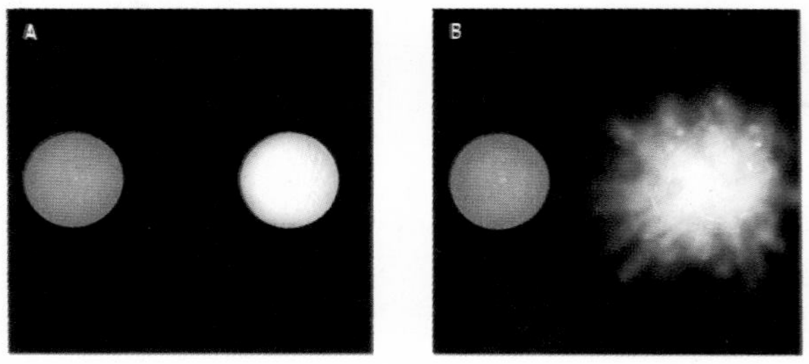

A
B

A violent beginning *above* One of the theories of how the solar system came to be formed assumes that the Sun once had a binary companion star. This exploded as a supernova (above) and was blown off as a white dwarf

16 As the 'fuel' runs out, the radiation pressure falls, and under internal gravity the Sun will collapse inwards changing in only 50000 years from a red giant into a super-dense white dwarf.

15 By now all the inner planets will have long since been destroyed. The Sun will become unstable, reaching the most violent stage of its career as a red giant, with a vast, relatively cool surface and an intensely hot, dense core.

14 When the center of the Sun has reached another critical temperature, the helium will begin to 'burn' giving the so-called 'helium flash'. After a temporary contraction the Sun will then swell out to a diameter 400 times that at present.

17 As a white dwarf, the Sun will continue to radiate feebly for an immense period. At last all radiation must cease, and the Sun will remain as a dead, dark globe - a black dwarf.

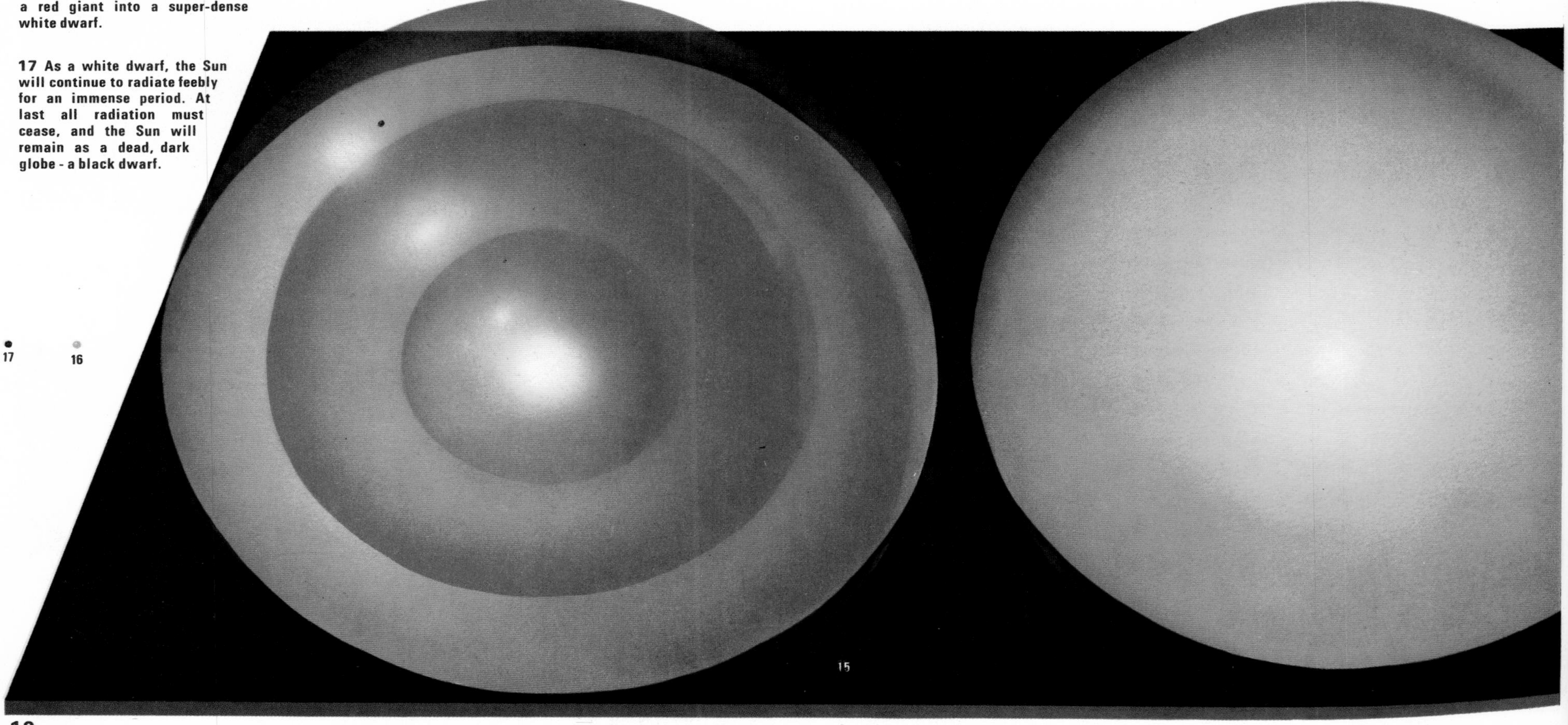

17
16
15

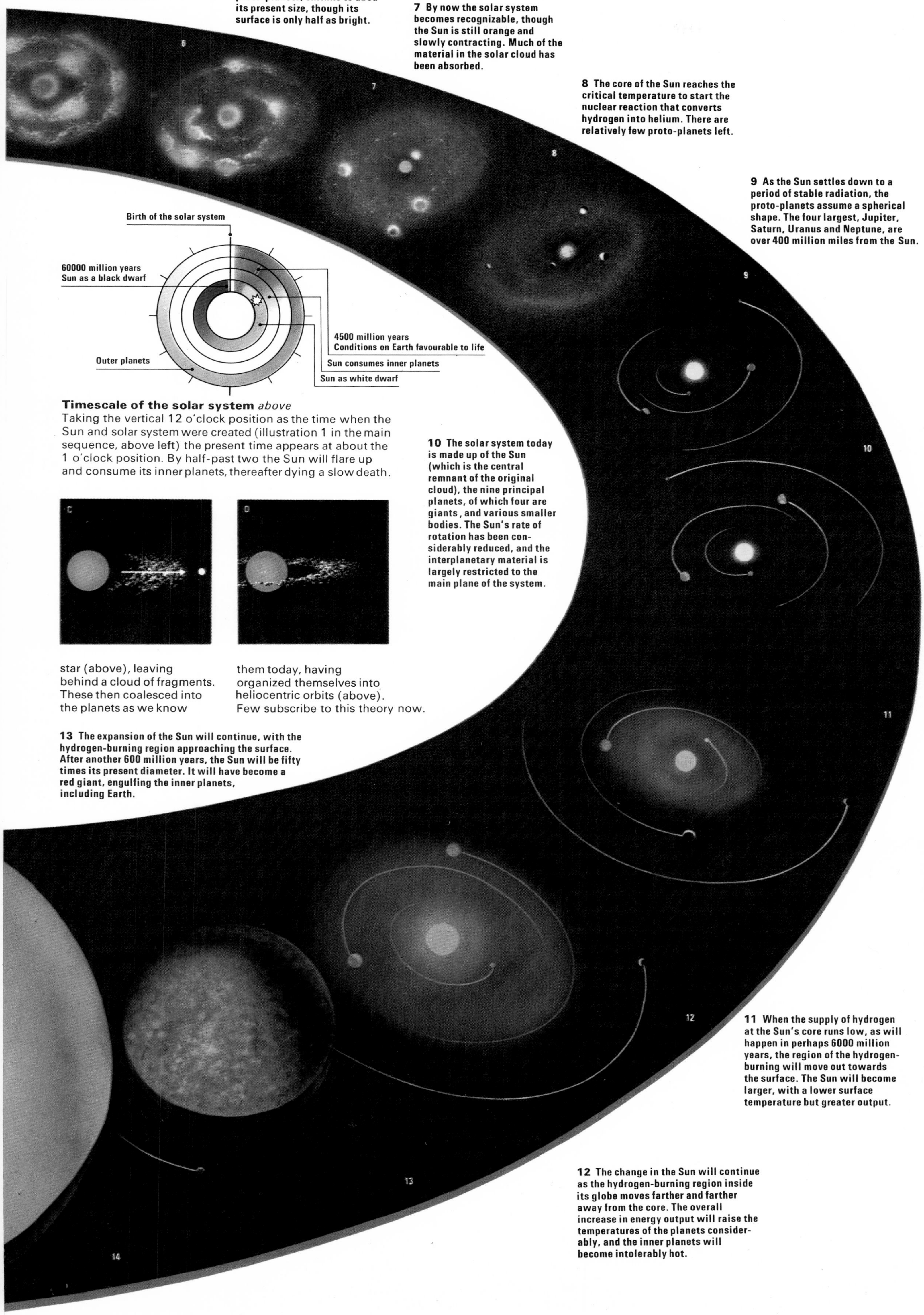
6
7
8
9
10
11
12
13
14
Birth of the solar system
60000 million years
Sun as a black dwarf
4500 million years
Conditions on Earth favourable to life
Sun consumes inner planets
Sun as white dwarf
Outer planets
C
D

5 The Sun, still contracting, continues to radiate because of gravitational effects. More and more of the solar cloud collects into the condensations.

6 The Sun, surrounded by a system of regularly-shaped proto-planets, shrinks to abou its present size, though its surface is only half as bright.

7 By now the solar system becomes recognizable, though the Sun is still orange and slowly contracting. Much of the material in the solar cloud has been absorbed.

8 The core of the Sun reaches the critical temperature to start the nuclear reaction that converts hydrogen into helium. There are relatively few proto-planets left.

9 As the Sun settles down to a period of stable radiation, the proto-planets assume a spherical shape. The four largest, Jupiter, Saturn, Uranus and Neptune, are over 400 million miles from the Sun.

Timescale of the solar system *above*
Taking the vertical 12 o'clock position as the time when the Sun and solar system were created (illustration 1 in the main sequence, above left) the present time appears at about the 1 o'clock position. By half-past two the Sun will flare up and consume its inner planets, thereafter dying a slow death.

star (above), leaving behind a cloud of fragments. These then coalesced into the planets as we know them today, having organized themselves into heliocentric orbits (above). Few subscribe to this theory now.

13 The expansion of the Sun will continue, with the hydrogen-burning region approaching the surface. After another 600 million years, the Sun will be fifty times its present diameter. It will have become a red giant, engulfing the inner planets, including Earth.

10 The solar system today is made up of the Sun (which is the central remnant of the original cloud), the nine principal planets, of which four are giants, and various smaller bodies. The Sun's rate of rotation has been considerably reduced, and the interplanetary material is largely restricted to the main plane of the system.

11 When the supply of hydrogen at the Sun's core runs low, as will happen in perhaps 6000 million years, the region of the hydrogen-burning will move out towards the surface. The Sun will become larger, with a lower surface temperature but greater output.

12 The change in the Sun will continue as the hydrogen-burning region inside its globe moves farther and farther away from the core. The overall increase in energy output will raise the temperatures of the planets considerably, and the inner planets will become intolerably hot.

The lifespan of the Earth

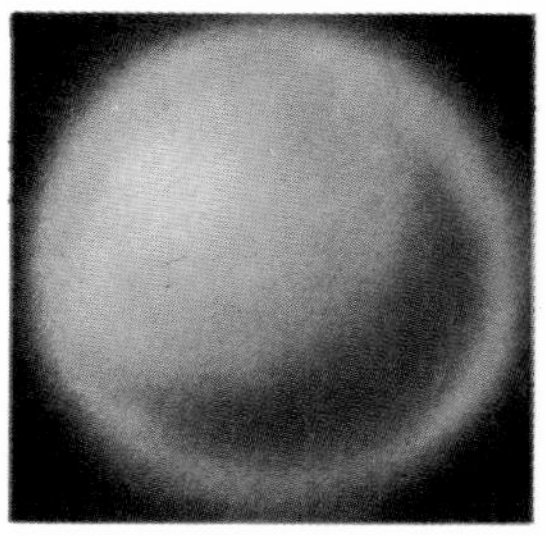

The Earth was produced from the solar cloud (1-6 on main diagram). It had no regular form, but, as more and more material was drawn in, it began to assume a spherical shape (7-8).

When it had reached its present size (9), the Earth had a dense atmosphere; not the original hydrogen atmosphere but one produced by gas from the interior. Life had not started.

The Earth today (10), moving in a stable orbit, has an equable temperature and oxygen-rich atmosphere, so that it alone of all the planets in the solar system is suitable for life.

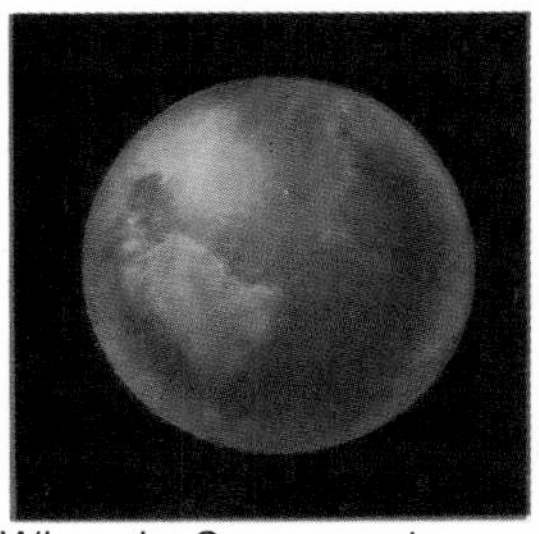

When the Sun nears the red giant stage (11-13), the Earth will be heated to an intolerable degree. The atmosphere will be driven off, the oceans will boil and life must come to an end.

As the Sun reaches the peak of its violence (14-15), it will swell out until the Earth is engulfed. Its natural life is probably no more than 8000 million years: its end is certain

The Solar System

The Sun is the controlling body of the solar system and is far more massive than all its planets combined. Even Jupiter, much the largest of the planets, has a diameter only about one-tenth that of the Sun. The solar system is divided into two main parts. The inner region includes four relatively small, solid planets: Mercury, Venus, the Earth and Mars. Beyond the orbit of Mars comes a wide gap in which move many thousands of small minor planets or asteroids, some of which are little more than rocks. Further out come the four giants: Jupiter, Saturn, Uranus and Neptune. Pluto, on the fringe of the system, is a curious little planet; it appears to be in a class of its own, but at present very little is known about it and even its size is a matter for conjecture. Maps of the solar system can be misleading in that they tend to give a false idea about distance. The outer planets are very widely separated. For example, Saturn is further away from Uranus than it is from the Earth.

The contrasting planets

The inner, or terrestrial, planets have some points in common, but a greater number of differences. Mercury, the planet closest to the Sun, has no atmosphere and that of Mars is very thin; but Venus, strikingly similar to the Earth in size and mass, has a dense atmosphere made up chiefly of carbon dioxide, and a surface temperature of over 400°C. The giant planets are entirely different. At least in their outer layers they are made up of gas, like a star; but, unlike a star, they have no light of their own and shine only by reflecting the light of their star, the Sun. Several of the planets have moons. The Earth has one (or it may be our partner in a binary system), Jupiter has 12, Saturn 10 (discounting its rings), Uranus five and Neptune two. Mars also has two satellites but these are less than 15 mi (24 km) in diameter and of a different type from the Earth's Moon. The Earth is unique in the solar system in having oceans on its surface and an atmosphere made up chiefly of nitrogen and oxygen. It is the only planet suited to life of terrestrial type. It is not now believed that highly evolved life can exist on any other planet in the Sun's family, though it it still possible that some primitive life forms may exist on Mars.

Observing the planets

Five of the planets, Mercury, Venus, Mars, Jupiter and Saturn, were known to the inhabitants of the Earth in very ancient times. They are starlike in aspect but easy to distinguish because, unlike the stars, they seem to wander slowly about the sky whereas the true stars appear to hold their position for century after century. The so-called proper motions of the stars are too slight to be noticed by the naked eye, but they can be measured by modern techniques. Mercury and Venus always appear to be in the same part of the sky as the Sun. Mercury is never prominent but Venus is dazzlingly bright, partly because its upper clouds are highly reflective and partly because it is close; it can come within 25,000,000 mi (40,000,000 km), only about 100 times as far as the Moon. Jupiter is generally very bright, as is Mars when it is well placed. Saturn is also conspicuous to the naked eye, but Uranus is only just visible and Neptune and Pluto are much fainter.

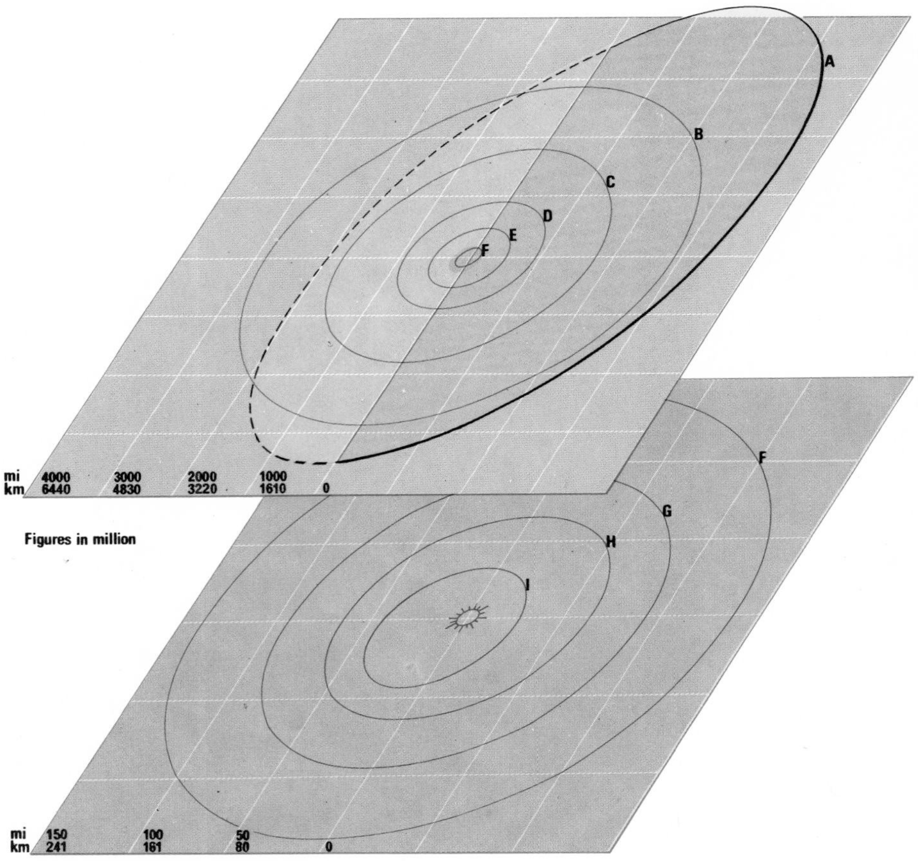

A
B
C
D
E
F
mi 4000 3000 2000 1000 0
km 6440 4830 3220 1610
Figures in million
F
G
H
I
mi 150 100 50 0
km 241 161 80

Orbits around the Sun *above*
The Sun's nine known planets, and the asteroids, describe heliocentric orbits in the same direction. But some planetary orbits are highly eccentric, while some asteroids are both eccentric and steeply inclined. The outermost planet, Pluto, passes within the orbit of Neptune, while one asteroid reaches almost to the radius of Saturn. Over 350 years ago Johannes Kepler showed that the planets do not move in perfect circles, and found that the line joining each planet to the Sun sweeps out a constant area in a given time, so that speed is greatest close to the Sun.

A Pluto
B Neptune
C Uranus
D Saturn
E Jupiter
F Mars
G Earth
H Venus
I Mercury

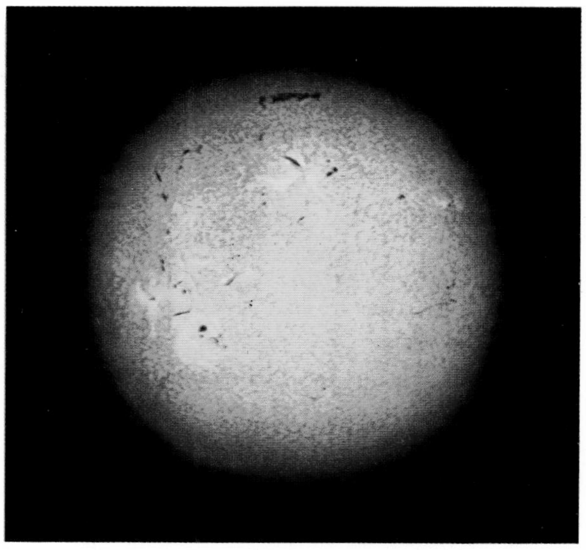

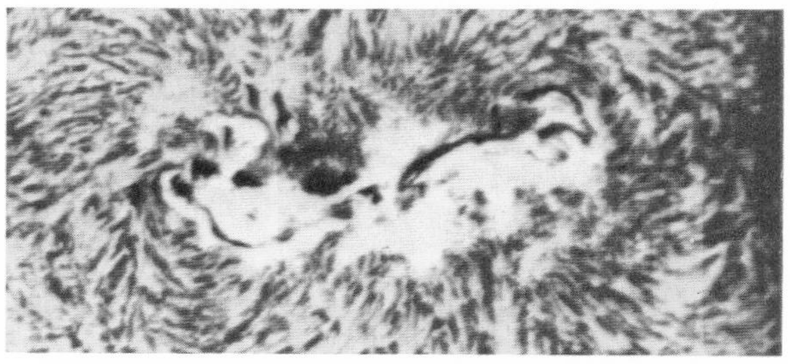

The Sun's active surface *right*
The structure of a star, such as the Sun, is immensely complex. The very concept of its surface is hard to define, and the size of the Sun depends on the wavelength of the light with which it is viewed. Using the 'hydrogen alpha' wavelength the bright surface of the Sun, known as the photosphere, appears as shown right, above. The surface, at about 6000 °C, is dotted with light and dark patches as a result of the violent upcurrents of hotter gas and cooler areas between them. Larger, darker regions are sunspots (right), temporary but very large disturbances.

1,250,000
2,000,000
A
B
432,475
695,800
400,000
640,000
C
350,000
560,000
300,000
480,000
250,000
400,000
D
200,000
320,000
150,000
240,000
E
100,000
160,000
mi 50 000
km 80 000

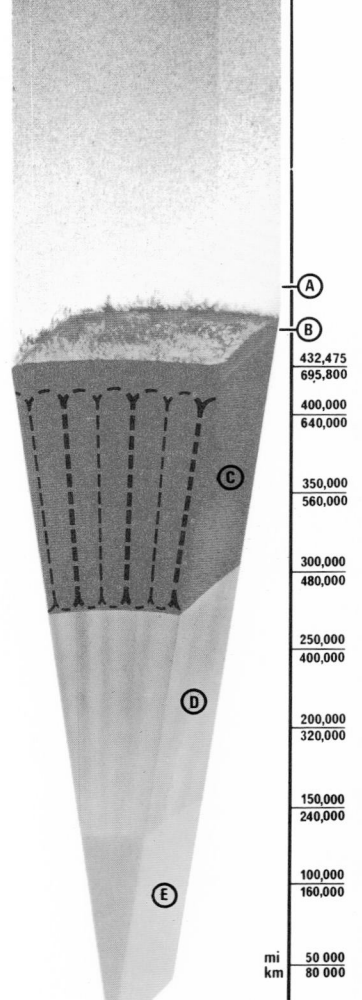

The Sun's structure *right*
The Sun is made up of highly dissimilar regions. This narrow sector includes the inner part of the corona (A) which, though very diffuse, has a temperature of some 1,000,000 °C. Into it leap solar prominences, 'flames' thousands of miles long which arch along the local magnetic field from the chromosphere (B), the outer layer of the Sun proper, which covers the visible photosphere with a layer of variable, highly mobile and rarefied gas about 6000 mi (10000 km) thick. Inside the Sun the outer layer (C) of gas is in constant movement and transfers heat from the interior. Inner region D is thought to transfer energy mainly by radiation. The innermost zone of all (E), the conditions of which can only be surmised but are thought to include a temperature of some 14,000,000 °C, sustains the energy of the Sun (and its planets) by continuous fusion of hydrogen into helium.

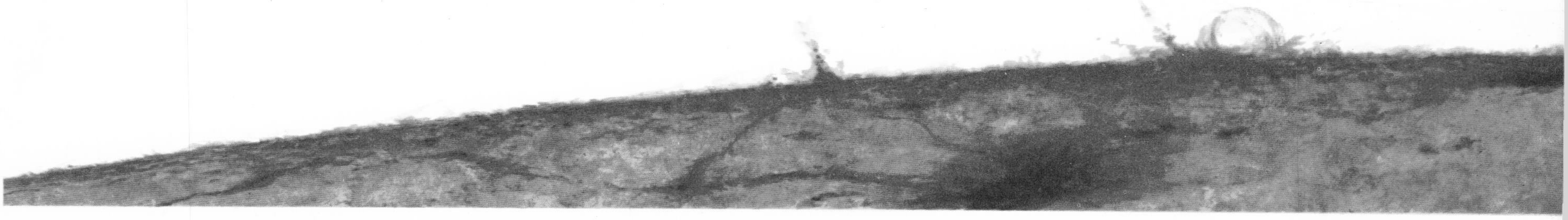

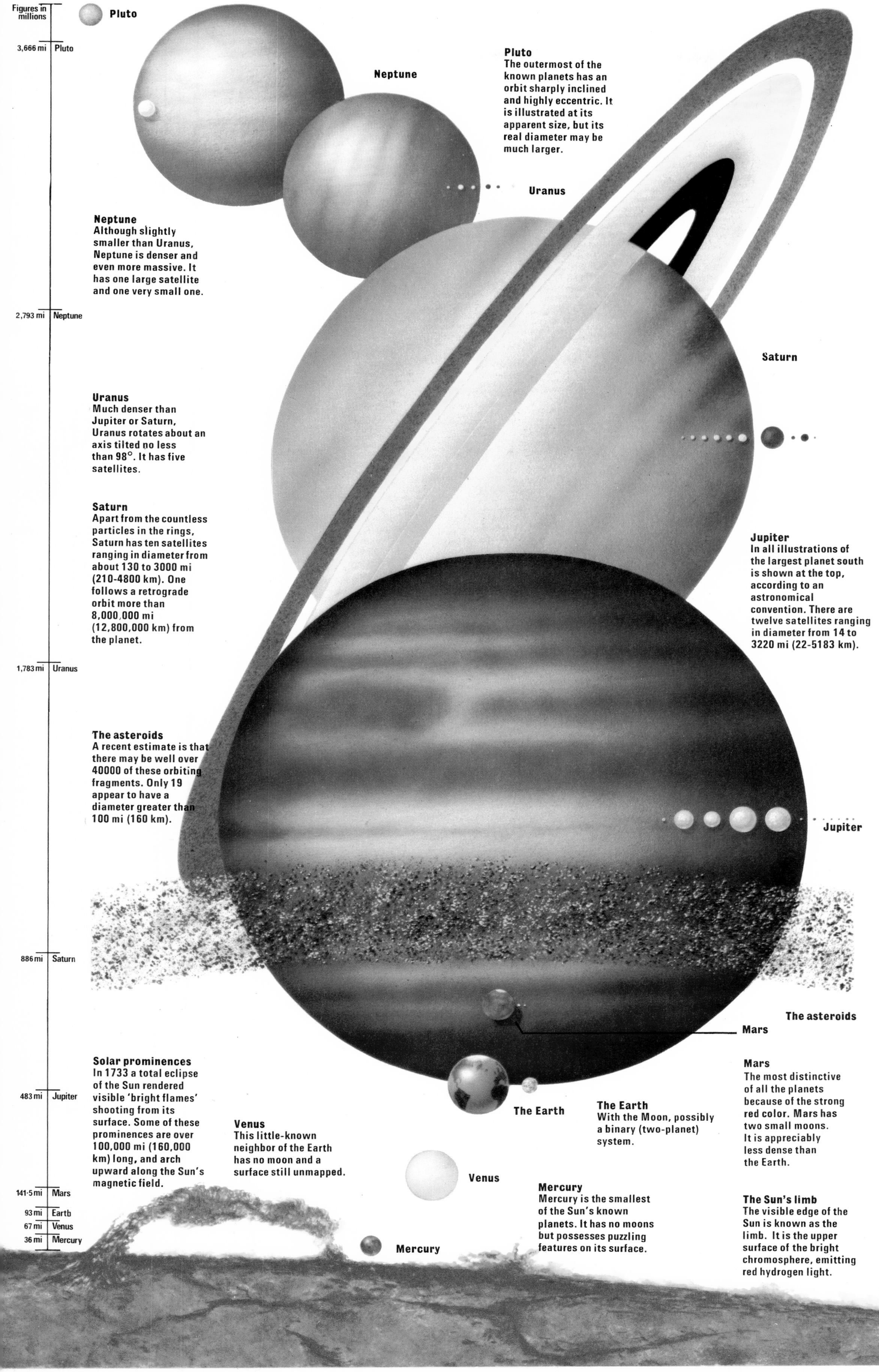
Figures in millions
3,666 mi Pluto
2,793 mi Neptune
1,783 mi Uranus
886 mi Saturn
483 mi Jupiter
141·5 mi Mars
93 mi Earth
67 mi Venus
36 mi Mercury
Pluto
Neptune
Uranus
Saturn
Jupiter
The asteroids
Mars
The Earth
Venus
Mercury

Pluto
The outermost of the known planets has an orbit sharply inclined and highly eccentric. It is illustrated at its apparent size, but its real diameter may be much larger.

Neptune
Although slightly smaller than Uranus, Neptune is denser and even more massive. It has one large satellite and one very small one.

Uranus
Much denser than Jupiter or Saturn, Uranus rotates about an axis tilted no less than 98°. It has five satellites.

Saturn
Apart from the countless particles in the rings, Saturn has ten satellites ranging in diameter from about 130 to 3000 mi (210-4800 km). One follows a retrograde orbit more than 8,000,000 mi (12,800,000 km) from the planet.

Jupiter
In all illustrations of the largest planet south is shown at the top, according to an astronomical convention. There are twelve satellites ranging in diameter from 14 to 3220 mi (22-5183 km).

The asteroids
A recent estimate is that there may be well over 40000 of these orbiting fragments. Only 19 appear to have a diameter greater than 100 mi (160 km).

Solar prominences
In 1733 a total eclipse of the Sun rendered visible 'bright flames' shooting from its surface. Some of these prominences are over 100,000 mi (160,000 km) long, and arch upward along the Sun's magnetic field.

Venus
This little-known neighbor of the Earth has no moon and a surface still unmapped.

The Earth
With the Moon, possibly a binary (two-planet) system.

Mars
The most distinctive of all the planets because of the strong red color. Mars has two small moons. It is appreciably less dense than the Earth.

Mercury
Mercury is the smallest of the Sun's known planets. It has no moons but possesses puzzling features on its surface.

The Sun's limb
The visible edge of the Sun is known as the limb. It is the upper surface of the bright chromosphere, emitting red hydrogen light.

The solar system *left*
The Sun is the major body in the solar system. It lies 30000 light-years from the center of our galaxy and takes 225 million years to complete one journey around it. There are nine planets and their satellites in the system, as well as comets and various minor bodies such as meteoroids. The diagram on the left shows the upper limb of the Sun (bottom) and the main constituent members of the solar system very greatly condensed into a smaller space. To indicate the amount of the radial compression, the limb of the Sun is drawn for a near-sphere of 5 ft (1.52 m) diameter. On this scale the Earth would be about 420 ft (127 m) away and the outermost planet Pluto, no less than 3 mi (4.9 km) distant.

Pluto, discovered in 1930, has a very eccentric orbit, with a radius varying between 2766 and 4566 million mi (4500 and 7400 million kilometers). Being so far from the Sun, it is extremely cold, and probably has no atmosphere.

Neptune, discovered in 1846, has a diameter of 31500 mi (50700 km) and is made up of gas, although little is known of its interior. It orbits the Sun once in 164¾ years. Seen through binoculars it is a small bluish disk.

Uranus, discovered in 1781, is apparently similar to Neptune, but less massive. Although faintly visible to the naked eye, even large telescopes show little detail upon its greenish surface.

Saturn is the second largest planet, its equatorial diameter being 75100 mi (122,300 km). Visually it is unlike any other heavenly body, because of its equatorial system of rings made up of particles of various sizes. The planet itself is less dense than water and at least its outer layers are gaseous.

Jupiter, the largest planet, has an equatorial diameter of 88700 mi (142,750 km), but its rapid spin, once every 9¾ hours, makes it very flattened at the poles. It appears to have cloud belts, possibly of liquid ammonia, and various spots, of which the great red spot seems to be semi-permanent.

The asteroids, a mass of apparent planetary material ranging in size from dust up to one lump about as large as the British Isles, orbit mainly between Mars and Jupiter, though some have eccentric orbits which approach the Earth.

Mars is about 4200 mi (6760 km) in diameter. It has a thin atmosphere, mainly of carbon dioxide, and its surface is pitted with Moon-like craters. It is not thought today that the planet contains any life.

The Earth/Moon system is today regarded as a double planet rather than a planet and satellite. The Moon has an average distance from Earth of 239,000 mi (385,000 km) and it is now known that it has never contained life.

Venus is almost the twin of the Earth in size and mass. It is too hot to contain life, and its very dense atmosphere is mainly carbon dioxide. It has a 'year' of 224¾ Earth days, and it spins on its axis once every 243 Earth days.

Mercury, the innermost planet, is only about 3000 mi (4800 km) in diameter, and has lost whatever atmosphere it had. Like Venus it shows phases, but it is always close to the Sun when viewed from the Earth and cannot be seen clearly.

The Sun's Influence on Earth

We depend entirely upon the Sun. It sends us virtually all our light and heat, and without it no life could exist on Earth. Fortunately for us, the Sun has throughout the Earth's lifetime behaved as a stable star. Its output of energy has remained much the same, though minor fluctuations may possibly have caused the Ice Ages which have affected the Earth's climate at intervals up to about 12000 years ago. Some of this energy, captured in the fossil remains of ancient plants, provides man's modern fuels in the form of coal, petroleum and gas. Even today the Sun continues to be the driving force that maintains all life on the Earth.

The Earth moves round the Sun at a mean distance of 92,957,000 miles (149,590,000 km) in an orbit which is not very far from being a true circle. The seasonal variation of climate on the Earth is due to the fact that the Earth's axis of rotation is not perpendicular to the plane of its orbit but inclined at an angle of $23\frac{1}{2}°$. The fact that we are three million miles (4.8 million km) closer to the Sun in the northern winter than in the northern summer has only a minor effect.

The Sun's surface is far from featureless. The relatively dark areas known as sunspots (pages 14-15) are not truly black but appear so because their temperature of some 4000°C is 2000° cooler than the surrounding photosphere. These spots occur at any time but their number varies according to a cycle of eleven years. At a time of spot maximum, as in 1957-58 and 1968-69, many groups may be seen simultaneously; at spot minimum there may be short periods with none at all. Few spots last longer than a few days, and none longer than a month or two.

Sunspots are the centers of strong magnetic storms and are often associated with brief, violent outbreaks known as flares. These send out streams of charged particles which reach beyond the orbit of the Earth and interact with the Earth's own powerful magnetic field. The result is visible phenomena, such as the aurorae, and interference with man's radio signals. On the other hand, it is no longer believed that sunspots and flares have any significant influence upon the Earth's weather.

Even when it is 'quiet' the Sun sends out streams of low-energy particles in all directions, generating the solar wind. Recent studies of it have been carried out, mainly by means of interplanetary probes and Earth satellites carrying instruments. In addition, the Sun emits radiations at all wavelengths from the long-wavelength radio waves down to the very short X-rays and gamma rays. The Sun is also one of the sources of cosmic rays.

Most of the short-wave radiation from the Sun is blocked out by layers in the Earth's upper atmosphere. But for this screening effect it is very unlikely that life could have developed on Earth (pages 50-51), because intense emissions of many of the short-wave radiations are lethal to terrestrial life. They may, too, prove to be a hazard to astronauts who spend long periods in space or on the surface of the airless Moon, outside the protective layers of the Earth's atmosphere (pages 26-27).

The magnetosphere *right*
The Earth is much more than a mere solid sphere travelling through a near-vacuum. The solar wind interacts with the Earth's magnetic field and rarefied outer atmosphere in a way that until very recently was almost unknown. The two Van Allen radiation belts around the Earth were not suspected until 1958. These belts appear in the illustration in bright orange. Both are closed orbits in which high-energy particles oscillate to and fro along the lines of the Earth's magnetic field. Both are dangerous to humans exposed within them for more than a brief period. The innermost belt (A) is 3000 mi (4800 km) above the equator. It is apparently caused by the impact of cosmic rays with atoms in the outer atmosphere. The collisions generate free neutrons which decay into protons and electrons which are at once trapped by the magnetic field. The outer zone (B) appears to be populated by energetic electrons thought to be supplied by the solar wind. The broken line shows an energetic particle from the Sun becoming influenced by the Earth's magnetic field and spiralling into the outer radiation belt, there to remain for several hundred years. The only regions of the Earth's magnetosphere which can readily be penetrated by all particles is that above each magnetic pole, where the field lines arch down to the surface. The upper trajectory is thought to be typical of a particle caused by a solar flare, of the type which gives rise to aurorae. The outer, less intense zones of the magnetosphere are distorted by the solar wind into a teardrop shape with a tail pointing away from the Sun. On the sunward side of the Earth the interaction between solar wind and magnetosphere gives rise to a shockwave at which the incoming particles are deflected past the Earth. On the shadow side the long tail of the magnetosphere may extend half a million miles.

A
B

Radiation belts *right*
These great rings of high-energy radiation girdle the globe. They are in fact distorted by the solar wind (see main illustration below) but have a theoretical form as shown here, the plan view being a toroidal ring when viewed from above either magnetic pole. The immediate effect of the belts extends out to at least six Earth radii above the equator (scale of figures). Although the Earth's axis of rotation passes through the geographic poles (axis X-X) the radiation belts are positioned in space by the magnetic field which is displaced (axis N-S, the position of which varies).

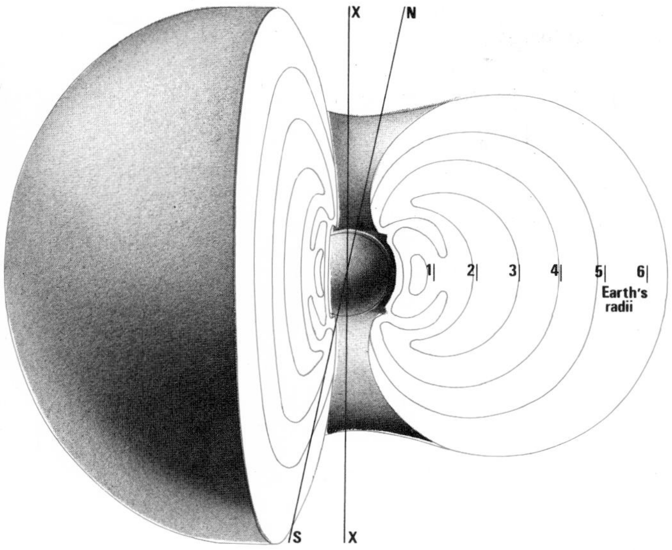
X
N
S
X
1
2
3
4
5
6
Earth's radii

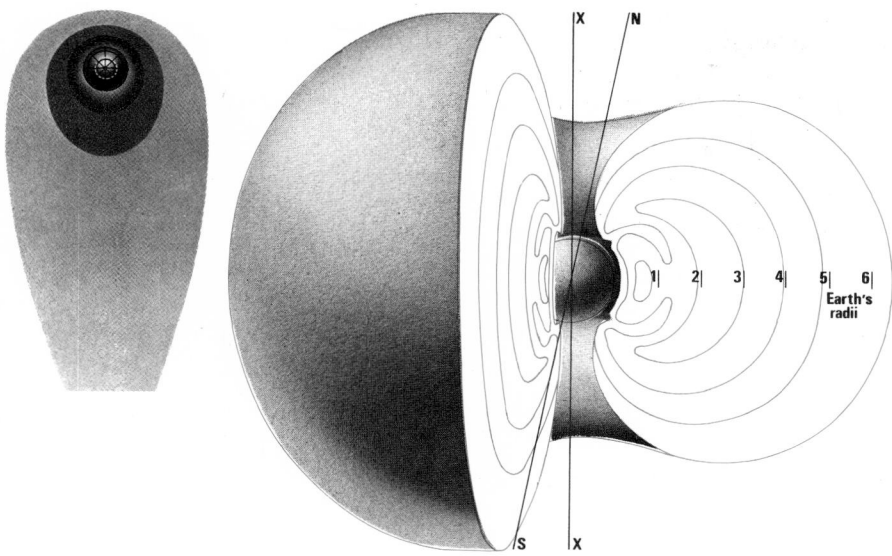

The ecosphere *below*
The ecosphere is the region of the solar system within which a planet or other environment is likely to be neither too hot nor too cold for life to exist. It is a comparatively narrow zone. Venus, at a mean radius from the Sun of about 67,200,000 mi (108,148,000 km), is near its inner boundary. Mars, at approximately 141,500,000 mi (227,724,000 km), is close to the outer edge. Only the Earth lies near the middle of the ecosphere, which is one of the main reasons why it is the only planet in the Sun's family which is suitable for life of terrestrial type. The ecosphere has no sharp boundaries, and the sizes and masses of the planets are important factors. Mars, for instance, may be said to lie within the ecosphere, but it has such a small mass and escape velocity that it has not been able to retain much of an atmosphere. Venus, also within the ecosphere, is very much of a mystery. Instruments carried by interplanetary probes indicate that this planet has a dense atmosphere made up almost wholly of carbon dioxide and having a temperature, near the planetary surface, as high as 400-530°C. There is little doubt that the underlying cause of the apparent high temperature is the relative proximity of Venus to the Sun.

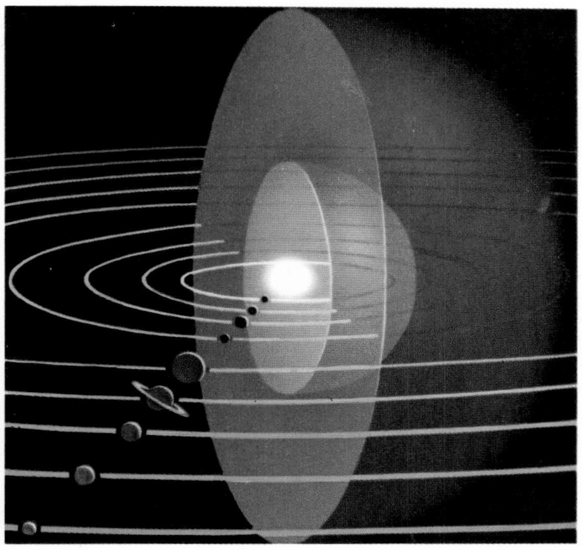

The aurora *below*
It has been known for many decades that this beautiful spectacle is caused by the influence of the Sun. The aurora is most widespread at times of maximum solar activity, when the Sun's surface is dotted with sunspots and flares. The mechanism is an interaction between charged solar particles, free electrons and gas atoms in the outer atmosphere. The Earth's magnetic field arches in to the terrestrial sphere to foci near the geographic poles, and it is rare to see aurorae except at high latitudes. They persist from seconds to days.

A diffuse curtain *right*
Aurorae occur in the upper atmosphere at heights from about 600 mi (960 km) down to as low as 60 mi. The curtain-like form visible in the two upper photographs is typical of the majority of aurorae; colors range from blue through white to gold and red.

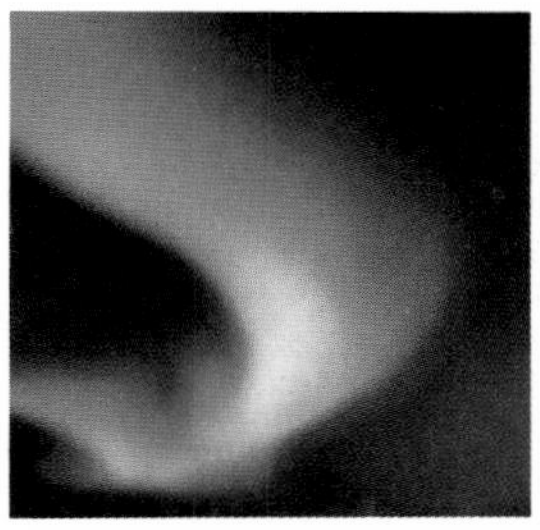

A later stage *right*
This photograph was taken shortly after the one above and shows a slightly later development of the same aurora. Most aurorae pulsate, becoming alternately brighter and dimmer; the display is sometimes unexpectedly and suddenly terminated.

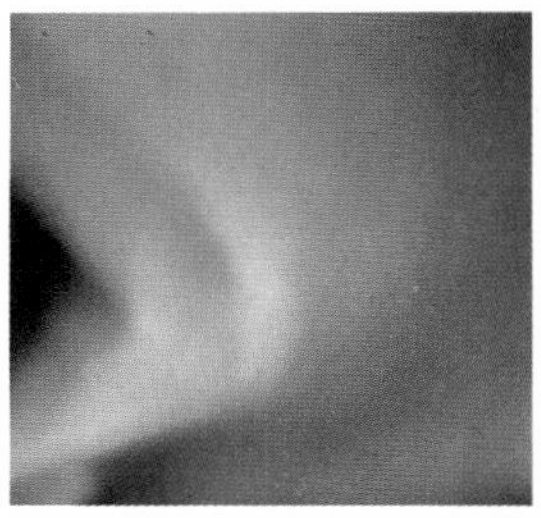

Far from the pole *right*
Nearly all auroral displays occur at high latitudes, the northern display being known as the Northern Lights or Aurora Borealis and the southern as Aurora Australis. This display was seen from only 39°N at Washington DC.

Earth's Companion: The Moon

The Moon is our companion in space. Its mean distance from the Earth is less than a quarter of a million miles – it varies between 221,460 miles (356,410 km) and 252,700 miles (406,685 km) – and it was the first world other than our Earth to come within the range of man's space probes. At first mere masses, these then became instrument packages and finally spacecraft carrying men. With their aid our knowledge of the Moon has been vastly increased in the past decade. Astronauts Neil Armstrong and Edwin Aldrin made the first human journey to the lunar surface in July 1969, and the Moon has since been subjected to detailed and direct investigation.

The mean diameter of the Moon is 2158 miles (3473 km), and its mass is 1/81st as much as that of the Earth. Despite this wide difference the ratio is much less than that between other planets and their moons, and the Earth/Moon system is now widely regarded as a double planet rather than as a planet and satellite. The Moon's mean density is less than that of the Earth, and it may lack a comparable heavy core. Escape velocity from the lunar surface is only 1.5 mi/sec (2.4 km/sec), and this is so low that the Moon has lost any atmosphere it may once have had. To Earth life it is therefore an extremely hostile world. Analysis of lunar rock brought back to Earth laboratories and investigated by Soviet probes on the Moon has so far revealed no trace of any life. The Moon appears to have always been sterile.

Much of the surface of the Moon comprises large grey plains, mis-called 'mare' (seas), but most of it is extremely rough. There are great ranges of mountains, isolated peaks and countless craters which range from tiny pits up to vast enclosures more than 150 miles (240 km) in diameter. Many of the craters have central mountains or mountain-groups. Some of the larger craters show signs of having been produced by volcanic action, while others appear to have resulted from the impacts of meteorites.

The Moon rotates slowly, performing one complete turn on its axis every 27.3 days. This is the same as its period of revolution around the Earth, so it always presents the same face to us. But in October 1959 the Soviet probe *Lunik 3* photographed the hidden rear hemisphere and it has since been mapped in detail. It contains no large 'seas'. The appearance of the lunar surface depends strongly on the angle at which it is viewed and the direction of solar illumination. In the photograph on the right, taken from a height of about 70 miles (115 km) with the Earth having once more come into full view ahead, the lunar surface looks deceptively smooth; in fact, there is practically no level ground anywhere in the field of vision. The lunar horizon is always sharply defined, because there is no atmosphere to cause blurring or distortion. For the same reason, the sky seen from the Moon is always jet black.

Full Moon *below*
This striking photograph was taken by the *Apollo 11* astronauts in July 1969. It shows parts of both the Earth-turned and far hemispheres. The dark plain near the center is the Mare Crisium.

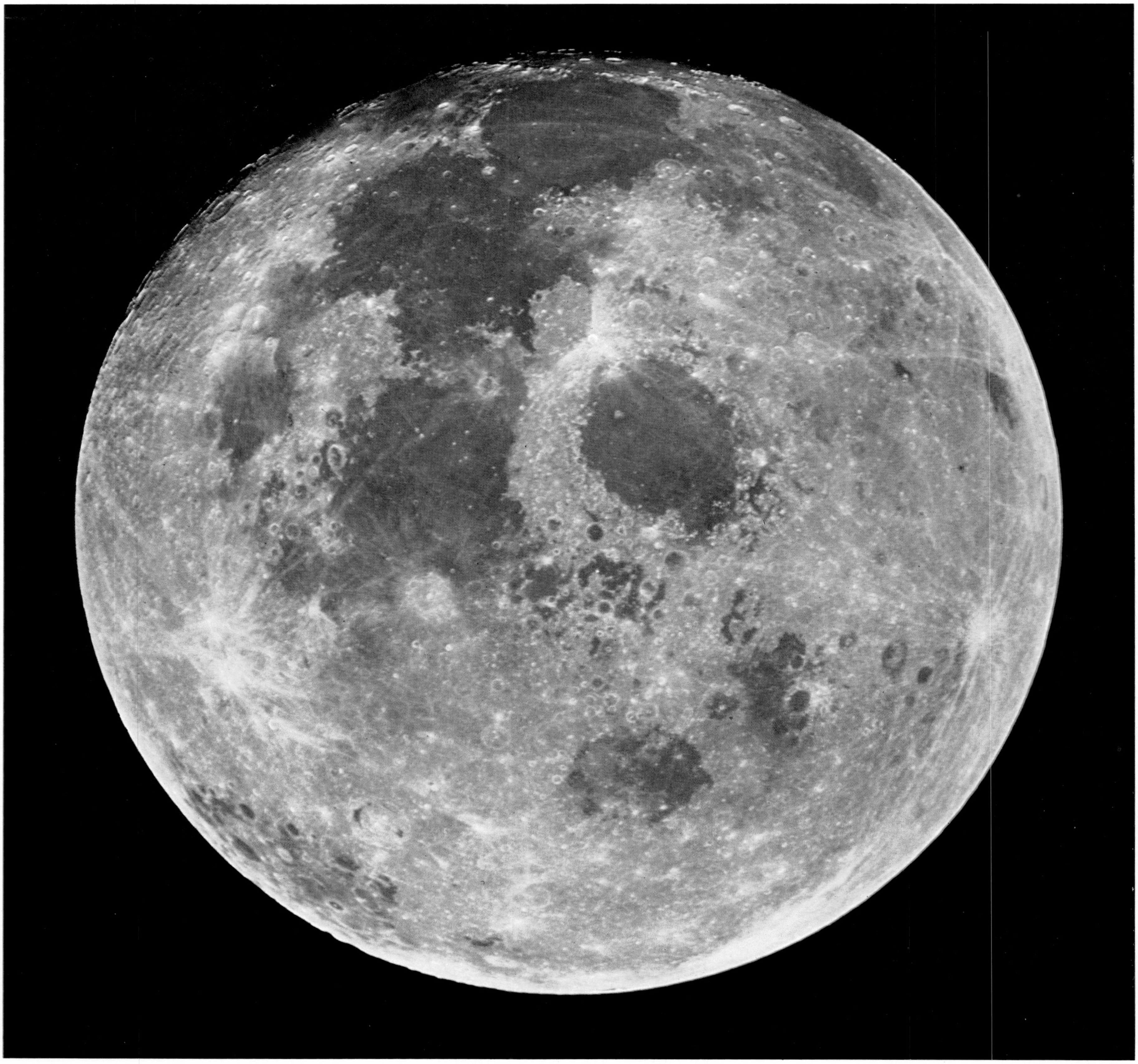

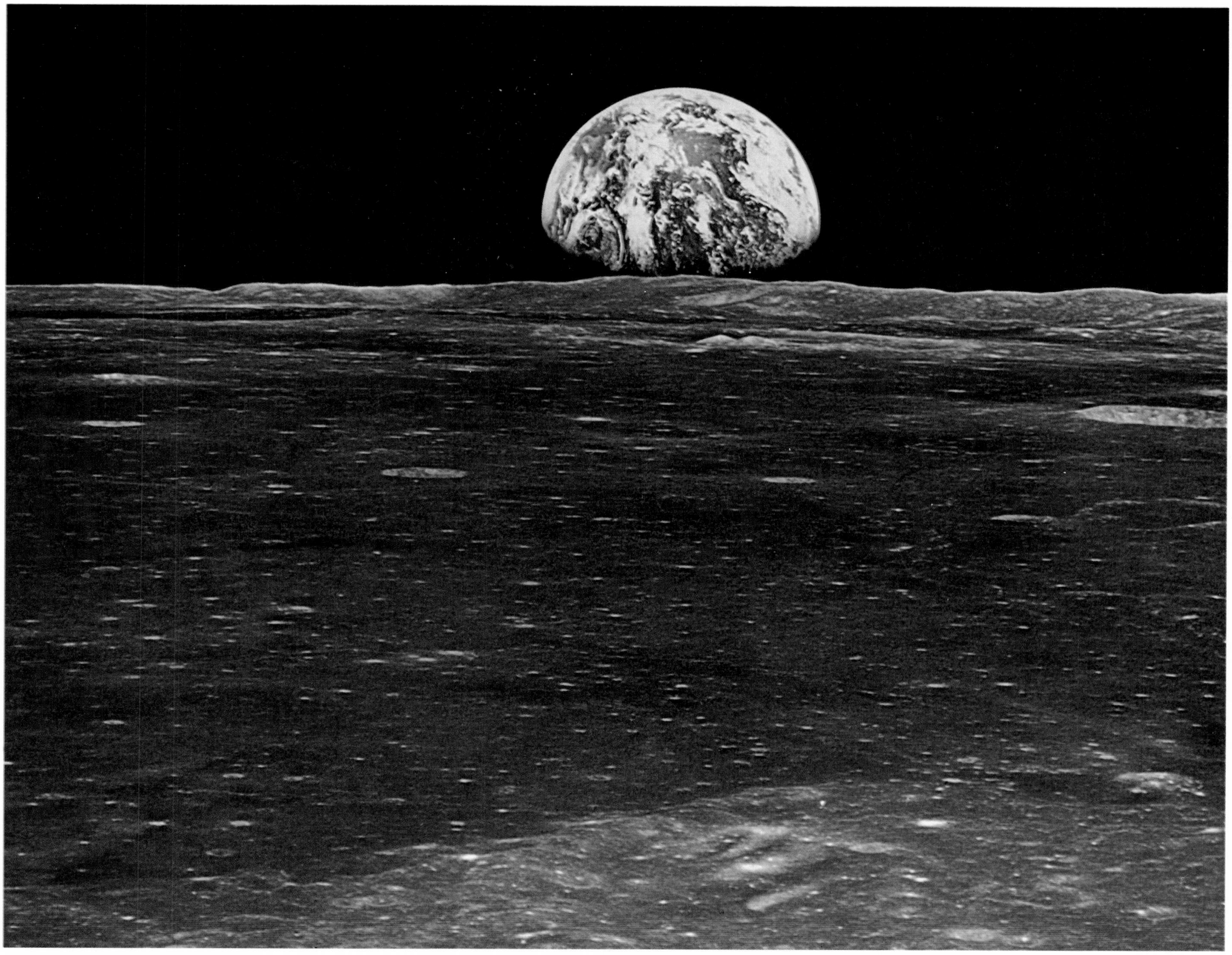

Earthrise *above*
This view of the Earth rising was visible to the crew of *Apollo 10* in May 1969 as they orbited the Moon 70 miles (115 km) above the surface. They had just come round from the Moon's rear hemisphere.

Eclipses

Once regarded as terrifying actions of angry gods, eclipses are today merely useful. They provide a different view of the Sun and Moon that opens up fresh information. In a lunar eclipse the Earth passes directly between the Sun and Moon; in a solar eclipse the Moon passes between Sun and Earth. Both the Earth and Moon constantly cast a shadow comprising a dark inner cone surrounded by a region to which part of the sunlight penetrates. A body passing through the outer shadow experiences a partial eclipse, while the inner cone causes a total eclipse in which all direct sunlight is cut off.

A total solar eclipse is magnificent. The bright star is blocked out by a black Moon, but around it the Sun's atmosphere flashes into view. The pearly corona of thin gas can be seen extending a million miles from the Sun. Closer to the surface huge 'prominences' of red hydrogen leap into space and curve back along the solar magnetic field. In a partial solar eclipse these things cannot be seen, while in a total eclipse caused by the Moon at its greatest distance from Earth a ring of the Sun is left visible. As the Moon's orbit is not in the same plane as the Earth's, total solar eclipses occur very rarely, on occasions when the tip of the Moon's dark shadow crosses the Earth as a spot 169 miles (272 km) wide.

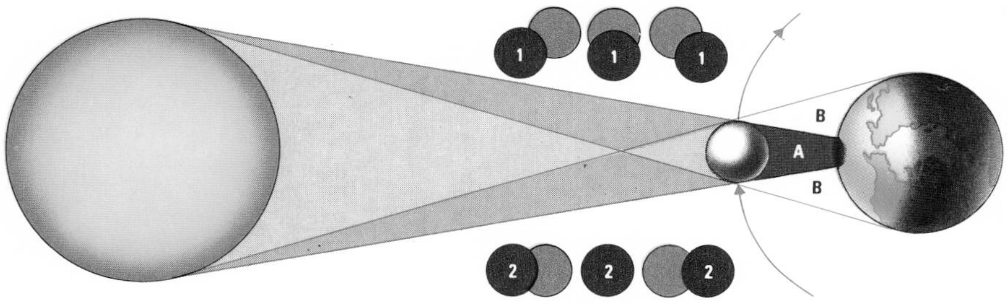
1 1 1
B
A
B
2 2 2

Eclipses *left and below*
When the Moon passes in front of the Sun as in sequence 1 its shadow B causes a partial solar eclipse (below, left, taken 21 November 1966).
But in the case of sequence 2, shadow cone A gives a total eclipse (below, right, 15 February 1961).

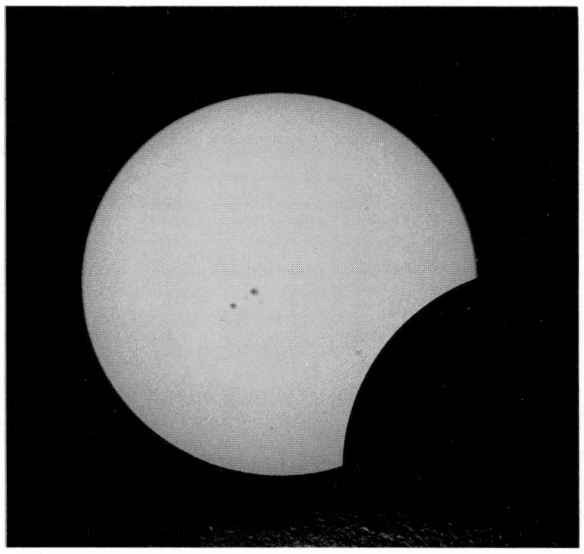

Earth from Space: 1

From a distance the Earth looks one of the most interesting objects in the solar system. This is largely because it has an atmosphere that provides highly variable cloud cover which frequently enables a distant observer to see through to the planet beneath. Astronaut Neil Armstrong said that the Earth 'looks like a beautiful jewel in space'. Its predominant color is bluish, and the albedo, the Earth's power to reflect visible light, is as high as about 40 per cent, compared with the Moon's ability to reflect only seven per cent of the light falling upon it. From a very great distance the Earth would appear to be a bright bluish disk. A human observer on Mars would see it as a star, but from Jupiter and the more distant planets the Earth would be practically invisible without a telescope because it would always be in the same area of sky as the Sun. And an observer living on a planet in orbit around another star would never see the Earth at all, even with the most powerful telescope (unless he had a vastly superior technology), and would know nothing of human life.

Full Earth *above*
At 22,300 miles (35,900 km) a satellite hovers over the same place on Earth. At noon each day the whole hemisphere is visible.

Crescent Earth *left*
From Apollo 4, 10000 mi (16000 km) away, this photograph was taken looking southwest over Africa and S America.

Andean sunset *right*
A much less distant view of Earth, this photograph was taken from Gemini 7 in 1965. The camera was over Bolivia, looking south.

Earth from Space: 2

Southern North America *above*
This photograph was taken from the Apollo 11 spacecraft in its translunar trajectory in July 1969, at the beginning of man's first voyage to the lunar surface.
The area covered (key below) is approximately 1,000,000 sq mi (2,590,000 km^2). Some 200 mi (320 km) west of Mexico is a gyrating cyclone, and northward from this a cloud layer extends as far as Los Angeles. Much of the land is clear of cloud, although fine-weather cumulus is widespread, and it is possible to see the interplay of land, sea, wind and cloud.

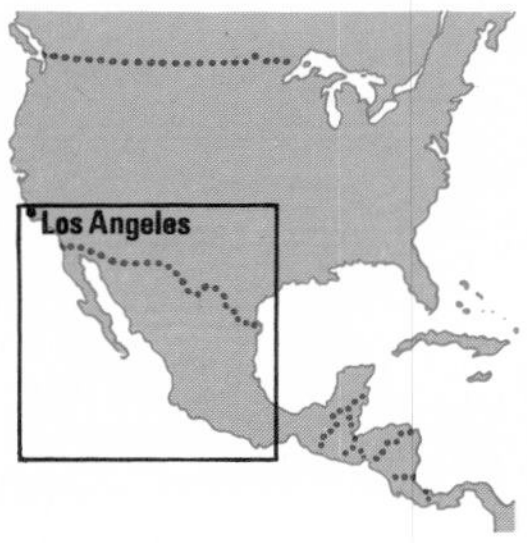

Los Angeles

The area covered *left*
The photograph above portrays the region within the black square at left. Vertical and near-vertical photography from space makes it possible for maps to be kept constantly up to date. So far most manned photography has been within 30° of the equator.

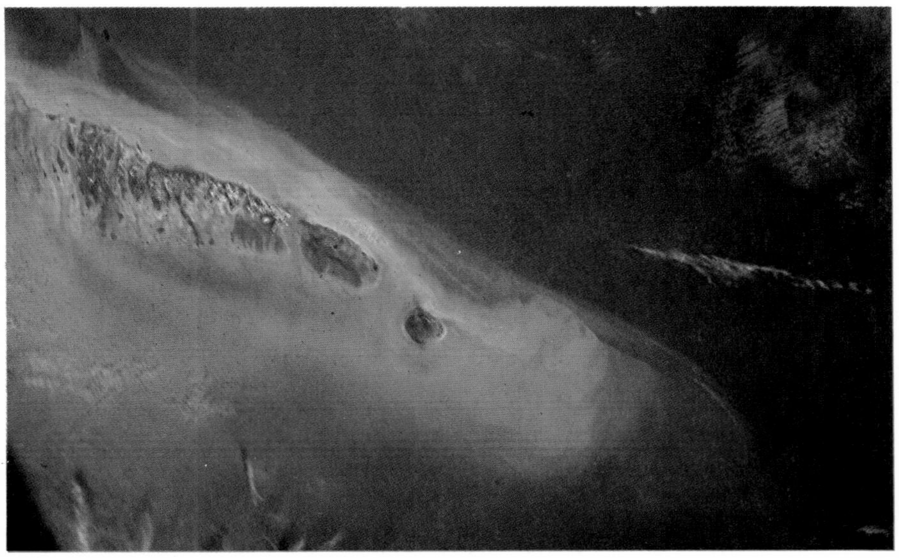

Great Barrier Reef *left*
Some of the most beautiful space photographs are those of shallow seas and reefs. The Great Barrier Reef extends more than 1000 mi (1600 km) from 20–150 mi (32–240 km) off the northeast coast of Australia. In this nearly vertical view the deep water appears dark and the shallows around the coral much lighter. Such pictures are of value to oceanographers because they reveal submarine detail, such as channels newly cut by hurricanes. Surface reflectance patterns disclose local sea state, current and the presence of slicks of oil or organic matter.

Rocky Mountains *right*
Rather more northerly than most manned spacecraft pictures of the Earth, this photograph was taken from Apollo 9 in March 1969. It shows northern New Mexico and, at the top, a narrow strip of Colorado. Down the center the valley of the Rio Grande stands out clearly against the rugged terrain, with the city of Albuquerque at the center of the bottom edge. The very large circular formation above the center is Redondo Peak, while at the right are the Sangre de Cristo mountains, one of the major elements of the Rocky Mountain chain.

Color at sunset *above*
The film used here aboard Apollo 7 was sensitive to visible light, not infra-red, and the color – due to diffusion of the inclined sunlight by atmospheric dust – is real. The ocean is mainly cloud covered, but the bright bluish haze belt on the horizon is always seen.

Hurricane *below*
The largest tropical cyclonic storms are so big nothing but a spacecraft can see the whole structure at once. This view of Bernice – called a typhoon, the word more common for Pacific storms – was seen by the first explorers of the Moon aboard Apollo 11.

Reflectance *below*
This computer print-out is the graphical presentation of data sent back from the unmanned Nimbus 3 in May 1969. It shows sunlight reflectance from parts of Africa (left), the Red Sea (dark) and Arabia, over wavelengths from 0.7–1.3 microns.

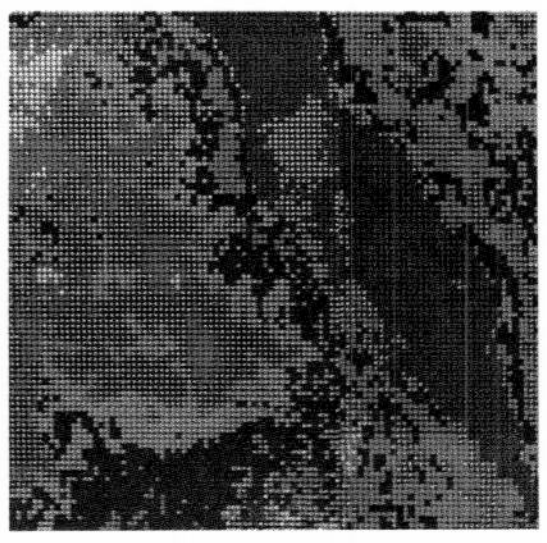

Infra-red survey *right*
Today man is beginning to use spacecraft as platforms for working tools, and one of the most valuable of these is the infra-red camera. Some of the first infra-red pictures were taken from Nimbus weather satellites, which recorded temperature as shades of grey. The picture at right, from the Mississippi-Louisiana border with the Mississippi river top right, uses infra-red film to record land use in fine detail. Such film is sensitive to differences not discernible at visible light wavelengths: such as diseased trees, variations in crops, and the salinity and temperature of water.

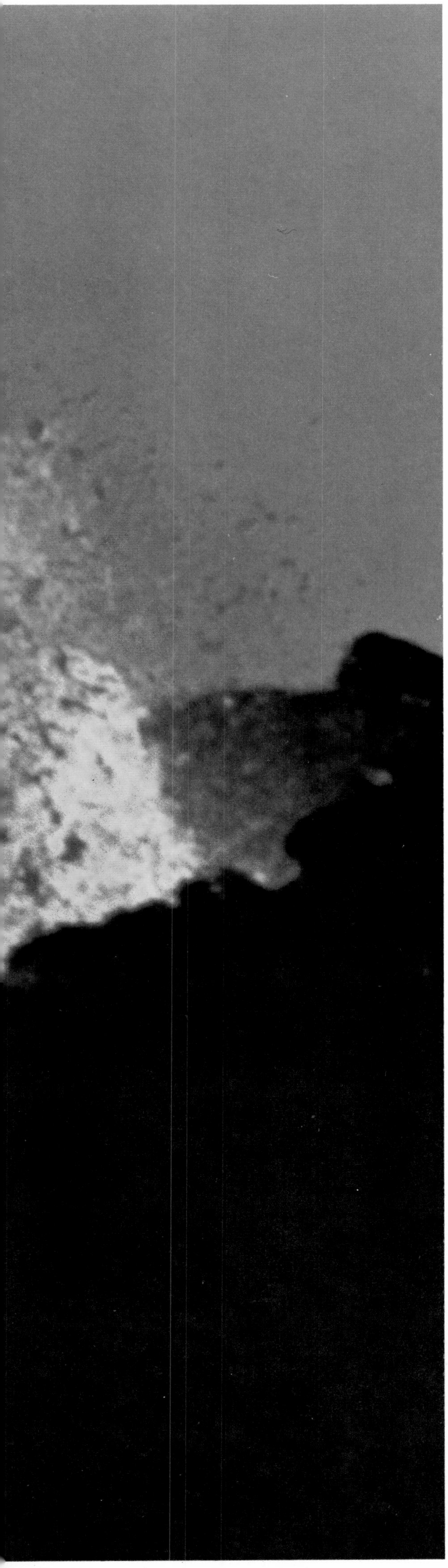

The Structure of the Earth

The Earth's first rocks were formed about 3500 million years ago. Since that time the planet's surface has been ceaselessly altered and its present physical features are the result of numerous processes which interact with each other, usually very slowly but sometimes very violently, on a scale man can never hope to rival. The land is eroded by the wind and rain, washed away by the rivers and seas, and reduced to sediment which builds up elsewhere. The records of all these cyclic processes can be seen both in the rocks themselves and in the evidence of more spectacular changes such as explosive volcanic eruptions and vast outpourings of molten lava. On the continents thick sequences of rock strata and the relationship each layer bears to those above and below retain the evidence of events that happened millions of years ago just as effectively as a slow-moving tape recorder through most of the Earth's history. The story of these processes and the slow evolution of the world forms the subject of this section.

The violent Earth
All Earth life exists around a very thin skin enclosing a sphere hotter than molten steel. At intervals the merest suspicions of the interior energy escape through the crust, as in the Askja eruption in central Iceland in 1961.

The Atmosphere

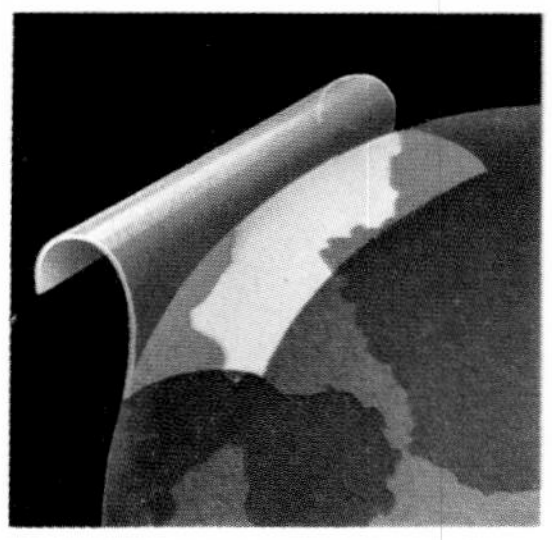

A thin coating *left*
The protective atmospheric shell around the Earth is proportionally no thicker than the skin of an apple. Gravity compresses the air so that half its mass lies within 3.5 miles (5.5 km) of the surface and all the weather within an average depth of 12 miles (20 km).

Space exploration has enabled man to stand back and take a fresh look at his Earth. Even though we, like all Earth life, have evolved to suit the Earth environment, we can see today as never before how miraculous that environment is. And by far the most important single factor in determining that environment is the atmosphere.

The Earth orbits round the Sun in a near-total vacuum. So rarefied is the interplanetary medium that it contains little heat energy, but the gas molecules that are present are vibrating so violently that their individual temperature is over 2000°C. And the surface of the Sun, at some 6000°C, would melt almost everything on the surface of the Earth, while the tenuous chromosphere around the Sun is as hot as 1,000,000°C. From the chromosphere, and from millions of other stars and heavenly objects, come radio waves. Various places in the universe, most of them far beyond the solar system, send us a penetrating kind of radiation known as cosmic rays. The Earth also receives gamma rays, X-rays and ultraviolet radiation, and from the asteroid belt in the solar system (see pages 14-15) comes a stream of solid material. Most of these are small micrometeorites, no more than flying specks, but the Earth also receives meteors and meteorites.

A meteorite is a substantial mass that strikes the Earth; fortunately, none has yet hit in a populous area. Apart from these extremely rare objects, every other influence from the environment that would be dangerous to life is filtered out by the atmosphere. Meteors burn up through friction as they plunge into the upper parts of the atmosphere. To avoid burning up in the same way, spacecraft designed to return to the Earth from lunar or interplanetary flight require a special re-entry shield.

Much of the ultraviolet radiation is arrested many miles above the Earth and creates ionized layers known as the ionosphere which man uses to reflect radio waves. Much of the infra-red (heat) radiation is likewise absorbed, lower down in the atmosphere, and most of the cosmic radiation is broken up by collisions far above the ground into such particles as 'mu-mesons'. Only a few cosmic rays, harmless radio waves and visible light penetrate the blanket of air to reach the planetary surface and its teeming life.

Credit for our vital atmosphere rests with the Earth's gravitational attraction, which both prevents the molecules and atoms in the atmosphere from escaping into space and also pulls them down tightly against the Earth. As a result nearly all the atmosphere's mass is concentrated in a very thin layer; three-quarters of it lies below 29000 feet (8840 m), the height of Mount Everest. The highest-flying aircraft, 19 miles (30 km) up, are above 99 per cent of the atmosphere. The total weight of the atmosphere is of the order of 5000 million million tons. In the lower parts are some 17 million million tons of water vapor.

The water vapor plays a great part in determining the weather on Earth, the only way in which the atmosphere consciously affects daily human life. All the weather is confined to the lower parts of the atmosphere below the tropopause. In this region, called the troposphere, temperature falls away sharply with increasing altitude. The Sun heats up the Earth's surface, water is evaporated from the surface of the oceans and an immensely complicated pattern of global and local weather systems is set up. Every part of the air in the troposphere is in motion. Sometimes the motion is so slow as to be barely perceptible, while on other occasions, or at the same time in other places, the air roars over the surface with terrifying force at speeds of 200 miles (320 km) per hour or more. It erodes the land, lashes the surface with rain and clogs cold regions with snow. Yet it is man's shield against dangers, an ocean of air without which we could not exist.

Characteristics of the atmosphere *right*
Basically the Earth's atmosphere consists of a layer of mixed gases covering the surface of the globe which, as a result of the Earth's gravitational attraction, increases in density as the surface is approached. But there is very much more to it than this. Temperature, composition and physical properties vary greatly through the depth of the atmosphere. The Earth's surface is assumed to lie along the bottom of the illustration, and the various major regions of the atmosphere—which imperceptibly merge into each other—are indicated by the numbers on the vertical scale on the facing page.

Exosphere (1)
This rarefied region is taken to start at a height of some 400 miles (650 km) and to merge above into the interplanetary medium. Atomic oxygen exists up to 600 mi (1000 km); from there up to about 1500 mi (2400 km) helium and hydrogen are approximately equally abundant, with hydrogen becoming dominant above 1500 mi. The highest auroras are found in this region. Traces of the exosphere extend out to at least 5000 mi (8000 km).

Ionosphere (2)
This contains electrically conducting layers capable of reflecting radio waves and thus of enabling radio signals to be received over great distances across the Earth. The major reflecting layers, designated D, E, F1 and F2, are at the approximate heights shown. Meteors burn up brightly at heights of around 100 mi (160 km). Charged particles coming in along the lines of force of the Earth's magnetic field produce aurorae in the ionosphere at high latitudes, some of them of the corona type with a series of radial rays; and the ionosphere's structure alters from day to night and according to the influence of the solar wind and incoming streams of other particles and radiation.

Stratosphere (3)
This lies above the tropopause which varies in altitude from about 10 mi (16 km) over the equator to just below 7 mi (11 km) in temperate latitudes. The lower stratosphere has a constant temperature of -56°C up to 19 mi (30 km); higher still the 'mesosphere' becomes warmer again. One of the vital properties of the stratosphere is its minute ozone content which shields the Earth life from some harmful short-wave radiations which, before the Earth's atmosphere had developed, penetrated to the surface.

Troposphere (4)
Within this relatively very shallow layer is concentrated about 80 per cent of the total mass of the atmosphere, as well as all the weather and all the Earth's life. The upper boundary of the troposphere is the tropopause, which is about 36000 ft (11000 m) above the surface in temperate latitudes; over the tropics it is higher, and therefore colder, while it is at a lower altitude over the poles. Air temperature falls uniformly with increasing height until the tropopause is reached; thereafter it remains constant in the stratosphere. Composition of the troposphere is essentially constant, apart from the vital factor of clouds and humidity.

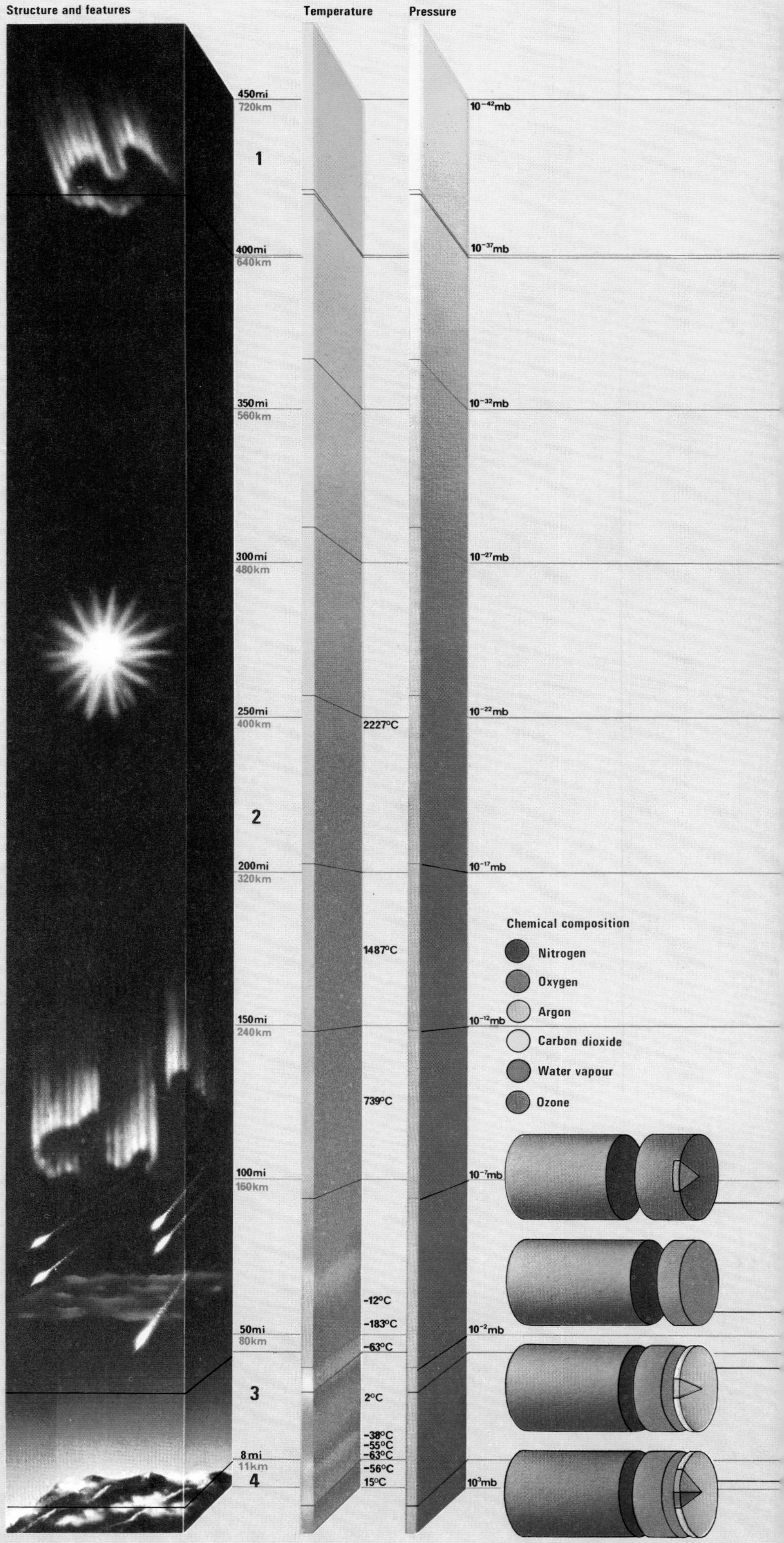

Structure and features
Temperature
Pressure
450mi
720km
1
400mi
640km
350mi
560km
300mi
480km
250mi
400km
2
200mi
320km
150mi
240km
100mi
160km
50mi
80km
3
8 mi
11km
4
2227°C
1487°C
739°C
-12°C
-183°C
-63°C
2°C
-38°C
-55°C
-63°C
-56°C
15°C
10^{-42}mb
10^{-37}mb
10^{-32}mb
10^{-27}mb
10^{-22}mb
10^{-17}mb
10^{-12}mb
10^{-7}mb
10^{-2}mb
10^{3}mb
Chemical composition
Nitrogen
Oxygen
Argon
Carbon dioxide
Water vapour
Ozone

Temperature
The mean temperature at the Earth's surface is about 15°C. As height is gained the temperature falls swiftly, to —56°C at the tropopause. It remains at this value to 19 miles (30 km), becomes warmer again, and then falls to a very low value around 60 miles (100 km). It rises once again in space.

Pressure
At sea level the pressure is some 1000 millibars, or about 14.7 pounds per square inch. The total force acting on the surface of an adult human body is thus of the order of 20 tons. But only 10 miles (16 km) above the Earth the pressure, and the atmospheric density, have both fallen by some 90 per cent.

Composition
Chemical composition of the atmosphere varies considerably with altitude. In the troposphere the mixture of nitrogen, oxygen and other gases is supplemented by water vapor, which exerts a profound influence on the weather. Ozone in the stratosphere shields life from harmful ultraviolet rays.

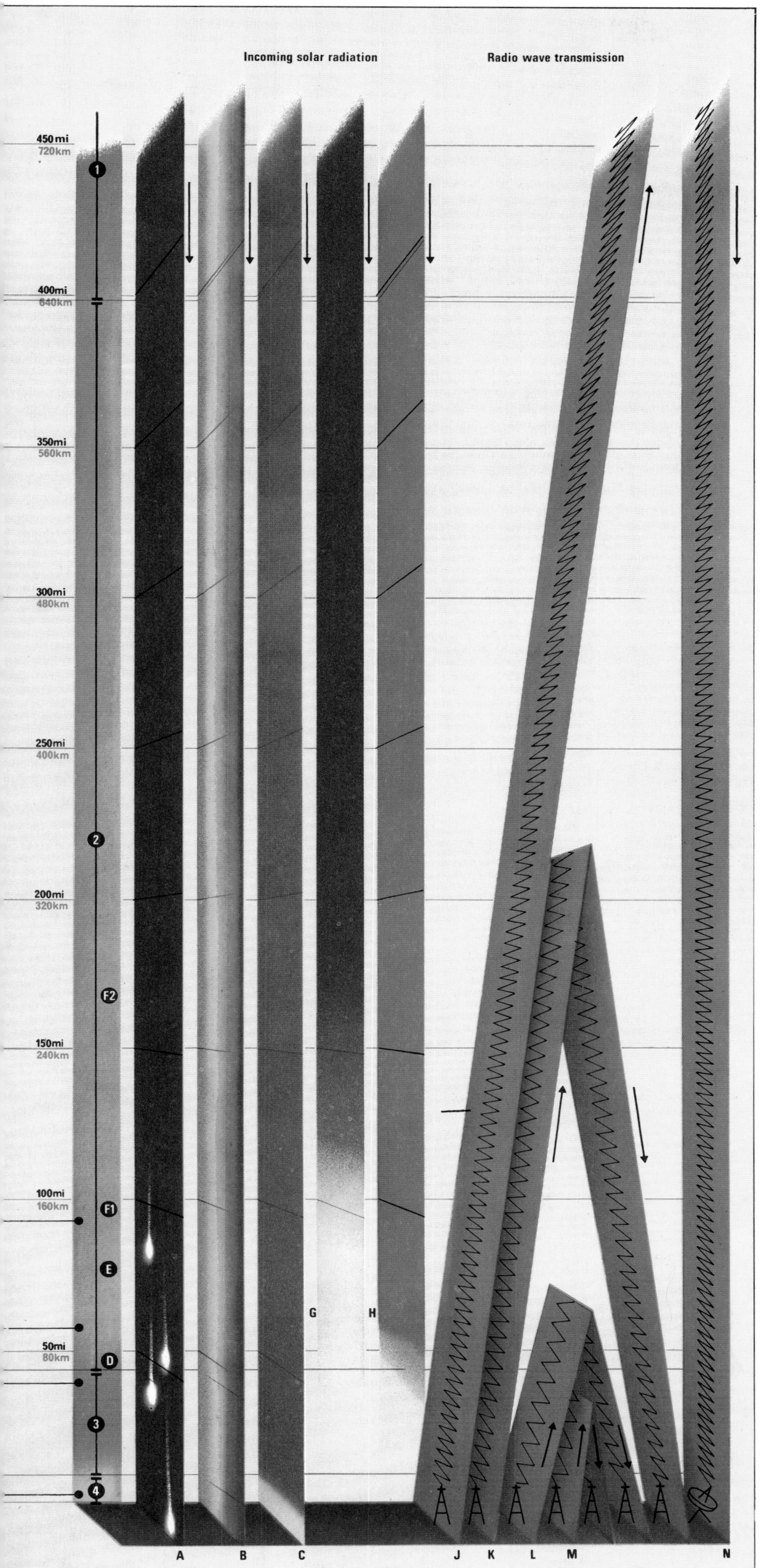

Incoming solar radiation
Radio wave transmission
450mi
720km
400mi
640km
350mi
560km
300mi
480km
250mi
400km
200mi
320km
150mi
240km
100mi
160km
50mi
80km
1
2
F2
F1
E
D
3
4
G
H
A
B
C
J
K
L
M
N

A particle shield
The Earth is continuously bombarded with solid particles from elsewhere in the solar system and possibly from more distant parts of the universe. Only the largest meteors (A) reach the surface. Small meteorites generally burn up through friction caused by passage through the thin air more than 40 miles (65 km) up.

A radiation shield
Most of the Sun's visible light (B) can penetrate the whole of the atmosphere right down to the Earth's surface, except where cloud intervenes. But only some of the infra-red radiation gets through (C); the rest (G) is cut off, along with the harmful ultraviolet radiation (H), by atmospheric gases.

Radio waves
Very-high-frequency radio waves (VHF) can penetrate the whole depth of the atmosphere (J), but short-wave transmissions are reflected by the Appleton F2 layer (K). Medium (L) and long waves (M) are reflected at lower levels by the D, E or F1 layers. Yet radio waves from distant stellar sources can be received (N).

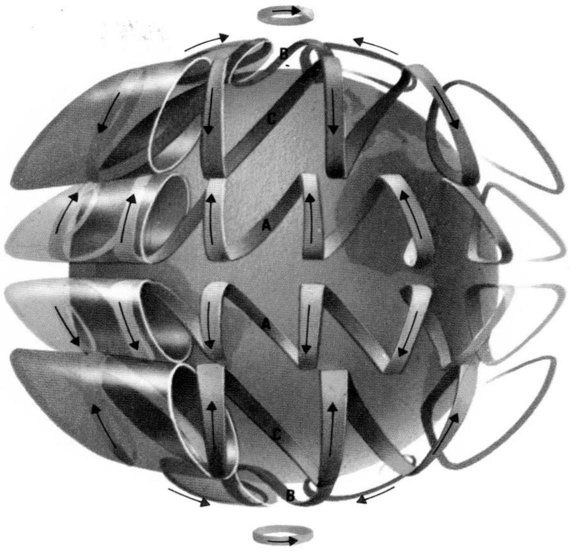

The circulation of the atmosphere *left*
The atmosphere maintains its equilibrium by transferring heat, moisture and momentum from low levels at low latitudes to high levels at high latitudes where the heat is radiated to space. This circulation appears to comprise three distinct 'cells' in each hemisphere. In the tropical (A) and polar (B) cells the circulations are thermally direct – warm air rises and cold air sinks – but the mid-latitude circulation, the Ferrel cell (C), is distorted by the polar front as shown in greater detail below.

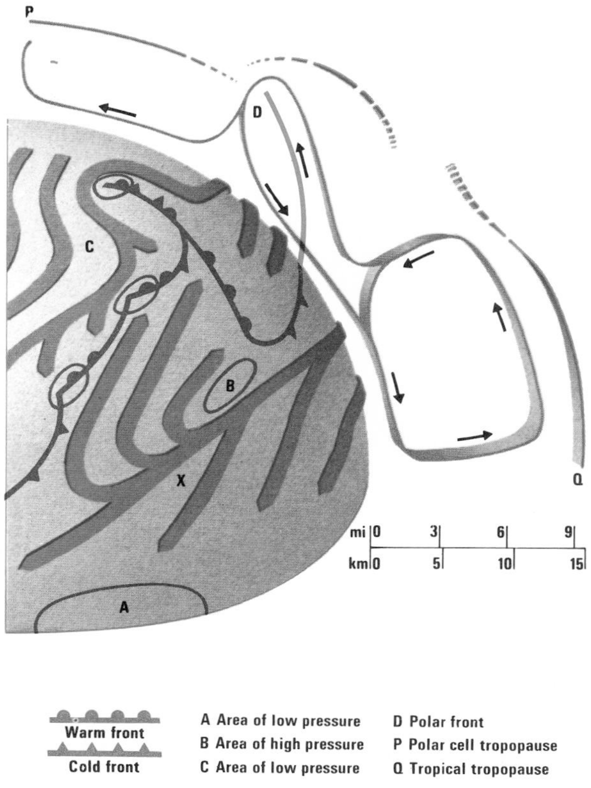

P
D
C
B
X
A
Q
mi 0 3 6 9
km 0 5 10 15
Warm front
Cold front
A Area of low pressure
B Area of high pressure
C Area of low pressure
D Polar front
P Polar cell tropopause
Q Tropical tropopause

Frontal systems *left*
Although the figure above shows a true general picture, the actual circulation is more complicated. A portion of the Earth on a larger scale shows how frontal systems develop between the polar and tropical air masses. The tropopause, the demarcation between the troposphere in which temperature falls with height, and the stratosphere above, is much higher in the tropics than in the polar cell. Between the cells the polar front causes constant successions of warm and cold fronts and changeable weather. Surface winds are shown, together with areas of low pressure and high pressure. The scale along the bottom, although exaggerated, indicates the greater height of the tropical tropopause compared with that in polar regions. Conventional symbols indicate warm and cold fronts.

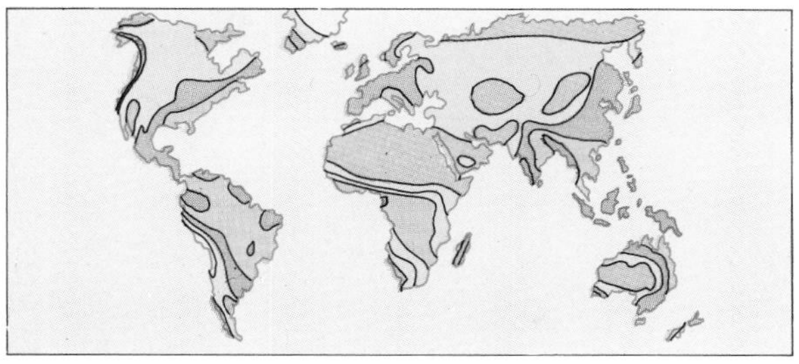

Precipitation *left*
This map shows the mean annual rain, hail and snow over the Earth.

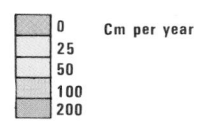

Cm per year
0
25
50
100
200

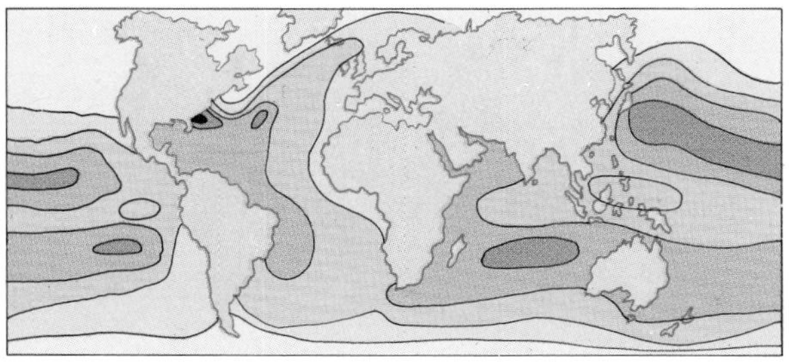

Evaporation *left*
Accurate estimates of evaporation can be made only over the oceans.

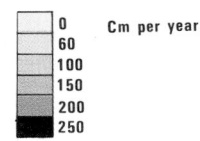

Cm per year
0
60
100
150
200
250

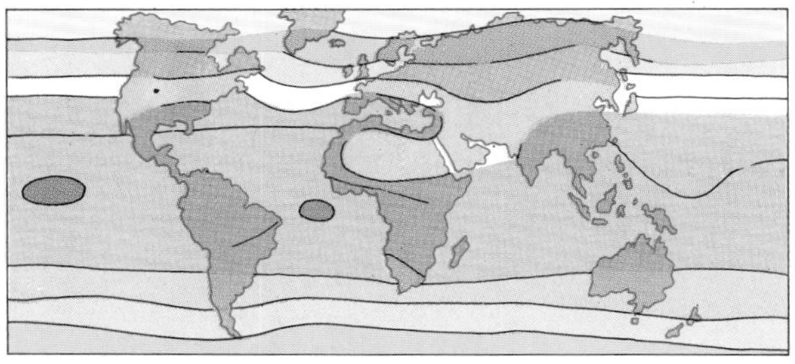

Surface radiation *left*
Variations in heat output over the Earth's surface affect air and ocean circulations.

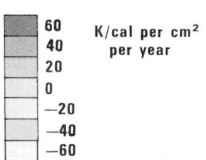

K/cal per cm^2 per year
60
40
20
0
–20
–40
–60

The Structure of Weather Systems

Until recently there were few scientists in the tropics or the polar regions, and the science of meteorology therefore evolved in the mid-latitudes. Likewise, the early concepts of meteorology were all based on observations of the mid-latitude atmosphere. Originally only two types of air mass were recognized: polar and tropical. Today a distinct equatorial air mass has been identified, as well as Arctic and Antarctic masses at latitudes even higher than the original polar ones. The concept of a 'front' between dissimilar air masses dates from as recently as 1919, and three years later the development of a cyclone – a large system of air rotating around an area of low pressure–was first described. Today satellite photographs have confirmed the validity of these early studies and enable the whole Earth's weather to be watched on daily computer processed photo-charts as it develops.

Why the weather varies

Anywhere in the Earth's mid-latitudes the climate is determined mainly by the frequency and intensity of the cyclones, with their frontal systems and contrasting air masses, which unceasingly alter the local temperature, wind velocity, air pressure and humidity. In turn, the frequency of the cyclonic visits is governed principally by the behavior of the long waves in the upper westerlies. When these waves change their shape and position the cyclonic depressions follow different paths. The major changes are seasonal, but significant variations also occur on a cycle of 5–6 weeks. It is still proving difficult to investigate the long wave variations. As a front passes, a fairly definite sequence of cloud, wind, humidity, temperature, precipitation and visibility can be seen. The most obvious change is the type of cloud, of which nine are shown opposite. Each cyclone contains numerous cloud types in its structure. Within these clouds several forms of precipitation can form; raindrops are the most common, but ice precipitation also forms, with snow in winter and hail in the summer when intense atmospheric instability produces towering cumulonimbus clouds topped by an 'anvil' of ice crystals.

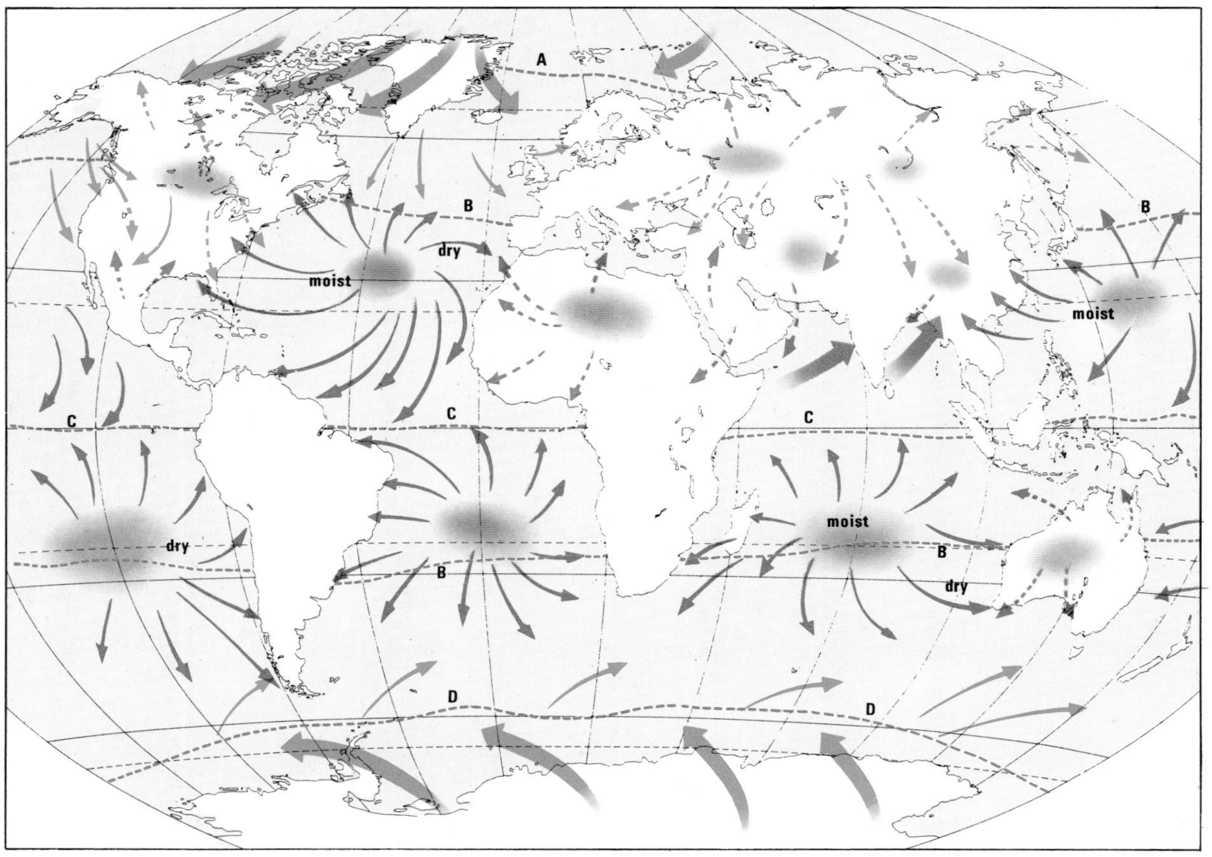

A
B
C
D
moist
dry
Arctic
Polar maritime
Polar continental
Cold air masses
Equatorial
Tropical maritime
Tropical continental
Warm air masses

Air masses and convergences *above*
An air mass is an extensive portion of the atmosphere in which, at any given altitude, the moisture and temperature are almost uniform. Such a mass generally arises when the air rests for a time on a large area of land or water which has uniform surface conditions. There are some 20 source regions throughout the world. A second pre-requisite is large-scale subsidence and divergence over the source region. The boundary between air masses is a convergence or front. (A Arctic, B Polar, C Equatorial, D Antarctic.) The polar front is particularly important in governing much of the weather in mid-latitudes. The pattern depicted provides a raw framework for the world's weather. It is considerably modified by the air's vertical motion, by surface friction, land topography, the Earth's rotation and other factors.

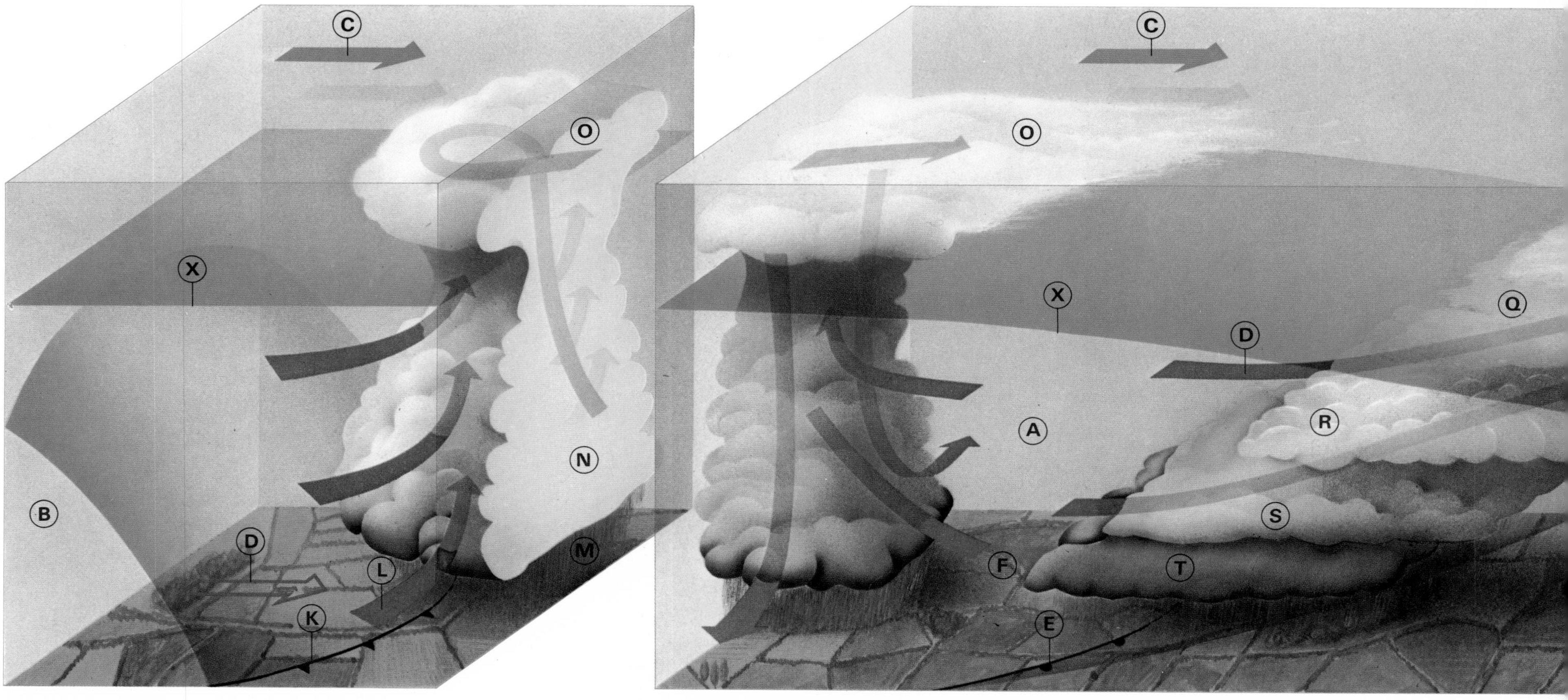

A
B
C
D
E
F
K
L
M
N
O
Q
R
S
T
X

Anatomy of a depression
Seen in cross section, a mature mid-latitude cyclone forms a large system which always follows basically the same pattern. Essentially it comprises a wedge of warm air (A) riding over, and being undercut by, cold air masses (B). (Page 30 shows full development.) The entire cyclone is moving from left to right, and this is also the basic direction of the winds (C) and (D). To an observer on the ground the warm front (E) may take 12-24 hours to pass, followed by the warm sector (F) perhaps 180 miles (300 km) wide.

The cold front (K)
As this frontal zone, about one mile (1-2 km) wide, passes overhead the direction of the wind alters (L) and precipitation (M) pours from cumuliform clouds (N). If the air above the frontal surface is moving upwards then giant cumulonimbus (O) may grow, with heavy rain or hail. Cirrus clouds then form in air above the freezing level (X). Sometimes the front is weak with subsidence of air predominant on both sides of it. In this case there is little cloud development and near-zero surface precipitation.

The warm front (E)
The front is first heralded by cirrus clouds (P), followed by cirrostratus (Q), altocumulus (R), stratus (S) and finally nimbostratus (T). The descending layers are due partly to humidity distribution and partly to the warm air rising over the sloping frontal surface. Precipitation may be steady and last for hours. Alternatively some warm fronts have a predominantly subsident air motion, with the result that there is only a little thin cloud and negligible precipitation. Air temperature increases as the front passes.

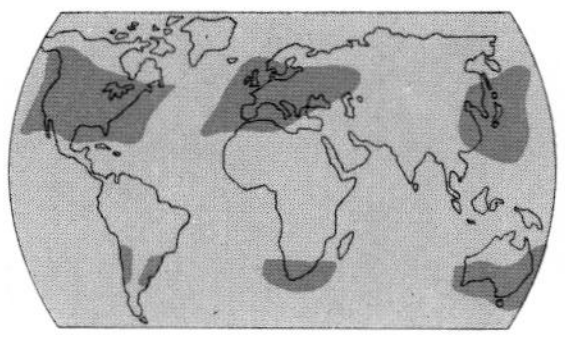

Development of a depression *right*
Most mid-latitude depressions (cyclones) develop on the polar front (map above). An initial disturbance along this front causes a fall in pressure and a confluence at the surface, deforming the front into a wave (1, right). The confluence and thermal structure accelerate the cyclonic spin into a fully developed depression (2). The depression comprises a warm sector bounded by a sharp cold front (A) and warm front (B). The fast-moving cold front overtakes the warm front and eventually the warm sector is lifted completely clear of the ground resulting in an occlusion (3). The continued overlapping of the two wedges of cold air eventually fills up the depression and causes it to weaken and disperse (4). By the time this occurs the warm sector has been lifted high in the atmosphere. In this way, depressions fulfil an essential role in transferring heat from low to high levels and from low to high latitudes.

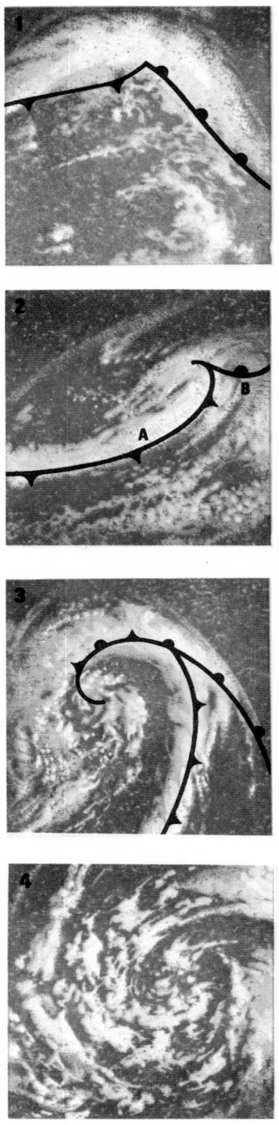

1
2
A
B
3
4

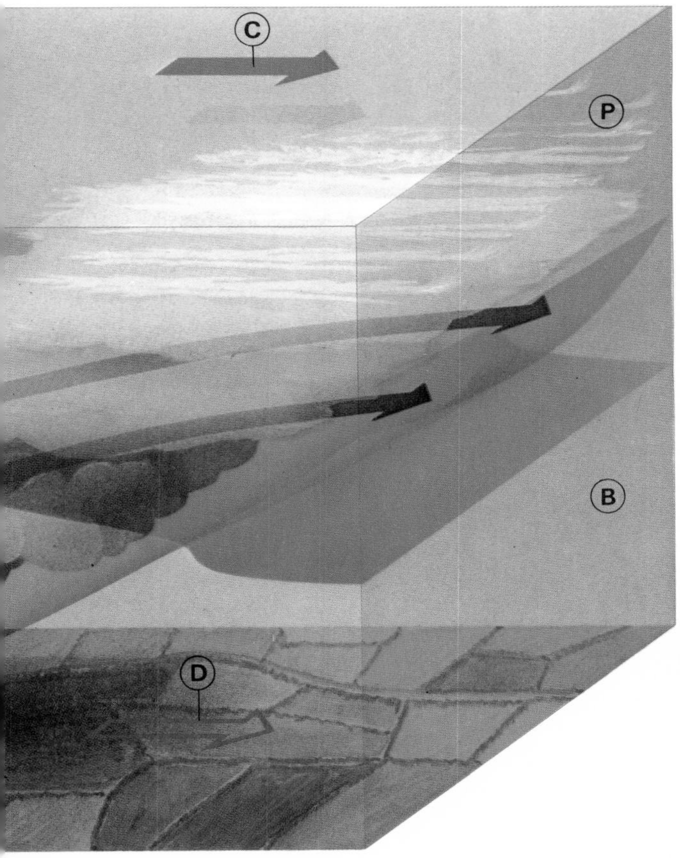

C
P
B
D

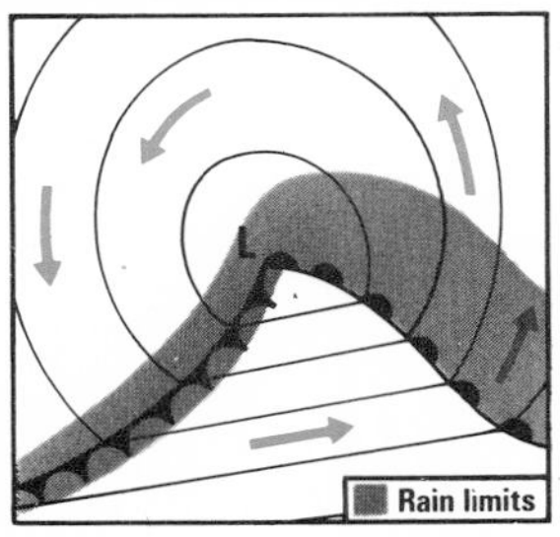

L
Rain limits

Plan view *left*
A developing cyclone will appear this way on the 'synoptic' weather chart. Lines of equal pressure (isobars) are nearly straight within the warm sector but curve sharply in the cold sector to enclose the low pressure focus of the system.

Examples of the three major cloud groups

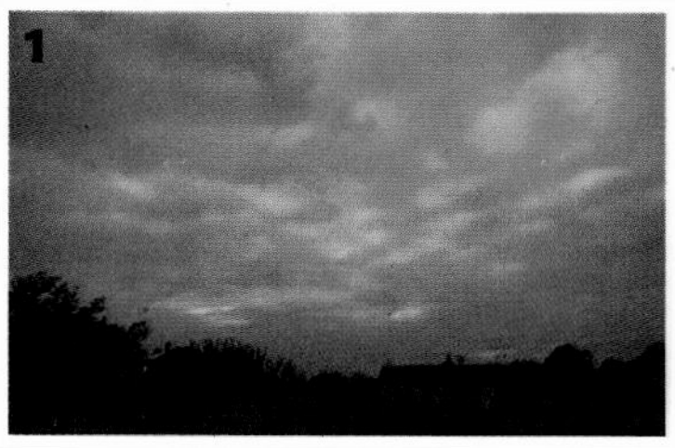

1

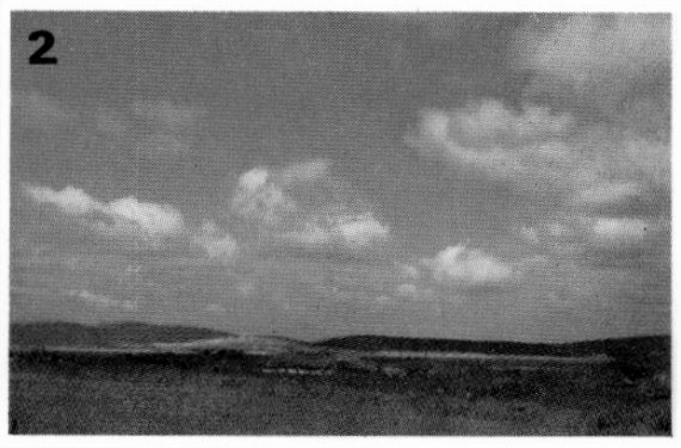

2

3

4

Low cloud *top*
Stratocumulus (1) is a grey or white layer of serried masses or rolls. Cumulus (2) is the familiar white cauliflower. It can develop into cumulonimbus (3), a large, threatening cloud, characterized by immense vertical development topped by an 'anvil' of ice crystals. These produce heavy rain or hail.

7

5

Medium cloud *left*
Nimbostratus (4) is a ragged grey layer producing drizzle or snow. Altocumulus (5) comprises rows of 'blobs' of ice and water forming a sheet at a height of 1.5-4.5 miles (2-7 km). Altostratus (6) occurs at similar heights but is a water/ice sheet either uniform, striated or fibrous in appearance.

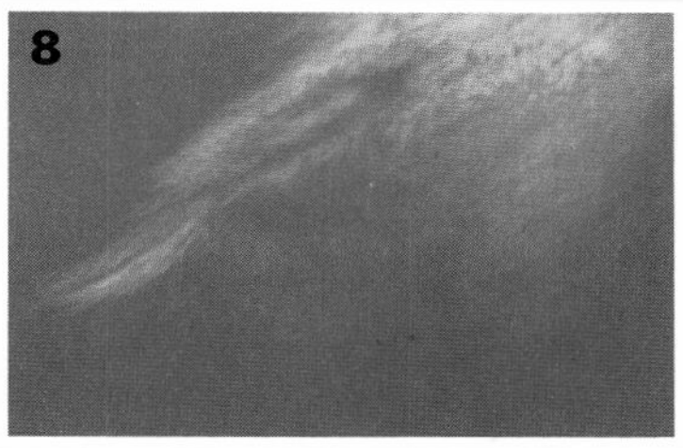

8

6

High cloud *right*
Cirrus (7) is the highest cloud and appears as fine white ice filaments at 8–10 miles (13–16 km), often hair-like or silky. Cirro-cumulus (8) forms into thin white layers made up of very numerous icy globules or ripples. Cirrostratus (9) is a high-level veil of ice crystals often forming a halo round the Sun.

9

Four kinds of precipitation

Rain
Most rain results from the coalescence of microscopic droplets (1) which are condensed from vapor onto nuclei in the atmosphere. The repeated merging of small droplets eventually forms water droplets (2) which are too large to be kept up by the air currents. Rain drops may also form from melting of ice crystals in the atmosphere.

Glaze
In completely undisturbed air it is possible for water to remain liquid even at temperatures well below freezing point. So air above the freezing level (X) may contain large quantities of this 'supercooled water'. This can fall as rain and freeze on impact with objects, coating them with ice.

Dry snow
The origin of snow differs from that of rain in that the vapor droplets (1) settle on microscopic crystals of ice and freeze. The result is the growth of a white or translucent ice crystal having a basically hexagonal form (photomicrograph below). The crystals then agglomerate into flakes (2).

Hail
In cumulonimbus clouds raindrops (formed at 1,2) may encounter up-currents strong enough to lift them repeatedly back through a freezing level (X). On each pass (3) a fresh layer of ice is collected. The hailstone builds up like an onion until it is so heavy (4) that it falls to the ground.

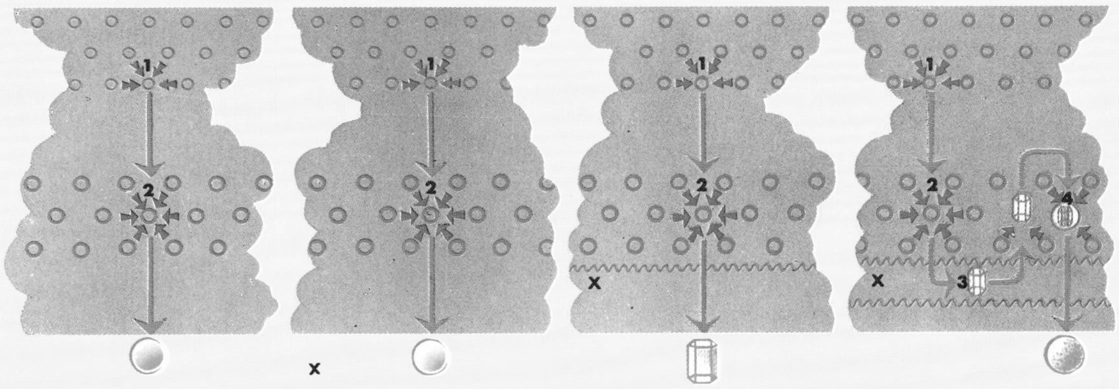

1
2
X
3
4

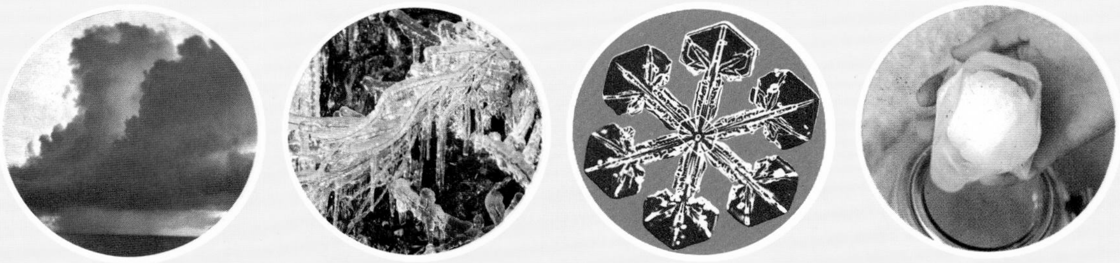

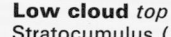

Extremes of Weather

Tropical weather, between the Tropic of Cancer at 23½°N and the Tropic of Capricorn at 23½°S, differs fundamentally from that at higher latitudes. Overall there is a considerable surplus of heat, giving high mean temperatures; and the 'Coriolis force' due to the Earth's rotation, which deflects air currents to the right in the northern hemisphere and to the left in the southern, is almost non-existent. As a result, tropical weather hardly ever contains distinct air masses, fronts and cyclones. Instead the region is occupied mainly by the tradewinds, which are laden with moisture and potentially unstable. Thunderstorms are frequent, especially over land, and the pattern of land and sea leads to local anomalies, such as the monsoon of southeast Asia. This particular anomaly, too big to be called local, changes the prevailing wind over a vast area. It is superimposed on the apparently simple global circulation near the Equator.

Polar weather

At very high latitudes the atmosphere radiates heat to space. The Arctic is essentially an ocean surrounded by land, whereas the Antarctic is land surrounded by ocean. The land around the Arctic quickly takes up solar heat but the southern oceans transfer heat to deeper water to make the Antarctic the coldest region on Earth. Because the air is so intensely cold it can hold very little moisture, so the south polar region is a freezing desert with exceptionally clean air.

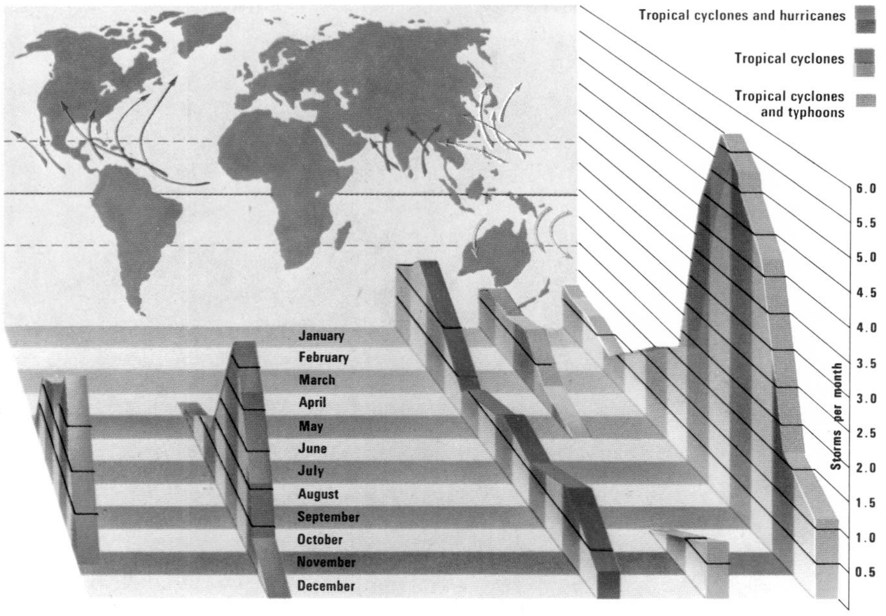

Tropical cyclones and hurricanes
Tropical cyclones
Tropical cyclones and typhoons
January
February
March
April
May
June
July
August
September
October
November
December
Storms per month
6.0
5.5
5.0
4.5
4.0
3.5
3.0
2.5
2.0
1.5
1.0
0.5

The afflicted areas *above*
Tropical cyclones build up over the warm oceans, and many of them—about half over the Caribbean and four-fifths over the western Pacific—develop into hurricanes. Precisely how a hurricane is triggered is still not fully known, but there is no doubt it is a thermodynamic engine on a giant scale which either misfires completely or runs with catastrophic effect.

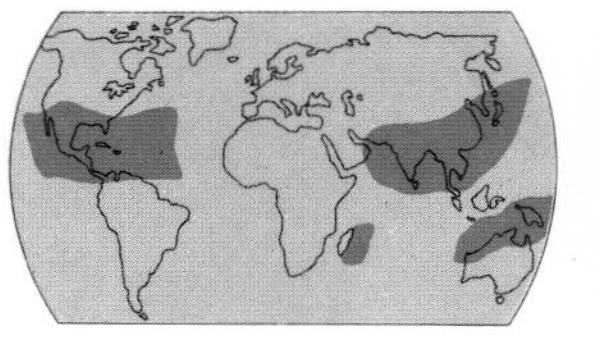

Hurricanes *left*
These violent storms form over ocean warm enough (27°C) to maintain strong vertical circulation, except for the belt closest to the equator where lack of a Coriolis force prevents cyclonic spin from building up. Condensation of the moisture taken up from the ocean surface releases latent heat and thus provides energy to drive the storm. The daily energy can be equivalent to that released by several hundred H bombs. Despite their formidable power hurricanes are penetrated by specially equipped aircraft whose mission is both to provide early warning and to gather data enabling the storm's mechanism to be better understood.

Hurricane structure
A Spiral rainbands.
B High-altitude winds.
C Easterly tradewinds.

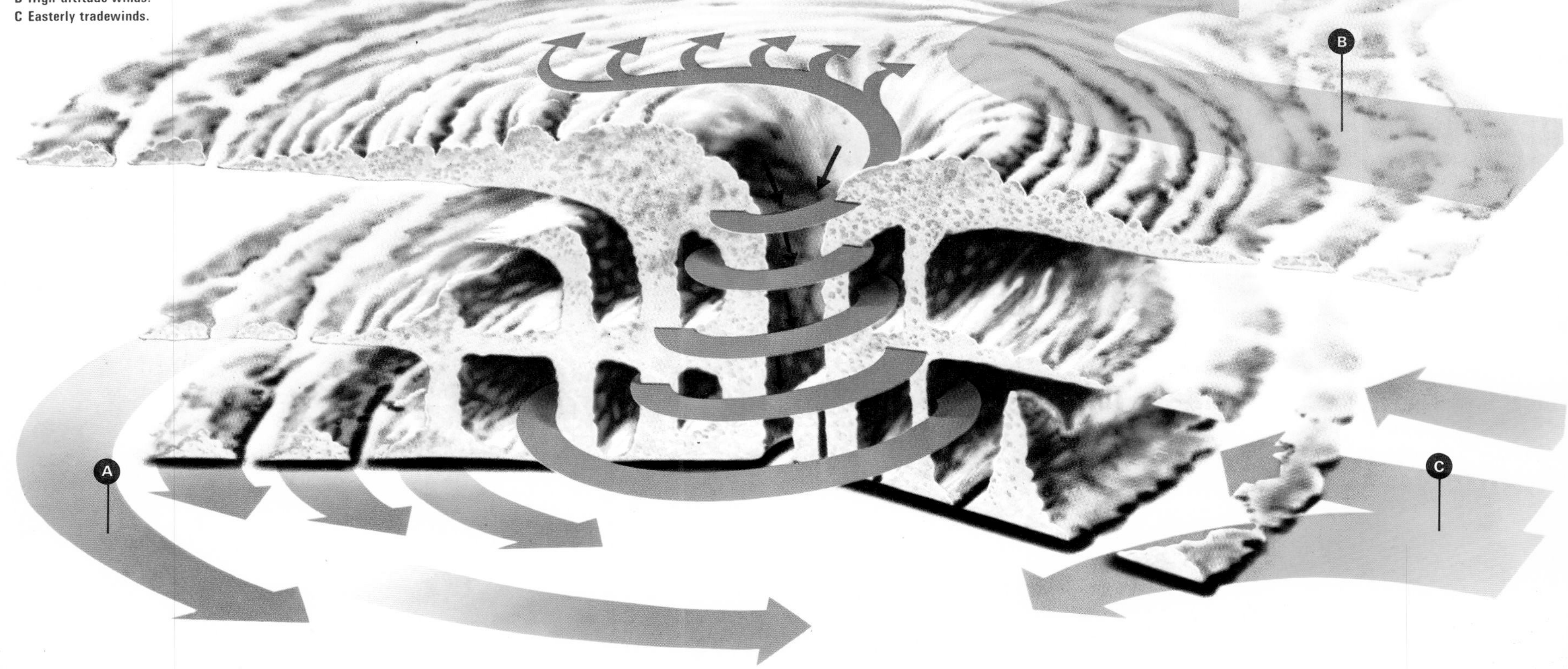

A
B
C

Structure of a hurricane *above*
A hurricane consists of a huge swirl of clouds rotating around a calm center known as the eye. This cyclonic circulation may be as much as 250 miles (400 km) in diameter, and it extends right through the troposphere which is about 9-12 miles (15-20 km) thick. The clouds, nearly all of the cumulonimbus type, are arranged in bands around the eye. The largest form the wall of the eye and it is here that precipitation is heaviest. The whole system is usually capped by streamers of cirrus. Wind speeds range from about 110 mph (180 kmh) at 20–25 miles (30–40 km) from the eye wall down to about 45 mph (72 kmh) at a distance of 90 miles (140 km). Warm, calm air in the eye is sucked downwards.

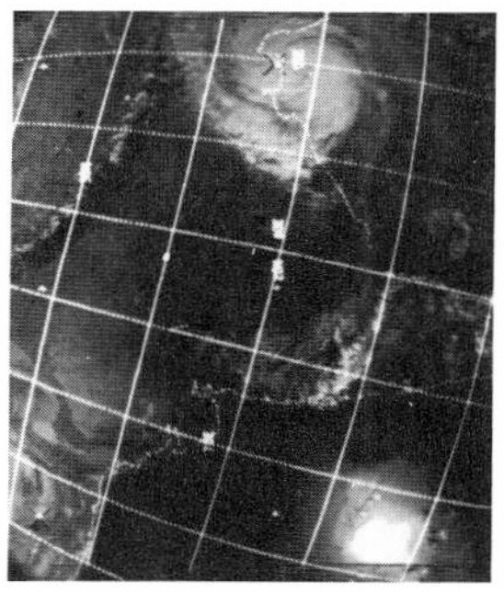

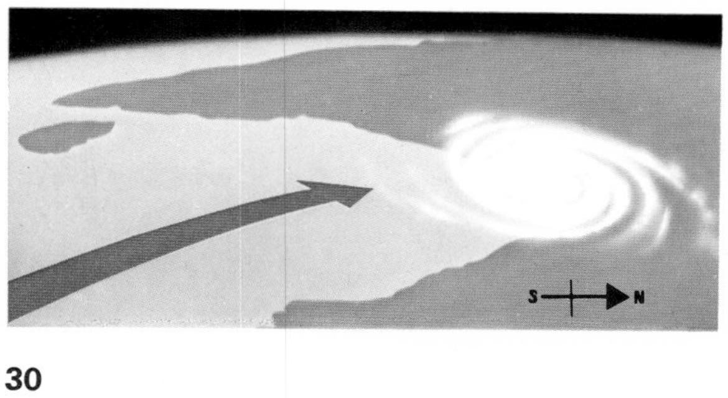

S N

Nature's giant energy *left and above*
A hurricane such as that which killed over half a million people in East Pakistan in November 1970 (left) dissipates thousands of millions of horsepower. The spiral structure is clearly visible from a satellite (above).

Hurricane development *below*

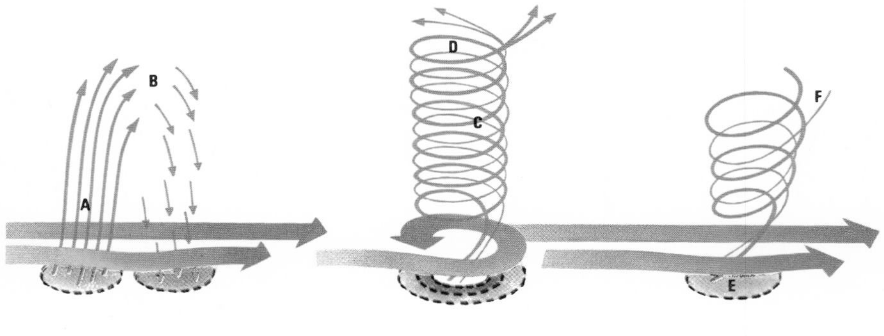

A
B
C
D
E
F

Birth of a storm.
Hurricanes usually have their origin in a low-pressure disturbance directing part of an easterly wind (A) to the north. The air rises to some 40,000 ft (12 km) where it releases heat and moisture (B) before descending.

The young hurricane
The Earth's rotation imparts a twist to the rising column which becomes a cylinder (C) spiralling round a relatively still core (D). Warm, moist air off the sea picks up speed and feeds energy at a very high rate to intensify the rising column.

Dying of starvation
The hurricane does not begin to die until it moves over colder water or over land (E). Then, cut off from its supply of energy, the speed of the spiralling winds falls away. The eye begins to fill with clouds, the hurricane expands (F) and dissipates.

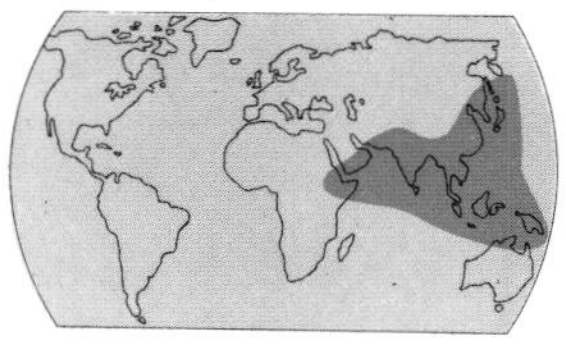

The monsoon *right*
In principle the processes which give rise to the monsoon are the same as those causing a sea breeze but on a vastly larger scale in space and time. In southeast Asia each May and June warm, moist air streams in from the south causing heavy rain and occasional violent storms. In winter the circulation is reversed and winds come mainly from high pressure over Siberia. In detail the monsoon is considerably modified by the Himalayas and the positions of the waves in the westerlies in the atmosphere's upper levels, but its mechanism is not fully known.

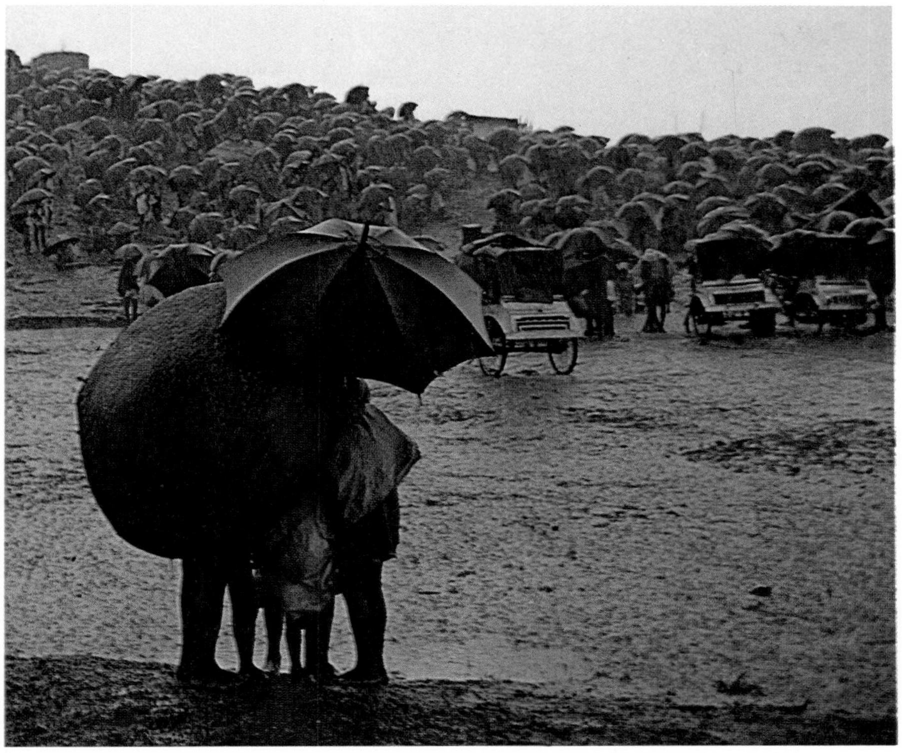

The monsoon seasons *below*
In summer an intense low-pressure area over northwest India overcomes the equatorial low pressure region. In winter an intense high over central Asia blows cold, dry air in the reverse direction.

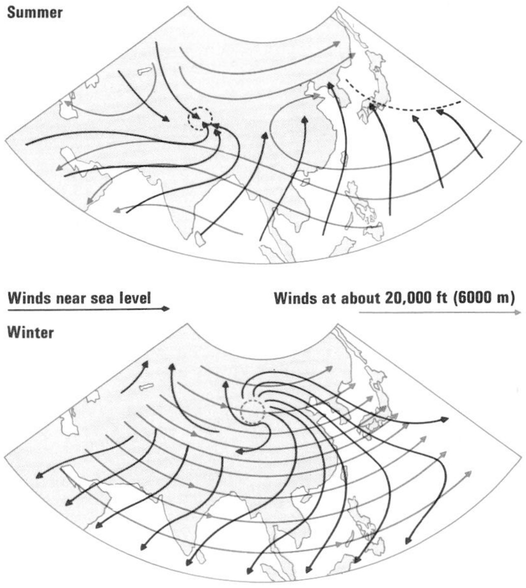
Summer
Winds near sea level
Winds at about 20,000 ft (6000 m)
Winter

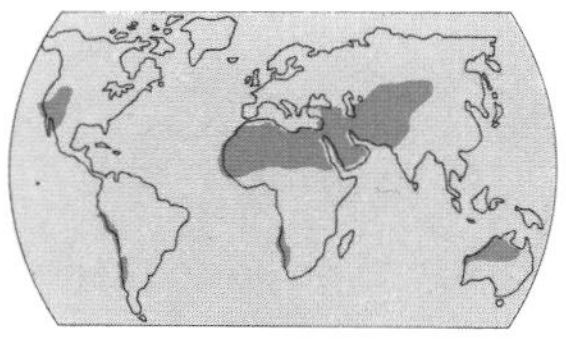

Duststorm *right*
In arid regions strong wind circulations can become filled with dust and extend over considerable areas. The storm typically arrives in the form of an advancing wall of dust possibly five miles (8 km) long and 1000 ft (300 m) high. The haboobs of the Sudan, a recurrent series of storms, are most frequent from May to September and can approach from almost any direction. They usually occur, after a few days of rising temperature and falling pressure, where the soil is very dry. Dust-devils, small local whirlwinds forming pillars of sand, can dot the land.

Flash flood *below*
In historic times floods have drowned millions. Even in a modern advanced country a major flood is a national disaster. The scene below is a flooded crossing on the road from Lake Grace to Dumbleyung, W Australia. It is a 'flash flood', caused by heavy rain and poor drainage.

After the hurricane *left*
Whereas a tornado can cause buildings to explode, as a result of the sudden violent difference in pressure between inside and outside, a hurricane just blows. But the wind can demolish sound houses, such as this residence in Biloxi, Mississippi.

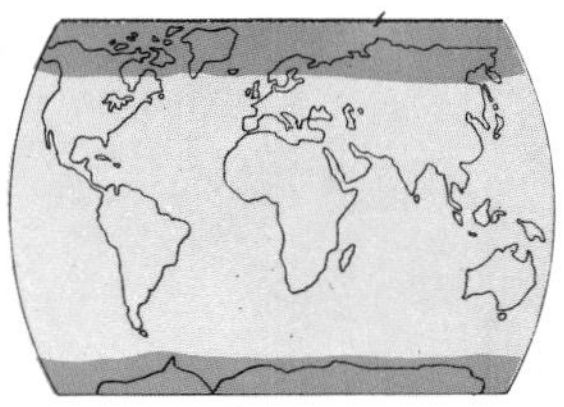

Nacreous cloud *right*
At high latitudes, when the Sun is below the horizon, these clouds sometimes come into view as fine filmy areas containing regions of bright spectral color. They look rather like a form of cirrus, but are far higher. Nacreous cloud in the Antarctic—such as that in the photograph, taken in Grahamland—has been measured at heights from 8.5 to 19 miles (13.5-30 km), and Scandinavian observations lie in the 20-30 km range. Despite their great altitude, nacreous clouds are undoubtedly formed as a result of air being lifted by passage across high mountains.

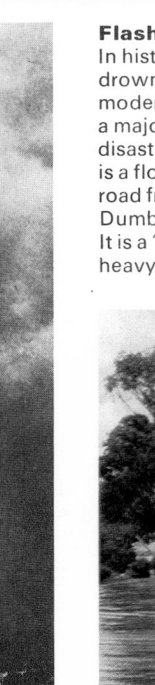

Blown snow *above*
When the wind blows in polar regions it soon begins to lift dry powdery snow and ice granules from the surface. As the wind increases in strength this drifting snow forms a thicker layer, as at this British base in Antarctica. When the entrained material reaches eye level it is known as blown snow. Any further rise in wind velocity swiftly increases the concentration of particulate matter, causing the visibility rapidly to fall to zero. When this is the case the term blizzard is appropriate, as it also is when high winds are combined with a heavy snowfall.

The Active Oceans

The surface of the oceans presents an infinite variety of contrasts ranging from glassy calm to terrifying storms with towering waves and wind-whipped wraiths of spray. But no part of the oceans is ever really still. Together the oceans comprise 300 million cubic miles (1250 million km^3) of ever-active water. The whole mass ebbs and flows on a global scale with the tides. The surface is disturbed by winds into great patterns of waves which eventually break on the shores of the land. And the largest and most far-reaching movements of all are the ocean currents, some on or near the surface and others at great depths, which profoundly alter not only the oceans but also the weather.

Best known of all these currents is the Gulf Stream, which was discovered in late medieval times when early navigators found that their ships were consistently not in the place predicted by their calculations of course and estimated speed. Some 500 years ago it had become customary for Spanish captains voyaging to the New World to keep well south of the Gulf Stream on their outward journey and then use its swift four or five knot (8–9 km/hr) current to help them along on the return. The Gulf Stream brings mild weather to northwest Europe, and a corresponding role is played on the other side of the globe by the Kuroshio, a warm current which flows northeastward off Japan. Conversely, in the southeastern Pacific the Peru Current brings cold water from the sub-Antarctic region northward towards the equator. The surface flow is accompanied during most months of the year by an 'upwelling' of water rich in nutrients along the coast of Chile and Peru, and this, like many other cold currents elsewhere, supports great fisheries.

In coastal seas the water movements are often dominated by the currents that accompany the rise and fall of the tide. Because of the friction of the tides, the Moon is moving slowly further from the Earth.

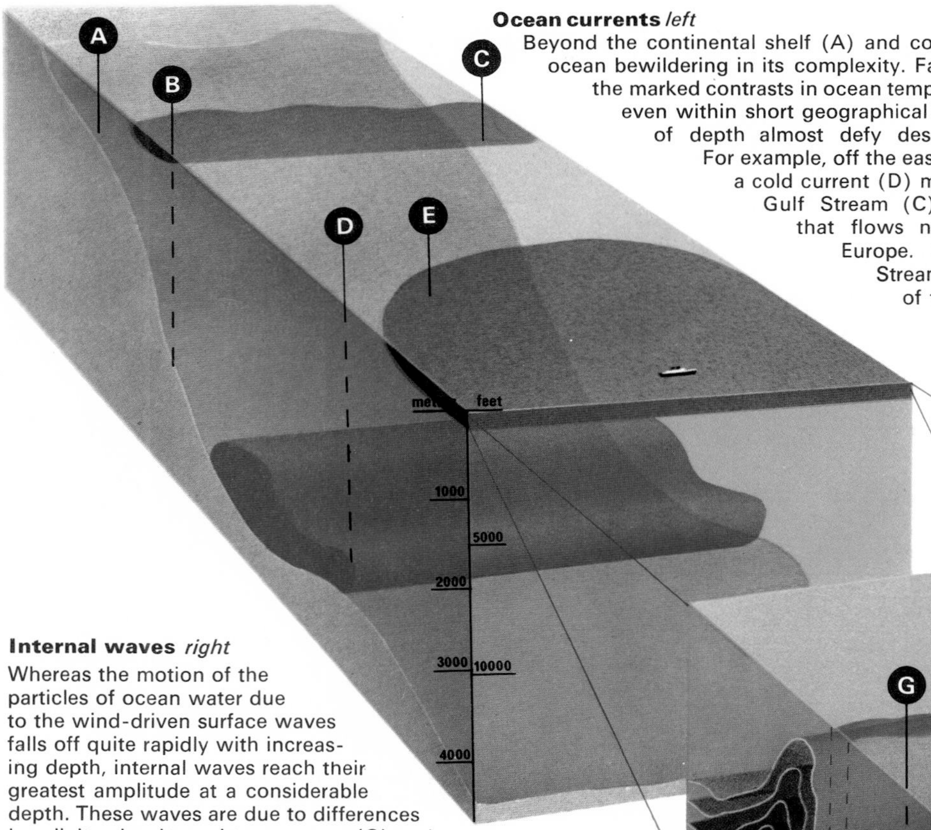
A
B
C
D
E
metres
feet
1000
5000
2000
3000
10000
4000

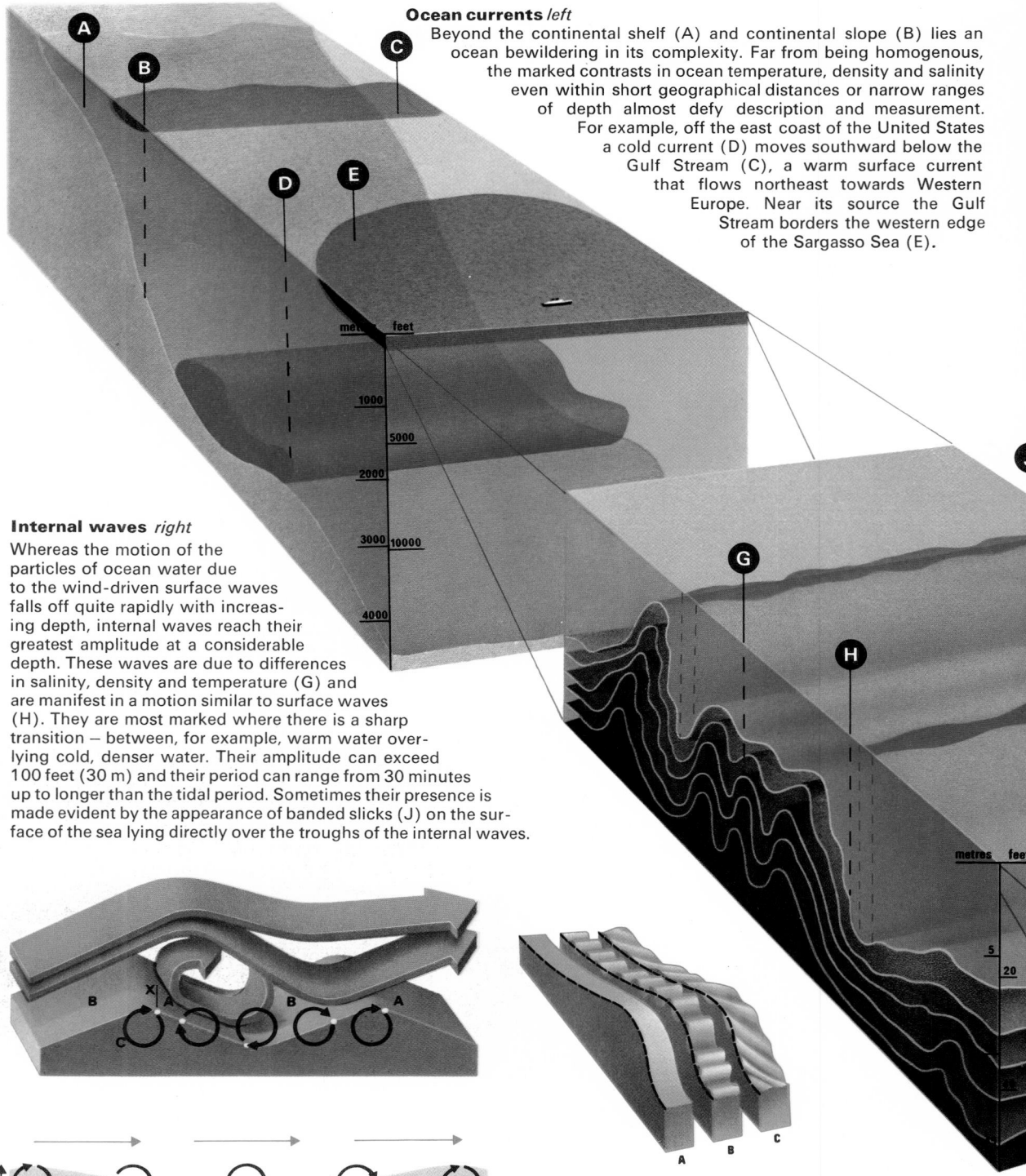

Ocean currents *left*
Beyond the continental shelf (A) and continental slope (B) lies an ocean bewildering in its complexity. Far from being homogenous, the marked contrasts in ocean temperature, density and salinity even within short geographical distances or narrow ranges of depth almost defy description and measurement. For example, off the east coast of the United States a cold current (D) moves southward below the Gulf Stream (C), a warm surface current that flows northeast towards Western Europe. Near its source the Gulf Stream borders the western edge of the Sargasso Sea (E).

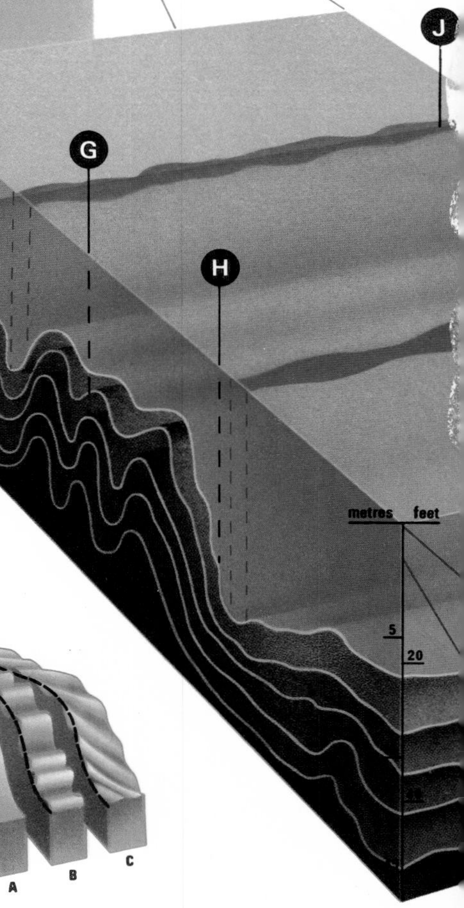
J
G
H
metres
feet
5
20

Internal waves *right*
Whereas the motion of the particles of ocean water due to the wind-driven surface waves falls off quite rapidly with increasing depth, internal waves reach their greatest amplitude at a considerable depth. These waves are due to differences in salinity, density and temperature (G) and are manifest in a motion similar to surface waves (H). They are most marked where there is a sharp transition – between, for example, warm water overlying cold, denser water. Their amplitude can exceed 100 feet (30 m) and their period can range from 30 minutes up to longer than the tidal period. Sometimes their presence is made evident by the appearance of banded slicks (J) on the surface of the sea lying directly over the troughs of the internal waves.

Wave generation *right*
Waves are generated on the surface by the wind. Once a slight undulation has been formed it will react on the air flow so that an eddying motion, with a reduced pressure, is produced on the lee side (A) of each crest. Combined with the wind pressure on the windward side (B), this causes the waves to grow in height. The wave travels forward in the direction of the wind, but the individual water particles (X) move in almost closed orbits (C).

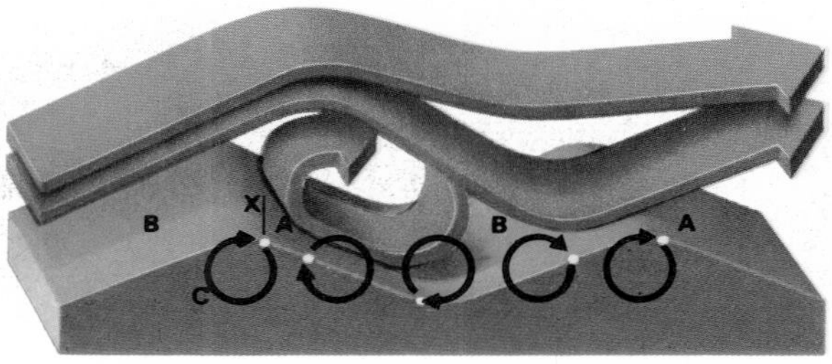
B
X
A
C
B
A

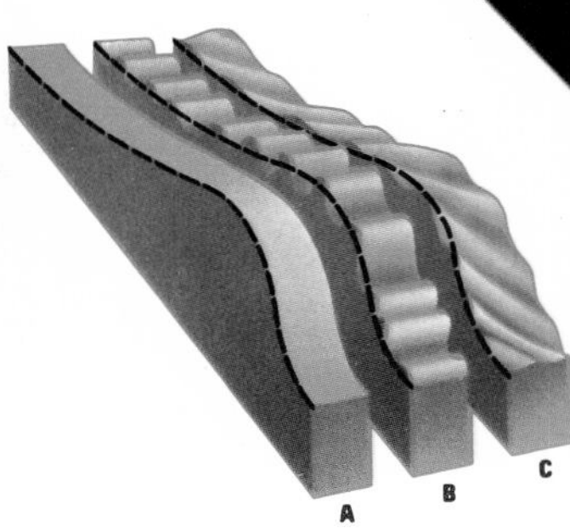
A
B
C

Internal motion *right*
On the surface of deep water these orbits are almost circular. Below the surface the radii of the orbits decrease with depth and become very small at a depth equal to half a wavelength. In shallow water the orbits are ellipses, becoming flatter towards the bottom.

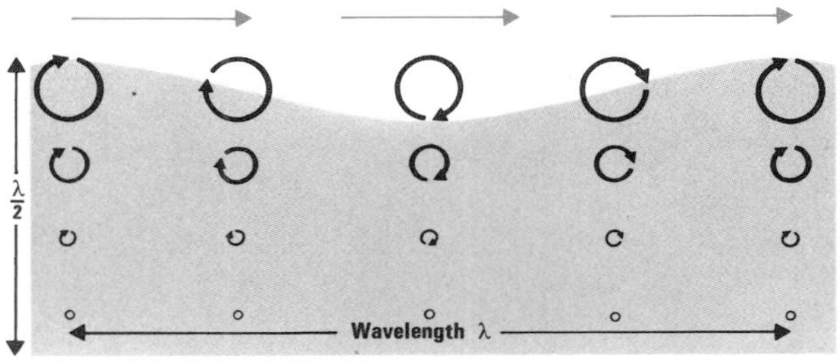
λ/2
Wavelength λ

Waves and swell *above*
Ocean swell (A) is invariably present and travels hundreds of miles. On it the wind can superimpose small waves (B), which die out relatively rapidly. These smaller waves may be at any angle to the original swell (C).

Shore and rip currents *below*
In addition to its circular movement, each water particle slowly moves in the direction of propagation. When waves approach a coast water tends to pile up at the shoreline. This leads to a return flow seaward (X) which is concentrated in narrow, fast-flowing rip currents (Y). Beyond the breaker zone these spread out into a head and gradually disperse (Z).

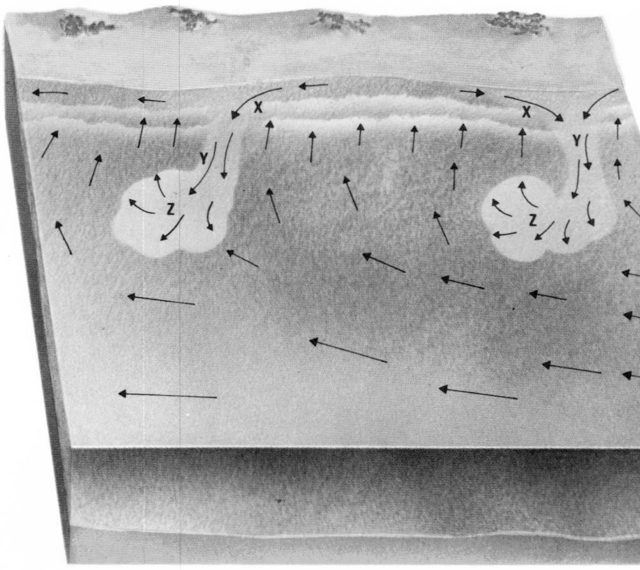
X
X
Y
Y
Z
Z

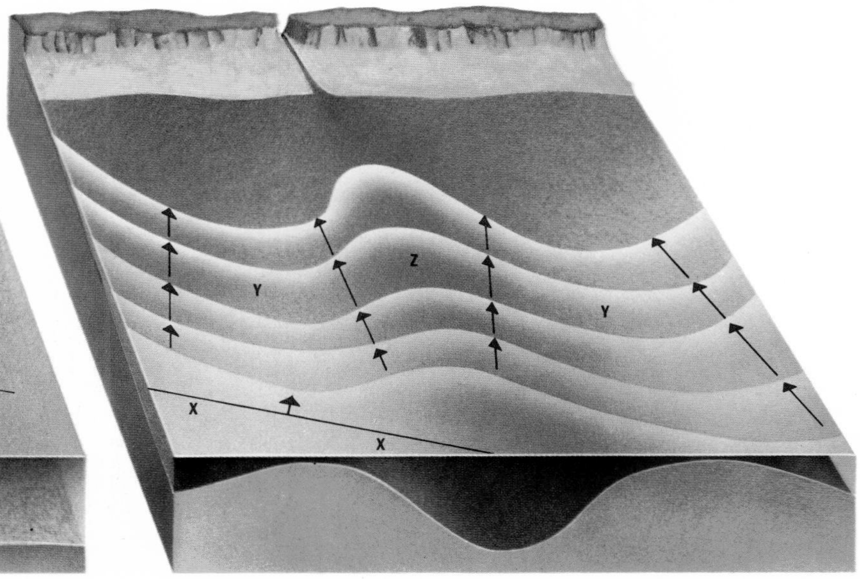
Z
Y
Y
X
X

Change of wave front *left, below*
When waves from the open sea pass into a region of shallow water where the depth is less than about half a wavelength their forward velocity is progressively reduced. One consequence of this is that the wave fronts are refracted so that they turn towards the shallower water, and the wave crests tend to line up parallel to the shore. In the diagram X-X is the original frontal axis of the waves coming in from the ocean. When the depth of water varies along a coast, waves tend to become focused on the shallower areas (Y) and to diverge from the deeper ones such as the head of a submarine valley or canyon (Z). For the same reason large waves can often be seen breaking on a headland while the breakers in an area of originally deeper water, leading to a bay, are relatively much smaller.

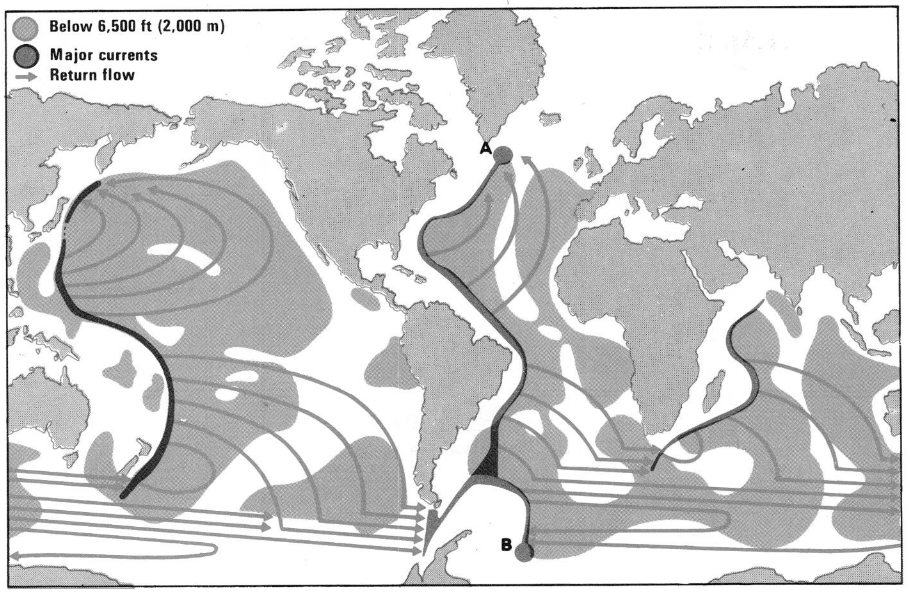
Below 6,500 ft (2,000 m)
Major currents
Return flow
A
B

Surface currents *right*
The pattern in which ocean currents flow results from several factors – friction or drag between prevailing winds and water; differences in density of water; 'Coriolis effect' of Earth's rotation; position and configuration of land masses. Trade winds in tropical latitudes (between X and Y), and westerlies farther poleward are the most significant winds that affect broad current circulation patterns (A and B). Along the eastern coast of North America the Gulf Stream is 30 to 50 miles (50-80 km) wide and flows at speeds up to 5 to 6 knots (9-11 Kmh).

A
X
B
Y

Deep ocean currents *above*
The deep layers of the oceans, below about 6500 feet (2000 m), are filled with dense, cold water which has been formed by cooling and then sinking in the polar regions. Nearly all of this deep water is formed in one of two areas: the Labrador Sea and Greenland area of the North Atlantic (A) and the Weddell Sea in the Antarctic (B). The above diagram shows in a simplified form how the water from these two regions spreads out to fill all the Earth's deep ocean basins.

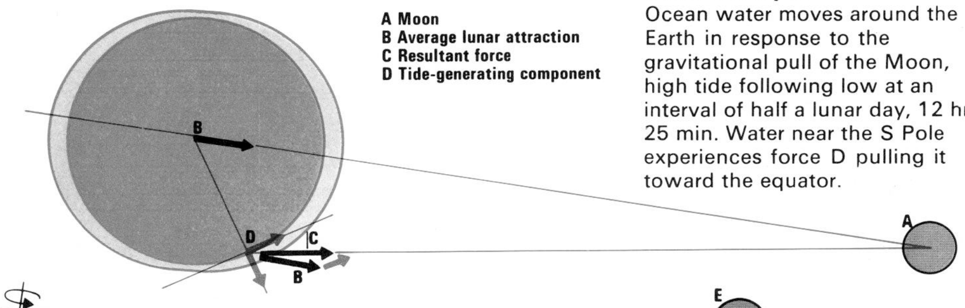
A Moon
B Average lunar attraction
C Resultant force
D Tide-generating component

Tidal theory *left*
Ocean water moves around the Earth in response to the gravitational pull of the Moon, high tide following low at an interval of half a lunar day, 12 hr 25 min. Water near the S Pole experiences force D pulling it toward the equator.

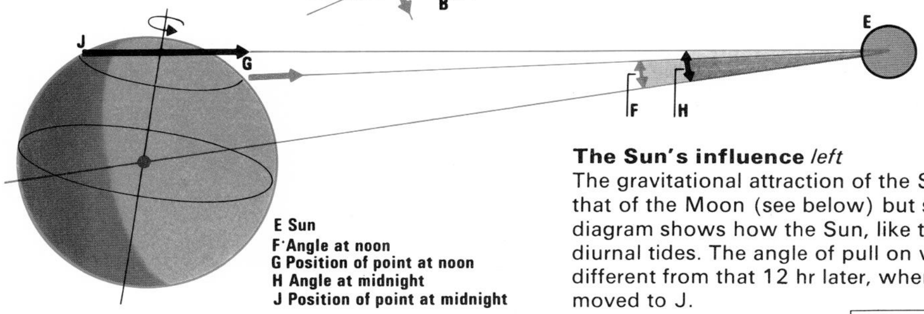
E Sun
F Angle at noon
G Position of point at noon
H Angle at midnight
J Position of point at midnight

The Sun's influence *left*
The gravitational attraction of the Sun is weaker than that of the Moon (see below) but still significant. This diagram shows how the Sun, like the Moon, causes diurnal tides. The angle of pull on water at G is quite different from that 12 hr later, when the water has moved to J.

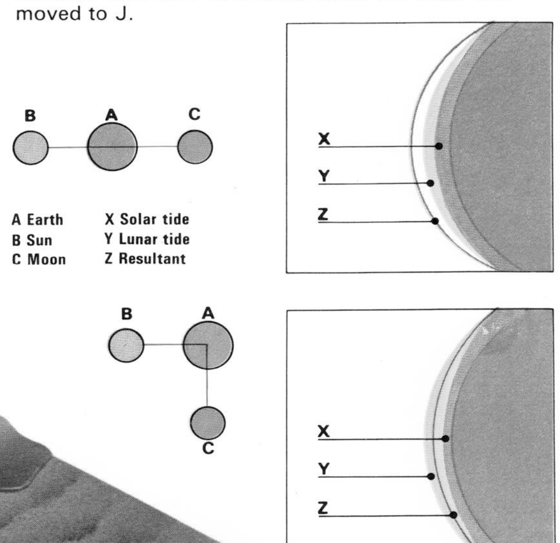
A Earth
B Sun
C Moon
X Solar tide
Y Lunar tide
Z Resultant

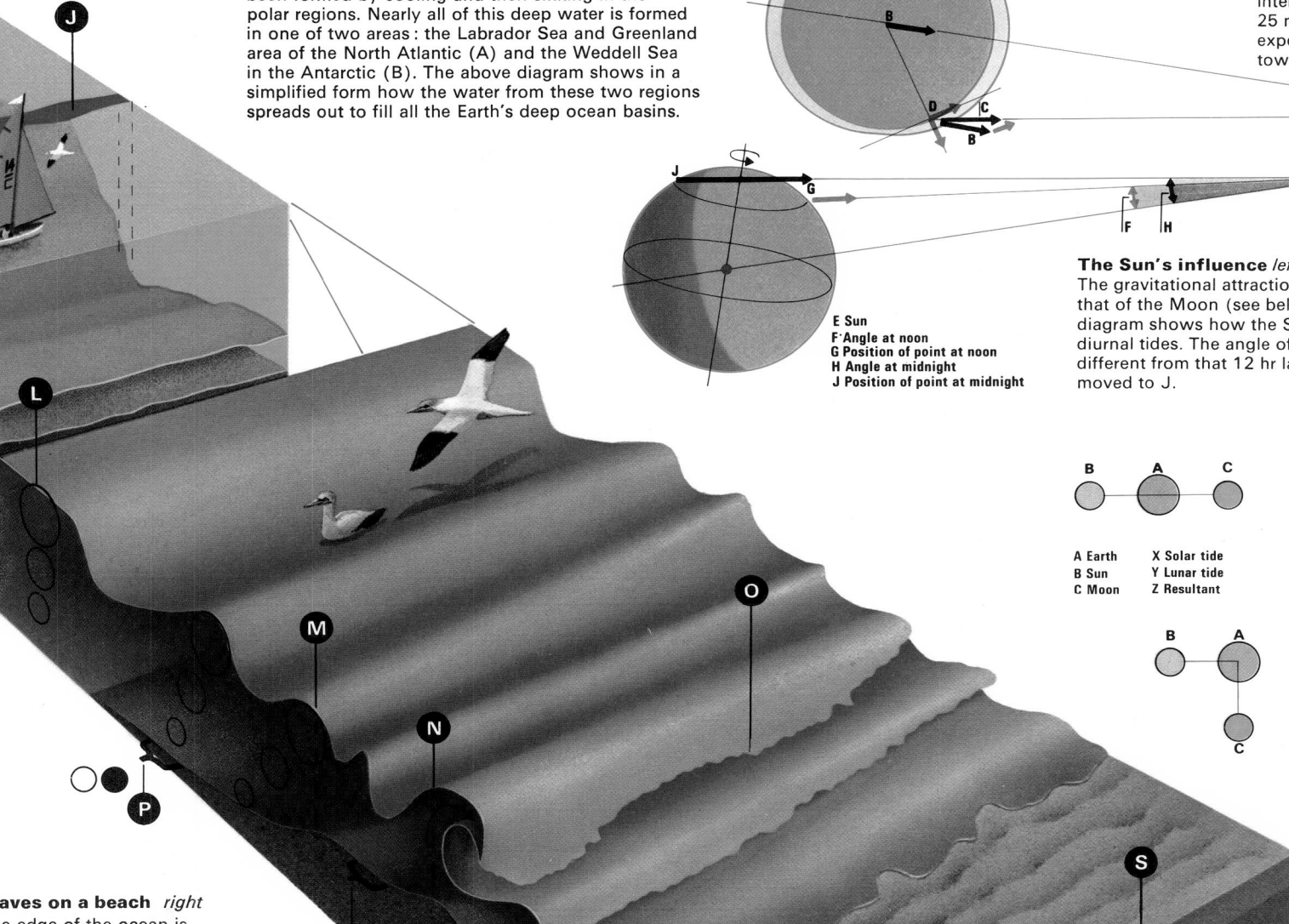

Neap and spring tides *above*
The Sun (B) also gives rise to a gravitational force which affects the Earth's waters but, because of its much greater distance, its attraction is less than half as powerful. When the solar and lunar tides reinforce one another, as they do near new and full Moon, the high spring tides (upper figure) result. Neap tides occur near the Moon's first and third quarters when the solar and lunar effects are out of phase. In coastal seas many tidal variations result from the individual response of each body of water.

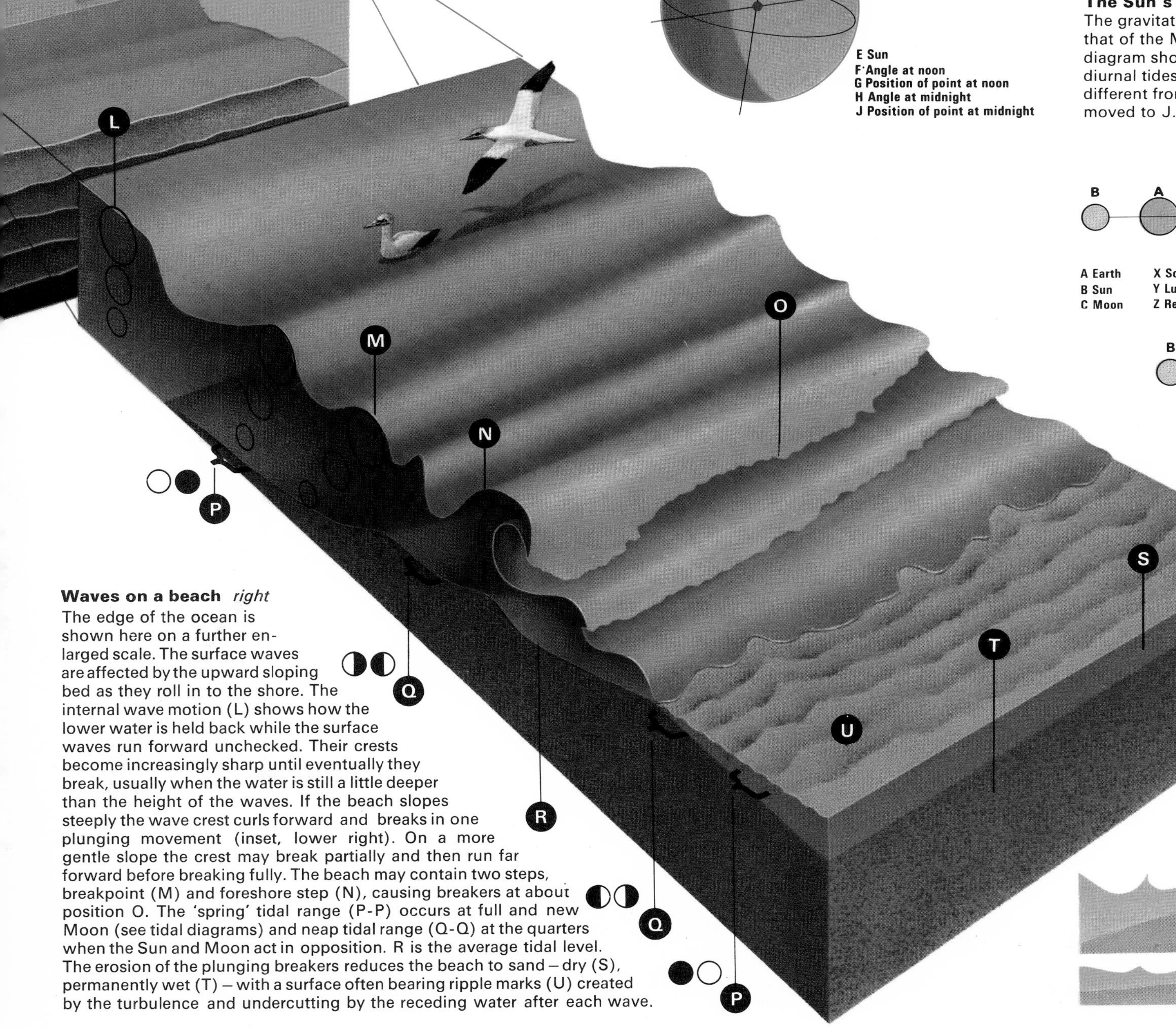
J
L
M
N
O
P
Q
R
S
T
U

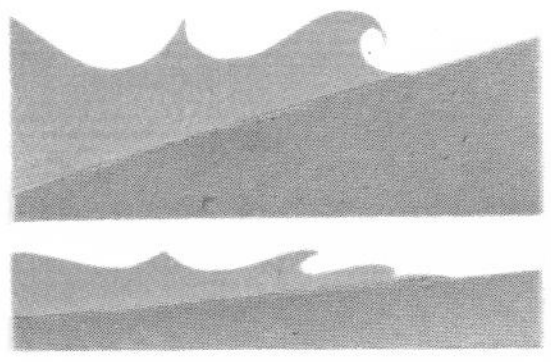

Waves on a beach *right*
The edge of the ocean is shown here on a further enlarged scale. The surface waves are affected by the upward sloping bed as they roll in to the shore. The internal wave motion (L) shows how the lower water is held back while the surface waves run forward unchecked. Their crests become increasingly sharp until eventually they break, usually when the water is still a little deeper than the height of the waves. If the beach slopes steeply the wave crest curls forward and breaks in one plunging movement (inset, lower right). On a more gentle slope the crest may break partially and then run far forward before breaking fully. The beach may contain two steps, breakpoint (M) and foreshore step (N), causing breakers at about position O. The 'spring' tidal range (P-P) occurs at full and new Moon (see tidal diagrams) and neap tidal range (Q-Q) at the quarters when the Sun and Moon act in opposition. R is the average tidal level. The erosion of the plunging breakers reduces the beach to sand – dry (S), permanently wet (T) – with a surface often bearing ripple marks (U) created by the turbulence and undercutting by the receding water after each wave.

The Earth under the Sea

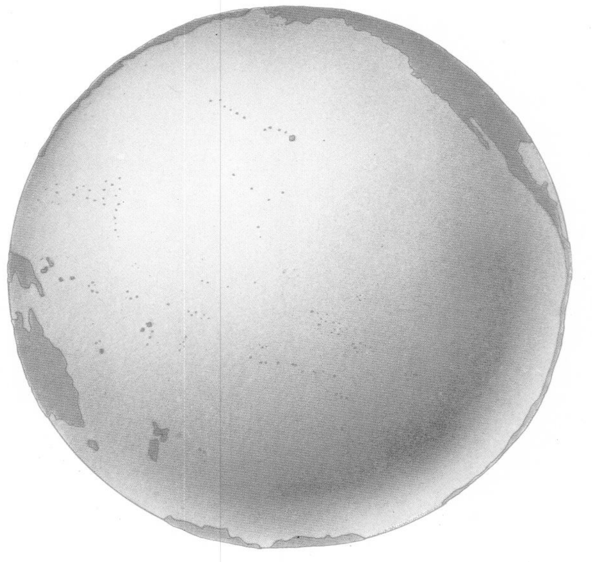

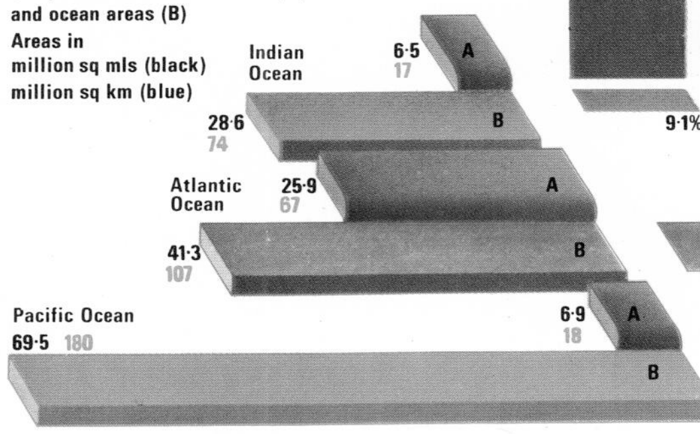
Comparison of drained areas. (A)
and ocean areas (B)
Areas in
million sq mls (black)
million sq km (blue)
Indian Ocean
6·5
17
A
28·6
74
B
Atlantic Ocean
25·9
67
A
41·3
107
B
Pacific Ocean
69·5 180
6·9
18
A
B

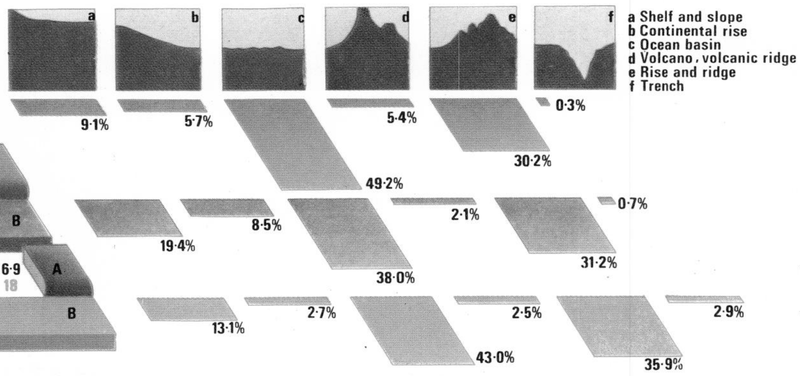
a
b
c
d
e
f
a Shelf and slope
b Continental rise
c Ocean basin
d Volcano, volcanic ridge
e Rise and ridge
f Trench
9·1%
5·7%
49·2%
5·4%
30·2%
0·3%
19·4%
8·5%
38·0%
2·1%
31·2%
0·7%
13·1%
2·7%
43·0%
2·5%
35·9%
2·9%

The water planet *left*
From directly over Tahiti the Earth appears to be covered by water. The Pacific averages 2.5 miles (4 km) deep, with great mountains and trenches.

Ocean drainage *above*
The ratio between the areas of the oceans and the land they drain varies greatly. Many large rivers feed the Atlantic but few discharge into the Pacific.

Ocean proportions *above*
The major oceans show a similarity in the proportions of their submarine topography. By far the greatest areas contain deep plains with rises and ridges. More prominent features, the mid-ocean volcanic ridges and trenches, occupy much smaller areas. About one tenth of each ocean is continental shelf.

At present the sea covers about 71 per cent of the Earth's surface. But if the continents could be sliced away and put into the deep oceans to make a perfectly uniform sphere the sea would have an average depth of about 8000 feet (2500 m) over the whole planet. In the distant past the level of the sea has fluctuated violently. The main cause has been the comings and goings of the ice ages. Glaciers and ice-caps lock up enormous volumes of water and the advance and recession of ice has alternately covered the continental shelves with shallow seas and revealed them as dry land. If the Earth's present polar ice-caps and glaciers were to melt, the mean sea level would rise by about 200 feet (60 m), which would submerge half the world's population. Average depth of the sea is more than 12000 feet (3600 m), five times the average height of the land above sea level.

The deep oceans

Below the level of the continental shelf lies the deep ocean floor with great topographical contrasts ranging from abyssal plains at a depth of about 13000 feet (4 km) to towering submarine mountain ranges of the mid-ocean ridges which reach far up toward the surface. Great advances have recently been made in exploring the ocean floors which were previously unknown. Most of the ocean area is abyssal plain which extends over about 78 million square miles (200 million km^2). But a more remarkable feature of the deep ocean is the almost continuous mid-ocean mountain range which sweeps 40000 miles (64000 km) around the globe and occasionally – as at Iceland – is seen above sea level in the form of isolated volcanic islands. The basic symmetry of the oceans is the central ridge flanked by abyssal plain sloping up to the continental shelves. On the deep floor sediments accumulate at a rate of 30–35 feet (10 m) per million years; they also build up more slowly at the central ridges. No ocean sediments have been found older than 150 million years, which suggests that the material which now makes up the floors of the deep oceans was formed comparatively recently. Exploration and detailed mapping of the ocean bed is still in its infancy.

Submarine relief *below*
The bottom of the sea is very far from being flat. If the ocean waters were removed a new landscape would become visible, with immense relief features.

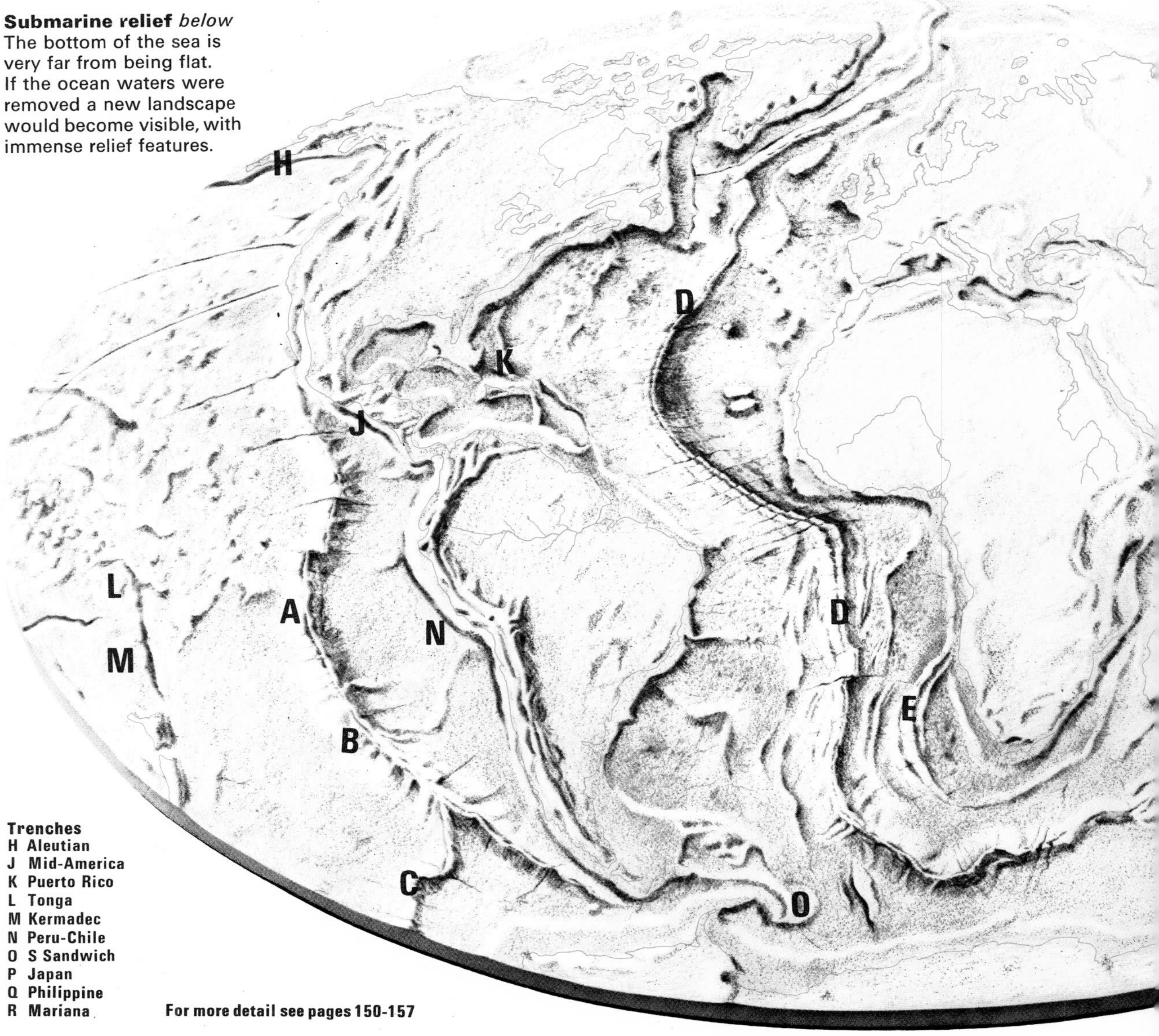
H
D
K
J
L
A
N
D
M
E
B
C
O

Trenches
H Aleutian
J Mid-America
K Puerto Rico
L Tonga
M Kermadec
N Peru-Chile
O S Sandwich
P Japan
Q Philippine
R Mariana

For more detail see pages 150-157

Submarine landscape
Principal features of the bed of the oceans can be grouped into a much smaller space than they would actually occupy. Although each ocean differs in detail, all tend to conform to the general layout of a central volcanic ridge (which can break the surface in places), broad abyssal plains with occasional deep trenches and shallow slopes and shelves bordering the continents.

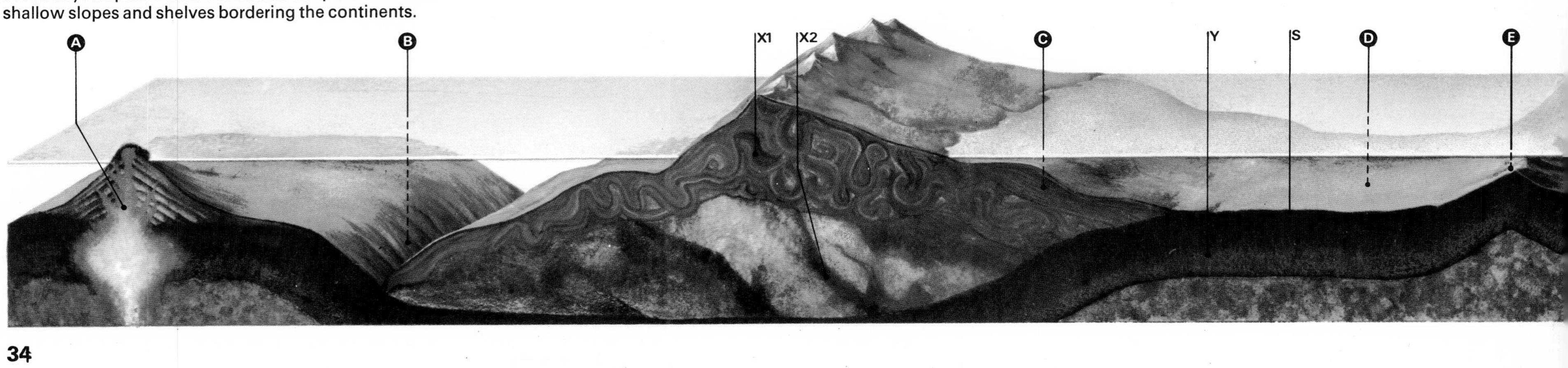
A
B
X1
X2
C
Y
S
D
E

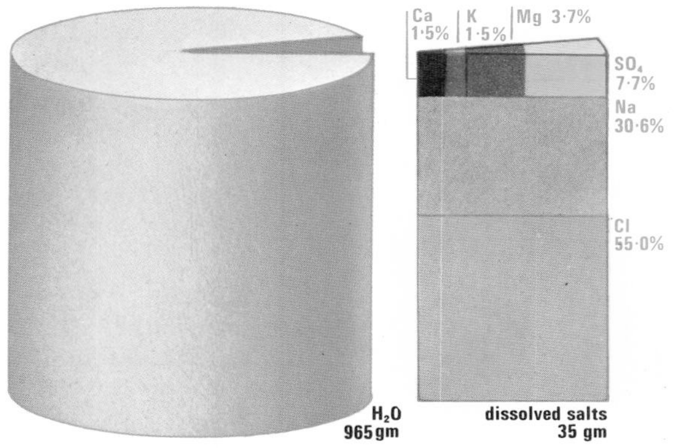
Ca 1·5%
K 1·5%
Mg 3·7%
SO_4 7·7%
Na 30·6%
Cl 55·0%
H_2O 965gm
dissolved salts 35 gm

Composition of sea-water *above*
The water of the Earth's oceans is an exceedingly complex solution of many organic and inorganic salts, together with suspended solid matter. In a typical kilogram of sea-water there are 35 grams of chlorine, sodium, sulphates, magnesium, potassium and calcium.

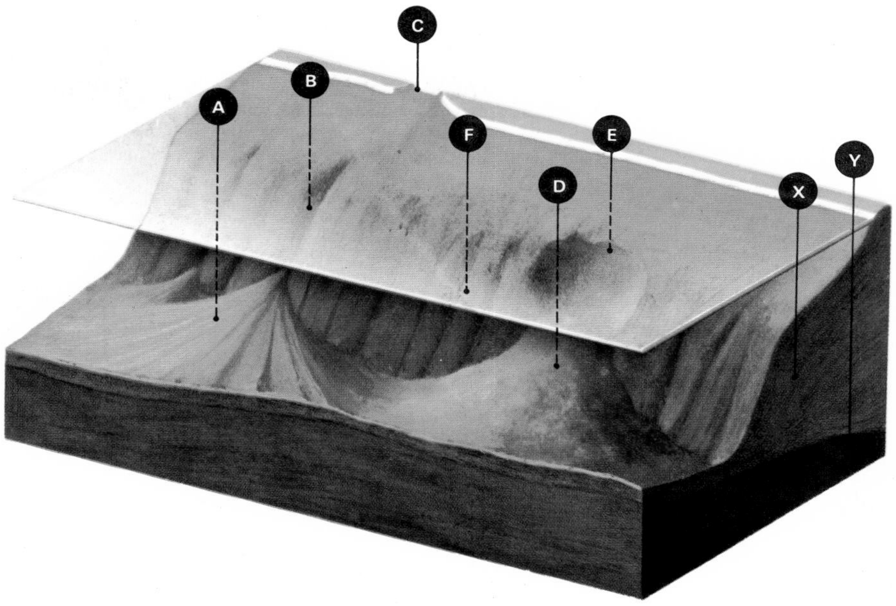
A
B
C
D
E
F
X
Y

Continental shelf *left*
The submerged continental fringes lie at depths to about 450 feet (135 m) and have a total area of some 11 million square miles (28 million km²). The surface of the land is eroded and carried by rivers to form sedimentary deposits on the shelf. At its outer margin it slopes down to the abyssal plains of the deep ocean at about 2½ miles (4 km) below sea level.

A Scree fan
B Gully opposite river
C River delta
D Slump (turbidite) mass
E Scar left by (D)
F Continental slope
X Granite
Y Basalt

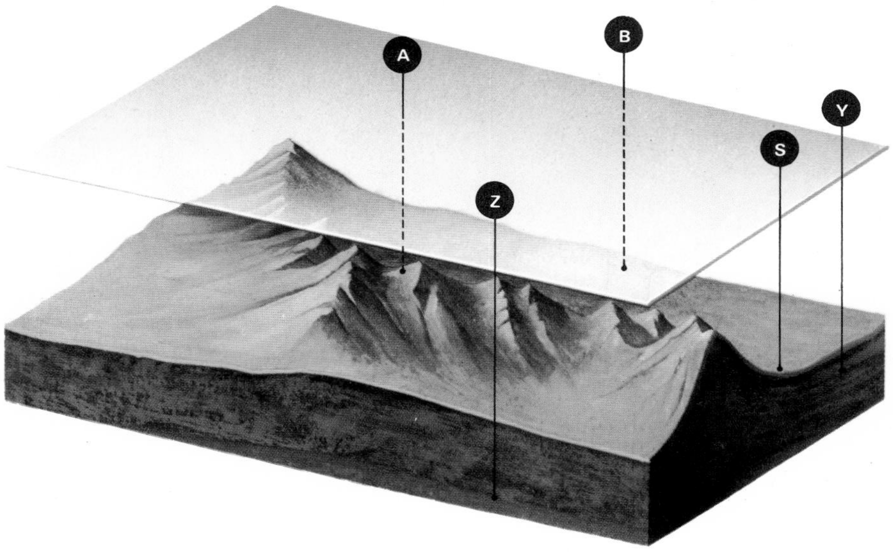
A
B
S
Y
Z

Mid-ocean ridge *left*
Well-marked ridges are found along the centers of the major oceans and form an extensive worldwide system. The central part of the ridge may have a double crest with an intervening deep trough forming a rift valley, or there may be several ridges. They are volcanic in nature and along them is generated new basaltic ocean crust. The volcanoes become progressively younger as the mid-ocean ridge is approached.

A Mid-ocean ridge
B Abyssal plain
S Ocean floor sediments
Y Basalt crust
Z Mantle

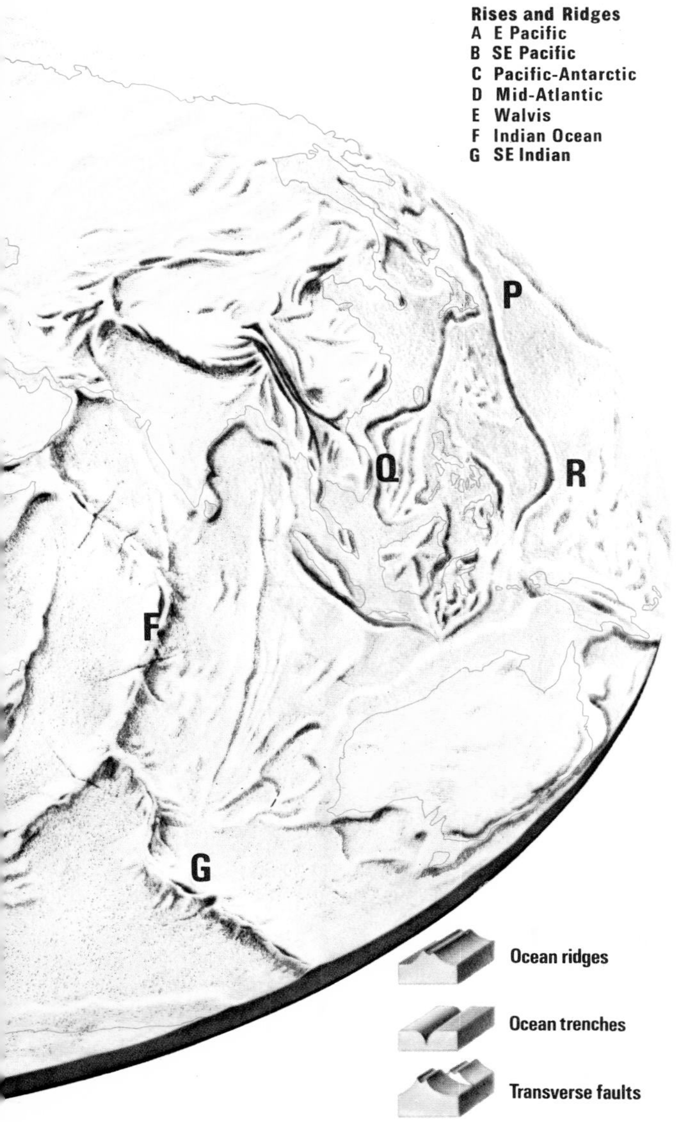
Rises and Ridges
A E Pacific
B SE Pacific
C Pacific-Antarctic
D Mid-Atlantic
E Walvis
F Indian Ocean
G SE Indian
P
Q
R
F
G
Ocean ridges
Ocean trenches
Transverse faults

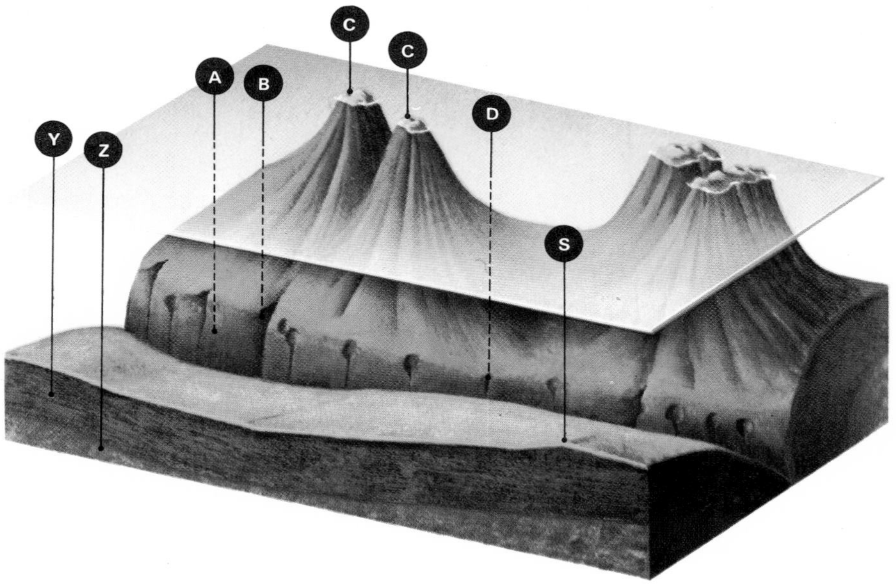
A
B
C
C
D
S
Y
Z

Oceanic trench *left*
These long and relatively narrow depressions are the deepest portions of the oceans, averaging over 30,000 feet (10 km) below sea level. Around the Pacific they lie close to the continental margins and in the western Pacific are often associated with chains of volcanic islands. Some trenches are slowly becoming narrower as the ocean floor plates on either side converge.

A Trench wall
B Canyon
C Island arc
D Trench
S Sediment
Y Basalt
Z Mantle

A Volcano in mid-ocean ridge
B Deep oceanic trench
C Continental shelf
D Abyssal plain
E Mid-ocean ridge
F Guyots
G Oceanic islands
X1 Upper granitic crust and sediments
X2 Lower granitic crust
Y Basaltic crust
Z Mantle

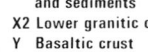

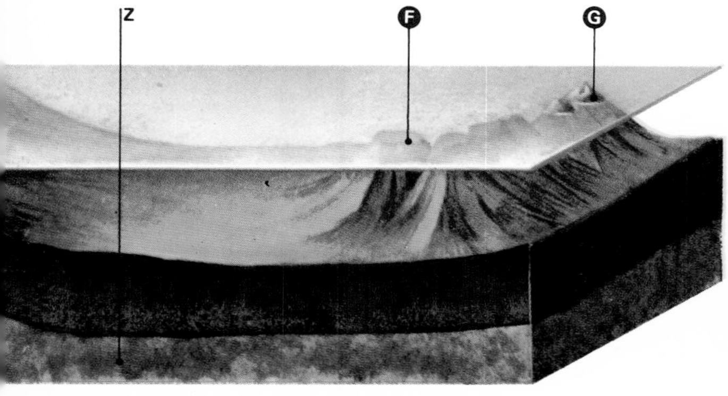
Z
F
G

A sinking island *below*
A pre-requisite to the formation of a coral atoll is an island that is becoming submerged by the sea. Such islands are formed by the peaks of the volcanic mountains which are found on the flanks of the great mid-oceanic ridges.

Coral grows *below*
Millions of polyps, small marine animals, secrete a substance which forms the hard and often beautiful coral. The structure grows round the island in shallow water and extends above the sinking island to form an enclosed and shallow salt-water lagoon.

The mature atoll *below*
Continued submergence of the volcano results in the disappearance of the original island, but the upward growth of the coral continues unabated. The reef is then worn away by the sea and the coral debris fills in the central part of the lagoon.

A guyot *below*
Eventually the coral atoll itself begins to sink beneath the ocean surface. By this time the lagoon is likely to have become completely filled in by debris eroded from the reef, and the result is a submerged flat island, known as a guyot.

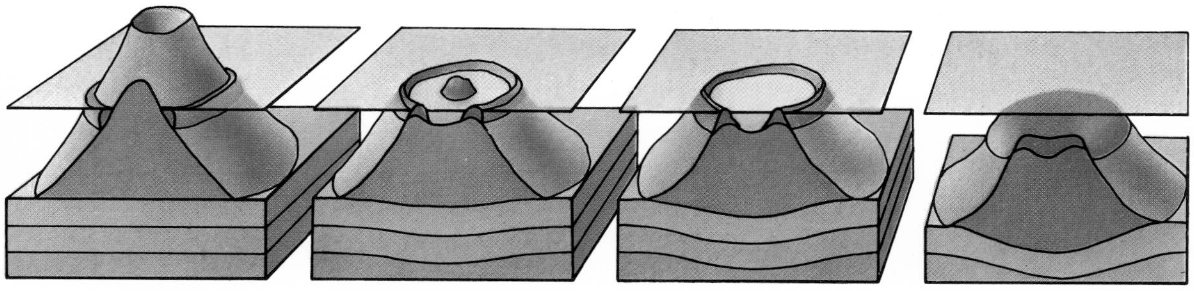

The Evolution of Land and Sea

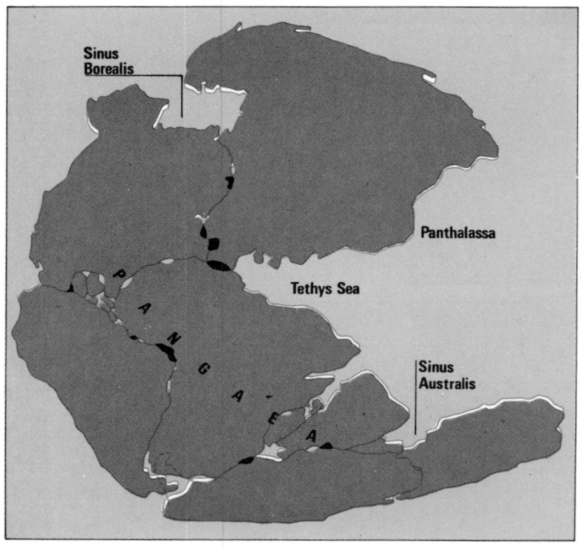

Sinus Borealis
Panthalassa
Tethys Sea
P A N G A E A
Sinus Australis

Pangaea *above*
About 200 million years ago there was only a single land mass on Earth, named Pangaea. The map shows how today's continents can be fitted together, with the aid of a computer, at the edge of the continental shelf at a depth of 1000 fathoms (6000 ft, 1830 m).

Although land and water first appeared on the Earth's surface several thousand million years before anyone could be there to watch, modern man has a very good idea of how it came about. The Earth's gravitational field caused the lighter, more volatile elements gradually to move outwards through the mantle and form a solid crust on the surface. By far the largest proportion of material newly added to the crust is basaltic volcanic rock derived from partial melting of the mantle beneath; in fact the oceanic crust which underlies the Earth's great water areas is made of almost nothing else. So the earliest crust to form was probably volcanic and of basaltic composition.

Air and water appear

The earliest records of the existence of an atmosphere of air and a hydrosphere of water are to be found in sediments laid down some 3300 million years ago from the residue of erosion of previously existing rocks. These sediments could not have been formed without atmospheric weathering, water transport and water deposition. The atmosphere was probably originally similar to the fumes which today issue from volcanoes and hot springs and which are about three-quarters water vapor. Once formed, the primitive atmosphere and oceans could erode the crust to produce vast layers of sediments of new chemical compositions. Gradually the oceans deepened and the land took on a more varied form. Convection in the mantle produced mountain ranges which in turn eroded to generate new sedimentary rocks. The ceaseless cycles of growth and decay had started, causing continually changing patterns of seas, mountains and plains. And in the past few years man has discovered how the continents and oceans have developed over the most recent 200 million years of geological time. The results of this research are to be seen in the maps on this page.

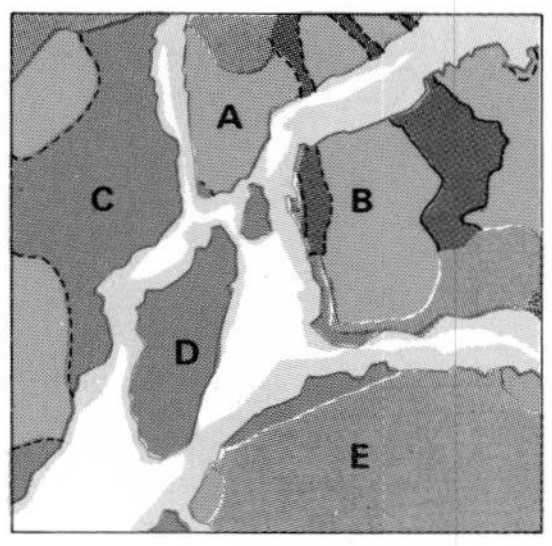

A
B
C
D
E

Another arrangement *left*
India (A) may have been separated by Australia (B) from East Antarctica (E) more than 200 million years ago on the evidence of today's geological deposition zones. Africa (C) and Madagascar (D) complete this convincing fit.

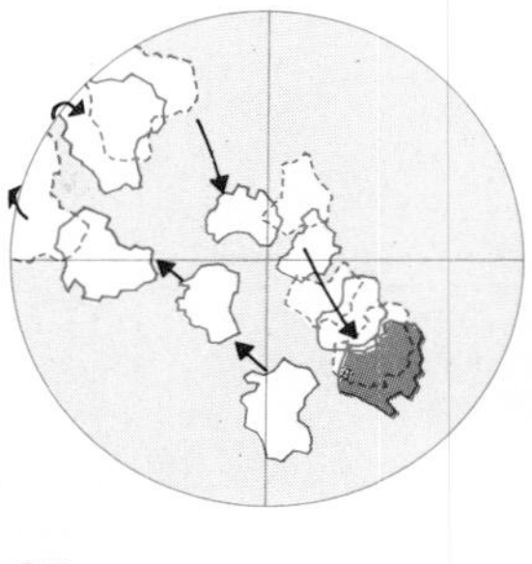

Migrant Australia *left*
By measuring the direction of magnetization of old Australian rocks it is possible to trace successive positions of that continent with respect to the Earth's magnetic pole. It appears to have moved across the world and back during the past 1000 million years.

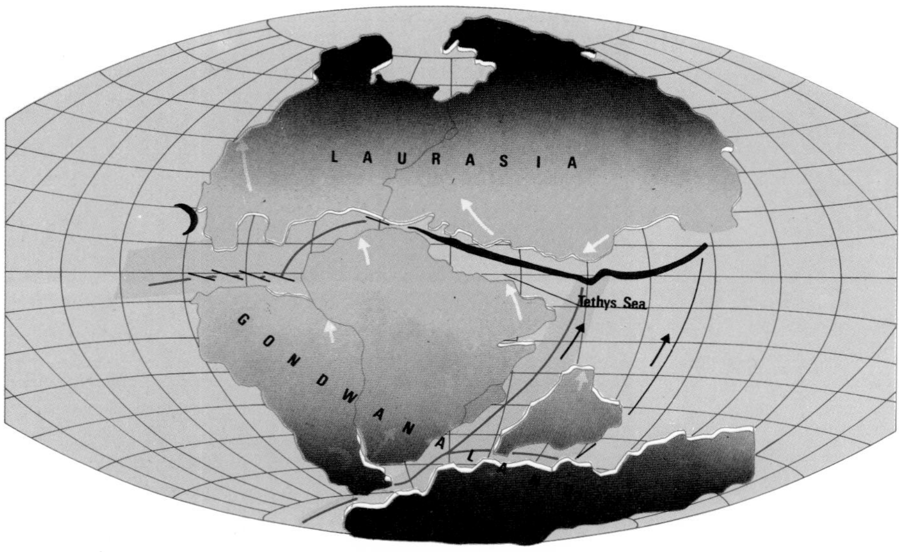

L A U R A S I A
Tethys Sea

180 million years ago
At this time the original Pangaea land mass had just begun to break up. The continents first split along the lines of the North Atlantic and Indian Oceans. North America separated from Africa and so did India and Antarctica. The Tethys Sea, between Africa and Asia, closed somewhat, and the super continents of Laurasia to the north and Gondwanaland to the south became almost completely separated. In effect the Earth possessed three super landmasses, plus an India that had already begun to move strongly northward.

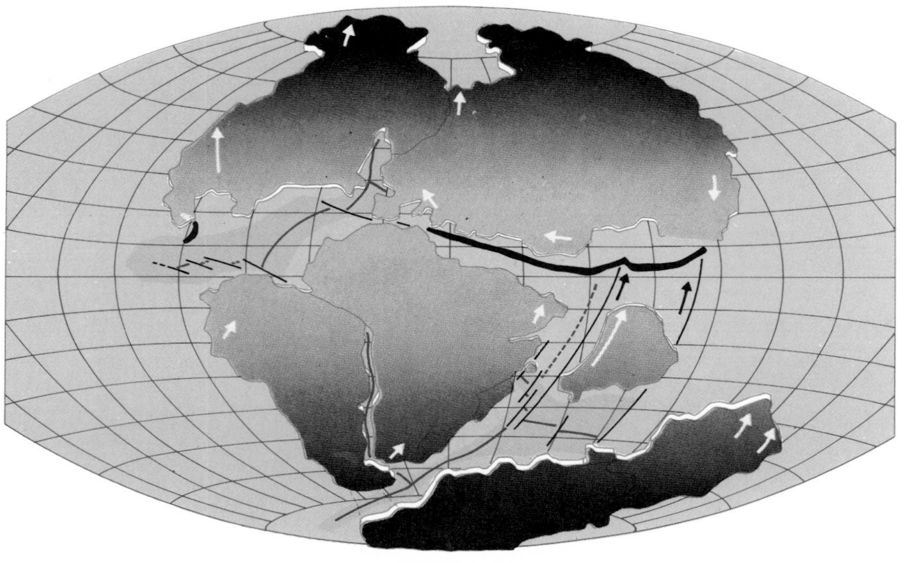

135 million years ago
After a further 45 million years of drifting, the world map had still not taken on a form that looks familiar today. But the two original splits, the North Atlantic and the Indian Ocean, have continued to open out. The North Atlantic is now about 600–650 miles (1000 km) wide. Rifting is extending towards the split which opened up the Labrador Sea and this will eventually separate Greenland from North America. India has firmly launched itself on its collision course with the southern coast of Asia, which is still 2000 miles (3200 km) away.

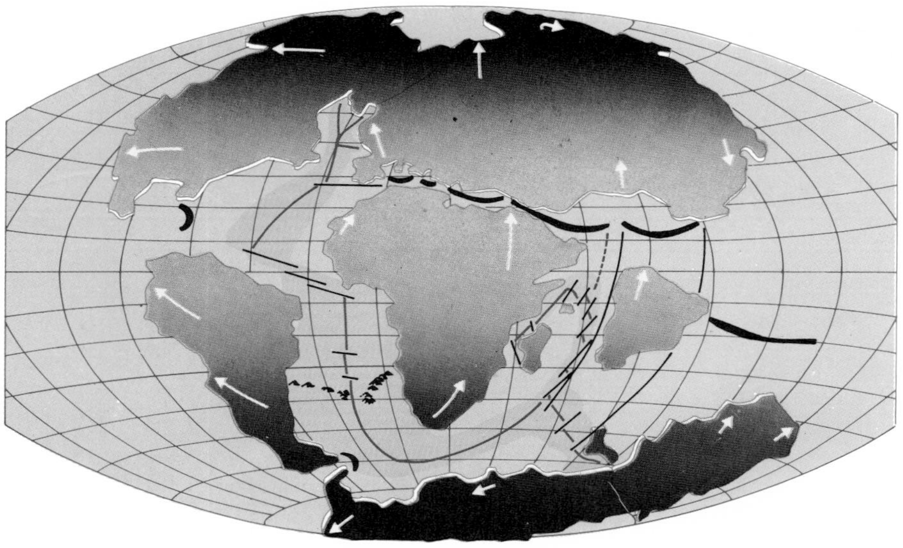

65 million years ago
Some 135 million years after the start of the drifting process the continents have begun to assume their present configuration. South America has at last separated from Africa and in Gondwanaland only Australia and Antarctica have yet to move apart. A continuation of the North Atlantic rifting will shortly bring about another big separation in Laurasia. Greenland will move apart from Europe and eventually North America will separate completely from the Eurasian landmass. The pink area (below) shows the extent of the crustal movements.

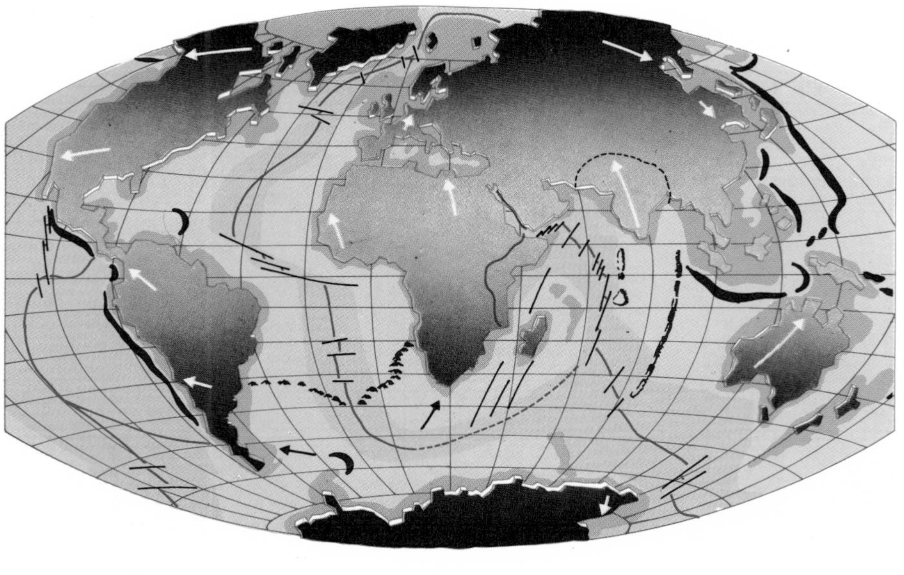

Today's positions
The Atlantic is now a wide ocean from Arctic to Antarctic, the Americas have joined and Australia has separated from Antarctica and moved far to the north. India has likewise moved northwards and its collision with Asia and continued movement has given rise to the extensive uplift of the Himalayas. All the continents which formerly made up the great land mass of Pangaea are now separated by wide oceans. Comparison of areas shows how much of India has been submerged by sliding underneath the crust of Asia (see facing page, far right).

Plate tectonics

This theory has revolutionized the way the Earth's crust – continents and oceans – is interpreted on a global scale. The crust is regarded as being made up of huge plates which converge or diverge along margins marked by earthquakes, volcanoes and other seismic activity. Major divergent margins are the mid-ocean ridges where molten lava forces its way upward and escapes. This causes vast regions of crust to move apart at a rate of an inch or two (some centimeters) per year. When sustained for up to 200 million years this means movements of thousands of miles or kilometers. The process can be seen in operation today in and around Iceland. Oceanic trenches are margins where the plates are moving together and the crust is consumed downward. The overall result is for the crustal plates to move as relatively rigid entities, carrying the continents along with them as if they were on a giant conveyor belt. Over further considerable periods of geologic time this will markedly change today's maps.

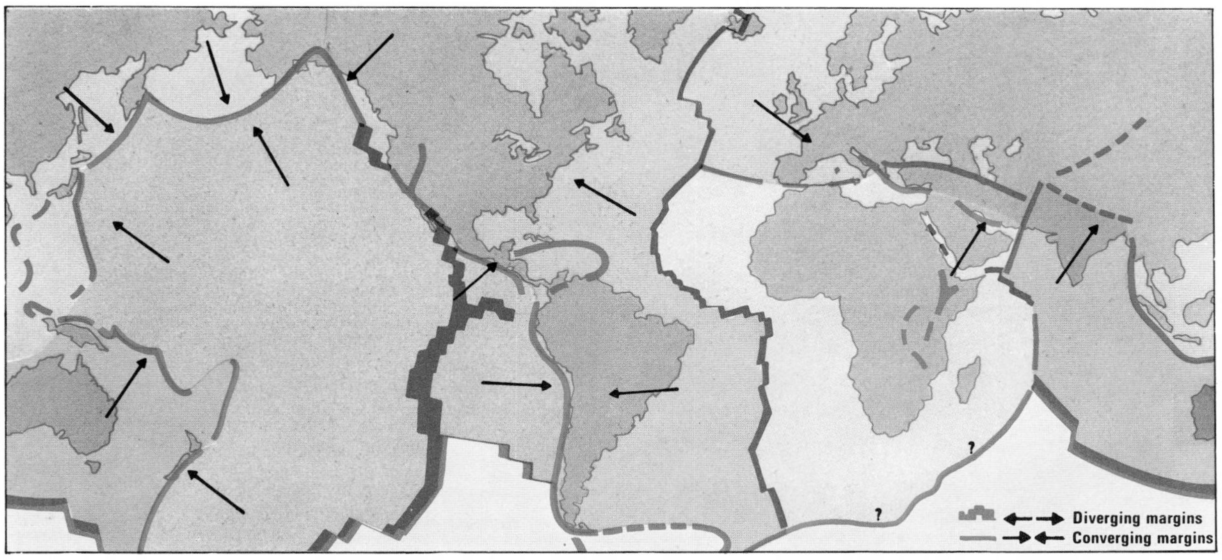
?
?
Diverging margins
Converging margins

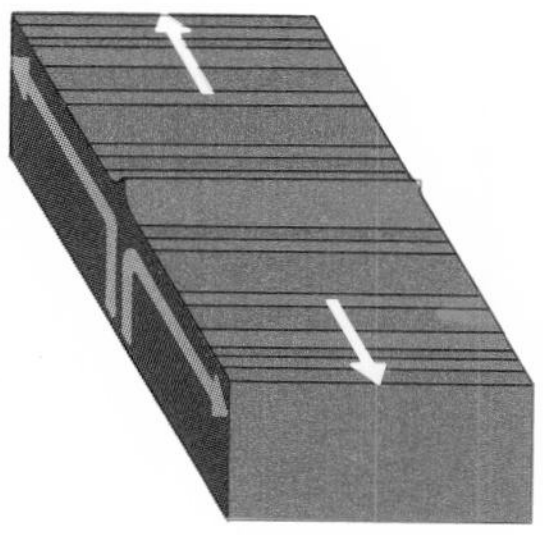

Sea-floor spreading *left*
Arrows show how the lava flows on the ocean bed spread out on each side of a mid-ocean ridge. Evidence for such movement is provided by the fact the rock is alternately magnetized in opposing directions (coloured stripes).

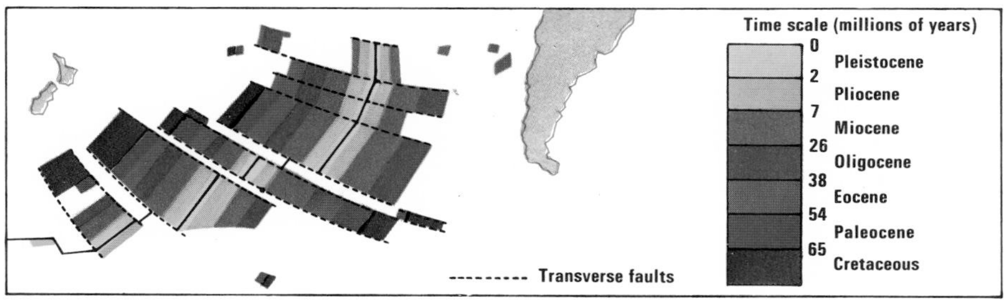
Time scale (millions of years)
0
Pleistocene
2
Pliocene
7
Miocene
26
Oligocene
38
Eocene
54
Paleocene
65
Cretaceous
Transverse faults

Plate movements
above and left
The Earth's crust is a series of large plates 'floating' on the fluid mantle. At their edges the plates are either growing or disappearing. Magnetic measurements in the S. Pacific (left) show rock ages on each side of the mid-ocean ridges.

2
1
3
1
4
6
7
5

Plate movements in cross-section *above*
The basic mechanism of plate movements is illustrated above in simplified form with the vertical scale greatly exaggerated. This figure is explained in detail in both of the captions below.

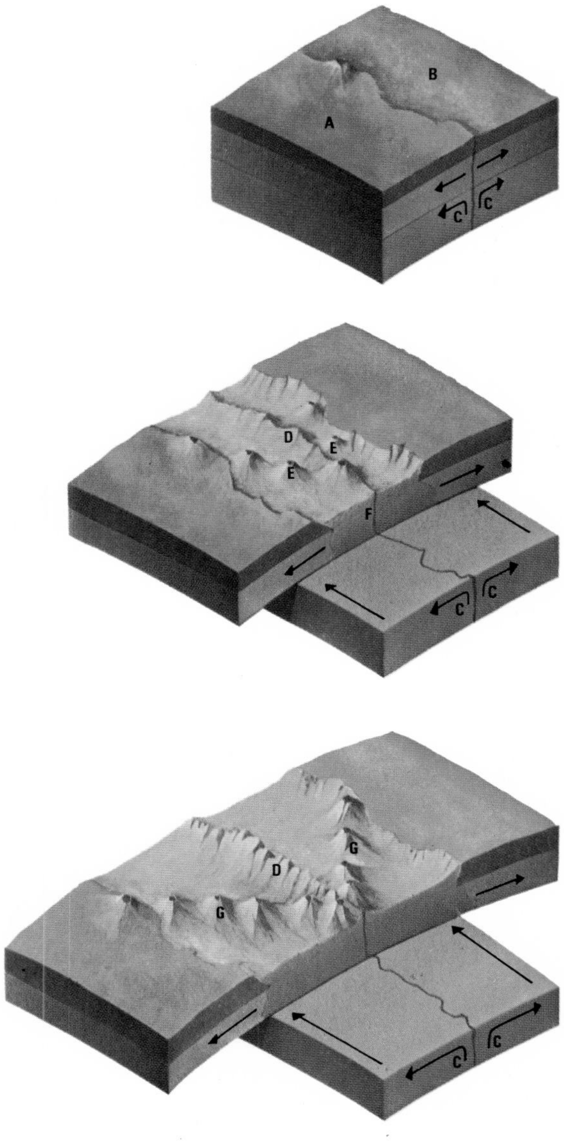
A
B
C
C
D
E
E
F
C
C
D
G
G
C
C

Crustal divergence
above and right
The Earth's crust (1) behaves as a series of rigid plates which move on top of the fluid mantle (2). At their mating edges some of these plates are moving apart (3). This was the mechanism that separated North America (A) from Europe (B). The plates moved to the north and also away from each other under the influence of convection currents in the mantle (C). Between the land areas appeared an oceanic gap with a mid-ocean ridge (D) and lateral ridges (E). The movements continued for some 200 million years, fresh volcanoes being generated by igneous material escaping through the plate joint (F) to add to the lateral ridges which today cross the Atlantic (G). The volcanoes closest to the median line in mid-Atlantic are still young and active — as witness the scene on page 24 – whereas those nearer to the continents are old and extinct.

Crustal convergence
above and right
Diverging plate margins occur only in the centers of the major oceans (see map above) but plates are converging on both sea and land. Where an oceanic plate (4, above) is under-riding a continental plate (5) a deep ocean trench is the result (6). Such trenches extend around much of the Pacific; those around the northwest Pacific include the deepest on Earth where the sea bed is almost seven miles below the ocean surface. The continental margin is squeezed upward to form mountains such as the Andes or Rockies (7). If continental masses converge, such as India (A, right) and Asia (B), the convection in the mantle (C) pulls the plates together so hard that the upper crust crumples (D). Sedimentary deposits between the plates (E) are crushed and squeezed out upward (F), while the mantle on each side is turned downward, one side being forced under the other (G). Continued movement causes gross deformation at the point of collision. The static or slow-moving crust is crushed and tilted, and giant young mountains (the Himalayas, H) are thrust upward along the collision just behind the edge of the crumpled plate.

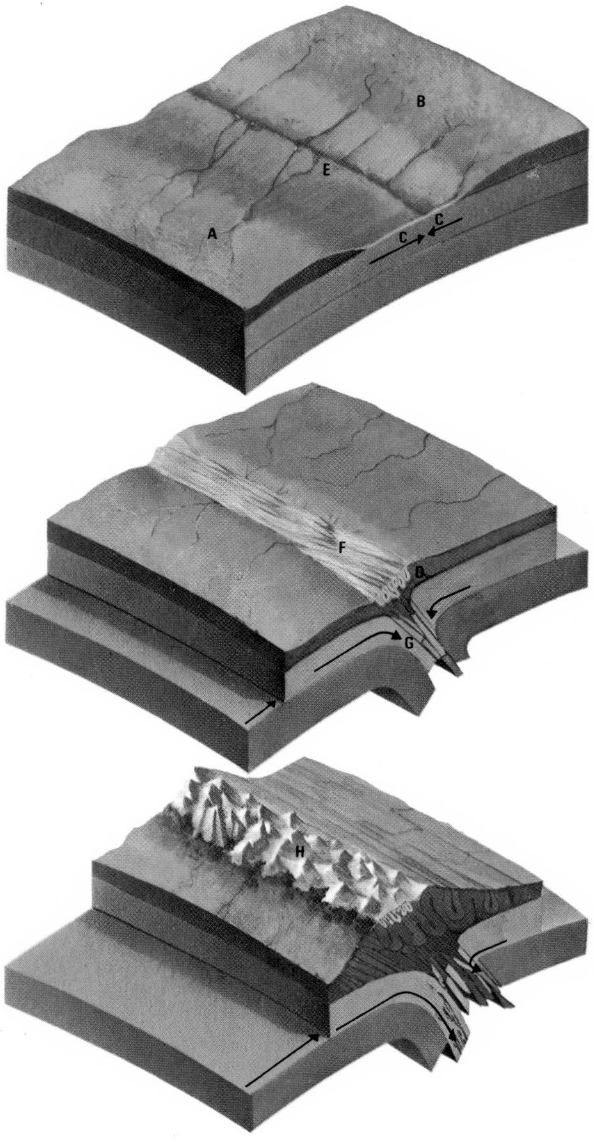
B
E
A
C
C
F
D
G
H

The Active Earth

Man's most powerful nuclear weapons pale into insignificance beside the violence of an earthquake or the destructive and indiscriminate force of a volcano. These cataclysmic phenomena frequently occur along the same belts of instability in the Earth's crust and are often only different manifestations of the same fundamental processes. About 800 volcanoes are known to have been active in historical times, and many are extremely active today. All the mid-ocean ridges are volcanic in origin, and many underwater eruptions occur along these submarine mountain ranges. Spectacular volcanic eruptions sometimes break the ocean surface, such as during the formation in 1963 of the island of Surtsey, south of Iceland (photograph, right). Some islands, such as Iceland itself, are the products of continued outpourings of lava along the crest of the mid-ocean ridge.

Oceanic earthquakes caused by sudden sea-floor displacements may result in tsunamis or giant sea waves. About 80 per cent of the shallow earthquakes and almost all deep ones take place along the belt around the Pacific. Clear evidence of the large scale movements of the mantle are provided by the zones within which earthquake shocks are generated along some Pacific island arc systems. These zones plunge down from sea-floor level to depths of 440 miles (700 km) beneath the adjacent continents and mark the positions of downward flow of the mantle convection currents (page 41). The corresponding upwelling regions lie along the mid-ocean ridges, where new basic volcanic material is continually being added to the ocean crust as outward movement takes place away from the ridges.

These sea-floor spreading movements act as 'conveyor belts' for the continents, and constitute the basic mechanism for the large displacements involved in continental drifting. Geological data confirm the former close fits of the margins of the reassembled continental jig-saw puzzle, and also corroborate the detailed paleomagnetic evidence visible in today's rocks of the movements of the continents relative to the geographic poles.

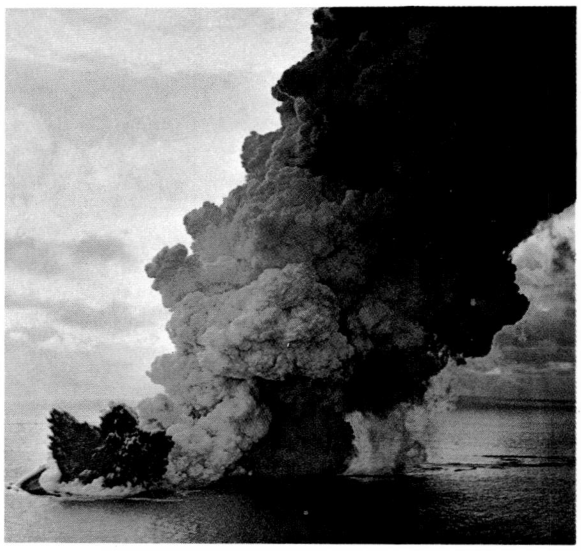

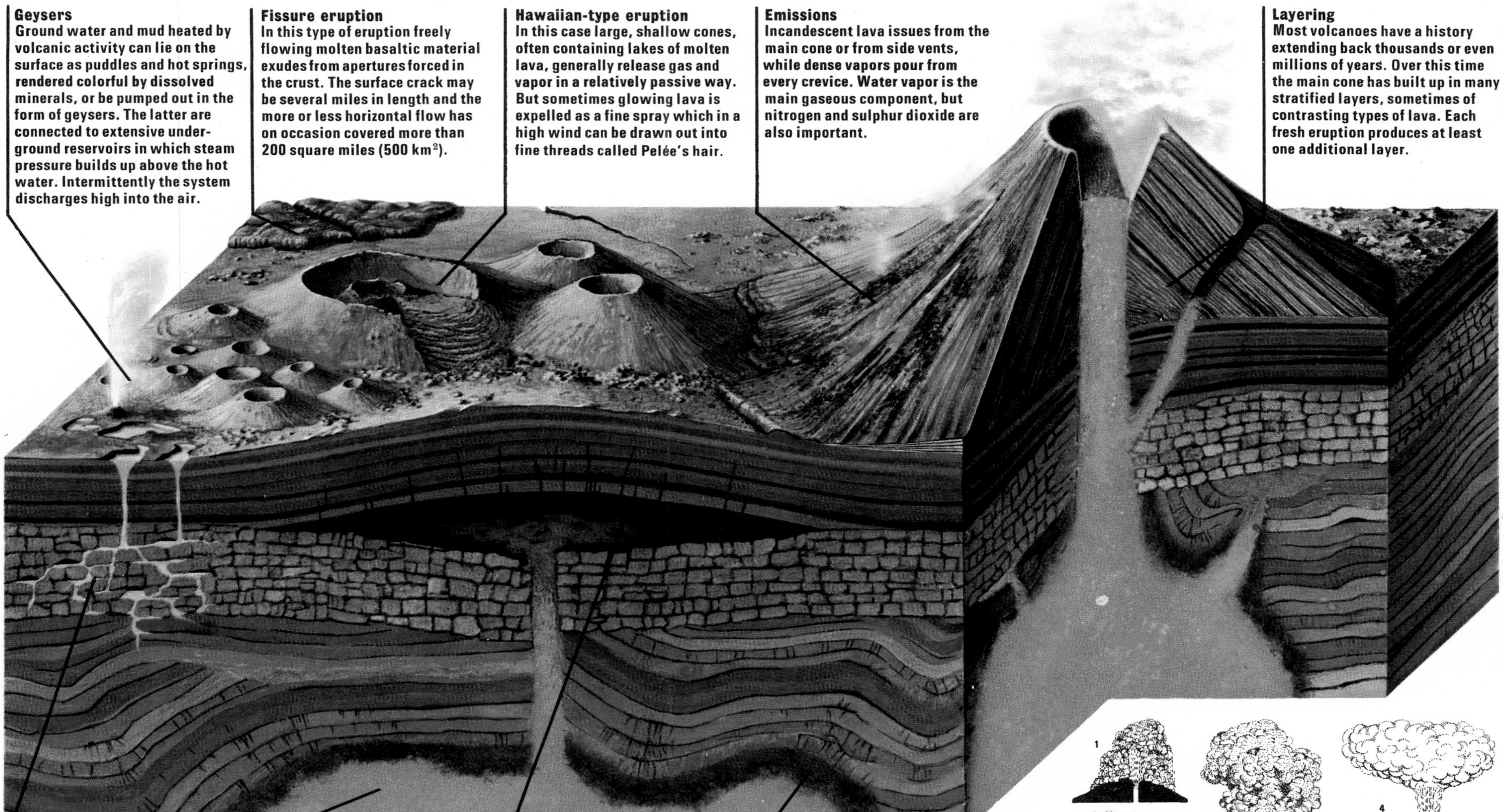

Geysers
Ground water and mud heated by volcanic activity can lie on the surface as puddles and hot springs, rendered colorful by dissolved minerals, or be pumped out in the form of geysers. The latter are connected to extensive underground reservoirs in which steam pressure builds up above the hot water. Intermittently the system discharges high into the air.

Fissure eruption
In this type of eruption freely flowing molten basaltic material exudes from apertures forced in the crust. The surface crack may be several miles in length and the more or less horizontal flow has on occasion covered more than 200 square miles (500 km^2).

Hawaiian-type eruption
In this case large, shallow cones, often containing lakes of molten lava, generally release gas and vapor in a relatively passive way. But sometimes glowing lava is expelled as a fine spray which in a high wind can be drawn out into fine threads called Pelée's hair.

Emissions
Incandescent lava issues from the main cone or from side vents, while dense vapors pour from every crevice. Water vapor is the main gaseous component, but nitrogen and sulphur dioxide are also important.

Layering
Most volcanoes have a history extending back thousands or even millions of years. Over this time the main cone has built up in many stratified layers, sometimes of contrasting types of lava. Each fresh eruption produces at least one additional layer.

Underground water
Heated beyond normal boiling point, the pressurized water issues in a rush when pressure is relieved.

Magma chamber
Underlying every volcano is a volume of intensely hot fluid under high pressure.

Laccolith
Above the pipes and sills of the hot magma lies a giant lens-shaped intrusion of cold rock.

Metamorphic rock
The strata adjacent to the fiery magma are physically and chemically altered by the heat.

1
2
3
4

Types of eruption *above*
Volcanic cones differ in both shape and activity. The Strombolian (1) erupts every few minutes or hours; the Peléan form (2) gives a hot avalanche; the Vesuvian (3) is a fierce upward expulsion, while the Plinian (4) is the extreme form.

Where the Earth seems active *right*
Although we live on a white-hot globe with a thin cool crust, the fierce heat and energy of the interior is manifest only along fairly clearly defined belts. Around the Pacific, volcanoes and earthquakes are frequent. Another belt traverses the mountains from southeast Asia through the Middle East to the Mediterranean. Every site is an external expression of activity within the crust and upper mantle. The underlying cause is a slow flowing of the rocks of the mantle in response to changes in temperature and density.

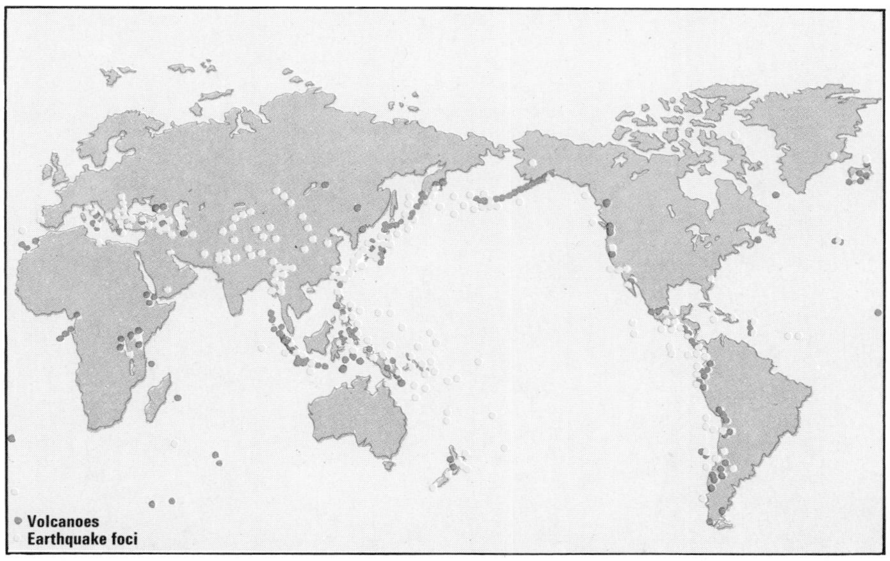
Volcanoes
Earthquake foci

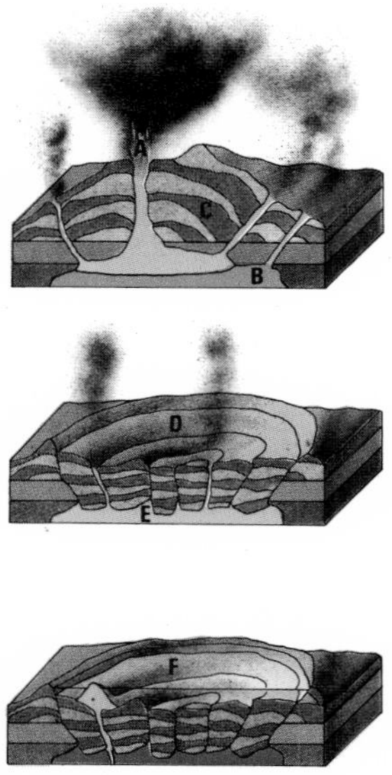
A
B
C
D
E
F

A caldera *left*
Expulsion of lava (A) from the magma chamber (B) may leave the central core (C) without support. A collapse results in a large, steep-sided caldera (D). The magma chamber may cool and solidify (E), and water may collect inside the caldera (F).

Earthquake *right*
Along lines of potential movement, such as fault planes, stresses may build up over many years until the breaking strength of some part of the rock is exceeded (A). A sudden break occurs and the two sides of the fault line move, generating shock-waves which travel outward in all directions from the focus at the point of rupture (B). The point on the surface directly above the focus is the epicenter (C). While the fault movement reaches its fullest extent, the shockwaves reach the surface (D). Far right the aftermath of an earthquake.

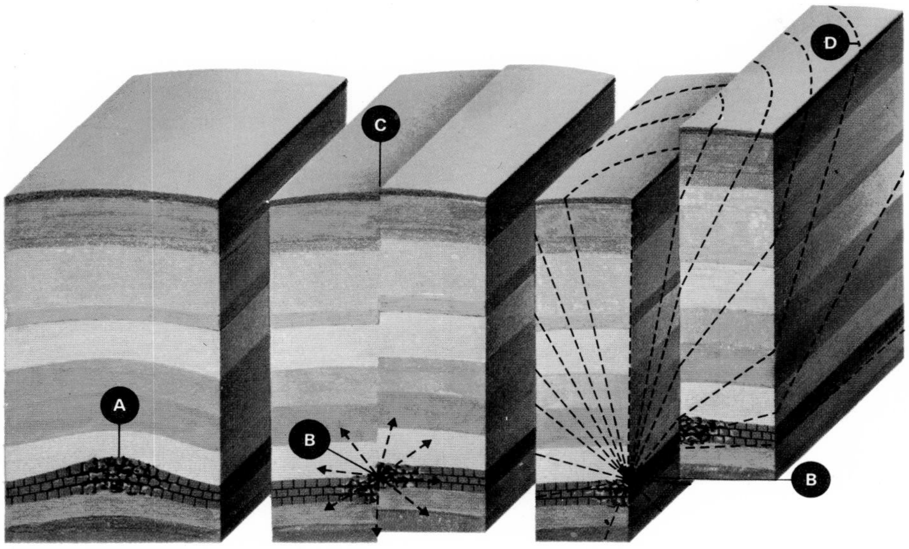
A
B
C
D
B

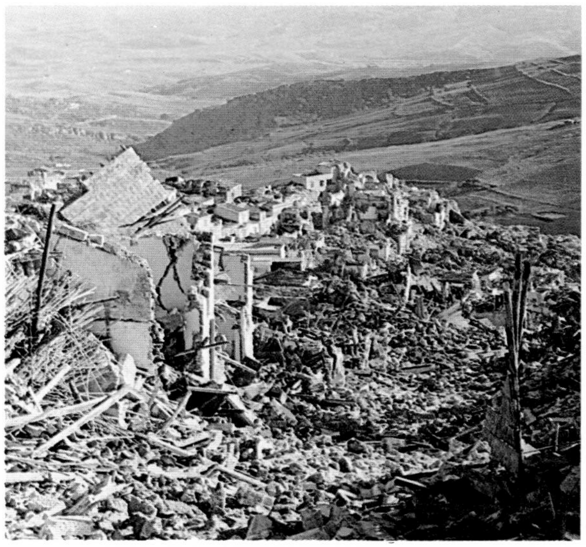

Destructive waves *right*
The Japanese, who have suffered severely from them, have given the name tsunami to the terrifying waves which follow earthquakes. Their character depends on the cause. In the case of a sudden rift and slump in the ocean bed (A) the wave at the surface is initially a trough, which travels away to both sides followed by a crest and subsequent smaller waves (B). A fault causing a sudden changed level of sea bed (C) can generate a tsunami that starts with a crest (D). Travelling at 400 miles (650 km) per hour or more the tsunami arrives at a beach as a series of waves up to 200 feet (60 m) high (E), the 'trough first' variety being heralded by a sudden withdrawal of the ocean from the shore. Warning stations ring the Pacific (far right) and the concentric rings show tsunamic travel time from an earthquake site to Hawaii at the center.

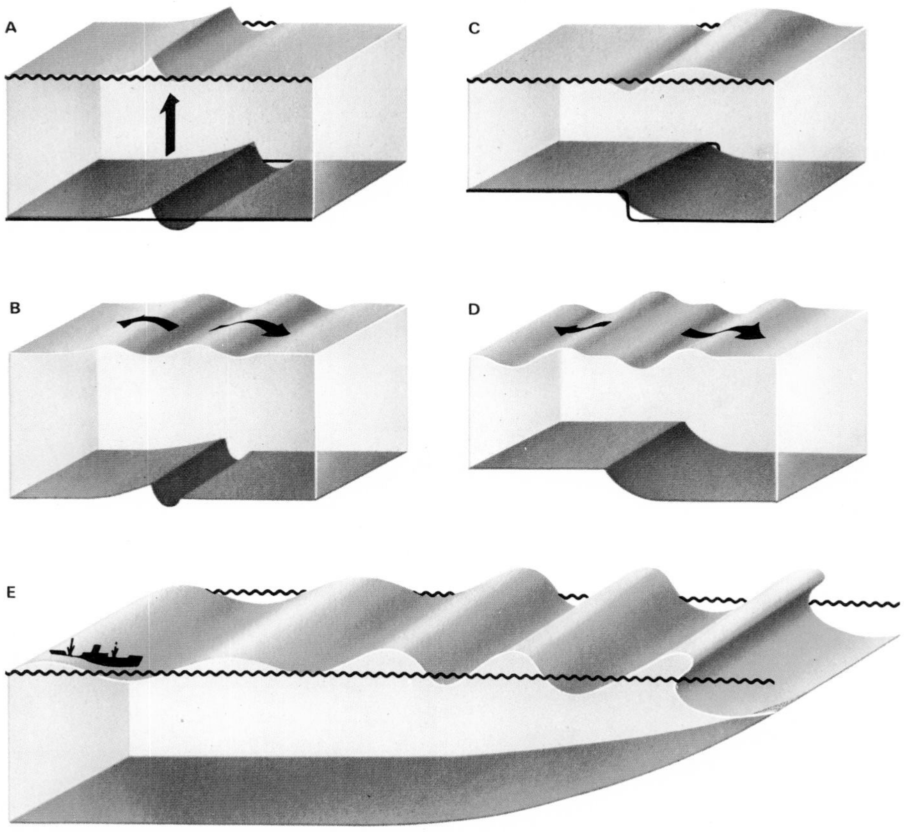
A
C
B
D
E

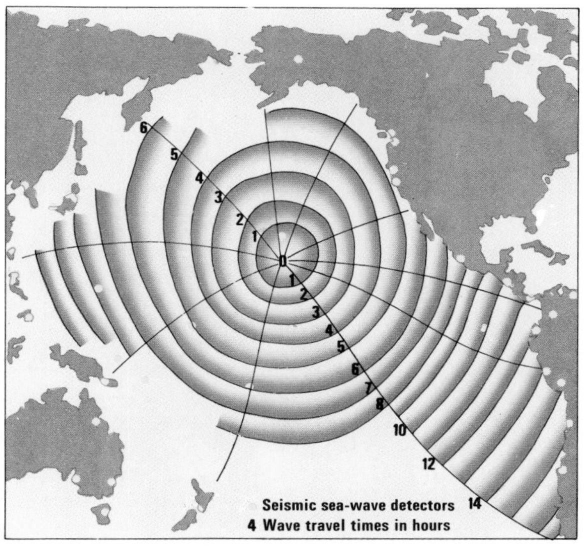
Seismic sea-wave detectors
4 Wave travel times in hours

Tsunami warning *above*
Numerous seismographic warning stations around the earthquake belt of the Pacific Ocean maintain a continuous alert for earthquake shocks and for the tsunami waves that may follow it. Possible recipients of such waves plot a series of concentric rings, such as these centered on the Hawaiian Islands, which show the time in hours that would be taken for a tsunami to travel from any earthquake epicenter. Aircraft and satellites are increasingly helping to create a globally integrated life-saving system.

Seismic waves *right*
An earthquake caused by a sudden movement in the crust at the focus (A) sends out a pattern of shock waves radiating like ripples in a pond. These waves are of three kinds. Primary (P) waves (full lines) vibrate in the direction of propagation, and thus are a rapid succession of high and low pressures. Secondary (S) waves (broken lines), which travel only 60 per cent as fast, shake from side to side. Long waves (L) travel round the crust. In a belt around the world only waves of the L-type occur, giving rise to the concept of a shadow zone (B and shaded belt in inset at lower right). But intermittent records of P waves in this zone led seismologists to the belief that the Earth must have a very dense fluid core (D, lower drawing) capable of strongly refracting P waves like a lens. Seismic waves are almost man's only source of knowledge about the Earth's interior.

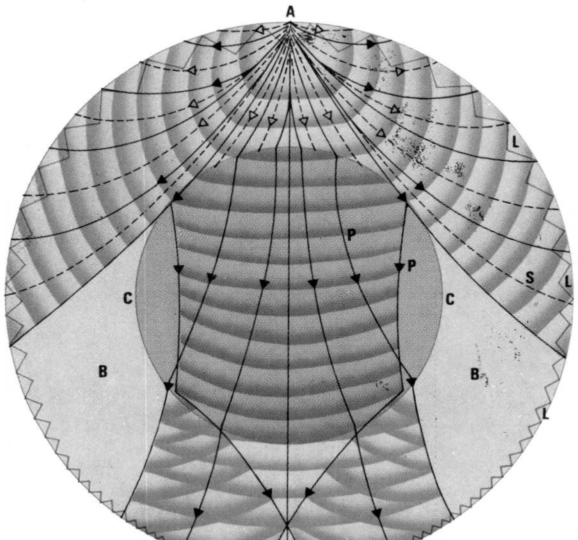
A
L
P
P
S
C
C
B
B
L

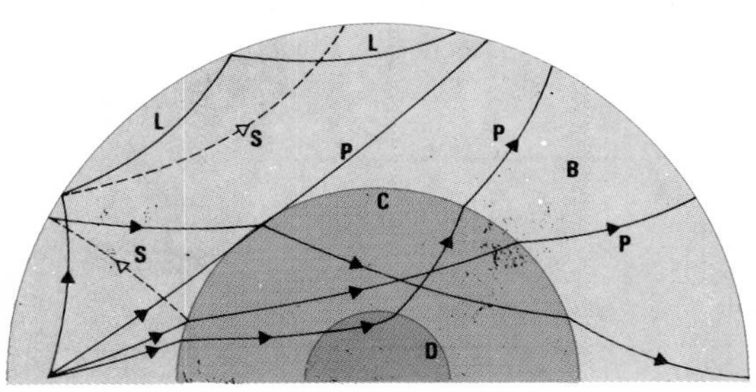
L
L
S
P
P
B
C
S
P
D

Seismology *right*
Seismic waves of all three types (P, S and L) are detected and recorded by seismographs. Usually these contain a sprung mass which, when an earthquake shock passes, stays still while the rest of the instrument moves. Some seismographs detect horizontal waves (A) while others detect vertical ones (B). The pen in the instrument leaves a distinctive trace (P-S-L). P (primary) waves are a succession of rarefactions and compressions, denoted by the packing of the dots; S (secondary) waves are a sideways shaking, shown here in plan view.

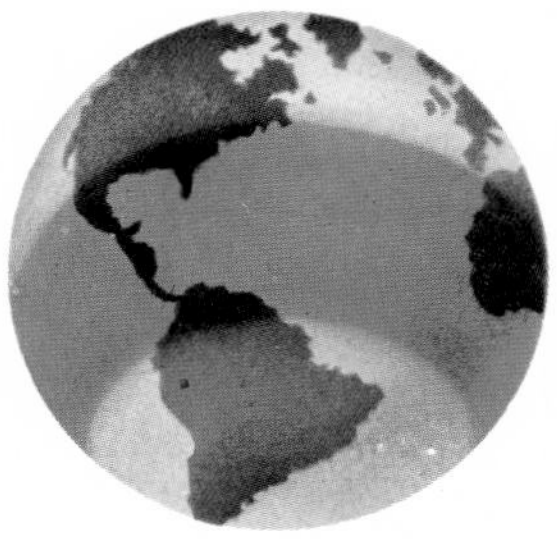

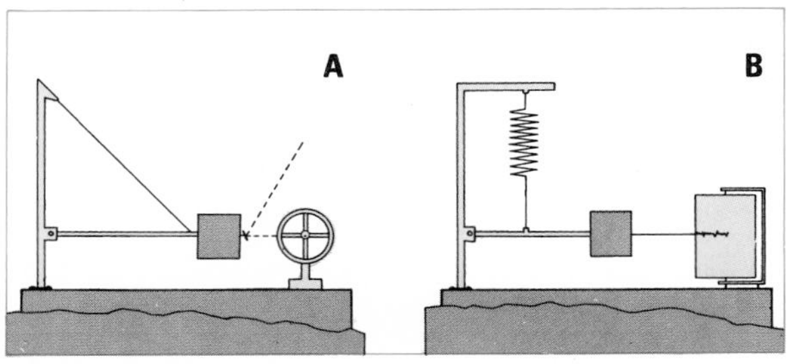
A
B

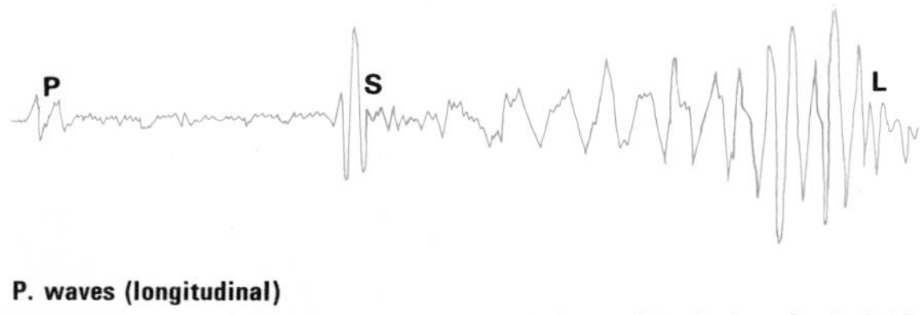
P
S
L

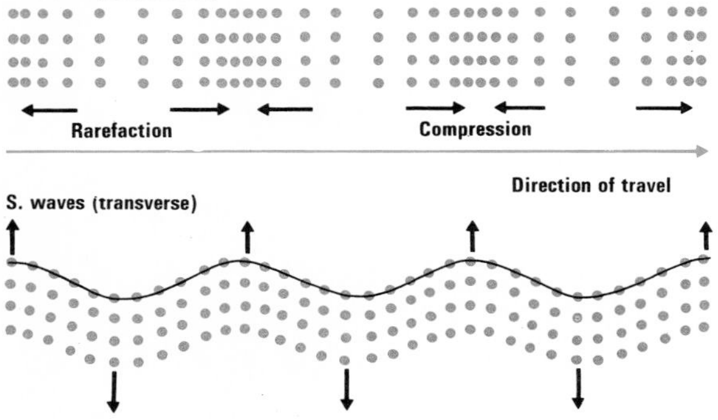
P. waves (longitudinal)
Rarefaction
Compression
Direction of travel
S. waves (transverse)

Anatomy of the Earth

A fundamental mystery that still confronts science even today is the detailed internal structure of the planet on which we live. Although Jules Verne's intrepid Professor Otto Lindenbrock was able to journey to the center of the Earth, this is one scientific fantasy that will never be achieved. The deepest boreholes and mines do little more than scratch the surface and so, deprived of direct observation, the geologist is forced to rely almost entirely on indirect evidence (pages 38-39) to construct his picture of the Earth's anatomy. In spite of these drawbacks, he can outline with some confidence the story of the planet's development from the time of its formation as a separate body in space some 4550 million years ago.

Since that time the Earth has been continuously evolving. The crust, mantle and inner core developed during its first 1000 million years, but there is only scant evidence of how they did so. Probably the original homogenous mass then partly or completely melted, whereupon gravitational attraction caused the densest material to form a part-liquid, part-solid central core overlaid by the less dense mantle. The extremely thin outermost layer of 'scum' began to form at an early stage and as long ago as 3500 million years parts of it had reached almost their present state. But most of the crust evolved in a complex way through long-term cyclic changes spanning immense periods of time. The evidence of today's rocks can be interpreted in different ways; for example, the core, mantle and crust could have separated out quickly at an early stage or gradually over a longer period.

Today's restless Earth

Many of the changes which have taken place in the Earth's structure and form have been very gradual. For example, although it may well be that our planet has been getting larger (as illustrated below), the rate of increase in radius has been no more rapid than 2½ inches (65 mm) per century. But this does not alter the fact that the Earth is very far from being a mere inert sphere of matter. Although it is not possible faithfully to portray it, almost the whole globe is at brilliant white heat. If the main drawing were true to life it would contain no color except for a thin band, about as thick as cardboard, around the outer crust in which the color would change from white through yellow and orange to red. With such high temperatures the interior of the Earth is able to flow under the influence of relatively small differences in density and stress. The result is to set up convection currents which are now believed to be the main driving force behind the formation of mountain ranges and the drifting apart of continents. But the fact remains that our knowledge of the interior of our planet is derived almost entirely from indirect evidence, such as the passage of earthquake shock waves through the mantle (see page 39). Direct exploration is confined to the surface and to boreholes which so far have never penetrated more than about five miles (8 km) into the crust. It is difficult to imagine how man could ever devise experiments that would greatly enhance and refine his knowledge of the Earth's interior. Indeed, he knows as much about the Moon and other much more distant heavenly bodies as he does about the Earth below a depth of a mere 20 miles (32 km).

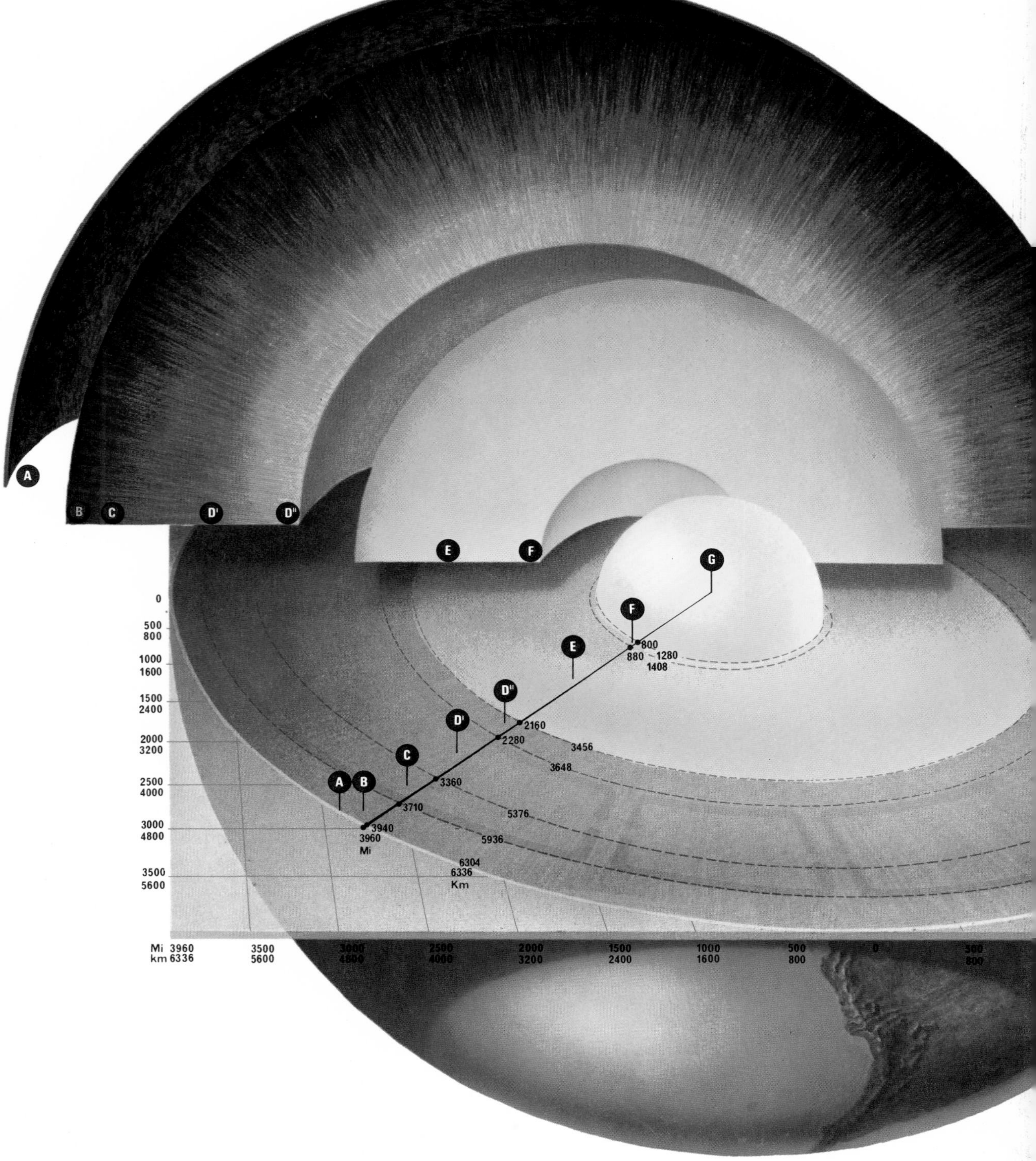

A
B
C
D'
D''
E
F
G
0
500
800
1000
1600
1500
2400
2000
3200
2500
4000
3000
4800
3500
5600
3960
Mi
3940
3710
3360
2280
2160
880
800
1280
1408
3456
3648
5376
5936
6304
6336
Km
Mi 3960
km 6336

The crust (A)
This varies in thickness from 25 miles (40 km) in continental regions, where it is largely granitic, to 3 miles (5 km) under the oceans, where it is basaltic.

The upper mantle (B, C)
From the crust down to 375 miles (600 km), this layer is divided into upper and lower zones with differing P wave speeds (see page 39).

The lower mantle (D¹, D²)
Made of peridotite, as is the upper mantle, this zone extends down to a depth of 1800 miles (2900 km). P wave speeds increase still further.

The outer core (E, F)
Largely iron and nickel, this molten zone reaches to 2900 miles (4700 km). Dynamo action of convection currents may cause the Earth's magnetic field.

Not a true sphere *below*
The Earth's shape is controlled by equilibrium between inward gravitational attraction and outward centrifugal force. This results in the average radius at the equator of 3963 miles (6378 km) slightly exceeding that at the poles of 3950 miles (6356 km).

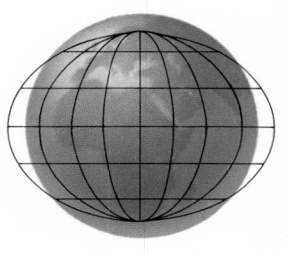

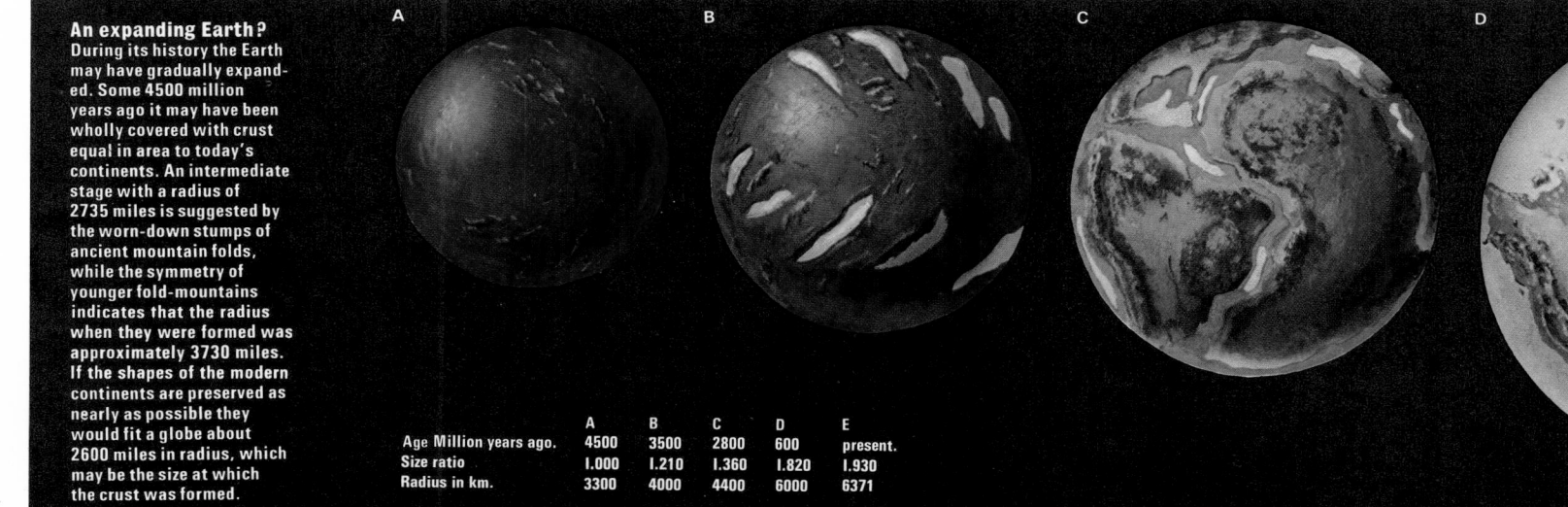

An expanding Earth?
During its history the Earth may have gradually expanded. Some 4500 million years ago it may have been wholly covered with crust equal in area to today's continents. An intermediate stage with a radius of 2735 miles is suggested by the worn-down stumps of ancient mountain folds, while the symmetry of younger fold-mountains indicates that the radius when they were formed was approximately 3730 miles. If the shapes of the modern continents are preserved as nearly as possible they would fit a globe about 2600 miles in radius, which may be the size at which the crust was formed.

A
B
C
D

	A	B	C	D	E
Age Million years ago.	4500	3500	2800	600	present.
Size ratio	1.000	1.210	1.360	1.820	1.930
Radius in km.	3300	4000	4400	6000	6371

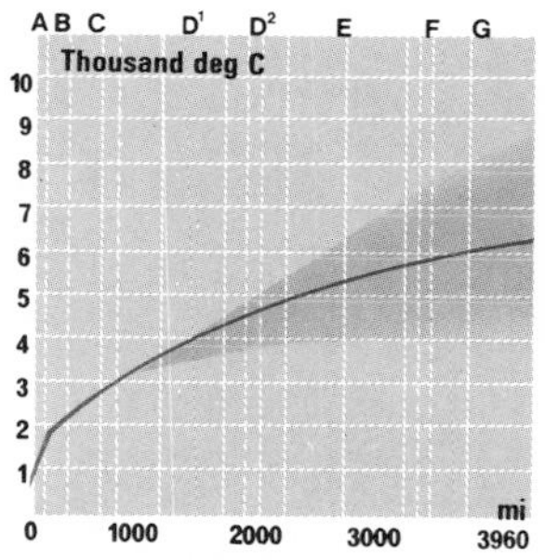
A B C D¹ D² E F G
Thousand deg C
10
9
8
7
6
5
4
3
2
1
0 1000 2000 3000 3960 mi

Temperature *left*
Temperature inside the Earth increases with depth, initially at a rate of 48°C per mile (30°C/km) so that 60 miles (100 km) down it is white hot. The rate of increase then falls, and the shaded area indicates how uncertain is man's knowledge of great depths.

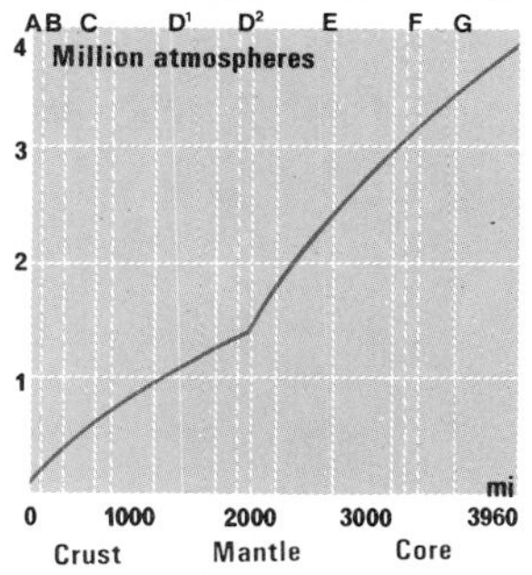
A B C D¹ D² E F G
Million atmospheres
4
3
2
1
0 1000 2000 3000 3960 mi
Crust
Mantle
Core

Pressure *left*
This likewise increases with depth. Only 200 miles (320 km) down it reaches 100,000 atmospheres, 1200 times the pressure at the deepest point in the ocean. A change of state at the discontinuity between the mantle and core shows as a kink on the graph.

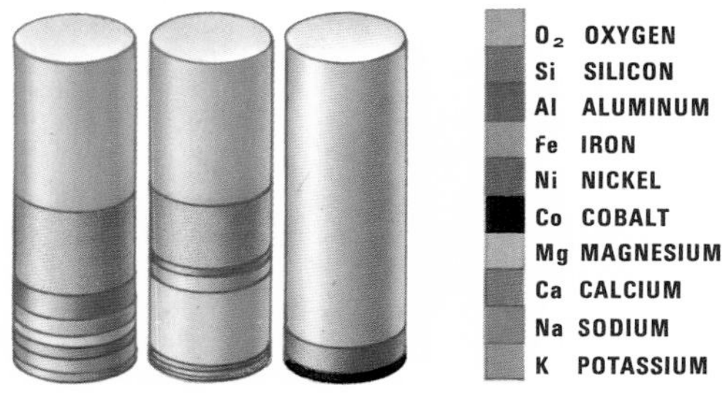
O_2 OXYGEN
Si SILICON
Al ALUMINUM
Fe IRON
Ni NICKEL
Co COBALT
Mg MAGNESIUM
Ca CALCIUM
Na SODIUM
K POTASSIUM

Chemical composition *above*
The crust is made of mainly light elements and has relatively low density. Towards the base of the crust the composition is probably richer in iron and magnesium. The mantle is composed of heavier elements and the core is probably of iron and nickel.

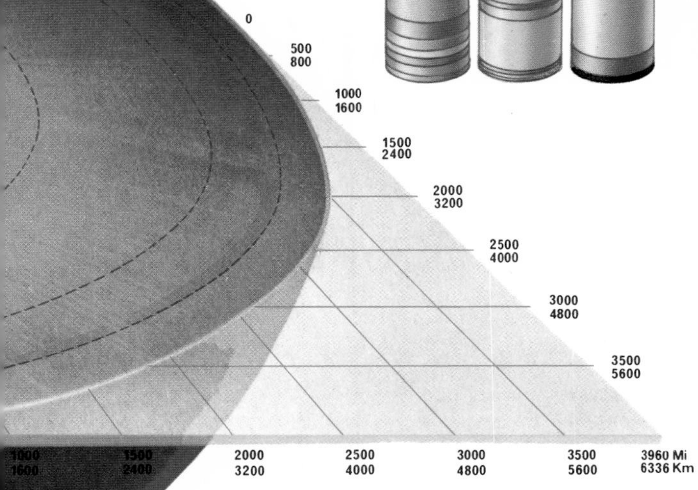
0
500
800
1000
1600
1500
2400
2000
3200
2500
4000
3000
4800
3500
5600
1000
1600
1500
2400
2000
3200
2500
4000
3000
4800
3500
5600
3960 Mi
6336 Km

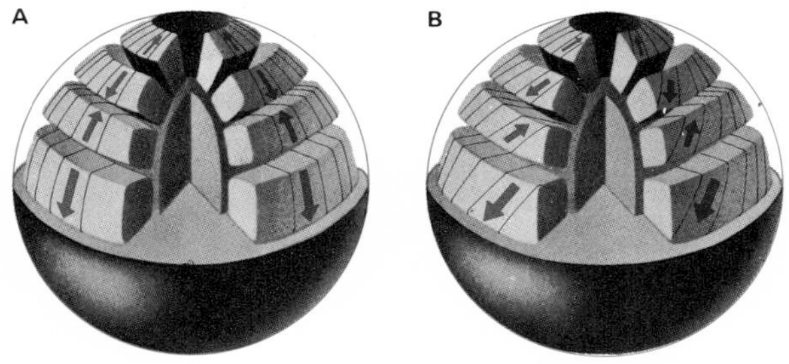
A
B

Convection currents
The fundamental pattern of movement in the mantle (A) is modified by the Earth's rotation (B) and also by friction between adjacent cells as shown in the main figure, below, in which core (X) and mantle (Y) are shown but crust (Z) is removed.

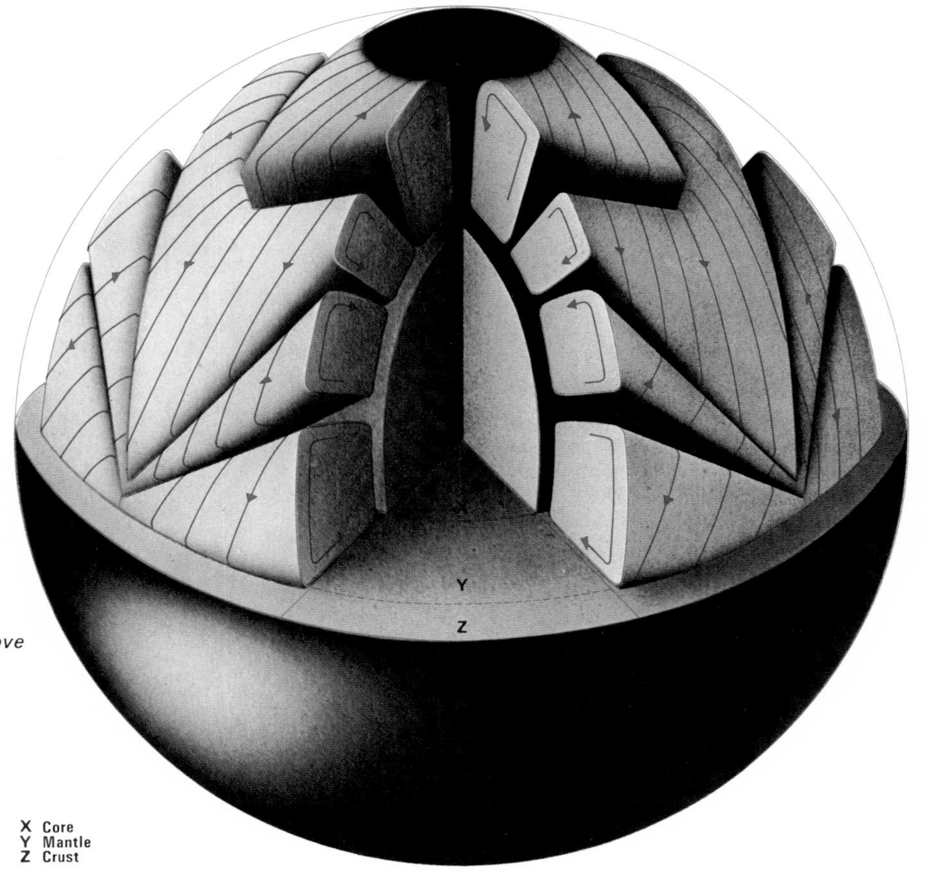
Y
Z

X Core
Y Mantle
Z Crust

Convection theory

Geologists and geophysicists are not unanimous on the question of whether there are convection currents present in the Earth's mantle or not, nor on the part these could play in providing the driving mechanism for major movements of the continents. Slow movement of 'solid' rocks can occur over long periods of time when the temperature is high and only relatively small density differences would be required to trigger them. Another matter for debate is whether convection is confined to the upper mantle or is continuous throughout the whole. It is not certain whether changes of physical state at different levels would constitute barriers to mantle-wide convection. The convection cells above are highly schematic but could largely explain the formation of some of the major geosynclinal fold mountains in the crust over the past thousand million years. Large-scale convection current systems in the mantle could also be the driving force for sea floor spreading and the associated continental drift.

The watery Earth *below*
Almost three-quarters of the Earth is covered by water. Basically the continents are rafts of relatively light crust 'floating' on generally denser oceanic crust. They comprise not only the visible land but also the adjacent continental shelves covered by shallow water. Oceanic crust underlies the deep sea platforms and ocean trenches. The areas of the major lands and seas (below, left) do not take into account the continental shelves but are the gross areas reckoned in terms of the land and water distribution at mean sea level. Extra area due to terrain is not included.

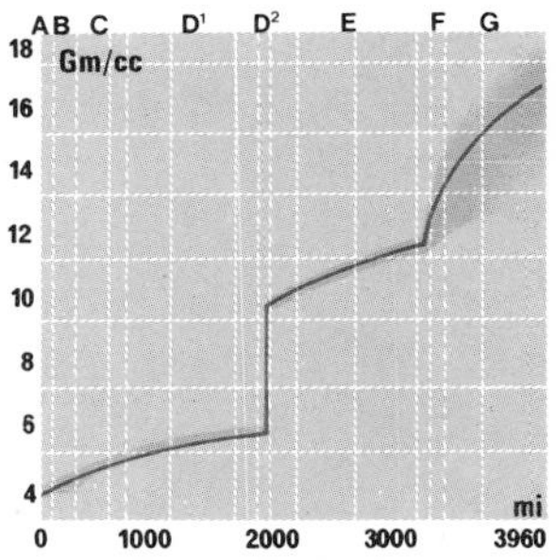
A B C D¹ D² E F G
Gm/cc
18
16
14
12
10
8
6
4
0 1000 2000 3000 3960 mi

The inner core (G)
The pressure of 3½ million atmospheres (35000 kg/mm²) keeps this a solid ball of 750 miles (1200 km) radius. Its density varies from 14 to about 16.

Density *left*
Virtually all man's knowledge of the interior of the Earth stems from measuring the transit of earthquake waves. The resulting data indicate sharp increases in density at the boundaries of both the outer core and the 'solid' inner core, with several intermediate zones.

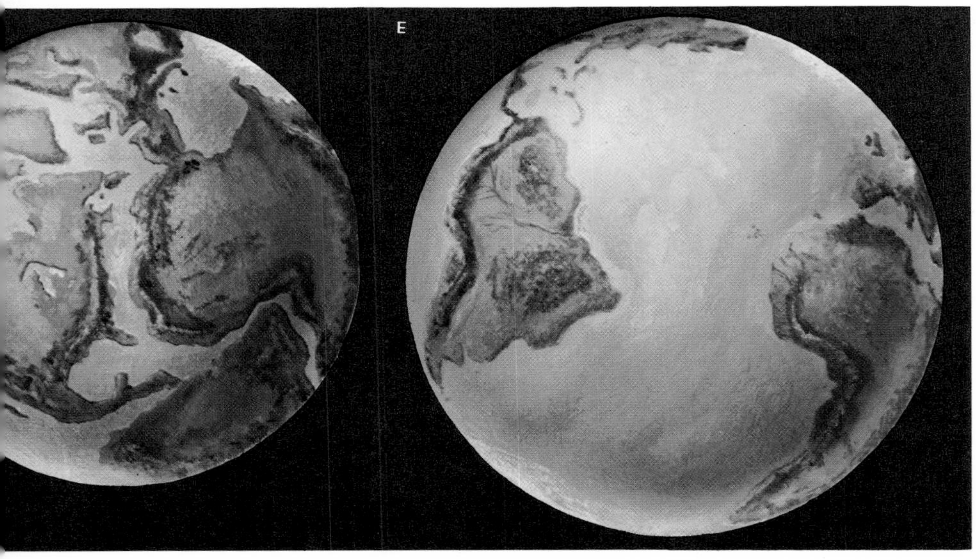
E

The watery Earth *right*
Key to numbered areas.

Oceans	Area (x1000) Sq mi	km²
1 Arctic	5541	14350
2 Pacific	63986	165750
3 Atlamtic	31530	81660
4 Indian	28350	73430
Continents		
5 Americas	16241	42063
6 Europe (excluding USSR)	1903	4929
7 Asia (excluding USSR)	10661	27611
8 USSR	8649	22402
9 Africa	11683	30258
10 Oceania	3286	8510
11 Antarctica	5500	14245

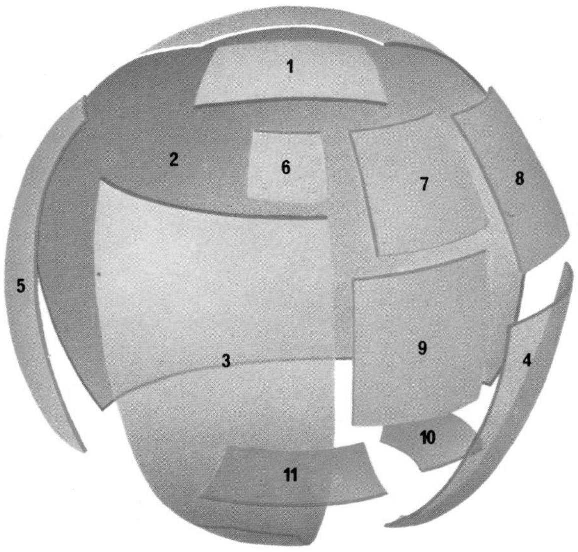
1
2
6
7
8
5
3
9
4
10
11

Forces that Shape the Land

Measured against the time standards of everyday life, the major forces that shape the face of the Earth seem to act almost unbelievably slowly. But in geological terms the erosion of rock formations by river, marine or ice action is in fact rather rapid. Indeed in isolated locations, on coasts or below waterfalls, visible erosion can take place in a period of months or even days.

Over large regions of the Earth the rates of river erosion, expressed as the mass of material removed from each unit of land area in a given time, range between about 30 and 6000 tons per square mile per year (12–2300 tonnes/km^2/year). The main factor determining the rate at any place is the climate. The average rate of erosion for Eurasia, Africa, the Americas and Australia, a land area of some 50 million square miles (130 million km^2), has been calculated to be of the order of 350 tons per square mile per year (135 tonnes/km^2/year). This corresponds to a general lowering of the surface of the land by about 40 inches (one meter) every 22000 years. At this rate these continents would be worn down to sea level in less than 20 million years, which in geological terms is a fairly short span of time.

In practice, the surface of the land would be most unlikely to suffer such a fate. Although isolated areas could be worn away, worldwide erosion on this scale and at a steady rate would be balanced or prevented by a number of factors, one of which is the continuing large-scale uplift of the land in other regions. Nevertheless long-term estimates do emphasize the cumulative effects of the apparently slow processes of erosion. Even man's own structures wear away. Already the portland stone of St. Paul's cathedral in London has lost half an inch (13 mm) overall in 250 years, aided by the additional force of atmospheric pollution.

Where do all the products of this erosion go? By far the largest accumulations of sediments occur in river deltas, and at many periods in the geological past great thicknesses of such deposits have been laid down in extensive subsiding troughs called geosynclines. A rate of deposition of 1/250 inch (0.1 millimeter per year is enough to lay down 12 miles (20 km) of strata in 200 million years.

The cycle of rock change

The agents of weathering
Gross break-up of the Earth's surface rocks is caused by earthquakes, the ceaseless cycle of diurnal and annual heating and cooling, and by the freezing of water trapped in fissures and crevices. The water of the seas, rivers and rain dissolves some rocks and in others leaches out particular minerals. Water is especially powerful as a weathering agent when it contains dissolved acidic chemicals. Today's main sources are plants and animals (1), but in the primeval world such chemicals were evolved mainly by volcanoes (2).

Erosion of the land
Only the material exposed at the surface of the Earth by volcanic action (2) or uplift (3) is subjected to erosion, but this material is constantly changing. Chemical erosion is an extension of the weathering process, converting the surface material into different and usually physically degraded substances. Physical erosion (4) is effected by running water and the wind (in both cases accelerated by the presence of an abrasive load) and by ice action and frost shattering.

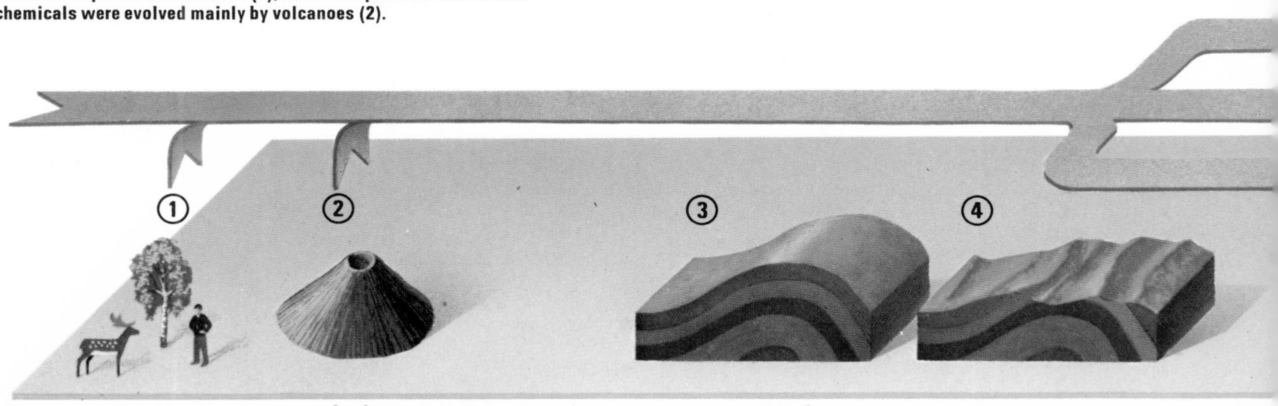

1
2
3
4

Extrusions (15)
Most lavas are at a temperature of 900-1200°C. Acidic (granitic) lava is fairly viscous, but basic (basalt) lava flows relatively freely and when extruded from surface fissures or volcanoes can cover large areas (15). Lavas which have originated from partial melting of crustal rocks can also be erupted.

Intrusions (13)
Contact metamorphism is a form of baking and re-crystallization caused by the intrusion of hot magma into existing strata (13).

Slow uplift (11)
Strata can be slowly uplifted (11) until they once more appear at the surface; continued or violent uplift results in mountain-building. In either case, erosion begins afresh.

Basic magmas (14)
Basic magma generated by partial melting in the mantle (14) may rise into and through the crust to be extruded from surface volcanoes. Basic magmas are the hottest, as well as the most freely flowing, and are often generated at very considerable depth. In their ascent they can intrude large areas of the crust and finally extrude through fissures in the surface.

Granitic magmas (12)
Partial melting deep in the crust generates new granitic magma—hot, rather viscous molten rock of an acidic nature which is able to migrate both upwards and laterally (12). This may then inject and mix with the surrounding rocks to form a migmatite complex.

Deep metamorphism (10)
If the strata are depressed far down, to depths up to about 25 miles (40 km), deep metamorphism at high pressures and high temperatures (10) results in complete re-crystallization. This gradually converts the original sediments into a complex of new rock types.

Erosion

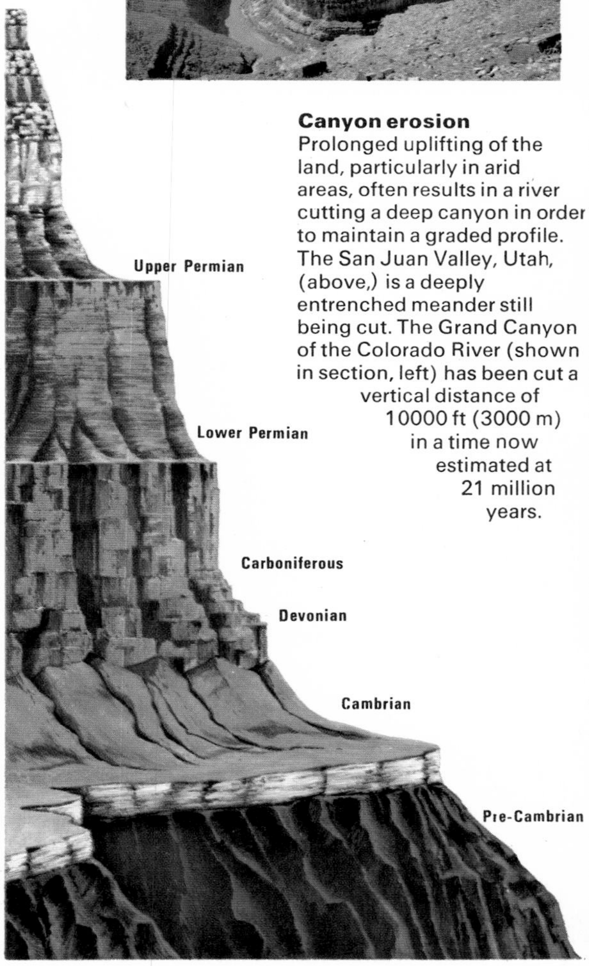

Upper Permian
Lower Permian
Carboniferous
Devonian
Cambrian
Pre-Cambrian

Canyon erosion
Prolonged uplifting of the land, particularly in arid areas, often results in a river cutting a deep canyon in order to maintain a graded profile. The San Juan Valley, Utah, (above,) is a deeply entrenched meander still being cut. The Grand Canyon of the Colorado River (shown in section, left) has been cut a vertical distance of 10000 ft (3000 m) in a time now estimated at 21 million years.

Wind erosion
Laden with grains of sand and other air-transportable debris, the wind exerts a powerful sculpturing effect. Rate of erosion varies with rock hardness, giving rise to odd effects (Mushroom Rock, Death Valley, California, left). Desert sand forms 'barchan' dunes (right), which slowly travel points-first.

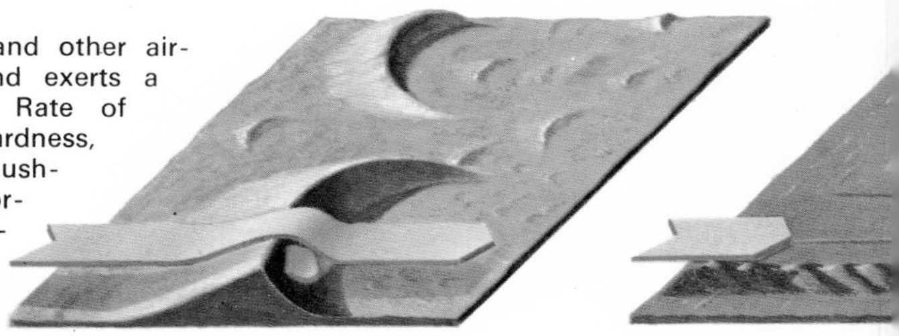

Sculpture by the sea
The ocean shapes the land by the pounding of the waves, scouring by the currents, chemical solution and deposition of debris. Around the Atlantic coast of the Portuguese Algarve are particularly fine wave-eroded rocks (at Piedade, left) while some of the principle mechanisms and coastal features are seen at right (key, far right).

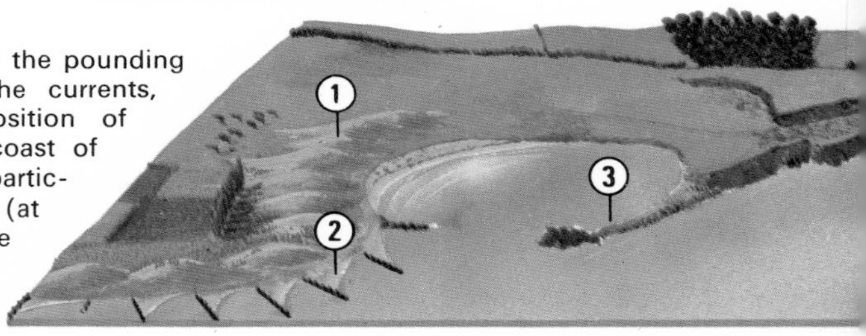

1
2
3

River development
The youthful river flows fast, eroding a narrow channel in an otherwise unchanged landscape. In maturity the channel is wider; flow is slower and some transported debris is deposited. The old river meanders across a broad flood plain (River Wye near Goodrich, left), some meanders becoming cut off as ox-bow lakes.

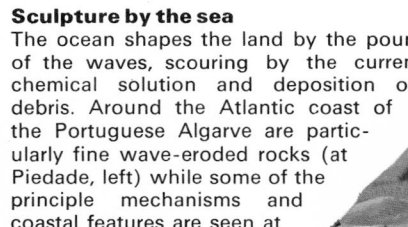

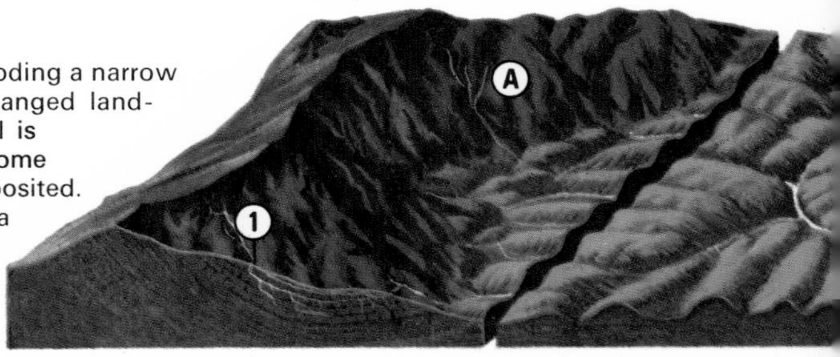

A
1

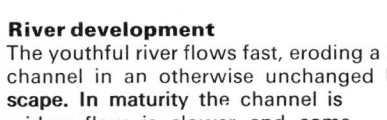

Glacial action
Briksdal Glacier, Norway (left), is a remnant of the Ice Ages, carving U-shaped valleys (2) in the pre-glacial rock (1). The bergschrund (3) forms close to the back wall, while other crevasses (4) form at gradient changes. Eroded rocks form a longitudinal moraine (5).

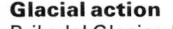

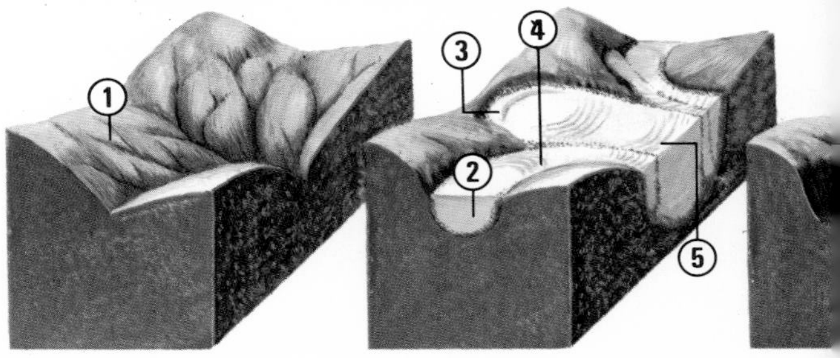

1
2
3
4
5

Transportation
As material is worn away from the surface rocks it is carried away by various processes. The most important transport system is flowing water (5), which can move sediments in suspension, in solution or carried along the beds of river channels. In open country, and especially over deserts, much solid debris is blown by the wind (6). Even slow-moving glaciers (7) perform a significant erosion and transport role by bearing heavy burdens of rock debris.

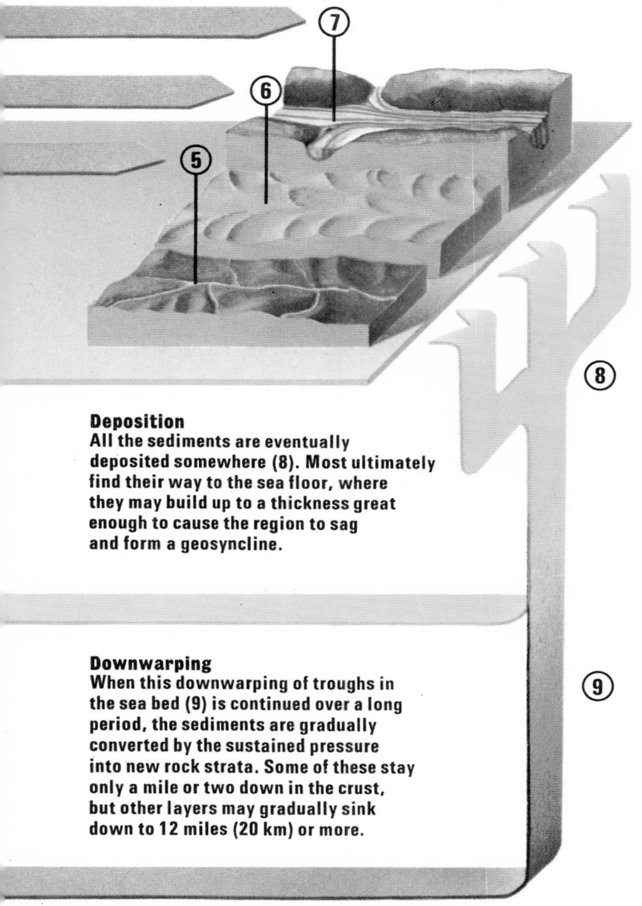

7
6
5
8

Deposition
All the sediments are eventually deposited somewhere (8). Most ultimately find their way to the sea floor, where they may build up to a thickness great enough to cause the region to sag and form a geosyncline.

Downwarping
When this downwarping of troughs in the sea bed (9) is continued over a long period, the sediments are gradually converted by the sustained pressure into new rock strata. Some of these stay only a mile or two down in the crust, but other layers may gradually sink down to 12 miles (20 km) or more.

9

250 million years ago

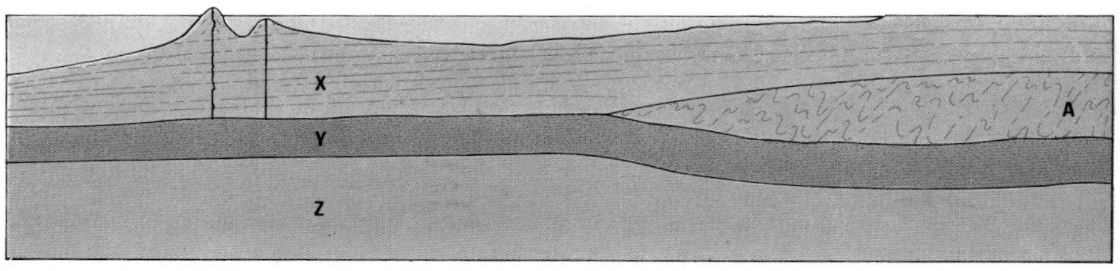

X
Y
Z
A

Late Paleozoic *left*
The formation of a geosyncline begins with the laying down of heavy sediments. In the creation of the Sierra Nevada range sediments X were deposited by the primeval ocean on top of Precambrian rock A, basalt crust Y and peridotite mantle Z.

180 million years ago

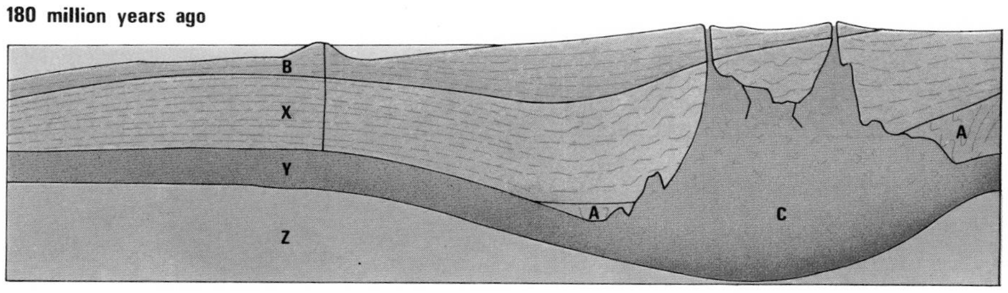

B
X
Y
Z
A
C
A

Jurassic *left*
Downwarping of the crust causes the deposition of Mesozoic sediments B and carries the lower basalt crust and sediments into the zone of the mantle's influence. The bottom of the bulge is gradually converted into hot, fluid magma C.

100 million years ago

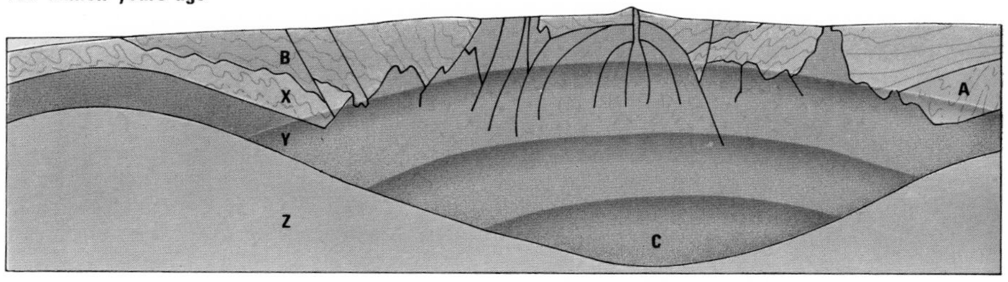

B
X
Y
Z
C
A

Cretaceous *left*
In this period the geosynclinal process is in a mature stage. The inner rocks reach their maximum downward penetration into the mantle and are metamorphosed by high temperature and pressure. The deep metamorphism spreads (curved shading).

Present day

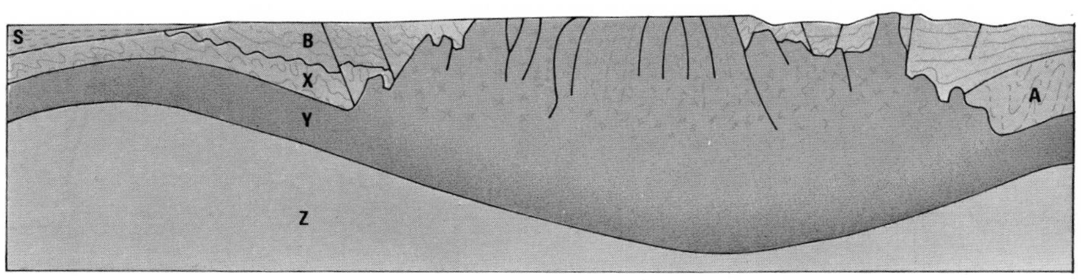

S
B
X
Y
Z
A

Present day *left*
Uplift and cooling opens the way to a new cycle of formation. The metamorphic rocks are exposed at the surface and subsequently eroded to yield today's complex landscape structure. Final withdrawal of the sea exposes marine sediments S.

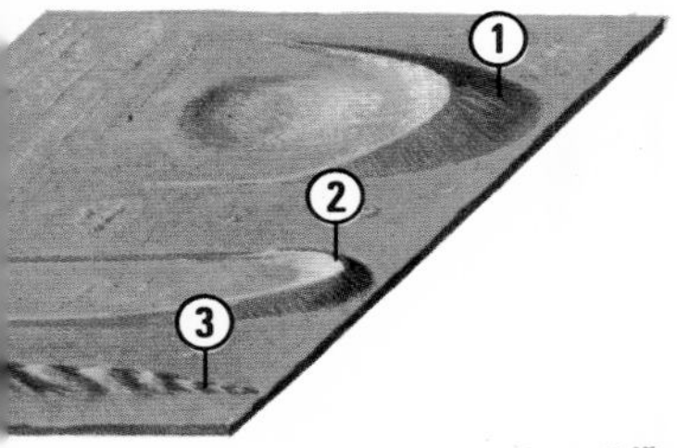

1
2
3

Wind-blown sand *left*
Sand deserts exhibit dunes of various forms. Unlike a barchan the parabolic blowout (1) travels with points trailing. In elongated form this becomes a parabolic hairpin (2), and a third form is the longitudinal ridge (3), known in the Sahara as a seif dune.

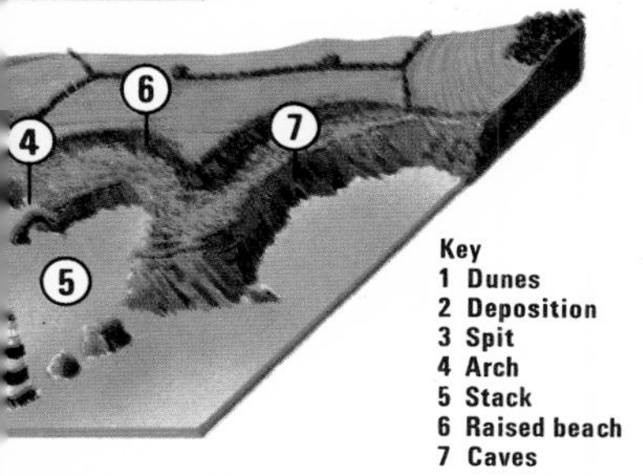

6
7
4
5

Key
1 Dunes
2 Deposition
3 Spit
4 Arch
5 Stack
6 Raised beach
7 Caves

Emerging coastline *right*
Where the shoreline is rising, the continental shelf becomes exposed. River silt accumulates and forms an offshore bar, pierced by the river flow. Eventually infilling forms a tidal salt marsh through which the braided river reaches a new shore. Spain (far right) and Italy provide good examples.

Key
A Initial stage
B Late youth
C Early maturity
1 Cut-off
2 Spit
3 4 Bars
5 Lagoon

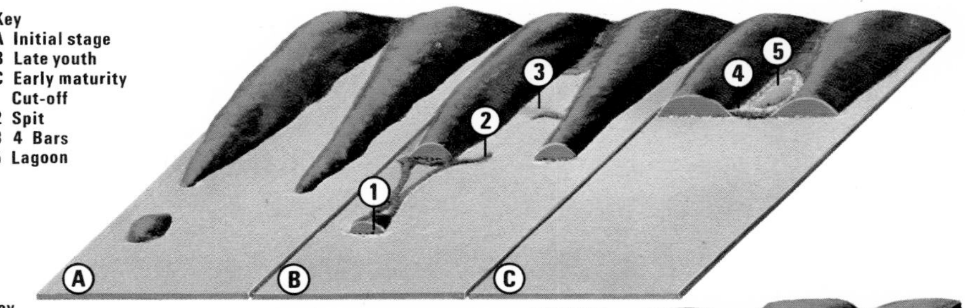

1
2
3
4
5
A
B
C

Subsiding coastline *left*
Most coastal regions undergoing submergence are highly irregular. Drowned hills are eroded by the waves to form cliff headlands, or cut-offs; spits and bars cross the submerged valleys, enclose them and form lagoons. Finally all these features wear back to a new shoreline.

Key
A Initial stage
B Bar development
C Emergence complete

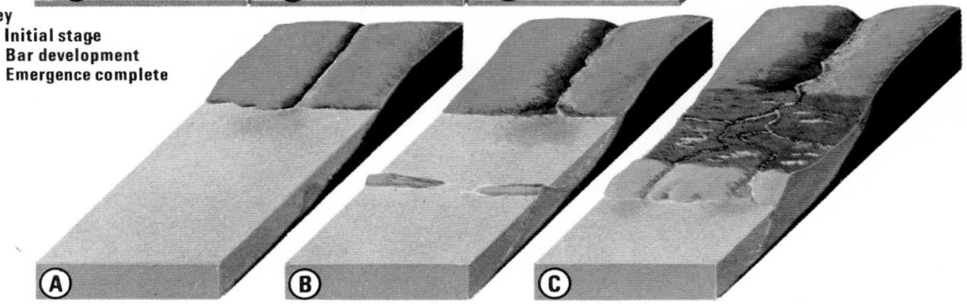

A
B
C

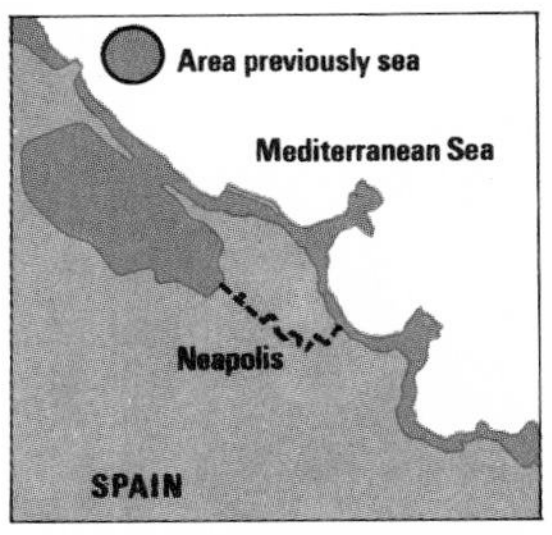

Area previously sea
Mediterranean Sea
Neapolis
SPAIN

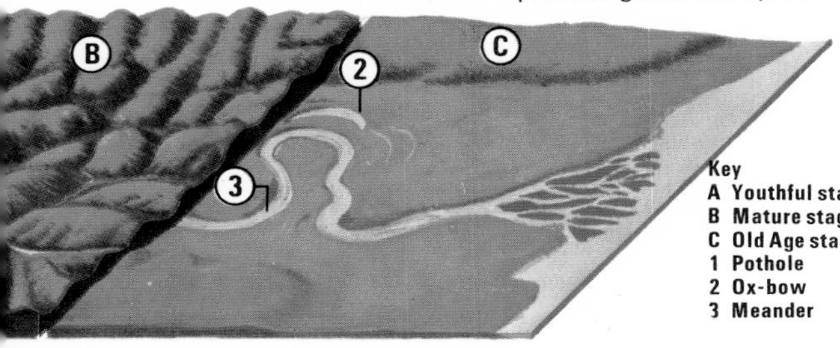

B
2
C
3

Key
A Youthful stage
B Mature stage
C Old Age stage
1 Pothole
2 Ox-bow
3 Meander

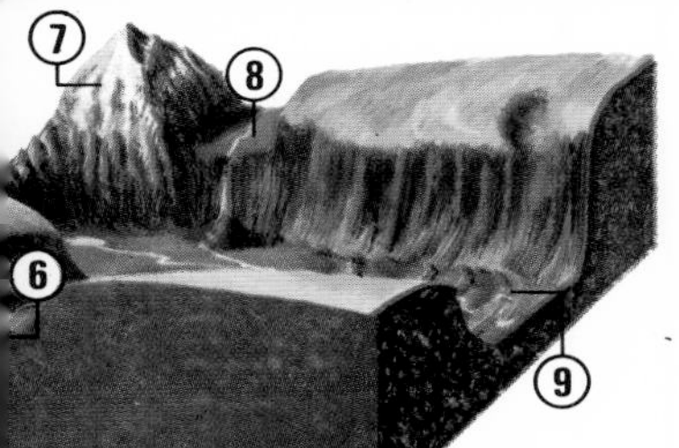

7
8
6
9

Glaciated landscape *left*
The landscape shows evidence of former ice coverage. Broken rock debris forms valley-floor moraines (6), the peaks are sharp and knife-edged (7), and hanging valleys (8) mark the entry of the glacier's tributaries. Terminal moraines (9) are a characteristic feature.

Key
1 Esker
2 Recessional moraine
3 Drumlin
4 Lake
5 Terminal moraine
6 Outwash delta
7 Lake deposits
8 Kettle lake
9 Outwash plain
10 Kettle hole

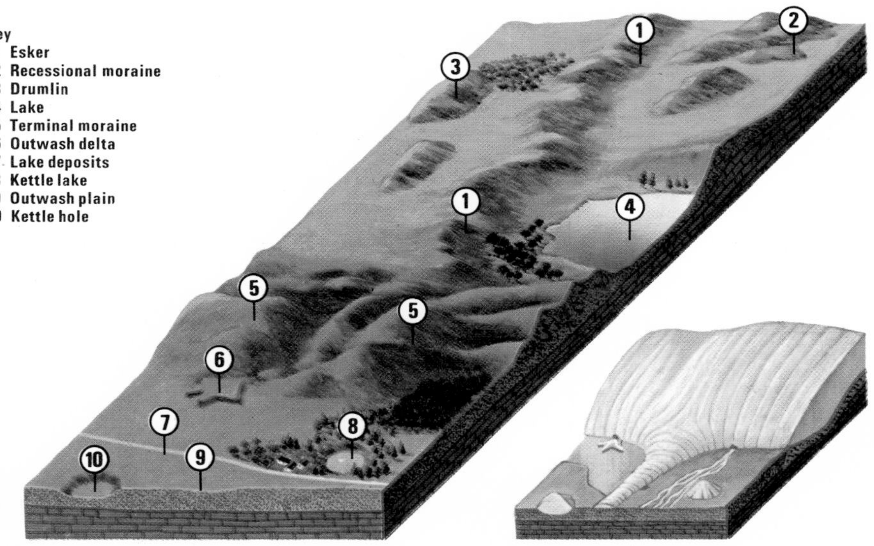

1
2
3
1
4
5
5
6
7
8
9
10

Glaciated landforms *left*
Throughout a vast area of the temperate lands evidence of past glacial action is abundant. A geomorphologist, studying the landscape shown in the larger illustration, would deduce the former glacial situation depicted in the inset. Weight and sculpture by the ice carved out characteristic depressions, some later filled with water. Subglacial streams left alluvial deposits in the form of eskers and an outwash fan or delta, while the limit of the glacier is suggested by rocks deposited as a terminal moraine. Kettle holes result from the melting of ice within moraine debris.

The Record in the Rocks

All the past history of the Earth since the original formation of the crust is there to be discovered in the rocks existing today if only the appropriate techniques are used to find it. Sedimentary, igneous and metamorphic – the three basic types of rock – all have an enormous amount of information stored within them on such diverse aspects of the Earth's history as, for example, the variations of past climates in space and in time, the incidence of ice ages and the positions of former mountain ranges. The migrations of the ancient geo-magnetic poles at different periods of time can be discovered by studying some sedimentary and igneous rocks, while other types can yield their ages of formation or metamorphism – their changed character over long periods. The prevailing wind directions over certain regions, the direction of stream flow in river deltas that have long since vanished, or the ways in which the ice flowed in some past ice age are all there to be discovered. So are the past distributions of land and sea, areas of deposition, periods of uplift and the raising of great mountain chains (page 37). Even lightning strikes millions of years old can be clearly seen.

The first task of the geologist is to make a map showing the positions and relative ages of the various rock types in a region. It is around this basic information incorporated into the geological map that all else is built, whether it is to be studies of the geological history and evolution of the region, or detailed investigations of the flora and fauna, or any of many other lines of research – such as the disentangling of various periods of deformation which have affected the region during which the rocks may have been folded or faulted (foot of this page) or eroded down to sea level. Two of the most important methods of dating, by which the age of rock is determined, are the study of fossils and the use of radiometric methods in which age is calculated by analyzing radioactive minerals having a known half-life (opposite page). Using a combination of 'correlation' techniques and either method of dating it is possible for a skilled geologist to compare the relative time sequences of geological events in any regions in the world.

How the story unfolds *right*
The complex 3500 million year story of the rocks is very far from being superficially obvious. Even a skilled geologist can do no more than study the land as it is today, plot a geological map and then try to think backward over periods of millions of years in an endeavor to determine the sequences which produced the present terrain. On the right is depicted such a sequence, which might reasonably be arrived at after studying the map below, left.
The history begins (A) with the landmass rising and the sea retreating, leaving behind 'off-lap' sediments. The landmass continues to rise and is folded by compressive forces, the fold tops then being eroded (B). Over a long period the landmass then subsides and tilts; the sea once more advances, laying down 'on-lap' sediments (C). Then a great upheaval causes the sea to retreat completely.
The landmass is strongly uplifted and faulted, and the higher mass is at once attacked by erosion (D). Continued erosion gradually reduces the region to a more or less common level. Rivers, formed at stage C, carry eroded materials away and deposit them at lower levels (left side of E). Finally, the northeast part of the region is invaded by an extrusive mass of volcanic material. Of course, the processes of change would continue even now.

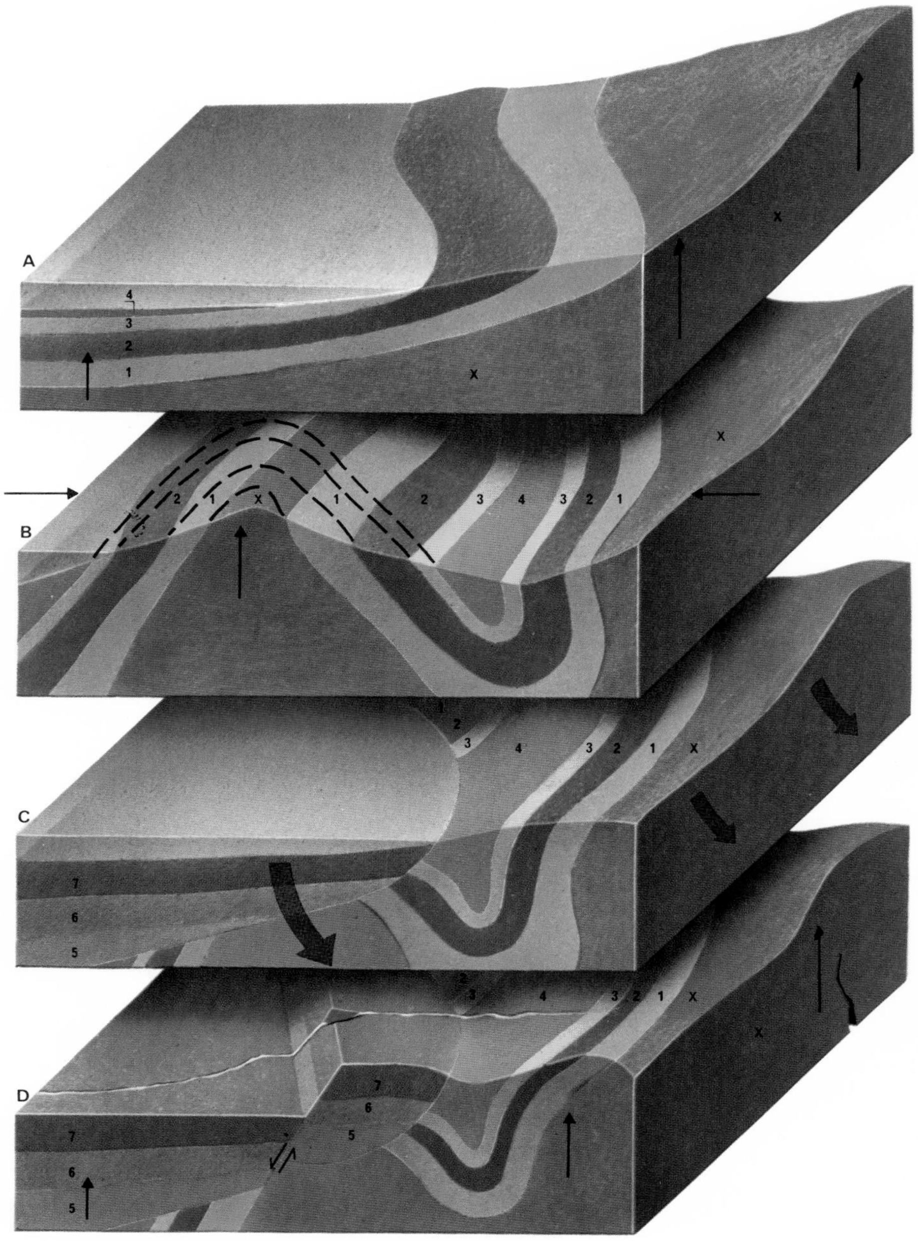

A
B
C
D

A geological map *below*
A geological map records the outcrop pattern and the structural features of each region as they are today, corresponding with the final stage of the reconstruction—right.

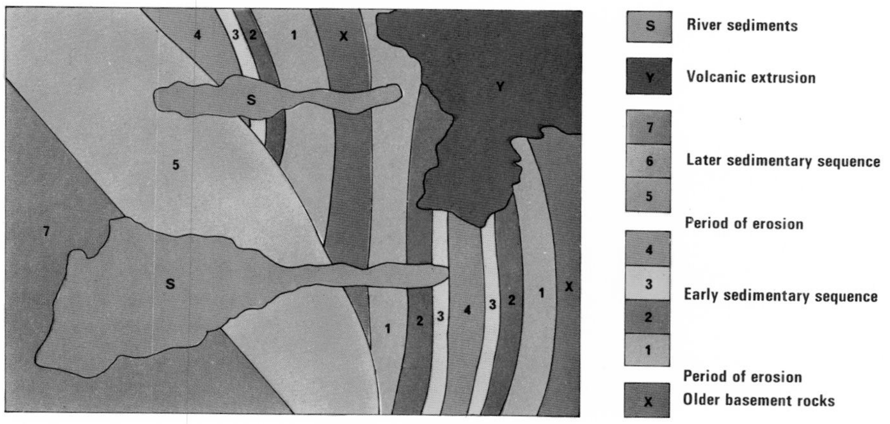

S River sediments
Y Volcanic extrusion
7 6 5 Later sedimentary sequence
Period of erosion
4 3 2 1 Early sedimentary sequence
Period of erosion
X Older basement rocks

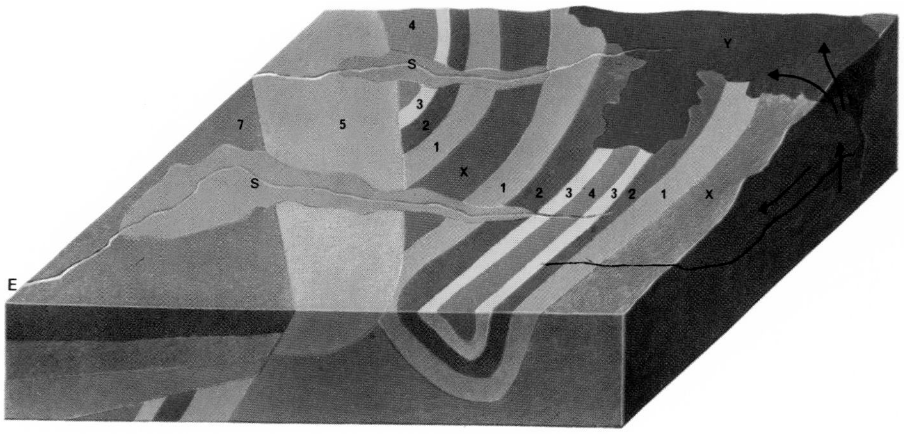

E

The language of geology
Plane of movement of a normal fault (1) displacing strata to right (downthrow side) relative to left (upthrow side).

Block of strata (2) dropped between two tensional faults forming a rift valley. Other strata are compressional.

Normal anticline (3) and syncline (4) with symmetrically dipping limbs on either side of the axial plane of the strata.

Positions of the axial planes (5, 6) passing through an asymmetrical anticline (5) and an asymmetrical syncline (6).

Compressional reversed fault (7). In this case the left side of the fault is over-riding basically horizontal strata on the right.

Monoclinal fold (8), with a relatively steep limb separating basically horizontal areas of strata at two levels.

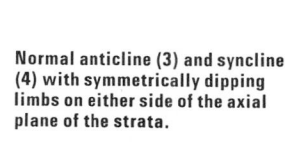

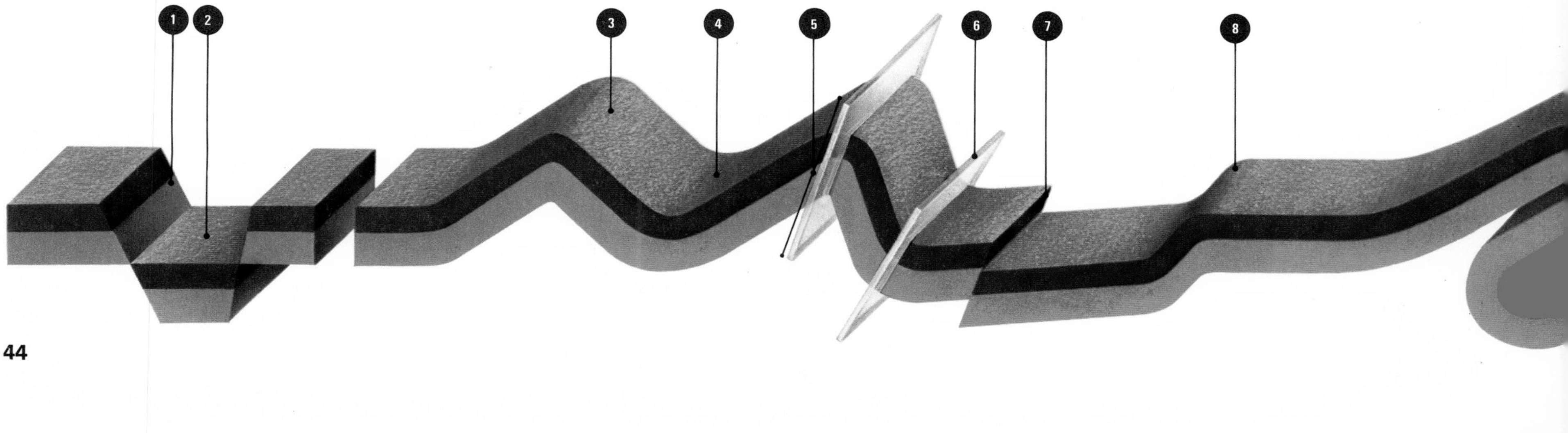

1
2
3
4
5
6
7
8

Geological dating

The relative dating of geological strata is found from the sequence in which the layers were deposited, the oldest being at the base of a local sequence and the youngest at the top. On this basis, together with correlations over wide areas based on the fossil evidence of the forms of life at different stages of the 'geological column', the main periods and subdivisions can be worked out.

Prior to the Cambrian, the oldest epoch of the Paleozoic era (see scale at right), evidence of life is seldom found in the rocks. The extremely primitive earliest forms of life have generally not been preserved in the form of fossils, and so correlations by palaeontological methods cannot be applied to the Precambrian.

In recent years the progressive evolution of radiometric dating has enabled geologists to assign actual dates to the relative sequences of strata. Since the formation of the Earth's crust various isotopes have been present in it which are radioactive, spontaneously decaying over a precisely fixed period of time into a different element. For example a large number of geological dates have been based on the decay of potassium (K^{40}) to argon (A^{40}) and on that of rubidium (Rb^{87}) to strontium (Sr^{87}). The manner in which these valuable geological time-clocks decay over many millions of years is depicted below. No radioactive isotope is ever completely used up; millions of years later atoms are still present of both the original isotope and the end-product of its disintegration.

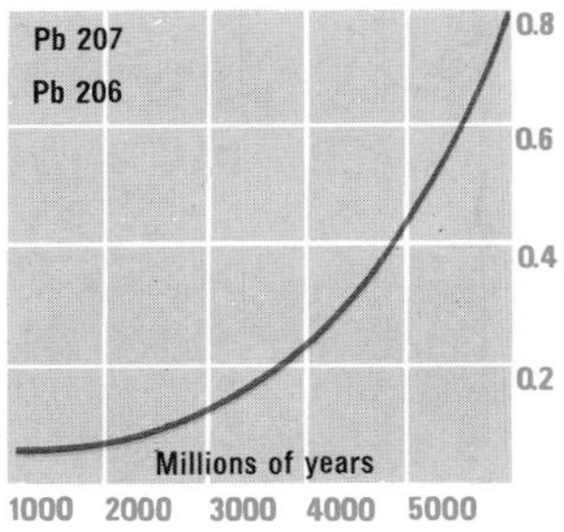

Pb 207
Pb 206
0.8
0.6
0.4
0.2
Millions of years
1000 2000 3000 4000 5000

Half-life *left*
Radioactive materials decay according to a law. Each isotope has a characteristic half-life, the time required for the number of radioactive atoms to decay to half the original number. The half-life for each element is unalterable.

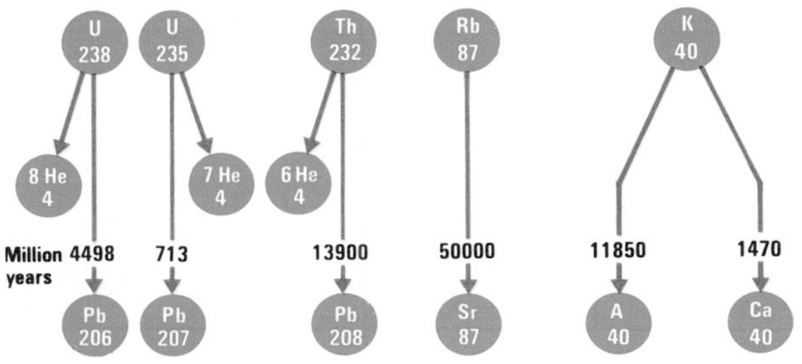

U 238
U 235
Th 232
Rb 87
K 40
8 He 4
7 He 4
6 He 4
Million years 4498
713
13900
50000
11850
1470
Pb 206
Pb 207
Pb 208
Sr 87
A 40
Ca 40

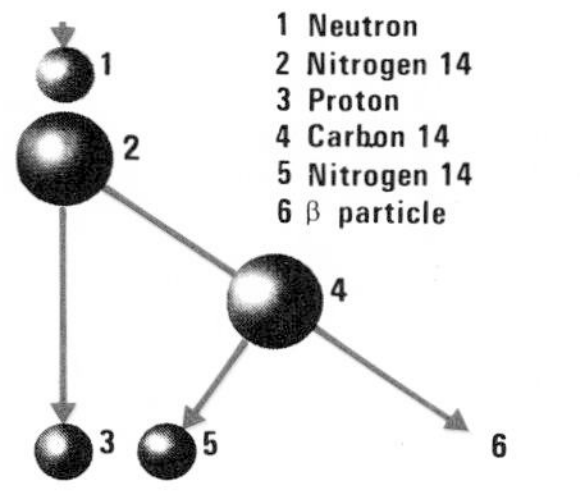

1 Neutron
2 Nitrogen 14
3 Proton
4 Carbon 14
5 Nitrogen 14
6 β particle
1
2
3
4
5
6

Degeneration
above and left
Some of the isotopes, shown above with their half-lives and end-products can be used for dating over the whole age of the Earth. For more recent dating, radio-carbon with a half-life of 5570 years is used (left).

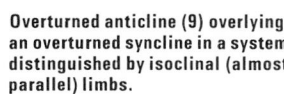

Overturned anticline (9) overlying an overturned syncline in a system distinguished by isoclinal (almost parallel) limbs.

Plane of thrusting (10) causes the overturned anticline (11) to ride over lower strata in form of a horizontally displaced 'nappe'.

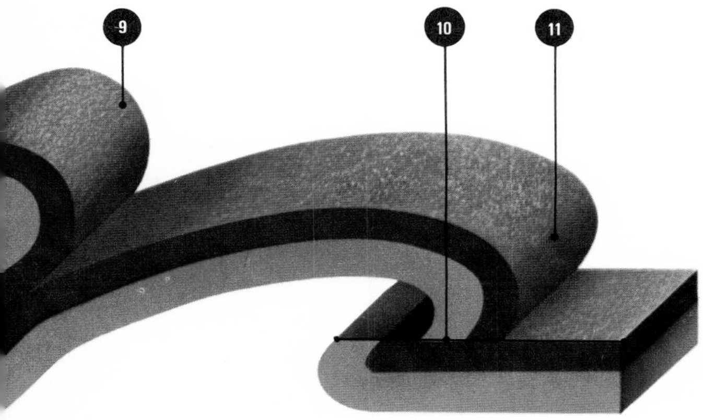

9
10
11

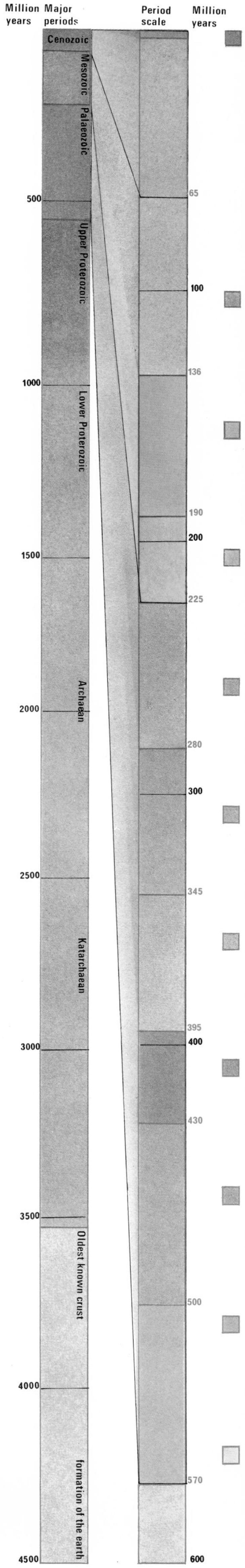

Million years
Major periods
Period scale
Million years
Cenozoic
Mesozoic
Palaeozoic
Upper Proterozoic
Lower Proterozoic
Archaean
Katarchaean
Oldest known crust
formation of the earth
500
1000
1500
2000
2500
3000
3500
4000
4500
65
100
136
190
200
225
280
300
345
395
400
430
500
570
600

Period

Quaternary
This most recent period of geological history leads up to the appearance of man and the present day. Changes of climate took place which brought on the great ice ages with glacial periods alternating with warmer sequences between them. And, of course, the period is still in progress.

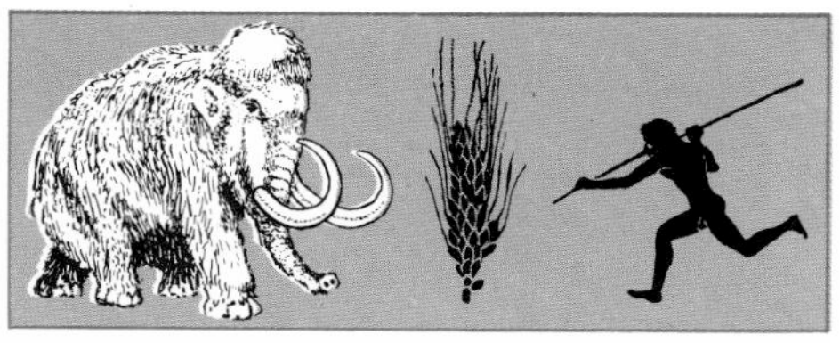

Tertiary
A complex history of changes took place, each epoch of the Tertiary period from Paleocene to Pliocene showing a diverse sequence of volcanism and mountain-building in different regions. Shallow seas alternated with sub-tropical delta flats harboring the precursors of today's life.

Cretaceous
The Tethys Sea spread over large areas of the adjacent continents. Fossil evidence reveals a diverse flora and fauna. The South Atlantic reached a width of some 1900 miles (3000 km) and only Antarctica and Australia and the northern lands of the North Atlantic remained unseparated.

Jurassic
The North Atlantic had opened to a width of some 600 miles (1000 km). Sedimentary deposits formed marginal belts around the continents which had separated, and deeper-water sediments were deposited in the Tethys Sea. Extensive eruption of basalts accompanied the rifting of the South Atlantic.

Triassic
This was the period in which the continental drift began. The progressive opening of the North Atlantic was accompanied by rift-valley faulting and large outpourings of basalt along the eastern seaboard of what is today North America. Gondwanaland in the south began to break up.

Permian
Many areas were characterized by arid or semi-arid climates, with frequent salt lakes giving rise to evaporite deposits and red desert sandstones. Much volcanic activity took place on a local scale. This was the last period in which Pangaea remained a single continental mass. New flora were abundant.

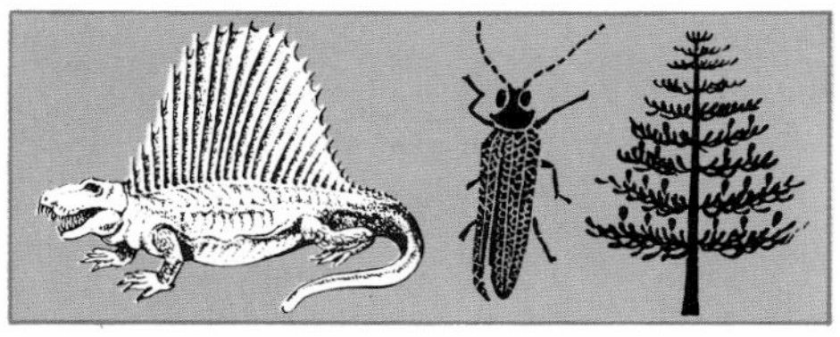

Carboniferous
Extensive forest and deltaic swamp conditions led to the eventual formation of coal basins in North America and Europe. Phases of folding and mountain formation occurred in many places. In Gondwanaland widespread glaciation occurred, with glaciers radiating from a great central ice-cap.

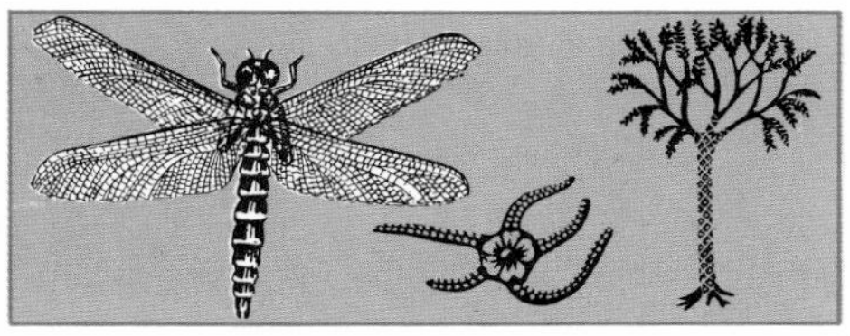

Devonian
Large areas of arid continental and sandstone deposits formed, partly as the products of erosion of the mountains formed previously. Intervening basins of shallow sea or lagoonal deposits occurred, with abundant fossil fish. Distinct faunal provinces have been recognized from this period.

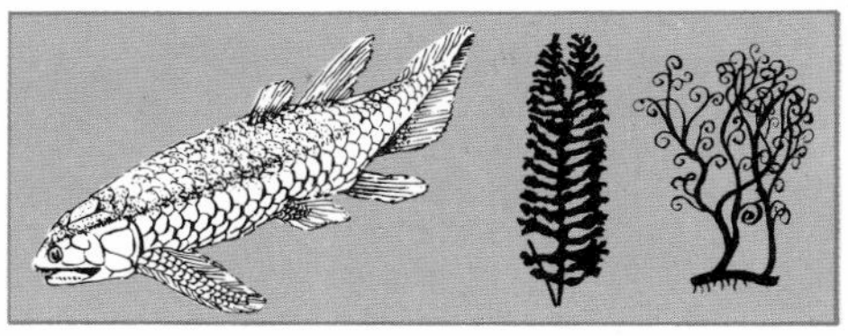

Silurian
In this period further widespread basins of thick sedimentary deposits were laid down. Many of these are characterized by the abundance of marine fossils, including corals. The Caledonian mountains were formed in Laurasia in which enormous volumes of granitic rocks were later emplaced.

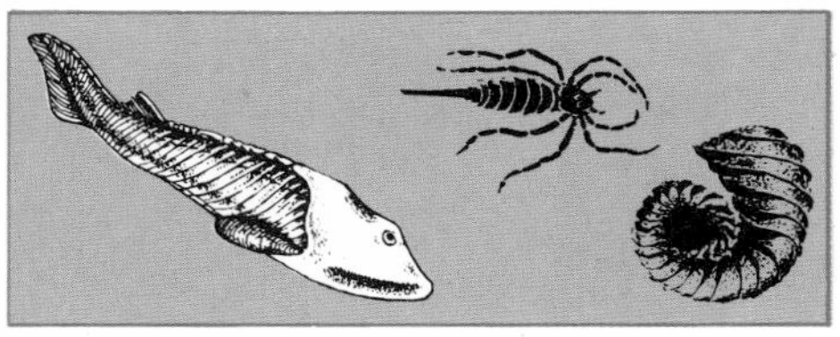

Ordovician
Graptolites and trilobites continued to be important forms of marine life. Thick marine sediments continued to be laid down, and there were extensive and widespread outbursts of volcanic activity. In some regions deformation and uplift of the rocks created major mountain ranges.

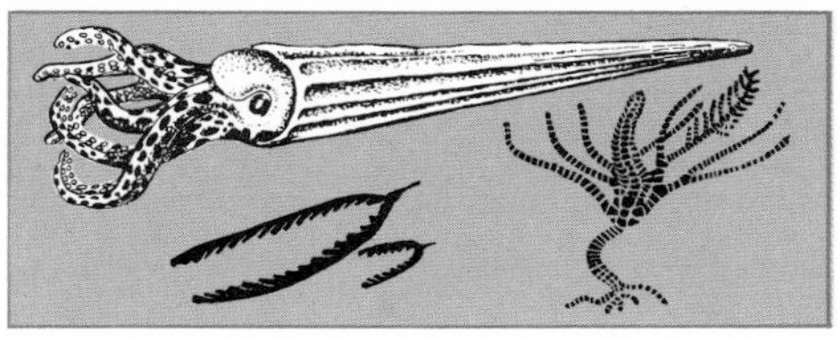

Cambrian
Rocks of this period contain the earliest fossilized remnants of more complex forms of life such as graptolites, brachiopods, trilobites and gastropods. In many regions the Cambrian period was characterized by the deposition of thick sequences of sedimentary rocks, usually on an eroded basement.

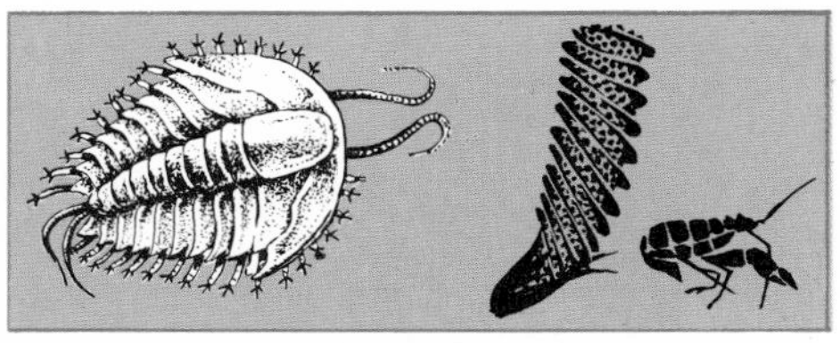

Precambrian
By far the longest period of geological time is included in the Precambrian. This encompasses a complex history of sedimentation, mountain-building, volcanism, and granitic intrusions. Precambrian rocks form basements to many sedimentary deposits, and make up the nuclei of continents.

The Treasures of the Earth

One of the wonders of the Earth must be the subtle interplay between light and structure that transforms common minerals into precious jewels. In most cases man's hand can be detected in their creation, but even in the natural state many minerals have a range of color, shape, texture and form that makes them the treasures of the Earth.

By popular definition, anything that is mined is called a mineral and on this basis coal and oil are the most important minerals (pages 100-101). However, geologists reserve the term for naturally occurring materials which have an unvarying chemical composition and crystalline structure. The basic structural elements are arranged in a rigid pattern within three-dimensional crystal matrices.

Each crystal grows from a nucleus by adding atoms layer by layer. A freely growing crystal assumes one of seven basic forms, depending on the relative angles of its faces and the distances between opposite parallel pairs. But in practice the shape of naturally occurring crystals is generally influenced by the space in which it is constrained to grow. Thus in nature crystals develop characteristic habits or overall shapes. The faces may be all of the same size or unequal. They may occur in narrow layers or grow like a bunch of grapes.

Minerals can be identified by their structure, habit, hardness, density, and the ease with which they can be cleaved along particular planes. Hardness, for example, is normally measured against a scale of increasing hardness from talc to diamond, devised in 1822 by the Austrian mineralogist, F. Mohs. Color is frequently the result of minute proportions of impurities. These often result in minerals of such startling beauty that they are coveted by man as gemstones. The brilliance of transparent gems is due to the way light is reflected inside the stone, and man has learned how to cut gems to enhance their optical properties. The stone is cut or ground to a precise external form with face angles arranged to insure the maximum brilliance based on the refractive index of the material. Rocks (below) are composed of different combinations of a limited number of minerals.

Basic igneous rock
Dolerite, a basic igneous rock, is composed of laths of plagioclase (grey and black), pyroxene (yellow and orange) and oxides of iron and titanium (blackish regions).

Sedimentary rock *above*
Limestone is composed of finely crystalline calcite. It shows the fossilized remains of foraminifera.

Acid igneous rock *below*
Granite is a hard igneous rock made up of quartz, potassium feldspar and red-brown crystals of biotite.

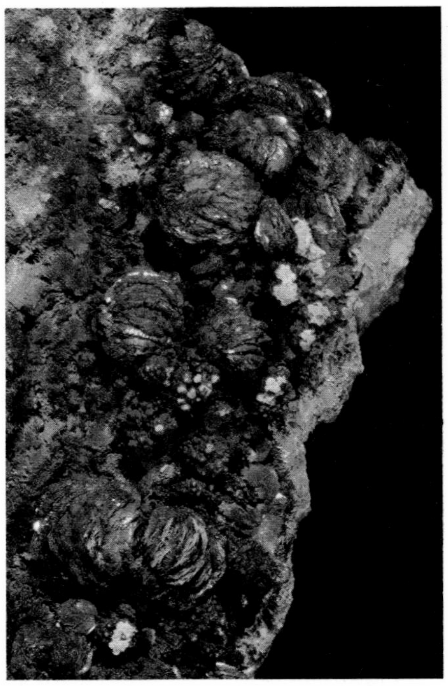

Azurite
Carbonate of copper, possibly the first metal used by man.

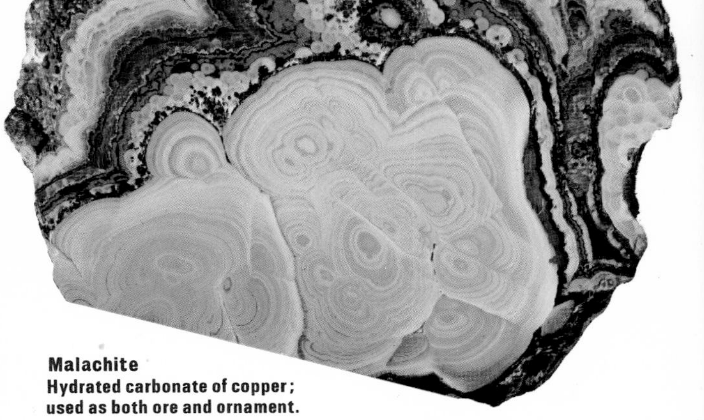

Malachite
Hydrated carbonate of copper; used as both ore and ornament.

Opal
Amorphous silicon dioxide with a variable content of water.

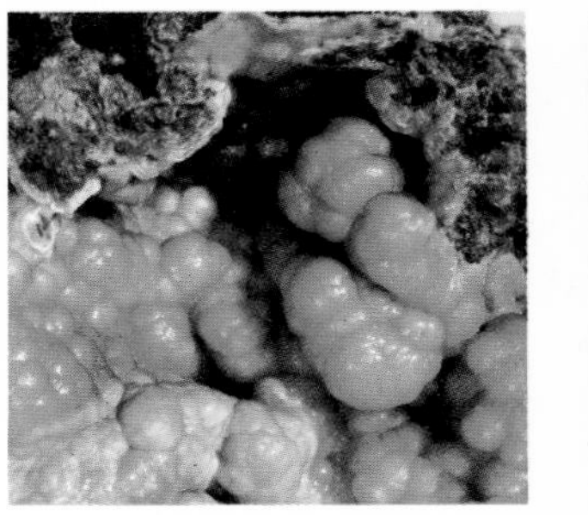

Hemimorphite
A zinc silicate, botryoidal crystal found with other zinc deposits.

Cerussite
Very clearly defined crystals of lead carbonate.

Pyromorphite
A bed of fine hexagonal columns of lead chlorophosphate.

Sphene
Silicates are abundant; sphene is calcium titanium silicate.

Crystal size
Although crystal shapes are governed by internal structure, individual sizes are controlled only by conditions of growth. For example, plates of mica—seen as minute biotite flakes in granite sections (lower left)—have reached 33ft (10m) by 14ft (4.3m) wide as in one 90-ton example discovered in Canada.

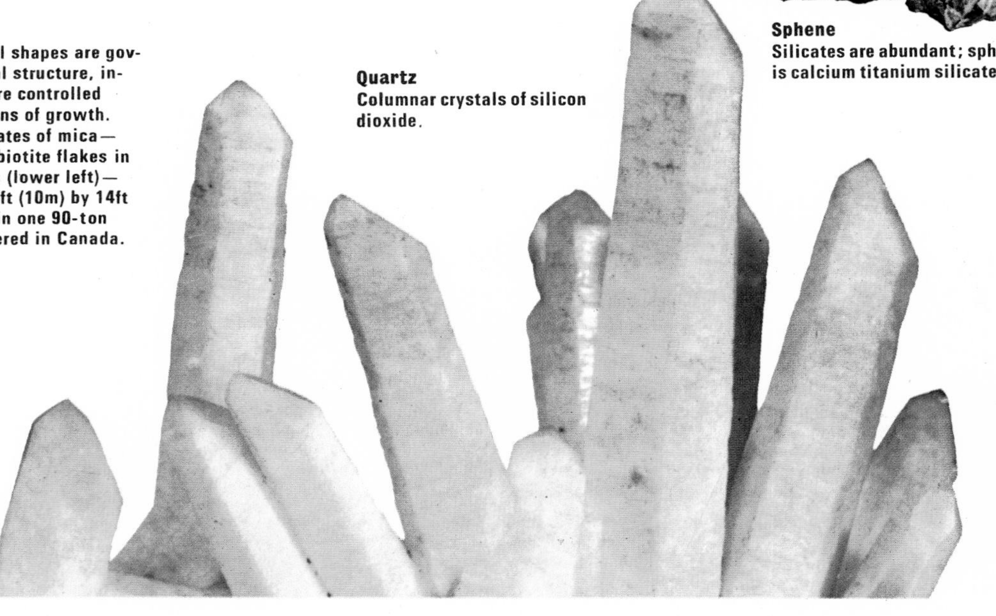

Quartz
Columnar crystals of silicon dioxide.

Torbernite
Hydrous copper uranium phosphate; a uranium source.

Beryl
Beryllium aluminium silicate is known in crystals of 25 tons.

Pyrite on calcite
Crystals of iron disulphide, on calcium carbonate.

Calcite
Often occurs as stalactites and stalagmites.

Wavelite
Crystals of hydrous basic aluminium phosphate.

Cassiterite
Tin was one of man's earliest metals; this is the dioxide ore.

Diamonds in kimberlite
Native diamonds (crystalline carbon) in their original rock.

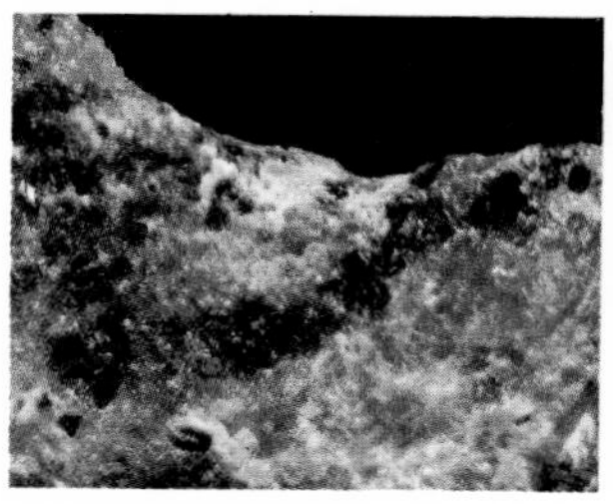

Ruby in host rock
The deep red variety of corundum (aluminium oxide).

Citrine
The yellowish variety of quartz (silicon dioxide).

Polished diamond
For use as a gemstone the diamond is skilfully cut.

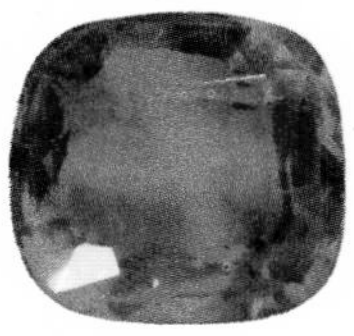

Polished ruby
Large rubies are among the most precious of all gemstones.

Sulphur
Crystalline sulphur (brimstone) occurs in nature.

Blue John
Calcium fluoride (fluorite), occurs in various colorful forms.

Galena
Cubic crystals of lead sulphide, a major ore of lead.

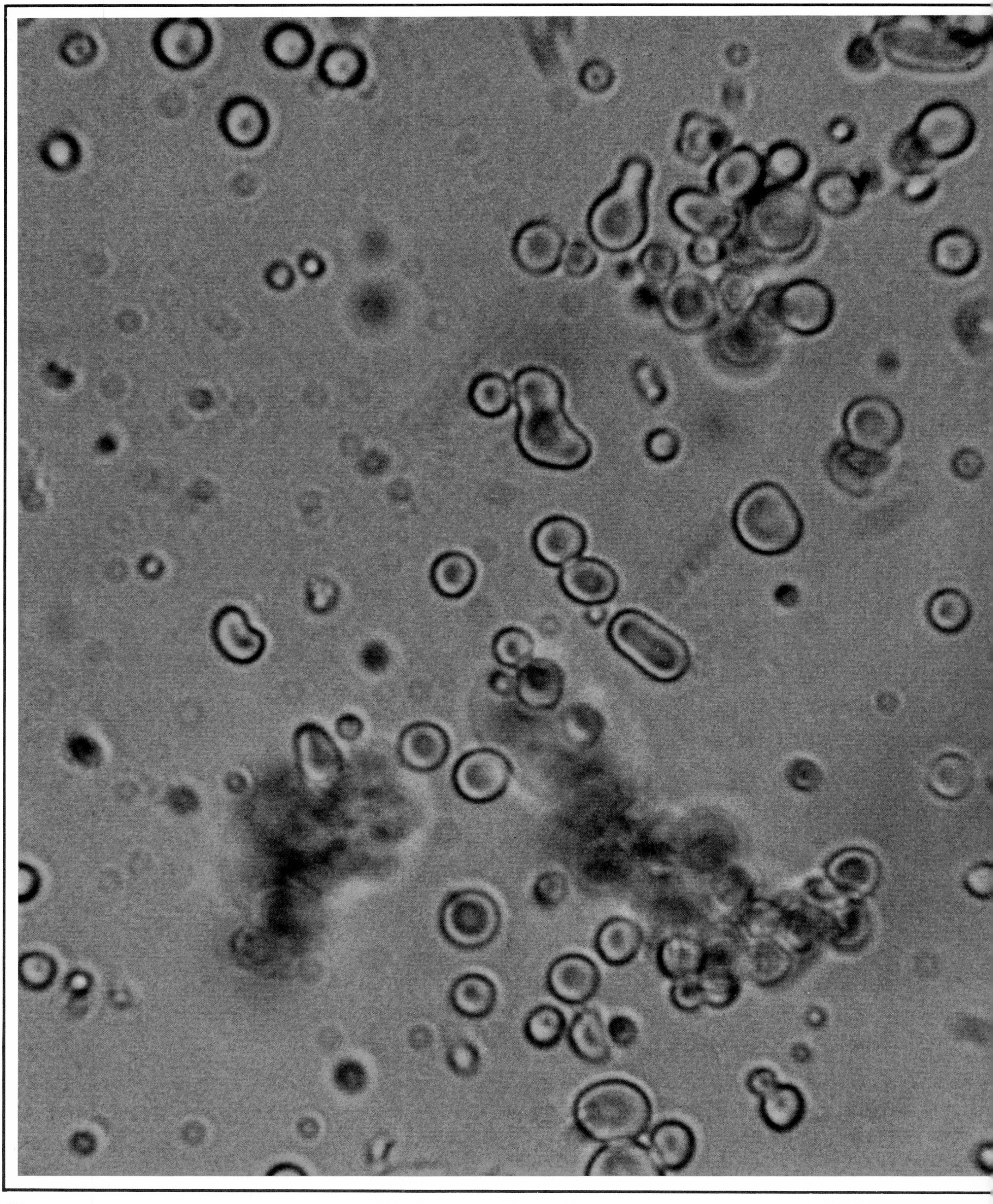

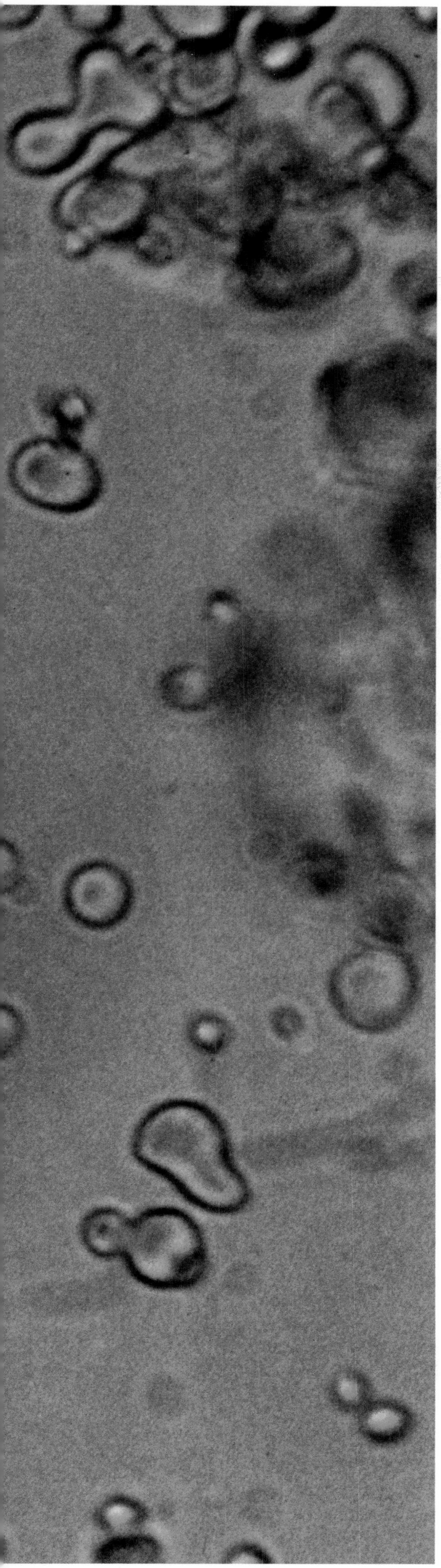

Life on Earth

No one will ever know exactly how or when life first appeared on Earth. But one thing is certain : the planet upon which life glimmered into being was very different from the world we know now. Barren rock, heaving with earthquakes and volcanic eruptions ; the shores echoing discordantly to the crash of a sterile sea ; violent thunderstorms and heavy cloud flickering across the face of a harsh, blinding Sun ; and a choking, noxious atmosphere : these are the fierce and unlikely conditions that nourished life into existence. Ironically, they were tamed by those first primitive specks of living matter to which they had given birth. With agonizing slowness, through hundreds of millions of years, life gradually began to fashion its own environment. The struggle to stay alive produced new plants and animals of many millions of varieties, from the tiniest bug to giant whales and from speck-like algae to towering trees, crowded together into a thin film of life smeared over the surface of the planet. And it was into this world that man eventually emerged.

The dawn of life
Exactly how, where and when terrestrial life began will probably never be known. But it is certain that all Earth life stemmed from primitive cells such as these microspheres grown in the laboratory from artificial chains of amino-acids. (Magnified over 5000 times)

Life Begins

Dawn of life *left*
It was probably upon primitive estuarine shores such as these that most of the key chemical reactions which were to precede the emergence of life took place. Chain-like chemicals dissolved in the seas were concentrated in and upon the mud of such estuaries. Here the alternation of wet and dry, the fierce heat of an unshielded Sun and the catalytic effects of the mud combined to promote the chemical rearrangements needed to make primeval proteins and nucleic acids. Associations of such molecules then formed the first primitive living cells.

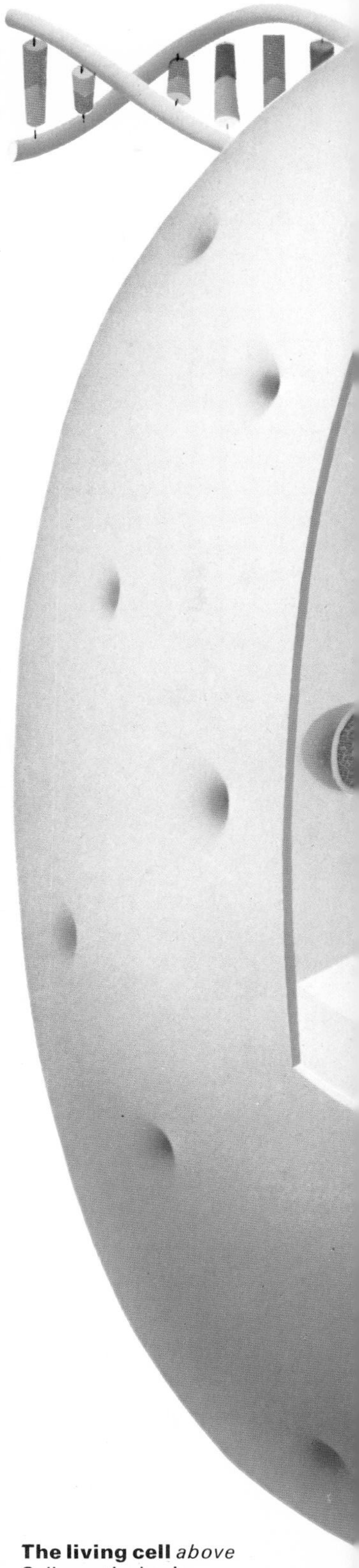

For something like half of its existence the Earth has been devoid of life. Perhaps the most important characteristic of the primitive Earth was that its atmosphere contained no oxygen, the vital element that makes today's life possible. It was this absence during at least the first 2000 million years of the Earth's history that allowed the chemical reactions to take place that were necessary for life to evolve.

The primordial atmosphere contained such gases as methane and ammonia which, under the action of a glaring Sun, formed new compounds, including the poisonous hydrogen cyanide, which could link together to form chemical chains. These then dissolved in the oceans and became concentrated in the sea foam and on the shores. Some of these chain-like chemicals must have been similar to present-day proteins, which play such an important role in living things. Other primordial molecules were undoubtedly crude versions of the so-called nucleic acids, the best known of which – DNA, deoxyribonucleic acid – functions as the material of inheritance as illustrated in the main figure opposite.

Over millions of years such chemicals were made and destroyed under the fierce rays of the Sun. But, as time went by, some of these molecules acquired a totally new characteristic: they became able to an increasing degree to organize their own manufacture. Such molecules, which were probably nucleic acids, fared better than the others which were made completely by accident, and so increased at the latter's expense. Then some of these nucleic acids became able to use proteins in constructing themselves, and began to organize them also. Thus a close and interdependent relationship sprang up between the two classes of molecule. Separated from the rest of the world by their surrounding membrane, such interrelated proteins and nucleic acids formed the first living cells.

Certain cells, by making a dye known as chlorophyll, became able to use sunlight more efficiently and in so doing pumped oxygen into the atmosphere. For 1000 million years this oxygen was soaked up by the rocks of the Earth; then it slowly began to accumulate in the atmosphere. Oxygen that rose to great altitudes became converted by the Sun into ozone which gradually formed a protective screen for the Earth by filtering out some of the Sun's harshest rays which previously reached the surface. At this point life began in earnest. The oxygen went on increasing, and evolutionary expansion had begun.

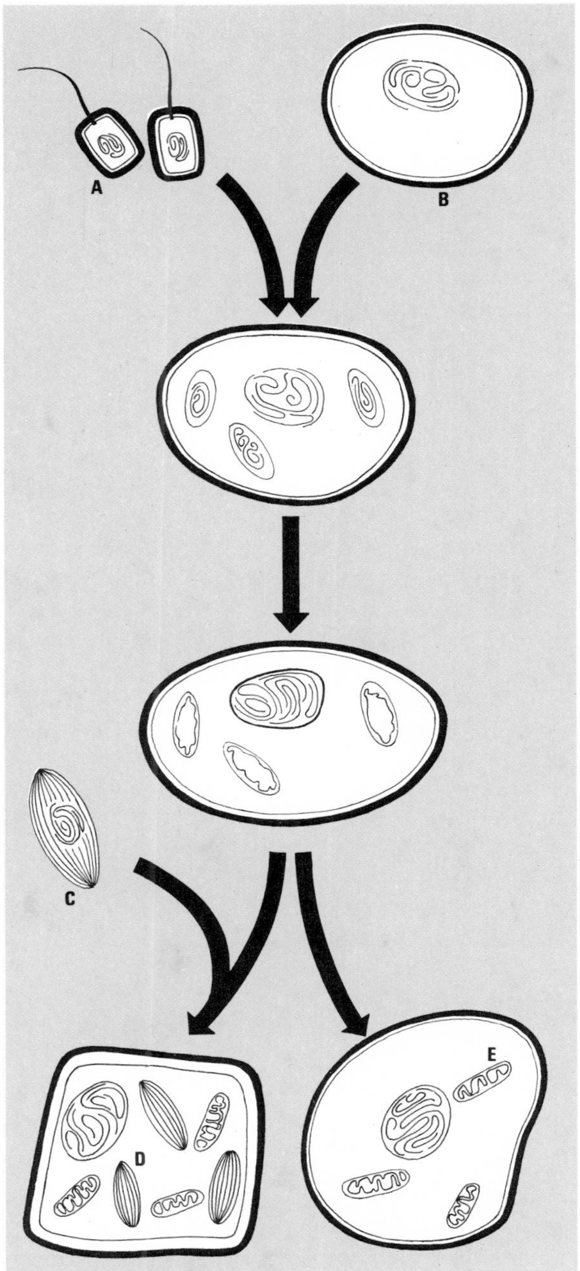

A
B
C
D
E

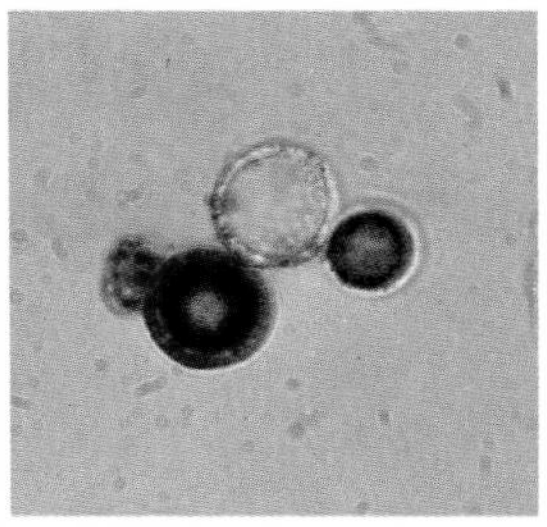

From microsphere to cell *left*
That objects looking very like cells can be formed merely by dissolving protein-like molecules in water is shown by the photograph of a 'microsphere' (above). Of course, such microspheres lack the complex internal organization of real cells (right), many of which contain a nucleus and other internal structures or 'organelles'. Nuclei were formed by creating a wall around the hereditary material, the DNA, but the organelles were probably acquired by engulfing other types of cell (left). Some of these were bacteria (A) very efficient at burning sugars to produce energy. Their engulfment by larger cells (B) meant that they were assured of a steady sugar supply, and the cells were in turn provided with built-in miniature 'power plants'. The organelles descended from these bacteria are mitochondria. Algae (C) taken into the cell were able to make sugars using the energy of the Sun and gave rise to chloroplasts (D). Animal cells contain mitochondria (E) only; plant cells contain chloroplasts as well.

The living cell *above*
Cells are the basic building blocks from which all but the most primitive forms of Earth life are constructed. Strictly speaking, a bird's egg could be defined as a cell, but most cells are microscopic. The illustration above is 100,000 times life size.

The struggle for life *right*
This time scale shows the gradual evolution of terrestrial life forms from simple chemicals, and the concomitant evolution of the Earth's atmosphere. The primitive atmosphere was totally devoid of oxygen, and consisted almost entirely of methane and ammonia. It was life itself, by producing oxygen which became ozone, that made conditions safer for life.

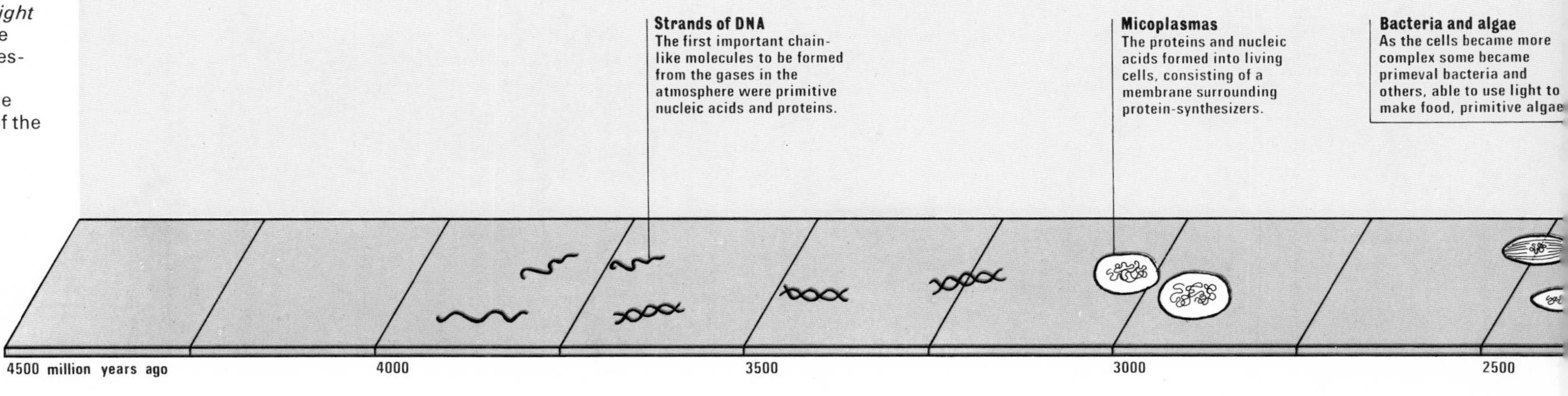

Strands of DNA
The first important chain-like molecules to be formed from the gases in the atmosphere were primitive nucleic acids and proteins.
Micoplasmas
The proteins and nucleic acids formed into living cells, consisting of a membrane surrounding protein-synthesizers.
Bacteria and algae
As the cells became more complex some became primeval bacteria and others, able to use light to make food, primitive algae
4500 million years ago
4000
3500
3000
2500

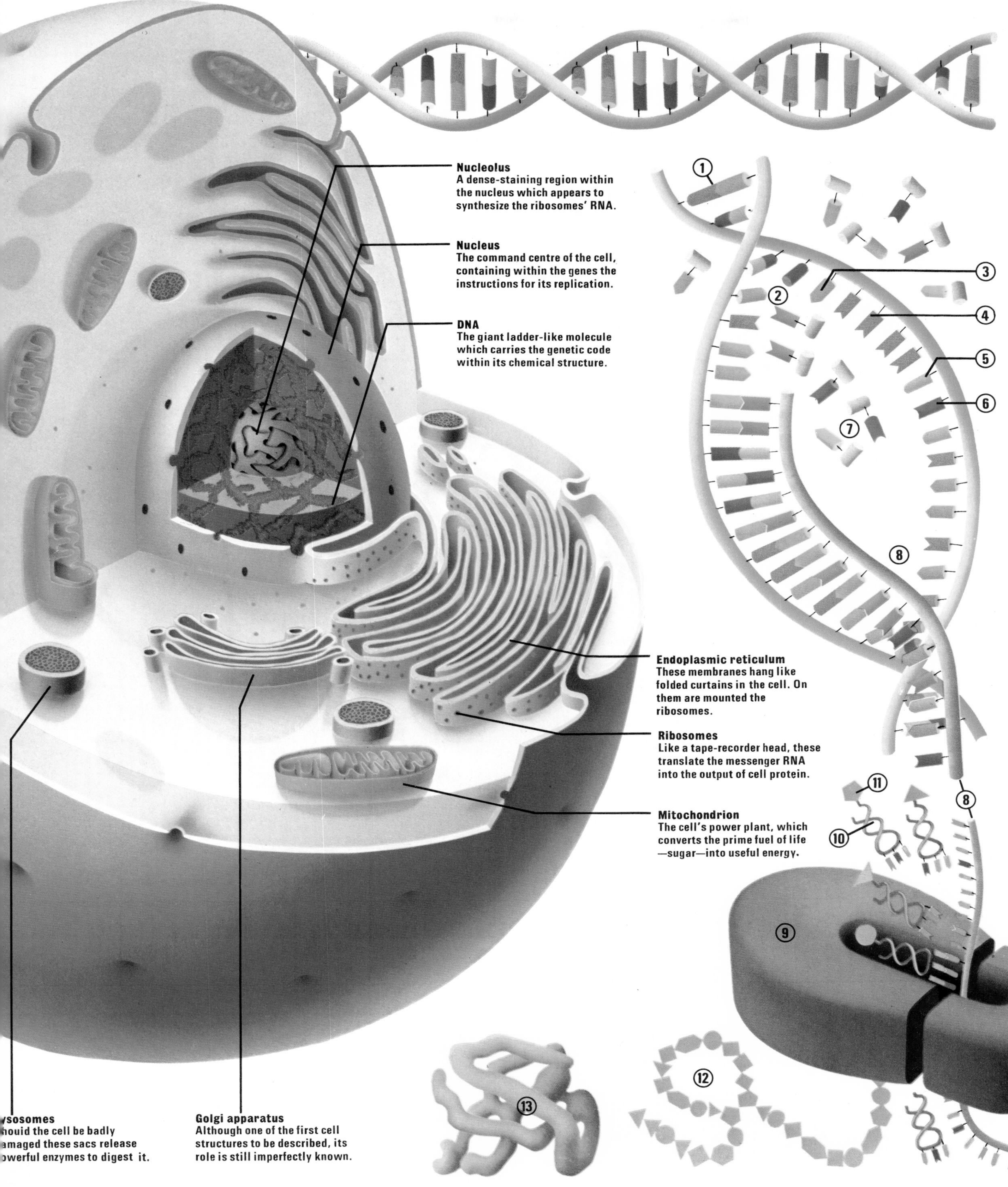

Nucleolus
A dense-staining region within the nucleus which appears to synthesize the ribosomes' RNA.
Nucleus
The command centre of the cell, containing within the genes the instructions for its replication.
DNA
The giant ladder-like molecule which carries the genetic code within its chemical structure.
Endoplasmic reticulum
These membranes hang like folded curtains in the cell. On them are mounted the ribosomes.
Ribosomes
Like a tape-recorder head, these translate the messenger RNA into the output of cell protein.
Mitochondrion
The cell's power plant, which converts the prime fuel of life —sugar—into useful energy.
ysosomes
hould the cell be badly
amaged these sacs release
owerful enzymes to digest it.
Golgi apparatus
Although one of the first cell structures to be described, its role is still imperfectly known.
1
2
3
4
5
6
7
8
8
9
10
11
12
13

The double helix *left*
DNA, the incredible 'material of inheritance' is now known to be structured in the form of a double helix. Rather like a programming tape fed into a computer, this controls the amazing sequence of proteins made by the cell.

How the cell works *left*
The DNA in the nucleus of the cell exists in the form of a ladder twisted into a double helix. The rungs of this ladder (1) contain the vital coding information needed to construct the fresh protein. The DNA ladder first splits down the centers of the rungs (2). There are four types of half-rung (3,4,5,6,) and the exact order in which they are arranged is vital. This order is copied by messenger RNA (7) which builds itself into a continuous filament (8) and passes out of the nucleus into a ribosome (9). These are protein-synthesizing machines scattered throughout the cell. Tiny 'adapter plugs' called transfer RNA (10) bring the amino acids (11) from which a protein is made. The transfer RNAs can fit on to the messenger RNA only in the correct sequence of three half-rungs. Each triplet is linked to one of 20 kinds of amino acid, which are thus linked in the correct order to make the protein (12). Once completed, the protein folds up (13) into the shape that fits it for its job of controlling the cell's chemistry, including the synthesis of new DNA.

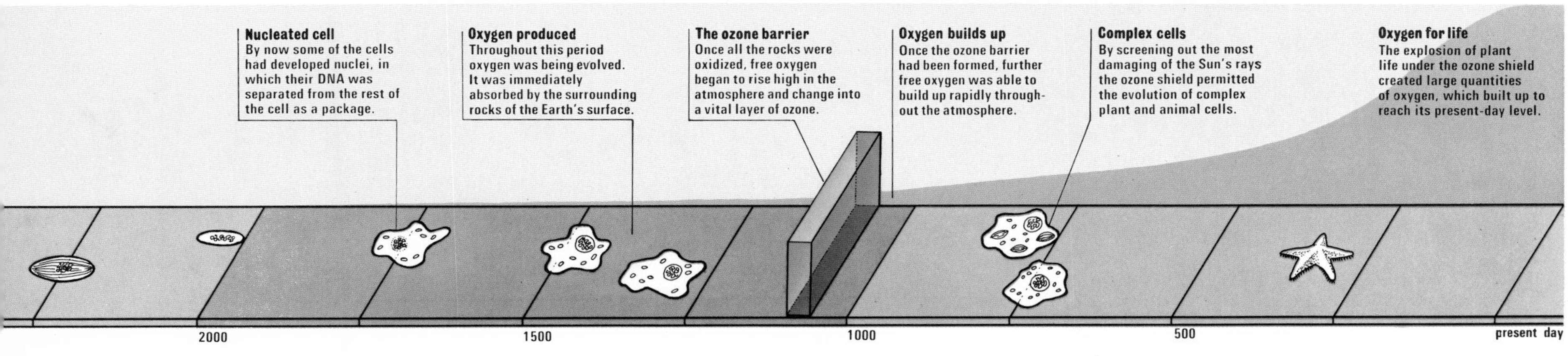

Nucleated cell
By now some of the cells had developed nuclei, in which their DNA was separated from the rest of the cell as a package.
Oxygen produced
Throughout this period oxygen was being evolved. It was immediately absorbed by the surrounding rocks of the Earth's surface.
The ozone barrier
Once all the rocks were oxidized, free oxygen began to rise high in the atmosphere and change into a vital layer of ozone.
Oxygen builds up
Once the ozone barrier had been formed, further free oxygen was able to build up rapidly throughout the atmosphere.
Complex cells
By screening out the most damaging of the Sun's rays the ozone shield permitted the evolution of complex plant and animal cells.
Oxygen for life
The explosion of plant life under the ozone shield created large quantities of oxygen, which built up to reach its present-day level.
2000
1500
1000
500
present day

The Ocean Cradle

Early life probably derived its energy not directly from the Sun or atmosphere, but by breaking down compounds as some bacteria do today. The arrival of chlorophyll marked the appearance of the first real plants able to synthesize food out of sunlight, carbon dioxide and water (photosynthesis). Thereafter there was abundant food on the Earth to support all types of animals. Some fed directly on, or in, plants. Others fed on the plant-eaters, or in them as parasites. The result was a vast chain of animal energy-dissipators all depending on the primary producers, the green plants.

Since the lack of oxygen in the primeval atmosphere meant that the surface of the Earth was flooded with far more ultraviolet light from the Sun than it is today, early life could not leave the protection of the water. So the first great evolution of living things was confined to the oceans – not the great depths where there is no light, but the surface, inshore waters and tidal pools. Later even the depths could be colonized, as life near the surface became so abundant that dead plants and animals, mainly microscopic, perpetually rained down into the depths to provide food there.

A few fossils, mainly algae, are known to date from 2700 million years ago. But the earliest plentiful fossils, in the Cambrian rocks, are already highly evolved: true arthropods (jointed-legged animals), true mollusks, true echinoderms (related to starfish), rather odd corals and other forms all nearing the end of their branches on the evolutionary thicket. Even today it is tempting to think of mammals, birds and perhaps reptiles as the higher animals and to dismiss fishes and the remainder as very lowly. But within that remainder there is far more diversity than within all the vertebrates.

True vertebrates appear in the fossil record only in the Ordovician (about 400 million years ago). But their evolution is then rapid, and by the Devonian (300 million) true sharks, bony fishes and lung fishes have appeared. Quickly thereafter (250 million) the first four-legged beasts are abundant. They first appeared at the end of the Carboniferous, when the advance to the land had begun.

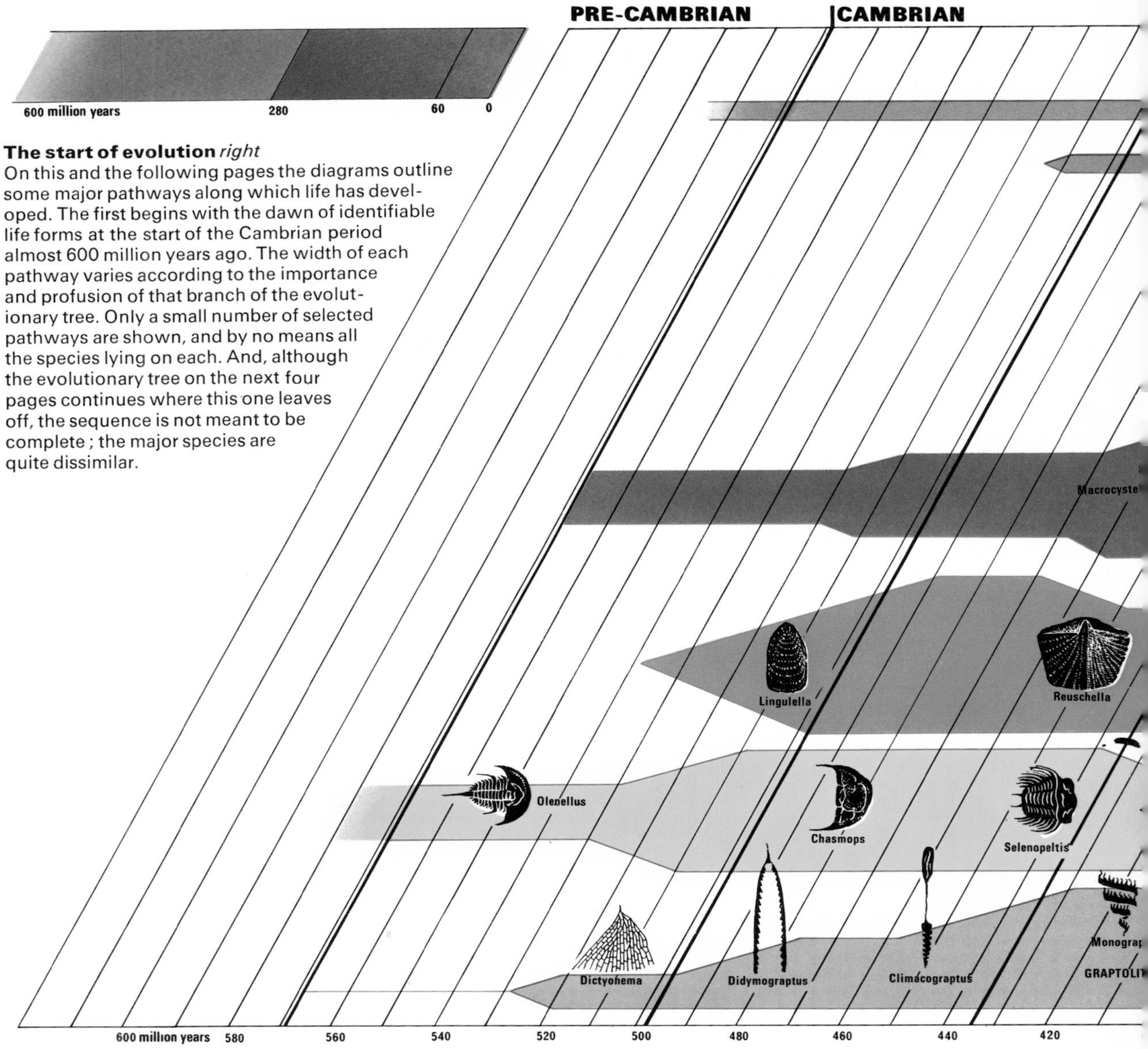

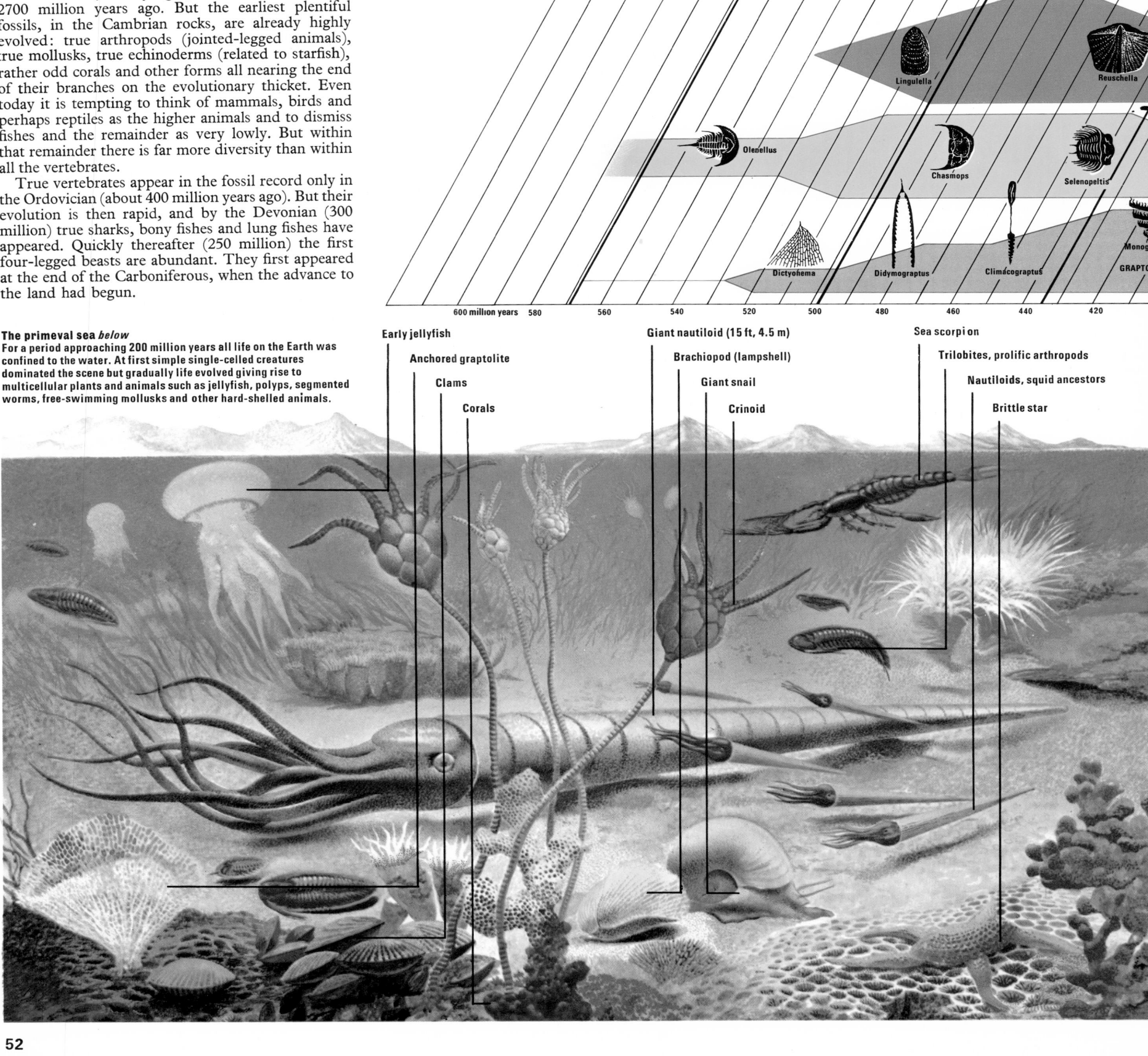

PRE-CAMBRIAN
CAMBRIAN
600 million years
280
60
0
Lingulella
Reuschella
Olenellus
Chasmops
Selenopeltis
Dictyonema
Didymograptus
Climacograptus
600 million years
580
560
540
520
500
480
460
440
420

The start of evolution *right*
On this and the following pages the diagrams outline some major pathways along which life has developed. The first begins with the dawn of identifiable life forms at the start of the Cambrian period almost 600 million years ago. The width of each pathway varies according to the importance and profusion of that branch of the evolutionary tree. Only a small number of selected pathways are shown, and by no means all the species lying on each. And, although the evolutionary tree on the next four pages continues where this one leaves off, the sequence is not meant to be complete; the major species are quite dissimilar.

The primeval sea *below*
For a period approaching 200 million years all life on the Earth was confined to the water. At first simple single-celled creatures dominated the scene but gradually life evolved giving rise to multicellular plants and animals such as jellyfish, polyps, segmented worms, free-swimming mollusks and other hard-shelled animals.

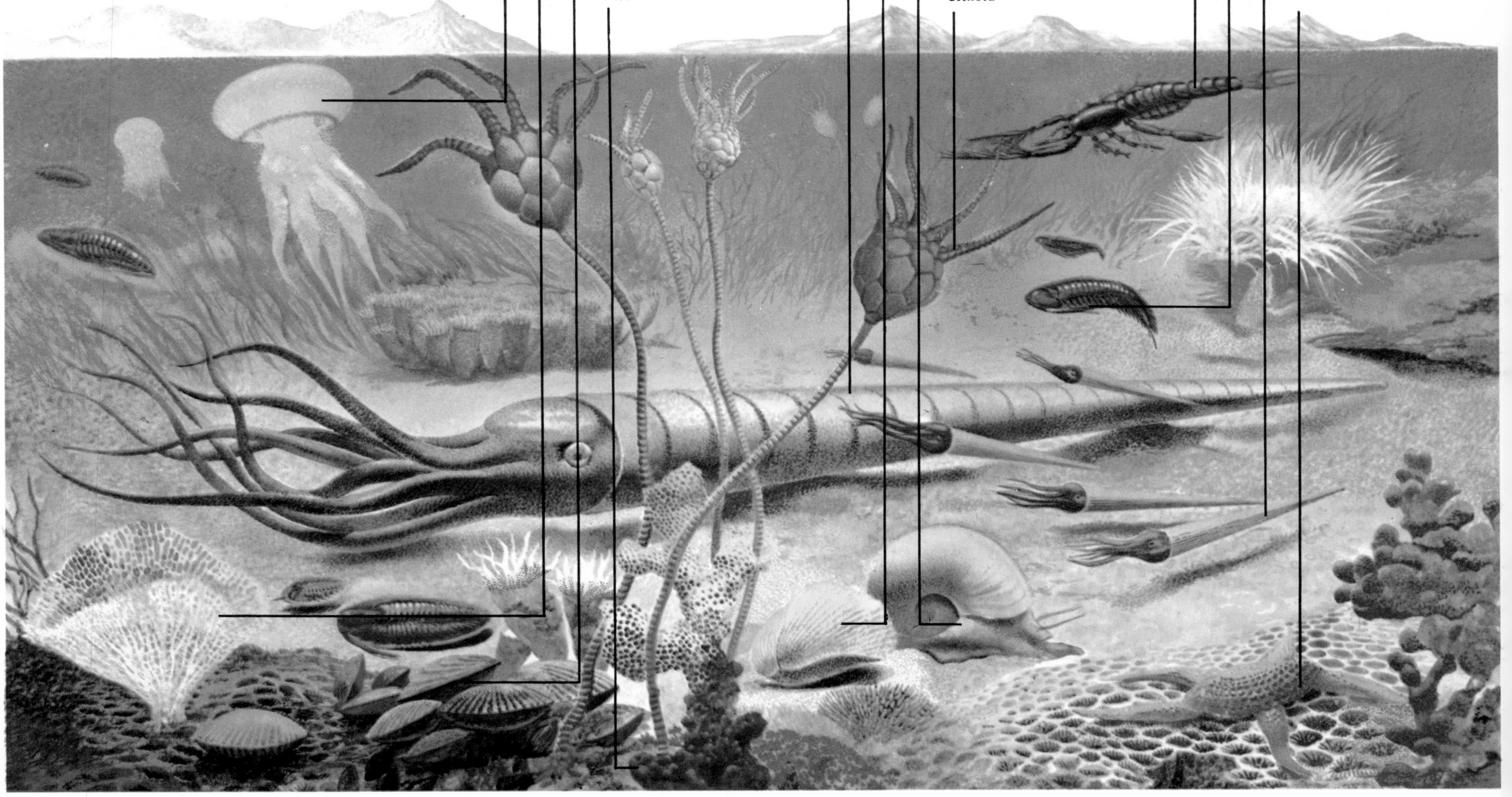

Early jellyfish
Anchored graptolite
Clams
Corals
Giant nautiloid (15 ft, 4.5 m)
Brachiopod (lampshell)
Giant snail
Crinoid
Sea scorpion
Trilobites, prolific arthropods
Nautiloids, squid ancestors
Brittle star

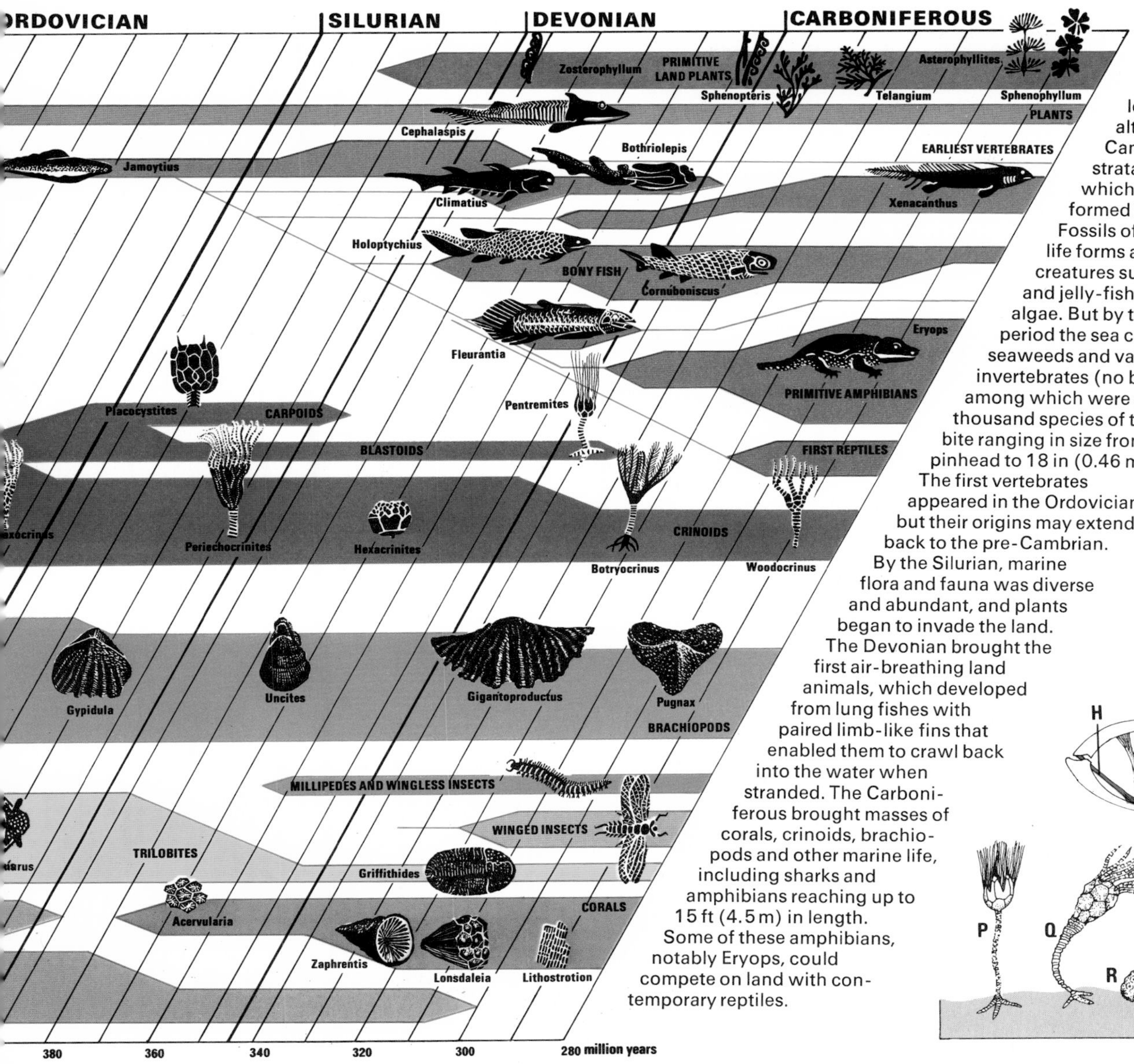

ORDOVICIAN
SILURIAN
DEVONIAN
CARBONIFEROUS
Zosterophyllum
PRIMITIVE LAND PLANTS
Asterophyllites
Sphenopteris
Telangium
Sphenophyllum
PLANTS
Cephalaspis
Bothriolepis
EARLIEST VERTEBRATES
Jamoytius
Climatius
Xenacanthus
Holoptychius
BONY FISH
Cornuboniscus
Eryops
Fleurantia
PRIMITIVE AMPHIBIANS
Placocystites
CARPOIDS
Pentremites
BLASTOIDS
FIRST REPTILES
Periechocrinites
Hexacrinites
CRINOIDS
Botryocrinus
Woodocrinus
Gypidula
Uncites
Gigantoproductus
Pugnax
BRACHIOPODS
MILLIPEDES AND WINGLESS INSECTS
WINGED INSECTS
TRILOBITES
Griffithides
CORALS
Acervularia
Zaphrentis
Lonsdaleia
Lithostrotion
380
360
340
320
300
280 million years

The earliest life forms, which probably dwelt in water devoid of free oxygen, have left no traces whatever, although many pre-Cambrian rocks contain strata of lime carbonates which may have been formed by bacteria or algae. Fossils of pre-Cambrian life forms are of soft-bodied creatures such as worms and jelly-fish and primitive algae. But by the Cambrian period the sea contained seaweeds and various invertebrates (no backbone) among which were some thousand species of trilobite ranging in size from a pinhead to 18 in (0.46 m). The first vertebrates appeared in the Ordovician, but their origins may extend back to the pre-Cambrian. By the Silurian, marine flora and fauna was diverse and abundant, and plants began to invade the land. The Devonian brought the first air-breathing land animals, which developed from lung fishes with paired limb-like fins that enabled them to crawl back into the water when stranded. The Carboniferous brought masses of corals, crinoids, brachiopods and other marine life, including sharks and amphibians reaching up to 15 ft (4.5 m) in length. Some of these amphibians, notably Eryops, could compete on land with contemporary reptiles.

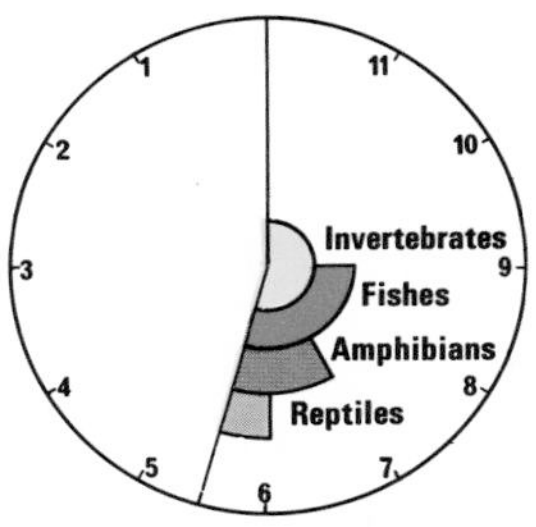

Invertebrates
Fishes
Amphibians
Reptiles

Evolutionary countdown 1
The count begins at 600 million years ago with early invertebrates.

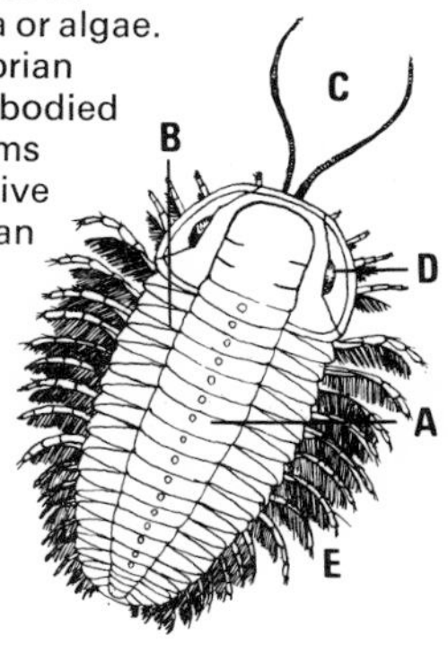

A trilobite *left and below*
These arthropods derive their name from their three-lobed structure, central lobe A being flanked by lateral lobes B. Other features include antennae C, eyes D, thoracic appendages E and heart F.

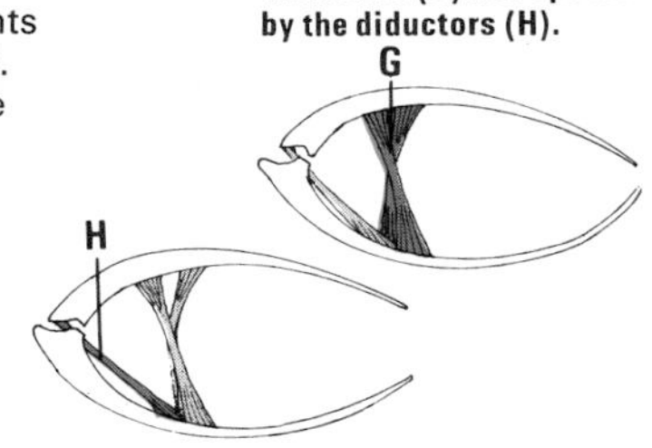

A brachiopod *below*
The two hinged shells are closed by tension in the adductors (G) and opened by the diductors (H).

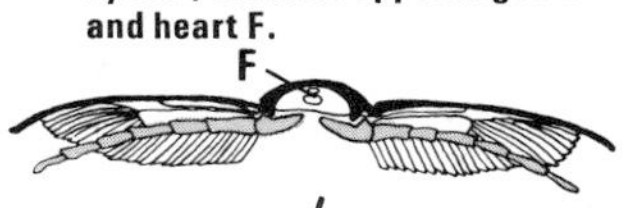

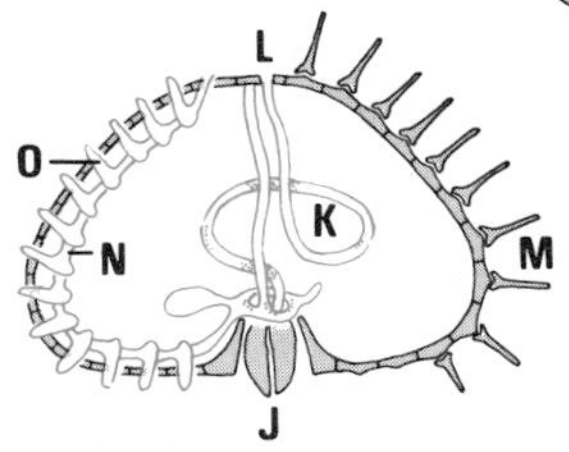

An echinoid *above*
These widespread animals survive today in the form of the familiar sea urchin. A modern example is shown sectioned: J, mouth; K, intestine; L, anus; M, spines; N, water vessel; O, extendible tube feet.

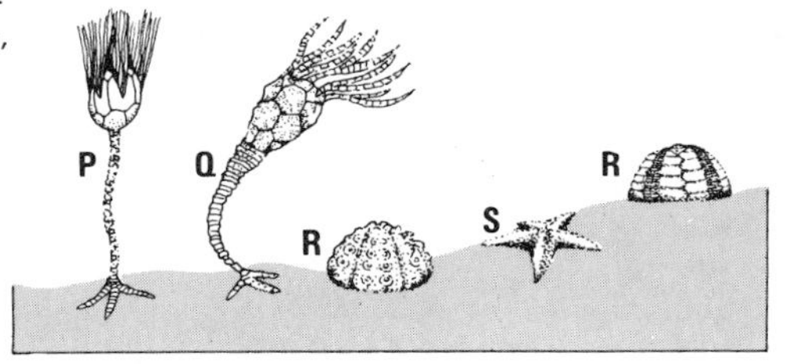

Contrasting living habits *left*
The echinoderms swiftly adapted to a variety of living conditions. The eocrinoid P and blastoid Q are both anchored to the sea floor; echinoids R and brittle star S crawl about the bottom.

The first fishes *below*
There is evidence that the first fishes originated in inland waters and only later migrated to the oceans. Some of the earliest were devoid of a proper jaw but instead sifted small organisms from the water in the same way that many modern marine animals eat plankton. The first fish with jaws, the Acanthodians, appeared late in the Silurian period.

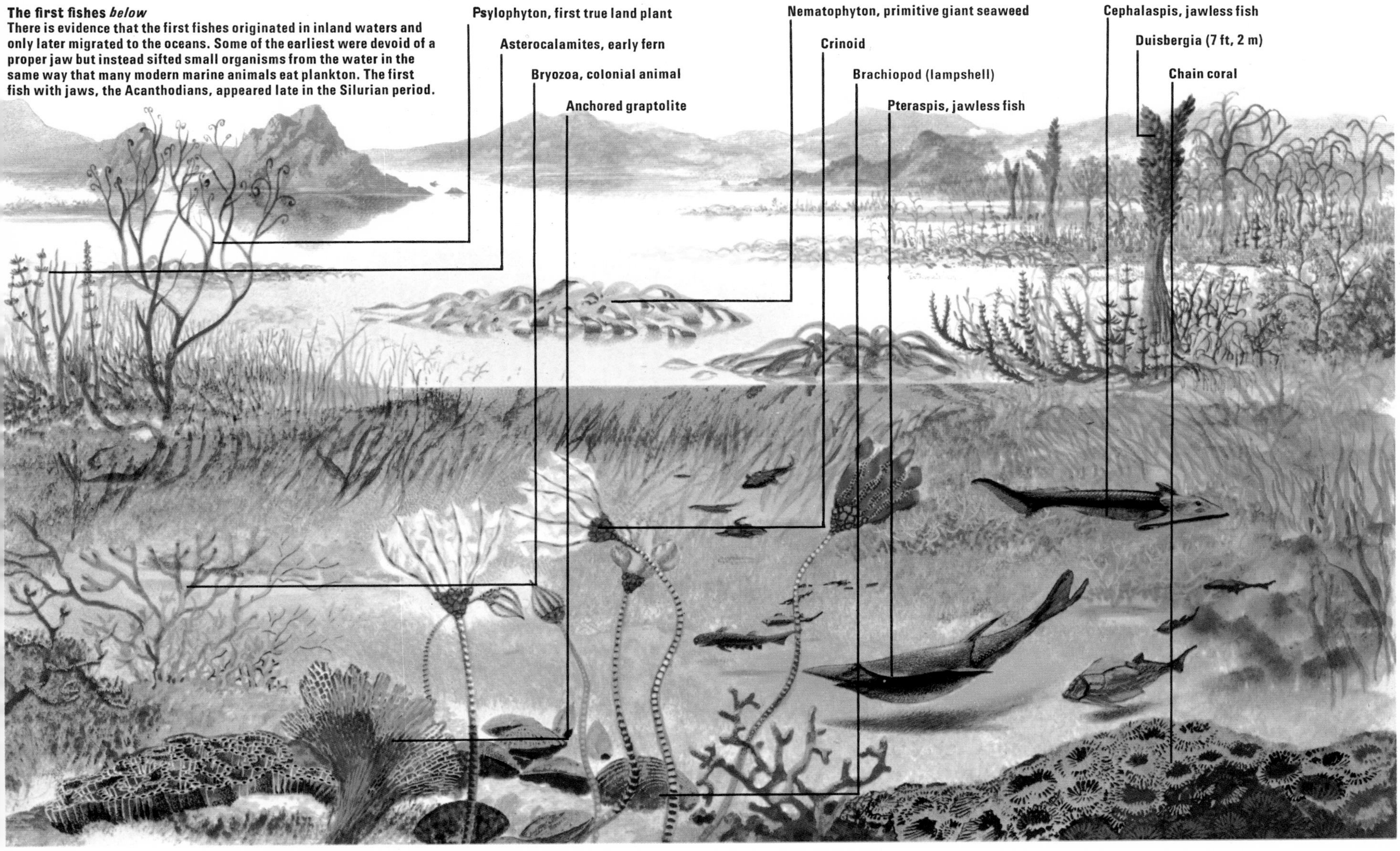

Psylophyton, first true land plant
Asterocalamites, early fern
Bryozoa, colonial animal
Anchored graptolite
Nematophyton, primitive giant seaweed
Crinoid
Brachiopod (lampshell)
Pteraspis, jawless fish
Cephalaspis, jawless fish
Duisbergia (7 ft, 2 m)
Chain coral

Advance to the Land

As soon as the land was inhabitable it was invaded by many different sorts of living things. First came the essential plants; as the vegetation spread it was followed by animals. Fresh water had been colonized quite early and some animals came to the land from there instead of directly from the seas. In swampy places in the Carboniferous period tree-ferns, horsetails and clubmosses had produced real forests. These supported many insects, some scorpions, myriapods and other jointed-legged animals. There were probably worms and other soil animals, but these are not easily fossilized. The advance to the land happened many times over, in many groups. For example, the land snails belong to at least two distinct stocks, one of which invaded the land via fresh water while the other, related to the winkles, may have come straight from the sea.

Primitive fishes possibly evolved under fresh water or estuarine conditions, and invaded the sea soon after. As early as the Devonian period amphibians had been produced, resembling fishes but with four legs instead of paired fins. They probably arose in rivers and pools subjected to seasonal drought, and it has been suggested that their legs were just for walking to the next puddle. By the Carboniferous they had given rise to the reptiles, which produce eggs that can develop on land.

The reptiles soon split up into diverse types, filling all the places that mammals do today. They produced everything from tiny lizards to immense plant-eating armored monsters and carnivores of all sizes up to the huge Tyrannosaurus. Many of the earlier carnivores and herbivores that flourished in the Permian and Triassic periods died out, but not before they had given rise to successful lines of descendants leading to today's mammals. The later ones include the two main groups of dinosaurs, as well as the flying pterodactyls, the marine ichthyosaurs – so like modern porpoises and dolphins – and the fish- or mollusk-eating plesiosaurs which resembled large turtles with long necks. Crocodile-like forms were produced several times independently, and from one of the primitive dinosaur stocks arose the true birds.

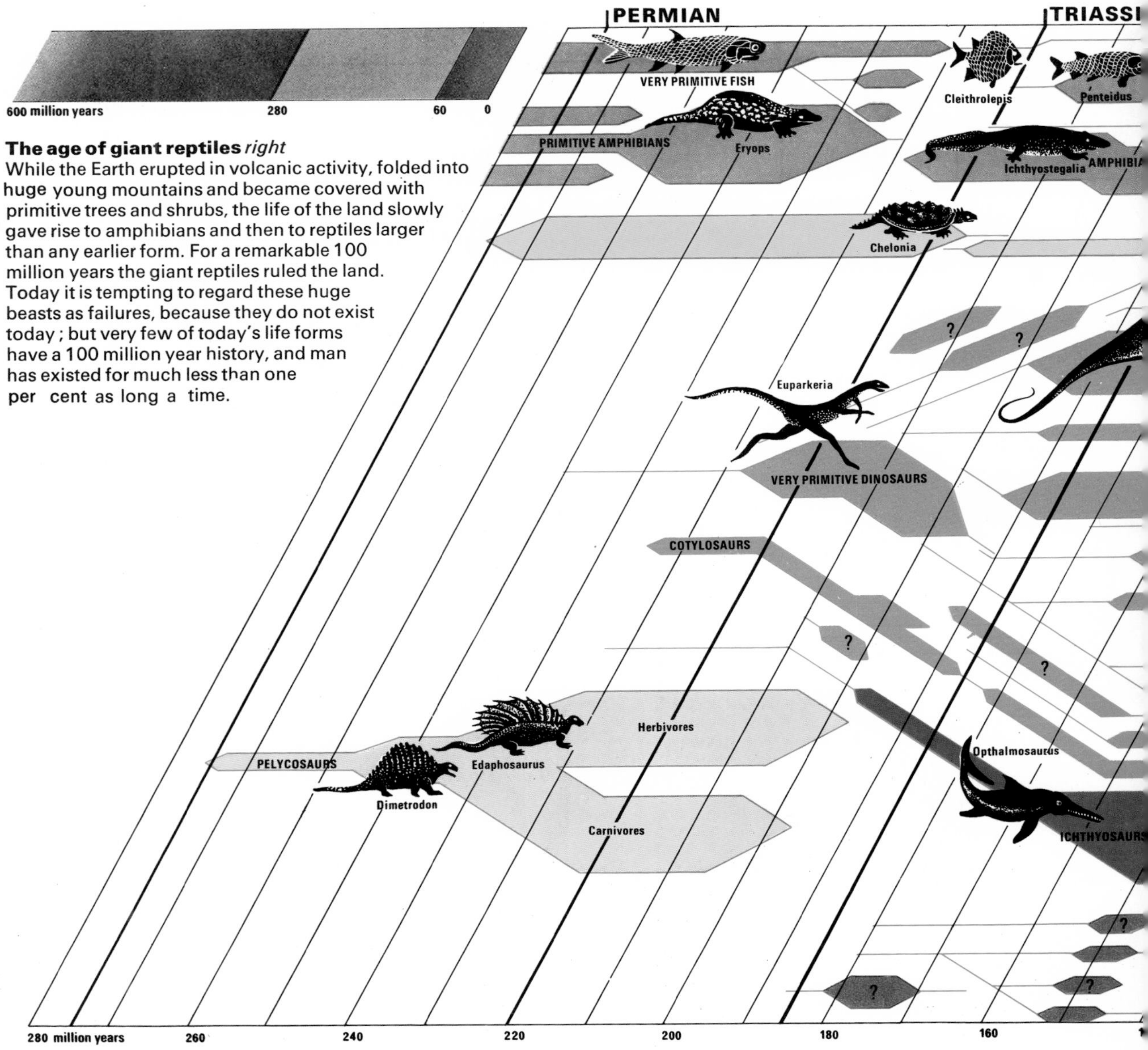

PERMIAN
TRIASSI
600 million years
280
60
0
VERY PRIMITIVE FISH
Cleithrolepis
Pteroidus
PRIMITIVE AMPHIBIANS
Eryops
Ichthyostegalia
AMPHIBIA
Chelonia
Euparkeria
VERY PRIMITIVE DINOSAURS
COTYLOSAURS
Herbivores
PELYCOSAURS
Edaphosaurus
Dimetrodon
Carnivores
Opthalmosaurus
ICHTHYOSAURS
280 million years
260
240
220
200
180
160

The age of giant reptiles *right*
While the Earth erupted in volcanic activity, folded into huge young mountains and became covered with primitive trees and shrubs, the life of the land slowly gave rise to amphibians and then to reptiles larger than any earlier form. For a remarkable 100 million years the giant reptiles ruled the land. Today it is tempting to regard these huge beasts as failures, because they do not exist today; but very few of today's life forms have a 100 million year history, and man has existed for much less than one per cent as long a time.

Life inherits the land *below*
The first life forms to colonize the land were probably marine plants, perhaps seaweeds growing at the water's edge, which were forced to survive periods when the water was absent. By 250 million years ago the Earth was clothed in green, mainly as a result of soft, pithy trees and giant ferns. Amphibians, reptiles and flying insects appeared.

Sigillaria, early tree
Lepidodendron (over 120 ft, 37 m)
Sphenacodon, probable carnivore
Meganeuron, giant dragonfly
Edaphosaurus, a 'finback' herbivore
Seymouria, only about 30 in (0.75 m)
Calamites
Dimetrodon, hunter of Edaphosaurus
Eryops, dwelt mainly on land
Limnoscelis
Araucarioxylon, a conifer

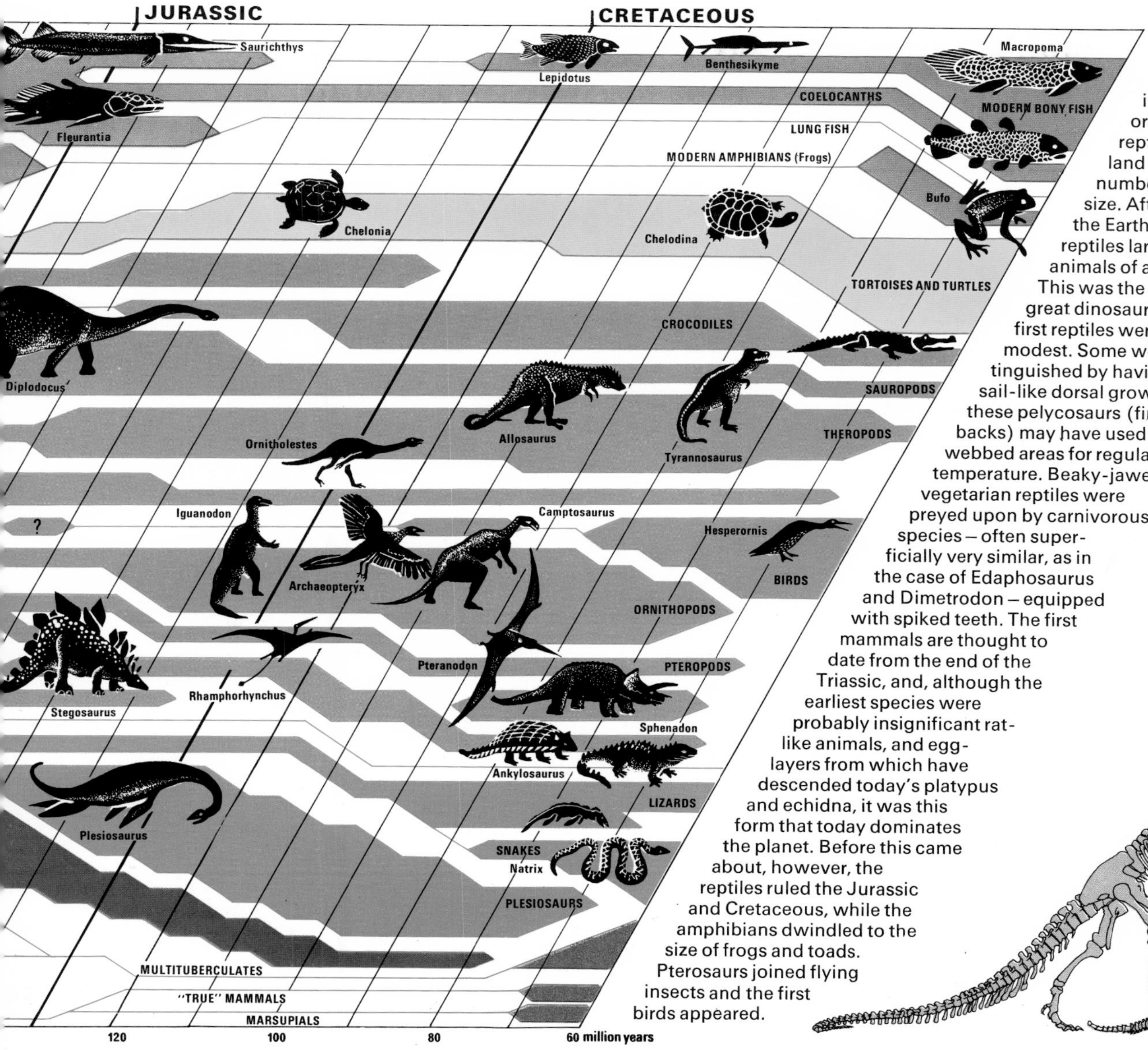
JURASSIC
CRETACEOUS
Saurichthys
Lepidotus
Benthesikyme
Macropoma
Fleurantia
COELOCANTHS
LUNG FISH
MODERN BONY FISH
MODERN AMPHIBIANS (Frogs)
Bufo
Chelonia
Chelodina
TORTOISES AND TURTLES
CROCODILES
Diplodocus
SAUROPODS
Ornitholestes
Allosaurus
Tyrannosaurus
THEROPODS
?
Iguanodon
Camptosaurus
Hesperornis
BIRDS
Archaeopteryx
ORNITHOPODS
Pteranodon
PTEROPODS
Stegosaurus
Rhamphorhynchus
Sphenodon
Ankylosaurus
LIZARDS
Plesiosaurus
SNAKES
Natrix
PLESIOSAURS
MULTITUBERCULATES
"TRUE" MAMMALS
MARSUPIALS
120
100
80
60 million years

While marine flora and fauna changed dramatically, largely as a result of increasing salinity, the new orders of amphibians and reptiles spread across the land and grew both in numbers and in individual size. After 100 million years the Earth was inhabited by reptiles larger than any land animals of any other period. This was the age of the great dinosaurs. But the first reptiles were more modest. Some were distinguished by having large sail-like dorsal growths; these pelycosaurs (finbacks) may have used their webbed areas for regulating temperature. Beaky-jawed vegetarian reptiles were preyed upon by carnivorous species – often superficially very similar, as in the case of Edaphosaurus and Dimetrodon – equipped with spiked teeth. The first mammals are thought to date from the end of the Triassic, and, although the earliest species were probably insignificant rat-like animals, and egg-layers from which have descended today's platypus and echidna, it was this form that today dominates the planet. Before this came about, however, the reptiles ruled the Jurassic and Cretaceous, while the amphibians dwindled to the size of frogs and toads. Pterosaurs joined flying insects and the first birds appeared.

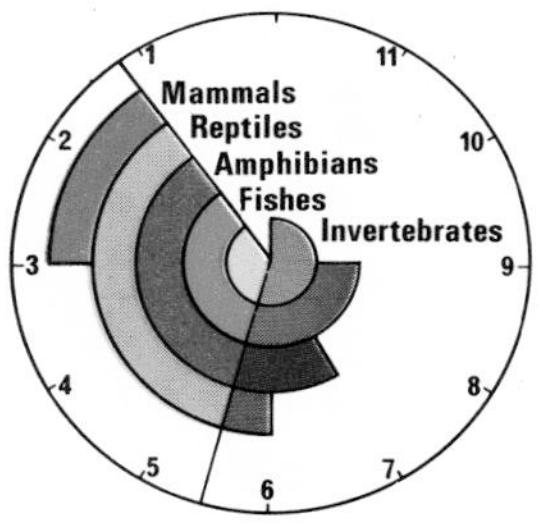
Mammals
Reptiles
Amphibians
Fishes
Invertebrates
1
2
3
4
5
6
7
8
9
10
11

Evolutionary countdown 2
The final form of Earth life, mammals, emerged about 200 million years ago.

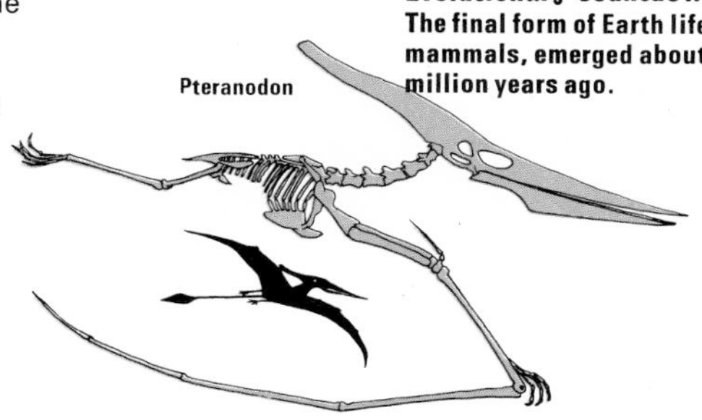
Pteranodon

Contrasting large reptiles
During the Cretaceous period the pterosaurs, the flying reptiles, increased in size to a maximum wingspan of 27 ft (8.2 m) in the impressive Pteranodon (fossil part skeleton above), which was equipped with a toothless beak and a long bony crest extending behind the head. This appears to have been the last of the pterosaurs. But land reptiles survived the Cretaceous, even though such animals as Tyrannosaurus, Camptosaurus and Centrosaurus (below, left to right) were unsuccessful. The first was a biped, the second had useful front limbs and the third was a quadruped.

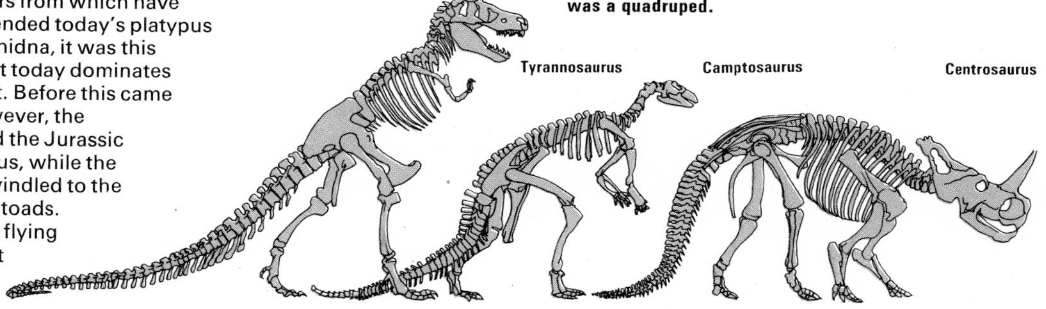
Tyrannosaurus
Camptosaurus
Centrosaurus

The great dinosaurs *below*
The largest land creatures that ever lived emerged at a time of violent mountain building, extremes of climate, and fluctuating sea levels. It was an age of reptiles, some carnivorous and some vegetarian, some grotesquely armoured and some soft-skinned, some walking on four legs, some on two and others airborne on leathery wings.

Fan palm
Triceratops – three horned
Brontosaurus, 30 tons, 70 ft (21 m)
Stegosaurus, 10 tons, 20 ft (6 m)
Tyrannosaurus, 50 ft (15 m), the largest land carnivore
Rhamphorhynchus, one of the leathery-skin flying lizards
Ankylosaurus, with heavy armour
Archaeopteryx, the apparent forerunner of the birds which combined feathers and wings with a reptile's jaws and tail

The Age of Mammals

At the end of the Cretaceous period something happened that involved a great change in the environment – a change so far-reaching that all the large reptiles died out. However, snakes, lizards, turtles, crocodiles and birds survived, and so did the primitive small mammals who now got the chance of their evolutionary life. They blossomed out into all the modes of life of the great reptiles, as well as into new ones. Plant eaters, carnivores, insectivores and omnivores (plant and meat eaters) arose in all sizes. By this time the continents had drifted far apart, so that usually only very small mammals could disperse across the sea on driftwood. As a result the mammals show many examples of 'convergent evolution' in which different species in widely separated but similar places become remarkably alike.

For example, South America was for about 70 million years an island continent. It had room for horses, for camels, for elephants, for pigs of all kinds, and for lions and tigers to eat them. What actually happened was that three or four sorts of primitive mammals managed to get in, and proceeded to evolve to fill all these niches, independently of how they were being filled elsewhere. A one-toed horse and a three-toed variety thus appeared in S America quite independently of the evolution, from a similar stock, of the 'true' horses in N America. Even more remarkable was the emergence of 'weasels', 'dogs' and 'cats' – even 'great cats' and a 'saber-tooth tiger' – from a stock of primitive marsupials (pouched mammals) that reached there very early. Similarly, in Australia the marsupials independently produced forms that resembled cats, dogs, wolves, rabbits, shrews and moles, as well as all the wallabies and kangaroos. And in Madagascar the lemurs produced independent goat-like and chimpanzee-like forms.

When S America became joined to N America vast invasions took place and most of the S American specialities became extinct. Then came the great ice ages, shaking the whole world including the tropics, and many more mammals vanished. Only in small parts of Africa can we today get any idea of what evolution has produced in the mammal line.

Mammals come into the ascendancy *right*
In this evolutionary tree the major lines of development are those of the Old World, with the exception of the blue pathway at the bottom which divides into a lower South American branch and an upper line leading to today's marsupials of Australasia. As in the earlier trees, many branches begin with insignificant or even unknown species, while other lines terminate abruptly, gradually peter out or thin down to a reduced number of survivors. The period shown extends up to the present, and the final 36 million years are shown on pages 58-59 on a larger scale to illustrate the evolution of man.

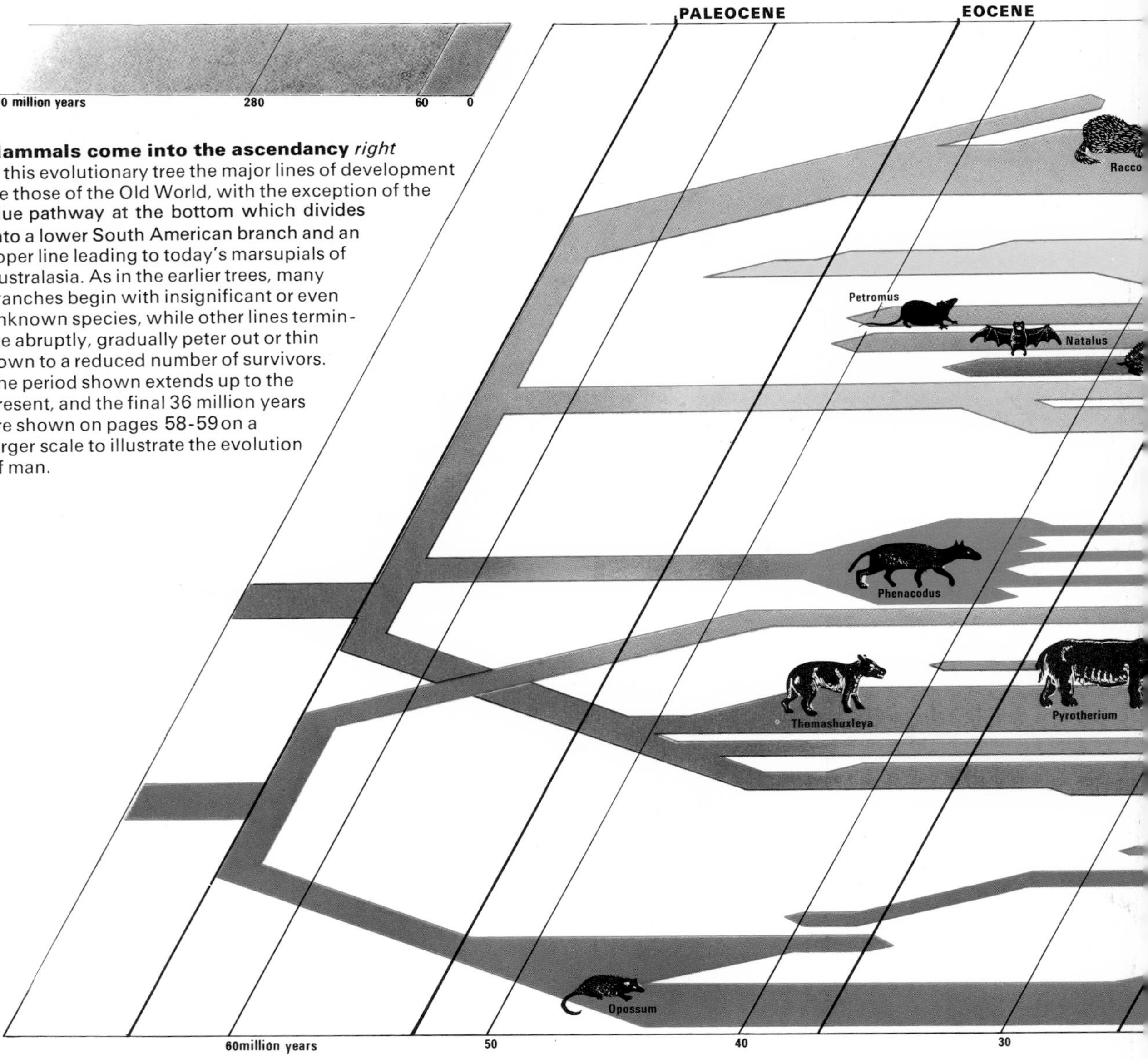

600 million years
280
60
0
PALEOCENE
EOCENE
Racco
Petromus
Natalus
Phenacodus
Thomashuxleya
Pyrotherium
Opossum
60million years
50
40
30

Replacing the reptiles *below*
As the Paleocene epoch dawned, the life of the land underwent a great change. After dominating their rivals for the remarkable period of over 100 million years, the dinosaurs faded away almost completely. In their place developed a new major group: the warm-blooded mammals, bearing living young. But there was no clue to the development of man.

Diatryma, a 7 ft (2 m) bird

Mesonyx, a successful carnivore

Palaeosyops, unsuccessful herbivore

Eohippus, ancestor of the horse (see facing page)

Uintatherium, a herbivore with many horns

Coryphodon, an ungulate (hoofed animal)

Hyrachyus, ancestor of the rhino

Eocene trees were in many respects the same as those of today, although grass did not evolve until later

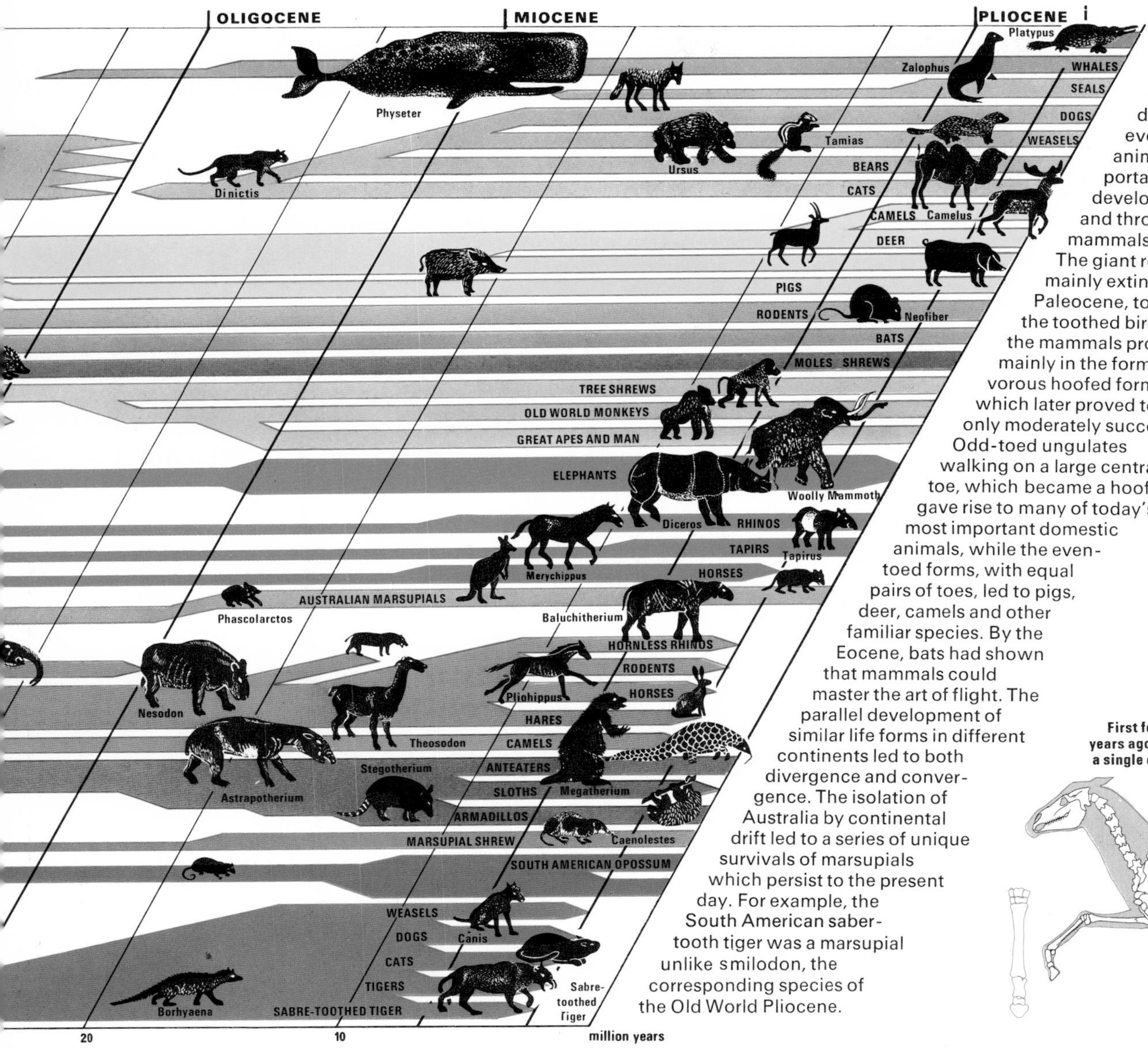

OLIGOCENE
MIOCENE
PLIOCENE
Platypus
Zalophus
WHALES
SEALS
DOGS
WEASELS
Physeter
Tamias
Ursus
BEARS
CATS
Dinictis
CAMELS
Camelus
DEER
PIGS
RODENTS
Neofiber
BATS
MOLES SHREWS
TREE SHREWS
OLD WORLD MONKEYS
GREAT APES AND MAN
ELEPHANTS
Woolly Mammoth
Diceros
RHINOS
TAPIRS
Tapirus
HORSES
Merychippus
AUSTRALIAN MARSUPIALS
Phascolarctos
Baluchitherium
HORNLESS RHINOS
RODENTS
HORSES
Pliohippus
HARES
Nesodon
Theosodon
CAMELS
ANTEATERS
Stegotherium
SLOTHS
Megatherium
Astrapotherium
ARMADILLOS
MARSUPIAL SHREW
Caenolestes
SOUTH AMERICAN OPOSSUM
WEASELS
DOGS
Canis
CATS
TIGERS
Sabre-toothed Tiger
Borhyaena
SABRE-TOOTHED TIGER
20
10
million years

Throughout the Tertiary the flora was similar to that of the modern world. Insects were also highly developed and embraced every modern order. But animal life still had very important evolutionary development to undergo, and throughout the period mammals became dominant. The giant reptiles were mainly extinct by the Paleocene, together with the toothed birds. At first the mammals proliferated mainly in the form of herbivorous hoofed forms, which later proved to be only moderately successful. Odd-toed ungulates walking on a large central toe, which became a hoof, gave rise to many of today's most important domestic animals, while the even-toed forms, with equal pairs of toes, led to pigs, deer, camels and other familiar species. By the Eocene, bats had shown that mammals could master the art of flight. The parallel development of similar life forms in different continents led to both divergence and convergence. The isolation of Australia by continental drift led to a series of unique survivals of marsupials which persist to the present day. For example, the South American sabertooth tiger was a marsupial unlike smilodon, the corresponding species of the Old World Pliocene.

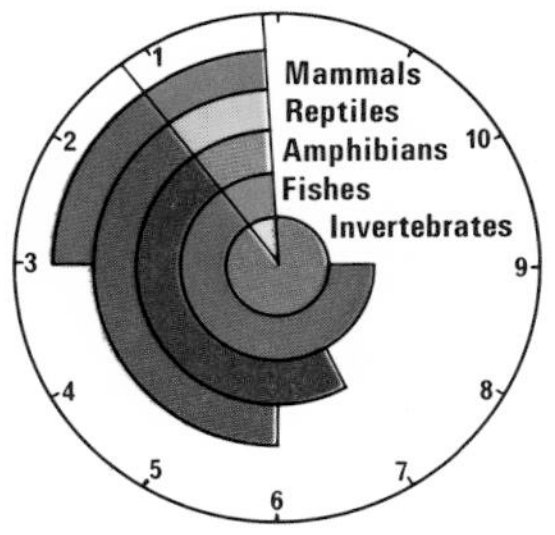

Mammals
Reptiles
Amphibians
Fishes
Invertebrates
1
2
3
4
5
6
7
8
9
10

Evolutionary countdown 3
The final 65 million years brings life of profuse variety—and man.

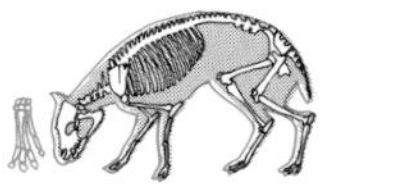

Eohippus *left*
The horse began to evolve about 60 million years ago. At first it was about as large as a big cat, with long legs having four-toed front feet and three-toed rear feet.

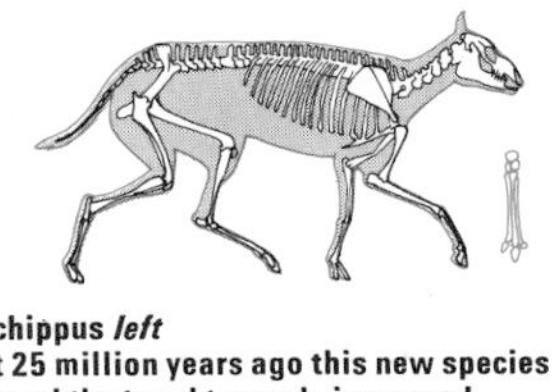

Mesohippus *right*
Eohippus evolved into this new species, roughly the size of a large dog, about 40 million years ago. It had three-toed feet.

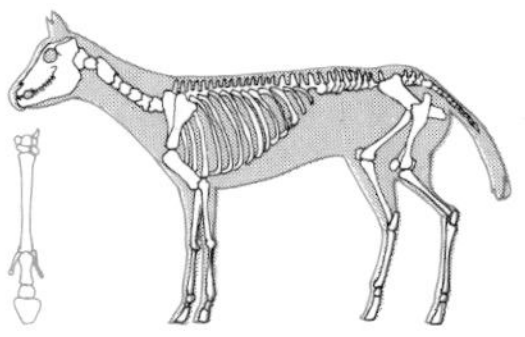

Merychippus *left*
About 25 million years ago this new species continued the trend towards increased size and began to lose its two side toes.

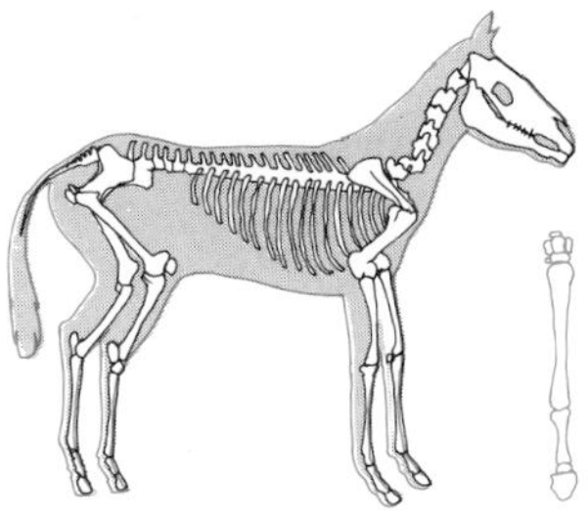

Pliohippus *right*
First found in fossils dating from about 11 million years ago, Pliohippus was the first horse to stand on a single central toe. It could run fast on firm ground.

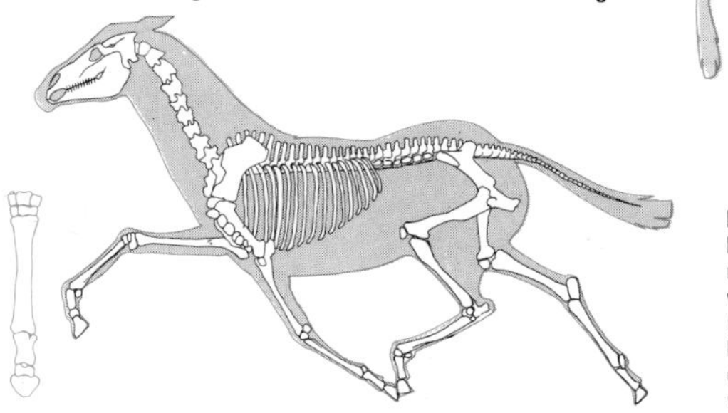

Equus *left*
Pliohippus survived until about one million years ago. By this time it was being replaced by Equus, the modern horse. Curiously, the horse became extinct in the seemingly ideal environment of N America, where it was re-introduced by the Spanish.

Rivals of the first men *below*
In and between the ice ages the mammals spread and diversified. Many roamed across new land links from one continent to another; the mastodon penetrated deep into N America from Egypt. But at the end of the ice ages scores of the mammal species vanished. How far early man's wasteful hunting was to blame is a matter for conjecture.

Woolly mammoth, contributor of half the world's ivory bank

Megatherium, giant ground sloth

Castoroides, a bear-size beaver

Canis dirus, a 6 ft (1.8 m) wolf

Smilodon, the saber-tooth tiger

Musk ox survives today

Mastodon, hunted in large numbers by early man

Bison, another ice age survivor

The Evolution of Man

Man has a history of at least 70 million years of development. During the first half of this period various monkey groups evolved, and probably about 35 million years ago one of the more advanced of these gave rise to the first hominoids, the primitive stock from which sprang today's pongids (great apes) and hominids (humans). Practically no fossil record survives of this period, but fragments exist of Ramapithecus, a probable hominid dating from 14 million years ago found in India and Africa. Then there is a gap until the first undeniable hominid group, Australopithecus, is found from five to three million years ago. He was an ape-man who may have lingered on until 500,000 years ago or later.

During this group's evolutionary lifetime major structural changes occurred which were critical to the success and survival of the hominids. These changes were centered in the regions of the pelvis, thighs, feet, and head, and resulted in the great advantage of upright stance. Although there was at this stage little parallel advance in brain power, the improved skeleton led about 500,000 years ago to a new stock, *Homo erectus*. He did show a marked advance in brain size, and he also used well-shaped stone tools and roasted his meat by the fire. By 250,000 years ago a further advance had taken place, as exemplified by the Swanscombe skull from the Thames Valley and the Steinheim skull from Germany. The immediate forebears of *Homo sapiens* are still unknown. The final forms of *Homo erectus* could have given rise to the Upper Paleolithic people; equally, the large-brained Neanderthal man could have done so.

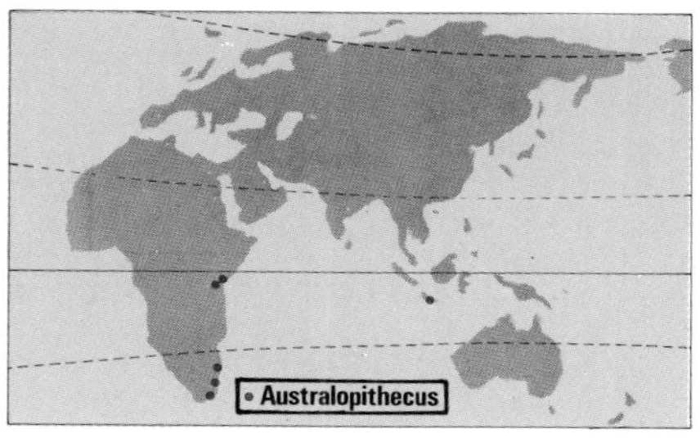

Australopithecus

Australopithecus *left*
Man did not suddenly appear; many kinds of men evolved in many places over several million years. Remains of the earliest indisputable hominid group, Australopithecus, were discovered first in S Africa. So far, only one find, still disputed, is outside Africa.

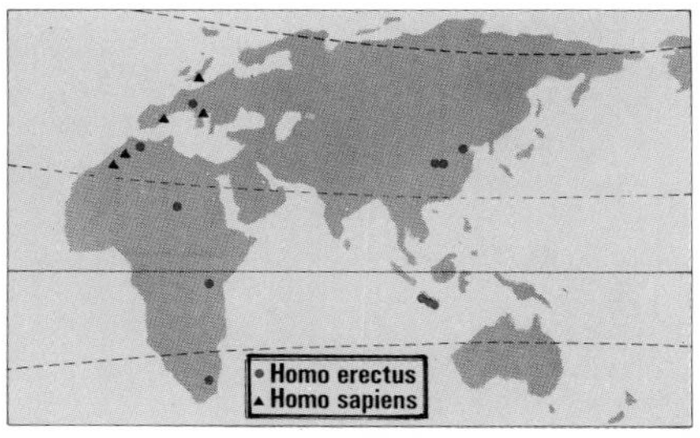

Homo erectus
Homo sapiens

The tree of man *right*
Continuing the story of the previous pages, these were the main pathways to modern man.

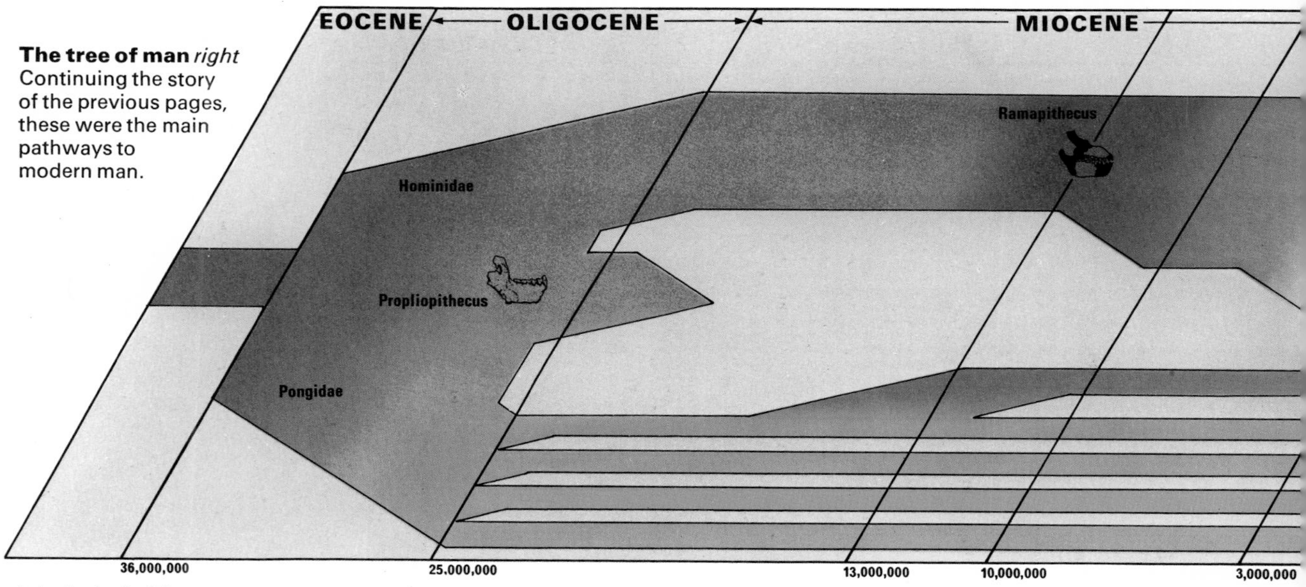

EOCENE
OLIGOCENE
MIOCENE
Ramapithecus
Hominidae
Propliopithecus
Pongidae
36,000,000
25,000,000
13,000,000
10,000,000
3,000,000

Early Australopithecus
2,500,000 years ago
Ten million and more years later than Ramapithecus and other 'ape men', the Australopithecines were the first true hominids. They walked upright, lived on the ground and used primitive tools such as the broken piece of bone below. While hominids are all erect man-like creatures, Australopithecus is more correctly described as a pre-man, for he lacked modern man's brain-power and versatility. Knowledge of the earliest hominids is sparse. Their remains are usually in deep strata, and their tools difficult to distinguish from natural bones and stones. But the finds that have been made cover a very wide area of the Earth, mainly in Africa, and have revealed some sub-species differing in body size, possibly in diet and certainly in jaw and skull geometry and chewing strength.

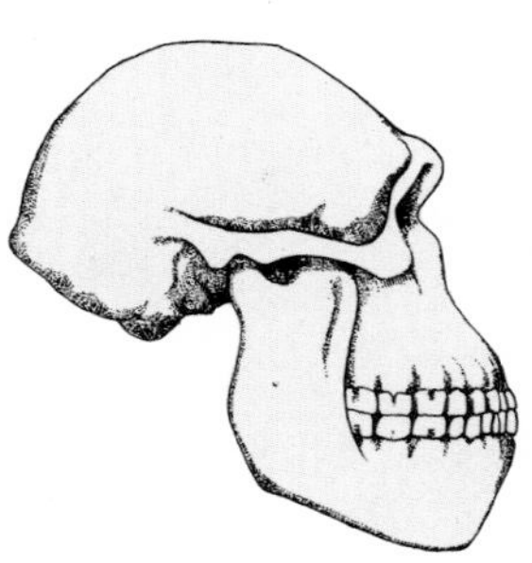

A primitive skull
In 1925 Raymond Dart discovered a human ancestor who had a small brain-case; previously, a large brain was thought to be a fundamental characteristic of man. Dart had found the earliest Pleistocene hominid yet known: *Australopithecus africanus,* shown above.

Late Australopithecus
1,000,000 years ago
Another 1½ million years of development brought great advances and further diversification. *Australopithecus robustus,* whose massive dental equipment suggested he was a vegetarian, proved to be an evolutionary dead-end; but *A. africanus* and other early hominid lines appear to have become progressively larger in stature and particularly improved in brain size and power. Some of the most significant finds of these later Australopithecines have been made in Olduvai Gorge, Tanzania, where there is ready access to strata extending down over 300 feet (100 m), representing a time-span of more than 2,000,000 years. Forty years ago Louis Leakey found chipped stones in this gorge which he judged could not have happened by accident: they were apparently the oldest shaped tools on Earth.

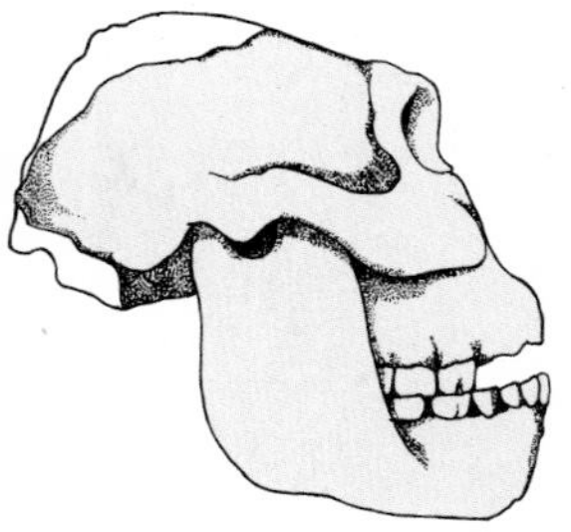

Cranium and mandible
The skull of *Australopithecus robustus* from Swartkrans, in South Africa, has been assembled from a cranium and mandible from two individuals of the same period. The main difference seen in *A. robustus* is a dental one, the cheek teeth being massive.

Homo erectus
500,000 years ago
There is no sharp dividing line between apes and men, but *Homo erectus* is possibly the first human ancestor that would be universally regarded by modern men as one of their own kind. First found, in differing forms, in Java and near Peking, his bones are much closer in geometry and proportion to those of modern man than are those of his predecessors. His lower legs, thighs, pelvic girdle and head are fully adapted to a life spent in an upright posture. His brain shows further growth, falling midway in capacity between that of a chimpanzee and that of an advanced modern man. His greatest known achievements are that he used fire and appears to have lived in communities larger than the family.

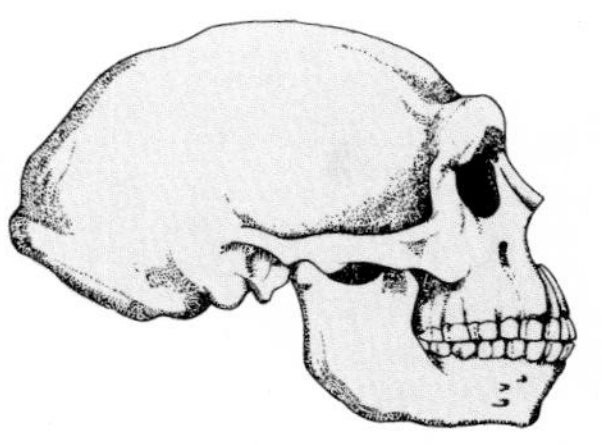

Peking man
Most initial finds of *Homo erectus* come from the neighbourhood of Peking. This skull was found at Lower Cave, Choukoutien, and dates from about 450,000 years ago.

The first men *left*
In 1891 fragments of an ape-man skeleton found in Java caused a sensation. They are now seen as the first clue to *Homo erectus* who has since been dug up in China and Tanzania. But his successor, *Homo sapiens*, was discovered first in Britain and Germany.

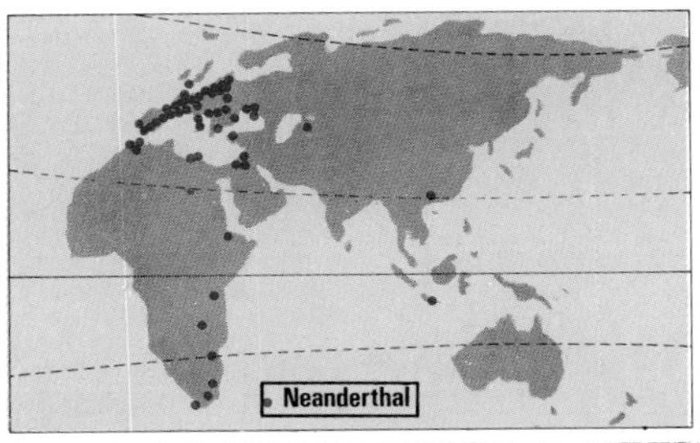
Neanderthal

Neanderthal man *left*
The best-known of primitive men, he dates from 110,000 to 35000 years ago and was found from the Atlantic to Iraq. Solo and Rhodesian man were his contemporaries. These men were thoughtful, superstitious, skillful and often artistic.

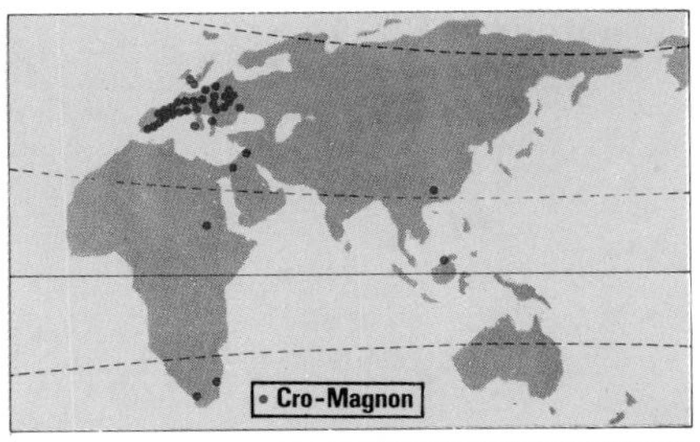
Cro-Magnon

Cro-Magnon man *left*
Over 25000 years ago these men sheltered from the Upper Palaeolithic ice in caves which preserved their remains for research today. While the greatest finds have been in the Dordogne, scattered caves have been found elsewhere, inhabited by related men.

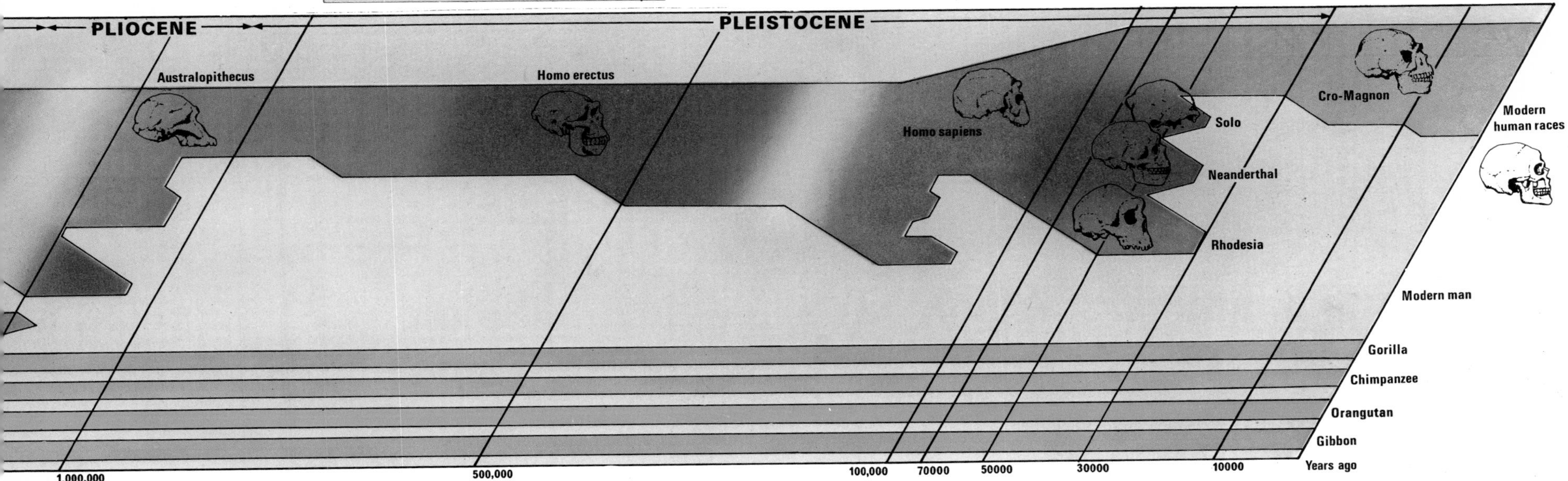
PLIOCENE
PLEISTOCENE
Australopithecus
Homo erectus
Homo sapiens
Solo
Neanderthal
Rhodesia
Cro-Magnon
Modern human races
Modern man
Gorilla
Chimpanzee
Orangutan
Gibbon
1,000,000
500,000
100,000
70000
50000
30000
10000
Years ago

Early Homo sapiens
200,000 years ago
Man was not the first animal to walk on two legs, but he remains the only species to do so while retaining the full use of powerful and dextrous hands. This, allied with his great brain power, enabled him to become the most widespread and dominant species on Earth. Of all his manifold assets one of the greatest is his capacity to think. *Homo sapiens* ('thinking man') is the species from which all modern men have sprung; indeed, all humans today are members of the high-browed subspecies *Homo sapiens sapiens*, no matter what their color. Solo man and Rhodesian man are examples of extinct species of *Homo sapiens*, but the illustration below is based on Swanscombe man who, with his contemporaries found at Steinheim and Montmaurin, shows many modern features.

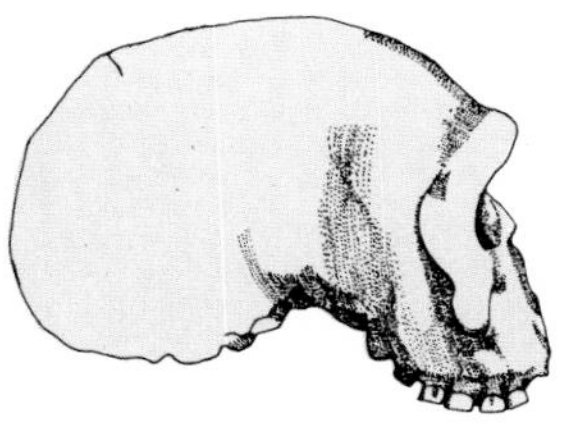

Steinheim man
The oldest fossils that can claim to be *Homo sapiens* were fragments found in Germany and in Britain.

Early Neanderthal
70,000 years ago
By this time man's history was becoming varied and complex. The people known as Neanderthal, from the German town where the first primitive man's skull was found, lived from 110,000 to 35000 years ago and were widely distributed throughout Europe and the Middle East, and to a lesser degree in N Africa and the Near East. Many sub-types of Neanderthaler are known. Most appear to have been squat, thick-set and powerful, with a craggy, beetle-browed face and a brain sometimes larger than that of modern men. The Neanderthaler is the archetype of Stone Age man. He was very far from being a crude, ignorant brute. Typically, he dwelt in a cave, wore clothing of skins and used highly sophisticated tools and weapons. He was the first man to leave behind substantial culture.

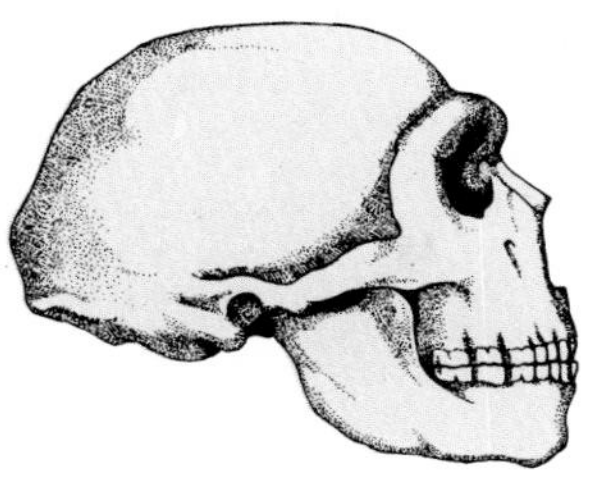

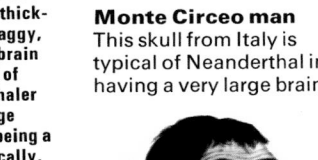

Monte Circeo man
This skull from Italy is typical of Neanderthal in having a very large brain.

Upper Paleolithic
30,000 years ago
The later forms of Neanderthal man were replaced by Cro-Magnon man a little more than 30000 years ago. Much of our knowledge of this period stems from a unique assortment of caves and other dwellings as in the Dordogne, in France (Cro-Magnon=big grotto). Here men have lived for more than 30000 years, and traces of their culture are everywhere. The man illustrated is not quite Cro-Magnon but is drawn from early skulls found in Eastern Europe. He wears a fur coat, skin shoes and leather girdle, and his dwelling and tools show marked advance on everything that went before. In cave paintings, the manufacture of ornaments and the use of early jewelry, the period is often remarkable. There is evidence such men had devised religions, and almost certainly spoken language.

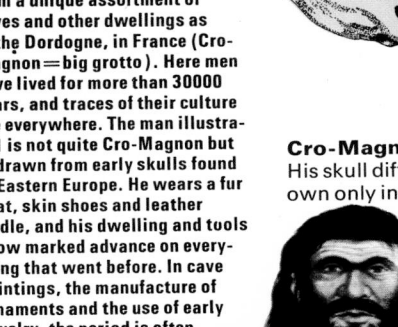

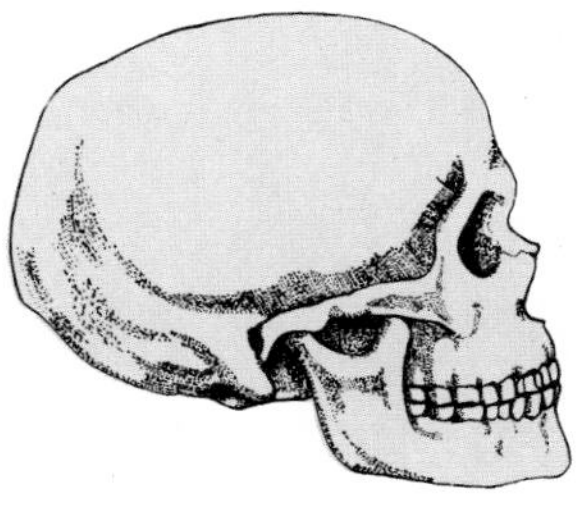

Cro-Magnon shape
His skull differed from our own only in detail.

Digging for Man's History

In 1833 Charles Lyell courageously proposed that the fragments of bones of animals and men that persistently cropped up in deep geological strata could mean only one thing: that the Earth had been created long before the date of 4004 BC accepted by Christianity. Since then practically the whole of our knowledge of man's early development has come from systematic digging. At first a lone archaeologist could do the whole job, but today digging for early man involves a team of specialized archaeologists, geologists, technologists and laboratory workers. They hope to identify everything significant, study it in relation to its resting place, the history of the region and nearby finds, and also subject chosen items to detailed laboratory tests – such as accurate age determination by the potassium/argon method (p. 45). A major dig needs experts on rocks, on soils and on plant pollen.

Although there are remarkable instances of well-preserved human bodies being found (for example, in peat bogs) and of woolly mammoths whose flesh could be eaten after a million years in frozen Siberia, almost all archaeology rests on bones and on man's artifacts. Gradually, from small fragments of jaw, teeth, skull and other bones, it has been possible to piece together what appears to be a fairly complete history of human evolution. The artist can then cover a deduced skeleton with tissue, as has been done in these pages. But pigmentation of skin and degree of hairiness is still a matter for conjecture.

Among the significant factors studied in early man are his brain size, jaw structure, posture and locomotion. Today's great apes have a stooping, occasionally four-legged posture. So did ape-men from 20 million down to five million years ago; then, gradually, the hominid line learned to walk upright. Its members also learned to use tools, and to make them progressively better. Even later, true men began to leave behind evidence of their growing culture in their burials, their artifacts and their art. All these things can be studied in bone caves, such as the imaginary one illustrated on the right, and in excavation sites.

The cave in use
The cave is modeled after European examples of the Upper Paleolithic period of the order of 25000 years ago. It was at about this time that cave paintings appear to have become widespread. The river was then close to its present level, but the rock falls and piles of debris were still to come.

A bone cave *above and right*
From about 100,000 years ago caves provided many types of early men with a ready-made refuge. Probably most of these caves still exist. Although many are buried under later strata, and virtually all are greatly changed by subsequent developments, it is still possible with experience to read the message contained in them.

A burrow in the cave
Here a small animal has burrowed into the floor. It was deflected sideways by the hard flowstone until it could continue on down, throwing fossil bones up on to the floor above. Finally it died at the end of its burrow.

A buzzard's nest?
Just inside the lip of the cave mouth a bird of prey built its nest. Directly beneath it on the slope of the rock debris are scattered small rodent bones.

River level
In general, the lowest geological sediments are the oldest, but it is unwise to jump to this conclusion. In this hypothetical cave the earliest of all the deposits is a river terrace A above the cave on the hillside, indicating that the whole cave was originally submerged. At about this period insoluble limestone residue was settling on the cave floor at B. As the river cut its valley its level fell to C, leaving silt bed D. Continued deepening of the valley brought the river to its present level, leaving the cave dry and eroding the thick layer of silt at the mouth of the cave.

An obstructed mouth
Early man sheltered in the mouth of the cave and lit fires there for warmth and to cook food. The ashes of these fires gradually accumulated in three main layers, each denoting a long period of use. The 'contemporary' inset illustrates the third of these periods. Later the cave was abandoned by man and the mouth gradually became blocked by a pile of rock debris.

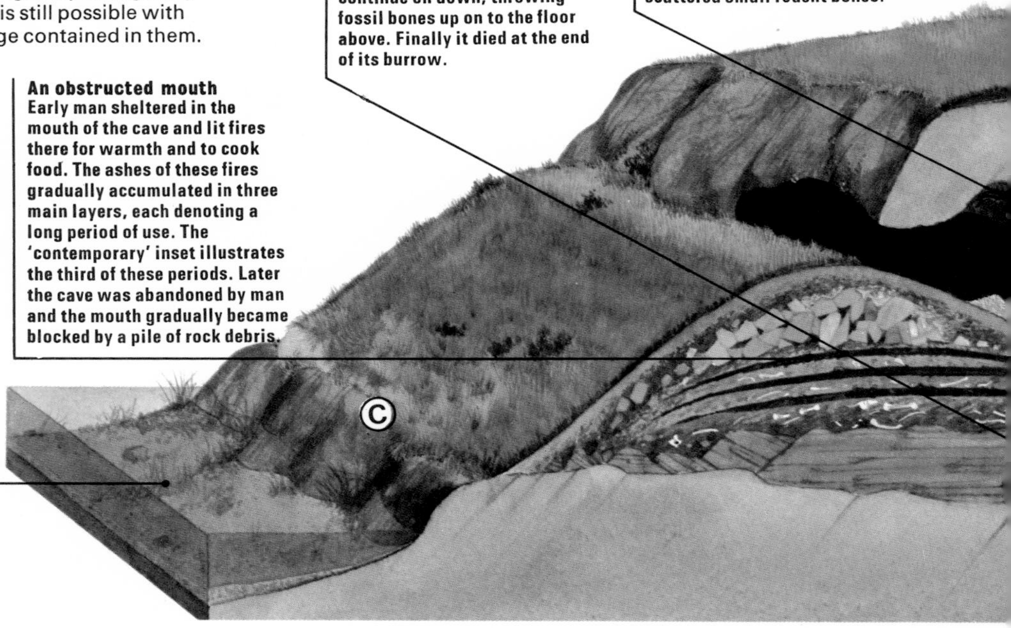
C

Mesolithic
About 10,000 years ago
About 20000 years ago the great ice sheets began slowly to recede, a process that is still continuing. As the climate grew warmer the Late Paleolithic people gave way to the Mesolithic (transitional) about the year 8000 BC. Milder conditions allowed man to exploit the rivers and seas, using fishing nets and even elaborate barricades and weirs made of woven saplings. The family had by now become a firm social unit, while people also explored the territory of their neighbors. For the first time there is evidence of large groups combining in habitation, hunting, art and making useful articles. Although farming of crops and animals had yet to come, the Mesolithic period saw a great enrichment of life and—probably—the development of a social conscience.

Neolithic
8000 years ago
The scene below depicts the greatest revolution ever wrought on Earth. The Neolithic ('new stone') people discovered some of the basic secrets of life—how animals can be reared in captivity and how plants can be grown from seed. The keeping of pets by children may have provided the key to animal husbandry by their parents. As a result men no longer had to risk their lives in finding and killing their prey; they kept them in a herd. And the organized growing of crops at last freed man from the role of passive and often desperate scavenger, and instead set him on his great path leading to mastery over his environment. Unlike all other Earth life he became able to shape the whole world around him and, to an increasing degree, become master of his life and future destiny. Many of the inhabitants of today's world still live in a basically Neolithic way.

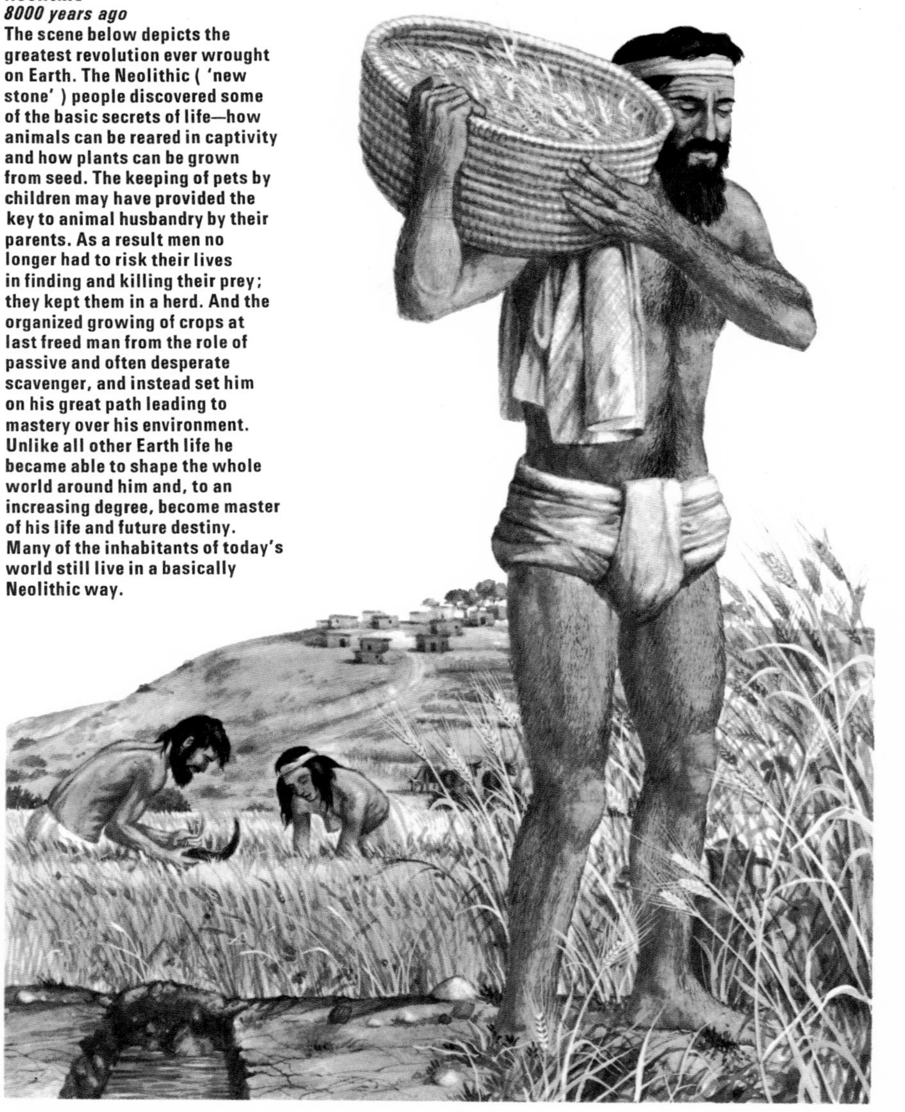

Cave art
Many well preserved cave paintings are masterpieces. Most show animals being hunted by early man, and their power, color and dynamic energy can be startling. But they are often in difficult, inaccessible places, and appear to have been part of the hunter's semi-religious efforts to insure his success and safety in finding and then killing a powerful and dangerous opponent.

The bear cult
Another manifestation of early man's hunting superstitions is to be found in carefully prepared arrangements of cave bear skulls, leg bones and other fragments. Men could hardly have chosen a more dangerous opponent, and they could find meat much more easily; yet the cave bear cult is evident in many forms, such as this stone compartment filled with skulls.

Human burial
Early men buried their own kind in various ways. Some societies buried skulls only, arrayed with possessions or ornaments; others buried men but left female corpses on refuse heaps. This skeleton shows evidence of careful burial in a sleeping posture similar to that of the Grimaldi remains in the Grotte des Enfants, Monaco. Later the grave was overlain by rock debris, here removed.

Petrification
Even the interior of a structurally stable cave changes over a long period, and in this case a sudden gross alteration has resulted from a large fall of rock from the roof. Subsequent to this, slow seepage through the limestone roof of water containing dissolved minerals, especially calcium carbonate, caused gradual growth of pendulous stalactites and upright stalagmites.

Animal remains
The cave is littered to a depth of well over a foot (0.3 m) with the debris of the food and other refuse of carnivores. The great cone above the fall of rock is littered with the remains of animals which fell in through the hole above; and on top of the cone is a pile of bat dung.

A rock fall
A massive collapse of the cave roof left a pile of rock on the floor of the cave and a gaping open shaft above. New layers of flowstone accumulated, earth and rock debris built up above the rock pile and ultimately the growing cone reached the roof. Sediments then filled the shaft.

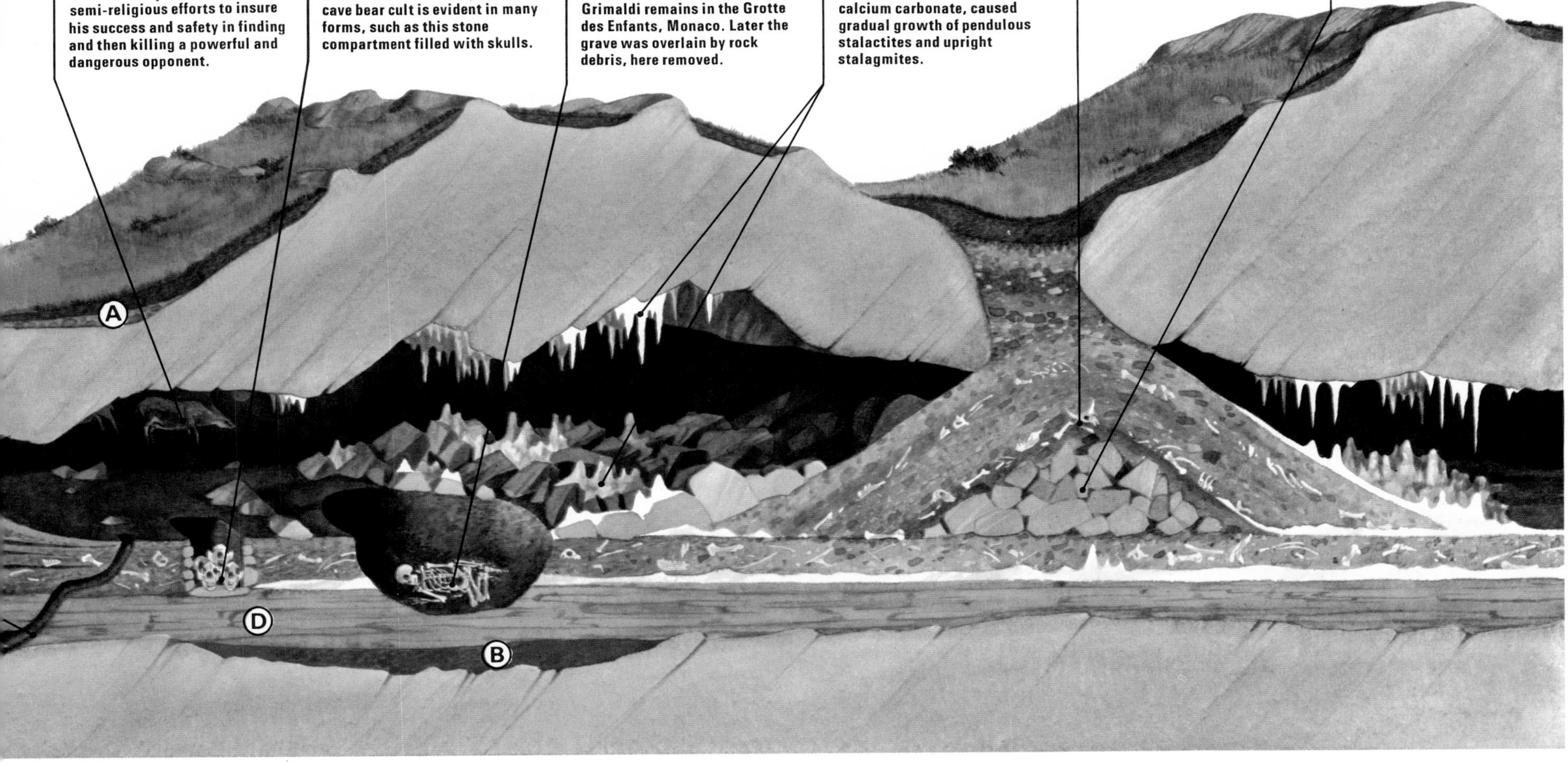

A
D
B

	LOWER PALEOLITHIC Over 2 million yrs AUSTRALOPITHECUS	500,000 yrs HOMO ERECTUS	MIDDLE PALEOLITHIC 100,000 yrs H. SAPIENS NEANDERTHALENSIS	UPPER PALEOLITHIC 40000 yrs H. SAPIENS SAPIENS (MODERN MAN)	MESOLITHIC 10000 yrs
Hunting and fishing methods	Food gathering (roots, berries, grubs, eggs). Hunting small game. Killing with stones and stabbing sticks.		Food gathering. Hunting large game. Use of fire hardened spears and stone clubs. Group hunting using ambush and stampede.	Food gathering, fowling and fishing. More specialized hunting of herd animals using traps and falls.	Food gathering, fowling and fishing with traps. Collection of shell fish. Beginnings of agriculture and domestication of animals.
Material culture	Oldowan pebble tools. 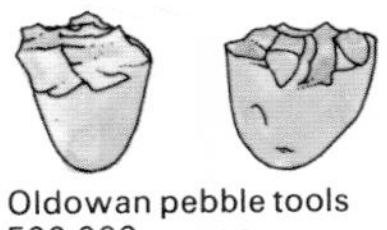 Oldowan pebble tools 500,000 yrs ago	Chopping tools and hand axes. Wooden spears. Use of fire (Pekin man). 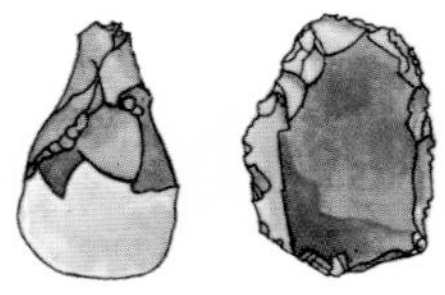 Hand axe — Tortoise core tool	Development of varied stone tool kits (scrapers, burins points, blades). 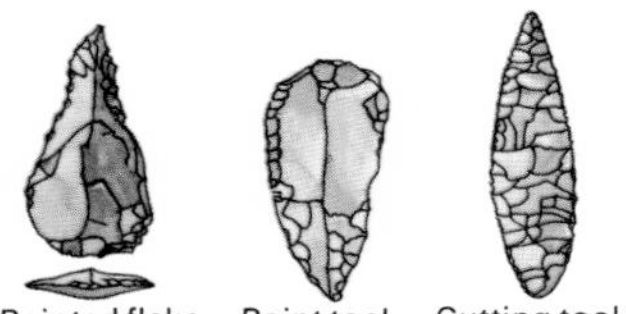 Pointed flake tool — Point tool — Cutting tool	Throwing spears with separate heads. Harpoons and fish-spears. Implements of bone, horn and ivory. Microlith arrowhead Flint point 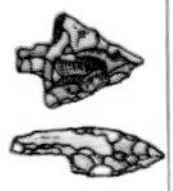 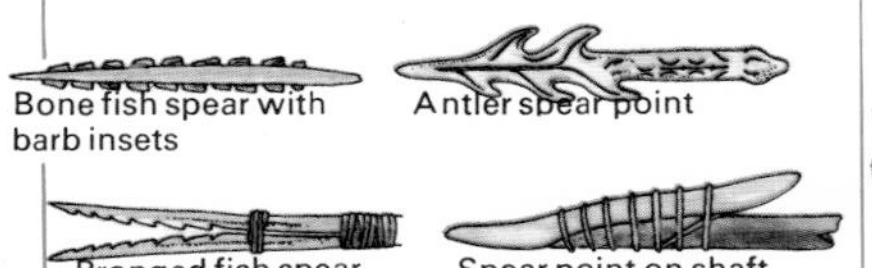 Bone fish spear with barb insets — Antler spear point Pronged fish spear — Spear point on shaft	Use of bow and arrows. Transport by canoe, skis, and sledges. Development of basketry and pottery. Fishhook and net making needle Fish gorge 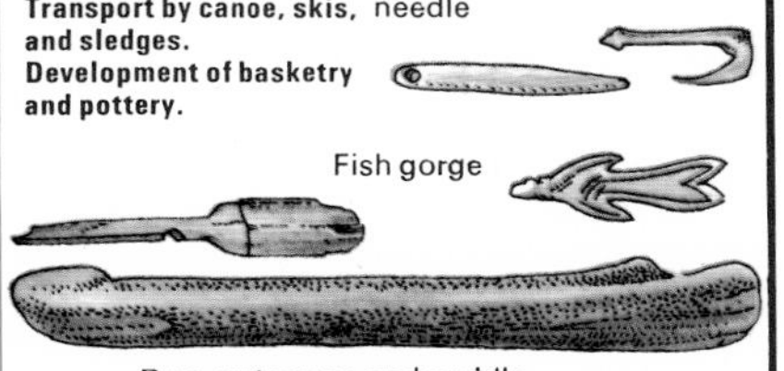 Dug-out canoe and paddle
Dwellings	Wind breaks, hunting hides and temporary shelters.	Use of caves, usually as temporary dwelling. Better shelters constructed.	Permanent cave dwellings and more sophisticated shelters.		Evidence of village communities, particularly in coastal areas.
Intellectual and religious activities		Possible existence of cannibalism. Skull: evidence of cannibalism. 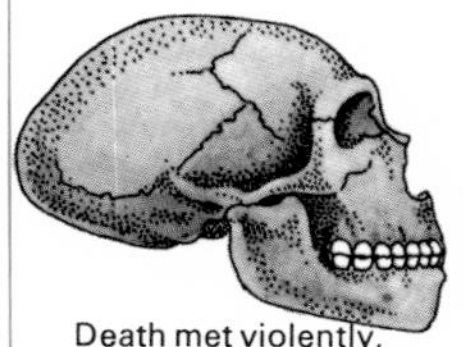 Death met violently, hole in skull base to extract brain.	Ritual burial (La Ferrassie). Possible cannibalism (Solo man). Growth of religious beliefs. 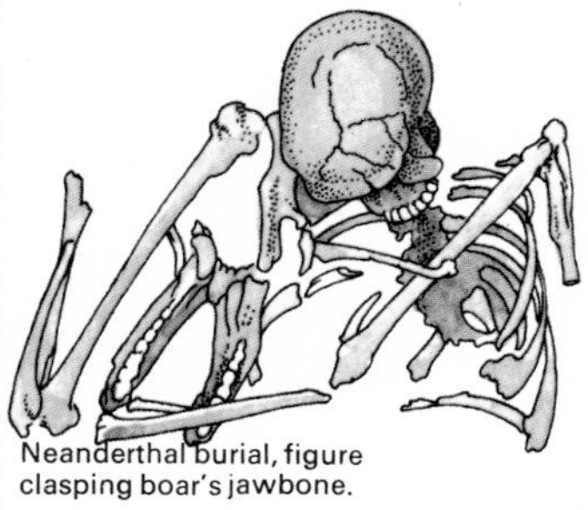 Neanderthal burial, figure clasping boar's jawbone.	Personal adornment and ritual mutilation. Development of cave painting and sculpture.  Carved antler (art) 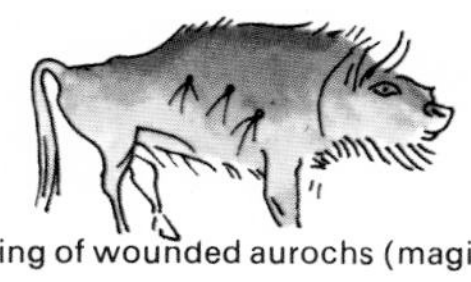 Engraving of wounded aurochs (magic)	Carved ivory figurine (magic) 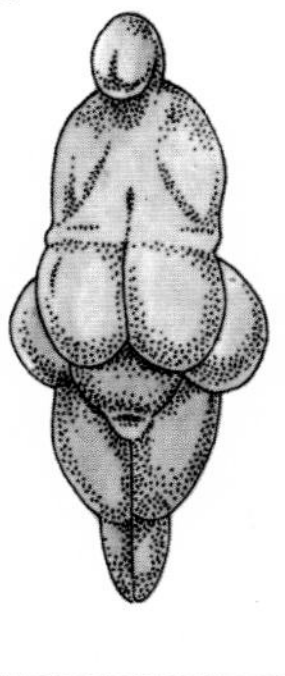 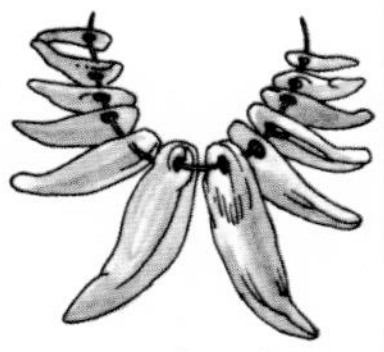 Necklace of carnivore canines (personal adornment)

The Origin of Species

When Charles Darwin published his book, 'Origin of Species', in 1859, it seemed to strike at the very foundations of human life and beliefs. Even now there are people who steadfastly refuse to believe that evolution has ever occurred and, directly related to this, that new species can arise without Divine intervention. Bishop Wilberforce, carrying the banner of the Church, was among the first to set out to destroy the proposal that evolution by natural selection had led to the tremendous diversity of living things and the exchanges between him and Darwin's steadfast supporter, Thomas Henry Huxley, have become classics of satire and rhetoric.

Starting point for Charles Darwin's theory was his experience as a naturalist on the *Beagle* during a five year trip that took him to South America and, of course, the Galapagos Islands. In South America he found fossils of large animals with bony armor like that of the armadillos still living there. The immutability of species, embodied in the then extant theory of creation, could provide no explanation as to why these animals built on a similar plan had become extinct. At the same time, he was impressed by the close similarity of animals occupying particular niches in neighboring regions. However, it was in the Galapagos Islands that he found a perfect microcosm embodying many of the features that had been puzzling him during his travels.

On the islands he found species of finches that not only provided a gradation of form and habit, but also resembled some species on the neighbouring mainland. On the other hand, the fauna showed no resemblance to other oceanic islands with similar physical conditions that he had visited. Indeed, each island had its own peculiar, but related, animal populations. The comparative newness of the volcanic islands and the sparsity of forms that had colonized them provided a laboratory of evolution which in its simplicity emphasized the inadequacy of existing ideas on the creation of life.

On his return to England in 1836 the young Darwin set about collecting evidence from many different sources starting from a working hypothesis that species have undergone evolution and have originated by descent from an ancestral species. The stage had been set for the theory of evolution and the Galapagos Archipelago with its bizarre animal life was to gain a remarkable place in the development of man's ideas about both himself and his place in nature. He ceased to occupy a special place in the scheme of things, but came to represent a stage in the evolution of a particular line of mammals. Man was placed in the milieu of his territorial environment, a point that even today is only just being fully appreciated.

The world's only sea-going lizards *above*
Looking like miniature dinosaurs, marine iguanas swarm over the rough volcanic rock of the Galapagos Islands. Despite their formidable appearance, they are strictly vegetarian.

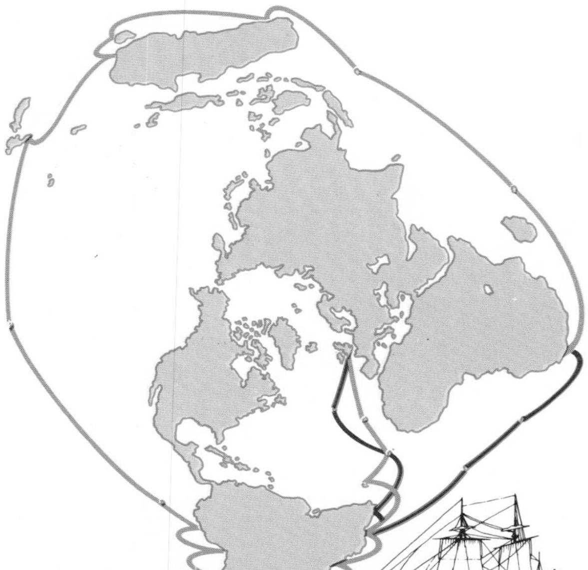

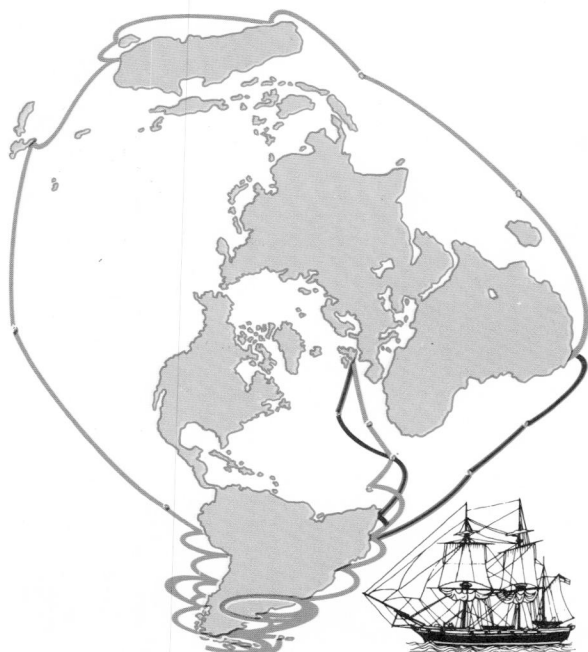

Voyage of the Beagle *above*
On 27th December, 1831, the *Beagle* (above, right) set out under Captain Robert Fitzroy on a scientific expedition that was not to end until 2nd October, 1836. As naturalist and companion, Fitzroy selected a young Cambridge graduate, Charles Darwin. During the voyage Darwin collected evidence that led to his revolutionary theory of evolution.

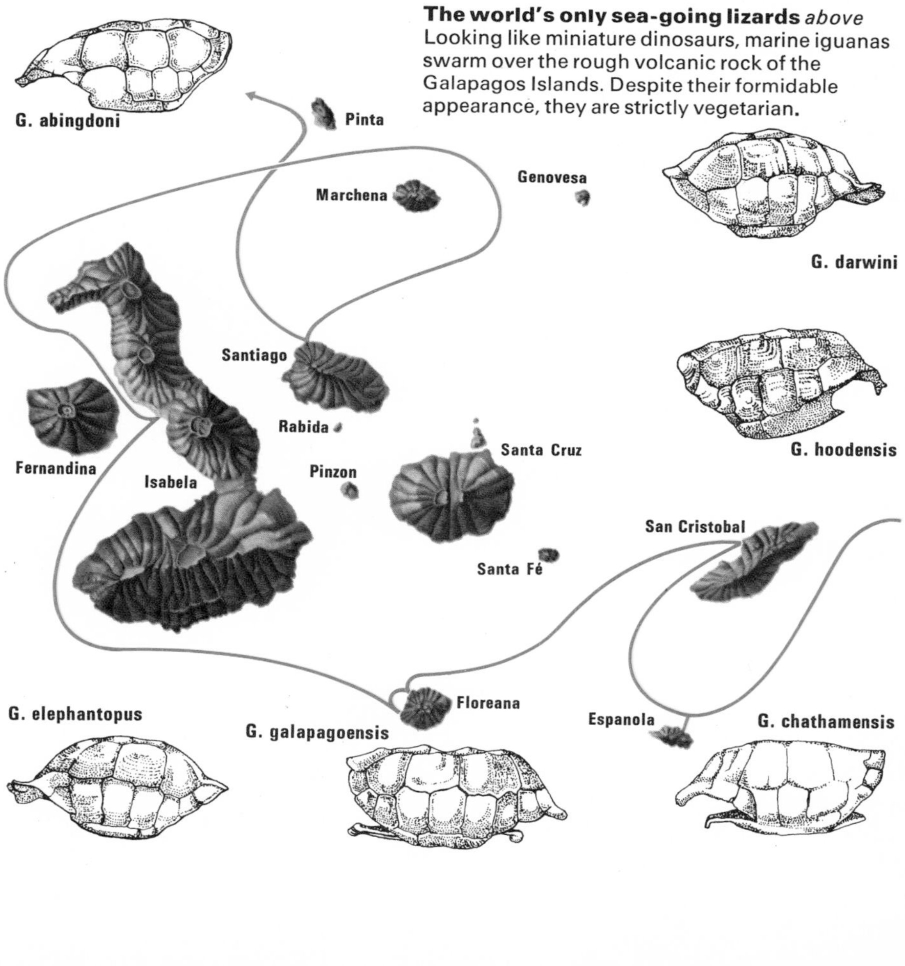
G. abingdoni
Pinta
Marchena
Genovesa
G. darwini
Santiago
Rabida
Fernandina
Isabela
Pinzon
Santa Cruz
G. hoodensis
San Cristobal
Santa Fé
Floreana
G. elephantopus
G. galapagoensis
Espanola
G. chathamensis

Darwin in the Galapagos
above and right
Although Charles Darwin had already begun to question the existing theory of creation early in his travels, it was the strange creatures that he found on the Galapagos Islands that finally convinced him of the need for a new explanation. Each of the islands, for example, had its own species of giant tortoise (the shells of six are shown here) although all were clearly related. If such creatures had been separately created, why should there have been such a prodigal expenditure of 'creation' and why were the animals so similar?

Evidence for natural selection *below*
The finches of the Galapagos Islands are famous as the birds that, in 1835, provided Charles Darwin with the most significant single clue supporting his theory of the origin of species. They are a perfect example of the results of natural evolution in a small localized population. All the modern Galapagos finches are descended from a single ancestral line of birds that long ago rafted over from the mainland of South America. At the time of their immigration there were no indigenous finches on the islands. The invading finches were seed-eaters, and they rapidly spread throughout all of the available space. Soon they were competing with each other for food and territory. Some adopted a tree habitat, others preferred cactus and others the ground. The different populations adopted different food preferences which are now reflected in the shape of their beak (see below). The ecological and geographical isolation of each group restricted the opportunities for interbreeding, allowing them to evolve independently along individual paths. Today they cannot interbreed and the islands contain 14 species. Nevertheless, the stability of the present population could be disturbed by a new influx of mainland birds.

Woodpecker finch *left*
Camarrhynchus pallidus is perhaps the most unusual of the Galapagos finches. The woodpecker finch has adopted the useful trick of digging insect grubs out of crevices in tree bark with the aid of a spine broken from a large cactus plant.

Darwin's finches

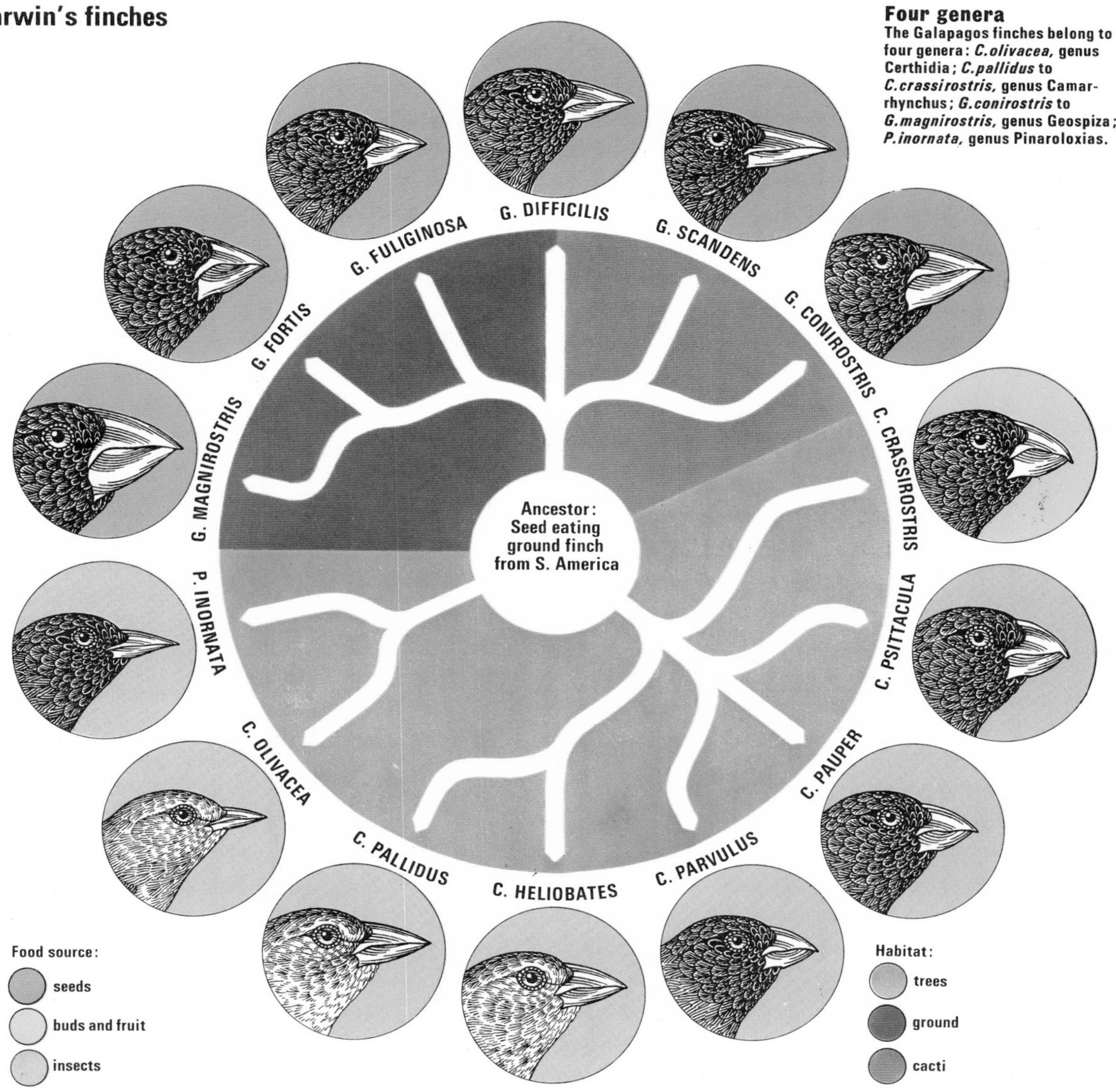
G. DIFFICILIS
G. SCANDENS
G. CONIROSTRIS
C. CRASSIROSTRIS
C. PSITTACULA
C. PAUPER
C. PARVULUS
C. HELIOBATES
C. PALLIDUS
C. OLIVACEA
P. INORNATA
G. MAGNIROSTRIS
G. FORTIS
G. FULIGINOSA
Ancestor: Seed eating ground finch from S. America
Food source:
seeds
buds and fruit
insects
Habitat:
trees
ground
cacti

Four genera
The Galapagos finches belong to four genera: *C.olivacea*, genus Certhidia; *C.pallidus* to *C.crassirostris*, genus Camarhynchus; *G.conirostris* to *G.magnirostris*, genus Geospiza; *P.inornata*, genus Pinaroloxias.

Galapagos penguin is the most northern member of its group. Sea lions breed on the islands.

Cold water animals
above and left
The presence of the penguin (above) and the sea lion (left) on the Galapagos Islands is explained by the fact that the cold Humboldt Current flows westward by them. Although sea lions have a wide range, they usually return to the same beaches on which they were born, to breed. In this way distinct species can evolve.

Unique island forms
above and right
The giant tortoise (above) gave its Spanish name, galápago, to the islands. The giant reptile may weigh as much as 500 lb (226 kg), with a shell as big as a bathtub. They are the largest animal on the islands. Besides the reptiles, the islands also support large numbers of birds. One of the rarest birds in the world, a flightless cormorant (right) occurs on two islands. Like many other creatures on the Galapagos Islands, these animals have not learned to fear man, and in the past they fell easy victims to the sailors who landed in search of fresh meat.

The man-o'-war bird *above and right*
The frigate bird received its nickname because it robs other birds of food. Masters of the air with an 8 ft (2.4 m) wingspan they pursue until the bird regurgitates its food.

The male frigate bird attracts a mate by inflating its vivid red throat sac.

Colorful animals
The blue-footed booby (above) has vivid 'gaiters'. The red land crabs (right) have deserted the sea.

Species and Variety

The variety of nature has as its basis the fact that the giant molecules of life do not always copy themselves precisely. All the instructions for a creature's construction are carried within its DNA, and this DNA is passed on to its offspring. If the copying process by which DNA is replicated was not very nearly perfect, life would soon become impossible for each new generation would receive garbled instructions from its parents. Equally, if the copying was always without blemish, the existing forms of life would remain in an unchangeable rut.

In fact, the tiny errors that creep in allow life to perform an experiment with every new generation. Most of the differences in the inherited instructions have no effect on the creature's ability to survive. Nearly all the remainder make it less fit for its environment, but a minute proportion improve its performance. These are the successful experiments with the environment. Because they are successful, the altered DNA that caused them is passed on to more descendants than is the case with the neutral or failed experiments. Thus nature tends to select the more successful varieties.

This process of natural selection has been going on since life began, and it is unlikely ever to end. It has enabled every possible niche for life to be explored and then exploited. When two organisms that have descended from the same ancestor have become so different, as a result of the accumulation through successive generations of differences in their DNA, that they can no longer breed together – and thus mix their DNA – they are said to belong to different species. For the DNA differences to accumulate, the two lines of descendants must be prevented from interbreeding by some form of impenetrable barrier. Sometimes this is of a geographical nature, but it can arise from increasingly incompatible styles of life.

Today man is usurping the role of the environment by imposing his own selection process on domestic plants and animals. To widen his range of choice he deliberately increases the variety of these species by artificially increasing the level of errors in the replication process.

Sexual reproduction: the key to natural diversity
In the 'dance' of the chromosomes genetic material inherited from both parents is shuffled in the process of creating new sex cells or gametes. For clarity the male nucleus in this diagram is assumed to have only six chromosomes while the maternal and paternal genetic information is shown by different colours. During the process, known as meiosis. which leads to the production of gametes, the hereditary information carried on the chromosomes is exchanged between like pairs, while the overall number of chromosomes is halved. A similar process takes place within the female so that when fertilization takes place the full complement of chromosomes is restored and a new, different, individual develops.

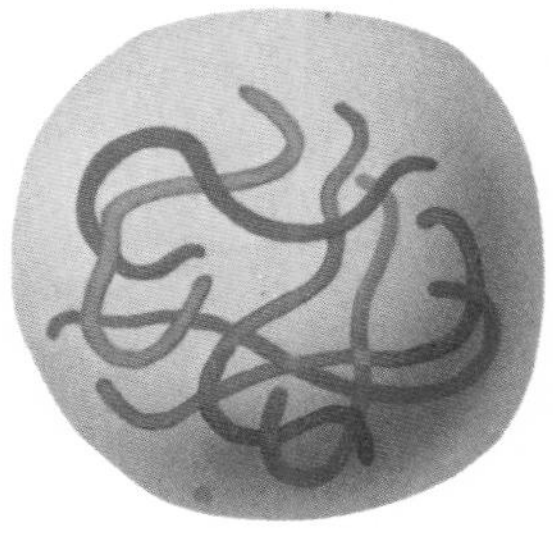

In the resting nucleus chromosomes which carry the genetic instructions from generation to generation are not visible. Only prior to cell division are thin strands seen.

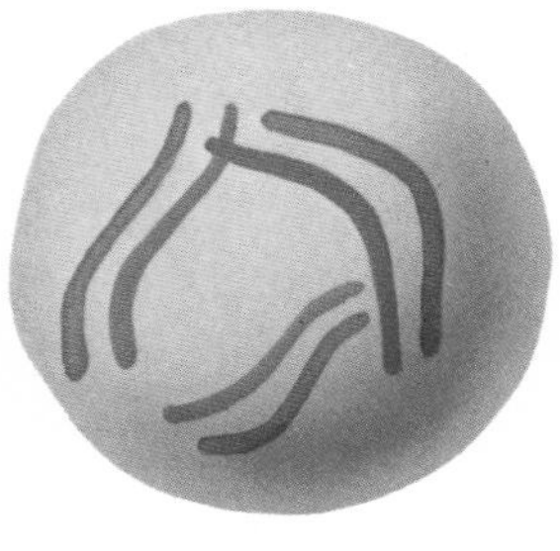

At first the chromosomes are thin and intertwined, but gradually they become thicker and align in pairs. Each pair consists of similar, but not identical, chromosomes.

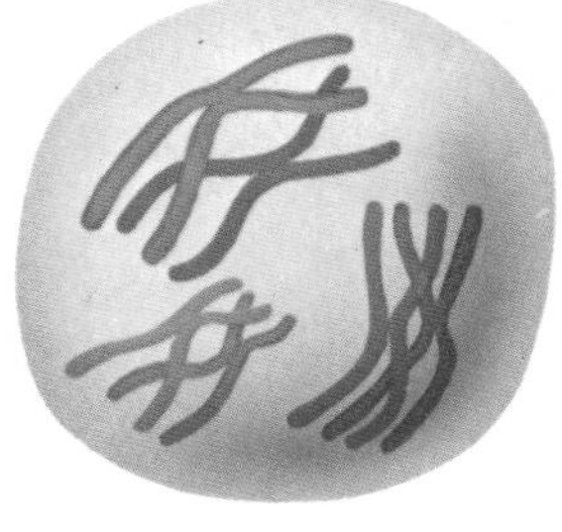

Later in the process each member of the pair itself splits lengthwise with each part connected at one point only. Each chromosome still appears as one under the microscope.

At this stage, 'crossing over' occurs causing an exchange of segments of genetic material. This is the key to the diversity of the next generation once fertilization occurs.

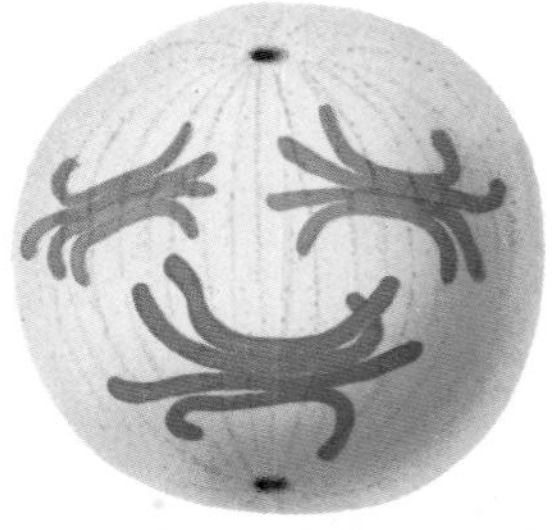

The chromosome pairs now align themselves around the equator of a spindle-like structure. Slowly the paired chromosomes separate. The nuclear membrane has completely disappeared.

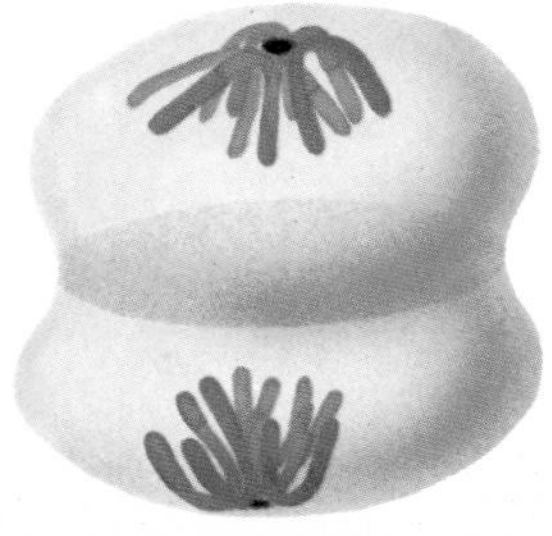

Each of the paired chromosomes migrates towards a pole of the spindle. They are apparently pulled there by the contraction of spindle fibers attached at a single point.

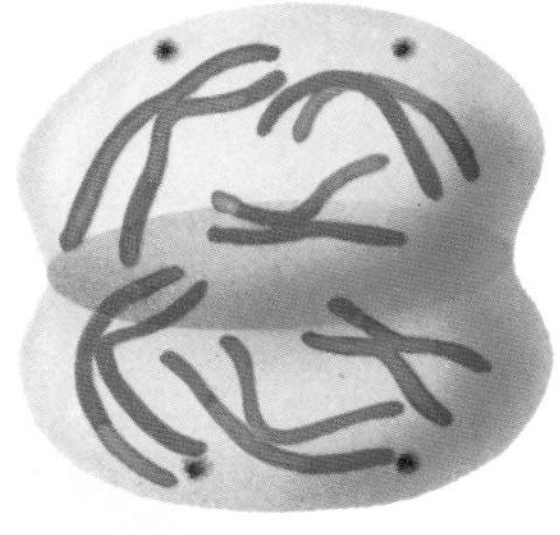

At this stage—a resting phase for the chromosomes in some cases—the poles of the spindle split and separate to the east and west extremities of the two halves of the cell.

Unlike the earlier division, the final one does not involve exchange of any genetic material. New nuclear membranes form around the four clusters of chromosomes.

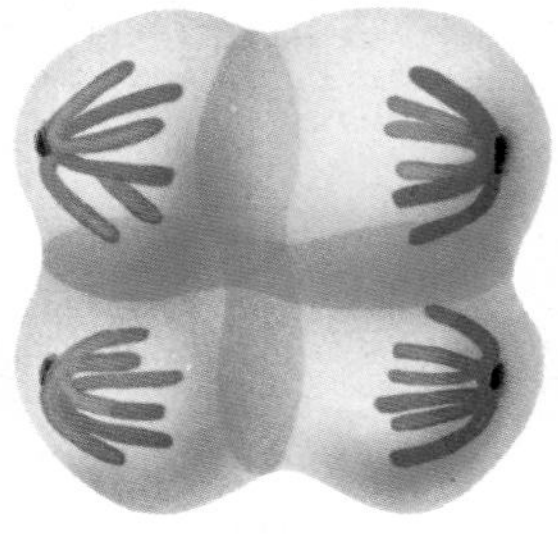

With the formation of new spindles, the double chromosomes align themselves once again at the equators. They then separate with each half moving to opposite poles.

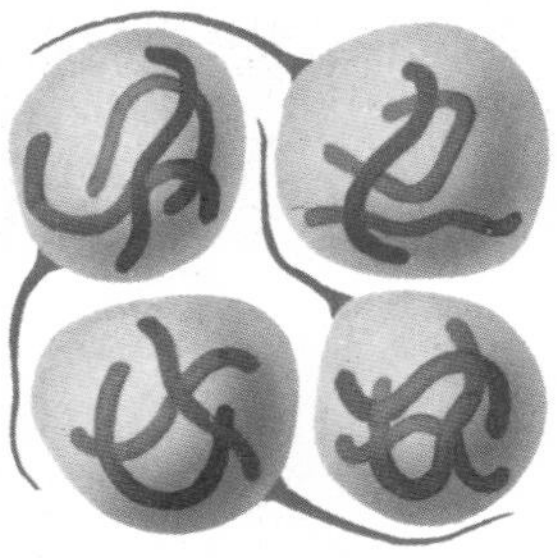

The final step leads to the production of four sperm with half the body's number of chromosomes, each of which has different proportions of hereditary material to transmit.

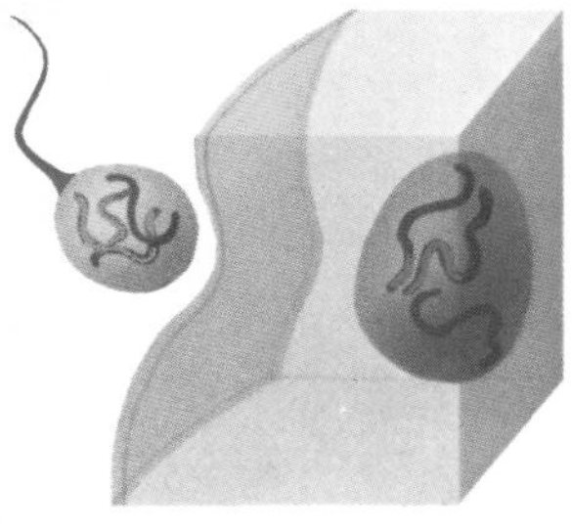

A similar 'reduction' division takes place in the female ovary, but only one of the four cells survives to become an egg ready for fertilization by a single sperm in due course.

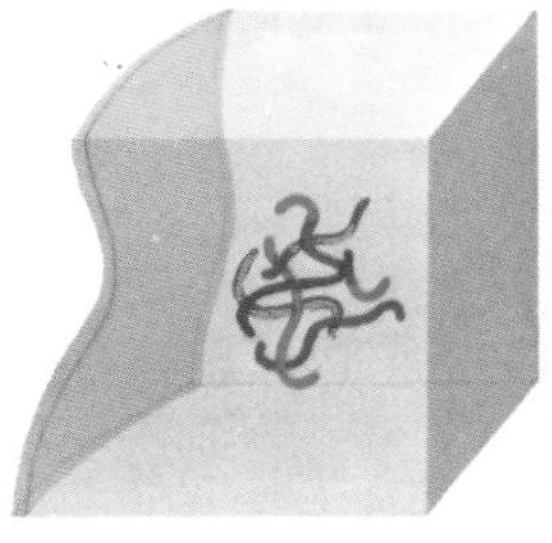

After fertilization, this first cell of a new individual contains a mix of genetic material inherited equally from both parents and passing on some from all four grandparents.

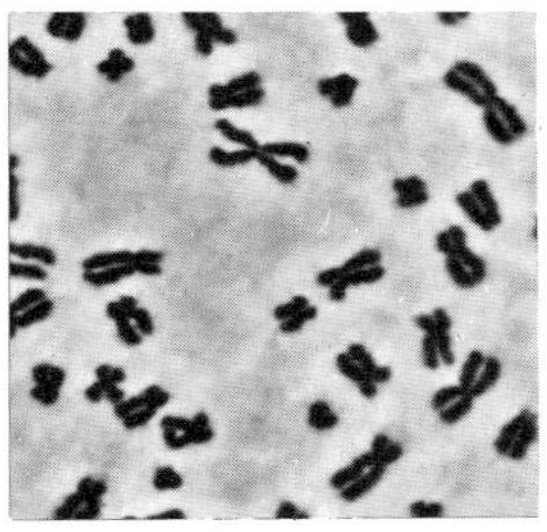

Chromosomes *right*
The normal human cell has 23 pairs of chromosomes. The members of each pair are similar in all except one pair – the so-called 'sex chromosomes'. Female cells contain two similar X chromosomes, but males have only one X with a Y chromosome.

- Parus major major
- Area of gradual transition between P.m. major and P.m. cinereus (P.m. intermedius)
- Area of overlap between P.m. major and P.m. cinereus with no interbreeding
- P.m. cinereus
- Area of gradual transition between P.m. cinereus and P.m. minor (P.m. commixtus)
- P.m. minor
- Area of overlap between P.m. minor and P.m. major with no interbreeding

Ring species *right*
The distribution of the great tit *Parus major* throughout Europe and Asia affords an outstanding example of the way geography can give rise to variety. In Europe, Asia Minor and Siberia the great tit has a green back and yellow belly, and interbreeds freely throughout the whole area. The result is that the gene 'pool' of the species is kept continually stirred, and local differences quickly become eliminated. To the south this tit overlaps and interbreeds with another variety which has a grey back and white belly. But the overlap is not sufficient to allow the gene pool to flow freely, and so the distinctive characteristics of the species are maintained. A similar transition occurs in Vietnam, where the local species has a pale green back and white belly. But this species cannot interbreed with the European, and so the two behave as separate species. A similar overlap occurs in mid-Siberia.

Barriers to breeding *right*
A singularly colorful illustration of speciation is provided by the salamanders of the US west coast. The salamanders that today inhabit this large area are descendants of a species that migrated southwards. In doing so the population was split into two by the hot, dry barrier of the Great Valley of California. The western arm, the coastal races, overlap and interbreed; so do the inland races. The distinctive coloration and eye size of the different forms is adaptive: after random genetic experimentation with the environment they have emerged as the best adapted to the local conditions. The most southerly race of the inland series, *Ensatina klauberi*, has become geographically isolated from its cousins to the north. Since its individuals do not interbreed with their coastal neighbors they are in effect a new species. Speciation appears to be a never-ending process.

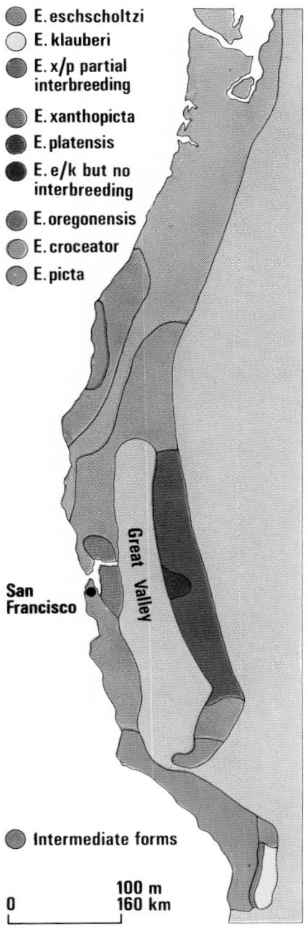
E. eschscholtzi
E. klauberi
E. x/p partial interbreeding
E. xanthopicta
E. platensis
E. e/k but no interbreeding
E. oregonensis
E. croceator
E. picta
Great Valley
San Francisco
Intermediate forms
0
100 m
160 km

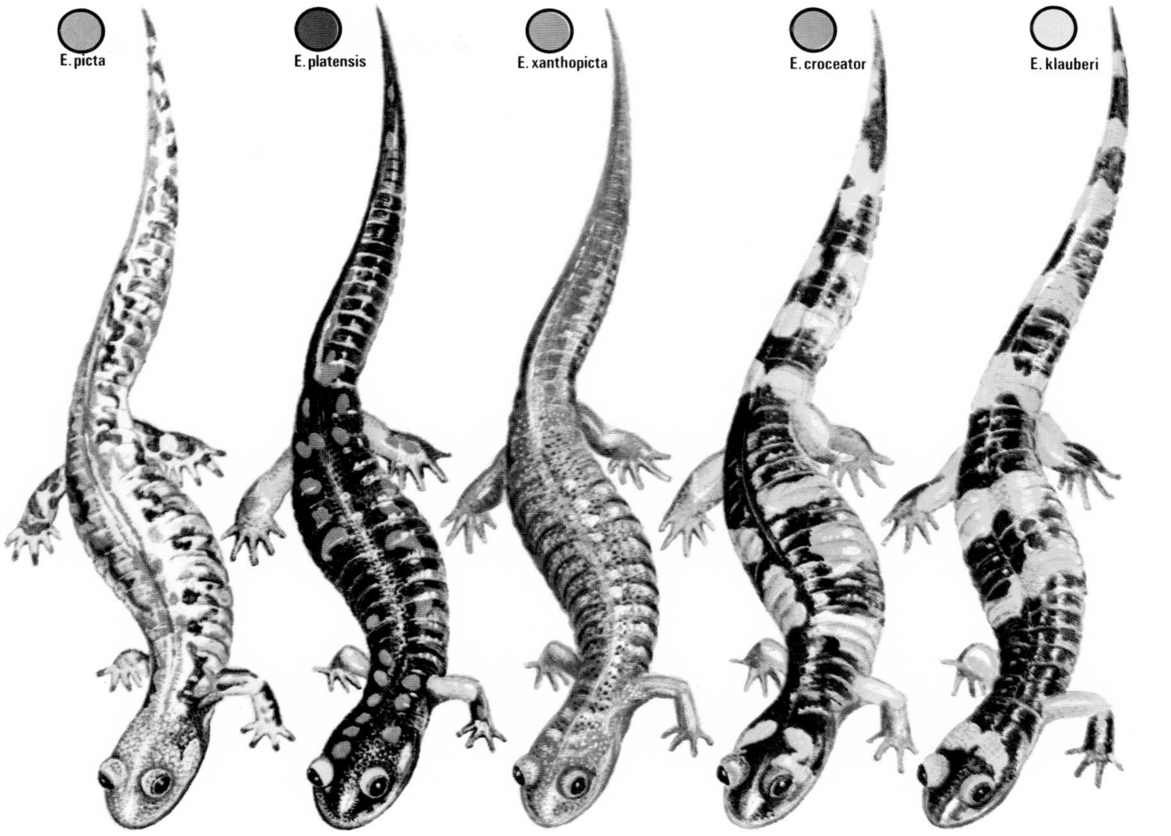
E. picta
E. platensis
E. xanthopicta
E. croceator
E. klauberi

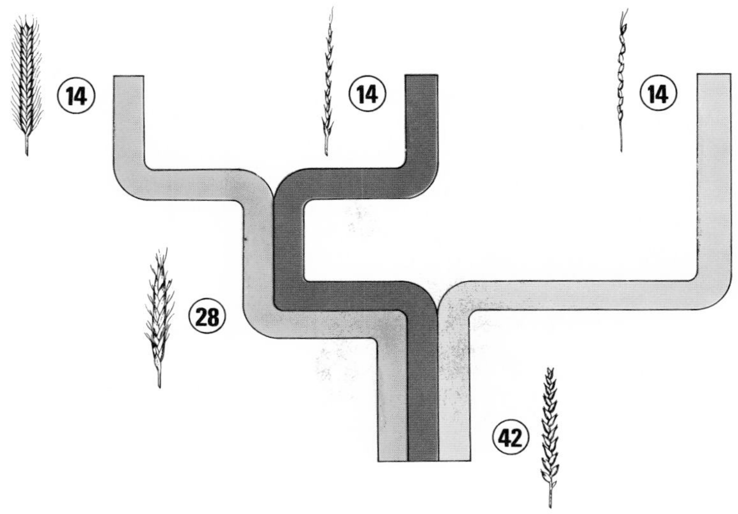
14
14
14
28
42

Cattle *below*
Like crop plants, domesticated animals have been produced by selecting from a wild population those individuals possessing the desired characteristics, and breeding from these. Thus the gene pool of the species is dammed and subdivided into carefully separated 'ponds'. The range of different races this can produce is shown below for cattle. By interbreeding selected animals, and thus demolishing the artificial barriers, it has been possible to re-create the aurochs, primitive ancestor of many breeds.

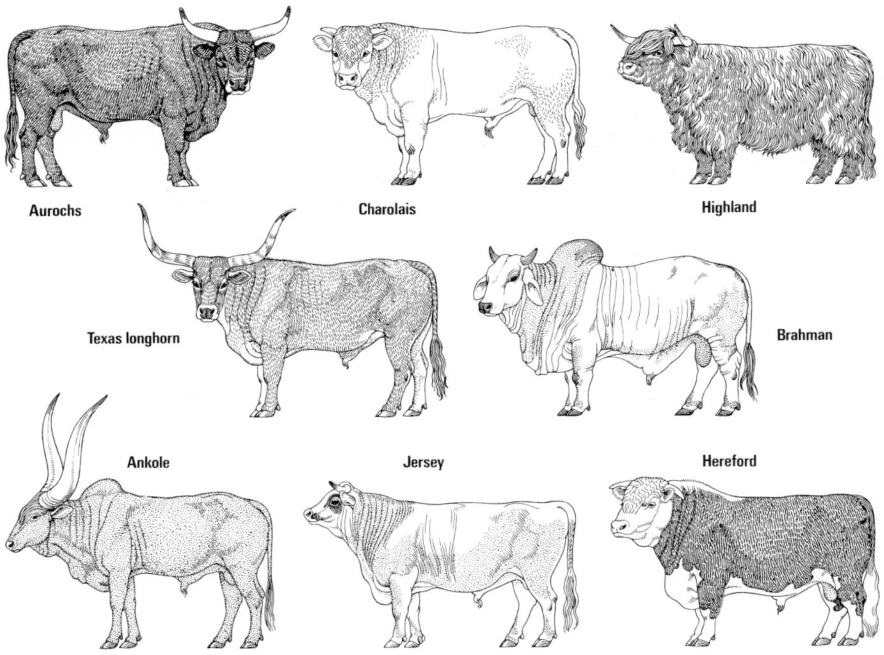
Aurochs
Charolais
Highland
Texas longhorn
Brahman
Ankole
Jersey
Hereford

Tailoring cereals to man *above and left*
Bread wheat has three ancestors. *Triticum monococcum* (above, top left) a primitive wheat, has 14 chromosomes; *Aegilops speltoides* (top center) and *Aegilops squarrosa* (top right) are grasses, each again having 14 chromosomes. Hybridization of the wheat with the grass *A. speltoides* produced *Triticum dicoccoides*, with 28 chromosomes, which when crossed with *A. squarrosa* resulted in modern bread wheat, *Triticum aestivum*, with 42 chromosomes. To produce a cereal for poor soils, *T. aestivum* (far left) has been crossed with rye (left, center) to give a hybrid (near left).

Strains of wheat *right*
Man has cultivated wheat for at least 10000 years. For a considerable proportion of this time he picked the seeds from the best of the crop for the next year's sowing, without understanding the principles involved. Modern bread wheat is designed by man, using as raw material the random experiments provided by nature (upper sequence) or the greater variety resulting from artificial irradiation (lower), and applying his own criteria to select the best strains (colored panels). The modern *Triticum aestivum* is the result of double hybridization.

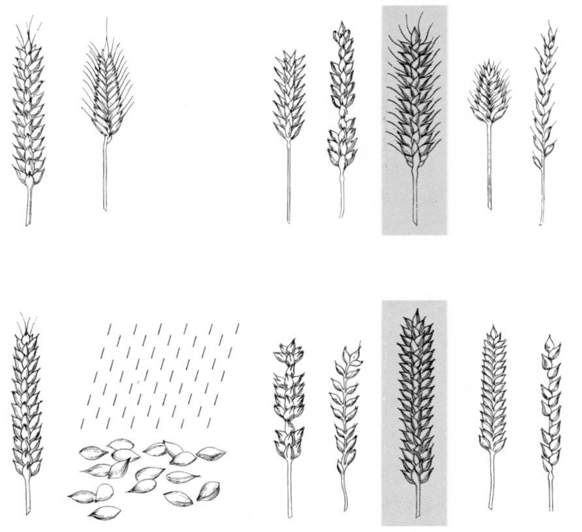

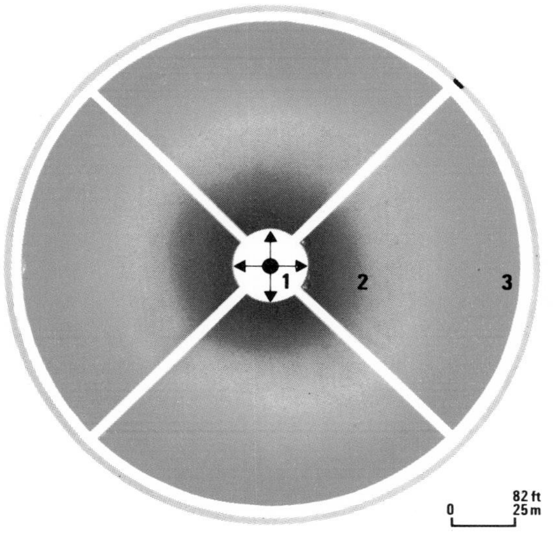
1
2
3
0
82 ft
25 m

Irradiated growth *left*
Most of the mutations caused in plants by deliberate irradiation are the result of a single intense exposure, but in this 656 ft (200 m) diameter field in Japan plants are subjected to a sustained dose from a cobalt 60 source mounted on a tower at the center (1). Most of the resulting mutations are harmful (2), but a small proportion of the plants contain DNA altered in a favorable manner (3). The result is new and improved varieties of crops which are already playing a part in the 'green revolution'—the high yielding varieties considered to be an essential factor in feeding the world.

Earth's Diverse Environments

To survive, animals must be adapted to their environment. They must be able to resist cold if they live in polar regions, drought if they live in deserts. They must find food, escape from predators and reproduce. Their offspring must mature and reproduce in turn. Adaptations of anatomy, physiology and behavior have evolved, so that today animals are found in all the Earth's diverse environments.

Ecologists divide the Earth into natural zones or 'biomes', each with its own highly adapted and integrated animal and plant communities. Inside each broad climatic zone animals have become adapted to various local environments or habitats. In tropical forests, for example, there are several layers of vegetation from the ground up to the tallest trees, and different animals with contrasting ways of life live in different layers. One species eats leaves and another eats berries, and so they avoid competition. Indeed the animals and plants of a community are interdependent. Herbivores eat plants, and carnivores eat herbivores. Food chains and the whole balance of a natural community can be altered by destroying one part of it. Thus, insecticides kill insects but also poison other animals in the area and the predators which prey on them.

Today's animals and plants are those whose ancestors survived immense changes. Continents drifted apart and moved together, seas rose and fell, mountains erupted and were levelled by erosion, glaciers advanced and retreated. Life evolved. Some animals became extinct; others adapted to the changes and spread to new areas. Sometimes they met impassable oceans, mountains and deserts. Groups of animals then became isolated and continued to evolve independently. Marsupials, mammals with pouches, were isolated in Australia before placental mammals, whose young are nourished for a long time in the mother's uterus, evolved in Europe and Asia. Placental mammals then supplanted marsupials everywhere but in Australia. Scientists divide the world into six zoogeographical realms each containing animals not found elsewhere. Some animals mix in transitional zones such as the Sahara Desert and the Himalayas.

Environmental factors

Climate is determined by the Sun's radiation on the Earth's atmosphere, oceans and continents. It varies with the time of day and season. Winds generated by the solar heating carry moisture inland, and heat away from the tropics. Ocean currents affect the prevailing temperature over large regions. Solar radiation, winds and ocean currents, together with latitude, altitude and the form of the land, combine to produce each local climate.

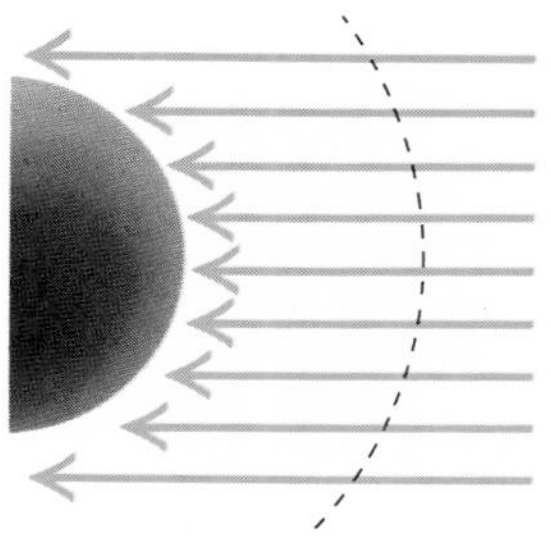

Solar heating *left*
The tropics are hotter than the poles because the Sun's rays pass almost vertically through a shallower depth of atmosphere and so are less attenuated. The Sun's vertical rays shift seasonally between the Tropics of Cancer and Capricorn, altering the length of daylight.

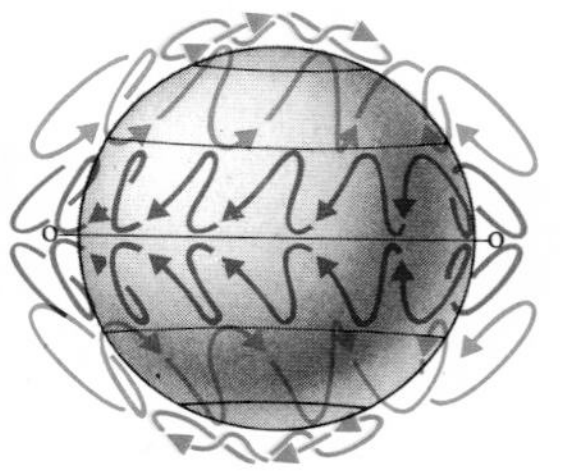

Wind and weather *left*
Hot air at the equator rises and moves north and south to higher latitudes. It subsides, producing trade winds, deflected by the rotation of the Earth, back again to the tropics. Westerly winds blow from the sub-tropics highs poleward toward the sub-polar lows.

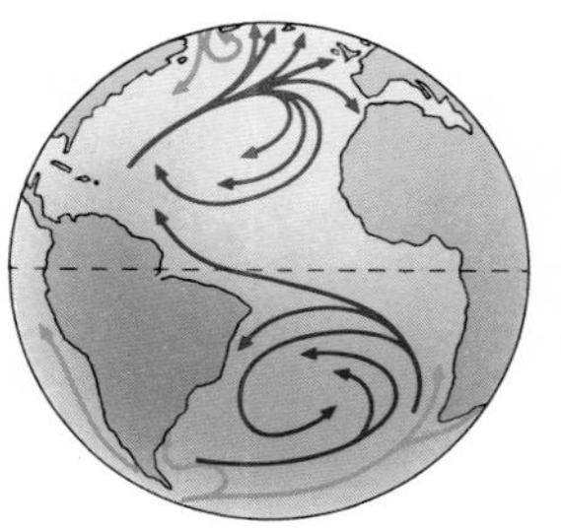

Oceans *left*
Surface currents created by prevailing winds and variations in the density of the water are deflected by landmasses and the Coriolis effect' of rotation. Onshore winds across ocean currents are a major climatic control.

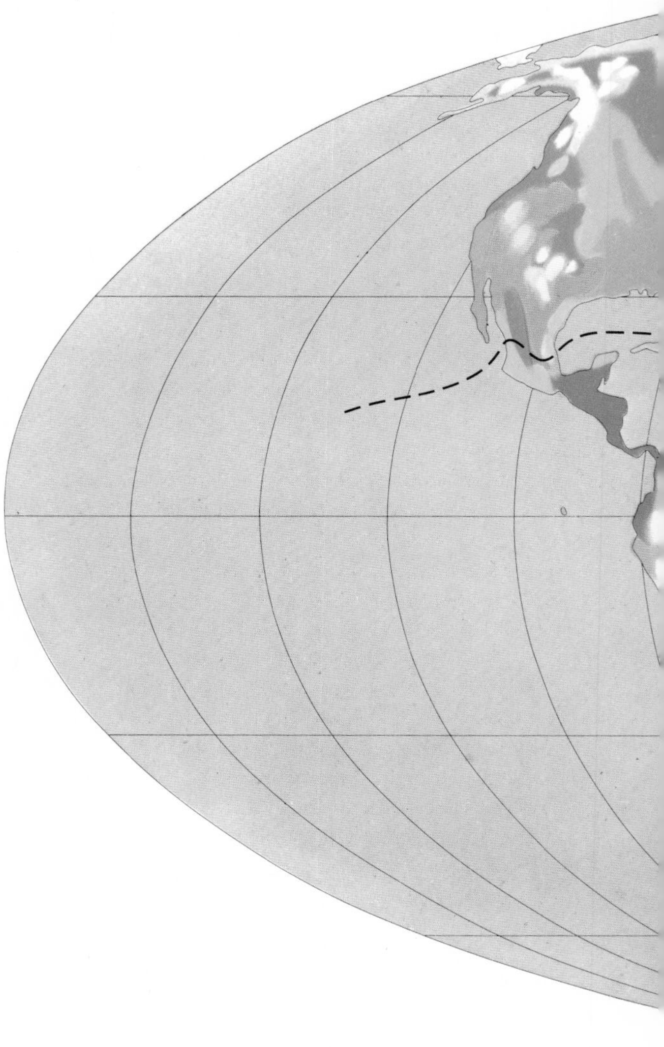

The zoogeographical classification of environments

Roe deer
Flycatcher
Warbler
Dunnock
Wild ass
Hedgehog
Edible dormouse
Wild Sheep

Palearctic (A)
This zoogeographical realm, the extent of which is shown on the map at right, is often grouped with the Nearctic to form the so-called Holarctic region. Roe deer, hedgehogs, dormice and the Asian wild ass are all unique here. Ancestors of modern horses crossed into it from North America during an ice age when the continents were bridged with ice.

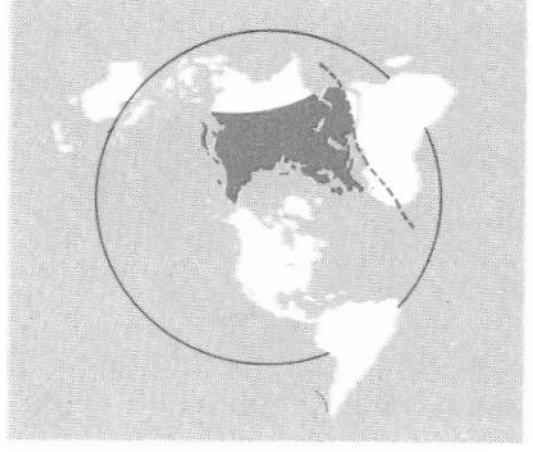

Beaver
Tiger salamander
Pronghorn
Skunk
Mocking bird
Bison
Turkey
Rattlesnake

Nearctic (B)
Covering the whole of North America from Greenland to the high plateau of Mexico, this realm contains beavers, elk and caribou. The prairie buffalo, which were slaughtered in their millions by 19th century man, have been saved from total extinction. And the American wild turkey has now been very successfully domesticated.

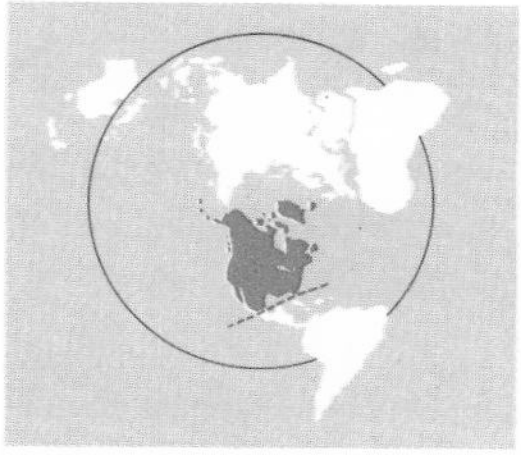

Orangutan
Tree shrew
Gibbon
Fairy bluebird
Tiger
Peacock
Indian elephant

Oriental (C)
Comprising the southern part of Asia, Indonesia and the Philippines, this realm is largely isolated from the Palearctic realm to the north by the great folded barrier of the Himalayas, thrown up when the Indian subcontinent collided with Asia. Indigenous animals include tree shrews, tarsiers, gibbons, orangutans and the Indian elephant.

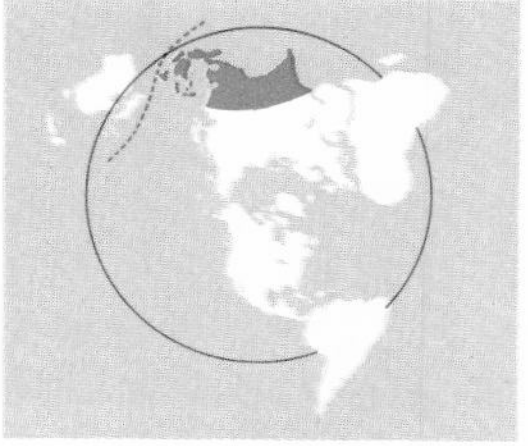

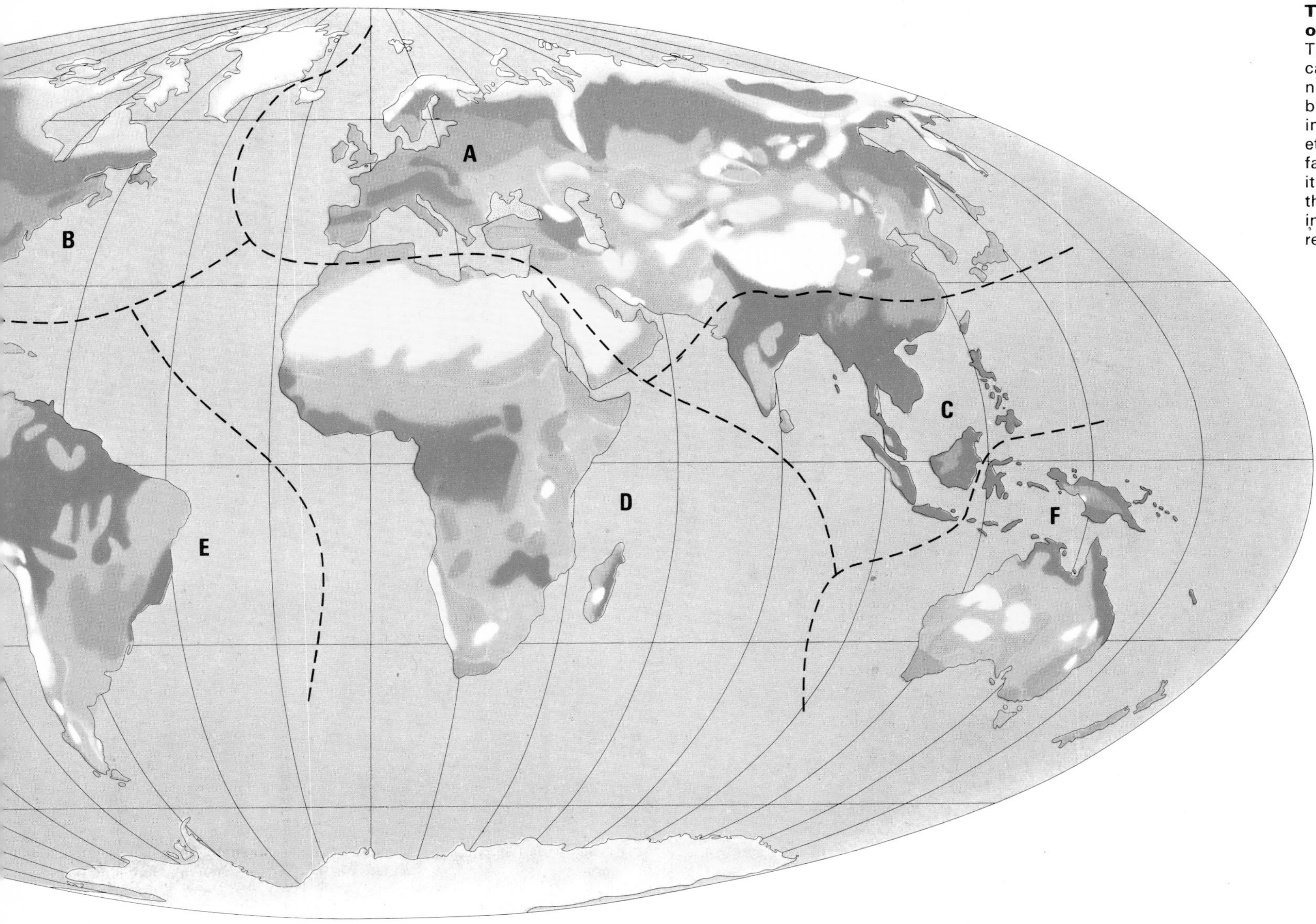
A
B
C
D
E
F

The ecological classification of environments *left*
The living world of the Earth can be divided into at least nine broad ecological zones or biomes (key, below) each distinguished by its climate, vegetation and other environmental factors. In the following pages it is this system of classification that is followed. The letters indicate the zoogeographical regions shown in detail below.

Key to zones

- Permanent ice
- Tundra
- Mountains
- Coniferous forest
- Temperate forest
- Grasslands
- Tropical forest
- Thorn scrub and semi-desert
- Desert

Secretary bird
Sable
African elephant
Potto
Zebra
Gorilla

Ethiopian (D)
Africa south of the Sahara, the southern part of Arabia and Madagascar are the main areas of this realm. It contains the giraffe, hippopotamus, lion, chimpanzee and gorilla. The Old World monkeys, of which there are many species in African tropical forests, often have highly colored buttocks but never prehensile tails capable of gripping.

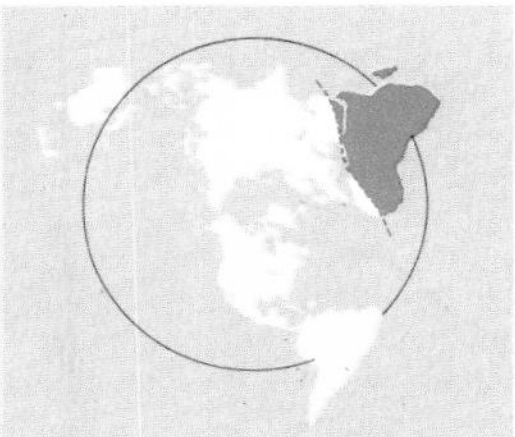

Anteater
Toucan
Howler monkey
Guinea pig
Humming bird
Tapir
Sloth
Rhea

Neotropical (E)
Covering the whole of South America, the Caribbean area and Central America, this realm is the only one containing the curious sloths which hang upside-down from tree branches. Another unique series of mammals is grouped under the title of New World monkeys, which are well adapted for climbing and have prehensile tails.

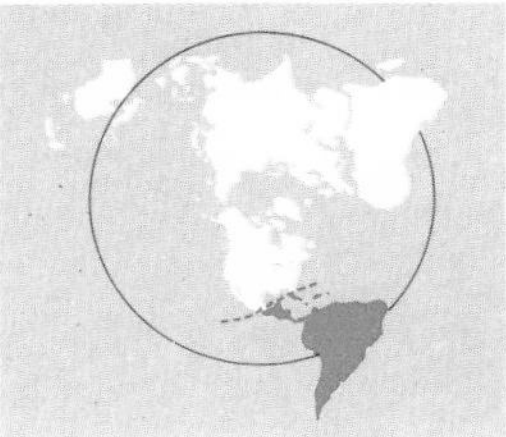

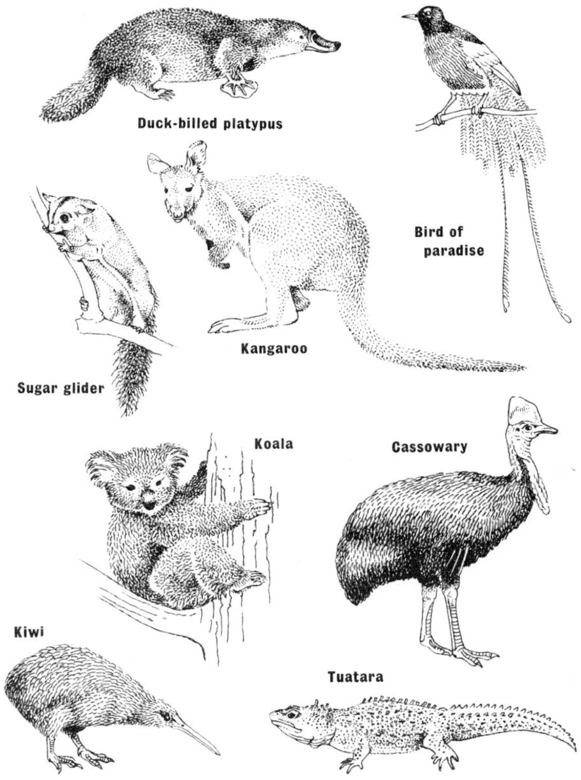
Duck-billed platypus
Bird of paradise
Sugar glider
Kangaroo
Koala
Cassowary
Kiwi
Tuatara

Australian (F)
Quite distinct from all other realms, and covering a large area of the Earth's surface, this is the home of the marsupials, which adapted to different environments in parallel with the placental mammals elsewhere. Carnivores include a cat and the thylacine (Tasmanian wolf), an arboreal opossum and marsupial mole. Kangaroos are herbivores.

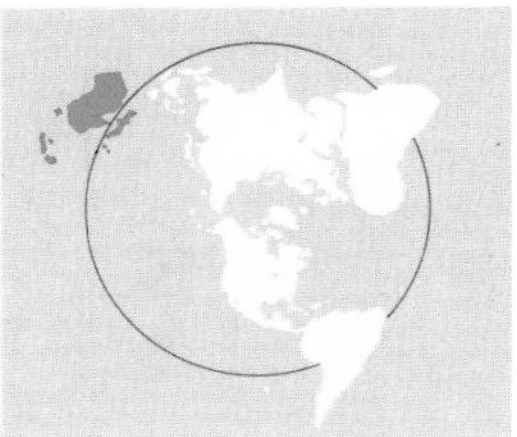

The Polar Caps: Arctic

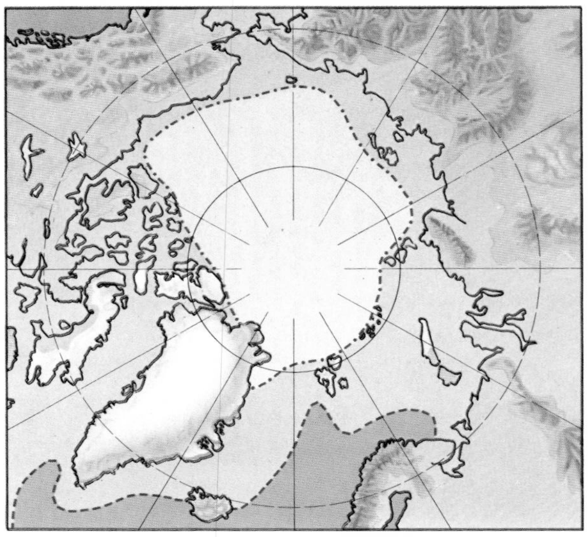

Pack ice limit
Drifting ice limit

The Arctic ice cap is the opposite of Antarctica in much more than mere location. It is principally an area of permanently frozen sea ice, although it also includes part of Greenland. It has an indigenous human population, despite the average annual temperature of −24°F on the Greenland ice cap, who have managed to adapt themselves to a ferocious environment by copying the animals around them. Just as the seals and polar bears shelter under the snow, bearing their cubs in dens, the Eskimos developed the igloo built from blocks of wind-packed snow. These ice homes are windproof and the temperature inside can rise to 59°F.

Fur and feathers are good heat insulators because each hair or feather is surrounded by air, which conducts heat poorly and thus lessens the amount of body heat escaping. Polar animals have very thick fur. Eskimos wear two layers of skins, one fur side in and the other fur side out. But fur is less efficient if it is wet, so seals and walruses have a thick layer of fatty blubber under the skin. Fat, like air, is a poor heat conductor. Circulation can be restricted so that some animals maintain two body temperatures: one normally warm-blooded inside the body and one as cold as the environment in the feet, flippers and nostrils, which must be free of fur or blubber to function. Extremities from which heat is easily lost, such as ears, are small in polar bears and absent in seals. Heat lost through radiation is proportional to the body's surface. Relative to its volume, a large animal has less surface area than a small one. So a large animal will lose heat more slowly. Polar bears, for instance, are bigger than bears in more temperate regions.

Few eskimos are still hunters of seals, walruses and whales. There has been mass slaughter of seals for their skins, and the population has rapidly declined. Life in the Arctic is changing. Uranium, titanium and other minerals have been discovered. In Alaska oil is bringing prosperity and industrialization. Much of the energy devoted to opening up these great 'lands of tomorrow' has been triggered by military needs. Now the main spur is becoming an economic one.

Polar bears
Bigger animals have less surface area for each unit of body weight than small animals, and thus lose heat less rapidly. Polar bears are larger than all other bears. The adult male (top right) can be 11 feet (3.4 m) long, compared with the 9-10 ft (2.7-3 m) of the brown grizzly (center right) and 4-4.5ft (1.3m) of the sun bear (bottom right). Most polar bears winter in a den roughly eight feet (2.4 m) long, but two-room dens have been found.

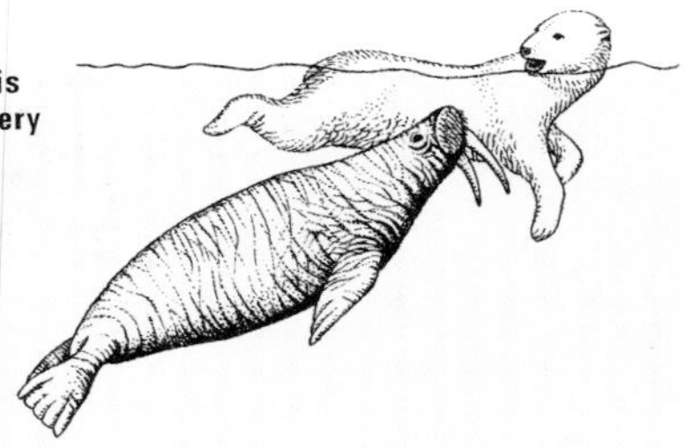

Vulnerable *right*
On land the polar bear is supreme, even on slippery ice. But if a bear is forced to enter deep water it becomes much more vulnerable and can be harried even by young seals. A big bull walrus, illustrated, can kill it swiftly.

Walrus bulls *below*
Weighing up to a ton, the 12 foot (3.7 m) bull walrus uses its tusks for digging out shellfish, breaking air-holes in the ice and fighting. One-third of its weight is blubber, in a 2½ inch (63.5 mm) thick layer under the skin (right).

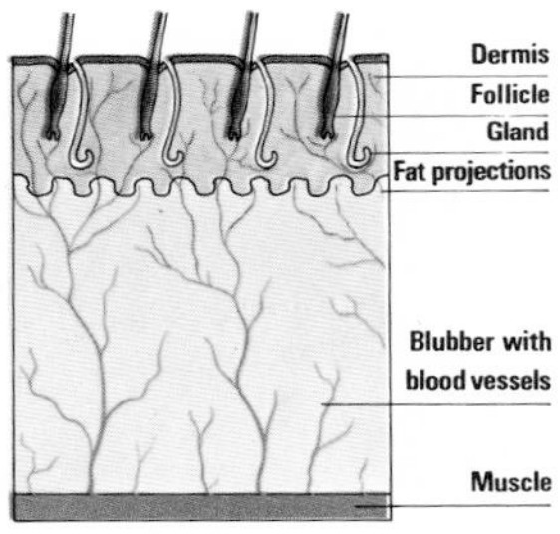

Dermis
Follicle
Gland
Fat projections
Blubber with blood vessels
Muscle

Pack ice *above*
Open pack ice, stretching as far as the eye can see, reflects the pink rays of the low Sun. Such ice is seldom more than one year old and usually gets crushed or melted in a shorter time. Unlike the dangerous bergs, it is no hazard to navigation.

Seal and tern *below*
The shores of the Irish Sea are among the wide areas of rocky coast on both sides of the North Atlantic inhabited by the grey seal (female illustrated : the male is larger) and sandwich tern (once common at Sandwich in Kent).

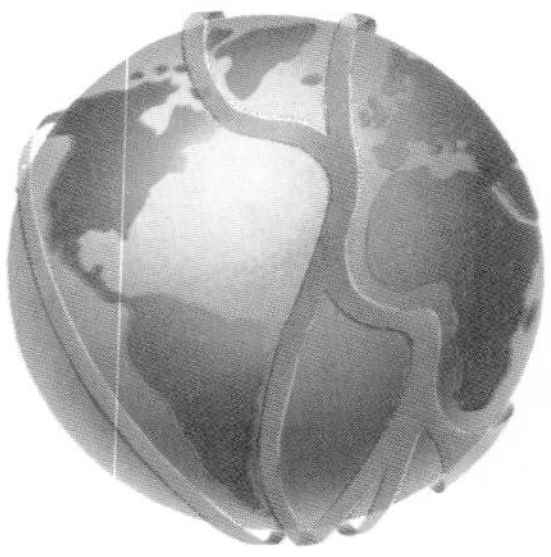

Arctic tern *below*
Distinguished from other terns by its vivid beak and feet, the Arctic tern migrates down the coasts of Europe and Africa to the Antarctic before returning to the Arctic to nest.
The round trip (left) can be a remarkable 24000 miles (39000 km).

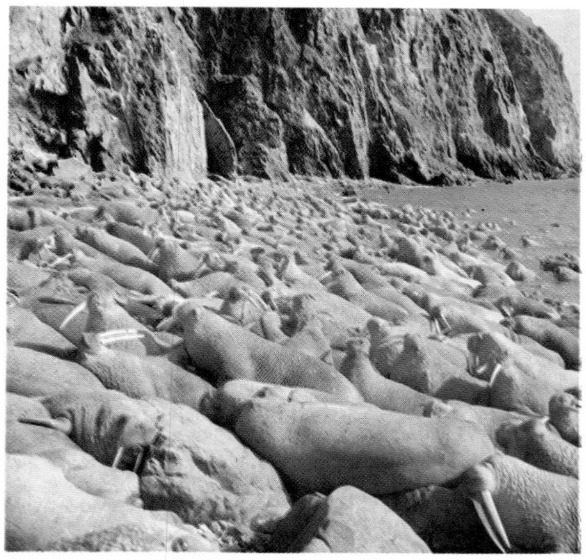

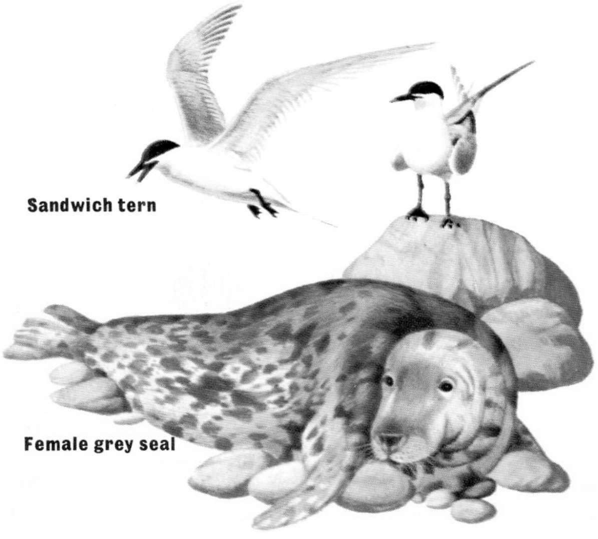

Sandwich tern
Female grey seal

Antarctic

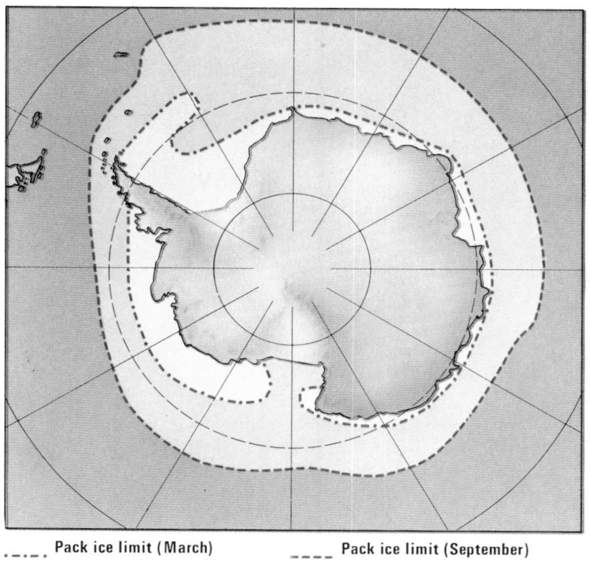
Pack ice limit (March)
Pack ice limit (September)

In complete contrast to the North Polar region, the Antarctic is a frozen continent encircled by ocean. Mountains surround low-lying land covered with ice so thick that it forms a high plateau. It is the coldest region on Earth. Throughout almost all of Antarctica no monthly average temperature exceeds 0°C, and the average annual temperature at the South Pole is –60°C. Blizzards blow when a shallow layer of colder air over the ice-sheet flows downslope, and the snow is packed into a hard pavement.

Around the continental edges, icebergs up to 1000 feet (300 m) thick break off the ice caps or valley glaciers and fall into the sea. The ice, formed of compacted and recrystallized snow, is only slightly less dense than sea-water, so icebergs float low in the ocean with five-sixths to eight-ninths of their bulk below the surface. The Antarctic icebergs are tabular, with flat tops and cliff-like sides; Arctic bergs from the Greenland ice cap are peaked and rarely break off in the sizes common in Antarctica, where the floating ice islands can be as much as ten miles (16 km) long.

Until 450 million years ago the Earth had no ice caps. In the Antarctic, ice formed in the center of the continent and moved out towards the sea. Cooling at the North Pole probably occurred later.

In summer, when the ice breaks up and the amount of daylight increases, there is a rapid growth of tiny floating plants called phytoplankton. These plants provide 'grazing' for the zooplankton, small animals of which the shrimp-like krill are the most numerous, which in turn are eaten by the larger animals, among them seals and whalebone whales. One of these whales, the blue whale, is the largest animal ever to inhabit the Earth. A variety of birds live in the Antarctic, including penguins and the skuas which prey on them, snow petrels and albatrosses. These warm-blooded animals all have to keep their body temperature well above that of the environment. Many birds avoid the polar winter by migrating to temperate lands. But emperor penguins stay, and in an Antarctic blizzard colonies of them huddle tightly together to reduce the exposed surface area of their bodies.

18in, 45cm

Adélie penguins *above*
They make devoted parents and may, as shown here, produce two chicks at different times in one season.

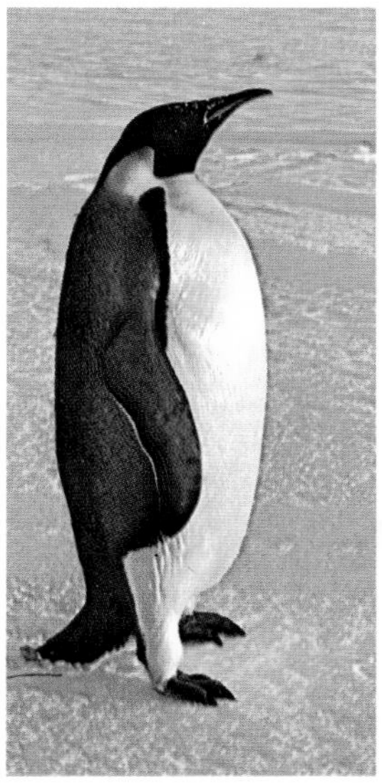

Emperor penguin *right*
Easily the largest penguin, the emperor (41 in, 104 cm) breeds on Antarctic sea ice and coasts (see below).

Seals *left and below*
Seals abound in the Antarctic. The crab-eater (left) bears the scars of an encounter with a killer whale. The Weddell seal (below left) is guarding its three-week pup. South Georgia elephant seals (below) are wallowing among tussock grass.

Fjord *above*
A scene of rare beauty north of Marguerite Bay in the Antarctic Peninsula (Grahamland). Here the rock of the continent is visible, with a glacier at the right and brash ice at the left floating on water ruffled only by the gentle passage of the ship.

Incubating *above*
The male emperor hatches the eggs, which rest on the feet beneath a warm brood flap of fatty skin.

Macaroni *left*
There are several species of crested penguins. Tallest is the macaroni, here seated on its nest. (18 in, 45 cm)

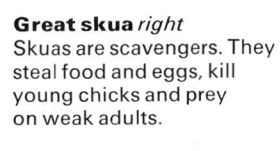

Great skua *right*
Skuas are scavengers. They steal food and eggs, kill young chicks and prey on weak adults.

Lichen *below*
The red lichen on this rock could be 1000 years old. Its slow metabolism survives the cold.

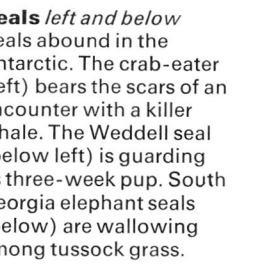

The Cold Lands: Tundra

The cold lands *above*
In the northern hemisphere there are vast areas of land at latitudes higher than 60°. The warmer parts of these regions are colonized by immense numbers of conifers (facing page) which extend right across the Earth's widest land mass. Where the climate is too severe for trees, the forest gives way to tundra.

Surrounding the Arctic Ocean are the Arctic tundra and, further south, the coniferous forest. There is no land at such high latitude (60°-70°) in the southern hemisphere. Seasonal changes are extreme. The Sun may shine continuously in summer and not at all in mid-winter. Winter cold and summer heat are greatest in the continental interiors, where it is also drier than around the coasts. Interaction between polar and tropical air masses causes storms.

In the treeless tundra the average temperature of the warmest month is below 10°C. The land is forested where the average for at least one month is above that temperature. In some places the tundra and forest are divided by a distinct tree-line; in other regions the true coniferous forest is preceded by grasses, sedges and lichens. The soils are affected by 'permafrost' and are almost permanently frozen. In summer the surface becomes waterlogged and often flooded, but the seasonal thaw reaches a depth of only 4-24 inches (100-600 mm). Soil water under the plants melts, and a thick mud forms which may flow downslope making bulging terraces. Because of recent glaciation there are many lakes and swamps, called muskeg in Canada.

Lemmings feed on the vegetation of the tundra. In winter they dig for roots in an underground network of tunnels where it is about 10°C warmer than on the surface. If their population increases so much that there is competition for space, masses of lemmings move into the forest and cross streams, lakes and rivers as they go. Many drown.

Herds of American caribou and closely related European reindeer migrate up to several hundred miles from their summer pasture on the tundra to find winter food on the forest fringes. Nomadic Lapps follow the reindeer and use them for transport, food and clothing. They milk them and make cheese. In contrast, the caribou have never been domesticated: the Indians of northern Canada were hunters. Their skill as trappers was exploited by the European fur trade. And in the Siberian tundra every resource is being vigorously exploited; a new land is opening up.

Permanent residents of the tundra

Life is hard in the Arctic tundra, but a great variety of animal life is adapted to it. Grass and other plant food grows for no more than two out of each 12 months, but many animals live off it all the year round and even eat the roots while the surface is covered with snow. Carnivores depend to a great degree on the population of lemmings (below) which reaches a peak about every third year. In spring the land becomes ablaze with flowers, and birds abound.

Lemmings
These small rodents are about five inches (125 mm) long. They have short tails, and ears hidden by thick fur. Every three or four years a population explosion triggers a mass migration in which thousands of lemmings die.

Winter and summer *above and left*
In winter the cold lands are dull and seemingly barren, although at the edges of the tundra stunted conifers are dotted among the lakes. But in summer the plant life flourishes. Reindeer graze among flowers from Norway to the Pacific.

Early blooms *above*
The Pasque flower is in evidence throughout Alaska as early as May.

Seasonal plumage
Many of the Arctic birds and animals change their appearance to blend into the contrasting summer and winter backgrounds. For example, the rock ptarmigan is mottled brown in July (left) but white in winter until May (below). Both hunted animals, such as the Arctic hare, and their predators change their color. The Arctic fox, which preys on the rock ptarmigan, is white or very pale in winter (above) but changes into a summer coat which is usually brown but in the so-called "blue-foxes" is deep blue-grey (right).

Arctic color *below*
Tundra is not always dull. In the Alaskan September plant life is in full bloom.

Coniferous forest

Except for the Siberian larch, which sheds its needles in winter, the trees of the coniferous forest are evergreen. Spruce, fir, pine and hemlock (associated near water with mountain ash, poplar, balsam, willow and birch) are widespread through Eurasia and North America. The similarity between the distribution of plants and animals is the result of frequent freezing of the Bering Strait which allowed migration between the continents.

The forest animals depend on the trees for food. Beavers eat bark, and squirrels and birds eat buds and seeds. In summer, when there is more food, multitudes of birds migrate to the forest to nest.

The cold forests are of enormous extent. Lumbering is a major industry, and the numerous rivers are used to transport the logs to the sawmills. Great volumes of softwoods are consumed every year, mainly in the building industry and for papermaking. Minerals are now being mined in the cold lands. Iron ore is mined in Labrador and Quebec, and Alaska's gold, copper, iron, oil and gas are being exploited.

The beaver's handiwork
Throughout northern America, and in northern Europe and Asia, the beaver gnaws through trees to secure the soft inner bark from the upper branches. It stores these in a still pool formed by damming a river, and nearby constructs a remarkable lodge with as many as eight underwater entrances.

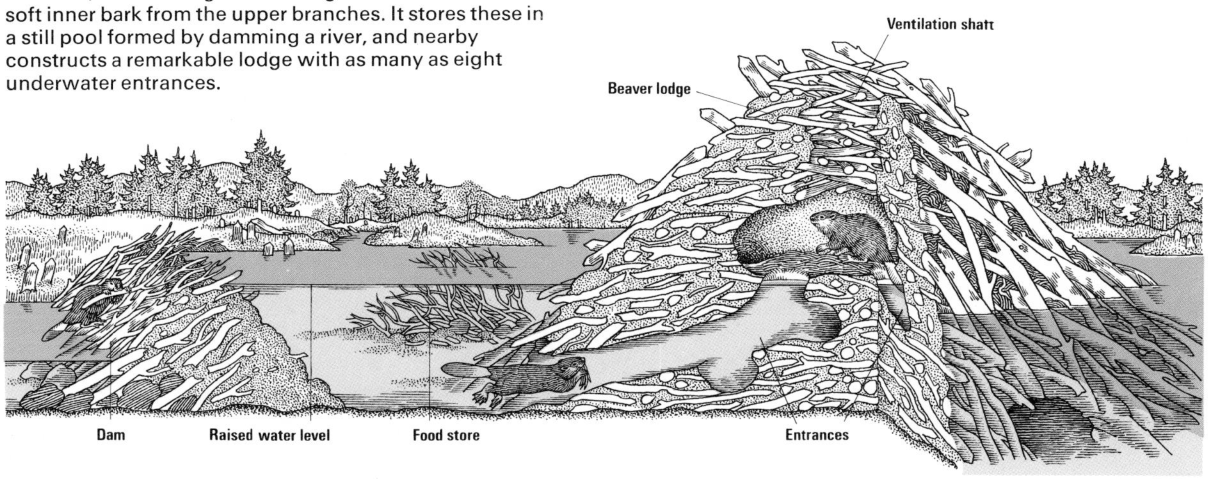
Ventilation shaft
Beaver lodge
Dam
Raised water level
Food store
Entrances

Tree types *above*
Temperate broad-leaved trees could not survive the northern winter. Most cold forest trees are conifers, with needle-like leaves. From the left : scots pine ; larch, which sheds its leaves ; Norway spruce ; Douglas fir.

Contrasting diets
above and right
Despite its formidable appearance the moose lives on small plants, berries and tree shoots. Only the male has antlers. But the lynx (right) is a carnivore, whose population follows that of its principal prey, the hare.

Burrowers *right and below*
The woodchuck (right) is one of the cold forest dwellers that hibernates. Its winter metabolism falls almost to a standstill ; then it awakens in March and is busy until fall. The European polecat (below) sometimes kills marmots and uses their burrows.

Grizzlies *above*
Although a carnivore, the giant brown bear often digs for roots, as here.

Ground squirrel *below*
The striped ground squirrel does not climb trees but eats roots, leaves and insects.

The Temperate Forests

South of the coniferous forest is extensive deciduous woodland of oak, beech and chestnut which flourishes wherever there is an annual rainfall of 30-60 inches (750-1500mm) distributed throughout the year. Woodland once covered large areas of the northern hemisphere, but most has now been cleared for agriculture. There are different mid-latitude climates on the east and west sides of continents: east coast climates are continental, with hot summers and cold winters, while winds blowing off the ocean bring rain to the more equable west coasts.

In winter the deciduous trees shed their broad leaves which would be vulnerable to frost. The leaves slowly rot to a rich humus, and in boggy places peat forms. Nutrients circulate by water draining through the soil and then being drawn up by evaporation and transpiration through the leaves.

Tree types

In North America and Asia the oak, beech, hickory and maple dominate; in Europe the oak, ash, lime and chestnut, with beech in cool moist areas. On damp ground near rivers willow, alder, ash and elm are found. Conifers grow faster so that they often supplant deciduous trees in managed forests. They form the natural forest on the west coast of North America, where some of the largest trees are found.

Near the tropics are the broadleaf evergreen forests. In Japan and the southeast of the United States there are evergreen oaks, laurel and magnolia, with palms, bays and ferns in the swamps of the Mississippi delta. The warm wet forest of New Zealand's South Island contains conifers, podocarp and evergreen beeches, with tree ferns, palms and bamboos. In a Mediterranean type of climate the summers are hot and dry. Cork oaks have hard, leathery leaves covered with a thick cuticle to minimize water loss. The Mediterranean forest is now only a narrow coastal belt. Tree felling and frequent summer fires have left scrub known as the maquis. The chaparral of California and Mexico is similar.

Redwoods *above*
Along the west coast of the United States is a foggy coastal belt where the redwood forests flourish. The giant redwoods and sequoias may be several thousand years old and up to 400 feet (120 m) high. They are among the Earth's oldest living things.

Beechwoods *left*
Typical of the cool northern deciduous forest, Burnham Beeches, near London, generates millions of beech leaves each year. Littering the ground, they decompose into a rich humus which overlies the soil and supports plant life, worms and a variety of insects.

Little owl *above*
Predator of woodland animals, its forward-facing eyes give good binocular vision for judging distance in dim light.

Luna moth *above*
Found in American deciduous forest, the moth prefers a diet of rhododendrons. India has a tropical variety.

Animal variety
above and left
Woodland inhabitants of the New England states are the box turtle and wood frog (above). The Yugoslavian four-lined snake (left) has the slender body and angled scales common to snakes which need to obtain purchase on bark.

Forest birds
The crossbill (left) can pry open tough pine cones; the pheasant (below,) of which there are 49 species, is concealed on the ground by its camouflage.

The ecology of an oak

Oaks of various subspecies are among the most important trees in the northern deciduous forests, and they play a major role in local wildlife. Oaks have a history dating back over 50 million years, and 7000 years ago covered vast tracts of temperate land. Throughout recorded history man has prized the oak for its hard, durable wood, which has been favored above all others for making houses, ships, furniture and other artifacts. The oak population has thus dwindled, and in modern managed forests the faster-growing conifers are preferred. But each remaining oak is a microcosm of nature. The autumn leaf-fall returns valuable nutrients to the soil, providing a source of humus. In the spring up to a quarter of a million new leaves grow, providing an area for photosynthesis as great as 10000 sq ft (930 m^2). Small streamers of flowers are pollinated by wind-borne pollen, leading in midsummer to the crop of acorns which are stored by grey squirrels, badgers and many other animals for the coming winter. As many as 200 species of insect can feed on one tree. Largest is the leaf-eating stag beetle, and the most prominent the gall wasp whose marble gall houses the larva. The damage insects inflict often results in the tree producing a second crop of midsummer leaves. The serotine bat and tawny owl are the main nocturnal predators of the oak forest. The former takes winged insects in flight, while small rodents form the staple diet of the owl.

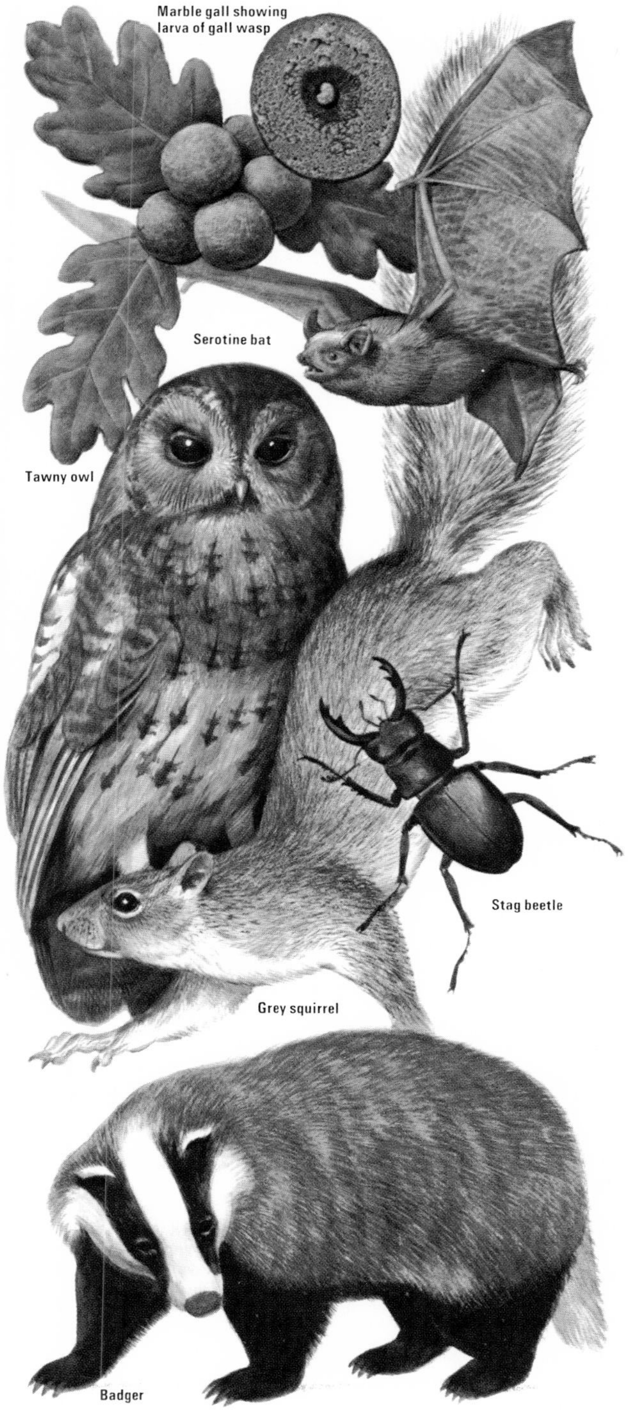
Marble gall showing larva of gall wasp
Serotine bat
Tawny owl
Stag beetle
Grey squirrel
Badger

The mature oak *right*
The extensive buttressed roots of an old oak can provide the portal through which a fox (1) tunnels to its lair. Low on the trunk a beefsteak fungus (2) may grow, providing fruiting bodies upon which feed many kinds of animals and insects. The trunk often decays locally (3), providing a home for both bats and owls. The fallow deer (female, 4) and jay (5) collect acorns, while in the branches a clump of mistletoe (6) grows, nurtured by the tree on which it is a parasite.

1
2
3
4
5

Record in the rings *above*
In deciduous trees each year's growth adds a ring of new tissue to the trunk, as shown by this section segment from an oak with an age of 24 years. Within the first five years is the dark heartwood (1). Between years 7-10 growth was slowed (2), possibly by drought or the crowding of other trees. Growth was also slow in years 19-22, and in the 21st year part of the tree was burned, leaving a scar (4) which gradually heals with further growth. Present growth takes place in the cambium (3) just inside the bark (5).

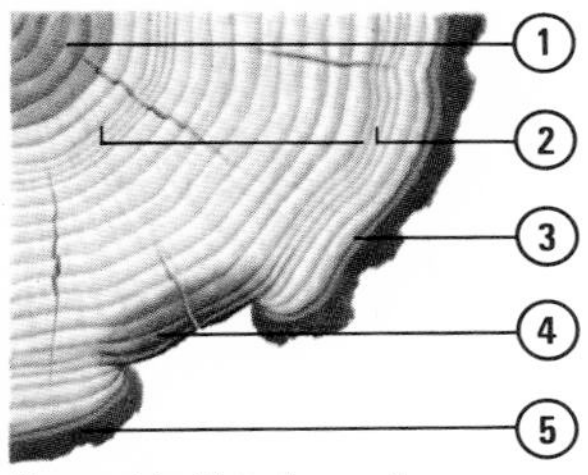
5
6
3
4
2
1

Paper wasp
The queen starts the football-like nest, which is made of chewed wood and has a paper-like consistency. Her subjects enlarge it.

Mole
Moles live in burrows excavated underground by their strong front claw-feet. Emerging into the open, their eyes see poorly.

Dormouse
Most of the forest rodents store food for the winter, but the dormouse hibernates, at a reduced body temperature.

Dormouse nest
Although the dormouse lives deep in the undergrowth, it is very agile, and builds a spherical nest above ground level.

Sparrowhawk
Like many birds of prey the sparrowhawk makes a substantial nest of twigs and forest debris high in a tree, where its young are safe.

Blue tit
A favorite choice of home for the blue tit is a hole in a tree. Inside the cavity it constructs a nest of moss and soft debris.

Common oak
Widespread and important to commerce and forest life, the oak grows slowly and is yielding to other species.

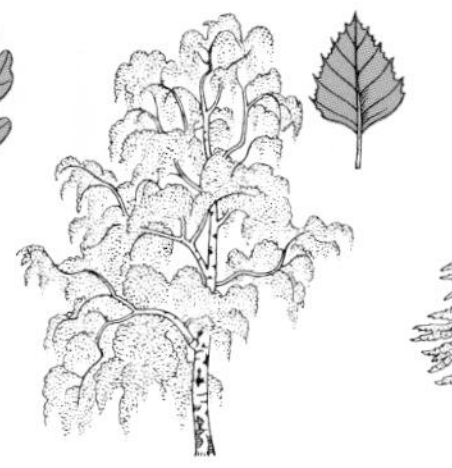

Silver birch
Mature at 50, the silver-barked birch is found in all temperate forest and extends far into the tundra.

Beech
Big and densely packed, the beech is very beneficial. Essentially a forest tree, it prefers drained chalky soil.

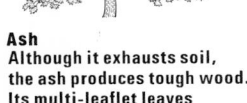

Ash
Although it exhausts soil, the ash produces tough wood. Its multi-leaflet leaves are one foot (0.25 m) long.

Sweet chestnut
Originally from Asia Minor, the sweet chestnut fruit is a preferred food of many forest animals.

Sycamore
One of the maple family, the sycamore prefers exposed positions where its seeds can travel on the wind.

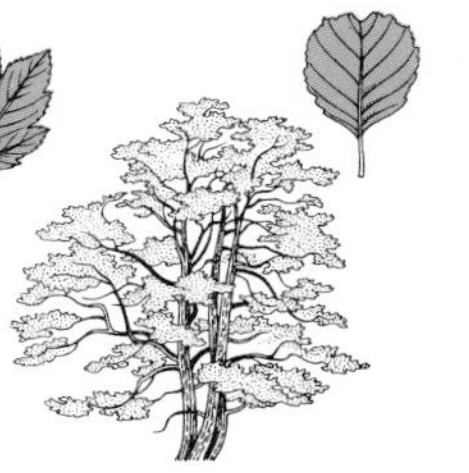

Alder
The inconspicuous alder prefers marshy ground and river banks. Although not a conifer, it bears cone fruit.

The Tropical Forests

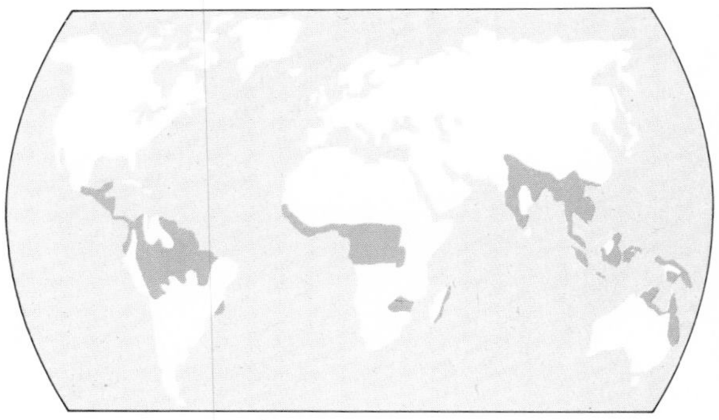

The hot, humid conditions in equatorial rainforests which encourage a profusion of life, change very little over the year, daily variations being greater than seasonal ones. The average temperature is about 27°C, while the rainfall, which is as high as 80-160 inches (2000-4000 mm) a year, falls regularly in heavy thunderstorms.

Tropical forests are the highest, densest and most varied on Earth, in spite of having infertile soil. This is because nutrients are contained in the plants which grow, flower and fruit throughout the year. As leaves and fruits fall to the ground and decay, the minerals are rapidly taken up again by the roots of the growing shrubs and trees. The crowns of the tall, broad-leaved trees form a canopy of foliage. Underneath, it is shady and the tree trunks are smooth and unbranched, while lianas and creepers thrust upwards to the light.

Forest animals find a variety of habitats in the different layers. Monkeys, apes, sloths, lizards and frogs are adapted to climbing or swinging through trees. Multitudes of birds feed on nectar, insects or fruit. Many animals browse on the forest floor, and a vast number of animal and plant species co-exist.

Lianas *below*
Long rope-like stems loop from tree to tree, ever climbing toward the light that pierces the canopy.

Deep rainforest *right*
The hot, humid atmosphere of tropical rainforest encourages most luxuriant plant growth.

Flowers *right and below*
Tropical blooms are famed for their size and beauty. The very small seasonal variation in climate means plants can germinate, grow and flower without interruption throughout the year. Right, blossoms of Royal Poinciana; below, Strelitzia, native to Africa.

Contrasting predators *right and below*
Tropical forests are the home of the largest spiders and largest snakes. But, whereas the monkey spider of Trinidad (right) kills its prey by a venomous bite, the 30 foot (10 m) royal python (below) crushes and suffocates its victim.

Butterflies *right and below*
There are more butterflies and moths in the rainforest than in all the rest of the Earth; typical species are the Ulysses butterfly (right), *Precis almana* (below right) and Rajah Brooke's bird-wing *Trogonoptera brookiana* (below).

Hovering jewel *right*
Hummingbirds, such as Pucheran's emerald variety illustrated here, are found only in the Americas. Their wings, which beat about 100 times a second and allow them to hover while drinking nectar, are covered with iridescent feathers of brilliant hues.

Forest reptiles *above and right*
As large as a man, the iguana (above) has feet with long digits provided with hard scales and curved claws adapted to tree-climbing. Another climber is the African grey tree frog (right) whose nest of foam overhangs the water.

White rumped swift
Spinetail swift
Indian crested swift
Harpy eagle

100 feet
30 m

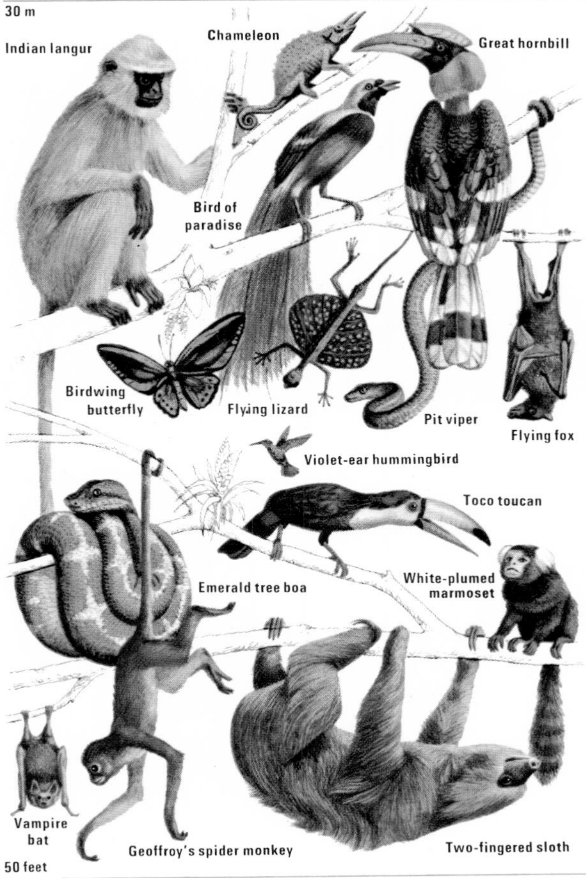
Chameleon
Indian langur
Great hornbill
Bird of paradise
Birdwing butterfly
Flying lizard
Pit viper
Flying fox
Violet-ear hummingbird
Toco toucan
Emerald tree boa
White-plumed marmoset
Vampire bat
Geoffroy's spider monkey
Two-fingered sloth

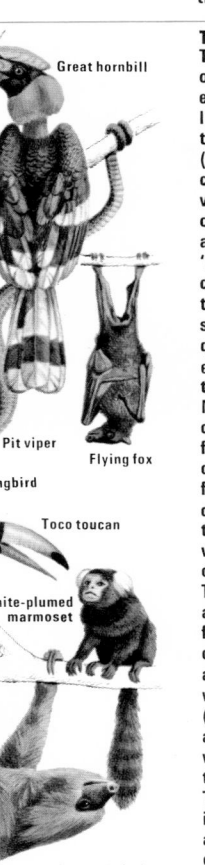

50 feet
15 m

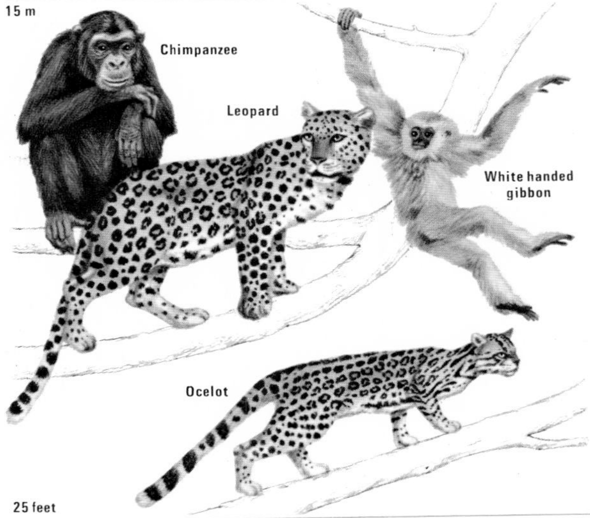
Chimpanzee
Leopard
White handed gibbon
Ocelot

25 feet
7.5 m

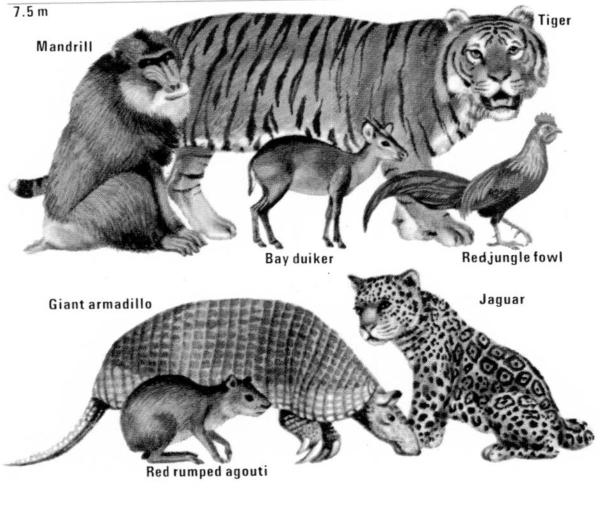
Tiger
Mandrill
Bay duiker
Redjungle fowl
Giant armadillo
Jaguar
Red rumped agouti

Life in the forest

The emergents
Some trees break through the canopy formed by the main tree population. Many of these emergent trees reach to 150 ft (46 m), although all tree heights are reduced with increasing altitude or distance from the equator. Life at this topmost level is almost wholly insects and birds. The swifts, which fly above the forest at up to 200 mph (320 kmh), catch insects on the wing. The harpy eagle preys on animals in the upper branches.

The canopy
This is one of the major life zones of the tropical forest, and it exerts a powerful effect on all the lower levels. Most of the forest trees grow to 100-120 ft (30-37 m) and form an almost continuous layer of leafy vegetation at this height, cutting off direct sunlight from below and markedly altering the climate 'inside' the forest to a shady coolness. Most of the trees of tropical forests have straight stems which do not branch until quite close to the canopy; emergent tree (1) passes straight through without branching. Many tropical trees are cauliflorous—they produce flowers which grow directly out of the trunks and branches and frequently dot the canopy with color (2). Inside the forest is a tangle of creepers and climbers which tend to bind the branches of the canopy into a tight mass. The fauna of the canopy is adapted to specialized feeding from particular flowers, fruit or other food. Winged insects and animals range readily through the whole stratum. Many of the birds (for example, the great hornbill and toucan) have long bills with which they can reach food through the mat of vegetation. The non-flying animals are invariably adapted to running along branches, swinging from one branch to another and even leaping 50 ft (15 m) or more.

The middle layer
There may be no sharp division between this layer and the canopy, but in general the middle is made up of smaller trees whose crowns do not form a continuous mat. In this layer are found nest epiphytes (3), non-parasitic plants growing in sunlight on trees where they seed in cracks in the bark. Some store water while others absorb it through hanging roots (4). Cauliflorous growths (5) hang from some trees, while many trunks are covered in vines and lianas (6). The trees are sturdy enough to bear heavy animals. Whereas many inhabitants of the canopy seldom if ever come down to ground level, a considerable proportion of the middle-level animals spend part of their life on the forest floor.

The lower levels
The bottom strata of the humid tropical forest can be divided into a shrub layer below 15 ft (4.5 m), a herb layer below 3 ft (1 m) and a fungus layer on the surface. The fallen tree (7) may have died from strangulation by parasitic vegetation. At the right air roots (8) pick up moisture, while a trunk (9) is almost hidden by two types of epiphyte. Fungi (10) cover the ground near a massive buttressed tree root (11), while in the rear is a stilt root (12) of a kind common in swamp forest. The ground here is covered in sparse vegetation (13) typical of the shady floor. The features illustrated are typical of hot rain forest throughout the tropics, but the elephant (14) is Indian.

1
2
3
4
3
3
5
6
3
7
8
9
14
11
12
13
10

The Grasslands

Flat or rolling grasslands lie between the forests and deserts in the dry interiors of all the continents, in the transitional zones where dry and moist climates merge into each other. There are two major types of grassland, the temperate which is hot in summer and cold in winter and the tropical which has a fairly uniform high temperature all the year round. The Russian steppe, North American prairie, South American pampas, South African veld and Australian downland are examples of temperate grassland, while more than one third of Africa is covered by tropical savanna.

The height of the grass is dependent upon the annual rainfall. There are few trees on these wide plains to break the wind or provide shelter. In spring or summer there is a short rainy season when the grasses and shrubs flourish and there is rich grazing; then the long dry season comes and growth halts as a severe drought develops. The grasslands may result from frequent fires during this period, which kill the trees and shrubs leaving grass-roots unharmed.

Animal life

Throughout most of the tropical grasslands the climate is semi-arid, the soil poor, yet their meager grazing supports a rich and varied assortment of animals. In most grassland regions the fauna has been used by man with care for the future, but in the biggest savanna of all, that of Africa, man has done little but misuse and destroy the grassland animals. To a considerable degree this has been the result of emphasis by both Africans and white ranchers, on domestic cattle. Such beasts graze only on certain species of grass, and have been bred principally for the temperate regions of Europe. In contrast, the natural fauna makes full use of the whole spectrum of vegetation, grazing selectively at different levels and in different places. As a result there is no deterioration of the environment despite the large numbers of animals supported by each area of land. Moreover, the wild animals need not be fed or sheltered, nor inoculated against the sleeping sickness carried by the tsetse fly which ravages cattle. Now that game can be seen to have a distinct commercial value the grassland animals, particularly easily domesticated species such as the eland, are at last being more generally preserved so that controlled game-cropping can provide an additional source of high quality protein.

The dust bowls

Man has often interfered in the grassland environment sometimes with disastrous consequences. The American grassland soil is rich and farmers have turned the wetter tall-grass prairie into the corn belt and the short-grass prairie into the wheat belt. Further west is the cattle country. But in years of drought crops fail and the valuable topsoil, lacking the protective cover of grass, blows away in great dust clouds, leaving behind large areas of barren land.

Venomous snakes *left*
Grasslands in every continent harbor dangerous snakes. The Egyptian cobra (far left) is the largest cobra in Africa. The prairie rattlesnake (near left) is the most common venomous snake in the United States and causes many deaths each year.

African savanna *above*
The Serengeti plains of Tanzania are among the most beautiful areas of big game country in the world. Here animals of a great range of species graze on fine grassland amongst the kopjes — rocky outcrops which are characteristic of central Africa.

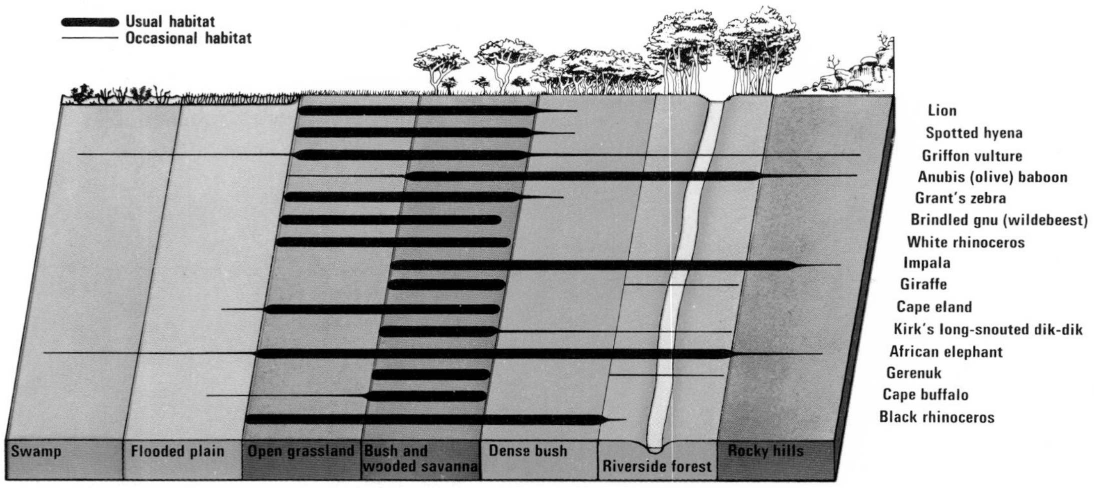
Usual habitat
Occasional habitat
Lion
Spotted hyena
Griffon vulture
Anubis (olive) baboon
Grant's zebra
Brindled gnu (wildebeest)
White rhinoceros
Impala
Giraffe
Cape eland
Kirk's long-snouted dik-dik
African elephant
Gerenuk
Cape buffalo
Black rhinoceros
Swamp
Flooded plain
Open grassland
Bush and wooded savanna
Dense bush
Riverside forest
Rocky hills

Ecological co-existence *above*
The African savanna supports a very large and varied animal population. Most of the animals are herbivores which have each adapted to a particular habitat and a particular section of the available food. These sections are divided geographically, as shown here, and also into different feeding levels above the ground.

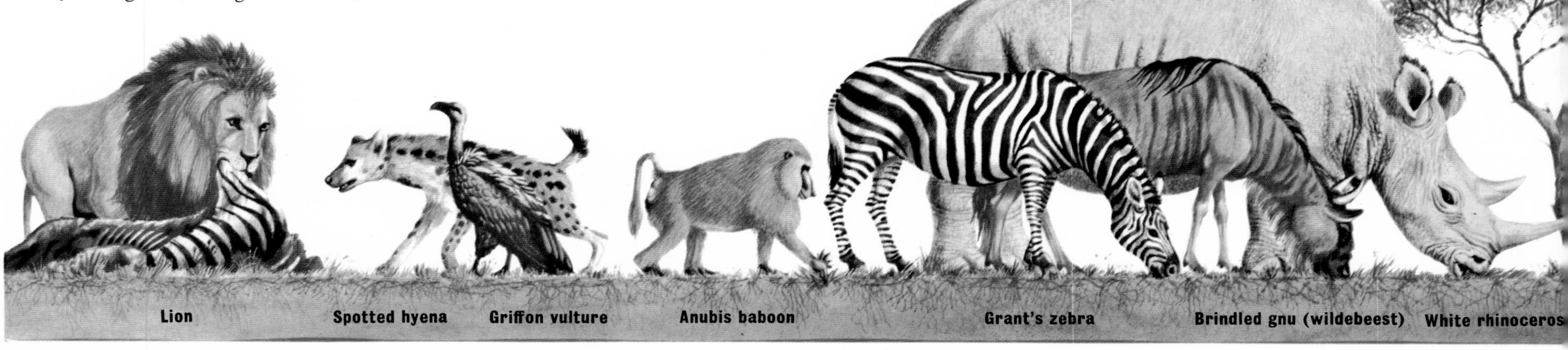
Lion
Spotted hyena
Griffon vulture
Anubis baboon
Grant's zebra
Brindled gnu (wildebeest)
White rhinoceros

Buffalo *above*
African buffalo at Manyara, Tanzania. Buffalo live in herds of up to 100 or more males and females of all ages, with a firm hierarchy among the males. They use their horns and horn-bosses in pushing contests that help to decide their ranks.

Impala *below*
African grassland has 72 species of antelope, weighing from a few pounds to 1800 lb (800 kg).

Tick bird *left*
The yellow-billed oxpecker rides on the backs of rhinos and other large animals and eats ticks and flies living in or on the hide. Sometimes the birds swoop off their perch to take large insects which have been disturbed by the animal.

Leopard *right*
Stealthy and athletic, the leopard is found through most of Africa and southern Asia. It often rests in trees, and this fine specimen has pulled its prey, a reedbuck, onto a high branch.

Giraffes *left*
Tallest of all land animals, the giraffe eats acacia leaves and other greenery high above the ground (see large illustration below). Here a group gallops past zebras across a bare patch of ground.

7ft, 213cm

Griffon vulture *left*
Vultures soar at high altitudes on their large wings while searching to the horizon for carrion.

Jackrabbit *above*
Big ears are not only for keen hearing: they help radiate heat and control body temperature.

Ostrich *below*
The tall ostrich can see for miles across the African plains and run swiftly from danger.

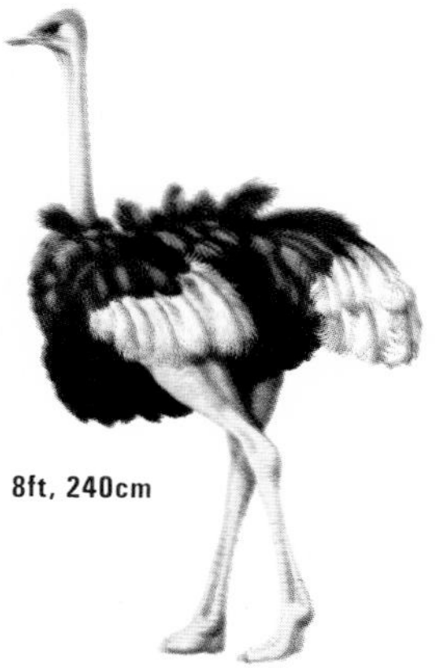
8ft, 240cm

Impala
Giraffe
Cape eland
Kirk's dik-dik
African elephant
Gerenuk
Cape buffalo
Black rhinoceros

Feeding habits
The great grasslands of Africa, and to a lesser degree those of other continents, teem with wild life of remarkable variety. In this wide open environment concealment is difficult and the majority of animals survive by having good long-distance vision and by being fleet of foot. Some of the smaller plant eaters escape their predators by burrowing. The key to the co-existence of the herbivores is that they tend to feed at different levels. The elephant can reach up to 15 feet (4·5 m) above the ground to tear at broad-leafed trees, while the giraffe can feed on its favored acacias at even higher levels. The rhino, buffalo, gerenuk and eland eat not only low shrubs and trees but also grass. Only the gnus, zebras and some rhinos compete for the same areas, but these areas are so large that there is little fear of over-grazing. The baboon delves for roots and whatever it can find, while the carnivores include the carrion-eating hyenas and vultures and the predatory lion, cheetah and leopard. Left to themselves, the wild animals of the savanna do little harm to their habitat, but the growing herds of domesticated cattle and goats pose a threat. Whereas the native fauna leaves living shoots which can sprout into a fresh plant, the cattle and goats eat the whole of the grass and tree shoots so that the vegetation is soon eradicated. Over-grazing and poor range management are encouraged by the fact that some African tribes still regard cattle as symbols of wealth. The value of the indigenous savanna animals has been forcefully demonstrated in parts of South Africa and Rhodesia where ranges run down by domestic cattle have been restored by grazing 10 to 12 varieties of antelope in their place.

The Deserts

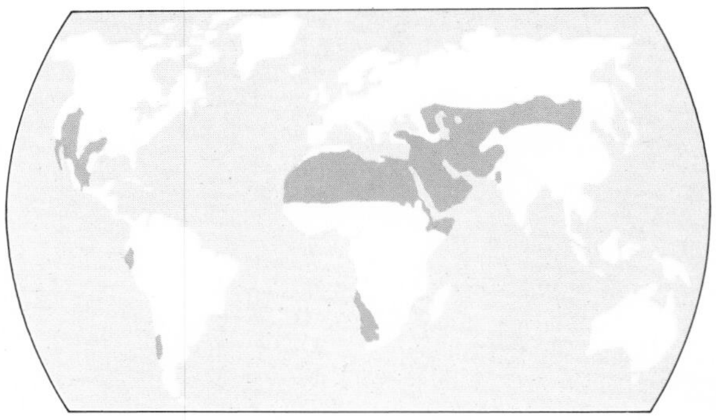

The desert is a harsh, arid and inhospitable environment of great variety where the average rainfall for a year is less than five inches (125 mm) and in some years there is none at all. The cloudless sky allows the Earth's surface to heat up to 30–40°C by day and cool near to freezing at night. Relative humidity is low. On the basis of temperature arid lands are divided into low-latitude hot deserts and mid-latitude deserts. The latter, in central Asia and the Great Basin of the United States, are bitterly cold in winter. In the coastal deserts of Peru and Chile the cold offshore current flowing northward from the Antarctic Ocean cools the moist air producing a swirling sea fog.

Landscapes are rocky, and weathered to strange shapes by the winds and sudden rains (page 42). Sand dunes shifted and shaped by the wind are common in Saudi Arabia and the Sahara. The dunes are almost sterile, but most deserts have some sparse plant cover. Stems and leaves are hard, to prevent loss of water and protect the plant from sand erosion. Succulent cacti and euphorbias store water in fleshy stems or leaves, and have widespread shallow roots to absorb the dew. Sahara oases were probably cultivated 7000 years ago, producing grain, olives, wine, figs and dates. The Egyptians channelled the waters of the flooding Nile to irrigate the land, and today the Imperial Valley of the Californian desert and the Arizona desert near Phoenix are highly productive agricultural land.

Water in the desert
Most of the world's deserts are neither billowing sand dunes (such as that on the opposite page) nor totally devoid of water. But in all deserts water, especially fresh water, is a precious commodity. In the great stony deserts brief rains allow stunted vegetation to provide a basis for animal life. The neighborhood of Monument Valley, Utah (above) is surprisingly full of life which has adapted to arid conditions. Some life is also found in the Sahara, where sudden torrential rains cause flash flood erosion (south of Ouargla, left) leaving smooth ridges and deep gullies Sometimes the water table is at the surface. The water may be brackish and undrinkable, as in Cyrenaica west of the Siwa Oasis (below), but the true oasis contains fresh water at which a camel can drink copiously (right). Even the meager dew is stored by plants – nothing is wasted.

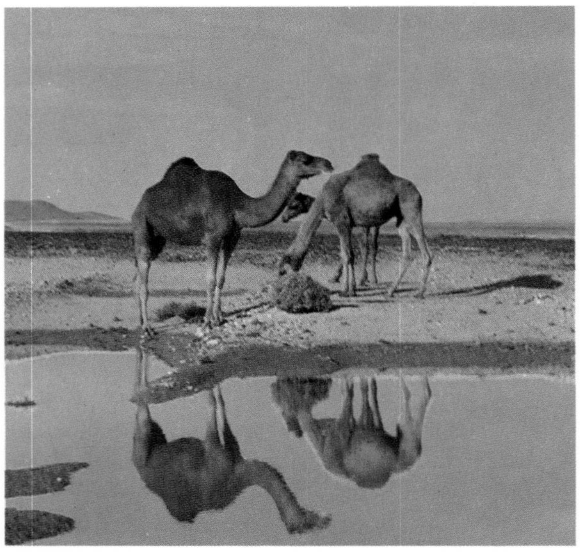

Desert plants *right*
Deserts test the ability of plants to adapt to a near absence of water. Plants survive by throwing out large catchment areas for dew at night, minimizing water loss by evaporation during the day, growing deep roots to find water far below the surface, storing what water they find, and in extreme cases by lying dormant during dry years and springing to life as soon as it rains.

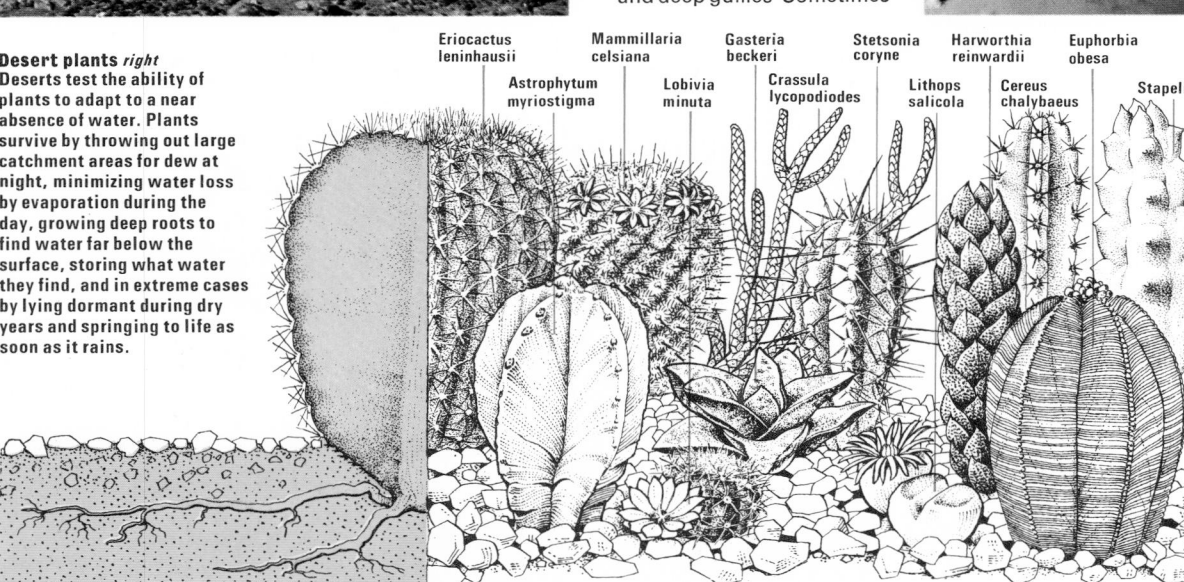

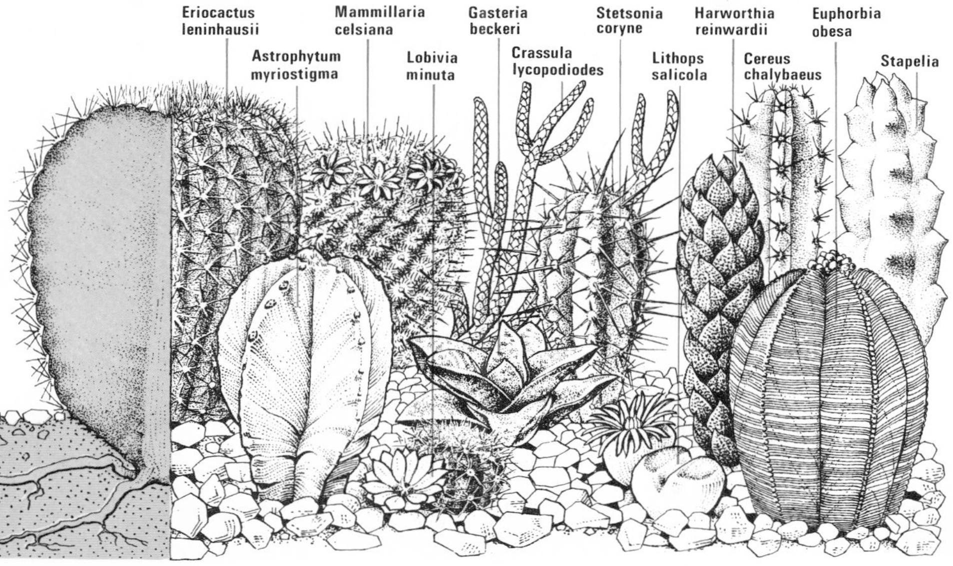
Eriocactus leninhausii
Astrophytum myriostigma
Mammillaria celsiana
Lobivia minuta
Gasteria beckeri
Crassula lycopodiodes
Stetsonia coryne
Lithops salicola
Harworthia reinwardii
Cereus chalybaeus
Euphorbia obesa
Stapelia

1 Agave
2 Aloe dichotoma
3 Opuntia
4 Ferocactus
5 Carnegia
6 Pachypodium
7 Haageocereus
8 Giant cereus

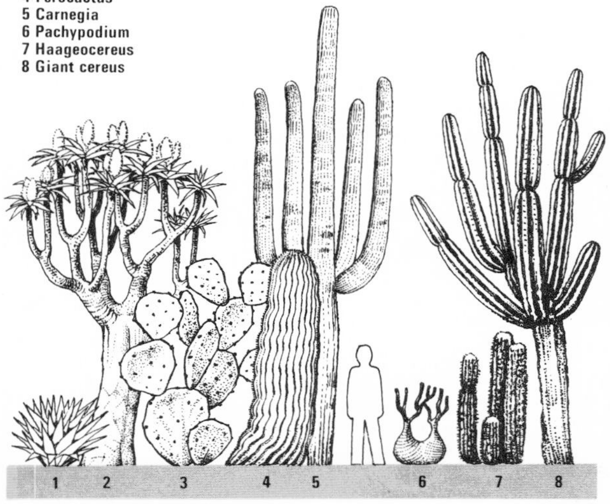
1
2
3
4
5
6
7
8

Desert animals

Many animals are so well adapted to retain water that they survive on the moisture in their food. Some, such as the armadillo lizard, scorpions, insects and spiders, have hard, impenetrable skins to reduce water loss. The urine of camels and gazelles is very concentrated to minimize excretion of water. Arabian camels can lose 30 per cent of their body weight (which would be lethal for a man) without distress, and then regain it by drinking up to 27 gallons (120 liters) at a time. This does not dilute their blood dangerously. A camel does not sweat until its body temperature reaches 40°C, and it loses heat easily during the cold night because it stores its fat in the hump and not as a layer under the skin. Its fur insulates against the heat, as do the loose clothes of the people. Snakes hide in crevices, and sand-swimming lizards burrow to avoid extreme temperatures. Jerboas and kangaroo rats hop along, and some lizards run on their hind legs to keep their bellies off the ground. As soon as it rains, swarms of dormant life surge into activity.

Desert Burrowers

White-footed mouse
Burrow taken over by horned lizard
Horned lizard
American badger
Pocket mouse
Kit fox
Kangaroo rat in nest
Green-collared lizard
Food store
Kangaroo rat

Ant lions *right and below*
Some types of ant lion catch their prey — mainly ants — by digging a smooth conical pit and waiting at the bottom; others bury themselves in the sand with only eyes and jaws protruding. The larval stage (right) precedes the winged adult (below).

Sand desert *above*
Only one-seventh of the Sahara looks like this Hollywood-style vista of giant dunes in Algeria.

Dung beetles *left*
These female scarabs are rolling a pellet of animal dung into a ball containing an egg.

8in, 21cm

Painted lady *above*
N African desert thistles provide nectar for their migration through Europe as far as Iceland.

20in, 51cm

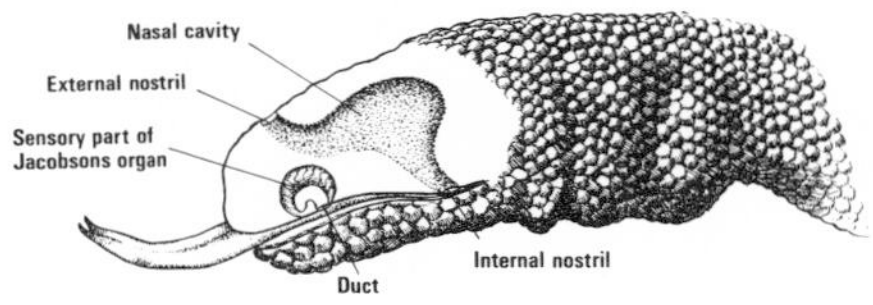
Nasal cavity
External nostril
Sensory part of Jacobsons organ
Duct
Internal nostril

Gila monster *right*
This venomous N American lizard tracks its prey with the aid of a sensor in its mouth (right, lower).

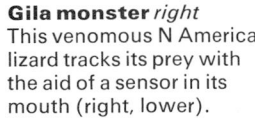

Scorpion and snake
When scorpions mate, the male deposits a patch of sperm on the ground and then contrives to maneuver a female over it in what looks like a square dance (above, left). The dangerous rattlesnake (above) senses the heat radiated by its prey using organs on its face.

Plants and predator
The leopard tortoise (left) enjoys a meal of cactus, a plant which stores water and minimizes evaporation (Ferocactus of Arizona, right). Other desert blooms include Echinopsis rhodatricia and Chamacerus silvestri (far right, upper and lower).

The Mountains

The mountain environment varies enormously with height and the direction of the prevailing wind. Temperature falls about 2°C (3.4°F) for each 1000 feet (300 m) increase in altitude. Barometric pressure also falls until lack of oxygen makes any human exertion cause shortness of breath. Before people adjust to the conditions they often suffer from mountain sickness —headache, weakness and nausea.

Sun temperature may be 28°C (83°F) hotter than in the shade or at night, and the slope of a mountain facing the equator is warmer than the other sides. Mountains force rain-bearing winds to rise, so that they cool and have to release moisture. Clouds form, and rain falls on the windward slope; on the opposite slope the descending winds are drying.

High-altitude life

Altitude has the same effect on vegetation as latitude. At about 5000 feet (1500 m) tropical rainforest changes to montane forest resembling a temperate rainforest. At twice this height the broad-leaved trees disappear but there are conifers and shrubs such as laurel. Above the treeline, where the average monthly temperature never exceeds 10°C, is alpine tundra or heath. The snowline at the equator is at about 15000 feet (4500 m). In Peru irrigated sugar and cacao cover the lower slopes, and above the timberline corn grows at 11000 feet, wheat at 12000, barley at 13000 and potatoes up to 14000 feet. The Incas had terraced the Andes and had an efficient agricultural system by 1000 AD.

The mountain life zone which is unique is that above the treeline. The animal communities are isolated, since mountains act as a barrier to migration. Most plants and insects on mountain tops can withstand freezing. Some animals burrow or shelter under rocks where temperature variations are smaller. Ibexes, yaks, deer and sheep all have thick coats but move down the mountain-side in winter. Mountain animals have enlarged hearts and lungs and extra oxygen-carrying red blood corpuscles to make the most of the thin air. The vicuna, for example, has nearly three times the number of red corpuscles per cubic millimeter of blood as man.

Near Murren *above right*
The environment on a high mountain is essentially polar, even in a tropical country. Above the timberline ice and snow replace animals and plants, and the conditions are further modified by intense solar radiation and low atmospheric pressure.

Lichens *above and right*
Lichens comprise a fungus and an alga in close association. The alga govern the color (page 69 for red lichen). The metabolism of lichens is exceedingly slow; barely alive, they can subsist on mountain rock in harsh conditions for hundreds of years.

Altitude and latitude *right*
At extreme latitudes – for example, in the Antarctic – the climate is so severe at sea level that no very pronounced change takes place even as one climbs a mountain, although the mountain's presence can strongly modify the local weather. In contrast, mountains near the equator rise from hot, steamy forests into freezing, arid peaks, with almost every kind of Earth environment in between. To most kinds of terrestrial life large mountains are barriers. As altitude increases, plants and animals become adapted to the environment and then peter out entirely.

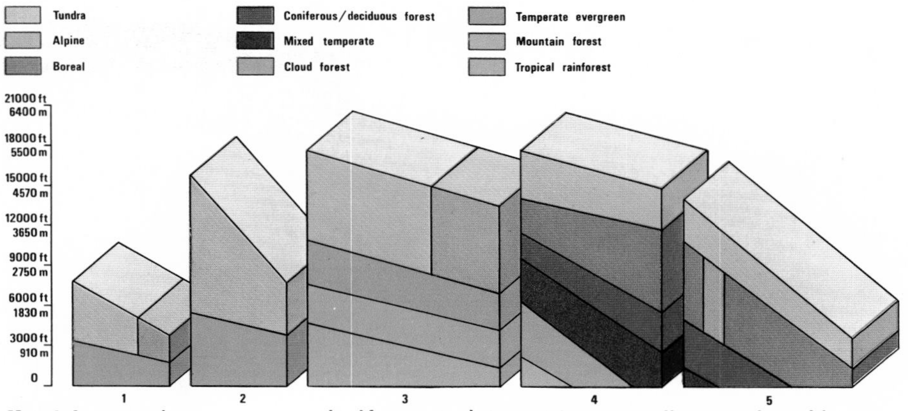
Tundra
Alpine
Boreal
Coniferous/deciduous forest
Mixed temperate
Cloud forest
Temperate evergreen
Mountain forest
Tropical rainforest
21000 ft
6400 m
18000 ft
5500 m
15000 ft
4570 m
12000 ft
3650 m
9000 ft
2750 m
6000 ft
1830 m
3000 ft
910 m
0
1
2
3
4
5

Mountain zones *above*
At high latitudes a mountain offers fewer contrasts; much of New Zealand (1) has cool, humid cloud forest, topped by alpine heath and tundra. In SE Australia, SE Africa and S Brazil (2) the cloud forest extends to a greater altitude, with only tundra above. The high tropical Andes (3) afford contrasts surpassed only by the mountainous regions of the eastern Himalayas and SE Asia (4), where six distinct regions overlie one another, with very local regions of tropical mountain forest. Mountains of Europe (5) lie in regions where there are already great contrasts in climate at sea level. Boreal is a north-facing mountain region.

Tortoise *above*
The margined tortoise is native to mountainous regions in Greece and the Balkans.

Plants *left*
Purple gentian and (upper) auricula are typical of mountain dwarf perennials; some can resist freezing.

Butterflies
Mountains are often rich in insects. The six-spot burnet (mating, left) is common. Some Apollo butterflies (below) are found above 17000 feet (5200 m) in the Himalayas. Erebia (right) is carrying an orange mite, a parasite which can survive freezing. Mountain insects rely for much of their food on pollen, seeds and even insects swept up in the frequent updraft of winds from the warm lowlands.

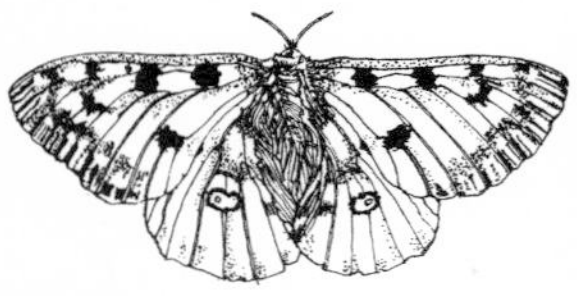

4in, 8cm

African birds of prey
Small mountain rodents make a tasty meal for the jackal buzzard (left), a bird with exceedingly acute vision. The black eagle (with three-week chick, right) lives on rats and lizards but can tackle animals as large as the 7 lb (3.2 kg) rock hyrax. It nests in July.

Rodents
Whereas the alpine marmot (below) hibernates in winter, the pika of Tibet (in group, below right) stores its supplies. The chinchilla and cavy both come from South America. Above 10000 ft (3000 m) rodents outnumber all other animals.

Chinchilla
Cavy
Pika

Salamander *right*
This Pyrenean salamander is climbing out of a cool mountain stream, but the true alpine salamander has had to become adapted to an arid habitat. Much darker than the lowland varieties, it does not lay its eggs in water but bears its young alive. It remains amphibious.

American cougar *left*
Also known as the puma or mountain lion, the cougar hunts by day above the timberline. When it makes a large kill it is able to store the carcass for weeks at sub-zero temperature. Most of these beasts range over a fixed area, although some wander down to lower levels.

Yak *right*
Domesticated in its native Tibet, the shaggy yak is still found in local wild herds in central Asia. It is a hardy animal, adapted to eating snow in the absence of water, and moss and lichens when no better vegetation is available. It is found up to 20000 ft (6000 m).

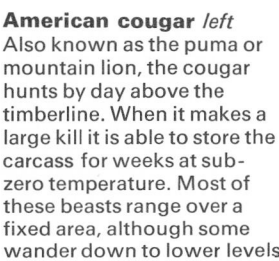

Grazers
Sure-footed, the mountain goat (left) inhabits the northern Rockies.
The chamoix (above) is scattered through mountain regions of southern Europe, while ibexes (right) are a very widespread family. Specialized sheep also graze at high altitudes.

The Lakes and the Rivers

Freshwater environments range from puddles to lakes which cover thousands of square miles, from small streams to rivers that stretch hundreds of miles from mountain source to the ocean. Together, they provide a diversity of habitats that supports a wide range of plant and animal life.

In rivers the type and variety of life is controlled by the depth and speed of water. Fast mountain streams have few plants and the fish are either fast swimmers or shelter among stones. The slower, wider lowland rivers are rich in vegetation and many of the fish have mouths adapted to sucking food from the rich silt of the river bed. In the brackish waters of the estuary few freshwater animals can survive because of the increasing salinity. But migratory fish, such as eels and Atlantic salmon, adapt to fresh and salt water at different stages of their life cycles.

In standing water the surface is often much warmer than the depths. This produces layers which are so distinct that separate habitats are created. The deeper waters may be completely devoid of oxygen because they do not mix with the well-aerated surface layers. Lakes go through three stages of development: oligotrophic with barren sides and clear water; eutrophic when the lake has begun to silt up and is rich in life; and, finally, dystrophic with decayed organic matter developing into swamp or peat bog. This natural process of eutrophication normally takes thousands of years, but man can, by his indiscriminate pollution and over-enrichment of some lakes condense this process dangerously into a few decades.

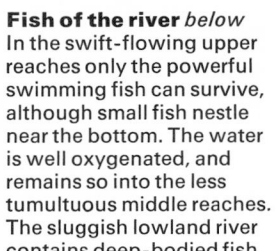

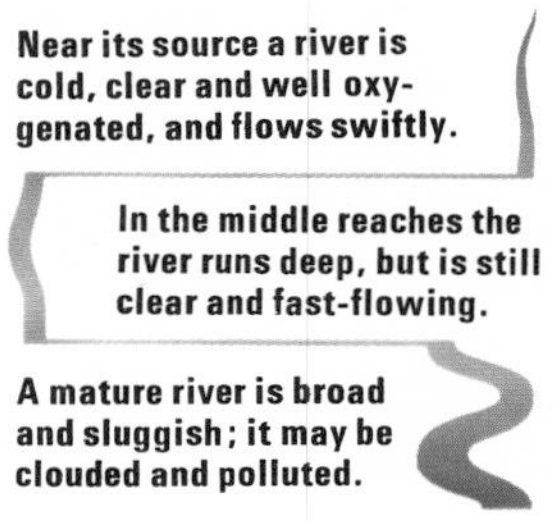
Near its source a river is cold, clear and well oxygenated, and flows swiftly.
In the middle reaches the river runs deep, but is still clear and fast-flowing.
A mature river is broad and sluggish; it may be clouded and polluted.

Fish of the river *below*
In the swift-flowing upper reaches only the powerful swimming fish can survive, although small fish nestle near the bottom. The water is well oxygenated, and remains so into the less tumultuous middle reaches. The sluggish lowland river contains deep-bodied fish.

Trout stream

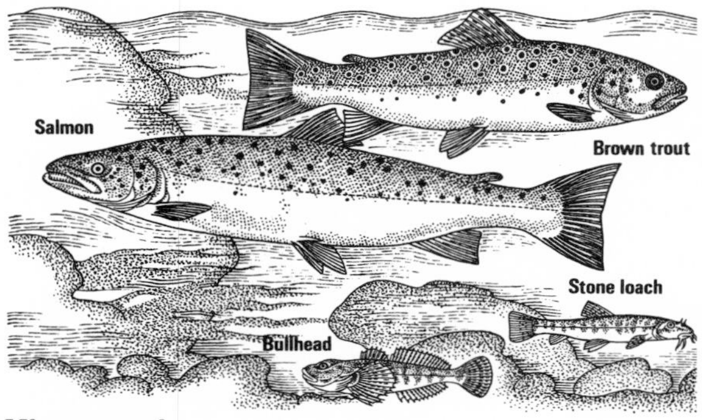
Salmon
Brown trout
Stone loach
Bullhead

Minnow reach

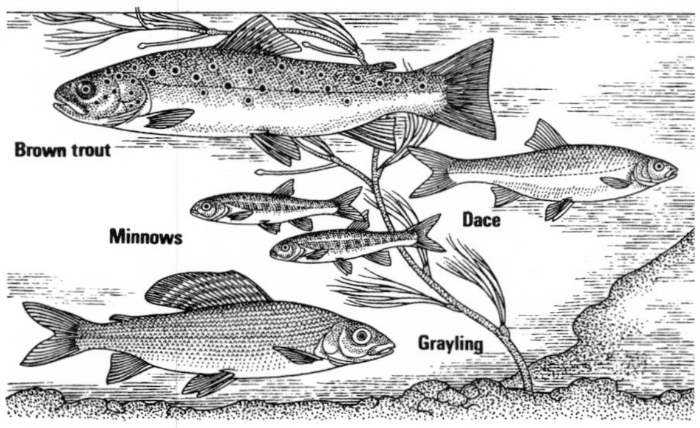
Brown trout
Minnows
Dace
Grayling

Lowland river

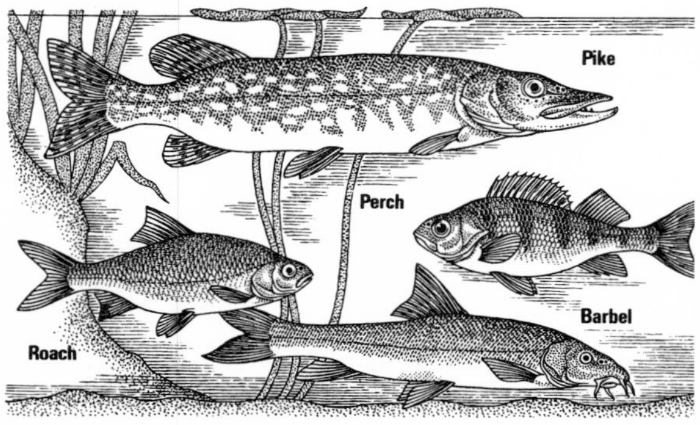
Pike
Perch
Barbel
Roach

Salmon leaping *above*
Mature salmon return from the ocean to the rivers in which they hatched. Swimming against the current, and leaping up rapids and waterfalls, they finally gain the upper reaches where they spawn. After 1-3 years, the next generation migrates to the sea.

Kingfisher *above*
These colorful birds are by far the most numerous of the many species that take fish while on the wing. Plunging across the surface in a shallow dive, they seize in their long beaks prey they had spotted while on the branch of a tree. Average size 7 in (18 cm).

Teeming with life *left*
Most lakes begin life in the oligotrophic stage, barren of life and with clear, bright waters. After a time the water is colonized, and gradually a community rich in plant and animal species occupies the freshwater habitat. Such a lake is eutrophic.

A swamp *left*
The Indian name of Lake Okeefenokee, Georgia, means 'land of trembling earth'. Measuring some 30 miles by 60 (50 by 100 km), it is a region of perfect mirror-like reflections and teeming wild life.

Swamp butterfly *above*
There are many sub-species of swallowtail; this is the eastern tiger swallowtail from the marshes of Georgia. Average size 4 in (10 cm).

Tree frog *above*
Devouring flies and gnats by the million, green tree frogs breed in the warm swamp waters. Average size is 2½in (6 cm).

Alligator *above*
Generally not aggressive, they keep open the channels in American swamps. Average size is 10 ft (3 m).

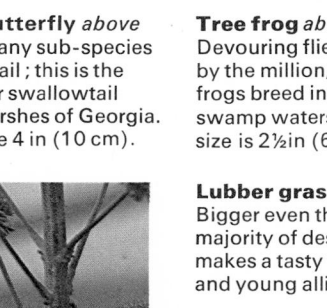

Lubber grasshopper *left*
Bigger even than the majority of desert locusts, it makes a tasty meal for birds and young alligators.

Terrapin *above*
The Suwannee river terrapin is sometimes found in the Gulf of Mexico. Average size is 7 in (18 cm).

Swamp turtle *above*
The soft-shelled turtles have a leathery skin without an outer covering of horny plates. Size 14 in (36 cm).

1
2
3
4
5
6
7
8
9
10
11

The pond environment *left*
1 Common frog (male, ×0.5)
2 Starwort (×0.5)
3 Water crowfoot (×0.25)
4 Aplecta hypnorum (×2)
5 Wandering snail (×0.75)
6 Keeled ramshorn snail (×0.5)
7 Curled pondweed (×0.25)
8 Bithynia (×1)
9 Ramshorn snail (×0.3)
10 Water lily root (×0.25)
11 Great pond snail (×0.8)

Pond life *below*
The essential characteristic of pond life is adaptation to a fresh-water environment without a flowing current. As in almost every other habitat on Earth the life is divided into distinct zones—atmosphere, surface film, middle depths and bed—although many species cross from one zone to another. The newt, for example, is active everywhere from the bed of a pond to dry land. Throughout the ecology of freshwater life all food is manufactured by green plants. First-order animals, such as zooplankton and many fish and insects, feed directly on the plants; everything else feeds on predators lower in the food chain or web. The water itself is very far from being a pure compound of hydrogen and oxygen. It contains dissolved oxygen and nitrogen salts and much organic material. The life of the pond establishes ecological cycles which constantly balance inputs and outputs between water, air, and life. For example, the supply of nitrates washed in from the land is augmented by the decomposition of dead organisms in the water itself.

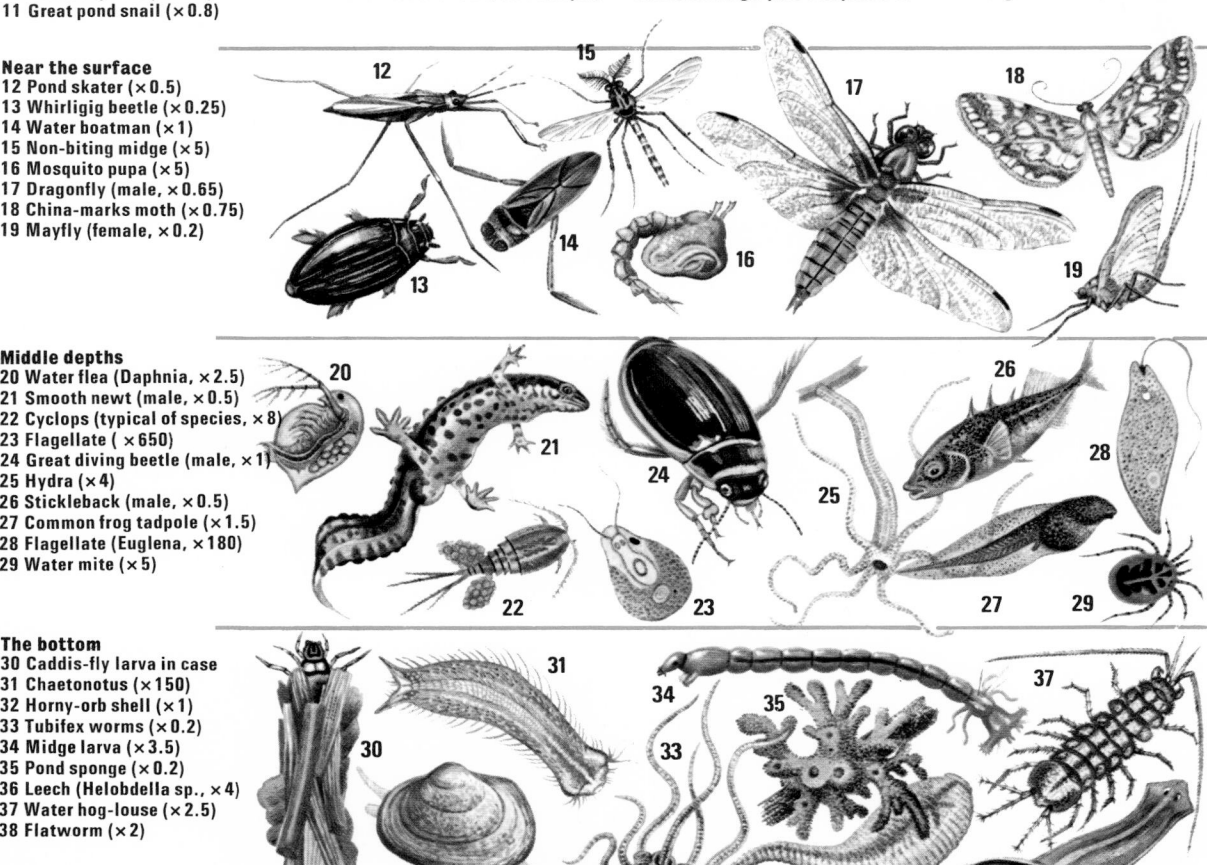

Near the surface
12 Pond skater (×0.5)
13 Whirligig beetle (×0.25)
14 Water boatman (×1)
15 Non-biting midge (×5)
16 Mosquito pupa (×5)
17 Dragonfly (male, ×0.65)
18 China-marks moth (×0.75)
19 Mayfly (female, ×0.2)

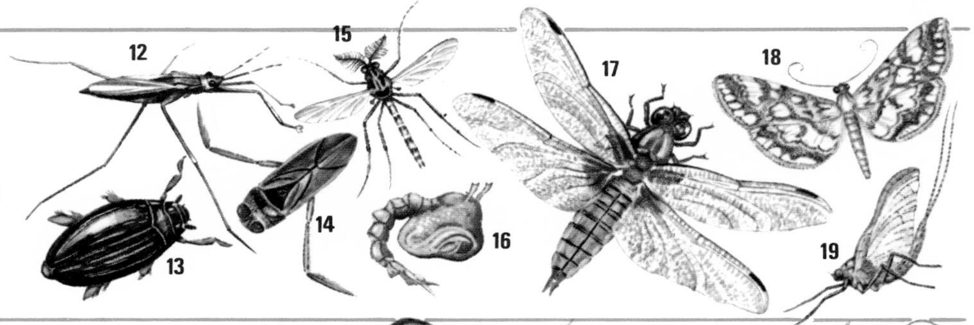

12
13
14
15
16
17
18
19

Middle depths
20 Water flea (Daphnia, ×2.5)
21 Smooth newt (male, ×0.5)
22 Cyclops (typical of species, ×8)
23 Flagellate (×650)
24 Great diving beetle (male, ×1)
25 Hydra (×4)
26 Stickleback (male, ×0.5)
27 Common frog tadpole (×1.5)
28 Flagellate (Euglena, ×180)
29 Water mite (×5)

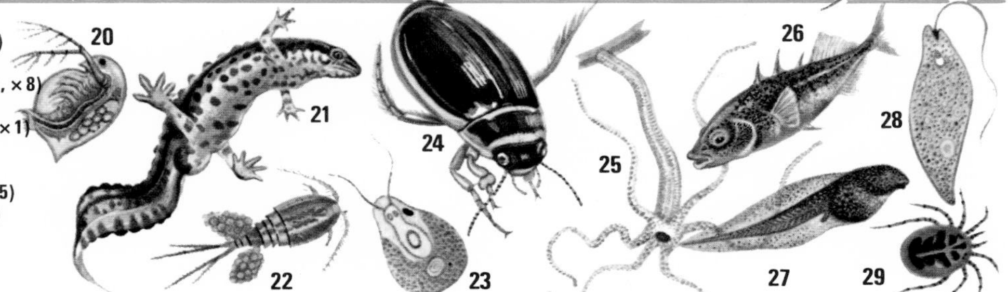

20
21
22
23
24
25
26
27
28
29

The bottom
30 Caddis-fly larva in case
31 Chaetonotus (×150)
32 Horny-orb shell (×1)
33 Tubifex worms (×0.2)
34 Midge larva (×3.5)
35 Pond sponge (×0.2)
36 Leech (Helobdella sp., ×4)
37 Water hog-louse (×2.5)
38 Flatworm (×2)

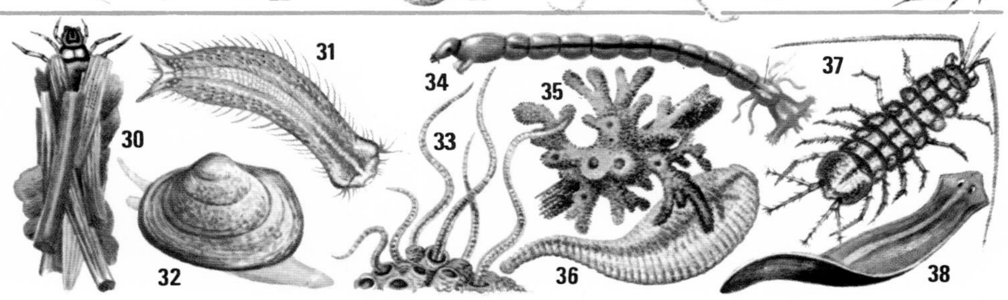

30
31
32
33
34
35
36
37
38

The Oceans

The oceans are a continuous mass of 5000 million million tons of water; but variations in light, pressure, salinity, temperature, currents, waves, and tides interact to create numerous regions each with its own typical forms of life.

Plants are the basis of ocean food chains, just as they are on land. Since all plants need sunlight they are found only in the upper layer of the sea. Myriads of tiny marine plants called phytoplankton are eaten by the small floating zooplankton and by tiny fish, which in turn support a succession of predators. Deep-water animals are adapted to great pressure and to darkness. Most are predators but some of them are scavengers which depend on a rain of food debris from above.

Some ocean islands are coral, built by millions of polyps resembling sea anemones which produce a hard stony skeleton (p.35). But most are thrust up by volcanic eruptions. They are completely isolated and were never joined to a continent. Such islands are usually wet and windswept.

Island plant and animal communities evolved from the few original forms which crossed the ocean and colonized. Island colonization is difficult, and is seldom accomplished by land mammals apart from bats, nor even by amphibians. Land and freshwater animals may have evolved from sea-dwelling ancestors. Once a species has colonized an island it interbreeds, because of its isolation, and adapts to its new conditions and competitors. Often new endemic species evolve.

The first colonizers are usually sea birds. They bring nutrients, so seeds and the spores of mosses, lichens and ferns carried by the wind can take root. The wind also brings insects, spiders and bats, and occasionally land birds in storms, but such birds rarely establish themselves. Reptiles and some land animals may cross the sea on driftwood rafts. Many island reptiles, perhaps because of the lack of mammals, have become unusually large. Examples include such creatures as the Komodo dragon and the giant tortoises of the Galapagos.

The ocean layers

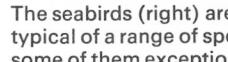

sea leve
1000 m
3300 ft
3000 m
10000 f
6000 m
20000 f

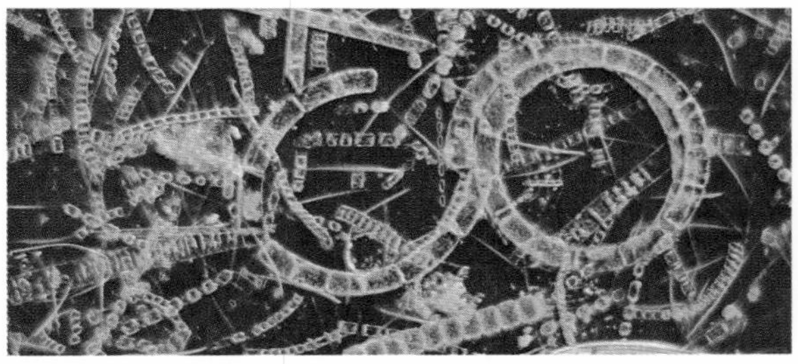

Phytoplankton *above*
All marine life depends ultimately on microscopic plant plankton, which is mostly single-celled. (x 20)

Tiger cowrie *right*
Cowries are tropical marine snails. This spotted example is feeding, with its mantle extended below.

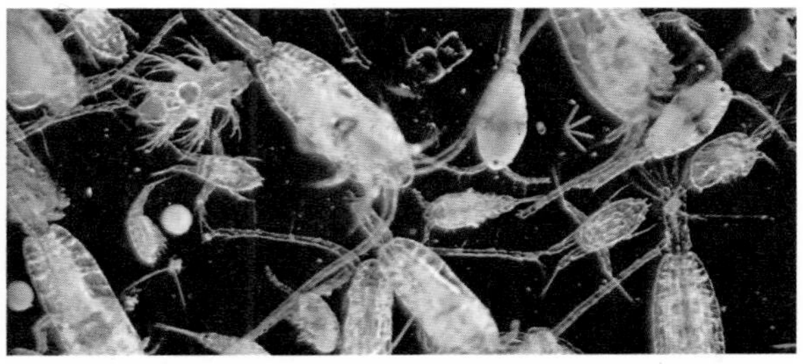

Zooplankton *above*
These microscopic animals feed on the phytoplankton and on each other. In turn they support fish. (x 8)

Leopard coral *right*
The derivation of the name of this hard coral is obvious. Each 'spot' is an individual in the colony.

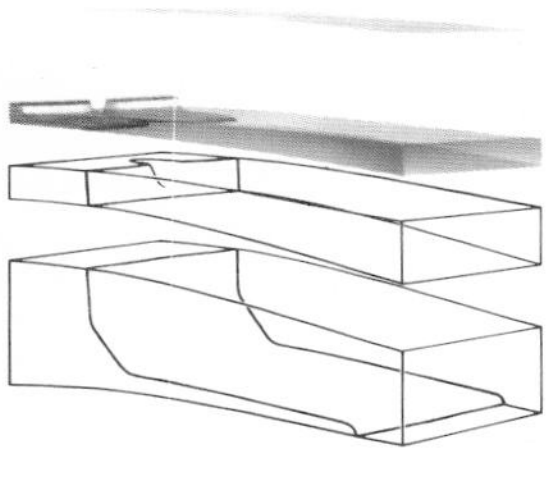

Near the surface
above and right
Seabirds generally keep below 1000 ft (300 m) but can be found much higher. The upper layer of ocean is taken to extend down to 3300 ft (1000 m). Water temperature is about 10 °C and sunlight may reach to 650 ft (200 m).

Air and surface life
The seabirds (right) are typical of a range of species, some of them exceptionally large birds, which navigate unerringly over thousands of miles of ocean. Most have wide wingspans and use favourable airflow over the waves to soar apparently without effort. Sunlight penetrates the warm upper layers of the ocean to provide energy for photosynthesis, permitting the prolific growth of the phytoplankton (plant life). This is the starting point for the whole complex web of marine life which leads ultimately to large predatory fish such as the tuna and marlin, and to human foods.

Soft coral *above*
Photographed in Mauritius, a bluish coral has almost finished reproducing by splitting into two.

Sea urchin *below*
This 'slate pencil' variety from Mozambique coral reefs contrasts with spiny types. Size 10 in (25 cm).

Sea slug *above*
Many of these marine relatives of land slugs are colorful. This one from the Indian Ocean is 4 in (10 cm).

Feather star *below*
Another of the starfish and sea urchin group from Mozambique, this has four inch (10 cm) arms.

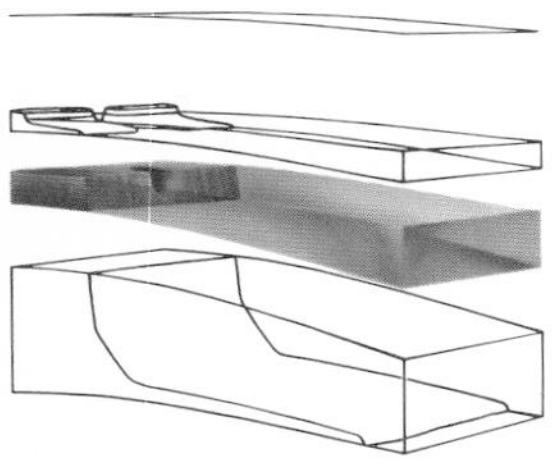

Middle depths
above and right
The horizontal 'slice' of ocean water in which live the middle-depth species illustrated opposite is taken to extend from 3300 down to 10000 ft (1000-3000 m). Here the temperature falls from 10 °C down to below 4 °C at the lower level.

Middle dwellers
In this range of depths, most of which (down to 6000 ft) is known as the bathyal or bathypelagic zone, the water cools to 4 °C, the temperature at which the density of water reaches its peak. Little or no light penetrates, and the life is made up of free-swimming fish, crustaceans and cephalopods (squids, for example) possessing body fluids at the same hydrostatic pressure as the environment and having approximately the same degree of salinity. At night some middle dwellers migrate to the surface to feed on other animals which in turn congregate to 'graze' on the plankton.

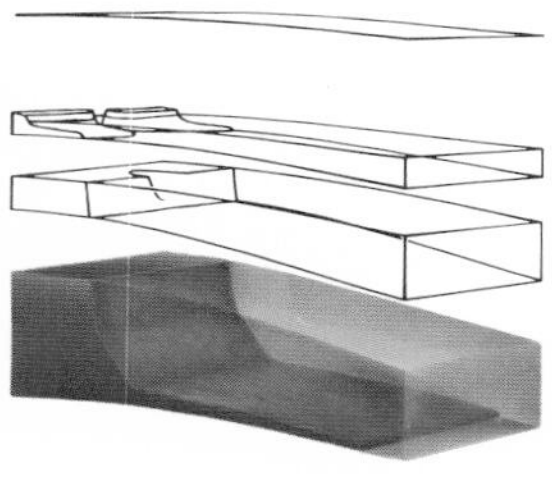

The abyss
above and right
The bottom layer of the ocean is here taken to extend down to about 20000 ft (6000 m). Temperature is always below 4 °C, hydrostatic pressure is enormous and the environment is perpetually devoid of sunlight.

Bottom dwellers
Below 3000 meters the life comprises a range of animals, most of them very small, adapted to living in near-freezing water at extremely high pressures. The only light in this region comes from the curious luminescent organs common to many deep-sea creatures. Although the deep waters contain abundant salts and nutrient minerals, these are useless without the energy of sunlight. Every abyssal organism is therefore either a scavenger, depending for its supply of food on a 'rain' of debris from above, or a predator. Yet the abyssal zone supports a surprising variety of life.

Great Shearwater
span 8½ in 0.2 m
Wandering albatross
span 11 ft 3.35 m
Red-billed tropic bird
span 1 ft 0.3 m
Magnificent frigate bird
span 8 ft 2.45 m
Portuguese man o'war
11 in 0.28 m
(tentacles 100 ft 30 m)
sea level
Flying fish
9 in 0.23 m
Marlin
10 ft 3 m
Ocean sunfish
10 ft 3 m
Anchovies
6 in 0.15 m
Basking shark
40 ft 12 m
Dolphin fish
4 ft 1.2 m
Squid
1 ft 0.3 m
Bluefin tuna
7 ft 2 m
Ocean bonito
2 ft 0.6 m
Diretmus argentus
2 in 0.05 m
Mackerel shark
12 ft 3.6 m
Lantern fish
3 in 0.075 m
Photostomias guerni
7 in 0.18 m
1000 m
3300 ft
Giant squid
55 ft 17 m
Hatchet fish
1 in 0.025 m
Oarfish
20 ft 6 m
Ghost shark
4 ft 1.2 m
Chiasmodus niger
3 in 0.075 m
Gulper eel
4 ft 6 in 1.4 m
3000 m
10000 ft
Angler fish
3 in 0.075 m
Deep sea swimming cucumber
4 in 0.1 m
Prawn
4 in 0.1 m
Viper fish
1 ft 0.3 m
Angler fish
2 in 0.05 m
Pelican eel
10 in 0.25 m
Deep sea jellyfish
3 in 0.075 m
Rat tail
18 in 0.45 m
Tripod fish
10 in 0.25 m
Abyssal octopus
4 in 0.1 m
Brotulid
6 in 0.15 m
Abyssal sea cucumber
¾ in 0.02 m
Sea snail
9 in 0.23 m
Brittle star 3 in 0.075 m

The Endangered Animals

As man's population soars towards 5000 million, other species sharing the planet with him are being driven to extinction. In biological terms, the disappearance of less efficient forms before more efficient or better adapted ones is not new. But the present situation is unparalleled because the endangered species, and those that have already vanished during the past 400 years, have not fallen before man's biological superiority. They are the victims of man's greed, stupidity and thoughtlessness.

Only about one quarter of the birds and mammals that have vanished since 1600 have done so through natural causes. Man is responsible for the plight of about 68 per cent of the endangered birds and 86 per cent of the mammals. Since 1600 at least 120 forms of mammals and 150 forms of birds have become extinct; and today at least a further 120 species of mammals and 187 species of birds are threatened with this fate. These figures represent almost seven per cent of the species in these two groups that existed in 1600.

1 Polar Bear ***(Thalarctos maritimus) above***
Circumpolar in distribution, the polar bear is larger than all other bears, and much more nomadic. Its main food is seals, especially those of the ringed type, but in summer it forages on land for carrion, birds, berries and roots. Man and his animals have increased its susceptibility to disease, and hunting has reduced the population to 5000-10000 animals.
Average size of male is 7 ft (2 m) and weight 1000 lbs (450 kg).

2 Audouin's gull
(Larus audouinii) above
Today there are believed to be fewer than 1000 of these birds, scattered around rocky coasts and islets in the Mediterranean. Fishermen eat their eggs and collectors also take them, while herring gulls prey on their nests.
Length from beak to tail is 19 in (48 cm).

3 Addax ***(Addax nasomaculatus) left***
Man bears sole responsibility for the near extinction of this fine beast. Perfectly adapted to deriving moisture solely from plants, it was once common throughout NW Africa. But hunting—often using machine guns—has left under 5000.
Average height of male 42 in (107 cm).

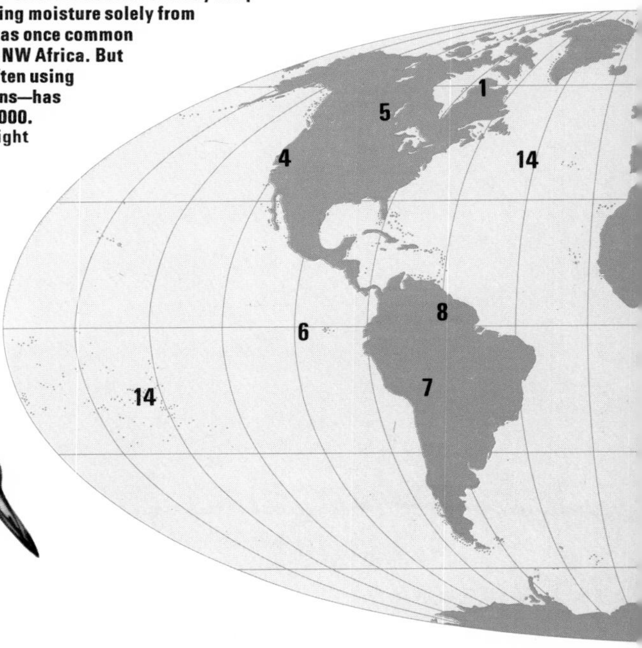
1
5
4
14
8
6
7
14

4 California condor
(Gymnogyps californianus) right
Until recently this great bird was found from the Columbia river, Washington, to Baja (lower) California. But in this region of booming development wild life has suffered. Condors have had their habitat disturbed or destroyed, and this, combined with shooting and accidental poisoning, has reduced their numbers to fewer than 50 birds.
Average wingspan is 9 ft (3 m).

5 Whooping crane
(Grus americana) left
Breeds in muskegs of Wood Buffalo Park, Alberta, and migrates to winter in an Aransas, Texas, refuge. Human exploitation of nesting areas and hunting reduced its numbers to 23 in 1941, but careful preservation has apparently saved the species and today there are believed to be at least 50.
Average height 50 in (127 cm).

6 Galapagos penguin
(Spheniscus mendiculus) below
This species lives on two islands of the Galapagos group—on the equator but on the cold Humboldt current. The total population is thought not to exceed 2000 birds. It is endangered by the collection of eggs and adult birds for food.
One of the smallest penguins, its average height is 20 in (51 cm).

7 Vicuna
(Vicugna vicugna) right
Found on grassy and arid plains of the Andes, the vicuna has retreated to higher altitudes in the face of flocks of man's domestic animals. In 1954 there were thought to be some 400,000, but by 1964 the total had dropped to no more than 11000. This appears to have been due mainly to poaching for the exceptionally fine wool.
Average height at shoulder is 32in (81 cm.)

8 Giant otter
(Pteronura brasiliensis) above
This is the largest otter in the world, found along the courses of rivers in northern South America. Hunting for its very valuable fur has devastated the population in Venezuela, and in Peru the species appears to be in imminent danger of extinction.
Average length from nose to the tip of the tail is 66 in (168 cm).

Depletion and extinction of a species can come about in many ways. Natural causes, such as the inability to adapt to changed circumstances, are inevitable. Uncontrolled hunting can have disastrous results. Habitat destruction and disturbance, particularly dangerous to birds, can be caused by tree felling and land clearance, or indirectly through overgrazing by domestic stock. And existing populations may have no defense against new predators, nor against disease brought in by the introduction of other animals.

In the late Pleistocene era, at the end of the ice ages some 15000 years ago, at least 200 species of large vertebrates vanished. To what extent the new predator, man, was responsible is unknown. What distinguishes the situation today is man's vastly greater power to change the environment and affect all of natural life on a huge scale. To some degree the problem is now being tackled by the creation of nature reserves, and by legislation to protect endangered species, but it may already be too late.

9 Mountain gorilla ***(Gorilla gorilla beringei) right***
Found in the mountainous regions of eastern Congo, SW Uganda and W Ruanda. The present population is thought to lie between 5000 and 15000 animals. Average height of male is 66 in (168 cm). The chief threat comes from habitat destruction by pastoralists and large herds of domestic animals.

10 Monkey-eating eagle
(Pithecophaga jefferyi) above
Long a fashionable trophy in the Philippine islands, this eagle was subjected to uncontrolled hunting by man. Late in 1964 it was estimated there were no more than 40, on two islands. Today urgent measures are being taken to try to insure their survival. Propaganda aimed at discrediting collection of trophies is linked with strict new legislation. Average wingspan 72 in (183 cm.).

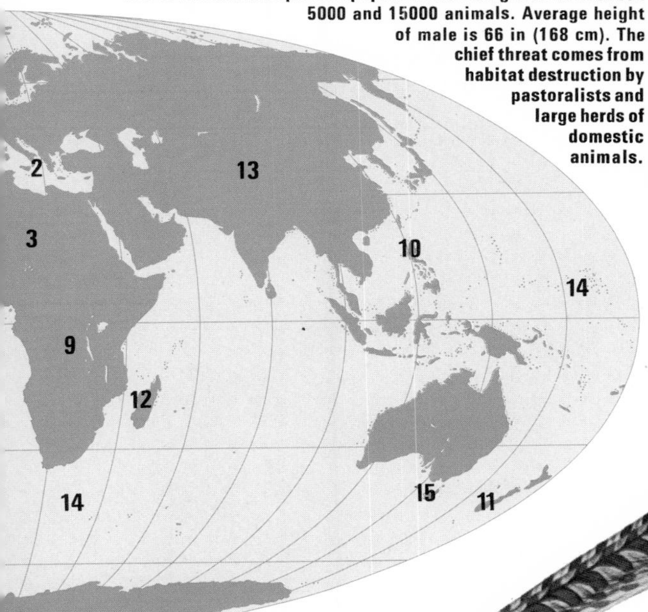
2
13
3
10
14
9
12
14
15
11

11 Kakapo
(Strigops habroptilus) right
Before the coming of man, New Zealand possessed a unique range of fauna. It included numerous flightless birds, but as soon as man and such imports as dogs, cats, rats and ferrets appeared in numbers, these unfortunate creatures found survival difficult or impossible. The kakapo, a stumpy-winged parrot, is on the verge of extinction; fewer than 100 are left. Average length 24in (61 cm).

12 Long-tailed ground roller
(Uratelornis chimaera) above
Another island having unique species is Madagascar. One is the ground roller, which searches for insects among dead leaves, and seldom flies. More than half its length is its eight inch (200 mm) tail. Destruction of its specialized habitat has confined the few survivors to a tiny coastal area.

13 Snow leopard ***(Panthera unica) left***
The range of this great cat extends over the entire mountainous zone of central Asia, from Afghanistan deep into China, and extends almost to 20000 ft (6000 m). Powerful and cunning, it can be a formidable predator of both wild and domestic animals, but it has been ruthlessly hunted for its valuable fur. Today its numbers do not exceed 400 and may not reach half this. Average length 84 in (312 cm).

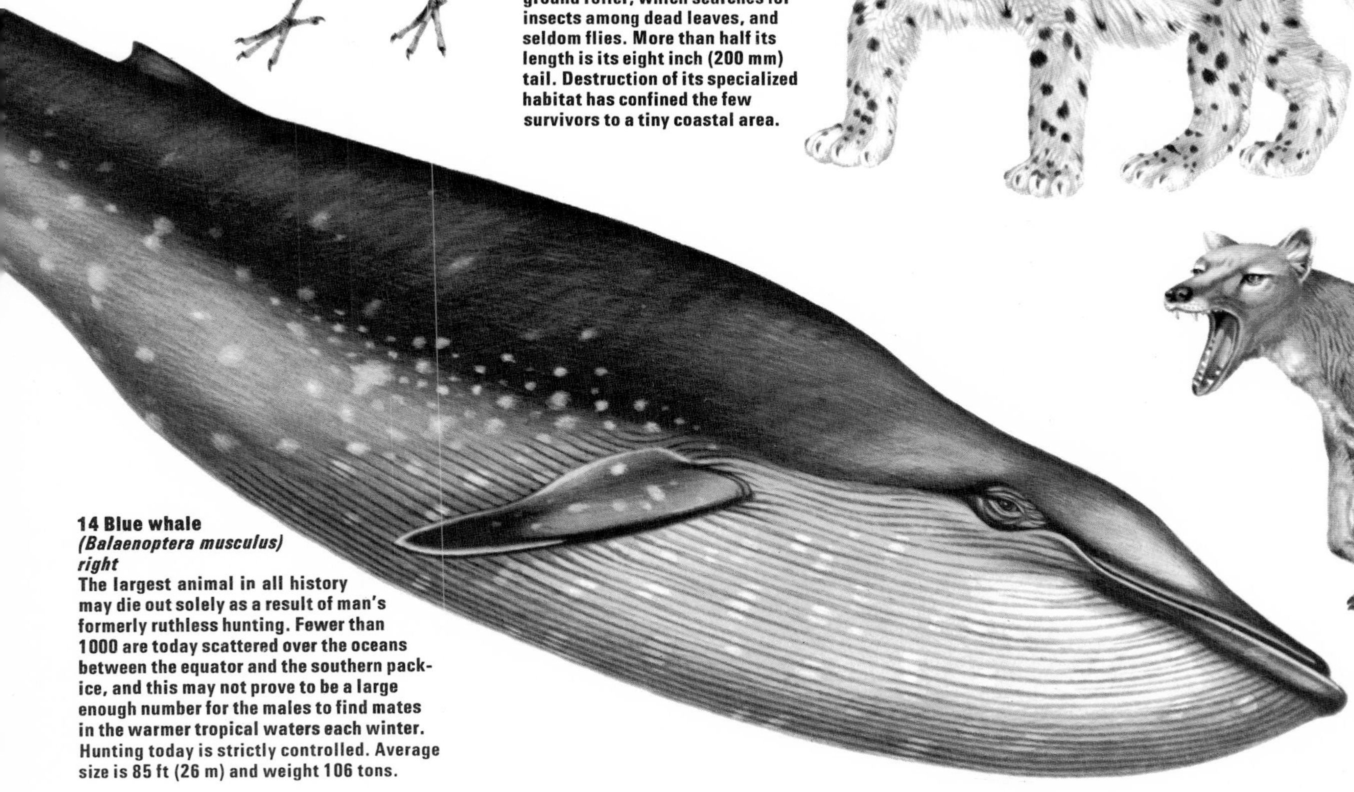

14 Blue whale
(Balaenoptera musculus) right
The largest animal in all history may die out solely as a result of man's formerly ruthless hunting. Fewer than 1000 are today scattered over the oceans between the equator and the southern pack-ice, and this may not prove to be a large enough number for the males to find mates in the warmer tropical waters each winter. Hunting today is strictly controlled. Average size is 85 ft (26 m) and weight 106 tons.

15 Thylacine ***(Thylacinus cynocephalus) above***
In many ways this species resembles the wolf, which developed in parallel on the other side of the world, but it differs basically in being a marsupial—it is the largest carnivorous marsupial on Earth. Once common throughout Australia, it was driven out by the dingo and is fighting for survival in Tasmania. Average length 60 in (152 cm).

The Resources of the Earth

The vast geographical expanse of the Earth has beguiled man into believing that its resources could never be exhausted. Only with the dramatic growth in man's industrial and agricultural demands has it become obvious that not only does his home planet have limits, but in some instances these limits are being fast approached. Of course some new supplies remain to be discovered and others will be replaced from man-made sources, but there is no room for complacency when man continues to squander his terrestrial heritage. If all nations were ever to enjoy the same standard of life as the privileged few, the demand for energy and minerals would generate an industrial 'famine' that would bring a world-wide crisis. Already excessive demands have led in some instances to over-exploitation and dereliction of the land. If a world disaster is to be averted, man must discover a new relationship with the Earth and learn to manage and to conserve its vital resources.

Monitoring Earth's resources
With Earth's known resources under pressure, a complete global picture of them, using techniques such as infra-red photography shown here, becomes urgent. In the photo, healthy vegetation is red, stubble in a harvested field pink over blue, while roads and buildings are blue.

From Landscape to Townscape

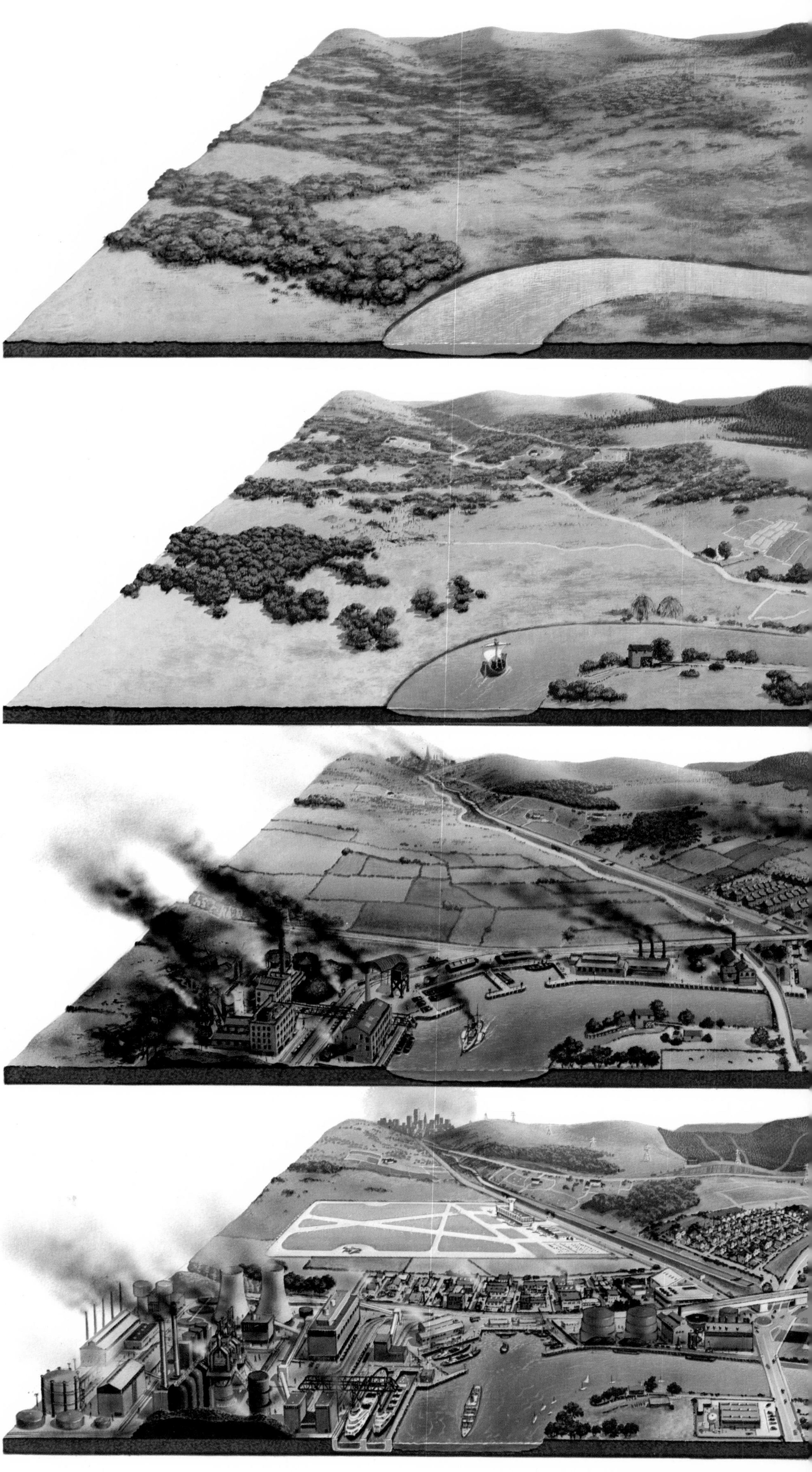

The story of man's use of the land is one of increasing diversity and complexity. Preagricultural man developed perhaps six land uses; hunting, trapping, fishing, gathering wild fruits, fashioning tools and sheltering in caves. Modern man has developed several thousand forms, and frequently concentrates hundreds within a single square mile. For most of them he has created distinctive environments; one can tell at a glance whether the land is being used to grow carrots, make cement, repair ships, treat sewage, sell antiques, mine coal or educate children.

Although every place is unique in the ways its land uses intermingle, we can nevertheless recognize five major land-use patterns. Each has sprung into prominence at some major crossroads in human history. The first of the five is wildscape, which man uses so lightly and so rarely that nature is still in chief control. Some of it is still almost wholly natural, as in the remote parts of the Antarctic icecap. Other areas have been quite profoundly changed, as on the Pennine moorlands where generations of sheep have nibbled away tree seedlings and prevented the regeneration of forest, or where polluted air is now preventing the growth of sphagnum moss. But these areas are still wildscape. Man uses their resources but he leaves nature to replenish them.

The rural landscape evolves

Farmscape dates from man's first great technical advance, the Neolithic agricultural revolution of about 8000 years ago. For the first time he began to alter the landscape and live with the results instead of moving on; he ploughed and harvested, enclosed fields and diverted water for irrigation. During subsequent millennia this more controlled form of land-use spread over enormous areas of every continent, with a cumulative stream of diversifications as man applied his ingenuity to it in different environments. The rural landscape was now distinctively divided into the wild and the cultivated.

Townscape also existed from an early date, but had to await man's second great technical advance before it could develop at all extensively. Not until the twin agrarian and industrial revolutions of the 18th century did agriculture develop sufficiently to support a vastly greater population than its own labor force, or industry develop sufficiently to be able to employ a vast non-agricultural population. Once this possibility was established as a world trend, townscape began to develop rapidly.

Conflicts in land use

There are now three 'scapes' of increasing artificiality and complexity, respectively dominated by nature, the individual farmer and the public authority. So different are these three 'scapes' that problems tend to arise where they confront and interact with each other. Unfortunately such fringes of conflict have been intensified as side effects of two otherwise beneficial transport revolutions.

The first, or long-distance, transport revolution began with the steamship and the train in the 19th century. It opened up competition in foodstuffs on a global scale: the benefit was cheaper food from more favored areas, and the cost was the decline of less-favored areas. Some farmscape reverted to wildscape, resolving the problem. Elsewhere, the land remained good enough to reclaim in times of booming prices but too poor to be profitable in times of recession. The result in such areas is recurrent farm poverty.

The long-distance transport revolution also had a similar effect upon less competitive mining areas which tended to become derelict as a result, forming rurban (rural-urban) fringe. The main growth of rurban fringe, however, was stimulated by the second, or personal, transport revolution, in which the car gave city workers the opportunity to live in the country and commute daily to a neighboring city. The result was an unprecedented intermingling of urban areas and farmland, and an unprecedented degree of conflict between the two. Farmland became fragmented and subjected to many kinds of urban pressures so that much of it became uneconomic to farm. The urban area, on the other hand, experienced many difficulties in service facilities, because its sprawling layout multiplied distances and costs. Thus both marginal fringe and rurban fringe have become areas of patchy, conflicting landuses.

Prehistoric landscape
The natural prehistoric landscape consisted of a series of wildscape ecosystems wherein all forms of life interacted in a stable balance of nature. The land falls from distant hills to a coastal plain where the river widens into a broad estuary. Woodlands partially cover the plains, thinning into scrub on the hills. Stone age man used this wildscape in diffuse and restricted ways. He roamed the forest and heath hunting game but, apart from a cave shelter or toolmaking floor, rarely set aside land for a particular use. He exerted no perceptible influence upon the landscape apart from the fact that grazing animals gradually retarded the regeneration of the forest and led to a more open vegetation. But the presence of flat land, water, coal, stone and good access were ideal for later man.

Medieval
After he had developed agriculture man was able to use the land in more ways. It is possible by this time to detect at least a dozen types of stable land use. This was basically an age of slowly developing farmscape, when wildscape was reclaimed for food production and most settlement was designed to serve agricultural communities. Villagers are cultivating open strip fields in rotation for winter corn, spring corn and fallowing, surrounded by common grazing lands. The improved standard of shelter is reflected in clearance of forest to obtain timber, and the land is quarried for clay (near left), stone (left) and iron ore (backgroupd). With such burdens man has improved his transport methods. And the river is now becoming polluted.

19th Century
The industrial revolution was a marked change in man's use of land. Coal was deep-mined as a source of unprecedented power which led to the concentration of crafts in large factories. Gasworks, flour mills and textile mills were basic industries, in turn leading to an industrial townscape. Different types of land use can be measured by the score. Building stone and brick-making continue to flourish, but imports have replaced the old ironworkings. Agriculture plays its part by more efficient production from larger fields to support the growing population. Greatly improved communications are evident. But there is marked pollution of both the river and the atmosphere, and filter beds and clean-water reservoirs are necessary.

Modern
Land uses are now so differentiated as to be countless. Many hundreds of new uses are service functions, ranging from financial institutions to children's playgrounds (the former brick pit) and hairdressers. Dwellings abound in great variety, many of them made of new materials by new methods Electricity has wrought a revolution that extends to virtually every human construction, and the urgent demand for better transport has led to a complete transformation of the scene on this ground alone. A more subtle effect of better transport is that uneconomic local farming has given way to imported food, and much of the land is being reforested. Perhaps most important of all is the fact that man has become concerned about his environment.

Battles for the Land

Land use involves environmental control. Even the primitive camel-drawn plough implies two major discoveries in the art of controlling nature: the removal of weeds that compete with the crop and the supplementation of human energy by that of animals. Contour plowing to prevent soil erosion is a more advanced technique, based upon scientific experiment in place of trial and error intuition, as is also the use of modern fertilizers and the realization that animal manures can offset the long-term defects of chemical fertilizers. The controlled supply of water reaches a sophisticated level in Asia where hill slopes are remodelled to facilitate the systematic irrigation and drainage of rice crops, and even more so in Holland where dike drainage operates against gravity. The Dutch not only create new land with controlled agricultural characteristics but also specialize in controlling crop climates by the artificial supply of water, warmth, and sometimes even light, in greenhouses — a technique certain to grow in importance.

But irrigation water may act as a medium for the upward movement of salts in toxic concentrations, and so destroy the resource it was designed to create. Clear-felling of mountain forests, or over-grazing by hill sheep, may expose slopes to soil erosion. Erosion is not usually a danger in long-grass country but experiments prove that cattle thrive less at the two bites a minute possible on long grass than at the 90 bites a minute possible on grass kept to 4 in (10 cm). Proper control of the environment is not possible without its proper understanding; nature can be coaxed but not bullied.

Rice terraces *left*
The hardy and versatile rice plant sustains half the world's population. Terraces such as these in Bali, Indonesia, hold the essential water in the rainy season. Cultivation in man-made shallow lakes is one of the most ancient methods of farming.

Sowing *above*
In the developing countries there is no alternative to the traditional methods of agriculture in which everything is done by animal power or by hand. In arid parts of India farmers use the camel as a draft animal for plowing and sowing.

Grain *right and below*
In North America cereals are grown by the most mechanized methods on the largest farms. Harvesting teams start in May in Texas. By August they reach Montana, where to conserve the limited supplies of water the land is farmed in rectangles on alternate years (right). In September the harvest reaches Alberta (below).

Greenhouses *right*
This vista of glass in the Netherlands is typical of large areas of northern Europe where man locally extends the growing season by protecting crops such as tomatoes, cucumbers and table grapes from the cold. Ultimately much larger areas may be enclosed under huge membranes inflated by air. Controlling the climate will become more common.

Livestock *above and below*
Domestic animals bring to an increasing share of the world's population the higher nutritive value of animal protein. In New Zealand beef cattle (above) are second in importance to sheep; the sheep below are in Turkey.

Abuse of the land
Man is gradually learning that some apparently advanced methods of using the land involve hidden penalties. For many years there has been a move to replace traditional 'organic' farming, using livestock and dung, with inorganic man-made fertilizers. But results from British farms show a reduction in yield for the inorganic method and a gain for its predecessor (below, left). Moreover, soil on an experimental farm where conditions are closely controlled appears to have suffered in reduced ability to hold water as a result of inorganic methods (below, right). The organic soil retains a high humus content and resists breakdown.

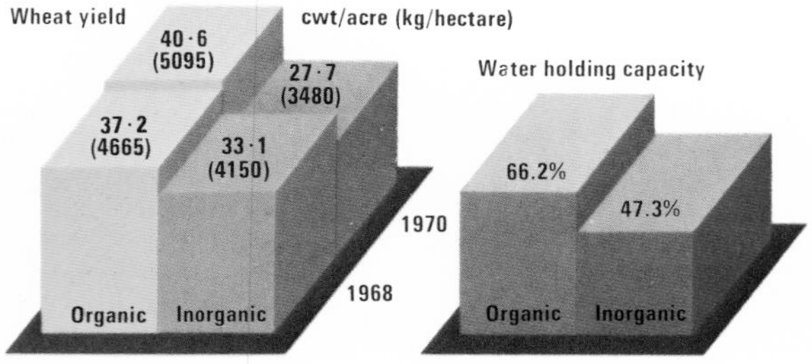
Wheat yield
cwt/acre (kg/hectare)
40·6
(5095)
27·7
(3480)
37·2
(4665)
33·1
(4150)
1970
1968
Organic
Inorganic
Water holding capacity
66.2%
47.3%
Organic
Inorganic

How the forest can be turned into Badlands.

Removal of forests by man can expose the topsoil to excessive erosion. If left unchecked, the soil is swept away leaving deep gullies as seen here (left) in California.

How poor irrigation can turn land into a salt pan.

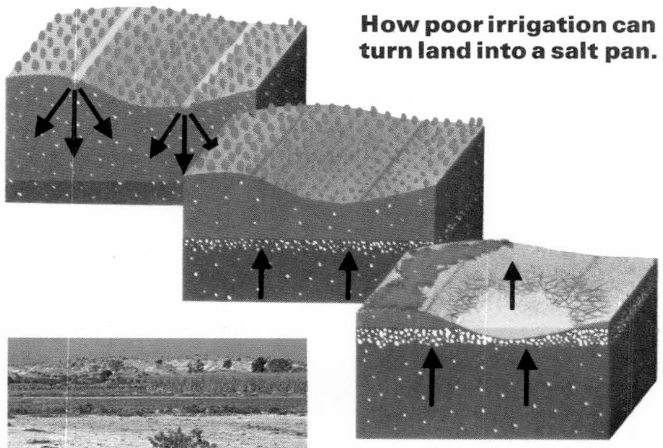

Lack of adequate drainage in irrigated areas causes the water table to rise, returning dissolved salts to the surface where they form a hard sterile crust as seen here (left) near Agra, India.

Reclaiming the land

Won from the sea *right*
For centuries the Dutch have fought the sea. At first all they could do was build hillocks to which they could retreat in times of flood. But after 1500 they discovered how to build secure embankments to keep out the water and also pump the water away and thus recover additional areas of land. This map (near right) shows the great area, half the total, that would be under salt water were it not for man-made dikes. On a larger scale (far right) are the remarkable polders which have won back 556,000 acres (225,000 hectares) from the sea since 1900.

Areas reclaimed: 13th to 19th centuries
Areas reclaimed: 20th century
Areas under preparation
Area protected by sea dikes

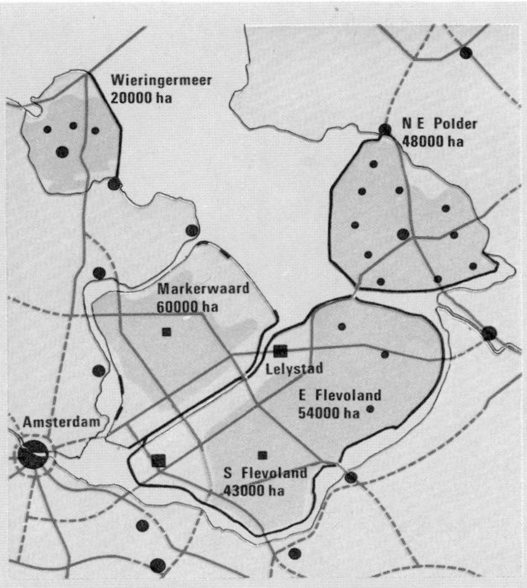

Wieringermeer
20000 ha
N E Polder
48000 ha
Markerwaard
60000 ha
Lelystad
E Flevoland
54000 ha
Amsterdam
S Flevoland
43000 ha
Existing towns
Existing villages
Planned towns
Planned villages
Completed dike
Major roads
Planned extensions
Agrarian areas

Building a polder dike
In reclaiming land by the Dutch polder method the initial operation is to dredge away soft, unstable silt (1). A suction dredger (2) then draws up sand which is positioned by barge (3) and dumped to provide an infill. Bucket dredgers then raise boulder clay which is placed by a floating crane to form a watertight dam (4) surrounding the dike. Sheet-steel piling (5) is used to form a retaining wall around the toe of the dike, on the sea side of which a watertight (continued below)

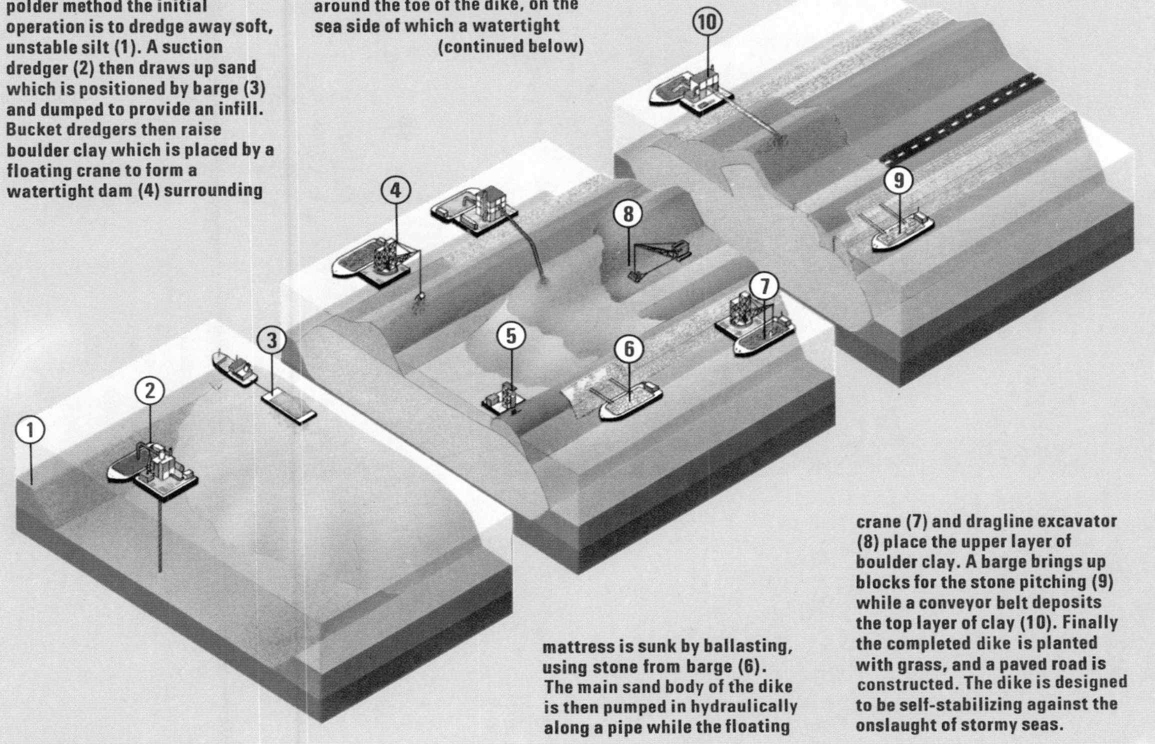

1
2
3
4
5
6
7
8
9
10

mattress is sunk by ballasting, using stone from barge (6). The main sand body of the dike is then pumped in hydraulically along a pipe while the floating crane (7) and dragline excavator (8) place the upper layer of boulder clay. A barge brings up blocks for the stone pitching (9) while a conveyor belt deposits the top layer of clay (10). Finally the completed dike is planted with grass, and a paved road is constructed. The dike is designed to be self-stabilizing against the onslaught of stormy seas.

Using new land
right and below
The Dutch polders are the only large man-made areas of land. All of them have been created in the center of one of the busiest and most densely populated areas on Earth, and putting them to use has posed exciting challenges. The north-east polder, Oostelijk Flevoland, shows how 118,000 acres (48000 hectares) have been parcelled up without creating a boring checkerboard effect, while linking up the surrounding transport systems. Particularly noteworthy is the amount of land that is devoted to recreation.

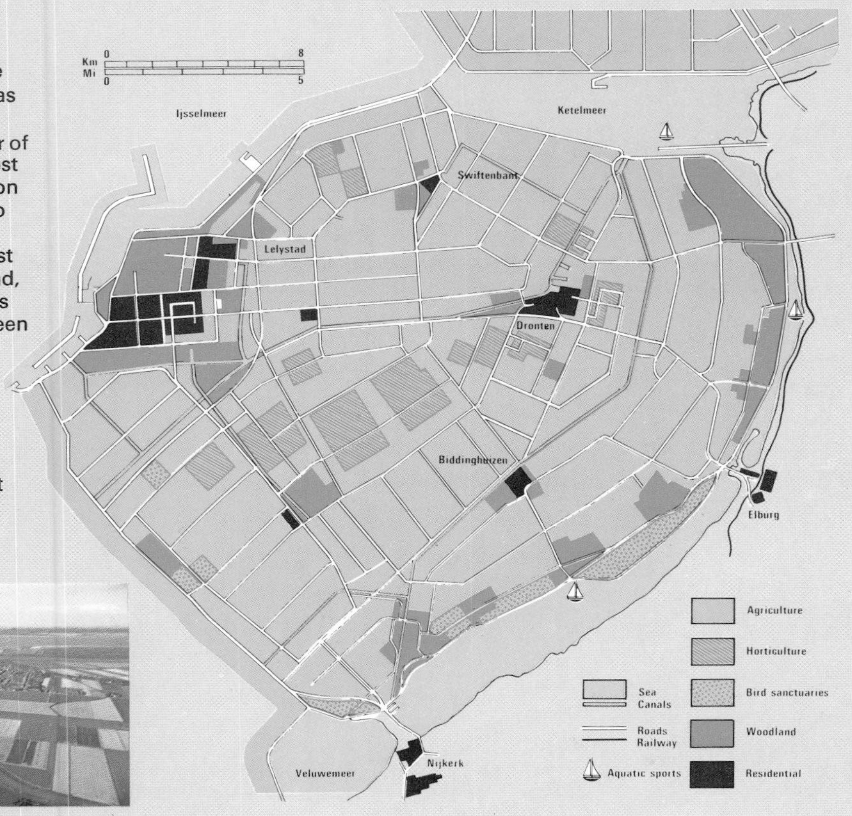

Km 0 8
Mi 0 5
IJsselmeer
Ketelmeer
Swiftenbant
Lelystad
Dronten
Biddinghuizen
Elburg
Veluwemeer
Nijkerk
Agriculture
Horticulture
Bird sanctuaries
Woodland
Residential
Sea
Canals
Roads
Railway
Aquatic sports

Primitive uses of Earth's materials

During the Paleolithic period, from about 100,000 years ago, men became increasingly curious about the materials they found around them. Many appeared to have possible uses as a fuel, a structure, a tool or a decoration. Early man clearly experimented. Such trial and error must have been often exciting, sometimes lethal and often the route to capabilities which are lost to modern man. Such enterprise has a snowball effect, each new discovery opening a path to others until by the end of the Mesolithic about 9000 years ago man had mastered nearly all the technologies not involving metals. Housing, clothing, tools, agriculture and the beginnings of mass production had reached stages still practiced today, as shown below. At the end of the Neolithic, possibly about 6000 years ago in what is today Iraq, men began to use native copper, silver and gold, and about 500 years later discovered how to make copper and tin into bronze. From the Mediterranean to China many utensils have improved little in 4000 years.

Pottery
Neolithic shards show that pottery was as important then as stone. The Indian village potter (right) is making beakers. Below, from the left, are an Algerian jug copied from a design of Neolithic Cyprus, and products of Spain, Palestine and the Cameroons.

Digging clay *left*
For about 100,000 years man has used the Earth as a construction material. One way of doing so is to choose wet earth having a high clay content and fashion this into bricks which dry almost rock hard. Using a mortar of mud these are then used for walls in the method known as adobe. Alternatively houses can be made of solid clay, with or without a skeleton of poles or laths.

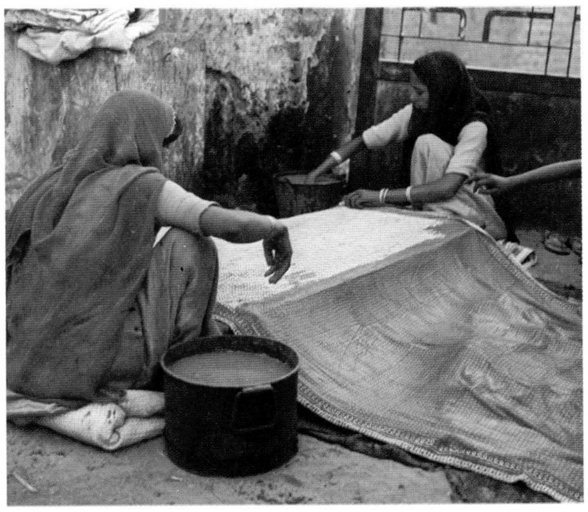

Mineral dyes

By the end of Neolithic times man was spinning a wide range of fibers into thread and rope. Settlements used different fibers and often dissimilar production methods. The girls above are dyeing cloth with a mineral dye, in Ahmadabad, India. The hand loom in Guatemala (left) is typical of American Indian designs for weaving.

Patterns of Land Use

Land-use surveys are inventories of the Earth intended both to increase academic knowledge and to resolve practical planning problems. Some have been of a specialized nature, such as detailed surveys made of dereliction in the English Midlands and of neglected land around Ottawa, but most are general and comprehensive. The first national survey in history was that of Britain directed by L. D. Stamp to study the plight of farming during the depression of the 1930s. It soon proved to have many unexpected uses. Its detailed record of farmscape aided the plow-up campaign during World War 2; its urban findings stimulated the growth of government planning; its wildscape commentary spurred the conservation movement and its derived statistics proved more accurate than many official records. A great advantage is the complete overview such surveys give.

Today most countries have undertaken detailed land-use surveys, using increasingly modern methods to secure more information. Aerial photography, using color and infra-red film, and other data-gathering methods are integrated to create a map recording vast amounts of factual data. Such maps have proved far more useful than generalized ones because different users can extract particular sets of information for their own analysis. Thus one user can trace the spread of crop disease while another designs the restoration of open-pit coal mines and quarries. Now the whole world is being surveyed in a series of maps by the UN Food and Agriculture Organization which will not merely record how man uses the Earth but will help him to use it better.

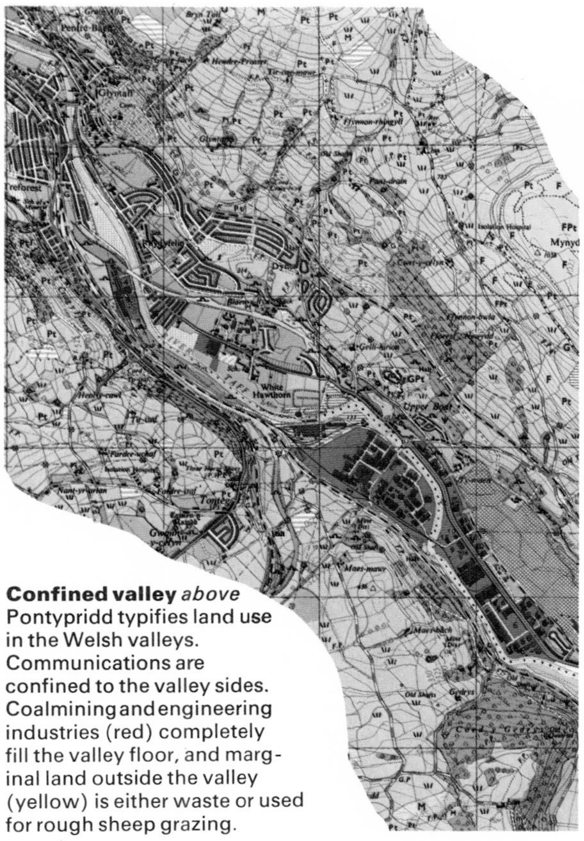

Confined valley *above*
Pontypridd typifies land use in the Welsh valleys. Communications are confined to the valley sides. Coalmining and engineering industries (red) completely fill the valley floor, and marginal land outside the valley (yellow) is either waste or used for rough sheep grazing.

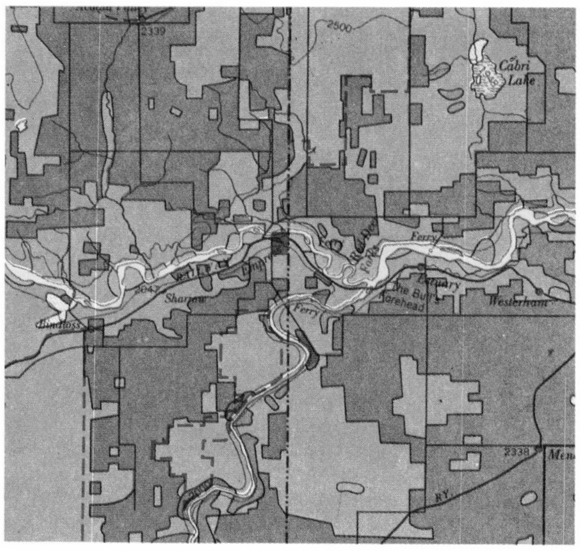

Wide open spaces *above*
Affording a total contrast with the Welsh valley, the region around the border between Alberta and Saskatchewan (left and right of vertical broken grey line) is vast and open. Roads run straight, north/south or east/west, and the fields show the large-scale rectilinear pattern of N American farming. Dark areas are spring wheat, pale regions grass for mixed farming and red lines the borders of co-operative pastures. Along the Red Deer and Saskatchewan rivers are natural, irregular scrub woodlands (green).

A dam and its problems

In 1954 the decision was taken to build the largest rockfill dam in the world near a small earlier dam at Aswan. The completion of this, one of man's greatest engineering triumphs, has brought many economic rewards—a vast increase in arable area, good flood control and a huge output of electricity. But there are many inherent environmental problems in a dam of this size—among others nutrient and silt holdback, bilharzia increase and a build-up of toxic mineral salts. The future will tell if these outweigh the advantages.

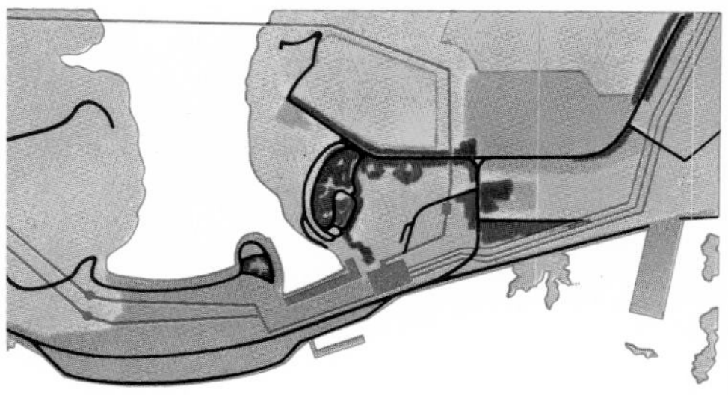

Building the dam *left*
This 1965 photograph shows concrete being placed on the main dam (left) with the power station in front. Three of the 12 turbine water tunnels, each 50 ft (15 m) in diameter, can be seen in the floor. Right, a plan of the dam site.

Abu Simbel *left*
The 3200-year-old temple of Rameses II was raised 200 ft at a cost of $40m.

The lake (1-4)
The High Dam (1) should allow two crops annually in Upper Egypt, irrigate 1,200,000 acres of new land and eliminate floods. Lake Nasser (2) will be 310 miles (500 km) long and should hold 157000 million m³. Filling is slowed by evaporation losses (3) and underground seepage (4).

Egypt's fisheries (5)
Nutrient losses have badly damaged offshore fisheries but by stocking coastal lakes and Lake Nasser the projected annual catch of 30000 tons may be attained.

The displaced people (6)
As villages are covered by the rising water 50000 Egyptian Nubians must be resettled in Nasser City, Kom Ombo and Kalabsha and 50000 in the Sudan.

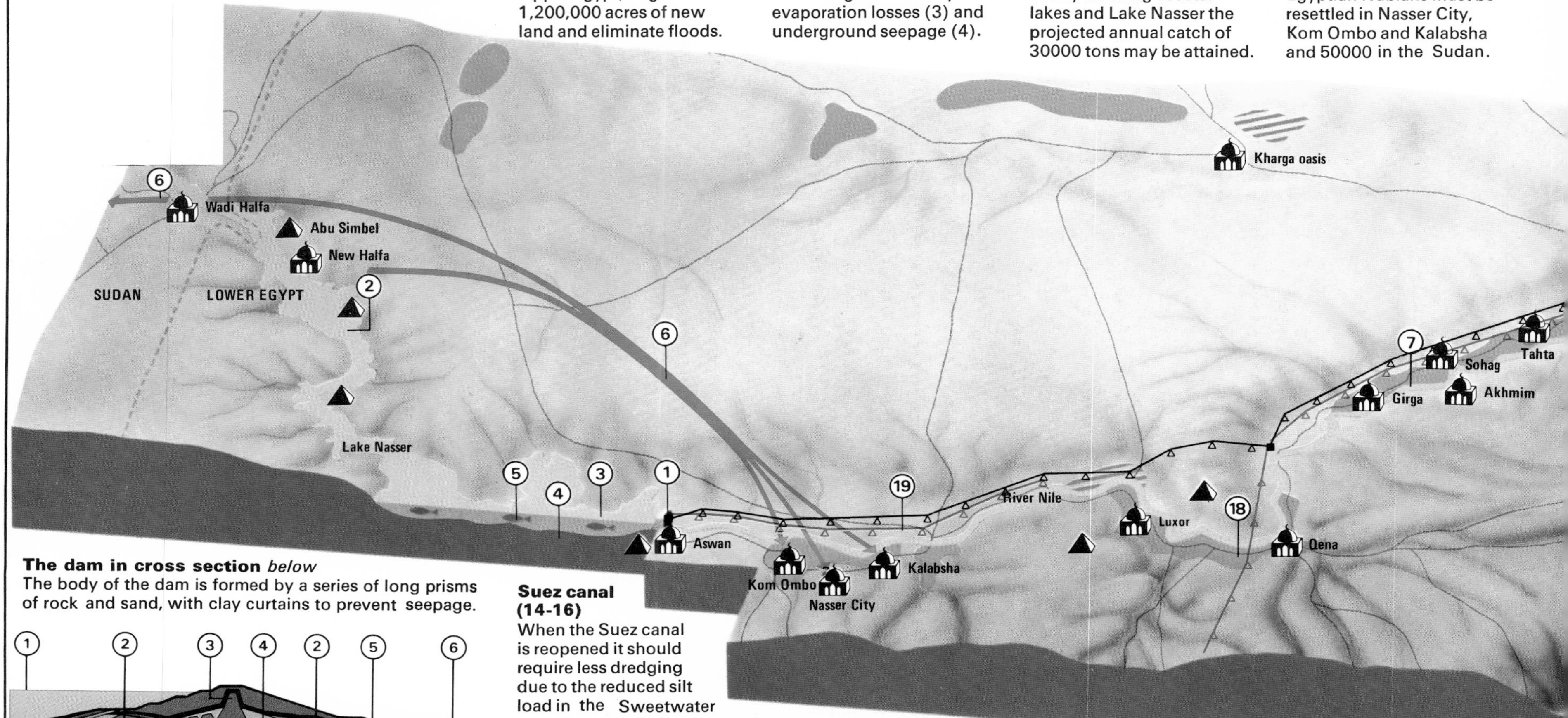

Kharga oasis
6
Wadi Halfa
Abu Simbel
New Halfa
2
SUDAN
LOWER EGYPT
6
Lake Nasser
5
4
3
1
Aswan
19
River Nile
Luxor
18
Qena
Kom Ombo
Nasser City
Kalabsha
7
Sohag
Tahta
Girga
Akhmim

The dam in cross section *below*
The body of the dam is formed by a series of long prisms of rock and sand, with clay curtains to prevent seepage.

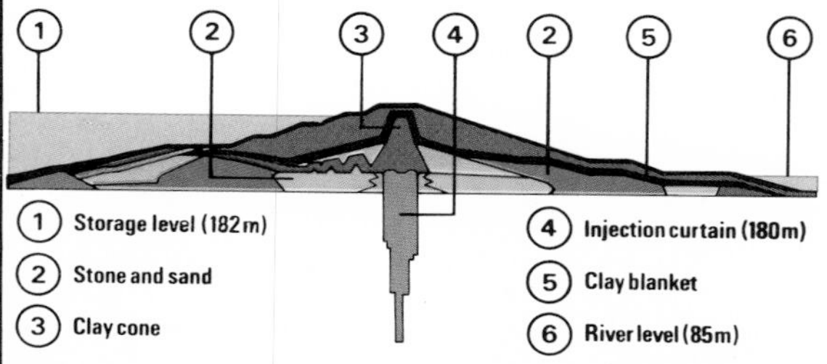

1 Storage level (182 m)
2 Stone and sand
3 Clay cone
4 Injection curtain (180 m)
5 Clay blanket
6 River level (85 m)

Suez canal (14-16)
When the Suez canal is reopened it should require less dredging due to the reduced silt load in the Sweetwater canal (14). Altered currents and the apparent reduction of the saline barrier of the Bitter Lakes (15) may allow northward migration of Red Sea species (16).

Power supply (19)
Once the power station is in full operation the annual power out-put will be 10000 million kilowatt hours. Although the project initially cost $1000 million, Egypt, already the second most industrialized country in Africa, is assured of a firm basis for development.

Hostilities (17)
Reclamation projects on the Sinai coast were halted by the 1967 war.

Crowded coast *left*
Japan's dense population is confined to a coastal strip by the steep, heavily forested hinterland (pale brown). The Hanshin urban region just west of the city of Kobe has large docks, a dense residential area (red), heavy industries (bright blue) and city-center offices (purple).

Tyneside *right*
This area in NE England has both river banks completely devoted to heavy industry, (red), as they have been for 150 years. Residential areas are set back from the river, and to the south are small mixed farms (brown) on scrub-land and some market gardening (pink).

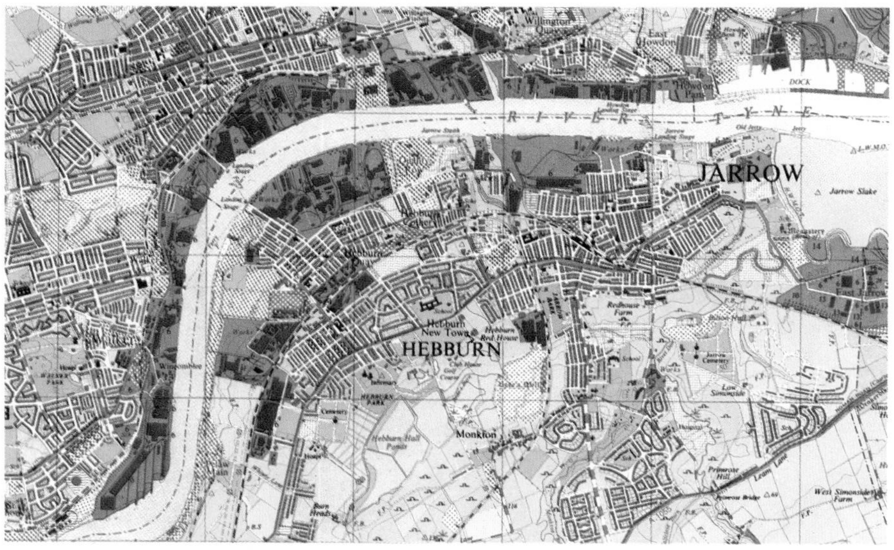

JARROW
HEBBURN

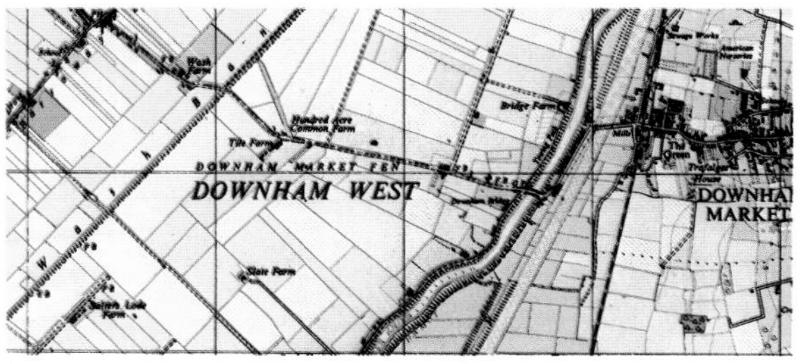

DOWNHAM WEST
DOWNHAM MARKET

The fens *left*
The low-lying flat country of East Anglia, England, was among the first ever to be artificially drained to avoid flooding and maintain high-yield arable land. Downham Market grew from a compact medieval village, and is surrounded by a varied pattern of fields all delineated by the drainage control scheme. The region produces vegetables, fruit, poultry, pigs and cereals, the latter on the larger, more modern fields which without drainage would be too wet. Many of the older plots still have the form of long, narrow rectangles of small area.

New and old *left and right*
The Aswan High Dam (under construction, left) succeeds 6000 or more years of irrigation by wells and the Archimedean screw (right). Hydro-electric power drives the new large pumps needed to handle the new irrigation flow.

Nile delta *right*
Throughout much longer than recorded history the delta of the Nile has been naturally fertile, in sharp contrast to the Sinai desert seen in the background beyond the Gulf of Suez. The dam promises to bring fertility to the arid Upper Nile region.

Control barrages (7)
Need rebuilding due to increased river erosion.

Coastal erosion (8)
The river will now carry less silt and expensive measures may be needed to control erosion. Silting, however, may continue to be a problem for the port at Damietta (9) where rebuilding plans appear to have been abandoned.

The delta (10, 11 and 13)
Fertility of delta soil (10) is now maintained not by silt but by chemical fertilizers. Plant at Aswan, Kafr-el-Zayat (13) and Suez produce 60% of requirements and it is hoped that enough fresh water will soon be available for a rice crop from a million acres of extra land (11).

Hazards (12 and 18)
Soil sterility due to accumulation of mineral salts (page 92) must be avoided by installing adequate drainage in irrigated areas (12). Bilharzia (18), a disease carried by freshwater snails, will increase but should be contained at a tolerable level.

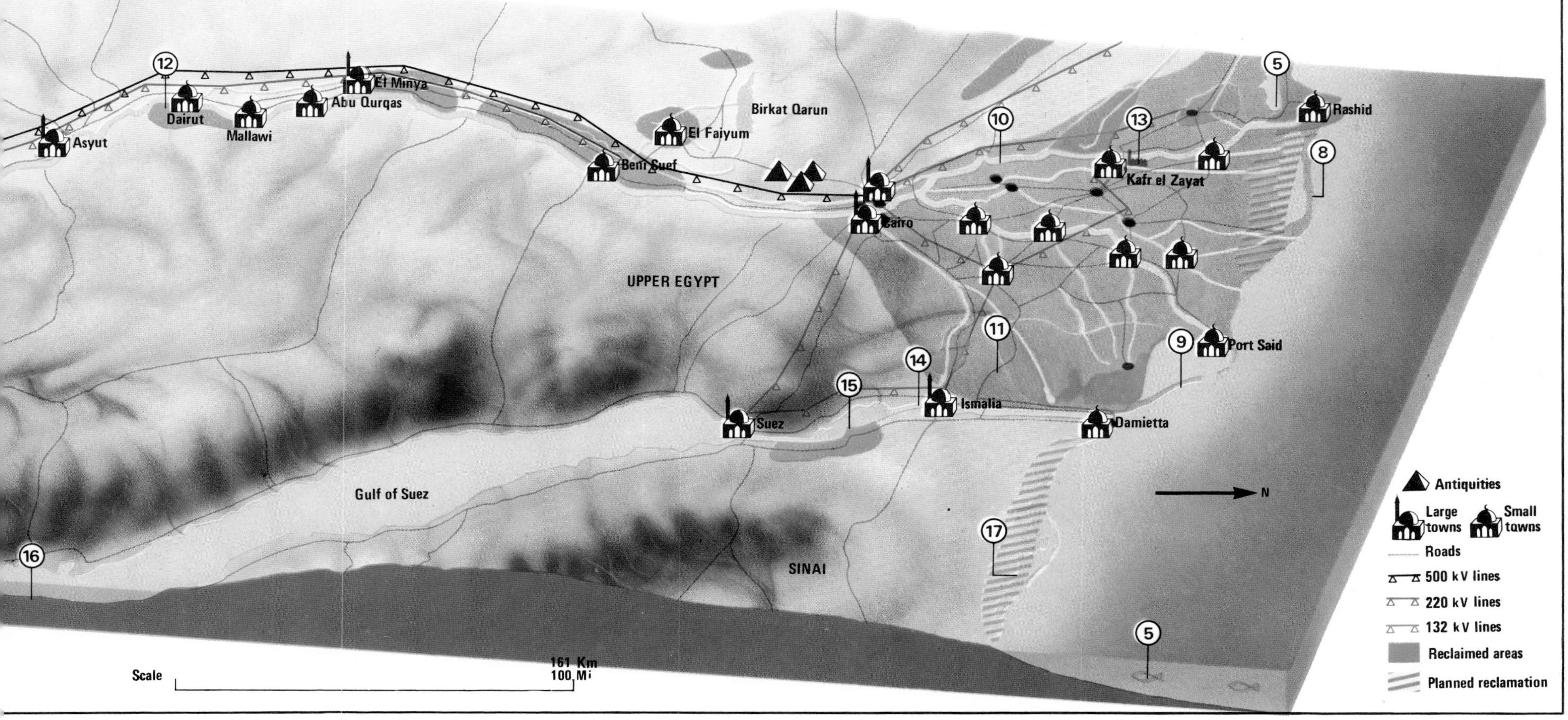

Asyut
Dairut
Mallawi
Abu Qurqas
El Minya
Birkat Qarun
El Faiyum
Beni Suef
Cairo
Rashid
Kafr el Zayat
UPPER EGYPT
Port Said
Suez
Ismalia
Damietta
Gulf of Suez
SINAI
N
Scale
161 Km
100 Mi
Antiquities
Large towns
Small towns
Roads
500 kV lines
220 kV lines
132 kV lines
Reclaimed areas
Planned reclamation

Prospecting for Minerals

Man's need for large workable deposits of mineral ores, oil and natural gas increases dramatically year by year, while the number of such deposits which can be found by ordinary surface prospecting grows smaller. Those deposits as yet unworked often lie in inaccessible parts of the Earth's crust and under many hundreds of feet of rock. Today geophysical exploration affords a means of conducting broad regional surveys so that the areas most likely to prove economically worthwhile can be selected for detailed survey and test drillings. Without these techniques vital minerals would be considerably more expensive.

Geophysical prospecting is based on the fact that minerals and rocks display a wide range of physical characteristics which can be recorded, both directly and by inference, at the surface. The three landscapes below show the three major techniques in common use today. The main properties exploited are: elasticity, which directly affects the speed of propagation of seismic waves (1); magnetic characteristics (2); and density, which causes local changes in the value of gravity (3). For example, a large dense ore body lying within a less dense geological formation could be recorded as an anomaly on a regional gravimetric survey, as would a strongly magnetized formation on a regional magnetic survey. Radioactive minerals, such as pitchblend, a major source of uranium, may be detected by a geiger counter sensing their particle emissions (page 45). In addition to these main techniques, particular minerals can be detected by other methods; for example, silver and mercury may be found by sensitive air 'sniffers'.

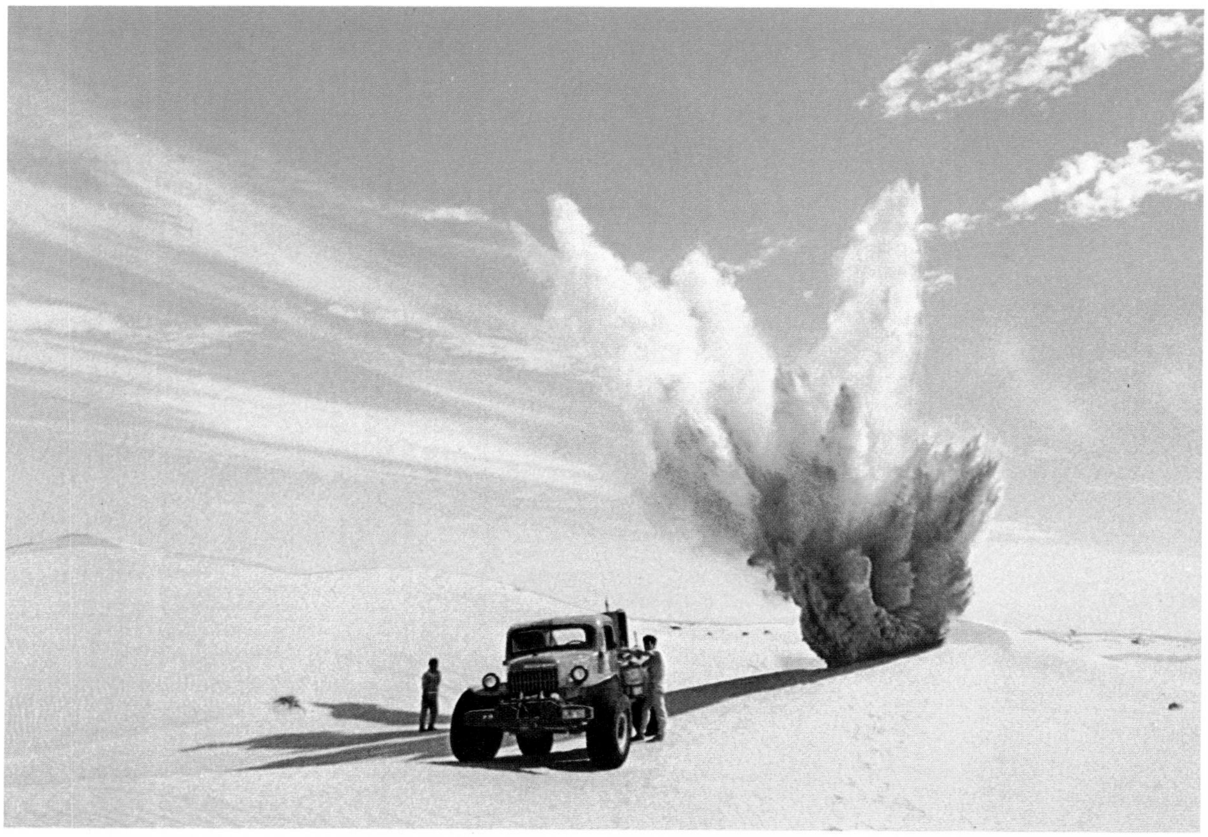

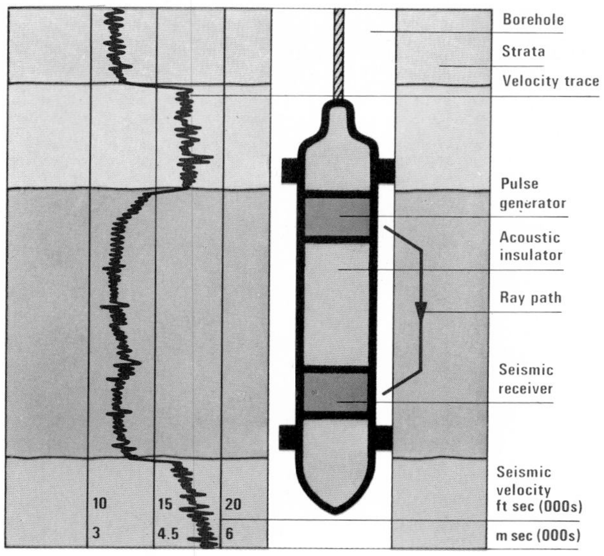

Borehole
Strata
Velocity trace
Pulse generator
Acoustic insulator
Ray path
Seismic receiver
Seismic velocity ft sec (000s)
m sec (000s)
10
15
20
3
4.5
6

Well logging *below*
Once a regional survey has shown a promising area, specific features in it can be resurveyed in detail. A well is bored at each selected location and into it is lowered a measuring instrument chosen to highlight the characteristic sought. The seismic unit (below) emits a series of shock waves as it is lowered down a borehole. The time taken by the waves to travel between the transmitter and receiver on the 4 ft (1.2 m) unit depends on the density of the surrounding rock so that the velocity trace (at left of diagram) provides a record of the successive strata.

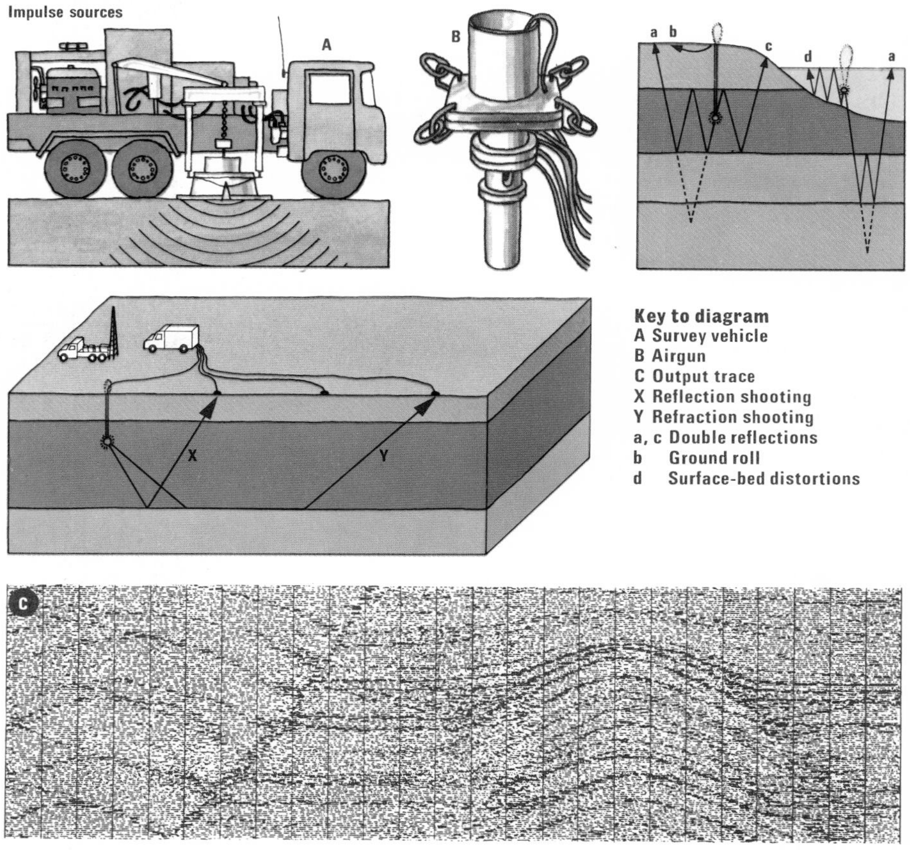

Impulse sources
A
B
a b c d a
X
Y
C
Key to diagram
A Survey vehicle
B Airgun
C Output trace
X Reflection shooting
Y Refraction shooting
a, c Double reflections
b Ground roll
d Surface-bed distortions

Seismic survey (1) *right*
Earthquake investigations have yielded knowledge of shock waves which is put to use in finding deposits. Shock waves are sound waves of high intensity that travel through the crust for great distances, being reflected as from a mirror by abrupt changes in the strata. A shockwave can be generated by various methods. A vibrator can be mounted on a vehicle; a high-energy spark discharge or explosive can be used, and at sea an airgun. The waves can be detected by geophones after reflection shooting (X) or refraction shooting (Y), taking care to avoid double reflections, ground roll and reflection between sea surface and bed. The output trace (C) from the survey below reveals a fault and a dome. The shockwave is here generated by an explosive charge, which sends out waves reflected off the dome to the four geophones. The received impulses are transmitted to a recording caravan.

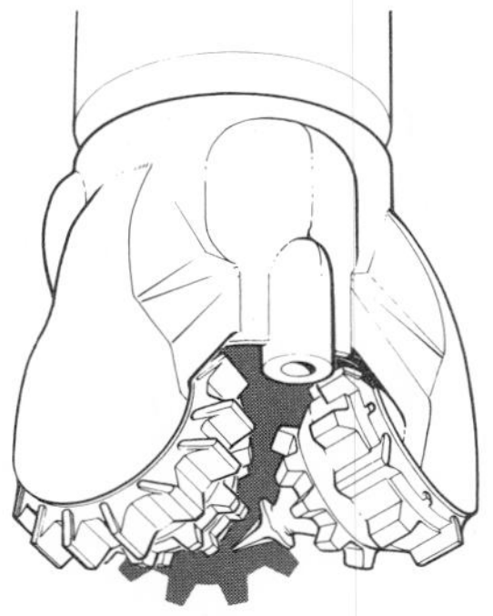

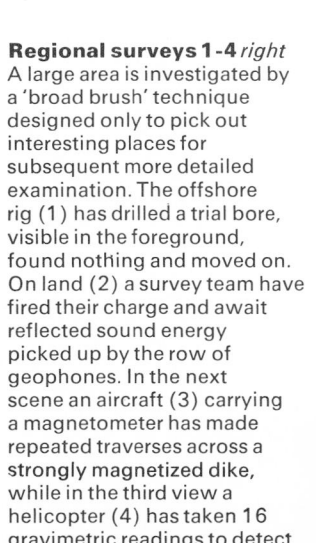

Drill bit *above*
The search for minerals has led to the development of many types of drill head but the most common rock bit (above) uses the weight of the rotating tubular drill string to force gear teeth into the rock.

Regional surveys 1-4 *right*
A large area is investigated by a 'broad brush' technique designed only to pick out interesting places for subsequent more detailed examination. The offshore rig (1) has drilled a trial bore, visible in the foreground, found nothing and moved on. On land (2) a survey team have fired their charge and await reflected sound energy picked up by the row of geophones. In the next scene an aircraft (3) carrying a magnetometer has made repeated traverses across a strongly magnetized dike, while in the third view a helicopter (4) has taken 16 gravimetric readings to detect a dense ore body.

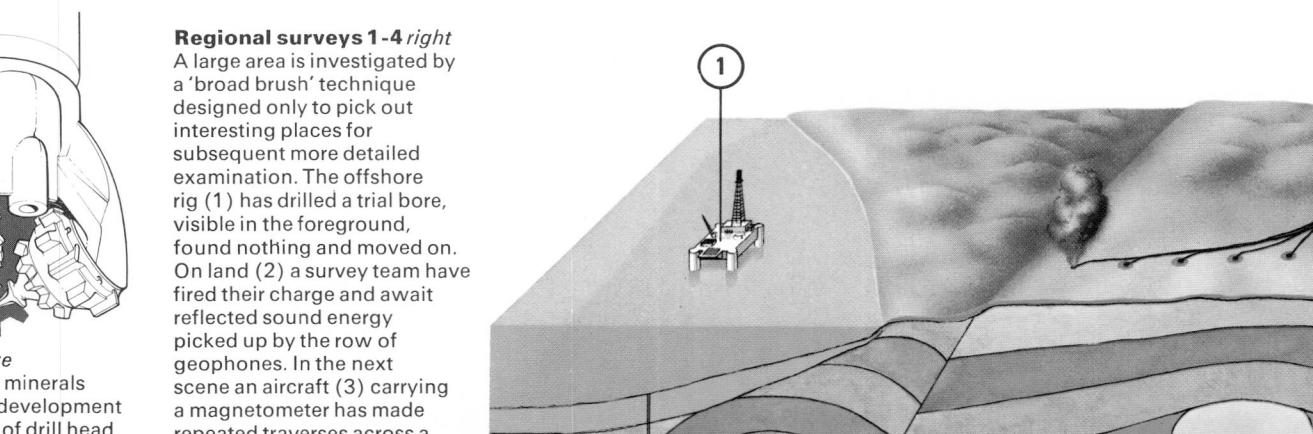

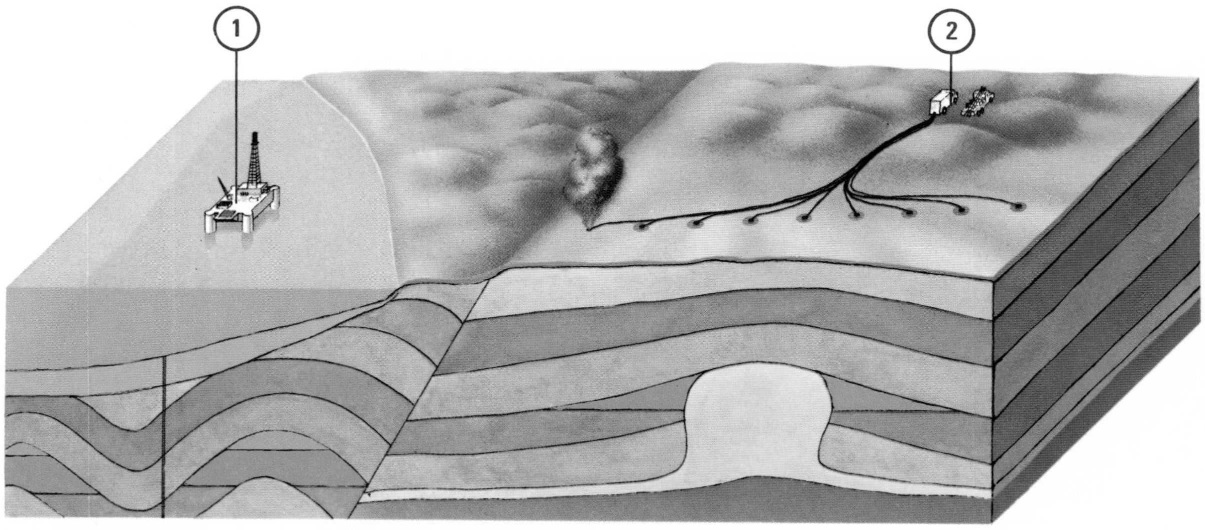

1
2

Contrasts in mining
Exploitation of the Earth's mineral resources frequently involves a compromise between ecological and visual despoliation and a profitable business. The vast machine seen in the background above is no longer used, because its trenching of the US Midwest in search of metal ores left a useless trail of processed overburden. In Zambia, open-pit copper mines (such as the Nchanga pit, right) leave huge scars on the landscape, but in Britain legislation now exists to ensure that after such mining operations the topsoil is returned. Modern coal mining (in Ayrshire, below) puts waste back underground.

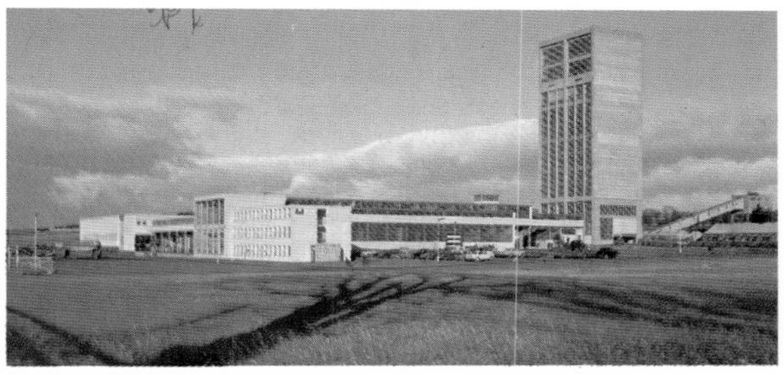

Magnetic survey (2) *right*
Regional magnetic surveys are carried out using an airborne magnetometer which measures the detailed strength and direction of the Earth's magnetic field. In this way local variations caused by the presence of magnetic minerals can be detected and their location determined accurately. An airborne magnetometer covers large areas of territory each day and accurate readings can be obtained in less than half a second. Flying over sloping strata with two strongly magnetized dikes projecting up to the surface would yield two clear peaks in the recorded trace, plotted in gammas (right). When the overall regional magnetic contours are plotted, the dike shows up clearly as if it were a mountain range. This provides a valuable coarse-scale indication of the location of a magnetic deposit, such as the iron ore known as magnetite. With this knowledge, borehole logging may be resorted to in carefully chosen places to refine the survey.

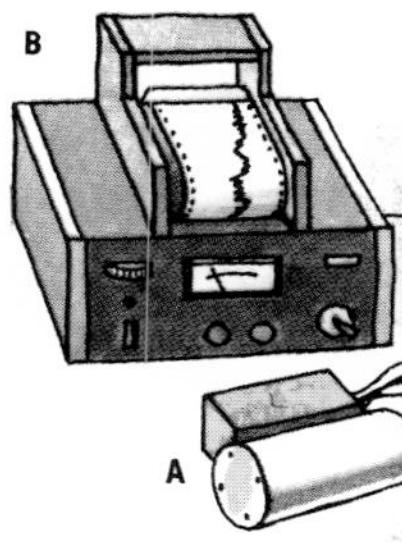
B
A

Magnetic readings
When a sensitive magnetometer (A) is passed across the surface it measures the vertical and horizontal components of the Earth's magnetic field and generates a varying output which can be plotted on a pen/chart recorder (B). During analysis the resulting readings may be 'screened' to remove regional field values and highlight local anomalies.

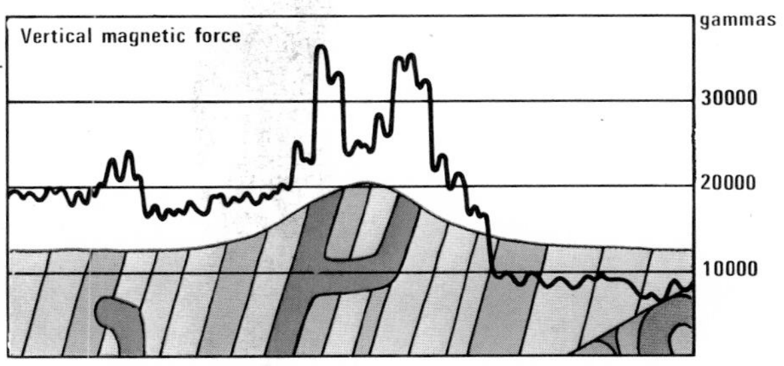
Vertical magnetic force
gammas
30000
20000
10000

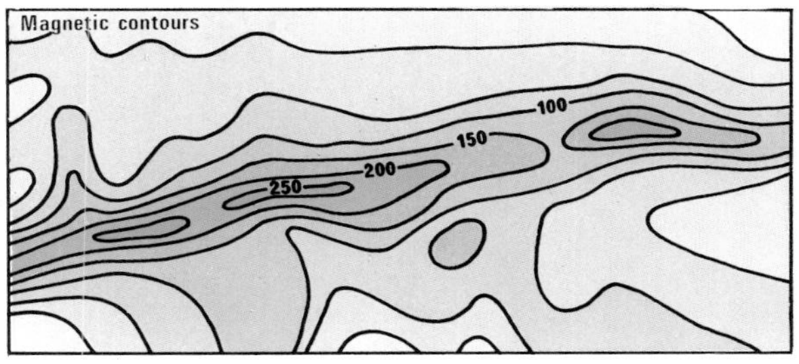
Magnetic contours
100
150
200
250

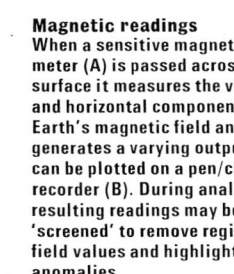

Gravimetric survey (3) *right*
Any mass of unusually high or low density, for example a salt dome, creates a localized anomaly in the gravity field. If known distortions caused by the Sun, Moon, latitude and height above sea level (h) are allowed for this small anomaly may disclose the presence of economically workable mineral deposits. In the Worden gravimeter (A) a vacuum flask (a) encloses a sensitive quartz mechanism (b) distorted by variations in the field. Its microscopic motions are magnified and read against a scale through an eyepiece. The regional field is first plotted (fine horizontal lines, right), perhaps by using a gravimeter placed at intervals by a helicopter (below). Any kinks in these lines (heavy lines on gravimetric plot, right) indicate a local anomaly. The position of the body causing the disturbance can then be indicated by plotting the discrepancies as a series of closed rings on the contours (right). The units are milligals (mgal).

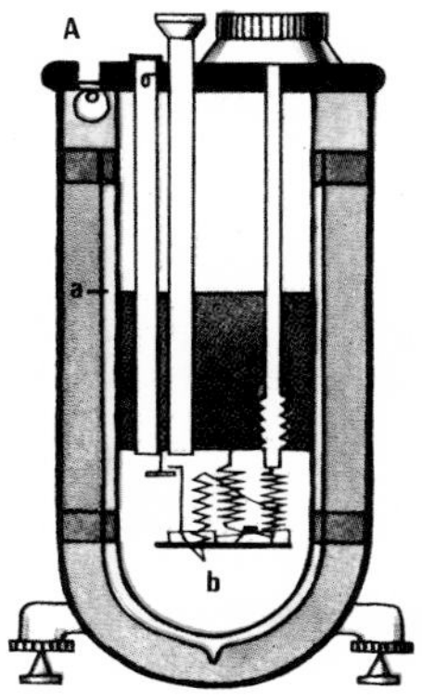
A
a
b

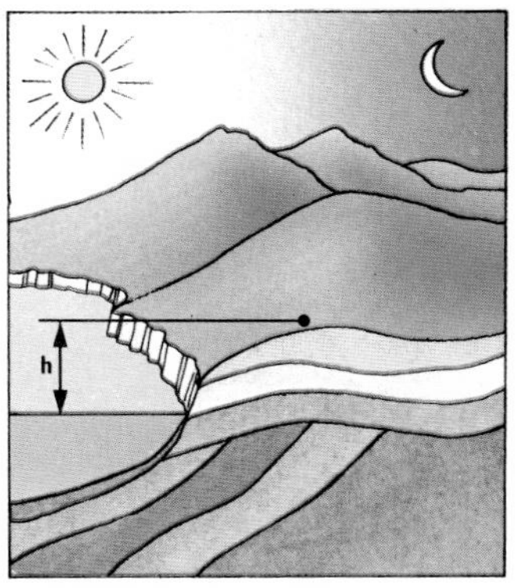
h

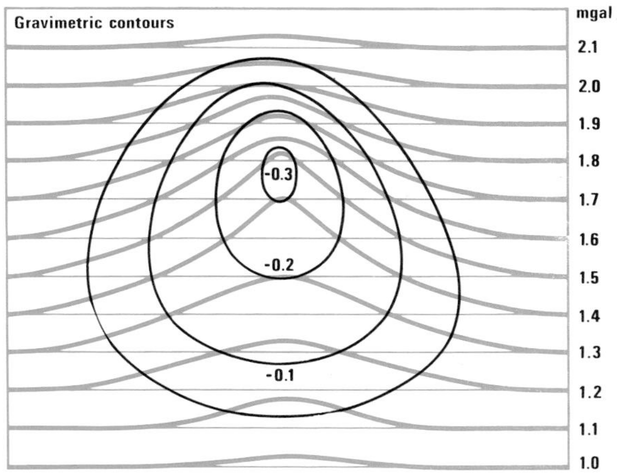
Gravimetric contours
mgal
2.1
2.0
1.9
1.8
1.7
1.6
1.5
1.4
1.3
1.2
1.1
1.0
-0.3
-0.2
-0.1

3

4

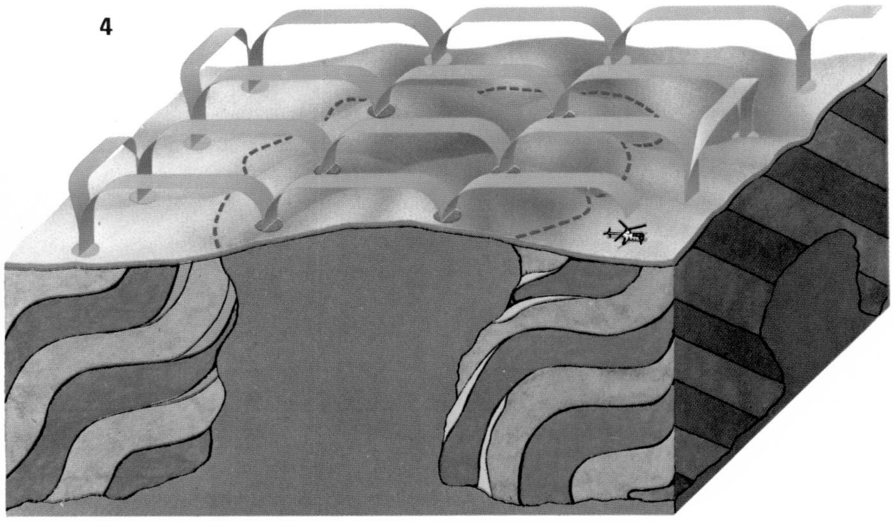

Minerals under the Land

Of about 2000 minerals in the Earth's crust only 100 or so are of economic importance. These are distributed very irregularly, so that no country today can boast all the minerals it needs. As a result minerals are a source of great national wealth, exploitation and even of rivalry. And the strife is likely to intensify as man's demands grow, because the total of the Earth's minerals is limited.

Against this background of uneven distribution, economic warfare and sharply increasing demand, man's use of minerals constantly changes. Coal, in 1920 the most important mineral in the world on a tonnage basis, is today unable to compete in several of its former markets because of the high cost of transporting it, and its use is increasingly changing from that of a fuel to that of a raw material for plastics and chemicals. Nitrates for fertilizers and explosives sustained the economy of Chile until 1914, when Germany found a way to 'fix' nitrogen from the atmosphere. Aluminum, one the most abundant minerals, was costly and little used until a large-scale refining process was discovered which made use of cheap hydroelectricity.

Taking the broad view, the Earth's minerals are seen as a stern test of man's ability to make proper use of the resources available to him. Already some nations have amassed enormous stockpiles of what are today considered to be strategically important minerals. Nickel is one such metal, and the bulk of the world's supply comes from Canada. Another is manganese, and in this case the dominant supplier is the Soviet Union; but manganese is one of the many minerals which might be dredged from the sea bed.

Uneven distribution of minerals is paralleled by uneven consumption. Paradoxically, the industrialized countries which owed their original development to the presence of mineral resources, particularly iron and coal, now rely for their continued prosperity on developing nations. If the latter were to develop a similar demand for materials a mineral famine would ensue which would have repercussions throughout the world.

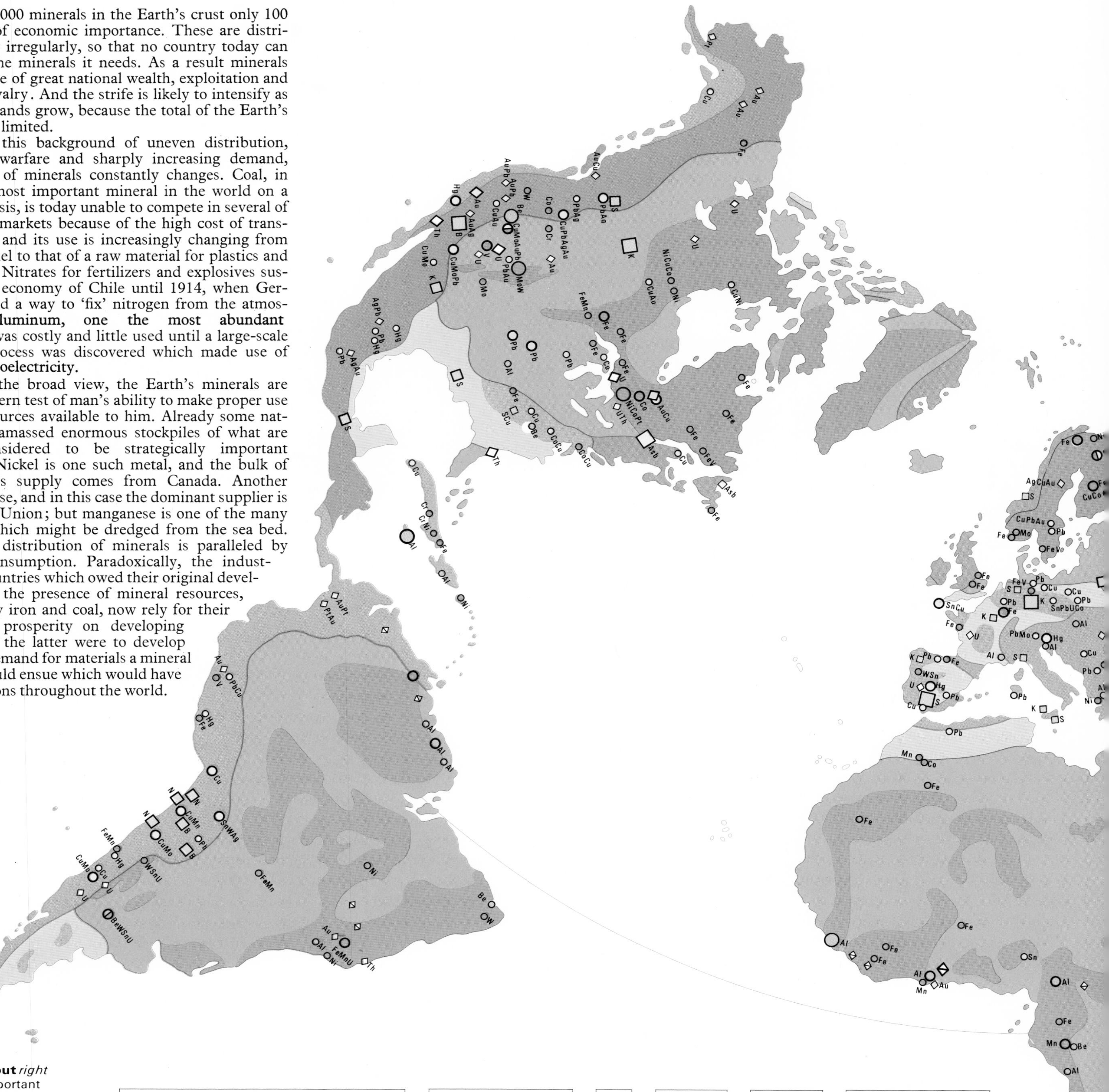

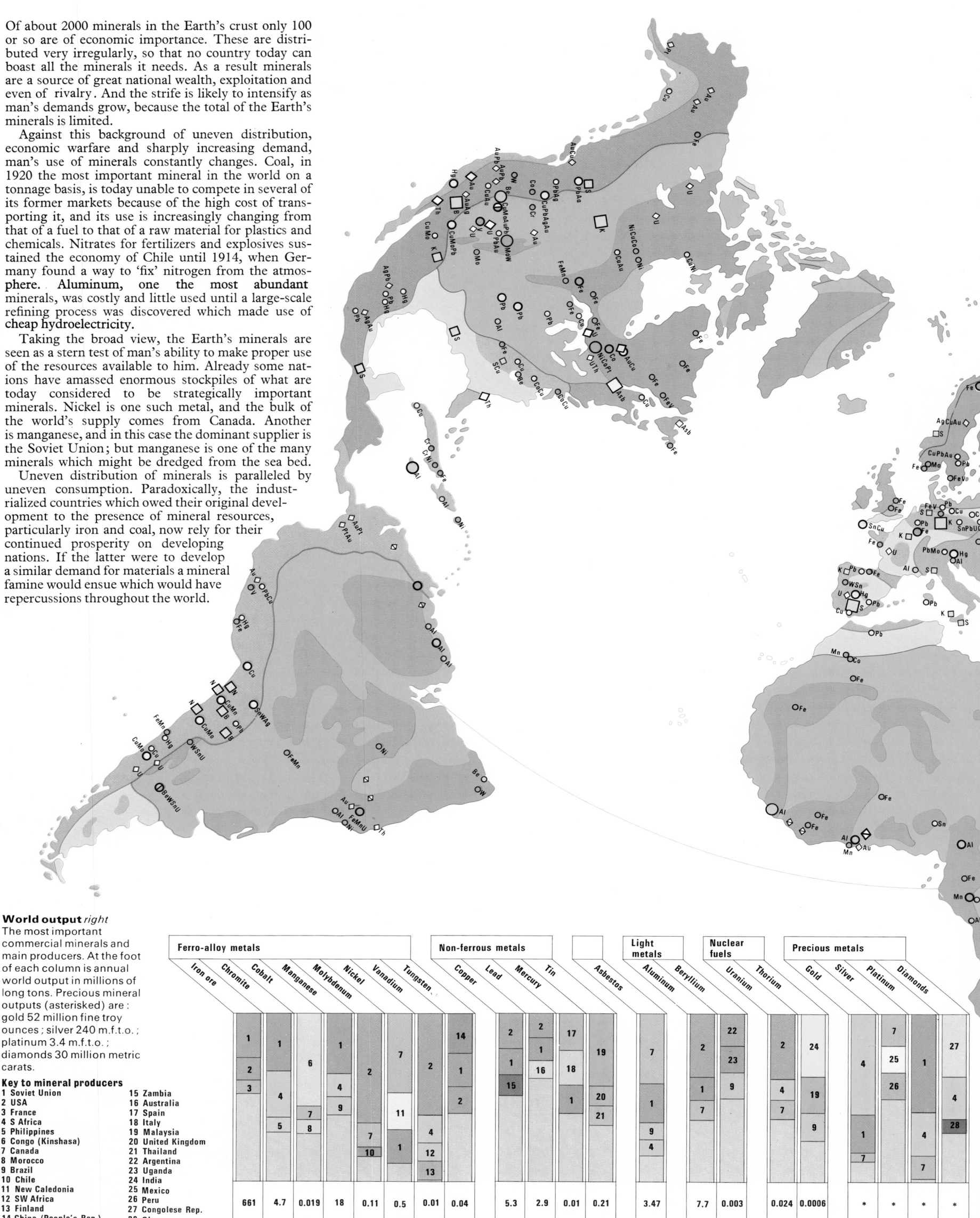

World output *right*
The most important commercial minerals and main producers. At the foot of each column is annual world output in millions of long tons. Precious mineral outputs (asterisked) are: gold 52 million fine troy ounces; silver 240 m.f.t.o.; platinum 3.4 m.f.t.o.; diamonds 30 million metric carats.

Key to mineral producers

1 Soviet Union
2 USA
3 France
4 S Africa
5 Philippines
6 Congo (Kinshasa)
7 Canada
8 Morocco
9 Brazil
10 Chile
11 New Caledonia
12 SW Africa
13 Finland
14 China (People's Rep.)
15 Zambia
16 Australia
17 Spain
18 Italy
19 Malaysia
20 United Kingdom
21 Thailand
22 Argentina
23 Uganda
24 India
25 Mexico
26 Peru
27 Congolese Rep.
28 Ghana

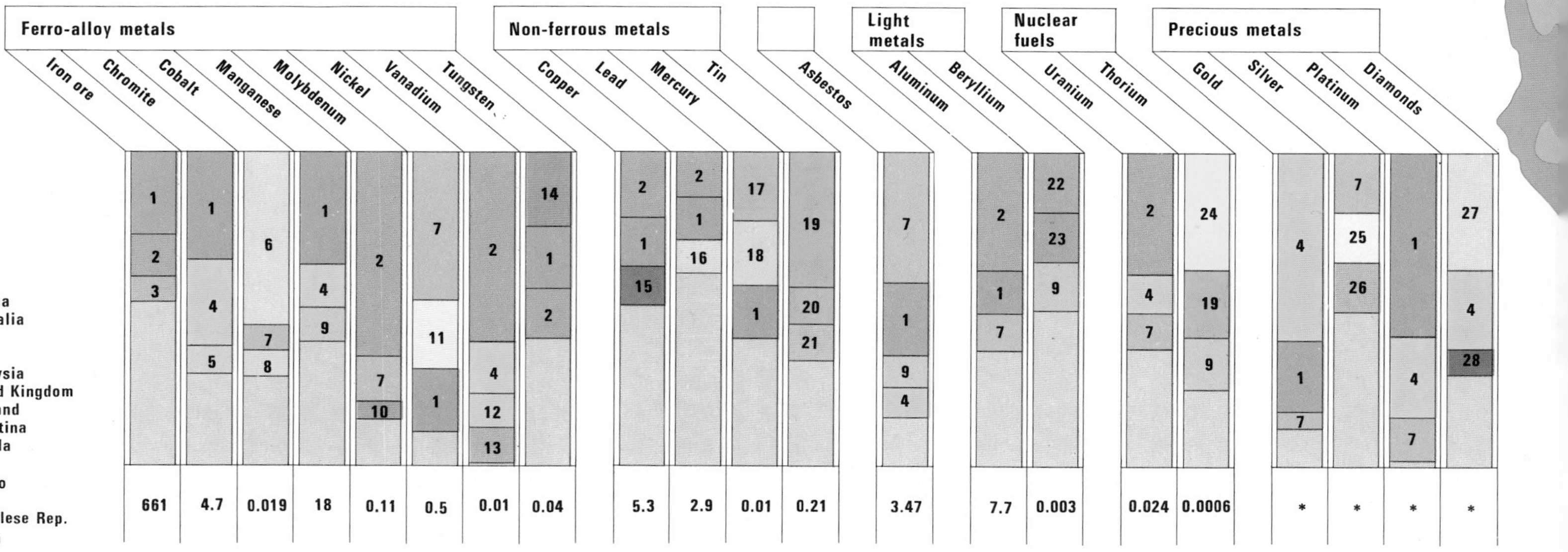

Ferro-alloy metals
Non-ferrous metals
Light metals
Nuclear fuels
Precious metals
Iron ore: 1, 2, 3 — 661
Chromite: 1, 4, 5 — 4.7
Cobalt: 6, 7, 8 — 0.019
Manganese: 1, 4, 9 — 18
Molybdenum: 2, 7, 10 — 0.11
Nickel: 7, 11, 1 — 0.5
Vanadium: 2, 4, 12, 13 — 0.01
Tungsten: 14, 1, 2 — 0.04
Copper: 2, 1, 15 — 5.3
Lead: 2, 1, 16 — 2.9
Mercury: 17, 18, 1 — 0.01
Tin: 19, 20, 21 — 0.21
Asbestos: 7, 1, 9, 4 — 3.47
Aluminum: 2, 1, 7 — 7.7
Beryllium: 22, 23, 9 — 0.003
Uranium: 2, 4, 7 — 0.024
Thorium: 24, 19, 9 — 0.0006
Gold: 4, 1, 7 — *
Silver: 7, 25, 26 — *
Platinum: 1, 4, 7 — *
Diamonds: 27, 4, 28 — *

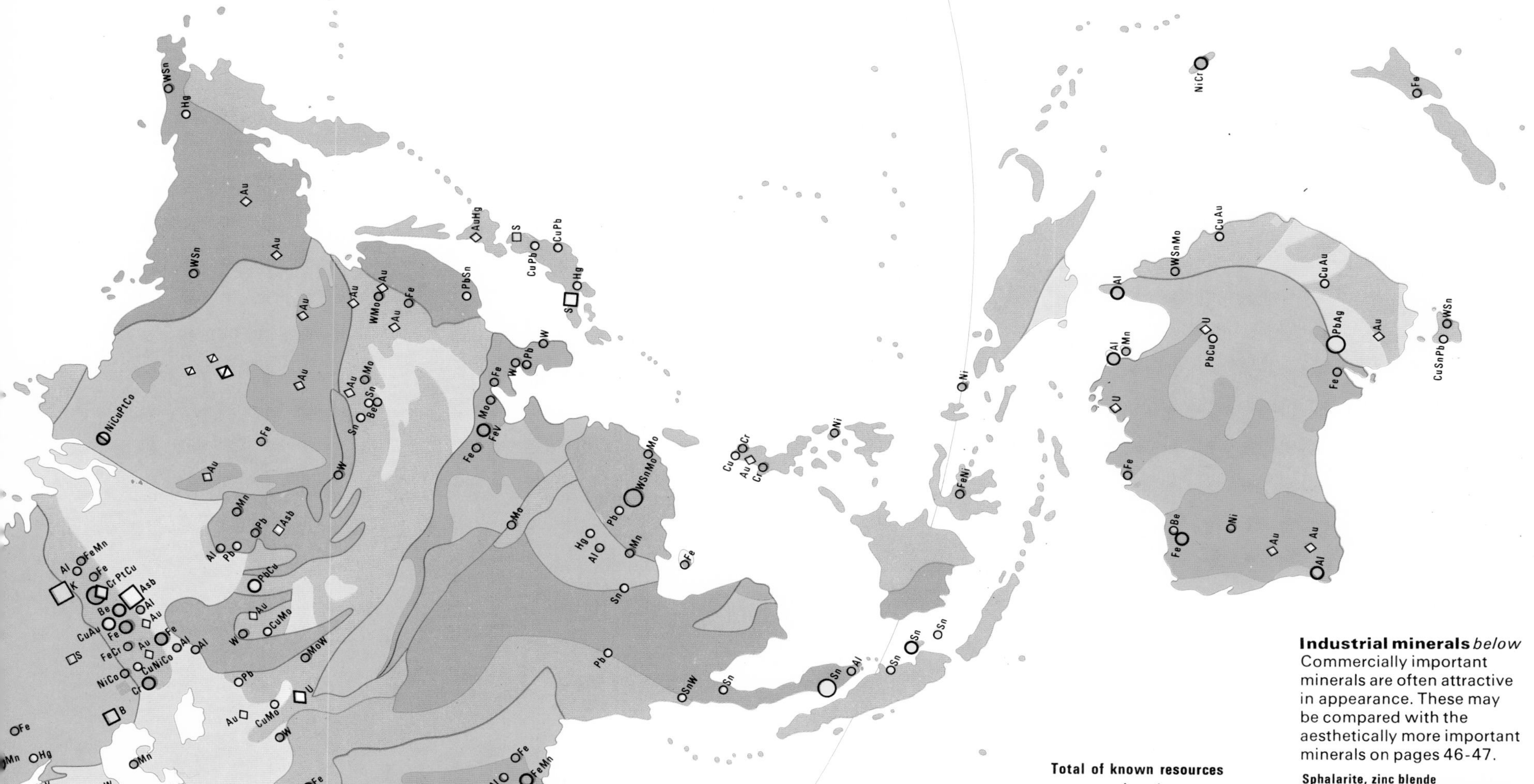
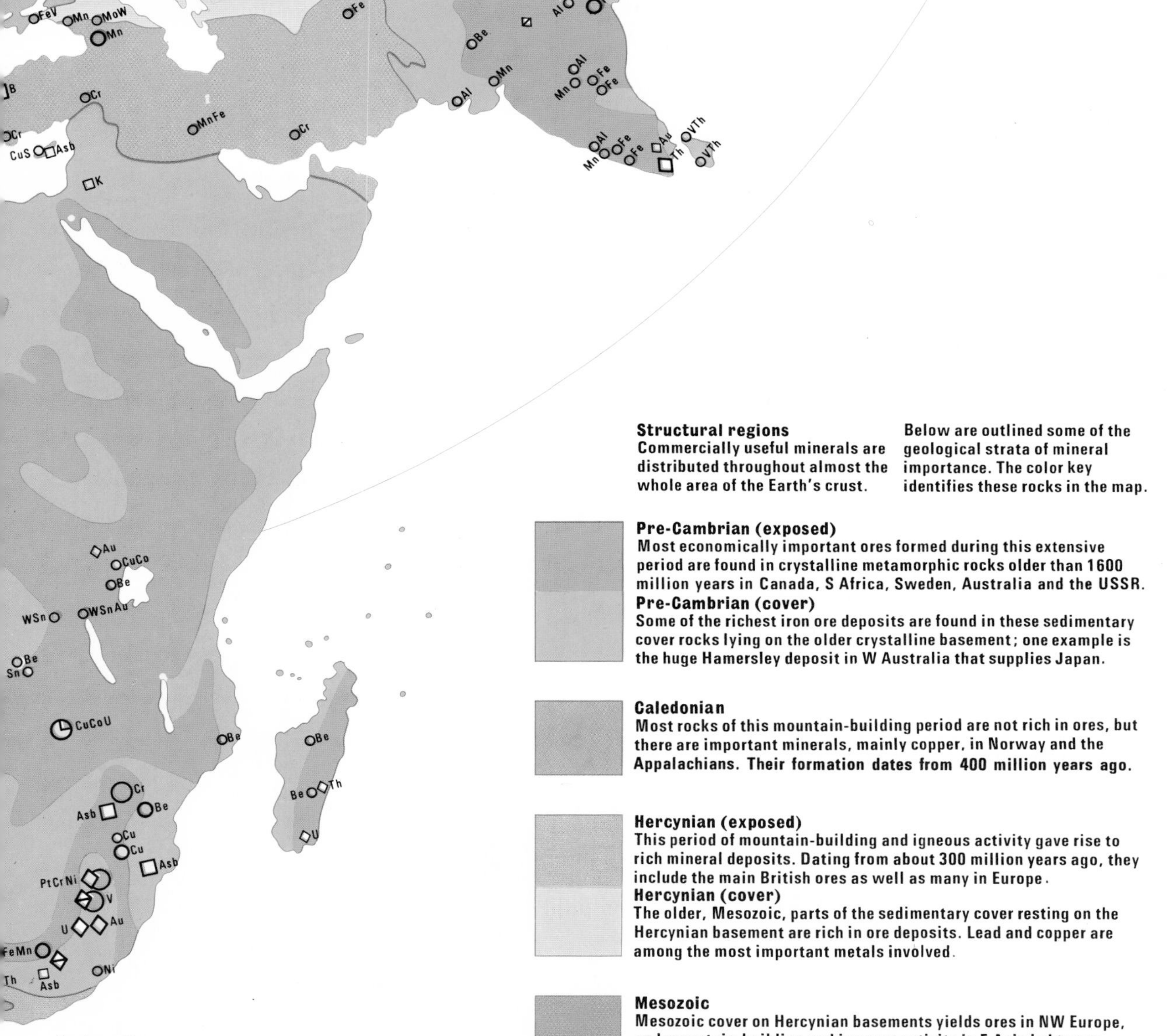

Structural regions

Commercially useful minerals are distributed throughout almost the whole area of the Earth's crust.

Below are outlined some of the geological strata of mineral importance. The color key identifies these rocks in the map.

Pre-Cambrian (exposed)
Most economically important ores formed during this extensive period are found in crystalline metamorphic rocks older than 1600 million years in Canada, S Africa, Sweden, Australia and the USSR.

Pre-Cambrian (cover)
Some of the richest iron ore deposits are found in these sedimentary cover rocks lying on the older crystalline basement; one example is the huge Hamersley deposit in W Australia that supplies Japan.

Caledonian
Most rocks of this mountain-building period are not rich in ores, but there are important minerals, mainly copper, in Norway and the Appalachians. Their formation dates from 400 million years ago.

Hercynian (exposed)
This period of mountain-building and igneous activity gave rise to rich mineral deposits. Dating from about 300 million years ago, they include the main British ores as well as many in Europe.

Hercynian (cover)
The older, Mesozoic, parts of the sedimentary cover resting on the Hercynian basement are rich in ore deposits. Lead and copper are among the most important metals involved.

Mesozoic
Mesozoic cover on Hercynian basements yields ores in NW Europe, and mountain-building and igneous activity in E Asia led to ore deposits of many kinds from E Siberia through China to Malaysia.

Tertiary
Many of the world's largest ore deposits are of this age, formed during mountain-building episodes such as the laramide and mid-tertiary in both the Americas. Copper, gold, zinc and uranium are found.

Antarctica

Surveying Antarctica is difficult since 97 per cent of the continent is under ice, but copper, iron and some radioactive minerals have been found, though whether in large enough quantities is not yet known. The world's largest coal field is thought to lie under eastern Antarctica.

Total of known resources

- ○ □ ◇ ◈ Over 20 per cent
- ○ □ ◇ ◈ 5-20 per cent
- ○ □ ◇ ◈ 1-4 per cent

Ferro-alloy metals

- Fe Iron
- Cr Chrome
- Co Cobalt
- Mn Manganese
- Mo Molybdenum
- Ni Nickel
- W Tungsten
- V Vanadium

Non-ferrous metals

- Cu Copper
- Pb Lead
- Hg Mercury
- Sn Tin

Light metals

- Al Aluminum
- Be Beryllium

Nuclear fuels

- Th Thorium
- U Uranium

Precious metals

- Au Gold
- Pt Platinum
- Ag Silver

Diamonds

Asb Asbestos

Chemicals and fertilizers

- B Borax
- N Nitrates
- K Potash
- S Sulphur

Industrial minerals *below*
Commercially important minerals are often attractive in appearance. These may be compared with the aesthetically more important minerals on pages 46-47.

Sphalarite, zinc blende

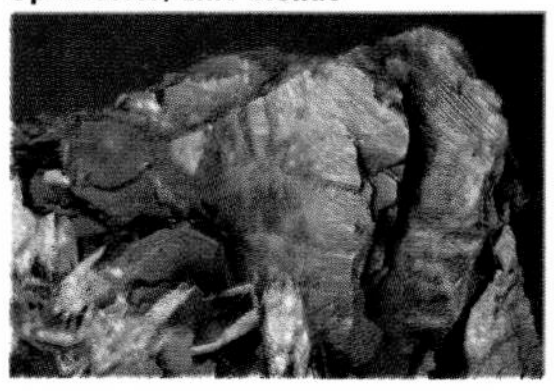

Muscovite, a mica

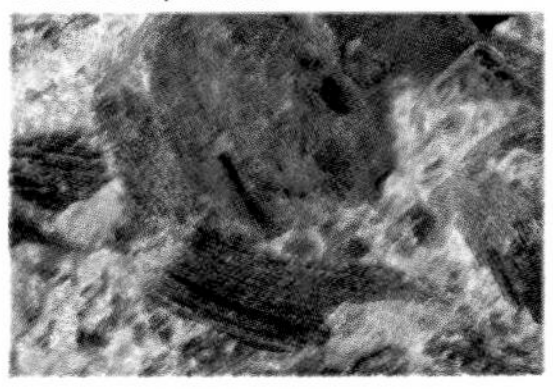

Specular haematite, iron ore

Gold in quartz

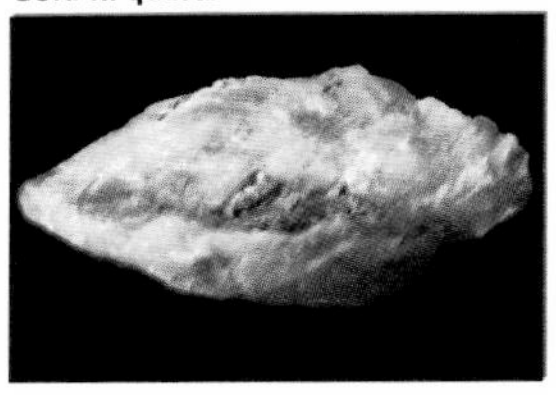

Asbestos

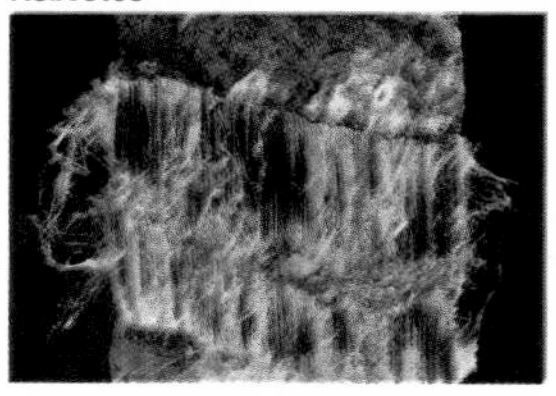

Sulphur

Earth's Energy Resources

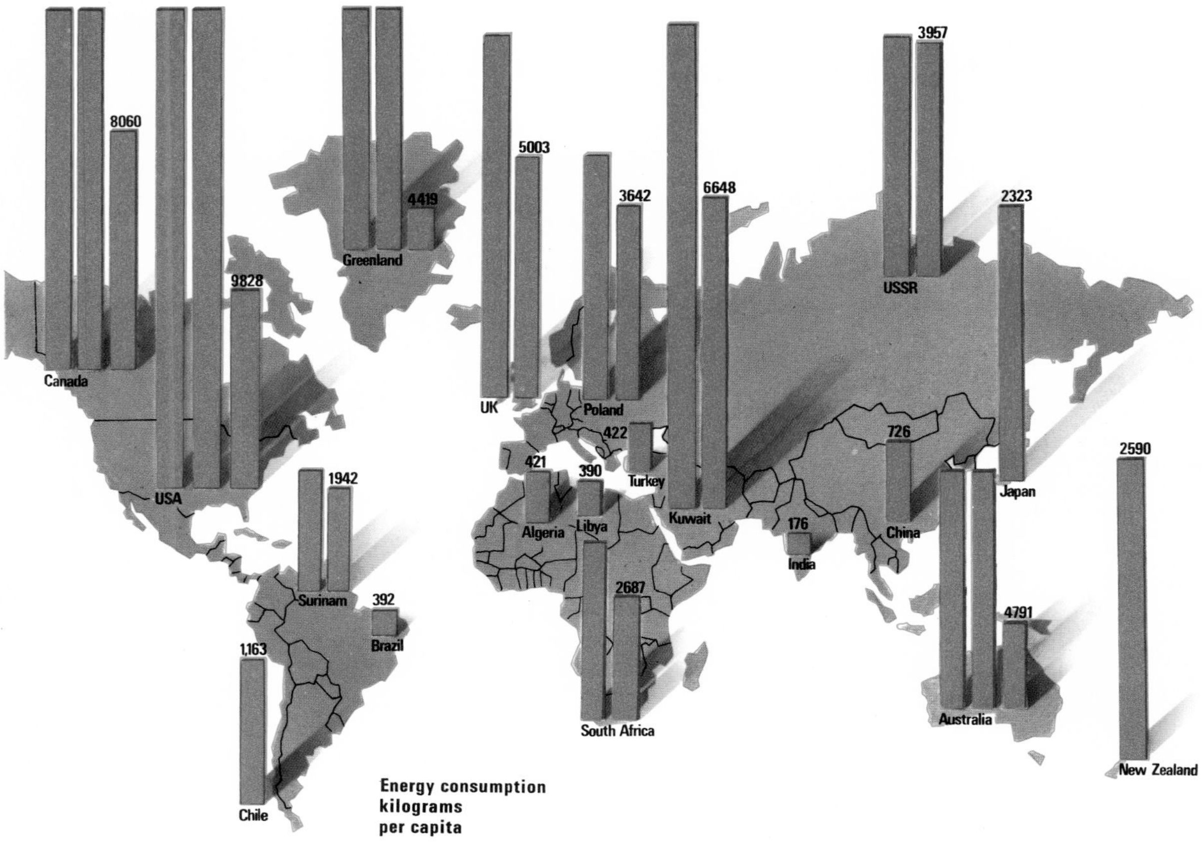

8060
Canada
4419
Greenland
9828
USA
5003
UK
3642
Poland
6648
Kuwait
3957
USSR
2323
Japan
726
China
2590
New Zealand
422
Turkey
421
Algeria
390
Libya
176
India
1942
Surinam
392
Brazil
1,163
Chile
2687
South Africa
4791
Australia
Energy consumption
kilograms
per capita

The concept of energy arose only very recently in the period of man's life on Earth, but already it dominates the whole quality of this life. Early man had no mechanical energy but that of his muscles. By about 2500 years ago he had learned to harness draft animals, such as the ox and horse, and to devise crude water wheels to harness part of the energy of the flow of water in a river. Soon afterwards he added sails to make the fickle wind propel his ships, and by 1000 years ago had started to dot his landscape with windmills. By this time he was adept at burning combustible materials, and during the past 500 years his energy has been increasingly based upon fire, first using wood, and subsequently coal, gas made from coal, petroleum, and natural gas.

All these energy sources, including animal muscle and the wind, are based on the energy radiated by the Sun. Although modern man has begun to use this energy directly in a few trivial installations in hot countries, almost all his energy is derived from solar heat locked up in fossil fuels. The known reserves of these fuels are tending to increase, as a result of prospecting, even faster than man is burning them up. But if no more were discovered most of man's world would come to a halt inside 20 years.

But there should be no energy gap. The promise of nuclear energy is such that, by using fast reactors that breed more fuel than they consume, energy should become one of the very few really plentiful and cheap commodities in man's world of the future. The challenges reside in extracting the fuels and using them effectively.

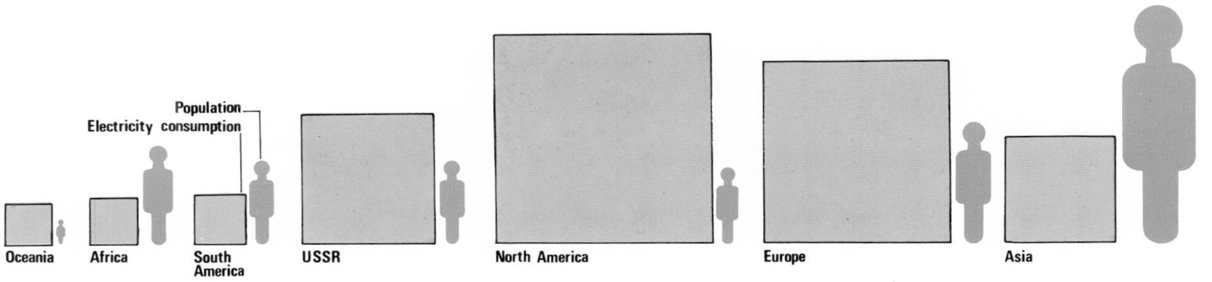

Electricity
Population consumption
Oceania
Africa
South America
USSR
North America
Europe
Asia

Power and people *above*
World consumption of energy is very uneven. One way of measuring it is to reduce all forms of energy to an equivalent weight of coal burned. The columns on the world map are proportional to the 'coal equivalent' of selected national consumptions expressed in kilograms per head. Electricity consumption is even more disproportionate, as witness the square areas and figure heights immediately above.

Fuels and energy *right*
The caloric value of a fuel is the quantity of heat generated by burning a unit mass. Figures are in British Thermal Units per pound. The surrounding curve shows the increase in the rate at which man is consuming energy; one joule (j) per second is equal to one watt.

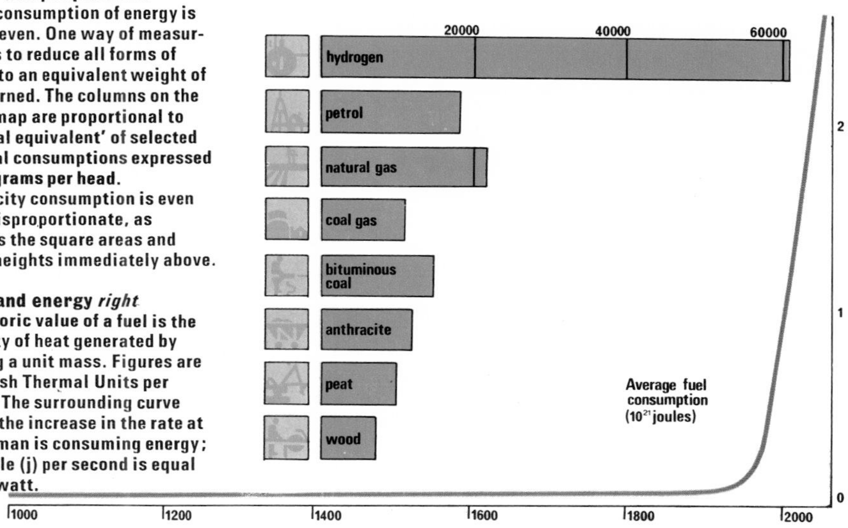

20000
40000
60000
hydrogen
petrol
natural gas
coal gas
bituminous coal
anthracite
peat
wood
Average fuel consumption (10^{21} joules)
2
1
0
1000
1200
1400
1600
1800
2000

Sources of power *below*
For many centuries the only alternative sources of power to muscles were wood fires, waterwheels and windmills – and the latter had too slight an effect to be shown on the figure below. The left portion shows the way in which, since 1850, the United States has enjoyed successive new sources of energy. In 1920 the US economy was not untypical in being based on coal, but since then more energetic, cleaner and more efficiently used fuels have dominated the picture. In the future, nuclear power, shown in the right-hand figure, promises to make good shortages of fossil fuels.

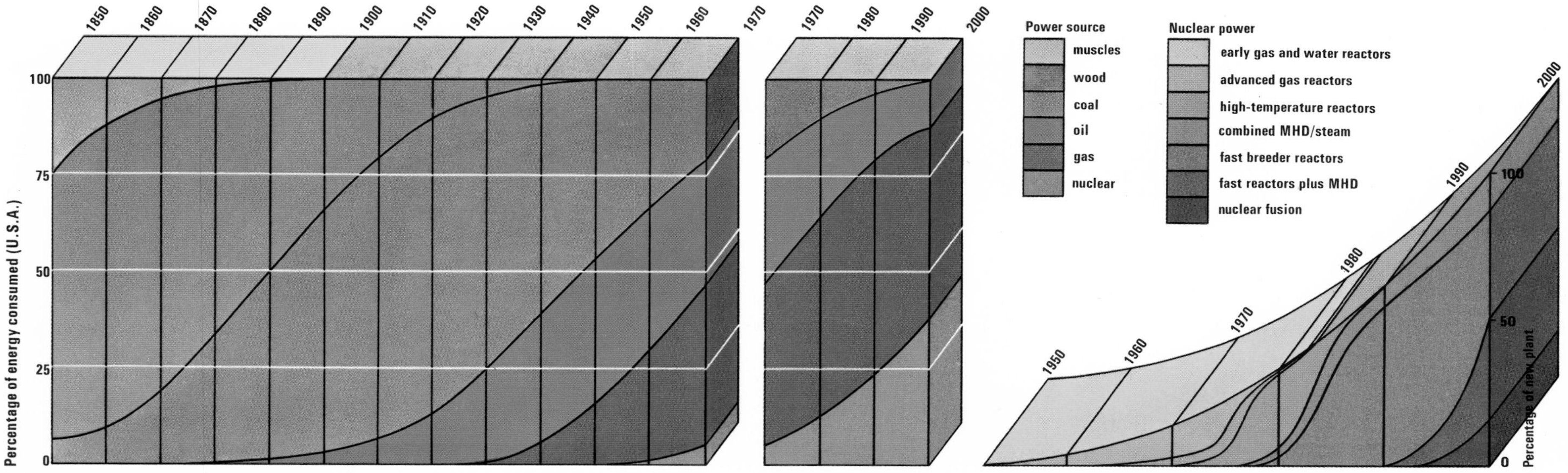

1850
1860
1870
1880
1890
1900
1910
1920
1930
1940
1950
1960
1970
1970
1980
1990
2000
100
75
50
25
0
Percentage of energy consumed (U.S.A.)
Power source
muscles
wood
coal
oil
gas
nuclear
Nuclear power
early gas and water reactors
advanced gas reactors
high-temperature reactors
combined MHD/steam
fast breeder reactors
fast reactors plus MHD
nuclear fusion
1950
1960
1970
1980
1990
2000
100
50
0
Percentage of new plant

Coal into electricity
To reduce costs modern coal-fired generating stations are sited on coalfields; Lea Hall colliery feeds Rugeley power station (background).

Coal

For three centuries the most important of the fossil fuels, coal is the result of some 300 million years of subterranean decay of vegetation. Many thousands of generations of the Carboniferous trees have become compressed and hardened, first into peat, then into lignite, then into bituminous coal and finally into anthracite. Until this century coal was used inefficiently as a source of heat. Today it is becoming equally important as a raw material producing plastics, heavy chemicals, insecticides, perfumes, antiseptics, road surfaces and many other products. Great advances have been made in automating the mining of coal, but it remains a laborious task and is therefore becoming increasingly expensive. However, coal mining remains a worldwide industry that passes on to modern man the products of the solar energy captured by a younger Earth.

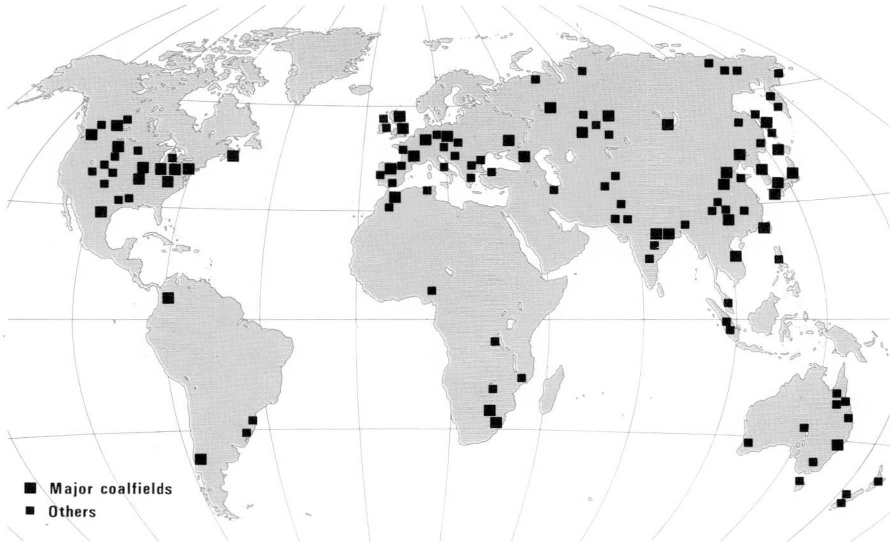
Major coalfields
Others

Flare in the desert
Once oil has been struck, harmful gases are burned off in the atmosphere. Similar 'flares' are a prominent feature of petroleum refineries.

Petroleum

Like coal, oil is a mixture of fossil remains, but yields few clues as to its origin. Crude oil, from the locations shown on the map at right, is carried by tanker ships to refineries in the user countries. Here it is heated in pipe stills until the various constituent 'fractions' are boiled off. The result is a wide range of products from gasoline through kerosene and gas oil to heavy fuel oils, lubricants and vaseline, with a wide range of other by-products used in many thousands of chemicals and plastics materials. Petroleum fuels are replacing coal in heating and transport applications, partly owing to their easier handling and partly to reduce air pollution by sulphurous compounds. LPG, liquefied pertroleum gas, is even cleaner burning and may become more important than gasoline and kerosene in road vehicles and aircraft over the next 25 years.

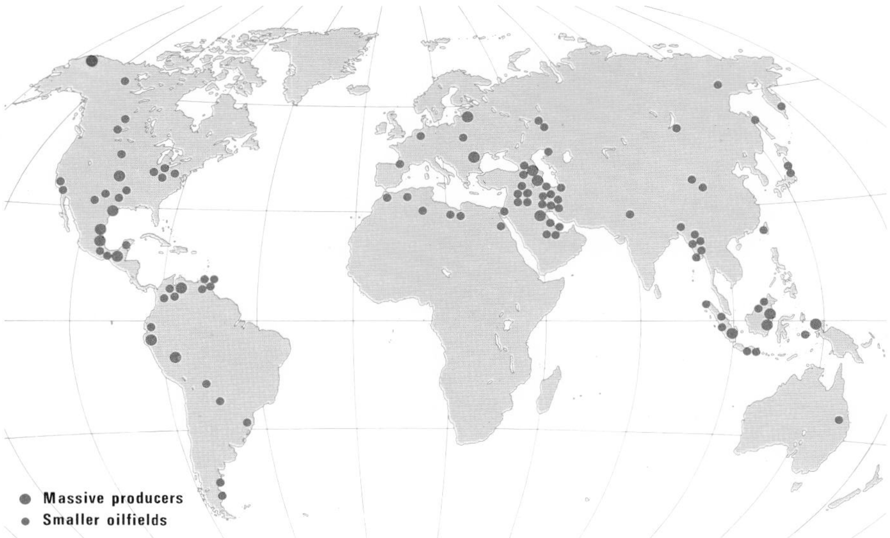
Massive producers
Smaller oilfields

Drilling for gas
To reach natural gas trapped in submarine strata a drill rig is used to bore a hole at a location determined by the prospectors

Gas

In 1807 a London street was lit by town gas, a mixture of hydrogen (about 50%), methane, carbon monoxide and dioxide and other gases, formed by cooking coal at high temperature in a retort. By 1950 this manufactured gas was an important fuel, but in many advanced countries its place is now being taken by natural gas, a primary fuel consisting mainly of methane piped straight from deposits sometimes conveniently sited from the user's point of view (right). Intensive prospecting is discovering natural gas faster than it is being used, and during the past 20 years natural gas has become man's largest single source of energy. In refrigerated form, as a compact liquid, it promises to become an attractive fuel for transport vehicles. A major benefit is that the exhaust from such a vehicle would contain less pollutants than from those using gasoline.

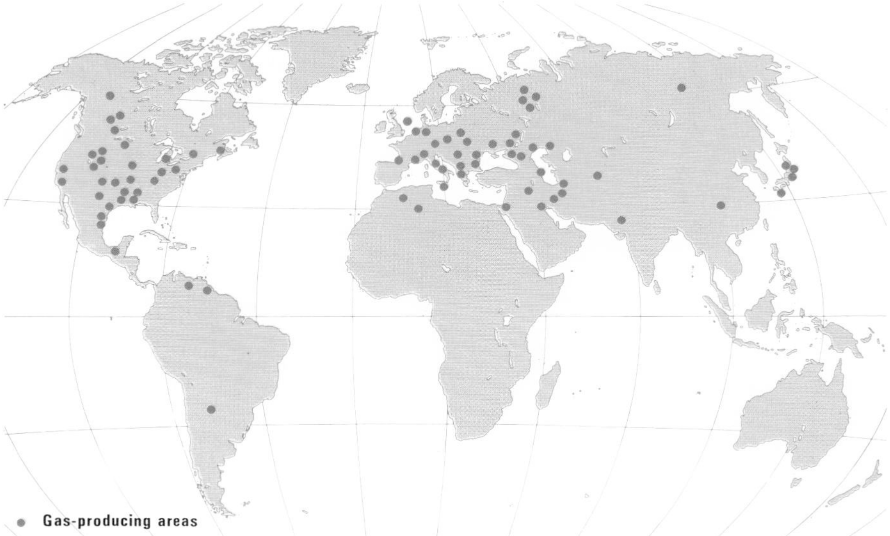
Gas-producing areas

Nuclear power station
Nearly all today's nuclear energy is used to generate electricity. One of the largest stations is Wylfa, Wales, rated at 1180 million watts.

Nuclear energy

In 1956 Britain opened the world's first electricity generating station using the heat of nuclear fission. It was fuelled with rods of natural uranium, a heavy silvery metal containing a small proportion of atoms capable of spontaneous fission when struck by a free neutron. Fission releases further neutrons capable of sustaining a continuous chain reaction. Such a reaction generates heat which is used to provide steam for turbines. The prime advantage of nuclear power is that the fuel is used extremely slowly. Now the fast reactor, which uses raw 'fast' neutrons instead of ones artificially slowed down, has been developed. Not only can the fast reactor generate great energy from a small bulk but it creates fresh fuel faster than the original (plutonium) fuel is consumed. Fast reactors, using uranium from granite, could provide limitless cheap energy.

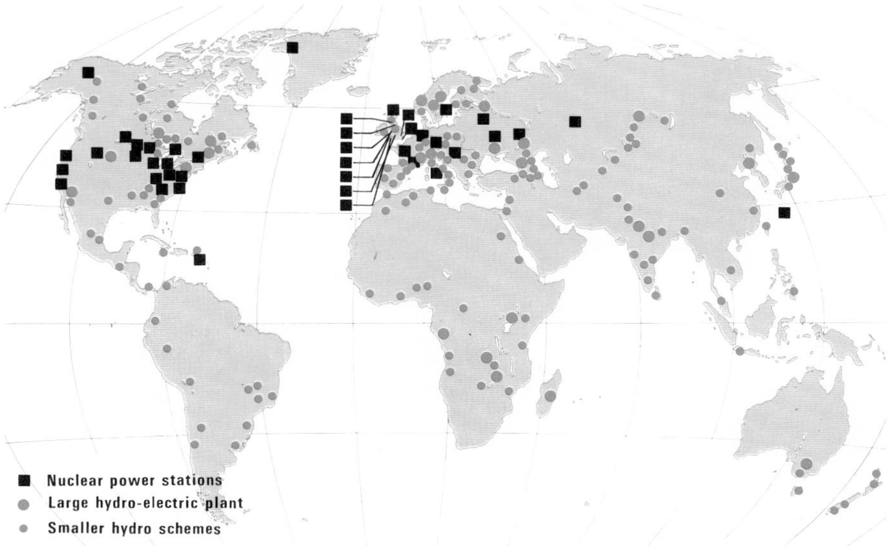
Nuclear power stations
Large hydro-electric plant
Smaller hydro schemes

Earth's Water Resources

Without water there would be no life as we know it on the Earth. Life began in the oceans (p.50) and the life of the land, both plant and animal, still remains utterly dependent on water for its survival. The atmosphere plays a vital role in the terrestrial water system. Spurred by the energy of the Sun, the moist layer surrounding the globe forms a vast heat engine, operating at a rate of billions of horsepower. All the exposed water surface is constantly being converted into vapor. Eventually the air holding the vapor cools, and the vapor condenses as rain, hail or snow. Most of this precipitation falls into the sea, but nearly a quarter of it falls on the land. Altogether about two-thirds of it evaporates back into the air, or is transpired by plants; the rest runs off in rivers, or filters through the ground to the water table beneath.

Satisfying the collective thirst of man and his industry grows daily more difficult. Almost always the demand is for fresh water; but the proportion of the Earth's water in rivers and streams is less than one part in a million. If the Antarctic ice cap were to melt, it would feed all the rivers for 800 years. Although schemes have been suggested for towing giant freshwater icebergs from Antarctica to the Californian coast, man is unlikely to make extensive use of the ice cap. Far more promising is the large supply of subterranean water. At the same time great strides are being made in desalination of sea water, using a variety of methods. Management of the Earth's water resources is seen ever more clearly as a technical challenge of the greatest magnitude.

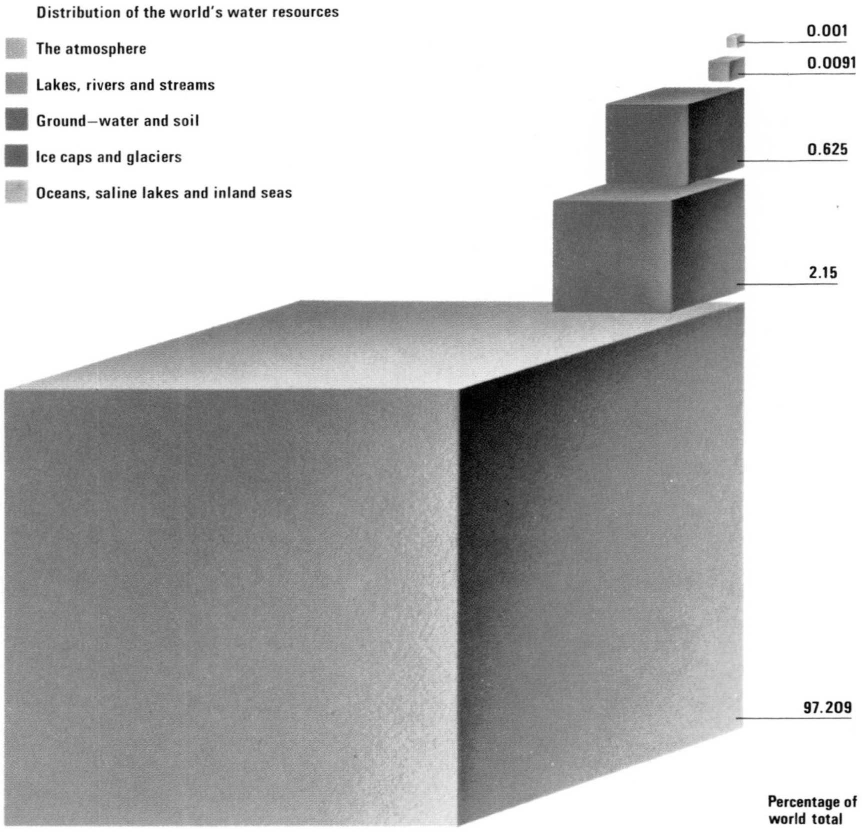
Distribution of the world's water resources
The atmosphere
Lakes, rivers and streams
Ground–water and soil
Ice caps and glaciers
Oceans, saline lakes and inland seas
0.001
0.0091
0.625
2.15
97.209
Percentage of world total

The world's water *left*
The total volume of the Earth's water is 317 million cubic miles (1330 million km^3). Practically all of it is in the oceans, in a form rich in dissolved salts. Solar heating is constantly evaporating this mass, converting it ultimately into precipitation of fresh water which falls back to the surface. Run-off from the surface in rivers and streams is one of the forms of terrestrial water most visible to man, but it accounts for a negligible fraction of the total. Some 80 times as much water lies in salt lakes and inland seas, 90 times as much in fresh-water lakes, more than 6000 times as much in ground water beneath the land surface, and almost a quarter-million times as much in ice caps and glaciers. So far man has made little attempt to use these sources of fresh water. Instead he interrupts the hydrologic cycle in the easy places: the rivers and lakes, where, because of the small volumes and flows available, he causes significant pollution.

A valued resource *above*
Shiupur head, the head-waters of the Gang canal in Rajasthan province, India. This and other canal systems are gradually bringing to this arid province an assured supply of irrigation water from the Himalayas.

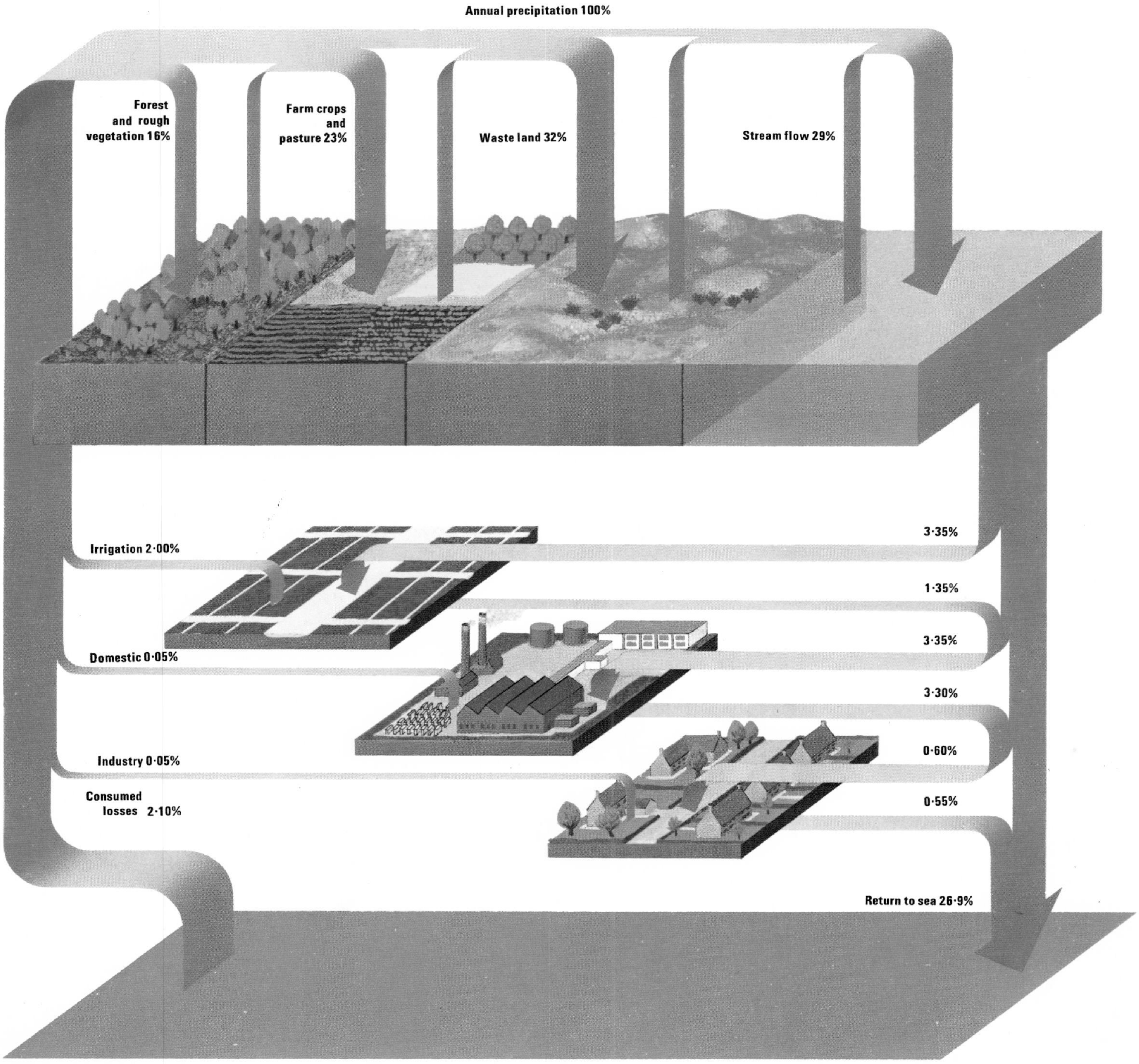
Annual precipitation 100%
Forest and rough vegetation 16%
Farm crops and pasture 23%
Waste land 32%
Stream flow 29%
Irrigation 2·00%
Domestic 0·05%
Industry 0·05%
Consumed losses 2·10%
3·35%
1·35%
3·35%
3·30%
0·60%
0·55%
Return to sea 26·9%

The hydrologic cycle *left*
This diagram is drawn for United States, but the basic features of the cycle are common to most of the Earth's land. Just over three-quarters of the rain snow and hail falls on the oceans. The usual measure for water in huge quantities is the acre-foot (one acre of water, one foot deep). Each year about 300 thousand million acre-feet of water falls on the oceans and 80 thousand million on the land. In the diagram all the figures are percentages. In the US, which is not unusual in its proportion of farmland, less than one-quarter of the water falling on the land falls directly on crops or pasture. A greater amount falls into rivers and streams, from which man takes varying small fractions for his own purposes. It can be seen that, even in the US, the total quantity of water withdrawn for use is only 7.3 per cent of the fraction of water falling on the land. Yet, to attain even this performance, Americans spend more than $10000 million each year on improving their water supplies.

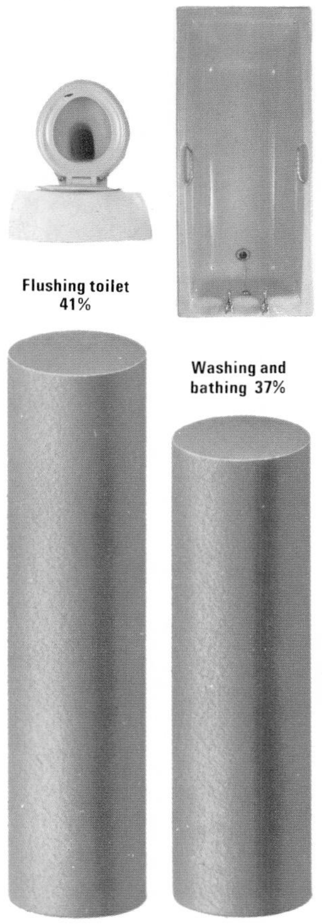

Flushing toilet
41%
Washing and bathing 37%

Domestic use of water

In some countries the total consumption of water is less than one gallon per head, but in the United States more than 70 US gallons are consumed by each person daily, on average, in domestic use alone. The way this consumption is split up varies greatly, but these percentages, for 'an average home in Akron, Ohio' are typical for modern urban areas having piped water to flush toilets. Total domestic water consumption in the industrially advanced countries is usually between five and 30 per cent of the national total.

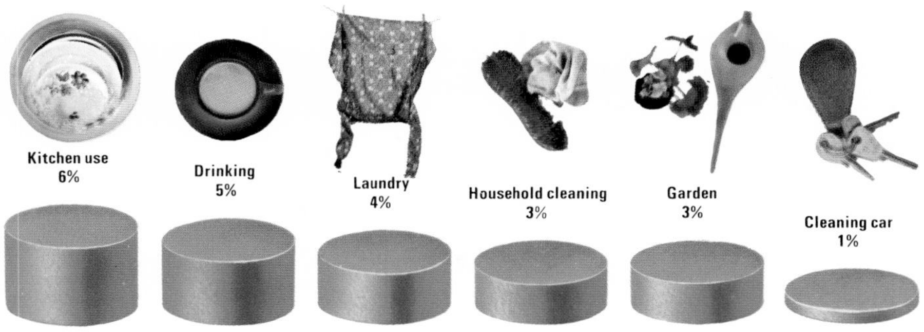

Kitchen use
6%
Drinking
5%
Laundry
4%
Household cleaning
3%
Garden
3%
Cleaning car
1%

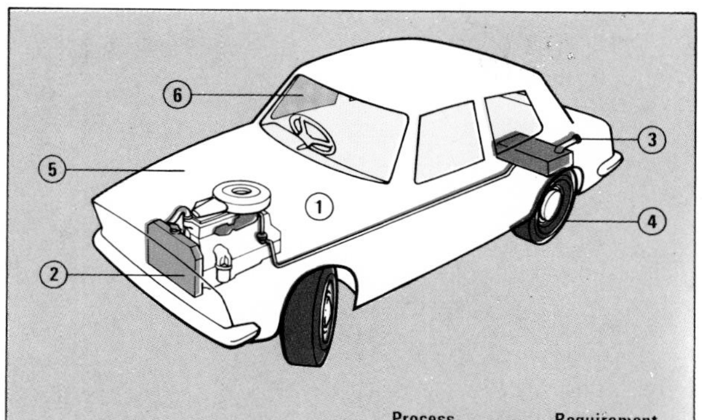

1
2
3
4
5
6

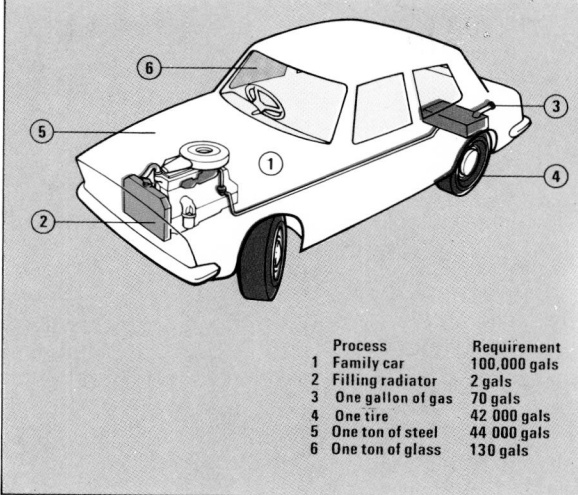

	Process	Requirement
1	Family car	100,000 gals
2	Filling radiator	2 gals
3	One gallon of gas	70 gals
4	One tire	42 000 gals
5	One ton of steel	44 000 gals
6	One ton of glass	130 gals

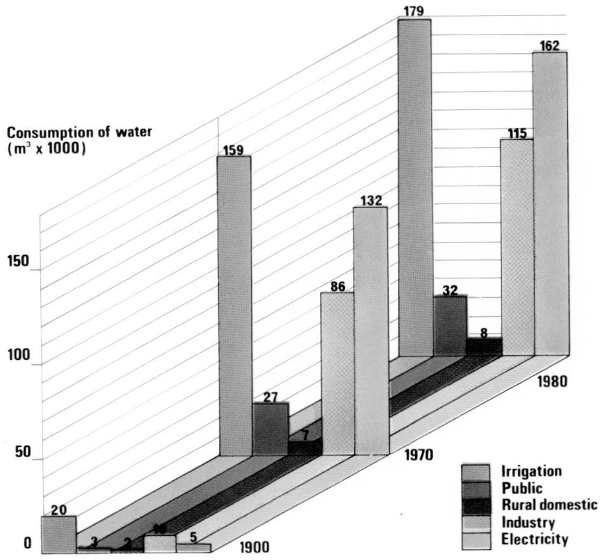

Consumption of water
(m³ x 1000)
150
100
50
0
20
3
2
5
1900
27
7
1970
159
86
132
32
8
179
115
162
1980
Irrigation
Public
Rural domestic
Industry
Electricity

Rising demand *above*
Civilized man needs more water every year. Plotted graphically, the rising demand for water in the United States is startling; the rate of increase is about three times the rate of population growth. Rural domestic supplies are from wells; others are piped.

Irrigation *below*
Irrigation of land by man is at least 7000 years old, yet still in its infancy. The grey areas on the world map are virtually without irrigation. The last column of data shows the percentage of each continent irrigated. Only Japan and the UAR exceed 50 per cent.

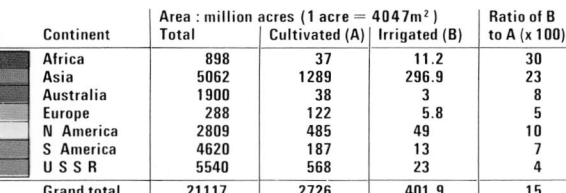

Continent	Area : million acres (1 acre = 4047m²) Total	Cultivated (A)	Irrigated (B)	Ratio of B to A (x 100)
Africa	898	37	11.2	30
Asia	5062	1289	296.9	23
Australia	1900	38	3	8
Europe	288	122	5.8	5
N America	2809	485	49	10
S America	4620	187	13	7
U S S R	5540	568	23	4
Grand total	21117	2726	401.9	15

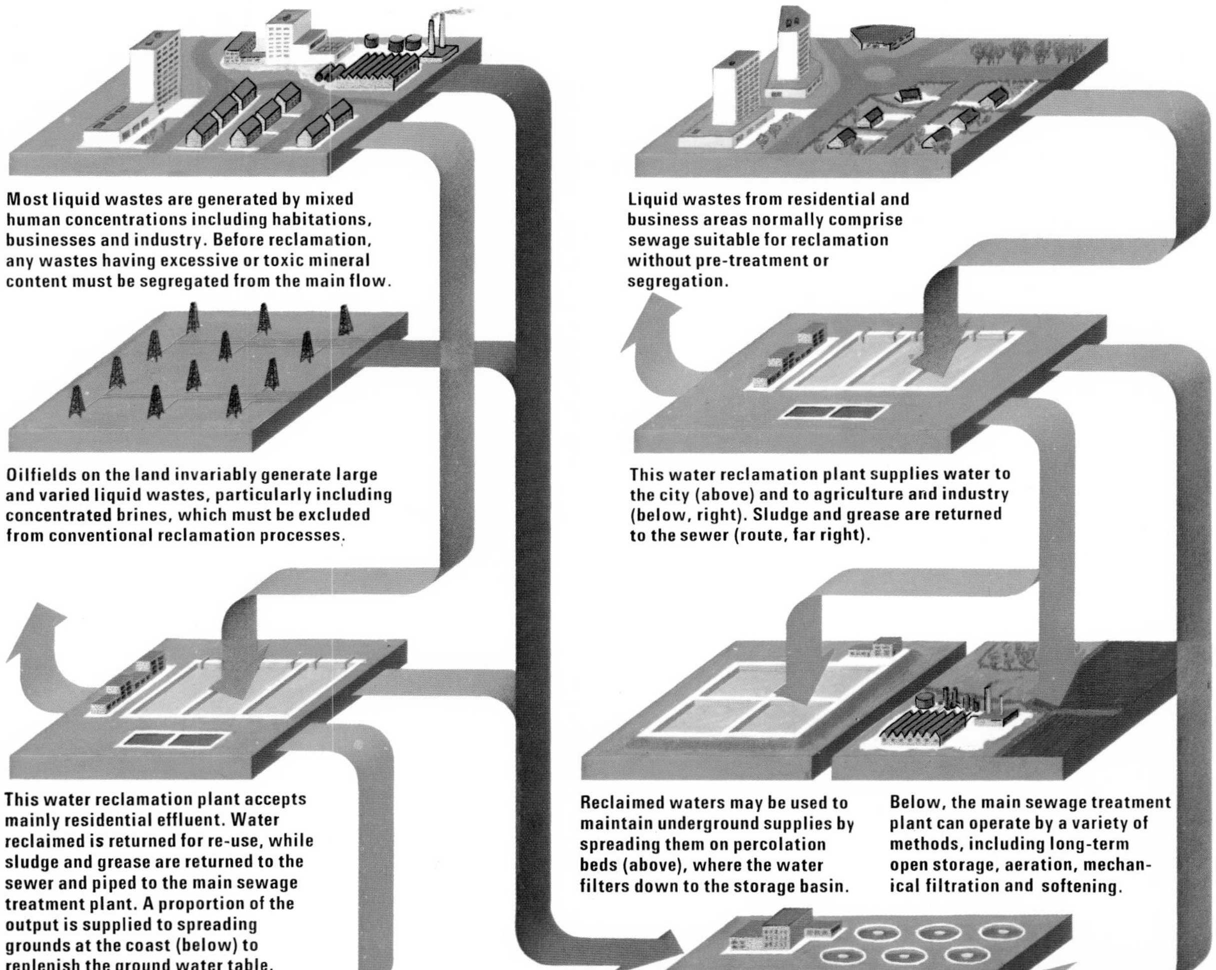

Most liquid wastes are generated by mixed human concentrations including habitations, businesses and industry. Before reclamation, any wastes having excessive or toxic mineral content must be segregated from the main flow.

Oilfields on the land invariably generate large and varied liquid wastes, particularly including concentrated brines, which must be excluded from conventional reclamation processes.

This water reclamation plant accepts mainly residential effluent. Water reclaimed is returned for re-use, while sludge and grease are returned to the sewer and piped to the main sewage treatment plant. A proportion of the output is supplied to spreading grounds at the coast (below) to replenish the ground water table.

Liquid wastes from residential and business areas normally comprise sewage suitable for reclamation without pre-treatment or segregation.

This water reclamation plant supplies water to the city (above) and to agriculture and industry (below, right). Sludge and grease are returned to the sewer (route, far right).

Reclaimed waters may be used to maintain underground supplies by spreading them on percolation beds (above), where the water filters down to the storage basin.

Below, the main sewage treatment plant can operate by a variety of methods, including long-term open storage, aeration, mechanical filtration and softening.

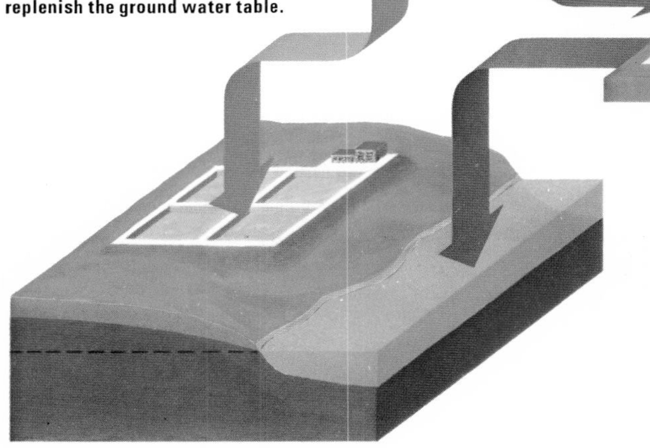

Reclaiming used water

In almost every country the quality of the water pumped into domestic supplies is subject to precise controls, and the proportion of some substances may not exceed one or two parts per million. National water systems make maximum use of water reclaimed close to the point of consumption by plant which returns the heavy sludges and greases to the sewer for treatment at a large sewage works. This facilitates effluent quality control and also provides an emergency outlet for a temporarily overloaded or faulty reclamation plant. In the example here the main treatment plant discharges wastes into an ocean outfall (left), while the fresh water spreading grounds just inshore replenish the water table and thus prevent infiltration by the ocean water.

Desalination

Man's growing demand for fresh water cannot readily be met without an enormous increase in his capacity to desalinate salt water. A choice between several ways of doing this is invariably made on economic grounds. Nearly all the large installations in use are multi-stage flash evaporators in which some form of heat – if possible, heat otherwise wasted - is used to convert sea water to steam which is condensed by the incoming salt water. But in some circumstances more economic results can be obtained by freezing, reverse osmosis or other methods.

GROWTH OF DESALTING CAPACITY 1961 TO 1968

Year Ending	Municipal water use M gal per day	Industrial/other uses M gal per day	Total
1961	17.6	42.2	59.8
1962	20.9	45.5	66.4
1963	28.4	50.4	78.8
1964	32.5	53.5	86.0
1965	39.3	58.9	98.2
1966	52.6	101.6	154.2
1967	102.2	115.3	217.5
1968	121.4	125.8	247.2
Historical annual growth %	32	17	23
Projection to 1975	835	415	1250
Projected annual growth %	32	19	26

SIZE RANGES OF THE WORLD'S DESALTING PLANTS

Size range M gal per day	Number of Plants	Total capacity M gal per day
0.025—0.1	351	17.8
0.1—0.3	218	35.3
0.3—0.5	34	13.0
0.5—1.0	31	21.3
1.0—5.0	46	95.4
5.0—7.5	3	17.5
over 7.5	3	46.9
TOTAL	686	247.2

The Oceans' Mineral Resources

A submerged land almost equal to the area of the Moon is being urgently explored for its store of minerals. The continental shelf around the Earth's land has the proportions of a seventh continent; around Britain or Japan its area is several times larger than that of the land itself. The shelf is rich in minerals, some of which are accumulating faster than man can at present use them.

By far the most important resources of the shallow seas are the deposits of oil and gas locked in the strata below the bed. About 200 drilling rigs are constantly looking for new deposits, and already nearly 20 per cent of the world's supplies, worth annually $4800 million, are taken from under the sea. Geologists estimate that oil and gas resources under the oceans are at least as great as those under the land. Next to oil and gas the most important marine minerals are lowly sand and gravel. It is becoming increasingly difficult and costly to extract these from the land, and marine deposits are fast becoming of great commercial importance. Often their extraction is combined with land reclamation. The Dutch, for example, have devised several systems that help to create new land and, as at Europoort, deep-water channels.

Last in importance, but very high in speculative interest, come the heavy minerals. Some, such as gravels rich in ilmenite, rutile and zircon, have been concentrated by the sorting action of the waves. Others, including tin, gold and diamonds, have been derived from igneous deposits. But in most cases these minerals can still be obtained more cheaply on land, except in one or two freak instances where concentrated deposits can be easily reached.

Exploiting the shallow sea

One of the most important recent discoveries of oil and natural gas has occurred in the North Sea, on the very doorstep of industrial Western Europe. The North Sea gas is found mainly in layers of a porous sandstone deposited under desert conditions. Since both natural gas and oil are thought to have originated from the compressed remains of animals and plants that swarmed in the warm seas of the Carboniferous period, the gas could not have formed in the rocks where it is now found.

Immediately below the sandstone lie thick coal measures, and the gas appears to have risen from these into the porous sandstone until halted by a thick layer of salt and limestone. Where the limestone is broken and porous, the gas has risen into it and become trapped under salt domes. In the Gulf of Mexico these domes have themselves become a source of minerals. While drilling down to a promising dome an oil company came across the third largest sulphur deposit in the United States.

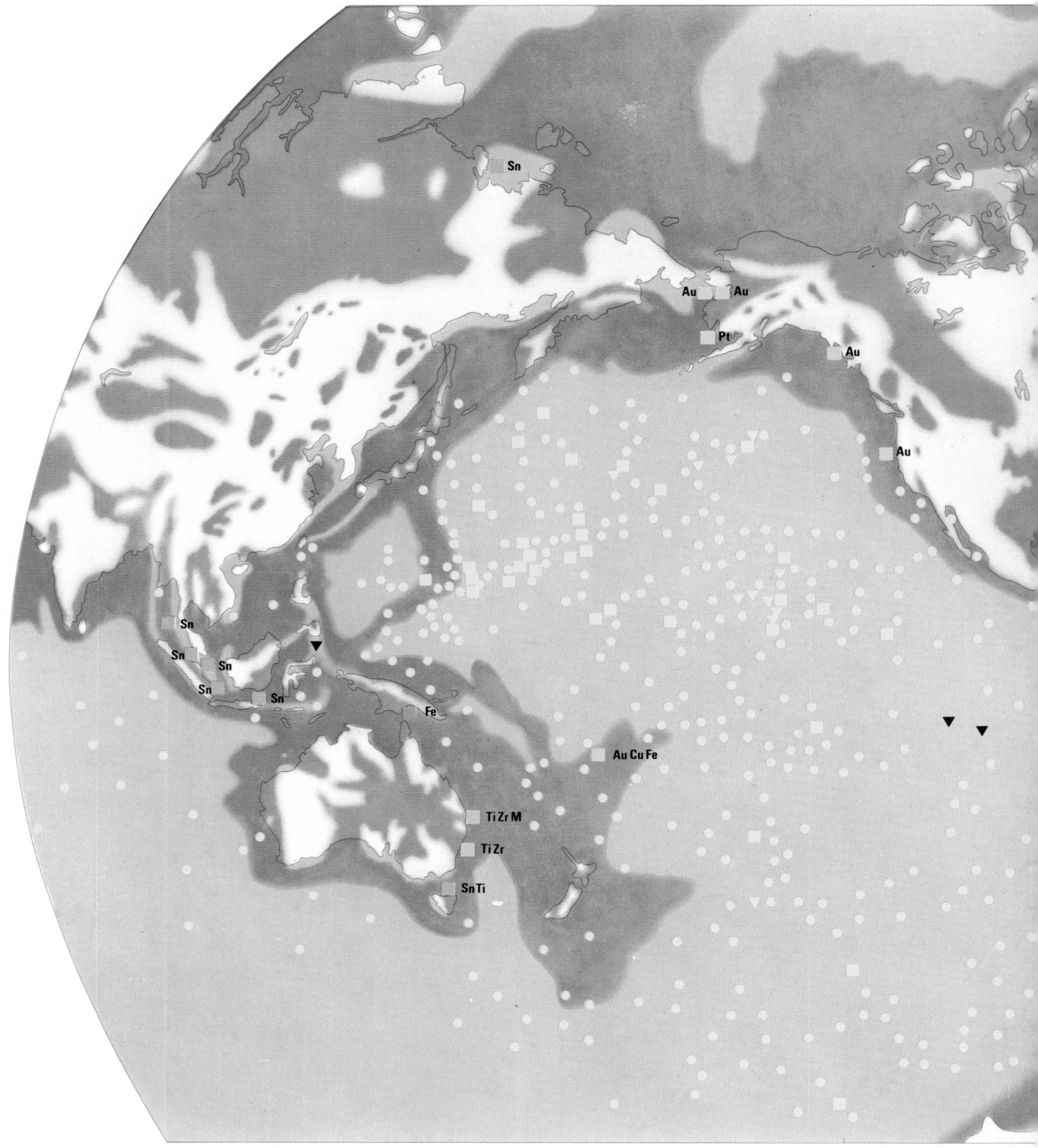
Sn
Au
Au
Pt
Au
Au
Sn
Sn
Sn
Sn
Sn
Fe
Au Cu Fe
Ti Zr M
Ti Zr
Sn Ti

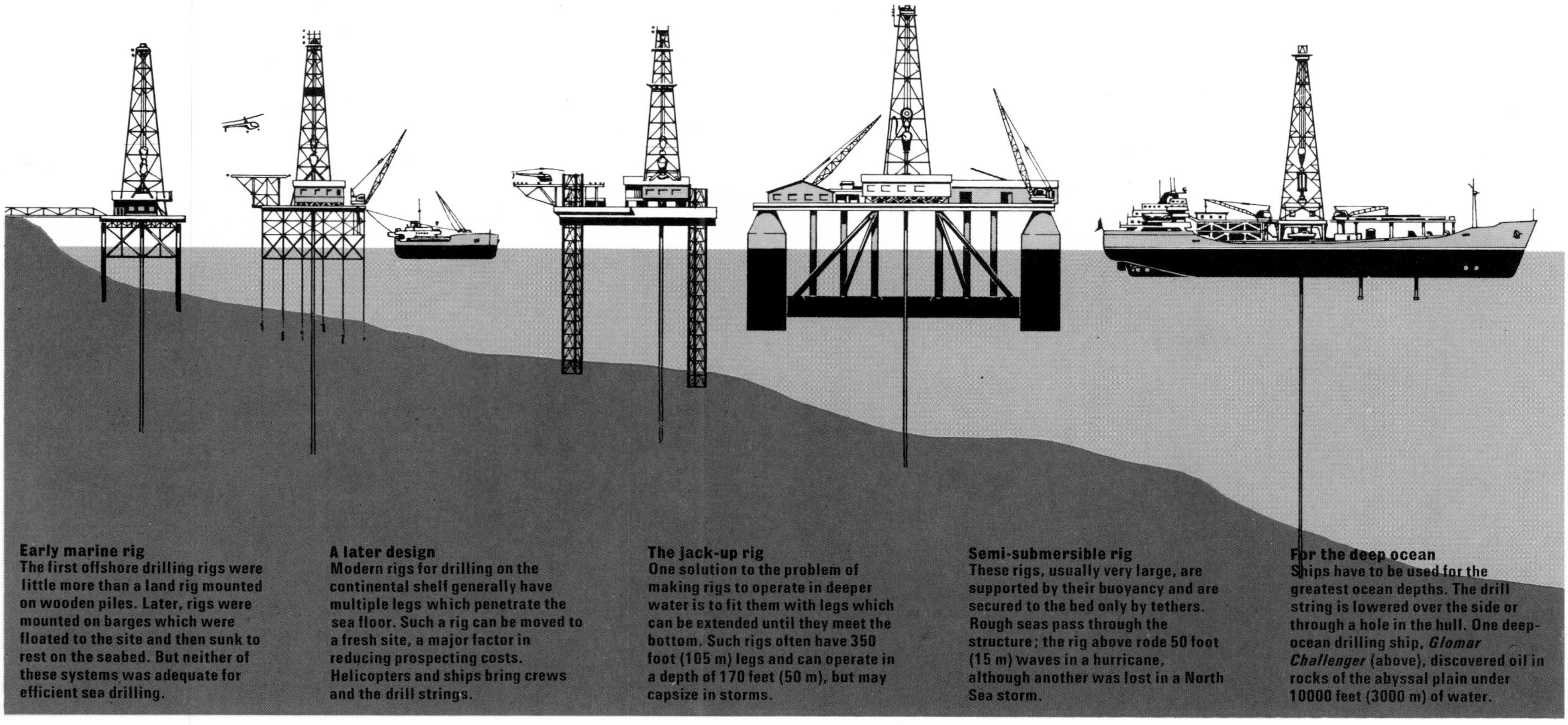

Early marine rig
The first offshore drilling rigs were little more than a land rig mounted on wooden piles. Later, rigs were mounted on barges which were floated to the site and then sunk to rest on the seabed. But neither of these systems was adequate for efficient sea drilling.

A later design
Modern rigs for drilling on the continental shelf generally have multiple legs which penetrate the sea floor. Such a rig can be moved to a fresh site, a major factor in reducing prospecting costs. Helicopters and ships bring crews and the drill strings.

The jack-up rig
One solution to the problem of making rigs to operate in deeper water is to fit them with legs which can be extended until they meet the bottom. Such rigs often have 350 foot (105 m) legs and can operate in a depth of 170 feet (50 m), but may capsize in storms.

Semi-submersible rig
These rigs, usually very large, are supported by their buoyancy and are secured to the bed only by tethers. Rough seas pass through the structure; the rig above rode 50 foot (15 m) waves in a hurricane, although another was lost in a North Sea storm.

For the deep ocean
Ships have to be used for the greatest ocean depths. The drill string is lowered over the side or through a hole in the hull. One deep-ocean drilling ship, *Glomar Challenger* (above), discovered oil in rocks of the abyssal plain under 10000 feet (3000 m) of water.

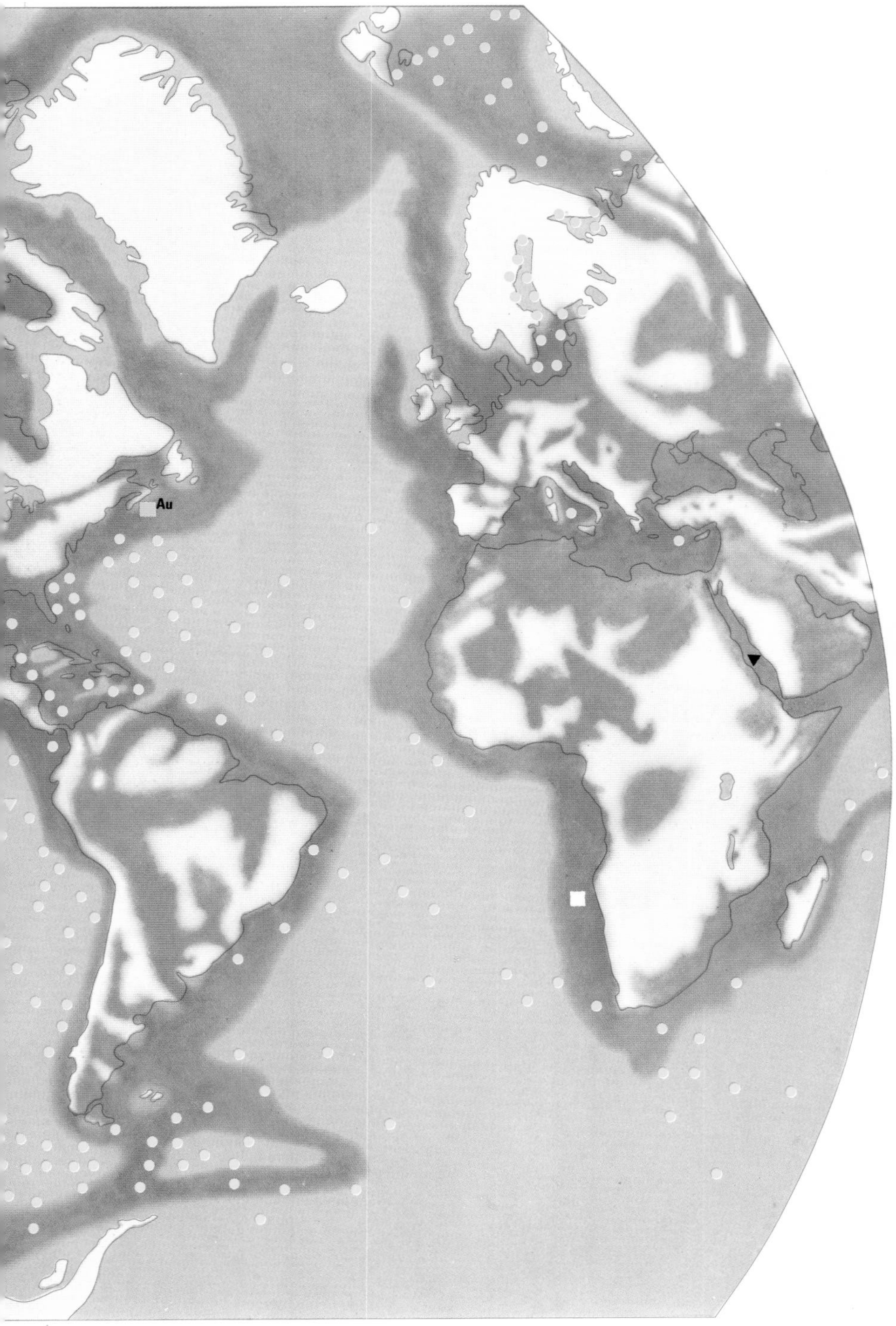
Au

Undersea resources *left*

- Deep ocean basins
- Sedimentary basins locally favourable for petroleum
- Au: gold
- Sn: tin
- Fe: iron
- Ti: titanium
- □ D: diamonds
- ○ Mn sampled
- □ Mn photo 25+ per cent.
- ▽ Mn photo 25— per cent.
- ▼ Metal-bearing muds

The large map gives a broad general picture of the distribution of petroleum resources, shown as favorable sedimentary basins, and of major subsea mineral deposits, but does not attempt to indicate commercial value or even which regions are worth exploiting. These are multi-billion dollar questions which are taxing mining companies in many countries. The manganese oxide deposits are shown only where they have been sampled or photographed (with symbols to indicate whether the nodules cover more or less than one-quarter of the sea floor). The metal-bearing muds are a recent exciting discovery. Deep down in the Red Sea, off Indonesia and elsewhere, prospectors have discovered concentrated brines rich in valuable industrial metals.

Mining the oceans *below*

For 20 years industry has been tantalized by the prospect of literally sucking or sweeping valuable minerals off the ocean floor. But the most widespread loose nodules (see photograph below) have a composition ill-matched to world demand (foot of page), and even the mining system sketched below, in which ships operate what is in effect a giant vacuum cleaner, has yet to be used on a commercial scale. The technical, economic and political problems associated with such ventures are immense: but the potential rewards are great enough to sustain interest.

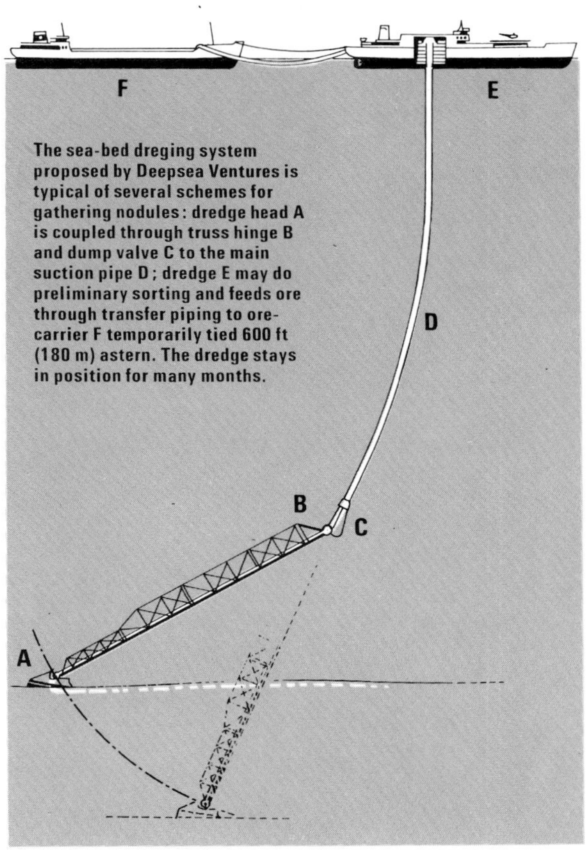
F
E
D
B
C
A

The sea-bed dreging system proposed by Deepsea Ventures is typical of several schemes for gathering nodules: dredge head A is coupled through truss hinge B and dump valve C to the main suction pipe D; dredge E may do preliminary sorting and feeds ore through transfer piping to ore-carrier F temporarily tied 600 ft (180 m) astern. The dredge stays in position for many months.

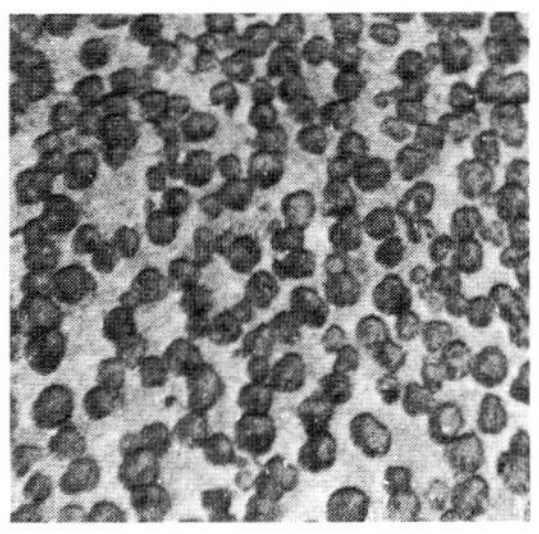

Manganese nodules

One of the most tempting concepts is to scoop minerals off the bed of the ocean. One of the few products which could thus be harvested is manganese, which is found in the form of potato-sized nodules scattered on the ocean floor. Unfortunately not only are there technical difficulties standing in the way of such an operation but production would be out of step with world needs. The undersea production of the world's needs of manganese, equivalent to more than 18.6 million tons of ore, would lead to a 453 per cent glut of cobalt. Similarly, if all the world demand for copper were met from the same source, the glut of cobalt would be no less than 11335 per cent (right).

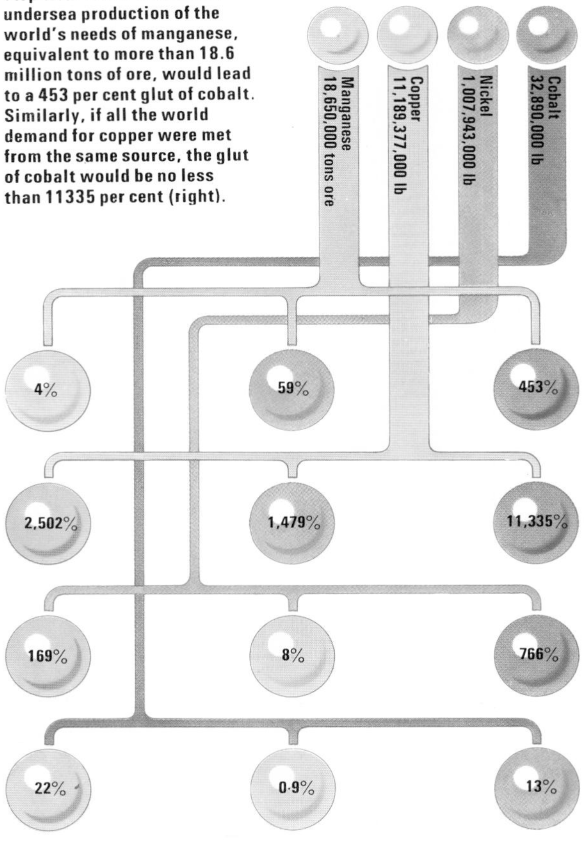
Manganese 18,650,000 tons ore
Copper 11,189,377,000 lb
Nickel 1,007,943,000 lb
Cobalt 32,890,000 lb
4%
59%
453%
2,502%
1,479%
11,335%
169%
8%
766%
22%
0·9%
13%

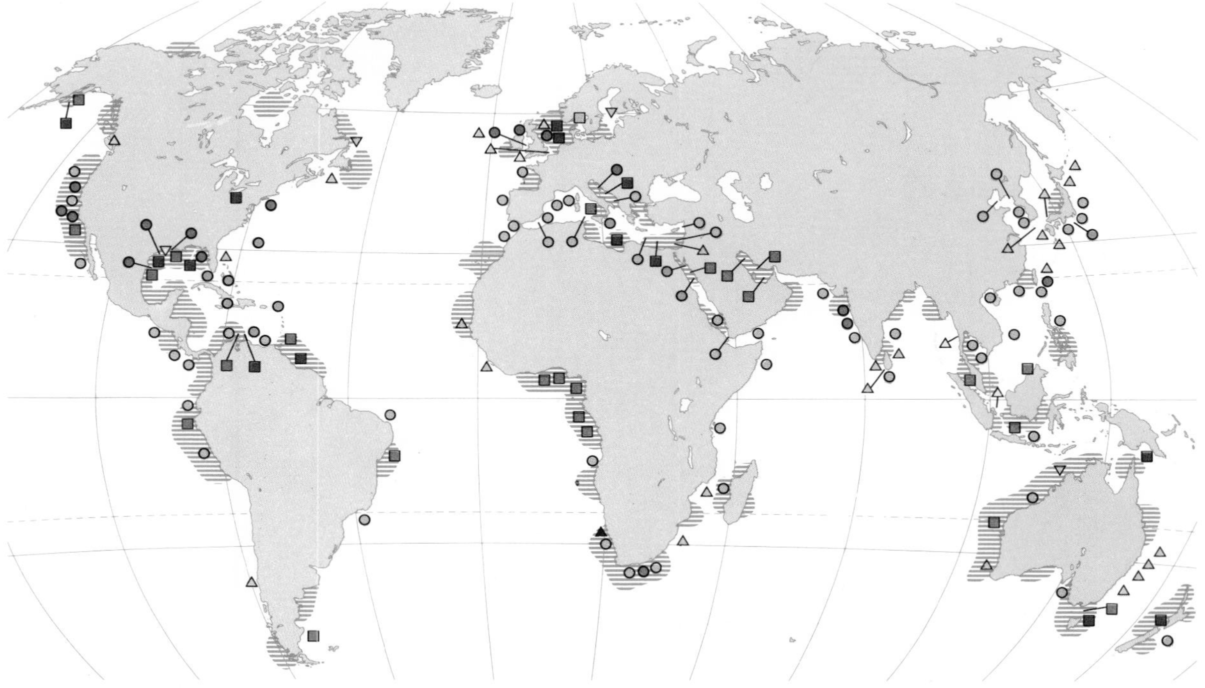

- ■ oil
- ■ gas
- △ tin
- ▽ iron
- △ coal
- ○ salt
- △ heavy minerals
- ▽ sulphur
- ▲ diamonds
- ■ magnesium
- ● fresh water
- ● other minerals
- oil and gas exploration

Undersea production

Man's commercial use of the ocean minerals is so far confined almost entirely to the continental shelves around the land.

The Oceans' Living Resources

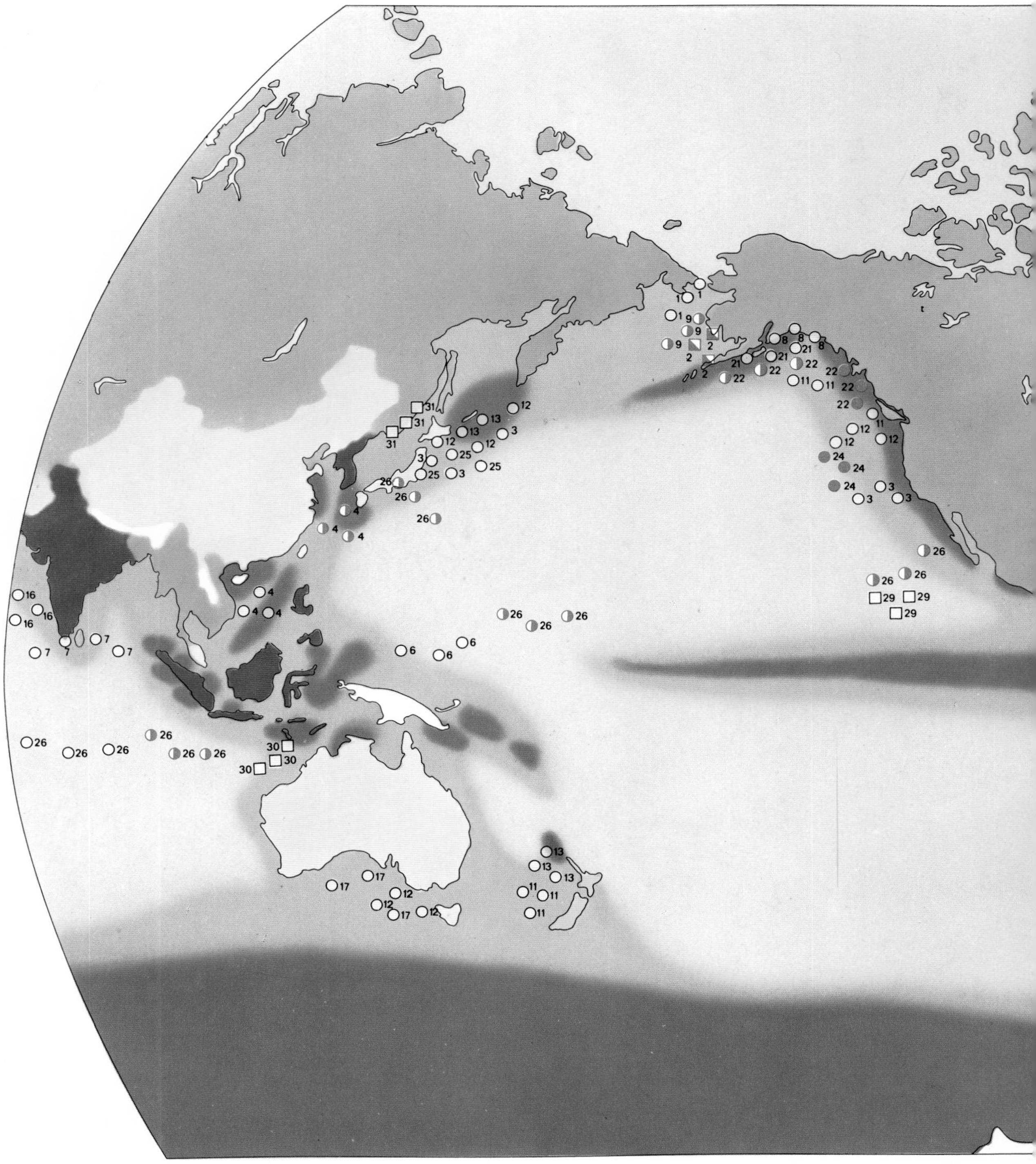

Fish and shellfish were probably the first marine resources to be exploited by man. Many of his early settlements in coastal and estuarine areas bear witness to this with their ancient mounds of oyster and mussel shells. Even now, coastal fisheries remain a vital source of high quality protein for numerous primitive communities. And yet, in spite of this long history of coastal fishing, the commercial fisheries have been dominated by a mere handful of nations until recent times. Three-quarters of the world fish catch is still accounted for by only 14 countries.

The world fish catch is the only source of food that has managed to increase dramatically since the end of World War 2. In the decade from 1958-68 alone, it rose from below 34 million tons to 64 million tons. Although the catch fell by two per cent in 1969, it is expected to continue to improve and may even top the 120 million ton mark by the mid-1980s.

The steady growth of the commercial fisheries since the war has relied on improvements in technology and boats, and the spread of these modern techniques from traditional northern fisheries to newer ones being developed in the southern oceans. Peru, for example, now has the world's largest single species fishery, catching some 10 million tons of anchoveta a year: in 1958 the catch was only 960,000 tons. However, the time is fast approaching when few fish stocks will remain unexploited.

Already many established fisheries are beginning to suffer from the effects of over-fishing with too many boats pursuing too few fish, leading to the capture of younger, smaller fish and a decline in the fish stocks and the fisheries that they support. Only the briefest respite may be needed for the fish to recover: a single female fish can lay thousands of eggs in a single season. Over-exploitation of the whales and turtles is a much more serious matter. Already several species of whale are on the verge of extinction and, with one young born to a female every two years, the prospects for their recovery are poor.

The living resources of the oceans must be conserved and managed if they are to continue to provide mankind with food. It is now clear that the world fish catch has a finite limit, possibly about 200 million tons. With adequate international agreement and controls, this limit might one day be approached. The productivity of the oceans could be increased further only by harvesting animals lower than fish in the marine food chain or by artificially fertilizing and farming the seas. Some of the first steps in this direction are now in progress. Perhaps in the future a new pattern of exploitation will emerge, with fleets harvesting the oceanic fish while other fish, shellfish and crustaceans such as lobster and prawn are farmed in the shallow coastal waters.

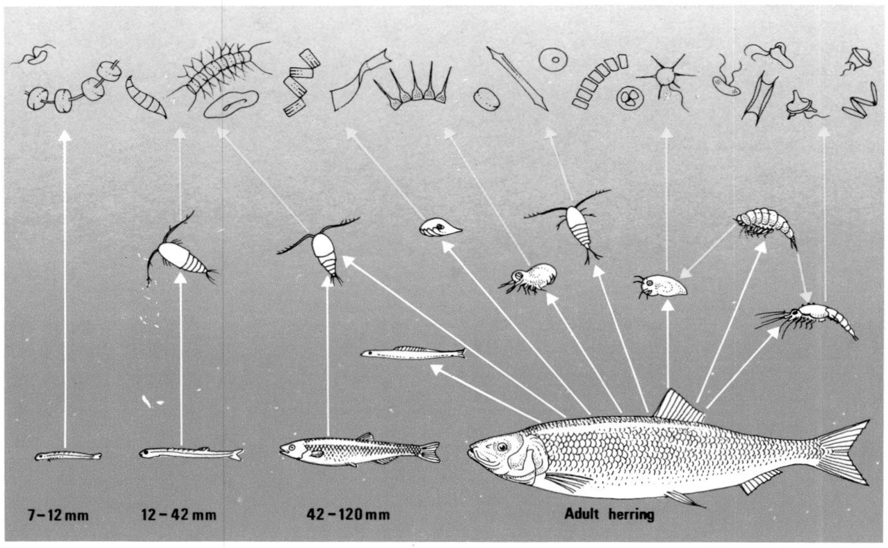
7–12 mm
12–42 mm
42–120 mm
Adult herring

Marine food web *above*
The path leading to food fish such as the herring involves a succession of feeding and energy levels. The plants drifting in the plankton first convert the Sun's energy into a usable form through the process of photosynthesis (top band). The plants are then eaten by small planktonic animals (middle band). These in turn are eaten by the fish during its growth (bottom band). However, as the arrows indicate, the path from plant to fish is far from simple. At each point in the web, energy is exchanged and lost so that the adult fish receives less than a thousandth of the original energy captured in photosynthesis. This loss of energy has prompted suggestions for short-circuiting the process by harvesting members of the plankton itself – either the plants or the small crustaceans and other animals that feed on them.

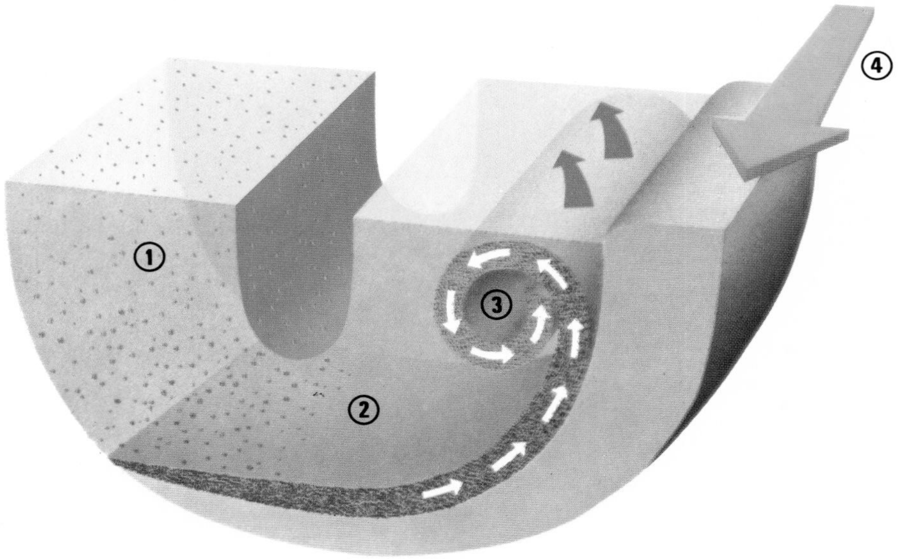
1
2
3
4

Upwelling *above*
Most of the world's great fisheries occur in regions of upwelling where nutrient-rich water rises to the surface and supports prolific marine life. Deep ocean waters accumulate the remains of dead and decaying organisms (1) that rain down from the surface. When this nutrient-rich water (2) rises to the surface (3) it contains all the minerals and salts necessary for plant growth in approximately the ratio best suited to stimulate maximum growth. The actual mechanism which causes the water to rise to the surface can vary, but a common source is the interaction between surface winds and ocean currents running along the edge of continents. The wind (4) causes the surface water to move away from the coast, enabling the deep water to swirl up to the surface where it renews the supplies of plant nutrients.

World fisheries *left*
With more nations claiming a share of the oceans' living resources few productive regions remain unexplored by fishing fleets. Already many fisheries show signs of over-exploitation and some coastal states are demanding exclusive rights to very large areas of sea, e.g. Iceland's demand for a 50 mile limit.

Biological productivity

- Very favorable conditions for the growth of marine life
- Moderately favorable conditions for the growth of marine life

Exploitation of fish stocks

- Over-exploited by 1949
- Over-exploited by 1968
- Under-exploited

Exploitation of crustaceans

- Over-exploited by 1968
- Under-exploited

Key to numbers

1 Alaska pollack	17 Pilchard
2 Anchoveta	18 Plaice
3 Anchovy	19 Pamfret
4 Demersal fish	20 Red fish
5 Capelin	21 Rock fish
6 Carangidae	22 Salmon
7 Clupeidae	23 Sand eel
8 Cod	24 Sardine
9 Flat fish	25 Saury
10 Haddock	26 Tuna
11 Hake	27 King crab
12 Herring	28 Krill
13 Jack mackerel	29 Red crab
14 Mackerel	30 Shrimp
15 Menhaden	31 Squid
16 Pelagic	

Fishing limits

- Nations claiming a 3 mile exclusive zone
- Nations claiming a 6 mile exclusive zone
- Nations claiming a 12 mile exclusive zone
- Nations claiming more than 12 miles

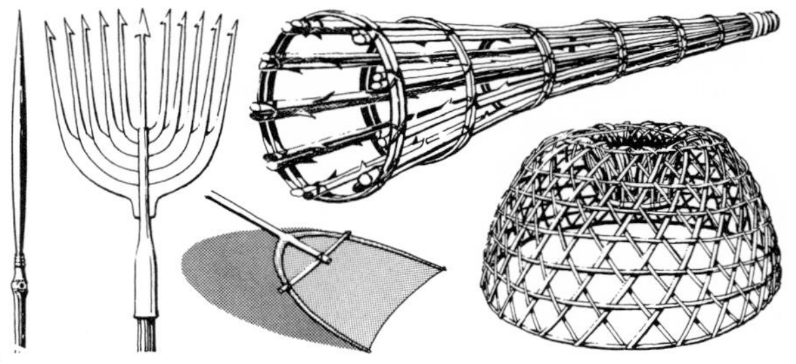

Fishing gear
Primitive fisheries use a wide range of techniques (above) including spears, nets and basket traps.

Mainstays of the modern commercial fisheries (below) are the gill net (top), the seine net and the otter trawl (bottom).

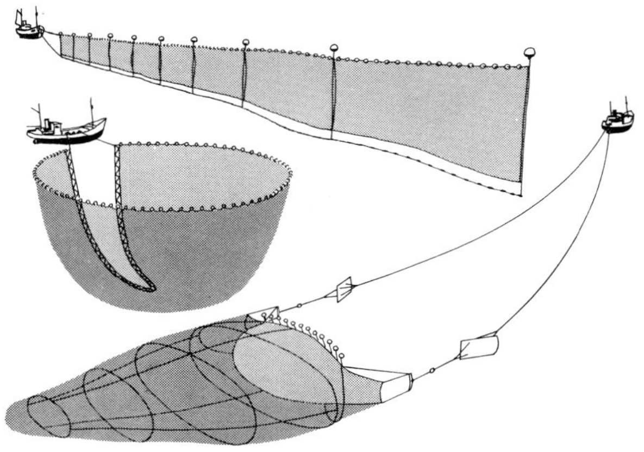

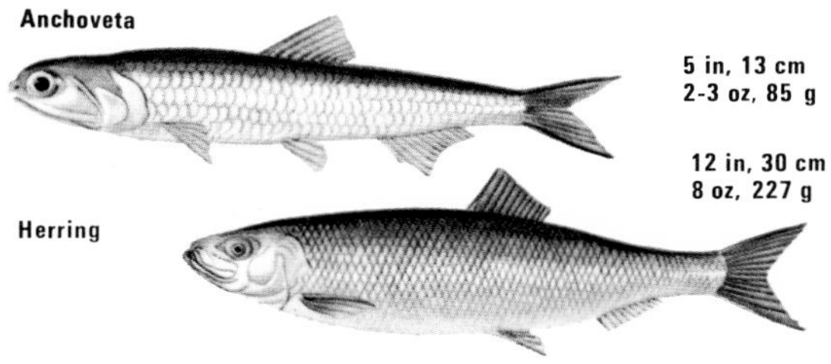

Anchoveta
5 in, 13 cm
2-3 oz, 85 g
Herring
12 in, 30 cm
8 oz, 227 g

Commercial fish
Although the oceans contain many thousands of different fish species, very few of these support large commercial fisheries. The anchoveta supplies the largest single species fishery in the world with an annual catch of about 10 million tons. This is slightly greater than the total catch of the other species illustrated here.

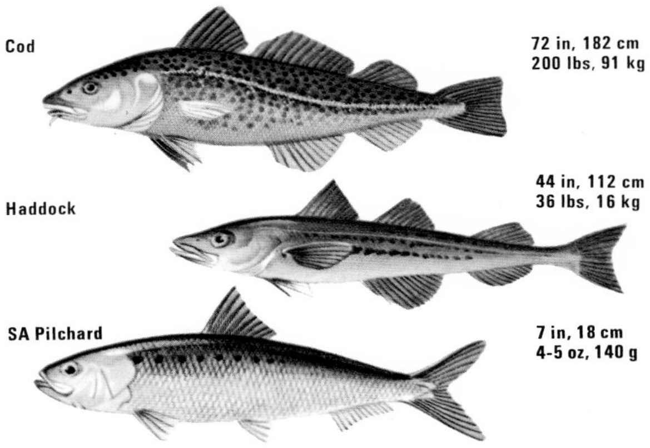

Cod
72 in, 182 cm
200 lbs, 91 kg
Haddock
44 in, 112 cm
36 lbs, 16 kg
SA Pilchard
7 in, 18 cm
4-5 oz, 140 g

The first marine farms, *right*
An early use of marine stockades was to keep alive fish caught at sea until they were needed for eating (A). An advance on this is to catch young fish and then fatten them in fertile coastal waters (B). But marine farming really begins with the production of 'seed fish' which can be reared until they are large enough to survive at sea (C). Such a scheme was proposed in the early 1900s as a means of increasing the productivity of the North Sea fisheries. The proposal was rejected, although marine fish hatcheries existed at the time. These hatcheries, however, were unable to feed their young fish once the yolk sacs had become exhausted. Success became possible with the discovery that brine shrimps, hatched in large numbers, could be used as fish food and that antibiotics would prevent marine bacteria from coating the eggs and killing or weakening the fish embryos inside. The point has now been reached at which fish farming is possible, although fish reared in this way are still too expensive to compete with those caught at sea. In one scheme, eggs collected from adult fish kept in ponds are hatched and the young fed on diatoms and brine shrimps until large enough to be put into marine enclosures (D).

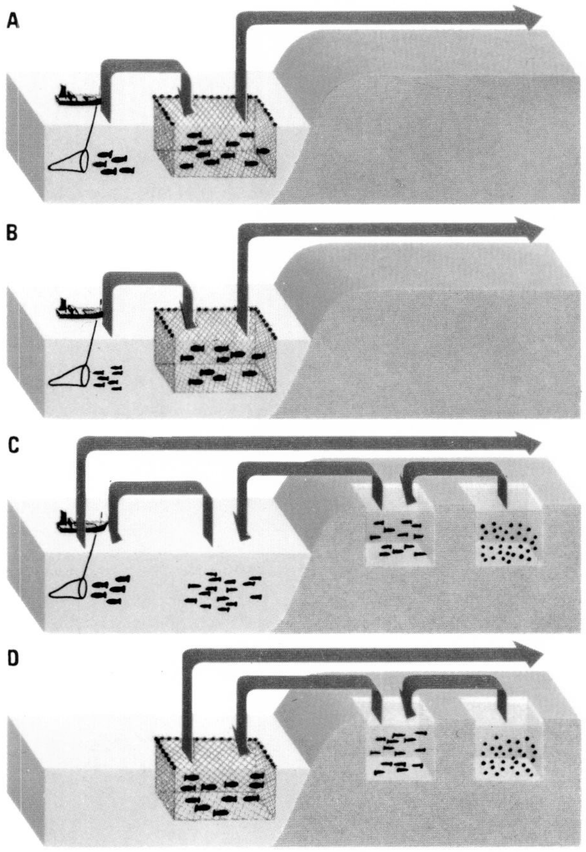

A
B
C
D

Enriching the sea *right, below*
Some marine farms in the future will exploit the store of nutrients that lie in the cold, deep ocean water. The value of this marine 'fertilizer' is clearly seen in areas where deep water rises to the surface. One project to create an artificial upwelling was started in the Virgin Islands in 1970. When completed it could include both a marine farm and provide fresh water supplies. In this system the cold nutrient-rich water (1) would be raised to the surface by a pump (2) driven by the warm, humid, prevailing winds (3). The cold water would then pass through a condenser (4) where it would be used to cool the wind and release its store of fresh water (5). Finally, the water, now warmed to the temperature of the surface waters, would be used to promote the growth of marine plants and animals such as shellfish, prawn and valuable food fish within net enclosures in the lagoon (6). Deep ocean water may also be used to combat thermal pollution, particularly in tropical areas where marine organisms live close to their upper temperature limit. The cold water would cool down the warm effluent discharged from power stations as well as provide valuable nutrients for marine aquiculture.

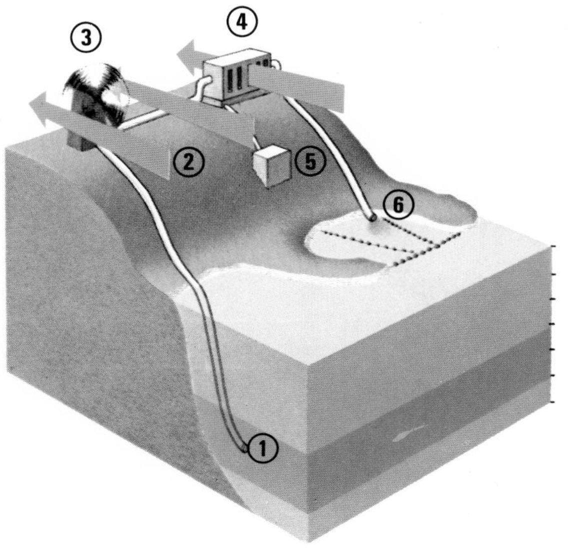

1
2
3
4
5
6

The Food Resource : 1

Combine harvester discharging wheat into trailer

Agriculture has always been a cornerstone of human civilization. Until man was able to give up the life of a nomadic hunter he could not be called civilized, and it was the settled life based on the land which enabled progress toward modern society to begin. Today agriculture is the occupation of more people than all other industries, but the pattern of their work varies greatly. In poor or developing lands as many as 90 per cent of the population live directly off the land, whereas in the most industrialized countries the proportion can be as low as three per cent.

The underlying purpose of farming is to convert the energy of sunlight into a form in which it can be assimilated by humans. Initially this can be done only by photosynthesis in green plants, and here the efficiency of the conversion process – expressed in terms of assimilable food energy obtained from a given amount of sunlight – varies from about two per cent down to less than one part in 1000. Further stages involve the consumption of plants by livestock to provide meat and other food for man, or the direct consumption of fruit, vegetables and cereals by man himself. Each additional step in this food chain involves large losses in energy, lowering the overall 'efficiency' of the process.

For many years research has led to improved methods of producing crops, by developing new plant strains with a higher edible yield or greater resistance to disease, by increasing both the area of land under cultivation and the nutritional value of the soil, by devising swifter and surer techniques of cultivation and by reducing the labor effort needed. Improved methods are especially needed in regions of poor farming. The 'Green Revolution' of SE Asia has already shown how yields can be increased dramatically, although at a greater cost in terms of agricultural chemicals and water supplies. Another promising way of increasing food supplies is to extract protein from plants such as soybean and even grass, and to convert them into forms that have the texture and taste of meat. For the more distant future there are prospects of growing single-cell protein and other revolutionary foods which in theory could at least double the Earth's ability to produce food.

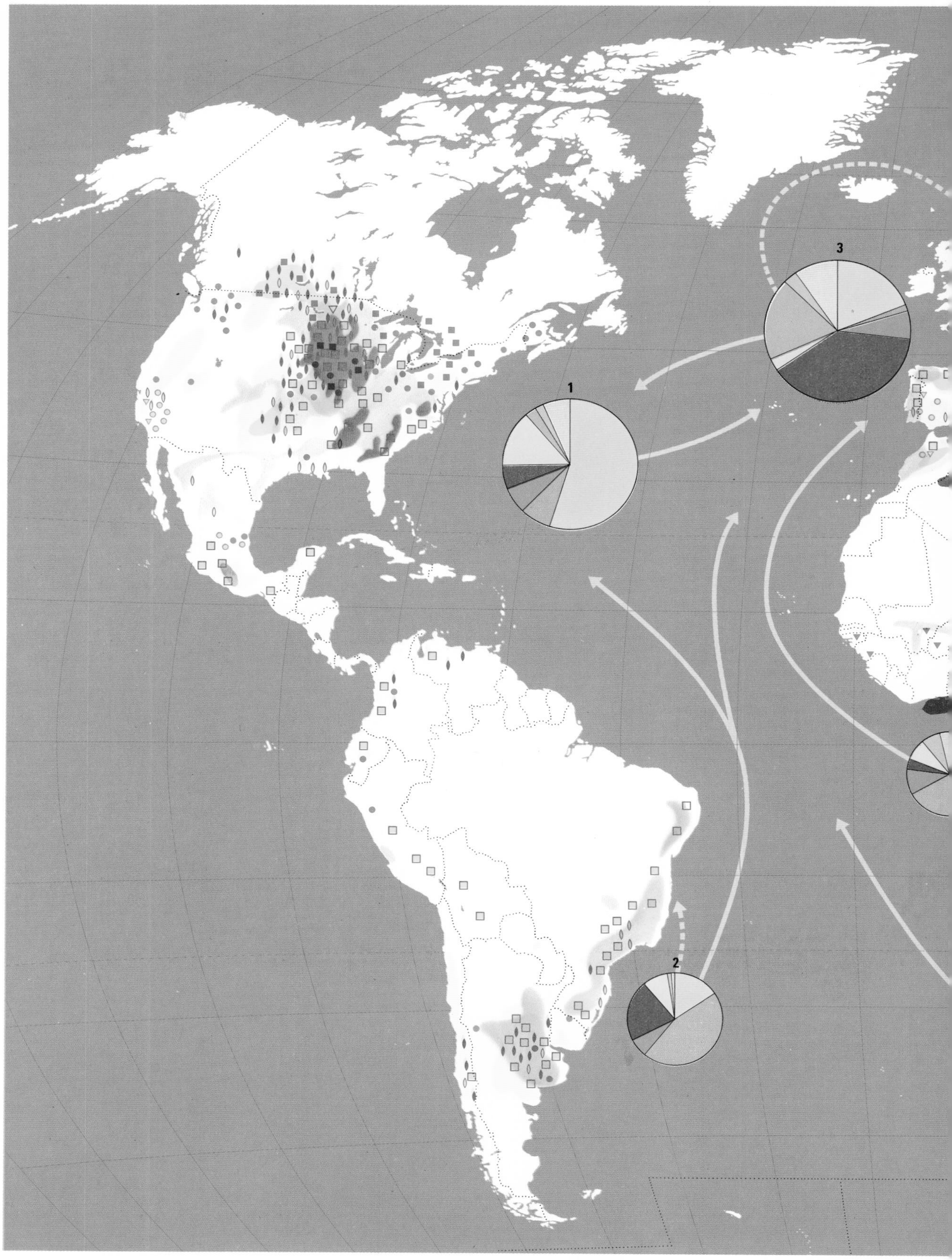

1
2
3

World crop production and trade *right above*
In the large map, symbols and shading indicate the pattern of distribution of a selection of the most important crops used for human food The distribution shown is that of growing area. This is often far removed from the plant's original center, and today the world crop pattern is being subjected to dramatic changes. For example, enormous increases have taken place in Italy's yield of maize (corn) and the United States' production of rice. Pie diagrams are used to show world crop trade, the pie area giving output and the color segments the products (key, far right).

Some important crops *right*
Eight of the world's chief human food crops are described individually at right. The figure below the name is the aggregate world production expressed in metric tons (1 m. ton is 0.984 British ton and 1.12 US tons). The pie diagrams in the form of segmented drums show the percentage of the world total raised by the three largest producing countries (in each case China is the People's Republic). The sketches illustrate the mature plant and its fruit, a form often unfamiliar to consumers. Similar panels on the next two pages deal with livestock, fish and oils.

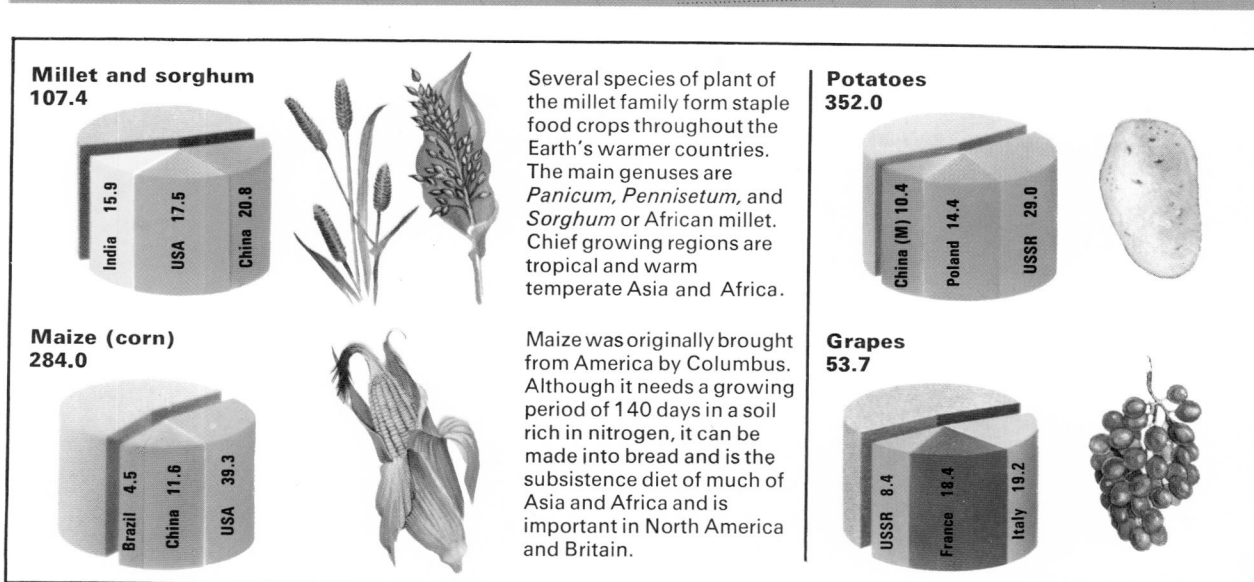

Millet and sorghum
107.4

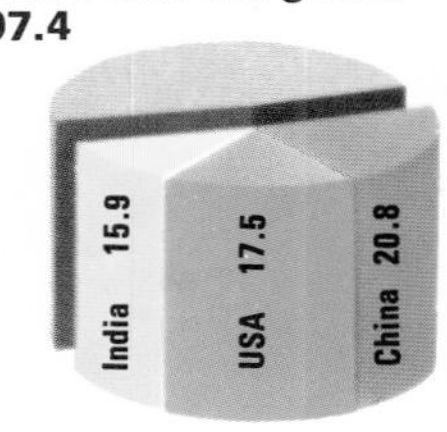

India 15.9
USA 17.5
China 20.8

Several species of plant of the millet family form staple food crops throughout the Earth's warmer countries. The main genuses are *Panicum, Pennisetum,* and *Sorghum* or African millet. Chief growing regions are tropical and warm temperate Asia and Africa.

Potatoes
352.0

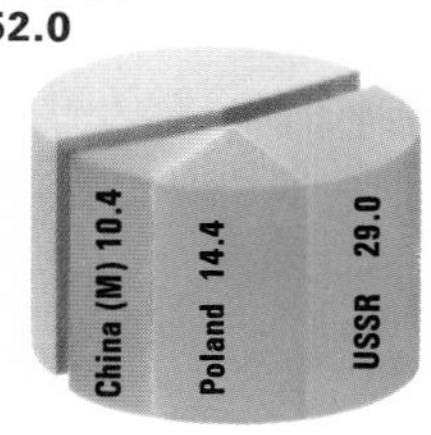

China (M) 10.4
Poland 14.4
USSR 29.0

Maize (corn)
284.0

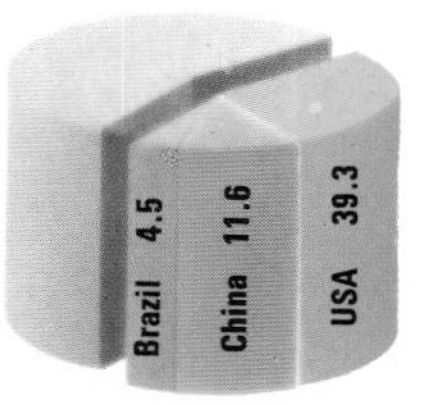

Brazil 4.5
China 11.6
USA 39.3

Maize was originally brought from America by Columbus. Although it needs a growing period of 140 days in a soil rich in nitrogen, it can be made into bread and is the subsistence diet of much of Asia and Africa and is important in North America and Britain.

Grapes
53.7

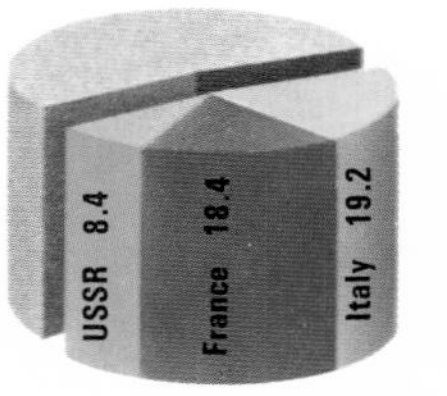

USSR 8.4
France 18.4
Italy 19.2

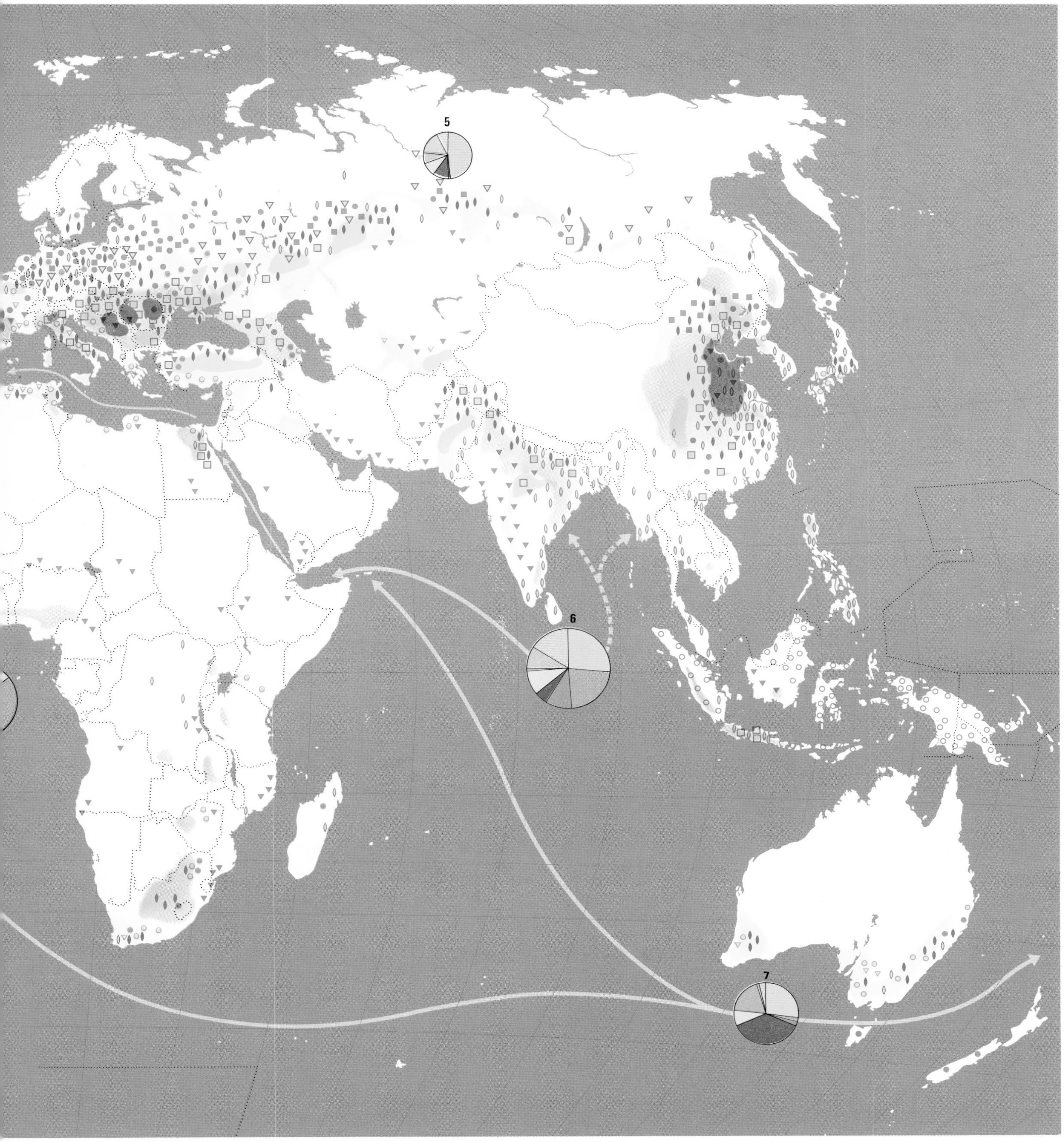
5
6
7

Cereals, predominantly wheat

Cereals, predominantly maize

Shading is proportional to intensity of cultivation.

- Wheat
- Barley
- Rye
- Corn (maize)
- Sago
- Sorghum
- Millet
- Rice
- Potatoes
- Apples
- Citrus fruit
- Grapes

The circular 'pie diagrams' depict world trade in selected agricultural products in 1968: 1 N and Central America; 2 S America 3 Europe 4 Africa; 5 Soviet Union 6 Asia 7 Oceania Products considered are cereals, beverages, meat and meat products, fish and fish products, dairy products, fruit and vegetables, vegetable oils and sugar.

- Cereals
- Beverages
- Fruit
- Meat and meat products
- Sugar
- Dairy products
- Vegetable oils
- Fish and fish products

Total trade US$ million

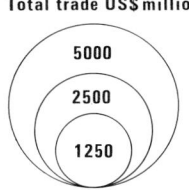

5000
2500
1250

Native to South America, the potato was introduced by Spanish explorers to an intrigued Europe about 1572. Although it needs a long, cool growing season, and a high nutrient level. it yields more food per area of land than cereals. It is a source of alcohol.

The vine thrives in warm, temperate areas, although the quality of its rootstock is critical to its nutrient demand and its resistance to disease and drought. About 80 per cent of the world crop is made into wine, but large quantities are dried for raisins.

Rice
284.2

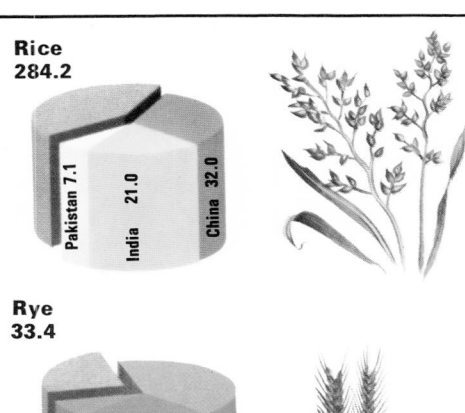

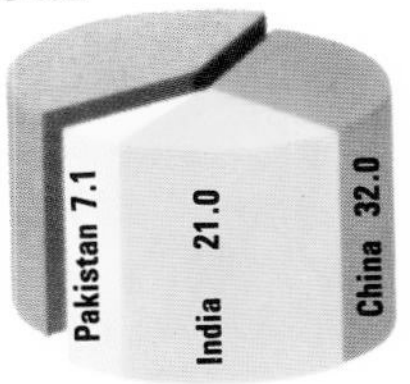
Pakistan 7.1
India 21.0
China 32.0

Grown in Asia for at least 5000 years, rice was introduced into Europe by the Arabs. Irrigation or a very heavy rainfall is essential for growing rice, with the fields being flooded for most of the season. The main source of vitamins, the husk, is removed in milling.

Rye
33.4

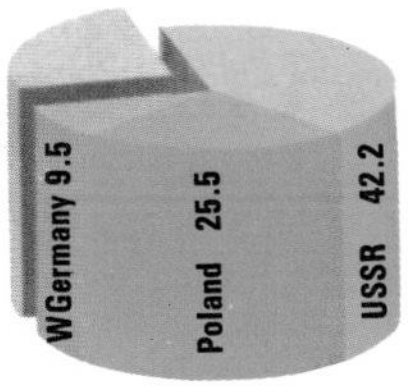
WGermany 9.5
Poland 25.5
USSR 42.2

Gradually giving way to other cereals, rye is important where soils are sandy and acid and the winters long and harsh. From Britain deep into Siberia it remains a staple foodstuff used for animal feeds, for various forms of bread and for whisky.

Wheat
332.5

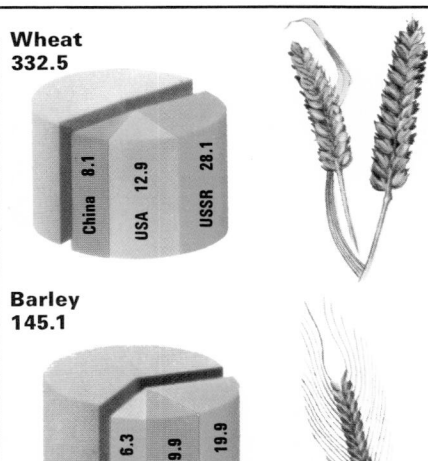

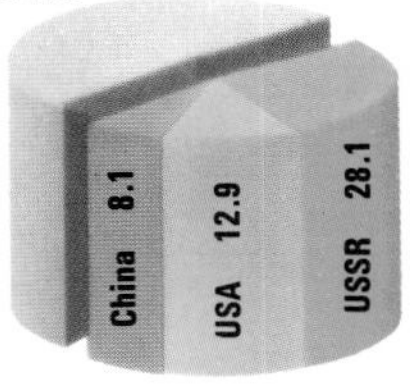
China 8.1
USA 12.9
USSR 28.1

Wheat is the most basic human food of the temperate zone. It flourishes in well-drained, fertile conditions, but can rapidly exhaust the soil. New breeds have been genetically tailored to improve yield and resistance to disease (p.65).

Barley
145.1

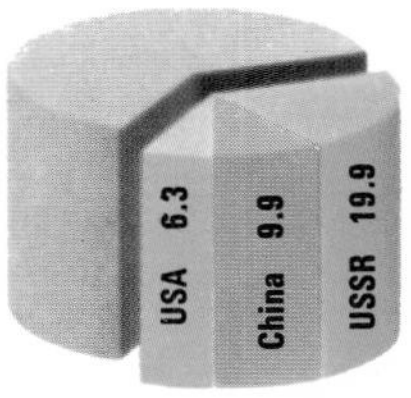
USA 6.3
China 9.9
USSR 19.9

Barley has a very short growing season and so can be produced further north and at a higher altitude than any other cereal. It needs good drainage and non-acid soil. More than half the world crop is eaten by livestock, and 12 per cent goes into making beer.

The Food Resource:2

Unloading frozen lamb carcasses.

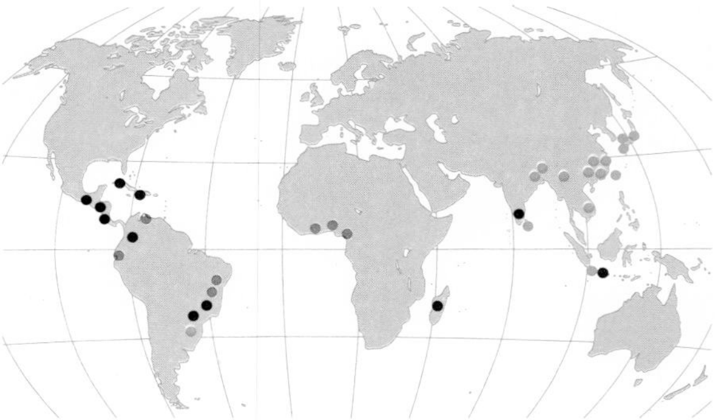

Beverages
Coffee, cocoa and tea are grown in the tropics for export to economically advanced countries where their chief role is to add flavor rather than to provide nutrition. Tea is the cheapest at present.

- Coffee
- Cocoa
- Tea

Spices
Invariably these are pungent, aromatic vegetable products. They have been important European imports since pre-Roman times, and a major source today is Indonesia. Spices are extracted from buds, bark and pods.

- Pimento
- Ginger
- Nutmeg
- Mace
- Pepper
- Cloves
- Cinnamon
- Cassia
- Vanilla

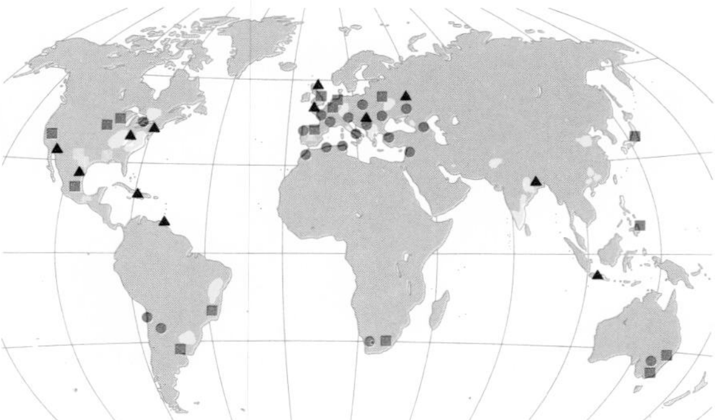

Alcohol and tobacco
Originally native to South America, tobacco was brought to Europe by the Spanish 400 years ago. Today, it is grown all over the world in various climates and soils. The US is the biggest producer.

- Beer
- Wine
- Spirits
- Tobacco

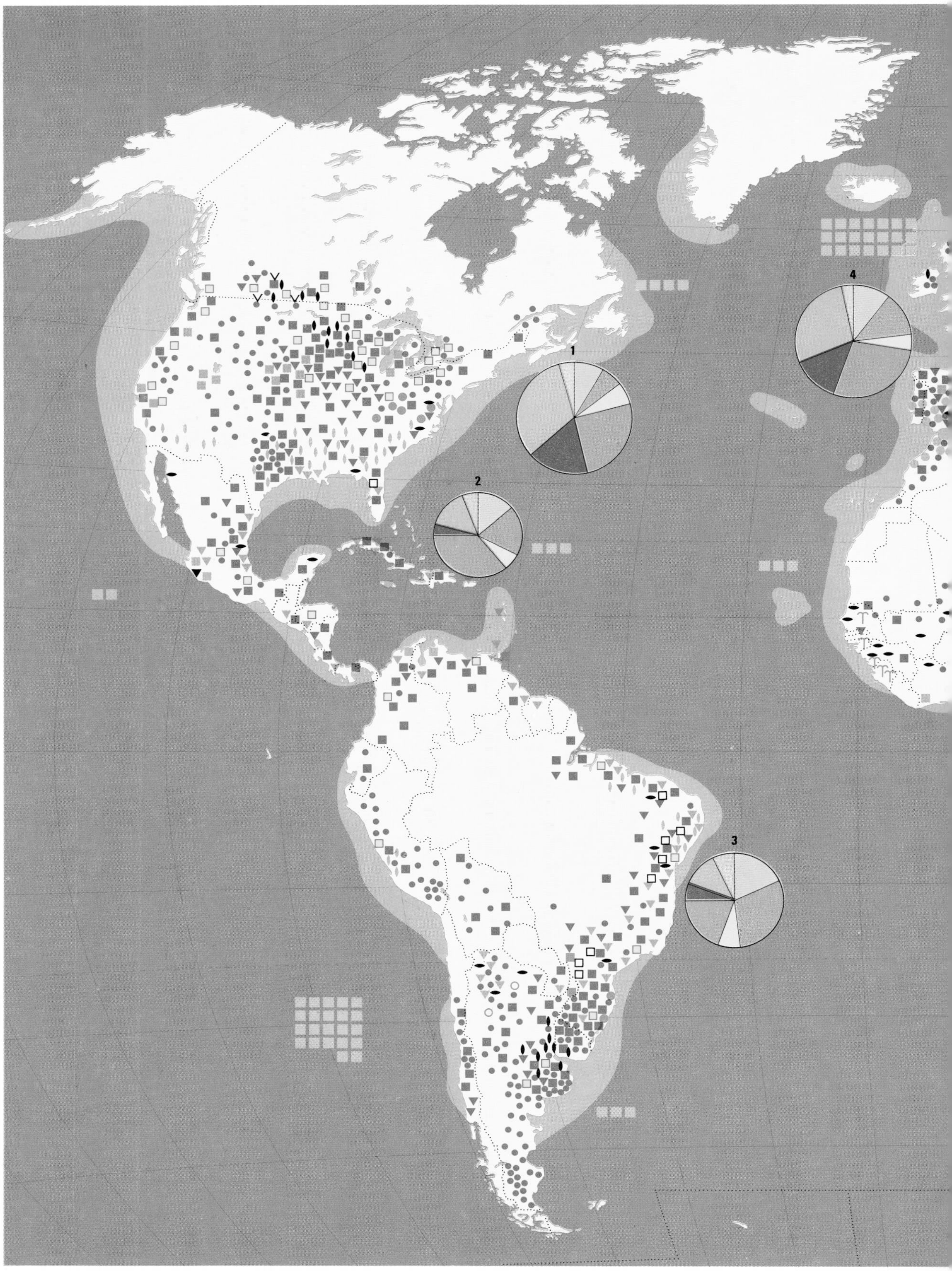

1
2
3
4

Beef cattle
Beef 29.7

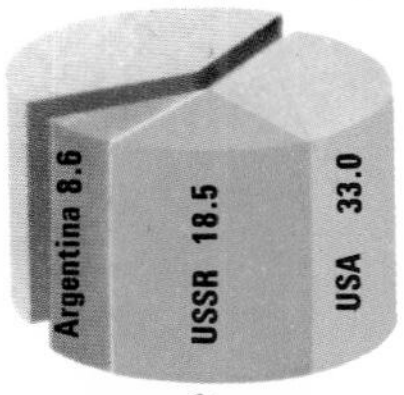

Argentina 8.6
USSR 18.5
USA 33.0

The two principal types of domestic cattle, the Eurpopean and the tropical Zebu or humped type, are found all over the world in every type of climate. There is an urgent need in the developing countries for better breeding, disease control and management.

Dairy cattle
415.8

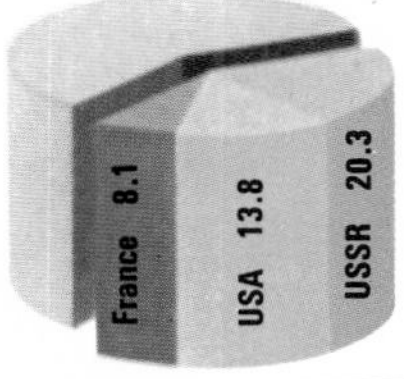

France 8.1
USA 13.8
USSR 20.3

Specialized dairy farming takes place mainly near densely populated urban areas with a high standard of living, though there is an increasing trend towards combined milk/meat herds. Various forms of processing, such as canning and freezing, extend product life.

Sheep
Mutton 4.5

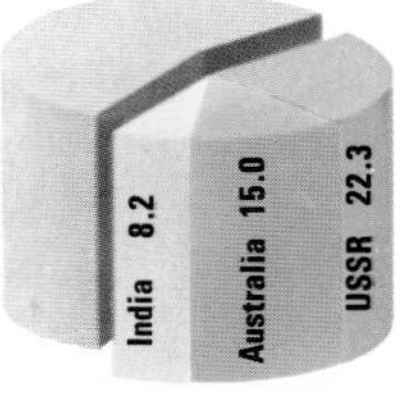

India 8.2
Australia 15.0
USSR 22.3

Sheep are kept mainly for meat and wool, although in southern Europe they may be milked and in the tropics the hides are the most important product. Sheep do not lend themselves readily to 'factory farming' and are raised on marginal land only.

Pigs
Pork 24.5

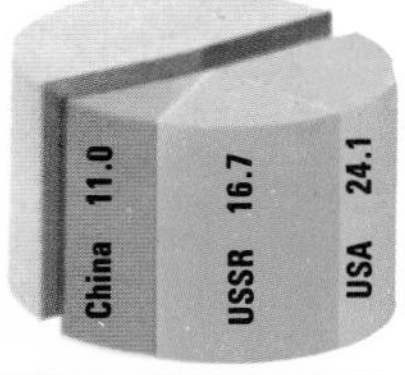

China 11.0
USSR 16.7
USA 24.1

Because they are often kept indoors, the distribution of pigs depends more on food supply than on the climate. They are often found on mixed farms where they are fed on by-products such as skim milk. Their breeding cycle is complete in about six months.

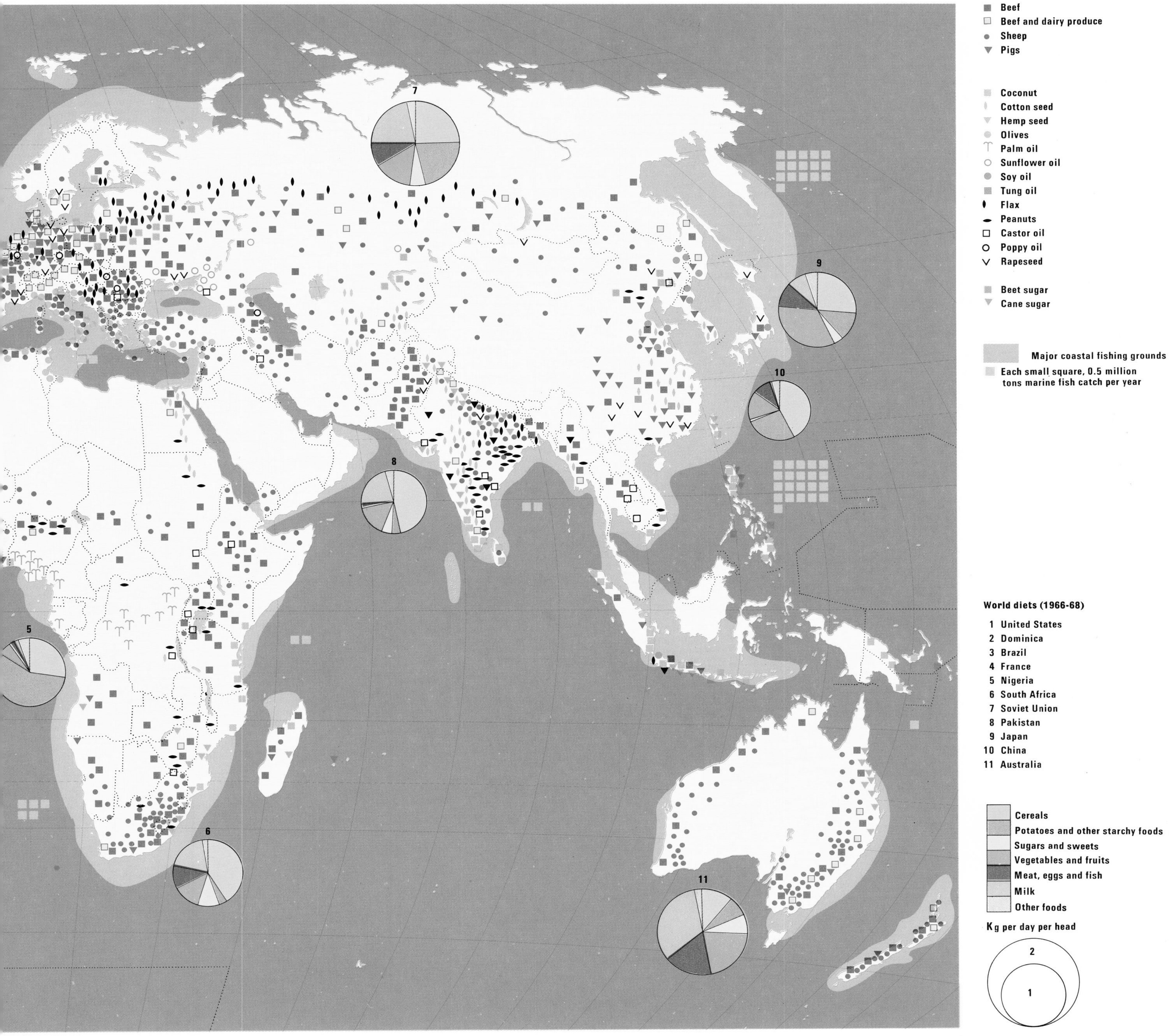

Beef
Beef and dairy produce
Sheep
Pigs
Coconut
Cotton seed
Hemp seed
Olives
Palm oil
Sunflower oil
Soy oil
Tung oil
Flax
Peanuts
Castor oil
Poppy oil
Rapeseed
Beet sugar
Cane sugar
Major coastal fishing grounds
Each small square, 0.5 million tons marine fish catch per year
World diets (1966-68)
1 United States
2 Dominica
3 Brazil
4 France
5 Nigeria
6 South Africa
7 Soviet Union
8 Pakistan
9 Japan
10 China
11 Australia
Cereals
Potatoes and other starchy foods
Sugars and sweets
Vegetables and fruits
Meat, eggs and fish
Milk
Other foods
Kg per day per head
2
1

Vegetable oils
20.7

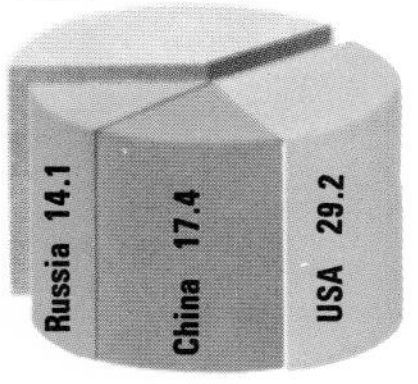

Russia 14.1
China 17.4
USA 29.2

The demand for vegetable oils, which are produced from plants found all over the world, has risen dramatically over the past 100 years, in parallel with the rise in prosperity and the discovery of new uses. The pattern of production has also altered markedly, with the United States changing from being a net importer to a net exporter, as a response to being cut off from supplies from China and Indonesia during World War 2. Vegetable oils are used in the manufacture of such products as margarine, soap and paint. They can be divided into three main categories : edible (for example, groundnut, rapeseed, olive and soy-bean), edible industrial (palm), and industrial (flax and castor). The oil is produced by crushing the seeds, and the residue often makes good cattle feed.

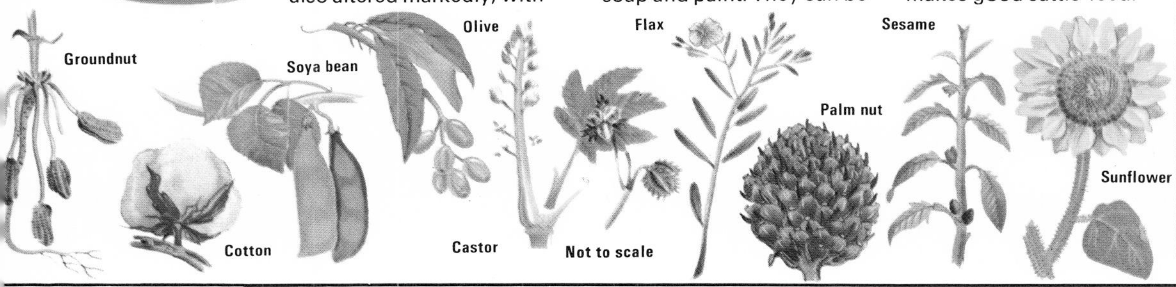

Groundnut
Soya bean
Olive
Flax
Sesame
Palm nut
Sunflower
Cotton
Castor
Not to scale

Sugar
79.2

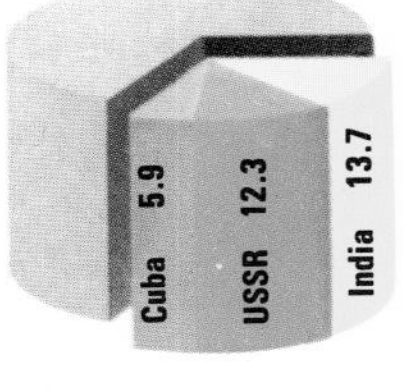

Cuba 5.9
USSR 12.3
India 13.7

There are two sources of sugar : cane and beet. Cane sugar is a perennial found in the warm tropics, while sugar-beet is produced mainly in Europe. As it is more expensive to produce than cane its production is often protected by tariffs.

Fish
64.0

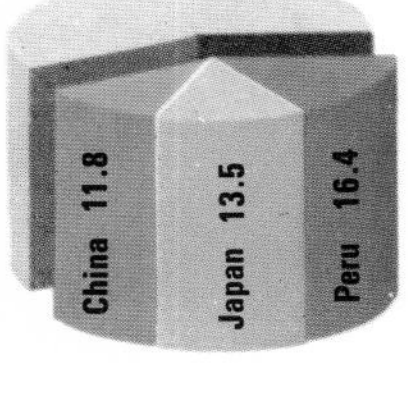

China 11.8
Japan 13.5
Peru 16.4

Fish are a valuable source of protein. As they putrify so easily and thus are subject to distribution problems, an increasing amount of the world catch is converted into meal for use in animal feeds. Most fish are caught near the coasts over the continental shelves.

Man on Earth

Throughout the history of the Earth no animal species has been as successful biologically as modern man *Homo sapiens sapiens.* Much of this success he owes to the remarkable nature of his body and mind. Compared with many animals, man has a primitive unspecialized body that can be turned to many uses. This, coupled with a brain of large size and complexity, has enabled man to develop a rich emotional and material life, leading to the intricate society of the world today. And yet, even in the midst of success come forebodings: man's rapid spread and growth in numbers could destroy by their excessive demands the environment that has nurtured him. If left unchecked, the twin perils of pollution and human conflict could remove man from the world that he has helped to shape. All that would remain of his brief trusteeship – less than 40000 years – would be the ruins of a spent civilization marking yet another unsuccessful experiment in the evolution of life on the planet Earth.

The diversity of man
The migrations of early man, which took him into all kinds of new environments, imposed the racial patterns that are apparent now. Only in recent times has man become free of these constraints through the agency of his knowledge and technical skills.

The Body of Man

The human form has long been an object of aesthetic pleasure and physical desire, but the actual workings of the body have remained very much a mystery until quite recent times. Although Leonardo da Vinci (1452-1519), Andreas Vesalius (1514-64) and others produced fine detailed anatomical drawings, the various functions of the body were still only poorly understood and were often grossly misinterpreted by the early physicians. Even now, there are gaps in medical knowledge, but our understanding is such that the emphasis of modern medical and biological research has moved from the broader subject of form and function to processes occurring within single cells and the relationship of these to disease and the physiology of the body.

Just how man came to be endowed with his unique physical and mental capabilities must remain a matter of speculation. However, an important 'breakthrough' which gave renewed potential to the body's evolutionary progress must have been the freeing of the forelimbs of ancestral man from the main task of helping to support his weight. This left the arms and the versatile hand free to make and to manipulate objects, in particular primitive tools. The jaw also began to recede allowing a reduction in the thick heavy cranium needed to anchor and support the jaw muscles. In consequence, the brain had room to expand and so provide for the fine control of his limbs. The enlarging of the brain also allowed the development of speech and the use of the muscles of the face as a further means of communication.

During the course of life, the human body is replenished and renewed by the repair of worn out tissues. Body proteins are replaced in this way every 28 days and calcium in the bones every 120 days. Man's body is thus completely changed every few months. Not all tissues have the same capacity for repair. Skin and muscle tissues repair quickly and easily, whereas cells in the brain, once they are damaged, show only minimal regeneration. However, in spite of the continual renewal of man's body, slow irreversible changes do occur which lead to its ageing. Should science ever discover a way of halting this process, there seems no reason why the body, with its own innate capacity for renewal, should not be able to survive indefinitely.

Taking in energy

The diagram below contains all the major elements of the human digestive system, the function of which is to assimilate the energy contained in food and transform its constituents into usable matter.

The digestive system

In the mouth food is chewed up and mixed with saliva containing an enzyme—a biological catalyst—which starts the process of chemical digestion. The tongue molds the food into a ball or bolus convenient for swallowing.

Rhythmic contractions in the wall of the esophagus (1) carry the food to the stomach (2).

Food stays three to five hours being churned by muscle (3) action and mixed with acid juices, and two further enzymes. The acid enables enzymes to act and also kills many of the microbes taken in with the food.

The partially digested food called chyme passes into the duodenum (4), the 10 in (250 mm) first section of the 22 ft long (6.7 m) small intestine. Alkaline secretions now neutralize the acid contents.

Bile, which contains no enzymes, is fed from the gall bladder (5) in the liver (6). It emulsifies fat and activates fat-splitting enzymes in the other secretions.

The pancreas (7) secretes enzymes that act on fat, protein and carbohydrate.

The wall of the small intestine (8) also releases enzymes that act on all types of food. Digestion is completed here. The food is reduced to chemicals that can be absorbed through the lining of the intestine. The journey through the small intestine takes about 4½ hours.

Approximately every four hours a valve (9) opens enabling material to enter the large intestine (10) which is about 5 ft (1.5 m) long. Here it stays for six to 20 hours while water is retrieved.

Only feces remain. These pass into the rectum (11) and are expelled through the anus (12).

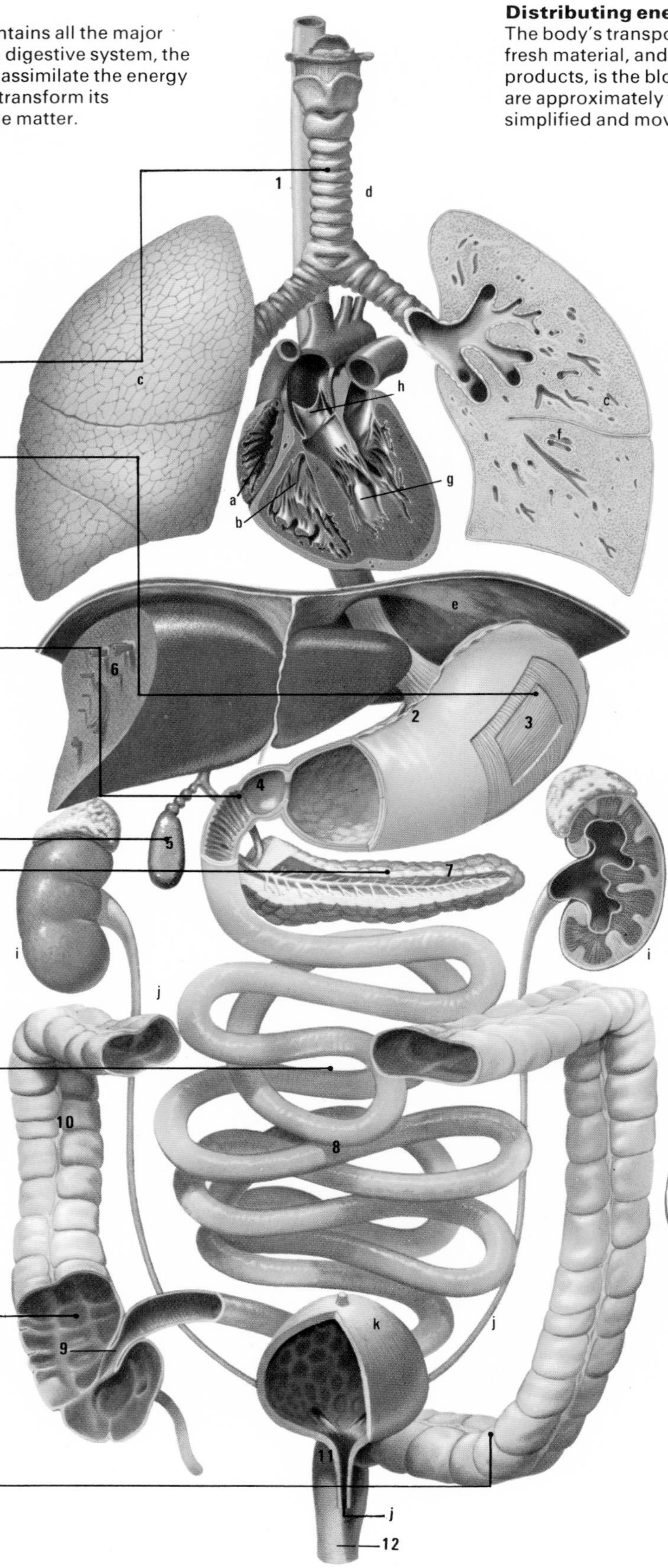

1
d
c
h
g
a
b
e
6
2
3
4
5
7
i
j
10
8
9
k
11
12

Distributing energy

The body's transport system for energy and fresh material, and for carrying away waste products, is the blood. All the organs shown are approximately to scale, but they are simplified and moved further apart for clarity.

The blood system

Most adults have about a gallon (4.5 litres) of blood. The key organ in its circulation is, of course, the heart. Stale venous blood from the body passes into its right auricle (a) and then through a one-way valve into the right ventricle (b). Strong contractions of the ventricle drive the blood to the lungs (c). Here air drawn down the trachea (d) by the expansion of the chest and downward movement of the diaphragm (e) is brought into close contact with the blood which sheds carbon dioxide and absorbs oxygen in the sac-like alveoli (f). The blood then returns to the left ventricle (g) via the left auricle (h). The ventricle pumps the oxygenated blood to all parts of the body via the arteries. Other wastes in the blood are removed by the kidneys (i) and excreted as urine which flows via the ureters (j) to the bladder (k). It remains there until voided down the urethra (l). Blood also goes to the small intestine (8) where it collects digested food substances and carries them to the liver (6) for processing or storage.

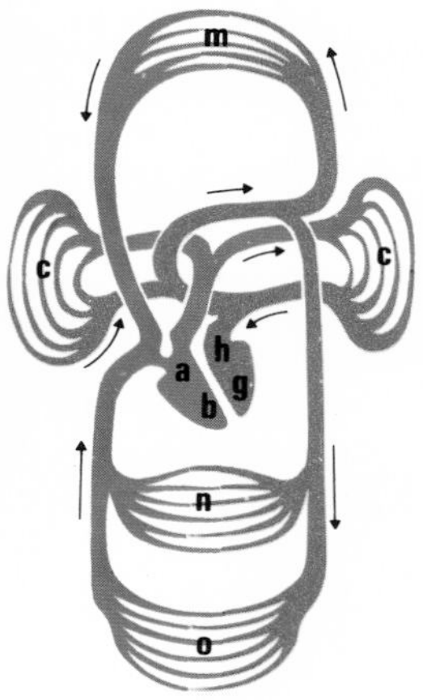

m
c
c
h
a
b
g
n
o

The heart pumps bl from left auricle (h) ventricle (g) through head and arms (m), lungs (c), trunk (n) and legs (o). Blood returns to the right auricle (a).

Nitrogen 34.0g
Phosphorus 12.0g
Calcium 22.4g
Sodium 1.84g
Chloride 1.77g
Potassium 2.5g
Water 720g
Magnesium 0.47g
Iron 74.0mg
Zinc 28.0mg
Copper 1.7mg
Barium 0.37mg
Cobalt 0.02mg

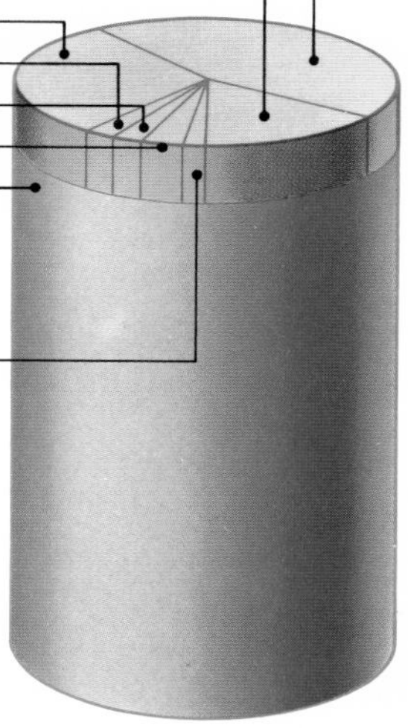

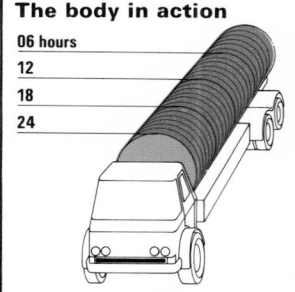

Chemical composition

A typical adult weighs about 154 lb (70 kg). The chemical make-up of a healthy body is depicted here, the predominance of water being obvious. About 43 per cent of the body is muscle, and 7 per cent skin.

The body in action

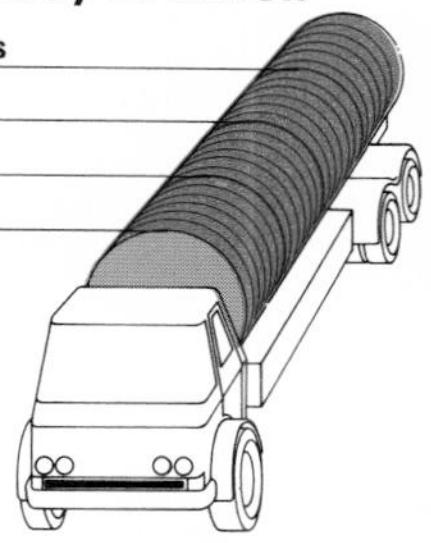

06 hours
12
18
24

The heart's output *above*

If an average adult heart continuously pumped fresh blood, it could in 24 hours fill this 2642 US gallon (10000 liter) tanker. It has also been calculated that the body's blood vessels total 65000 mi (100,000 km).

The following are average figures for a healthy adult male:

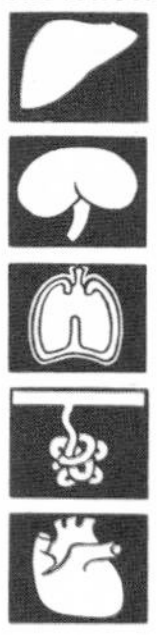

Liver Generates 0.5-1 quart of bile a day.

Kidneys Pass 159 quarts of dilute filtrate per day, of which 148.5 are re-absorbed and 1.5 emitted as urine.

Lungs Pump 407 cubic feet of air per day but can work at 30 times this rate for short periods.

Sweat Glands in the skin exude 0.6 quart per day but in extreme conditions can emit 9.5 quarts (7000 calories).

Heart Pumps 2642 gallons per day but can work six times this rate in extreme exercise.

Limits of endurance

Deprivation of food Total deprivation, (with water), 94 days; allowance of liquids of very small nutritive value, 382 days

Deprivation of air With previous hyperventilation with oxygen, 13.7 minutes; without, 5.7 minutes

Limits of internal body temperature For survival, approximately 15° - 43.5°C (59°-110°F); normal is 98.4°F (36.9°C)

Limits of performance

Fastest running
26.9 mph (43.3 kmh) May 1964

Longest jump
29 ft 2½ in (8.90 m) 18 October 1968

Fastest swimming
4.89 mph (7.88 kmh) 26 March 1964

Highest jump
7' 6¼" (2.29 m) 3 July 1971

Heaviest weight lifted In back lift, 6270 lb (2844 kg) 12 June 1957

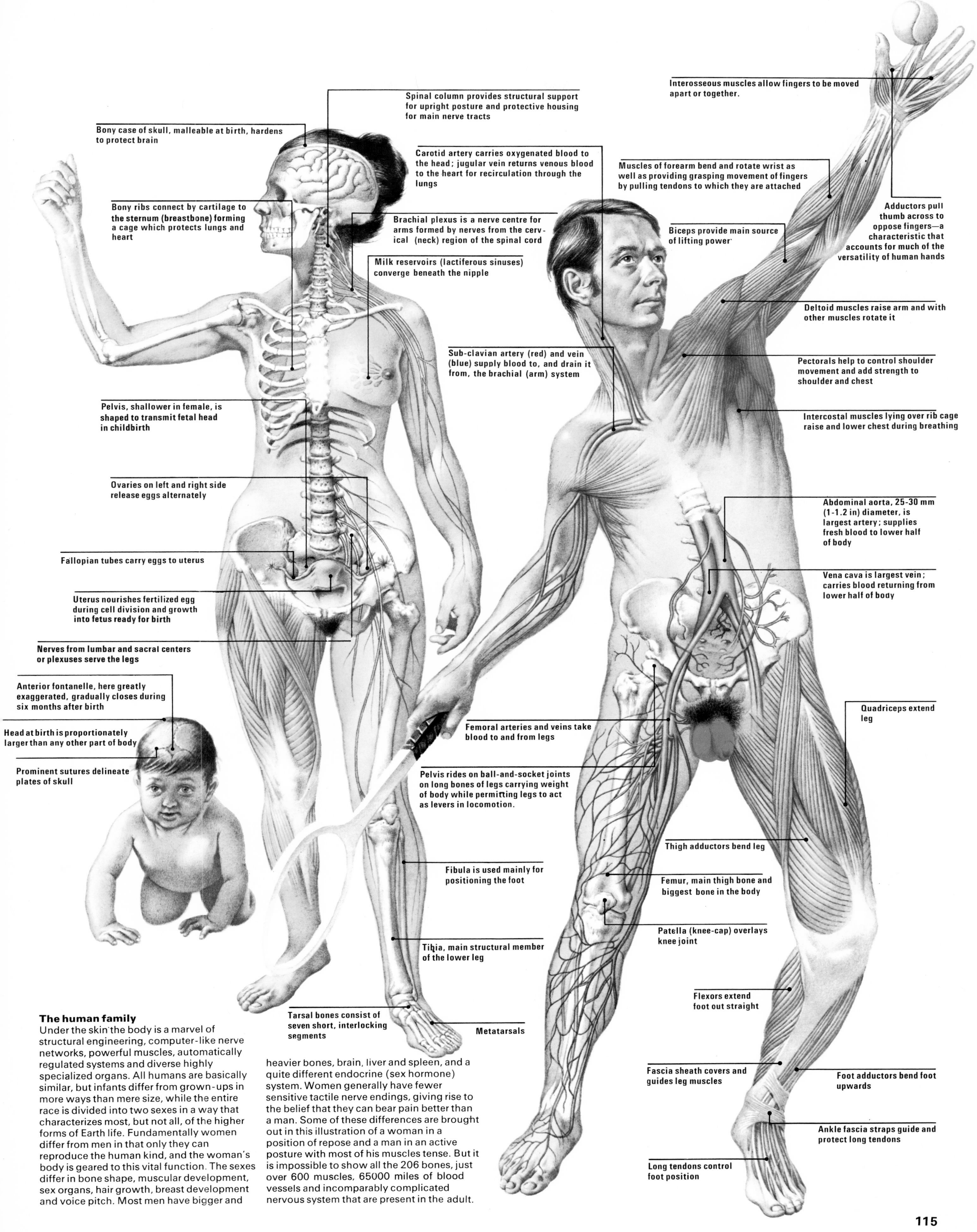

Spinal column provides structural support for upright posture and protective housing for main nerve tracts
Bony case of skull, malleable at birth, hardens to protect brain
Carotid artery carries oxygenated blood to the head; jugular vein returns venous blood to the heart for recirculation through the lungs
Bony ribs connect by cartilage to the sternum (breastbone) forming a cage which protects lungs and heart
Brachial plexus is a nerve centre for arms formed by nerves from the cervical (neck) region of the spinal cord
Milk reservoirs (lactiferous sinuses) converge beneath the nipple
Pelvis, shallower in female, is shaped to transmit fetal head in childbirth
Ovaries on left and right side release eggs alternately
Fallopian tubes carry eggs to uterus
Uterus nourishes fertilized egg during cell division and growth into fetus ready for birth
Nerves from lumbar and sacral centers or plexuses serve the legs
Anterior fontanelle, here greatly exaggerated, gradually closes during six months after birth
Head at birth is proportionately larger than any other part of body
Prominent sutures delineate plates of skull
Interosseous muscles allow fingers to be moved apart or together.
Muscles of forearm bend and rotate wrist as well as providing grasping movement of fingers by pulling tendons to which they are attached
Adductors pull thumb across to oppose fingers—a characteristic that accounts for much of the versatility of human hands
Biceps provide main source of lifting power
Deltoid muscles raise arm and with other muscles rotate it
Sub-clavian artery (red) and vein (blue) supply blood to, and drain it from, the brachial (arm) system
Pectorals help to control shoulder movement and add strength to shoulder and chest
Intercostal muscles lying over rib cage raise and lower chest during breathing
Abdominal aorta, 25-30 mm (1-1.2 in) diameter, is largest artery; supplies fresh blood to lower half of body
Vena cava is largest vein; carries blood returning from lower half of body
Quadriceps extend leg
Femoral arteries and veins take blood to and from legs
Pelvis rides on ball-and-socket joints on long bones of legs carrying weight of body while permitting legs to act as levers in locomotion.
Thigh adductors bend leg
Fibula is used mainly for positioning the foot
Femur, main thigh bone and biggest bone in the body
Patella (knee-cap) overlays knee joint
Tibia, main structural member of the lower leg
Flexors extend foot out straight
Tarsal bones consist of seven short, interlocking segments
Metatarsals
Fascia sheath covers and guides leg muscles
Foot adductors bend foot upwards
Ankle fascia straps guide and protect long tendons
Long tendons control foot position

The human family

Under the skin the body is a marvel of structural engineering, computer-like nerve networks, powerful muscles, automatically regulated systems and diverse highly specialized organs. All humans are basically similar, but infants differ from grown-ups in more ways than mere size, while the entire race is divided into two sexes in a way that characterizes most, but not all, of the higher forms of Earth life. Fundamentally women differ from men in that only they can reproduce the human kind, and the woman's body is geared to this vital function. The sexes differ in bone shape, muscular development, sex organs, hair growth, breast development and voice pitch. Most men have bigger and heavier bones, brain, liver and spleen, and a quite different endocrine (sex hormone) system. Women generally have fewer sensitive tactile nerve endings, giving rise to the belief that they can bear pain better than a man. Some of these differences are brought out in this illustration of a woman in a position of repose and a man in an active posture with most of his muscles tense. But it is impossible to show all the 206 bones, just over 600 muscles, 65000 miles of blood vessels and incomparably complicated nervous system that are present in the adult.

The Mind of Man

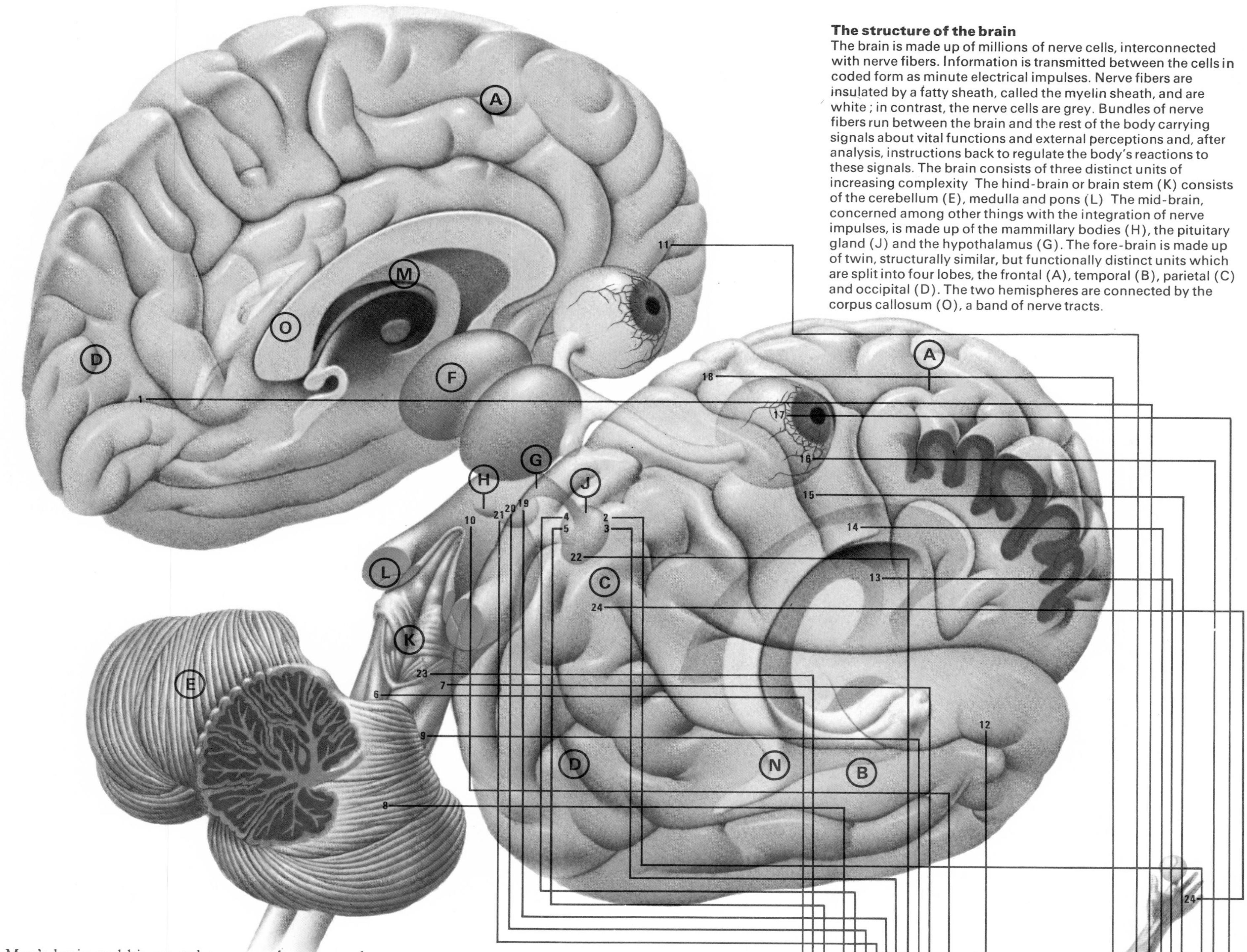

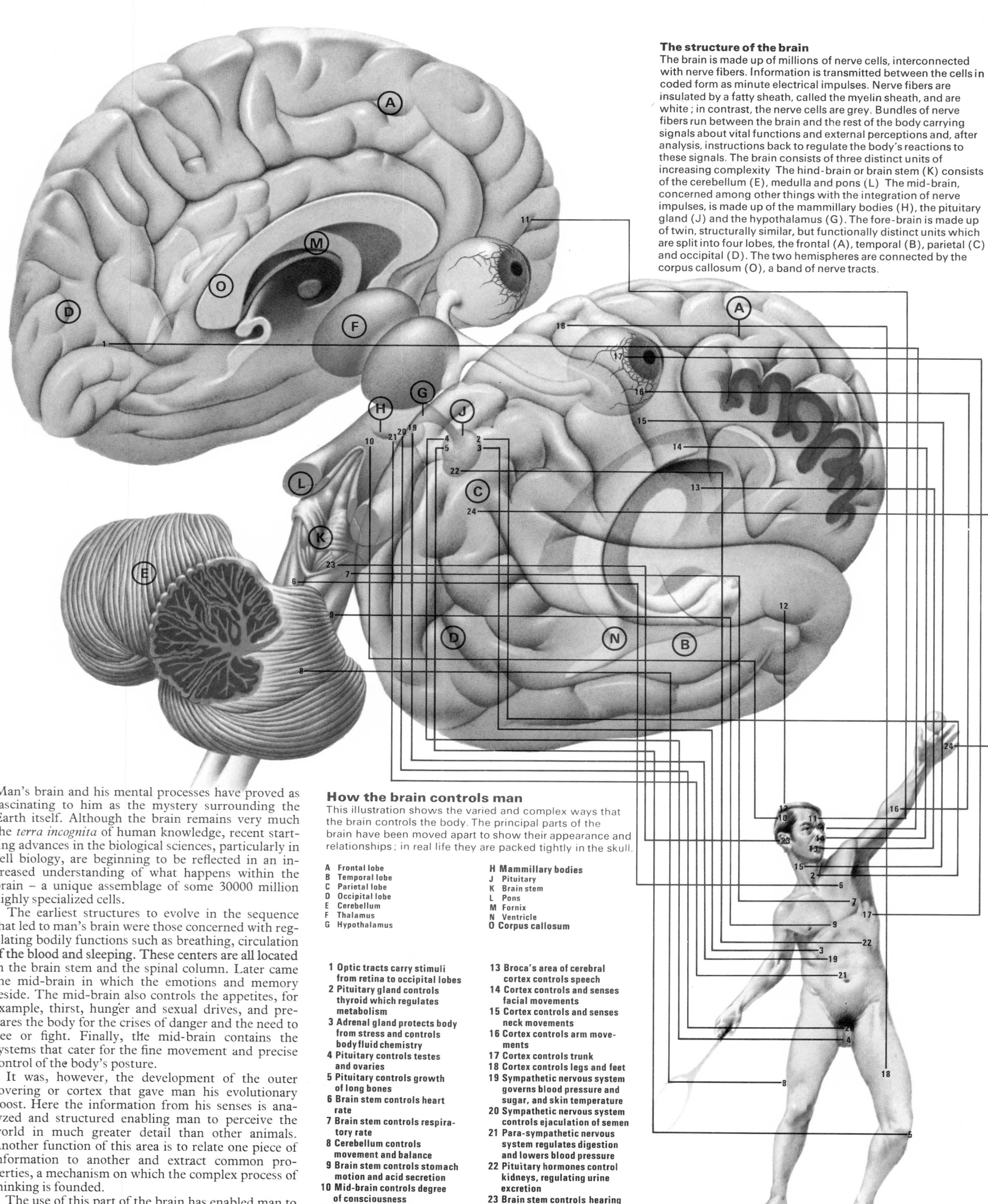

The structure of the brain

The brain is made up of millions of nerve cells, interconnected with nerve fibers. Information is transmitted between the cells in coded form as minute electrical impulses. Nerve fibers are insulated by a fatty sheath, called the myelin sheath, and are white; in contrast, the nerve cells are grey. Bundles of nerve fibers run between the brain and the rest of the body carrying signals about vital functions and external perceptions and, after analysis, instructions back to regulate the body's reactions to these signals. The brain consists of three distinct units of increasing complexity The hind-brain or brain stem (K) consists of the cerebellum (E), medulla and pons (L) The mid-brain, concerned among other things with the integration of nerve impulses, is made up of the mammillary bodies (H), the pituitary gland (J) and the hypothalamus (G). The fore-brain is made up of twin, structurally similar, but functionally distinct units which are split into four lobes, the frontal (A), temporal (B), parietal (C) and occipital (D). The two hemispheres are connected by the corpus callosum (O), a band of nerve tracts.

Man's brain and his mental processes have proved as fascinating to him as the mystery surrounding the Earth itself. Although the brain remains very much the *terra incognita* of human knowledge, recent startling advances in the biological sciences, particularly in cell biology, are beginning to be reflected in an increased understanding of what happens within the brain – a unique assemblage of some 30000 million highly specialized cells.

The earliest structures to evolve in the sequence that led to man's brain were those concerned with regulating bodily functions such as breathing, circulation of the blood and sleeping. These centers are all located in the brain stem and the spinal column. Later came the mid-brain in which the emotions and memory reside. The mid-brain also controls the appetites, for example, thirst, hunger and sexual drives, and prepares the body for the crises of danger and the need to flee or fight. Finally, the mid-brain contains the systems that cater for the fine movement and precise control of the body's posture.

It was, however, the development of the outer covering or cortex that gave man his evolutionary boost. Here the information from his senses is analyzed and structured enabling man to perceive the world in much greater detail than other animals. Another function of this area is to relate one piece of information to another and extract common properties, a mechanism on which the complex process of thinking is founded.

The use of this part of the brain has enabled man to evolve his higher mental life as well as create the technological basis of his society.

How the brain controls man

This illustration shows the varied and complex ways that the brain controls the body. The principal parts of the brain have been moved apart to show their appearance and relationships; in real life they are packed tightly in the skull.

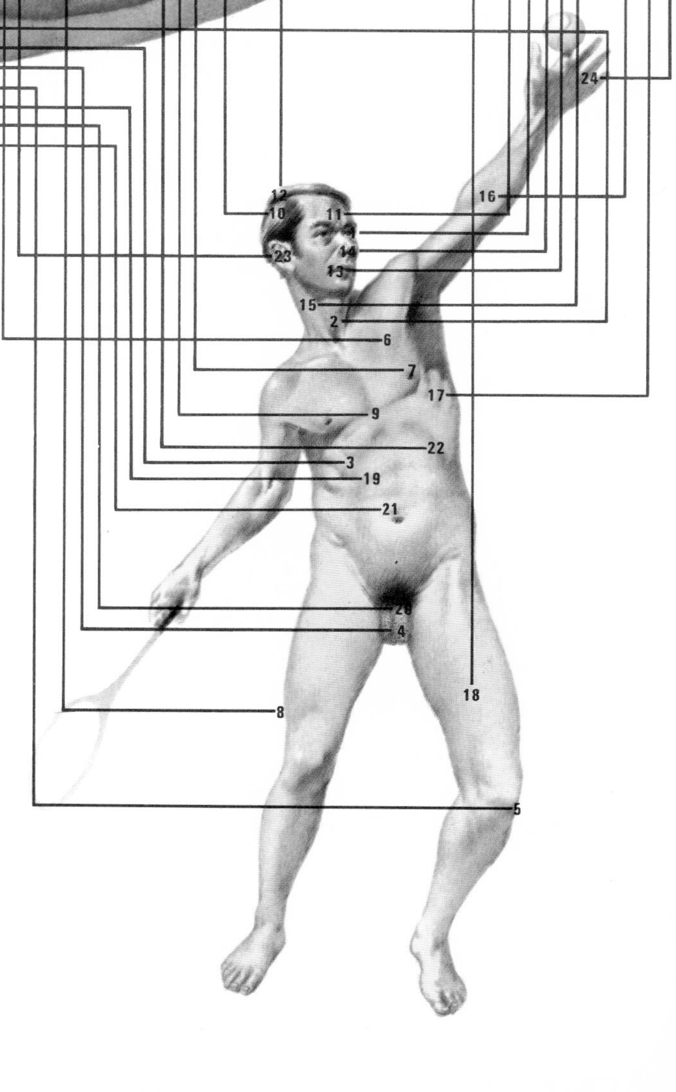

A Frontal lobe
B Temporal lobe
C Parietal lobe
D Occipital lobe
E Cerebellum
F Thalamus
G Hypothalamus
H Mammillary bodies
J Pituitary
K Brain stem
L Pons
M Fornix
N Ventricle
O Corpus callosum

1 Optic tracts carry stimuli from retina to occipital lobes
2 Pituitary gland controls thyroid which regulates metabolism
3 Adrenal gland protects body from stress and controls body fluid chemistry
4 Pituitary controls testes and ovaries
5 Pituitary controls growth of long bones
6 Brain stem controls heart rate
7 Brain stem controls respiratory rate
8 Cerebellum controls movement and balance
9 Brain stem controls stomach motion and acid secretion
10 Mid-brain controls degree of consciousness
11 Frontal lobes control judgement and personality
12 Temporal lobe, seat of memory
13 Broca's area of cerebral cortex controls speech
14 Cortex controls and senses facial movements
15 Cortex controls and senses neck movements
16 Cortex controls arm movements
17 Cortex controls trunk
18 Cortex controls legs and feet
19 Sympathetic nervous system governs blood pressure and sugar, and skin temperature
20 Sympathetic nervous system controls ejaculation of semen
21 Para-sympathetic nervous system regulates digestion and lowers blood pressure
22 Pituitary hormones control kidneys, regulating urine excretion
23 Brain stem controls hearing
24 Parietal lobe controls judgement of weight, shape, size and feel

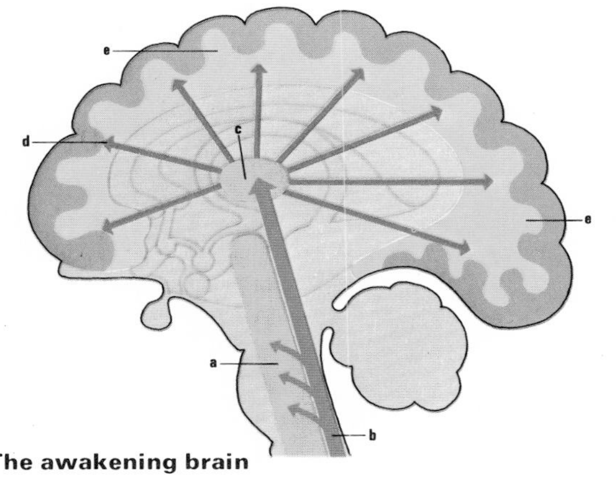
e
d
c
e
a
b

The awakening brain

Deep in the stem (a) is the reticular system which regulates the brain. Impulses from main tracts (b) carry sensory information to the sleeping brain, stimulating the reticular system to send showers of impulses to the thalamus (c). From here divergent tracts (d) arouse the cerebral cortex (e).

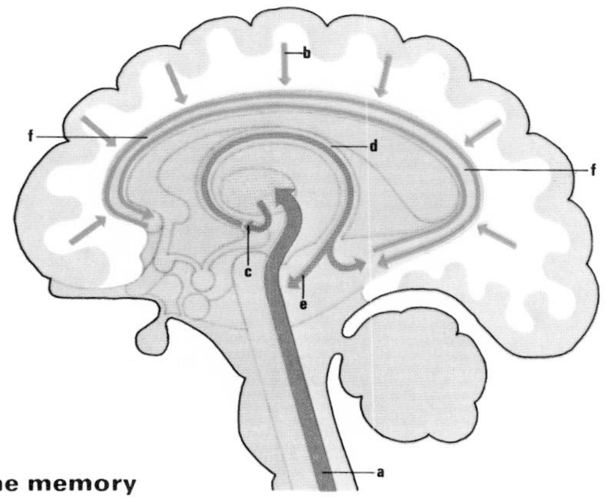
b
f
d
f
c
e
a

The memory

Impulses from the senses (a) and brain areas (b) enter the limbic system where information is filed and recalled. Impulses pass through mamillary body (c) around fornix (d) to the hippocampus (e) and cingulate gyrus (f). These limbic structures record the impressions and recall them.

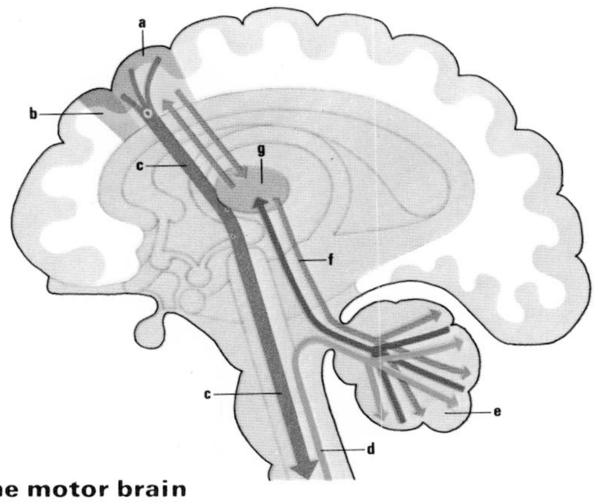
a
b
c
g
f
c
e
d

The motor brain

Movements start as complex signal patterns in motor area (a) that are modified by suppressor area (b) and transmitted via tracts (c) to spinal cord (d) and muscles. Return information via (d) reaches cerebellum (e) and then, via pathways (f) and thalamus (g), co-ordinate body movement.

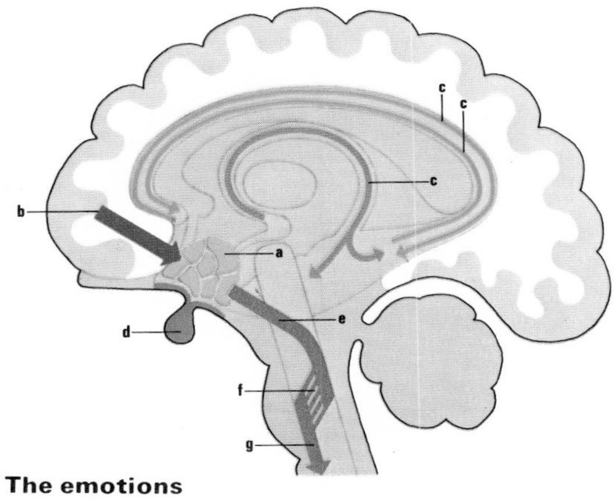
c
c
c
b
a
e
d
f
g

The emotions

Hypothalamus (a) controls appetite, sex drive, aggression and emotion generally. One input (b), from the frontal lobe, is integrated in the limbic system (c) and fed to pituitary gland (d). Limbic impulses via stem (e) control heart and lung rates (f) and other organs (g).

How man senses the world

This illustration shows the four human senses found in the head, with all organs in their correct relative location (the fifth sense, touch, is dealt with at the foot of the page). The organization of the brain is such that its computing power is greatest for the eyes, and considerably less for hearing and less still for smell and taste (inset below).

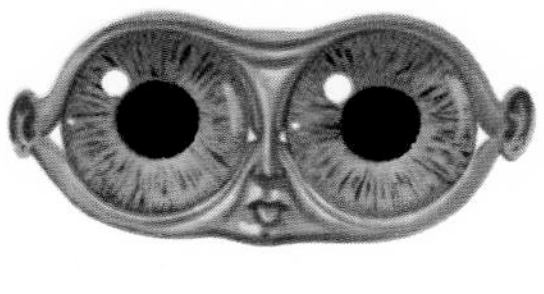

The senses present the brain with information about the outside world. They do this by means of nervous impulses that travel along separate tracts to a central nervous relay station, the thalamus, whence they pass to the cerebral cortex. The world we see and understand is wholly dependent on this sensory system. But the system has limitations For example, we cannot see X-rays, hear high-pitched sounds, or sense radio waves (except when translated into audible sound by a radio receiver), because these are beyond the parts of the spectrum to which our senses are tuned.

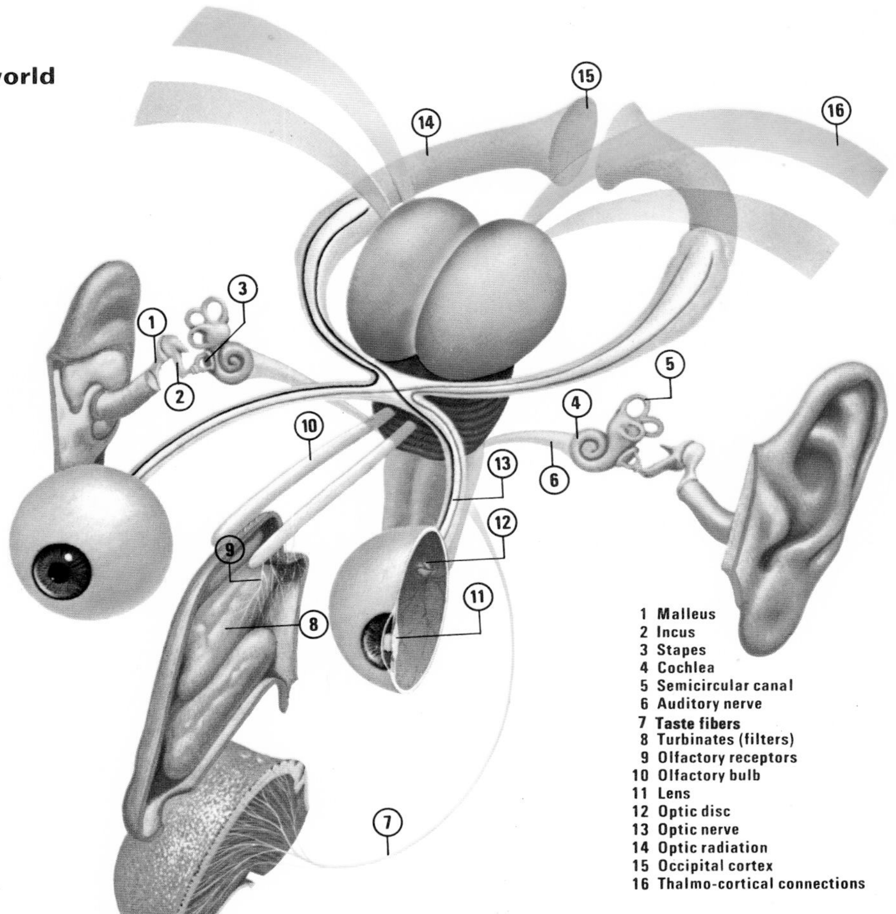
1
2
3
4
5
6
7
8
9
10
11
12
13
14
15
16

1 Malleus
2 Incus
3 Stapes
4 Cochlea
5 Semicircular canal
6 Auditory nerve
7 Taste fibers
8 Turbinates (filters)
9 Olfactory receptors
10 Olfactory bulb
11 Lens
12 Optic disc
13 Optic nerve
14 Optic radiation
15 Occipital cortex
16 Thalmo-cortical connections

Smell

The receptor cells lining the nose sense just four classes of odor: broad groups that resemble nail polish, gasoline, cedar wood and eucalyptus oil. All the countless smells of this world are derived from complex combinations of these basic chemical types.

Taste

Subtle distinctions of flavor are made mainly by smell. The tongue can distinguish only four main sensations: sweet, chiefly at the tip; sour, at the sides; bitter, at the back; and salt, all over but mainly at the front. The taste buds send impulses to the brain.

Sight

Light entering the eye pupils is focused by the lens to form an image on the retina. The retinal cones are packed so tightly that 150,000 would fit on a pin-head. The rods are so sensitive they can be stimulated by the smallest 'quantum' of light.

Hearing

The external ear and drum receive the air vibrations we call sound. These oscillate the drum, movements of which are magnified by a chain of small bones connected to the fluid-filled inner ear, where they disturb minute hairs lining the cochlea.

Nose

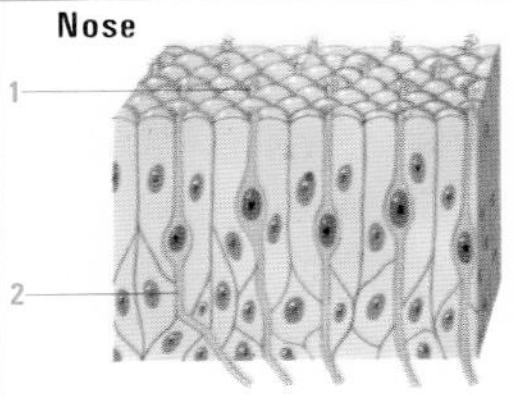
1
2

On each side of the nose cavity a peanut-size area contains receptors (1) feeding nerves (2).

Tongue

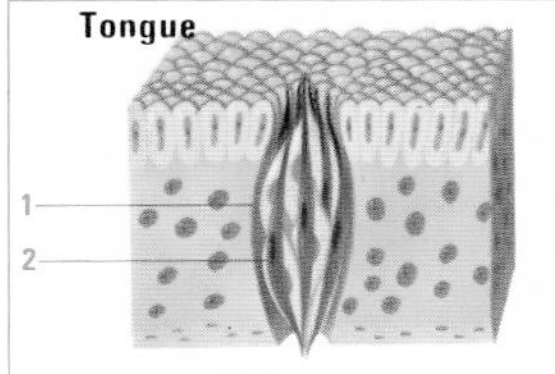
1
2

'Papillae' on the tongue contain some 10000 taste buds (1) each with about 12 gustatory cells (2).

Eye

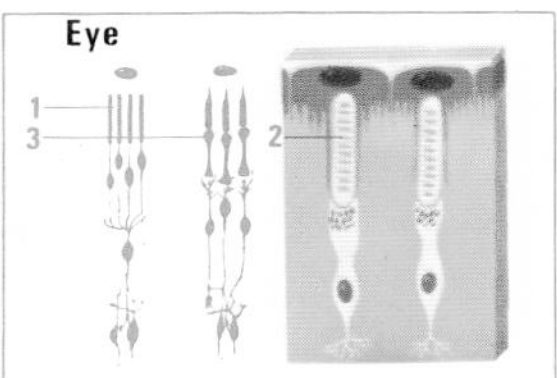
1
3
2

The retina houses some 130 million rods (1, enlarged at 2) for night vision, plus six million cones (3) for color.

Ear

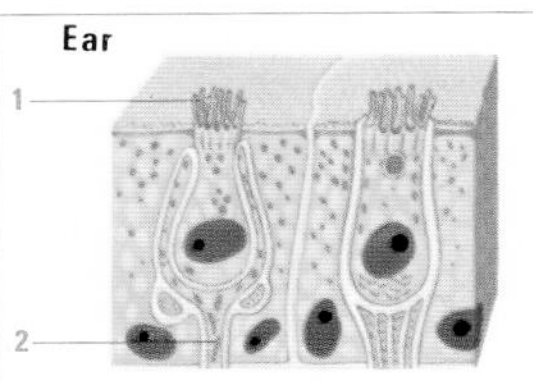
1
2

The spiral cochlea wall contains about 700,000 tiny hairs (1) which signal fluid motion to nerve (2).

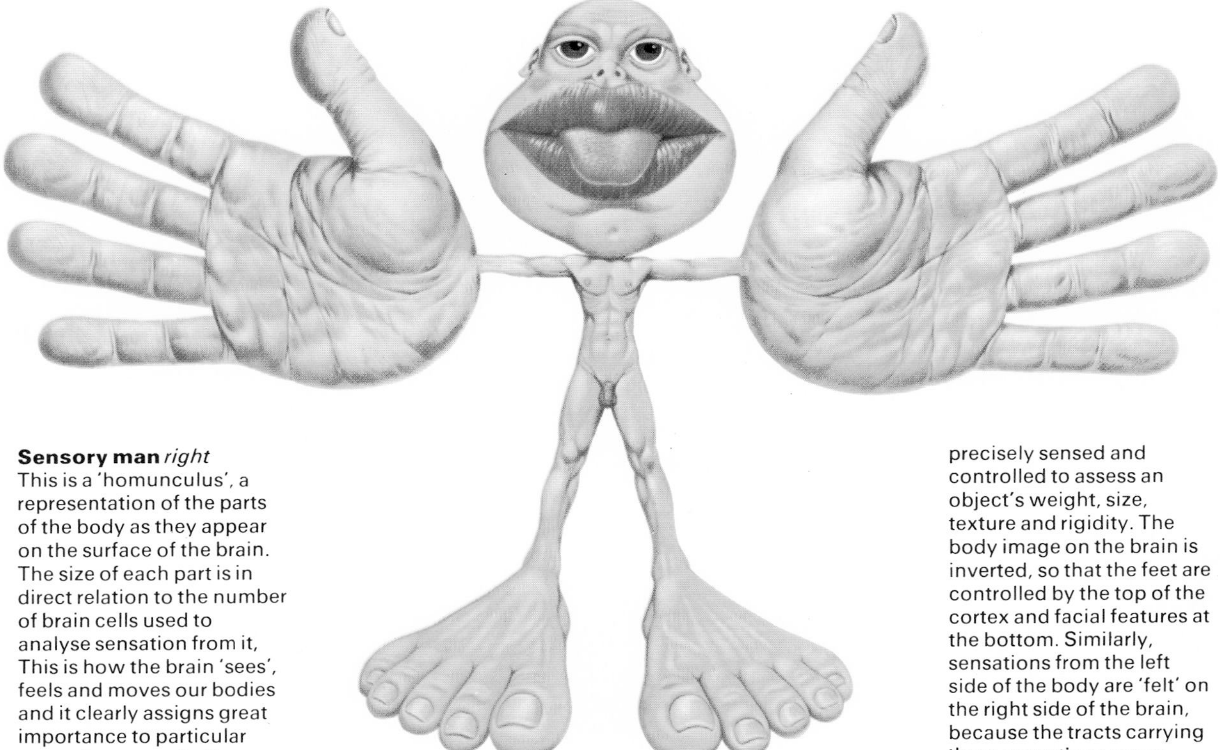

Sensory man *right*

This is a 'homunculus', a representation of the parts of the body as they appear on the surface of the brain. The size of each part is in direct relation to the number of brain cells used to analyse sensation from it. This is how the brain 'sees', feels and moves our bodies and it clearly assigns great importance to particular areas. For example, the hands and fingers are very precisely sensed and controlled to assess an object's weight, size, texture and rigidity. The body image on the brain is inverted, so that the feet are controlled by the top of the cortex and facial features at the bottom. Similarly, sensations from the left side of the body are 'felt' on the right side of the brain, because the tracts carrying these sensations cross-over in the brain.

The Family of Man: 1

The word 'race' is much maligned. It has long been made an excuse for bitter conflict among human groups. Outside the biological sciences it has been used loosely to mean many things. But, to an anthropologist, race is based on objective observations of the body: 'A race is a great subdivision of mankind, members of which, though varying individually, are characterized as a group by a certain combination of measurable features which have been derived from a common ancestor.' The criteria are bodily ones, such as color, stature, shape of head and type of hair; they are inherited and unlikely to change greatly in response to the environment.

Unfortunately the layman goes further. He adds such immeasurables as intelligence, cultural attitudes and morality. He makes snap judgments on the barest evidence, and tends to judge a whole race from one individual. He thinks, often literally, in black and white. It is important to recognize this, because this is how societies deal with classification.

A simple way to classify mankind is into three primary races: caucasoid (so-called white), mongoloid (yellow) and negroid (black). Each of these has its subdivisions. In northern Europe the Nordics are tall, slender, long-headed, big-boned, blue-eyed and fair, with blond wavy hair. The Alpines of central Europe are shorter, with broad heads, concave noses and a mass of dark wavy hair. From western Britain through Iberia to India the Mediterranean people are short and slight, with long heads and a dark complexion; they often have a hooked nose. Yet all these are caucasoids.

All mongoloids have yellowish, parchment-like skin, lank black hair and their eyes have an 'epicanthic' upper fold of skin which reduces the eye to a slit and often makes it appear slanted. Negroids, with very dark skin and woolly hair, are divided into negroes – tall, with bulging forehead and wide nose – and negrillos – very short, with rust-colored hair and almost reddish skin. In addition, there are many composite races. The S African Bushman and Hottentot may have features of very early man as well as of the negro, and their eyes have a slight epicanthic fold. Australoids have an archaic caucasoid base, and range from the yellow-brown Vedda of Ceylon to the very dark Aborigine. Pacific peoples are mainly mongoloid with some caucasoid, but Papuans and Melanesians are basically negroid.

Races tend to belong to one part of the Earth. But distribution maps usually show how things were in the 15th century. There were large movements before then – the whole of America was peopled by mongoloids – and migrations since then have changed the picture dramatically (pages 122-123). Caucasoids dominate in N America, much of S America and parts of S Africa and Australasia. Vast numbers of negroids were moved to N America. In Europe and North America constant large-scale movement, particularly of migrant labor, has blurred any boundaries that may once have existed, and the rapidly growing ease and popularity of world travel can only increase this tendency. This should emphasize the fallacy of thinking any 'pure' race exists at all.

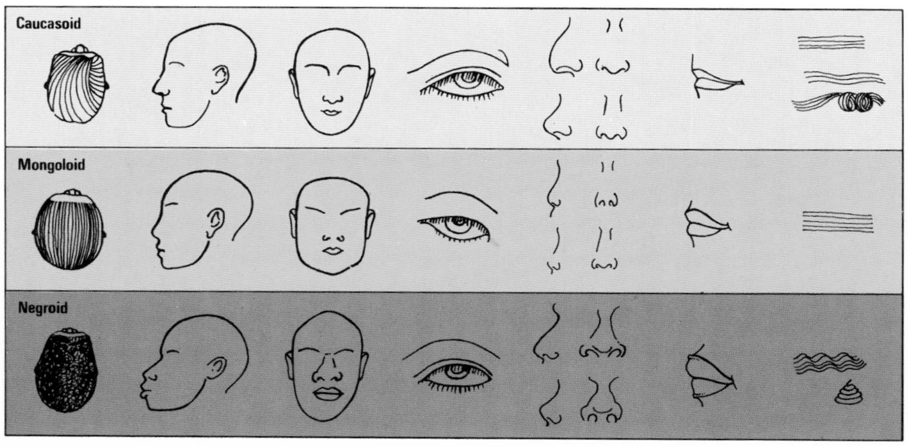
Caucasoid
Mongoloid
Negroid

The differences *above*
These pages clarify the differences that distinguish the races of man. Some of the more familiar of these characteristics are illustrated above. But there are very many other distinguishing traits, all stemming from the genetic material inherited by each child. The blood in every man's body is strongly characteristic of his race, in its grouping, Rhesus factor and Duffy factor. Some racial populations can taste bitter substances, while others cannot. Even wax in the ears is racially distinctive.

Pigmentation *right*
The color of the skin is a fundamental racial characteristic (see the Punjabi dancer, left). Scientific research has established that human skin is composed of the outer epidermis (A) overlying the dermis (B) or true skin. The outerlayer of epidermis is the horny corneum (C), underlain by the granular layer (D). Below is a germinative layer (E), and it is here that dark brown or black granules of melanin are packed between the cells in a density characteristic of each race.

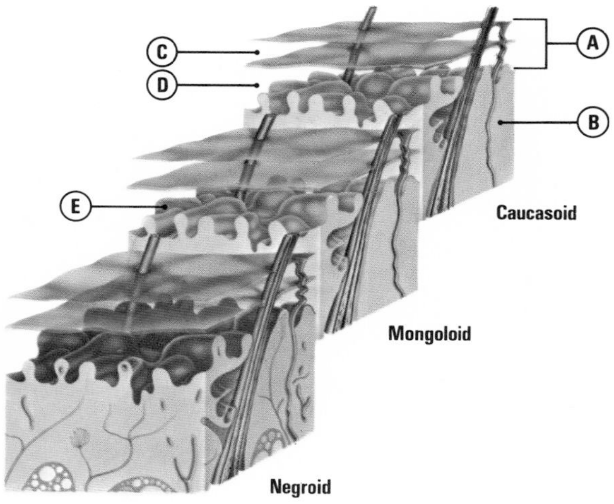
C
D
A
B
E
Caucasoid
Mongoloid
Negroid

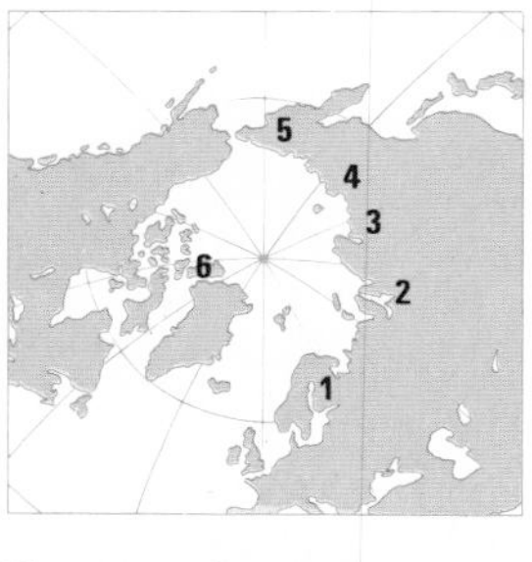
5
4
3
6
2
1

Circumpolar peoples
Unlike the Antarctic, which has no indigenous human inhabitants, the Arctic is an ocean surrounded by land which is everywhere sparsely inhabited. The peoples of these areas are a mixture of Mongoloid and Caucasoid types. All appear to have moved into their present habitat in relatively recent times, within a few thousand years at most; but this is quite long enough for each race to have become adapted to the environment. The Lapp (1, and located in Finland by the corresponding figure on the map, left) is a reindeer herdsman. The Vogul (2), of Siberia, is one of a mainly fishing people living east of the Samoyed on the opposite page. The Yukaghir (3,) with his reindeer, is a survivor of a group once widespread in central Siberia. The dress of the Tungus (4) shows a strong Japanese influence. The Siberian Eskimo (5) and his racial brother from Ellesmere Island (Canada) (6) are seal hunters.

1
2
3
4
5
6

Mongoloids

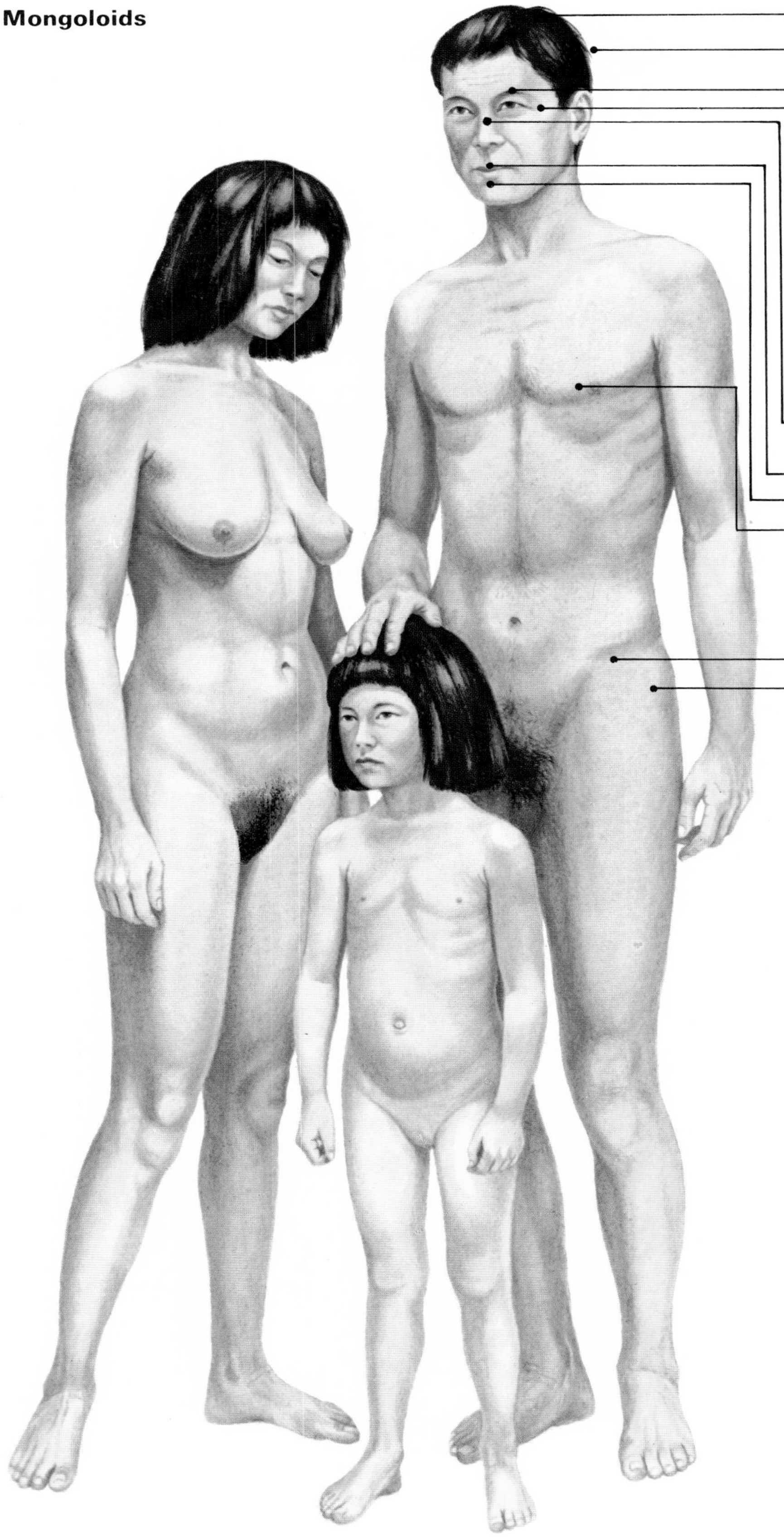

Physical characteristics
The term Mongoloid covers a wide range of general characteristics which are not all found in any one individual. This Japanese family (left) shows some of them.

hair : always black and straight with lank appearance

head : broad, forehead well rounded and brow ridges completely absent

eyes : epicanthic fold gives slanting appearance

cheekbones : strongly pronounced

nose : broad with a depressed base

lips : medium prominent

chin : well developed

hair : extremely sparse on both face and body, although some classic Mongols of central Asia grow a moustache or thin beard

build : slight

skin : 'yellow', although Eskimos have a reddish tinge and the North American Indians coppery brown. It has very little pigmentation and deep-seated blood vessels which give a characteristic parchment-like appearance.

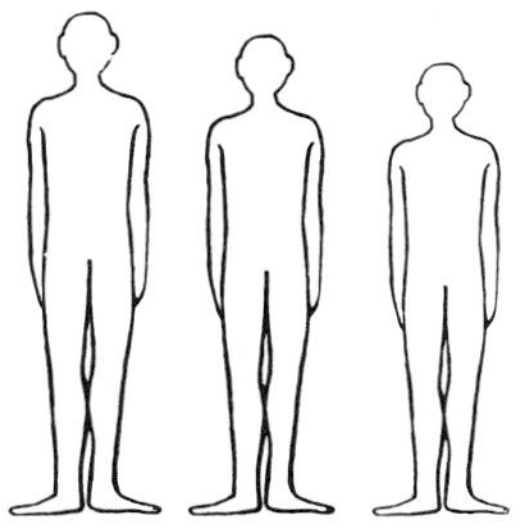

Height
Adult male Mongoloids cover a range of heights from approximately 5 ft 2 in (1.57 m) to 5 ft 8 in (1.73 m). At the lower end of the range are the Eskimos; Chinese generally come in the middle, and the North American Indian tribes are the tallest.

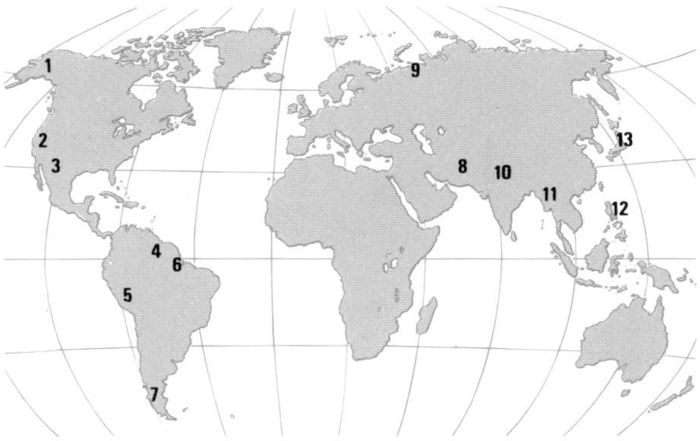

1
2
3
4
5
6
7
8
9
10
11
12
13

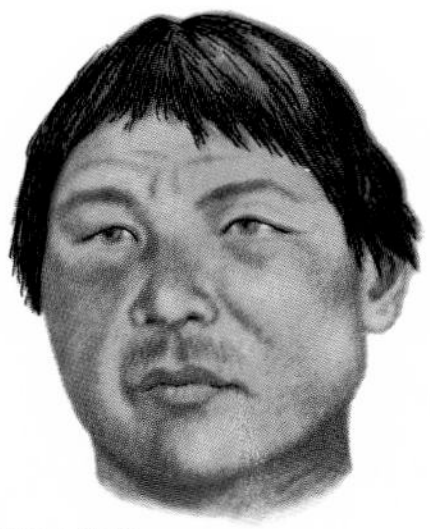

1 Eskimo *right*
The Mongoloid form, adapted to withstand severe cold, probably originated in Siberia. The Eskimos all of whom have similar features, culture and language crossed the Bering Strait about 3000 years ago.

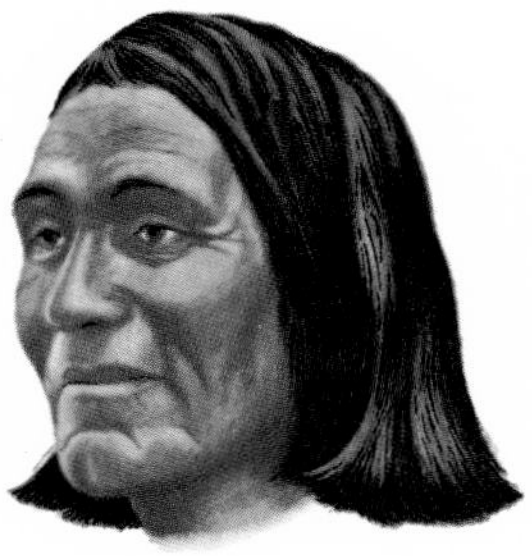

2 Hupa *left*
American Indians are descended from Mongoloids who crossed into the New World long before the Eskimo, probably about 25000 years ago before the Mongoliform face had fully developed.

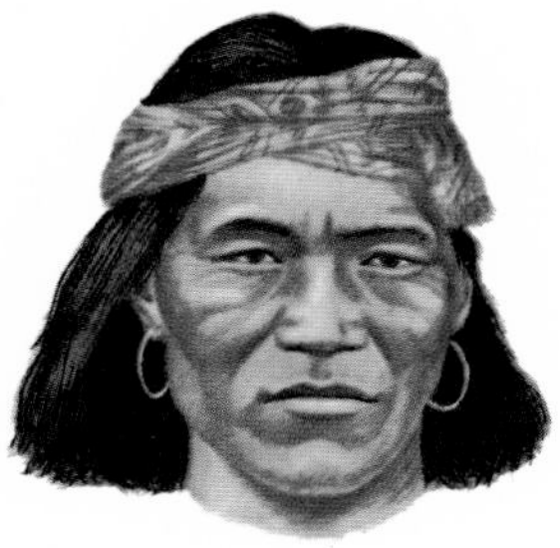

3 Pueblo Indian *right*
Unlike the tall copper-colored 'Red Indian', the Pueblo (Spanish = village) of Arizona and New Mexico are stocky Mongoloids with more yellowish skin. They still maintain an elaborate culture.

4 Wai Wai *left*
One of the least interbred of the Amerindian races, the Wai Wai **are centered in the remote jungles** of southern Guyana (British Guiana) and northern Brazil, and occupy a region once overrun by the cannibal Caribs.

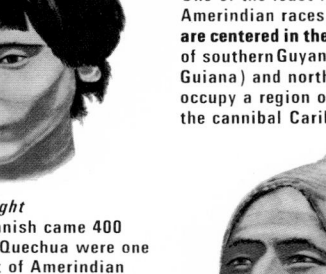

5 Quechua *right*
Before the Spanish came 400 years ago the Quechua were one of the greatest of Amerindian people. Numbering several million they were ruled by the Incas. Many pure Quechuas still inhabit the high Andes.

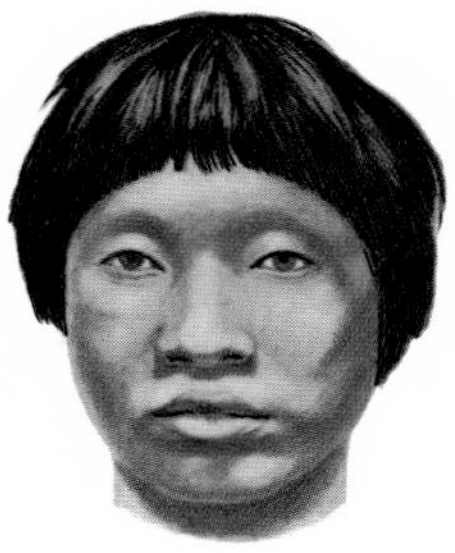

6 Wai Wai *left*
This second Wai Wai from northern Brazil shows even more clearly the facial features that betray Mongoloid ancestry. It has been assumed that the first men to enter the Americas from Asia were those that penetrated furthest south, but this is unproven.

7 Ona *right*
If this belief (No 6, above) were true, the Ona could, with the shorter Yaghan, claim to have been the first Americans. Their habitat is Patagonia, at the extreme southerly tip of S America in one of the most desolate and windswept regions of the Earth.

8 Kirghiz *left*
In the 12th century these people of Turkic Mongoloid stock fled from Mongolia before Genghis Khan and have since dwelt in the high Pamirs and Tienchan (Tien Shan) along the Sino-Soviet border. Their prominent features do not include the epicanthic eye fold.

9 Samoyed *above*
Classic Mongoloids, the **Samoyeds are centered on the** Arctic coastline of European Siberia. They show Caucasoid features, including fair hair and blue eyes; but their faces are wide, with flaring cheekbones, and they have the stocky, muscular Mongol build.

10 Tibetan *below*
Tibetans are a mix of Mongol and archaic White stock, resulting in a narrower, less fat face than the classic Mongoloid, and a prominent nose. The Mongol influence enables them to thrive at 12000 ft (3650 m).

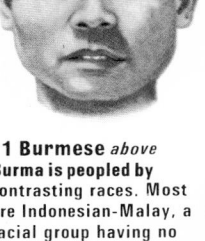

11 Burmese *above*
Burma is peopled by contrasting races. Most are Indonesian-Malay, a racial group having no relevance to modern politics. The Indonesian type is short and slim, while Malays are taller.

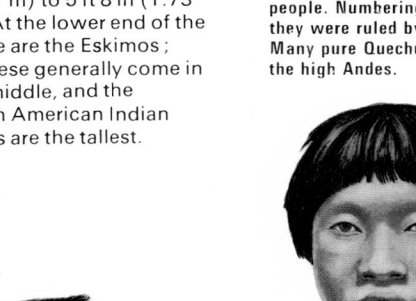

12 Filipino *below*
Most inhabitants of the Philippines are Malay type, but descended from an earlier group than today's Malays, distinguished by long heads, broad noses and stocky build—characteristics evident in this man from Luzon.

13 Japanese *above*
Anthropologists argue over the Japanese, who are either Malays from the Indonesian-Malay race or, like the Koreans, Mongoloids. Short and stocky, they have for 50 years been increasing in stature to a mean of 5 ft 4 in (1.63 m).

The Family of Man: 2

Negroids

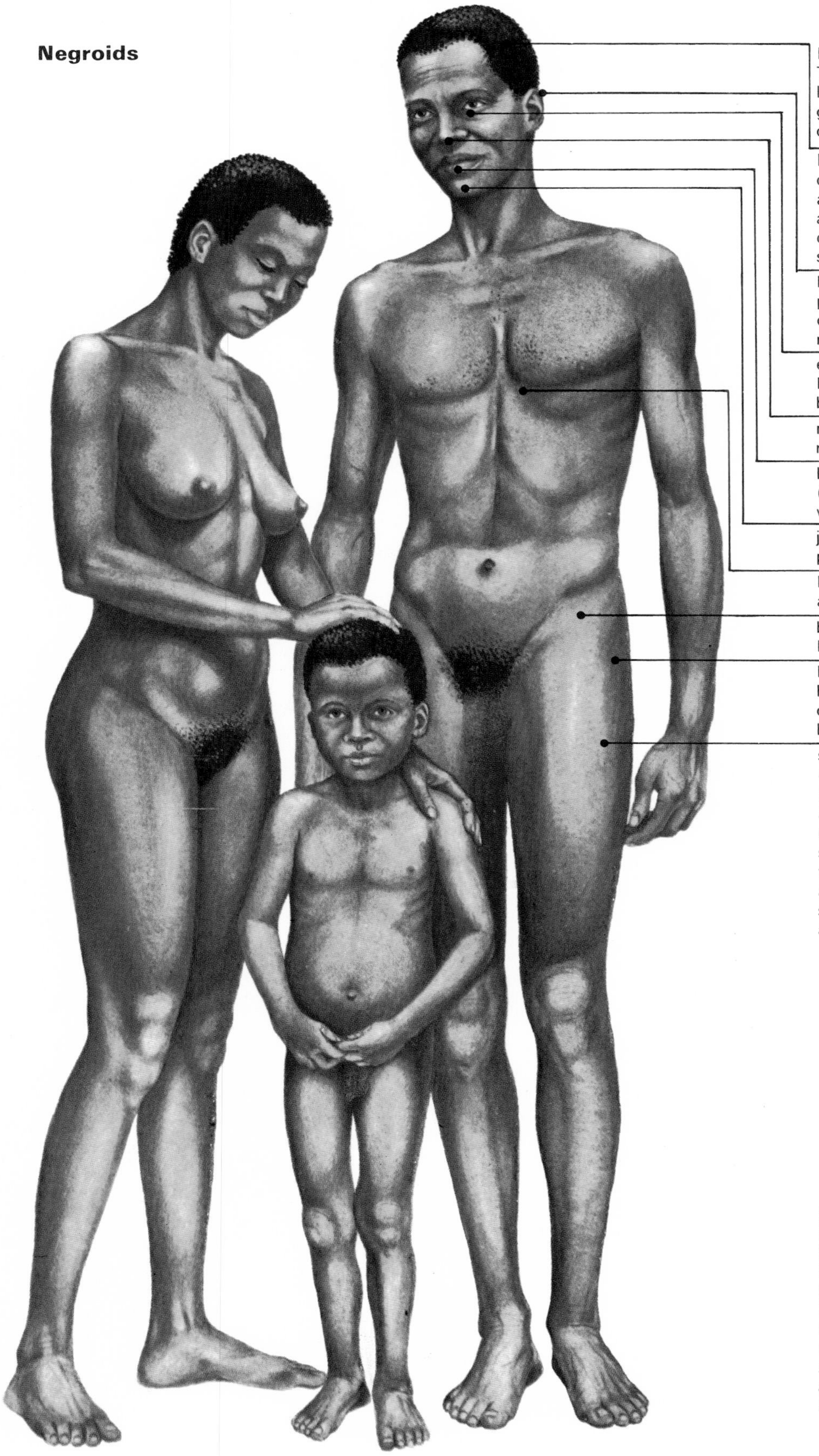

Physical characteristics
The Bantu family on the left exhibits some of the general Negroid characteristics.

hair : black, of flattened cross-section, resulting in a frizzy or woolly appearance and in extreme cases causing the hair to spiral into tufts.

head : long, with a prominent occiput (back of skull), little or no brow ridge

eyes : dark brown. In Bushmen they are overlain by an epicanthic fold

nose : broad with low roots

lips : thick and everted (showing pink inner portion when closed).

jaws : prominent but chin poorly developed

hair : sparse on both face and body

build : burly, except Bushmen

Bushmen are steatopygic, having large accumulations of fat on thighs and buttocks

skin : darkly pigmented, except for Bushmen and Papuans. Negroid skins absorb more visible radiation than do white skins but filter out ultra-violet so that in the absence of sustained sunshine negro children are deficient in Vitamin D

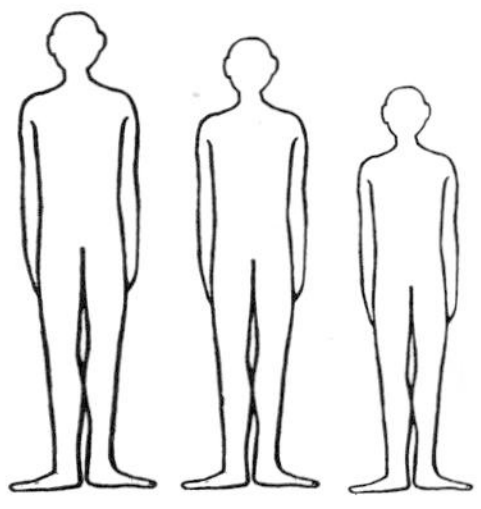

Height
Negroids vary enormously in height. Average adult Pygmies reach about 4 ft 8 in (1.42 m); Asiatic Negritos are one or two inches taller, while Bushmen reach 5 ft 2 in (1.57 m) Aborigines 5 ft 5 in (1.65 m), and the Nilotic races to 5 ft 10 in (1.78 m).

1 Shilluk *left*
A northern group of the Nilotes from the Sudan, the Shilluk average almost 6 ft (1.82 m) and have long heads and slender legs. This man has almost European features, but the Hamitic high-bridged nose and thin lips are common.

2 Amhara *right*
In Ethiopia eastern Mediterraneans are diluted by a negroid infusion giving variable hair type and skin color.

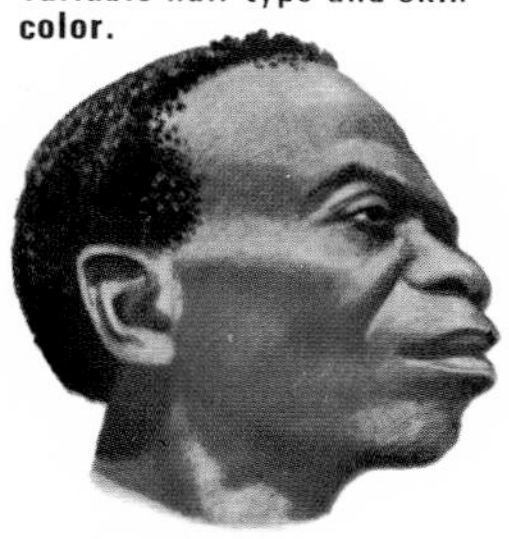

3 Ituri *left*
Pygmies of the Ituri basin have a mahogany skin and jutting upper lip. Other pygmies inhabit the Congo and Angola.

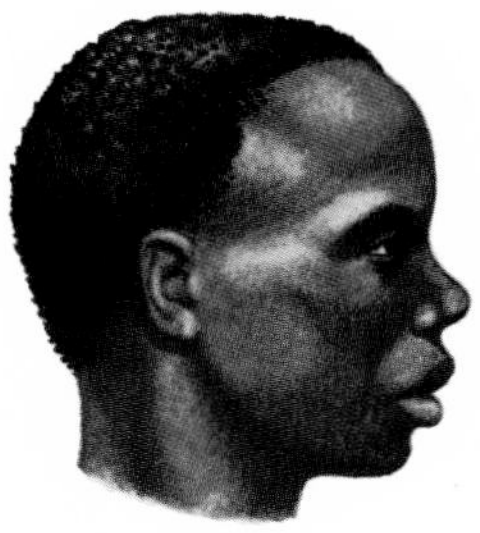

4 Dodoth *right*
The Negroid profile is exhibited by this Dodoth from Uganda. Bantu-speaking Negroids resemble many W Africans.

5 Samburu *left*
A Nilo-Hamite—Nilotic negro with Hamitic blood—this Samburu warrior from N Kenya is related to the Masai. Nilo-Hamites range from the Sudan to Tanzania.

6 Somali *right*
Hamitic Caucasoids, the Somali claim descent from Islamic missionaries. They have minimal Negroid influence and are unique in their fine features, straight hair, slim build, long legs and delicate hands and feet.

Khoisan peoples *below*
The Bushmen and Hottentots, collectively known as Khoisans, once covered much of southern Africa but have gradually been forced into isolated pockets. They differ from most Negroids.

Australoids *below*
Also called 'archaic White' and possibly descended direct from the first *Homo sapiens*, Australoids are widely distributed.

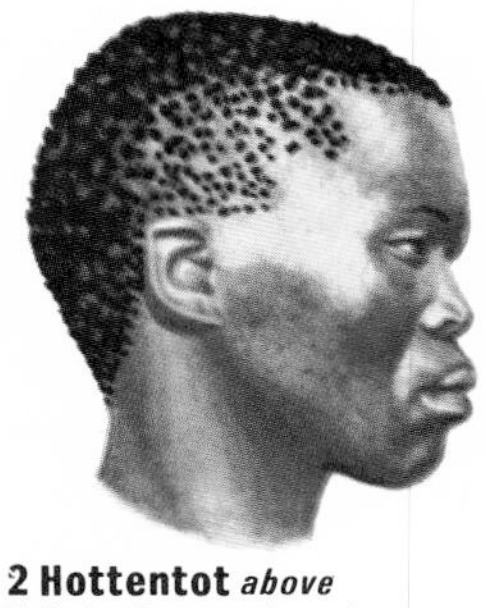

12 Hottentot *above*
Slightly shorter than the 5 ft 2 in (1.57 m) Bushmen, Hottentots use a 'clicking' language. Their skulls show Caucasoid influence absent from Bushmen.

11 Kalahari Bushman *above*
Related to the Hottentot, the Bushmen once occupied the whole of southern Africa but now possibly number fewer than 60000.

10 Fijian *above*
With the Papuans, the Fijians came from Asia via Malaysia. Their dark skin and frizzy hair give them a Negroid resemblance.

9 Aborigine *above*
Australoids evolved in SE Asia and Indonesia. The Australian aborigines are nearest to the Solo, Rhodesian and other men of the Upper Pleistocene.

8 Ainu *above*
The Ainu puzzle anthropologists who cannot decide where they came from. The head is often Australian but archaic White ancestry is certain.

7 Vedda *above*
Half way between Caucasoid and Australoid heartlands, the Veddas have inherited genes from both. They represent the oldest aboriginal population of India.

Caucasoids

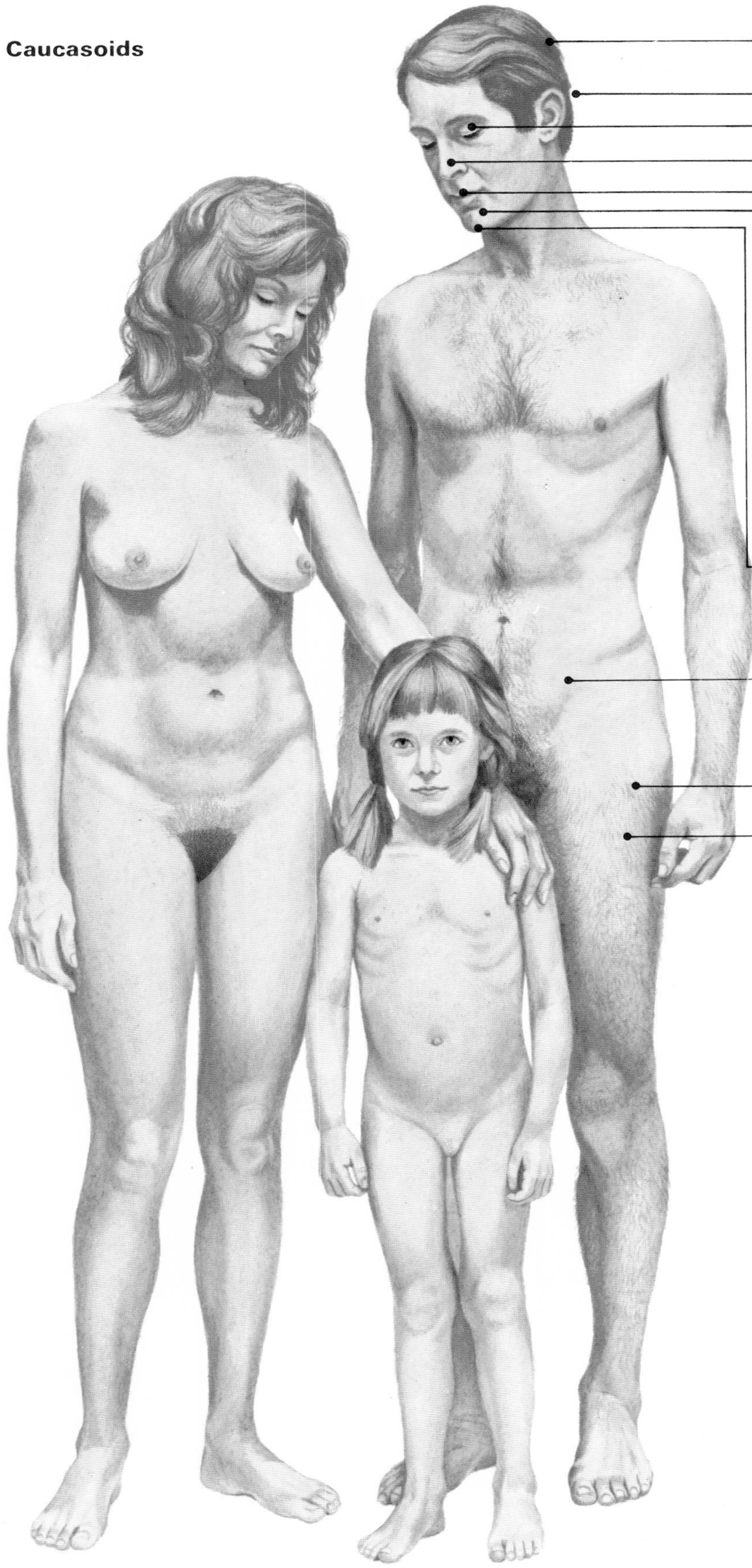

Physical characteristics
There is no such thing as a pure or even typical Caucasoid. The various members of a racial group for example, this Nordic family, show only some of the features.

hair : almost any color and form – from black and brown to blond

head : mostly broad (but Nordic and Mediterranean types are long), the cranium high and the brow ridges small

eyes : blue to dark brown

nose : usually long and high ridged and of various shapes

lips : thin

chin : well developed

facial shape : narrower than in other races and, except in round-faced Alpines, is of a straight form

hair : abundant on both face and body in the male a characteristic shared only with some of the archaic White Australoids

build : variable, but limbs normally long

skin : color is pale varying from near-white to olive brown. Caucasoids are generally thin-skinned and have little melanin pigment, so the blood vessels tinge the skin pink

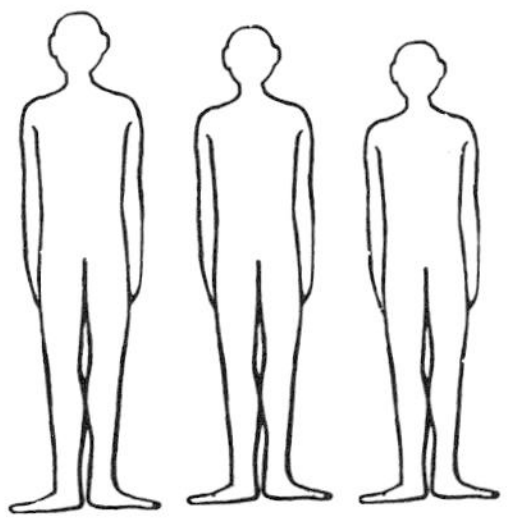

Height
Despite the great variety of Caucasoid types and colours the average adult height does not vary much. The Mediterranean group show a figure of about 5 ft 3 in (1.6 m), the Alpine group from two to four inches taller, and the Nordics an average of 5 ft 8 in (1.73 m)

1
2
3
4
5
6
7
8
9
10
11
12
13

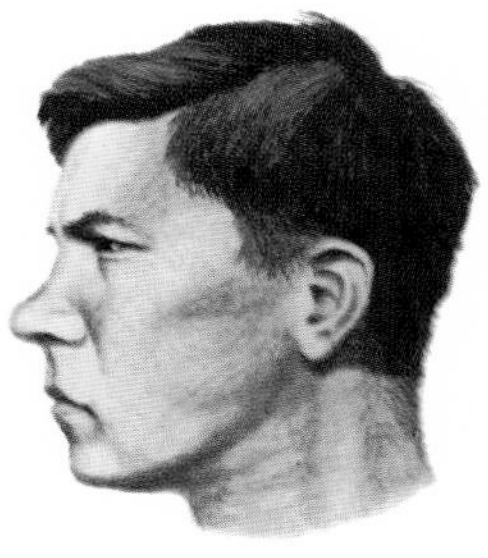

1 Lapp *right*
These people of northern Scandinavia often have a Mongol type of eye and yellowish skin, but are Caucasoids. They probably came from European Siberia. This boy is politically Norwegian.

2 Latvian *left*
Like most other E Baltic races the Latvians came from the Volga/Don region, reaching their present lands about 1000 years ago. They typify the fair-haired, blue-eyed groups of northern Europe.

3 English *right*
The Nordics typify what is considered to be a 'white' race, which in turn is a caricature of the Caucasoid. But, far from being 'pure', the people of Britain are an amalgam of numerous races.

4 Basque *left*
In many ways—language, blood group and Rhesus factor—the Basques are unlike other Europeans. Broad forehead, narrow chin and long nose are characteristics; the Berbers may be related.

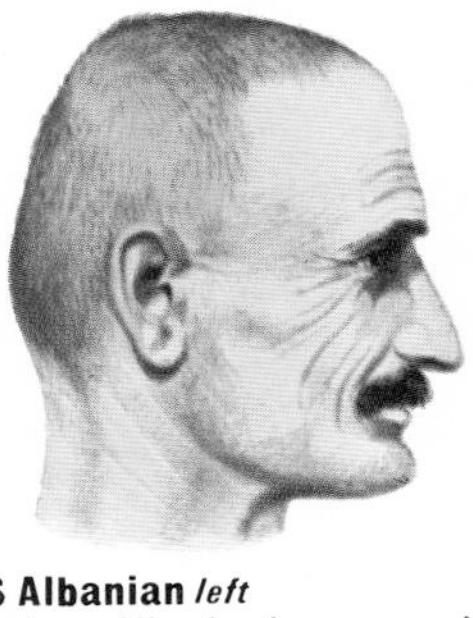

5 N Albanian *right*
Tall and straight-nosed, this man from the mountainous northern part of Albania shows the flattened rear of the skull caused by cradling. He is a typical Dinaric type.

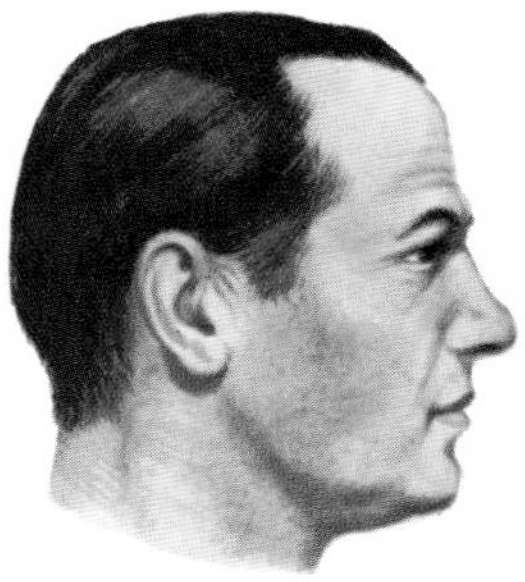

6 S Albanian *left*
Southern Albania shows a predominance of the round-headed Alpine type, which extends from France through Asia Minor into Russia. Round-headedness has increased in Europe for at least 1000 years.

7 Sicilian *right*
One of the Mediterranean group of Caucasoids, the people of southern Italy and Sicily are derived from the Near East and closely linked with Arabs and Spaniards. Greek and Armenian genes exert strong influences.

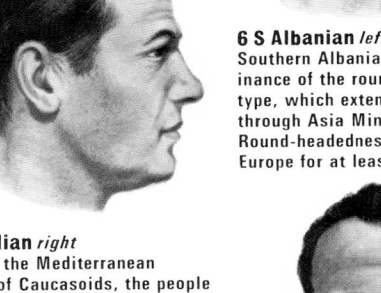

8 Tuareg *left*
The nobles of this northern group of African Caucasoids have kept their identity through centuries of Negroid proximity. This man shows the expected lean, aquiline head of these men of the Sahara.

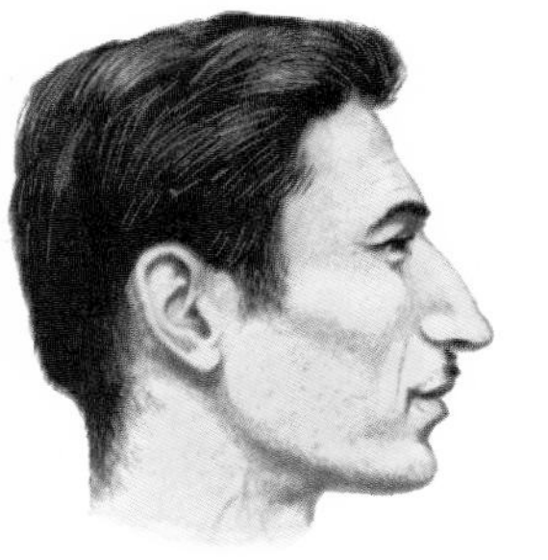

9 Arab *above*
The Arabs are typical of the Mediterranean Proper group of Caucasoids. Among the earliest of this group were Mesolithic people of what is now Israel, but today's racial nucleus is found in Yemen.

10 Armenian *below*
Armenians appear to have derived from the Hittites and possibly the Sumerians and Babylonians. This man from the Lake Van region shows the characteristic nose and flattened back of the head.

11 Tamil *above*
This Dravidian-speaking group has spread from south India to Ceylon and Malaysia. Although fully Caucasoids, superficially their dark skins make them look Veddoid.

12 Hindu *below*
One of the world's largest groups, the Hindu are lightly built Mediterranean types. The race is subdivided by a rigorous caste system and differing religions.

13 Tajik *above*
From northern Afghanistan, Tajiks are of the Irano-Afghan group in which Nordic and Mediterranean blood is mixed. Their round heads have Armenoid or Turkic features.

The Settled World

Man is the most mobile of animals and has adapted himself to life in almost every part of the Earth's land surface. The earliest adaptations involved bodily changes giving rise to three main racial groups: one was peculiar to Africa; a second group, adapted to colder conditions, arose in central and northern Asia and eventually spread to the Americas; and, finally, a third group ranged from northern Europe to Oceania. Nevertheless, this early settlement still remains a matter of debate. The more recent migrations of man are much easier to trace and to explain.

Although the expansion of population and the need for food are major underlying reasons for migration, the movement of people around the world is not always voluntary. The most spectacular forced movement was that of West Africans caught up in the slave trade. Anything from ten to fifteen millions reached America, but many millions more did not survive the journey. Only modern warfare has caused comparable movement. In World War 2 about 60 million people were forced to move by such means as deportation, evacuation and transfer of minority groups. After the partition of India, a million Hindus left Pakistan and almost as many Moslems left India. Forced movement has therefore played a large part in determining the shifting pattern of population.

In modern times the overwhelming movements are voluntary, whether for short distances or long. Although there are examples of small communities moving for ideological reasons, the vast majority of people move for economic or social reasons. Those who left Europe to live in the United States were generally seeking to escape oppression or looking for improved living conditions. Industrialization, which brought more prosperity to Europe, helped to stem the movement away. Even voluntary movement is generally controlled when it involves migration from one country to another. Sometimes states are reluctant to allow emigration because it depletes their manpower, while states often control immigration in an effort to protect the indigenous populations or to secure some particular social or economic goal.

Migrations bring many social problems. Migrants have to adapt to a new society and possibly learn a new language; and the problems are even worse for the society which receives them, especially if the migrants come from a variety of sources. In the past the United States has tried to absorb migrants completely, minimizing their differences, and aiming to Americanize them thoroughly. This was a difficult process when the differences were cultural. When they were racial as well, the difficulties were compounded.

Neanderthal man

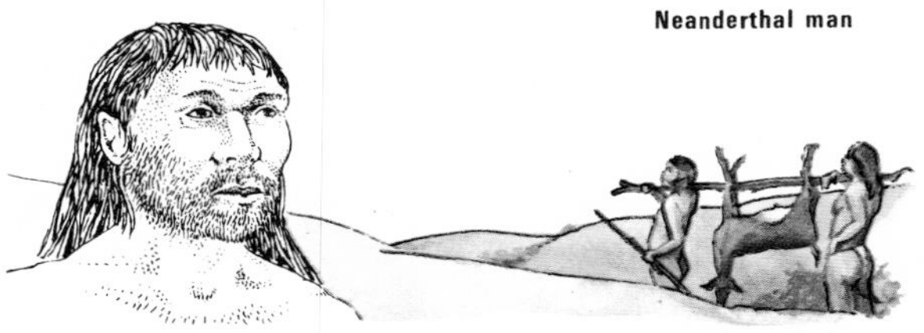

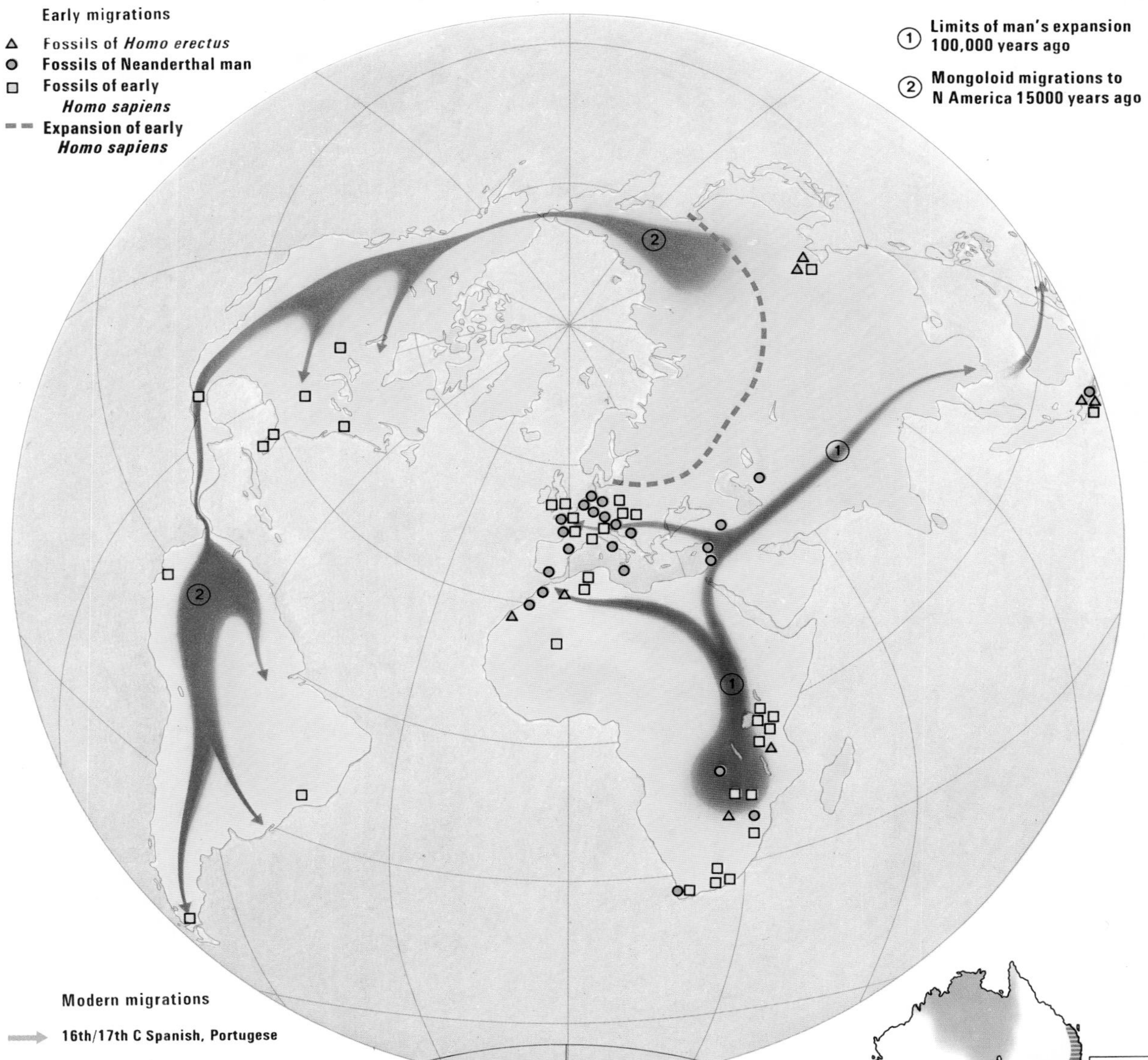
Early migrations
Fossils of *Homo erectus*
Fossils of Neanderthal man
Fossils of early *Homo sapiens*
Expansion of early *Homo sapiens*
1 Limits of man's expansion 100,000 years ago
2 Mongoloid migrations to N America 15000 years ago

The spread of mankind *right, above*
Early hominid fossils have been discovered throughout the eastern hemisphere, but on present evidence the birthplace of mankind appears to lie somewhere in central Africa. From here, and possibly from other centers, man has spread across the entire land surface of the Earth. Ancestral man may have been a relatively adaptable animal whose physical make-up changed according to climate. In Africa the negro is well adapted to strong sunlight, while Mongoloids appear to have been adapted to cold before they spread from Asia to the Americas.

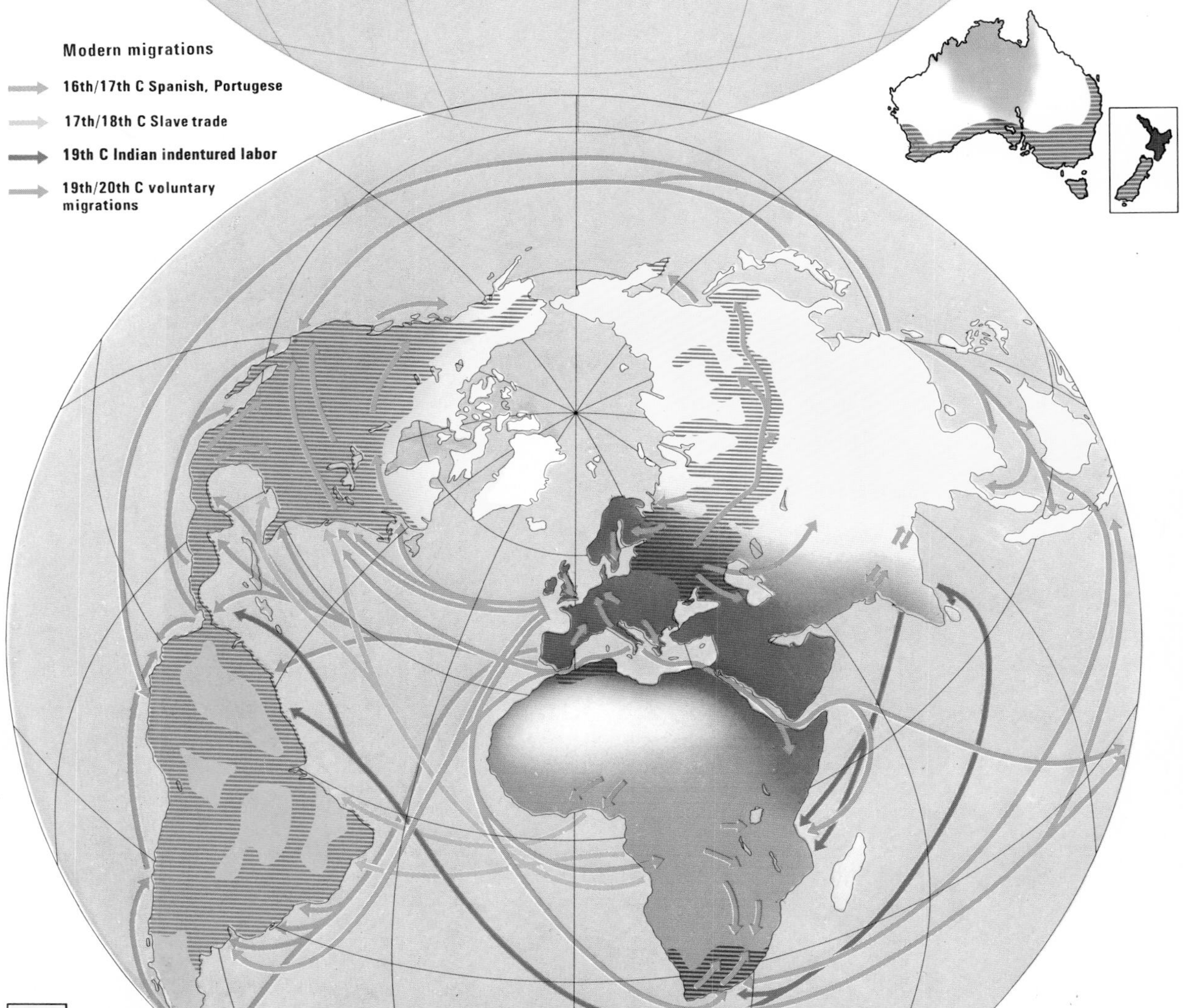
Modern migrations
16th/17th C Spanish, Portugese
17th/18th C Slave trade
19th C Indian indentured labor
19th/20th C voluntary migrations
Mongoloid
Negroid
American indian
Caucasoid
Significant Caucasoid settlement

The great migrations *right*
In historic times migrations were principally a story of the movement of people from heavily populated areas to relatively empty ones. Some of these great mass movements were forced, an outstanding example of this kind being the transport of millions of slaves from West Africa to North America. But overpopulation and economic pressure caused an even greater voluntary movement to the New World, in this case from Europe. It was by such migrations that man was able to open up the continental interiors in North America and Asiatic Russia.

Don Amigos
Slave trader

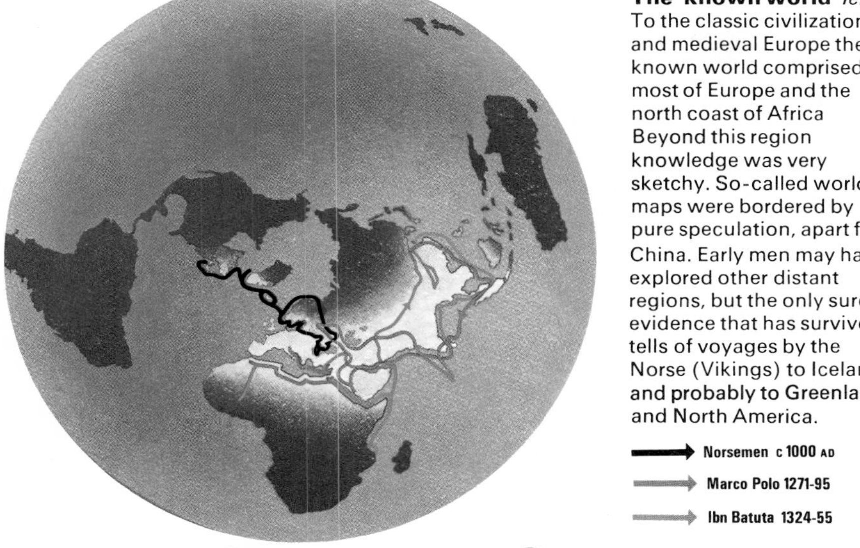

Norsemen c 1000 AD
Marco Polo 1271-95
Ibn Batuta 1324-55

The 'known world' *left*
To the classic civilizations and medieval Europe the known world comprised most of Europe and the north coast of Africa Beyond this region knowledge was very sketchy. So-called world maps were bordered by pure speculation, apart from China. Early men may have explored other distant regions, but the only sure evidence that has survived tells of voyages by the Norse (Vikings) to Iceland and probably to Greenland and North America.

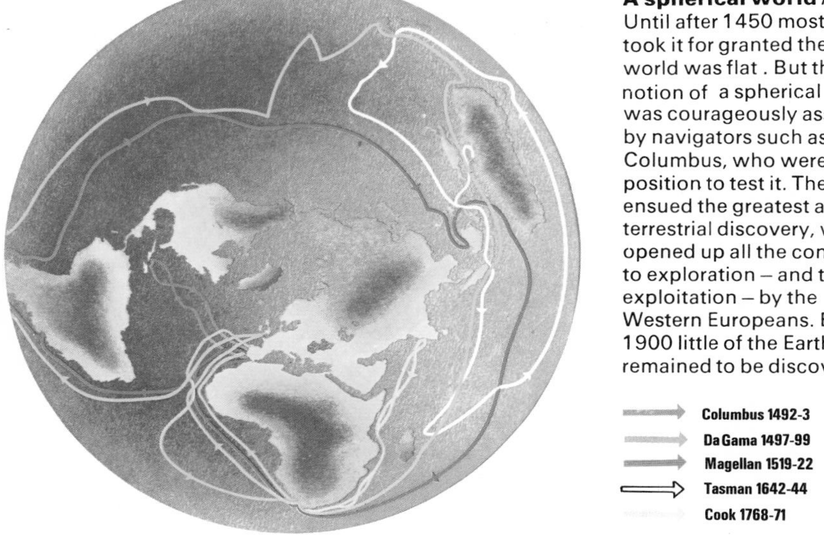

Columbus 1492-3
Da Gama 1497-99
Magellan 1519-22
Tasman 1642-44
Cook 1768-71

A spherical world *left*
Until after 1450 most men took it for granted the world was flat . But the notion of a spherical world, was courageously assumed by navigators such as Columbus, who were in a position to test it. There ensued the greatest age of terrestrial discovery, which opened up all the continents to exploration – and to exploitation – by the Western Europeans. By 1900 little of the Earth remained to be discovered.

Leif the Lucky
Norse longship
Marco Polo
Overland routes
Christopher Columbus
Santa Maria
Vasco da Gama
San Gabriel
Ferdinand Magellan
Victoria
James Cook
Endeavour

Great Britain

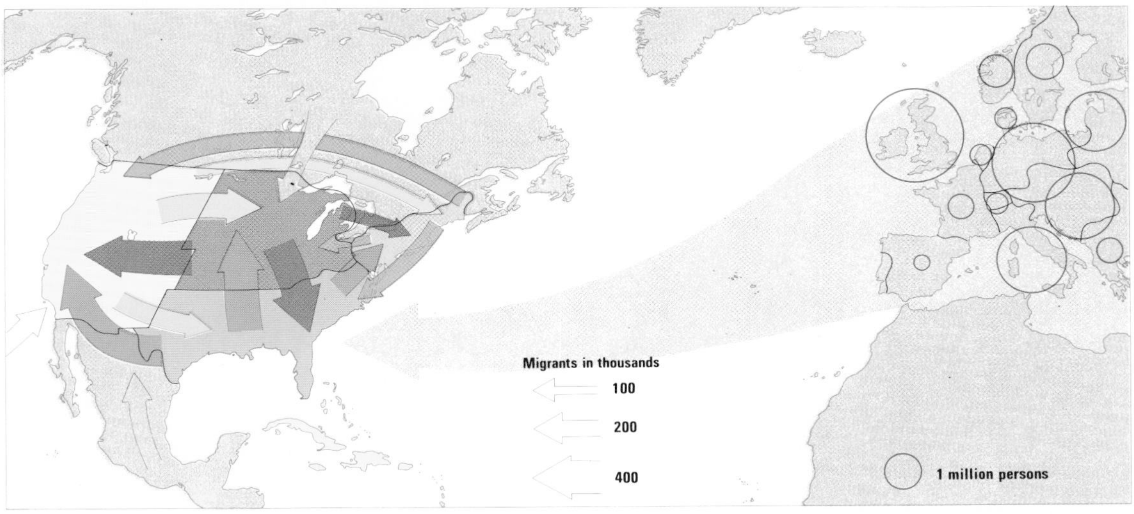

Migrants in thousands
100
200
400
1 million persons

Colonizing America *right and above*
The greatest voluntary movement in the history of man was the colonization of North America in the 19th century. It involved about 36 million people, and almost all of them came from Western Europe. Until the 1890s the majority came from the British Isles, Germany and Scandinavia, but in the early 20th century the main sources shifted to Eastern Europe and the Mediterranean. Within the US itself there has also been further massive migration.

Urbanization

Today there are several localized areas in which refugees are seeking to escape from war, civil strife or a discriminatory administration, but there are no massive population movements such as were common in the past. By far the biggest movement in terms of numbers and ultimate social consequence is the steady drift from the countryside to the cities. In 1900, about one person in every six in the so-called advanced countries lived in a large city; by 1950 the proportion had risen to one in three, and the movement had become worldwide. Until this century there were very few 'million cities', but today there are more than 130 distributed across the globe, with the fastest-growing examples often lying in developing lands. Until this century cities, such as Rome (above, left), grew naturally without imposing any insuperable problems. Today's cities, such as Tokyo (above, right), are the sites of problems of congestion, pollution, transport and almost every other facet of human life on a scale so large that there is no simple solution.

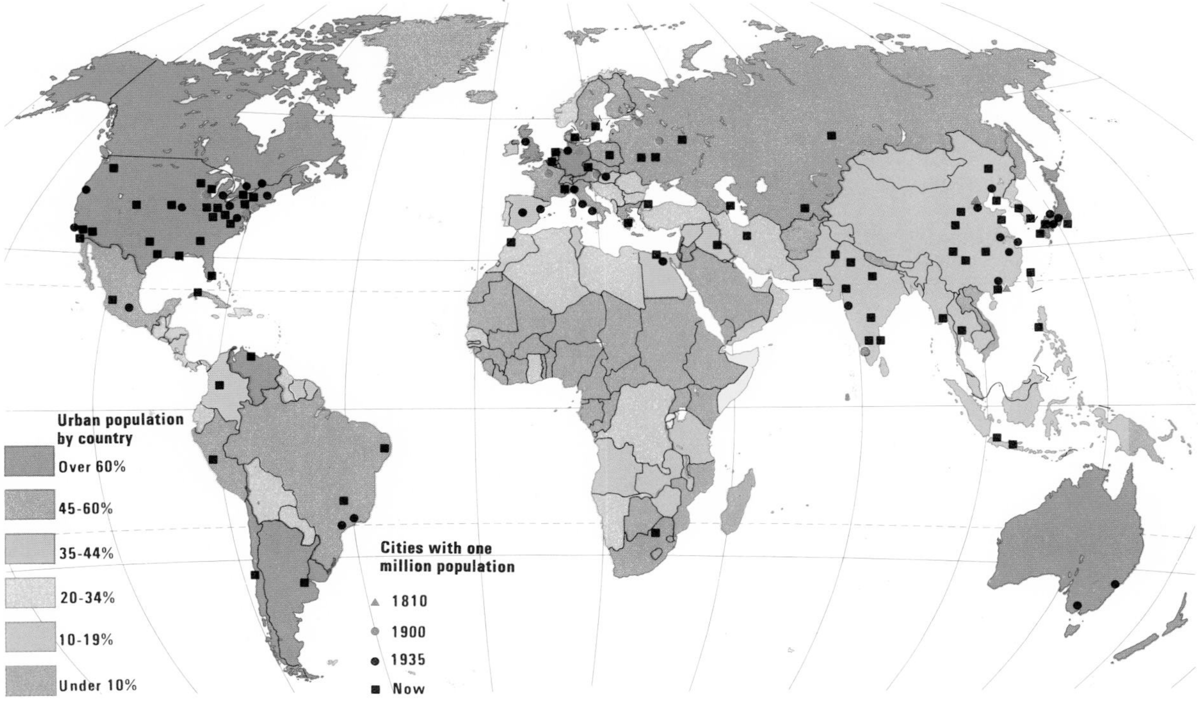

Urban population by country
Over 60%
45-60%
35-44%
20-34%
10-19%
Under 10%
Cities with one million population
1810
1900
1935
Now

The growing cities *above*
The biggest modern migration is the move from the country into the cities. Spurred by prospects of a richer life, this movement usually involves quite short distances but extremely large numbers of people. Ultimately nearly the entire human population will probably live in huge urban regions, each housing many millions, with the intervening spaces used for food production and leisure.

Religion

The earliest religions, still strong among pre-civilized peoples, were animistic and identified with the forces of nature. Even when these have crystallized into systems of beliefs centered on gods there often is still a close identification with a restricted territory. These ethnic religions are confined to specific peoples having a limited range of movement. Such a territorial concept of a deity is apparent in the earlier parts of Jewish and Christian scripture. In the religions of the East beliefs of this kind became more diffuse and the system more philosophical. The teaching of Gautama Buddha (563-483 BC) was a denial of materialism, in the face of the miseries of life in a part of the world where existence is still equated with hardship. Confucius (551-478 BC) was more concerned with defining social relationships and was able to absorb primitive ancestor worship, which still survives. In India Hinduism is a comprehensive system embracing a range of beliefs in numbers of gods but welding the whole together by fundamental attitudes such as the doctrine of rebirth, worship of cattle and the caste system. The last is a practical social element based on occupation and very different from the philosophical elements of Hinduism.

Ethnic religions in the Near East took on a totally different aspect by becoming monotheistic: the tribal god of the Jews became for them the only god. To Christianity, which emerged from Judaism, monotheism was central, and so it became in Islam, which owed much to both Judaism and Christianity. Judaism was dispersed, but retained its strength until Israel was re-established in 1948. But Christianity and Islam became the great 'saving' religions whose aim was the conversion of mankind. The early history of Christianity is of proselytizing, and later of conquest. And within a short time of the death of Mohammed (AD 632), his beliefs also had been carried far.

But a characteristic of both these religions is the deep schisms which have appeared. In Islam there is sharp disagreement between Sunni and Shia. Equally marked is the division of Christianity into Roman Catholics and Protestants, with a strong third element in the Eastern Orthodox Church.

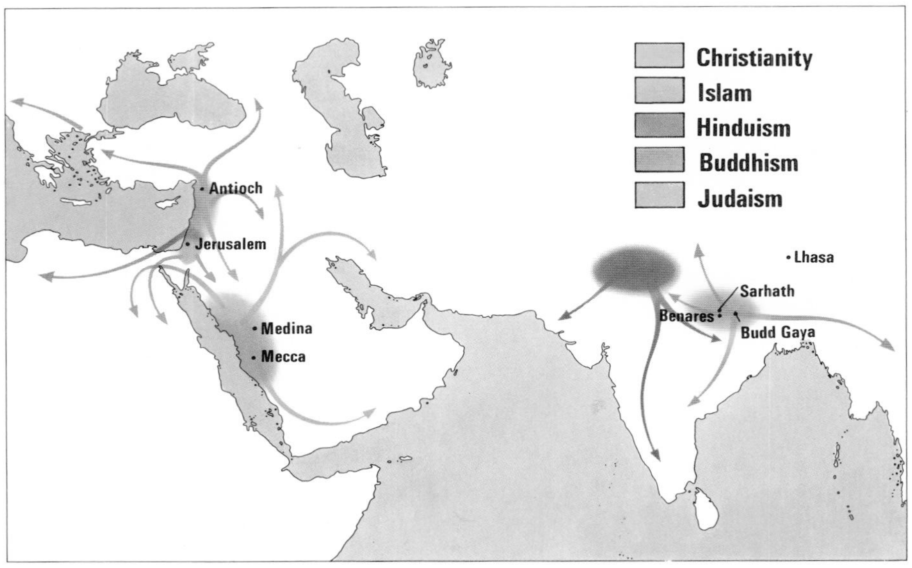
Christianity
Islam
Hinduism
Buddhism
Judaism
Antioch
Jerusalem
Medina
Mecca
Lhasa
Sarhath
Benares
Budd Gaya

Cradlelands *left*
Hinduism has its origins in earlier Indian civilizations. The quietism of Buddhism also owes much to them, although its origin can be pin-pointed. There was a very close association between the origins of Christianity and Islam and the older religion of Judaism in the same area. The foci of these religions are today places of pilgrimage for adherents throughout the world, despite the divisive and often abrasive effects of disagreements between sects. Perhaps the most remarkable facet of man's great religions is that they are so few. Future man may create new ones.

Hindu *left*
While most Hindus worship at home, often to local or to family deities, they may passively watch ceremonies conducted by priests in temples for their gods. In Jinja, Uganda, priests pour ghee (clarified butter) into a fire in supplication to the terrible god Amba (Durga).

Buddhism *left*
Buddhist temples are ornate and richly decorated. Here in Singapore an assistant priest studies the scriptures. His white robe distinguishes him from a monk who would wear saffron yellow (and be prohibited from having any possessions apart from vestments, razor and bowl).

Islam *left*
Seated in the open court-yard of a mosque an Indian reads the Koran. This holy book, about as long as the Christian New Testament, is the scripture revealed to Mohammed. It is the basis of Moslem teaching and social behaviour; mosques are also schools.

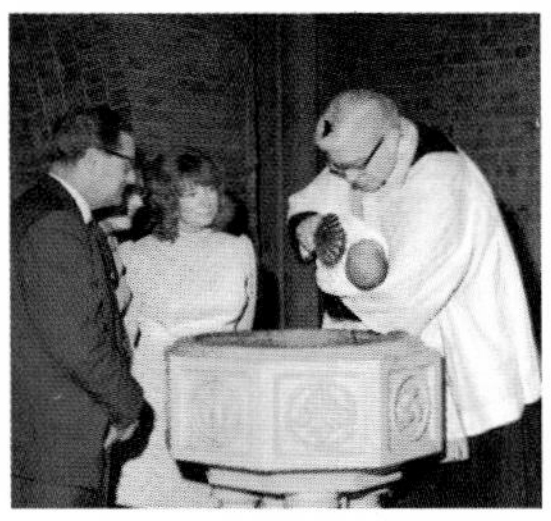

Christianity *left*
Central to the belief in Christianity is the observance of the sacraments, such as baptism, confirmation, matrimony, burials, and other rites considered to have been instituted by Jesus. Shown here is a baptism of baby being performed by a priest.

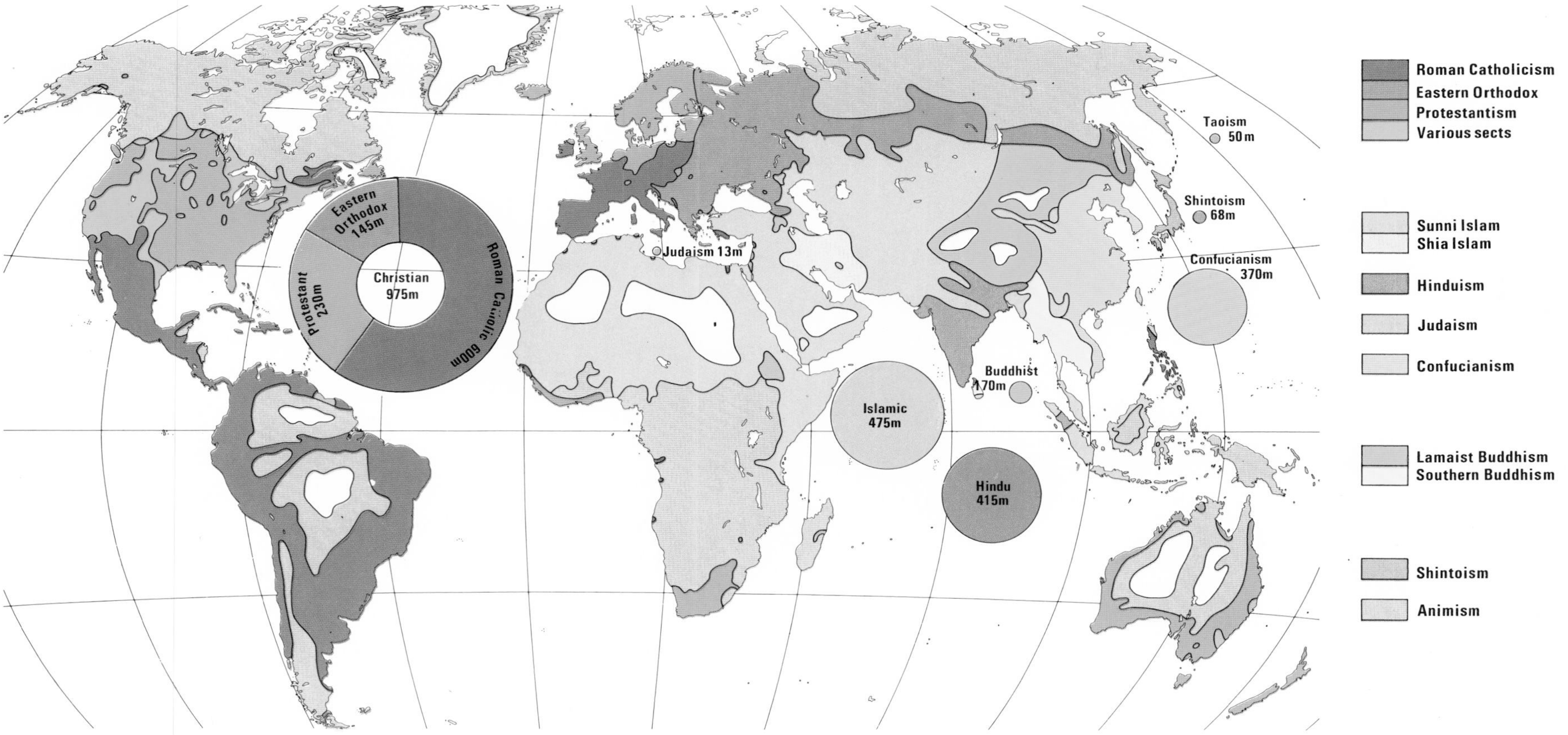
Eastern Orthodox 145m
Protestant 230m
Christian 975m
Roman Catholic 600m
Judaism 13m
Taoism 50m
Shintoism 68m
Confucianism 370m
Buddhist 170m
Islamic 475m
Hindu 415m
Roman Catholicism
Eastern Orthodox
Protestantism
Various sects
Sunni Islam
Shia Islam
Hinduism
Judaism
Confucianism
Lamaist Buddhism
Southern Buddhism
Shintoism
Animism

Contrasting beliefs
Christianity is numerically the strongest religion, with Roman Catholicism the largest of its many sects. Islam is next largest (overwhelmingly Sunni), and Hinduism is growing with the Indian population. Animism and ethnic religions prevail where Western influences are slight or where, as in Central Africa, there is a very large indigenous population. The most remarkable spread has been that of the great proselytizing religions, Christianity and Islam. The former is world-wide, while the latter is restricted to hot, dry lands of the Old World. Many minor sects are urban.

Shinto *left*
This religion is based on a multitude of small shrines dedicated to numerous deities. Its priests were government officials until 1945. The Japanese temple in the background contains an inner sanctuary where these priests recite, pray and conduct the purification rites.

Judaism *left*
Inside the West London Synagogue the Rabbi holds up the richly decorated Torah (Law) which contains the five Books of Moses. Behind him is the Ark. Judaism emphasizes the transcendence of God, whose name it avoids by substituting some epithet (such as 'the Holy One').

Language

Of all those things which tend to divide mankind into groups, language is possibly the most important. While it binds together those who speak a common language, it imposes a major handicap upon communication between different groups. Language is the medium by which ideas are transmitted, and this tends to give a cultural homogeneity to each language group. For example, the 'English-speaking world' identifies people with common culture and sympathetic beliefs. Language also has very strong emotional connotations, because it is associated with the individual's earliest memories. Consequently a great amount of tension can arise between contiguous language groups, or when a majority language is given precedence in a multi-language state. The subdivision of India, largely on a language basis, produced many riots. The dividing line between Flemish and Walloon in Belgium is marked by constant tensions. Language is the main basis of the claims of the French Canadians to independence.

World languages and their distribution are extremely complex. Even the major groups of languages, such as Latin or Teutonic, do not mean much in practical terms because to the layman it is the minor differences which count and not the basic similarities. Differences even of dialect are enough to divide people: the least nuance will serve to identify group antipathies. 'Speaking another language' can apply to subtleties of meaning even within one language. One way of overcoming this problem is to encourage second languages of international standing. Many of the world's peoples are bilingual—a fact which makes the mapping of distributions very difficult. Even so it is difficult to overcome a person's emotional link with his first language. There are over 30 languages in Europe alone. Many of the minor languages are in danger of disappearing. This is partly because they cannot cope with the language of modern technology, and partly because fluent knowledge of a major language is an essential. Within the British Isles, for example, the Celtic languages could not hope to compete with English and some such as Cornish and Manx have virtually disappeared.

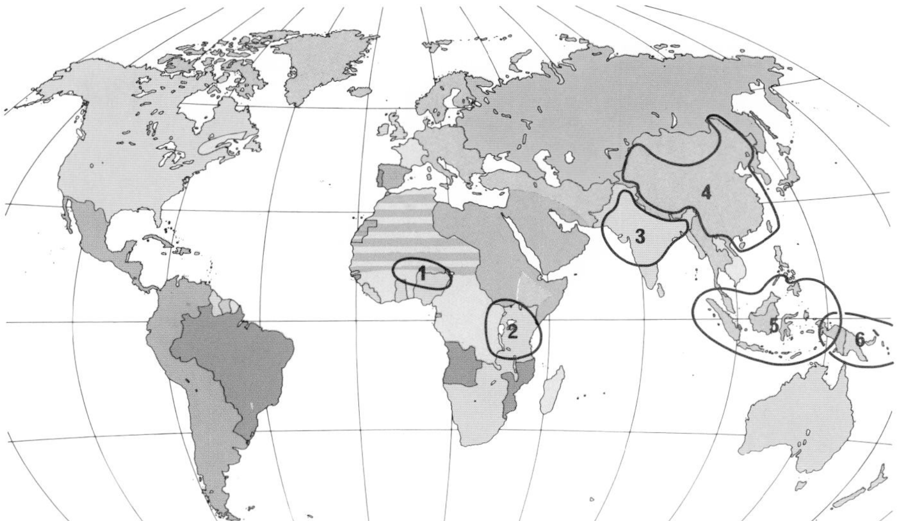

1
2
3
4
5
6

International languages
Superimposed on the thousands of local languages and dialects round the world are six major international languages—those of the colonialist powers. They are used for ease of communication in government and business, for example, India's retention of English as the official language.

Spanish
English
French
Portuguese
Russian
Arabic

1 Hausa
2 Swahili
3 Hindi/Urdu
4 Chinese
5 Malay
6 Melanesian pidgin

Russian

Л Идея использования квантовых систем для ге
радиоволн оказалась весьма плодотворной и
недостижимые для обычной радиотехники резу.

Burmese

ကြ ခပစ္စည်းကရိယာများ ရှိပြီးဖြစ်လေသည်။ အလယ်
ဝိုင်ရာ ပုဂ္ဂိုလ်များအတွက် အထူးသင်တန်းများ

Greek

λ ‘Ο ’Οδυσσεὺς καὶ οἱ σύντροφοι αὐτοῦ
πλοῖα, τὰ ὁποῖα ἦσαν πλήρη λαφύρων, ἀπ
Τρῳάδος, ἐπιθυμοῦντες νὰ φθάσωσιν ὅσο

Hebrew

ת : יְהוּדִים שֶׁמָּרְדוּ בָּךְ. כֵּן שֶׁהִגִּיעַ לְאַנְטִפַּטְרֶם זָרְחָה
וָן שֶׁרָאָה אֶת שִׁמְעוֹן הַצַּדִּיק יָרַד מִמֶּרְכַּבְתּוֹ וְהִשְׁתַּחֲוָה

Sanskrit

प संस्कृत नाम दैवी वाग् अन्वाख्याता महर्षिभि: । तद्भवस् तत्समो देशीत्य् अनेक:
प्राकृतक्रम:।। आभीरादिगिर: काव्येष्वपभ्रंश इति स्मृता:। शास्त्रे तु संस्कृताद्
अन्यद् अपभ्रंशतयोदितम् ।। श्लेष: प्रसाद: समता माधुर्यं सुकुमारता। अर्थव्यक्तिर्

Chinese

帶所及，使英國人的生活習慣也起了變化。
館子吃一頓的，現在大多數改爲吃自助餐，
習慣，一星期中，捱了幾天牛油麵包或三文
被迫產生的節約風氣所造成的後果是帶來不
至殃及學生們在假期中找臨時工作的出路。
貶值以來，英國的經濟衰退情形更嚴重。人
是情況都還不錯的華僑們所開設的中國
停業。光是倫敦一地，過去一年來停

The written word
left and foot of page
The invention of writing has proved one of the most potent of all human tools. Some of the earliest written forms show clear derivation from pictures; indeed Nasi (foot of page) is still a major language in the Yunnan province of China. But most modern languages have become streamlined into simpler forms. Even Chinese is being simplified, although its hieroglyphic form remains. Modern Burmese, based on curved characters, contrasts with the angular Sanskrit which is an ancient script pictorially resembling Hindi and other languages of modern India.

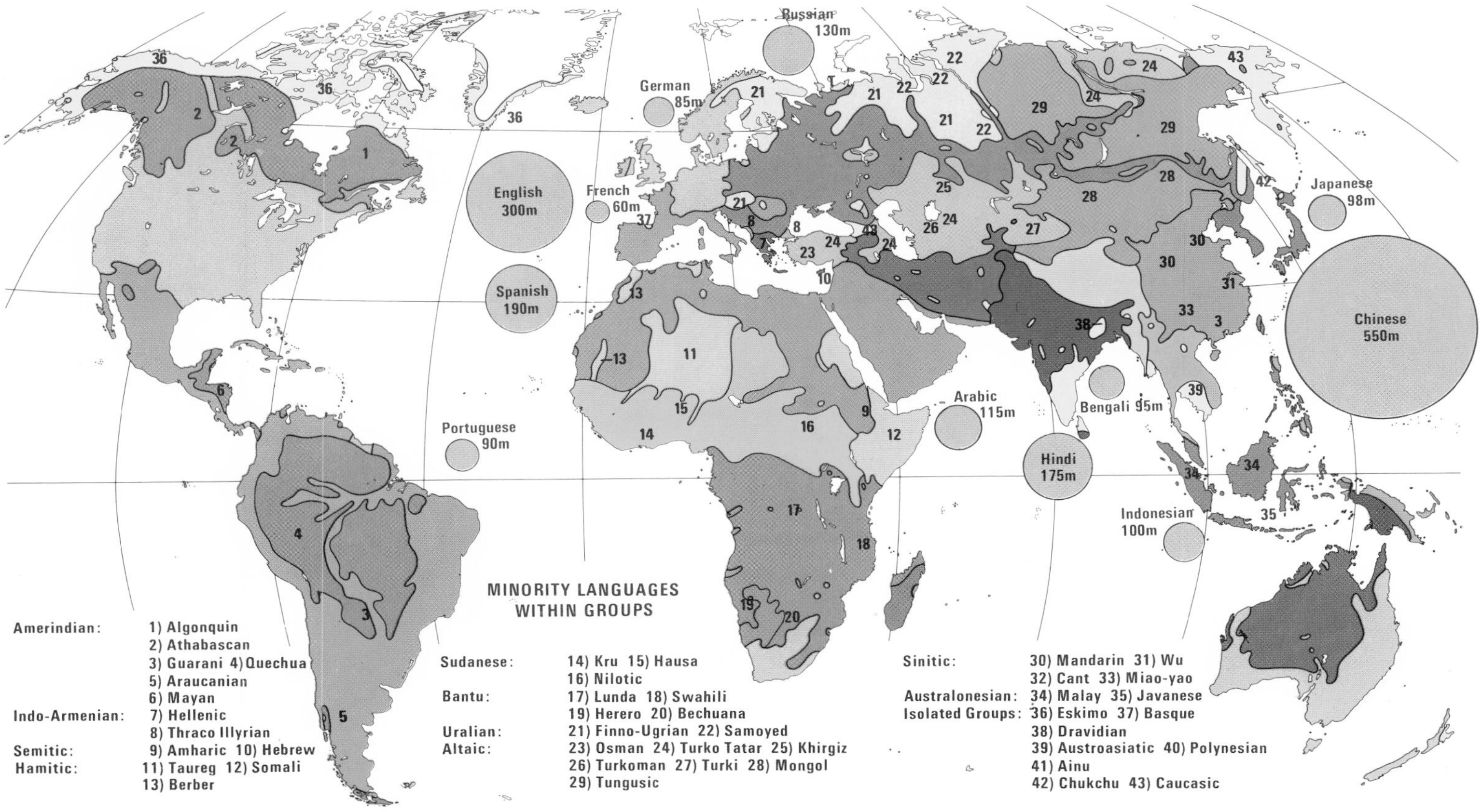

Russian 130m
German 85m
English 300m
French 60m
Spanish 190m
Portuguese 90m
Arabic 115m
Hindi 175m
Bengali 95m
Indonesian 100m
Japanese 98m
Chinese 550m
MINORITY LANGUAGES WITHIN GROUPS
Amerindian: 1) Algonquin
2) Athabascan
3) Guarani 4) Quechua
5) Araucanian
6) Mayan
Indo-Armenian: 7) Hellenic
8) Thraco Illyrian
Semitic: 9) Amharic 10) Hebrew
Hamitic: 11) Taureg 12) Somali
13) Berber
Sudanese: 14) Kru 15) Hausa
16) Nilotic
Bantu: 17) Lunda 18) Swahili
19) Herero 20) Bechuana
Uralian: 21) Finno-Ugrian 22) Samoyed
Altaic: 23) Osman 24) Turko Tatar 25) Khirgiz
26) Turkoman 27) Turki 28) Mongol
29) Tungusic
Sinitic: 30) Mandarin 31) Wu
32) Cant 33) Miao-yao
Australonesian: 34) Malay 35) Javanese
Isolated Groups: 36) Eskimo 37) Basque
38) Dravidian
39) Austroasiatic 40) Polynesian
41) Ainu
42) Chukchu 43) Caucasic

Teutonic
Latin
Slavonic
Indo-Armenian
Indo-Aryan

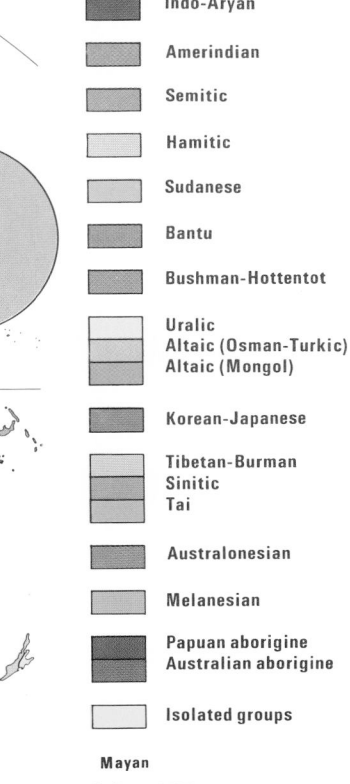

Amerindian

Semitic

Hamitic

Sudanese

Bantu

Bushman-Hottentot

Uralic
Altaic (Osman-Turkic)
Altaic (Mongol)

Korean-Japanese

Tibetan-Burman
Sinitic
Tai

Australonesian

Melanesian

Papuan aborigine
Australian aborigine

Isolated groups

Contrasting languages
The biggest language group is Chinese, but this is really a profusion of dialects. English, Spanish and Portuguese have spread with colonization, while Russian has become a uniform language from Europe to the Pacific. Easy communications will increase the domination of the great international languages for education, commerce and cultural exchange. This means that many more people will have to become at least bilingual, although minor languages may survive indefinitely. It is unlikely that cultural diversity, which depends so much on language, will be submerged.

Nasi

New Assyrian

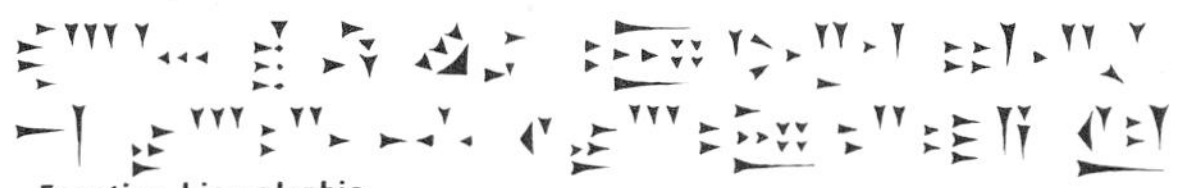

Egyptian hieroglyphic

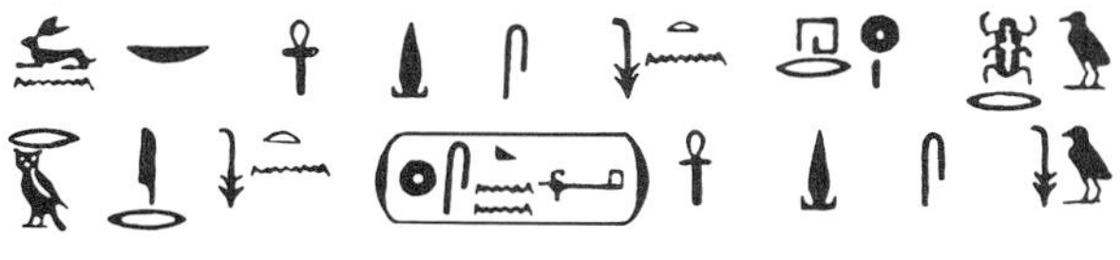

Mayan

The Health of Man

In the constitution of the World Health Organization 'health' is defined as 'a state of complete physical, mental and social well-being, and not merely the absence of disease or infirmity.' Such a definition sets a standard which man can seek to attain, but it is not yet possible to measure such an ideal state of life. In practice health is measured by the absence of disease. Indices based on mortality, such as crude and age-adjusted death rates, infant mortality rates, and the expectation of life at birth and different ages, are traditionally used as measures of health. Such indices take into account only the extreme situation – death – and afford no data on the amount of incapacitating illness (morbidity) in a community, which is of greater economic concern and a more useful measure of quality of life.

The picture of health and disease varies greatly throughout the world, but there is always a sharp distinction between that in the industrialized, developed countries and the picture in developing countries. Expectation of life at birth is much lower in the developing countries, where the main causes of death are infectious and parasitic diseases, invariably in inter-relation with malnutrition. The absence of any doctors over large areas results in 'fevers of unknown origin' appearing on many death certificates. Multiple pathology – the state of suffering from several diseases at once – is the rule rather than the exception among the population throughout the tropical developing nations. Malaria, measles, tuberculosis, diphtheria, smallpox, cholera, typhoid, dysentery, bilharzia, filariasis, trachoma, kwashiorkor, beri-beri and pellagra are widespread. In contrast, in the developed countries the dominant causes of death are cancer and cardiovascular diseases.

Nearly half the total of world deaths are of newborn babies and infants in Asia, Africa and Latin America. These underprivileged children, whose resistance is undermined by malnutrition, fall a ready prey to infection or die from so-called tropical diseases. Nevertheless, the swift rise in the world's population is due to the fact that infantile mortality is falling while the rate of conception is not.

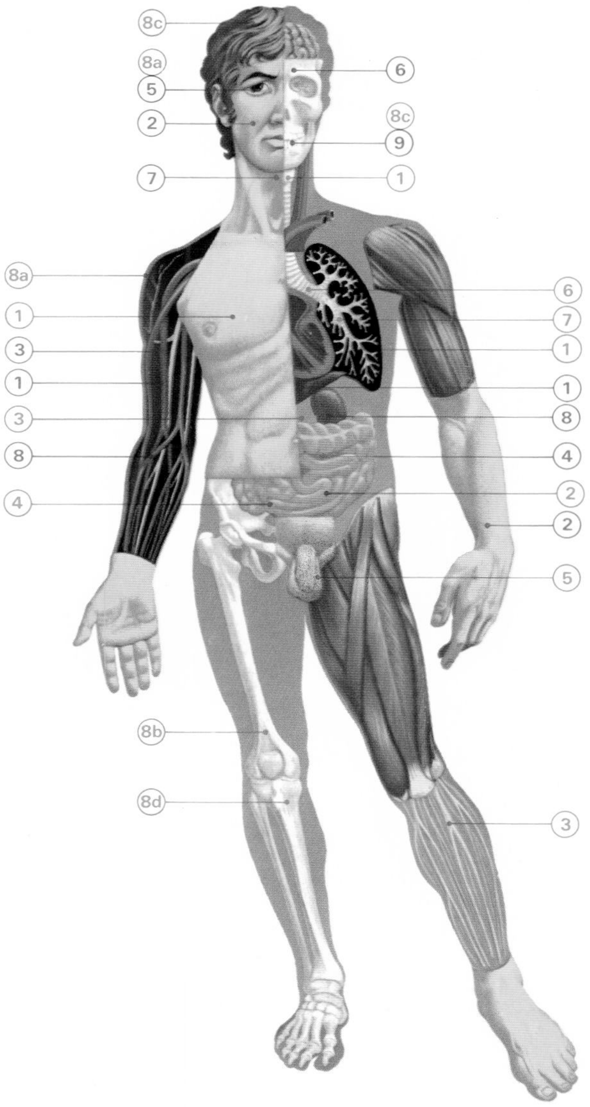
8c
8a
5
2
7
6
8c
9
1
8a
1
3
1
3
8
4
6
7
1
1
8
4
2
2
5
8b
8d
3

	Disease and cause	Carrier	Sites of infection
1	Malaria; parasites of genus Plasmodium	Anopheles mosquito	Blood stream; especially the liver
2	Smallpox; virus	Infected person or object	The skin; extensive pustular rash
3	Typhoid; bacteria of genus Salmonella	Infected water supply	Blood stream; build up of toxins
4	Dysentery; single celled organisms Shigella and Entamoeba	Flies and contaminated waste, excreta etc.	Intestine and bowels
5	Trachoma; virus	Flies	Eyes; severe conjunctivitis
6	Influenza; virus	Close contact with infected person	Head cold accompanied by fever
7	Diphtheria; bacteria of genus Corynebacterium	Contact with infected person or contaminated food	Throat
8	Yellow fever; virus	Flies; especially Aëdes mosquito	Blood supply; especially the kidneys
9	Dental caries	Lack of care and Vitamin C	Teeth and gums
1	Cancer; virus	Possible ties with polluted air, climate, smoking	Usually throat, lung, breast and cervix
2	Parasitic worms; adult and larvae	Lack of sanitation, contaminated water	Intestines, tissue and blood stream (eggs)
3	Polio; virus	Infected person	Nervous system; results in paralysis
4	Cholera	Contaminated food and water	Intestines
5	Syphilis; spiral protozoon, Spirochaeta pallida	Sexual intercourse, skin abrasions; may be inherited	Genitals; can spread to nervous system and brain
6	Pneumonia and bronchitis	Climatic conditions, polluted air	Bronchial tubes and lungs
7	Tuberculosis	Breath of infected person or animal	Lungs
8a	Keratomalacea	Vitamin C deficiency	Eyes and skin
8b	Beri-beri	Vitamin B deficiency	Muscular wasting
8c	Scurvy	Vitamin C deficiency	Gums, teeth and scalp
8d	Skull bossing	Vitamin D deficiency	Bone; affects skeletal development

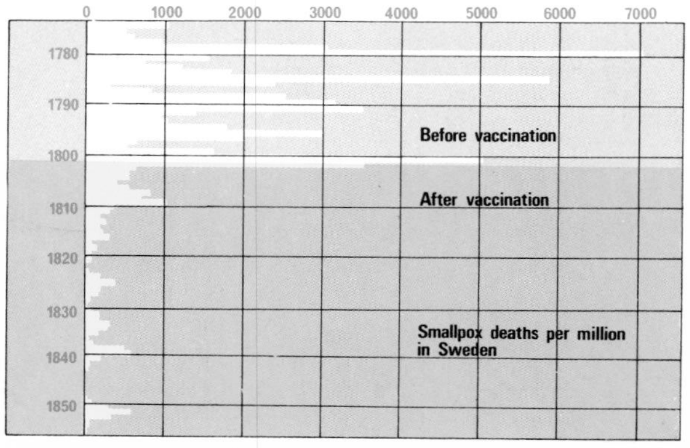
0
1000
2000
3000
4000
5000
6000
7000
1780
1790
1800
1810
1820
1830
1840
1850
Before vaccination
After vaccination
Smallpox deaths per million in Sweden

Smallpox *above*
Once a cause of wholesale death and disfigurement, smallpox was the first disease to be curbed and finally almost eradicated by vaccination, the deliberate introduction of 'antibodies' demonstrated by Dr Edward Jenner in 1798. Sweden was an early user.

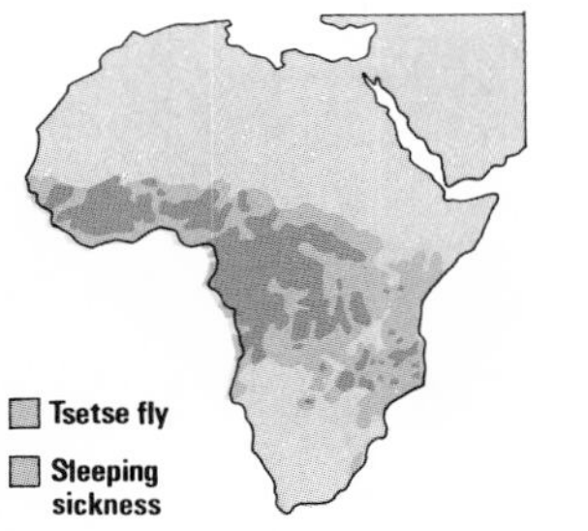
Tsetse fly
Sleeping sickness

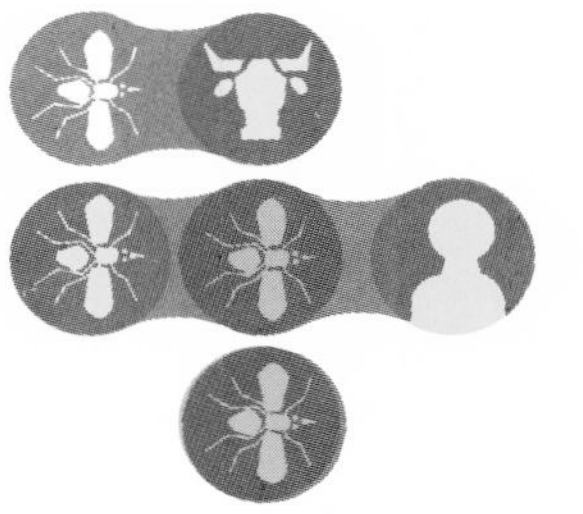

Sleeping sickness *left*
This virulent disease still ravages cattle and other domestic animals throughout a large area of tropical Africa (shaded region, left). The tsetse fly (top line, left) bites an infected animal, sucking in single-celled trypanosomes. These mature in its body before being passed on to the next victim, in this case a human (middle line). The fly is thereafter a carrier (bottom line). It is difficult to eradicate the fly population, but drugs have eased the menace where humans are concerned. Wild animals which carry the trypanosome provide a massive reservoir of infection.

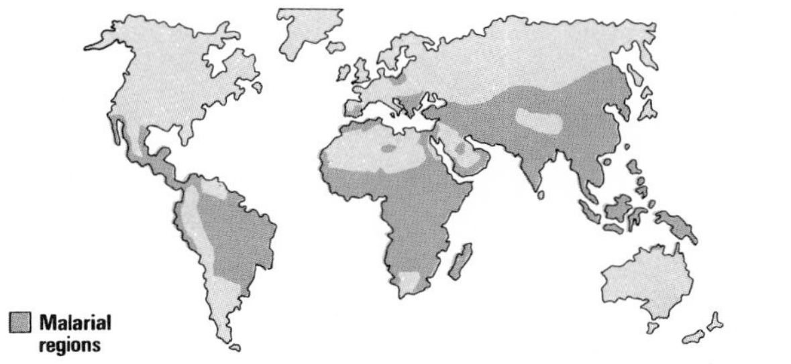
Malarial regions

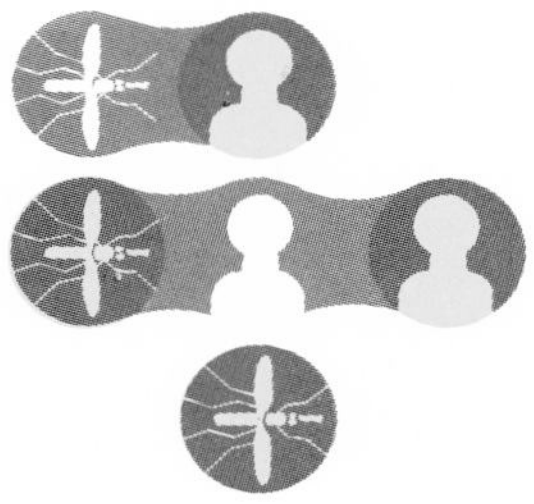

Malaria *above and left*
The malarial parasite (three types of *Plasmodium*) is carried in the bloodstream. When a mosquito (top line, left) bites an infected human, it becomes a carrier. The parasite multiplies then in the insect and anyone bitten by it is infected with the disease (middle line).

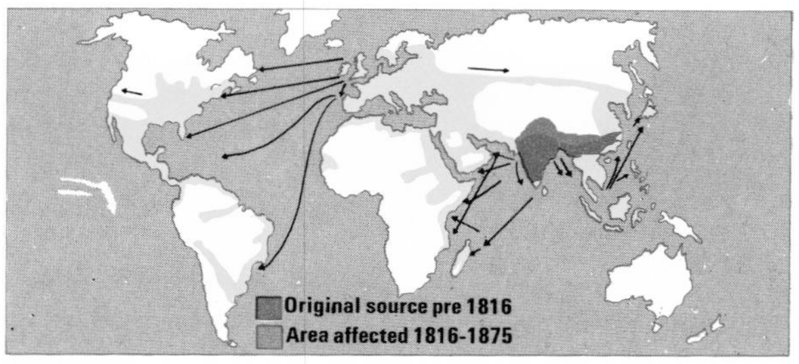
Original source pre 1816
Area affected 1816-1875

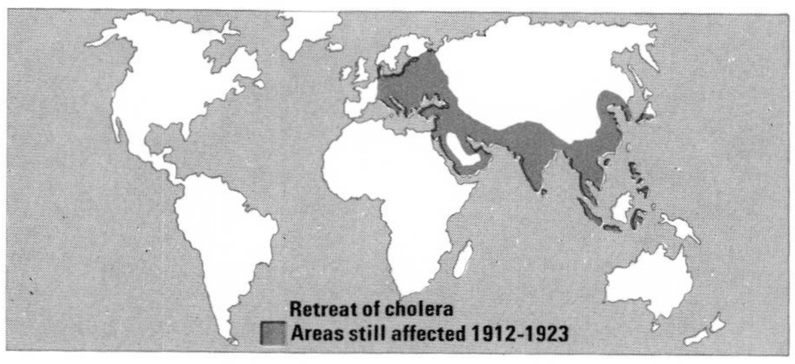
Retreat of cholera
Areas still affected 1912-1923

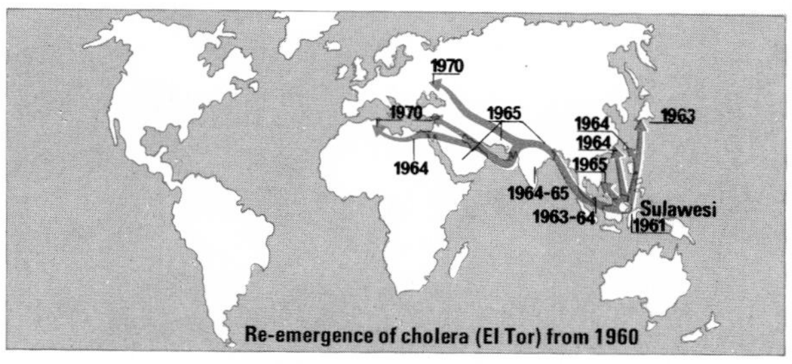
1970
1970
1965
1964
1963
1964
1965
1964
1964-65
1963-64
Sulawesi
1961
Re-emergence of cholera (El Tor) from 1960

The rise and fall of cholera
Cholera is an acute infectious disease characterized by violent purging, muscular cramps and rapid collapse. Its cause is a micro-organism, the cholera vibriola, which grows in the human alimentary canal. Wherever poor sanitation allows fecal material to contaminate drinking water, cholera can thrive. It has been endemic in India for centuries. In 1816, the disease swiftly spread to neighboring lands, and by 1850 was raging throughout the huge area indicated above. There were six of these pandemics which killed millions of people.

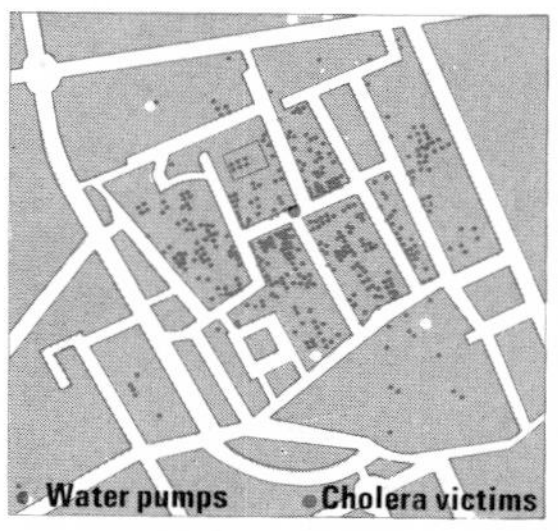
Water pumps
Cholera victims

Soho, 1848 *left*
In 1848 Dr John Snow, whose practice was in Soho, London, concluded cholera was transmitted through drinking impure water. He had the handle removed from a pump in the center of an epidemic (left), whereupon new cases ceased.

The threat returns
Apart from outbreaks in Iran in 1939 and Egypt in 1947, cholera has in recent years been confined to its historical home in and around India (above center). By 1954 it seemed to be disappearing even there, but in 1961 a new strain of the disease, known as El Tor, suddenly appeared from a focus in Sulawesi (Celebes). By the end of 1970 it had affected approximately 30 countries in Asia, Africa and Europe. Control measures have proved very difficult, and the vaccines in current use have all demonstrated very low effectiveness and a short duration.

The overall picture of world health *left and below*
Although disease is intensely personal it is possible in a few square inches to portray basic facts that affect the world population. In the table (left) are listed 17 important diseases, each identified by a number and a color. These numbers are repeated in the human figure (far left) to show the usual afflicted region of the body and their world incidence on the map (below).

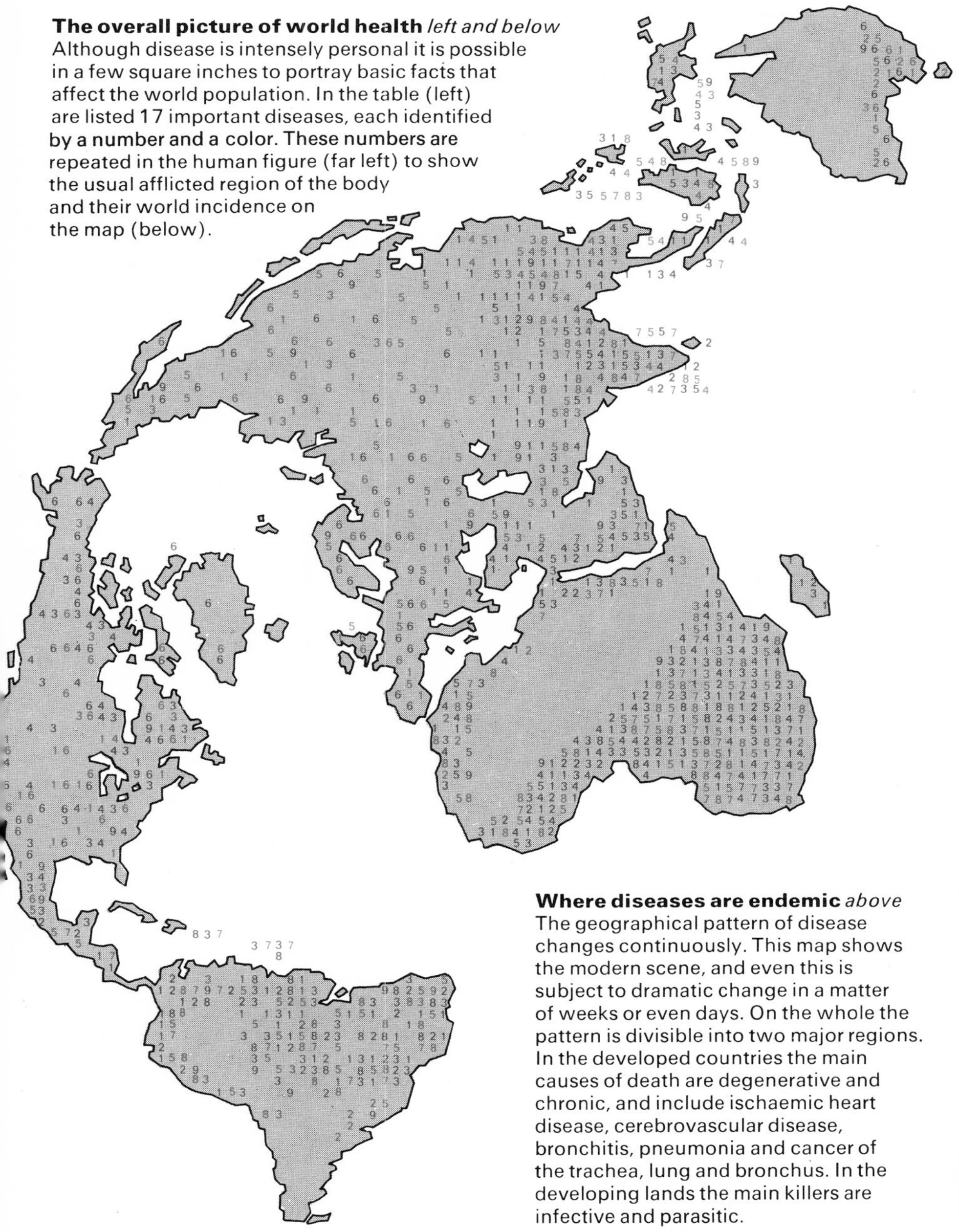

Where diseases are endemic *above*
The geographical pattern of disease changes continuously. This map shows the modern scene, and even this is subject to dramatic change in a matter of weeks or even days. On the whole the pattern is divisible into two major regions. In the developed countries the main causes of death are degenerative and chronic, and include ischaemic heart disease, cerebrovascular disease, bronchitis, pneumonia and cancer of the trachea, lung and bronchus. In the developing lands the main killers are infective and parasitic.

Mental hospitals *right*
Nearly all the 'civilized' countries used to treat the mentally ill as criminals or objects of derision. Today the gradual subjugation of physical disease is combined with sharply increased mental stress, with the result that mental illness is becoming a more and more important clinical condition, both in terms of numbers and therapy. Severe cases demand constant, skilled attention over a period which may be many years. In most of the advanced nations the job is assigned to specialist hospitals, which number five to ten per cent of the total.

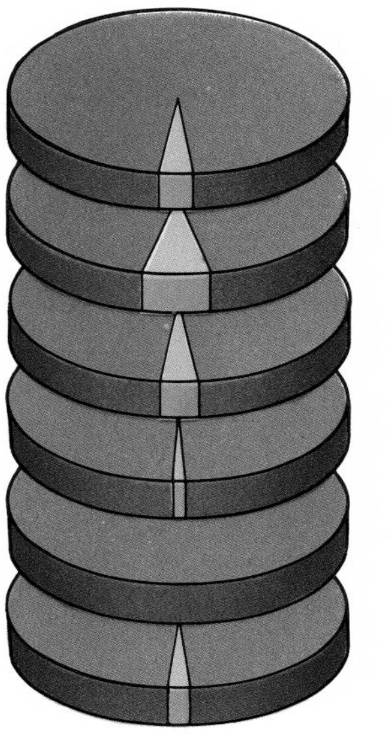
England and Wales
Total hospitals 2531
Specialist mental hospitals 152
Denmark
Total hospitals 170
Specialist mental hospitals 17
USA
Total hospitals 7172
Specialist mental hospitals 418
Japan
Total hospitals 35521
Specialist mental hospitals 769
France
Total hospitals 1097
Specialist mental hospitals 0
Peru
Total hospitals 282
Specialist mental hospitals 9

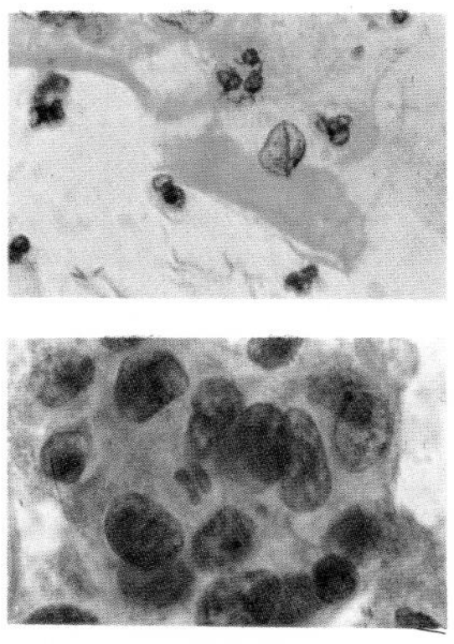

Cancer cells *above*
The upper photograph shows normal cells from a cervical smear. Immediately above are malignant cervical cells, to the same magnification (x 500).

Cancer in the US *below*
This map shows the distribution of deaths from lung cancer in the United States in 1966. The density of shading of each state is proportional to the incidence of such deaths per hundred thousand of population. It should be emphasized that the data are for lung cancer only.

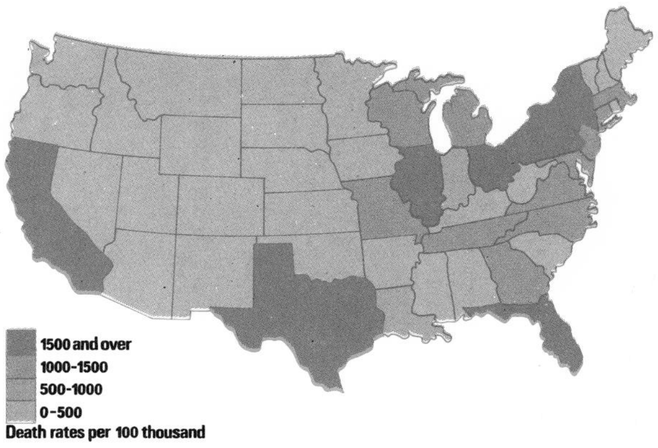
1500 and over
1000-1500
500-1000
0-500
Death rates per 100 thousand

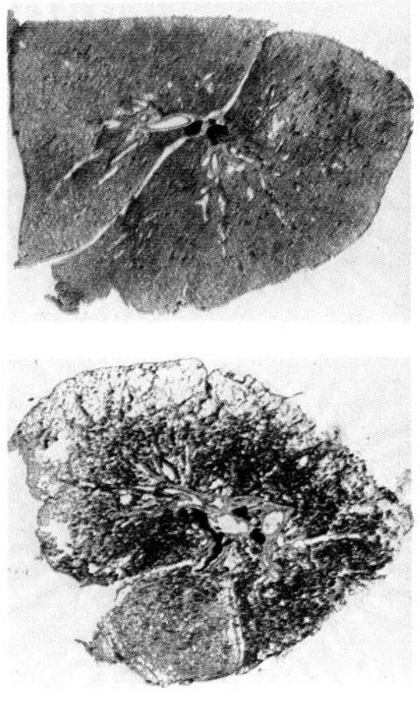

Diseased lungs *above*
Healthy (upper) and bronchitic tissues.

Bronchitis in Britain *right*
Often called 'the English disease' by other countries, bronchitis is typical of the disabling and killing afflictions that accompany a polluted industrial environment. The shading on the map shows the death rates for females in different areas, compared to a base index of 100 Figures for men are almost twice as high but follow the same pattern. Data for Manchester and London are more than three times the national average, and those for Eastbourne, Bournemouth and Canterbury are less than half the average.

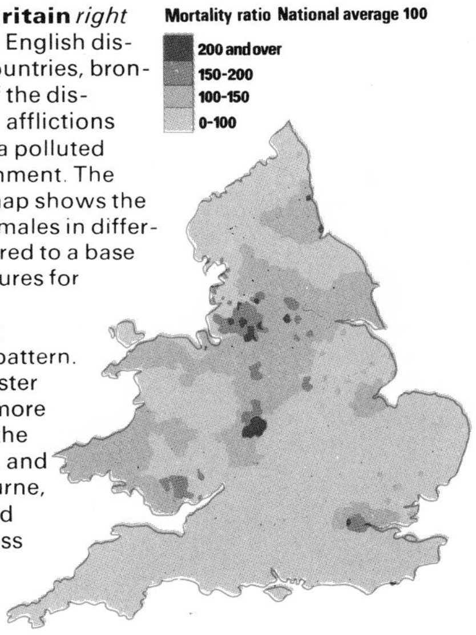
Mortality ratio National average 100
200 and over
150-200
100-150
0-100

The facilities available
Two of the most fundamental yardsticks for the measurement of national medical facilities are the number of people in the country for each hospital bed and for each doctor. These data are plotted here for some highly contrasting countries, illustrating the wide variation in facilities. In this figure 'China' signifies Taiwan; the figures for the Peoples' Republic are unknown.

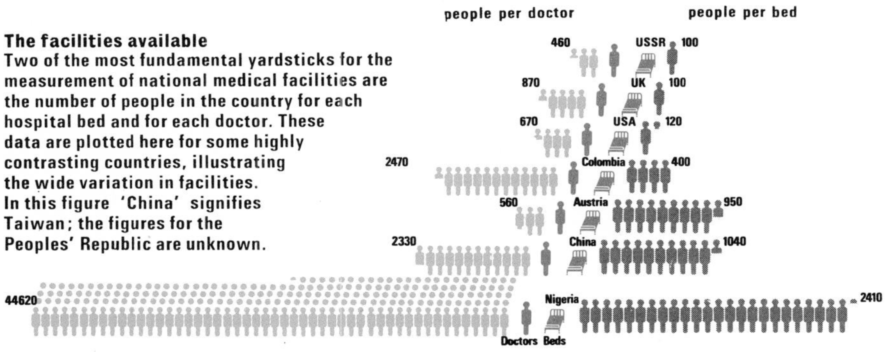
people per doctor
people per bed
460
USSR
100
870
UK
100
670
USA
120
2470
Colombia
400
560
Austria
950
2330
China
1040
44620
Nigeria
2410
Doctors Beds

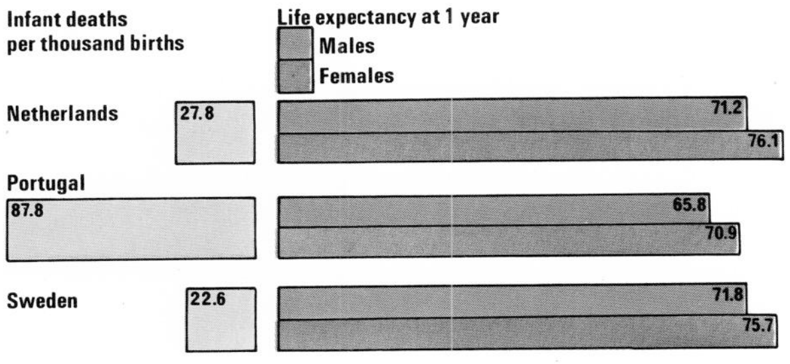
Infant deaths
per thousand births
Life expectancy at 1 year
Males
Females
Netherlands
27.8
71.2
76.1
Portugal
87.8
65.8
70.9
Sweden
22.6
71.8
75.7

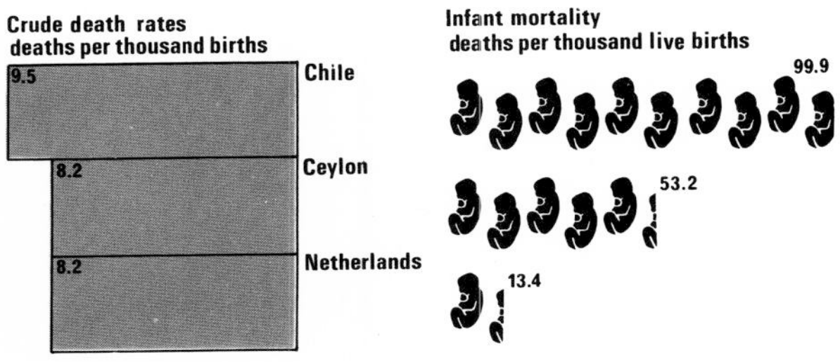
Crude death rates
deaths per thousand births
9.5
Chile
8.2
Ceylon
8.2
Netherlands
Infant mortality
deaths per thousand live births
99.9
53.2
13.4

Births and deaths *left*
Health statistics can be very misleading. The Netherlands, Portugal and Sweden all have a similar index of health in that the expectation of life of their citizens at the age of one is approximately the same. But the sum of late fetal deaths and those of children aged less than one year, the rate per 1000 live births is more than three times as high for one of the countries. Again, the crude death rates for the whole population for Chile, Ceylon and the Netherlands are similar, but their infant mortality figures, which reflect social conditions, show a great contrast.

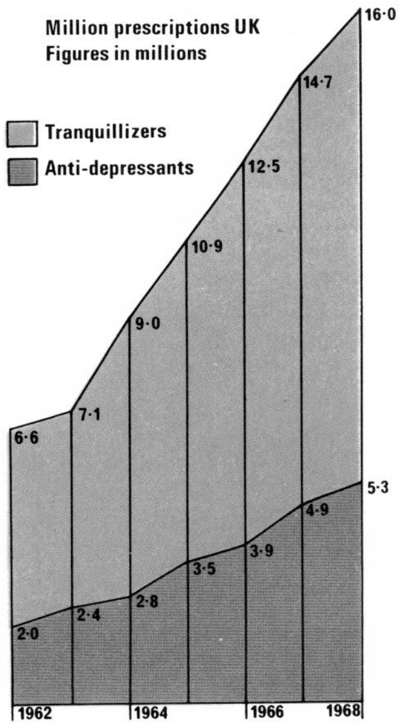
Million prescriptions UK
Figures in millions
Tranquillizers
Anti-depressants
6·6
7·1
9·0
10·9
12·5
14·7
16·0
2·0
2·4
2·8
3·5
3·9
4·9
5·3
1962
1964
1966
1968

Drugs *left and right*
Affluent societies seem to rely increasingly on drugs to cushion them from the stress of life. These graphs are plotted from data for the United Kingdom, a country which a generation ago regarded drug abuse as a problem for others. The rise in prescribed medicinal drugs (left) reflects not only occupational and domestic stress but increasing social and medical acceptance of drugs. The curve of drug addicts registered at the Home Office (right) tells a different story which many would consider horrifying. Rising addiction to 'hard' drugs is difficult to reverse.

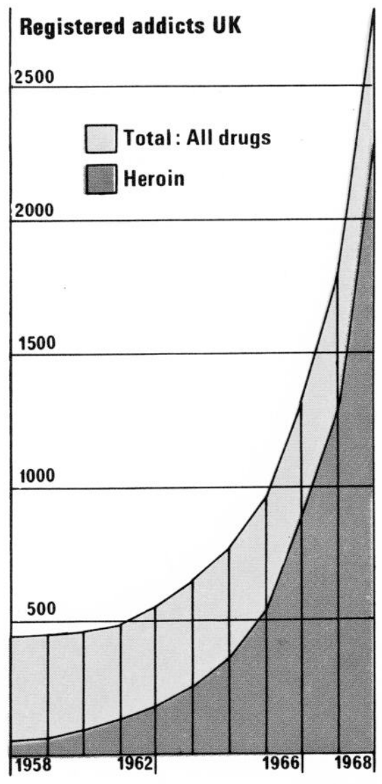
Registered addicts UK
2500
Total: All drugs
Heroin
2000
1500
1000
500
1958
1962
1966
1968

Human Nutrition

Man's existence depends on his capacity to produce, store, process and distribute food. Technically, an agreeable food consists of the non-toxic, socially acceptable, digestible, palatable and nutritive parts of plants and animals. At least 43 chemical compounds and elements are required in the human diet. Of these essential nutrients 17 are minerals such as calcium, iron and magnesium, while the remainder fall within four main groups: carbohydrates (sugars and starch); fats and fatty acids; proteins; and vitamins.

Proteins provide the very stuff of life—the variety of tissues that make up the healthy individual. For example, proteins are the key substance of heart and other muscles and of the corpuscles in the blood. They and their products are essential for digestion and many other body functions. Man needs protein to replace daily wear and tear and to repair tissues damaged by accident or disease. Pregnant women and growing children need extra protein to meet the demands of pregnancy, lactation and growth. Unfortunately, proteins vary in quality—measured in terms of the amino-acids of which they consist. Since the body cannot synthesize all these chemicals, some essential amino-acids must be received in the diet either as plants which can make them or as the meat of animals that have previously consumed them. Therefore meat products generally have a higher protein quality than plant foods, some of which are deficient in essential amino-acids. Vitamins and minerals are also essential in small amounts; and deficits lead to specific deficiency diseases. Energy foods—carbohydrates, fats and, if necessary, proteins—provide the power for internal work, such as pumping blood, and external work.

Human foods differ widely in their palatability and in their content of proteins, vitamins, minerals and energy sources. People can suffer from deficiencies in their diet simply because the staple food lacks essential nutritive ingredients. A good diet should be a mixture of food which is neither too bulky nor too liquid, is appetizing, and easy to cook and prepare for the table. This increases the likelihood that it will supply a balanced intake of the needed nutrients.

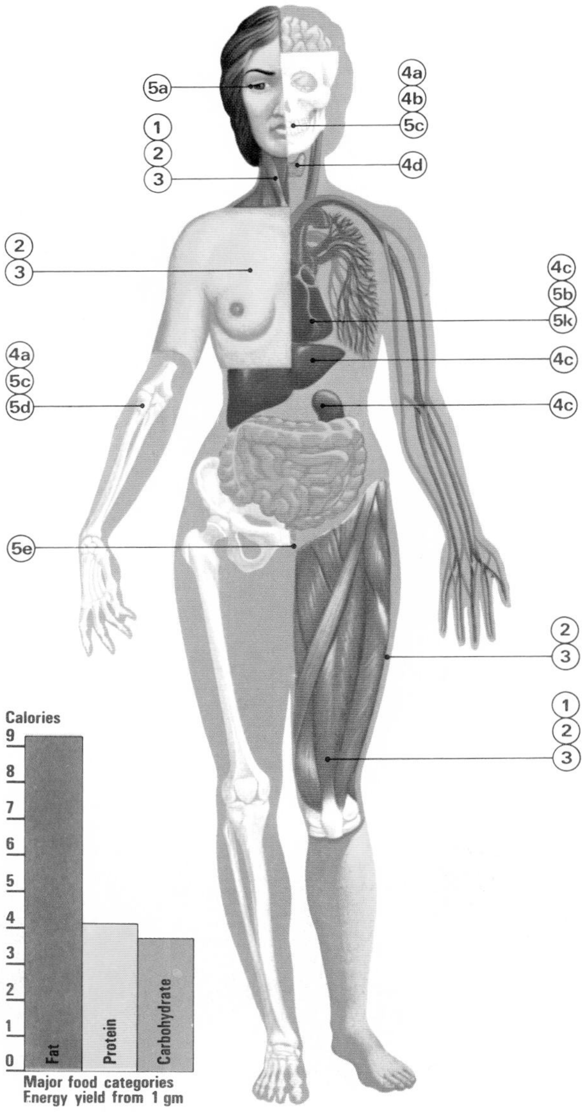
5a
1
2
3
4a
4b
5c
4d
2
3
4c
5b
5k
4c
4c
4a
5c
5d
5e
2
3
1
2
3
Calories
9
8
7
6
5
4
3
2
1
0
Fat
Protein
Carbohydrate
Major food categories
Energy yield from 1 gm

1 Protein	Meats, eggs, fish, milk	Basic body structural material: growth and repair of muscles and tissue: control of metabolism and muscular energy
2 Fats	Animal and vegetable oils animal fats, fish oils, butter	Body fat provides, with sugars, basic source of energy for body; also provides energy store and heat insulation
3 Carbohydrates	Starches, such as potatoes, sugars	Starch yields glycogen, mainly stored in liver and muscle; sugar is basic source of body energy
4 Minerals	4a Calcium: peas, beans, milk, meat, cheese	Essential for bone formation, including nails and teeth.
	4b Phosphorus: cheese, liver, eggs	Essential for energy transfer and health of teeth
	4c Iron: green vegetables	Blood hemoglobin, energy transport, liver and kidney function
	4d Iodine: fish, water	Thyroid gland; prevents goiter and cretinism
5 Vitamins	5a Animal fats, fish oils,	Eyes
Note: 5a=Vitamin A; 5k=Vitamin K	5b Grain products, meat, milk	Growth, circulatory system
	5c Fruit, vegetables	Bones, teeth, child growth
	5d Cod liver oil, liver of tuna, halibut	Bones, child skeletal development
	5e Fat content of food, egg yolks, liver	
	5k Green plants, liver	Blood clotting

How we use our food *left and below*
Human food is composed of at least 43 chemical elements and compounds, all of which are needed to sustain a healthy individual. Of these essential constituents, 17 are minerals; the rest are carbohydrates and fats (needed in substantial bulk) and proteins and vitamins (specialized chemicals needed in much smaller quantities yet nonetheless vital). The table below lists the principal constituents of each class of food and the parts of the body for which they are particularly needed; these locations are indicated in the keyed illustration of a typical white adult. In fact, of course, the interaction between food and the body is usually almost unbelievably complicated.

Physique and food *below*
Although there are numerous exceptions, human body shape is in general adapted to climate. The Watussi (below, right) from Entebbe, Uganda, is tall and slender, whereas the Eskimo from Angmagssalik is rotund and better shaped for conserving heat energy and avoiding frostbite.

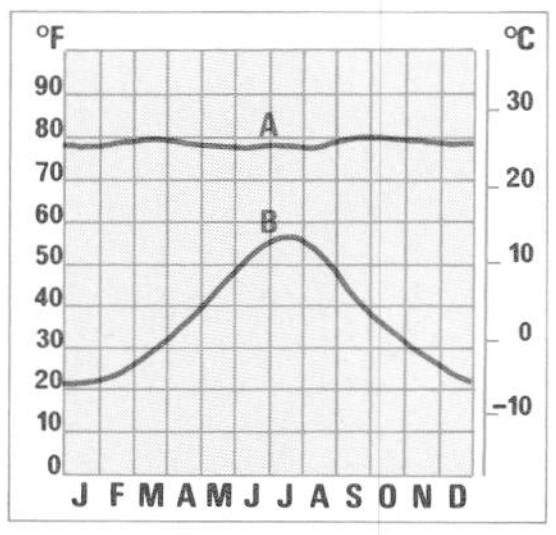
°F
°C
90
80
70
60
50
40
30
20
10
0
30
20
10
0
–10
A
B
J F M A M J J A S O N D

Temperature contrast
Temperature variation at Entebbe (A) is near zero, unlike Angmagssalik (B).

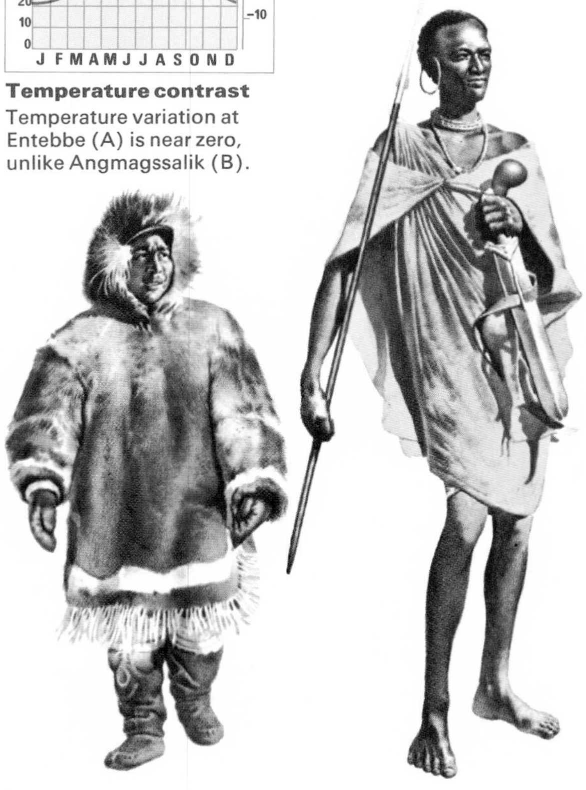

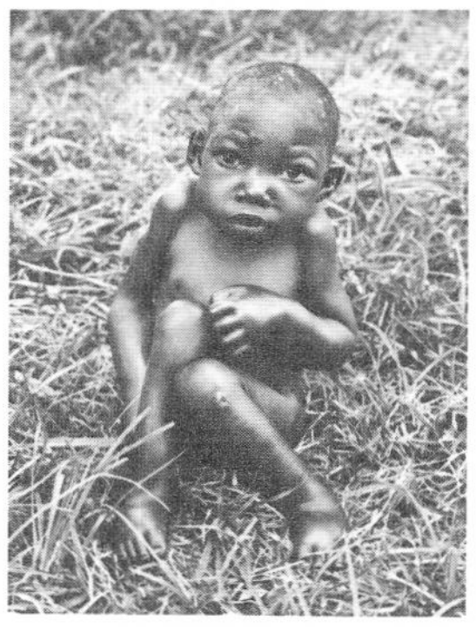

Kwashiorkor *above*
Widespread in Africa and SE Asia, this protein-deficiency disease is characterized by swollen stomach, wasted muscles and general retardation and susceptibility to other afflictions. The name means 'first-second', signifying a disease of the first child when the second is near.

The deficient profile *right*
Although malnutrition causes ill-health and death, large numbers of children (and adults) still die from a lack of food. This state of undernourishment, called marasmus, is reflected in the emaciated body. Gradually the body ceases to function and ultimately diarrhea and vomiting cause death from dehydration. In many cases, however, the sufferer falls victim to infections against which the weakened body no longer has any defense.

What do we need? *right*
Human need for food depends on our body size, how warm it is and what energy we expend in our daily life. Shown here are the daily requirements for different people in terms of kilogram calories of energy and grams per day of protein.

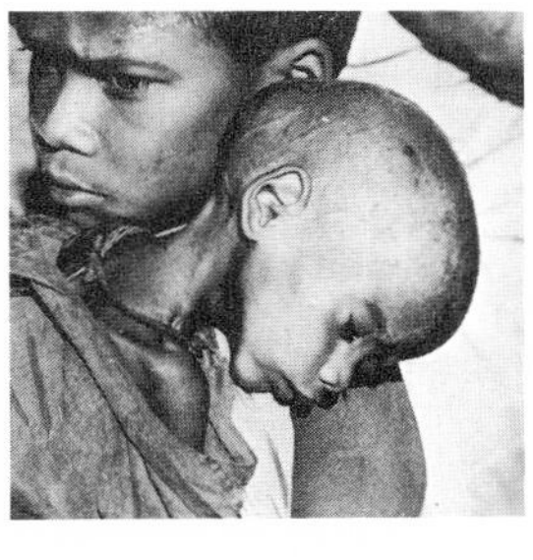

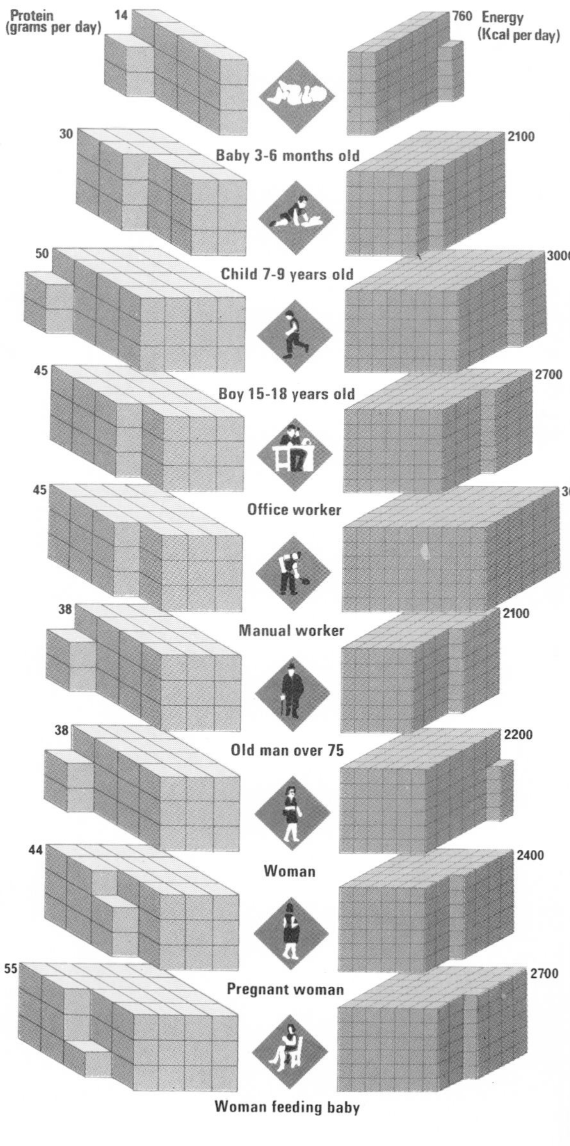
Protein (grams per day)
Energy (Kcal per day)
14
760
30
2100
Baby 3-6 months old
50
3000
Child 7-9 years old
45
2700
Boy 15-18 years old
45
3600
Office worker
38
2100
Manual worker
38
2200
Old man over 75
44
2400
Woman
55
2700
Pregnant woman
Woman feeding baby

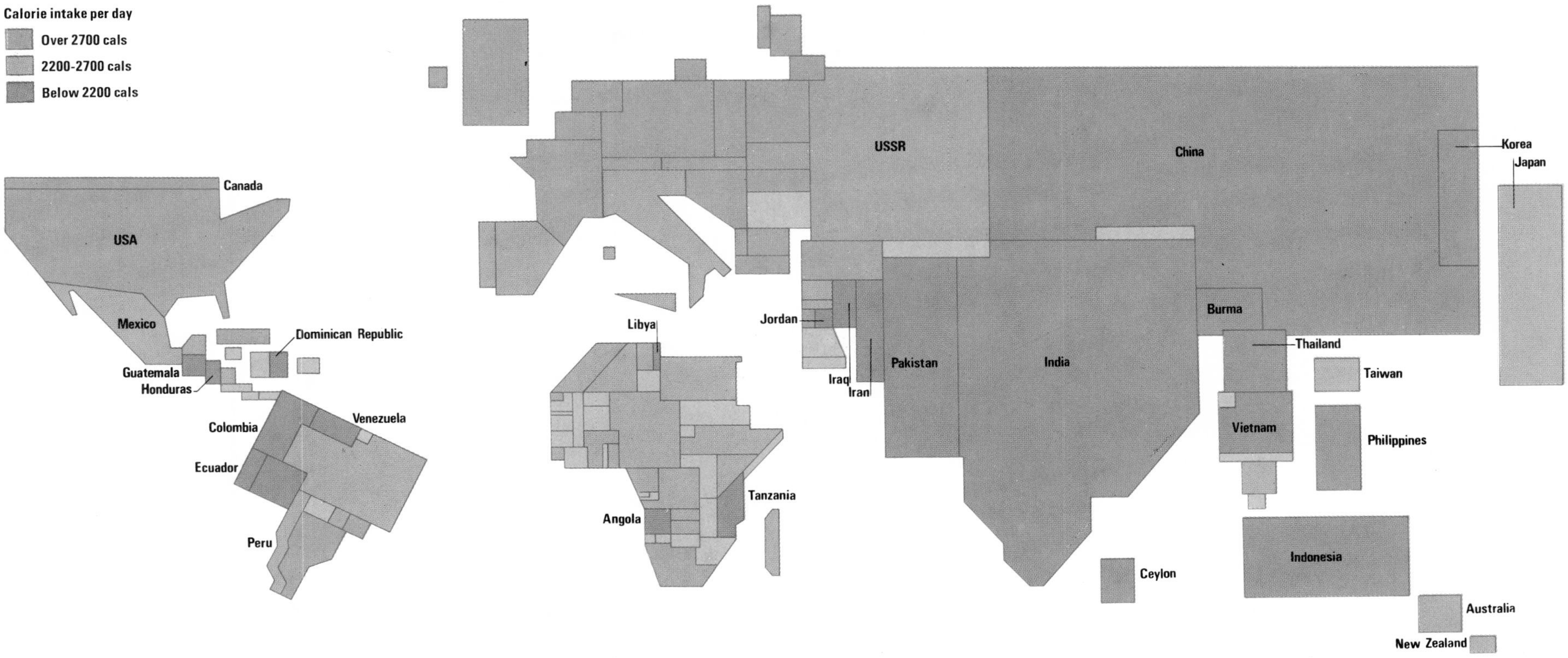
Calorie intake per day
Over 2700 cals
2200-2700 cals
Below 2200 cals
Canada
USA
Mexico
Dominican Republic
Guatemala
Honduras
Colombia
Venezuela
Ecuador
Peru
USSR
China
Korea
Japan
Libya
Jordan
Iraq
Iran
Pakistan
India
Burma
Thailand
Taiwan
Vietnam
Philippines
Angola
Tanzania
Ceylon
Indonesia
Australia
New Zealand

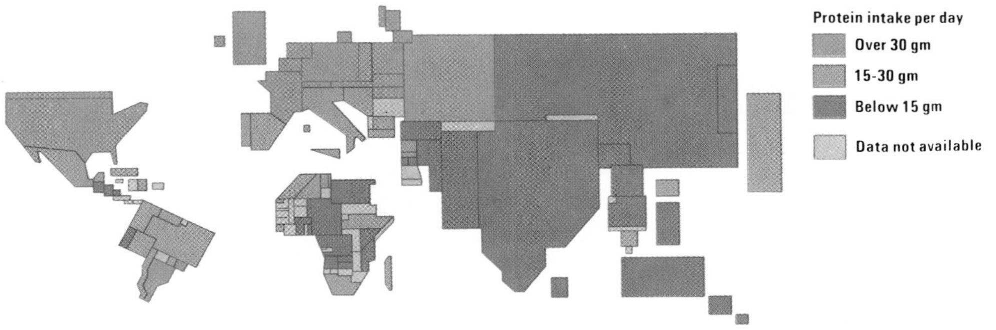
Protein intake per day
Over 30 gm
15-30 gm
Below 15 gm
Data not available

Population and food supply *above, right and below*
These maps are distorted to make the area of each country proportional to its population. The larger map indicates the supply of food available to each country in terms of calories per head per day; the smaller map shows available protein in terms of weight. Countries with little food also generally suffer from a poor quality diet, with ample starchy food but little meat; there is a sharp contrast in animal protein figures (below). Although some countries with modest food supplies do have adequate protein (Japan is one), others such as Spain and the Soviet Union still lack protein despite ample supplies of food.

Daily protein and calorie consumption per head

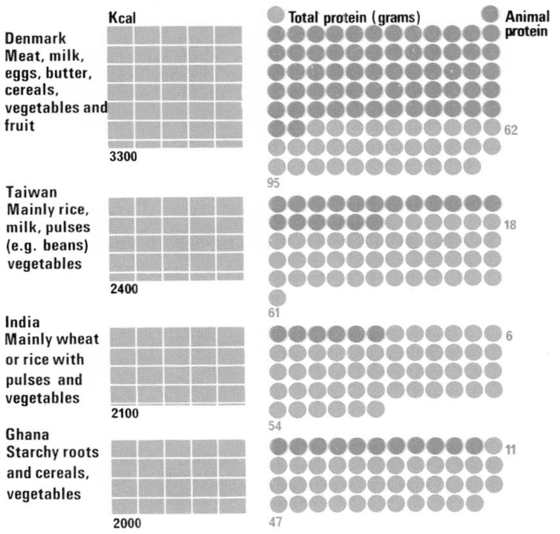
Kcal
Total protein (grams)
Animal protein
Denmark
Meat, milk, eggs, butter, cereals, vegetables and fruit
3300
62
95
Taiwan
Mainly rice, milk, pulses (e.g. beans) vegetables
2400
18
61
India
Mainly wheat or rice with pulses and vegetables
2100
6
54
Ghana
Starchy roots and cereals, vegetables
2000
11
47

Food and nutrition

All man's food depends ultimately on the capture of the Sun's energy by plants via the process of photosynthesis. When man eats these plants, he makes efficient use of the Earth's resources in terms of energy conversion. In fact, poorer peoples generally have little other choice, but richer ones favor meat in their diet. Not only do the animals consume foods unpalatable to man but their meat also has a much greater nutritive value, at the expense of an inefficient energy-conversion process. The basic energy released by eating food is expressed in calories. Different people need different amounts of energy(see facing page). In many countries hardly anyone can attain even this basic energy level. In most of the world stomachs are filled, but a more subtle form of hunger remains. Unless the body also receives adequate quantities of certain constituents of proteins, minerals and vitamins it cannot function properly. Disorders and disease are the inevitable result of this malnutrition.

The diet of the 'haves'

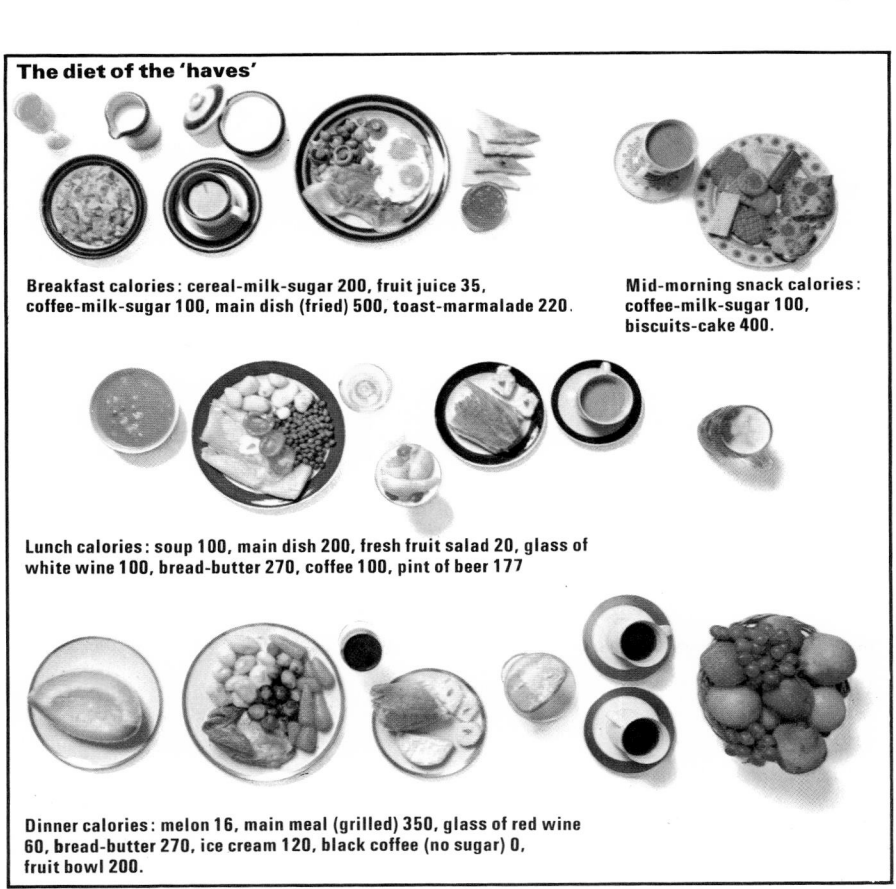

Breakfast calories: cereal-milk-sugar 200, fruit juice 35, coffee-milk-sugar 100, main dish (fried) 500, toast-marmalade 220.

Mid-morning snack calories: coffee-milk-sugar 100, biscuits-cake 400.

Lunch calories: soup 100, main dish 200, fresh fruit salad 20, glass of white wine 100, bread-butter 270, coffee 100, pint of beer 177

Dinner calories: melon 16, main meal (grilled) 350, glass of red wine 60, bread-butter 270, ice cream 120, black coffee (no sugar) 0, fruit bowl 200.

The diet of the 'have-nots'

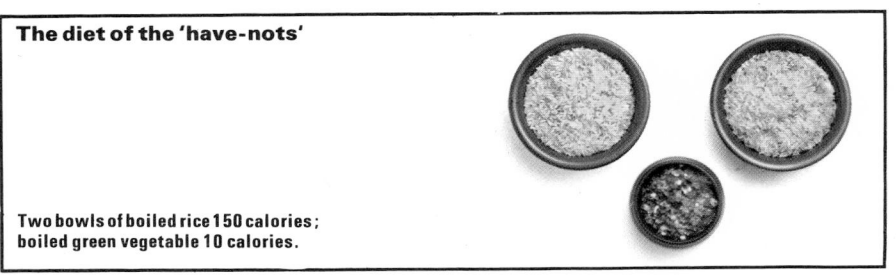

Two bowls of boiled rice 150 calories; boiled green vegetable 10 calories.

The haves and have-nots
Throughout a large and growing part of the Earth man is often found to suffer from a form of malnutrition caused not by starvation but by overeating. It is manifest in gross build-up of body fat leading to increased effort in walking and movement. In turn this leads to greater stress on the heart and a shorter life span. The food shown at left is not untypical of the daily consumption of adults in some of the world's more prosperous societies. The total number of calories is 3538, probably double the energy input needed and used mainly in new tissue formation. Protein input is substantially above requirement, and all vitamins are abundant. Vitamin A total amounts to more than 4000 international units, and thiamine, riboflavin, nicotinamide and ascorbic acid are all included in amounts which in aggregate are about double the body's needs. In contrast, the world's less advanced, poorer and hungrier nations have a diet that results in the more common type of malnutrition. Two small bowls of rice and a small quantity of vegetable such as cabbage, pulses or lentils form a common daily intake over a wide belt of tropical countries. Such fare is uninteresting, lacking in energy content and grossly deficient in proteins and vitamin content.

Man's Food Supplies

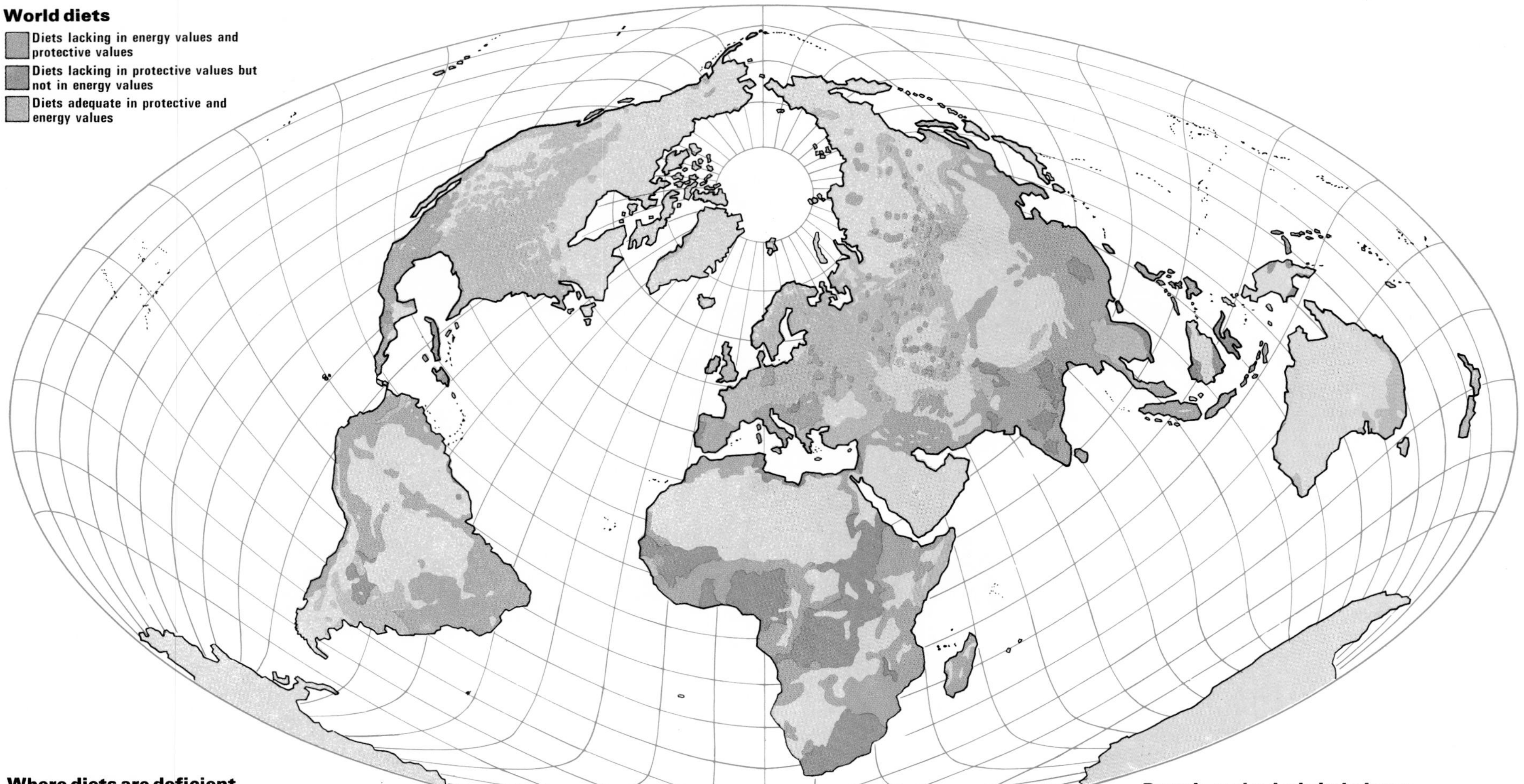
World diets
Diets lacking in energy values and protective values
Diets lacking in protective values but not in energy values
Diets adequate in protective and energy values

Where diets are deficient
Diets can lack energy, protective protein or both (above). Quantitative values for each continent (far right, below) show that Africa and the Far East are, on average, grossly deficient in both ; the protein figures are percentages and the calorie figures the number either over or under the average requirement per head. Diets are also deficient if they lack vitamins (map below, right).

Protein and calorie imbalance

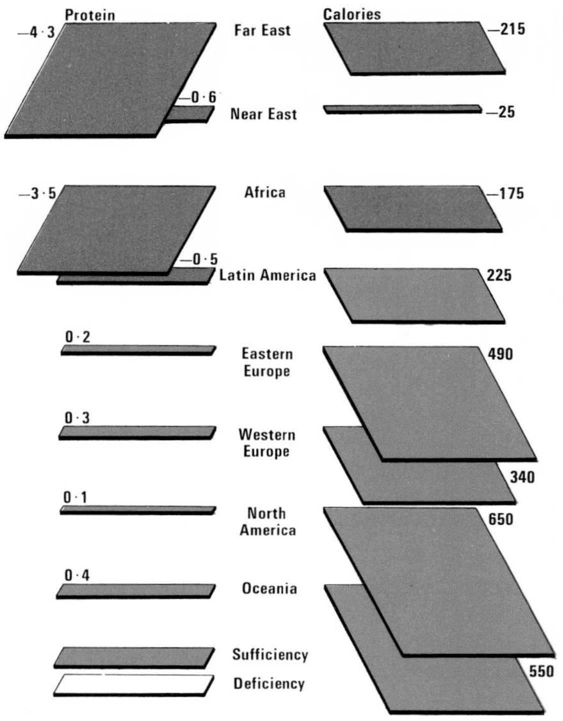
Protein
Calories
Far East
—4·3
—215
Near East
—0·6
—25
Africa
—3·5
—175
Latin America
—0·5
225
Eastern Europe
0·2
490
Western Europe
0·3
340
North America
0·1
650
Oceania
0·4
550
Sufficiency
Deficiency

Malnutrition

There has been no major famine since 1948, and almost nine out of every ten people on Earth have enough to eat. But only about half the world's population have an adequate balanced diet. On the previous two pages it was shown that shortage of minerals, carbohydrates, fats, proteins and vitamins can cause deficiency diseases. In a few parts of the world there is a shortage of calories, resulting in hunger and undernourishment (map above). In many other regions – nearly all in the hot, developing lands – there is a shortage of the other essentials (map right). Malnutrition hits children first, causing increased infant mortality, stunted growth and tragic physical symptoms (below). The worst problem is usually met at weaning, when the valuable milk falls short of the child's needs and there is nothing else available but starchy foods of low nutritive value. The answer for the future lies in increased understanding, and in wider introduction of protein-rich mixtures based on skim milk powder and selected vitamins.

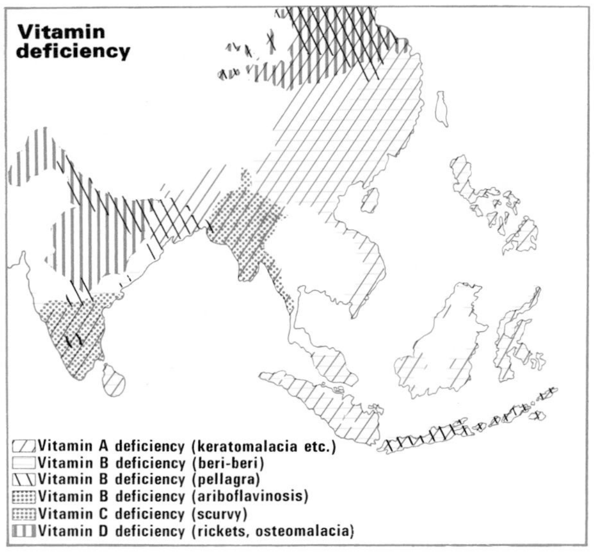
Vitamin deficiency
Vitamin A deficiency (keratomalacia etc.)
Vitamin B deficiency (beri-beri)
Vitamin B deficiency (pellagra)
Vitamin B deficiency (ariboflavinosis)
Vitamin C deficiency (scurvy)
Vitamin D deficiency (rickets, osteomalacia)

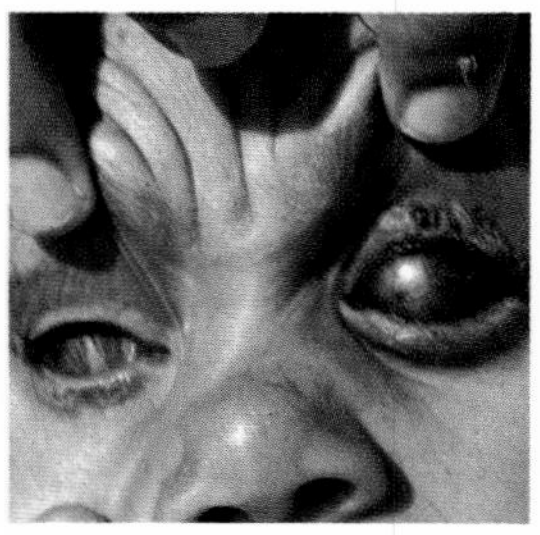

Keratomalacia
The only unequivocal signs of vitamin A deficiency are seen in the eyes. Deficiency of this vitamin can damage the retina, cornea and other parts. One of the most serious symptoms, keratomalacia affects the cornea and later the lens and iris.

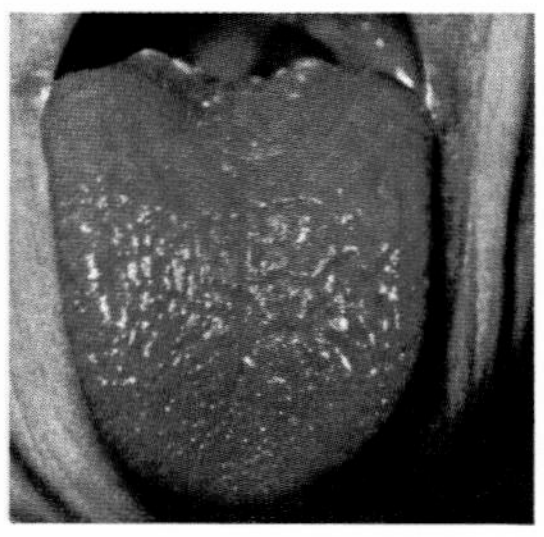

B2 deficiency
Early symptoms of riboflavine (vitamin B2) deficiency are soreness and burning of the lips, mouth and tongue, and difficulty in swallowing. The regions mentioned may suffer fissuring and ulceration. In this case the tongue has lost its original surface.

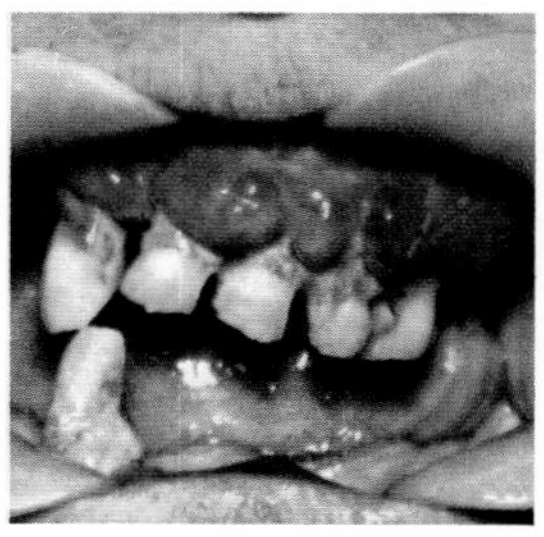

Scurvy
Gross deficiency of vitamin C, ascorbic acid, is the cause of scurvy. Lassitude, irritability, weakness and vague pains are followed by multiple haemorrhages. The first sure signs are usually bleeding gums and loose teeth, as in this sufferer.

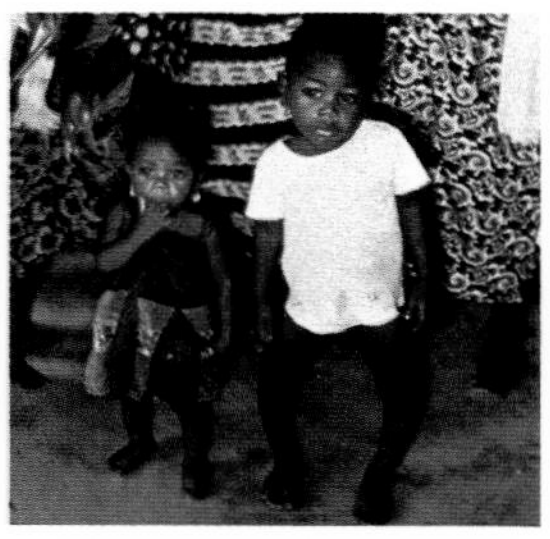

Rickets
Deficiency of vitamin D leads to rickets, a disease characterized by severe bone deformities. The deficiency is far less serious in adults where the skeleton is already formed, but it does lead to brittleness, particularly of the long bones of the limbs.

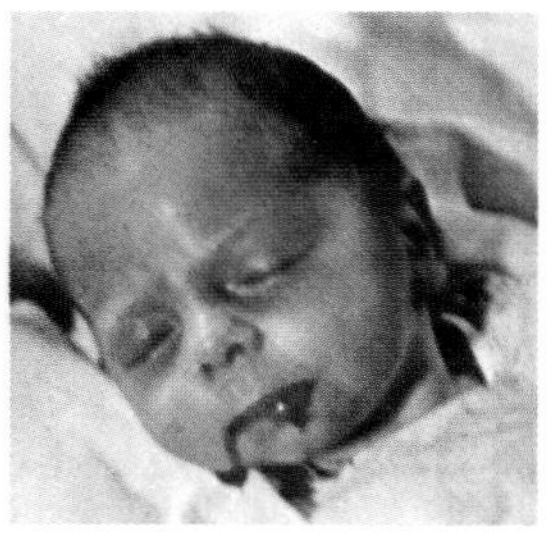

Haemorrhagia
Vitamin K is a group of quinone compounds which have anti-haemorrhagic properties. These are absorbed in the presence of bile salts, and this infant may suffer from a sterile gut. Obstructive jaundice, cirrhosis and anti-coagulants cause deficiency.

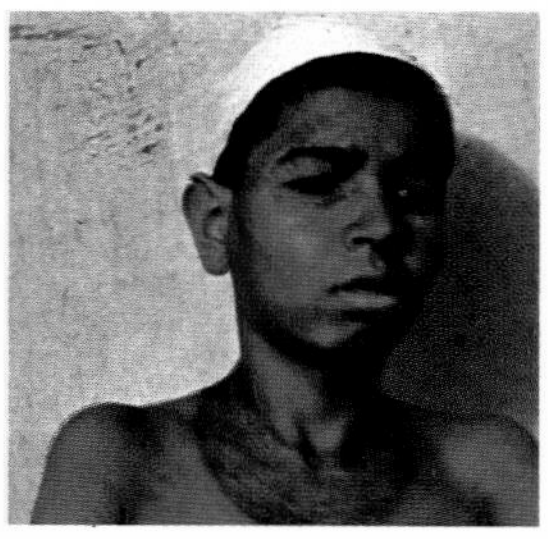

Pellagra
Nicotinic acid, niacin, is the PP (pellagra-preventive) factor. It is present in wheat, meat and fish, but where maize is the staple diet it may be present in a non-absorbable form. Pellagra starts with a redness like sunburn and progresses to severe purple eruptions.

1
2
3
4
5
6
7
8
9
10
11
12
13
14
15
16
17

The modern farm and its produce *left*
An idealized modern mixed farm in the temperate Western world and its varied products.

1 Beet or cabbage
2 Rye
3 Plowing/fallow field
4 Milk tanker
5 Pasture and cattle
6 Barley
7 Oats
8 Cultivation under glass
9 Pigs
10 Silo
11 Wheat
12 Fowl
13 Geese
14 Vetch
15 Orchards
16 Farmhouse
17 Market garden

The broad pattern *below*
Man has farmed the land for at least 10000 years. In that time farming methods have developed out of all recognition in the industrially advanced lands, while about one-third of the world's population still uses methods that are extremely primitive by comparison. The factors governing farming methods are complex and involve tradition, education, national wealth, competition, available labor and available land.

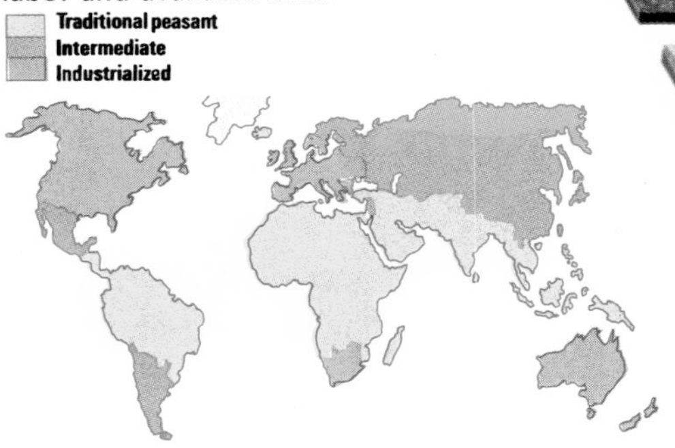
Traditional peasant
Intermediate
Industrialized

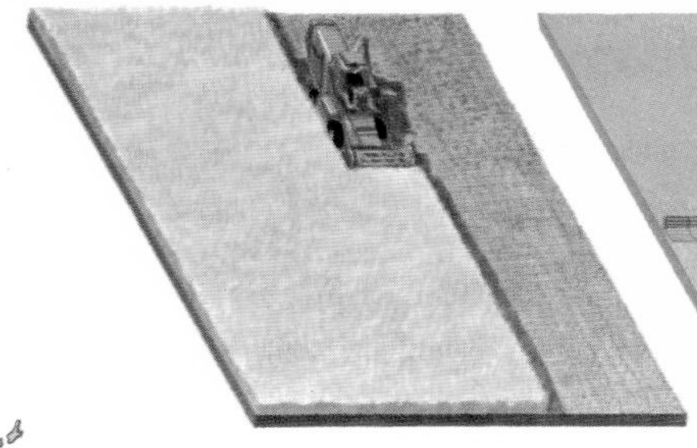

Industrial farming
The world's most efficient farming method applicable on a large scale appears to be the growing of crops on extremely large farms making the maximum possible use of mechanization. Although it calls for large capital resources, it must become universal.

Extensive grazing
This intermediate method is effective and valuable where capital resources are limited and, in particular, where the soil is relatively poor and the climate semi-arid. Sheep are especially adaptable to such conditions, which are prevalent in Australia and Argentina.

Rice growing
Although theoretically rice can be grown on vast mechanized farms, most of the world rice crop is still a product of labor-intensive plantations divided by 'bunds' (walls) of mud to control water level in small plots. Those above are typical of Malaysia.

Shifting cultivation
Throughout many tropical countries crops are planted, harvested and the land then abandoned. This 'shifting' cultivation' is little better than that of Mesolithic times. But it occupies at least 200 million people using some 30 per cent of the usable soil.

Farming efficiency

All farming is based on the fact that atmospheric carbon dioxide plus rain can be converted by green plant leaves on which the Sun is shining into simple sugars. These in turn can be converted into proteins, fats or complex sugars including starch. Green plants lie at the head of food chains. One such is: grass-cattle-milk-cheese. Each step in such a chain involves a loss, and a basic farming objective is to minimize losses and achieve the maximum quantity and quality of output for a given area of land and input in terms of chemicals and sunshine. Over the past 10000 years farming has developed from primitive peasant methods to a modern mechanized and partly automated industry producing much greater yield per acre while needing only a small fraction of the labor force. In parallel with improved methods, geneticists have selectively developed new strains of cereal, root crops and fruit and new breeds of livestock and other animals giving higher and more assured yields, higher quality and enhanced resistance to disease (page 65).

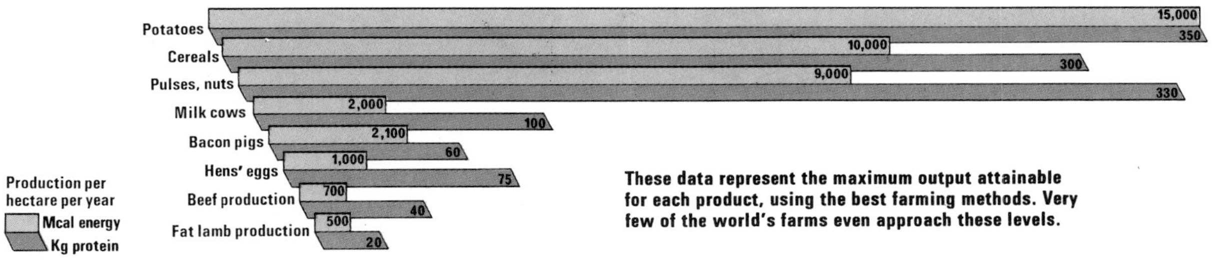
Potatoes
15,000
350
Cereals
10,000
300
Pulses, nuts
9,000
330
Milk cows
2,000
100
Bacon pigs
2,100
60
Hens' eggs
1,000
75
Beef production
700
40
Fat lamb production
500
20
Production per hectare per year
Mcal energy
Kg protein

These data represent the maximum output attainable for each product, using the best farming methods. Very few of the world's farms even approach these levels.

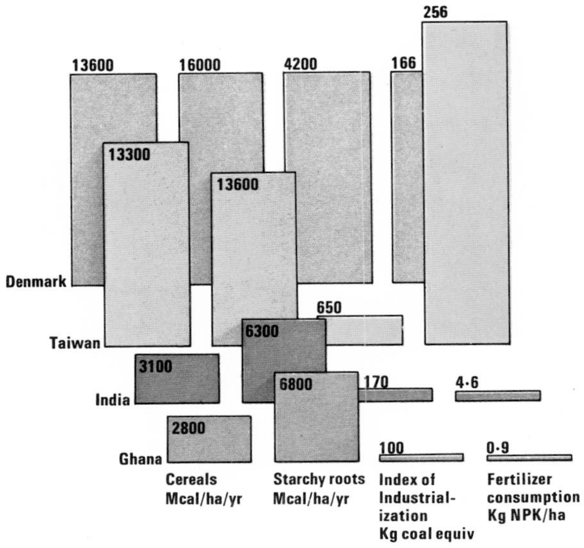
256
13600
16000
4200
166
13300
13600
Denmark
650
Taiwan
6300
3100
India
6800
170
4·6
2800
Ghana
100
0·9
Cereals Mcal/ha/yr
Starchy roots Mcal/ha/yr
Index of Industrialization Kg coal equiv
Fertilizer consumption Kg NPK/ha

Farming output *above*
No matter how good a farm may be, there are clear constraints on performance resulting from the inevitable losses in the food chain. Potatoes can yield 15000 million calories of energy per hectare of land per year, plus 350 kg (770 lb) protein.

Efficiency factors *left*
A yardstick of efficiency is the energy value of food produced per unit area of land ; these figures for four contrasting countries show the enormous variation, in millions of calories per hectare per year. Taiwan approaches Denmark by using much fertilizer.

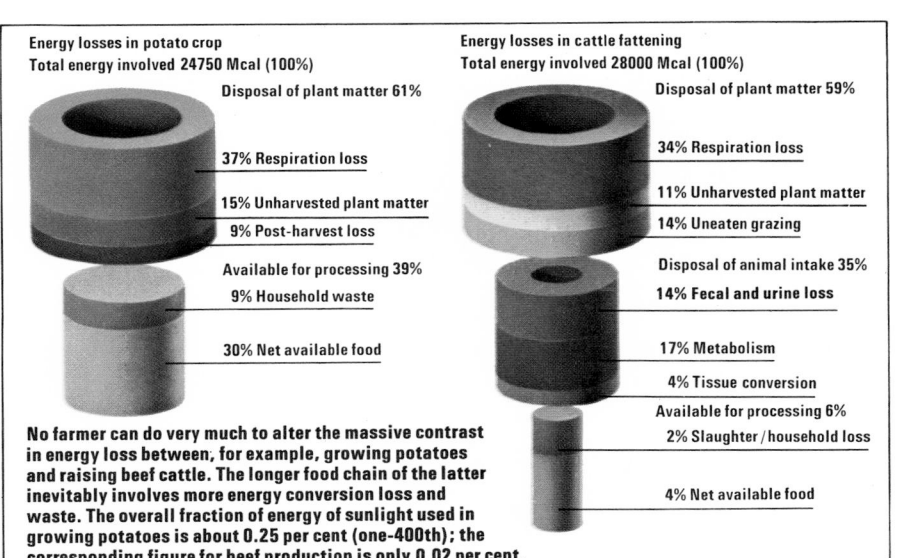

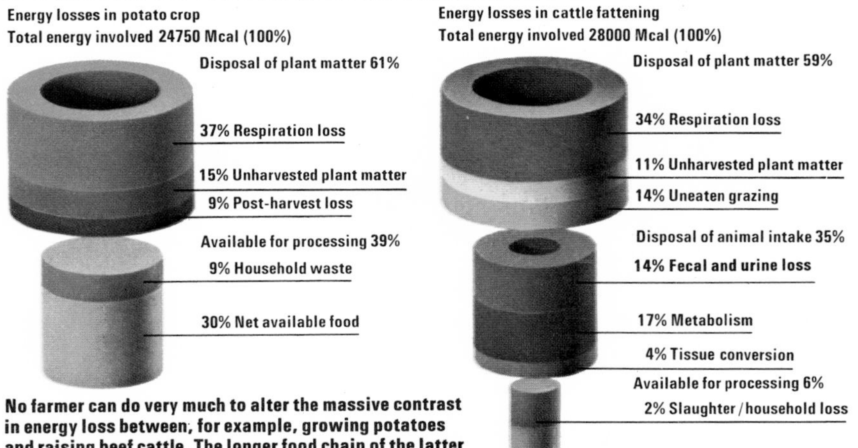
Energy losses in potato crop
Total energy involved 24750 Mcal (100%)
Disposal of plant matter 61%
37% Respiration loss
15% Unharvested plant matter
9% Post-harvest loss
Available for processing 39%
9% Household waste
30% Net available food
Energy losses in cattle fattening
Total energy involved 28000 Mcal (100%)
Disposal of plant matter 59%
34% Respiration loss
11% Unharvested plant matter
14% Uneaten grazing
Disposal of animal intake 35%
14% Fecal and urine loss
17% Metabolism
4% Tissue conversion
Available for processing 6%
2% Slaughter/household loss
4% Net available food

No farmer can do very much to alter the massive contrast in energy loss between, for example, growing potatoes and raising beef cattle. The longer food chain of the latter inevitably involves more energy conversion loss and waste. The overall fraction of energy of sunlight used in growing potatoes is about 0.25 per cent (one-400th); the corresponding figure for beef production is only 0.02 per cent.

The Population Problem

In the year 1000 there were about 300 million people. In the last century the population reached 1000 million. Today it exceeds 3600 million. In 2000 it is predicted to reach 7000 million, and in 2050 something between 12000 and 20000 million. The main reason is that even with generally improved survival rates for children, little attempt has been made in many countries to curb the size of families.

The distribution of humans over the Earth has always been grossly uneven, and it appears likely to stay that way. While man has never ceased to open up and exploit new regions, a process of urbanization has become clearly evident in recent years. The more advanced the development of a nation, the more its cities attract people from the surrounding countryside. In most industrialized countries the proportion of the population living in cities has risen to 60 or 70 per cent. Modern cities pose severe social and environmental problems; they have to be considered as living, adaptable organisms in themselves if human life is not to become increasingly frustrating.

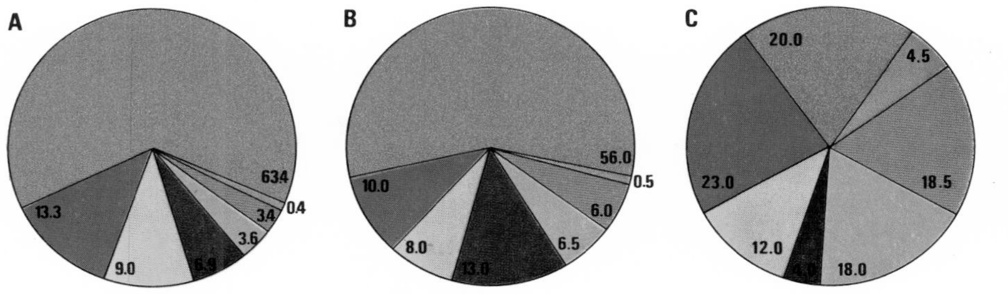

A
634
04
34
3.6
6.9
9.0
13.3
B
56.0
0.5
6.0
6.5
13.0
8.0
10.0
C
20.0
4.5
18.5
18.0
4.0
12.0
23.0

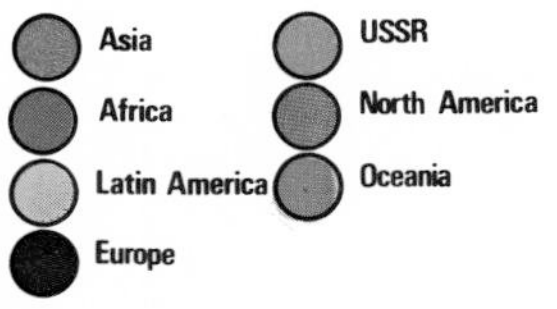

Asia
Africa
Latin America
Europe
USSR
North America
Oceania

People and land area *left*
Nearly two-thirds of the births (percentages per continent, A) and half the population (B) are in only quarter of the area (C).

World population density *below*
Humanity is distributed over the Earth's land surface in a most uneven way. Dividing the population of each country by its area yields such diverse figures (for 1965) as 3.8 inhabitants per square mile for Australia and almost 10000 per square mile for Hong Kong (1.46 and 3900 per square kilometer, respectively). This map indicates density in proportion to the heights of the columns.

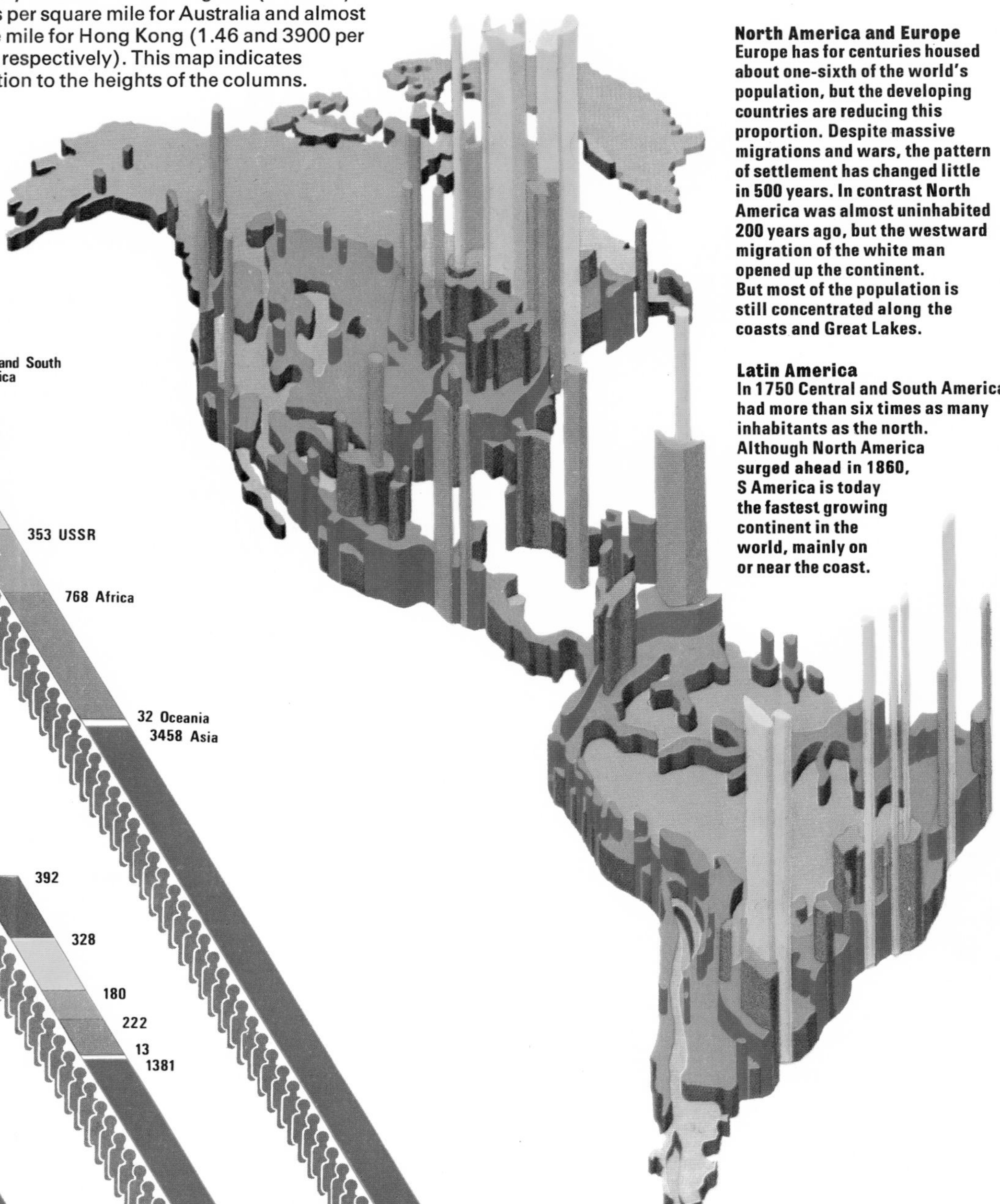

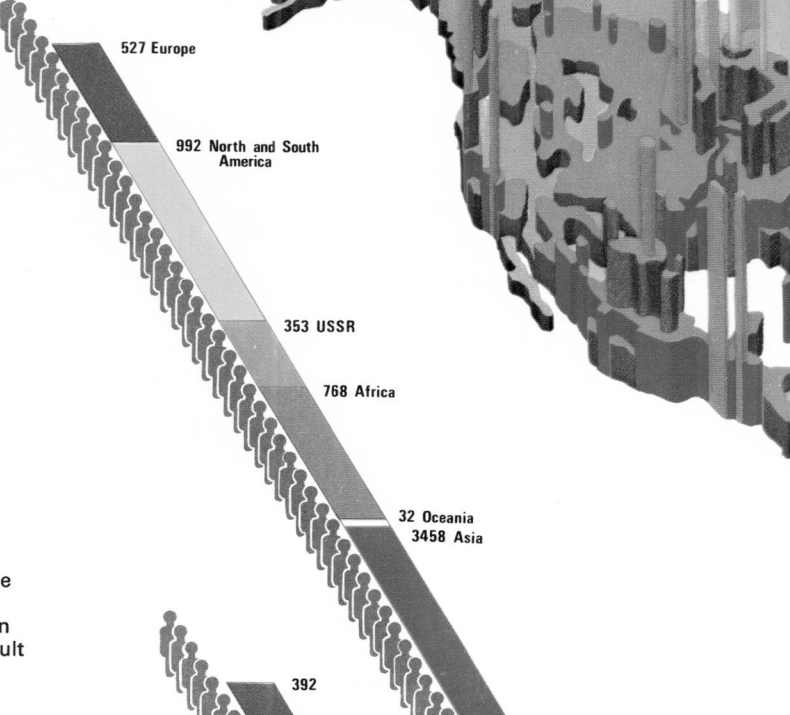

North America and Europe
Europe has for centuries housed about one-sixth of the world's population, but the developing countries are reducing this proportion. Despite massive migrations and wars, the pattern of settlement has changed little in 500 years. In contrast North America was almost uninhabited 200 years ago, but the westward migration of the white man opened up the continent.
But most of the population is still concentrated along the coasts and Great Lakes.

Latin America
In 1750 Central and South America had more than six times as many inhabitants as the north. Although North America surged ahead in 1860, S America is today the fastest growing continent in the world, mainly on or near the coast.

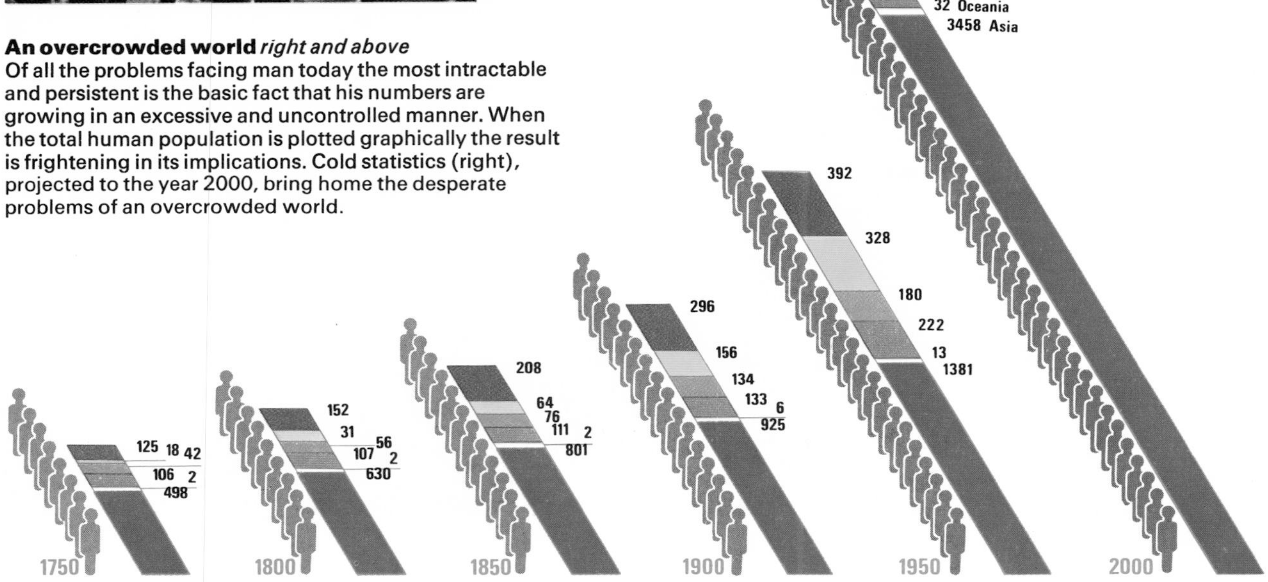

527 Europe
992 North and South America
353 USSR
768 Africa
32 Oceania
3458 Asia
392
328
180
222
13
1381
296
156
134
133
6
925
208
64
76
111
2
801
152
31
56
107
2
630
125
18
42
106
2
498
1750
1800
1850
1900
1950
2000

An overcrowded world *right and above*
Of all the problems facing man today the most intractable and persistent is the basic fact that his numbers are growing in an excessive and uncontrolled manner. When the total human population is plotted graphically the result is frightening in its implications. Cold statistics (right), projected to the year 2000, bring home the desperate problems of an overcrowded world.

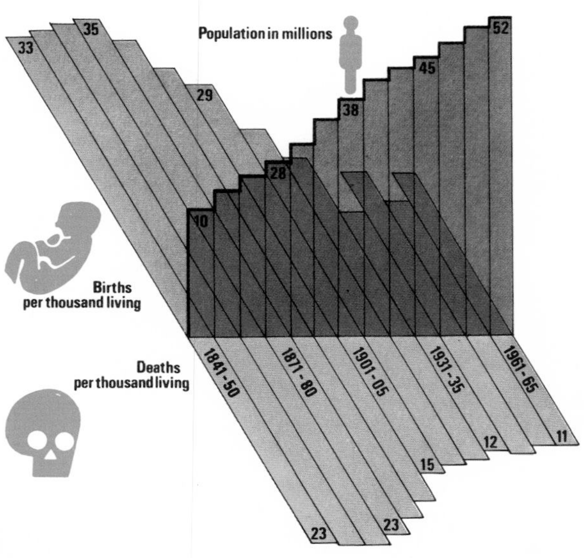

Population in millions
33
35
29
38
45
52
28
10
Births per thousand living
Deaths per thousand living
1841-50
1871-80
1901-05
1931-35
1961-65
12
11
15
23
23

UK births and deaths *left*
The basic reason for the population explosion is an excess of births over deaths. In the UK both birth and death rates have declined during the past 100 years, but over five year periods births have always exceeded deaths, though in the 1930s the margin was very small.

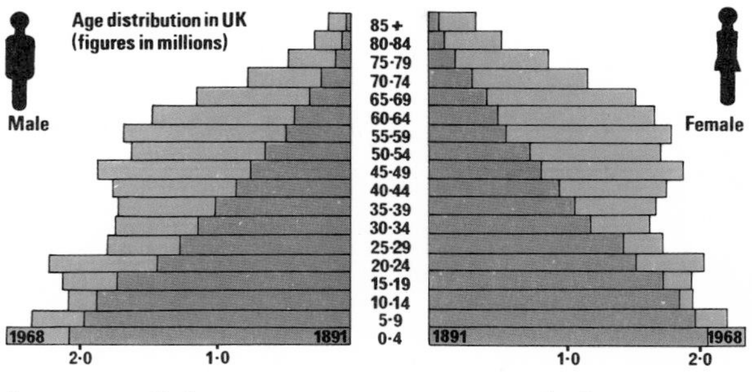

Age distribution in UK (figures in millions)
Male
Female
85+
80-84
75-79
70-74
65-69
60-64
55-59
50-54
45-49
40-44
35-39
30-34
25-29
20-24
15-19
10-14
5-9
0-4
1968
1891
2·0
1·0

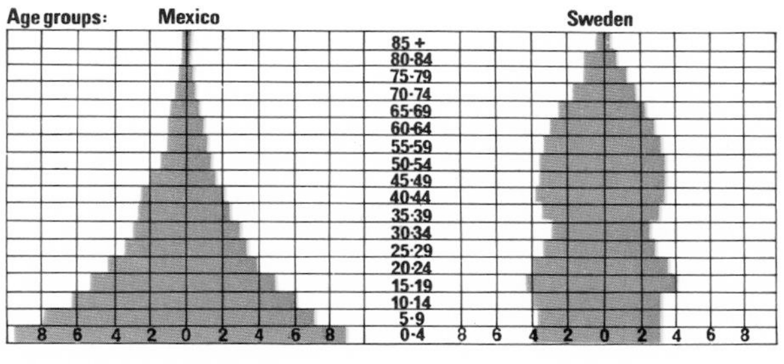

Age groups:
Mexico
Sweden
8 6 4 2 0 2 4 6 8

Age distribution *right*
British population growth is about 0.5 per cent, or 250,000 people, per year. This is a modest rate and gives an age distribution where the old are almost as numerous as the young (right above). Sweden (far right) is an even more marked case of slow growth.

Large families *above*
Big families are no longer common in the U.K. But in many parts of the world the tradition of large families persists. Allied with much lower child mortality, the result is booming population. The age distribution then looks like that of Mexico (left).

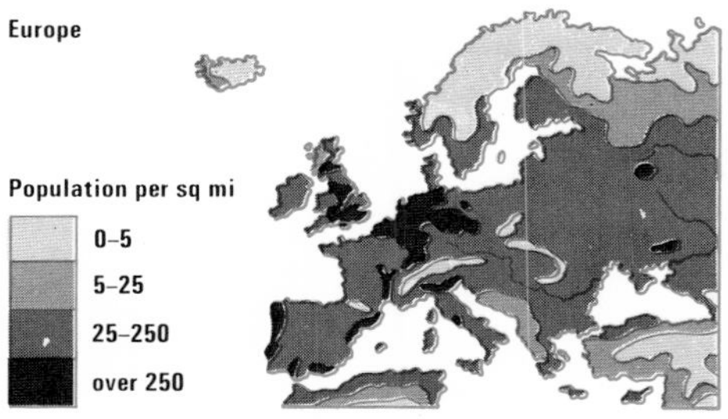

Europe
Population per sq mi
0–5
5–25
25–250
over 250

Migration to the cities

In every part of the world people are congregating in the cities, searching for a better standard of living. Many of the world's larger cities, unable to accommodate this rapid influx, have become marred by largely unplanned settlements. The most densely packed city in the world, Hong Kong, is home to over three million people. The fortunate ones live in tenements (right) ; the rest have built shanties (left). Man's population is thus becoming increasingly an urban one.

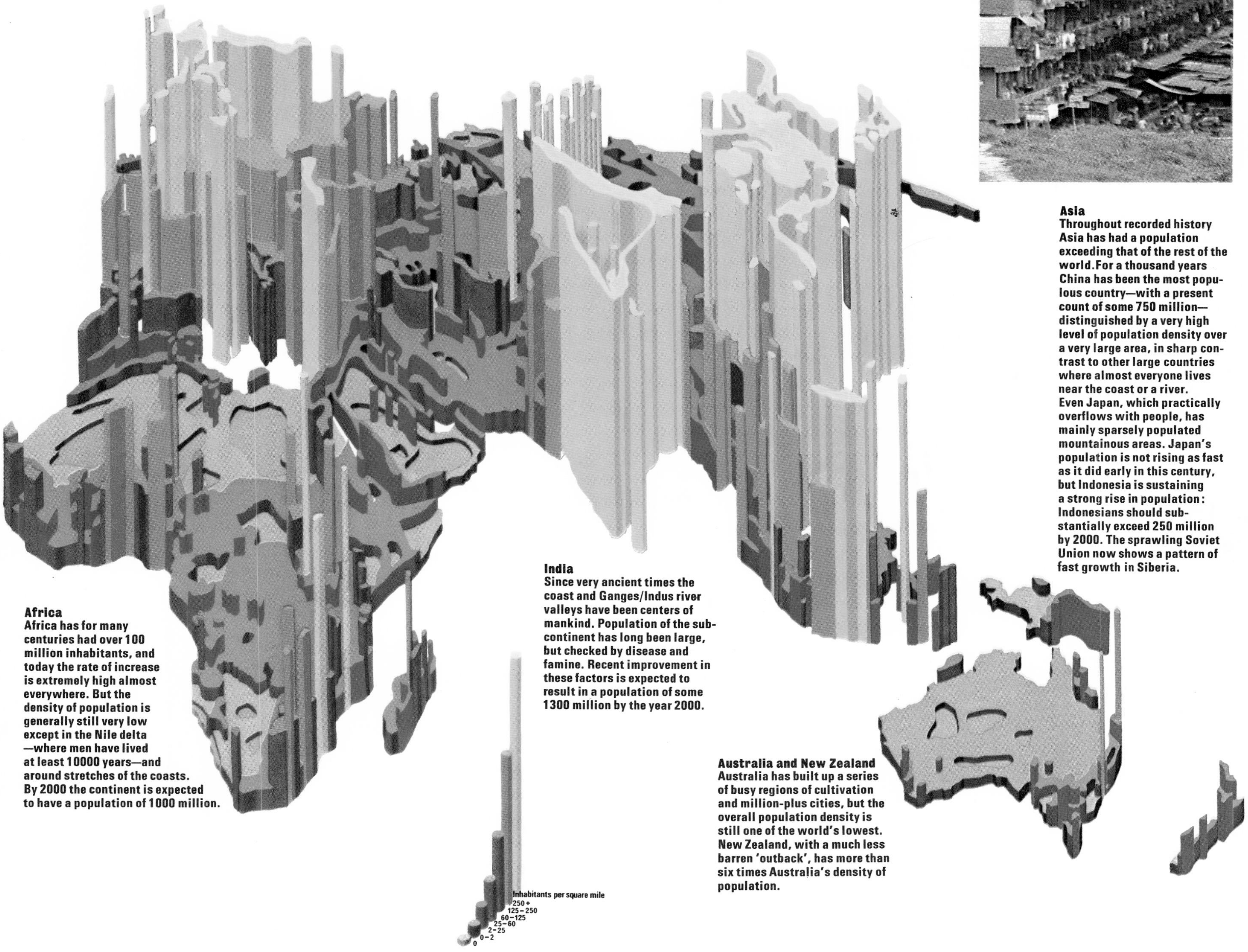

Inhabitants per square mile
250+
125–250
60–125
25–60
2–25
0–2
0

Asia
Throughout recorded history Asia has had a population exceeding that of the rest of the world. For a thousand years China has been the most populous country—with a present count of some 750 million—distinguished by a very high level of population density over a very large area, in sharp contrast to other large countries where almost everyone lives near the coast or a river. Even Japan, which practically overflows with people, has mainly sparsely populated mountainous areas. Japan's population is not rising as fast as it did early in this century, but Indonesia is sustaining a strong rise in population: Indonesians should substantially exceed 250 million by 2000. The sprawling Soviet Union now shows a pattern of fast growth in Siberia.

India
Since very ancient times the coast and Ganges/Indus river valleys have been centers of mankind. Population of the subcontinent has long been large, but checked by disease and famine. Recent improvement in these factors is expected to result in a population of some 1300 million by the year 2000.

Africa
Africa has for many centuries had over 100 million inhabitants, and today the rate of increase is extremely high almost everywhere. But the density of population is generally still very low except in the Nile delta —where men have lived at least 10000 years—and around stretches of the coasts. By 2000 the continent is expected to have a population of 1000 million.

Australia and New Zealand
Australia has built up a series of busy regions of cultivation and million-plus cities, but the overall population density is still one of the world's lowest. New Zealand, with a much less barren 'outback', has more than six times Australia's density of population.

Unless production rises faster than population, overall economic growth cannot be maintained.

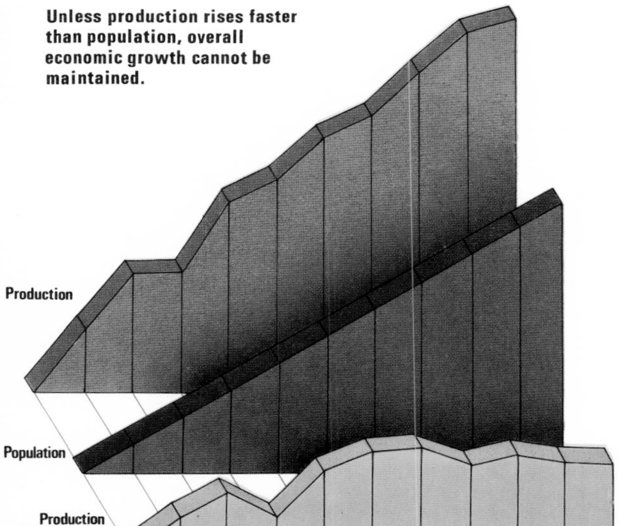

Production
Population
Production per head
years 1954–1964
54–55
55–56
56–57
57–58
58–59
59–60
60–61
61–62
62–63
63–64

People and prosperity
left and below

To a first-order approximation, man's standard of living depends on the total production per head, with especial importance being given to food. At present a fast rising population is countering all attempts to increase available resources (left). And this is particularly the case in the very countries which are most in need of an improved standard of living : those where gross national product per head per year is below the world average or less than 200 US dollars. These lands almost all lie in the tropics.

Above world mean
Underdeveloped
Underdeveloped and below world mean

Doubling time *below*
Excess of birth rate over death rate yields a rate of population growth which, in turn, governs the proportion of young people (percentage under 15) and time taken for population to double. Mexico and Pakistan are doubling every 21 years.

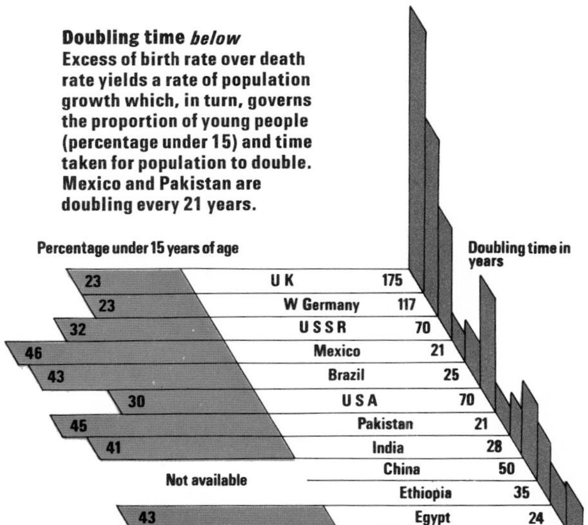

Percentage under 15 years of age
Doubling time in years
23 UK 175
23 W Germany 117
32 USSR 70
46 Mexico 21
43 Brazil 25
30 USA 70
45 Pakistan 21
41 India 28
Not available China 50
Ethiopia 35
43 Egypt 24
43 Nigeria 28

The Abuse of the Earth

Pollution is harmful waste. All living creatures produce waste, often with marked effects on the environment. Pine leaves blanket out the flowers which would otherwise grow on the forest floor; the droppings of seabirds can cover nesting islands meters deep in guano. Plants as well as road vehicles give off carbon dioxide; volcanoes as well as power stations emit sulphur dioxide.

What turns man's waste into pollution? First, we produce too much waste: only man lives in such vast communities that his excreta de-oxygenates whole rivers. Secondly, the unwanted by-products of man's industrial metabolism change so rapidly that the environment has little hope of accommodating it. African grassland has evolved over millions of years to accept piles of elephant dung, with many species of animals specially adapted to living inside dungheaps and helping to decompose them. But the ecosystem is often unable to cope with our latest pollutants: few bacteria are able to digest plastics. Thirdly, man's waste is often extremely persistent: DDT may remain unchanged for decades, passing from one animal to another, poisoning and weakening them all.

Pollution may harm man directly: smoke causes bronchitis, and fouled drinking water can spread typhoid. Pollution may harm us indirectly, reducing the capacity of the land, rivers and seas to supply us with food. But perhaps the most insidious effects are the least obvious. Small doses of separate pollutants, each harmless by itself, may together weaken wild populations of animals so that they cannot recover from natural disasters. Acute pollution kills tens of thousands of animals; chronic pollution gradually reduces the quality of the entire human environment.

Pollution is wasteful. Too often modern technology painstakingly extracts a metal from the crust, uses it once and then discards it. For example, once unwanted chromium or mercury is released into the seas it will be diluted many millions of times and is unlikely ever to be recoverable except at prohibitive expense. If man is not to face raw material famines in the foreseeable future, he must learn to recycle everything from air and water to the rarer elements.

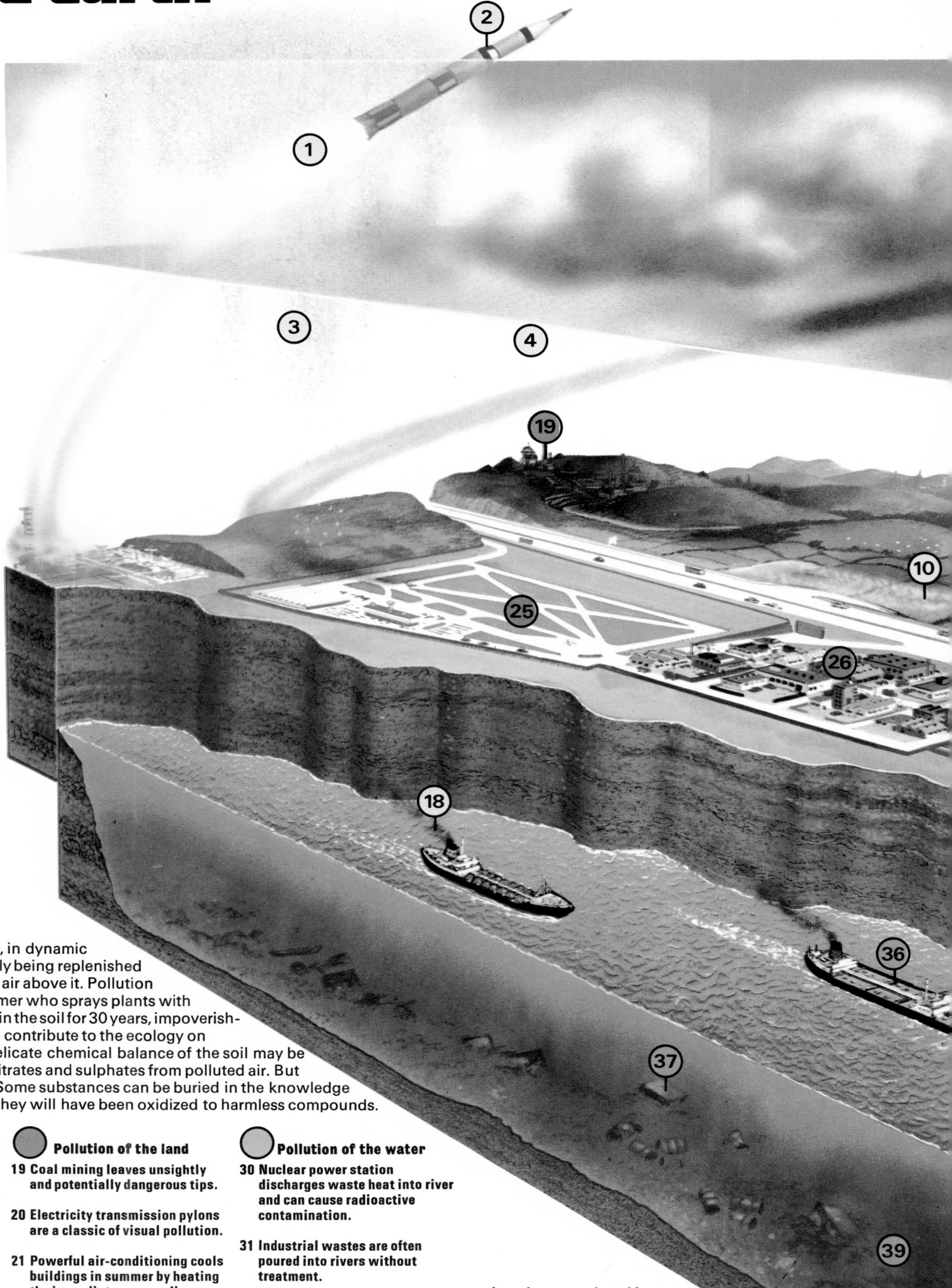

2
1
3
4
19
10
25
26
18
36
37
39

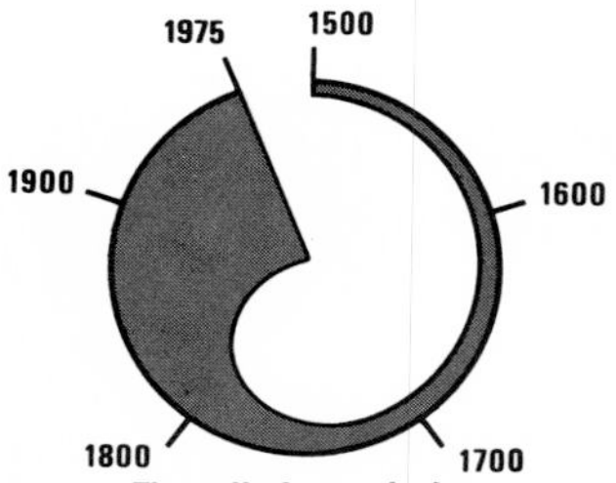

1975
1500
1600
1700
1800
1900

The pollution explosion

Pollution of the land
The soil is a living organic layer, in dynamic equilibrium with, and continually being replenished by, the rocks beneath it and the air above it. Pollution affects it in many ways. The farmer who sprays plants with insecticides may leave residues in the soil for 30 years, impoverishing the micro-organisms which contribute to the ecology on which his crops depend. The delicate chemical balance of the soil may be disrupted by rain loaded with nitrates and sulphates from polluted air. But the land is also a de-pollutant. Some substances can be buried in the knowledge that before they can re-appear they will have been oxidized to harmless compounds.

Pollution of the air

1 Rocket exhaust contains a variety of combustion products.

2 Space launchings leave jettisoned propellants and other debris orbiting above the atmosphere.

3 Nuclear weapon testing can leave fall-out on a global scale.

4 Increased air traffic creates noise pollution over wide areas.

5 Jet efflux contains kerosene combustion products, unburned fuel and particles of soot.

6 Nuclear weapons can cause radioactive contamination; together with chemical and biological devices they could eradicate all life on Earth.

7 Jet aircraft cause intense local noise, and supersonic aircraft create a shock-wave boom.

8 Large-scale aerial transport of pollutants distributes particles and gaseous matter.

9 Carbon dioxide build-up and 'greenhouse effect' traps solar heat within the atmosphere.

10 Pesticide spraying can cause widespread contamination, and organochlorine residues (such as DDT) can build up in animals and disrupt natural food chains.

11 Nuclear power station is potential source of escaping radioactive or liquid coolant.

12 Thermal (coal or oil fired) power station causes thermal and chemical pollution from exhaust stacks.

13 Power station cooling towers transfer waste heat to the air.

14 Sulphur dioxide from high roof-level chimneys falls into 'canyon streets' causing irritation to eyes and lungs.

15 Refinery waste gases burned in the air cause heavy pollution unless the flame is extremely hot.

16 Road vehicle exhausts and crankcase gases contain lead, unburned hydrocarbons, carbon monoxide and oxides of nitrogen, and can cause widespread pollution; action of sunlight on nitrogen oxides causes smog.

17 Most domestic fuels are very inefficiently burned, causing smoke and chemical pollution.

18 Steam boilers or diesel smoke can cause persistent trails of gaseous and particulate matter.

Pollution of the land

19 Coal mining leaves unsightly and potentially dangerous tips.

20 Electricity transmission pylons are a classic of visual pollution.

21 Powerful air-conditioning cools buildings in summer by heating the immediate surroundings.

22 Visual pollution of highways is accentuated by billboards.

23 Unreclaimed wastes are often dumped and not recycled.

24 Quarrying leaves unsightly scars.

25 Growth of air traffic is reflected in increasing size and number of airports which occupy otherwise valuable land.

26 Even modern industrial estates invariably cause chemical and thermal pollution, and pose waste-disposal problems.

27 Large motorways, especially intersections, occupy large areas of land.

28 Caravan and chalet sites may cause severe local chemical, as well as visual, pollution.

29 Modern litter includes high proportion of non-biodegradable plastics materials.

Pollution of the water

30 Nuclear power station discharges waste heat into river and can cause radioactive contamination.

31 Industrial wastes are often poured into rivers without treatment.

32 Cooling water from thermal power stations can cause very large-scale heating of rivers, changing or destroying the natural fauna and flora.

33 Refinery and other chemical plants generate waste heat and liquid refuse which may be discharged directly into the river.

34 Oil storage installation can cause intermittent pollution.

35 When it reaches the sea the river is heavily polluted by nitrates and phosphates from fertilizers and treated sewage, as well as by heavy toxic metals.

36 Tanker too close inshore risks severe beach pollution from accidental release of cargo.

37 Radioactive and corrosive wastes often dumped without enough knowledge of local conditions to insure that the containers will not leak before contents have decomposed; nothing should be dumped on continental shelf and adequate dilution is essential.

38 The main influx of pollutants into the sea is via rivers; typical categories include agricultural and industrial chemicals, waste heat, treated and untreated sewage and solid matter.

39 Excess nutrients from untreated sewage, agricultural chemicals and nuclear wastes can lead to 'blooms' of toxic marine plankton or, through their oxidation and decay, to severely reduced oxygen levels in the water.

40 Sewage sludge dumped at sea contains persistent chemicals such as PCB (polychlorinated biophenyl) compounds, toxic heavy metals and nutrients.

41 Large oil slicks are released by tanker accidents or deliberate washing at sea, and by oil-rig blow-outs.

42 Sediments stirred by mineral exploitation, dumped from ships or carried by rivers may form thick layers on the ocean floor which suffocate the organisms living there.

43 Clouds of particulate matter, both organic and inorganic wastes, reduce the penetration of sunlight and sharply curtail marine productivity.

44 Oil rigs suffer explosive blow-outs, a serious problem off the California coast.

45 In some waters wrecks, many of them uncharted, pose hazards to shipping which may lead to further pollution.

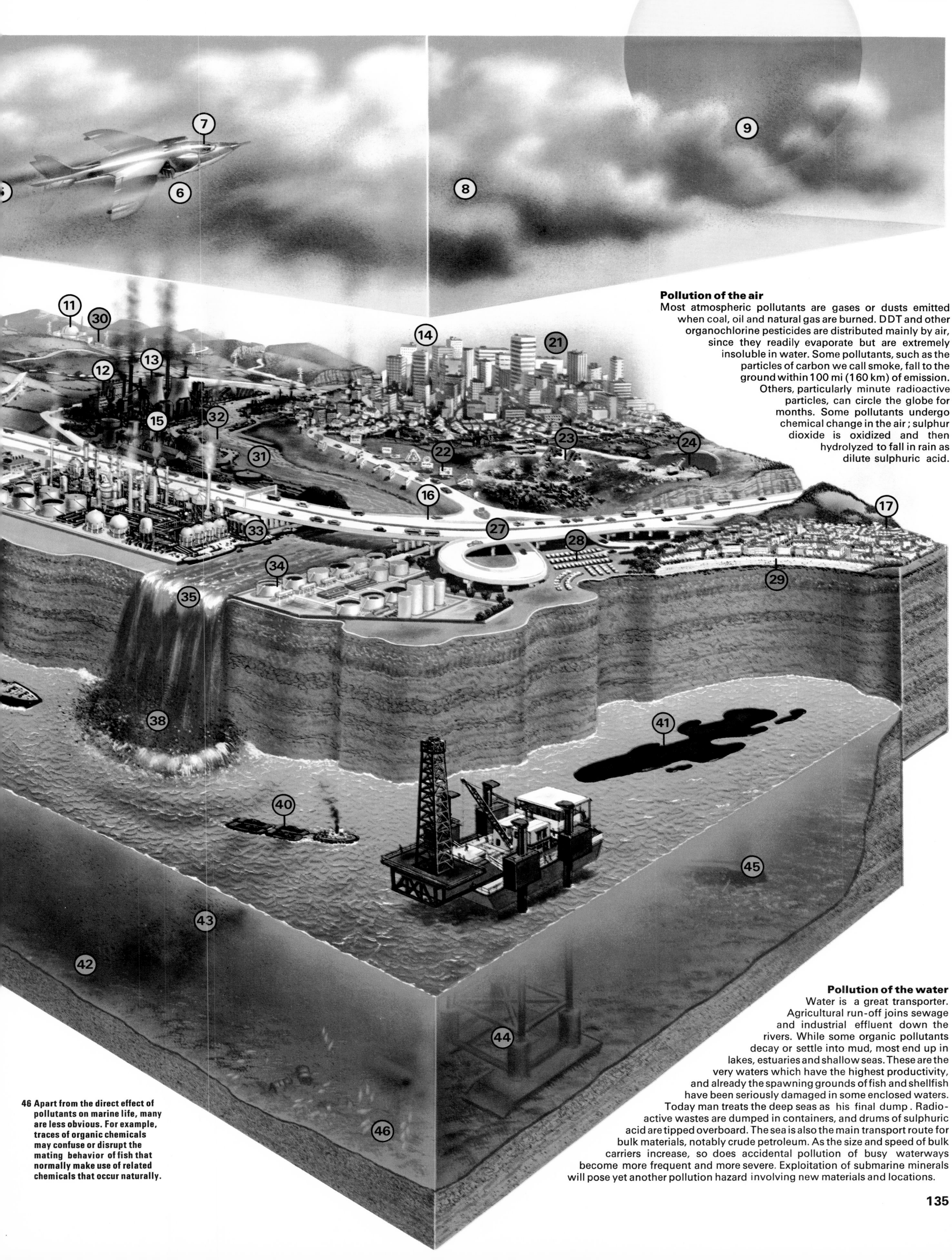
7
6
8
9
11
30
14
21
12
13
15
32
23
24
22
31
16
17
33
27
28
34
29
35
38
41
40
45
43
42
44
46

Pollution of the air
Most atmospheric pollutants are gases or dusts emitted when coal, oil and natural gas are burned. DDT and other organochlorine pesticides are distributed mainly by air, since they readily evaporate but are extremely insoluble in water. Some pollutants, such as the particles of carbon we call smoke, fall to the ground within 100 mi (160 km) of emission. Others, particularly minute radioactive particles, can circle the globe for months. Some pollutants undergo chemical change in the air; sulphur dioxide is oxidized and then hydrolyzed to fall in rain as dilute sulphuric acid.

Pollution of the water
Water is a great transporter. Agricultural run-off joins sewage and industrial effluent down the rivers. While some organic pollutants decay or settle into mud, most end up in lakes, estuaries and shallow seas. These are the very waters which have the highest productivity, and already the spawning grounds of fish and shellfish have been seriously damaged in some enclosed waters. Today man treats the deep seas as his final dump. Radioactive wastes are dumped in containers, and drums of sulphuric acid are tipped overboard. The sea is also the main transport route for bulk materials, notably crude petroleum. As the size and speed of bulk carriers increase, so does accidental pollution of busy waterways become more frequent and more severe. Exploitation of submarine minerals will pose yet another pollution hazard involving new materials and locations.

46 Apart from the direct effect of pollutants on marine life, many are less obvious. For example, traces of organic chemicals may confuse or disrupt the mating behavior of fish that normally make use of related chemicals that occur naturally.

Pathways of Pollution

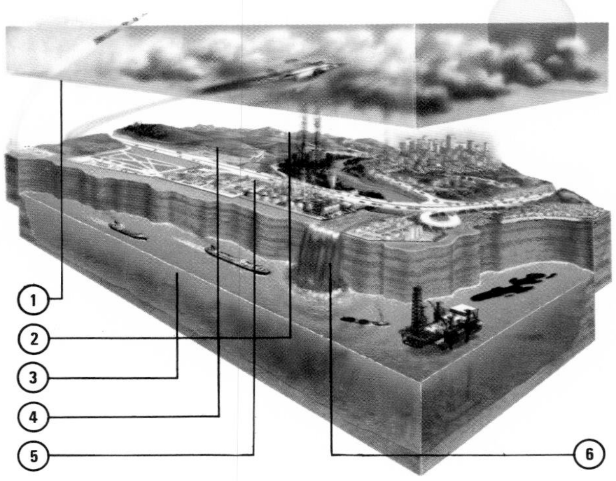
1
2
3
4
5
6

Pollution often travels along strange pathways, and these must be unravelled if the menace is to be controlled and its effects predicted. It is unwise ever to assume the obvious. DDT was found in the soil of apple orchards in Kent months after spraying, and it was also detected in local rivers. The obvious conclusion was that it was leaching down through the soil into the groundwater. But analysis of the springs and wells showed no DDT at all. In fact the insecticide was leaving the surface by evaporation and falling again as rain.

Pollution can be distributed over vast distances. The insecticide BHC is carried by the prevailing westerly winds from the Soviet Union across China and N America and to Europe. Water likewise carries contaminants down rivers to oceans. But the most important pathway is the food chain. A pollutant is released into the air, soil or sea. It is absorbed by plants. These are eaten by a herbivore, which in its turn is eaten by a carnivore which is itself eaten by a predator. The chain may have many links or only a few, but at every stage the pollutant is more concentrated. If a hawk eats 100 birds which each ate 100 insects it may die from pollution 10000 times the strength met by the insect.

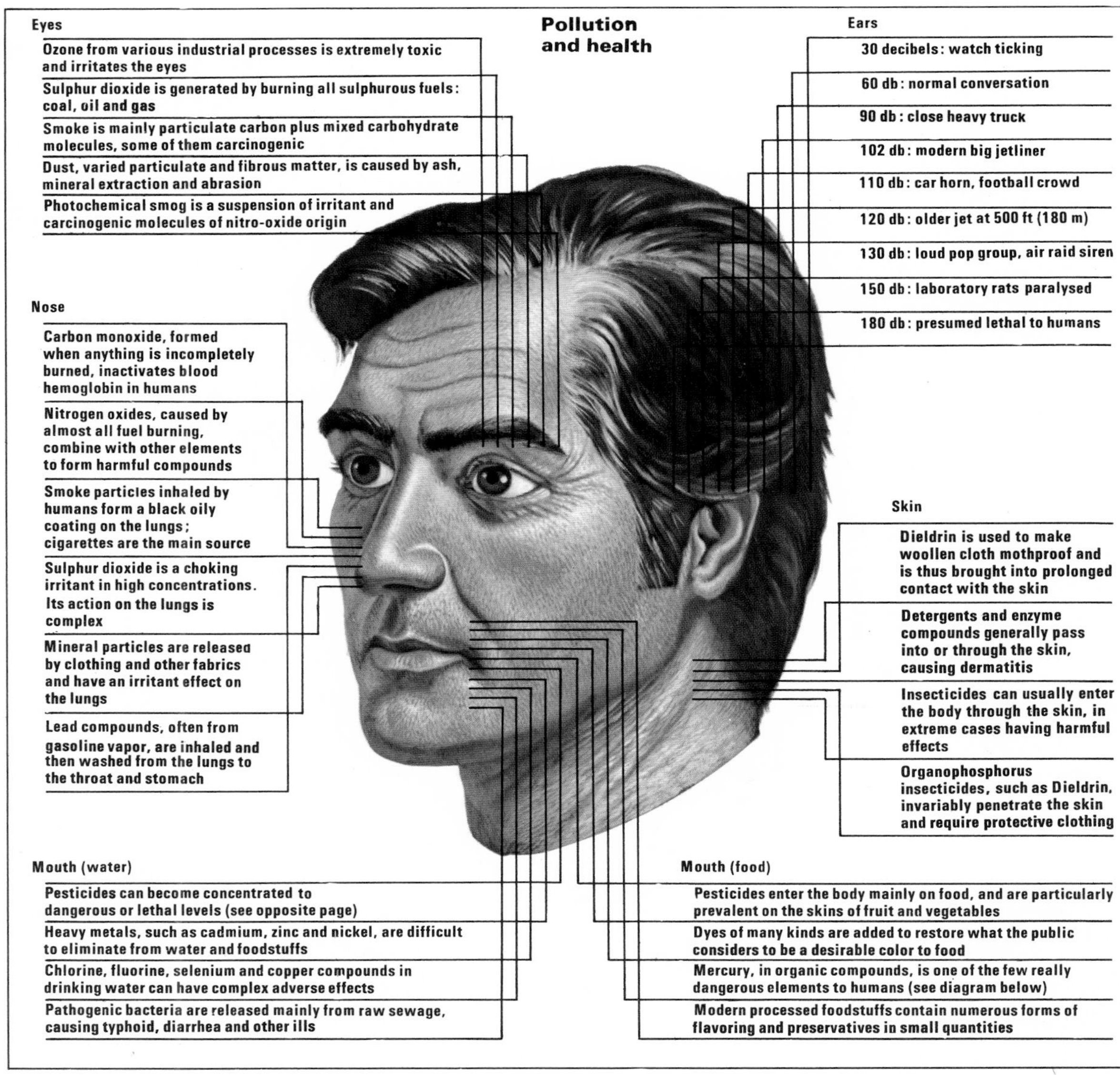
Pollution and health
Eyes
Ozone from various industrial processes is extremely toxic and irritates the eyes
Sulphur dioxide is generated by burning all sulphurous fuels: coal, oil and gas
Smoke is mainly particulate carbon plus mixed carbohydrate molecules, some of them carcinogenic
Dust, varied particulate and fibrous matter, is caused by ash, mineral extraction and abrasion
Photochemical smog is a suspension of irritant and carcinogenic molecules of nitro-oxide origin
Nose
Carbon monoxide, formed when anything is incompletely burned, inactivates blood hemoglobin in humans
Nitrogen oxides, caused by almost all fuel burning, combine with other elements to form harmful compounds
Smoke particles inhaled by humans form a black oily coating on the lungs; cigarettes are the main source
Sulphur dioxide is a choking irritant in high concentrations. Its action on the lungs is complex
Mineral particles are released by clothing and other fabrics and have an irritant effect on the lungs
Lead compounds, often from gasoline vapor, are inhaled and then washed from the lungs to the throat and stomach
Ears
30 decibels: watch ticking
60 db: normal conversation
90 db: close heavy truck
102 db: modern big jetliner
110 db: car horn, football crowd
120 db: older jet at 500 ft (180 m)
130 db: loud pop group, air raid siren
150 db: laboratory rats paralysed
180 db: presumed lethal to humans
Skin
Dieldrin is used to make woollen cloth mothproof and is thus brought into prolonged contact with the skin
Detergents and enzyme compounds generally pass into or through the skin, causing dermatitis
Insecticides can usually enter the body through the skin, in extreme cases having harmful effects
Organophosphorus insecticides, such as Dieldrin, invariably penetrate the skin and require protective clothing
Mouth (water)
Pesticides can become concentrated to dangerous or lethal levels (see opposite page)
Heavy metals, such as cadmium, zinc and nickel, are difficult to eliminate from water and foodstuffs
Chlorine, fluorine, selenium and copper compounds in drinking water can have complex adverse effects
Pathogenic bacteria are released mainly from raw sewage, causing typhoid, diarrhea and other ills
Mouth (food)
Pesticides enter the body mainly on food, and are particularly prevalent on the skins of fruit and vegetables
Dyes of many kinds are added to restore what the public considers to be a desirable color to food
Mercury, in organic compounds, is one of the few really dangerous elements to humans (see diagram below)
Modern processed foodstuffs contain numerous forms of flavoring and preservatives in small quantities

1 Radiation *right*
No pollutant has been so continuously monitored as nuclear radiation. But it is not a problem created solely by modern man. In the modern world nearly all the radioactivity issues from the rocks, and, as far as humans are concerned, from the body.

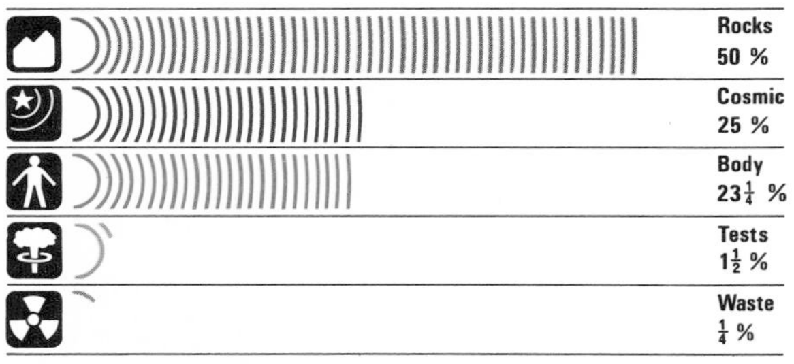
Rocks 50 %
Cosmic 25 %
Body 23¼ %
Tests 1½ %
Waste ¼ %

2 Radiation and life *right*
Living cells concentrate radiation. In an above-ground nuclear-weapon test all heavy radioactive particles drop within hours in a narrow region downwind of the explosion. Their residence time in the atmosphere varies from four weeks in the troposphere to ten years in the mesosphere. One such product, strontium 90, is taken up from the soil by plants. Eaten by cattle and released in their milk, it ends up in human bone where it is only slowly liquidated. As it decays it can destroy the marrow which produces red blood cells, in extreme cases causing death through pentaemia. Radiation pollution can also arise from power reactors or nuclear waste. Plankton can concentrate radioactivity a thousandfold. Fish eat plankton, and on migration can disperse the radiation far from its source. In the 1950s this mechanism caused radiation sickness in Japanese fishermen hundreds of miles from US test sites in the Pacific.

Concentration of atomic waste (phosphorus 32) in animal food chains

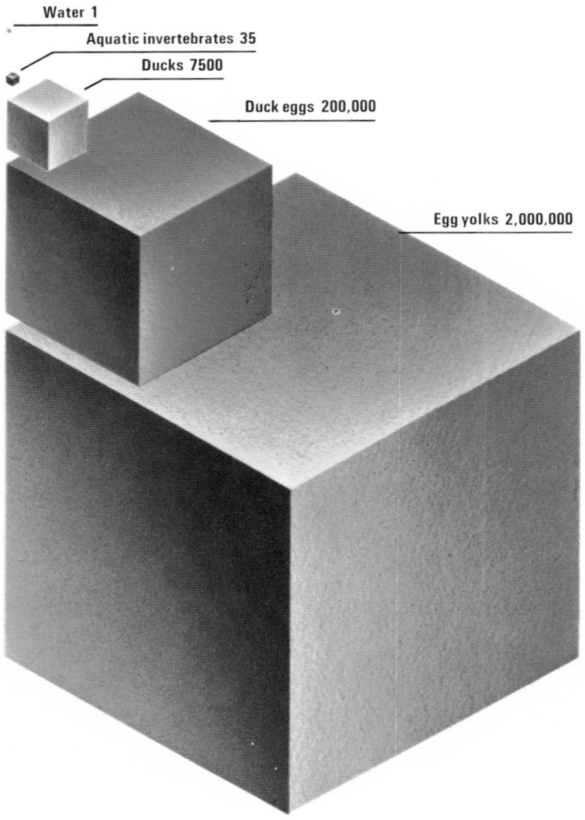
Water 1
Aquatic invertebrates 35
Ducks 7500
Duck eggs 200,000
Egg yolks 2,000,000

3 Deadly mercury *right*
Compounds of mercury have for 1000 years been known to be highly toxic. An industrial plant often discharges such compounds, but it was thought these rested at the sea bed. Man has now learned that bacteria can convert inorganic mercury compounds to deadly methyl mercury, which can then be successively concentrated in marine food chains. Shellfish are particularly good concentrators of methyl mercury. When eaten by humans they cause severe disabling of the central nervous system, and in extreme cases cause death (below).

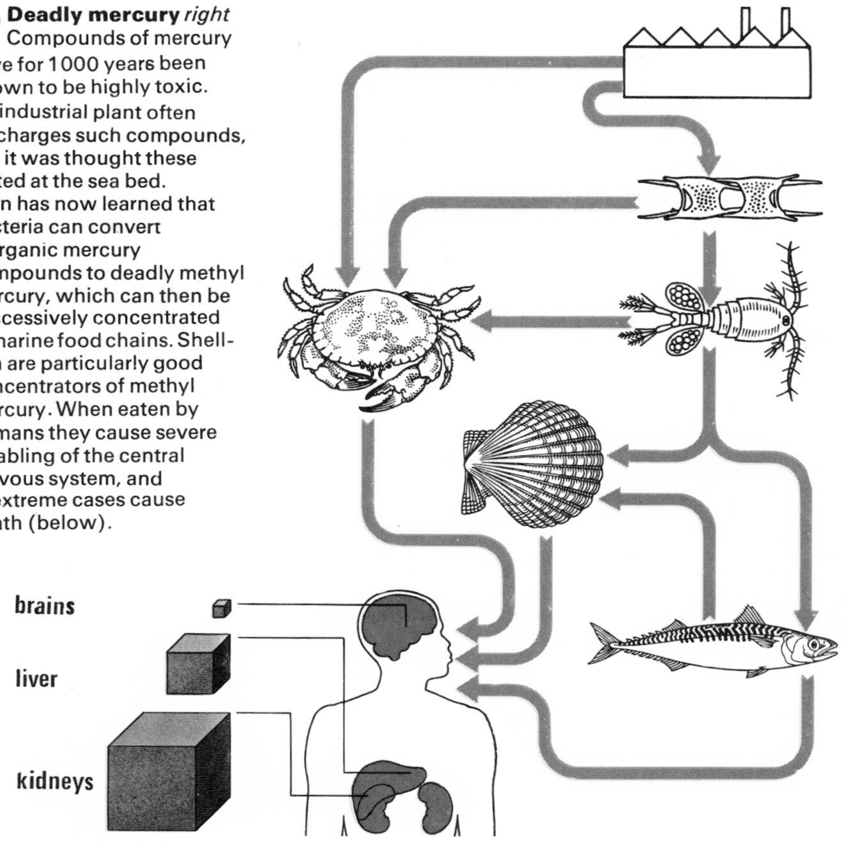
brains
liver
kidneys

Minimata tragedy *right*
In 1953 people living in this Japanese city became ill. Ultimately over 120 were afflicted, and 43 (black) died. The cause was methyl mercury concentrated in seafoods. Some acetaldehyde plants still emit methyl mercury.

④ **The DDT menace** *right*
Introduced during World War 2, DDT appeared to be ideal. It would kill lice on soldiers weeks after the treatment of their clothes. Houses sprayed against malaria remained lethal to mosquitoes long after the health teams had departed. But the persistence brought its own problems. DDT and other organochlorine pesticides, such as BHC, Dieldrin, Endosulfan and Heptachlor, are only slightly broken down by animal metabolism. An insect receiving a non-lethal dose of DDT retains it in its body and passes it on up the food chain. Animals at the head of the chain often build up large residues in their fatty tissues. Under stress these residues can be released and fatally damage the liver, kidney and brain. DDT can evaporate from soil, travelling round the globe, before being adsorbed on to dust and falling as rain. The organochlorines soon penetrate every corner of an ecosystem.

DIELDRIN

Seed that has been 'dressed' is eaten by a wood pigeon. The bird finds the seeds palatable, and may eat dozens to hundreds in a day.

The pigeon is devoured by a badger (or a cat, fox, hawk or other predator). The badger may build up poison from eating many pigeons.

In this case the pesticide-soaked grain is attractive to a yellowhammer, typical of many small birds which pick seeds off the land.

The yellowhammer has fallen prey to a sparrowhawk. In a few weeks dieldrin may build up causing death or inability to breed.

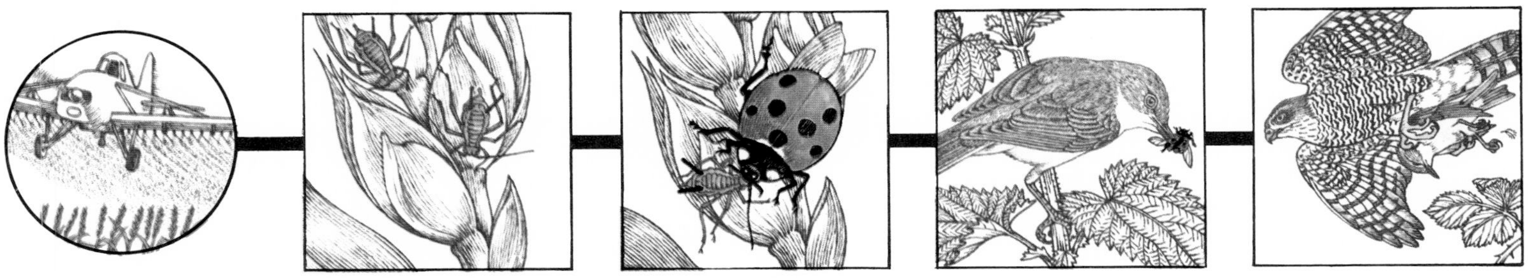

DDT

Sap-sucking insects, such as aphids, feed on sprayed wheat and build up a DDT concentration not sufficiently high to kill them.

A predator ladybird climbs wheat grain devouring aphids in large numbers. It soon builds up a very large residue of DDT in its body.

On a nettle at the edge of the field the ladybird is in turn eaten by a whitethroat, spotted flycatcher or other insect-eating bird.

Finally the bird, suffering from severe DDT toxicity, is devoured by a hawk. In many countries birds of prey have almost vanished.

⑥ **Misuse of a river by overloading** *above and left*
In moderation, man can safely pour his effluents into the rivers. A farmhouse beside a river (above) causes a little local pollution which is soon oxidized; the fish population does not suffer. A village causes no lasting pollution but merely a depression of the dissolved oxygen in the water for a mile or two downstream. But a large city pours out so much effluent that the river is completely de-oxygenated. All the fish and plants are killed and the river becomes foul in an irreversible way (left). Whereas a river may be capable of processing pollutants from 50000 people, pollutants from 100000 may destroy the ecological cycle.

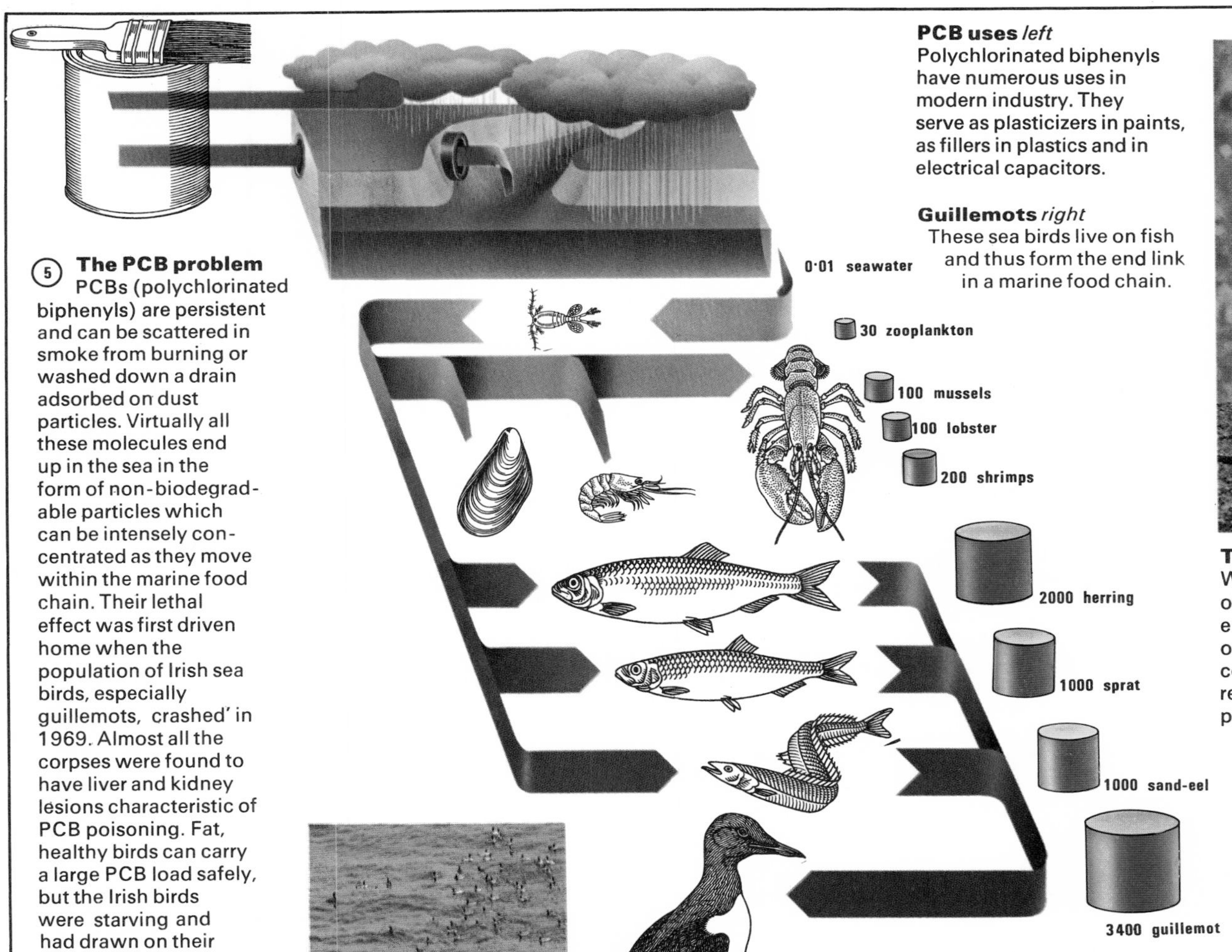
0·01 seawater
30 zooplankton
100 mussels
100 lobster
200 shrimps
2000 herring
1000 sprat
1000 sand-eel
3400 guillemot

PCB uses *left*
Polychlorinated biphenyls have numerous uses in modern industry. They serve as plasticizers in paints, as fillers in plastics and in electrical capacitors.

Guillemots *right*
These sea birds live on fish and thus form the end link in a marine food chain.

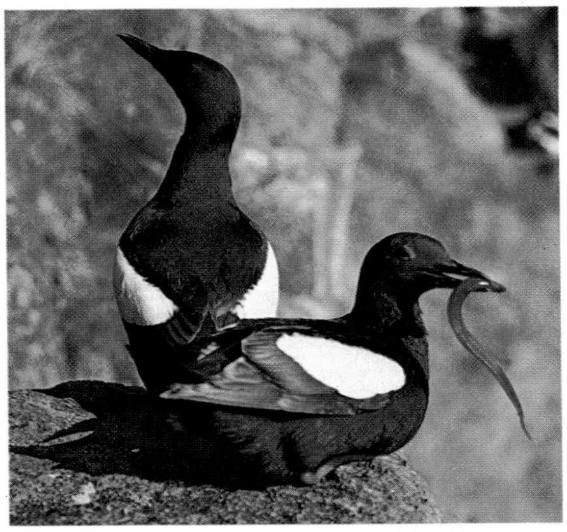

⑤ **The PCB problem**
PCBs (polychlorinated biphenyls) are persistent and can be scattered in smoke from burning or washed down a drain adsorbed on dust particles. Virtually all these molecules end up in the sea in the form of non-biodegradable particles which can be intensely concentrated as they move within the marine food chain. Their lethal effect was first driven home when the population of Irish sea birds, especially guillemots, crashed' in 1969. Almost all the corpses were found to have liver and kidney lesions characteristic of PCB poisoning. Fat, healthy birds can carry a large PCB load safely, but the Irish birds were starving and had drawn on their fatty reserves, where the PCB was stored. Passing into the circulation, the chemical accumulated in the birds' organs in lethal amounts.

Thin guillemot *below*
When a guillemot with 3400 ppb of PCB in its body becomes emaciated it draws on its reserves of fat. The chemical becomes concentrated in its organs, reaching a lethal level of 60000 ppb.

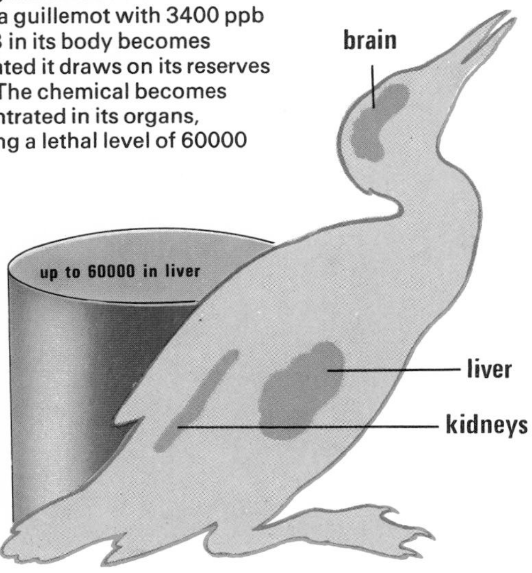
brain
up to 60000 in liver
liver
kidneys

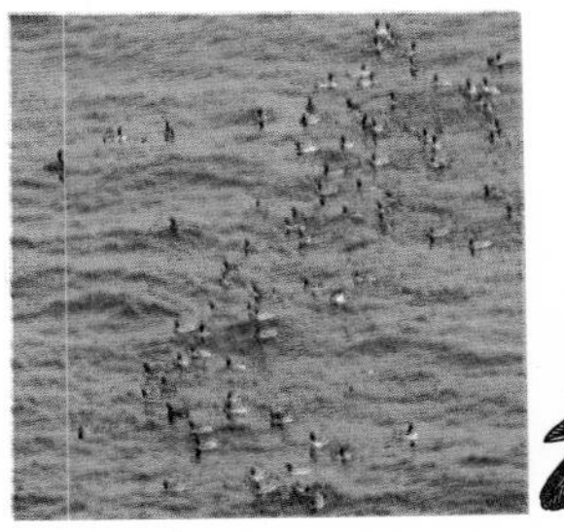

Fat guillemot *left*
Healthy guillemots (feeding at sea, far left) can have 3400 parts per billion (ppb) of PCBs in the body but only 400 in the liver.

Controlling Pollution

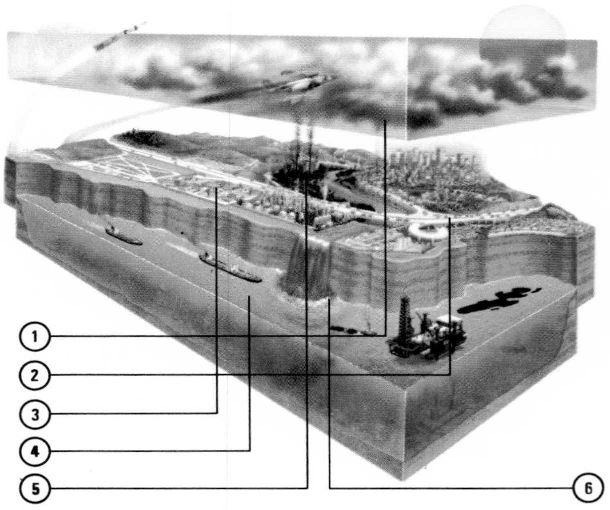

1
2
3
4
5
6

Pollution is a global problem. It affects the land, the sea and the atmosphere in an inter-related way that is incredibly complex and often very subtle. At least in the industrially developed countries man has learned that he must do better than merely bury his unwanted materials in the ground, pour them into the rivers or burn them to pollute the air. But learning the best ways of disposing of them – or, preferably, of storing them until they can be used again – is a difficult, long-term process; and time is not on man's side.

Once pollutants are dispersed, controlling them becomes extremely costly or even impossible. The answer is to prevent their release, wherever possible, into the arterial pathways of water and air. The growing awareness of this is reflected in the legislation of many countries. It is seen in the Clean Air Act of the UK, the German convention banning harmful detergents, the tight California restrictions on car exhaust gases, and so on. But this is only the start of the movement to clean-up the environment and conserve its resources.

Much of the action against pollution has been piecemeal in nature, often in response to particular disasters. Now comes the promise, in no small part due to the public mood, for more widespread action against pollutants that are already known to be harmful to the environment and man. For example, public health authorities in most countries are alive to the hazard of mercury contamination in fish and other foods. At the international level, the convention on oil pollution is being strengthened and the permissible levels of radioactive discharges reviewed. At the same time, industry is slowly becoming persuaded that waste should be regarded as a valued resource which is often capable of being recycled over and over again instead of discarded.

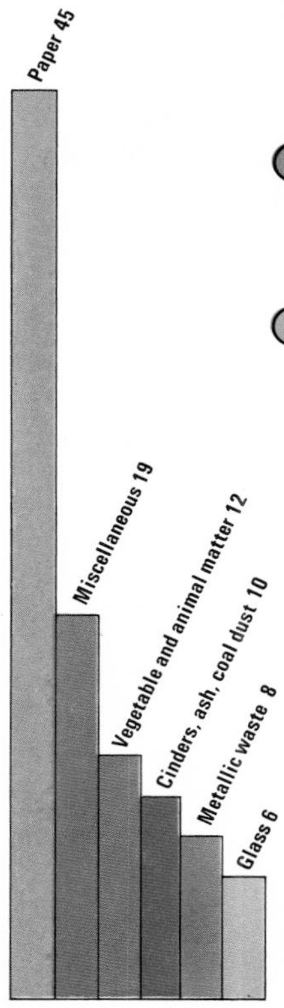

Paper 45
Miscellaneous 19
Vegetable and animal matter 12
Cinders, ash, coal dust 10
Metallic waste 8
Glass 6

Percentage composition of domestic waste in U S A

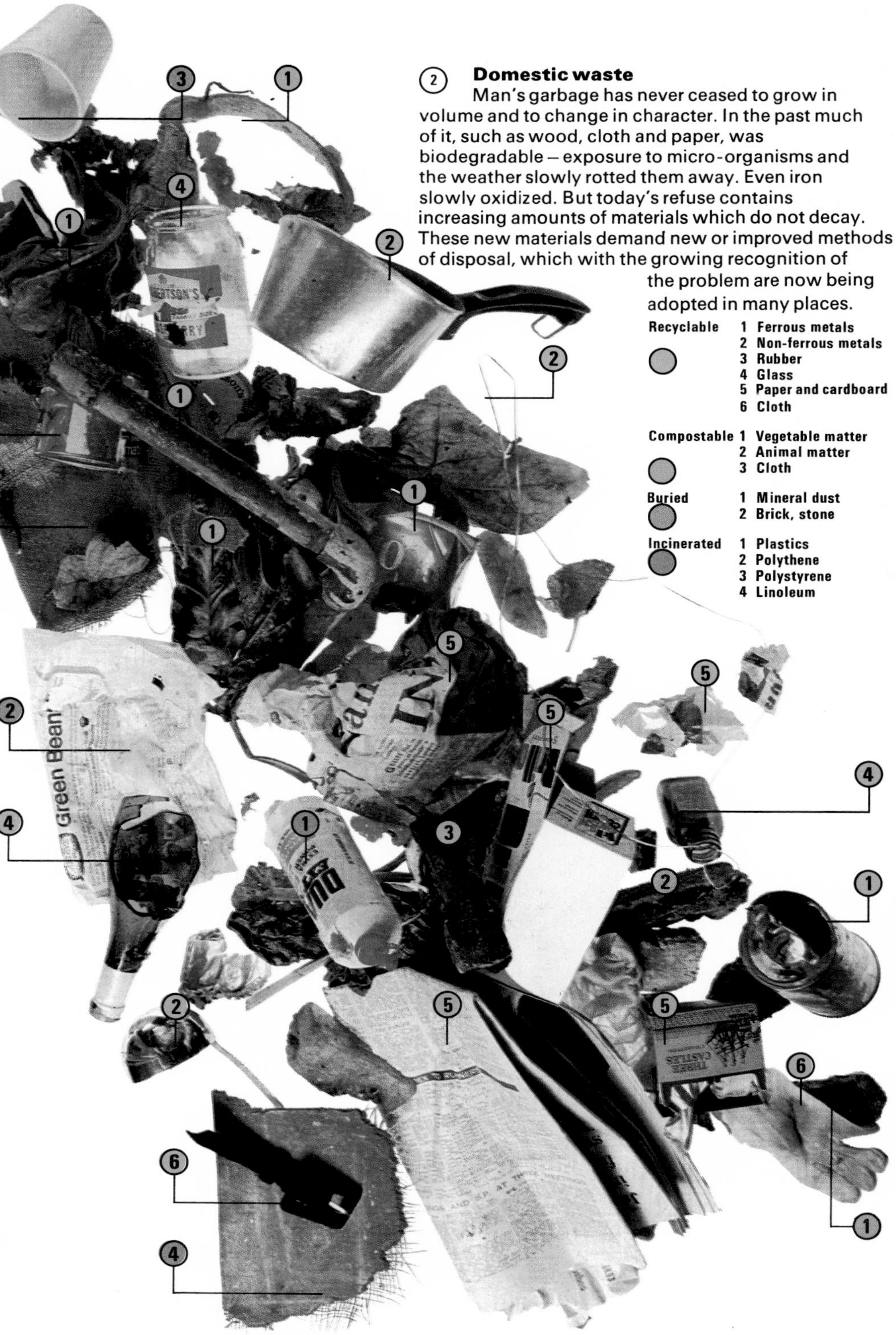

(2) Domestic waste

Man's garbage has never ceased to grow in volume and to change in character. In the past much of it, such as wood, cloth and paper, was biodegradable – exposure to micro-organisms and the weather slowly rotted them away. Even iron slowly oxidized. But today's refuse contains increasing amounts of materials which do not decay. These new materials demand new or improved methods of disposal, which with the growing recognition of the problem are now being adopted in many places.

Recyclable
1 Ferrous metals
2 Non-ferrous metals
3 Rubber
4 Glass
5 Paper and cardboard
6 Cloth

Compostable
1 Vegetable matter
2 Animal matter
3 Cloth

Buried
1 Mineral dust
2 Brick, stone

Incinerated
1 Plastics
2 Polythene
3 Polystyrene
4 Linoleum

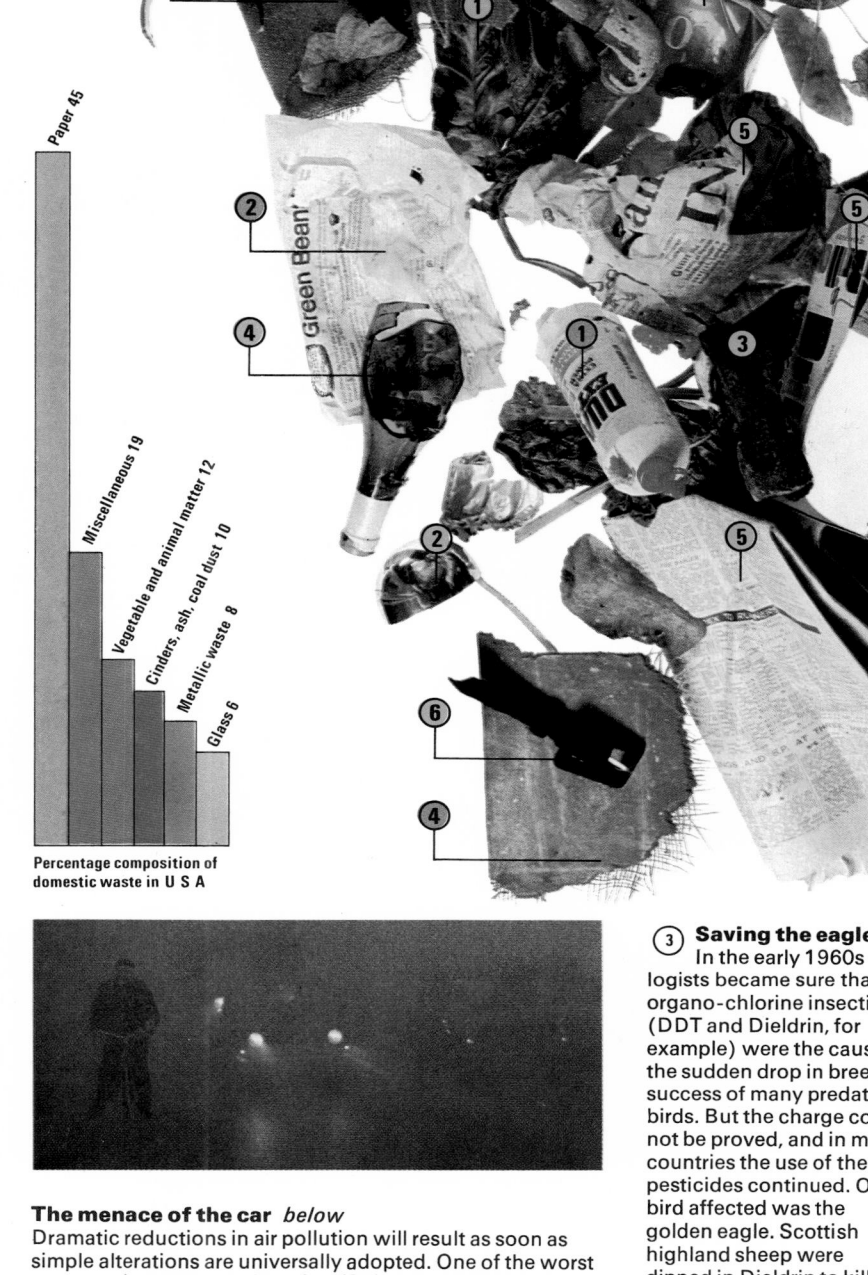

(1) Air pollution in cities

Smoke is one of the commonest, most dangerous and most visible of all air pollutants. It is the direct cause of bronchitis and other respiratory diseases. But many nations are cleaning their urban atmosphere by introducing smokeless zones. Since 1956 winter sunshine in British city centers has increased by over 50 per cent. Smoke from railways (violet segment, right) has dwindled as steam traction has been superseded. Industrial smoke has likewise been reduced, although iron oxide dust from steelworks (above) remains a problem as do domestic coal fires.

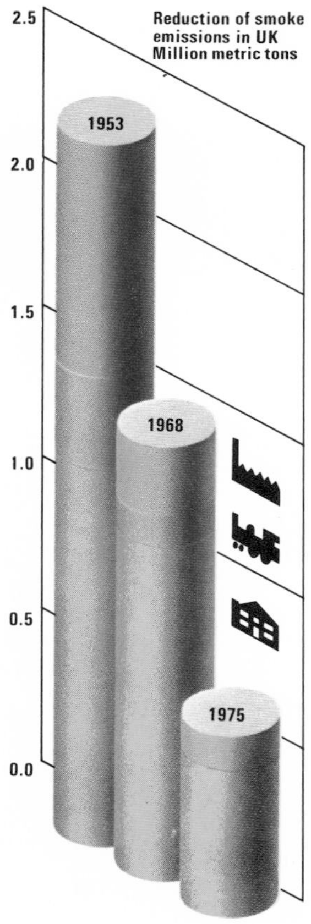

Reduction of smoke emissions in UK
Million metric tons
2.5
2.0
1.5
1.0
0.5
0.0
1953
1968
1975

The menace of the car *below*

Dramatic reductions in air pollution will result as soon as simple alterations are universally adopted. One of the worst sources, the crankcase breather (1), is not opened to the air but piped through a vacuum-sensing valve (2) back to the intake. Fuel-tank vapor (3) is filtered and similarly dealt with. The exhaust is made oxygen-rich with extra fresh air (4) to burn up all but a few combustion products; the residue is oxidized to harmless compounds by passage through a high temperature furnace (5) in the presence of a chemical catalyst which promotes the desired reactions.

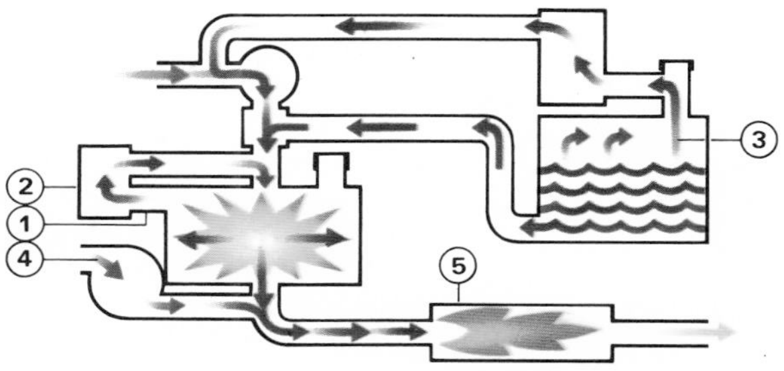

1
2
3
4
5

(3) Saving the eagle *right*

In the early 1960s ecologists became sure that organo-chlorine insecticides (DDT and Dieldrin, for example) were the cause of the sudden drop in breeding success of many predatory birds. But the charge could not be proved, and in most countries the use of these pesticides continued. One bird affected was the golden eagle. Scottish highland sheep were dipped in Dieldrin to kill ticks. The chemical became dissolved in the mutton fat, and this eagle lives largely on sheep carrion. In one area the proportion of eagle eyries producing young fell from 72 to 29 per cent, following the introduction of Dieldrin sheep dips in 1960. Scotland's 300 pairs of eagles seemed doomed. But in 1966 Britain banned Dieldrin sheep-dips. By the early 1970s more than enough young survived to maintain the eagle population.

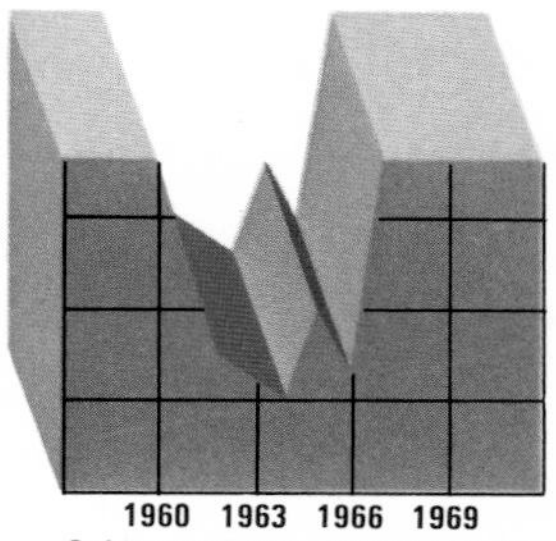

1960
1963
1966
1969

Golden eagle: percentage breeding successes

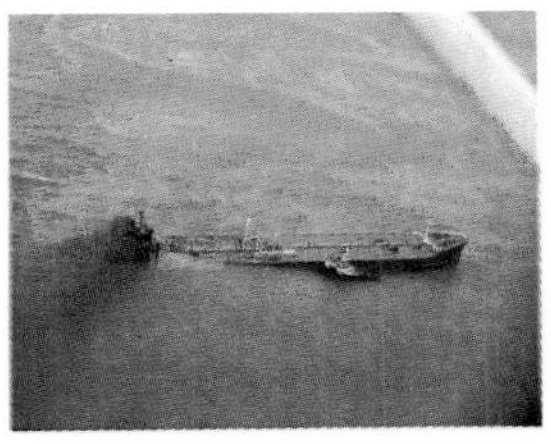

④ Oil pollution

Every year millions of tons of oil enter the oceans either directly through spills, accidents and deliberate discharge or indirectly via air and water from the land. Hardly any part of the ocean remains free from contamination. Some oil pollution is the disturbing result of industrial society's dependence on an oil-based technology. Equally, there is no doubt that much oil pollution is unnecessary and can be controlled or prevented. One of the earliest attempts to do this occurred in 1926 when the United States tried to obtan international agreement to limit the discharge of oil. This and later attempts by the United Kingdom failed and it was not until 1958 that the International Convention for the Preven-tionof Pollution of the Sea by Oil came into force – four years after it was agreed. Even then, the Convention did not ban completely the release of oil into the sea. This must be the ultimate goal. However, even if this is achieved, the problem will persist – oil pollution from sources on land is more than double that occurring directly at sea. One of the chief offenders are gasoline and diesel engines. The crankcases of such engines contribute at least 2.8 million metric tons of oil to the sea every year. A serious waste of a vital resource, steps are at last being taken in some countries to curb it.

The Torrey Canyon disaster
In 1967 the sea had its first major case of oil pollution when the Torrey Canyon ran aground off the Cornish coast (above left). Within a few days the first oil began to sweep onto the beaches. To disperse it, large quantities of detergent were sprayed both from boats (above) and on the shore, turning the sea creamy white with a froth of oily emulsion (center left). Unfortunately the use of these detergents probably caused more damage to marine life than did the oil – except for the early kill of seabirds (bottom left). The oil also drifted across to France coating the shore with congealed oil (right).

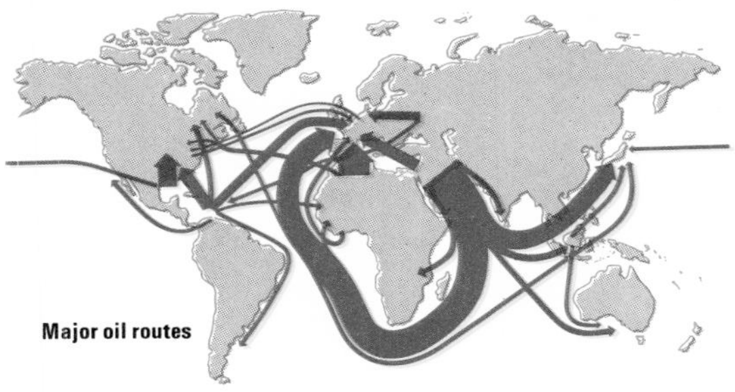
Major oil routes

Oil movements ***left***
Increased transport is reflected in the percentage growth of the world tanker fleet (below).

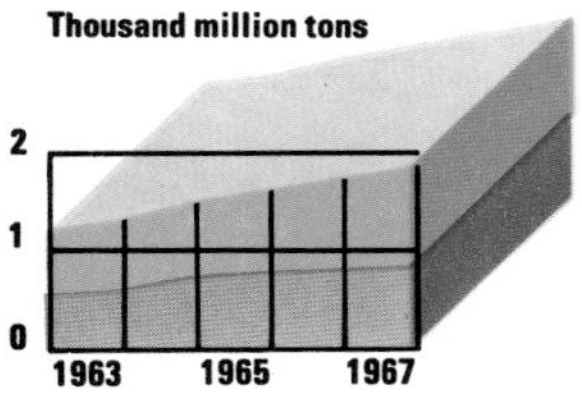
Thousand million tons
2
1
0
1963
1965
1967

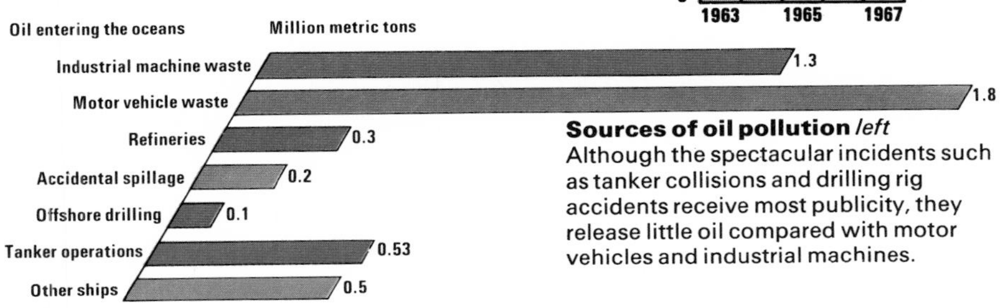
Oil entering the oceans
Million metric tons
Industrial machine waste
1.3
Motor vehicle waste
1.8
Refineries
0.3
Accidental spillage
0.2
Offshore drilling
0.1
Tanker operations
0.53
Other ships
0.5

Sources of oil pollution *left*
Although the spectacular incidents such as tanker collisions and drilling rig accidents receive most publicity, they release little oil compared with motor vehicles and industrial machines.

Oil tankers' new load-on-top system *below*
Before the introduction of this system, ballast water and tank washings, along with a hundred or so tons of oil which had originally stuck to the internal steelwork, were discharged into the sea before taking on a new cargo. In the load-on-top system, one cargo compartment (A) is used as a 'slop tank'. Water in a ballast tank (B) is run off until only oil and oily water remains (C). The residue together with washings from the tanks are collected in the slop tank (D). Here the mixture is finally separated before running clean water off (E). The load goes on top of the remaining oil.

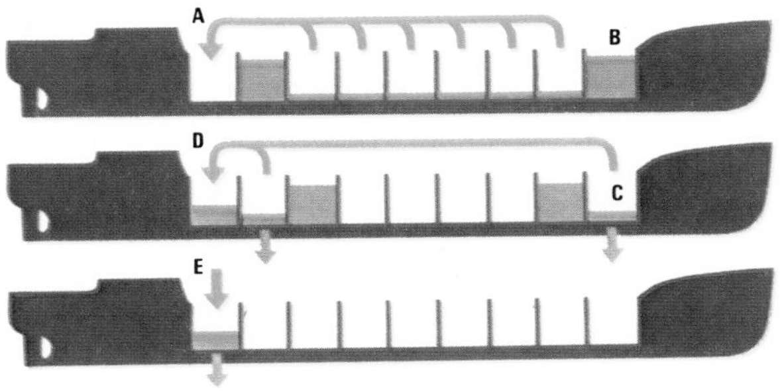
A
B
D
C
E

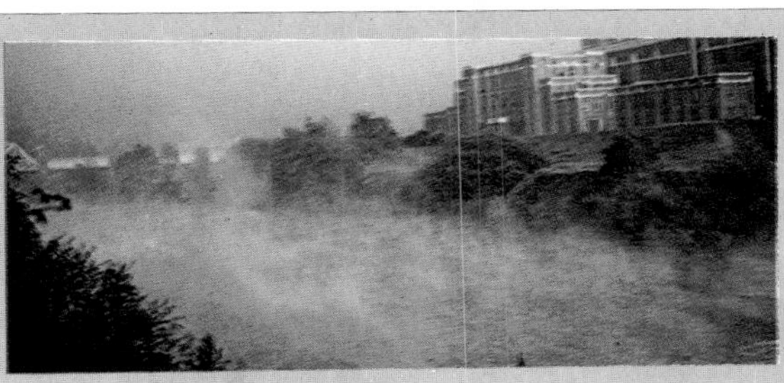

⑤ Thermal pollution ***above and below***
Man throws away a great deal of unwanted heat into rivers. This is done on the largest scale by electricity generating stations whose condensers cycle cooling water in vast quantities. In Britain the hot effluent is spread as a thin film on an otherwise cool river, causing visible steam (above, River Trent) but minimal disturbance to river life. The problem is accentuated by the spread of very large nuclear stations (in the US, below), which for safety reasons have so far generally been sited miles from urban areas on rivers which previously were quite unpolluted. In Britian all such stations are on the sea shore or wide estuaries.

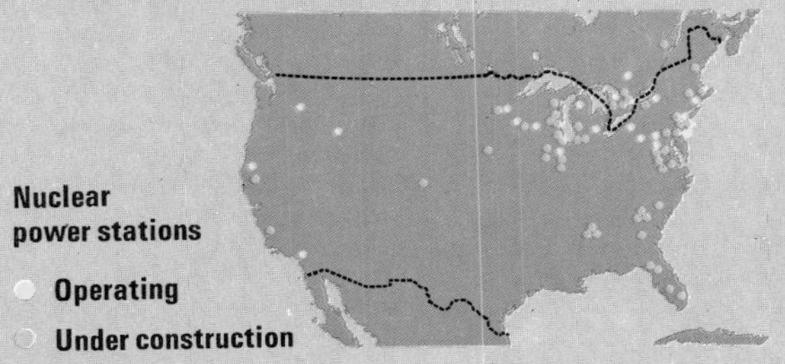
Nuclear
power stations
Operating
Under construction

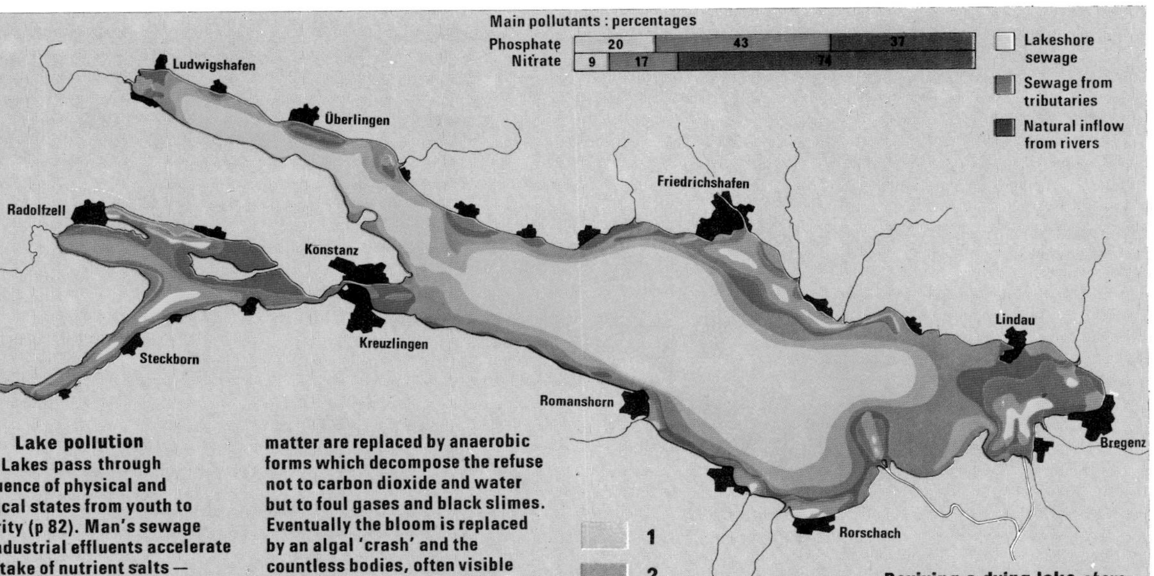
Main pollutants : percentages
Phosphate
20
43
37
Nitrate
9
17
74
Lakeshore sewage
Sewage from tributaries
Natural inflow from rivers
Ludwigshafen
Überlingen
Friedrichshafen
Radolfzell
Konstanz
Kreuzlingen
Steckborn
Romanshorn
Lindau
Bregenz
Rorschach

⑥ Lake pollution
Lakes pass through a sequence of physical and chemical states from youth to maturity (p 82). Man's sewage and industrial effluents accelerate the intake of nutrient salts – such as the phosphates and nitrates shown in the bar chart above the map – which feed the natural population of algae. Combined with sunny weather the result can be an algal 'bloom'. Billions of algae use up the water's dissolved oxygen, killing fish and other life. The aerobic (oxygen-breathing) bacteria needed to degrade sewage and other organic matter are replaced by anaerobic forms which decompose the refuse not to carbon dioxide and water but to foul gases and black slimes. Eventually the bloom is replaced by an algal 'crash' and the countless bodies, often visible as a colored tide, evolve toxic decomposition products which, concentrated in food chains, can prove lethal to sea birds and even humans. The answer is better water treatment plants, possibly combined with new forms of fertilizers, detergents and other products of modern civilization which contain smaller quantities of nutrient salts.

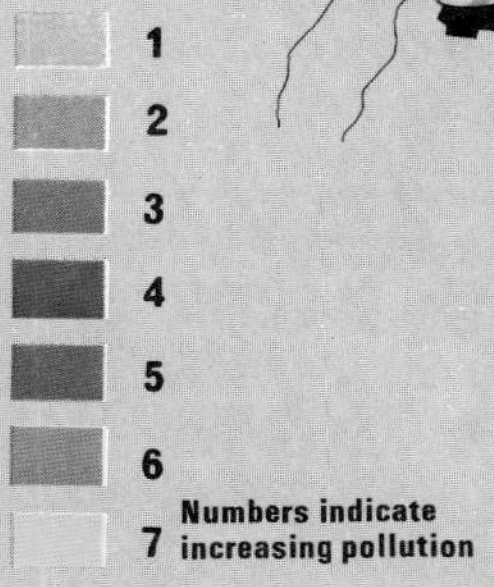
1
2
3
4
5
6
7
Numbers indicate increasing pollution

Reviving a dying lake ***above***
One of the largest European freshwater lakes, Lake Constance (Bodensee), is a prime example of how the increasing load of industrial and domestic effluent causes serious pollution. The aim now is to install treatment plant at source rather than use the lake as a liquid refuse dump.

Man the Aggressor

Human beings have always resorted to fighting as the final arbiter in settling disputes – a pre-disposition that encourages the view that man is naturally aggressive. Whereas, in general, other members of the animal kingdom are content with aggressive displays and rarely kill each other, man has no such scruples – he has even embarked on deliberate policies of genocide. Modern psychologists, however, believe that even though aggressive behavior is part of our animal inheritance, war is not an instinctive, ineradicable or uncontrollable facet of human nature.

Massive resources and great energy have been devoted to improving the destructive power of man's weapons of war. And three types – chemical, biological and nuclear – have been developed to such horrific levels of destructive power that unless arms races are soon brought under control, their widespread use could totally eliminate all life on the planet. This is particularly true for the nuclear arms race because these types of weapon are unique in that their destructive power is virtually unlimited. And an increasing number of nations are becoming able to produce them, once the decision to do so has been made.

Although wars can be limited, it only needs one to get out of hand to destroy us all and with armed conflicts becoming more and more frequent this is a very real threat. Between 1898 and 1950 there were 59 wars; between 1950 and 1970 there were 72, although their scale has become smaller and the major powers, except in Korea and Vietnam, have been reluctant to become involved.

Efforts to end the arms race, nuclear, biological and chemical, between the superpowers have been totally unsuccessful. Some international arms control agreements have been negotiated, but these are of trivial importance and have had little effect on the pace of the arms race let alone the number of nuclear weapons in the world's arsenals. There is, above all, the terrifying danger of a general nuclear war being started by accident, miscalculation or even madness. In the words of the late President Kennedy, 'Mankind must put an end to war or war will put an end to Mankind!'

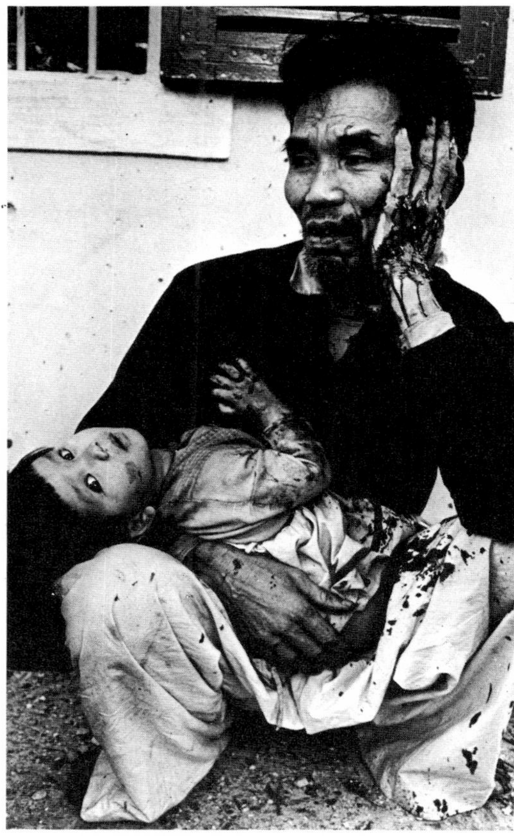

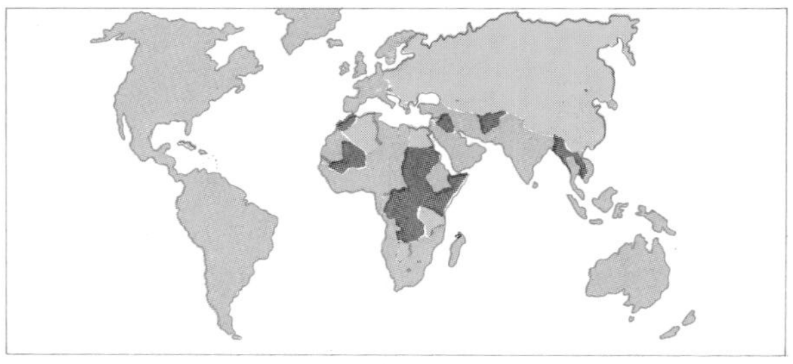
Western and affiliated countries including non-aligned countries with strong links with West
Communist bloc and non-aligned countries closely linked to it
Non-aligned countries

11
11
15
19

Is world conflict beyond control? *above and right*
The dramatic increase in the number of armed conflicts in modern times is clearly seen from the map(right). As more countries gain their independence the importance placed on sovereignty and nationalism has increased. There is little sign of any real move towards internationalism – the only way to obtain a secure and stable world. In the future, boundary disputes are likely to be an increasing cause of new conflicts. Meanwhile more and more non-combatant civilians are being directly involved in the reality of war (photograph above from Vietnam).

The man in battle *below*
The fire-power at the command of the individual soldier has increased considerably in recent times. Not only is he equipped with a large range of offensive and defensive weapons but he can also call on tactical back-up forces and air transport both locally and to distant combat points.

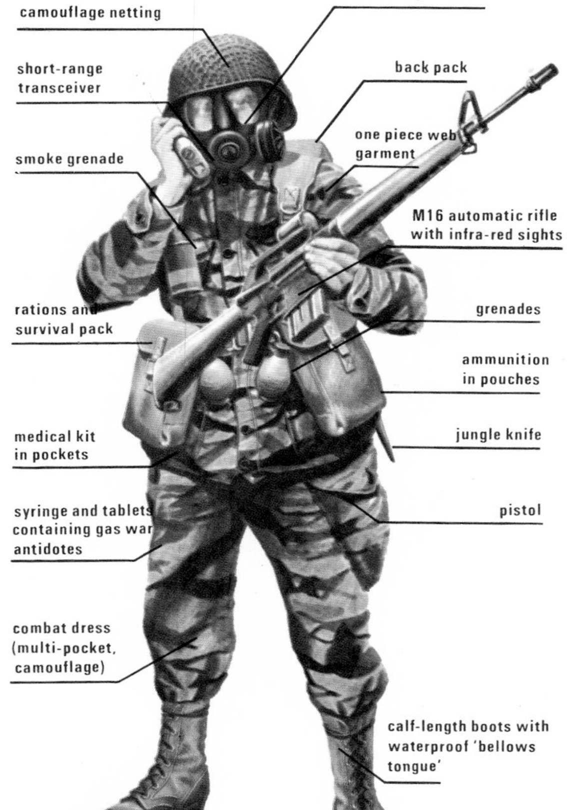
bullet-proof helmet with camouflage netting
gas mask
short-range transceiver
back pack
smoke grenade
one piece web garment
M16 automatic rifle with infra-red sights
rations and survival pack
grenades
ammunition in pouches
medical kit in pockets
jungle knife
syringe and tablets containing gas war antidotes
pistol
combat dress (multi-pocket, camouflage)
calf-length boots with waterproof 'bellows tongue'

Escalation in destructive power *below*
Since the 'Little Boy' A-bomb of 1945 the destructive power of nuclear weapons has been increased by more than 1500 times (compare areas of cirles).

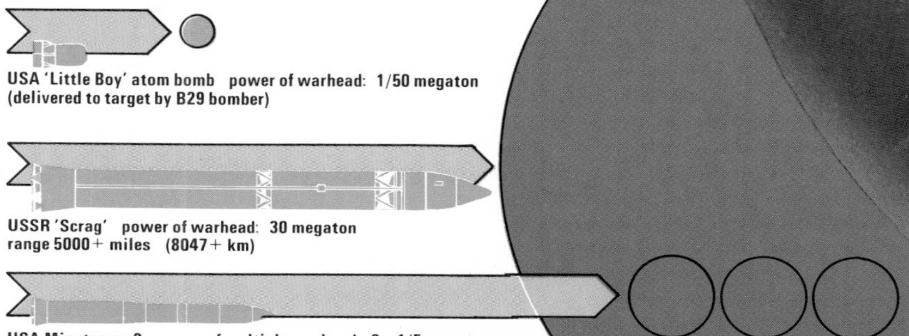
USA 'Little Boy' atom bomb power of warhead: 1/50 megaton (delivered to target by B29 bomber)
USSR 'Scrag' power of warhead: 30 megaton range 5000+ miles (8047+ km)
USA Minuteman 3 power of multiple warhead: 3 x 1/5 megaton range 6950+ miles (11195+ km)

Nuclear arms race
right and below
The super powers are now equipped with insanely large numbers of thermo-nuclear warheads. Thus in 1971 the USA could deliver more than 4000 of them onto the USSR – 1050 from land-based missiles, 2000 from bombers and about 1000 from nuclear submarines such as the 'George Washington' (below). New multiple warheads will increase the numbers by a factor of 2 or 3.

Delivery system	USA	USSR	UK	France	China
land based (ICBMs)	1054	1300			some
strategic bombers	500	200		45	
missile submarines	41	20-30	4		some

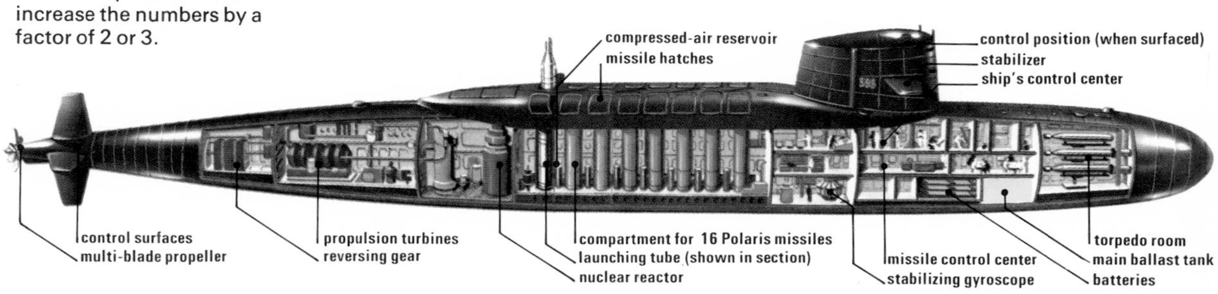
compressed-air reservoir
missile hatches
control position (when surfaced)
stabilizer
ship's control center
control surfaces
multi-blade propeller
propulsion turbines
reversing gear
compartment for 16 Polaris missiles
launching tube (shown in section)
nuclear reactor
missile control center
stabilizing gyroscope
torpedo room
main ballast tank
batteries

1 Ballistic-missile early-warning system (BMEWS)
2 Distant early-warning line (Dewline) against aircraft
3 Pinetree line; N American air defence (Norad) against aircraft
4 Mid-Canada line; Norad against aircraft
5 **Electronic fence; Norad space-defense system**
6 Tallinn line; surface-to-air missiles
7 Norad command center, inside Cheyenne Mountain
8 Titan 2 ICBM bases
9 Minuteman 3 ICBM bases
10 Soviet ICBM bases
11 Soviet IRBM units, silo-based and mobile
12 French SSBS silos
13 US ABM sites
14 Soviet ABM sites
15 Chinese IRBM bases
16 Soviet ballistic-missile submarines
17 US ballistic-missile submarines
18 French ballistic-missile submarines
19 Chinese ballistic-missile submarines?
20 US missile submarine bases
21 **NADGE (NATO air-defense ground environment)**
22 Norad space detection and tracking system radar fence

Power to the people? *above*
A new element in conflict is the involvement of whole or large segments of populations in civil uprisings, often provoked by repressive regimes or by religious or tribal antagonism. Such conflicts have been particularly vicious.

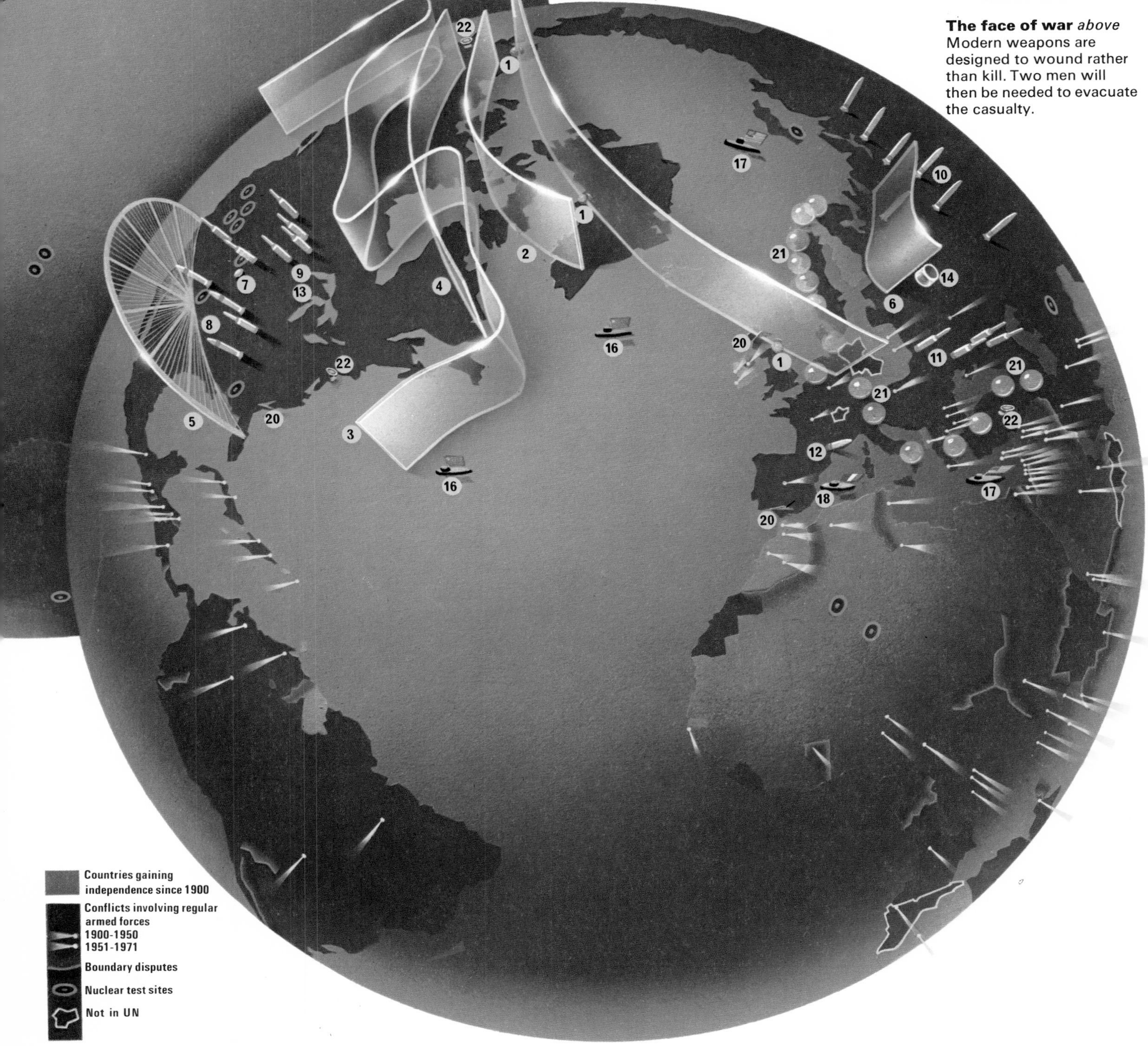

Countries gaining independence since 1900
Conflicts involving regular armed forces
1900-1950
1951-1971
Boundary disputes
Nuclear test sites
Not in UN

Rising toll in lives *right*
As international wars have become 'total' they have resulted in greatly enhanced casualty rates and extensive destruction.

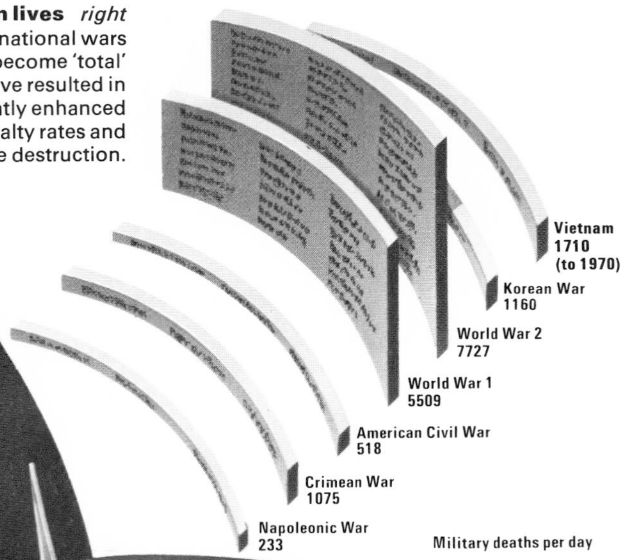

Vietnam 1710 (to 1970)
Korean War 1160
World War 2 7727
World War 1 5509
American Civil War 518
Crimean War 1075
Napoleonic War 233
Military deaths per day

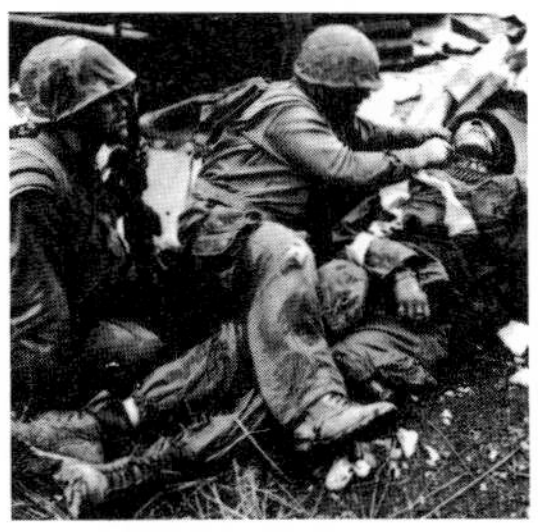

The face of war *above*
Modern weapons are designed to wound rather than kill. Two men will then be needed to evacuate the casualty.

World alliances *below*
The major alliance is the United Nations, but its peacekeeping role has often been hampered by the major powers. Even though, in theory, each state has an equal voice, they tend to form familiar groupings. Other main alliances are shown below.

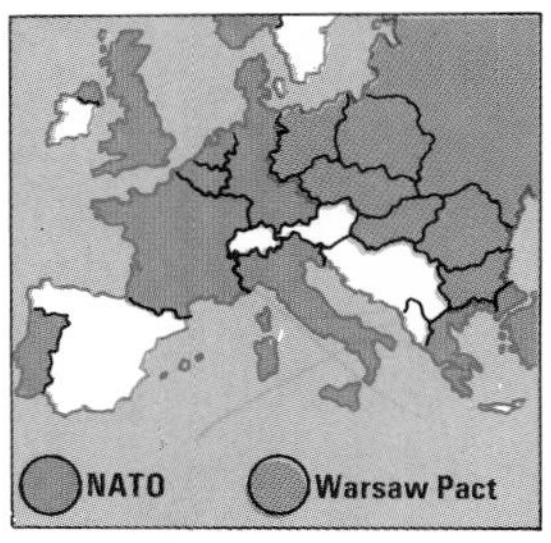

NATO
Warsaw Pact

In the heart of Europe 1.0 million NATO troops face 1.3 million Warsaw Pact troops in a state of combat readiness. The huge concentration of weaponry on each side includes a variety of tactical nuclear weapons, shells, howitzer projectiles and ground-to-ground missiles.

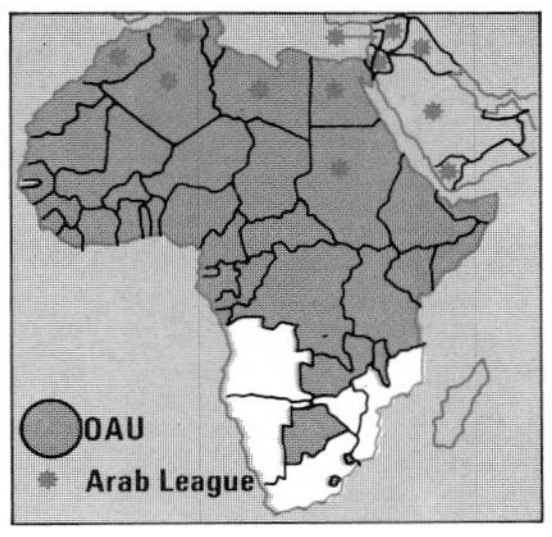

OAU
Arab League

The Organization of African Unity is designed to coordinate national policies for the benefit of the continent as a whole and to guarantee each member's independence. Some of the OAU are also members of the Arab League – a treaty for joint defense and economic cooperation.

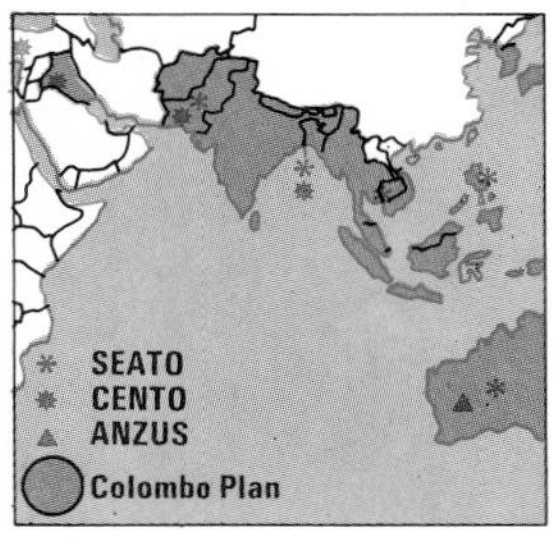

SEATO
CENTO
ANZUS
Colombo Plan

The South-East Asia Treaty Organization provides for collective action should external aggression or internal subversion threaten members within the general region of Southeast Asia. Although the Central Treaty Organization (CENTO) aims to provide for defense and security, it has been particularly beneficial in developing communications within the area. The ANZUS pact, which commits the USA to the defense of Australia and New Zealand, is fundamental to the defense policies of the two countries. Unlike the other three treaties, the Colombo Plan has, as its primary aim, economic cooperation and development.

... I have promises to keep,
And miles to go before I sleep,
And miles to go before I sleep.

(From 'Stopping by Woods on a Snowy Evening' by Robert Frost)

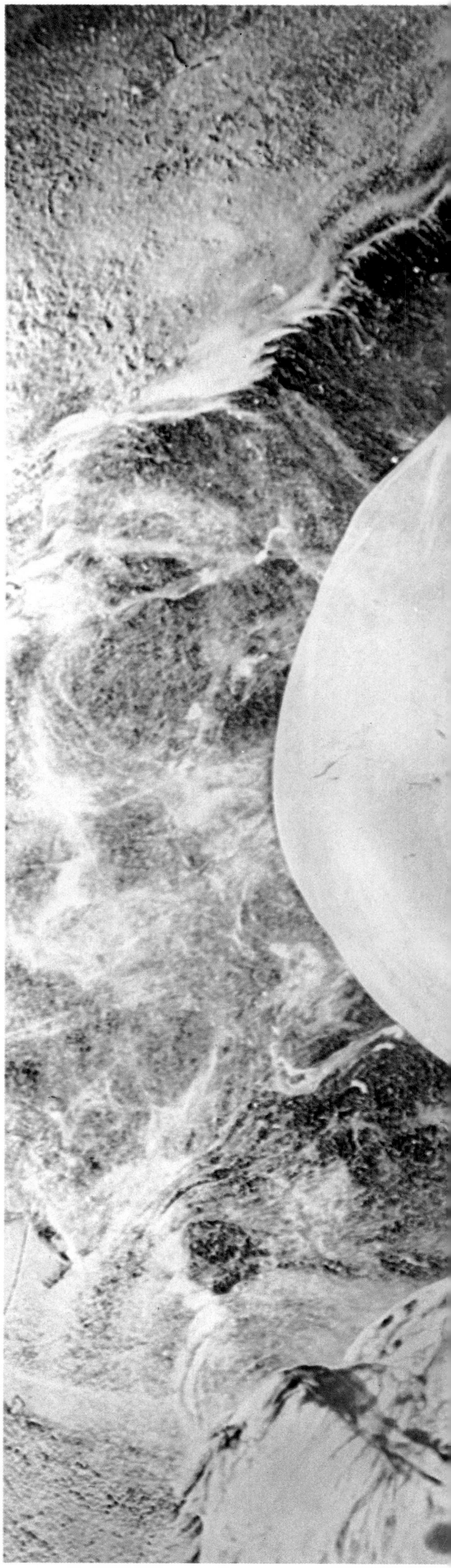

The object of The Good Earth has been to tell the story of our earthly home.

With a world as vast in its natural heritage and as bountiful in its resources, our ancestors could have been forgiven for some of the thoughtlessness with which they sometimes misused it.

They might have been forgiven, too, for ignoring the protestations of people who, like Malthus and others before him, warned that the Earth could sustain man only if man himself attempted to sustain the Earth.

But today there can be no excuses.

We live in an age when some of the worst fears concerning the future of the Earth and mankind appear to be coming to pass. Greed and mindless exploitation of the Earth's resources, both physical and living, are impoverishing the planet and will, unless halted, plunge us into an environmental catastrophe with man its ultimate victim.

Some people would claim that already it is too late and that the most mankind can hope for is a stay of execution.

The Editors of The Good Earth do not subscribe to such a fatalistic view. We conceived this book to awaken thinking people — you — to the fact that man, through the natural world, still has a magnificent inheritance.

It is a treasure to be preserved and conserved for future generations and not to be squandered within a few lifetimes.

Never before in the history of man has it been possible, as it is now possible, for him to correct some of the harm he has inflicted upon the Earth and its creatures in the past and to take steps to prevent further damage in the years to come.

In this sincere belief we dedicate this book to you, the reader. The challenge is now your challenge: the Earth, the good Earth, the prize.

The Editors

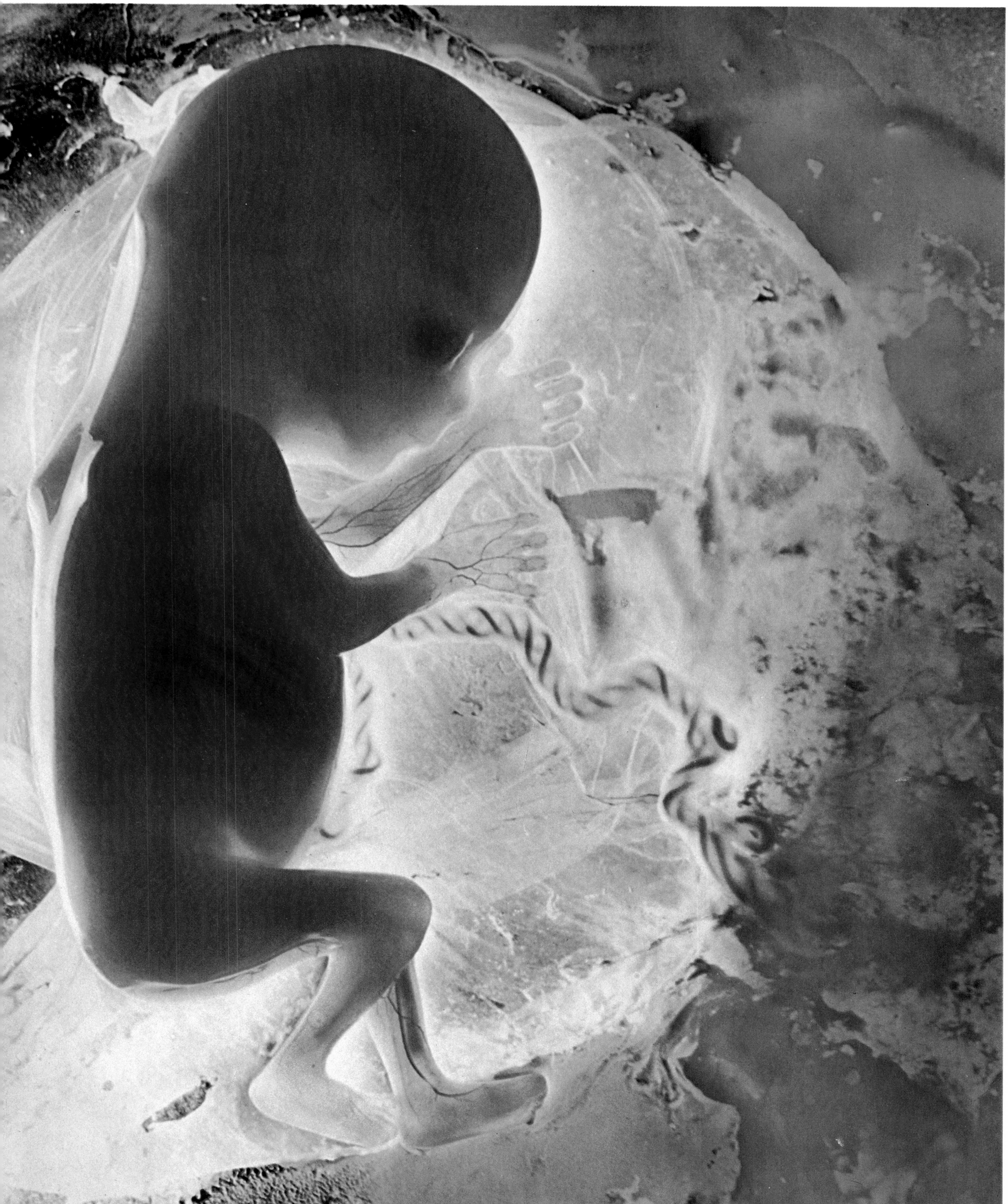

Maps

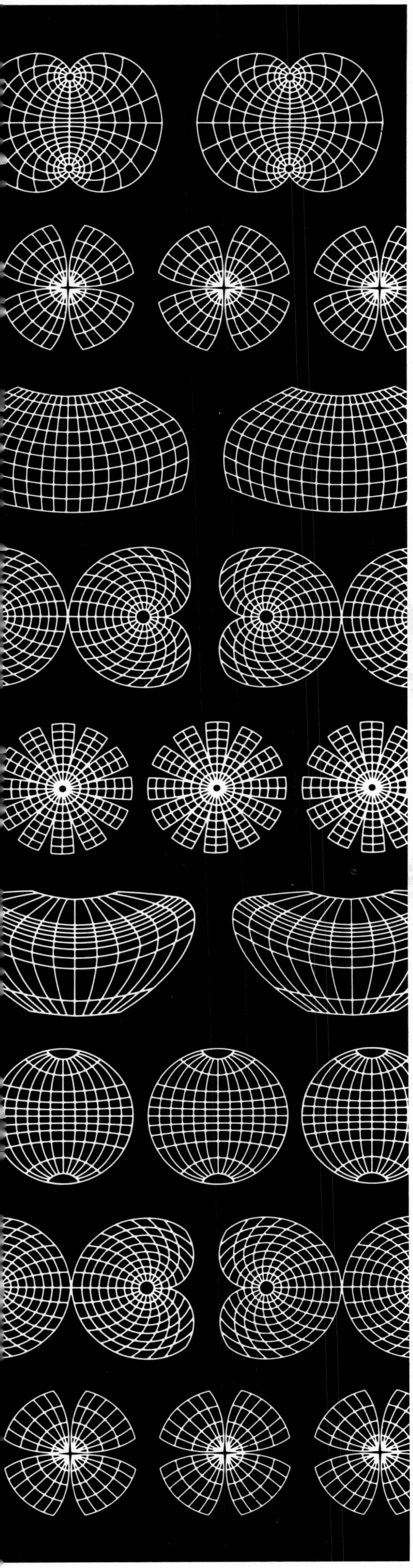

For many centuries, during the Age of Discovery, our earthly home seemed to be expanding. With each new voyage or exploration the known world became larger. In recent years, with the coming of air and space travel, our Earth seemed to shrink as the speed of flight increased.
Now the Earth can be encircled in minutes and full views of our planet have become a familiar sight.

In this section, except for the first group of specialized maps, the atlas maps emphasize national boundaries and the effects of man on the Earth spread out on the physical background provided by nature. The map selection also has been made with man in mind, and emphasis has been placed on the more congested areas of the world.
The major urbanized areas and communities contiguous to them are shown on a larger scale. These maps show transportation and drainage patterns in great detail plus a large number of place names.

The Spherical Earth Flattened
The curved surface of the Earth is transferred to a flat surface by means of a projection. This is an orderly system of parallels and meridians upon which a map can be drawn. Many different map projections are used today, and the most appropriate ones have been chosen for the maps that follow.

World Index Map

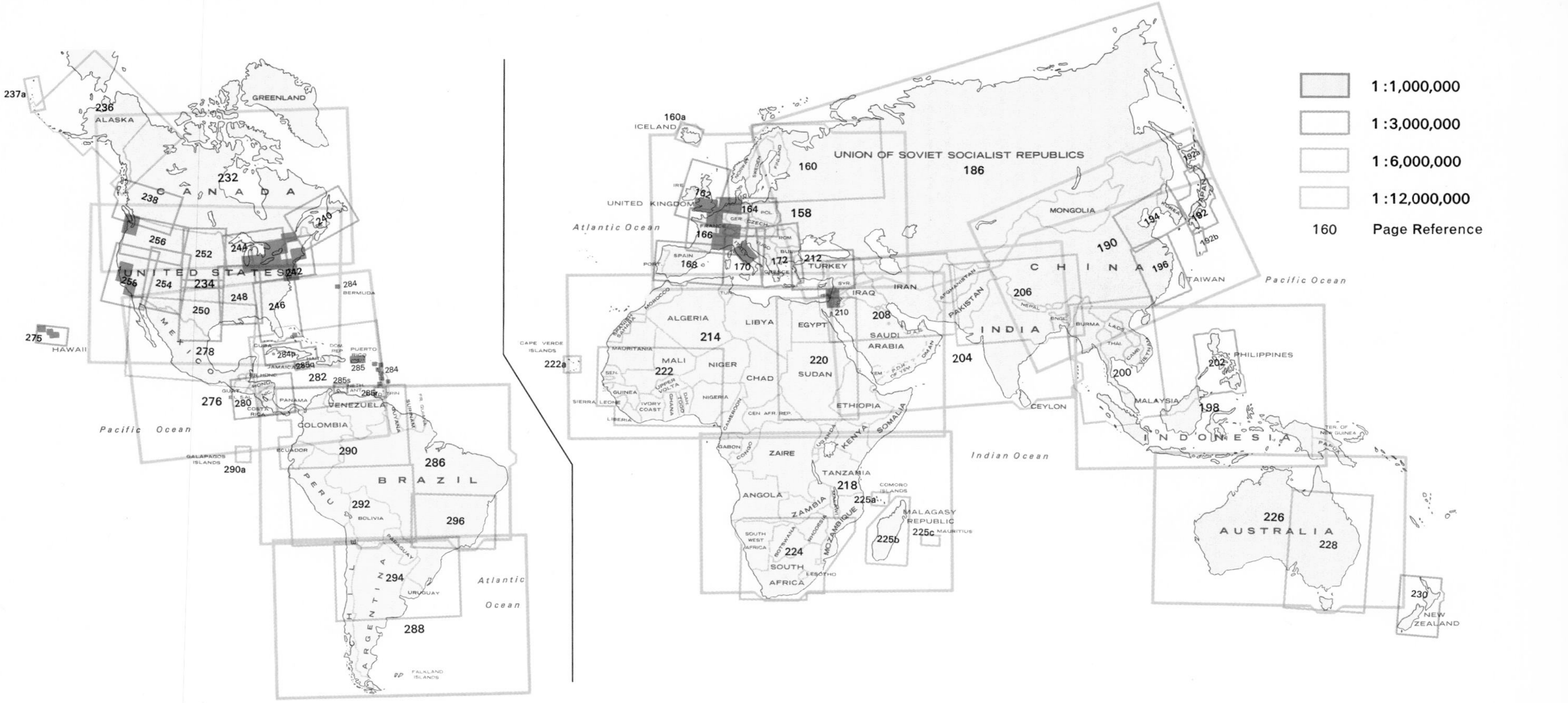
1:1,000,000
1:3,000,000
1:6,000,000
1:12,000,000
160 Page Reference
UNION OF SOVIET SOCIALIST REPUBLICS
CANADA
UNITED STATES
GREENLAND
ALASKA
HAWAII
MEXICO
BRAZIL
COLOMBIA
VENEZUELA
PERU
ARGENTINA
ICELAND
UNITED KINGDOM
ALGERIA
LIBYA
EGYPT
MALI
NIGER
CHAD
SUDAN
ETHIOPIA
ZAIRE
ANGOLA
TANZANIA
ZAMBIA
MOZAMBIQUE
SOUTH AFRICA
MALAGASY REPUBLIC
TURKEY
IRAN
IRAQ
SAUDI ARABIA
PAKISTAN
INDIA
CEYLON
CHINA
MONGOLIA
TAIWAN
PHILIPPINES
MALAYSIA
INDONESIA
AUSTRALIA
NEW ZEALAND
Pacific Ocean
Atlantic Ocean
Indian Ocean

Legend to Maps

Inhabited Localities

The symbol represents the number of inhabitants within the locality

Scale	Symbol	Inhabitants
1:1,000,000 / 1:3,000,000 / 1:6,000,000	•	0—10,000
	○	10,000—25,000
	⊙	25,000—100,000
	▣	100,000—250,000
	▣	250,000—1,000,000
	■	>1,000,000
1:12,000,000	•	0—50,000
	⊙	50,000—100,000
	▣	100,000—250,000
	▣	250,000—1,000,000
	■	>1,000,000

Urban Area (area of continuous industrial, commercial, and residential development)

The size of type indicates the relative economic and political importance of the locality

Écommoy Lisieux **Rouen**
Trouville **Orléans** **PARIS**

Hollywood, *Westminster* — Section of a City, Neighborhood

Bi'r Safājah — Inhabited Oasis   *Kumdah* — Uninhabited Oasis

Capitals of Political Units

BUDAPEST Independent Nation

Luanda Dependency (Colony, protectorate, etc.)

GALAPAGOS (Ecuador) Administering Country

Villarica State, Province, etc.

White Plains County, Oblast, etc.

Alternate Names

Basel (Bâle) **MOSKVA** (MOSCOW) English or second official language names are shown in reduced size lettering

Ventura (San Buenaventura) **Volgograd** (Stalingrad) Historical or other alternates in the local language are shown in parentheses

Political Boundaries

International (First-order political unit)

1:1,000,000 — 1:3,000,000, 1:6,000,000, 1:12,000,000

Demarcated, Undemarcated, and Administrative

Disputed de jure

Indefinite or Undefined

Demarcation Line (used in Germany, Korea, and Vietnam)

Internal

GUAIRA — State, Province, etc. (Second-order political unit)

WESTCHESTER — County, Oblast, etc. (Third-order political unit)

ANDALUCIA Historical Region (No boundaries indicated)

Miscellaneous Cultural Features

PARQUE NACIONAL CANAIMA — National or State Park or Monument

FORT CLATSOP NAT. MEM. — National or State Historic(al) Site, Memorial

BLACKFOOT IND. RES. — Indian Reservation

FORT DIX — Military Installation

TANGLEWOOD — Point of Interest (Battlefield, cave, historical site, etc.)

STEINHAUSEN — Church, Monastery

UXMAL — Ruins

WINDSOR CASTLE — Castle

AMISTAD DAM — Dam

Quarry or Surface Mine

Subsurface Mine

Regional Index Maps

CANADA
UNITED STATES
MEXICO
BRITISH COLUMBIA
ALBERTA
SASKATCHEWAN
MANITOBA
ONTARIO
QUEBEC
NEWFOUNDLAND
N. B.
P. E. I.
NOVA SCOTIA
WASH.
OREGON
IDAHO
MONTANA
WYOMING
NORTH DAKOTA
SOUTH DAKOTA
NEBRASKA
MINN.
WISCONSIN
MICHIGAN
IOWA
ILL.
IND.
OHIO
PA.
NEW YORK
VT.
N.H.
MAINE
MASS.
CONN.
N.J.
MD.
W. VA.
VIRGINIA
KENTUCKY
TENNESSEE
NORTH CAROLINA
SOUTH CAROLINA
GEORGIA
ALABAMA
MISS.
ARKANSAS
LOUISIANA
FLORIDA
MISSOURI
KANSAS
OKLAHOMA
TEXAS
NEW MEXICO
ARIZONA
COLORADO
UTAH
NEVADA
CALIFORNIA
BAJA CALIFORNIA
BAJA CAL. SUR
SONORA
CHIHUAHUA
COAHUILA
NUEVO LEON
TAMAULIPAS
SINALOA
DURANGO
NEW PROVIDENCE
236
238
240
242
244
246
248
250
252
254
256
258
260
261
262
264
266
268
270
272
274
278
282
284b

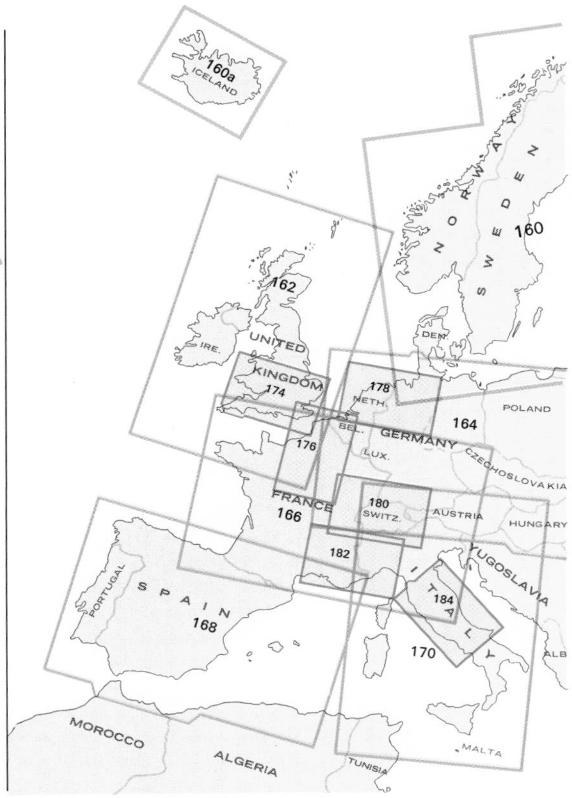
ICELAND
160a
NORWAY
SWEDEN
160
162
IRE.
UNITED KINGDOM
174
DEN.
178
NETH.
BEL.
LUX.
GERMANY
164
POLAND
CZECHOSLOVAKIA
176
FRANCE
166
180
SWITZ.
AUSTRIA
HUNGARY
182
YUGOSLAVIA
184
ITALY
170
PORTUGAL
SPAIN
168
MOROCCO
ALGERIA
TUNISIA
MALTA
ALB.

Transportation

1:12,000,000	1:3,000,000 / 1:6,000,000	1:1,000,000	
		PENNSYLVANIA TURNPIKE	Primary Road
			Secondary Road
			Tertiary Road
			Minor Road, Trail
		CANADIAN NATIONAL	Primary Railway
			Secondary Railway
		CHICAGO-MIDWAY AIRPORT	Airport

MACKINAC BRIDGE — Bridge

GREAT ST. BERNARD TUNNEL — Tunnel

TO CALAIS — Ferry

Shipping Channel

Canal du Midi — Navigable Canal

Intracoastal Waterway

Metric-English Equivalents

Areas represented by one square centimeter at various map scales

1:1,000,000 100 km² 39 square miles	1:6,000,000 3,600 km² 1,390 square miles
1:3,000,000 900 km² 348 square miles	1:12,000,000 14,400 km² 5,558 square miles

Meter=3.28 feet
Kilometer=0.62 mile

Meter² (m²)=10.76 square feet
Kilometer² (km²)=0.39 square mile

Hydrographic Features

Shoreline

Undefined or Fluctuating Shoreline

Amur — River, Stream

Intermittent Stream

Rapids, Falls

Irrigation or Drainage Canal

Reef

764 — Depth of Water

The Everglades — Swamp

SEWARD GLACIER — Glacier

L. Victoria — Lake, Reservoir

Tuz Gölü — Salt Lake

Intermittent Lake, Reservoir

Dry Lake Bed

(395) — Lake Surface Elevation

Topographic Features

Mt. Kenya 5199 — Elevation Above Sea Level

76 — Elevation Below Sea Level

Mount Cook 3764 — Highest Elevation in Country

Khyber Pass 1067 — Mountain Pass

133 — Lowest Elevation in Country

(106) — Elevation of City

Elevations and depths are given in meters

Highest Elevation and Lowest Elevation of a continent are underlined

Lava

Sand Area

Salt Flat

A N D E S
KUNLUNSHANMAI — Mountain Range, Plateau, Valley, etc.

BAFFIN ISLAND
NUNIVAK ISLAND — Island

POLUOSTROV
KAMČATKA
CABO DE HORNOS — Peninsula, Cape, Point, etc.

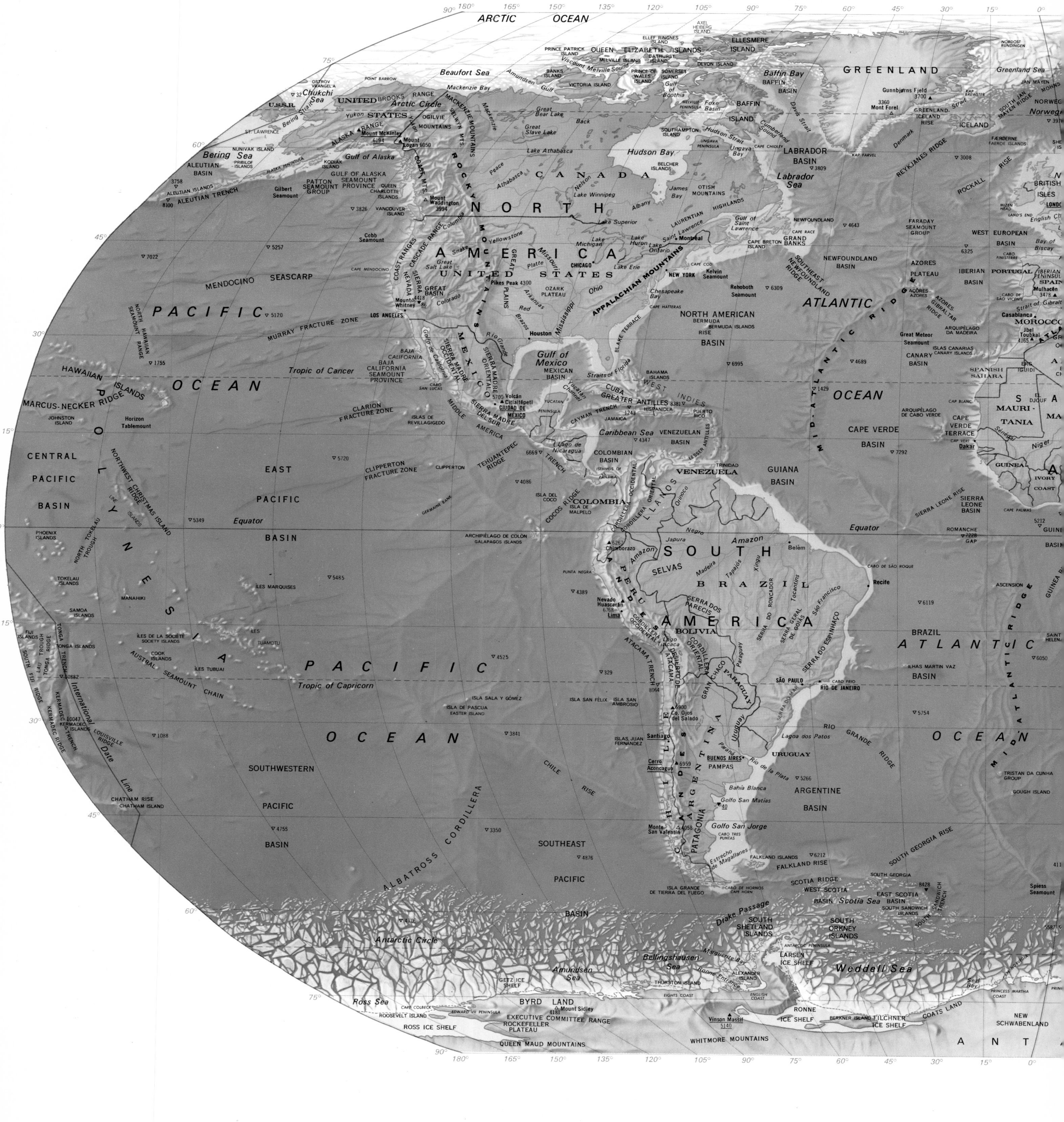

ARCTIC OCEAN
QUEEN ELIZABETH ISLANDS
ELLESMERE ISLAND
GREENLAND
Beaufort Sea
Baffin Bay
BAFFIN ISLAND
Chukchi Sea
U.S.S.R.
UNITED STATES
Arctic Circle
BROOKS RANGE
ALASKA RANGE
Mount McKinley 6194
Mount Logan 6050
Bering Sea
ALEUTIAN BASIN
ALEUTIAN TRENCH
Gulf of Alaska
GULF OF ALASKA SEAMOUNT PROVINCE
Hudson Bay
LABRADOR BASIN
Labrador Sea
Greenland Sea
ICELAND
REYKJANES RIDGE
CANADA
NORTH AMERICA
UNITED STATES
ROCKY MOUNTAINS
Lake Superior
Lake Michigan
APPALACHIAN MOUNTAINS
GREAT PLAINS
CASCADE RANGE
SIERRA NEVADA
GREAT BASIN
LOS ANGELES
CHICAGO
NEW YORK
Houston
MEXICO
Gulf of Mexico
MEXICAN BASIN
NORTH AMERICAN BASIN
NEWFOUNDLAND BASIN
ATLANTIC OCEAN
MID-ATLANTIC RIDGE
AZORES PLATEAU
IBERIAN BASIN
PORTUGAL
MOROCCO
CANARY BASIN
MENDOCINO SEASCARP
MURRAY FRACTURE ZONE
PACIFIC OCEAN
HAWAIIAN ISLANDS
MARCUS-NECKER RIDGE
Tropic of Cancer
CLARION FRACTURE ZONE
CLIPPERTON FRACTURE ZONE
CENTRAL PACIFIC BASIN
EAST PACIFIC BASIN
Equator
POLYNESIA
CUBA
GREATER ANTILLES
WEST INDIES
Caribbean Sea
VENEZUELAN BASIN
COLOMBIAN BASIN
VENEZUELA
COLOMBIA
GUIANA BASIN
CAPE VERDE BASIN
MAURITANIA
SOUTH AMERICA
Amazon
SELVAS
BRAZIL
BOLIVIA
PERU
ANDES
PARAGUAY
URUGUAY
ARGENTINA
PAMPAS
PATAGONIA
SÃO PAULO
RIO DE JANEIRO
BUENOS AIRES
Santiago
Lima
Recife
BRAZIL BASIN
ARGENTINE BASIN
RIO GRANDE RIDGE
Tropic of Capricorn
PACIFIC OCEAN
SOUTHWESTERN PACIFIC BASIN
SOUTHEAST PACIFIC BASIN
CHILE RISE
ALBATROSS CORDILLERA
International Date Line
KERMADEC TRENCH
TONGA TRENCH
Golfo San Jorge
FALKLAND ISLANDS
Drake Passage
Scotia Sea
SOUTH GEORGIA
SOUTH SHETLAND ISLANDS
SOUTH ORKNEY ISLANDS
Weddell Sea
Bellingshausen Sea
Amundsen Sea
Ross Sea
Antarctic Circle
BYRD LAND
ROSS ICE SHELF
QUEEN MAUD MOUNTAINS
WHITMORE MOUNTAINS
RONNE ICE SHELF
FILCHNER ICE SHELF
NEW SCHWABENLAND
ANT

ARCTIC OCEAN
SVALBARD
ZEML'A FRANCA-IOSIFA
SEVERNAJA ZEML'A
NOVOSIBIRSKIJE OSTROVA
Barents Sea
Karskoje More
More Laptevych
Vostočno-Sibirskoje More
East Siberian Sea
OSTROV VRANGEL'A
BARENTS TROUGH
NOVAJA ZEML'A
SEVERO-SIBIRSKAJA NIZMENNOST'
SREDNESIBIRSKOJE PLOSKOGORJE
ZAPADNO-SIBIRSKAJA NIZMENNOST'
Arctic Circle
UNION OF SOVIET SOCIALIST REPUBLICS
URAL'SKIJE GORY
URAL MOUNTAINS
NORWAY
SWEDEN
FINLAND
Gulf of Bothnia
Gulf of Finland
Baltic Sea
LENINGRAD
MOSKVA
Volga
BERLIN
POLAND
GER.
E U R O P E
CARPATHIAN MTS.
ROMANIA
YUGOSLAVIA
ITALY
Roma
Adriatic Sea
Tyrrhenian Sea
Ionian Sea
Aegean Sea
Mediterranean Sea
Black Sea
Istanbul
TURKEY
Caspian Sea
Aral'skoje More
PLATO UST'URT
KYZYLKUM
KARAKUMY
A S I A
SAYAN MTS.
ALTAI
Ozero Bajkal
MONGOLIA
GOBI
CHANGAJN NURUU
Sea of Okhotsk
OKHOTSK BASIN
POLUOSTROV KAMČATKA
OSTROV SACHALIN
Bering Sea
ALEUTIAN BASIN
ALEUTIAN ISLANDS
ALEUTIAN TRENCH
KURIL TRENCH
EMPEROR SEAMOUNT CHAIN
International Date Line
Pik Pobedy
Pik Kommunizma
TIEN SHAN
TALIMUPENDI
KUNLUNSHANMAI
C H I N A
TANGGULASHANMAI
HIMALAYAS
Mount Everest
PAMIR
HINDU KUSH
KARAKORAM RANGE
Godwin Austen
SYRIA
CYPRUS
ISRAEL
IRAQ
IRAN
Tehrān
DASHT-E KAVĪR
Zagros
Persian Gulf
SAUDI ARABIA
AN-NAFŪD
AL-QĀHIRAH
EGYPT
LIBYA
Red Sea
NUBIAN DESERT
SUDAN
CHAD
NIGER
Lake Chad
TIBESTI
Emi Koussi
ENNEDI
NIGERIA
Lagos
Gulf of Guinea
CEN. AFRICAN REPUBLIC
Congo
GABON
ZAIRE
Kinshasa
ANGOLA
ZAMBIA
Lake Kariba
RHODESIA
MOZAMBIQUE
Mozambique Channel
MADAGASCAR
MALAGASY REPUBLIC
BOTSWANA
KALAHARI DESERT
SOUTH WEST AFRICA
Johannesburg
SOUTH AFRICA
Cape Town
CAPE OF GOOD HOPE
DRAKENSBERG
ETHIOPIA
Addis Abeba
Ras Dashen
Gulf of Aden
SOMALIA
Lake Rudolf
Mount Elgon
Mount Kenya
Kilimanjaro
Lake Victoria
TANZANIA
Lake Tanganyika
Lake Nyasa
RIFT VALLEY
Arabian Sea
Gulf of Oman
Gulf of Kutch
Gulf of Cambay
BOMBAY
CALCUTTA
I N D I A
THAR DESERT
PAKISTAN
WESTERN GHATS
EASTERN GHATS
Bay of Bengal
CEYLON
ARABIAN BASIN
CARLSBERG RIDGE
SOMALI BASIN
SEYCHELLES
MID-INDIAN RIDGE
CENTRAL BASIN
INDIAN RIDGE
Equator
CHAGOS ARCHIPELAGO
MAURITIUS RIDGE
MASCARENE BASIN
Tropic of Capricorn
INDIAN OCEAN
WEST AUSTRALIAN BASIN
EAST INDIAN RIDGE
WEST INDIAN RIDGE
CROZET BASIN
MADAGASCAR BASIN
MADAGASCAR PLATEAU
MOZAMBIQUE PLATEAU
AGULHAS BASIN
CAPE BASIN
CAPE RISE
AMSTERDAM NATURALISTE RIDGE
ÎLE AMSTERDAM
ÎLE SAINT-PAUL
PRINCE EDWARD ISLANDS
ÎLES CROZET
ÎLES KERGUELEN
KERGUELEN GAUSSBERG RIDGE
McDONALD ISLANDS
ATLANTIC-INDIAN RIDGE
ATLANTIC-INDIAN BASIN
SOUTH INDIAN BASIN
AUSTRALIAN - ANTARCTIC RISE
BURMA
THAILAND
VIETNAM
CAMB.
Gulf of Siam
Andaman Sea
ANDAMAN BASIN
NICOBAR BASIN
MALAYSIA
Singapore
SUMATERA
BORNEO
South China Sea
SOUTH CHINA BASIN
PHILIPPINES
Philippine Sea
PHILIPPINE BASIN
Sulu Sea
Celebes Sea
CELEBES BASIN
SULAWESI
I N D O N E S I A
DJAKARTA
Laut Djawa
JAVA TRENCH
SUNDA
Yellow Sea
East China Sea
Sea of Japan
JAPAN BASIN
KOREA
JAPAN
TŌKYŌ
BEIJING
SHANGHAI
HONG KONG
Tropic of Cancer
PACIFIC OCEAN
MARIANA TRENCH
MARIANA BASIN
M I C R O N E S I A
WEST CAROLINE BASIN
EAST CAROLINE BASIN
NEW GUINEA
Arafura Sea
Timor Sea
Gulf of Carpentaria
Coral Sea
A U S T R A L I A
GREAT SANDY DESERT
GIBSON DESERT
GREAT VICTORIA DESERT
Lake Eyre
Perth
Sydney
Mount Kosciusko
GREAT DIVIDING RANGE
Great Australian Bight
SOUTH AUSTRALIAN BASIN
TASMANIA
Tasman Sea
TASMAN BASIN
NEW ZEALAND
NORTH ISLAND
SOUTH ISLAND
Mount Cook
SOLOMON ISLANDS
M E L A N E S I A
NEW HEBRIDES TRENCH
FIJI
Antarctic Circle
SHACKLETON ICE SHELF
WEST ICE SHELF
WILKES LAND
ENDERBY LAND
AMERICAN HIGHLAND
AMERY ICE SHELF
LAMBERT GLACIER
VICTORIA LAND
McMurdo Sound
Ross Sea
ROSS ICE SHELF
QUEEN MAUD MOUNTAINS
QUEEN MAUD LAND
A N T A R C T I C A
Copyright © by Rand McNally & Co.
Map prepared by Rand McNally & Co.
A-510000-764

Kilometers 0 1000 2000 3000 Km.

Statute Miles 0 1000 2000 3000 Mi.

One centimeter represents 750 kilometers.
One inch represents approximately 1200 miles.
Robinson Projection

Scale 1:75,000,000

The Ocean World

Dr. H. W. Menard, Scripps Institution of Oceanography, *Consultant*

The helpful assistance of Dr. Bruce C. Heezen of the Lamont-Doherty Geological Observatory and of the U.S. Naval Oceanographic Office in the preparation of this section must be gratefully acknowledged

Photographs of earth taken from space dramatize a salient fact: about three-fourths of the planet is covered by water. To be more precise, if all water bodies are counted, 77.2% of the earth's surface is water, with 71.2% being oceans and major seas. Long surrounded by mystery and myth, the oceans have played a vital role in shaping the destiny of man by influencing his settlement patterns, by offering routes of communications, and by providing food. While the impact on man appears most direct at the fringes of the sea, planetary water bodies play a decisive role in producing world climatic realms and thus affect the livelihood of man in virtually every part of the world. By the same token, ocean-influenced climates affect the patterns of growth of flora and fauna.

Despite a centuries-old preoccupation with the seas, man has only recently had the technology to explore the deeps, measure currents and temperatures, and chart the topography of the ocean floor. The vastness of the ocean world is such that despite new scientific tools, man's understanding of the seas still is puny. But every day sees new information added to a rapidly growing store of knowledge, and as a result important new theories have been advanced concerning the characteristics and origins, not only of the oceans, but also of the earth itself. Yet much remains to be done. In a world faced with dwindling resources, man is looking toward the oceans as an important supply of food and minerals. Scientific methods of raising and harvesting crops of fish and other marine life are being perfected. Efficient means for recovering known reserves of oil and mineral resources are being developed. One of the most dramatic results of deep-sea exploration has been the discovery of baseball-size nuggets of high-grade manganese lying on the ocean floor at great depths. It remains to be seen whether economic ways to gather these nodules can be developed. Without question, scientists must develop ways to exploit these resources without harming ecological balances.

Oceanographic research is also directed toward learning more about the seas' influence on climates, the mechanics of tidal movements, and how these and other elements of the sea can be controlled for man's benefit.

The following maps are intended to convey an impression of the physical nature of the world's sea floors, with the graphs and illustrations on the opposite page indicating some characteristics of the water envelope and of the nature of the sea bottom itself. From man's still-sketchy knowledge of the ocean environment some broad patterns of its physical form are emerging. Towering mountain ranges, vast canyons, broad plains, and a variety of physiographic features exceed in magnitude those found on the continents.

Scientific explorations of the last decade have revealed the existence of many distinctive features on the ocean floor, among them being a number of ridges. One of the most pronounced is the Mid-Atlantic Ridge, a lazy-S chain of mountains that bisects the Atlantic Ocean. A remarkable feature of such ridges is a trough that runs along the entire center, in effect producing twin ridge lines. Away from the center are a series of parallel and lower crests, while at right angles to them are numerous fracture zones. Measurements of temperatures and magnetism indicate that the troughs are younger in age than the paralleling ridges, whose ages increase with distance from the center. It is believed that the central troughs mark a line where molten materials from the earth's interior rise to the ocean floor where they form gigantic plates that move slowly apart. This theory suggests that continents are moving away from each other, having once been a single land mass in ancient times. The matching curves of the Atlantic shorelines of both South America and Africa have long given rise to such conjecture. The map below shows the world-wide distribution of these plates.

Where these subsea plates meet certain continental areas or island chains, they plunge downward to replenish the inner earth materials and form trenches of profound depths. Along the northern and western edge of the Pacific Ocean several lines of such gutters include some of the deepest known spots. Deep trenches also parallel the western coasts of Central and South America, the northern coast of Puerto Rico and the Virgin Islands, and other coastal areas.

Many other unique features have been identified. Great submarine canyons lead from the edges of continents. Seamounts rise miles above the ocean floor. Tablemounts are like seamounts, but culminate in plateau-like summits hundreds of feet below sea level. Continental shelves appear to be underwater extensions of land masses, and vary in shape from narrow fringes to broad plains. The deep floor of the sea itself shows a variety of characteristics. Muddy ooze, piles of rounded rock ("pillow" lava), sand, and coral formations are found in different locations.

With the accumulation of knowledge of the configuration and mechanics of the sea floor, more information about the characteristics of the sea itself is being added. Salinity, pressure, opacity, and temperature are studied to discover how and why they vary spatially and seasonally.

The scales and projections of the maps were selected to show major sea areas in the most optimal way. Thus scales of the Atlantic and Indian oceans are the same, with the Pacific Ocean being somewhat smaller. Coverage for the polar areas is at the same scale. Projections and dimensions maximize the water areas relative to land areas. In general, colors used are those thought to exist on the seafloors. For continental shelves or shallow inland seas, grayish green is used to correspond to terrigenous oozes, sediments washed from continental areas. In deeper parts of the oceans, calcareous oozes derived from the skeletons of marine life appear in various shades of white and the fine mud from land is red. In the Atlantic materials accumulate relatively rapidly, have a high iron content, and thus are a brighter red than elsewhere. Slower sedimentation in the Pacific and Indian oceans result in more manganese and darker colors. Undersea ridges are shown in black to suggest recent upwelling of molten rock. Small salt-and-pepper patches portray areas where manganese nodules are found. Around certain islands, white is used to show coral reefs. Land areas carry a generalized portrayal of continental land forms.

Colors otherwise do not coincide with specific depth zones, and differences in relief are conveyed through the technique of relief shading. The perspective of relief features is from directly above, so that the topmost part of, for example, a seamount corresponds to its actual geographic position.

World-Wide Distribution of Tectonic Plates

Credit: adapted from a drawing by Scripps Institution of Oceanography

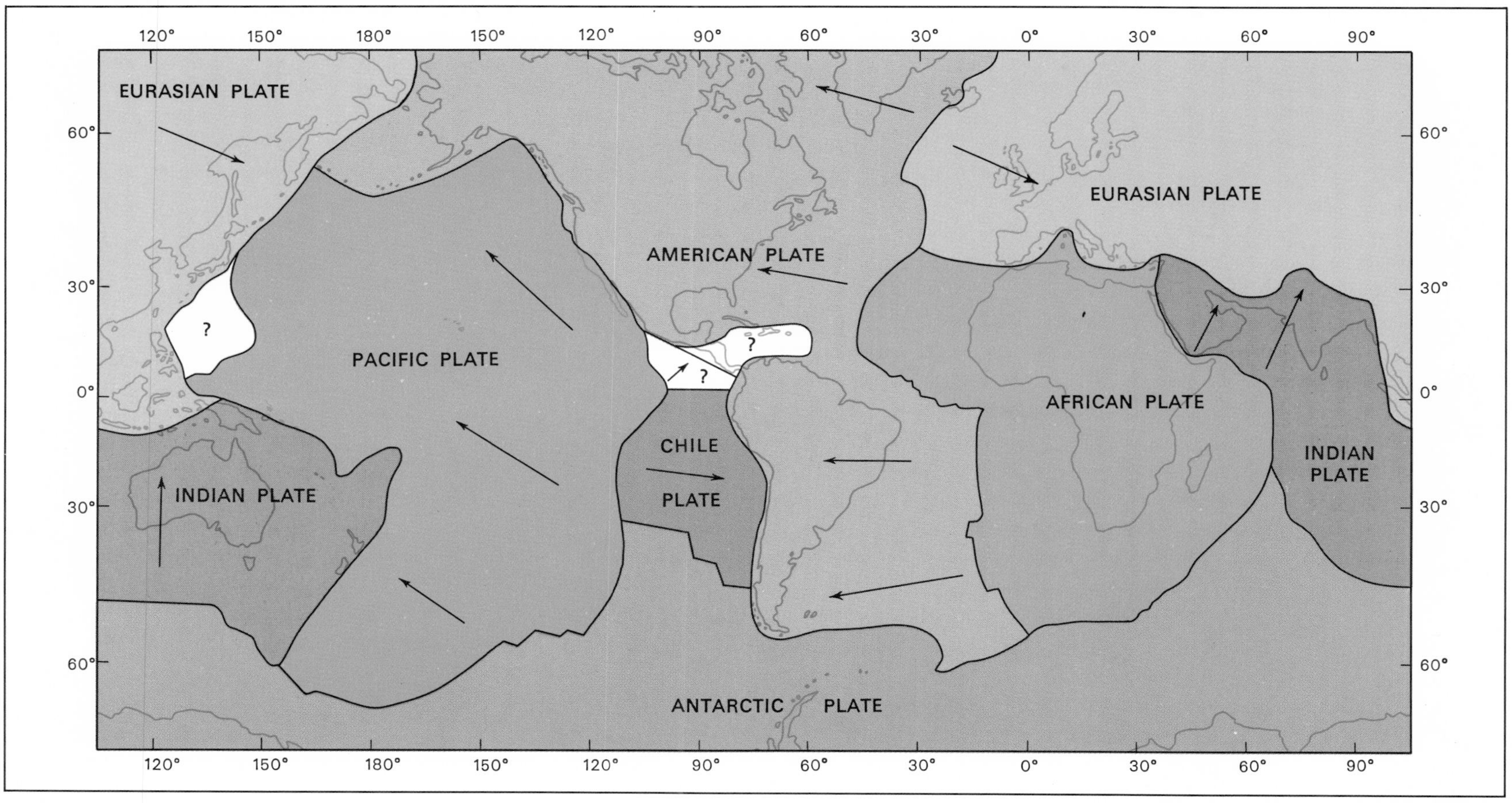
120°
150°
180°
150°
120°
90°
60°
30°
0°
30°
60°
90°
60°
30°
0°
30°
60°
EURASIAN PLATE
AMERICAN PLATE
EURASIAN PLATE
PACIFIC PLATE
?
?
?
AFRICAN PLATE
CHILE
PLATE
INDIAN PLATE
INDIAN
PLATE
ANTARCTIC PLATE

SEA-FLOOR TERMINOLOGY

This glossary should familiarize the reader with some of the important terms associated with undersea features. Because the development of terms describing sea-floor features is so recent, not all of them enjoy universal usage.

Abyssal Plain: a nearly flat area of the sea floor, smaller than a basin, and at a greater depth than surrounding features.

Basin: a depression of the sea floor usually of moderate or large extent.

Continental Shelf: a flat or gently sloping zone surrounding a landmass between the coast and the continental slope.

Continental Slope: a steep slope at the outer edge of the continental shelf.

Deep: the lowest recorded depth in a trench.

Fault: a fracture in the sea floor.

Fracture Zone: an extensive linear zone of irregular sea floor characterized by parallel faults, seamounts, ridges, and troughs.

Mid-Ocean Ridge: an extensive area of roughly parallel ridges and troughs, often crossed by fracture zones, with heights generally well above the surrounding sea floor. Example: Mid-Atlantic Ridge.

Ridge: a long narrow elevation of the sea floor with sides.

Seamount: an elevation rising 1,000 meters or more from the sea floor, and of limited areal extent at its summit. Several seamounts clustered together may be termed seamount chain, group, province, range, or line.

Tablemount: a seamount with a flat top (sometimes called a guyot).

Trench: a long, narrow, deep, steep-sided depression of the sea floor.

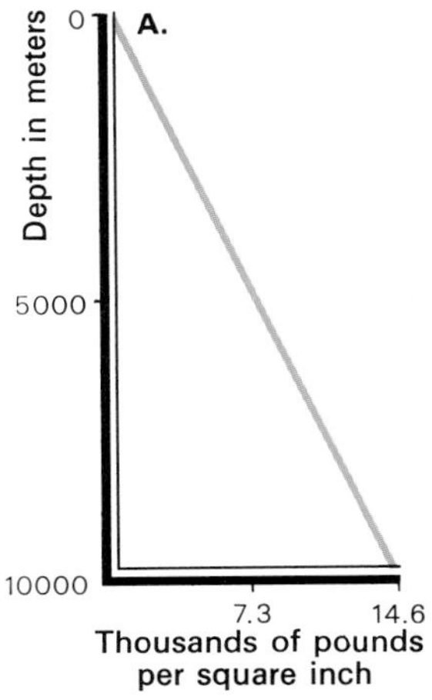
A.
Depth in meters
0
5000
10000
7.3
14.6
Thousands of pounds per square inch

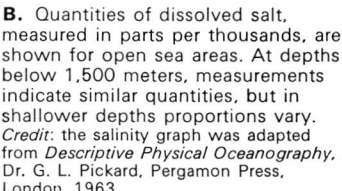

A. Pressure increases at a fairly constant rate with depth, although the rate is affected by salinity and temperature variations. At around 10,000 meters, corresponding to the deepest known spot in the ocean, the pressure is nearly 7 tons per square inch, or almost 1,000 times atmospheric pressures at sea level.

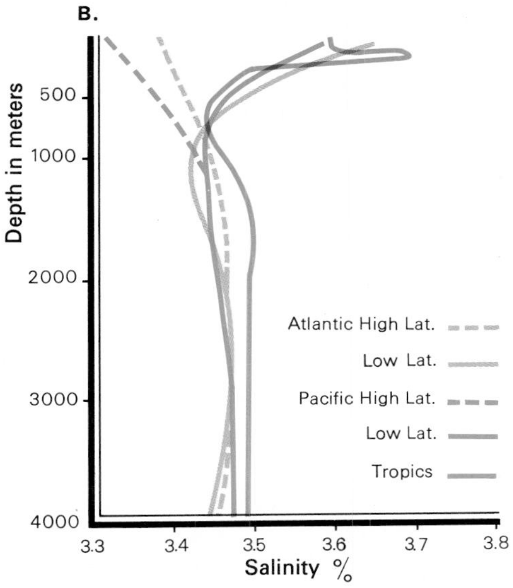
B.
Depth in meters
500
1000
2000
3000
4000
3.3
3.4
3.5
3.6
3.7
3.8
Salinity %
Atlantic High Lat.
Low Lat.
Pacific High Lat.
Low Lat.
Tropics

B. Quantities of dissolved salt, measured in parts per thousands, are shown for open sea areas. At depths below 1,500 meters, measurements indicate similar quantities, but in shallower depths proportions vary. *Credit*: the salinity graph was adapted from *Descriptive Physical Oceanography*, Dr. G. L. Pickard, Pergamon Press, London, 1963.

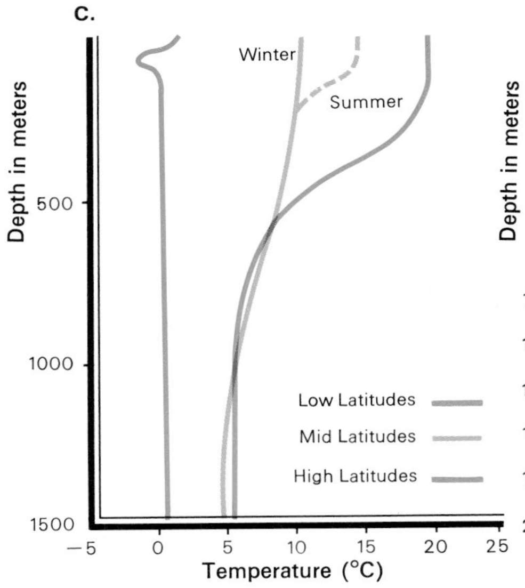
C.
Winter
Summer
Depth in meters
500
1000
1500
Low Latitudes
Mid Latitudes
High Latitudes
−5
0
5
10
15
20
25
Temperature (°C)

C. Temperatures in the open ocean show a range of some 17° C (63° F) on the surface, and even more at a depth of 100 meters or so, where, near polar regions, subsurface water can be a few degrees below 0° C (32° F). Because of salt content, ocean water does not freeze until temperatures of —10° C (14° F) are reached. *Credit*: the temperature graph was adapted from *Descriptive Physical Oceanography*, Dr. G. L. Pickard, Pergamon Press, London, 1963.

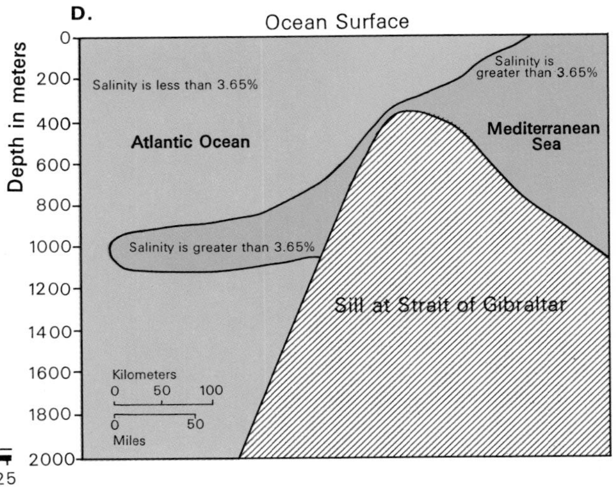
D.
Ocean Surface
Depth in meters
0
200
400
600
800
1000
1200
1400
1600
1800
2000
Salinity is less than 3.65%
Salinity is greater than 3.65%
Atlantic Ocean
Mediterranean Sea
Salinity is greater than 3.65%
Sill at Strait of Gibraltar
Kilometers
0 50 100
0 50
Miles

D. Because of high evaporation rates in the Mediterranean Sea, waters there are more saline than in the Atlantic Ocean. Thus, the denser Mediterranean waters which slip over the sill at the Strait of Gibraltar extend seaward into the Atlantic as a tongue, hundreds of meters below sea level. *Credit:* the illustration is adapted from *Geographie der Atlantischen Ozeans*, G. Schott, Verlag Boysen, Hamburg, 1942.

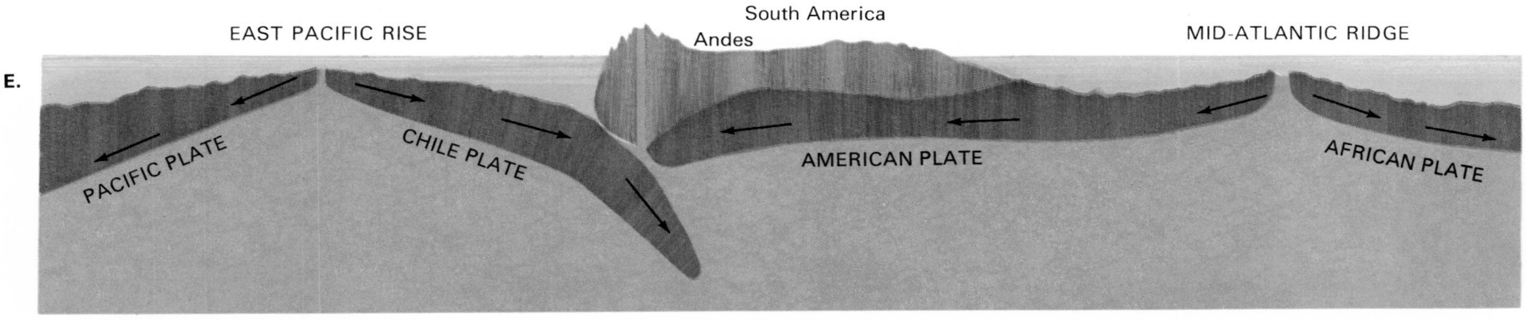
E.
EAST PACIFIC RISE
South America
Andes
MID-ATLANTIC RIDGE
PACIFIC PLATE
CHILE PLATE
AMERICAN PLATE
AFRICAN PLATE

E. A diagram of the earth's crust, including part of South America shows the mechanics of plate tectonics. Molten rock wells up to the center of mid-ocean ridges, and adds new material to plates that slowly move apart carrying land masses with them. Colliding plates may build volcanic mountains and deep trenches. *Credit*: adapted from an illustration by Dr. P. Vogt, U.S. Naval Oceanographic Office.

a. National Park Service

b. Johns Hopkins Press

c. U.S. Naval Oceanographic Office

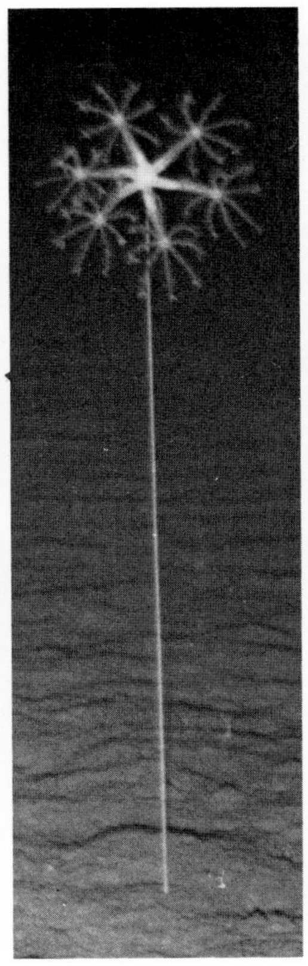

d. W. Jahn, U.S. Naval Oceanographic Office

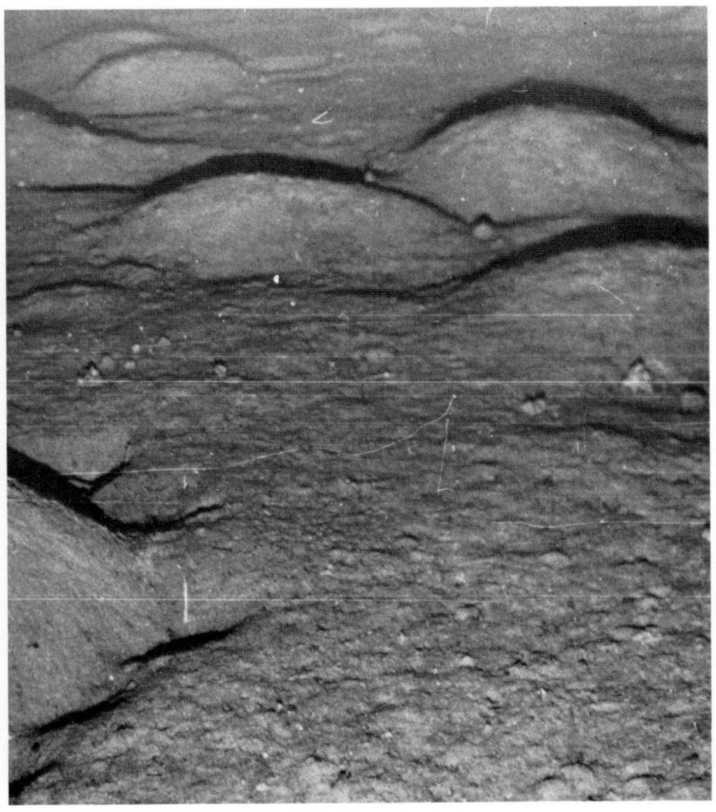

e. U.S. Naval Oceanographic Office

a. Where seas are shallow, filtering sunlight permits a rich variety of fish, coral, and other animal life. Often showing bright colors, sea life here produces a beautiful ocean world.

b. One of the results of deep-sea exploration is the discovery of widespread carpets of manganese nodules lying on the sea floor. Despite the high ore content, no economical method for recovery has been devised.

c. Molten rock issuing from deep water crevasses cools to form pillow lava. Found on or near underwater mountain chains, pillow lava is associated with activity that causes sea-floor spreading.

d. This deep-sea animal is related to living coral and was photographed at a depth of 5,300 meters on the sea bottom west of the African coast. It is approximately one meter in length and with a bulb-like foot imbedded in the soft-mud bottom, its tentacles capture food and pass it to its central mouth.

e. These mounds, found at a depth of 3,510 meters in the eastern Atlantic, are thought to be made by a bottom-dwelling animal that has yet to be photographed.

Atlantic Ocean Floor

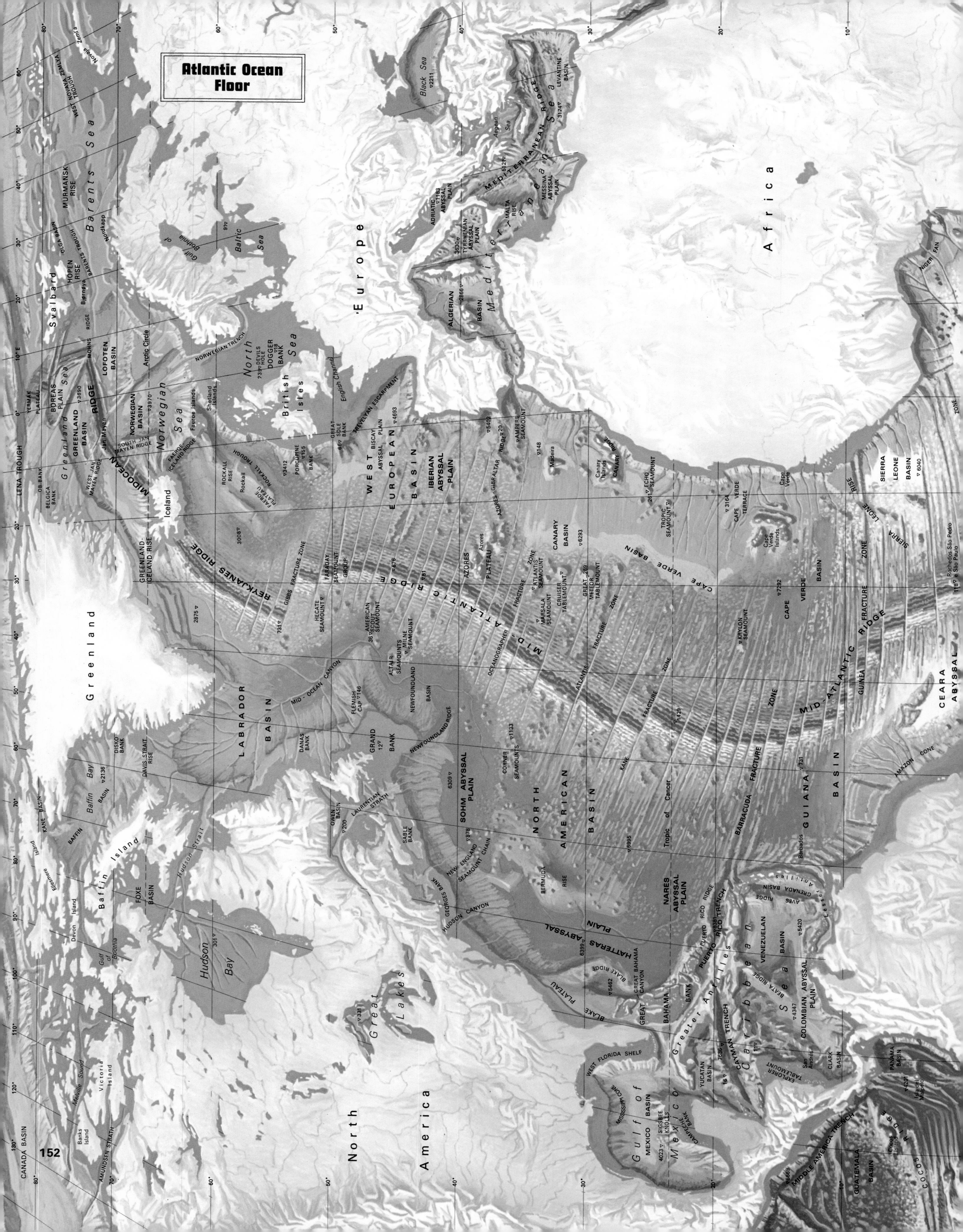

Europe
Africa
Greenland
North America
Iceland
British Isles
Svalbard
Barents Sea
Norwegian Sea
Greenland Sea
North Sea
Baltic Sea
Gulf of Bothnia
Black Sea
Aegean Sea
Mediterranean Sea
Hudson Bay
Hudson Strait
Baffin Bay
Baffin Island
Great Lakes
Gulf of Mexico
Caribbean Sea
Greater Antilles
Lesser Antilles
Arctic Circle
Tropic of Cancer
English Channel
Faeroe Islands
Shetland Islands
Madeira
Azores
Canary Islands
Cape Verde Islands
Bermuda
Barbados
MID-ATLANTIC RIDGE
REYKJANES RIDGE
MIDOCEAN RIDGE
LABRADOR BASIN
NORTH AMERICAN BASIN
WEST EUROPEAN BASIN
IBERIAN ABYSSAL PLAIN
CANARY BASIN
CAPE VERDE BASIN
GUIANA BASIN
SIERRA LEONE BASIN
CEARA ABYSSAL
SOHM ABYSSAL PLAIN
HATTERAS ABYSSAL PLAIN
NARES ABYSSAL PLAIN
NORWEGIAN BASIN
LOFOTEN BASIN
GREENLAND BASIN
BOREAS PLAIN
ALGERIAN BASIN
TYRRHENIAN ABYSSAL PLAIN
ADRIATIC ABYSSAL PLAIN
MESSINA ABYSSAL PLAIN
LEVANTINE BASIN
MEDITERRANEAN RIDGE
VENEZUELAN BASIN
COLOMBIAN ABYSSAL PLAIN
YUCATAN BASIN
CAYMAN TRENCH
PUERTO RICO TRENCH
MIDDLE AMERICA TRENCH
GUATEMALA BASIN
MEXICO BASIN
SIGSBEE KNOLLS
MISSISSIPPI CONE
WEST FLORIDA SHELF
BLAKE PLATEAU
BLAKE RIDGE
GREAT BAHAMA CANYON
GREAT BAHAMA BANK
NEW ENGLAND SEAMOUNT CHAIN
HUDSON CANYON
GEORGES BANK
SABLE BANK
LAURENTIAN STRATH
GRAND BANK
FLEMISH CAP
NEWFOUNDLAND RIDGE
NEWFOUNDLAND BASIN
MID-OCEAN CANYON
GIBBS FRACTURE ZONE
OCEANOGRAPHER FRACTURE ZONE
ATLANTIS FRACTURE ZONE
KANE FRACTURE ZONE
BARRACUDA FRACTURE ZONE
GUINEA FRACTURE ZONE
AZORES PLATEAU
AZORES GIBRALTAR RIDGE
AMPERE SEAMOUNT
GREAT METEOR TABLEMOUNT
CRUISER TABLEMOUNT
CORNER SEAMOUNTS
ROCKALL TROUGH
ROCKALL RISE
PORCUPINE BANK
GREAT SOLE BANK
TREVELYAN ESCARPMENT
BISCAY ABYSSAL PLAIN
FAEROE ICELAND RIDGE
GREENLAND ICELAND RISE
JAN MAYEN
NORWEGIAN TRENCH
DOGGER BANK
DAVIS STRAIT RISE
DISKO BANK
AMAZON CONE
NIGER FAN
CAPE VERDE TERRACE
TROPIC SEAMOUNT
ECHO SEAMOUNT
KRYLON SEAMOUNT
SIERRA LEONE RISE
Rochedos São Pedro e São Paulo
AVES RIDGE
BEATA RIDGE
GRENADA BASIN
FOXE BASIN
KANE BASIN
LENA TROUGH
CANADA BASIN
AMUNDSEN STRATH
COCOS RIDGE

South America
Antarctica
Antarctica
Pacific
Ocean
PERU BASIN
PERU - CHILE TRENCH
NAZCA RIDGE
SALA Y GOMEZ RIDGE
EASTER ISLAND FRACTURE ZONE
MERRIAM SPUR
Islas San Ambrosio
Isla San Felix
CHILE RISE
Islas Juan Fernandez
GIFFORD SEAMOUNT
MORNINGTON ABYSSAL PLAIN
SOUTHEAST PACIFIC
BELLINGSHAUSEN ABYSSAL PLAIN
BASIN
Bellingshausen Sea
Amundsen Sea
Peter I Island
Atol das Rocas
Fernando de Noronha
PERNAMBUCO ABYSSAL PLAIN
BRAZIL BASIN
STOCKS SEAMOUNT
GROLL SEAMOUNT
HOTSPUR SEAMOUNT
TRINIDAD SEAMOUNT LINE
Ilhas Martim Vaz
COLUMBIA SEAMOUNT
BROMLEY PLATEAU (RIO GRANDE RISE)
GARNET BANK
ARGENTINE ABYSSAL PLAIN
ARGENTINE BASIN
FALKLAND PLATEAU
FALKLAND FRACTURE ZONE
Falkland Islands
FALKLAND TROUGH
SCOTIA (SOUTH GEORGIA RIDGE) RIDGE
BURDWOOD BANK
Cabo de Hornos
WEST SCOTIA BASIN
South Georgia
EAST SCOTIA BASIN
SCOTIA RIDGE
SOUTH SANDWICH TRENCH
METEOR DEEP 8428
South Sandwich Islands
South Orkney Islands
South Shetland Islands
Larsen Ice Shelf
WEST ATLANTIC - INDIAN BASIN
BARTH SEAMOUNT
WEDDELL ABYSSAL PLAIN
Weddell Sea
Ronne Ice Shelf
Filchner Ice Shelf
CHAIN FRACTURE ZONE
GUINEA RISE
Ascension Island
St. Helena
MID-ATLANTIC RIDGE
Tropic of Capricorn
WALVIS RIDGE
EWING SEAMOUNT
VALDIVIA SEAMOUNT
ANGOLA BASIN
CONGO CANYON
VEMA SEAMOUNT
WÜST SEAMOUNT
CAPE BASIN
Tristan da Cunha
Gough Island
ZENKER SEAMOUNT
DISCOVERY TABLEMOUNT
HERDMAN SEAMOUNT
MERZ SEAMOUNT
METEOR SEAMOUNT
SPIESS SEAMOUNT
Bouvetøya
ATLANTIC-INDIAN RIDGE
CAPE RISE
AGULHAS BANK
AFRICANA SEAMOUNT
WYANDOT SEAMOUNT
NATAL SEAMOUNT
SCHMIDT-OTT SEAMOUNT
AGULHAS PLATEAU
AGULHAS BASIN
MOZAMBIQUE FRACTURE ZONE
PRINCE EDWARD FRACTURE ZONE
Prince Edward Islands
OB TABLEMOUNT
LENA TABLEMOUNT
ENDERBY ABYSSAL PLAIN
ATLANTIC-INDIAN BASIN
GUNNERUS BANK
MAUD SEAMOUNT
Antarctic Circle
4839
329
8066
5170
4876
5240
500
6537
6119
5754
5266
109
6212
2310
5769
84
2330
5574
6060
514
545
1531
411
5538
2310
315
560
413
5865
6972
247
840
4830
677
Kilometers 0 200 400 600 800 1000 Km
Statute Miles 0 200 400 600 800 1000 Mi
Scale 1:31,000,000 at Equator
One centimeter represents 310 kilometers
One inch represents approximately 500 miles
Depths in meters
Modified Cylindrical Projection

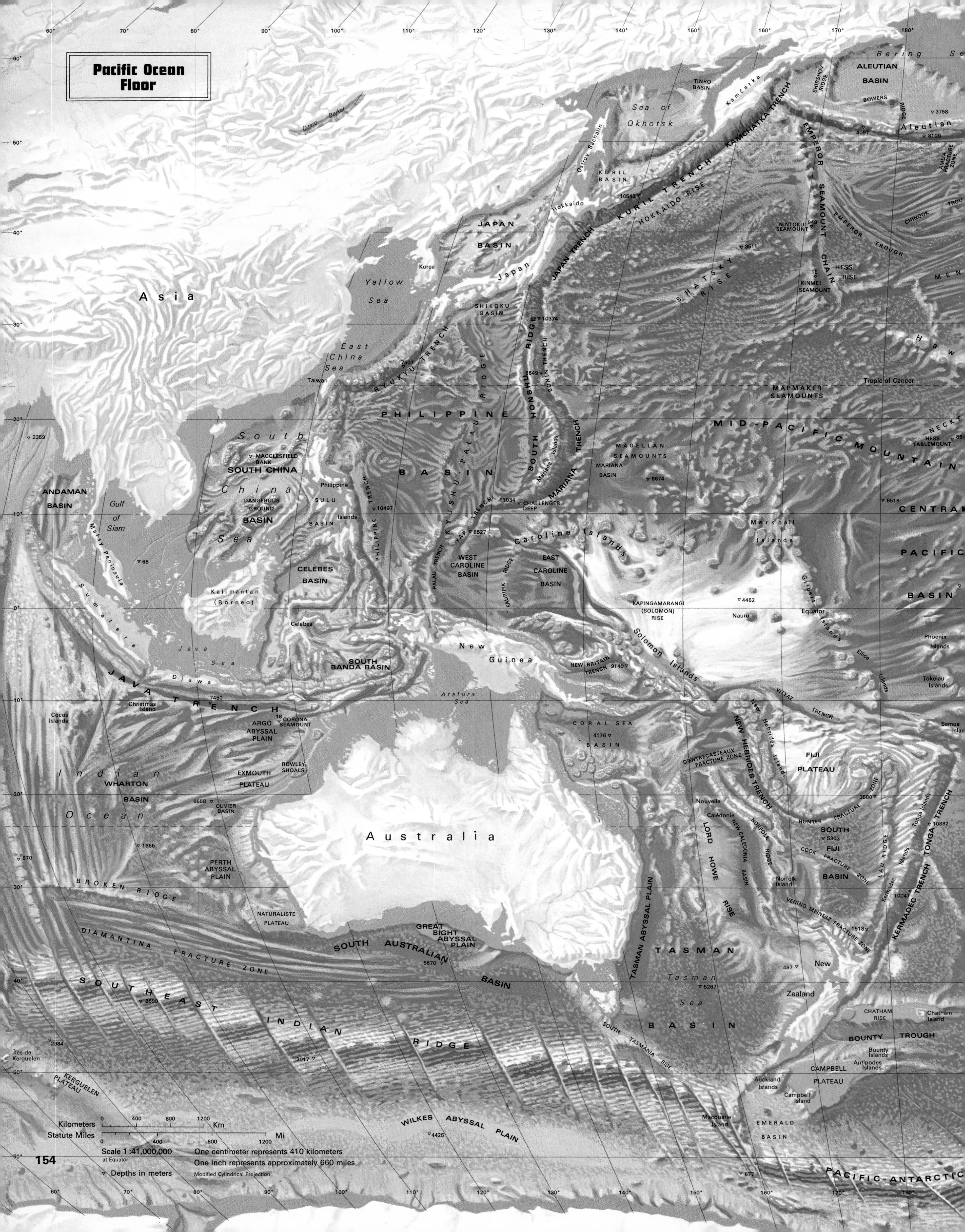
Pacific Ocean Floor
Asia
Ozero Bajkal
Sea of Okhotsk
Ostrov Sachalin
Kamčatka
TINRO BASIN
ALEUTIAN BASIN
SHIRSHOV RIDGE
BOWERS RIDGE
Bering Sea
Aleutian
KURIL BASIN
Hokkaido
KURIL TRENCH
KAMCHATKA TRENCH
HOKKAIDO RISE
EMPEROR SEAMOUNT CHAIN
EMPEROR TROUGH
CHINOOK
NINTOKU SEAMOUNT
HESS RISE
KINMEI SEAMOUNT
JAPAN BASIN
Korea
Japan
JAPAN TRENCH
SHATSKY RISE
Yellow Sea
SHIKOKU BASIN
East China Sea
Taiwan
RYUKYU TRENCH
KYUSHU-PALAU RIDGE
SOUTH HONSHU RIDGE
BONIN TRENCH
PHILIPPINE BASIN
Mariana Islands
MARIANA TRENCH
MAPMAKER SEAMOUNTS
Tropic of Cancer
MID-PACIFIC MOUNTAINS
HESS TABLEMOUNT
MAGELLAN SEAMOUNTS
MARIANA BASIN
CHALLENGER DEEP
South China Sea
MACCLESFIELD BANK
SOUTH CHINA BASIN
DANGEROUS GROUND
ANDAMAN BASIN
Gulf of Siam
Malay Peninsula
Philippine Islands
SULU BASIN
PHILIPPINE TRENCH
YAP TRENCH
PALAU TRENCH
WEST CAROLINE BASIN
EAST CAROLINE BASIN
EAURIPIK RIDGE
Caroline Islands
Marshall Islands
CENTRAL PACIFIC BASIN
CELEBES BASIN
Kalimantan (Borneo)
Sumatera
Celebes
KAPINGAMARANGI (SOLOMON) RISE
Nauru
Gilbert Islands
Equator
Java Sea
New Guinea
SOUTH BANDA BASIN
NEW BRITAIN TRENCH
Solomon Islands
Ellice Islands
Phoenix Islands
Tokelau Islands
Djawa
JAVA TRENCH
Christmas Island
Cocos Islands
Arafura Sea
ARGO ABYSSAL PLAIN
CORONA SEAMOUNT
CORAL SEA BASIN
VITYAZ TRENCH
New Hebrides Islands
NEW HEBRIDES TRENCH
D'ENTRECASTEAUX FRACTURE ZONE
FIJI PLATEAU
Samoa Islands
Indian Ocean
WHARTON BASIN
EXMOUTH PLATEAU
ROWLEY SHOALS
CUVIER BASIN
Australia
Nouvelle Calédonie
LORD HOWE RISE
NEW CALEDONIA BASIN
NORFOLK RIDGE
HUNTER FRACTURE ZONE
SOUTH FIJI BASIN
COOK FRACTURE ZONE
LAU RIDGE
Tonga Islands
TONGA TRENCH
Kermadec Islands
KERMADEC TRENCH
Norfolk Island
PERTH ABYSSAL PLAIN
BROKEN RIDGE
VENING MEINESZ FRACTURE ZONE
NATURALISTE PLATEAU
GREAT BIGHT ABYSSAL PLAIN
SOUTH AUSTRALIAN BASIN
TASMAN ABYSSAL PLAIN
TASMAN BASIN
Tasman Sea
New Zealand
DIAMANTINA FRACTURE ZONE
SOUTHEAST INDIAN RIDGE
SOUTH TASMANIA RISE
CHATHAM RISE
Chatham Island
BOUNTY TROUGH
Bounty Islands
Antipodes Islands
CAMPBELL PLATEAU
Auckland Islands
Campbell Island
Îles de Kerguelen
KERGUELEN PLATEAU
WILKES ABYSSAL PLAIN
Macquarie Island
EMERALD BASIN
PACIFIC-ANTARCTIC
Kilometers 0 400 800 1200 Km
Statute Miles 0 400 800 1200 Mi
Scale 1:41,000,000 at Equator
One centimeter represents 410 kilometers
One inch represents approximately 660 miles
Depths in meters
Modified Cylindrical Projection

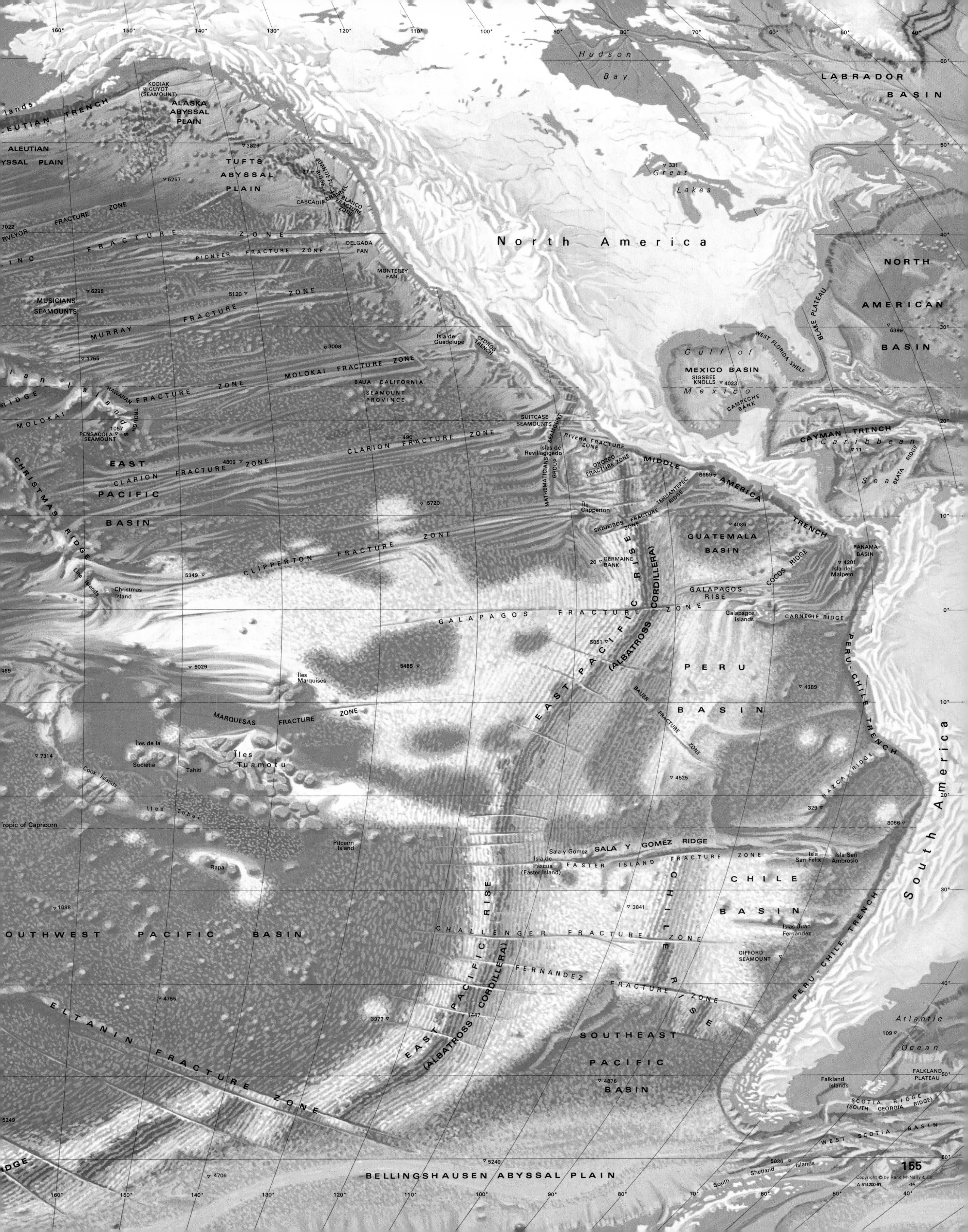
Hudson Bay
LABRADOR BASIN
KODIAK GUYOT (SEAMOUNT)
ALASKA ABYSSAL PLAIN
ALEUTIAN TRENCH
ALEUTIAN ABYSSAL PLAIN
TUFTS ABYSSAL PLAIN
JUAN DE FUCA RIDGE
CASCADIA CHANNEL
BLANCO FRACTURE ZONE
Great Lakes
North America
SURVEYOR FRACTURE ZONE
MENDOCINO FRACTURE ZONE
PIONEER FRACTURE ZONE
DELGADA FAN
MONTEREY FAN
NORTH AMERICAN BASIN
BLAKE PLATEAU
MUSICIANS SEAMOUNTS
MURRAY FRACTURE ZONE
Isla de Guadelupe
CEDROS TRENCH
WEST FLORIDA SHELF
Gulf of Mexico
MEXICO BASIN
SIGSBEE KNOLLS
CAMPECHE BANK
MOLOKAI FRACTURE ZONE
BAJA CALIFORNIA SEAMOUNT PROVINCE
HAWAIIAN FRACTURE ZONE
Hawaiian Islands
HAWAIIAN RIDGE
HAWAIIAN TROUGH
PENSACOLA SEAMOUNT
SUITCASE SEAMOUNTS
MOLOKAI
CLARION FRACTURE ZONE
RIVERA FRACTURE ZONE
Islas de Revillagigedo
MATHEMATICIANS SEAMOUNT GROUP
OROZCO FRACTURE ZONE
MIDDLE AMERICA TRENCH
CAYMAN TRENCH
Caribbean Sea
BEATA RIDGE
EAST PACIFIC BASIN
CHRISTMAS RIDGE
Île Clipperton
TEHUANTEPEC RIDGE
SIQUEIROS FRACTURE ZONE
GUATEMALA BASIN
PANAMA BASIN
COCOS RIDGE
Isla del Malpelo
CLIPPERTON FRACTURE ZONE
GERMAINE BANK
Line Islands
Christmas Island
GALAPAGOS RISE
Galapagos Islands
CARNEGIE RIDGE
GALAPAGOS FRACTURE ZONE
EAST PACIFIC RISE (ALBATROSS CORDILLERA)
PERU BASIN
PERU-CHILE TRENCH
Îles Marquises
MARQUESAS FRACTURE ZONE
BAUER FRACTURE ZONE
Îles de la Société
Tahiti
Îles Tuamotu
Cook Islands
Îles Tubai
NAZCA RIDGE
Tropic of Capricorn
Pitcairn Island
SALA Y GOMEZ RIDGE
Sala y Gomez
Isla de Pascua (Easter Island)
EASTER ISLAND FRACTURE ZONE
Isla San Felix
Isla San Ambrosio
Rapa
CHILE BASIN
CHILE RISE
South America
SOUTHWEST PACIFIC BASIN
CHALLENGER FRACTURE ZONE
Islas Juan Fernandez
GIFFORD SEAMOUNT
FERNANDEZ FRACTURE ZONE
Atlantic Ocean
ELTANIN FRACTURE ZONE
SOUTHEAST PACIFIC BASIN
Falkland Islands
FALKLAND PLATEAU
SCOTIA RIDGE (SOUTH GEORGIA RIDGE)
WEST SCOTIA BASIN
South Shetland Islands
BELLINGSHAUSEN ABYSSAL PLAIN
160° 150° 140° 130° 120° 110° 100° 90° 80° 70° 60° 50° 40°
60° 50° 40° 30° 20° 10° 0° 10° 20° 30° 40° 50° 60°
3828 5257 7022 6298 5120 1765 3008 1057 490 4809 5720 6669 11 4086 4201 20 5349 5851 5485 5029 4389 7314 4525 329 8066 3841 1088 4755 3977 1447 109 4876 5249 5240 4706 5036 331 4023 6399

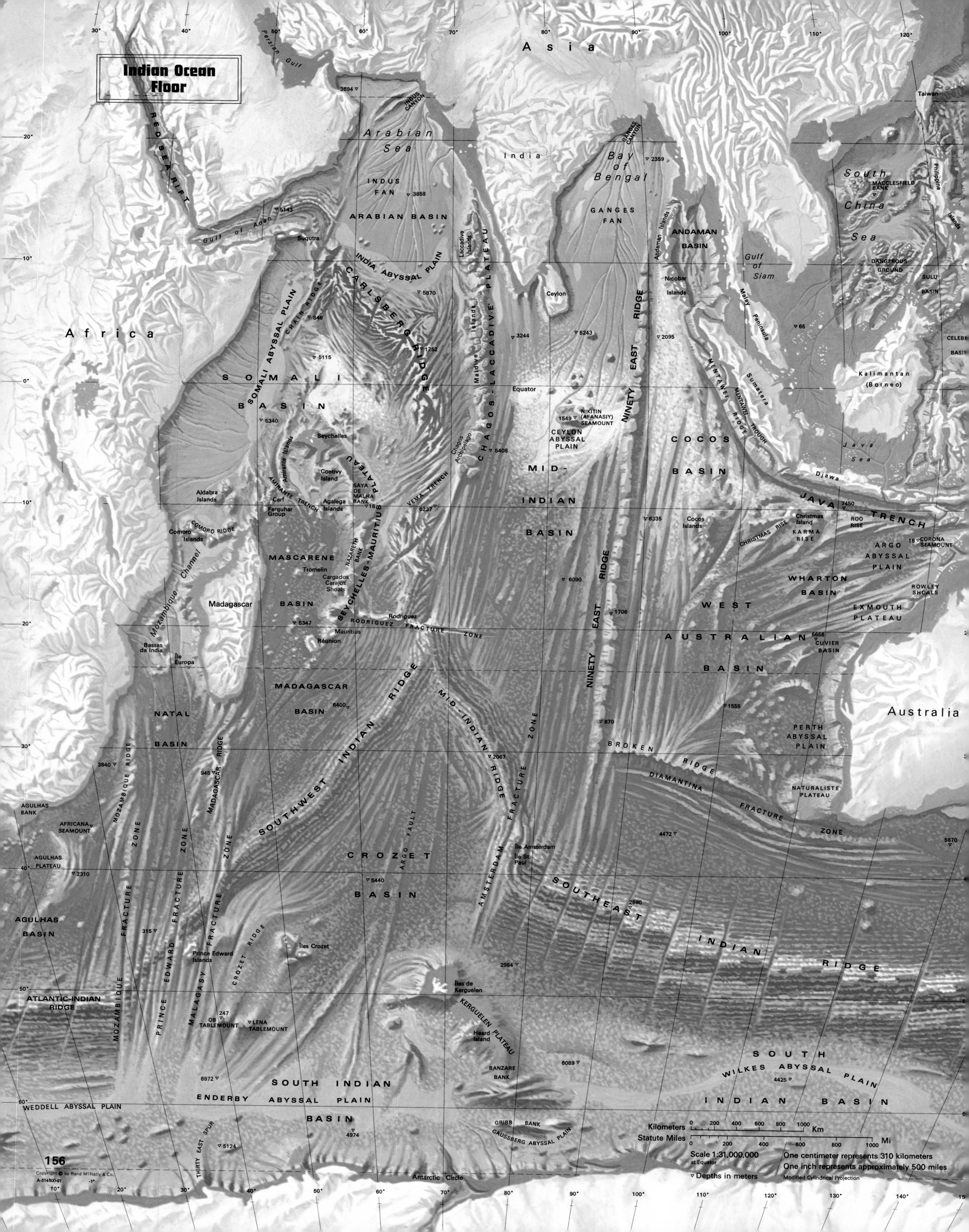
Indian Ocean Floor
Asia
Africa
India
Australia
Persian Gulf
Arabian Sea
Bay of Bengal
Gulf of Aden
Gulf of Siam
South China Sea
Java Sea
Mozambique Channel
RED SEA RIFT
INDUS CANYON
GANGES CANYON
INDUS FAN
GANGES FAN
ARABIAN BASIN
INDIA ABYSSAL PLAIN
CARLSBERG RIDGE
CHAIN RIDGE
SOMALI ABYSSAL PLAIN
SOMALI BASIN
CHAGOS-LACCADIVE PLATEAU
Lacadive Islands
Maldive Islands
Chagos Archipelago
VEMA TRENCH
Equator
NIKITIN (AFANASIY) SEAMOUNT
CEYLON ABYSSAL PLAIN
MID-INDIAN BASIN
NINETY EAST RIDGE
ANDAMAN BASIN
Andaman Islands
Nicobar Islands
Ceylon
Suqutra
Malay Peninsula
Sumatera
MENTAWEI RIDGE
MENTAWEI TROUGH
COCOS BASIN
Cocos Islands
Djawa
JAVA TRENCH
Christmas Island
CHRISTMAS RISE
KARMA RISE
ROO RISE
CORONA SEAMOUNT
ARGO ABYSSAL PLAIN
WHARTON BASIN
ROWLEY SHOALS
EXMOUTH PLATEAU
CUVIER BASIN
WEST AUSTRALIAN BASIN
PERTH ABYSSAL PLAIN
NATURALISTE PLATEAU
BROKEN RIDGE
DIAMANTINA FRACTURE ZONE
Taiwan
MACCLESFIELD BANK
DANGEROUS GROUND
SULU BASIN
Philippine Islands
CELEBES BASIN
Kalimantan (Borneo)
Seychelles
Amirante Islands
AMIRANTE TRENCH
Coetivy Island
SAYA DE MALHA BANK
Agalega Islands
Farquhar Group
Cerf
Aldabra Islands
Comoro Islands
COMORO RIDGE
MASCARENE PLATEAU
MASCARENE BASIN
NAZARETH BANK
SEYCHELLES-MAURITIUS PLATEAU
Tromelin
Cargados Carajos Shoals
Madagascar
Rodriguez
RODRIGUEZ FRACTURE ZONE
Mauritius
Réunion
Bassas da India
Île Europa
MADAGASCAR BASIN
NATAL BASIN
MADAGASCAR RIDGE
MOZAMBIQUE RIDGE
SOUTHWEST INDIAN RIDGE
MID-INDIAN RIDGE
FRACTURE ZONE
AGULHAS BANK
AFRICANA SEAMOUNT
AGULHAS PLATEAU
AGULHAS BASIN
MOZAMBIQUE FRACTURE ZONE
PRINCE EDWARD FRACTURE ZONE
MALAGASY FRACTURE ZONE
ARGO FAULT
CROZET BASIN
AMSTERDAM FRACTURE ZONE
Île Amsterdam
Île St. Paul
SOUTHEAST INDIAN RIDGE
Prince Edward Islands
CROZET RIDGE
Îles Crozet
ATLANTIC-INDIAN RIDGE
OB TABLEMOUNT
LENA TABLEMOUNT
Îles de Kerguelen
KERGUELEN PLATEAU
Heard Island
BANZARE BANK
SOUTH INDIAN BASIN
ENDERBY ABYSSAL PLAIN
WEDDELL ABYSSAL PLAIN
THIRTY EAST SPUR
GRIBB BANK
GAUSSBERG ABYSSAL PLAIN
SOUTH INDIAN BASIN
WILKES ABYSSAL PLAIN
Antarctic Circle
3694
5143
3858
5870
846
1752
5115
5340
3244
5243
2359
2095
65
1549
5408
6237
18
6335
7450
6090
1706
6658
5347
6400
1555
870
2067
3840
945
2310
4472
5670
5440
2690
315
2984
247
6972
6089
4425
4974
5124
Kilometers 0 200 400 600 800 1000 Km
Statute Miles 0 200 400 600 800 1000 Mi
Scale 1:31,000,000 at Equator
One centimeter represents 310 kilometers
One inch represents approximately 500 miles
▽ Depths in meters
Modified Cylindrical Projection
A-514800-91 -1^-

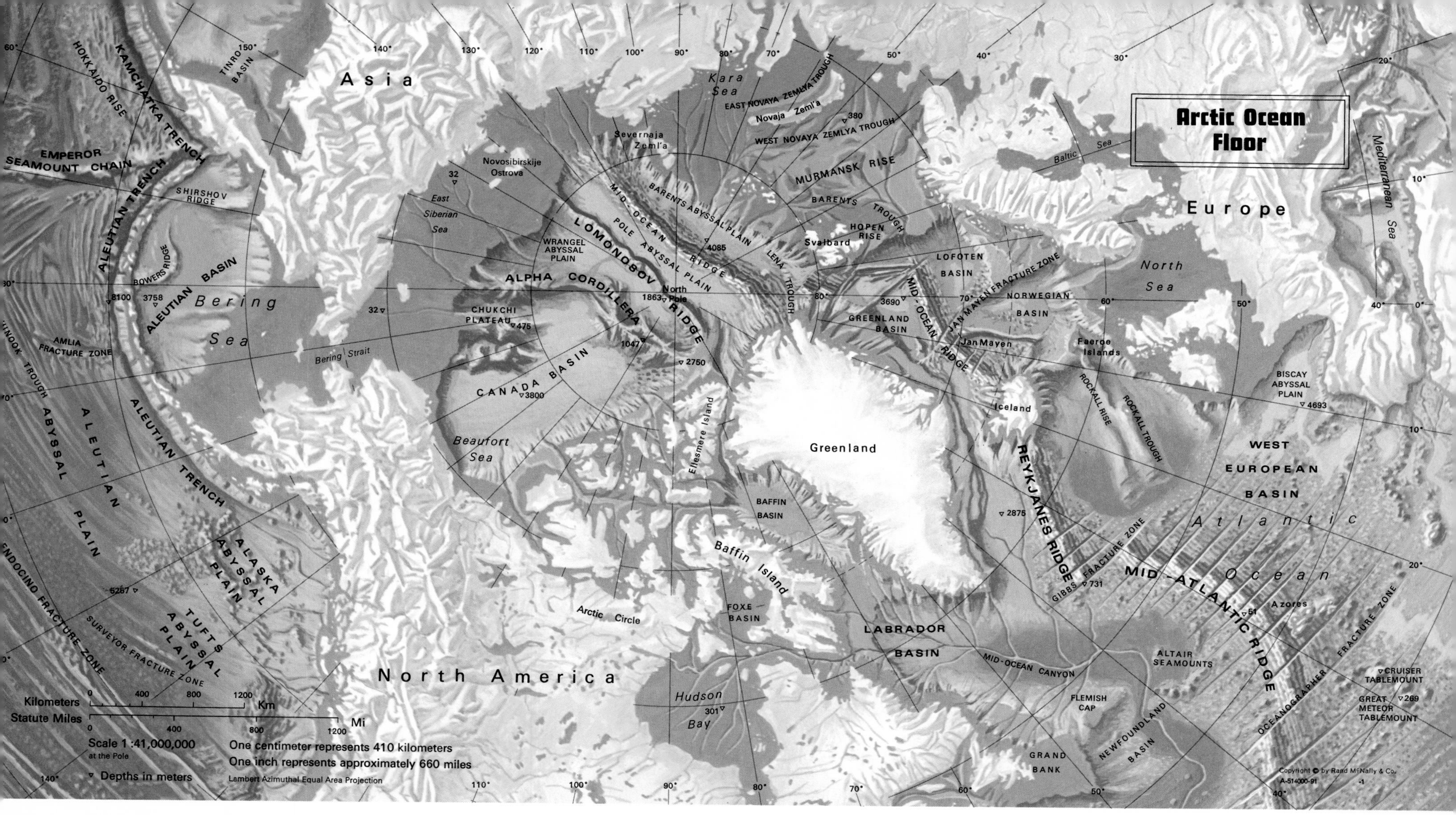
Arctic Ocean Floor
Asia
Europe
North America
Greenland
Kara Sea
Novaja Zeml'a
Severnaja Zeml'a
Novosibirskije Ostrova
East Siberian Sea
Bering Sea
Bering Strait
Beaufort Sea
Baltic Sea
North Sea
Mediterranean Sea
Hudson Bay
Baffin Island
Ellesmere Island
Svalbard
Iceland
Jan Mayen
Faeroe Islands
Azores
Arctic Circle
North Pole
KAMCHATKA TRENCH
HOKKAIDO RISE
TINRO BASIN
EMPEROR SEAMOUNT CHAIN
ALEUTIAN TRENCH
SHIRSHOV RIDGE
BOWERS RIDGE
ALEUTIAN BASIN
AMLIA FRACTURE ZONE
ALEUTIAN ABYSSAL PLAIN
ALASKA ABYSSAL PLAIN
TUFTS ABYSSAL PLAIN
SURVEYOR FRACTURE ZONE
MENDOCINO FRACTURE ZONE
CHUKCHI PLATEAU
CANADA BASIN
ALPHA CORDILLERA
WRANGEL ABYSSAL PLAIN
LOMONOSOV RIDGE
POLE ABYSSAL PLAIN
MID-OCEAN RIDGE
BARENTS ABYSSAL PLAIN
EAST NOVAYA ZEMLYA TROUGH
WEST NOVAYA ZEMLYA TROUGH
MURMANSK RISE
BARENTS TROUGH
HOPEN RISE
LENA TROUGH
LOFOTEN BASIN
JAN MAYEN FRACTURE ZONE
NORWEGIAN BASIN
GREENLAND BASIN
MID-OCEAN RIDGE
ROCKALL RISE
ROCKALL TROUGH
BISCAY ABYSSAL PLAIN
WEST EUROPEAN BASIN
REYKJANES RIDGE
GIBBS FRACTURE ZONE
MID-ATLANTIC RIDGE
Atlantic Ocean
BAFFIN BASIN
FOXE BASIN
LABRADOR BASIN
MID-OCEAN CANYON
ALTAIR SEAMOUNTS
CRUISER TABLEMOUNT
GREAT METEOR TABLEMOUNT
OCEANOGRAPHER FRACTURE ZONE
FLEMISH CAP
NEWFOUNDLAND BASIN
GRAND BANK
Kilometers 0 400 800 1200 Km
Statute Miles 0 400 800 1200 Mi
Scale 1:41,000,000 at the Pole
One centimeter represents 410 kilometers
One inch represents approximately 660 miles
Depths in meters
Lambert Azimuthal Equal Area Projection
Copyright © by Rand McNally & Co.

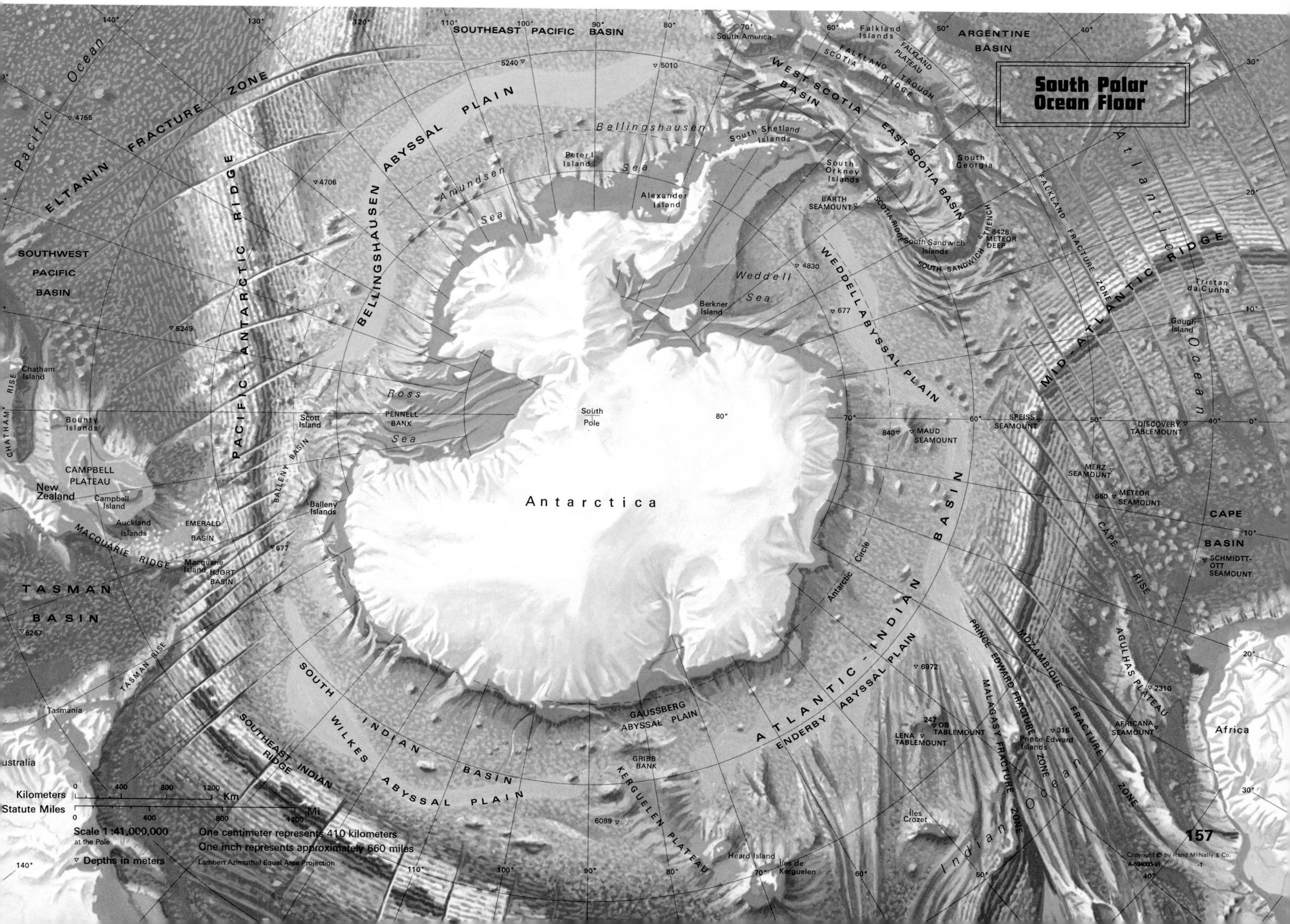
South Polar Ocean Floor
Antarctica
South Pole
South America
Africa
New Zealand
Tasmania
Pacific Ocean
Atlantic Ocean
Indian Ocean
Bellingshausen Sea
Amundsen Sea
Ross Sea
Weddell Sea
Falkland Islands
South Georgia
South Shetland Islands
South Orkney Islands
South Sandwich Islands
Peter I Island
Alexander Island
Berkner Island
Scott Island
Balleny Islands
Macquarie Island
Campbell Island
Auckland Islands
Chatham Island
Bounty Islands
Tristan da Cunha
Gough Island
Prince Edward Islands
Iles Crozet
Heard Island
Iles de Kerguelen
Antarctic Circle
SOUTHEAST PACIFIC BASIN
ARGENTINE BASIN
FALKLAND PLATEAU
FALKLAND TROUGH
WEST SCOTIA BASIN
EAST SCOTIA BASIN
SCOTIA RIDGE
SOUTH SANDWICH TRENCH
METEOR DEEP
BARTH SEAMOUNT
FALKLAND FRACTURE ZONE
ELTANIN FRACTURE ZONE
BELLINGSHAUSEN ABYSSAL PLAIN
PACIFIC-ANTARCTIC RIDGE
SOUTHWEST PACIFIC BASIN
WEDDELL ABYSSAL PLAIN
MID-ATLANTIC RIDGE
PENNELL BANK
BALLENY BASIN
CAMPBELL PLATEAU
EMERALD BASIN
MACQUARIE RIDGE
HJORT BASIN
TASMAN BASIN
TASMAN RISE
SPIESS SEAMOUNT
MAUD SEAMOUNT
DISCOVERY TABLEMOUNT
MERZ SEAMOUNT
METEOR SEAMOUNT
CAPE BASIN
CAPE RISE
SCHMIDTT-OTT SEAMOUNT
ATLANTIC-INDIAN BASIN
ENDERBY ABYSSAL PLAIN
PRINCE EDWARD FRACTURE ZONE
MOZAMBIQUE FRACTURE ZONE
MALAGASY FRACTURE ZONE
AGULHAS PLATEAU
AFRICANA SEAMOUNT
LENA TABLEMOUNT
OB TABLEMOUNT
GAUSSBERG ABYSSAL PLAIN
GRIBB BANK
KERGUELEN PLATEAU
SOUTH INDIAN BASIN
WILKES ABYSSAL PLAIN
SOUTHEAST INDIAN RIDGE
Kilometers 0 400 800 1200 Km
Statute Miles 0 400 800 1200 Mi
Scale 1:41,000,000 at the Pole
One centimeter represents 410 kilometers
One inch represents approximately 660 miles
Depths in meters
Lambert Azimuthal Equal Area Projection
Copyright © by Rand McNally & Co.

ICELAND
Reykjavik
Akureyri
Hekla
Arctic Circle
NORWEGIAN SEA
FAEROE ISLANDS (Den.)
Tórshavn
SHETLAND ISLANDS
Lerwick
ORKNEY ISLANDS
NORWAY
Trondheim
Bergen
Stavanger
Oslo
SWEDEN
Stockholm
Göteborg
DENMARK
København
Århus
Ålborg
Skagerrak
Kattegat
Baltic Sea
ATLANTIC OCEAN
NORTH SEA
IRELAND
Dublin
Cork
Limerick
NORTHERN IRELAND
Belfast
ISLE OF MAN
SCOTLAND
Glasgow
Edinburgh
Aberdeen
Dundee
Inverness
UNITED KINGDOM
Newcastle
Sunderland
Middlesbrough
Leeds
Manchester
Liverpool
Sheffield
Kingston upon Hull
Nottingham
Birmingham
Coventry
Leicester
Norwich
WALES
Cardiff
Swansea
Bristol
Oxford
ENGLAND
LONDON
Southampton
Portsmouth
Bournemouth
Plymouth
Brighton
English Channel
Saint George's Channel
Irish Sea
Strait of Dover
NETHERLANDS
Amsterdam
's-Gravenhage
The Hague
Rotterdam
Groningen
Antwerpen
Bruxelles
BELGIUM
Liège
LUXEMBOURG
Luxembourg
WEST GERMANY
Hamburg
Bremen
Hannover
Essen
Dortmund
Düsseldorf
Köln
Bonn
Frankfurt
Mannheim
Stuttgart
Nürnberg
München
EAST GERMANY
BERLIN
Leipzig
Dresden
Magdeburg
Rostock
Kiel
Lübeck
POLAND
Gdańsk
Gdynia
Szczecin
Poznań
Wrocław
CZECHOSLOVAKIA
Praha
Brno
Ostrava
Katowice
AUSTRIA
Wien
Innsbruck
Graz
Linz
Salzburg
HUNGARY
Budapest
Bratislava
SWITZERLAND
Zürich
Bern
Basel
Genève
Lausanne
FRANCE
PARIS
Le Havre
Rouen
Lille
Reims
Metz
Strasbourg
Nancy
Dijon
Lyon
Saint-Étienne
Grenoble
Marseille
Toulon
Nice
Montpellier
Toulouse
Bordeaux
Nantes
Rennes
Brest
Tours
Le Mans
Limoges
Clermont-Ferrand
MONACO
Bay of Biscay
ANDORRA
SPAIN
Madrid
Barcelona
Valencia
Zaragoza
Bilbao
Sevilla
Málaga
Córdoba
Granada
Murcia
Alicante
Valladolid
Oviedo
Gijón
La Coruña
Vigo
PORTUGAL
Lisboa
Porto
Gibraltar (U.K.)
ISLAS BALEARES
Palma
MALLORCA
ITALY
Milano
Torino
Genova
Venezia
Bologna
Firenze
Roma
Napoli
Bari
Taranto
Palermo
Messina
Catania
Reggio di Calabria
CORSE
SARDEGNA
Cagliari
SICILIA
Tyrrhenian Sea
Adriatic Sea
Ionian Sea
YUGOSLAVIA
Zagreb
Ljubljana
Rijeka
Split
Sarajevo
Trieste
MEDITERRANEAN SEA
MALTA
Valletta
TUNISIA
Tunis
ALGERIA
Alger
Oran
Constantine
Annaba
MOROCCO
Casablanca
Rabat
Fès
Tanger
Ceuta (Sp.)
Melilla (Sp.)
ATLAS MOUNTAINS
Copyright © by Rand McNally & Co.
Map prepared by Esselte Map Service AB, Stockholm.
A-550000-264

UNION OF SOVIET SOCIALIST REPUBLICS
ROSSIJSKAJA SOVETSKAJA FEDERATIVNAJA SOCIALISTIČESKAJA RESPUBLIKA
RUSSIAN SOVIET FEDERATED SOCIALIST REPUBLIC
URAL'SKIJE GORY
URAL MOUNTAINS
ZAPADNO-SIBIRSKAJA NIZMENNOST'
Barents Sea
Beloje More
White Sea
BLACK SEA
CASPIAN SEA
Aral'skoje More
BOL'ŠOJ KAVKAZ
CAUCASUS
FINLAND
TURKEY
IRAN
IRAQ
SYRIA
CYPRUS
BULGARIA
ROMANIA
MOSKVA
MOSCOW
LENINGRAD
Kijev
Char'kov
Gor'kij
Kujbyšev
Sverdlovsk
Volgograd
Baku
Tbilisi
İstanbul
Ankara
TEHRĀN
Baghdād
Bucureşti
Sofija
Helsinki
Minsk
Odessa
Rostov-na-Donu
Kazan'
Perm'
Čel'abinsk
Saratov
Astrachan'
Tallinn
Riga
Vilnius
Kišin'ov
Jerevan
Syktyvkar
Archangel'sk
Murmansk

Kilometers 0 200 400 600 Km.

Statute Miles 0 200 400 600 Mi.

Scale 1:12,000,000

One centimeter represents 120 kilometers.
One inch represents approximately 190 miles.

Miller Oblated Stereographic Projection

a

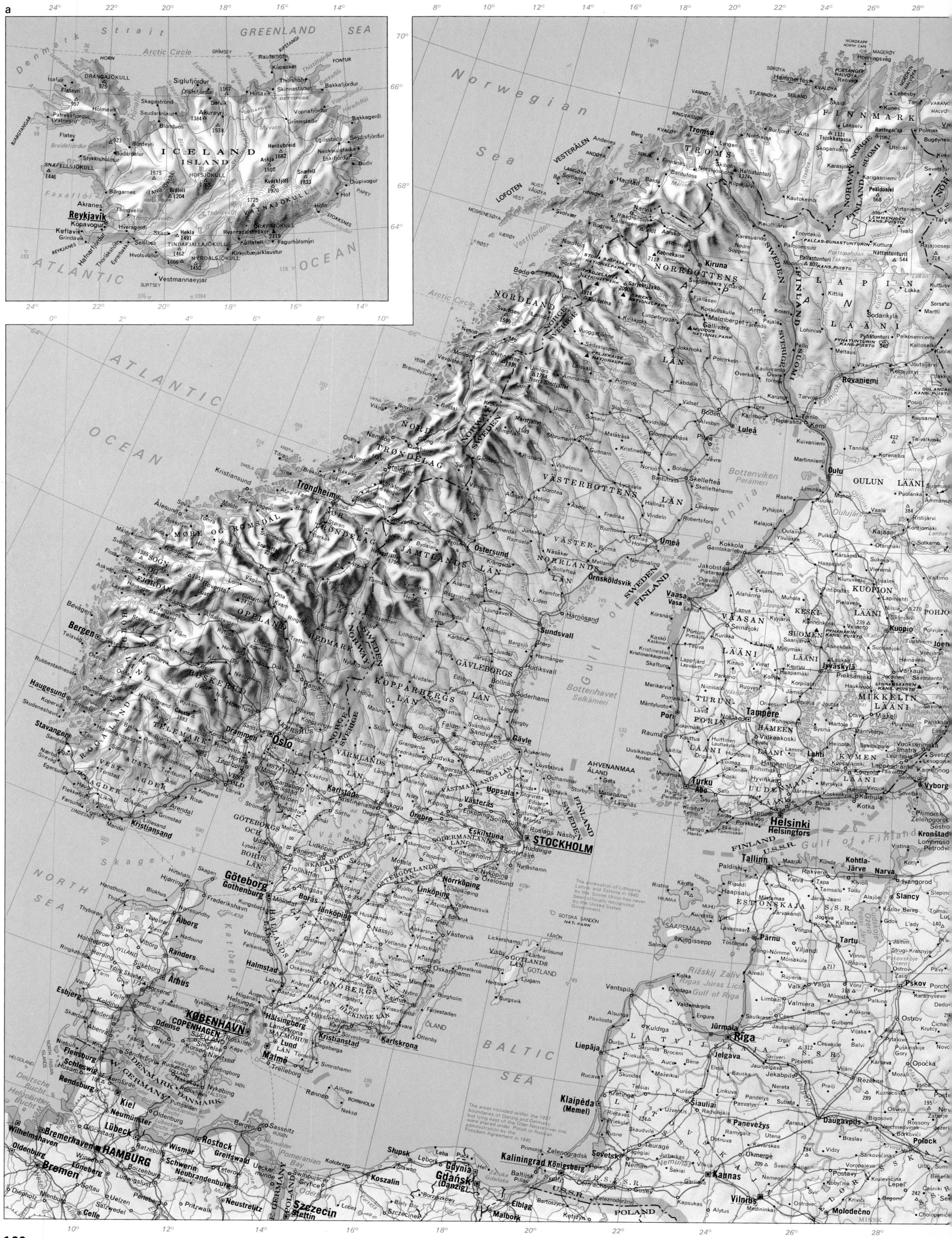
GREENLAND SEA
Denmark Strait
Arctic Circle
ICELAND
ISLAND
Reykjavík
Akureyri
VATNAJÖKULL
Hekla
ATLANTIC OCEAN
Vestmannaeyjar
Norwegian Sea
ATLANTIC OCEAN
NORTH SEA
Skagerrak
Kattegat
BALTIC SEA
Gulf of Bothnia
Gulf of Finland
Gulf of Riga
NORDLAND
NORRBOTTENS LÄN
LAPIN LÄÄNI
FINNMARK
TROMS
NORD TRØNDELAG
SØR TRØNDELAG
MØRE OG ROMSDAL
SOGN OG FJORDANE
HORDALAND
OPPLAND
HEDMARK
BUSKERUD
TELEMARK
ROGALAND
VEST AGDER
AUST AGDER
ØSTFOLD
VÄSTERBOTTENS LÄN
JÄMTLANDS LÄN
VÄSTERNORRLANDS LÄN
GÄVLEBORGS LÄN
KOPPARBERGS LÄN
VÄRMLANDS LÄN
GÖTEBORGS OCH BOHUS LÄN
OULUN LÄÄNI
VAASAN LÄÄNI
KESKI SUOMEN LÄÄNI
KUOPION LÄÄNI
MIKKELIN LÄÄNI
TURUN PORIN LÄÄNI
HÄMEEN LÄÄNI
KYMEN LÄÄNI
UUDENMAAN LÄÄNI
ESTONSKAJA S.S.R.
LATVIJSKAJA S.S.R.
LITOVSKAJA S.S.R.
Tromsø
Narvik
Kiruna
Bodø
Luleå
Oulu
Rovaniemi
Trondheim
Umeå
Östersund
Vaasa
Bergen
Sundsvall
Tampere
Oslo
Stavanger
Kristiansand
Drammen
Karlstad
Örebro
Västerås
Uppsala
Turku
Helsinki
Helsingfors
STOCKHOLM
Tallinn
Göteborg
Gothenburg
Jönköping
Linköping
Norrköping
Halmstad
Ålborg
Århus
KØBENHAVN
COPENHAGEN
Malmö
Lund
Kristianstad
Karlskrona
Visby
GOTLAND
ÖLAND
BORNHOLM
Riga
Liepāja
Klaipėda (Memel)
Kaunas
Vilnius
Kaliningrad Königsberg
Gdańsk (Danzig)
Gdynia
Szczecin Stettin
Rostock
Lübeck
Kiel
HAMBURG
Bremen
Bremerhaven
Tartu
Pärnu
Pskov
Daugavpils
The annexation of Lithuania, Latvia, and Estonia in 1940 by the Soviet Union has never been officially recognized by the United States Government.
The areas included within the 1937 boundaries of Danzig and Germany, but lying east of the Oder-Neisse river line, were placed under Polish or Russian administration by the Potsdam Agreement in 1945.

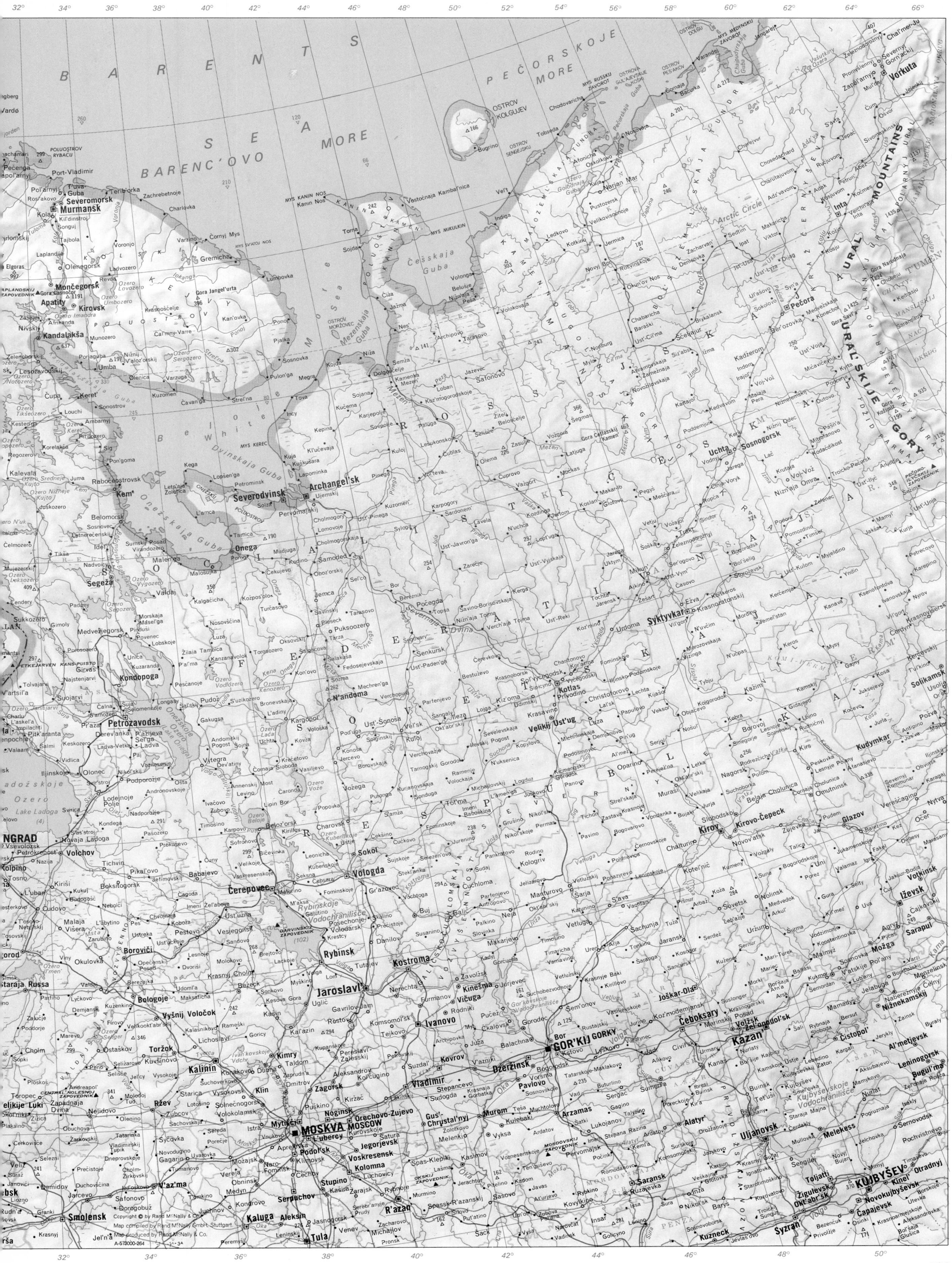
BARENTS SEA
BARENC'OVO MORE
PEČORSKOJE MORE
White Sea
Belo je More
Arctic Circle
URAL MOUNTAINS
URAL'SKIJE GORY
MOSKVA
MOSCOW
Archangel'sk
Murmansk
Severomorsk
Kandalakša
Apatity
Kirovsk
Severodvinsk
Onega
Petrozavodsk
Kondopoga
Syktyvkar
Kotlas
Vologda
Čerepovec
Jaroslavl
Kostroma
Ivanovo
GOR'KIJ
GORKY
Kazan'
Čeboksary
Joškar-Ola
Kirov
Kirovo-Čepeck
Glazov
Iževsk
Votkinsk
Sarapul
Al'met'evsk
Uljanovsk
KUJBYŠEV
Toljatti
Syzran'
Kuzneck
Saransk
Arzamas
Dzeržinsk
Vladimir
Rjazan'
Tula
Kaluga
Smolensk
Kalinin
Rybinsk
Pečora
Uchta
Sosnogorsk
Inta
Vorkuta
Nar'jan Mar
Solikamsk
Kudymkar
Nižnekamskij
Naberežnyje Čelny
Čistopol'
Melekess
Novokujbyševsk
Otradnyj
Čapajevsk
Kinel'
Zelenodol'sk
Volžsk
Sokol
Kimry
Dubna
Klin
Zagorsk
Orechovo-Zujevo
Noginsk
Kolomna
Serpuchov
Obninsk
Volchov
Kiriši
Ladoga
Ostrov Kolgujev
Češskaja Guba
Mezenskaja Guba
Dvinskaja Guba
Onežskaja Guba
Kanin Nos
Poluostrov Kanin
Kol'skij Poluostrov
Timanskij Kr'až
Pečora
Rybinskoje Vodochranilišče
Kujbyševskoje Vodochranilišče
Gor'kovskoje Vodochranilišče
Copyright © by Rand McNally & Co.
Map compiled by Rand McNally & Co.
Map compiled by Rand McNally GmbH, Stuttgart
Map produced by Rand McNally & Co.
A-573000-264

Kilometers 0 100 200 300 Km.

Statute Miles 0 100 200 300 Mi.

Scale 1:6,000,000

One centimeter represents 60 kilometers.

One inch represents approximately 95 miles.

Lambert Conformal Conic Projection

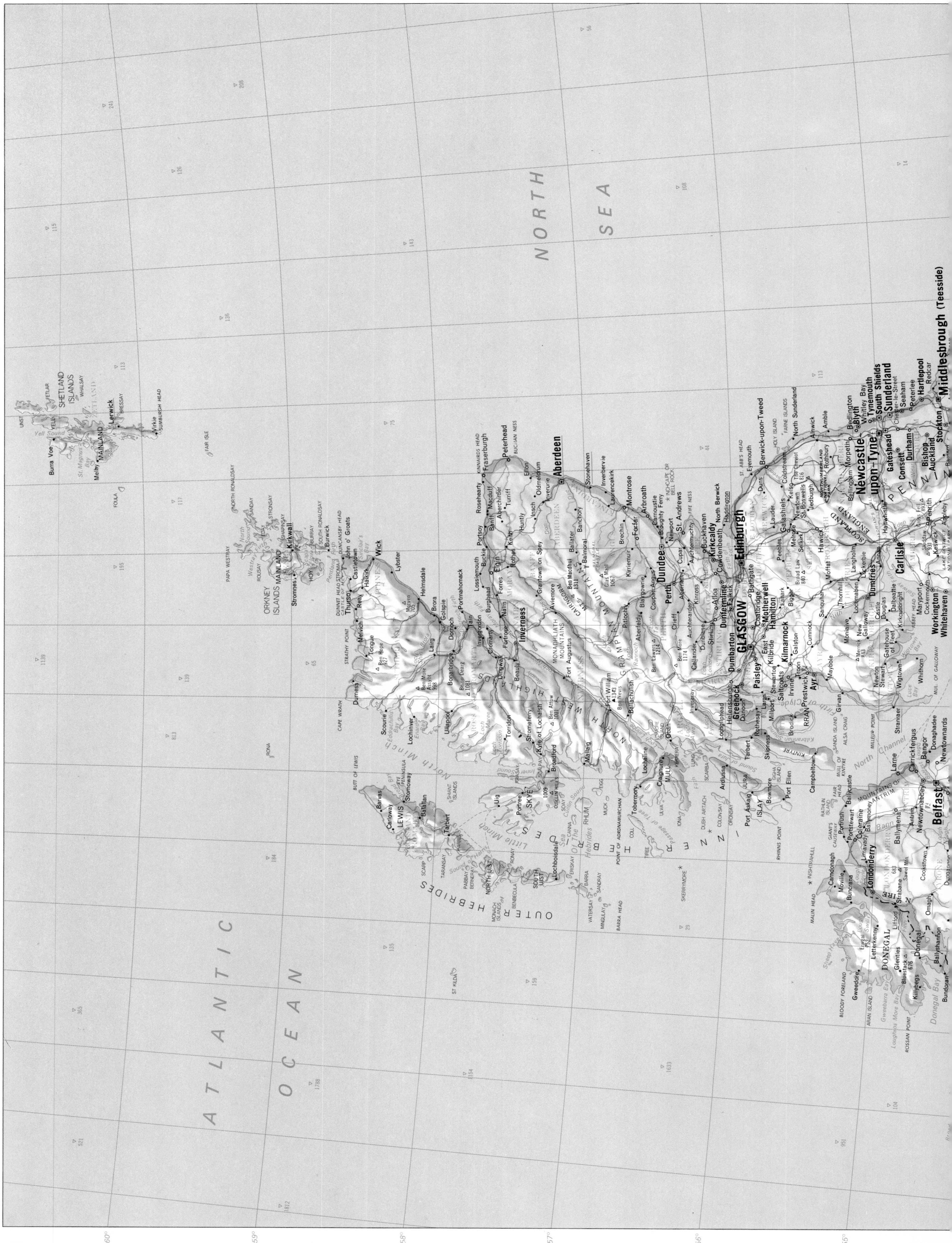
NORTH SEA
ATLANTIC OCEAN
SHETLAND ISLANDS
Lerwick
ORKNEY ISLANDS
Kirkwall
Stromness
Thurso
Wick
Inverness
Aberdeen
Peterhead
Fraserburgh
Dundee
Perth
Edinburgh
GLASGOW
Paisley
Greenock
Kilmarnock
Ayr
Stranraer
Dumfries
Carlisle
Newcastle upon-Tyne
Sunderland
Middlesbrough (Teesside)
Belfast
Londonderry
DONEGAL
LEWIS
Stornoway
SKYE
MULL
ISLAY
OUTER HEBRIDES
INNER HEBRIDES
Fort William
Oban
North Channel
Workington
Whitehaven

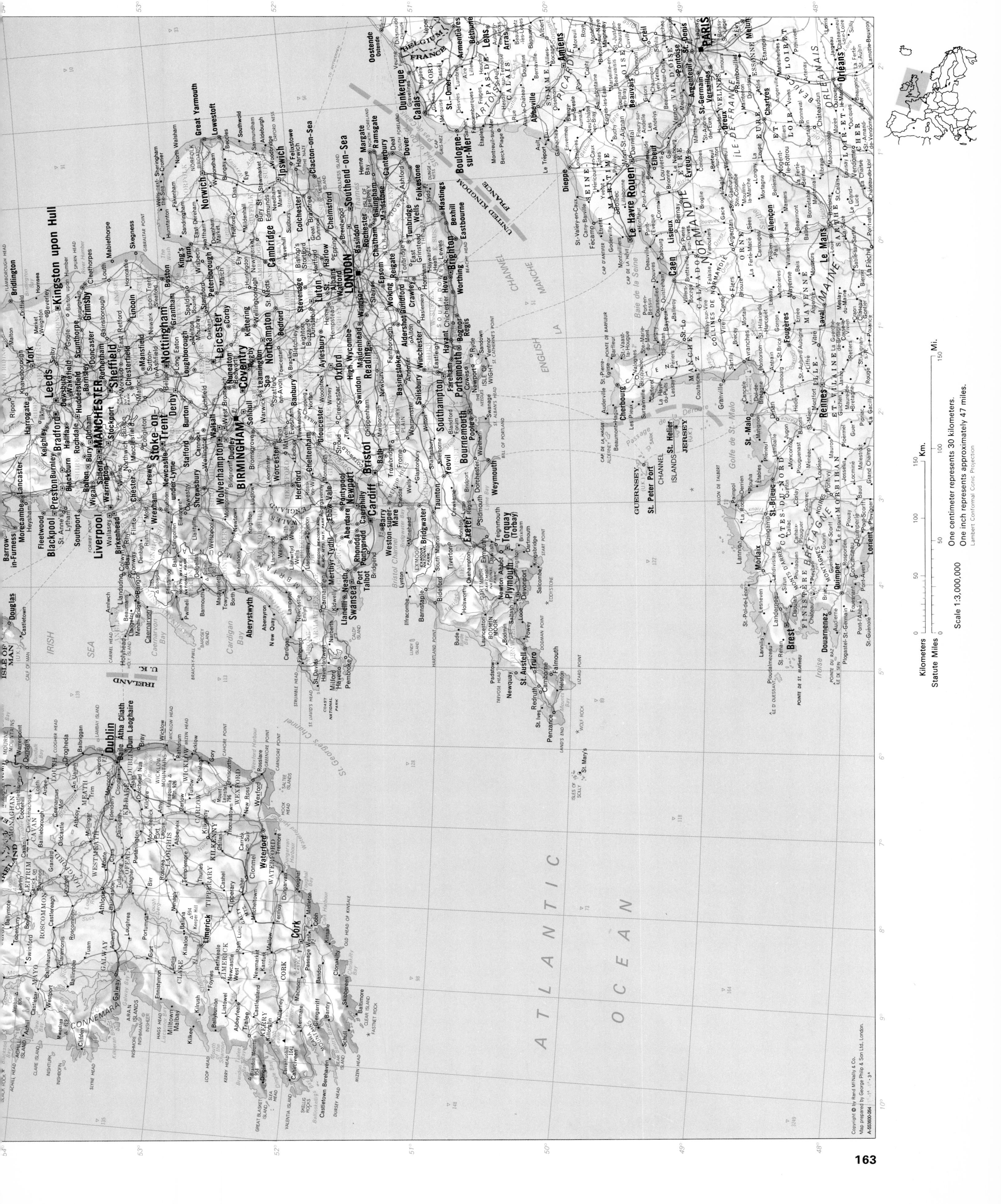
Kilometers 0 50 100 150 Km.
Statute Miles 0 50 100 150 Mi.
Scale 1:3,000,000
One centimeter represents 30 kilometers.
One inch represents approximately 47 miles.
Lambert Conformal Conic Projection
ATLANTIC OCEAN
ENGLISH CHANNEL
LA MANCHE
IRISH SEA
Copyright © by Rand McNally & Co.
Map prepared by George Philip & Son Ltd, London.

NORTH SEA
Deutsche Bucht
Helgoländer Bucht
NORTH FRISIAN ISLANDS
OSTFRIESISCHE INSELN
WESTFRIESE EILANDEN
DENMARK
WEST GERMANY
EAST GERMANY
NETHERLANDS
BELGIUM
FRANCE
LUXEMBOURG
SWITZERLAND
AUSTRIA
ITALY
LIECHTENSTEIN
AMSTERDAM
's-Gravenhage
The Hague
Rotterdam
Utrecht
Antwerpen
BRUXELLES
Lille
Liège
Luxembourg
Hamburg
Bremen
Hannover
Kiel
Lübeck
Flensburg
Rostock
Schwerin
Magdeburg
Düsseldorf
Köln
Essen
Dortmund
Bonn
Koblenz
Frankfurt a.M.
Mannheim
Stuttgart
Nürnberg
MÜNCHEN
MUNICH
Saarbrücken
Strasbourg
Metz
Nancy
Reims
Dijon
Besançon
Basel
Zürich
Bern
Lausanne
Genève
Innsbruck
Bolzano
Leipzig
Halle
Kassel
Erfurt
Würzburg
Augsburg
Freiburg
Karlsruhe
Heidelberg
Mulhouse
ALPS
Copyright by Rand McNally & Co.

Kilometers 0 50 100 150 Km.

Statute Miles 0 50 100 150 Mi.

Scale 1:3,000,000

One centimeter represents 30 kilometers.

One inch represents approximately 47 miles.

Conic Projection, Two Standard Parallels.

BALTIC SEA
Gulf of Danzig
The areas included within the 1937 boundaries of Danzig and Germany, but lying east of the Oder-Neisse river line, were placed under Polish or Russian administration by the Potsdam Agreement in 1945.
Pomeranian Bay
Kaliningrad
Königsberg
Gdańsk
(Danzig)
Gdynia
Szczecin
Stettin
Bydgoszcz
Toruń
Olsztyn
Białystok
Grodno
WARSZAWA WARSAW
Poznań
Łódź
Brest
Lublin
Radom
Kielce
Częstochowa
Wrocław
Breslau
Kraków
Katowice
Ostrava
Opava
Olomouc
Brno
PRAHA
PRAGUE
Dresden
BERLIN
Plzeň
České Budějovice
WIEN
VIENNA
Linz
Graz
Bratislava
Košice
Miskolc
BUDAPEST
Debrecen
Szeged
Pécs
Győr
Oradea
Arad
Subotica
Kikinda
Sombor
CARPATHIAN MOUNTAINS
POLAND
CZECHOSLOVAKIA
HUNGARY
U.S.S.R.
ROMANIA
YUGOSLAVIA
MAGYARORSZÁG
SRBIJA
SERBIA
HRVATSKA
CROATIA
Balaton
Tatabánya
Nitra
Žilina
Zakopane
Rzeszów
Przemyśl
Tarnów
Chełm
Siedlce
Płock
Kalisz
Opole
Gliwice
Zabrze
Bytom
Legnica
Zielona Góra
Koszalin
Słupsk
Elbląg
Grudziądz
Włocławek
Tarnobrzeg
Zamość
Sandomierz
Nowy Sącz
Bielsko-Biała
Prešov
Banská Bystrica
Trnava
Zlín
Gottwaldov
Pardubice
Hradec Králové
Jihlava
Liberec
Ústí nad Labem
Chomutov
Kladno
Cottbus
Frankfurt an der Oder
Neubrandenburg
Stralsund
Passau
Salzburg
Klagenfurt
Villach
Maribor
Sopron
Szombathely
Veszprém
Székesfehérvár
Kecskemét
Szolnok
Eger
Nyíregyháza
Satu Mare
Mukačevo
Užgorod
Kaposvár
Nagykanizsa
Zalaegerszeg
Dunaújváros
Hódmezővásárhely
Békéscsaba
Varaždin
14°
15°
16°
17°
18°
19°
20°
21°
22°
23°
24°
54°
53°
52°
51°
50°
49°
48°
47°
46°

English Channel
La Manche
ATLANTIC
OCEAN
Bay of Biscay
Golfe de Saint-Malo
Baie de la Seine
Strait of Dover
Pas de Calais
UNITED KINGDOM
FRANCE
PARIS
Southampton
Portsmouth
Brighton
Bournemouth
Plymouth
Exeter
Torquay (Torbay)
Dunkerque
Calais
Lille
Amiens
Rouen
Le Havre
Caen
Cherbourg
St. Peter Port
St. Helier
GUERNSEY
JERSEY
CHANNEL ISLANDS
Brest
Quimper
Lorient
Vannes
Rennes
St.-Brieuc
St.-Malo
Nantes
Angers
Le Mans
Tours
Orléans
Chartres
Blois
Poitiers
La Rochelle
Rochefort
Niort
Limoges
Angoulême
Bordeaux
Périgueux
Clermont-Ferrand
Toulouse
Montpellier
Carcassonne
Perpignan
Pau
Tarbes
Bayonne
Biarritz
Agen
Montauban
Bourges
Nevers
Auxerre
Vichy
Moulins
Montluçon
Châteauroux
Santander
Bilbao
San Sebastián
Vitoria
Pamplona
Burgos
Logroño
ANDORRA
PYRÉNÉES
BRETAGNE
NORMANDIE
MASSIF CENTRAL
LIMOUSIN
GASCOGNE
LANDES
ARMAGNAC
BÉARN

MEDITERRANEAN SEA
LIGURIAN SEA
ADRIATIC SEA
Gulf of Venice
Golfo di Genova
ALPS
APPENNINO
München
MUNICH
Stuttgart
Frankfurt a. M.
Nürnberg
Zürich
Basel
Bern
Genève
Lausanne
Strasbourg
MILANO
MILAN
Torino
Turin
Genova
Genoa
Venezia
Venice
Firenze
Florence
Bologna
Marseille
Nice
PRAHA
PRAGUE
Copyright © by Rand McNally & Co.
Map prepared by Rand McNally GmbH, Stuttgart.
A-559495-264

Kilometers 0 50 100 150 Km.

Statute Miles 0 50 100 150 Mi.

Scale 1:3,000,000

One centimeter represents 30 kilometers.

One inch represents approximately 47 miles.

Lambert Conformal Conic Projection

Bay of Biscay
ATLANTIC
OCEAN
ATLANTIC
OCEAN
MADRID
LISBOA
LISBON
Porto
La Coruña
Santiago de Compostela
Vigo
Oviedo
Gijón
Santander
Bilbao
San Sebastián
León
Burgos
Valladolid
Salamanca
Zamora
Palencia
Segovia
Ávila
Toledo
Coimbra
Badajoz
Mérida
Cáceres
Sevilla
Córdoba
Granada
Málaga
Cádiz
Huelva
Almería
Jaén
Ciudad Real
Albacete
Cuenca
Gibraltar (U.K.)
Algeciras
Tanger
Tétouan
Ceuta
Melilla
MOROCCO
AL MAGHREB
PORTUGAL
SPAIN
ESPAÑA
CORDILLERA CANTABRICA
SIERRA MORENA
SIERRA NEVADA
Golfo de Cádiz
Strait of Gibraltar
Copyright © by Rand McNally & Co.
Map prepared by Rand McNally GmbH, Stuttgart.

Toulouse
Montpellier
Nîmes
Avignon
Arles
Marseille
Toulon
Nice
Cannes
Antibes
Grasse
Fréjus
Hyères
La Seyne
La Ciotat
Aix-en-Provence
Béziers
Sète
Narbonne
Carcassonne
Perpignan
Albi
Castres
Montauban
Tarbes
Pau
Bayonne
Biarritz
Lourdes
Andorra
PYRENEES
PIRINEOS
CATALUÑA
Lérida
Gerona
Manresa
Sabadell
Tarrasa
Mataró
Badalona
BARCELONA
Hospitalet
Villanueva y Geltrú
Tarragona
Reus
Tortosa
Delta del Ebro
Zaragoza
Huesca
Teruel
Castellón de la Plana
Sagunto
Valencia
Golfo de Valencia
Alcira
Gandía
Alcoy
Elda
Elche
Alicante
Orihuela
Murcia
Cartagena
Torrevieja
Golfe du Lion
MENORCA
MINORCA
Ciudadela
Mahón
MALLORCA
MAJORCA
Palma
Inca
Manacor
BALEARES
ISLAS BALEARES
BALEARIC ISLANDS
IBIZA
Ibiza
FORMENTERA
San Antonio Abad
MEDITERRANEAN SEA
ALGER
ALGIERS
Blida
Médéa
Tizi-Ouzou
Bejaïa (Bougie)
Djidjelli
Sétif
El Asnam (Orléansville)
Mostaganem
Oran (Ouahran)
Sidi bel Abbès
ATLAS
TELL ATLAS
KABYLIE
ALGERIA
ALGÉRIE
Bou Saâda
Batna
PLAINE DU HODNA
M'Sila
Bordj Bou Arreridj

Kilometers 0 50 100 150 Km.

Statute Miles 0 50 100 150 Mi.

Scale 1:3,000,000

One centimeter represents 30 kilometers.
One inch represents approximately 47 miles.
Lambert Conformal Conic Projection

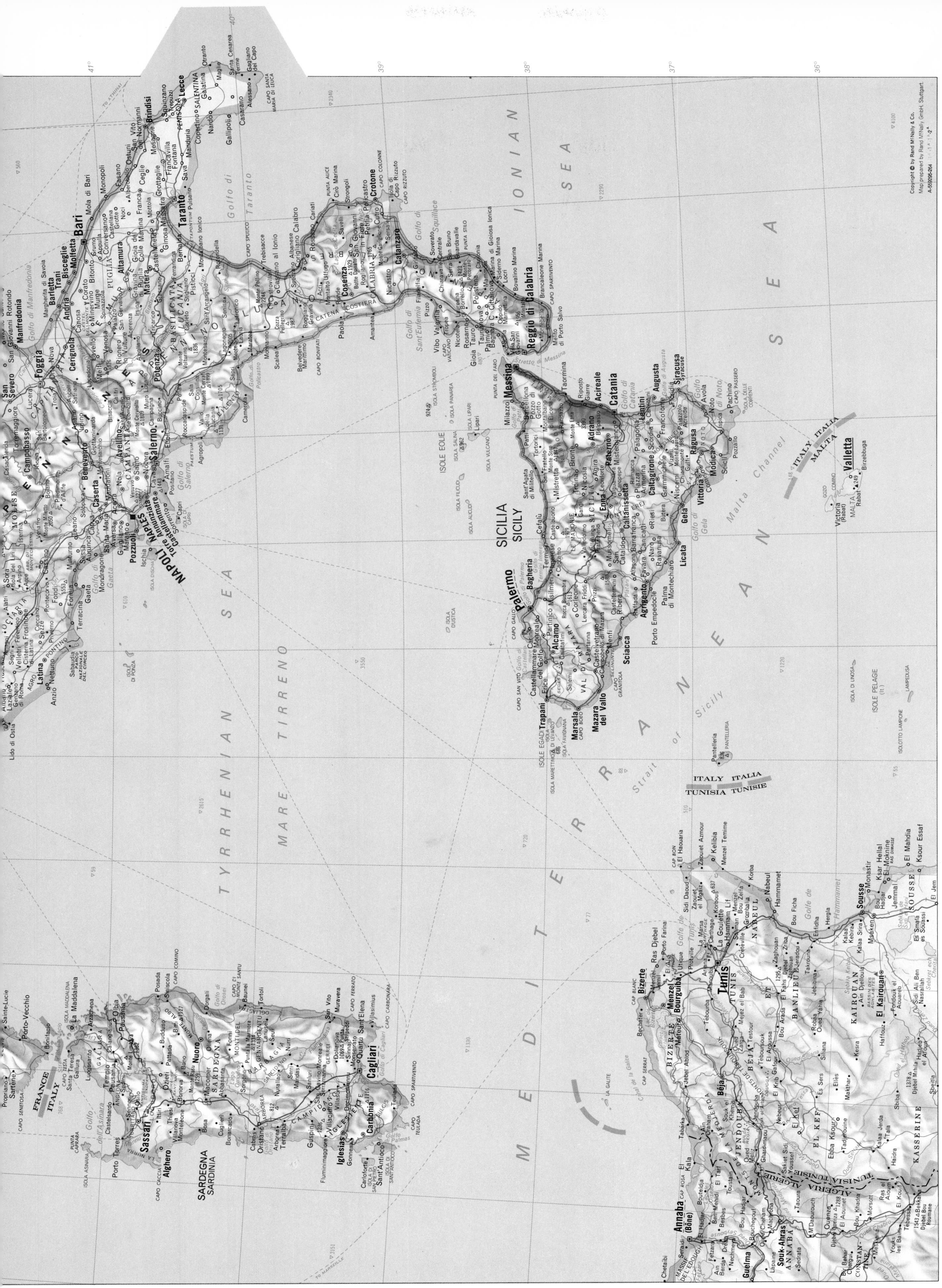
TYRRHENIAN SEA
MARE TIRRENO
IONIAN SEA
MEDITERRANEAN SEA
Golfo di Taranto
Strait of Sicily
Malta Channel
SICILIA
SICILY
SARDEGNA
SARDINIA
ITALY ITALIA
TUNISIA TUNISIE
ITALY ITALIA
MALTA
FRANCE
ITALY
ISOLE EOLIE
ISOLE EGADI
ISOLE PELAGIE (It.)
NAPOLI
NAPLES
Salerno
Potenza
Foggia
Bari
Taranto
Brindisi
Lecce
Otranto
Cosenza
Catanzaro
Crotone
Reggio di Calabria
Messina
Catania
Siracusa
Palermo
Trapani
Marsala
Agrigento
Caltanissetta
Enna
Ragusa
Gela
Cagliari
Sassari
Nuoro
Oristano
Iglesias
Carbonia
Alghero
Olbia
Valletta
Tunis
Bizerte
Sousse
Annaba (Bône)
Béja
Jendouba
El Kef
Kairouan
Guelma
Souk-Ahras
Pantelleria
Lampedusa
Ustica
Capri
Ischia

Kilometers	0	50	100	150 Km.
Statute Miles	0	50	100	150 Mi.

Scale 1:3,000,000

One centimeter represents 30 kilometers.

One inch represents approximately 47 miles.

Lambert Conformal Conic Projection

BLACK SEA
CARPATHIAN MOUNTAINS
BUCUREȘTI
BUDAPEST
Beograd
Sofija
Kišin'ov
Sarajevo
Danube
Cluj
Brașov
Ploiești
Constanța
Varna
Burgas
Debrecen
Szeged
Timișoara
Oradea
Craiova
Galați
Brăila
Iași
Sibiu
Arad
Pécs
Novi Sad
Niš
Ruse
Pleven
Skopje
Tuzla
Osijek
Miskolc
Košice
Uzhgorod
Odessa
Tiraspol'
Bendery
Izmail
Tulcea
Titograd
Dubrovnik
Zenica

Kilometers 0 50 100 150 Km.
Statute Miles 0 50 100 150 Mi.
Scale 1:3,000,000
One centimeter represents 30 kilometers.
One inch represents approximately 47 miles.
Lambert Conformal Conic Projection

AEGEAN SEA
MEDITERRANEAN SEA
IONIAN SEA
ADRIATIC SEA
Strait of Otranto
Sea of Crete
Kritikón Pélagos
Marmara Denizi
Sea of Marmara
IONIAN ISLANDS
KIKLÁDHES
CYCLADES
D'HODHEKÁNISOS
DODECANESE
KRÍTI
CRETE
ATHÍNAI
ATHENS
Piraiévs
Thessaloníki
Salonika
İSTANBUL
Bursa
İzmir
Manisa
Denizli
Aydın
Tirana
Durrës
Vlorë
Kérkira
Pátrai
Lárisa
Vólos
Kalámai
Iráklion
Khaniá
Ródhos
Rhodes
Mitilíni
Khíos
Limnos
Edirne
Kavála
Komotiní
Bitola
Ioánnina
ITALY
Otranto
TURKEY
TÜRKİYE
GREECE
HELLAS
Copyright © by Rand McNally & Co.
Map prepared by Rand McNally GmbH, Stuttgart.

London—Birmingham—Cardiff

Caernarvon Bay
Saint George's Channel
Cardigan Bay
Carmarthen Bay
Bristol Channel
Bridgwater Bay
Lyme Bay
CAMBRIAN MOUNTAINS
BLACK MOUNTAINS
BRECON BEACONS
EXMOOR
DARTMOOR
BODMIN MOOR
LLEYN PENINSULA
LUNDY ISLAND
BARDSEY ISLAND
ISLE OF PORTLAND
WALES
ENGLAND
ENGL
Caernarvon
Wrexham
Crewe
Stoke-on-Trent
Shrewsbury
Stafford
Wolverhampton
BIRMINGH
Aberystwyth
Kidderminster
Worcester
Hereford
Gloucester
Cheltenha
Swansea
Neath
Port Talbot
Rhondda
Merthyr Tydfil
Pontypridd
Caerphilly
Newport
Cardiff
Penarth
Barry
Bristol
Bath
Weston-super-Mare
Pembroke
Milford Haven
Haverfordwest
Carmarthen
Llanelli
Bridgwater
Taunton
Yeovil
Barnstaple
Bideford
Exeter
Exmouth
Newton Abbot
Torquay (Torbay)
Paignton
Plymouth
Devonport
Newquay
Saint Austell
Truro
Falmouth
Dorchester
Weymouth
Poole
Bourneme
5°
4° 30'
4°
3° 30'
3°
2° 30'
2°
53°
52° 30'
52°
51° 30'
51°
50° 30'

NORTH SEA
The Wash
LONDON
Birmingham
Nottingham
Derby
Leicester
Coventry
Northampton
Peterborough
Cambridge
Norwich
Great Yarmouth
Lowestoft
Ipswich
Colchester
Chelmsford
Southend-on-Sea
Oxford
Reading
Luton
Bedford
Boston
King's Lynn
Canterbury
Dover
Folkestone
Margate
Maidstone
Brighton
Eastbourne
Hastings
Portsmouth
Southampton
Winchester
Chichester
Worthing
Guildford
Boulogne-sur-Mer
Strait of Dover
Pas de Calais
UNITED KINGDOM
FRANCE
CHANNEL
Copyright © by Rand McNally & Co.
Map prepared by George Philip & Son Ltd., London.
1° 30'
1°
0° 30' West
0°
0° 30' East
53°
52° 30'
52°
51° 30'
51°
50° 30'

Kilometers 0 10 20 30 40 50 Km.

Statute Miles 0 10 20 30 40 50 Mi.

Scale 1:1,000,000

One centimeter represents 10 kilometers.

One inch represents approximately 16 miles.

Lambert Conformal Conic Projection

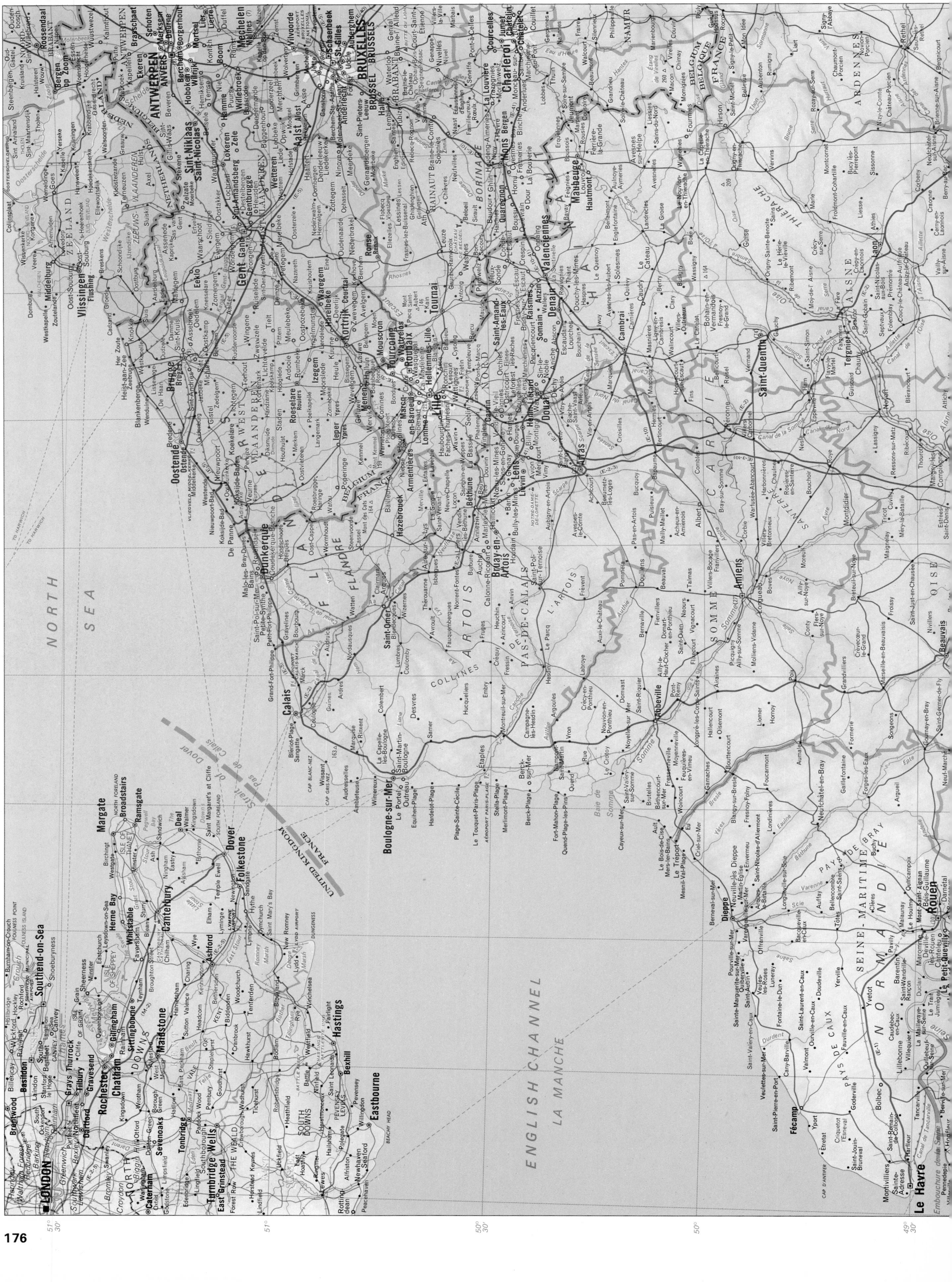
NORTH SEA
ENGLISH CHANNEL
LA MANCHE
Strait of Dover
Pas de Calais
UNITED KINGDOM
FRANCE
BELGIQUE
BELGIUM
LONDON
Southend-on-Sea
Margate
Ramsgate
Canterbury
Dover
Folkestone
Ashford
Maidstone
Hastings
Eastbourne
Brighton
ANTWERPEN
ANVERS
BRUXELLES
BRUSSEL
BRUSSELS
Gent
Brugge
Oostende
Kortrijk
Tournai
Mons
Charleroi
Lille
Roubaix
Tourcoing
Valenciennes
Douai
Arras
Cambrai
Saint-Quentin
Amiens
Abbeville
Boulogne-sur-Mer
Calais
Dunkerque
Saint-Omer
Béthune
Lens
Beauvais
Laon
Dieppe
Rouen
Fécamp
Le Havre
ARTOIS
PICARDIE
NORMANDIE
SEINE-MARITIME
SOMME
AISNE
OISE
NORD
PAS-DE-CALAIS
ARDENNES
THIÉRACHE

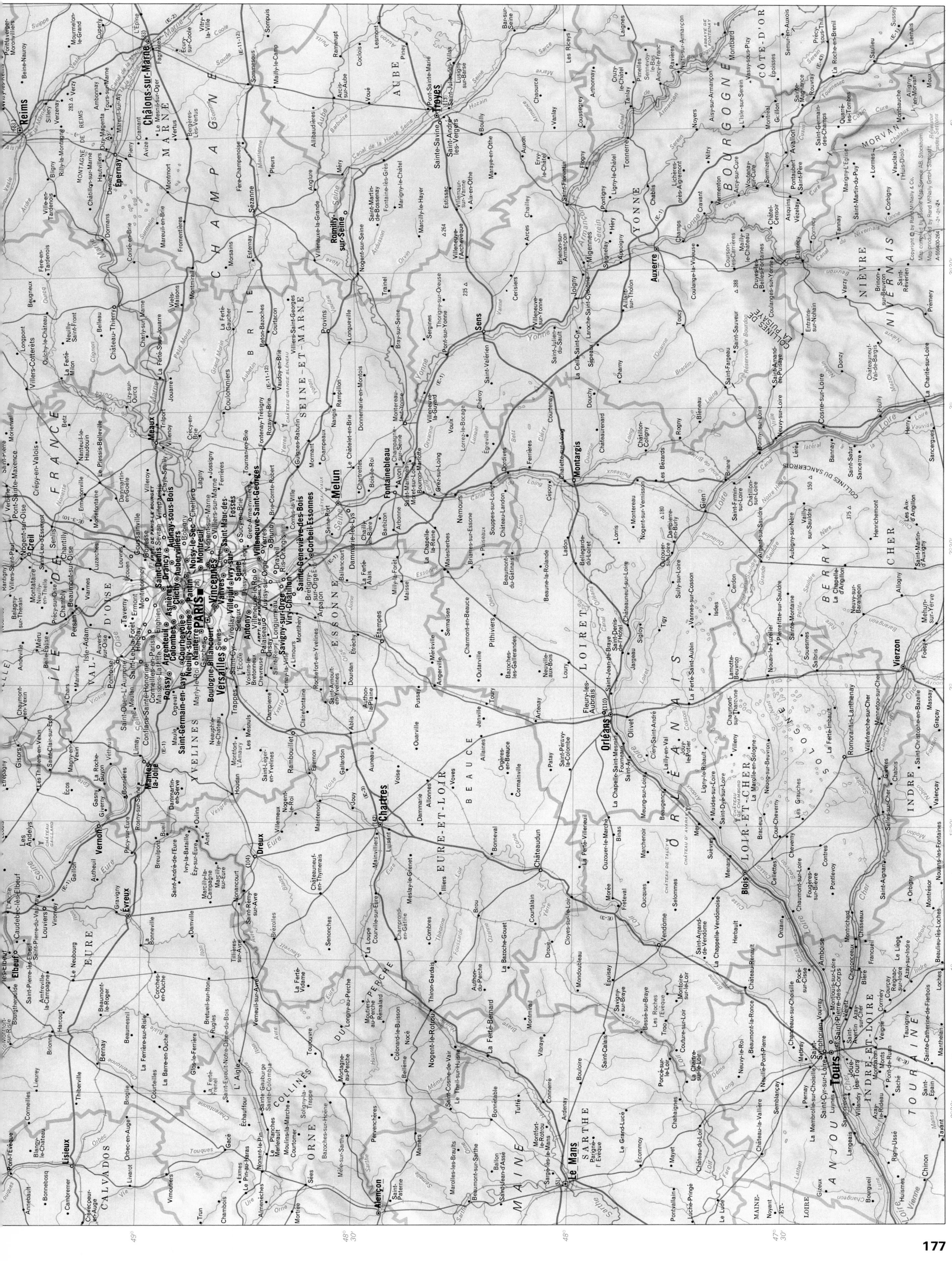
Reims
Châlons-sur-Marne
Épernay
Troyes
Sens
Auxerre
Montargis
Orléans
Blois
Tours
Le Mans
Alençon
Chartres
Dreux
Évreux
Vernon
Versailles
PARIS
Melun
Fontainebleau
Meaux
Vierzon
C H A M P A G N E
B O U R G O G N E
O R L É A N A I S
Y O N N E
L O I R E T
S O L O G N E
B E R R Y
C H E R
N I È V R E
N I V E R N A I S
C Ô T E - D ' O R
A U B E
M A R N E
S E I N E - E T - M A R N E
E S S O N N E
Y V E L I N E S
E U R E - E T - L O I R
B E A U C E
L O I R - E T - C H E R
I N D R E - E T - L O I R E
T O U R A I N E
I N D R E
S A R T H E
M A I N E
O R N E
E U R E
C A L V A D O S
A N J O U
Kilometers
Statute Miles
Km.
Mi.
Scale 1:1,000,000
One centimeter represents 10 kilometers.
One inch represents approximately 16 miles.
Lambert Conformal Conic Projection

NORTH SEA
FRISIAN
WESTFRIESE EILANDEN
Waddenzee
TEXEL
VLIELAND
TERSCHELLING
AMELAND
SCHIERMONNIKOOG
BORKUM
WEST GERMANY
NETHERLANDS
NEDERLAND
Den Helder
IJsselmeer (Zuiderzee)
MARKERWAARD
NOORDOOST POLDER
OOSTELIJK FLEVOLAND
ZUIDELIJK FLEVOLAND
FRIESLAND
DRENTHE
OVERIJSSEL
GELDERLAND
VELUWE
SALLAND
DE GRAAFSCHAP
BETUWE
MEIERIJ
NOORD-BRABANT
ZEELAND
ZEEUWS-VLAANDEREN
LIMBURG
ANTWERPEN
KEMPEN
FLANDERS
OOST-VLAANDEREN
BELGIUM
BELGIË
Groningen
Leeuwarden
Drachten
Assen
Sneek
Harlingen
Meppel
Emmen
Coevorden
Hoogeveen
Kampen
Zwolle
Alkmaar
Hoorn
Enkhuizen
IJmuiden
Haarlem
Zaandam
AMSTERDAM
Hilversum
Amersfoort
Apeldoorn
Deventer
Almelo
Hengelo
Enschede
Zutphen
Arnhem
Nijmegen
Ede
Utrecht
Leiden
'S-Gravenhage
The Hague
Delft
Gouda
ROTTERDAM
Schiedam
Vlaardingen
Dordrecht
Gorinchem
Tiel
Breda
Tilburg
's-Hertogenbosch
Oss
Eindhoven
Helmond
Venlo
Roosendaal
Bergen op Zoom
Middelburg
Vlissingen
Flushing
ANTWERPEN
ANVERS
Sint-Niklaas
Mechelen
Malines
Lier
Herentals
Turnhout
Geel
Mol
Gent
Gand
Lokeren
Weert
Roermond
Mönchen-gladbach
Rheydt
Krefeld
Duisburg
Moers
Kleve
Emmerich
Wesel
Bocholt
Neuss
Viersen
TO HARWICH
TO HARWICH, TILBURG, HULL
3° 30′
4°
4° 30′
5°
5° 30′
6°
6° 30′
53° 30′
53°
52° 30′
52°
51° 30′

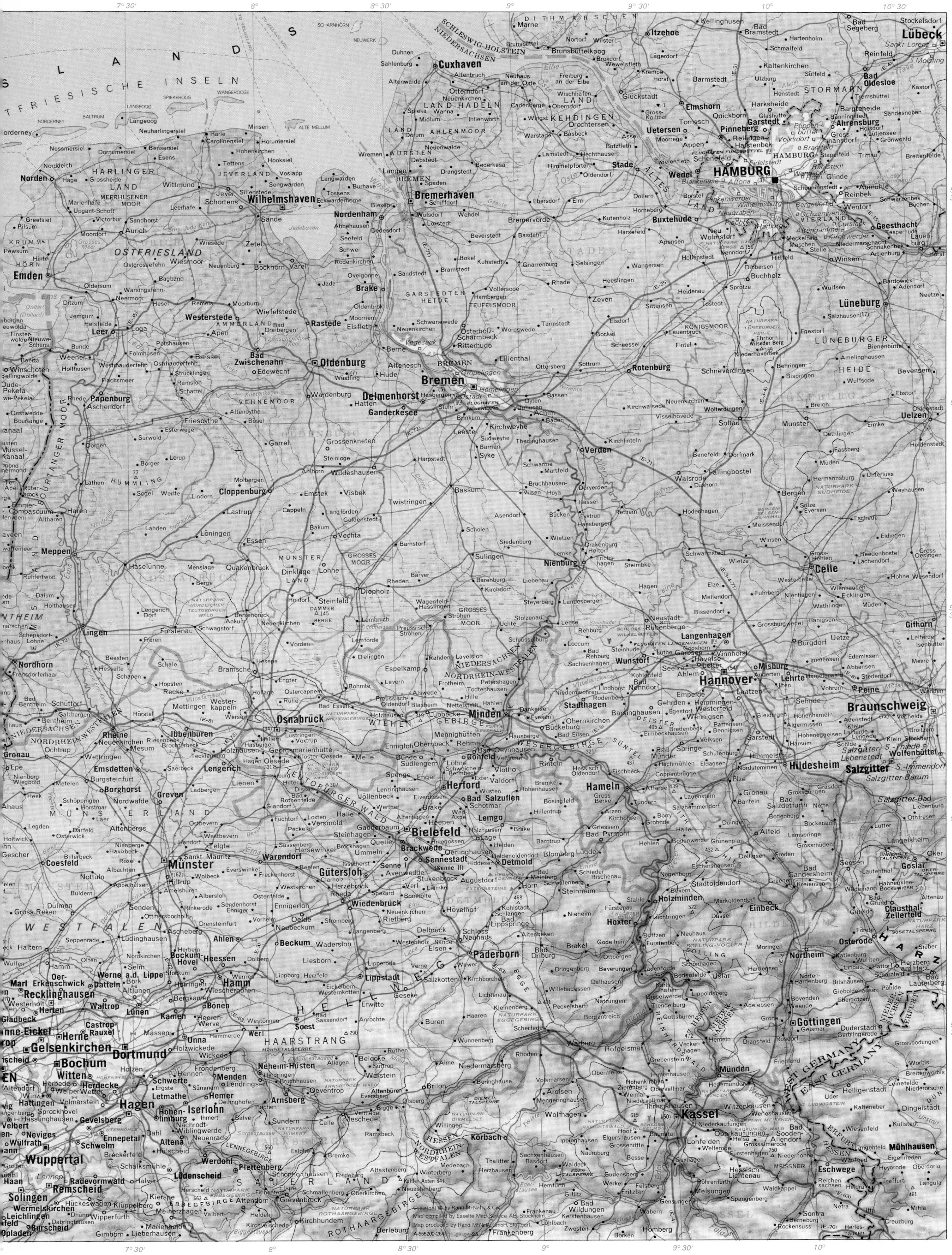
Lübeck
Itzehoe
Cuxhaven
HAMBURG
Bremerhaven
Wilhelmshaven
Emden
Oldenburg
Bremen
Delmenhorst
Lüneburg
Uelzen
Celle
Verden
Nienburg
Hannover
Braunschweig
Hildesheim
Salzgitter
Osnabrück
Minden
Bielefeld
Herford
Münster
Paderborn
Hameln
Göttingen
Kassel
Dortmund
Bochum
Gelsenkirchen
Hagen
Wuppertal
Lingen
Meppen
Cloppenburg
Gifhorn
Wolfenbüttel
Mühlhausen
Eschwege
OSTFRIESISCHE INSELN
OSTFRIESLAND
LÜNEBURGER HEIDE
TEUTOBURGER WALD
HARZ
WEST GERMANY
EAST GERMANY
NIEDERSACHSEN
NORDRHEIN-WESTFALEN
SCHLESWIG-HOLSTEIN
HESSEN
WESTFALEN
SAUERLAND
7° 30'
8°
8° 30'
9°
9° 30'
10°
10° 30'
53° 30'
53°
52° 30'
52°
51° 30'
Copyright by Rand McNally & Co.
Map produced by Esselte Map Service AB, Stockholm
Map produced by Rand McNally GmbH, Stuttgart

Kilometers 0 10 20 30 40 50 Km.

Statute Miles 0 10 20 30 40 50 Mi.

Scale 1:1,000,000

One centimeter represents 10 kilometers.
One inch represents approximately 16 miles.

Lambert Conformal Conic Projection

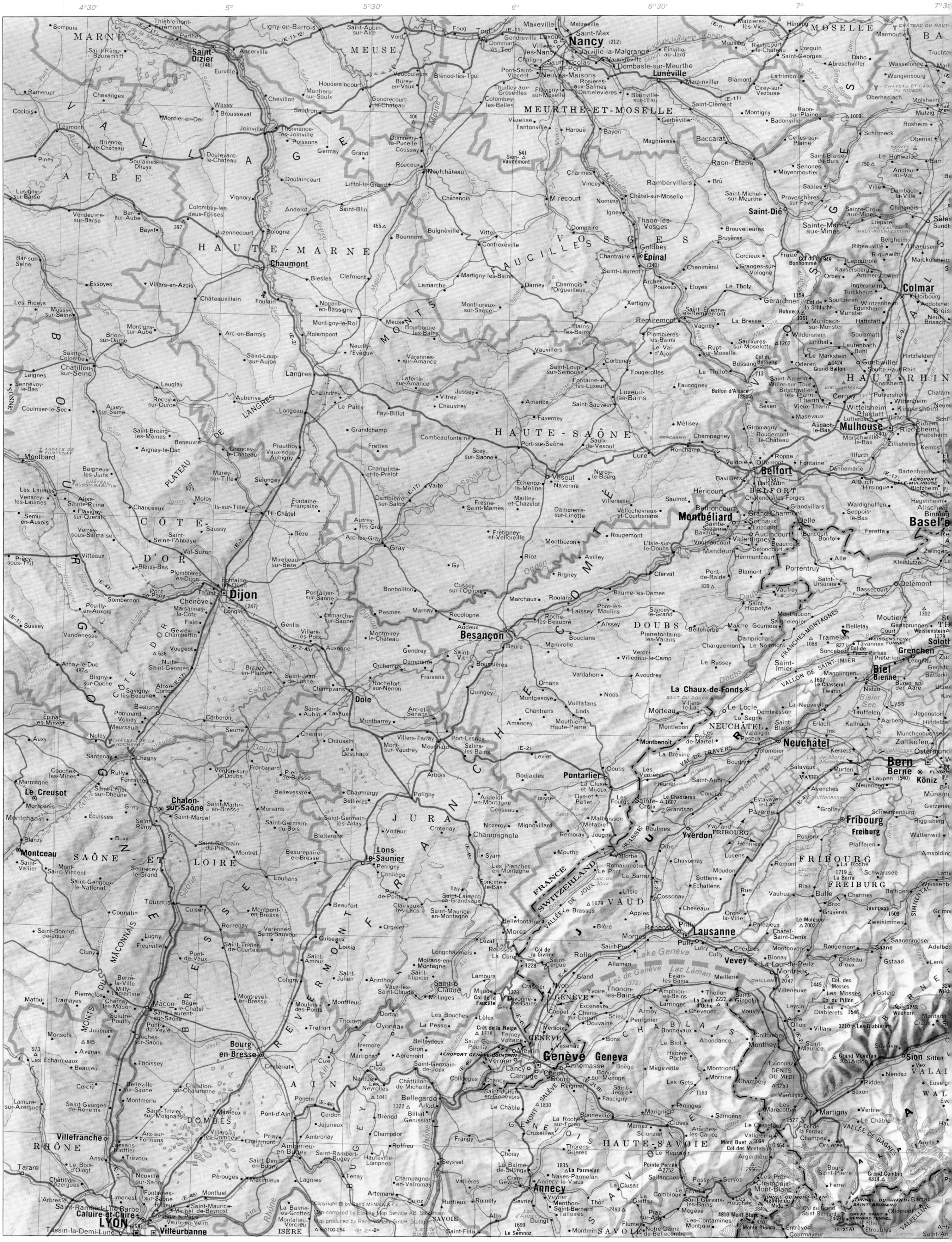
Nancy
Lunéville
Épinal
Colmar
Mulhouse
Belfort
Montbéliard
Basel
Dijon
Besançon
Chaumont
Langres
Vesoul
Dole
Lons-le-Saunier
Bourg-en-Bresse
Chalon-sur-Saône
Mâcon
LYON
Villeurbanne
Genève
Geneva
Lausanne
Annecy
Neuchâtel
Bern
Biel
Fribourg
La Chaux-de-Fonds
Pontarlier
MARNE
MEUSE
MEURTHE-ET-MOSELLE
MOSELLE
VOSGES
HAUTE-MARNE
HAUTE-SAÔNE
HAUT-RHIN
CÔTE-D'OR
DOUBS
JURA
SAÔNE-ET-LOIRE
AIN
HAUTE-SAVOIE
SAVOIE
RHÔNE
AUBE
VAUD
FRIBOURG
FRANCE
SWITZERLAND
Lake Geneva
Lac Léman
Copyright © by Rand McNally & Co.

Strasbourg
Freiburg im Breisgau
Stuttgart
Tübingen
Reutlingen
Ulm
Neu-Ulm
Augsburg
Kempten
Konstanz
Schaffhausen
Winterthur
Zürich
Luzern
Sankt Gallen
Bregenz
Lindau
Feldkirch
Vaduz
Chur
Lugano
Como
Varese
Lecco
Sondrio
Domodossola
Verbania
Bellinzona
Locarno
Friedrichshafen
Ravensburg
Memmingen
Kaufbeuren
Biberach an der Riss
Offenburg
Lahr
Rottweil
Tuttlingen
Singen (Hohentwiel)
Baden
Aarau
Olten
Zug
Dornbirn
Sigmaringen
Heidenheim an der Brenz
Göppingen
Böblingen
Sindelfingen
WEST GERMANY
SWITZERLAND
AUSTRIA
ITALY
FRANCE
Bodensee
Lake Constance
SCHWÄBISCHE ALB
SCHWARZWALD
GRAUBÜNDEN
TICINO
GLARUS
URI
SCHWYZ
LUZERN
ZÜRICH
AARGAU
THURGAU
APPENZELL
SANKT GALLEN
LIECHTENSTEIN
VORARLBERG
TIROL
LOMBARDIA
BAYERN
SCHWABEN
BADEN-WÜRTTEMBERG
8°
8°30′
9°
9°30′
10°
10°30′
11°
48° 30′
48°
47° 30′
47°
46° 30′
46°

Kilometers 0 10 20 30 40 50 Km.

Statute Miles 0 10 20 30 40 50 Mi.

Scale 1:1,000,000

One centimeter represents 10 kilometers.
One inch represents approximately 16 miles.
Lambert Conformal Conic Projection

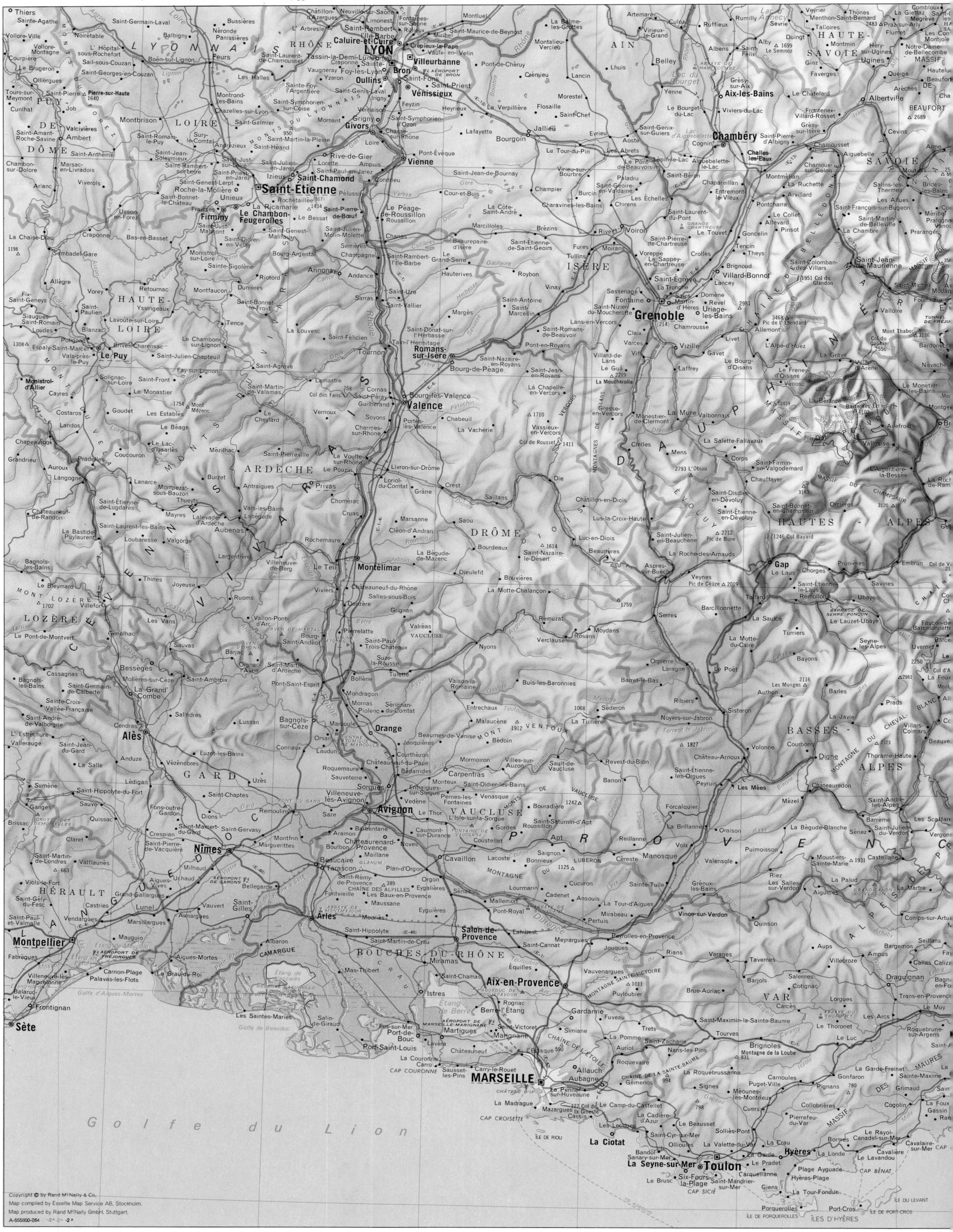

4°
4°30'
5°
5°30'
6°
6°30'
45° 30'
45°
44° 30'
44°
43° 30'
43°
LYON
Villeurbanne
Vénissieux
Oullins
Bron
Caluire-et-Cuire
Givors
Vienne
Saint-Étienne
Saint-Chamond
Firminy
Rive-de-Gier
Annonay
Le Puy
Valence
Romans-sur-Isère
Bourg-de-Péage
Tournon
Privas
Montélimar
Orange
Avignon
Carpentras
Cavaillon
Nîmes
Alès
Arles
Tarascon
Beaucaire
Lunel
Montpellier
Sète
Frontignan
Salon-de-Provence
Aix-en-Provence
Martigues
Marignane
MARSEILLE
Aubagne
La Ciotat
La Seyne-sur-Mer
Toulon
Hyères
Draguignan
Brignoles
Manosque
Digne
Sisteron
Gap
Grenoble
Voiron
Vizille
Chambéry
Aix-les-Bains
Bourgoin
Albertville
Saint-Jean-de-Maurienne
Embrun
Briançon
Die
Crest
Nyons
Vaison-la-Romaine
Apt
Pertuis
Istres
Miramas
Aigues-Mortes
Les Saintes-Maries
LYONNAIS
RHÔNE
LOIRE
HAUTE-LOIRE
ARDÈCHE
DRÔME
ISÈRE
AIN
HAUTE-SAVOIE
SAVOIE
DAUPHINÉ
HAUTES-ALPES
BASSES-ALPES
VAUCLUSE
GARD
LOZÈRE
HÉRAULT
BOUCHES-DU-RHÔNE
VAR
PROVENCE
LANGUEDOC
VIVARAIS
CAMARGUE
MONTS DU LYONNAIS
MONTS DU VIVARAIS
CÉVENNES
MONT VENTOUX
LUBERON
Golfe du Lion
Golfe d'Aigues-Mortes
Golfe de Beauduc
CAP COURONNE
CAP CROISETTE
CAP SICIÉ
CAP BÉNAT
ÎLE DE PORQUEROLLES
ÎLES D'HYÈRES
ÎLE DE PORT-CROS
ÎLE DU LEVANT

7°
7°30'
8°
8°30'
9°
9°30'
45° 30'
45°
44° 30'
44°
43° 30'
43°
MILANO
MILAN
TORINO TURIN
GENOVA
GENOA
Bergamo
Lecco
Como
Varese
Monza
Novara
Vercelli
Biella
Ivrea
Aosta
Chivasso
Asti
Alessandria
Pavia
Piacenza
Lodi
Crema
Voghera
Tortona
Novi Ligure
Acqui Terme
Alba
Bra
Cuneo
Savigliano
Saluzzo
Pinerolo
Carmagnola
Casale Monferrato
Vigevano
Busto Arsizio
Gallarate
Legnano
Savona
Rapallo
Chiavari
Sestri Levante
La Spezia
Imperia
San Remo
Ventimiglia
Menton
Monaco
MONACO
Nice
Cannes
Antibes
Grasse
Cagnes-sur-Mer
Villefranche-sur-Mer
Albenga
Alassio
Finale Ligure
Varazze
ALPI MARITTIME
MARITTIME ALPS
ALPES MARITIMES
APPENNINO
APPENNINES
MONFERRATO
LANGHE
RIVIERA DI PONENTE
RIVIERA DI LEVANTE
CÔTE D'AZUR
Golfo di Genova
Ligurian Sea
Mar Ligure
MEDITERRANEAN SEA
AEROPORTO DELLA MALPENSA
AEROPORTO DI LINATE
AEROPORTO CRISTOFORO COLOMBO
AÉROPORT DE NICE-CÔTE D'AZUR
TUNNEL DU GRAND-SAINT-BERNARD
TUNNEL DE TENDE
FRANCE
ITALIA
ITALY

Kilometers 0 10 20 30 40 50 Km.

Statute Miles 0 10 20 30 40 50 Mi.

Scale 1:1,000,000

One centimeter represents 10 kilometers.
One inch represents approximately 16 miles.
Lambert Conformal Conic Projection

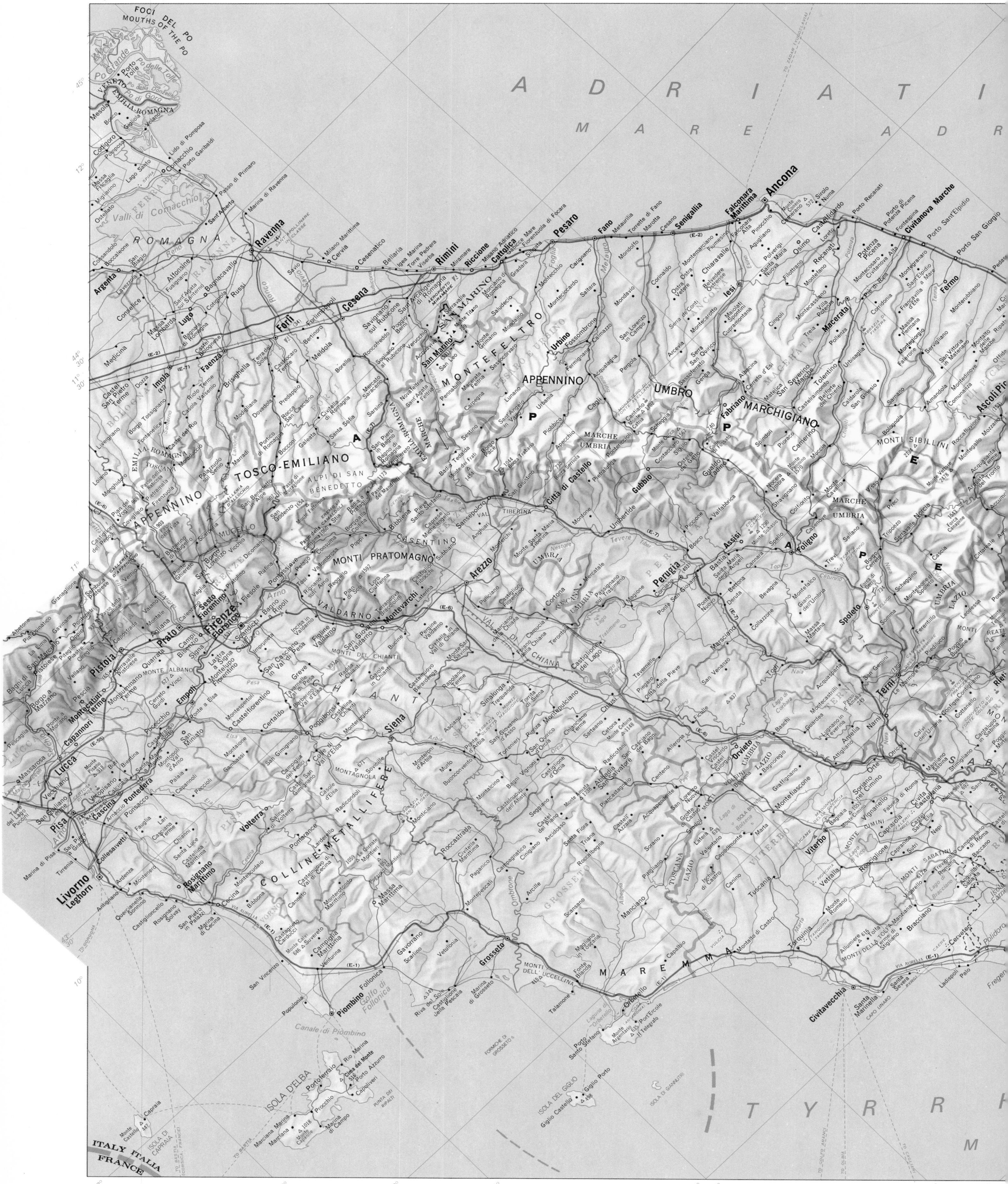
A D R I A T I
M A R E A D R
FOCI DEL PO
MOUTHS OF THE PO
Ravenna
Rimini
Riccione
Cattolica
Pesaro
Fano
Senigallia
Ancona
Falconara Marittima
Civitanova Marche
Fermo
Cesena
Forlì
Faenza
Imola
Lugo
Argenta
SAN MARINO
San Marino
Urbino
Iesi
Macerata
MONTEFELTRO
APPENNINO
UMBRO
MARCHIGIANO
TOSCO-EMILIANO
APPENNINO
ALPI DI SAN BENEDETTO
MONTI SIBILLINI
Fabriano
Gubbio
Città di Castello
Perugia
Assisi
Foligno
Spoleto
Terni
Ascoli Piceno
Rieti
MONTI PRATOMAGNO
CASENTINO
MUGELLO
VALDARNO
Arezzo
Montevarchi
Firenze
Florence
Prato
Pistoia
Lucca
Pisa
Livorno
Leghorn
Empoli
Siena
Cascina
Pontedera
Volterra
Rosignano Marittimo
Montecatini Terme
MONTI DEL CHIANTI
COLLINE METALLIFERE
Cortona
Chiusi
Orvieto
Viterbo
Montefiascone
Grosseto
Piombino
Follonica
Orbetello
Civitavecchia
Santa Marinella
Cerveteri
Ladispoli
Bracciano
MAREMMA
MONTI DELL' UCCELLINA
Golfo di Follonica
Canale di Piombino
ISOLA D'ELBA
Portoferraio
Capraia
ISOLA DI CAPRAIA
ISOLA DEL GIGLIO
Giglio Porto
Porto Santo Stefano
Talamone
T Y R R H
M
ITALY ITALIA
FRANCE

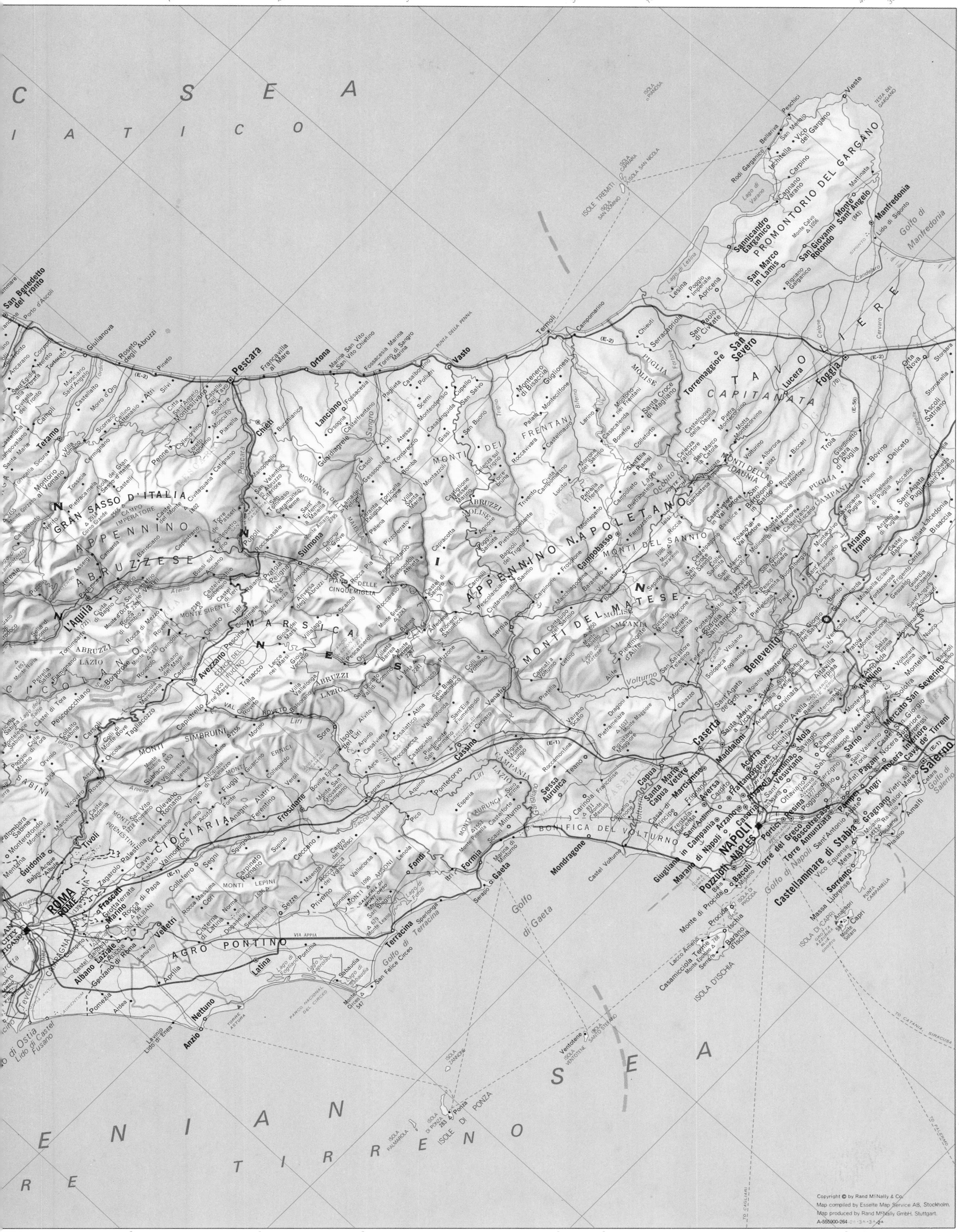

MARE ADRIATICO
ADRIATIC SEA
MAR TIRRENO
TYRRHENIAN SEA
PROMONTORIO DEL GARGANO
Golfo di Manfredonia
TAVOLIERE
CAPITANATA
ISOLE TREMITI
APPENNINO NAPOLETANO
APPENNINO ABRUZZESE
GRAN SASSO D'ITALIA
MONTI DEL MATESE
MONTI DEL SANNIO
MONTI DELLA DAUNIA
MONTI DEI FRENTANI
MONTI SIMBRUINI
MONTI LEPINI
MONTI AUSONI
MONTI AURUNCI
CIOCIARIA
MARSICA
AGRO PONTINO
BONIFICA DEL VOLTURNO
CAMPANIA
MOLISE
PUGLIA
LAZIO
ABRUZZI
Golfo di Gaeta
Golfo di Napoli
Golfo di Salerno
Golfo di Terracina
ISOLA D'ISCHIA
ISOLA DI CAPRI
ISOLE DI PONZA
ISOLA VENTOTENE
ISOLA ZANNONE
ISOLA PALMAROLA
ROMA
ROME
NAPOLI
NAPLES
Pescara
Chieti
Teramo
L'Aquila
Avezzano
Sulmona
Lanciano
Ortona
Vasto
Termoli
Campobasso
Isernia
Foggia
Lucera
San Severo
Manfredonia
Vieste
Benevento
Avellino
Salerno
Caserta
Capua
Aversa
Pozzuoli
Sorrento
Castellammare di Stabia
Torre Annunziata
Torre del Greco
Gaeta
Formia
Terracina
Latina
Anzio
Nettuno
Frosinone
Cassino
Sora
Tivoli
Frascati
Velletri
Fondi
San Benedetto del Tronto
Giulianova
Mondragone
Ariano Irpino
Vesuvio

Kilometers 0 10 20 30 40 50 Km.
Statute Miles 0 10 20 30 40 50 Mi.

Scale 1:1,000,000

One centimeter represents 10 kilometers.
One inch represents approximately 16 miles.
Lambert Conformal Conic Projection

Soviet Union

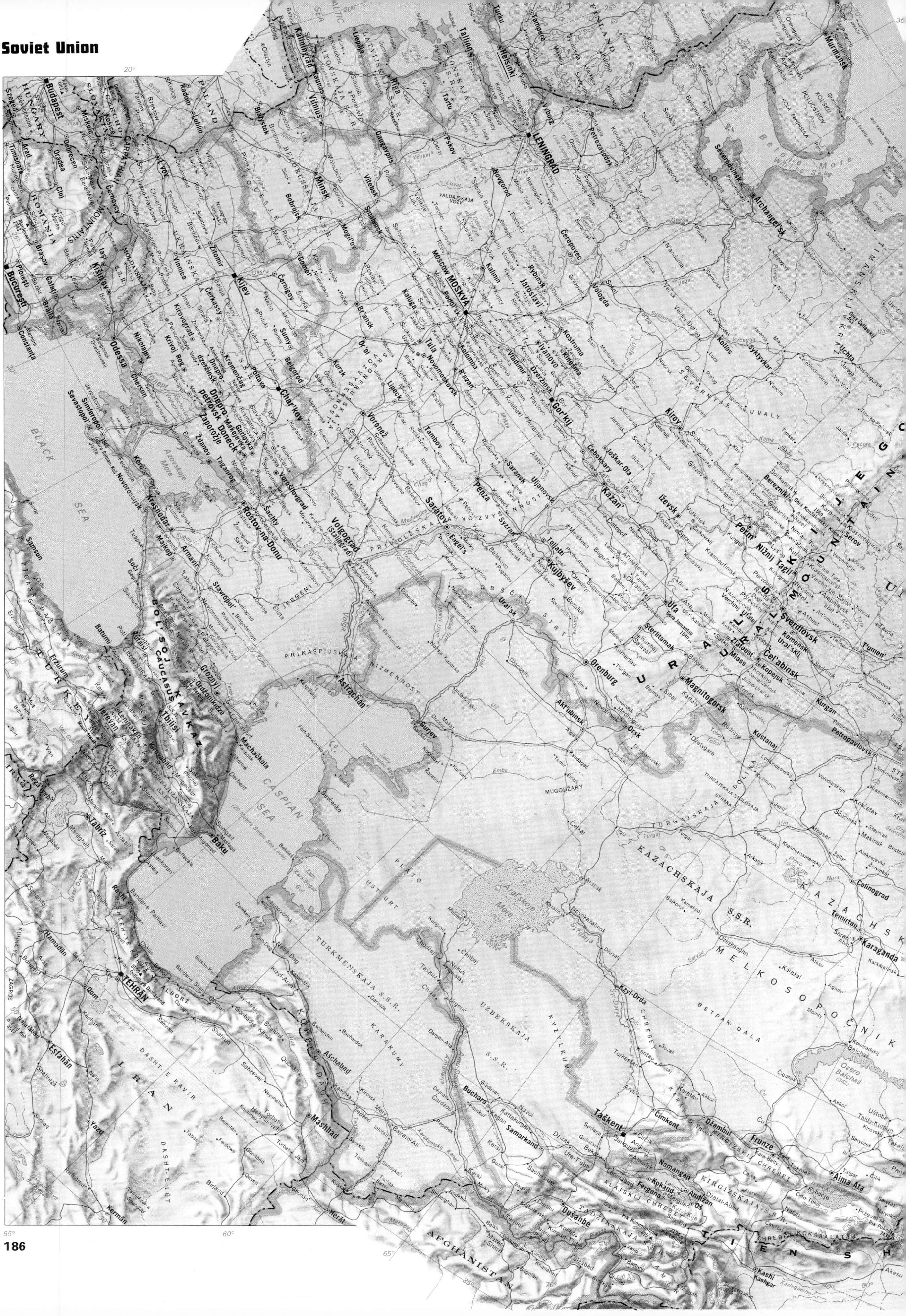

LENINGRAD
MOSCOW MOSKVA
Kijev
Minsk
Riga
Tallinn
Helsinki
Vilnius
Budapest
București
Odessa
Char'kov
Volgograd (Stalingrad)
Rostov-na-Donu
Saratov
Kujbyšev
Kazan'
Gor'kij
Sverdlovsk
Čel'abinsk
Perm'
Orenburg
Astrachan'
Baku
Tbilisi
Jerevan
TEHRAN
Mashhad
Herat
Ašchabad
Taškent
Samarkand
Dušanbe
Frunze
Alma-Ata
Karaganda
Celinograd
Archangel'sk
Murmansk
BLACK SEA
CASPIAN SEA
Aral'skoje More
Azovskoje More
Beloje More
White Sea
KAZACHSKAJA S.S.R.
TURKMENSKAJA S.S.R.
UZBEKSKAJA S.S.R.
POLAND
HUNGARY
ROMANIA
TURKEY
IRAN
AFGHANISTAN
FINLAND
CARPATHIAN MOUNTAINS
BOL'ŠOJ KAVKAZ
CAUCASUS
URAL'SKIJE GORY
KARAKUMY
KYZYLKUM
USTJURT
PRIKASPIJSKAJA NIZMENNOST'
MUGODŽARY

ALASKA
UNITED STATES
Chukchi Sea
Bering Strait
OSTROV VRANGEL'A
SAINT LAWRENCE ISLAND
NUNIVAK ISLAND
SAINT MATTHEW ISLAND
ČUKOTSKIJ POLUOSTROV
EKIATAPSKIJ CHREBET
Arctic Circle
Anadyrskij Zaliv
Zaliv Kresta
VOSTOČNO-SIBIRSKOJE MORE
EAST SIBERIAN SEA
OSTROVA DE-LONGA
OSTROV NOVAJA SIBIR'
OSTROV BOL'ŠOJ L'ACHOVSKIJ
MEDVEŽ'I OSTROVA
AN'UJSKIJ CHREBET
ANADYRSKOJE PLOSKOGORJE
KOLYMSKAJA NIZMENNOST
JUKAGIRSKOJE PLOSKOGORJE
KORJAKSKOJE NAGORJE
PENŽINSKIJ CHREBET
Bering Sea
MOMSKIJ CHREBET
CHREBET ČERSKOGO
Gora Pobeda 3147
CHREBET SUNTAR-CHAJATA
CHREBET SETTE-DABAN
Gora Mus-Chaja 2959
Pik Aborigen 2586
Zaliv Šelichova
Magadan
Ochotsk
SREDINNYJ CHREBET
POLUOSTROV KAMČATKA
Petropavlovsk-Kamčatskij
Kl'učevskaja Sopka 4750
KOMANDORSKIJE OSTROVA
SEA OF OKHOTSK
OCHOTSKOJE MORE
CHREBET DŽUGDŽUR
Gora Topko 1906
ŠANTARSKIJE OSTROVA
OSTROV SACHALIN
SAKHALIN
Gora Lopatina 1609
KURIL'SKIJE OSTROVA
KURIL ISLANDS
Habomai, Shikotan, Kunashiri, and Etorofu, occupied by the U.S.S.R. since 1945, are claimed by Japan pending a final peace treaty.
Južno-Sachalinsk
La Perouse Strait
Komsomol'sk-na-Amure
BUREINSKIJ CHREBET
Gora Tardoki-Jani 2077
SICHOTE-ALIN'
Chabarovsk
Blagoveščensk
XIAOXINGANLINGSHANMAI
HEILONGJIANG
Qiqihaer Tsitsihar
CHINA
MANCHURIA
Haerbin
Yichun
Hegang
Jiamusi
Shuangyashan
Mudanjiang
Ussurijsk
Vladivostok
JILIN
Nachodka
SEA OF JAPAN
Wakkanai
Asahikawa
Sapporo
Otaru
Muroran
Kushiro
Nemuro
HOKKAIDO
Hakodate
Aomori
Hachinohe
HONSHU
Akita
Morioka
JAPAN
PACIFIC OCEAN

KARSKOJE MORE
KARA SEA
MORE LAPTEVYCH
LAPTEV SEA
NOVAJA ZEML'A
SEVERNAJA ZEML'A
OSTROV KOMSOMOLEC
OSTROV OKT'ABR'SKOJ REVOL'UCII
OSTROV BOL'ŠEVIK
POLUOSTROV TAJMYR
GORY BYRRANGA
SEVERO - SIBIRSKAJA NIZMENNOST'
POLUOSTROV JAMAL
GYDANSKIJ POLUOSTROV
PLATO PUTORANA
SREDNE-SIBIRSKOJE PLOSKOGORJE
CENTRAL SIBERIA
ZAPADNO-SIBIRSKAJA NIZMENNOST'
ROSSIJSKAJA SOVETSKAJA FEDERATIVNAJA SOCIALISTIČESKAJA RESPUBLIKA
RUSSIAN SOVIET FEDERATED SOCIALIST REPUBLIC
SOVIET SOCIALIST REPUBLICS
STANOVOJE NAGORJE
STANOVOY MOUNTAINS
JABLONOVYJ CHREBET
YABLONOVY RANGE
VOSTOČNYJ SAJAN
ZAPADNYJ SAJAN
SAYAN MOUNTAINS
SAJANY
ALTAJ
CHINA
MONGOLIA
XINJIANG WEIWUER ZIZHIQU
SINKIANG
ZHUANGAERPENDI
DAXINGANLINGSHANMAI
Ozero Bajkal
Lake Baykal
Ob'
Jenisej
Lena
Vorkuta
Noril'sk
Dudinka
Igarka
Surgut
Tomsk
Novosibirsk
Barnaul
Kemerovo
Novokuzneck
Krasnojarsk
Bratsk
Irkutsk
Angarsk
Ulan-Ude
Čita
Ulaanbaatar
Darchan
Semipalatinsk
Ust'-Kamenogorsk
Bijsk
Rubcovsk
Abakan
Kyzyl
Mirnyj
Nordvik
Chatanga
Tiksi
Copyright © by Rand McNally & Co.
Map prepared by Esselte Map Service AB, Stockholm.

Kilometers 0 200 400 600 Km.

Statute Miles 0 200 400 600 Mi.

Scale 1:12,000,000

One centimeter represents 120 kilometers.
One inch represents approximately 190 miles.
Lambert Conformal Conic Projection

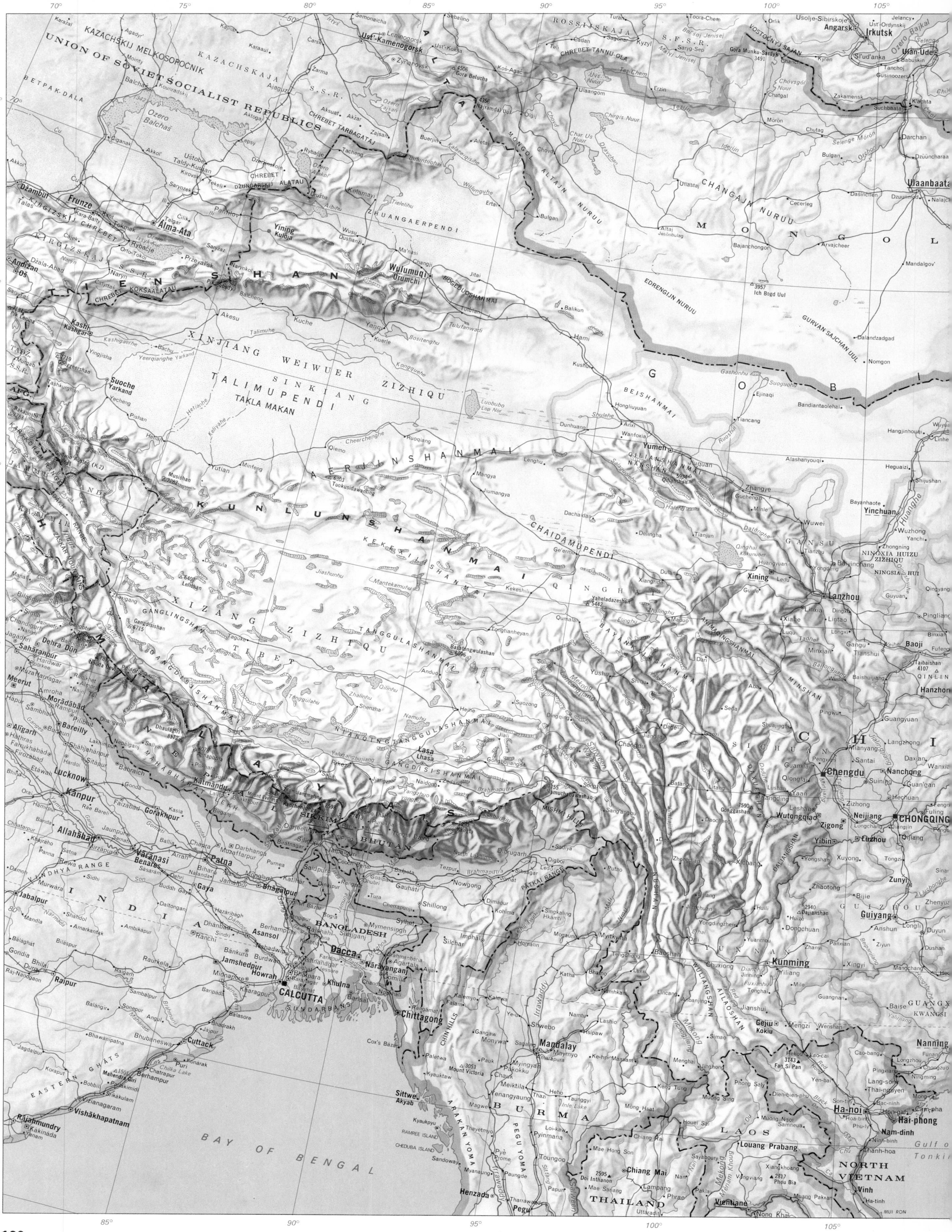
UNION OF SOVIET SOCIALIST REPUBLICS
KAZACHSKIJ MELKOSOPOCNIK
KAZACHSKAJA S.S.R.
BETPAK-DALA
ROSSIJSKAJA S.F.S.R.
Ozero Balchaš
Alma-Ata
Frunze
Džambul
Ust'-Kamenogorsk
Irkutsk
Angarsk
Ulan-Ude
Ozero Bajkal
Ulaanbaatar
CHANGAJN NURUU
MONGOL
MONGOL ALTAJN NURUU
EDRENGIJN NURUU
GURVAN SAJCHAN UUL
GOBI
ZHUANGAERPENDI
Wulumuqi
Urumchi
TIEN SHAN
XINJIANG WEIWUER ZIZHIQU
SINKIANG
TALIMUPENDI
TAKLA MAKAN
Kashi
Kashgar
Suoche
Yarkand
Hami
BEISHANMAI
Yumen
QILIANSHANMAI
NANSHAN
AERJINSHANMAI
KUNLUNSHANMAI
CHAIDAMUPENDI
QINGHAI
GANSU
Xining
Lanzhou
NINGXIA HUIZU ZIZHIQU
XIZANG ZIZHIQU
TIBET
TANGGULASHANMAI
GANGLINGSHAN
NIANQINGTANGGULASHANMAI
GANGDISISHANMAI
Lasa
Lhasa
HIMALAYAS
Katmandu
SIKKIM
BHUTAN
BANGLADESH
Dacca
CALCUTTA
INDIA
Lucknow
Kanpur
Allahabad
Varanasi
Benares
Patna
Meerut
Dehra Dun
Raipur
Jabalpur
Cuttack
Vishakhapatnam
Rajahmundry
EASTERN GHATS
BAY OF BENGAL
Chittagong
Mandalay
BURMA
ARAKAN YOMA
PEGU YOMA
Sittwe
Akyab
Henzada
Pegu
SICHUAN
Chengdu
CHONGQING
Kunming
YUNNAN
GUIZHOU
Guiyang
Zunyi
Baoji
Nanning
GUANGXI
Ha-noi
Hai-phong
NORTH VIETNAM
LAOS
Louang Prabang
Vientiane
THAILAND
Chiang Mai
Gulf of Tonkin

U. S. S. R.
ROSSIJSKAJA S.F.S.R.
Blagoveščensk
Chabarovsk
Južno-Sachalinsk
OSTROV SACHALIN
SAKHALIN
SEA OF OKHOTSK
La Perouse Strait
HOKKAIDŌ
Sapporo
Asahikawa
Kushiro
Hakodate
Aomori
Hachinohe
Morioka
Akita
Sendai
Niigata
JAPAN
TŌKYŌ
Yokohama
Kawasaki
Nagoya
Kyōto
Kōbe
ŌSAKA
Hiroshima
Kitakyūshū
Fukuoka
Nagasaki
Kumamoto
Kagoshima
SHIKOKU
KYŪSHŪ
HONSHŪ
SEA OF JAPAN
Vladivostok
Ussurijsk
Nachodka
MANCHURIA
HEILONGJIANG
Harbin
Qiqihaer
Tsitsihar
Changchun
Jilin
SHENYANG
MUKDEN
Fushun
Anshan
Dalian
Lüda
Dairen
NORTH KOREA
P'yŏngyang
SOUTH KOREA
SOUL
SEOUL
Pusan
Inch'ŏn
Taegu
Kwangju
CHEJU-DO
(S. Korea)
NEIMENGGU ZIZHIQU
INNER MONGOLIA
DA HINGGAN LING
BEIJING
PEKING
TIANJIN
TIENTSIN
Baotou
Huhehaote
Datong
Taiyuan
Shijiazhuang
Jinan
Tsinan
Qingdao
Tsingtao
SHANDONG
Bohai
Yellow Sea
Zhengzhou
Kaifeng
Luoyang
Xuzhou
Nanjing
SHANGHAI
Hangzhou
Ningbo
Hefei
WUHAN
Nanchang
Changsha
Fuzhou
Xiamen
Amoy
GUANGZHOU
CANTON
Shantou
Swatow
Kowloon
Victoria
HONG KONG
Macau
Aomen
Haikou
HAINANDAO
TAIWAN
FORMOSA
T'aipei
Kaohsiung
T'ainan
EAST CHINA SEA
RYUKYU ISLANDS (Jap.)
NANSEI-SHOTŌ
OKINAWA-JIMA
Naha
SAKISHIMA-SHOTŌ
Tropic of Cancer
PACIFIC OCEAN
PHILIPPINE SEA
SOUTH CHINA SEA
Bashi Channel
BATAN ISLANDS
BABUYAN ISLANDS
PHILIPPINES
LUZON
PRATAS ISLANDS
(China)
Copyright © by Rand McNally & Co.
Map prepared by Esselte Map Service AB, Stockholm.

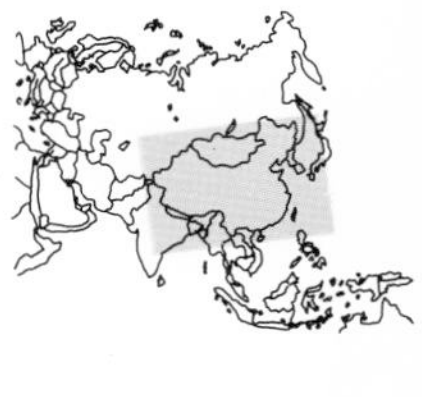

Kilometers 0 200 400 600 Km.

Statute Miles 0 200 400 600 Mi.

Scale 1:12,000,000

One centimeter represents 120 kilometers.

One inch represents approximately 190 miles.

Lambert Conformal Conic Projection

PACIFIC OCEAN
HONSHŪ
HOKKAIDŌ
SEA OF JAPAN
NIHON-KAI
SEA OF OKHOTSK
KURIL ISLANDS
OSTROV SACHALIN
SAKHALIN
La Perouse Strait
Tsugaru-kaikyō
Sado-kaikyō
Sapporo
Otaru
Asahikawa
Kitami
Obihiro
Kushiro
Nemuro
Muroran
Hakodate
Wakkanai
Aomori
Hachinohe
Morioka
Akita
Sendai
Yamagata
Niigata
Fukushima
Kōriyama
Mito
Hitachi
Utsunomiya
Maebashi
Nagano
Toyama
Kanazawa
Chiba
Tōkyō
Yokohama
Kawasaki
Chōshi
U.S.S.R.
JAPAN
NIHON

SEA OF JAPAN
NIHON-KAI
OKI-GUNTŌ
ULLŪNG-DO (S. Korea)
TOK-DO (S. Korea)
TSUSHIMA
Tsushima-kaikyō Eastern Channel
Genkai-nada
GOTO-RETTŌ
FUKUE-SHIMA
KYŪSHŪ
AMAKUSA-SHOTŌ
KOSHIKIJIMA-RETTŌ
Ōsumi-kaikyō
TANEGA-SHIMA
SHIKOKU
PACIFIC OCEAN
Tosa-wan
Kii-suidō
Kumano-nada
Enshū-nada
IZU-SHOTŌ
Shimonoseki
Kitakyūshū
Fukuoka
Nagasaki
Sasebo
Kumamoto
Kagoshima
Miyazaki
Ōita
Beppu
Hiroshima
Kure
Okayama
Kurashiki
Matsuyama
Takamatsu
Tokushima
Kōchi
Kōbe
Himeji
ŌSAKA
Kyōto
Nara
Wakayama
NAGOYA
Shizuoka
Hamamatsu
Toyohashi
Tsu
Gifu
Matsue
Tottori
Ube
Shimonoseki
CHŪGOKU
SHIKOKU
KII-HANTŌ
Copyright © by Rand McNally & Co.
Map prepared by Teikoku-Shoin Co., Ltd., Tokyo.

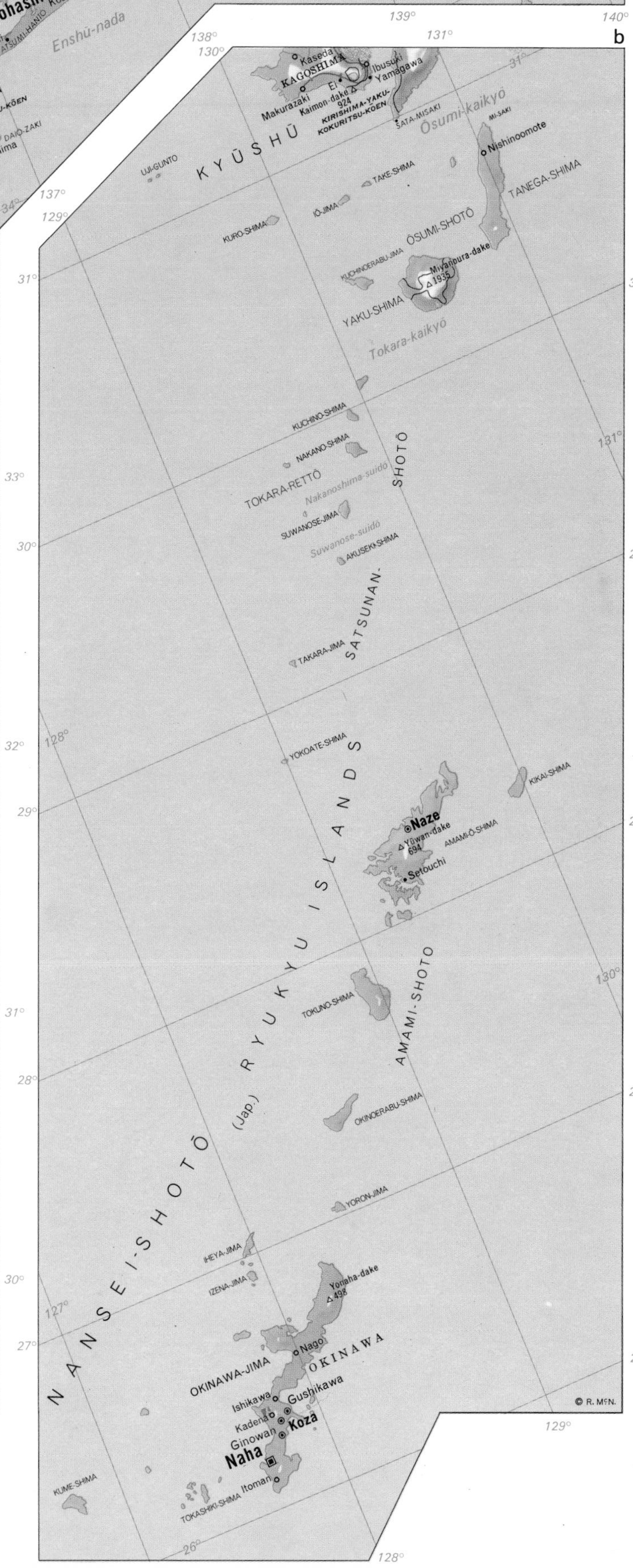
b
KYŪSHŪ
KAGOSHIMA
ŌSUMI-SHOTŌ
TANEGA-SHIMA
YAKU-SHIMA
Tokara-kaikyō
TOKARA-RETTŌ
SATSUNAN-SHOTŌ
RYUKYU ISLANDS
NANSEI-SHOTŌ (Jap.)
AMAMI-SHOTŌ
Naze
OKINAWA
OKINAWA-JIMA
Naha
Koza
© R. McN.

Kilometers 0 50 100 150 Km.
Statute Miles 0 50 100 150 Mi.

Scale 1:3,000,000
One centimeter represents 30 kilometers.
One inch represents approximately 47 miles.
Lambert Conformal Conic Projection

Northeast China and Korea

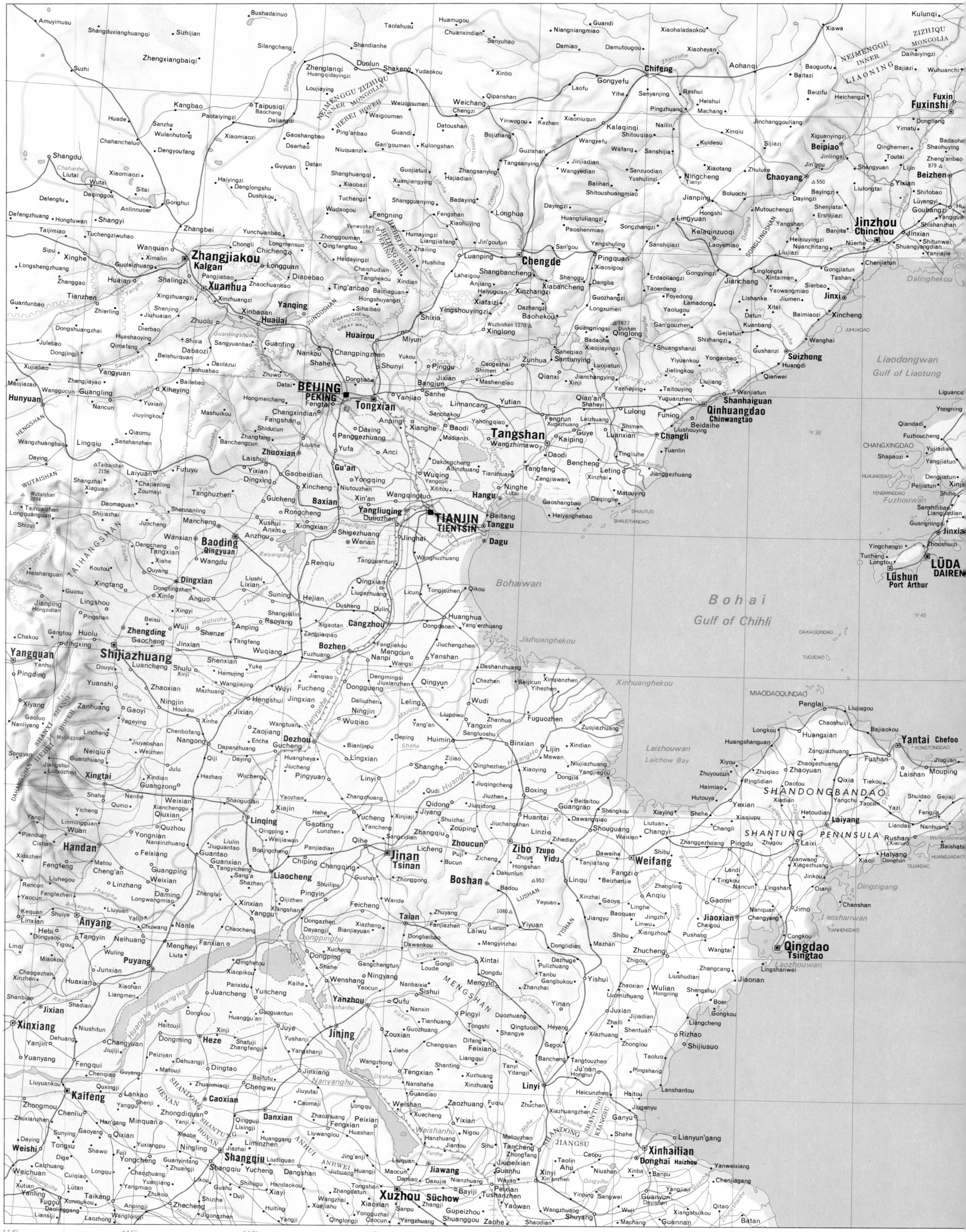

Zhangjiakou
Kalgan
Xuanhua
Chengde
Chifeng
Jinzhou
Chinchou
Fuxinshi
Beipiao
Chaoyang
Beijing
Peking
Tongxian
Tianjin
Tientsin
Tanggu
Dagu
Tangshan
Qinhuangdao
Chinwangtao
Shanhaiguan
Baoding
Qingyuan
Dingxian
Shijiazhuang
Xingtai
Handan
Anyang
Cangzhou
Dezhou
Jinan
Tsinan
Zibo
Weifang
Yantai
Chefoo
Qingdao
Tsingtao
Lüda
Dairen
Lüshun
Port Arthur
Xinxiang
Kaifeng
Shangqiu
Xuzhou
Süchow
Jining
Linyi
Heze
Xinhailian
Lianyun'gang
Bohai
Gulf of Chihli
Bohaiwan
Liaodongwan
Gulf of Liaotung
Laizhouwan
Laichow Bay
Shandong Bandao
Shantung Peninsula
Taihangshan
Yanshan
Great Wall
Neimenggu Zizhiqu
Inner Mongolia
Hebei
Hopeh
Liaoning
Shanxi
Henan
Honan
Anhui
Jiangsu
Shandong
Huanghe
Hwang Ho
Grand Canal

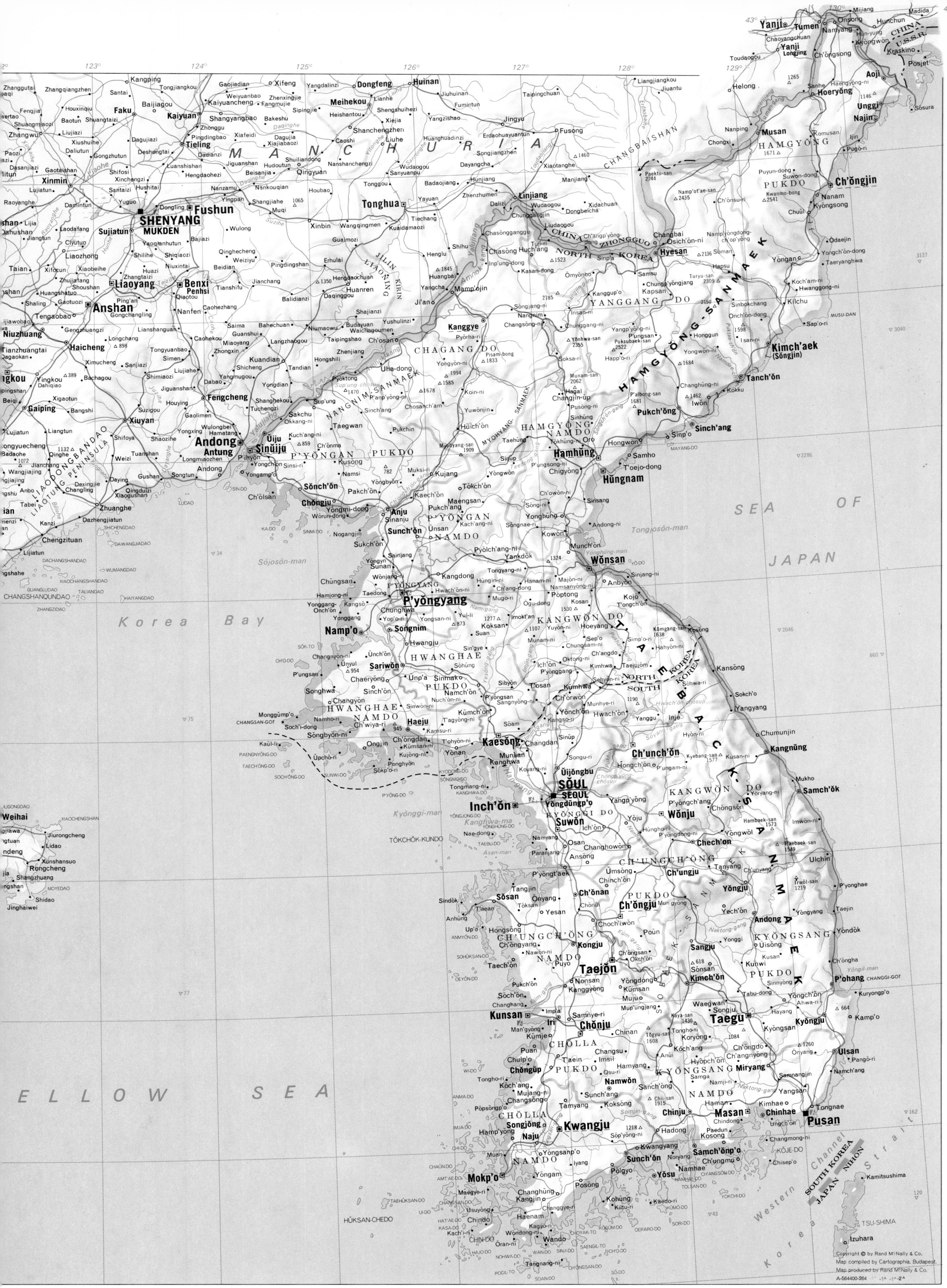
MANCHURIA
CHINA
U.S.S.R.
NORTH KOREA
SOUTH KOREA
JAPAN
NIHON
SEA OF JAPAN
YELLOW SEA
Korea Bay
Korea Strait
Western Channel
SHENYANG
MUKDEN
Fushun
Anshan
Liaoyang
Benxi
Andong
Antung
Sinŭiju
P'yŏngyang
Nampo
Hamhŭng
Hŭngnam
Ch'ŏngjin
Kimch'aek
Wŏnsan
Kaesŏng
SŎUL
SEOUL
Inch'ŏn
Suwŏn
Taejŏn
Taegu
Kwangju
Pusan
Masan
Mokp'o
Ulsan
Kunsan
Chŏnju
Ch'ŏngju
Ch'unch'ŏn
Wŏnju
Kangnŭng
HAMGYŎNG PUKDO
HAMGYŎNG NAMDO
YANGGANG DO
CHAGANG DO
P'YŎNGAN PUKDO
P'YŎNGAN NAMDO
HWANGHAE PUKDO
HWANGHAE NAMDO
KANGWŎN DO
KYŎNGGI DO
CH'UNGCH'ŎNG PUKDO
CH'UNGCH'ŎNG NAMDO
KYŎNGSANG PUKDO
KYŎNGSANG NAMDO
CHŎLLA PUKDO
CHŎLLA NAMDO
HAMGYŎNG-SANMAEK
T'AEBAEK-SANMAEK
SOBAEK-SANMAEK
NANGNIM-SANMAEK
CHANGBAISHAN
LIAODONG BANDAO
LIAOTUNG PENINSULA
Copyright © by Rand McNally & Co.
Map compiled by Cartographia, Budapest.
Map produced by Rand McNally & Co.
A-564400-264

Kilometers 0 50 100 150 Km.

Statute Miles 0 50 100 150 Mi.

Scale 1:3,000,000

One centimeter represents 30 kilometers.
One inch represents approximately 47 miles.

Lambert Conformal Conic Projection

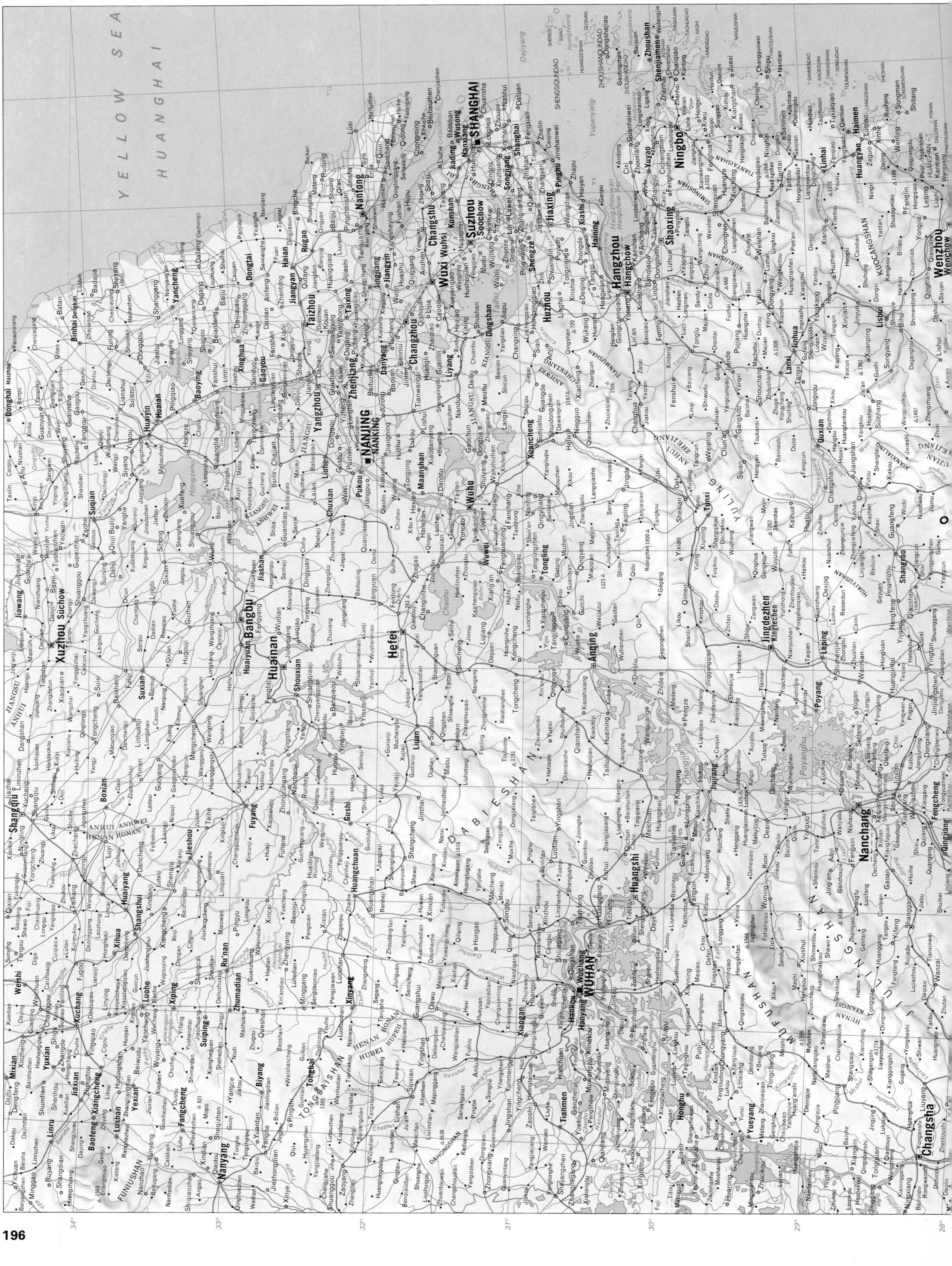
YELLOW SEA
HUANGHAI
SHANGHAI
NANJING
NANKING
WUHAN
Suzhou
Soochow
Hangzhou
Hangchow
Ningbo
Wuxi
Changzhou
Zhenjiang
Yangzhou
Nantong
Xuzhou
Suchow
Bengbu
Huainan
Hefei
Anqing
Wuhu
Nanchang
Changsha
Jiujiang
Huangshi
Jingdezhen
Kingtechen
Shaoxing
Huzhou
Jiaxing
Wenzhou
Wenchow
Shangqiu
Nanyang
Xinyang
Zhumadian
Kaifeng
DABIESHAN
TONGBAISHAN
FUNIUSHAN
JIANGSU
ANHUI
ANHWEI
HENAN
HONAN
HUBEI
HUPEH
HUNAN
JIANGXI
ZHEJIANG

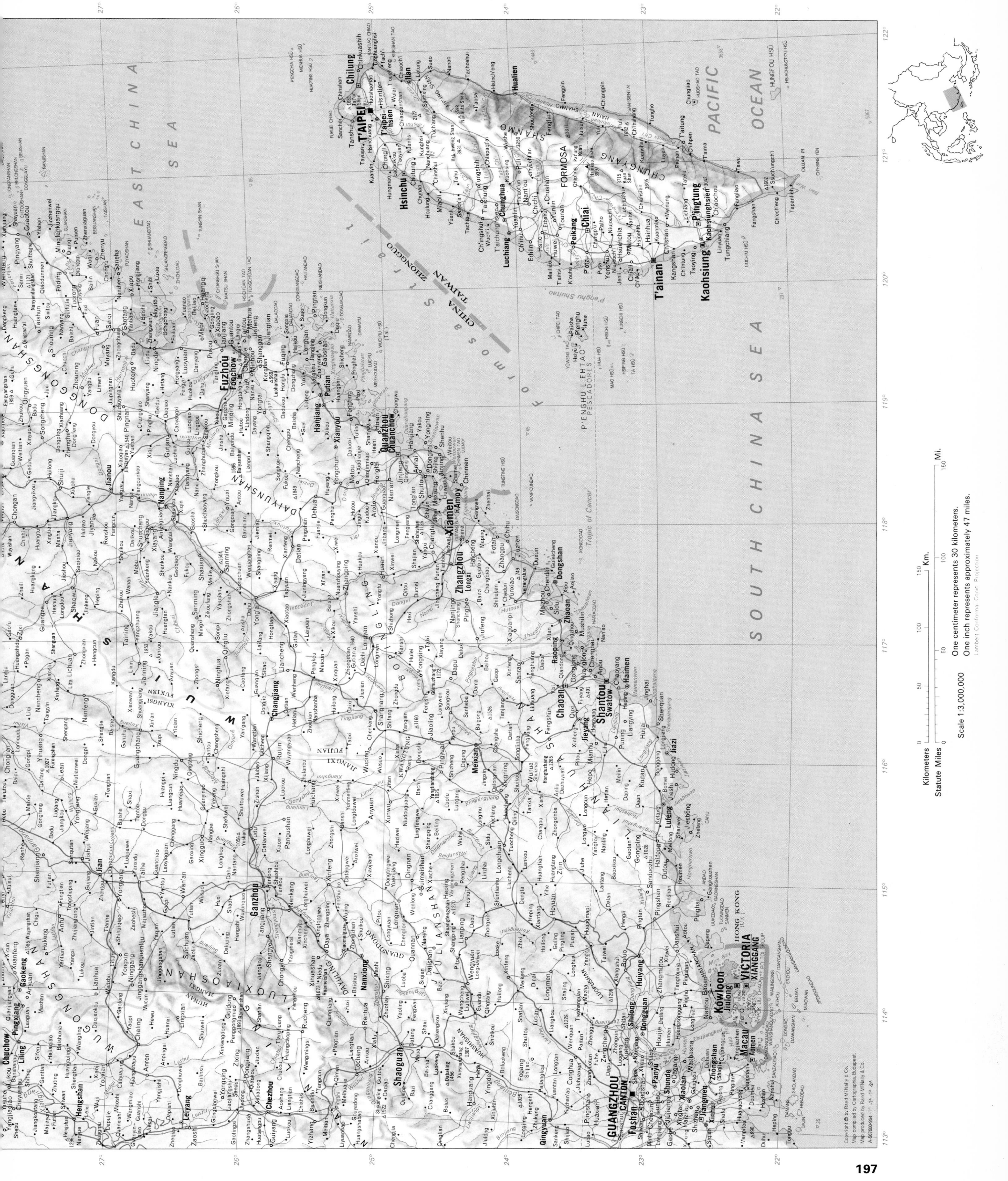
EAST CHINA SEA
Formosa Strait
TAIWAN
PACIFIC OCEAN
SOUTH CHINA SEA
FORMOSA
T'AIPEI
Fuzhou
Foochow
Xiamen
Amoy
Shantou
Swatow
GUANGZHOU
CANTON
HONG KONG
VICTORIA
Kowloon
Macau
Kaohsiung
T'ainan
Tropic of Cancer
Kilometers 0 50 100 150 Km.
Statute Miles 0 50 100 150 Mi.
Scale 1:3,000,000
One centimeter represents 30 kilometers.
One inch represents approximately 47 miles.
Lambert Conformal Conic Projection
Copyright © by Rand McNally & Co.
Map compiled by Cartographia, Budapest.
Map produced by Rand McNally & Co.

CHINA
YUNNAN
GUANGDONG
GUANGZHOU
CANTON
GUANGXI ZHUANG
Nanning
Kowloon Jiulong
Victoria Xianggang
HONG KONG (U.K.)
Aomen Macau
Shantou
Swatow
INDIA
Chittagong
BANGLADESH
Mandalay
BURMA
Sittwe (Akyab)
BAY OF BENGAL
Henzada
Bassein
Rangoon
Pegu
Moulmein
Tavoy
Gulf of Martaban
Preparis North Channel
Preparis South Channel
ANDAMAN ISLANDS (India)
NORTH ANDAMAN
MIDDLE ANDAMAN
SOUTH ANDAMAN
Port Blair
LITTLE ANDAMAN
ANDAMAN SEA
Ten Degree Channel
NICOBAR ISLANDS (India)
CAR NICOBAR
LITTLE NICOBAR
GREAT NICOBAR
Great Channel
LAOS
Louang Prabang
Vientiane
Chiang Mai
THAILAND
Nakhon Sawan
Nakhon Ratchasima
KRUNG THEP
BANGKOK
Thon Buri
Gulf of Siam
Ha-noi
Hai-phong
Gulf of Tonkin
NORTH VIETNAM
Vinh
Hue
Da-nang
SOUTH VIETNAM
Haikou
HAINANDAO
Zhanjiang
Beihai
CAMBODIA
Phnum Penh
Bătdâmbâng
SAI-GON
Gia-dinh
Nha-trang
Phan-thiet
Can-tho
SOUTH CHINA SEA
PALAWAN
Surat Thani
Nakhon Si Thammarat
Phuket
Songkhla
Hat Yai
Kota Bharu
Alor Setar
Pinang (George Town)
Kuala Trengganu
Ipoh
MALAYSIA
MALAYA
Kuantan
Kuala Lumpur
Kelang
Seremban
Malacca
Johore Bahru
SINGAPORE
Banda Atjeh (Kutaradja)
Medan
Pematangsiantar
PULAU SIMEULUE
PULAU NIAS
Equator
SUMATERA
SUMATRA
Pakanbaru
Padang
KEPULAUAN BATU
KEPULAUAN MENTAWAI
Djambi
Palembang
Bengkulu
Telukbetung
Pangkalpinang
BANGKA
BELITUNG
KEPULAUAN RIAU
KEPULAUAN LINGGA
NATUNA BESAR
BRUNEI
Bandar Seri Begawan
Kota Kinabalu (Jesselton)
Mount Kinabalu
Kuching
Sibu
Pontianak
BORNEO
KALIMANTAN
Samarinda
Balikpapan
Bandjarmasin
GREATER SUNDA ISLANDS
INDONESIA
LAUT DJAWA
JAVA SEA
DJAKARTA
Bogor
Bandung
Tjirebon
Semarang
Surakarta
Jogjakarta
Surabaja
Malang
MADURA
DJAWA JAVA
BALI
Denpasar
LOMBOK
SUMBAWA
INDIAN OCEAN
CHRISTMAS ISLAND (Austr.)
Copyright © by Rand McNally & Co.
Map prepared by Esselte Map Service AB, Stockholm.

PHILIPPINE SEA
PACIFIC OCEAN
Tropic of Cancer
TAIWAN
FORMOSA
Hualien
Chiai
Hsinkao Shan
T'aitung
P'ingtung
Bashi Channel
BATAN ISLANDS
Basco
Luzon
Strait
Balintang Channel
BABUYAN ISLANDS
Laoag
Aparri
Tuguegarao
Vigan
Bontoc
SIERRA MADRE
Ilagan
San Fernando
Mount Pulog
LUZON
Baguio
Dagupan
San Carlos
Cabanatuan
Tarlac
Dingalan Bay
Angeles
POLILLO ISLANDS
PHILIPPINES
MANILA
Quezon City
Cavite
Manila Bay
Lamon Bay
Tagaytay
Lipa
San Pablo
Lucena
Batangas
Daet
CATANDUANES ISLAND
Naga
Virac
Mayon Volcano
Calapan
MARINDUQUE ISLAND
Legazpi
Sorsogon
Mamburao
MINDORO
San Bernardino Strait
Sibuyan
Sea
San Jose
Mindoro Strait
Bulan
Laoang
Catarman
Calbayog
SAMAR
MASBATE ISLAND
Masbate
Kalibo
Roxas
PANAY
Visayan Sea
Catbalogan
Tacloban
Guiuan
Ormoc
Bogo
LEYTE
Iloilo
Bacolod
San Carlos
Leyte Gulf
Panay Gulf
Cebu
Tabilaran
Liloan
DINAGAT ISLAND
NEGROS
BOHOL
Surigao
SIARGAO ISLAND
Dumaguete
Santander
SIQUIJOR ISLAND
Mindanao Sea
Tandag
Butuan
Dipolog
Cagayan de Oro
SULU SEA
Ozamiz
Liloy
Pagadian
Malaybalay
Bislig
Siocon
MINDANAO
Malabang
Cotabato
Zamboanga
Moro Gulf
Datu Piang
Mount Apo
Davao
Isabela (Basilan)
BASILAN ISLAND
Davao Gulf
Lebak
Kiamba
CAPE SAN AGUSTIN
Jolo
SULU ARCHIPELAGO
TAWITAWI ISLAND
TINACA POINT
SARANGANI ISLANDS
PULAU MIANGAS
PULAU KARAKELONG
KEPULAUAN TALAUD
PULAU SALEBABU
PULAU KABURUANG
Tahuna
PULAU SANGIHE
CELEBES SEA
KEPULAUAN SANGIHE
PULAU SIAU
PULAU TAHULANDANG
PULAU BIARO
TANDJUNG TORAWITAN
Manado
Bitung
Gunung Klabat
Tondano
MINAHASA
Kotamobagu
Tolitoli
Bukit Malino
Gorontalo
Tomini
Moutong
Teluk Tomini
KEPULAUAN TOGIAN
Luwuk
Poso
PULAU PELENG
Banggai
KEPULAUAN BANGGAI
Teluk Tolo
SULAWESI
CELEBES
Teluk Bone
Kendari
Kolaka
Watampone
PULAU WOWONI
PULAU BUTUNG
Makasar
Sindjai
Bulukumba
Bonthain
Baubau
PULAU MUNA
PULAU KABAENA
KEPULAUAN TUKANGBESI
PULAU BINONGKO
PULAU SELAJAR
Morotai
Wajabula
Galela
Tobelo
HALMAHERA
Djailolo
Ternate
Tidore
Weda
MOLUCCAS
LAUT MALUKU
MOLUCCA SEA
PULAU GEBE
Laut Halmahera
PULAU KASIRUTA
PULAU MANDIOLI
PULAU BATJAN
Labuha
PULAU BISA
PULAU OBILATU
PULAU MANGOLE
PULAU TALIABU
KEPULAUAN SULA
PULAU SANANA
KEPULAUAN OBI
LAUT SERAM
CERAM SEA
Namlea
BURU
SERAM
Piru
Wahai
Bula
Ambon
PULAU AMBON
PULAU AMBELAU
Geser
PULAU MANUI
KEPULAUAN WATUBELA
KEPULAUAN BANDA
LAUT BANDA
BANDA SEA
KEPULAUAN LUCIPARA
KEPULAUAN PENJU
KEPULAUAN KAI
Tual
KAI BESAR
KAI KETJIL
PULAU SERUA
PULAU NILA
PULAU TEUN
PULAU DAMAR
KEPULAUAN BARAT DAJA
PULAU ROMANG
PULAU WETAR
PULAU KISAR
PULAU MOA
KEPULAUAN LETI
KEPULAUAN SERMATA
PULAU BABAR
KEPULAUAN BABAR
Tepa
PULAU WULIARU
PULAU SELU
Saumlaki
PULAU JAMDENA
KEPULAUAN TANIMBAR
PULAU LARAT
PULAU SELARU
PULAU MOLU
PULAU WAIGEO
Selat Dampier
PULAU SALAWATI
PULAU BATANTA
Sorong
DJAZIRAH DOBERAI
Teminabuan
PULAU MISOOL
Inanwatan
Manokwari
PULAU NUMFOOR
Ransiki
BIAK
Bosnik
PULAU JAPEN
Serui
TANDJUNG PERKAMI
Sarmi
Steenkool
Babo
Teluk Berau
Wasior
Teluk Sarera
Waren
PEGUNUNGAN VAN REES
Fakfak
Nabire
Kaimana
Karufa
PULAU ADI
Teluk Kamrau
Modowi
PEGUNUNGAN MAOKE
Puntjak Djaja
Puntjak Trikora
Puntjak Mandala
Kokonau
Dobo
PULAU WOKAM
PULAU KOBROOR
PULAU MAIKOOR
PULAU TRANGAN
KEPULAUAN ARU
Kepi
Mapi
Digul
PULAU DOLAK
Okaba
Merauke
TANDJUNG VALS
NEW GUINEA
Tanahmerah
Demta
Djajapura (Sukarnapura)
Vanimo
TERRITORY OF NEW GUINEA
(Austl. Trust.)
Aitape
Dagua
Wewak
Sepik
Ambunti
Angoram
Telefomin
BISMARCK RANGE
Wabag
Mount Hagen
Mount Giluwe
Mendi
Mount Bosavi
Mount Wilhelm
Goroka
Lake Murray
Fly
PAPUA
(Austl.)
Kikori
Balimo
Gulf of Papua
Daru
BOIGU ISLAND
SAIBAI ISLAND
WARRIOR REEFS
Torres Strait
BANKS ISLAND
PRINCE OF WALES ISLAND
CAPE YORK
Endeavour Strait
CAPE YORK PENINSULA
ARAFURA SEA
AUSTRALIA
CAPE WESSEL
CAPE CROKER
TIMOR SEA
TIMOR
PORTUGUESE TIMOR
Dili
Monte Tata Mailau
Ocussi (Port. Timor)
Soe
Kupang
PULAU ROTI
PULAU SAWU
PULAU SEMAU
Savu Sea
Laut Sawu
SUMBA
Waingapu
Baing
SUNDA ISLANDS
FLORES
Ruteng
Reo
Ende
Maumere
Larantuka
PULAU ADONARA
PULAU LOMBLEN
PULAU PANTAR
PULAU ALOR
Kalabahi
Ilwaki
ILHA DE ATAÚRO
Flores Sea
PULAU KALAOTOA
PARECE VELA (Japan)
FARALLON DE PAJAROS
MAUG ISLANDS
ASUNCION ISLAND
AGRIHAN
PAGAN
MARIANA ISLANDS
ALAMAGAN
GUGUAN
PACIFIC ISLANDS TRUST TERRITORY
(U.S.)
SARIGAN
ANATAHAN
FARALLON DE MEDINILLA
SAIPAN
TINIAN
AGUIJAN
ROTA
Agana
GUAM
(U.S.)
ULITHI
FAIS
YAP
GAFERUT
NGULU
SOROL
FARAULEP
KAYANGEL ISLANDS
PALAU ISLANDS
BABELTHUAP
URUKTHAPEL
Koror
PELELIU
EIL MALK
ANGAUR
OLIMARAO
WOLEAI
FALIK
EAURIPIK
CAROLINE ISLANDS
SONSOROL ISLANDS
PULO ANNA
MERIR
TOBI
HELEN ISLAND
KEPULAUAN ASIA
KEPULAUAN AJU
KEPULAUAN MAPIA
Equator
NINIGO ISLANDS
WUVULU
120°
125°
130°
135°
140°
145°
20°
15°
10°
5°
0°
5°
10°

Kilometers 0 200 400 600 Km.

Statute Miles 0 200 400 600 Mi.

Scale 1:12,000,000

One centimeter represents 120 kilometers.
One inch represents approximately 190 miles.
Lambert Conformal Conic Projection

Burma, Thailand and Indochina

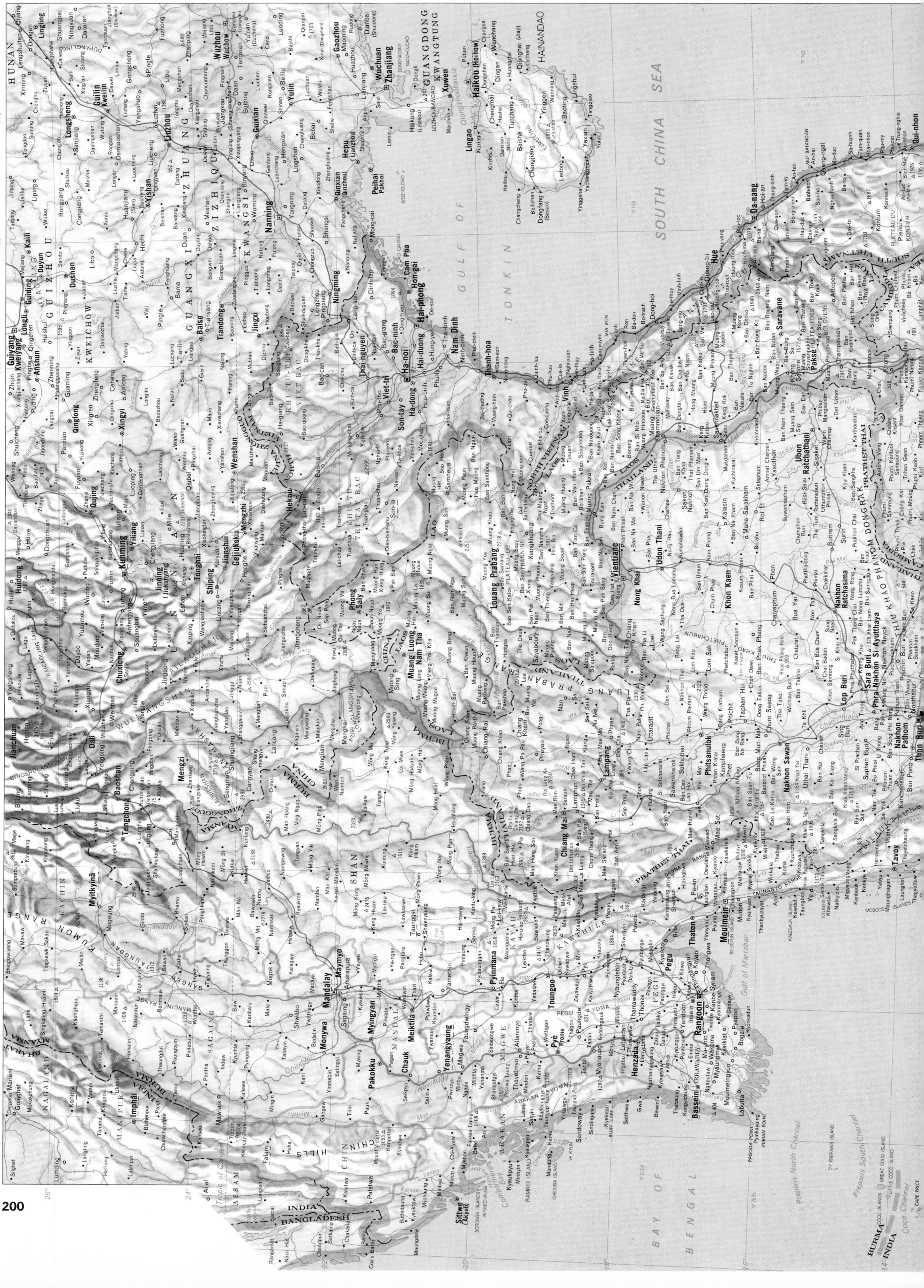

Kilometers 0 100 200 300 Km.
Statute Miles 0 100 200 300 Mi.

Scale 1:6,000,000
One centimeter represents 60 kilometers.
One inch represents approximately 95 miles.
Lambert Conformal Conic Projection

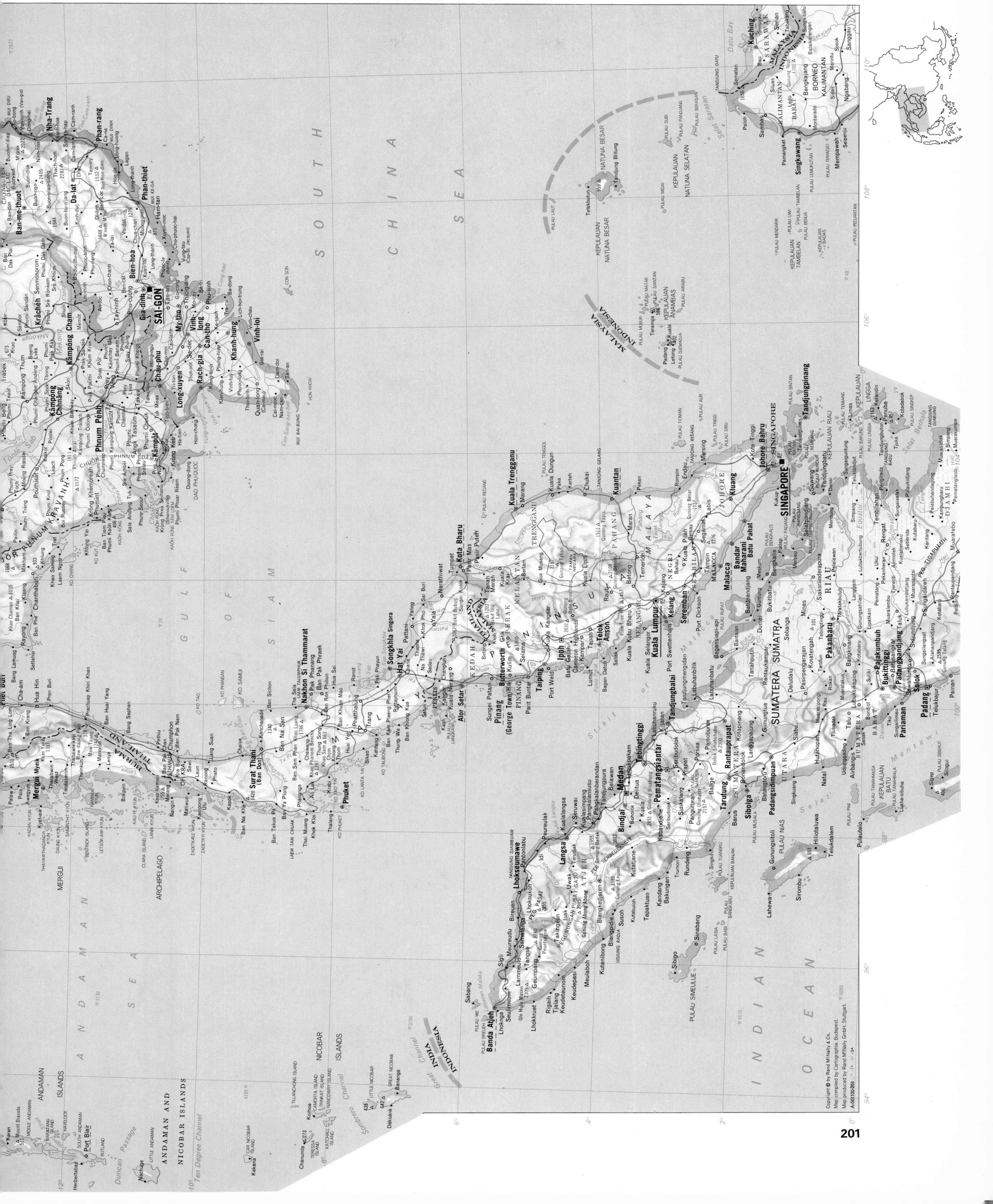
SOUTH CHINA SEA
GULF OF SIAM
ANDAMAN SEA
INDIAN OCEAN
Strait of Malacca
MERGUI ARCHIPELAGO
ANDAMAN AND NICOBAR ISLANDS
ANDAMAN ISLANDS
NICOBAR ISLANDS
Ten Degree Channel
Duncan Passage
Great Channel
Sombrero Channel
KEPULAUAN NATUNA BESAR
KEPULAUAN NATUNA SELATAN
KEPULAUAN ANAMBAS
KEPULAUAN RIAU
KEPULAUAN LINGGA
MALAYSIA
INDONESIA
INDIA
THAILAND
BURMA
SINGAPORE
SUMATERA
BORNEO
KALIMANTAN
SAIGON
Gia-dinh
Phnum Penh
Kampong Chhnang
Kampong Cham
Kratie
Ban-me-thuot
Da-lat
Nha-Trang
Phan-rang
Phan-thiet
Bien-hoa
My-tho
Vinh-long
Can-tho
Long-xuyen
Rach-gia
Khanh-hung
Vinh-loi
Chau-phu
Kampot
Chanthaburi
Rayong
Hua Hin
Prachuap Khiri Khan
Chumphon
Surat Thani (Ban Don)
Nakhon Si Thammarat
Songkhla
Hat Yai
Phuket
Ranong
Mergui
Port Blair
Kuala Trengganu
Kota Bharu
Kuantan
Alor Setar
Pinang (George Town)
Butterworth
Taiping
Ipoh
Teluk Anson
Kuala Lumpur
Kelang
Seremban
Malacca
Johore Bahru
Kluang
Medan
Pematangsiantar
Tebingtinggi
Tanjungbalai
Rantauprapat
Sibolga
Padangsidimpuan
Tarutung
Langsa
Lhokseumawe
Banda Atjeh
Bukittinggi
Padang
Pakanbaru
Tandjungpinang
Kuching
Singkawang
Copyright © by Rand McNally & Co.
Map compiled by Cartographia, Budapest.
Map produced by Rand McNally GmbH, Stuttgart.

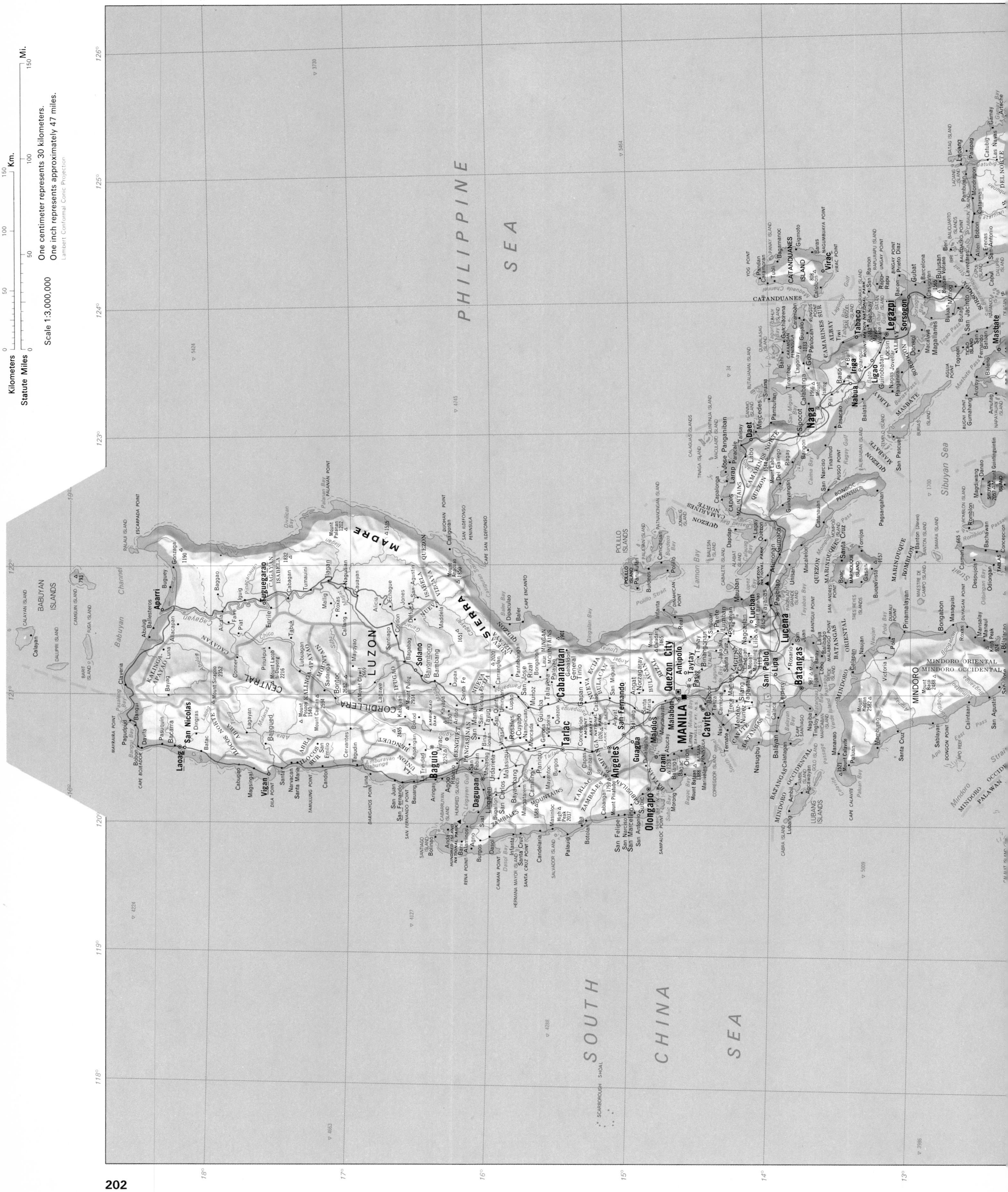
Kilometers
Statute Miles
Km.
Mi.
Scale 1:3,000,000
One centimeter represents 30 kilometers.
One inch represents approximately 47 miles.
Lambert Conformal Conic Projection
PHILIPPINE SEA
SOUTH CHINA SEA
Sibuyan Sea
LUZON
SIERRA MADRE
CORDILLERA CENTRAL
BABUYAN ISLANDS
Babuyan Channel
MANILA
Quezon City
MINDORO
CATANDUANES

SULU SEA
CELEBES SEA
Mindanao Sea
Visayan Sea
Camotes Sea
Moro Gulf
Davao Gulf
Panay Gulf
Illana Bay
Iligan Bay
Leyte Gulf
MINDANAO
NEGROS
PANAY
BOHOL
CEBU
LEYTE
SAMAR
PALAWAN
BORNEO
KALIMANTAN
SULU ARCHIPELAGO
ZAMBOANGA PENINSULA
PHILIPPINES PILIPINAS
MALAYSIA
SABAH NORTH BORNEO
Cebu
Iloilo
Bacolod
Tacloban
Catbalogan
Davao
Zamboanga
Cagayan de Oro
Butuan
Surigao
Cotabato
General Santos (Dadiangas)
Dumaguete
Ozamiz
Dipolog
Pagadian
Marawi
Jolo
Isabela (Basilan)
Puerto Princesa
Sandakan
Roxas (Capiz)
Ormoc
Dapitan
Tagbilaran
Copyright © by Rand McNally & Co.
Map prepared by Rand McNally & Co.
A-563100-264

UNION OF SOVIET SOCI
TURKMENSKAJA S.S.R.
KARAKUMY
UZBEKSK
CASPIAN SEA
TURKEY
ASIA MINOR
SYRIA
LEBANON
ISRAEL
JORDAN
CYPRUS
MEDITERRANEAN SEA
EGYPT
IRAQ
MESOPOTAMIA
BADIYAT ASH-SHAM
IRAN
DASHT-E KAVIR
DASHT-E LUT
KUHHA-YE ZAGROS
KUWAIT
NEUTRAL ZONE
AN-NAFUD
SAUDI ARABIA
AL-HIJAZ
AD-DAHNA
BAHRAIN
QATAR
UNITED ARAB EMIRATES
OMAN
Gulf of Oman
Tropic of Cancer
AR-RAB' AL-KHALI
RED SEA
YEMEN
PEOPLE'S DEMOCRATIC REPUBLIC OF YEMEN
HADRAMAWT
SUDAN
ERITREA
ETHIOPIA
AFARS AND ISSAS
SOMALIA
Gulf of Aden
ARABI
INDIAN O
Tbilisi
Jerevan
Baku
Ankara
Konya
Adana
Halab Aleppo
Dimashq Damascus
Bayrut
Tel Aviv-Yafo
Yerushalayim Jerusalem
'Amman
Baghdad
Al-Kuwayt
Ar-Riyad Riyadh
Makkah Mecca
Al-Madinah Medina
Juddah Jidda
San'a'
Aden
Djibouti
Asmera
Hargeysa
Muqdisho
TEHRAN
Tabriz
Esfahan
Shiraz
Mashhad
Kerman
Ad-Dawhah Doha
Al-Manamah
Abu Zaby
Dubayy
Masqat Muscat
Sugutra
Tropic of Cancer
35°
40°
45°
50°
55°
60°
30°
25°
20°
15°
10°

Kilometers 0 200 400 600 Km.

Statute Miles 0 200 400 600 Mi.

Scale 1:12,000,000

One centimeter represents 120 kilometers.

One inch represents approximately 190 miles.

Lambert Conformal Conic Projection

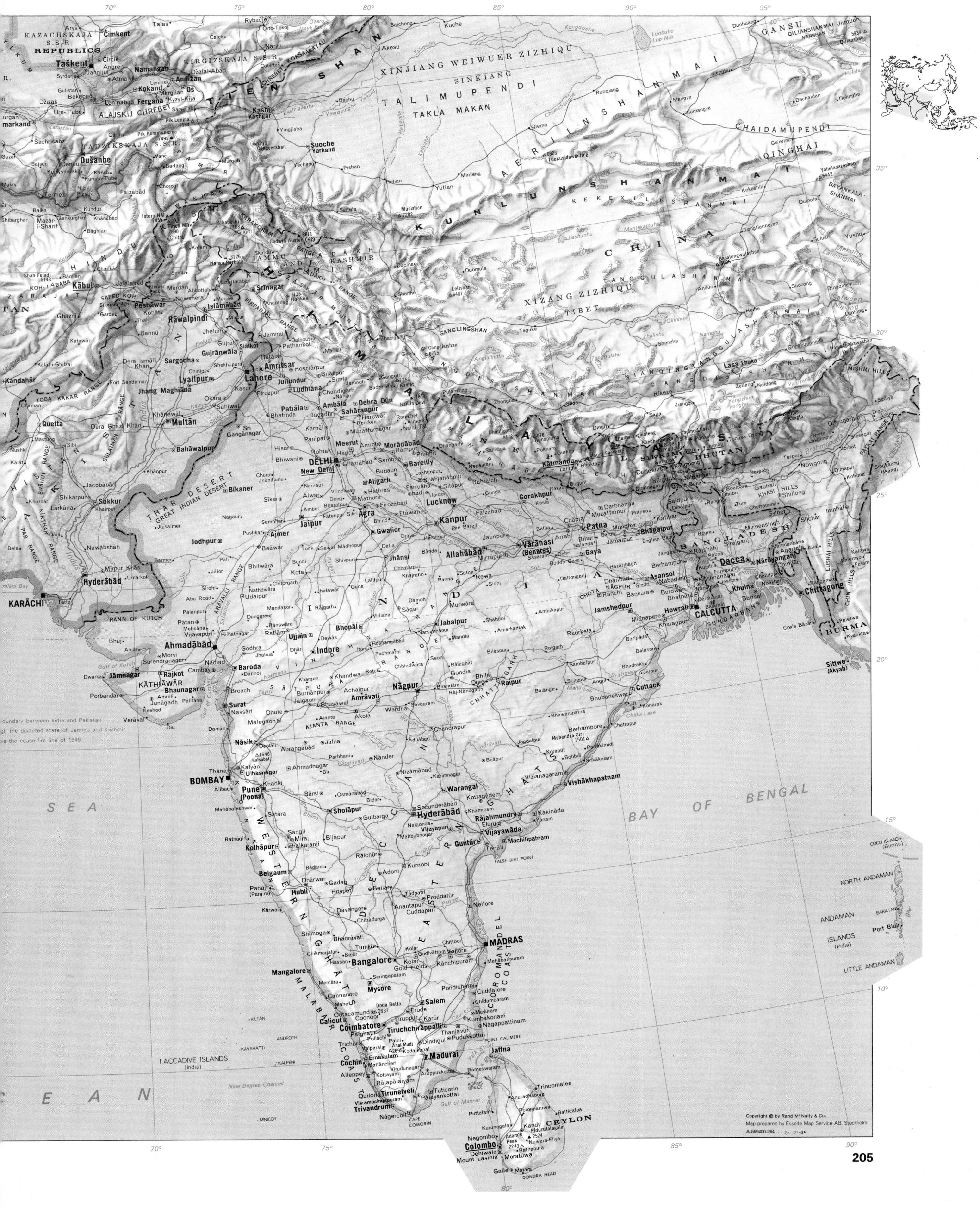

KAZACHSKAJA S.S.R.
REPUBLICS
Taškent
Čimkent
KIRGIZSKAJA S.S.R.
TIEN SHAN
XINJIANG WEIWUER ZIZHIQU
SINKIANG
TALIMUPENDI
TAKLA MAKAN
Namangan
Andižan
Kokand
Fergana
Leninabad
ALAJSKIJ CHREBET
Kashi
Kashgar
Suoche
Yarkand
TADZIKSKAJA S.S.R.
Dušanbe
Termez
Mazār-i-Sharif
Kunduz
Faizābād
Hotan
Yutian
Minfeng
Qiemo
Ruoqiang
Kuche
Aksu
Luobubo
Lop Nor
Dunhuang
GANSU
QILIANSHANMAI
NANSHAN
CHAIDAMUPENDI
QINGHAI
ARJINSHANMAI
KUNLUNSHANMAI
KEKEXILISHANMAI
BAYANKALA SHANMAI
Yushu
CHINA
TANGGULASHANMAI
XIZANG ZIZHIQU
TIBET
GANGDISISHANMAI
NIANQINGTANGGULASHANMAI
Lasa Lhasa
Rikeze
HINDU KUSH
KARAKORAM
Godwin Austen (K2) 8611
JAMMU AND KASHMIR
LADAKH RANGE
Srīnagar
Kābul
Peshāwar
Islāmābād
Rāwalpindi
SAFED KOH
Ghazni
Kandahār
Quetta
TOBA KAKAR RANGE
SULAIMAN RANGE
Multān
Lahore
Amritsar
Lyallpur
Jhelum
Gujrānwāla
Sargodha
Bahāwalpur
Sukkur
Jacobābād
KIRTHAR RANGE
Hyderābād
KARĀCHI
THAR DESERT
GREAT INDIAN DESERT
Bīkaner
Jodhpur
Ajmer
Jaipur
Agra
Mathura
DELHI
New Delhi
Meerut
Morādābād
Bareilly
Lucknow
Kānpur
Allahābād
Vārānasi (Benares)
Gorakhpur
Patna
Gaya
Bhāgalpur
Kātmāndu
NEPAL
SIKKIM
BHUTAN
HIMALAYA
Dārjeeling
BANGLADESH
Dacca
Nārāyanganj
Chittagong
Khulna
Sylhet
Mymensingh
Shillong
Imphāl
BURMA
Sittwe (Akyab)
CALCUTTA
Howrah
Asansol
Jamshedpur
Rānchi
CHOTA NĀGPUR
SUNDARBANS
Cuttack
Puri
Bhubaneswar
Gwalior
Jhānsi
Bhopāl
Ujjain
Indore
Jabalpur
VINDHYA RANGE
SĀTPURA RANGE
Ahmadābād
Baroda
Rājkot
Bhāvnagar
Jāmnagar
KĀTHIĀWĀR
RANN OF KUTCH
Gulf of Kutch
Gulf of Cambay
Surat
Nāgpur
Amrāvati
Raipur
CHHATTĪSGARH
AJANTA RANGE
Nāsik
Aurangābād
BOMBAY
Thāna
Pune (Poona)
Sholāpur
Hyderābād
Secunderābād
Warangal
Vishākhapatnam
Rājahmundry
Kākināda
Vijayawāda
Guntūr
Machilīpatnam
DECCAN
EASTERN GHATS
WESTERN GHATS
Kolhāpur
Belgaum
Hubli
Panaji (Panjim)
Bellary
Kurnool
Nellore
MADRAS
Bangalore
Mysore
Mangalore
Calicut
Coimbatore
Salem
Tiruchchirāppalli
Pondicherry
Cochin
Madurai
Tirunelveli
Trivandrum
MALABAR COAST
COROMANDEL COAST
CAPE COMORIN
Jaffna
Trincomalee
Anurādhapura
Kandy
Colombo
Galle
CEYLON
DONDRA HEAD
Palk Strait
Gulf of Mannar
LACCADIVE ISLANDS (India)
Nine Degree Channel
BAY OF BENGAL
SEA
OCEAN
ANDAMAN ISLANDS (India)
NORTH ANDAMAN
LITTLE ANDAMAN
Port Blair
COCO ISLANDS (Burma)
Boundary between India and Pakistan through the disputed state of Jammu and Kashmir shows the cease-fire line of 1949
70°
75°
80°
85°
90°
95°
35°
30°
25°
20°
15°
10°

Northern India and Pakistan

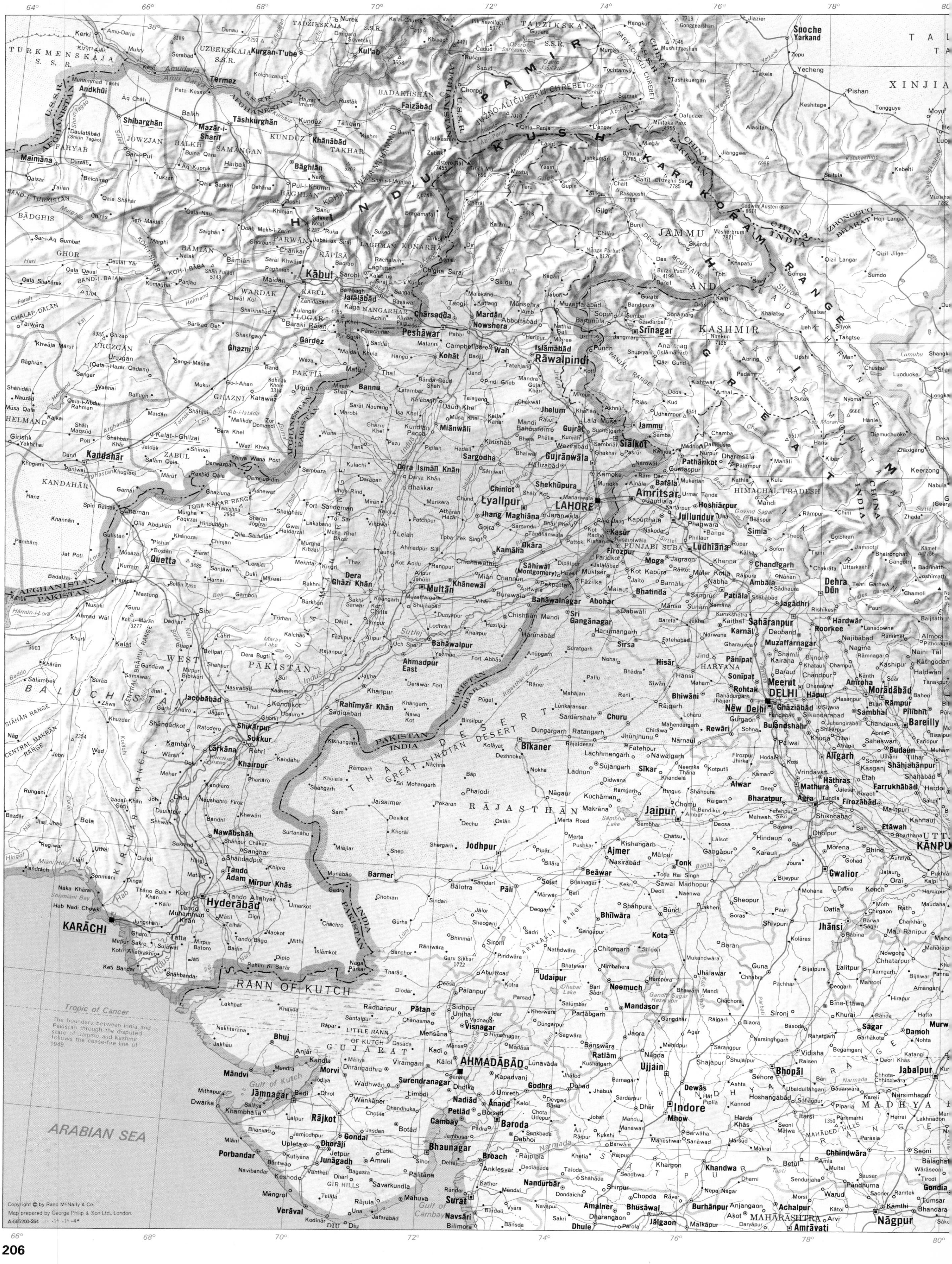

TURKMENSKAJA S.S.R.
UZBEKSKAJA S.S.R.
TADŽIKSKAJA S.S.R.
AFGHANISTAN
PAMIR
HINDU KUSH
KARAKORAM RANGE
JAMMU AND KASHMIR
XINJIANG
HIMACHAL PRADESH
PUNJABI SUBA
HARYANA
WEST PĀKISTĀN
BALUCHISTAN
THAR DESERT
GREAT INDIAN DESERT
RĀJASTHĀN
RANN OF KUTCH
LITTLE RANN OF KUTCH
GUJARAT
MAHĀRĀSHTRA
MADHYA PRADESH
ARABIAN SEA
Gulf of Kutch
Gulf of Cambay
Tropic of Cancer
Kābul
Kandahār
Quetta
Peshāwar
Rāwalpindi
Islāmābād
Srīnagar
Lahore
Amritsar
Lyallpur
Multān
Hyderābād
Karāchi
Sukkur
Delhi
New Delhi
Jaipur
Jodhpur
Bikaner
Ajmer
Ahmadābād
Baroda
Surat
Rājkot
Indore
Bhopāl
Gwalior
Nāgpur
Kānpur
Simla
Ambāla
Meerut
Agra
Aligarh
Bareilly
Jabalpur
Ujjain
The boundary between India and Pakistan through the disputed state of Jammu and Kashmir follows the cease-fire line of 1949

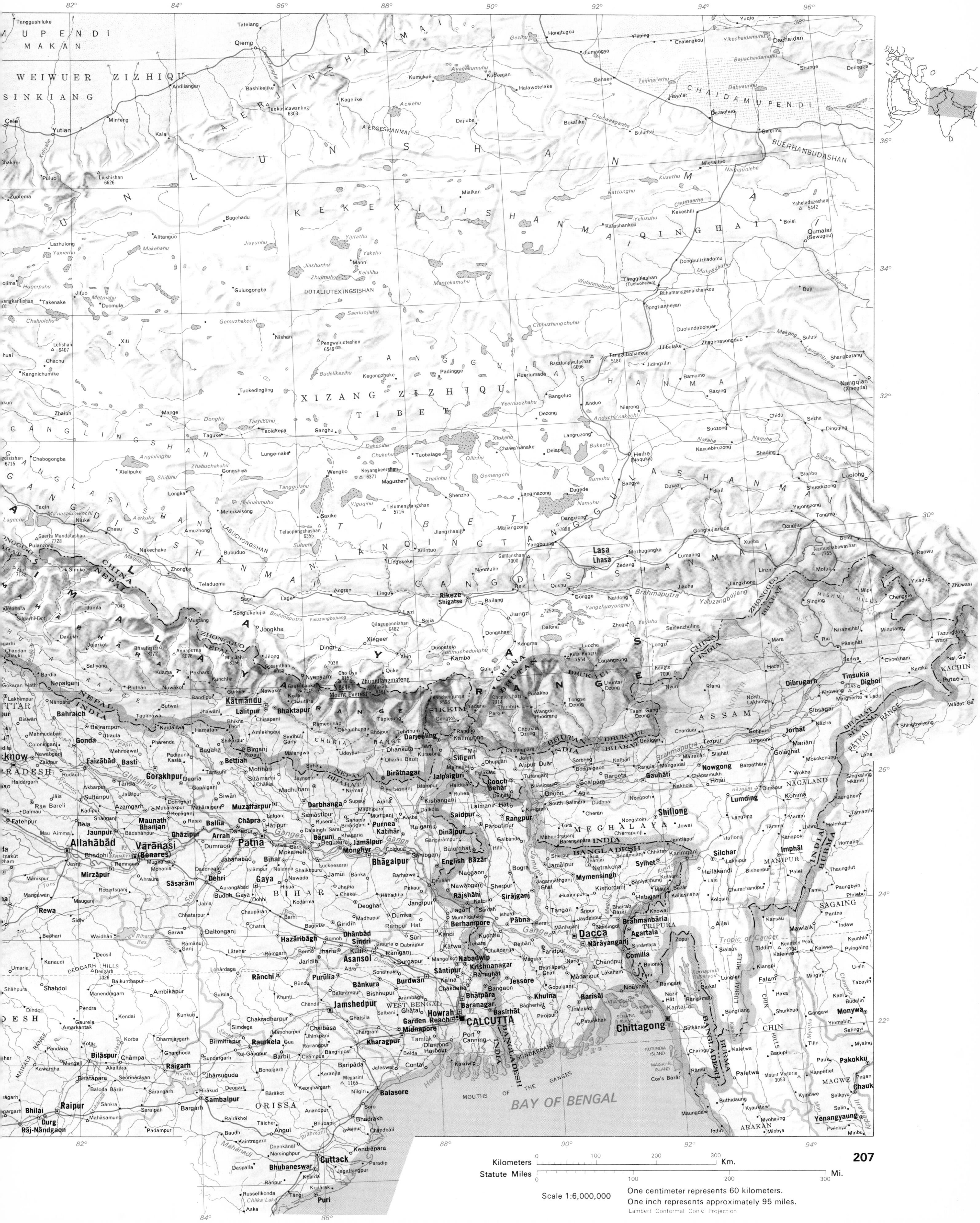

WEIWUER ZIZHIQU
SINKIANG
CHAIDAMUPENDI
XIZANG ZIZHIQU
TIBET
KEKEXILISHAN
TANGGULASHAN
GANGDISISHAN
NIANQINGTANGGULASHAN
HIMALAYAS
NEPAL
BHUTAN
SIKKIM
BANGLADESH
INDIA
CHINA
BURMA
ASSAM
MEGHALAYA
NAGALAND
MANIPUR
TRIPURA
BIHAR
ORISSA
WEST BENGAL
BAY OF BENGAL
MOUTHS OF THE GANGES
Lasa
Lhasa
Rikeze
Shigatse
Kātmāndu
Mount Everest
Darjeeling
Gangtok
Thimbu
Patna
Vārānasi
(Benares)
Allahābād
CALCUTTA
Howrah
Dacca
Chittagong
Cuttack
Bhubaneswar
Puri
Ranchi
Jamshedpur
Gauhāti
Shillong
Imphāl
Dibrugarh
Brahmaputra
Ganges
Tropic of Cancer
Mekong
Salween
Irrawaddy

Kilometers 0 100 200 300 Km.

Statute Miles 0 100 200 300 Mi.

Scale 1:6,000,000

One centimeter represents 60 kilometers.

One inch represents approximately 95 miles.

Lambert Conformal Conic Projection

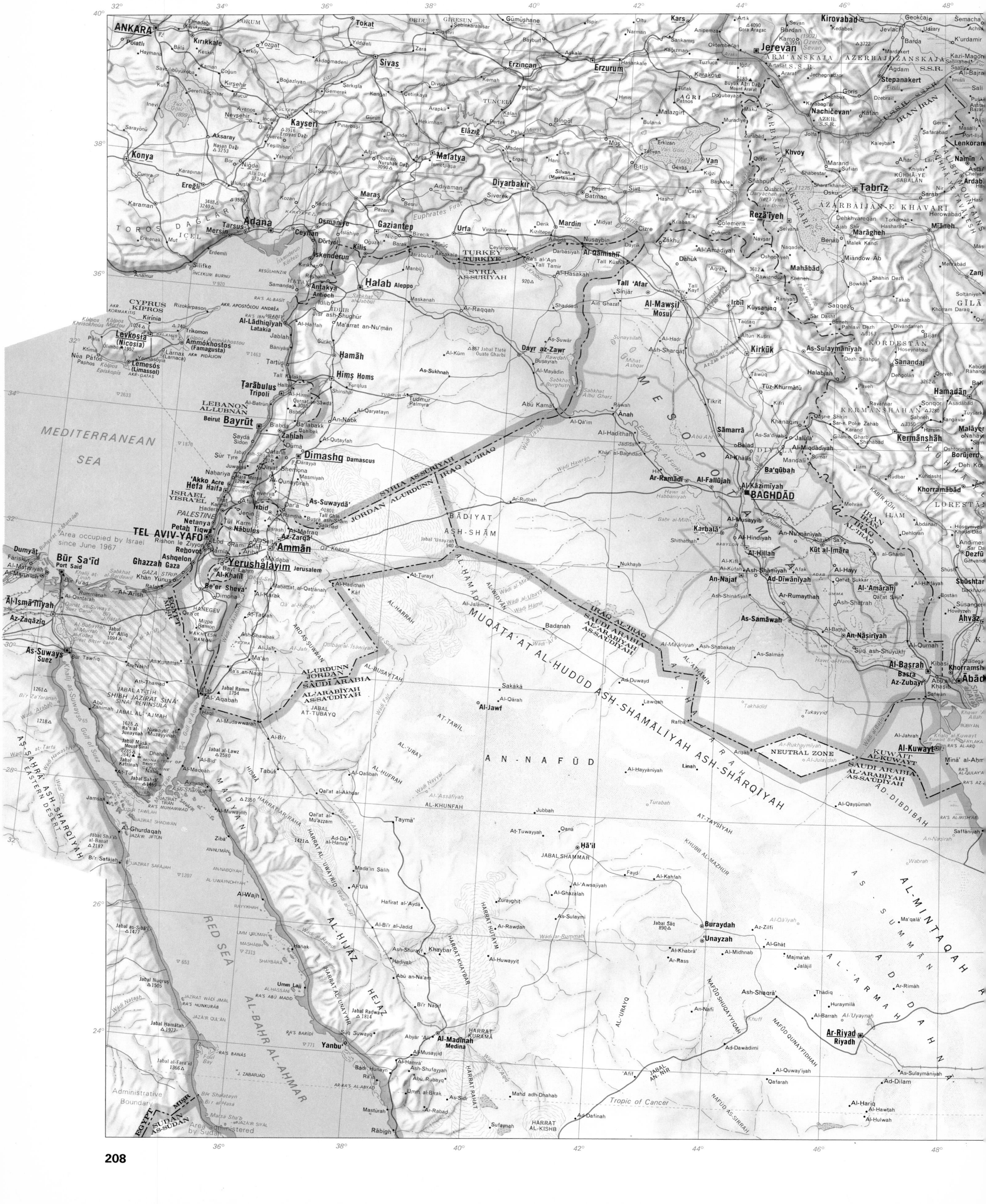
ANKARA
Konya
Adana
Kayseri
Sivas
Malatya
Erzurum
Diyarbakır
Gaziantep
TURKEY
TÜRKİYE
SYRIA
AS-SŪRIYAH
Ḥalab Aleppo
Dimashq Damascus
Ḥamāh
Ḥimṣ Homs
Dayr az-Zawr
LEBANON
AL-LUBNĀN
Bayrūt
Beirut
CYPRUS
KIPROS
Levkosía
(Nicosia)
ISRAEL
YISRA'EL
TEL AVIV-YAFO
Yerushalayim
Jerusalem
JORDAN
AL-URDUNN
'Ammān
IRAQ
AL-'IRĀQ
BAGHDĀD
Al-Mawṣil
Mosul
Kirkūk
Al-Baṣrah
Basra
Al-Kuwayt
KUWAIT
AL-KUWAYT
NEUTRAL ZONE
SAUDI ARABIA
AL-'ARABĪYAH AS-SA'ŪDĪYAH
Ar-Riyāḍ
Riyadh
Al-Madīnah
Medina
Ḥā'il
Buraydah
Yanbu'
Tabūk
Jerevan
Tabrīz
Kermānshāh
EGYPT
MIṢR
Būr Sa'īd
Port Said
As-Suways
Suez
MEDITERRANEAN SEA
RED SEA
AL-BAḤR AL-AḤMAR
AN-NAFŪD
AL-ḤIJĀZ
Euphrates
Tigris
Tropic of Cancer
Area occupied by Israel since June 1967
Administrative Boundary

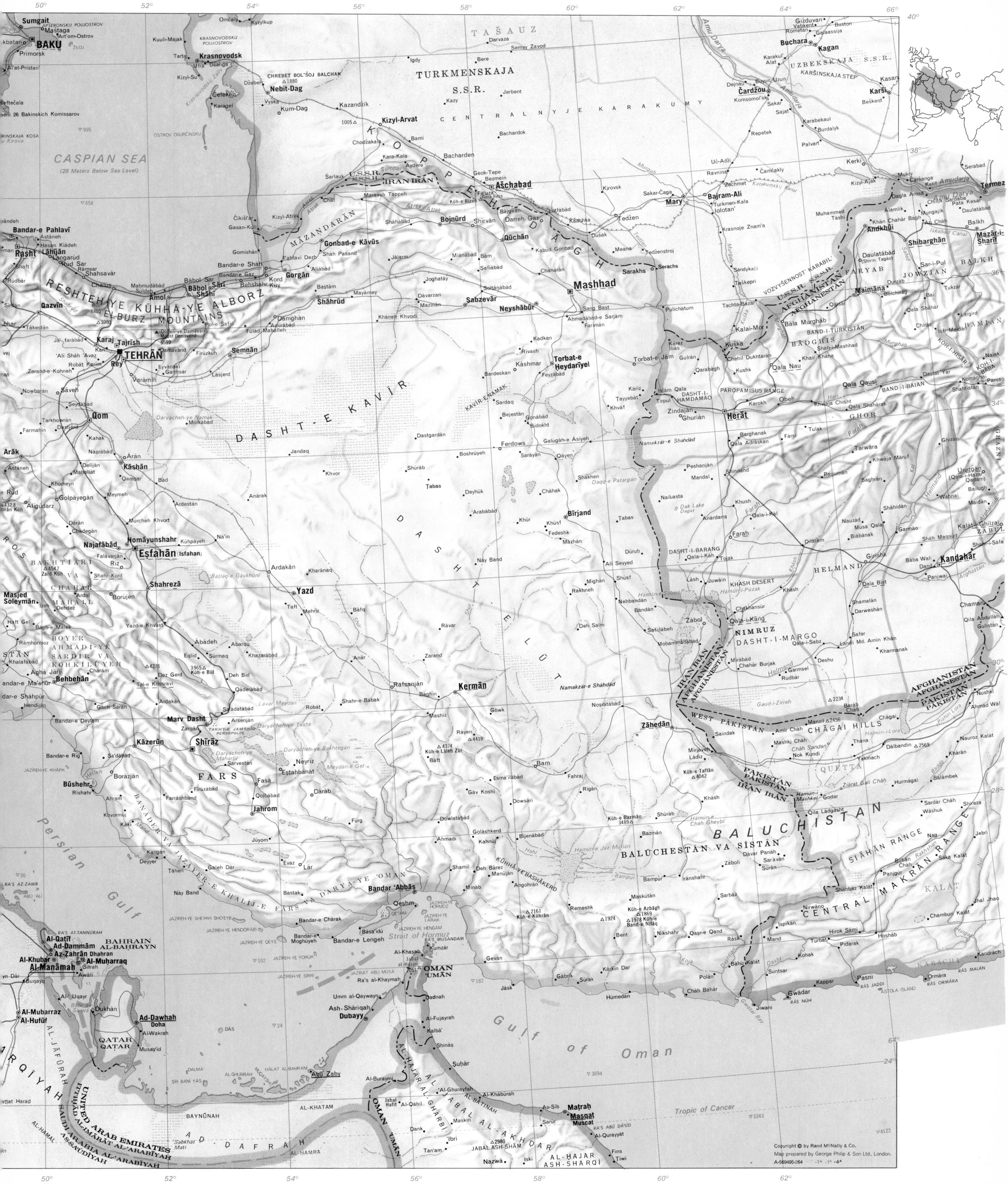
CASPIAN SEA
(28 Meters Below Sea Level)
TURKMENSKAJA S.S.R.
CENTRALNYJE KARAKUMY
UZBEKSKAJA S.S.R.
KOPPEH DĀGH
RESHTEH-YE KŪHHĀ-YE ALBORZ
ELBURZ MOUNTAINS
DASHT-E KAVĪR
DASHT-E LŪT
MĀZANDARĀN
FĀRS
BALUCHISTAN
BALŪCHESTĀN VA SĪSTĀN
NIMRUZ
DASHT-I-MARGO
HELMAND
CHĀGAI HILLS
CENTRAL MAKRAN RANGE
SIAHAN RANGE
Persian Gulf
Gulf of Oman
Strait of Hormuz
Tropic of Cancer
BAKU
Krasnovodsk
Nebit-Dag
Kizyl-Arvat
Aśchabad
Mary
Čardžou
Buchara
Rasht
Gorgān
Sārī
Bābol
Qazvīn
TEHRĀN
Semnān
Dāmghān
Shāhrūd
Sabzevār
Neyshābūr
Mashhad
Torbat-e Heydarīyeh
Qom
Arāk
Kāshān
Esfahān (Isfahan)
Yazd
Kermān
Shīrāz
Būshehr
Bandar-e 'Abbās
Zāhedān
Bīrjand
Herāt
Farah
Kandahar
Mazār-i-Sharif
Maimāna
Shibarghān
Andkhui
Termez
Karši
Zabol
Chāh Bahār
Gwadar
Jiwani
Pasni
Ormāra
Masqat
Matrah
Ṣuḥār
Dubayy
Abū Zaby
Ad-Dawhah
Doha
QATAR
Al-Manāmah
BAHRAIN
Ad-Dammām
Al-Hufūf
OMAN 'UMĀN
UNITED ARAB EMIRATES
AL-HAJAR AL-GHARBĪ
JABAL AL-AKHDAR
IRAN
AFGHANISTAN
PAKISTAN
WEST PAKISTAN
U.S.S.R.
50° 52° 54° 56° 58° 60° 62° 64° 66°
40° 38° 36° 34° 32° 30° 28° 26° 24°
Copyright © by Rand McNally & Co.
Map prepared by George Philip & Son Ltd., London.

Kilometers 0 100 200 300 Km.

Statute Miles 0 100 200 300 Mi.

Scale 1:6,000,000

One centimeter represents 60 kilometers.

One inch represents approximately 95 miles.

Lambert Conformal Conic Projection

MEDITERRANEAN
SEA
Dimashq Damascus
Bayrūt Beirut
Yerushalayim Jerusalem
TEL AVIV-YAFO
Hefa Haifa
'Ammān
Irbid
Nābulus
Teverya Tiberias
Şaydā Sidon
Şūr Tyre
Netanya
Ashdod
Al-Qunayţirah
As-Suwaydā'
Dar'ā
Az-Zarqā'
As-Salţ
SYRIA AS-SURIYAH
JORDAN AL-URDUNN
LEBANON AL-LUBNAN
ISRAEL YISRA'EL

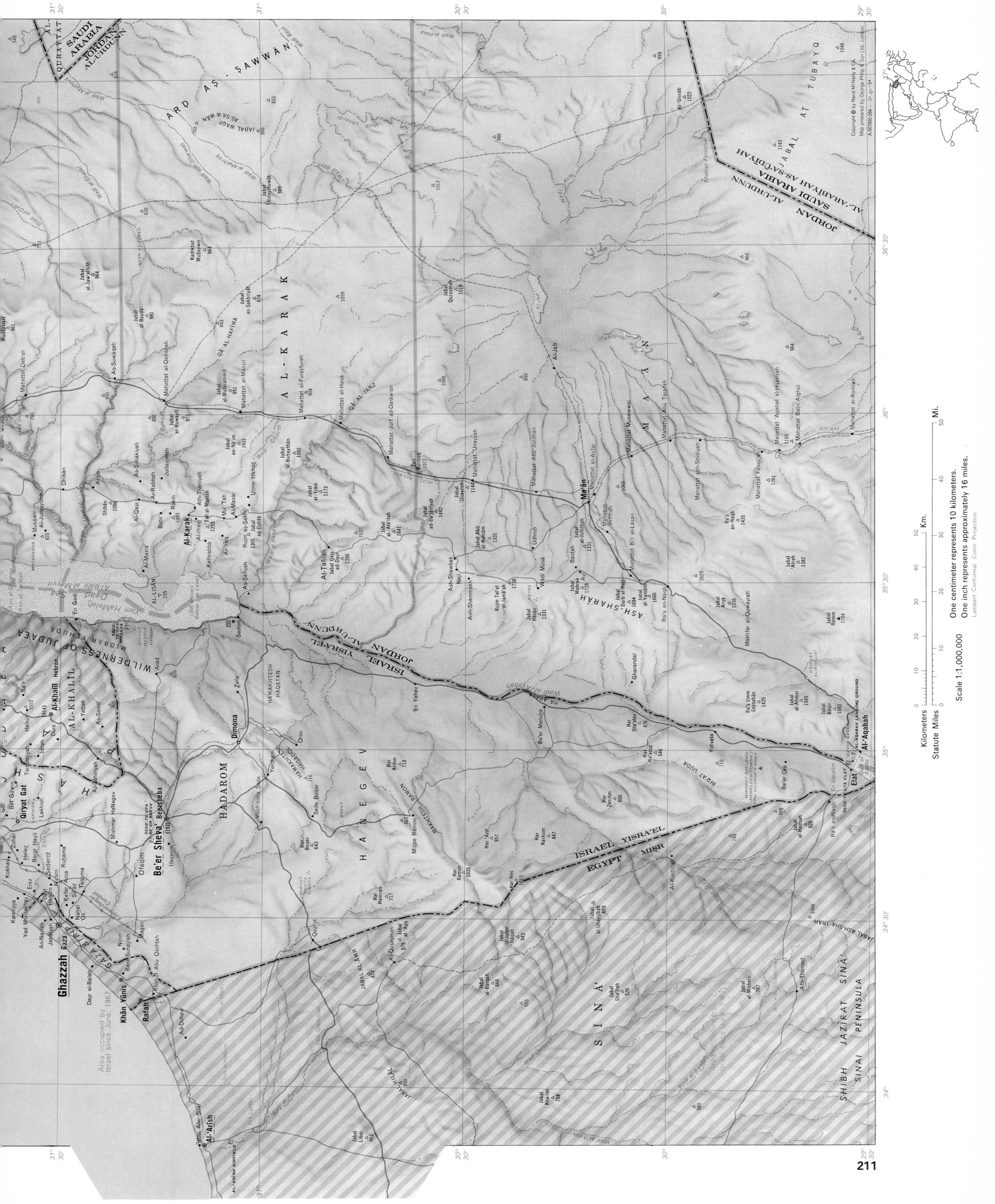

JORDAN AL-URDUNN
SAUDI ARABIA AL-'ARABIYAH AS-SA'ŪDIYAH
ISRAEL YISRA'EL
EGYPT MIṢR
ARḌ AṢ-ṢAWWĀN
AL-KARAK
MA'ĀN
HANEGEV
HADAROM
SĪNĀ'
SHIBH JAZĪRAT SĪNĀ'
SINAI PENINSULA
WILDERNESS OF JUDAEA
GAZA STRIP
Dead Sea
Al-Baḥr al-Mayyit
Yam HaMelaḥ
Ma'ān
Al-Karak
Aṭ-Ṭafīlah
Be'er Sheva' Beersheba
Dimona
Elat
Al-'Aqabah
Ghazzah Gaza
Khān Yūnis
Rafaḥ
Al-'Arīsh
Ḥebron
Al-Khalīl
Area occupied by Israel since June, 1967
Kilometers
Statute Miles
Scale 1:1,000,000
One centimeter represents 10 kilometers.
One inch represents approximately 16 miles.
Lambert Conformal Conic Projection
Copyright © by Rand McNally & Co.
Map prepared by George Philip & Son Ltd., London.

Turkey and Cyprus

B L A C K
M E D I T E R R A N E A N
S E A
İSTANBUL
ANKARA
İzmir
Bursa
Eskişehir
Konya
Antalya
Adapazarı
İzmit (Kocaeli)
Afyonkarahisar
Kütahya
Balıkesir
Manisa
Aydın
Denizli
Burdur
İsparta
Bolu
Zonguldak
Kastamonu
Karabük
Çankırı
Kırıkkale
Kırşehir
Aksaray
Karaman
Uşak
Edirne
Kırklareli
Tekirdağ
Çanakkale
Muğla
Rhodos
Rhodes
RÓDHOS
RHODES
KÁRPATHOS
CYPRUS
KIPROS
Levkosía (Nicosia)
Lemesós (Limassol)
Lárnax (Larnaca)
Néa Páfos (Paphos)
BULGARIA
GREECE
TURKEY
TÜRKİYE
ELLÁS
LÉSVOS
LESBOS
KHÍOS
CHIOS
SÁMOS
KRÍTI
CRETE
D H O D H E K Á N I S O S
D O D E C A N E S E
Marmara Denizi
Sea of Marmara
Antalya Körfezi
Gulf of Antalya
TAURUS MOUNTAINS
T O R O S D A Ğ L
P A P H L A G O N I A
B I T H Y N I A
M Y S I A
L Y D I A
C A R I A
L Y C I A
P I S I D I A
P A M P H Y L I A
P H R Y G I A
G A L A T I A
L Y C A O N I A
T H R A C E
Tuz Gölü
Beyşehir Gölü
Eğridir
EMIR DAĞLARI
BOZ DAĞLAR
AYDIN DAĞLARI
BEY DAĞLARI
SAKARYA
KOCAELI
26°
27°
28°
29°
30°
31°
32°
33°
34°
35°
36°
37°
38°
39°
40°
41°
42°

SEA
Sinop
Samsun
Bafra
Çarşamba
Ordu
Giresun
Trabzon
Rize
Poti
Batumi
Achalciche
U.S.S.R.
TURKEY
Kars
Artvin
Amasya
Tokat
Merzifon
Çorum
Zile
Turhal
Sivas
Yozgat
Erzincan
Erzurum
Gümüşhane
Bayburt
Tunceli
Elâzığ
Malatya
Bingöl
Muş
Bitlis
Siirt
Batman
Diyarbakır
Mardin
Kayseri
Nevşehir
Niğde
Kozan
Adana
Mersin
Tarsus
Ceyhan
Osmaniye
Gaziantep
Maraş
Adıyaman
Urfa
Siverek
Nizip
Kilis
İskenderun
Kırıkhan
Antakya
Antioch
Halab
Aleppo
Idlib
Al-Lādhiqīyah
Latakia
Ḥamāh
Ḥimṣ
Homs
Ṭarābulus
Tripoli
Bayrūt
Beirut
Zaḥlah
DIMASHQ
LEBANON
AL-LUBNĀN
Tudmur
Palmyra
Ar-Raqqah
Dayr az-Zawr
Al-Ḥasakah
Al-Qāmishlī
Abū Kamāl
Euphrates
SYRIA
IRAQ
MESOPOTAMIA
AL-MAWSIL
AR-RAMĀDI
TARAQ AL-'ULAB

Kilometers 0 50 100 150 Km.

Statute Miles 0 50 100 150 Mi.

Scale 1:3,000,000

One centimeter represents 30 kilometers.

One inch represents approximately 47 miles.

Conic Projection, Two Standard Parallels

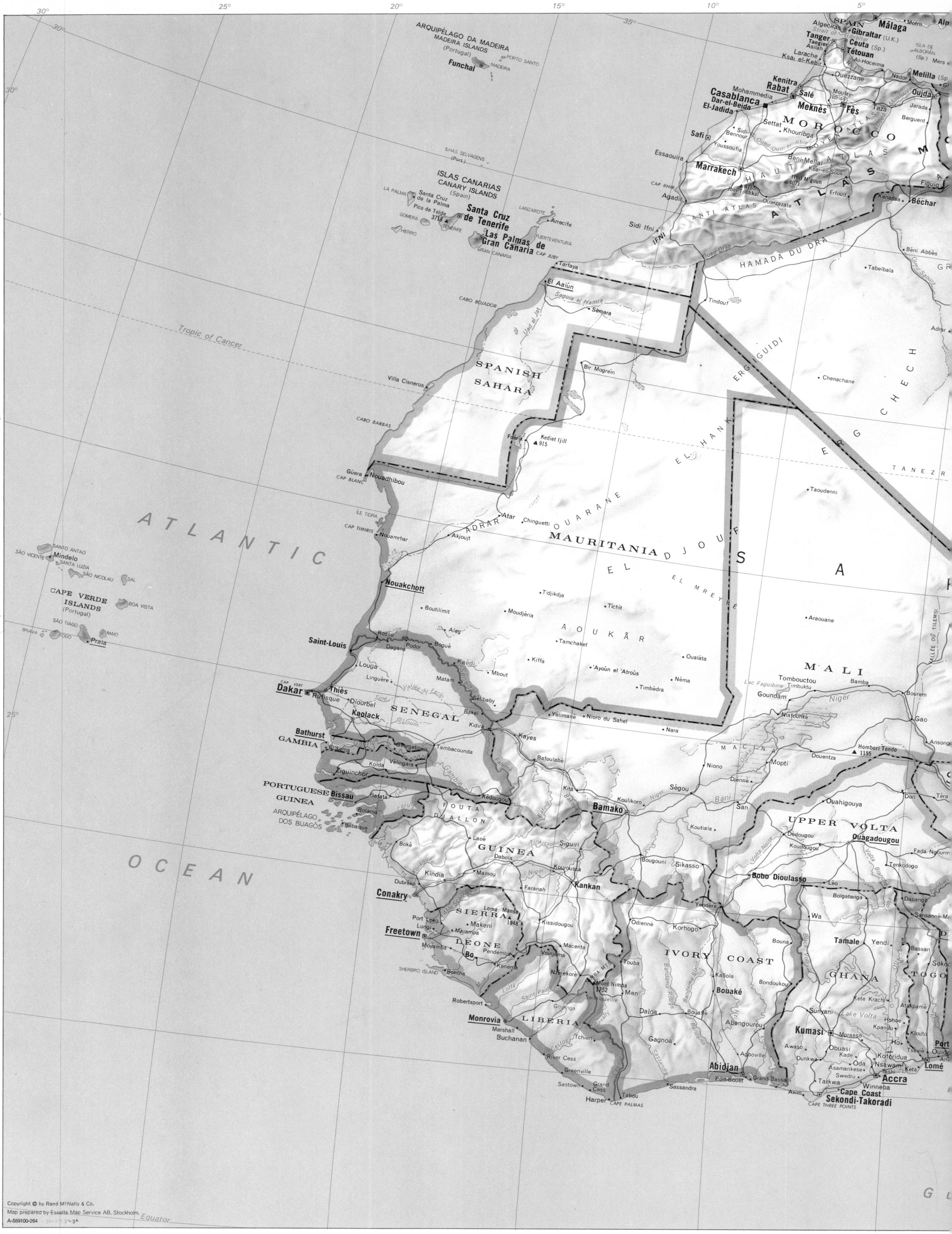

ARQUIPÉLAGO DA MADEIRA
MADEIRA ISLANDS
(Portugal)
Funchal
PORTO SANTO
MADEIRA
ILHAS SELVAGENS
(Port.)
ISLAS CANARIAS
CANARY ISLANDS
(Spain)
LA PALMA
Santa Cruz de la Palma
Pico de Teide 3718
GOMERA
HIERRO
TENERIFE
Santa Cruz de Tenerife
Las Palmas de Gran Canaria
GRAN CANARIA
LANZAROTE
Arrecife
FUERTEVENTURA
CAP JUBY
Tarfaya
El Aaiún
Saguia el Hamra
Semara
CABO BOJADOR
Tropic of Cancer
SPANISH SAHARA
Villa Cisneros
Bir Mogreïn
CABO BARBAS
Fdérik
Kediet Ijill 915
Güera
CAP BLANC
Nouadhibou
ÎLE TIDRA
CAP TIMIRIS
Nouamrhar
Akjoujt
Atar
Chinguetti
ADRAR
OUARANE
MAURITANIA
DJOUF
EL MREYYÉ
Nouakchott
Boutilimit
Tidjikdja
Moudjéria
Tichit
AOUKÂR
Tamchakett
Kiffa
'Ayoûn el 'Atroûs
Oualâta
Néma
Timbédra
Aleg
Rosso
Dagana
Podor
Bogué
Kaédi
Mbout
Saint-Louis
Louga
Linguère
Matam
Sélibaby
CAP VERT
Dakar
Thiès
Rufisque
Diourbel
Kaolack
SENEGAL
Bakel
Kidira
Bathurst
GAMBIA
Georgetown
Tambacounda
Kolda
Vélingara
Ziguinchor
PORTUGUESE GUINEA
Bissau
Bafatá
Bolama
ARQUIPÉLAGO DOS BIJAGÓS
Bubaque
Kédougou
FOUTA DJALLON
Labé
Boké
GUINEA
Dabola
Kindia
Mamou
Faranah
Kouroussa
Siguiri
Kankan
Dubréka
Conakry
Port Loko
Lungi
SIERRA LEONE
Makeni
Loma Mansa 1948
Freetown
Moyamba
Bo
Pendembu
Kenema
SHERBRO ISLAND
Bonthe
Kissidougou
Macenta
Voinjama
Nzérékoré
Mont Nimba 1752
Robertsport
Monrovia
Marshall
Buchanan
LIBERIA
Tchien
River Cess
Greenville
Sastown
Grand Cess
Harper
CAPE PALMAS
Tabou
Sassandra
Abidjan
Port-Bouët
Grand-Bassam
IVORY COAST
Odienné
Korhogo
Touba
Man
Katiola
Bouaké
Daloa
Bouaflé
Gagnoa
Abengourou
Agboville
Bondoukou
Kayes
Bafoulabé
Kita
Bamako
Koulikoro
Ségou
Niono
Djenné
Mopti
Bougouni
Sikasso
Koutiala
MALI
Yélimané
Nioro du Sahel
Nara
Tombouctou
Timbuktu
Goundam
Lac Faguibine
Niafounké
Bamba
Bourem
Gao
Ansongo
Douentza
Hombori Tondo 1155
Araouane
Taoudenni
Chenachane
ERG CHECH
ERG IGUIDI
EL HANK
TANEZROUFT
HAMADA DU DRA
Tindouf
Tabelbala
Béni Abbès
Adrar
Béchar
Kenadsa
Figuig
Erfoud
Ouarzazate
ANTI ATLAS
HAUT ATLAS
Jbel Toubkal 4165
Irhil M'goun 4071
Ksar-es-Souk
Beni-Mellal
Khouribga
Settat
MOYEN ATLAS
MOROCCO
Marrakech
Essaouira
Safi
Sidi-Bennour
Youssoufia
El-Jadida
Casablanca
Dar-el-Beida
Mohammedia
Rabat
Salé
Kenitra
Meknès
Fès
Taza
Oujda
Jerada
Berguent
Nador
Melilla (Sp.)
Al-Hoceima
Ouezzane
Larache
Ksar el-Kebir
Asilah
Tanger
Tangier
Ceuta (Sp.)
Tétouan
Strait of Gibraltar
Algeciras
Gibraltar (U.K.)
SPAIN
Málaga
Motril
ISLA DE ALBORÁN (Sp.)
Agadir
CAP RHIR
Sidi Ifni
IFNI
Oued Dra
UPPER VOLTA
Ouahigouya
Dori
Téra
Dédougou
Koudougou
Ouagadougou
Tenkodogo
Fada Ngourma
Bobo Dioulasso
Léo
Yendéré
Bolgatanga
Wa
Dapango
Tamale
Yendi
Bassari
TOGO
GHANA
Kete Krachi
Sunyani
Lake Volta
Kumasi
Obuasi
Atakpamé
Kpandu
Ho
Tsévié
Awaso
Dunkwa
Oda
Koforidua
Nsawam
Asamankese
Swedru
Tarkwa
Winneba
Accra
Cape Coast
Sekondi-Takoradi
Axim
CAPE THREE POINTS
Lomé
ATLANTIC
OCEAN
SANTO ANTÃO
SÃO VICENTE
Mindelo
SANTA LUZIA
SÃO NICOLAU
SAL
CAPE VERDE ISLANDS
(Portugal)
BOA VISTA
SÃO TIAGO
MAIO
BRAVA
FOGO
Praia
Equator
30°
25°
20°
15°
10°
5°
0°
35°
Copyright © by Rand McNally & Co.
Map prepared by Esselte Map Service AB, Stockholm.
A-589100-264

40°
45°
50°
55°
60°
25°
20°
15°
10°
5°
0°
35°
Equator
MESOPOTAMIA
IRAQ
Baghdād
Al-Mawṣil
Irbil
Kirkūk
As-Sulaymānīyah
Sanandaj
Hamadān
Qom
Kāshān
Kermānshāh
Khorramābād
Borūjerd
Eṣfahān
Yazd
IRAN
DASHT-E LŪT
KŪHHĀ-YE ZĀGROS
Shahreza
Dezfūl
Ahvāz
Khorramshahr
Ābādān
Al-Baṣrah
Shīrāz
Kermān
Rafsanjān
Jahrom
Būshehr
Lār
Bandar-e 'Abbās
Jāsk
Zāhedān
Nehbandān
AFGHANISTAN
PAKISTAN
Chāh Bahār
Bampūr
Īrānshahr
Aleppo
Euphrates
SYRIA
Dayr az-Zawr
Tudmur
Palmyra
Damascus
BĀDIYAT ASH-SHĀM
Ar-Ramādī
Karbalā'
Al-Ḥillah
An-Najaf
Ad-Dīwānīyah
As-Samāwah
An-Nāṣirīyah
Al-'Amārah
Kūt al-Imāra
Ar-Ruṭbah
Jerusalem
JORDAN
AL-ḤAMĀD
Badanah
Sakākā
Al-Jawf
Rafḥā
KUWAIT
Al-Kuwayt
NEUTRAL ZONE
AN-NAFŪD
Tabūk
Ḥā'il
Taymā'
Buraydah
'Unayzah
Az-Zilfī
Al-Wajh
Muwayliḥ
Al-Madīnah
Medina
Yanbu'
Mahd adh-Dhahab
AL-ḤIJĀZ
Rābigh
Juddah
Jidda
Makkah Mecca
Aṭ-Ṭā'if
Al-Līth
Al-Qunfudhah
'ASĪR
Abhā
Qal'at Bīshah
As-Sulayyil
Al-Līdam
Ar-Riyāḍ
Riyadh
Ash-Shaqrā'
Ad-Dawādimī
Al-Kharj
Al-Hufūf
Al-Mubarraz
Ad-Dammām
Aẓ-Ẓahrān
Al-Qaṭīf
Al-Manāmah
BAHRAIN
QATAR
Ad-Dawḥah Doha
SAUDI ARABIA
AD-DAHNĀ'
NAFŪD AD-DAHY
JABAL ṬUWAYQ
Al-Mubarraz
Jabrīn
Al-'Ubaylah
AR-RUB' AL-KHĀLĪ
Persian Gulf
Strait of Hormuz
UNITED ARAB EMIRATES
Abū Ẓaby
Dubayy
Ash-Shāriqah
Umm al-Qaywayn
OMAN
Gulf of Oman
Masqaṭ
Muscat
Maṭraḥ
Ṣuḥār
AL-JABAL AL-AKHḌAR
Jabal ash-Shām 2980
Tropic of Cancer
Ra's al-Ḥadd
'Ādam
OMAN
Jūwāra
Ṣalālah
Mirbāṭ
KHURIYĀN MURIYĀN
KURIA MURIA ISLANDS
ARABIAN SEA
P.D.R. OF YEMEN
Al-Ghayḍah
Ra's Fartak
Qishn
Sayḥūt
Shibām
Say'ūn
HAḌRAMAWT
Ash-Shiḥr
Al-Mukallā
Al-Ḥawrah
Aḥwar
Shuqrā
Lawdar
Aden
Shaykh 'Uthmān
Laḥij
Ṣa'dah
Ṣan'ā'
YEMEN
Dhamār
Yarīm
Ibb
Ta'izz
Al-Mukhā
Al-Ḥudaydah
Zabīd
Jīzān
Qīzān
Gulf of Aden
Bab el-Mandeb
SUQUṬRĀ SOCOTRA
(P.D.R. of Yem.)
Tamrida
'ABD AL-KŪRĪ
THE BROTHERS
RED SEA
DAHLAK ARCHIPELAGO
Mesewa
Massaua
Asmera
Keren
Akordat
Kassalā
ERITREA
Adigrat
Aksum
Adwa
Mek'ele
Ras Dashen
Gonder
Lake Tana
Debre Tabor
Bahir Dar
Dese
Debre Markos
Blue Nile
ETHIOPIA
Addis Abeba
Nekemte
Dire Dawa
Harer
AHMAR MTS.
Jijiga
Awash
DANAKIL PLAIN
AFARS AND ISSAS
Djibouti
Tadjoura
Obock
Dikhil
Zeila
Berbera
Hargeysa
Burao
Borama
Erigavo
Las Anod
Karin
Bosaso
Qandala
'Alula
RAS ASIR
CAPE GUARDAFUI
Hando
RAS HAFUN
Gardo
Eil
SOMALIA
Galka'yo
Obbia
Mareg
Beled Weyne
Kelafo
Degeh-Bur
Kebri Dehar
Imi
Domo
INDIAN OCEAN
Mogadisho
Marka
Brava
Afgoi
Johar
Baidoa
Bardera
Lugh Ganane
Dolo
Shebelle
Juba
Ginir
Goba
Dodola
Sodo
Arba Minch
Kibre Mengist
Negele
Mega
Moyale
Gore
Gambela
Jima
Hosaina
Waka
Bako
Maji
Lake Rudolf
CHALBI DESERT
Marsabit
Wajir
Lodwar
KENYA
Bur Sudan
Port Sudan
Suakin
Sawakin
Tawkar
Kassala
Adarama
Halā'ib
Jabal Oda 2259

Kilometers 0 200 400 600 Km.

Statute Miles 0 200 600 Mi.

Scale 1:12,000,000

One centimeter represents 120 kilometers.

One inch represents approximately 190 miles.

Miller Oblated Stereographic Projection

0°
5°
10°
15°
20°
25°
30°
35°
MEDITERRANEAN SEA
IONIAN SEA
Palermo
Messina
Reggio di Calabria
ITALY
Catania
Siracusa
SICILIA
SICILY
Trapani
Marsala
Ragusa
MALTA
Valletta
Alger
Algiers
Blida
El Asnam
Bejaïa
Skikda
Annaba
(Bône)
Constantine
Sétif
Batna
Tébessa
Biskra
Bizerte
Tunis
Sousse
Sfax
Gabès
Gafsa
TUNISIA
El Kairouan
Touggourt
El Oued
Ghardaïa
Laghouat
Ouargla
Hassi Messaoud
El Goléa
ALGERIA
GRAND ERG OCCIDENTAL
GRAND ERG ORIENTAL
PLATEAU DU TINRHERT
In Salah
In Amenas
Djanet
Tamanrasset
Tahat
3003
AHAGGAR
TASSILI N'AJJER
In Guezzam
Athínai
Athens
Piraiévs
Pátrai
GREECE
PELOPÓNNISOS
KIKLÁDHES
Iráklion
KRÍTI
Kritikón Pélagos
Ródhos
TURKEY
Izmir
Konya
Adana
Mersin
Antalya
Levkosía
CYPRUS
Lemesós
Bayrūt
LEBANON
Tarābulus
Tripoli
Hefa
ISRAEL
Tel Aviv-Yafo
Yerushalayim
Ṭarābulus
Tripoli
Al-Khums
Misrātah
Zuwārah
Banghāzī
Darnah
Tubruq
Ajdābiyah
Khalīj Surt
BARQAH
CYRENAICA
ṬARĀBULUS
TRIPOLITANIA
Ghudāmis
Ghāt
Sabhah
Awbārī
Marzūq
FAZZĀN
FEZZAN
LIBYA
Waw al-Kabīr
Al-Jawf
Al-Jaghbūb
Al-Iskandarīyah
Alexandria
Būr Sa'īd
Port Said
Dumyāṭ
Ṭanṭā
Al-Manṣūrah
Al-Ismā'īlīyah
As-Suways
Suez
AL-QĀHIRAH
CAIRO
Al-Jīzah
Al-Fayyūm
Banī Suwayf
Al-Minyā
Asyūṭ
Sawhāj
Qinā
Al-Uqṣur
Luxor
Aswān
Lake Nasser
Siwah
Marsā Maṭrūḥ
AṢ-ṢAḤRĀ AL-GHARBĪYAH
WESTERN DESERT
EGYPT
AS-SAHRĀ AL-LĪBĪYAH
LIBYAN DESERT
AṢ-ṢAḤRĀ ASH-SHARQĪYAH
EASTERN DESERT
Wādī Halfā'
NUBIAN DESERT
SAHARA
TIBESTI
Emi Koussi
3415
Pic Toussidé
3315
Bardaï
Zouar
Mont Gréboun
2000
AÏR
NIGER
Agadez
Bilma
GRAND ERG DE BILMA
TÉNÉRÉ
DÉPRESSION DU MOURDI
ENNEDI
Fada
BODÉLÉ
CHAD
Largeau
Abéché
Ati
Fort-Lamy
Lake Chad
Lac Tchad
Mao
Mongo
Am Timan
Fort-Archambault
Moundou
SUDAN
Umm Durmān
Omdurman
Al-Khurṭūm
Khartoum
Wad Madanī
Al-Ubayyiḍ
Al-Fāshir
Jabal Marrah
3088
Nyala
An-Nuhūd
Kūstī
Malakal
Wāw
Juba
Dunqulah
Atbarah
Shandī
Abū Ḥamad
SUDAN
Zinder
Maradi
Tahoua
Niamey
Sokoto
Katsina
Kano
Maiduguri
Zaria
Kaduna
Jos
Bauchi
Minna
NIGERIA
Ilorin
Oshogbo
Ibadan
Abeokuta
Ijebu-Ode
Lagos
Benin City
Sapele
Warri
Enugu
Onitsha
Makurdi
Aba
Calabar
Port Harcourt
Yola
ADAMAWA
Garoua
Maroua
CAMEROON
Douala
Yaoundé
Bamenda
Foumban
Ngaoundéré
Bertoua
Mont Cameroun
4070
Santa Isabel
FERNANDO PÓO
EQUAT. GUINEA
Bight of Biafra
PRÍNCIPE
EQUAT. GUINEA
GABON
CONGO
CENTRAL AFRICAN REPUBLIC
Bangui
Bambari
Bouar
Berbérati
Bossangoa
ZAIRE
Bumba
Buta
Isiro
Bondo
UGANDA

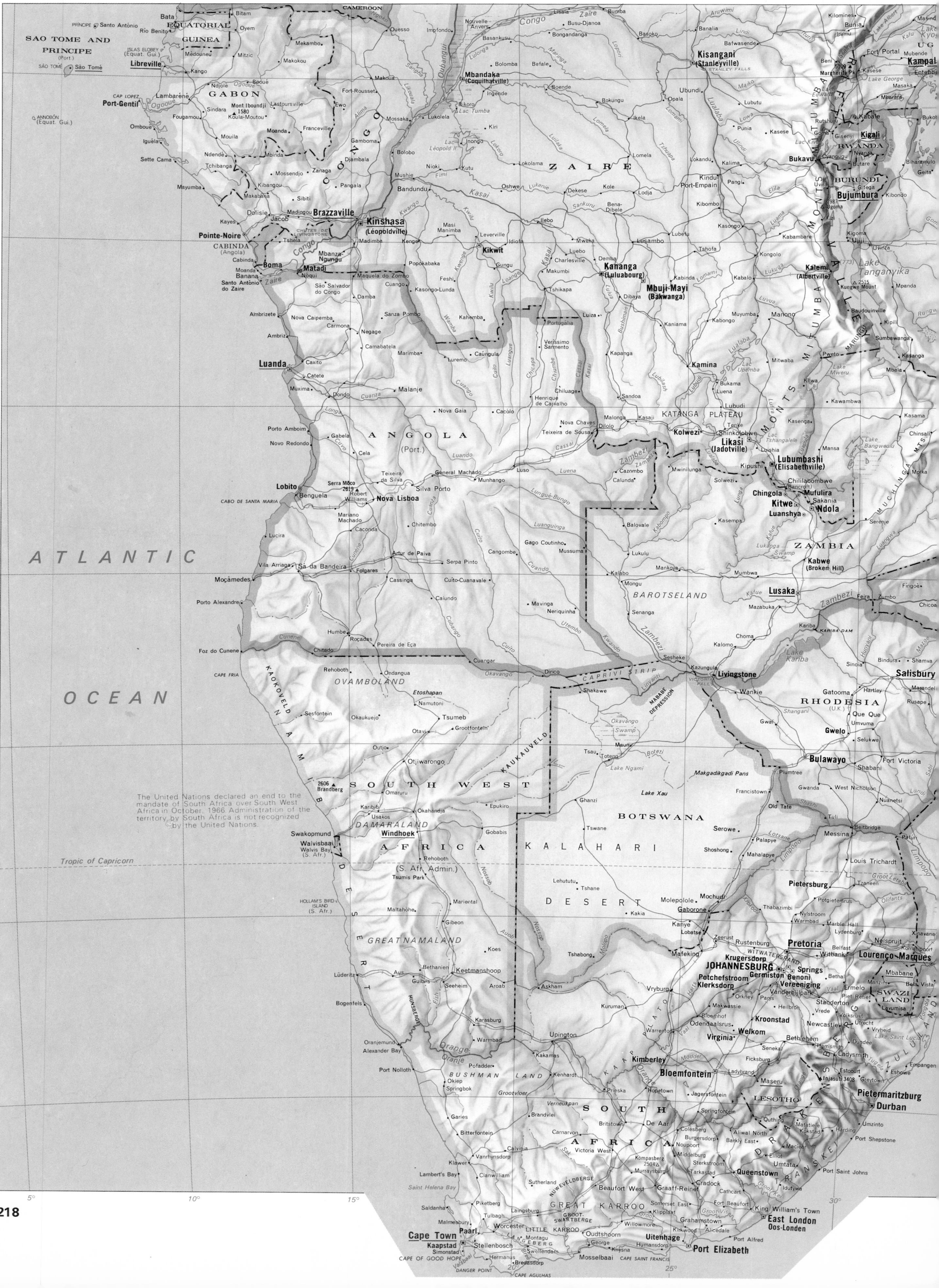
SAO TOME AND PRINCIPE
EQUATORIAL GUINEA
GABON
CAMEROON
CONGO
ZAIRE
ANGOLA
(Port.)
CABINDA
(Angola)
SOUTH WEST AFRICA
(S. Afr. Admin.)
BOTSWANA
ZAMBIA
RHODESIA
(U.K.)
RWANDA
BURUNDI
LESOTHO
SWAZILAND
SOUTH AFRICA
ATLANTIC
OCEAN
KALAHARI DESERT
NAMIB DESERT
KAOKOVELD
OVAMBOLAND
DAMARALAND
GREAT NAMALAND
BUSHMAN LAND
BAROTSELAND
KATANGA PLATEAU
GREAT KARROO
LITTLE KARROO
CAPRIVI STRIP
Tropic of Capricorn
The United Nations declared an end to the mandate of South Africa over South West Africa in October, 1966. Administration of the territory by South Africa is not recognized by the United Nations.
Libreville
Port-Gentil
Brazzaville
Kinshasa
(Léopoldville)
Pointe-Noire
Matadi
Boma
Luanda
Lobito
Benguela
Nova Lisboa
Silva Porto
Moçâmedes
Sá da Bandeira
Kananga
(Luluabourg)
Mbuji-Mayi
(Bakwanga)
Kisangani
(Stanleyville)
Mbandaka
(Coquilhatville)
Kikwit
Kamina
Kolwezi
Likasi
(Jadotville)
Lubumbashi
(Elisabethville)
Kalemi
(Albertville)
Bukavu
Kigali
Bujumbura
Kampala
Chingola
Mufulira
Kitwe
Ndola
Luanshya
Kabwe
(Broken Hill)
Lusaka
Livingstone
Salisbury
Gwelo
Bulawayo
Swakopmund
Walvis Bay
Windhoek
Tsumeb
Lüderitz
Keetmanshoop
Gaborone
Mafeking
Pretoria
JOHANNESBURG
Lourenço Marques
Kimberley
Bloemfontein
Pietermaritzburg
Durban
East London
Port Elizabeth
Cape Town
Kaapstad
Stellenbosch
Paarl
Worcester
CAPE OF GOOD HOPE
CAPE AGULHAS
Lake Tanganyika
Lake Kariba
Lake Ngami
Okavango Swamp
Zambezi
Congo
Orange
Limpopo
Kasai
Cuanza
Cunene
Molopo
Vaal
5°
10°
15°
20°
25°
30°

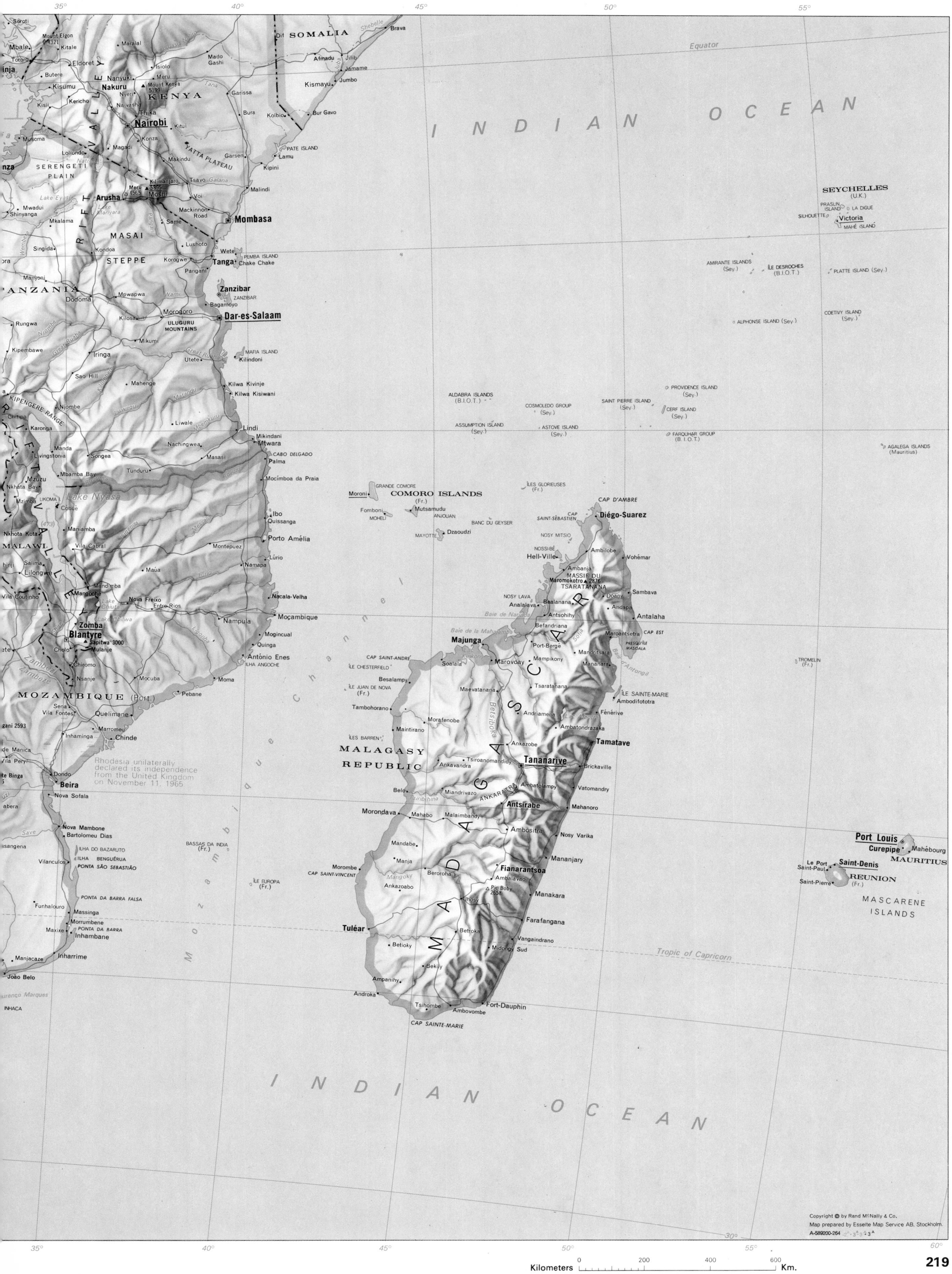

SOMALIA
KENYA
Nairobi
Mombasa
Kismayu
INDIAN OCEAN
Equator
SEYCHELLES (U.K.)
Victoria
MAHÉ ISLAND
AMIRANTE ISLANDS (Sey.)
ÎLE DESROCHES (B.I.O.T.)
PLATTE ISLAND (Sey.)
ALPHONSE ISLAND (Sey.)
COETIVY ISLAND (Sey.)
PROVIDENCE ISLAND (Sey.)
ALDABRA ISLANDS (B.I.O.T.)
COSMOLEDO GROUP (Sey.)
SAINT PIERRE ISLAND (Sey.)
CERF ISLAND (Sey.)
ASSUMPTION ISLAND (Sey.)
ASTOVE ISLAND (Sey.)
FARQUHAR GROUP (B.I.O.T.)
AGALEGA ISLANDS (Mauritius)
MASAI STEPPE
SERENGETI PLAIN
Kilimanjaro
Tanga
Zanzibar
Dar-es-Salaam
TANZANIA
MAFIA ISLAND
Kilwa Kivinje
Lindi
Mtwara
CABO DELGADO
Lake Nyasa
MALAWI
Lilongwe
Zomba
Blantyre
Moroni
COMORO ISLANDS (Fr.)
GRANDE COMORE
MAYOTTE
Dzaoudzi
ÎLES GLORIEUSES (Fr.)
CAP D'AMBRE
Diégo-Suarez
Hell-Ville
Majunga
Moçambique
Nampula
Porto Amélia
MOZAMBIQUE (Port.)
Quelimane
Beira
Inhambane
Chinde
Rhodesia unilaterally declared its independence from the United Kingdom on November 11, 1965
Mozambique Channel
MALAGASY REPUBLIC
MADAGASCAR
Tananarive
Tamatave
Antsirabe
Fianarantsoa
Tuléar
Morondava
Fort-Dauphin
CAP SAINTE-MARIE
BASSAS DA INDIA (Fr.)
ÎLE EUROPA (Fr.)
ÎLE JUAN DE NOVA (Fr.)
TROMELIN (Fr.)
Port Louis
MAURITIUS
Saint-Denis
REUNION (Fr.)
MASCARENE ISLANDS
Tropic of Capricorn

A-589200-264

Kilometers 0 200 400 600 Km.
Statute Miles 0 200 400 600 Mi.

Scale 1:12,000,000

One centimeter represents 120 kilometers.
One inch represents approximately 190 miles.
Miller Oblated Stereographic Projection

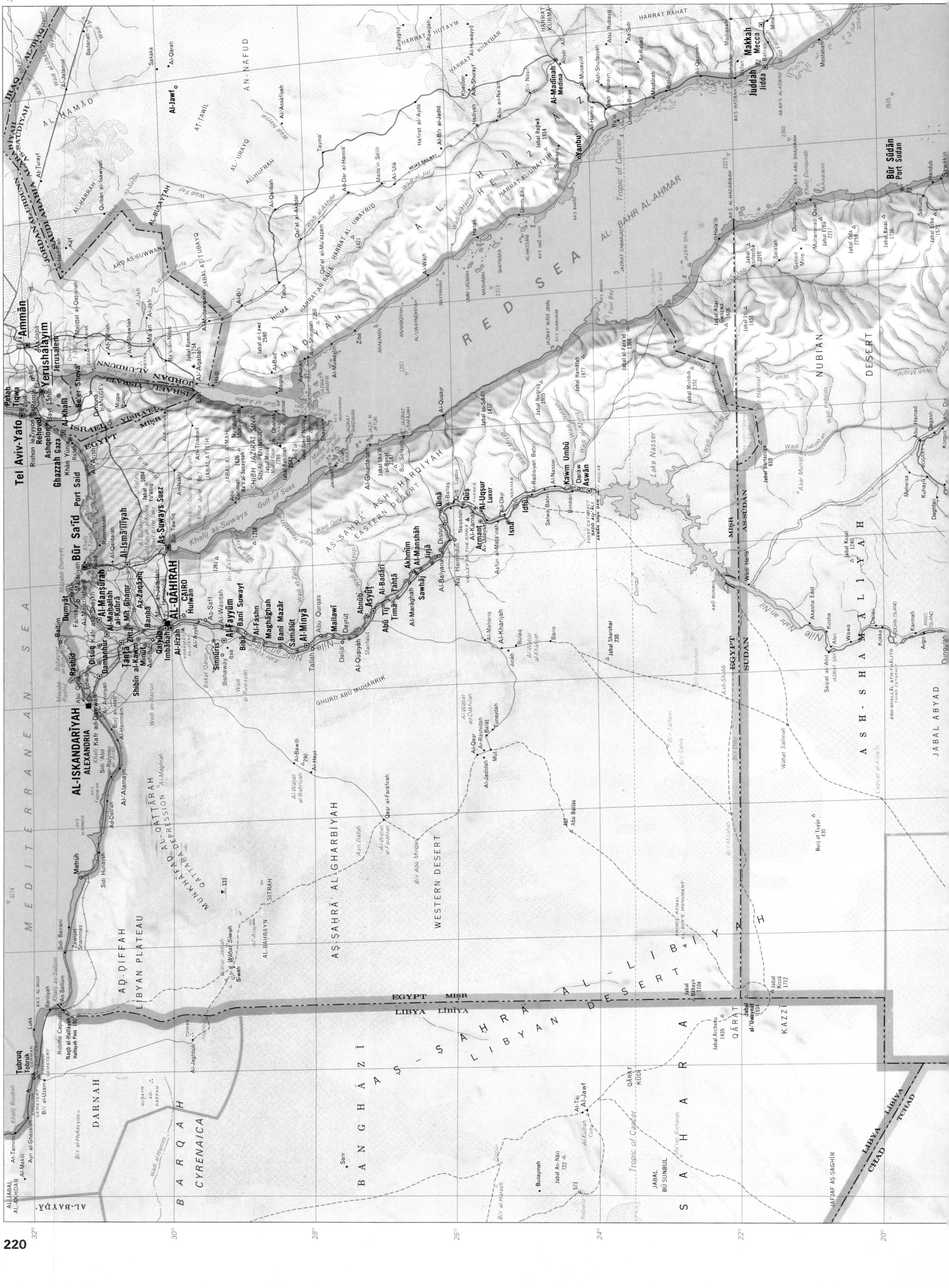
MEDITERRANEAN SEA
RED SEA
AL-BAHR AL-AHMAR
AL-ISKANDARIYAH
ALEXANDRIA
AL-QAHIRAH
CAIRO
Bur Sa'id
Port Said
As-Suways Suez
Al-Jizah
Tanta
Al-Mansurah
Dumyat
Rashid
Al-Fayyum
Bani Suwayf
Al-Minya
Asyut
Sawhaj
Qina
Al-Uqsur
Luxor
Aswan
Lake Nasser
Matruh
As-Sallum
Tubruq
Tobruk
Siwah
Al-Kharijah
Ammān
Yerushalayim
Jerusalem
Tel Aviv-Yafo
Ghazzah Gaza
Al-Madinah
Medina
Makkah
Mecca
Juddah
Jidda
Yanbu'
Bur Sudan
Port Sudan
Wadi Halfa
WESTERN DESERT
EASTERN DESERT
LIBYAN DESERT
NUBIAN DESERT
LIBYAN PLATEAU
QATTARA DEPRESSION
AS-SAHRA' AL-GHARBIYAH
AS-SAHRA' ASH-SHARQIYAH
AS-SAHRA' AL-LIBIYAH
ASH-SHAMALIYAH
CYRENAICA
BARQAH
BANGHAZI
DARNAH
SAHARA
AL-HIJAZ
MIDYAN
EGYPT MISR
LIBYA LIBIYA
SUDAN AS-SUDAN
ISRAEL YISRA'EL
JORDAN AL-URDUNN
SAUDI ARABIA
IRAQ AL-IRAQ
CHAD TCHAD
Tropic of Cancer
Gulf of Suez
Gulf of Aqaba
Nile

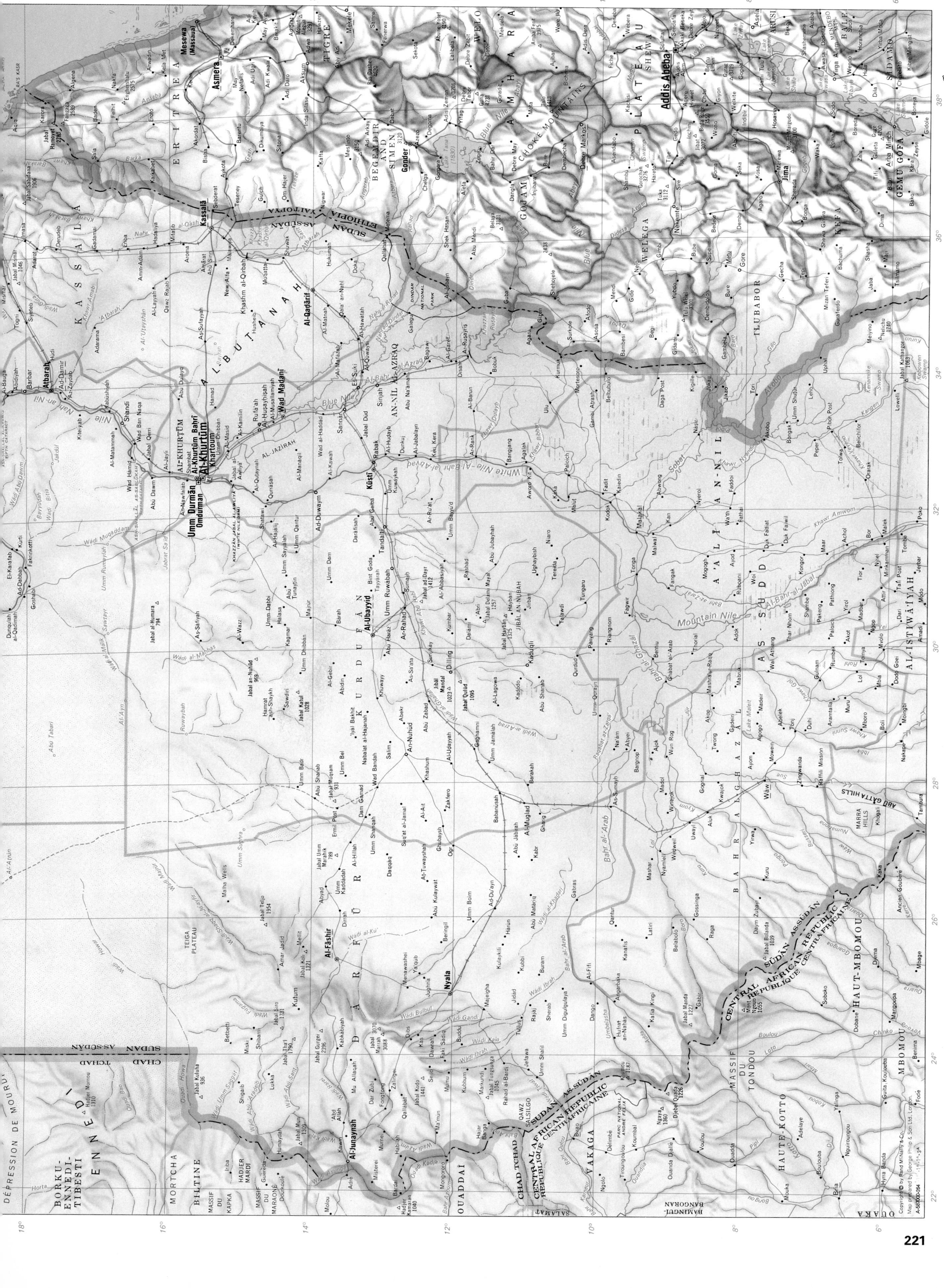
Kilometers
Km.
Statute Miles
Mi.
Scale 1:6,000,000
One centimeter represents 60 kilometers.
One inch represents approximately 95 miles.
Lambert Azimuthal Equal-Area Projection
Al-Khurṭūm
Khartoum
Umm Durmān
Omdurman
Addis Abeba
Asmera
Mesewa (Massaua)
Kassalā
Atbarah
Wad Madanī
Al-Qaḍārif
Kūstī
Al-Ubayyiḍ
Al-Fāshir
Nyala
Al-Junaynah
Malakāl
Wāw
Jima
Gonder
Nekemte
ERITREA
TIGRE
BEGEMDIR AND SIMEN
GOJAM
SHEWA
WELEGA
ILUBABOR
KEFA
GEMU GOFA
SIDAMO
ARUSI
BALE
WELO
KASSALĀ
AL-BUṬĀNAH
KURDUFĀN
DĀR FŪR
AṢ-ṢUDD
BAḤR AL-GHAZĀL
AL-ISTIWĀʾIYAH
AN-NĪL AL-AZRAQ
ETHIOPIA
SUDAN
AS-SŪDĀN
CHAD
TCHAD
CENTRAL AFRICAN REPUBLIC
RÉPUBLIQUE CENTRAFRICAINE
BORKU-ENNEDI-TIBESTI
OUADDAÏ
BILTINE
HAUT-MBOMOU
HAUTE-KOTTO
VAKAGA
Blue Nile
White Nile
Mountain Nile
Bahr al-Arab
CHOKE MOUNTAINS
Lake Tana
Copyright © by Rand McNally & Co.
Map prepared by George Philip & Son Ltd., London

ATLANTIC OCEAN
GRAIN COAST
IVORY COAST
Nouakchott
Saint-Louis
Dakar
Rufisque
Thiès
Kaolack
Bathurst
Ziguinchor
Bissau
Conakry
Freetown
Monrovia
Buchanan
Greenville
Harper
Bamako
Ségou
Kayes
Kankan
Labé
Sikasso
Korhogo
Bouaké
Abidjan
Sassandra
Atar
Akjoujt
Tidjikdja
Kiffa
Néma
Mopti
TRARZA
AOUKÂR
HODH
AFFOLLE
ADÂFER EL ABIOD
EL DJOUF
EL MREYYÉ
DHAR TICHIT
DHAR TAGNANT
AKLÉ AOUÂNA
FLEUVE
DIOURBEL
FERLO
SINE-SALOUM
CASAMANCE
SÉNÉGAL ORIENTAL
GAMBIA
SENEGAL
PORT. GUINEA
GUINÉE
MALI
MAURITANIA
MAURITANIE
SIERRA LEONE
LIBERIA
IVORY COAST
CÔTE D'IVOIRE
UPPER VOLTA
HAUTE-VOLTA
FOUTA DJALLON
KINDIA
BOKÉ
BOFFA
FORÉCARIAH
FARANAH
KOUROUSSA
SIGUIRI
KISSIDOUGOU
BEYLA
MACENTA
NZÉRÉKORÉ
NIMBA
GRAND BASSA
SINOE
MARYLAND
ODIENNÉ
SÉGUÉLA
KATIOLA
MAN
DALOA
GAGNOA
DIVO
WESTERN AREA
NORTHERN
SOUTHERN
EASTERN
BAMAKO
SIKASSO
SÉGOU
KAYES
ARQUIPÉLAGO DOS BIJAGÓS
a
CAPE VERDE ISLANDS
ARQUIPÉLAGO DE CABO VERDE
(Port.)
SANTO ANTÃO
SÃO VICENTE
SÃO NICOLAU
SAL
BOA VISTA
MAIO
SÃO TIAGO
FOGO
BRAVA
Praia
ATLANTIC
OCEAN
Copyright © by Rand McNally & Co.
Map prepared by George Philip & Son Ltd. London.
A-589792-264

ALGERIA
ALGÉRIE
MALI
NIGER
NIGERIA
UPPER VOLTA
HAUTE-VOLTA
DAHOMEY
TOGO
GHANA
IVORY COAST
CÔTE D'IVOIRE
CAMEROON
EQUATORIAL GUINEA
ADRAR DES IFORAS
TIMÉTRINE MONTS
MASSIF DE TAZARIT
MONTS TAMGAK
AGADEZ
AÏR
MASSIF DE TAROUADJI
GAO
TAHOUA
ZINDER
MARADI
NIAMEY
DOSSO
SOKOTO
KANO
NORTH-WESTERN
NORTH-CENTRAL
NORTH EASTERN
BENUE-PLATEAU
KWARA
WESTERN
MID-WESTERN
EAST-CENTRAL
RIVERS
SOUTH-EASTERN
NORTHERN
UPPER
BRONG-AHAFO
ASHANTI
EASTERN
CENTRAL
VOLTA
CENTRE
EST
BORGOU
ATAKORA
ZOU
MONO
CAMEROUN OCCIDENTAL
CAMEROUN ORIENTAL
Niger
Lake Volta
Kainji Lake
Benue
SLAVE COAST
Bight of Benin
Bight of Biafra
GOLD COAST
GULF OF GUINEA
NIGER DELTA
Tessalit
Kidal
Gao
Bourem
Tombouctou
Ansongo
Tillia
Tchin Tabaraden
Agadez
I-n-Gall
Iferouâne
Assodé
Tahoua
Birni Nkonni
Maradi
Zinder
Niamey
Dosso
Tillabéry
Ouagadougou
Koudougou
Fada Ngourma
Tenkodogo
Tamale
Yendi
Bolgatanga
Kumasi
Sunyani
Accra
Tema
Winneba
Cape Coast
Sekondi-Takoradi
Lomé
Anécho
Cotonou
Porto-Novo
Abomey
Parakou
Natitingou
Djougou
Kandi
Sokodé
Lama-Kara
Lagos
Ibadan
Abeokuta
Ogbomosho
Oshogbo
Ilorin
Ife
Ondo
Akure
Ado-Ekiti
Benin City
Sapele
Warri
Onitsha
Enugu
Aba
Port Harcourt
Owerri
Calabar
Opobo
Lokoja
Makurdi
Bida
Minna
Kaduna
Zaria
Kano
Katsina
Sokoto
Gusau
Kaura Namoda
Birnin Kebbi
Jos
Bauchi
Lafia
Keffi
Douala
Buea
Victoria
Santa Isabel
Mont Cameroun 4070
FERNANDO POO

Kilometers 0 100 200 300 Km.

Statute Miles 0 100 200 300 Mi.

Scale 1:6,000,000

One centimeter represents 60 kilometers.

One inch represents approximately 95 miles.

Lambert Azimuthal Equal-Area Projection

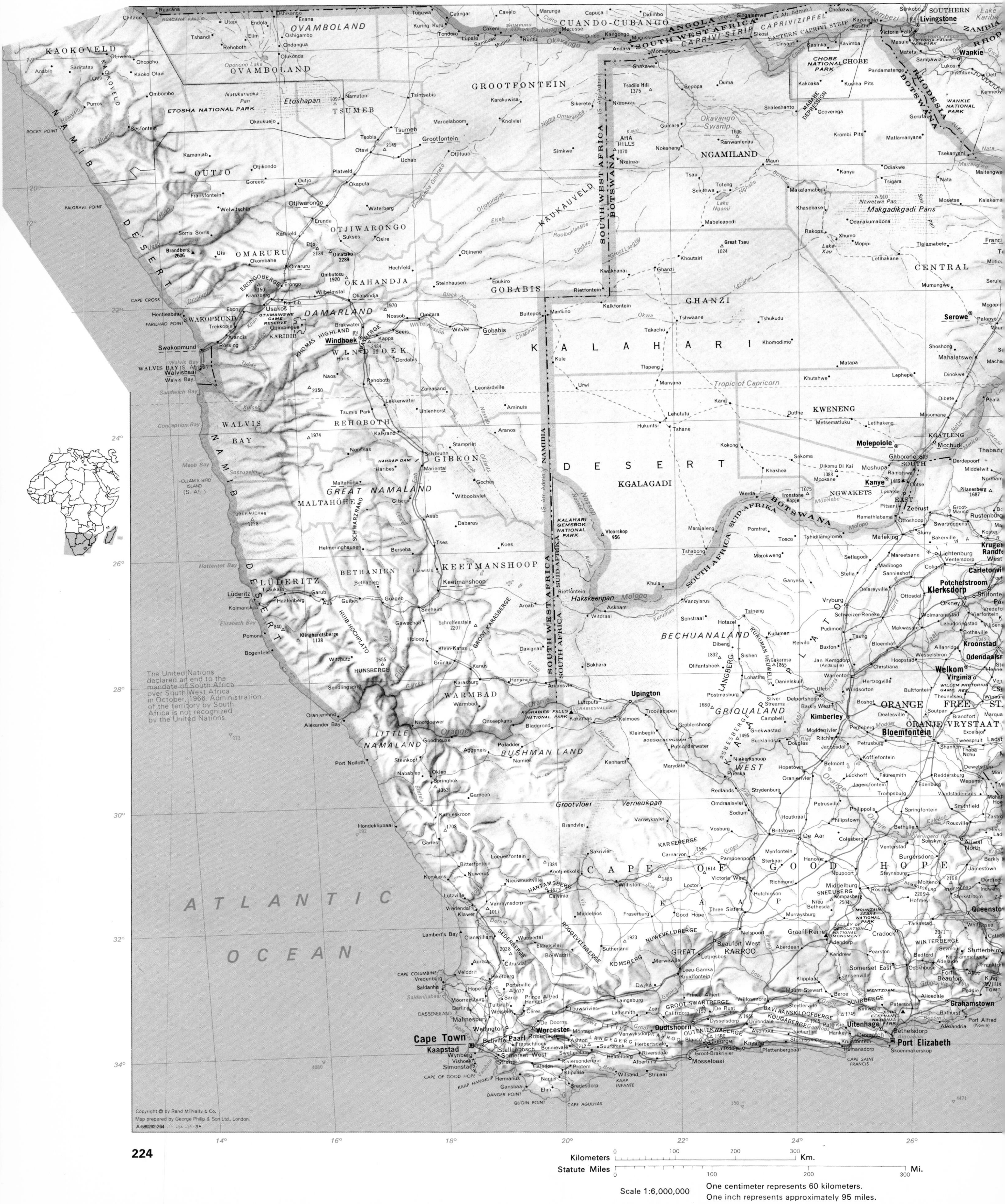
14°
16°
18°
20°
22°
24°
26°
KAOKOVELD
OVAMBOLAND
ETOSHA NATIONAL PARK
Etoshapan
TSUMEB
GROOTFONTEIN
CUANDO-CUBANGO
ANGOLA
SOUTH WEST AFRICA
CAPRIVI STRIP
EASTERN CAPRIVI STRIP
CHOBE NATIONAL PARK
CHOBE
Livingstone
ZAMBIA
RHODESIA
BOTSWANA
WANKIE NATIONAL PARK
Okavango Swamp
NGAMILAND
Lake Ngami
Makgadikgadi Pans
CENTRAL
OUTJO
OTJIWARONGO
KAUKAUVELD
OMARURU
OKAHANDJA
GOBABIS
GHANZI
DAMARLAND
Swakopmund
SWAKOPMUND
Windhoek
WINDHOEK
KALAHARI
WALVIS BAY (S. Afr.)
Walvisbaai
Walvis Bay
Tropic of Capricorn
REHOBOTH
KWENENG
NAMIB DESERT
WALVIS BAY
GIBEON
DESERT
KGALAGADI
Molepolole
Gaborone
Kanye
NGWAKETS
HOLLAM'S BIRD ISLAND (S. Afr.)
GREAT NAMALAND
MALTAHÖHE
KALAHARI GEMSBOK NATIONAL PARK
SOUTH AFRICA
SUID-AFRIKA
Mafeking
BETHANIEN
KEETMANSHOOP
Keetmanshoop
LÜDERITZ
Lüderitz
Molopo
Hakskeenpan
BECHUANALAND
Kimberley
Klerksdorp
Kroonstad
Welkom
Upington
WARMBAD
GRIQUALAND WEST
ORANGE FREE STATE
ORANJE-VRYSTAAT
Bloemfontein
Orange
Oranjemund
Alexander Bay
LITTLE NAMALAND
BUSHMAN LAND
Port Nolloth
Grootvloer
Verneukpan
De Aar
CAPE OF GOOD HOPE
KAAP
ATLANTIC OCEAN
Queenstown
GREAT KARROO
Beaufort West
Cradock
Graaff-Reinet
Grahamstown
Saldanha
Cape Town
Kaapstad
Worcester
Paarl
Stellenbosch
Oudtshoorn
George
Mosselbaai
Uitenhage
Port Elizabeth
CAPE OF GOOD HOPE
CAPE AGULHAS
The United Nations declared an end to the mandate of South Africa over South West Africa in October, 1966. Administration of the territory by South Africa is not recognized by the United Nations.

Kilometers 0 100 200 300 Km.

Statute Miles 0 100 200 300 Mi.

Scale 1:6,000,000

One centimeter represents 60 kilometers.
One inch represents approximately 95 miles.

Lambert Azimuthal Equal-Area Projection

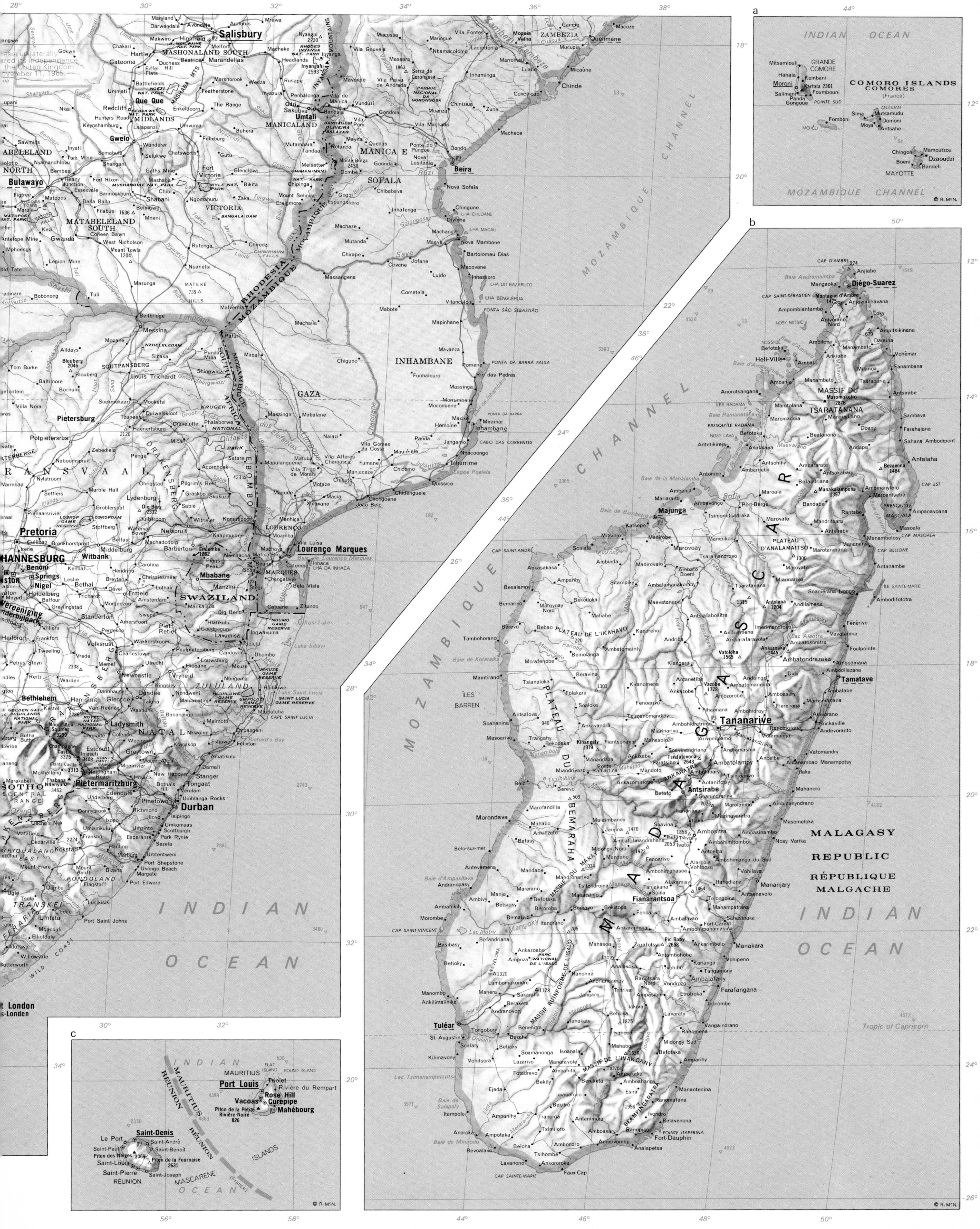
a
INDIAN OCEAN
COMORO ISLANDS
COMORES
(France)
GRANDE COMORE
Moroni
MOHÉLI
ANJOUAN
MAYOTTE
MOZAMBIQUE CHANNEL
b
MADAGASCAR
MALAGASY REPUBLIC
RÉPUBLIQUE MALGACHE
INDIAN OCEAN
MOZAMBIQUE CHANNEL
Tropic of Capricorn
Diégo-Suarez
Majunga
Tamatave
Tananarive
Antsirabe
Fianarantsoa
Tuléar
Morondava
Fort-Dauphin
Manakara
MASSIF DU TSARATANANA
PLATEAU DE L'IKAHAVO
PLATEAU DU BEMARAHA
c
INDIAN OCEAN
MAURITIUS
Port Louis
Mahébourg
Curepipe
Rose Hill
Vacoas
RÉUNION
Saint-Denis
Saint-Pierre
MASCARENE ISLANDS
(France)
Salisbury
Bulawayo
Umtali
Beira
Quelimane
RHODESIA
MOZAMBIQUE
SOUTH AFRICA
TRANSVAAL
NATAL
SWAZILAND
Mbabane
Pretoria
Lourenço Marques
Pietermaritzburg
Durban
Ladysmith
Pietersburg
INHAMBANE
GAZA
SOFALA
MANICA E
ZAMBEZIA
MOZAMBIQUE CHANNEL
INDIAN OCEAN
© R. McN.

INDONESIA
DJAWA
JAVA
Tasikmalaja
Tjilatjap
Jogjakarta
Surakarta
Madiun
Kediri
Malang
Blitar
Djember
Banjuwangi
Singaradja
BALI
Denpasar
Mataram
Sumbawa Besar
SUMBAWA
LOMBOK
LESSER SUNDA ISLANDS
FLORES
Waikabubak
Waingapu
SUMBA
Baing
Laut Sawu
SAWU
PULAU SEMAU
PULAU ROTI
Kupang
TIMOR
Soe
Ocussi
(Port. Timor)
PORTUGUESE TIMOR
Timor Sea
Ara
HIBERNIA REEF
ASHMORE REEF
CARTIER ISLAND
(Austl.)
SANDY ISLET
(Austl.)
SCOTT REEF
BROWSE ISLAND
BONAPARTE ARCHIPELAGO
York Sound
Admiralty Gulf
CAPE LONDONDERRY
Joseph Bonaparte Gulf
BATHURST ISLAND
MELVILLE ISLAND
CAPE CROKER
COBOURG PENINSULA
Van Diemen Gulf
Beagle Gulf
Clarence Strait
Darwin
POINT BLAZE
Rum Jungle
ARNHEM L.
Pine Creek
Katherine
Daly
Wyndham
Kununurra
Victoria
Victoria River Downs
Daly Waters
LYNHER REEF
ADELE ISLAND
BEAGLE BANK
Collier Bay
BUCCANEER ARCHIPELAGO
Yampi Sound
CAPE LEVEQUE
King Sound
Derby
KIMBERLEY PLATEAU
KING LEOPOLD RANGES
936
Mount Ord
DURACK RANGE
Ord
Fitzroy
Fitzroy Crossing
Halls Creek
Gordon Downs
Wave Hill
Newcastle Waters
Powell Cr
INDIAN OCEAN
ROWLEY SHOALS
Broome
CAPE LATOUCHE TREVILLE
La Grange
EIGHTY MILE BEACH
TANAMI DESERT
NORTHERN TERRITORY
Gregory Lake
Lake White
(Dry)
Barrow
DAMPIER ARCHIPELAGO
MONTE BELLO ISLANDS
Port Hedland
Dampier
Roebourne
De Grey
GREAT SANDY DESERT
Marble Bar
BARROW ISLAND
Nullagine
THROSSELL RANGE
Lake Dora
(Dry)
Lake Auld
(Dry)
Lake Mackay
(Dry Salt Lake)
MUIRON ISLANDS
NORTH WEST CAPE
Exmouth Gulf
Onslow
Fortescue
HAMERSLEY RANGE
Wittenoom
Mount Brockman
1114
1227
Mount Bruce
ROBERTSON RANGE
Lake Disappointment
(Dry Salt Lake)
Lake Macdonald
(Dry)
Mount Leisler
1006
Mount Zeil
1510
MACDONNELL
POINT CLOATES
Ashburton
BARLEE RANGE
WESTERN AUSTRALIA
GIBSON DESERT
RAWLINSON RANGE
Lake Amadeus
(Dry)
Mount Olga
1069
Ayers Rock
867
CAPE CUVIER
Lake McLeod
1106
Mount Augustus
Tropic of Capricorn
910
Mount Essendon
AUST
Geographe Channel
BERNIER ISLAND
DORRE ISLAND
Carnarvon
Gascoyne
Peak Hill
ROBINSON RANGES
Lake Carnegie (Dry)
Lake Gillen
(Dry)
BARROW RANGE
Mount Aloysius
987
MUSGRAVE RANGES
1440
Mount Woodroffe
Naturaliste Channel
Shark Bay
Wooramel
DIRK HARTOG ISLAND
STEEP POINT
Wiluna
Lake Wells
(Dry)
Meekatharra
Murchison
Nannine
Cue
Lake Austin
(Dry)
Sandstone
Boogardie
Mount Magnet
Agnew
Mount Redcliffe
576
Lake Yeo
(Dry)
GREAT VICTORIA DESERT
Laverton
Malcolm
Leonora
Northampton
Mullewa
Yalgoo
Lake Carey
(Dry Salt Lake)
Lake Ballard
Lake Raeside
(Dry)
Lake Minigwal
(Dry)
Lake Maurice
(Dry)
SOU
Maralinga
Ooldea
HOUTMAN ROCKS
Geraldton
Lake Monger
(Dry)
Lake Barlee
(Dry Salt Lake)
Dongara
Three Springs
Lake Moore
(Dry)
Kanowna
Kalgoorlie
Coolgardie
Boulder
Zanthus
Rawlinna
Haig
Forrest
Deakin
NULLARBOR PLAIN
GREEN HEAD
Dalwallinu
Bonnie Rock
Bencubbin
Bullfinch
Southern Cross
Moora
Lake Lefroy
(Dry)
Eucla
Lake Cowan
(Dry Salt Lake)
Eyre
RED POINT ROCK
CAPE ADIEU
SAINT PETER ISLA
DARLING RANGE
Muchea
Northam
York
Merredin
Kellerberrin
Norseman
Perth
Fremantle
Pinjarra
Beverley
Brockton
Hyden
The Johnston Lakes
(Dry)
Lake Dundas
(Dry)
POINT CULVER
Narrogin
Newdegate
Wagin
Ravensthorpe
Hopetoun
Esperance
CAPE ARID
Great Australian Bight
Bunbury
Collie
Geographe Bay
CAPE NATURALISTE
Busselton
Bridgetown
Manjimup
Nyabing
Katanning
Gnowangerup
STIRLING RANGE
HOOD POINT
CAPE KNOB
Esperance Bay
ARCHIPELAGO OF THE RECHERCHE
SALISBURY ISLAND
Augusta
CAPE LEEUWIN
Pemberton
Mount Barker
Albany
Denmark
CAPE VANCOUVER
King George Sound
POINT D'ENTRECASTEAUX
TORBAY HEAD
INDIAN OCE
105°
110°
115°
120°
125°
130°
10°
15°
20°
25°
30°
35°
40°
Copyright © by Rand McNally & Co.
Map prepared by Esselte Map Service AB, Stockholm
A-590200-264

NEW GUINEA
PAPUA (Austl.)
Port Moresby
Gulf of Papua
Torres Strait
Coral Sea
PACIFIC OCEAN
Tasman Sea
Solomon Sea
BRITISH SOLOMON ISLANDS
Gulf of Carpentaria
GREAT BARRIER REEF
GREAT DIVIDING RANGE
GREAT ARTESIAN BASIN
QUEENSLAND
NEW SOUTH WALES
VICTORIA
TASMANIA
SOUTH AUSTRALIA
SIMPSON DESERT
STURT DESERT
CAPE YORK PENINSULA
Tropic of Capricorn
Brisbane
Cairns
Townsville
Mackay
Rockhampton
Toowoomba
Ipswich
Newcastle
SYDNEY
Wollongong
Canberra
A.C.T.
MELBOURNE
Geelong
Ballarat
Bendigo
Broken Hill
Elizabeth
Adelaide
Launceston
Hobart
Mount Isa
Lake Eyre (North) (Dry Salt Lake)
Lake Eyre (South)
Lake Torrens (Dry Salt Lake)
Lake Gairdner (Dry Salt Lake)
Lake Frome (Dry Salt Lake)
FLINDERS RANGES
MAIN BARRIER RANGE
GREY RANGE
SELWYN RANGE
GREGORY RANGE
BARKLY TABLELAND
Bass Strait
KING ISLAND
FLINDERS ISLAND
FURNEAUX GROUP
KANGAROO ISLAND
FRASER ISLAND
LORD HOWE ISLAND (N.S.W.)
BALLS PYRAMID (N.S.W.)
ÎLES CHESTERFIELD (N. Cal.)
Mount Kosciusko 2230
Scale 1:12,000,000

Kilometers 0 200 400 600 Km.

Statute Miles 0 200 400 600 Mi.

Scale 1:12,000,000 One centimeter represents 120 kilometers. One inch represents approximately 190 miles. Lambert Conformal Conic Projection

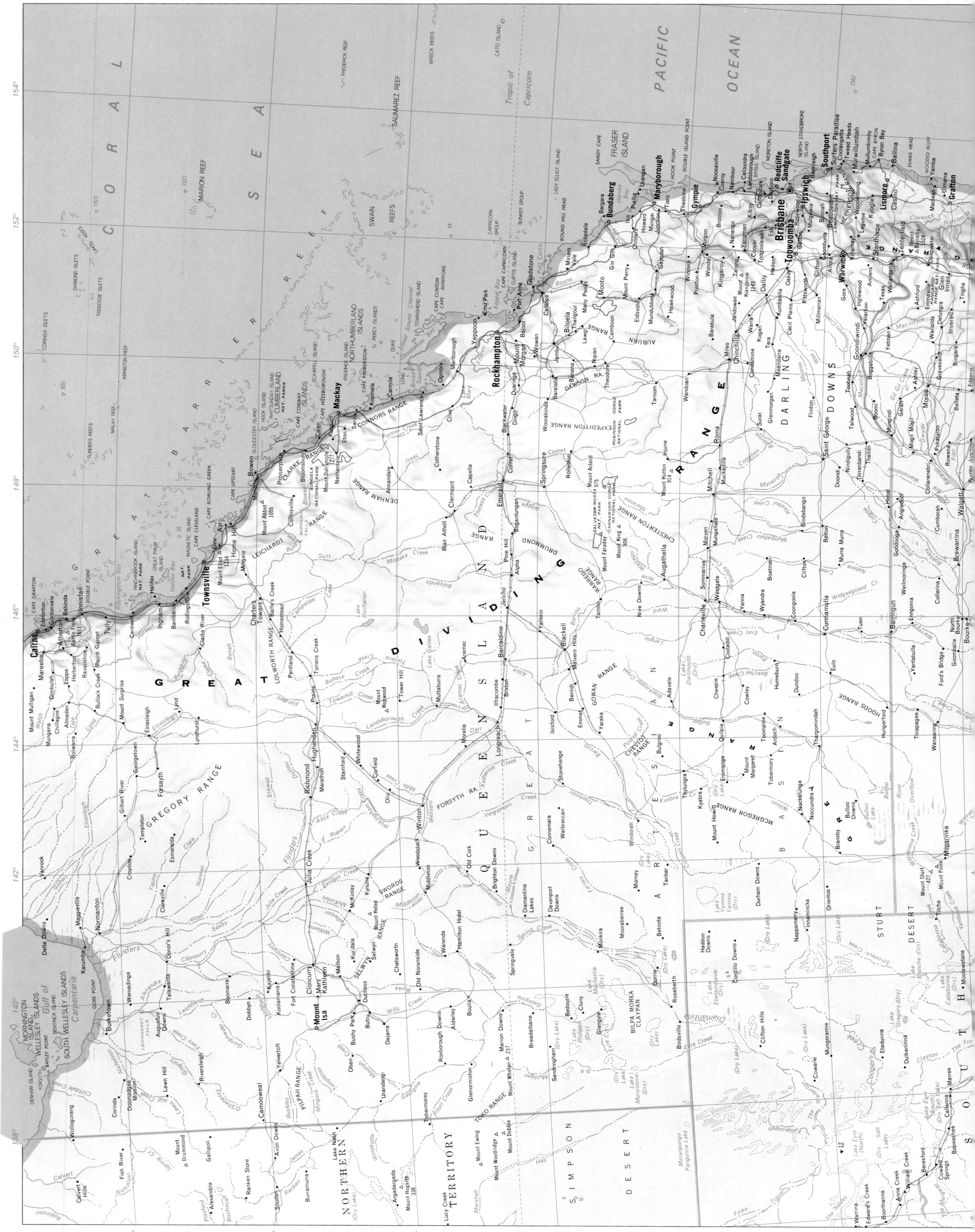
CORAL SEA
PACIFIC OCEAN
GREAT BARRIER REEF
Tropic of Capricorn
GREAT DIVIDING RANGE
QUEENSLAND
GREAT ARTESIAN BASIN
DARLING DOWNS
SIMPSON DESERT
STURT DESERT
NORTHERN TERRITORY
Gulf of Carpentaria
MORNINGTON ISLAND
WELLESLEY ISLANDS
SOUTH WELLESLEY ISLANDS
FRASER ISLAND
SWAIN REEFS
MARION REEF
SAUMAREZ REEF
CUMBERLAND ISLANDS
NORTHUMBERLAND ISLANDS
Cairns
Townsville
Mackay
Rockhampton
Gladstone
Bundaberg
Maryborough
Gympie
Brisbane
Ipswich
Toowoomba
Southport
Warwick
Lismore
Grafton
Mount Isa
Longreach
Charleville
Roma
Cunnamulla
Birdsville
Boulia
Winton
Hughenden
Charters Towers
Bowen
Emerald
Barcaldine
Cloncurry
Normanton
Burketown
Camooweal
GREGORY RANGE
SELWYN RANGE
CONNORS RANGE
DAWSON RA
EXPEDITION RANGE
WARREGO RANGE
GOWAN RANGE
GREY RANGE
MCGREGOR RANGE
FORSYTH RA
CHESTERTON RANGE
DENHAM RANGE
CLARKE RANGE
LEICHHARDT RANGE
AUBURN RANGE
TOKO RANGE
PILPAH RANGE
SWORDS RANGE
BILPA MOREA CLAYPAN
Lake Eyre (North)

NEW SOUTH WALES
VICTORIA
TASMANIA
AUSTRALIA
GREAT DIVIDING RANGE
AUSTRALIAN CAPITAL TERRITORY
COMMONWEALTH TERRITORY (ACT)
TASMAN SEA
INDIAN OCEAN
Bass Strait
Spencer Gulf
Investigator Strait
KANGAROO ISLAND
KING ISLAND
FURNEAUX GROUP
FLINDERS ISLAND
RIVERINA
SYDNEY
MELBOURNE
Canberra
Adelaide
Hobart
Newcastle
Wollongong
Geelong
Ballarat
Bendigo
Launceston
Broken Hill
Mildura
Wagga Wagga
Albury
Dubbo
Tamworth
Port Augusta
Port Lincoln
Whyalla
Port Pirie
Mount Gambier
Warrnambool
Portland
Orange
Bathurst
Goulburn
Shepparton
Wangaratta
Devonport
Burnie
Murray
Darling
Lachlan
Murrumbidgee

Kilometers 0 100 200 300 Km.

Statute Miles 0 100 200 300 Mi.

Scale 1:6,000,000

One centimeter represents 60 kilometers.

One inch represents approximately 95 miles.

Lambert Conformal Conic Projection

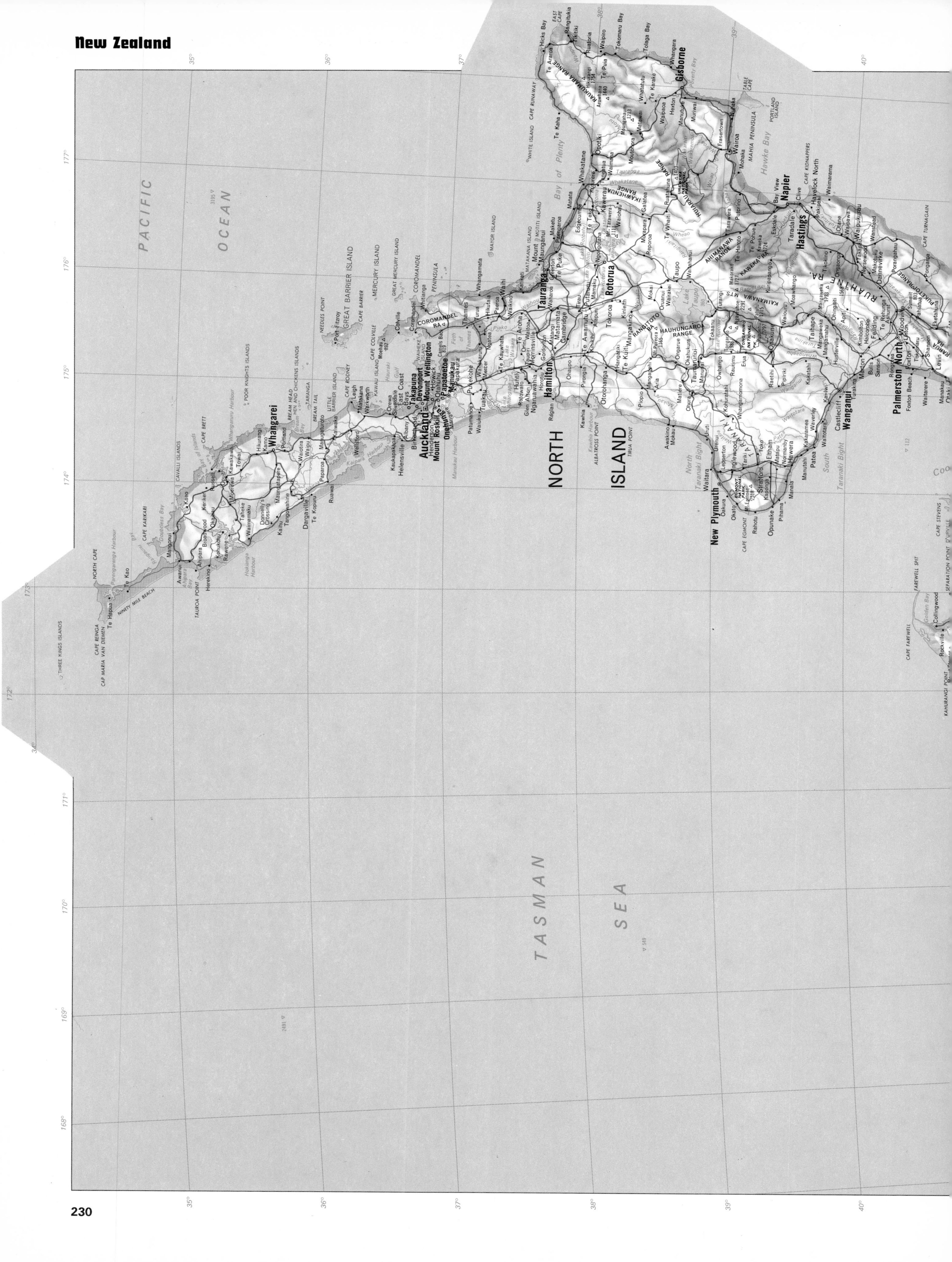
PACIFIC
OCEAN
TASMAN
SEA
NORTH
ISLAND
Auckland
Whangarei
Hamilton
Tauranga
Rotorua
Gisborne
Napier
Hastings
New Plymouth
Wanganui
Palmerston North
Taupo
Lake Taupo
Bay of Plenty
Hawke Bay
Firth of Thames
Hauraki Gulf
GREAT BARRIER ISLAND
NORTH CAPE
EAST CAPE
CAPE EGMONT
THREE KINGS ISLANDS
North Taranaki Bight
South Taranaki Bight
RUAHINE RA.
KAIMANAWA MTS.
COROMANDEL PENINSULA
MAHIA PENINSULA
NINETY MILE BEACH
Kaipara Harbour
Manukau Harbour
FAREWELL SPIT
CAPE FAREWELL

PACIFIC
OCEAN
SOUTH
ISLAND
STEWART
ISLAND
Tasman Bay
Karamea Bight
Pegasus Bay
Canterbury Bight
Palliser Bay
Foveaux Strait
BANKS PENINSULA
KAIKOURA PENINSULA
OTAGO PENINSULA
CAPE FOULWIND
CAPE CAMPBELL
CAPE PALLISER
CAPE JACKSON
ABUT HEAD
GILLESPIE POINT
OPEN BAY ISLANDS
JACKSON HEAD
CASCADE POINT
AWARUA POINT
MOERAKI POINT
NUGGET POINT
CHASLANDS MISTAKE
SOLANDER ISLAND
CODFISH ISLAND
RUAPUKE ISLAND
CENTRE ISLAND
LONG ISLAND
SOUTHWEST CAPE
WEST CAPE
Milford Sound
Bligh Sound
George Sound
Caswell Sound
Charles Sound
Thompson Sound
Doubtful Sound
Dagg Sound
Breaksea Sound
Mason Bay
Doughboy Bay
Port Pegasus
Halfmoon Bay
SOUTHERN ALPS
CANTERBURY PLAINS
NELSON
MARLBOROUGH
OTAGO
TASMAN MTS.
RICHMOND RANGE
KAIKOURA RA.
INLAND KAIKOURA RA.
SEAWARD KAIKOURA RANGE
SPENSER MTS.
VICTORIA RA.
PAPAROA RANGE
BEN OHAU RANGE
TWO THUMB RA.
KIRKLISTON RANGE
THE HUNTERS HILLS
HAWKDUN RA.
KAKANUI MTS.
DUNSTAN MTS.
GARVIE MTS.
EYRE MTS.
THE REMARKABLES
HARRIS MOUNTAINS
RICHARDSON MTS.
HUMBOLDT MTS.
OLIVINE RANGE
YOUNG RANGE
LIVINGSTONE MTS.
TAKITIMU MTS.
HUNTER MTS.
CAMERON MTS.
FRANKLIN MTS.
STUART MTS.
MURCHISON MTS.
AORANGI MTS.
Wellington
Porirua
Upper Hutt
Lower Hutt
Masterton
Carterton
Martinborough
Nelson
Richmond
Motueka
Blenheim
Picton
Westport
Greymouth
Hokitika
Kaikoura
Christchurch
Kaiapoi
Ashburton
Timaru
Oamaru
Dunedin
Port Chalmers
Mosgiel
Balclutha
Gore
Invercargill
Bluff
Queenstown
Alexandra
Cromwell
Te Anau
Franz Josef Glacier
Fox Glacier
Haast
Geraldine
Temuka
Waimate
Winton
Riverton

Kilometers 0 50 100 150 Km.
Statute Miles 0 50 100 150 Mi.

Scale 1:3,000,000
One centimeter represents 30 kilometers.
One inch represents approximately 47 miles.
Lambert Conformal Conic Projection

Beaufort Sea
PACIFIC OCEAN
Gulf of Alaska
UNITED STATES
CANADA
ALASKA RANGE
BROOKS RANGE
BRITISH MOUNTAINS
RICHARDSON MTS.
OGILVIE MTS.
MACKENZIE MTS.
SELWYN MTS.
PELLY MOUNTAINS
DAWSON RANGE
COAST MOUNTAINS
ROCKY MOUNTAINS
CASCADE RANGE
SIERRA NEVADA
COAST RANGES
BLUE MTS.
BITTERROOT RANGE
SALMON RIVER MTS.
LEWIS RANGE
BIGHORN MTS.
NORTHWEST TERRITORIES
ALBERTA
SASKATCHEWAN
MANITOBA
BRITISH COLUMBIA
WASHINGTON
OREGON
IDAHO
MONTANA
WYOMING
NORTH DAKOTA
SOUTH DAKOTA
MINNESOTA
NEBRASKA
IOWA
NEVADA
UTAH
COLORADO
CALIFORNIA
VICTORIA ISLAND
BANKS ISLAND
MELVILLE ISLAND
PRINCE OF WALES ISLAND
Great Bear L.
Great Slave Lake
Lake Athabasca
Lake Winnipeg
Fairbanks
Anchorage
Whitehorse
Dawson
Yellowknife
Fort Smith
Prince Rupert
Prince George
Edmonton
Calgary
Saskatoon
Regina
Winnipeg
Vancouver
Victoria
Seattle
Tacoma
Spokane
Portland
Salem
Eugene
Boise
Missoula
Great Falls
Helena
Butte
Billings
Bismarck
Fargo
Grand Forks
Minneapolis
St. Paul
Duluth
Rapid City
Sioux Falls
Salt Lake City
Ogden
Reno
Sacramento
SAN FRANCISCO
Oakland
San Jose
Fresno
Cheyenne
Casper

Baffin Bay
Davis Strait
GREENLAND (Denmark)
Labrador Sea
ATLANTIC OCEAN
Hudson Bay
Foxe Basin
Hudson Strait
Ungava Bay
James Bay
DEVON ISLAND
Lancaster Sound
BAFFIN ISLAND
PENNY HIGHLANDS
MELVILLE PENINSULA
SOUTHAMPTON ISLAND
UNGAVA PENINSULA
LABRADOR
NEWFOUNDLAND
QUÉBEC
ONTARIO
NEW BRUNSWICK
NOVA SCOTIA
PRINCE EDWARD ISLAND
ÎLE ANTICOSTI
Gulf of St. Lawrence
ST. PIERRE AND MIQUELON
CAPE BRETON ISLAND
NOTRE DAME MTS.
APPALACHIAN MTS.
TORNGAT MOUNTAINS
OTISH MTS.
MAINE
VERMONT
N.H.
MASS.
CONN.
NEW YORK
PENNSYLVANIA
NEW JERSEY
MICHIGAN
WISCONSIN
ILLINOIS
OHIO
IND.
St. John's
Halifax
Québec
MONTREAL
Ottawa
TORONTO
BOSTON
NEW YORK
PHILADELPHIA
DETROIT
CHICAGO
Cleveland
Buffalo
All islands within Hudson Bay, James Bay, and Ungava Bay lie within Northwest Territories
Copyright © by Rand McNally & Co.
Map prepared by Rand McNally & Co.
A-520200-264

Kilometers 0 200 400 600 Km.

Statute Miles 0 200 400 600 Mi.

Scale 1:12,000,000

One centimeter represents 120 kilometers.

One inch represents approximately 190 miles.

Lambert Conformal Conic Projection

United States (excluding Alaska and Hawaii)

CANADA
UNITED STATES
MEXICO
PACIFIC OCEAN
VANCOUVER ISLAND
BRITISH COLUMBIA
ALBERTA
SASKATCHEWAN
MANITOBA
WASHINGTON
OREGON
IDAHO
MONTANA
WYOMING
NORTH DAKOTA
SOUTH DAKOTA
NEBRASKA
KANSAS
OKLAHOMA
TEXAS
NEW MEXICO
ARIZONA
UTAH
COLORADO
NEVADA
CALIFORNIA
ROCKY MOUNTAINS
CASCADE RANGE
SIERRA NEVADA
GREAT BASIN
COAST RANGES
SALMON RIVER MOUNTAINS
BLUE MOUNTAINS
BITTERROOT RANGE
SIERRA MADRE OCCIDENTAL
SIERRA MADRE ORIENTAL
Tropic of Cancer
Edmonton
Calgary
Vancouver
Victoria
Seattle
Tacoma
Spokane
Portland
Salem
Eugene
Boise
Helena
Butte
Great Falls
Billings
Regina
Saskatoon
Winnipeg
Bismarck
Fargo
Rapid City
Salt Lake City
Ogden
Provo
Reno
Sacramento
SAN FRANCISCO
Oakland
San Jose
Fresno
Bakersfield
LOS ANGELES
Long Beach
Anaheim
San Diego
Tijuana
Mexicali
Las Vegas
Phoenix
Tucson
Flagstaff
Albuquerque
Santa Fe
El Paso
Ciudad Juárez
Denver
Colorado Springs
Pueblo
Cheyenne
Lubbock
Amarillo
Wichita
Oklahoma City
Fort Worth
Odessa
Midland
Abilene
Waco
Austin
San Antonio
Laredo
Nuevo Laredo
Monterrey
Saltillo
Torreón
Chihuahua
Hermosillo
Culiacán
Mazatlán
Durango
Zacatecas
Aguascalientes
San Luis Potosí
Guadalajara
León
Tampico
La Paz
Copyright © by Rand McNally & Co.
Map prepared by Rand McNally & Co.

ONTARIO
QUÉBEC
James Bay
Gulf of Saint Lawrence
NEW BRUNSWICK
NOVA SCOTIA
PRINCE EDWARD ISLAND
NEWFOUNDLAND
CAPE BRETON ISLAND
Halifax
Saint John
Québec
MONTRÉAL
Ottawa
TORONTO
Superior
Thunder Bay
Duluth
Minneapolis
St. Paul
MINNESOTA
WISCONSIN
MICHIGAN
Lake Michigan
Lake Huron
Lake Erie
CHICAGO
DETROIT
Milwaukee
Cleveland
Pittsburgh
Buffalo
Rochester
Syracuse
Albany
BOSTON
NEW YORK
PHILADELPHIA
Baltimore
WASHINGTON
Richmond
Norfolk
APPALACHIAN MOUNTAINS
ADIRONDACK MTS.
Indianapolis
Cincinnati
Columbus
Louisville
St. Louis
Kansas City
Des Moines
IOWA
ILLINOIS
INDIANA
OHIO
PENNSYLVANIA
NEW YORK
KENTUCKY
TENNESSEE
MISSOURI
ARKANSAS
VIRGINIA
WEST VIRGINIA
NORTH CAROLINA
SOUTH CAROLINA
GEORGIA
ALABAMA
MISSISSIPPI
LOUISIANA
FLORIDA
MAINE
Nashville
Memphis
Knoxville
Chattanooga
Atlanta
Birmingham
Charlotte
Little Rock
Jackson
Shreveport
New Orleans
Mobile
Jacksonville
Savannah
Charleston
Tampa
Orlando
Miami
Houston
Galveston
MISSISSIPPI DELTA
GULF OF MEXICO
ATLANTIC OCEAN
BERMUDA (U.K.)
Hamilton
BAHAMAS
Nassau
Tropic of Cancer
Straits of Florida
WEST INDIES
CUBA
La Habana Havana
Santiago de Cuba
Guantánamo
CAYMAN IS. (U.K.)
CARIBBEAN SEA
Yucatan Channel
YUCATAN PENINSULA
Mérida
TURKS AND CAICOS ISLANDS (U.K.)
HAITI
DOMINICAN REPUBLIC
Port-au-Prince
Santo Domingo
HISPANIOLA
95°
90°
85°
80°
75°
70°
65°
60°
45°
40°
35°
30°
25°
20°

Kilometers 0 200 400 600 Km.
Statute Miles 0 200 400 600 Mi.

Scale 1:12,000,000
One centimeter represents 120 kilometers.
One inch represents approximately 190 miles.
Albers Conical Equal-Area Projection

Alaska and Yukon

ARCTIC
Chukchi Sea
BERING SEA
PACIFIC
UNION OF SOVIET SOCIALIST REPUBLICS
UNITED STATES
Arctic Circle
International Date Line
Bering Strait
Norton Sound
Bristol Bay
Kuskokwim Bay
Kotzebue Sound
Anadyrskij Zaliv
ANADYRSKOJE PLOSKOGORJE
ČUKOTSKIJ POLUOSTROV
SEWARD PENINSULA
BROOKS
BAIRD MOUNTAINS
SCHWATKA MOUNTAINS
WARING MOUNTAINS
DE LONG MOUNTAINS
LOOKOUT RIDGE
KAIYUH MOUNTAINS
KUSKOKWIM
BEAVER MOUNTAINS
TAYLOR MOUNTAINS
KILBUCK MOUNTAINS
AHKLUN MOUNTAINS
NUSHAGAK PENINSULA
ALASKA PENINSULA
ALEUTIAN ISLANDS
ANDREANOF ISLANDS
ISLANDS OF THE FOUR MOUNTAINS
FOX ISLANDS
KRENITZIN ISLANDS
SHUMAGIN ISLANDS
PRIBILOF ISLANDS
SAINT LAWRENCE ISLAND
SAINT MATTHEW ISLAND
NUNIVAK ISLAND
NELSON ISLAND
UNIMAK ISLAND
UNALASKA ISLAND
UMNAK ISLAND
ATKA ISLAND
ADAK ISLAND
KATMAI NATIONAL MONUMENT
Barrow
Wainwright
Point Hope
Kivalina
Noatak
Kotzebue
Kiana
Noorvik
Selawik
Shungnak
Kobuk
Ambler
Shishmaref
Deering
Candle
Buckland
Wales
Brevig Mission
Teller
Nome
White Mountain
Golovin
Elim
Moses Point
Koyuk
Shaktoolik
Unalakleet
Saint Michael
Stebbins
Kotlik
Emmonak
Alakanuk
Hamilton
Mountain Village
Saint Marys
Pilot Station
Russian Mission
Scammon Bay
Hooper Bay
Chevak
Bethel
Akiak
Kwethluk
Napakiak
Tununak
Toksook Bay
Mekoryuk
Kipnuk
Quinhagak
Goodnews Bay
Platinum
Togiak
Dillingham
Aleknagik
Manokotak
Ekuk
Naknek
King Salmon
Egegik
Pilot Point
Ugashik
Port Heiden
Chignik
Perryville
Port Moller
Cold Bay
King Cove
Sand Point
False Pass
Akutan
Unalaska
Dutch Harbor
Nikolski
Adak
Atka
Galena
Nulato
Kaltag
Koyukuk
Hughes
Huslia
Ruby
Anvik
Grayling
Holy Cross
Shageluk
Flat
McGrath
Takotna
Sleetmute
Stony River
Crooked Creek
Aniak
Kalskag
Napamute
Nondalton
Iliamna
Newhalen
Kakhonak
Levelock
Koliganek
New Stuyahok
Ekwok
Gambell
Savoonga
Northeast Cape
Saint Paul Island
Saint George
Anadyr'
Providenija
Uelen
Lavrentija
Egvekinot
Pevek
Mys Šmidta
Vankarem
Beringovskij
Meynypilgino
Tumanskij
Krasneno
Kivak
Lorino
Enmelen
Nunligran
Sireniki
Little Diomede Island
Diomede
King Island
Sledge Island
Stuart Island
Hall Island
Kodiak
Shishaldin Volcano 2857
Pavlof Volcano 2714
Mount Veniaminof 2507
Mount Katmai 2047
Makushin Volcano 2036
Korovin Volcano 1533
Tanaga Volcano 1805
Kanaga Volcano 1307
Mount Vsevidof 2109
Mount Dutton 1473
Pyre Peak 1054
Mount Chiginagak 2126
Mount Hamlet 620
Tingmerkpuk Mountain 1057
Mishegak Mountain 1489
Tututalak Mountain 1364
Cone Mountain 1372
Granite Mountain 867
Mount Bendeleben 1137
Traverse Peak 865
Christmas Mountain 694
Debauch Mountain 1040
Tetson Mountain 827
Von Frank Mountain 1374
Cloudy Mountain 1291
Camelback Mountain 840
Mount Hamilton 1111
Cairn Mountain 1158
Finn Mountain 756
Roberts Mountain 511
Seemalik Butte 264
Jagged Mountain 703
Ikuktlitlig Mountain 789
North Peak 535
Bonasila Dome 551
Cape Lisburne
Cape Krusenstern
Cape Espenberg
Cape Prince of Wales
Cape Rodney
Cape Darby
Cape Denbigh
Cape Romanzof
Cape Vancouver
Cape Mohican
Cape Mendenhall
Cape Corwin
Cape Newenham
Cape Peirce
Cape Constantine
Cape Rozhnoi
Point Barrow
Point Franklin
Icy Cape
Point Spencer
Rocky Point
Sheldon Point
Northwest Cape
Southwest Cape
Southeast Cape
Chirikof Island
Semidi Islands
Mitrofania Island
Unga Island
Sanak Islands
Amak Island
Amlia Island
Seguam Island
Yunaska Island
Chuginadak Island
Kagamil Island
Carlisle Island
Herbert Island
Amukta Island
Amukta Pass
Seguam Pass
Unimak Pass
Umnak Pass
Akutan Pass
Bechevin Bay
Hazen Bay
Etolin Strait
Kuskokwim
Yukon
Noatak
Kobuk
Koyuk
Nushagak
Iliamna Lake
Becharof Lake
Lake Clark
Tikchik Lakes
Upnuk Lake
Chikuminuk Lake
Imuruk Lake
Whitefish Lake
Selawik Lake
Kgun Lake
Aropuk Lake

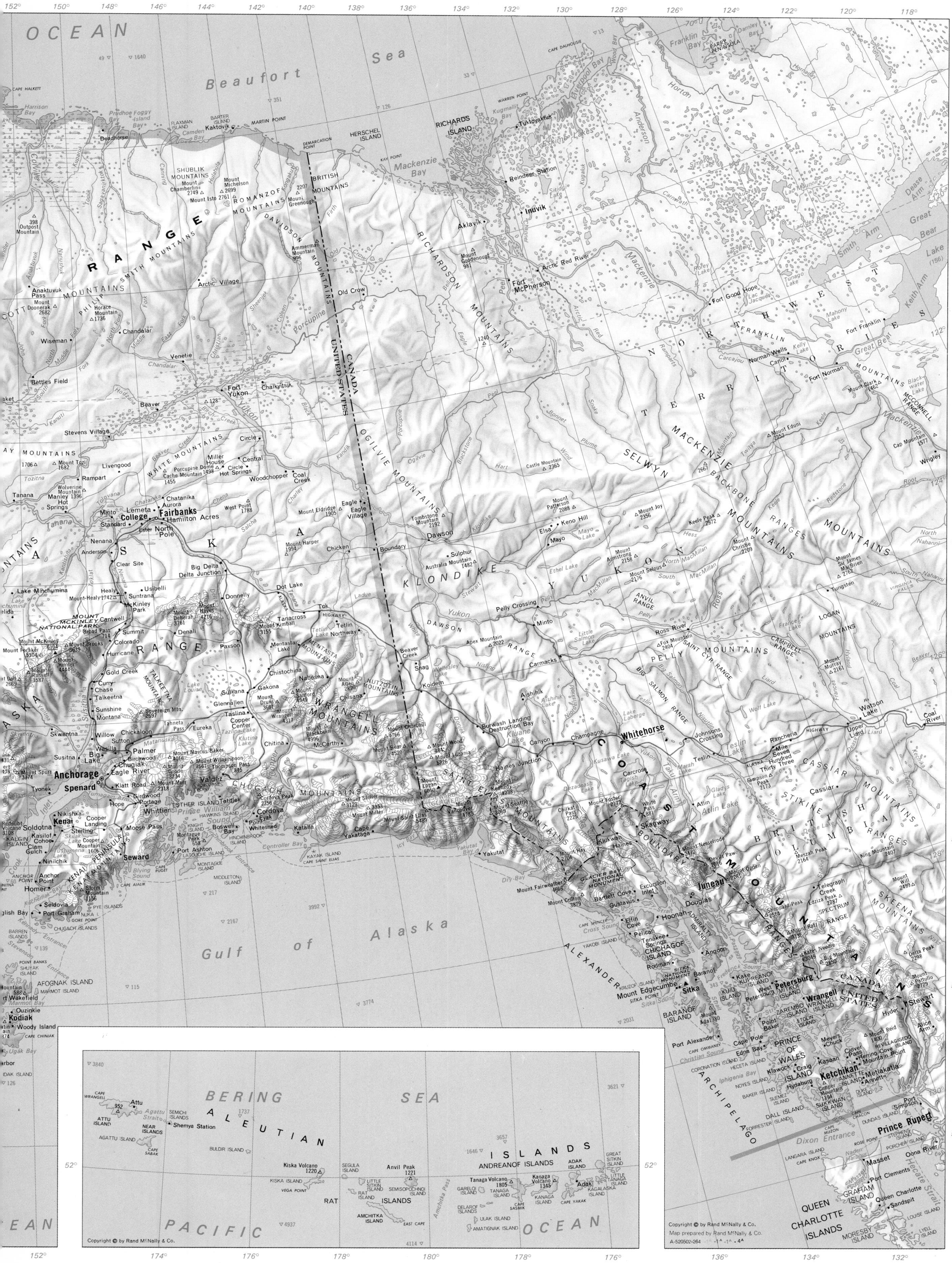

OCEAN
Beaufort Sea
Gulf of Alaska
ALEXANDER ARCHIPELAGO
BROOKS RANGE
ALASKA RANGE
WRANGELL MOUNTAINS
CHUGACH MOUNTAINS
SAINT ELIAS MOUNTAINS
COAST MOUNTAINS
BRITISH MOUNTAINS
RICHARDSON MOUNTAINS
OGILVIE MOUNTAINS
SELWYN MOUNTAINS
MACKENZIE MOUNTAINS
CASSIAR MOUNTAINS
PELLY MOUNTAINS
KLONDIKE
YUKON
NORTHWEST TERRITORIES
BRITISH COLUMBIA
CANADA
UNITED STATES
Anchorage
Fairbanks
Juneau
Whitehorse
Dawson
Inuvik
Ketchikan
Sitka
Prince Rupert
Kodiak
QUEEN CHARLOTTE ISLANDS
Dixon Entrance
BERING SEA
ALEUTIAN ISLANDS
RAT ISLANDS
ANDREANOF ISLANDS
PACIFIC OCEAN
Copyright © by Rand McNally & Co.
Map prepared by Rand McNally & Co.
A-520502-264

Kilometers 0 100 200 300 Km.

Statute Miles 0 100 200 300 Mi.

Scale 1:6,000,000

One centimeter represents 60 kilometers.

One inch represents approximately 95 miles.

Lambert Conformal Conic Projection

PACIFIC
OCEAN
Queen Charlotte Sound
Hecate Strait
Dixon Entrance
QUEEN CHARLOTTE ISLANDS
GRAHAM ISLAND
MORESBY ISLAND
PRINCE OF WALES ISLAND
REVILLAGIGEDO ISLAND
DALL ISLAND
U.S.
CANADA
UNITED STATES
ALASKA
BRITISH COLUMBIA
COAST MOUNTAINS
PACIFIC RANGES
KITIMAT RANGES
SKEENA MOUNTAINS
OMINECA MOUNTAINS
NECHAKO PLATEAU
FRASER PLATEAU
TWEEDSMUIR PROVINCIAL PARK
STRATHCONA PROVINCIAL PARK
GARIBALDI PROVINCIAL PARK
VANCOUVER ISLAND
VANCOUVER ISLAND RANGES
Prince Rupert
Kitimat
Terrace
Smithers
Prince George
Quesnel
Williams Lake
Powell River
Courtenay
Port Alberni
Nanaimo
VANCOUVER
New Westminster
North Vancouver
Burnaby
Victoria
Esquimalt
Bellingham
Port Angeles
Ketchikan
Stewart
Hyder
Bella Coola
Ocean Falls
Port Hardy
Campbell River
Strait of Juan de Fuca
Strait of Georgia
Queen Charlotte Strait
Copyright © by Rand McNally & Co.
Map prepared by Rand McNally & Co.
A-520220-264

121°
120°
119°
118°
117°
116°
115°
114°
113°
112°
111°
Fort St. John
Peace River
Dawson Creek
Grande-Prairie
Lesser Slave Lake
Athabasca
Edmonton
St. Albert
Sherwood Park
Red Deer
Calgary
Lethbridge
Medicine Hat
Jasper
Banff
Golden
Revelstoke
Kamloops
Vernon
Kelowna
Penticton
Nelson
Trail
Cranbrook
Kimberley
Kalispell
Whitefish
Colville
Omak
Sandpoint
ROCKY MOUNTAINS
COLUMBIA MOUNTAINS
MONASHEE MOUNTAINS
SELKIRK MOUNTAINS
PURCELL MOUNTAINS
CASCADE RANGE
JASPER NATIONAL PARK
BANFF NATIONAL PARK
GLACIER NATIONAL PARK
WATERTON-GLACIER INTERNATIONAL PEACE PARK
LEWIS RANGE
SWAN RANGE
BRITISH COLUMBIA
ALBERTA
WASHINGTON
IDAHO
MONTANA
CANADA
UNITED STATES
SWAN HILLS
56°
55°
54°
53°
52°
51°
50°
49°
48°

Kilometers 0 50 100 150 Km.

Statute Miles 0 50 100 150 Mi.

Scale 1:3,000,000

One centimeter represents 30 kilometers.

One inch represents approximately 47 miles.

Lambert Conformal Conic Projection

72°
71°
70°
69°
68°
67°
66°
65°
64°
63°
51°
50°
49°
48°
47°
46°
45°
44°
Lac Manicouagan
Mont de Babel 952
Lac Plétipi
Réservoir Pipmouacane
DANIEL-JOHNSON DAM
Sept-Îles
Moisie
Baie Moisie
Clarke City
Port-Cartier
Baie Sainte-Marguerite
Rivière-Pentecôte
Islets-Caribou
Baie-Trinité
POINTE DES MONTS
Godbout
Baie-Comeau
Hauterive
Betsiamites
BERSIMIS INDIAN RESERVE
POINT BETSIAMITES
Forestville
Portneuf-sur-Mer
Sault-au-Mouton
Tadoussac
Magpie
Mingan
Rivière-au-Tonnerre
Havre-St-Pierre
Baie-Johan-Beetz
Aguanish
ÎLES DE MINGAN
Lac Allard
Passage de Jacques-Cartier
POINTE OUEST
CAP HENRY
Baie-Ste-Claire
Port-Menier
ÎLE ANTICOSTI
POINTE SUD-OUEST
Détroit de Gaspé
Rivière-de-la-Chaloupe
Saint Lawrence River
Fleuve Saint-Laurent
Alma
Kénogami
Arvida
Jonquière
Chicoutimi
Rivière-du-Moulin
Bagotville
Port-Alfred
Laterrière
Saguenay
RÉSERVE DE CHICOUTIMI
PARC DES LAURENTIDES
LAURENTIDES PROVINCIAL PARK
Clermont
La Malbaie
St-Urbain-de-Charlevoix
Baie-St-Paul
ÎLE AUX COUDRES
St-Tite-des-Caps
Ste-Anne-de-Beaupré
Beaupré
Château-Richer
Montmorency
ÎLE AUX DIES
ÎLE D'ORLÉANS
Québec
Lauzon
Lévis
Ste-Foy
St-Romuald-d'Etchemin
St-Anselme
Montmagny
St-Pamphile
Lac-Frontière
Dubergen
La Pocatière
St-Jean-Port-Joli
St-Pacôme
St-Pascal
St-Alexandre-de-Kamouraska
Ste-Eleuthère
Cabano
Ste-Rose-du-Dégelé
Rivière-Bleue
Rivière-du-Loup
St-Éloi
Rivière-Trois-Pistoles
St-Fabien
Bic
Rimouski
Mont-Joli
St-Léandre
Matane
Ste-Félicité
Rivière-Matane
Amqui
Causapscal
Routhierville
Pointe-à-la-Garde
Matapédia
Cap-Chat
Ste-Anne-des-Monts
Ste-Marthe-de-Gaspé
Rivière-à-Claude
Madeleine-Centre
Pointe-à-la-Frégate
St-Yvon
Rivière-au-Renard
Fontenelle
Gaspé
CAP GASPÉ
Baie de Gaspé
Barachois-de-Malbaie
St-Gabriel-de-Gaspé
Percé
ÎLE BONAVENTURE
Grande-Rivière
Chandler
Newport
POINTE AU MAQUEREAU
Mont Jacques-Cartier 1268
SHICKSHOCK
MONTS NOTRE DAME
PÉNINSULE DE GASPÉ
PARC DE LA GASPÉSIE
GASPESIAN PROVINCIAL PARK
RÉSERVE DE LA PETITE-CASCAPÉDIA
LITTLE CASCAPEDIA RIVER RESERVE
RÉSERVE PORT-DANIEL
New Richmond
Caplan
Bonaventure
Nouvelle
New Carlisle
Dalhousie
Campbellton
Squaw Cap Mountain 483
Blue Mountain 528
Jacquet River
Chaleur Bay
MISCOU POINT
Miscou Centre
MISCOU ISLAND
SHIPPEGAN ISLAND
Lamèque
Shippegan
Grande-Anse
Caraquet
Bathurst
Kedgwick
St-Quentin
Mount Carleton 820
St-Isidore
Upper Sheila
Tracadie
Brantville
Lavillette
Neguac
Big Bald Mountain 672
Miramichi Bay
Newcastle
Chatham
Chatham Head
POINT ESCUMINAC
QUÉBEC
NEW BRUNSWICK
MAINE
UNITED STATES
CANADA
APPALACHIAN MOUNTAINS
NOTRE DAME MOUNTAINS
Edmundston
Madawaska
St-Basile
Ste-Anne-de-Madawaska
St-Léonard
Van Buren
Fort Kent
McClean Mountain 596
Soldier Pond
Eagle Lake
Stockholm
Grand Falls
Limestone
Caribou
Washburn
Plaster Rock
Fort Fairfield
Presque Isle
Perth
Ashland
Peaked Mountain 689
Mars Hill
Bridgewater
Bath
Juniper
Hartland
Stanley
Houlton
Oakfield
Woodstock
Mount Chase 744
BAXTER STATE PARK
Mount Katahdin 1606
Patten
Island Falls
Meductic
Nashwaaksis
Marysville
Fredericton
Oromocto
Canterbury
Peekaboo Mtn. 331
Danforth
Millinocket
East Millinocket
Mattawamkeag
White Cap Mountain 1111
Moosehead L.
Mount Kineo
Greenville
Jackman
Sandy Bay Mtn. 974
Big Squaw Mountain
Coburn Mountain 1133
Caribou Mtn.
Brownville
Rockwood
Lac-Mégantic
Lac-Etchemin
St-Joseph-de-Beauce
St-Prosper-de-Dorchester
Beauceville-Est
Ville St-Georges
La Guadeloupe (St. Évariste)
Stratton
Rangeley
Sugarloaf Mountain 1291
Kingfield
BLUE MOUNTAINS
Phillips
Jackson Mtn.
Elephant Mtn.
North Anson
Madison
Skowhegan
Bingham
Farmington
Wilton
Rumford
Mexico
Bethel
Livermore Falls
Norway
South Paris
Mechanic Falls
Auburn
Lewiston
Winthrop
Augusta
Hallowell
Gardiner
Richmond
Lisbon Falls
Bath
Brunswick
Wiscasset
Boothbay Harbor
North Windham
Westbrook
Yarmouth
Falmouth
Portland
South Portland
Cape Elizabeth
Old Orchard Beach
Saco
Biddeford
Kennebunk
Ogunquit
Waterville
Fairfield
Clinton
Oakland
Pittsfield
Newport
Dexter
Dover-Foxcroft
Guilford
Howland
Lincoln
Bangor
Old Town
Orono
Brewer
Aurora
Bucksport
Brooks
Belfast
Ellsworth
Blue Hill
Bar Harbor
ACADIA NATIONAL PARK
Southwest Harbor
Camden
Rockland
Thomaston
Stonington
Vinalhaven
ISLE AU HAUT
MATINICUS ISLAND
Harrington
Machias
Eastport
Lubec
Calais
St. Stephen
St. Andrews
Princeton
Woodland
Passadumkeag Mountain 446
CAMPOBELLO ISLAND
ROOSEVELT-CAMPOBELLO INTERNATIONAL PARK
GRAND MANAN
Seal Cove
Blacks Harbour
St. George
Pembroke
Wilsons Beach
McAdam
Welsford
Fredericton Junction
Geary
Gagetown
Rothesay
Hampton
Grand Bay
Saint John
Lancaster
CAPE SPENCER
POINT LEPREAU
Sussex
Norton
FUNDY NATIONAL PARK
Alma
Petitcodiac
Moncton
Dieppe
Riverview
Turtle Creek
Hillsborough
Dorchester
Sackville
Amherst
Harvey
Joggins
River Hebert
Springhill
COBEQUID MOUNTAINS
Parrsboro
Five Islands
Bass River
Advocate Harbour
Port Greville
CAPE CHIGNECTO
Minas Basin
Minas Channel
Bay of Fundy
Truro
Brookfield
Maitland
Walton
Kennetcook
Gore
Canning
Kentville
Wolfville
Hantsport
Windsor
Berwick
Waterville
Kingston
Torbrook
Middleton
Bridgetown
Annapolis Royal
Clementsport
Digby
DIGBY NECK
Bear River
LONG ISLAND
Freeport
Westport
Weymouth
Meteghan
Hectanooga
Yarmouth
Port Maitland
CAPE SAINT MARY
Wedgeport
Pubnico
Lower West Pubnico
Lower Woods Harbour
Barrington
Clark's Harbour
CAPE SABLE ISLAND
Shelburne
Lockeport
Jordan Bay
Liverpool
Brooklyn
Port Mouton
MOUTON ISLAND
Bridgewater
Lunenburg
Mahone Bay
Chester Basin
Hubbards
Hemford
Western Shore
New Germany
Springfield
Caledonia
New Ross
KEJIMKUJIK NATIONAL PARK
NOVA SCOTIA
Halifax
Dartmouth
Bedford
Lakeside
Herring Cove
Terence Bay
BIG TANCOOK ISLAND
PENNANT POINT
Hatchet Lake
Three Mile Plains
Mount Uniacke
Elmsdale
Milford Station
Stewiacke
Upper Musquodoboit
Middle Musquodoboit
Musquodoboit Harbour
Meaghers Grant
Sheet Harbour
Middle Stewiacke
Shediac
Cap-Pelé
Shemogue
Cape Tormentine
Port Elgin
Pugwash
Malagash
Oxford
Westchester Station
Wentworth
Londonderry
Belmont
Tatamagouche
River John
Pictou
Westville
Stellarton
New Glasgow
Trenton
Lismore
Thorburn
Scotsburn
Sunnybrae
Rexton
Richibucto
Buctouche
St.-Louis-de-Kent
St.-Ignace
Rogersville
Renous
Doaktown
Upper Blackville
Boiestown
St. Anthony
Notre-Dame
Dorchester Crossing
Lewisville
Point Sapin
Kouchibouguac Bay
Tignish
Alberton
CAPE KILDARE
NORTH POINT
O'Leary Station
Campbellton
Conway Station
Wellington Station
Port Hill
Kensington
North Rustico
Summerside
St. Eleanors
Borden
Victoria
Bonshaw
Charlottetown
Hunters River
Sherwood
Parkdale
Mount Stewart
Morell
St. Peters Bay
Souris East
Vernon River
Cardigan
Georgetown
Montague
Murray River
Murray Harbour
Flat River
Wood Island
PRINCE EDWARD ISLAND
PRINCE EDWARD ISLAND NATIONAL PARK
Malpeque Bay
Bedeque Bay
Egmont Bay
Northumberland Strait
Amet Sound
Ecum Secum
Sherbrooke
Tangier
Halifax Harbour
HALIFAX CITADEL NATIONAL HISTORIC PARK
PORT ROYAL NATIONAL HISTORIC PARK
FORT ANNE NATIONAL HISTORIC PARK
GRAND PRÉ NATIONAL HISTORIC PARK
FORT BEAUSÉJOUR NATIONAL HISTORIC PARK
FORT AMHERST NATIONAL HISTORIC PARK
ST. CROIX ISLAND NATIONAL MONUMENT
ÎLE AUX MEULES
Grindstone Isl.
ÎLE AMHERST

LABRADOR SEA
ATLANTIC OCEAN
NEWFOUNDLAND
Gulf of St. Lawrence
Cabot Strait
SAINT PIERRE AND MIQUELON (France)
SAINT-PIERRE-ET-MIQUELON
MIQUELON
LANGLADE
Saint-Pierre
SAINT-PIERRE
NEWFOUNDLAND
CANADA
QUEBEC
NEWF.
Corner Brook
St. John's
Sydney
Glace Bay
CAPE BRETON ISLAND
CAPE BRETON HIGHLANDS NATIONAL PARK
SABLE ISLAND (N.S.)
ST. PAUL ISLAND (N.S.)
AVALON PENINSULA
BURIN PENINSULA
TERRA NOVA NATIONAL PARK
LONG RANGE MOUNTAINS
ANNIEOPSQUOTCH MOUNTAINS
LEWIS HILLS
BLUE HILLS OF COUTEAU
Red Bay
West St.-Modeste
Cook's Harbour
Raleigh
St. Anthony
Forteau
Blanc Sablon
Flower's Cove
Brig Bay
Bartlett's Harbour
Port Saunders
River of Ponds
Daniel's Harbour
Parson's Pond
Cow Head
Rocky Harbour
Trout River
Norris Point
Woody Point
Deer Lake
Pasadena
Howley
Stephenville
Stephenville Crossing
Port-au-Port
St. George's
Flat Bay
Robinson
St. David's
Codroy Pond
South Branch
Codroy
Doyles
Tompkins
Channel-Port-aux-Basques
Burnt Islands
Isle-aux-Morts
Rose-Blanche
Grand-Bruit
Burgeo
Ramea
François
Cape La Hune
Harbour Breton
Hermitage
Pass Island
Grand Bank
Fortune
Lawn
Lamaline
St. Lawrence
Burin
Creston
Marystown
Garnish
Belleoram
Placentia Bay
Fortune Bay
St. Mary's Bay
Trinity Bay
Conception Bay
Bonavista Bay
Notre Dame Bay
White Bay
Bay of Islands
Saint George's Bay
Placentia
Argentia
Dunville
Ship Cove
Branch
St. Bride's
St. Mary's
St. Vincent's
St. Shott's
Trepassey
Portugal Cove South
Renews
Ferryland
Cape Broyle
Tors Cove
Witless Bay
Bay Bulls
Petty Harbour
Pouch Cove
Torbay
Wabana
Carbonear
Harbour Grace
Bay Roberts
Brigus
Whitbourne
Long Harbour
Sunnyside
Come by Chance
Clarenville
Hickman's Harbour
Old Perlican
Bay de Verde
Hant's Harbour
Winterton
Heart's Content
Bonavista
Elliston
Little Catalina
Catalina
Port Union
Port Rexton
Keels
Salvage
Eastport
Glovertown
Gambo
Gander
Glenwood
Lumsden
Newtown
Wesleyville
Valleyfield
Greenspond
Doting Cove
Carmanville
Gander Bay
Fogo
Joe Batt's Arm
Change Islands
Twillingate
Durrell
Summerford
Boyd's Cove
Birchy Bay
Lewisporte
Campbellton
Botwood
Northern Arm
Norris Arm
Bishop's Falls
Grand Falls
Windsor
Badger
Millertown
Millertown Junction
Buchans
Springdale
King's Point
Hampden
Jackson's Arm
Westport
Seal Cove
Baie Verte
La Scie
Shoe Cove
Round Harbour
Pacquet
Fleur-de-Lys
Harbour Deep
Little Harbour Deep
Williamsport
Hooping Harbour
Englee
Roddickton
Conche
Main Topsail 555
Mount Sylvester 376
Mount Saint Gregory 686
Gros Morne 806
Table Mountain 587
Blue Mountain 649
Old Man Mountain 496
Hodges Hill 570
Grand L.
Red Indian L.
Sandy L.
Gander L.
Meelpaeg L.
Victoria L.
Terra Nova L.
Head Bay d'Espoir
St. Alban's
Conne River
Milltown
Rencontre East
Bay L'Argent
Terrenceville
Davis Cove
Swift Current
Baie des Ha! Ha!
La Tabatière
Mutton Bay
Tête-à-la-Baleine
Pointe-à-Maurier
Washicouta
Kegaska
Gethsemani
Wolf Bay
St.-Augustin-Saguenay
Shekatika Bay
Old Fort Bay
Middle Bay
Salmon Bay
Port St. Servan
Bradore Bay
Dingwall
Ingonish
Pleasant Bay
Chéticamp
Grand-Étang
Margaree Harbour
Margaree
Inverness
Strathlorne
Mabou
Whycocomagh
Judique
Baddeck
Iona
Sydney Mines
North Sydney
New Waterford
Dominion
Port-Morien
Louisbourg
Gabarouse
Fourchu
St. Peter's
L'Ardoise
Arichat
Louisdale
West Bay
Port Hawkesbury
Guysborough
Canso
Queensport
Larry's River
Grand-Entrée
ÎLE DE LA MADELEINE (Que.)
CAPE RACE
CAPE SPEAR
CAPE BONAVISTA
CAPE FREELS
CAPE SAINT JOHN
CAPE SAINT FRANCIS
CAPE SAINT MARY'S
CAPE RAY
CAPE ANGUILLE
CAPE SAINT GEORGE
CAPE NORTH
CAPE SAINT LAWRENCE
BELLE ISLE
FUNK ISLAND
FOGO ISLAND
GROAIS ISLAND
BELL ISLAND
PENGUIN ISLANDS
RAMEA ISLANDS
BRUNETTE ISLAND
GREY ISLANDS
Copyright © by Rand McNally & Co.
Map prepared by Rand McNally & Co.
A-520219-264

Kilometers 0 50 100 150 Km.

Statute Miles 0 50 100 150 Mi.

Scale 1:3,000,000

One centimeter represents 30 kilometers.
One inch represents approximately 47 miles.

Lambert Conformal Conic Projection

LAKE MICHIGAN
LAKE HURON
Georgian Bay
LAKE ONTARIO
LAKE ERIE
CANADA
UNITED STATES
MICHIGAN
ONTARIO
NEW YORK
PENNSYLVANIA
OHIO
INDIANA
WEST VIRGINIA
MARYLAND
KENTUCKY
VIRGINIA
QUÉBEC
DETROIT
TORONTO
CLEVELAND
BUFFALO
PITTSBURGH
CINCINNATI
WASHINGTON
Toledo
Columbus
Dayton
Akron
Lansing
Flint
Saginaw
Bay City
Grand Rapids
Fort Wayne
Erie
Rochester
London
Hamilton
Kitchener
Windsor
Charleston
Lexington
Huntington
Youngstown
Canton
Wheeling
Johnstown
Altoona
Sarnia
Port Huron
Ann Arbor
Jackson
Battle Creek
Springfield
Mansfield
Lima
Zanesville
Parkersburg
Morgantown
Clarksburg
Cumberland
Hagerstown
Frederick
Winchester
Harrisonburg
Staunton
Charlottesville
Ashland
Portsmouth
Chillicothe
Marion
Findlay
Sandusky
Lorain
Sudbury
North Bay
Pembroke
Barrie
Orillia
Peterborough
Oshawa
Owen Sound
St. Catharines
Niagara Falls
Lockport
Jamestown
Bradford
Olean
Midland
Alpena
Traverse City
Petoskey
Cheboygan
MANITOULIN ISLAND
ALLEGHENY MOUNTAINS
APPALACHIAN PLATEAU

ATLANTIC
OCEAN
MONTREAL
Ottawa
Trois-Rivières
Sherbrooke
QUEBEC
VERMONT
MAINE
N.H.
NEW YORK
BOSTON
Providence
Hartford
Springfield
Worcester
New Haven
Bridgeport
Albany
Schenectady
Syracuse
Utica
Binghamton
Scranton
Wilkes-Barre
Allentown
Reading
Lancaster
PHILADELPHIA
Trenton
Camden
Wilmington
Atlantic City
Newark
Paterson
Jersey City
Elizabeth
Portland
Lewiston
Augusta
Bangor
Burlington
Montpelier
Concord
Manchester
Nashua
Lowell
Cambridge
Brockton
New Bedford
Fall River
Cape Cod Bay
Massachusetts Bay
Long Island Sound
Nantucket Sound
Block Island Sound
Rhode Island Sound
Chesapeake Bay
Delaware Bay
ADIRONDACK MOUNTAINS
CATSKILL MOUNTAINS
WHITE MOUNTAINS
GREEN MOUNTAINS
Mount Washington 1917
Mount Marcy 1629
Copyright © by Rand McNally & Co.
Map prepared by Rand McNally & Co.
A-520596-264

Kilometers 0 50 100 150 Km.
Statute Miles 0 50 100 150 Mi.

Scale 1:3,000,000

One centimeter represents 30 kilometers.
One inch represents approximately 47 miles.
Albers Conical Equal-Area Projection

Thunder Bay
(Fort William-Port Arthur)
LAKE SUPERIOR
(183 Meters Above Sea Level)
ISLE ROYALE
CANADA
UNITED STATES
ONTARIO
MICHIGAN
MINNESOTA
WISCONSIN
IOWA
ILLINOIS
MISSOURI
MINNEAPOLIS
St. Paul
Duluth
Superior
LAKE MICHIGAN
(176 Meters Above Sea Level)
MILWAUKEE
CHICAGO
Madison
Green Bay
Des Moines
Cedar Rapids
Davenport
Rock Island
Moline
Rockford
Peoria
Grand Rapids
Kalamazoo
South Bend
Gary
Marquette
Escanaba
Rochester
La Crosse
Eau Claire
Dubuque
Waterloo
St. Cloud
Muskegon
Map prepared by Rand McNally & Co.

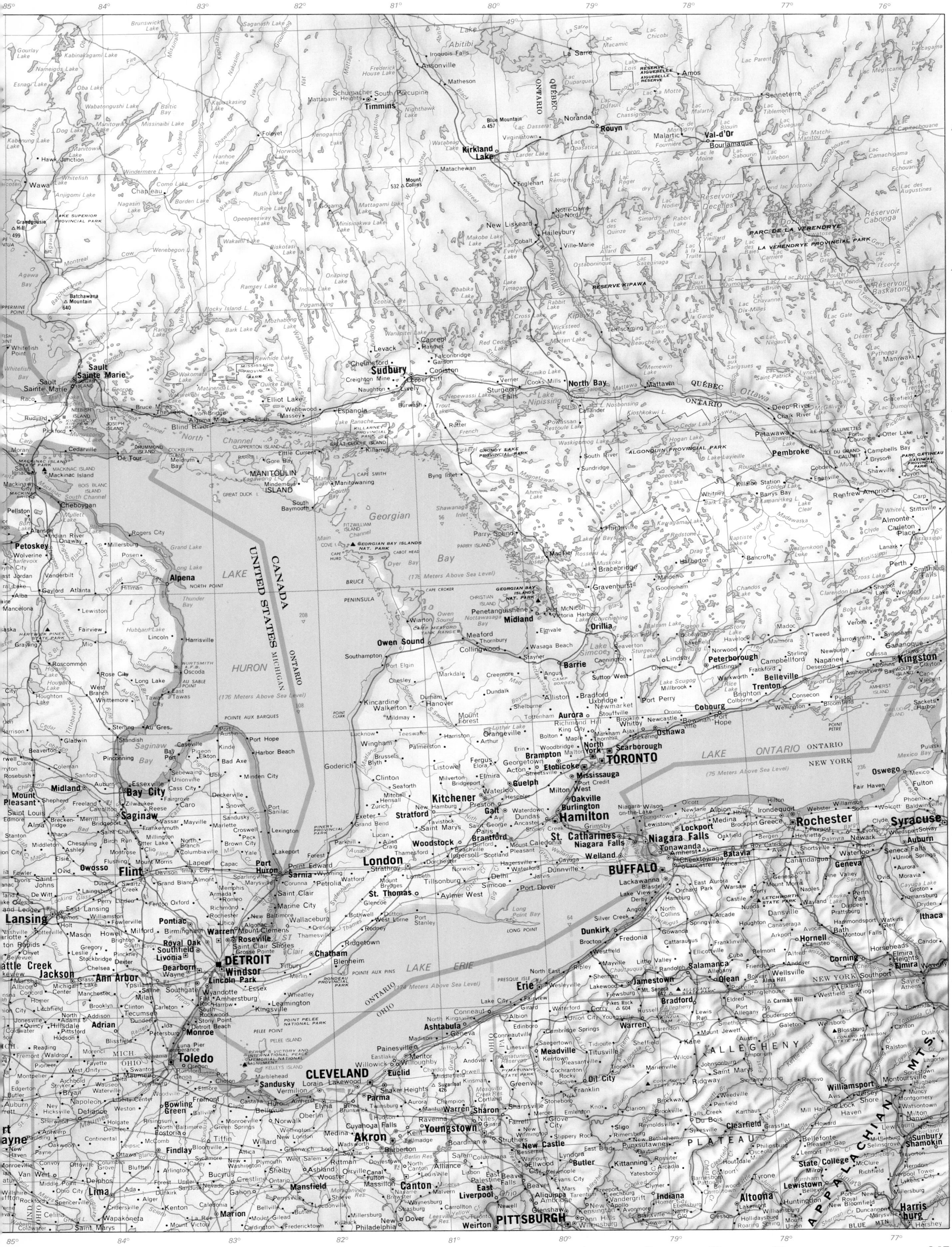
LAKE HURON
LAKE ONTARIO
LAKE ERIE
Georgian Bay
(176 Meters Above Sea Level)
(75 Meters Above Sea Level)
(174 Meters Above Sea Level)
CANADA
UNITED STATES
ONTARIO
QUÉBEC
MICHIGAN
NEW YORK
OHIO
ALLEGHENY
PLATEAU
APPALACHIAN MTS.
TORONTO
DETROIT
BUFFALO
CLEVELAND
PITTSBURGH
Hamilton
London
Windsor
Toledo
Rochester
Syracuse
Kingston
Sudbury
North Bay
Sault Sainte Marie
Timmins
Rouyn
Val-d'Or
Kirkland Lake
Pembroke
Peterborough
Barrie
Kitchener
St. Catharines
Niagara Falls
Erie
Akron
Youngstown
Canton
Lansing
Flint
Saginaw
Bay City
Jackson
Ann Arbor
Lima
Altoona
Williamsport
Harrisburg
Ithaca
Elmira
Jamestown
ALGONQUIN PROVINCIAL PARK
LA VERENDRYE PROVINCIAL PARK
MANITOULIN ISLAND
Lake Nipissing
Lake Simcoe
Lake Timiskaming
85°
84°
83°
82°
81°
80°
79°
78°
77°
76°
48°
47°
46°
45°
44°
43°
42°
41°

Kilometers 0 50 100 150 Km.

Statute Miles 0 50 100 150 Mi.

Scale 1:3,000,000

One centimeter represents 30 kilometers.

One inch represents approximately 47 miles.

Albers Conical Equal-Area Projection

Kilometers 0 50 100 150 Km.

Statute Miles 0 50 100 150 Mi.

Scale 1:3,000,000

One centimeter represents 30 kilometers.
One inch represents approximately 47 miles.

Albers Conical Equal-Area Projection

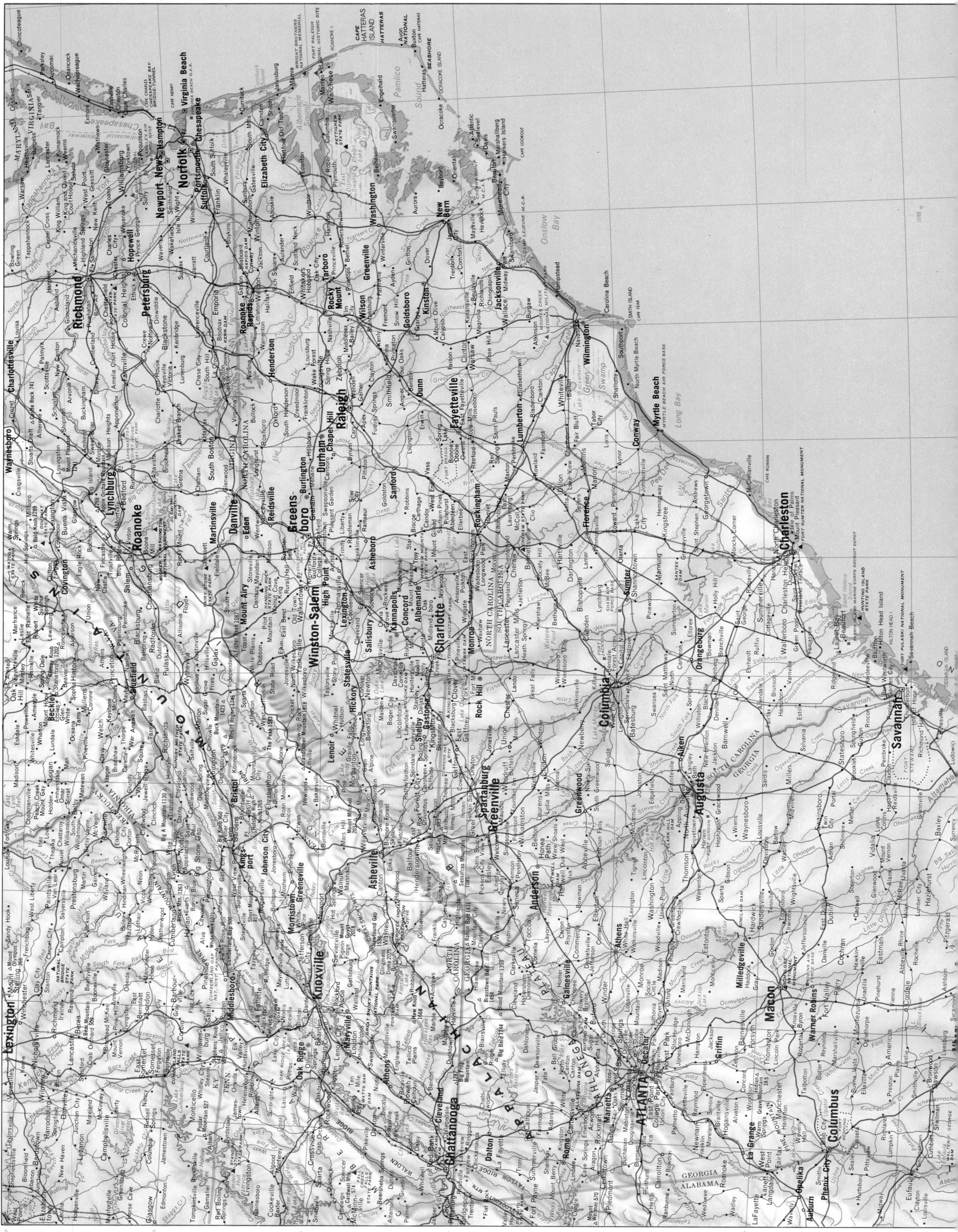
Richmond
Norfolk
Virginia Beach
Chesapeake
Portsmouth
Newport News
Hampton
Petersburg
Lynchburg
Roanoke
Danville
Greensboro
Winston-Salem
Durham
Raleigh
Fayetteville
Wilmington
Charlotte
Rock Hill
Spartanburg
Greenville
Columbia
Florence
Myrtle Beach
Charleston
Savannah
Augusta
Athens
Atlanta
Macon
Columbus
Chattanooga
Knoxville
Asheville
Bristol
Lexington
VIRGINIA
NORTH CAROLINA
SOUTH CAROLINA
GEORGIA
ALABAMA
TENN.
KENTUCKY
MARYLAND

ATLANTIC
OCEAN
GULF OF MEXICO
Straits of Florida
FLORIDA KEYS
Northwest Providence Channel
Northeast Providence Channel
UNITED STATES
BAHAMAS (U.K.)
GRAND BAHAMA
GREAT ABACO
LITTLE ABACO ISLAND
BERRY ISLANDS
ANDROS ISLAND
ELEUTHERA
NEW PROVIDENCE
BIMINI ISLANDS
Nassau
Freeport
West End
Alice Town
Jacksonville
St. Augustine
Daytona Beach
Orlando
Tampa
St. Petersburg
Clearwater
Sarasota
Fort Myers
West Palm Beach
Fort Lauderdale
MIAMI
Key West
Tallahassee
Gainesville
Ocala
Valdosta
Lake Okeechobee
The Everglades
Copyright © by Rand McNally & Co.
Map prepared by Rand McNally & Co.

CHICAGO
INDIANAPOLIS
ST. LOUIS
KANSAS CITY
Louisville
Nashville
Evansville
Springfield
Peoria
Des Moines
Omaha
Topeka
Fort Wayne
South Bend
Terre Haute
Jefferson City
MISSOURI
KANSAS
OKLAHOMA
ARKANSAS

GULF OF MEXICO
ARKANSAS
OKLAHOMA
TEXAS
LOUISIANA
MISSISSIPPI
ALABAMA
FLORIDA
TENNESSEE
GEORGIA
OUACHITA MOUNTAINS
Memphis
Little Rock
Shreveport
Jackson
Birmingham
Montgomery
Mobile
NEW ORLEANS
Baton Rouge
HOUSTON
Beaumont
Galveston
Huntsville
Chattanooga
Pensacola
Tuscaloosa
Alexandria
Monroe
Texarkana
Lake Charles
Lafayette
Gulfport
MISSISSIPPI DELTA
Copyright © by Rand McNally & Co.
Map prepared by Rand McNally & Co.
A-501292-264

Kilometers 0 50 100 150 Km.

Statute Miles 0 50 100 150 Mi.

Scale 1:3,000,000

One centimeter represents 30 kilometers.

One inch represents approximately 47 miles.

Albers Conical Equal-Area Projection

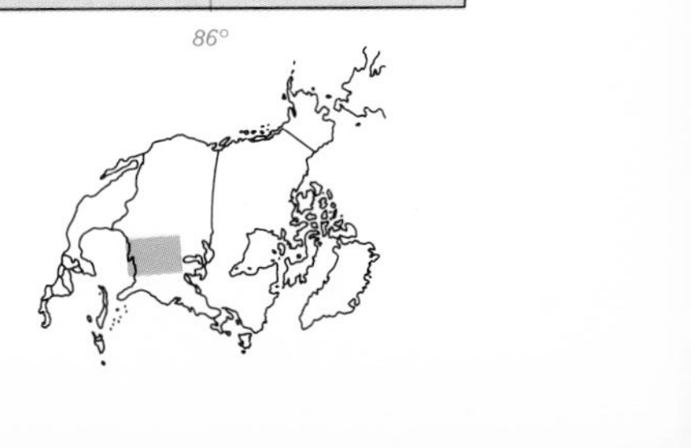

Southern Great Plains

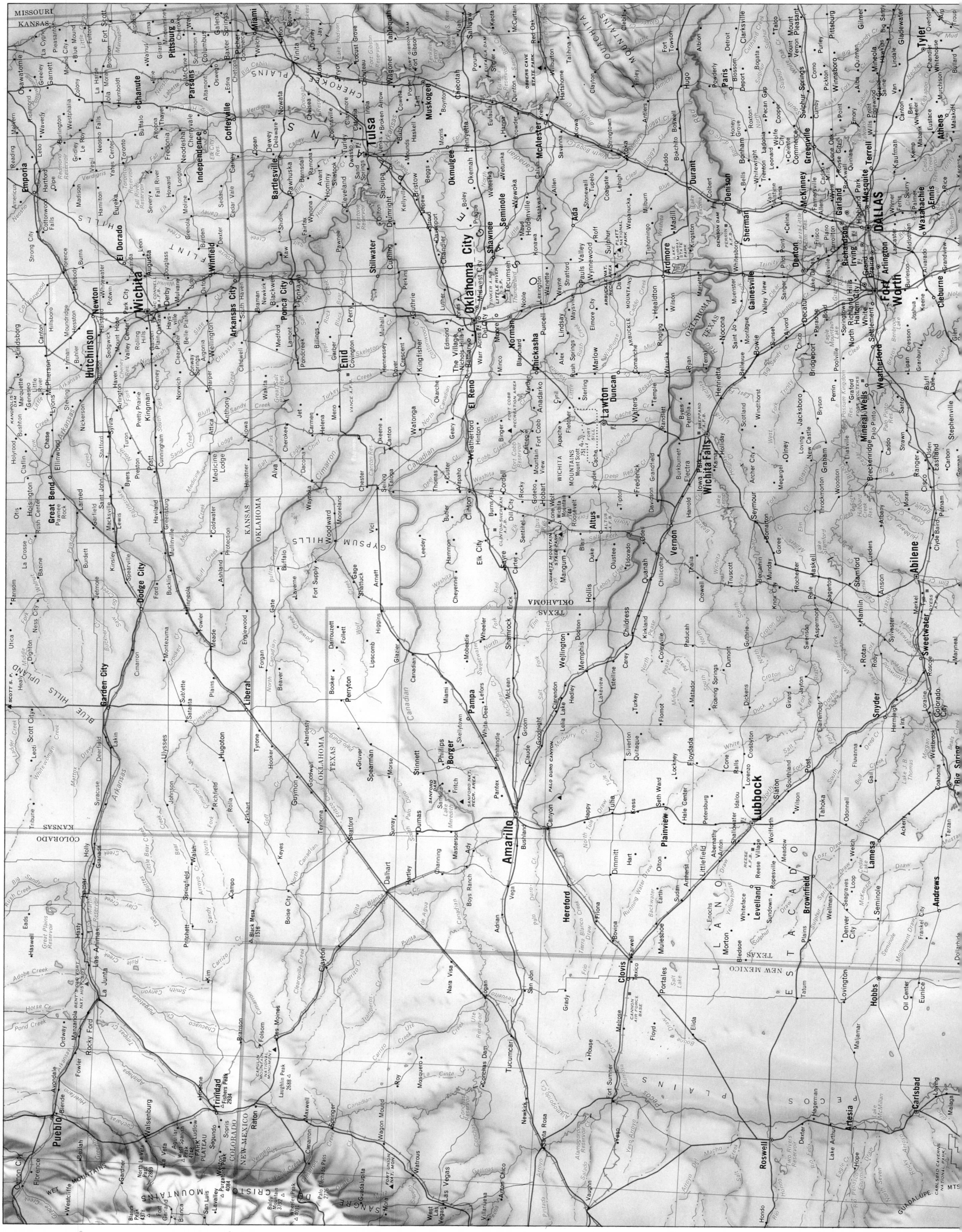

MISSOURI
KANSAS
OKLAHOMA
TEXAS
COLORADO
NEW MEXICO
FLINT HILLS
GYPSUM HILLS
BLUE HILLS UPLAND
CHEROKEE PLAINS
OUACHITA MOUNTAINS
WICHITA MOUNTAINS
ARBUCKLE MOUNTAINS
SANGRE DE CRISTO MOUNTAINS
LLANO ESTACADO
Wichita
Hutchinson
Emporia
Dodge City
Garden City
Tulsa
Oklahoma City
Enid
Lawton
Muskogee
McAlester
Dallas
Fort Worth
Denton
Wichita Falls
Abilene
Amarillo
Lubbock
Pampa
Borger
Pueblo
Trinidad
Raton
Clovis
Roswell
Hobbs
Carlsbad
Tucumcari
Las Vegas

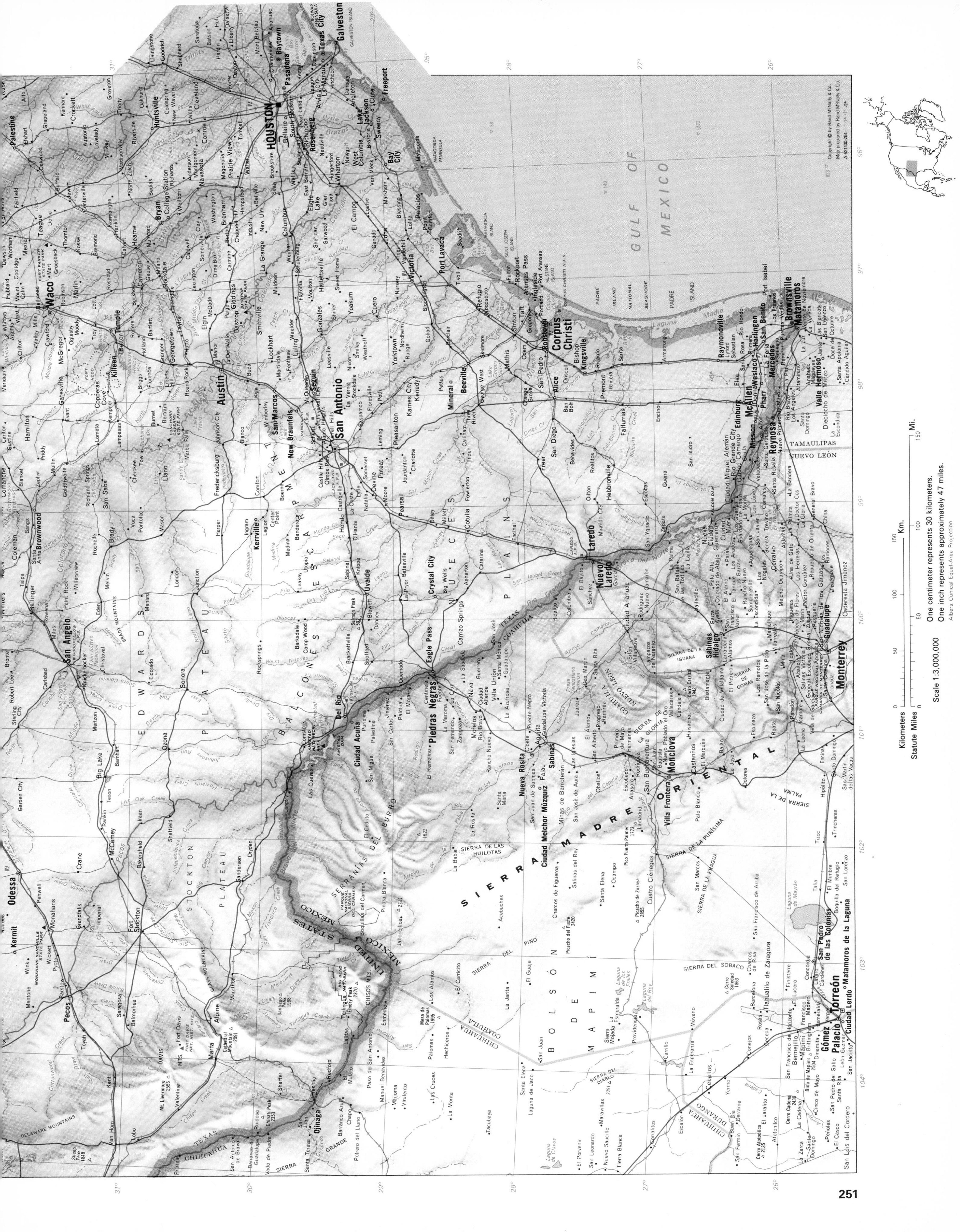
Kilometers 0 50 100 150 Km.
Statute Miles 0 50 100 150 Mi.
Scale 1:3,000,000
One centimeter represents 30 kilometers.
One inch represents approximately 47 miles.
Albers Conical Equal-Area Projection
Copyright © by Rand McNally & Co.
Map prepared by Rand McNally & Co.
GULF OF MEXICO
EDWARDS PLATEAU
STOCKTON PLATEAU
BALCONES ESCARPMENT
NUECES PLAINS
SIERRA MADRE ORIENTAL
BOLSÓN DE MAPIMÍ
SERRANÍAS DEL BURRO
UNITED STATES
MEXICO
TEXAS
CHIHUAHUA
COAHUILA
NUEVO LEÓN
TAMAULIPAS
DURANGO
PADRE ISLAND NATIONAL SEASHORE
Laguna Madre
Rio Grande
Bravo del Norte
Houston
San Antonio
Austin
Corpus Christi
Galveston
Waco
San Angelo
Odessa
Laredo
Nuevo Laredo
Brownsville
Matamoros
Monterrey
Torreón
Gómez Palacio
Ciudad Lerdo
Piedras Negras
Eagle Pass
Del Rio
Ciudad Acuña
Reynosa
McAllen
Harlingen
Monclova
Ojinaga
Presidio
Pecos
Fort Stockton
Kerrville
New Braunfels
San Marcos
Victoria
Killeen
Temple
Bryan
Huntsville
Kingsville
Brownwood
Alpine
Marfa

CANADA
UNITED STATES
MANITOBA
SASKATCHEWAN
ONTARIO
MINNESOTA
NORTH DAKOTA
SOUTH DAKOTA
MONTANA
WYOMING
Winnipeg
Brandon
Minot
Williston
Grand Forks
Fargo
Moorhead
Jamestown
Bismarck
Mandan
Dickinson
Aberdeen
Watertown
Brookings
Huron
Mitchell
Pierre
Rapid City
Miles City
Glendive
St. Cloud
Brainerd
Bemidji
Fergus Falls
Willmar
Mankato
New Ulm
Worthington
Fairmont
Kenora
MISSOURI
COTEAU
BADLANDS
BLACK HILLS

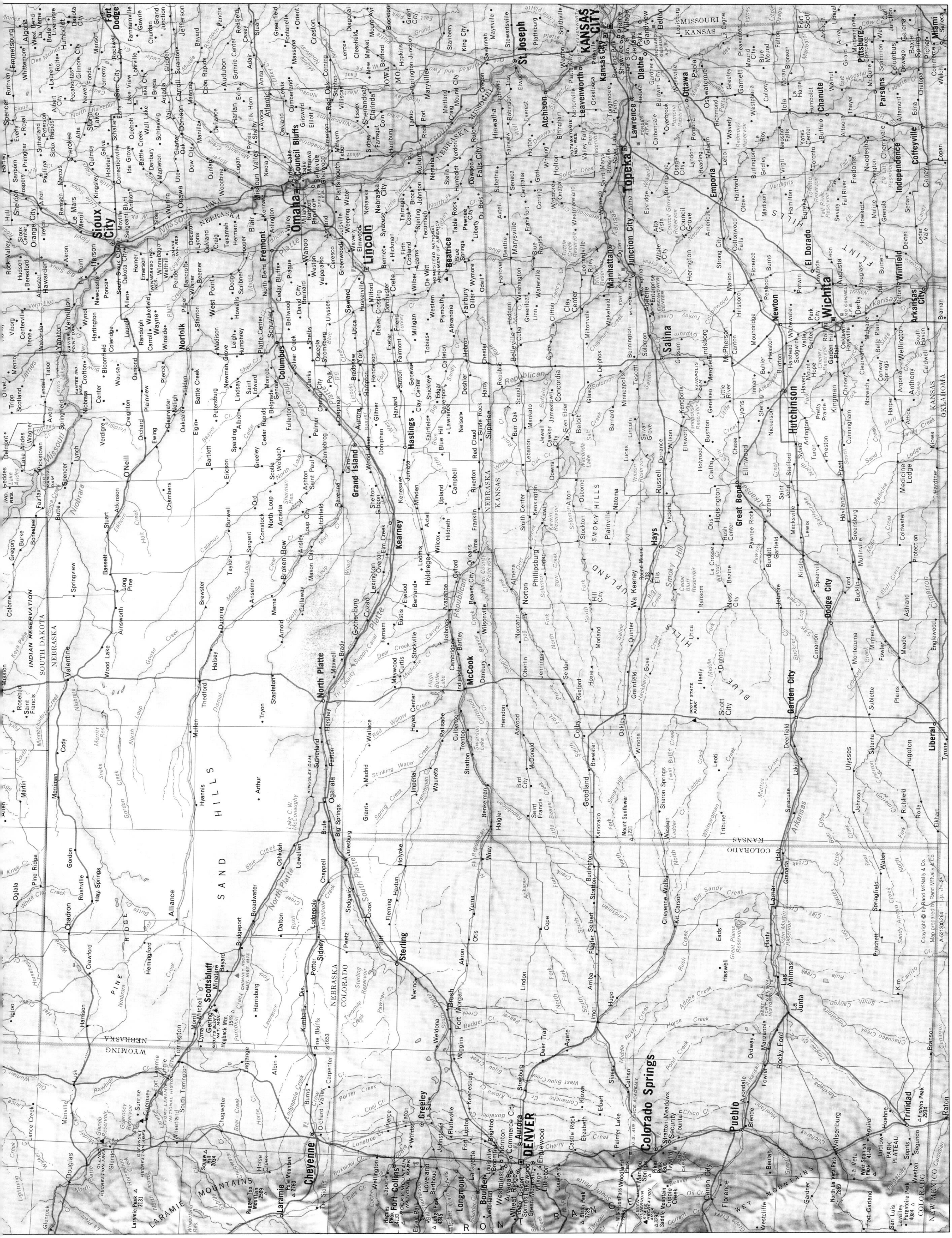
Kilometers 0 50 100 150 Km.
Statute Miles 0 50 100 150 Mi.
Scale 1:3,000,000
One centimeter represents 30 kilometers.
One inch represents approximately 47 miles.
Albers Conical Equal-Area Projection
Copyright © by Rand McNally & Co.
Map prepared by Rand McNally & Co.

DENVER
Aurora
Colorado Springs
Pueblo
Cheyenne
Casper
Laramie
Fort Collins
Greeley
Boulder
Longmont
Rock Springs
Grand Junction
Salt Lake City
Ogden
Provo
Logan
Brigham City
Pocatello
Idaho Falls
Twin Falls
Mountain Home
ROCKY MOUNTAINS
FRONT RANGE
PARK RANGE
WYOMING
COLORADO
UTAH
IDAHO
NEVADA
GREAT SALT LAKE DESERT
Great Salt Lake
SNAKE RIVER PLAIN
WYOMING RANGES
WASATCH RANGE
UINTA MOUNTAINS
MEDICINE BOW MOUNTAINS
LARAMIE MOUNTAINS
WIND RIVER RANGE
SAWATCH RANGE
BOOK CLIFFS
ROAN PLATEAU
UNCOMPAHGRE PLATEAU
SAN JUAN MOUNTAINS
SANGRE DE CRISTO MOUNTAINS
WET MOUNTAINS
SHOSHONE BASIN
OWL CREEK MOUNTAINS
BIG HORN MTS.
Bonneville Salt Flats
Utah Lake
Flaming Gorge Reservoir
Bear Lake

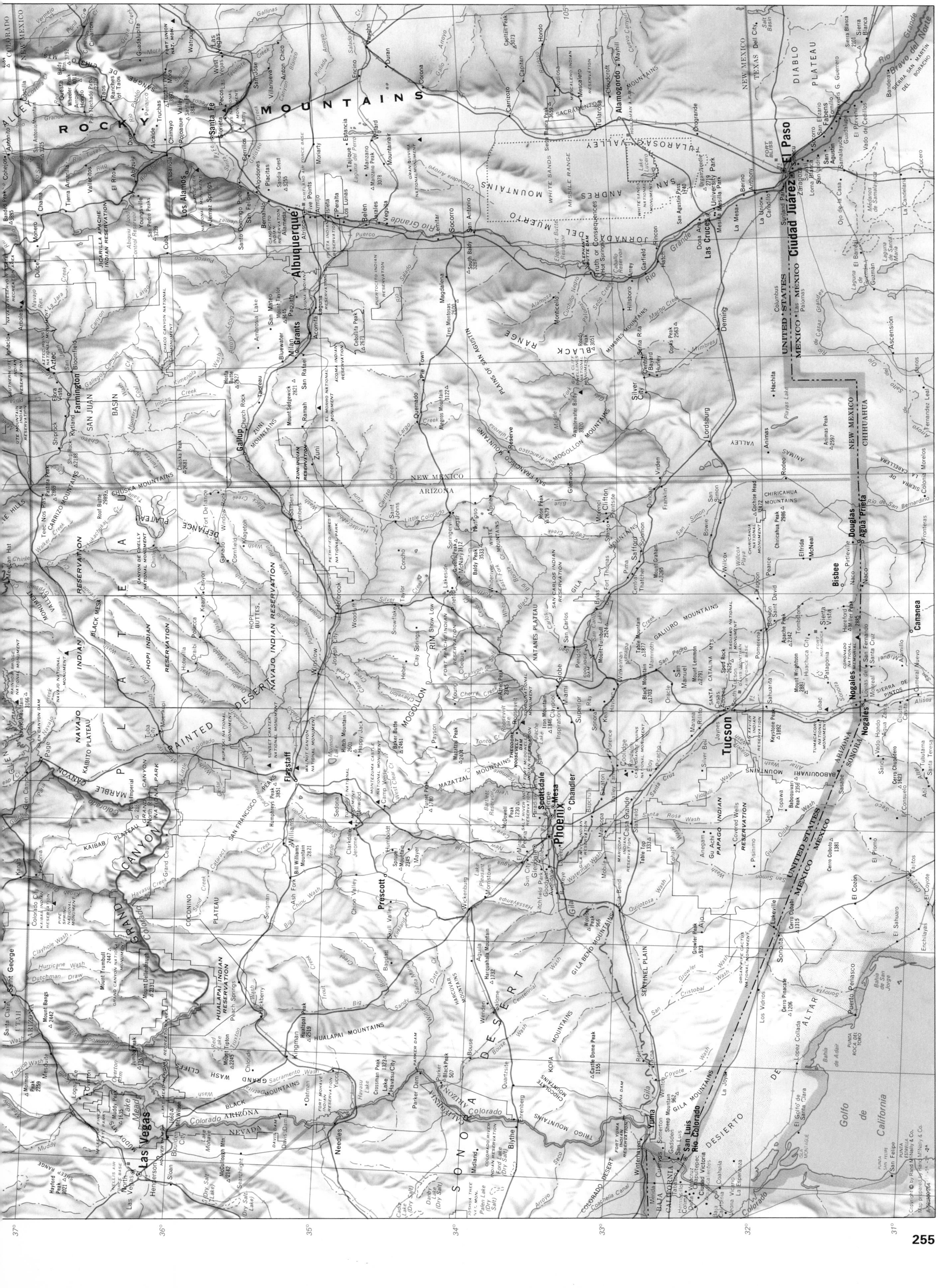
ROCKY MOUNTAINS
NEW MEXICO
ARIZONA
COLORADO
UTAH
NEVADA
TEXAS
CALIFORNIA
BAJA CALIFORNIA
SONORA
CHIHUAHUA
UNITED STATES
MEXICO
Santa Fe
Albuquerque
Los Alamos
Gallup
Farmington
Grants
Socorro
Las Cruces
El Paso
Ciudad Juárez
Alamogordo
Deming
Lordsburg
Silver City
Flagstaff
Prescott
Phoenix
Scottsdale
Tempe
Mesa
Chandler
Tucson
Nogales
Douglas
Bisbee
Agua Prieta
Cananea
Yuma
San Luis Río Colorado
Kingman
Las Vegas
Needles
Blythe
GRAND CANYON
PAINTED DESERT
SONORA DESERT
MOGOLLON RIM
Golfo de California
Copyright © by Rand McNally & Co.

Kilometers 0 50 100 150 Km.
Statute Miles 0 50 100 150 Mi.

Scale 1:3,000,000
One centimeter represents 30 kilometers.
One inch represents approximately 47 miles.
Albers Conical Equal-Area Projection

Vancouver
Victoria
Bellingham
Everett
SEATTLE
Tacoma
Olympia
Bremerton
Aberdeen
Hoquiam
Port Angeles
Wenatchee
Ellensburg
Yakima
Richland
Kennewick
Pasco
Walla Walla
Spokane
Coeur d'Alene
Lewiston
Moscow
Pullman
Pendleton
The Dalles
PORTLAND
Salem
Albany
Corvallis
Eugene
Springfield
Bend
Roseburg
Coos Bay
Grants Pass
Medford
Ashland
Klamath Falls
Eureka
Boise
Nampa
Caldwell
Penticton
Nelson
Trail
BRITISH COLUMBIA
CANADA
UNITED STATES
WASHINGTON
OREGON
IDAHO
CALIFORNIA
NEVADA
PACIFIC OCEAN
OLYMPIC MTS.
COLUMBIA BASIN
BLUE MOUNTAINS
CASCADE RANGE
COAST RANGES
KLAMATH MOUNTAINS
GREAT SANDY DESERT
HARNEY BASIN
OWYHEE PLATEAU
SNAKE RIVER PLAIN
Columbia
Snake
Strait of Juan de Fuca
Puget Sound
125°
124°
123°
122°
121°
120°
119°
118°
117°
116°
49°
48°
47°
46°
45°
44°
43°
42°
41°

CANADA
UNITED STATES
ALBERTA
SASKATCHEWAN
MONTANA
WYOMING
IDAHO
UTAH
COLORADO
Great Falls
Helena
Butte
Missoula
Bozeman
Billings
Havre
Kalispell
Miles City
Sheridan
Casper
Cody
Idaho Falls
Pocatello
Logan
Ogden
Rock Springs
Yellowstone National Park
Fort Peck Reservoir
Great Salt Lake
GREAT SALT LAKE DESERT
BIG HORN BASIN
WIND RIVER RANGE
BIG HORN MOUNTAINS
Copyright © by Rand McNally & Co.
Map prepared by Rand McNally & Co.
A-520607-264

Kilometers 0 50 100 150 Km.

Statute Miles 0 50 100 150 Mi.

Scale 1:3,000,000

One centimeter represents 30 kilometers.

One inch represents approximately 47 miles.

Albers Conical Equal-Area Projection

SAN FRANCISCO
Oakland
San Jose
Sacramento
Stockton
Reno
Carson City
Eureka
Redding
Medford
Klamath Falls
Grants Pass
Roseburg
Coos Bay
Twin Falls
Mountain Home
Elko
Winnemucca
Fallon
Modesto
Merced
SNAKE RIVER PLAIN
GREAT SALT LAKE DESERT
COLUMBIA PLATEAU
GREAT BASIN
CASCADE RANGE
COAST RANGES
SIERRA NEVADA
KLAMATH MOUNTAINS
SACRAMENTO VALLEY
SAN JOAQUIN
RUBY MOUNTAINS
BLACK ROCK DESERT
WARNER MOUNTAINS
IDAHO
NEVADA
OREGON
CALIFORNIA
UTAH

PACIFIC
OCEAN
LOS ANGELES
SAN DIEGO
Las Vegas
Fresno
Bakersfield
Santa Barbara
San Bernardino
Riverside
Long Beach
Santa Ana
Anaheim
Pasadena
Tijuana
Mexicali
Ensenada
Salinas
Monterey
San Luis Obispo
Ventura
Oxnard
Barstow
Lancaster
Victorville
Needles
Yuma
MOJAVE DESERT
CHANNEL ISLANDS
Gulf of Santa Catalina
COAST RANGES
TEMBLOR RANGE
IMPERIAL VALLEY
DESIERTO DE ALTAR
BAJA CALIFORNIA
SONORA
ARIZONA
NEVADA
CALIFORNIA
MEXICO

Kilometers 0 50 100 150 Km.

Statute Miles 0 50 100 150 Mi.

Scale 1:3,000,000

One centimeter represents 30 kilometers.
One inch represents approximately 47 miles.

Albers Conical Equal-Area Projection

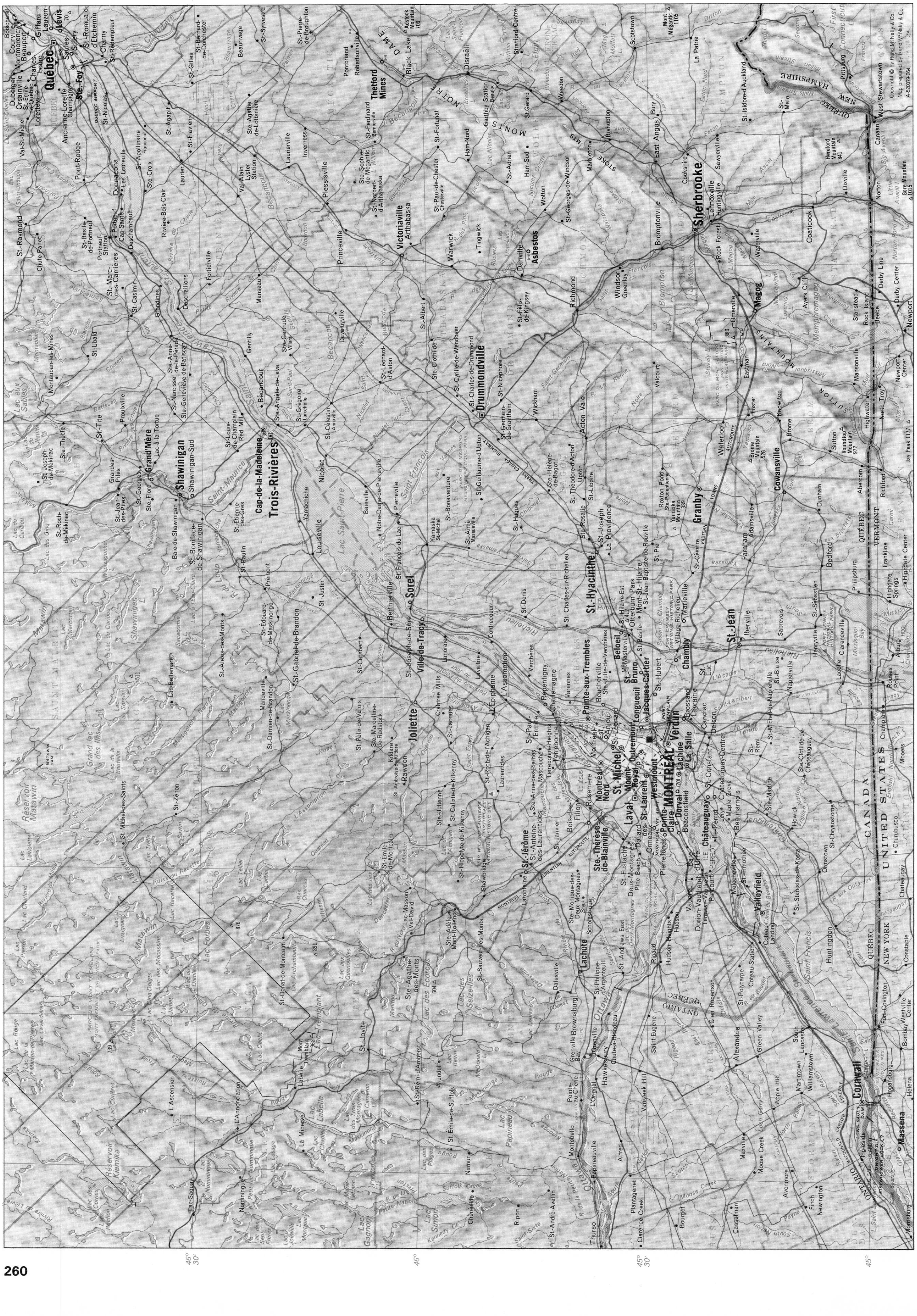

Kilometers 0 10 20 30 40 50 Km.
Statute Miles 0 10 20 30 40 50 Mi.
Scale 1:1,000,000
One centimeter represents 10 kilometers.
One inch represents approximately 16 miles.
Lambert Conformal Conic Projection
Québec
Lévis
Ste-Foy
Trois-Rivières
Cap-de-la-Madeleine
Shawinigan
Grand'Mère
Victoriaville
Drummondville
Sherbrooke
Magog
Granby
St-Hyacinthe
Sorel
Joliette
St-Jérôme
Laval
MONTRÉAL
St-Jean
Valleyfield
Cornwall
Massena
Lachute
Thetford Mines
Asbestos
Cowansville
QUÉBEC
ONTARIO
NEW YORK
VERMONT
NEW HAMPSHIRE
CANADA
UNITED STATES

Boston—New York—Albany

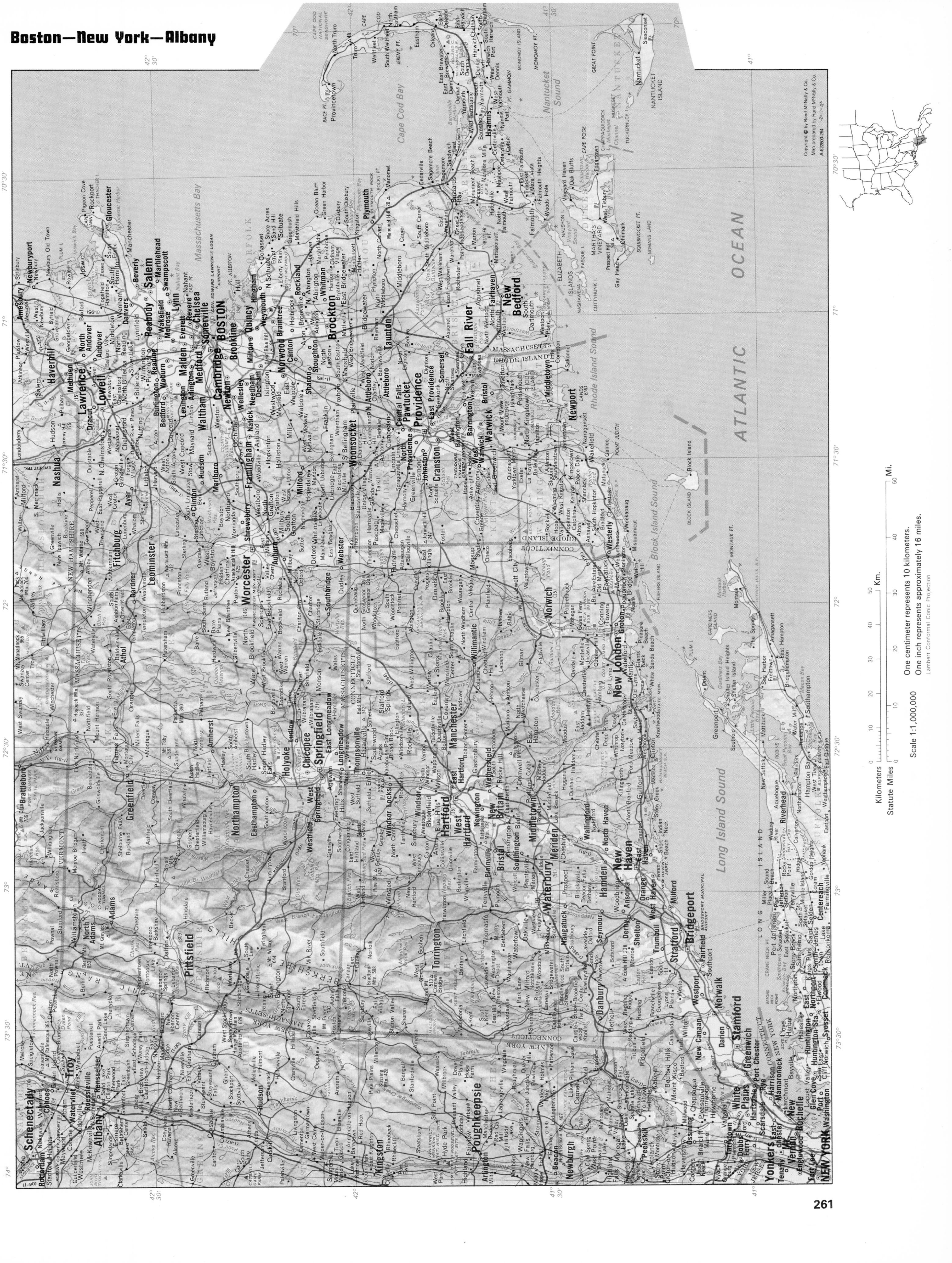
ATLANTIC OCEAN
Long Island Sound
Rhode Island Sound
Block Island Sound
Nantucket Sound
Cape Cod Bay
Massachusetts Bay
Scale 1:1,000,000
One centimeter represents 10 kilometers.
One inch represents approximately 16 miles.
Lambert Conformal Conic Projection
Kilometers
Statute Miles
Copyright © by Rand McNally & Co.
Map prepared by Rand McNally & Co.

NEW YORK
NEWARK
Jersey City
Elizabeth
Bayonne
Perth Amboy
New Brunswick
Trenton
Princeton
Asbury Park
Atlantic City
Vineland
PHILADELPHIA
Camden
Chester
Wilmington
Dover
Allentown
Bethlehem
Easton
Reading
Lancaster
Harrisburg
York
Pottsville
Hanover
Frederick
BALTIMORE
Annapolis
WASHINGTON
Alexandria
Arlington
Delaware Bay
NEW JERSEY
PENNSYLVANIA
DELAWARE
MARYLAND
VIRGINIA
APPALACHIAN
MOUNTAINS

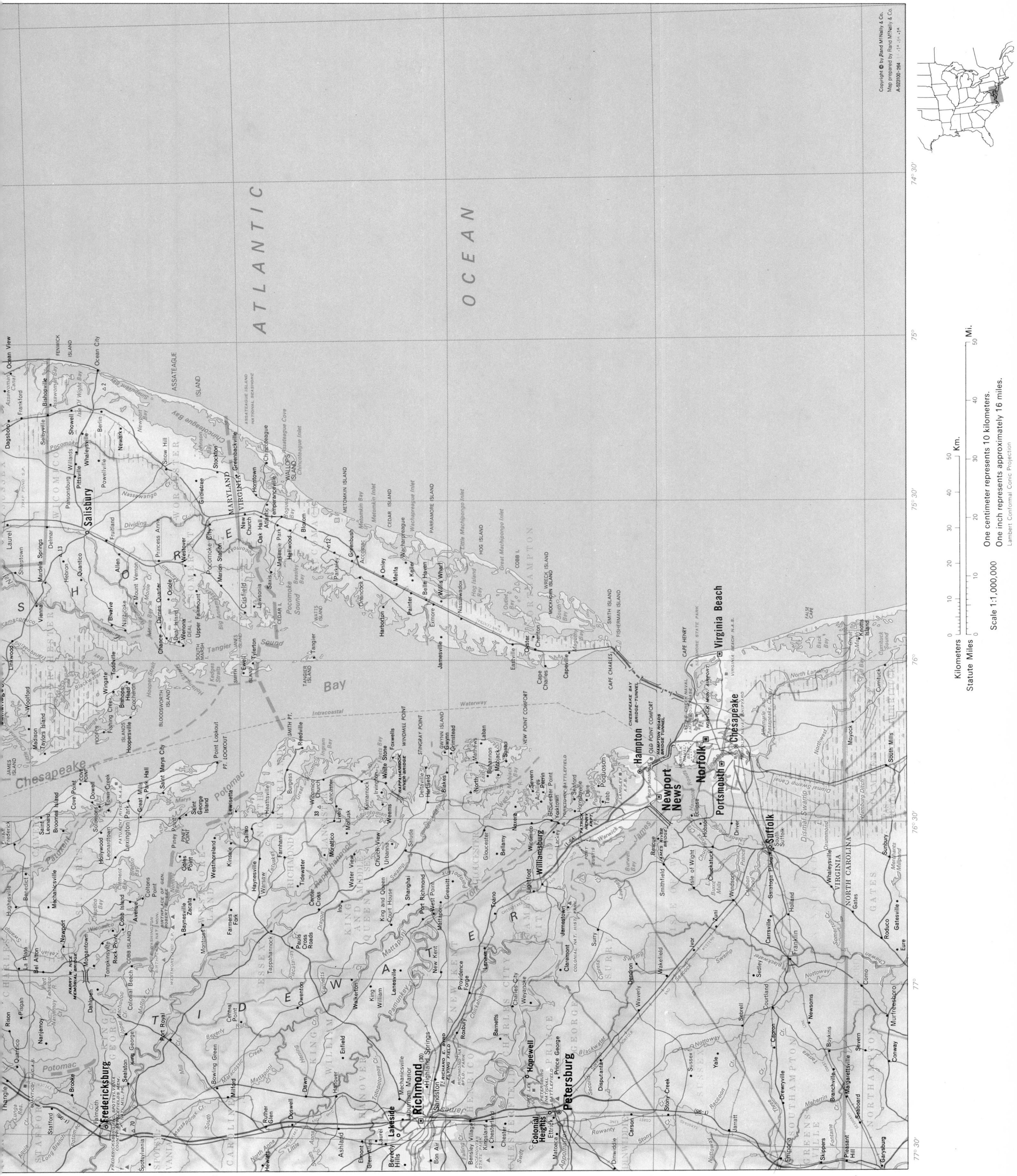
ATLANTIC
OCEAN
Chesapeake
Bay
Potomac
Richmond
Petersburg
Fredericksburg
Norfolk
Portsmouth
Chesapeake
Virginia Beach
Newport News
Hampton
Suffolk
Williamsburg
Salisbury
Colonial Heights
Hopewell
Lakeside
MARYLAND
VIRGINIA
NORTH CAROLINA
Copyright © by Rand McNally & Co.
Map prepared by Rand McNally & Co.
Scale 1:1,000,000
One centimeter represents 10 kilometers.
One inch represents approximately 16 miles.
Lambert Conformal Conic Projection
Kilometers
Statute Miles
Km.
Mi.

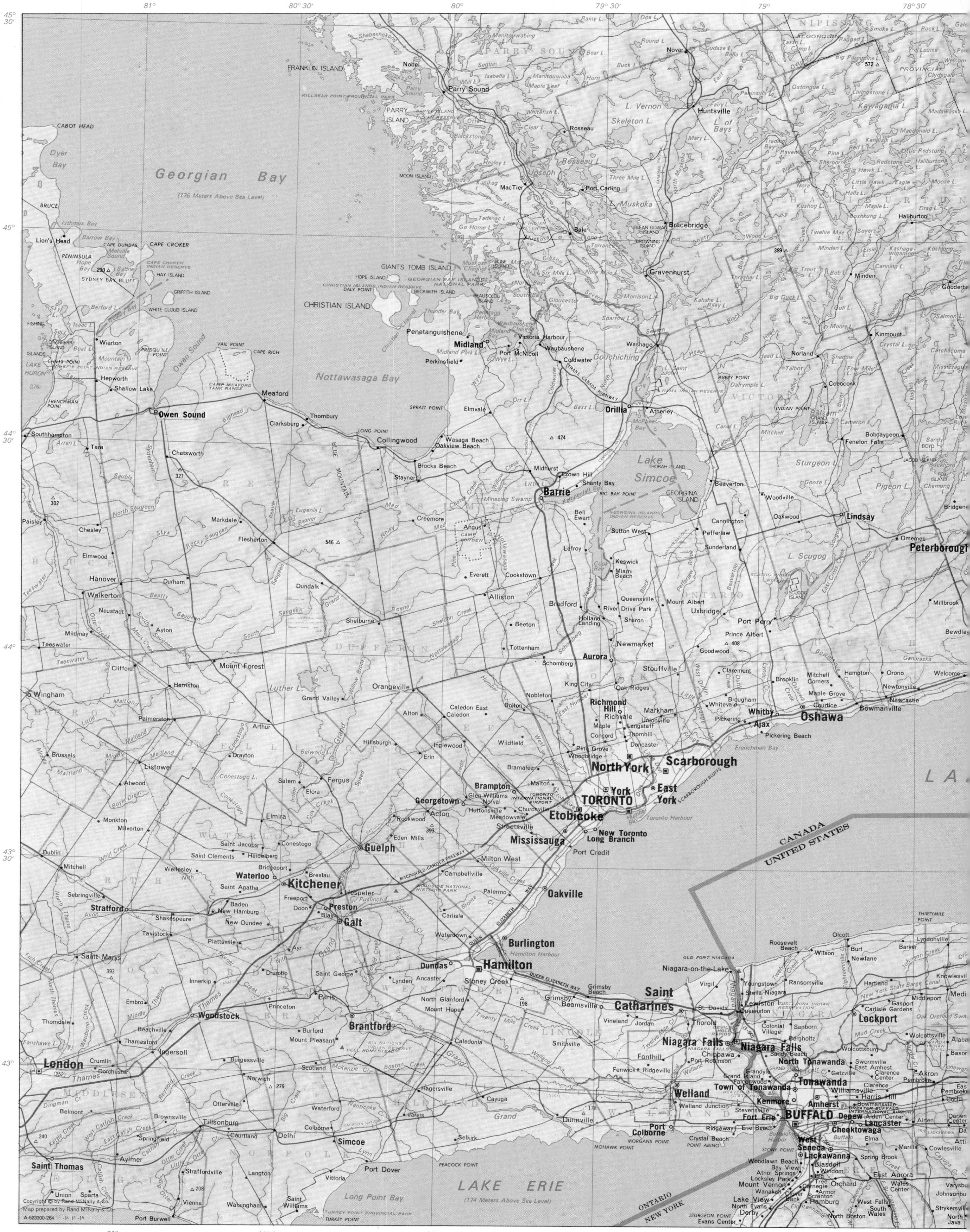

Georgian Bay
(176 Meters Above Sea Level)
Nottawasaga Bay
LAKE ERIE
(174 Meters Above Sea Level)
Long Point Bay
Lake Simcoe
CANADA
UNITED STATES
ONTARIO
NEW YORK
TORONTO
North York
Scarborough
East York
York
Etobicoke
Mississauga
New Toronto
Long Branch
Toronto Harbour
Hamilton
Hamilton Harbour
Burlington
Oakville
Kitchener
Waterloo
Guelph
Galt
Preston
Brantford
London
Woodstock
Stratford
Saint Thomas
Simcoe
Saint Catharines
Niagara Falls
Welland
BUFFALO
Lockport
Barrie
Orillia
Oshawa
Whitby
Ajax
Peterborough
Lindsay
Owen Sound
Collingwood
Midland
Parry Sound
Huntsville
Bracebridge
Gravenhurst
Port Colborne
Dunnville
Port Dover
Tillsonburg
Aylmer
Ingersoll
Listowel
Walkerton
Hanover
Orangeville
Brampton
Georgetown
Aurora
Newmarket
Richmond Hill
Markham
Bowmanville
Port Perry
Uxbridge
Grimsby
Dundas
Stoney Creek
Tonawanda
North Tonawanda
Cheektowaga
Lackawanna
West Seneca
Amherst
Lancaster
Depew
Fort Erie
Niagara-on-the-Lake
CHRISTIAN ISLAND
GIANTS TOMB ISLAND
FRANKLIN ISLAND
CABOT HEAD
CAPE CROKER
BRUCE
PENINSULA
Lake Huron
Muskoka
Lake of Bays
Lake Scugog
Copyright © by Rand McNally & Co.
Map prepared by Rand McNally & Co.
45° 30'
45°
44° 30'
44°
43° 30'
43°
81°
80° 30'
80°
79° 30'
79°
78° 30'

78°
77°30'
77°
76°30'
76°
75°30'
45° 30'
45°
44° 30'
44°
43° 30'
43°
Ottawa
Hull
Gatineau
Pointe-Gatineau
Eastview
Renfrew
Arnprior
Almonte
Carleton Place
Smiths Falls
Perth
Brockville
Ogdensburg
Prescott
Kingston
Belleville
Trenton
Picton
Cobourg
Gananoque
Napanee
Watertown
Oswego
Fulton
Rome
Utica
Oneida
Syracuse
Auburn
Geneva
Rochester
Irondequoit
Greece
Gates
Brighton
Batavia
ONTARIO
(75 Meters Above Sea Level)
ONTARIO
NEW YORK
Wellington Bay
Mexico Bay
Bay of Quinte
Rice L.
Oneida L.
Seneca L.
Cayuga L.
Skaneateles L.
Owasco L.
Canandaigua L.
AMHERST ISLAND
WOLFE ISLAND
THOUSAND ISLANDS
St. Lawrence
Rideau
Mississippi
Ottawa
FREEWAY
TRANS CANADA HIGHWAY
THRUWAY
NEW YORK STATE

Kilometers 0 10 20 30 40 50 Km.

Statute Miles 0 10 20 30 40 50 Mi.

Scale 1:1,000,000

One centimeter represents 10 kilometers.

One inch represents approximately 16 miles.

Lambert Conformal Conic Projection

LAKE HURON
LAKE ERIE
(175 Meters Above Sea Level)
Lake Saint Clair
CANADA
UNITED STATES
ONTARIO
OHIO
MICHIGAN
Port Huron
Sarnia
Point Edward
BLUE WATER BRIDGE
Pontiac
Troy
Warren
Royal Oak
DETROIT
Dearborn
Windsor
Livonia
Westland
Wyandotte
Southgate
Monroe
Toledo
Maumee
Oregon
Sandusky
Fremont
Tiffin
Fostoria
Lorain
Elyria
CLEVELAND
Lakewood
Parma
Euclid
Mentor
Painesville
Ashtabula
Akron
Cuyahoga Falls
Barberton
Canton
Massillon
Wooster
Mansfield
Ashland
Bucyrus
Marion
Delaware
Columbus
Worthington
Newark
Mount Vernon
Coshocton
New Philadelphia
Dover
Steubenville
Youngstown
Warren
Niles
Alliance
East Liverpool
Chatham
Wallaceburg
Leamington
Kingsville
Amherstburg
Tilbury
Saint Thomas
Tillsonburg
Port Stanley
Port Burwell
Pelee Island
Kelleys Island
Put-in-Bay
Pelee Passage
POINT PELEE NATIONAL PARK
Rondeau Provincial Park
LAMBTON
KENT
ESSEX
ELGIN
MIDDLESEX
OXFORD
WAYNE
MONROE
LUCAS
OTTAWA
SANDUSKY
ERIE
HURON
LORAIN
CUYAHOGA
SUMMIT
PORTAGE
MEDINA
WAYNE
STARK
TUSCARAWAS
HOLMES
KNOX
LICKING
COSHOCTON
MUSKINGUM
RICHLAND
CRAWFORD
WYANDOT
MARION
MORROW
DELAWARE
UNION
HARRISON
CARROLL
COLUMBIANA
MAHONING
TRUMBULL
GEAUGA
LAKE
ASHTABULA
Copyright © by Rand McNally & Co.
Map prepared by Rand McNally & Co.
A-523500-264
83°30′
83°
82°30′
82°
81°30′
81°
42°30′
42°
41°30′
41°
40°30′

BUFFALO
PITTSBURGH
Erie
Jamestown
Olean
Bradford
Warren
Meadville
Oil City
Franklin
New Castle
Butler
Kittanning
Indiana
Johnstown
Altoona
State College
Greensburg
McKeesport
Washington
Dunkirk
Hornell
Clearfield
Du Bois
CANADA
UNITED STATES
ONTARIO
NEW YORK
PENNSYLVANIA
Long Point Bay
A L L E G H E N Y
P L A T E A U
ALLEGHENY
APPALACHIAN
MOUNTAINS
Allegheny Reservoir
80°
79°30′
79°
78°30′
78°
42° 30′
42°
41° 30′
41°
40° 30′

Kilometers 0 10 20 30 40 50 Km.

Statute Miles 0 10 20 30 40 50 Mi.

Scale 1:1,000,000

One centimeter represents 10 kilometers.

One inch represents approximately 16 miles.

Lambert Conformal Conic Projection

LAKE MICHIGAN
(176 Meters Above Sea Level)
ILLINOIS
INDIANA
WISCONSIN
Madison
Janesville
Beloit
Rockford
Elgin
De Kalb
Aurora
Joliet
Kankakee
Ottawa
La Salle
Streator
Pontiac
Bloomington
Normal
Rantoul
MILWAUKEE
Waukesha
Racine
Kenosha
Waukegan
Evanston
CHICAGO
Oak Park
Cicero
Gary
Hammond
East Chicago
Michigan City
La Porte
Valparaiso
Lafayette
West Lafayette
Logansport
Saint Joseph
Benton Harbor
Muskegon
JEFFERSON
WAUKESHA
WALWORTH
RACINE
KENOSHA
ROCK
GREEN
WINNEBAGO
BOONE
MC HENRY
LAKE
COOK
DU PAGE
KANE
DE KALB
OGLE
LEE
LA SALLE
KENDALL
GRUNDY
WILL
KANKAKEE
LIVINGSTON
IROQUOIS
FORD
MC LEAN
WOODFORD
CHAMPAIGN
VERMILION
DE WITT
PIATT
NEWTON
JASPER
BENTON
WARREN
TIPPECANOE
WHITE
CARROLL
PULASKI
STARKE
LA PORTE
PORTER
FOUNTAIN
89°
88°30′
88°
87°30′
87°
86°30′
43°
42°30′
42°
41°30′
41°
40°30′
Copyright © by Rand McNally & Co.
Map prepared by Rand McNally & Co.
A-523000-264

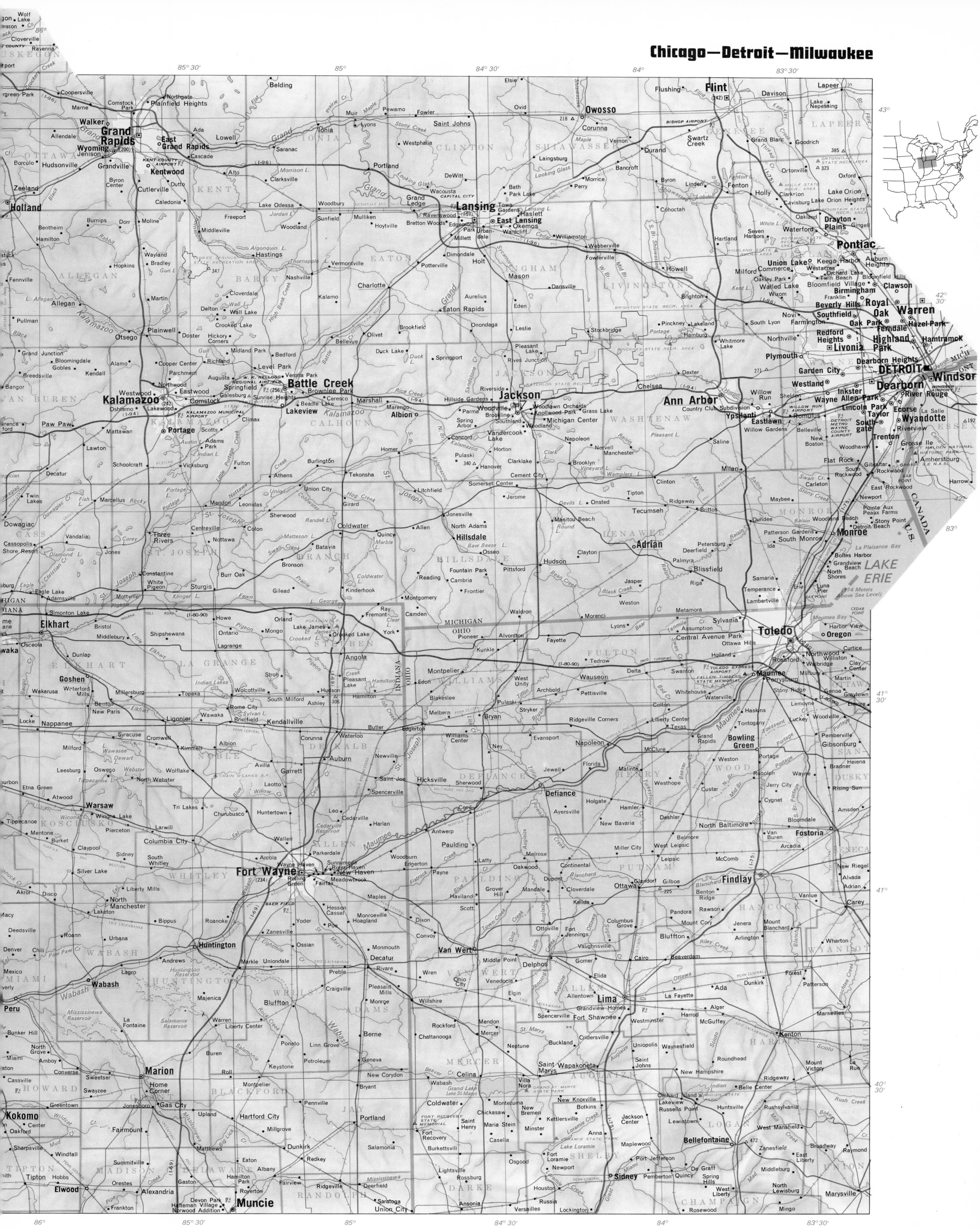
Flint
Owosso
Lansing
East Lansing
Grand Rapids
Kalamazoo
Battle Creek
Jackson
Ann Arbor
Pontiac
Warren
DETROIT
Windsor
Dearborn
Livonia
Toledo
Adrian
Monroe
Fort Wayne
Elkhart
Goshen
Findlay
Lima
Marion
Muncie
Kokomo
Huntington
Wabash
Defiance
Bowling Green
LAKE ERIE
MICHIGAN
OHIO
INDIANA
CANADA
U.S.
85° 30'
85°
84° 30'
84°
83° 30'
86°
43°
42° 30'
42°
41° 30'
41°
40° 30'
83°

Kilometers 0 10 20 30 40 50 Km.

Statute Miles 0 10 20 30 40 50 Mi.

Scale 1:1,000,000

One centimeter represents 10 kilometers.
One inch represents approximately 16 miles.
Lambert Conformal Conic Projection

VANCOUVER
North Vancouver
New Westminster
Port Coquitlam
Port Moody
Chilliwack
Abbotsford
Mission City
White Rock
BRITISH COLUMBIA
WASHINGTON
CANADA
UNITED STATES
Strait of Georgia
Strait of Juan de Fuca
Haro Strait
Victoria
Oak Bay
Esquimalt
Nanaimo
VANCOUVER ISLAND
SEYMOUR RANGE
Port Alberni
Port Renfrew
Bellingham
Anacortes
Mount Vernon
SAN JUAN ISLANDS
WHIDBEY ISLAND
Everett
Edmonds
SEATTLE
Bellevue
Renton
Kent
Auburn
Tacoma
Bremerton
Port Angeles
Port Townsend
Puget Sound
OLYMPIC MOUNTAINS
CASCADE MOUNTAINS
WENATCHEE MOUNTAINS
ENTIAT MOUNTAINS
Mt. Baker 3285
Neah Bay
Forks
La Push
Clallam Bay

PACIFIC OCEAN
WASHINGTON
OREGON
Olympia
Aberdeen
Hoquiam
Centralia
Chehalis
Kelso
Longview
Astoria
Vancouver
PORTLAND
Hillsboro
Beaverton
Lake Oswego
Oregon City
Milwaukie
Salem
McMinnville
Tillamook
The Dalles
Hood River
White Salmon
Goldendale
Mt. Rainier
Mt. St. Helens
Mt. Adams
Mt. Hood
CASCADE RANGE
COAST RANGE
Kilometers
Statute Miles
Km.
Mi.
Scale 1:1,000,000
One centimeter represents 10 kilometers.
One inch represents approximately 16 miles.
Lambert Conformal Conic Projection

Reno
Sparks
Carson City
South Lake Tahoe
Lake Tahoe
SIERRA NEVADA
CARSON RANGE
PINE NUT MOUNTAINS
Yerington
Sacramento
North Highlands
Citrus Heights
Roseville
Auburn
Placerville
Marysville
Yuba City
Oroville
Woodland
Davis
West Sacramento
Stockton
Lodi
Modesto
Manteca
Tracy
Turlock
Sonora
Livermore
Fairfield
Vacaville
Napa
Vallejo
Santa Rosa
Petaluma
Novato
San Rafael
Berkeley
Oakland
Alameda
San Leandro
Hayward
Fremont
San Mateo
Palo Alto
SAN FRANCISCO
Daly City
Pacifica
Concord
Walnut Creek
Antioch
Pittsburg
Martinez
Willows
Colusa
SACRAMENTO VALLEY
YOSEMITE NATIONAL PARK
CATHEDRAL RANGE
DESERT MTNS
SONOMA MOUNTAINS

PACIFIC OCEAN
Scale 1:1,000,000
One centimeter represents 10 kilometers.
One inch represents approximately 16 miles.
Lambert Conformal Conic Projection
Kilometers
Statute Miles
Km.
Mi.
Copyright © by Rand McNally & Co.
Map prepared by Rand McNally & Co.
SAN JOAQUIN VALLEY
DIABLO RANGE
COAST RANGES
SANTA LUCIA RANGE
SANTA CRUZ MOUNTAINS
GABILAN RANGE
TEMBLOR RANGE
KETTLEMAN HILLS
SIERRA DE SALINAS
CHOLAME HILLS
Monterey Bay
Fresno
Bakersfield
Salinas
Monterey
Santa Cruz
San Luis Obispo
Visalia
Hanford
Tulare
Madera
Delano
Paso Robles
King City
Hollister
Watsonville
Los Banos
Coalinga
Carmel
Pacific Grove
Seaside
Morro Bay
Oildale
Corcoran
Wasco
Gilroy
Los Gatos
Saratoga
Campbell
Chowchilla
Kerman
Selma
Dinuba
Reedley
Sanger
Lemoore
Kingsburg

Los Angeles—San Diego

119°
118°30'
118°
117°30'
117°
35°
34° 30'
34°
33° 30'
33°
32° 30'
Bakersfield
Hillcrest Center
Kern City
Vista Park
Lamont
Pumpkin Center
Delkern
Di Giorgio
Edmondson Acres
Arvin
Caliente
Loraine
Keene
Eagle Peak 1668
2109 Bear Mtn.
Cache Peak 2005
SIERRA NEVADA
Tehachapi
Monolith
Tehachapi Pass 1158
SAN JOAQUIN VALLEY
Buena Vista Lake
Cummings Mtn. 2367
Double Mtn. 2433
Wheeler Ridge
TEHACHAPI MTS.
Mojave
Cantil
Koehn Dry Lake
FREMONT VALLEY
California City
MOJAVE
North Edwards
Boron
Randsburg
Johannesburg
Red Mountain 1606
CHINA LAKE NAVAL ORDNANCE TEST STATION
Cuddeback Lake (Dry)
Fremont Peak 1397
Slocum Mtn. 1562
Superior Lake (Dry)
Black Mountain 1201
Lane Mtn. 1378
Harper Lake (Dry)
Goldstone L.
Hinkley
Edwards
Rogers Dry Lake
EDWARDS AIR FORCE BASE
Rosamond Lake (Dry)
Rosamond
Willow Springs
Buckhorn Lake (Dry)
Lenwood
Barstow
Daggett
Lebec
Frazier Park
Mt. Pinos 2692
Tejon Pass 1273
Frazier Mtn. 2442
Gorman
Castaic Lake
ANTELOPE VALLEY
Antelope Acres
Lancaster
Hi Vista
DESERT
Helendale
Stoddard Mtn. 1492
SAN BERNARDINO
ORD MOUNTAINS
Reyes Peak 2289
Cobblestone Mtn. 2051
Lake Hughes
Quartz Hill
Desert View Highland
Sun Village
Palmdale
Mirage L. (Dry)
Adelanto
Oro Grande
Bell Mountain
Victorville
Apple Valley
Littlerock
Pearblossom
Mountain View Acres
Hines Peak 2043
Meiners Oaks
West Hills
Ojai
Mira Monte
Woodland Acres
Oak View
Casitas Springs
Foster Park
Castaic
Val Verde Park
Agua Dulce
Acton
Soledad Pass 983
Mint Canyon
North Fillmore
Fillmore
Piru
Valyermo
Phelan
Hesperia
Lucerne Valley
Rabbit L. (Dry)
Saugus
Newhall
SAN GABRIEL MTS.
Pacifico Mtn. 2171
Wrightwood
Cajon Summit 1298
Summit
Cajon Pass 1166
Ventura (San Buenaventura)
Santa Paula
Sespe
Saticoy
Moorpark
Community Center
Santa Susana
San Fernando
Waterman Mtn. 2450
Mt. Baden-Powell 2865
Mt. San Antonio 3068
SAN BERNARDINO MTS.
Big Bear City
Big Bear Lake
Montalvo
El Rio
Somis
Simi
Santa Susana Knolls
Camarillo Heights
Camarillo
Oxnard
Oxnard Beach
Nyland Acres
Port Hueneme
Thousand Oaks
Newbury Park
La Crescenta
Montrose
La Canada
Flintridge
Altadena
Burbank
Sierra Madre
Monrovia
Duarte
Glendora
Crestline
Twin Peaks
Lake Arrowhead
Blue Jay
Running Springs
Valley View Park
Devore
Cucamonga Peak 2270
Arrowhead Peak 1291
Keller Peak 2402
Del Rosa
Highland
San Bernardino
Anderson Peak 3311
Glendale
Pasadena
Arcadia
Temple City
Azusa
Covina
San Dimas
Claremont
Upland
Alta Loma
Etiwanda
Muscoy
Rialto
Fontana
Cucamonga
San Antonio Heights
Hidden Hills
Agoura
Cornell
Topanga
West Hollywood
Hollywood
Beverly Hills
San Gabriel
Alhambra
Baldwin Park
Monterey Park
El Monte
West Covina
La Puente
Diamond Bar
Walnut
Pomona
Montclair
Ontario
Chino
Bloomington
Colton
Loma Linda
Redlands
Mentone
Yucaipa
Dunlap Acres
Calimesa
Malibu
Santa Monica
LOS ANGELES
East Los Angeles
Culver City
Montebello
Huntington Park
Bell Gardens
Pico Rivera
Whittier
Hacienda Heights
Los Serranos
Glen Avon Heights
Rubidoux
Riverside
Highgrove
Grand Terrace
Sunnymead
Cherry Valley
Beaumont
Banning
Venice
Inglewood
South Gate
Florence
Downey
Los Nietos
La Habra
Brea
Norco
Pedley
Edgemont
Moreno
El Segundo
Lennox
Hawthorne
Lynwood
Norwalk
La Mirada
Fullerton
Yorba Linda
Home Gardens
Corona
Woodcrest
Lakeview
Gilman Hot Springs
Manhattan Beach
Hermosa Beach
Redondo Beach
Lawndale
Compton
Gardena
Bellflower
Paramount
Buena Park
Placentia
Torrance
Lakewood
Anaheim
Nuevo
San Jacinto
Palos Verdes Estates
Lomita
Carson
Long Beach
Stanton
Garden Grove
Villa Park
El Modeno
Orange
Perris
Romoland
Winchester
Hemet
Valle Vista
Miraleste
San Pedro
Westminster
Seal Beach
Santa Ana
Tustin
Silverado
Santiago Peak 1733
Quail Valley
Sun City
Alberhill
Lake Elsinore
Elsinore
Sedco Hills
Fountain Valley
Irvine
Huntington Beach
Santa Ana Heights
Costa Mesa
Newport Beach
El Toro
Lakeland Village
Laguna Beach
South Laguna
Murrieta
Temecula
Dana Point
San Juan Capistrano
Capistrano Beach
San Clemente
Margarita Peak 972
SANTA MARGARITA MTS.
San Onofrio Mtn. 526
Fallbrook
Rainbow
Pala
Agua Tibia 1457
Bonsall
San Luis Rey
Oceanside
North Carlsbad
Vista
Valley Center
Carlsbad
San Marcos
Burnt Mtn. 651
Escondido
Leucadia
Encinitas
Del Dios
Cardiff-by-the-Sea
Rancho Santa Fe
Ramona
Solana Beach
Black Mtn. 476
Poway
Del Mar
Carmel Mtn. 129
Eucalyptus Hills
Lakeside
Santee
Winter Gardens
La Jolla
El Cajon
Grossmont
La Mesa
Spring Valley
Vista La Mesa
Lemon Grove
San Diego
San Miguel Mtn. 782
Coronado
La Presa
National City
Lincoln Acres
Chula Vista
Castle Park
Harbor Side
Otay
Imperial Beach
U.S.
MEXICO
Tijuana
Santa Monica Bay
San Pedro Bay
San Pedro Channel
Gulf of Santa Catalina
PACIFIC OCEAN
Outer Santa Barbara Passage
SANTA BARBARA ISLAND
CHANNEL ISLANDS NAT. MON.
Black Point
Silver Peak 550
SANTA CATALINA ISLAND
613
Avalon
SAN CLEMENTE ISLAND
198
599
Pyramid Head
Copyright © by Rand McNally & Co.
Map prepared by Rand McNally & Co.
A-522600-264

Kilometers 0 10 20 30 40 50 Km.

Statute Miles 0 10 20 30 40 50 Mi.

Scale 1:1,000,000

One centimeter represents 10 kilometers.
One inch represents approximately 16 miles.
Lambert Conformal Conic Projection

a

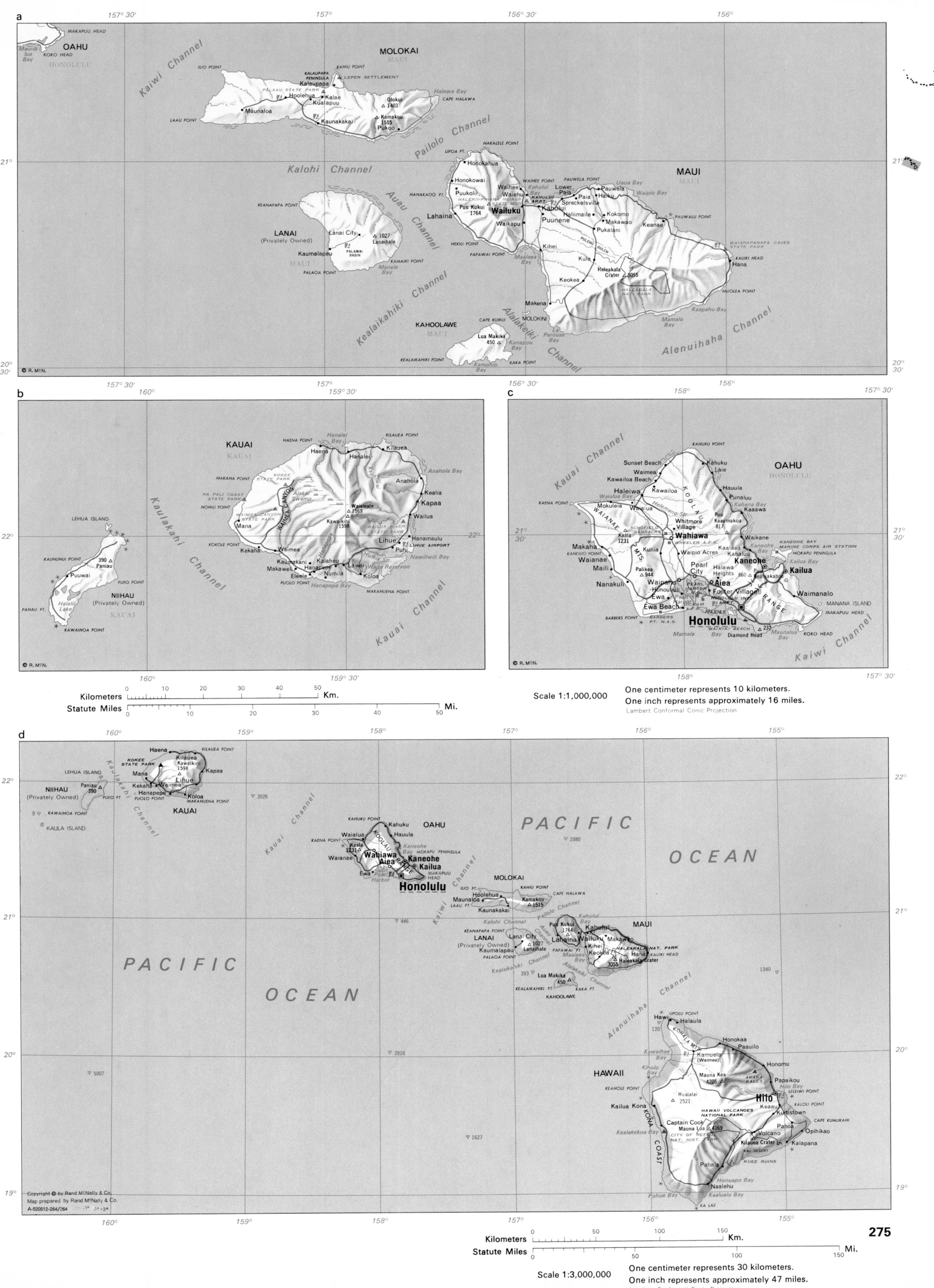

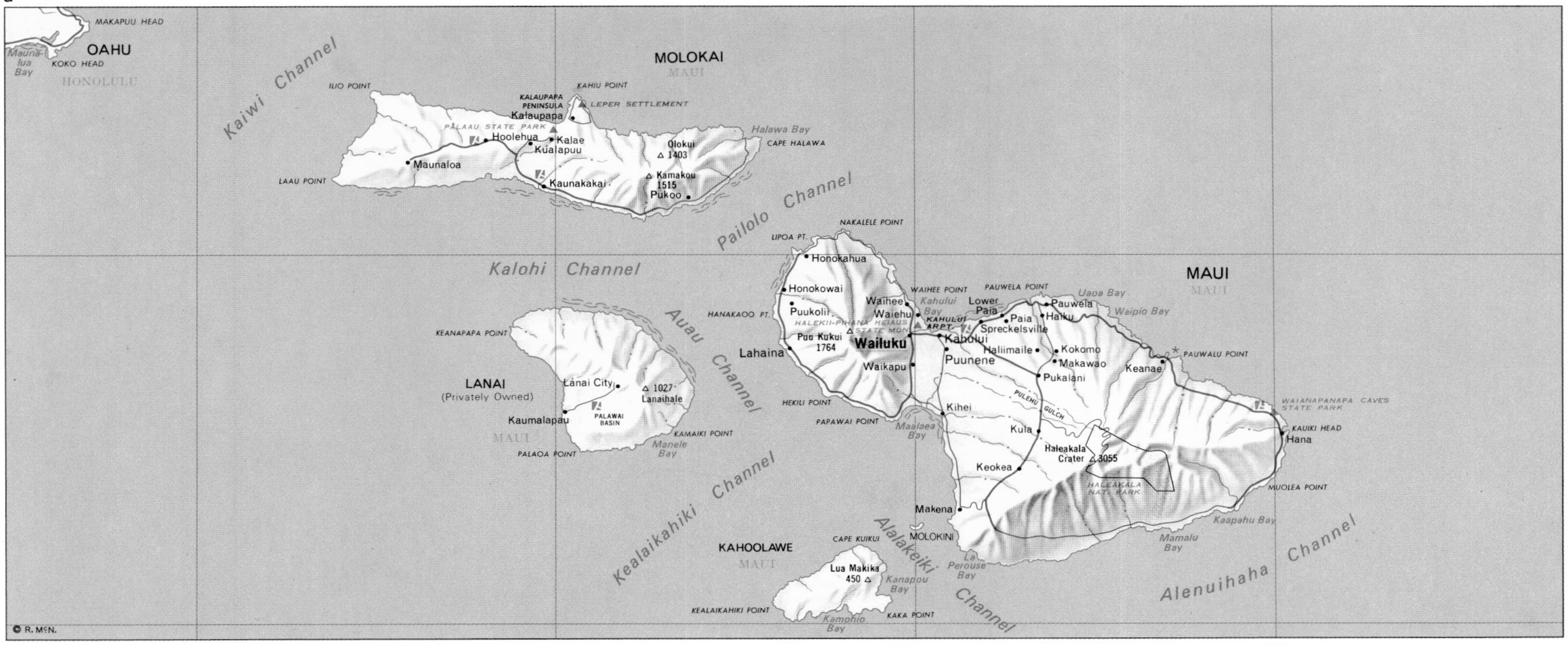
OAHU
HONOLULU
MOLOKAI
MAUI
Kaiwi Channel
Kalaupapa
Hoolehua
Kalae
Kualapuu
Maunaloa
Kaunakakai
Olokui 1403
Kamakou 1515
Pukoo
Pailolo Channel
Kalohi Channel
LANAI
(Privately Owned)
Lanai City
1027 Lanaihale
Kaumalapau
Auau Channel
Honokahua
Honokowai
Puukolii
Lahaina
Puu Kukui 1764
Wailuku
Waikapu
Waihee
Waiehu
Kahului
Paia
Haiku
Pauwela
Makawao
Pukalani
Kokomo
Keanae
Kihei
Kula
Haleakala Crater 3055
Keokea
Makena
Hana
MOLOKINI
KAHOOLAWE
Lua Makika 450
Kealaikahiki Channel
Alalakeiki Channel
Alenuihaha Channel
© R. McN.

b

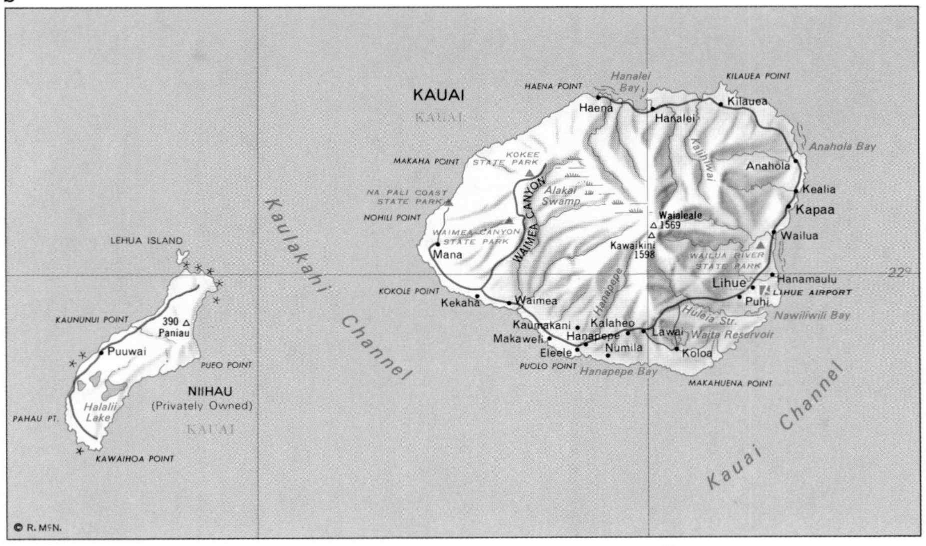
KAUAI
Hanalei
Haena
Kilauea
Anahola
Kealia
Kapaa
Wailua
Waialeale 1569
Kawaikini 1598
Hanamaulu
Lihue
Puhi
Koloa
Lawai
Kalaheo
Numila
Eleele
Hanapepe
Makaweli
Kaumakani
Waimea
Kekaha
Mana
WAIMEA CANYON
LEHUA ISLAND
NIIHAU
(Privately Owned)
390 Paniau
Puuwai
Kaulakahi Channel
Kauai Channel
© R. McN.

c

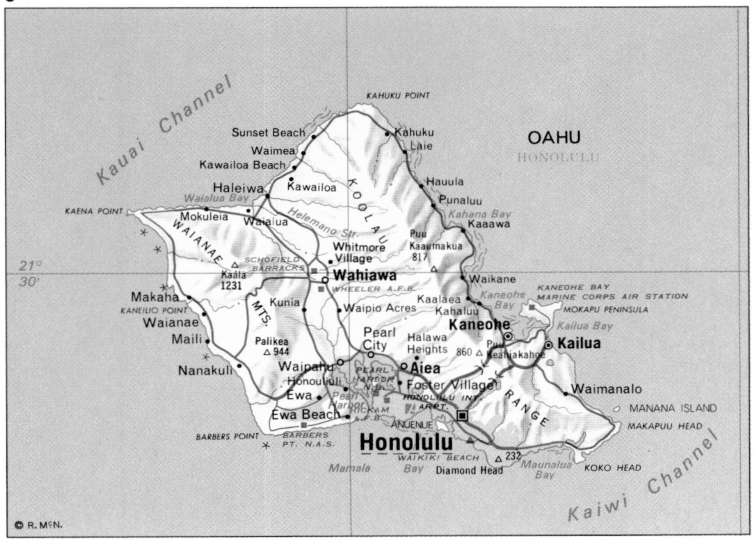
OAHU
HONOLULU
Kauai Channel
Sunset Beach
Waimea
Kawailoa Beach
Haleiwa
Kawailoa
Waialua
Mokuleia
Kahuku
Laie
Hauula
Punaluu
Kaaawa
Wahiawa
Whitmore Village
Kaala 1231
Makaha
Waianae
Maili
Nanakuli
Kunia
Waipio Acres
Palikea 944
Waipahu
Pearl City
Aiea
Ewa
Ewa Beach
Kaneohe
Kailua
Halawa Heights
Foster Village
Waimanalo
Honolulu
Diamond Head 232
Kaiwi Channel
© R. McN.

Kilometers 0 10 20 30 40 50 Km.
Statute Miles 0 10 20 30 40 50 Mi.

Scale 1:1,000,000
One centimeter represents 10 kilometers.
One inch represents approximately 16 miles.
Lambert Conformal Conic Projection

d

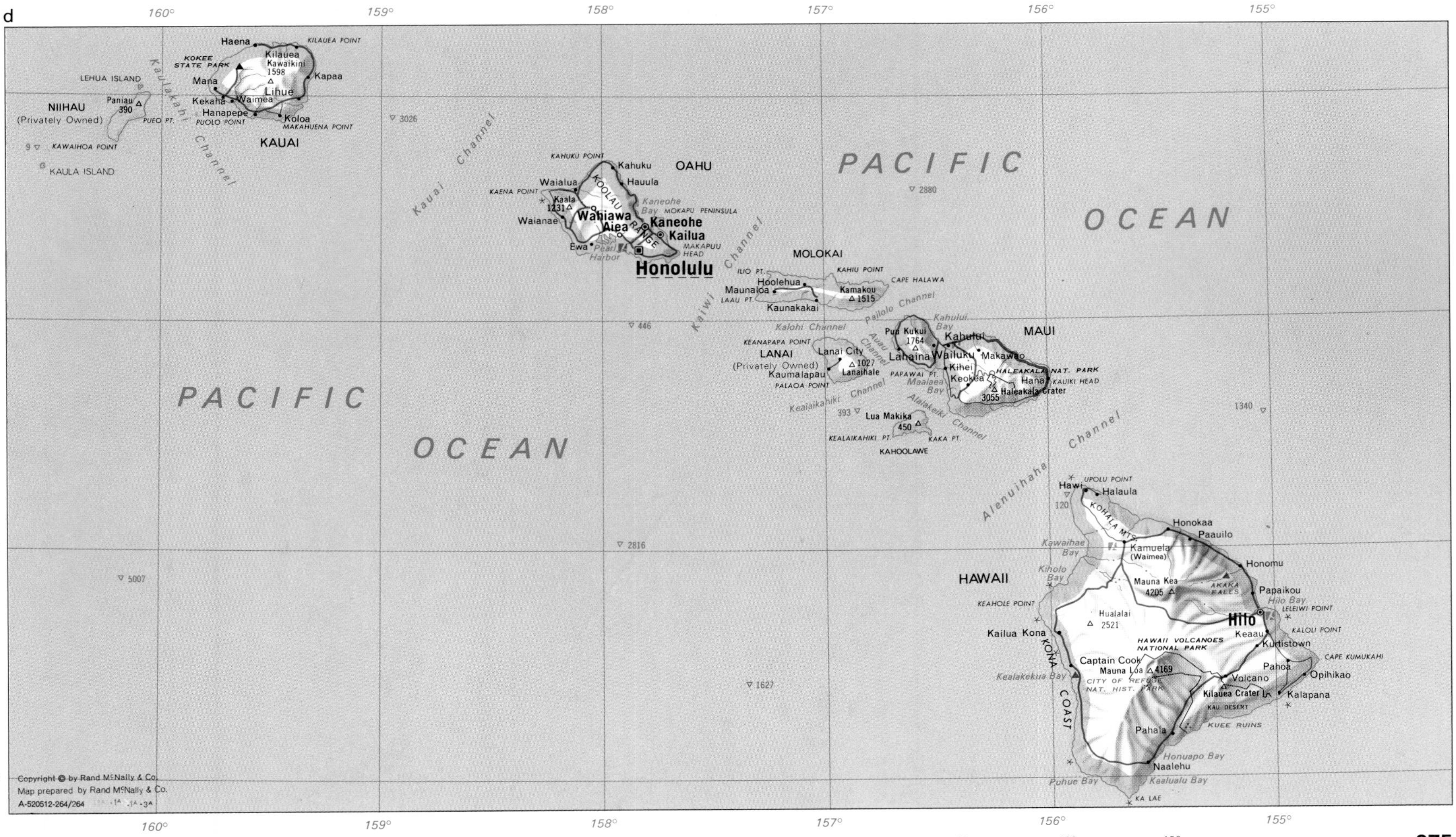
PACIFIC OCEAN
PACIFIC OCEAN
NIIHAU
(Privately Owned)
KAUAI
Lihue
OAHU
Honolulu
MOLOKAI
MAUI
LANAI
KAHOOLAWE
HAWAII
Hilo
Kailua Kona
Mauna Kea 4205
Mauna Loa 4169
Hualalai 2521
Kilauea Crater
Hawi
Honokaa
Kamuela (Waimea)
Pahala
Naalehu
Kaiwi Channel
Kauai Channel
Kaulakahi Channel
Alenuihaha Channel
Copyright © by Rand McNally & Co.
Map prepared by Rand McNally & Co.
A-520512-264/264

Kilometers 0 50 100 150 Km.
Statute Miles 0 50 100 150 Mi.

Scale 1:3,000,000
One centimeter represents 30 kilometers.
One inch represents approximately 47 miles.
Lambert Conformal Conic Projection

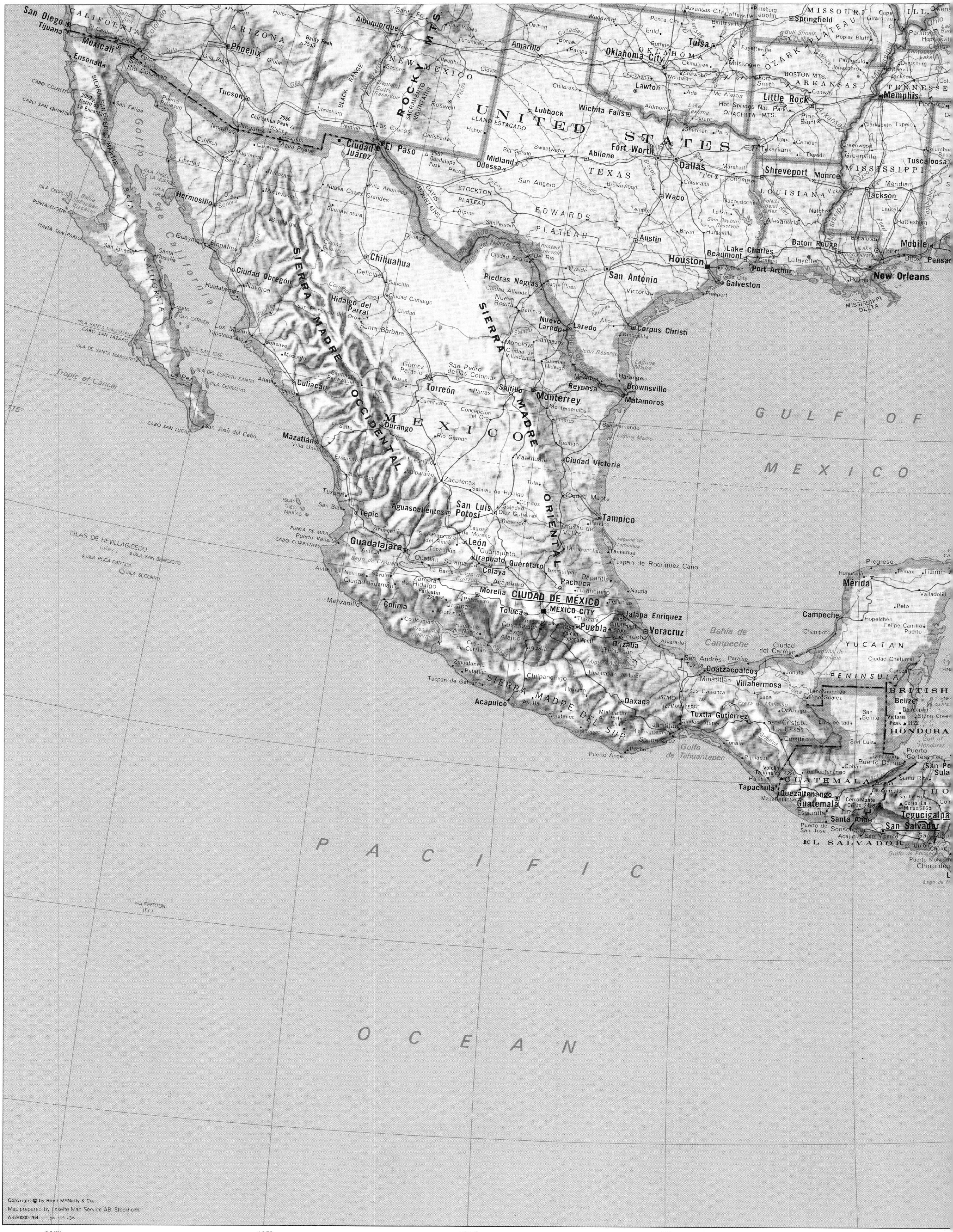
UNITED STATES
MEXICO
GULF OF MEXICO
PACIFIC OCEAN
SIERRA MADRE OCCIDENTAL
SIERRA MADRE ORIENTAL
SIERRA MADRE DEL SUR
ROCKY MTS.
EDWARDS PLATEAU
LLANO ESTACADO
OZARK PLATEAU
Golfo de California
BAJA CALIFORNIA
Tropic of Cancer
Bahía de Campeche
Golfo de Tehuantepec
PENINSULA YUCATAN
GUATEMALA
EL SALVADOR
BRITISH
HONDURA
ISLAS DE REVILLAGIGEDO
CLIPPERTON (Fr.)
San Diego
Tijuana
Mexicali
Ensenada
Phoenix
Tucson
Albuquerque
El Paso
Ciudad Juárez
Hermosillo
Chihuahua
Ciudad Obregón
Culiacán
Mazatlán
Durango
Torreón
Monterrey
Saltillo
Nuevo Laredo
Laredo
San Antonio
Austin
Houston
Dallas
Fort Worth
Oklahoma City
Tulsa
Little Rock
Memphis
Shreveport
Jackson
Baton Rouge
New Orleans
Mobile
Corpus Christi
Brownsville
Matamoros
Tampico
San Luis Potosí
Aguascalientes
Guadalajara
León
Querétaro
Morelia
CIUDAD DE MÉXICO
MEXICO CITY
Puebla
Veracruz
Acapulco
Oaxaca
Coatzacoalcos
Villahermosa
Tuxtla Gutiérrez
Campeche
Mérida
Belize
Guatemala
Tegucigalpa
San Salvador
Tapachula
Quezaltenango

A-530000-264

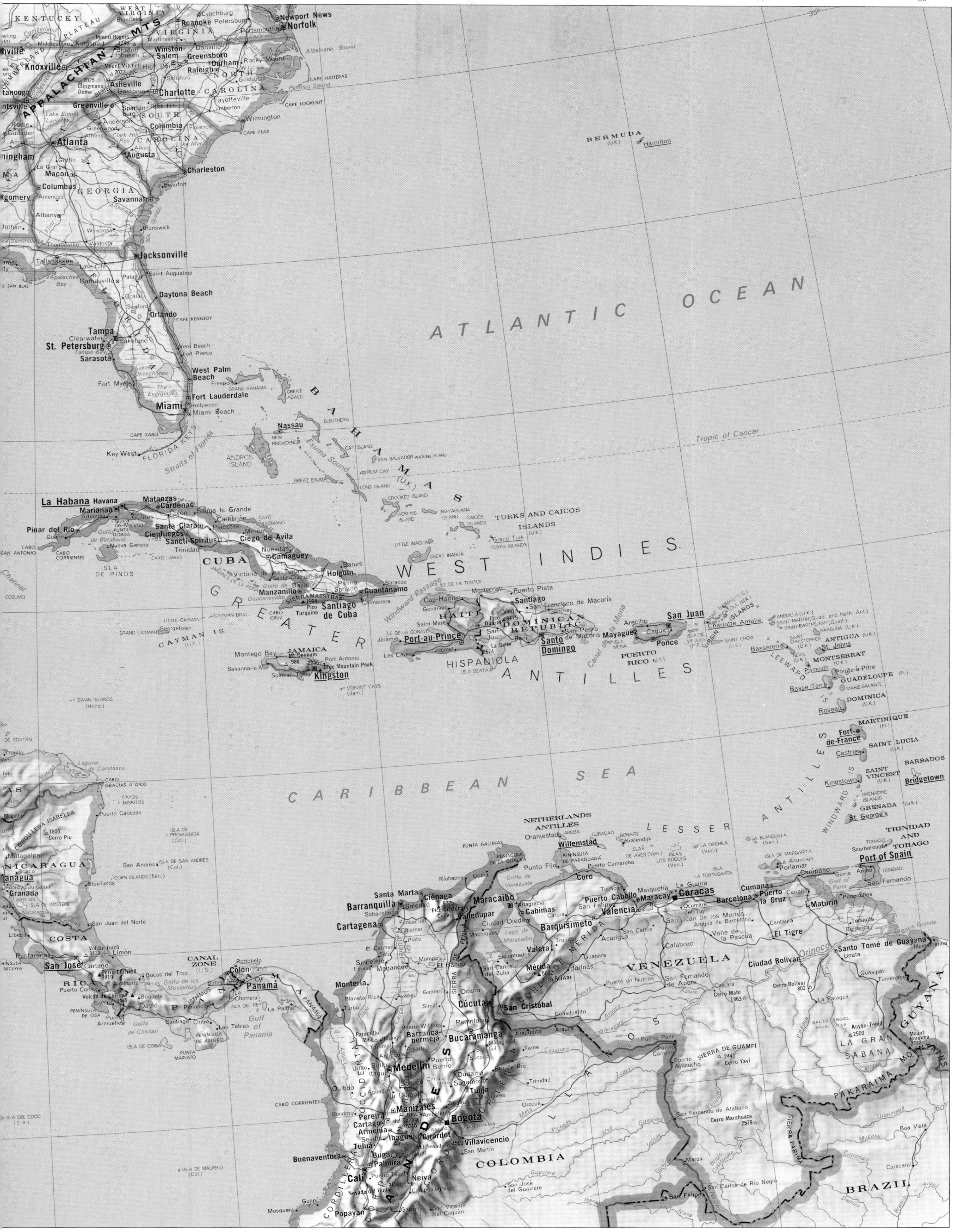
ATLANTIC OCEAN
WEST INDIES
GREATER ANTILLES
LESSER ANTILLES
CARIBBEAN SEA
BAHAMAS (U.K.)
BERMUDA (U.K.)
Hamilton
TURKS AND CAICOS ISLANDS (U.K.)
Tropic of Cancer
CUBA
La Habana Havana
Matanzas
Cárdenas
Pinar del Río
Cienfuegos
Santa Clara
Sancti-Spíritus
Ciego de Ávila
Camagüey
Holguín
Guantánamo
Santiago de Cuba
Manzanillo
ISLA DE PINOS
CAYMAN IS. (U.K.)
JAMAICA
Montego Bay
Kingston
HISPANIOLA
HAITI
Port-au-Prince
Cap-Haïtien
DOMINICAN REPUBLIC
Santo Domingo
Santiago
PUERTO RICO (U.S.)
San Juan
Ponce
Mayagüez
Charlotte Amalie
Basseterre
ANTIGUA (U.K.)
St. Johns
MONTSERRAT (U.K.)
GUADELOUPE (Fr.)
Basse-Terre
DOMINICA (U.K.)
Roseau
MARTINIQUE (Fr.)
Fort-de-France
SAINT LUCIA (U.K.)
Castries
BARBADOS
Bridgetown
SAINT VINCENT (U.K.)
Kingstown
GRENADA (U.K.)
St. George's
TRINIDAD AND TOBAGO
Port of Spain
NETHERLANDS ANTILLES
Oranjestad
Willemstad
LEEWARD ISLANDS
WINDWARD ISLANDS
KENTUCKY
VIRGINIA
NORTH CAROLINA
SOUTH CAROLINA
GEORGIA
FLORIDA
APPALACHIAN MTS
Norfolk
Newport News
Knoxville
Charlotte
Atlanta
Augusta
Columbia
Charleston
Savannah
Jacksonville
Macon
Columbus
Tallahassee
Daytona Beach
Orlando
Tampa
St. Petersburg
Sarasota
West Palm Beach
Fort Lauderdale
Miami
Key West
Nassau
Straits of Florida
NICARAGUA
Managua
Granada
COSTA RICA
San José
PANAMÁ
Panamá
Colón
CANAL ZONE (U.S.)
Gulf of Panama
COLOMBIA
Bogotá
Medellín
Cali
Barranquilla
Cartagena
Santa Marta
Cúcuta
Bucaramanga
Manizales
Pereira
Ibagué
Villavicencio
Neiva
Popayán
Buenaventura
VENEZUELA
Caracas
Maracaibo
Valencia
Barquisimeto
Maracay
Barcelona
Cumaná
Maturín
Ciudad Bolívar
Santo Tomé de Guayana
San Cristóbal
Mérida
LLANOS
Orinoco
GUYANA
BRAZIL
LA GRAN SABANA
PAKARAIMA MOUNTAINS
ANDES
85°
80°
75°
70°
65°
60°
55°
35°
30°
25°
20°
15°
10°
5°

Kilometers 0 200 400 600 Km.

Statute Miles 0 200 400 600 Mi.

Scale 1:12,000,000

One centimeter represents 120 kilometers.
One inch represents approximately 190 miles.

Oblique Conic Conformal Projection

116°
114°
112°
110°
108°
106°
104°
32°
30°
28°
26°
24°
22°
20°
18°
16°
San Diego
Tijuana
Mexicali
Yuma
San Luis Río Colorado
Ensenada
ARIZONA
NEW MEXICO
Tucson
Nogales
Las Cruces
El Paso
Ciudad Juárez
Carlsbad
Hobbs
Odessa
UNITED STATES
MEXICO
Puerto Peñasco
Hermosillo
SONORA
Guaymas
Ciudad Obregón
Navojoa
Los Mochis
Culiacán
Mazatlán
Chihuahua
Delicias
Hidalgo del Parral
Durango
Gómez Palacio
Torreón
Zacatecas
Fresnillo
Tepic
NAYARIT
Guadalajara
JALISCO
Ocotlán
Sahuayo
Ciudad Guzmán
Colima
Manzanillo
SINALOA
BAJA CALIFORNIA
BAJA CALIFORNIA SUR
SIERRA SAN PEDRO MÁRTIR
SIERRA DE LA GIGANTA
SIERRA MADRE OCCIDENTAL
BOLSÓN DE MAPIMÍ
Golfo de California
Santa Rosalía
Mulegé
Loreto
La Paz
Todos Santos
San José del Cabo
San Lucas
CABO SAN LUCAS
ISLA CEDROS
ISLA TIBURÓN
Bahía Sebastián Vizcaíno
Tropic of Cancer
PACIFIC
OCEAN
ISLAS TRES MARÍAS
ISLAS DE REVILLAGIGEDO (Mex.)
ISLA SOCORRO
ISLA SAN BENEDICTO
ISLA ROCA PARTIDA
ISLA CLARIÓN (Mex.)
Copyright © by Rand McNally & Co.
Map prepared by Rand McNally & Co.
A-531600-264

Kilometers 0 100 200 300 Km.

Statute Miles 0 100 200 300 Mi.

Scale 1:6,000,000

One centimeter represents 60 kilometers.
One inch represents approximately 95 miles.
Lambert Conformal Conic Projection

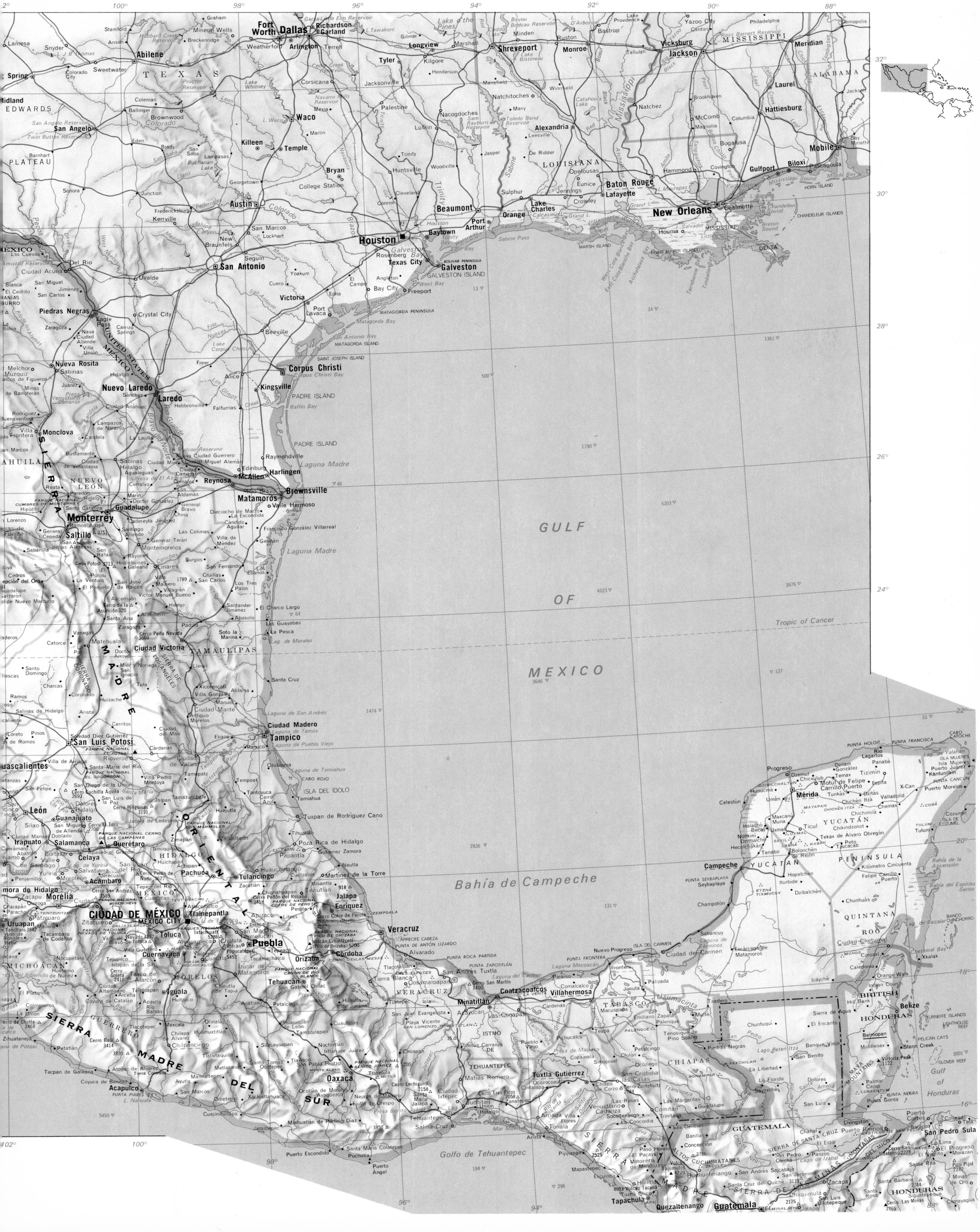

GULF
OF
MEXICO
Bahía de Campeche
Golfo de Tehuantepec
Gulf of Honduras
Tropic of Cancer
TEXAS
LOUISIANA
MISSISSIPPI
ALABAMA
TAMAULIPAS
NUEVO LEÓN
YUCATÁN
CAMPECHE
QUINTANA ROO
TABASCO
CHIAPAS
VERACRUZ
OAXACA
GUERRERO
MICHOACÁN
HIDALGO
MÉXICO
MORELOS
GUATEMALA
BRITISH HONDURAS
HONDURAS
SIERRA MADRE ORIENTAL
SIERRA MADRE DEL SUR
UNITED STATES
MEXICO
EDWARDS PLATEAU
Fort Worth
Dallas
Richardson
Garland
Arlington
Abilene
San Angelo
Waco
Killeen
Temple
Bryan
Austin
San Antonio
Houston
Galveston
Texas City
Baytown
Beaumont
Port Arthur
Orange
Lake Charles
Lafayette
Baton Rouge
New Orleans
Shreveport
Alexandria
Monroe
Vicksburg
Jackson
Meridian
Laurel
Hattiesburg
Mobile
Gulfport
Biloxi
Tyler
Longview
Corpus Christi
Kingsville
Laredo
Nuevo Laredo
McAllen
Harlingen
Brownsville
Matamoros
Reynosa
Monterrey
Saltillo
Monclova
Piedras Negras
Del Rio
Ciudad Acuña
Ciudad Victoria
Ciudad Madero
Tampico
San Luis Potosí
Aguascalientes
León
Guanajuato
Irapuato
Salamanca
Celaya
Querétaro
Morelia
Uruapan
CIUDAD DE MÉXICO
MEXICO CITY
Tlalnepantla
Toluca
Cuernavaca
Puebla
Pachuca
Tulancingo
Jalapa Enríquez
Veracruz
Orizaba
Córdoba
Tehuacán
Oaxaca
Acapulco
Chilpancingo
Iguala
Coatzacoalcos
Minatitlán
Villahermosa
Tuxtla Gutiérrez
Tapachula
Ciudad del Carmen
Campeche
Mérida
Progreso
Cozumel
Chetumal
Belize
Belmopan
Quezaltenango
Guatemala
Tuxpan de Rodríguez Cano
Poza Rica de Hidalgo
Salina Cruz
Juchitán
Tehuantepec

92°
91°
90°
89°
88°
87°
16°
15°
14°
13°
12°
11°
10°
9°
8°
MEXICO
MÉXICO
GUATEMALA
BELIZE
HONDURAS
EL SALVADOR
CHIAPAS
SIERRA MADRE
ALTOS CUCHUMATANES
EL PETÉN
ALTA VERAPAZ
BAJA VERAPAZ
SIERRA DE CHAMÁ
SIERRA DE LAS MINAS
SIERRA DE CHUACÚS
EL QUICHÉ
HUEHUETENANGO
SAN MARCOS
QUEZALTENANGO
TOTONICAPÁN
SOLOLÁ
CHIMALTENANGO
RETALHULEU
SUCHITEPÉQUEZ
ESCUINTLA
SANTA ROSA
JUTIAPA
JALAPA
CHIQUIMULA
ZACAPA
EL PROGRESO
IZABAL
OCOTEPEQUE
COPÁN
SANTA BÁRBARA
CORTÉS
YORO
ATLÁNTIDA
COMAYAGUA
INTIBUCÁ
LEMPIRA
LA PAZ
FRANCISCO MORAZÁN
EL PARAÍSO
VALLE
CHOLUTECA
MADRIZ
NUEVA SEGOVIA
ESTELÍ
CHINANDEGA
LEÓN
MANAGUA
MASAYA
CARAZO
GRANADA
ISLAS DE LA BAHÍA
ISLA DE ROATÁN
Roatán
Utila
La Ceiba
Gulf of Honduras
Bahía de Amatique
Puerto Barrios
Livingston
Puerto Cortés
San Pedro Sula
El Progreso
Tegucigalpa
Comayagua
Danlí
Choluteca
Golfo de Fonseca
San Miguel
Usulután
San Vicente
Zacatecoluca
San Salvador
Nueva San Salvador
Santa Ana
Sonsonate
Acajutla
Ahuachapán
Chalchuapa
Guatemala
Antigua Guatemala
Escuintla
Puerto de San José
Quezaltenango
Tapachula
Comitán
Huehuetenango
Cobán
Zacapa
Chiquimula
Jalapa
Jutiapa
Chinandega
Corinto
León
Managua
Masaya
Jinotepe
Lago de Managua
Lago de Izabal
Lago de Atitlán
Lago de Amatitlán
Lago de Güija
Lago de Ilopango
Lago de Yojoa
Monkey River
Punta Gorda
Poptún
San Luis
PACIFIC
OCEAN
Copyright © by Rand McNally & Co.
Map prepared by Rand McNally & Co.
A-533600-264

85°
84°
83°
82°
81°
80°
15°
14°
13°
12°
11°
10°
9°
8°
CARIBBEAN
SEA
SERRANILLA BANK
(Claimed by Col. and U.S.)
CAYOS CAJONES
CAYOS BECERRO
CAYOS VIVORILLO
CAYOS COCOROCUMA
ARRECIFE DE LA MEDIA LUNA
CABO FALSO
CABO GRACIAS A DIOS
Cabo Gracias a Dios
EDINBURGH REEF
Edinburgh Channel
MISKITOS REEF
CAYOS MISKITOS
QUITA SUEÑO BANK
(Claimed by Col. and U.S.)
SERRANA BANK
(Claimed by Col. and U.S.)
RONCADOR BANK
(Claimed by Col. and U.S.)
ISLA DE PROVIDENCIA
SAN ANDRÉS Y PROVIDENCIA
(Colombia)
ISLA DE SAN ANDRÉS
San Andrés
CAYOS DEL ESTE SUDESTE
CAYOS DE ALBUQUERQUE
CORN ISLANDS
(Nic.)
CABO CAMARÓN
Santa Rosa de Aguán
Limón
Iriona
PUNTA PATUCA
Laguna de Brus
Brus Laguna
Cerro Payas
1128
COLÓN
Paya
GRACIAS A DIOS
ISLA DE TANSÍN
Laguna de Caratasca
MONTAÑAS DE COLÓN
Dulce Nombre de Culmí
Guanpata
Camacosni
Valencia
San Ramón
Bilwascarma
Waspán
Raiti
Bocay
Cerro Yelucá
1128
HONDURAS
NICARAGUA
Güina
Bonanza
Rosita
Yablis
Puerto Cabezas
MOSQUITOS
JINOTEGA
Bahá
Siuna
Cerro Piu
1800
Huaunta
Laguna Huaunta
Prinzapolca
Tungla
El Garrobo
CORDILLERA ISABELLA
Cerro Kilambé
1750
Cerro Peñas Blancas 1745
Los Angeles
San Pedro del Norte
La Cruz de Río Grande
Río Grande de Matagalpa
CORDILLERA DE DARIÉN
ZELAYA
Matiguás
MATAGALPA
Tarica
Río Grande
El Camarón
Laguna de Perlas
COSTA
Los Encuentros
BOACO
MONTAÑAS DE HUAPI
PUNTA COCA
PUNTA DE PERLAS
Cerro Mombachito 1040
Camoapa
Comalapa
Santo Domingo
Rama
CHONTALES
Juigalpa
La Libertad
Villa Somoza
Santo Tomás
Muelle de los Bueyes
El Bluff
Bluefields
Laguna de Bluefields
ISLA VENADO
Acoyapa
PUNTA MAYALES
San Ubaldo
Lago de Nicaragua
ISLA ZAPATERA
Concepción 1610
Alta Gracia
ISLA DE OMETEPE
Volcán Madera 1394
Morrito
Jesús María
CORDILLERA DE YOLAINA
PUNTA MICO
Punta Gorda
PUNTA GORDA
ISLA SAN BERNARDO
San Miguelito
La Flor
(32 Meters Above Sea Level)
Bahía de San Juan del Norte
Cárdenas
ISLAS SOLENTINAME
ISLA MANCORNADO
ISLA VENADA
RÍO SAN JUAN
Los Chiles
El Castillo
San Juan del Norte
La Cruz
Volcán Orosí 1487
Caño Negro
Santa Rosa
Upala
NICARAGUA
COSTA RICA
Colorado
Curubande
Volcán Miravalles 2028
Hacienda Miravalles
ALAJUELA
Liberia
Bagaces
Altamira
HEREDIA
Sardinal
Tilarán
Arenal
La Fortuna
Volcán Arenal 1633
Venecia
Puerto Viejo
Filadelfia
Cañas
GUANACASTE
Portegolpe
Quesada
Las Juntas
Guápiles
Santa Cruz
Veintisiete de Abril
San Antonio
Nicoya
Zarcero
Volcán Poás 2704
Volcán Barba 2906
Parismina
Siquirres
Cerro Brujo 982
La Mansión
Miramar
Lagarto
San Ramón
Naranjo
Grecia
Alajuela
Heredia
Volcán Turrialba 3329
Volcán Irazú 3432
PUNTARENAS
Puntarenas
Esparta
San José
Guadalupe
Turrialba
Moravia
Limón
PENÍNSULA DE NICOYA
Lepanto
Cerro Azul 1018
Paquera
Carrillo
Orotina
Santiago
Cartago
Tres Ríos
Juan Viñas
Paraíso
Cerro Matama 2251
Vesta
PUNTA COYOTE
San Francisco
Tambor
Golfo de Nicoya
PUNTA LEONA
Cerro Turrubares 1756
Playa Bonita
San Ignacio
Cerro Caraigres 2505
San Marcos
CARTAGO
CORDILLERA DE TALAMANCA
LIMÓN
PUNTA CAHUITA
Puerto Viejo
PUNTA MONA
Cabuya
CABO BLANCO
PUNTA JUDAS
Parrita
Santa María
Cerro Chirripó 3819
Cerro Buenavista 3491
SAN JOSÉ
Suretka
Amubri
Guabito
ISLA COLÓN
ARCHIPIÉLAGO DE BOCAS DEL TORO
Bocas del Toro
ISLA BASTIMENTOS
BOCAS DEL TORO
Almirante
Quepos
San Isidro del General
Palmares
Convento
Cerro Kamuk 3554
Buenos Aires
COSTA RICA
PANAMÁ
Cusapin
PUNTA VALIENTE
PENÍNSULA VALIENTE
ISLA ESCUDO DE VERAGUAS
Golfo de los Mosquitos
Dominical
PUNTA DOMINICAL
PUNTA MALA
Bahía de Coronado
ISLA VIOLÍN
Puerto Cortés
Boruca
Potrero Grande
Cerro Fábrega 3335
Palmar Sur
Cerro Pando 2468
Volcán de Chiriquí (Volcán Barú) 3475
Chiriquí Grande
Laguna de Chiriquí
BOCAS DEL TORO
PUNTARENAS
Las Cruces
San Vito
Cerro 1683
Hato del Volcán
Boquete
Cerro Chorcha 2238
Piedra Roja
Santa Catalina
ISLA DEL CAÑO
Rincón
Golfito
Plaza de Caisán
San Andrés
Potrerillos Arriba
Río Grande
SERRANÍA DE TABASARÁ
PENÍNSULA DE OSA
Cerro Tigre 782
Puerto Jiménez
Golfo Dulce
La Unión de Coto
La Cuesta
Concepción
Boquerón
Gualaca
Cerro Santiago 2826
Peña Blanca
Santa Fe
PUNTA SAN PEDRO
PUNTA SALSIPUEDES
CABO MATAPALO
PUNTA BANCO
Divalá
Alanje
David
CHIRIQUÍ
Dolega
Boca del Monte
Chiriquí
Pedregal
Horconcitos
Las Lajas
Chichica
Tolé
Remedios
Canazas
VERAGUAS
Calobre
San Francisco
Pocrí
Pico Burica 708
Puerto Armuelles
ISLA SEVILLA
ISLA BOCA BRAVA
ISLA PARIDA
Bahía de Charco Azul
Golfo de Chiriquí
ISLAS SECAS
PUNTA BURICA
Las Palmas
La Mesa
Santiago
Soná
Río de Jesús
Montijo
Atalaya
Ocú
HERRERA
Monagrillo
La Arena
Pesé
Chitré
LOS SANTOS
Santa María
Aguadulce
Bahía de Parita
PUNTA LISA
Gulf of Panama
Natá
Antón
Río Hato
Ola
Penonomé
El Valle
Tranquilla
San Carlos
Chame
COCLÉ
Cerro Gaital 1185
La Pintada
Bejuco
COLÓN
La Chorrera
PANAMÁ
Lídice
Capira
Panamá
Balboa
Balboa Heights
Taboga
Bay of Panama
PUNTA CHAME
ISLA OTOQUE
ISLA BONÁ
CANAL ZONE
(U.S.)
Colón
Cristóbal
GATUN LOCKS
Gatún L.
Rainbow City
Puerto Pilón
ISTHMUS OF PANAMA
Portobelo
PUNTA MANZANILLO
Nombre de Dios
Cerro Bruja 979
Palmas Bellas
Nuevo Chagres
Miguel de la Borda
Escobal
Gamboa
Paraíso
Madden L.
MIRAFLORES LOCKS
RODMAN NAVAL STATION

Kilometers 0 50 100 150 Km.

Statute Miles 0 50 100 150 Mi.

Scale 1:3,000,000

One centimeter represents 30 kilometers.

One inch represents approximately 47 miles.

Lambert Conformal Conic Projection

Caribbean Region

GULF OF MEXICO
UNITED STATES
FLORIDA
The Everglades
Fort Myers
Belle Glade
West Palm Beach
Palm Beach
Lake Worth
Delray Beach
Boca Raton
Pompano Beach
Fort Lauderdale
Hollywood
Hialeah
MIAMI
Miami Beach
Coral Gables
Homestead
Naples
Everglades
CAPE SABLE
EVERGLADES NATIONAL PARK
Florida Bay
FLORIDA KEYS
Key Largo
Key West
DRY TORTUGAS
MARQUESAS KEYS
Straits of Florida
West End
Freeport
GRAND BAHAMA
Marsh Harbour
GREAT ABACO
Cherokee Sound
Alice Town
BIMINI ISLANDS
Northwest Providence Channel
Northeast Providence Channel
BERRY ISLANDS
Nassau
NEW PROVIDENCE
Nicolls Town
Adelaide
ANDROS ISLAND
Andros Town
Tongue of the Ocean
Kemps Bay
ELEUTHERA
Governors Harbour
Rock Sound
Dunmore Town
BAHAMAS (U.K.)
Exuma Sound
Arthurs Town
CAT ISLAND
The Bight
Old Bight
GREAT EXUMA
RUM CAY
LONG ISLAND
Deadmans Cay
Clarence Town
CROOKED ISLAND
RAGGED ISLAND
SALINA POINT
CAY SAL BANK
GREAT BAHAMA BANK
Old Bahama Channel
Nicholas Channel
ARCHIPIÉLAGO DE SABANA
LA HABANA
HAVANA
Mariano
Guanabacoa
Matanzas
Cárdenas
Guanajay
Artemisa
San Antonio de los Baños
Jovellanos
Güines
Colón
Sagua la Grande
Camajuaní
Caibarién
Santa Clara
Placetas
Cienfuegos
Trinidad
Sancti-Spíritus
Ciego de Ávila
Morón
Florida
Camagüey
Nuevitas
Puerto Manatí
Vertientes
Victoria de las Tunas
Puerto Padre
Holguín
Gibara
Banes
Bayamo
Manzanillo
Palma Soriano
Santiago de Cuba
Guantánamo
Baracoa
SIERRA MAESTRA
Pico Turquino 1994
CABO CRUZ
Golfo de Guacanayabo
JARDINES DE LA REINA
Golfo de Ana María
Pinar del Río
Golfo de Batabanó
Golfo de Guanahacabibes
CABO SAN ANTONIO
ISLA DE PINOS
ISLE OF PINES
Nueva Gerona
Santa Fé
CAYO LARGO
CUBA
CAYMAN ISLANDS (U.K.)
Georgetown
GRAND CAYMAN
LITTLE CAYMAN
CAYMAN BRAC
WEST INDIES
GREATER
JAMAICA
Montego Bay
Falmouth
Ocho Rios
Saint Ann's Bay
Port Maria
Savanna-la-Mar
Mandeville
Mount Denham 986
Kingston
Blue Mountain Peak 2256
Port Antonio
Morant Bay
Spanish Town
May Pen
PORTLAND POINT
MORANT CAYS
NAVASSA ISLAND (U.S.)
Jamaica Channel
Windward
Yucatan Channel
YUCATAN PENINSULA
YUCATÁN
MEXICO
MÉXICO
QUINTANA ROO
Isla Mujeres
Puerto Juárez
PUNTA CANCÚN
Puerto Morelos
Cozumel
ISLA DE COZUMEL
Tulum
Chemax
Kantunilkín
CABO CATOCHE
BANCO CHINCHORRO
Bahía de la Ascensión
Bahía del Espíritu Santo
LIGHTHOUSE REEF
GLOVER REEF
MISTERIOSA BANK
ROSARIO BANK
SWAN ISLANDS (Hond.)
THUNDER KNOLL
ROSALIND BANK
SERRANILLA BANK (Claimed by Col. and U.S.)
Gulf of Honduras
ISLAS DE LA BAHÍA
Roatán
Guanaja
Utila
CABO DE HONDURAS
CABO CAMARÓN
PUNTA PATUCA
Trujillo
La Ceiba
Tela
El Triunfo
Colorado
Balfate
Tocoa
Limón
Olanchito
Yoro
Cerro Payas 1128
Brus Laguna
Paya
CORDILLERA DE AGALTA
Guanpata
Catacamas
Juticalpa
Minas de Oro
Salamá
San Ignacio
Guaimaca
MONTAÑAS DE COMAYAGUA
Tegucigalpa
Yuscarán
Danlí
Güinope
Sabanagrande
HONDURAS
NICARAGUA
Cerro Yelucá 1128
CORDILLERA ISABELLA
Cerro Mogotón 2107
Ocotal
Somoto
Cerro Kilambé 1750
Cerro Piu 1800
Bonanza
Siuna
Choluteca
San Marcos de Colón
Condega
Estelí
San Rafael del Norte
Jinotega
Matagalpa
CORDILLERA DE DARIÉN
Sébaco
Ciudad Darío
Boaco
Puerto Morazán
El Sauce
El Viejo
Chinandega
León
Volcán San Cristóbal 1745
Volcán Momotombo 1491
La Paz Centro
Nagarote
Managua
Tipitapa
Masaya
Granada
Diriamba
Masatepe
Nandaime
Juigalpa
Santo Tomás
Acoyapa
Jesús María
La Libertad
Santo Domingo
Villa Somoza
Rama
Muelle de los Bueyes
La Flor
SIERRA DE AMERIQUE
Lago de Nicaragua
Volcán Concepción 1610
ISLA DE OMETEPE
Belén
Rivas
San Juan del Sur
San Carlos
El Castillo
San Juan del Norte
Colorado
Bahía de San Juan del Norte
Punta Gorda
Bluefields
El Bluff
Laguna de Perlas
Río Grande
Prinzapolca
Huaunta
Tungla
La Cruz
Puerto Cabezas
Yablis
Waspán
Bilwaskarma
San Ramón
Bocay
CABO GRACIAS A DIOS
CAYOS MISKITOS
PUNTA GORDA
ARRECIFE DE LA MEDIA LUNA
QUITA SUEÑO BANK (Claimed by Col. and U.S.)
SERRANA BANK (Claimed by Col. and U.S.)
RONCADOR BANK (Claimed by Col. and U.S.)
ISLA DE PROVIDENCIA
SAN ANDRÉS Y PROVIDENCIA (Col.)
ISLA DE SAN ANDRÉS
San Andrés
CORN ISLANDS (Nic.)
CAYOS DE ALBUQUERQUE
CARIBBEAN
COSTA RICA
CORDILLERA DE GUANACASTE
Volcán Miravalles 2028
Golfo del Papagayo
CABO VELAS
Liberia
Bagaces
Cañas
Santa Cruz
Nicoya
PENÍNSULA DE NICOYA
Cerro Azul 1018
Golfo de Nicoya
CABO BLANCO
Puntarenas
Esparza
La Fortuna
Venecia
San Ramón
Puerto Viejo
Alajuela
Heredia
Guápiles
Siquirres
Limón
Volcán Irazú 3432
San José
Cartago
Juan Viñas
Cerro Chirripó 3819
Vesta
Cerro Buenavista 3491
San Isidro
CORDILLERA DE TALAMANCA
Buenos Aires
Puerto Cortés
Bahía de Coronado
PUNTA MONA
PANAMA
Cerro Kamuk 3554
Almirante
Bocas del Toro
Laguna de Chiriquí
Volcán de Chiriquí 3475
Boquete
Chiriquí Grande
PENÍNSULA VALIENTE
Golfo de los Mosquitos
CANAL ZONE (U.S.)
Colón
Portobelo
Nombre de Dios
Palmas Bellas
Cristóbal
Gatun Lake
Gamboa
Balboa
Panamá
Madden Lake
CORDILLERA DE SAN BLAS
ISTHMUS OF PANAMA
Golfo de San Blas
Ustupo
Playón Grande
Ailigandí
PUNTA MOSQUITO
Mulatupo
PACIFIC OCEAN
Santa Marta
CABO DE LA AGUJA
Barranquilla
Ciénaga
Soledad
Puerto Colombia
ATLÁNTICO
Cartagena
Turbaco
Arjona
Calamar
BOLÍVAR
San Onofre
San Jacinto
El Carmen de Bolívar
Golfo de Morrosquillo
Tolú
Sincelejo
Corozal
Magangué
CÓRDOBA
Sahagún
SUCRE
San Bernardo del Viento
Lorica
ISLAS DE SAN BERNARDO
ISLAS DEL ROSARIO
Copyright © by Rand McNally & Co.
Map prepared by Rand McNally & Co.
A-530100-264

ATLANTIC
OCEAN
Tropic of Cancer
WEST
INDIES
ANTILLES
SEA
TURKS AND CAICOS ISLANDS
(U.K.)
CAICOS ISLANDS
TURKS ISLANDS
Grand Turk
GREAT INAGUA
MAYAGUANA
SILVER BANK
MOUCHOIR BANK
HAITI
HAÏTI
HISPANIOLA
Cap-Haïtien
Gonaïves
Port-au-Prince
Les Cayes
Jacmel
Santiago
Puerto Plata
San Francisco de Macorís
Santo Domingo
La Romana
Higüey
San Pedro de Macorís
DOMINICAN REPUBLIC
REPÚBLICA DOMINICANA
PUERTO RICO
(U.S.)
San Juan
Arecibo
Aguadilla
Mayagüez
Ponce
Caguas
Bayamón
Guayama
VIRGIN ISLANDS
(U.S.)
(U.K.)
Charlotte Amalie
Road Town
Christiansted
Frederiksted
SAINT CROIX
Anegada Passage
SOMBRERO
ANGUILLA
(U.K.)
Marigot
Philipsburg
SAINT MARTIN
SINT MAARTEN
(Guad and Neth Ant.)
SAINT BARTHÉLEMY
(Guad.)
SABA
(Neth.Ant.)
SINT EUSTATIUS
(Neth.Ant.)
SAINT CHRISTOPHER
(SAINT KITTS)
Basseterre
Charlestown
NEVIS
SAINT KITTS-NEVIS-ANGUILLA
(U.K.)
ANTIGUA
(U.K.)
Saint Johns
BARBUDA
LEEWARD ISLANDS
REDONDA
MONTSERRAT
(U.K.)
Plymouth
LESSER ANTILLES
GRANDE-TERRE
Pointe-à-Pitre
Le Moule
GUADELOUPE
Basse-Terre
BASSE-TERRE
MARIE GALANTE
Grand-Bourg
LES DES SAINTES
DOMINICA
(U.K.)
Roseau
Marigot
Dominica Channel
Montagne Pelée
Fort-de-France
MARTINIQUE
(Fr.)
Saint Lucia Channel
Castries
SAINT LUCIA
(U.K.)
Vieux Fort
Saint Vincent Passage
Kingstown
SAINT VINCENT
(U.K.)
Bridgetown
BARBADOS
WINDWARD ISLANDS
GRENADINES
CARRIACOU
GRENADA
(U.K.)
Saint George's
TOBAGO
TRINIDAD AND TOBAGO
Port of Spain
San Fernando
NETHERLANDS ANTILLES
NEDERLANDSE ANTILLEN
Oranjestad
ARUBA
Willemstad
CURAÇAO
BONAIRE
ISLAS DE AVES (Ven.)
ISLAS LOS ROQUES (Ven.)
LA ORCHILA (Ven.)
LA BLANQUILLA (Ven.)
ISLAS LOS HERMANOS (Ven.)
ISLAS LOS TESTIGOS (Ven.)
ISLA DE MARGARITA
LA GUAJIRA
Riohacha
COLOMBIA
VENEZUELA
Maracaibo
Golfo de Venezuela
Lago de Maracaibo
Cabimas
Punto Fijo
Coro
FALCÓN
Barquisimeto
LARA
ZULIA
TRUJILLO
Valera
Puerto Cabello
Valencia
Maracay
CARACAS
La Guaira
Maiquetía
MIRANDA
ARAGUA
CARABOBO
San Juan de los Morros
GUÁRICO
COJEDES
PORTUGUESA
Acarigua
Barcelona
Puerto la Cruz
Cumaná
SUCRE
Carúpano
ANZOÁTEGUI
MONAGAS
Maturín
El Tigre
DELTA AMACURO
72°
70°
68°
66°
64°
62°
60°
24°
22°
20°
18°
16°
14°
12°
10°

Kilometers 0 100 200 300 Km.

Statute Miles 0 100 200 300 Mi.

Scale 1:6,000,000

One centimeter represents 60 kilometers.
One inch represents approximately 95 miles.
Lambert Conformal Conic Projection

a

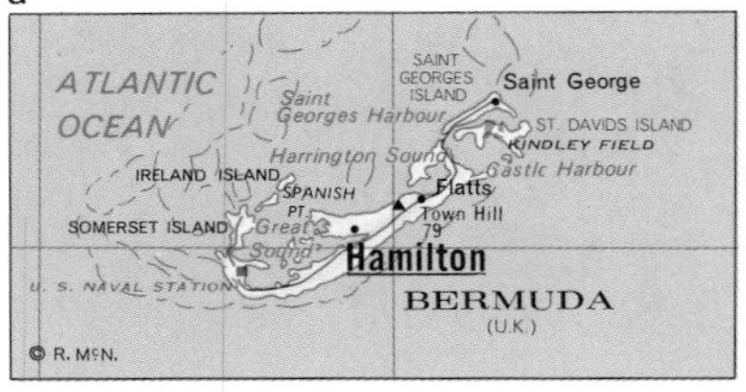
ATLANTIC
OCEAN
Saint George
ST. DAVIDS ISLAND
KINDLEY FIELD
Castle Harbour
Harrington Sound
IRELAND ISLAND
Flatts
Town Hill
SOMERSET ISLAND
Great Sound
Hamilton
BERMUDA
(U.K.)
64° 45′
32° 15′
65°

b

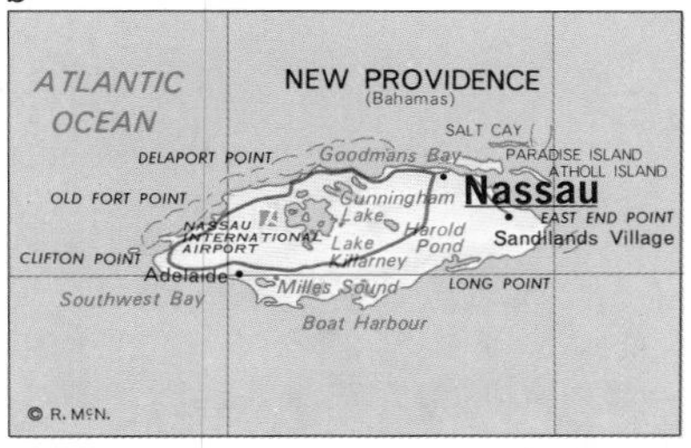
ATLANTIC
OCEAN
NEW PROVIDENCE
(Bahamas)
SALT CAY
DELAPORT POINT
PARADISE ISLAND
ATHOLL ISLAND
OLD FORT POINT
Nassau
EAST END POINT
CLIFTON POINT
Sandilands Village
Adelaide
LONG POINT
Southwest Bay
Boat Harbour
25°
77° 30′
77° 15′

c

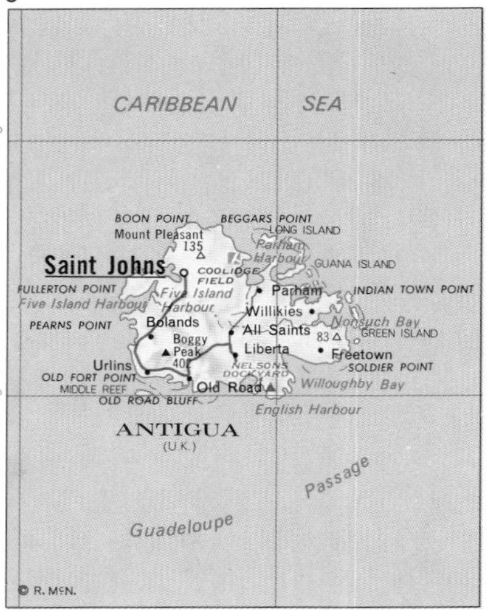
CARIBBEAN
SEA
61° 45′
17° 15′
BOON POINT
BEGGARS POINT
Mount Pleasant
LONG ISLAND
Saint Johns
GUANA ISLAND
FULLERTON POINT
Five Island Harbour
PEARNS POINT
Parham
INDIAN TOWN POINT
Willikies
Bolands
All Saints
GREEN ISLAND
Liberta
Freetown
Urlins
SOLDIER POINT
OLD FORT POINT
Old Road
Willoughby Bay
English Harbour
ANTIGUA
(U.K.)
17°
Passage
Guadeloupe
62°

d

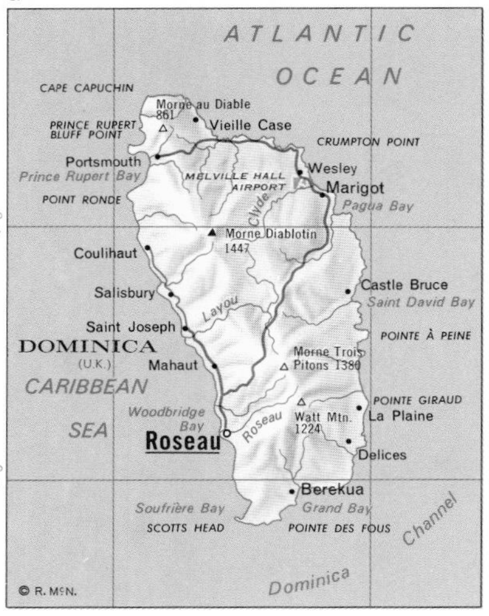
ATLANTIC
OCEAN
61° 30′
61° 15′
CAPE CAPUCHIN
Morne au Diable
Vieille Case
PRINCE RUPERT BLUFF POINT
CRUMPTON POINT
Portsmouth
Prince Rupert Bay
Wesley
Marigot
POINT RONDE
Pagua Bay
Morne Diablotin
1447
Coulihaut
Castle Bruce
Saint David Bay
Salisbury
Saint Joseph
POINTE À PEINE
DOMINICA
(U.K.)
Mahaut
Morne Trois Pitons 1390
CARIBBEAN
SEA
Watt Mtn.
1224
POINTE GIRAUD
La Plaine
Roseau
Delices
Berekua
Grand Bay
Soufrière Bay
SCOTTS HEAD
POINTE DES FOUS
Dominica
Channel
15° 30′
15° 15′

e

ATLANTIC
OCEAN
Dominica Channel
Grand Rivière
POINTE DU MACOUBA
CAP SAINT-MARTIN
Basse-Pointe
Le Lorrain
Montagne Pelée
1397
Le Prêcheur
POINTE LA MARE
Morne-Rouge
Sainte-Marie
La Trinité
Saint-Pierre
Le Carbet
Gros-Morne
Bellefontaine
Le Robert
Case-Pilote
Saint Joseph
Fort-de-France
Le Lamentin
Le François
MARTINIQUE
(Fr.)
Ducos
Le Saint-Esprit
Le Vauclin
Trois-Îlets
Rivière-Salée
CAP SALOMON
Les Anses-d'Arlets
Le Diamant
Sainte-Luce
Rivière-Pilote
Le Marin
Sainte-Anne
CARIBBEAN
SEA
Saint Lucia Channel
61° 15′
61°
60° 45′
14° 45′
14° 30′

m

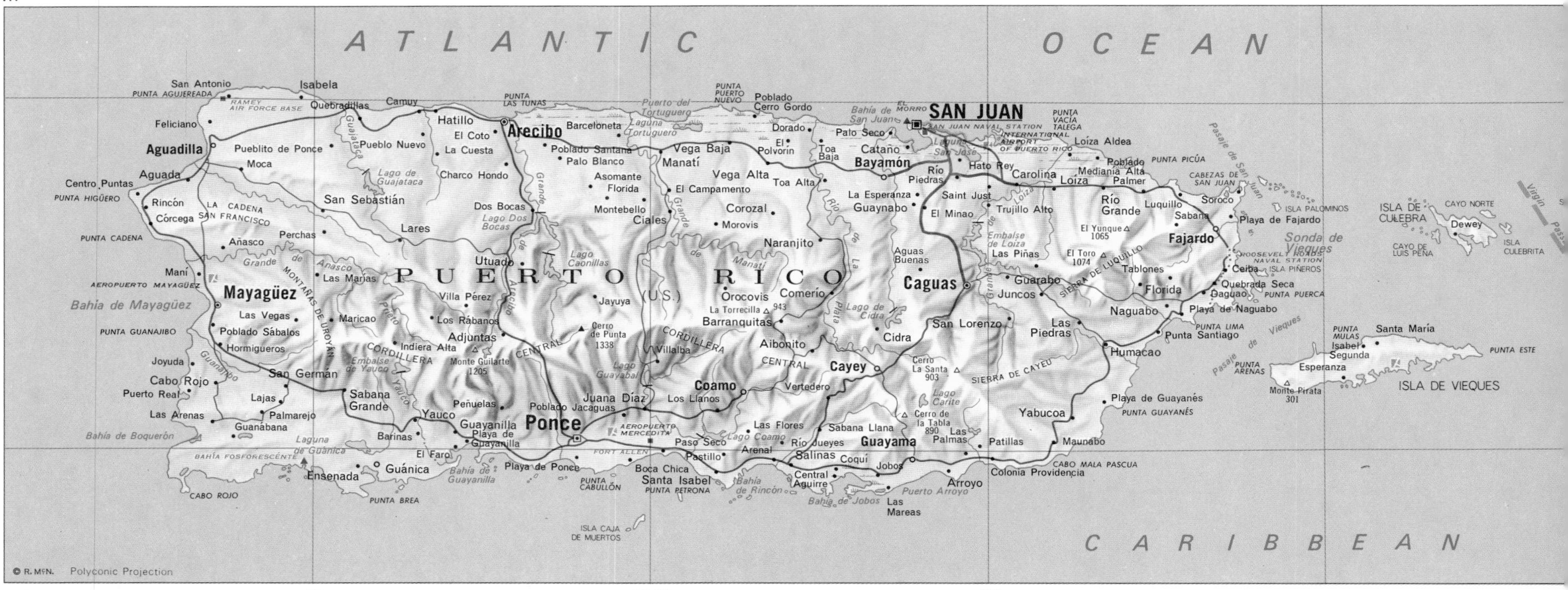
ATLANTIC
OCEAN
SAN JUAN
Isabela
Camuy
Hatillo
Arecibo
Aguadilla
Barceloneta
Manatí
Vega Baja
Vega Alta
Dorado
Cataño
Bayamón
Carolina
Loiza
Río Grande
Luquillo
Fajardo
Rincón
Mayagüez
San Sebastián
Lares
Utuado
Ciales
Corozal
Naranjito
Caguas
Humacao
PUERTO RICO
(U.S.)
Cayey
Coamo
Juana Díaz
Ponce
Guayanilla
Yauco
San Germán
Cabo Rojo
Guánica
Salinas
Guayama
Arroyo
Patillas
Maunabo
Yabucoa
Santa Isabel
ISLA DE CULEBRA
ISLA DE VIEQUES
Isabel Segunda
CARIBBEAN
Polyconic Projection
67°
66° 30′
66°
65° 30′
18° 30′
18°

p

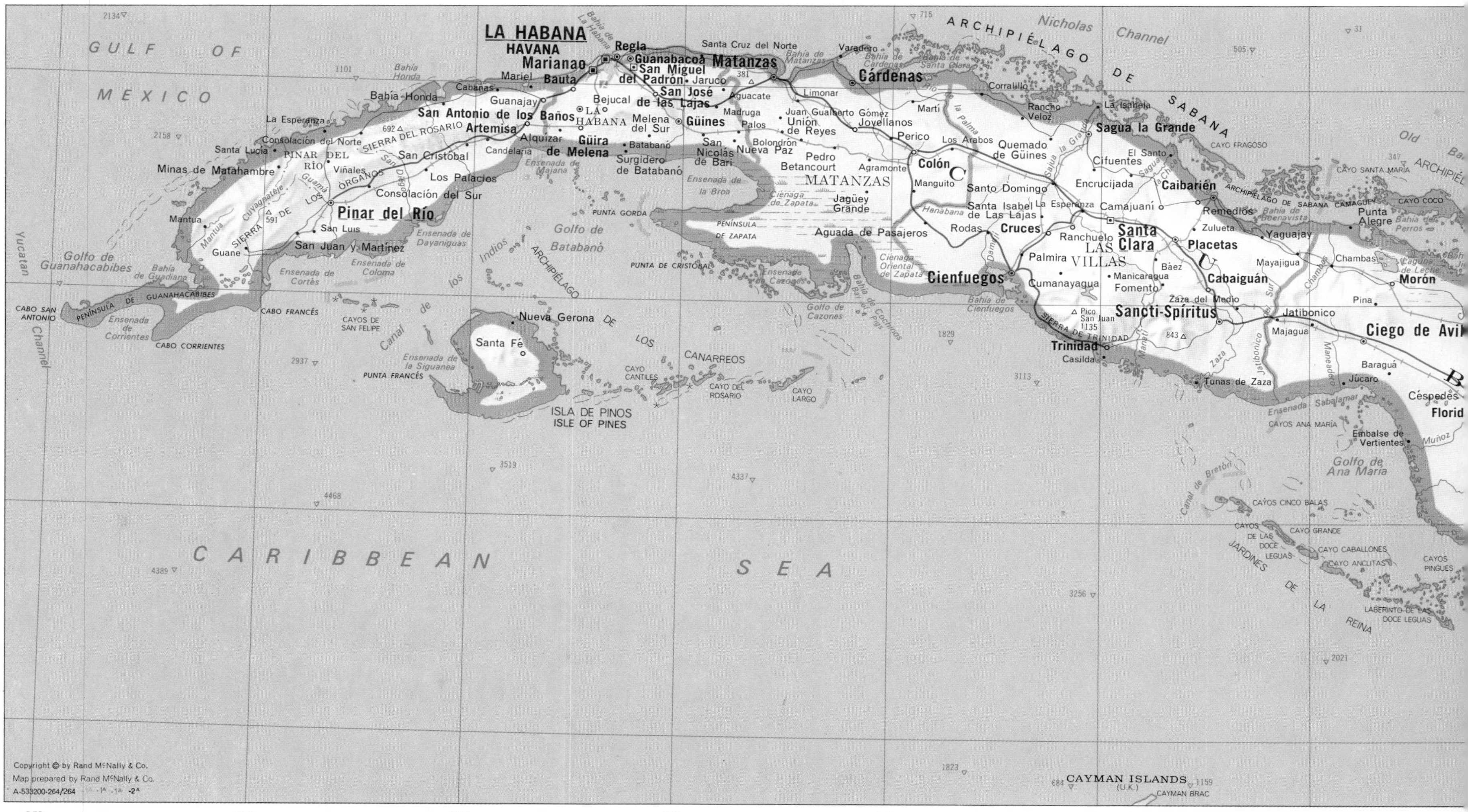
GULF OF MEXICO
LA HABANA
HAVANA
Marianao
Regla
Guanabacoa
Matanzas
Cárdenas
Bahía Honda
Artemisa
San Antonio de los Baños
Güines
Pinar del Río
PINAR DEL RÍO
LA HABANA
MATANZAS
Colón
Sagua la Grande
Caibarién
Santa Clara
LAS VILLAS
Cienfuegos
Trinidad
Sancti-Spíritus
Cabaiguán
Placetas
Morón
Ciego de Avila
Nueva Gerona
ISLA DE PINOS
ISLE OF PINES
ARCHIPIÉLAGO DE SABANA
Nicholas Channel
Golfo de Batabanó
CARIBBEAN SEA
CAYMAN ISLANDS
(U.K.)
Yucatan Channel
Golfo de Guanahacabibes
Golfo de Ana María
JARDINES DE LA REINA
85°
84°
83°
82°
81°
80°
79°
23°
22°
21°
20°

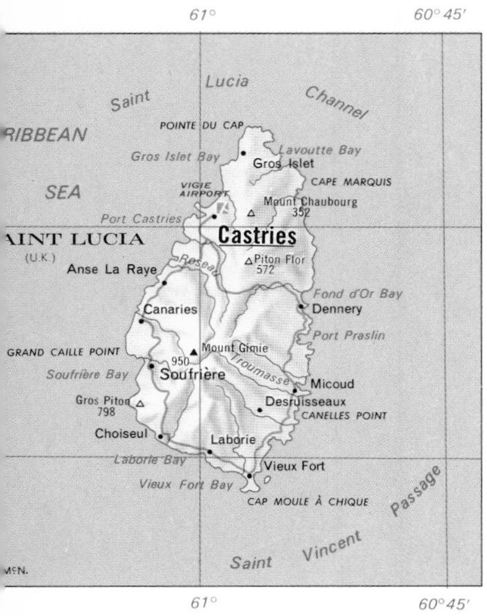
SAINT LUCIA
(U.K.)
Castries
Saint Lucia Channel
Gros Islet
Soufrière
Vieux Fort
Saint Vincent Passage
CARIBBEAN SEA

g

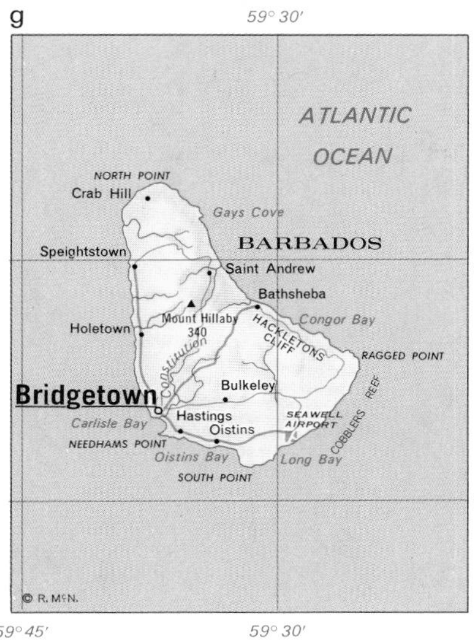
ATLANTIC OCEAN
BARBADOS
Bridgetown
Speightstown
Holetown
Bathsheba
Mount Hillaby
340
Oistins

h

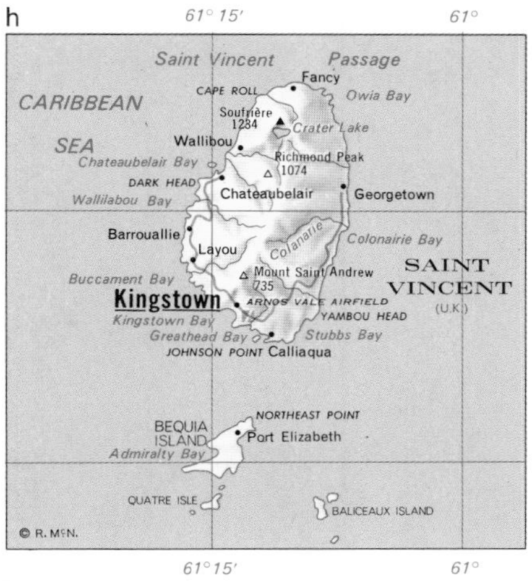
Saint Vincent Passage
CARIBBEAN SEA
SAINT VINCENT
(U.K.)
Kingstown
Georgetown
Chateaubelair
Soufrière
1234
BEQUIA ISLAND
Port Elizabeth

k

CARIBBEAN SEA
GRENADA
(U.K.)
St. George's
Grenville
Gouyave
Victoria
Sauteurs

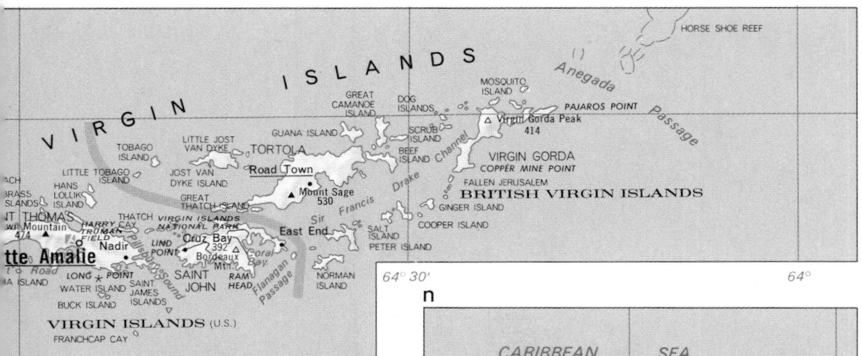
VIRGIN ISLANDS
BRITISH VIRGIN ISLANDS
VIRGIN ISLANDS (U.S.)
TORTOLA
Road Town
VIRGIN GORDA
Anegada Passage
Charlotte Amalie
SAINT JOHN
SAINT THOMAS
SEA

n

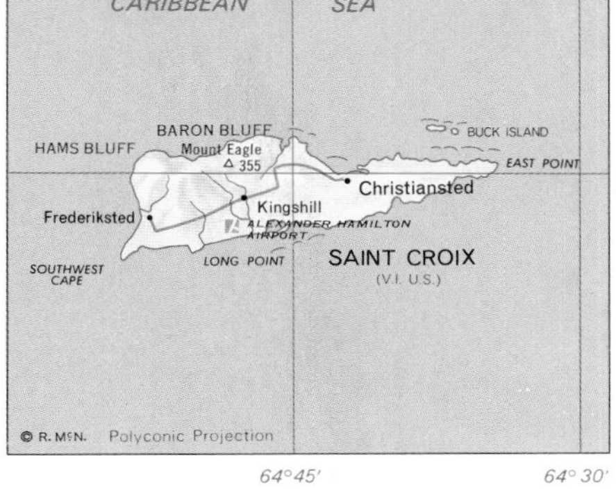
CARIBBEAN SEA
SAINT CROIX
(V.I. U.S.)
Christiansted
Frederiksted
Kingshill
Polyconic Projection

o

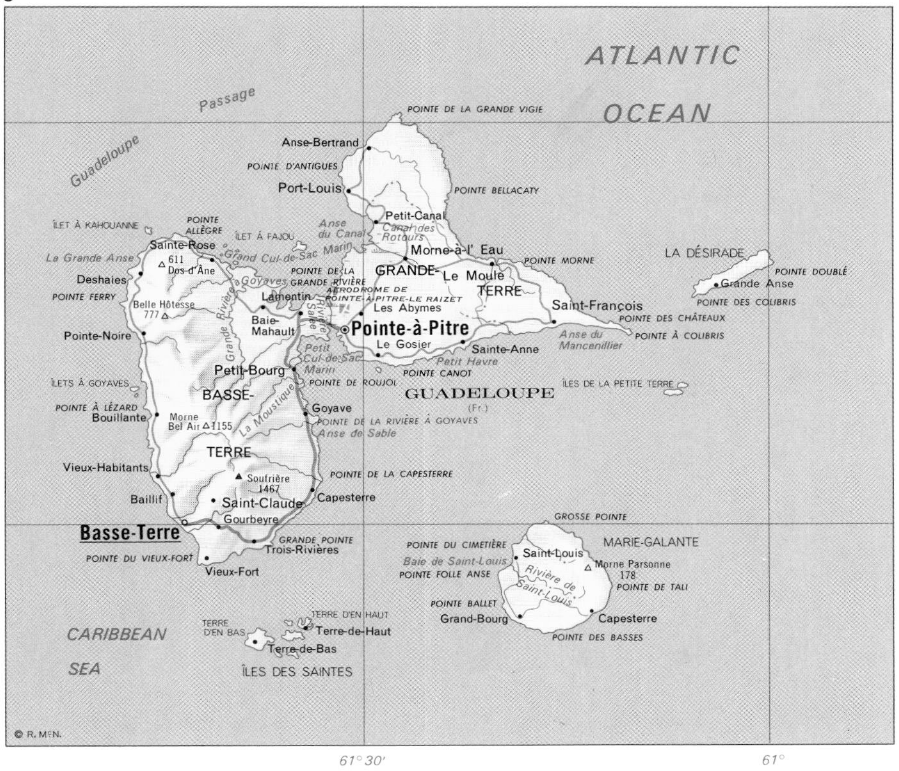
ATLANTIC OCEAN
GUADELOUPE
(Fr.)
Basse-Terre
Pointe-à-Pitre
GRANDE-TERRE
BASSE-TERRE
MARIE-GALANTE
LA DÉSIRADE
ÎLES DES SAINTES
CARIBBEAN SEA
Guadeloupe Passage

Kilometers 0 10 20 30 40 50 Km.
Statute Miles 0 10 20 30 40 50 Mi.

Scale 1:1,000,000
One centimeter represents 10 kilometers.
One inch represents approximately 16 miles.
Transverse Mercator Projection (except as noted)

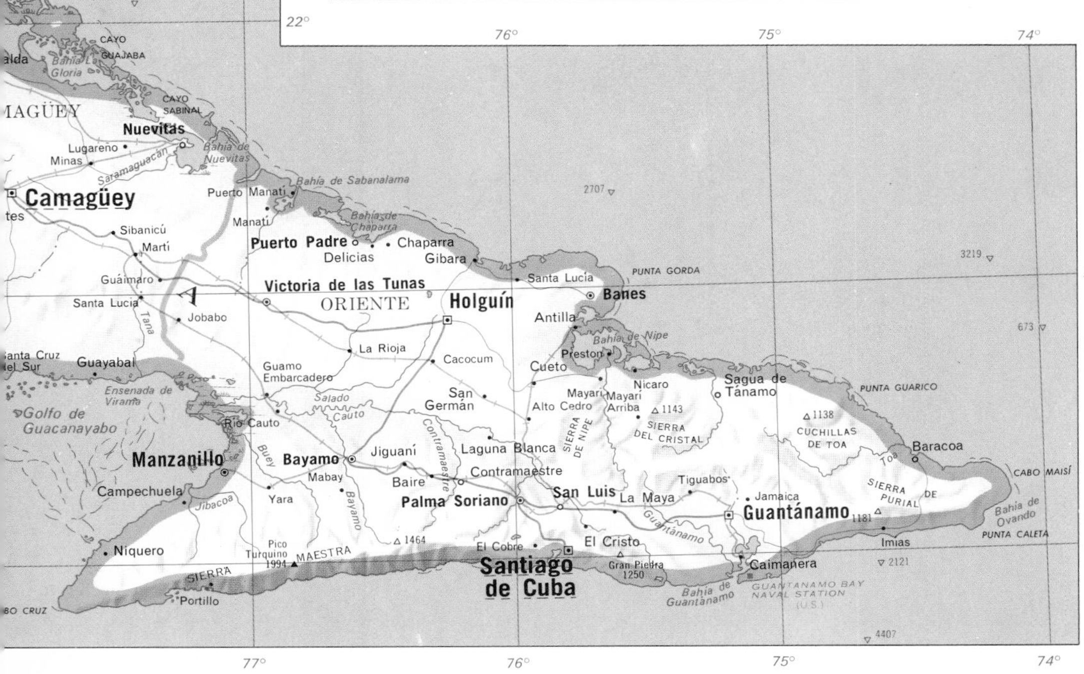
ATLANTIC OCEAN
Camagüey
Nuevitas
Holguín
ORIENTE
Victoria de las Tunas
Puerto Padre
Banes
Manzanillo
Bayamo
Palma Soriano
Santiago de Cuba
Guantánamo
Baracoa
Golfo de Guacanayabo
SIERRA MAESTRA

q

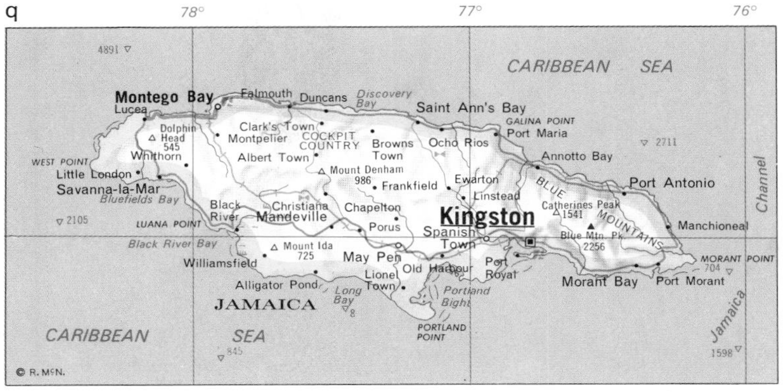
CARIBBEAN SEA
JAMAICA
Kingston
Montego Bay
Spanish Town
Mandeville
Port Antonio
Savanna-la-Mar
BLUE MOUNTAINS
Jamaica Channel

r

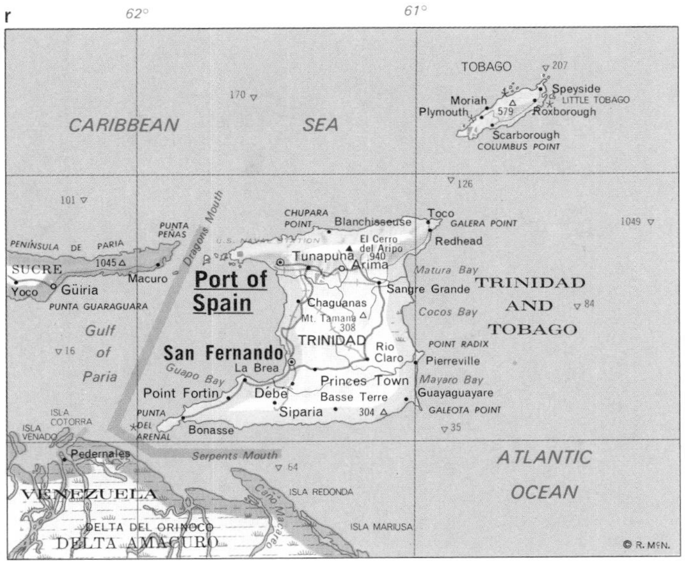
CARIBBEAN SEA
TRINIDAD AND TOBAGO
TOBAGO
TRINIDAD
Port of Spain
San Fernando
Scarborough
Gulf of Paria
ATLANTIC OCEAN
VENEZUELA

s

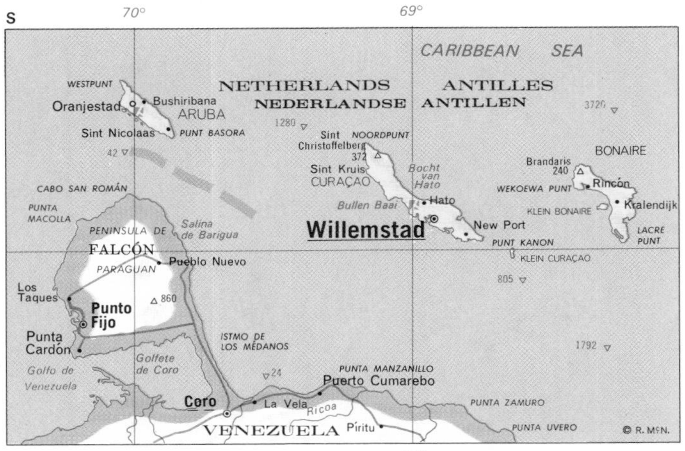
CARIBBEAN SEA
NETHERLANDS ANTILLES
NEDERLANDSE ANTILLEN
ARUBA
Oranjestad
CURAÇAO
Willemstad
BONAIRE
Kralendijk
FALCÓN
Punto Fijo
Coro
VENEZUELA

Kilometers 0 50 100 150 Km.
Statute Miles 0 50 100 150 Mi.

Scale 1:3,000,000
One centimeter represents 30 kilometers.
One inch represents approximately 47 miles.
Lambert Conformal Conic Projection

Northern South America

CARIBBEAN SEA
PACIFIC OCEAN
NICARAGUA
COSTA RICA
PANAMA
COLOMBIA
VENEZUELA
ECUADOR
PERU
BOLIVIA
CHILE
ARGENTINA
NETHERLANDS ANTILLES
LESSER ANTILLES
TRINIDAD
CANAL ZONE
Managua
Granada
San José
Colón
Panamá
Barranquilla
Cartagena
Santa Marta
Maracaibo
Caracas
Valencia
Barquisimeto
Maracay
Medellín
Bogotá
Cali
Manizales
Bucaramanga
Cúcuta
Quito
Guayaquil
Cuenca
Iquitos
Lima
Callao
Trujillo
Chiclayo
Piura
Arequipa
Cuzco
La Paz
Cochabamba
Oruro
Sucre
Potosí
Santa Cruz
Arica
Iquique
Ciudad Bolívar
Amazon
Orinoco
Equator
Gulf of Panama
ISTHMUS OF PANAMA
CORDILLERA OCCIDENTAL
CORDILLERA CENTRAL
CORDILLERA ORIENTAL
CORDILLERA BLANCA
CORDILLERA NEGRA
CORDILLERA REAL
ALTIPLANO
LLANOS
SELVA
LLANOS DE MOXOS
LA GRAN SABANA
DESIERTO DE ATACAMA
SIERRA PARIMA
SERRA DOS PACAÁS NOVOS
Lago de Maracaibo
Lago Titicaca
Salar de Uyuni
Salar de Coipasa
Lago de Poopó
Iquitos
Leticia
Pucallpa
Huancayo
Ayacucho
Tumbes
Chimbote
Ica
Nazca
Tacna
Puno
Juliaca
Riobamba
Ambato
Esmeraldas
Manta
Buenaventura
Pasto
Popayán
Ibagué
Neiva
Villavicencio
Mérida
San Cristóbal
Cumaná
Barcelona
Maturín
Valledupar
Porto Velho
Rio Branco
Trinidad
Tarija
Copyright © by Rand McNally & Co.
Map prepared by Esselte Map Service AB, Stockholm.
A-549100-264

Kilometers 0 200 400 600 Km.
Statute Miles 0 200 400 600 Mi.

Scale 1:12,000,000 One centimeter represents 120 kilometers.
One inch represents approximately 190 miles.
Oblique Conic Conformal Projection

ATLANTIC OCEAN
Equator
Tropic of Capricorn
BRAZIL
SURINAM
FRENCH GUIANA
Georgetown
Paramaribo
Cayenne
New Amsterdam
Nieuw Nickerie
Nieuw Amsterdam
Moengo
Albina
Saint-Laurent-du-Maroni
Sinnamary
ÎLE DU DIABLE
Kourou
Brokopondo
Saint-Élie
Matoury
Régina
Saint-Georges
Oiapoque
CABO ORANGE
Saül
Julianatop 1280
WILHELMINA GEBERGTE
ORANJE GEBERGTE
TUMUC-HUMAC MOUNTAINS
ACARAÍ MOUNTAINS
Cunani
Calçoene
Amapá
ILHA DE MARACÁ
Serra do Navio
ILHA BAILIQUE
ILHA CURUÁ
ILHA JANAUCU
ILHA CAVIANA
ILHA MEXIANA
Macapá
Mazagão
CABO MAGUARINHO
ILHA DE MARAJÓ
Belém
Bragança
Carutapera
Breves
Gurupá
Porto de Moz
Amazonas
Amazon
Óbidos
Oriximiná
Alenquer
Monte Alegre
Santarém
Faro
Parintins
Maués
Itaituba
Altamira
Tucuruí
Cametá
Camiranga
Turiaçu
Alcântara
São Luís
Pinheiro
São Bento
Viana
Rosário
Itapecuru-Mirim
Tutóia
Camocim
Parnaíba
Acaraú
Fortaleza
Maranguape
Parangaba
Baturité
Sobral
Brejo
Barras
Codó
Caxias
Bacabal
Pedreiras
Monção
Teresina
Campo Maior
Crateús
Quixadá
Russas
Aracati
Areia Branca
Mossoró
Macau
CABO DE SÃO ROQUE
Ceará-Mirim
Natal
Angicos
Lajes
Caicó
Currais Novos
Nova Cruz
Iguatu
Icó
Sousa
Cajazeiras
Patos
Crato
Juazeiro do Norte
Campina Grande
Guarabira
Rio Tinto
Cabedelo
João Pessoa
Goiana
Olinda
Recife
Jaboatão
Cabo
Caruaru
Pesqueira
Arcoverde
Sertânia
Flores
Serra Talhada
Garanhuns
Palmares
Barreiros
Porto de Pedras
União dos Palmares
Palmeira dos Índios
Arapiraca
Rio Largo
Maceió
Penedo
Propriá
Coruripe
Paulo Afonso
Petrolina
Juazeiro
Remanso
Aracaju
São Cristóvão
Estância
Itabaiana
Serrinha
Alagoinhas
Feira de Santana
Cachoeira
Santo Amaro
Salvador
Nazaré
Valença
Jequié
Ilhéus
Itabuna
Vitória da Conquista
Canavieiras
Belmonte
Porto Seguro
Caravelas
Alcobaça
Prado
Nanuque
São Mateus
Vitória
Vila Velha
Cachoeiro de Itapemirim
Campos
CABO DE SÃO TOMÉ
CABO FRIO
Petrópolis
Niterói
RIO DE JANEIRO
Volta Redonda
Juiz de Fora
Barbacena
Belo Horizonte
Governador Valadares
Teófilo Otoni
Diamantina
Montes Claros
Pirapora
Uberaba
Uberlândia
Araguari
Patos de Minas
Brasília
Goiânia
Anápolis
Ribeirão Prêto
Franca
São José do Rio Prêto
Araçatuba
Marília
Bauru
Araraquara
São Carlos
Campinas
Jundiaí
Piracicaba
Sorocaba
SÃO PAULO
Santos
São Vicente
Presidente Prudente
Campo Grande
Corumbá
Cuiabá
Cáceres
Rondonópolis
Aquidauana
Porto Murtinho
Puerto Casado
Bela Vista
Dourados
PLANALTO DO MATO GROSSO
PLANALTO CENTRAL
SERRA DO CACHIMBO
SERRA DOS CARAJÁS
SERRA DO GURUPI
SERRA DO TIRACAMBU
CHAPADA DAS MANGABEIRAS
SERRA DO URUÇUÍ
SERRA DA TABATINGA
SERRA DO RONCADOR
SERRA DO ESTRONDO
SERRA DOURADA
SERRA GERAL DE GOIÁS
SERRA DO ESPINHAÇO
SERRA DOS AIMORÉS
SERRA DA MANTIQUEIRA
SERRA DA CANASTRA
SERRA CAIAPÓ
SERRA FORMOSA
SERRA DOS CAIABIS
SERRA DO TOMBADOR
SERRA DOS APIACÁS
SERRA DO NORTE
ILHA DO BANANAL
Tocantins
Araguaia
Xingu
Tapajós
São Francisco
Paraná
Paranaíba
Pantanal de São Lourenço
Pico da Bandeira 2890
Pico das Agulhas Negras 2787
ATOL DAS ROCAS
ILHA FERNANDO DE NORONHA (Brazil)
ILHA DE SÃO SEBASTIÃO
ILHA GRANDE
55°
50°
45°
40°
35°
10°
5°
0°
15°
20°

PACIFIC OCEAN
CHILE
ARGENTINA
BOLIVIA
PARAGUAY
GRAN CHACO
PAMPAS
PATAGONIA
ANDES
FALKLAND ISLANDS (U.K.)
WEST FALKLAND
EAST FALKLAND
Mount Adam 695
JASON ISLANDS
Tropic of Capricorn
ISLA SAN FÉLIX (Chile)
ISLA SAN AMBROSIO (Chile)
ISLAS JUAN FERNÁNDEZ (Chile)
ISLA ALEJANDRO SELKIRK
ISLA MÁS AFUERA
ISLA SANTA CLARA
ISLA RÓBINSON CRUSOE
ISLA MÁS A TIERRA
ISLA MOCHA
ISLA DE CHILOÉ
ARCHIPIÉLAGO DE LOS CHONOS
PENÍNSULA DE TAITAO
Golfo de Penas
ISLA WELLINGTON
ISLA DESOLACIÓN
ISLA GRANDE DE TIERRA DEL FUEGO
Estrecho de Magallanes
ISLA DE LOS ESTADOS
Estrecho de Le Maire
CABO DE HORNOS (CAPE HORN)
ISLAS DIEGO RAMÍREZ
Tocopilla
Antofagasta
Taltal
Chañaral
Copiapó
Vallenar
La Serena
Coquimbo
Ovalle
Valparaíso
Viña del Mar
SANTIAGO
Rancagua
Talca
Chillán
Concepción
Talcahuano
Los Angeles
Temuco
Valdivia
Osorno
Puerto Montt
Puerto Aisén
Coihaique
Puerto Natales
Punta Arenas
Ushuaia
Salta
San Salvador de Jujuy
San Miguel de Tucumán
Santiago del Estero
Catamarca
La Rioja
San Juan
Mendoza
San Rafael
Córdoba
Río Cuarto
Santa Fe
Paraná
Rosario
BUENOS AIRES
La Plata
Mar del Plata
Bahía Blanca
Neuquén
San Carlos de Bariloche
Trelew
Rawson
Puerto Madryn
Comodoro Rivadavia
Puerto Deseado
San Julián
Santa Cruz
Río Gallegos
Río Grande
Asunción
Resistencia
Corrientes
Formosa
Concordia
Salto
Paysandú
Cerro Aconcagua 6959
Cerro Ojos del Salado 6863
Monte Fitzroy 3375
Copyright © by Rand McNally & Co.
Map prepared by Esselte Map Service AB, Stockholm
A-549200-264

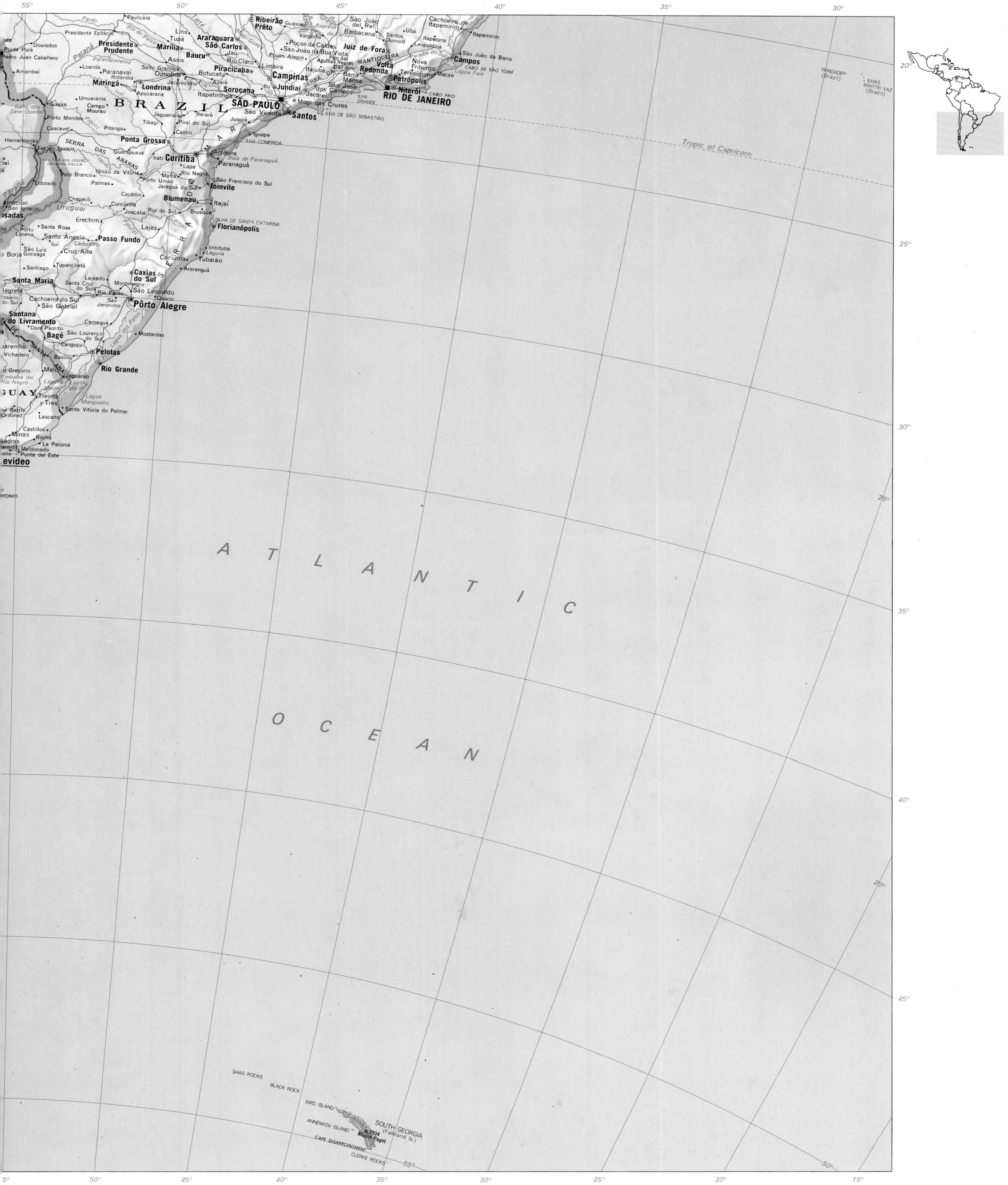
BRAZIL
SÃO PAULO
RIO DE JANEIRO
Santos
Campinas
Jundiaí
Sorocaba
Piracicaba
Ribeirão Prêto
Araraquara
São Carlos
Bauru
Marília
Presidente Prudente
Londrina
Maringá
Ponta Grossa
Curitiba
Paranaguá
Joinvile
Blumenau
Itajaí
Florianópolis
Tubarão
Criciúma
Lajes
Passo Fundo
Caxias do Sul
Pôrto Alegre
Santa Maria
Pelotas
Rio Grande
Bagé
Santana do Livramento
Juiz de Fora
Volta Redonda
Petrópolis
Niterói
Campos
Nova Friburgo
São José dos Campos
Mogi das Cruzes
São Vicente
ILHA DE SÃO SEBASTIÃO
CABO FRIO
CABO DE SÃO TOMÉ
ILHA DE SANTA CATARINA
Tropic of Capricorn
Lagoa dos Patos
Lagoa Mirim
Lagoa Mangueira
Maldonado
Punta del Este
La Paloma
Rocha
Castillos
TRINDADE (Brazil)
ILHAS MARTIN VAZ (Brazil)
ATLANTIC OCEAN
SHAG ROCKS
BLACK ROCK
BIRD ISLAND
ANNENKOV ISLAND
SOUTH GEORGIA (Falkland Is.)
Mount Paget
2934
CAPE DISAPPOINTMENT
CLERKE ROCKS
55°
50°
45°
40°
35°
30°
25°
20°
15°

Kilometers 0 200 400 600 Km.
Statute Miles 0 200 400 600 Mi.

Scale 1:12,000,000

One centimeter represents 120 kilometers.
One inch represents approximately 190 miles.
Oblique Conic Conformal Projection

CARIBBEAN SEA
PACIFIC OCEAN
NICARAGUA
CANAL ZONE (U.S.)
Colón
Panamá
Golfo de Panamá
Golfo de los Mosquitos
ARCH. DE LAS PERLAS
ISLA DE COIBA
PENÍNSULA DE AZUERO
Golfo de Chiriquí
Golfo de Urabá
Golfo de Venezuela
Lago de Maracaibo
LA GUAJIRA
Riohacha
Santa Marta
Barranquilla
Ciénaga
Cartagena
Valledupar
Maracaibo
Cabimas
Ciudad Ojeda
Valera
Mérida
Barinas
San Cristóbal
Cúcuta
Ocaña
Pamplona
Bucaramanga
Barrancabermeja
Montería
Sincelejo
Medellín
Itagüí
Envigado
Quibdó
Manizales
Pereira
Armenia
Ibagué
Girardot
BOGOTÁ
Tunja
Sogamoso
Duitama
Villavicencio
Neiva
Buenaventura
Cali
Palmira
Tuluá
Popayán
Pasto
Tumaco
Florencia
Esmeraldas
Ibarra
Quito
Latacunga
Ambato
Riobamba
Manta
Portoviejo
Guayaquil
Milagro
Cuenca
Machala
Loja
Tumbes
Talara
Sullana
Iquitos
Golfo de Guayaquil
ANTIOQUIA
CHOCÓ
CALDAS
RISARALDA
CUNDINAMARCA
BOYACÁ
SANTANDER
NORTE DE SANTANDER
META
HUILA
CAUCA
NARIÑO
PUTUMAYO
CAQUETÁ
VAUPÉS
AMAZONAS
ZULIA
ESMERALDAS
IMBABURA
PICHINCHA
MANABÍ
COTOPAXI
NAPO
PASTAZA
MORONA-SANTIAGO
GUAYAS
AZUAY
EL ORO
LOJA
LORETO
PACIFIC OCEAN
ARCHIPIÉLAGO DE COLÓN
GALAPAGOS ISLANDS
ISLA ISABELA
ISLA FERNANDINA
ISLA SANTA CRUZ
ISLA SAN CRISTÓBAL
ISLA SANTA MARÍA
ISLA ESPAÑOLA
ISLA PINTA
ISLA MARCHENA
ISLA GENOVESA
Equator
Copyright © by Rand McNally & Co.
Map prepared by Rand McNally & Co.
A-549700-264

ATLANTIC
OCEAN
NETHERLANDS ANTILLES
NEDERLANDSE ANTILLEN
Kralendijk
BONAIRE
ISLAS DE AVES (Ven.)
ISLA LA ORCHILA (Ven.)
ISLAS LOS ROQUES (Ven.)
LA BLANQUILLA (Ven.)
ISLAS LOS HERMANOS (Ven.)
ISLAS LOS TESTIGOS
CARRIACOU
GRENADINE ISLANDS
Victoria
Saint George's
GRENADA (U.K.)
TOBAGO
Speyside
Scarborough
TRINIDAD
TRINIDAD AND TOBAGO
Port of Spain
Arima
Sangre Grande
San Fernando
Point Fortin
Princes Town
Rio Claro
Siparia
GALERA POINT
GALEOTA POINT
Gulf of Paria
Serpent's Mouth
NUEVA ESPARTA
ISLA DE MARGARITA
La Asunción
Porlamar
Juangriego
Punta Piedras
Boca del Pozo
ISLA CUBAGUA
ISLA COCHE
ISLA LA TORTUGA (Ven.)
Carúpano
Río Caribe
Cumaná
Araya
Puerto la Cruz
Barcelona
Maturín
SUCRE
MONAGAS
ANZOÁTEGUI
DISTRITO FEDERAL
Maiquetía
La Guaira
CARACAS
Los Teques
MIRANDA
Petare
Guarenas
Guatire
Puerto Cabello
Valencia
Maracay
San Felipe
Barquisimeto
Acarigua
San Juan de los Morros
Calabozo
Valle de la Pascua
GUÁRICO
El Tigre
Anaco
Cantaura
Zaraza
Tucupita
DELTA AMACURO
Boca Grande
Punta Barima
Santo Tomé de Guayana
San Félix
Puerto Ordaz
Ciudad Bolívar
Soledad
Upata
El Callao
Tumeremo
Guasipati
El Dorado
Ciudad Piar
San Fernando de Apure
APURE
Caicara
Cabruta
La Urbana
Puerto Páez
Puerto Carreño
VENEZUELA
COLOMBIA
Meta
Orinoco
Caroní
Caura
Puerto Ayacucho
Samariapo
Puerto Nariño
San Fernando de Atabapo
BOLÍVAR
SIERRA DE GUAMPI
Cerro Guaiquinima 2100
Auyán-Tepuí 2500
ANGEL FALLS
LA GRAN SABANA
PARQUE NACIONAL CANAIMA
Mount Roraima 2772
Santa Elena de Uairén
Luepa
Cerro Yaví 2441
Cerro Yumari 2262
AMAZONAS
Cerro Marahuaca 2579
Cerro Duida 2400
Esmeralda
SIERRA PARIMA
SIERRA DE CURUPIRA
Pico Tamacuari 2340
San Carlos de Río Negro
San Felipe
Santa Rosa de Amanadona
Cucuí
Maroa
Yavita
Victorino
GUYANA
Georgetown
New Amsterdam
Morawhanna
Mabaruma
NORTH WEST
ESSEQUIBO
ESSEQUIBO ISLANDS
Charity
Queenstown
Suddie
Bartica
Parika
Vreed en Hoop
EAST DEMERARA
WEST DEMERARA
WEST BERBICE
MAZARUNI
POTARO
EAST BERBICE
Rockstone
Linden
Mackenzie
Wismar
Tumatumari Fall
Potaro Landing
KAIETEUR FALL
Issano
Holmia
Orinduik
PAKARAIMA MOUNTAINS
RUPUNUNI
KANUKU MOUNTAINS
KAMOA MOUNTAINS
Lethem
Saint Ignatius Mission
Dadanawa
Isherton
Skeldon
Corriverton
Nieuw Nickerie
CORONIE
NICKERIE
SARAMACCA
WILHELMINA GEB.
Julianatop 1280
SURINAM
SURINAME
ACARAI MOUNTAINS
BRAZIL
RORAIMA
Boa Vista
Caracaraí
São Bento
Uraricoera
Conceição do Maú
ILHA DE MARACÁ
São José de Anauá
Equator
Catrimani
Branco
Negro
Uaupés
Barcelos
Moura
Carvoeiro
Airão
Manaus
Manacapuru
Itacoatiara
Parintins
Amazonas
Amazon
Solimões
Japurá
Içá
Juruá
Purus
Madeira
Tefé
Coari
Codajás
Borba
Maués
Urucará
Nhamundá
Faro
Oriximiná
Trombetas
PARÁ
AMAZONAS
Santo Antônio do Içá
Tonantins
Fonte Boa
Juruá
Carauari
Alvarães
Nova Olinda do Norte
Autazes
Careiro
Novo Aripuanã
ARQUIPÉLAGO DAS ANAVILHANAS
ILHA DE SERPA
ILHA DA BOTIJA
ILHA GRANDE DA BOTIJA
Lago Grande de Manacapuru
Lago Badajós
Lago Piorini
Lago Coari
Lago Jamari
Lago Erepecu
Cachoeira do Aripuanã
TREZE QUEDAS

Kilometers 0 100 200 300 Km.
Statute Miles 0 100 200 300 Mi.

Scale 1:6,000,000
One centimeter represents 60 kilometers.
One inch represents approximately 95 miles.
Oblique Conic Conformal Projection

Peru, Bolivia and Western Brazil

PACIFIC
OCEAN
ANDES
CORDILLERA CENTRAL
CORDILLERA OCCIDENTAL
CORDILLERA ORIENTAL
CORDILLERA AZUL
CORDILLERA BLANCA
CORDILLERA NEGRA
CORDILLERA VILCABAMBA
CORDILLERA ULTRAORIENTAL
CORDILLERA DE CARABAYA
CORDILLERA DE HUANZO
CORDILLERA DE CHILCA
PAMPA DEL SACRAMENTO
SERRA DO DIVISOR
DESIERTO DE SECHURA
DESIERTO DE ATACAMA
PAMPA DE HUAYURI
GRAN PAJONAL
AMAZONAS
LORETO
SAN MARTÍN
CAJAMARCA
LAMBAYEQUE
PIURA
LA LIBERTAD
ANCASH
HUÁNUCO
PASCO
JUNÍN
LIMA
HUANCAVELICA
AYACUCHO
APURÍMAC
CUZCO
MADRE DE DIOS
PUNO
AREQUIPA
MOQUEGUA
TACNA
ICA
ACRE
TARAPACÁ
ANTOFAGASTA
PERU
BRAZIL
BRASIL
CHILE
EC.
Sullana
Piura
Castilla
Chulucanas
Chiclayo
Cajamarca
Trujillo
Chimbote
Huaraz
Huánuco
Cerro de Pasco
La Oroya
Huancayo
Huancavelica
Ayacucho
Cuzco
Callao
LIMA
Vitarte
Chosica
Pisco
Ica
Nazca
Arequipa
Mollendo
Puno
Juliaca
Tacna
Arica
Iquique
Tocopilla
Yurimaguas
Tarapoto
Moyobamba
Pucallpa
Tingo María
Chachapoyas
Jaén
Huacho
Barranca
Chincha Alta
Cañete
Mala
Jauja
Tarma
Sicuani
Ilo
Moquegua
Camaná
Requena
Lagunas
Jeberos
Contamana
Orellana
Cruzeiro do Sul
Tarauacá
Feijó
Envira
Eirunepé
Manuel Urbano
Inapari
Puerto Portillo
Puerto Bermúdez
Puerto Victoria
Atalaya
Satipo
Quillabamba
Paucartambo
Marañón
Huallaga
Ucayali
Urubamba
Apurímac
Mantaro
Madre de Dios
Purus
Juruá
Javari
Yavari
Lago Titicaca
Bahía de Paita
Bahía de Sechura
Bahía de Chimbote
Bahía de Pisco
Bahía de la Independencia
PUNTA AGUJA
PUNTA NEGRA
ISLA LOBOS DE TIERRA
ISLAS LOBOS DE AFUERA
ISLA SAN LORENZO
PENÍNSULA PARACAS
80°
78°
76°
74°
72°
70°
82°
6°
8°
10°
12°
14°
16°
18°
20°
Copyright © by Rand McNally & Co.
Map prepared by Rand McNally & Co.

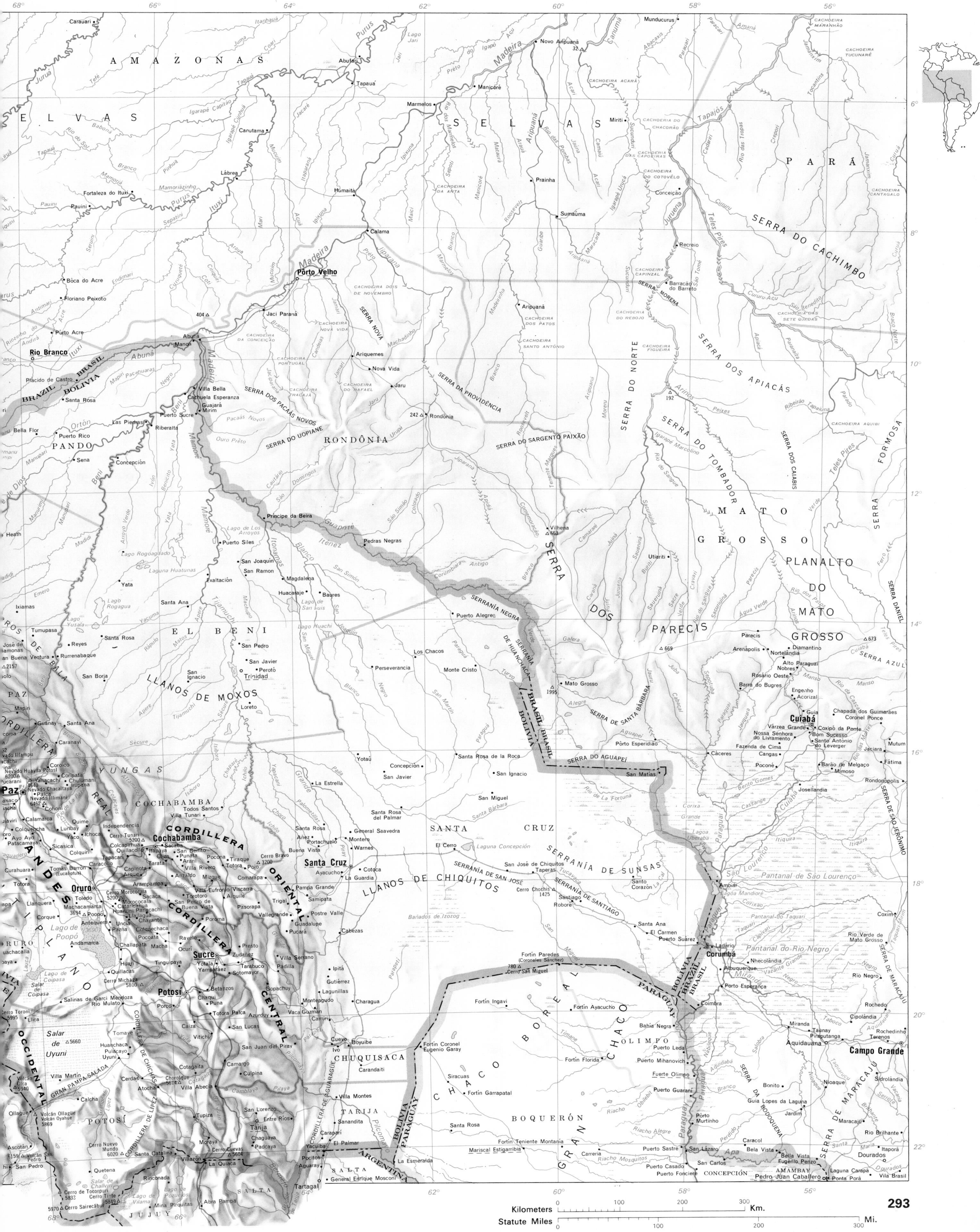
AMAZONAS
SELVAS
PARÁ
RONDÔNIA
PANDO
EL BENI
LLANOS DE MOXOS
MATO GROSSO
PLANALTO DO MATO GROSSO
SERRA DOS PARECIS
SERRA DO CACHIMBO
SERRA DOS APIACÁS
SERRA DO NORTE
SERRA DO TOMBADOR
SERRA FORMOSA
SERRA DOS PACAÁS NOVOS
SERRA DO UOPIANE
SERRA DA PROVIDÊNCIA
SERRA DO SARGENTO PAIXÃO
SERRANÍA NEGRA
SERRANÍA DE HUANCHACA
SERRA DO AGUAPEÍ
SERRA DE SANTA BÁRBARA
SERRANÍA DE SUNSAS
SERRANÍA DE SAN JOSÉ
SERRANÍA DE SANTIAGO
LLANOS DE CHIQUITOS
SANTA CRUZ
COCHABAMBA
CHUQUISACA
TARIJA
POTOSÍ
ORURO
YUNGAS
CORDILLERA REAL
CORDILLERA ORIENTAL
CORDILLERA CENTRAL
CORDILLERA OCCIDENTAL
ANDES
ALTIPLANO
CHACO BOREAL
GRAN CHACO
OLIMPO
BOQUERÓN
Pantanal de São Lourenço
Pantanal do Rio Negro
SERRA DE MARACAJU
SERRA DA BODOQUENA
SERRA DE SÃO JERÔNIMO
SERRA DANIEL
BRAZIL
BOLIVIA
BRASIL
PARAGUAY
ARGENTINA
SALTA
JUJUY
AMAMBAY
CONCEPCIÓN
Pôrto Velho
Rio Branco
Cuiabá
Corumbá
Campo Grande
Cochabamba
Santa Cruz
Sucre
Potosí
Oruro
Trinidad
Tarija
Humaitá
Manicoré
Lábrea
Guajará Mirim
Vilhena
Cáceres
Ladário
Porto Esperança
Aquidauana
Dourados
Ponta Porã
Pedro Juan Caballero
Puerto Suárez
Yacuiba
Villazón
La Quiaca
Tartagal
Salar de Uyuni
Lago de Poopó
Salar de Coipasa
68° 66° 64° 62° 60° 58° 56°
6° 8° 10° 12° 14° 16° 18° 20° 22°

Kilometers 0 100 200 300 Km.
Statute Miles 0 100 200 300 Mi.

Scale 1:6,000,000
One centimeter represents 60 kilometers.
One inch represents approximately 95 miles.
Oblique Conic Conformal Projection

PACIFIC
OCEAN
Tropic of Capricorn
A N D E S
ANTOFAGASTA
ATACAMA
COQUIMBO
ACONCAGUA
O'HIGGINS
COLCHAGUA
TALCA
MAULE
LINARES
ÑUBLE
ARAUCO
BÍO-BÍO
MALLECO
CAUTÍN
POTOSÍ
TARIJA
BOLIVIA
CHILE
ARGENTINA
JUJUY
SALTA
PUNA DE ATACAMA
CATAMARCA
TUCUMÁN
SANTIAGO DEL ESTERO
LA RIOJA
SAN JUAN
CÓRDOBA
SANTA FE
SAN LUIS
MENDOZA
LA PAMPA
NEUQUÉN
RÍO NEGRO
BUENOS
BOQUERÓN
CHACO AUSTRAL
GRAN CHACO
Antofagasta
Tocopilla
Chuquicamata
Calama
Copiapó
La Serena
Coquimbo
Ovalle
Viña del Mar
Valparaíso
San Antonio
Santiago
Puente Alto
San Bernardo
Rancagua
Curicó
Talca
Linares
Chillán
Talcahuano
Concepción
Coronel
Lota
Los Angeles
Temuco
San Salvador de Jujuy
Salta
San Miguel de Tucumán
Santiago del Estero
Catamarca
La Rioja
San Juan
Mendoza
Godoy Cruz
Guaymallén
Las Heras
San Rafael
San Luis
Mercedes
Río Cuarto
Córdoba
Villa María
Rafaela
San Francisco
Santa Rosa
Neuquén
Cipolletti
General Roca
Bahía Blanca
Punta Alto
Bahía Blanca
Copyright © by Rand McNally & Co.
Map prepared by Rand McNally & Co.
A-540191-264

ATLANTIC
OCEAN
MATO GROSSO
SÃO PAULO
PARANÁ
SANTA CATARINA
RIO GRANDE DO SUL
CORRIENTES
MISIONES
CONCEPCION
AMAMBAY
SAN PEDRO
ALTO PARANÁ
CAAGUAZU
CORDILLERA
CENTRAL
GUAIRA
ITAPÚA
NEEMBUCÚ
PRESIDENTE HAYES
Asunción
Concepción
Encarnación
Posadas
Corrientes
Formosa
Uruguaiana
Alegrete
Santa Maria
Pôrto Alegre
Pelotas
Rio Grande
Bagé
Rivera
Salto
Concordia
Paysandú
Gualeguaychú
Mercedes
Melo
Minas
MONTEVIDEO
BUENOS AIRES
La Plata
Mar del Plata
Tandil
Necochea
Dolores
Curitiba
Florianópolis
Blumenau
Joinvile
Lajes
Passo Fundo
Santos
SÃO PAULO
Campinas
Sorocaba
Londrina
Maringá
Ponta Grossa
Paranaguá
Bauru
Marília
Presidente Prudente
Lagoa dos Patos
Lagoa Mirim
Bahía Samborombón
Río de la Plata
58°
56°
54°
52°
50°
48°
46°
44°
22°
24°
26°
28°
30°
32°
34°
36°
38°

Kilometers 0 100 200 300 Km.

Statute Miles 0 100 200 300 Mi.

Scale 1:6,000,000

One centimeter represents 60 kilometers.

One inch represents approximately 95 miles.

Oblique Conic Conformal Projection

Southeastern Brazil

ATLANTIC
OCEAN
Salvador
Vitória
Belo Horizonte
RIO DE JANEIRO
SÃO PAULO
Santos
Brasília
Goiânia
Campo Grande
MINAS GERAIS
BAHIA
ESPÍRITO SANTO
GOIÁS
MATO GROSSO
SÃO PAULO
PARANÁ
Tropic of Capricorn

Kilometers 0 100 200 300 Km.
Statute Miles 0 100 200 300 Mi.
Scale 1:6,000,000
One centimeter represents 60 kilometers.
One inch represents approximately 95 miles.
Oblique Conic Conformal Projection

Geographical Facts, Figures and Information about the World and the United States

In the 56 pages that follow, the editors of the atlas have provided information of geographic interest on the World, the continents, individual foreign countries, and the 50 states of the United States. Presenting these facts in tabular form, the pages are designed to supplement the political maps, listing data not readily available from the maps themselves. Here will be found answers to many of the questions raised by those who use the atlas, particularly questions that ask "how large?" or "how many?"

The first of the tables is the World Political Information Table. For each political unit listed it specifies the 1972 estimated population, area in square miles, population density, capital, largest city, and principal languages. In addition, the table designates the precise political or administrative status of the units listed and classifies them into major types.

Following the World Political Information Table is a table giving current population figures for the world's major metropolitan areas and cities. The data for metropolitan areas have been especially prepared by Rand McNally to make possible accurate comparisons of size among the world's great urban centers.

The next 17 pages are devoted to a table of major world cities and their populations (excluding those in the United States). Arranged alphabetically by country, it includes every important foreign urban center. Major political subdivisions (states, provinces, etc.) are also listed for the leading countries. This concludes the section devoted to world information.

The next two tables are devoted to information relating to the United States. The first lists the populations of U.S. cities and towns, counties, and states. Arranged alphabetically by state, the table includes every U.S. city, village, or unincorporated community with 1,000 or more population, as well as many smaller communities. The counties or equivalent subdivisions of each state are also listed. The second table ranks the largest metropolitan areas, based on 1972 population figures, and gives the populations for the central cities of these areas.

This brief summary indicates the vast store of information to be found in the pages ahead, and the tables and lists will be a ready reference source for every user of this atlas.

World Political Information Table

This table lists all countries and dependencies in the world, U.S. States, Canadian provinces, and other important regions and political subdivisions. Besides specifying the form of government for all political areas, the table classifies them into six groups according to their political status. Units labeled **A** are independent sovereign nations. (Several of these are designated as members of the British Commonwealth of Nations.) Units labeled **B** are independent as regards internal affairs, but for purposes of foreign affairs they are under the protection of another country. Areas under military government are also labeled **B.** Units labeled **C** are colonies, overseas territories, dependencies, etc., of other countries. Together the **A, B,** and **C** areas comprise practically the entire inhabited area of the world. The areas labeled **D** are physically separate units, such as groups of islands, which are *not* separate countries, but form part of a nation or dependency. Units labeled **E** are States, provinces, Soviet Republics, or similar major administrative subdivisions of important countries. Units in the table with no letter designation are regions or other areas that do not constitute separate political units by themselves.

Region or Political Division	Area in sq. miles	Estimated Population 1/1/1972	Pop. per sq. mi.	Form of Government and Ruling Power	Capital; Largest City (unless same)	Predominant Languages
Afars & Issas (French Somaliland)	8,900	130,000	15	Overseas Territory (France)....C	Djibouti	Somali, French
Afghanistan†	250,000	17,700,000	71	Monarchy....A	Kābul	Pushtu (Afghan), Persian
Africa	11,685,000	363,800,000	31	...	........; Al-Qāhirah (Cairo)	...
Alabama	51,609	3,482,000	67	State (U.S.)....E	Montgomery; Birmingham	...
Alaska	586,412	318,000	0.5	State (U.S.)....E	Juneau; Anchorage	English, Indian, Eskimo
Albania†	11,100	2,300,000	207	People's Republic....A	Tiranë	Albanian
Alberta	255,285	1,658,000	6.5	Province (Canada)....E	Edmonton	English
Algeria†	919,595	14,800,000	16	Republic....A	Alger (Algiers)	Arabic, French
American Samoa	76	28,000	368	Unincorporated Territory (U.S.)....C	Pago Pago	Polynesian, English
Andaman & Nicobar Is.	3,215	120,000	37	Territory (India)....D	Port Blair	Andaman, Nicobar Malay
Andorra	175	22,000	126	Principality....A	Andorra	Catalan
Angola	481,353	5,750,000	12	Overseas Province (Portugal)....C	Luanda	Bantu languages
Antarctica	5,100,000	...	...	...	...	...
Antigua (incl. Barbuda)	171	65,000	380	Associated State (U.K.)....B	St. Johns	English
Arabian Peninsula	1,145,636	17,210,000	15	...	........; Ar-Riyāḍ (Riyadh)	Arabic
Argentina†	1,072,162	23,800,000	22	Federal Republic....A	Buenos Aires	Spanish
Arizona	113,909	1,906,000	17	State (U.S.)....E	Phoenix	...
Arkansas	53,104	1,953,000	37	State (U.S.)....E	Little Rock	...
Arm'anskaja (Armenia) S.S.R.	11,500	2,600,000	226	Soviet Socialist Republic (U.S.S.R.)....E	Jerevan	Armenian
Aruba	69	62,000	899	Division of Netherlands Antilles (Neth.)....D	Oranjestad	Dutch, Spanish, English, Papiamento
Ascension I.	34	1,300	38	Dependency of St. Helena (U.K.)....D	Georgetown	English
Asia	17,085,000	2,172,300,000	127	...	........; Tōkyō	...
Australia†	2,967,909	12,870,000	4.3	Monarchy (Federal) (Br. Comm. of Nations)....A	Canberra; Sydney	English
Australian Capital Territory	939	149,000	159	Federal Territory (Australia)....E	Canberra	English
Austria†	32,374	7,463,000	231	Federal Republic....A	Wien (Vienna)	German
Azerbajdžanskaja (Azerbaidzhan) S.S.R.	33,450	5,320,000	159	Soviet Socialist Republic (U.S.S.R.)....E	Baku	Turkic languages, Russian, Armenian
Azores Is.	894	337,000	377	Part of Portugal (3 Districts)....D	........; Ponta Delgada	Portuguese
Baden-Württemberg	13,803	9,075,000	657	State (Germany, West)....E	Stuttgart	German
Bahama Is.	4,403	179,000	41	Colony (U.K.)....C	Nassau	English
Bahrain†	231	220,000	952	Sheikdom....A	Al-Manāmah	Arabic
Balearic Is.	1,936	542,000	280	Part of Spain (Baleares Province)....D	Palma	Catalan
Baltic Republics	67,150	6,985,000	104	Union of Soviet Socialist Republics....	........; Rīga	Lithuanian, Latvian, Estonian, Russian
Bangladesh	55,126	73,000,000	1,324	Republic (Br. Comm. of Nations)....A	Dacca	Bengali
Barbados†	166	239,000	1,440	Self-governing Member (Br. Comm. of Nations).A	Bridgetown	English
Basutoland, see Lesotho	...	...	...	...	...	...
Bayern (Bavaria)	27,239	10,625,000	390	State (Germany, West)....E	München (Munich)	German
Bechuanaland, see Botswana	...	...	...	...	...	...
Belgium†	11,781	9,722,000	825	Monarchy....A	Bruxelles (Brussels)	Flemish, French
Belorusskaja (Byelorussia) S.S.R.†	80,150	9,160,000	114	Soviet Socialist Republic (U.S.S.R.)....E	Minsk	Byelorussian, Polish
Benelux	28,549	23,313,000	817	...	Bruxelles (Brussels)	Dutch, Flemish, French, Luxembourgeois
Berlin, West	185	2,115,000	11,432	State (Germany, West)....E	Berlin (West)	German
Bermuda	21	55,000	2,619	Colony (U.K.)....C	Hamilton	English
Bhutan†	18,200	800,000	44	Monarchy (Indian protection)....B	Paro and Thimbu	Tibetan dialects
Bismarck Archipelago	18,965	275,000	15	Part of Australian Trust Ter. of New Guinea (3 Districts)....D	........; Rabaul	Malay-Polynesian and Papuan languages
Bolivia†	424,164	5,150,000	12	Republic....A	Sucre and La Paz; La Paz	Spanish, Quechua, Aymará, Guaraní
Borneo, Indonesian (Kalimantan)	208,286	5,500,000	26	Part of Indonesia (4 Provinces)....D	........; Bandjarmasin	Bahasa Indonesia (Indonesian)
Botswana (Bechuanaland)†	231,805	630,000	2.7	Republic (Br. Comm. of Nations)....A	Gaborone; Serowe	Bechuana, other Bantu languages
Brazil†	3,286,487	96,000,000	29	Federal Republic....A	Brasília; São Paulo	Portuguese
Bremen	156	720,000	4,615	State (Germany, West)....E	Bremen	German
British Antarctic Territory (excl. Antarctic mainland)	2,040	Winter pop. 100	...	Colony (U.K.)....C	Stanley, Falkland Islands	...
British Columbia	366,255	2,237,000	6.1	Province (Canada)....E	Victoria; Vancouver	English
British Commonwealth of Nations	10,675,407	885,314,000	83	...	London	...
British Guiana, see Guyana	...	...	...	...	...	...
British Honduras	8,867	125,000	14	Colony (U.K.)....C	Belmopan; Belize	English, Spanish, Indian languages
British Indian Ocean Territory	29	2,000	69	Colony (U.K.)....C	Victoria, Seychelles	Creole, English, French
Brunei	2,226	220,000	99	Sultanate (U.K. protection)....B	Bandar Seri Begawan	Malay-Polynesian languages
Bulgaria†	42,823	8,580,000	200	People's Republic....A	Sofija (Sofia)	Bulgarian
Burma†	261,790	28,500,000	109	Federal Republic....A	Rangoon	Burmese, English
Burundi (Urundi)†	10,747	3,650,000	340	Republic....A	Bujumbura	Bantu and Hamitic languages
California	158,693	20,444,000	129	State (U.S.)....E	Sacramento; Los Angeles	...
Cambodia†	69,898	7,050,000	101	Republic....A	Phnum Pénh	Cambodian (Khmer), French
Cameroon†	183,569	6,000,000	33	Federal Republic....A	Yaoundé; Douala	Native languages, French
Canada†	3,851,809	21,870,000	5.7	Monarchy (Federal) (Br. Comm. of Nations)....A	Ottawa; Montréal	English, French
Canal Zone	558	45,000	81	Under U.S. Jurisdiction....C	Balboa Heights; Balboa	Spanish, English
Canary Is.	2,808	1,145,000	408	Part of Spain (2 Provinces)....D	........; Las Palmas de Gran Canaria	Spanish
Canton & Enderbury	27	...	...	U.K.-U.S. Administration....C	Canton Island	Malay-Polynesian languages, English
Cape Verde Is.	1,557	260,000	167	Overseas Province (Portugal)....C	Paria; Mindelo	Portuguese
Caroline Is.	463	59,000	127	Part of U.S. Pacific Is. Trust Ter. (4 Districts)...D	...	Malay-Polynesian languages
Cayman Is.	100	11,000	110	Colony (U.K.)....C	Georgetown	English
Celebes (Sulawesi)	72,987	9,500,000	130	Part of Indonesia (2 Provinces)....D	........; Makasar	Malay-Polynesian languages
Central African Republic†	240,535	1,660,000	6.9	Republic....A	Bangui	Bantu languages, French
Central America	202,063	17,585,000	87	...	........; Guatemala	Spanish, Indian languages
Central Asia, Soviet	493,950	21,100,000	43	Union of Soviet Socialist Republics....	........; Taškent	Uzbek, Russian, Kirghiz, Turkoman, Tadzhik
Ceylon†	25,332	12,925,000	510	Commonwealth (Br. Comm. of Nations)....A	Colombo	Sinhalese, Tamil, English
Chad†	495,800	3,850,000	7.8	Republic....A	Fort-Lamy	Hamitic languages, Arabic, French
Channel Is. (Guernsey, Jersey, etc.)	75	126,000	1,680	...	........; St. Helier	English, French
Chile†	292,258	10,100,000	35	Republic....A	Santiago	Spanish
China (excl. Taiwan)†	3,691,500	779,000,000	211	People's Republic....A	Beijing (Peking); Shanghai	Chinese, Mongolian, Turkish, Tungus
China (Nationalist), see Taiwan	...	...	...	...	...	...
Christmas I. (Indian Ocean)	52	3,500	67	External Territory (Australia)....C	...	Chinese, Malay, English
Cocos (Keeling) Is.	5	700	120	External Territory (Australia)....C	...	Malay, English
Colombia†	439,737	22,100,000	47	Republic....A	Bogotá	Spanish

† Member of the United Nations (1971).

World Political Information Table (Continued)

Region or Political Division	Area in sq. miles	Estimated Population 1/1/1972	Pop. per sq. mi.	Form of Government and Ruling Power	Capital; Largest City (unless same)	Predominant Languages
Colorado	104,247	2,313,000	22	State (U.S.) E	Denver	
Commonwealth of Nations, see Br. Commonwealth of Nations						
Comoro Is.	838	280,000	334	Overseas Territory (France) C	Moroni	Malagasy, French
Congo†	132,000	970,000	7.3	Republic A	Brazzaville	Bantu languages, French
Congo, The, see Zaire						
Connecticut	5,009	3,088,000	616	State (U.S.) E	Hartford	
Cook Is.	93	22,000	237	Self-governing Territory, (New Zealand) C	Avarua	Malay-Polynesian languages
Corsica	3,352	222,000	66	Part of France (Corse Department) D	Ajaccio; Bastia	French, Italian
Costa Rica†	19,650	1,780,000	91	Republic A	San José	Spanish
Cuba†	44,218	8,750,000	198	Republic A	La Habana (Havana)	Spanish
Curaçao	173	148,000	855	Division of Netherlands Antilles (Neth.) D	Willemstad	Dutch, Spanish, English, Papiamento
Cyprus†	3,572	642,000	180	Republic (Br. Comm. of Nations) A	Levkósía (Nicosia)	Greek, Turkish, English
Czechoslovakia†	49,373	14,530,000	294	People's Republic A	Praha (Prague)	Czech, Slovak
Dahomey†	43,484	2,800,000	64	Republic A	Porto-Novo; Cotonou	Native languages, French
Delaware	2,057	566,000	275	State (U.S.) E	Dover; Wilmington	
Denmark†	16,629	4,965,000	299	Monarchy A	København (Copenhagen)	Danish
Denmark and Possessions	857,169	5,053,000	5.9		København (Copenhagen)	Danish, Faeroese, Greenlandic
District of Columbia	67	755,000	11,269	District (U.S.) E	Washington	
Dominica	290	72,000	248	Associated State (U.K.) B	Roseau	English, French
Dominican Republic†	18,816	4,475,000	238	Republic A	Santo Domingo	Spanish
Ecuador†	109,483	6,400,000	58	Republic A	Quito; Guayaquil	Spanish, Quechua
Egypt (United Arab Republic)†	386,900	34,550,000	89	Republic‡‡ A	Al-Qāhirah (Cairo)	Arabic
El Salvador†	8,260	3,725,000	451	Republic A	San Salvador	Spanish
England (excl. Monmouthshire)	50,332	46,155,000	917	United Kingdom	........; London	English
England & Wales	58,348	48,885,000	838	Administrative division of United Kingdom E	London	English, Welsh
Equatorial Guinea†	10,830	295,000	27	Republic A	Santa Isabel	Bantu languages, Spanish
Estonskaja (S.S.R.)	17,400	1,390,000	80	Soviet Socialist Republic (U.S.S.R.) E	Tallinn	Estonian, Russian
Ethiopia†	471,778	26,100,000	55	Monarchy A	Addis Abeba	Amharic and other Semitic languages English, various Hamitic languages
Eurasia	20,910,000	2,806,500,000	134		........; Tōkyō	
Europe	3,825,000	634,200,000	166		........; London	
Faeroe Is.	540	38,000	70	Self-governing Territory (Denmark) C	Tórshavn	Danish, Faeroese
Falkland Is. (Is. Malvinas) (excl. Deps)	4,618	2,100	0.5	Colony (U.K.) C	Stanley	English
Fernando Poo	785	82,000	104	Part of Equatorial Guinea D	Santa Isabel	Bantu languages, Spanish
Fiji†	7,055	535,000	76	Monarchy (Federal) (Br. Comm. of Nations) A	Suva	Malaya-Polynesian languages, English, Hindi
Finland†	130,129	4,685,000	36	Republic A	Helsinki (Helsingfors)	Finnish, Swedish
Florida	58,560	7,186,000	123	State (U.S.) E	Tallahassee; Miami	
France†	210,039	51,500,000	245	Republic A	Paris	French
France and Possessions	239,575	53,397,600	223		Paris	
Franklin	549,253	9,400	0.02	District of Northwest Territories, Canada E	........; Cambridge Bay	English, Eskimo, Indian
French Guiana	35,100	54,000	1.5	Overseas Department (France) C	Cayenne	French
French Polynesia	1,550	123,000	79	Overseas Territory (France) C	Papeete	Malay-Polynesian languages, French
French Somaliland, see Afars & Issas						
French Southern & Antarctic Ter. (excl. Adélie Coast)	2,918	200	0.07	Overseas Territory (France) C		French
French West Indies	1,112	688,000	619		........; Fort-de-France	French
Gabon†	103,347	520,000	5.0	Republic A	Libreville	Bantu languages, French
Galápagos Is. (Colon, Archipélago de)	3,075	3,300	1.1	Province (Ecuador) D	Puerto Baquerizo Moreno	Spanish
Gambia†	4,361	375,000	86	Republic (Br. Comm. of Nations) A	Bathurst	Mandingo, Fula, English
Georgia	58,876	4,728,000	80	State (U.S.) E	Atlanta	
Germany (Entire)	137,727	79,475,000	577		........; Berlin	German
Germany, East	41,768	17,050,000	408	People's Republic A	Ost-Berlin	German
Germany, West (incl. West Berlin)	95,959	61,300,000	639	Federal Republic A	Bonn; West Berlin	German
Ghana†	92,100	8,850,000	96	Republic (Br. Comm. of Nations) A	Accra	Twi, Fanti, Ewe-Fon, English
Gibraltar	2	27,000	13,500	Colony (U.K.) C	Gibraltar	Spanish, English
Gilbert & Ellice Is.	283	57,000	201	Colony (U.K.) C	Tarawa	Malay-Polynesian languages
Great Britain & Northern Ireland, see United Kingdom						
Greece†	50,944	8,775,000	172	Monarchy A	Athínai (Athens)	Greek
Greenland	840,000	50,000	0.06	Overseas Territory (Denmark) C	Godthåb	Greenlandic, Danish, Eskimo
Grenada	133	96,000	722	Associated State (U.K.) B	Saint George's	English
Gruzinskaja (Georgia) S.S.R.	26,900	4,780,000	178	Soviet Socialist Republic (U.S.S.R.) E	Tbilisi	Georgic, Armenian, Russian
Guadeloupe (incl. Dependencies)	687	335,000	488	Overseas Department (France) C	Basse-Terre; Pointe-à-Pitre	French
Guam	212	88,000	415	Unincorporated Territory (U.S.) C	Agana	English, Chamorro
Guatemala†	42,042	5,625,000	134	Republic A	Guatemala	Spanish, Indian languages
Guernsey (incl. Dependencies)	30	53,000	1,767	Bailiwick (U.K.) C	St. Peter Port	English, French
Guinea†	94,926	4,060,000	43	Republic A	Conakry	Native languages, French
Guyana†	83,000	744,000	9.0	Republic (Br. Comm. of Nations) A	Georgetown	English
Haiti†	10,714	5,025,000	469	Republic A	Port-au-Prince	Creole, French
Hamburg	288	1,785,000	6,198	State (Germany, West) E	Hamburg	German
Hawaii	6,450	796,000	123	State (U.S.) E	Honolulu	English, Japanese, Hawaiian
Hessen (Hesse)	8,150	5,465,000	671	State (German, West) E	Wiesbaden; Frankfurt am Main	German
Hispaniola	29,530	9,500,000	322		........; Santo Domingo	French, Spanish
Holland, see Netherlands						
Honduras†	43,277	2,710,000	63	Republic A	Tegucigalpa	Spanish
Hong Kong	399	4,020,000	10,075	Colony (U.K.) C	Victoria (Xianggang)	Chinese, English
Hungary†	35,920	10,385,000	289	People's Republic A	Budapest	Hungarian
Iceland†	39,800	207,000	5.2	Republic A	Reykjavík	Icelandic
Idaho	83,557	723,000	8.7	State (U.S.) E	Boise (Boise City)	
Illinois	56,400	11,239,000	199	State (U.S.) E	Springfield; Chicago	
India (incl. part of Kashmir)†	1,226,466	557,000,000	454	Republic (Br. Comm. of Nations) A	New Delhi; Calcutta	Hindi and other Indo-Aryan languages, Dravidian languages, English
Indiana	36,291	5,282,000	146	State (U.S.) E	Indianapolis	
Indonesia (incl. West Irian)†	735,271	127,600,000	174	Republic A	Djakarta	Bahasa Indonesia (Indonesian), Chinese, English
Iowa	56,290	2,842,000	50	State (U.S.) E	Des Moines	
Iran (Persia)†	636,300	30,300,000	48	Monarchy A	Tehrān	Persian, Turkish dialects, Kurdish
Iraq†	167,925	9,800,000	58	Republic A	Baghdād	Arabic, Kurdish
Ireland†	27,137	2,985,000	110	Republic A	Dublin (Baile Átha Cliath)	English, Irish
Isle of Man	227	50,000	220	Possession (U.K.) C	Douglas	English
Israel†	8,019	3,060,000	382	Republic‡‡ A	Yerushalayim; Tel Aviv-Yafo	Hebrew, Arabic
Italy†	116,313	55,050,000	473	Republic A	Roma (Rome)	Italian
Ivory Coast†	124,504	4,460,000	36	Republic A	Abidjan	French, native languages
Jamaica†	4,232	1,910,000	451	Self-governing Member (Br. Comm. of Nations). A	Kingston	English
Japan†	143,706	106,250,000	739	Monarchy A	Tōkyō	Japanese
Java (Djawa) (incl. Madura)	51,040	82,000,000	1,607	Part of Indonesia (5 Provinces) D	........; Djakarta	Bahasa Indonesia (Indonesian), Chinese, English
Jersey	45	73,000	1,622	Bailiwick (U.K.) C	St. Helier	English, French
Jordan†	37,738	2,475,000	66	Monarchy‡‡ A	'Ammān	Arabic
Kansas	82,264	2,257,000	27	State (U.S.) E	Topeka; Wichita	

† Member of the United Nations (1971).
‡‡ As of late 1967, the Gaza Strip was under Israeli military occupation. Data for Egypt, Israel, Jordan and Syria do not reflect de facto changes which took place during 1967.

World Political Information Table (Continued)

Region or Political Division	Area in sq. miles	Estimated Population 1/1/1972	Pop. per sq. mi.	Form of Government and Ruling Power	Capital; Largest City (unless same)	Predominant Languages
Kashmir, Jammu &	86,024	5,800,000	67	In dispute (India & Pakistan)	Srīnagar	Kashmiri, Punjabi
Kazachskaja (Kazakh) S.S.R.	1,048,300	13,250,000	13	Soviet Socialist Republic (U.S.S.R.)....E	Alma-Ata	Turkic languages, Russian
Keewatin	228,160	3,600	0.02	District of Northwest Territories, Canada....E	........; Baker Lake	English, Eskimo, Indian
Kentucky	40,395	3,268,000	81	State (U.S.)....E	Frankfort; Louisville	....
Kenya†	224,960	11,900,000	53	Republic (Br. Comm. of Nations)....A	Nairobi	Swahili and other Bantu languages, English
Kerguelen	2,700	90	0.03	Part of French Southern & Antarctic Ter (Fr.)...D	....	French
Kirgizskaja (Kirghiz) S.S.R.	76,650	3,075,000	40	Soviet Socialist Republic (U.S.S.R.)....E	Frunze	Turkic languages, Persian
Korea (Entire)	85,049‡	47,250,000	556	....	........; Sŏul (Seoul)	Korean
Korea, North	46,540	14,450,000	310	People's Republic....A	P'yŏngyang	Korean
Korea, South	38,022	32,800,000	863	Republic....A	Sŏul (Seoul)	Korean
Kuwait†	6,200	860,000	139	Shiekdom....A	Al-Kuwayt	Arabic
Labrador	112,826	27,000	0.2	Part of Newfoundland Province, Canada....D	........; Labrador City	English, Eskimo
Laos†	91,400	3,060,000	33	Monarchy....A	Vientiane	Lao, French
Latin America	7,924,731	290,699,900	37	....	........; São Paulo	....
Latvijskaja (Latvia) S.S.R.	24,600	2,405,000	98	Soviet Socialist Republic (U.S.S.R.)....E	Rīga	Latvian, Russian
Lebanon†	3,950	2,930,000	742	Republic....A	Bayrūt (Beirut)	Arabic, French, English
Lesotho (Basutoland)†	11,720	920,000	78	Monarchy (Br. Comm. of Nations)....A	Maseru	Kaffir, other Bantu languages
Liberia†	43,000	1,200,000	30	Republic....A	Monrovia	Native languages, English
Libya†	679,362	2,050,000	3.0	Republic....A	Ṭarābulus and Banghāzi; Ṭarābulus	Arabic
Liechtenstein	62	22,000	355	Principality....A	Vaduz	German
Litovskaja (Lithuania) S.S.R.	25,150	3,190,000	127	Soviet Socialist Republic (U.S.S.R.)....E	Vilnius	Lithuanian, Polish, Russian
Louisiana	48,523	3,727,000	77	State (U.S.)....E	Baton Rouge; New Orleans	....
Luxembourg†	998	341,000	342	Grand Duchy....A	Luxembourg	Luxembourgeois, French
Macau	6	252,000	42,000	Overseas Province (Portugal)....C	Macau	Chinese, Portuguese
Mackenzie	527,490	24,000	0.05	District of Northwest Territories, Canada....E	........; Yellowknife	English, Eskimo, Indian
Madeira Is.	308	270,000	877	Part of Portugal (Funchal District)....D	Funchal	Portuguese
Maine	33,215	1,001,000	30	State (U.S.)....E	Augusta; Portland	....
Malagasy Republic (Madagascar)†	226,658	6,975,000	31	Republic....A	Tananarive	French, Malagasy
Malawi (Nyasaland)†	45,747	4,600,000	101	Republic (Br. Comm. of Nations)....A	Zomba; Blantyre	Bantu languages
Malaya	50,700	9,080,000	179	Part of Malaysia	Kuala Lumpur	Malay, Chinese, English
Malaysia†	128,430	10,800,000	84	Self-governing Member (Br. Comm. of Nations).A	Kuala Lumpur	Malay, Chinese, English
Maldives†	115	116,000	1,009	Republic....A	Male	Arabic
Mali†	478,655	5,225,000	11	Republic....A	Bamako	Native languages, French, Arabic
Malta†	122	322,000	2,639	Self-governing Member (Br. Comm. of Nations).A	Valletta	English, Maltese
Manitoba	251,000	989,000	3.9	Province (Canada)....E	Winnipeg	English
Mariana Is. (excl. Guam)	184	10,000	54	District of U.S. Pacific Is. Trust Ter....D	Saipan	Malay-Polynesian languages
Maritime Provinces (excl. Newfoundland)	51,963	1,517,000	29	Canada	........; Halifax	English
Marshall Is.	70	23,000	329	District of U.S. Pacific Is. Trust Ter....D	Majuro	Malay-Polynesian languages
Martinique	425	353,000	831	Overseas Department (France)....C	Fort-de-France	French
Maryland	10,577	4,052,000	383	State (U.S.)....E	Annapolis; Baltimore	....
Massachusetts	8,257	5,791,000	701	State (U.S.)....E	Boston	....
Mauritania†	397,950	1,220,000	3.1	Republic....A	Nouakchott	Arabic, French
Mauritius (incl. Dependencies)†	789	862,000	1,093	Self-governing Member (Br. Comm. of Nations).A	Port Louis	Indo-Aryan languages, French, Creole, English
Mexico†	761,604	51,800,000	68	Federal Republic....A	Ciudad de México (Mexico City)	Spanish
Michigan	58,216	9,040,000	155	State (U.S.)....E	Lansing; Detroit	....
Middle America	1,054,731	95,199,900	90	....	........; Ciudad de México (Mexico City)	....
Midway Is.	2	2,200	1,100	Possession (U.S.)....C	....	English
Minnesota	84,068	3,877,000	46	State (U.S.)....E	St. Paul; Minneapolis	....
Mississippi	47,716	2,257,000	47	State (U.S.)....E	Jackson	....
Missouri	69,686	4,746,000	68	State (U.S.)....E	Jefferson City; St. Louis	....
Moldavskaja (Moldavia) S.S.R.	13,000	3,625,000	279	Soviet Socialist Republic (U.S.S.R.)....E	Kišin'ov (Kishinev)	Moldavian, Russian, Ukrainian
Monaco	0.6	25,000	41,667	Principality....A	Monaco	French, Italian
Mongolia†	604,200	1,300,000	2.2	People's Republic....A	Ulaanbaatar (Ulan Bator)	Mongolian
Montana	147,138	701,000	4.8	State (U.S.)....E	Helena; Billings	....
Montserrat	39	12,400	318	Colony (U.K.)....C	Plymouth	English
Morocco†	172,415	16,300,000	95	Monarchy....A	Rabat; Casablanca	Arabic, Berber, French
Mozambique	303,771	8,500,000	28	Overseas Province (Portugal)....C	Lourenço Marques	Bantu Languages, Portuguese
Nauru	8	7,000	875	Republic (Br. Comm. of Nations)....A	....	Malay-Polynesian languages, Chinese, English
Nebraska	77,227	1,503,000	19	State (U.S.)....E	Lincoln; Omaha	....
Nepal†	54,362	11,350,000	209	Monarchy....A	Kātmāndu	Nepali, Tibeto-Burman languages
Netherlands†	15,770	13,250,000	840	Monarchy....A	Amsterdam and 's-Gravenhage (The Hague) Amsterdam	Dutch
Netherlands and Possessions	79,178	13,897,000	176	....	Amsterdam and 's-Gravenhage; Amsterdam	....
Netherlands Antilles	371	227,000	612	Self-governing Territory (Netherlands)....C	Willemstad	Dutch, Spanish, English, Papiamento
Netherlands Guiana, see Surinam	....	....	....			
Nevada	110,540	534,000	4.8	State (U.S.)....E	Carson City; Las Vegas	....
New Brunswick	28,354	634,000	22	Province (Canada)....E	Fredericton; Saint John	English, French
New Caledonia (incl. Deps.)	7,358	115,000	16	Overseas Territory (France)....C	Nouméa	Malay-Polynesian languages, French
New England	66,608	12,065,000	181	United States	........; Boston	English
Newfoundland	156,185	527,000	3.4	Province (Canada)....E	St. John's	English
Newfoundland (excl. Labrador)	43,359	500,000	12	....	........; St. John's	English
New Guinea, North-East	69,095	1,480,000	21	Part of Australian Trust Ter. of New Guinea (3 Districts)....D	........; Lae	Papuan and Negrito languages
New Guinea, Ter. of	92,160	1,850,000	20	Trust Territory (Austl.; administered from Papua)....C	Port Moresby, Papua; Lae	Papuan and Negrito languages, English
New Hampshire	9,304	765,000	82	State (U.S.)....E	Concord; Manchester	....
New Hebrides	5,700	87,000	15	Condominium (France-U.K.)....C	Vila	Malay-Polynesian languages, French
New Jersey	7,836	7,311,000	933	State (U.S.)....E	Trenton; Newark	....
New Mexico	121,666	1,035,000	8.5	State (U.S.)....E	Santa Fe; Albuquerque	....
New South Wales	309,433	4,670,000	15	State (Australia)....E	Sydney	English
New York	49,576	18,423,000	372	State (U.S.)....E	Albany; New York	....
New Zealand†	103,736	2,890,000	28	Monarchy (Br. Comm. of Nations)....A	Wellington; Auckland	English
Nicaragua†	50,200	2,090,000	42	Republic....A	Managua	Spanish
Niedersachsen (Lower Saxony)	18,299	7,140,000	390	State (Germany, West)....E	Hannover	German
Niger†	489,200	4,180,000	8.5	Republic....A	Niamey	Hausa, Arabic, French
Nigeria†	356,669	57,000,000	160	Republic (Br. Comm. of Nations)....A	Lagos	Hausa, Ibo, Yoruba, English
Niue	100	5,200	52	Island Territory (New Zealand)....C	Alofi	Malay-Polynesian languages, English
Nordrhein-Westfalen (North Rhine Westphalia)	13,145	17,075,000	1,299	State (Germany, West)....E	Düsseldorf; Köln	German
Norfolk Island	14	1,500	107	External Territory (Australia)....C	Kingston	English
North America	9,420,000	325,300,000	35	....	........; New York	....

† Member of the United Nations (1971).
‡ Includes 487 sq. miles of demilitarized zone, not included in North or South Korea figures.

World Political Information Table (Continued)

Region or Political Division	Area in sq. miles	Estimated Population 1/1/1972	Pop. per sq. mi.	Form of Government and Ruling Power	Capital; Largest City (unless same)	Predominant Languages
North Borneo, see Sabah						
North Carolina	52,586	5,175,000	98	State (U.S.)...E	Raleigh; Charlotte	
North Dakota	70,665	623,000	8.8	State (U.S.)...E	Bismarck; Fargo	
Northern Ireland	5,452	1,530,000	281	Administrative division of United Kingdom...E	Belfast	English
Northern Rhodesia, see Zambia						
Northern Territory	520,280	88,000	0.2	Territory (Australia)...E	Darwin	English, Aboriginal languages
North Polar Regions						
Northwest Territories	1,304,903	37,000	0.03	Territory (Canada)...E	Yellowknife	English, Eskimo, Indian
Norway†	125,050	3,920,000	31	Monarchy...A	Oslo	Norwegian (Riksmål and Landsmål)
Nova Scotia	21,425	772,000	36	Province (Canada)...E	Halifax	English
Nyasaland, see Malawi						
Oceania (incl. Australia)	3,295,000	19,900,000	6.0		........; Sydney	
Ohio	41,222	10,817,000	262	State (U.S.)...E	Columbus; Cleveland	
Oklahoma	69,919	2,613,000	37	State (U.S.)...E	Oklahoma City	
Oman†	82,030	690,000	8.4	Sultanate...A	Masqaṭ; Maṭraḥ	Arabic
Ontario	412,582	7,931,000	19	Province (Canada)...E	Toronto	English
Oregon	96,981	2,155,000	22	State (U.S.)...E	Salem; Portland	
Orkney Is.	376	17,200	46	Part of Scotland, U.K. (Orkney County)...D	Kirkwall	English
Pacific Islands Trust Territory	717	92,000	128	Trust Territory (U.S.)...C	Saipan	Malay-Polynesian languages, English
Pakistan (incl. part of Kashmir)†	345,753	63,000,000	182	Federal Republic...A	Islāmābād; Karāchī	Urdu, English
Palestine (Gaza Strip)	146	330,000	2,260	Military Government (Egypt)‡‡...B	Ghazzah (Gaza)	Arabic
Panama†	29,209	1,485,000	51	Republic...A	Panamá	Spanish
Papua (excl. New Guinea, Ter. of)	86,100	700,000	8.1	External Territory (Australia)...C	Port Moresby	Papuan and Negrito languages, English
Paraguay†	157,048	2,500,000	16	Republic...A	Asunción	Spanish, Guaraní
Pennsylvania	45,333	11,908,000	263	State (U.S.)...E	Harrisburg; Philadelphia	
Persia, see Iran						
Peru†	496,224	14,350,000	29	Republic...A	Lima	Spanish, Quechua
Philippines†	115,831	38,500,000	332	Republic...A	Quezon City; Manila	Tagalog and other Malay-Polynesian languages, English
Pitcairn (excl. Dependencies)	2	100	50	Colony (U.K.)...C	Adamstown	English
Poland†	120,725	32,950,000	273	People's Republic...A	Warszawa (Warsaw)	Polish
Portugal†	35,553	9,760,000	275	Republic...A	Lisboa (Lisbon)	Portuguese
Portugal and Possessions	842,323	25,779,000	31		Lisboa (Lisbon)	
Portuguese Guinea	13,948	570,000	41	Overseas Province (Portugal)...C	Bissau	Native languages, Portuguese
Portuguese Timor	5,763	620,000	108	Overseas Province (Portugal)...C	Dili	Malay, Papuan languages, Portuguese
Prairie Provinces	757,985	3,565,000	4.7	Canada	........; Winnipeg	English
Prince Edward Island	2,184	111,000	51	Province (Canada)...E	Charlottetown	English
Puerto Rico	3,435	2,761,000	804	Commonwealth (U.S.)...C	San Juan	Spanish, English
Qatar†	8,500	90,000	11	Shiekdom...A	Ad-Dawḥah (Doha)	Arabic
Quebec	594,860	6,038,000	10	Province (Canada)...E	Québec; Montréal	French, English
Queensland	667,000	1,840,000	2.8	State (Australia)...E	Brisbane	English
Reunion	969	460,000	457	Overseas Department (France)...C	St. Denis	French
Rheinland-Pfalz (Rhineland-Palatinate)	7,657	3,670,000	479	State (Germany, West)...E	Mainz; Ludwigshafen	German
Rhode Island	1,214	964,000	794	State (U.S.)...E	Providence	
Rhodesia	150,804	5,550,000	37	Self-governing Colony (U.K.)*...C	Salisbury	Bantu languages, English
Rio Muni, see Equatorial Guinea						
Rodrigues	42	25,000	595	Dependency of Mauritius (U.K.)...D	Port Mathurin	English, French
Romania†	91,699	20,625,000	225	People's Republic...A	Bucureşti (Bucharest)	Romanian, Hungarian
Rossijskaja Sovetskaja Federativnaja Socialističeskaja Respublika	6,592,850	131,400,000	20	Soviet Federated Socialist Republic (U.S.S.R.)..E	Moskva (Moscow)	Russian, Finno-Ugric languages, various Turkic, Iranian, and Mongol languages
Rossijskaja S.F.S.R. in Europe	1,527,350	97,250,000	64	Union of Soviet Socialist Republics	........; Moskva (Mowcow)	Russian, Finno-Ugric languages
Rwanda†	10,169	3,900,000	384	Republic...A	Kigali	Bantu and Hamitic languages
Saarland (Saar)	991	1,115,000	1,125	State (Germany, West)...E	Saarbrücken	German
Sabah (North Borneo)	29,388	690,000	23	Administrative division of Malaysia...E	Kota Kinabalu; Sandakan	Malay, Chinese
St. Helena (incl. Dependencies)	162	6,500	40	Colony (U.K.)...C	Jamestown	English
St. Kitts-Nevis-Anguilla	138	60,000	435	Associated State (U.K.)...B	Basseterre	English
St. Lucia	238	104,000	437	Associated State (U.K.)...B	Castries	English
St. Pierre & Miquelon	93	5,400	58	Overseas Territory (France)...C	St. Pierre	French
St. Vincent	150	91,000	607	Associated State (U.K.)...B	Kingstown	English
Samoa (Entire)	1,173	176,000	150		........; Apia	Malay-Polynesian languages, English
San Marino	24	19,000	792	Republic...A	San Marino	Italian
Sao Tome & Principe	372	67,000	180	Overseas Province (Portugal)...C	São Tomé	Bantu languages, Portuguese
Sarawak	48,342	1,030,000	21	Administrative division of Malaysia...E	Kuching	Malay, Chinese, English
Sardinia	9,301	1,508,000	162	Part of Italy (3 Provinces)...D	........; Cagliari	Italian
Saskatchewan	251,700	918,000	3.6	Province (Canada)...E	Regina	English
Saudi Arabia†	830,000	7,650,000	9.2	Monarchy...A	Ar-Riyāḍ (Riyadh)	Arabic
Scandinavia (incl. Finland and Iceland)	509,899	21,955,000	43		........; København (Copenhagen)	Swedish, Danish, Norwegian, Finnish, Icelandic
Schleswig-Holstein	6,046	2,515,000	416	State (Germany, West)...E	Kiel	German
Scotland	30,414	5,235,000	172	Administrative division of United Kingdom...E	Edinburgh; Glasgow	English
Senegal†	75,955	3,990,000	53	Republic...A	Dakar	Wolof, Poular French
Seychelles	145	52,000	359	Colony (U.K.)...C	Victoria	French, Creole, English
Shetland Is.	550	17,500	32	Part of Scotland, U.K. (Zetland County)...D	Lerwick	English
Siam, see Thailand						
Sicily	9,926	4,890,000	493	Part of Italy (Sicilia Autonomous Region)...D	Palermo	Italian
Sierra Leone†	27,699	2,620,000	95	Monarchy (Br. Comm. of Nations)...A	Freetown	Temne, Mende, English
Sikkim	2,744	200,000	73	Monarchy (Indian protection)...B	Gangtok	Tibeto-Burman languages
Singapore†	224	2,240,000	10,000	Republic (Br. Comm. of Nations)...A	Singapore	Chinese, Malay, English
Solomon Is. (Austl. Trust)	4,100	95,000	23	Part of Australian Trust Terr. of New Guinea (Bougainville District)...D	Sohano; Kieta	Malay-Polynesian languages
Solomon Is., British	11,500	170,000	15	Protectorate (U.K.)...C	Honiara	Malay-Polynesian languages
Somalia†	246,201	2,880,000	12	Republic...A	Mogadisho	Somali
South Africa (incl. Walvis Bay)†	471,879	20,850,000	44	Federal Republic...A	Pretoria and Cape Town; Johannesburg	English, Afrikaans, Bantu languages
South America	6,870,000	195,500,000	28		........; São Paulo	
South Australia	380,070	1,189,000	3.1	State (Australia)...E	Adelaide	English
South Carolina	31,055	2,643,000	85	State (U.S.)...E	Columbia	
South Dakota	77,047	669,000	8.7	State (U.S.)...E	Pierre; Sioux Falls	
Southern Rhodesia, see Rhodesia						
Southern Yemen, see Yemen, People's Democratic Republic of						
South Georgia	1,450	20	0.01	Dependency of Falkland Is. (U.K.)...D	Grytviken	English, Norwegian
South Polar Regions						
South West Africa (excl. Walvis Bay)	317,827	755,000	2.4	Mandate (South Africa)**...C	Windhoek	Bantu languages, Hottentot, Bushman, Afrikaans, English

† Member of the United Nations (1971).
* Rhodesia unilaterally declared its independence from the United Kingdom on November 11, 1965.
** The United Nations declared an end to the mandate of South Africa over South West Africa in October 1966. Administration of the territory by South Africa is not recognized by the United Nations.

World Political Information Table (Continued)

Region or Political Division	Area in sq. miles	Estimated Population 1/1/1972	Pop. per sq. mi.	Form of Government and Ruling Power	Capital; Largest City (unless same)	Predominant Languages
Spain†	194,885	34,300,000	176	Monarchy (Regency) A	Madrid	Spanish, Catalan, Galician, Basque
Spain and Possessions	297,597	34,495,000	116	...	Madrid	...
Spanish Possessions in North Africa	12	125,000	10,417	Five Possessions (no central government) (Spain) C	........; Melilla	Spanish, Arabic, Berber
Spanish Sahara	102,700	70,000	0.7	African Province (Spain) C	Aaiun	Arabic, Spanish
Spitsbergen, see Svalbard	...	...	...	...	...	...
Sudan†	967,499	16,300,000	17	Republic A	Al-Khurṭūm (Khartoum)	Arabic, native languages, English
Sumatra (Sumatera)	182,860	21,000,000	115	Part of Indonesia (6 Provinces) D	........; Medan	Bahasa Indonesia, English, Chinese
Surinam (Neth. Guiana)	63,037	420,000	6.7	Self-governing Territory (Netherlands) C	Paramaribo	Dutch, Indo-Aryan languages
Svalbard (Spitsbergen) and Jan Mayen	24,102	Winter pop. 3,000	...	Dependency (Norway) C	Longyearbyen	Norwegian, Russian
Swaziland†	6,705	420,000	63	Monarchy (Br. Comm. of Nations) A	Mbabane	Swazi and other Bantu languages, English
Sweden†	173,649	8,140,000	47	Monarchy A	Stockholm	Swedish
Switzerland	15,941	6,340,000	398	Federal Republic A	Bern (Berne); Zürich	German, French, Italian
Syria†	71,498	6,550,000	92	Republic‡‡ A	Dimashq (Damascus)	Arabic
Tadžikskaja (Tadzhik) S.S.R.	55,250	3,075,000	56	Soviet Socialist Republic (U.S.S.R.) E	Dušhanbe	Tadzhik, Turkic languages, Russian
Taiwan (Formosa) (Nationalist China)	13,885	15,300,000	1,102	Republic A	T'aipei	Chinese
Tanganyika, see Tanzania	...	...	...	...	...	...
Tanzania (Tanganyika & Zanzibar)†	364,900	13,800,000	38	Republic (Br. Comm. of Nations) A	Dar es Salaam	Swahili and other Bantu languages, English Arabic
Tasmania	26,383	399,000	15	State (Australia) E	Hobart	English
Tennessee	42,244	3,993,000	95	State (U.S.) E	Nashville; Memphis	...
Texas	267,339	11,569,000	43	State (U.S.) E	Austin; Houston	...
Thailand (Siam)†	198,500	35,500,000	179	Monarchy A	Krung Thep (Bangkok)	Thai, Chinese
Tibet (Xizang Zizhiqu)	471,700	1,500,000	3.2	Autonomous Region (China) E	Lasa (Lhasa)	Tibetan
Togo†	21,600	2,030,000	94	Republic A	Lomé	Native languages, French
Tokelau (Union) Is.	4	1,700	425	Island Territory (New Zealand) C	........; Fakaofu	Malay-Polynesian languages
Tonga	270	90,000	333	Monarchy (Br. Comm. of Nations) A	Nukualofa	Malay-Polynesian languages, English
Transcaucasia	71,850	12,700,000	177	Union of Soviet Socialist Republics	........; Tbilisi	...
Trinidad & Tobago†	1,980	965,000	487	Self-governing Member (Br. Comm. of Nations) A	Port of Spain	English, Spanish
Tristan da Cunha	40	300	7.5	Dependency of St. Helena (U.K.) D	Edinburgh	English
Trucial States, see United Arab Emirates	...	...	...	...	...	...
Tunisia†	63,379	5,350,000	84	Republic A	Tunis	Arabic, French
Turkey†	301,382	36,750,000	122	Republic A	Ankara; İstanbul	Turkish
Turkey in Europe	9,121	3,300,000	362	Turkey	........; İstanbul	Turkish
Turkmenskaja (Turkmen) S.S.R.	188,450	2,290,000	12	Soviet Socialist Republic (U.S.S.R.) E	Aščhabad	Turkic languages, Russian
Turks & Caicos Is.	166	5,500	33	Colony (U.K.) C	Grand Turk	English
Uganda†	91,076	10,150,000	111	Republic (Br. Comm. of Nations) A	Kampala	Bantu languages
Ukrainskaja (Ukraine) S.S.R.†	233,100	47,780,000	205	Soviet Socialist Republic (U.S.S.R.) E	Kijev (Kiev)	Ukrainian, Russian
Union of Soviet Socialist Republics (Soviet Union)†	8,600,350	246,000,000	29	Federal Soviet Republics A	Moskva (Moscow)	Russian and other Slavic languages, various Finno-Ugric, Turkic and Mongol languages, Caucasian languages, Persian
Union of Soviet Socialist Republics in Europe	1,920,750	164,800,000	86	Union of Soviet Socialist Republics	........; Moskva (Moscow)	Russian, Ruthenian, various Finno-Ugric and Caucasian languages
United Arab Emirates (Trucial States)	32,300	200,000	6.2	Self-governing Union A	Abū Ẓaby	Arabic
United Arab Republic, see Egypt	...	...	...	...	...	...
United Kingdom of Great Britain & Northern Ireland†	94,214	55,650,000	591	Monarchy (Br. Comm. of Nations) A	London	English, Welsh, Gaelic
United Kingdom & Possessions	287,229	66,906,700	233	...	London	...
United States†	*3,675,545	‡208,120,000	57	Federal Republic A	Washington; New York	English
United States and Possessions	3,680,713	211,161,900	57	...	Washington; New York	English, Spanish
Upper Volta†	105,800	5,530,000	57	Republic A	Ouagadougou	Voltaic and Mande languages, French
Uruguay†	68,536	2,930,000	57	Republic A	Montevideo	Spanish
Utah	84,916	1,100,000	13	State (U.S.) E	Salt Lake City	...
Uzbekskaja (Uzbek) S.S.R.	173,600	12,660,000	73	Soviet Socialist Republic (U.S.S.R.) E	Taškent	Turkic languages, Sarṭ, Russian
Vatican City (Holy See)	0.2	1,000	5,000	Ecclesiastical State A	Città del Vaticano (Vatican City)	Italian, Latin
Venezuela†	352,144	10,950,000	31	Federal Republic A	Caracas	Spanish
Vermont	9,609	456,000	47	State (U.S.) E	Montpelier; Burlington	...
Victoria	87,884	3,515,000	40	State (Australia) E	Melbourne	English
Vietnam (Entire)	128,402	40,800,000	318	...	........; Sai-gon	Annamese, Chinese
Vietnam, North	61,294	21,800,000	356	People's Republic A	Ha-noi	Annamese, Chinese
Vietnam, South	67,108	19,000,000	283	Republic A	Sai-gon	Annamese, Chinese
Virginia	40,817	4,773,000	117	State (U.S.) E	Richmond; Norfolk	...
Virgin Is., British	59	11,000	186	Colony (U.K.) C	Road Town	English
Virgin Is. of the U.S.	133	68,000	511	Unincorporated Territory (U.S.) C	Charlotte Amalie	English
Wake I.	3	1,700	567	Possession (U.S.) C	...	English
Wales (incl. Monmouthshire)	8,016	2,730,000	341	United Kingdom	Cardiff	English, Welsh
Wallis & Futuna	98	9,000	92	Overseas Territory (France) C	Mata-Utu	Malay-Polynesian languages
Washington	68,192	3,468,000	51	State (U.S.) E	Olympia; Seattle	...
Western Australia	975,920	1,020,000	1.0	State (Australia) E	Perth	English
Western Samoa	1,097	148,000	135	Constitutional Monarchy (Br. Comm. of Nations) A	Apia	Malay-Polynesian languages, English
West Indies	91,064	25,814,900	283	...	........; La Habana (Havana)	...
West Virginia	24,181	1,737,000	72	State (U.S.) E	Charleston	...
White Russia, see Belorusskaja	...	...	...	...	...	...
Wisconsin	56,154	4,493,000	80	State (U.S.) E	Madison; Milwaukee	...
World	57,280,000	3,711,000,000	65	...	........; Tōkyō	...
Wyoming	97,914	335,000	3.4	State (U.S.) E	Cheyenne	...
Yemen†	75,300	6,000,000	80	Republic A	Ṣan'ā'	Arabic
Yemen, People's Democratic Republic of,†	111,075	1,500,000	14	People's Republic A	Aden	Arabic; English
Yugoslavia†	98,766	20,675,000	209	Socialist Federal Republic A	Beograd (Belgrade)	Serbo-Croatian-Slovenian, Macedonian
Yukon	207,076	18,000	0.09	Territory (Canada) E	Whitehorse	English, Eskimo, Indian
Zaire (Congo, The)†	905,567	22,900,000	25	Republic A	Kinshasa	Bantu languages, French
Zambia (Northern Rhodesia)†	290,586	4,500,000	15	Republic (Br. Comm. of Nations) A	Lusaka	Bantu languages, English
Zanzibar	1,020	380,000	373	Part of Tanzania D	........; Zanzibar	Arabic, English

† Member of the United Nations (1971).
‡‡ As of late 1967, the Gaza Strip was under Israeli military occupation. Data for Egypt, Israel, Jordan and Syria do not reflect de facto changes which took place during 1967.
* Total area of the United States includes 3,536,855 square miles of land; 78,268 square miles of inland water; and 60,422 square miles of Great Lakes area, not included in any State.
‡ 1972 estimated population including armed forces overseas.

Largest Metropolitan Areas and Cities of the World, 1968‡

This table lists every metropolitan area in the world with 1,000,000 or more population. For ease of comparison, each metropolitan area has been defined by Rand McNally & Company according to consistent rules. A metropolitan area includes a central city, neighboring communities linked to it by continuous built-up areas, and more distant communities if the bulk of their population is supported by commuters to the central city.

As a further aid to comparability, all populations are estimates for a single date, January 1, 1968. The "city proper" figures refer to the area locally considered to be the city, provided it is under a single municipal government. Some metropolitan areas, such as Tōkyō-Yokohama and Minneapolis-St. Paul, have more than one central city; in such cases the population and rank listed for the "city proper" refer to the first-named city only.

Rank 1968	Metropolitan Area, Country	POPULATION 1/1/1968 Metropolitan Area	City Proper	Rank of City Proper
1	Tōkyō–Yokohama, Japan	20,500,000	8,950,000†	2
	Yokohama		*1,975,000*	*36*
2	New York, United States	16,900,000	8,000,000	3
3	Ōsaka–Kōbe–Kyōto, Japan	12,300,000	3,100,000	17
	Kōbe		*1,250,000*	*67*
	Kyōto		*1,400,000*	*57*
4	London, United Kingdom	10,950,000	7,775,000	5
5	Moskva (Moscow), U.S.S.R.	9,150,000	6,466,000†	6
6	Buenos Aires, Argentina	8,600,000	2,900,000	23
7	Paris, France	8,575,000	2,600,000	28
8	Los Angeles, United States	8,455,000	2,810,000	25
9	Calcutta, India	7,900,000	3,000,000	20
10	Shanghai, China	7,800,000	10,700,000▲	1
11	Chicago, United States	7,435,000	3,460,000	14
12	Ciudad de México (Mexico City), Mexico	7,200,000	3,200,000	16
13	São Paulo, Brazil	6,600,000	5,200,000	7
14	Rio de Janeiro, Brazil	6,100,000	4,000,000	10
15	Al-Qāhirah (Cairo), Egypt	5,900,000	4,500,000	9
16	Bombay, India	5,650,000	5,000,000	8
17	Essen–Dortmund–Duisburg (The Ruhr), West Germany	5,150,000	705,000	
18	Philadelphia–Trenton–Wilmington, United States	5,025,000	2,015,000	34
19	Beijing (Peking), China	4,750,000	7,800,000▲	4
20	Detroit–Windsor, United States–Canada	4,625,000	1,575,000	50
21	Leningrad, Soviet Union	4,350,000	3,338,000†	15
22	Sŏul (Seoul), South Korea	4,175,000	3,950,000	11
23	San Francisco–Oakland–San Jose, United States	4,150,000	710,000	
24	Berlin, Germany (West and East)	3,975,000		
	Berlin, West		*2,163,000*	*30*
	Berlin, Ost–		*1,082,000*	*85*
25	Djakarta, Indonesia	3,750,000	3,750,000	13
26	Delhi–New Delhi, India	3,750,000	3,000,000	18
27	Boston, United States	3,575,000	595,000	
28	Victoria, Hong Kong	3,500,000	560,000	
29	Tianjin (Tientsin), China	3,500,000	3,900,000▲	12
30	Milano (Milan), Italy	3,365,000	1,684,000	46
31	Tehrān, Iran	3,250,000	2,875,000	24
32	Manila, Philippines	3,200,000	1,400,000	55
33	Madrid, Spain	3,075,000	2,950,000	21
34	Shenyang (Mukden), China	3,000,000	3,000,000	19
35	Nagoya, Japan	2,925,000	2,100,000	31
36	Wuhan, China	2,900,000	2,900,000	22
37	Manchester, United Kingdom	2,890,000	611,000	
38	Roma (Rome), Italy	2,810,000	2,631,000	26
39	Santiago, Chile	2,725,000	635,000	
40	Krung Thep (Bangkok), Thailand	2,700,000	1,975,000	37
41	Washington, United States	2,695,000	815,000	
42	Birmingham, United Kingdom	2,645,000	1,090,000	84
43	Chongqing (Chungking), China	2,600,000	2,600,000	27
44	Barcelona, Spain	2,600,000	1,738,000	44
45	Sydney, Australia	2,600,000	156,000	
46	Lima, Peru	2,550,000	335,000	
47	Johannesburg, South Africa	2,550,000	600,000	
48	Montréal, Canada	2,540,000	1,225,000	69
49	Karāchi, Pakistan	2,400,000	1,700,000	45
50	Madras, India	2,350,000	1,975,000	38
51	Budapest, Hungary	2,350,000	1,990,000	35
52	Hamburg, West Germany	2,335,000	1,833,000	41
53	İstanbul, Turkey	2,325,000	1,850,000	40
54	Melbourne, Australia	2,300,000	76,000	
55	Toronto, Canada	2,275,000	690,000	
56	St. Louis, United States	2,255,000	675,000	
57	Sai-gon, South Vietnam	2,250,000	1,640,000	47
58	Guangzhou (Canton), China	2,250,000	2,250,000	29
59	Cleveland, United States	2,250,000	780,000	
60	Bogotá, Colombia	2,200,000	2,075,000	33
61	Caracas, Venezuela	2,150,000	1,450,000	53
62	Haerbin (Harbin), China	2,100,000	2,100,000	32
63	Athínai (Athens), Greece	2,100,000	660,000	
64	Al-Iskandarīyah (Alexandria), Egypt	2,075,000	1,875,000	39
65	Bruxelles (Brussels), Belgium	2,070,000	169,000	
66	Katowice–Bytom–Gliwice, Poland	2,025,000	292,000	
67	Wien (Vienna), Austria	2,020,000	1,640,000	48
68	T'aipei, Taiwan	2,000,000	1,275,000	65
69	Singapore, Singapore	1,980,000	1,150,000	74
70	Pittsburgh, United States	1,920,000	540,000	
71	Baghdād, Iraq	1,900,000	1,200,000	70
72	Doneck–Makejevka, U.S.S.R.	1,875,000	855,000	
73	Napoli (Naples), Italy	1,875,000	1,263,000	66
74	Glasgow, United Kingdom	1,860,000	950,000	
75	Amsterdam–Haarlem, Netherlands	1,805,000	858,000	
76	Baltimore, United States	1,785,000	915,000	
77	La Habana (Havana), Cuba	1,765,000	990,000	
78	Xi'an (Sian), China	1,750,000	1,750,000	42
79	Nanjing (Nanking), China	1,750,000	1,750,000	43
80	Warszawa (Warsaw), Poland	1,700,000	1,283,000	64
81	Liverpool, United Kingdom	1,685,000	695,000	
82	Lahore, Pakistan	1,675,000	1,575,000	49
83	Köln (Cologne), West Germany	1,655,000	855,000	
84	München (Munich), West Germany	1,625,000	1,244,000	68
85	Minneapolis–St. Paul, United States	1,615,000	445,000	
86	Ahmadābād, India	1,600,000	1,350,000	60
87	Kijev (Kiev), U.S.S.R.	1,590,000	1,456,000	52
88	Houston, United States	1,575,000	1,150,000	73
89	București (Bucharest), Romania	1,550,000	1,400,000†	56
90	Gor'kij (Gorky), U.S.S.R.	1,535,000	1,139,000	79
91	Leeds–Bradford, United Kingdom	1,530,000	507,000	
92	Montevideo, Uruguay	1,525,000	1,325,000	62
93	Frankfurt am Main, West Germany	1,520,000	662,000	
94	Miami–Fort Lauderdale, United States	1,515,000	320,000	
95	Lisboa (Lisbon), Portugal	1,500,000	820,000	
96	Torino (Turin), Italy	1,480,000	1,132,000	80
97	Recife, Brazil	1,475,000	1,050,000	89
98	Pusan, South Korea	1,475,000	1,475,000	51
99	Stuttgart, West Germany	1,470,000	614,000	
100	Kitakyūshū–Shimonoseki, Japan	1,465,000	1,055,000	88
101	Bangalore, India	1,450,000	1,025,000	93
102	Chengdu (Chengtu), China	1,450,000	1,450,000	54
103	Hyderābād, India	1,450,000	1,025,000	94
104	Taškent, U.S.S.R	1,440,000	1,295,000	63
105	Char'kov (Kharkov), U.S.S.R.	1,425,000	1,148,000	78
106	Newcastle–Sunderland, United Kingdom	1,400,000	250,000	
107	København (Copenhagen), Denmark	1,385,000	655,000	
108	Buffalo–Niagara Falls, United States–Canada	1,372,000	460,000	
109	Milwaukee, United States	1,370,000	745,000	
110	Fushun, China	1,350,000	1,350,000	58
111	Taiyuan, China	1,350,000	1,350,000	59
112	Qingdao (Tsingtao), China	1,350,000	1,350,000	61
113	Baku, U.S.S.R.	1,335,000	790,000†	
114	Dallas, United States	1,325,000	795,000	
115	San Diego–Tijuana, United States–Mexico	1,325,000	670,000	
116	Cincinnati, United States	1,325,000	495,000	
117	Guadalajara, Mexico	1,300,000	1,125,000	81
118	Atlanta, United States	1,300,000	510,000	
119	Stockholm, Sweden	1,275,000	768,000	
120	Bandung, Indonesia	1,225,000	1,150,000	75
121	Surabaja, Indonesia	1,225,000	1,150,000	76
122	Kansas City, United States	1,215,000	550,000	
123	Mannheim–Ludwigshafen–Heidelberg, West Germany	1,210,000	324,000	
124	Medellín, Colombia	1,200,000	910,000	
125	Kujbyšev, U.S.S.R	1,200,000	1,014,000	95
126	Kānpur, India	1,200,000	1,060,000	87
127	Dnepropetrovsk, U.S.S.R.	1,200,000	837,000	
128	Changchun, China	1,200,000	1,200,000	71
129	Casablanca, Morocco	1,200,000	1,170,000	72
130	Lüda (Dairen), China	1,200,000	1,150,000†	77
131	Alger (Algiers), Algeria	1,175,000	1,000,000	97
132	Pôrto Alegre, Brazil	1,175,000	850,000	
133	Sverdlovsk, U.S.S.R.	1,160,000	981,000	
134	Novosibirsk, U.S.S.R.	1,160,000	1,079,000	86
135	Belo Horizonte, Brazil	1,150,000	1,000,000	96
136	Praha (Prague), Czechoslovakia	1,150,000	1,035,000	92
137	Hiroshima–Kure, Japan	1,100,000	530,000	
138	Seattle, United States	1,100,000	550,000	
139	Jinan (Tsinan), China	1,100,000	1,100,000	82
140	Kunming, China	1,100,000	1,100,000	83
141	Rotterdam, Netherlands	1,095,000	711,000	
142	Lyon, France	1,090,000	530,000	
143	Fukuoka, Japan	1,085,000	805,000	
144	Düsseldorf, West Germany	1,075,000	689,000	
145	Monterrey, Mexico	1,050,000	900,000	
146	Ankara, Turkey	1,050,000	1,035,000	91
147	Dacca–Nārāyanganj, Bangladesh	1,050,000	425,000	
148	Anshan, China	1,050,000	1,050,000	90
149	New Orleans, United States	1,040,000	655,000	
150	Antwerpen (Anvers), Belgium	1,040,000	240,000	
151	Čel'abinsk, U.S.S.R.	1,035,000	851,000	
152	Marseille, France	1,005,000	880,000	
153	Denver, United States	1,000,000	480,000	

▲ *Municipal boundaries include extensive rural areas, which have been excluded in estimating the metropolitan population.* † *Population within city limits, excluding areas beyond limits but administered by the city government.*

‡ *For 1972 estimates for United States metropolitan areas, see tables on pages 321–352 and 353. For latest official figures for foreign areas, see the World Cities table (pages 304–320).*

Population of Foreign Cities and Towns, Countries and Important Political Divisions

This table includes every urban center of 50,000 or more population in the world (excluding the United States), as well as many other important or well-known cities and towns. The table also lists major political subdivisions (states, provinces, etc.) of the leading countries.

The population figures are all from recent censuses (designated C) or official estimates (designated E), except for a few cities for which only unofficial estimates are available (designated UE). The date of the census or estimate is specified for each country. Individual exceptions are dated in parentheses or with a symbol (‡ or †).

For many cities, a second population figure is given accompanied by a star (★). The starred population refers to the city's entire metropolitan area, including suburbs. These metropolitan areas have been defined by Rand McNally & Company, following consistent rules to facilitate comparisons among the urban centers of various countries. Where a place is part of the metropolitan area of another city, that city's name is specified in parentheses preceded by (★). Some important places that are secondary central cities of their areas are designated by (★★) preceding the name of the metropolitan area's main city. A population marked with a triangle (▲) refers to an entire municipality, commune, or other district, which includes rural areas in addition to the urban center itself. In such entries the population for the city proper is often a Rand McNally estimate, because recent official data are only available for the larger area.

The names of capital cities appear in CAPITALS; the largest city in each country is designated by the symbol •. Designations in italics are used either to identify cities located in remote island groups such as the Azores, or to distinguish between cities with identical names by specifying their state or province location.

For more recent population totals for countries, see the Rand McNally 1972 population estimates in the table on pages 298–302. For lists of the largest metropolitan areas, see pages 303 (world) and 353 (United States). For a list of U.S. cities and towns, see pages 321–352.

AFARS & ISSAS / Afars et Issas

1970 E.......95,000

•DJIBOUTI.......62,000

AFGHANISTAN / Afghānestān

1971 E.......17,480,280

Andkhūi (1959 E).......30,000
Bāghlān (1959 E).......25,000
Chārikār (1959 E).......18,000
Faizābād (1959 E).......30,000
Farah (1959 E).......12,000
Gardez (1959 E).......20,000
Ghazni (1959 E).......30,000
Herāt.......103,915
Jalālābād (1959 E).......25,000
•KĀBUL (★498,800).......318,094
Kandahār.......133,799
Khānābād (1959 E).......30,000
Maimāna (1959 E).......30,000
Mazār-i-Sharīf (1969 E).......43,197
Pul-i-Khumri (1959 E).......20,000
Shibarghān (1959 E).......25,000
Tāshkurghān (1959 E).......30,000

ALBANIA / Shqipëri

1967 E.......1,964,800

Berat.......23,900
Durrës (1970 E).......53,800
Elbasan.......33,900
Fier.......19,700
Gjinokastër.......15,600
Kavajë.......18,800
Korçë (1970 E).......47,300
Lushnje.......17,500
Shkodër (1970 E).......55,300
Stalin (Kuçovë).......13,500
•TIRANË (1970 E).......171,300
Vlorë (Valona) (1970 E).......50,000

ALGERIA / Algérie

1966 C.......12,101,994

Aïn Beïda.......30,757
Aïn Benian (★Alger).......17,653
Aïn M'Lila (44,662▲).......12,632
Aïn Taya (★Alger).......22,542
Aïn Témouchent.......33,481
•ALGER (ALGIERS) (★1,116,493).943,142
Annaba (Bône).......168,790
Arzew.......13,080
Barika (40,957▲).......13,689
Batna (69,090▲).......54,924
Béchar (Colomb-Béchar).......46,505
Bejaïa (Bougie) (64,876▲).......49,930
Béni Saf (23,368▲).......18,507
Birkhadem (★Alger).......16,871
Biskra.......59,275
Blida.......99,238
Bordj Bou Arreridj (43,494▲).......33,780
Bordj Menaïel (32,411▲).......14,284
Boufarik (33,881▲).......24,108
Bouguerra (21,401▲).......13,373
Bouira (31,036▲).......16,615
Bou Ismaïl (29,648▲).......12,370
Bou Saâda.......26,262
Chelghoum el Aïd (27,985▲).......15,031
Cherchel (27,464▲).......11,667
Collo (31,285▲).......10,803
Constantine.......253,649
Dellys (23,718▲).......10,268
Djelfa (30,304▲).......25,472
Djidjelli (35,371▲).......25,007
Douéra.......20,039
El Affroun (14,920▲).......10,484
El Arba (22,857▲).......14,415
El Asnam (Orléansville) (69,745▲).......49,109
El Bayadh (24,770▲).......15,592
El Eulma (33,550▲).......25,590
El Goléa.......13,708
El Meghaier (23,506▲).......11,324
El Oued (43,547▲).......11,429
Fouka.......10,208
Frenda.......12,480
Ghardaïa (46,609▲).......30,167
Ghazaouet (20,785▲).......11,671
Guelma.......39,817
Guerrara.......12,546
Hadjout (16,038▲).......13,454
Hamma Bouziane (21,040▲).......11,472
Hammam Bou Hadjar (14,637▲).......11,219
Ighil Izane.......43,547
Khemis Miliana (36,530▲).......23,887
Khenchela (34,712▲).......28,421
Koléa (21,383▲).......15,941
Ksar el Boukhari (30,338▲).......15,127
Laghouat (38,166▲).......26,553
Lakhdaria (18,013▲).......10,321
Maghnia (35,137▲).......24,310
Mascara (43,108▲).......36,930
Mecheria.......12,151
Médéa (53,567▲).......36,992
Mers el Kébir (★Oran) (20,193▲).......5,624
Metlili Chaamba (17,999▲).......10,200
Mila (33,007▲).......12,733
Miliana (28,410▲).......16,735
Mohammadia (38,441▲).......23,182
Mostaganem.......75,332
M'Sila (36,930▲).......19,883
Nedroma (19,783▲).......12,137
Oran (Ouahran) (★369,462).......328,257
Ouargla (48,323▲).......18,206
Ouenza (29,069▲).......18,501
Ouled Djellal (15,632▲).......13,866
Saïda (38,348▲).......33,497
Sedrata (22,383▲).......14,156
Sétif.......98,337
Sfizef (16,305▲).......11,359
Sidi bel Abbès.......91,527
Sig (32,257▲).......26,192
Skikda (Philippeville).......72,742
Sougueur (14,494▲).......12,762
Souk Ahras (42,680▲).......34,397
Tébessa.......46,148
Ténès (22,881▲).......11,724
Tiaret.......40,934
Tighennif (25,839▲).......11,834
Tissemsilt (14,961▲).......11,381
Tizi-Ouzou (53,546▲).......25,852
Tlemcen.......87,210
Touggourt (50,159▲).......26,486

AMERICAN SAMOA

1970 C.......27,159

•PAGO PAGO.......2,451

ANDORRA

1971 C.......20,550

•ANDORRA.......2,000

ANGOLA

1970 C.......5,673,046

Benguela (1960 C).......23,256
Lobito (1960 C).......50,164
•LUANDA.......475,328
Nova Lisboa (1960 C).......38,745

ANTIGUA

1960 C.......54,304

•ST. JOHNS.......21,595

ARGENTINA

1970 C.......23,364,431

Provinces

Buenos Aires.......8,774,529
Capital Federal (Federal District).......2,972,453
Catamarca.......172,323
Chaco.......566,613
Chubut.......189,920
Córdoba.......2,060,065
Corrientes.......564,147
Entre Ríos.......811,691
Formosa.......234,075
Jujuy.......302,436
La Pampa.......172,029
La Rioja.......136,237
Mendoza.......973,075
Misiones.......443,020
Neuquén.......154,570
Río Negro.......262,622
Salta.......509,803
San Juan.......384,284
San Luis.......183,460
Santa Cruz.......84,457
Santa Fe.......2,135,583
Santiago del Estero.......495,419
Tierra del Fuego (Ter.).......15,658
Tucumán.......765,962

Cities

Almirante Brown (★Buenos Aires).......245,017
Avellaneda (★Buenos Aires).......337,538
Azul.......37,000
Bahía Blanca.......155,000
Balcarce.......21,000
Barranqueras (★Resistencia).......23,000
Bell Ville.......21,000
Berazategui (★Buenos Aires).......80,000
Berisso (★La Plata).......58,833
Bolívar.......16,500
Bragado.......22,000
•BUENOS AIRES (★8,625,000).2,972,453
Campana (★Buenos Aires).......35,000
Cañada de Gómez.......23,000
Caseros (Tres de Febrero) (★Buenos Aires).......313,460
Catamarca.......55,000
Chivilcoy.......35,000
Cipolletti.......30,000
Comodoro Rivadavia.......55,000
Concepción del Uruguay.......38,000
Concordia.......65,000
Córdoba (★825,000).......798,663
Corrientes.......128,000
Cruz del Eje.......24,000
Ensenada (★La Plata).......39,154
Esquel.......14,000
Esteban Echeverría (★Buenos Aires).......55,000
Florencio Varela (★Buenos Aires).......50,000
Formosa.......55,000
General Pico.......22,500
General Roca.......32,000
General San Martín (★Buenos Aires).......360,573
General Sarmiento (★Buenos Aires).......313,457
Godoy Cruz (★Mendoza).......105,000
Goya.......34,000
Gualeguaychú.......31,000
Guaymallén (★Mendoza).......110,000
Junín.......56,000
La Banda (★Santiago del Estero).......27,000
Lanús (★Buenos Aires).......449,824
La Plata (★510,000).......408,300
La Rioja.......43,000
Las Heras (★Mendoza).......48,000
Lomas de Zamora (★Buenos Aires).......410,806
Luján (★Buenos Aires).......33,500
Maipú.......18,000
Mar del Plata.......302,000
Mendoza (★400,000).......118,568
Mercedes.......42,000
Merlo (★Buenos Aires).......188,868
Moreno (★Buenos Aires).......114,041
Morón (★Buenos Aires).......485,983
Necochea.......35,000
Neuquén.......30,000
Olavarría.......45,000
Paraná.......120,000
Pergamino.......48,000
Posadas.......95,000
Punta Alta.......51,000
Quilmes (★Buenos Aires).......355,265
Rafaela.......43,000
Rawson.......5,500
Reconquista.......21,000
Resistencia (★135,000).......112,000
Río Cuarto.......78,000
Río Gallegos.......26,000
Río Tercero.......22,000
Rosario (★875,000).......705,000
Salta.......172,000
San Carlos de Bariloche.......23,000
San Fernando (★Buenos Aires).119,565
San Francisco.......44,000
San Isidro (★Buenos Aires).......250,008
San Juan (★210,000).......112,500
San Justo (★Buenos Aires).......659,193
San Lorenzo (★Rosario).......28,000
San Luis.......50,000
San Martín.......26,000
San Miguel de Tucumán.......310,000
San Nicolás de los Arroyos.......64,000
San Pedro.......19,000
San Rafael.......54,000
San Salvador de Jujuy.......67,000
Santa Fe.......245,000
Santa Rosa.......35,000
Santiago del Estero (★135,000).......105,000
Tafí Viejo.......25,000
Tandil.......54,000
Tartagal.......22,000
Tigre (★Buenos Aires).......152,335
Trelew.......21,000
Tres Arroyos.......37,000
Ushuaia.......5,500
Venado Tuerto.......30,000
Vicente López (★Buenos Aires).285,178
Viedma.......12,500
Villa María.......48,000
Zárate.......51,000

AUSTRALIA

1971 C.......12,728,461

States

Australian Capital Territory (Ter.).......143,843
New South Wales.......4,589,556
Northern Territory (Ter.).......85,519
Queensland.......1,823,362
South Australia.......1,172,774
Tasmania.......389,874
Victoria.......3,496,161
Western Australia.......1,027,372

Cities

Adelaide (★842,611).......16,331
Albury (★38,931).......28,398
Alice Springs.......11,118
Altona (★Melbourne).......30,397
Ashfield (★Sydney).......44,322
Auburn (★Sydney).......48,568
Ballarat (★58,854).......39,605
Bankstown (★Sydney).......162,310
Bendigo (★46,564).......31,972
Blacktown (★Sydney).......156,619
Blue Mountains (★Sydney).......36,627
Botany (★Sydney).......38,180
Box Hill (★Melbourne).......54,583
Brighton (★Melbourne).......39,103
Brisbane (★866,207).......699,371
Broadmeadows (★Melbourne).......100,873
Broken Hill.......29,743
Brunswick (★Melbourne).......51,424
Bundaberg.......27,394
Burnside (★Adelaide).......39,379
Burwood (★Sydney).......32,245
Cairns.......30,059
Camberwell (★Melbourne).......98,227
Campbelltown (★Adelaide).......37,953
Campbelltown (★Sydney).......34,207
CANBERRA (★158,594).......141,575
Canterbury (★Sydney).......130,334
Caulfield (★Melbourne).......81,705
Cessnock (★★Newcastle).......16,141
Chelsea (★Melbourne).......26,275
Coburg (★Melbourne).......65,428
Collingwood (★Melbourne).......20,906
Concord (★Sydney).......25,903
Dandenong (★Melbourne).......40,842
Darwin (★36,828).......31,687
Doncaster and Templestowe (★Melbourne).......64,298
Drummoyne (★Sydney).......31,209
Elizabeth (★Adelaide).......33,363
Enfield (★Adelaide).......77,555
Essendon (★Melbourne).......57,578
Fairfield (★Sydney).......112,862
Fitzroy (★Melbourne).......25,405
Footscray (★Melbourne).......57,710
Frankston (★Melbourne).......59,308
Fremantle (★Perth).......25,990
Geelong (★121,966).......17,775
Goulburn.......21,568
Hawthorn (★Melbourne).......37,476
Heidelberg (★Melbourne).......67,943
Hobart (★153,024).......52,425
Holroyd (★Sydney).......77,210
Hurstville (★Sydney).......67,070
Ipswich (★Brisbane).......61,514
Kalgoorlie (★20,784).......9,170
Keilor (★Melbourne).......55,538
Kew (★Melbourne).......32,574
Knox (★Melbourne).......56,778
Kogarah (★Sydney).......47,088
Ku-ring-gai (★Sydney).......98,435
Lane Cove (★Sydney).......28,577
Launceston (★62,181).......35,001
Leichhardt (★Sydney).......70,540
Lismore.......20,901
Liverpool (★Sydney).......82,270
Mackay (★28,416).......19,101
Maitland (★Newcastle).......30,963
Malvern (★Melbourne).......50,569
Manly (★Sydney).......39,250
Marion (★Adelaide).......67,591
Marrickville (★Sydney).......96,331
Maryborough.......19,304
Melbourne (★2,497,993).......74,877
Melville (★Perth).......52,877
Mitcham (★Adelaide).......54,347
Moe (★44,000).......15,524
Moorabbin (★Melbourne).......109,543
Mordialloc (★Melbourne).......29,652
Mosman (★Sydney).......29,220
Mount Isa.......26,213
Nedlands (★Perth).......22,586
Newcastle (★351,010).......145,718
Northcote (★Melbourne).......59,162
North Sydney (★Sydney).......52,920
Nunawading (★Melbourne).......90,686
Oakleigh (★Melbourne).......57,248
Orange.......23,143
Parramatta (★Sydney).......110,717
Penrith (★Sydney).......60,242
Perth (★701,392).......97,242
Port Adelaide (★Adelaide).......39,039
Prahran (★Melbourne).......56,493
Preston (★Melbourne).......91,663
Randwick (★Sydney).......123,404
Redcliffe (★Brisbane).......34,441
Richmond (★Melbourne).......27,849
Ringwood (★Melbourne).......34,928
Rockdale (★Sydney).......83,995
Rockhampton.......49,141
Ryde (★Sydney).......88,622
St. Kilda (★Melbourne).......60,742
Salisbury (★Adelaide).......56,290
Sandringham (★Melbourne).......35,404
Shellharbour (★Wollongong).......31,137
Shepparton.......19,409
South Melbourne (★Melbourne).26,813
South Perth (★Perth).......31,657
Southport (Gold Coast).......66,558
South Sydney (Northcott) (★Sydney).......38,816
Springvale (★Melbourne).......58,365
Sunshine (★Melbourne).......76,521
•Sydney (★2,799,634).......61,940
Tamworth.......24,076
Tea Tree Gully (★Adelaide).......36,687
Toowoomba.......59,476
Townsville.......71,109
Unley (★Adelaide).......39,906
Wagga Wagga.......28,814
Warrnambool.......18,663
Waverley (★Melbourne).......96,999
Waverley (★Sydney).......65,192
West Torrens (★Adelaide).......50,026
Whyalla.......31,568
Williamstown (★Melbourne).......29,983
Willoughby (★Sydney).......53,758
Wollongong (★198,768).......160,902
Woodville (★Adelaide).......72,703
Woollahra (★Sydney).......59,533

AUSTRIA / Österreich

1971 C.......7,456,745

States

Burgenland.......272,119
Kärnten (Carinthia).......525,728
Niederösterreich (Lower Austria).......1,414,161
Oberösterreich (Upper Austria).......1,223,444
Salzburg.......401,766
Steiermark (Styria).......1,192,442
Tirol (Tyrol).......540,771
Vorarlberg.......271,473
Wien (Vienna).......1,614,841

Cities

Amstetten.......13,334
Baden (★Wien).......22,629
Bad Ischl.......12,735
Bludenz.......12,262
Braunau [am Inn].......16,414
Bregenz.......23,171
Bruck an der Mur (★50,000).......16,369
Dornbirn.......34,772
Eisenerz.......11,528
Eisenstadt.......10,073
Feldkirch.......21,776
Fohnsdorf.......11,165
Gmunden.......12,211
Graz (★270,000).......249,211
Hallein.......14,090
Innsbruck (★140,000).......115,293
Kapfenberg (★★Bruck).......26,006
Kitzbühel.......8,003
Klagenfurt (★90,000).......74,618
Klosterneuburg (★Wien).......21,989
Knittelfeld.......14,494
Köflach.......12,569
Krems an der Donau.......21,643
Kufstein.......12,503
Leoben (★48,000).......35,122
Lienz.......11,713
Linz (★275,000).......204,627
Lustenau.......15,419
Mödling (★Wien).......18,792
Mürzzuschlag.......11,494
Neunkirchen.......10,929
Salzburg (★150,000).......127,455
Sankt Pölten.......43,229
Sankt Viet an der Glan.......11,058
Solbad Hall in Tirol.......12,209
Spittal an der Drau.......12,556
Steyr (★54,000).......40,587
Stockerau (★Wien).......12,564
Traun (★Linz).......20,838
Villach (★45,000).......34,593
Wels (★59,000).......47,081
•WIEN (VIENNA) (★1,940,000).......1,614,841
Wiener Neustadt (★41,000).......34,707

BAHAMA IS.

1970 C.......168,812

Dunmore Town (1963 C).......1,103
Eight Mile Rock (1963 C).......1,288
Freeport.......15,286
Matthew Town (1963 C).......1,258
•NASSAU (★95,000).......8,000

C Census. E Official estimate. UE Unofficial estimate.
L Population within municipal limits of year specified. • Largest city in country.

★ Population or designation of metropolitan area, including suburbs (see headnote).
▲ Population of an entire municipality, commune, or district, including rural area.
‡† Year of information specified at start of country.

BAHRAIN / Al-Baḥrayn

1971 C ... 216,078
•AL-MANĀMAH (*145,000) ... 89,112
Al-Muḥarraq (*Al-Manāmah) ... 37,577

BANGLADESH

1961 C ... 50,840,235
Barisāl ... 69,936
Bogra ... 33,784
Brāhmanbāria ... 44,784
Chāndpur ... 34,837
Chittagong ... 364,205
Comilla ... 54,504
•DACCA (*830,000) ... 362,006
Dinājpur ... 37,711
Farīdpur ... 28,333
Jamālpur ... 37,988
Jessore (*46,366) ... 39,304
Khulna (*127,970) ... 80,917
Kishorganj ... 24,031
Kushtia ... 24,952
Mādārīpur ... 25,328
Mymensingh ... 53,256
Nārāyanganj (**Dacca) ... 125,792
Nawābganj ... 29,725
Pābna ... 40,792
Pārbatipur ... 27,188
Rājshāhi (Rampur Boalia) ... 56,885
Rangpur ... 40,634
Saidpur ... 60,628
Sātkhira ... 20,169
Sherpur ... 24,924
Sirājganj ... 47,152
Sylhet ... 37,740
Tangail ... 23,688

BARBADOS

1970 C ... 238,141
•BRIDGETOWN (*115,000) ... 8,789

BELGIUM / Belgique / België

1970 E ... 9,690,991

Provinces
Antwerpen (Anvers) ... 1,535,680
Brabant ... 2,177,975
Hainaut (Henegouwen) ... 1,330,789
Liège (Luik) ... 1,015,309
Limburg (Limbourg) ... 656,477
Luxembourg (Luxemburg) ... 219,186
Namur (Namen) ... 384,689
Oost-Vlaanderen; Flandre Orientale (East Flanders) ... 1,314,031
West-Vlaanderen; Flandre Occidentale (West Flanders) ... 1,056,855

Cities
Aalst (Alost) (*Bruxelles) ... 46,744
Anderlecht (*Bruxelles) ... 103,753
Antwerpen (Anvers) (*1,050,000) ... 226,570
Arlon ... 14,343
Auderghem (*Bruxelles) ... 33,994
Bastogne ... 6,821
Berchem (*Antwerpen) ... 50,528
Borgerhout (*Antwerpen) ... 48,967
Brasschaat (*Antwerpen) ... 28,614
Brugge (Bruges) (*120,000) ... 51,303
•BRUXELLES (BRUSSEL) (BRUSSELS) (*2,000,000) ... 161,089
Charleroi (*380,000) ... 23,324
Dendermonde ... 9,154
Deurne (*Antwerpen) ... 80,112
Dinant ... 9,862
Eeklo ... 19,306
Ekeren (*Antwerpen) ... 27,636
Etterbeek (*Bruxelles) ... 51,386
Eupen ... 14,938
Evere (*Bruxelles) ... 26,943
Forest (Vorst) (*Bruxelles) ... 55,211
Geel ... 29,270
Genk ... 58,240
Gent (Gand) (*320,000) ... 149,265
Halle (Hal) (*Bruxelles) ... 20,205
Hasselt ... 39,673
Herentals ... 18,736
Herstal (*Liège) ... 29,718
Hoboken (*Antwerpen) ... 33,811
Huy ... 12,931
Ieper (Ypres) ... 18,837
Ixelles (*Bruxelles) ... 87,524
Izegem ... 22,958
Jette (*Bruxelles) ... 39,619
Jumet (*Charleroi) ... 27,845
Kortrijk (Courtrai) (*167,000) ... 44,998
La Louvière (*158,000) ... 23,711
Leuven (Louvain) (*109,000) ... 32,189
Liège (Luik) (*550,000) ... 147,277
Lier (*Antwerpen) ... 28,341
Lokeren ... 26,824
Lommel ... 21,961
Maaseik ... 8,732
Marcinelle (*Charleroi) ... 27,756
Mechelen (Malines) ... 65,620
Menen ... 22,141
Merksem (*Antwerpen) ... 39,785
Mol ... 28,475
Molenbeek St.-Jean (Sint-Jans-Molenbeek) (*Bruxelles) ... 68,756
Mons (Bergen) (*171,000) ... 28,727
Mortsel (*Antwerpen) ... 27,984
Mouscron (Moeskroen) (*Lille, France) ... 37,450
Namur (*88,000) ... 32,507
Nivelles ... 16,196
Oostende (Ostende) (*79,000) ... 56,167
Oudenaarde ... 22,079
Roeselare (Roulers) ... 40,587
Ronse (Renaix) ... 25,063
Saint-Gilles (Sint-Gillis) (*Bruxelles) ... 52,414
Schaerbeek (Schaarbeek) ... 118,947
Seraing (*Liège) ... 40,524
Sint-Amandsberg (*Gent) ... 25,049
Sint-Niklaas (St.-Nicolas) ... 49,294
Sint-Truiden (St.-Trond) ... 21,369
Soignies ... 12,075
Spa ... 9,586
Tielt ... 14,172
Tienen (Tirlemont) ... 22,518
Tongeren (Tongres) ... 17,226
Tournai (Doornik) ... 33,545
Turnhout ... 38,011
Uccle (Ukkel) (*Bruxelles) ... 78,645
Verviers (*82,000) ... 33,616
Veurne (Furnes) ... 7,607
Vilvoorde (*Bruxelles) ... 34,369
Waterloo (*Bruxelles) ... 17,711
Watermael-Boitsfort (*Bruxelles) ... 25,150
Wetteren ... 20,826
Wilrijk (*Antwerpen) ... 43,738
Woluwe-St.-Lambert (*Bruxelles) ... 46,913
Woluwe-St.-Pierre (*Bruxelles) ... 39,867

BERMUDA

1970 C ... 52,700
•HAMILTON (*18,000) ... 2,127
St. George (1960 C) ... 1,869

BHUTAN / Druk-Yul

1968 E ... 750,000
PARO ...
THIMBU ...

BOLIVIA

1967 E ... 4,561,400

Departments
Beni ... 181,000
Chuquisaca ... 427,400
Cochabamba ... 741,100
La Paz ... 1,433,000
Oruro ... 317,700
Pando ... 29,900
Potosí ... 807,400
Santa Cruz ... 432,300
Tarija ... 191,600

Cities (1969 E)
Cobija ... 3,000
Cochabamba ... 157,000
•LA PAZ ... 525,000
Oruro ... 91,000
Potosí ... 64,000
Santa Cruz ... 108,700
SUCRE ... 48,000
Tarija ... 23,000
Trinidad ... 17,000

BOTSWANA

1971 C ... 625,893
Francistown ... 19,680
GABORONE (GABERONES) ... 17,698
Kanye (1964 C) ... 34,045
Mahalapye (1964 C) ... 13,199
Mochudi (1964 C) ... 17,712
Molepolole (1964 C) ... 29,625
Moshupa (1964 C) ... 12,892
•Serowe (1964 C) ... 34,182

BRAZIL / Brasil

1970 C ... 93,215,301

States
Acre ... 216,200
Alagoas ... 1,589,605
Amapá (Ter.) ... 114,687
Amazonas ... 955,394
Bahia ... 7,508,779
Ceará ... 4,366,970
Distrito Federal (Brasília) ... 538,351
Espírito Santo ... 1,600,305
Fernando de Noronha (Ter.) ... 1,239
Goiás ... 2,941,107
Guanabara ... 4,252,009
Maranhão ... 2,997,576
Mato Grosso ... 1,600,494
Minas Gerais ... 11,497,574
Pará ... 2,161,316
Paraíba ... 2,384,615
Paraná ... 6,936,743
Pernambuco ... 5,166,554
Piauí ... 1,680,954
Rio de Janeiro ... 4,746,848
Rio Grande do Norte ... 1,552,158
Rio Grande do Sul ... 6,670,382
Rondônia (Ter.) ... 113,659
Roraima (Ter.) ... 40,915
Santa Catarina ... 2,903,360
São Paulo ... 17,775,889
Sergipe ... 901,618

Cities
Alagoinhas ... 53,891
Alegrete ... 45,522
Americana ... 62,387
Anápolis ... 89,405
Apucarana ... 41,800
Aracaju ... 179,512
Araçatuba ... 85,660
Araguari ... 48,702
Araraquara ... 82,607
Assis ... 45,531
Bagé ... 57,036
Barbacena ... 57,766
Barra do Piraí ... 42,713
Barra Mansa (**Volta Redonda) ... 75,006
Barretos ... 53,050
Bauru ... 120,178
Belém (*660,000) ... 565,097
Belford Roxo (*Rio de Janeiro) ... 173,427
Belo Horizonte (*1,550,000) ... 1,235,001
Blumenau ... 85,942
Boa Vista ... 16,720
Botucatu ... 42,252
Bragança Paulista ... 39,573
BRASÍLIA (*495,000) ... 272,002
Cabedelo (*João Pessoa) ... 12,811
Cachoeira do Sul ... 50,001
Cachoeiro de Itapemirim ... 58,968
Campina Grande ... 163,206
Campinas ... 328,629
Campo Grande ... 130,792
Campos ... 153,310
Campos Elyseos (*Rio de Janeiro) ... 104,636
Canoas (*Pôrto Alegre) ... 148,798
Carapicuíba (*São Paulo) ... 54,907
Caruaru ... 101,006
Cascatinha (*Rio de Janeiro) ... 28,576
Catanduva ... 48,446
Cavaleiro (*Recife) ... 58,811
Caxias do Sul ... 107,487
Coelho da Rocha (*Rio de Janeiro) ... 100,781
Colatina ... 46,012
Conselheiro Lafaiete ... 44,894
Corumbá ... 48,607
Crato ... 36,836
Criciuma ... 50,430
Cruz Alta ... 43,568
Cruzeiro ... 42,366
Cubatão (*Santos) ... 37,255
Cuiabá ... 83,621
Curitiba (*680,000) ... 483,038
Diadema (*São Paulo) ... 68,552
Diamantina ... 17,551
Divinópolis ... 69,872
Duque de Caxias (*Rio de Janeiro) ... 256,582
Feira de Santana ... 127,105
Florianópolis ... 115,665
Fortaleza (*910,000) ... 859,135
Franca ... 86,852
Garanhuns ... 49,579
Goiânia ... 362,152
Governador Valadares ... 125,174
Guaratinguetá ... 55,069
Guarujá (*Santos) ... 30,741
Guarulhos (*São Paulo) ... 221,639
Ilhéus ... 58,529
Ipiíba (*Rio de Janeiro) ... 55,486
Itabira ... 40,143
Itabuna ... 89,928
Itajaí ... 54,135
Itajubá ... 42,485
Itapetininga ... 42,331
Itaquari (*Vitória) ... 64,559
Ituiutaba ... 46,784
Jaboatão (*Recife) ... 52,537
Jacareí ... 48,684
Jaú ... 40,989
Jequié ... 62,341
João Monlevade ... 38,689
João Pessoa (*310,000) ... 197,398
Joinvile ... 77,760
Juàzeiro do Norte ... 79,796
Juiz de Fora ... 218,832
Jundiaí ... 145,785
Lajes ... 82,235
Limeira ... 77,243
Lins ... 38,080
Londrina ... 156,670
Lorena ... 39,655
Macapá ... 51,563
Maceió ... 242,867
Manaus ... 284,118
Marília ... 73,165
Maringá ... 51,620
Mauá (*São Paulo) ... 101,569
Mesquita (*Rio de Janeiro) ... 93,926
Mogi das Cruzes (*São Paulo) ... 90,330
Monjolo (*Rio de Janeiro) ... 46,793
Montes Claros ... 81,572
Mossoró ... 77,251
Muribeca dos Guararapes (*Recife) ... 74,963
Natal ... 250,787
Neves (*Rio de Janeiro) ... 112,912
Nilópolis (*Rio de Janeiro) ... 86,720
Niterói (*Rio de Janeiro) ... 291,970
Nova Friburgo ... 65,732
Nova Iguaçu (*Rio de Janeiro) ... 331,457
Nova Lima (*Belo Horizonte) ... 27,386
Nôvo Hamburgo ... 81,248
Olinda (*Recife) ... 187,553
Olinda (*Rio de Janeiro) ... 41,378
Osasco (*São Paulo) ... 283,303
Ourinhos ... 40,733
Ouro Prêto ... 24,050
Paranaguá ... 51,510
Parnaíba ... 57,031
Parque Industrial (*Belo Horizonte) ... 80,572
Passo Fundo ... 69,135
Passos ... 39,184
Patos ... 39,850
Patos de Minas ... 42,215
Paulo Afonso ... 38,494
Pelotas ... 150,278
Petrolina ... 37,801
Petrópolis (*Rio de Janeiro) ... 116,080
Pinheirinho (*Curitiba) ... 50,302
Piracicaba ... 125,490
Poços de Caldas ... 51,844
Ponta Grossa ... 92,344
Pôrto Alegre (*1,375,000) ... 885,564
Pôrto Velho ... 41,146
Presidente Prudente ... 91,188
Queimados (*Rio de Janeiro) ... 62,560
Recife (*1,750,000) ... 1,060,752
Ribeirão Prêto ... 190,897
Rio Branco ... 34,531
Rio Claro ... 69,240
Rio de Janeiro (*7,000,000) ... 4,252,009
Rio Grande ... 98,863
Salvador (*1,020,000) ... 1,007,744
Santa Maria ... 120,667
Santana do Livramento ... 48,448
Santarém ... 51,123
Santo André (*São Paulo) ... 415,025
Santos (*610,000) ... 341,317
São Bernardo do Campo (*São Paulo) ... 187,368
São Caetano do Sul (*São Paulo) ... 150,171
São Carlos ... 74,835
São Gonçalo (*Rio de Janeiro) ... 161,392
São João da Boa Vista ... 33,051
São João del Rei ... 45,019
São João de Meriti (*Rio de Janeiro) ... 163,934
São José do Rio Prêto ... 108,319
São José dos Campos ... 130,118
São Leopoldo (*Pôrto Alegre) ... 62,861
São Luís ... 167,529
•São Paulo (*8,050,000) ... 5,921,796
São Vicente (*Santos) ... 116,075
Sete Lagoas ... 61,063
Sete Pontes (*Rio de Janeiro) ... 53,766
Sobral ... 51,864
Sorocaba ... 165,990
Taubaté ... 98,933
Téofilo Otoni ... 64,568
Teresina ... 181,071
Teresópolis ... 53,462
Três Lagoas ... 40,157
Três Rios ... 31,733
Tubarão ... 51,121
Uberaba ... 108,576
Uberlândia ... 110,463
Uruguaiana ... 60,667
Vicente de Carvalho (*Santos) ... 59,767
Vila Velha (Espírito Santo) (*Vitória) ... 43,177
Vitória (*345,000) ... 121,978
Vitória da Conquista ... 82,477
Vitória de Santo Antão ... 41,130
Volta Redonda (*205,000) ... 120,645

BRITISH HONDURAS

1970 C ... 119,863
BELMOPAN (1971 E) ... 5,000
•Belize ... 39,332
Cayo (San Ignacio) ... 4,335
Corozal ... 4,674
Punta Gorda ... 2,123
Stann Creek ... 6,979

BRITISH SOLOMON ISLANDS
See Solomon Islands, British

BRITISH VIRGIN ISLANDS
See Virgin Islands, British

BRUNEI

1960 C ... 83,877
•BANDAR SERI BEGAWAN (BRUNEI) (*22,939) ... 9,702

BULGARIA / Bâlgarija

1969 E ... 8,464,300

Districts
Blagoevgrad ... 310,600
Burgas ... 404,200
Gabrovo ... 188,400
Haskovo (Khaskovo) ... 289,500
Jambol ... 217,200
Kârdžali ... 296,400
Kjustendil ... 197,500
Loveč ... 221,300
Michajlovgrad ... 236,900
Pazardžik ... 306,200
Pernik ... 181,400
Pleven ... 349,800
Plovdiv ... 658,300
Razgrad ... 200,600
Ruse ... 285,900
Silistra ... 171,800
Sliven ... 233,300
Smoljan ... 177,000
Sofija (Sofia) ... 317,500
Sofija (Sofia) (City) ... 973,500
Stara Zagora ... 373,700
Šumen (Shumen) ... 249,200
Târgovište ... 175,400
Tolbuhin ... 239,300
Varna ... 397,800
Veliko Târnovo ... 333,200
Vidin ... 175,600
Vraca ... 302,800

Cities
Ajtos ... 18,700
Asenovgrad ... 38,500
Bjala Slatina ... 16,500
Blagoevgrad (Gorna Dzhumaya) ... 36,500
Botevgrad ... 14,000
Burgas ... 131,700
Dimitrovgrad ... 44,200
Gabrovo ... 71,800
Goce Delčev ... 15,500
Gorna Orjachovica ... 28,300
Harmanli (Kharmanli) ... 16,000
Haskovo (Khaskovo) ... 66,900
Jambol (Yambol) ... 70,300
Kârdžali ... 41,500
Karlovo ... 22,900
Karnobat ... 20,500
Kazanlâk ... 50,300
Kjustendil ... 43,700
Kneža ... 14,500
Lom ... 29,100
Loveč ... 40,000
Mihajlovgrad ... 34,200
Nova Zagora ... 21,000
Panagjurište ... 21,800
Pazardžik ... 61,400
Pernik (Dimitrovo) ... 79,900
Peštera ... 15,300
Petrič ... 21,900
Pleven ... 92,500
Plovdiv ... 247,500
Popovo ... 17,400
Provadija ... 13,800
Razgrad ... 35,600
Ruse ... 149,600
Samokov ... 23,800
Sevlievo ... 21,900
Silistra ... 37,400
Sliven ... 81,100
Smoljan ... 20,300
•SOFIJA (SOFIA) (*973,500) ... 868,200
Stanke Dimitrov ... 37,800
Stara Zagora ... 109,100
Šumen (Shumen) (Kolarovgrad) ... 69,600
Svištov ... 22,900
Tolbuhin (Dobrich) ... 64,100
Târgovište ... 31,100
Varna ... 219,000
Veliko Târnovo (Tŭrnovo) ... 43,700
Vidin ... 42,600
Vraca (Vratsa) ... 47,600

BURMA / Myanma

1969 E ... 26,980,000
Bassein ... 133,000
Bogale (1953 C) ... 23,211
Chauk (1953 C) ... 24,466
Henzada ... 83,000
Mandalay ... 393,000
Ma-ubin (1953 C) ... 23,362
Meiktila (1953 C) ... 25,180
Merqui (1953 C) ... 33,697
Monywa (1953 C) ... 26,172
Moulmein ... 169,000
Myaungmya (1953 C) ... 24,532
Myingyan ... 63,500
Myitkyina (1953 C) ... 12,833
Pakokku (1953 C) ... 30,943
Pegu ... 122,000
Pyè (Prome) ... 64,000
Pyinmana (1953 C) ... 22,066
•RANGOON (1968E) ... 1,717,600
Sagaing (1953 C) ... 15,439
Sittwe (Akyab) ... 81,000
Tavoy ... 52,000
Thaton (1953 C) ... 38,047
Toungoo (1953 C) ... 31,589
Yenangyaung (1953 C) ... 24,416

BURUNDI

1970 E ... 3,540,000
•BUJUMBURA (*100,000) ... 80,000

CAMBODIA / Kampuchea

1962 C ... 5,728,711
Bătdâmbâng ... 38,780
Kâmpóng Cham ... 28,532
•PHNUM PÉNH ... 393,995
Takêv ... 7,308

CAMEROON / Cameroun

1970 E ... 5,836,000
•Douala ... 230,000
YAOUNDÉ (1969 E) ... 165,800

CANADA

1971 C ... 21,568,311

CANADA/ALBERTA ... 1,627,874
Banff (1966 C) ... 2,896
Barrhead ... 2,786
Bonnyville ... 2,536
Brooks ... 3,999
Calgary ... 400,154
Camrose ... 8,648
Cardston ... 2,744
Claresholm ... 2,957
Coaldale ... 2,795
Drayton Valley ... 3,916
Drumheller ... 5,428
Edmonton (*490,811) ... 434,116
Edson ... 3,817
Fort MacLeod ... 2,725
Fort Saskatchewan ... 5,743
Grand Cache ... 2,605
Grande-Prairie ... 12,797
Hanna ... 2,561
High Prairie ... 2,329
High River ... 2,663
Hinton ... 4,916
Innisfail ... 2,468
Jasper (1966 C) ... 2,505
Lacombe ... 3,407
Leduc ... 3,994
Lethbridge ... 40,706
McMurray ... 6,749
Medicine Hat ... 26,048
Olds ... 3,378
Peace River ... 4,951
Pincher Creek ... 3,231
Ponoka ... 4,422
Redcliff ... 2,266
Red Deer ... 27,428

(Canada/Alberta continued)

C Census. E Official estimate. UE Unofficial estimate.
L Population within municipal limits of year specified. • Largest city in country.
★ Population or designation of metropolitan area, including suburbs (see headnote).
▲ Population of an entire municipality, commune, or district, including rural area.
‡† Year of information specified at start of country.

(Canada/Alberta continued)

Rocky Mountain House...2,975
St.-Albert (*Edmonton)...11,800
St. Paul...4,171
Sherwood Park (*Edmonton) (1966 C)...6,339
Spruce Grove (*Edmonton)...3,012
Stettler...4,106
Taber...4,790
Vegreville...3,696
Vermilion...2,900
Wainwright...3,791
Westlock...3,265
Wetaskiwin...6,266
Whitecourt...3,200

CANADA/ BRITISH COLUMBIA...2,184,621

Burnaby (*Vancouver)...124,216
Campbell River (1966 C)...4,971
Castlegar...3,068
Chilliwack...8,848
Comox...3,884
Courtenay...6,968
Cranbrook...11,710
Creston...3,175
Dawson Creek...11,488
Duncan...4,391
Esquimalt (*Victoria)...12,895
Fernie...4,170
Fort St. John...8,243
Golden...2,929
Grand Forks...3,169
Haney (1966 C)...2,441
Hope...3,067
Kamloops...25,599
Kelowna...19,089
Kimberley...7,441
Kinnaird...2,838
Kitimat...11,813
Ladysmith...3,656
Lake Cowichan...2,368
Langley...4,634
Merritt...5,161
Mission City (1966 C)...3,412
Nanaimo...14,762
Nelson...9,168
New Westminster (*Vancouver)...42,083
North Vancouver (*Vancouver)...31,863
Oak Bay (*Victoria)...18,364
Ocean Falls (1966 C)...2,896
Penticton...17,702
Port Alberni...19,749
Port Coquitlam (*Vancouver)...19,570
Port Moody (*Vancouver)...10,780
Powell River...13,714
Prince George...32,755
Prince Rupert...15,355
Quesnel...6,224
Revelstoke...4,717
Richmond (*Vancouver)...61,376
Rossland...3,911
Sidney (*Victoria)...4,859
Smithers...3,772
Summerland...5,358
Terrace (1966 C)...6,889
Trail...10,843
Valley View...3,700
Vancouver (*1,071,081)...422,278
Vernon...12,921
Victoria (*193,512)...60,897
West Vancouver (*Vancouver)...36,273
White Rock (*Vancouver)...10,244
Williams Lake...4,071

CANADA/MANITOBA...988,247

Beauséjour...2,225
Brandon...30,832
Dauphin...8,860
East Kildonan (*Winnipeg)...29,722
Flin Flon *(Man. and Sask.)*...9,307
Minnedosa...2,629
Morden...3,276
Neepawa...3,216
Portage-la-Prairie...12,722
St. Boniface (*Winnipeg)...46,661
St. James-Assiniboia (*Winnipeg)...70,768
St. Vital (*Winnipeg)...32,613
Selkirk...9,158
Steinbach...5,161
Swan River...3,487
The Pas...6,072
Thompson...16,219
Transcona (*Winnipeg)...22,085
Tuxedo (*Winnipeg)...3,245
Virden...2,778
West Kildonan (*Winnipeg)...23,278
Winkler...2,942
Winnipeg (*534,685)...243,208

CANADA/ NEW BRUNSWICK...634,557

Bathurst...16,404
Campbellton...10,232
Caraquet...3,411
Chatham...7,812
Dalhousie...6,247
Dieppe (*Moncton)...4,261
Edmundston...12,089
Fredericton...23,612
Grand Falls...4,364
Lewisville (*Moncton)...3,710
Marysville...3,802
Moncton (*65,000)...47,781
Nashwaaksis...7,197
Newcastle...6,347
Oromocto...11,518
Riverview Heights (*Moncton)...6,411
Sackville...3,176
Saint John (*105,227)...87,910
St. Stephen...3,300
Sussex...3,840
Tracadie...2,188
Woodstock...4,775

CANADA/ NEWFOUNDLAND...522,104

Baie Verte...2,406
Bay Roberts...3,629
Bishop's Falls...4,108
Bonavista...4,217
Botwood...4,109
Carbonear...4,673
Channel-Port-aux-Basques...5,870
Corner Brook...25,929
Deer Lake...4,403
Gander...7,720
Grand Bank...3,465
Grand Falls...7,659
Happy Valley...4,954
Harbour Grace...2,726
Labrador City...7,641
Lewisporte...3,166
Marystown...4,982
Mount Pearl Park (*St. John's)...7,110
St. John's (*129,304)...86,290
St. Lawrence...2,147
Springdale...3,221
Stephenville...7,723
Wabana (Bell Island)...5,256
Wabash...3,390
Windsor...6,651

CANADA/ NORTHWEST TERRITORIES...34,807

Aklavik (1966 C)...611
Fort Smith...2,372
Frobisher Bay (1966 C)...1,631
Hay River...2,420
Inuvik...2,672
Yellowknife...5,867

CANADA/NOVA SCOTIA...788,960

Amherst...9,898
Antigonish...5,403
Bible Hill (1966 C)...2,901
Bridgewater...5,197
Dartmouth (*Halifax)...64,002
Digby...2,324
Dominion (*Glace Bay)...2,860
Florence (*Sydney Mines) (1966 C)...2,059
Glace Bay (*43,500)...22,276
Halifax (*220,350)...121,086
Kentville...5,129
Liverpool...3,610
Louisbourg...1,578
Lower Sackville (1966 C)...2,613
Lunenburg...3,201
New Glasgow...10,792
New Waterford (*Glace Bay)...9,549
North Sydney (**Sydney Mines)...8,498
Pictou...4,247
Reserve Mines (*Glace Bay) (1966 C)...2,710
Shelburne...2,699
Springhill...5,195
Stellarton...5,334
Sydney (*44,000)...32,459
Sydney Mines (*23,000)...8,957
Trenton...3,319
Truro...12,968
Westville...3,844
Windsor...3,626
Wolfville...2,831
Yarmouth...8,291

CANADA/ONTARIO...7,703,106

Acton...5,033
Ajax (*Toronto)...12,509
Alexandria...3,230
Alliston...3,174
Almonte...3,708
Amherstburg...5,115
Ansonville (1966 C)...3,037
Arnprior...6,017
Atikokan (1966 C)...6,240
Aurora...13,534
Aylmer West...4,697
Barrie...26,985
Belleville...34,498
Blenheim...3,483
Blind River...3,393
Bowmanville...8,894
Bracebridge...6,936
Bradford...3,390
Bramalea (*Toronto) (1966 C)...8,846
Brampton (*Toronto)...41,238
Brantford (*65,000)...62,853
Brighton...2,953
Brockville...19,707
Burlington (*Hamilton)...86,125
Caledonia...3,184
Campbellford...3,470
Capreol...3,471
Carleton Place...5,044
Chapleau...3,365
Chatham...34,601
Clinton...3,113
Cobourg...11,214
Cochrane...4,926
Collingwood...9,719
Cornwall...46,429
Deep River...5,661
Delhi...3,837
Dryden...6,935
Dundas (*Hamilton)...17,211
Dunnville...5,509
East York (*Toronto)...104,919
Elliot Lake (1966 C)...6,640
Elmira...4,722
Espanola...6,059
Essex...4,034
Etobicoke (*Toronto)...282,244
Exeter...3,379
Fergus...5,415
Fort Erie (*Buffalo, N.Y.)...23,099
Fort Frances...9,698
Galt (*Kitchener)...38,134
Gananoque...5,072
Garson (*Sudbury) (1966 C)...3,901
Georgetown...15,793
Geraldton...3,145
Goderich...6,804
Gravenhurst...7,101
Grimsby...15,742
Guelph...58,364
Gwillimbury (1966 C)...4,528
Haileybury...5,257
Hamilton (*495,864)...307,473
Hanmer (1966 C)...3,619
Hanover...5,034
Hawkesbury...9,256
Hearst...3,484
Hespeler (*Kitchener)...6,252
Huntsville...9,577
Ingersoll...7,780
Iroquois Falls...7,248
Kapuskasing...12,789
Kenora...10,889
Kincardine...3,200
Kingston (*77,000)...61,870
Kingsville...4,078
Kirkland Lake (1966 C)...14,008
Kitchener (*224,390)...109,954
Lambeth (*London) (1966 C)...3,056
Leamington...10,589
Levack...2,943
Lincoln (*Buffalo, N.Y.)...14,262
Lindsay...12,705
Listowel...4,677
Lively (*Sudbury)...2,988
London (*284,469)...221,430
Manitouwadge (1966 C)...2,983
Markham (*Toronto)...36,636
Mattawa...2,878
Meaford...4,055
Midland...10,995
Milton West (*Toronto)...7,023
Mississauga (*Toronto)...155,667
Mitchell...2,549
Mount Forest...3,031
Napanee...4,600
New Hamburg...2,998
New Liskeard...5,487
Newmarket...18,974
Niagara Falls (**Buffalo, N.Y.)...65,271
Niagara-on-the-Lake (*Buffalo, N.Y.)...12,501
North Bay...49,063
North York (*Toronto)...504,453
Oakville (*Toronto)...61,365
Orangeville...8,030
Orillia...24,016
Oshawa (*119,000)...91,113
OTTAWA (*596,176)...298,087
Owen Sound...18,281
Paris...6,474
Parry Sound...5,840
Pelham (*Buffalo, N.Y.)...9,949
Pembroke...16,130
Penetanguishene...5,491
Perth...5,539
Petawawa...5,657
Peterborough...57,498
Petrolia...4,030
Picton...4,860
Point Edward (*Sarnia)...2,780
Port Colborne (*Buffalo, N.Y.)...21,388
Port Credit (*Toronto)...9,433
Port Dover...3,403
Port Hope...8,747
Port Perry...2,977
Prescott...5,178
Preston (*Kitchener)...16,530
Renfrew...9,048
Richmond Hill (*Toronto)...32,399
Ridgetown...2,836
Rockland...3,654
St. Catharines (**Buffalo, N.Y.)...109,636
St. Marys...4,569
St. Thomas...25,062
Sarnia (*137,300)...56,727
Sault Ste. Marie (*95,300)...78,175
Scarborough (*Toronto)...332,118
Simcoe...10,800
Sioux Lookout...2,495
Smiths Falls...9,598
South Porcupine (*Timmins) (1966 C)...4,912
Stoney Creek (*Hamilton)...8,364
Stratford...23,863
Strathroy...6,594
Streetsville (*Toronto)...6,833
Sturgeon Falls...6,661
Sudbury (*172,456)...89,898
Tecumseh (*Detroit, Mich.)...5,157
Thorold (*Buffalo, N.Y.)...15,042
Thunder Bay (*111,492)...107,805
Tilbury...3,626
Tillsonburg...6,611
Timmins (*39,000)...28,252
Toronto (*2,609,638)...698,634
Trenton...14,405
Uxbridge...3,068
Vanier (Eastview) (*Ottawa)...21,859
Vaughan (*Toronto)...15,839
Walkerton...4,364
Wallaceburg...10,553
Waterloo (*Kitchener)...37,245
Wawa (Jamestown) (1966 C)...4,577
Welland (**Buffalo, N.Y.)...44,222
Whitby (*Oshawa)...25,291
Whitchurch-Stouffville (*Toronto)...11,277
Windsor (**Detroit, Mich.)...199,784
Wingham...2,910
Woodstock...25,559
York (*Toronto)...147,062

CANADA/PRINCE EDWARD ISLAND...111,641

Charlottetown...18,631
Kensington...1,079
Montague...1,594
Parkdale...2,321
St. Eleanors...1,611
Sherwood...3,792
Souris East...1,365
Summerside...9,315

CANADA/QUEBEC/ QUÉBEC...6,027,764

Acton Vale...4,572
Alma...22,353
Amos...6,845
Amqui...3,777
Ancienne-Lorette (Notre-Dame-de-Lorette) (*Québec)...8,282
Anjou (*Montréal)...33,842
Arthabaska...4,483
Arvida (*Chicoutimi)...18,433
Asbestos...9,760
Aylmer East (*Ottawa)...7,160
Bagotville...6,019
Baie-Comeau...12,108
Baie-d'Urfé (*Montréal)...3,886
Baie-St. Paul...4,156
Beaconsfield (*Montréal)...19,328
Beauharnois...8,141
Beauport (*Québec)...14,739
Beaupré...2,853
Bécancour...8,163
Bedford...2,789
Bélair...4,485
Beloeil...12,248
Berthierville...4,076
Black Lake...4,140
Blainville...9,641
Bois-des-Filion...4,060
Boucherville (*Montréal)...20,000
Bromptonville...2,766
Brossard (*Montréal)...23,421
Brownsburg...3,387
Buckingham...7,267
Cabano...3,055
Candiac (*Montréal)...5,189
Cap-Chat...3,855
Cap-de-la-Madeleine (*Trois-Rivières)...31,120
Carignan...3,333
Causapscal...2,974
Chambly...11,466
Chandler...3,842
Chapais...2,906
Charlemagne (*Montréal)...4,174
Charlesbourg (*Québec)...33,484
Charny (*Québec)...5,192
Châteauguay (*Montréal)...15,759
Châteauguay-Centre (*Montréal)...17,897
Château-Richer...3,099
Chibougamau...9,741
Chicoutimi (*131,924)...32,990
Chicoutimi-Nord (*Chicoutimi)...14,058
Clermont...3,386
Coaticook...6,566
Contrecoeur...2,688
Côte-St.-Luc (*Montréal)...24,358
Courville (*Québec)...6,217
Cowansville...11,906
Danville...2,589
Deux-Montagnes (*Montréal)...8,598
Disraëli...3,394
Dolbeau...7,656
Dollard-des-Ormeaux (*Montréal)...25,284
Donnacona...5,846
Dorion-Vaudreuil (Dorion) (*Montréal)...6,195
Dorval (*Montréal)...20,471
Drummondville (*42,500)...31,537
Drummondville-Sud (*Drummondville)...9,003
East Angus...4,747
Farnham...6,462
Gagnon...3,773
Gaspé...16,842
Gatineau (*Ottawa)...22,356
Giffard (*Québec)...13,087
Granby...33,958
Grand'Mère (*Shawinigan)...17,144
Greenfield Park (*Montréal)...15,277
Hampstead (*Montréal)...7,035
Hauterive...13,204
Hudson...4,321
Hull (*Ottawa)...62,842
Huntingdon...3,069
Iberville (*St.-Jean)...9,300
Île-Perrot (*Montréal)...4,043
Joliette...19,497
Jonquière (**Chicoutimi)...28,080
Kénogami (*Chicoutimi)...10,955
Lac-Brome...4,071
Lac-Etchemin...2,789
Lachine (*Montréal)...44,345
Lachute...11,789
Lac-Mégantic...6,756
Laflèche (Mackayville) (*Montréal)...15,036
La Malbaie...4,032
La Pocatière...4,246
Laprairie (*Montréal)...8,310
La Providence...4,671
La Salle (*Montréal)...72,916
La Sarre...5,095
L'Assomption...4,885
La Tuque...13,071
Lauzon (*Québec)...12,801
Laval (Ville de Laval) (*Montréal)...228,101
LeMoyne (*Montréal)...8,162
Lennoxville (*Sherbrooke)...3,867
L'Épiphanie...2,757
Lévis (*Québec)...16,566
Longueuil (*Montréal)...97,483
Loretteville (*Québec)...11,646
Louiseville...4,015
McMasterville...2,502
Magog...13,280
Malartic...5,357
Maniwaki...6,457
Marieville...4,521
Mascouche (*Montréal)...8,783
Matane...11,826
Mercier (Ste.-Philomène)...4,007
Mistassini...3,607
Mont-Joli...6,707
Mont-Laurier...8,196
Montmagny...12,378
Montmorency (*Québec)...4,947
•Montréal (*2,720,413)...1,197,753
Montréal-Est (*Montréal)...5,048
Montréal-Nord (*Montréal)...88,038
Montréal-Ouest (*Montréal)...6,364
Mont-St.-Hilaire...5,966
Mount-Royal (*Montréal)...21,470
Murdochville...2,858
Napierville...1,993
New Richmond...3,942
Nicolet...4,716
Noranda...10,670
Notre-Dame-des-Laurentides...5,087
Orsainville (*Québec)...12,561
Otterburn Park...3,506
Outremont (*Montréal)...28,402
Percé...5,598
Pierrefonds (*Montréal)...33,046
Pincourt (*Montréal)...5,903
Plessisville...7,224
Pointe-aux-Trembles (*Montréal)...35,521
Pointe-Claire (*Montréal)...27,310
Pointe-Gatineau (*Ottawa)...15,607
Pont-Rouge...3,226
Port Alfred...9,191
Port-Cartier...3,738
Price...2,752
Princeville...3,827
Québec (*476,232)...182,418
Rawdon...2,752
Repentigny (*Montréal)...19,441
Richmond...4,275
Rimouski...26,546
Rivièra (1966 C)...3,552
Rivière-du-Loup...12,423
Rivière-du-Moulin (*Chicoutimi)...4,391
Roberval...8,286
Rosemère (*Montréal)...6,727
Rouyn...17,804
Roxboro (*Montréal)...7,654
Ste.-Adèle (1966 C)...2,675
Ste.-Agathe-des-Monts...5,525
Ste.-Anne-de-Beaupré...1,778
Ste.-Anne-de-Bellevue (*Montréal)...4,932
Ste.-Anne-des-Monts...5,577
St.-Antoine (*Ste.-Jérôme)...5,828
St.-Basile-le-Grand...4,383
St.-Boniface-de-Shawinigan (*Shawinigan)...2,586
St.-Bruno (*Montréal)...15,822
St.-Césaire...2,273
St.-David-de-l'Auberivière (*Québec)...3,808
St.-Eustache (*Montréal)...9,464
St.-Félicien...4,955
St.-Ferdinand (Bernierville)...2,405
Ste.-Foy (*Québec)...67,834
St.-Gabriel...3,362
Ste.-Geneviève (*Montréal)...2,847
St.-Georges-Ouest...6,002
St.-Hubert (*Montréal)...21,753
St.-Hyacinthe...24,192
St.-Jacques...1,973
St.-Jean (*48,000)...32,484
St.-Jérôme (*35,000)...26,131
St.-Joseph...4,944
St.-Joseph-de-Beauce...2,886
St.-Joseph-de-Sorel...3,279
St.-Jovite...2,844
St.-Lambert (*Montréal)...18,590
St.-Laurent (*Montréal)...63,067
St.-Léonard (*Montréal)...52,013
St.-Luc (*St.-Jean)...4,852
St.-Marc-des-Carrières...2,664
Ste.-Marie-de-Beauce...4,308
St.-Pamphile...3,553
St.-Paul-l'Ermite (1966 C)...3,175
St.-Pierre (*Montréal)...6,762
St.-Raymond...4,000
St.-Rémi...2,297
St.-Romuald-d'Etchemin (*Québec)...8,439
Ste.-Scholastique...14,778
Ste.-Thérèse (*Montréal)...17,161
Ste.-Thérèse-Ouest (*Montréal)...7,282
St.-Tite...3,136
Sayabec...1,799
Schefferville...3,277
Senneterre...4,305
Sept-Îles (Seven Islands)...24,289
Shawinigan (*61,500)...27,502
Shawinigan-Sud (*Shawinigan)...11,452
Sherbrooke (*85,000)...80,457
Sillery (*Québec)...13,950
Sorel...19,317
Témiscaming...2,430
Templeton (*Ottawa)...3,696
Terrebonne...9,208
Thetford Mines...21,662
Thurso...3,243

C Census. E Official estimate. UE Unofficial estimate.
L Population within municipal limits of year specified. • Largest city in country.

* Population or designation of metropolitan area, including suburbs (see headnote).
▲ Population of an entire municipality, commune, or district, including rural area.
‡‡ Year of information specified at start of country.

Trois-Pistoles ... 4,654
Trois-Rivières (★95,000) ... 55,240
Trois-Rivières-Ouest (★Trois-Rivières) ... 8,071
Valcourt ... 2,505
Val-d'Or ... 17,419
Valleyfield (Salaberry-de) (★35,000) ... 29,776
Vanier (Québec-Ouest) (★Québec) ... 9,716
Varennes ... 2,368
Vaudreuil ... 3,831
Verdun (★Montréal) ... 74,520
Victoriaville ... 22,088
Ville-de-Tracy ... 11,845
Villeneuve (★Québec) ... 4,044
Ville-St.-Georges ... 7,570
Warwick ... 2,841
Waterloo ... 4,949
Westmount (★Montréal) ... 23,570
Windsor ... 6,047

CANADA/ SASKATCHEWAN ... 926,242

Assiniboia ... 2,609
Biggar ... 2,598
Canora ... 2,612
Esterhazy ... 2,886
Estevan ... 8,930
Humboldt ... 3,989
Kamsack ... 2,779
Kindersley ... 3,402
Lloydminster (*Sask. and Alta.*) ... 8,542
Maple Creek ... 2,268
Meadow Lake ... 3,426
Melfort ... 4,740
Melville ... 5,243
Moose Jaw ... 31,284
Moosomin ... 2,359
Nipawin ... 4,060
North Battleford ... 12,453
Prince Albert ... 27,613
Regina (★138,956) ... 137,759
Rosetown ... 2,543
Saskatoon ... 125,079
Shaunavon ... 2,253
Swift Current ... 15,048
Tisdale ... 2,789
Unity ... 2,295
Weyburn ... 8,576
Yorkton ... 13,149

CANADA/YUKON ... 18,388

Dawson ... 745
Whitehorse ... 11,084

CANAL ZONE

1970 C ... 44,198

•Balboa (★Panamá) ... 2,569
BALBOA HEIGHTS (★Panamá) ... 232
Cristóbal (★Colón) ... 388
Paraiso ... 1,659
Rainbow City (★Colón) ... 2,375

CAPE VERDE IS. / Cabo Verde

1970 C ... 272,071

•Mindelo ... 28,797
PRAIA ... 21,494

CAYMAN IS.

1970 C ... 10,652

•GEORGETOWN ... 3,975

CENTRAL AFRICAN REPUBLIC / République centrafricaine

1966 E ... 1,437,000

•BANGUI ... 150,000

CEYLON / Sihala / Ilam

1963 C ... 10,582,064

Anuradhapura ... 29,426
Badulla ... 27,115
•COLOMBO (1968 E) (★910,000) ... 558,500
Dehiwala-Mount Lavinia (★Colombo) (1968 E) ... 122,500
Galle ... 65,236
Jaffna (1968 E) ... 101,700
Kandy ... 68,202
Kegalla ... 11,427
Kotte (★Colombo) ... 73,838
Matale ... 25,609
Matara ... 32,541
Moratuwa ... 77,833
Negombo ... 46,908
Puttalam ... 13,195
Ratnapura ... 21,592
Trincomalee ... 34,817

CHAD / Tchad

1968 E ... 3,460,000

Abéché (1968 C) ... 19,700
Fort-Archambault (1968 C) ... 35,000
•FORT-LAMY (1968 C) ... 126,500
Mondou (1968 C) ... 34,100

CHILE

1970 C ... 8,836,223

Provinces

Aconcagua ... 169,821
Aisén ... 51,082
Antofagasta ... 250,665
Arauco ... 97,720
Atacama ... 152,326
Bío-Bío ... 193,027
Cautín ... 420,682
Chiloé ... 110,728
Colchagua ... 167,899
Concepción ... 638,118
Coquimbo ... 336,821
Curicó ... 113,710
Linares ... 189,030
Llanquihue ... 197,986
Magallanes ... 88,244
Malleco ... 176,060
Maule ... 82,339
Ñuble ... 314,738
O'Higgins ... 306,863
Osorno ... 158,673
Santiago ... 3,218,155
Talca ... 231,008
Tarapacá ... 174,730
Valdivia ... 274,642
Valparaíso ... 721,156

Cities (†1970 C or 1960 C)

Angol ... 18,637
Antofagasta (1969 E) ... 132,500
Apoquindo (★Santiago) ... 41,983
Arica ... 43,344
Calama ... 26,166
Cauquenes ... 17,836
Chillán ... 65,112
Chuquicamata ... 24,798
Concepción (1969 E) (★400,000) ... 191,700
Conchalí (★Santiago) ... †244,229
Copiapó ... 30,123
Coquimbo ... 33,749
Coronel ... 33,870
Curicó ... 32,562
Iquique ... 50,655
La Calera ... 18,134
La Cisterna (★Santiago) ... †247,448
La Granja (★Santiago) ... †160,981
La Serena ... 40,854
Lebu ... 6,248
Linares ... 27,568
Lo Prado Arriba (★Santiago) ... 49,396
Los Andes ... 20,448
Los Ángeles ... 35,511
Lota ... 48,693
Ñuñoa (★Santiago) ... †279,279
Osorno ... 55,091
Ovalle ... 25,282
Penco (★Concepción) ... 15,483
Providencia (★Santiago) ... †85,704
Puente Alto (★Santiago) ... 43,557
Puerto Aisén ... 5,488
Puerto Montt ... 41,681
Puerto Natales ... 9,399
Punta Arenas ... 49,504
Quillota ... 29,447
Quilpué (★Valparaíso) ... 26,588
Quinta Normal (★Santiago) ... †137,225
Rancagua ... 53,318
Renca (★Santiago) ... †67,168
San Antonio ... 26,917
San Bernardo (★Santiago) ... 45,207
San Carlos ... 16,097
San Felipe ... 19,048
San Fernando ... 21,774
San Miguel (★Santiago) ... †320,029
•SANTIAGO (★2,900,000) ... †510,246
Talca ... 68,148
Talcahuano (★★Concepción) (1969 E) ... 112,100
Temuco (1969 E) ... 101,000
Tocopilla ... 21,580
Tomé ... 26,942
Valdivia ... 61,334
Vallenar ... 15,693
Valparaíso (1969 E) (★540,000) ... 289,500
Viña del Mar (★Valparaíso) (1969 E) ... 149,300

CHINA / Zhongguo

1957 E ... 646,530,000

Provinces

Anhui (Anhwei) ... 33,560,000
Beijing Shi (Peking Auton. City) ... 6,230,000
Fujian (Fukien) ... 14,650,000
Gansu (Kansu) ... 12,800,000
Guangdong (Kwangtung) ... 37,960,000
Guangxi Zhuang Zizhiqu (Kwangsi Chuang Auton. Region) ... 19,390,000
Guizhou (Kweichow) ... 16,890,000
Hebei (Hopeh) ... 42,500,000
Heilongjiang (Heilungkiang) ... 14,860,000
Henan (Honan) ... 48,670,000
Hubei (Hupeh) ... 30,790,000
Hunan ... 36,220,000
Jiangsu (Kiangsu) ... 42,630,000
Jiangxi (Kiangsi) ... 18,610,000
Jilin (Kirin) ... 12,550,000
Liaoning ... 24,090,000
Neimenggu Zizhiqu (Inner Mongolia Auton. Region) ... 9,200,000
Ningxia Huizu Zizhiqu (Ningsia Hui Auton. Region) ... 1,810,000
Quinghai (Tsinghai) ... 2,050,000
Shandong (Shantung) ... 54,030,000
Shanghai Shi (Shanghai Auton. City) ... 9,500,000
Shānxi (Shansi) ... 15,960,000
Shănxi (Shensi) ... 18,130,000
Sichuan (Szechwan) ... 72,160,000
Xinjiang Weiwuer Zizhiqu (Sinkiang Uighur Auton. Region) ... 5,640,000
Xizang Zizhiqu (Tibet Auton. Region) ... 1,270,000
Yunnan (Yünnan) ... 19,100,000
Zhejiang (Chekiang) ... 25,280,000

Cities (1953 C or ‡1958 UE)

Andong (Antung) ... ‡370,000
Anqing (Anking) ... 105,300
Anshan ... ‡833,000
Anyang ... 124,900
Baiyinchang (Paiyin) ... ‡50,000
Bangbu (Pengpu) ... ‡330,000
Baoding (Paoting) (1957 E) ... 265,000
Baoji (Paoki) ... ‡180,000
Baotou (Paotow) ... ‡490,000
Beian (Peian) (1953 UE) ... 70,000
Beihai (Pakhoi) ... 80,000
BEIJING (Peking) (6,230,000▲) ... ‡3,500,000
Benxi (Penki) ... 449,000
Boshan (Tzupo) (875,000▲) ... ‡250,000
Boxian (Pohsien) (1953 UE) ... 90,000
Cangzhou (Tsanghsien) (1953 UE) ... 60,000
Changchun (Hsinking) ... ‡988,000
Changde (Changte) ... 94,800
Changsha ... ‡709,000
Changshu ... 101,400
Changzhi (Changchih) ... ‡180,000
Changzhou (Changchow) ... ‡300,000
Chaoan ... ‡101,300
Chengde (Chengteh) ... ‡120,000
Chengdu (Chengtu) ... ‡1,135,000
Chifeng (Chihfeng) ... 49,000
Chongqing (Chungking) ... ‡2,165,000
Datong (Tatung) ... 228,500
Duyun (Tuyün) ... ‡60,000
Foshan (Fatshan) ... ‡120,000
Fuling (Fowling) (1953 UE) ... 60,000
Fushun ... ‡1,019,000
Fuxian (Fuhsien) (1953 UE) ... 70,000
Fuxinshi (Fusin) ... ‡290,000
Fuyang (Fowyang) (1953 UE) ... 65,000
Fuzhou (Foochow) ... ‡623,000
Ganzhou (Kanchow) ... 98,600
Gejiu (Kokiu) ... ‡180,000
Guangzhou (Canton) ... ‡1,867,000
Guilin (Kweilin) ... ‡170,000
Guiyang (Kweiyang) ... ‡530,000
Haerbin (Harbin) (1959 E) ... 1,814,000
Haicheng (1953 UE) ... 80,000
Haikou (Hoihow) ... ‡402,000
Hailaer (Hailar) ... ‡60,000
Handan (Hantan) ... ‡380,000
Hangu (Hanku) (1953 UE) ... 50,000
Hangzhou (Hangchow) ... ‡794,000
Hanzhong (Hanchung) ... 70,000
Hechuan (Hochwan) (1953 UE) ... 50,000
Hefei (Hofei) ... ‡360,000
Hegang (Hokang) ... ‡200,000
Hengyang ... ‡240,000
Huaian (Hwaian) (1953 UE) ... 55,000
Huaide (Hwaite) ... ‡60,000
Huainan (Hwainan) ... ‡280,000
Huaiyin (Hwaiyin) ... 77,000
Huangshi (Hwangshih) ... 110,500
Huhehaote (Kweisui) ... ‡320,000
Huiyang (Waiyeung) ... ‡73,000
Hulan (1953 UE) ... 60,000
Huzhou (Huchow) ... ‡120,000
Jiamusi (Kiamusze) ... ‡232,000
Ji'an (Kian) ... 52,800
Jiangmen (Kongmoon) ... ‡110,000
Jiaoxian (Kiaochow) (1953 UE) ... 40,000
Jiaozuo (Tsiaotso) ... ‡250,000
Jiaxing (Kashing) ... ‡132,000
Jieyang (Kityang) (1953 UE) ... 55,000
Jilin (Kirin) ... ‡583,000
Jinan (Tsinan) ... ‡882,000
Jingdezhen (Kingtechen) ... ‡266,000
Jinhua (Kinhwa) ... 46,200
Jining ... ‡100,000
Jining (Tsining) ... 86,200
Jinshi (Tsingshih) (1953 UE) ... 50,000
Jinxian (Chinhsien) (1953 UE) ... 60,000
Jinzhou (Chinchow) ... ‡400,000
Jiujiang (Kiukiang) ... 64,600
Jixi (Chihsi) ... ‡253,000
Kaifeng ... 299,100
Kashi (Kashgar) ... ‡100,000
Kelamayi (Karamai) ... ‡43,000
Kunming ... ‡900,000
Lanzhou (Lanchow) ... ‡732,000
Lasa (Lhasa) ... 70,000
Leshan (Loshan) (1953 UE) ... 60,000
Liaoyang ... ‡169,000
Liaoyuan (Shwangliao) ... ‡177,000
Linxia (Linsia) (1953 UE) ... 50,000
Linyi (Lini) (1953 UE) ... 40,000
Liuzhou (Liuchow) ... ‡190,000
Luda (Dairen) (1,590,000▲) ... ‡1,000,000
Luohe (Loho) (1953 UE) ... 50,000
Luoyang (Loyang) ... ‡500,000
Lüshun (Port Arthur) ... 126,000
Luzhou (Luchow) ... ‡130,000
Manzhouli (Manchouli) ... 30,000
Meixian (Meihsien) (1953 UE) ... 45,000
Mudanjiang (Mutankiang) ... ‡251,000
Nanchang ... ‡520,000
Nanchong (Nanchung) ... 164,700
Nanjing (Nanking) ... ‡1,455,000
Nanning (1957 E) ... 264,000
Nantong (Nantung) ... ‡240,000
Nanyang (1953 UE) ... 50,000
Neijiang (Neikiang) ... ‡180,000
Ningbo (Ningpo) ... ‡280,000
Pingdingshan ... ‡70,000
Pingliang ... 60,000
Qingdao (Tsingtao) ... ‡1,144,000
Qinhuangdao (Chinwangtao) ... ‡210,000
Qiqihaer (Tsitsihar) ... ‡704,000
Quanzhou (Chüanchow) ... ‡110,000
Rugao (Jukao) (1953 UE) ... 40,000
•Shanghai (1957 E) (9,500,000▲) ... 6,900,000
Shangqiu (Shangkiu) ... 134,400
Shangrao (Shangjao) (1953 UE) ... 50,000
Shangshui (Chowkiakow) ... 85,500
Shantou (Swatow) ... ‡250,000
Shaoguan (Kükong) ... 81,700
Shaoxing (Shaohing) ... 130,600
Shaoyang ... ‡170,000
Shashi (Shasi) ... 85,800
Shenyang (Mukden) ... ‡2,423,000
Shijiazhuang (Shihkiachwang) ... ‡623,000
Shuangcheng (1953 UE) ... 80,000
Shuangyashan ... ‡110,000
Siping (Szeping) ... ‡130,000
Suihua (Suihwa) (1953 UE) ... 55,000
Suining (1953 UE) ... 50,000
Suoche (Yarkand) ... 80,000
Suzhou (Soochow) ... ‡651,000
Taiyuan (Taiyüan) ... ‡1,053,000
Taizhou (Taichow) ... 159,800
Tangshan ... ‡812,000
Taoan (1953 UE) ... 65,000
Tianjin (Tientsin) (3,278,000▲) ... ‡2,900,000
Tianshui (Tienshui) ... 63,000
Tieling (Tiehling) (1953 UE) ... 65,000
Tonghua (Tunghwa) ... 129,100
Tongxian (Tunghsien) (1953 UE) ... 55,000
Tunxi (Tunki) (1953 UE) ... 50 000
Wanxian (Wanhsien) (1953 UE) ... 90,000
Weifang ... ‡190,000
Weihai (Weihaiwei) (1953 UE) ... 45,000
Wenzhou (Wenchow) ... ‡210,000
Wuhan (Hankow) ... ‡2,226,000
Wuhu ... ‡240,000
Wulanhaote (Ulanhot) ... 51,400
Wulumuqi (Urumchi) ... ‡320,000
Wutongqiao (Wutungkiao) ... ‡140,000
Wuxi (Wusih) ... ‡616,000
Wuzhou (Wuchow) ... ‡120,000
Xiamen (Amoy) ... ‡308,000
Xi'an (Sian) ... ‡1,368,000
Xiangfan (Siangfan) ... 73,300
Xiangtan (Siangtan) ... ‡247,000
Xianyang (Sienyang) ... 70,000
Xinghua (Hinghwa) (1953 UE) ... 85,000
Xingtai (Singtai) (1953 UE) ... 70,000
Xinhailian (Sinhailien) ... ‡210,000
Xining (Sining) (1957 E) ... 300,000
Xinxiang (Sinsiang) ... ‡203,000
Xinyang (Sinyang) (1953 UE) ... 50,000
Xuanhua (Süanhwa) ... 114,100
Xuchang (Hsüchang) ... 58,000
Xuzhou (Süchow) ... ‡710,000
Yaan ... 55,200
Yancheng (1953 UE) ... 50,000
Yangjiang (Yeungkong) (1953 UE) ... 50,000
Yangquan (Yangchüan) ... ‡200,000
Yangzhou (Yangchow) ... ‡160,000
Yanji (Yenki) ... ‡80,000
Yantai (Chefoo) ... ‡140,000
Yibin (Ipin) ... ‡190,000
Yichang (Ichang) (1953 UE) ... 85,000
Yichun (Ichun) ... ‡200,000
Yinchuan (Yinchwan) ... ‡91,000
Yingkou (Yingkow) ... 131,400
Yining (Kuldja) ... ‡85,000
Yiyang (Iyang) (1953 UE) ... 80,000
Yuci (Yütze) ... ‡100,000
Yumen (Yümen) ... ‡200,000
Zhangjiakou (Kalgan) (480,000▲) ... ‡350,000
Zhangzhou (Changchow) ... 81,200
Zhanjiang (Tsamkong) ... ‡170,000
Zhaoqing (Kaoyao) ... ‡70,000
Zhengzhou (Chengchow) ... ‡785,000
Zhenjiang (Chinkiang) ... ‡190,000
Zhongshan (Shekki) ... 93,000
Zhuzhou (Chuchow) ... ‡190,000
Zigong (Tzekung) ... ‡280,000
Zunyi (Tsunyi) ... ‡200,000

COLOMBIA

1968 E ... 19,829,400

Departments

Amazonas (Comisaría) ... 14,900
Antioquia ... 2,828,000
Arauca (Intendencia) ... 28,900
Atlántico ... 833,900
Bolívar ... 791,900
Boyacá ... 1,144,400
Caldas ... 775,400
Caquetá (Intendencia) ... 136,900
Cauca ... 664,000
Chocó ... 199,700
Córdoba ... 695,400
Cundinamarca ... 3,313,500
El Cesar ... 334,600
Guainía (Comisaría) ... 4,100
Huila ... 460,000
La Guajira ... 201,300
Magdalena ... 627,000
Meta ... 216,000
Nariño ... 757,600
Norte de Santander ... 585,800
Putumayo (Comisaría) ... 67,900
Quindío ... 331,200
Risaralda ... 483,500
San Andrés y Providencia (Intendencia) ... 23,100
Santander ... 1,087,500
Sucre ... 343,200
Tolima ... 879,800
Valle del Cauca ... 1,973,800
Vaupés (Comisaría) ... 15,800
Vichada (Comisaría) ... 10,300

Cities

Arjona (1964 C) ... 16,510
Armenia ... 156,100
Armero (1964 C) ... 17,495
Barrancabermeja (81,400▲) ... 68,300
Barranquilla (★640,000) ... 590,300
Bello (★Medellín) ... 118,100
•BOGOTÁ (★2,250,000) ... 2,148,400
Bucaramanga ... 264,900
Buenaventura (108,600▲) ... 78,700
Buga (85,800▲) ... 74,000
Caicedonia (1964 C) ... 16,327
Calarcá (1964 C) (54,834▲) ... 31,089
Caldas (1964 C) ... 17,704
Cali ... 772,000
Cartagena ... 285,100
Cartago (71,100▲) ... 60,500
Chinchiná (1964 C) ... 15,944
Chiquinquirá (1964 C) ... 16,926
Ciénaga (135,600▲) ... 57,200
Cúcuta ... 199,400
Duitama (1964 C) (52,537▲) ... 31,865
El Banco (1964 C) ... 14,889
El Carmen de Bolívar (1964 C) ... 19,196
Envigado (★Medellín) (1964 C) (61,546▲) ... 40,686
Espinal (1964 C) ... 22,791
Facatativá (1964 C) ... 20,742
Florencia (1964 C) ... 17,709
Fusagasugá (1964 C) ... 18,755
Girardot (82,300▲) ... 71,200
Honda (1964 C) ... 19,945
Ibagué (172,100▲) ... 131,700
Ipiales (1964 C) ... 23,320
Itagüí (★Medellín) ... 92,200
La Dorada (1964 C) ... 26,168
Líbano (1964 C) (54,574▲) ... 18,640
Lorica (1964 C) (54,750▲) ... 12,880
Magangué (1964 C) (64,651▲) ... 27,354
Manizales ... 256,300
Medellín (★1,240,000) ... 913,000
Montería (161,300▲) ... 90,000
Neiva (107,000▲) ... 90,400
Ocaña (1964 C) ... 28,028
Palmira (157,600▲) ... 119,100
Pamplona (1964 C) ... 25,502
Pasto (120,100▲) ... 87,800
Pereira (216,200▲) ... 169,300
Popayán (85,700▲) ... 65,500
Puerto Berrío (1964 C) ... 15,812
Quibdó (1964 C) (42,926▲) ... 19,989
Ríohacha (1964 C) ... 11,708
Sabanalarga (1964 C) ... 20,254
San Andrés (1964 C) ... 9,040
San Gil (1964 C) ... 18,518
Santa Marta ... 129,200
Santa Rosa de Cabal (1964 C) (74,223▲) ... 31,646
Sevilla (1964 C) ... 26,757
Sincelejo (63,000▲) ... 49,800
Sogamoso (1964 C) (51,639▲) ... 32,274
Soledad (★Barranquilla) (1964 C) ... 37,617
Sonsón (1964 C) ... 16,955
Tuluá (84,400▲) ... 59,300
Tumaco (1964 C) (71,427▲) ... 25,145
Tunja (1964 C) (68,905▲) ... 40,451
Valledupar (110,500▲) ... 61,300
Villavicencio (80,700▲) ... 62,500
Yarumal (1964 C) ... 16,823
Yumbo (1964 C) ... 15,270
Zarzal (1964 C) ... 17,768
Zipaquirá (1964 C) ... 22,648

COMORO IS. / Comores

1970 E ... 267,000

Dzaoudzi (1966 C) ... 196
•MORONI ... 14,000

CONGO (REP. OF CONGO)

1970 C ... 1,089,300

•BRAZZAVILLE ... 175,000
Dolisie (1969 E) ... 15,000
Jacob (1969 E) ... 18,000
Pointe-Noire ... 135,000

COOK IS.

1966 C ... 19,251

•AVARUA (1961 E) ... 4,000

COSTA RICA

1970 E ... 1,710,000

Alajuela ... 29,200
Cartago ... 22,400
Guadalupe (★San José) ... 28,100
Heredia ... 24,000
Liberia (14,100▲) ... 8,800
Limón (36,400▲) ... 24,500
Puntarenas (31,200▲) ... 23,500
•SAN JOSÉ (★395,400) ... 205,700
San Pedro (★San José) ... 21,400

CUBA

1970 C ... 8,553,400

Provinces

Camagüey ... 813,200
Habana ... 2,335,300
Las Villas ... 1,362,200
Matanzas ... 501,300
Oriente ... 2,999,000
Pinar del Río ... 542,400

Cities

Amancio Rodríguez (37,900▲) ... 12,300
Artemisa ... 31,200
Banes (39,300▲) ... 27,100
Baracoa (35,600▲) ... 20,900
Batabanó (17,000▲) ... 11,500
Bauta (★La Habana) (25,400▲) ... 21,100
Bayamo (92,700▲) ... 71,700
Bejucal (17,200▲) ... 15,400
Cabaiguán (34,500▲) ... 21,700
Caibarién (31,200▲) ... 27,000
Caimanera (6,800▲) ... 5,500
Camagüey ... 196,900
Camajuaní (32,300▲) ... 15,900
Cárdenas (55,700▲) ... 55,200
Ciego de Avila (70,200▲) ... 60,900

(Cuba continued)

C Census. E Official estimate. UE Unofficial estimate.
L Population within municipal limits of year specified. • Largest city in country.
★ Population or designation of metropolitan area, including suburbs (see headnote).
▲ Population of an entire municipality, commune, or district, including rural area.
‡† Year of information specified at start of country.

(Cuba continued)

Cienfuegos (90,700▲) 85,200
Colón (40,800▲) 26,000
Consolación del Sur (42,000▲) 15,100
Contramaestre (43,900▲) 22,900
Cruces (32,100▲) 19,100
Florida (37,500▲) 32,700
Fomento (33,600▲) 12,900
Gibara (29,800▲) 12,100
Guanabacoa (★La Habana) 69,700
Guanajay (22,000▲) 18,800
Guantánamo (131,500▲) 130,100
Güines (45,300▲) 41,400
Güira de Melena (26,700▲) 19,900
Holguín (163,100▲) 131,500
Jaruco (13,700▲) 10,000
Jiguaní (27,300▲) 10,800
Jovellanos (23,900▲) 16,500
•LA HABANA (HAVANA)
(★1,800,000) 1,755,400
Los Palacios (22,900▲) 10,200
Manicaragua (28,100▲) 10,700
Manzanillo (88,900▲) 77,900
Matanzas 85,400
Mayarí (34,000▲) 17,600
Moa (22,400▲) 15,000
Morón (31,100▲) 29,000
Niquero (36,500▲) 11,300
Nueva Gerona (20,100▲) 17,200
Nuevitas (21,500▲) 20,700
Palma Soriano (59,600▲) 41,200
Palmira (19,000▲) 10,900
Pedro Betancourt (18,900▲) 11,000
Perico (19,400▲) 10,500
Pinar del Río 73,200
Placetas (48,400▲) 32,300
Puerto Padre (23,300▲) 16,500
Ranchuelo (24,300▲) 13,000
Remedios (20,900▲) 13,100
Sagua de Tánamo (40,100▲) 9,600
Sagua la Grande (41,900▲) 35,800
San Antonio de los Baños
(30,000▲) 25,300
San Cristóbal (25,300▲) 15,700
Sancti-Spíritus (66,500▲) 57,700
San Germán (30,200▲) 12,400
San José de las Lajas (33,600▲) 24,900
San Juan y Martínez (45,700▲) 11,100
San Luis (35,000▲) 17,400
San Nicolás de Bari (17,800▲) 11,000
Santa Clara (154,500▲) 131,500
Santa Cruz del Sur 10,800
Santiago de Cuba 276,000
Trinidad (37,000▲) 31,500
Vertientes (32,600▲) 14,000
Victoria de las Tunas (65,000▲) 53,700

CYPRUS / Kípros / Kıbrıs

1970 E 633,000

Ammókhostos (Famagusta) 42,500
Kirínia 4,900
Lárnax (Larnaca) 21,400
Lemesós (Limassol) 51,500
•LEVKOSÍA (NICOSIA)
(★115,000) 50,000
Páfos 11,800

CZECHOSLOVAKIA / Československo

1970 C 14,357,557

Historic Provinces and Regions

BOHEMIA (ČECHY) 6,077,430
Jihočeský 653,116
Plzeň (Pilsen) (City) 148,032
Praha (Prague) (City) 1,078,096
Severočeský 1,102,559
Středočeský 1,191,901
Východočeský 1,202,405
Západočeský 701,321
MORAVIA (MORAVA) 3,738,035
Brno (City) 335,918
Jihomoravský 1,601,877
Ostrava (City) 278,737
Severomoravský 1,521,503
SLOVAKIA (SLOVENSKO) 4,542,092
Bratislava (City) 283,539
Stredoslovenský 1,402,974
Východoslovenský 1,256,209
Západoslovenský 1,599,370

Cities (‡1970 C or 1969 E)

Banská Bystrica 40,082
Beroun (★24,000) 17,809
Bratislava .... ‡283,539
Brno .... ‡335,918
České Budějovice (Budweis) 76,945
Český Těšín 16,503
Cheb 26,098
Chomutov 40,078
Děčín 44,228
Frýdek-Místek (★Ostrava) 37,025
Gottwaldov (Zlín) 65,310
Havířov (★Ostrava) 82,157
Hodonín 20,834
Hradec Králové 68,160
Jablonec [nad Nisou] 34,082
Jihlava 40,463
Karlovy Vary (Karlsbad)
(★58,000) 45,102
Karviná (★★Ostrava) 77,117
Kladno (★73,000) 56,935
Kolín 26,519
Komárno 27,282
Košice 142,233
Krnov 23,054
Kroměříž 22,132
Liberec (★87,000) 73,444
Litoměřice 19,713
Litvínov 23,549
Lučenec 20,427
Mariánské Lázně (Marienbad) 13,581
Martin 32,435
Mladá Boleslav 29,687
Most 55,364
Náchod 19,019
Nitra 43,596
Nové Zámky 24,628
Nový Jičín 19,740
Olomouc 80,563
Opava 47,909
Ostrava (★670,000) .... ‡278,737
Pardubice 70,777
Piešťany 22,601
Písek 22,719
Plzeň (Pilsen) .... ‡148,032
Poprad 20,349
•PRAHA (PRAGUE)
(★1,175,000) .... ‡1,078,096
Přerov 38,963
Prešov 41,163
Příbram 29,724
Prievidza 27,825
Prostějov 36,980
Ružomberok 21,380
Sokolov 20,009
Spišská Nová Ves 22,554
Šumperk 23,080
Tábor 21,949
Teplice 52,982
Trenčín (★39,000) 28,746
Třinec 30,368
Trnava (★46,000) 38,634
Trutnov 24,666
Uherské Hradiště (★32,000) 15,796
Ústí nad Labem (★93,000) 74,425
Vsetín 22,092
Žilina 41,806
Znojmo 25,905
Zvolen 25,354

DAHOMEY

1965 E 2,300,000

•Cotonou 111,100
PORTO-NOVO 74,500

DENMARK / Danmark

1970 E 4,932,982

Åbenrå 20,370
Ålborg 153,978
Århus 236,129
Ballerup-Måløv (★København) 50,628
Brøndbyerne (★København) 33,073
Esbjerg 76,192
Fredericia 43,754
Frederiksberg (★København) 101,449
Frederikshavn 32,983
Gentofte (★København) 77,858
Gladsakse (★København) 74,519
Glostrup (★København) 28,236
Haderslev 29,593
Helsingør (Elsinore) 52,377
Herning 52,598
Hillerød 29,989
Høje Tåstrup (★København) 30,443
Holbæk 26,081
Holstebro 33,078
Horsens 52,023
Hvidovre (★København) 45,264
Kolding 52,408
•KØBENHAVN (COPENHAGEN)
(★1,460,000) 627,800
Lyngby (Kongens Lyngby)-
Tårbæk (★København) 61,474
Middelfart 16,262
Næstved 41,546
Nakskov 17,106
Nykøbing [på Falster] 25,700
Odense 164,679
Randers 63,996
Rødovre (★København) 44,703
Rønne 15,501
Roskilde 49,968
Silkeborg 43,039
Skagen 13,515
Skive 25,414
Slagelse 32,121
Søllerød (★København) 31,028
Sønderborg 29,527
Svendborg 35,810
Tårnby (★København) 45,724
Vejle 49,834
Viborg 36,214

DOMINICA

1970 C 70,302

•ROSEAU 10,157

DOMINICAN REPUBLIC / República Dominicana

1970 C 4,011,800

Baní 23,700
Barahona 37,900
Bonao 20,200
Higüey 21,700
La Romana 36,700
La Vega 31,100
Mao (Valverde) 27,100
Puerto Plata 32,200
San Cristóbal 25,800
San Francisco de Macorís 43,900
San Juan [de la Maguana] 32,200
San Pedro de Macorís 42,500
Santiago [de los Caballeros] 155,200
•SANTO DOMINGO 671,400

ECUADOR

1967 E 5,585,500

Provinces

Archipiélago de Colón
(Galápagos Islands) (Ter.) 3,100
Azuay 305,400
Bolívar 165,100
Cañar 128,700
Carchi 111,600
Chimborazo 342,300
Cotopaxi 223,600
El Oro 208,700
Esmeraldas 157,000
Guayas 1,238,800
Imbabura 200,900
Loja 345,500
Los Ríos 314,800
Manabí 743,200
Morona-Santiago 34,700
Napo 33,000
Pastaza 18,600
Pichincha 749,300
Tungurahua 245,600
Zamora-Chinchipe 15,600

Cities

Ambato (1970 E) 75,300
Azogues 8,800
Babahoyo 20,300
Chone (1962 C) 12,832
Cuenca (1970 E) 77,300
Esmeraldas (1970 E) 59,000
Guaranda 11,000
•Guayaquil (1970 E) 794,300
Ibarra 32,800
Jipijapa (1962 C) 13,367
Latacunga 16,400
Loja 33,900
Machala (1970 E) 58,700
Manta (1962 C) 33,622
Milagro (1962 C) 28,148
Portoviejo (1970 E) 47,500
Quevedo (1962 C) 20,602
QUITO (1970 E) 528,100
Riobamba (1970 E) 53,700
Tulcán 20,300

EGYPT / Miṣr

1966 C 30,083,419

Abnūb 31,195
Abū Kabīr 41,789
Abū Tīj 28,161
Akhmīm 44,829
Al-'Arīsh .... ††40,338
Al-Badārī 26,531
Al-Fashn 27,746
Al-Fayyūm (1970 E) 151,000
Al-Ghurdaqah 2,082
Al-Ḥawāmidīyah (★Al-Qāhirah) 36,227
Al-Iskandarīyah (Alexandria)
(1970 E) (★2,250,000) 2,032,000
Al-Ismā'īlīyah (Ismailia)
(★180,000) 144,163
Al-Jīzah (Giza) (★Al-Qāhirah)
(1970 E) 712,000
Al-Khānkah (★Al-Qāhirah) 28,084
Al-Khārijah 15,719
Al-Maḥallah al Kubrá (1970 E) 256,000
Al-Maḥmūdīyah 17,241
Al-Manshāh 25,027
Al-Manṣūrah (El Mansura)
(1970 E) (★238,000) 212,000
Al-Manzilah 33,298
Al-Maṭarīyah 41,105
Al-Minyā (1970 E) 122,000
•AL-QĀHIRAH (CAIRO)
(1970 E) (★6,600,000) 4,961,000
Al-Qaṣr 3,321
Al-Quṣayr 5,525
Al-Quṣīyah 25,991
Al-Uqṣur (Luxor) 77,578
Armant 38,308
Ashmūn 32,168
As-Sallūm 2,483
As-Sinbillāwayn 40,686
As Suways (Suez) 264,098
Aswān (1970 E) 202,000
Asyūṭ (1970 E) 176,000
Az-Zaqāzīq (1970 E) 173,000
Banhā 63,849
Banī Mazār 34,053
Banī Suwayf 90,425
Bilbays 58,070
Bilqās Qism Awwal 41,067
Biyalā 33,008
Būlāq ad Dakrūr (★Al-Qāhirah) 75,130
Būr Sa'īd (Port Said) 282,977
Damanhūr (1970 E) 161,000
Dayr Mawās 16,947
Dayrūṭ 27,646
Disūq 45,580
Dumyāṭ (Damietta) 86,327
Fāqūs 40,561
Fuwah 30,654
Ḥawsh 'Īsá 30,006
Hihyā 17,696
Idfū 27,326
Idkū 42,239
Isnā 27,383
Jirjā 44,150
Kafr ad-Dawwār
(★Al-Iskandarīyah) 41,560
Kafr ash-Shaykh 51,544
Kafr az-Zayyāt 34,084
Kafr Salīm (★Al-Iskandarīyah) 40,381
Kawm Umbū 27,227
Maghāghah 33,211
Mallawī 59,938
Manfalūṭ 34,132
Maṭāy 17,014
Maṭrūḥ 11,039
Minūf 48,256
Minya al-Qamḥ 31,533
Mīt Ghamr (★82,000) 43,665
Nafīshah (★Al-Ismā'īlīyah) 29,483
Qalyūb 49,303
Qinā 68,536
Qūṣ 27,462
Ras Gharib 9,638
Rashīd (Rosetta) 36,711
Samālūṭ 37,861
Samannūd 29,749
Sawhāj 74,753
Shibīn al-Kawm 66,290
Shirbīn 25,089
Shubrā al-Khaymah
(★Al-Qāhirah) (1970 E) 253,000
Sinnūris 34,855
Sirs al-Layyānah 16,000
Sīwah 3,569
Ṭahṭā 39,815
Ṭalā 25,448
Ṭanṭā (1970 E) 254,000
Ṭimā 29,293
Ṭūkh 15,610
Warraq al-Arab (★Al-Qāhirah) 31,263
Ziftá (★★Mīt Ghamr) 37,883

††31,733 per 1967 census taken by Israeli occupation authorities.

EL SALVADOR

1971 C 3,541,010

Ahuachapán 17,242
Chalchuapa 19,631
Cojutepeque 20,615
Cuscatancingo 18,711
Ilopango 18,997
La Unión 17,207
Mejicanos (★San Salvador) 54,916
Nueva San Salvador 35,106
Quezaltepeque 12,641
San Marcos 22,722
San Miguel 59,304
•SAN SALVADOR (★600,000) 337,171
Santa Ana 96,306
San Vicente 18,872
Sonsonate 33,562
Usulután 19,616
Villa Delgado (★San Salvador) 44,367
Zacatecoluca 15,718

EQUATORIAL GUINEA / Guinea Ecuatorial

1965 C 254,684

Bata (1960 C) (27,024▲) 4,000
•SANTA ISABEL (37,152▲) 17,500

ETHIOPIA / Yaitopya

1970 E 24,319,000

•ADDIS ABEBA 795,900
Adwa 15,712
Akaki Beseka 17,326
Asela 17,106
Asmera 218,360
Bahir Dar 22,192
Debre Markos 27,170
Debre Zeyt 27,627
Dese 45,731
Dire Dawa 60,925
Gonder 35,331
Harer 45,033
Jima 41,848
Mekele 27,895
Mesewa (Massaua) 18,490
Nazeret 39,359
Nekemte 16,105

FAEROE IS. / Føroyar

1969 E 38,000

•TÓRSHAVN 10,188

FALKLAND ISLANDS

1970 E 2,045

•STANLEY 1,080

FIJI

1966 C 476,727

Lautoka (★21,221) 11,287
•SUVA (★80,269) 54,157

FINLAND / Suomi

1971 E 4,682,567

Provinces

Ahvenanmaa (Åland) 21,521
Häme 643,012
Keski-Suomi 243,563
Kuopio 258,646
Kymi 347,316
Lappi 209,855
Mikkeli 219,908
Oulu (Uleåborg) 409,704
Pohjois-Karjala 185,591
Turku-Pori 683,464
Uusimaa (Nyland) 1,029,788
Vaasa (Vasa) 430,199

Cities

Espoo (Esbo) (★Helsinki) 98,900
Hämeenlinna 38,117
•HELSINKI (HELSINGFORS)
(★765,000) 528,800
Hyvinkää 34,473
Iisalmi 20,695
Imatra 34,807
Jakobstad (Pietarsaari) 19,747
Järvenpää 16,636
Joensuu 36,708
Jyväskylä (★75,000) 58,621
Kajaani 19,514
Karhula (★★Kotka) 22,143
Kemi 29,165
Kerava 14,350
Kokkola (Gamlakarleby) 20,740
Kotka (★58,000) 34,154
Kouvola (★50,000) 26,330
Kuopio 65,063
Kuusankoski (★★Kouvola) 22,341
Lahti 90,593
Lappeenranta 51,513
Mariehamn (Maarianhamina) 8,855
Mikkeli 25,841
Nokia 19,580
Nurmijärvi 16,846
Oulu 86,916
Pori 74,271
Porvoo 17,104
Rauma 25,769
Riihimäki 23,097
Rovaniemi 29,191
Savonlinna 18,065
Seinäjoki 20,334
Tampere (★200,000) 157,810
Turku (Åbo) (★204,000) 156,882
Vaasa (Vasa) 49,605
Varkaus 24,618

FRANCE

1971 E 51,029,500

Regions and Departments

ALSACE 1,453,900
Bas-Rhin 852,400
Haut-Rhin 601,500
AQUITAINE 2,491,700
Dordogne 369,300
Gironde 1,029,200
Landes 281,200
Lot-et-Garonne 292,100
Pyrénées-Atlantiques
(Basses-Pyrénées) 519,900
AUVERGNE 1,329,000
Allier 386,900
Cantal 167,600
Haute-Loire 207,000
Puy-de-Dôme 567,500
BASSE-NORMANDIE 1,284,800
Calvados 538,600
Manche 453,200
Orne 293,000
BOURGOGNE 1,533,600
Côte-d'Or 437,700
Nièvre 248,000
Saône-et-Loire 558,000
Yonne 289,900
BRETAGNE 2,503,400
Côtes-du-Nord 508,000
Finistère 778,600
Ille-et-Vilaine 672,100
Morbihan 544,700
CENTRE 2,056,000
Cher 309,200
Eure-et-Loir 315,200
Indre 244,200
Indre-et-Loire 459,300
Loiret 451,800
Loir-et-Cher 276,300
CHAMPAGNE 1,315,300
Ardennes 312,400
Aube 277,400
Haute-Marne 216,400
Marne 509,100
CORSE (CORSICA) 218,100
FRANCHE-COMTÉ 1,025,800
Belfort, Territoire de 123,600
Doubs 450,700
Haute-Saône 215,300
Jura 236,200
HAUTE-NORMANDIE 1,546,700
Eure 395,300
Seine-Maritime 1,151,400
LANGUEDOC-ROUSSILLON 1,741,500
Aude 276,300
Gard 490,200
Hérault 615,600
Lozère 72,800
Pyrénées-Orientales 286,600
LIMOUSIN 739,500
Corrèze 237,900
Creuse 153,900
Haute-Vienne 347,700
LORRAINE 2,323,200
Meurthe-et-Moselle 721,700
Meuse 205,600
Moselle 1,002,500
Vosges 393,400
MIDI-PYRÉNÉES 2,208,200
Ariège 136,700
Aveyron 274,500
Gers 179,100
Haute-Garonne 722,300
Hautes-Pyrénées 228,500
Lot 150,600
Tarn 333,600
Tarn-et-Garonne 182,900
NORD 3,864,300
Nord 2,465,900
Pas-de-Calais 1,398,400
PAYS DE LA LOIRE 2,637,300
Loire-Atlantique 887,100
Maine-et-Loire 598,400
Mayenne 254,600
Sarthe 471,000
Vendée 426,200
PICARDIE 1,623,000
Aisne 531,100
Oise 568,600
Somme 523,300
POITOU-CHARENTES 1,496,000
Charente 332,300
Charente-Maritime 490,000
Deux-Sèvres 329,300
Vienne 344,400
PROVENCE-CÔTE D'AZUR 3,408,300
Alpes-de-Haute-Provence
(Basses-Alpes) 106,800
Alpes-Maritimes 747,100
Bouches-du-Rhône 1,517,100
Hautes-Alpes 90,900
Var 579,700
Vaucluse 366,700

C Census. E Official estimate. UE Unofficial estimate.
L Population within municipal limits of year specified. • Largest city in country.
★ Population or designation of metropolitan area, including suburbs (see headnote).
▲ Population of an entire municipality, commune, or district, including rural area.
‡† Year of information specified at start of country.

RÉGION PARISIENNE	9,638,100
Essonne	778,100
Hauts-de-Seine	1,491,400
Paris	2,488,600
Seine-et-Marne	639,500
Seine-Saint-Denis	1,329,000
Val-de-Marne	1,198,000
Val-d'Oise	769,000
Yvelines	944,500
RHÔNE-ALPES	4,591,800
Ain	348,800
Ardèche	259,700
Drôme	359,000
Haute-Savoie	401,900
Isère	797,800
Loire	729,700
Rhône	1,396,400
Savoie	298,500

Cities (1968 C)

Abbeville	23,999
Agen	34,949
Aigues-Mortes	4,197
Aix-en Provence	89,566
Aix-les-Bains	20,627
Ajaccio	40,834
Albi	42,930
Alençon	31,656
Alès	42,818
Alfortville (★Paris)	35,023
Amiens (★138,000)	117,888
Angers (★165,000)	128,533
Angoulême (★92,000)	47,822
Annecy (★82,000)	54,484
Annonay	20,757
Antibes (★★Cannes)	47,547
Antony (★Paris)	56,638
Arcachon (★39,000)	14,986
Argenteuil (★Paris)	90,480
Arles (45,774▲)	33,576
Armentières (★55,000)	26,916
Arras (★72,000)	49,144
Asnières [-sur-Seine] (★Paris)	80,113
Aubervilliers (★Paris)	73,695
Auch	21,462
Aulnay-sous-Bois (★Paris)	61,521
Aurillac	28,226
Autun	18,398
Auxerre	35,784
Avignon	86,096
Avranches	9,775
Bagneux (★Paris)	42,006
Bagnolet (★Paris)	34,038
Barentin (★16,000)	9,790
Bar-le-Duc	19,159
Bastia	49,375
Bayeux	11,451
Bayonne (★110,000)	42,743
Beaune	16,874
Beauvais	46,777
Belfort (★72,000)	53,214
Bergerac	27,165
Besançon	113,220
Béthune (★56,000)	27,154
Béziers	80,492
Biarritz (★★Bayonne)	26,750
Blois	42,264
Bobigny (★Paris)	39,453
Bondy (★Paris)	51,652
Bordeaux (★560,000)	266,662
Boulogne-Billancourt (★Paris)	109,008
Boulogne-sur-Mer (★106,000)	49,276
Bourg-en-Bresse	37,887
Bourges	70,814
Brest	154,023
Briançon	8,215
Brive-la-Gaillarde	46,561
Bron (★Lyon)	41,619
Bruay-en-Artois (★115,000)	28,628
Caen (★155,000)	110,262
Cahors	19,203
Calais (★94,000)	74,624
Caluire-et-Cuire (★Lyon)	37,603
Cambrai (★48,000)	37,532
Cannes (★175,000)	67,152
Carcassonne	43,616
Carmaux (★24,500)	14,755
Castres	40,457
Châlons-sur-Marne	50,764
Chalon-sur-Saône	50,589
Chambéry (★76,000)	51,066
Chamonix-Mont-Blanc	5,942
Champigny-sur-Marne (★Paris)	70,419
Chantilly	10,246
Charleville-Mézières	55,543
Chartres (★59,000)	34,469
Châteauroux	49,138
Châtellerault	35,337
Chaumont	25,779
Chauny (★20,000)	13,920
Chelles (★Paris)	33,281
Cherbourg (★79,000)	38,243
Chinon (7,735▲)	5,435
Choisy-le-Roi (★Paris)	41,440
Cholet	41,766
Clamart (★Paris)	54,906
Clermont-Ferrand (★205,000)	148,896
Clichy (★Paris)	52,477
Cognac	22,062
Colmar	59,550
Colombes (★Paris)	80,357
Compiègne (★48,000)	29,700
Concarneau	17,801
Corbeil-Essonnes	32,192
Courbevoie (★Paris)	58,118
Coutances	9,061
Creil (★67,000)	32,544
Créteil (★Paris)	49,197
Dax (★26,000)	19,348
Deauville	5,232
Decazeville (★26,000)	10,532
Denain (★130,000)	27,973
Dieppe (★40,000)	29,970
Digne (14,661▲)	12,478
Dijon (★185,000)	145,357
Dinard	9,052
Dives-sur-Mer (★11,500)	6,299
Dole	27,188
Douai (★180,000)	49,187
Douarnenez	19,705
Drancy (★Paris)	69,444
Dreux	29,408
Dunkerque (1970 L) (★145,000)	42,727
Elbeuf (★47,000)	19,407
Épernay	26,583
Épinal (★48,000)	36,856
Épinay-sur-Seine (★Paris)	41,774
Escoublac-La-Baule (★St.-Nazaire)	13,336
Étaples (★19,000)	9,095
Eu (★19,000)	8,079
Évreux	42,550
Évry (★Paris)	7,113
Falaise	7,180
Fécamp	21,406
Firminy (★St. Étienne)	24,924
Foix	9,331
Fontainebleau (★35,000)	18,094
Fontenay-sous-Bois (★Paris)	38,962
Forbach (★58,000)	23,120
Fougères	26,045
Fréjus (★41,500)	23,629
Gagny (★Paris)	35,780
Gap	23,994
Gennevilliers (★Paris)	46,074
Givors (★34,000)	19,048
Granville	12,715
Grasse	30,907
Grenoble (★335,000)	161,616
Guebwiller (★20,500)	10,840
Guéret	12,849
Haguenau	22,944
Hayange (1970 L) (★75,000)	13,678
Hendaye	8,006
Hénin-Beaumont (Hénin-Liétard) (★★Lens) (1970 L)	26,846
Hyères	34,875
Issy-les-Moulineaux (★Paris)	50,442
Ivry-sur-Seine (★Paris)	60,455
Joeuf (★31,000)	12,305
La Ciotat (23,916▲)	19,485
La Courneuve (★Paris)	43,318
La Grand' Combe (★20,000)	13,240
Laon	26,316
La Rochelle (★88,000)	73,347
La Roche-sur-Yon	36,067
La Seyne-sur-Mer (★Toulon)	43,783
Laval	45,674
Le Blanc-Mesnil (★Paris)	48,487
Le Creusot	34,102
Le Havre (★250,000)	199,509
Le Mans	143,246
Lens (★330,000)	41,874
Le Puy-en-Velay (★39,000)	26,389
Les Sables-d'Olonne (★28,000)	18,093
Levallois-Perret (★Paris)	58,941
Le Vésinet (★Paris)	18,459
Libourne	22,123
Liévin (★Lens)	35,853
Lille (★950,000)	190,546
Limoges	132,935
Lisieux	23,830
Livry-Gargan (★Paris)	32,063
Loches	6,359
Lomme (★Lille)	29,315
Longwy (★82,000)	21,087
Lons-le-Saunier	18,769
Lorient (★98,000)	66,444
Lourdes	17,939
Lunéville	23,177
Lyon (★1,100,000)	527,800
Mâcon	33,445
Maisons-Alfort (★Paris)	53,149
Mantes-la-Jolie (★58,000)	26,058
Marcq-en-Baroeul (★Lille)	35,136
Marignane (★Marseille)	20,044
Marseille (★1,015,000)	889,029
Martigues (27,945▲)	17,826
Massy (★Paris)	37,055
Maubeuge (★99,000)	32,028
Mazamet (★28,000)	16,171
Meaux	30,167
Melun (★60,000)	34,518
Mende	9,713
Menton (★34,000)	25,040
Mérignac (★Bordeaux)	45,951
Metz (★165,000)	107,537
Meudon (★Paris)	50,623
Millau	22,595
Montargis (★45,000)	18,225
Montauban (45,895▲)	34,513
Montbéliard (★115,000)	23,908
Montceau-les-Mines (★50,000)	27,421
Mont-de-Marsan	24,458
Montélimar	26,748
Montereau-faut-Yonne	19,789
Montluçon	57,871
Montmorency (★Paris)	18,691
Montpellier	161,910
Montreuil-sous-Bois (★Paris)	95,714
Montrouge (★Paris)	44,922
Morlaix	19,919
Moulins (★40,000)	25,979
Moyeuvre-Grande (★78,000)	14,568
Mulhouse (★200,000)	116,336
Nancy (★260,000)	123,428
Nanterre (★Paris)	90,332
Nantes (★400,000)	259,208
Narbonne	38,441
Neuilly-sur-Seine (★Paris)	70,995
Nevers (★55,000)	42,422
Nice (★400,000)	322,442
Nîmes	123,292
Niort (1969 L)	53,394
Noisy-le-Sec (★Paris)	34,079
Noyon	11,603
Orange (24,562▲)	18,616
Orléans (★170,000)	95,828
Orly (★Paris)	30,202
Oullins (★Lyon)	26,604
Oyonnax	19,777
Pantin (★Paris)	47,607
Paray-le-Monial	10,716
•PARIS (1971 E) (★9,000,000)	2,488,600
Pau (★110,000)	74,005
Périgueux (★57,000)	37,450
Perpignan	102,191
Pessac (★Bordeaux)	36,986
Poissy (★Paris)	33,555
Poitiers	70,681
Pont-à-Mousson (★20,000)	13,406
Pontoise (★Paris)	17,509
Privas	10,080
Puteaux (★Paris)	37,946
Quimper	52,496
Reims (1970 L)	154,534
Rennes	180,943
Rezé (★Nantes)	33,509
Riom	15,467
Rive-de-Gier (★35,000)	16,855
Roanne (★78,000)	53,373
Rochefort	29,226
Rodez (★31,000)	23,328
Romans-sur-Isère (★43,000)	31,545
Rosny-sous-Bois (★Paris)	30,705
Roubaix (★★Lille)	114,547
Rouen (★370,000)	120,471
Royan (★27,000)	17,292
Rueil-Malmaison (★Paris)	60,804
St.-Avold (★25,000)	16,280
St.-Brieuc	50,281
St.-Chamond	37,728
St.-Cloud (★Paris)	28,162
St.-Cyr-l'École (★Paris)	16,001
St.-Denis (★Paris)	99,268
St.-Dié	25,117
St.-Dizier	36,616
Saintes	26,507
St.-Étienne (1969 L) (★330,000)	222,536
St.-Étienne-du-Rouvray (★Rouen)	34,713
St.-Germain-en-Laye (★Paris)	38,308
St.-Jean-de-Luz (★21,000)	10,841
St.-Lô	18,615
St.-Malo	42,297
St.-Martin-d'Hères (★Grenoble)	33,605
St.-Maur-des-Fossés (★Paris)	77,251
St.-Nazaire (★110,000)	63,289
St.-Omer (★27,000)	18,205
St.-Ouen (★Paris)	48,886
St.-Quentin	64,196
St.-Tropez (6,130▲)	5,184
Salon-de-Provence (30,722▲)	25,174
Sarcelles (★Paris)	51,674
Sarreguemines	23,284
Sartrouville (★Paris)	40,277
Saumur (★33,000)	21,551
Savigny-sur-Orge (★Paris)	32,075
Schiltigheim (★Strasbourg)	29,198
Sedan	23,037
Senlis	11,169
Sens	23,035
Sète	40,476
Sèvres (★Paris)	20,083
Soissons (★40,000)	25,890
Sotteville (★Rouen)	34,495
Stains (★Paris)	32,169
Strasbourg (★355,000)	249,396
Suresnes (★Paris)	40,616
Talence (★Bordeaux)	29,161
Tarbes (★73,000)	55,375
Thann (★26,000)	8,318
Thionville (1970 L) (★65,000)	40,254
Thonon-les-Bains	20,700
Toul (★20,000)	14,780
Toulon (★340,000)	174,746
Toulouse (★440,000)	370,796
Tourcoing (★★Lille)	98,755
Tours (★205,000)	128,120
Trouville-sur-Mer (★15,000)	6,429
Troyes (★115,000)	74,898
Tulle	20,016
Valence (★92,000)	62,358
Valenciennes (★240,000)	46,626
Vannes	36,576
Vénissieux (★Lyon)	47,613
Verdun-sur-Meuse	22,013
Versailles (★Paris)	90,829
Vesoul	16,352
Vichy (★57,000)	33,506
Vienne	29,057
Vierzon	33,775
Villefranche (★Nice)	6,790
Villefranche-sur-Saône (★36,000)	26,338
Villejuif (★Paris)	51,120
Villeneuve-d'Ascq (★Lille) (1970 L)	26,178
Villeneuve-St.-Georges (★Paris)	30,488
Villeurbanne (★Lyon)	119,879
Vincennes (★Paris)	49,143
Vitry-le-François	16,879
Vitry-sur-Seine (★Paris)	77,846
Voiron (★27,000)	17,587
Wattrelos (★Lille)	43,754

FRENCH GUIANA / Guyane francaise

1967 C	**44,392**
•CAYENNE	24,518
St.-Laurent-du-Maroni (4,993▲)	3,897

FRENCH POLYNESIA / Polynésie française

1962 C	**84,551**

Island Groups

Clipperton Island	None
Marquesas Islands	4,838
Society Islands (incl. Tahiti and Leeward Islands)	68,245
Tuamotu (Low) Archipelago	7,097
Tubuai Islands	4,371

Cities

•PAPEETE (1971 C) (★63,000)	24,000

GABON

1969 E	**485,000**
•LIBREVILLE (1969 C)	73,000
Port-Gentil (1964 E)	25,000

GAMBIA

1971 E	**374,770**
•BATHURST (★52,640)	36,570

GAZA STRIP

1967 C	**356,261**
•GHAZZAH (GAZA)	118,272
Jabālyah	43,604
Khān Yūnus	52,997
Rafaḥ	49,812

GERMANY, EAST / Deutsche Demokratische Republik

1971 C	**17,040,926**

Districts

Berlin, East (City)	1,084,866
Cottbus	860,929
Dresden	1,871,463
Erfurt	1,255,186
Frankfurt	678,666
Gera	738,727
Halle	1,922,353
Karl-Marx-Stadt (Chemnitz)	2,044,762
Leipzig	1,489,594
Magdeburg	1,317,154
Neubrandenburg	636,930
Potsdam	1,131,023
Rostock	860,472
Schwerin	596,538
Suhl	552,263

Cities (1971 C or ‡1970 E)

Altenburg	‡46,737
Annaberg-Buchholz	‡27,892
Apolda	‡29,087
Arnstadt	‡28,762
Aschersleben	‡37,196
Aue	‡30,930
Bautzen	‡43,670
•BERLIN, OST- (EAST BERLIN) (★Berlin)	1,084,866
Bernburg	‡45,322
Bitterfeld (★115,000)	‡28,964
Blankenburg	‡19,603
Brandenburg	93,916
Burg [bei Magdeburg]	‡29,994
Cottbus	83,354
Crimmitschau	‡29,932
Dessau (★130,000)	98,121
Döbeln	‡27,754
Dresden (★635,000)	500,051
Eberswalde	‡46,090
Eisenach	‡50,906
Eisenhüttenstadt	44,885
Eisleben	‡30,386
Erfurt	196,198
Falkensee (★Berlin)	‡25,891
Forst	‡29,284
Frankfurt an der Oder	62,019
Freiberg	‡50,272
Freital (★Dresden)	‡42,159
Fürstenwalde	‡30,830
Gera	111,534
Glauchau	‡32,127
Görlitz	87,211
Gotha	‡57,328
Greifswald	‡47,083
Greiz	‡39,058
Güstrow	‡37,213
Halberstadt	‡46,774
Halle (★455,000)	257,337
Halle-Neustadt (★Halle)	35,132
Hettstedt	‡20,160
Hoyerswerda	‡58,663
Jena	88,270
Johanngeorgenstadt	‡10,872
Karl-Marx-Stadt (Chemnitz) (★455,000)	298,335
Köthen	‡36,587
Lauchhammer	‡27,458
Leipzig (★745,000)	583,311
Leuna (★Halle)	‡11,168
Limbach-Oberfrohna (★Karl-Marx-Stadt)	‡25,460
Luckenwalde	‡28,984
Magdeburg (★375,000)	270,503
Meerane	‡24,933
Meiningen	‡25,357
Meissen	‡45,571
Merseburg (★★Halle)	‡55,986
Mühlhausen	‡45,385
Naumburg	‡37,636
Neubrandenburg	45,601
Neuruppin	‡22,258
Neustrelitz	‡27,788
Nordhausen	‡44,505
Pirna	‡47,468
Plauen	81,944
Potsdam (★Berlin)	110,817
Quedlinburg	‡30,829
Radebeul (★Dresden)	‡39,626
Rathenow	‡29,823
Reichenbach	‡28,818
Riesa	‡49,746
Rostock	200,982
Rudolstadt	‡31,539
Saalfeld	‡33,405
Salzwedel	‡19,960
Sangerhausen	‡32,312
Sassnitz	‡13,456
Schmalkalden	‡14,103
Schönebeck	‡46,146
Schwedt	34,244
Schwerin	96,929
Senftenberg	‡24,301
Sondershausen	‡22,880
Sonneberg	‡29,767
Stassfurt	‡25,695
Stendal	‡36,478
Stralsund	71,345
Suhl	31,589
Tangermünde	‡13,087
Torgau	‡21,688
Weimar	63,677
Weissenfels	‡46,120
Werdau	‡23,023
Wernigerode	‡32,662
Wilhelm-Pieck-Stadt Guben	‡29,521
Wismar	56,263
Wittenberg	‡47,151
Wittenberge	‡33,028
Wolfen (★★Bitterfeld)	‡26,941
Wurzen	‡24,164
Zeitz	‡46,736
Zerbst	‡19,589
Zittau	‡43,087
Zwickau (★180,000)	126,902

GERMANY, WEST / Bundesrepublik Deutschland

1969 E	**61,194,600**

States and Government Districts

BADEN-WÜRTTEMBERG	8,909,700
Nordbaden	1,909,400
Nordwürttemberg	3,487,500
Südbaden	1,885,300
Südwürttemberg-Hohenzollern	1,627,500
BAYERN (BAVARIA)	10,568,900
Mittelfranken	1,491,000
Niederbayern	1,005,100
Oberbayern	3,310,900
Oberfranken	1,113,900
Oberpfalz	954,400
Schwaben	1,501,000
Unterfranken	1,192,600
BERLIN (WEST)	2,134,300
BREMEN	756,000
HAMBURG	1,817,100
HESSEN (HESSE)	5,422,600
Darmstadt	4,064,300
Kassel	1,358,300
NIEDERSACHSEN (LOWER SAXONY)	7,100,400
Aurich	402,700
Braunschweig	865,900
Hannover	1,538,000
Hildesheim	972,900
Lüneburg	1,071,800
Oldenburg	849,100
Osnabrück	772,900
Stade	627,100
NORDRHEIN-WESTFALEN (NORTH RHINE-WESTPHALIA)	17,129,700
Aachen	1,030,600
Arnsberg	3,759,200
Detmold	1,754,200
Düsseldorf	5,690,800
Köln	2,477,000
Münster	2,417,900
RHEINLAND-PFALZ (RHINE-LAND-PALATINATE)	3,671,300
Koblenz	1,377,000
Rheinhessen-Pfalz	1,820,700
Trier	473,600
SAARLAND	1,127,400
SCHLESWIG-HOLSTEIN	2,557,200

Cities (‡1970 C or 1969 E)

Aachen (★475,000)	177,600
Aalen	35,100
Ahlen	50,400
Ahrensburg (★Hamburg)	25,800
Alsdorf (★Aachen)	31,700
Altena	31,200
Amberg	42,100
Andernach (★★Neuwied)	22,400
Ansbach	30,100
Arnsberg	22,600
Aschaffenburg (★120,000)	56,200
Augsburg (★365,000)	214,400
Aurich	12,300
Backnang	28,100
Baden-Baden	38,900
Bad Hersfeld	23,500
Bad Homburg (★Frankfurt)	41,200
Bad Honnef am Rhein	20,600
Bad Kissingen	12,700
Bad Kreuznach	42,700
Bad Neuenahr-Ahrweiler	25,400
Bad Oldesloe	18,900
Bad Reichenhall	14,900
Bad Salzuflen	49,000
Bad Vilbel (★Frankfurt)	18,300
Bamberg (★106,000)	68,700
Bayreuth	63,400
Beckum	26,800
Bensberg (★Köln)	41,100
Bensheim	27,500
Berchtesgaden (1966 E)	4,100
Bergisch Gladbach (★Köln)	50,100
Bergkamen (★Essen)	43,700
•Berlin, West- (★3,960,000)	‡2,121,000
Biberach	25,600
Bielefeld (★330,000)	169,300
Bietigheim	22,500
Bingen	24,500
Böblingen (★Stuttgart)	36,600
Bocholt	48,100
Bochum (★★Essen)	346,900
BONN (★510,000)	299,400
Borken	30,600
Bornheim (★Bonn)	30,500
Bottrop (★Essen)	108,200
Brackwede (★Bielefeld)	40,300
Brake	19,400
Braunschweig (Brunswick) (★355,000)	225,200
Bremen (★810,000)	‡582,300
Bremerhaven (★195,000)	148,800
Bruchsal	27,100
Brühl (★Köln)	41,800
Bünde	41,100
Buxtehude	23,100
Castrop-Rauxel (★Essen)	83,400

(Germany, West continued)

C Census. E Official estimate. UE Unofficial estimate.
L Population within municipal limits of year specified. • Largest city in country.

★ Population or designation of metropolitan area, including suburbs (see headnote).
▲ Population of an entire municipality, commune, or district, including rural area.
‡† Year of information specified at start of country.

(Germany, West continued)

Celle...56,300
Cloppenburg...18,200
Coburg...41,400
Coesfeld...26,600
Cuxhaven...45,200
Dachau (★München)...33,100
Darmstadt (★265,000)...141,100
Datteln (★Essen)...34,900
Deggendorf...18,600
Delmenhorst (★★Bremen)...63,700
Detmold...64,500
Dillingen (★Saarlouis)...22,000
Dinkelsbühl (1966 E)...8,100
Dinslaken (★Essen)...54,500
Dormagen (★Köln)...31,800
Dorsten (★Essen)...39,400
Dortmund (★★Essen)...648,900
Dudweiler (★Saarbrücken)...30,100
Duisburg (★★Essen)...457,900
Dülmen...21,100
Düren (★98,000)...54,900
Düsseldorf (★1,090,000)...‡663,600
Ebingen...22,000
Eckernförde...22,000
Einbeck...18,600
Elmshorn...41,400
Emden...48,300
Emmerich...24,500
Emsdetten...29,000
Ennepetal (★Essen)...37,200
Erftstadt...34,900
Erlangen (★118,000)...85,700
Eschwege...22,200
Eschweiler (★★Aachen)...39,600
Essen (★5,475,000)...704,800
Esslingen (★Stuttgart)...86,500
Ettlingen (★Karlsruhe)...21,300
Euskirchen...42,000
Fellbach (★Stuttgart)...29,300
Flensburg (★113,000)...96,800
Forchheim...21,600
Frankenthal (★Mannheim)...40,500
Frankfurt am Main (★1,660,000).660,400
Frechen (★Köln)...30,800
Freiburg (★195,000)...166,000
Freising...30,300
Friedrichshafen...42,500
Fulda (★76,000)...44,300
Fürstenfeldbruck (★München)..22,500
Fürth (★★Nürnberg)...94,300
Garbsen (★Hannover)...26,800
Garmisch-Partenkirchen...27,300
Geislingen...27,200
Gelsenkirchen (★Essen)...348,600
Gevelsberg (★Essen)...35,900
Giessen (★145,000)...74,700
Gifhorn...23,000
Gladbeck (★Essen)...83,300
Goch...27,700
Göppingen (★140,000)...46,900
Goslar...41,700
Göttingen...115,200
Greven...26,400
Grevenbroich...28,200
Gronau (★Enschede, Netherlands)...26,600
Gummersbach...45,000
Gütersloh...76,300
Hagen (★★Essen)...203,000
Hamburg (★2,350,000)...‡1,794,000
Hameln (★67,000)...47,100
Hamm (★162,000)...84,300
Hanau [am Main] (★Frankfurt)..55,700
Hannover (★830,000)...‡523,900
Hattingen (★Essen)...60,500
Heide...23,400
Heidelberg (★★Mannheim)...121,900
Heidenheim (★93,000)...50,200
Heilbronn (★210,000)...99,400
Heiligenhaus (★Essen)...28,700
Helmstedt...27,200
Hemer (★Iserlohn)...25,300
Hennef...26,600
Herford (★121,000)...67,300
Herne (★Essen)...100,800
Herten (★Essen)...52,400
Hilden (★Düsseldorf)...50,000
Hildesheim (★132,000)...95,900
Hof...54,800
Hohenlimburg (★Essen)...26,300
Holzminden...22,300
Homberg (★Essen)...35,200
Homburg...32,300
Höxter...32,800
Hückelhoven...25,100
Hürth (★Köln)...52,000
Husum...25,000
Hüttental (★Siegen)...40,300
Idar-Oberstein...32,600
Ingolstadt (★113,000)...72,000
Iserlohn (★87,000)...57,800
Itzehoe...35,700
Jülich...20,200
Kaiserslautern (★130,000)...99,900
Kamen (★Essen)...41,100
Kamp-Lintfort (★Essen)...38,400
Karlsruhe (★445,000)...257,100
Kassel (★335,000)...213,500
Kaufbeuren...39,900
Kempen (★Essen)...41,000
Kempten...44,600
Kevelaer...20,300
Kiel (★340,000)...‡271,700
Kirchheim...28,900
Kleve (Cleves)...44,200
Koblenz (★167,000)...106,200
Köln (Cologne) (★1,715,000)...866,300
Königswinter (★Bonn)...32,000
Konstanz...61,600
Kornwestheim (★Stuttgart)...28,600
Krefeld (★★Essen)...228,700
Kreuztal...27,700
Kulmbach...22,800
Lage...30,900
Lahnstein (★Koblenz)...20,100
Lahr...25,000
Lampertheim (★Mannheim)...24,100
Landau...32,300
Landshut...51,400
Langen (★Frankfurt)...30,200
Langenfeld (★Wuppertal)...45,300
Langenhagen (★Hannover)...37,100
Leer...29,900
Lehrte...21,800
Lemgo...38,500
Lengerich...21,500
Lennestadt...26,100
Leonberg (★Stuttgart)...25,600
Letmathe (★Essen)...27,900
Leverkusen (★Köln)...111,600
Lindau...26,300
Lingen...25,800
Lippstadt...42,300
Löhne...37,200
Lörrach (★Basel, Switzerland)...32,900
Lövenich (★Köln)...26,900
Lübeck (★285,000)...242,200
Lüdenscheid...80,100
Ludwigsburg (★Stuttgart)...79,500
Ludwigshafen (★★Mannheim)..174,700
Lüneburg...59,900
Lünen (★Essen)...72,200
Mainz (★★Wiesbaden)...‡172,200
Mannheim (★1,250,000)...330,900
Marburg an der Lahn...51,400
Marl (★Essen)...75,800
Meerbusch (★Düsseldorf)...47,000
Memmingen...35,500
Menden...30,800
Mettmann (★Wuppertal)...30,200
Minden (★96,000)...51,500
Moers (★Essen)...51,300
Mönchengladbach (★365,000)..152,200
Monheim (★Düsseldorf)...35,800
Mülheim an der Ruhr (★Essen)...191,100
München (Munich) (★1,735,000)...‡1,293,600
Münster (★245,000)...204,600
Neckarsulm (★Heilbronn)...18,500
Neheim-Hüsten...36,900
Nettetal...37,200
Neuburg an der Donau...18,500
Neu Isenburg (★Frankfurt)...36,000
Neumarkt in der Oberpfalz...18,900
Neumünster...84,700
Neunkirchen (★125,000)...44,300
Neuss (★Düsseldorf)...117,600
Neustadt an der Weinstrasse...51,100
Neu-Ulm (★Ulm)...27,700
Neuwied (★135,000)...31,400
Nienburg...22,500
Nordenham (★★Bremerhaven)..27,400
Norderstadt (★Hamburg)...54,700
Nordhorn...42,900
Nördlingen...14,200
Northeim...19,200
Nürnberg (★835,000)...477,100
Nürtingen...21,300
Oberammergau (1966 E)...4,600
Oberhausen (★Essen)...249,000
Oberursel (★Frankfurt)...24,900
Oelde...21,400
Offenbach (★Frankfurt)...118,800
Offenburg...32,600
Oldenburg...131,400
Olpe...22,100
Opladen (★Köln)...43,500
Osnabrück (★240,000)...141,000
Paderborn...68,700
Passau...31,600
Peine...30,900
Pelkum (★Hamm)...25,100
Pforzheim (★200,000)...90,800
Pinneberg (★Hamburg)...36,400
Pirmasens...56,200
Plettenberg...30,200
Porz (★Köln)...78,100
Radevormwald...22,100
Rastatt...29,100
Ratingen (★Düsseldorf)...43,400
Ravensburg...31,800
Recklinghausen (★Essen)...125,500
Regensburg (★170,000)...128,100
Remagen...13,600
Remscheid (★★Wuppertal)...137,400
Rendsburg...35,500
Reutlingen (★134,000)...77,900
Rheda-Wiedenbrück...36,900
Rheine...51,200
Rheinhausen (★Essen)...71,700
Rheinkamp (★Essen)...43,200
Rheydt (★★Mönchengladbach).100,600
Rietberg...20,900
Rodenkirchen (★Köln)...41,000
Rosenheim...36,400
Rothenburg ob der Tauber...11,600
Rottweil...19,900
Rüsselsheim (★★Wiesbaden)...57,300
Saarbrücken (★385,000)...‡128,000
Saarlouis (★94,000)...36,300
Salzgitter...118,000
Sankt Augustin (★Bonn)...32,800
Sankt Ingbert...28,800
Schleswig...33,300
Schorndorf...21,000
Schramberg...19,100
Schwabach (★Nürnberg)...25,800
Schwäbisch Gmünd...44,600
Schwäbisch Hall...23,800
Schweinfurt (★100,000)...59,300
Schwelm (★Wuppertal)...34,200
Schwenningen...35,500
Schwerte (★Essen)...24,400
Selb...18,500
Sennestadt (★Bielefeld)...20,500
Siegburg (★★Bonn)...34,600
Siegen (★152,000)...58,000
Sindelfingen (★Stuttgart)...41,000
Singen...39,700
Soest...40,600
Solingen (★★Wuppertal)...175,900
Speyer...42,300
Stade...31,600
Stolberg (★★Aachen)...39,600
Straubing...36,900
Stuttgart (★1,615,000)...‡633,200
Sulzbach-Rosenberg...18,700
Trier...103,400
Troisdorf (★Bonn)...50,300
Tübingen...56,000
Tuttlingen...26,600
Uelzen...23,800
Ulm (★172,000)...92,500
Unna (★Essen)...50,400
Velbert (★Essen)...57,000
Viernheim (★Mannheim)...28,100
Viersen (★★Mönchengladbach).84,000
Villingen...37,700
Voerde (★Essen)...27,800
Völklingen (★★Saarbrücken)...39,800
Walsum (★Essen)...48,600
Waltrop (★Essen)...25,100
Wanne-Eickel (★Essen)...99,900
Wattenscheid (★Essen)...80,500
Wedel (★Hamburg)...31,100
Weiden...43,100
Weinheim...29,500
Werdohl...23,900
Werl...25,200
Wermelskirchen (★Wuppertal)..26,500
Wesel...44,700
Wetter (★Essen)...30,600
Wetzlar (★94,000)...37,200
Wiesbaden (★620,000)...‡250,100
Wilhelmshaven...103,200
Willich (★Essen)...38,700
Witten (★Essen)...97,800
Wolfenbüttel (★★Braunschweig)...41,200
Wolfsburg (★126,000)...89,400
Worms...78,000
Wuppertal (★920,000)...414,700
Würzburg (★168,000)...120,300
Zweibrücken...32,900

GHANA

1970 C...8,545,561

•ACCRA (★736,718)...633,880
Bolgatanga...18,719
Cape Coast...71,594
Ho...22,446
Keta...16,100
Koforidua...44,768
Kumasi...342,986
Nsawam...25,618
Obuasi...31,018
Oda...24,770
Sekondi-Takoradi...161,071
Sunyani...23,872
Swedru...19,280
Tamale...81,612
Tarkwa...11,001
Winneba...30,800

GIBRALTAR

1970 C...27,965

•GIBRALTAR (★100,000)...27,965

GREECE / Ellás

1971 C...8,745,084

Agrínion (★41,518)...30,905
Aiyáleo (★Athínai)...80,271
Aíyion (★23,656)...18,733
Akharnaí (Acharnae)...24,362
Alexandroúpolis...23,042
Amaliás...14,143
Árgos...18,966
Árta...19,322
•ATHÍNAI (ATHENS) (★2,530,207)...862,133
Dráma...29,655
Édhessa...13,904
Elevsís (Eleusis)...18,642
Ermoúpolis (Síros) (★16,038)...13,461
Flórina (Phlorina)...11,185
Grevená...8,011
Ioánnina (Yanina)...39,814
Iráklion (Candia) (★84,304)...76,787
Kalámai (★40,290)...39,346
Kálimnos...9,434
Kallithéa (★Athínai)...82,108
Kardhítsa...25,378
Kariaí (1961 C)...429
Kastoría...15,355
Kateríni (★30,328)...28,634
Kavála...46,103
Keratsínion (★Athínai)...67,457
Kérkira (Corfu)...26,658
Khalkís (Chalcis)...36,381
Khaniá (Canea) (★53,376)...40,452
Khíos (Chios) (★30,011)...24,074
Komotiní...28,789
Kórinthos (Corinth)...20,819
Kozáni...23,108
Lamía...37,817
Lárisa...72,332
Levádhia (Lebadea)...15,202
Mégara...17,260
Mesolóngion...11,220
Mitilíni (Mytilene)...23,447
Náousa...17,324
Návplion (Nauplia)...9,252
Néa Ionía (★Athínai)...54,994
Néa Liósia (★Athínai)...56,302
Níkaia (★Athínai)...86,304
Pátrai (Patras) (★119,956)...110,632
Peristérion (★Athínai)...118,765
Piraiévs (Piraeus) (★★Athínai)..186,223
Pírgos (Pyrgos)...20,442
Ródhos (Rhodes)...31,812
Salamís...18,317
Sérrai...39,863
Spárti (Sparta) (★13,414)...10,523
Thessaloníki (Salonika) (★550,563)...339,496
Thívai (Thebes)...15,899
Tírnavos...10,459
Tríkkala...34,243
Trípolis (Tripolitza)...20,327
Vathí...2,490
Véroia...29,447
Víron (★Athínai)...47,025
Vólos (★88,065)...51,340
Xánthi...23,079
Zákinthos...9,281
Zografós (★Athínai)...56,663

GREENLAND / Grønland

1965 C...39,600

Angmagssalik (1960 C)...612
Egedesminde...2,495
Frederikshåb (1960 C)...1,038
•GODTHÅB (1968E)...6,790
Holsteinsborg...2,495
Jakobshavn (1960 C)...1,293
Julianehåb...2,198
K'utdligssat (1960 C)...1,760
Narssak (1960 C)...1,061
Sukkertoppen (1960 C)...1,635
Thule (1960 C)...206

GRENADA

1970 C...94,500

•ST. GEORGE'S (1966E) (★21,730)...8,099

GUADELOUPE

1967 C...312,724

BASSE-TERRE (★24,000)...15,690
Capesterre (17,912▲)...6,790
•Pointe-à-Pitre (★49,000)...29,522

GUAM

1970 C...84,996

•AGANA (★29,000)...2,119

GUATEMALA

1964 C...4,284,473

Amatitlán...12,225
Antigua Guatemala...13,576
Chimaltenango...9,077
Chiquimula...14,760
Coatepeque...13,657
Cobán...9,073
Escuintla...24,832
•GUATEMALA (1971E) (★825,000)...731,000
Huehuetenango...10,185
Jalapa...10,035
Jutiapa...7,747
Mazatenango...19,506
Puerto Barrios (1971E)...29,400
Quezaltenango (1971E)...54,500
Retalhuleu...14,366
San Marcos...5,569
Santa Cruz del Quiché...6,472
Tiquisate...10,348
Totonicapán...7,292
Zacapa...11,173

GUERNSEY

1971 C...53,734

•ST. PETER PORT (★36,000)...16,303

GUINEA / Guinée

1967 E...3,702,000

•CONAKRY (1967 C)...197,267
Kankan (1959 E)...29,000
Kindia (1959 E)...25,000
Labé (1959 E)...12,500
Macenta (1959 E)...10,500
Nzérékoré (1959 E)...10,500
Siguiri (1959 E)...12,700

GUYANA

1970 C...714,233

•GEORGETOWN (★167,078)...66,070
New Amsterdam...18,199

HAITI / Haïti

1950 C...3,097,304

Cap-Haïtien (1971C)...43,600
Gonaïves...13,634
Jacmel...8,643
Jérémie...11,048
Les Cayes...11,608
Pétionville...9,417
•PORT-AU-PRINCE (1971C) (★448,800)...419,900
Port-de-Paix...6,405
St.-Marc...9,401

HONDURAS

1967 E...2,445,000

Choluteca...15,900
Comayagua...11,700
El Progreso...17,500
La Ceiba (1970E)...36,900
La Lima...12,000
Puerto Cortés...21,600
San Pedro Sula (1970 E)...102,500
•TEGUCIGALPA (1970 E)...232,300
Tela...15,000

HONG KONG

1971 C...3,950,802

Aberdeen (★Victoria) (1961 C)...44,169
Kowloon (★★Victoria)...715,440
New Kowloon (★Victoria)...1,479,417
North Point (★Victoria) (1966E)...350,000
Tai Wan Tsun (Ngau Tau Kok) (★Victoria) (1961 C)...53,836
Tsun Wan (★Victoria)...267,670
•VICTORIA (HONG KONG) (★3,575,000)...521,612

HUNGARY / Magyarország

1970 C...10,315,597

Counties

Bács-Kiskun...572,988
Baranya...279,715
Békés...447,196
Borsod-Abaúj-Zemplén...608,368
Budapest (Independent City).1,940,212
Csongrád...323,229
Debrecen (City)...155,122
Fejér...388,910
Győr-Sopron...404,698
Hajdu-Bihar...375,371
Heves...348,395
Komárom...301,853
Miskolc (City)...172,952
Nógrád...241,122
Pécs (City)...145,307
Pest...869,864
Somogy...363,510
Szabolcs-Szatmár...592,186
Szeged (City)...118,490
Szolnok...449,827
Tolna...259,267
Vas...280,842
Veszprém...408,989
Zala...267,184

Cities

Baja...34,360
Békéscsaba (55,408▲)...48,261
•BUDAPEST (★2,325,000)...1,940,212
Cegléd (38,082▲)...30,933
Debrecen...155,122
Dunaújváros...44,200
Eger...45,229
Esztergom...26,955
Gyöngyös...33,149
Győr...100,065
Hódmezővásárhely (52,797▲)...44,219
Kaposvár...58,099
Kazincbarcika...25,884
Kecskemét (77,484▲)...61,784
Komárom...11,271
Makó...30,097
Miskolc...172,952
Nagykanizsa...39,411
Nyíregyháza (70,640▲)...55,805
Orosháza (33,346▲)...29,146
Ózd...38,637
Pápa...27,775
Pécs...145,307
Salgótarján...37,212
Sopron...44,950
Szeged...118,490
Székesfehérvár...72,490
Szentes (32,492▲)...28,336
Szolnok...61,418
Szombathely...64,745
Tatabánya...65,130
Vác...27,946
Várpalota...24,527
Veszprém...35,158
Zalaegerszeg...39,176

ICELAND / Ísland

1971 E...206,818

Akureyri...10,898
Hafnarfjördür (★Reykjavík)...10,071
•REYKJAVÍK (★109,500)...82,693

INDIA / Bhārat

1971 C...547,367,926

States

Andaman and Nicobar Islands (Ter.)...115,090
Andhra Pradesh...43,394,951
Assam...14,952,108
Bihār...56,332,246
Chandīgarh (Ter.)...256,979
Dādra and Nagar Haveli (Ter.)...74,165
Delhi (Ter.)...4,044,338
Goa, Damān and Diu (Ter.)...857,180
Gujarāt...26,687,186
Haryana...9,971,165
Himāchal Pradesh...3,424,332
Jammu and Kashmīr...4,615,176
Kerala...21,280,397
Laccadive, Minicoy & Amīndīvi Islands (Ter.)...31,798
Madhya Pradesh...41,650,684
Mahārāshtra...50,335,492
Manipur (Ter.)...1,069,555
Meghalaya...983,336
Mysore...29,263,334
Nāgāland...515,561
North-East Frontier Agency (Ter.)...444,744
Orissa...21,934,827
Pondicherry (Ter.)...471,347
Punjab...13,472,972
Rājasthān...25,724,142
Tamil Nadu (Madras)...41,103,125
Tripura (Ter.)...1,556,822
Uttar Pradesh...88,364,779
West Bengal...44,440,095

C Census. E Official estimate. UE Unofficial estimate.
L Population within municipal limits of year specified. • Largest city in country.

★ Population or designation of metropolitan area, including suburbs (see headnote).
▲ Population of an entire municipality, commune, or district, including rural area.
‡† Year of information specified at start of country.

Cities

Abohar	58,912
Achalpur (Ellichpur) (★66,422)	42,333
Ādoni	85,314
Agartala	59,682
Āgra (★637,785)	594,858
Ahmadābād (★1,950,000)	1,588,378
Ahmadnagar (★147,444)	117,275
Ajmer	262,480
Akola	168,454
Alandur (★Madras)	64,221
Alīgarh	254,008
Alīpur Duār (★55,224)	36,667
Allahābād (★513,997)	491,702
Alleppey	160,064
Alwar	100,791
Amalner	55,524
Ambālā (★186,168)	83,649
Ambāla Cantonment (★Ambālā)	102,519
Ambarnāth (★Bombay)	56,461
Āmbūr	54,022
Amrāvati (Amraoti) (★221,119)	193,636
Amreli	43,788
Amritsar (★455,755)	432,663
Amroha	82,692
Anakapalle	57,220
Ānand	59,069
Anantapur	80,072
Arcot	30,229
Arrah	92,670
Aruppukkottai	62,227
Asansol (★925,000)	157,388
Aurangābād (★165,275)	150,514
Avadi (★Madras)	53,338
Badagara	53,916
Bāgalkot	51,765
Bahraich	73,925
Baidyabāti (★Calcutta)	54,555
Ballia	47,080
Bālurghāt	66,541
Bānda	50,543
Bangalore (★1,750,000)	1,500,000
Bangaon	50,335
Bānkura	79,243
Bansbāria (★Calcutta)	61,601
Baranagar (★Calcutta)	131,431
Bareilly (★326,127)	296,093
Baroda	467,422
Barrackpore (★Calcutta)	97,169
Bārsi	62,389
Bāruni (★61,562)	41,750
Basīrhāt	63,282
Basti	49,645
Batāla	76,410
Beāwar	66,110
Behāla (South Suburban) (★Calcutta)	273,762
Belgaum (★213,830)	185,000
Bellary	125,127
Berhampore (★79,686)	73,380
Berhampur	117,635
Bettiah	51,076
Bhadrāvati (★101,315)	35,000
Bhadreswar (★Calcutta)	45,018
Bhāgalpur	172,700
Bharatpur	69,442
Bhatinda	64,162
Bhātpāra (★Calcutta)	205,303
Bhaunagar	226,072
Bhilai (★245,333)	158,464
Bhīlwāra	82,101
Bhīmavaram	63,773
Bhiwandi (★Bombay)	79,523
Bhiwāni	73,065
Bhopāl (★392,077)	302,618
Bhubaneswar	105,514
Bhuj	52,869
Bhusāwal (★104,589)	96,236
Bīdar	50,677
Bihar	100,052
Bijāpur	103,308
Bīkaner	188,598
Bilāspur (★130,804)	107,883
Bīr	50,015
Bodināyakkanūr	54,118
Bokāro Steel City (★108,012)	94,311
Bombay (★6,750,000)	5,968,546
Broach	92,263
Budaun	72,109
Budge Budge (★Calcutta)	51,979
Bulandshahr	59,682
Bulsār	43,497
Burdwān	144,970
Burhānpur (★105,349)	105,260
•Calcutta (★9,100,000)	3,141,180
Calicut (Kozhikode)	333,980
Cambay	62,133
Cannanore (★59,860)	55,111
Champdāni (★Calcutta)	58,425
Chandannagar (Chandernagore) (★Calcutta)	75,960
Chandausi	53,390
Chandīgarh (★233,004)	218,807
Chandrapur	74,994
Changanācheri	48,552
Chāpra (★98,634)	83,166
Chhindwāra	53,489
Chidambaram	48,819
Chīralā	54,461
Chitradurga	50,275
Chittoor	63,041
Churu	52,491
Cochin (★438,420)	40,000
Coimbatore (★560,000)	353,469
Cooch Behār (★62,703)	53,734
Coonoor (★64,343)	37,663
Cuddalore	101,345
Cuddapah	66,238
Cuttack	194,036
Damoh	59,993
Dānāpur (★Patna)	42,688
Darbhanga	132,129
Darjeeling	42,662
Dāvangere	121,018
Dehra Dún (★199,443)	166,436
Dehri	46,038
Delhi (★4,475,000)	3,694,451
Delhi Cantonment (★Delhi)	57,030
Deoghar (★45,088)	40,395
Deolāli (★★Nāsik)	55,461
Dewās	51,882
Dhānbād (★600,000)	79,545
Dhārwār (★★Hubli)	110,000
Dhorāji	60,046
Dhrāngadhra	40,798
Dhule	137,089
Dibrugarh	80,344
Digboi (★32,231)	16,605
Dindigul	127,406
Dohad	51,409
Dombivli (★Bombay)	51,203
Durg (★Bhilai)	70,776
Durgapur	207,232
Elūru (Ellore)	127,047
English Bāzār	61,713
Ernākulam (★★Cochin) (1961C)	117,253
Erode (★140,783)	103,704
Etāwah	85,900
Faizābād (★109,765)	102,794
Farīdābād New Township (★Delhi)	85,819
Farrukhābād (★111,373)	103,282
Fatehpur	54,647
Fīrozābād	133,945
Fīrozpur (Ferozepore) (★97,444)	51,187
Gadag	95,381
Garden Reach (★Calcutta)	155,520
Gauhāti	122,981
Gaya	179,826
Ghāziābād (★Delhi)	119,199
Ghāzīpur	45,636
Giridih	40,331
Godhra	66,414
Gonda	52,647
Gondal	55,346
Gondia	77,999
Gorakhpur	230,701
Govindpura (★Bhopāl)	53,927
Gudivada	61,085
Gudiyāttam	63,007
Gulbarga	145,630
Guntakal	65,885
Guntūr	269,941
Gurgaon	57,085
Gwalior (★406,755)	379,145
Hābra (★87,917)	51,726
Hājīpur	41,864
Haldwāni	52,396
Hālisahar (★Calcutta)	68,997
Hāpur	71,249
Hardoi	46,665
Hardwār (★79,353)	77,940
Hassan	51,329
Hāthras	69,052
Hazāribāgh	54,703
Hinganghāt	44,328
Hisār	89,463
Hooghly-Chinsurà (★Calcutta)	105,341
Hoshiārpur	57,700
Hospet	65,342
Howrah (★Calcutta)	740,622
Hubli (★379,555)	265,000
Hyderābād (★2,000,000)	1,798,910
Ichalkaranji	87,727
Imphāl	100,605
Indore (★572,622)	543,797
Jabalpur (★533,751)	425,122
Jabalpur Cantonment (★Jabalpur)	50,400
Jagādhri (★107,726)	35,096
Jagannāthnagar (★Rānchī)	55,691
Jaipur	613,144
Jālgaon	106,739
Jālna	91,048
Jalpaiguri	55,345
Jamālpur (★★Monghyr)	62,302
Jammu (★161,553)	155,249
Jāmnagar (★227,460)	214,853
Jamshedpur (★465,200)	340,564
Jaunpur	76,040
Jetpur	41,874
Jhānsi (★198,101)	173,255
Jharia (★★Dhānbād)	45,248
Jodhpur	318,894
Jorhāt	30,486
Jullundur (★330,178)	296,103
Junāgadh	95,945
Kadaiyanallūr	50,258
Kaithal	45,231
Kākināda	164,172
Kālol (★Ahmadābād)	50,331
Kalyān (★Bombay)	99,480
Kamarhati (★Calcutta)	169,222
Kāmthi (★Nāgpur)	53,327
Kānchipuram (Conjeeveram)	110,505
Kānchrāpāra (★Calcutta)	79,019
Kānpur (★1,320,000)	1,151,975
Kānpur Cantonment (★Kānpur)	69,401
Kāraikkudi	55,450
Kārikāl	26,082
Karīmnagar	48,729
Karnāl	92,835
Karūr	65,526
Kāsganj	46,462
Katihār (★80,121)	67,035
Kayankulam	53,912
Kerkend (★Dhānbād)	51,316
Khadki (Kirkee) (★Pune)	65,551
Khāmgaon	53,698
Khammam	56,962
Khandwa	85,513
Kharagpur	161,911
Khurja	50,242
Kolar	43,345
Kolar Gold Fields	76,143
Kolhāpur (★267,533)	259,068
Kota	213,005
Kot Kapūra	34,107
Kottagūdem	75,527
Kottayam	59,718
Krishnanagar	86,354
Kulti	29,858
Kumbakonam (★119,499)	112,971
Kurnool	136,682
Lātūr	70,147
Lucknow (★850,000)	750,512
Lucknow Cantonment (★Lucknow)	50,324
Ludhiāna	401,124
Machilīpatnam (Bandar)	112,636
Madras (★3,000,000)	2,470,288
Madurai (★675,000)	548,298
Mahbūbnagar	51,775
Mālegaon	191,784
Mandasor	57,008
Mandaya (★72,058)	60,000
Mangalore (★214,093)	180,000
Mannārgudi	42,785
Mathura (★140,468)	131,813
Mattāncheri (★Cochin) (1961C)	83,896
Maunath Bhanjan	64,072
Māyūram	60,196
Meerut (★367,821)	271,325
Meerut Cantonment (★Meerut)	85,151
Mehsāna	51,705
Mhow	63,755
Midnapore	71,521
Miraj (★★Sāngli)	77,612
Mirzāpur	105,920
Moga	61,647
Mokameh	38,251
Monghyr (★164,764)	102,462
Morādābād (★272,355)	258,251
Morvi	61,161
Motihāri (★40,380)	37,058
Murwāra (Katni) (★67,817)	62,677
Muzaffarnagar	114,859
Muzaffarpur	127,045
Mysore	355,636
Nabadwip	93,986
Nābha	35,224
Nadiad	108,268
Nāgappattinam	68,015
Nagercoil	141,207
Nāgpur (★950,000)	866,144
Naihati (★Calcutta)	81,782
Nander	126,400
Nandurbār	54,058
Nandyāl	63,199
Nāsik (★271,370)	176,187
Navsāri	73,103
Neemuch	49,773
Nellore	133,607
NEW DELHI (★★Delhi)	292,857
Neyveli	58,289
Nizāmābād	114,868
North Barrackpore (★Calcutta)	76,651
North Dum-Dum (★Calcutta)	63,114
Nowgong	52,892
Ongole	53,337
Ootacamund	63,003
Outer Burnpur (★Asansol)	57,177
Pālayankottai (★★Tirunelveli)	70,050
Pālghāt	95,765
Pallavaram (★Madras)	50,165
Palni (★70,000)	49,576
Panaji (Panjim) (Nova Goa)	59,149
Pandharpur	53,634
Pānihāti (★Calcutta)	148,121
Pānīpat	88,017
Parbhani	61,477
Pātan	64,618
Pathānkot	78,197
Patiāla	151,903
Patna (★625,000)	472,051
Periyakulam	41,515
Petlad	39,539
Phagwāra	50,858
Pīlībhīt	68,380
Pimpri-Chinchwad (★Pune)	83,552
Pollāchi	68,589
Pondicherry (★155,000)	90,639
Porbandar	96,756
Port Blair	26,212
Proddatūr	70,855
Pudukkottai	66,388
Pune (Poona) (★1,175,000)	853,226
Pune Cantonment (★Pune)	77,776
Puri	72,712
Purnea (★71,629)	56,541
Purūlia	57,721
Quilon	124,072
Rae-Bareli	38,762
Rāichūr	79,519
Raigarh	48,046
Raipur (★205,909)	174,382
Rājahmundry (★188,841)	165,900
Rājapālaiyam	86,946
Rājkot	300,152
Rāj-Nāndgaon	55,782
Rāmpur	161,802
Ranaghat	47,956
Rānchī (★256,011)	176,225
Rānīganj (★★Asansol)	39,039
Ratlām (★118,625)	106,039
Ratnāgiri	37,579
Raurkela (★172,536)	125,427
Rewa	69,197
Rewāri	43,900
Rishra (★Calcutta)	63,582
Rohtak	124,783
Roorkee (★62,932)	47,731
Sāgar (★154,811)	118,589
Sahāranpur	225,698
Salem	308,303
Sambalpur	64,603
Sambhal	86,319
Sāngli (★192,664)	115,052
Sāntipur	61,201
Sāsarām	48,215
Sātāra	66,431
Satna	60,944
Secunderābād Cantonment (★Hyderābād)	94,324
Serampore (★Calcutta)	101,597
Shāhjahānpur (★144,058)	135,492
Shillong (★122,651)	73,529
Shimoga	102,703
Shivpuri	50,858
Sholāpur	398,122
Sidhpur	40,416
Sīkar	70,983
Silchar	52,612
Silīguri	97,462
Simla	55,326
Sindri (★★Dhānbād)	46,159
Singānallūr (★Coimbatore)	113,397
Sirsa	48,801
Sītāpur	66,663
Sivakāsi	44,868
Sonīpat	62,378
South Dum-Dum (★Calcutta)	174,538
Sri Gangānagar	90,053
Srīkākulam	45,173
Srīnagar (★411,614)	403,612
Srīrangam (★Tiruchchirāppalli)	51,066
Srivilliputtūr	53,859
Sūjāngarh	39,066
Surat (★492,691)	471,815
Surendranagar	66,630
Tāmbaram (★Madras)	54,050
Tellicherry	68,736
Tenāli	102,943
Tenkāsi	42,611
Tezpur	39,915
Thāna (★Bombay)	170,167
Thanjāvúr (Tanjore)	140,470
Tindivanam	45,028
Tinsukia	55,392
Tiruchchirāppalli (Trichinopoly) (★450,000)	306,247
Tirunelveli (★250,000)	108,509
Tirupati (★71,677)	65,847
Tiruppattūr	40,300
Tiruppur	113,171
Tiruvannāmalai	60,478
Tiruvottiyūr (★Madras)	82,415
Titāgarh (★Calcutta)	88,318
Tonk	55,867
Trichūr	76,248
Trivandrum	409,761
Tumkūr	70,475
Tuticorin (★157,951)	154,804
Udaipur	162,934
Ujjain (★209,118)	207,511
Ulhāsnagar (★Bombay)	168,128
Uttarpara-Kotrung (★Calcutta)	68,315
Valparai	94,939
Vāniyambādi (★57,659)	51,795
Vārānasi (Benares) (★582,915)	560,296
Vellore (★150,190)	138,220
Verāval (★77,158)	59,685
Vijayawāda (★343,664)	316,448
Vikramasingapuram (★89,338)	40,076
Villupuram	60,237
Viramgām	44,095
Virudunagar	61,904
Vishākhapatnam (★362,270)	351,249
Vizianagaram	86,548
Warangal	207,130
Wardha	68,990
Yamunānagar (★★Jagādhri)	72,630
Yavatmāl	64,829

INDONESIA

1961 C....................95,939,000

(includes West Irian, incorporated into Indonesia in August, 1969)

Island Groups and Provinces

BORNEO, INDONESIAN (KALIMANTAN)	4,067,000
Kalimantan Barat (West Borneo)	1,569,000
Kalimantan Selatan (South Borneo)	1,515,000
Kalimantan Tengah (Central Borneo)	476,000
Kalimantan Timur (East Borneo)	507,000
CELEBES	6,571,000
Sulawesi Selatan (South Celebes)	4,617,000
Sulawesi Utara (North Celebes)	1,954,000
JAVA AND MADURA	62,733,000
Djakarta Raja (Greater Djakarta)	2,922,000
Djawa Barat (West Java)	17,504,000
Djawa Tengah (Central Java)	18,331,000
Djawa Timur (East Java)	21,792,000
Jogjakarta	2,184,000
LESSER SUNDA ISLANDS	5,521,000
Bali	1,775,000
Nusa Tenggara Barat (West Nusa Tenggara)	1,804,000
Nusa Tenggara Timur (East Nusa Tenggara)	1,942,000
MOLUCCAS	1,608,000
Irian Barat (1961 E)	811,000
Maluku (Moluccas)	797,000
SUMATRA	15,439,000
Atjeh	1,502,000
Djambi	656,000
Riau	1,232,000
Sumatera Barat (West Sumatra)	2,311,000
Sumatera Selatan (South Sumatra)	4,826,000
Sumatera Utara (North Sumatra)	4,912,000

Cities

Amahai	18,256
Ambon (Amboina)	56,037
Amuntai	27,383
Balikpapan	91,706
Banda Atjeh (Kutaradja)	40,067
Bandjarmasin	214,096
Bandjarnegara	13,351
Bandung (1971E) (★1,175,000)	1,114,000
Bangil	28,275
Bangkalan	22,514
Banjuwangi	72,467
Bantul	30,572
Baubau	21,060
Bekasi	32,012
Bengkulu	25,330
Bindjai	45,235
Blitar	62,972
Blora	29,201
Bodjonegoro	40,976
Bogor	154,092
Bondowoso	35,760
Brebes	36,851
Bukittinggi	51,456
Denpasar	56,780
Djajapura (Sukarnapura) (1961 E)	14,500
•DJAKARTA (1971E) (★6,050,000)	5,899,000
Djember	94,089
Djepara	18,921
Djombang	68,963
Ende	26,843
Garut	76,244
Gorontalo	71,378
Gresik	38,998
Indramaju	25,710
Jogjakarta	312,698
Kandangan	26,112
Kebumen	25,125
Kediri	158,918
Kendari	11,672
Klaten	33,400
Kotabumi	37,496
Krawang	49,567
Kualakapuas	18,573
Kudus	74,911
Kuningan	21,542
Kupang	29,831
Lahat	21,416
Langsa	36,752
Lawang	35,852
Lumadjang	39,536
Madiun	123,373
Madjalengka	14,361
Madjene	24,259
Magelang	96,454
Magetan	26,818
Makale	32,578
Makasar	384,159
Malang	341,452
Manado	129,912
Martapura	44,608
Mataram	17,601
Medan	479,098
Modjokerto	51,732
Ngawi	29,220
Padang	143,699
Padangpandjang	25,521
Padangsidempuan	46,496
Pajakumbuh	21,031
Pakanbaru	70,821
Palangkaraja	6,860
Palembang	474,971
Palopo	29,724
Palu	16,977
Pamekasan	36,121
Pangkalpinang	60,283
Parepare	67,992
Pasuruan	63,408
Pati	38,246
Pekalongan	102,380
Pemalang	42,533
Pematangsiantar	114,870
Perabumulih	41,951
Pinrang	23,818
Ponorogo	59,952
Pontianak	150,220
Praja	26,729
Probolinggo	68,328
Purbolinggo	22,698
Purwakarta	45,610
Purwokerto	80,556
Purworedjo	32,119
Raba	29,881
Rangkasbitung	30,822
Rantauprapat	25,707
Rembang	22,985
Salatiga	58,135
Samarinda	69,715
Sampit	24,876
Semarang	503,153
Serang	40,956
Sibolga	38,655
Sidoardjo	33,414
Sindjai	18,390
Singaradja	33,252
Singkawang	35,169
Situbondo	34,483
Solok	81,909
Sragen	25,685
Subang	33,649
Sukabumi	80,438
Sumedang	27,891
Sumenep	26,823
Sungaipenuh	36,766
Surabaja (1971E) (★1,325,000)	1,273,000
Surakarta	367,626
Tandjungbalai	29,152
Tandjungpandan	29,412
Tandjungpinang	37,638
Tangerang	36,349
Tarutung	24,998
Tasikmalaja	125,525
Tebingtinggi	26,228
Tegal	89,016
Telanaipura (Djambi)	113,080
Telukbetung	133,091
Ternate	24,287
Tidore	26,160
Tjiamis	35,189
Tjiandjur	62,546
Tjilatjap	55,333
Tjimahi	64,226
Tjirebon	158,299
Tual	38,403
Tuban	38,575
Tulungagung	62,069
Watampone	32,461

C Census. E Official estimate. UE Unofficial estimate.
L Population within municipal limits of year specified. • Largest city in country.

★ Population or designation of metropolitan area, including suburbs (see headnote).
▲ Population of an entire municipality, commune, or district, including rural area.
‡† Year of information specified at start of country.

IRAN / Īrān

1966 C ... **25,323,064**

Ābādān ... 272,962
Ahvāz ... 206,375
Āmol ... 40,076
Arāk ... 71,925
Ardabīl ... 83,596
Bābol ... 49,973
Bam ... 21,761
Bandar 'Abbās ... 34,627
Bandar-e Pahlavī (Pahlavī) ... 41,785
Behbehān ... 39,874
Behshahr ... 26,032
Bīrjand ... 25,854
Bojnūrd ... 31,248
Borūjerd ... 71,486
Dezfūl ... 84,499
Eşfahān (Isfahan) ... 424,045
Gonbad-e Kāvūs ... 40,667
Gorgān ... 51,181
Hamadān ... 124,167
Homāyunshahr ... 46,836
Jahrom ... 38,236
Karaj ... 44,243
Kāshān ... 58,468
Kāzerūn ... 39,758
Kermān ... 85,404
Kermānshāh ... 187,930
Khorramābād ... 59,578
Khorramshahr ... 88,536
Khvoy ... 47,648
Lāhījān ... 25,725
Mahābād ... 28,610
Malāyer ... 28,434
Marāgheh ... 54,106
Marv Dasht ... 25,498
Mashhad (Meshed) ... 409,616
Masjed Soleymān ... 64,488
Mīāneh ... 28,447
Najafābād ... 43,384
Neyshābūr ... 33,482
Qazvīn ... 88,106
Qom ... 134,292
Qūchān ... 29,133
Rasht ... 143,557
Rey (★Tehrān) ... 102,825
Reẕā'īyeh ... 110,749
Sabzevār ... 42,415
Sanandaj ... 54,578
Sārī ... 44,547
Semnān ... 31,058
Shāhī ... 38,898
Shahreẕā ... 34,220
Shāhrūd ... 30,767
Shīrāz ... 269,865
Tabrīz ... 403,413
Tajrīsh (★Tehrān) ... 157,486
•TEHRĀN (★3,075,000) ... 2,719,730
Torbat-e Ḩeydarīyeh ... 30,106
Yazd ... 93,241
Zāhedān ... 39,732
Zanjān ... 58,714

IRAQ / Al-'Irāq

1970 E ... **9,465,800**

Ad-Dīwānīyah ... 62,300
Al-'Amārah ... 80,100
Al-Başrah (Basra) ... 370,900
Al-Fallūjah (1965 C) ... 38,072
Al-Ḩillah (Hilla) ... 128,800
Al-Kūfah (1965 C) ... 30,862
Al-Mawşil (Mosul) ... 293,100
An-Najaf ... 179,200
An-Nāşirīyah ... 62,400
Ar-Ramādī (1965 C) ... 28,723
As-Samāwah (1965 C) ... 33,473
As-Sulaymānīyah ... 98,100
Az-Zubayr (1965 C) ... 41,408
•BAGHDĀD (★2,183,800) ... 1,300,000
Ba'qūbah (1965 C) ... 34,575
Irbīl ... 107,400
Karbalā' ... 107,500
Khānaqīn (1965 C) ... 23,522
Kirkūk ... 207,900
Kūt al-Imāra (Al-Kūt) (1965 C) ... 42,116
Sāmarrā (1965 C) ... 24,746
Tall 'Afar (1965 C) ... 36,837

IRELAND / Eire

1971 C ... **2,971,230**

Provinces and Counties

CONNACHT ... 389,763
Galway ... 148,220
Leitrim ... 28,313
Mayo ... 109,497
Roscommon ... 53,497
Sligo ... 50,236
LEINSTER ... 1,494,544
Carlow ... 34,025
Dublin ... 849,542
Kildare ... 71,522
Kilkenny ... 61,811
Laoighis ... 45,349
Longford ... 28,227
Louth ... 74,899
Meath ... 71,616
Offaly ... 51,834
Westmeath ... 53,557
Wexford ... 85,892
Wicklow ... 66,270
MUNSTER ... 880,018
Clare ... 74,844
Cork ... 351,735
Kerry ... 112,941
Limerick ... 140,370
Tipperary ... 123,196
Waterford ... 76,932
ULSTER ... 206,905
Cavan ... 52,674
Donegal ... 108,000
Monaghan ... 46,231

Cities

Arklow (Inbhear Mór) ... 6,750
Athlone (Áth Luain) ... 9,821
Bray (Brí Chualann) ... 14,458
Carlow (Ceatharlach) (★11,500) ... 9,384
Clonmel (Cluain Meala) ... 11,630
Cobh ... 6,049
Cork (Corcaigh) (★132,000) ... 128,235
Drogheda (Droichead Átha) ... 19,744
•DUBLIN (BAILE ÁTHA CLIATH) (★815,000) ... 566,034
Dundalk (Dún Dealgan) ... 21,718
Dún Laoghaire (★Dublin) ... 52,990
Galway (Gaillimh) ... 26,896
Kilkenny (CillChoinnigh) ... 10,292
Killarney (Cill Áirne) ... 7,179
Limerick (Luimneach) ... 57,137
New Ross (Ros Mhic Treoin) ... 4,775
Sligo (Sligeach) ... 14,071
Thurles (Durlas Éile) ... 6,790
Tipperary (Tiobrad Árann) ... 4,592
Tralee (Tráighlí) ... 12,227
Tullamore (Tulach Mhór) ... 6,810
Waterford (Port Láirge) ... 31,695
Wexford (Loch Garman) ... 11,744

ISLE OF MAN

1971 C ... **56,248**

•DOUGLAS (★28,000) ... 20,385
Peel ... 3,081
Ramsey ... 5,048

ISRAEL / Yisra'el

1969 E ... **†2,918,600**

Districts

HaDarom (Southern) ... 320,000
HaMerkaz (Central) ... 521,500
HaẔafon (Northern) ... 447,300
Ḩefa (Haifa) ... 455,100
Tel Aviv ... 860,500
Yerushalayim (Jerusalem) ... 314,200

†Includes entire city of Jerusalem, but excludes population of other areas occupied by Israel in 1967 (1969 estimate):
West Bank (from Jordan) ... *599,600*
Gaza Strip and Al 'Arish Area (from Egypt) ... 365,500
Golan Heights (from Syria) (1967 census) ... *6,396*

Cities

'Afula ... 16,700
'Akko (Acre) (★Ḩefa) ... 33,500
Ashdod ... 35,600
Ashqelon ... 39,200
Bat Yam (★Tel Aviv-Yafo) ... 76,600
Be'er Sheva' (Beersheba) ... 74,500
Bene Beraq (★Tel Aviv-Yafo) ... 69,700
Dimona ... 21,600
Elat (Elath) ... 13,200
Giv'atayim (★Tel Aviv-Yafo) ... 44,400
Ḩadera ... 30,500
Ḩefa (Haifa) (★350,000) ... 214,500
Herzliyya (★Tel Aviv-Yafo) ... 37,300
Ḩolon (★Tel Aviv-Yafo) ... 84,700
Kefar Sava ... 23,700
Lod (Lydda) ... 28,000
Nahariya ... 21,100
Naẕerat (Nazareth) (★47,000) ... 32,900
Naẕerat 'Illit (★Naẕerat) ... 13,200
Nes Ẕiyyona ... 12,000
Netanya ... 62,500
Or Yehuda (★Tel Aviv-Yafo) ... 12,000
Petaḩ Tiqwa (★Tel Aviv-Yafo) ... 80,000
Qiryat Ata (★Ḩefa) ... 25,000
Qiryat Bialik (★Ḩefa) ... 13,900
Qiryat Gat ... 17,400
Qiryat Motzkin (★Ḩefa) ... 14,500
Qiryat Ono (★Tel Aviv-Yafo) ... 14,200
Qiryat Shemona ... 15,400
Qiryat Yam (★Ḩefa) ... 16,500
Ramat Gan (★Tel Aviv-Yafo) ... 112,600
Ramat HaSharon (★Tel Aviv-Yafo) ... 16,600
Ramla ... 29,900
Reḩovot ... 35,600
Rishon leẔiyyon (★Tel Aviv-Yafo) ... 44,100
•Tel Aviv-Yafo (Tel Aviv-Jaffa) (★1,025,000) ... 382,900
Teverya (Tiberias) ... 23,600
Tirat Karmel (★Ḩefa) ... 13,200
YERUSHALAYIM (AL-QUDS) (JERUSALEM) *(includes Old City area occupied in 1967)* (★300,000) ... 283,100
Ẕefat ... 13,100

ITALY / Italia

1970 E ... **54,683,136**

Regions and Provinces

ABRUZZI ... 1,201,498
Chieti ... 366,959
L'Aquila ... 304,409
Pescara ... 266,511
Teramo ... 263,619
APULIA, see PUGLIA
BASILICATA (LUCANIA) ... 620,731
Matera ... 200,948
Potenza ... 419,783
CALABRIA ... 2,048,655
Catanzaro ... 734,342
Cosenza ... 715,699
Reggio di Calabria ... 598,614
CAMPANIA ... 5,191,450
Avellino ... 446,167
Benevento ... 303,509
Caserta ... 706,486
Napoli (Naples) ... 2,756,570
Salerno ... 978,718
EMILIA-ROMAGNA ... 3,858,756
Bologna ... 916,461
Ferrara ... 387,451
Forlì ... 568,137
Modena ... 552,924
Parma ... 399,070
Piacenza ... 287,802
Ravenna ... 353,743
Reggio nell'Emilia ... 393,168
FRIULI-VENEZIA GIULIA ... 1,232,399
Gorizia ... 143,235
Pordenone ... 257,754
Trieste ... 305,381
Udine ... 526,029
LAZIO (LATIUM) ... 4,705,121
Frosinone ... 436,568
Latina ... 381,491
Rieti ... 148,010
Roma (Rome) ... 3,479,172
Viterbo ... 259,880
LIGURIA ... 1,881,952
Genova ... 1,111,313
Imperia ... 229,631
La Spezia ... 247,942
Savona ... 293,066
LOMBARDIA (LOMBARDY) ... 8,442,914
Bergamo ... 826,314
Brescia ... 958,440
Como ... 709,333
Cremona ... 336,548
Mantova ... 379,476
Milano ... 3,817,873
Pavia ... 529,489
Sondrio ... 171,274
Varese ... 714,167
MARCHE (MARCHES) ... 1,368,765
Ancona ... 417,887
Ascoli Piceno ... 344,270
Macerata ... 288,343
Pesaro e Urbino ... 318,265
MOLISE ... 331,257
Campobasso ... 235,194
Isernia ... 96,063
PIEMONTE (PIEDMONT) ... 4,433,593
Alessandria ... 485,878
Asti ... 219,682
Cuneo ... 542,290
Novara ... 496,500
Torino (Turin) ... 2,280,587
Vercelli ... 408,656
PUGLIA (APULIA) ... 3,642,464
Bari ... 1,361,164
Brindisi ... 373,524
Foggia ... 668,075
Lecce ... 727,286
Taranto ... 512,435
SARDEGNA (SARDINIA) ... 1,501,749
Cagliari ... 814,532
Nuoro ... 282,651
Sassari ... 404,566
SICILIA (SICILY) ... 4,882,718
Agrigento ... 482,385
Caltanissetta ... 296,812
Catania ... 969,657
Enna ... 209,295
Messina ... 686,196
Palermo ... 1,177,203
Ragusa ... 260,700
Siracusa ... 370,240
Trapani ... 430,230
TOSCANA (TUSCANY) ... 3,479,585
Arezzo ... 307,537
Firenze ... 1,140,362
Grosseto ... 217,734
Livorno ... 337,385
Lucca ... 381,705
Massa-Carrara ... 204,941
P sa ... 375,864
Pistoia ... 253,819
Siena ... 260,238
TRENTINO-ALTO ADIGE ... 844,743
Bolzano ... 415,618
Trento ... 429,125
UMBRIA ... 782,621
Perugia ... 557,518
Terni ... 225,103
VALLE D'AOSTA ... 109,963
VENETO (VENETIA) ... 4,122,202
Belluno ... 228,197
Padova ... 759,561
Rovigo ... 253,616
Treviso ... 666,577
Venezia (Venice) ... 809,685
Verona ... 730,028
Vicenza ... 674,538

Cities

Abano Terme (13,505▲) ... 7,700
Acireale (48,729▲) ... 30,000
Adrano ... 32,635
Afragola (★Napoli) ... 52,165
Agrigento (52,142▲) ... 46,000
Alassio ... 13,539
Albano Laziale (★Roma) (25,383▲) ... 20,000
Alcamo ... 42,967
Alessandria (100,649▲) ... 89,000
Alghero (32,250▲) ... 27,000
Altamura ... 46,315
Amalfi (7,116▲) ... 5,000
Ancona ... 110,438
Andria ... 77,307
Anzio (23,335▲) ... 18,000
Aosta ... 36,324
Arezzo (87,061▲) ... 64,000
Ariano Irpino (24,510▲) ... 10,700
Ascoli Piceno (55,818▲) ... 43,000
Assisi (24,382▲) ... 5,000
Asti (76,203▲) ... 61,000
Augusta ... 32,779
Avellino (51,753▲) ... 46,000
Aversa ... 48,426
Avezzano (32,397▲) ... 26,000
Bagheria ... 37,133
Barcellona Pozzo di Gotto (34,871▲) ... 24,000
Bari ... 356,250
Barletta ... 76,744
Bassano del Grappa (35,891▲) ... 31,000
Benevento (60,636▲) ... 49,000
Bergamo (★310,000) ... 126,504
Biella ... 54,850
Bisceglie ... 44,837
Bitonto ... 42,629
Bollate (★Milano) ... 42,638
Bologna (★540,000) ... 493,070
Bolzano ... 106,009
Bordighera (12,108▲) ... 9,700
Brescia ... 209,659
Bressanone (15,615▲) ... 11,800
Brindisi ... 82,712
Busto Arsizio (★Milano) ... 77,834
Cagliari (★270,000) ... 225,812
Caltagirone (42,428▲) ... 36,000
Caltanissetta (63,756▲) ... 52,000
Camerino (8,784▲) ... 3,700
Campobasso (41,426▲) ... 36,500
Cantù ... 31,963
Capannori (41,617▲) ... 23,500
Capua (19,292▲) ... 16,400
Carbonia ... 32,357
Carpi (54,812▲) ... 36,000
Carrara (★★Massa) ... 68,070
Casale Monferrato (44,288▲) ... 40,000
Caserta (61,739▲) ... 55,000
Casoria (★Napoli) ... 46,534
Castel Gandolfo (★Roma) (4,980▲) ... 2,900
Castellammare di Stabia ... 71,301
Castelvetrano ... 31,587
Catania ... 414,619
Catanzaro ... 82,905
Cattolica ... 15,513
Cava de' Tirreni (★Salerno) (47,246▲) ... 40,000
Cefalù (13,120▲) ... 11,200
Cerignola (47,626▲) ... 42,000
Cesena (86,654▲) ... 55,000
Cesenatico (18,714▲) ... 9,500
Chiavari ... 29,236
Chieti (54,177▲) ... 47,000
Chioggia (49,471▲) ... 26,500
Cinisello Balsamo (★Milano) ... 74,315
Cittadella (15,715▲) ... 6,500
Città di Castello (36,385▲) ... 15,200
Civitanova Marche (32,382▲) ... 25,000
Civitavecchia ... 43,781
Collegno (★Torino) ... 39,806
Cologno Monzese (★Milano) ... 43,918
Como (★146,000) ... 95,552
Corato ... 39,377
Corsico (★Milano) ... 34,892
Cortina d'Ampezzo ... 8,308
Cortona (22,939▲) ... 3,000
Cosenza ... 97,558
Cremona ... 82,014
Crotone (50,647▲) ... 43,000
Cuneo (53,989▲) ... 42,000
Desio (★Milano) ... 29,393
Domodossola ... 19,399
Empoli (43,833▲) ... 34,000
Enna ... 28,937
Ercolano (Resina) (★Napoli) ... 52,451
Este (17,370▲) ... 12,200
Faenza (54,907▲) ... 32,500
Fano (47,585▲) ... 31,500
Ferrara (155,793▲) ... 118,000
Fiesole (★Firenze) (13,953▲) ... 4,400
Firenze (Florence) (★620,000) ... 460,944
Foggia ... 141,400
Foligno (50,429▲) ... 33,500
Forlì (105,420▲) ... 78,000
Frascati (★Roma) (18,574▲) ... 14,700
Frattamaggiore (★Napoli) ... 35,505
Gaeta ... 23,385
Gallarate (★Milano) ... 42,913
Gallipoli ... 18,077
Gela ... 66,638
Genova (Genoa) (★890,000) ... 842,114
Gorizia ... 43,918
Gravina in Puglia ... 33,372
Grosseto (62,439▲) ... 47,000
Grugliasco (★Torino) ... 30,459
Gubbio (30,807▲) ... 9,500
Iesi (Jesi) (39,374▲) ... 29,000
Iglesias ... 28,368
Imola (56,717▲) ... 36,000
Imperia ... 40,254
Isernia (15,212▲) ... 11,000
Ivrea ... 28,900
L'Aquila (59,347▲) ... 47,000
La Spezia (★197,000) ... 128,255
Latina (76,513▲) ... 54,000
Lecce ... 82,598
Lecco ... 52,745
Legnago ... 25,971
Legnano (★Milano) ... 47,370
Lentini ... 32,708
Licata ... 40,491
Livorno (Leghorn) ... 175,280
Lodi ... 43,864
Loreto (9,518▲) ... 5,300
Lucca (91,582▲) ... 74,000
Lucera (29,312▲) ... 25,000
Lugo (34,900▲) ... 20,500
Macerata (43,260▲) ... 33,000
Maddaloni (33,867▲) ... 27,000
Magenta ... 23,030
Manfredonia (45,859▲) ... 40,500
Mantova ... 66,595
Marino (★Roma) (46,741▲) ... 40,000
Marsala (83,322▲) ... 42,500
Martina Franca (39,464▲) ... 29,000
Massa (★139,000) ... 63,377
Matera ... 45,171
Mazara del Vallo ... 40,876
Merano (Meran) ... 34,106
Messina ... 274,740
•Milano (Milan) (★3,565,000) ... 1,713,539
Milazzo (26,154▲) ... 17,500
Modena ... 170,450
Modica (44,993▲) ... 23,500
Molfetta ... 65,390
Moncalieri (★Torino) ... 53,035
Monfalcone ... 29,077
Monopoli ... 42,626
Monreale (25,709▲) ... 20,500
Montecatini Terme (20,396▲) ... 18,500
Montepulciano (14,663▲) ... 3,300
Monte Sant'Angelo ... 19,376
Monza (★Milano) ... 110,429
Napoli (Naples) (★1,940,000) ... 1,278,051
Nardò (30,555▲) ... 24,000
Nettuno (24,333▲) ... 21,000
Nicastro (Lamezia Terme) (56,317▲) ... 27,000
Nichelino (★Torino) ... 42,567
Nocera Inferiore (50,123▲) ... 45,000
Nola (27,453▲) ... 21,000
Novara ... 100,795
Novi Ligure ... 33,098
Nuoro ... 30,252
Oristano (27,075▲) ... 20,500
Orvieto (23,867▲) ... 9,200
Otranto (4,505▲) ... 4,100
Padova ... 228,854
Pagani (30,185▲) ... 27,000
Palermo ... 663,776
Parma ... 174,553
Paternò ... 47,967
Pavia ... 86,230
Perugia (128,343▲) ... 92,000
Pesaro (83,542▲) ... 69,000
Pescara ... 120,473
Piacenza ... 105,233
Piazza Armerina ... 22,372
Pietrasanta (25,552▲) ... 22,000
Pinerolo (37,239▲) ... 33,000
Piombino ... 40,162
Pisa ... 103,223
Pistoia (92,520▲) ... 71,000
Pompei (22,659▲) ... 12,500
Pontedera (26,352▲) ... 22,500
Pordenone ... 46,397
Portici (★Napoli) ... 72,340
Portoferraio (10,830▲) ... 6,500
Portofino (942▲) ... 600
Potenza (54,229▲) ... 46,500
Pozzuoli (★Napoli) (63,064▲) ... 54,000
Prato (★181,000) ... 142,463
Ragusa (61,119▲) ... 54,000
Rapallo ... 26,630
Ravello (2,493▲) ... 1,500
Ravenna (132,172▲) ... 82,500
Recoaro Terme ... 8,453
Reggio di Calabria (167,087▲) ... 139,500
Reggio nell'Emilia (128,717▲) ... 100,000
Rho (★Milano) ... 45,975
Riccione ... 27,945
Rieti (39,763▲) ... 31,000
Rimini (118,938▲) ... 99,000
Riva [del Garda] (12,090▲) ... 8,500
Rivoli (★Torino) ... 45,208
ROMA (ROME) (★2,980,000) ... 2,778,872
Rosignano Marittimo (29,465▲) ... 24,000
Rovereto ... 28,852
Rovigo (49,126▲) ... 39,500
Ruvo di Puglia ... 23,325
Salerno (★225,000) ... 152,780
Salsomaggiore (17,622▲) ... 11,000
San Donà di Piave (28,579▲) ... 20,000
San Gimignano (7,856▲) ... 3,000
San Giorgio a Cremano (★Napoli) ... 36,689
San Remo (64,996▲) ... 51,000
San Severo ... 52,130
Santa Maria Capua Vetere ... 32,107
Sarno (30,733▲) ... 24,500
Saronno ... 32,203
Sassari (109,152▲) ... 93,000
Savona (★115,000) ... 79,192
Scandicci (★Firenze) (45,257▲) ... 11,000
Schio ... 35,120
Sciacca (33,944▲) ... 30,000
Senigallia (37,647▲) ... 25,500
Seregno (★Milano) ... 34,197
Sesto Fiorentino (★Firenze) ... 40,268
Sesto San Giovanni (★Milano) ... 89,431
Sestri Levante ... 21,027
Settimo Torinese (★Torino) ... 39,390
Siena (66,321▲) ... 54,500
Siracusa (107,529▲) ... 90,000
Sondrio ... 23,185
Sorrento (14,974▲) ... 11,000
Spoleto (36,690▲) ... 26,000
Sulmona (21,944▲) ... 19,000
Taormina (9,351▲) ... 6,500
Taranto ... 223,392
Tarquinia (12,507▲) ... 9,500
Teramo (47,735▲) ... 35,000
Termini Imerese ... 25,094
Terni ... 107,321
Terracina (33,805▲) ... 23,000
Tivoli (★Roma) ... 41,891
Todi (17,772▲) ... 4,000
Torino (Turin) (★1,595,000) ... 1,190,688
Torre Annunziata ... 62,563
Torre del Greco (★Napoli) (94,326▲) ... 83,000
Tortona (29,213▲) ... 23,500
Trani ... 41,672
Trapani (76,156▲) ... 66,000
Trento ... 91,017
Treviglio (25,798▲) ... 22,000
Treviso ... 90,368
Trieste ... 277,133
Udine (★118,000) ... 98,034
Urbino (16,392▲) ... 7,000
Varese ... 82,462
Velletri (38,398▲) ... 23,000
Venezia (Venice) (★420,000) ... 367,528
Ventimiglia (25,878▲) ... 21,000
Verbania ... 34,874
Vercelli ... 56,734
Verona ... 262,014
Viareggio ... 55,825
Vibo Valentia (28,649▲) ... 23,000
Vicenza ... 114,349
Vigevano ... 67,657
Viterbo (53,418▲) ... 38,000
Vittoria ... 47,234
Vittorio Veneto (30,295▲) ... 24,500
Voghera (40,920▲) ... 36,000
Volterra (16,556▲) ... 10,500

C Census. E Official estimate. UE Unofficial estimate.
L Population within municipal limits of year specified. • Largest city in country.
★ Population or designation of metropolitan area, including suburbs (see headnote).
▲ Population of an entire municipality, commune, or district, including rural area.
‡† Year of information specified at start of country.

IVORY COAST / Côte d'Ivoire

1963 C … 3,712,200

Abengourou … 15,825
•ABIDJAN (1969 E) … 510,000
Agboville … 18,068
Bouaké (1969 E) … 161,300
Daloa (1965 E) … 30,000
Danané … 17,240
Dimbokro … 15,281
Divo … 19,551
Gagnoa (1965 E) … 22,000
Grand-Bassam … 22,994
Korhogo … 23,766
Man (1965 E) … 27,000
Séguéla … 11,017

JAMAICA

1970 C … 1,861,300

•KINGSTON … 550,100
Mandeville … 13,100
May Pen … 26,200
Montego Bay … 42,800
Ocho Rios … 6,900
Port Antonio … 10,400
Savanna-la-Mar … 12,000
Spanish Town … 41,600

JAPAN

1970 C … 104,665,171

Districts and Prefectures

CHUBU … 18,091,285
Aichi … 5,386,163
Fukui … 744,230
Gifu … 1,758,954
Ishikawa … 1,002,420
Nagano … 1,956,917
Niigata … 2,360,982
Shizuoka … 3,089,895
Toyama … 1,029,695
Yamanashi … 762,029
CHUGOKU … 6,996,961
Hiroshima … 2,436,135
Okayama … 1,707,026
Shimane … 773,575
Tottori … 568,777
Yamaguchi … 1,511,448
HOKKAIDŌ … 5,184,287
Hokkaidō … 5,184,287
KANTŌ (KWANTŌ) … 29,495,895
Chiba … 3,366,624
Gumma … 1,658,909
Ibaraki … 2,143,551
Kanagawa … 5,472,247
Saitama … 3,866,472
Tochigi … 1,580,021
Tōkyō … 11,408,071
KINKI … 18,944,242
Hyōgo … 4,667,928
Kyōto … 2,250,087
Mie … 1,543,083
Nara … 930,160
Ōsaka … 7,620,480
Shiga … 889,768
Wakayama … 1,042,736
KYŪSHŪ … 13,017,290
Fukuoka … 4,027,416
Kagoshima … 1,729,150
Kumamoto … 1,700,229
Miyazaki … 1,051,105
Nagasaki … 1,570,245
Ōita … 1,155,566
Okinawa … 945,111
Saga … 838,468
SHIKOKU … 3,904,014
Ehime … 1,418,124
Kagawa … 907,897
Kōchi … 786,882
Tokushima … 791,111
TŌHOKU … 9,031,197
Akita … 1,241,376
Aomori … 1,427,520
Fukushima … 1,946,077
Iwate … 1,371,383
Miyagi … 1,819,223
Yamagata … 1,225,618

Cities

Abashiri (43,904▲) … 35,000
Ageo (★Tōkyō) … 110,792
Aioi … 40,657
Aizu-wakamatsu … 104,065
Akashi (★Ōsaka) … 206,525
Akishima (★Tōkyō) … 75,662
Akita … 235,873
Akō … 45,942
Amagasaki (★Ōsaka) … 553,696
Anan (58,467▲) … 36,000
Anjō … 94,307
Aomori … 240,063
Arao (★Ōmuta) (55,452▲) … 45,000
Asahikawa … 288,492
Asaka (★Tōkyō) … 67,938
Ashibetsu (42,730▲) … 34,000
Ashikaga … 156,004
Ashiya (★Ōsaka) … 70,938
Atami … 51,281
Atsugi (★Tōkyō) … 82,888
Beppu … 123,786
Bibai (47,369▲) … 36,000
Bisai … 51,337
Chiba (★Tōkyō) … 482,133
Chichibu … 60,867
Chigasaki (★Tōkyō) … 129,621
Chitose … 56,118
Chōfu (★Tōkyō) … 157,488
Chōshi … 90,415
Daitō (★Ōsaka) … 93,136
Ebetsu … 63,762
Fuchū (★Tōkyō) … 163,173
Fuji (★265,000) … 180,639
Fujieda (78,750▲) … 56,000
Fujiidera (★Ōsaka) … 50,414
Fujimi (★Tōkyō) … 52,011
Fujinomiya (★★Fuji) (88,880▲) … 69,000
Fujisawa (★Tōkyō) … 228,978
Fuji-yoshida … 50,046
Fukaya (60,609▲) … 42,500
Fukuchiyama (57,174▲) … 41,000
Fukui … 200,509
Fukuoka (★1,185,000) … 853,270
Fukuoka (★Tōkyō) … 51,747
Fukuroi (38,999▲) … 23,500
Fukushima … 227,451
Fukuyama … 255,086
Funabashi (★Tōkyō) … 325,426
Furukawa (52,518▲) … 30,000
Gamagōri … 82,868
Gifu … 385,727
Ginowan (*Ryukyu Is.*) … 39,390
Goshogawara (47,567▲) … 23,000
Gotemba (55,997▲) … 44,000
Gushikawa (*Ryukyu Is.*) … 37,292
Gyōda … 60,135
Habikino (★Ōsaka) … 77,134
Hachinohe … 208,801
Hachiōji (★Tōkyō) … 253,527
Hadano (★Tōkyō) … 75,226
Hagi (52,541▲) … 42,000
Hakodate … 241,663
Hakone … 21,299
Hamada … 49,407
Hamakita (59,592▲) … 44,000
Hamamatsu … 432,221
Hanamaki (63,753▲) … 37,000
Handa … 80,663
Hannō (★Tōkyō) … 52,066
Hanyū (45,001▲) … 31,000
Hashima (48,075▲) … 37,000
Hatogaya (★Tōkyō) … 51,377
Hekinan … 56,933
Higashikurume (★Tōkyō) … 78,075
Higashimatsuyama … 50,383
Higashimurayama (★Tōkyō) … 96,545
Higashiōsaka (★Ōsaka) … 500,173
Hikari (★Tokuyama) … 45,716
Hikone … 78,753
Himeji … 408,353
Himi (60,883▲) … 38,000
Hino (★Tōkyō) … 98,557
Hirakata (★Ōsaka) … 217,369
Hiratsuka (★Tōkyō) … 163,671
Hirosaki (157,603▲) … 102,000
Hiroshima (★1,175,000) … 541,998
Hita (64,866▲) … 48,000
Hitachi … 193,210
Hitoyoshi (42,196▲) … 30,000
Hōfu (97,009▲) … 76,000
Honjō … 47,116
Hōya (★Tōkyō) … 86,194
Hyūga (47,420▲) … 36,000
Ibaraki (★Ōsaka) … 163,903
Ichihara (★Tōkyō) (156,016▲) … 116,000
Ichikawa (★Tōkyō) … 261,055
Ichinomiya … 219,274
Ichinoseki (55,830▲) … 34,000
Iida (77,261▲) … 52,000
Iizuka (★100,000) … 75,643
Ikeda (★Ōsaka) … 94,333
Imabari … 111,125
Imari (61,561▲) … 37,000
Ina (51,922▲) … 31,000
Inazawa (★Nagoya) … 78,180
Innoshima … 41,729
Inuyama (★Nagoya) … 50,594
Iruma … 65,369
Isahaya (65,261▲) … 44,000
Ise (Uji-yamada) … 103,576
Isesaki … 91,277
Ishinomaki … 106,681
Itami (★Ōsaka) … 153,763
Itō … 63,003
Itoigawa (38,395▲) … 22,000
Iwaki (Taira) (327,164▲) … 260,000
Iwakuni … 106,116
Iwamizawa (68,712▲) … 54,000
Iwata … 63,002
Iwatsuki (★Tōkyō) (56,449▲) … 41,000
Iyo-mishima … 38,071
Izumi (★Ōsaka) … 95,987
Izumi-ōtsu (★Ōsaka) … 59,437
Izumi-sano (★Ōsaka) … 77,000
Izumo (69,078▲) … 46,000
Kadoma (★Ōsaka) … 141,041
Kaga (56,514▲) … 43,500
Kagamigahara … 78,109
Kagoshima … 403,340
Kainan … 53,370
Kaizuka (★Ōsaka) … 73,366
Kakegawa (59,153▲) … 37,000
Kakogawa (★Ōsaka) … 127,112
Kamaishi … 72,923
Kamakura (★Tōkyō) … 139,249
Kameda (★Hakodate) … 50,623
Kanazawa … 361,379
Kanoya (66,995▲) … 38,000
Kanuma (77,746▲) … 53,000
Karatsu … 74,233
Kariya (★Nagoya) … 87,671
Karuizawa … 13,373
Kasai (48,354▲) … 29,500
Kasaoka (62,405▲) … 42,000
Kashihara (★Ōsaka) … 75,508
Kashiwa (★Tōkyō) … 150,635
Kashiwara (★Ōsaka) … 53,104
Kashiwazaki (73,569▲) … 49,000
Kasugai (★Nagoya) … 161,835
Kasukabe (★Tōkyō) … 84,919
Katsuta … 66,754
Kawachi-nagano (★Ōsaka) … 51,994
Kawagoe (★Tōkyō) … 171,038
Kawaguchi (★Tōkyō) … 305,886
Kawanishi (★Ōsaka) … 87,127
Kawasaki (★Tōkyō) … 973,486
Kesennuma … 63,265
Kimitsu … 70,440
Kiryū … 132,000
Kisarazu … 73,319
Kishiwada (★Ōsaka) … 162,022
Kitaibaraki (48,323▲) … 36,500
Kitakami (44,919▲) … 26,000
Kitakyūshū (★1,450,000) … 1,042,321
Kitami (82,727▲) … 66,000
Kiyose (★Tōkyō) … 51,911
Kōbe (★★Ōsaka) … 1,288,937
Kōchi … 240,481
Kodaira (★Tōkyō) … 137,373
Kōfu … 182,669
Koga (★Tōkyō) … 54,173
Koganei (★Tōkyō) … 94,448
Kokubunji (★Tōkyō) … 81,259
Komae (★Tōkyō) … 60,297
Komaki (★Nagoya) … 79,606
Komatsu … 95,684
Kōnan … 77,996
Kōnosu (★Tōkyō) … 41,990
Kōriyama (241,673▲) … 165,000
Koshigaya (★Tōkyō) … 139,368
Koza (*Ryukyu Is.*) … 58,658
Kudamatsu (★★Tokuyama) … 49,627
Kumagaya (★Tōkyō) … 120,841
Kumamoto … 440,020
Kunitachi (★Tōkyō) … 59,709
Kurashiki … 339,799
Kurayoshi (49,629▲) … 34,000
Kure (★★Hiroshima) … 235,193
Kurume … 194,178
Kusatsu (★Ōsaka) … 46,409
Kushiro … 191,948
Kuwana … 81,015
Kyōto (★★Ōsaka) … 1,419,165
Machida (★Tōkyō) … 202,801
Maebashi … 233,632
Maizuru (95,895▲) … 81,000
Marugame … 59,214
Masuda (50,071▲) … 34,000
Matsubara (★Ōsaka) … 111,562
Matsudo (★Tōkyō) … 253,591
Matsue … 118,005
Matsumoto … 162,931
Matsuyama … 322,902
Matsuzaka (102,138▲) … 74,000
Mihara … 82,621
Mikasa … 40,553
Minamata (38,109▲) … 28,500
Minō (★Ōsaka) … 57,414
Misawa (35,343▲) … 27,000
Mishima (★★Numazu) … 78,141
Mitaka (★Tōkyō) … 155,693
Mito … 173,789
Mitsuke (41,057▲) … 31,000
Miura … 45,532
Miyako … 59,063
Miyakonojō (114,802▲) … 74,000
Miyata … 27,945
Miyazaki … 202,862
Mizusawa (48,267▲) … 32,000
Mobara … 48,495
Mombetsu (35,110▲) … 30,000
Moriguchi (★Ōsaka) … 184,466
Morioka … 196,036
Muroran (★210,000) … 162,059
Musashino (★Tōkyō) … 136,959
Nagahama … 51,027
Nagano (285,355▲) … 215,000
Nagaoka … 162,262
Nagareyama (★Tōkyō) … 56,485
Nagasaki … 421,114
Nagoya (★3,200,000) … 2,036,053
Naha (*Ryukyu Is.*) … 276,380
Nakatsu (57,461▲) … 43,000
Nakatsugawa (48,656▲) … 35,000
Nanao (47,855▲) … 37,500
Naoetsu … 45,357
Nara (★Ōsaka) … 208,266
Narashino (★Tōkyō) … 99,951
Naruto (60,634▲) … 49,500
Naze (*Ryukyu Is.*) … 44,491
Nemuro … 45,381
Neyagawa (★Ōsaka) … 206,961
Nichinan (53,288▲) … 39,000
Niigata … 383,919
Niihama … 126,033
Niitsu (57,089▲) … 41,500
Niiza (★Tōkyō) … 77,704
Nikkō … 28,502
Nishinomiya (★Ōsaka) … 377,043
Nishio (75,193▲) … 57,000
Nishiwaki … 37,934
Nobeoka … 128,292
Noboribetsu … 46,526
Noda (★Tōkyō) … 68,641
Nōgata … 55,615
Noshiro (59,795▲) … 44,000
Numata (43,898▲) … 33,000
Numazu (★375,000) … 189,038
Obihiro … 131,568
Ōdate (72,958▲) … 51,000
Odawara (★Tōkyō) … 156,654
Ōfunato (38,804▲) … 32,000
Oga (40,907▲) … 25,000
Ōgaki … 134,942
Oita … 260,584
Ojiya (44,581▲) … 27,000
Ōkawa … 51,637
Okaya … 60,350
Okayama … 375,106
Okazaki … 210,515
Ōme (★Tōkyō) … 70,954
Ōmiya (★Tōkyō) … 268,777
Ōmura (56,538▲) … 41,000
Ōmuta (★230,000) … 175,143
Onoda (★Ube) … 42,041
Onomichi … 101,363
Ōsaka (★13,350,000) … 2,980,487
Ōta … 98,257
Ōtake … 37,637
Otaru … 191,856
Ōtsu (★Ōsaka) … 171,777
Oyama (105,346▲) … 68,000
Rumoi … 38,691
Sabae (52,614▲) … 42,000
Saga … 143,454
Sagamihara (★Tōkyō) … 278,326
Saijō (51,127▲) … 38,000
Saiki (50,689▲) … 40,500
Saito (38,509▲) … 16,000
Sakai (★Ōsaka) … 594,367
Sakaide … 64,147
Sakata (96,072▲) … 70,000
Saku (55,214▲) … 32,000
Sakura (60,433▲) … 46,000
Sakurai (52,081▲) … 41,000
Sanjō … 77,814
Sano … 71,573
Sapporo … 1,010,123
Sasebo … 247,898
Sawara (46,761▲) … 25,000
Sayama (★Tōkyō) … 60,886
Seki … 49,078
Sendai (*Kagoshima pref.*) (62,374▲) … 35,000
Sendai (*Miyagi pref.*) (★690,000) … 545,065
Sennan (★Ōsaka) … 38,206
Seto … 92,681
Settsu (★Ōsaka) … 59,758
Shibata (74,459▲) … 49,000
Shibetsu (33,004▲) … 17,000
Shibukawa … 44,531
Shimabara (44,475▲) … 33,500
Shimada … 66,489
Shimizu (★★Shizuoka) … 234,966
Shimminato (★Takaoka) … 45,701
Shimodate (53,863▲) … 34,000
Shimonoseki (★★Kitakyūshū) … 258,425
Shingū … 38,808
Shiogama (★Sendai) … 58,772
Shizuoka (★680,000) … 416,378
Sōka (★Tōkyō) … 123,269
Suita (★Ōsaka) … 259,619
Sukagawa (53,761▲) … 33,000
Sumoto (44,499▲) … 36,000
Suwa … 48,125
Suzaka … 41,538
Suzuka (121,185▲) … 85,000
Tachikawa (★Tōkyō) … 117,057
Tajimi … 63,522
Takada (75,063▲) … 56,000
Takaishi (★Ōsaka) … 61,442
Takamatsu … 274,367
Takaoka (★205,000) … 159,664
Takarazuka (★Ōsaka) … 127,179
Takasago (★Ōsaka) … 68,900
Takasaki … 193,072
Takatsuki (★Ōsaka) … 231,129
Takawa … 64,233
Takayama (62,019▲) … 56,459
Takefu (62,019▲) … 46,500
Takikawa … 43,535
Tamano … 68,446
Tanabe (63,368▲) … 49,000
Tanashi (★Tōkyō) … 58,466
Tatebayashi … 61,130
Tateyama (55,236▲) … 40,000
Tendō (44,758▲) … 26,000
Tenri (57,020▲) … 41,000
Tochigi … 78,345
Toda (★Tōkyō) … 69,511
Tokai (★Nagoya) … 86,608
Tōkamachi (49,619▲) … 33,000
Toki … 60,786
Tokoname … 54,168
Tokorozawa (★Tōkyō) … 136,611
Tokushima … 223,451
Tokuyama (★185,000) … 98,520
•TŌKYŌ (★22,200,000) … 8,840,942
Tomakomai … 101,573
Tomioka (45,638▲) … 28,500
Tondabayashi (★Ōsaka) … 75,754
Tosu … 47,369
Tottori … 113,151
Towada (50,601▲) … 26,000
Toyama … 269,276
Toyohashi … 258,547
Toyokawa … 85,860
Toyonaka (★Ōsaka) … 368,498
Toyooka (44,094▲) … 31,500
Toyota … 197,193
Tsu … 125,203
Tsubame … 42,427
Tsuchiura … 89,958
Tsuruga … 56,445
Tsuruoka (95,136▲) … 74,000
Tsushima … 51,441
Tsuyama (76,368▲) … 54,000
Ube (★203,000) … 152,935
Ueda … 93,198
Ueno (57,666▲) … 41,000
Uji (★Ōsaka) … 103,497
Uozu … 47,124
Urawa (★Tōkyō) … 269,397
Usa (51,942▲) … 26,000
Usuki (38,890▲) … 28,000
Utsunomiya … 301,231
Uwajima … 64,262
Wakayama … 365,267
Wakkanai … 54,493
Warabi (★Tōkyō) … 77,225
Yachiyo (★Tōkyō) … 66,630
Yaizu … 82,737
Yamagata … 204,127
Yamaguchi (101,041▲) … 73,000
Yamato (★Tōkyō) … 102,760
Yamato-kōriyama (★Ōsaka) … 57,456
Yamato-takada (★Ōsaka) … 53,475
Yanagawa (45,789▲) … 32,000
Yao (★Ōsaka) … 227,778
Yatsushiro (101,866▲) … 76,000
Yawatahama (46,903▲) … 36,000
Yokkaichi … 229,234
Yokohama (★★Tōkyō) … 2,238,264
Yokosuka (★Tōkyō) … 347,576
Yokote (43,363▲) … 28,000
Yonago … 109,096
Yonezawa (92,764▲) … 72,000
Yono (★Tōkyō) … 62,802
Yūbari … 69,871
Yukuhashi (47,843▲) … 35,000
Zama (★Tōkyō) … 56,727
Zushi (★Tōkyō) … 48,242

JERSEY

1971 C … 72,629

•ST. HELIER (★45,000) … 28,135

JORDAN / Al-Urdunn

1970 E … 2,348,000

Al-'Aqabah ('Aqaba) (1961 C) … 8,908
Al-Karak (1961 C) … 7,422
Al-Khalīl (Hebron) (††1967 C) … 38,348
Al-Quds (Jerusalem, Old City) (★Yerushalayim, Israel) (††1961 C) … 60,488
• AMMĀN … 570,000
Arīḥā (Jericho) (††1967 C) … 6,829
As-Salt (1961 C) … 16,176
Az-Zarqā' … 200,000
Bayt Laḥm (Bethlehem) (††1967 C) … 16,313
Irbid … 120,000
Janīn (††1967 C) … 13,365
Ma'ān (1961 C) … 6,643
Nābulus (††1967 C) … 44,223
Ṭūl Karm (††1967 C) … 15,275

††Located in area occupied by Israel in 1967. See note under Israel.

KENYA

1970 E … 11,247,000

Eldoret (1962 C) … 19,605
Kisumu (1969 C) … 30,570
Mombasa … 255,400
•NAIROBI … 535,200
Nakuru (1969 C) … 47,010

KOREA, NORTH / Chosŏn Minjujuŭi In'min Konghwaguk

1966 E … 12,640,000

Provinces

Chagang Do (Jagang) … 739,000
Hamgyŏng Namdo (South Hamgyeong) … 1,699,000
Hamgyŏng Pukto (North Hamgyeong) … 1,333,000
Hwanghae Namdo (South Hwanghae) … 1,301,000
Hwanghae Pukto (North Hwanghae) … 993,000
Kaesŏng (Gaeseong) (City) … 265,000
Kangwŏn Do (Gangweon) … 1,050,000
P'yŏngan Namdo (South Pyeongan) … 1,875,000
P'yŏngan Pukto (North Pyeongan) … 1,599,000
P'yŏngyang (Pyeongyang) (City) … 1,364,000
Yanggang Do … 422,000

Cities (1967 E or †1944 C)

Anak … †25,185
Anju … †21,861
Aoji … †39,616
Chaeryŏng … †22,227
Ch'ŏngjin … 265,000
Haeju … 115,000
Hamhŭng … †112,184
Hoeryŏng … †24,330
Hongwŏn … †25,663
Hŭngnam … †143,600
Kaesŏng … 140,000
Kanggye … †30,013
Kilchu … †30,026
Kimch'aek (Sŏngjin) … 265,000
Kyŏngsŏng … †25,925
Najin … †34,338
Namp'o (Chinnamp'o) … 130,000
Ongjin (1949 C) … 32,965
Pukch'ŏng … †30,709
•P'YŎNGYANG … 840,000
Sariwŏn … †42,957
Sinp'o … †26,086
Sinŭiju … 165,000
Songnim … †53,035
Tanch'ŏn … †32,761
Ŭiju … †27,378
Wŏnsan … 215,000

KOREA, SOUTH / Taehan-Min'guk

1970 C … 31,469,132

Provinces

Cheju Do (Jeju) … 365,522
Chŏlla Namdo (South Jeonla) … 4,005,735
Chŏlla Pukto (North Jeonla) … 2,434,522
Ch'ungch'ŏng Namdo (South Chungcheong) … 2,860,690
Ch'ungch'ŏng Pukto (North Chungcheong) … 1,481,566
Kangwŏn Do (Gangweon) … 1,866,928
Kyŏnggi Do (Gyeonggi) … 3,358,105
Kyŏngsang Namdo (South Gyeongsang) … 3,119,393
Kyŏngsang Pukto (North Gyeongsang) … 4,559,584
Pusan (Busan) (City) … 1,880,710
Sŏul (Seoul) (City) … 5,536,377

Cities

Andong (76,434▲) … 64,000
Chech'ŏn (62,249▲) … 43,000
Cheju (106,456▲) … 58,000
Chinhae … 91,947
Chinju (121,622▲) … 95,000
Choch'iwŏn (27,996▲) … 20,000
Ch'ŏnan (78,316▲) … 55,000
Ch'ŏngju … 143,944
Chŏngŭp (49,667▲) … 34,000
Chŏnju … 262,816
Ch'unch'ŏn … 122,672
Ch'ungju (87,727▲) … 61,000
Chungmu (54,974▲) … 46,000

(Korea, South continued)

C Census. E Official estimate. UE Unofficial estimate.
L Population within municipal limits of year specified. •Largest city in country.

★ Population or designation of metropolitan area, including suburbs (see headnote).
▲ Population of an entire municipality, commune, or district, including rural area.
‡† Year of information specified at start of country.

(Korea, South continued)

Inch'ŏn	646,013
Iri (86,770▲)	72,000
Kangnŭng (74,489▲)	49,000
Kimch'ŏn (62,157▲)	47,000
Kunsan	112,453
Kwangju	502,753
Kyŏngju (92,093▲)	55,000
Masan	190,992
Mokp'o	177,801
Namwŏn (46,532▲)	32,000
P'ohang (79,451▲)	65,000
Pusan	1,880,710
Samch'ŏnp'o (54,945▲)	33,000
Sangju (52,504▲)	28,000
Sŏkch'o	73,096
•SŎUL (SEOUL) (★5,900,000)	5,536,377
Sunch'ŏn (90,910▲)	61,000
Suwŏn (170,518▲)	140,000
Taegu	1,082,750
Taejŏn	414,598
Ŭijŏngbu (★Sŏul)	94,518
Ulsan (159,340▲)	108,000
Wŏnju	111,972
Yŏngju (58,527▲)	42,000
Yŏsu	113,651

KUWAIT / Al-Kuwayt

1970 C	**738,663**
•AL-KUWAYT (★560,000)	80,008

LAOS / Lao

1970 E	**3,033,000**
Louang Prabang	25,000
Muang Khammouan (1968 C)	12,676
Paksé (1968 C)	34,774
Savannakhet (1967 C)	35,682
•VIENTIANE	150,000

LEBANON / Al-Lubnān

1964 E	**2,179,600**
•BAYRŪT (BEIRUT) (★893,000)	450,500
Ṣaydā (Sidon)	35,600
Ṭarābulus (Tripoli)	127,600
Zaḥlah	57,700

LESOTHO

1971 E	**1,064,000**
•MASERU (★29,000)	16,000

LIBERIA

1970 E	**1,200,000**
•MONROVIA	100,000

LIBYA / Lībiyā

1970 E	**1,938,000**
Ajdābiyah (1964 C)	15,400
Al-Marj (1964 C)	10,600
BANGHĀZĪ (BENGASI)	170,000
Darnah (Derna) (1964 C)	21,400
Misrātah	44,000
•ṬARĀBULUS (TRIPOLI)	264,000
Tubruq (Tobruk) (1964 C)	15,900
Zāwiyat al-Bayḍā' (Beida) (1964 C)	12,800

LIECHTENSTEIN

1970 C	**21,078**
•VADUZ	3,790

LUXEMBOURG

1970 C	**339,848**
Clervaux	1,430
Diekirch	5,056
Differdange (★Esch-sur-Alzette)	17,963
Dudelange	14,612
Echternach	3,792
Esch-sur-Alzette (★96,000)	27,575
Ettelbruck	5,998
•LUXEMBOURG (★100,000)	76,143
Pétange (★★Longwy, France)	11,844
Vianden	1,519

MACAU

1970 C	**248,316**
•MACAU (MACAO) (★248,316)	226,710

MALAGASY REPUBLIC / République malgache

1969 E	**7,198,600**
Antsirabe (55,900▲)	32,100
Diégo-Suarez (Antsirane)	41,200
Fianarantsoa	47,300
Majunga	49,800
Tamatave	54,700
•TANANARIVE	334,800
Tuléar	33,800

MALAWI

1971 E	**4,552,000**
•Blantyre	169,000
Lilongwe (1966 C)	19,200
Mzuzu	8,200
ZOMBA	20,000

MALAYSIA

1964 E	**9,136,500**

States

Johore	1,179,200
Kedah	849,900
Kelantan	618,900
Malacca	372,100
Negri Sembilan	466,300
Pahang	387,400
Perak	1,508,000
Perlis	109,100
Pinang	697,000
Sabah (North Borneo)	506,600
Sarawak	819,800
Selangor	1,276,200
Trengganu	346,000

Cities (‡1970 C or 1957 C)

Alor Setar	‡66,179
Ayer Hitam	22,369
Bandar Maharani	39,046
Batu Pahat	39,294
Bentong	18,845
Bukit Mertajam	24,663
Butterworth (★Pinang)	45,504
Ipoh	‡247,689
Johore Bahru (★Singapore)	‡135,936
Kampar	24,602
Kangar	6,064
Kelang (1968 E)	91,974
Keluang	31,181
Kota Bharu	‡55,052
Kota Kinabalu (Jesselton)	‡41,830
Kuala Lipis	8,753
•KUALA LUMPUR (★706,997)	‡451,728
Kuala Trengganu	‡53,353
Kuantan	23,034
Kuching	‡63,491
Kulim	17,605
Malacca (Melaka)	‡86,357
Miri (1960 C)	13,350
Pinang (George Town) (★395,000)	‡270,019
Sandakan (1960 C)	28,806
Segamat	18,445
Seremban	‡79,915
Sibu (1960 C)	29,630
Sungai Petani	22,916
Taiping	48,206
Telok Anson	37,042

MALDIVES

1970 C	**114,469**
•MALE	13,610

MALI

1969 E	**4,929,000**
•BAMAKO	189,200
Gao	13,700
Goundam	6,100
Kati	12,100
Kayes	29,900
Kita	10,200
Koulikoro	12,600
Koutiala	12,800
Mopti	34,000
Nioro du Sahel	11,600
San	14,400
Ségou	31,900
Sikasso	23,300
Tombouctou (Timbuktu)	10,400

MALTA

1967 C	**314,200**
Birkirkara (★Valletta)	17,200
Cospicua (★Valletta)	9,100
Hamrun (★Valletta)	14,800
Msida (★Valletta)	11,400
Paola (★Valletta)	11,800
Qormi (★Valletta)	15,400
Rabat (*Gozo I.*)	12,200
Sliema (★Valletta)	21,000
•VALLETTA (1969 E) (★204,000)	15,500
Victoria	5,500
Zabbar (★Valletta)	10,200
Zejtun	10,400

MARTINIQUE

1967 C	**320,030**
•FORT-DE-FRANCE (★110,000)	96,943
Le Lamentin (18,553▲)	6,776
Saint-Pierre (6,559▲)	5,556
Schœlcher (★Fort-de-France) (13,241▲)	10,819

MAURITANIA / Mauritanie

1966 E	**1,100,000**
Aleg (1961/62 C)	1,360
Atar (1965 E)	8,600
'Ayoûn el 'Atroûs (1961/62 C)	4,877
Kaédi	10,000
Kiffa (1961/62 C)	4,359
Néma (1961/62 C)	3,893
Nouadhibou	11,000
•NOUAKCHOTT (1971 E)	35,000
Rosso (1961/62 C)	4,811

MAURITIUS

1970 E	**811,280**
Beau Bassin (★Port Louis)	71,285
Curepipe (★Port Louis)	52,010
•PORT LOUIS (★370,000)	139,700
Quatre Bornes (★Port Louis)	45,525
Vacoas-Phoenix (★Port Louis)	49,045

MEXICO / México

1970 C	**48,377,363**

States

Aguascalientes	338,142
Baja California	870,421
Baja California Sur (Ter.)	128,019
Campeche	251,556
Chiapas	1,569,053
Chihuahua	1,612,525
Coahuila	1,114,956
Colima	241,153
Distrito Federal (Federal District)	6,874,165
Durango	939,208
Guanajuato	2,270,370
Guerrero	1,597,360
Hidalgo	1,193,845
Jalisco	3,296,587
México	3,833,187
Michoacán	2,320,042
Morelos	616,119
Nayarit	544,031
Nuevo León	1,694,689
Oaxaca	2,171,733
Puebla	2,508,226
Querétaro	485,523
Quintana Roo (Ter.)	88,150
San Luis Potosí	1,281,996
Sinaloa	1,266,528
Sonora	1,098,720
Tabasco	768,327
Tamaulipas	1,456,858
Tlaxcala	420,638
Veracruz	3,815,419
Yucatán	758,355
Zacatecas	951,462

Cities (‡1970 C or 1960 C)

Acámbaro	26,187
Acapulco [de Juárez]	‡174,378
Acayucan	12,831
Agrícola Oriental (★Ciudad de México)	43,417
Agua Prieta	15,339
Aguascalientes	‡181,277
Alvarado	12,548
Ameca	17,588
Apizaco	‡21,189
Arandas	17,071
Atlixco	30,650
Atotonilco el Alto	14,430
Autlán de Navarro	17,017
Azcapotzalco (★Ciudad de México)	63,857
Caborca	9,338
Campeche	‡69,506
Cananea	19,683
Celaya	‡79,977
Chihuahua	‡257,000
Chilpancingo [de los Bravos]	‡36,193
Cholula [de Rivadabia]	12,833
Ciudad Acuña	20,048
Ciudad Camargo	18,951
Ciudad Chetumal	‡23,685
Ciudad del Carmen	‡34,656
•CIUDAD DE MÉXICO (MEXICO CITY) (★9,000,000)	‡2,902,969
Ciudad de Valles	‡47,587
Ciudad Guzmán	30,941
Ciudad Hidalgo	17,155
Ciudad Jiménez	14,904
Ciudad Juárez (★★El Paso, Tex.)	‡407,000
Ciudad Lerdo (★Torreón)	‡19,803
Ciudad Madero (★Tampico)	‡91,000
Ciudad Mante	‡51,247
Ciudad Mendoza (★Orizaba)	16,051
Ciudad Obregón	‡114,000
Ciudad Serdán	9,942
Ciudad Victoria	‡84,000
Coatepec	18,022
Coatzacoalcos	‡70,000
Colima	‡58,450
Comitán [de Domínguez]	15,409
Córdoba	‡78,000
Cortazar	17,925
Cosamaloapan [de Carpio]	16,944
Coyoacán (★Ciudad de México)	54,866
Cuauhtémoc	14,686
Cuautla	12,427
Cuernavaca	‡134,117
Culiacán	‡168,000
Delicias	‡52,000
Dolores Hidalgo	12,311
Durango	‡150,541
Ecatepec de Morelos (★Ciudad de México)	4,632
Empalme	18,964
Ensenada	‡77,687
Etzatlán	8,796
Fortín de las Flores	6,328
Fresnillo [de González Echeverría] (101,300▲)	‡45,000
Gertrudis Sánchez (★Ciudad de México)	28,808
Gómez Palacio (★★Torreón)	‡79,650
Guadalajara (★1,500,000)	‡1,194,646
Guadalupe (★Monterrey)	‡51,899
Guanajuato	28,212
Guasave	‡26,080
Guaymas	‡57,000
Gustavo A. Madero (★Ciudad de México) (1965 E)	134,300
Hermosillo	‡177,000
Hidalgo del Parral	‡58,000
Huajuapan de León	8,531
Huixtla	12,327
Iguala	‡45,355
Irapuato	‡116,651
Ixtacalco (★Ciudad de México)	25,546
Ixtapalapa (★Ciudad de México)	25,517
Izúcar de Matamoros	16,556
Jacona de Plancarte	13,101
Jalapa Enríquez	‡122,000
Jalostotitlán	13,675
Jerez de García Salinas	15,016
Juchitán [de Zaragoza]	‡30,218
La Barca	16,273
Lagos de Moreno	23,636
La Paz	‡46,011
La Piedad [Cavadas]	24,377
Las Choapas	11,189
León [de los Aldamas]	‡364,990
Linares	13,592
Loma Bonita	9,789
Los Mochis	‡67,953
Magdalena	9,445
Manzanillo	19,950
Martínez de la Torre	14,615
Mártires de Río Blanco (★Ciudad de México)	23,336
Matamoros (★★Brownsville, Tex.)	‡138,000
Matamoros de la Laguna	13,770
Matehuala	‡28,799
Matías Romero	10,187
Mazatlán	‡120,000
Meoqui	10,287
Mérida	‡212,944
Mexicali (★280,000)	‡267,000
Minatitlán	‡68,000
Mineral del Monte	10,061
Molino de Rosas (★Ciudad de México)	10,235
Monclova	‡78,134
Montemorelos	11,641
Monterrey (★1,200,000)	‡858,107
Morelia	‡162,458
Moroleón	17,954
Motul de Felipe Carrillo Puerto	10,351
Naucalpan (★Ciudad de México)	10,365
Navojoa	30,560
Netzahualcóyotl (★Ciudad de México)	‡580,436
Nogales (*Sonora*)	‡52,000
Nogales (*Veracruz*) (★Orizaba)	11,219
Nueva Atzacoalco (★Ciudad de México)	31,688
Nueva Casas Grandes	11,687
Nueva Rosita	34,302
Nueva Santa María (★Ciudad de México)	29,848
Nuevo Laredo (★★Laredo, Tex.)	‡149,000
Oaxaca [de Juárez]	‡99,509
Ocotlán	25,416
Orizaba (★210,000)	‡93,000
Pachuca [de Soto]	‡83,892
Pantitlán (★Ciudad de México)	17,314
Papantla [de Olarte]	18,865
Parras de la Fuente	19,768
Pátzcuaro	14,324
Pénjamo	11,429
Piedras Negras	44,992
Poza Rica de Hidalgo	‡120,000
Progreso	13,694
Pro-Hogar (★Ciudad de México)	27,682
Puebla [de Zaragoza]	‡401,603
Puerto Vallarta	7,484
Puruándiro	11,480
Querétaro	‡112,993
Reynosa	‡137,000
Río Blanco (★Orizaba)	11,918
Río Bravo	17,500
Ríoverde	14,825
Romita	11,912
Rosario	11,703
Sabinas	16,076
Sabinas Hidalgo	11,598
Sahuayo	25,661
Salamanca	‡61,039
Salina Cruz	14,897
Saltillo	‡161,000
Salvatierra	14,451
San Andrés Tetepilco (★Ciudad de México)	24,555
San Andrés Tuxtla	20,256
San Cristóbal las Casas	23,343
San Francisco del Oro	11,333
San Francisco del Rincón	20,878
San Juan de los Lagos	14,319
San Juan del Río	‡15,422
San Luis Potosí	‡230,039
San Luis Río Colorado	28,545
San Martín Texmelucan	13,786
San Miguel de Allende	14,891
San Miguel el Alto	10,074
San Nicolás de los Garzas (★Monterrey)	15,437
San Pedro de las Colonias	26,018
Santa Ana Chiautempan	11,296
Santa Bárbara	15,846
Santa Cruz de Juventino Rosas	11,917
Santa Inés Zacatelco	11,303
Santa Rosalía	5,361
Santiago Ixcuintla	11,017
Sayula	11,616
Silao	24,229
Tala	12,547
Tamazula de Gordiano	10,672
Tamazunchale	8,687
Tampico (★305,000)	‡180,000
Tangancícuaro [de Arista]	9,355
Tapachula	‡61,000
Taxco de Alarcón	‡27,089
Tecate	6,588
Tecomán	16,162
Tecuala	10,868
Tehuacán	31,897
Tehuantepec	13,458
Tepatitlán [de Morelos]	19,835
Tepic	‡87,540
Texcoco [de Mora]	11,215
Teziutlán	17,400
Ticul	10,893
Tierra Blanca	16,556
Tijuana (★★San Diego, Calif.)	‡277,000
Tizapán (★Ciudad de México)	15,314
Tizimín	15,723
Tlalnepantla (★Ciudad de México)	25,868
Tlalpan (★Ciudad de México)	22,957
Tlapacoyan	8,580
Tlaquepaque (★Guadalajara)	‡59,760
Tlatilco (★Ciudad de México)	10,423
Tlaxcala [de Xicoténcatl]	7,545
Toluca [de Lerdo]	‡114,079
Tonalá	13,208
Torreón (★410,000)	‡223,000
Tulancingo	‡35,999
Tuxpan (*Jalisco*)	10,833
Tuxpan (*Nayarit*)	‡20,332
Tuxpan de Rodríguez Cano	23,262
Tuxtla Gutiérrez	‡67,000
Umán	6,495
Uriangato	10,068
Uruapan [del Progreso]	‡83,480
Valladolid	9,297
Valle de Santiago	21,795
Valle Hermoso	15,769
Venustiano Carranza	10,729
Veracruz [Llave] (★270,000)	‡214,000
Vicente Guerrero (*Tlaxcala*)	10,678
Vicente Guerrero (*Veracruz*) (★Orizaba)	8,747
Villa Frontera	14,297
Villahermosa	‡99,565
Villa Obregón (★Ciudad de México)	31,416
Xicotepec de Juárez	9,618
Yautepec	9,205
Yurécuaro	12,084
Yuriria	10,167
Zaachila	6,177
Zacapu	22,200
Zacatecas	‡50,000
Zacatepec	13,475
Zacoalco de Torres	8,988
Zamora de Hidalgo	‡57,775
Zapopan (★Guadalajara)	19,138
Zapotiltic	9,023
Zihuatanejo	1,619
Zitácuaro	23,883
Zumpango	8,371

MONACO

1970 E	**23,600**
•MONACO (★46,000)	23,600

MONGOLIA / Mongol Ard Uls

1969 E	**1,197,200**
Cecerleg (Tsetserleg) (1966 E)	14,000
Chovd (1959 E)	5,800
Cojbalsan (Bajan Tümen) (1967 E)	10,900
Darchan (1968 E)	25,000
Süchbaatar (1967 E)	12,000
•ULAANBAATAR (ULAN BATOR)	262,600

MONTSERRAT

1970 C	**12,302**
•PLYMOUTH	3,500

MOROCCO / Al-Magreb

1970 E	**15,433,000**
Agadir (1960 C)	16,695
Al-Hoceima (1960 C)	11,262
Beni-Mellal (1960 C)	28,933
Berkane (1960 C)	20,496
•Casablanca (Dar-el-Beida) (1970 C) (★1,550,000)	1,500,100
El-Jadida (Mazagan) (1960 C)	40,302
Essaouira (Mogador) (1960 C)	26,392
Fès (Fez)	290,000
Jerada (1960 C)	18,872
Kenitra	130,000
Khenifra	18,503
Khouribga (1960 C)	40,838
Ksar-el-Kebir (1960 C)	34,035
Ksar-es-Souk (1960 C)	6,554
Larache (1960 C)	30,763
Marrakech	305,000
Meknès	245,000
Mohammedia (Fedala) (1960 C)	35,010
Nador (1960 C)	17,583
Ouarzazate (1960 C)	4,200
Oued-Zem (1960 C)	18,640
Ouezzane (1960 C)	26,203
Oujda	160,000
RABAT (1970 C) (★480,000)	374,800
Safi	130,000
Salé (★★Rabat) (1960 C)	75,799
Sefrou (1960 C)	21,478
Settat (1960 C)	31,667
Sidi Ifni (1966 E)	15,700
Sidi-Kacem (1960 C)	19,478
Tanger (Tangier)	170,000
Taza (1960 C)	31,667
Tétouan	125,000

MOZAMBIQUE / Moçambique

1970 C	**8,233,800**
António Enes (1960 UE)	15,000
Beira (1970 UE)	90,000
Inhambane (1970 UE)	20,000
•LOURENÇO MARQUES (★354,700)	110,000
Moçambique (1960 C)	12,166

NEPAL / Nepāl

1971 C	**11,289,968**
Bhaktapur (1961 C)	37,100
Birātnagar (1961 C)	33,300
Bīrganj (1961 C)	10,800
•KĀTMĀNDU (★210,000)	153,405
Lalitpur (★Kātmāndu) (1961 C)	48,600
Nepālganj (1961 C)	15,800

C Census. E Official estimate. UE Unofficial estimate.
L Population within municipal limits of year specified. • Largest city in country.

★ Population or designation of metropolitan area, including suburbs (see headnote).
▲ Population of an entire municipality, commune, or district, including rural area.
‡† Year of information specified at start of country.

NETHERLANDS / Nederland

1971 E 13,119,430
(*incl. 3,586 persons with no fixed residence in any province*)

Provinces

Drenthe 372,580
Friesland 526,749
Gelderland 1,533,740
Groningen 522,425
Limburg 1,012,357
Noord-Brabant (North Brabant) 1,819,459
Noord-Holland (North Holland) 2,259,955
Overijssel 932,946
Zuidelijke IJsselmeerpolders (Southern IJsselmeer Polders) 17,211 (not part of any province)
Zuid-Holland (South Holland) 2,991,735
Utrecht 816,369
Zeeland 310,318

Cities

Aalsmeer 19,019
Alkmaar (★89,000) 51,643
Almelo 59,426
Alphen aan den Rijn 34,571
Amersfoort (★116,000) 78,908
Amstelveen (★Amsterdam) 70,202
• AMSTERDAM (★1,810,000) 820,406
Apeldoorn 126,266
Arnhem (★274,384) 132,330
Assen 40,471
Baarn 24,315
Bergen op Zoom 39,612
Beverwijk (★Amsterdam) 41,029
Breda (★149,535) 122,068
Brunssum 26,060
Bussum (★Amsterdam) 41,372
De Bilt (★Utrecht) 29,514
Delft (★ 's-Gravenhage) 86,189
Delfzijl 22,217
Den Helder 61,052
Deventer 66,318
Doetinchem (31,639▲) 21,500
Dordrecht (★171,841) 100,935
Edam (18,495▲) 5,300
Ede (74,511▲) 38,000
Eindhoven (★341,068) 189,613
Emmen (80,713▲) 21,000
Enschede (★260,000) 141,204
Ermelo (38,215▲) 10,200
Franeker 9,765
Geleen (★169,579) 36,892
Goes 26,522
Gorinchem 26,972
Gouda 46,718
Groningen (★204,767) 171,334
Haarlem (★★Amsterdam) 172,612
Haarlemmermeer (60,042▲) 6,800
Harlingen 12,707
Heerenveen (31,817▲) 15,000
Heerlen (★264,911) 75,058
Helmond 58,003
Hengelo (★★Enschede) 69,685
Hilversum (★Amsterdam) 98,948
Hoogeveen (38,451▲) 22,500
Hoorn 19,204
Huizen (★Amsterdam) 21,843
IJmuiden (Velsen) (★Amsterdam) 67,501
Kampen 29,087
Katwijk aan Zee 36,914
Kerkrade (★★Heerlen) 47,753
Leeuwarden 88,644
Leiden (★164,751) 100,135
Maassluis (★Rotterdam) 27,369
Maastricht (★155,000) 112,465
Middelburg 30,873
Nijmegen (★206,277) 150,185
Oldenzaal 23,434
Oss 41,047
Papendrecht (★Dordrecht) 18,311
Purmerend 25,715
Renkum (★Arnhem) (33,685▲) 12,100
Rheden (★Arnhem) (50,210▲) 10,500
Ridderkerk (★Rotterdam) 43,552
Rijswijk (★'s-Gravenhage) 50,482
Roermond 36,715
Roosendaal 46,764
Rotterdam (★1,125,000) 679,032
Schiedam (★Rotterdam) 83,313
's-GRAVENHAGE (THE HAGUE) (★825,000) 537,643
's-Hertogenbosch (★169,013) 81,401
Sittard (★★Geleen) 34,395
Sliedrecht 20,202
Sneek 27,129
Soest (★Amersfoort) 37,469
Tegelen (★Venlo) 18,429
Terneuzen (31,334▲) 17,000
Tiel 21,934
Tilburg (★205,606) 153,734
Utrecht (★459,470) 278,417
Valkenswaard (★Eindhoven) 23,800
Veendam 23,974
Veenendaal 30,311
Veldhoven (★Eindhoven) 27,744
Venlo (★86,000) 63,077
Vlaardingen (★Rotterdam) 81,097
Vlissingen (Flushing) 41,085
Volendam 12,300
Voorburg (★'s-Gravenhage) 44,207
Vught (★'s-Hertogenbosch) 22,962
Waalwijk 23,934
Wageningen 27,050
Wassenaar (★'s-Gravenhage) 27,623
Weert (35,657▲) 24,200
Winschoten 17,799
Woerden 19,275
Zaandam (★Amsterdam) 65,981
Zeist (★Utrecht) 56,187
Zutphen 27,871
Zwijndrecht (★★Dordrecht) 32,412
Zwolle 77,047

NETHERLANDS ANTILLES / Nederlandse Antillen

1960 C 188,914

Islands

Aruba 53,199
Bonaire 5,812
Curaçao 125,181
Saba 980
Sint Eustatius 1,014
Sint Maarten (St. Martin) (part) 2,728

Cities

Kralendijk (*Bonaire*) (1953 E) 600
Oranjestad (*Aruba*) (1965 E) 14,700
• WILLEMSTAD (*Curaçao*) (★94,133) 43,547

NEW CALEDONIA / Nouvelle-Calédonie

1971 E 113,700

• NOUMÉA (★57,800) 49,300

NEW GUINEA, TERRITORY OF

1966 C 1,578,500

Island Groups

Bismarck Archipelago 225,100
Northeast New Guinea 1,280,900
Solomon Islands (Austl. Trust) 72,500

Cities (1971 C)

CAPITAL: Port Moresby, Papua
• Lae 34,699
Madang 15,751
Rabaul 24,778
Wewak 12,154

NEW HEBRIDES / Nouvelles-Hébrides

1971 E 86,000

• VILA 5,000

NEW ZEALAND

1971 C 2,860,475

Islands

North Island 2,050,208
South Island 810,267

Cities

Ashburton 13,299
• Auckland (★670,000) 151,567
Blenheim 14,760
Christchurch (★284,000) 165,198
Dunedin (★111,512) 82,289
Gisborne (★30,392) 26,709
Hamilton (★80,780) 74,762
Hastings (★★Napier) 29,736
Invercargill (★50,670) 47,092
Lower Hutt (★Wellington) 58,549
Manukau (★Auckland) 104,096
Masterton 18,556
Mount Albert (★Auckland) 26,150
Mount Roskill (★Auckland) 33,842
Napier (★89,000) 40,181
Nelson (★37,985) 29,270
New Plymouth (★38,626) 34,165
Palmerston North (★57,037) 51,859
Papatoetoe (★Auckland) 21,804
Porirua (★Wellington) 30,345
Rotorua (★39,658) 31,230
Takapuna (★Auckland) 24,031
Tauranga (★40,288) 28,126
Timaru (★28,962) 28,327
Wanganui (★37,994) 35,794
WELLINGTON (★323,809) 135,515
Whangarei (★34,040) 30,749

NICARAGUA

1971 C 1,911,543

Bluefields 14,542
Chinandega (1969 E) 34,500
Diriamba (1969 E) 15,100
Estelí (1969 E) 17,700
Granada 34,976
Jinotega (1969 E) 9,500
León 55,625
• MANAGUA 398,514
Masaya 30,753
Matagalpa (1969 E) 23,500
Rivas (1969 E) 12,800

NIGER

1968 E 3,806,000

• NIAMEY 79,000

NIGERIA

1963 C 55,670,052

Aba 131,003
Abeokuta 187,292
Ado-Ekiti 157,519
Afikpo 36,096
Agege 45,986
Akure 71,106
Awka 48,725
Bauchi 37,778
Benin City 100,694
Bida 55,007
Calabar 76,418
Deba 60,679
Ede 134 550
Effon-Alaiye 67,090
Enugu 138,457
Epe 44,268
Gombe 47,265
Gusau 69,231
Ibadan (1970 E) 746,000
Ife 130,050
Ihiala 40,198
Ijebu-Igbo 43,180
Ijebu-Ode 68,543
Ikare 61,696
Ikerre 107,216
Ikire 54,022
Ikirun 79,516
Ikorodu 81,024
Ikot Ekpene 38,107
Ila 114,688
Ilawe 80,833
Ilesha 165,822
Ilobu 87,223
Ilorin 208,546
Inisa 52,482
Iseyin 95,220
Iwo 158,583
Jimeta 36,291
Jos 90,402
Kaduna 149,910
Kano 295,432
Katsina 90,538
Kumo 64,878
Lafia 53,667
• LAGOS (1970 E) (★1,200,000) 875,000
Maiduguri 139,965
Makurdi 52,967
Minna 59,988
Mushin (★Lagos) 145,976
Nguru 43,234
Offa 86,425
Ogbomosho 319,881
Oka 62,761
Ondo 74,343
Onitsha 163,032
Opobo 35,458
Oshogbo 208,966
Owo 89,693
Oyo 112,349
Port Harcourt 179,563
Potiskum 30,998
Sapele 61,007
Shagamu 51,371
Shaki 76,290
Shomolu (★Lagos) 64,731
Sokoto 89,817
Ugep 44,945
Warri 55,254
Zaria 166,170

NORWAY / Norge

1971 E 3,891,739

Counties

Akershus 324,896
Aust-Agder 80,857
Bergen 113,489
Buskerud 199,063
Finmark 76,354
Hedmark 179,384
Hordaland 260,799
Møre og Romsdal 223,889
Nordland 241,213
Nord-Trøndelag 118,088
Oppland 172,763
Oslo 481,204
Østfold 221,656
Rogaland 269,051
Sogn og Fjordane 101,061
Sør-Trøndelag 234,216
Telemark 156,814
Troms 137,063
Vest-Agder 124,352
Vestfold 175,527

Cities

Ålesund 39,534
Arendal (★19,000) 11,710
Bergen (★234,000) 113,489
Bodø 29,144
Drammen (★68,000) 49,847
Fredrikstad (★49,000) 30,069
Gjøvik 25,295
Halden 26,744
Hamar 15,744
Hammerfest 7,125
Harstad 19,982
Haugesund 27,212
Horten 14,271
Kongsberg 18,491
Kristiansand 56,975
Kristiansund 18,515
Larvik (★18,000) 10,253
Lillehammer 20,576
Lillestrøm (★Oslo) (1960 C) 10,547
Mo (1960 C) 8,348
Molde 19,210
Moss 25,238
Namsos 11,203
Narvik 13,150
Notodden 13,324
Odda 10,064
• OSLO (★720,000) 481,204
Porsgrunn (★★Skien) 31,567
Ringerike 29,240
Sandefjord 32,060
Sandnes (★Stavanger) 30,750
Sarpsborg (★36,000) 13,338
Skien (★77,065) 45,498
Stavanger (★113,000) 82,079
Steinkjer 20,170
Tønsberg (★34,500) 10,889
Tromsø 39,126
Trondheim 127,699
Vadsø 5,591

OMAN / 'Umān

1962 E 565,000

MASQAT (MUSCAT) 6,000
• Maṭraḥ 14,000

PACIFIC ISLANDS TRUST TERRITORY

1970 C 90,940

Island Groups

Caroline Islands 58,412
Mariana Islands (excl. Guam) 9,640
Marshall Islands 22,888

PAKISTAN / Pākistān

1961 C 42,880,378
(*excl. approx. 1,000,000 in section of Jammu and Kashmir occupied by Pakistan*)

Abbottābād (★31,036) 15,955
Ahmadpur East 32,423
Bahāwalnagar 36,290
Bahāwalpur 84,377
Bannu (★31,623) 23,859
Chārsadda 37,396
Chiniot 47,099
Dera Ghāzi Khān 47,105
Dera Ismāīl Khān (★46,140) 44,319
Gojra 29,665
Gujrānwāla 196,154
Gujrāt 59,608
Hāfizābād 34,576
Hyderābād (★460,000) 416,441
ISLĀMĀBĀD (1967 E) 50,000
Jacobābād 35,278
Jhang Maghiāna 94,971
Jhelum (★52,585) 41,160
Kalāt 5,321
Kamālia 35,248
• Karāchi (★1,912,598) 1,447,419
Kasūr 74,546
Khairpur 34,144
Khānewāl 49,093
Khānpur 31,465
Kohāt (★49,854) 36,016
Lahore (★1,325,000) 1,227,996
Lahore Cantonment (★Lahore) 68,481
Lārkāna 48,008
Lyallpur 425,248
Mardān (★77,932) 73,246
Miānwāli 31,398
Mīrpur-Khās 60,861
Multān (★358,201) 340,399
Nawābshāh 45,651
Nowshera (★43,757) 21,516
Okāra 68,299
Peshāwar (★218,691) 166,273
Quetta (★106,633) 79,493
Rahīmyār Khān 43,548
Rāwalpindi (★340,175) 197,370
Rāwalpindi Cantonment (★Rāwalpindi) 142,805
Sāhiwāl (Montgomery) 75,180
Sargodha (★129,291) 83,141
Shekhūpura 41,635
Shikārpur 53,910
Siālkot (★164,346) 143,889
Sukkur 103,216
Tando Ādam 31,246

PANAMA / Panamá

1970 C 1,428,082

Bocas del Toro 2,511
Chitré 12,379
Colón (★76,000) 67,695
David 35,677
La Chorrera 25,873
La Palma 1,742
Las Tablas 3,852
• PANAMA (★465,000) 348,704
Penonomé 5,066
San Miguelito (★Panama) 68,400

PAPUA

1970 E 669,000

• PORT MORESBY (1971 C) 66,244

PARAGUAY

1969 E 2,314,200

Departments

Alto Paraná 55,300
Amambay 57,400
Asunción (Distrito Federal) 424,300
Boquerón 47,700
Caaguazú 216,200
Caazapá 100,900
Central 254,800
Concepción 106,800
Cordillera 199,100
Guairá 128,300
Itapúa 197,600
Misiones 69,700
Ñeembucú 65,000
Olimpo 4,800
Paraguarí 226,700
Presidente Hayes 41,000
San Pedro 118,600

Cities (1962 C)

• ASUNCIÓN (1970 E) (★550,000) 385,000
Caacupé 6,329
Concepción (1970 E) 17,200
Coronel Oviedo 9,468
Encarnación (1970 E) 21,900
Luque (★Asunción) 11,008
Paraguarí 4,880
Pedro Juan Caballero 10,355
Pilar 5,317
San Juan Bautista 5,972
Santísima Trinidad (★Asunción) 17,353
Villa Hayes 4,712
Villarrica (1970 E) 18,300

PERU / Perú

1970 E 13,586,300

Departments

Amazonas 171,100
Ancash 744,700
Apurímac 330,400
Arequipa 518,300
Ayacucho 474,100
Cajamarca 1,007,600
Callao (Province) 335,400
Cuzco (Cusco) 756,100
Huancavelica 367,100
Huánuco 430,100
Ica 362,700
Junín 699,100
La Libertad 784,900
Lambayeque 485,500
Lima 3,155,800
Loreto 504,600
Madre de Dios 24,200
Moquegua 68,800
Pasco 188,000
Piura 922,300
Puno 848,200
San Martín 229,400
Tacna 93,900
Tumbes 84,000

Cities (1961 C)

Abancay 9,053
Arequipa (1970 E) 195,000
Ayacucho 23,768
Barranco (★Lima) 42,449
Barrio Obrero Industrial (★Lima) 90,645
Bellavista (★Lima) 43,128
Breña (★Lima) 99,810
Cajamarca 22,705
Callao (★Lima) (1970 E) 250,000
Castilla (★Piura) 29,541
Cerro de Pasco 21,363
Chachapoyas 6,860
Chiclayo (1970 E) 140,000
Chimbote (1970 UE) 90,000
Chincha Alta 20,817
Chorrillos (★Lima) 31,703
Chosica 25,248
Chulucanas 19,714
Cuzco (1970 E) 110,000
Huacho 22,806
Huancavelica 11,039
Huancayo (1970 E) 95,000
Huánuco 24,646
Huaraz 20,345
Ica (1970 E) 70,000
Iquitos (1970 E) 75,000
Jesús María (★Lima) (1966 C) 75,720
Lambayeque 10,629
La Oroya 24,724
La Victoria (★Lima) 203,442
• LIMA (1970 E) (★2,925,000) 300,000
Lince (★Lima) 82,393
Magdalena del Mar (★Lima) 55,737
Miraflores (★Lima) 88,446
Mollendo 12,483
Moquegua 7,795
Moyobamba 8,373
Pisco 22,112
Piura (1970 E) (★110,000) 70,000
Pucallpa 26,391
Pueblo Libre (★Lima) (1963 L) 51,500
Puerto Maldonado 3,518
Rímac (★Lima) 144,121
San Isidro (★Lima) 37,832
Sullana (★53,000) 34,501
Surco (★Lima) 45,661
Surquillo (★Lima) 70,757
Tacna 27,499
Talara 27,957
Trujillo (1970 E) 155,000
Tumbes 20,885
Vitarte (★Lima) 62,971
Yurimaguas 11,655

PHILIPPINES / Pilipinas

1960 C 27,087,685

Angeles (1968 E) (102,400▲) 80,000
Bacolod (1968 E) (156,900▲) 124,000
Bago (58,834▲) 6,396
Baguio 50,436
Batangas (1966 E) (102,100▲) 43,000
Butuan (1968 E) (110,100▲) 48,000
Cabanatuan (69,580▲) 38,379
Cadiz (1968 E) (118,200▲) 21,000
Cagayan de Oro (68,274▲) 34,672
Calbayog (1968 E) (103,100▲) 12,000
Caloocan (★Manila) (1968 E) 194,600
Catbalogan (34,873▲) 19,360
Cavite 54,891
Cebu (1968 E) 332,100
Cotabato (37,499▲) 27,980
Dadiangas (1968 E) (114,000▲) 18,000
Daet 20,956
Dagupan (63,191▲) 34,484
Davao (1968 E) (337,000▲) 135,000
Dumaguete (35,282▲) 24,062
Gingoog (52,677▲) 9,152
Iligan (58,433▲) 14,281
Iloilo (1968 E) 201,000
Iriga (1968 E) (101,000▲) 36,000
Isabela (Basilan) (1968 E) (209,100▲) 16,000
Jolo 33,259
La Carlota (56,772▲) 15,286
Laoag 25,105
Legazpi (60,593▲) 36,374
Lipa (69,036▲) 17,470
Lucena (49,264▲) 40,652
Makati (★Manila) 114,540
Malabon (★Manila) 76,438
Mandaluyong (★Manila) 71,619
• Manila (1970 C) (★4,000,000) 1,310,600

(Philippines continued)

C Census. E Official estimate. UE Unofficial estimate.
L Population within municipal limits of year specified. • Largest city in country.
★ Population or designation of metropolitan area, including suburbs (see headnote).
▲ Population of an entire municipality, commune, or district, including rural area.
‡† Year of information specified at start of country.

(Philippines continued)

Naga	55,506
Olongapo	45,330
Ormoc (62,764▲)	13,640
Ozamiz (44,091▲)	17,940
Parañaque (★Manila)	61,898
Pasay (★Manila) (1968 E)	174,100
Pasig (★Manila)	62,130
QUEZON CITY (★MANILA) (1968 E)	545,500
Roxas (Capiz) (49,326▲)	30,033
San Carlos (1968 E) (165,200▲)	30,000
San Fernando (56,861▲)	33,335
San Juan del Monte (★Manila)	56,861
San Pablo (70,680▲)	29,990
Silay (60,324▲)	19,569
Tacloban (53,551▲)	35,974
Tagaytay	7,203
Tagbilaran (20,250▲)	7,206
Tarlac (1966 E) (121,400▲)	51,000
Toledo (63,881▲)	4,913
Trece Martires	4,422
Tuguegarao	23,584
Zamboanga (1968 E) (176,800▲)	70,000

POLAND / Polska

1970 C 32,589,000

Voivodships

Białystok	1,173,000
Bydgoszcz	1,912,000
Gdańsk	1,465,000
Katowice	3,691,000
Kielce	1,889,000
Koszalin	793,000
Kraków	2,181,000
Kraków (City)	583,000
Łódź	1,670,000
Łódź (City)	762,000
Lublin	1,922,000
Olsztyn	978,000
Opole	1,057,000
Poznań	2,190,000
Poznań (City)	469,000
Rzeszów	1,757,000
Szczecin	897,000
Warszawa	2,514,000
Warszawa (City)	1,308,000
Wrocław	1,973,000
Wrocław (City)	523,000
Zielona Góra	882,000

Cities

Będzin (★Katowice)	42,700
Biała Podlaska	26,100
Białystok	166,600
Bielawa (Langenbielau) (★★Dzierżoniów)	30,900
Bielsko-Biała	105,600
Bolesławiec (Bunzlau)	30,500
Brzeg (Brieg)	30,700
Bydgoszcz	280,400
Bytom (Beuthen) (★★Katowice)	186,900
Chełm	38,700
Chojnice	23,500
Chorzów (★★Katowice)	151,300
Chrzanów	28,500
Ciechanów	23,200
Cieszyn	25,200
Czechowice-Dziedzice	25,400
Czeladź (★Katowice)	31,800
Częstochowa	187,600
Dąbrowa Górnicza (★Katowice)	61,600
Dzierżoniów (Reichenbach) (★73,000)	32,800
Elbląg (Elbing)	89,800
Ełk (Lyck)	27,100
Gdańsk (Danzig) (★670,000)	364,200
Gdynia (★★Gdańsk)	190,100
Gliwice (Gleiwitz) (★★Katowice)	170,900
Gniezno	50,600
Gorzów Wielkopolski (Landsberg)	74,200
Grudziądz	75,500
Gubin	14,600
Inowrocław	54,800
Jaworzno	63,200
Jelenia Góra (Hirschberg) (★82,000)	55,700
Kalisz	81,200
Katowice (★2,060,000)	303,200
Kędzierzyn	32,400
Kielce	125,900
Kłodzko (Glatz)	26,000
Konin	40,600
Koszalin (Köslin)	64,400
Kraków	583,400
Legnica (Liegnitz)	75,800
Leszno	33,800
Łódź (★930,000)	761,700
Łomża	25,500
Lubin	28,400
Lublin	235,900
Malbork (Marienburg)	30,900
Mysłowice (★Katowice)	44,700
Nowa Sól (Neusalz)	33,300
Nowy Sącz	41,100
Nysa (Neisse)	31,800
Olsztyn (Allenstein)	94,100
Opole (Oppeln)	86,500
Ostrowiec Świętokrzyski	49,900
Ostrów Wielkopolski	49,500
Oświęcim	39,600
Otwock (★Warszawa)	39,800
Pabianice (★Łódź)	62,200
Piekary Śląskie (★Katowice)	36,300
Piła (Schneidemühl)	43,700
Piotrków Trybunalski	59,600
Płock	71,700
Poznań (★525,000)	469,000
Pruszków (★Warszawa)	42,900
Przemyśl	53,200
Puławy	34,800
Racibórz (Ratibor)	40,400
Radom	158,600
Radomsko	31,100
Ruda Śląska (★Katowice)	142,400
Rybnik	43,400
Rzeszów	82,100
Siedlce	38,900
Siemianowice Śląskie (★Katowice)	67,200
Skarżysko-Kamienna	39,100
Słupsk (Stolp)	68,300
Sopot (Zoppot) (★Gdańsk)	47,500
Sosnowiec (★★Katowice)	144,600
Stalowa Wola	29,700
Starachowice	42,800
Stargard Szczeciński	44,400
Starogard Gdański	33,400
Świdnica (Schweidnitz)	47,500
Świętochłowice (★Katowice)	57,600
Świnoujście (Swinemünde)	27,900
Szczecin (Stettin)	337,200
Szczecinek (Neustettin)	28,600
Tarnów	85,500
Tarnowskie Góry (★Katowice)	34,200
Tczew	40,700
Tomaszów Mazowiecki	54,900
Toruń	129,100
Tychy (★Katowice)	71,300
Wałbrzych (Waldenburg) (★160,000)	125,000
•WARSZAWA (WARSAW) (★1,760,000)	1,308,100
Wejherowo	33,600
Włocławek	77,100
Wrocław (Breslau)	523,300
Zabrze (Hindenburg) (★★Katowice)	197,200
Zakopane	27,000
Zamość	34,700
Żary (Sorau)	28,300
Zawiercie	39,400
Zduńska Wola	29,000
Zgierz (★Łódź)	42,800
Zgorzelec	28,400
Zielona Góra (Grünberg)	73,100
Żyrardów	33,100
Żywiec	22,400

PORTUGAL

1968 E 9,496,800

Regions

Alentejo	685,200
Algarve	315,300
Azores (Archipelago)	334,300
Beira	2,105,400
Entre Minho e Douro	2,297,400
Estremadura	2,904,000
Madeira (Archipelago)	268,700
Trás-os-Montes	586,500

Cities (1960 C)

Almada (★Lisboa)	30,688
Angra do Heroísmo (*Azores Is.*)	13,502
Aveiro	16,011
Barreiro (★Lisboa)	30,399
Beja	15,702
Braga	40,977
Bragança	8,075
Coimbra	46,313
Évora	24,144
Faro	18,909
Funchal (*Madeira Is.*)	43,301
Ílhavo	6,346
•LISBOA (LISBON) (1969 E) (★1,525,000)	830,600
Matozinhos (★Porto)	37,694
Ponta Delgada (*Azores Is.*)	22,316
Portimão	12,129
Porto (1969 E) (★860,000)	325,400
Santarem	16,449
Setúbal	44,435
Sintra (★Lisboa)	7,705
Vila Nova de Gaia (★Porto)	45,479
Viseu	16,961

PORTUGUESE GUINEA / Guiné

1960 C	**521,336**
•BISSAU (1950 C)	18,309

PORTUGUESE TIMOR / Timor

1970 C	**610,541**
•DILI	29,312

PUERTO RICO

1970 C 2,712,033

Adjuntas (18,691▲)	5,319
Aguadilla (51,355▲)	21,031
Aibonito (20,044▲)	7,582
Arecibo (73,468▲)	35,484
Bayamón (★San Juan)	147,552
Cabo Rojo (26,060▲)	7,181
Caguas (95,661▲)	63,215
Carolina (★San Juan)	94,271
Cataño (★San Juan)	26,459
Cayey (38,432▲)	21,562
Cidra (23,892▲)	6,306
Coamo (26,468▲)	12,077
Comerío (18,819▲)	6,297
Corozal (24,545▲)	5,211
Fajardo (23,032▲)	18,249
Guánica (14,889▲)	8,979
Guayama (36,249▲)	20,318
Guayanilla (18,144▲)	5,189
Guaynabo (★San Juan)	55,310
Gurabo (18,289▲)	6,290
Hormigueros (10,827▲)	6,531
Humacao (36,023▲)	12,411
Isabela (30,430▲)	9,515
Juana Díaz (36,270▲)	8,765
Juncos (21,814▲)	7,985
Levittown (★San Juan)	17,079
Manatí (30,559▲)	13,483
Mayagüez (85,857▲)	68,872
Ponce (158,981▲)	128,233
Sabana Grande (16,343▲)	5,561
San Germán (27,990▲)	11,613
•SAN JUAN (★936,693)	452,749
San Lorenzo (27,755▲)	7,702
San Sebastian (30,157▲)	7,169
Utuado (35,494▲)	11,573
Vega Alta (22,810▲)	8,688
Vega Baja (35,327▲)	17,089
Yabucoa (30,165▲)	5,119
Yauco (35,103▲)	12,922

QATAR / Qaṭar

1971 E	**160,000**
•AD-DAWḤAH (DOHA)	95,000

REUNION / Réunion

1971 E	**455,200**
Le Port (1967 C) (19,768▲)	17,297
Le Tampon (1967 C) (31,321▲)	13,909
•ST. DENIS (94,100▲)	85,400
St. Pierre (1967 C) (40,355▲)	18,867

RHODESIA

1969 C	**5,099,344**
Bulawayo (★245,040)	65,998
Fort Victoria (★11,380)	6,088
Gatooma (★20,940)	3,963
Gwelo (★46,170)	17,066
Harari (★Salisbury)	58,007
Highfield (★Salisbury)	52,560
Que Que (★32,880)	13,505
•SALISBURY (★386,040)	85,674
Shabani (★15,820)	1,520
Sinoia (★13,360)	4,503
Umtali (★45,610)	16,819
Wankie (★20,190)	10,276

ROMANIA / România

1970 E	**20,252,541**
Alba-Iulia	27,547
Arad	137,194
Bacău (★114,333)	91,045
Baia-Mare	76,855
Bîrlad	47,371
Bistrița	27,832
Botoșani	40,387
Brăila	151,650
Brașov	182,105
•BUCUREȘTI (BUCHAREST) (★1,574,536)	1,475,050
Buzău	71,300
Călărași	40,004
Cîmpulung	26,675
Cluj	202,715
Constanța (★205,000)	172,464
Craiova	175,454
Dej	30,869
Deva	38,579
Focșani	39,629
Galați	179,189
Gheorghe Gheorghiu-Dej	40,563
Giurgiu	43,701
Hunedoara	77,292
Iași	183,776
Lugoj	39,052
Lupeni	30,350
Medgidia	33,629
Mediaș	55,924
Oradea	137,662
Petroșeni (★79,000)	39,706
Piatra-Neamț (★67,295)	53,630
Pitești	74,237
Ploiești (★217,341)	162,937
Reșița	67,980
Rîmnicu-Sărat	24,481
Rîmnicu-Vîlcea	34,668
Roman	43,188
Satu-Mare	78,812
Sfîntu Gheorghe	24,975
Sibiu	120,118
Sighet	33,361
Sighișoara	29,090
Suceava	44,941
Tecuci	31,007
Timișoara	192,616
Tîrgoviște	33,359
Tîrgu-Jiu	42,935
Tîrgu-Mureș (★120,725)	98,201
Tulcea	41,981
Turda	50,113
Turnu-Măgurele	29,988
Turnu-Severin	54,619

RWANDA

1970 E	**3,736,000**
•KIGALI	60,000

ST. HELENA
(excl. Dependencies)

1966 C	**4,649**
•JAMESTOWN	1,475

ST. KITTS-NEVIS-ANGUILLA

1970 C	**47,457**
•BASSETERRE (*St. Kitts*)	13,055
Charlestown (*Nevis*)	1,880
South Hill (*Anguilla*) (1960 C)	617

ST. LUCIA

1970 C	**101,064**
•CASTRIES	39,132

ST. PIERRE & MIQUELON / Saint-Pierre-et-Miquelon

1967 C	**5,186**
•ST.-PIERRE	4,565

ST. VINCENT

1970 C	**89,129**
•KINGSTOWN (★23,782)	17,258

SAN MARINO

1970 E	**17,726**
•SAN MARINO	4,195

SAO TOME & PRINCIPE / São Tomé e Príncipe

1960 C	**64,406**
•SÃO TOMÉ	5,714

SAUDI ARABIA / Al-'Arabīyah as-Sa'ūdīyah

1965 E or †1961 UE	**6,750,000**
Abhā	†25,000
Ad-Dammām	†40,000
Al-Hufūf (Hofuf)	†85,000
Al-Jawf	†20,000
Al-Khubar	†35,000
Al-Madīnah (Medina)	†60,000
Al-Mubarraz	†40,000
Al-Qaṭīf	†30,000
•AR-RIYĀḌ (RIYADH)	225,000
Aṭ-Ṭā'if	†30,000
Aẓ-Ẓahrān (Dhahran)	†12,500
Buraydah	†50,000
Ḥā'il	†30,000
Juddah (Jidda)	194,000
Makkah (Mecca)	185,000
Qal'at Bīshah	†20,000
'Unayzah	†50,000
Yanbu'	†20,000

SENEGAL / Sénégal

1970 E	**3,925,000**
•DAKAR (★650,000)	581,000
Diourbel	36,000
Kaolack	96,300
Rufisque (★Dakar) (1960/61 E)	49,700
Saint-Louis	81,200
Thiès	90,700
Ziguinchor	45,800

SEYCHELLES

1971 C	**52,437**
•VICTORIA	13,622

SIERRA LEONE

1963 C	**2,180,355**
Bo	26,613
Bonthe	6,230
•FREETOWN (1970 E) (★225,000)	178,600
Kenema	13,246
Kissy (★Freetown)	13,143
Koidu	11,706
Lunsar	12,132
Makeni	12,304
Port Loko	5,809

SIKKIM

1971 E	**196,852**
•GANGTOK (1968 E)	9,000

SINGAPORE

1970 C	**2,122,466**
•SINGAPORE (★2,250,000)	2,122,466

SOLOMON IS., BRITISH

1970 C	**160,998**
•HONIARA	11,191

SOMALIA / Somaliya

1967 E	**2,610,000**
Afgoi (1964 C)	16,575
Berbera (1966 E)	14,000
Hargeysa (1966 E)	42,000
Kismayu (1968 C)	17,872
Marka	17,700
•MOGADISHO	172,700

SOUTH AFRICA / Suid-Afrika

1960 C 15,995,312

Provinces

Cape of Good Hope (Kaap)	5,355,368
Natal	2,979,920
Orange Free State (Oranje-Vrystaat)	1,386,547
Transvaal	6,273,477

Cities

Alexandra (★Johannesburg)	63,486
Aliwal North	10,762
Beaufort West	16,467
Bellville (★Cape Town)	27,924
Benoni (★Johannesburg)	122,502
Bethlehem	24,125
Bloemfontein (★145,273)	112,606
Boksburg (★Johannesburg)	71,029
Brakpan (★Johannesburg)	77,777
CAPE TOWN (KAAPSTAD) (★807,211)	508,341
Carletonville	56,246
Constantia	15,501
Cradock	19,561
Durban (★681,492)	560,010
East London (Oos-Londen) (★116,056)	113,746
Edendale (★Pietermaritzburg)	32,362
Ermelo	17,025
Evaton	38,973
George	14,759
Germiston (★★Johannesburg)	148,102
Goodwood (★Cape Town)	71,407
Graaff-Reinet	16,936
Grahamstown	32,611
Harrismith	13,924
•Johannesburg (★2,075,000)	594,290
Kempton Park	17,763
Kimberley (★79,031)	75,376
Klerksdorp	43,726
Kroonstad	42,438
Krugersdorp (★Johannesburg)	89,947
Ladysmith	22,955
Mafeking	8,362
Mamelodi (★Pretoria)	48,129
Meadowlands (★Johannesburg)	41,798
Mosselbaai	12,225
Nelspruit	15,498
Newcastle	17,554
Nigel	34,008
Nyanga (★Cape Town)	21,757
Odendaalsrus (★21,268)	15,126
Orkney	22,425
Oudtshoorn	22,229
Paarl	41,540
Parow (★Cape Town)	39,737
Parys	12,683
Pietermaritzburg (★128,598)	91,988
Pietersburg	28,071
Port Elizabeth (★290,693)	249,211
Potchefstroom	41,927
Potgietersrus	11,491
PRETORIA (★422,590)	303,684
Queenstown	33,182
Randfontein (★Johannesburg)	41,499
Roodepoort-Maraisburg (★Johannesburg)	95,211
Rustenburg	21,016
Springs (★Johannesburg)	137,253
Standerton	16,897
Stellenbosch	22,333
Uitenhage	48,755
Umtata	12,221
Upington	20,366
Vanderbijlpark (★★Vereeniging)	41,415
Vereeniging (★130,000)	78,835
Virginia (★41,057)	18,273
Walmer (★Port Elizabeth)	24,969
Welkom (★97,614)	48,069
Westonaria (★Johannesburg)	26,640
Witbank	25,881
Worcester	32,274

SOUTH WEST AFRICA

1970 C	**722,867**
Gobabis	4,428
Keetmanshoop	10,297
Lüderitz	6,642
Mariental	4,629
Otjiwarongo	8,018
Rehoboth	5,363
Swakopmund	5,681
Tsumeb	12,338
•WINDHOEK	61,260

SOVIET UNION
See Union of Soviet Socialist Republics

SPAIN / España

1970 C 33,918,032

Regions and Provinces

ANDALUCÍA (ANDALUSIA)	5,991,076
Almería	377,639
Cádiz	878,602
Córdoba	731,317
Granada	741,659
Huelva	403,405
Jaén	668,206
Málaga	853,579
Sevilla	1,336,669
ARAGÓN (ARAGON)	1,153,055
Huesca	221,761
Teruel	173,861
Zaragoza	757,433
ASTURIAS	1,052,048
Oviedo	1,052,048
BALEARES (BALEARIC IS.)	532,946
Baleares	532,946
CANARIAS (CANARY IS.)	1,125,442
Las Palmas	548,984
Santa Cruz de Tenerife	576,458
CASTILLA LA NUEVA (NEW CASTILE)	5,153,324
Ciudad Real	512,821
Cuenca	251,619
Guadalajara	149,804
Madrid	3,761,348
Toledo	477,732

C Census. E Official estimate. UE Unofficial estimate.
L Population within municipal limits of year specified. • Largest city in country.

★ Population or designation of metropolitan area, including suburbs (see headnote).
▲ Population of an entire municipality, commune, or district, including rural area.
‡† Year of information specified at start of country.

CASTILLA LA VIEJA (OLD CASTILE)	2,170,568
Ávila	211,556
Burgos	361,181
Logroño	234,628
Palencia	201,532
Santander	469,077
Segovia	162,106
Soria	117,462
Valladolid	413,026
CATALUÑA (CATALONIA)	5,107,606
Barcelona	3,915,010
Gerona	412,357
Lérida	347,101
Tarragona	433,138
EXTREMADURA (ESTREMADURA)	1,169,396
Badajoz	701,709
Cáceres	467,687
GALICIA	2,676,403
La Coruña	1,030,745
Lugo	423,064
Orense	441,260
Pontevedra	781,334
LEÓN (LEON)	1,201,426
León	562,766
Salamanca	380,133
Zamora	258,527
MURCIA	1,172,767
Albacete	340,720
Murcia	832,047
NAVARRA (NAVARRE)	466,593
Navarra	466,593
VALENCIA	3,078,095
Alicante	922,027
Castellón	386,516
Valencia	1,769,552
VASCONGADAS (BASQUE PROVINCES)	1,867,287
Álava	199,777
Guipúzcoa	626,049
Vizcaya	1,041,461

Cities (1970 C or †1960 C)

Albacete (93,062▲)	79,000
Alcalá [de Guadaira] (31,004▲)	†27,378
Alcalá de Henares (★Madrid)	57,354
Alcalá la Real (23,314▲)	†8,351
Alcázar de San Juan	†24,963
Alcira	†26,669
Alcoy	61,061
Algeciras	79,997
Alicante	181,550
Almadén	†13,443
Almería	114,298
Andújar (32,185▲)	†23,897
Antequera (42,327▲)	†28,400
Aranjuez	†27,251
Ávila	30,080
Avilés (★120,000)	82,433
Badajoz (100,551▲)	75,000
Badalona (★Barcelona)	163,374
Baracaldo (★Bilbao)	109,185
Barcelona (★2,800,000)	1,741,979
Baza (20,440▲)	†13,323
Bilbao (★810,000)	405,908
Burgos	116,797
Cabra (20,739▲)	†15,688
Cáceres	55,341
Cádiz	134,342
Carmona	†28,216
Cartagena (143,466▲)	118,000
Castellón de la Plana	92,777
Chiclana [de la Frontera]	†21,524
Ciudad Real	41,036
Córdoba	232,343
Cornellá (★Barcelona)	76,387
Cuenca	33,571
Daimiel	†19,625
Don Benito	†25,248
Dos Hermanas (27,696▲)	†21,517
Éibar	†31,725
Elche (123,716▲)	90,000
Elda	†28,151
El Ferrol del Caudillo (★106,000)	80,194
El Puerto de Santa María	†35,505
Gerona	47,747
Getafe (★Madrid)	69,396
Gijón	184,698
Granada	186,160
Granollers	†20,194
Guadalajara	31,640
Guadix (24,704▲)	†15,897
Guernica y Luno (7,847▲)	†4,855
Hellín (27,242▲)	†17,071
Hospitalet (★Barcelona)	240,630
Huelva	96,347
Huesca	31,552
Ibiza	†11,259
Igualada	†19,866
Irún	†29,814
Jaén	77,317
Jerez de la Frontera (149,337▲)	110,000
La Coruña	189,467
La Línea (★Gibraltar)	52,749
La Orotava (*Canarias*) (22,371▲)	†8,019
Las Palmas de Gran Canaria (*Canarias*)	263,407
Leganés (★Madrid)	56,279
León (★126,000)	105,243
Lérida (88,897▲)	73,000
Linares (51,883▲)	43,000
Logroño	82,821
Loja (25,976▲)	†11,441
Lorca (60,286▲)	21,000
Lucena	†19,975
Lugo (63,604▲)	50,000
• MADRID (★3,525,000)	3,120,941
Mahón	†16,619
Málaga	361,282
Manacor	†19,224
Manresa	58,110
Martos (23,990▲)	†16,442
Mataró	73,125
Mérida	†34,297
Mieres (65,923▲)	19,000
Miranda de Ebro	†27,881
Morón de la Frontera (35,248▲)	†29,096
Motril	†18,264
Murcia (243,687▲)	160,000
Orense (73,145▲)	50,000
Orihuela (44,830▲)	†15,873
Oviedo	152,453
Palencia	56,816
Palma [de Mallorca]	217,525
Pamplona	145,026
Peñarroya-Pueblonuevo	†24,152
Plasencia	†21,297
Ponferrada	†37,053
Pontevedra (52,562▲)	21,000
Portugalete (★Bilbao)	†22,584
Priego [de Córdoba] (25,168▲)	†13,469
Puente-Genil (30,185▲)	†24,836
Puertollano	53,674
Reus	59,904
Ronda	†17,703
Sabadell	158,311
Sagunto	†40,293
Salamanca	122,241
Sama de Langreo (Langreo) (59,465▲)	11,000
San Cristóbal de la Laguna (*Canarias*) (77,704▲)	21,000
San Fernando	57,235
Sanlúcar (40,335▲)	†32,580
San Sebastián (★240,000)	161,293
Santa Coloma de Gramanet (★Barcelona)	105,880
Santa Cruz de Tenerife (*Canarias*)	142,305
Santander	148,845
Santiago de Compostela (65,270▲)	45,000
Segovia	40,816
Sevilla (Seville)	545,692
Soria	24,455
Sueca	†20,612
Talavera de la Reina	†31,900
Tarragona	77,275
Tarrasa	136,952
Telde (*Canarias*) (32,177▲)	†11,761
Teruel	20,668
Toledo	44,190
Tomelloso	†27,815
Torrente (★Valencia)	†24,042
Tortosa (43,267▲)	†18,674
Úbeda	†28,956
Utrera (41,126▲)	†25,935
Valdepeñas	†25,706
Valencia (★890,000)	648,003
Valladolid	233,974
Vélez-Málaga (35,061▲)	†14,348
Vich	†20,303
Vigo	198,815
Villanueva y Geltrú	†25,669
Villarreal [de los Infantes] (24,516▲)	†20,025
Vitoria	132,963
Zamora	48,691
Zaragoza (Saragossa)	469,366

SPANISH NORTH AFRICA / Plazas de Soberanía en el Norte de África

1970 C	**124,000**
• Ceuta	62,607
Melilla	60,843

SPANISH SAHARA / Sahara Español

1970 C	**76,092**
• EL AAIÚN (AIÚN)	24,048

SUDAN / As-Sūdān

1965 E	**13,198,000**

Provinces

A'ālī an-Nīl (Upper Nile)	1,142,000
Al-Istiwā'īyah (Equatoria)	1,161,000
Al-Khurṭūm (Khartoum)	771,000
An-Nīl-al-Azraq (Blue Nile)	2,801,000
Ash-Shamalīyah (Northern)	1,009,000
Bahr-al-Ghazāl	1,274,000
Dārfūr	1,509,000
Kassalā	1,452,000
Kurdufān (Kordofan)	2,079,000

Cities

Al-Fāshir	40,500
Al-Junaynah	20,700
• AL-KHURṬŪM (KHARTOUM) (1970 E) (★675,000)	261,840
Al-Khurṭūm Bahrī (Khartoum North (★Al-Khurṭūm) (1970 E)	127,672
Al-Qaḍārif (1968 E)	55,430
Al-Ubayyiḍ (El Obeid) (1968 E)	66,270
An-Nuhūd	19,800
'Atbarah (1968 E)	53,110
Barbar	12,900
Būr-Sūdān (Port Sudan) (1970 E)	110,091
Kassalā (1968 E)	81,230
Kūstī	37,900
Nyala	26,200
Sannār	17,600
Sinjah	15,500
Ṭawkar	14,700
Umm Durmān (Omdurman) (★★Al-Khurṭūm) (1970 E)	258,532
Umm Ruwābah	14,200
Wad Madanī (1968 E)	71,030

SURINAM / Suriname

1964 C	**324,211**
• PARAMARIBO	110,867

SWAZILAND

1966 C	**374,697**
Manzini	6,081
• MBABANE	13,803

SWEDEN / Sverige

1970 E	**8,091,782**

Historic Provinces

Ångermanland	165,764
Blekinge	153,784
Bohuslän	198,404
Dalarna	279,221
Dalsland	54,309
Gästrikland	150,005
Gotland	53,835
Halland	199,587
Hälsingland	144,512
Härjedalen	11,629
Jämtland	112,033
Lappland	127,273
Medelpad	123,759
Närke	172,009
Norrbotten	178,821
Öland	20,307
Östergötland	380,115
Skåne	985,421
Småland	697,129
Södermanland	962,446
Uppland	1,003,835
Värmland	335,171
Västerbotten	167,319
Västergötland	1,122,459
Västmanland	292,635

Counties

Älvsborg	403,897
Blekinge	153,784
Gävleborg	293,906
Göteborg och Bohus	717,243
Gotland	53,835
Halland	193,487
Jämtland	125,302
Jönköping	306,589
Kalmar	241,119
Kopparberg	278,192
Kristianstad	264,713
Kronoberg	166,950
Malmöhus	721,821
Norrbotten	255,694
Örebro	277,003
Östergötland	383,319
Skaraborg	257,670
Södermanland	248,657
Stockholm	1,477,234
Uppsala	218,635
Värmland	285,031
Västerbotten	233,134
Västernorrland	274,108
Västmanland	260,459

Cities

Arvika (27,409▲)	18,482
Avesta (28,249▲)	21,799
Boden	27,149
Borås (★95,798)	74,545
Borlänge	43,989
Enköping (31,919▲)	23,167
Eskilstuna	94,076
Eslöv (26,205▲)	14,892
Falun (46,846▲)	37,080
Gällivare (25,417▲)	21,773
Gävle	84,625
Göteborg (Gothenburg) (★625,000)	451,806
Halmstad (★61,323)	47,298
Hälsingborg	100,559
Härnösand (27,057▲)	23,776
Huddinge (★Stockholm) (54,588▲)	46,000
Järfälla (★Stockholm) (49,397▲)	10,500
Jönköping (★107,768)	88,481
Kalmar (52,774▲)	44,598
Karlshamn (31,915▲)	14,747
Karlskoga	39,508
Karlskrona (★49,160)	36,405
Karlstad	72,467
Kiruna (30,623▲)	25,838
Kristianstad (55,403▲)	43,214
Landskrona	34,590
Lidingö (★Stockholm)	36,308
Lindesberg (24,205▲)	10,191
Linköping	104,642
Ludvika (33,489▲)	21,578
Luleå	58,946
Lund (★65,176)	55,986
Malmö (★295,000)	265,505
Mölndal (★Göteborg)	44,884
Motala (37,841▲)	31,896
Nacka (★Stockholm)	48,532
Norrköping	115,766
Nyköping (46,772▲)	36,399
Örebro	115,695
Örnsköldsvik (★60,521)	36,183
Östersund (★49,672)	42,957
Piteå (32,829▲)	13,919
Ronneby (29,712▲)	15,986
Sandviken	43,663
Skellefteå (61,912▲)	40,793
Skövde	43,625
Södertälje (★Stockholm)	75,980
Sollentuna (★Stockholm)	38,004
Solna (★Stockholm)	55,578
• STOCKHOLM (★1,344,748)	740,486
Sundbyberg (★Stockholm)	28,178
Sundsvall (★96,801)	64,920
Täby (★Stockholm)	38,892
Trelleborg (36,167▲)	29,526
Trollhättan	48,156
Uddevalla	47,724
Umeå	56,151
Uppsala	127,448
Västerås	116,763
Västervik (42,322▲)	21,845
Växjö (59,028▲)	41,795
Visby (53,835▲)	22,800

SWITZERLAND / Schweiz / Suisse / Svizzera

1970 C	**6,269,783**

Cantons

Aargau	433,284
Appenzell (Ausser-Rhoden)	49,023
Appenzell (Inner-Rhoden)	13,124
Basel-Land	204,889
Basel-Stadt	234,945
Bern (Berne)	983,296
Fribourg (Freiburg)	180,309
Genève	331,599
Glarus	38,155
Graubünden (Grisons)	162,086
Luzern (Lucerne)	289,641
Neuchâtel	169,173
Nidwalden	25,634
Obwalden	24,509
Sankt Gallen	384,475
Schaffhausen	72,854
Schwyz	92,072
Solothurn	224,133
Thurgau	182,835
Ticino (Tessin)	245,458
Uri	34,091
Valais (Wallis)	206,563
Vaud (Waadt)	511,851
Zug	67,996
Zürich	1,107,788

Cities

Aarau (★49,445)	16,881
Altdorf	8,647
Appenzell	5,217
Arbon (★14,818)	12,227
Arosa	2,717
Baar	14,074
Baden (★55,829)	14,115
Basel (Bâle) (★555,000)	212,857
Bellinzona (★29,620)	16,979
BERN (BERNE) (★272,000)	162,405
Biel (Bienne) (★89,315)	64,333
Brugg	8,635
Bülach	11,043
Burgdorf (★18,903)	15,888
Chateau d'Oex	3,203
Chiasso	8,868
Chur (Coire)	31,193
Davos	10,238
Delémont	11,797
Dietikon (★Zürich)	22,705
Einsiedeln	10,020
Emmen (★Luzern)	22,040
Frauenfeld	17,576
Fribourg (Freiburg) (★51,212)	39,695
Genève (Geneva) (★380,000)	173,618
Glarus	6,189
Grenchen (★24,097)	20,051
Grindelwald	3,511
Herisau	14,597
Horgen (★Zürich)	15,691
Interlaken	4,735
Köniz (★Bern)	32,505
Kreuzlingen	15,760
Kriens (★Luzern)	20,409
La Chaux-de-Fonds	42,347
Langenthal (★18,670)	13,007
Lausanne (★219,216)	137,383
Lauterbrunnen	3,431
Le Locle	14,452
Liestal (★Basel)	12,500
Locarno (★23,461)	14,143
Lugano (★58,324)	22,280
Luzern (Lucerne) (★148,926)	69,879
Martigny	10,478
Meiringen	3,759
Montreux (★21,331)	20,421
Morges	11,931
Neuchâtel (Neuenburg) (★56,454)	38,784
Nyon	11,424
Olten (★49,026)	21,209
Renens (★Lausanne)	17,391
Riehen (★Basel)	21,026
Rorschach (★24,723)	11,963
Sankt Gallen (St.-Gall) (★114,000)	80,852
Sankt Moritz	5,699
Sarnen	6,952
Schaffhausen (Schaffhouse) (★57,037)	37,035
Schwyz	12,194
Sierre	11,017
Sion (Sitten)	21,925
Solothurn (Soleure) (★36,477)	17,708
Stans	5,180
Thun (Thoune) (★60,632)	36,523
Uster	21,819
Vevey (★31,054)	17,957
Wädenswil	15,695
Wettingen (★Baden)	19,900
Wetzikon	13,469
Wil	14,646
Winterthur (★114,000)	92,722
Wohlen	12,024
Yverdon (Iferten)	20,538
Zermatt	3,101
Zug (Zoug)	22,972
• Zürich (★770,000)	422,640

SYRIA / As-Sūrīyah

1970 C	**6,294,000**
Al-Ḥasakah	32,495
Al-Lādhiqīyah (Latakia)	125,657
Al-Qāmishlī	48,084
Ar-Raqqah	37,186
As-Suwaydā'	29,598
Dayr az-Zawr	66,143
• DIMASHQ (DAMASCUS)	836,179
Dūmā	30,954
Ḥalab (Aleppo)	639,361
Ḥamāh	137,584
Ḥimṣ (Homs)	215,526
Idlib	34,518

TAIWAN / T'aiwan

1970 E	**14,505,400**
Changhua (135,400▲)	97,000
Chiai	236,500
Chilung (Keelung)	320,900
Chungli (Chunli) (127,200▲)	98,500
Hsinchu	204,900
Hualien	92,400
Ilan (71,100▲)	51,500
Kaohsiung (★910,000)	806,300
Kaohsiunghsien (Fengshan) (★Kaohsiung)	99,200
Lotung	40,500
Luchiang	36,000
Miaoli	35,000
Nant'ou	27,000
Peikang	35,000
P'enghu	24,000
P'ingtung	163,500
Sanch'ung (★T'aipei)	228,500
T'aichung (438,300▲)	337,000
T'aichunghsien (Fengyüan)	73,000
T'ainan	468,300
T'ainanhsien (Hsinying)	47,500
• T'AIPEI (★2,490,000)	1,740,800
T'aipeihsien (Panch'iao) (★T'aipei)	107,800
T'aitung	59,500
T'aoyüan	87,500
Yungho (★T'aipei)	86,700
Yünlin	43,000

TANZANIA

1967 C	**12,313,469**
Arusha	32,452
Bukoba	8,141
• DAR-ES-SALAAM (1970 E)	344,900
Dodoma	23,559
Iringa	21,746
Lindi	13,351
Mbeya	12,479
Morogoro	25,262
Moshi	26,864
Mtwara	20,413
Musoma	15,412
Mwanza	34,861
Tabora	21,012
Tanga	61,058
Ujiji	21,369
Zanzibar	68,490

THAILAND / Prathet Thai

1967 E	**32,680,000**
Ban Pong (1964 E)	18,700
Chachoengsao (1964 E)	21,100
Chiang Mai	81,600
Chon Buri	42,900
Hat Yai	49,300
Khon Kaen	28,400
• KRUNG THEP (BANGKOK) (★2,750,000)	2,008,000
Lampang	40,500
Lop Buri	30,400
Nakhon Pathom	35,100
Nakhon Ratchasima	73,000
Nakhon Sawan	44,900
Nakhon Si Thammarat	39,400
Narathiwat (1964 E)	19,100
Nong Khai	26,500
Nonthaburi (1964 E)	18,600
Pattani (1964 E)	19,900
Phayao (1964 E)	20,100
Phet Buri	26,700
Phitsanulok	39,200
Phra Nakhon Si Ayutthaya (Ayutthaya)	38,400
Phuket	33,900
Rat Buri	30,700
Samut Prakan	38,200
Samut Sakhon	34,500
Sara Buri	28,000
Songkhla	40,700
Surat Thani (Ban Don)	32,000
Thon Buri (★Krung Thep)	606,300
Trang (1964 E)	19,700
Ubon Ratchathani	34,600
Udon Thani	46,700
Yala	31,500

TOGO

1970 C	**1,955,916**
• LOMÉ	148,443
Palimé	19,801
Sokodé	29,623

TONGA

1966 C	**77,429**
• NUKUALOFA	15,545

TRINIDAD & TOBAGO

1960 C	**827,957**
Arima	10,982
Barataria (★Port of Spain)	10,478
Chaguanas	3,509
Débé (★Port of Spain)	11,823
Morvant (★Port of Spain)	5,805
Point Fortin	8,753
• PORT OF SPAIN (1970 C) (★310,000)	67,867
Princes Town	6,681
Rio Claro	2,174
San Fernando (1970 C) (★68,000)	37,313
Sangre Grande	5,087
San Juan (★Port of Spain)	30,270
Scarborough (*Tobago*)	1,931
Siparia	4,174
Tunapuna (★Port of Spain)	11,287

C Census. E Official estimate. UE Unofficial estimate.
L Population within municipal limits of year specified. • Largest city in country.

★ Population or designation of metropolitan area, including suburbs (see headnote).
▲ Population of an entire municipality, commune, or district, including rural area.
‡† Year of information specified at start of country.

TUNISIA / Tunisie

1966 C	**4,533,351**
Ariana (★Tunis)	22,026
Béja	28,145
Binzert (Bizerte)	51,708
El Kairouan	46,199
El Kasserine	9,847
El Kef	23,244
Gabès	32,330
Hammam Lif (★Tunis)	25,091
Jendouba (Souk el Arba)	14,778
Kalaa Kébira	18,760
La Goulette (★Tunis)	31,830
La Manouba (★Tunis)	18,732
Le Bardo (★Tunis)	40,714
Médenine	7,931
Menzel Bourguiba	33,780
Moknine	20,485
Monastir	20,366
Msaken	28,130
Nabeul	34,134
Sfax	70,472
Sousse	58,161
•TUNIS (★685,000)	468,997

TURKEY / Türkiye

1970 C	**35,667,100**

(Cities designated (E) are in Turkey in Europe)

Adana	351,700
Adapazari	101,600
Adiyaman	31,500
Afyonkarahisar	51,700
Akhisar	47,900
Aksaray	30,000
Akşehir	32,500
Amasya	38,600
ANKARA (★1,240,000)	1,208,800
Antakya (Antioch)	66,400
Antalya	95,200
Artvin	13,100
Aydin	50,600
Bafra	29,200
Balikesir	85,000
Bandirma	39,600
Batman	44,900
Bayburt	20,300
Bergama	27,000
Bingöl (Çapakçur)	17,300
Bitlis	20,600
Bolu	27,600
Bolvadin	25,300
Bornova (★İzmir)	33,000
Burdur	32,700
Bursa	275,900
Çanakkale	27,100
Çankiri	26,500
Çarşamba	20,700
Ceyhan	50,300
Çorlu (E)	30,300
Çorum	55,900
Denizli	83,600
Diyarbakir	138,700
Düzce	28,100
Edirne (E)	54,900
Elâziğ	108,300
Ereğli *(Konya prov.)*	46,100
Ereğli *(Zonguldak prov.)*	28,000
Erzincan	58,100
Erzurum	134,700
Eskişehir	216,300
Gaziantep	225,900
Gelibolu (Gallipoli) (E)	14,600
Giresun	30,700
Gölcük	29,300
Gümüşane	13,000
İnegöl	31,900
İskenderun (Alexandretta)	81,600
İsparta	51,100
•İstanbul (E) (★2,800,000)	2,247,600
İzmir (Smyrna) (★760,000)	520,700
İzmit (Kocaeli)	123,000
Kadirli	27,800
Kâğithane (E) (★İstanbul) (1965 C)	56,157
Karabük	64,800
Karaköse (Ağri)	30,600
Karaman	35,000
Kars	53,500
Kartal (★İstanbul)	29,800
Kastamonu	29,300
Kayseri	167,700
Keşan (E)	22,500
Kilis	43,600
Kirikhan	32,100
Kirikkale	91,700
Kirklareli (E)	28,300
Kirşehir	32,600
Konya	200,800
Kozan	26,100
Kütahya	62,100
Lüleburgaz (E)	27,500
Malatya	130,300
Manisa	70,000
Maraş	105,200
Mardin	33,600
Mersin	114,300
Merzifon	28,100
Muğla	18,600
Muş	23,500
Mustafakemalpasa	25,700
Nazilli	45,700
Nevşehir	25,600
Niğde	26,800
Nizip	30,200
Ödemiş	35,000
Ordu	38,500
Osmaniye	45,700
Polatli	32,400
Reyhanli	20,500
Rize	31,300
Sağmalcilar (E) (★İstanbul) (1965 C)	69,064
Salihli	38,200
Samsun	134,300
Siirt	29,400
Sinop	15,100
Sivas	132,500
Siverek	35,100
Söke	30,200
Soma	20,900
Tarsus	78,000
Tekirdağ (E)	33,100
Tire	28,300
Tokat	44,800
Trabzon	81,500
Turgutlu	40,500
Turhal	29,100
Urfa	100,200
Uşak	46,800
Uzunköprü (E)	23,500
Van	47,100
Yozgat	27,800
Zile	27,600
Zonguldak (★140,000)	72,700

TURKS & CAICOS IS.

1970 C	**5,675**
•GRAND TURK	2,300

UGANDA

1959 C	**6,538,031**
Arua	4,645
Entebbe	10,941
Fort Portal	8,317
Gulu	4,770
Jinja (★32,392)	29,741
Kabale	10,919
•KAMPALA (1969 C)	331,889
Lugazi	8,105
Masaka	4,782
Mbale	13,569
Soroti	6,645
Tororo	6,365

UNION OF SOVIET SOCIALIST REPUBLICS / Sojuz Sovetskich Socialističeskich Respublik

1970 C	**241,720,000**

UNION OF SOVIET SOCIALIST REPUBLICS IN EUROPE

UNION OF SOVIET SOCIALIST REPUBLICS IN EUROPE	**162,579,000**

Soviet Socialist Republics

Byelorusskaja S.S.R. (Byelorussia) (White Russia)	9,002,000
Estonskaja S.S.R. (Estonia)	1,356,000
Latvijskaja S.S.R. (Latvia)	2,364,000
Litovskaja S.S.R. (Lithuania)	3,128,000
Moldavskaja S.S.R. (Moldavia)	3,569,000
Rossijskaja S.F.S.R. (Russian Soviet Federated Socialist Republic) (part)	96,034,000
Ukrainskaja S.S.R. (Ukraine)	47,126,000

Cities

Abdulino	26,000
Achtubinsk	43,000
Achtyrka	41,000
Alatyr'	43,000
Aleksandrija	69,000
Aleksandrov	50,000
Aleksin	61,000
Al'metjevsk	87,000
Alytus	27,900
Antracit (★★Krasnyj Luč)	55,000
Apatity	46,000
Aral'sk	38,000
Archangel'sk (Archangel)	343,000
Armavir	145,000
Art'omovsk (Artemovsk)	82,000
Arzamas	67,000
Astrachan'	410,000
Azov	59,000
Bachčisaraj (Bakhchisaray)	16,000
Balakovo	103,000
Balašicha (Balashikha) (★Moskva)	92,000
Balašov (Balashov)	83,000
Baranoviči (Baranovichi)	101,000
Batajsk (★Rostov-na-Donu)	85,000
Belaja Cerkov'	109,000
Bel'cy (Bel'tsy)	101,000
Belgorod	151,000
Belgorod-Dnestrovskij	33,000
Belorečensk (Belorechensk)	36,000
Beloreck (Beloretsk)	67,000
Beloz'orsk (1959 C)	11,000
Bendery	72,000
Berd'ansk (Berdyansk)	100,000
Berdičev (Berdichev)	71,000
Berezniki	146,000
Bobrujsk (Bobruysk)	138,000
Bogorodick (Bogoroditsk)	32,000
Bogorodsk (★Gor'kij)	37,000
Bor (★Gor'kij)	55,000
Borislav	34,000
Borisoglebsk	64,000
Borisov	84,000
Boroviči (Borovichi)	55,000
Br'anka (Bryanka) (★Kadijevka)	71,000
Br'ansk (Bryansk)	318,000
Brest	122,000
Bugul'ma	72,000
Buguruslan	49,000
Bujnaksk (Buynaksk)	38,000
Buzuluk	67,000
Čajkovskij (Chaykovskij)	48,000
Čapajevsk (Chapayevsk)	86,000
Čeboksary (Cheboksary)	216,000
Čechov (Chekhov)	38,000
Čerepovec (Cherepovets)	188,000
Čerkassy (Cherkassy)	158,000
Čerkessk (Cherkessk)	67,000
Čern'achovsk (Insterburg)	33,000
Černigov (Chernigov)	159,000
Černovcy (Chernovtsy)	187,000
Červonograd (Chervonograd)	44,000
Charcyzsk (★Doneck)	51,000
Char'kov (Kharkov) (1971 E) (★1,480,000)	1,248,000
Chasavjurt (Khasavyurt)	54,000
Cherson (Kherson)	261,000
Chimki (Khimki) (★Moskva)	87,000
Chmel'nickij (Khmel'nitskiy)	113,000
Čistopol' (Chistopol')	60,000
Čusovoj (Chusovoy)	58,000
Daugavpils	100,000
Debal'cevo (Debaltsevo)	35,000
Derbent	57,000
Dmitrov	44,000
Dneprodzeržinsk (★★Dnepropetrovsk)	227,000
Dnepropetrovsk (★1,225,000)	862,000
Dolgoprudnyj (★Moskva)	53,000
Doneck (Donetsk) (★1,850,000)	879,000
Drogobyč (Drogobych)	56,000
Družkovka (★Kramatorsk)	53,000
Dubna	44,000
Džankoj (Dzhankoy)	43,000
Dzeržinsk (★Gor'kij)	221,000
Dzeržinsk (★Gorlovka)	47,000
Elektrostal'	123,000
Elista	50,000
Engel's (★★Saratov)	130,000
Fastov	42,000
Feodosija	65,000
Furmanov	40,000
Galič (Galich)	19,000
Gatčina (★Leningrad)	63,000
Georgiu-Dež (Liski)	49,000
Georgijevsk	44,000
Glazov	68,000
Gomel'	272,000
Gor'kij (Gorky) (1971 E) (★1,635,000)	1,189,000
Gorlovka (★690,000)	335,000
Gorodec (Gorodets)	34,000
Grodno	132,000
Groznyj (Groznyy)	341,000
Gubacha	33,000
Gubkin	54,000
Gukovo	65,000
Gus'-Chrustal'nyj	65,000
Gusev (Gumbinnen)	22,000
Inta	50,000
Išimbaj (Ishimbay)	54,000
Ivano-Frankovsk	105,000
Ivanovo	420,000
Iževsk (Izhevsk)	422,000
Izmail	70,000
Iz'um (Izyum)	52,000
Jalta (Yalta)	62,000
Jarcevo (Yartsevo)	37,000
Jaroslavl' (Yaroslavl')	517,000
Jasinovataja (Yasinovataya)	37,000
Jefremov (Yefremov)	48,000
Jegorjevsk (Yegor'yevsk)	67,000
Jejsk (Yeysk)	64,000
Jēkabpils	22,500
Jelec (Yelets)	101,000
Jelgava	55,000
Jenakijevo (Yenakiyevo) (★★Gorlovka)	92,000
Jessentuki (Yessentuki)	65,000
Jevpatorija (Yevpatoriya)	79,000
Joškar-Ola (Yoshkar-Ola)	166,000
Jūrmala (★Rīga)	54,000
Kachovka (Kakhovka)	29,000
Kadijevka (★585,000)	137,000
Kalinin	345,000
Kaliningrad (★Moskva)	106,000
Kaliningrad (Königsberg)	297,000
Kaluga	211,000
Kamenec-Podol'skij	57,000
Kamensk-Šachtinskij	68,000
Kamyšin (Kamyshin)	97,000
Kanaš (Kanash)	41,000
Kandalakša (Kandalaksha)	43,000
Kapsukas	28,700
Kasimov	33,000
Kašira (Kashira)	39,000
Kaspijsk	39,000
Kaunas	305,000
Kazan'	869,000
Kerč' (Kerch)	128,000
Kijev (Kiev) (1971 E) (★1,850,000)	1,693,000
Kimovsk	44,000
Kimry	53,000
Kinešma (Kineshma)	96,000
Kirov	333,000
Kirovo-Čepeck	51,000
Kirovograd	189,000
Kirovsk *(Murmansk obl.)*	38,000
Kirovsk (★Kadijevka) *(Vorošilovgrad obl.)*	45,000
Kišin'ov (Kishinev) (1971 E)	374,000
Kislovodsk	90,000
Kizel	46,000
Klaipėda (Memel)	140,000
Klimovsk (★Moskva)	43,000
Klin	81,000
Klincy (Klintsy)	58,000
Kohtla-Järve	68,000
Kol'čugino	42,000
Kolomna	136,000
Kolomyja	41,000
Kolpino (★Leningrad) (1969 E)	62,000
Kommunarsk (★★Kadijevka)	123,000
Konotop	68,000
Konstantinovka	105,000
Korosten'	56,000
Kostroma	223,000
Kotlas	56,000
Kotovsk	33,000
Kovel'	33,000
Kovrov	123,000
Kramatorsk (★375,000)	150,000
Krasnoarmejsk (★135,000)	55,000
Krasnodar	464,000
Krasnodon	69,000
Krasnogorsk (★Moskva)	63,000
Krasnoje Selo (★Leningrad)	27,000
Krasnokamsk	55,000
Krasnyj Luč (★210,000)	103,000
Krasnyj Sulin	42,000
Kremenčug (Kremenchug)	148,000
Krivoj Rog (Krivoy Rog)	573,000
Kronštadt (Kronshtadt) (★Leningrad) (1959 C)	40,000
Kropotkin	68,000
Krymsk (Krymskaya)	41,000
Kstovo (★Gor'kij)	48,000
Kudymkar	26,000
Kujbyšev (Kuybyshev) (1971 E) (★1,250,000)	1,069,000
Kulebaki	46,000
Kumertau	44,000
Kungur	74,000
Kursk	284,000
Kuzneck (Kuznetsk)	84,000
Labinsk	50,000
Leningrad (1971 E) (★4,675,000)	3,560,000
Leninogorsk	47,000
Lida	48,000
Liepāja	93,000
Lipeck (Lipetsk)	289,000
Lisičansk (★320,000)	118,000
Livny	37,000
Lomonosov (★Leningrad)	40,000
L'ubercy (Lyubertsy) (★Moskva)	139,000
Lubny	40,000
Luck (Lutsk)	94,000
L'vov	553,000
Lys'va	73,000
Machačkala (Makhachkala)	186,000
Majkop (Maykop)	110,000
Makejevka (★★Doneck)	392,000
Marganec (Marganets)	46,000
Marks	17,000
Mednogorsk	38,000
Melekess	81,000
Melitopol'	137,000
Michajlovka	50,000
Mičurinsk (Michurinsk)	94,000
Millerovo	35,000
Mineral'nyje Vody	55,000
Minsk (1971 E) (★970,000)	945,000
Mogil'ov (Mogilev)	202,000
Molodečno (Molodechno)	50,000
Mončegorsk (Monchegorsk)	46,000
Moršansk (Morshansk)	44,000
•MOSKVA (MOSCOW) (1971 E) (★10,000,000)	7,040,000
Mozdok	32,000
Mozyr'	49,000
Mukačevo (Mukachevo)	57,000
Murmansk	309,000
Murom	99,000
Mytišči (Mytishchi) (★Moskva)	119,000
Naberežnyje Čelny	38,000
Nal'čik (Nal'chik)	146,000
Narjan-Mar (Naryan-Mar)	17,000
Naro-Fominsk	49,000
Narva	58,000
Neftekamsk	46,000
Nevinnomyssk	85,000
Nežin (Nezhin)	56,000
Nikolajev (Nikolayev)	331,000
Nikopol'	125,000
Nižnekamskij	49,000
Noginsk	104,000
Novgorod	128,000
Novgorod-Severskij (1959 C)	11,249
Novočerkassk (Novocherkassk)	162,000
Novoekonomičeskoje (★★Krasnoarmejsk)	31,000
Novograd-Volynskij	41,000
Novokujbyševsk (★Kujbyšev)	104,000
Novomoskovsk *(Dnepropetrovsk obl.)*	61,000
Novomoskovsk *(Tula obl.)* (★340,000)	134,000
Novopolock (Novopolotsk)	40,000
Novorossijsk	133,000
Novošachtinsk (Novoshakhtinsk)	102,000
Novotroick (Novotroitsk)	83,000
Obninsk	49,000
Odessa	892,000
Odincovo (★Moskva)	67,000
Okt'abr'skij (Oktyabrskiy)	77,000
Ordžonikidze (Ordzhonikidze)	236,000
Orechovo-Zujevo (★180,000)	120,000
Orenburg	344,000
Or'ol (Orel)	232,000
Orša (Orsha)	101,000
Orsk	225,000
Otradnyj	44,000
Panevėžys	73,000
Pärnu	46,000
P'atigorsk (Pyatigorsk)	93,000
Pavlograd	80,000
Pavlovo	63,000
Pavlovskij Posad	66,000
Pečora (Pechora)	38,000
Penza	374,000
Perejaslav-Chmel'nickij	21,000
Pereslavl'-Zalesskij	30,000
Perm'	850,000
Pervomajsk (★Kadijevka) *(Vorovšilovgrad obl.)*	46,000
Pervomajsk *(Nikolajev obl.)*	59,000
Petrodvorec (★Leningrad) (1959 C)	21,700
Petrozavodsk	184,000
Pinsk	62,000
Podol'sk (★Moskva)	169,000
Polock (Polotsk)	64,000
Poltava	220,000
Priluki	57,000
Prochladnyj	40,000
Pskov	127,000
Pugačov (Pugachev)	34,000
Puškin (★Leningrad) (1969 E)	73,000
Puškino (Pushkino)	48,000
Ramenskoje (★Moskva)	61,000
Rasskazovo	40,000
R'azan' (Ryazan)	350,000
Rečica (Rechitsa)	48,000
Reutov (★Moskva)	50,000
Rīga (1971 E) (★810,000)	743,000
Romny	48,000
Roslavl'	49,000
Rostov	31,000
Rostov-na-Donu (★905,000)	789,000
Roven'ki	61,000
Rovno	116,000
Rtiščevo (Rtishchevo)	37,000
Rubežnoje (★★Lisičansk)	58,000
Ruzajevka	41,000
Rybinsk	218,000
Rybnica (Rybnitsa)	32,400
Ržev (Rzhev)	61,000
Šach'torsk (Shakhtersk) (★★Torez)	65,000
Šachty (Shakhty)	205,000
Safonovo	46,000
Salavat	114,000
Sal'sk	50,000
Saransk	191,000
Sarapul	97,000
Saratov (★935,000)	757,000
Ščelkovo (★Moskva)	78,000
Ščokino (Shchekino)	61,000
Šepetovka (Shepetovka)	39,000
Serpuchov	124,000
Sestroreck (Sestroretsk) (★Leningrad) (1959 C)	25,200
Sevastopol'	229,000
Severodoneck (★★Lisičansk)	90,000
Severodvinsk	145,000
Severomorsk	41,000
Šiauliai	93,000
Simferopol'	249,000
Slancy (Slantsy)	41,000
Slav'ansk (★★Kramatorsk)	124,000
Slav'ansk-na-Kubani	52,000
Smela	55,000
Smolensk	211,000
Snežnoje (★Torez)	64,000
Soči (Sochi)	224,000
Sokol	48,000
Soligorsk	38,000
Solikamsk	89,000
Šostka (Shostka)	64,000
Sovetsk (Tilsit)	38,000
Staraja Russa (Staraya Russa)	35,000
Staryj Oskol (Staryy Oskol)	52,000
Stavropol'	198,000
Sterlitamak	185,000
Stryj	48,000
Stupino	59,000
Šuja (Shuya)	69,000
Sumy	159,000
Suzdal' (1959 C)	9,000
Sverdlovsk	68,000
Svetlogorsk	40,000
Svetlovodsk (Kremges)	34,000
Syktyvkar	125,000
Syzran'	173,000
Taganrog	254,000
Tallinn (1971 E)	371,000
Tambov	230,000
Tartu	90,000
Tejkovo	42,000
Ternopol'	85,000
Tichoreck (Tikhoretsk)	60,000
Tiraspol'	105,000
Tokmak	36,000
Toljatti (Togliatti)	251,000
Torez (Thorez) (★275,000)	93,000
Toržok	46,000
Tuapse	51,000
Tula (★545,000)	462,000
Uchta (Ukhta)	63,000
Ufa	771,000
Uglic (Uglich)	35,000
Uljanovsk (Ulyanovsk)	351,000
Uman'	63,000
Ur'upinsk (Uryupinsk)	38,000
Užgorod (Uzhgorod)	65,000
Uzlovaja (Uzlovaya) (★★Novomoskovsk)	62,000
V'az'ma (Vyazma)	44,000
V'azniki (Vyazniki)	43,000
Velikije Luki (Velikiye Luki)	85,000
Velikij Ust'ug (Velikiy Ustyug)	37,000
Ventspils	40,000
Vičuga (Vichuga)	53,000
Vilnius (1971 E)	386,000
Vinnica (Vinnitsa)	212,000
Vitebsk	231,000
Vladimir	234,000
Volchov	47,000
Volgograd (Stalingrad) (★1,015,000)	818,000
Vologda	178,000
Vol'sk	69,000
Volžsk	43,000
Volžskij (★Volgograd)	142,000
Vorkuta	90,000
Voronež (Voronezh)	660,000
Vorošilovgrad (Lugansk)	383,000
Voskresensk	67,000
Votkinsk	74,000
Vyborg	65,000
Vyksa	46,000
Vyšnij Voločok	74,000
Zagorsk	92,000
Zaporožje (Zaporozhye)	658,000
Ždanov (Zhdanov)	417,000
Zelenograd (1969 E)	61,000
Železnodorožnyj (★Moskva)	57,000
Zel'onodol'sk (Zelenodolsk)	77,000
Žigulevsk (Zhigulevsk)	52,000
Žitomir (Zhitomir)	161,000
Žlobin (Zhlobin)	25,000
Žoltyje Vody (Zheltyye Vody)	40,000
Žukovskij (Zhukovskiy)	74,000

C Census. E Official estimate. UE Unofficial estimate.
L Population within municipal limits of year specified. • Largest city in country.

★ Population or designation of metropolitan area, including suburbs (see headnote).
▲ Population of an entire municipality, commune, or district, including rural area.
‡† Year of information specified at start of country.

UNION OF SOVIET SOCIALIST REPUBLICS IN ASIA ... 79,141,000

Soviet Socialist Republics

Arm'anskaja S.S.R. (Armenia) 2,492,000
Azerbajdžanskaja S.S.R. (Azerbaidzhan) 5,117,000
Gruzinskaja S.S.R. (Georgia) 4,686,000
Kazachskaja S.S.R. (Kazakh S.S.R.) 12,849,000
Kirgizskaja S.S.R. (Kirghiz S.S.R.) 2,933,000
Rossiskaja S.F.S.R. (Russian Soviet Federated Socialist Republic) (part) 34,045,000
Tadžikskaja S.S.R. (Tadzhik S.S.R.) 2,900,000
Turkmenskaja S.S.R. (Turkmen S.S.R.) 2,159,000
Uzbekskaja S.S.R. (Uzbek S.S.R.) 11,960,000

Cities

Abakan 90,000
Achalciche (Akhaltsikhe) 19,000
Ačinsk (Achinsk) 97,000
Agdam 21,300
Ajaguz (Ayaguz) 36,000
Akt'ubinsk (Aktyubinsk) 150,000
Alapajevsk 52,000
Aleksandrovsk-Sachalinskij 20,000
Ali-Bajramly 34,000
Alma-Ata (1971 E) 753,000
Almalyk 81,000
Andižan (Andizhan) 188,000
Angarsk 203,000
Angren 76,000
Anžero-Sudžensk 106,000
Arsenjev 47,000
Art'om (Artem) 61,000
Art'omovskij (Artemovskiy) 38,000
Arys' 26,000
Aša (Asha) 37,000
Asbest 76,000
Asčhabad (Ashkhabad) (1971 E) 259,000
Atbasar 37,000
Bajram-Ali (Bayram-Ali) 32,000
Baku (1971 E) (*1,435,000) 870,000
Balchaš (Balkhash) 76,000
Barabinsk 37,000
Barnaul (*495,000) 439,000
Batumi 101,000
Bekabad (Begovat) 58,000
Belogorsk 57,000
Belovo 108,000
Berdsk (*Novosibirsk) 53,000
Bijsk (Biysk) 186,000
Birobidžan (Birobidzhan) 56,000
Blagoveščensk (Blagoveshchensk) 128,000
Bratsk 155,000
Buchara (Bukhara) 112,000
Čardžou (Chardzhou) 96,000
Cchinvali (Tskhinvali) 30,000
Čel'abinsk (Chelyabinsk) (*1,050,000) 875,000
Celinograd (Tselinograd) 180,000
Čeremchovo (Cheremkhovo) 99,000
Černogorsk (Chernogorsk) 60,000
Chabarovsk (Khabarovsk) 436,000
Chanty-Mansijsk 25,000
Chiva (Khiva) 24,000
Chodžejli (Khodzheyli) 36,000
Cholmsk (Kholmsk) 37,000
Chorog (Khorog) 12,000
Čimkent (Chimkent) 247,000
Čirčik (Chirchik) (*Taškent) 107,000
Čita (Chita) 241,000
Ču (Chu) 34,000
Dudinka 20,000
Dušanbe (Dushanbe) (1971 E) 388,000
Džalal-Abad (Dzhalal-Abad) 44,000
Džambul (Dzhambul) 187,000
Džezkazgan (Dzhezkazgan) 62,000
Ečmiadzin (Echmiadzin) 32,000
Ekibastuz 44,000
Fergana 111,000
Frunze (1971 E) 442,000
Gagra 23,000
Geokčaj (Geokchay) 25,900
Gori 48,000
Gorno-Altajsk 34,000
Gulistan 31,000
Gurjev 114,000
Igarka 16,000
Irbit 49,000
Irkutsk 451,000
Išim (Ishim) 56,000
Iskitim 45,000
Jakutsk (Yakutsk) 108,000
Jangijul' (Yangiyul') 55,000
Jemanželinsk (Yemanzhelinsk) 33,000
Jenisejsk (Yeniseysk) 20,000
Jerevan (Yerevan) (1971 E) 791,000
Jevlach (Yevlakh) 29,400
Jurga (Yurga) 62,000
Južno-Sachalinsk (Yuzhno-Sakhalinsk) 106,000
K'achta (Kyakhta) 15,000
Kagan 34,000
Kamen'-na-Obi 36,000
Kamensk-Ural'skij 169,000
Kansk 95,000
Karaganda 523,000
Karpinsk 38,000
Karši (Karshi) 71,000
Kartaly 43,000
Kattakurgan 44,000
Kemerovo 385,000
Kentau 55,000
Kirovabad 190,000
Kirovakan 107,000
Kisel'ovsk (Kiselevsk) (**Prokopjevsk) 127,000
Kokand 133,000
Kokčetav (Kokchetav) 81,000
Komsomol'sk-na-Amure 218,000
Kopejsk (Kopeysk) (*Čel'abinsk) 156,000
Korkino 71,000
Krasnojarsk (Krasnoyarsk) 648,000
Krasnoturjinsk 59,000
Krasnoufimsk 38,000
Krasnoural'sk 40,000
Krasnovodsk 49,000
Kujbyšev (Kuybyshev) 40,000
Kul'ab (Kulyab) 39,600
Kurgan 244,000
Kurgan-T'ube (Kurgan-Tyube) 35,000
Kustanaj (Kustanay) 124,000
Kušva (Kushva) 44,000
Kutaisi 161,000
Kyštym (Kyshtym) 36,000
Kyzyl 52,000
Kyzyl-Kija 32,000
Kyzl-Orda 122,000
Leninabad 103,000
Leninakan 165,000
Leninogorsk 72,000
Leninsk-Kuzneckij 128,000
Lenkoran' 36,000
Lensk 17,000
Lesozavodsk 35,000
Magadan 92,000
Magnitogorsk 364,000
Margilan (Margelan) 95,000
Mariinsk 40,000
Mary 62,000
Meždurečensk (Mezhdurechensk) 82,000
Miass 131,000
Mingečaur (Mingechaur) 43,000
Minusinsk 41,000
Mirnyj 24,000
Mogoča (Mogocha) 18,000
Myski 36,000
Nachičevan' (Nakhichevan) 33,000
Nachodka (Nakhodka) 104,000
Namangan 175,000
Naryn 21,000
Navoi 61,000
Nazarovo 44,000
Nebit-Dag 56,000
Nikolajevsk-na-Amure 30,000
Nižneudinsk (Nizhneudinsk) 40,000
Nižnij Tagil (Nizhniy Tagil) 378,000
Noril'sk 135,000
Novoaltajsk (*Barnaul) 49,000
Novokazalinsk (1959 C) 19,499
Novokuzneck (Novokuznetsk) 499,000
Novosibirsk (1971 E) (*1,285,000) 1,180,000
Nukus 74,000
Ocha (Okha) 31,000
Omsk 821,000
Oš (Osh) 120,000
Osinniki 62,000
Pavlodar 187,000
Pervoural'sk 117,000
Petropavlovsk 173,000
Petropavlovsk-Kamčatskij 154,000
Polevskoj (Polevskoy) 58,000
Poti 46,000
Prokopjevsk (*405,000) 274,000
Prževal'sk 42,000
Revda 59,000
Rubcovsk (Rubtsovsk) 145,000
Rudnyj (Rudnyy) 96,000
Rustavi (*Tbilisi) 98,000
Šachtinsk (Shakhtinsk) 40,000
Šadrinsk (Shadrinsk) 75,000
Salechard 22,000
Samarkand 267,000
Saran' 49,000
Satka 44,000
Ščučinsk (Shchuchinsk) 40,000
Šeki (Nucha) 43,000
Semipalatinsk 236,000
Serov 101,000
Ševčenko (Shevchenko) 59,000
Sovetskaja Gavan' 28,000
Spassk-Dal'nij 45,000
Stepanakert 30,000
Sučan (Suchan) 48,000
Suchumi (Sukhumi) 102,000
Sumgait (*Baku) 124,000
Sverdlovsk (1971 E) (*1,230,000) 1,048,000
Svobodnyj 63,000
Taldy-Kurgan 61,000
Tašauz (Tashauz) 63,000
Taškent (Tashkent) (1971 E) (*1,590,000) 1,424,000
Tavda 47,000
Tbilisi (1971 E) (*1,025,000) 907,000
Temirtau 166,000
Termez 35,000
Tobol'sk 49,000
Tokmak 42,000
Tomsk 338,000
Troick (Troitsk) 85,000
Tulun 49,000
T'umen' (Tyumen) 269,000
Turkestan 54,000
Ulan-Ude 254,000
Ural'sk 134,000
Ura-T'ube (Ura-Tyube) 33,000
Urgenč (Urgench) 76,000
Usolje-Sibirskoje 87,000
Ussurijsk 128,000
Ust'-Kamenogorsk 230,000
Ust-Kut 33,000
Uzgen 23,000
V'azemskij (Vyazemskiy) 18,000
Verchn'aja Salda 45,000
Verchnij Ufalej 38,000
Vladivostok 441,000
Zima 42,000
Zlatoust 180,000
Zugdidi 40,000
Zyr'anovsk (Zyryanovsk) 56,000

UNITED ARAB EMIRATES / Ittiḥād al-Imārāt al-'Arabīyah

1968 C ... 180,200

ABŪ ẒABY 22,000
'Ajmān 3,725
Al Fujayrah 760
Ash Shāriqah 19,200
•Dubayy 57,500
Ra's al Khaymah 5,300
Umm al Qaywayn 2,900

UNITED KINGDOM

1971 E ... 55,575,000

Political Divisions

ENGLAND 46,089,820
WALES 2,725,180
SCOTLAND 5,230,000
NORTHERN IRELAND 1,530,000

ENGLAND

Counties

Bedford 465,300
Berks 647,010
Buckingham 592,750
Cambridge & Isle of Ely 304,570
Cheshire 1,551,350
Cornwall 379,480
Cumberland 291,090
Derby 884,950
Devon 899,420
Dorset 364,420
Durham 1,413,590
Essex 1,359,260
Gloucester 1,079,840
Greater London (Metropolis) 7,418,020
Hampshire 1,687,010
  Hampshire 1,579,950
  Wight, Isle of 107,060
Hereford 139,070
Hertford 930,390
Huntingdon & Peterborough 205,780
Kent 1,408,820
Lancashire 5,109,800
Leicester 771,900
Lincoln 812,310
  Holland, Part of 105,600
  Kesteven, Parts of 234,290
  Lindsey, Parts of 472,420
Norfolk 616,570
Northampton 470,380
Northumberland 795,850
Nottingham 972,130
Oxford 388,190
Rutland 29,230
Shropshire 341,960
Somerset 686,230
Stafford 1,860,200
Suffolk 553,980
  East 385,240
  West 168,740
Surrey 1,011,230
Sussex 1,244,560
  East 751,850
  West 492,710
Warwick 2,081,690
Westmorland 71,830
Wilts 489,370
Worcester 695,760
York 5,064,530
  East Riding 544,190
  North Riding 728,320
  West Riding 3,792,020

Cities

Abingdon (*Oxford) 18,820
Accrington (**Blackburn) 36,870
Aldershot (*210,000) 33,900
Aldridge-Brownhills (*Birmingham) 88,200
Altrincham (*Manchester) 41,010
Andover 26,070
Arnold (*Nottingham) 33,130
Ashford 35,680
Ashton-under-Lyne (**Manchester) 48,620
Aycliffe (1971 C) 20,190
Aylesbury 41,100
Banbury 29,320
Banstead (*London) 45,030
Barnsley (*199,000) 75,040
Barnstaple 17,590
Barrow-in-Furness 63,860
Basildon (*London) 129,900
Basingstoke 53,080
Bath 85,600
Batley (*Leeds) 42,300
Battle (1961 C) 4,517
Bebington (*Liverpool) 61,960
Bedford 72,880
Bedworth (*Coventry) 40,740
Beeston & Stapleford (*Nottingham) 63,630
Benfleet (*London) 48,140
Berkhamsted (*London) 15,820
Berwick-upon-Tweed 11,650
Bexhill-on-Sea 33,330
Bingley (*Leeds) 26,530
Birkenhead (*Liverpool) 138,090
Birmingham (*2,630,000) 1,013,420
Bishop Auckland 33,320
Bishop's Stortford (*London) 22,120
Blackburn (*230,000) 101,130
Blackpool (*275,000) 149,770
Blaydon (*Newcastle) 32,070
Bletchley 30,820
Blyth 34,800
Bodmin 9,260
Bognor Regis 33,890
Bolton (**Manchester) 154,360
Bootle (*Liverpool) 74,310
Boston 26,030
Bournemouth (*298,000) 148,990
Bracknell (*London) (1971 C) 33,953
Bradford (**Leeds) 294,740
Bradford-on-Avon 7,920
Braintree 24,480
Brentwood (*London) 58,060
Bridgwater 26,740
Bridlington 26,770
Brighouse (*Halifax) 34,370
Brighton (*430,000) 163,860
Bristol (*635,000) 426,170
Bromsgrove (*Birmingham) 40,730
Burnham-on-Sea 12,480
Burnley (*166,000) 76,130
Burton-upon-Trent 50,540
Bury (**Manchester) 68,130
Bury St. Edmunds 25,890
Buxton 19,880
Camborne-Redruth 41,930
Cambridge 99,600
Cannock (*Birmingham) 55,870
Canterbury 35,530
Canvey Island (*London) 26,920
Carlisle 71,820
Carlton (*Nottingham) 44,960
Castleford (*Leeds) 38,140
Caterham & Warlingham (*London) 36,770
Chadderton (*Manchester) 32,480
Chalfont St. Giles (1961 C) 5,597
Chatham (*235,000) 57,760
Cheadle and Gatley (*Manchester) 61,170
Chelmsford 58,050
Cheltenham 75,500
Chertsey (*London) 45,830
Cheshunt (*London) 44,930
Chester 62,700
Chesterfield (*128,000) 69,960
Chichester 20,830
Chigwell (*London) 54,620
Chippenham 18,680
Chorley (**Preston) 31,470
Christchurch (*Bournemouth) 31,040
Cirencester 13,420
Clacton-on-Sea 37,880
Cleethorpes (*Grimsby) 35,920
Coalville 28,360
Colchester 76,710
Congleton 20,370
Consett 35,390
Corby 47,940
Coventry (*640,000) 333,000
Cowes 18,970
Crawley (*London) 67,340
Crewe 51,250
Crosby (*Liverpool) 57,790
Darlington 85,900
Dartford (*London) 45,110
Dartmouth 6,570
Darwen (*Blackburn) 29,110
Dawley 26,460
Deal 25,770
Dearne 25,090
Denton (*Manchester) 38,360
Derby (*270,000) 219,320
Dewsbury (**Leeds) 51,130
Doncaster (*158,000) 81,060
Dorchester 13,720
Dorking (*London) 22,680
Dover 34,210
Dudley (**Birmingham) 185,390
Dunstable (*Luton) 31,790
Durham 29,100
Eastbourne 68,810
East Grinstead (*London) 18,850
Eastleigh (*Southampton) 45,490
East Retford 18,340
Eccles (*Manchester) 38,430
Egham (*London) 31,470
Ellesmere Port (*Liverpool) 61,830
Ely 10,270
Epsom and Ewell (*London) 72,120
Esher (*London) 64,760
Eton (*London) 5,180
Evesham 13,910
Exeter 93,800
Exmouth 25,470
Falmouth 17,960
Fareham (*Portsmouth) 83,570
Farnborough (**Aldershot) 41,900
Farnham (*Aldershot) 31,300
Farnworth (*Manchester) 26,270
Faversham 14,830
Felixstowe 19,120
Felling (*Newcastle) 38,570
Fleet (*Aldershot) 21,000
Fleetwood (**Blackpool) 29,270
Folkestone 44,810
Formby (*Liverpool) 23,800
Frimley & Camberley (*Aldershot) 45,960
Frome 13,490
Gainsborough 17,580
Gateshead (*Newcastle) 94,680
Gillingham (**Chatham) 88,480
Glastonbury 6,530
Glossop (*Manchester) 24,360
Gloucester (*111,000) 89,980
Goole 18,020
Gosforth (*Newcastle) 27,140
Gosport (*Portsmouth) 78,900
Grantham 27,890
Gravesend (*London) 53,600
Great Yarmouth 49,920
Grimsby (*149,000) 95,610
Guildford (*London) 58,090
Halesowen (*Birmingham) 53,990
Halifax (*164,000) 91,040
Haltemprice (*Hull) 53,220
Harlow (*London) 77,920
Harrogate 63,470
Hartlepool (**Middlesbrough) 97,110
Harwich 14,830
Haslemere 13,440
Hastings 72,770
Hatfield (*London) (1971 C) 25,211
Havant and Waterloo (*Portsmouth) 108,810
Haverhill 12,470
Hazel Grove & Bramhall (*Manchester) 39,870
Heanor 24,300
Hebburn (*Newcastle) 23,560
Hemel Hempstead (*London) 69,720
Hemsworth 14,740
Henley-on-Thames 11,550
Hereford 46,920
Herne Bay 25,370
Hertford 20,770
Hexham 9,950
Heywood (*Manchester) 30,450
High Wycombe 59,930
Hinckley (**Coventry) 48,170
Hitchin 28,670
Horsham (*London) 26,710
Houghton-le-Spring (*Newcastle) 32,900
Hove (*Brighton) 72,010
Hoylake (*Liverpool) 32,950
Hucknall (*Nottingham) 26,360
Huddersfield (*209,000) 130,560
Huntingdon & Godmanchester 16,570
Huyton-with-Roby (*Liverpool) 67,200
Hyde (*Manchester) 37,520
Hythe 11,870
Ilkeston (*Nottingham) 34,210
Ilkley (*Leeds) 21,990
Ipswich 122,700
Irlam (*Manchester) 20,750
Jarrow (*Newcastle) 29,050
Keighley (**Leeds) 55,720
Kendal 21,410
Kenilworth (*Coventry) 19,980
Keswick 4,820
Kettering 42,530
Kidderminster 47,640
King's Lynn 30,200
Kingston-upon-Hull (Hull) (*355,000) 284,680
Kingswood (*Bristol) 30,400
Kirkby (*Liverpool) 60,170
Lancaster (*99,000) 49,300
Leamington Spa (**Coventry) 45,010
Leatherhead (*London) 41,050
Leeds (*1,550,000) 501,080
Leek 19,340
Leicester (*475,000) 282,000
Leigh (*Manchester) 46,180
Letchworth 31,300
Lewes 14,080
Leyland (*Preston) 23,370
Lichfield 22,920
Lincoln 74,090
Littlehampton 18,730
Liverpool (*1,615,000) 603,210
•LONDON (*10,700,000) 7,418,020
Longbenton (*Newcastle) 49,180
Long Eaton (*Nottingham) 33,630
Loughborough 48,180
Lowestoft 52,120
Ludlow (1966 E) 7,100
Luton (*205,000) 160,730
Lymington 35,830
Lytham St. Annes (*Blackpool) 40,180
Macclesfield 44,030
Maidenhead (*London) 46,530
Maidstone 71,250
Malvern 30,380
Manchester (*2,875,000) 542,430
Mansfield (*197,000) 57,820
Margate 49,680
Market Harborough 14,440
Marlborough 6,120
Matlock 20,180
Melton Mowbray 19,840
Middlesbrough (Teesside) (*580,000) 395,530
Middleton (*Manchester) 54,270
Morecambe [& Heysham] (**Lancaster) 41,620
Morley (*Leeds) 44,660
Nelson (**Burnley) 31,560
Newark-upon-Trent 24,540
Newburn (*Newcastle) 39,260
Newbury 23,940
Newcastle-under-Lyme (**Stoke-on-Trent) 77,320
Newcastle-upon-Tyne (*1,365,000) 221,390
Newmarket 13,040
Newport 21,870
Newton Abbot 19,680
Newton-le-Willows 22,330
Northampton 126,250
Northfleet (*London) 26,660
Northwich 18,190
Norwich (*197,000) 120,740
Nottingham (*650,000) 296,750
Nuneaton (**Coventry) 66,860
Oakengates 16,760
Oakham 6,810
Oldham (**Manchester) 105,530
Ormskirk (*Liverpool) 27,720
Oxford (*210,000) 110,630
Penrith 11,470
Penzance 19,060
Peterborough 69,800
Peterlee (1971 C) 21,836
Plymouth (*275,000) 246,850
Pontefract (*Leeds) 31,120
Poole (**Bournemouth) 106,610
Portland 13,740
Portsmouth (*485,000) 204,280
Potters Bar (*London) 24,750
Preston (*240,000) 96,790
Prestwich (*Manchester) 33,310
Pudsey (*Leeds) 38,240
Queenborough-in-Sheppey 31,050
Radcliffe (*Manchester) 29,510
Ramsgate 39,770
Rawtenstall 21,200
Rayleigh (*London) 26,390
Reading (*195,000) 133,360
Redditch (*Birmingham) 41,160
Reigate (*London) 56,320

(England continued)

C Census. E Official estimate. UE Unofficial estimate.
L Population within municipal limits of year specified. • Largest city in country.

* Population or designation of metropolitan area, including suburbs (see headnote).
▲ Population of an entire municipality, commune, or district, including rural area.
‡† Year of information specified at start of country.

(England continued)

Rickmansworth (★London)	29,670
Ripon	11 800
Rochdale (★★Manchester)	91,470
Rochester (★★Chatham)	55,700
Rotherham (★★Sheffield)	84,500
Rothwell (★Leeds)	28,260
Rugby	59,110
Rugeley	22,410
Runcorn	36,340
Ryde	22,790
Rye	4,410
Saint Albans (★London)	52,690
St. Austell [with Fowey]	32,000
Saint Helens (★158,000)	104,050
Sale (★Manchester)	56,560
Salford (★Manchester)	131,330
Salisbury	35,550
Sandwich	4,500
Scarborough	43,070
Scunthorpe	70,480
Seaham (★Newcastle)	23,650
Seaton Valley (★Newcastle)	32,460
Selby	11,620
Sevenoaks (★London)	18,280
Sheffield (★725,000)	515,950
Shipley (★Leeds)	28,570
Shrewsbury	56,630
Sittingbourne & Milton	31,180
Skelmersdale [& Holland] (★Manchester)	31,120
Slough (★London)	87,660
Smethwick (Warley) (★Birmingham)	163,270
Solihull (★Birmingham)	107,460
Southampton (★390,000)	213,550
Southend-on-Sea (★London)	162,420
Southport (★★Liverpool)	84,870
South Shields (★★Newcastle)	100,220
Spalding	16,970
Spenborough (★Leeds)	41,120
Spennymoor	19,070
Stafford	54,120
Staines (★London)	56,370
Stalybridge (★Manchester)	22,860
Stamford	14,310
Stanley (★Newcastle)	42,090
Stevenage	67,620
Stockport (★Manchester)	139,530
Stoke-on-Trent (★445,000)	263,610
Stourbridge (★Birmingham)	54,700
Stratford-on-Avon	19,280
Stretford (★Manchester)	54,220
Stroud	19,150
Sudbury	8,280
Sunbury-on-Thames (★London)	39,990
Sunderland (★★Newcastle)	215,650
Sutton Coldfield (★Birmingham)	83,550
Sutton-in-Ashfield (★★Mansfield)	40,240
Swadlincote	20,240
Swindon	90,670
Swinton & Pendlebury (★Manchester)	40,070
Tamworth	40,940
Taunton	38,640
Tewkesbury	8,780
Thetford	13,630
Thurrock (★London)	125,030
Tiverton	15,660
Todmorden	15,040
Tonbridge	31,110
Torquay (Torbay)	105,050
Trowbridge	19,380
Truro	15,100
Tunbridge Wells	44,610
Tynemouth (★Newcastle)	68,740
Ulverston	12,010
Urmston (★Manchester)	44,400
Wakefield (★★Leeds)	59,410
Wallasey (★Liverpool)	97,470
Wallsend (★Newcastle)	45,950
Walsall (★★Birmingham)	184,380
Walton and Weybridge (★London)	51,850
Walton-le-Dale (★Preston)	26,780
Warrington (★135,000)	67,890
Warwick (★★Coventry)	18,040
Washington (★Newcastle)	24,330
Watford (★London)	78,010
Wellingborough	37,960
Wells	8,590
Welwyn Garden City (★London)	40,390
West Bridgford (★Nottingham)	28,420
West Bromwich (★★Birmingham)	166,560
Weston-super-Mare	49,540
Weymouth and Melcombe Regis	41,420
Whickham (★Newcastle)	28,730
Whitby	12,850
Whitefield (★Manchester)	21,850
Whitehaven	26,420
Whitley Bay (★Newcastle)	37,890
Whitstable	25,240
Widnes	56,960
Wigan (★★Manchester)	81,140
Wigston (★Leicester)	30,140
Wilmslow (★Manchester)	29,330
Winchester	31,670
Windermere	7,710
Windsor (New Windsor) (★London)	30,900
Winsford	24,840
Wirral (★Liverpool)	27,110
Woking (★London)	76,260
Wokingham	21,300
Wolverhampton (★★Birmingham)	268,380
Worcester	72,970
Workington	28,540
Worksop	36,110
Worsley (★Manchester)	49,800
Worthing (★★Brighton)	87,780
Yeovil	25,760
York (★140,000)	105,210

WALES

Counties

Anglesey	60,170
Brecknock (Brecon)	52,910
Caernarvon	122,410
Cardigan	56,160
Carmarthen	163,170
Denbigh	184,830
Flint	176,830
Glamorgan	1,252,970
Merioneth	34,810
Monmouth	461,670
Montgomery	43,110
Pembroke	97,870
Radnor	18,270

Cities

Aberdare	37,780
Aberystwyth	12,150
Bangor	15,730
Barry (★Cardiff)	41,910
Brecon	6,260
Caernarvon	9,370
Caerphilly (★Cardiff)	40,750
•CARDIFF (★615,000)	276,790
Carmarthen	13,430
Colwyn Bay	25,480
Cwmbran (★Newport)	31,650
Ebbw Vale	26,030
Flint	14,740
Llandudno	17,360
Llanelli	26,260
Merthyr Tydfil	55,100
Milford Haven	13,840
Monmouth	6,680
Neath (★★Swansea)	28,210
Newport (★315,000)	111,810
Pembroke	14,200
Pontypool (★★Newport)	36,850
Pontypridd (★Cardiff)	34,530
Port Talbot (★131,000)	50,310
Rhondda (★★Cardiff)	88,990
Swansea (★270,000)	171,320
Wrexham	38,650

SCOTLAND

Counties (1971 C)

Aberdeen	319,887
Angus	279,396
Argyll	59,909
Ayr	361,074
Banff	43,501
Berwick	20,750
Bute	13,237
Caithness	27,754
Clackmannan	45,553
Dumfries	88,215
Dunbarton	237,518
East Lothian	55,891
Fife	326,989
Inverness	89,545
Kincardine	26,050
Kinross	6,422
Kirkcudbright	27,450
Lanark	1,524,175
Midlothian	595,631
Moray	51,485
Nairn	11,049
Orkney	17,075
Peebles	13,675
Perth	127,138
Renfrew	362,144
Ross & Cromarty	58,267
Roxburgh	41,942
Selkirk	20,868
Stirling	208,956
Sutherland	13,053
West Lothian	108,474
Wigtown	27,335
Zetland (Shetland)	17,298

Cities (1971 C)

Aberdeen (★210,000)	182,006
Airdrie (★Glasgow)	37,736
Alloa	14,110
Arbroath	22,585
Ardrossan (★★Irvine)	10,569
Ayr (★96,000)	47,884
Clydebank (★Glasgow)	48,296
Coatbridge (★Glasgow)	52,131
Cumbernauld (★Glasgow)	31,787
Dumbarton (★Glasgow)	25,640
Dumfries	29,384
Dundee (★205,000)	182,084
Dunfermline (★125,000)	49,882
East Kilbride (★Glasgow)	63,505
EDINBURGH (★645,000)	453,422
Elgin	16,401
Falkirk (★140,000)	37,587
Forfar	10,500
•Glasgow (★2,030,000)	896,958
Glenrothes (★★Kirkcaldy)	27,137
Grangemouth (★★Falkirk)	24,572
Greenock (★104,000)	69,004
Hamilton (★Glasgow)	46,347
Helensburgh (★Glasgow)	12,874
Inverness	34,870
Irvine (★80,000)	23,011
Kilmarnock (★79,000)	48,785
Kirkcaldy (★139,000)	50,338
Kirkwall	4,618
Lerwick	6,107
Montrose	9,963
Motherwell (★Glasgow)	74,184
Oban	6,910
Paisley (★★Glasgow)	95,344
Perth	43,051
Peterhead	14,164
Port Glasgow (★Greenock)	22,399
Prestwick (★Ayr)	13,441
St. Andrews	11,633
Stirling (★56,000)	29,769
Stranraer	9,853
Thurso	9,074
Wick	7,613

NORTHERN IRELAND

Counties (1971 C)

Antrim	352,549
Armagh	133,196
Belfast (County Borough)	360,150
Down	310,617
Fermanagh	49,960
Londonderry	130,296
Londonderry (County Borough)	51,850
Tyrone	138,975

Cities (1971 C)

Armagh	12,297
Bangor (★Belfast)	35,178
•BELFAST (★720,000)	360,150
Enniskillen	6,553
Larne	18,242
Lisburn (★Belfast)	27,405
Londonderry (★85,000)	51,850
Lurgan (★59,000)	24,055
Newry	11,393
Newtownabbey (★Belfast)	57,908
Omagh	11,953
Portadown (★★Lurgan)	21,906

UPPER VOLTA / Haute-Volta

1970 E	**5,485,981**
Bobo Dioulasso	77,385
Koudougou (1966 E)	31,000
•OUAGADOUGOU	110,000

URUGUAY

1963 C	**2,595,510**

Departments

Artigas	52,843
Canelones	258,195
Cerro Largo	71,023
Colonia	105,350
Durazno	53,635
Flores	23,530
Florida	63,987
Lavalleja	65,823
Maldonado	61,259
Montevideo	1,202,757
Paysandú	88,029
Río Negro	46,861
Rivera	77,086
Rocha	55,097
Salto	92,183
San José	79,563
Soriano	77,906
Tacuarembó	76,964
Treinta y Tres	43,419

Cities

Artigas	23,781
Canelones	14,180
Colonia del Sacramento	12,839
Durazno	22,495
Florida	20,923
Fray Bentos	20,755
Las Piedras (★Montevideo)	41,509
Melo	33,378
Mercedes	31,352
Minas	31,388
•MONTEVIDEO (★1,300,000)	1,202,757
Paysandú	52,472
Punta del Este	5,272
Rivera	41,263
Salto	57,958
San José de Mayo	27,478
Tacuarembó	29,058
Treinta y Tres	22,422

VATICAN CITY / Città del Vaticano

1964 E	**1,000**

VENEZUELA

1961 C	**7,555,799**

(incl. 31,800 jungle natives, not included in state figures)

States

Amazonas (Ter.)	11,757
Anzoátegui	382,002
Apure	117,577
Aragua	313,274
Barinas	139,271
Bolívar	213,543
Carabobo	381,636
Cojedes	72,652
Delta Amacuro (Ter.)	33,979
Dependencias Federales (Los Roques) (Dependency)	861
Distrito Federal (Federal District)	1,257,515
Falcón	340,450
Guárico	244,966
Lara	489,140
Mérida	270,668
Miranda	492,349
Monagas	246,217
Nueva Esparta	89,492
Portuguesa	203,707
Sucre	401,992
Táchira	399,163
Trujillo	326,634
Yaracuy	175,291
Zulia	919,863

Cities

Acarigua	30,683
Altagracia de Orituco	13,013
Anaco	23,105
Araure	12,316
Bachaquero	14,492
Barcelona	42,379
Barinas	25,748
Barquisimeto (1969 E)	280,100
Baruta (★Caracas)	45,565
Cabimas (1969 E)	141,300
Cagua	16,233
Calabozo	15,739
Cantaura	14,068
•CARACAS (1969 E) (★2,300,000)	1,600,000
Caripito	21,598
Carora	23,227
Carúpano	38,197
Chacao (★Caracas)	64,006
Ciudad Bolívar (1969 E)	103,700
Ciudad Ojeda (Lagunillas)	53,745
Coro	45,506
Cumaná	69,937
El Tigre	41,961
El Tocuyo	14,560
Guanare	18,452
La Guaira (★Caracas)	20,497
La Victoria	22,293
Los Dos Caminos (★Caracas)	44,412
Los Teques	36,073
Maiquetía (★Caracas)	75,687
Maracaibo (1969 E)	625,100
Maracay (1969 E)	185,700
Maturín	54,362
Mérida	46,339
Ocumare del Tuy	15,006
Petare (★Caracas)	77,631
Porlamar	21,787
Puerto Cabello	52,493
Puerto la Cruz	59,033
Punto Fijo	34,457
San Antonio del Táchira	14,247
San Carlos	11,934
San Carlos del Zulia	14,480
San Cristóbal (1969 E)	149,100
San Felipe	28,744
San Félix	29,497
San Fernando de Apure	24,470
San José de Guanipa	20,746
San Juan de los Morros	28,556
Santo Tomé de Guayana (Ciudad Guayana) (1969 E)	127,700
Trujillo	18,957
Valencia (1969 E)	224,600
Valera	46,643
Valle de la Pascua	24,308
Villa de Cura	19,945
Yaritagua	14,740

VIETNAM, NORTH / Viet-nam Dan-chu Cong-hoa

1960 C	**15,916,955**
Bac-giang	15,738
Bac-ninh	22,520
Cam-pha	32,228
Ha-dong	25,001
Hai-douong	24,752
Hai-phong (369,248▲)	182,496
•HA-NOI (★643,576)	414,620
Hon-gai	35,412
Lang-son	15,071
Nam-dinh	86,132
Phu-tho	10,888
Son-tay	19,213
Thai-binh	14,739
Thai-nguyen	21,846
Thanh-hoa	31,211
Viet-tri	21,501
Vinh	43,954

VIETNAM, SOUTH / Viet-nam Cong-hoa

1967 E	**16,973,000**
Ban-me-thuot	37,500
Bien-hoa	52,200
Cam-ranh	46,600
Can-tho	61,100
Chau-phu	32,200
Da-lat (1968 E)	83,700
Da-nang (1968 E)	334,200
Gia-dinh (★Sai-gon) (1968 E)	151,100
Hue (1968 E)	156,500
Khanh-hung	40,300
Kontum	18,700
Long-xuyen	45,800
My-tho	62,700
Nha-trang	59,600
Phan-rang	21,900
Phan-thiet	58,300
Phu-vinh	35,300
Pleiku	23,700
Quang-tri	11,300
Quang-long	33,500
Qui-nhon	50,000
Rach-gia	56,000
•SAI-GON (1968 E) (★2,300,000)	1,681,900
Tam-ky	10,200
Tuy-hoa	24,300
Vinh-loi	41,700
Vinh-long	28,800
Vung-tau	54,200

VIRGIN ISLANDS, BRITISH

1970 C	**10,484**
•ROAD TOWN	2,183

VIRGIN ISLANDS OF THE U.S.

1970 C	**62,468**
•CHARLOTTE AMALIE	12,220
Christiansted	3,020

WESTERN SAMOA

1971 E	**148,565**
•APIA	30,593

YEMEN / Al-Yaman

1970 E	**5,728,000**
Al-Ḥudaydah (Hodeida)	50,000
•ṢAN'Ā' (1970 C)	120,800
Ta'izz	48,000

YEMEN, PEOPLE'S DEMOCRATIC REPUBLIC OF / Al-Yaman ash-Sha'bīyah

1970 E	**1,436,000**
•ADEN	250,000
Al-Mukallā	65,000
Madīnat ash-Sha'b (Al-Ittiḥad) (1966 UE)	10,000

YUGOSLAVIA / Jugoslavija

1971 C	**20,504,516**

People's Republics

Bosnia-Hercegovina (Bosna i Hercegovina)	3,742,852
Croatia (Hrvatska)	4,422,564
Macedonia (Makedonija)	1,647,104
Montenegro (Crna Gora)	530,361
Serbia (Srbija)	8,436,547
Slovenia (Slovenija)	1,725,088

Cities (1961 C)

Banja Luka (1971 C) (157,515▲)	62,000
•BEOGRAD (BELGRADE) (1971 C) (1,204,271▲)	800,000
Bitola	49,001
Bor	18,496
Čačak	27,642
Cetinje	9,359
Djakovica	20,778
Dubrovnik	23,059
Karlovac	40,180
Kikinda	34,059
Kosovska Mitrovica	26,721
Kragujevac (1971 C) (130,396▲)	68,000
Kranj	21,477
Kruševac	21,957
Kumanovo	30,762
Leskovac	34,396
Ljubljana (1971 C) (257,640▲)	172,000
Maribor (1971 C) (172,155▲)	95,000
Mostar	35,284
Nikšik	20,166
Niš (1971 C) (193,320▲)	112,000
Novi Pazar	20,706
Novi Sad (1971 C) (214,048▲)	140,000
Osijek (1971 C) (143,109▲)	92,000
Pančevo	40,570
Peć	28,351
Požarevac	24,269
Prilep	37,459
Priština	38,593
Prizren	28,062
Pula	37,403
Rijeka (1971 C) (160,630▲)	130,000
Šabac	30,352
Sarajevo (1971 C) (292,241▲)	210,000
Senta	25,062
Šibenik	24,800
Sisak	26,647
Skopje (1971 C) (387,889▲)	250,000
Slavonski Brod	28,781
Smederevo	27,182
Sombor	37,760
Split (1971 C) (183,912▲)	142,000
Štip	20,269
Subotica (1971 C) (146,755▲)	82,000
Svetozarevo	19,872
Tetovo	25,357
Titograd	29,217
Titovo Užice	20,060
Titov Veles	27,050
Tuzla	37,760
Valjevo	22,132
Varaždin	26,460
Vinkovci	23,192
Vršac	31,620
Vukovar	23,740
Zadar	25,243
Zagreb (1971 C) (602,058▲)	565,000
Zenica	32,536
Zrenjanin	49,020

ZAIRE / Zaïre

1970 C	**21,637,876**
Bandundu	74,467
Boma (1958 E)	31,500
Bukavu	134,861
Kalemi (Albertville) (1958 E)	29,500
Kamina (1953 E)	32,100
Kikwit	111,960
•KINSHASA (LÉOPOLDVILLE)	1,323,039
Kisangani (Stanleyville)	229,596
Kolwezi (1958 E)	48,000
Likasi (Jadotville)	146,934
Lubumbashi (Élisabethville)	318,000
Luluabourg	428,960
Matadi	110,436
Mbandaka (Coquilhatville)	107,910
Mbuji-Mayi (Bakwanga)	256,154

ZAMBIA

1969 C	**4,054,000**
Chililabombwe (Bancroft)	39,900
Chingola	92,800
Kabwe (Broken Hill)	67,200
Kalulushi	24,300
Kitwe	179,300
Livingstone	43,000
Luanshya	90,400
•LUSAKA	238,200
Mufulira	101,200
Ndola	150,800

C Census. E Official estimate. UE Unofficial estimate.
L Population within municipal limits of year specified. • Largest city in country.

★ Population or designation of metropolitan area, including suburbs (see headnote).
▲ Population of an entire municipality, commune, or district, including rural area.
‡† Year of information specified at start of country.

Population of U.S. Cities and Towns, Counties and States

This table includes all incorporated cities, towns, and villages with 600 or more population, and all unincorporated communities of 1,000 or more. Many smaller places are also included. The population figures are from the 1970 Census, except for some unincorporated places that the census does not report separately. The populations for these are Rand McNally estimates.

For some cities and towns, the population is from a local census taken since the national enumeration; the date of the local census is specified in parentheses preceded by a dagger symbol (†).

For many larger cities, a second population figure is given accompanied by a star (*). The starred figure refers to the 1970 population of the city's entire metropolitan area, as defined by Rand McNally & Company. For a list of the largest Metro. Areas, see the table on page 353.

Where a place is part of the metropolitan area of another city, the Metro. Area name is designated in abbreviated form in parentheses, preceded by (*). Some important places such as Newark, N.J., and Oakland, Calif. are considered to be secondary central cities of their Metro. Areas and are designated by (**). To aid in identification, the abbreviations are also given in the entry for the chief city of each Metro. Area.

A population marked with a triangle (▲) refers to an entire township or New England "town", and therefore includes separate communities and rural areas in addition to the main community whose population is given at the end of the entry. A few townships are listed without any community population because they contain no place with the same name as the township.

ALABAMA

1970 C....3,444,165

Counties

Autauga....25,460
Baldwin....59,382
Barbour....22,543
Bibb....13,812
Blount....26,853
Bullock....11,824
Butler....22,007
Calhoun....103,092
Chambers....36,356
Cherokee....15,606
Chilton....25,180
Choctaw....16,589
Clarke....26,724
Clay....12,636
Cleburne....10,996
Coffee....34,872
Colbert....49,632
Conecuh....15,645
Coosa....10,662
Covington....34,079
Crenshaw....13,188
Cullman....52,445
Dale....52,938
Dallas....55,296
De Kalb....41,981
Elmore....33,535
Escambia....34,906
Etowah....94,144
Fayette....16,252
Franklin....23,933
Geneva....21,924
Greene....10,650
Hale....15,888
Henry....13,254
Houston....56,574
Jackson....39,202
Jefferson....644,991
Lamar....14,335
Lauderdale....68,111
Lawrence....27,281
Lee....61,268
Limestone....41,699
Lowndes....12,897
Macon....24,841
Madison....186,540
Marengo....23,819
Marion....23,788
Marshall....54,211
Mobile....317,308
Monroe....20,883
Montgomery....167,790
Morgan....77,306
Perry....15,388
Pickens....20,326
Pike....25,038
Randolph....18,331
Russell....45,394
St. Clair....27,956
Shelby....38,037
Sumter....16,974
Talladega....65,280
Tallapoosa....33,840
Tuscaloosa....116,029
Walker....56,246
Washington....16,241
Wilcox....16,303
Winston....16,654

Cities

Abbeville....2,996
Adamsville (*BIR)....2,412
Addison....692
Airport Highlands (*BIR)....2,000
Akron....535
Alabaster (*BIR)....2,642
Albertville....9,963
Alexander City....12,358
Aliceville....2,851
Altoona....781
Andalusia....10,092
Anniston (*94,900; ANNI)....31,533
Arab....4,399
Ardmore....761
Ariton....643
Ashford....1,980
Ashland....1,921
Ashville....986
Athens (*HNTS)....14,360
Atmore....8,293
Attalla (*GAD)....7,510
Auburn (**OP-AU)....22,767
Autaugaville....870
Bay Minette....6,727
Bayou la Batre....2,664
Bay View (*BIR)....1,200
Berry....679
Bessemer (*BIR)....33,663
Birmingham (*647,400; BIR)....300,910
Blountsville....1,254
Bluff Park (*BIR)....12,372
Boaz....5,635
Boylston (*MTGY)....2,000
Brantley....1,066
Brent....2,093
Brewton....6,747
Bridgeport....2,908
Brighton (*BIR)....2,277
Brilliant....726
Brookside (*BIR)....990
Brownville (*BIR)....501
Brundidge....2,709
Butler....2,064
Bynum (*ANNI)....900
Cahaba Heights (*BIR)....4,000
Calera....1,655
Camden....1,742
Camp Hill....1,554
Carbon Hill....1,929
Carrollton....923
Carrville....895
Castleberry....666
Cedar Bluff....956
Center Point (*BIR)....15,675
Centre....2,418
Centreville....2,233
Chatom....1,059
Cherokee....1,484
Chickasaw (*MOB)....8,447
Childersburg....4,831
Citronelle....1,935
Clanton....5,868
Clayton....1,626
Clio....1,065
Collinsville....1,300
Columbia....891
Columbiana....2,248
Cordova....2,750
Cottondale (*TUSC)....1,500
Cottonwood....1,149
Courtland....547
Crossville....1,035
Cullman....12,601
Dadeville....2,847
Daleville....5,182
Daphne (*MOB)....2,382
Decatur (*52,800; DEC)....38,044
Demopolis....7,651
Docena (*BIR)....1,140
Dolomite (*BIR)....2,500
Dora....1,862
Dothan....36,733
Double Springs....957
East Brewton....2,336
Eastern Valley (*BIR)....1,500
Eclectic....1,184
Edgewater (*BIR)....1,800
Elba....4,634
Enterprise....15,591
Eufaula....9,102
Eutaw....2,805
Evergreen....3,924
Fairfax....2,772
Fairfield (*BIR)....14,369
Fairfield Highlands (*BIR)....3,000
Fairhope (*MOB)....5,720
Falkville....946
Fayette....4,568
Flomaton....1,584
Florala....2,701
Florence (*88,100; FLO-)....34,031
Foley....3,368
Forestdale (*BIR)....1,800
Fort Deposit....1,438
Fort Payne....8,435
Frisco City....1,286
Fulton....628
Fultondale (*BIR)....5,163
Gadsden (*81,500; GAD)....53,928
Garden City....745
Gardendale (*BIR)....6,537
Geneva....4,398
Georgiana....2,148
Geraldine....610
Glencoe (*GAD)....2,901
Good Hope....840
Goodwater....2,172
Gordo....1,991
Grasselli (*BIR)....1,300
Graysville (*BIR)....3,182
Greensboro....3,371
Greenville....8,033
Grove Hill....1,825
Guin....2,220
Gulf Shores....909
Guntersville....6,491
Gurley....647
Hackleburg....726
Haleyville....4,190
Hamilton....3,088
Hanceville....2,027
Harpersville....639
Hartford....2,648
Hartselle....7,355
Headland....2,545
Heflin (*ANNI)....2,872
Helena (*BIR)....1,110
Henager....812
Hillman Gardens (*BIR)....1,200
Hillview (*BIR)....2,000
Hobson City (*ANNI)....1,124
Hokes Bluff (*GAD)....2,133
Holt (*TUSC)....3,800
Homewood (*BIR)....21,137
Hoover (*BIR)....1,393
Hueytown (*BIR)....8,673
Huguley....2,000
Huntsville (*206,800; HNTS)....137,802
Hurtsboro....937
Industrial City (*BIR)....1,000
Irondale (*BIR)....3,166
Ishkooda (*BIR)....1,000
Jackson....5,957
Jacksonville (*ANNI)....7,715
Jasper....10,798
Jemison....1,423
Killen (*FLO-)....683
Kimberly (*BIR)....847
Kinston....540
Lafayette....3,530
Lanett....6,908
Langdale....2,235
Leeds (*BIR)....6,991
Leighton (*FLO-)....1,231
Level Plains....950
Lincoln....1,127
Linden....2,697
Lineville....1,984
Lipscomb (*BIR)....3,225
Lisman....628
Littleville (*FLO-)....858
Livingston....2,358
Lockhart....698
Louisville....785
Loxley....859
Luverne....2,440
McDonald Chapel (*BIR)....2,000
Madison (*HNTS)....3,086
Maplesville....596
Margaret....685
Marion....4,289
Maytown (*BIR)....667
Midfield (*BIR)....6,340
Midland City....1,172
Midway....558
Mignon....1,726
Millbrook (*MTGY)....1,200
Millport....1,070
Millry....911
Minor (*BIR)....1,200
Mobile (*303,500; MOB)....190,026
Monroeville....4,846
Montevallo....3,719
Montgomery (*188,200; MTGY)....133,386
Moody....504
Morris (*BIR)....519
Moulton....2,470
Moundville....996
Mountain Brook (*BIR)....19,509
Mount Olive (*BIR)....1,000
Mount Vernon....1,079
Mulga (*BIR)....582
Muscle Shoals (*FLO-)....6,907
Napier (Napier Field)....572
New Brockton....1,374
New Castle (*BIR)....1,000
New Hope (*HNTS)....1,300
Newton....1,865
Normal (*HNTS)....2,600
Northport (*TUSC)....9,435
Notasulga....833
Oakman....853
Odenville....533
Oneonta....4,390
Opelika (*45,000; OP-AU)....19,027
Opp....6,493
Owens Cross Roads (*HNTS)....767
Oxford (*ANNI)....4,361
Ozark....13,555
Parrish....1,742
Pelham (*BIR)....931
Pell City....5,602
Phenix City (*COL)....25,281
Phil Campbell....1,230
Piedmont....5,063
Pinckard....609
Pine Hill....697
Pinson (Mount Pinson) (*BIR)....1,600
Pisgah....519
Plant City....1,500
Pleasant Grove (*BIR)....5,090
Powderly Hills (*BIR)....1,000
Prattville (*MTGY)....13,116
Prichard (*MOB)....41,578
Ragland....1,239
Rainbow City (*GAD)....3,107
Rainsville....2,099
Red Bay....2,464
Red Level....616
Reform....1,893
River Falls....580
River View (Riverview)....1,109
Roanoke....5,251
Robertsdale....2,078
Robinwood (*BIR)....1,500
Rockford....603
Rocky Ridge (*BIR)....4,000
Roebuck Plaza (*BIR)....1,000
Rogersville....950
Roosevelt City (*BIR)....3,663
Russellville....7,814
Samson....2,257
Sandusky (*BIR)....1,500
Saraland (*MOB)....7,840
Satsuma (*MOB)....2,035
Scottsboro....9,324
Section....702
Selma....27,379
Selmont....2,270
Semmes (*MOB)....1,000
Shawmut....2,181
Sheffield (**FLO-)....13,115
Siluria (*BIR)....678
Silverhill....552
Sipsey....608
Slocomb....1,883
Southside (*GAD)....983
Spanish Fort (*MOB)....2,364
Springville....1,153
Steele....798
Stevenson....2,390
Sulligent....1,762
Sumiton....2,374
Summerdale....550
Sylacauga....12,255
Talladega....17,662
Tallassee....4,809
Tarrant (Tarrant City) (*BIR)....6,835
Thomaston....824
Thomasville....3,769
Thorsby....944
Tillmans Corner (*MOB)....5,000
Town Creek....1,203
Trafford (*BIR)....628
Trinity (*DEC)....881
Troy....11,482
Trussville (*BIR)....2,985
Tuscaloosa (*98,200; TUSC)....65,773
Tuscumbia (*FLO-)....8,828
Tuskegee....11,028
Union Springs....4,324
Uniontown....2,133
Vernon....2,190
Vestavia Hills (*BIR)....8,311
Vincent....1,419
Vredenburgh....622
Wadley....626
Warrior (*BIR)....2,621
Weaver (*ANNI)....2,091
Wedowee....842
Wenonah (*BIR)....1,200
West Blocton....1,172
West End Anniston (*ANNI)....5,515
Wetumpka (*MTGY)....3,912
Wilsonville....659
Wilton....573
Winfield....3,292
Woodward (*BIR)....1,000
York....3,044

ALASKA

1970 C....302,361

Census Divisions

Aleutian Islands....8,057
Anchorage....126,333
Angoon....503
Barrow....2,663
Bethel....7,767
Bristol Bay Borough....1,147
Bristol Bay....3,485
Cordova-McCarthy....1,857
Fairbanks....45,864
Haines....1,504
Juneau....13,556
Kenai-Cook Inlet....14,250
Ketchikan....10,041
Kobuk....4,434
Kodiak....9,409
Kuskokwim....2,306
Matanuska-Susitna....6,509
Nome....5,749
Outer Ketchikan....1,676
Prince of Wales....2,106
Seward....2,336
Sitka....6,109
Skagway-Yakutat....2,157
Southeast Fairbanks....4,179
Upper Yukon....1,684
Valdez-Chitina-Whittier....3,098
Wade Hampton....3,917
Wrangell-Petersburg....4,913
Yukon-Koyukuk....4,752

Cities

Akiachak....312
Akolmiut....526
Anchorage (*122,000; ANCH)....48,081
Angoon....400
Aurora....1,000
Barrow....2,104
Bethel....2,416
Birchwood (*ANCH)....1,219
Butte....448
Chevak....387
Chugiak (*ANCH)....489
College....3,000
Cordova....1,164
Delta Junction....703
Dillingham....914
Eagle River (*ANCH)....2,437
Emmonak....439
Eyak....340
Fairbanks....14,771
Fire Lake (*ANCH)....475
Fort Yukon....448
Galena....302
Gambell....372
Glennallen....363
Graehl....349
Haines....1,093
Homer....1,083
Hoonah....748
Hooper Bay....490
Johnston....365
Juneau....13,556
Kake....448
Kenai....3,533
Ketchikan....6,994
Kipnuk....325
Kodiak....3,798
Kotzebue....1,696
Kwethluk....408
Lemeta....1,318
Metlakatla....1,050
Mountain Point....459
Mountain Village....419
Mount Edgecumbe....835
Nenana....362
Nome....2,488
Noorvik....462
Nulato....308
Palmer....1,140
Petersburg....2,042
Point Hope....386
Quinhagak....340
St. Marys....384
St. Paul Island....450
Sand Lake (*ANCH)....4,168
Sand Point....360
Savoonga....364
Selawik....429
Seldovia....437
Seward....1,587
Sitka....3,370
Skagway....675
Soldotna....1,202
Spenard (*ANCH)....18,089
Thorne Bay....443
Togiak....383
Totem Park....450
Unalakleet....434
Valdez....1,005
Wainwright....315
Wrangell....2,029

ARIZONA

1970 C....1,772,482

Counties

Apache....32,304
Cochise....61,910
Coconino....48,326
Gila....29,255
Graham....16,578
Greenlee....10,330
Maricopa....968,487
Mohave....25,857
Navajo....47,559
Pima....351,667
Pinal....68,579
Santa Cruz....13,966
Yavapai....36,837
Yuma....60,827

Cities

Ajo....5,881
Apache Junction (*PHOE)....2,390
Avondale (*PHOE)....6,626
Bagdad....2,079
Benson....2,839
Bisbee....8,328
Buckeye....2,599
Buckhorn (*PHOE)....2,000
Bullhead City....1,500
Bylas....1,125
Casa Grande....10,536
Casas Adobes (*TUC)....3,000
Cashion (*PHOE)....2,705
Catalina Foothills (*TUC)....1,100
Central Heights....1,300
Chandler (*PHOE)....13,763
Clarkdale....892
Claypool....2,245
Clifton....5,087
Coolidge....5,314
Cottonwood....2,815
Crane (*YUMA)....3,500
Desert Sage (*PHOE)....1,500
Douglas....12,462

(Arizona continued)

* Population or designation of metropolitan area, including suburbs (see headnote).
▲ Population of entire "town" or township, including other communities and rural areas.
† Population is from a local census taken at date specified.

(Arizona continued)

Dreamland Villa (★PHOE) 2,000
Duncan 773
Eagar 1,279
El Mirage (★PHOE) 3,258
Eloy 5,381
Flagstaff 26,117
Flecha Caida Estates (★TUC) 1,000
Florence 2,173
Fort Defiance 950
Fredonia 798
Gila Bend (Gila) 1,795
Gilbert (★PHOE) 1,971
Glendale (★PHOE) 36,228
Globe 7,333
Goodyear (★PHOE) 2,140
Grand Canyon 1,101
Green Valley 2,000
Guadalupe (★PHOE) 3,500
Hayden 1,283
Holbrook 4,759
Huachuca City 1,241
Indian Ridge Estates (★TUC) 1,200
Kearny 2,829
Kingman 7,312
Lake Havasu City 2,500
Litchfield Park (★PHOE) 1,664
Mammoth 1,953
Mesa (★PHOE) 62,853
Miami 3,394
Midland City 1,000
Morenci 900
Nogales 8,946
Page 1,439
Paradise Valley (★PHOE) 7,155
Parker 1,948
Patagonia 630
Payson 1,490
Peoria (★PHOE) 4,792
Phoenix (★947,800; PHOE) 581,562
Pima 1,184
Plantsite 1,077
Prescott 13,283
Safford 5,333
St. Johns 1,320
San Carlos 2,542
San Manuel 4,332
Scottsdale (★PHOE) 67,823
Sedona 2,022
Show Low 2,129
Sierra Vista (Garden Canon) 6,689
Snowflake 1,977
Somerton 2,225
South Tucson (★TUC) 6,220
Springerville 1,151
Stargo 1,194
Sun City (★PHOE) 13,670
Superior 4,975
Surprise (★PHOE) 2,427
Taylor 888
Tempe (★PHOE) 63,550
Thatcher 2,320
Tolleson (★PHOE) 3,881
Tombstone 1,241
Tucson (★325,000; TUC) 262,933
Velda Rose Estates (★PHOE) 1,000
Wickenburg 2,698
Willcox 2,568
Williams 2,386
Winkelman 974
Winslow 8,066
Youngtown (★PHOE) 1,886
Yuma (★41,100; YUMA) 29,007

ARKANSAS

1970 C 1,923,295

Counties

Arkansas 23,347
Ashley 24,976
Baxter 15,319
Benton 50,476
Boone 19,073
Bradley 12,778
Calhoun 5,573
Carroll 12,301
Chicot 18,164
Clark 21,537
Clay 18,771
Cleburne 10,349
Cleveland 6,605
Columbia 25,952
Conway 16,805
Craighead 52,068
Crawford 25,677
Crittenden 48,106
Cross 19,783
Dallas 10,022
Desha 18,761
Drew 15,157
Faulkner 31,572
Franklin 11,301
Fulton 7,699
Garland 54,131
Grant 9,711
Greene 24,765
Hempstead 19,308
Hot Spring 21,963
Howard 11,412
Independence 22,723
Izard 7,381
Jackson 20,452
Jefferson 85,329
Johnson 13,630
Lafayette 10,018
Lawrence 16,320
Lee 18,884
Lincoln 12,913
Little River 11,194
Logan 16,789
Lonoke 26,249
Madison 9,453
Marion 7,000
Miller 33,385
Mississippi 62,060
Monroe 15,657
Montgomery 5,821
Nevada 10,111
Newton 5,844
Ouachita 30,896
Perry 5,634
Phillips 40,046
Pike 8,711
Poinsett 26,822
Polk 13,297
Pope 28,607
Prairie 10,249
Pulaski 287,189
Randolph 12,645
St. Francis 30,799
Saline 36,107
Scott 8,207
Searcy 7,731
Sebastian 79,237
Sevier 11,272
Sharp 8,233
Stone 6,838
Union 45,428
Van Buren 8,275
Washington 77,370
White 39,253
Woodruff 11,566
Yell 14,208

Cities

Alma (★FTSM) 1,613
Altheimer 1,037
Amity 614
Arkadelphia 9,841
Arkansas City 615
Ashdown 3,522
Atkins 2,015
Augusta 2,777
Bald Knob 2,094
Barling (★FTSM) 1,739
Batesville 7,209
Bay 751
Bearden 1,272
Beebe 2,805
Benton 16,499
Bentonville 5,508
Berryville 2,271
Blytheville 24,752
Booneville 3,239
Bradford 826
Bradley 706
Brinkley 5,275
Bryant 1,199
Cabot (★L.R.) 2,903
Calico Rock 723
Camden 15,147
Cammack Village (Cammack) (★L.R.) 1,165
Caraway 952
Carlisle 2,048
Cave City 807
Center Hill 1,201
Charleston 1,497
Cherokee Village 1,200
Clarendon 2,563
Clarksville 4,616
Clinton 1,029
Coal Hill 733
College City 645
College Heights 900
Conway 15,510
Corning 2,705
Cotter 858
Cotton Plant 1,657
Crawfordsville 831
Crossett 6,191
Danville (†12/1/71) 1,558
Dardanelle 3,297
Decatur 847
De Queen 3,863
Dermott 4,250
Des Arc 1,714
De Valls Bluff 622
De Witt 3,728
Dierks 1,159
Dover 662
Dumas 4,600
Earle 3,146
Elaine 1,210
El Dorado 25,283
England 3,075
Eudora 3,687
Eureka Springs 1,670
Farmington (★FAY-) 908
Fayetteville (★63,900; FAY-) 30,729
Flippin 626
Fordyce 4,837
Foreman 1,173
Forrest City 12,521
Fort Smith (★85,300; FTSM) 62,802
Genevia (★L.R.) 3,500
Gentry 1,022
Gillett 860
Glenwood 1,212
Gosnell (†10/4/71) 1,786
Gould 1,683
Grady 688
Gravette 1,154
Green Forest 1,354
Greenland (★FAY-) 650
Greenwood 2,156
Gurdon 2,075
Hamburg 3,102
Hampton 1,252
Hardy 692
Harrisburg 1,931
Harrison 7,239
Hartford 616
Hazen 1,605
Heber Springs 2,497
Helena (†12/7/71) 10,201
Holly Grove 840
Hope 8,810
Horatio 852
Horseshoe Bend (†11/29/71) 604
Hot Springs National Park (Hot Springs) (★47,900; HTSPR) 35,631
Hoxie 2,265
Hughes 1,872
Humphrey 818
Huntington 627
Huntsville 1,287
Huttig 822
Jacksonville (★L.R.) 19,832
Joiner 839
Jonesboro 27,050
Judsonia 1,667
Junction City 763
Keiser 688
Kensett 1,444
Kibler (★FTSM) 611
Lake City 948
Lake Village 3,310
Lamar 589
Lavaca (★FTSM) 532
Leachville 1,582
Lepanto 1,846
Lewisville 1,653
Lincoln 1,023
Little Rock (★293,700; L.R.) 132,483
Lockesburg 620
Lonoke 3,140
Lowell (★FAY-) 653
Luxora 1,566
McAlmont (★L.R.) 1,800
McNeil 684
McRae 643
McCrory 1,378
McGehee 4,683
Madison 984
Magazine 677
Magnolia 11,303
Malvern 8,739
Mammoth Spring 1,072
Manila 1,961
Mansfield 981
Marianna 6,196
Marion (★MEM) (†12/27/71) 1,620
Marked Tree 3,208
Marmaduke 821
Marshall 1,397
Marvell 1,980
Melbourne 1,043
Mena 4,530
Mineral Springs 761
Monette 1,076
Monticello 5,085
Montrose 558
Morrilton 6,814
Mountain Home 3,936
Mountain Pine 1,127
Mountain View 1,866
Mount Ida 819
Mulberry 1,340
Murfreesboro 1,350
Nashville 4,016
Newark 849
Newport 7,725
Norphlet 755
North Crossett 2,891
North Little Rock (★L.R.) 60,040
Oil Trough 524
Ola 1,029
Osceola 7,204
Ozark 2,592
Palestine 755
Pangburn 654
Paragould 10,639
Paris 3,646
Parkin (†8/23/71) 2,055
Pea Ridge 1,088
Perryville 815
Piggott 3,087
Pine Bluff (★69,800; PNBLF) 57,389
Plainview 677
Plumerville 724
Pocahontas 4,544
Portland 662
Prairie Grove 1,582
Prescott 3,921
Rector 1,990
Rison 1,214
Rogers 11,050
Russellville 11,750
Salem 1,277
Searcy 9,040
Sheridan 2,480
Sherwood (★L.R.) 2,754
Siloam Springs 6,009
Smackover 2,058
Sparkman 663
Springdale (★★FAY-) 16,783
Stamps 2,448
Star City 2,032
Stephens 1,184
Strong 965
Stuttgart 10,477
Sweet Home (★L.R.) 900
Swifton 703
Sylvan Hills (★L.R.) 3,000
Taylor 671
Texarkana (★★TEXR-) 21,682
Thornton 746
Trumann 6,023
Tuckerman 1,731
Turrell 783
Van Buren (★FTSM) 8,373
Wabbaseka 644
Waldo 1,658
Waldron 2,132
Walnut Ridge 3,800
Ward 619
Warren 6,433
Watson Chapel (★PNBLF) 900
Weiner 715
West End (★PNBLF) 1,000
West Fork (†11/4/71) 1,007
West Helena 11,007
West Memphis (★MEM) 26,070
Whitehall (★PNBLF) 1,300
Wilmar 653
Wilmot 1,132
Wilson 1,009
Wynne 6,696
Yellville 860

CALIFORNIA

1970 C 19,963,945

Counties

Alameda 1,073,184
Alpine 484
Amador 11,821
Butte 101,969
Calaveras 13,585
Colusa 12,430
Contra Costa 555,805
Del Norte 14,580
El Dorado 43,833
Fresno 413,329
Glenn 17,521
Humboldt 99,692
Imperial 74,492
Inyo 15,571
Kern 329,271
Kings 66,717
Lake 19,548
Lassen 16,796
Los Angeles 7,036,887
Madera 41,519
Marin 206,758
Mariposa 6,015
Mendocino 51,101
Merced 104,629
Modoc 7,469
Mono 4,016
Monterey 247,450
Napa 79,140
Nevada 26,346
Orange 1,420,690
Placer 77,632
Plumas 11,707
Riverside 459,074
Sacramento 634,190
San Benito 18,226
San Bernardino 681,535
San Diego 1,357,854
San Francisco 715,674
San Joaquin 289,564
San Luis Obispo 105,690
San Mateo 556,601
Santa Barbara 264,324
Santa Clara 1,066,421
Santa Cruz 123,790
Shasta 77,640
Sierra 2,365
Siskiyou 33,225
Solano 171,815
Sonoma 204,885
Stanislaus 194,506
Sutter 41,935
Tehama 29,517
Trinity 7,615
Tulare 188,322
Tuolumne 22,169
Ventura 378,497
Yolo 91,788
Yuba 44,736

Cities

Adelanto 2,115
Alameda (★SF-O-) 70,968
Alamo (★SF-O-) 4,560
Albany (★SF-O-) 14,674
Alhambra (★L.A.) 62,125
Alondra (Alondra Park) (★L.A.) 12,193
Alpine (★SDGO) 1,570
Altadena (★L.A.) 42,415
Alta Hill 1,185
Alta Loma (★L.A.) 4,000
Altaville 900
Alturas 2,799
Alum Rock (★SF-O-) 18,355
Anaheim (★L.A.) 166,408
Anderson (★REDD) 5,492
Angels Camp (Angels) 1,710
Angwin 2,690
Antioch (★62,500; ANT-P) 28,060
Apple Valley 6,702
Aptos (★S.CRZ) 8,704
Arbuckle 1,037
Arcade (★SAC) 37,000
Arcadia (★L.A.) 43,237
Arcata (★EUR) 8,985
Arden (★SAC) 45,500
Argus 1,130
Armona 1,392
Arroyo Grande 7,454
Artesia (★L.A.) 14,757
Arvin 5,199
Ashland (★SF-O-) 14,810
Atascadero 10,290
Atherton (★SF-O-) 8,085
Atwater 11,640
Auburn (★SAC) 6,570
August School Area (★STOC) 6,293
Avalon 1,520
Avenal 3,035
Avocado Heights (★L.A.) 9,810
Azusa (★L.A.) 25,217
Bakersfield (★194,900; BAK) 69,515
Bakersfield East (★BAK) 19,000
Bakersfield South (★BAK) 24,000
Baldwin Park (★L.A.) 47,285
Banning 12,034
Barron Park (★SF-O-) 3,500
Barstow 17,442
Bayview (★EUR) 1,300
Bayview Park (★SF-O) 1,500
Baywood Park 1,500
Beaumont 5,484
Bell (★L.A.) 21,836
Bellflower (★L.A.) 51,454
Bell Gardens (★L.A.) 29,308
Bel Marin Keys (★SF-O-) 900
Belmont (★SF-O-) 23,667
Belvedere (★SF-O-) 2,599
Benicia (★SF-O-) 7,349
Ben Lomond (★S.CRZ) 2,793
Berkeley (★SF-O-) 116,716
Bethel Island 1,398
Beverly Hills (★L.A.) 33,416
Big Bear Lake 2,800
Biggs 1,115
Big Sur 150
Bishop 3,498
Bloomington (★SBDO-) 11,957
Blue Lake 1,112
Blythe 7,047
Bonita (★SDGO) 4,000
Bonnyview (★REDD) 4,882
Boonville 950
Boron 1,999
Boulder Creek (★S.CRZ) 1,806
Boyes Hot Springs (★SF-O-) 3,558
Bradbury (★L.A.) 1,098
Brawley 13,746
Brea (★L.A.) 18,447
Brentwood 2,649
Brisbane (★SF-O-) 3,003
Broadmoor (★SF-O-) 6,000
Broderick (★SAC) 10,000
Bryte (★SAC) 2,780
Buckeye (★REDD) 950
Buellton 1,402
Buena Park (★L.A.) 63,646
Burbank (★L.A.) 88,871
Burbank (★SF-O-) 5,000
Burkett Acres (★STOC) 1,400
Burkett Gardens (★STOC) 4,000
Burlingame (★SF-O-) 27,320
Burney 2,190
Buttonwillow 1,193
Cabazon 598
Calaveras Yacht and Country Club Estates (★STOC) 1,500
Calavo Gardens (★SDGO) 3,500
Calexico (★10,900; CLEX) 10,625
California City (†3/15/71) 1,900
Calimesa (★SBDO) 3,000
Calipatria 1,824
Calistoga 1,882
Calwa (★FRES) 5,198
Camarillo (★V-OX) 19,219
Camarillo Heights (★V-OX) 3,800
Cambria 1,716
Cambrian Park (★SF-O-) 5,316
Campbell (★SF-O-) 24,770
Campton Heights 1,500
Capistrano Beach (★L.A.) 4,149
Capistrano Highlands (★L.A.) 1,680
Capitola (★S.CRZ) 5,080
Cardiff by the Sea (Cardiff-by-the-Sea) (★SDGO-) 5,724
Carlsbad (★OC-V) 14,944
Carmel (★MTRY) 4,525
Carmel Valley 3,026
Carmel Woods (★MTRY) 2,200
Carmichael (★SAC) 37,625
Carpinteria (★S.BAR) 6,982
Carson (★L.A.) 71,150
Caruthers 900
Casitas Springs (★V-OX) 1,113
Castaic 900
Castle Park (★SDGO) 2,500
Castro Valley (★SF-O-) 44,760
Castroville (★MTRY) 3,235
Cathedral City 3,640
Cayucos 1,772
Central Valley (★REDD) 2,361
Ceres (★MOD) 6,029
Cerritos (★L.A.) 15,856
Chapmantown (Mulberry) (★CHICO) 1,795
Chapman Woods (★L.A.) 2,000
Charter Oak (★L.A.) 5,000
Cherryland (★SF-O-) 9,969
Cherry Valley 3,165
Chester 1,531
Chico (★44,600; CHICO) 19,580
Chico North (★CHICO) 6,656
Chico Vecino (Chico West) (★CHICO) 4,787
Chino (★L.A.) 20,411
Chowchilla 4,349
Chula Vista (★SDGO) 67,901
Citrus Heights (★SAC) 21,760
City of Industry (Industry) (★L.A.) 714
Claremont (★L.A.) 23,464
Clayton 1,385
Clearlake Highlands 2,836
Clearlake Oaks 950
Clifton (★L.A.) 1,800
Cloverdale 3,251
Clovis (★FRES) 13,856
Coachella 8,353
Coalinga 6,161
Colfax 798
Colma (★SF-O-) 537
Colton (★SBDO-) 20,016
Colusa 3,842
Commerce (★L.A.) 10,536
Compton (★L.A.) 78,611
Compton East (East Compton) (★L.A.) 5,853
Compton West (West Compton) (★L.A.) 5,748
Concord (★SF-O-) 85,164
Corcoran 5,249
Corning 3,573
Corona (★L.A.) 27,519
Coronado (★SDGO) 20,910
Corralitos 950
Corte Madera (★SF-O-) 8,464
Costa Mesa (★L.A.) 72,660
Cotati (★SF-O-) 1,368
Cottonwood (★REDD) 1,288
Covelo 950
Covina (★L.A.) 30,380
Cowan Heights (★L.A.) 1,400
Crescent City 2,586
Crescent North 3,053
Crestline (Crest Forest) 3,509
Crockett (★SF-O-) 3,300
Cucamonga (★L.A.) 5,796
Cudahy (★L.A.) 16,998
Culver City (★L.A.) 34,526
Cupertino, (★SF-O-) 18,216
Cutler 2,503

★ Population or designation of metropolitan area, including suburbs (see headnote).
▲ Population of entire "town" or township, including other communities and rural areas.
† Population is from a local census taken at date specified.

Cutten (★EUR)...2,228
Cypress (★L.A.)...31,569
Daly City (★SF-O-)...66,922
Dana Point (★L.A.)...4,745
Danville (★SF-O-)...9,500
Davis...23,488
Del Aire (★L.A.)...5,500
Delano...14,559
Delhi...2,063
Del Mar (★SDGO-)...3,956
Del Monte Park (★MTRY)...1,500
Del Rey (★FRES)...900
Del Rey Oaks (★MTRY)...1,823
Denair...1,128
Desert Hot Springs...2,738
Desert View Highlands (★LANC)...2,172
Diablo (★SF-O-)...800
Diamond Bar (★L.A.)...12,234
Diamond Springs...900
Dinuba...7,917
Dixon...4,432
Dominguez (★L.A.)...3,680
Dorris...840
Dos Palos...2,496
Downey (★L.A.)...88,445
Duarte (★L.A.)...14,981
Dublin (★SF-O-)...13,641
Dunlap Acres (★SBDO-)...5,000
Dunsmuir...2,214
Durham (★CHICO)...950
Eagle Mountain...2,453
Earlimart...3,080
East Blythe...1,252
East Los Angeles (★L.A.)...105,033
Easton (★FRES)...1,065
East Palo Alto (★SF-O-)...17,897
East Porterville...4,042
East Quincy...1,500
East Richmond (★SF-O-)...5,000
East Tustin (★L.A.)...11,000
East View (★L.A.)...4,000
Edgemont (★SBDO-)...3,500
El Cajon (★SDGO)...52,273
El Centro...19,272
El Cerrito (★SF-O-)...25,190
El Dorado Hills (★SAC)...1,500
El Encanto Heights (★S.BAR)...6,225
El Granada (★SF-O-)...1,473
Elk Grove (★SAC)...3,721
El Monte (★L.A.)...69,852
El Porto Beach (★L.A.)...1,200
El Rio (★V-OX)...6,173
El Segundo (★L.A.)...15,620
Elsinore...3,530
El Sobrante (★SF-O-)...12,500
El Toro (★L.A.)...8,654
El Verano (★SF-O-)...1,753
Emerald Bay (★L.A.)...1,000
Emeryville (★SF-O-)...2,681
Empire (★MOD)...2,016
Encinitas (★SDGO-)...5,375
Enterprise (★REDD)...11,486
Escalon...2,366
Escondido (★SDGO)...36,792
Esparto...1,088
Etna...667
Eureka (★65,400; EUR)...24,337
Exeter...4,475
Fairfax (★SF-O-)...7,661
Fairfield (★70,600; FRFL-)...44,146
Fairmont Terrace (★SF-O-)...2,000
Fair Oaks (★SAC)...11,256
Fallbrook (★OC-V)...6,945
Farmersville...3,456
Fellows...950
Felton (★S.CRZ)...2,062
Ferndale...1,352
Fig Garden (★FRES)...9,000
Fillmore...6,285
Firebaugh (†8/2/71)...3,215
Flintridge (★L.A.)...2,650
Florence (★L.A.)...34,400
Florin (★SAC)...9,646
Folsom (★SAC)...5,810
Fontana (★SBDO-)...20,673
Foothill Farms (★SAC)...14,000
Fort City...3,503
Foresthill...900
Fort Bragg...4,455
Fort Jones...515
Fortuna...4,203
Foster City (★SF-O-)...9,327
Fountain Valley (★L.A.)...31,886
Fowler (★FRES)...2,239
Frazier Park...1,167
Freedom...5,563
Fremont (★SF-O-)...100,869
French Camp (★STOC)...2,500
Fresno (★309,200; FRES)...165,972
Fullerton (★L.A.)...85,987
Galt...3,200
Gardena (★L.A.)...41,021
Garden Acres (★STOC)...2,400
Garden Gate Village (★SF-O-)...1,300
Garden Grove (★L.A.)...121,371
Gilroy...12,665
Glen Avon Heights (Glen Avon) (★SBDO-)...5,759
Glendale (★L.A.)...132,752
Glendora (★L.A.)...31,349
Goleta (★S.BAR)...8,000
Gonzales...2,575
Goshen...1,324
Graham (★L.A.)...8,500
Grand Terrace (★SBDO-)...5,901
Grandview-Palos Verdes (★L.A.)...5,000
Grass Valley...5,149
Graton (★S.ROS)...900
Greenacres (★BAK)...2,116
Greenbrae (★SF-O-)...3,500
Greenfield...2,608
Greenville...1,073
Gridley...3,534
Grossmont (★SDGO)...2,000
Grover City...5,939
Guadalupe...3,145
Guerneville...900
Gustine...2,793
Hacienda Heights (★L.A.)...35,969
Half Moon Bay (★SF-O-)...4,023
Hanford...15,179
Hanford South...2,494
Harbor Side (★SDGO)...2,000
Hatton Fields (★MTRY)...2,400
Hawaiian Gardens (★L.A.)...9,019
Hawthorne (★L.A.)...53,304
Hayfork...950
Hayward (★SF-O-)...93,058
Healdsburg...5,438
Hemet...12,252
Hermosa Beach (★L.A.)...17,412
Hesperia...4,592
Hidden Hills (★L.A.)...1,529
Highgrove (★SBDO-)...2,800
Highland (★SBDO-)...12,669
Highway City (★FRES)...1,100
Hillcrest Center (★BAK)...27,500
Hillcrest Park (★SF-O-)...1,200
Hillsborough (★SF-O-)...8,753
Hollister...7,663
Holtville...3,496
Home Gardens (★L.A.)...5,116
Homeland...1,187
Homestead Valley (★SF-O-)...1,500
Hope Ranch (★S.BAR)...2,500
Hopland...900
Hughson (★MOD)...2,144
Huntington Beach (★L.A.)...115,960
Huntington Park (★L.A.)...33,744
Huron...1,525
Idyllwild...900
Idylwood Acres (★SF-O-)...1,100
Ignacio (★SF-O-)...3,200
Imperial...3,094
Imperial Beach (★SDGO)...20,244
Independence...950
Indian Wells...760
Indio...14,459
Inglewood (★L.A.)...89,985
Ione...2,369
Irvine (★L.A.)...7,000
Irwindale (★L.A.)...784
Isla Vista (★S.BAR)...13,441
Isleton...909
Ivanhoe...1,595
Jackson...1,924
Jamestown...950
Joshua Tree...1,211
Kensington (★SF-O-)...5,823
Kentfield (★SF-O-)...5,500
Kent Woodlands (★SF-O-)...1,500
Kerman...2,667
Kern City (★BAK)...900
Kernville...900
Keyes (★MOD)...1,875
King City...3,717
Kings Beach...2,000
Kingsburg...3,843
La Canada (★L.A.)...18,000
La Crescenta (★L.A.)...13,600
Ladera (★SF-O-)...2,000
Ladera Heights (★L.A.)...6,079
Lafayette (★SF-O-)...20,484
Laguna Beach (★L.A.)...14,550
Laguna Hills (★L.A.)...12,000
Laguna Niguel (★L.A.)...4,644
La Habra (★L.A.)...41,350
La Habra Heights (★L.A.)...4,500
Lakeland Village...1,724
Lakeport...3,005
Lake San Marcos (★SDGO)...1,400
Lakeside (★SDGO)...11,991
Lakewood (★L.A.)...82,973
La Mesa (★SDGO)...39,178
La Mirada (★L.A.)...30,808
La Mirada East (★L.A.)...12,339
Lamont (★BAK)...7,007
Lancaster (★68,100; LANC)...32,570
La Palma (★L.A.)...9,687
La Puente (★L.A.)...31,092
Larchmont Riviera (★SAC)...2,500
Larkfield (★S.ROS)...1,000
Larkspur (★SF-O-)...10,487
La Selva Beach (★S.CRZ)...1,171
Las Posas Estates (★V-OX)...2,100
Lathrop (★STOC)...2,137
Laton...1,071
La Verne (★L.A.)...12,965
Lawndale (★L.A.)...24,825
Le Grand...900
Lemon Grove (★SDGO)...19,690
Lemon Heights (★L.A.)...1,500
Lemoore (†5/10/71)...4,810
Lennox (★L.A.)...16,121
Lenwood...3,834
Leucadia (★SDGO)...5,600
Liberty Acres (★L.A.)...6,500
Lincoln...3,176
Lincoln Acres (★SDGO)...1,000
Lincoln Village (★STOC)...6,722
Lincoln Village (★L.A.)...2,300
Lincoln Village (★SAC)...1,500
Linda (★MRYS-)...7,731
Lindsay...5,206
Little Lake...3,500
Littlerock (★LANC)...1,500
Live Oak (★S.CRZ)...5,400
Livermore (★SF-O-)...37,703
Livingston...2,588
Lodi (★STOC)...28,691
Loma Linda (★SBDO-)...9,797
Lomita (★L.A.)...19,784
Lompoc (★46,600; LOMP)...25,284
Lone Pine...1,800
Long Beach (★L.A.)...358,633
Loomis (★SAC)...1,108
Los Alamitos (★L.A.)...11,346
Los Altos (★SF-O-)...24,726
Los Altos Hills (★SF-O-)...6,865
Los Angeles (★8,716,000; L.A.)...2,809,596
Los Banos (†8/6/71)...10,031
Los Gatos (★SF-O-)...23,735
Los Molinos...900
Los Nietos (★L.A.)...7,845
Los Osos...2,000
Los Ranchitos (★SF-O-)...2,300
Los Serranos (★L.A.)...1,700
Loyalton...945
Lucas Valley (★SF-O-)...1,650
Lucerne...1,300
Lucerne Valley...1,000
Lynwood (★L.A.)...43,353
McCloud...1,643
McFarland...4,177
McKinley (★EUR)...2,000
McMillan Manor (★V-OX)...1,000
Madera...16,044
Malaga (★FRES)...1,000
Malibu (★L.A.)...7,000
Malibu Canyon Homes (★L.A.)...1,000
Manhattan Beach (★L.A.)...35,352
Manteca (★STOC)...13,845
Maricopa...740
Marina (★MTRY)...8,343
Marina Del Rey (★L.A.)...3,300
Marin City (★SF-O-)...1,650
Marinwood (★SF-O-)...4,500
Martinez (★SF-O-)...16,506
Marysville (★67,300; MRYS-)...9,353
Maywood (★L.A.)...16,996
Meiners Oaks (★V-OX)...5,000
Mendocino...950
Mendota...2,705
Menlo Park (★SF-O-)...26,906
Mentone (★SBDO-)...3,800
Merced (†5/11/71)...26,191
Michillinda (★L.A.)...3,000
Midway City (★L.A.)...5,200
Millbrae (★SF-O-)...20,920
Mill Valley (★SF-O-)...12,942
Milpitas (★SF-O-)...27,149
Mint Canyon (★L.A.)...1,500
Miraleste (★L.A.)...3,500
Mira Loma (★SBDO-)...8,482
Mission Hills (Lompoc North) (★LOMP)...2,699
Mission Viejo (★L.A.)...11,933
Modesto (★135,100; MOD)...61,712
Mojave...2,573
Monrovia (★L.A.)...30,015
Montague (†12/6/71)...889
Montalvin Manor (★SF-O-)...2,300
Montara (★SF-O-)...1,459
Monta Vista (★SF-O-)...1,000
Montclair (★L.A.)...22,546
Montebello (★L.A.)...42,807
Montecito (★S.BAR)...7,000
Monterey (★135,000; MTRY)...26,302
Monterey Park (★L.A.)...49,166
Monte Rio...900
Monte Sereno (★SF-O-)...3,089
Montrose (★L.A.)...6,000
Moonridge...1,000
Moorpark (★L.A.)...3,380
Morada (★STOC)...2,936
Moraga (★SF-O-)...6,000
Morgan Hill (★SF-O-)...6,485
Morro Bay...7,109
Mountain View (★SF-O-)...54,206
Mountain View Acres...1,000
Mount Helix (★SDGO)...1,500
Mount Shasta...2,256
Mount View (★SF-O-)...3,000
Murphys...950
Muscoy (★SBDO-)...7,091
Myrtletowne (Ryans Slough) (★EUR)...3,922
Napa (★SF-O-)...35,978
Narod (★L.A.)...1,000
National City (★SDGO)...43,184
Needles...4,051
Nevada City...2,314
Newark (★SF-O-)...27,153
Newbury Park (★L.A.)...9,000
Newhall (★L.A.)...9,651
Newman...2,505
Newport Beach (★L.A.)...49,422
Niland...950
Nipomo (★S.MAR)...3,642
Norco (★L.A.)...14,511
North Fair Oaks (★SF-O-)...9,740
North Highlands (★SAC)...31,854
North Oaks (★L.A.)...4,50
North Richmond (★SF-O-)...4,000
Norwalk (★L.A.)...91,827
Novato (★SF-O-)...31,006
Nyland Acres (★V-OX)...1,200
Oakdale...6,594
Oak Knolls (★S.MAR)...3,000
Oakland (★★SF-O-)...361,561
Oakley...1,306
Oak Valley (★L.A.)...1,000
Oak View (★V-OX)...4,872
Oceano...2,564
Oceanside (★131,200; OC-V)...40,494
Oildale (★BAK)...20,879
Ojai (★V-OX)...5,591
Olivehurst (★MRYS-)...8,100
Ontario (★L.A.)...64,118
Opal Cliffs (★S.CRZ)...5,425
Orange (★L.A.)...77,365
Orange Cove...3,392
Orangevale (★SAC)...16,493
Orcutt (★S.MAR)...1,700
Orick...900
Orinda (★SF-O-)...15,000
Orland...2,884
Orosi...2,757
Oroville...7,536
Otay (★SDGO)...3,500
Oxnard (★★V-OX)...71,225
Oxnard Beach (★V-OX)...2,000
Pacheco (★SF-O-)...2,500
Pacifica (★SF-O-)...36,020
Pacific Gardens (★STOC)...3,500
Pacific Grove (★MTRY)...13,505
Pajaro...1,407
Palermo...1,966
Palm City...1,200
Palmdale (★LANC)...8,511
Palm Desert...5,000
Palm Springs...20,936
Palo Alto (★SF-O-)...56,181
Palomar Park (★SF-O-)...900
Palos Verdes Estates (★L.A.)...13,631
Paradise...14,539
Paramount (★L.A.)...34,734
Parkway (★SAC)...13,000
Parlier...1,993
Pasadena (★L.A.)...112,981
Pasatiempo (★S.CRZ)...1,115
Paso Robles (El Paso de Robles)...7,168
Patterson (†8/18/71)...3,743
Pearblossom...900
Pebble Beach (★MTRY)...1,000
Pedley (★SBDO-)...4,500
Perris...4,228
Petaluma (★SF-O-)...24,870
Pico Rivera (★L.A.)...54,170
Piedmont (★SF-O-)...10,917
Pinedale (★FRES)...3,000
Pine Hills...1,000
Pinole (★SF-O-)...13,266
Pioneer Point...1,200
Piru...900
Pismo Beach...4,043
Pittsburg (★★ANT-P)...20,651
Pixley...1,584
Placentia (★L.A.)...21,948
Placerville...5,416
Planada...2,506
Pleasant Hill (★SF-O-)...24,610
Pleasanton (★SF-O-)...18,328
Plymouth...501
Pomona (★L.A.)...87,384
Polar...1,239
Porterville...12,602
Porterville Northwest...2,517
Porterville West...6,200
Port Hueneme (★V-OX)...14,295
Portola...1,625
Portola Valley (★SF-O-)...4,943
Portuguese Bend (★L.A.)...3,000
Poway (★SDGO)...9,422
Project City (★REDD)...1,431
Quartz Hill (★LANC)...4,935
Quincy...2,500
Ramona (★SDGO)...3,554
Rancho Cordova (Mills) (★SAC)...30,451
Rancho Del Mar (★SF-O-)...2,200
Rancho Mirage...1,298
Rancho Rinconado (★SF-O-)...5,149
Rancho Santa Fe (★SDGO)...3,000
Red Bluff...7,676
Redding (★58,800; REDD)...16,659
Red Hill (★L.A.)...1,600
Redlands (★SBDO-)...36,355
Redondo Beach (★L.A.)...57,425
Redwood City (★SF-O-)...55,686
Redwood Estates (★SF-O-)...1,100
Reedley...8,131
Rialto (★SBDO-)...28,370
Richgrove...1,023
Richmond (★SF-O-)...79,043
Ridgecrest...7,629
Rio Dell...2,817
Rio Linda (★SAC)...7,524
Rio Vista...3,135
Ripon...2,679
Riverbank (★MOD)...3,949
Riverdale...1,722
Riverside (★★SBDO-)...140,089
Rocklin (★SAC)...3,039
Rodeo (★SF-O-)...5,356
Rohnert Park (★SF-O-)...6,133
Rohnerville...1,300
Rolling Hills (★L.A.)...2,050
Rolling Hills Estates (★L.A.)...6,735
Rolling Hills Riviera (★L.A.)...3,000
Rollingwood (★SF-O-)...3,000
Roosevelt Terrace (★SF-O-)...2,200
Rosamond...2,281
Roseland (★S.ROS)...5,105
Rosemead (★L.A.)...40,972
Rosemont (★SAC)...4,000
Roseville (★SAC)...18,221
Ross (★SF-O-)...2,742
Rossmoor (★L.A.)...12,922
Rowland Heights (★L.A.)...16,881
Rubidoux (★SBDO-)...12,000
Sacramento (★703,200; SAC)...257,105
Sacramento South (★SAC)...15,500
St. Helena...3,173
Salida (★MOD)...1,456
Salinas (★68,100; SLNS)...58,896
San Andreas...1,564
San Anselmo (★SF-O-)...13,031
San Antonio Heights (★L.A.)...2,000
San Bernardino (★573,400; SBDO-)...104,783
San Bruno (★SF-O-)...36,254
San Carlos (★SF-O-)...25,924
San Clemente (★L.A.)...17,063
San Diego (★1,207,300; SDGO)...697,027
San Dimas (★L.A.)...15,692
San Fernando (★L.A.)...16,571
San Francisco (★4,283,100; SF-O-)...715,674
San Gabriel (★L.A.)...29,336
Sanger (★FRES)...10,088
San Jacinto...4,385
San Joaquin...1,506
San Jose (★SF-O-)...445,779
San Juan Bautista...1,164
San Juan Capistrano (★L.A.)...3,781
San Leandro (★SF-O-)...68,698
San Leandro South (★SF-O-)...2,000
San Lorenzo (★SF-O-)...24,633
San Luis Obispo...28,036
San Marcos (★SDGO)...3,896
San Marino (★L.A.)...14,177
San Martin (★SF-O-)...1,392
San Mateo (★SF-O-)...78,991
San Pablo (★SF-O-)...21,461
San Rafael (★SF-O-)...38,977
San Ramon (★SF-O-)...5,000
Santa Ana (★L.A.)...156,786
Santa Barbara (★147,400; S.BAR)...70,215
Santa Clara (★SF-O-)...87,717
Santa Cruz (★91,600; S.CRZ)...32,076
Santa Cruz Gardens (★S.CRZ)...1,000
Santa Fe Springs (★L.A.)...14,750
Santa Margarita...950
Santa Maria (★54,300; S.MAR)...32,749
Santa Maria South (★S.MAR)...7,129
Santa Monica (★L.A.)...88,289
Santa Paula (★V-OX)...18,001
Santa Rosa (★103,900; S.ROS)...50,006
Santa Venetia (★SF-O-)...4,000
Santee (★SDGO)...21,107
Saratoga (★SF-O-)...27,110
Saticoy (★V-OX)...2,250
Saugus (★L.A.)...5,100
Sausalito (★SF-O-)...6,158
Scotia...950
Scotts Valley (★S.CRZ)...3,621
Seal Beach (★L.A.)...24,441
Seaside (★MTRY)...35,935
Sebastopol (★S.ROS)...3,993
Selma...7,459
Shafter...5,327
Shore Acres (★ANT-P)...4,000
Short Acres (★Hanford Northwest)...1,476
Sierra Madre (★L.A.)...12,140
Signal Hill (★L.A.)...5,582
Simi (Simi Valley) (★L.A.)...59,832
Sleepy Hollow (★SF-O-)...1,200
Solana Beach (★SDGO)...5,023
Soledad...4,222
Solvang...2,004
Sonoma (★SF-O-)...4,112
Sonora...3,100
Soquel (★S.CRZ)...5,795
South El Monte (★L.A.)...13,443
South Gate (★L.A.)...56,909
South Laguna (★L.A.)...2,566
South Lake Tahoe...12,921
South Modesto (★MOD)...7,889
South Oroville...3,100
South Park (★S.ROS)...900
South Pasadena (★L.A.)...22,979
South San Francisco (★SF-O-)...46,646
South San Gabriel (★L.A.)...5,051
South San Jose Hills (★L.A.)...12,386
South Taft...2,214
South Turlock...1,762
South Whittier (★L.A.)...46,641
Spring Valley (★SDGO)...29,742
Springville...950
Stanford (★SF-O-)...8,691
Stanton (★L.A.)...18,186
Stockton (★242,500; STOC)...109,963
Strathmore...1,221
Strawberry Point (★SF-O-)...3,300
Suisun City (★FRFL-)...2,917
Summerland (★S.BAR)...1,000
Summit City (★REDD)...1,000
Sun City...5,519
Sun Crest (★SDGO)...2,000
Sunnymead (★SBDO-)...6,708
Sunnyside (★FRES)...2,000
Sunnyslope (★SBDO-)...2,000
Sunnyvale (★SF-O-)...95,408
Sunset Beach (★L.A.)...1,500
Sunshine Homes (★L.A.)...1,500
Sun Village (★LANC)...1,000
Susanville...6,608
Sutter (★MRYS-)...1,488
Sutter Creek...1,508
Taft...4,285
Taft Heights...2,108
Tahoe City...1,394
Tamalpais Valley (★SF-O-)...5,000
Tara Hills (★SF-O-)...4,000
Tehachapi...4,211
Temple City (★L.A.)...31,040
Terra Bella...1,037
Terra Linda (★SF-O-)...5,000
Thermalito...4,217
Thousand Oaks (★L.A.)...35,873
Tiburon (★SF-O-)...6,209
Topanga (★L.A.)...1,800
Torrance (★L.A.)...134,584
Tracy...14,724
Trona...1,500
Truckee...1,392
Tulare...16,235
Tulare East...2,361
Tulare Northwest...1,950
Tulelake...857
Tuolumne...1,365
Turlock...13,992
Tustin (★L.A.)...21,178
Tuxedo Country Club Estates (★STOC)...3,300
Twain Harte...1,484
Twentynine Palms...5,667
Twin Lakes (★S.CRZ)...2,300
U C D (U. Cal. Davis)...4,000
Ukiah...10,095
Union City (★SF-O-)...14,724
University (★S.BAR)...4,500
University Heights (★SF-O-)...5,000
Upland (★L.A.)...32,551
Vacaville (★★FRFL-)...21,690
Valencia (★L.A.)...4,243
Valinda (★L.A.)...18,837
Vallejo (★SF-O-)...71,710
Valle Vista...1,500
Valleydale (★L.A.)...1,500
Vandenberg Village (Lompoc Northwest) (★LOMP)...4,874
Ventura (San Buenaventura) (★246,800; V-OX)...57,964
Vernon (★L.A.)...261
Victorville...10,845
View Park (★L.A.)...5,000
Villa Park (★L.A.)...2,723
Villa Verona...1,000
Vine Hill (Martinez East) (★SF-O-)...2,000
Visalia...27,268
Vista (★★OC-V)...24,688
Vista La Mesa (★SDGO)...2,000
Vista Park (★BAK)...2,000

(California continued)

★ Population or designation of metropolitan area, including suburbs (see headnote).
▲ Population of entire "town" or township, including other communities and rural areas.
† Population is from a local census taken at date specified.

(California continued)

Walnut (★L.A.) 5,992
Walnut Creek (★SF-O-) 39,844
Walnut Creek West (★SF-O-) 8,330
Walnut Grove (★SAC) 900
Walnut Park (★L.A.) 8,925
Wasco 8,269
Waterford (★MOD) 2,243
Watsonville 14,569
Weaverville 1,489
Weed 2,983
West Athens (★L.A.) 8,000
West Carson (★L.A.) 15,501
West Covina (★L.A.) 68,034
Westfield (★L.A.) 1,500
West Hollywood (★L.A.) 34,625
Westlake Village (★L.A.) 4,000
Westminster (★L.A.) 59,874
West Modesto (★MOD) 6,135
Westmont (★L.A.) 29,310
Westmorland 1,175
West Pittsburg (★ANT-P) 5,969
West Point 900
West Puente Valley (★L.A.) 20,733
West Sacramento (★SAC) 12,002
West Whittier (★L.A.) 13,000
Westwood 1,862
Wheatland 1,280
Whittier (★L.A.) 72,863
Williams 1,571
Willits 3,091
Willow Brook (Willowbrook) (★L.A.) 28,705
Willows 4,085
Windsor 2,359
Windsor Hills (★L.A.) 7,270
Winterhaven (★YUMA) 800
Winters 2,419
Winton 3,393
Woodacre (★SF-O-) 1,000
Woodbridge (★STOC) 1,397
Woodcrest (★SBDO-) 900
Woodlake 3,371
Woodland 20,677
Woodside (★SF-O-) 4,734
Woodville 1,031
Wrightwood 1,000
Yermo 1,304
Yorba Linda (★L.A.) 11,856
Yosemite National Park 900
Yountville (★SF-O-) 2,332
Yreka (Yreka City) 5,394
Yuba City (★★MRYS-) 13,986
Yuba City South (South Yuba City) (★MRYS-) 5,352
Yucaipa (★SBDO-) 14,300
Yucca Valley 3,893

COLORADO

1970 C 2,207,259

Counties

Adams 185,789
Alamosa 11,422
Arapahoe 162,142
Archuleta 2,733
Baca 5,674
Bent 6,493
Boulder 131,889
Chaffee 10,162
Cheyenne 2,396
Clear Creek 4,819
Conejos 7,846
Costilla 3,091
Crowley 3,086
Custer 1,120
Delta 15,286
Denver 514,678
Dolores 1,641
Douglas 8,407
Eagle 7,498
Elbert 3,903
El Paso 235,972
Fremont 21,942
Garfield 14,821
Gilpin 1,272
Grand 4,107
Gunnison 7,578
Hinsdale 202
Huerfano 6,590
Jackson 1,811
Jefferson 233,031
Kiowa 2,029
Kit Carson 7,530
Lake 8,282
La Plata 19,199
Larimer 89,900
Las Animas 15,744
Lincoln 4,836
Logan 18,852
Mesa 54,374
Mineral 786
Moffat 6,525
Montezuma 12,952
Montrose 18,366
Morgan 20,105
Otero 23,523
Ouray 1,546
Park 2,185
Phillips 4,131
Pitkin 6,185
Prowers 13,258
Pueblo 118,238
Rio Blanco 4,842
Rio Grande 10,494
Routt 6,592
Saguache 3,827
San Juan 831
San Miguel 1,949
Sedgwick 3,405
Summit 2,665
Teller 3,316
Washington 5,550
Weld 89,297
Yuma 8,544

Cities

Adams City (★DEN) 1,500
Aguilar 699
Akron 1,775
Alamosa 6,985
Altura (★DEN) 900
Antonito 1,113
Applewood (★DEN) 5,700
Arvada (★DEN) 46,814
Aspen 2,437
Ault 841
Aurora (★DEN) 74,974
Bennett 613
Berthoud 1,446
Black Forest (★CSPG) 2,000
Blende (★PUEB) 2,000
Boulder (★80,100; BOUL) 66,870
Bow Mar (★DEN) 945
Breckenridge 548
Brighton (★DEN) 8,309
Broadmoor (★CSPG) 3,500
Broadway Estates (★DEN) 2,500
Broomfield (★DEN) 7,261
Brush 3,377
Buena Vista 1,962
Burlington 2,828
Canon City 9,206
Carbondale 726
Castle Rock 1,531
Cedaredge 581
Center 1,470
Cherry Hills Village (★DEN) 4,605
Cherry Knolls (★DEN) 3,000
Cheyenne Canon (★CSPG) 1,600
Cheyenne Wells 982
Colorado Springs (★229,300; CSPG) 135,060
Columbine (★DEN) 4,000
Commerce City (★DEN) 17,407
Coronado (★DEN) 2,500
Cortez 6,032
Craig 4,205
Creede 653
Del Norte 1,569
Delta 3,694
Denver (★1,105,400; DEN) 514,678
Dolores 820
Dove Creek 619
Dream House Acres (★DEN) 1,500
Dupont (★DEN) 1,500
Durango 10,333
Eads 795
Eagle 790
East Alamosa (Alamosa East) 1,040
East Canon 1,805
Eaton 1,389
Eckert (Orchard City) 1,163
Edgewater (★DEN) 4,866
Englewood (★DEN) 33,695
Erie 1,090
Estes Park 1,616
Evans (★GRLY) 2,570
Evergreen (★DEN) 2,321
Federal Heights (★DEN) 1,502
Firestone 570
Flagler 615
Florence 2,846
Fort Collins (★55,000; FTCL) 43,337
Fort Lupton (Lupton) (★DEN) 2,489
Fort Morgan 7,594
Fountain (★CSPG) 3,515
Fowler 1,241
Frederick 696
Fruita 1,822
Georgetown 542
Glendale (★DEN) 765
Glenwood Springs 4,106
Golden (★DEN) 9,817
Granada 551
Granby 554
Grand Junction (★43,400; GDJC) 20,170
Greeley (★48,900; GRLY) 38,902
Greenwood Village (★DEN) 3,095
Gunnison 4,613
Haxtun 899
Hayden 763
Holly 993
Holyoke 1,640
Hotchkiss 507
Hudson 518
Hugo 759
Idaho Springs 2,003
Ignacio 613
Ivywild (★CSPG) 4,000
Johnstown 1,191
Julesburg 1,578
Kremmling 764
Lafayette (★DEN) 3,498
La Jara 768
La Junta 7,938
Lakewood (★DEN) 92,787
Lamar 7,797
La Salle (★GRLY) 1,227
Las Animas 3,148
La Veta 589
Leadville 4,314
Limon 1,814
Lincoln Park 2,984
Littleton (★DEN) 26,466
Longmont 23,209
Louisville (★BOUL) 2,409
Loveland 16,220
Lyons 958
Manassa 814
Mancos 709
Manitou Springs (Manitou) (★CSPG) 4,278
Meeker 1,597
Milliken 702
Minturn 706
Monte Vista 3,909
Montrose 6,496
Mountain View (★DEN) 706
Mountain View (★FTCL) 1,693
Naturita 820
Nob Hill (★DEN) 900
Northglenn (★DEN) 27,937
North La Junta 1,249
North Washington Heights (★DEN) 1,500
Nucla 949
Olathe 756
Orchard Mesa (★GDJC) 5,824
Ordway 1,017
Otis 521
Ouray 741
Pagosa Springs 1,360
Palisade 874
Palmer Lake (★CSPG) 947
Paonia 1,161
Perl-Mack (★DEN) 7,576
Platteville 683
Pleasant View (★DEN) 2,500
Pueblo (★111,600; PUEB) 97,453
Rangely 1,591
Redcliff 621
Rifle 2,150
Rocky Ford 4,859
Saguache 642
Salida 4,355
Sanford 638
San Luis 781
Security (★CSPG) 9,500
Shaw Heights (★DEN) 2,000
Shaw Heights Mesa (★DEN) 1,000
Sheridan (★DEN) 4,787
Sherrelwood (★DEN) 7,700
Silverton 797
Skyline (★DEN) 3,000
Skyway (★CSPG) 2,000
Southglenn (★DEN) 4,500
Southwood (★DEN) 1,200
Springfield 1,660
Steamboat Springs 2,340
Sterling 10,636
Stratmoor Hills (★CSPG) 1,000
Stratton 790
Stratton Meadows (★CSPG) 6,223
Telluride 553
Thornton (★DEN) 13,326
Trinidad 9,901
United States Air Force Academy (★CSPG) 9,000
Walden 907
Walnut Hills (★DEN) 1,600
Walsenburg 4,329
Walsh 989
Wellington 691
Western Hills (★DEN) 4,000
Westminster (★DEN) 19,432
Wheat Ridge (★DEN) 29,795
Widefield (★CSPG) 5,700
Windsor 1,564
Woodland Park 1,022
Wray 1,953
Yuma 2,259

CONNECTICUT

1970 C 3,032,217

Counties

Fairfield 792,814
Hartford 816,737
Litchfield 144,091
Middlesex 115,018
New Haven 744,948
New London 230,654
Tolland 103,440
Windham 84,515

Cities

Ansonia (★BRDG) 21,160
Avon (★H-NB) (8,352▲) 900
Baltic (★N.LON-) 900
Bantam 881
Beacon Falls (★WATB) (3,546▲) 1,900
Berlin (★H-NB) (14,149▲) 3,000
Bethany (3,857▲) 800
Bethel (★DANB) 10,945
Bloomfield (★H-NB) (18,301▲) 9,000
Blue Hills (★H-NB) 3,500
Bolton (★H-NB) (3,691▲) 150
Branford (★N.HAV-) (20,444▲) 2,080
Bridgeport (★457,200; BRDG) 156,542
Bristol (★H-NB) 55,487
Broad Brook (★H-NB) 1,548
Brookfield (★DANB) (9,688▲) 800
Brooklyn (4,965▲) 800
Burlington (★H-NB) (4,070▲) 500
Canaan (Canaan Center) 1,083
Candlewood Shores (★DANB) 1,000
Cannondale (★N.Y.) 300
Canterbury (2,673▲) 120
Canton (★H-NB) (6,868▲) 800
Cheshire (★N.HAV-) (19,051▲) 10,300
Chester (2,982▲) 1,569
Clinton (★N.HAV-) 10,267
Colchester (★H-NB) (6,603▲) 3,529
Collinsville (★H-NB) 2,897
Columbia (★H-NB) (3,129▲) 200
Conning Towers (★N.LON-) 1,500
Coventry (South Coventry) (★H-NB) (8,140▲) 3,735
Cromwell (★H-NB) 7,400
Danbury (★79,900; DANB) 50,781
Danielson 4,580
Darien (★N.Y.) 20,411
Deep River (3,690▲) 2,333
Derby (★BRDG) 12,599
Dolphin Gardens (★N.LON-) 2,000
Durham (★N.HAV-) (4,489▲) 900
East Berlin (★H-NB) 950
East Brooklyn 1,377
East Farmington Heights (★H-NB) 1,600
East Granby (★H-NB) (3,532▲) 250
East Haddam (4,676▲) 500
East Hampton (★H-NB) (7,078▲) 3,497
East Hartford (★H-NB) 57,583
East Haven (★H-NB) 25,120
East Lyme (★N.LON-) (11,399▲) 700
Easton (★BRDG) (4,885▲) 400
East Windsor (★H-NB) (8,513▲) ...
Ellington (★H-NB) (7,707▲) 600
Enfield (★H-NB) (46,189▲) 3,500
Essex (Essex Center) (4,911▲) 2,473
Fairfield (★BRDG) 56,487
Farmington (★H-NB) (14,390▲) 2,500
Field Crest Estates (★N.LON-) 900
Georgetown (★N.Y.) 1,600
Glastonbury (★H-NB) (20,651▲) 8,000
Granby (★H-NB) (6,150▲) 700
Green Manorville (★H-NB) 2,500
Greenwich (★N.Y.) 59,755
Griswold (7,763▲) ...
Groton (★N.LON-) (38,244▲) 8,933
Guilford (★N.HAV-) (12,033▲) 3,632
Haddam (★H-NB) (4,934▲) 500
Hamden (★N.HAV-) 49,357
Hartford (★1,036,900; H-NB) 158,017
Harwinton (4,318▲) 900
Hazardville (★H-NB) 10,000
Hebron (★H-NB) (3,815▲) 250
Hitchcock Lake (★WATB) 1,500
Ivoryton 950
Jewett City (★N.LON-) 3,372
Kensington (★H-NB) 5,500
Killingly (13,573▲) ...
Lakeville 900
Lebanon (3,804▲) 3,007
Ledyard (★N.LON-) (14,837▲) 150
Lisbon (2,808▲) 50
Litchfield (7,399▲) 1,559
Madison (★N.HAV-) (9,768▲) 4,310
Manchester (★H-NB) 47,994
Mansfield (★H-NB) (19,994▲) 600
Marlboro (★H-NB) (2,991▲) 400
Meriden (★★N.HAV-) 55,959
Middlebury (★WATB) (5,542▲) 1,200
Middlefield (★H-NB) (4,132▲) 600
Middletown (★H-NB) 36,924
Milford (★BRDG) 50,858
Milldale (★H-NB) 900
Mohegan 800
Monroe (★BRDG) (12,047▲) 950
Montville (★N.LON-) (15,662▲) 1,688
Moodus (★H-NB) 1,352
Moosup 3,376
Mystic (★N.LON-) 4,850
Naugatuck (★WATB) 23,034
Nautilus Park (★N.LON-) 6,300
New Britain (★★H-NB) 83,441
New Canaan (★N.Y.) 17,455
New Fairfield (★DANB) (6,991▲) 200
New Hartford (★H-NB) (3,970▲) 1,076
New Haven (★493,400; N.HAV-) 137,707
Newington (★H-NB) 26,037
New London (★239,000; N.LON-) 31,630
New Milford (14,601▲) 4,606
Newtown (★BRDG) (16,942▲) 1,963
Niantic (★N.LON-) 4,000
Noank (★N.LON-) 1,371
Norfolk 900
North Branford (★N.HAV-) (10,778▲) 4,000
North Canaan (3,045▲) ...
North Grosvenor Dale 2,156
North Haven (★N.HAV-) 22,194
North Stonington (★N.LON-) (3,748▲) 110
Norwalk (★N.Y.) 79,113
Norwich (★★N.LON-) 41,739
Oakville (★WATB) 8,000
Old Lyme (★N.LON-) (4,964▲) 400
Old Saybrook (8,468▲) 2,281
Orange (★N.HAV-) 13,524
Oxford (★BRDG) (4,480▲) 400
Pawcatuck (★N.LON-) 5,255
Plainfield (Plainfield Center) (11,957▲) 2,923
Plainville (★H-NB) 16,733
Plantsville (★H-NB) 6,000
Pleasure Beach (★N.LON-) 1,394
Plymouth (★WATB) (10,321▲) 1,000
Pomfret (2,529▲) 500
Poquonock Bridge (★N.LON-) 2,500
Portland (★H-NB) 8,812
Preston (★N.LON-) (3,593▲) 200
Prospect (★WATB) 6,543
Putnam (8,598▲) 6,918
Quaker Hill (★N.LON-) 2,068
Redding (5,590▲) 200
Reynolds Bridge (★WATB) 1,400
Ridgefield (Ridgefield Center) (★N.Y.) (18,188▲) 5,878
Rockfall (★H-NB) 500
Rocky Hill (★H-NB) 11,103
Salisbury (3,573▲) 800
Seymour (★BRDG) 12,776
Shelton (★BRDG) 27,165
Sherwood Manor (★H-NB) 1,400
Short Beach (★N.HAV-) 1,500
Simsbury (Simsbury Center) (★H-NB) (17,475▲) 4,994
Somers (★H-NB) (6,893▲) 1,274
Southbury (★WATB) (7,852▲) 600
South Glastonbury (★H-NB) 1,400
Southington (★H-NB) (30,946▲) 16,000
South Windsor (★H-NB) (15,553▲) 9,500
Southwood Acres (★H-NB) 10,000
Sport Hill (★BRDG) 1,200
Sprague (★N.LON-) (2,912▲) ...
Stafford Springs (★H-NB) (8,680▲) 3,339
Stamford (★N.Y.) 108,798
Stonington (★N.LON-) (15,940▲) 1,413
Storrs (★H-NB) 10,691
Stratford (★BRDG) 49,775
Suffield (★H-NB) (8,634▲) 1,500
Talcottville (★H-NB) 1,000
Tariffville (★H-NB) 1,337
Terryville (★H-NB) 5,500
Thomaston (★WATB) (6,233▲) 4,700
Thompson (7,580▲) 500
Thompsonville (★H-NB) 15,000
Tolland (★H-NB) (7,857▲) 300
Torrington 31,952
Trumbull (★BRDG) 31,394
Uncasville (★N.LON-) 1,350
Unionville (★H-NB) 3,000
Vernon (★H-NB) 27,237
Wallingford (★N.HAV-) 35,714
Washington (3,121▲) 500
Waterbury (★203,400; WATB) 108,033
Waterford (★N-LON) (17,227▲) 4,400
Watertown (★WATB) (18,610▲) 6,500
Weatogue (★H-NB) 2,396
Westbrook (3,820▲) 1,509
West Hartford (★H-NB) 68,031
West Haven (★N.HAV-) 52,851
West Mystic (★N.LON-) 1,150
Weston (7,417▲) 700
Westport (★N.Y.) 27,414
West Simsbury (★H-NB) 1,419
Wethersfield (★H-NB) 26,662
Whitacres (★H-NB) 1,600
Willimantic (★H-NB) 14,402
Willington (3,755▲) ...
Wilton (★N.Y.) (13,572▲) 2,500
Winchester Center (Winchester) (11,106▲) 170
Windham (★H-NB) (19,626▲) 500
Windsor (★H-NB) 18,000
Windsor Locks (★H-NB) 15,080
Winsted 8,954
Wolcott (★WATB) (12,495▲) 4,500
Woodbridge (★N.HAV-) 7,673
Woodbury (Woodbury Center) (★WATB) (5,869▲) 1,342
Woodstock (4,311▲) 400

DELAWARE

1970 C 548,104

Counties

Kent 81,892
New Castle 385,856
Sussex 80,356

Cities

Arden (★PHIL-) 555
Bellefonte (★PHIL-) 1,442
Belvidere (★PHIL-) 1,500
Birchwood Park (★PHIL-) 1,500
Blades 632
Brack-Ex (★PHIL-) 2,000
Bridgeville 1,317
Brookland Terrace (★PHIL-) 2,500
Brookside (Brookside Park) (★PHIL-) 7,856
Camden 1,241
Castle Hills (★PHIL-) 2,000
Chelsea Estates (★PHIL-) 1,300
Chestnut Hill Estates (★PHIL-) 1,500
Claymont (★PHIL-) 15,000
Clayton 1,015
Collins Park (★PHIL-) 2,600
Cranston Heights (★PHIL-) 1,500
Delaware City (★PHIL-) 2,024
Delmar 943
Dover 17,488
Dupont Manor 1,256
Elsmere (★PHIL-) 8,415
Fairfax (★PHIL-) 4,000
Frankford 635
Frederica 878
Garfield Park (★PHIL-) 2,000
Georgetown 1,844
Greenwood 654
Harmony Hills (★PHIL-) 1,700
Harrington 2,407
Hillside Heights (★PHIL-) 1,000
Holloway Terrace (★PHIL-) 2,000
Holly Oak (★PHIL-) 1,000
Jefferson Farms (★PHIL-) 1,000
Kynlyn (★PHIL-) 1,000
Laurel 2,408
Leedom Estates (★PHIL-) 1,200
Lewes 2,563
Marshallton (★PHIL-) 9,000
Meadowood (★PHIL-) 2,000
Middletown 2,644
Milford 5,314
Millsboro 1,073
Milton 1,490
Minquadale (★PHIL-) 1,300
Newark (★PHIL-) 21,078
New Castle (★PHIL-) 4,814
Newkirk Estates (★PHIL-) 1,600
Newport (★PHIL-) 1,366
Odessa 547
Penny Hill (★PHIL-) 1,000
Rambleton Acres (★PHIL-) 1,000
Rehoboth Beach 1,614
Richardson Park (★PHIL-) 4,000
Rodney Village 2,127
Roselle (★PHIL-) 1,200
Seaford 5,537
Selbyville 1,099
Smyrna 4,243
Stanton (★PHIL-) 3,000
Swanwyck Estates (★PHIL-) 1,500
Talleyville (★PHIL-) 5,000
Todd Estates (★PHIL-) 1,500
Townsend 505
Wilmington (★★PHIL-) 80,386
Wilmington Manor (★PHIL-) 1,200
Wilmington Manor Gardens (★PHIL-) 1,700
Windy Hills (★PHIL-) 1,000
Wyoming 1,062

DISTRICT OF COLUMBIA

1970 C 756,510

Cities

Washington (★2,964,500; WASH) 756,510

★ Population or designation of metropolitan area, including suburbs (see headnote).
▲ Population of entire "town" or township, including other communities and rural areas.
† Population is from a local census taken at date specified.

FLORIDA

1970 C 6,789,443

Counties

Alachua 104,764
Baker 9,242
Bay 75,283
Bradford 14,625
Brevard 230,006
Broward 620,100
Calhoun 7,624
Charlotte 27,559
Citrus 19,196
Clay 32,059
Collier 38,040
Columbia 25,250
Dade 1,267,792
De Soto 13,060
Dixie 5,480
Duval 528,865
Escambia 205,334
Flagler 4,454
Franklin 7,065
Gadsden 39,184
Gilchrist 3,551
Glades 3,669
Gulf 10,096
Hamilton 7,787
Hardee 14,889
Hendry 11,859
Hernando 17,004
Highlands 29,507
Hillsborough 490,265
Holmes 10,720
Indian River 35,992
Jackson 34,434
Jefferson 8,778
Lafayette 2,892
Lake 69,305
Lee 105,216
Leon 103,047
Levy 12,756
Liberty 3,379
Madison 13,481
Manatee 97,115
Marion 69,030
Martin 28,035
Monroe 52,586
Nassau 20,626
Okaloosa 88,187
Okeechobee 11,233
Orange 344,311
Osceola 25,267
Palm Beach 348,753
Pasco 75,955
Pinellas 522,329
Polk 227,222
Putnam 36,290
St. Johns 30,727
St. Lucie 50,836
Santa Rosa 37,741
Sarasota 120,413
Seminole 83,692
Sumter 14,839
Suwannee 15,559
Taylor 13,641
Union 8,112
Volusia 169,487
Wakulla 6,308
Walton 16,087
Washington 11,453

Cities

Alachua 2,252
Altamonte Springs (★ORL) 4,391
Andover Golf Estates (★MIA-) 1,000
Anna Maria (★SAR-B) 1,137
Apalachicola 3,102
Apollo Beach 1,042
Apopka (★ORL) 4,045
Arcadia 5,658
Archer 898
Auburndale (★WNHV) 5,386
Avon Park 6,712
Azalea Park (★ORL) 7,367
Bal Harbour (★MIA-) 2,038
Bartow 12,891
Bay Harbor Islands (★MIA-) 4,619
Bayshore Gardens (★SAR-B) 9,255
Bayview (★PNCY) 696
Beacon Squier 2,927
Bellair (★JAX) 1,100
Belleair (★ST.PET-) 2,962
Belleair Bluffs (★ST.PET-) 1,910
Belleaire Beach (★ST.PET-) 952
Belle Glade 15,949
Belle Glade Camp 1,892
Belle Isle (★ORL) 2,705
Belleview 916
Belvedere Homes (★WPB) 2,600
Biscayne Gardens (★MIA-) 9,000
Biscayne Park (★MIA-) 2,717
Bithlo 684
Blountstown 2,384
Boca Raton 28,506
Bonifay 2,068
Bonita Springs 1,932
Bowling Green 1,357
Boynton Beach 18,115
Bradenton (★★SAR-B) 21,040
Bradenton Beach (★SAR-B) 1,370
Bradenton South (★SAR-B) 10,820
Bradley (Bradley Junction) 1,276
Brandon (★TAM) 12,749
Branford 820
Brent (★PENS) 4,000
Bristol 626
Broadview Country Club Estates (★MIA-) 2,000
Broadview Park (★MIA-) 6,049
Bronson 698
Brooksville 4,060
Browardale (★MIA-) 10,000
Brownsville (Browns Village) (★MIA-) 23,442
Buccaneer Estates (★MIA-) 1,000
Buena Vista 3,407
Bunche Park (★MIA-) 5,773
Bunnell 1,687
Callahan 772
Calloway (Callaway) (★PNCY) 3,240
Canova Beach (★MELB) 2,500
Cantonment (★PENS) 2,740
Cape Canaveral (★COCO) 4,258
Cape Coral 10,193
Carol City (★MIA-) 23,000
Carrabelle 1,044
Carrollwood (★TAM) 2,000
Carver Ranch Estates (★MIA-) 5,515
Caryville 724
Casselberry (★ORL) 9,438
Cedar Grove (★PNCY) 689
Cedar Key 714
Century 2,679
Chattahoochee 7,944
Chiefland 1,965
Chipley 3,347
Clair-Mel City (★TAM) 5,300
Clearwater (★★ST.PET-) 52,074
Clermont 3,661
Clewiston 3,896
Cocoa (★93,200; COCO) 16,110
Cocoa Beach (★COCO) 9,952
Cocoa West (★COCO) 5,779
Coconut Creek (★MIA-) 1,359
Coleman 614
Collier (★MIA-) 1,200
Collier Manor (★MIA-) 1,200
Colonial Hills 2,193
Conway (★ORL) 8,642
Copper City (★MIA-) 2,535
Coral Cove (★SAR-B) 1,520
Coral Gables (★MIA-) 42,494
Coral Springs (★MIA-) 1,489
Coral Way Village (★MIA-) 1,200
Cottondale 765
Country Club Estates (*Columbia co.*) 1,500
Country Club Estates (★LKLD) 4,000
Country Estates 1,950
Crescent City 1,734
Cresthaven (★MIA-) 6,000
Crestview (★MIA-) 4,300
Crestview 7,952
Cross City 2,268
Crystal Lake (Lake Holloway) (★LKLD) 6,227
Crystal River 1,696
Cutler Ridge (★MIA-) 17,441
Cypress Gardens (★WNHV) 2,460
Cypress Quarters 1,310
Dade City 4,241
Dade City East 1,163
Dade City North 1,837
Dania (★MIA-) 9,013
Davenport 1,303
Davie (★MIA-) 4,977
Daytona Beach (★103,000; D.BCH) 45,327
Daytona Beach Shores (★D.BCH) 768
De Bary 3,154
Deerfield Beach 16,662
De Funiak Springs 4,966
De Land 11,641
De Leon Springs 1,134
Delray Beach 19,366
Deltona 4,868
Destin (★FTWL) 1,536
Dover 2,094
Dundee 1,660
Dunedin (★ST.PET-) 17,639
Dunnellon 1,146
Eagle Lake (★WNHV) 1,373
East Auburndale (★WNHV) 2,621
East Lake Park (★TAM) 1,000
East Naples 6,152
East Palatka 1,446
Eastpoint 1,188
East Winter Haven (★WNHV) 1,148
Eatonville (★ORL) 2,024
Edgewater 3,348
Ellenton (★SAR-B) 1,421
Eloise (★WNHV) 1,504
Eloise Woods (★WNHV.) 1,300
El Portal (★MIA-) 2,068
El Ranchero Village (★SAR-B) 1,859
Englewood 5,108
Ensley (★PENS) 2,200
Eustis 6,722
Fairview Shores (★ORL) 3,500
Fairvilla (★ORL) 1,500
Fellsmere 813
Fernandina Beach 6,955
Fern Crest Village (★MIA-) 1,009
Fern Park (★ORL) 2,000
Five Points 1,214
Flagler Beach 1,042
Florida City (★MIA-) 5,133
Florida Ridge 1,338
Forest Hills 1,215
Forest Hills (★TAM) 3,500
Fort Lauderdale (★★MIA-) 139,590
Fort Meade 4,374
Fort Myers (★66,500; FTMY) 27,351
Fort Myers Beach 4,305
Fort Myers Southeast (★FTMY) 3,150
Fort Myers Southwest (★FTMY) 5,086
Fort Myers Villas (★FTMY) 2,000
Fort Pierce (★47,600; FTPI) 29,721
Fort Walton Beach (★70,800; FTWL) 19,994
Freeport 900
Frostproof 2,814
Fruitland Park 1,359
Fruitville (★SAR-B) 1,531
Gainesville (★82,100; GAIN) 64,510
Gibsonton (★TAM) 2,500
Gifford 5,772
Glenvar Heights (★MIA-) 1,500
Golden Beach (★MIA-) 849
Goldenrod (★ORL) 1,000
Goulds (★MIA-) 6,690
Graceville 2,560
Grand Ridge 512
Greenacres City (★WPB) 1,731
Green Cove Springs 3,857
Green Hills (★MIA-) 2,600
Greensboro 716
Greenville 1,141
Greenwood 1,130
Gretna 883
Grove City 1,252
Groveland 1,928
Grove Park Estates (★TAM) 2,400
Gulf Breeze (★PENS) 4,190
Gulf Gate Estates (★SAR-B) 5,874
Gulf Harbors 1,177
Gulfport (★ST.PET-) 9,730
Haines City 8,956
Hallandale (★MIA-) 23,849
Harbor Bluffs (★ST.PET-) 1,200
Harlem 2,006
Havana 2,022
Haverhill (★WPB) 1,034
Hawthorne (Hawthorn) 1,126
Hernando 524
Hialeah (★MIA-) 102,452
Highland City (★LKLD) 1,300
High Springs 2,787
Hiland Park (★PNCY) 3,691
Hilliard 1,205
Hillsboro Beach (★MIA-) 713
Hobe Sound 2,029
Holden Heights (★ORL) 6,206
Holiday Gardens 2,132
Holiday Hills 1,657
Holly Hill (★D.BCH) 8,191
Hollywood (★MIA-) 106,873
Holmes Beach (★SAR-B) 2,699
Homestead (★MIA-) 13,674
Hudson 2,278
Immokalee 3,764
Indialantic (★MELB) 2,685
Indian Harbour Beach (★MELB) 5,371
Indian Rocks Beach (★ST.PET-) 2,666
Indian Rocks Beach South Shore (★ST.PET-) 791
Indiantown 2,283
Inverness 2,299
Inwood (West Winter Haven) (★WNHV) 7,716
Islamorada 1,251
Ives Estates (★MIA-) 2,400
Jacksonville (★548,500; JAX) 528,865
Jan-Phyl Village (★WNHV) 1,340
Jasmine Estates 2,967
Jasper 2,221
Jay 646
Jennings 582
June Park (★MELB) 3,090
Juno Beach (★WPB) 747
Jupiter (★WPB) 3,136
Kendall (★MIA-) 25,000
Kenneth City (★ST.PET-) 3,862
Kensington Park (★SAR-B) 3,138
Key Biscayne (★MIA-) 4,500
Key Largo 2,866
Keystone Heights 800
Key West 29,312
Kissimmee 7,119
La Belle 1,823
Lacoochee 1,380
Lake Alfred (★WNHV) 2,847
Lake Butler 1,598
Lake City 10,575
Lake Clarke Shores (★WPB) 2,328
Lake Forest (★MIA-) 5,216
Lake Hamilton 836
Lake Helen 1,303
Lakeland (★88,600; LKLD) 41,550
Lake Lucerne (★MIA-) 1,250
Lake Magdalene (★TAM) 9,266
Lake Park (★WPB) 6,993
Lake Placid 656
Lake Shipp Heights (★WNHV) 1,114
Lake Wales 8,240
Lake Worth (★WPB) 23,714
Lantana (★WPB) 7,126
Largo (★ST.PET-) 22,031
Lauderdale-by-the-Sea (★MIA-) 2,879
Lauderdale Isles (★MIA-) 2,000
Lauderdale Lakes (★MIA-) 10,577
Lauderhill (★MIA-) 8,465
Laurel 1,000
Lawtey 636
Lealman (Lellman) (★ST.PET-) 19,000
Leesburg 11,869
Lehigh Acres 4,394
Leisure City (★MIA-) 4,500
Lighthouse Point (★MIA-) 9,071
Live Oak 6,830
Lockhart (★ORL) 5,809
Longboat Key (★SAR-B) 2,850
Longwood (★ORL) 3,203
Lynn Haven (★PNCY) 4,044
MacClenny 2,733
Madeira Beach (★ST.PET-) 4,342
Madison 3,737
Maitland (★ORL) 7,157
Malabar (★MELB) 634
Malone 667
Mangonia Park (★WPB) 827
Marathon 4,397
Margate (★MIA-) 8,867
Marianna 6,741
Mary Esther (★FTWL) 3,192
Mascotte 966
Mayo 793
Meadowbrook (★JAX) 2,000
Meadow Park (★WPB) 700
Melbourne (★93,600; MELB) 40,236
Melbourne Beach (★MELB) 2,262
Melbourne Village (★MELB) 597
Melrose Park (★MIA-) 6,111
Memphis (★SAR-B) 3,207
Merritt Island (★COCO) 29,223
Mexico Beach 588
Miami (★1,864,200; MIA-) 334,859
Miami Beach (★MIA-) 87,072
Miami Lakes (★MIA-) 3,000
Miami Shores (★MIA-) 9,425
Miami Springs (★MIA-) 13,279
Micanopy 759
Midway 2,060
Milton 5,360
Mims (★TITUS) 8,309
Minneola 878
Miramar (★MIA-) 23,973
Monticello 2,473
Moore Haven 974
Mount Dora 4,543
Mulberry 2,701
Myrtle Grove (★PENS) 16,186
Naples 12,042
Naples Park 1,522
Naranja (★MIA-) 2,500
Newberry 1,247
New Port Richey 6,098
New Port Richey East 2,758
New Smyrna Beach 10,580
Niceville (★FTWL) 4,024
Nokomis 2,240
Norland (★MIA-) 18,000
North Andrews Gardens (North Andrews Terrace) (★MIA-) 7,082
North Bay Village (North Bay) (★MIA-) 4,831
North Fort Myers (★FTMY) 8,798
North Lauderdale (★MIA-) 1,213
North Miami (★MIA-) 34,767
North Miami Beach (★MIA-) 30,723
North Naples 3,201
North Orlando (★ORL) 1,161
North Palm Beach (★WPB) 9,035
North Port Charlotte 2,244
North Winter Haven (★WNHV) 1,659
Oak Hill 747
Oakland 672
Oakland Park (★MIA-) 16,261
Ocala 22,583
Ocala West (West End) 5,289
Ocean Breeze Park (Ocean Breeze) 714
Ocean City (★FTWL) 5,267
Ocean Ridge 1,074
Ocoee (★ORL) 3,937
Ojus (★MIA-) 2,000
Okeechobee 3,715
Oldsmar (★TAM) 1,538
Olympia Heights (★MIA-) 8,000
Oneco (★SAR-B) 3,246
Opa Locka (Opa-Locka) (★MIA-) 11,902
Orange City 1,777
Orange Park (★JAX) 7,619
Orient Park (★TAM) 1,700
Orlando (★363,700; ORL) 99,006
Orlovista (★ORL) 3,800
Ormond Beach (★D.BCH) 14,063
Ormond-by-the-Sea (★D.BCH) 6,002
Osprey (★SAR-B) 1,115
Oviedo 1,870
Ozona (★ST.PET-) 1,000
Pace 1,776
Pahokee 5,663
Palatka 9,444
Palma Sola (★SAR-B) 1,745
Palm Bay (★MELB) 7,199
Palm Beach (★WPB) 9,086
Palm Beach Gardens (★WPB) 6,102
Palm Beach Shores (★WPB) 1,241
Palm City 950
Palmetto (★SAR-B) 7,422
Palmetto Estates (★MIA-) 4,000
Palm Harbor (★ST.PET-) 3,000
Palm River (★TAM) 3,200
Palm Springs (★WPB) 4,340
Palm Springs North (★MIA-) 3,000
Panama City (★70,700; PNCY) 32,096
Panama City Beach (★PNCY) 1,370
Parker (★PNCY) 4,212
Pembroke Park (★MIA-) 2,949
Pembroke Pines (★MIA-) 15,520
Penney Farms 561
Pensacola (★196,100; PENS) 59,507
Perrine (★MIA-) 10,257
Perry 7,701
Pierson 654
Pine Castle (★ORL) 4,500
Pinecraft (Pine Craft) (★SAR-B) 1,208
Pine Crest (Leto) (★TAM) 8,458
Pine Hills (★ORL) 13,882
Pinellas Park (★ST.PET-) 22,287
Pine Shores (★SAR-B) 1,145
Pinewood (★MIA-) 7,000
Plantation (★MIA-) 23,523
Plant City 15,451
Pomona Park 578
Pompano Beach (★MIA-) 38,544
Pompano Beach Highlands (★MIA-) 5,014
Ponte Vedra Beach (★JAX) 1,300
Port Charlotte 10,769
Port Orange (★D.BCH) 3,781
Port Richey 1,259
Port Saint Joe 4,401
Port Salerno (Salerno) 1,161
Princeton (★MIA-) 1,800
Progress Village (★TAM) 2,573
Punta Gorda 3,879
Quincy 8,334
Redington Beach (★ST.PET-) 1,583
Redington Shores (★ST.PET-) 1,733
Richmond Heights (★MIA-) 6,663
Ridge Wood Heights (★SAR-B) 2,528
Riverland Village (★MIA-) 3,500
Riverview (★TAM) 2,225
Riviera Beach (★WPB) 21,401
Rockdale Keys (★MIA-) 1,500
Rock Island Village (★MIA-) 2,000
Rockledge (★COCO) 10,523
Rocky Creek (★TAM) 3,000
Ruskin 2,414
Safety Harbor (★ST.PET-) 3,103
St. Augustine 12,352
St. Cloud 5,041
St. Leo 1,145
St. Petersburg (★509,300; ST.PET-) 216,232
St. Petersburg Beach (★ST.PET-) 8,024
Samoset (★SAR-B) 4,070
Sanford 17,393
Sarasota (★187,800; SAR-B) 40,237
Sarasota North (★SAR-B) 1,737
Sarasota South (★SAR-B) 3,730
Saratoga Springs (★SAR-B) 4,405
Satellite Beach (★MELB) 6,558
Sea Ranch Lakes (★MIA-) 660
Sebastian 825
Sebring 7,223
Seminole (★ST.PET-) 20,000
Seminole Park (★ST.PET-) 3,500
Siesta Key (★SAR-B) 4,460
Sky Lake (★ORL) 3,500
Snapper Creek Park (★MIA-) 1,600
Sneads 1,550
Solana 1,286
South Apopka (★ORL) 2,293
South Bay 2,958
South Daytona (Blake) (★D.BCH) 4,979
Southgate (Sarasota Southeast) (★SAR-B) 6,885
South Gate Ridge (★SAR-B) 940
South Miami (★MIA-) 11,780
South Miami Heights (★MIA-) 5,000
South Pasadena (★ST.PET-) 2,063
South Patrick Shores (★MELB) 10,313
South Peninsula (★D.BCH) 3,302
Southport (★PNCY) 1,560
South Venice 1,800
Springfield (★PNCY) 5,949
Starke 4,848
Stuart 4,820
Sun City Center 2,143
Sunrise Golf Village (★MIA-) 7,403
Surfside (★MIA-) 3,614
Sweetwater (★MIA-) 3,357
Sweetwater Creek (★TAM) 10,000
Taft (★ORL) 1,183
Tahitian Gardens 1,286
Tallahassee (★92,900; TALL) 72,586
Tamarac (★MIA-) 5,078
Tampa (★439,400; TAM) 277,767
Tangelo Park (★ORL) 2,000
Tarpon Springs 7,118
Tavares 3,261
Temple Terrace (★TAM) 7,347
Tequesta (★WPB) 2,642
Tice (★FTMY) 7,254
Titusville (★41,800; TITUS) 30,515
Trailer Estates (★SAR-B) 1,759
Treasure Island (★ST.PET-) 6,120
Trenton 1,074
Tri Par Estates (★SAR-B) 1,080
Uleta (★MIA-) 2,500
Umatilla 1,600
Union Park (★ORL) 3,166
University of South Florida (University) (★TAM) 10,039
University Park 1,032
Valparaiso (★FTWL) 6,504
Venice Gardens 1,500
Venice (Venice City) 6,648
Vernon 691
Vero Beach 11,908
Vero Beach South 7,330
Virginia Gardens (★MIA-) 2,524
Wahneta (★WNHV) 2,733
Waldo 800
Warrington (★PENS) 15,848
Washington Park (★MIA-) 5,000
Wauchula 3,007
Waverly 1,172
Webster 739
West Auburndale (★WNHV) 2,148
West Bradenton (★SAR-B) 6,162
Westchester (★MIA-) 2,000
West Eau Gallie (★MELB) 2,705
Westgate (★WPB) 3,000
West Hollywood (★MIA-) 3,900
West Melbourne (★MELB) 3,050
West Miami (★MIA-) 5,494
West Palm Beach (★232,900; WPB) 57,375
West Pensacola (★PENS) 20,924
Westview (★MIA-) 4,000
Westwood Lakes (★MIA-) 12,811
Wewahitchka 1,733
White Springs 767
Whitefield Estates (★SAR-B) 1,362
Wildwood 2,082
Williston 1,939
Wilton Manors (★MIA-) 10,948
Windermere (★ORL) 894
Winston (★LKLD) 4,505
Winter Garden 5,153
Winter Haven (★60,700; WNHV) 16,136
Winter Park (★ORL) 21,895
Zephyrhills 3,369
Zolfo Springs 1,117

GEORGIA

1970 C 4,589,575

Counties

Appling 12,726
Atkinson 5,879
Bacon 8,233
Baker 3,875
Baldwin 34,240
Banks 6,833
Barrow 16,859
Bartow 32,663
Ben Hill 13,171
Berrien 11,556
Bibb 143,418
Bleckley 10,291
Brantley 5,940

(Georgia continued)

★ Population or designation of metropolitan area, including suburbs (see headnote).
▲ Population of entire "town" or township, including other communities and rural areas.
† Population is from a local census taken at date specified.

(Georgia continued)

Brooks	13,739
Bryan	6,539
Bulloch	31,585
Burke	18,255
Butts	10,560
Calhoun	6,606
Camden	11,334
Candler	6,412
Carroll	45,404
Catoosa	28,271
Charlton	5,680
Chatham	187,767
Chattahoochee	25,813
Chattooga	20,541
Cherokee	31,059
Clarke	65,177
Clay	3,636
Clayton	98,043
Clinch	6,405
Cobb	196,793
Coffee	22,828
Colquitt	32,200
Columbia	22,327
Cook	12,129
Coweta	32,310
Crawford	5,748
Crisp	18,087
Dade	9,910
Dawson	3,639
Decatur	22,310
De Kalb	415,387
Dodge	15,658
Dooly	10,404
Dougherty	89,639
Douglas	28,659
Early	12,682
Echols	1,924
Effingham	13,632
Elbert	17,262
Emanuel	18,189
Evans	7,290
Fannin	13,357
Fayette	11,364
Floyd	73,742
Forsyth	16,928
Franklin	12,784
Fulton	607,592
Gilmer	8,956
Glascock	2,280
Glynn	50,528
Gordon	23,570
Grady	17,826
Greene	10,212
Gwinnett	72,349
Habersham	20,691
Hall	59,405
Hancock	9,019
Haralson	15,927
Harris	11,520
Hart	15,814
Heard	5,354
Henry	23,724
Houston	62,924
Irwin	8,036
Jackson	21,093
Jasper	5,760
Jeff Davis	9,425
Jefferson	17,174
Jenkins	8,332
Johnson	7,727
Jones	12,218
Lamar	10,688
Lanier	5,031
Laurens	32,738
Lee	7,044
Liberty	17,569
Lincoln	5,895
Long	3,746
Lowndes	55,112
Lumpkin	8,728
Mc Duffie	15,276
Mc Intosh	7,371
Macon	12,933
Madison	13,517
Marion	5,099
Meriwether	19,461
Miller	6,397
Mitchell	18,956
Monroe	10,991
Montgomery	6,099
Morgan	9,904
Murray	12,986
Muscogee	167,377
Newton	26,282
Oconee	7,915
Oglethorpe	7,598
Paulding	17,520
Peach	15,990
Pickens	9,620
Pierce	9,281
Pike	7,316
Polk	29,656
Pulaski	8,066
Putnam	8,394
Quitman	2,180
Rabun	8,327
Randolph	8,734
Richmond	162,437
Rockdale	18,152
Schley	3,097
Screven	12,591
Seminole	7,059
Spalding	39,514
Stevens	20,331
Stewart	6,511
Sumter	26,931
Talbot	6,625
Taliaferro	2,423
Tattnall	16,557
Taylor	7,865
Telfair	11,381
Terrell	11,416
Thomas	34,515
Tift	27,288
Toombs	19,151
Towns	4,565
Treutlen	5,647
Troup	44,466
Turner	8,790
Twiggs	8,222
Union	6,811
Upson	23,505
Walker	50,691
Walton	23,404
Ware	33,525
Warren	6,669
Washington	17,480
Wayne	17,858
Webster	2,362
Wheeler	4,596
White	7,742
Whitfield	55,108
Wilcox	6,998
Wilkes	10,184
Wilkinson	9,393
Worth	14,770

Cities

Abbeville	781
Acworth (★ATL)	3,929
Adairsville	1,676
Adel	4,972
Adrian	705
Alamo	833
Alapaha	633
Albany (★87,600; ALB)	72,623
Alma (★ALB)	3,765
Alpharetta (★ATL)	2,455
Americus	16,091
Arlington	1,698
Arrowhead Village (★ATL)	1,200
Ashburn	4,209
Athens (★75,000; ATH)	44,342
Atlanta (★1,513,600; ATL)	497,421
Augusta (★218,800; AUG)	59,864
Austell (★ATL)	2,632
Avondale Estates (★ATL)	1,735
Baconton	710
Bainbridge	10,887
Baldwin	772
Ball Ground	617
Barnesville	4,935
Baxley	3,503
Belvedere Park (★ATL)	22,500
Beverly Hills (★CHTN)	1,200
Bibb City (★COL)	812
Blackshear	2,624
Blackwells (★ATL)	2,500
Blakely	5,267
Bloomingdale (★SAV)	1,588
Blue Ridge	1,602
Bogart (★ATH)	667
Boston	1,443
Bowdon	1,753
Bowman	724
Bremen	3,484
Brooklet	683
Brookwood (★ATL)	3,200
Broxton	957
Brunswick (★47,600; BRUNS)	19,587
Buchanan	800
Buena Vista	1,486
Buford	4,640
Butler	1,589
Byron (★MAC-)	1,368
Cairo	8,061
Calhoun	4,748
Camilla	4,987
Canon	709
Canton	3,654
Carnesville	510
Carrollton	13,520
Cartersville	9,929
Cave Spring (Cave Springs)	1,305
Cedartown	9,253
Centerville (★MAC-)	1,725
Chamblee (★ATL)	9,127
Chatsworth	2,706
Chickamauga (★CHTN)	1,842
Clarkesville	1,294
Clarkston (★ATL)	3,127
Claxton	2,669
Clayton	1,569
Cleveland	1,353
Cochran	5,161
College Park (★ATL)	18,203
Colquitt	2,026
Columbus (★232,500; COL)	166,565
Comer (★COL)	828
Commerce	3,702
Conyers (★ATL)	4,890
Coolidge	717
Cordele	10,733
Cornelia	3,014
Covington (★ATL)	10,267
Crawford	624
Crawfordville	735
Cumming (★ATL)	2,031
Cusseta (★COL)	1,251
Cuthbert	3,972
Dacula	782
Dahlonega	2,658
Dallas (★ATL)	2,133
Dalton	18,872
Danville	515
Darien	1,826
Dawson	5,383
Decatur (★ATL)	21,943
Deenwood	1,500
Deerwood Park (★ATL)	2,800
Demorest	1,070
Dock Junction (★BRUNS)	6,009
Doerun	1,157
Donalsonville	2,907
Doraville (★ATL)	9,157
Douglas	10,195
Douglasville (★ATL)	5,472
Druid Hills (★ATL)	3,000
Dublin	15,143
Duluth (★ATL)	1,810
Dunaire (★ATL)	5,500
Duncan Park (★CHTN)	1,600
Dunwoody (★ATL)	2,500
East Dublin	1,986
East Griffin	1,479
Eastman	5,416
East Marietta (★ATL)	5,500
East Newnan	1,634
East Point (★ATL)	39,315
Eatonton	4,125
Edison	1,210
Elberton	6,438
Elizabeth (★ATL)	1,700
Ellaville	1,391
Ellijay	1,326
Embry Hills (★ATL)	2,000
Emerson	813
Emory University (★ATL)	3,500
Enigma	505
Experiment	2,000
Fairburn (★ATL)	3,143
Fairmount	623
Fair Oaks (★ATL)	12,500
Fairview (★CHTN)	3,500
Fayetteville (★ATL)	2,160
Fitzgerald	8,187
Flowery Branch	779
Folkston	2,112
Forest Park (★ATL)	19,994
Forsyth	3,736
Fort Gaines	1,255
Fort Oglethorpe (★CHTN)	3,869
Fort Valley	9,251
Franklin	749
Gainesville	15,459
Gainesville Cotton Mills	2,060
Garden City (★SAV)	5,790
Garden Lakes (★ROME)	2,500
Georgetown	860
Gibson	701
Glen Haven (★ATL)	3,000
Glennville	2,965
Glenwood	670
Gordon	2,553
Grantville	1,128
Gray (★MAC-)	2,014
Greensboro	2,583
Greenville	1,085
Gresham Park (★ATL)	5,000
Griffin	22,734
Grovetown (★AUG)	3,169
Guyton	742
Hahira	1,326
Hampton (★ATL)	1,551
Hapeville (★ATL)	9,567
Hardwick	3,500
Harlem (★AUG)	1,540
Hartwell	4,865
Hawkinsville	4,077
Hazlehurst	4,065
Hebardville	1,000
Helena	1,230
Hephzibah	987
Hinesville	4,115
Hogansville	3,075
Holly Springs (★ATL)	575
Homeland	595
Homerville	3,025
Hoschton	509
Ideal	543
Irwinton	757
Isle of Hope (★SAV)	2,000
Jackson	3,778
Jasper	1,202
Jefferson	1,647
Jeffersonville	1,302
Jekyll Island (★BRUNS)	250
Jesup	9,091
Jonesboro (★ATL)	4,105
Kennesaw (★ATL)	3,548
Kingsland	1,831
Kingston	714
Lafayette	6,044
La Grange	23,301
Lake City (★ATL)	2,306
Lakeland	2,569
Lakeview (★CHTN)	7,000
Lakeview Estates (★ATL)	1,000
La Vista (★ATL)	5,000
Lavonia	2,044
Lawrenceville (★ATL)	5,115
Leary	907
Leesburg	996
Lenox	860
Leslie	562
Lilburn (★ATL)	1,668
Lincoln Park	1,852
Lincolnton	1,442
Lindale (★ROME)	2,768
Linwood	588
Lithia Springs (★ATL)	3,500
Lithonia (★ATL)	2,270
Locust Grove (★ATL)	642
Loganville (★ATL)	1,318
Lookout Mountain (★CHTN)	1,538
Louisville	2,691
Ludowici	1,419
Lula	736
Lumber City	1,377
Lumpkin	1,431
Lyons	3,739
Mableton (★ATL)	11,500
McCaysville	1,619
McDonough (★ATL)	2,675
Macon (★212,800; MAC-)	122,423
McRae (★MAC)	3,151
Madison	2,890
Manchester	4,779
Marietta (★ATL)	27,216
Marshallville	1,376
Maysville	553
Meigs	1,226
Menlo	593
Metter	2,912
Midville	665
Milan	1,084
Milledgeville	11,601
Millen	3,713
Milstead (★ATL)	1,157
Monroe	8,071
Montezuma	4,125
Monticello	2,132
Morrow (★ATL)	3,708
Moultrie	14,400
Mountain City	594
Mountain View (★ATL)	2,330
Mount Vernon	1,579
Nahunta	974
Nashville	4,323
Nelson	613
Newnan	11,205
Newton	624
Nicholls	1,150
Norcross (★ATL)	2,755
Norman Park	912
North Atlanta (★ATL)	16,500
North Decatur (★ATL)	11,000
North Druid Hills (★ATL)	5,000
Oak Grove (★ATL)	3,500
Ochlocknee	611
Ocilla	3,185
Oglethorpe	1,286
Omega	831
Oxford (★ATL)	1,373
Palmetto (★ATL)	2,045
Panthersville (★ATL)	13,000
Paradise Park (★SAV)	1,000
Patterson	788
Pavo	775
Peach Orchard (★AUG)	9,000
Peachtree City	793
Pearson	1,700
Pelham	4,539
Pembroke	1,361
Pendley Hills (★ATL)	4,500
Perry (★MAC-)	7,771
Phillipsburg	2,335
Pine Lake (★ATL)	866
Pine Mountain	862
Pineview	528
Plains	683
Pooler (★SAV)	1,517
Portal	643
Porterdale (★ATL)	1,773
Port Wentworth (★SAV)	3,905
Poulan	766
Powder Springs (★ATL)	2,559
Quitman	4,818
Raoul	950
Ray City	617
Red Oak (★ATL)	1,200
Rehoboth (★ATL)	1,500
Reidsville	1,806
Reynolds	1,253
Richland	1,823
Rincon (★SAV)	1,854
Ringgold (★CHTN)	1,331
Riverdale (★ATL)	2,521
Riverside (★ROME)	1,159
Roberta	746
Rochelle	1,380
Rockmart	3,857
Rome (★64,900; ROME)	30,759
Rosemont Park (★ROME)	900
Rossville (★CHTN)	3,957
Roswell (★ATL)	5,430
Royston	2,428
Rutledge	628
St. Marys	3,408
St. Simons Island (St. Simons) (★BRUNS)	5,346
Sandersville	5,546
Sandy Springs (★ATL)	11,000
Sardis	643
Sargent	900
Savannah (★193,400; SAV)	118,349
Savannah Beach (★SAV)	1,786
Scottdale (★ATL)	9,200
Screven	936
Senoia	910
Shannon (★ROME)	1,563
Shellman	1,166
Skyland (★ATL)	4,500
Smithville	713
Smyrna (★ATL)	19,157
Snellville (★ATL)	1,990
Social Circle	1,961
Soperton	2,596
South Cobb (★ATL)	1,500
South Decatur (★ATL)	22,000
Sparks	1,337
Sparta	2,172
Spencer Hills (★CHTN)	900
Springfield	1,001
State College (★SAV)	1,000
Statesboro	14,616
Statham	817
Stockbridge (★ATL)	1,561
Stone Mountain (★ATL)	1,899
Sugar Hill	1,745
Summerville	5,043
Suwanee (★ATL)	615
Swainsboro	7,325
Sycamore	547
Sylvania	3,199
Sylvester	4,226
Talbotton	1,045
Tallapoosa	2,896
Tate	900
Temple	864
Tennille	1,753
Thomaston	10,024
Thomasville	18,155
Thomson	6,503
Thunderbolt (★SAV)	2,750
Tifton	12,179
Tignall	756
Toccoa	6,971
Toco Hills (★ATL)	5,000
Toomsboro	682
Trenton (★CHTN)	1,523
Trion	1,965
Tucker (★ATL)	11,000
Tunnel Hill	1,146
Twin City	1,119
Unadilla	1,457
Union City (★ATL)	3,031
Union Point	1,624
Unionville	1,646
Uvalda	663
Valdosta (★46,300; VALD)	32,303
Vidalia	9,507
Vienna	2,341
Villa Rica	3,922
Vist-Grove (★ATL)	1,000
Wadley	1,989
Warm Springs	523
Warner Robins (★★MAC-)	33,491
Warrenton	2,073
Washington	4,094
Watkinsville (★ATH)	986
Waverly Hall	671
Waycross	18,996
Waynesboro	5,530
Westoak (★ATL)	1,500
West Point	4,232
Westside (★CHTN)	1,000
Westside *(Hall co.)*	900
Whitesburg	720
Willacoochee	1,210
Wilmington Island (★SAV)	3,284
Wilshire (★SAV)	1,200
Winder	6,605
Windsor Forest (★SAV)	7,288
Winterville (★ATH)	551
Woodbine	1,002
Woodbury	1,422
Woodland	689
Woodstock (★ATL)	870
Wrens	2,204
Wrightsville	2,106
Young Harris	544
Zebulon	776

HAWAII

1970 C **769,913**

Counties

Hawaii	63,468
Honolulu	630,528
Kauai	29,761
Maui	46,156

Cities

Aiea (★HON)	12,560
Anahola	638
Captain Cook	1,263
Eleele	758
Ewa (★HON)	2,906
Ewa Beach (★HON)	7,765
Foster Village (★HON)	3,755
Haiku	464
Hakalau	742
Halaula	450
Halawa Heights (★HON)	5,809
Haleiwa	2,626
Haliimaile	638
Hana	459
Hanamaulu	2,461
Hanapepe	1,388
Hauula (★HON)	2,048
Hawi	797
Hilo	26,353
Holualoa	700
Honokaa	1,555
Honokahua	431
Honolulu (★620,000; HON)	324,871
Honomu (★HON)	737
Honouliuli (★HON)	350
Kaaawa (★HON)	848
Kahaluu (★HON)	1,657
Kahuku (★HON)	917
Kahului	8,280
Kailua (★HON)	33,783
Kailua Kona	365
Kainaliu	500
Kalaheo	1,514
Kamuela	756
Kaneohe (★HON)	29,903
Kapaa	3,794
Kaumakani	1,014
Kaunakakai	1,070
Kawailoa Beach	375
Keaau	951
Kealakekua	740
Kealia	600
Kekaha	2,404
Keokea	500
Kihei	900
Kilauea	671
Koloa	1,368
Kualapuu	441
Kukuihaele	310
Kula	350
Kunia (★HON)	500
Kurtistown	700
Lahaina	3,718
Laie (★HON)	3,009
Lanai City	2,122
Laupahoehoe	452
Lawai	600
Lihue	3,124
Lower Paia	1,105
Maili (★HON)	4,397
Makaha (★HON)	4,644
Makakilo City (★HON)	3,499
Makawao	1,066
Makaweli	500
Maunaloa	872
Maunawili (★HON)	5,303
Mililani Town (★HON)	2,035
Mountainview	419
Naalehu	1,014
Nanakuli (★HON)	6,506
Ookala	486
Paauhau	450
Paauilo	710
Pacific Palisades (★HON)	7,846
Pahala	1,507
Pahoa	924
Paia	541
Papaaloa	319
Papaikou	1,888
Pauwela	355
Pearl City (★HON)	19,552
Pepeekeo Mill Camp	400

★ Population or designation of metropolitan area, including suburbs (see headnote).
▲ Population of entire "town" or township, including other communities and rural areas.
† Population is from a local census taken at date specified.

Poipu	466
Pomoho	340
Puhi	772
Pukalani	1,629
Punaluu (★HON)	300
Puunene	1,132
Sunset Beach	500
Volcano	300
Wahiawa (★HON)	17,598
Waialua	4,047
Waianae (★HON)	3,302
Waihee	346
Waikapu	598
Wailua	1,379
Wailuku	7,979
Waimalu (★HON)	2,982
Waimanalo (★HON)	2,081
Waimanalo Beach (★HON)	3,045
Waimea	1,569
Waipahu (★HON)	24,150
Waipio Acres (★HON)	2,146
Whitmore Village (★HON)	2,015

IDAHO

1970 C **713,008**

Counties

Ada	112,230
Adams	2,877
Bannock	52,200
Bear Lake	5,801
Benewah	6,230
Bingham	29,167
Blaine	5,749
Boise	1,763
Bonner	15,560
Bonneville	52,457
Boundary	5,484
Butte	2,925
Camas	728
Canyon	61,288
Caribou	6,534
Cassia	17,017
Clark	741
Clearwater	10,871
Custer	2,967
Elmore	17,479
Franklin	7,373
Fremont	8,710
Gem	9,387
Gooding	8,645
Idaho	12,891
Jefferson	11,740
Jerome	10,253
Kootenai	35,332
Latah	24,891
Lemhi	5,566
Lewis	3,867
Lincoln	3,057
Madison	13,452
Minidoka	15,731
Nez Perce	30,376
Oneida	2,864
Owyhee	6,422
Payette	12,401
Power	4,864
Shoshone	19,718
Teton	2,351
Twin Falls	41,807
Valley	3,609
Washington	7,633

Cities

Aberdeen	1,542
American Falls	2,769
Ammon (★IDFL)	2,545
Arco	1,244
Ashton	1,187
Bellevue	537
Blackfoot	8,716
Boise (★106,100; BOIS)	74,990
Bonners Ferry	1,909
Buhl	2,975
Burley	8,279
Caldwell	14,219
Cascade	833
Challis	784
Chubbuck (★POC)	2,924
Coeur d'Alene	16,228
Collister (★BOIS)	2,000
Cottonwood	867
Council	899
Craigmont	554
Dalton Gardens	1,559
Downey	586
Driggs	727
Emmett	3,945
Filer	1,173
Fruitland	1,576
Garden City (★BOIS)	2,368
Genesee	619
Glenns Ferry	1,386
Gooding	2,599
Grace	826
Grangeville	3,636
Hailey	1,425
Hayden	1,285
Heyburn	1,637
Homedale	1,411
Horse Shoe Bend	511
Idaho Falls (★45,500; IDFL)	35,776
Inkom	522
Iona (★IDFL)	890
Jerome	4,183
Kamiah	1,307
Kellogg	3,811
Ketchum	1,454
Kimberly	1,557
Kooskia	809
Kuna	593
Lava Hot Springs	516
Lewiston	26,068
McCall	1,758
McCammon	623
Mackay	539
Malad City	1,848
Marsing	610
Menan	545
Meridian (★BOIS)	2,616
Middleton	739
Montpelier	2,604
Moscow	14,146
Mountain Home	6,451
Mullan	1,279
Nampa	20,768
New Meadows	605
New Plymouth	986
Nezperce	555
Oakley	656
Orofino	3,883
Osburn	2,248
Paris	615
Parma	1,228
Paul	911
Payette	4,521
Pierce	1,218
Pinehurst (Pine Creek)	1,934
Pocatello (★45,000; POC)	40,036
Post Falls	2,371
Potlach	871
Preston	3,310
Priest River	1,493
Rathdrum	741
Rexburg	8,272
Rigby	2,293
Riggins	533
Ririe	575
Rupert	4,563
St. Anthony	2,877
St. Maries	2,571
Salmon	2,732
Sandpoint	4,144
Shelley	2,614
Shoshone	1,233
Smelterville	967
Soda Springs	2,977
Spirit Lake	622
Sugar City	617
Troy	541
Twin Falls	21,914
Ucon	664
Wallace	2,206
Weiser	4,108
Wendell	1,122
Wilder	564

ILLINOIS

1970 C **11,113,976**

Counties

Adams	70,861
Alexander	12,015
Bond	14,012
Boone	25,440
Brown	5,586
Bureau	38,541
Calhoun	5,675
Carroll	19,276
Cass	14,219
Champaign	163,281
Christian	35,948
Clark	16,216
Clay	14,735
Clinton	28,315
Coles	47,815
Cook	5,492,369
Crawford	19,824
Cumberland	9,772
De Kalb	71,654
De Witt	16,975
Douglas	18,997
Du Page	491,882
Edgar	21,591
Edwards	7,090
Effingham	24,608
Fayette	20,752
Ford	16,382
Franklin	38,329
Fulton	41,890
Gallatin	7,418
Greene	17,014
Grundy	26,535
Hamilton	8,665
Hancock	23,645
Hardin	4,914
Henderson	8,451
Henry	53,217
Iroquois	33,532
Jackson	55,008
Jasper	10,741
Jefferson	31,446
Jersey	18,492
Jo Daviess	21,766
Johnson	7,550
Kane	251,005
Kankakee	97,250
Kendall	26,374
Knox	61,280
Lake	382,638
La Salle	111,409
Lawrence	17,522
Lee	37,947
Livingston	40,690
Logan	33,538
McDonough	36,653
McHenry	111,555
McLean	104,389
Macon	125,010
Macoupin	44,557
Madison	250,934
Marion	38,986
Marshall	13,302
Mason	16,161
Massac	13,889
Menard	9,685
Mercer	17,294
Monroe	18,831
Montgomery	30,260
Morgan	36,174
Moultrie	13,263
Ogle	42,867
Peoria	195,318
Perry	19,757
Piatt	15,509
Pike	19,185
Pope	3,857
Pulaski	8,741
Putnam	5,007
Randolph	31,379
Richland	16,829
Rock Island	166,734
St. Clair	285,176
Saline	25,721
Sangamon	161,335
Schuyler	8,135
Scott	6,096
Shelby	22,589
Stark	7,510
Stephenson	48,861
Tazewell	118,649
Union	16,071
Vermilion	97,047
Wabash	12,841
Warren	21,595
Washington	13,780
Wayne	17,004
White	17,312
Whiteside	62,877
Will	249,498
Williamson	49,021
Winnebago	246,623
Woodford	28,012

Cities

Abingdon	3,936
Addison (★CHI) (†6/15/71)	24,200
Albany (★CLNT)	942
Albers	656
Albion	1,791
Aledo	3,325
Alexis	946
Algonquin (★CHI)	3,515
Alhambra	594
Alorton (★ST.L.)	3,573
Alpha	771
Alsip (★CHI)	11,141
Altamont	1,929
Alton (★ST.L.)	39,700
Altona	542
Amboy	2,184
Andalusia (★D-RI-M)	950
Anna	4,766
Annawan	787
Antioch (★CHI)	3,189
Arbury Hills (★CHI)	1,291
Arcola	2,276
Argenta (★DEC)	1,034
Arlington Heights (★CHI)	64,884
Aroma Park (★KANK)	896
Aroma Park Northwest (★KANK)	2,010
Arthur	2,214
Ashland	1,128
Ashley	655
Ashton	1,112
Assumption	1,487
Astoria	1,281
Athens	1,158
Atkinson	1,053
Atlanta	1,640
Atwood	1,264
Auburn	2,594
Augusta	824
Aurora (★CHI)	74,182
Ava	728
Aviston	828
Avon	1,013
Bannockburn (★CHI)	1,359
Barrington (★CHI)	8,674
Barrington Hills (★CHI) (†8/4/71)	2,920
Barry	1,444
Bartlett (★CHI)	3,501
Bartonville (★PEOR)	7,221
Batavia (★CHI)	8,994
Beach (★CHI)	3,000
Beardstown	6,222
Beckemeyer	1,069
Bedford Park (★CHI)	583
Beecher	1,770
Belleville (★St.L.)	41,699
Bellevue (★PEOR)	1,189
Bellwood (★CHI) (†8/2/71)	21,473
Belvidere (★RKFD)	14,061
Bement	1,638
Benld	1,736
Bensenville (★CHI)	12,956
Benton	6,833
Berkeley (★CHI)	6,152
Berwyn (★CHI)	52,502
Bethalto (★ST.L.) (†9/21/71)	7,332
Bethany	1,235
Blandinsville	922
Bloomingdale (★CHI) (†10/21/71)	4,434
Bloomington (★72,400; BLMNG)	39,992
Blue Island (★CHI)	22,958
Blue Mound	1,181
Bluffs	866
Bolingbrook (★CHI)	7,643
Boulder Hill (★CHI)	4,000
Bourbonnais (★KANK)	5,909
Braceville	668
Bradford	885
Bradley (★KANK)	9,881
Braidwood	2,323
Brandywine (★CHI)	5,000
Breese	2,885
Bridgeport	2,262
Bridgeview (Bridge View) (★CHI)	12,522
Brighton (★ST.L.)	1,889
Brimfield	729
Broadview (★CHI) (†9/28/71)	9,470
Brookfield (★CHI)	20,284
Brookport (★PAD)	1,046
Brownstown	689
Buckley	680
Buda	675
Buffalo Grove (P.O.) (★CHI)	11,799
Bunker Hill (†5/24/71)	1,670
Burbank (★CHI)	26,608
Burnham (★CHI)	3,634
Burr Ridge (★CHI)	1,637
Bushnell	3,703
Butterfield (★CHI)	3,000
Butterfield West (★CHI)	1,500
Byron	1,749
Cahokia (★ST.L.)	20,649
Cairo	6,277
Calumet City (★CHI)	33,107
Calumet Park (★CHI)	10,069
Cambria	798
Cambridge	2,095
Camelot (★CHI)	1,000
Camp Point	1,143
Canton	14,217
Capron	654
Carbon Cliff (★D-RI-M)	1,369
Carbondale	22,816
Carlinville	5,675
Carlyle	3,139
Carmi	6,033
Carol Stream (★CHI) (†3/7/72)	6,193
Carpentersville (★CHI)	24,059
Carriers Mills (Carrier Mills)	2,013
Carrollton	2,866
Carterville	3,061
Carthage	3,350
Cary (★CHI)	4,358
Casey	2,994
Caseyville (★ST.L.)	3,411
Catlin (★DANV)	2,093
Cave in Rock	503
Cedarville	578
Central City	1,377
Centralia	15,217
Central Park (★DANV)	1,500
Centreville (★ST.L.)	11,378
Cerro Gordo	1,368
Chadwick	605
Champaign (★119,400; CH-U)	56,532
Chandlerville	762
Channahon (★CHI) (†2/1/72)	2,690
Channel Lake (★CHI)	600
Chapin	552
Charleston	16,421
Chatham (★SPRG)	2,788
Chatsworth	1,255
Chebanse (★KANK)	1,185
Chenoa	1,860
Cherry	551
Cherry Valley (★RKFD)	952
Chester	5,310
Chicago (★7,585,300; CHI)	3,369,359
Chicago Heights (★CHI)	40,900
Chicago Ridge (★CHI) (†7/23/71)	9,847
Chillicothe (★PEOR)	6,052
Chrisman	1,285
Christopher	2,910
Cicero (★CHI)	67,058
Cisne	615
Cissna Park	773
Clarendon Hills (★CHI)	6,750
Clay City	1,049
Clayton	727
Clifton	1,339
Clinton	7,570
Cloverleaf (★ST.L.)	1,000
Coal City	3,040
Coal Valley (★D-RI-M)	3,088
Cobden	1,114
Coffeen	641
Colchester	1,747
Colfax	935
Collinsville (★ST.L.)	18,015
Colona (★D-RI-M)	1,293
Colonial Heights (★CHI)	1,200
Colonial Ridge (★CHI)	1,500
Columbia (★ST.L.)	4,188
Cordova (★D-RI-M)	589
Cornell	532
Cortland (★DKLB)	541
Cottage Hills (★ST.L.)	1,261
Coulterville	1,186
Country Club Hills (★CHI)	6,920
Countryside (★CHI)	2,864
Cowden	537
Crainville	549
Creal Springs	830
Crescent City	597
Crest Hill (★CHI)	7,460
Creston	595
Crestwood (★CHI)	5,770
Crete (★CHI)	4,656
Creve Coeur (★PEOR)	6,440
Crossville	860
Crystal Lake (★CHI)	14,541
Crystal Lawns (★CHI)	1,700
Cuba	1,581
Cullom	572
Cutler	508
Dallas City	1,284
Dalzell	579
Danvers	854
Danville (★73,500; DANV)	42,570
Darien (★CHI)	7,789
Davis	525
Decatur (★115,900; DEC)	90,397
Deer Creek	647
Deerfield (★CHI)	18,876
Deer Park (★CHI)	834
De Kalb (★46,600; DKLB)	32,949
Delavan	1,844
Depue	1,919
De Soto	723
De Soto	966
Des Plaines (★CHI)	57,239
Diamond Lake (★CHI)	1,343
Dieterich	532
Divernon	1,010
Dixmoor (★CHI)	4,735
Dixon	18,147
Dolton (★CHI)	25,937
Dongola	825
Downers Grove (★CHI)	32,751
Downs	651
Dundee (West Dundee) (★CHI)	3,295
Dunlap	656
Dupo (★ST.L.)	2,842
Du Quoin	6,691
Durand	972
Dwight	3,841
Eagle Park (★St.L.)	1,300
Earlville	1,410
East Alton (★ST.L.)	7,309
East Chicago Heights (★CHI)	5,000
East Dubuque (★DUB)	2,408
East Dundee (★CHI)	2,920
East Galesburg (★GLSB)	706
East Hazelcrest (★CHI)	1,885
East Moline (★D-RI-M)	20,832
East Peoria (★PEOR)	18,455
East St. Louis (★ST.L.)	69,996
Edinburg	1,153
Edwardsville (★ST.L.)	11,070
Effingham	9,458
Elburn (★CHI)	1,122
Eldorado	3,876
Elgin (★CHI)	55,691
Elizabeth	707
Elk Grove Village (★CHI)	21,907
Elkville	850
Elmhurst (★CHI)	48,887
Elmwood	2,014
Elmwood Park (★CHI)	26,160
El Paso	2,291
Elsah (★ST.L.)	928
Elwood	794
Energy	812
Enfield	764
Equality	732
Erie	1,566
Eureka (★PEOR)	3,028
Evanston (★CHI)	79,808
Evansville	838
Evergreen Park (★CHI) (†7/20/71)	25,981
Fairbury	3,359
Fairfield	5,897
Fairmont (★CHI)	1,500
Fairmont City (★ST.L.)	2,769
Fairmount (★ST.L.)	1,521
Fairmount	785
Fairview	601
Fairview Gardens (★CHI)	1,000
Fairview Heights (★ST.L.)	8,625
Farina	634
Farmer City	2,217
Farmington	2,959
Fernway (★CHI)	1,000
Findlay	809
Fisher	1,525
Fithian	562
Flanagan	878
Flat Rock	504
Flora	5,283
Flossmoor (★CHI)	7,846
Forest Lake (★CHI)	1,000
Forest Park (★CHI)	15,472
Forest View (★CHI)	927
Forrest	1,219
Forreston	1,227
Foxcroft (★CHI)	1,000
Fox Lake (★CHI)	4,511
Fox Lake Hills (★CHI)	1,869
Fox River (★CHI)	1,067
Fox River Grove (★CHI)	2,245
Frankfort (★CHI)	2,325
Franklin	565
Franklin Grove	968
Franklin Park (★CHI)	20,348
Freeburg (★ST.L.)	2,495
Freeport	27,736
French Village (★ST.L.)	1,500
Fruitland (★D-RI-M)	1,000
Fulton (★CLNT)	3,630
Gages Lake (★CHI)	2,000
Galatia	792
Galena	3,930
Galesburg (★43,500; GLSB) (†6/8/71)	34,501
Galva	3,061
Garden Homes (★CHI)	1,000
Gardner	1,212
Geneseo	5,840
Geneva (★CHI)	9,115
Genoa	3,003
Georgetown (★DANV)	3,984
Germantown	1,108
Gibson City	3,454
Gifford	814
Gillespie	3,457
Gilman	1,786
Girard	1,881
Glasford (★PEOR)	1,066
Glen Carbon (★ST.L.)	1,897
Glencoe (★CHI)	10,675
Glendale Heights (★CHI)	11,406
Glen Ellyn (★CHI)	21,909
Glen Ellyn Countryside (★CHI)	2,000
Glenview (★CHI)	24,880
Glenview Countryside (★CHI)	2,500
Glenwood (★CHI)	7,416
Godfrey (★ST.L.)	1,261
Golconda	922
Golden	571
Golf Park Terrace (★CHI)	1,000
Goreville	1,109
Grafton	1,018
Grand Ridge	698
Grand Tower (†9/13/71)	786
Grandview (★SPRG)	2,242
Granite City (★ST.L.)	40,440
Grant Park	914
Granville	1,232
Grayslake (Grays Lake) (★CHI)	4,907
Grayville	2,035
Greenfield	1,179
Green Oaks (★CHI)	659
Green Rock (★D-RI-M)	2,744
Greenup	1,618
Green Valley	617
Greenview	740
Greenville	4,631
Gridley	1,007

(Illinois continued)

★ Population or designation of metropolitan area, including suburbs (see headnote).
▲ Population of entire "town" or township, including other communities and rural areas.
† Population is from a local census taken at date specified.

(Illinois continued)

Griggsville....1,245
Gurnee (★CHI)....2,738
Hamilton....2,764
Hampshire....1,611
Hampton (★D-RI-M)....1,612
Hanna City (★PEOR)....1,282
Hanover....1,243
Hanover Park (★CHI)....11,916
Hardin....1,035
Harrisburg....9,535
Hartford (★ST.L.)....2,243
Harvard....5,177
Harvey (★CHI)....34,636
Harwood Heights (★CHI) (†7/7/71)....8,837
Havana....4,376
Hawthorn Woods (★CHI)....939
Hazel Crest (★CHI) (†1/4/72)....11,657
Hebron....781
Hegeler (★DANV)....1,595
Hennepin....535
Henry....2,610
Herrick....537
Herrin....9,623
Herscher....988
Heyworth....1,441
Hickory Hills (★CHI)....13,176
Highland....5,981
Highland Hills (★CHI)....1,800
Highland Park (★CHI)....32,263
Highwood (★CHI)....4,973
Hillcrest....630
Hillsboro....4,267
Hillsdale....539
Hillside (★CHI) (†6/2/71)....9,466
Hinckley....1,053
Hinsdale (★CHI)....15,918
Hodgkins (★CHI)....2,270
Hoffman Estates (★CHI) (†9/29/71)....28,512
Hollywood Heights (★ST.L.)....1,500
Homer....1,354
Hometown (★CHI)....6,729
Homewood (★CHI)....18,871
Hoopeston....6,461
Hopedale....923
Hudson....802
Hull....585
Huntley (★CHI)....1,432
Hurst....934
Hutsonville....544
Illiopolis....1,122
Industry....558
Ingalls Park (★CHI)....4,000
Ingleside (★CHI)....1,621
Inverness (★CHI)....1,674
Ipava....608
Irving....599
Island Lake (★CHI)....1,973
Itasca (★CHI)....4,638
Jacksonville....20,553
Jerome (★SPRG)....1,673
Jerseyville....7,446
Johnston City....3,928
Joliet (★CHI)....78,887
Jonesboro....1,676
Joppa....531
Joy....513
Justice (★CHI)....9,473
Kankakee (★74,900; KANK)....30,944
Kansas....779
Karnak....641
Keithsburg....836
Kenilworth (★CHI)....2,980
Ken Rock (★RKFD)....5,945
Kewanee....15,762
Kildeer (★CHI)....643
Kincaid....1,424
Kinmundy....759
Kirkland....1,138
Kirkwood....817
Knollwood (★CHI)....1,200
Knoxville (★GLSB)....2,930
Lacon....2,147
Ladd....1,328
La Grange (★CHI)....17,814
La Grange Highlands (★CHI)....6,920
La Grange Park (★CHI)....15,459
La Harpe....1,240
Lake Bluff (★CHI)....5,008
Lake Catherine (★CHI)....620
Lake Forest (★CHI)....15,642
Lake in the Hills (★CHI)....3,240
Lakemoor (★CHI)....797
Lake Villa (★CHI)....1,090
Lakewood (★CHI)....782
Lake Zurich (★CHI) (†10/13/71)....5,461
La Moille....669
Lanark....1,495
Lansing (★CHI)....25,805
La Salle....10,736
Lawrenceville....5,863
Leaf River....633
Lebanon (★ST.L.)....3,564
Leland....743
Leland Grove (★SPRG)....1,624
Lemont (★CHI)....5,080
Lena....1,722
Le Roy (Leroy)....2,435
Lewistown....2,706
Lexington....1,615
Libertyville (★CHI)....11,684
Lincoln....17,582
Lincolnshire (★CHI)....2,531
Lincolnwood (★CHI)....12,929
Lindenhurst (★CHI)....3,141
Lisle (★CHI) (†10/19/71)....6,921
Litchfield....7,190
Livingston....916
Loami....537
Lockport (★CHI)....9,985
Lomax....565
Lombard (★CHI) (†8/23/71)....37,052
London Mills....610
Long Grove (★CHI)....1,196
Long Lake (★CHI)....1,500

Louisville....1,020
Lovejoy (Brooklyn) (★ST.L.)....1,702
Loves Park (★RKFD)....12,390
Lovington....1,303
Lyndon....673
Lynwood (★CHI)....1,042
Lyons (★CHI)....11,124
McCullom Lake (★CHI)....873
McHenry (★CHI)....6,772
Mackinaw....1,293
McLean....820
McLeansboro....2,630
Macomb....19,643
Macon (★DEC)....1,249
Madison (★ST.L.)....7,042
Mahomet (★CH-U)....1,296
Malta....961
Manhattan....1,530
Manito....1,334
Mansfield....870
Manteno....2,864
Maple Park....660
Marengo....4,235
Marine....882
Marion (†3/22/72)....12,899
Marissa....2,004
Markham (★CHI)....15,987
Maroa....1,467
Marquette Heights (★PEOR)....2,758
Marseilles....4,320
Marshall....3,468
Martinsville....1,374
Maryville (★ST.L.) (†6/28/71)....1,290
Mascoutah (★ST.L.)....5,045
Mason City....2,611
Matherville....699
Matteson (★CHI)....4,741
Mattoon....19,681
Maywood (★CHI)....29,019
Mazon....727
Meadowbrook (★ST.L.)....1,295
Medinah (★CHI)....2,000
Medora....505
Melrose Park (★CHI)....22,716
Mendon....883
Mendota....6,902
Meredosia....1,178
Merrionette Park (★CHI)....2,303
Metamora (★PEOR)....2,176
Metropolis....6,940
Meyers Bay (★CHI)....1,055
Middletown....626
Midlothian (★CHI)....15,939
Milan (★D-RI-M)....4,873
Mildred (★SPRG)....1,400
Milford....1,656
Milledgeville....1,130
Millstadt (★ST.L.)....2,168
Minier....986
Minonk....2,267
Minooka (★CHI)....768
Mitchell (★ST.L.)....1,500
Moecherville (★CHI)....1,300
Mokena (★CHI)....1,643
Moline (★★D-RI-M)....46,237
Momence....2,836
Monee (★CHI)....940
Monmouth....11,022
Montgomery (★CHI)....3,278
Monticello....4,130
Mooseheart (★CHI)....1,200
Morris (†1/18/72)....8,435
Morrison....4,387
Morrisonville....1,178
Morristown (★RKFD)....669
Morton (★PEOR)....10,419
Morton Grove (★CHI)....26,369
Mound City....1,177
Mounds....1,718
Mount Auburn....520
Mount Carmel....8,096
Mount Carroll....2,143
Mount Morris....3,173
Mount Olive....2,288
Mount Prospect (★CHI)....34,995
Mount Pulaski....1,677
Mount Sterling....2,182
Mount Vernon....16,382
Mount Zion (★DEC)....2,343
Moweaqua....1,687
Mulberry Grove....697
Mundelein (★CHI)....16,128
Murphysboro....10,013
Murrayville....595
Naperville (★CHI)....23,885
Naplate....686
Nashville....3,027
Nauvoo....1,047
Neoga....1,270
Neponset....507
Newark....590
New Athens....2,000
New Baden....1,953
New Berlin....754
New Boston....706
New Haven....606
New Lenox (★CHI)....2,855
Newman....1,018
New Milford (★RKFD)....1,500
Newton....3,024
New Windsor....723
Niantic....705
Niles (★CHI) (†6/15/71)....32,432
Noble....719
Nokomis....2,532
Normal (★BLMNG)....26,396
Norridge (★CHI) (†5/25/71)....18,043
Norris City....1,319
North Aurora (★CHI)....4,833
North Barrington (★CHI)....1,411
Northbrook (★CHI)....27,297
North Chicago (★CHI)....47,275
Northfield (★CHI)....5,010
Northfield Woods (★CHI)....1,000
North Glen Ellyn (★CHI)....3,000
Northlake (North Lake) (★CHI)....14,212
North Park (★RKFD)....15,679
North Pekin (★PEOR)....1,886

North Riverside (★CHI) (†10/5/71)....7,849
North Shore Trace (★CHI)....4,000
Norwood (★PEOR)....632
Nottingham Park (★CHI)....900
Oak Brook (★CHI)....4,164
Oakbrook Terrace (★CHI)....1,126
Oak Forest (★CHI)....17,870
Oak Hills (★ST.L.)....1,000
Oakland....1,012
Oak Lawn (★CHI)....60,305
Oak Park (★CHI)....62,511
Oakwood (★DANV)....1,367
Oblong....1,860
Odell....1,076
Odin....1,263
O'Fallon (★ST.L.)....7,268
Ogden....703
Oglesby....4,175
Ohio....506
Okawville....992
Olney....8,974
Olympia Fields (★CHI)....3,478
Onarga....1,436
Oneida....728
Oquawka....1,352
Orangeville....538
Oreana (★DEC)....1,092
Oregon....3,539
Orient....502
Orion....1,801
Orland Park (★CHI) (†6/2/71)....7,297
Oswego (★CHI)....1,862
Ottawa....18,716
Palatine (★CHI)....25,904
Palestine....1,640
Palmyra....776
Palos Heights (★CHI)....9,915
Palos Hills (★CHI)....6,629
Palos Park (★CHI)....3,297
Pana....6,326
Paris....9,971
Park City (★CHI)....2,855
Park Forest (★CHI)....30,638
Park Forest South (★CHI)....1,748
Park Ridge (★CHI)....42,614
Park Ridge Manor (★CHI)....900
Patoka....562
Pawnee....1,936
Pawpaw....846
Paxton....4,373
Payson....589
Pearl City....535
Pecatonica....1,781
Pekin (★PEOR)....31,375
Pembroke (★KANK)....2,671
Peoria (★299,800; PEOR)....126,963
Peoria Heights (★PEOR)....7,943
Peotone....2,345
Percy....967
Peru....11,772
Pesotum....536
Petersburg....2,632
Petite Lake (★CHI)....1,275
Philo (★CH-U)....1,022
Phoenix (★CHI)....3,596
Pinckneyville....3,377
Piper City....817
Pittsburg....509
Pittsfield....4,244
Plainfield (★CHI)....2,928
Plano (★CHI)....4,664
Pleasant Hill....1,064
Pleasant Plains....644
Plymouth....740
Pocahontas....764
Polo....2,542
Pontiac....10,595
Pontoon Beach (★ST.L.)....2,448
Poplar Grove....607
Port Byron (★D-RI-M)....1,222
Posen (★CHI)....5,498
Potomac....909
Prairie City....630
Prairie Du Rocher....658
Preston Heights (★CHI)....1,000
Princeton....6,959
Princeville....1,455
Prophetstown....1,915
Prospect Heights (★CHI)....13,333
Quincy (★55,700; QUIN)....45,288
Ramsey....830
Randwood (★CHI)....1,000
Rankin....727
Rantoul....25,562
Rapids City (★D-RI-M)....656
Raymond....890
Red Bud....2,559
Reynolds (★D-RI-M)....610
Richmond (★CHI)....1,153
Richton Park (★CHI) (†3/13/72)....4,786
Ridge Farm....1,015
Ridgewood (★CHI) *(Cook co.)*....1,000
Ridgewood (★CHI) *(Will co.)*....3,500
Ridgway....1,160
Riverdale (★CHI)....15,806
River Forest (★CHI)....13,402
River Grove (★CHI)....11,465
Riverside (★CHI)....10,432
Riverton (★SPRG)....2,090
Riverwoods (★CHI)....1,571
Roanoke....2,040
Robbins (★CHI)....9,641
Robein (★PEOR)....1,000
Roberts....506
Roberts Park (★CHI)....1,750
Robinson....7,178
Rochelle....8,594
Rochester (★SPRG)....1,667
Rockdale (★CHI)....2,085
Rock Falls....10,287
Rockford (★244,900; RKFD)....147,370
Rock Island (★★D-RI-M)....50,166
Rockton (★BLOIT)....2,099
Rolling Meadows (★CHI)....19,178
Rome (★PEOR)....1,919
Romeoville (★CHI) (†10/15/71)....15,336
Roodhouse....2,357
Roscoe (★RKFD)....1,070

Roselle (★CHI)....6,207
Rosemont (★CHI)....4,360
Roseville....1,111
Rosewood Heights (★ST.L.)....6,620
Rosiclare....1,421
Rossville....1,420
Round Lake (★CHI)....1,531
Round Lake Beach (★CHI)....5,717
Round Lake Heights (★CHI)....1,144
Round Lake Park (★CHI)....3,148
Roxana (★ST.L.)....1,882
Royalton....1,166
Rushville....3,300
St. Anne (★KANK)....1,271
St. Charles (★CHI)....12,928
St. David....773
St. Elmo....1,676
St. Francisville....997
St. Jacob....659
St. Joseph (★CH-U)....1,554
Salem....6,187
Sandoval....1,332
Sandwich (★CHI)....5,056
San Jose....681
Sauk Village (★CHI)....7,479
Savanna....4,942
Savoy (★CH-U)....592
Saybrook....814
Schaumburg (★CHI)....18,730
Schiller Park (★CHI)....12,712
Schram City....657
Seneca....1,781
Sesser....2,125
Shabbona....730
Shannon....848
Shaw (★CHI)....1,329
Shawneetown....1,742
Sheffield....1,038
Shelbyville....4,597
Sheldon....1,455
Sheridan....724
Sherrard....808
Shiloh (★ST.L.)....945
Shorewood (★CHI)....1,749
Sidell....645
Sidney....915
Signal Hill (★ST.L.)....1,000
Silvis (★D-RI-M)....5,907
Silvis Heights (★D-RI-M)....2,000
Skokie (★CHI) (†6/28/71)....68,911
Sleepy Hollow (★CHI)....1,729
Smithton....847
Somonauk....1,112
Sorento....625
South Beloit (★BLOIT)....3,804
South Chicago Heights (★CHI)....4,923
South Elgin (★CHI)....4,289
Southern View (★SPRG)....1,504
South Holland (★CHI)....23,931
South Jacksonville....2,950
Southlawn (★SPRG)....3,000
South Park (★CHI)....2,500
South Pekin (★PEOR)....955
South Roxana (★ST.L.)....2,241
South Streator....1,869
South Wilmington....725
Sparland....585
Sparta....4,307
Springfield (★137,400; SPRG)....91,753
Spring Valley....5,605
Stanford....657
State Park Place (★ST.L.)....3,000
Staunton....4,396
Steeleville....1,957
Steger (★CHI)....8,104
Sterling....16,113
Sterling West....2,171
Stewardson....729
Stickney (★CHI)....6,601
Stillman Valley....871
Stockton....1,930
Stone Park (★CHI)....4,429
Stonington....1,096
Streamwood (★CHI)....18,176
Streator....15,600
Streator East....1,660
Stronghurst....836
Sugar Grove (★CHI)....1,230
Sullivan....4,112
Summit (★CHI)....11,569
Sumner....1,201
Sunny Crest (★CHI)....930
Sunnyland (★PEOR)....4,000
Sunset Trailer Park (★CHI)....1,100
Swansea (★ST.L.)....5,432
Sycamore (★DKLB)....7,843
Tallula....643
Tamaroa....799
Tamms....645
Tampico....838
Taylor Springs....620
Taylorville....10,927
Teutopolis....1,249
Thayer....616
Thomasboro (★CH-U)....806
Thomson....617
Thornton (★CHI)....3,714
Tilden....909
Tilton (★DANV)....2,544
Tinley Park (★CHI)....12,382
Tiskilwa....973
Toledo....1,068
Tolono (★CH-U)....2,027
Toluca....1,319
Tonica....821
Toulon....1,207
Towanda....578
Tower Hill....683
Tower Lakes (★CHI)....932
Tremont (★PEOR)....1,942
Trenton....2,328
Tristate Village (★CHI)....1,700
Troy (★ST.L.)....2,144
Truro....537
Tuscola....3,917
Ullin....546
Union....579
Urbana (★★CH-U)....32,800

Utica (North Utica)....974
Valier....628
Valley View (★CHI)....1,723
Valmeyer....733
Vandalia....5,160
Venetian Village (★CHI)....2,554
Venice (★ST.L.)....4,680
Vermont....947
Vernon Hills (★CHI)....1,056
Vicic (★PEOR)....900
Vienna....1,325
Villa Grove....2,605
Villa Hills (★ST.L.)....1,585
Villa Park (★CHI) (†7/7/71)....25,546
Viola....946
Virden....3,504
Virginia....1,814
Wadsworth (★CHI)....756
Walnut....1,295
Wamac....1,347
Wapella....572
Warren....1,523
Warrensburg....738
Warrenville (★CHI)....3,268
Warsaw....1,758
Washburn....1,173
Washington (★PEOR)....6,790
Washington Park (★ST.L.)....9,524
Wataga....570
Waterloo (★ST.L.)....4,546
Waterman....990
Watseka....5,294
Wauconda (★CHI)....5,460
Waukegan (★CHI)....65,269
Waverly....1,442
Wayne (★CHI)....572
Wayne City....985
Waynesville....522
Weldon....553
Wenona....1,080
Westchester (★CHI)....20,033
West Chicago (★CHI)....10,111
West City....637
Westdale (★CHI)....3,500
West End (★RKFD)....7,054
Western Springs (★CHI)....13,029
Westfield....678
West Frankfort....8,854
Westmont (★CHI)....8,920
West Peoria (★PEOR)....6,873
West Salem....979
West Vermilion Heights (★DANV)....1,000
Westville (★DANV)....3,655
Wheaton (★CHI)....31,138
Wheeling (★CHI)....14,746
White Hall....2,979
Wildwood (★CHI)....3,000
Williamsfield....552
Williamsville....923
Willisville....659
Willowbrook (★CHI)....1,169
Willow Springs (★CHI)....3,318
Wilmette (★CHI)....32,134
Wilmington....4,335
Wilsonville....691
Winchester....1,788
Windsor....1,126
Winfield (★CHI)....4,285
Winnebago (★RKFD)....1,285
Winnetka (★CHI)....13,998
Winthrop Harbor (★CHI)....4,794
Witt....1,040
Wonder Lake (★CHI)....4,806
Wood Dale (Wooddale) (★CHI)....8,831
Woodhull....898
Woodridge (★CHI)....11,028
Wood River (★ST.L.)....13,186
Woodstock....10,226
Worden....1,091
Worth (★CHI) (†4/30/71)....12,153
Wyanet....1,005
Wyoming....1,563
Yates City....840
York Center (★CHI)....1,700
Yorkfield (★CHI)....1,000
Yorkville (★CHI)....2,049
Zeigler....1,940
Zion (★CHI)....17,268

INDIANA

1970 C....5,193,669

Counties

Adams....26,871
Allen....280,455
Bartholomew....57,022
Benton....11,262
Blackford....15,888
Boone....30,870
Brown....9,057
Carroll....17,734
Cass....40,456
Clark....75,876
Clay....23,933
Clinton....30,547
Crawford....8,033
Daviess....26,602
Dearborn....29,430
Decatur....22,738
De Kalb....30,837
Delaware....129,219
Dubois....30,934
Elkhart....126,529
Fayette....26,216
Floyd....55,622
Fountain....18,257
Franklin....16,943
Fulton....16,984
Gibson....30,444
Grant....83,955
Greene....26,894
Hamilton....54,532
Hancock....35,096
Harrison....20,423
Hendricks....53,974

★ Population or designation of metropolitan area, including suburbs (see headnote).
▲ Population of entire "town" or township, including other communities and rural areas.
† Population is from a local census taken at date specified.

Henry	52,603
Howard	83,198
Huntington	34,970
Jackson	33,187
Jasper	20,429
Jay	23,575
Jefferson	27,006
Jennings	19,454
Johnson	61,138
Knox	41,546
Kosciusko	48,127
La Grange	20,890
Lake	546,253
La Porte	105,342
Lawrence	38,038
Madison	138,451
Marion	792,299
Marshall	34,986
Martin	10,969
Miami	39,246
Monroe	84,849
Montgomery	33,930
Morgan	44,176
Newton	11,606
Noble	31,382
Ohio	4,289
Orange	16,968
Owen	12,163
Parke	14,600
Perry	19,075
Pike	12,281
Porter	87,114
Posey	21,740
Pulaski	12,534
Putnam	26,932
Randolph	28,915
Ripley	21,138
Rush	20,352
St. Joseph	245,045
Scott	17,144
Shelby	37,797
Spencer	17,134
Starke	19,280
Steuben	20,159
Sullivan	19,889
Switzerland	6,306
Tippecanoe	109,378
Tipton	16,650
Union	6,582
Vanderburgh	168,772
Vermillion	16,793
Vigo	114,528
Wabash	35,553
Warren	8,705
Warrick	27,972
Washington	19,278
Wayne	79,109
Wells	23,821
White	20,995
Whitley	23,395

Cities

Advance	561
Akron	1,019
Albany (★MUN)	2,293
Albion	1,498
Alexandria (★AND)	5,168
Anderson (★142,100; AND)	70,787
Andrews	1,207
Angola	5,117
Arcadia	1,338
Ardmore (★S.B.-)	1,900
Argos	1,393
Ashley	721
Atlanta	620
Attica	4,262
Auburn	7,388
Aurora	4,293
Austin	4,902
Avilla	881
Bainbridge	703
Bargersville (★IND)	873
Batesville	3,799
Battle Ground (★LAF)	818
Bedford	13,087
Beech Grove (★IND)	13,832
Berne	2,988
Beverly Shores (★CHI)	946
Bicknell	3,717
Black Oak (★CHI)	9,624
Bloomfield	2,565
Bloomington (★75,300; BLMNG)	42,890
Bluffton	8,297
Boonville	5,736
Boswell	998
Bourbon	1,606
Brazil	8,163
Bremen	3,487
Bristol (★S.B.-)	1,100
Broadview (★BLMNG)	2,362
Brook	919
Brooklyn (★IND)	911
Brookston	1,232
Brookville	2,864
Brownsburg (★IND)	5,751
Brownstown	2,376
Bruceville	627
Bunker Hill	956
Burlington	685
Burnettsville	510
Burns Harbor (★CHI)	1,284
Butler	2,394
Cambridge City	2,481
Camden	577
Campbellsburg	678
Cannelton	2,280
Carlisle	714
Carmel (★IND)	6,568
Carthage	946
Cayuga	1,090
Cedar Lake (★CHI)	7,589
Centerville (★RICH)	2,380
Chalmers	544
Chandler (★EV)	2,032
Charlestown (★LOU)	5,933
Chesterfield (★AND)	3,001
Chesterton (★CHI)	6,177
Chrisney	550
Churubusco	1,528
Cicero	1,378
Clarks Hill	741
Clarksville (★LOU)	13,806
Clay City	900
Clayton (★IND)	736
Clinton (★T.H.)	5,340
Cloverdale	870
Colfax	633
College Meadows (★IND)	1,000
Columbia City	4,911
Columbus (★53,500; COL)	26,457
Connersville	17,604
Converse	1,163
Corydon	2,719
Covington	2,641
Crawfordsville	13,842
Creston (★MUN)	900
Crothersville	1,663
Crown Point (★CHI)	10,931
Culver	1,783
Cynthiana	793
Dale	1,113
Daleville (★AND)	1,730
Dana	720
Danville (★IND)	3,771
Darlington	802
Dayton	850
Decatur	8,445
Delphi	2,582
De Motte (★CHI)	1,697
Denver	566
Devon Park (★MUN)	1,000
Dillsboro	840
Dublin	1,021
Dugger	1,150
Dunkirk	3,465
Dunlap (★S.B.-)	3,500
Dyer (★CHI)	4,906
East Chicago (★CHI)	46,982
East Gary (★CHI)	9,858
Eaton	1,594
Edgewood (★AND)	2,326
Edinburg	4,906
Elberfeld	834
Elizabethtown (★COL)	519
Elkhart (★★S.B.-)	43,152
Ellettsville (★BLMNG)	1,627
Elnora	873
Elwood (★AND)	11,196
Englewood	1,219
English	664
Etna Green	516
Evansville (★204,200; EV)	138,764
Fairmount (★MRN)	3,427
Fairview Park (★T.H.)	1,067
Farmersburg	962
Farmland (★MUN)	1,262
Ferdinand	1,432
Fishers (★IND)	628
Fish Lake	900
Flora	1,877
Fort Branch	2,535
Fortville (★IND)	2,460
Fort Wayne (★274,400; FTWA)	178,021
Fountain City (★RICH)	852
Fowler	2,643
Francesville	1,015
Francisco	621
Frankfort	14,956
Franklin	11,477
Frankton (★AND)	1,796
Fremont	1,043
French Lick	2,059
Galveston	1,284
Garrett	4,715
Gary (★CHI)	175,415
Gas City (★MRN)	5,742
Gaston	928
Geneva	1,100
Georgetown (★LOU)	1,273
Gilmer Park (★S.B.-)	1,850
Glen Park West (★CHI)	5,940
Goodland	1,176
Goshen	18,004
Gosport	692
Grabill (★FTWA)	570
Grandview	696
Greencastle	8,852
Greendale	3,783
Greenfield (★IND)	9,986
Greensburg	8,620
Greentown (★KOK)	1,870
Greenville (★LOU)	611
Greenwood (★IND)	11,408
Griffith (★CHI)	18,168
Hagerstown	2,059
Halteman Village (★MUN)	1,000
Hamilton	537
Hamlet	761
Hammond (★CHI)	107,790
Hanover	3,018
Harmony	750
Hartford City	8,207
Haubstadt (★EV)	1,171
Hebron (★CHI)	1,624
Highland (★CHI)	24,947
Hillsboro	505
Hobart (★CHI)	21,485
Holland	662
Home Corner (★MRN)	900
Home Place (★IND)	1,000
Hope (★COL)	1,603
Hudson Lake	1,134
Huntertown (★FTWA)	775
Huntingburg	4,794
Huntington	16,217
Hymera	907
Independence Hill (★CHI)	900
Indianapolis (★976,900; IND)	745,739
Indian Heights (★KOK)	4,000
Ingalls (★AND)	888
Jamestown	938
Jasonville	2,335
Jasper	8,641
Jeffersonville (★LOU)	20,008
Jonesboro (★MRN)	2,466
Kendallville	6,838
Kennard	518
Kentland	1,864
Kewanna	614
Kingman	530
Kingsford Heights	1,200
Kirklin	736
Knightstown	2,456
Knightsville	788
Knox	3,519
Kokomo (★81,200; KOK)	44,042
Koontz Lake	900
Kouts	1,388
La Crosse	696
Ladoga	1,099
Lafayette (★101,000; LAF)	44,955
La Fontaine	793
Lagrange	2,053
Lagro	552
Lakeville (★S.B.-)	712
Lanesville	586
Lapaz (La Paz)	604
Lapel (★AND)	1,796
La Porte	22,140
Laurel	753
Lawrence (★IND)	16,646
Lawrenceburg	4,636
Lebanon	9,766
Leesburg	561
Lewisville	530
Liberty	1,831
Ligonier	3,034
Linden	713
Linden Park (★MUN)	1,000
Linton	5,450
Liverpool (★CHI)	2,200
Logansport	19,255
Long Beach (★MICH)	2,740
Loogootee	2,953
Lowell (★CHI)	3,839
Lydick (★S.B.-)	1,341
Lynn	1,360
Lynnville	556
Lyons	702
Madison	13,081
Marengo	767
Marion (★70,700; MRN)	39,607
Markle	963
Martinsville	9,723
Matthews	728
Mayfield (★MUN)	2,500
Meadowbrook (★FTWA)	2,300
Medaryville	732
Medora	788
Mentone	830
Merrillville (★CHI)	15,918
Michigan City (★60,400; MICH)	39,369
Middlebury	1,055
Middletown (★AND)	2,046
Middletown Park (★MUN)	1,200
Milan	1,260
Millersburg	618
Milltown	829
Milton	694
Mishawaka (★S.B.-)	35,517
Mitchell	4,092
Monon	1,548
Monroe	622
Monroe City	603
Monroeville	1,353
Montezuma	1,192
Monticello	4,869
Montpelier	2,093
Moores Hill	616
Mooresville (★IND)	5,800
Morgantown	1,134
Morningside (★MUN)	1,700
Morocco	1,285
Morristown	838
Mount Vernon	6,770
Mulberry	1,075
Muncie (★122,300; MUN)	69,082
Munster (★CHI)	16,514
Nappanee	4,159
Nashville	527
New Albany (★LOU)	38,402
Newburgh (★EV)	2,302
New Carlisle	1,434
New Castle	21,215
New Chicago (★CHI)	2,231
New Elliott (★CHI)	1,500
New Harmony	971
New Haven (★FTWA)	5,728
New Market	640
New Palestine (★IND)	863
New Paris	1,080
Newport	708
New Whiteland (★IND)	4,200
Noblesville (★IND)	7,548
North Judson	1,738
North Liberty	1,259
North Manchester	5,791
North Salem	601
North Terre Haute (★T.H.)	2,500
North Vernon	4,582
Norwood Addition (★MUN)	1,000
Notre Dame (★S.B.-)	7,700
Oakland City	3,289
Oak Park (★LOU)	800
Oaktown	726
Odon	1,433
Ogden Dunes (★CHI)	1,361
Oldenburg	758
Oolitic	1,155
Oregon Heights (★CHI)	1,500
Orestes (★AND)	519
Orleans	1,834
Osceola (★S.B.-)	1,572
Osgood	1,346
Ossian (★FTWA)	1,538
Otterbein	899
Owensville	1,056
Oxford	1,098
Paoli	3,281
Paragon	538
Parkerdale (★FTWA)	1,000
Parker (Parker City) (★MUN)	1,179
Patoka	529
Pekin (New Pekin)	912
Pendleton (★AND)	2,243
Pennville	798
Perrysville	510
Peru	14,139
Petersburg	2,697
Pierceton	1,175
Pine Lake	1,500
Pittsboro (★IND)	867
Plainfield (★IND)	8,211
Plainville	538
Plymouth	7,661
Portage (★CHI)	19,127
Porter (★CHI)	3,058
Portland	7,115
Poseyville	1,035
Princes Lakes	597
Princeton	7,431
Purdue University (★LAF)	12,000
Red Key	1,667
Remington	1,127
Rensselaer	4,688
Reynolds	641
Richland	550
Richmond (★64,900; RICH)	43,999
Ridgeville	924
Rising Sun	2,305
Roachdale	1,004
Roann	509
Roanoke	858
Rochester	4,631
Rockport	2,565
Rockville	2,820
Rome City	1,354
Rosedale	817
Roseland (★S.B.-)	895
Rossville	830
Royal Center	987
Rushville	6,686
Russiaville (★KOK)	844
St. Bernice	900
St. Joe	564
St. Marys (Holy Cross) (★S.B.-)	1,500
St. Paul	785
Salem	5,041
Sandborn	528
Schererville (★CHI)	3,663
Scottsburg	4,791
Seelyville (★T.H.)	1,195
Sellersburg (★LOU)	3,177
Selma (★MUN)	890
Seymour	13,352
Sharpsville (★KOK)	672
Shelburn	1,281
Shelbyville	15,094
Sheridan	2,137
Shirley (★AND)	958
Shoals	1,039
Silver Lake	588
Smith Valley (★IND)	1,679
South Bend (★380,800; S.B.-)	125,580
South Haven (★CHI)	5,500
Southport (★IND)	2,317
South Whitley	1,362
Speedway (★IND)	15,056
Spencer	2,553
Spiceland	957
Star City	500
Staunton (★T.H.)	582
Sullivan	4,683
Summitville	1,104
Sunman	707
Swayzee	1,073
Sweetsers (★MRN)	1,076
Syracuse	1,546
Tell City	7,933
Terre Haute (★117,700; T.H.)	70,335
Thorntown	1,399
Tipton	5,313
Topeka	677
Town of Pines (★CHI)	1,007
Trail Creek (★MICH)	2,697
Tri Lakes	1,193
Troy	575
Union City	3,995
Upland	3,202
Valparaiso (★CHI)	20,020
Van Buren	1,057
Veedersburg	2,198
Versailles	1,020
Vevay	1,463
Vincennes	19,867
Wabash	13,379
Wakarusa	1,160
Waldron	700
Walkerton	2,006
Wallen (★FTWA)	900
Walton	1,054
Warren	1,229
Warsaw	7,506
Washington	11,358
Waterloo	1,876
Waveland	557
Waynetown	993
West Baden Springs	930
West College Corner	709
Westfield (★IND)	1,837
West Lafayette (★LAF)	19,157
West Lebanon	899
Westport	1,170
West Terre Haute (★T.H.)	2,704
Westville	2,614
Wheatfield	713
Wheatland	562
Whiteland (★IND)	1,492
Whitestown (★IND)	569
Whiting (★CHI)	7,247
Williamsport	1,661
Winamac	2,341
Winchester	5,493
Windfall	946
Winona Lake	2,811
Winslow	1,030
Wolcott	894
Wolcottville	915
Woodburn (★FTWA)	688
Worthington	1,691
Yorktown (★MUN)	1,673
Zionsville (★IND)	1,857

IOWA

1970 C ... 2,825,041

Counties

Adair	9,487
Adams	6,322
Allamakee	14,968
Appanoose	15,007
Audubon	9,595
Benton	22,885
Black Hawk	132,916
Boone	26,470
Bremer	22,737
Buchanan	21,746
Buena Vista	20,693
Butler	16,953
Calhoun	14,287
Carroll	22,912
Cass	17,007
Cedar	17,655
Cerro Gordo	49,335
Cherokee	17,269
Chickasaw	14,969
Clarke	7,581
Clay	18,464
Clayton	20,606
Clinton	56,749
Crawford	19,116
Dallas	26,085
Davis	8,207
Decatur	9,737
Delaware	18,770
Des Moines	46,982
Dickinson	12,565
Dubuque	90,609
Emmet	14,009
Fayette	26,898
Floyd	19,860
Franklin	13,255
Fremont	9,282
Greene	12,716
Grundy	14,119
Guthrie	12,243
Hamilton	18,383
Hancock	13,330
Hardin	22,248
Harrison	16,240
Henry	18,114
Howard	11,442
Humboldt	12,519
Ida	9,190
Iowa	15,419
Jackson	20,839
Jasper	35,425
Jefferson	15,774
Johnson	72,127
Jones	19,868
Keokuk	13,943
Kossuth	22,937
Lee	42,996
Linn	163,213
Louisa	10,682
Lucas	10,163
Lyon	13,340
Madison	11,558
Mahaska	22,177
Marion	26,352
Marshall	41,076
Mills	11,832
Mitchell	13,108
Monona	12,069
Monroe	9,357
Montgomery	12,781
Muscatine	37,181
O'Brien	17,522
Osceola	8,555
Page	18,507
Palo Alto	13,289
Plymouth	24,312
Pocahontas	12,729
Polk	286,101
Pottawattamie	86,991
Poweshiek	18,803
Ringgold	6,373
Sac	15,573
Scott	142,687
Shelby	15,528
Sioux	27,996
Story	62,783
Tama	20,147
Taylor	8,790
Union	13,557
Van Buren	8,643
Wapello	42,149
Warren	27,432
Washington	18,967
Wayne	8,405
Webster	48,391
Winnebago	12,990
Winneshiek	21,758
Woodbury	103,052
Worth	8,968
Wright	17,294

Cities

Ackley	1,794
Adair	750
Adel	2,419
Afton	823
Agency	610
Akron	1,324
Albert City	683
Albia	4,151
Albion	772
Alden	876
Algona	6,032
Allerton	643
Allison	1,071
Alta	1,717
Alton	1,018
Altoona (★DES)	2,854
Amana	550
Ames (★45,600; AMES)	39,505
Anamosa	4,389
Anita	1,101

(Iowa continued)

★ Population or designation of metropolitan area, including suburbs (see headnote).
▲ Population of entire "town" or township, including other communities and rural areas.
† Population is from a local census taken at date specified.

(Iowa continued)

Ankeny (★DES) 9,151
Anthon 711
Aplington 936
Armstrong 1,061
Arnolds Park 970
Atkins 581
Atlantic 7,306
Audubon 2,907
Aurelia 1,065
Avoca 1,535
Bancroft 1,103
Batavia 525
Battle Creek 837
Baxter 788
Bayard 628
Bedford 1,733
Belle Plaine 2,810
Bellevue 2,336
Belmond 2,358
Bettendorf (★D-RI-M) 22,126
Blairstown 612
Bloomfield 2,718
Blue Grass (★D-RI-M) 1,032
Bonaparte 517
Boone 12,468
Boyden 670
Breda 518
Brighton 632
Britt 2,069
Brooklyn 1,410
Buffalo (★D-RI-M) 1,513
Buffalo Center 1,118
Burlington (★40,500; BUR) 32,366
Burt 608
Calmar 1,008
Camanche (★CLNT) 3,470
Cambridge 661
Capitol Heights (★DES) 1,000
Carlisle (★DES) 2,246
Carroll 8,716
Carson 756
Carter Lake (★OMA-) 3,268
Cascade 1,744
Casey 561
Cedar Falls (★WATL) 29,597
Cedar Rapids (★147,700; CEDR) 110,642
Center Point 1,456
Centerville 6,531
Central City 1,116
Chariton 5,009
Charles City 9,268
Charter Oak 715
Cherokee 7,272
Churdan 598
Cincinnati 570
Clarence 915
Clarinda 5,420
Clarion 2,972
Clarksville 1,360
Clear Lake 6,430
Clermont 582
Clinton (★44,200; CLNT) 34,719
Clive (★DES) 3,005
Coggon 656
Colfax 2,293
Colo 606
Columbus Junction 1,205
Conrad 932
Coon Rapids 1,381
Coralville (★IACY) 6,130
Corning 2,095
Correctionville 870
Corydon 1,745
Council Bluffs (★★OMA-) 60,348
Cresco 3,927
Creston 8,234
Dakota City 746
Dallas Center 1,128
Danbury 527
Danville (★BUR) 948
Davenport (★301,000; D-RI-M) 98,469
Dayton 909
Decorah 7,458
Delhi 527
Delmar 599
Denison 6,300
Denver (★WATL) 1,169
Des Moines (★291,900; DES) 201,404
De Witt 3,647
Dexter 652
Dike 794
Donnellson 798
Dow City 571
Dows 777
Dubuque (★75,200; DUB) 62,309
Dumont 724
Dunkerton 563
Dunlap 1,292
Durant 1,472
Dyersville 3,437
Dysart 1,251
Eagle Grove 4,489
Earlham 974
Earling 573
Earlville 751
Early 727
Eddyville (†11/30/71) 970
Edgewood 786
Eldon 1,319
Eldora 3,223
Eldridge (★D-RI-M) 1,535
Elgin 613
Elkader 1,592
Elk Horn 667
Elk Run Heights (★WATL) 1,175
Elma 601
Emmetsburg 4,150
Epworth 1,132
Essex 770
Estherville 8,108
Evansdale (★WATL) 5,038
Everly 699
Exira 966
Fairbank 810
Fairfax (★CEDR) 635
Fairfield 8,715
Farley 1,096
Farmington 800
Farragut 521
Fayette 1,947
Fonda 980
Fontanelle 752
Forest City 3,841
Fort Dodge 31,263
Fort Madison 13,996
Fredericksburg 912
Garnavillo 634
Garner 2,257
Garwin 563
George 1,194
Gilbert (★AMES) 521
Gilbertville (★WATL) 655
Gilman 513
Gilmore City 766
Gladbrook 961
Glenwood 4,421
Glidden 964
Goldfield 722
Gowrie 1,225
Graettinger 907
Grand Junction 967
Grand Mound 627
Granger 661
Greene 1,363
Greenfield 2,212
Grimes (★DES) 834
Grinnell 8,402
Griswold 1,181
Grundy Center 2,712
Guthrie Center 1,834
Guttenberg 2,177
Hamburg 1,649
Hampton 4,376
Harlan 5,049
Hartford 582
Hartley 1,694
Hawarden 2,789
Hawkeye 529
Hazleton 626
Hedrick 790
Hiawatha (★CEDR) 2,416
Hills 507
Holstein 1,445
Hopkinton 800
Hospers 646
Hubbard 846
Hudson 1,535
Hull 1,523
Humboldt 4,665
Humeston 673
Huxley (★AMES) 937
Ida Grove 2,261
Independence 5,910
Indianola 8,852
Inwood 644
Iowa City (★57,000; IACY) 46,850
Iowa Falls 6,454
Ireton 582
Janesville (★WATL) 741
Jefferson 4,735
Jesup 1,662
Jewell 1,152
Kalona 1,488
Kanawha 822
Kellogg 607
Keokuk 14,631
Keosauqua 1,018
Keota 707
Keystone 549
Kingsley 1,097
Klemme 554
Knoxville 7,755
Lake City 1,910
Lake Mills 2,124
Lake Park 918
Lake View 1,249
Lamoni 2,540
Lansing 1,218
La Porte City 2,256
Larchwood 611
Laurens 1,756
Lawler 513
Le Claire (★D-RI-M) 2,520
Le Grand 565
Lehigh 739
Le Mars 8,159
Lenox 1,215
Leon 2,142
Lewis 526
Lisbon 1,329
Little Rock 531
Livermore 510
Logan 1,526
Lohrville 553
Lone Tree 834
Lost Nation 547
Lovilia 640
Lovington (★DES) 800
Lowden 667
McGregor 990
Madrid 2,448
Malvern 1,158
Manchester 4,641
Manilla 943
Manly 1,294
Manning 1,656
Manson 1,993
Mapleton 1,647
Maquoketa 5,677
Marcus 1,272
Marengo 2,235
Marion (★CEDR) 18,028
Marquette 509
Marquisville (★DES) 700
Marshalltown 26,219
Mason City 30,379
Maxwell 758
Maynard 503
Mechanicsville 989
Mediapolis 1,242
Melbourne 661
Melcher 913
Merrill 790
Milford 1,668
Milo 561
Milton 567
Missouri Valley 3,519
Mitchellville (★DES) 1,341
Monona 1,395
Monroe 1,389
Montezuma 1,353
Monticello 3,509
Montrose 735
Moravia 699
Morning Sun 906
Moulton 763
Mount Ayr 1,762
Mount Pleasant 7,007
Mount Vernon 3,018
Moville 1,198
Murray 620
Muscatine 22,405
Mystic 696
Nashua 1,712
Neola 968
Nevada 4,952
New Albin 644
Newell 877
Newhall 701
New Hampton 3,621
New Hartford 690
New London 1,900
New Market 501
New Sharon 944
Newton 15,619
Nora Springs 1,337
North Cedar (★WATL) 1,900
North English 965
North Liberty (★IACY) 1,055
Northwood 1,950
Norwalk (★DES) 1,745
Norway 554
Norwoodville (★DES) 1,500
Oakland 1,603
Ocheyedan 545
Odebolt 1,323
Oelwein 7,735
Ogden 1,661
Olin 710
Onawa 3,154
Orange City 3,572
Osage 3,815
Osceola 3,124
Oskaloosa 11,224
Ossian 847
Otho 581
Ottumwa 29,610
Oxford 666
Oxford Junction 666
Pacific Junction 505
Panora 982
Parkersburg 1,631
Paullina 1,257
Pella 6,668
Perry 6,906
Pleasant Hill (★DES) 1,535
Pleasantville 1,297
Pocahontas 2,338
Polk City (★DES) 715
Pomeroy 765
Postville 1,546
Prairie City 1,141
Preston 950
Primghar 995
Princeton 633
Radcliffe 548
Raymond (★WATL) 582
Readlyn 616
Redfield 921
Red Oak 6,210
Reinbeck 1,711
Remsen 1,367
Riceville 877
Richland 595
Ringsted 509
Riverdale (★D-RI-M) 684
Riverside 758
Robins (★CEDR) 663
Rockford 902
Rock Rapids 2,632
Rock Valley 2,205
Rockwell 923
Rockwell City 2,396
Roland 803
Rolfe 767
Rossville 5,150
Russell 591
Ruthven 708
Sabula 845
Sac City 3,268
St. Ansgar 994
Sanborn 1,465
Saydel (★DES) 1,200
Schaller 835
Schleswig 875
Scranton 751
Sergeant Bluff (★SXCY) (†11/16/71) 2,054
Seymour 931
Sheffield 1,070
Shelby 537
Sheldon 4,535
Shell Rock 1,159
Shellsburg 740
Shenandoah 5,968
Sibley 2,749
Sidney 1,061
Sigourney 2,319
Sioux Center 3,450
Sioux City (★99,600; SXCY) 85,925
Sioux Rapids 813
Slater (★AMES) 1,094
Sloan 799
Solon (★CEDR) 837
Spencer 10,278
Spirit Lake 3,014
Springville 970
Stacyville 598
Stanton 574
Stanwood 642
State Center 1,232
Storm Lake 8,591
Story City 2,104
Stratford 710
Strawberry Point 1,281
Stuart 1,354
Sully 685
Sumner 2,174
Sutherland 875
Swea City 774
Tabor 957
Tama 3,000
Thompson 600
Tipton 2,877
Titonka 599
Toledo 2,361
Traer 1,682
Tripoli 1,345
University Heights (★IACY) 1,265
University Park 534
Urbana 552
Urbandale (★DES) 14,434
Ute 512
Van Horne 613
Ventura 543
Victor 949
Villisca 1,402
Vinton 4,845
Walcott (★D-RI-M) 989
Walker 622
Wall Lake 936
Walnut 870
Wapello 1,873
Washburn (★WATL) 1,408
Washington 6,317
Waterloo (★125,200; WATL) 75,533
Waukee (★DES) 1,577
Waukon 3,883
Waverly 7,205
Wayland 702
Webster City 8,488
Wellman 977
Wellsburg 754
Wesley 548
West Bend 865
West Branch 1,322
West Burlington (★BUR) 3,139
West Des Moines (★DES) 16,441
West Liberty 2,296
West Point 1,045
West Union 2,624
What Cheer 868
Wheatland 832
Whiting 590
Whittemore 658
Williamsburg 1,544
Wilton Junction (Wilton) 1,873
Windsor Heights (★DES) 6,303
Winfield 897
Winterset 3,654
Winthrop 750
Woodbine 1,349
Woodward 1,010
Wyoming 746
Zearing 535

KANSAS

1970 C 2,249,071

Counties

Allen 15,043
Anderson 8,501
Atchison 19,165
Barber 7,016
Barton 30,663
Bourbon 15,215
Brown 11,685
Butler 38,658
Chase 3,408
Chautauqua 4,642
Cherokee 21,549
Cheyenne 4,256
Clark 2,896
Clay 9,890
Cloud 13,466
Coffey 7,397
Comanche 2,702
Cowley 35,012
Crawford 37,850
Decatur 4,988
Dickinson 19,993
Doniphan 9,107
Douglas 57,932
Edwards 4,581
Elk 3,858
Ellis 24,730
Ellsworth 6,146
Finney 19,029
Ford 22,587
Franklin 20,007
Geary 28,111
Gove 3,940
Graham 4,751
Grant 5,961
Gray 4,516
Greeley 1,819
Greenwood 9,141
Hamilton 2,747
Harper 7,871
Harvey 27,236
Haskell 3,672
Hodgeman 2,662
Jackson 10,342
Jefferson 11,945
Jewell 6,099
Johnson 220,073
Kearny 3,047
Kingman 8,886
Kiowa 4,088
Labette 25,775
Lane 2,707
Leavenworth 53,340
Lincoln 4,582
Linn 7,770
Logan 3,814
Lyon 32,071
McPherson 24,778
Marion 13,935
Marshall 13,139
Meade 4,912
Miami 19,254
Mitchell 8,010
Montgomery 39,949
Morris 6,432
Morton 3,576
Nemaha 11,825
Neosho 18,812
Ness 4,791
Norton 7,279
Osage 13,352
Osborne 6,416
Ottawa 6,183
Pawnee 8,484
Phillips 7,888
Pottawatomie 11,755
Pratt 10,056
Rawlins 4,393
Reno 60,765
Republic 8,498
Rice 12,320
Riley 56,788
Rooks 7,628
Rush 5,117
Russell 9,428
Saline 46,592
Scott 5,606
Sedgwick 350,694
Seward 15,744
Shawnee 155,322
Sheridan 3,859
Sherman 7,792
Smith 6,757
Stafford 5,943
Stanton 2,287
Stevens 4,198
Sumner 23,553
Thomas 7,501
Trego 4,436
Wabaunsee 6,397
Wallace 2,215
Washington 9,249
Wichita 3,274
Wilson 11,317
Woodson 4,789
Wyandotte 186,845

Cities

Abilene 6,661
Alma 905
Altamont 845
Andale 500
Andover (★WICH) 1,880
Anthony 2,653
Argonia 591
Arkansas City 13,216
Arlington 503
Arma 1,348
Ashland 1,244
Atchison 12,565
Attica 639
Atwood 1,658
Augusta (★WICH) 5,977
Baldwin City (Baldwin) 2,520
Basehor 724
Baxter Springs 4,489
Belle Plaine (★WICH) 1,553
Belleville 3,063
Beloit 4,121
Bennington 561
Benton 517
Bird City 671
Blue Rapids 1,148
Bonner Springs (★K.C.) 3,662
Bucklin 771
Buhler 1,019
Burden 503
Burlingame 999
Burlington 2,099
Burrton 808
Caldwell 1,540
Caney 2,192
Canton 893
Carbondale 1,041
Cawker City 726
Cedar Vale 665
Centralia 511
Chanute 10,341
Chapman 1,132
Chase 800
Cheney 1,160
Cherokee 790
Cherryvale 2,609
Chetopa 1,596
Cimarron 1,373
Claflin 887
Clay Center 4,963
Clearwater 1,435
Clifton 718
Clyde 946
Coffeyville 15,116
Colby 4,658
Coldwater 1,016
Columbus 3,356
Colwich 879
Concordia 7,221
Conway Springs 1,153
Cottonwood Falls 987
Council Grove 2,403
Delphos 599
Derby (★WICH) 7,947
De Soto 1,839
Dighton 1,540
Dodge City 14,127
Douglass 1,126
Downs 1,268
Eastborough (★WICH) 1,141
Edgerton 513
Edwardsville (★K.C.) 619
Effingham 605
El Dorado 12,308
Elkhart 2,089
Ellinwood 2,416
Ellis 2,137
Ellsworth 2,080
Elwood (★ST.JO) 1,283

★ Population or designation of metropolitan area, including suburbs (see headnote).
▲ Population of entire "town" or township, including other communities and rural areas.
† Population is from a local census taken at date specified.

Enterprise ... 868
Erie ... 1,414
Eskridge ... 589
Eudora ... 2,071
Eureka ... 3,576
Fairway (★K.C.) ... 5,133
Florence ... 716
Fort Scott ... 8,967
Fowler ... 588
Frankfort ... 960
Fredonia ... 3,080
Frontenac ... 2,223
Galena (★JOP) ... 3,712
Galva ... 522
Garden City ... 14,790
Garden Plain ... 678
Gardner (★K.C.) ... 1,839
Garnett ... 3,169
Girard ... 2,591
Glasco ... 767
Goddard (★WICH) ... 955
Goodland ... 5,510
Grandview Plaza ... 734
Great Bend ... 16,133
Greensburg ... 1,907
Halstead ... 1,716
Hanover ... 793
Harper ... 1,665
Haven ... 1,146
Haviland ... 705
Hays ... 15,396
Haysville (★WICH) ... 6,483
Herington ... 3,165
Hesston ... 1,926
Hiawatha ... 3,365
Highland ... 899
Hill City ... 2,071
Hillsboro ... 2,730
Hoisington ... 3,710
Holmdel Gardens (★HUCH) ... 1,960
Holton ... 3,063
Holyrood ... 593
Horton ... 2,177
Howard ... 918
Hoxie ... 1,419
Hugoton ... 2,739
Humboldt ... 2,249
Hutchinson (★46,600; HUCH) ... 36,885
Independence ... 10,347
Inman ... 836
Iola ... 6,493
Jetmore ... 936
Jewell ... 569
Johnson (Johnson City) ... 1,038
Junction City ... 19,018
Kanopolis ... 626
Kansas City (★K.C.) ... 168,213
Kensington ... 653
Kingman ... 3,622
Kinsley ... 2,212
Kiowa ... 1,414
La Crosse ... 1,583
La Cygne ... 989
La Harpe ... 509
Lake Quivira (★K.C.) ... 1,200
Lakin ... 1,570
Lansing (★LEAV) ... 3,797
Larned ... 4,567
Lawrence (★46,900; LAWR) ... 45,698
Leavenworth (★43,000; LEAV) ... 25,147
Leawood (★K.C.) ... 10,349
Lebanon ... 517
Lebo ... 589
Lenexa (★K.C.) ... 5,242
Leon ... 510
Leoti ... 1,916
Le Roy ... 551
Lewis ... 525
Liberal ... 13,789
Lincoln (Lincoln Center) ... 1,582
Lindsborg ... 2,764
Logan ... 760
Louisburg ... 1,033
Lucas ... 524
Lyndon ... 958
Lyons ... 4,355
McClouth ... 623
McPherson ... 10,851
Madison ... 1,061
Maize (★WICH) ... 785
Manhattan ... 27,575
Mankato ... 1,287
Marion ... 2,052
Marquette ... 639
Marysville ... 3,588
Meade ... 1,899
Medicine Lodge ... 2,545
Merriam (★K.C.) ... 10,851
Miltonvale ... 718
Minneapolis ... 1,971
Minneola ... 630
Mission (★K.C.) ... 8,376
Mission Hills (★K.C.) ... 4,177
Moline ... 555
Montezuma ... 606
Moran ... 550
Mound City ... 714
Moundridge (Mound Ridge) ... 1,271
Mount Hope ... 665
Mulberry ... 622
Mulvane (★WICH) ... 3,185
Natoma ... 603
Neodesha ... 3,295
Ness City ... 1,756
Newton ... 15,439
Nickerson ... 1,187
North Newton ... 963
Norton ... 3,627
Nortonville ... 727
Oaklawn (★WICH) ... 5,000
Oakley ... 2,327
Oberlin ... 2,291
Ogden (Ogdensburg) ... 1,491
Olathe (★K.C.) ... 17,917
Onaga ... 761
Osage City ... 2,600
Osawatomie ... 4,294
Osborne ... 1,980
Oskaloosa ... 955
Oswego ... 2,200
Ottawa ... 11,036
Overbrook ... 748
Overland Park (★K.C.) ... 79,034
Oxford ... 1,113
Paola ... 4,622
Park City (★WICH) ... 2,529
Parsons ... 13,015
Peabody ... 1,368
Perry ... 664
Phillipsburg ... 3,241
Pittsburg ... 20,171
Plains (West Plains) ... 857
Plainville ... 2,627
Pleasanton ... 1,216
Pomona ... 541
Prairie Village (★K.C.) ... 28,138
Pratt ... 6,736
Pretty Prairie ... 561
Protection ... 673
Quinter ... 930
Riley ... 668
Riverview (★WICH) ... 1,700
Roeland Park (★K.C.) ... 9,974
Rossville ... 934
Russell ... 5,371
Sabetha ... 2,376
St. Francis ... 1,725
St. John ... 1,477
St. Marys ... 1,434
St. Paul ... 804
Salina (★41,300; SLN) ... 37,714
Satanta ... 1,161
Scandia ... 567
Scott City ... 4,001
Scranton ... 575
Sedan ... 1,555
Sedgwick ... 1,083
Seneca ... 2,182
Sharon Springs ... 1,012
Shawnee (★K.C.) ... 20,482
Silver Lake (★TOP) ... 811
Smith Center ... 2,389
Solomon ... 973
South Hutchinson (★HUCH) ... 1,879
Spearville ... 738
Spring Hill ... 1,186
Stafford ... 1,414
Sterling ... 2,312
Stockton ... 1,818
Strong City ... 545
Sublette ... 1,208
Sunflower ... 1,744
Syracuse ... 1,720
Tonganoxie ... 1,717
Topeka (★149,700; TOP) ... 125,011
Towanda ... 1,190
Tribune ... 1,013
Troy ... 1,047
Udall ... 668
Ulysses ... 3,779
Valley Center (★WICH) ... 2,551
Valley Falls ... 1,169
Victoria ... 1,246
Wakeeney ... 2,334
Wakefield ... 583
Wamego ... 2,507
Washington ... 1,584
Waterville ... 632
Wathena ... 1,150
Waverly ... 510
Weir ... 740
Wellington ... 8,072
Wellsville ... 1,183
Westwood (★K.C.) ... 2,329
Whitewater ... 520
Wichita (★349,600; WICH) ... 276,554
Wilson ... 870
Winfield ... 11,405
Yates Center ... 1,967

KENTUCKY

1970 C ... 3,219,311

Counties

Adair ... 13,037
Allen ... 12,598
Anderson ... 9,358
Ballard ... 8,276
Barren ... 28,677
Bath ... 9,235
Bell ... 31,087
Boone ... 32,812
Bourbon ... 18,476
Boyd ... 52,376
Boyle ... 21,090
Bracken ... 7,227
Breathitt ... 14,221
Breckinridge ... 14,789
Bullitt ... 26,090
Butler ... 9,723
Caldwell ... 13,179
Calloway ... 27,692
Campbell ... 88,561
Carlisle ... 5,354
Carroll ... 8,523
Carter ... 19,850
Casey ... 12,930
Christian ... 56,224
Clark ... 24,090
Clay ... 18,481
Clinton ... 8,174
Crittenden ... 8,493
Cumberland ... 6,850
Daviess ... 79,486
Edmonson ... 8,751
Elliott ... 5,933
Estill ... 12,752
Fayette ... 174,323
Fleming ... 11,366
Floyd ... 35,889
Franklin ... 34,481
Fulton ... 10,183
Gallatin ... 4,134
Garrard ... 9,457
Grant ... 9,999
Graves ... 30,939
Grayson ... 16,445
Green ... 10,350
Greenup ... 33,192
Hancock ... 7,080
Hardin ... 78,421
Harlan ... 37,370
Harrison ... 14,158
Hart ... 13,980
Henderson ... 36,031
Henry ... 10,910
Hickman ... 6,264
Hopkins ... 38,167
Jackson ... 10,005
Jefferson ... 695,055
Jessamine ... 17,430
Johnson ... 17,539
Kenton ... 129,440
Knott ... 14,698
Knox ... 23,689
Larue ... 10,672
Laurel ... 27,386
Lawrence ... 10,726
Lee ... 6,587
Leslie ... 11,623
Letcher ... 23,165
Lewis ... 12,355
Lincoln ... 16,663
Livingston ... 7,596
Logan ... 21,793
Lyon ... 5,562
McCracken ... 58,281
McCreary ... 12,548
McLean ... 9,062
Madison ... 42,730
Magoffin ... 10,443
Marion ... 16,714
Marshall ... 20,381
Martin ... 9,377
Mason ... 17,273
Meade ... 18,796
Menifee ... 4,050
Mercer ... 15,960
Metcalfe ... 8,177
Monroe ... 11,642
Montgomery ... 15,364
Morgan ... 10,019
Muhlenberg ... 27,537
Nelson ... 23,477
Nicholas ... 6,508
Ohio ... 18,790
Oldham ... 14,687
Owen ... 7,470
Owsley ... 5,023
Pendleton ... 9,949
Perry ... 26,259
Pike ... 61,059
Powell ... 7,704
Pulaski ... 35,234
Robertson ... 2,163
Rockcastle ... 12,305
Rowan ... 17,010
Russell ... 10,542
Scott ... 17,948
Shelby ... 18,999
Simpson ... 13,054
Spencer ... 5,488
Taylor ... 17,138
Todd ... 10,823
Trigg ... 8,620
Trimble ... 5,349
Union ... 15,882
Warren ... 57,432
Washington ... 10,728
Wayne ... 14,268
Webster ... 13,282
Whitley ... 24,145
Wolfe ... 5,669
Woodford ... 14,434

Cities

Adairville ... 973
Albany ... 1,891
Alexandria (★CIN-) ... 3,844
Allen ... 724
Anchorage (★LOU) ... 1,477
Arlington ... 549
Ashland (★★HNTG-) ... 29,245
Auburn ... 1,160
Audubon Park (★LOU) ... 1,862
Augusta ... 1,434
Barbourmeade (★LOU) ... 884
Barbourville ... 3,549
Bardstown ... 5,816
Bardwell ... 1,049
Barlow ... 746
Beattyville ... 923
Beaver Dam ... 2,622
Bedford ... 780
Beechwood Village (★LOU) ... 1,788
Bellefonte (★HNTG-) ... 966
Bellemeade (★LOU) ... 576
Bellevue (★CIN-) ... 8,847
Benham ... 1,000
Benton ... 3,652
Berea ... 6,956
Bloomfield ... 1,072
Blue Ridge Manor (★LOU) ... 596
Bowling Green (★42,900; BOWLG) ... 36,253
Brandenburg ... 1,637
Brodhead ... 769
Bromley (★CIN-) ... 1,069
Brooksville ... 609
Brownsboro Farm (★LOU) ... 823
Brownsville ... 542
Buechel (★LOU) ... 9,000
Burgin ... 1,002
Burkesville ... 1,717
Burnside ... 586
Butler ... 558
Cadiz ... 1,987
Calhoun ... 901
Calvert City (★PAD) ... 2,104
Campbellsville ... 7,598
Caneyville ... 530
Carlisle ... 1,579
Carrollton ... 3,884
Catlettsburg (★HNTG-) ... 3,420
Cave City ... 1,818
Central City ... 5,450
Clarkson ... 660
Clay ... 1,426
Clay City ... 983
Clinton ... 1,618
Cloverport ... 1,388
Cold Spring (★CIN-) ... 1,406
Colonial Terrace (★LOU) ... 1,200
Columbia ... 3,234
Corbin ... 7,317
Corydon ... 880
Covington (★CIN-) ... 52,535
Crab Orchard ... 861
Crescent Park (★CIN-) ... 598
Crescent Springs (★CIN-) ... 1,662
Crestview (★CIN-) ... 659
Crestview Hills (★CIN-) ... 1,114
Crofton ... 631
Cumberland ... 3,624
Cynthiana ... 6,356
Danville ... 11,542
Dawson Springs ... 3,009
Dayton (★CIN-) ... 8,751
Devondale (★LOU) ... 1,071
Dixon ... 572
Drakesboro ... 907
Dry Ridge ... 1,100
Earlington ... 2,321
Eddyville ... 1,981
Edgewood (★CIN-) ... 4,139
Edmonton ... 958
Elizabethtown ... 11,748
Elkhorn City ... 1,081
Elkton ... 1,612
Elsmere (★CIN-) ... 5,161
Eminence ... 2,225
Erlanger (★CIN-) ... 12,676
Evarts ... 1,182
Fairdale (★LOU) ... 2,500
Falmouth ... 2,593
Ferguson ... 507
Fern Creek (★LOU) ... 6,000
Flatwoods (★HNTG-) ... 7,380
Flemingsburg ... 2,483
Florence (★CIN-) ... 11,661
Fort Mitchell (★CIN-) ... 6,982
Fort Thomas (★CIN-) ... 16,338
Fort Wright-Lookout Heights (★CIN-) ... 4,819
Frankfort ... 21,902
Franklin ... 6,553
Fulton ... 3,250
Gardenside (★LEX-) ... 9,000
Georgetown (★LEX) ... 8,629
Glasgow ... 11,301
Glengary (★LOU) ... 1,500
Graymoor (★LOU) ... 1,419
Grayson (★HNTG-) ... 2,184
Greensburg ... 1,990
Greenup ... 1,284
Greenville ... 3,875
Guthrie ... 1,200
Hamilton Park (★LEX) ... 1,400
Hardin ... 522
Hardinsburg ... 1,547
Harlan ... 3,318
Harrodsburg ... 6,741
Hartford ... 1,868
Hawesville ... 1,262
Hazard ... 5,459
Henderson (★EV) ... 22,976
Hickman ... 3,048
Highland Heights (★CIN) ... 4,400
Highview (★LOU) ... 5,000
Hinda Heights (★LEX) ... 1,000
Hindman ... 808
Hodgenville ... 2,562
Hollyvilla (★LOU) ... 907
Hopkinsville ... 21,250
Horse Cave ... 2,068
Houston Acres (★LOU) ... 684
Independence (★CIN-) ... 1,784
Indian Hills (★LOU) ... 600
Irvine ... 2,918
Irvington ... 1,300
Jackson ... 1,887
Jamestown ... 1,027
Jeffersontown (★LOU) ... 9,701
Jenkins ... 2,552
Junction City ... 1,046
Keeneland (★LOU) ... 587
Kenwick (★LEX) ... 1,500
Kingsley (★LOU) ... 504
La Center ... 1,044
La Grange ... 1,713
Lakeside Park (★CIN-) ... 2,511
Lancaster ... 3,230
Lansdowne (★LEX) ... 2,300
Lawrenceburg ... 3,579
Lebanon ... 5,528
Lebanon Junction ... 1,571
Leitchfield ... 2,983
Lewisburg ... 651
Lewisport ... 1,595
Lexington (★217,900; LEX) ... 108,137
Liberty ... 1,765
Livermore ... 1,594
London ... 4,337
Lone Oak (★PAD) ... 3,759
Loretto ... 985
Louisa ... 1,781
Louisville (★840,000; LOU) ... 361,958
Loyall ... 1,212
Ludlow (★CIN-) ... 5,815
Lynch ... 1,700
Lynnview (★LOU) ... 1,494
McRoberts ... 1,037
Madisonville ... 15,332
Manchester ... 1,664
Marion ... 3,008
Martin ... 786
Mayfield ... 10,724
Maysville ... 7,411
Meadowthorpe (★LEX) ... 1,000
Meadow Vale (★LOU) ... 1,231
Middlesboro (Middlesborough) ... 11,878
Middletown (★LOU) ... 3,500
Midway (★LEX) ... 1,278
Millersburg ... 788
Milton ... 756
Minor Lane Heights (★LOU) ... 2,217
Monticello ... 3,618
Moorland (★LOU) ... 705
Morehead ... 7,191
Morganfield ... 3,563
Morgantown ... 1,394
Mortons Gap ... 1,169
Mount Sterling ... 5,083
Mount Vernon ... 1,639
Mount Washington (★LOU) ... 2,020
Muldraugh ... 1,773
Munfordville ... 1,233
Murray ... 13,537
Neon ... 705
Newburg (★LOU) ... 4,000
New Castle ... 755
New Haven ... 977
Newport (★CIN-) ... 25,998
Nicholasville (★LEX) ... 5,829
Nortonville ... 699
Okolona (★LOU) ... 17,643
Olive Hill ... 1,197
Owensboro (★61,600; OWNS) ... 50,329
Owensboro East (★OWNS) ... 2,500
Owenton ... 1,280
Owingsville ... 1,381
Paducah (★64,500; PAD) ... 31,627
Paintsville ... 3,868
Paris ... 7,823
Park City ... 567
Park Hills (★CIN-) ... 3,999
Parkway Village (★LOU) ... 829
Pembroke ... 634
Perryville ... 730
Pewee Valley (★LOU) ... 950
Phelps ... 770
Pikeville ... 4,899
Pineville ... 2,817
Plantation (★LOU) ... 895
Pleasure Ridge Park (★LOU) ... 18,000
Pleasureville ... 747
Powderly ... 631
Prairie Village (★LOU) ... 3,000
Prestonsburg ... 3,422
Princeton ... 6,292
Providence ... 4,270
Raceland (★HNTG-) ... 1,857
Radcliff ... 7,881
Ravenna ... 784
Richlawn (★LOU) ... 578
Richmond ... 16,861
Rolling Fields (★LOU) ... 737
Rolling Hills (★LOU) ... 1,313
Russell (★HNTG-) ... 1,982
Russell Springs ... 1,641
Russellville ... 6,456
St. Dennis Center (★LOU) ... 1,500
St. Matthews (★LOU) ... 13,152
St. Regis Park (★LOU) ... 1,527
Salyersville ... 1,196
Scottsville ... 3,584
Sebree ... 1,092
Seneca Gardens (★LOU) ... 822
Shelbyville ... 4,182
Shepherdsville (★LOU) ... 2,769
Shively (★LOU) ... 19,150
Silver Grove (★CIN-) ... 1,365
Simpsonville ... 628
Smithland ... 514
Smiths Grove ... 756
Somerset ... 10,436
South Dixie (★LOU) ... 1,000
Southgate (★CIN-) ... 3,212
South Shore (★PTSM) ... 676
Springfield ... 2,961
Springlee (★LOU) ... 583
Stanford ... 2,474
Stanton ... 2,037
Stonewall Estates (★LEX) ... 2,000
Strathmoor Village (★LOU) ... 540
Sturgis ... 2,210
Taylor Mill (★CIN-) ... 3,194
Taylorsville ... 897
Tompkinsville ... 2,207
Twin Oaks (★LEX) ... 1,200
Uniontown ... 1,255
Upton ... 552
Valley Station (★LOU) ... 17,000
Valley Village (★LOU) ... 3,500
Vanceburg ... 1,773
Van Lear ... 1,033
Versailles (★LEX) ... 5,679
Villa Hills (★CIN-) ... 1,647
Vine Grove ... 2,987
Walton (★CIN-) ... 1,801
Warsaw ... 1,232
Wellington (★LOU) ... 727
West Buechel (★LOU) ... 1,581
West Liberty ... 1,387
West Point ... 1,741
Westwood (★HNTG-) ... 5,500
Westwood (★LOU) ... 777
Wheelwright ... 793
Whipps Millgate (★LOU) ... 529
White Plains ... 729
Whitesburg ... 1,137
Whitesville ... 752
Whitley City ... 1,060
Wickliffe ... 1,211
Wilders (★CIN-) ... 823
Williamsburg ... 3,687
Williamstown ... 2,063
Wilmore (★LEX) ... 3,466
Winchester ... 13,402
Windy Hills (★LOU) ... 1,692
Wingo ... 593
Winston Park (★CIN-) ... 1,108
Woodland Hills (★LOU) ... 1,233
Woodlawn (★CIN-) ... 525
Woodlawn Park (★LOU) ... 1,237
Worthington (★HNTG-) ... 1,364
Wurtland (★HNTG-) ... 1,000
Zandale (★LEX) ... 2,000

★ Population or designation of metropolitan area, including suburbs (see headnote).
▲ Population of entire "town" or township, including other communities and rural areas.
† Population is from a local census taken at date specified.

LOUISIANA

1970 C ... 3,643,180

Parishes

Acadia ... 52,109
Allen ... 20,794
Ascension ... 37,086
Assumption ... 19,654
Avoyelles ... 37,751
Beauregard ... 22,888
Bienville ... 16,024
Bossier ... 63,703
Caddo ... 230,184
Calcasieu ... 145,415
Caldwell ... 9,354
Cameron ... 8,194
Catahoula ... 11,769
Claiborne ... 17,024
Concordia ... 22,578
De Soto ... 22,764
East Baton Rouge ... 285,167
East Carroll ... 12,884
East Feliciana ... 17,657
Evangeline ... 31,932
Franklin ... 23,946
Grant ... 13,671
Iberia ... 57,397
Iberville ... 30,746
Jackson ... 15,963
Jefferson ... 338,229
Jefferson Davis ... 29,554
Lafayette ... 111,745
Lafourche ... 68,941
La Salle ... 13,295
Lincoln ... 33,800
Livingston ... 36,511
Madison ... 15,065
Morehouse ... 32,463
Natchitoches ... 35,219
Orleans ... 593,471
Ouachita ... 115,387
Plaquemines ... 25,225
Pointe Coupee ... 22,002
Rapides ... 118,078
Red River ... 9,226
Richland ... 21,774
Sabine ... 18,638
St. Bernard ... 51,185
St. Charles ... 29,550
St. Helena ... 9,937
St. James ... 19,733
St. John the Baptist ... 23,813
St. Landry ... 80,364
St. Martin ... 32,453
St. Mary ... 60,752
St. Tammany ... 63,585
Tangipahoa ... 65,875
Tensas ... 9,732
Terrebonne ... 76,049
Union ... 18,447
Vermilion ... 43,071
Vernon ... 53,794
Washington ... 41,987
Webster ... 39,939
West Baton Rouge ... 16,864
West Carroll ... 13,028
West Feliciana ... 11,376
Winn ... 16,369

Cities

Abbeville ... 10,996
Abita Springs (★N.O.) ... 839
Addis (★B.R.) ... 724
Albany ... 700
Alexandria (★93,500; ALEX) ... 41,557
Amelia ... 2,292
Amite (Amite City) ... 3,593
Anandale (★ALEX) ... 1,779
Arabi (★N.O.) ... 12,500
Arcadia ... 2,970
Arnaudville ... 1,673
Avondale (★N.O.) ... 4,000
Baker (★B.R.) ... 8,281
Baldwin ... 2,117
Basile ... 1,779
Bastrop ... 14,713
Baton Rouge (★336,600; B.R.) ... 165,963
Bawcomville (★MONR) ... 1,500
Bayou Cane ... 9,077
Bayou Vista ... 5,121
Belle Chasse (★N.O.) ... 2,000
Benton ... 1,493
Bernice ... 1,794
Berwick ... 4,168
Blanchard (★SHRE) ... 806
Bogalusa ... 18,412
Bonita ... 533
Bossier City (★SHRE) ... 41,595
Boyce ... 1,240
Breaux Bridge (★LAF) ... 4,942
Bridge City (★N.O.) ... 3,500
Broussard (★LAF) ... 1,707
Brownfields (★B.R.) ... 2,000
Brownsville (★MONR) ... 3,000
Brusly (★B.R.) ... 1,282
Bunkie ... 5,395
Buras ... 2,500
Campti ... 1,078
Carencro (★LAF) ... 2,302
Carville ... 950
Chalmette (★N.O.) ... 20,000
Chatham ... 827
Cheneyville ... 1,082
Choudrant ... 555
Church Point ... 3,865
Clarks ... 889
Clayton ... 1,103
Clinton ... 1,884
Colfax ... 1,892
Columbia ... 1,000
Cooper Road (North Shreveport) (★SHRE) ... 9,034
Cottonport ... 1,924
Cotton Valley ... 1,261
Coushatta ... 1,492
Covington (★N.O.) ... 7,170
Crowley ... 16,104
Cullen ... 1,956
Cut Off ... 950
Delcambre ... 1,975
Delhi ... 2,887
Denham Springs (★B.R.) ... 6,752
De Quincy ... 3,448
De Ridder ... 8,030
Des Allemands (Allemands) ... 2,318
Donaldsonville ... 7,367
Doyline ... 716
Dubach ... 1,096
Dupont (Plaquemine Southwest) ... 1,224
Duson ... 1,190
East Bank (Little Farms) (★N.O.) ... 15,713
Elizabeth ... 504
Elton ... 1,598
Erath ... 2,024
Estherwood ... 661
Eunice ... 11,390
Farmerville ... 3,416
Ferriday ... 5,239
Florien ... 639
Forest Park (★MONR) ... 1,000
Fountain Place (★B.R.) ... 4,000
Franklin ... 9,325
Franklinton ... 3,562
French Settlement ... 600
Galliano ... 1,200
Garyville ... 2,474
Gibsland ... 1,380
Gilbert ... 746
Glenmora ... 1,651
Golden Meadow ... 2,681
Gonzales (★B.R.) ... 4,512
Grambling ... 4,407
Gramercy ... 2,567
Grand Coteau ... 1,301
Grand Isle ... 2,236
Grayson ... 516
Greensburg ... 652
Gretna (★N.O.) ... 24,875
Grosse Tete ... 710
Gueydan ... 1,984
Hahnville (★N.O.) ... 2,483
Hammond ... 12,487
Hammond East ... 1,342
Harahan (★N.O.) ... 13,037
Harrisonburg ... 626
Harvey (★N.O.) ... 10,000
Haughton (★SHRE) ... 885
Haynesville ... 3,055
Hodge ... 818
Hollywood (★LKCH) ... 2,328
Homer ... 4,483
Hornbeck ... 525
Houma ... 30,922
Independence ... 1,770
Inniswold (★B.R.) ... 1,200
Iota ... 1,271
Iowa ... 1,944
Jackson ... 4,697
Jeanerette ... 6,322
Jefferson (Jefferson Heights) (★N.O.) ... 16,489
Jena ... 2,431
Jennings ... 11,783
Jonesboro ... 5,072
Jonesville ... 2,761
Junction City ... 733
Kaplan ... 5,540
Kennedy Heights (★N.O.) ... 2,000
Kenner (★N.O.) ... 29,858
Kentwood ... 2,736
Kinder ... 2,307
Kiroli Woods (★MONR) ... 1,000
Krotz Springs ... 1,435
Lacombe (★N.O.) ... 1,100
Lafayette (★114,400; LAF) ... 68,908
Lafitte ... 1,223
Lake Arthur ... 3,551
Lake Charles (★124,100; LKCH) ... 77,998
Lake Providence ... 6,183
Lakeshore (★MONR) ... 2,000
Lakeview (★SHRE) ... 1,000
Laplace (La Place) ... 5,953
Larose ... 4,267
Lecompte ... 1,518
Leesville ... 8,928
Live Oak Manor (★N.O.) ... 1,500
Livingston ... 1,398
Livonia ... 611
Lockport ... 2,398
Logansport ... 1,330
Loreauville ... 728
Luling (★N.O.) ... 3,255
Lutcher ... 3,911
Madisonville (★N.O.) ... 801
Magnolia Woods (★B.R.) ... 1,000
Mamou ... 3,275
Mandeville (★N.O.) ... 2,571
Mangham ... 544
Mansfield ... 6,432
Mansura ... 1,699
Many ... 3,112
Maringouin ... 1,365
Marion ... 796
Marksville ... 4,519
Marrero (★N.O.) ... 29,015
Melville ... 2,076
Mermentau ... 756
Mer Rouge ... 819
Merryville ... 1,286
Metairie (★N.O.) ... 136,477
Mimosa Park (★N.O.) ... 1,624
Minden ... 13,996
Monroe (★105,000; MONR) ... 56,374
Montgomery ... 923
Mooringsport (★SHRE) ... 830
Moreauville ... 807
Morgan City ... 16,586
Morganza ... 836
Morse ... 759
Moss Bluff (★LKCH) ... 1,000
Mossville (★LKCH) ... 1,000
Napoleonville ... 1,008
Natchitoches ... 15,974
Newellton ... 1,403
New Iberia ... 30,147
Newllano ... 1,800
New Orleans (★1,051,800; N.O.) ... 593,471
New Roads ... 3,945
New Sarpy (★N.O.) ... 1,643
Norco (★N.O.) ... 4,773
North Hodge ... 640
North Merrydale (★B.R.) ... 1,200
Oakdale ... 7,301
Oak Grove ... 1,980
Oberlin ... 1,857
Oil City ... 907
Olla ... 1,387
Opelousas ... 20,387
Patterson ... 4,409
Pearl River (★N.O.) ... 1,361
Pine Prairie ... 515
Pineville (★ALEX) ... 8,951
Plain Dealing ... 1,300
Plaquemine ... 7,739
Pleasant Hill ... 826
Ponchatoula ... 4,545
Port Allen (★B.R.) ... 5,728
Port Barre ... 2,133
Port Sulphur ... 3,022
Provencal ... 530
Raceland ... 4,880
Rayne ... 9,510
Rayville ... 3,962
Red Oaks (★B.R.) ... 2,000
Reserve ... 6,381
Ridgecrest ... 1,076
Ringgold ... 1,731
Roseland ... 1,273
Rosepine ... 587
Ruston ... 17,365
St. Francisville ... 1,603
St. Joseph ... 1,864
St. Martinville ... 7,153
St. Rose (★N.O.) ... 2,106
Samtown (★ALEX) ... 3,750
Sarepta ... 882
Scotlandville (Scotland) (★B.R.) ... 22,557
Scott (★LAF) ... 1,334
Seymourville ... 2,506
Shreveport (★263,800; SHRE) ... 182,064
Sibley ... 869
Sicily Island ... 630
Siegle (★MONR) ... 2,000
Simmesport ... 2,027
Slaughter ... 580
Slidell (★N.O.) ... 16,101
Sorrento ... 1,182
South Acres (Sulphur South) (★LKCH) ... 1,108
Springhill ... 6,496
Sterlington (★MONR) ... 1,118
Sulphur (★LKCH) ... 15,247
Sunset ... 1,675
Tallulah ... 9,643
Terrytown (Terry Town) (★N.O.) ... 13,832
Thibodaux ... 15,028
Timberlande (★N.O.) ... 1,000
Tioga (★ALEX) ... 1,200
Triumph ... 1,600
Tullos ... 600
Urania ... 874
Vacherie ... 2,145
Vidalia ... 5,538
Ville Platte ... 9,692
Vinton ... 3,454
Violet (★N.O.) ... 1,300
Vivian ... 4,046
Waggaman (★N.O.) ... 1,000
Walker (★B.R.) ... 1,363
Wardville (★ALEX) ... 1,087
Washington ... 1,473
Waterproof ... 1,438
Welsh ... 3,203
Westlake (West Lake) (★LKCH) ... 4,082
Westminster (★B.R.) ... 1,000
West Monroe (★MONR) ... 14,868
Westwego (★N.O.) ... 11,402
White Castle ... 2,206
Wilson ... 606
Winnfield ... 7,142
Winnsboro ... 5,349
Wisner ... 1,339
Youngsville (★LAF) ... 1,002
Zachary (★B.R.) ... 4,964
Zwolle ... 2,169

MAINE

1970 C ... 993,663

Counties

Androscoggin ... 91,279
Aroostook ... 94,078
Cumberland ... 192,528
Franklin ... 22,444
Hancock ... 34,590
Kennebec ... 95,247
Knox ... 29,013
Lincoln ... 20,537
Oxford ... 43,457
Penobscot ... 125,393
Piscataquis ... 16,285
Sagadahoc ... 23,452
Somerset ... 40,597
Waldo ... 23,328
Washington ... 29,859
York ... 111,576

Cities

Anson (2,168▲) ... 870
Auburn (★★LEW-) ... 24,151
Augusta ... 21,945
Baileyville (2,167▲) ...
Bangor (★78,400; BANG) ... 33,168
Bar Harbor (Bar Harbor Center) (3,716▲) ... 2,392
Bath ... 9,679
Belfast ... 5,957
Berwick (Berwick Center) (★DOV-) (3,136▲) ... 1,765
Bethel (2,220▲) ... 950
Biddeford (★POR) ... 19,983
Bingham (Bingham Center (1,254▲) ... 1,184
Boothbay Harbor (2,320▲) ... 1,800
Brewer (★BANG) ... 9,300
Bridgton (2,967▲) ... 1,779
Brunswick (Brunswick Center) (16,195▲) ... 12,546
Bucksport (3,756▲) ... 2,456
Buxton Center (Buxton) (3,135▲) ... 100
Calais ... 4,044
Camden (Camden Center) (4,115▲) ... 3,492
Cape Elizabeth (★POR) ... 7,873
Caribou ... 10,419
Castine ... 700
Chelsea (2,095▲) ... 125
Chisholm ... 1,530
Clinton (Clinton Center) ... 1,124
Cumberland Center (4,096▲) ... 700
Dexter (Dexter Center) (3,725▲) ... 2,732
Dixfield (2,188▲) ... 1,535
Dover-Foxcroft (Dover-Foxcroft Center) (4,178▲) ... 3,102
East Millinocket ... 2,567
Eastport ... 1,989
Eliot (★PTSM) (3,497▲) ... 2,000
Ellsworth ... 4,603
Fairfield (5,684▲) ... 3,694
Falmouth (★POR) ... 6,291
Farmingdale (Farmingdale Center) (2,423▲) ... 1,832
Farmington (Farmington Center) (5,657▲) ... 3,096
Fort Fairfield (Fort Fairfield Center) (4,859▲) ... 2,322
Fort Kent (Fort Kent Center) (4,575▲) ... 2,876
Freeport (Freeport Center) (4,781▲) ... 1,822
Fryeburg (2,208▲) ... 1,075
Gardiner ... 6,685
Gorham (Gorham Center) (★POR) (7,839▲) ... 3,337
Gray (★POR) (2,939▲) ... 700
Greenville (Greenville Center) (1,894▲) ... 1,320
Guilford (1,694▲) ... 1,216
Hallowell ... 2,814
Hampden (★BANG) (4,693▲) ... 1,400
Harpswell (2,552▲) ... 130
Hartland (1,414▲) ... 950
Hermon (2,376▲) ... 300
Houlton (Houlton Center) (8,111▲) ... 6,760
Howland ... 1,468
Jay (3,954▲) ... 350
Jonesport (1,326▲) ... 1,073
Kennebunk (Kennebunk Center) (5,646▲) ... 2,764
Kennebunkport (Kennebunkport Center) ... 1,097
Kittery (Kittery Center) (★PTSM) (11,028▲) ... 7,363
Kittery Point (★PTSM) ... 1,172
Lewiston (★75,900; LEW-) ... 41,779
Limestone (Limestone Center) (10,360▲) ... 1,572
Lincoln (4,759▲) ... 3,482
Lisbon (★LEW-) (6,544▲) ... 1,100
Lisbon Falls (★LEW-) ... 3,257
Livermore Falls (3,450▲) ... 2,378
Lubec ... 950
Machias (2,441▲) ... 1,368
Madawaska (5,585▲) ... 4,452
Madison (4,278▲) ... 2,920
Mars Hill (1,875▲) ... 1,384
Mechanic Falls ... 2,193
Mexico (4,309▲) ... 3,325
Milford (★BANG) (1,828▲) ... 1,519
Millinocket ... 7,742
Milo (Milo Center) (2,572▲) ... 1,514
Monmouth (2,062▲) ... 500
New Gloucester (2,811▲) ... 200
Newport (2,260▲) ... 1,588
Norridgewock (1,964▲) ... 1,067
North Anson ... 700
North Berwick (2,224▲) ... 1,449
North Windham (★POR) ... 900
Norway (3,595▲) ... 2,430
Oakland (3,535▲) ... 2,261
Ogunquit ... 800
Old Orchard Beach (★POR) ... 5,404
Old Town (★BANG) ... 9,057
Orono (★BANG) ... 9,989
Orrington (Orrington Corner) (★BANG) (2,702▲) ... 240
Paris (3,739▲) ... 250
Patten (Patten Center) ... 1,068
Pittsfield (Pittsfield Center) (4,274▲) ... 3,398
Poland (2,015▲) ... 250
Portland (★192,700; POR) ... 65,116
Presque Isle ... 11,452
Richmond (2,168▲) ... 1,449
Randolph ... 1,741
Rockland ... 8,505
Rockport (2,067▲) ... 900
Rumford (9,363▲) ... 6,198
Saco (★POR) ... 11,678
Sanford (Sanford Center) (15,812▲) ... 10,457
Scarborough (Scarboro) (★POR) (7,845▲) ... 800
Searsport (1,951▲) ... 1,110
Skowhegan (7,601▲) ... 6,571
South Berwick (★DOV-) (3,488▲) ... 1,863
South Paris ... 2,315
South Portland (★POR) ... 23,267
Southwest Harbor (1,657▲) ... 900
South Windham (★POR) ... 1,453
Springvale ... 2,914
Standish (3,122▲) ... 300
Thomaston (2,646▲) ... 2,160
Topsham (5,022▲) ... 2,700
Turner (2,246▲) ... 350
Van Buren (Van Buren Center) (3,971▲) ... 3,429
Vassalboro (Vassalborough) (2,618▲) ... 100
Veazie (★BANG) ... 1,556
Vinalhaven (1,135▲) ... 800
Waldoboro (3,146▲) ... 850
Washburn (1,914▲) ... 1,098
Waterville ... 18,192
Wells (4,448▲) ... 600
Westbrook (★POR) ... 14,444
Wilton (Wilton Center) (3,802▲) ... 2,225
Windham Center (Windham) (★POR) (6,593▲) ... 100
Winslow (Winslow Center) (7,299▲) ... 5,389
Winthrop (4,335▲) ... 2,571
Wiscasset (2,244▲) ... 950
Woodland ... 1,534
Yarmouth (★POR) (4,854▲) ... 2,421
York (★PTSM) (5,690▲) ... 1,900
York Beach (★PTSM) ... 900
York Harbor (★PTSM) ... 1,000

MARYLAND

1970 C ... 3,922,399

Counties

Allegany ... 84,044
Anne Arundel ... 297,539
Baltimore (county) ... 621,077
Calvert ... 20,682
Caroline ... 19,781
Carroll ... 69,006
Cecil ... 53,291
Charles ... 47,678
Dorchester ... 29,405
Frederick ... 84,927
Garrett ... 21,476
Harford ... 115,378
Howard ... 61,911
Kent ... 16,146
Montgomery ... 522,809
Prince Georges ... 660,567
Queen Annes ... 18,422
St. Marys ... 47,388
Somerset ... 18,924
Talbot ... 23,682
Washington ... 103,829
Wicomico ... 54,236
Worcester ... 24,442
Baltimore (Independent City) ... 905,759

Cities

Aberdeen ... 12,375
Adelphi (★WASH) ... 12,000
Allview Estates (★WASH) ... 1,300
Annapolis (★50,100; ANPLS) ... 30,095
Ardmore (★WASH) ... 1,000
Aspen Hill Park (★WASH) ... 900
Avondale (★WASH) ... 2,000
Baltimore (★1,892,800; BAL) ... 905,759
Baltimore Highlands (★BAL) ... 7,000
Barton (★CUMB) ... 723
Beacon Heights (★WASH) ... 1,300
Bel Air (★BAL) ... 6,307
Bellemead (★WASH) ... 1,000
Beltsville (★WASH) ... 8,912
Berkshire (★WASH) ... 4,000
Berlin ... 1,942
Berwyn Heights (★WASH) ... 3,934
Bethesda (★WASH) ... 71,621
Birchwood City (★WASH) ... 4,400
Bladensburg (★WASH) ... 7,488
Boonsboro ... 1,410
Boulevard Heights (★WASH) ... 2,000
Bowie (★WASH) ... 35,028
Bowling Green (★CUMB) ... 1,000
Bradbury Heights (★WASH) ... 1,000
Brentwood (★WASH) ... 3,426
Brinkley Manor (★WASH) ... 2,500
Brooklyn (★BAL) ... 13,896
Brunswick ... 3,566
Burnt Mills Hills (★WASH) ... 800
Burtonsville (★WASH) ... 1,100
Cabin John (★WASH) ... 2,500
Calverton (★WASH) ... 6,543
Cambridge ... 11,595
Camp Springs (★WASH) ... 2,800
Cape St. Claire (★BAL) ... 2,689
Capitol Heights (★WASH) ... 2,852
Carmody Hills (★WASH) ... 2,400
Carole Highlands (★WASH) ... 4,300
Catonsville (★BAL) ... 46,500
Catonsville Manor (★BAL) ... 3,500
Cecilton ... 581
Cedar Heights (★WASH) ... 2,200
Cedarhurst (★BAL) ... 1,100
Centreville ... 1,853
Chadwick Manor (★BAL) ... 2,000
Charlestown (★PHIL-) ... 721
Chesapeake Beach (★WASH) ... 934
Chesapeake City ... 1,031
Chestertown ... 3,476
Cheverly (★WASH) ... 6,808
Cheverly Manor (★WASH) ... 1,500
Chevy Chase (★WASH) ... 16,424
Chevy Chase Section Four (★WASH) ... 2,266
Chevy Chase View (★WASH) ... 1,200
Chillum (★WASH) ... 15,000
Clinton (★WASH) ... 4,700
Cockeysville (★BAL) ... 4,500
Colesville (★WASH) ... 9,455
College Park (★WASH) ... 26,156
Colmar Manor (★WASH) ... 1,715
Columbia (★WASH) ... 8,815
Columbia Park (★WASH) ... 1,500
Coral Hills (★WASH) ... 1,700
Cottage City (★WASH) ... 993
Cresaptown (★CUMB) ... 1,731
Crisfield ... 3,078
Crofton (★WASH) ... 4,478

★ Population or designation of metropolitan area, including suburbs (see headnote).
▲ Population of entire "town" or township, including other communities and rural areas.
† Population is from a local census taken at date specified.

Cumberland (★82,100; CUMB)...29,724
Damascus (★WASH)...2,638
Deale (★WASH)...1,059
Defense Heights (★WASH)...1,500
Delmar...1,191
Dennis Grove Apartments (★WASH)...2,500
Denton...1,561
District Heights (★WASH)...8,424
Dodge Park (★WASH)...2,500
Dundalk (★BAL)...85,377
Easton...6,809
East Pines (★WASH)...3,000
Edgemere (★BAL)...7,000
Edgewood (★BAL)...8,000
Edmonston (★WASH)...1,441
Ednor (★WASH)...900
Elkridge (Elk Ridge) (★BAL)...2,000
Elkton (★PHIL-)...5,362
Ellicott City (★BAL)...2,000
Emmitsburg...1,532
English Manor (★WASH)...2,000
Essex (★BAL)...38,193
Fairmount Heights (★WASH)...1,972
Fairview (★WASH)...1,000
Federalsburg...1,917
Ferndale (★BAL)...3,000
Fernglen Manor (★BAL)...900
Forest Heights (★WASH)...3,600
Forest Manor (★WASH)...2,000
Forestville (★WASH)...9,000
Fort Washington Forest (★WASH)...1,500
Fountain Head (★HAG)...2,029
Frederick...23,641
Friendsville...566
Frostburg (★CUMB)...7,327
Fruitland (★SLSB)...2,315
Funkstown (★HAG)...1,051
Gaithersburg (★WASH)...8,344
Garland (★BAL)...1,000
Garrett Park (★WASH)...1,258
Garrett Park Estates (★WASH)...3,000
Glassmanor (★WASH)...4,300
Glenarden (★WASH)...4,502
Glen Burnie (★BAL)...32,000
Glen Burnie Park (★BAL)...4,000
Glen Echo Heights (★WASH)...1,100
Glen Hills (★WASH)...1,600
Glenmore (★BAL)...1,000
Glyndon (★BAL)...900
Good Luck (★WASH)...10,584
Grantsville...517
Grasonville...1,182
Greenbelt (★WASH)...18,199
Green Haven (★BAL)...2,700
Green Meadows (★WASH)...1,500
Greensboro...1,173
Hagerstown (★82,700; HAG)...35,862
Halethorpe (★BAL)...22,745
Halfway (★HAG)...6,106
Hampstead (★BAL)...961
Hancock...1,832
Havre De Grace...9,791
Heather Hill Apartments (★WASH)...1,700
Hebron...705
Herald Harbor (★BAL)...1,000
Hillandale (★WASH)...3,000
Hillandale Forest (★WASH)...2,000
Hillandale Heights (★WASH)...1,600
Hillcrest Heights (★WASH)...24,037
Hillside (★WASH)...1,900
Hillsmere Shores (★ANPLS)...1,200
Homewood (★WASH)...1,800
Hurlock...1,056
Hyattsville (★WASH)...14,998
Indian Head (★WASH)...1,350
Jefferson Heights (★HAG)...950
Jessup (★BAL)...1,000
Joppa (Joppatowne) (★BAL)...9,092
Kemp Mill (★WASH)...10,037
Kensington (★WASH)...2,322
Kensington Estates (★WASH)...2,500
Kentland (★WASH)...2,500
Kent Village (★WASH)...1,500
Kerby Hills (★WASH)...900
Kirkwood (★WASH)...2,500
Knollwood (★WASH)...1,000
Lake Shore (★BAL)...2,000
Landover (★WASH)...1,000
Landover Estates (★WASH)...1,500
Landover Hills (★WASH)...2,409
Langley Park (★WASH)...11,564
Lanham (★WASH)...6,700
Lansdowne (★BAL)...10,000
La Plata (★WASH)...1,561
Laurel (★WASH)...10,525
La Vale (★CUMB)...3,971
Leisure World (★WASH)...1,000
Leonardtown...1,406
Lewisdale (★WASH)...5,000
Lexington Park...9,136
Linthicum Heights (Linthicum) (★BAL)...12,700
Lochearn (★BAL)...5,000
Loch Lynn Heights...507
Lonaconing (★CUMB)...1,572
Londontowne (Woodland Beach) (★WASH)...2,750
Lutherville-Timonium (★BAL)...24,055
Lynn Acres (★BAL)...3,500
McAlpine (★BAL)...2,500
Manchester (★BAL)...1,466
Manor Park (★WASH)...1,000
Marley (★BAL)...2,500
Maryland City (★WASH)...4,000
Maryland Park (★WASH)...2,000
Maugansville (★HAG)...1,069
Mayo (★WASH)...2,154
Middle River (★BAL)...19,935
Middleton Farm (★WASH)...1,500
Middletown...1,262
Midland (★CUMB)...665
Milford (★BAL)...2,000
Montgomery White Oak (★WASH)...1,400
Morningside (★WASH)...1,665
Mountain Lake Park...1,263
Mount Airy (★BAL)...1,825
Mount Rainier (★WASH)...8,180
Mount Savage (★CUMB)...1,413
Naval Academy (★ANPLS)...5,487
New Carrollton (Carrollton) (★WASH)...14,870
New Hampshire Estates (★WASH)...3,500
New Windsor...788
North Beach (★WASH)...761
North Brentwood (★WASH)...758
North East (★PHIL-)...1,818
Northwest Park Apartments (★WASH)...4,000
Oakland...1,786
Oakland (★BAL)...1,256
Oak View (★WASH)...3,000
Ocean City...1,493
Odenton (★BAL)...5,989
Old Farm (★WASH)...1,500
Olney (★WASH)...2,138
Orchard Beach (★BAL)...1,700
Overlea (★BAL)...13,086
Owings Mills (★BAL)...7,360
Oxford...750
Oxon Hill (★WASH)...1,500
Palmer Park (★WASH)...8,172
Parkside (★WASH)...3,500
Parkview Gardens (★WASH)...2,000
Parkville (★BAL)...33,589
Parkwood (★WASH)...2,800
Pasadena (★BAL)...1,500
Pepper Mill Village (★WASH)...3,440
Perry Hall (Fullerton) (★BAL)...5,446
Perryville...2,091
Pikesville (★BAL)...25,395
Pleasantville (★BAL)...1,500
Pocomoke City (Pocomoke)...3,573
Port Deposit...906
Potomac (★WASH)...1,000
Potomac Heights (★WASH)...1,983
Potomac Park (★CUMB)...1,250
Powder Mill Village (★WASH)...2,800
Preston...509
Princess Anne...975
Pumphrey (★BAL)...3,500
Radiant Valley (★WASH)...1,500
Randallstown (★BAL)...15,000
Randolph Hills (★WASH)...4,500
Regency Estates (★WASH)...1,500
Reisterstown (★BAL)...13,000
Ridgley...822
Rising Sun...956
Riverdale (★WASH)...5,724
Riverdale Heights (★WASH)...1,100
Riviera Beach (★BAL)...7,464
Rock Creek Highlands (★WASH).1,300
Rock Creek Hills (★WASH)...2,000
Rockdale (★BAL)...2,500
Rock Hall...1,125
Rockville (★WASH)...41,564
Rogers Heights (★WASH)...3,200
Rolling Terrace (★WASH)...1,500
Rosecroft Park (★WASH)...1,100
Rosedale (★BAL)...19,417
Rossville (★BAL)...1,500
St. Michaels...1,456
Salisbury (★39,800; SLSB)...15,252
Savage (Savage Factory) (★BAL).2,116
Seabrook (★WASH)...6,500
Seat Pleasant (★WASH)...7,217
Severna Park (★BAL)...16,358
Shady Side (★WASH)...1,562
Sharpsburg (★HAG)...833
Sharptown...660
Silver Hill (★WASH)...5,000
Silver Spring (★WASH)...77,496
Smithsburg (★HAG)...671
Snow Hill...2,201
Somerset (★WASH)...1,303
Southern Garden Apartments (★WASH)...1,500
South Gate (★BAL)...5,360
South Laurel (★WASH)...13,345
Southlawn (★WASH)...2,800
Southview Apartments (★WASH)...3,500
Sparrows Point (★BAL)...2,750
Suitland (★WASH)...25,000
Sykesville (★BAL)...1,399
Takoma Park (★WASH)...18,455
Taneytown...1,731
Tantallon (★WASH)...1,500
Temple Hills Park (★WASH)...3,500
Templeton Knolls (★WASH)...1,000
Templeton Manor (★WASH)...1,800
Thurmont...2,359
Tilden Woods (★WASH)...1,200
Towson (★BAL)...77,799
Tuxedo (★WASH)...1,000
Union Bridge...904
University Gardens (★WASH)...1,200
University Hills (★WASH)...2,000
University Park (★WASH)...2,926
Upper Marlboro (★WASH)...646
Villa Nova (★BAL)...3,200
Waldorf (★WASH)...6,000
Walker Mill (★WASH)...6,322
Walkersville...1,269
Washington Grove (★WASH)...688
Westchester Estates (★WASH)...1,800
West Edmondale (★BAL)...2,500
Westernport...3,106
West Lanham Hills (★WASH)...1,200
West Laurel (★WASH)...4,478
Westminster (★BAL)...7,207
Westminster South (★BAL)...2,242
Wheaton (★WASH)...66,247
White Oaks (★WASH)...1,500
White Plains (★WASH)...1,370
Williamsport (★HAG)...2,270
Woodberry Forest (★WASH)...1,500
Woodlawn (★WASH)...3,000
Woodlawn (★BAL)...7,500
Woodlawn Heights (★BAL)...2,000
Woodmoor (★BAL)...6,000

MASSACHUSETTS

1970 C...5,689,170

Counties

Barnstable...96,656
Berkshire...149,402
Bristol...444,301
Dukes...6,117
Essex...637,887
Franklin...59,210
Hampden...459,050
Hampshire...123,981
Middlesex...1,398,355
Nantucket...3,774
Norfolk...604,854
Plymouth...333,314
Suffolk...735,190
Worcester...637,079

Cities

Abington (★BOS) (12,334▲)...4,700
Acton (★BOS) (14,770▲)...2,500
Acushnet (★N.BED) (7,767▲)...4,000
Adams (★PTSF)...11,772
Agawam (★SPRG) (21,717▲)...10,000
Amesbury (★BOS)...11,388
Amherst (26,331▲)...17,926
Andover (★BOS) (23,695▲)...5,500
Arlington (★BOS)...53,534
Ashburnham (★FTCH-) (3,484▲)...1,013
Ashland (★BOS)...8,882
Assinippi (★BOS)...900
Athol...11,185
Attleboro (★PROV-)...32,907
Auburn (★WORC)...15,347
Avon (★BOS)...5,295
Ayer...8,283
Baldwinville...1,739
Ballardvale (★BOS)...1,500
Barnstable (19,842▲)...1,202
Barre (3,825▲)...1,098
Bedford (★BOS)...13,513
Belchertown (★SPRG-) (5,936▲)...2,636
Bellingham (★BOS) (13,967▲)...4,228
Belmont (★BOS)...28,285
Beverly (★BOS)...38,348
Billerica (★BOS) (31,648▲)...4,500
Blackstone (★PROV-) (6,566▲)...5,000
Bondsville (★SPRG-)...1,657
Boston (★3,762,900; BOS)...641,071
Bourne (12,636▲)...500
Boxford (★BOS) (4,032▲)...2,026
Boylston (★WORC) (2,774▲)...600
Braintree (★BOS)...35,050
Bridgewater (★BOS) (11,829▲)...4,032
Brockton (★★BOS)...89,040
Brookfield (★WORC)...1,197
Brookline (★BOS)...58,689
Brookville (★BOS)...2,000
Burlington (★BOS)...21,980
Buzzards Bay...2,422
Cambridge (★BOS)...100,361
Canton (★BOS)...17,100
Carlisle (★BOS) (2,871▲)...350
Centerville...2,000
Chaffins (Chaffinville) (★WORC)...3,000
Charlton (Charlton Center) (★WORC) (4,654▲)...300
Charlton City (★WORC)...900
Chatham (4,554▲)...1,652
Chelmsford (★BOS) (31,432▲)...6,000
Chelsea (★BOS)...30,625
Cherry Valley (★WORC)...2,300
Cheshire (★PTSF) (3,006▲)...1,021
Chicopee (★SPRG-)...66,676
Clinton...13,383
Cochituate (★BOS)...5,000
Chohasset (★BOS) (6,954▲)...4,500
Collinsville (BOS)...5,000
Concord (★BOS) (16,148▲)...6,000
Cotuit...900
Dalton (★PTSF)...7,505
Danvers (★BOS)...26,151
Dartmouth (★N.BED.) (18,800▲)...200
Dedham (★BOS)...26,938
Deerfield (3,850▲)...500
Dennis (6,454▲)...600
Dennis Port...1,410
Dighton (★TAUN) (4,667▲)...700
Douglas (2,947▲)...300
Dorothy Pond (★WORC)...1,000
Dover (★BOS) (4,529▲)...1,881
Dracut (★BOS) (18,214▲)...8,000
Dudley (8,087▲)...3,470
Duxbury (★BOS) (7,636▲)...2,000
East Billerica (★BOS)...1,500
East Bridgewater (★BOS) (8,347▲)...3,000
East Brookfield (★WORC) (1,800▲)...1,392
East Chelmsford (★BOS)...2,000
East Douglas...1,763
East Falmouth...2,971
East Hampton (★SPRG-)...13,012
East Longmeadow (★SPRG-)...13,029
East Millbury (★WORC)...1,000
Easton (★BOS) (12,157▲)...250
East Pepperell (★BOS)...1,500
East Sudbury (★BOS)...2,500
East Templeton...900
East Walpole (★BOS)...3,500
East Wareham...900
Edgartown...1,006
Egypt (★BOS)...1,500
Essex (★BOS) (2,670▲)...930
Everett (★BOS)...42,485
Fairhaven (★N.BED.)...16,332
Fall River (★150,400; F.R.)...96,898
Falmouth (15,942▲)...4,000
Fayville (★BOS)...900
Feeding Hills (★SPRG-)...6,000
Fiskdale...1,612
Fitchburg (★100,100; FTCH-)...43,343
Forge Village (★BOS)...950
Foxboro (Foxborough) (★BOS) (14,218▲)...4,090
Framingham (★BOS)...64,048
Franklin (★BOS) (17,830▲)...8,863
Freetown (★F.R., ★N.BED.) (4,270▲)...
Gardner...19,748
Georgetown (★BOS) (5,290▲)...3,000
Gilbertville...1,247
Gloucester (★BOS)...27,941
Grafton (★WORC) (11,659▲)...1,300
Granby (Granby Center) (★SPRG-) (5,473▲)...1,354
Graniteville (★BOS)...950
Great Barrington (7,537▲)...3,203
Greenfield...18,116
Groton (5,109▲)...1,314
Groveland (★BOS) (5,382▲)...2,500
Hadley (3,750▲)...800
Halifax (★BOS) (3,537▲)...600
Hamilton (★BOS) (6,373▲)...900
Hampden (★SPRG-) (4,572▲)...400
Hanover (★BOS) (10,107▲)...1,500
Hanson (★BOS) (7,148▲)...800
Hardwick (2,379▲)...1,200
Harvard (12,536▲)... 65
Harwich (5,892▲)...1,000
Harwich Port...1,700
Hatfield (2,825▲)...1,380
Haverhill (★★BOS)...46,120
Hingham (★BOS) (18,845▲)...13,500
Hinsdale (★PTSF)...900
Holbrook (★BOS) (11,775▲)...9,750
Holden (★WORC) (12,564▲)...2,200
Holliston (★BOS) (12,069▲)...6,000
Holyoke (★★SPRG-)...50,112
Hopedale (★BOS)...4,292
Hopkinton (★BOS) (5,981▲)...3,300
Housatonic...1,344
Hudson (★BOS)...16,084
Hull (★BOS)...9,961
Huntington (1,593▲)...850
Hyannis...6,500
Ipswich (★BOS) (10,750▲)...5,022
Islington (★BOS)...4,500
Kenwood (★BOS)...2,000
Kingston (★BOS) (5,999▲)...3,772
Lakeville (★BOS) (4,376▲)...1,432
Lancaster (6,095▲)...750
Lanesboro (★PTSF) (2,972▲)...900
Lawrence (★★BOS)...66,915
Lee (★PTSF) (6,426▲)...3,389
Leicester (★WORC) (9,140▲)...3,173
Lenox (★PTSF) (5,804▲)...2,208
Leominster (★★FTCH-)...32,939
Lexington (★BOS)...31,886
Lincoln (★BOS) (7,567▲)...1,500
Linwood...1,100
Littleton (Littleton Common) (★BOS) (6,380▲)...2,764
Longmeadow (★SPRG-)...15,630
Lowell (★★BOS)...94,239
Ludlow (★SPRG-) (17,580▲)...12,500
Lunenburg (★FTCH-) (7,419▲)...950
Lynn (★BOS)...90,294
Lynnfield (★BOS)...10,826
Malden (★BOS)...56,127
Manchaug...900
Manchester (★BOS)...5,151
Manomet (★BOS)...500
Mansfield (★BOS) (9,939▲)...4,778
Marblehead (★BOS)...21,295
Marion (★N.BED.) (3,466▲)...1,262
Marlborough (Marlboro) (★BOS)...27,936
Marshfield (★BOS) (15,223▲)...2,562
Marshfield Hills (★BOS)...1,350
Matfield (★BOS)...900
Mattapoisett (★N.BED.) (4,500▲)...2,188
Maynard (★BOS)...9,710
Medfield (★BOS) (9,821▲)...2,900
Medford (★BOS)...64,397
Medway (★BOS) (7,938▲)...3,716
Melrose (★BOS)...33,180
Mendon (★BOS) (2,524▲)...900
Merrimac (★BOS) (4,245▲)...2,400
Methuen (★BOS)...35,456
Middleboro (★BOS) (13,607▲)...6,259
Middleton (★BOS)...4,044
Milford (★BOS)...19,352
Millbury (★WORC) (11,987▲)...6,000
Millers Falls...1,186
Millis (★BOS) (5,686▲)...3,217
Millville...1,764
Milton (★BOS)...27,190
Monson (★SPRG-) (7,355▲)...1,110
Montague (8,451▲)...600
Monument Beach...1,000
Morningdale (★WORC)...900
Nabnasset (★BOS)...2,700
Nahant (★BOS)...4,119
Nantucket (3,774▲)...2,461
Natick (★BOS)...31,057
Needham (★BOS)...29,748
New Bedford (★158,900; N.BED).101,777
Newbury (★BOS) (3,804▲)...800
Newburyport (★BOS)...15,807
Newton (★BOS)...91,263
Norfolk (★BOS) (4,656▲)...400
North Abington (★BOS)...3,600
North Adams...19,195
North Amherst...2,854
Northampton...29,664
North Andover (★BOS)...16,284
North Attleboro (★PROV-)...18,665
North Billerica (★BOS)...5,000
Northboro (★WORC) (9,218▲)...2,650
Northbridge (★WORC) (11,795▲)...3,100
North Brookfield (★WORC) (3,967▲)...2,677
North Chelmsford (★BOS)...6,000
North Dartmouth (★N.BED.)...6,000
North Dighton (★TAUN)...1,264
North Easton (★BOS)...4,500
Northfield (2,631▲)...1,191
North Grafton (★WORC)...4,300
North Oxford (★WORC)...1,550
North Pembroke (★BOS)...2,881
North Reading (★BOS)...11,264
North Scituate (★BOS)...4,000
North Tewksbury (★BOS)...900
North Uxbridge...1,360
North Wilbraham (★SPRG-)...1,000
North Wilmington (★BOS)...4,000
Norton (★PROV-) (9,487▲)...2,073
Norwell (★BOS) (7,796▲)...600
Norwood (★BOS)...30,815
Nutting Lake (★BOS)...1,500
Oak Bluffs...1,385
Ocean Grove (★F.R.)...2,500
Onset...1,771
Orange (6,104▲)...3,847
Orleans (3,055▲)...950
Osterville...1,286
Oxford (★WORC) (10,345▲)...6,109
Palmer (★SPRG-) (11,680▲)...3,649
Paxton (★WORC) (3,731▲)...1,500
Peabody (★BOS)...48,080
Pembroke (★BOS) (11,193▲)...650
Pepperell (★BOS) (5,887▲)...600
Pigeon Cove (★BOS)...1,466
Pinehurst (★BOS)...5,681
Pittsfield (★101,300; PTSF)...57,020
Plainville (★PROV-)...4,953
Plymouth (★BOS) (18,606▲)...10,374
Pocasset...900
Point Independence...900
Provincetown...2,911
Quincy (★BOS)...87,966
Randolph (★BOS)...27,035
Raynham (North Raynham) (★TAUN-) (6,705▲)...800
Raynham Center (★TAUN-)...2,526
Reading (★BOS)...22,539
Rehoboth (★PROV-) (6,512▲)...300
Revere (★BOS)...43,159
River Pines (★BOS)...3,000
Rochdale (★WORC)...1,320
Rockland (★BOS)...15,674
Rockport (★BOS) (5,636★)...4,166
Rowley (★BOS) (3,040▲)...1,325
Rutland (★WORC) (3,198▲)...1,751
Sagamore...1,007
Salem (★★BOS)...40,556
Salisbury (★BOS) (4,179▲)...1,500
Sand Hill (★BOS)...1,750
Sandwich (5,239▲)...1,305
Saugus (★BOS)...25,110
Scituate (★BOS) (16,973▲)...3,000
Seekonk (★PROV-)...11,116
Sharon (★BOS)...12,367
Shawsheen Village (★BOS)...5,000
Shelburne Falls...2,183
Sherborn (★BOS) (3,309▲)...500
Shirley (4,909▲)...1,718
Shore Acres (★BOS)...1,200
Shrewsbury...19,196
Silver Lake (★BOS)...5,000
Somerset (★F.R.)...18,088
Somerville (★BOS)...88,779
Southampton (★SPRG-) (3,069▲)...400
South Acton (★BOS)...3,000
South Ashburnham (★FTCH-)...1,181
South Bellingham (★PROV-)...3,000
Southboro (★BOS) (5,798▲)...1,500
Southbridge...17,057
South Chelmsford (★BOS)...3,000
South Dartmouth (★N.BED.)...7,000
South Deerfield...1,628
South Dennis...1,000
South Duxbury (★BOS)...2,075
South Grafton (Fisherville) (★WORC)...3,000
South Hadley (★SPRG-) (17,033▲)...6,000
South Hadley Falls (★SPRG-)...9,000
South Hamilton (★BOS)...3,500
South Hingham (★BOS)...5,000
South Lancaster...2,679
South Monson (★SPRG-)...1,200
South Swansea (★F.R.)...1,500
Southwick (★SPRG-) (6,330▲)...1,263
South Yarmouth...5,380
Spencer (★WORC) (8,779▲)...5,895
Springfield (★500,000; SPRG-)..163,905
Sterling (★WORC) (4,247▲)...950
Stockbridge (★PTSF) (2,312▲)...1,147
Stoneham (★BOS)...20,725
Stoughton (★BOS)...23,459
Stow (★BOS) (3,984▲)...950
Sturbridge (4,878▲)...800
Sudbury (★BOS) (13,506▲)...2,500
Sudbury Center (★BOS)...2,000
Sutton (★WORC) (4,590▲)...500
Swampscott (★BOS)...13,578
Swansea (12,640▲)...300
Taunton (★57,200; TAUN)...43,756
Teaticket...1,800
Templeton (5,863▲)...750
Tewksbury (★BOS) (22,755▲)...4,000
Thorndike (★SPRG-)...900
Three Rivers (★SPRG-)...3,366
Topsfield (★BOS) (5,225▲)...2,200
Townsend (★FTCH-) (4,281▲)...1,329
Truro (1,234▲)...400
Turners Falls...4,470
Upton (★BOS) (3,484▲)...1,130
Uxbridge (8,253▲)...3,380
Vineyard Haven (Tisbury)...2,257
Wakefield (★BOS)...25,402
Walpole (★BOS) (18,149▲)...8,500
Waltham (★BOS)...61,582
Wamesit (★BOS)...3,000
Ware (8,187▲)...6,509
Wareham (11,492▲)...2,024
Warren (★SPRG-) (3,633▲)...1,688
Watertown (★BOS)...39,307
Wayland (★BOS) (13,469▲)...4,000
Webster...14,917
Wellesley (★BOS)...28,051
Wellfleet...900
Wenham (★BOS)...3,849
West Abington (★BOS)...1,500
West Acton (★BOS)...4,000

(Massachusetts continued)

★ Population or designation of metropolitan area, including suburbs (see headnote).
▲ Population of entire "town" or township, including other communities and rural areas.
† Population is from a local census taken at date specified.

(Massachusetts continued)

West Andover (★BOS)...3,000
West Billerica (★BOS)...1,200
Westborough (★WORC) (12,594▲)...4,474
West Boylston (★WORC) (6,369▲)...3,400
West Bridgewater (★BOS) (7,152▲)...1,920
West Brookfield (2,653▲)...1,536
West Chelmsford (★BOS)...2,500
West Concord (★BOS)...4,000
West Dennis...1,400
Westfield (★SPRG-)...31,433
West Hanover (★BOS)...1,500
Westlands (★BOS)...4,000
West Medway (★BOS)...2,269
Westminster (★FTCH-) (4,273▲)...1,200
Weston (★BOS)...10,870
Westport (★F.R.) (9,791▲)...1,500
West Springfield (★SPRG-)...28,461
West Upton (★BOS)...1,000
West Warren (★SPRG-)...1,237
Westwood (★BOS) (12,750▲)...8,000
West Yarmouth...3,699
Weymouth (★BOS)...54,610
Whalom (★FTCH-)...1,400
Whitinsville...5,210
Whitman (★BOS)...13,059
Wilbraham (★SPRG-) (11,984▲)...2,500
Williamstown (8,454▲)...4,285
Wilmington (★BOS) (17,102▲)...4,500
Winchendon (6,635▲)...3,997
Winchester (★BOS)...22,269
Winthrop (★BOS)...20,335
Woburn (★BOS)...37,406
Woods Hole...900
Worcester (★334,000; WORC)...176,572
Wrentham (★BOS) (7,315▲)...1,723

MICHIGAN

1970 C...8,879,862

Counties

Alcona...7,113
Alger...8,568
Allegan...66,575
Alpena...30,708
Antrim...12,612
Arenac...11,149
Baraga...7,789
Barry...38,166
Bay...117,339
Benzie...8,593
Berrien...163,875
Branch...37,906
Calhoun...141,963
Cass...43,312
Charlevoix...16,541
Cheboygan...16,573
Chippewa...32,412
Clare...16,695
Clinton...48,492
Crawford...6,482
Delta...35,924
Dickinson...23,753
Eaton...68,892
Emmet...18,331
Genesee...445,589
Gladwin...13,471
Gogebic...20,676
Grand Traverse...39,175
Gratiot...39,246
Hillsdale...37,171
Houghton...34,652
Huron...34,083
Ingham...261,039
Ionia...45,848
Iosco...24,905
Iron...13,813
Isabella...44,594
Jackson...143,274
Kalamazoo...201,550
Kalkaska...5,272
Kent...411,044
Keweenaw...2,264
Lake...5,661
Lapeer...52,361
Leelanau...10,872
Lenawee...81,951
Livingston...58,967
Luce...6,789
Mackinac...9,660
Macomb...625,309
Manistee...20,094
Marquette...64,686
Mason...22,612
Mecosta...27,992
Menominee...24,587
Midland...63,769
Missaukee...7,126
Monroe...118,479
Montcalm...39,660
Montmorency...5,247
Muskegon...157,426
Newaygo...27,992
Oakland...907,871
Oceana...17,984
Ogemaw...11,903
Ontonagon...10,548
Osceola...14,838
Oscoda...4,726
Otsego...10,422
Ottawa...128,181
Presque Isle...12,836
Roscommon...9,892
Saginaw...219,743
St. Clair...120,175
St. Joseph...47,392
Sanilac...35,181
Schoolcraft...8,226
Shiawassee...63,075
Tuscola...48,603
Van Buren...56,173
Washtenaw...234,103
Wayne...2,669,604
Wexford...19,717

Cities

Addison...595
Adrian...20,382
Akron...525
Albion...12,112
Algonac (★DET)...3,684
Allegan...4,516
Allen Park (★DET)...40,747
Alma...9,790
Almont (★DET)...1,634
Alpena...13,805
Anchor Bay Gardens (★DET)...1,000
Ann Arbor (★★DET)...99,797
Armada (★DET)...1,352
Athens...996
Auburn (★BC-M)...1,919
Auburn Heights (★DET)...6,000
Au Gres...564
Augusta (★B.CK)...1,025
Au Sable...1,305
Bad Axe...2,999
Baldwin...612
Bancroft (★FLN)...724
Bangor...2,050
Bangor Township (★BC-M)...15,896
Baraga...1,116
Battle Creek (★110,000; B.CK)...38,931
Bay City (★175,100; BC-M)...49,449
Beaverton...954
Beecher (★FLN)...15,500
Beechwood (★HLND)...2,714
Belding...5,121
Bellaire...897
Belleville (★DET)...2,406
Bellevue...1,297
Benton Harbor (★98,200; BNTH-)...16,481
Benton Heights (★BNTH-)...6,000
Berkley (★DET)...21,879
Berrien Springs (★S.B.-)...1,951
Bertrand (★S.B.-)...3,500
Bessemer...2,805
Beverly Hills (★DET)...13,598
Big Rapids...11,995
Bingham Farms...566
Birch Run (★FLN)...932
Birmingham (★DET)...26,170
Birmingham Farms (★DET)...1,200
Blissfield...2,753
Bloomfield Highlands (★DET)...1,500
Bloomfield Hills (★DET)...3,672
Bloomfield Village (★DET)...4,000
Boyne City...2,969
Breckenridge...1,257
Bridgeport (★SAG)...1,900
Bridgman (★BNTH-)...1,621
Brighton (★DET)...2,457
Britton...697
Bronson...2,390
Brooklands (★DET)...2,500
Brooklyn (★JAC)...1,112
Brown City...1,142
Brownlee Park (★B.CK)...2,985
Buchanan (★S.B.-)...4,645
Bunny Run (★DET)...1,391
Burr Oak...873
Byron...655
Byron Center (★GD.R)...900
Cadillac...9,990
Caledonia (★GD.R)...716
Calumet...1,007
Capac...1,279
Carleton (★DET)...1,503
Caro...3,701
Carrollton (★SAG)...8,526
Carson City...1,217
Carsonville...621
Caseville...607
Caspian...1,165
Cass City...1,974
Cassopolis...2,108
Cedar Springs (★GD.R)...1,807
Cement City (★JAC)...531
Center Line (★DET)...10,379
Central Lake...741
Centreville...1,044
Charlevoix...3,519
Charlotte...8,244
Cheboygan...5,553
Chelsea (★DET)...3,858
Chesaning (★FLN)...2,876
Clair Haven West (★DET)...1,367
Clare...2,639
Clarenceville (★DET)...3,500
Clarkston (★DET)...1,034
Clawson (★DET)...17,617
Clayton...505
Climax (★B.CK)...594
Clinton...1,677
Clinton Township (★DET)...48,865
Clintonville (★DET)...900
Clio (★FLN)...2,357
Cloverville (★MUS)...1,000
Coldwater...9,155
Coleman...1,295
Coloma (★BNTH-)...1,814
Colon...1,172
Columbiaville (★FLN)...935
Commerce (★DET)...3,500
Comstock (★KZOO)...3,650
Comstock Park (★GD.R)...3,370
Concord...983
Constantine...1,733
Coopersville...2,129
Corunna...2,829
Crescent Lake Estates (★DET)...2,000
Croswell...1,954
Crystal Falls...2,000
Cutlerville (★GD.R)...6,267
Davison (★FLN)...5,259
Dearborn (★DET)...104,199
Dearborn Heights (★DET)...80,069
Decatur...1,764
Deckerville...817
Deerfield...834
Detroit (★4,489,100; DET)...1,513,601
Detroit Beach (★MONR)...2,053
DeWitt (★LANS)...1,829
Dexter (★DET)...1,729
Dimondale (★LANS)...970
Douglas...813
Dowagiac...6,583
Drayton Plains (★DET)...16,462
Dryden...654
Dundee...2,472
Durand (★FLN)...3,678
East Detroit (★DET)...45,920
East Grand Rapids (★GD.R)...12,565
East Jordan...2,041
East Kingsford...1,155
Eastlake...512
East Lansing (★LANS)...47,540
East Tawas...2,372
Eastwood (★KZOO)...9,682
Eaton Rapids...4,494
Eau Claire (★S.B.-)...527
Ecorse (★DET)...17,515
Edgemont Park (★LANS)...1,500
Edmore...1,149
Edwardsburg (★S.B.-)...1,107
Elberta...542
Elizabeth Lake Estates (★DET)...3,000
Elk Rapids...1,249
Elkton...973
Elsie...988
Escanaba...15,368
Essexville (★BC-M)...4,990
Euclid Center (★BNTH-)...2,000
Evart...1,707
Fairgrove...629
Fair Plain (★BNTH-)...8,176
Farmington (★DET)...10,329
Farwell...777
Fennville...811
Fenton (★FLN)...8,284
Ferndale (★DET)...30,850
Ferrysburg (★MUS)...2,196
Flat Rock (★DET)...5,643
Flint (★522,000; FLN)...193,317
Flushing (★FLN)...7,190
Forest Hills (★GD.R)...1,600
Fowler...1,020
Fowlerville...1,978
Frankenmuth (★SAG)...2,834
Frankfort...1,660
Franklin (★DET)...3,344
Fraser (★DET)...11,868
Freeland (★BC-M)...1,303
Freeport...501
Fremont...3,465
Fruitport (★MUS)...1,409
Galesburg (★KZOO)...1,355
Galien...691
Garden City (★DET)...41,864
Gaylord...3,012
Genesee (★FLN)...800
Gibraltar (★DET)...3,842
Gladstone...5,237
Gladwin...2,071
Gobles...801
Goodrich (★FLN)...774
Grand Blanc (★FLN)...5,132
Grand Haven (★MUS)...11,844
Grand Ledge (★LANS)...6,032
Grand Rapids (★444,300; GD.R)...197,649
Grandville (★GD.R)...10,764
Grant...772
Grass Lake (★JAC)...1,061
Grayling...2,143
Greenville...7,493
Grosse Ile (★DET)...8,306
Grosse Pointe (★DET)...6,637
Grosse Pointe Farms (★DET)...11,701
Grosse Pointe Park (★DET)...15,585
Grosse Pointe Shores (★DET)...3,042
Grosse Pointe Woods (★DET)...21,878
Gwinn...1,054
Hagar Shores (Lake Michigan Beach) (★BNTH-)...1,201
Hamtramck (★DET)...27,245
Hancock...4,820
Hanover (★JAC)...513
Harbor Beach...2,134
Harbor Springs...1,662
Harper Woods (★DET)...20,186
Harrison...1,460
Harrisville...541
Hart...2,139
Hartford (★BNTH-)...2,508
Haslett (★LANS)...4,000
Hastings...6,501
Hazel Park (★DET)...23,784
Hesperia...877
Highland Park (★DET)...35,444
Hillsdale...7,728
Holland (★55,900; HLND)...26,337
Holly (★FLN)...4,355
Holt (★LANS)...6,980
Homer...1,617
Hopkins...566
Hopwood Acres (★LANS)...2,000
Houghton...6,067
Houghton Lake Heights...1,252
Howard City...1,060
Howell (★DET)...5,224
Hubbell...1,251
Hudson...2,618
Hudsonville (★GD.R)...3,523
Huntington Woods (★DET)...8,536
Huron Gardens (★DET)...5,000
Imlay City...1,980
Indian Lake...700
Inkster (★DET)...38,595
Ionia...6,361
Iron Mountain...8,702
Iron River...2,684
Ironwood...8,711
Ishpeming...8,245
Ithaca...2,749
Jackson (★133,000; JAC)...45,484
Jenison (★GD.R)...11,266
Jonesville...2,081
Kalamazoo (★208,800; KZOO)...85,555
Kalkaska...1,475
Keego Harbor (★DET)...3,092
Kent City...686
Kentwood (★GD.R)...20,310
Kinde...618
Kingsford...5,276
Kingsley...632
Laingsburg...1,159
Lake Angelus (★DET)...573
Lake City...704
Lake Fenton (★FLN)...2,101
Lake Linden...1,214
Lake Odessa...1,924
Lake Orion (★DET)...2,921
Lake Orion Heights (★DET)...2,552
Lakeview (★B.CK)...16,222
Lakeview...1,118
Lakewood (★KZOO)...1,420
Lakewood Club (★MUS)...590
Lambertville (★TOL)...5,721
L'Anse...2,538
Lansing (★303,200; LANS)...131,546
Lapeer (★FLN)...6,314
Lapeer Heights (★FLN)...4,000
La Salle Gardens (★DET)...1,500
Lathrup Village (★DET)...4,676
Laurium...2,868
Lawrence...790
Lawton...1,358
Leslie...1,894
Level Park (★B.CK)...3,080
Lexington...834
Lincoln Park (★DET)...52,984
Linden (★FLN)...1,546
Litchfield...1,167
Livonia (★DET)...110,109
Lottivue (★DET)...1,270
Lowell (★GD.R)...3,068
Ludington...9,021
Luna Pier (★TOL)...1,418
Lyons...758
McBain...520
Mackinac Island...517
Mackinaw City...810
Madison Heights (★DET)...38,599
Mancelona...1,255
Manchester...1,650
Manistee...7,723
Manistique...4,324
Manitou Beach...1,892
Manton...1,107
Maple Rapids...683
Marcellus...1,139
Marine City...4,567
Marion...891
Marlette...1,706
Marquette...21,967
Marshall...7,253
Martin...502
Marysville (★PT.H)...5,610
Mason (★LANS)...5,468
Mattawan (★KZOO)...1,569
Mayville...872
Melvindale (★DET)...13,862
Memphis...1,121
Mendon...949
Menominee...10,748
Merrill (★BC-M)...961
Michigan Center (★JAC)...5,000
Middleville (★GD.R)...1,865
Midland (★★BC-M)...35,176
Milan (★DET)...4,533
Milford (★DET)...4,699
Millington (★FLN)...1,099
Monroe (★56,100; MONR)...23,894
Montague (★MUS)...2,396
Montrose (★FLN)...1,789
Morenci...2,132
Morrice (★LANS)...734
Mount Clemens (★DET)...20,476
Mount Clemens Southeast (★DET)...5,800
Mount Morris (★FLN)...3,778
Mount Pleasant...20,504
Muir...617
Munising...3,677
Muskegon (★178,400; MUS)...44,631
Muskegon Heights (★MUS)...17,304
Nashville...1,558
Negaunee...5,248
Newaygo...1,381
New Baltimore (★DET)...4,132
Newberry...2,334
New Boston (★DET)...1,500
New Buffalo...2,784
New Haven (★DET)...1,855
New Lothrop...596
Niles (★S.B.-)...12,988
North Adams...574
North Farmington (Quakertown North) (★DET)...7,101
North Muskegon (★MUS)...4,243
Northport...594
Northville (★DET)...5,400
Northville (★GD.R)...1,700
Northwood (★KZOO)...1,500
Norton Shores (★MUS)...22,271
Norway...3,033
Novi (★DET)...9,668
Oakley Park (★DET)...1,500
Oak Park (★DET)...36,762
Okemos (★LANS)...7,770
Olivet...1,629
Onaway...1,262
Onekama...638
Onsted...555
Ontonagon...2,432
Orchard Lake (★DET)...1,487
Ortonville (★DET)...983
Oscoda...2,170
Otisville (★FLN)...724
Otsego (★KZOO)...3,957
Otter Lake (★FLN)...551
Ovid...1,650
Owosso...17,179
Oxbow (★DET)...2,000
Oxford (★DET)...2,536
Parchment (★KZOO)...2,027
Parma...880
Patterson Gardens (★MONR)...1,000
Paw Paw...3,160
Paw Paw Lake (★BNTH-)...3,726
Pearl Beach (★DET)...1,744
Peck...580
Pentwater...993
Perry (★LANS)...1,531
Petersburg...1,227
Petoskey...6,342
Pigeon...1,174
Pinckney (★DET)...921
Pinconning (★BC-M)...1,320
Plainfield Heights (★GD.R)...3,500
Plainwell (★KZOO)...3,195
Pleasant Ridge (★DET)...3,989
Plymouth (★DET)...11,758
Pontiac (★DET)...85,279
Portage (★KZOO)...33,590
Port Austin...706
Port Huron (★67,300; PT.H)...35,794
Portland...3,817
Potterville (★LANS)...1,280
Powers...560
Quakertown (★DET)...837
Quincy...1,540
Ramsay...1,068
Ravenswood (★LANS)...1,200
Reading...1,125
Redford Township (★DET)...71,901
Reed City...2,286
Reese...1,050
Richland (★KZOO)...728
Richmond (★DET)...3,234
River Rouge (★DET)...15,947
Riverview (★DET)...11,342
Rochester (★DET)...7,054
Rockford (★GD.R)...2,428
Rockwood (★DET)...3,225
Rogers City...4,275
Romeo (★DET)...4,012
Romulus (★DET)...22,879
Roosevelt Park (★MUS)...4,176
Roscommon...810
Rose City...530
Roseville (★DET)...60,529
Royal Oak (★DET)...86,238
Royal Oak Township (★DET)...6,326
Saginaw (★181,600; SAG)...91,849
St. Charles (★SAG)...2,046
St. Clair...4,770
St. Clair Haven (Clair Haven) (★DET)...2,177
St. Clair Shores (★DET)...88,093
St. Ignace...2,892
St. Johns...6,672
St. Joseph (★★BNTH-)...11,042
St. Louis...4,101
Saline (★DET)...4,811
Sandusky...2,071
Sanford (★BC-M)...818
Saranac...1,223
Saugatuck...1,022
Sault Ste. Marie (★16,800; SOO)...15,136
Schoolcraft (★KZOO)...1,277
Scottville...1,202
Sebewaing...2,053
Sebille Manor (★DET)...1,694
Seven Harbors (★DET)...3,170
Shelby...1,703
Shelby Village (★DET)...1,200
Sheldon (★DET)...750
Shepherd...1,416
Sheridan...653
Shields (★SAG)...1,000
Shoreham (★BNTH-)...666
Southfield (★DET)...69,285
Southgate (★DET)...33,909
South Haven...6,471
Southland (★JAC)...2,000
South Lyon (★DET)...2,675
South Monroe (★MONR)...1,200
South Range...898
South Rockwood (★DET)...1,477
Sparlingville (★PT.H)...1,845
Sparta (★GD.R)...3,094
Spring Arbor (★JAC)...1,832
Springfield (★B.CK)...3,994
Spring Lake (★MUS)...3,034
Springport...723
Stambaugh...1,458
Standish...1,184
Stanton...1,089
Stephenson...800
Sterling...507
Sterling Heights (★DET)...61,365
Stevensville (★BNTH-)...1,107
Stockbridge...1,190
Stony Point (★MONR)...1,000
Sturgis...9,295
Sunrise Heights (★B.CK)...1,626
Suttons Bay...522
Swartz Creek (★FLN)...4,928
Sylvan Lake (★DET)...2,219
Tawas City...1,666
Taylor (★DET)...70,020
Tecumseh...7,120
Tekonsha...739
Temperance (★TOL)...3,000
Three Oaks...1,750
Three Rivers...7,355
Towar Gardens (★LANS)...1,500
Traverse City...18,048
Trenton (★DET)...24,127
Trips Subdivision (★DET)...1,000
Troy (★DET)...39,419
Twin Beach (★DET)...1,000
Ubly...899
Union City...1,740
Union Lake (★DET)...9,000
Unionville...647
Urbandale (★LANS)...1,000
Utica (★DET)...3,504
Vanderbilt...522
Vandercook Lake (★JAC)...5,000
Vassar...2,802
Vermontville...857

★ Population or designation of metropolitan area, including suburbs (see headnote).
▲ Population of entire "town" or township, including other communities and rural areas.
† Population is from a local census taken at date specified.

Vernon (★FLN)........818
Vernon........754
Verona Park (★B.CK)........2,107
Vicksburg (★KZOO)........2,139
Wakefield........2,757
Waldron........564
Walker (★GD.R)........11,492
Walled Lake (★DET)........3,759
Walnut Lake (★DET)........1,200
Warren (★DET)........179,260
Washington (★DET)........1,563
Waterford (★DET)........8,000
Watervliet (★BNTH-)........2,059
Waverly (★LANS)........8,000
Wayland........2,054
Wayne (★DET)........21,054
Webberville........1,251
Wells........1,085
Westacres (★DET)........1,000
West Branch........1,912
Westchester Village (★DET)........1,200
Westgate (★GD.R)........2,400
Westland (★DET)........86,749
Westphalia........806
West Willow (★DET)........3,000
Westwood (★KZOO)........9,143
White Cloud........1,044
Whitehall (★MUS)........3,017
White Lake (★DET)........1,330
White Pigeon........1,455
White Pine........1,218
Whitmore Lake (★DET)........2,763
Williamston (★LANS)........2,600
Willow Run (★DET)........5,000
Windemere (★LANS)........2,500
Wixom (★DET)........2,010
Wolf Lake (★MUS)........2,258
Wolverine Lake (★DET)........4,301
Wood Creek Farms (★DET)........1,090
Woodhaven (★DET)........3,566
Woodland Beach (★MONR)........2,249
Woodville (★JAC)........2,700
Wyandotte (★DET)........41,061
Wyoming (★GD.R)........56,560
Yale........1,505
Ypsilanti (★DET)........29,538
Ypsilanti East (★DET)........20,000
Zeeland (★HLND)........4,734
Zilwaukee (★SAG)........2,072

MINNESOTA

1970 C........3,805,069

Counties

Aitkin........11,403
Anoka........154,556
Becker........24,372
Beltrami........26,373
Benton........20,841
Big Stone........7,941
Blue Earth........52,322
Brown........28,887
Carlton........28,072
Carver........28,310
Cass........17,323
Chippewa........15,109
Chisago........17,492
Clay........46,585
Clearwater........8,013
Cook........3,423
Cottonwood........14,887
Crow Wing........34,826
Dakota........139,808
Dodge........13,037
Douglas........22,892
Faribault........20,896
Fillmore........21,916
Freeborn........38,064
Goodhue........34,763
Grant........7,462
Hennepin........960,080
Houston........17,556
Hubbard........10,583
Isanti........16,560
Itasca........35,530
Jackson........14,352
Kanabec........9,775
Kandiyohi........30,548
Kittson........6,853
Koochiching........17,131
Lac qui Parle........11,164
Lake........13,351
Lake of the Woods........3,987
Le Sueur........21,332
Lincoln........8,143
Lyon........24,273
McLeod........27,662
Mahnomen........5,638
Marshall........13,060
Martin........24,316
Meeker........18,810
Mille Lacs........15,703
Morrison........26,949
Mower........43,783
Murray........12,508
Nicollet........24,518
Nobles........23,208
Norman........10,008
Olmsted........84,104
Otter Tail........46,097
Pennington........13,266
Pine........16,821
Pipestone........12,791
Polk........34,435
Pope........11,107
Ramsey........476,255
Red Lake........5,388
Redwood........20,024
Renville........21,139
Rice........41,582
Rock........11,346
Roseau........11,569
St. Louis........220,693
Scott........32,423
Sherburne........18,344
Sibley........15,845
Stearns........95,400
Steele........26,931
Stevens........11,218
Swift........13,177
Todd........22,114
Traverse........6,254
Wabasha........17,224
Wadena........12,412
Waseca........16,663
Washington........82,948
Watonwan........13,298
Wilkin........9,389
Winona........44,409
Wright........38,933
Yellow Medicine........14,516

Cities

Ada........2,076
Adams........771
Adrian........1,350
Aitkin........1,553
Albany........1,599
Albert Lea........19,418
Alden........713
Alexandria........6,973
Amboy........571
Annandale........1,234
Anoka (★MPLS-)........13,489
Appleton........1,789
Apple Valley (★MPLS-)........8,502
Arden Hills (★MPLS-)........4,975
Argyle........739
Arlington........1,823
Arnold (★DUL-)........1,000
Atwater........956
Aurora........2,531
Austin........25,074
Avon........725
Babbitt........3,076
Bagley........1,314
Balaton........649
Bald Eagle (★MPLS-)........2,000
Barnesville........1,782
Battle Lake........772
Baudette........1,547
Baxter........1,556
Bayport (★MPLS-)........2,987
Belgrade........713
Bellaire (★MPLS-)........1,000
Belle Plaine........2,328
Bemidji........11,490
Benson........3,484
Bertha........512
Big Falls........534
Big Lake (★MPLS-)........1,015
Birchwood (★MPLS-)........926
Bird Island........1,309
Biwabik........1,483
Blackduck........595
Blaine (★MPLS-)........20,625
Blooming Prairie........1,804
Bloomington (★MPLS-)........81,970
Blue Earth........3,965
Bovey........858
Braham........744
Brainerd........11,667
Branch........880
Breckenridge........4,200
Brewster........563
Brooklyn Center (★MPLS-)........35,173
Brooklyn Park (★MPLS-)........26,230
Brooten........615
Browerville........665
Brownsdale........625
Browns Valley........906
Brownton........688
Buffalo (★MPLS-)........3,275
Buffalo Lake........758
Buhl........1,303
Burnsville (★MPLS-)........19,940
Butterfield........619
Byron (★ROCH)........1,419
Caledonia........2,619
Cambridge........2,720
Canby........2,147
Cannon Falls........2,072
Carlton........884
Carver (★MPLS-)........669
Cass Lake........1,317
Cedar Grove (★MPLS-)........3,000
Centerville (★MPLS-)........534
Champlin (★MPLS-)........4,704
Chanhassen (★MPLS-) (†11/1/71)........5,054
Chaska (★MPLS-)........4,352
Chatfield........1,885
Chisago City (★MPLS-)........1,068
Chisholm........5,913
Circle Pines (★MPLS-)........3,918
Clara City........1,491
Claremont........520
Clarissa........599
Clarkfield........1,084
Clearbrook........599
Clinton........608
Cloquet........8,699
Cohasset........536
Cokato........1,735
Cold Spring........2,006
Coleraine........1,086
Collegeville (P. O.)........1,500
Cologne........518
Columbia Heights (★MPLS-)........23,837
Comfrey........525
Cook........687
Coon Rapids (★MPLS-)........30,505
Corcoran (★MPLS-)........1,656
Cosmos........570
Cottage Grove (★MPLS-)........13,419
Cottonwood........794
Crookston........8,312
Crosby........2,241
Crystal (★MPLS-)........30,925
Dassel........1,058
Dawson........1,699
Dayton........517
Deephaven (★MPLS-)........3,853
Deer River........815
Delano (★MPLS-)........1,851
Dellwood (★MPLS-)........524
Detroit Lakes........5,797
Dilworth (★FAR-)........2,321
Dodge Center........1,603
Duluth (★155,000; DUL-)........100,578
Eagle Bend........557
Eagle Lake (★MNKT)........839
East Bethel (★MPLS-)........2,586
East Grand Forks (★GDFK)........7,607
Eden Prairie (★MPLS-)........6,938
Eden Valley........776
Edgerton........1,119
Edina (★MPLS-)........44,046
Elbow Lake........1,484
Elgin........580
Elk River (★MPLS-)........2,252
Ellendale........569
Ellsworth........588
Elmore........910
Ely........4,904
Erskine........571
Evansville........553
Eveleth........4,721
Excelsior (★MPLS-)........2,563
Eyota........639
Fairfax........1,432
Fairmont........10,751
Falcon Heights (★MPLS-)........5,641
Faribault........16,595
Farmington (★MPLS-)........3,104
Fergus Falls........12,443
Fertile........955
Floodwood........650
Foley........1,271
Forest Lake (★MPLS-)........3,207
Fosston........1,684
Frazee........1,015
Freeport........593
Fridley (★MPLS-)........29,233
Fulda........1,226
Gaylord........1,720
Gibbon........877
Gilbert........2,287
Glencoe........4,217
Glenville........740
Glenwood........2,584
Glyndon........674
Golden Valley (★MPLS-)........24,246
Goodhue........539
Goodview........1,829
Graceville........735
Grand Marais........1,301
Grand Meadow........869
Grand Rapids........7,247
Granite Falls........3,225
Greenbush........787
Greenfield (★MPLS-)........977
Greenwood (★MPLS-)........587
Grove City........502
Hallock........1,477
Halstad........598
Hamel (Medina) (★MPLS-)........2,396
Hancock........806
Harmony........1,130
Harris........559
Hastings (★MPLS-)........12,195
Hawley........1,371
Hayfield........939
Hector........1,178
Henderson........730
Hendricks........712
Henning........850
Herman........619
Hermantown (★DUL-)........900
Heron Lake........777
Hibbing........16,104
Hills........571
Hilltop (★MPLS-)........1,015
Hinckley........885
Hoffman........627
Hokah........697
Holdingford........551
Hopkins (★MPLS-)........13,428
Houston........1,090
Howard Lake........1,162
Hoyt Lakes........3,634
Hugo (★MPLS-)........751
Hutchinson........8,031
Independence (★MPLS-)........1,993
International Falls........6,439
Inver Grove Heights (Inver Grove) (★MPLS-)........12,148
Ironton........562
Isanti........679
Isle........551
Ivanhoe........738
Jackson........3,550
Janesville........1,557
Jasper........754
Jordan (★MPLS-)........1,836
Karlstad........727
Kasota........732
Kasson........1,883
Keewatin........1,382
Kenyon........1,575
Kerkhoven........641
Kiester........681
Kimball........567
La Crescent (★LACRO)........3,296
Lake Benton........759
Lake City........3,594
Lake Crystal........1,807
Lake Elmo (★MPLS-)........4,032
Lakefield........1,820
Lakeland (★MPLS-)........962
Lake Park........658
Lake St. Croix Beach (★MPLS-)........1,111
Lakeville (★MPLS-)........7,556
Lamberton........962
Landfall (★MPLS-)........671
Lanesboro........850
Lauderdale (★MPLS-)........2,571
Le Center........1,890
Le Roy........870
Lester Prairie........1,162
Le Sueur........3,745
Lewiston........1,000
Lexington (★MPLS-)........2,140
Lilydale (★MPLS-)........664
Lindstrom (★MPLS-)........1,260
Lino Lakes (★MPLS-)........3,692
Litchfield........5,262
Little Canada (★MPLS-)........3,481
Little Falls........7,467
Littlefork........824
Long Lake (★MPLS-)........1,506
Long Prairie........2,416
Lonsdale........622
Luverne........4,703
Lyle........522
Mabel........888
McIntosh........753
Madelia........2,316
Madison........2,242
Madison Lake........587
Mahnomen........1,313
Mahtomedi (★MPLS-)........2,640
Mankato (★45,000; MNKT)........30,895
Maple Grove (★MPLS-)........6,275
Maple Lake........1,124
Maple Plain (★MPLS-)........1,169
Mapleton........1,307
Maplewood (★MPLS-)........25,222
Marble........682
Marine on St. Croix........513
Marshall........9,886
Medford........690
Melrose........2,273
Menahga........835
Mendota Heights (★MPLS-)........6,165
Milaca........1,940
Minneapolis (★1,875,200; MPLS-)........434,400
Minneota........1,320
Minnesota Lake........738
Minnetonka (★MPLS-)........35,737
Minnetonka Beach (★MPLS-)........586
Minnetrista (★MPLS-)........2,878
Montevideo........5,661
Montgomery........2,281
Monticello........1,636
Moorhead (★★FAR-)........29,687
Moose Lake........1,400
Mora........2,582
Morgan........972
Morris........5,366
Morristown........659
Morton........591
Mound (★MPLS-)........7,572
Mounds View (★MPLS-)........10,641
Mountain Iron........1,698
Mountain Lake........1,986
Nashwauk........1,341
New Brighton (★MPLS-)........19,507
New Hope (★MPLS-)........23,180
New London........736
Newport (★MPLS-)........2,922
New Prague........2,680
New Richland........1,113
New Ulm........13,051
New York Mills........791
Nicollet........618
Nisswa........1,011
North Branch........1,106
Northfield........10,235
North Mankato (★MNKT)........7,347
North Oaks (★MPLS-)........2,002
North St. Paul (★MPLS-)........11,950
Norwood........1,058
Oakdale (★MPLS-)........7,304
Oak Park Heights (★MPLS-)........1,238
Oklee........536
Olivia........2,553
Onamia........670
Orono (★MPLS-)........6,787
Oronoco........564
Ortonville........2,665
Osakis........1,306
Osseo (★MPLS-)........2,908
Owatonna........15,341
Parkers Prairie........882
Park Rapids........2,772
Paynesville........1,920
Pelican Rapids........1,835
Perham........1,933
Pierz........893
Pike Lake (★DUL-)........900
Pine City........2,143
Pine Island........1,640
Pine River........803
Pipestone........5,328
Plainview........2,093
Plymouth (★MPLS-)........18,077
Preston........1,413
Princeton........2,531
Prior Lake (★MPLS-)........1,114
Proctor (★DUL-)........3,123
Randall........536
Raymond........589
Red Lake Falls........1,740
Red Wing........10,441
Redwood Falls........4,774
Renville........1,252
Richfield (★MPLS-)........47,231
Richmond........866
Robbinsdale (★MPLS-)........16,845
Rochester (★73,300; ROCH)........53,766
Rockford (★MPLS-)........730
Rogers (★MPLS-)........544
Roseau........2,552
Rosemount (★MPLS-)........1,337
Roseville (★MPLS-)........34,518
Round Lake........506
Royalton........534
Rush City........1,130
Rushford........1,318
Rushford Village........601
Sacred Heart........707
St. Anthony (★MPLS-)........9,239
St. Bonifacius (★MPLS-)........685
St. Charles........1,942
St. Cloud (★63,900; ST.CLD)........39,691
St. Francis........897
St. James........4,027
St. Joseph (★ST. CLD)........1,786
St. Louis Park (★MPLS-)........48,922
St. Michael........1,021
St. Paul (★★MPLS-)........309,828
St. Paul Park (★MPLS-)........5,587
St. Peter........8,339
Sanborn........505
Sandstone........1,641
Sartell (★ST.CLD)........1,323
Sauk Centre........3,750
Sauk Rapids (★ST.CLD)........5,051
Savage (★MPLS-)........3,611
Scanlon........1,132▲
Sebeka........668
Shakopee (★MPLS-)........6,876
Sherburn........1,190
Shoreview (★MPLS-)........10,995
Shorewood (★MPLS-)........4,223
Silver Bay........3,504
Silver Lake........694
Slayton........2,351
Sleepy Eye........3,461
South International Falls........2,116
South St. Paul (★MPLS-)........25,016
Spicer........586
Springfield........2,530
Spring Grove........1,290
Spring Lake Park (★MPLS-)........6,417
Spring Park (★MPLS-)........1,087
Spring Valley........2,572
Staples........2,657
Starbuck........1,138
Stephen........904
Stewart........666
Stewartville (★ROCH)........2,802
Stillwater (★MPLS-)........10,191
Taylors Falls........587
Thief River Falls........8,618
Tonka Bay (★MPLS-)........1,397
Tower........699
Tracy........2,516
Trimont........835
Truman........1,137
Twin Valley........868
Two Harbors........4,437
Tyler........1,069
Vadnais Heights (★MPLS-)........3,391
Verndale........570
Victoria (★MPLS-)........850
Virginia........12,450
Wabasha........2,371
Wabasso........738
Waconia (★MPLS-)........2,445
Wadena........4,640
Waite Park (★ST.CLD)........2,824
Walker........1,073
Walnut Grove........756
Wanamingo........574
Warren........1,999
Warroad........1,086
Waseca........6,789
Watertown (★MPLS-)........1,390
Waterville........1,539
Watkins........785
Waverly........573
Wayzata (★MPLS-)........3,700
Welcome........694
Wells........2,791
Westbrook........990
West Concord........718
West St. Paul (★MPLS-)........18,799
Wheaton........2,029
White Bear Lake (★MPLS-)........23,313
Willernie (★MPLS-)........697
Willmar........12,869
Windom........3,952
Winnebago........1,791
Winona........26,438
Winsted........1,266
Winthrop........1,391
Woodbury (★MPLS-)........6,184
Woodland (★MPLS-)........544
Worthington........9,916
Wyoming (★MPLS-)........695
Young America........611
Zumbrota........1,929

MISSISSIPPI

1970 C........2,216,912

Counties

Adams........37,293
Alcorn........27,179
Amite........13,763
Attala........19,570
Benton........7,505
Bolivar........49,409
Calhoun........14,623
Carroll........9,397
Chickasaw........16,805
Choctaw........8,440
Claiborne........10,086
Clarke........15,049
Clay........18,840
Coahoma........40,447
Copiah........24,749
Covington........14,002
De Soto........35,885
Forrest........57,849
Franklin........8,011
George........12,459
Greene........8,545
Grenada........19,854
Hancock........17,387
Harrison........134,582
Hinds........214,973
Holmes........23,120
Humphreys........14,601
Issaquena........2,737
Itawamba........16,847
Jackson........87,975
Jasper........15,994
Jefferson........9,295
Jefferson Davis........12,936
Jones........56,357
Kemper........10,233

(Mississippi continued)

★ Population or designation of metropolitan area, including suburbs (see headnote).
▲ Population of entire "town" or township, including other communities and rural areas.
† Population is from a local census taken at date specified.

(Mississippi continued)

Lafayette...24,181
Lamar...15,209
Lauderdale...67,087
Lawrence...11,137
Leake...17,085
Lee...46,148
Leflore...42,111
Lincoln...26,198
Lowndes...49,700
Madison...29,737
Marion...22,871
Marshall...24,027
Monroe...34,043
Montgomery...12,918
Neshoba...20,802
Newton...18,983
Noxubee...14,288
Oktibbeha...28,752
Panola...26,829
Pearl River...27,802
Perry...9,065
Pike...31,756
Pontotoc...17,363
Prentiss...20,133
Quitman...15,888
Rankin...43,933
Scott...21,369
Sharkey...8,937
Simpson...19,947
Smith...13,561
Stone...8,101
Sunflower...37,047
Tallahatchie...19,338
Tate...18,544
Tippah...15,852
Tishomingo...14,940
Tunica...11,854
Union...19,096
Walthall...12,500
Warren...44,981
Washington...70,581
Wayne...16,650
Webster...10,047
Wilkinson...11,099
Winston...18,406
Yalobusha...11,915
Yazoo...27,304

Cities

Aberdeen...6,507
Ackerman...1,502
Amory...7,236
Anguilla...612
Arcola...517
Baldwyn...2,366
Batesville...3,796
Bay St. Louis...6,752
Bay Springs...1,801
Bear Town (McComb South)...1,085
Beaumont...1,061
Belmont...968
Belzoni...3,394
Bentonia...544
Biloxi (★GUL-B)...48,486
Blue Mountain...677
Bolton...787
Booneville...5,895
Boyle...861
Brandon (★JAC)...2,685
Brookhaven...10,700
Brooksville...978
Bruce...2,033
Bude...1,146
Byhalia...702
Calhoun City...1,847
Candlestick (★JAC)...5,000
Canton...10,503
Carthage...3,031
Cary...517
Centreville...1,819
Charleston...2,821
Clarksdale...21,673
Cleveland...13,327
Clinton (★JAC)...7,289
Coffeeville...1,024
Coldwater...1,450
Collins...1,934
Columbia...7,587
Columbus (★40,700; COL)...25,795
Como...1,003
Corinth...11,581
Crenshaw...1,271
Crowder...815
Crystal Springs...4,195
Decatur...1,311
DeKalb...1,072
Derma...660
D'Iberville (★GUL-B)...7,288
Drew...2,574
Duck Hill...809
Duncan...599
Durant...2,752
Edwards...1,236
Ellisville (★LAUR)...4,643
Escatawpa (★PSCG)...1,579
Ethel...560
Eupora...1,792
Fayette...1,725
Flora...987
Forest...4,085
Friars Point...1,177
Fulton...2,899
Gautier (★PSCG)...2,087
Gloster...1,401
Goodman...1,194
Greenville (★48,600; GRNV)...39,648
Greenville North (★GRNV)...2,154
Greenwood...22,400
Grenada...9,944
Gulfport (★151,300; GUL-B)...40,791
Gunnison...545
Hattiesburg (★54,900; HATT)...38,277
Hazlehurst...4,577
Heidelberg...1,112
Hernando (★MEM)...2,499
Hickory...570
Hollandale...3,260
Holly Springs...5,728
Houlka...646
Houston...2,720
Indianola...8,947
Inverness...1,119
Itta Bena...2,489
Iuka...2,389
Jackson (★239,100; JAC)...153,968
Jonestown...1,110
Kilmichael...543
Kosciusko...7,266
Lambert...1,511
Laurel (★41,600; LAUR)...24,145
Leakesville...1,090
Leland...6,000
Lexington...2,756
Liberty...612
Long Beach (★GUL-B)...6,170
Louisville...6,626
Lucedale...2,083
Lumberton...2,084
Maben...862
McLain...632
McComb...11,969
Macon...2,612
Madison (★JAC)...853
Magee...2,973
Magnolia...1,970
Marks...2,609
Mathiston...570
Meadville...594
Mendenhall...2,402
Meridian (★55,200; MRID)...45,083
Merigold...772
Monticello...1,790
Moorhead...2,284
Morgantown...2,008
Morton...2,672
Moss Point (★PSCG)...19,321
Mound Bayou...2,134
Mount Olive...923
Natchez...19,704
Nettleton...1,591
New Albany...6,426
New Augusta...511
Newton...3,556
North Carrollton...611
North Gulfport (★GUL-B)...4,000
North Tunica (Tunica North)...1,325
Noxapater...554
Ocean Springs (★GUL-B)...9,580
Okolona...3,002
Olive Branch (★MEM)...1,513
Orange Grove (★GUL-B)...2,000
Osyka...628
Oxford...13,846
Pace...629
Palmers Crossing (Palmer) (★HATT)...2,000
Pascagoula (★57,100; PSCG)...27,264
Pass Christian (★GUL-B)...2,979
Pearl (★JAC)...9,603
Pelahatchie...1,306
Petal (★HATT)...6,986
Philadelphia...6,274
Picayune...10,467
Pickens...1,012
Plain (★JAC)...900
Plantersville...910
Pontotoc...3,453
Poplarville...2,312
Port Gibson...2,589
Prentiss...1,789
Purvis...1,860
Quitman...2,702
Raleigh...1,018
Raymond (★JAC)...1,620
Richton...1,110
Ridgeland (★JAC)...1,650
Ripley...3,482
Rolling Fork...2,034
Rosedale...2,599
Roxie...662
Ruleville...2,351
Saltillo...836
Sandersville (★LAUR)...694
Sardis...2,391
Scooba...626
Senatobia...4,247
Shannon...575
Shaw...2,513
Shelby...2,645
Shubuta...602
Shuqualak...591
Sledge...516
Smithville...552
Southaven (★MEM)...8,931
Starkville...11,369
State College...4,595
State Line...598
Stonewall...1,161
Summit...1,640
Sumner...533
Sumrall...955
Sunflower...983
Taylorsville...1,299
Tchula...1,729
Terry (★JAC)...546
Tougaloo (★JAC)...1,000
Tunica...1,685
Tupelo...20,471
Tutwiler...1,103
Tylertown...1,736
Union...1,856
Utica...1,019
Vaiden...716
Vancleave...900
Van Winkle (★JAC)...2,000
Vardaman...777
Verona...1,877
Vicksburg...25,478
Water Valley...3,285
Waveland...3,108
Waynesboro...4,368
Webb...751
Weir...573
Wesson...1,253
West Point...8,714
Wiggins...2,995
Winona...5,521
Winstonville...536
Woodville...1,734
Yazoo City...10,796

MISSOURI

1970 C...4,677,399

Counties

Adair...22,472
Andrew...11,913
Atchison...9,240
Audrain...25,362
Barry...19,597
Barton...10,431
Bates...15,468
Benton...9,695
Bollinger...8,820
Boone...80,911
Buchanan...86,915
Butler...33,529
Caldwell...8,351
Callaway...25,950
Camden...13,315
Cape Girardeau...49,350
Carroll...12,565
Carter...3,878
Cass...39,448
Cedar...9,424
Chariton...11,084
Christian...15,124
Clark...8,260
Clay...123,644
Clinton...12,462
Cole...46,228
Cooper...14,732
Crawford...14,828
Dade...6,850
Dallas...10,054
Daviess...8,420
DeKalb...7,305
Dent...11,457
Douglas...9,268
Dunklin...33,742
Franklin...55,116
Gasconade...11,878
Gentry...8,060
Greene...152,929
Grundy...11,819
Harrison...10,257
Henry...18,451
Hickory...4,481
Holt...6,654
Howard...10,561
Howell...23,521
Iron...9,529
Jackson...654,558
Jasper...79,852
Jefferson...105,248
Johnson...34,172
Knox...5,692
Laclede...19,944
Lafayette...26,626
Lawrence...24,585
Lewis...10,993
Lincoln...18,041
Linn...15,125
Livingston...15,368
McDonald...12,357
Macon...15,432
Madison...8,641
Maries...6,851
Marion...28,121
Mercer...4,910
Miller...15,026
Mississippi...16,647
Moniteau...10,742
Monroe...9,542
Montgomery...11,000
Morgan...10,068
New Madrid...23,420
Newton...32,901
Nodaway...22,467
Oregon...9,180
Osage...10,994
Ozark...6,226
Pemiscot...26,373
Perry...14,393
Pettis...34,137
Phelps...29,567
Pike...16,928
Platte...32,081
Polk...15,415
Pulaski...53,967
Putnam...5,916
Ralls...7,764
Randolph...22,434
Ray...17,599
Reynolds...6,106
Ripley...9,803
St. Charles...92,954
St. Clair...7,667
St. Francois...36,818
St. Louis (county)...951,353
Ste. Genevieve...12,867
Saline...24,837
Schuyler...4,665
Scotland...5,499
Scott...33,250
Shannon...7,196
Shelby...7,906
Stoddard...25,771
Stone...9,921
Sullivan...7,572
Taney...13,023
Texas...18,320
Vernon...19,065
Warren...9,699
Washington...15,086
Wayne...8,546
Webster...15,562
Worth...3,359
Wright...13,667
St. Louis (Independent City)...622,236

Cities

Adrian...1,259
Advance...903
Affton (★ST.L.)...24,067
Albany...1,804
Alton...715
Anderson...1,065
Anniston...515
Appleton City...1,058
Arbor Terrace (★ST.L.)...1,440
Arbyrd...575
Arcadia...627
Archie...525
Arnold (★ST.L.)...2,000
Ash Grove...934
Ashland...769
Aurora...5,359
Auxvasse...808
Ava...2,504
Avondale (★K.C.)...512
Ballwin (★ST.L.)...10,656
Bella Villa (★ST.L.)...1,018
Belle...1,133
Bellefontaine Neighbors (★ST.L.)...13,987
Bel-Nor (★ST.L.)...2,085
Bel-Ridge (★ST.L.)...5,561
Belton (★K.C.)...12,179
Benton...640
Berkeley (★ST.L.)...19,743
Bernie...1,641
Bertrand...604
Bethany...2,914
Beverly Hills (★ST.L.)...846
Bevier...806
Billings...760
Birch Tree...573
Bismarck...1,387
Bland...621
Bloomfield...1,584
Blue Springs (★K.C.)...6,779
Blue Summit (★K.C.)...1,283
Bolivar...4,769
Bonne Terre...3,622
Boonville...7,514
Bourbon...955
Bowling Green...2,936
Branson...2,175
Braymer...919
Breckenridge...598
Breckenridge Hills (★ST.L.)...7,011
Brentwood (★ST.L.)...11,248
Bridgeton (★ST.L.)...19,992
Brookfield...5,491
Brunswick...1,370
Bucklin...654
Buckner (★K.C.)...1,695
Buffalo...1,915
Burke City (★ST.L.)...1,800
Burlington Junction...634
Butler...3,984
Cabool...1,848
California...3,105
Calverton Park (★ST.L.)...2,025
Camdenton...1,636
Cameron...3,960
Campbell...1,979
Canton...2,680
Cape Girardeau...31,282
Cardwell...859
Carl Junction (★JOP)...1,661
Carrollton...4,847
Carterville (★JOP)...1,716
Carthage...11,035
Caruthersville...7,350
Cassville...1,910
Center...588
Centralia...3,618
Chaffee...2,793
Chamois...615
Charlack (★ST.L.)...1,872
Charleston...5,131
Chillicothe...9,519
Clarence...1,050
Clarksville...668
Clarkton...1,177
Claycomo (★K.C.)...1,841
Clayton (★ST.L.)...16,222
Clinton...7,504
Cole Camp...1,038
Columbia (★63,800; COL)...58,804
Concord (★ST.L.)...21,217
Concordia...1,854
Conway...547
Cool Valley (★ST.L.)...2,059
Country Club Hills (★ST.L.)...1,644
Country Club Village (★ST.JO)...943
Crane...1,003
Crestwood (★ST.L.)...15,123
Creve Coeur (★ST.L.)...8,967
Crocker...814
Crystal City (★ST.L.)...3,898
Cuba...2,070
Dearborn...543
Deepwater...565
Dellwood (★ST.L.)...7,137
Desloge...2,818
De Soto (★ST.L.)...5,984
Des Peres (★ST.L.)...5,333
Dexter...6,024
Diamond...608
Dixon...1,387
Doniphan...1,850
Doolittle...509
Drexel...723
Duenweg (★JOP)...656
Duquesne (★JOP)...738
East Prairie...3,275
Edina...1,574
Edmundson (★ST.L.)...2,298
Eldon...3,520
El Dorado Springs...3,300
Ellington...1,094
Ellisville (★ST.L.)...4,681
Elsberry...1,398
Elvins...1,660
Eminence...520
Esther...1,040
Eureka (★ST.L.)...2,384
Excelsior Springs (★K.C.)...9,411
Fairfax...835
Farmington...6,590
Fayette...3,520
Fenton (★ST.L.)...2,275
Ferguson (★ST.L.)...28,759
Festus (★ST.L.)...7,530
Fisk...503
Flat River...4,550
Flordell Hills (★ST.L.)...989
Florissant (★ST.L.)...65,908
Forsyth...803
Fredericktown...3,799
Freeburg...577
Frontenac (★ST.L.)...3,920
Fulton...12,248
Gainesville...627
Gallatin...1,833
Garden City...633
Gerald...762
Gideon...1,112
Gladstone (★K.C.)...23,422
Glasgow...1,336
Glenaire (★K.C.)...505
Glendale (★ST.L.)...6,891
Golden City...810
Goodfellow Terrace (★ST.L.)...744
Goodman...565
Gower...758
Grain Valley (★K.C.)...709
Granby...1,678
Grandview (★K.C.)...17,456
Grant City...1,095
Grantwood (★ST.L.)...994
Green City...632
Greendale (★ST.L.)...972
Greenfield...1,172
Greenwood (★K.C.)...925
Hallsville...790
Hamilton...1,645
Hanley Hills (★ST.L.)...2,726
Hannibal...18,698
Hardin...683
Harrisonville...4,928
Hartville...524
Hayti...3,841
Hazelwood (★ST.L.)...14,082
Herculaneum (★ST.L.)...1,885
Hermann...2,658
Higbee...641
Higginsville...4,318
Hillsboro (★ST.L.)...831
Hillsdale (★ST.L.)...2,599
Holcomb...593
Holden...2,089
Hollister...906
Hopkins...656
Hornersville...693
Houston...2,178
Howardville...500
Humansville...825
Huntleigh (★ST.L.)...714
Huntsville...1,442
Iberia...741
Illmo...1,232
Independence (★K.C.)...111,630
Ironton...1,452
Jackson...5,896
Jamesport...614
Jasper...796
Jefferson City...32,407
Jennings (★ST.L.)...19,379
Joplin (★64,900; JOP)...39,256
Kahoka...2,207
Kansas City (★1,206,500; K.C.)...507,330
Kearney...984
Kennett...10,090
Keytesville...730
King City...1,023
Kinloch (★ST.L.)...5,629
Kirksville...15,560
Kirkwood (★ST.L.)...31,769
Knob Noster...2,264
La Belle...848
Laddonia...745
Ladue (★ST.L.)...10,594
La Grange...1,237
Lake Lotawana (★K.C.)...1,786
Lake Ozark...507
Lakeshire (★ST.L.)...1,186
Lake Waukomis (★K.C.)...1,105
Lamar...3,760
La Monte...814
Lancaster...821
La Plata...1,377
Lathrop...1,268
Lawson...1,034
Leadwood...1,397
Lebanon...8,616
Lee's Summit (★K.C.)...16,230
Lemay (Luxemburg) (★ST.L.)...26,000
Lewistown...615
Lexington...5,388
Liberal...644
Liberty (★K.C.)...13,704
Licking...1,002
Lilbourn...1,152
Lincoln...574
Linn...1,289
Lockwood...887
Louisiana...4,533
Lucas and Hunt Village (★ST.L.)...1,800
Lutesville...626
Macon...5,301
Madison...540
Malden...5,374
Manchester (★ST.L.)...5,031
Mansfield...1,056
Maplewood (★ST.L.)...12,785
Marceline...2,622
Marionville...1,496
Marlborough (★ST.L.)...1,459
Marshall...12,051
Marshfield...2,961
Marston...666
Maryland Heights (★ST.L.)...8,805

★ Population or designation of metropolitan area, including suburbs (see headnote).
▲ Population of entire "town" or township, including other communities and rural areas.
† Population is from a local census taken at date specified.

Mary Ridge (★ST.L.)....602
Maryville....9,970
Mattese (★ST.L.)....500
Matthews....538
Maysville....1,045
Mehlville (★ST.L.)....14,000
Memphis....2,081
Mexico....11,807
Milan....1,794
Miller....676
Miner....640
Moberly....12,988
Moline Acres (★ST.L.)....3,722
Monett....5,937
Monroe City....2,456
Montgomery City....2,187
Montrose....531
Morehouse....1,332
Morley....528
Mound City....1,202
Mountain Grove....3,377
Mountain View....1,320
Mount Vernon....2,600
Murphy (★ST.L.)....800
Naylor....586
Neosho....7,517
Nevada....9,736
Newburg....806
New Florence....635
New Franklin....1,122
New Haven....1,474
New London....967
New Madrid....2,719
Nixa (★SPRG)....1,636
Noel....924
Norborne....950
Normandy (★ST.L.)....6,183
North Kansas City (★K.C.)....5,183
Northmoor (★K.C.)....562
Northwoods (★ST.L.)....4,611
Novinger....547
Oak Grove (★K.C.)....2,025
Oakland (★ST.L.)....1,609
Oakview (★K.C.)....541
Oakville (★ST.L.)....1,000
Odessa....2,839
O'Fallon (★ST.L.)....7,018
Olivette (★ST.L.)....9,238
Oran....1,226
Oregon....789
Orrick....883
Osage Beach....1,091
Osceola....874
Otto (★ST.L.)....706
Overland (★ST.L.)....24,949
Owensville....2,416
Ozark (★SPRG)....2,384
Pacific (★ST.L.)....3,247
Pagedale (★ST.L.)....5,083
Palmyra....3,188
Paris....1,442
Parkdale (★ST.L.)....836
Parkville (★K.C.)....1,253
Parma....1,051
Pasadena Hills (★ST.L.)....1,337
Pasadena Park (★ST.L.)....760
Pattonsburg....540
Peculiar (★K.C.)....705
Perry....839
Perryville....5,149
Pevely (★ST.L.)....517
Piedmont....1,906
Pierce City....1,097
Pilot Grove....701
Pilot Knob....582
Pine Lawn (★ST.L.)....5,773
Platte City....2,022
Plattsburg....1,832
Pleasant Hill....3,396
Pleasant Valley (★K.C.)....1,535
Point Lookout....900
Poplar Bluff....16,653
Portage Des Sioux....509
Portageville....3,117
Potosi....2,761
Princeton....1,328
Purdy....588
Puxico....759
Queen City....588
Raymore (★K.C.)....587
Raytown (★K.C.)....33,306
Republic....2,411
Rich Hill....1,661
Richland....1,783
Richmond....4,948
Richmond Heights (★ST.L.)....13,802
Riverside (★K.C.)....2,123
Riverview (★ST.L.)....3,741
Rock Hill (★ST.L.)....6,815
Rock Port....1,575
Rogersville....574
Rolla....13,245
Russellville....557
St. Ann (★ST.L.)....18,215
St. Charles (★ST.L.)....31,834
St. Clair (★ST.L.)....2,978
Ste. Genevieve....4,468
St. George (★ST.L.)....2,033
St. James....2,873
St. Johns (St. John) (★ST.L.)....8,960
St. Joseph (★83,000; ST.JO)....72,691
St. Louis (★2,300,100; ST.L.)....622,236
St. Marys....645
St. Robert....1,465
Salem....4,363
Salisbury....1,960
Sappington (★ST.L.)....10,603
Sarcoxie....1,175
Savannah....3,324
Scott City....2,464
Sedalia....22,847
Senath....1,484
Seneca....1,577
Seymour....1,208
Shelbina....2,060
Shelbyville....601
Shrewsbury (★ST.L.)....5,896
Sikeston....14,699
Slater....2,576
Smithville....1,785
Spanish Lake (★ST.L.)....15,647
Springfield (★137,200; SPRG)....120,096
Springtown....500
Stanberry....1,479
Steele....2,107
Steelville....1,392
Stewartsville....634
Stockton....1,063
Stover....849
Sturgeon....787
Sugar Creek (★K.C.)....4,755
Sullivan....5,111
Sunset Hills (★ST.L.)....4,126
Sweet Springs....1,716
Sycamore Hills (★ST.L.)....821
Tarkio....2,517
Thayer....1,609
Times Beach (★ST.L.)....1,265
Tipton....1,914
Town and Country (★ST.L.)....2,645
Trenton....6,063
Troy....2,538
Union (★ST.L.)....5,183
Unionville....2,075
University City (★ST.L.)....46,309
Uplands Park (★ST.L.)....695
Valley Park (★ST.L.)....3,662
Van Buren....714
Vandalia....3,160
Velda (★ST.L.)....2,112
Velda Village Hills (★ST.L.)....1,179
Verona....515
Versailles....2,244
Viburnum....520
Vienna....505
Vinita Park (★ST.L.)....3,657
Warrensburg....13,125
Warrenton....2,057
Warsaw....1,423
Warson Woods (★ST.L.)....2,544
Washington....8,499
Waverly....827
Waynesville....3,375
Weatherby Lake (★K.C.)....832
Webb City (★JOP)....6,923
Webster Groves (★ST.L.)....27,455
Wellington....720
Wellston (★ST.L.)....7,050
Wellsville....1,565
Wentzville (★ST.L.)....3,223
Weston....1,267
West Plains....6,893
Wilber Park (★ST.L.)....692
Willard....1,018
Willow Springs....2,045
Winchester (★ST.L.)....2,329
Windsor....2,734
Winfield....620
Winona....973
Woodson Terrace (★ST.L.)....5,880
Wright City....943
Wyatt....562

MONTANA

1970 C....694,409

Counties

Beaverhead....8,187
Big Horn....10,057
Blaine....6,727
Broadwater....2,526
Carbon....7,080
Carter....1,956
Cascade....81,804
Chouteau....6,473
Custer....12,174
Daniels....3,083
Dawson....11,269
Deer Lodge....15,652
Fallon....4,050
Fergus....12,611
Flathead....39,460
Gallatin....32,505
Garfield....1,796
Glacier....10,783
Golden Valley....931
Granite....2,737
Hill....17,358
Jefferson....5,238
Judith Basin....2,667
Lake....14,445
Lewis and Clark....33,281
Liberty....2,359
Lincoln....18,063
McCone....2,875
Madison....5,014
Meagher....2,122
Mineral....2,958
Missoula....58,263
Musselshell....3,734
Park....11,197
Petroleum....675
Phillips....5,386
Pondera....6,611
Powder River....2,862
Powell....6,660
Prairie....1,752
Ravalli....14,409
Richland....9,837
Roosevelt....10,365
Rosebud....6,032
Sanders....7,093
Sheridan....5,779
Silver Bow....41,981
Stillwater....4,632
Sweet Grass....2,980
Teton....6,116
Toole....5,839
Treasure....1,069
Valley....11,471
Wheatland....2,529
Wibaux....1,465
Yellowstone....87,367
Yellowstone National Park (part)....64

Cities

Anaconda....9,771
Baker....2,584
Belgrade....1,307
Belt....656
Big Sandy....827
Big Timber....1,592
Billings (★74,800; BIL)....61,581
Billings Heights (★BIL)....900
Black Eagle (★GTFA)....2,200
Boulder....1,342
Bozeman....18,670
Bridger....717
Broadus....799
Browning....1,700
Butte (★40,000; BUT)....23,368
Cascade....714
Centerville (★BUT)....1,200
Chester....936
Chinook....1,813
Choteau....1,586
Circle....964
Columbia Falls....2,652
Columbus....1,173
Conrad....2,770
Culbertson....821
Cut Bank....4,004
Darby....538
Deer Lodge....4,306
Dillon....4,548
East Helena....1,651
Ekalaka....663
Ennis....501
Eureka....1,195
Evergreen....1,000
Fairfield....638
Fairview....956
Floral Park (★BUT)....5,113
Forsyth....1,873
Fort Benton....1,863
Glasgow....4,700
Glendive....6,305
Great Falls (★74,500; GTFA)....60,091
Hamilton....2,499
Hardin....2,733
Harlem....1,094
Harlowton....1,375
Havre....10,558
Helena....22,730
Hot Springs....664
Jordan....529
Kalispell....10,526
Laurel....4,454
Lewistown....6,437
Libby....3,286
Livingston....6,883
Lodge Grass....806
McGlone Heights (★BUT)....1,100
Malta....2,195
Manhattan....816
Miles City....9,023
Missoula (★51,700; MSLA)....29,497
Missoula Southwest (★MSLA)....4,000
Nashua....513
North Havre (Havre North)....1,073
Orchard Homes (★MSLA)....3,500
Philipsburg....1,128
Plains....1,046
Plentywood....2,381
Polson....2,464
Poplar....1,389
Rattlesnake (★MSLA)....1,492
Red Lodge....1,844
Ronan....1,347
Roundup....2,116
St. Ignatius....925
Scobey....1,486
Shelby....3,111
Sheridan....636
Sidney....4,543
Silver Bow Park (★BUT)....5,524
Stanford....505
Stevensville....829
Sunburst....604
Superior....993
Terry....870
Thompson Falls....1,356
Three Forks....1,188
Townsend....1,371
Troy....1,046
Twin Bridges....613
Valier....651
Walkerville (★BUT)....1,097
West Yellowstone....756
Whitefish....3,349
Whitehall....1,035
White Sulphur Springs....1,200
Wibaux....644
Wolf Point....3,095

NEBRASKA

1970 C....1,483,772

Counties

Adams....30,553
Antelope....9,047
Arthur....606
Banner....1,034
Blaine....847
Boone....8,190
Box Butte....10,094
Boyd....3,752
Brown....4,021
Buffalo....31,222
Burt....9,247
Butler....9,461
Cass....18,076
Cedar....12,192
Chase....4,129
Cherry....6,846
Cheyenne....10,778
Clay....8,266
Colfax....9,498
Cuming....12,034
Custer....14,092
Dakota....13,137
Dawes....9,761
Dawson....19,537
Deuel....2,717
Dixon....7,453
Dodge....34,782
Douglas....389,455
Dundy....2,926
Fillmore....8,137
Franklin....4,566
Frontier....3,982
Furnas....6,897
Gage....25,719
Garden....2,929
Garfield....2,411
Gosper....2,178
Grant....1,019
Greeley....4,000
Hall....42,851
Hamilton....8,867
Harlan....4,357
Hayes....1,530
Hitchcock....4,051
Holt....12,933
Hooker....939
Howard....6,807
Jefferson....10,436
Johnson....5,743
Kearney....6,707
Keith....8,487
Keya Paha....1,340
Kimball....6,009
Knox....11,723
Lancaster....167,972
Lincoln....29,538
Logan....991
Loup....854
Mc Pherson....623
Madison....27,402
Merrick....8,751
Morrill....5,813
Nance....5,142
Nemaha....8,976
Nuckolls....7,404
Otoe....15,576
Pawnee....4,473
Perkins....3,423
Phelps....9,553
Pierce....8,493
Platte....26,544
Polk....6,468
Red Willow....12,191
Richardson....12,277
Rock....2,231
Saline....12,809
Sarpy....64,889
Saunders....17,018
Scotts Bluff....36,432
Seward....14,460
Sheridan....7,285
Sherman....4,725
Sioux....2,034
Stanton....5,758
Thayer....7,779
Thomas....954
Thurston....6,942
Valley....5,783
Washington....13,310
Wayne....10,400
Webster....5,396
Wheeler....1,047
York....13,685

Cities

Ainsworth....2,073
Albion....2,074
Alliance....6,862
Alma....1,299
Ansley....631
Arapahoe....1,147
Arlington....910
Arnold....752
Ashland....2,176
Atkinson....1,406
Auburn....3,650
Aurora....3,180
Axtell....500
Bancroft....545
Bassett....983
Battle Creek....771
Bayard....1,338
Beatrice....12,389
Beaver City....802
Beemer....699
Bellevue (★OMA-)....21,953
Benkelman....1,349
Bennington (★OMA-)....683
Bertrand....662
Blair....6,106
Bloomfield....1,287
Blue Hill....784
Boys Town (★OMA-)....989
Bridgeport....1,490
Broken Bow....3,734
Burwell....1,341
Butte....575
Cairo....686
Callaway....523
Cambridge....1,145
Cedar Bluffs....616
Central City....2,803
Chadron....5,921
Chappell....1,204
Clarkson....805
Clay Center....952
Coleridge....608
Columbus....15,471
Cozad....4,219
Crawford....1,291
Creighton....1,461
Crete....4,444
Crofton....677
Culbertson....801
Curtis....1,166
Dakota City (★SXCY)....1,057
David City....2,380
Decatur....679
Deshler....937
De Witt....651
Dodge....704
Doniphan....542
Edgar....707
Elgin....917
Elkhorn (★OMA-)....1,184
Elm Creek....798
Elmwood....548
Elwood....601
Emerson....850
Ewing....552
Exeter....759
Fairbury....5,265
Fairmont....761
Falls City....5,444
Fort Calhoun....642
Franklin....1,193
Fremont....22,962
Friend....1,126
Fullerton....1,444
Geneva....2,275
Genoa....1,174
Gering....5,639
Gibbon....1,388
Gordon....2,106
Gothenburg....3,154
Grand Island....31,269
Grant....1,099
Greeley (Greeley Center)....580
Greenwood....506
Gretna....1,557
Hartington....1,581
Harvard....1,230
Hastings....23,580
Hay Springs....682
Hebron....1,667
Hemingford....734
Henderson....901
Hershey....526
Holdrege....5,635
Hooper....895
Howells....682
Humboldt....1,194
Humphrey....862
Imperial....1,589
Indianola....672
Kearney....19,181
Kenesaw....728
Kimball....3,680
Laurel....1,009
La Vista (★OMA-) (†9/14/71)....6,388
Leigh....501
Lexington....5,618
Lincoln (★158,100; LINC)....149,518
Louisville....1,036
Loup City....1,456
Lyman....561
Lyons....1,177
McCook....8,285
Madison....1,595
Milford....1,846
Minatare....939
Minden....2,669
Mitchell....1,842
Morrill....937
Mullen....667
Nebraska City....7,441
Neligh....1,764
Nelson....746
Newman Grove....863
Niobrara....602
Norfolk....16,607
North Bend....1,350
North Platte....19,447
Oakland....1,355
Offutt West (★OMA-)....8,445
Ogallala....4,976
Omaha (★521,500; OMA-)....346,929
O'Neill....3,753
Ord....2,439
Orleans....592
Osceola....923
Oshkosh....1,067
Osmond....883
Overton....538
Oxford....1,116
Papillion (★OMA-)....5,606
Parkview....1,089
Pawnee City....1,267
Paxton....503
Pender....1,229
Peru....1,380
Pierce....1,360
Plainview....1,494
Plattsmouth (★OMA-)....6,371
Ponca....984
Ralston (★OMA-)....4,731
Randolph....1,130
Ravenna....1,356
Red Cloud....1,531
Rushville....1,137
St. Edward....853
St. Paul....2,026
Sargent....789
Schuyler....3,597
Scottsbluff....14,507
Scribner....1,031
Seward....5,294
Shelby....647
Shelton....1,028
Sidney....6,403
South Sioux City (★SXCY)....7,920
Spalding....676
Spencer....606
Springfield....795
Stanton....1,363
Stromsburg....1,215
Stuart....561
Superior....2,779
Sutherland....840
Sutton....1,361
Syracuse....1,562
Tecumseh....2,058
Tekamah....1,848
Terrytown....747
Tilden....947

(Nebraska continued)

★ Population or designation of metropolitan area, including suburbs (see headnote).
▲ Population of entire "town" or township, including other communities and rural areas.
† Population is from a local census taken at date specified.

(Nebraska continued)

Trenton....770
Utica....602
Valentine....2,662
Valley....1,595
Verdigre....570
Wahoo....3,835
Wakefield....1,160
Walthill....897
Wauneta....738
Wausa....720
Waverly (★LINC)....1,152
Wayne....5,379
Weeping Water....1,143
West Point....3,385
Wilber....1,483
Winnebago....675
Wisner....1,315
Wood River....1,147
Wymore....1,790
York....6,778
Yutan....507

NEVADA

1970 C....488,738

Counties

Churchill....10,513
Clark....273,288
Douglas....6,882
Elko....13,958
Esmeralda....629
Eureka....948
Humboldt....6,375
Lander....2,666
Lincoln....2,557
Lyon....8,221
Mineral....7,051
Nye....5,599
Pershing....2,670
Storey....695
Washoe....121,068
White Pine....10,150
Carson City (Independent City)....15,468

Cities

Babbitt....1,579
Battle Mountain....1,856
Boulder City....5,223
Caliente....916
Carlin....1,313
Carson City....15,468
East Ely....1,992
East Las Vegas (★LASV)....6,501
Elko....7,621
Ely....4,176
Fallon....2,959
Gabbs....874
Hawthorne....3,539
Henderson (★LASV)....16,395
Las Vegas (★261,900; LASV)....125,787
Lovelock....1,571
McGill....2,164
North Las Vegas (★LASV)....36,216
Paradise (★LASV)....24,477
Reno (★118,000; RENO)....72,863
Sparks (★RENO)....24,187
Stateline (State Line)....900
Sunrise Manor (★LASV)....10,886
Sun Valley (★RENO)....2,414
Tonopah....1,716
Vegas Creek (★LASV)....8,970
Wells....1,081
Winchester (★LASV)....13,981
Winnemucca....3,587
Yerington....2,010
Zephyr Cove....900

NEW HAMPSHIRE

1970 C....737,681

Counties

Belknap....32,367
Carroll....18,548
Cheshire....52,364
Coos....34,291
Grafton....54,914
Hillsborough....223,941
Merrimack....80,925
Rockingham....138,951
Strafford....70,431
Sullivan....30,949

Cities

Allentown (★MNCH) (2,732▲)....
Amherst (★NSHUA) (4,605▲)....500
Antrim (2,122▲)....800
Ashland (1,599▲)....1,391
Atkinson (★BOS) (2,291▲)....700
Auburn (★MNCH) (2,035▲)....250
Bedford (★MNCH) (5,859▲)....1,000
Belmont (2,493▲)....600
Berlin....15,256
Boscawen (3,162▲)....350
Bow (2,479▲)....400
Bristol (1,670▲)....1,080
Charlestown (3,274▲)....1,285
Claremont....14,221
Colebrook (2,094▲)....1,070
Concord....30,022
Conway (4,865▲)....1,489
Derry (★MCNH) (11,712▲)....6,090
Dover (★54,400; DOV-)....20,850
Durham (8,869▲)....7,221
Enfield (2,345▲)....1,408
Epping (2,356▲)....1,097
Exeter (8,892▲)....6,439
Farmington (3,588▲)....2,884
Franklin....7,292
Goffstown (★MNCH) (9,284▲)....2,272
Gorham (2,998▲)....2,020
Greenville (★FTCH-) (1,587▲)....1,332
Groveton....1,597
Hampton (★PTSM) (8,011▲)....5,407
Hanover (8,494▲)....6,147
Haverhill (3,090▲)....300
Henniker (2,348▲)....900
Hillsboro (Hillsborough) (2,775▲)....1,784
Hinsdale (3,276▲)....1,059
Hollis (★NSHUA) (2,616▲)....250
Hooksett (★MNCH) (5,564▲)....1,303
Hopkinton (3,007▲)....700
Hudson (★NSHUA) (10,638▲)....5,500
Jaffrey (3,353▲)....1,922
Keene....20,467
Kingston (★BOS) (2,882▲)....600
Laconia....14,888
Lancaster (3,166▲)....2,120
Lebanon....9,725
Lincoln (1,341▲)....800
Lisbon (1,480▲)....1,247
Littleton (5,290▲)....4,180
Londonderry (★MNCH) (5,346▲)....700
Manchester (★137,800; MNCH)....87,754
Marlborough (1,671▲)....1,231
Meredith (2,904▲)....1,017
Merrimack (★NSHUA) (8,595▲)....400
Milford (★NSHUA) (6,622▲)....4,997
Nashua (★92,300; NSHUA)....55,820
New Castle (★PTSM)....975
New London (2,236▲)....1,347
Newmarket (★PTSM) (3,361▲)....2,645
Newport (5,899▲)....3,296
North Conway....1,723
Northfield (2,193▲)....1,315
North Hampton (★PTSM) (3,259▲)....900
Northumberland (2,493▲)....100
North Walpole....900
Pelham (★BOS) (5,408▲)....200
Pembroke (4,261▲)....
Peterborough (Peterboro) (3,807▲)....1,780
Pinardville (★MNCH)....4,000
Pittsfield (2,517▲)....1,662
Plaistow (★BOS) (4,712▲)....1,500
Plymouth (4,225▲)....3,109
Portsmouth (★71,800; PTSM)....25,717
Raymond (★MNCH) (3,003▲)....900
Rindge (2,175▲)....140
Rochester (★★DOV-)....17,938
Rollinsford (Salmon Falls) (★DOV-) (2,273▲)....900
Rye (4,083▲)....600
Salem (★BOS)....10,000
Seabrook (★BOS) (3,053▲)....700
Somersworth (★DOV-)....9,026
South Hooksett (★MNCH)....1,500
Suncook (★MNCH)....4,280
Swanzey Center (Swanzey) (4,254▲)....700
Tilton (2,579▲)....1,105
Troy (1,713▲)....1,123
Walpole (2,966▲)....600
West Swanzey....900
Whitefield....1,093
Wilton (★NSHUA) (2,276▲)....1,161
Winchester (2,889▲)....900
Windham (★BOS) (3,008▲)....100
Wolfeboro (3,036▲)....1,500
Woodsville....1,336

NEW JERSEY

1970 C....7,172,164

Counties

Atlantic....175,043
Bergen....897,148
Burlington....323,132
Camden....456,291
Cape May....59,554
Cumberland....121,374
Essex....932,299
Gloucester....172,681
Hudson....609,266
Hunterdon....69,718
Mercer....303,968
Middlesex....583,813
Monmouth....461,849
Morris....383,454
Ocean....208,470
Passaic....460,782
Salem....60,346
Somerset....198,372
Sussex....77,528
Union....543,116
Warren....73,960

Cities

Absecon (★AT.CY)....6,094
Adamston (★N.Y.)....900
Allendale (★N.Y.)....6,240
Allenhurst (★N.Y.)....1,012
Allentown (★PHIL-)....1,603
Almonesson (★PHIL-)....2,000
Alpha (★AL-B-E)....2,829
Alpine (★N.Y.)....1,344
Andover (★N.Y.)....813
Arrowhead Village (★N.Y.)....1,300
Asbury Park (★N.Y.)....16,533
Ashland (★PHIL-)....1,500
Atco (★PHIL-)....2,100
Atlantic City (★153,200; AT.CY)....47,859
Atlantic Highlands (★N.Y.)....5,102
Audubon (★PHIL-)....10,802
Audubon Park (★PHIL-)....1,492
Avalon....1,283
Avenel (★N.Y.)....10,000
Avon by the Sea (★N.Y.)....2,163
Barnegat Light....554
Barrington (★PHIL-)....8,409
Basking Ridge (★N.Y.)....4,000
Bay Head (★N.Y.)....1,083
Bayonne (★N.Y.)....72,743
Bay Shore (★N.Y.)....800
Bayville (★N.Y.)....900
Beach Haven....1,488
Beachwood (★N.Y.)....4,390
Belford (★N.Y.)....6,500
Belleville (★N.Y.)....34,772
Bellmawr (★PHIL-)....15,618
Bells Lake (★PHIL-)....2,000
Belmar (★N.Y.)....5,782
Belvidere....2,722
Bergenfield (★N.Y.)....29,000
Berkeley Heights (★N.Y.)....13,078
Berlin (★PHIL-)....4,997
Bernardsville (★N.Y.)....6,652
Beverly (★PHIL-)....3,105
Birchwood Park (★N.Y.)....1,400
Blackwood (★PHIL-)....4,000
Blackwood Terrace (★PHIL-)....2,000
Blenheim (★PHIL-)....1,000
Bloomfield (★N.Y.)....52,029
Bloomingdale (★N.Y.)....7,797
Bloomsbury....879
Bogota (★N.Y.)....8,960
Boonton (★N.Y.)....9,261
Bordentown (★PHIL-)....4,490
Bossert Estates (★PHIL-)....1,300
Bound Brook (★N.Y.)....10,450
Bradley Beach (★N.Y.)....4,163
Bradley Gardens (★N.Y.)....3,500
Branchville....911
Breton Woods (★N.Y.)....1,200
Brick Town (★N.Y.)....2,000
Bridgeton (★35,800; BRDGT)....20,435
Brielle (★N.Y.)....3,594
Brigantine (★AT.CY)....6,741
Brooklawn (★PHIL-)....2,870
Brookside (★N.Y.)....800
Brookwood (★N.Y.)....4,000
Browns Mills....7,144
Browntown (★N.Y.)....3,500
Budd Lake (★N.Y.)....3,168
Buena (★VINL-)....3,283
Burlington (★PHIL-)....11,991
Butler (★N.Y.)....7,051
Caldwell (★N.Y.)....8,719
Califon (★N.Y.)....970
Camden (★PHIL-)....102,551
Candlewood (★N.Y.)....2,000
Cap May....4,392
Cape May Court House....2,062
Carlstadt (★N.Y.)....6,724
Carneys Point (★PHIL-)....3,000
Carteret (★N.Y.)....23,137
Cedar Grove (★N.Y.)....15,582
Cedar Knolls (★N.Y.)....3,200
Cedarwood Park (★N.Y.)....1,300
Central Park (★N.Y.)....1,600
Centre City (★PHIL-)....1,800
Chatham (★N.Y.)....9,566
Cheesequake (★N.Y.)....2,200
Cherry Hill (★PHIL-)....64,395
Chesilhurst (★PHIL-)....801
Chester (★N.Y.)....1,299
Cinnaminson (★PHIL-)....16,962
Clark (★N.Y.)....18,829
Clayton (★PHIL-)....5,193
Clementon (★PHIL-)....4,492
Cliffside Park (★N.Y.)....18,891
Cliffwood (★N.Y.)....2,700
Cliffwood Beach (★N.Y.)....6,000
Clifton (★N.Y.)....82,437
Clinton (★N.Y.)....1,742
Closter (★N.Y.)....8,604
Collingswood (★PHIL-)....17,422
Collinsville (★N.Y.)....3,500
Colonia (★N.Y.)....17,800
Colonial Manor (★PHIL-)....1,000
Convent Station (★N.Y.)....1,500
Cranbury (Cranbury Center) (★N.Y.)....1,253
Cranford (★N.Y.)....27,391
Cresskill (★N.Y.)....8,298
Crestwood Village (★N.Y.)....2,000
Deal (★N.Y.)....2,401
Delanco (★PHIL-)....4,157
Delran (★PHIL-)....10,065
Demarest (★N.Y.)....5,133
Denville (★N.Y.)....14,045
Deptford (★PHIL-)....3,500
Dover (★N.Y.)....15,039
Dumont (★N.Y.)....20,155
Dunellen (★N.Y.)....7,072
East Brunswick (★N.Y.)....27,000
East Hanover (★N.Y.)....7,734
East Keansburg (★N.Y.)....3,500
East Millstone (★N.Y.)....600
East Newark (★N.Y.)....1,922
East Orange (★N.Y.)....75,471
East Paterson (★N.Y.)....20,511
East Rutherford (★N.Y.)....8,536
East Windsor (★N.Y.)....10,000
Eatontown (★N.Y.)....14,619
Edgewater (★N.Y.)....4,987
Edgewater Park (★PHIL-)....7,412
Edison (★N.Y.)....67,120
Egg Harbor City (Egg Harbor) (★AT.CY)....4,304
Eldridge Park (★PHIL-)....1,300
Elizabeth (★N.Y.)....112,654
Elmer (★PHIL-)....1,592
Emerson (★N.Y.)....8,428
Englewood (★N.Y.)....24,985
Englewood Cliffs (★N.Y.)....5,938
Englishtown (★N.Y.)....1,048
Erial (★PHIL-)....900
Essex Fells (★N.Y.)....2,541
Estell Manor....539
Ewing Township (★PHIL-)....32,831
Fairfield (★N.Y.)....6,731
Fair Haven (★N.Y.)....6,142
Fair Lawn (★N.Y.)....37,975
Fairton (★BRDGT)....700
Fairview (★N.Y.)....10,698
Fairview (★N.Y.)....5,000
Fanwood (★N.Y.)....8,920
Far Hills (★N.Y.)....780
Farmingdale (★N.Y.)....1,148
Fieldsboro (★PHIL-)....615
Finderne (★N.Y.)....6,000
Flemington (★N.Y.)....3,917
Florence (★PHIL-)....4,000
Florham Park (★N.Y.)....8,094
Folsom....1,767
Fords (★N.Y.)....14,800
Forked River....1,422
Fort Lee (★N.Y.)....30,631
Franklin (★N.Y.)....4,236
Franklin Lakes (★N.Y.)....7,550
Franklin Park (★N.Y.)....900
Franklinville (★PHIL-)....900
Freehold (★N.Y.)....10,545
Freewood Acres (★N.Y.)....1,000
Frenchtown....1,459
Garfield (★N.Y.)....30,797
Garwood (★N.Y.)....5,260
Gibbsboro (★PHIL-)....2,634
Gibbstown (Greenwich) (★PHIL-)....5,676
Gilford Park (★N.Y.)....3,200
Gillette (★N.Y.)....2,500
Gladstone (Peapack-Gladstone) (★N.Y.)....1,924
Glassboro (★PHIL-)....12,938
Glendola (★N.Y.)....2,000
Glendora (★PHIL-)....5,000
Glen Gardner (★N.Y.)....874
Glen Ridge (★N.Y.)....8,518
Glen Rock (★N.Y.)....13,011
Gloucester City (★PHIL-)....14,707
Green Brook (★N.Y.)....4,302
Greenfields Village (★PHIL-)....2,500
Green Knoll (★N.Y.)....3,000
Groveville (★PHIL-)....2,500
Guttenberg (★N.Y.)....5,754
Hackensack (★N.Y.)....36,008
Hackettstown (★N.Y.)....9,472
Haddonfield (★PHIL-)....13,118
Haddon Heights (★PHIL-)....9,365
Haddon Hills (★PHIL-)....1,700
Haddon Leigh (★PHIL-)....2,300
Hainesport (★PHIL-)....900
Haledon (★N.Y.)....6,767
Hamburg (★N.Y.)....1,820
Hamilton Square (★PHIL-)....10,000
Hammonton....11,464
Hampton (★N.Y.)....1,386
Harrington Park (★N.Y.)....4,841
Harrison (★N.Y.)....11,811
Hasbrouck Heights (★N.Y.)....13,651
Haworth (★N.Y.)....3,760
Hawthorne (★N.Y.)....19,173
Hazlet (★N.Y.)....18,000
Helmetta (★N.Y.)....955
High Bridge (★N.Y.)....2,606
Highland Park (★N.Y.)....14,385
Highlands (★N.Y.)....3,916
Hightstown (★N.Y.)....5,431
Highview Park (★N.Y.)....1,000
Hillsdale (★N.Y.)....11,768
Hillside (★N.Y.)....21,636
Hilltop (★PHIL-)....1,500
Hi-Nella (★PHIL-)....1,195
Hoboken (★N.Y.)....45,380
Ho-Ho-Kus (★N.Y.)....4,348
Holiday City (★N.Y.)....3,000
Hopatcong (★N.Y.)....9,052
Hopelawn (★N.Y.)....2,000
Hopewell (★PHIL-)....2,271
Interlaken (★N.Y.)....1,182
Ironia (★N.Y.)....900
Irvington (★N.Y.)....59,743
Iselin (★N.Y.)....20,800
Island Heights (★N.Y.)....1,397
Jamesburg (★N.Y.)....4,584
Jericho (★PHIL-)....500
Jersey City (★N.Y.)....260,545
Keansburg (★N.Y.)....9,720
Kearny (★N.Y.)....37,585
Keasbey (★N.Y.)....1,000
Kendall Park (★N.Y.)....7,412
Kenilworth (★N.Y.)....9,165
Kenvil (★N.Y.)....2,000
Keyport (★N.Y.)....7,205
Kinnelon (★N.Y.)....7,600
Lake Hiawatha (★N.Y.)....11,389
Lake Hopatcong (Esponong) (★N.Y.)....1,941
Lakehurst (★N.Y.)....2,641
Lake Ridge (★N.Y.)....1,200
Lake Riviera (★N.Y.)....1,200
Lake Telemark (★N.Y.)....1,086
Lakewood (★N.Y.)....25,223
Lambertville (★PHIL-)....4,359
Landing (Shore Hills) (★N.Y.)....3,064
Laurel Springs (★PHIL-)....2,566
Laurence Harbor (★N.Y.)....5,000
Lavallette (★N.Y.)....1,509
Lawnside (★PHIL-)....2,757
Lawrenceville (★PHIL-)....3,000
Lebanon (★N.Y.)....885
Ledgewood (★N.Y.)....1,700
Leisure World (★N.Y.)....900
Leonardo (★N.Y.)....4,000
Leonia (★N.Y.)....8,847
Lincoln Park (★N.Y.)....9,034
Lincroft (★N.Y.)....5,000
Linden (★N.Y.)....41,409
Lindenwold (★PHIL-)....12,199
Linwood (★AT.CY)....6,159
Little Falls (★N.Y.)....11,727
Little Ferry (★N.Y.)....9,042
Little Silver (★N.Y.)....6,010
Livingston (★N.Y.)....30,127
Lodi (★N.Y.)....25,213
Long Branch (★N.Y.)....31,774
Longport (★AT.CY)....1,225
Long Valley (★N.Y.)....1,645
Lyndhurst (★N.Y.)....22,729
Madison (★N.Y.)....16,710
Madison Park (★N.Y.)....2,800
Magnolia (★PHIL-)....5,893
Mahwah (★N.Y.)....6,000
Manahawkin....1,278
Manasquan (★N.Y.)....4,971
Manasquan Shores (★N.Y.)....1,200
Mantua (★PHIL-)....2,000
Manville (★N.Y.)....13,029
Maple Shade (★PHIL-)....16,464
Maplewood (★N.Y.)....24,932
Margate City (Margate) (★AT.CY)....10,576
Marlton (★PHIL-)....10,180
Masonville (★PHIL-)....900
Matawan (★N.Y.)....9,136
Mays Landing....1,272
Maywood (★N.Y.)....11,087
Medford Lakes (★PHIL-)....4,792
Medford (Medford Center) (★PHIL-)....1,448
Mendham (★N.Y.)....3,729
Menlo Park Terrace (★N.Y.)....2,800
Mercerville (★PHIL-)....14,500
Merchantville (★PHIL-)....4,425
Metuchen (★N.Y.)....16,031
Middlebush (★N.Y.)....1,000
Middlesex (★N.Y.)....15,038
Middletown (★N.Y.)....15,000
Midland Park (★N.Y.)....8,159
Milford....1,230
Millbrook (★N.Y.)....1,500
Millburn (★N.Y.)....21,307
Millington (★N.Y.)....2,000
Millstone (★N.Y.)....630
Milltown (★N.Y.)....6,470
Millville (★★VINL-)....21,366
Mine Hill (★N.Y.)....3,557
Monmouth Beach (★N.Y.)....2,042
Montclair (★N.Y.)....44,043
Montvale (★N.Y.)....7,327
Montville (★N.Y.)....2,500
Moonachie (★N.Y.)....2,951
Moorestown (★PHIL-)....15,577
Morris Plains (★N.Y.)....5,540
Morristown (★N.Y.)....17,662
Mountain Lakes (★N.Y.)....4,739
Mountainside (★N.Y.)....7,520
Mount Arlington (★N.Y.)....3,590
Mount Ephraim (★PHIL-)....5,625
Mount Fern (★N.Y.)....1,000
Mount Freedom (★N.Y.)....1,621
Mount Holly (★PHIL-)....12,713
National Park (★PHIL-)....3,730
Navesink (★N.Y.)....1,500
Neptune (★N.Y.)....21,800
Neptune City (★N.Y.)....5,502
Netcong (★N.Y.)....2,858
Newark (★★N.Y.)....382,288
New Brunswick (★N.Y.)....41,885
New Egypt....1,769
Newfield (★VINL-)....1,487
New Milford (★N.Y.)....19,149
New Providence (★N.Y.)....13,796
New Shrewsbury (★N.Y.)....8,395
Newton (★N.Y.)....7,297
North Arlington (★N.Y.)....18,096
North Bergen (★N.Y.)....47,751
North Branch (★N.Y.)....2,500
North Brunswick (★N.Y.)....16,691
North Caldwell (★N.Y.)....6,425
North Cape May....3,812
Northfield (★AT.CY)....8,875
North Haledon (★N.Y.)....7,614
North Plainfield (★N.Y.)....21,796
Northvale (★N.Y.)....5,177
North Wildwood....3,914
Norwood (★N.Y.)....4,398
Nutley (★N.Y.)....31,913
Oakhurst (★N.Y.)....4,660
Oakland (★N.Y.)....14,420
Oaklyn (★PHIL-)....4,626
Oak Valley (★PHIL-)....5,000
Oakview (★PHIL-)....2,400
Ocean City (★AT.CY)....10,575
Ocean Gate (★N.Y.)....1,081
Ocean Grove (★N.Y.)....6,000
Oceanport (★N.Y.)....7,503
Ogdensburg (★N.Y.)....2,222
Old Bridge (★N.Y.)....15,200
Old Tappan (★N.Y.)....3,917
Oradell (★N.Y.)....8,903
Orange (★N.Y.)....32,566
Oxford (Oxford Furnace)....1,411
Palisades Park (★N.Y.)....13,351
Palmyra (★PHIL-)....6,969
Paramus (★N.Y.)....28,381
Park Ridge (★N.Y.)....8,709
Parkway Pines (★N.Y.)....1,500
Parsippany (Lake Parsippany) (★N.Y.)....7,488
Passaic (★N.Y.)....55,124
Paterson (★★N.Y.)....144,824
Paulsboro (★PHIL-)....8,084
Pemberton....1,344
Pennington (★PHIL-)....2,151
Pennsauken (★PHIL-)....36,394
Penns Grove (★PHIL-)....5,727
Pennsville (★PHIL-)....11,014
Pequannock (★N.Y.)....5,000
Perth Amboy (★N.Y.)....38,798
Phillipsburg (★AL-B-E)....17,849
Pine Beach (★N.Y.)....1,395
Pine Hill (★PHIL-)....5,132
Piscataway (★N.Y.)....36,418
Pitman (★PHIL-)....10,257
Plainfield (★N.Y.)....46,862
Pleasantville (★AT.CY)....13,778
Point Pleasant (★N.Y.)....15,968
Point Pleasant Beach (★N.Y.)....4,882
Point Pleasant Manor (★N.Y.)....1,200
Pompton Lakes (★N.Y.)....11,397
Pompton Plains (★N.Y.)....9,500
Port Monmouth (★N.Y.)....4,500
Port Norris....1,955
Port Reading (★N.Y.)....4,500
Port Republic (★AT.CY)....586
Princeton....12,311
Princeton Township....13,651
Prospect Park (★N.Y.)....5,176
Rahway (★N.Y.)....29,114
Rainbow Lakes (★N.Y.)....1,000
Ramblewood (★PHIL-)....5,556
Ramsey (★N.Y.)....12,571
Rancocas Woods (★PHIL-)....1,200
Raritan (★N.Y.)....6,691
Red Bank (★N.Y.)....12,847
Ridgefield (★N.Y.)....11,308
Ridgefield Park (★N.Y.)....13,990
Ridgewood (★N.Y.)....27,547
Ringwood (★N.Y.)....10,393
Rio Grande....1,203

★ Population or designation of metropolitan area, including suburbs (see headnote).
▲ Population of entire "town" or township, including other communities and rural areas.
† Population is from a local census taken at date specified.

Riverdale (★N.Y.)....2,729
River Edge (★N.Y.)....12,850
River Plaza (★N.Y.)....3,500
Riverside (★PHIL-)....8,591
Riverton (★PHIL-)....3,412
River Vale (★N.Y.)....8,883
Riviera Beach (★N.Y.)....2,000
Rochelle Park (★N.Y.)....6,380
Rockaway (★N.Y.)....6,383
Rockaway Neck (★N.Y.)....3,000
Rocky Hill....917
Roebling (★PHIL-)....3,600
Roosevelt....814
Roseland (★N.Y.)....4,453
Roselle (★N.Y.)....22,585
Roselle Park (★N.Y.)....14,277
Rumson (★N.Y.)....7,421
Runnemede (★PHIL-)....10,475
Rutherford (★N.Y.)....20,802
Saddle Brook (★N.Y.)....15,975
Saddle River (★N.Y.)....2,437
Salem (★PHIL-)....7,648
Salem Hills (★N.Y.)....1,800
Sayreville (★N.Y.)....32,508
Sayre Woods South (★N.Y.)....7,500
Scotch Plains (★N.Y.)....22,279
Sea Bright (★N.Y.)....1,339
Seabrook (Seabrook Farms) (★BRDGT)....1,569
Sea Girt (★N.Y.)....2,207
Sea Girt Estates (★N.Y.)....1,300
Sea Isle City....1,712
Seaside Heights (★N.Y.)....1,248
Seaside Park (★N.Y.)....1,432
Secaucus (★N.Y.)....13,228
Sedgefield (★N.Y.)....800
Sewaren (★N.Y.)....2,000
Sewell (★PHIL-)....1,900
Shark River Manor (★N.Y.)....1,500
Shiloh (★BRDGT)....573
Ship Bottom....1,079
Shrewsbury (★N.Y.)....3,315
Silverton (★N.Y.)....1,500
Sky Manor (★N.Y.)....900
Slackwood (★PHIL-)....1,400
Somerdale (★PHIL-)....6,510
Somerset (★N.Y.)....18,000
Somers Point (★AT.CY)....7,919
Somerville (★N.Y.)....13,652
South Amboy (★N.Y.)....9,338
South Belmar (★N.Y.)....1,490
South Bound Brook (★N.Y.)....4,525
South Hackensack (★N.Y.)....2,384
South Orange (★N.Y.)....16,971
South Plainfield (★N.Y.)....21,142
South River (★N.Y.)....15,428
South Toms River (★N.Y.)....3,981
Sparta (Lake Mohawk) (★N.Y.)....6,262
Spotswood (★N.Y.)....7,891
Springfield (★N.Y.)....15,740
Spring Lake (★N.Y.)....3,896
Spring Lake Heights (★N.Y.)....4,602
Springside (★PHIL-)....1,000
Stanhope (★N.Y.)....3,040
Stirling (★N.Y.)....2,000
Stockton (★PHIL-)....619
Stone Harbor....1,089
Stratford (★PHIL-)....9,801
Strathmore (★N.Y.)....7,674
Succasunna (★N.Y.)....4,000
Summit (★N.Y.)....23,620
Surf City....1,129
Sussex....2,038
Swedesboro (★PHIL-)....2,287
Tabor (Mount Tabor) (★N.Y.)....1,500
Teaneck (★N.Y.)....42,355
Tenafly (★N.Y.)....14,827
Thorofare (★PHIL-)....1,200
Titusville (★PHIL-)....1,000
Toms River (★N.Y.)....7,303
Totowa (★N.Y.)....11,580
Towaco (★N.Y.)....3,000
Trenton (★★PHIL-)....104,638
Trenton East (★PHIL-)....25,000
Troy Hills (★N.Y.)....4,000
Tuckerton....1,926
Twin Rivers (★N.Y.)....1,500
Union (Unionbury) (★N.Y.)....53,077
Union Beach (★N.Y.)....6,472
Union City (★N.Y.)....58,537
Upper Greenwood Lake (★N.Y.)....1,505
Upper Saddle River (★N.Y.)....7,949
Vail Homes (Shrewsbury)(★N.Y.)....1,164
Ventnor City (Ventnor) (★AT.CY)....10,385
Verona (★N.Y.)....15,067
Victory Gardens (★N.Y.)....1,027
Villas....3,155
Vineland (★86,800; VINL-)....47,399
Waldwick (★N.Y.)....12,313
Wallington (★N.Y.)....10,284
Wanamassa (★N.Y.)....6,000
Wanaque (Wanaque-Midvale) (★N.Y.)....8,636
Washington....5,943
Washington Township (★N.Y.)....10,577
Washington Valley (★N.Y.)....1,000
Watchung (★N.Y.)....4,750
Wayne (★N.Y.)....49,141
Weehawken (★N.Y.)....13,383
Wenonah (★PHIL-)....2,364
West Allenhurst (★N.Y.)....1,000
West Belmar (★N.Y.)....3,000
West Berlin (★PHIL-)....3,800
West Caldwell (★N.Y.)....11,887
West Cape May....1,005
West Collingswood Heights (★PHIL-)....1,300
Westfield (★N.Y.)....33,720
West Keansburg (★N.Y.)....4,000
West Long Branch (★N.Y.)....6,845
West Milford (★N.Y.)....900
Westmont (★PHIL-)....8,000
West New York (★N.Y.)....40,627
West Orange (★N.Y.)....43,715
West Paterson (★N.Y.)....11,692
Westville (★PHIL-)....5,170
Westville Grove (★PHIL-)....3,000
Westwood (★N.Y.)....11,105
Wharton (★N.Y.)....5,535
Whippany (★N.Y.)....7,500
White Horse (★PHIL-)....11,500
White House Station (White House sta.) (★N.Y.)....1,019
White Meadow Lake (★N.Y.)....6,000
Whitman Square (★PHIL-)....2,500
Wildwood....4,110
Wildwood Crest....3,483
Williamstown (★PHIL-)....4,075
Willingboro (Levittown) (★PHIL-)....43,386
Winfield (★N.Y.)....2,184
Woodbine....2,625
Woodbridge (★N.Y.)....21,800
Woodbury (★PHIL-)....12,408
Woodbury Heights (★PHIL-)....3,621
Woodcliff Lake (★N.Y.)....5,506
Woodlynne (Wood-Lynne) (★PHIL-)....3,101
Wood-Ridge (★N.Y.)....8,311
Woodstown (★PHIL-)....3,137
Wrightstown....2,719
Wyckoff (★N.Y.)....16,039
Yardville (★PHIL-)....7,200

NEW MEXICO

1970 C....1,016,000

Counties

Bernalillo....315,774
Catron....2,198
Chaves....43,335
Colfax....12,170
Curry....39,517
De Baca....2,547
Dona Ana....69,773
Eddy....41,119
Grant....22,030
Guadalupe....4,969
Harding....1,348
Hidalgo....4,734
Lea....49,554
Lincoln....7,560
Los Alamos....15,198
Luna....11,706
McKinley....43,208
Mora....4,673
Otero....41,097
Quay....10,903
Rio Arriba....25,170
Roosevelt....16,479
Sandoval....17,492
San Juan....52,517
San Miguel....21,951
Santa Fe....53,756
Sierra....7,189
Socorro....9,763
Taos....17,516
Torrance....5,290
Union....4,925
Valencia....40,539

Cities

Adobe Acres (★ALBU)....1,400
Alameda (★ALBU)....6,000
Alamogordo....23,035
Albuquerque (★327,700; ALBU)....243,751
Anthony....1,728
Armijo (★ALBU)....9,000
Artesia....10,315
Atrisco (★ALBU)....5,000
Aztec....3,354
Bayard....2,908
Belen....4,823
Bernalillo (★ALBU)....2,016
Bloomfield....1,574
Carlsbad....21,297
Carrizozo....1,123
Central....1,864
Chama....899
Cimarron....927
Clayton....2,931
Cloudcroft....525
Clovis....28,495
Corrales (★ALBU)....1,500
Deming....8,343
Dexter....746
Espanola....4,528
Estancia....721
Eunice....2,641
Farmington....21,979
Five Points (★ALBU)....4,000
Fort Sumner....1,615
Gallup....14,596
Grants....8,768
Hagerman....953
Hatch....867
Hobbs....26,025
Hurley....1,796
Isleta (Isleta Pueblo) (★ALBU)....1,080
Jal....2,602
Jemez Pueblo....1,197
La Huerta....950
Las Cruces (★48,000; LSCR)....37,857
Las Vegas....13,835
Lordsburg....3,429
Los Alamos....15,198
Los Lunas (★ALBU)....973
Los Padillas (★ALBU)....2,000
Los Ranchos (★ALBU)....2,500
Los Ranchos de Albuquerque (★ALBU)....1,900
Loving....1,192
Lovington....8,915
Magdalena....652
Melrose....636
Mesilla (La Mesilla) (★LSCR)....1,713
Milan....2,185
Moriarty....758
Mountainair....1,022
Mountain View (★ALBU)....1,500
Pajarito (★ALBU)....2,500
Paradise Hills (★ALBU)....2,000
Portales....10,554
Questa....1,095
Ranchos of Taos (Ranchos de Taos)....900
Raton....6,962
Rio Rancho Estates (★ALBU)....1,000
Roswell....33,908
Ruidoso....2,216
Ruidoso Downs....702
San Felipe Pueblo (San Felipe)....1,187
Santa Fe (★43,800; S.FE)....41,167
Santa Rosa....2,485
Santo Domingo Pueblo....1,662
Silver City....7,751
Socorro....5,849
Springer....1,574
Sunland Park (Meadow Vista) (★ELP)....1,402
Taos....2,475
Taos Pueblo....1,030
Tatum....982
Texico....772
Truth or Consequences....4,656
Tucumcari....7,189
Tularosa....2,851
University Park (★LSCR)....3,700
Vaughn....867
Wagon Mound....630
Zuni (Zuni Pueblo)....3,958

NEW YORK

1970 C....18,241,266

Counties

Albany....286,742
Allegany....46,458
Bronx....1,471,701
Broome....221,815
Cattaraugus....81,666
Cayuga....77,439
Chautauqua....147,305
Chemung....101,537
Chenango....46,368
Clinton....72,934
Columbia....51,519
Cortland....45,894
Delaware....44,718
Dutchess....222,295
Erie....1,113,491
Essex....34,631
Franklin....43,931
Fulton....52,637
Genesee....58,722
Greene....33,136
Hamilton....4,714
Herkimer....67,633
Jefferson....88,508
Kings....2,602,012
Lewis....23,644
Livingston....54,041
Madison....62,864
Monroe....711,917
Montgomery....55,883
Nassau....1,428,838
New York....1,539,233
Niagara....235,720
Oneida....273,037
Onondaga....472,835
Ontario....78,849
Orange....221,657
Orleans....37,305
Oswego....100,897
Otsego....56,181
Putnam....56,696
Queens....1,987,174
Rensselaer....152,510
Richmond....295,443
Rockland....229,903
St. Lawrence....111,991
Saratoga....121,764
Schenectady....161,078
Schoharie....24,750
Schuyler....16,737
Seneca....35,083
Steuben....99,546
Suffolk....1,127,030
Sullivan....52,580
Tioga....46,513
Tompkins....77,064
Ulster....141,241
Warren....49,402
Washington....52,725
Wayne....79,404
Westchester....894,406
Wyoming....37,688
Yates....19,831

Cities

Adams....1,951
Addison....2,104
Afton....1,064
Airmont (★N.Y.)....1,000
Akron (★BUF-)....2,863
Albany (★683,000; A-S-T)....115,781
Albertson (★N.Y.)....11,420
Albion....5,122
Alden (★BUF-)....2,651
Alexandria Bay....1,440
Alfred....3,804
Allegany....2,050
Almond....658
Altamont (A-S-T)....1,561
Amagansett....1,500
Amenia....1,157
Amherst (★BUF-)....62,000
Amityville (★N.Y.)....9,794
Amsterdam (★A-S-T)....25,524
Andover....1,214
Angelica....948
Angola (★BUF-)....2,676
Angola on the Lake (★BUF-)....1,200
Antwerp....872
Apalachin (★BING)....1,233
Arcade....1,972
Ardsley (★N.Y.)....4,470
Arkport....984
Arlington (★POK)....11,203
Arlyn Oaks (★N.Y.)....1,500
Armonk (★N.Y.)....5,000
Armor (★BUF-)....2,000
Asharoken (★N.Y.)....540
Athens....1,718
Athol Springs (★BUF)....800
Atlantic Beach (★N.Y.)....1,640
Attica....2,911
Auburn (★46,100; AUB)....34,599
Auburn Southeast Melrose Park) (★AUB)....2,189
Aurora....1,072
Au Sable Forks....2,100
Averill Park (★A-S-T)....1,471
Avoca....1,153
Avon (★ROCH)....3,260
Babylon (★N.Y.)....12,897
Bainbridge....1,674
Baldwin (★N.Y.)....34,525
Baldwinsville (★SYR)....6,298
Ballston Lake (★A-S-T)....930
Ballston Spa....4,968
Balmville (★NWBG)....3,214
Bardonia (★N.Y.)....1,500
Batavia....17,338
Bath....6,053
Baxter Estates (★N.Y.)....1,026
Bayberry (★SYR)....2,500
Bay Park (★N.Y.)....3,000
Bayport (★N.Y.)....8,232
Bay Shore (★N.Y.)....35,600
Bayville (N.Y.)....6,147
Beacon (★NWBG)....13,255
Bedford (★N.Y.)....900
Bedford Hills (★N.Y.)....3,500
Belfast....900
Bellerose (★N.Y.)....1,136
Bellerose Terrace (★N.Y.)....2,000
Bellmore (★N.Y.)....18,431
Bellport (★N.Y.)....3,046
Belmont....1,102
Bergen (★ROCH)....1,018
Bethpage (★N.Y.)....29,300
Big Flats (★ELM-)....2,509
Big Tree (★BUF-)....1,600
Billington Heights (★BUF-)....1,278
Binghamton (★243,400; BING)....64,123
Black River (★WATN)....1,307
Blasdell (★BUF-)....3,910
Blauvelt (★N.Y.)....5,426
Bloomingdale....536
Blue Point (★N.Y.)....3,100
Bohemia (★N.Y.)....8,926
Bolivar....1,379
Boonville....2,488
Bowmansville (★BUF-)....900
Brentwood (★N.Y.)....41,000
Brewerton (★SYR)....1,985
Brewster (★N.Y.)....1,638
Brewster Heights (★N.Y.)....1,265
Briarcliff Manor (N.Y.)....6,521
Bridgehampton....900
Brighton (★ROCH)....35,065
Brightwaters (★N.Y.)....3,808
Broadalbin (★A-S-T)....1,452
Brockport (★ROCH)....7,878
Brocton....1,370
Bronxville (★N.Y.)....6,674
Brookhaven (★N.Y.)....900
Brookville (★N.Y.)....3,212
Brownville (★WATN)....1,187
Brushton....547
Buchanan (★N.Y.)....2,110
Buffalo (★1,280,000; BUF-)....462,768
Caledonia (★ROCH)....2,327
Cambridge....1,769
Camden....2,936
Camillus (★SYR)....1,534
Canajoharie....2,686
Canandaigua....10,488
Canaseraga....750
Canastota....5,033
Candor....939
Canisteo....2,772
Canton....6,398
Cape Vincent....820
Carle Place (★N.Y.)....6,326
Carmel (★N.Y.)....3,395
Carthage....3,889
Cassadaga....905
Castile....1,330
Castleton-on-Hudson (★A-S-T)....1,730
Catskill....5,317
Cattaraugus....1,200
Cayuga....693
Cayuga Heights (★ITH)....3,130
Cazenovia (★SYR)....3,031
Cedarhurst (★N.Y.)....6,941
Celoron (★JMST)....1,456
Centereach (★N.Y.)....15,700
Center Moriches (★N.Y.)....3,802
Centerport (★N.Y.)....5,000
Central Islip (★N.Y.)....25,500
Central Nyack (★N.Y.)....1,300
Central Square (★SYR)....1,298
Chadwicks (Chadwick) (★UT-R)....1,200
Champlain....1,426
Chappaqua....6,500
Chateaugay....976
Chatham....2,239
Chaumont....567
Cheektowaga (★BUF-)....89,000
Chenango Bridge (★BING)....2,500
Cherry Creek....658
Cherry Valley....661
Chester (★N.Y.)....1,627
Chili Center (★ROCH)....2,000
Chittenango (★SYR)....3,605
Churchville (★ROCH)....1,065
Clarence (★BUF-)....2,014
Clarence Center (★BUF-)....1,332
Clark Mills (★UT-R)....1,206
Clayton....1,970
Clayville (★UT-R)....535
Cleveland (★SYR)....821
Clifton Heights (★BUF-)....1,500
Clifton Knolls (★A-S-T)....5,771
Clifton Springs (★ROCH)....2,058
Clinton (★UT-R)....2,271
Clyde....2,828
Cobleskill....4,368
Cohocton....897
Cohoes (★A-S-T)....18,653
Cold Brook Estates (★A-S-T)....2,000
Cold Spring (★N.Y.)....2,083
Cold Spring Harbor (★N.Y.)....2,800
Colonie (★A-S-T)....8,701
Commack (★N.Y.)....22,507
Congers (★N.Y.)....5,928
Conklin (★BING)....1,500
Cooperstown....2,403
Copenhagen....734
Copiague (★N.Y.)....19,632
Coram (★N.Y.)....3,300
Corfu (★BUF-)....722
Corinth....3,267
Corning (★★ELM-)....15,792
Cornwall on the Hudson (Cornwall) (★NWBG)....3,131
Cornwall P.O. (★NWBG)....4,025
Cortland....19,621
Country Knolls (★A-S-T)....2,082
Coxsackie....2,399
Crestview Heights (★BING)....1,500
Croghan....765
Croton Falls (★N.Y.)....1,200
Croton-on-Hudson (★N.Y.)....7,523
Crown Village (★N.Y.)....1,700
Crugers (★N.Y.)....1,500
Cuba....1,735
Dannemora....3,735
Dansville....5,436
Deer Park (★N.Y.)....29,000
Delevan....994
Delhi....3,017
Delmar (★A-S-T)....7,300
Denton Hills (★N.Y.)....1,000
Depew (★BUF-)....22,158
Deposit....2,061
Derby (★BUF-)....3,000
De Ruyter....643
De Witt (★SYR)....10,032
Dexter (★WATN)....1,061
Dix Hills (★N.Y.)....10,050
Dobbs Ferry (★N.Y.)....10,353
Dolgeville....2,872
Dryden (★ITH)....1,490
Dundee....1,539
Dunkirk....16,855
Earlville....1,050
East Atlantic Beach (★N.Y.)....1,500
East Aurora (★BUF-)....7,033
East Bloomfield (★ROCH)....643
East Cayuga Heights (★ITH)....2,611
Eastchester (★N.Y.)....21,330
East Farmingdale (★N.Y.)....3,000
East Glenville (★A-S-T)....8,000
East Greenbush (★A-S-T)....1,325
East Hampton....1,753
East Herkimer (★UT-R)....1,135
East Hills (★N.Y.)....8,675
East Huntington (★N.Y.)....3,000
East Islip (★N.Y.)....13,300
East Meadow (★N.Y.)....46,252
East Moriches (★N.Y.)....1,702
East Northport (★N.Y.)....20,317
East Norwich (★N.Y.)....3,600
East Patchogue (★N.Y.)....8,092
Eastport (★N.Y.)....1,308
East Quogue....1,143
East Randolph....636
East Rochester (★ROCH)....8,347
East Rockaway (★N.Y.)....10,323
East Setauket (★N.Y.)....1,400
East Syracuse (★SYR)....4,333
East Vestal (★BING)....5,000
East White Plains (★N.Y.)....5,000
East Williston (★N.Y.)....2,808
Eden (★BUF-)....2,962
Edgemont (★N.Y.)....2,800
Edwards....576
Elba....752
Elbridge (★SYR)....1,040
Elizabethtown....607
Ellenville....4,482
Ellicottville....955
Elma (★BUF-)....2,784
Elmira (★128,200; ELM-)....39,945
Elmira Heights (★ELM-)....4,906
Elmira Heights North (★ELM-)....2,906
Elmont (★N.Y.)....29,363
Elmsford (★N.Y.)....3,911
Elmsmere (★A-S-T)....4,600
Elwood (★N.Y.)....15,031
Endicott (★BING)....16,556
Endwell (Hooper) (★BING)....15,999
Evans Mills....714
Fair Haven....859
Fairmount (★SYR)....15,317
Fairport (★ROCH)....6,474
Fairview (★POK)....8,517
Fairview (★N.Y.)....3,000
Falconer (★JMST)....2,983
Falconwood (★BUF-)....2,100
Farmingdale (★N.Y.)....9,297
Farmingville (★N.Y.)....6,600
Farnham (★BUF-)....546
Fayetteville (★SYR)....4,996
Fernwood (★GLFLS)....3,659
Fillmore....537
Fishkill (★NWBG)....913
Flanders....1,905
Floral Park (★N.Y.)....18,466
Florida....1,674
Flower Hill (★N.Y.)....4,486
Fonda....1,120
Forestville....908
Fort Covington....983
Fort Edward (★GLFLS)....3,733
Fort Johnson (★A-S-T)....711
Fort Plain....2,809
Fort Salonga (★N.Y.)....1,604
Frankfort (★UT-R)....3,305

(New York continued)

★ Population or designation of metropolitan area, including suburbs (see headnote).
▲ Population of entire "town" or township, including other communities and rural areas.
† Population is from a local census taken at date specified.

(New York continued)

Franklin	552
Franklin Park (*SYR)	1,800
Franklin Square (*N.Y.)	32,156
Franklinville	1,948
Fredonia	10,326
Freeport (*N.Y.)	40,374
Freetown	1,543
Freeville (*ITH)	664
Frewsburg (*JMST)	1,772
Friendship	1,285
Fulton (*SYR)	14,003
Fultonville	812
Galeville (*SYR)	1,000
Gang Mills (*ELM-)	1,258
Garden City (*N.Y.)	25,373
Garden City Park (*N.Y.)	7,488
Garden City South (*N.Y.)	4,700
Gardnertown (*NWBG)	4,614
Gates (*ROCH)	26,442
Geneseo	5,714
Geneva	16,793
Getzville (*BUF-)	2,000
Gilbertsville	552
Glasco (*KNGST)	1,169
Glen Cove (*N.Y.)	25,770
Glenham (*NWBG)	2,720
Glen Head (*N.Y.)	4,300
Glen Park (*WATN)	587
Glens Falls (*58,800; GLFLS)	17,222
Glenwood Landing (*N.Y.)	3,800
Gloversville	19,677
Golden's Bridge (*N.Y.)	1,101
Gordon Heights (*N.Y.)	1,000
Goshen (*MIDD)	4,342
Gouverneur	4,574
Gowanda	3,110
Grandyle (*BUF-)	1,700
Granville	2,784
Great Neck Estates (*N.Y.)	3,131
Great Neck P.O. (Great Neck Plaza) (*N.Y.)	5,921
Great Neck (village) (*N.Y.)	10,731
Great River (*N.Y.)	1,700
Greece (*ROCH)	38,000
Greene	1,874
Green Island (*A-S-T)	3,297
Greenlawn (*N.Y.)	8,493
Greenport	2,481
Greenvale (*N.Y.)	1,050
Greenville (*N.Y.)	5,500
Greenwich	2,092
Greenwood Lake (*N.Y.)	2,262
Groton	2,112
Guilderland (*A-S-T)	1,000
Hagaman (*A-S-T)	1,410
Hagerman (*N.Y.)	3,000
Halesite (*N.Y.)	4,400
Half Hollows (Half Hollow Hills) (*N.Y.)	12,081
Hamburg (*BUF-)	10,215
Hamilton	3,636
Hammondsport	1,066
Hampton Bays	1,862
Hampton Manor (*A-S-T)	2,000
Hancock	1,688
Hannibal	686
Harbor Hills (*N.Y.)	1,300
Harbor Isle (*N.Y.)	1,300
Harriman (*N.Y.)	955
Harris Hill (*BUF-)	5,000
Harrison (*N.Y.)	13,200
Harrisville	836
Hartsdale (*N.Y.)	12,226
Hastings-on-Hudson (*N.Y.)	9,479
Hauppauge (*N.Y.)	13,957
Haverstraw (*N.Y.)	8,198
Hawthorne (*N.Y.)	5,000
Head of the Harbor (*N.Y.)	943
Hempstead (*N.Y.)	39,411
Herkimer (*UT-R)	8,960
Heuvelton	770
Hewlett (*N.Y.)	6,796
Hewlett Bay Park (*N.Y.)	586
Hewlett Harbor (*N.Y.)	1,545
Hewlett Neck (*N.Y.)	529
Hicksville (*N.Y.)	48,075
Highland (*POK)	2,184
Highland Falls	4,638
Hillburn (*N.Y.)	1,058
Hillcrest (*N.Y.)	5,357
Hillcrest (*BING)	1,500
Hillside Manor (*N.Y.)	12,000
Hilton (*ROCH)	2,440
Holbrook (*N.Y.)	13,200
Holcomb (*ROCH)	778
Holland (*BUF-)	950
Holland Patent (*UT-R)	556
Holley (*ROCH)	1,868
Holtsville (*N.Y.)	4,000
Homer	4,143
Homewood (*SYR)	1,400
Honeoye Falls (*ROCH)	2,248
Hoosick Falls	3,897
Hopewell Junction (*POK)	2,055
Hornell	12,144
Horseheads (*ELM-)	7,989
Houghton	1,620
Hudson	8,940
Hudson Falls (*GLFLS)	7,917
Huntington (*N.Y.)	12,601
Huntington Bay (*N.Y.)	1,789
Huntington Beach (*N.Y.)	2,000
Huntington Station (*N.Y.)	28,817
Hurley	4,081
Hyde Park (*POK)	2,805
Ilion (*UT-R)	9,808
Interlaken	733
Inwood (*N.Y.)	8,433
Irondequoit (*ROCH)	63,675
Irvington (*N.Y.)	5,878
Island Park (*N.Y.)	5,396
Islip (*N.Y.)	13,100
Islip Terrace (*N.Y.)	5,100
Ithaca (*64,700; ITH)	26,226
Ithaca College (*ITH)	3,600
Jamestown (*68,900; JMST)	39,795
Jamesville (*SYR)	1,000
Jericho (*N.Y.)	14,010
Johnson City (*BING)	18,025
Johnstown	10,045
Jordan (*SYR)	1,493
Katonah (*N.Y.)	3,000
Keeseville	2,122
Kenmore (*BUF-)	20,980
Kensington (*N.Y.)	1,582
Kerhonkson	1,243
Keuka Park	900
Kinderhook (*A-S-T)	1,233
Kings Park (*N.Y.)	5,555
Kings Point (*N.Y.)	5,614
Kingston (*89,900; KNGST)	25,544
Lackawanna (*BUF-)	28,657
Lacona	556
Lake Carmel (*N.Y.)	4,796
Lake Delta Area (*UT-R)	2,300
Lake Erie Beach (*BUF-)	3,467
Lake George	1,046
Lake Grove (*N.Y.)	8,133
Lake Katrine (*KNGST)	1,092
Lakeland (*SYR)	2,500
Lake Placid	2,731
Lake Ronkonkoma (*N.Y.)	8,250
Lake Secor (*N.Y.)	900
Lake Success (*N.Y.)	3,254
Lake View (*BUF-)	1,500
Lakewood (*JMST)	3,864
Lancaster (*BUF-)	13,365
Larchmont (*N.Y.)	7,203
Larchmont North (*N.Y.)	9,500
Latham (*A-S-T)	9,661
Lattingtown (*N.Y.)	1,773
Laurel Hollow (*N.Y.)	1,401
Lawrence (*N.Y.)	6,566
Le Roy	5,118
Levittown (*N.Y.)	65,440
Lewiston (*BUF-)	3,292
Liberty	4,293
Lido Beach (*N.Y.)	1,400
Lima (*ROCH)	1,686
Limestone	535
Lincoln Park (*KNGST)	1,100
Lindenhurst (*N.Y.)	28,359
Little Falls	7,629
Little Valley	1,340
Liverpool (*SYR)	3,307
Livingston Manor	1,522
Livonia (*ROCH)	1,278
Lloyd Harbor (*N.Y.)	3,371
Lockport (*62,000; LOCK)	25,399
Locust Grove (*N.Y.)	11,626
Locust Valley (*N.Y.)	3,900
Long Beach (*N.Y.)	33,127
Long Branch (*SYR)	1,500
Lorenz Park	1,995
Loudonville (*A-S-T)	9,299
Lowville	3,671
Lynbrook (*N.Y.)	23,776
Lyndon (*SYR)	2,400
Lyndonville	888
Lynwood Estates (*A-S-T)	1,500
Lyons	4,496
Lyons Falls	852
Macedon (*ROCH)	1,168
McGraw	1,319
McKownville (*A-S-T)	3,500
Mahopac (*N.Y.)	5,265
Malone	8,048
Malverne (*N.Y.)	10,036
Mamaroneck (*N.Y.)	18,909
Manchester (*ROCH)	1,305
Manhasset (*N.Y.)	8,541
Manlius (*SYR)	4,295
Manorhaven (*N.Y.)	5,488
Marathon	1,053
Marcellus (*SYR)	2,017
Margaretville	816
Marlboro (*POK)	1,580
Maryknoll (*N.Y.)	800
Massapequa (*N.Y.)	26,821
Massapequa Park (*N.Y.)	22,112
Massena	14,042
Mastic (*N.Y.)	4,700
Mastic Beach (*N.Y.)	4,870
Matinecock (*N.Y.)	841
Mattituck	1,995
Mattydale (*SYR)	8,292
Maybrook (*NWBG)	1,536
Mayfield	981
Mayville	1,567
Maywood (*A-S-T)	3,000
Mechanicstown (East Middletown) (*MIDD)	2,640
Mechanicville (*A-S-T)	6,247
Medford Station (Medford) (*N.Y.)	4,500
Medina	6,415
Melville (*N.Y.)	8,500
Menands (*A-S-T)	3,449
Merrick (*N.Y.)	25,904
Mexico	1,555
Middleburg	1,410
Middle Hope (*NWBG)	2,327
Middle Island (*N.Y.)	950
Middleport (*LOCK)	2,132
Middletown (*52,400; MIDD)	22,607
Middleville	725
Millbrook	1,735
Miller Place (*N.Y.)	2,900
Millerton	1,042
Mill Neck (*N.Y.)	982
Mineola (*N.Y.)	21,845
Mineville	1,000
Minoa (*SYR)	2,245
Mohawk (*UT-R)	3,301
Mohegan Lake (*N.Y.)	2,000
Monroe (*N.Y.)	4,439
Monsey (*N.Y.)	8,797
Montgomery (*NWBG)	1,533
Monticello	5,991
Montour Falls	1,534
Montrose (*N.Y.)	2,200
Mooers	536
Moravia	1,642
Morris	675
Morrisonville	1,276
Morrisville	2,296
Mountain Dale	900
Mount Kisco (*N.Y.)	8,172
Mount Morris	3,417
Mount Vernon (*BUF-)	3,200
Mount Vernon (*N.Y.)	72,778
Munsey Park (*N.Y.)	2,980
Muttontown (*N.Y.)	2,081
Nanuet (*N.Y.)	10,447
Napanoch	950
Naples	1,324
Nassau (*A-S-T)	1,466
Nassau Shores (*N.Y.)	5,500
Nazareth College (*ROCH)	1,400
Nedrow (*SYR)	3,500
Nelliston	716
Nelsonville (*N.Y.)	583
Nesconset (*N.Y.)	7,500
Newark	11,644
Newark Valley (*BING)	1,286
New Berlin	1,369
Newburgh (*138,900; NWBG)	26,219
New Cassel (*N.Y.)	8,554
New City (*N.Y.)	27,344
Newfane (*LOCK)	2,588
New Hamburg (*POK)	1,064
New Hartford (*UT-R)	2,433
New Hempstead (*N.Y.)	2,000
New Hyde Park (*N.Y.)	10,116
New Paltz	6,058
Newport	908
New Rochelle (*N.Y.)	75,385
New Square (*N.Y.)	1,156
Newtonville (*A-S-T)	1,500
New Windsor (*NWBG)	8,803
New York (*17,306,500; N.Y.)	7,895,563
New York Mills (*UT-R)	3,805
Niagara Falls (**BUF-)	85,615
Niagara University (*BUF-)	2,000
Nichols (*BING)	638
Nimmonsburg (*BING)	1,500
Nissequogue (*N.Y.)	1,120
Norfolk (Norfolk Center)	1,379
North Amityville (*N.Y.)	11,905
North Babylon (*N.Y.)	25,726
North Bellmore (*N.Y.)	22,893
North Bellport (*N.Y.)	3,000
North Boston (*BUF-)	1,635
North Chili (*ROCH)	3,163
North Collins (*BUF-)	1,675
Northeast Henrietta (*ROCH)	9,800
North Great River (*N.Y.)	12,080
North Haven	694
North Hornell	919
North Lindenhurst (*N.Y.)	11,117
North Long Beach (*N.Y.)	1,300
North Lynbrook (*N.Y.)	900
North Massapequa (*N.Y.)	23,123
North Merrick (*N.Y.)	13,650
North New Hyde Park (*N.Y.)	15,000
North Patchogue (*N.Y.)	7,178
North Pelham (*N.Y.)	5,184
Northport (*N.Y.)	7,494
North Syracuse (*SYR)	8,687
North Tarrytown (*N.Y.)	8,334
North Tonawanda (*BUF-)	36,012
North Valley Stream (*N.Y.)	14,881
Northville	1,192
North Wantagh (*N.Y.)	15,053
Norwich	8,843
Norwood	2,098
Nunda	1,254
Nyack (*N.Y.)	6,659
Oakdale (*N.Y.)	7,334
Oakfield	1,964
Oceanside (*N.Y.)	35,028
Odessa	606
Ogdensburg	14,554
Olcott (*LOCK)	1,592
Old Bethpage (*N.Y.)	7,084
Old Brookville (*N.Y.)	1,785
Old Field (*N.Y.)	812
Old Westbury (*N.Y.)	2,667
Olean	19,169
Oneida	11,658
Oneida Castle	788
Oneonta	16,030
Onondaga (*SYR)	1,500
Oot Park (*SYR)	2,000
Orangeburg (*N.Y.)	3,500
Orchard Park (*BUF-)	3,732
Orchard Village (*SYR)	2,000
Oriskany (*UT-R)	1,627
Oriskany Falls	927
Ossining (*N.Y.)	21,659
Oswego	20,913
Otego	956
Otisville (*MIDD)	933
Ovid	779
Owego (*BING)	5,152
Oxford	1,944
Oyster Bay (*N.Y.)	6,800
Oyster Bay Cove (*N.Y.)	1,320
Painted Post (*ELM-)	2,496
Palatine Bridge	601
Palisades (*N.Y.)	1,000
Palmyra (*ROCH)	3,776
Parish	634
Park Hill (*SYR)	3,000
Patchogue (*N.Y.)	11,582
Patterson (*N.Y.)	900
Pawling	1,914
Pearl River (*N.Y.)	17,146
Peekskill (*N.Y.)	19,283
Pelham (*N.Y.)	2,076
Pelham Manor (*N.Y.)	6,673
Penfield (*ROCH)	8,500
Penn Yan	5,293
Perry	4,538
Peru	1,261
Phelps	1,989
Philadelphia	858
Philmont	1,674
Phoenix (*SYR)	2,617
Piermont (*N.Y.)	2,386
Pine Bush	1,183
Pinehurst (*BUF-)	1,000
Pine Plains	900
Pittsford (*ROCH)	1,755
Plainview (*N.Y.)	33,440
Plandome (*N.Y.)	1,593
Plandome Heights (*N.Y.)	1,032
Plandome Manor (*N.Y.)	835
Plattsburg	18,715
Pleasant Valley (*POK)	1,372
Pleasantville (*N.Y.)	7,110
Point Lookout (*N.Y.)	1,500
Poland	629
Pomona (*N.Y.)	1,792
Ponquogue	1,474
Port Byron	1,330
Port Chester (*N.Y.)	25,803
Port Crane (*BING)	1,200
Port Dickinson (*BING)	2,132
Port Ewen (*KNGST)	2,882
Port Henry	1,532
Port Jefferson (*N.Y.)	5,515
Port Jefferson Station (*N.Y.)	7,405
Port Jervis	8,852
Port Leyden	862
Portville	1,304
Port Washington (*N.Y.)	15,923
Port Washington North (*N.Y.)	2,883
Potsdam	9,985
Poughkeepsie (*150,100; POK)	32,029
Prattsburg	765
Pulaski	2,480
Purchase (*N.Y.)	2,500
Putnam Lake (*N.Y.)	1,425
Putnam Valley (*N.Y.)	950
Quogue	865
Randolph	1,498
Ransomville (*BUF-)	1,034
Ravena (*A-S-T)	2,797
Red Creek	626
Red Hook (*KNGST)	1,680
Red Oaks Mill (*POK)	3,919
Remsen (*UT-R)	602
Rensselaer (*A-S-T)	10,136
Rhinebeck (*KNGST)	2,336
Richfield Springs	1,540
Richmondville	826
Ridgemont (*ROCH)	8,000
Ridgewood (*UT-R)	2,000
Ripley	1,173
Riverhead	7,585
Riverside (*ELM-)	911
Rochdale (*POK)	1,849
Rochester (*793,500; ROCH)	296,233
Rockville Centre (*N.Y.)	27,444
Rocky Point (*N.Y.)	3,500
Roessleville (*A-S-T)	5,476
Rome (**UT-R)	50,148
Ronkonkoma (*N.Y.)	15,000
Roosevelt (*N.Y.)	15,008
Rosendale (*KNGST)	1,220
Roslyn (*N.Y.)	2,546
Roslyn Estates (*N.Y.)	1,420
Roslyn Harbor (*N.Y.)	977
Roslyn Heights (*N.Y.)	7,142
Rotterdam (South Schenectady) (*A-S-T)	26,500
Round Lake (*A-S-T)	886
Rouses Point	2,250
Russel Gardens (*N.Y.)	1,174
Rye (*N.Y.)	15,869
Sackets Harbor	1,202
Saddle Rock (*N.Y.)	895
Sag Harbor	2,363
St. Bonaventure	1,800
St. James (*N.Y.)	10,500
St. Johnsville	2,089
St. Regis Falls	950
Salamanca	7,877
Salem	1,025
Sanborn (*BUF-)	900
Sand Ridge (*SYR)	1,109
Sands Point (*N.Y.)	2,916
Sandy Beach (*BUF-)	1,691
Sandy Creek	731
San Remo (*N.Y.)	8,700
Saranac Lake	6,086
Saratoga Springs	18,845
Saugerties (*KNGST)	4,190
Saugerties South (*KNGST)	3,159
Sauquoit (*UT-R)	2,100
Savannah	636
Savona	933
Sayville (*N.Y.)	15,300
Scarsdale (*N.Y.)	19,229
Schaghticoke (*A.S.T)	860
Schenectady (**A-S-T)	77,958
Schenectady East (Niskayuna) (*A-S-T-)	6,186
Schenevus	540
Schoharie	1,125
Schuylerville	1,402
Scotchtown (*MIDD)	2,119
Scotia (*A-S-T)	8,224
Scottsville (*ROCH)	1,967
Scranton (*BUF-)	1,100
Sea Cliff (*N.Y.)	5,890
Seaford (*N.Y.)	17,379
Selden (*N.Y.)	18,300
Seneca Falls	7,794
Setauket (*N.Y.)	2,000
Shenorock (Lake Shenorock) (*N.Y.)	1,600
Sherburne	1,613
Sherman	769
Sherrill	2,986
Shirley (*N.Y.)	6,280
Shoreham (*N.Y.)	524
Shortsville (*ROCH)	1,516
Shrub Oak (*N.Y.)	2,200
Sidney	4,789
Silver Creek (*BUF-)	3,182
Silver Springs	823
Sinclairville	772
Skaneateles (*SYR)	3,055
Slingerlands (*A-S-T)	1,500
Sloan (*BUF-)	5,216
Sloatsburg (*N.Y.)	3,134
Smithtown (*N.Y.)	12,000
Smithtown Pines (*N.Y.)	2,500
Sodus	1,813
Sodus Point	1,172
Solvay (*SYR)	8,280
Sound Beach (*N.Y.)	4,900
Southampton	4,904
South Corning (*ELM-)	1,414
South Dayton	688
South Fallsburg	1,590
South Farmingdale (*N.Y.)	20,464
South Floral Park (*N.Y.)	1,032
South Glens Falls (*GLFLS)	4,013
South Hempstead (*N.Y.)	3,000
South Hudson Falls (*GLFLS)	2,097
South Huntington (*N.Y.)	9,115
South Lockport (*LOCK)	1,341
South Nyack (*N.Y.)	3,435
Southold	2,030
Southport (Elmira Southeast) (*ELM-)	8,685
South Setauket (*N.Y.)	4,900
South Stony Brook (*N.Y.)	15,329
South Valley Stream (*N.Y.)	6,595
South Westbury (*N.Y.)	10,978
Sparkill (*N.Y.)	1,200
Spencer (*N.Y.)	854
Spencerport (*ROCH)	2,929
Spring Valley (*N.Y.)	18,112
Springville	4,350
Stamford	1,286
Stanford Heights (*A-S-T)	3,000
Stanley Manor (*SYR)	1,100
Stewart Manor (*N.Y.)	2,183
Stillwater (*A-S-T)	1,428
Stony Brook (*N.Y.)	6,391
Stony Point (*N.Y.)	8,270
Stottville	1,106
Suffern (*N.Y.)	8,273
Sycaway (*A-S-T)	1,800
Syosset (*N.Y.)	10,084
Syracuse (*532,600; SYR)	197,297
Tannersville	650
Tappan (*N.Y.)	7,424
Tarrytown (*N.Y.)	11,115
Taunton (*SYR)	1,000
Terryville (*N.Y.)	5,600
Theresa	985
Thomaston (*N.Y.)	2,486
Thornwood (*N.Y.)	4,500
Ticonderoga	3,268
Tillson (*KNGST)	1,256
Tivoli (*KNGST)	739
Tonawanda (*BUF-)	21,898
Tonetta Lake Heights (Brewster Hill) (*N.Y.)	1,745
Town of Tonawanda (*BUF-)	86,300
Tribes Hill (*A-S-T)	1,184
Troy (**A-S-T)	62,918
Trumansburg (*ITH)	1,803
Tuckahoe (*N.Y.)	6,236
Tully (*SYR)	899
Tupper Lake	4,854
Tuxedo Park (*N.Y.)	861
Twin Orchards (*BING)	1,500
Unadilla	1,489
Union Center (*BING)	1,000
Uniondale (*N.Y.)	22,077
Union Springs	1,183
Unionville (*MIDD)	576
University Gardens (*N.Y.)	1,000
Upper Brookville (*N.Y.)	1,182
Upper Nyack (*N.Y.)	2,096
Utica (*283,400; UT-R)	91,611
Vails Gate (*NWBG)	900
Valatie (A-S-T)	1,288
Valhalla (*N.Y.)	5,500
Valley Cottage (*N.Y.)	6,007
Valley Falls (*A-S-T)	681
Valley Stream (*N.Y.)	40,413
Van Cortlandtville (*N.Y.)	900
Van Etten	522
Verdoy (*A-S-T)	1,000
Vernon	1,108
Verplanck (*N.Y.)	2,400
Vestal (*BING)	6,800
Vestal Center (*BING)	900
Victor (*ROCH)	2,187
Victory Mills	718
Village of the Branch (*N.Y.)	1,675
Viola (*N.Y.)	5,136
Voorheesville (*A-S-T)	2,826
Waddington	955
Wading River	900
Walden (*NWBG)	5,277
Wallkill (*NWBG)	1,849
Walton	3,744
Wampsville	586
Wanakah (*BUF-)	1,500
Wantagh (*N.Y.)	21,873
Wappingers Falls (*POK)	5,607
Wappingers Falls East (*POK)	2,017
Warrensburg (Warrensburg Center)	2,743
Warsaw	3,619
Warwick	3,604
Washington Heights (*MIDD)	1,204
Washingtonville (*NWBG)	1,887
Waterford (*A-S-T)	2,879
Waterloo	5,418
Watertown (*42,800; WATN)	30,787
Waterville (*UT-R)	1,808
Watervliet (*A-S-T)	12,404
Watkins Glen	2,716
Waverly	5,261
Wayland	2,022
Webster (*ROCH)	5,037
Weedsport (*SYR)	1,900
Wellsburg (*ELM-)	779
Wellsville	5,815
West Amityville (*N.Y.)	6,424
West Babylon (*N.Y.)	26,500
West Bay Shore (*N.Y.)	8,800
Westbury (*N.Y.)	15,362
West Carthage	2,047
West Corners (*BING)	3,000
West Ellicott (*JMST)	2,491
West Elmira (*ELM-)	5,901
West End	1,692
West Endicott (*BING)	3,000

* Population or designation of metropolitan area, including suburbs (see headnote).
▲ Population of entire "town" or township, including other communities and rural areas.
† Population is from a local census taken at date specified.

Westfield 3,651
West Genesee Terrace (★SYR) 1,100
West Glens Falls (★GLFLS) 3,363
Westhampton 1,156
Westhampton Beach 1,926
West Haverstraw (★N.Y.) 8,558
West Hempstead (★N.Y.) 25,850
West Hills (★N.Y.) 800
West Huntington (★N.Y.) 4,000
West Islip (★N.Y.) 25,000
Westmere (★A-S-T) 6,364
West Nyack (★N.Y.) 5,510
Westons Mills 900
West Point 5,200
Westport 673
West Sand Lake (★A-S-T) 1,875
West Sayville (★N.Y.) 3,650
West Seneca (★BUF) 48,404
Westvale (★SYR) 7,253
West Webster (★ROCH) 9,000
West Winfield 1,018
Whitehall 3,764
White Plains (★N.Y.) 50,346
Whitesboro (★UT-R) 4,805
Whitney Estates (★A-S-T) 1,300
Whitney Point 1,058
Williamson (Williamson Center) (★ROCH) 1,991
Williamsville (★BUF-) 6,835
Williston Park (★N.Y.) 9,154
Willow Point (★BING) 3,000
Wilson (★LOCK) 1,284
Windsor (★BING) 1,098
Witherbee 960
Wolcott 1,617
Woodbourne 1,155
Woodbury (★N.Y.) 3,900
Woodlawn Beach (★BUF-) 2,000
Woodmere (★N.Y.) 19,831
Woodridge 1,071
Woodsburgh (★N.Y.) 817
Woodstock 1,073
Wurtsboro 732
Wyandanch (★N.Y.) 16,200
Wynantskill (★A-S-T) 2,000
Wyoming 514
Yaphank (★N.Y.) 2,000
Yonkers (★N.Y.) 204,297
Yorktown (★N.Y.) 4,000
Yorktown Heights (★N.Y.) 6,805
Yorkville (★UT-R) 3,425
Youngstown (★BUF-) 2,169

NORTH CAROLINA

1970 C 5,082,059

Counties

Alamance 96,362
Alexander 19,466
Alleghany 8,134
Anson 23,488
Ashe 19,571
Avery 12,655
Beaufort 35,980
Bertie 20,528
Bladen 26,477
Brunswick 24,223
Buncombe 145,056
Burke 60,364
Cabarrus 74,629
Caldwell 56,699
Camden 5,453
Carteret 31,603
Caswell 19,055
Catawba 90,873
Chatham 29,554
Cherokee 16,330
Chowan 10,764
Clay 5,180
Cleveland 72,556
Columbus 46,937
Craven 62,554
Cumberland 212,042
Currituck 6,976
Dare 6,995
Davidson 95,627
Davie 18,855
Duplin 38,015
Durham 132,681
Edgecombe 52,341
Forsyth 214,348
Franklin 26,820
Gaston 148,415
Gates 8,524
Graham 6,562
Granville 32,762
Greene 14,967
Guilford 288,590
Halifax 53,884
Harnett 49,667
Haywood 41,710
Henderson 42,804
Hertford 23,529
Hoke 16,436
Hyde 5,571
Iredell 72,197
Jackson 21,593
Johnston 61,737
Jones 9,779
Lee 30,467
Lenoir 55,204
Lincoln 32,682
McDowell 30,648
Macon 15,788
Madison 16,003
Martin 24,730
Mecklenburg 354,656
Mitchell 13,447
Montgomery 19,267
Moore 39,048
Nash 59,122
New Hanover 82,996
Northampton 24,009
Onslow 103,126
Orange 57,707
Pamlico 9,467
Pasquotank 26,824
Pender 18,149
Perquimans 8,351
Person 25,914
Pitt 73,900
Polk 11,735
Randolph 76,358
Richmond 39,899
Robeson 84,842
Rockingham 72,402
Rowan 90,035
Rutherford 47,337
Sampson 44,954
Scotland 26,929
Stanly 42,822
Stokes 23,782
Surry 51,415
Swain 7,861
Transylvania 19,713
Tyrrell 3,806
Union 54,714
Vance 32,691
Wake 228,453
Warren 15,810
Washington 14,038
Watauga 23,404
Wayne 85,408
Wilkes 49,524
Wilson 57,486
Yadkin 24,599
Yancey 12,629

Cities

Aberdeen 1,592
Ahoskie 5,105
Albemarle 11,126
Alexander Mills 988
Allen Jay (★GRNS-) 800
Alliance 577
Andrews 1,384
Angier (★RAL) 1,431
Ansonville 694
Apex (★RAL) 2,192
Archdale (★GRNS-) 4,844
Arlington 711
Asheboro 10,797
Asheboro South 1,998
Asheboro West 1,158
Asheville (★126,600; ASHE) 57,681
Aulander 947
Aurora 620
Ayden 3,450
Badin 1,626
Bailey 724
Banner Elk 754
Bannertown 1,138
Barker Heights 2,933
Battleboro (★RKYMT) 562
Bayboro 665
Beaufort 3,368
Belhaven 2,259
Belmont (★CHRLT) 5,054
Belmont South (★CHRLT) 2,125
Benson 2,267
Bessemer City (★GAST) 4,991
Bethel 1,514
Beulaville 1,156
Biltmore Forest (★ASHE) 1,298
Biscoe 1,244
Black Mountain 3,204
Bladenboro 783
Blowing Rock 801
Boger City 2,203
Boiling Springs 2,284
Bolton 534
Bonnie Doone (★FAY) 3,500
Boone 8,754
Boonville 687
Brentwood (★RAL) 3,000
Brevard 5,243
Bridgeton 520
Brightwood (★GRNS-) 1,000
Broadway 694
Brookford (★HICK) 590
Bryson City 1,290
Buies Creek 2,024
Burgaw 1,744
Burlington (★88,900; BUR) 35,930
Burnsville 1,348
Butner 3,538
Candor 561
Canton 5,158
Cape Carteret 616
Carolina Beach (★WILM) 1,663
Carrboro (★DUR-) 5,058
Carthage 1,034
Cary (★RAL) 7,430
Catawba 565
Catawba Heights (★CHRLT) 3,000
Chadbourn 2,213
Chapel Hill (★★DUR-) 25,537
Charlotte (★416,800; CHRLT) 241,178
Cherryville 5,258
China Grove (★KANN-) 1,788
Chocowinity 566
Claremont 788
Clarkton 662
Clayton (★RAL) 3,103
Clemmons (★WNS) 1,500
Cleveland 614
Clinton 7,157
Clyde 900
Coats 1,051
College Downs (★CHRLT) 1,500
College Lakes (★FAY) 2,000
Columbia 902
Columbus 731
Concord (★★KANN-) 18,464
Conover 3,355
Conway 694
Cooleemee 1,800
Cornelius (★CHRLT) 1,296
Cottonade (★FAY) 1,500
Cramerton (★GAST) 2,142
Creedmoor 1,405
Creswell 633
Cross Mill 1,000
Cullowhee 2,000
Dallas (★GAST) 4,059
Davidson (★CHRLT) 2,931
Denton 1,017
Derita (★CHRLT) 4,000
Dobson 933
Dover 585
Drake Park (★FAY) 1,500
Drexel 1,431
Druid Hills 1,500
Dunn 8,302
Durham (★170,000; DUR) 95,438
East Fayetteville (★FAY) 3,500
East Flat Rock 2,627
East Hickory (Hickory East) (★HICK) 4,181
East Rockingham 2,858
East Spencer (★SLSB) 2,217
Echo Heights (★RAL) 1,100
Eden 15,871
Edenton 4,956
Elizabeth City 14,381
Elizabethtown 1,418
Elkin 2,899
Elk Mountain (★ASHE) 1,000
Elk Park 503
Ellerbe 913
Elm City 1,201
Elon College (★BUR) 2,150
Enfield 3,272
Enka (★ASHE) 1,000
Erwin 2,852
Fair Bluff 1,039
Fair Grove (★GRNS-) 1,100
Fairmont 2,827
Fairview 1,000
Faison 598
Faith (★SLSB) 506
Farmville 4,424
Fayetteville (★202,700; FAY) 53,510
Flat Rock 1,688
Fletcher 998
Forest City 7,179
Four Oaks 1,057
Franklin 2,336
Franklinton 1,459
Franklinville 794
Fremont 1,596
Fuquay-Varina (Fuquay Springs) (★RAL) 3,576
Garland 656
Garner (★RAL) 4,923
Gaston 1,105
Gastonia (★113,600; GAST) 47,142
Gastonia East (★GAST) 2,370
Gastonia North (★GAST) 1,316
Gibson 502
Gibsonville (★BUR) 2,019
Glen Alpine 797
Glen Raven (★BUR) 2,848
Goldsboro (★58,600; GLDS) 26,810
Goldsboro South (South Goldsboro) (★GLDS) 2,094
Graham (★BUR) 8,172
Granite Falls (★HICK) 2,388
Granite Quarry (★SLSB) 1,344
Greenbrier Estates (★RAL) 1,000
Greensboro (★334,100; GRNS-) 144,076
Greenville 29,063
Grifton 1,860
Grover 555
Guilford (★GRNS-) 1,200
Hamilton 579
Hamlet 4,627
Harkers Island 1,633
Havelock 5,283
Haw River (★BUR) 1,542
Hazelwood 2,057
Henderson 13,896
Hendersonville 6,443
Henrietta 1,200
Hertford 2,023
Hickory (★71,000; HICK) 20,569
Hickory Grove (★CHRLT) 4,000
Highlands 583
High Point (★★GRNS-) 63,259
Hillsborough 1,444
Hobgood 530
Holly Springs (★RAL) 697
Hope Mills (★FAY) 1,866
Hot Springs 653
Hudson 2,820
Huntersville (★CHRLT) 1,538
Idlewild (★CHRLT) 3,000
Jackson 762
Jackson Park (★KANN-) 2,000
Jacksonville (★82,800; JAC) 16,289
Jamestown (★GRNS-) 1,297
Jamesville 533
Jefferson 943
Jonesville 1,659
Kannapolis (★87,500; KANN-) 36,293
Kenansville 762
Kenly 1,370
Kernersville (★WNS) 4,815
King (★WNS) 1,033
Kings Mountain (★GAST) 8,465
Kinston 23,020
Knightdale (★RAL) 815
Kornbow (★FAY) 2,000
Lafayette (★FAY) 2,500
La Grange 2,679
Lake Waccamaw 924
Landis (★KANN-) 2,297
Lansdowne (★CHRLT) 1,200
Laurel Hill 1,215
Laurel Park 581
Laurinburg 8,859
Laurinburg West 1,156
Lawndale 544
Lenoir 14,705
Lexington 17,205
Liberty 2,167
Lilesville 641
Lillington 1,155
Lincolnton 5,293
Littleton 903
Longhurst 1,485
Long View (★HICK) 3,360
Longwood Park 1,284
Louisburg 2,941
Lowell (★GAST) 3,307
Lucama 610
Lumberton 16,961
McAdenville (★GAST) 950
Macclesfield 536
Madison 2,018
Magnolia 614
Maiden 2,416
Manteo 547
Marion 3,335
Marion East (East Marion) 2,600
Marshall 982
Mars Hill 1,623
Marshville 1,405
Matthews (★CHRLT) 783
Maxton 1,885
Mayodan 2,875
Maysville 912
Mebane (★BUR) 2,433
Methodist College (★FAY) 1,000
Middlesex 729
Mint Hill (★CHRLT) 1,000
Misenheimer (Misenheimer Springs) 1,250
Mocksville 2,529
Monroe (★CHRLT) 11,282
Montreat 581
Mooresville 8,808
Morehead City 5,233
Morganton 13,625
Morgantown (★BUR) 1,500
Morlan Park (★SLSB) 950
Morven 562
Mount Airy 7,325
Mount Gilead 1,286
Mount Holly (★CHRLT) 5,107
Mount Olive 4,914
Mount Olive (★HICK) 2,000
Mount Pleasant (★KANN-) 1,174
Murfreesboro 3,508
Murphy 2,082
Nashville (★RKYMT) 1,670
Neuse Forest 1,500
New Bern 14,660
New Hope (★RAL) 1,000
Newland 524
Newport 1,735
Newton 7,857
Newton Grove 546
Norlina 969
North Asheboro (Balfours) 4,836
North Belmont (★CHRLT) 4,000
North Henderson (Henderson North) 1,997
North Wilkesboro 3,357
Norwood 1,896
Oakboro 568
Oak City 559
Oak Ridge (★GRNS-) 900
Old Fort 676
Oteen (★ASHE) 2,000
Oxford 7,178
Parkton 550
Parkwood (★DUR-) 2,267
Paw Creek (Thrift) (★CHRLT) 1,200
Peachland 556
Pembroke 1,982
Pikeville 580
Pilot Mountain 1,309
Pinebluff 570
Pinehurst 1,056
Pine Level 983
Pinetops 1,379
Pineville (★CHRLT) 1,948
Pink Hill 522
Pittsboro 1,447
Pleasant Garden (★GRNS-) 1,000
Plymouth 4,774
Polkton 845
Princeton 1,044
Princeville 654
Raeford 3,180
Raleigh (★216,900; RAL) 123,793
Ramseur 1,328
Randleman 2,312
Rankin (★GRNS-) 1,200
Ranlo (★GAST) 2,092
Red Springs 3,383
Reidsville 13,636
Rhodhiss (★HICK) 784
Richlands 935
Richmond Hill (★BUR) 1,500
Rich Square 1,254
Roanoke Rapids 13,508
Roanoke Rapids West (Belmont-South Rosemary) 2,260
Robbins 1,059
Robbinsville 777
Robersonville 1,910
Rockingham 5,852
Rockwell (★SLSB) 999
Rocky Mount (★57,600; RKYMT) 34,284
Rolesville (★RAL) 529
Roper 649
Roseboro 1,235
Rose Hill 1,448
Rowan Mill (★SLSB) 1,184
Rowland 1,358
Roxboro 5,370
Royal Pines (★ASHE) 2,041
Rural Hall (★WNS) 2,338
Rutherfordton 3,245
St. Pauls (St. Paul) 2,011
Salemburg 669
Salisbury (★54,700; SLSB) 22,515
Saluda 546
Sanford 11,716
Scotland Neck 2,869
Seaboard 611
Seagate (★WILM) 1,200
Selma 4,356
Shallotte 597
Sharpsburg (★RKYMT) 789
Shaw Heights (★FAY) 1,500
Shelby 16,328
Siler City 4,689
Skyland (★ASHE) 2,177
Smithfield 6,677
Snow Hill 1,359
Southern Pines 5,937
South Gastonia (Gastonia South) (★GAST) 3,718
South Henderson (Henderson South) 1,843
Southport 2,220
South Salisbury (★SLSB) 2,199
South Weldon 1,630
Sparta 1,304
Spencer (★SLSB) 3,075
Spindale 3,848
Spring Hope 1,334
Spring Lake (★FAY) 3,968
Spruce Pine 2,333
Stanley (★CHRLT) 2,336
Stanleyville (★WNS) 2,362
Stantonsburg 869
Star 892
Statesville 19,996
Statesville West 1,905
Stedman 505
Stonehaven (★CHRLT) 1,200
Stoneville 1,030
Stony Point 1,001
Swannanoa (★ASHE) 1,966
Swansboro 1,207
Sylva 1,561
Tabor City 2,400
Tarboro 9,425
Taylorsville 1,231
Thomasville (★GRNS-) 15,230
Toast 2,635
Trenton 539
Trentwoods (Trent Woods) 719
Trinity (★GRNS-) 950
Troutman 797
Troy 2,429
Tryon 1,951
Valdese 3,182
Vanceboro 758
Vass 885
Wadesboro 3,977
Wagram 718
Wake Forest (★RAL) 3,148
Walkertown (★WNS) 1,652
Wallace 2,095
Walnut Cove 1,213
Warrenton 1,035
Warsaw 2,701
Washington 8,961
Washington Park 517
Waxhaw 1,248
Waynesville 6,488
Weaverville (★ASHE) 1,280
Weldon 2,304
Welmar Heights (★FAY) 1,200
Wendell 1,929
West Burlington (★BUR) 1,471
West Concord (★KANN-) 3,400
West Jefferson 889
West Marion 2,000
Whitakers 926
Whiteville 4,195
Wilkesboro 1,974
Williamston 6,570
Wilmington (★83,000; WILM) 46,169
Wilson 29,347
Windsor 2,199
Winfall 581
Wingate (★CHRLT) 2,569
Winston-Salem (★235,900; WNS) 134,676
Winter Park (★WILM) 1,300
Winterville 1,437
Winton 917
Woodfin (★ASHE) 3,300
Woodland 744
Woodrow 900
Wrightsville Beach (★ WILM) 1,701
Yadkinville 2,232
Yanceyville 1,274
Yorkmont Park (★CHRLT) 1,500
Youngsville 555
Zebulon 1,839

NORTH DAKOTA

1970 C 617,761

Counties

Adams 3,832
Barnes 14,669
Benson 8,245
Billings 1,198
Bottineau 9,496
Bowman 3,901
Burke 4,739
Burleigh 40,714
Cass 73,653
Cavalier 8,213
Dickey 6,976
Divide 4,564
Dunn 4,895
Eddy 4,103
Emmons 7,200
Foster 4,832
Golden Valley 2,611
Grand Forks 61,102
Grant 5,009
Griggs 4,184
Hettinger 5,075
Kidder 4,362
La Moure 7,117
Logan 4,245
McHenry 8,977
McIntosh 5,545
McKenzie 6,127
McLean 11,251
Mercer 6,175
Morton 20,310
Mountrail 8,437
Nelson 5,776

(North Dakota continued)

★ Population or designation of metropolitan area, including suburbs (see headnote).
▲ Population of entire "town" or township, including other communities and rural areas.
† Population is from a local census taken at date specified.

(North Dakota continued)

Oliver 2,322
Pembina 10,728
Pierce 6,323
Ramsey 12,915
Ransom 7,102
Renville 3,828
Richland 18,089
Rolette 11,549
Sargent 5,937
Sheridan 3,232
Sioux 3,632
Slope 1,484
Stark 19,613
Steele 3,749
Stutsman 23,550
Towner 4,645
Traill 9,571
Walsh 16,251
Ward 58,560
Wells 7,847
Williams 19,301

Cities

Ashley 1,236
Beach 1,408
Belfield 1,130
Beulah 1,344
Bismarck (★47,200; BIS-) 34,703
Bottineau 2,760
Bowbells 584
Bowman 1,762
Cando 1,512
Carrington 2,491
Casselton 1,485
Cavalier 1,381
Center 619
Cooperstown 1,485
Crosby 1,545
Devils Lake 7,078
Dickinson 12,405
Drake 636
Drayton 1,095
Dunseith 811
Edgeley 888
Elgin 839
Ellendale 1,517
Emerado (†12/7/71) 864
Enderlin 1,343
Fargo (★94,800; FAR-) 53,365
Fessenden 815
Finley 809
Forman 596
Fort Yates 1 153
Garrison 1,614
Glen Ullin 1,070
Grafton 5,946
Grand Forks (★48,500; GDFK) (†10/7/71) 40,060
Gwinner 623
Hankinson 1,125
Harvey 2,361
Hatton 808
Hazen 1,240
Hebron 1,103
Hettinger 1,655
Hillsboro 1,309
Jamestown (†11/30/71) 15,078
Kenmare (†7/19/71) 1,937
Killdeer 615
Kulm 625
Lakota (†8/3/71) 1,144
La Moure 951
Langdon (†7/19/71) 3,923
Larimore 1,469
Leeds 626
Lidgerwood 1,000
Linton 1,695
Lisbon 2,090
McClusky 664
McVille 583
Maddock 708
Mandan (★★BIS-) 11,093
Mayville 2,554
Milnor 645
Minot (★35,400; MINO) 32,290
Minto 636
Mohall 950
Mott 1,368
Napoleon 1,036
New England 906
New Rockford 1,969
New Salem 943
New Town 1,428
Northwood 1,189
Oakes 1,742
Park River 1,680
Parshall 1,246
Pembina 741
Portland 534
Powers Lake 523
Ray 776
Richardton 799
Riverdale 700
Rolette 579
Rolla 1,458
Rugby 2,889
Stanley 1,581
Stanton 517
Steele 696
Strasburg 642
Tioga 1,667
Towner 870
Turtle Lake 712
Underwood 781
Valley City 7,843
Velva 1,241
Wahpeton 7,076
Walhalla 1,471
Washburn 804
Watford City 1,768
West Fargo (★FAR-) 5,161
Westhope 705
Williston 11,280
Wilton 695
Wishek 1,275
Wyndmere 516

OHIO

1970 C 10,657,296

Counties

Adams 18,957
Allen 111,144
Ashland 43,303
Ashtabula 98,237
Athens 55,747
Auglaize 38,602
Belmont 80,917
Brown 26,635
Butler 226,207
Carroll 21,579
Champaign 30,491
Clark 157,115
Clermont 95,887
Clinton 31,464
Columbiana 108,310
Coshocton 33,486
Crawford 50,364
Cuyahoga 1,721,300
Darke 49,141
Defiance 36,949
Delaware 42,908
Erie 75,909
Fairfield 73,301
Fayette 25,461
Franklin 833,249
Fulton 33,071
Gallia 25,239
Geauga 62,977
Greene 125,057
Guernsey 37,665
Hamilton 924,018
Hancock 61,217
Hardin 30,813
Harrison 17,013
Henry 27,058
Highland 28,996
Hocking 20,322
Holmes 23,024
Huron 49,587
Jackson 27,174
Jefferson 96,193
Knox 41,795
Lake 197,200
Lawrence 56,868
Licking 107,799
Logan 35,072
Lorain 256,843
Lucas 484,370
Madison 28,318
Mahoning 304,545
Marion 64,724
Medina 82,717
Meigs 19,799
Mercer 35,558
Miami 84,342
Monroe 15,739
Montgomery 608,413
Morgan 12,375
Morrow 21,348
Muskingum 77,826
Noble 10,428
Ottawa 37,099
Paulding 19,329
Perry 27,434
Pickaway 40,071
Pike 19,114
Portage 125,868
Preble 34,719
Putnam 31,134
Richland 129,997
Ross 61,211
Sandusky 60,983
Scioto 76,951
Seneca 60,696
Shelby 37,748
Stark 372,210
Summit 553,371
Trumbull 232,579
Tuscarawas 77,211
Union 23,786
Van Wert 29,194
Vinton 9,420
Warren 85,505
Washington 57,160
Wayne 87,123
Williams 33,669
Wood 89,722
Wyandot 21,826

Cities

Aberdeen 1,165
Academia 1,447
Ada 5,309
Addyston (★CIN-) 1,336
Adena 1,134
Akron (★633,000; AKR) 275,425
Albany 899
Alexandria 588
Alger 1,071
Alliance (★51,900; ALLI) 26,547
Amanda 788
Amberley (★CIN-) 4,761
Amelia (★CIN-) 820
Amherst (★CLEV) 9,902
Amlin Heights (★DAY-) 900
Amsterdam 882
Andover 1,179
Anna 792
Ansonia 1,044
Antwerp (★FTWA) 1,735
Apple Creek 784
Arcadia 689
Arcanum 1,993
Archbold 3,047
Arlington (★DAY-) 1,066
Arlington Heights (★CIN-) 1,476
Ashland 19,872
Ashley 1,034
Ashtabula (★44,700; ASHT) 24,313
Ashville (★COL) 1,772
Athens 24,168
Attica 1,005
Aurora (★CLEV) 6,549
Aurora East (★CLEV) 900
Austintown (★YNGS-) 21,500
Avon (★CLEV) 7,214
Avondale (★CAN-) 1,500
Avondale (★DAY-) 5,195
Avon Lake (★CLEV) 12,261
Bainbridge 1,057
Ballville 1,652
Baltic 571
Baltimore 2,418
Barberton (★AKR) 33,052
Barnesville 4,292
Batavia (★CIN-) 1,894
Bay View (★SNDSK) 798
Bay Village (★CLEV) 18,163
Beach City 1,133
Beachwood (★CLEV) 9,631
Bedford (★CLEV) 17,552
Bedford Heights (★CLEV) 13,063
Beechcrest (★AKR) 900
Bellaire (★WHL) 9,655
Bellbrook (★DAY-) 1,268
Belle Center 985
Bellefontaine 11,255
Belleview Acres (★DAY-) 5,000
Bellevue 8,604
Bellville (★MANS) 1,685
Belmont 666
Beloit (★ALLI) 921
Belpre (★PRKB) 7,189
Berea (★CLEV) 22,396
Bergholz 914
Berlin Heights (★CLEV) 828
Bethel (★CIN-) 2,214
Bethesda 1,157
Bettsville 833
Beverly 1,396
Beverly Gardens (★DAY-) 2,400
Bexley (★COL) 14,888
Blacklick Estates (★COL) 7,200
Blanchester 3,080
Bloomdale 727
Bloomingburg 895
Bloomville 884
Blue Ash (★CIN-) 8,324
Bluffton 2,935
Boardman (★YNGS-) 30,852
Bolivar (★CAN-) 1,084
Boston Heights (★CLEV) 846
Botkins 1,057
Bowling Green 21,760
Bradford 2,163
Bradner 1,140
Bratenahl (★CLEV) 1,613
Brecksville (★CLEV) 9,137
Bremen 1,413
Brentwood (★CIN-) 12,000
Brentwood Estates (★STU-) 1,200
Brewster 2,020
Briarwood Beach (★CLEV) 508
Bridgeport (★WHL) 3,001
Bridgetown (★CIN-) 7,350
Brilliant (★STU-) 2,178
Brimfield (★AKR) 900
Broadview Heights (★CLEV) 11,463
Brooklyn (★CLEV) 13,142
Brooklyn Heights (★CLEV) 1,527
Brook Park (★CLEV) 30,774
Brookside (★WHL) 939
Brookside Estates (★COL) 2,000
Brookville (★DAY-) 4,403
Brunswick (★CLEV) 15,852
Bryan 7,008
Buchtel 592
Buckeye Lake (★NWRK) 2,961
Bucyrus 13,111
Burlington (★HNTG-) 1,400
Burton (★CLEV) 1,214
Butler (★MANS) 1,502
Byesville 2,097
Cadiz 3,060
Cain Heights (★E.LIV-) 1,100
Cairo 587
Calcutta (★E.LIV-) 3,000
Caldwell 2,082
Caledonia (★MRN) 792
Cambridge 13,656
Camden 1,507
Campbell (★YNGS-) 12,577
Canal Fulton (★AKR) 2,367
Canal Winchester (★COL) 2,412
Canfield (★YNGS-) 4,997
Canton (★311,100; CAN-) 110,053
Cardington 1,730
Carey 3,523
Carlisle (★MIDD) 3,821
Carroll 614
Carrollton 2,817
Castalia (★SNDSK) 1,045
Cedarville 2,342
Celina 8,072
Centerburg 1,038
Centerville (★DAY-) 10,333
Chagrin Falls (★CLEV) 4,848
Champion (★YNGS-) 5,000
Chardon (★CLEV) 3,991
Chauncey 1,117
Cherry Grove (★CIN-) 2,500
Chesapeake (★HNTG-) 1,364
Chesterland (★CLEV) 1,500
Cheviot (★CIN-) 11,135
Chillicothe 24,842
Christiansburg 724
Churchill (★YNGS-) 7,457
Cincinnati (★1,421,600; CIN-) 452,524
Circleville 11,687
Clarksville 574
Clayton (★DAY-) 773
Clearview (★CLEV) 4,000
Cleveland (★2,361,100; CLEV) 750,879
Cleveland Heights (★CLEV) 60,767
Cleves (★CIN-) 2,044
Clinton (★AKR) 1,335
Clyde 5,503
Coal Grove (★HNTG-) 2,759
Coalton 550
Coldwater 3,533
Colerain Heights (★CIN-) 3,000
Columbiana 4,959
Columbus (★886,500; COL) 540,025
Columbus Grove 2,290
Conneaut 14,552
Continental 1,185
Convoy 991
Cool Ridge Heights (★MANS) 1,100
Coolville 672
Copley (★AKR) 7,000
Corning 838
Cortland (★YNGS-) 2,525
Coshocton 13,747
Country Acres (★DAY-) 2,000
Covedale (★CIN-) 6,639
Covington 2,575
Craig Beach (★YNGS-) 1,451
Crestline 5,947
Creston 1,792
Cridersville (★LIMA) 1,103
Crooksville 2,828
Crystal Lakes (★DAY-) 2,000
Cuyahoga Falls (★AKR) 49,678
Cuyahoga Heights (★CLEV) 866
Cygnet 629
Dalton (★CAN-) 1,177
Danville 1,025
Darbydale (★COL) 743
Day Heights (★CIN-) 1,500
Dayton (★934,000; DAY-) 243,601
Deer Park (★CIN-) 7,415
Defiance 16,281
De Graff 1,117
Delaware 15,008
Delhi Hills (★CIN-) 9,000
Delphos 7,608
Delta 2,544
Dennison 3,506
Deshler 1,938
DeVola (★MRIET) 1,989
Dillonvale 1,095
Dover 11,516
Doylestown (★AKR) 2,373
Dresden 1,516
Drexel (★DAY-) 4,000
Dublin (★COL) 681
Dunkirk 1,036
East Alliance (★ALLI) 1,175
East Canton (★CAN-) 1,631
East Carlisle (★CLEV) 1,800
East Cleveland (★CLEV) 39,600
Eastlake (★CLEV) 19,690
East Liverpool (★65,800; E.LIV-) 20,020
East Palestine 5,604
East Sparta (★CAN-) 959
Eastview (★DAY-) 5,200
Eaton (★DAY-) 6,020
Eaton Estates (★CLEV) 2,076
Edgemont (★CIN-) 1,300
Edgerton 2,126
Edgewood (★ASHT) 3,437
Edison 569
Edon 803
Elida (★LIMA) 1,211
Elmore 1,316
Elmwood Place (★CIN-) 3,525
Elyria (★CLEV) 53,427
Englewood (★DAY-) 7,885
Enon (★DAY-) 1,929
Euclid (★CLEV) 71,552
Evendale (★CIN-) 1,967
Fairborn (★DAY-) 32,267
Fairfax (★CIN-) 2,705
Fairfield (★CIN-) 14,680
Fairhope (★CAN-) 2,200
Fairlawn (★AKR) 6,102
Fairport Harbor (Fairport) (★CLEV) 3,665
Fairview Lanes (★SNDSK) 1,000
Fairview Park (★CLEV) 21,681
Farmersville (★DAY-) 865
Fayette 1,175
Felicity 786
Findlay (★42,000; FIND) 35,800
Finneytown (★CIN-) 3,000
Fletcher 539
Flushing 1,207
Forest 1,535
Forest Park (★CIN-) 15,139
Forest Park (★DAY-) 1,370
Fort Jennings 533
Fort Loramie 744
Fort McKinley (★DAY-) 11,536
Fort Recovery 1,348
Fort Shawnee (★LIMA) 3,436
Fostoria 16,037
Frankfort 949
Franklin (★MIDD) 10,075
Frazeysburg 941
Fredericksburg 601
Fredericktown 1,935
Fremont 18,490
Frontier Town (★YNGS-) 1,500
Gahanna (★COL) 12,400
Galion 13,123
Gallipolis 7,490
Gambier 1,571
Garfield Heights (★CLEV) 41,417
Garrettsville 1,718
Gates Mills (★CLEV) 2,378
Geneva 6,449
Geneva-on-the-Lake 877
Genoa (★TOL) 2,139
Georgetown 2,949
Germantown (★DAY-) 4,088
Gettysburg 526
Gibsonburg 2,585
Girard (★YNGS-) 14,119
Glandorf 732
Glendale (★CIN-) 2,690
Glenmoor (★E.LIV-) 2,000
Glenwillow (★CLEV) 526
Glouster 2,121
Gnadenhutten 1,466
Golf Manor (★CIN-) 5,170
Goshen (★CIN-) 1,174
Grafton (★CLEV) 1,771
Grand Rapids 976
Grand River (★CLEV) 613
Grandview Heights (★COL) 8,460
Granville (★NWRK) 3,963
Gratis 621
Green Camp 537
Greenfield 4,780
Greenhills (★CIN-) 6,092
Green Springs 1,279
Greenville 12,380
Greenwich 1,473
Groesbeck (★CIN-) 6,000
Grove City (★COL) 13,911
Groveport (★COL) 2,490
Grover Hill 536
Hamden 953
Hamersville (★CIN-) 567
Hamilton (★★CIN-) 67,865
Hamilton Meadows (★COL) 1,000
Hamler 681
Hanover (★NWRK) 626
Harrisburg (★COL) 556
Harrison (★CIN-) 4,408
Harrod (★LIMA) 533
Hartville (★CAN-) 1,752
Haskins 549
Hayesville 506
Heath (★NWRK) 6,768
Hebron (★NWRK) 1,699
Hicksville 3,461
Highland Heights (★CLEV) 5,926
Highpoint (★CIN-) 1,100
Hillcrest (★YNGS-) 1,000
Hilliard (★COL) 8,369
Hillsboro 5,584
Hiram 1,484
Holgate 1,541
Holland (★TOL) 1,108
Homedale (★COL) 2,000
Homewood (★CIN-) 2,200
Hopedale 916
Hubbard (★YNGS-) 8,583
Huber Heights (★DAY-) 18,943
Huber Ridge (★COL) 2,700
Huber South (★DAY-) 5,000
Hudson (★CLEV) 3,933
Hunting Valley (★CLEV) 797
Huron (★SNDSK) 6,896
Hyde Park (★DAY-) 1,400
Independence (★CLEV) 7,034
Indian Hill (★CIN-) 5,651
Indian Ridge (★CIN) 1,000
Irondale (★E.LIV-) 602
Ironton (★HNTG-) 15,030
Jackson 6,843
Jackson Center 1,119
Jacksonville 545
Jamestown 1,790
Jefferson 2,472
Jeffersonville 1,031
Jeromesville 559
Jewett 901
Johnstown (★COL) 3,208
Junction City 732
Kalida 900
Kendall Heights (★CAN-) 1,000
Kent (★AKR) 28,183
Kenton 8,315
Kenwood (★CIN-) 15,789
Kettering (★DAY-) 71,864
Killbuck 893
Kingsgate (★CIN-) 1,000
Kingston 1,157
Kingsville (★ASHT) 1,129
Kirkersville (★COL) 578
Kirtland (★CLEV) 5,530
Knollwood (★DAY-) 5,513
Krumroy (★AKR) 1,600
LaGrange (★CLEV) 1,074
Lake Cable (★CAN-) 1,500
Lake Milton (★YNGS-) 900
Lakemore (★AKR) 2,708
Lakeview 1,026
Lakewood (★CLEV) 70,173
Lancaster (★46,800; LANC) 32,911
Lansing (★WHL) 1,000
La Rue 867
Laurelville 624
Lawrenceville (★DAY-) 687
Leavittsburg (★YNGS-) 3,000
Lebanon (★DAY-) 7,934
Leesburg 984
Leetonia 2,342
Leipsic 2,072
Leroy (★CLEV) 715
Lewisburg 1,553
Lexington (★MANS) 2,972
Liberty Center 1,007
Lima (★100,300; LIMA) 53,734
Limecrest (★DAY-) 1,000
Lincoln Heights (★CIN-) 6,099
Lincoln Heights (★MANS) 1,500
Lincoln Village (★COL) 11,215
Lindsey 652
Lisbon 3,521
Lithopolis (★COL) 705
Little Farms (★COL) 2,200
Lockland (★CIN-) 5,288
Lodi (★CLEV) 2,399
Logan 6,269
London 6,481
Lorain (★CLEV) 78,185
Loudonville 2,865
Louisville (★CAN-) 6,298
Loveland (★CIN-) 7,144
Loveland Park (★CIN-) 1,000
Lowell 852
Lowellville (★YNGS-) 1,836
Lucas (★MANS) 771
Luckey (★TOL) 996
Lynchburg 1,186
Lyndhurst (★CLEV) 19,749
Lyons 630
McArthur 1,543
McClure 699
McGuffey 704
McComb 1,329
McConnelsville 2,107
McDonald (★YNGS-) 3,177
Macedonia (★CLEV) 6,375

★ Population or designation of metropolitan area, including suburbs (see headnote).
▲ Population of entire "town" or township, including other communities and rural areas.
† Population is from a local census taken at date specified.

Mack (★CIN-)...6,000
McKinley Heights (★YNGS-)...1,700
Madeira (★CIN-)...6,713
Madison (★CLEV)...1,678
Madison North (★CLEV)...6,882
Madison-on-the-Lake (★CLEV)...900
Magnolia...1,064
Malta...1,017
Malvern...1,256
Manchester...2,195
Manchester (★AKR)...1,000
Mansfield (★111,100; MANS)...55,047
Mantua (★CLEV)...1,199
Maple Heights (★CLEV)...34,093
Marble Cliff (★COL)...715
Marblehead...726
Mariemont (★CIN-)...4,540
Marietta (★29,500; MRIET)...16,861
Marion (★53,800; MRN)...38,646
Marion East (★MRN)...1,079
Marshallville (★AKR)...693
Martins Ferry (★WHL)...10,757
Martinsville...500
Marysville...5,744
Mason (★CIN-)...5,677
Massillon (★★CAN-)...32,539
Masury (★SHAR)...5,180
Maumee (★TOL)...15,937
Mayfield (★CLEV)...3,548
Mayfield Heights (★CLEV)...22,139
Mechanicsburg...1,686
Medina (★CLEV)...10,913
Medway (★DAY-)...900
Mendon...672
Mentor (★CLEV)...36,912
Mentor-on-the-Lake (★CLEV)...6,517
Metamora...594
Miamisburg (★DAY-)...14,797
Middleburgh Heights (★CLEV)...12,367
Middlefield (★CLEV)...1,726
Middle Point (Middlepoint)...543
Middleport...2,784
Middletown (★101,900; MIDD)...48,767
Midvale...636
Milan (★SNDSK)...1,862
Milford (★CIN-)...4,828
Milford Center...753
Millbury (★TOL)...771
Millersburg...2,979
Millersport...777
Millville (★CIN-)...697
Mineral City...860
Mineral Ridge (★YNGS-)...2,100
Minerva...4,359
Minerva Park (★COL)...1,402
Mingo Junction (★STU-)...5,278
Minster (★CAN-)...2,405
Mogadore (★AKR)...4,825
Monfort Heights (★CIN-)...8,000
Monroe (★MIDD)...3,492
Monroeville...1,455
Monterey (★CIN-)...1,500
Montgomery (★CIN-)...5,683
Montpelier...4,184
Moraine (★DAY-)...4,898
Moreland Hills (★CLEV)...3,000
Morrow (★CIN-)...1,486
Mount Carmel Heights (★CIN-)...1,450
Mount Gilead...2,971
Mount Healthy (★CIN-)...7,446
Mount Healthy Heights (★CIN-)...1,000
Mount Orab (★CIN-)...1,306
Mount Pleasant...635
Mount Sterling (★COL)...1,536
Mount Vernon...13,373
Mount Victory...633
Munroe Falls (★AKR)...3,794
Napoleon...7,791
Navarre (★CAN-)...1,607
Nelsonville...4,812
Nevada...917
Newark (★76,500; NWRK)...41,836
New Boston (★PTSM)...3,325
New Bremen...2,185
Newburgh Heights (★CLEV)...3,396
New Burlington (★CIN-)...4,000
New Carlisle (★DAY-)...6,112
Newcomerstown...4,155
New Concord...2,318
New Holland...796
New Knoxville...852
New Lebanon (★DAY-)...4,248
New Lexington...4,921
New London...2,336
New Madison...959
New Matamoras...940
New Miami (★CIN-)...3,273
New Middletown (★YNGS-)...1,664
New Paris (★RICH)...1,692
New Philadelphia...15,184
New Richmond (★CIN-)...2,650
New Straitsville...947
Newton Falls (★YNGS-)...5,378
Newtown (★CIN-)...2,047
New Vienna...849
New Washington...1,251
New Waterford...735
Niles (★YNGS-)...21,581
North Baltimore...3,143
North Bend (★CIN-)...638
Northbrook (★CIN-)...6,000
North Canton (★CAN-)...15,228
North College Hill (★CIN-)...12,363
North Fairfield...540
Northfield (★CLEV)...4,283
Northfield Center (★CLEV)...4,364
North Fork Village
(Chillicothe West)...1,122
North Industry (★CAN-)...1,500
North Kingsville (★ASHT)...2,458
North Lewisburg...840
North Olmsted (★CLEV)...34,861
North Perry (★CLEV)...851
North Randall (★CLEV)...1,212
Northridge (★DAY-)...4,500
Northridge (★DAY-)...17,000
North Ridgeville (★CLEV)...13,152
North Royalton (★CLEV)...12,807

Northwood (★TOL)...4,222
Norton (★AKR)...12,308
Norwalk...13,386
Norwood (★CIN-)...30,420
Oak Harbor...2,807
Oak Hill...1,642
Oakwood (★DAY-)...10,095
Oakwood (★CLEV)...3,127
Oakwood...804
Oberlin (★CLEV)...8,761
Obetz (★COL)...2,248
Ohio City...816
Olmsted (★CLEV)...6,318
Olmsted Falls (★CLEV)...2,504
Oneida (★MIDD)...1,500
Ontario (★MANS)...4,345
Orange (★CLEV)...2,112
Oregon (★TOL)...16,563
Orrville...7,408
Orwell...965
Ottawa...3,622
Ottawa Hills (★TOL)...4,270
Ottoville...914
Overlook Homes (★DAY-)...2,600
Owensville (★CIN-)...707
Oxford...15,868
Page Manor (★DAY-)...7,500
Painesville (★CLEV)...16,536
Painesville Northeast (★CLEV)...2,000
Painesville Southwest (★CLEV)...5,461
Pandora...857
Park Layne (★DAY-)...4,800
Parma (★CLEV)...100,216
Parma Heights (★CLEV)...27,192
Pataskala (★COL)...1,831
Paulding...2,983
Payne...1,351
Peebles...1,629
Pemberville...1,301
Peninsula (★CLEV)...692
Pepper Pike (★CLEV)...5,933
Perry (★CLEV)...917
Perry Heights (★CAN-)...5,000
Perrysburg (★TOL)...7,693
Perrysville (★MANS)...752
Petersburg (★YNGS-)...800
Phillipsburg (★DAY-)...831
Philo (★ZAN)...846
Pickerington (★COL)...696
Piketon...1,347
Pioneer...968
Piqua...20,741
Pisgah (★CIN-)...900
Plain City...2,254
Pleasant Hill...1,025
Pleasant Run Farms (★CIN-)...6,000
Pleasantville (★LANC)...754
Plymouth...1,993
Poland (★YNGS-)...3,097
Pomeroy...2,672
Portage Lakes (★AKR)...20,000
Port Clinton...7,202
Portsmouth (★65,400; PTSM)...27,633
Powhatan Point...2,167
Proctorville (★HNTG-)...881
Prospect...1,031
Quaker City...510
Quincy...686
Racine...583
Ravenna (★AKR)...11,780
Rayland (★WHL)...617
Reading (★CIN-)...14,303
Redbird (★CLEV)...900
Reedurban (★CAN-)...4,500
Reno Beach (★TOL)...1,049
Rensselaer Park (★CIN-)...1,700
Republic...705
Reynoldsburg (★COL)...13,921
Richfield (West Richfield)
(★CLEV)...3,228
Richmond (★STU-)...777
Richmond Heights (★CLEV)...9,220
Richwood...2,072
Ridgewood Heights (★DAY-)...2,000
Rio Grande...814
Ripley...2,745
Risingsun (Rising Sun)...730
Rittman...6,308
River Edge (★CLEV)...632
Riverside (★DAY-)...778
Rock Creek...731
Rockford...1,207
Rocky River (★CLEV)...22,958
Roseland (★MANS)...3,000
Rosemount (★PTSM)...1,786
Roseville...1,767
Ross (★CIN-)...1,661
Rossford (★TOL)...5,302
Rushsylvania...526
Russels Point...1,104
Rutland...663
Sabina...2,160
Sagamore Hills (★CLEV)...6,000
St. Bernard (★CIN-)...6,080
St. Clairsville (★WHL)...4,754
St. Henry...1,276
St. Marys...7,699
St. Paris...1,646
Salem...14,186
Salineville...1,686
Sandusky (★61,100; SNDSK)...32,674
Sardinia...824
Saville Estates (★DAY-)...1,000
Sawyerwood (★AKR)...3,000
Scio...1,002
Seaman...866
Sebring (★ALLI)...4,954
Seven Hills (★CLEV)...12,700
Seven Hills (★CIN-)...2,000
Seven Mile (★CIN-)...699
Seville...1,402
Shadyside (★WHL)...5,070
Shaker Heights (★CLEV)...36,306
Sharonville (★CIN-)...10,985
Shawnee...914
Sheffield (★CLEV)...1,730
Sheffield Lake (★CLEV)...8,734
Shelby...9,847

Sherwood...784
Shiloh (★DAY-)...10,000
Shiloh...817
Shreve...1,635
Sidney...16,332
Silver Lake (★AKR)...3,637
Silverton (★CIN-)...6,588
Singing Hills (★DAY-)...1,850
Skyline Acres (★CIN-)...1,800
Smithfield (★STU-)...1,245
Smithville...1,278
Solon (★CLEV)...11,519
Somerset...1,417
South Amherst (★CLEV)...2,913
South Bloomfield (★COL)...610
South Charleston...1,500
South Euclid (★CLEV)...29,579
South Lebanon (★CIN-)...3,014
South Lorain (★CLEV)...1,000
South Point (★HNTG-)...2,243
South Russell (★CLEV)...2,673
South Vernon (South Mount
Vernon)...1,044
South Vienna (Vienna)...545
South Webster...825
South West Hubbard (★YNGS-)...1,500
South Zanesville (★ZAN)...1,436
Spencer...758
Spencerville...2,241
Springboro (★DAY-)...2,799
Springdale (★CIN-)...8,127
Springfield (★★DAY-)...81,941
Spring Valley...667
Steubenville (★138,200; STU-)...30,771
Stony Prairie...1,913
Stoutsville...573
Stow (★AKR)...19,847
Strasburg...1,874
Streetsboro (★CLEV)...7,966
Strongsville (★CLEV)...15,182
Struthers (★YNGS-)...15,343
Stryker...1,296
Sugarcreek...1,771
Summerside Estates (★CIN-)...1,500
Sunbury (★COL)...1,820
Swanton (★TOL)...2,927
Sycamore...1,096
Sylvania (★TOL)...12,031
Syracuse...684
Tallmadge (★AKR)...15,274
Terrace Park (★CIN-)...2,266
The Plains...1,568
Thornville...679
Tiffin...21,596
Tiltonsville (★WHL)...2,454
Timberlake (★CLEV)...964
Tipp City (★DAY-)...5,090
Toledo (★566,700; TOL)...383,818
Toronto (★STU-)...7,705
Trenton (★MIDD)...5,278
Trimble...542
Trotwood (★DAY-)...6,997
Troy...17,186
Tuscarawas...803
Twin Lakes (★AKR)...1,200
Twinsburg (★CLEV)...6,432
Twinsburg Heights (★CLEV)...1,200
Uhrichsville...5,731
Union (★DAY-)...3,654
Union City...1,808
Uniontown (★AKR)...900
University Heights (★CLEV)...17,055
University View (★COL)...1,000
Upper Arlington (★COL)...38,630
Upper Sandusky...5,645
Urbana...11,237
Urbancrest (★COL)...754
Utica...1,977
Valleydale (★CIN-)...1,300
Valley View (★CLEV)...1,422
Valley View (★COL)...909
Valleywood (★DAY-)...2,000
Vandalia (★DAY-)...10,796
Vanlue...539
Van Wert...11,320
Vermilion (★CLEV)...9,872
Verona (★DAY-)...593
Versailles...2,441
Viking Village (★CIN-)...1,000
Vincent (★CLEV)...1,700
Wadsworth (★AKR)...13,142
Waite Hill (★CLEV)...514
Wakeman (★CLEV)...822
Walbridge (★TOL)...3,208
Walton Hills (★CLEV)...2,508
Wapakoneta (★LIMA)...7,324
Warren (★★YNGS-)...63,494
Warrensville (★CLEV)...2,160
Warrensville Heights (★CLEV)...18,925
Warsaw...725
Washington Court House...12,495
Washingtonville...747
Waterville (★TOL)...2,940
Wauseon...4,932
Waverly...4,858
Wayne...921
Waynesburg...1,337
Waynesfield...704
Waynesville (★DAY-)...1,638
Wellington...4,137
Wellington Park (★CIN-)...1,000
Wellston...5,410
Wellsville (★E.LIV)...5,891
West Alexandria (★DAY-)...1,553
West Carrollton (★DAY-)...10,748
Westerville (★COL)...12,530
West Farmington...650
West Jefferson (Jefferson)
(★COL)...3,664
West Lafayette...1,719
Westlake (★CLEV)...15,689
West Liberty...1,580
West Mansfield...753
West Milton (★DAY-)...3,696
Weston...1,269
West Portsmouth (★PTSM)...3,396
West Salem...1,058
West Union...1,951

West Unity...1,589
Westview (★CLEV)...2,523
Westview (★CLEV)...1,200
Wheelersburg (★PTSM)...3,709
Whitehall (★COL)...25,263
Whitehouse (★TOL)...1,542
White Oak (★CIN-)...1,000
Wickliffe (★CLEV)...21,354
Wickliffe (★YNGS-)...7,900
Wilberforce (★DAY-)...4,400
Willard...5,510
Williamsburg (★CIN-)...2,054
Williamsport...857
Willoughby (★CLEV)...18,634
Willoughby Hills (★CLEV)...5,247
Willowick (★CLEV)...21,237
Willshire...623
Wilmington...10,051
Winchester...760
Windham...3,360
Wintersville (★STU-)...4,921
Withamsville (★CIN-)...3,000
Woodbourne (★DAY-)...4,000
Woodlawn (★CIN-)...3,251
Woodmere (★CLEV)...976
Woodsfield...3,239
Woodville...1,834
Woodworth (★YNGS-)...1,054
Wooster...18,703
Wooster Heights (★MANS)...1,100
Worthington (★COL)...15,326
Wyoming (★CIN-)...9,089
Xenia (★DAY-)...25,373
Yellow Springs (★DAY-)...4,624
Yorkville (WHL)...1,656
Youngstown (★501,500; YNGS-)...140,909
Zanesville (★55,800; ZAN)...33,045

OKLAHOMA

1970 C...2,559,253

Counties

Adair...15,141
Alfalfa...7,224
Atoka...10,972
Beaver...6,282
Beckham...15,754
Blaine...11,794
Bryan...25,552
Caddo...28,931
Canadian...32,245
Carter...37,349
Cherokee...23,174
Choctaw...15,141
Cimarron...4,145
Cleveland...81,839
Coal...5,525
Comanche...108,144
Cotton...6,832
Craig...14,722
Creek...45,532
Custer...22,665
Delaware...17,767
Dewey...5,656
Ellis...5,129
Garfield...56,343
Garvin...24,874
Grady...29,354
Grant...7,117
Greer...7,979
Harmon...5,136
Harper...5,151
Haskell...9,578
Hughes...13,228
Jackson...30,902
Jefferson...7,125
Johnston...7,870
Kay...48,791
Kingfisher...12,857
Kiowa...12,532
Latimer...8,601
Le Flore...32,137
Lincoln...19,482
Logan...19,645
Love...5,637
McClain...14,157
McCurtain...28,642
McIntosh...12,472
Major...7,529
Marshall...7,682
Mayes...23,302
Murray...10,669
Muskogee...59,542
Noble...10,043
Nowata...9,773
Okfuskee...10,683
Oklahoma...526,805
Okmulgee...35,358
Osage...29,750
Ottawa...29,800
Pawnee...11,338
Payne...50,654
Pittsburg...37,521
Pontotoc...27,867
Pottawatomie...43,134
Pushmataha...9,385
Roger Mills...4,452
Rogers...28,425
Seminole...25,144
Sequoyah...23,370
Stephens...35,902
Texas...16,352
Tillman...12,901
Tulsa...400,709
Wagoner...22,163
Washington...42,277
Washita...12,141
Woods...11,920
Woodward...15,537

Cities

Ada...14,859
Afton...1,022
Allen...974
Altus...23,302
Alva...7,440
Anadarko...6,682
Antlers...2,685
Apache...1,421
Arapaho...531
Ardmore...20,881
Arkoma (★FTSM)...2,098
Arnett...711
Atoka...3,346
Barnsdall...1,579
Bartlesville...29,683
Beaver...1,853
Beggs...1,107
Bethany (★O.C.)...21,785
Bethel Acres (★O.C.)...1,083
Billings...618
Binger...730
Bixby (★TUL)...3,973
Blackwell...8,645
Blair...1,114
Blanchard (★O.C.)...1,580
Boise City...1,993
Bokchito...607
Bokoshe...588
Boley...514
Boswell...755
Boynton...522
Bristow...4,653
Broken Arrow (★TUL)...11,787
Broken Bow...2,980
Buffalo...1,579
Burns Flat...988
Cache...1,106
Caddo...886
Calera...1,063
Canton...844
Carmen...519
Carnegie...1,723
Catoosa (★TUL)...970
Cement...892
Chandler...2,529
Checotah...3,074
Chelsea...1,622
Cherokee...2,119
Cheyenne...892
Chickasha...14,194
Choctaw (★O.C.)...4,750
Chouteau...1,046
Claremore (★TUL)...9,084
Clayton...718
Cleveland...2,573
Clinton...8,513
Coalgate...1,859
Colbert...814
Collinsville (★TUL)...3,009
Comanche...1,862
Commerce...2,593
Copan...675
Cordell (New Cordell)...3,261
Covington...605
Coweta (★TUL)...2,457
Cowlington...751
Crescent...1,568
Cushing...7,529
Cyril...1,302
Davenport...831
Davidson...515
Davis...2,223
Delaware...534
Del City (★O.C.)...27,133
Depew...739
Dewar...933
Dewey...3,958
Dickson...798
Dill City...578
Drumright...2,931
Duncan...19,718
Durant...11,118
Dustin...502
Edmond (★O.C.)...16,633
Eldorado...737
Elgin...840
Elk City...7,323
Elmore City...653
El Reno...14,510
Enid (★47,400; ENID)...44,986
Erick...1,285
Eufaula...2,355
Fairfax...1,889
Fairland...814
Fairview...2,894
Fletcher...950
Forest Park (★O.C.)...835
Fort Cobb...722
Fort Gibson...1,418
Fort Supply...550
Frederick...6,132
Gage...536
Garber...1,011
Geary...1,380
Geronimo...587
Glenpool (★TUL)...770
Goodwell...1,467
Grandfield...1,524
Granite...1,808
Grove...2,000
Guthrie...9,575
Guymon...7,674
Haileyville...928
Hammon...677
Harrah (★O.C.)...1,931
Hartshorne...2,121
Haskell...2,063
Healdton...2,324
Heavener...2,566
Helena...769
Hennessey...2,181
Henryetta...6,430
Hinton...889
Hobart...4,638
Holdenville...5,181
Hollis...3,150
Hominy...2,274
Hooker...1,615
Hugo...6,585
Hulbert...505
Hydro...805

(Oklahoma continued)

★ Population or designation of metropolitan area, including suburbs (see headhote).
▲ Population of entire "town" or township, including other communities and rural areas.
† Population is from a local census taken at date specified.

(Oklahoma continued)

Idabel 5,946
Inola 948
Jay 1,594
Jenks (★TUL) 1,997
Jones (★O.C.) 1,666
Kellyville 685
Keota 685
Keyes 569
Kiefer (★TUL) 803
Kingfisher 4,042
Kingston 710
Kiowa 754
Konawa 1,719
Krebs 1,515
Laverne 1,373
Lawton (★96,500; LAWT) 74,470
Lexington 1,516
Lindsay 3,705
Locust Grove 1,090
Lone Grove 1,240
Lone Wolf 584
Luther (★O.C.) 836
McAlester 18,802
McCloud (★O.C.) 2,159
McCurtain 575
Madill 2,875
Mangum 4,066
Mannford 892
Marietta 2,013
Marlow 3,995
Maud 1,143
Maysville 1,380
Medford 1,304
Meeker 683
Miami 13,880
Midwest City (★O.C.) 48,212
Minco 1,129
Moore (★O.C.) 18,761
Mooreland 1,196
Morris 1,119
Mounds (★TUL) 766
Mountain View 1,110
Muldrow 1,680
Muskogee 37,331
Mustang (★O.C.) 2,637
New Castle (★O.C.) 1,271
Newkirk 2,173
Nichols Hills (★O.C.) 4,478
Nicoma Park (★O.C.) 2,560
Noble (★O.C.) 2,241
Norman (★O.C.) 52,117
North Enid (★ENID) 730
Nowata 3,679
Oakhurst (★TUL) 2,000
Oilton 1,087
Okarche 826
Okeene 1,421
Okemah 2,913
Oklahoma City
(★627,300; O.C.) 368,856
Okmulgee 15,180
Olustee 819
Owasso (★TUL) 3,491
Panama 1,121
Pauls Valley 5,769
Pawhuska 4,238
Pawnee 2,443
Perkins 1,029
Perry 5,341
Picher 2,363
Pocola 1,840
Ponca City 25,940
Pondcreek 903
Porter 624
Porum 658
Poteau 5,500
Prague 1,802
Pryor (Pryor Creek) 7,057
Purcell 4,076
Quapaw 967
Quinton 1,262
Ramona 600
Red Oak 609
Ringling 1,206
Roff 632
Roland 827
Rush Springs 1,381
Ryan 1,011
Salina 1,024
Sallisaw 4,888
Sand Springs (★TUL) 10,565
Sapulpa (★TUL) 15,159
Savanna 948
Sayre 2,712
Seiling 1,033
Seminole 7,878
Sentinel 984
Shattuck 1,546
Shawnee 25,075
Shidler 717
Skiatook (★TUL) 2,930
Snyder 1,671
South Coffeyville 646
Spencer (★O.C.) 3,714
Sperry (★TUL) 1,123
Spiro 2,057
Sterling 675
Stigler 2,347
Stillwater 31,126
Stilwell 2,134
Stonewall 653
Stratford 1,278
Stroud 2,502
Sulphur 5,158
Taft 525
Tahlequah 9,254
Talihina 1,227
Tecumseh 4,451
Temple 1,354
Terral 636
Texhoma 921
The Village (★O.C.) 13,695
Thomas 1,336
Tipton 1,206
Tishomingo 2,663
Tonkawa 3,337
Tulsa (★460,300; TUL) 330,350
Turley (★TUL) 6,300
Tuttle 1,640
Valley Brook (★O.C.) 1,197
Valliant 840
Velma 611
Vian 1,131
Vici 694
Vinita 5,847
Wagoner 4,959
Walters 2,611
Warner 1,217
Warr Acres (★O.C.) 9,887
Watonga 3,696
Waukomis 842
Waurika 1,833
Wayne 618
Waynoka 1,444
Weatherford 7,959
Welch 651
Weleetka 1,199
Wellston 789
Westville 934
Wetumka 1,687
Wewoka 5,284
Wilburton 2,504
Wilson 1,569
Wister 927
Woodward 9,412
Wright City 1,068
Wynnewood 2,374
Wynona 547
Yale 1,239
Yukon (★O.C.) 8,411

OREGON

1970 C 2,091,533

Counties

Baker 14,919
Benton 53,776
Clackamas 166,088
Clatsop 28,473
Columbia 28,790
Coos 56,515
Crook 9,985
Curry 13,006
Deschutes 30,442
Douglas 71,743
Gilliam 2,342
Grant 6,996
Harney 7,215
Hood River 13,187
Jackson 94,533
Jefferson 8,548
Josephine 35,746
Klamath 50,021
Lake 6,343
Lane 215,401
Lincoln 25,755
Linn 71,914
Malheur 23,169
Marion 151,309
Morrow 4,465
Multnomah 554,668
Polk 35,349
Sherman 2,139
Tillamook 18,034
Umatilla 44,923
Union 19,377
Wallowa 6,247
Wasco 20,133
Washington 157,920
Wheeler 1,849
Yamhill 40,213

Cities

Agate Beach 900
Albany 18,181
Aloha (★POR) 5,000
Altamont 15,746
Amity 708
Ashland 12,342
Astoria 10,244
Athena 872
Aumsville (★SAL) 590
Baker 9,354
Bandon 1,832
Barview 1,388
Battin (★POR) 3,000
Bay City 898
Beaverton (★POR) 18,577
Bend 13,710
Brookings 2,720
Brownsville 1,034
Bunker Hill 1,549
Burns 3,293
Canby (★POR) 3,813
Cannon Beach 779
Canyonville 940
Carlton 1,126
Cascade Locks 574
Cedar Hills (★POR) 7,500
Cedar Mill (★POR) 3,000
Central Point (★MEDF) 4,004
Central Point West (★MEDF) 1,988
Chenoweth 2,329
Chiloquin 826
Clackamas (★POR) 1,500
Clackamas Heights (★POR) 1,200
Clatskanie 1,286
Coburg 713
Columbia City (★POR) 537
Concord (★POR) 2,000
Condon 973
Coos Bay 13,466
Coquille 4,437
Cornelius (★POR) 1,903
Corvallis (★44,200; CORV) 35,056
Cottage Grove 6,004
Creswell (★EUG) 1,199
Dallas 6,361
Dayton 949
Drain 1,204
Dunes 976
Eagle Point (★MEDF) 1,241
East Parkrose (★POR) 2,500
Eastside 1,331
Elgin 1,375
Enterprise 1,680
Errol Heights (★POR) 8,400
Estacada 1,164
Eugene (★171,100; EUG) 78,389
Fairview (★POR) 1,045
Falcon Heights 1,389
Falls City 745
Florence 2,246
Forest Grove (★POR) 8,275
Fossil 511
Four Corners (★SAL) 6,199
Fruitdale 2,655
Garden Home (★POR) 4,700
Garibaldi 1,083
Gearhart 829
Gervais (★SAL) 746
Gilbert (★POR) 3,300
Gladstone (★POR) 6,237
Glendale 709
Glendoveer (★POR) 4,900
Glenwood (★EUG) 2,000
Gold Beach 1,554
Gold Hill 603
Grants Pass 12,455
Grants Pass Southwest 3,431
Green 1,612
Gresham (★POR) 10,030
Hammond 500
Happy Valley (★POR) 1,392
Harrisburg 1,311
Hayesville (★SAL) 5,518
Hazelwood (★POR) 4,900
Heppner 1,429
Hermiston 4,893
Hillsboro (★POR) 14,675
Hines 1,407
Hood River 3,991
Hubbard (★POR) 975
Huntington 507
Independence (★SAL) 2,594
Jacksonville (★MEDF) 1,611
Jefferson (★SAL) 936
Jennings Lodge (★POR) 3,000
John Day 1,566
Joseph 839
Junction City (★EUG) 2,373
Keizer (★SAL) 11,405
Kendall (★POR) 3,400
King City (★POR) 1,427
Klamath Falls 15,775
Lafayette 786
La Grande 9,645
Lake Oswego (★POR) 14,573
Lakeview 2,705
Lebanon 6,636
Lebanon South 2,229
Lincoln City 4,198
Lowell 567
Lyons 645
McMinnville 10,125
McNulty (★POR) 1,017
Madras 1,689
Mapleton 900
Marlene Village (★POR) 1,000
May Park 1,466
Maywood Park (★POR) 1,230
Medford (★63,300; MEDF) 28,454
Medford West (★MEDF) 3,919
Merrill 722
Metzger (★POR) 4,200
Mill City 1,451
Milton-Freewater 4,105
Milwaukie (★POR) 16,379
Molalla 2,005
Monmouth (★SAL) 5,237
Mount Angel 1,973
Myrtle Creek 2,733
Myrtle Point 2,511
Newberg (★POR) 6,507
Newport 5,188
North Bend 8,553
North Plains (★POR) 690
Nyssa 2,620
Oak Grove (★POR) 6,000
Oakland 1,010
Oakridge 3,422
Ontario 6,523
Oregon City (★POR) 9,176
Parkrose (★POR) 22,500
Pendleton 13,197
Philomath (★CORV) 1,688
Phoenix (★MEDF) 1,287
Pilot Rock 1,612
Portland (★983,600; POR) 380,620
Port Orford 1,037
Powellhurst (★POR) 8,100
Powers 842
Prairie City 867
Prineville 4,101
Rainier (★LNGV) 1,731
Raleigh Hills (★POR) 8,000
Redmond 3,721
Reedsport 4,039
Riddle 1,042
River Grove (★POR) 1,500
River Road (★EUG) 9,000
Rockaway 665
Rockwood (★POR) 9,700
Rogue River 841
Roseburg 14,461
Russellville (★POR) 4,500
St. Helens (★POR) 6,212
Salem (★141,300; SAL) 68,856
Sandy (★POR) 1,544
Santa Clara (★EUG) 5,000
Scappoose (★POR) 1,859
Seaside 4,402
Sheridan 1,881
Sherwood (★POR) 1,396
Siletz 596
Silverton 4,301
Sisters 516
South Medford (Medford South)
(★MEDF) 3,497
Springfield (★EUG) 27,047
Stanfield 891
Stayton 3,170
Sublimity 634
Sutherlin 3,070
Sweet Home 3,799
Sylvan (★POR) 1,000
Talent (★MEDF) 1,389
The Dalles 10,423
Tigard (★POR) 5,302
Tillamook 3,968
Toledo 2,818
Tri City (Myrtle Creek South) 1,039
Troutdale (★POR) 1,661
Tualatin (★POR) 952
Turner (★SAL) 846
Umatilla 679
Union 1,531
Vale 1,448
Veneta (★EUG) 1,377
Vernonia 1,643
Waldport 700
Wallowa 811
Warrenton 1,825
West Haven (★POR) 3,000
West Linn (★POR) 7,091
Weston 660
West Powellhurst (★POR) 2,600
West Slope (★POR) 8,000
Westwood (★POR) 5,000
Willamina 1,193
Wilsonville (★POR) 1,001
Winston 2,468
Woodburn (★SAL) 7,495
Wood Village (★POR) 1,533
Yoncalla 675

PENNSYLVANIA

1970 C 11,797,463

Counties

Adams 56,937
Allegheny 1,605,133
Armstrong 75,590
Beaver 208,418
Bedford 42,353
Berks 296,382
Blair 135,356
Bradford 57,962
Bucks 415,056
Butler 127,941
Cambria 186,785
Cameron 7,096
Carbon 50,573
Centre 99,267
Chester 278,311
Clarion 38,414
Clearfield 74,619
Clinton 37,721
Columbia 55,114
Crawford 81,342
Cumberland 158,177
Dauphin 223,834
Delaware 601,425
Elk 37,770
Erie 263,654
Fayette 154,667
Forest 4,926
Franklin 100,833
Fulton 10,776
Greene 36,090
Huntingdon 39,108
Indiana 79,451
Jefferson 43,695
Juniata 16,712
Lackawanna 234,107
Lancaster 320,079
Lawrence 107,374
Lebanon 99,665
Lehigh 255,304
Luzerne 342,301
Lycoming 113,296
McKean 51,915
Mercer 127,225
Mifflin 45,268
Monroe 45,422
Montgomery 623,921
Montour 16,508
Northampton 214,368
Northumberland 99,190
Perry 28,615
Philadelphia 1,950,098
Pike 11,818
Potter 16,395
Schuylkill 160,089
Snyder 29,269
Somerset 76,037
Sullivan 5,961
Susquehanna 34,344
Tioga 39,691
Union 28,603
Venango 62,353
Warren 47,682
Washington 210,876
Wayne 29,581
Westmoreland 376,935
Wyoming 19,082
York 272,603

Cities

Abington (★PHIL-) 8,594
Acmetonia (★PGH) 1,500
Adamstown 1,202
Akron 3,149
Albion 1,768
Alburtis (★AL-B-E) 1,142
Aldan (★PHIL-) 5,001
Aliquippa (★PGH) 22,277
Allenport (★MNSN-) 762
Allentown (★502,000; AL-B-E) 109,527
Allison 1,040
Allison Park (★PGH) 10,000
Altoona (★102,800; ALT) 63,115
Ambler (★PHIL-) 7,800
Ambridge (★PGH) 11,324
Ambridge Heights (Harmony)
(★PGH) 5,022
Andalusia (★PHIL-) 4,300
Annville (★LEB) 4,704
Apollo 2,308
Applewold 515
Archbald (★SCR) 6,118
Ardmore (★PHIL-) 16,500
Ardsley (★PHIL-) 4,100
Arendtsville 589
Arnold (★PGH) 8,174
Ashland 4,737
Ashley (★WLKS) 4,095
Askam (★WLKS) 1,500
Aspinwall (★PGH) 3,541
Aston (★PHIL-) 2,000
Atglen (★COAT) 740
Athens 4,173
Atlas 1,527
Auburn 895
Audubon (★PHIL-) 2,500
Austin 626
Avalon (★PGH) 7,010
Avella 1,109
Avis 1,749
Avoca (★SCR) 3,543
Avon (★LEB) 1,271
Avondale (★PHIL-) 1,025
Avonmore 1,267
Baden (★PGH) 5,536
Bala-Cynwyd (Cynwyd) (★PHIL-) 9,500
Baldwin (★PGH) 26,729
Baldwin Township (★PGH) 2,598
Bally 1,197
Bangor 5,425
Baresville (★HANV) 1,700
Barnesboro 2,708
Bath (★AL-B-E) 1,829
Bath Addition (★PHIL-) 1,200
Bauerstown (★PGH) 3,000
Beaver (★PGH) 6,100
Beaverdale 1,579
Beaver Falls (★PGH) 14,375
Beaver Meadows (★HAZ) 1,274
Beavertown 783
Bechtelsville 728
Bedford 3,302
Beech Creek 639
Bell Acres (★PGH) 1,264
Bellefonte 6,828
Belle Vernon (★MNSN-) 1,496
Belleville 1,817
Bellevue (★PGH) 11,586
Bellwood (★ALT) 2,395
Belmont (★JNST) 2,000
Belmont Hills (★PHIL-) 1,200
Ben Avon (★PGH) 2,713
Bendersville 528
Bentleyville 2,714
Benton 1,027
Berlin 1,766
Bernville 848
Berwick 12,274
Berwyn (★PHIL-) 9,000
Bessemer 1,427
Bethel Park (Bethel) (★PGH) 34,791
Bethlehem (★★AL-B-E) 72,686
Big Beaver (★PGH) 2,739
Biglerville 977
Big Run 826
Birdsboro 3,196
Black Lick 1,074
Blaine Hill (★PGH) 1,000
Blairsville 4,411
Blakely (★SCR) 6,391
Blandon (★READ) 1,113
Blawnox (★PGH) 1,907
Bloomsburg 11,652
Blossburg 1,753
Blossom Hill (★LANC) 1,200
Blue Bell (★PHIL-) 1,000
Bobtown 1,055
Boiling Springs 1,521
Bolivar (★PGH) 668
Bonneauville 819
Boothwyn (★PHIL-) 6,500
Boston (★PGH) 4,000
Boswell 1,529
Bowmanstown (★AL-B-E) 864
Boyertown 4,428
Brackenridge (★PGH) 4,796
Braddock (★PGH) 8,795
Braddock Hills (★PGH) 2,459
Bradenville 1,200
Bradford 12,672
Bradfordwoods (★PGH) 970
Brentwood (★PGH) 13,732
Bressler (★HRBG) 1,800
Briarcliff (★PHIL-) 7,000
Bridgeport (★PHIL-) 5,630
Bridgeville (★PGH) 6,717
Bristol (★PHIL-) 12,085
Brockway 2,529
Brookhaven (★PHIL-) 7,370
Brookville 4,314
Broomall (Marple) (★PHIL-) 25,040
Broughton (★PGH) 2,800
Brownstown (★JNST) 1,035
Brownsville 4,856
Brownsville Township 875
Bruin 673
Bryn Athyn (★PHIL-) 970
Bryn Mawr (★PHIL-) 11,000
Burgettstown 2,118
Burnham 2,607
Butler (★66,000; BUTL) 18,691
Butztown (★AL-B-E) 900
Cadogan 563
California 6,635
Cambridge Springs 1,998
Campbelltown (★HRBG) 1,355
Camp Hill (★HRBG) 9,931
Canonsburg (★PGH) 11,439
Canton 2,037
Carbondale 12,808
Carlisle 18,079
Carmichaels 608
Carnegie (★PGH) 10,864
Carnot (★PGH) 4,000
Carroll Park (★PHIL-) 1,500

★ Population or designation of metropolitan area, including suburbs (see headnote).
▲ Population of entire "town" or township, including other communities and rural areas.
† Population is from a local census taken at date specified.

Carrolltown 1,507
Castanea 1,279
Castle Shannon (★PGH) 11,899
Catasauqua (★AL-B-E) 5,702
Catawissa 1,701
Cedar Cliff Manor (★HRBG) 1,300
Cementon (★AL-B-E) 1,200
Centerville 4,175
Central City 1,547
Central Highlands (★PGH) 1,000
Centralia 1,165
Centre Hall 1,282
Chalfant (★PGH) 1,370
Chalfont (★PHIL-) 2,366
Chambersburg 17,315
Chambers Hill (★HARB) 1,500
Charleroi (★★MNSN-) 6,723
Chatwood (★PHIL-) 1,000
Cheltenham (★PHIL-) 7,000
Cherokee Ranch (★READ) 1,200
Cherry City (★PGH) 4,000
Chester (★PHIL-) 56,331
Chester Heights (★PHIL-) 749
Chester Hill 868
Chester Township 5,708
Cheswick (★PGH) 2,580
Chevy Chase Heights 1,185
Chicora 1,166
Chinchilla (★SCR) 1,100
Christiana 1,132
Churchill (★PGH) 4,690
Churchville 2,600
Clairton (★PGH) 15,051
Clarendon 735
Claridge (★PGH) 1,100
Clarion 6,095
Clarks Green (★SCR) 1,674
Clarks Summit (★SCR) 5,376
Claysburg 1,516
Claysville (★WASH) 951
Clearfield 8,176
Clearview (★LANC) 1,200
Cleona (★LEB) 2,040
Clifton Heights (★PHIL-) 8,348
Clymer 2,054
Coaldale 3,023
Coalport 796
Coatesville (★64,100; COAT) 12,331
Cochranton 1,229
Codorus (Jefferson) 540
Cokeburg 845
Collegeville (★PHIL-) 3,191
Collingdale (★PHIL-) 10,605
Colonial Park (★HRBG) 9,000
Columbia 11,237
Colver 1,175
Colwyn (★PHIL-) 3,169
Conemaugh (East Conemaugh) (★JNST) 2,710
Confluence 954
Conneaut Lake 745
Conneautville 1,032
Connellsville 11,643
Connoquenessing (★BUTL) 553
Conshohocken (★PHIL-) 10,195
Conway (★PGH) 2,822
Conyngham (★HAZ) 1,850
Coopersburg (★AL-B-E) 2,326
Copperstown 1,300
Coplay (★AL-B-E) 3,642
Coraopolis (★PGH) 8,435
Coraopolis Heights (★PGH) 1,500
Cornwall (★LEB) 2,111
Cornwells Heights (★PHIL-) 8,200
Corry 7,435
Coudersport 2,831
Coulters (South Versailles) (★PGH) 558
Courtdale (★WLKS) 1,027
Crabtree 1,021
Crafton (★PGH) 8,233
Cranesville 705
Creighton (East Deer) (★PGH) 2,081
Cresson 2,446
Cressona (★PTSVL) 1,814
Croydon (★PHIL-) 9,800
Crum Creek Manor (★PHIL-) 900
Crum Lynne (★PHIL-) 3,700
Cuddy (★PGH) 1,400
Cumberland Park (★HRBG) 2,000
Curtisville (★PGH) 1,337
Curwensville 3,189
Daisytown 1,400
Dale (★JNST) 2,274
Dallas (★WLKS) 2,913
Dallastown (★YORK) 3,560
Dalton (★SCR) 1,282
Danville 6,176
Danville East (Mechanicsville) 2,046
Darby (★PHIL-) 13,729
Dauphin (★HRBG) 998
Davidson Heights (★PGH) 2,000
Davisville (★PHIL-) 1,600
Dawson 676
Dawson Ridge (★PGH) 1,200
Dayton 715
Deemston 711
Delaware Water Gap 533
Delmont (New Salem) (★PGH) 1,934
Delta 778
Denver 2,248
Derry 3,338
Deshon Manor 1,500
Devon (★PHIL-) 4,500
Dickson City (★SCR) 7,698
Dillsburg (★HRBG) 1,441
Dixonville 900
Donaldson (Frailey) 570
Donora (★MNSN-) 8,825
Dormont (★PGH) 12,856
Dover 1,168
Downingtown (★COAT) 7,437
Doylestown (★PHIL-) 8,270
Dravosburg (★PGH) 2,916
Dresher (★PHIL-) 1,000
Drexel Hill (★PHIL-) 31,000
Drexel Plaza (★PHIL-) 1,000
Dublin (★PHIL-) 657

Du Bois 10,112
Duboistown (★WMSPT) 1,468
Dunbar 1,499
Duncannon (★HRBG) 1,739
Duncansville (★ALT) 1,427
Dunlo 950
Dunmore (★SCR) 17,300
Dupont (★WLKS) 3,431
Duquesne (★PGH) 11,410
Duryea (★SCR) 5,264
Dushore 718
Eagleville (★PHIL-) 1,000
East Bangor 905
East Berlin 1,086
East Berwick 2,090
East Brady 1,218
East Butler (★BUTL) 919
East Faxon (★WMSPT) 4,175
East Greenville 2,003
East Lansdowne (★PHIL-) 3,186
East Lawn (★AL-B-E) 800
East McKeesport (★PGH) 3,233
East Norriton (★PHIL-) 11,837
Easton (★★AL-B-E) 30,256
East Petersburg (★LANC) 3,407
East Pittsburgh (★PGH) 3,006
East Prospect 547
East Rochester (★PGH) 920
East Springfield 593
East Stroudsburg 7,984
East Uniontown (★UNTN) 2,333
East Vandergrift 1,167
East Washington (★WASH) 2,198
East York (★YORK) 8,000
Ebensburg 4,318
Economy (★PGH) 7,176
Eddystone (★PGH) 2,706
Edgely (★PHIL-) 1,600
Edgewood (★PGH) 5,138
Edgewood (*Northumberland co.*) 3,186
Edgeworth (★PGH) 2,200
Edinboro 4,871
Edwardsville (★WLKS) 5,633
Egypt (★AL-B-E) 2,200
Eldred 1,092
Elim (★JNST) 1,200
Elizabeth (★PGH) 2,273
Elizabethtown (★HRBG) 8,072
Elizabethville 1,629
Elkins Park (★PHIL-) 10,000
Elkland 1,942
Ellport 1,350
Ellsworth 1,268
Ellwood City 10,857
Elmhurst (★SCR) 799
Elmora (Bakerton) 950
Elverson 509
Elwyn (★PHIL-) 1,500
Elysburg 1,337
Emlenton 854
Emmaus (★AL-B-E) 11,511
Emporium 3,074
Emsworth (★PGH) 3,345
Enhaut (★HRBG) 2,000
Enola (★HRBG) 7,000
Ephrata 9,662
Erdenheim (★PHIL-) 3,700
Erie (★225,900; ERIE) 129,231
Erlen (★PHIL-) 1,000
Espy 1,652
Essington (★PHIL-) 2,900
Etna (★PGH) 5,819
Etters (Goldsboro) (★HRBG) 576
Evans City (Evansburg) (★BUTL) 2,144
Everett 2,243
Everson 1,143
Exeter (★WLKS) 4,670
Export (★PGH) 1,402
Exton (★PHIL-) 2,000
Factoryville (★SCR) 922
Fairchance (★UNTN) 1,906
Fairdale 1,621
Fairfield (★ERIE) 900
Fairfield (*Adams co.*) 547
Fairhope (★MNSN-) 2,500
Fairless Hills (★PHIL-) 12,000
Fairoaks (Leet) (★PGH) 1,646
Fairview (*Northumberland co.*) 2,023
Fairview (★ERIE) 1,707
Fairview Knolls (★AL-B-E) 1,000
Falls Creek 1,255
Fallston (★PGH) 571
Farrell (★SHAR) 11,022
Faxon (★WMSPT) 1,946
Fayette City (★MNSN-) 968
Fayetteville 2,449
Feasterville (★PHIL-) 10,400
Fellsburg (★MNSN-) 1,092
Ferndale (★JNST) 2,482
Ferndale (*Northumberland co.*) 1,700
Fern Village (★PHIL-) 800
Fernway (★PGH) 1,200
Fisher Heights (★MNSN-) 1,000
Fleetwood 3,064
Flemington 1,519
Flourtown (★PHIL-) 5,000
Folcroft (★PHIL-) 9,610
Folsom (★PHIL-) 7,000
Ford City 4,749
Ford Cliff 526
Forest City 2,322
Forest Grove (★PGH) 2,500
Forest Hills (★PGH) 9,561
Fort Washington (★PHIL-) 4,000
Forty Fort (★WLKS) 6,114
Fountain Hill (★AL-B-E) 5,384
Fox Chapel (★PGH) 4,684
Fox Chase Hills (★PHIL-) 1,000
Frackville 5,445
Franklin (★JNST) 864
Franklin (*Venango co.*) 8,629
Franklin Park (★PGH) 5,310
Frazer (★PHIL-) 2,000
Fredericktown 1,067
Fredonia 731
Freeburg 636
Freedom (★PGH) 2,643
Freeland (★HAZ) 4,784

Freemansburg (★AL-B-E) 1,681
Freeport (★PGH) 2,375
Friedens 900
Fulmor Heights (★PHIL-) 1,200
Galeton 1,552
Gallitzin 2,496
Gap 1,022
Garden City (★PHIL-) 2,000
Garden View (★WMSPT) 2,662
Garrett 616
Geistown (★JNST) 3,633
Gettysburg 7,275
Gibsonia (★PGH) 2,065
Gilberton 1,293
Girard (★ERIE) 2,613
Girardville 2,450
Gladwyne (★PHIL-) 3,800
Glassport (★PGH) 7,450
Glendon (★AL-B-E) 637
Glen Lyon 3,408
Glen Moore (★LANC) 1,000
Glenolden (★PHIL-) 8,697
Glen Riddle (★PHIL-) 800
Glen Rock 1,600
Glenshaw (★PGH) 18,000
Glenside (★PHIL-) 17,500
Glenwillard (★PGH) 1,300
Gordon 856
Grampian 511
Grandview Heights (★LANC) 2,600
Grangeville (★HANV) 1,100
Grapeville (★PGH) 1,200
Gratz 675
Great Bend 826
Greencastle 3,293
Green Lane (★PHIL-) 543
Green Ridge (★PHIL-) 2,500
Greensburg (★PGH) 15,870
Green Tree (★PHIL-) 1,000
Green Tree (★PGH) 6,441
Greenville 8,704
Greenwood (★ALT) 2,000
Gringo (★PGH) 900
Grove City 8,312
Groveton (★PGH) 1,000
Gunnison Acres (★AL-B-E) 900
Halifax 907
Hallstead 1,447
Hamburg 3,909
Hamilton Park (★LANC) 3,500
Hanover (★41,900; HANV) 15,623
Hanover Green (★WLKS) 1,000
Harford Heights (★PGH) 900
Harleysville (★PHIL-) 1,448
Harmarville (★PGH) 1,300
Harmony 1,207
Harrisburg (★355,100; HRBG) 68,061
Harrison City (★PGH) 950
Harrisville 944
Harveys Lake 1,693
Harwick (★PGH) 1,200
Hastings 1,791
Hatboro (★PHIL-) 8,880
Hatfield (★PHIL-) 2,385
Haverford (★PHIL-) 7,000
Havertown (★PHIL-) 36,500
Hawley 1,331
Hawthorn 552
Hazleton (★65,900; HAZ) 30,426
Heidelberg (★PGH) 2,034
Hellam (Hallam) (★YORK) 1,825
Hellertown (★AL-B-E) 6,613
Herminie (★PGH) 2,000
Herndon 507
Hershey (★HRBG) 7,407
Hickory Township (★SHAR) 15,399
Highcliff (★PGH) 1,300
Highland Park (★HRBG) 2,100
Highland Park (*Mifflin co.*) 1,704
Highland Park (★AL-B-E) 1,300
High Spire (Highspire) (★HRBG) 2,947
Hiller 1,688
Hillsville 915
Hokendauqua (★AL-B-E) 2,500
Holland (★PHIL-) 3,500
Hollidaysburg (★ALT) 6,262
Hollsopple (★JNST) 900
Hollywood (★PHIL-) 2,000
Holmes (★PHIL-) 3,000
Homeacre (★BUTL) 2,500
Homer City 2,465
Homestead (★PGH) 6,309
Hometown 1,013
Honesdale 5,224
Honey Brook (★COAT) 1,115
Hooversville 962
Hopwood (★UNTN) 2,190
Horsham (★PHIL-) 8,000
Houston (★PGH) 1,812
Houtzdale 1,193
Howard 751
Hudson (★WLKS) 900
Hughestown (★WLKS) 1,407
Hughesville 2,249
Hulmeville (★PHIL-) 908
Hummelstown (★HRBG) 4,723
Huntingdon 6,987
Huntingdon Valley (★PHIL-) 9,700
Hyde Park (★PGH) 2,700
Hyde Villa (★READ) 1,500
Hyde Park 729
Hydetown 725
Hyndman 1,151
Imperial (★PGH) 2,385
Indiana 16,100
Industry (★E.LIV) 2,442
Ingomar (★PGH) 1,000
Ingram (★PGH) 4,902
Inkerman (★WLKS) 1,000
Irvona 714
Irwin (★PGH) 4,059
Ivyland (★PHIL-) 600
Jacktown Acres (★PGH) 1,200
Jacobus (★YORK) 1,360
Jamestown 937
Jeannette (★PGH) 15,209
Jefferson (★PGH) 8,512
Jenkintown (★PHIL-) 5,990

Jennerstown 621
Jermyn (★SCR) 2,435
Jerome (★JNST) 1,158
Jersey Shore (★WMSPT) 5,322
Jessup (★SCR) 4,948
Jim Thorpe (Mauch Chunk) 5,456
Johnsonburg 4,304
Johnstown (★112,300; JNST) 42,476
Jones Terrace (★AL-B-E) 1,500
Jonestown (★LEB) 954
Juniata Terrace 733
Kane 5,001
Keiser (Marion Heights) 958
Kenhorst (★READ) 3,482
Kenmawr (★PGH) 5,000
Kennett Square (★PHIL-) 4,876
King of Prussia (Brandywine Village (★PHIL-) 11,411
Kingston (★WLKS) 18,325
Kingswood Park (★PHIL-) 1,700
Kirwan Heights (★PGH) 1,000
Kittanning 6,231
Kittanning Heights 1,347
Knox 1,306
Knoxville 698
Koppel (★PGH) 1,312
Kulpmont 4,026
Kutztown 4,166
Lafayette Hill (★PHIL-) 5,500
Lake City (★ERIE) 2,117
Lakemont (★ALT) 2,500
La Mott (★PHIL-) 1,500
Lancaster (★171,600; LANC) 57,690
Landis Farms (★LANC) 1,500
Landisville (★LANC) 2,000
Lanesboro 550
Langeloth 1,200
Langhorne (★PHIL-) 1,889
Langhorne Manor (★PHIL-) 1,505
Langhorne Terrace (★PHIL-) 2,000
Lansdale (★PHIL-) 18,451
Lansdowne (★PHIL-) 14,090
Lansford 5,168
Larimer (★PGH) 1,800
Larksville (★WLKS) 3,937
Latrobe 11,749
Laureldale (★READ) 4,519
Laurel Gardens (★PGH) 1,800
Laverock (★PHIL-) 1,500
Lawnton (★HRBG) 2,500
Lawrence (★PGH) 1,100
Lawrence Park (★ERIE) 4,517
Lawrenceville 605
Lawson Heights 3,000
Lebanon (★74,900; LEB) 28,572
Lebanon South (★LEB) 3,457
Leechburg 2,999
Leedon Estates (★PHIL-) 1,800
Lee Park (★WLKS) 3,500
Leesport (★READ) 1,158
Leetsdale (★PGH) 1,862
Lehighton (★AL-B-E) 6,095
Lemont (★STCOL) 2,547
Lemoyne (★HRBG) 4,625
Leola (★LANC) 1,500
Lester (★PHIL-) 1,500
Level Green (★PGH) 3,000
Levittown (★PHIL-) 76,865
Lewisburg 6,376
Lewis Run 756
Lewistown 11,098
Liberty (★PGH) 3,594
Library (★PGH) 4,200
Ligonier 2,258
Lilly 1,429
Lincoln 1,885
Lincoln Heights (★PGH) 1,500
Lincoln Park (★READ) 1,500
Lincoln Park (★PHIL-) 1,500
Lincoln University 900
Linesville 1,265
Linglestown (★HRBG) 3,000
Linntown 1,851
Linwood (Lower Chichester) (★PHIL-) 4,009
Lititz (★LANC) 7,072
Littlestown 3,026
Liverpool 847
Lock Haven 11,427
Loganville (★YORK) 921
Long Branch (★MNSN-) 582
Lorain (★JNST) 972
Loretto 1,661
Lower Burrell (★PGH) 13,654
Lucernemines (Lucerne) 1,380
Lucknow (★HRBG) 900
Luzerne (★WLKS) 4,504
Lykens 2,506
Lyndora (★BUTL) 5,700
Lynnewood Gardens (★PHIL-) 4,000
Lynnwood (★WLKS) 1,200
Lynnwood (★MNSN-) 1,600
Lyon Station 589
McAdoo (★HAZ) 3,326
McClure 1,094
McConnellsburg 1,228
McDonald (★PGH) 2,879
McGovern (★PGH) 1,500
McKeesport (★PGH) 37,977
McKees Rocks (★PGH) 11,901
McKnight Village (★PGH) 1,700
McMurray (★PGH) 1,500
McSherrystown 2,773
Macungie (★AL-B-E) 1,414
Mahanoy City 7,257
Malvern (★PHIL-) 2,583
Manchester (★YORK) 2,391
Manheim 5,434
Manor (★PGH) 2,276
Mansfield 4,114
Maple Glen (★PHIL-) 2,000
Mapleton Depot 661
Maplewood Park (★PHIL-) 1,800
Marcus Hook (★PHIL-) 3,041
Marianna 875
Marietta 2,838
Marion Hill (Pulaski) (★PGH) 2,126
Markvue Manor (★PGH) 1,400

Mars (★PGH) 1,488
Marshallton 1,802
Martinsburg 2,088
Marysville (★HRBG) 2,328
Masontown 4,226
Matamoras 2,244
Mayfield (★SCR) 2,176
Meadowbrook (★PHIL-) 1,800
Meadow Lands (★PGH) 1,500
Meadville 16,573
Mechanicsburg (★HRBG) 9,385
Mechanicsville (★PTSVL) 663
Media (★PHIL-) 6,444
Melrose Park (★PHIL-) 4,200
Mercer 2,773
Mercersburg 1,727
Meridian (★BUTL) 2,234
Merion Station (★PHIL-) 6,800
Meyersdale 2,648
Middleburg 1,369
Middleport 609
Middletown (★HRBG) 9,080
Midland (★★E.LIV-) 5,271
Midway (★PGH) 1,188
Midway (*Adams co.*) (★HANV) 1,636
Mifflin 640
Mifflinburg 2,607
Mifflintown 828
Mifflinville 1,074
Milesburg 1,196
Milford 1,190
Millbourne (★PHIL-) 637
Millcreek Township (★ERIE) 36,946
Miller Heights (★AL-B-E) 1,500
Millersburg 3,074
Millerstown 612
Millersville (★LANC) 6,396
Mill Hall 1,838
Millheim 871
Millsboro 950
Millvale (★PGH) 5,815
Millville 896
Milmont Park (★PHIL-) 3,000
Milroy 1,575
Milton 7,723
Minersville (★PTSVL) 6,012
Mocanaqua 950
Modena (★COAT) 867
Mohnton (★READ) 2,153
Monaca (★PGH) 7,486
Monessen (★63,200; MNSN-) 15,216
Moninger (★PGH) 900
Monongahela (★PGH) 7,113
Monroeton 627
Monroeville (★PGH) 29,011
Mont Alto 1,532
Mont Clare (★PHIL-) 1,274
Montgomery 1,902
Montoursville (★WMSPT) 5,985
Montrose (★READ) 1,500
Montrose (*Susquehanna co.*) 2,058
Montrose Hill (★PGH) 2,000
Moon Crest (★PGH) 2,000
Moon Run (★PGH) 1,500
Moosic (★SCR) 4,273
Moreland Manor (★PHIL-) 1,000
Morgan (★PGH) 1,000
Morrisville (*Greene co.*) 1,232
Morrisville (★PHIL-) 11,309
Morton (★PHIL-) 2,602
Moscow (★SCR) 1,430
Mountain Top (★WLKS) 1,800
Mount Allen (★HRBG) 900
Mount Carmel 9,317
Mount Holly Springs 2,009
Mount Jewett 1,060
Mount Joy 5,041
Mount Lebanon (★PGH) 39,596
Mount Nebo (★PGH) 1,000
Mount Oliver (★PGH) 5,487
Mount Penn (★READ) 3,465
Mount Pleasant 5,895
Mount Pocono 1,019
Mount Union 3,662
Mount Vernon (★PGH) 1,000
Mountville 1,454
Mount Wolf (★YORK) 1,811
Moylan (★PHIL-) 1,500
Muhlenberg Park (★READ) 1,000
Muncy 2,872
Munhall (★PGH) 16,574
Murrysville (★PGH) 1,000
Muse (★PGH) 1,358
Myerstown (★LEB) 3,645
Nanticoke (★WLKS) 14,632
Nanty Glo 4,298
Narberth (★PHIL-) 5,151
Natrona Heights (Harrison) (★PGH) 14,448
Nazareth (★AL-B-E) 5,815
Neffsville (★LANC) 1,300
Nemacolin 1,273
Nescopeck 1,897
Nesquehoning 3,338
Neville Island (Neville) (★PGH) 2,017
New Alexandria 690
New Beaver (★PGH) 1,426
New Berlin 821
New Berlinville 1,145
New Bethlehem 1,406
New Bloomfield (Bloomfield) 1,032
New Brighton (★PGH) 7,637
New Britain (★PHIL-) 2,428
New Castle (★72,800; NWCS) 38,559
New Castle Northwest (★NWCS) 1,974
New Castle West (★NWCS) 3,094
New Cumberland (★HRBG) 9,803
New Eagle (★PGH) 2,497
Newell 650
New Florence 929
New Freedom 1,495
New Galilee (★PGH) 624
New Holland 3,971
New Hope 978
New Kensington (★PGH) 20,312
Newmanstown 1,532

(Pennsylvania continued)

★ Population or designation of metropolitan area, including suburbs (see headnote).
▲ Population of entire "town" or township, including other communities and rural areas.
† Population is from a local census taken at date specified.

(Pennsylvania continued)

New Milford ... 1,143
New Oxford (*HANV) ... 1,495
New Philadelphia ... 1,528
Newport ... 1,747
Newportville (*PHIL-) ... 1,200
New Sheffield (*PGH) ... 1,500
New Stanton (*PGH) ... 1,793
Newtown (*PHIL-) ... 2,216
Newtown (*WLKS) ... 2,400
Newtown Square (Newtown) (*PHIL-) ... 11,081
Newville ... 1,631
New Wilmington ... 2,721
Nicholson ... 877
Norristown (*PHIL-) ... 38,169
Northampton (*AL-B-E) ... 8,389
North Apollo ... 1,618
North Belle Vernon (*MNSN-) ... 2,916
North Braddock (*PGH) ... 10,838
North Catasauqua (*AL-B-E) ... 2,941
North Charleroi (*MNSN-) ... 1,964
North East (*ERIE) ... 3,846
North Hills (*PHIL-) ... 5,000
North Irwin (*PGH) ... 1,306
Northumberland ... 4,102
North Vandergrift ... 1,000
North Versailles (*PGH) ... 13,400
North Wales (*PHIL-) ... 3,911
North Warren ... 1,360
North York (*YORK) ... 2,032
Norvelt (*PGH) ... 1,800
Norwood (*PHIL-) ... 7,229
Nottingham (*PHIL-) ... 2,900
Oakdale (*PGH) ... 2,136
Oakford (*PHIL-) ... 1,000
Oakland (*Lawrence co.*) (*NWCS) ... 2,135
Oakland (*Susquehanna co.*) ... 817
Oakleigh (*HRBG) ... 1,000
Oakmont (*PGH) ... 7,550
Oberlin (*HRBG) ... 2,500
Ogden (*PHIL-) ... 1,600
Ohioville (*E.LIV) ... 3,918
Oil City ... 15,033
Oklahoma ... 1,084
Old Forge (*SCR) ... 9,522
Old Orchard (*AL-B-E) ... 1,500
Oliver (*UNTN) ... 1,500
Olyphant (*SCR) ... 5,422
Orbisonia ... 554
Orchard Hills ... 1,300
Oreland (*PHIL-) ... 9,114
Orwigsburg (*PTSVL) ... 2,661
Osborne (*PGH) ... 579
Osceola Mills (Osceola) ... 1,671
Overbrook Hills (*PHIL-) ... 1,000
Oxford ... 3,658
Paint ... 1,233
Palmdale (*HRBG) ... 1,724
Palmer Heights (*AL-B-E) ... 1,500
Palmerton (*AL-B-E) ... 5,620
Palmyra (*HRBG) ... 7,615
Palo Alto (*PTSVL) ... 1,428
Paoli (*PHIL-) ... 7,000
Parker ... 843
Parkersburg (*COAT) ... 2,701
Parkland (*PHIL-) ... 1,200
Parkside (*PHIL-) ... 2,343
Parkview (*PGH) ... 1,000
Parkville (*HANV) ... 1,300
Parryville (*AL-B-E) ... 528
Patterson Heights (*PGH) ... 777
Patterson Township (*PGH) ... 3,442
Patton ... 2,762
Paxtang (*HRBG) ... 2,160
Peely (Warrior Run) (*WLKS) ... 816
Pen Argyl ... 3,668
Penbrook (*HRBG) ... 3,379
Penn (*PGH) ... 735
Penndel (*PHIL-) ... 2,248
Penn Hills (Penn) (*PGH) ... 62,886
Pennsburg ... 2,260
Pennside (*READ) ... 3,000
Penns Woods (*PGH) ... 900
Penn Valley (*PHIL-) ... 3,800
Pennville (*HANV) ... 1,100
Penn Wynne (*PHIL-) ... 4,000
Perkasie (*PHIL-) ... 5,451
Perrymount (*PGH) ... 900
Perryopolis (*PGH) ... 2,043
Perrysville (*PGH) ... 5,500
Petersburg ... 555
Philadelphia (*5,282,200; PHIL-) ... 1,950,098
Phillipsburg ... 3,700
Phoenixville (*PHIL-) ... 14,823
Picture Rocks ... 570
Pilgrim Gardens (*PHIL-) ... 10,000
Pine Grove ... 2,197
Pitcairn (*PGH) ... 4,741
Pittsburgh (*2,142,700; PGH) ... 520,117
Pittston (*WLKS) ... 11,113
Plains (*WLKS) ... 6,606
Pleasant Gap ... 1,773
Pleasant Hill (*LEB) ... 1,071
Pleasant Hills (*PGH) ... 10,409
Pleasant Unity (*PGH) ... 900
Pleasantville ... 1,005
Pleasureville (*YORK) ... 3,000
Plum (*PGH) ... 21,922
Plymouth (*WLKS) ... 9,536
Plymouth Meeting (*PHIL-) ... 4,000
Plymouth Valley (*PHIL-) ... 7,000
Plymptonville ... 1,040
Point Marion ... 1,750
Polk ... 3,673
Portage ... 4,151
Port Allegany ... 2,703
Port Carbon (*PTSVL) ... 2,717
Port Griffith (*WLKS) ... 1,500
Portland ... 612
Port Matilda ... 680
Port Royal ... 829
Port Vue (*PGH) ... 5,862
Pottstown (*60,200; PTSTN) ... 25,355
Pottsville (*57,400; PTSVL) ... 19,715
Pricedale (*MNSN-) ... 1,600
Primos (*PHIL-) ... 1,000
Pringle (*WLKS) ... 1,155
Progress (*HRBG) ... 4,800
Prospect (*BUTL) ... 973
Prospect Heights (*AL-B-E) ... 900
Prospect Park (Moore) (*PHIL-) ... 7,250
Punxsutawney ... 7,792
Quaker Hills (*LANC) ... 950
Quakertown ... 7,276
Quarryville ... 1,571
Radnor (*PHIL-) ... 1,000
Ramey ... 542
Rankin (*PGH) (†5/3/71) ... 3,550
Ranshaw ... 950
Reading (*204,100; READ) ... 87,643
Reamstown ... 1,050
Red Hill ... 1,201
Red Lion (*YORK) ... 5,645
Reedsville ... 950
Reiffton (*READ) ... 1,800
Renovo ... 2,620
Republic ... 1,500
Reserve Township (*PGH) ... 4,151
Reynoldsville ... 2,771
Richland ... 1,444
Richlandtown ... 856
Ridgway ... 6,022
Ridley Acres (*PHIL-) ... 900
Ridley Farms (*PHIL-) ... 1,500
Ridley Park (*PHIL-) ... 9,025
Ridley Parkview (*PHIL-) ... 1,400
Riegelsville (*AL-B-E) ... 1,050
Rillton (*PGH) ... 900
Rimersburg ... 1,146
Ringtown ... 880
Riverside (South Danville) ... 1,905
Roaring Spring ... 2,811
Robesonia ... 1,685
Rochester (*PGH) ... 4,819
Rochester Township) (*PGH) ... 4,089
Rockledge (*PHIL-) ... 2,564
Rockwood ... 1,051
Roscoe (*MNSN-) ... 1,176
Rosemont (*PHIL-) ... 4,000
Roseto ... 1,538
Rose Valley (*PHIL-) ... 1,349
Roslyn (*PHIL-) ... 10,000
Rosslyn Farms (Rosslyn) (*PGH) ... 608
Rossmoyne (*HRBG) ... 1,200
Rothsville (*LANC) ... 1,318
Rouseville ... 877
Rouzerville ... 1,419
Royalton (*HRBG) ... 1,040
Royersford (*PHIL-) ... 4,235
Rural Valley ... 962
Russellton (*PGH) ... 1,597
Rutherford Heights (*HRBG) ... 2,700
Rutledge (*PHIL-) ... 1,167
Rydal (*PHIL-) ... 2,000
Saegertown ... 1,348
St. Clair (*PTSVL) ... 4,576
St. Davids (*PHIL-) ... 1,500
St. Lawrence (*READ) ... 1,256
St. Marys ... 7,470
St. Michael ... 1,248
Salisbury ... 895
Saltsburg ... 1,037
Sandy ... 2,000
Sandy Lake ... 772
Sankertown ... 881
Saxonburg (*PGH) ... 1,191
Saxton ... 858
Sayre ... 7,473
Scalp Level ... 1,353
School Lane Hills (*LANC) ... 950
Schuylkill Haven (*PTSVL) ... 6,125
Schwenksville (*PHIL-) ... 809
Scottdale ... 5,818
Scott Township (*PGH) ... 21,856
Scranton (*225,500; SCR) ... 103,564
Secane (*PHIL-) ... 2,000
Selinsgrove ... 5,116
Sellersville (*PHIL-) ... 2,829
Seneca ... 980
Seven Valleys (*YORK) ... 688
Seward ... 746
Sewickley (*PGH) ... 5,660
Sewickley Heights (*PGH) ... 797
Shalecrest (*PGH) ... 1,000
Shamokin ... 11,719
Shamokin Dam ... 1,562
Sharon (*82,700; SHAR) ... 22,653
Sharon Hill (*PHIL-) ... 7,464
Sharpsburg (*PGH) ... 5,453
Sharpsville (*SHAR) ... 6,126
Shavertown (*WLKS) ... 1,500
Sheffield ... 1,564
Shenandoah ... 8,287
Shenandoah Heights ... 1,471
Shickshinny ... 1,685
Shillington (*READ) ... 6,249
Shiloh (*YORK) ... 3,000
Shinglehouse ... 1,320
Shippensburg ... 6,536
Shippenville ... 602
Shiremanstown (*HRBG) ... 1,773
Shoemakersville ... 1,427
Shrewsbury ... 1,716
Silverdale (*PHIL-) ... 545
Simpson ... 1,700
Sinking Spring (*READ) ... 2,862
Slatington (*AL-B-E) ... 4,687
Slickville (*PGH) ... 1,066
Sligo ... 825
Slippery Rock ... 4,949
Smethport ... 1,883
Smithfield (*Fayette co.*) ... 969
Smithfield (South Huntingdon) ... 2,488
Smithton (*PGH) ... 552
Smock ... 950
Snow Shoe ... 874
Somerset ... 6,269
Souderton (*PHIL-) ... 6,366
Southampton (*PHIL-) ... 9,000
South Bethlehem ... 500
South Coatesville (*COAT) ... 1,583
South Connellsville ... 2,385
South Fork ... 1,661
South Greensburg (*PGH) ... 3,288
South Heights ... 799
Southmont (*JNST) ... 2,653
South New Castle (*NWCS) ... 940
South Renovo ... 662
South Temple (*READ) ... 1,500
South Uniontown (*UNTN) ... 3,546
South Waverly ... 1,307
Southwest Greensburg (*PGH) ... 3,186
South Williamsport (*WMSPT) ... 7,153
Spangler ... 3,109
Speers (*MNSN-) ... 1,408
Springboro ... 584
Spring City (*PHIL-) ... 3,578
Springdale (*PGH) ... 5,202
Springfield (*PHIL-) ... 29,006
Spring Garden Township (*YORK) ... 12,443
Spring Grove (*YORK) ... 1,669
Spring House (*PHIL-) ... 900
Springmont (*READ) ... 1,000
Spry (*YORK) ... 3,000
Stanwood Gardens (*PHIL-) ... 1,000
Starjunction (*PGH) ... 1,150
State College (*52,200; STCOL) ... 33,778
Steelton (*HRBG) ... 8,556
Stewartstown (*YORK) ... 1,157
Stiles (*AL-B-E) ... 1,000
Stockdale (*MNSN-) ... 720
Stockertown (*AL-B-E) ... 753
Stoneboro ... 1,129
Stony Creek Mills (*READ) ... 2,800
Stowe (West Pottsgrove) (*PTSTN) ... 4,038
Stowe Township (*PGH) ... 10,119
Strabane (*PGH) ... 1,700
Stafford (*PHIL-) ... 3,000
Strasburg (*LANC) ... 1,897
Strattanville ... 559
Stroudsburg ... 5,451
Stroudsburg West ... 1,777
Sugar Creek ... 5,944
Sugargrove ... 701
Sugar Notch (*WLKS) ... 1,333
Summerdale (*HRBG) ... 1,500
Summerhill ... 726
Summerville ... 859
Summit Hill ... 3,811
Sunbury ... 13,025
Sunset Hills (*PGH) ... 900
Susquehanna (Susquehanna Depot) ... 2,319
Sutersville (*PGH) ... 830
Swarthmore (*PHIL-) ... 6,156
Swedeland ... 950
Swedesburg (*PHIL-) ... 950
Swissvale (*PGH) ... 13,819
Swoyerville (Swoyersville) (*WLKS) ... 6,786
Sykesville ... 1,311
Tamaqua ... 9,246
Tarentum (*PGH) ... 7,379
Tatamy (*AL-B-E) ... 891
Taylor (*SCR) ... 6,977
Telford (*PHIL-) ... 3,409
Temple (*READ) ... 1,667
Terre Hill ... 1,129
Tharptown (Uniontown) ... 950
Thompsontown ... 677
Thornburg (*PGH) ... 617
Thorndale (*COAT) ... 1,606
Throop (*SCR) ... 4,307
Tidioute ... 939
Tioga ... 624
Tionesta ... 711
Titusville ... 7,331
Tobyhanna ... 900
Topton (*AL-B-E) ... 1,744
Toughkenamon (*PHIL-) ... 900
Towanda ... 4,224
Tower City ... 1,774
Trafford (*PGH) ... 4,383
Trainer (*PHIL-) ... 2,336
Trappe (*PHIL-) ... 1,676
Tremont ... 1,833
Tresckow (*HAZ) ... 1,146
Trevorton ... 2,196
Trevose (*PHIL-) ... 5,500
Trevose Heights (*PHIL-) ... 1,500
Trooper (*PHIL-) ... 3,500
Troy ... 1,315
Trucksville (*WLKS) ... 1,000
Trumbauersville ... 831
Tullytown (*PHIL-) ... 2,194
Tunkhannock ... 2,251
Tunnelhill ... 508
Turbotville ... 627
Turtle Creek (*PGH) ... 8,308
Twin Oaks (*PHIL-) ... 1,600
Twin Rocks ... 950
Tyrone ... 7,072
Ulysses ... 590
Union City ... 3,631
Uniontown (*47,900; UNTN) ... 16,282
Uniontown North (*UNTN) ... 1,500
Upland (*PHIL-) ... 3,930
Upper Darby (*PHIL-) ... 43,500
Upper Saint Clair (*PGH) ... 15,457
Valley Forge Estates (*PHIL-) ... 1,200
Valley View ... 1,585
Vanderbilt ... 755
Vandergrift ... 7,873
Vandling ... 633
Vanport (Borough) (*PGH) ... 2,122
Verona (*PGH) ... 3,737
Versailles (*PGH) ... 2,754
Vestaburg ... 950
Village Green (*PHIL-) ... 1,000
Villanova (*PHIL-) ... 6,000
Vintondale ... 812
Wall (*PGH) ... 1,265
Wallingford (*PHIL-) ... 4,000
Walnutport (*AL-B-E) ... 1,942
Wampum (*PGH) ... 1,189
Warminster (*PHIL-) ... 34,900
Warren ... 12,998
Warrendale (*PGH) ... 800
Warrington (*PHIL-) ... 4,600
Washington (*47,900; WASH) ... 19,827
Washington North (*WASH) ... 2,855
Washington West (*WASH) ... 3,297
Waterford (*Erie) ... 1,468
Watsontown ... 2,514
Waymart ... 1,122
Wayne (*PHIL-) ... 8,200
Wayne Heights ... 1,005
Waynesboro ... 10,011
Waynesburg ... 5,152
Weatherly ... 2,554
Webster (*MNSN-) ... 950
Weigelstown (*YORK) ... 2,500
Weissport (*AL-B-E) ... 561
Wellsboro ... 4,003
Wernersville (*READ) ... 1,761
Wesleyville (*ERIE) ... 3,920
West Ambler (*PHIL-) ... 800
West Bridgewater (Bridgewater) (*PGH) ... 966
West Bristol (*PHIL-) ... 4,300
Westbrook Park (*PHIL-) ... 5,500
West Brownsville ... 1,426
West Catasauqua (*AL-B-E) ... 1,300
West Chester (*PHIL-) ... 19,301
West Conshohocken (*PHIL-) ... 2,194
West Easton (*AL-B-E) ... 1,123
West Elizabeth (*PGH) ... 848
West Fairview (*HRBG) ... 1,388
Westfield ... 1,273
West Grove (*PHIL-) ... 1,870
West Hazleton (*HAZ) ... 6,059
West Homestead (*PGH) ... 3,789
West Kittanning ... 956
West Lancaster (*LANC) ... 1,500
West Lawn (*READ) ... 1,973
West Lebanon (*LEB) ... 986
West Leechburg ... 1,422
West Manayunk (*PHIL-) ... 2,800
West Mayfield (*PGH) ... 2,152
West Middlesex (*SHAR) ... 1,293
West Mifflin (*PGH) ... 28,070
Westmont (*JNST) ... 6,673
Westmoreland City (*PGH) ... 1,200
West Nanticoke (*WLKS) ... 1,000
West Newton (*PGH) ... 3,648
West Norriton (*PHIL-) ... 12,546
Westover ... 501
West Pittston (*WLKS) ... 7,074
West Reading (*READ) ... 4,578
West View (*PGH) ... 8,312
Westwood (*JNST) ... 2,500
West Wyoming (WLKS) ... 3,659
West Wyomissing (*READ) ... 3,000
West York (*YORK) ... 5,314
Wheatland (*SHAR) ... 1,421
Wheatland Hills (*LANC) ... 1,200
Whitaker (*PGH) ... 1,797
Whitehall (*AL-B-E) ... 7,908
Whitehall (*PGH) ... 16,551
White Haven ... 2,134
White Oak (*PGH) ... 9,304
White Township (*PGH) ... 1,747
Whitfield (*READ) ... 2,000
Wickerham Manor (*PGH) ... 1,000
Wiconisco ... 1,236
Wilkes-Barre (*244,000; WLKS) ... 58,856
Wilkes-Barre Township (*WLKS) ... 3,535
Wilkinsburg (*PGH) ... 26,780
Wilkins Township (*PGH) ... 8,749
Williamsburg ... 1,704
Williamsport (*85,200; WMSPT) ... 37,918
Williamstown ... 1,919
Willow Grove (*PHIL-) ... 20,000
Wilmerding (*PGH) ... 3,218
Wilson (*AL-B-E) ... 8,482
Windber ... 6,332
Windgap (Wind Gap) ... 2,270
Windsor (*YORK) ... 1,298
Wolfdale (*Wash) ... 1,202
Womelsdorf ... 1,551
Woodland ... 1,264
Woodland View (*YORK) ... 2,500
Woodlyn (*PHIL-) ... 6,000
Wormleysburg (*HRBG) ... 3,192
Worthington ... 816
Wrightsville ... 2,668
Wyalusing ... 723
Wyncote (*PHIL-) ... 6,000
Wyndmoor (*PHIL-) ... 5,800
Wynnewood (*PHIL-) ... 7,500
Wyoming (*WLKS) ... 4,195
Wyomissing (*READ) ... 7,136
Wyomissing Hills (*READ) ... 1,744
Yardley (*PHIL-) ... 2,616
Yeadon (*PHIL-) ... 12,136
Yeagertown ... 1,363
Yoe (*YORK) ... 790
York (*177,500; YORK) ... 50,335
York Haven (*HRBG) ... 671
Youngsville ... 2,158
Youngwood (*PGH) ... 3,057
Yukon (*PGH) ... 1,100
Zelienople ... 3,602

RHODE ISLAND

1970 C ... 949,723

Counties

Bristol ... 45,937
Kent ... 142,382
Newport ... 94,228
Providence ... 581,470
Washington ... 85,706

Cities

Allenton (*PROV-) ... 900
Anthony (*PROV-) ... 5,000
Ashaway (*N.LON-) ... 1,559
Ashton (*PROV-) ... 2,000
Barrington (*PROV-) (17,554▲) ... 13,500
Berkeley (*PROV-) ... 2,000
Block Island (New Shoreham) ... 489
Bradford (*N-LON-) ... 1,333
Bristol (*PROV-) ... 17,860
Burrillville (*PROV-) (10,087▲) ...
Central Falls (*PROV-) ... 18,716
Charlestown (2,863▲) ... 600
Coventry (*PROV-) (22,947▲) ... 6,500
Cranston (*PROV-) ... 74,287
Cumberland (*PROV-) (26,605▲) ...
Cumberland Hill (*PROV-) ... 3,000
Diamond Hill (*PROV-) ... 1,700
East Greenwich (*PROV-) ... 9,577
East Providence (*PROV-) ... 48,207
Esmond (*PROV-) ... 4,500
Exeter (3,245▲) ... 100
Foster (Foster Center) (2,626▲) ... 125
Glocester (*PROV-) (5,160▲) ...
Greenville (*PROV-) ... 3,000
Hamilton (*PROV-) ... 900
Harris (*PROV-) ... 1,500
Harrisville (*PROV-) ... 1,053
Hope Valley ... 1,326
Hopkinton (*N.LON-) (5,392▲) ... 100
Island Park (*NWPT) ... 1,350
Jamestown (*PROV-) ... 2,911
Johnston (*PROV-) ... 22,037
Kingston ... 5,601
La Fayette (*PROV-) ... 900
Lincoln (*PROV-) (16,182▲) ...
Little Compton (*F.R.) (2,385▲) ... 250
Lonsdale (*PROV-) ... 5,500
Manville (*PROV-) ... 3,500
Middletown (*NWPT) ... 29,290
Narragansett (Narragansett Pier) (7,138▲) ... 2,686
Newport (*76,700; NWPT) ... 34,562
North Kingstown (Wickford) (*PROV-) (29,793▲) ... 4,500
North Providence (*PROV-) ... 24,337
North Smithfield (*PROV-) (9,349▲) ...
Pascoag (*PROV-) ... 3,132
Pawtucket (**PROV-) ... 76,984
Peace Dale ... 3,000
Portsmouth (*NWPT) (12,521▲) ... 3,000
Providence (*892,800; PROV-) ... 179,116
Quidnick (*PROV-) ... 3,000
Richmond (2,625▲) ...
Saylesville (*PROV-) ... 3,200
Scituate (*PROV-) (7,489▲) ...
Slatersville (*PROV-) ... 2,000
Smithfield (*PROV-) (13,468▲) ...
South Kingstown (*PROV-) (16,913▲) ...
Tiverton (*F.R.) (12,559▲) ... 7,500
Union Village (*PROV-) ... 1,500
Valley Falls (*PROV-) ... 7,000
Wakefield ... 3,300
Warren (*PROV-) ... 10,523
Warwick (*PROV-) ... 83,694
West Barrington (*PROV-) ... 4,000
Westerly (*N.LON-) (17,248▲) ... 13,654
West Warwick (*PROV-) ... 24,323
Woonsocket (**PROV-) ... 46,820
Yorktown Manor (*PROV-) ... 900

SOUTH CAROLINA

1970 C ... 2,590,516

Counties

Abbeville ... 21,112
Aiken ... 91,023
Allendale ... 9,692
Anderson ... 105,474
Bamberg ... 15,950
Barnwell ... 17,176
Beaufort ... 51,136
Berkeley ... 56,199
Calhoun ... 10,780
Charleston ... 247,650
Cherokee ... 36,791
Chester ... 29,811
Chesterfield ... 33,667
Clarendon ... 25,604
Colleton ... 27,622
Darlington ... 53,442
Dillon ... 28,838
Dorchester ... 32,276
Edgefield ... 15,692
Fairfield ... 19,999
Florence ... 89,636
Georgetown ... 33,500
Greenville ... 240,546
Greenwood ... 49,686
Hampton ... 15,878
Horry ... 69,992
Jasper ... 11,885
Kershaw ... 34,727
Lancaster ... 43,328
Laurens ... 49,713
Lee ... 18,323
Lexington ... 89,012
McCormick ... 7,955
Marion ... 30,270
Marlboro ... 27,151
Newberry ... 29,273
Oconee ... 40,728
Orangeburg ... 69,789
Pickens ... 58,956
Richland ... 233,868
Saluda ... 14,528
Spartanburg ... 173,724
Sumter ... 79,425
Union ... 29,230
Williamsburg ... 34,243
York ... 85,216

Cities

Abbeville ... 5,515
Aiken ... 13,436
Aiken West ... 2,689
Allendale ... 3,620
Anderson (*57,600; AND) ... 27,556
Andrews ... 2,879
Appleton Mills (*AND) ... 900
Arcadia (*SPRT) ... 1,885
Arcadia Lakes (*COL) ... 741
Ardincaple (*COL) ... 726
Ariail (*GRNV) ... 1,150

* Population or designation of metropolitan area, including suburbs (see headnote).
▲ Population of entire "town" or township, including other communities and rural areas.
† Population is from a local census taken at date specified.

Arkwright (*SPRT) 1,300
Arthurtown (*COL) 1,500
Aynor 536
Bamberg 3,406
Barnwell 4,439
Batesburg 4,036
Bath (*AUG) 1,576
Beaufort 9,434
Belton 5,257
Belvedere (*AUG) 3,500
Bendale (*COL) 1,500
Bennettsville 7,468
Berea (*GRNV) 7,186
Bethune 506
Bishopville 3,404
Blacksburg 1,977
Blackville 2,395
Bluffton 529
Bowman 1,095
Branchville 1,011
Brandon (*GRNV) 2,200
Breeze Hill (*AUG) 950
Brooklyn 2,000
Brunson 559
Buffalo 1,461
Calhoun Falls 2,234
Camden 8,532
Campobello 530
Capitol View (*COL) 1,000
Carlisle 670
Cayce (*COL) 9,967
Central 1,550
Charleston (*280,000; CHAS) 66,945
Cheraw 5,627
Cherokee Forest (*GRNV) 2,000
Chesnee 1,069
Chester 7,045
Chesterfield 1,667
City View (*GRNV) 2,497
Clearwater (*AUG) 4,000
Clemson 5,578
Clifton (*SPRT) 900
Clinton 8,138
Clio 936
Clover 3,506
Columbia (*284,100; COL) 113,542
Conway 8,151
Cowpens (*SPRT) 2,109
Cross Hill 579
Darlington 6,990
Denmark 3,571
Denny Terrace (*COL) 2,000
Dentsville (*COL) 2,700
Dillon 6,735
Doneraile 1,417
Drayton (*SPRT) 1,400
Due West 1,380
Duncan (*SPRT) 1,266
Dunean (*GRNV) 3,000
Dupont (*CHAS) 4,600
Easley (*GRNV) 11,175
East Gaffney 3,750
East Gantt (*GRNV) 2,000
East Greer 1,000
Eastover 817
Edgefield 2,750
Estill 1,954
Evergreen Hills (*AND) 1,300
Fairfax 1,937
Fairforest (*SPRT) 900
Florence (*47,500; FLO) 25,997
Folly Beach (*CHAS) 1,157
Forest Acres (*COL) 6,808
Fort Lawn 510
Fort Mill 4,505
Fountain Inn 3,391
Gaffney 13,253
Gantt (*GRNV) 900
Georgetown 10,449
Gloverville (*AUG) 1,682
Gooches 1,300
Goose Creek (*CHAS) 3,656
Graniteville (*AUG) 2,464
Gray Court 859
Great Falls 2,727
Greeleyville 542
Greenview (*COL) 4,000
Greenville (*232,800; GRNV) 61,436
Greenwood 21,069
Greer 10,642
Hampton 2,845
Hampton Heights (*GRNV) 1,800
Hanahan (*CHAS) 8,376
Hardeeville 853
Harleyville 704
Hartsville 8,017
Hayne (*SPRT) 1,200
Heath Springs 955
Hemingway 1,026
Holly Hill 1,178
Homeland Park (*AND) 3,600
Honea Path 3,707
Industrial (*RKHL) 900
Inman (*SPRT) 1,661
Inman Mills (*SPRT) 1,811
Irmo (*COL) 517
Irwin 1,424
Isle of Palms (*CHAS) 2,657
Iva 1,114
Jackson 1,928
James Island (*CHAS) 13,500
Jefferson 709
Joanna 1,631
Johnsonville 1,267
Johnston 2,552
Jonesville 1,447
Judson (*GRNV) 4,000
Judson No. 2 (*GRNV) 1,000
Kathwood (*COL) 2,000
Kershaw 1,818
Kingstree 3,381
Ladson (*CHAS) 3,000
Lake City 6,247
Lake Forest (*GRNV) 1,200
Lake View 949
Lamar 1,250
Lancaster 9,186
Lando 850
Landrum 1,859
Lane 517
Langley (*AUG) 1,400
Latta 1,764
Laurel Bay 4,490
Laurens 10,298
Leesville 1,907
Lexington (*COL) 969
Liberty 2,860
Lincolnville (*CHAS) 504
Loris 1,741
Lugoff 1,500
Lydia Mills 950
Lyman (*SPRT) 1,159
Lynchburg 546
McBee 592
McColl 2,524
Manning 4,025
Marietta 1,000
Marion 7,435
Mauldin (*GRNV) 3,797
Mayesville (*SUMT) 757
Monarch (Monarch Mills) 1,726
Moncks Corner 2,314
Montmorenci 900
Mount Pleasant (*CHAS) 6,691
Mullins 6,006
Myrtle Beach 9,035
Newberry 9,218
New Ellenton 2,546
New Town 900
Nichols 549
Ninety Six 2,166
Norris 757
North 1,076
North Augusta (*AUG) 12,883
North Charleston (*CHAS) 78,000
North Hartsville 1,485
North Myrtle Beach 1,957
Norway 579
Olanta 640
Olympia (*COL) 2,000
Orangeburg 13,252
Orrville (*AND) 1,800
Pacolet 1,418
Pacolet Mills 1,504
Pageland 2,122
Pamplico 1,068
Paris (*GRNV) 1,000
Park Place (*GRNV) 2,500
Pelzer (unincorporated) 2,100
Pendleton (*AND) 2,615
Pickens (*GRNV) 2,954
Piedmont 2,242
Pineridge (*COL) 633
Pinewood 687
Poe (*GRNV) 900
Poovey Estate 1,000
Port Royal 2,865
Prosperity 762
Quinby (*FLO) 788
Ravenel 931
Ridgeland 1,165
Ridge Spring 644
Ridgeville 563
Ridgewood (*COL) 1,700
Riverside (*GRNV) 2,200
Rock Hill (*51,100; RKHL) 33,846
Roebuck (*SPRT) 800
St. Andrews (*CHAS) 5,500
St. Andrews (*COL) 5,000
St. George 1,806
St. Matthews 2,403
St. Stephen (St. Stephens) 1,506
Saluda 2,442
Sans Souci (*GRNV) 4,500
Saxon (*SPRT) 1,100
Scranton 732
Sellers 561
Seneca 6,382
Shannontown (*SUMT) 7,491
Simpsonville (*GRNV) 3,308
Socaste 900
Society Hill 806
South Congaree (*COL) 1,434
Southern Shops (*SPRT) 2,864
Spartanburg (*125,000; SPRT) 44,546
Springdale (*COL) 2,638
Springfield 724
Startex (*SPRT) 1,203
Sullivans Island (*CHAS) 1,426
Summerton 1,305
Summerville (*CHAS) 3,839
Sumter (*66,500; SUMT) 24,555
Sunnyside 1,000
Surfside Beach 1,329
Swansea 691
Taylors (*GRNV) 6,831
Timmonsville 2,246
Travelers Rest (*GRNV) 2,241
Una (*SPRT) 2,000
Union 10,775
Union Bleachery (*GRNV) 2,000
Utica 1,218
Varnville 1,555
Wagener 723
Walhalla 3,662
Walterboro 6,257
Ware Shoals 2,480
Warrenville (*AUG) 1,059
Welcome (*GRNV) 1,600
Wellford (*SPRT) 1,298
West Columbia (*COL) 7,838
Westminster 2,521
West Pelzer 861
West View (*SPRT) 1,105
Westville (*GRNV) 2,000
Whitmire 2,226
Whitney (*SPRT) 1,100
Williamston 3,991
Williston 2,594
Windy Hill (*FLO) 1,671
Winnsboro 3,411
Winnsboro Mills 2,312
Woodfield (*COL) 3,000
Woodruff 4,576
Yemassee 745
York 5,081

SOUTH DAKOTA

1970 C 666,257

Counties

Aurora 4,183
Beadle 20,877
Bennett 3,088
Bon Homme 8,577
Brookings 22,158
Brown 36,920
Brule 5,870
Buffalo 1,739
Butte 7,825
Campbell 2,866
Charles Mix 9,994
Clark 5,515
Clay 12,923
Codington 19,140
Corson 4,994
Custer 4,698
Davison 17,319
Day 8,713
Deuel 5,686
Dewey 5,170
Douglas 4,569
Edmunds 5,548
Fall River 7,505
Faulk 3,893
Grant 9,005
Gregory 6,710
Haakon 2,802
Hamlin 5,520
Hand 5,883
Hanson 3,781
Harding 1,855
Hughes 11,632
Hutchinson 10,379
Hyde 2,515
Jackson 1,531
Jerauld 3,310
Jones 1,882
Kingsbury 7,657
Lake 11,456
Lawrence 17,453
Lincoln 11,761
Lyman 4,060
McCook 7,246
McPherson 5,022
Marshall 5,965
Meade 17,020
Mellette 2,420
Miner 4,454
Minnehaha 95,209
Moody 7,622
Pennington 59,349
Perkins 4,769
Potter 4,449
Roberts 11,678
Sanborn 3,697
Shannon 8,198
Spink 10,595
Stanley 2,457
Sully 2,362
Todd 6,606
Tripp 8,171
Turner 9,872
Union 9,643
Walworth 7,842
Washabaugh 1,389
Yankton 19,039
Ziebach 2,221

Cities

Aberdeen 26,476
Alcester 627
Alexandria 598
Arlington 954
Armour 925
Avon 610
Belle Fourche 4,236
Beresford 1,655
Big Stone City 631
Bowdle 667
Box Elder (*RAP) 607
Brandon (*SXFL) 1,431
Bridgewater 633
Britton 1,465
Brookings 13,717
Bryant 502
Burke 892
Canistota 636
Canton 2,665
Castlewood 523
Centerville 910
Chamberlain 2,626
Clark 1,356
Clear Lake 1,157
Colton 601
Corsica 615
Custer 1,597
Deadwood 2,409
Dell Rapids 1,991
De Smet 1,336
Dupree 523
Eagle Butte 530
Edgemont 1,174
Elk Point 1,372
Elkton 541
Estelline 624
Eureka 1,547
Faith 576
Faulkton 955
Flandreau 2,027
Fort Pierre 1,448
Freeman 1,357
Garretson 847
Gettysburg 1,915
Gregory 1,756
Groton 1,021
Hartford 800
Herreid 672
Highmore 1,173
Hot Springs 4,434
Hoven 671
Howard 1,175
Huron 14,299
Ipswich 1,187
Kadoka 815
Keystone 500
Kimball 825
Lake Andes 948
Lake Preston 812
Lead 5,420
Lemmon 1,997
Lennox 1,487
Leola 787
McCook Lake (McCook) (*SXCY) 500
McIntosh 563
McLaughlin 863
Madison 6,315
Marion 844
Martin 1,248
Menno 796
Milbank 3,727
Miller 2,148
Mission 739
Mitchell 13,425
Mobridge 4,545
Murdo 865
Newell 664
North Eagle Butte 1,351
North Shore 400
North Sioux City (*SXCY) 860
Onida 785
Parker 1,005
Parkston 1,611
Philip 983
Pickstown 400
Pierre 9,699
Plankinton 613
Platte 1,351
Presho 922
Rapid City (*59,800; RAP) 43,836
Redfield 2,943
Renel Heights (*RAP) 1,300
Salem 1,391
Scotland 984
Selby 957
Sioux Falls (*81,800; SXFL) 72,488
Sisseton 3,094
Skyway (*RAP) 1,400
Spearfish 4,661
Springfield 1,566
Sturgis 4,536
Timber Lake 625
Tripp 851
Tyndall 1,245
Valley Springs 566
Vermillion 9,128
Viborg 662
Volga 982
Wagner 1,655
Wall 786
Watertown 13,388
Waubay 696
Webster 2,252
Wessington Springs 1,300
White River 617
Whitewood 689
Wilmot 518
Winner 3,789
Woonsocket 852
Yankton 11,919

TENNESSEE

1970 C 3,924,164

Counties

Anderson 60,300
Bedford 25,039
Benton 12,126
Bledsoe 7,643
Blount 63,744
Bradley 50,686
Campbell 26,045
Cannon 8,467
Carroll 25,741
Carter 43,259
Cheatham 13,199
Chester 9,927
Claiborne 19,420
Clay 6,624
Cocke 25,283
Coffee 32,572
Crockett 14,402
Cumberland 20,733
Davidson 447,877
Decatur 9,457
De Kalb 11,151
Dickson 21,977
Dyer 30,427
Fayette 22,692
Fentress 12,593
Franklin 27,244
Gibson 47,871
Giles 22,138
Grainger 13,948
Greene 47,630
Grundy 10,631
Hamblen 38,696
Hamilton 254,236
Hancock 6,719
Hardeman 22,435
Hardin 18,212
Hawkins 33,726
Haywood 19,596
Henderson 17,291
Henry 23,749
Hickman 12,096
Houston 5,845
Humphreys 13,560
Jackson 8,141
Jefferson 24,940
Johnson 11,569
Knox 276,293
Lake 7,896
Lauderdale 20,271
Lawrence 29,097
Lewis 6,761
Lincoln 24,318
Loudon 24,266
McMinn 35,462
McNairy 18,369
Macon 12,315
Madison 65,727
Marion 20,577
Marshall 17,319
Maury 44,028
Meigs 5,219
Monroe 23,475
Montgomery 62,721
Moore 3,568
Morgan 13,619
Obion 29,936
Overton 14,866
Perry 5,238
Pickett 3,774
Polk 11,669
Putnam 35,487
Rhea 17,202
Roane 38,881
Robertson 29,102
Rutherford 59,428
Scott 14,762
Sequatchie 6,331
Sevier 28,241
Shelby 722,014
Smith 12,509
Stewart 7,319
Sullivan 127,329
Sumner 56,106
Tipton 28,001
Trousdale 5,155
Unicoi 15,254
Union 9,072
Van Buren 3,758
Warren 26,972
Washington 73,924
Wayne 12,365
Weakley 28,827
White 16,355
Williamson 34,330
Wilson 36,999

Cities

Adamsville 1,344
Alamo 2,499
Alcoa (*KNOX-) 7,739
Alexandria 680
Algood 1,808
Allardt 610
Altamont 546
Ardmore 601
Arlington 1,349
Ashland City (*NASH) 2,027
Athens 11,790
Atwood 937
Bartlett (*MEM) 1,150
Baxter 1,229
Beersheba Springs 560
Bells 1,474
Bemis (*JAC) 1,883
Benton 749
Berry's Chapel (*NASH) 1,345
Bethel Springs 781
Big Sandy 539
Bloomingdale (*KNGSP) 8,000
Blount Hills (*KNOX-) 900
Bluff City (*BRIS-) 985
Bolivar 6,674
Bradford 968
Brentwood (*NASH) 4,099
Brighton 952
Bristol (*65,800; BRIS-) 20,064
Brownsville 7,011
Bruceton 1,450
Bullsgap 774
Byrdstown 582
Calhoun 624
Camden 3,052
Carthage 2,491
Caryville 648
Celina 1,370
Centerville 2,592
Chapel Hill 752
Charleston 792
Charlotte 610
Chattanooga (*311,100; CHTN) 119,082
Church Hill (*KNGSP) 2,822
Clarksville (*64,500; CLRKV) 31,719
Cleveland 20,651
Cleveland South (South Cleveland) 5,070
Clifton 737
Clinton (*KNOX-) 4,794
Coalmont 518
Collegedale (*CHTN) 3,031
Collierville (*MEM) 3,651
Collinwood 922
Colonial Heights (*KNGSP) 3,021
Columbia 21,471
Cookeville 14,270
Copperhill 563
Cornersville 655
Covington 5,801
Cowan 1,772
Crossville 5,381
Cumberland City (†1971) 564
Dandridge 1,270
Dayton 4,361
Decatur 698
Decaturville 958
Decherd 2,148
Dickson 5,665
Dover 1,179
Doyle 472
Dresden 1,939
Ducktown 562
Dunlap 1,672
Dyer 2,501
Dyersburg 14,523
Eagleton Village (*KNOX-) 3,000
East Brainerd (*CHTN) 1,700
East Cleveland 1,870
East Ridge (*CHTN) 21,799
Elizabethton (**JNSC-) 12,269
Ellendale (*MEM) 900
Englewood 1,878
Erin 1,165

(Tennessee continued)

* Population or designation of metropolitan area, including suburbs (see headnote).
▲ Population of entire "town" or township, including other communities and rural areas.
† Population is from a local census taken at date specified.

(Tennessee continued)

Erwin 4,715
Erwin South (Banner Hill) 2,517
Estill Springs 919
Etowah 3,736
Fairview (*NASH) 1,630
Fayetteville 7,030
Franklin (*NASH) 9,497
Gainesboro 1,101
Gallatin 13,271
Gates 523
Gatlinburg 2,329
Germantown (*MEM) 3,474
Gleason 1,314
Gordonsville 601
Graysville 951
Greater Hendersonville (*NASH) 11,996
Green Brier (Greenbrier) (*NASH) 2,279
Greeneville 13,722
Greenfield 2,050
Halls 2,323
Hampton (*JNSC-) 1,000
Harriman 8,734
Harrogate 1,100
Hartsville 2,243
Henderson 3,581
Henning 605
Hixson (Hixon) (*CHTN) 6,188
Hohenwald 3,385
Hollow Rock 722
Humboldt 10,066
Huntingdon 3,661
Huntland 849
Jacksboro 689
Jackson (*52,300; JAC) 39,996
Jamestown 1,899
Jasper 1,931
Jefferson City 5,124
Jellico 2,235
Johnson City (*93,500; JNSC-) 33,770
Jonesboro (*JNSC-) 1,510
Karns (Byington) (*KNOX-) 1,105
Kenton 1,439
Kimball 807
Kingsport (*100,900; KNGSP) 31,938
Kingston (*KNOX-) 4,142
Knoxville (*415,800; KNOX-) 174,587
Lafayette 2,583
La Follette 6,902
Lake City (*KNOX-) 1,923
Lake Hills (*CHTN) 1,800
La Vergne (*NASH) 2,825
Lawrenceburg 8,889
Lebanon 12,492
Lenoir City (*KNOX-) 5,324
Lewisburg 7,207
Lexington 5,024
Linden 1,062
Livingston 3,050
Lobelville 773
Long Island (*KNGSP) 1,352
Lookout Mountain (*CHTN) 1,741
Lookout Valley (*CHTN) 2,500
Loretto 1,375
Loudon 3,728
Luttrell 819
Lynchburg 538
Lynn Garden (*KNGSP) 7,000
McEwen 1,237
McKenzie 4,873
McMinnville 10,662
Madisonville 2,614
Manchester 6,208
Martin 7,781
Maryville (**KNOX-) 13,808
Maury City 813
Maynardville 702
Medina 755
Memphis (*770,300; MEM) 623,530
Middleton 654
Milan 7,313
Milligan College (*JNSC-) 1,000
Millington (*MEM) 21,177
Monteagle 934
Monterey 2,351
Morristown 20,318
Mountain City 1,883
Mount Carmel (*KNGSP) 2,821
Mount Pleasant 3,530
Munford (*MEM) 1,281
Murfreesboro 26,360
Nashville (*521,300; NASH) 447,877
Newbern 2,124
New Johnsonville 970
Newport 7,328
New Tazewell (Tazewell) 1,192
Nicta 629
Norris (*KNOX-) 1,359
Oak Ridge (**KNOX-) 28,319
Obion 1,010
Old Hometown (*MEM) 2,000
Oliver Springs (*KNOX-) 3,405
Oneida 2,602
Orebank (*KNGSP) 1,111
Palmer 898
Paris 9,892
Parsons 2,167
Philadelphia 554
Pigeon Forge 1,361
Pikeville 1,454
Portland 2,872
Pulaski 6,989
Raleigh (*MEM) 6,000
Red Bank (*CHTN) 12,715
Red Boiling Springs 726
Ridgely 1,657
Ridgetop (*NASH) 810
Ripley 4,794
Rockford (*KNOX-) 900
Rockwood 5,259
Rogersville 4,076
Rutherford 1,385
Rutledge 863
Rydall Springs (*CHTN) 1,000
St. Joseph 637
Savannah 5,576
Scotts Hill 638
Selmer 3,495
Sevierville 2,661
Sewanee 1,886
Sharon 1,188
Shelbyville 12,262
Signal Mountain (*CHTN) 4,839
Smithville 2,997
Smyrna (*NASH) 5,698
Sneedville 874
Soddy-Daisy (*CHTN) 7,569
Somerville 1,816
South Carthage 859
South Clinton (*KNOX-) 1,484
South Fulton 3,122
South Pittsburg 3,613
Sparta 4,930
Spencer 1,179
Spring City 1,756
Springfield 9,720
Spring Hill 685
Surgoinsville 1,285
Sweetwater 4,340
Tazewell 1,860
Tellico Plains 773
Tennessee Ridge 664
Tiftona (*CHTN) 3,000
Tiptonville 2,424
Tracy City 1,388
Trenton 4,226
Trezevant 877
Trimble 675
Troy 826
Tullahoma 15,311
Tusculum College (Tusculum) 1,157
Tyner (*CHTN) 1,200
Union City 11,925
Wartrace 616
Watertown 1,061
Waverly 3,794
Waynesboro 1,983
Westmoreland 1,423
White Bluff 1,163
White House (†1971) 740
White Pine 1,532
Whiteville 992
Whitwell 1,669
Winchester 5,256
Woodbury 1,725
Y Section (Embreeville Junction) (*JNSC-) 1,293

TEXAS

1970 C 11,196,730

Counties

Anderson 27,789
Andrews 10,372
Angelina 49,349
Aransas 8,902
Archer 5,759
Armstrong 1,895
Atascosa 18,696
Austin 13,831
Bailey 8,487
Bandera 4,747
Bastrop 17,297
Baylor 5,221
Bee 22,737
Bell 124,483
Bexar 830,460
Blanco 3,567
Borden 888
Bosque 10,966
Bowie 67,813
Brazoria 108,312
Brazos 57,978
Brewster 7,780
Briscoe 2,794
Brooks 8,005
Brown 25,877
Burleson 9,999
Burnet 11,420
Caldwell 21,178
Calhoun 17,831
Callahan 8,205
Cameron 140,368
Camp 8,005
Carson 6,358
Cass 24,133
Castro 10,394
Chambers 12,187
Cherokee 32,008
Childress 6,605
Clay 8,079
Cochran 5,326
Coke 3,087
Coleman 10,288
Collin 66,920
Collingsworth 4,755
Colorado 17,638
Comal 24,165
Comanche 11,898
Concho 2,937
Cooke 23,471
Coryell 35,311
Cottle 3,204
Crane 4,172
Crockett 3,885
Crosby 9,085
Culberson 3,429
Dallam 6,012
Dallas 1,327,321
Dawson 16,604
Deaf Smith 18,999
Delta 4,927
Denton 75,633
De Witt 18,660
Dickens 3,737
Dimmit 9,039
Donley 3,641
Duval 11,722
Eastland 18,092
Ector 91,805
Edwards 2,107
Ellis 46,638
El Paso 359,291
Erath 18,141
Falls 17,300
Fannin 22,705
Fayette 17,650
Fisher 6,344
Floyd 11,044
Foard 2,211
Fort Bend 52,314
Franklin 5,291
Freestone 11,116
Frio 11,159
Gaines 11,593
Galveston 169,812
Garza 5,289
Gillespie 10,553
Glasscock 1,155
Goliad 4,869
Gonzales 16,375
Gray 26,949
Grayson 83,225
Gregg 75,929
Grimes 11,855
Guadalupe 33,554
Hale 34,137
Hall 6,015
Hamilton 7,198
Hansford 6,351
Hardeman 6,795
Hardin 29,996
Harris 1,741,912
Harrison 44,841
Hartley 2,782
Haskell 8,512
Hays 27,642
Hemphill 3,084
Henderson 26,466
Hidalgo 181,535
Hill 22,596
Hockley 20,396
Hood 6,368
Hopkins 20,710
Houston 17,855
Howard 37,796
Hudspeth 2,392
Hunt 47,948
Hutchinson 24,443
Irion 1,070
Jack 6,711
Jackson 12,975
Jasper 24,692
Jeff Davis 1,527
Jefferson 244,773
Jim Hogg 4,654
Jim Wells 33,032
Johnson 45,769
Jones 16,106
Karnes 13,462
Kaufman 32,392
Kendall 6,964
Kenedy 678
Kent 1,434
Kerr 19,454
Kimble 3,904
King 464
Kinney 2,006
Kleberg 33,166
Knox 5,972
Lamar 36,062
Lamb 17,770
Lampasas 9,323
La Salle 5,014
Lavaca 17,903
Lee 8,048
Leon 8,738
Liberty 33,014
Limestone 18,100
Lipscomb 3,486
Live Oak 6,697
Llano 6,979
Loving 164
Lubbock 179,295
Lynn 9,107
McCulloch 8,571
McLennan 147,553
McMullen 1,095
Madison 7,693
Marion 8,517
Martin 4,774
Mason 3,356
Matagorda 27,913
Maverick 18,093
Medina 20,249
Menard 2,646
Midland 65,433
Milam 20,028
Mills 4,212
Mitchell 9,073
Montague 15,326
Montgomery 49,479
Moore 14,060
Morris 12,310
Motley 2,178
Nacogdoches 36,362
Navarro 31,150
Newton 11,657
Nolan 16,220
Nueces 237,544
Ochiltree 9,704
Oldham 2,258
Orange 71,170
Palo Pinto 28,962
Panola 15,894
Parker 33,888
Parmer 10,509
Pecos 13,748
Polk 14,457
Potter 90,511
Presidio 4,842
Rains 3,752
Randall 53,885
Reagan 3,239
Real 2,013
Red River 14,298
Reeves 16,526
Refugio 9,494
Roberts 967
Robertson 14,389
Rockwall 7,046
Runnels 12,108
Rusk 34,102
Sabine 7,187
San Augustine 7,858
San Jacinto 6,702
San Patricio 47,288
San Saba 5,540
Schleicher 2,277
Scurry 15,760
Shackelford 3,323
Shelby 19,672
Sherman 3,657
Smith 97,096
Somervell 2,793
Starr 17,707
Stephens 8,414
Sterling 1,056
Stonewall 2,397
Sutton 3,175
Swisher 10,373
Tarrant 716,317
Taylor 97,853
Terrell 1,940
Terry 14,118
Throckmorton 2,205
Titus 16,702
Tom Green 71,047
Travis 295,516
Trinity 7,628
Tyler 12,417
Upshur 20,976
Upton 4,697
Uvalde 17,348
Val Verde 27,471
Van Zandt 22,155
Victoria 53,766
Walker 27,680
Waller 14,285
Ward 13,019
Washington 18,842
Webb 72,859
Wharton 36,729
Wheeler 6,434
Wichita 121,862
Wilbarger 15,355
Willacy 15,570
Williamson 37,305
Wilson 13,041
Winkler 9,640
Wise 19,687
Wood 18,589
Yoakum 7,344
Young 15,400
Zapata 4,352
Zavala 11,370

Cities

Abernathy 2,625
Abilene (*92,100; ABIL) 89,653
Acre Homes (*HOU) 19,500
Addison (*DAL) 595
Agua Dulce 742
Alamo (*MCAL) 4,291
Alamo Heights (*SANT) 6,933
Albany 1,978
Aldine (*HOU) 2,500
Aledo (*FTWO) 620
Alice 20,121
Alice Southwest 1,908
Alief (*HOU) 1,100
Allen (*DAL) 1,940
Alpine 5,971
Alta Loma (*GLV-) 1,536
Alto 1,045
Alvarado 2,129
Alvin (*HOU) 10,671
Alvord 791
Amarillo (*132,200; AMA) 127,010
Amherst 825
Anahuac 1,881
Andrews 8,625
Angleton (*FREP-) 9,770
Angleton South (*FREP-) 1,017
Anna 736
Anson 2,615
Anthony 2,154
Anton 1,034
Aransas Pass (*CRPX) 5,813
Archer City 1,722
Arlington (*DAL) 89,723
Arp 816
Asherton 1,645
Aspermont 1,198
Athens 9,582
Atlanta 5,007
Aubrey 731
Austin (*296,600; AUS) 251,808
Avinger 642
Azle (*FTWO) 4,493
Bacliff (*HOU) 2,000
Baird 1,538
Balch Springs (*DAL) 10,464
Balcones Heights (*SANT) 2,504
Ballinger 4,203
Balmorhea 655
Bandera 891
Bangs 1,214
Barrett (*HOU) 2,750
Barstow 614
Bartlett 1,622
Bastrop 3,112
Bay City 11,733
Baytown (*HOU) 43,980
Beaumont (*266,300; B-PA) 117,548
Beaumont Place (*HOU) 1,600
Beauxart Gardens (*B-PA) 1,000
Beckville 582
Bedford (*FTWO) 10,049
Beeville 13,506
Bellaire (*HOU) 19,009
Bellmead (*WACO) 7,698
Bells 778
Bellville 2,371
Belton (*TMPL) 8,696
Benavides 2,112
Benbrook (*FTWO) 8,169
Beverly (Beverly Hills) (*WACO) 2,289
Bevil Oaks (*B-PA) 663
Big Lake 2,489
Big Sandy 1,022
Big Spring 28,735
Big Wells 711
Bishop 3,466
Blanco 1,022
Blooming Grove 740
Bloomington 1,676
Blossom 816
Blue Mound (*FTWO) 1,283
Boerne 2,432
Bogata 1,287
Bonham 7,698
Booker 904
Borger 14,195
Bovina 1,428
Bowie 5,185
Boyd (*FTWO) 695
Brackettville 1,539
Brady 5,557
Brazoria (*FREP-) 1,681
Breckenridge 5,944
Bremond 822
Brenham 8,922
Bridge City (*ORNG) 8,164
Bridgeport 3,614
Bronte 925
Brookshire 1,683
Brookside Village (*Brookside) (*HOU) 1,507
Brownfield 9,647
Brownsville (*62,100; BRNS) 52,522
Brownwood 17,368
Bryan (*53,700; BRY) 33,719
Buffalo 1,242
Bullard 573
Buna 1,649
Bunavista 1,402
Bunker Hill (*HOU) 3,977
Burkburnett (*WI.F) 9,230
Burleson (*FTWO) 7,713
Burnet 2,864
Byers 553
Cactus 644
Caddo Mills 935
Caldwell 2,308
Calvert 2,072
Cameron 5,546
Camp Wood 660
Canadian 2,292
Canton 2,283
Canutillo (*ELP) 1,588
Canyon 8,333
Carrizo Springs 5,374
Carrollton (*DAL) 13,855
Carthage 5,392
Castle Hills (*SANT) 5,311
Castroville 1,893
Cedar Hill (*DAL) 2,610
Celeste 736
Celina 1,272
Center 4,989
Centerville 831
Central Gardens (*B-PA) 1,700
Chandler 765
Channelview (*HOU) 12,000
Charlotte 1,329
Chico 723
Childress 5,408
Chillicothe 1,116
Cisco 4,160
Clarendon 1,974
Clarksville 3,346
Claude 992
Clear Lake City (*HOU) 9,000
Clear Lake Shores (*HOU) 865
Cleburne (*FTWO) 16,015
Cleveland 5,627
Clifton 2,578
Cloverleaf (*HOU) 4,000
Clute (Clute City) (*FREP-) 6,023
Clyde 1,635
Coahoma 1,158
Cockrell Hill (*DAL) 3,515
Coleman 5,608
College Station (*BRY) 17,676
Colleyville (*FTWO) 3,368
Collinsville 768
Colorado City 5,227
Columbus 3,342
Comanche 3,933
Combes (*HRL) 689
Commerce 9,534
Conroe (*HOU) 11,969
Converse (*SANT) 1,383
Coolidge 786
Cooper 2,258
Coppell (*DAL) 1,728
Copperas Cove (*KILL) 10,818
Corpus Christi (*244,600; CRPX) 204,525
Corrigan 1,304
Corsicana 19,972
Cotulla 3,415
Cove City (*ORNG) 1,578
Crandall 774
Crane 3,427
Crockett 6,616
Crosby (*HOU) 1,118
Crosbyton 2,251
Cross Plains 1,192
Crowell 1,399
Crowley (*FTWO) 2,662
Crystal City 8,104
Cuero 6,956
Cumby 628
Daingerfield 2,630
Daisetta 1,084
Dalhart 5,705
Dallas (*1,580,600; DAL) 844,401
Dalworthington Gardens (*DAL) 757
Danbury 807
Dawson 848
Dayton 3,804
Decatur 3,240
Deer Park (*HOU) 12,773

* Population or designation of metropolitan area, including suburbs (see headnote).
▲ Population of entire "town" or township, including other communities and rural areas.
† Population is from a local census taken at date specified.

De Kalb 2,197
De Leon 2,170
Del Rio 21,330
Denison (**SHRM-) 24,923
Denton (*DAL) 39,874
Denver City 4,133
Deport 761
De Soto (*DAL) 6,617
Detroit 668
Devine 3,311
Diboll 3,557
Dickinson (*HOU) 10,776
Dilley 2,362
Dimmitt 4,327
Donna 7,365
Driscoll 626
Dublin 2,810
Dumas 9,771
Duncanville (*DAL) 14,105
Eagle Lake 3,587
Eagle Pass 15,364
Early 1,097
Earth 1,152
East Bernard 1,159
Eastland 3,178
Ector 549
Edcouch 2,656
Eden 1,291
Edgecliff Village (*FTWO) 1,143
Edgewood 1,176
Edinburg (*19,700; EDIN) 17,163
Edna 5,332
El Campo 9,332
El Campo South 1,880
Eldorado 1,446
Electra 3,895
Elgin 3,832
Elkhart 997
El Lago (*HOU) 2,298
El Paso (*350,900; ELP) 322,261
Elsa 4,400
Emory 693
Ennis 11,046
Euless (*FTWO) 19,316
Everman (*FTWO) 4,570
Eylau (*TEXR-) 1,000
Fabens 3,241
Fairfield 2,074
Falfurrias 6,355
Farmers Branch (*DAL) 27,492
Farmersville 2,311
Farwell 1,185
Ferris (*DAL) 2,180
Flatonia 1,108
Florence 672
Floresville 3,707
Flower Mound (*DAL) 1,685
Floydada 4,109
Forest Hill (*FTWO) 8,236
Forney (*DAL) 1,745
Fort Stockton 8,283
Fort Worth (*674,000; FTWO) 393,476
Franklin 1,063
Frankston 1,056
Fredericksburg 5,326
Freeport (*56,500; FREP-) 11,997
Freer 2,804
Friendswood (*HOU) 5,675
Friona 3,111
Frisco (*DAL) 1,845
Fritch 1,778
Frost 548
Fulton 1,101
Gainesville 13,830
Galena Park (*HOU) 10,479
Galveston (*132,500; GLV-) 61,809
Ganado 1,640
Garland (*DAL) 81,437
Garrison 1,082
Gatesville 4,683
Georgetown 6,395
George West 2,022
Giddings 2,783
Gilmer 4,196
Gladewater 5,574
Glen Rose 1,554
Godley 533
Goldthwaite 1,693
Goliad 1,709
Gonzales 5,854
Goree 538
Gorman 1,236
Graford 613
Graham 7,477
Granbury 2,473
Grandfalls 622
Grand Prairie (*DAL) 50,904
Grand Saline 2,257
Grandview 935
Granger 1,256
Grant Garden (*ODES) 1,700
Grapeland 1,211
Grapevine (*FTWO) 7,023
Greenville 22,043
Gregory (*CRPX) 2,246
Griffing Park (*B-PA) 2,075
Groesbeck 2,396
Groom 808
Groves (*B-PA) 18,067
Groveton 1,219
Grulla (La Grulla) 1,194
Gruver 1,265
Gunter 647
Hale Center 1,964
Hallettsville 2,712
Hallsville 1,038
Haltom City (*FTWO) 28,127
Hamilton 2,760
Hamlin 3,325
Happy 672
Harker Heights (*KILL) 4,216
Harlingen (*56,800; HRL) 33,503
Hart 905
Haskell 3,655
Hawkins 977
Hearne 4,982
Heath 520
Hebbronville 4,097

Hedwig Village (*HOU) 3,255
Hemphill 1,005
Hempstead 1,891
Henderson 10,187
Henrietta 2,897
Hereford 13,414
Hewitt (*WACO) 569
Hico 975
Hidalgo 1,289
Hidden Valley (*HOU) 1,200
Higgins 582
Highland Park (*DAL) 10,133
Highlands (*HOU) 3,462
Highland Village (*DAL) 516
Hill Country Village (*SANT) 636
Hillcrest (*HOU) 650
Hillsboro 7,224
Hilshire Village (*HOU) 627
Hitchcock (*GLV-) 5,565
Holland 723
Holliday 1,048
Hollywood Park (*SANT) 2,299
Hondo 5,487
Honey Grove 1,853
Hooks 2,545
Houmont Park (*HOU) 1,000
Houston (*1,847,900; HOU) 1,232,802
Howe (*SHRM-) 1,359
Hubbard 1,572
Hughes Springs 1,701
Humble (*HOU) 3,278
Hunters Creek Village (*HOU) 3,959
Huntington 1,192
Huntsville 17,610
Hurst (*FTWO) 27,215
Hutchins (*DAL) 1,755
Hutto (*AUS) 545
Idalou (*LUB) 1,729
Ingleside (*CRPX) 3,763
Iowa Park (*WI.F) 5,796
Iraan 996
Irving (*DAL) 97,260
Italy 1,309
Itasca 1,483
Jacinto City (*HOU) 9,563
Jacksboro 3,554
Jacksonville 9,734
Jasper 6,251
Jayton 703
Jefferson 2,866
Jersey Village (*HOU) 765
Joaquin 819
Johnson City 767
Jones Creek (*FREP-) 1,268
Joshua (*FTWO) 924
Jourdanton 1,841
Junction 2,654
Justin 741
Karnes City 2,926
Katy 2,923
Kaufman (*DAL) 4,012
Keene (*FTWO) 2,440
Keller (*FTWO) 1,474
Kemah (*HOU) 1,144
Kemp 999
Kenedy 4,156
Kennedale (*FTWO) 3,076
Kerens 1,446
Kermit 7,884
Kerrville 12,672
Kilgore 9,495
Killeen (*85,900; KILL) 35,507
Kingsville 28,915
Kinwood (*HOU) 1,800
Kirby (*SANT) 2,558
Kirbyville 1,869
Kleberg (*DAL) 4,768
Knox City 1,536
Kountze 2,173
Kress 578
Kyle 1,629
La Coste 768
Lacy-Lakeview (*WACO) 2,558
Ladonia 757
La Feria 2,642
La Grange 3,092
La Joya 1,217
Lake Barbara (*FREP-) 605
Lake Dallas (*DAL) 1,431
Lake Jackson (**FREP-) 13,376
Lakeside (*FTWO) 988
Lakeview (*B-PA) 3,567
Lake Worth Village (*FTWO) 4,958
La Marque (*GLV-) 16,131
Lamesa 11,559
Lampasas 5,922
Lancaster (*DAL) 10,522
La Porte (*HOU) 7,149
Laredo (*70,800; LAR) 69,024
La Villa 1,255
League City (*HOU) 10,818
Lefors 816
Leonard 1,423
Leon Valley (*SANT) 1,960
Levelland 11,445
Lewisville (*DAL) 9,264
Lexington 719
Liberty 5,591
Lindale 1,631
Linden 2,264
Littlefield 6,738
Live Oak (*SANT) 2,779
Livingston 3,965
Llano 2,608
Lockhart 6,489
Lockney 2,094
Lomax (*HOU) 894
Lometa 633
Lone Oak 518
Lone Star 1,760
Longview (*60,700; LNGV) 45,547
Loraine 700
Lorenzo 1,206
Los Fresnos 1,297
Lott 799
Lubbock (*164,300; LUB) 149,101
Lucas (*DAL) 540
Lueders 511

Lufkin 23,049
Luling 4,719
Lyford 1,425
Lytle (*SANT) 1,271
Mabank 1,239
McAllen (*86,700; MCAL) 37,636
McCamey 2,647
McGregor 4,365
McKinney (*DAL) 15,193
McLean 1,183
McNair (*HOU) 2,039
Madisonville 2,881
Malakoff 2,045
Manor (*AUS) 940
Mansfield (*FTWO) 3,658
Marble Falls 2,209
Marfa 2,682
Marion (*SANT) 655
Marlin 6,351
Marshall 22,937
Mart 2,183
Mason 1,806
Matador 1,091
Mathis 5,351
Maud 1,107
Memphis 3,227
Menard 1,740
Mercedes 9,355
Meridian 1,162
Merkel 2,163
Mertzon 513
Mesquite (*DAL) 55,131
Mexia 5,943
Miami 611
Midland (*63,300; MIDL) 59,463
Midlothian (*DAL) 2,322
Miles 631
Milford 664
Mineola 3,926
Mineral Wells 18,411
Mission (*MCAL) 13,043
Missouri City (*HOU) 4,136
Monahans 8,333
Mont Belvieu 1,144
Moody 1,286
Morgans Point (*HOU) 593
Morton 2,738
Moulton 968
Mount Houston (*HOU) 2,000
Mount Pleasant 9,459
Mount Vernon 1,806
Muenster 1,411
Muleshoe 4,525
Munday 1,726
Nacogdoches 22,544
Naples 1,726
Nash (*TEXR-) 1,961
Nassau Bay (*HOU) 4,000
Natalia 1,296
Navasota 5,111
Nederland (*B-PA) 16,810
Needville 1,024
New Boston 4,034
New Braunfels 17,859
Newcastle 624
New London 899
Newton 1,529
Nixon 1,925
Nocona 2,871
Nolanville (*KILL) 902
Normangee 657
Northcrest (*WACO) 1,669
North Houston (*HOU) 2,700
Northline Terrace (*HOU) 1,000
North Oaks (*AUS) 1,000
North Richland Hills (*FTWO) 16,514
Oakwood 547
Odem 2,130
Odessa (*89,500; ODES) 78,380
O'Donnell 1,148
Olmos Park (*SANT) 2,250
Olney 3,624
Olton 1,782
Omaha 898
Orange (*50,400; ORNG) 24,457
Orange Grove 1,075
Ore City 830
Overton 2,084
Ozona 2,864
Paducah 2,052
Palacios 3,642
Palestine 14,525
Palmer 601
Pampa 21,726
Panhandle 2,141
Pantego (*DAL) 1,812
Paris 23,441
Pasadena (*HOU) 89,277
Patton 667
Pearland (*HOU) 6,444
Pear Ridge (*B-PA) 3,697
Pearsall 5,545
Pecos 12,682
Perryton 7,810
Petersburg 1,300
Petrolia 584
Pflugerville (*AUS) 549
Pharr (*MCAL) 15,829
Phillips 2,515
Pilot Point 1,663
Pine Forest (*B-PA) 512
Pinehurst (*ORNG) 2,198
Pineland 1,127
Piney Point (Piney Point Village) (*HOU) 2,548
Pittsburg 3,844
Plains 1,087
Plainview 19,096
Plano (*DAL) 17,872
Pleasanton 5,407
Point Comfort 1,446
Port Aransas 1,218
Port Arthur (**B-PA) 57,371
Port Isabel 3,067
Portland (*CRPX) 7,302
Port Lavaca 10,491
Port Neches (*B-PA) 10,894
Portway Acres (*BRNS) 1,000

Post 3,854
Poteet 3,013
Poth 1,296
Pottsboro (*SHRM-) 748
Prairie View 3,589
Premont 3,282
Primera (*HRL) 902
Princeton (*DAL) 1,105
Quanah 3,948
Queen City 1,227
Quinlan 844
Quitaque 601
Quitman 1,494
Ralls 1,962
Ranger 3,094
Rankin 1,105
Raymondville 7,987
Red Oak (*DAL) 767
Reese Village (*LUB) 1,470
Refugio 4,340
Reno (*FTWO) 688
Richardson (*DAL) 48,582
Richland Hills (*FTWO) 8,865
Richmond 5,777
Richwood Village (*FREP-) 1,452
Riesel 503
Rio Grande City 5,676
Rio Hondo (*HRL) 1,167
Rising Star 1,009
River Oaks (*FTWO) 8,193
Roanoke (*FTWO) 817
Robert Lee 1,119
Robinson (*WACO) 3,807
Robstown (*CRPX) 11,217
Roby 784
Rochester 529
Rockdale 4,655
Rockport 3,879
Rocksprings 1,221
Rockwall (*DAL) 3,121
Rogers 1,030
Rollingwood (*AUS) 780
Roma (Roma-Los Saenz) 2,154
Roscoe 1,580
Rosebud 1,597
Rosenberg 12,098
Rotan 2,404
Round Rock (*AUS) 2,811
Rowlett (*DAL) 2,579
Royse City (*DAL) 1,535
Rule 1,024
Runge 1,147
Rusk 4,914
Sabinal 1,554
Sachse (*DAL) 777
Saginaw (*FTWO) 2,382
St. Jo 1,054
San Angelo (*65,900; SANG) 63,884
San Antonio (*835,200; SANT) 654,153
San Augustine 2,539
San Benito (*HRL) 15,176
Sanderson 1,229
San Diego 4,490
Sanger 1,603
San Juan (*MCAL) 5,070
San Marcos 18,860
San Pedro (*CRPX) 5,294
San Saba 2,555
Sansom Park Village (*FTWO) 4,771
Santa Anna 1,310
Santa Rosa 1,466
Savoy 756
Schertz (*SANT) 4,061
Schulenburg 2,294
Seabrook (*HOU) 3,811
Seadrift 1,092
Seagoville (*DAL) 4,390
Seagraves 2,440
Sealy 2,685
Seguin 15,934
Seminole 5,007
Seymour 3,469
Shallowater (*LUB) 1,339
Shamrock 2,644
Shavano Park (*SANT) 881
Sheldon (*HOU) 1,665
Shepherd 928
Sherman (*63,100; SHRM-) 29,061
Shiner 2,102
Shoreacres (*HOU) 1,872
Silsbee 7,271
Silverton 1,026
Sinton 5,563
Skellytown 716
Slaton 6,583
Smithville 2,959
Snyder 11,171
Somerset 950
Somerville 1,250
Sonoma 678
Sonora 2,149
Sourlake 1,694
South Houston (Dumont) (*HOU) 11,527
Southlake (*FTWO) 2,031
South Side Place (*HOU) 1,466
Spearman 3,435
Springtown (*FTWO) 1,194
Spring Valley (*HOU) 3,170
Spur 1,747
Stafford (*HOU) 2,906
Stamford 4,558
Stanton 2,117
Stephenville 9,277
Sterling City 780
Stinnett 2,014
Stockdale 1,132
Stratford 2,139
Strawn 786
Sudan 976
Sugar Land (*HOU) 3,318
Sulphur Springs 10,642
Sundown 1,129
Sunnyvale (*DAL) 995
Sunray 1,854
Sunrise 1,213
Sunset Heights (*ODES) 1,500
Sweeny 3,191

Sweetwater 12,020
Taft 3,274
Taft Southwest 2,026
Tahoka 2,956
Talco 837
Tatum 684
Taylor 9,616
Taylor Lake Village (*HOU) 1,004
Teague 2,867
Temple (*46,600; TMPL) 33,431
Tenaha 1,094
Terrell (*DAL) 14,182
Terrell Hills (*SANT) 5,225
Texarkana (*69,600; TEXR-) 30,497
Texas City (**GLV-) 38,908
Thorndale 1,031
Thrall 619
Three Rivers 1,761
Throckmorton 1,105
Timpson 1,254
Tomball (*HOU) 2,734
Tom Bean 540
Trenton 599
Trinidad 1,079
Trinity 2,512
Troup 1,668
Troy (*TMPL) 542
Tulia 5,294
Turkey 680
Tye (*ABIL) 857
Tyler (*77,100; TYL) 57,770
Universal City (*SANT) 7,613
University Park (*DAL) 23,498
Uvalde 10,764
Valley Mills 1,022
Van 1,593
Van Alstyne 1,981
Van Horn 2,889
Van Vleck 1,051
Vega 839
Vernon 11,454
Victoria (*43,800; VICT) 41,349
Vidor (*B-PA) 9,738
Waco (*127,700; WACO) 95,326
Waelder 1,138
Wake Village (*TEXR-) 2,408
Waller 1,123
Wallis 1,028
Waskom 1,460
Watauga (*FTWO) 3,778
Waxahachie 13,452
Weatherford (*FTWO) 11,750
Webster (*HOU) 2,231
Weimar 2,104
Wellington 2,884
Wells 671
Weslaco 15,313
West 2,406
West Carlisle (*LUB) 1,200
West Columbia 3,335
West Lake Hills (*AUS) 1,488
West Orange (*ORNG) 4,820
West University Place (*HOU) 13,317
Westworth Village (*FTWO) 4,578
Wharton 7,881
Wheeler 1,116
White Deer 1,092
Whitehouse (*TYL) 1,245
White Oak (*LNGV) 2,300
Whitesboro 2,927
White Settlement (*FTWO) 13,449
Whitewright 1,742
Whitney 1,371
Wichita Falls (*115,000; WI.F) 96,265
Wickett 598
Willis 1,577
Wills Point 2,636
Wilmer (*DAL) 1,922
Windcrest (*SANT) 3,371
Wink 1,023
Winnie 1,543
Winnsboro 3,064
Winters 2,907
Wolfe City 1,433
Wolfforth (*LUB) 1,090
Woodsboro 1,839
Woodville 2,662
Woodway (*WACO) 4,819
Wortham 1,036
Wylie (*DAL) 2,675
Yoakum 5,755
Yorktown 2,411
Zapata 2,102

UTAH

1970 C 1,059,273

Counties

Beaver 3,800
Box Elder 28,129
Cache 42,331
Carbon 15,647
Daggett 666
Davis 99,028
Duchesne 7,299
Emery 5,137
Garfield 3,157
Grand 6,688
Iron 12,177
Juab 4,574
Kane 2,421
Millard 6,988
Morgan 3,983
Piute 1,164
Rich 1,615
Salt Lake 458,607
San Juan 9,606
Sanpete 10,976
Sevier 10,103
Summit 5,879
Tooele 21,545
Uintah 12,684
Utah 137,776
Wasatch 5,863

(Utah continued)

* Population or designation of metropolitan area, including suburbs (see headnote).
▲ Population of entire "town" or township, including other communities and rural areas.
† Population is from a local census taken at date specified.

(Utah continued)

Washington 13,669
Wayne 1,483
Weber 126,278

Cities

Alpine (★PRVO) 1,047
American Fork (★PRVO) 7,713
Beaver 1,453
Blanding 2,250
Bountiful (★S.L.C.) 27,956
Brigham City 14,007
Castle Dale 541
Cedar City 8,946
Centerville (★S.L.C.) 3,268
Clearfield (★OGD) 13,316
Clinton (★OGD) 1,768
Coalville 864
Cottonwood (★S.L.C.) 8,431
Cottonwood Heights (★S.L.C.) 4,500
Delta 1,610
Dragerton 1,614
Draper (★S.L.C.) 900
Duchesne 1,094
East Layton (★OGD) 763
Eastwood Hills (★S.L.C.) 1,200
Enterprise 844
Ephraim 2,127
Escalante 638
Eureka 753
Fairview 696
Farmington (★S.L.C.) 2,526
Ferron 663
Fillmore 1,411
Fruit Heights (★OGD) 800
Garland 1,187
Granger (★S.L.C.) 12,000
Granite Park (★S.L.C.) 9,573
Grantsville 2,931
Green River 1,033
Gunnison 1,073
Harrisville (★OGD) (†4/5/71) 867
Heber 3,245
Helper 1,964
Holladay (★S.L.C.) 23,014
Honeyville 640
Huntington 857
Huntsville 553
Hurricane 1,408
Hyde Park 1,025
Hyrum 2,340
Kamas 806
Kanab 1,381
Kaysville (★OGD) 6,192
Kearns (★S.L.C.) 17,071
Layton (★OGD) 13,603
Lehi (★PRVO) 4,659
Lewiston 1,244
Lindon (★PRVO) 1,644
Logan 22,333
Maeser 1,248
Magna (★S.L.C.) 5,509
Manti 1,803
Mapleton (★PRVO) 1,980
Midvale (★S.L.C.) 7,840
Midway 804
Milford 1,304
Millcreek (East Millcreek) (★S.L.C.) 26,579
Moab 4,793
Monroe 918
Monticello 1,431
Morgan (Morgan City) 1,586
Moroni 894
Mount Olympus (★S.L.C.) 5,909
Mount Pleasant 1,516
Murray (★S.L.C.) 21,206
Nephi 2,699
North Logan 1,405
North Ogden (★OGD) 5,257
North Salt Lake (★S.L.C.) 2,143
Ogden (★175,600; OGD) 69,478
Orangeville 511
Orem (★PRVO) 25,729
Panguitch 1,318
Park City 1,193
Park Terrace (★S.L.C.) 1,300
Parowan 1,423
Payson (★PRVO) 4,501
Perry 909
Peruvian Park (★S.L.C.) 1,000
Plain City (★OGD) 1,543
Pleasant Grove (★PRVO) 5,327
Pleasant View (★OGD) 2,028
Price 6,218
Providence 1,608
Provo (★134,800; PRVO) 53,131
Randolph 500
Redwood (★S.L.C.) 3,500
Richfield 4,471
Richmond 1,000
Riverdale (★OGD) 3,704
River Heights 1,008
Riverton (★S.L.C.) 2,820
Roosevelt 2,005
Roy (★OGD) 14,356
St. George 7,097
Salem (★PRVO) 1,081
Salina 1,494
Salt Lake City (★503,000; S.L.C.) 175,885
Sandy (Sandy City) (★S.L.C.) 6,438
Santaquin (★PRVO) 1,236
Smithfield 3,342
South Cottonwood (★S.L.C.) 4,800
South Jordan (★S.L.C.) 2,942
South Ogden (★OGD) 9,991
South Salt Lake (★S.L.C.) 7,810
South Weber (★OGD) 1,073
Spanish Fork (Spanish Fork City) (★PRVO) 7,284
Springville (★PRVO) 8,790
Sunset (★OGD) 6,268
Syracuse (★OGD) 1,843
Taylorsville (★S.L.C.) 4,500
Tooele 12,539
Tremonton 2,794
Union (★S.L.C.) 2,500
Val Verda (★S.L.C.) 1,200
Vernal 3,908
Vernon (Onaqui) 541
Washington 750
Washington Terrace (★OGD) 7,241
Wellington 922
Wellsville 1,267
Wendover 781
West Bountiful (★S.L.C.) 1,246
West Jordan (★S.L.C.) 4,221
West Point (★OGD) 1,020
White City (★S.L.C.) 6,402
Willard 1,045
Woods Cross (★S.L.C.) 3,124

VERMONT

1970 C 444,732

Counties

Addison 24,266
Bennington 29,282
Caledonia 22,789
Chittenden 99,131
Essex 5,416
Franklin 31,282
Grand Isle 3,574
Lamoille 13,309
Orange 17,676
Orleans 20,153
Rutland 52,637
Washington 47,659
Windham 33,476
Windsor 44,082

Cities

Alburg 520
Arlington 800
Barre 10,209
Barre (6,509▲)
Barton 1,051
Bellows Falls 3,505
Bennington (14,586▲) 7,950
Bradford 709
Brandon (Brandon Center) 1,720
Brattleboro 12,239
Bristol (2,744▲) 1,737
Burlington (★92,200; BUR) 38,633
Derby (Derby Center) (3,252▲) 547
Derby Line 834
Enosburg Falls 1,266
Essex Junction (★BUR) 6,511
Fair Haven 2,777
Hardwick (2,466▲) 1,503
Island Pond 1,123
Johnson 1,296
Ludlow (2,463▲) 1,508
Lyndonville 1,415
Manchester Center 1,060
Middlebury (6,532▲) 4,000
Milton (4,495▲) (★BUR) 1,164
Montpelier 8,609
Morrisville 2,116
Newport 4,664
North Bennington 984
Northfield (4,870▲) 2,139
North Troy 774
Orleans 1,138
Pittsford (2,306▲) 682
Plainfield 949
Poultney (3,217▲) 1,914
Proctor 2,095
Proctorsville 512
Randolph (3,882▲) 2,115
Richford (2,116▲) 1,527
Richmond (2,249▲) (★BUR) 935
Rutland 19,293
Rutland (2,248▲)
St. Albans 8,082
St. Albans (3,270▲)
St. Johnsbury (8,409▲) 6,400
Saxtons River 581
Shaftsbury (2,411▲) 700
Shelburne (★BUR) (3,728▲) 200
South Burlington (★BUR) 10,032
Springfield (Springfield Center) (10,063▲) 5,632
Swanton (4,622▲) 2,630
Vergennes 2,242
Waterbury (4,614▲) 2,840
Weathersfield (2,040▲)
West Rutland 2,381
White River Junction 2,379
Wilder 1,328
Wilmington (1,586▲) 544
Windsor (4,158▲) 3,000
Winooski (★BUR) 7,309
Woodstock (2,608▲) 1,154

VIRGINIA

1970 C 4,651,448

Counties

Accomack 29,004
Albemarle 37,780
Alleghany 12,461
Amelia 7,592
Amherst 26,072
Appomattox 9,784
Arlington 174,284
Augusta 44,220
Bath 5,192
Bedford 26,728
Bland 5,423
Botetourt 18,193
Brunswick 16,172
Buchanan 32,071
Buckingham 10,597
Campbell 43,319
Caroline 13,925
Carroll 23,092
Charles City 6,158
Charlotte 12,366
Chesterfield 77,046
Clarke 8,102
Craig 3,524
Culpeper 18,218
Cumberland 6,179
Dickenson 16,077
Dinwiddie 25,046
Essex 7,099
Fairfax 455,021
Fauquier 26,375
Floyd 9,775
Fluvanna 7,621
Franklin 28,163
Frederick 28,893
Giles 16,741
Gloucester 14,059
Goochland 10,069
Grayson 15,439
Greene 5,248
Greensville 9,604
Halifax 30,076
Hanover 37,479
Henrico 154,364
Henry 50,901
Highland 2,529
Isle of Wight 18,285
James City 17,853
King and Queen 5,491
King George 8,039
King William 7,497
Lancaster 9,126
Lee 20,321
Loudoun 37,150
Louisa 14,004
Lunenberg 11,687
Madison 8,638
Mathews 7,168
Mecklenburg 29,426
Middlesex 6,295
Montgomery 47,157
Nansemond 35,166
Nelson 11,702
New Kent 5,300
Northampton 14,442
Northumberland 9,239
Nottoway 14,260
Orange 13,792
Page 16,581
Patrick 15,282
Pittsylvania 58,789
Powhatan 7,696
Prince Edward 14,379
Prince George 29,092
Prince William 111,102
Pulaski 29,564
Rappahannock 5,199
Richmond 6,504
Roanoke 67,339
Rockbridge 16,637
Rockingham 47,890
Russell 24,533
Scott 24,376
Shenandoah 22,852
Smyth 31,349
Southampton 18,582
Spotsylvania 16,424
Stafford 24,587
Surry 5,882
Sussex 11,464
Tazewell 39,816
Warren 15,301
Washington 40,835
Westmoreland 12,142
Wise 35,947
Wythe 22,139
York 33,203

Independent Cities

Alexandria 110,938
Bedford 6,011
Bristol 14,857
Buena Vista 6,425
Charlottesville 38,880
Chesapeake 89,580
Clifton Forge 5,501
Colonial Heights 15,097
Covington 10,060
Danville 46,391
Emporia 5,300
Fairfax 21,970
Falls Church 10,772
Franklin 6,880
Fredericksburg 14,450
Galax 6,278
Hampton 120,779
Harrisonburg 14,605
Hopewell 23,471
Lexington 7,597
Lynchburg 54,083
Martinsville 19,653
Newport News 138,177
Norfolk 307,951
Norton 4,172
Petersburg 36,103
Portsmouth 110,963
Radford 11,596
Richmond 249,430
Roanoke 92,115
Salem 21,982
South Boston 6,889
Staunton 24,504
Suffolk 9,858
Virginia Beach 172,106
Waynesboro 16,707
Williamsburg 9,069
Winchester 14,643

Cities

Abingdon 4,376
Alexandria (★WASH) 110,938
Altavista 2,708
Amherst 1,108
Annalee Heights (★WASH) 2,000
Annandale (★WASH) 27,405
Appalachia 2,161
Appomattox 1,400
Arlington (★WASH) 174,284
Ashland (★RICH) 2,934
Baileys Crossroads (★WASH) 6,000
Bassett (★MRTNV) 3,058
Battlefield Park (★PET-) 1,000
Bedford 6,011
Bel Air (★WASH) 1,200
Belle Haven 504
Belle Haven (★WASH) 1,200
Belle View (★WASH) 4,000
Bellwood (★RICH) 1,100
Belvedere (★WASH) 1,500
Bensley (★RICH) 1,900
Berryville 1,569
Bethel Manor (★NN-H) 2,500
Beverly Hills (★RICH) 2,700
Big Stone Gap 4,153
Blacksburg 9,384
Blackstone 3,412
Bluefield 5,286
Blue Ridge Farms (★LYNCH) 1,400
Bon Air (★RICH) 10,771
Bowling Green 528
Boydton 541
Boykins 742
Bren Mar Park (★WASH) 2,200
Bridgewater 2,828
Brighton Square Apartments (★WASH) 1,200
Bristol (★★BRIS-) 14,857
Broadway 887
Brodnax 569
Brookneal 1,037
Broyhill Park (★WASH) 4,000
Buchanan 1,326
Bucknell Manor (★WASH) 2,500
Buena Vista 6,425
Burkeville 703
Camelot (★WASH) 1,000
Canterbury Woods (★WASH) 1,300
Cape Charles 1,689
Cave Spring (★ROAN) 1,500
Cedar Bluff 1,050
Central Gardens (★RICH) 1,500
Chamberlayne Farms (★RICH) 1,400
Chamberlayne Heights (★RICH) 1,000
Charlottesville (★53,700; CHRLTV) 38,880
Chase City 2,909
Chatham 1,801
Cheriton 655
Chesapeake (★NORF-) 89,580
Chester (★RICH) 5,556
Chesterbrook Woods (★WASH) 1,300
Chilhowie 1,317
Chincoteague 1,867
Christiansburg 7,857
Clarksville 1,641
Clifton Forge 5,501
Clintwood 1,320
Coeburn 2,362
Collinsville (★MRTNV) 6,015
Colonial Beach 2,058
Colonial Heights (★PET-) 15,097
Courtland 899
Covington 10,060
Craigsville 988
Crestview (★RICH) 2,000
Crewe 1,797
Crozet 1,433
Culmore (★WASH) 2,900
Culpeper 6,056
Dale City (★WASH) 13,857
Damascus 1,230
Dante 1,153
Danville (★69,700; DANV) 46,391
Dayton 978
Donna Lee Gardens (★WASH) 1,500
Drakes Branch 702
Dublin 1,653
Dumfries (★WASH) 1,890
Dunn Loring (★WASH) 1,100
Dunn Loring Woods (★WASH) 2,000
East Highland Park (★RICH) 4,000
Edinburg 766
Edsall Park (★WASH) 1,700
Elkton 1,511
Emporia 5,300
Engleside (★WASH) 15,000
Ettrick (★PET-) 3,500
Exmore 1,421
Fairfax (★Wash) 21,970
Fairfax Villa (★WASH) 2,100
Fair Haven (★WASH) 1,000
Fairlawn 1,767
Falls Church (★WASH) 10,772
Falls Hill (★WASH) 1,300
Farmington (★RICH) 2,500
Farmville 5,127
Ferry Farms 1,170
Fieldale (★MRTNV) 1,337
Fort Hill (★RICH) 2,500
Franklin 6,880
Franklin Park (★WASH) 1,000
Fredericksburg 14,450
Fries 885
Front Royal 8,211
Galax 6,278
Gate City (★KNGSP) 1,914
Glade Spring 1,615
Glasgow 1,304
Glen Allen (★RICH) 1,200
Glenwood (★DANV) 1,295
Glenwood Farms (★RICH) 3,200
Gordonsville 1,253
Greenbriar (★WASH) 3,200
Greenway Downs (★WASH) 1,500
Gretna 986
Grindall Creek (★RICH) 1,000
Grottoes 1,166
Groveton (★WASH) 4,500
Grundy 2,054
Halifax 899
Hampton (★★NN-H) 120,779
Harrisonburg 14,605
Herndon (★WASH) 4,301
Highland Springs (★RICH) 7,345
Hillsville 1,149
Hillwood (★WASH) 1,500
Hollin Hall Village (★WASH) 2,900
Hollins (★ROAN) 5,000
Hollywood 1,500
Holmes Run Acres (★WASH) 1,400
Holmes Run Park (★WASH) 950
Honaker 911
Hopewell (★★PET-) 23,471
Huntingdon (★WASH) 4,500
Hurt 1,434
Hybla Valley (★WASH) 4,000
Independence 673
Iron Gate 692
Irvington 504
Jarratt 591
Jefferson Apartments (★WASH) 1,800
Jefferson Manor (★WASH) 2,300
Jefferson Village (★WASH) 2,500
Jonesville 700
Kenbridge 1,223
Keysville 818
Kilmarnock 841
Kingsland (★RICH) 1,000
Kings Park (★WASH) 3,500
Laburnum Manor (★RICH) 2,000
La Crosse 674
Lake Barcroft (★WASH) 3,000
Lakeside (★RICH) 11,137
Lawrenceville 1,636
Lebanon 2,272
Lee Boulevard Heights (★WASH) 2,000
Leesburg (★WASH) 4,821
Lewis Gardens (★RICH) 1,450
Lexington 7,597
Lincolnia Heights (★WASH) 1,200
Lloyd Place 1,200
Louisa 633
Luray 3,612
Lynchburg (★96,600; LYNCH) 54,083
McLean (★WASH) 17,698
McLean Hamlet (★WASH) 1,500
Madison Heights (★LYNCH) 3,000
Manassas (★WASH) 9,164
Manassas Park (★WASH) 6,844
Mantua Hills (★WASH) 1,200
Marion 8,158
Martinsville (★61,900; MRTNV) 19,653
Matoaca (★PET-) 1,500
Mechanicsville (★RICH) 5,189
Middleburg 833
Middletown 507
Montezuma Gardens (★RICH) 1,000
Monticello Woods (★WASH) 1,200
Montrose (★RICH) 2,400
Monument Heights (★RICH) 3,500
Mount Jackson 681
Narrows 2,421
Nassawadox 591
New Market 718
Newport News (★296,800; NN-H) 138,177
Norfolk (★683,000; NORF-) 307,951
North Springfield (★WASH) 8,631
Norton 4,172
Occoquan (★WASH) 975
Old Creek Estates (★WASH) 1,500
Onancock 1,614
Orange 2,768
Orleans Village Apartments (★WASH) 2,000
Parklawn (★WASH) 1,800
Parksley 903
Pearisburg 2,169
Pembroke 1,095
Pennington Gap (Pennington) 1,886
Petersburg (★128,600; PET-) 36,103
Pimmit Hills (★WASH) 7,600
Pinecrest (★WASH) 1,000
Pocahontas 891
Poplar Heights (★WASH) 1,100
Poquoson (★NN-H) 5,441
Portsmouth (★★NORF-) 110,963
Pound 995
Pulaski 10,279
Pulaski North (North Pulaski) 1,315
Purcellville 1,775
Quantico (★WASH) 719
Radford 11,596
Raven 1,819
Ravensworth (★WASH) 3,600
Ravenwood (★WASH) 1,200
Reston (★WASH) 5,723
Rich Creek 729
Richland Hills (★LYNCH) 1,500
Richlands 4,843
Richmond (★489,500; RICH) 249,430
Ridgeway (★MRTNV) 624
Roanoke (★192,900; ROAN) 92,115
Rocky Mount 4,002
Rose Hill (★WASH) 14,492
Roslyn Hills (★RICH) 1,600
Round Hill 581
Rural Retreat 872
St. Paul 948
Salem (★ROAN) 21,982
Saltville 2,527
Sandston (★RICH) 5,000
Saratoga Place 1,200
Seaford (★NN-H) 1,200
Shenandoah 1,714
Skipwith Farms (★RICH) 1,000
Sleepy Hollow (★WASH) 1,200
Sleepy Hollow Estates (★RICH) 1,300
Smithfield 2,713
South Boston 6,889
South Hill 3,858
South Suffolk 1,000
South Woodley (★WASH) 1,200
Springfield (★WASH) 11,613
Springfield Estates (★WASH) 1,800
Stanley 1,208
Staunton 24,504
Stephens City 802
Sterling (★WASH) 8,321
Stonewall Manor (★WASH) 1,400
Strasburg 2,431
Stuart 947
Suburban Apartments (★RICH) 1,500
Suffolk 9,858
Sugar Loaf (★ROAN) 3,000
Tangier 814

★ Population or designation of metropolitan area, including suburbs (see headnote).
▲ Population of entire "town" or township, including other communities and rural areas.
† Population is from a local census taken at date specified.

Tappahannock...1,111
Tauxemont (★WASH)...1,300
Tazewell...4,168
Timberlake (★ LYNCH)...2,500
Timberville...959
Triangle (★ WASH)...3,021
Troutville (★ROAN)...522
Tyler Park (★WASH)...1,650
Varina (★RICH)...2,300
Victoria...1,408
Vienna (★WASH)...17,146
Vinton (★ROAN)...6,347
Virginia Beach (★NORF-)...172,106
Virginia Hills (★WASH)...2,500
Vista Acres (★LYNCH)...900
Wakefield...942
Warrenton (★WASH)...4,027
Warsaw...511
Waverly...1,717
Waynesboro...16,707
Waynewood (★WASH)...4,100
Weber City (Moccasin Gap) (★KNGSP)...1,676
Westbourne (★RICH)...1,000
West End Manor (★RICH)...1,200
West Gate of Lomond (★WASH)...2,250
Westham (★RICH)...2,800
West Lawn (★WASH)...1,700
Westover Hills (★DANV)...950
West Point...2,600
West Springfield (★WASH)...14,143
Westwood (★RICH)...1,400
Westwood Park (★WASH)...1,000
Weyanoke (★WASH)...1,400
Wildwood (★RICH)...1,600
Williamsburg...9,069
Willow Lawn (★RICH)...1,000
Willston (★WASH)...3,000
Winchester...14,643
Windsor...685
Wise...2,891
Woodbridge (★WASH)...25,412
Woodley Hills (★WASH)...1,200
Woodstock...2,338
Wytheville...6,069
Yorkshire (★WASH)...2,400

WASHINGTON

1970 C...3,409,169

Counties

Adams...12,014
Asotin...13,799
Benton...67,540
Chelan...41,355
Clallam...34,770
Clark...128,454
Columbia...4,439
Cowlitz...68,616
Douglas...16,787
Ferry...3,655
Franklin...25,816
Garfield...2,911
Grant...41,881
Grays Harbor...59,553
Island...27,011
Jefferson...10,661
King...1,156,633
Kitsap...101,732
Kittitas...25,039
Klickitat...12,138
Lewis...45,467
Lincoln...9,572
Mason...20,918
Okanogan...25,867
Pacific...15,796
Pend Oreille...6,025
Pierce...411,027
San Juan...3,856
Skagit...52,381
Skamania...5,845
Snohomish...265,236
Spokane...287,487
Stevens...17,405
Thurston...76,894
Wahkiakum...3,592
Walla Walla...42,176
Whatcom...81,950
Whitman...37,900
Yakima...144,971

Cities

Aberdeen...18,489
Airway Heights (★SPOK)...744
Albion...687
Alderwood Manor (★SEAT-)...6,000
Algona (★SEAT-)...1,276
Anacortes...7,701
Arlington (★SEAT-)...2,261
Armar (★SEAT-)...1,000
Arrowhead (★SEAT-)...1,400
Asotin...637
Auburn (★SEAT-)...21,817
Battle Ground (★POR)...1,438
Beacon Hill (★LNGV)...1,263
Bellevue (★SEAT-)...61,102
Bellingham (★54,900; BELNG)...39,375
Benton City...1,070
Bingen...671
Black Diamond (★SEAT-)...1,160
Blaine...1,955
Bonney Lake (★SEAT-)...2,700
Bothell (★SEAT-)...4,883
Bremerton (★87,700; BREM)...35,307
Bremerton East (Enetai) (★BREM)...2,878
Brewster...1,059
Bridgeport...952
Brier (★SEAT-)...3,093
Bryn Mawr (★SEAT-)...2,300
Buckley (★SEAT-)...3,446
Burien (★SEAT-)...15,000
Burlington...3,138
Camas...5,790
Carnation...530
Cashmere...1,976
Castle Rock...1,647
Cathlamet...647
Centralia...10,054
Central Park...2,720
Chehalis...5,727
Chelan...2,684
Cheney...6,358
Chewelah...1,365
Clarkston...6,312
Clarkston Heights...1,000
Cle Elum...1,725
Clyde Hill (★SEAT-)...2,987
Colfax...2,664
College Place...4,510
Columbia Heights (★LNGV)...1,572
Colville...3,742
Concrete...573
Connell...1,161
Cosmopolis...1,599
Coulee City...558
Coulee Dam...1,425
Country Homes (★SPOK)...4,000
Coupeville...678
Darrington...1,094
Davenport...1,363
Dayton...2,596
Deer Park...1,295
Des Moines (★SEAT-)...4,099
Dishman (★SPOK)...14,500
Duvall (★SEAT-)...607
Eastgate (★SEAT-)...5,000
East Wenatchee...913
East Wenatchee North (East Wenatchee Bench)...2,327
Eatonville...852
Edmonds (★SEAT-)...23,998
Electric City...651
Ellensburg...13,568
Ellsworth (★POR)...1,000
Elma...2,227
Enumclaw (★SEAT-)...4,703
Ephrata...5,255
Erlands Point (★BREM)...1,017
Everett (★★SEAT-)...53,622
Everson...633
Fairview (★YAK)...2,111
Fall City...1,300
Federal Way (★SEAT-)...18,500
Ferndale (★BELNG)...2,164
Fife (★SEAT-)...1,458
Fircrest (★SEAT-)...5,651
Fords Prairie...2,250
Forks...1,682
Friday Harbor...803
Fruitvale (★YAK)...3,275
Garfield...610
Geiger Heights (★SPOK)...1,424
Gig Harbor (★SEAT-)...1,657
Gold Bar...504
Goldendale...2,484
Grand Coulee...1,302
Grandview...3,605
Granger...1,567
Granite Falls (★SEAT-)...813
Greenacres (Green Acres) (★SPOK)...2,324
Hazel Dell (★POR)...3,500
Hoquiam...10,466
Hunts Point (★SEAT-)...578
Ilwaco...506
Inglewood (★SEAT-)...3,000
Ione...529
Issaquah (★SEAT-)...4,313
Juanita (★SEAT-)...3,000
Kalama...1,106
Kelso (★LNGV)...10,296
Kenmore (★SEAT-)...8,000
Kennewick (★★P-K-R)...15,212
Kent (★SEAT-)...16,275
Kettle Falls...893
Kingsgate (★SEAT-)...1,000
Kirkland (★SEAT-)...15,249
Kittitas...637
Lacey (★OLYM)...9,696
La Conner...639
Lake Forest Park (★SEAT-)...2,530
Lakeridge (★SEAT-)...2,500
Lake Shore (★POR)...1,000
Lake Stevens (★SEAT-)...1,283
Lakewood Center (Lakes District) (★SEAT-)...48,195
Langley (SEAT-)...547
Leavenworth...1,322
Lind...622
Linwood (Town and Country) (★SPOK)...6,484
Long Beach...968
Longview (★56,200; LNGV)...28,373
Lynden...2,808
Lynwood (★SEAT-)...16,919
Mabton...926
McCleary...1,265
Marysville (★SEAT-)...4,343
Mead (★SPOK)...1,099
Medical Lake...3,529
Medina (★SEAT-)...3,455
Mercer Island (★SEAT-)...19,819
Midland (★SEAT-)...3,000
Millwood (★SPOK)...1,770
Milton (★SEAT-)...2,607
Minnehaha (★POR)...2,000
Monroe (★SEAT-)...2,687
Monta Vista (★SEAT-)...1,500
Montesano...2,847
Moorlands (★SEAT-)...2,000
Morgan Acres (★SPOK)...2,500
Morton...1,134
Moses Lake...10,310
Moses Lake North...2,672
Mountlake Terrace (★SEAT-)...16,600
Mount Vernon...8,804
Moxee City...600
Mukilteo (★SEAT-)...1,369
Naches...666
Navy Yard City (★BREM)...2,827
Newport...1,418
Newport Hills (★SEAT-)...6,000
Normandy Park (★SEAT-)...4,202
North Bend...1,625
North City (★SEAT-)...6,500
North Lynnwood (★SEAT-)...1,200
Oak Harbor...9,167
Ocean Shores (†1970)...918
Odessa...1,074
Okanogan...2,015
Olympia (★63,000; OLYM)...23,111
Omak...4,164
Opportunity (★SPOK)...16,604
Oroville...1,555
Orting (★SEAT-)...1,643
Othello...4,122
Otis Orchards (★SPOK)...1,200
Pacific (★SEAT-)...1,831
Packwood...900
Palouse...948
Parkland (★SEAT-)...21,012
Parkwater (★SPOK)...4,500
Parkwood (★BREM)...900
Pasadena Park (★SPOK)...2,200
Pasco (★75,300; P-K-R)...13 920
Pe Ell...582
Pomeroy...1,823
Port Angeles...16,367
Port Orchard (★BREM)...3,904
Port Townsend...5,241
Poulsbo (★BREM)...1,856
Prosser...2,954
Pullman...20,509
Puyallup (★SEAT-)...14,742
Queensborough (★SEAT-)...1,300
Queensgate (★SEAT-)...1,200
Quincy...3,237
Raymond...3,126
Redmond (★SEAT-)...11,031
Renton (★SEAT-)...26,229
Republic...862
Richland (★★P-K-R)...26,290
Richmond Beach (★SEAT-)...8,000
Richmond Highlands (★SEAT-)...20,000
Ridgecrest (★SEAT-)...4,500
Ridgefield (★POR)...1,004
Ritzville...1,876
Riverton Heights (★SEAT-)...34,000
Riverview (Pasco West) (★P-K-R)...3,809
Rocky Point (★BREM)...1,733
Rosalia...569
Rose Hill (★SEAT-)...3,000
Roslyn...1,031
Ruston (★SEAT-)...668
St. John...575
Seahurst (★SEAT-)...3,000
Seattle (★1,816,100; SEAT-)...530,831
Sedro Woolley (Sedro-Woolley)...4,598
Selah (★YAK)...3,070
Sequim...1,549
Shelton...6,515
Sheridan Beach (★SEAT-)...2,000
Shoultes (★SEAT-)...2,000
Silver Lake (★SEAT-)...1,300
Skyway (★SEAT-)...9,000
Snohomish (★SEAT-)...5,174
Snoqualmie...1,260
Soap Lake...1,064
South Bend...1,795
South Broadway (★YAK)...3,298
Spanaway (★SEAT-)...5,768
Spokane (★259,000; SPOK)...170,516
Sprague...550
Stanwood (★SEAT-)...1,347
Steilacoom (★SEAT-)...2,850
Stevenson...916
Sultan...1,119
Sumas...689
Summit (★SEAT-)...2,000
Sumner (★SEAT-)...4,325
Sunnydale (★SEAT-)...2,000
Sunnyside...6,751
Sunnyside (★SEAT-)...1,000
Suquamish (★BREM)...900
Tacoma (★★SEAT-)...154,581
Tanglewild (★OLYM)...2,000
Tekoa...808
Tenino...962
Terrace Heights (★YAK)...1,033
Thompson Place (★OLYM)...1,200
Toledo...654
Tonasket...951
Toppenish...5,744
Tracyton (★BREM)...1,413
Trentwood (★SPOK)...1,800
Tukwila (★SEAT-)...3,496
Tumwater (★OLYM)...5,373
Twisp...756
Union Gap (★YAK)...2,040
University Place (★SEAT-)...9,500
Vancouver (★POR)...41,859
Veradale (Vera) (★SPOK)...2,400
Vineland...1,000
Waitsburg...953
Walla Walla...23,619
Walla Walla East...2,840
Walla Walla West (Garrett)...1,586
Walnut Grove (★POR)...1,000
Wapato...2,841
Warden...1,254
Washougal...3,388
Waterville...919
Wenatchee...16,912
West Clarkston...2,000
Westport...1,364
West Richland (★P-K-R)...1,107
West Wenatchee...2,134
White Center (★SEAT-)...19,000
White Salmon (Bingen-White Salmon)...1,585
Wilbur...1,074
Winlock...890
Winslow (★SEAT-)...1,461
Woodland...1,622
Woodmont Beach (★SEAT-)...900
Woodway (★SEAT-)...879
Yakima (★78,300; YAK)...45,588
Yarrow Point (★SEAT-)...1,103
Yelm...628
Zillah...1,138

WEST VIRGINIA

1970 C...1,744,237

Counties

Barbour...14,030
Berkeley...36,356
Boone...25,118
Braxton...12,666
Brooke...29,685
Cabell...106,918
Calhoun...7,046
Clay...9,330
Doddridge...6,389
Fayette...49,332
Gilmer...7,782
Grant...8,607
Greenbrier...32,090
Hampshire...11,710
Hancock...39,749
Hardy...8,855
Harrison...73,028
Jackson...20,903
Jefferson...21,280
Kanawha...229,515
Lewis...17,847
Lincoln...18,912
Logan...46,269
McDowell...50,666
Marion...61,356
Marshall...37,598
Mason...24,306
Mercer...63,206
Mineral...23,109
Mingo...32,780
Monongalia...63,714
Monroe...11,272
Morgan...8,547
Nicholas...22,552
Ohio...64,197
Pendleton...7,031
Pleasants...7,274
Pocahontas...8,870
Preston...25,455
Putnam...27,625
Raleigh...70,080
Randolph...24,596
Ritchie...10,145
Roane...14,111
Summers...13,213
Taylor...13,878
Tucker...7,447
Tyler...9,929
Upshur...19,092
Wayne...37,581
Webster...9,809
Wetzel...20,314
Wirt...4,154
Wood...86,818
Wyoming...30,095

Cities

Alderson...1,278
Anawalt...801
Anmoore (★CLRKB)...944
Ansted...1,511
Athens...967
Barboursville (★HNTG-)...2,279
Barrackville (★FAIRM)...1,596
Beaver (Glen Hedrick) (★BECK)...1,500
Beckley (★46,000; BECK)...19,884
Beech Bottom (★STU-)...544
Belington...1,567
Belle (★CHAS)...1,786
Belmont...802
Benwood (★WHL)...2,737
Berkeley Springs (Bath)...944
Bethany (★STU-)...602
Bethlehem (★WHL)...2,461
Bluefield...15,921
Bolivar...943
Boomer...1,000
Bradshaw...1,048
Bramwell...1,125
Bridgeport (★CLRKB)...4,777
Buchannon...7,261
Buffalo...831
Burnsville...591
Cameron...1,537
Cedar Grove...1,275
Ceredo (★HNTG-)...1,583
Chapmanville...1,175
Charleston (★219,400; CHAS)...71,505
Charles Town...3,023
Chattaroy...1,145
Chelyan...900
Chesapeake (★CHAS)...2,428
Chester (★E.LIV-)...3,614
Clarksburg (★49,200; CLRKB)...24,864
Clearview (★WHL)...512
Clendenin (Clendennin)...1,438
Coal City...1,000
Coal Fork (★CHAS)...900
Coalwood...950
Colliers (★STU-)...900
Colored Hill...1,031
Crab Orchard (★BECK)...1,758
Cross Lanes (★CHAS)...2,500
Culloden (★CHAS)...1,033
Danville...580
Davis...868
Davy...993
Delbarton...903
Despard (★CLRKB)...1,400
Dunbar (★CHAS)...9,151
Eastbank (East Bank)...1,025
East Pea Ridge (★HNTG-)...1,500
East View (★CLRKB)...1,618
Eccles (★BECK)...1,105
Eleanor (★CHAS)...1,035
Elizabeth...821
Elkhorn...900
Elkins...8,287
Elkview (★CHAS)...1,486
Enterprise...900
Fairlea...900
Fairmont (★47,800; FAIRM)...26,093
Fairview...640
Farmington...595
Fayetteville...1,712
Follansbee (★STU-)...3,883
Fort Ashby (★CUMB)...900
Fort Gay...792
Franklin...695
Gary...2,800
Gassaway...1,253
Gauley Bridge...950
Gilbert...778
Glasgow...904
Glen Dale (Glendale) (★WHL)...2,105
Glenville...2,183
Grafton...6,433
Grantsville...795
Grant Town...946
Granville (★MORG)...1,027
Hamlin...1,024
Harrisville...1,464
Hartford...527
Henlawson...900
Hico...800
Hinton...4,503
Holden...2,325
Hooverson Heights (★STU-)...1,800
Huntington (★242,700; HNTG-)...74,315
Hurricane (★CHAS)...3,491
Iaeger...822
Institute (★CHAS)...2,700
Itmann...900
Junior...513
Kenova (★HNTG-)...4,860
Kermit...716
Keyser...6,586
Keystone...1,008
Kimball...962
Kingwood...2,550
Kopperston...900
Lester...507
Lewisburg...2,407
Lilly Grove...1,655
Logan...3,311
Lost Creek...571
Lower Belle (★CHAS)...1,000
Lumberport...957
Mabscott (★BECK)...1,254
MacArthur (★BECK)...1,614
McComas...900
McMechen (★WHL)...2,808
Madison...2,342
Malden (★CHAS)...1,000
Man...1,201
Mannington...2,747
Marlinton...1,286
Marmet (★CHAS)...2,339
Martinsburg...14,626
Mason (Mason City)...1,319
Masontown...868
Matewan...651
Matoaka...608
Middlebourne...814
Mill Creek...800
Milton (★HNTG-)...1,597
Mitchell Heights...524
Monongah (★FAIRM)...1,194
Montgomery...2,525
Moorefield...2,124
Morgantown (★52,700; MORG)...29,431
Moundsville (★WHL)...13,560
Mount Gay...2,300
Mount Hope...1,829
Mullens...2,967
New Cumberland (★STU-)...1,865
Newell (★E.LIV-)...2,300
New Haven...1,538
New Martinsville...6,528
Nitro (★CHAS)...8,019
Northfork...737
North Matewan...900
Nutter Fort (★CLRKB)...2,379
Oak Hill...4,738
Oceana...1,580
Omar...900
Paden City...3,674
Parkersburg (★87,600; PRKB)...44,208
Parsons...1,784
Paw Paw...706
Pennsboro...1,614
Petersburg...2,177
Peterstown...563
Philippi...3,002
Piedmont...1,763
Pine Grove...630
Pineville...1,187
Poca (★CHAS)...772
Point Pleasant...6,122
Powellton...950
Pratt...671
Princeton...7,253
Rainelle...1,826
Rand (★CHAS)...3,000
Ranson...2,189
Ravenswood...4,240
Red Jacket...850
Rhodell...500
Richwood...3,717
Ridgeley (Ridgely) (★CUMB)...1,112
Ripley...3,244
Rivesville (★FAIRM)...1,108
Roderfield...1,000
Romney...2,364
Ronceverte...1,981
Rowlesburg...829
Rupert...1,027
St. Albans (★CHAS)...14,356
St. Marys...2,348
Salem...2,597
Shepherdstown...1,688
Shinnston...2,576
Sistersville...2,246
Smithers...2,020
Sophia (★BECK)...1,303
South Charleston (★CHAS)...16,333
Spencer...2,271
Sprague (★BECK)...1,500
Spring Valley (★HNTG-)...1,000

(West Virginia continued)

★ Population or designation of metropolitan area, including suburbs (see headnote).
▲ Population of entire "town" or township, including other communities and rural areas.
† Population is from a local census taken at date specified.

(West Virginia continued)

Squire....900
Stanaford (★BECK)....950
Star City (★MORG)....1,312
Stonewood (★CLRKB)....1,950
Summersville....2,429
Sutton....1,031
Switzer....900
Terra Alta....1,474
Thomas....713
Triadelphia (★WHL)....547
Tyler Heights (★CHAS)....2,400
Union....566
Valley Grove (★WHL)....509
Verdunville....900
Vienna (★PRKB)....11,549
War....2,004
Wayne....1,385
Webster Springs (Addison)....1,038
Weirton (★★STU-)....27,131
Welch....4,149
Wellsburg (★STU-)....4,600
West Dunbar (★CHAS)....1,000
West Hamlin....715
West Liberty (★WHL)....2,400
West Logan....685
Weston....7,323
Westover (★MORG)....5,086
West Union....1,141
Wheeling (★157,500; WHL)....48,188
White Sulphur Springs....2,869
Whitesville....781
Williamson....5,831
Williamstown (★MRIET)....2,743
Windsor Heights (★STU-)....800

WISCONSIN

1970 C....4,417,933

Counties

Adams....9,234
Ashland....16,743
Barron....33,955
Bayfield....11,683
Brown....158,244
Buffalo....13,743
Burnett....9,276
Calumet....27,604
Chippewa....47,717
Clark....30,361
Columbia....40,150
Crawford....15,252
Dane....290,272
Dodge....69,004
Door....20,106
Douglas....44,657
Dunn....29,154
Eau Claire....67,219
Florence....3,298
Fond du Lac....84,567
Forest....7,691
Grant....48,398
Green....26,714
Green Lake....16,878
Iowa....19,306
Iron....6,533
Jackson....15,325
Jefferson....60,060
Juneau....18,455
Kenosha....117,917
Kewaunee....18,961
La Crosse....80,468
Lafàyette....17,456
Langlade....19,220
Lincoln....23,499
Manitowoc....82,294
Marathon....97,457
Marinette....35,810
Marquette....8,865
Menominee....2,607
Milwaukee....1,054,249
Monroe....31,610
Oconto....25,553
Oneida....24,427
Outagamie....119,356
Ozaukee....54,461
Pepin....7,319
Pierce....26,652
Polk....26,666
Portage....47,541
Price....14,520
Racine....170,838
Richland....17,079
Rock....131,970
Rusk....14,238
St. Croix....34,354
Sauk....39,057
Sawyer....9,670
Shawano....32,650
Sheboygan....96,660
Taylor....16,958
Trempealeau....23,344
Vernon....24,557
Vilas....10,958
Walworth....63,444
Washburn....10,601
Washington....63,839
Waukesha....231,338
Waupaca....37,780
Waushara....14,795
Winnebago....129,934
Wood....65,362

Cities

Abbotsford....1,375
Adams....1,440
Albany....875
Algoma....4,023
Allouez (★GRBY)....13,753
Alma....956
Altoona (★EAUC-)....2,842
Amery....2,126
Amherst....585
Antigo....9,005
Appleton (★152,000; APP)....57,143
Arcadia....2,159
Argyle....673
Ashland....9,615
Ashwaubenon (★GRBY)....10,042
Athens....856
Augusta....1,242
Baldwin....1,399
Balsam Lake....648
Bangor....974
Baraboo....7,931
Barneveld....528
Barron....2,337
Bayfield....874
Bayside (★MILW)....4,461
Bear Creek....520
Beaver Dam....14,265
Belgium....809
Belleville....1,063
Belmont....688
Beloit (★57,800; BLOIT)....35,729
Beloit North (Perrygo Place) (★BLOIT)....5,912
Beloit West (★BLOIT)....1,903
Benton....873
Berlin....5,338
Big Bend (★MILW)....1,148
Birnamwood....632
Biron....771
Black Creek....921
Black Earth....1,114
Black River Falls....3,273
Blair....1,036
Blanchardville....794
Bloomer....3,143
Bloomington....719
Bohners Lake....1,417
Bonduel....995
Boscobel....2,510
Boyceville....725
Boyd....574
Brandon....872
Brillion....2,588
Brodhead....2,515
Brookfield (★MILW)....32,140
Brooklyn....565
Brown Deer (★MILW)....12,582
Browns Lake (Cedar Park)....1,669
Bruce....799
Buffalo....671
Burlington....7,479
Butler (★MILW)....2,261
Cadott....977
Cambria....631
Cambridge....689
Cameron....893
Campbellsport....1,681
Camp Douglas....547
Carol Beach Estates (★CHI)....800
Cascade....603
Cashton....824
Cassville....1,343
Cedarburg (★MILW)....7,697
Cedar Grove....1,276
Centuria....632
Chenequa (★MILW)....642
Chetek....1,630
Chilton....3,030
Chippewa Falls (★★EAUC-)....12,351
Clear Lake....721
Cleveland....761
Clinton....1,333
Clintonville....4,600
Cochrane....506
Colby....1,178
Coleman....683
Colfax....1,026
Columbus....3,789
Combined Locks (★APP)....2,734
Como....1,132
Coon Valley....596
Cornell....1,616
Crandon....1,582
Crestview (★RAC)....1,100
Cross Plains....1,478
Cuba City....1,993
Cudahy (★MILW)....22,078
Cumberland....1,839
Darien....839
Darlington....2,351
Deerfield....1,067
DeForest (★MAD)....1,911
Delafield (★MILW)....3,182
Delavan....5,526
Delavan Lake....2,124
Denmark....1,364
De Pere (★GRBY)....13,309
Dickeyville....1,057
Dodgeville....3,255
Dresser....533
Durand....2,103
Eagle....745
Eagle River....1,326
East Troy (★MILW)....1,711
Eau Claire (★78,000; EAUC-)....44,619
Eau Claire Southeast (★EAUC-)....2,316
Edgar....928
Edgerton....4,118
Eleva....574
Elkhart Lake....787
Elkhorn....3,992
Ellsworth....1,983
Elm Grove (★MILW)....7,201
Elmwood....737
Elroy....1,513
Evansville....2,992
Fairchild....562
Fall Creek....825
Fall River....633
Fennimore....1,861
Fond du Lac (★47,700; FDLC)....35,515
Fontana (Fontana on Geneva Lake)....1,464
Footville....698
Fort Atkinson....9,164
Fountain City....1,017
Fox Lake....1,242
Fox Point (★MILW)....7,939
Franklin (★MILW)....12,247
Frederic....908
Fredonia (★MILW)....1,045
Fremont....598
French Island (★LACRO)....2,800
Friendship....641
Galesville....1,162
Gays Mills....623
Genoa City (★CHI)....1,085
Germantown (★MILW)....6,974
Gillett....1,288
Glendale (★MILW)....13,426
Glenwood City....822
Glidden....700
Grafton (★MILW)....5,998
Grantsburg....930
Green Bay (★140,000; GRBY)....87,809
Greendale (★MILW)....15,089
Greenfield (★MILW)....24,424
Green Lake....1,109
Greenwood....1,036
Hales Corners (★MILW)....7,771
Hallie (★EAUC-)....1,223
Hammond....768
Hartford....6,499
Hartland (★MILW)....2,763
Hayward....1,457
Hazel Green....982
Highland....785
Hilbert....896
Hillsboro....1,231
Holmen (★LACRO)....1,081
Horicon....3,356
Hortonville....1,524
Howard (★GRBY)....4,911
Howards Grove-Millersville (★SHEB)....998
Hudson (★MPLS-)....5,049
Hurley....2,418
Hustisford....789
Independence....1,036
Iola....900
Jackson (★MILW)....561
Janesville (★59,200; JNSV)....46,426
Jefferson....5,429
Johnson Creek....790
Juneau....2,043
Kaukauna (★APP)....11,292
Kenosha (★104,500; KEN)....78,805
Kewaskum....1,926
Kewaunee....2,901
Kiel....2,848
Kimberly (★APP)....6,131
Kohler (★SHEB)....1,738
La Crosse (★74,800; LACRO)....51,153
Ladysmith....3,674
La Farge....748
Lake Butte des Morts (★OSH)....1,111
Lake Delton....1,059
Lake Geneva....4,890
Lake Mills....3,556
Lake Nebagamon....523
Lake Wazeecha....1,285
Lake Wissota (★EAUC-)....1,419
Lancaster....3,756
Lannon (★MILW)....1,056
Laona....700
Lena....569
Little Chute (★APP)....5,365
Livingston....503
Lodi....1,831
Lomira....1,084
Lone Rock....506
Loyal....1,126
Luck....848
Luxemburg....853
Lyndon Station....533
McFarland (★MAD)....2,386
Madison (★248,100; MAD)....172,007
Manawa....1,105
Manitowoc (★57,300; MNTW-)....33,430
Maple Bluff (★MAD)....1,974
Marathon (Marathon City)....1,214
Marinette....12,696
Marion....1,218
Markesan....1,378
Marshall....1,043
Marshfield....15,619
Mauston....3,466
Mayville....4,139
Mazomanie....1,217
Medford....3,454
Mellen....1,168
Melrose....505
Menasha (★APP)....14,905
Menomonee Falls (★MILW)....31,697
Menomonie....11,275
Mequon (★MILW)....12,150
Merrill....9,502
Merrillan....612
Merton (★MILW)....646
Middleton (★MAD)....8,286
Milltown....634
Milton (★JNSV)....3,699
Milwaukee (★1,379,000; MILW)....717,372
Mineral Point....2,305
Mishicot (★MNTW-)....938
Mondovi....2,338
Monona (★MAD)....10,420
Monroe....8,654
Montello....1,082
Montfort....518
Monticello....870
Montreal....877
Mosinee....2,395
Mount Calvary....942
Mount Horeb....2,402
Mukwonago (★MILW)....2,367
Muscoda....1,099
Muskego (★MILW)....11,573
Necedah....740
Neenah (★APP)....22,892
Neillsville....2,750
Nekoosa....2,409
Neopit....1,122
New Berlin (★MILW)....26,910
New Glarus....1,454
New Holstein....3,012
New Lisbon....1,361
New London....5,801
New Richmond....3,707
Niagara....2,347
North Fond du Lac (★FDLC)....3,286
North Freedom....596
North Hudson (★MPLS-)....1,547
North Lake (★MILW)....500
North Prairie (★MILW)....669
Oak Creek (★MILW)....13,928
Oakfield....918
Oak Grove Town of....890
Oconomowoc (★MILW)....8,741
Oconomowoc Lake (★MILW)....599
Oconomowoc Lake South (★MILW)....1,473
Oconto....4,667
Oconto Falls....2,517
Okauchee (★MILW)....1,740
Okauchee Lake (★MILW)....1,400
Omro (★OSH)....2,341
Onalaska (★LACRO)....4,909
Oostburg....1,309
Oregon (★MAD)....2,553
Orfordville....888
Osceola....1,152
Oshkosh (★70,100; OSH)....53,221
Osseo....1,356
Owen....1,031
Paddock Lake (★CHI)....1,470
Palmyra....1,341
Pardeeville....1,507
Park Falls....2,953
Park Ridge....817
Pell Lake (★CHI)....1,284
Pepin....747
Peshtigo....2,836
Pewaukee (★MILW)....3,271
Pewaukee West (★MILW)....3,401
Phillips....1,511
Pittsville....708
Plain....688
Plainfield....642
Platteville....9,599
Pleasant View....750
Plover....950
Plymouth....5,810
Portage....7,821
Port Edwards....2,126
Port Washington (★MILW)....8,752
Potosi....713
Poynette....1,118
Prairie du Chien....5,540
Prairie du Sac....1,902
Prentice....519
Prescott (★MPLS-)....2,331
Princeton....1,446
Pulaski....1,717
Racine (★132,300; RAC)....95,162
Randolph....1,582
Random Lake....1,068
Redgranite....645
Reedsburg....4,585
Reedsville....994
Reeseville....566
Rhinelander....8,218
Rib Lake....782
Rice Lake....7,278
Richland Center....5,086
Rio....792
Ripon....7,053
River Falls....7,238
River Hills (★MILW)....1,561
Rothschild (★WAUS)....3,141
St. Cloud....550
St. Croix Falls....1,425
St. Francis (★MILW)....10,489
St. Nazianz....718
Sauk City....2,385
Saukville (★MILW)....1,389
Schofield (★WAUS)....2,577
Seymour....2,194
Sharon....1,216
Shawano....6,488
Sheboygan (★70,500; SHEB)....48,484
Sheboygan Falls (★SHEB)....4,771
Sheboygan South (★SHEB)....1,920
Sheboygan West (★SHEB)....1,361
Shell Lake....928
Shiocton....830
Shorewood (★MILW)....15,576
Shorewood Hills (★MAD)....2,206
Shullsburg....1,376
Silver Lake (★CHI)....1,210
Siren....639
Slinger (★MILW)....1,022
Soldiers Grove....514
Solon Springs....598
Somerset....778
South Kenosha (★KEN)....600
South Milwaukee (★MILW)....23,297
Sparta....6,258
Spencer....1,181
Spooner....2,444
Spring Green....1,199
Spring Valley....995
Stanley....2,049
Stevens Point....23,479
Stockbridge....582
Stoddard....750
Stoughton....6,096
Stratford....1,239
Strum....738
Sturgeon Bay....6,776
Sturtevant (★RAC)....3,376
Sun Prairie (★MAD)....9,935
Superior (★★DUL-)....32,237
Suring....499
Sussex (★MILW)....2,758
Theresa....611
Thiensville (★MILW)....3,182
Thorp....1,469
Tichigan (★MILW)....900
Tigerton....742
Tomah....5,647
Tomahawk....3,419
Trempealeau....743
Turtle Lake....637
Twin Lakes (★CHI)....2,276
Two Rivers (★★MNTW-)....13,553
Union Grove (★KEN)....2,703
Valders....821
Verona (★MAD)....2,334
Viola....659
Viroqua....3,739
Wales (★MILW)....691
Walworth....1,637
Washburn....1,957
Waterford (★MILW)....1,922
Waterloo....2,253
Watertown....15,683
Waukesha (★MILW)....40,274
Waunakee (★MAD)....2,181
Waupaca....4,342
Waupun....7,946
Wausau (★56,600; WAUS)....32,806
Wausaukee....557
Wausau West (★WAUS)....6,399
Wautoma....1,624
Wauwatosa (★MILW)....58,676
Webster....502
West Allis (★MILW)....71,649
West Baraboo....563
West Bend....16,555
Westby....1,568
Westfield....884
West Milwaukee (★MILW)....4,405
Weston (★WAUS)....3,375
West Salem....2,180
Weyauwega....1,377
Whitefish Bay (★MILW)....17,402
Whitehall....1,486
Whitelaw....557
Whitewater....12,038
Whiting....1,782
Wild Rose....585
Williams Bay....1,554
Wilton....516
Wind Lake (★MILW)....2,000
Wind Point (★RAC)....1,251
Winneconne (★OSH)....1,611
Wisconsin Dells....2,401
Wisconsin Rapids....18,587
Wittenberg....895
Wonewoc....835
Woodruff....900
Woodville....522
Wrightstown (★APP)....1,020
Wyocena....809

WYOMING

1970 C....332,416

Counties

Albany....26,431
Big Horn....10,202
Campbell....12,957
Carbon....13,354
Converse....5,938
Crook....4,535
Fremont....28,352
Goshen....10,885
Hot Springs....4,952
Johnson....5,587
Laramie....56,360
Lincoln....8,640
Natrona....51,264
Niobrara....2,924
Park....17,752
Platte....6,486
Sheridan....17,852
Sublette....3,755
Sweetwater....18,391
Teton....4,823
Uinta....7,100
Washakie....7,569
Weston....6,307

Cities

Afton....1,290
Basin....1,145
Big Piney....570
Buffalo....3,394
Casper (★47,500; CASP)....39,361
Cheyenne (★51,500; CHEY)....40,914
Cody....5,161
Douglas....2,677
Dubois....898
Evanston....4,462
Evansville (★CASP)....832
Gillette....7,194
Glenrock....1,515
Green River....4,196
Greybull....1,953
Guernsey....793
Jackson....3,196
Jeffrey City....700
Kemmerer....2,292
Lander....7,125
Laramie....23,143
Lovell....2,371
Lusk....1,495
Lyman....643
Mills (★CASP)....1,724
Moorcroft....981
Mountain View (★CASP)....1,641
Newcastle....3,432
Orchard Valley (★CHEY)....1,015
Paradise Valley (★CASP)....1,764
Pine Bluffs....937
Pinedale....948
Powell....4,807
Rawlins....7,855
Riverton....7,995
Rock Springs....11,657
Saratoga....1,181
Sheridan....10,856
Shoshoni....562
Sundance....1,056
Thermopolis....3,063
Torrington....4,237
Upton....987
West Laramie....700
Wheatland....2,498
Worland....5,055

★ Population or designation of metropolitan area, including suburbs (see headnote).
▲ Population of entire "town" or township, including other communities and rural areas.
† Population is from a local census taken at date specified.

Largest Metro. Areas of the United States, 1972

To facilitate comparisons among major urban areas, Rand McNally has defined Metro. Areas around each large city. A Metro. Area includes one or more central cities, and neighboring communities that are linked to them by continuous built-up areas. More distant communities are also included if the bulk of their population is supported by commuters to the central cities or their immediate environs. For additional Metro. Area populations, see the Population of U.S. Cities and Towns table on pages 321–352.

Rank 1972		ESTIMATED POPULATION 1/1/1972 Metro. Area	City Proper
1	New York, New York	17,500,000	7,895,000
	Newark, New Jersey		378,000
	Paterson, New Jersey		145,000
2	Los Angeles, California	8,825,000	2,800,000
3	Chicago, Illinois	7,680,000	3,330,000
4	Philadelphia, Pennsylvania–	5,370,000	1,945,000
	Trenton, New Jersey–		104,500
	Wilmington, Delaware		78,000
5	Detroit, Michigan	4,560,000	1,490,000
	Ann Arbor, Michigan		103,000
	incl. Windsor, Ontario	*4,820,000*	
6	San Francisco, California–	4,365,000	701,000
	Oakland, California–		355,000
	San Jose, California		470,000
7	Boston, Massachusetts	3,835,000	637,000
	Lowell, Massachusetts		95,500
	Lawrence, Massachusetts		66,500
	Brockton, Massachusetts		93,000
	Salem, Massachusetts		41,000
	Haverhill, Massachusetts		46,000
8	Washington, D.C.	3,090,000	755,000
9	Cleveland, Ohio	2,380,000	733,000
10	St. Louis, Missouri	2,330,000	605,000
11	Pittsburgh, Pennsylvania	2,155,000	512,000
12	Miami, Florida–	1,990,000	345,000
	Fort Lauderdale, Florida		148,000
13	Houston, Texas	1,965,000	1,295,000
14	Baltimore, Maryland	1,945,000	900,000
15	Minneapolis, Minnesota–	1,940,000	427,000
	St. Paul, Minnesota		311,000
16	Seattle, Washington–	1,830,000	522,000
	Tacoma, Washington–		155,500
	Everett, Washington		54,000
17	Dallas, Texas	1,700,000	875,000
18	Atlanta, Georgia	1,605,000	498,000
19	Cincinnati, Ohio–	1,442,000	447,000
	Hamilton, Ohio		67,500
20	Milwaukee, Wisconsin	1,397,000	713,000
21	Buffalo, New York–	1,288,000	455,000
	Niagara Falls, New York		84,000
	incl. St. Catharines– Niagara Falls, Ontario	*1,593,000*	
22	San Diego, California	1,280,000	729,000
	incl. Tijuana, Mexico	*1,650,000*	
23	Kansas City, Missouri	1,238,000	510,000
24	Denver, Colorado	1,165,000	517,000
25	New Orleans, Louisiana	1,083,000	587,000
26	Hartford, Connecticut–	1,052,000	157,500
	New Britain, Connecticut		83,500
27	Phoenix, Arizona	1,040,000	615,000
28	Portland, Oregon	1,022,000	382,000
29	Indianapolis, Indiana	1,002,000	755,000
30	Dayton, Ohio–	964,000	241,000
	Springfield, Ohio		82,500
31	Columbus, Ohio	917,000	554,000
32	Providence, Rhode Island–	905,000	176,500
	Pawtucket, Rhode Island–		76,500
	Woonsocket, Rhode Island		47,000
33	San Antonio, Texas	868,000	666,000
34	Louisville, Kentucky	865,000	358,000
35	Rochester, New York	811,000	293,000
36	Memphis, Tennessee	795,000	632,000
37	Sacramento, California	732,000	260,000
38	Norfolk, Virginia–	699,000	305,000
	Portsmouth, Virginia		110,000
39	Fort Worth, Texas	697,000	400,000
40	Albany, New York–	695,000	113,000
	Schenectady, New York–		77,000
	Troy, New York		63,000
41	Oklahoma City, Oklahoma	659,000	378,000
42	Birmingham, Alabama	654,000	296,000
43	Honolulu, Hawaii	645,700	330,000
44	Akron, Ohio	642,000	272,000
45	San Bernardino, California–	586,000	106,000
	Riverside, California		142,000
46	Toledo, Ohio	576,000	383,000
47	Jacksonville, Florida	567,000	546,000
48	St. Petersburg, Florida–	555,000	225,000
	Clearwater, Florida		57,000
49	Flint, Michigan	543,000	193,000
50	Omaha, Nebraska–	540,000	358,000
	Council Bluffs, Iowa		61,500
51	Syracuse, New York	535,000	193,500
52	Nashville, Tennessee	534,000	454,000
53	Salt Lake City, Utah	527,000	175,000
54	Allentown, Pennsylvania–	510,000	110,000
	Bethlehem, Pennsylvania–		72,000
	Easton, Pennsylvania		29,800
55	Youngstown, Ohio–	508,000	138,000
	Warren, Ohio		63,500
56	Springfield, Massachusetts–	507,000	163,000
	Holyoke, Massachusetts		49,500
57	Richmond, Virginia	505,000	250,000
58	New Haven, Connecticut–	500,000	135,500
	Meriden, Connecticut		56,500
59	Tulsa, Oklahoma	478,000	342,000
60	Bridgeport, Connecticut	463,000	156,500
61	Tampa, Florida	460,000	283,000
62	Grand Rapids, Michigan	455,000	196,500
63	Charlotte, North Carolina	444,000	251,000
64	Knoxville, Tennessee–	421,000	174,000
	Maryville, Tennessee–		16,300
	Oak Ridge, Tennessee		27,900
65	Orlando, Florida	389,000	100,500
66	South Bend, Indiana–	386,000	124,500
	Elkhart, Indiana		43,700
67	El Paso, Texas	363,000	335,000
	incl. Ciudad Juárez, Mexico	*810,000*	
68	Harrisburg, Pennsylvania	360,000	66,500
69	Tucson, Arizona	350,000	273,000
70	Baton Rouge, Louisiana	348,000	168,000
71	Greensboro, North Carolina–	345,000	151,000
	High Point, North Carolina		64,300
72	Albuquerque, New Mexico	343,000	255,000
73	Wichita, Kansas	338,000	264,000
74	Worcester, Massachusetts	336,500	175,000
75	Fresno, California	320,000	172,500
76	Chattanooga, Tennessee	320,000	119,500
77	Canton, Ohio–	317,000	109,500
	Massillon, Ohio		32,700
78	Austin, Texas	314,000	265,000
79	Lansing, Michigan	311,000	133,000
80	Newport News, Virginia–	308,500	143,000
	Hampton, Virginia		126,000
81	Mobile, Alabama	308,000	193,000
82	Little Rock, Arkansas	305,000	135,000
83	Peoria, Illinois	304,500	126,500
84	Davenport, Iowa–	303,500	99,500
	Rock Island, Illinois–		49,800
	Moline, Illinois		45,800
85	Des Moines, Iowa	299,000	200,000
86	Columbia, South Carolina	298,000	113,000
87	Las Vegas, Nevada	294,000	135,000
88	Charleston, South Carolina	288,000	66,000
89	Utica, New York–	286,000	90,500
	Rome, New York		50,700
90	Fort Wayne, Indiana	280,000	176,000
91	Shreveport, Louisiana	274,000	187,000
92	Beaumont, Texas–	269,500	116,500
	Port Arthur, Texas		56,800
93	Spokane, Washington	266,500	171,000
94	Ventura, California–	264,000	60,500
	Oxnard, California		75,500
95	Madison, Wisconsin	257,000	175,500
96	Stockton, California	252,000	113,000
97	West Palm Beach, Florida	251,000	57,500
98	Jackson, Mississippi	250,000	156,000
99	Corpus Christi, Texas	249,000	207,000
100	Rockford, Illinois	247,500	147,000
101	Colorado Springs, Colorado	247,000	153,000
102	New London, Connecticut–	246,500	31,200
	Norwich, Connecticut		42,100
103	Huntington, West Virginia–	245,500	73,500
	Ashland, Kentucky		29,200
104	Wilkes-Barre, Pennsylvania	245,000	59,000
105	Binghamton, New York	244,000	62,000
106	Greenville, South Carolina	243,000	63,000
107	Winston-Salem, North Carolina	243,000	134,000
108	Columbus, Georgia	236,500	175,000
109	Raleigh, North Carolina	233,000	130,500
110	Lexington, Kentucky	231,000	117,000
111	Erie, Pennsylvania	228,500	128,000
112	Scranton, Pennsylvania	226,000	102,000
113	Charleston, West Virginia	221,000	71,500
114	Augusta, Georgia	219,500	58,000
115	Macon, Georgia–	218,500	123,000
	Warner Robins, Georgia		35,500
116	Kalamazoo, Michigan	214,000	86,000
117	Huntsville, Alabama	212,500	140,500
118	Waterbury, Connecticut	208,000	109,000
119	Reading, Pennsylvania	206,000	86,000
120	Evansville, Indiana	205,500	138,000
121	Pensacola, Florida	204,500	60,000
122	Roanoke, Virginia	201,500	92,500
123	Bakersfield, California	201,000	72,000
124	Sarasota, Florida–	200,500	41,000
	Bradenton, Florida		21,800
125	Savannah, Georgia	198,500	120,000
126	Portland, Maine	194,500	64,000
127	Montgomery, Alabama	193,500	135,000
128	Fayetteville, North Carolina	192,000	54,200
129	Saginaw, Michigan	184,500	91,000
130	Ogden, Utah	182,000	69,500
131	York, Pennsylvania	182,000	49,700
132	Muskegon, Michigan	181,000	44,500
133	Eugene, Oregon	178,000	81,500
134	Bay City, Michigan–	177,500	48,500
	Midland, Michigan		35,500
135	Lancaster, Pennsylvania	176,500	57,200
136	Durham, North Carolina–	176,000	96,000
	Chapel Hill, North Carolina		26,500
137	Lubbock, Texas	171,500	155,000
138	Gulfport, Mississippi–	167,000	46,000
	Biloxi, Mississippi		51,500
139	New Bedford, Massachusetts	161,000	102,000
140	Lincoln, Nebraska	160,800	151,000
141	Appleton, Wisconsin	157,500	59,500
142	Wheeling, West Virginia	156,900	47,500
143	Atlantic City, New Jersey	155,500	46,000
144	Santa Barbara, California	155,000	72,000
145	Duluth, Minnesota–	155,000	100,000
	Superior, Wisconsin		32,200
146	Poughkeepsie, New York	154,000	31,400
147	Fall River, Massachusetts	153,000	97,000
148	Topeka, Kansas	151,600	125,500
149	Cedar Rapids, Iowa	150,800	112,500
150	Salem, Oregon	148,500	70,500
151	Green Bay, Wisconsin	145,500	90,500
152	Newburgh, New York	144,000	26,300
153	Springfield, Missouri	143,200	124,500
154	Provo, Utah	143,000	56,200
155	Anderson, Indiana	142,600	70,500
156	Modesto, California	142,500	70,000
157	Manchester, New Hampshire	141,000	87,700
158	Springfield, Illinois	140,000	93,000
159	Steubenville, Ohio–	138,300	30,500
	Weirton, West Virginia		26,700
160	Oceanside, California–	136,500	44,000
	Vista, California		26,200
161	Racine, Wisconsin	135,000	95,500
162	Galveston, Texas–	134,200	61,500
	Texas City, Texas		39,500
163	Amarillo, Texas	133,000	126,500
164	Anchorage, Alaska	132,500	51,500
165	Jackson, Michigan	132,500	44,500
166	Waco, Texas	130,000	96,500
167	Spartanburg, South Carolina	129,200	45,500
168	Asheville, North Carolina	129,000	57,100
169	Elmira, New York–	129,000	39,000
	Corning, New York		15,500
170	Petersburg, Virginia–	129,000	36,300
	Hopewell, Virginia		23,800
171	Lake Charles, Louisiana	127,500	79,500
172	Reno, Nevada	126,500	76,500
173	Waterloo, Iowa	126,200	75,000
174	Muncie, Indiana	125,500	69,500
175	Lafayette, Louisiana	124,200	74,000
176	Champaign, Illinois–	123,500	58,000
	Urbana, Illinois		33,500
177	Terre Haute, Indiana	118,600	70,000
178	Gastonia, North Carolina	118,000	48,500
179	Decatur, Illinois	117,700	91,500
180	Monterey, California	117,500	26,600
181	Wichita Falls, Texas	116,800	97,200
182	Mansfield, Ohio	114,500	55,800
183	Pueblo, Colorado	114,300	99,500
184	Boise, Idaho	111,000	78,500
185	Johnstown, Pennsylvania	111,000	41,200
186	Battle Creek, Michigan	110,700	38,200
187	Santa Rosa, California	110,000	55,500
188	Daytona Beach, Florida	108,000	45,600
189	Kenosha, Wisconsin	107,500	80,500
190	Monroe, Louisiana	107,000	57,000
191	Middletown, Ohio	104,200	48,500
192	Lafayette, Indiana	103,200	44,800
193	Kingsport, Tennessee	103,000	32,000
194	Altoona, Pennsylvania	103,000	62,500
195	Pittsfield, Massachusetts	102,200	57,000
196	Tallahassee, Florida	102,000	76,500
197	Lima, Ohio	101,600	53,300
198	Fitchburg, Massachusetts–	101,500	43,200
	Leominster, Massachusetts		33,800
199	Lynchburg, Virginia	100,000	54,500
200	Benton Harbor, Michigan–	100,000	16,200
	St. Joseph, Michigan		10,900
201	Tuscaloosa, Alabama	100,000	66,300
202	Sioux City, Iowa	99,500	85,500
203	Nashua, New Hampshire	98,700	58,500
204	Melbourne, Florida	98,000	42,000
205	Fargo, North Dakota–	97,500	55,000
	Moorhead, Minnesota		29,800
206	Burlington, Vermont	97,000	39,000
207	Johnson City, Tennessee–	96,000	34,900
	Elizabethton, Tennessee		12,200
208	Lawton, Oklahoma	96,000	75,500
209	Santa Cruz, California	95,500	33,200
210	Anniston, Alabama	95,500	30,900
211	Cocoa, Florida	95,000	16,700
212	Alexandria, Louisiana	94,700	41,800
213	Kingston, New York	92,800	25,700
214	Albany, Georgia	92,200	75,500
215	Bremerton, Washington	92,200	36,500
216	Lakeland, Florida	91,700	41,800
217	Vineland, New Jersey–	91,000	50,500
	Millville, New Jersey		22,200
218	Abilene, Texas	91,000	88,000
219	Odessa, Texas	90,800	79,000
220	Burlington, North Carolina	90,700	36,600

Subject Index

A

Aborigine, characteristics, 118, 120
Abu Simbel, 94
Abyssal plain, 34
Acanthodians, 53
Accretion theory for origin of solar system, 12
Acervularia, 53
Addax nasomaculatus, 86
Adobe, 93
Aegilops speltoides, 65
  squarrosa, 65
Africa, grassland wild life, 76–7
  mountains, 80
  population, 133
  savanna, 76–7
Age, determination of rocks, 44–5, 60
  distribution of population, 132
Aggression in man, 140
Agouti, 75
Agriculture, farming types, 131
  land use, 92
  world production, 108
Ainu, characteristics, 120
Air, composition, 26–7
  masses, 28
  origins, 36
Albanian, characteristics, 121
Albatross, 69, 85
Albuquerque, from space-craft, 23
Aldebaran, 11
Alder, 73
Aldrin, Edwin, 18
Algae, 50
  in lichens, 80
  population boom and crash, 139
Alliances, world, 141
Alligator, 83
Alpine, characteristics, 118
Altitude, effects on life, 80
Aluminum, in Earth, 41
  world production, 98
America, colonization, 123
  See also United States
Amhara, characteristics, 120
Amino-acids, in cells, 49, 51
  in food, 128
Ammonia, in primordial atmosphere, 50
Amphibians, evolution, 53–5
Anchored graptolite, 52–3
Anchoveta, 107
Anchovies, 85
Andean sunset, 20
Andes, vegetation zones, 80
Andromeda nebula in, 10
Angmagssalik, height of Eskimos in, 128
Angler fish, 85
Animals,
  endangered species, 86–7
  environment adaptation, 66–7
  evolution, 54
  modern species and environments, 66–85
Animism, 124
Ankle fascia, 115
Ankylosaurus, 55
Ant lion, 79
Antarctic, 69
  weather, 30–1
Antares, 11
Anteater, 67
Antelope, 77
Anticline, defined, 44–5
Anus, human, 114
ANZUS pact, 141
Ape, 58, 60
Ape-man, 58, 60
Aphid, 137
Aplecta hypnorum, 83
Apollo-4, 20
Apollo-7, 23
Apollo-9, 23
Apollo-10, 19
Apollo-11, 18, 22–3
Arab, characteristics, 121
Arab League, 141
Araucarioxylon, 54
Archeology, techniques in, 60
Archaeopteryx, 55
Arctic, 68
  weather, 30
  people, 118
Argon in atmosphere, 26
Armadillo, 75, 62
Armenian, characteristics, 121
Arms race, 140
Armstrong, Neil, 18, 20
Art of cave dwellers, 61
Arteries, human, 115
Arthropods, 53
Asbestos, world production, 99
Ash (tree), 73
Asia, population, 133
Askja eruption, 25
Ass, wild, 66
Asterocalamites, 53
Asteroids, 14–15
  belt, 26
Asterophyllites, 53
Astronauts, 18, 20
Aswan High Dam, construction, advantages and hazards, 94–5
Atmosphere, 26
  circulation, 27
  composition, 26
  evolution, 36
  pressure, 26
  primitive Earth, 50
  primordial, 50
  temperature, 26
Atoll formation, 35
Audouin's gull, 86
Auricula, 80
Aurochs, 65
Aurora, 16–17, 26
  Australis, 17
  Borealis, 17
Australia, animals, 67
  mountains, 80
  population, 132–3
Australian zoogeographical realm, 67
Australoids, 118, 120
Australopithecus, 58, 61
Australopithecus africanus, 58
  robustus, 58
Azurite, crystals of, 46

B

Baboon, 76–7
Bacteria, in cell evolution, 50
Badger, 73, 79
Balaenoptera musculus, 87
Bantu, characteristics, 120
Barbel, 82
Barley, at high altitude, 80
  world production, 109
Barnard's star, 11
Basic magmas, 42
Basque, characteristics, 121
Bat, Eocene, 57
  serotine, 73
  vampire, 75
Bathyal zone, 84
Bathypelagic zone, 84
Batuta, John, 123
Beagle, voyage of, 62
Bear, Alaskan, 71
Bear cult, of primitive man, 61
Beaver, lodge, 71
  modern, 66, 71
  prehistoric, 57
Beech, 73
Beechwoods, 72
Beer, world production, 110
Beetle, dung, 79
  freshwater, 83
  stag, 73
Bering Strait, 71
Beryl, crystals of, 47
Beverages, world production, 110
BHC, as a pollutant, 136
Bile, human, 114
Bilharzia, 126
  in Egypt, 94–5
Biloxi, Mississippi, hurricane damage, 31
Biomes, Earth's natural zones, 66
Birds, 66–85
  endangered species, 86
  forerunners, 54–5
  of Paradise, 67, 75
  of prey, 81
Bison, 66
  prehistoric, 57
Bithynia, freshwater snail, 83
Blizzards, 31
Blood and race, 118
Blue-footed booby, 63
Blue John, crystals of, 47
Blue tit, 73
Body of man, 114–15
Bones, 115
Bonito, 85
Boreal mountain zone, 80
Bothriolepis, 53
Botryocrinites, 53
Box turtle, 72
Brachial plexus, human, 115
Brachiopods, 45, 52–3
Brain, 116
  development, 58
  pathway, 10
Brazil, mountain zones, 80
Bread wheat, development, 65
Bricks, from clay, 93
Brinksdal Glacier, 42
Brittle star, modern, 85
  prehistoric, 52
Bronchitis, 127, 138
Brontosaurus, 55
Brotulid, 85
Bryozoa, 53
Buddha, 124
Buddhism, 124
Buffalo, 66, 76
  African, 77
Bullhead, fish, 82
Burial, early human, 61
Burmese, characteristics, 119
Bushman, characteristics, 118, 120
Butterflies, mountain, 80
  swamp, 83
  tropical, 74–5
Buzzard, 81
  nest, 60

C

Cacao, world production, 110
Cactus, 78–9
Caddis-fly larva, 83
Calamites, 54
Calcite, crystals of, 47
Calcium, fluoride crystals, 47
  in Earth, 41
Caldera, 38
Caledonian, mountains, 45
  period, 99
California, bad land use, 92
Californian condor, 86
Calories, 129–30
Camarrhynchus pallidus, 63
Cambrian period, 45, 52
  and life forms, 52
  rocks, 52
Camel, 79
  plowing, 92
Camptosaurus, 55
Canada, mineral output, 98
Canals and water resources, 102
Cancer, human, 127
Canis dirus, 57
Canopy, of forest, 75
Canyon erosion, 42
Carbohydrates and nutrition, 128, 130
Carbon dioxide, in atmosphere, 26
Carboniferous period, 45
  and life forms, 52–4
  and today's minerals, 104
Caribou, 66, 70
Carnivores, 66
  polar, 70
  grassland, 77
Carotid artery, 115
Carpoids, 53
Cassia, world production, 110
Cassiterite, crystals of, 47
Cassowary, 67
Caste system in India, 124
Castoroides, 57
Cat, Australian, 67
  prehistoric, 56
Cattle, breeding, 65
  savanna, 77
  world production, 110
Caucasoids, characteristics, 118, 121–2
Cave, bear cults, 61
  early habitation, 60
  paintings, 61
Cavy, 81
Cells, brain, 116
  human, 64
  living, 50–1
  primitive, 49–50
Central Treaty Organization (CENTO), 141
Centrosaurus, 55
Cephalaspis, 53
Cephalopods, 84
Cereals, agriculture, 92
  mutations, 65
  world production, 108–9
Cerebral cortex, 117
Certhidia, 63
Cerussite, crystals of, 46
Chaetonotus, 83
Chain coral, 53
Chameleon, 75
Chamoix, home, 81
Chasmops, 52
Cheetah, 77
Chemicals, as pollutants, 135
  sources and production, 99
Chestnut, 73
Chiasmodus niger, 85
Chimpanzee, 67, 75
Chinchilla, 81
Chlorophyll, significance, 50,
Chloroplasts, 50
Cholera, incidence, 126
Christianity, 124
Chromosomes, inheritance from, 64
Chromosphere, 14, 26
Chyme, 114
Cinnamon, world production, 110
Cities, modern, 123
Citrine, crystals of, 47
Civil uprisings, 141
Clams, 52
Clay, as useful mineral, 93
Clean Air Act (UK), 138
Climacograptus, 52
Climate, 16
  and animal environment, 66
  and physique, 128
  and weather systems, 28–31
Climatius, 53
Cloud, 28, 30
  nacreous, 31
  types, 29
Cloves, world production, 110
Coal, 100–1
  undersea, 105
Coastline development, 43
Cobalt, in Earth, 41
  related to manganese, 105
  world production, 105
Cobra, 76
Cocoa, world production, 110
Cod, Atlantic, 107
Coelacanths, 55
Coffee, world production, 110
Cold front, 28–9
Colds lands environment, 70
Collieries, 101
Colombo Plan, 141
Colonization of America, 123
Columbus, Christopher, 123
Condor, 86
Confucius, 124
Confucianism, 124
Coniferous forest environment, 71
Conservation, 94
Constance, Lake, pollution of, 139
Contact metamorphism, 42
Continental, drift, 7, 36, 41, 45
  shelf, 32, 34–5, 43
  and minerals, 104
  slope, 32
Continents, areas, 41
Convection currents in Earth's mantle, 41
Cook, James, 123
Copper, related to manganese nodules, 105
  world output, 98–9
Coral, atoll, 35
  islands, formation, 84
Corals, ocean, 84
  primitive, 52–3
Coriolis force, 30
Corn, at high altitudes, 80
  world production, 108
Cornuboniscus, 53
Cortex, 116
Coryphodon, 56
Cosmic rays, 16, 26
Cotylosaurs, 54
Cougar, 81
Cowries, 84
Crab, red land, 63
Crane, 86
Cranium, 58
Crankcase breather, 138
Cretaceous period, 43, 45
  and crustal movement, 37
  life forms, 55–6
Crinoid, 52–3
Cro-magnon man, 59
Crops, Neolithic, 60
  species development, 65
  world production, 108–9
Crossbill, 72
Crustaceans, 84
Crustal convergence and divergence, 37
Crystals, 46
Cucumber, abyssal and deep-sea swimming, 85
Cuvier, Georges, 7
Cyclones, development, 28–30
Cyclops, 83
Cyrenaica, oasis, 78

D

Dace, 82
da Gama, Vasco, 123
Dairy farming, world production, 110
Dams, consequences, 94–5
Dart, Raymond, 58
Darwin, Charles, 7, 62–3
Dating methods, rock 44–5, 60
  radio-carbon, 45
  radiometric, 44–5
da Vinci, Leonardo, 114
DDT and pollution, 136–7
Deer, 73
Deficiency diseases, 130
Delta, formation, 43
  of Nile, 95
Depression, atmospheric, 28–9
Desalination of sea-water, 102–3
Desert, 78–9
  animals, 79
  erosion, 42–3
  irrigation, 94–5
  plants, 78
  water, 78
Destructive waves, tsunami, 39
Detergents and pollution, 138
Devonian period, 45
  animals, 52–4
Diamond, crystals of, 47
  world production, 98
Diatryma, 56
Dictyonema, 52
Didymograptus, 52
Dieldrin and pollution, 137–8
Diet, and nutrition, 128–9
  by continents, 110–11
  deficient, 130
  world, 130
Digestive system, human, 114
Dik-dik, 76
Dimetrodon, 54–5
Dinosaurs, 54–6
Diretmus argentus, 85
Diseases, 126
  deficiency, 130
  endemic, 127
Displaced people, 94
DNA (deoxyribonucleic acid), 50–1
  species variation, 64–5
Dodoth, characteristics, 120
Dolerite, crystals of, 46
Dolphin, 85
Don Amigos, ship, 122
Dordogne cave dwellings, 59
Dormouse, 73
  nest, 73
Double helix of DNA, 51
Downham Market, English fenland, 95
Downwarping, 43
Dragonfly, 83
Dredging, for minerals, 105
  in land reclamation, 93
Drill, bit, 96
  rigs, 104
Drilling for natural gas, 101
Drug addiction, 127
Drugs, 127
Duck-billed platypus, 67
Duffy factor, 118
Duiker, 75
Duisbergia, 53
Dung beetles, 79
Dunnock, 66
Duodenum, 114
Dust bowls, 76
Duststorm, 31
Dyes, fabric, 93
Dikes, land reclamation, 93

E

Eagle, and insecticides, 138
  black, 81
  monkey-eating, 87
  tropical harpy, 75
Ear, structure of, 117
Earth, abuse, 93, 134
  activity, 38
  anatomy, 40
  changes in structure and form, 40
  chemical composition of crust, mantle and core, 41
  convection currents in mantle, 41
  crust, 37
  density of interior, 41
  development of crust, mantle and core, 40
  environment, 26
  evolution, 40
  expansion, 40
  forces shaping, 42
  in solar system, 14
  in space, 9
  interior, 40
  life on, 49
  lifespan, 13
  magnetic field, 97
  origin, 12
  pressure of interior, 41
  resources 89 et seq
  monitoring, 89
  primitive uses of, 93
  rising, view from Moon, 19
  sphericity, 7, 13, 40
  structure, 25 et seq
  Sun's influence on, 16
  temperature of interior, 41
  treasures of (minerals), 46
  under the sea, 34
  view from space, 20, 22
  water coverage, 41
Earthquakes, 38–9
Echinoderms, 53
Echinoid, 53
Echinopsis, 79
Eclipses, 19
Ecosphere, 17
Edaphosaurus, 54–5
Edible dormouse, 66
Eel, gulper, 85
  pelican, 85
Efficiency of farming, 131
Egypt, Aswan High Dam, 94
Eland, 76–7
Electricity, 91
  consumption, 100
  from nuclear energy, 101
Elephant, African, 67, 76–7
  Indian, 66, 75
Elk, 66
Emotions, control, 117
Encrinurus, 53
Endeavour, Cook's ship, 123
Endoplasmic reticulum, 51
Energy, consumption, 100
  resources, 100–1
English, language, 125
  race, 121
Ensatina, salamanders, 65
Entebbe, Uganda, temperature and population physique, 128
Environment, adaptation to, 66
  control of in agriculture, 92
  zoogeographical classification, 66
Enzymes, 114
Eocene period, 56–7
  and crustal movement, 37
  and life forms, 56–8
  trees, 56
Eohippus, 56–7
Epiphyte, 75
Epsilon Eridani, 11
Equator, snowline, 80
Equus, 57
Erebia, 80
Erosion, earth, 42–3
  of Egyptian coast, 95
Eryops, 53–4
Eskimos, 68
  characteristics, 118–19
  stature and food, 128
Ethiopian zoogeographical realm, 67
Euglena, 83
Euphorbias, 78
Europe, population, 132
Europoort, 104
Eutrophication of lakes and rivers, 139
Evaporation into atmosphere, 27
Evolution, of Earth, 40
  of land and sea, 36
  of man, 58–62
  of terrestrial life, 7, 50
Exhaust, road vehicle, 134, 138
Exosphere, 26
Eyes, 117
  and disease, 130

F

Fairy bluebird, 66
Fallopian tubes, 115
Family of man, 118–21
Fan palm, 55
Farm produce, 131
Farming, efficiency, 131
  output, 108–10
Farmscape, 90–1
  survey of, 94
Fascia sheath, 115
Fats and fatty acids, 128, 130
Faults, in Earth's crust, 44
Feather star, 84
Femur, 115
Fens, 95
Ferrel cell of atmosphere, 27
Ferro-alloy metals, sources, 99
Fertilization, of cell, 64

Fertilizers, chemical, in
Egypt, 95
inorganic, 92
mineral, 98
Fibers and weaving, 93
Fibula, 115
Fijian, characteristics, 120
Filipino, characteristics, 119
Finches, Darwin's, and
natural selection, 63
Fish, commercial, 106–7, 111
earliest, 52–3
farms, 107
flying, 85
freshwater, 82
ocean, 84–5
pollution, 135–6
primitive, 54
Fisheries, 106–7
Egyptian, 94
Fishing gear, 107
Fissure eruption, 38
Fitzroy, Captain Robert, 62
Fjord, 69
Flagellate, 83
Flash flood, causes, 31
Flatworm, 83
Fleurantia, 51
Floods, effects, 31
Flowers, Arctic, 70
mountain, 80
tropical, 74
Flycatcher, 66
Flying fish, 85
Food, 128
and concentration of
pollution, 136–7
and nutrition, 129
and population, 129
chains, 131
energy value, 131
from oceans, 106–7
human, digestion, 114
need for, 128
principal constituents, 128
resources of Earth, 108–10
supplies and malnutrition, 130
world production, 108–11
Forests, broadleaf evergreen,
72
coniferous, 71
montane, 80
prehistoric, 54
temperate, 72
tropical, 74–5
Fossils, earliest, 52
hominid, 58, 60, 122
pre-Cambrian life forms, 53
Fox, 73
flying, 75
kit, 79
Frigate bird, 63, 85
Frog, common, 83
grey tree, 74
Frontal systems, atmospheric,
27–9
Frost, Robert, 142
Fuels, 101
and energy, 100
nuclear, 98, 101
Fungus, and lichen, 80
on oak, 73
tropical forest, 75

G

Galapagos Islands, 62–3
penguin, 86
Galaxies, 8–11
Gall, bladder, 114
wasp, 73
Game-cropping, 76
Gametes, production, 64
Gang Canal, India, 102
Garbage, 138
Gas, fuels, 101
in primordial atmosphere, 50
natural resources, 104
Gastropods, 45
Gazelle, 79
Gemini-7, 20
Gemstones, structure, 46
Gentian, 80
Geoffroy's spider monkey, 75
Geological map, 44
Geology, language of, 44
mapping, 96–7
Geophones, uses, 96
Geophysical exploration, 96
George Washington, nuclear
submarine, 140
Geospiza, 63
Geosyncline, defined, 43
Gerenuk, 76–7
Geysers, 38
Giant nautiloid, 52
otter, 86
snail, 52
squid, 85
tortoise, 63
Gibbon, 66, 75
Gigantoproductus, 53
Gila monster, 79
Ginger, world production, 110
Giraffe, 67, 76–7
Glaciers, 34
erosion by, 42–3
prehistoric, 45
Gland, pituitary, 116
Glaze, ice accretion, 29
Glomar Challenger, drilling
ship, 104
Gnu, 76–7
Goat, African grassland, 77
mountain, 81
Gold, 98–9
Gondwanaland, 36, 45
Gorilla, 67
mountain, 87
Gorilla gorilla beringei, 87
Grahamland, fjord, 69
nacreous cloud, 69
Grain, in N America, 92
world sources and
production, 108–9
Grand Canyon, 42
Granite, 46
Grapes, world production,
108–9
Graptolites, 45, 52–3
Grasshopper, lubber, 83
Grasslands, 76
Gravel resources, 104
Gravimeter, 97
Gravimetric surveys, 97
Gravity, and atmospheric
pressure, 26
and tides, 33
during formation of Earth, 36
Grayling, 82
Great Barrier Reef, 22
Great Britain, ship, 123
Great, hornbill, 75
tit, 64
Greenhouses, 92
Greenland, 68
and continental drift, 36
ocean currents, 33
Griffon vulture, 77
Ground roller, long-tailed, 87
Grus americana, 86
Guillemot, and pollution, 137
Guinea pig, 67
Gulf Stream, 32–3
Gull, Audouin's, 86
Guyot, development, 35
Gymnogyps californianus, 86
Gypidula, 53

H

Haboob, dust storm, 31
Hail, 28–9
Half-life (radioactive decay)
45
Hardness scale of minerals, 46
Hare, 71
Hatchet fish, 85
Hawaiian Islands, and
tsunamis, 39
Health of man, 126–7
Hearing, 117
Heart, 114
daily output, 114
Hedgehog, 66
Helium flash, 12
Hematite, iron ore, 99
Hemimorphite, crystals of, 46
Hemorrhagia, causes, 130
Herbivores, 66
savanna, 76–7
Hercynian period, 99
Herring, 106–7
Hexacrinites, 53
High altitudes, life forms
at, 80
Himalayas, 80
formation, 37
Hindu, characteristics, 121
Hinduism, 124
Hippocampus and human
memory, 117
Hippopotamus, 67
Holarctic zoogeographical
region, 66
Holland, *See* Netherlands
Holoptychius, 53
Hominids, 58
Hominoids, 58
Homo erectus, 58–9, 122
sapiens, 58–9, 122
sapiens Neanderthalensis, 61
sapiens sapiens, 59, 61, 113
Homonunculus, 117
Hong Kong, population
density, 132–3
Horny-orb shell, 83
Horse, one-toed, 56–7
three-toed, 56–7
Hospitals, mental, 127
Hottentot, characteristics,
118, 120
Howler monkey, 67
Human, body structure,
114–15
burial, prehistoric, 61
cell, 64
diseases, 114–15
Humboldt current, 63
Humming bird, 67, 74–5
Hupa, characteristics, 119
Hurricanes, 23
damage caused by, 31
structure, 30
Huxley, Sir Julian, 6–7
Huxley, Thomas Henry, 7, 62
Hydra, 83
Hydro-electric plant, 101
Hydro-electricity, Aswan, 94
Hydrogen cyanide in primtive
atmosphere, 50
Hydrologic cycle, 102
Hydrosphere, 36
Hyena, 76–7
Hypothalamus and emotion
control, 117
Hyrachyus, 56
Hyrax, 81

I

Ibex, 81
Ice Ages, 16, 34
and life forms, 56
Icebergs, 69
Ice-caps, 34
Greenland, 68
Antarctic, 69
Iceland, eruption, 25
formation, 34, 37–8
Ichthyosaurs, 54
Iguana, 62, 74
Impala, 76–7
Inca agriculture, 80
Incubation of penguin eggs,
69
India, and continental
drift, 36–7
population, 133
water resources, 102
Indian, N American,
characteristics, 119, 122
Industrial revolution, 91
Infra-red photography, 23, 89
Inheritance, mechanism of,
7, 64–5
Insecticides and pollution,
134, 136, 138
Insects, freshwater, 83
mountain, 80
on oak tree, 73
prehistoric, 54, 57
Intestines, functions and
structure of, 114
Invertebrates, early, 53
Ionosphere, 26
Iron, in Earth, 41
ore deposits, 99
Irradiation and mutations, 65
Irrigation, 92
in Egypt, 94
world map, 103
Islam, 124
Island, submerged, 35
Italy, emerging coastline, 43
Ituri, characteristics, 120

J

Jaguar, 75
Jamoytius, 53
Japan, diet, 129
land use map, 95
Japanese, characteristics, 119
Java man, 59
Jay, 73
Jeans, Sir James, 12
Jellyfish, deep-sea, 85
prehistoric, 52
Jenner, Dr. Edward, 126
Jewels, 46
Jews and Judaism, 124
Jupiter, 13–15
Jurassic period, 43, 45
and life forms, 55

K

Kakapo, 87
Kalahari Bushman,
characteristics, 120
Kangaroo, 67
rat, 79
Kepler, Johannes, 14
Keratomalacia, causes, 130
Kettle holes, 43
Khoisans, characteristics, 120
Kimberlite, crystals of, 47
Kingfisher, 82
Kirghiz, characteristics, 119
Kiwi, 67
Knee-cap, 115
Koala, 67
Krill, 69
Kuroshio current, 32
Kwashiorkor, effects, 128

L

Labrador Sea, source of deep
ocean water, 33
Laccolith, 38
Lactiferous sinuses, 115
Lake Constance, pollution
of, 139
Lake Nasser and Aswan
High Dam, 94
Lake Okeefenokee, 83
Lakes, and eutrophication, 82
and pollution, 139
Lamarck, Jean-Baptiste
Pierre, 7
Lamb, frozen carcasses, 110
Land, abuse, 92, 134
evolution, 36
invasion by living things, 54
reclamation from sea, 93,
104
use, by man, 90, 92
patterns of (maps), 94
surveys, 23, 94
Landscape, medieval, 90-1
modern, 90–1
19th century, 90–1
prehistoric, 90–1
submarine, 34
Languages of man, 125
Langur, Indian, 75
Lantern fish, 85
Laplace, Pierre Simon, 12
Lapp, characteristics, 118, 121
Latin America, animals of, 67
population, 132
Latitude and altitude, effect
on life, 80
Latvian, characteristics, 121
Laurasia and continental
drift, 36
Lava, 38, 42
Leakey, Dr. Louis, 58
Leech, 83
Leif the Lucky (Viking
explorer), 123
Lemming, 70
Lemur, 56
Leopard, 75, 77
coral, 84
snow, 87
Lepidodendron, 54
Lianas, 74–5
Lichen, 69, 80
Life, dawn of, 49–50
earliest fossil forms, 53
evolution, 7
final forms, 55
human, 112–21
Lightning, shown in fossils,
44
Limbic system, human, 117
Limestone, 46
Limnoscelis, 54
Lion, 67, 76–7
Lithostrotion, 53
Liver, 114
Livestock, 92
world production, 110–11
Lizard, 79
flying, 75
horned, 79
primitive, 55
sea-going (marine iguana),
62
Loach, 82
Long-tailed ground roller, 87
Lonsdaleia, 53
Lubber grasshopper, 83
Lumbering, in northern
coniferous forest, 71
Lung cancer in the US, 127
Lunik-3, 18
Lyell, Charles, 60
Lynx, 71

M

Macrocystella, 52
Macaroni penguin, 69
Mace, world production, 110
Madagascar, fauna, 56
Magellan, Ferdinand, 123
Magellanic clouds, 10
Magic, and early man, 61
Magma, 38, 42
Magnesium, in earth, 41
world production, 105
Magnetic, field of Earth,
16–17
surveys in mineral
prospecting, 97
Magnetometer, 97
Maize, world production, 108
Malachite, crystals of, 46
Malaria, 126
DDT against, 137
Malnutrition, 128, 130
Mamillary bodies, 116
Mammals, Age of, 56
placental, 66
Man, 113 *et seq*
and agriculture, 108–11
and pollution, 134–39
as aggressor, 140
body, 114–15
diversity, 113, 118–21
effects on land, 90–3
evolution, 58–62
family, 118–21
health, 126–7
language and religion,
124–5
mental processes, 116
migration, 122–3
mind, 116–7
nutrition, 128–9
performance limits, 114
precursors, 58
racial patterns, 113, 118–21
structure, 114–17
Mandible of early man, 58
Mandrill, 75
Manganese, mining of
nodules, 105
oxide, 105
world production, 98
Mankind, spread, 122
Man-o'-war bird, 63
Maps, geological, 44
land-use survey, 94–5
Marasmus, 128
Marlin, 85
Marmoset, 75
Marmot, 71
Alpine, 81
Mars, 14–15, 17
Marsupials, distribution, 67
evolution, 56, 66
Mastodon, 57
Meat, products and
nutrition, 128
types and world production,
110
Meganeuron, 54
Megatherium, 57
Melanesians, characteristics,
118
Memory, human, 117
Mendel, Abbé, 7
Mental, hospitals, 127
processes of man, 116
Mercury, compounds and
pollution, 136
contamination, 138
planet, 14–15
Merychippus, 57
Mesohippus, 57
Mesolithic period, 60–1, 93
Mesonyx, 56
Mesosphere, 26
Mesozoic period, 99
Messenger RNA, 51
Metal-bearing muds, 105
Metals, mining techniques,
97
non-ferrous, 98
precious, 98–9
production, 98–9
prospecting for, 96–7
Metamorphism of rocks, 42–4
Metatarsals, 115
Meteorites, 26–7
Meteorology, 28
Meteors, 26–7
Methane, in primitive
atmosphere, 50
Methylmercury and
pollution, 136
Mexico, age distribution, 132
Mica, thin section, 46
world production, 99
Micrometeorites, 26
Microspheres, 49–50
Mid-brain, 116
Midge, 83
larva, 83
Migration, of birds, 68
of man, 122
Milk reservoirs, human, 115
Millet, world production, 108
Mind of man, 116–17
Minerals, and mineral
resources, 98–9
crystals, 46
in cold lands, 71
in food, 128, 130
ocean resources, 104
prospecting for, 96–7
under land, 98–9
Minimata, tragedy, 136
Mining, in tundra, 71
contrasts in, 97
Minnow, 82
Miocene period, and animal
life, 57–8
and crustal movement, 37
Missiles, 140
Mistletoe, 73
Mitochondria, 50–1
Mocking bird, 66
Mohammed and Islam, 124
Mohs' hardness scale, 46
Mole, 67, 73
Molecules, primordial, 50
Mongoloids, characteristics,
118–19
migrations, 122
Monkey (see under different
species)
howler, 67
New World, 67
Monoclinal fold, 44
Monograptus, 52
Monsoon, 31
Montane forest, 80
Monte Circeo man, 59
Monument Valley, Utah, 78
Moon, 18
eclipse, 19
influence on Earth's tides, 33
man's landing on, 18
moth, 72
Moose, 71
Morgan, T.H., 7
Moslem, 124
Mosquito and malaria, 126
pupa, 83
Moths, 72, 74, 83
Motor brain, 116–17
Mountain, animals, 80
building, 37, 42
flora and fauna, 80–1
gorilla, 87
insects, 80
lion, 81
plants, 80
Mouse, 79
Mu-mesons, 26
Muller, H.J., 7
Munich 15040 (Barnard's
star), 11
Muscles, of man, 115
Muscovite, 99
Mushroom Rock, Death
Valley, California, 42
Musk ox, 57
Muskeys, 70
Mutton, world output, 110
Mycoplasmas, 50
Myriapods, 54

N

Nappe, 45
Nasser, Lake, 94
NATO, 141
Natural, gas, 101, 104
selection, 7, 63–5
and Darwin, 62
Nautiloids, 52
Nchanga Pit, 97
Neanderthal man, 58–9
distribution, 122
Nearctic zoogeographical
realm, 66
Nebulae, 8–11
Nebular hypothesis, 12
Negrillo, characteristics, 118
Negro, characteristics, 118
slave movement, 122
Negroid, types, 118, 120
Nematophyton, 53
Neolithic period, 60, 93
Neotropical zoogeographical
realm, 67
Neptune, 13–15
Nerves, human, 115
Nest epiphytes, 75
Netherlands, land use and
reclamation, 92–3
New Mexico, from spacecraft,
23
New Zealand, cattle, 92
endangered animals, 87
mountains, 80
population, 133
Newt, 83
Niacin, 130
Nickel, in Earth, 41

Subject Index

related to manganese, 105
world production, 98
Nicotinic acid and health, 130
Nile delta, 95
Nimbus weather satellites, 23
Nimbus-3, 23
Nitrogen, atmospheric, 26
Non-ferrous metals, 98–9
Nordics, characteristics, 118, 121
Norsemen, exploration, 123
North America, population, 132
Nose, human, 117
Nuclear, energy, 100–1
fission, 101
fuels, 99, 101
power station, 101
and thermal pollution, 134, 139
radiation, 136
reactors, 101
submarine, 140
weapons, 134, 136, 140–1
Nucleic acids, 50
Nucleus of cell, 51, 64
Nutmeg, world production, 110
Nutrition, human, 128–30

O

Oak, ecology of, 73
growth and rings, 73
Oarfish, 85
Occlusion, 29
Ocean, areas, 41
as cradle of life, 52
currents, 32–3, 66
drainage of land, 34, 102
Earth under the, 34–5
evolution, 36, 52
floor, 34
layers, 84
life forms in, 84
living resources, 106
mineral resources, 104
primeval, 52
proportions, 34
rises and ridges, 35
swell, 32
trenches, 34–5, 37
water, composition, 35
cycle, 102
desalination, 102–3
Oceanic crust, 41
Ocelot, 75
Octopus, abyssal, 85
Oil, 101
movements by tanker, 139
pollution, 138–9
resources, 104–5
Oilfields, 103
Okeefenokee, Lake, 83
Olduvai Gorge, 58
Olenellus, 52
Oligocene epoch, and animal life, 57–8
and crustal movement, 37
Ona, characteristics, 119
Opal, crystals of, 46
Open-cast mines, 97
Opossum, 67
Orangutan, 66
Orbits, of solar system, 12
Ordovician period, 45
and life forms, 52–3
Ore deposits, 99
Organelles and living cells, 50
Organic chemicals and pollution, 135
Organization of African Unity (OAU), 141
Organochlorine pesticides and pollution, 137–8
Oriental zoogeographical realm, 66
Origin of Species, 62
Ostrich, 77
Otter, Giant, 36
Ovaries, human, 64, 115
Owl, 72–3
Oxygen, and life, 50
in atmosphere, 26
in Earth, 41
Ozone, 26
and evolution of life, 51–1

P

P waves, seismic, 39
Pack ice, 68
Painted lady, butterfly, 79
Pakistan, hurricane, 30
Palearctic zoogeographical realm, 66
Paleocene epoch, 56
and crustal movement, 37
Paleolithic period, 60-1, 93
Paleosyops, 56
Paleozoic period,43
Pancreas, 114
Pangaea, 36, 45
Panicum, 108
Panthera unica, 87
Papillae, 117
Papuans, characteristics, 118
Particle shield, role of atmosphere as, 27
Parus major, 64
Pasque flower, 70
Patella, 115
PCB (polychlorinated biphenyl) and pollution, 137
Peacock, 66
Peking man, 58
Pelagic zone, 106–7
Pelée's hair 38
Pellagra and nutrition, 130
Pelvis, 115
Pelycosaurs, 54–5
Penguin, Antarctic, 69
endangered, 86
Galapagos, 63
Pennisetum, 108
Pentremites, 53
Pepper, world production, 110
Perch, 82
Periechocrimites, 53
Permafrost, 70
Permian period, 45
and life forms, 54
Peru, Current, 32
fisheries, 106
Pesticides and pollution, 134–5, 137
Petrel, 69
Petrification, in cave, 61
Petroleum, *See* Oil
Pheasant, 72
Philippine Islands, endangered eagle, 87
Photography, infra-red, 23, 89
Photostomias guerni, 85
Photosynthesis, and human food, 108, 129
in oceans, 84, 106
Phytoplankton, 69, 84
Piedade, coastal feature, 42
Pigs, world production, 110
Pika, 81
Pike, 82
Pilchard, 107
Pimento, world production, 110
Pinaroloxias, 63
Pitchblend world output, 96
Pithecophaga jefferyi, 87
Pituitary gland, 116
Placental mammals, 66
Placocystites, 53
Planets, 9–15
Plankton, and fisheries, 106
and pollution, 136
Antarctic, 69
oceanic, 84
Plants, as human food, 128
desert, 78
DNA in, 65
evolution, 52, 54
floating, 69
food resources, 108, 129
marine, 84
mountain, 80
Neolithic, 60
Plate, movements, 37
tectonics, 37
Platinum, world production, 98
Pleistocene period, and crustal movement, 37
and life forms, 59
Plesiosaurs, 54–5
Pliocene period, and animal life, 57–8
and crustal movement, 37
Pliohippus, 57
Plumage, seasonal, 70
Pluto, 14–15
Polar bear, habitat, 68
endangered, 86
Polar, caps, 68
cell, 27
water content, 102
weather, 30–1
Polders, 93
Polecat, 71
Poles, migration of geo-magnetic, 44
Pollack, Alaska Walleye, 107
Pollution, 134–9
air, 134–5, 138
control, 138–9
global problem, 138
land, 134
oil, 138–9
pathways, 136
radiation, 136
river, 137, 139
thermal, 134, 139
water, 134–7
Polo, Marco, 123
Polyps, 35
Pond, environment, 83
life, 83
skater, 83
sponge, 83
weed, 83
Pongids and evolution, 58
Pontypridd, land use map, 94
Population, 132
and food supply, 129
and land area, 132
density, 132
explosion, 132
Pork, world production, 110
Portuguese man-o'-war, 85
Potassium, in Earth, 41
world production, 98–9
Potatoes, at high altitude, 80
world production, 108
yield per hectare, 131
Pottery, 93
Potto, 67
Power, sources, 100
stations, 101
and pollution, 134, 139
nuclear, 101
supply from Aswan, 94
PP factor, 130
Prawn, 85
Pre-Cambrian period, 45
and minerals, 99
fossils of life forms, 52–3
Precious metals, 98–9
Precipitation, atmospheric, 27–9
Precis almana, 74
Procyon, 11
Pronghorn, 66
Prospecting for minerals, 96–7
Protaxocrinus, 53
Proteins, and food production, 108
and nutrition 128–30
evolution, 50–1
Proxima Centauri, 11
Psylophyton, 53
Ptarmigan, rock, 70
Pteranodon, 55
Pteraspis, 53
Pterodactyls, 54
Pteronura brasiliensis, 86
Pterosaurs, 55
Pueblo Indian, characteristics, 119
Pugnax, 53
Pulsars, 10–11
Puma, 81
Pygmies, characteristics, 120
Pyrites, crystals of, 47
Pyromorphite, crystals of, 46

Q

Quartz, crystals of, 46
Quaternary period, 45
Quechua, characteristics, 119

R

Rabbit, 77
Races, 118–21
Caucasoids, 121
distinguishing features, 118
Mongoloids, 119
Negroids, 120
Racial patterns, 113
Radiation, and pollution, 136
belts (Van Allen), 17
filtration by atmosphere, 26–7
shield, 27
sickness, 136
solar, 16
Radio-carbon dating, 45
Radio waves, 26–7
Radioactive, contamination, 134
isotopes, 45
materials, 96
wastes, 135
Radioactivity, and pollution, 136
Radiometric dating, 44–5
Rain, 28–9
Rainfall, 27
in hydrologic cycle, 102
Ramapithecus, 58
Rat tail, fish, 85
Rattlesnake, 66
desert, 79
prairie, 76
Raw material famines, 134
Reclamation, of land, 93 104
of water, 103
Rectum, 114
Recycling of refuse, 138
Red land crabs, 63
Red Sea, 105
Redondo Peak, from spacecraft, 23
Redwoods, 72
Reedbuck, 77
Refuse, domestic, 138
recycling, 138
Reindeer, 70
Religion, 124–5
Reptiles, flying, 54–5
giant, 54–5
modern, 66–86
prehistoric, 54–5
Resources, Earth's, 89
energy, 100–1
food, 108–11
minerals, 98–9
monitoring, 89
ocean, foodstuffs, 105–6
minerals, 104–5
primitive uses, 93
water, 102–3
Reticular system, 117
Retina, 117
Reuschella, 52
Rhamphorhynchus, 55
Rhea, 67
Rhesus factor, 118
Rhinoceros, 76–7
Rhodatricia, 79
Ribosome, 51
Ribs, 115
Rice, cultivation, 131
in Nile delta, 95
terraces, 92
world production, 108–9
Rickets, causes, 130
Rigel, 11
Ring species, 64
Rio Grande, from spacecraft, 23
Rip currents, 32
River, development, 42
levels in caves, 60
life forms, 82
pollution, 137, 139
water resources, 102
River Wye, 42
RNA, messenger, 51
transfer, 51
Roach, 82
Road vehicle exhausts, 134, 138
Rock, age and dating, 44–5
and mineral resources, 99
Cambrian, 52
cycle, 42–3
Earth's history recorded in, 44
fall in cave, 61
formation, 25
geosyncline formation, 43
igneous, 44, 46
metamorphic, 38, 44
periods, geological, 45
sedimentary, 44, 46
strata, 25
interpretation,' 44
Rodents, high altitude species, 81
Roe deer, 66
Rome, and city development, 123
Royal Poinciana, 74
Ruby, crystals of ,47
Rurban (rural-urban) fringe, 90
Russia, *See* Soviet Union
Rye, world production, 109

S

S waves, seismic, 39
Sable, 67
Saber-tooth tiger, 56-7
Sagittarius, 9
Sahara, 78–9
St. Paul's cathedral, erosion effects, 42
Salamander, Pyrenean, 81
speciation in western US, 65
Salmon, 82
Samburu, characteristics, 120
Samoyed, characteristics, 119
San Gabriel, ship, 123
San Juan Valley, erosion, 42
Sand, dunes, 42–3, 78
resources, marine, 104
Sangre de Cristo mountains, from spacecraft,-23
Santa Maria, ship, 123
Sargasso Sea, 32
Saturn, 13–15
Scorpion, 79
prehistoric, 54
Scurvy, 130
Sea, *See also* Oceans
floor movements, 37
lion, 63
pollution of, 137
scorpion, prehistoric, 52
slug, 84
snail, 85
urchin, 84
water, composition, 35
desalination, 102–3
Seabirds, 84–5
Seals, 68–9
Seaweeds, prehistoric, 53
Secretary bird, 67
Sediments, and minerals, 99
deposition, 43
formation on, 42
mapping, 44
transportation, 43
Seismic, mineral prospecting, 96
survey, 96
waves, 39
Seismographs, 39
Seismology, 39
Selenopeltis, 52
Senses, 117
Sequoias, 72
Serengeti plains, 76
Sewage, sludge and pollution, 134
treatment, 103
Sex cells, human, 64
Sexual reproduction, 64
Seymouria, 54
Sharks, basking, 85
ghost, 85
prehistoric, 53
Shearwater, Great, 85
Sheep, mountain, 81
wild, 66
world production, 110
Sheep-dips and pollution, 138
Shellfish, and pollution, 135–6
farming, 106
Shilluk, characteristics, 120
Shinto, 124
Shiupur head, 102
Shock waves, seismic, 96
Sicilian, characteristics, 121
Sierra Nevada, geosyncline formation, 43
Sight, human, 117
Sigillaria, 54
Silicon, in Earth, 41
Silurian period, 45
and life forms, 53
Silver, birch, 73
world production, 98
Sinai desert, 95
Sirius, 11
Skin color, 118
Skua, 69
Skull, bones of, 115
primitive, 58–9
Skunk, 66
Sleeping sickness, and cattle 76
spread, 126
Sloth, 67, 75
Smallpox, 126
Smell, cells sensitive to, 117
Smilodon, 57
Smoke control, and pollution, 138
Snails, freshwater, 83
Snakes, grassland, 76
primitive, 55
temperate forest, 72
tropical forest, 74–5
Snow, 28–9
blown, and blizzard, 31
leopard, 87
Snow, John, 126
Sodium, in Earth, 41
Soil, erosion, 92
sterility, 95
type, 92
Solar, *See also* Sun
heating, 66
prominences, 15
system, 12–15
timescale, 13
wind, 16–17
Soldier, and equipment, 140
Somali, characteristics, 120
Sorghum and millet, world production, 108
South America, prehistoric life forms, 56
South-East Asia Treaty Organization (SEATO), 141
Soviet Union, diet in, 129
mineral production, 98
Space, Earth in, 9
view of Earth from, 20–3
Spacecraft, 18
See under type names,
Spain, coastal changes, 43
diet, 129
Sparrowhawk, 73
Speciation by natural selection, 65
Species and variety, 64
Sperm, 64
Sphalarite, 99
Sphenacodon, 54
Sphene, crystals of, 46
Spheniscus mendiculus, 86
Sphenopteris, 53
Spices, world production, 110
Spiders, 74
Spine, human, 115
Spinning, 93
Spiral wall, cochlea, 117
Spirits, potable, 110
Squid, 85
primitive form, 52
Squirrel, 71, 73
Stag beetle, 73
Stalactite, 61
Stalagmite, 61
Stamp, L. D., 94
Standard of living, 133
Stars, 9–11
evolutionary sequence, 11
Starwort, 83
Stegosaurus, 55
Steinheim man, 59
Stickleback, 83
Stilt root, 75
Stomach, human, 114
Stone Age, 59
Stopping by Woods on a Snowy Evening (extract from), 142
Strata, *See* Rock strata
Stratosphere, 26–7
Strelitzia, 74
Strigops habroptilus, 87
Strontium-90, 136
Submarine, nuclear, 140
Sudan, duststorms, 31
Suez canal, 94
Sugar, glider, 67
in Peru, 80
world production, 111
Sulphur, 47
dioxide and pollution, 134–5
sources and production, 98–9
Sun, *See also* Solar
and early life, 50–2
and food production, 129, 131
and its neighbors, 11
collapse, 12
eclipse, 19
influence on Earth, 16
influence on tides, 33
limb of, 15
orbits around, 14
size, 11
structure, 14
surface, 14, 16
Sunfish, ocean, 85
Sunlight reflectance, 23
Sunset, Andean, 20
Sunspots, 16
Surtsey Island, volcanic formation, 38
Surveys, gravimetric, 97
land use, 94–5
magnetic, 97
regional, 96–7
Swamp ecology, 82–3
Swanscombe man, 59
Sweden, smallpox mortality, 126
Swifts, 75
Swiss alps, 80
Sycamore, 73
Syncline, 44–5

T

Tadpole, 83
Tahiti, 34
Taiga, 70
Tajik, characteristics, 121
Tamil, characteristics, 121
Tanzania, Serengeti plains, 76
Tapir, 67
Tarsal bones, 115
Tarsiers, 66
Tasman, Abel, 123
Tasmanian wolf (thylacine), 67, 87
Taste, cells sensitive to, 117
Tea, world production, 110
Telangium, 53
Temperate forests 72–3
Tendons, 115
Tern, Arctic, 68
Terrapin, 83
Tertiary period, 45
and minerals, 99
Tethys Sea, 36, 45

Textiles, 93
Thalamus, 117
Thalarctos maritimus, 86
Thermal pollution, 139
Thunderstorm, 30
Thylacinus cynocephalus, 67, 87
Tibetan, characteristics, 119
Tibia, 115
Tidal theories of Earth's origin, 12
Tides, 33
Tiger, 66, 75
  cowrie, 84
  saber-tooth, 56–7
  salamander, 66
Tobacco, world production, 110
Tokyo, and urban development, 123
Tongue, human, 117
Tools, oldest, 58
  primitive, 61
Torbernite, 47
Torrey Canyon tanker disaster, 139
Tortoise, Galapagos, 63
  leopard, 79
  mountain, 80
Toucan, 67, 75
Townscape, 90
Tradewinds, 30, 33
Transfer RNA, 51
Transport revolution, 90
Tree, frog, 83
  shrew, 66
Trees, cauliflorous, 75
  coniferous, 71
  deciduous, 72
  Eocene, 56
Trenches, ocean, 34–5, 37
Triassic period, 45
  and life forms, 54–5
Triceratops, 55
Trifid nebula, 9
Trilobites, 45, 52–3
Tripod fish, 85
Triticum aestivium, 65
  dicoccoides, 65
  monococcum,65
Trogonoptera brookiana, 74
Tropic, bird, 85
  of Cancer, 30
  of Capricorn, 30
Tropical, cell of atmosphere, 27
  forests, 74–5
  weather, 30
Tropopause, 26–7
Troposphere, 26–7
Trout, 82
Tsetse fly, 76
  and malaria, 126
Tsunami, 38–9
Tuareg, characteristics, 121
Tuatara, 67
Tuna, 85
Tundra, 70
Tungus, characteristics, 118
Turkey, wild, 66
  sheep in (country), 92
Turtle, box, 72
  exploitation of, 106
  soft-shelled swamp, 83
Tyneside, land use map, 95
Typhoon, 23
Tyrannosaurus, 54–5

U

Uintatherium, 56
Ulysses butterfly, 74
Uncites, 53
Underground water, 38
  quantity of, 102
Ungulates, 57
United Kingdom, births and deaths, 132
  bronchitis, 129
United Nations, 141
United States, energy resources, 100
  lung cancer deaths, 127
  water resources, 102–3
Universe, scale of, 10
Upper Paleolithic period, 59
Upwelling, of ocean water, 106
Uranium, and nuclear power, 101
  from pitchblende, 96
Uranus, 13–15
Uratelornis chimaera, 87
Urbanization, 123
  and population density, 132
Ussher, Archbishop, 12
USSR, *See* Soviet Union
Uterus, human, 115

V

Vanilla, world production, 110
Variety and species, 64
Vedda, characteristics, 118, 120
Vegetable oils, world production, 111
Veins, human, 115
Venus, 14–15, 17
Vertebrates, 52–3
Vesalius, Andreas, 114
Victoria, ship, 123
Vicugna vicugna (vicuna), 80, 86
Vietnam, great tit species, 64
  war, 140
Vines, 75
  and wine production, 108–9
Viper fish, 85
Virgin Islands, fisheries project, 107
Vitamins and nutrition, 128–30
Vogul, characteristics, 118
Volcanoes, 25
  forming atoll, 35
  types of eruption, 38
Vulture, 76–7

W

Wai Wai, characteristics, 119
Wallace, Alfred Russel, 7
Walrus, 68
War, 140–1
  and balance of power, 140–1
  trends in, 140
Warbler, 66
Warm front, 28–9
Warsaw Pact, 141
Wasp, paper, 73
Wastes, and pollution, 134
  and waste products, 103
  domestic, 138
  industrial, 134
Water, *See also* Oceans
  boatman, 83
  consumption, 103
  coverage of Earth, 41
  crowfoot, 83
  desert, 78
  domestic use, 103
  flea, 83
  fresh, modern life, 82–3
    prehistoric life, 54
  hog-louse, 83
  lily root, 83
  mite, 83
  origins, 36
  pollution, 134–5
  reclamation, 130
  resources, 102–3
  underground, 38, 102
  vapor, 26
Watussi, characteristics, 128
Wave, fronts, ocean, 32
Wavelite, crystals of, 47
Waves, destructive, 39
  generation, 32
  on beach, 33
  radio, 26–7
  seismic, 39, 96
Weasels, 56
Weather, 26
  and wind, 66
  chart, 29
  extremes, 30–1
  polar, 30
  systems, 28
  tropical, 30
Weathering of rocks, 42
Weaving, 93
Weddell Sea, source of cold water, 33
Wegener, Alfred, 7
Well logging, 96
Welsh valleys, map of land use, 94
Whale, blue, 87
  over-exploitation, 106
Wheat, at high altitude, 80
  strains, 65
  world production, 109
Whirligig beetle, 83
Whooping crane, 86
Wilberforce, Bishop, 62
Wild, ass, 66
  sheep, 66
  turkey, 66
Wildebeest, 76
Wildscape, 90–1, 94
Wind, and duststorm, 31
  and weather, 66
  erosion, 42
Wine, world production, 110
Wolf-359, 11
Wood frog, 72
Woodchuck, 71
Woodocrinus, 53
Woodpecker finch, 63
Woolly mammoth, 57
Worden gravimeter, 97
World Health Organisation (WHO), 126
Worms, freshwater, 83
  prehistoric, 54
Wye River, 42

X

Xenacanthus, 53

Y

Yak, 81
Yellow-billed oxpecker, 77
Yukaghir, characteristics, 118

Z

Zambia, copper mine, 97
Zaphrentis, 53
Zebra, 67, 76–7
Zinc blende, world production, 99
Zoogeographical realms, 66
Zooplankton, 69, 84
Zosterophyllum, 53

Acknowledgments

A great many people and institutions have given advice and assistance during the preparation of this book. The publishers wish to extend their thanks to them all, and in particular to the following:

Air Pollution Research Unit (M.R.C.), London. Bedford College, London. British Antarctic Survey. British Leyland, Coventry. British Museum of Natural History. Brookhaven National Laboratory, U.S.A. California Academy of Sciences. Chevron Oil (U.K.) Ltd. Cranfield Institute of Technology. *The Daily Telegraph*. Deep Sea Venture Inc. (U.S.A.). Directorate of Overseas Surveys (U.K.). *The Economist*. The Economist Intelligence Unit, London. Embassies and Cultural Offices of Australia, Canada, Denmark, Finland, India, Japan, Netherlands, New Zealand, Pakistan, South Africa, U.A.R., U.S.A., U.S.S.R. Environmental Science Services Administration (U.S.A.). Fairey Surveys Ltd, Maidenhead. *The Financial Times*. Food and Agricultural Organization (U.N.). The Galton Foundation, London. *Geographical Magazine*. Geological Survey and Museum, London. The Hale Observatories (Mt. Wilson and Palomar, U.S.A.,) The Harvard Center for Population Studies, U.S.A. Huntings Surveys Ltd. London. Imperial Chemical Industries, London. Institute of Psychiatry, London. Laboratory of Human Mechanics (M.R.C.), London. The Laboratory of Molecular Evolution, Miami, U.S.A. London School of Economics. The London School of Hygiene and Tropical Medicine. Lowestoft Seal Research Unit. Marine Biological Association of the United Kingdom. Medical Research Council, London. Meteorological Office, London. Ministries of H.M. Government. Monks Wood Experimental Station, England. Nature Conservancy. National Aeronautics and Space Administration (U.S.A.). National Coal Board. The National Institute of Oceanography, Surrey. *New Scientist and Science Journal. The Observer*. The Ordnance Survey of Great Britain. Pilkington Bros. Ltd., London. Queen Mary College, London. Royal Aircraft Establishment, Farnborough. The Royal Astronomical Society, London. Royal Institute of Netherlands Architects. The Royal Society for the Protection of Birds, London. The Science Museum, London. *Scientific American*. Shell Petroleum Co., London. Short Bros., Belfast. The Soil Association, Suffolk. The Stockholm Peace Research Institute. Survival Service Commission of the International Union for the Conservation of Nature. Unilever, London. Union for the Conservation of Nature. United Kingdom Atomic Energy Authority. United States Department of the Interior. United States Geological Survey. Universities of Cambridge, Liverpool, Newcastle-upon-Tyne, Oxford, Reading, Sheffield, Strathclyde. The Water Research Association. The White Fish Authority (U.K.). World Health Organization (U.N.). *Weather Magazine*. The Zoological Society of London.

The Ordnance Survey of Great Britain and the Landuse Surveys of Japan and Canada for permission to reproduce the landuse maps on pp 94–5.

Artists' credits

Section symbols throughout by Jim Bulman
10–11 Diagram 12–13 Diagram 14–15 Diagram, Colin Rose (time clock) 16–17 Diagram, Colin Rose (line drawing 19 Diagram 22 Colin Rose 26–7 Diagram 28 David Fryer & Centrum (map), Richard Lewis 29 David Fryer & Centrum (map), Centrum (clouds), Eric Jewel, Colin Rose 30 David Fryer & Centrum (map), Centrum, Eric Jewel 31 David Fryer & Centrum (maps), Eric Jewel 32–3 Diagram 34–5 Diagram 36–7 Diagram 38–9 Diagram, Sheilagh Noble (line drawing) 40–1 Diagram 42–3 Diagram 44–5 Diagram 50 Karel Thole/Artist Partners, Michael Ricketts, Richard Lewis 51 Richard Lewis 52 Diagram, Karel Thole/Artist Partners 53 Diagram, Sheilagh Noble, Karel Thole/Artist Partners 54–5 Diagram, Karel Thole/Artist Partners 56–7 Diagram, Karel Thole/Artist Partners 58–9 Colin Rose (maps), Diagram, Michael Ricketts, Peter Barrett/Artist Partners 60–1 Peter Barrett/Artist Partners, David Cook (chart) 62 Colin Rose (maps), Michael Ricketts 63 Harry Titcombe (birds), Colin Rose (diagram) 64 Richard Lewis, Colin Rose (map), John Norris Wood 65 Colin Rose (map), John Norris Wood, Charles Matheson (grasses), Harry Titcombe, Centrum and Colin Rose (diagrams) 66–7 Rex Gray, David Cook (animals) 68–9 Richard Lewis (maps), Peter Barrett/Artist Partners, Colin Rose (diagrams) 70–1 David Fryer & Centrum (map), Harry Titcombe, Anthony Joyce/Garden Studios 72 David Fryer & Centrum (map), John Norris Wood 73 Barry Driscoll/Artist Partners, Colin Rose (diagram), Harry Titcombe 74–5 David Fryer & Centrum (map), Peter Barrett/Artist Partners 76–7 David Fryer & Centrum (map), Colin Rose (diagram), Peter Barrett/Artist Partners 78 David Fryer & Centrum (map), Ian Garrard/Linden Studios 79 Richard Orr/Linden Studios 80 Richard Lewis, Victoria Gordon (violet), Catherine Bradbury/Garden Studios 81 Anthony Joyce/Garden Studios 82–3 Colin Rose (diagram), Harry Titcombe, John Norris Wood 84 Colin Rose 85 David Cook 86–7 David Fryer (map), Peter Barrett/Artist Partners 90–1 Roy Coombs/Artist Partners, Centrum (maps) 92 Richard Lewis 93 Richard Lewis, Sheilagh Noble (line drawings), Charles Matheson 94–5 Colin Rose (diagrams), Richard Lewis 96–7 Richard Lewis 98–9 David Fryer 100 Diagram 101 David Fryer 102 Colin Rose, Richard Lewis 103 Colin Rose, Richard Lewis 104–5 David Fryer & Centrum (map), Malcom Topp (line drawings), David Fryer (map), Centrum 106 David Fryer & Centrum (map), Richard Lewis, David Cook (line drawings) 107 Malcolm Topp, David Cook (fish), Richard Lewis 108–9 David Fryer, Centrum (diagrams), David Cook 110–11 David Fryer, Centrum (diagrams), David Cook 114 Giovanni Casselli/Artist Partners, Colin Rose (diagrams), Michael Ricketts 115 Charles Pickard/Creative Presentations 116 Charles Pickard/Creative Presentations 117 Richard Lewis (brains), Giovanni Casselli/Artist Partners 118–19 Colin Rose (diagram & maps), Peter Barrett/Artist Partners 120–1 Peter Barrett/Artist Partners, Colin Rose (maps) 122–3 David Fryer & Centrum (maps), David Cook 124–5 David Fryer 126–7 Giovanni Casselli/Artist Partners, Diagram 128–9 Giovanni Casselli/Artist Partners, Colin Rose, Diagram 130–1 Diagram, map based on American Geographical Society map Colin Rose 132 Diagram 133 Colin Rose (map), Diagram 134–5 Colin Rose (time scale), Roy Coombs/Artist Partners 136 Roy Coombs/Artist Partners, Giovanni Casselli/Artist Partners, Colin Rose, Harry Titcombe 137 Harry Titcombe (line drawings), Colin Rose (diagrams) 138 Roy Coombs/Artist Partners, Colin Rose, Richard Lewis, Harry Titcombe 139 Richard Lewis, Colin Rose 140–1 Diagram, Malcolm McGregor/PDA Illustration

Photographic credits

Photographs on each page are credited in descending order of the base line of each photograph. Where two or more photographs rest on the same level credits read left to right.
1 John Moyes 2–3 John Moyes 4–5 John Moyes 6 Camera Press Ltd, John Moyes 7 The Mansell Collection 8–9 The Hale Observatories (Mt. Wilson and Palomar) 11 The Royal Greenwich Observatory 12 The Hale Observatories (Mt. Wilson and Palomar) 17 National Aeronautics and Space Administration, U.S.A. (N.A.S.A.) A. H. Mikesell 18 N.A.S.A. 19 N.A.S.A., H. Brinton, W. Zunti 20 all N.A.S.A. 21 N.A.S.A. 22 all N.A.S.A. 23 all N.A.S.A. 24–5 Solarfilma (Iceland) 29 Ken Pillsbury, Ken Pillsbury Ken Pillsbury, M. J. Bramwell/N.H.P.A., Ken Pillsbury, Ken Pillsbury, Ken Pillsbury, M. J. Bramwell/N.H.P.A., Ken Pillsbury, J. Allan Cash, Picturepoint Ltd, Frank Lane, Ken Pillsbury 30 Associated Press 31 Brian Blake/Magnum, Barnabys Picture Library, U.S. Dept of Agriculture (Soil Conservation Service), Barnabys Picture Library, Picturepoint Ltd, M. J. Bramwell/N.H.P.A. 38 Solarfilma (Iceland) 39 Gerald Warhurst/Associated Press 42 Picturepoint Ltd, Barnabys Picture Library, Spectrum Colour Library, Spectrum Colour Library, Spectrum Colour Library 46–7 N.E.R.C. copyright: Reproduced by permission of the Director of the Institute of Geological Sciences, London 48–9 Institute of Molecular Evolution (University of Miami) 50 Institute of Molecular Evolution (University of Miami) 62 Francisco Erize/B. Coleman 63 Frances Perry, Sven Gillsater/B. Coleman, D. and J. Bartlett/B. Coleman, Tony Beamish/B. Coleman, D. & J. Bartlett B. Coleman, George Laycock/B. Coleman, D. and J. Bartlett/B. Coleman, Francisco Erize/B. Coleman, M. P. Harris/B. Coleman 64 Ken Moreman 68 M. J. Bramwell/N.H.P.A., Leonard Lee Rue/B. Coleman, Stephen Dalton/N.H.P.A. 69 all M. J. Bramwell/N.H.P.A. except lichen/British Antarctic Survey 70 Eric Hosking, Peter Keen, Eric Hosking, remainder C. Ott/B. Coleman 71 C. Ott/B. Coleman, National Film Board of Canada, Philip Wayre/N.H.P.A., Philip Wayre/N.H.P.A., Stephen Dalton/N.H.P.A., A. Huxley/N.H.P.A. 72 L. Willingen/Camera Press, J. N. Wood, J. N. Wood, Picturepoint Ltd. J. N. Wood, Eric Hosking, Eric Hosking 73 Stephen Dalton/N.H.P.A., J. Blossom/N.H.P.A., I. Beames/N.H.P.A., Walter Murray/N.H.P.A., J. Good/N.H.P.A., Stephen Dalton/N.H.P.A. 74 Gordon de'lisle/Picturepoint Ltd. Douglas Dickens/N.H.P.A., Russ Kine/B. Coleman, Paul Popper, John Markham, Russ Kine/B. Coleman, L. H. Newman/N.H.P.A., F. Baillie/N.H.P.A., John Markham, Anthony Bannister/N.H.P.A. 76 Heather Angel, Anthony Bannister/N.H.P.A., James Simon/B. Coleman 77 Heather Angel, R. J. Griffith, James Simon/B. Coleman, R. J. Griffith, Norman Myers/B. Coleman 78 Picturepoint Ltd, Middle East Archive, R. J. Griffith, Middle East Archive 79 Anthony Bannister/N.H.P.A., Anthony Bannister/N.H.P.A., Picturepoint Ltd., L. H. Newman/N.H.P.A., Anthony Bannister/N.H.P.A., John Markham, N. A. Callow/N.H.P.A., Anthony Bannister/N.H.P.A., E. Elkan/N.H.P.A., N. A. Callow/N.H.P.A. 80 G. W. Dowcra/N.H.P.A., R. Bock/B. Coleman, Heather Angel, L. H. Newman/N.H.P.A., J. N. Wood, Stephen Dalton/N.H.P.A., W. Zepf/N.H.P.A. 81 Peter Johnson/N.H.P.A., Jim Rowbotton/N.H.P.A., Peter Johnson/N.H.P.A., Heather Angel, Dick Robinson/B. Coleman, John Massey Stewart, C. Ott/B. Coleman, Brian Hawkes/N.H.P.A. 82 Ronald Thompson/F. W. Lane, John Markham, Heather Angel 83 all J. N. Wood 84 D. P. Wilson, D. P. Wilson, remainder Anthony Bannister/N.H.P.A. 88–9 Fairey Surveys Ltd. 92 T. Loftas, Picturepoint Ltd., Picturepoint Ltd., National Film Board of Canada, Adam Woolfitt, Picturepoint Ltd., Edward S. Ross/California Academy of Sciences, T. Loftas 93 Picturepoint Ltd., T. Loftas, Picturepoint Ltd., Susan Griggs, Picturepoint Ltd. 94 Colorific Photo Library 95 Prof. G. S. Nelson/London School of Tropical Medicine, W. MacQuitty, N.A.S.A. 96 British Petroleum Ltd. 97 U.S. Dept. of the Interior, National Coal Board, Picturepoint Ltd. 99 N.E.R.C. copyright: Reproduced by permission of the Director of the Institute of Geological Sciences, London 100 Picturepoint Ltd. 101 National Coal Board, Peter Keen, Shell International Petroleum Co., U.K.A.E.A. 102 T. Loftas 105 National Institute of Oceanography 108 Picturepoint Ltd. 110 Picturepoint Ltd. 112–13 John Hedgecoe 114 Bob Estall 118 Picturepoint Ltd. 123 The Mansell Collection, Spectrum Colour Library 124 Picturepoint Ltd. Spectrum Colour Library, remainder Picturepoint Ltd. 127 James Webb, James Webb, From the Diana Wyllie filmstrip/slide set on Air Pollution 128 John Moss/Oxfam, Gerard Klijn-Novib/Oxfam, Gerard Klijn-Novib/Oxfam 129 Mike Busselle 130 London School of Tropical Medicine, Dr. Geoffrey Taylor, Dr. Hansell, Westminster Hospital, London School of Tropical Medicine, London School of Tropical Medicine 132 *Daily Telegraph*, The Mansell Collection 133 Tom Kay 137 Mondadori Press, Ardea Photographics, Ardea Photographics 138 Mike Busselle, Prof. R. S. Scorer, From the Diana Wyllie filmstrip/slide set on Air Pollution Mondadori Press 139 L. R. Beynon, *Daily Telegraph*, L. R. Beynon, *Daily Telegraph*, L. R. Beynon, Prof. R. S. Scorer, From the Diana Wyllie filmstrip/slide set on Air Pollution 140 Don McCullin/Magnum 141 U.P.I., Don McCullin/Magnum 142–3 Transworld

Introduction to the Index

The Index includes in a single alphabetical list some 70,000 names appearing on the maps. Each name is followed by a page reference to one or more maps and by the location of the feature on the map, in coordinates of latitude and longitude. If a page contains several maps, a lowercase letter identifies the particular map. The page reference for two-page maps is always to the left-hand page.

Most map features are indexed to the largest-scale map on which they appear. Countries, mountain ranges, and other extensive features are generally indexed to the map that shows them in their entirety.

The features indexed are of three types: *point*, *areal*, and *linear*. For *point* features (for example, cities, mountain peaks, dams), latitude and longitude coordinates give the location of the point on the map. For *areal* features (countries, mountain ranges, etc.), the coordinates generally indicate the approximate center of the feature. For *linear* features (rivers, canals, aqueducts), the coordinates locate a terminating point—for example, the mouth of a river, or the point at which a feature reaches the map margin.

NAME FORMS Names in the Index, as on the maps, are generally in the local language and insofar as possible are spelled according to official practice. Diacritical marks are included, except that those used to indicate tone, as in Vietnamese, are usually not shown. Most features that extend beyond the boundaries of one country have no single official name, and these are usually named in English. Many local country name forms and conventional English names are cross referenced to the primary map name. All cross references are indicated by the symbol →. A name that appears in a shortened version on the map due to space limitations is given in full in the Index, with the portion that is omitted on the map enclosed in brackets, for example, Acapulco [de Juárez].

TRANSLITERATION For names in languages not written in the Roman alphabet, the locally official transliteration system has been used where one exists. Thus, names in the Soviet Union and Bulgaria have been transliterated according to the systems adopted by the academies of science of these countries. Similarly, the transliteration for mainland Chinese names follows the Pinyin system, which has been officially adopted in mainland China. For languages with no one locally accepted transliteration system, notably Arabic, transliteration in general follows closely a system adopted by the United States Board on Geographic Names.

ALPHABETIZATION Names are alphabetized in the order of the letters of the English alphabet. Spanish *ll* and *ch*, for example, are not treated as distinct letters. Furthermore, diacritical marks are disregarded in alphabetization—German or Scandinavian *ä* or *ö* are treated as *a* or *o*.

The names of physical features may appear inverted, since they are always alphabetized under the proper, not the generic, part of the name, thus: "Gibraltar, Strait of ." Otherwise every entry, whether consisting of one word or more, is alphabetized as a single continuous entity. "Lakeland," for example, appears after "La Crosse" and before "La Salle." Names beginning with articles (Le Havre, Den Helder, Al-Qāhirah, As-Suways) are not inverted. Names beginning "Mc" are alphabetized as though spelled "Mac," and names beginning "St." and "Sainte" as though spelled "Saint."

In the case of identical names, towns are listed first, then political divisions, then physical features. Entries that are completely identical (including symbols, discussed below) are distinguished by abbreviations of their official country names and are sequenced alphabetically by country name. The many duplicate names in Canada, the United Kingdom, and the United States are further distinguished by abbreviations of the names of their primary subdivisions. (See list of abbreviations on pages 359 and 360).

ABBREVIATION AND CAPITALIZATION Abbreviation and styling have been standardized for all languages. A period is used after every abbreviation even when this may not be the local practice. The abbreviation "St." is used only for "Saint." "Sankt" and other forms of the term are spelled out.

All names are written with an initial capital letter except for a few Dutch names, such as 's-Gravenhage. Capitalization of noninitial words in a name generally follows local practice.

SYMBOL The symbols that appear in the Index graphically represent the broad categories of the features named, for example, ∧ for mountain (Everest, Mount ∧). Superior numbers following some symbols in the Index indicate finer distinctions, for example, ∧¹ for volcano (Fuji-san ∧¹). A complete list of the symbols and those with superior numbers is given on page 360.

LIST OF ABBREVIATIONS

	LOCAL NAME	ENGLISH
Afg.	Afghānestān	Afghanistan
Afr.	—	Africa
A./I.	Afars et Issas	Afars and Issas
Ala., U.S.	Alabama	Alabama
Alaska, U.S.	Alaska	Alaska
Alg.	Algérie	Algeria
Alta., Can.	Alberta	Alberta
Am. Sam.	American Samoa	American Samoa
And.	Andorra	Andorra
Ang.	Angola	Angola
Ant.	—	Antarctica
Antig.	Antigua	Antigua
Arc. O.	—	Arctic Ocean
Arg.	Argentina	Argentina
Ariz., U.S.	Arizona	Arizona
Ark., U.S.	Arkansas	Arkansas
Ar. Sa.	Al-'Arabīyah as-Sa'ūdīyah	Saudi Arabia
As.	—	Asia
Atl. O.	—	Atlantic Ocean
Austl.	Australia	Australia
Ba.	Bahamas	Bahamas
Baḥr.	Al-Baḥrayn	Bahrain
Barb.	Barbados	Barbados
B.A.T.	British Antarctic Territory	British Antarctic Territory
B.C., Can.	British Columbia	British Columbia
Bdi.	Burundi	Burundi
Bel.	Belgique België	Belgium
Ber.	Bermuda	Bermuda
Ber. S.	—	Bering Sea
Bhārat	Bhārat	India
B.I.O.T.	British Indian Ocean Territory	British Indian Ocean Territory
Blg.	Bâlgarija	Bulgaria
Bngl.	Bangladesh	Bangladesh
Bol.	Bolivia	Bolivia
Bots.	Botswana	Botswana
Bra.	Brasil	Brazil
B.R.D.	Bundesrepublik Deutschland	West Germany
Br. Hond.	British Honduras	British Honduras
Br. Sol. Is.	British Solomon Islands	British Solomon Islands
Bru.	Brunei	Brunei
Br. Vir. Is.	British Virgin Islands	British Virgin Islands
Calif., U.S.	California	California
Cam.	Cameroun	Cameroon
Can.	Canada	Canada
Can./End.	Canton and Enderbury	Canton and Enderbury
Carib. S.	—	Caribbean Sea
Cay. Is.	Cayman Islands	Cayman Islands
Centraf.	République centrafricaine	Central African Republic
Česko.	Československo	Czechoslovakia
Chile	Chile	Chile
Christ. I.	Christmas Island	Christmas Island
C. Iv.	Côte d'Ivoire	Ivory Coast
C.M.I.K.	Chosŏn Minjujuŭi In'min Konghwaguk	North Korea
Cocos Is.	Cocos (Keeling) Islands	Cocos (Keeling) Islands
Col.	Colombia	Colombia
Colo., U.S.	Colorado	Colorado
Comores	Comores	Comoro Islands
Congo	Congo	Congo
Conn., U.S.	Connecticut	Connecticut
Cook Is.	Cook Islands	Cook Islands
C.R.	Costa Rica	Costa Rica
Cuba	Cuba	Cuba
C.V.	Cabo Verde	Cape Verde Islands
C.Z.	Canal Zone	Canal Zone
Dah.	Dahomey	Dahomey
Dan.	Danmark	Denmark
D.C., U.S.	District of Columbia	District of Columbia
D.D.R.	Deutsche Demokratische Republik	East Germany
Del., U.S.	Delaware	Delaware
Den.	Danmark	Denmark
Dom.	Dominica	Dominica
D.Y.	Druk-Yul	Bhutan
Ec.	Ecuador	Ecuador
Eire	Eire	Ireland
Ellás	Ellás	Greece
El Sal.	El Salvador	El Salvador
Eng., U.K.	England	England
Esp.	España	Spain
Eur.	—	Europe
Falk. Is.	Falkland Islands	Falkland Islands (Islas Malvinas)
Fiji	Fiji	Fiji
Fla., U.S.	Florida	Florida
Før.	Føroyar	Faeroe Islands
Fr.	France	France
Ga., U.S.	Georgia	Georgia
Gabon	Gabon	Gabon
Gam.	Gambia	Gambia
Gaza	—	Gaza Strip
G./E. Is.	Gilbert and Ellice Islands	Gilbert and Ellice Islands
Ghana	Ghana	Ghana
Gib.	Gibraltar	Gibraltar
Gren.	Grenada	Grenada
Grn.	Grønland	Greenland
Guad.	Guadeloupe	Guadeloupe
Guam	Guam	Guam
Guat.	Guatemala	Guatemala
Guer.	Guernsey	Guernsey
Gui. Ecu.	Guinea Ecuatorial	Equatorial Guinea
Guin.	Guinée	Guinea
Guiné	Guiné	Portuguese Guinea
Guy.	Guyana	Guyana
Guy. fr.	Guyane française	French Guiana
Haï.	Haïti	Haiti
Haw., U.S.	Hawaii	Hawaii
H.K.	Hong Kong	Hong Kong
Hond.	Honduras	Honduras
H. Vol.	Haute-Volta	Upper Volta
Idaho, U.S.	Idaho	Idaho
I.I.A.	Ittiḥād al-Imārāt al-'Arabīyah	United Arab Emirates
Ill., U.S.	Illinois	Illinois
Ind., U.S.	Indiana	Indiana
Ind. O.	—	Indian Ocean
Indon.	Indonesia	Indonesia
I. of Man	Isle of Man	Isle of Man
Iowa, U.S.	Iowa	Iowa
Īrān	Īrān	Iran
'Irāq	Al-'Irāq	Iraq
Ísland	Ísland	Iceland
It.	Italia	Italy
Jam.	Jamaica	Jamaica
Jersey	Jersey	Jersey
Jugo.	Jugoslavija	Yugoslavia
Kam.	Kampuchea	Cambodia
Kans., U.S.	Kansas	Kansas
Kenya	Kenya	Kenya
Kípros	Kípros Kıbrıs	Cyprus
Kuwayt	Al-Kuwayt	Kuwait
Ky., U.S.	Kentucky	Kentucky
La., U.S.	Louisiana	Louisiana
Lao	Lao	Laos
Leso.	Lesotho	Lesotho
Liber.	Liberia	Liberia
Lībiyā	Lībiyā	Libya
Liech.	Liechtenstein	Liechtenstein
Lubnān	Al-Lubnān	Lebanon
Lux.	Luxembourg	Luxembourg
Macau	Macau	Macau
Magreb	Al-Magreb	Morocco
Magy.	Magyarország	Hungary
Maine, U.S.	Maine	Maine
Malawi	Malawi	Malawi
Malay.	Malaysia	Malaysia
Mald.	Maldives	Maldives
Malg.	République malgache	Malagasy Republic
Mali	Mali	Mali
Malta	Malta	Malta
Man., Can.	Manitoba	Manitoba
Mart.	Martinique	Martinique
Mass., U.S.	Massachusetts	Massachusetts
Maur.	Mauritanie	Mauritania
Maus.	Mauritius	Mauritius
Md., U.S.	Maryland	Maryland
Medit. S.	—	Mediterranean Sea
Méx.	México	Mexico
Mich., U.S.	Michigan	Michigan
Mid. Is.	Midway Islands	Midway Islands
Minn., U.S.	Minnesota	Minnesota
Miṣr	Miṣr	Egypt
Miss., U.S.	Mississippi	Mississippi
Mo., U.S.	Missouri	Missouri
Moç.	Moçambique	Mozambique
Monaco	Monaco	Monaco
Mong.	Mongol Ard Uls	Mongolia
Mont., U.S.	Montana	Montana
Monts.	Montserrat	Montserrat
Mya.	Myanma	Burma
N.A.	—	North America
Nauru	Nauru	Nauru
N.B., Can.	New Brunswick	New Brunswick
N.C., U.S.	North Carolina	North Carolina
N. Cal.	Nouvelle-Calédonie	New Caledonia
N. Dak., U.S.	North Dakota	North Dakota
Nebr., U.S.	Nebraska	Nebraska
Ned.	Nederland	Netherlands
Ned. Ant.	Nederlandse Antillen	Netherlands Antilles
Nepāl	Nepāl	Nepal
Nev., U.S.	Nevada	Nevada
Newf., Can.	Newfoundland	Newfoundland
N.G. Ter.	Territory of New Guinea	Territory of New Guinea
N.H., U.S.	New Hampshire	New Hampshire
N. Heb.	New Hebrides Nouvelles-Hébrides	New Hebrides
Nic.	Nicaragua	Nicaragua
Nig.	Nigeria	Nigeria
Niger	Niger	Niger
Nihon	Nihon	Japan
N. Ire., U.K.	Northern Ireland	Northern Ireland
Niue	Niue	Niue
N.J., U.S.	New Jersey	New Jersey
N. Mex., U.S.	New Mexico	New Mexico
Nor.	Norge	Norway
Norf. I.	Norfolk Island	Norfolk Island
N.S., Can.	Nova Scotia	Nova Scotia
N.W. Ter., Can.	Northwest Territories	Northwest Territories
N.Y., U.S.	New York	New York
N.Z.	New Zealand	New Zealand
Oc.	—	Oceania
Ohio, U.S.	Ohio	Ohio
Okla., U.S.	Oklahoma	Oklahoma
Ont., Can.	Ontario	Ontario
Oreg., U.S.	Oregon	Oregon
Öst.	Österreich	Austria
Pa., U.S.	Pennsylvania	Pennsylvania
Pac. O.	—	Pacific Ocean
Pāk.	Pākistān	Pakistan
Pan.	Panamá	Panama
Papua	Papua	Papua
Para.	Paraguay	Paraguay
P.E.I., Can.	Prince Edward Island	Prince Edward Island
Perú	Perú	Peru
Pil.	Pilipinas	Philippines
Pit.	Pitcairn	Pitcairn
P.I.T.T.	Pacific Islands Trust Territory	Pacific Islands Trust Territory
Pol.	Polska	Poland
Poly. fr.	Polynésie française	French Polynesia
Port.	Portugal	Portugal
P.R.	Puerto Rico	Puerto Rico
P.S.N.Á.	Plazas de Soberanía en el Norte de África	Spanish North Africa
Qaṭar	Qaṭar	Qatar
Que., Can.	Québec	Quebec
Rep. Dom.	República Dominicana	Dominican Republic
Réu.	Réunion	Reunion
Rh.	Rhodesia	Rhodesia
R.I., U.S.	Rhode Island	Rhode Island
Rom.	România	Romania
Rw.	Rwanda	Rwanda
S.A.	—	South America
S. Afr.	South Africa Suid-Afrika	South Africa
Sah. Esp.	Sahara Español	Spanish Sahara
Sask., Can.	Saskatchewan	Saskatchewan
S.C., U.S.	South Carolina	South Carolina
S. Ch. S.	—	South China Sea
Schw.	Schweiz; Suisse; Svizzera	Switzerland
Scot., U.K.	Scotland	Scotland
S. Dak., U.S.	South Dakota	South Dakota
Sén.	Sénégal	Senegal
Sey.	Seychelles	Seychelles
Shq.	Shqipëri	Albania
Sih.	Sihala; Ilam	Ceylon
Sik.	Sikkim	Sikkim
Sing.	Singapore	Singapore
S.L.	Sierra Leone	Sierra Leone
S. Mar.	San Marino	San Marino
Som.	Somaliya	Somalia
Sp.	España	Spain
S.S.R.	Sovetskaja Socialističeskaja Respublika	Soviet Socialist Republic
S.S.S.R.	Sojuz Sovetskich Socialističeskich Respublik	Union of Soviet Socialist Republics
St. Hel.	St. Helena	St. Helena
St. K.-N.-A.	St. Kitts-Nevis-Anguilla	St. Kitts-Nevis-Anguilla
St. Luc.	St. Lucia	St. Lucia
S. Tom./P.	São Tomé e Príncipe	Sao Tome and Principe
St. P./M.	St.-Pierre-et-Miquelon	St. Pierre and Miquelon
St. Vin.	St. Vincent	St. Vincent
Sūd.	As-Sūdān	Sudan
Suomi	Suomi	Finland
Sur.	Suriname	Surinam
Sūriy.	As-Sūrīyah	Syria
Sval.	Svalbard og Jan Mayen	Svalbard and Jan Mayen
Sve.	Sverige	Sweden
S.W. Afr.	South West Africa	South West Africa
Swaz.	Swaziland	Swaziland
T.a.a.f.	Terres australes et antarctiques françaises	French Southern and Antarctic Territories
Taehan	Taehan-Min'guk	South Korea
T'aiwan	T'aiwan	Taiwan
Tan.	Tanzania	Tanzania
Tchad	Tchad	Chad
T./C. Is.	Turks and Caicos Islands	Turks and Caicos Islands
Tenn., U.S.	Tennessee	Tennessee
Tex., U.S.	Texas	Texas
Thai.	Prathet Thai	Thailand
Timor	Timor	Portuguese Timor
Togo	Togo	Togo
Tok. Is.	Tokelau Islands	Tokelau Islands
Tonga	Tonga	Tonga
Trin.	Trinidad and Tobago	Trinidad and Tobago
Tun.	Tunisie	Tunisia
Tür.	Türkiye	Turkey
Ug.	Uganda	Uganda
U.K.	United Kingdom	United Kingdom
'Umān	'Umān	Oman
Ur.	Uruguay	Uruguay
Urd.	Al-Urdunn	Jordan
U.S.	United States	United States

LIST OF ABBREVIATIONS CON'T.

	LOCAL NAME	ENGLISH
U.S.S.R.	Sojuz Sovetskich Socialističeskich Respublik	Union of Soviet Socialist Republics
Utah, U.S.	Utah	Utah
Va., U.S.	Virginia	Virginia
Vat.	Città del Vaticano	Vatican City
Ven.	Venezuela	Venezuela
Viet. N.	Viet-nam Dan-chu Cong-hoa	North Vietnam
Viet. S.	Viet-nam Cong-hoa	South Vietnam
Vir. Is., U.S.	Virgin Islands	Virgin Islands (U.S.)
Vt., U.S.	Vermont	Vermont
Wake I.	Wake Island	Wake Island
Wales, U.K.	Wales	Wales
Wal./F.	Wallis et Futuna	Wallis and Futuna
Wash., U.S.	Washington	Washington
Wis., U.S.	Wisconsin	Wisconsin
W. Sam.	Western Samoa	Western Samoa
W. Va., U.S.	West Virginia	West Virginia
Wyo., U.S.	Wyoming	Wyoming
Yai.	Yaitopya	Ethiopia
Yaman	Al-Yaman	Yemen
Yam. S.	Al-Yaman ash-Sha'bīyah	People's Democratic Republic of Yemen
Yis.	Yisra'el	Israel
Yukon, Can.	Yukon	Yukon
Zaïre	Zaïre	Zaire
Zam.	Zambia	Zambia
Zhg.	Zhongguo	China

KEY TO SYMBOLS

- ∧ **Mountain**
- ∧1 Volcano
- ∧2 Hill
- ∧∧ **Mountains**
- ∧∧1 Plateau
- ∧∧2 Hills
-)(**Pass**
- ∨ **Valley, Canyon**
- ≚ **Plain**
- ≚1 Basin
- ≚2 Delta
- ≻ **Cape**
- ≻1 Peninsula
- ≻2 Spit, Sand Bar
- I **Island**
- I1 Atoll
- I2 Rock
- II **Islands**
- II1 Rocks
- • **Other Topographic Features**
- •1 Continent
- •2 Coast, Beach
- •3 Isthmus
- •4 Cliff
- •5 Cave, Caves
- •6 Crater
- •7 Depression
- •8 Dunes
- •9 Lava Flow
- ≏ **River**
- ≏1 River Channel
- ≋ **Canal**
- ≋1 Aqueduct
- ⌊ **Waterfall, Rapids**
- ⊔ **Strait**
- C **Bay, Gulf**
- C1 Estuary
- C2 Fjord
- C3 Bight
- ◎ **Lake, Lakes**
- ◎1 Reservoir
- ≡ **Swamp**
- ⊓ **Ice Features, Glacier**
- ⊤ **Other Hydrographic Features**
- ⊤1 Ocean
- ⊤2 Sea
- ⊤3 Anchorage
- ⊤4 Oasis, Well, Spring
- ✣ **Submarine Features**
- ✣1 Depression
- ✣2 Reef, Shoal
- ✣3 Mountain, Mountains
- ✣4 Slope, Shelf
- □ **Political Unit**
- □1 Independent Nation
- □2 Dependency
- □3 State, Canton, Republic
- □4 Province, Region, Oblast
- □5 Department, District, Prefecture
- □6 County
- □7 City, Municipality
- □8 Miscellaneous
- □9 Historical
- ʊ **Cultural Institution**
- ʊ1 Religious Institution
- ʊ2 Educational Institution
- ʊ3 Scientific, Industrial Facility
- ⊥ **Historical Site**
- ♠ **Recreational Site**
- ⊠ **Airport**
- ▪ **Military Installation**
- ⊸ **Miscellaneous**
- ⊸1 Region
- ⊸2 Desert
- ⊸3 Forest, Moor
- ⊸4 Reserve, Reservation
- ⊸5 Transportation
- ⊸6 Dam
- ⊸7 Mine, Quarry
- ⊸8 Neighborhood
- ⊸9 Shopping Center

Index

Name	Page	Lat°′	Long°′
A			
Aachen	164	50.47 N	6.05 E
Aachen □5	178	50.30 N	6.15 E
Aalen	164	48.50 N	10.05 E
A'alī an-Nīl □4	220	9.00 N	32.00 E
Aalsmeer	178	52.16 N	4.45 E
Aalst (Alost)	176	50.56 N	4.02 E
Aalten	178	51.56 N	6.35 E
Aalter	176	51.05 N	3.27 E
Äänekoski	160	62.36 N	25.44 E
Aarau	180	47.23 N	8.03 E
Aarburg	180	47.19 N	7.54 E
Aare ≏	166	47.37 N	8.13 E
Aargau □3	180	47.30 N	8.10 E
Aarschot	164	50.59 N	4.50 E
Aazanèn	168	35.13 N	3.10 W
Aba, Nig.	222	5.06 N	7.21 E
Aba, Zhg.	190	33.06 N	101.59 E
'Abā, Ṭiwāl al- ∧	212	36.20 N	39.22 E
Abacaxis ≏	290	3.54 S	58.47 W
Abadab, Jabal ∧	220	18.53 N	35.59 E
Ābādān	208	30.20 N	48.16 E
Ābādeh	208	31.10 N	52.37 E
Abadia dos Dourados	296	18.28 S	47.24 W
Abadiânia	296	16.06 S	48.48 W
Abaeté	296	19.09 S	45.27 W
Abaeté ≏	296	18.02 S	45.12 W
Abaetetuba	286	18.02 S	45.12 W
Abagaqi	190	43.41 N	114.40 E
Abai, Malay.	202	5.41 N	118.23 E
Abaí, Para.	294	25.58 S	55.57 W
Abaj	186	49.38 N	72.52 E
Abajo Mountains ∧∧	254	37.50 N	109.25 W
Abajo Peak ∧	254	37.51 N	109.28 W
Abakaliki	222	6.21 N	8.06 E
Abakan	186	53.43 N	91.26 E
Abakan ≏	186	53.43 N	91.30 E
Abalemma, Vallée d' ∨	222	15.34 N	6.23 E
Abancay	292	13.35 S	72.55 W
Abashiri	192a	44.01 N	144.17 E
Abasolo, Méx.	250	27.12 N	101.24 W
Abasolo, Méx.	250	25.57 N	100.24 W
Abasolo, Méx.	258	32.39 N	115.21 W
Abasolo, Méx.	278	24.04 N	98.22 W
Abasolo, Méx.	278	20.27 N	101.32 W
Abasolo, Méx.	278	25.18 N	104.40 W
Abatiá	296	23.19 S	50.18 W
Abaya, Lake ◎	214	6.20 N	37.55 E
Abayita, Lake ◎	214	7.37 N	38.35 E
Abaza	186	52.39 N	90.06 E
Abbadia San Salvatore	184	42.53 N	11.41 E
Abbasanta	170	40.08 N	8.50 E
Abbeville, Fr.	176	50.06 N	1.50 E
Abbeville, Ala., U.S.	248	31.34 N	85.15 W
Abbeville, Ga., U.S.	246	31.59 N	83.18 W
Abbeville, La., U.S.	248	29.58 N	92.08 W
Abbeville, Miss., U.S.	248	34.25 N	89.37 W
Abbeville, S.C., U.S.	246	34.11 N	82.23 W
Abbeyfeale	162	52.24 N	9.18 W
Abbey Head ≻	162	54.46 N	3.58 W
Abbeyleix	162	52.55 N	7.20 W
Abbiategrasso	182	45.24 N	8.54 E
Abbot, Mount ∧	228	20.03 S	147.45 E
Abbotsford, B.C., Can.	238	49.03 N	122.17 W
Abbotsford, Wis., U.S.	244	44.57 N	90.19 W
Abbottābād	204	34.09 N	73.13 E
Abbott Butte ∧	256	42.57 N	122.33 W
Abbottstown	262	39.53 N	76.59 W
'Abd al-'Azīz, Jabal ∧∧	212	36.25 N	40.20 E
'Abd al-Kūrī I	204	12.12 N	52.15 E
'Abd Allāh, Khawr ⊔	208	29.50 N	48.20 E
Ábdēra ⊥	172	40.59 N	24.58 E
Abdulino	158	53.42 N	53.40 E
Abe, Lake ◎	214	11.06 N	41.50 E
Abéché	214	13.49 N	20.49 E
Abegondo	168	43.13 N	8.17 W
Abéjar	168	41.48 N	2.47 W
Abejonal, Cerro ∧	280	11.39 N	86.10 W
Abejorral	290	5.47 N	75.26 W
Abelardo L. Rodríguez, Presa ◎1	278	29.03 N	110.52 W
Abel Tasman National Park ♠	230	40.55 S	173.00 E
Abengourou	222	6.44 N	3.29 W
Abengourou □5	222	6.30 N	3.30 W
Abenójar	168	38.53 N	4.21 W
Åbenrå	160	55.02 N	9.26 E
Abensberg	164	48.49 N	11.51 E
Abeokuta	222	7.10 N	3.26 E
Aberaman	174	51.42 N	3.25 W
Aberayron	162	52.15 N	4.15 E
Abercarn	174	51.39 N	3.08 W
Aberchirder	162	57.33 N	2.38 W
Abercorn, Qué., Can.	260	45.03 N	72.40 W
Abercorn → Mbala, Zam.	218	8.50 S	31.22 E
Aberdare	174	51.43 N	3.27 W
Aberdeen, Scot., U.K.	162	57.10 N	2.04 W
Aberdeen, Idaho, U.S.	256	42.57 N	112.50 W
Aberdeen, Md., U.S.	262	39.30 N	76.10 W
Aberdeen, Miss., U.S.	248	33.49 N	88.33 W
Aberdeen, N.C., U.S.	246	35.08 N	79.26 W
Aberdeen, S. Dak., U.S.	252	45.28 N	98.29 W
Aberdeen, Wash., U.S.	270	46.59 N	123.50 W
Aberdeen □6	162	57.18 N	2.25 W
Aberdeen Lake ◎	232	64.27 N	99.00 W
Aberfeldy	162	56.37 N	3.54 W
Abergavenny	174	51.50 N	3.00 W
Abernant	248	33.17 N	87.12 W
Abernathy	250	33.50 N	101.51 W
Abernethy	162	56.20 N	3.19 W
Abersychan	174	51.44 N	3.04 W
Abert, Lake ◎	256	42.38 N	120.13 W
Abertillery	174	51.45 N	3.09 W
Aberystwyth	174	52.25 N	4.05 W
Abetone	170	44.08 N	10.40 E
Abez'	160	66.32 N	61.42 E
Abhā	214	18.13 N	42.30 E
Abhar	208	36.09 N	49.13 E
Abidjan	222	5.19 N	4.02 W
Abidjan □5	222	5.30 N	4.30 W
Āb-i-Istāda ◎	206	32.30 N	67.55 E
Abilene, Kans., U.S.	252	38.55 N	97.13 W
Abilene, Tex., U.S.	250	32.27 N	99.44 W
Abingdon, Eng., U.K.	174	51.41 N	1.17 W
Abingdon, Ill., U.S.	244	40.48 N	90.24 W
Abingdon, Va., U.S.	246	36.43 N	81.59 W
Abington, Conn., U.S.	261	41.52 N	72.01 W
Abington, Mass., U.S.	261	42.07 N	70.57 W
Abington, Pa., U.S.	262	40.07 N	75.08 W
Abington Reef ✣2	228	18.00 S	149.36 E
Āb-i-Panja (P'andž) ≏	206	37.06 N	68.20 E
Abiquiu	254	36.12 N	106.19 W
Abiquiu Flood Control Reservoir ◎1	254	36.18 N	106.32 W
Abisko	160	68.20 N	18.51 E
Abita Springs	248	30.29 N	90.02 W
Abitibi ≏	232	51.03 N	80:55 W
Abitibi, Lake ◎	244	48.42 N	79.45 W
Ablis	166	48.31 N	1.50 E
Abnūb	220	27.16 N	31.09 E
Åbo → Turku	160	60.27 N	22.17 E
Abohar	206	30.08 N	74.12 E
Aboisso	222	5.28 N	3.12 W
Aboisso □5	222	5.30 N	3.15 W
Abomey	222	7.11 N	1.59 E
Abong Abong, Gunung ∧	200	4.15 N	96.47 E
Abong Mbang	214	3.59 N	13.10 E
Abony	164	47.11 N	20.01 E
Aborigen, Pik ∧	186	61.59 N	149.19 E
Aborlan	202	9.26 N	118.33 E
Abou Deïa	214	11.27 N	19.17 E
Abra □4	202	17.35 N	120.50 E
Abra ≏	202	17.32 N	120.24 E
Abramovskaja	160	65.11 N	51.43 E
Abrantes	168	39.28 N	8.12 W
Abra Pampa	294	22.43 S	65.42 W
Abre Campo	296	20.18 S	42.29 W
Ábrego	290	8.05 N	73.13 W
Abreojos, Punta ≻	278	26.45 N	113.40 W
Abrud	172	46.17 N	23.04 E
Abruzzi □4	184	42.20 N	13.45 E
Abruzzo, Parco Nazionale d' ♠	170	41.45 N	13.45 E
Absaroka Range ∧∧	256	44.45 N	109.50 W
Absarokee	256	45.31 N	109.27 W
Absecon	262	39.26 N	74.30 W
Abtenau	164	47.33 N	13.21 E
Abū Ahl ⊤4	208	34.06 N	43.45 E
Abū 'Alī I	208	27.20 N	49.33 E
Abū al-Khaṣīb	208	30.27 N	47.59 E
Abū 'Aradeib, Wādī ∨	220	14.12 N	23.06 E
Abū Ballās ∧2	220	24.26 N	27.39 E
Abucay	202	14.43 N	120.32 E
Abū Dā'ūd, Ra's ≻	208	23.20 N	58.55 E
Abū Dawm, Wādī ∨	220	18.28 N	31.49 E
Abufari	292	5.25 S	62.59 W
Abū Gatta Hills ∧∧2	220	6.06 N	27.44 E
Abū Ḥabl, Khawr ∨	220	12.49 N	31.15 E
Abū Ḥamad	214	19.32 N	33.19 E
Abū Kamāl	208	34.27 N	40.55 E
Abukuma ≏	192	38.02 N	140.56 E
Abukuma-sanchi ∧∧	192	37.30 N	140.45 E
Abulug	202	18.27 N	121.27 E
Abulug ≏	202	18.27 N	121.27 E
Abū Madd, Ra's ≻	208	24.50 N	37.07 E
Abū Minqār, Bi'r ⊤4	220	26.30 N	27.35 E
Abū Muḥarrik, Ghurd •8	220	27.50 N	29.40 E
Abū Mūsā, Jazīrat I	208	25.52 N	55.03 E
Abunã	292	9.42 S	65.23 W
Abuná ≏	292	9.41 S	65.23 W
Abū Qurqāṣ	220	27.56 N	30.50 E
Abū Rujmayn, Jabal ∧∧	212	34.52 N	38.20 E
Abū Sanṭ, Wādī ∨	220	14.11 N	23.06 E
Abū Shajarah, Ra's ≻	220	21.04 N	37.14 E
Abū Shaykhāt, Ḍahr ∧2	212	36.36 N	39.40 E
Abū Sunbul ⊥	220	22.22 N	31.38 E
Abuta	192a	42.33 N	140.46 E
Abū Ṭabarī ⊤4	220	17.35 N	28.31 E
Abut Head ≻	230	43.06 S	170.15 E
Abū Tīj	220	27.02 N	31.19 E
Abuyog	202	10.45 N	125.01 E
Abū Ẓaby	208	24.28 N	54.22 E
Aby, Lagune C	222	5.15 N	3.14 W
Acacías	290	3.59 N	73.46 W
Acacio	278	24.50 N	102.44 W
Academia	266	40.25 N	82.28 W
Academy Corners	262	41.57 N	77.23 W
Acadia National Park ♠	242	44.18 N	68.15 W
Acahay	294	25.55 S	57.09 W
Acajutla	280	13.36 N	89.50 W
Acámbaro	278	20.02 N	100.44 W
Acampo	272	38.10 N	121.13 W
Acandí	290	8.32 N	77.14 W
Acaponeta	278	22.30 N	105.22 W
Acaponeta, Río de ≏	278	22.22 N	105.37 W
Acapulco [de Juárez]	278	16.51 N	99.55 W
Acará, Cachoeira ⌊	292	5.47 S	59.12 W
Acará, Lago ◎	290	3.39 S	62.40 W
Acarai Mountains ∧∧	290	1.59 N	57.40 W
Acaraú	286	2.53 S	40.07 W
Acaray ≏	294	25.29 S	54.42 W
Acarí	292	15.25 S	74.36 W
Acarí, Río de ≏	292	15.38 S	74.40 W
Acarigua	290	9.33 N	69.12 W
Acatlán de Juárez	278	20.26 N	103.38 W
Acatlán [de Osorio]	278	18.12 N	98.03 W
Acay, Nevado de ∧	294	24.22 S	66.10 W
Acayucan	278	17.57 N	94.55 W
Aččen, Mys ≻	236	64.45 N	175.30 W
Accokeek	262	38.40 N	77.02 W
Accomac	262	37.43 N	75.40 W
Accomack □6	262	37.45 N	75.40 W
Accoville	246	37.46 N	81.50 W
Accra	222	5.33 N	0.13 W
Acebal	294	33.15 S	60.50 W
Acebuches	278	28.15 N	102.43 W
Aceguá	294	31.52 S	54.12 W
Acerenza	170	40.48 N	15.57 E
Acerra	184	40.57 N	14.22 E
Acevedo	294	33.46 S	60.27 W
Achacachi	292	16.03 S	68.43 W
Achaguas	290	7.46 N	68.14 W
Achalpur	206	21.16 N	77.31 E
Achar	294	32.25 S	56.10 W
Acheng	190	45.32 N	126.59 E
Achern	164	48.37 N	8.04 E
Achí	290	8.34 N	74.33 W
Achiguate ≏	280	13.55 N	90.55 W
Achill	162	53.56 N	9.54 W
Achilles	262	37.17 N	76.27 W
Achill Head ≻	162	53.59 N	10.13 W
Achill Island I	162	54.00 N	10.00 W
Achim	178	53.00 N	9.02 E
Achiras	294	33.10 S	64.59 W
Achtuba ≏	158	46.42 N	48.00 E
Achtubinsk	158	48.17 N	46.10 E
Achtyrka	158	50.19 N	34.55 E
Achuapa	280	13.06 N	86.37 W
Acı Göl ◎	212	37.50 N	29.54 E
Acikehu ◎	206	37.05 N	88.05 E
Ačinsk	186	56.17 N	90.30 E
Acıpayam	172	37.25 N	29.22 E
Acireale	170	37.37 N	15.10 E
Acîş	172	47.33 N	22.47 E
Ačisaj	186	43.35 N	68.53 E
Ackerly	250	32.32 N	101.43 W
Ackerman	248	33.19 N	89.10 W
Ackley	244	42.33 N	93.03 W
Acklins, The Bightof C3	282	22.25 N	74.10 W
Acklins Island I	282	22.25 N	74.00 W
Aclan Point ≻	202	11.45 N	122.22 E
Acme, Alta., Can.	238	51.30 N	113.30 W
Acme, Pa., U.S.	266	40.08 N	79.26 W
Acme, Wash., U.S.	270	48.43 N	122.12 W
Acobamba	292	12.52 S	74.35 W
Acolla	292	11.44 S	75.32 W
Acoma Indian Reservation ⊸4	254	34.52 N	107.40 W
Acomayo, Perú	292	9.45 S	76.04 W
Acomayo, Perú	292	13.55 S	71.38 W
Acomita	254	35.03 N	107.35 W
Aconcagua □4	294	32.15 S	70.50 W
Aconcagua, Cerro ∧	294	32.39 S	70.00 W
Aconchi	278	29.50 N	110.12 W
Aconquija, Sierra del ∧∧	294	27.10 S	66.00 W
Açores (Azores) II	148	38.30 N	28.00 W
Acoria	292	12.34 S	74.52 W
Acorizal	292	15.12 S	56.22 W
Acosta	266	40.07 N	79.04 W
Acoyapa	280	11.57 N	85.12 W
Acquapendente	170	42.44 N	11.52 E
Acquasanta Terme	170	42.46 N	13.24 E
Acqui Terme	182	44.41 N	8.28 E
Acre → 'Akko	210	32.55 N	35.04 E
Acre □3	292	9.00 S	70.00 W
Acre ≏	292	8.45 S	67.22 W
Acri	170	39.29 N	16.23 E
Acrotambo, Cumbre de ∧	292	8.47 S	76.54 W
Acton, Ont., Can.	264	43.37 N	80.02 W
Acton, Calif., U.S.	274	34.26 N	118.09 W
Acton, Mass., U.S.	261	42.29 N	71.26 W
Acton Vale	260	45.39 N	72.34 W
Actopan	278	20.16 N	98.56 W
Açucena	296	19.04 S	42.32 W
Acuña	294	29.54 S	57.57 W
Acuracay	292	5.35 S	74.10 W
Acushnet	261	41.41 N	70.55 W
Acworth	246	34.04 N	84.41 W
Ada, Jugo.	172	45.48 N	20.08 E
Ada, Mich., U.S.	268	42.57 N	85.29 W
Ada, Minn., U.S.	252	47.18 N	96.31 W
Ada, Ohio, U.S.	268	40.46 N	83.49 W
Ada, Okla., U.S.	250	34.46 N	96.41 W
Ada, Mount ∧	236	56.41 N	134.41 W
Adab ⊥	208	31.59 N	45.45 E
Adâfer el Abiod ⊸1	222	19.30 N	10.00 W
Adagide	172	38.06 N	28.02 E
Adair, Iowa, U.S.	252	41.30 N	94.39 W
Adair, Okla., U.S.	250	36.26 N	95.16 W
Adair, Bahía de C	278	31.30 N	113.50 W
Adair, Cape ≻	232	71.24 N	71.13 W
Adairsville	246	34.22 N	84.56 W
Adairville	248	36.40 N	86.51 W
Adaja ≏	168	41.32 N	4.52 W
Adak, S.S.S.R.	160	66.30 N	59.38 E
Adak, Alaska, U.S.	236	51.54 N	176.35 W
Adak Island I	236	51.45 N	176.40 W
Adala	172	38.34 N	28.17 E
Ādam	204	22.24 N	57.32 E
Adam, Mount ∧	288	51.34 S	60.04 W
Adamantina	296	21.42 S	51.04 W
Adamawa ∧∧	214	7.00 N	12.00 E
Adamclisi	172	44.05 N	27.57 E
Adamów	164	51.45 N	22.17 E
Adams, Mass., U.S.	261	42.37 N	73.07 W
Adams, Minn., U.S.	244	43.34 N	92.43 W
Adams, Nebr., U.S.	252	40.28 N	96.31 W
Adams, N. Dak., U.S.	252	48.25 N	98.05 W
Adams, N.Y., U.S.	264	43.49 N	76.01 W
Adams, Tenn., U.S.	248	36.35 N	87.04 W
Adams, Wis., U.S.	244	43.58 N	89.49 W
Adams □6, Ind., U.S.	268	40.50 N	84.56 W
Adams □6, Pa., U.S.	262	39.48 N	77.15 W
Adams ≏	238	50.52 N	119.35 W
Adams, Mount ∧, N.Z.	230	41.19 S	175.46 E
Adams, Mount ∧, Wash., U.S.	256	46.12 N	121.28 W
Adams Bridge ✣2	204	9.04 N	79.37 E
Adams Center	264	43.52 N	76.00 W
Adams Lake ◎	238	51.13 N	119.33 W
Adams Mills	266	40.09 N	81.57 W
Adams Park	268	42.08 N	85.29 W
Adamston	262	40.03 N	74.04 W
Adamstown, Md., U.S.	262	39.19 N	77.29 W
Adamstown, Pa., U.S.	262	40.15 N	76.03 W
Adamsville, Qué., Can.	260	45.17 N	72.47 W
Adamsville, Ala., U.S.	248	33.36 N	86.57 W
Adamsville, Mich., U.S.	268	41.47 N	86.00 W
Adamsville, Ohio, U.S.	266	40.04 N	81.53 W
Adamsville, Pa., U.S.	266	41.31 N	80.22 W
Adamsville, Tenn., U.S.	248	35.14 N	88.23 W
Adana	212	37.01 N	35.18 E
Adanero	168	40.56 N	4.36 W
Adapazarı	212	40.46 N	30.24 E
Adarama	214	17.05 N	34.54 E
Adare, Cape ≻	148	71.17 S	170.14 E
Adavale	226	25.55 S	144.36 E
Adda ≏, It.	170	45.08 N	9.53 E
Adda ≏, Sūd.	220	9.51 N	24.50 E
Ad-Dabbah	214	18.03 N	30.57 E
Aḍ-Ḍafrah ⊸1	208	23.25 N	53.25 E
Ad-Dahnā' ⊸2	208	24.30 N	48.10 E
Ad-Dāmir	214	17.35 N	33.58 E
Ad-Dammām	208	26.26 N	50.07 E
Ad-Dawādimī	214	24.28 N	44.18 E
Ad-Dawḥah (Doha)	208	25.17 N	51.32 E
Ad-Dibdibah ⊸1	208	28.00 N	46.30 E
Aḍ-Ḍiffah ∧∧1	220	30.30 N	25.30 E
Ad-Dilam	208	23.59 N	47.12 E
Addis	248	30.21 N	91.16 W
Addis Abeba	214	9.00 N	38.50 E
Addison, Ala., U.S.	248	34.12 N	87.11 W
Addison, Ill., U.S.	268	41.55 N	88.00 W
Addison, Mich., U.S.	244	41.59 N	84.21 W
Ad-Dīwānīyah	208	31.59 N	44.56 E
Addo Elephant National Park ♠	224	33.29 S	25.46 E
Ad-Duwaym	220	14.00 N	32.19 E
Adegem	176	51.12 N	3.29 E
Adel, Ga., U.S.	246	31.08 N	83.25 W
Adel, Iowa, U.S.	244	41.37 N	94.01 W
Adel, Oreg., U.S.	256	42.11 N	119.54 W
Adelaide, Austl.	228	34.55 S	138.35 E
Adelaide, Ba.	284b	25.00 N	77.31 W
Adelaide Peninsula ≻1	232	68.09 N	97.45 W
Adelanto	274	34.35 N	117.24 W
Adèle Island I	226	15.32 S	123.09 E
Adélie Coast •2	148	67.00 S	139.00 E
Adelphia	262	40.13 N	74.15 W
Aden	214	12.45 N	45.12 E
Aden, Gulf of C	204	12.30 N	48.00 E
Adena	266	40.13 N	80.53 W
Ader ∧∧1	222	14.10 N	5.05 E
Adger	248	33.23 N	87.06 W
Adi, Pulau I	198	4.18 S	133.26 E
Adigrat	214	14.18 N	39.31 E
Adimi	190	47.20 N	138.56 E
Adin	258	41.12 N	120.57 W
Adirondack Mountains ∧∧	242	44.00 N	74.00 W
Adıyaman	212	37.46 N	38.17 E
Adjud	172	46.04 N	27.11 E
Adjuntas	284m	18.10 N	66.43 W
Adliswil	180	47.19 N	8.32 E
Admiralty Bay C	236	70.53 N	155.45 W
Admiralty Gulf C	226	14.20 S	125.50 E
Admiralty Inlet C	232	73.00 N	86.00 W
Admiralty Island I, N.W. Ter., Can.	232	69.30 N	101.00 W
Admiralty Island I, Alaska, U.S.	236	57.50 N	134.30 W
Adna	270	46.38 N	123.04 W
Ado-Ekiti	222	7.38 N	5.12 E
Adolfo López Mateos, Presa ◎1	278	25.13 N	107.25 W
Adolfo Ruíz Cortines	278	25.40 N	108.40 W
Adonara, Pulau I	198	8.20 S	123.10 E
Ado-Odo	222	6.36 N	2.56 E
Adoua, Vallée d' ∨	222	14.37 N	6.40 E
Adour ≏	166	43.32 N	1.32 E
Adra	168	36.44 N	3.01 W
Adrano	170	37.40 N	14.50 E
Adrar	214	27.51 N	0.19 W
Adrar ⊸1	214	20.30 N	13.30 W
Adria	170	45.03 N	12.03 E
Adrian, Ga., U.S.	246	32.32 N	82.35 W
Adrian, Mich., U.S.	268	41.54 N	84.02 W
Adrian, Minn., U.S.	252	43.38 N	95.56 W
Adrian, Mo., U.S.	248	38.24 N	94.21 W
Adrian, Ohio, U.S.	266	41.03 N	83.20 W
Adrian, Oreg., U.S.	256	43.44 N	117.04 W
Adrian, Pa., U.S.	266	40.53 N	79.32 W
Adrian, Tex., U.S.	250	35.16 N	102.40 W
Adrian, W. Va., U.S.	242	38.54 N	80.17 W
Adrianople → Edirne	212	41.40 N	26.34 E
Adriatic Sea ⊤2	158	42.30 N	16.00 E
Adronamurchan, Point of ≻	162	56.44 N	6.12 W
Advance	248	37.06 N	89.55 W
Advocate Harbour	240	45.20 N	64.47 W
Adwa	214	14.10 N	38.55 E
Ady	250	35.29 N	102.08 W
Adyča ≏	186	68.13 N	134.41 E
Adzopé □5	222	6.00 N	3.30 W
Adz'va ≏	160	66.36 N	59.28 E
Adz'vavom	160	66.36 N	59.12 E
Aegean Sea ⊤2	172	38.30 N	25.00 E
Aegina → Aíyina I	172	37.46 N	23.26 E
A'ergeshanmai ∧∧	206	36.40 N	88.00 E
A'erjinshanmai ∧∧	190	37.30 N	86.30 E
Aerkuhu ◎	206	30.43 N	82.55 E
Ærø I	164	54.53 N	10.20 E
Ærøskøbing	164	54.53 N	10.25 E
Aershan	190	47.11 N	119.57 E
Aesculapium ⊥	212	39.10 N	27.13 E
Aetna	238	49.08 N	113.15 W
Afadjoto ∧2	222	7.05 N	0.35 E
Afanasjevo	160	58.52 N	53.12 E
Afars and Issas □2	214	11.30 N	43.00 E
Affollé ∧∧2	222	16.55 N	10.25 W
Affton	248	38.33 N	90.20 W
Afghānestān → Afghanistan □1	204	34.00 N	66.00 E
Afghanistan □1	204	34.00 N	66.00 E
Afgoi	214	2.10 N	45.09 E
Afikpo	222	5.53 N	7.56 E
Åfjord	160	63.58 N	10.12 E
Afmadu	218	0.32 N	42.10 E
Afognak Island I	236	58.15 N	152.30 W
Afonicha	160	68.13 N	53.17 E
Afonso Cláudio	296	20.05 S	41.08 W
'Afrā', Wādī ∨	208	30.59 N	35.38 E
Afragola	184	40.55 N	14.18 E
Afram ≏	222	7.00 N	0.52 E
Afram Plains ≚	222	6.50 N	0.10 W
Africa •1	148	10.00 N	22.00 E
Afrikanda	160	67.25 N	32.43 E
Afton, Iowa, U.S.	248	41.02 N	94.12 W
Afton, N.Y., U.S.	242	42.14 N	75.32 W
Afton, Okla., U.S.	250	36.42 N	94.58 W
Afton, Wis., U.S.	268	42.36 N	89.04 W
Afton, Wyo., U.S.	254	42.44 N	110.56 W
'Afula	210	32.36 N	35.17 E
Afyon □4	212	38.40 N	30.30 E
Afyonkarahisar	212	38.45 N	30.33 E
Aga	160	60.18 N	6.36 E
Agadez	222	16.58 N	7.59 E
Agadez □5	222	19.45 N	12.00 E
Agadir	214	30.26 N	9.36 W
Agadyr'	186	48.17 N	72.53 E
Agalega Islands II	218	10.24 S	56.37 E
Agalta, Cordillera de ∧∧	280	15.00 N	85.53 W
Agan ≏	186	61.23 N	74.35 E
Agana	198	13.28 N	144.45 E
Agano ≏	192	37.57 N	139.08 E
Agapa	186	71.27 N	89.15 E
Agartala	206	23.50 N	91.16 E
Agassiz	238	49.14 N	121.46 W
Agate	252	39.28 N	103.56 W
Agattu Island I	237a	52.25 N	173.35 E
Agattu Strait ⊔	237a	52.35 N	173.25 E
Agawa ≏	244	47.21 N	84.38 W
Agawa Bay C	244	47.20 N	84.42 W
Agawam, Mass., U.S.	261	42.05 N	72.37 W
Agawam, Mont., U.S.	238	48.00 N	112.10 W
Agboville	214	5.56 N	4.13 W
Agboville □5	222	5.45 N	4.10 W
Agcawayan	202	13.46 N	120.16 E
Agdam	208	40.00 N	46.56 E
Agde	166	43.19 N	3.28 E
Agde, Cap d' ≻	166	43.16 N	3.30 E
Agege	222	6.37 N	3.20 E
Agen	166	44.12 N	0.37 E
Agency	244	41.00 N	92.18 W
Agency Lake ◎	256	42.32 N	121.58 W
Aggtelek •5	164	48.30 N	20.32 E
Āghā Jārī	208	30.42 N	49.50 E
Aginskoje	186	55.15 N	94.55 E
Agira	170	37.39 N	14.32 E
Agliana	184	43.54 N	11.00 E
Agly ≏	166	42.47 N	3.02 E
Agnano Terme ⊸8	184	40.47 N	14.11 E
Agnes Lake ◎	244	48.13 N	91.21 W
Agnew	226	28.01 S	120.30 E
Agnita	172	45.59 N	24.38 E
Agno	202	16.07 N	119.48 E
Agno ≏	202	16.02 N	120.13 E
Agnone	170	41.48 N	14.22 E
Ago	192	34.20 N	136.51 E
Agogo	222	6.47 N	1.04 W
Agoo	202	16.20 N	120.22 E
Agordat → Akordat	214	15.35 N	37.54 E
Agordo	170	46.17 N	12.02 E
Agoura	274	34.08 N	118.45 W
Agout ≏	166	43.47 N	1.41 E
Agoza ⊥	220	18.30 N	23.45 E
Āgra	206	27.12 N	77.59 E
Agraciada	294	33.48 S	58.15 W
Agrado	290	2.15 N	75.46 W
Agram → Zagreb	170	45.48 N	15.58 E
Agramonte	284p	22.41 N	81.07 W
Agrate Brianza	182	45.34 N	9.21 E
Ágreda	168	41.51 N	1.56 W
Ağrı □4	212	39.30 N	43.15 E
Agri ≏	170	40.13 N	16.44 E
Agricola	248	30.44 N	88.37 W
Agrigento	170	37.18 N	13.35 E
Agrihan I	198	18.46 N	145.40 E
Agrínion	172	38.37 N	21.24 E
Agropoli	170	40.21 N	15.00 E
Agryz	160	56.33 N	53.00 E
Agsumal, Sebjet ◎	214	24.21 N	12.52 W
Agtuuganon, Mount ∧	202	7.50 N	126.10 E
Agua, Volcán de ∧1	280	14.28 N	90.45 W
Água Boa	296	17.59 S	42.24 W
Agua Caliente	278	23.20 N	105.20 W
Agua Caliente, Cerro ∧	278	26.27 N	106.12 W
Agua Caliente de Chínipas	278	27.27 N	108.32 W
Agua Caliente Grande	278	26.31 N	108.22 W
Aguacate	284p	22.59 N	81.49 W
Aguachica	290	8.19 N	73.38 W
Água Clara	296	20.27 S	52.52 W
Água Comprida	296	20.04 S	48.08 W
Aguada	284m	18.23 N	67.11 W
Aguada de Pasajeros	284p	22.23 N	80.51 W
Aguadas	290	5.37 N	75.27 W

Name	Page	Lat°′	Long°′
Agua de Dios	290	4.23 N	74.40 W
Aguadilla	284m	18.26 N	67.09 W
Água Doce	294	27.00 S	51.33 W
Aguadulce, Pan.	280	8.15 N	80.32 W
Agua Dulce, Calif., U.S.	274	34.30 N	118.23 W
Agua Fría ≃, C.R.	280	10.35 N	83.30 W
Agua Fria ≃, Ariz., U.S.	254	33.23 N	112.21 W
Aguaí	296	22.04 S	46.58 W
Agualeguas	278	26.18 N	99.34 W
Água Limpa	296	18.06 S	48.46 W
Aguán ≃	280	15.58 N	85.44 W
Aguanaval ≃	278	25.28 N	102.53 W
Aguanish	240	50.16 N	62.10 W
Aguanus ≃	240	50.12 N	62.10 W
Aguapeí ≃	292	15.53 S	58.25 W
Aguapeí, Serra do ⛰	292	16.00 S	59.35 W
Aguapepito	278	24.33 N	107.39 W
Aguapey ≃	294	29.07 S	56.36 W
Agua Prieta	278	31.18 N	109.34 W
Aguaragüe, Cordillera de ⛰	292	21.30 S	63.40 W
Aguaray	294	22.15 S	63.45 W
Aguarico ≃	290	0.59 S	75.11 W
Aguaruto	278	24.47 N	107.29 W
Aguas ≃	168	37.09 N	1.49 W
Aguasabon ≃	244	48.46 N	87.07 W
Aguas Buenas	284m	18.15 N	66.06 W
Aguascalientes, Méx.	254	32.18 N	115.10 W
Aguascalientes, Méx.	278	21.53 N	102.18 W
Águas Formosas	296	17.05 S	40.57 W
Aguayo	294	31.42 S	65.54 W
Agua Zarca	254	31.10 N	110.59 W
Agu Bay C	232	70.18 N	86.30 W
Agudo	294	29.38 S	53.15 W
Agudos	296	22.28 S	49.00 W
Águeda	168	40.34 N	8.27 W
Águeda ≃	168	41.02 N	6.56 W
Aguenier, Lac ⊜	240	50.42 N	68.13 W
Aguijan I	198	14.51 N	145.34 E
Aguila	254	33.56 N	113.11 W
Águila, Cerro del Λ	278	26.50 N	112.28 W
Aguilar, Esp.	168	37.31 N	4.39 W
Aguilar, Colo., U.S.	252	37.24 N	104.46 W
Aguilar, Salar de ≚	294	25.49 S	68.53 W
Aguilares, Arg.	294	27.26 S	65.35 W
Aguilares, El Sal.	280	13.58 N	89.12 W
Águilas	168	37.24 N	1.35 W
Aguililla	278	18.44 N	102.44 W
Aguja, Punta ➤	292	5.48 S	81.06 W
Aguja Point ➤	202	12.41 N	123.23 E
Agujita	250	27.53 N	101.09 W
Agulhas, Cape ➤	224	34.52 S	20.00 E
Agulhas Basin ✢[1]	148	45.00 S	25.00 E
Agulhas Negras, Pico das Λ	296	22.23 S	44.38 W
Agusan □[4]	202	80.40 N	125.40 E
Agusan ≃	202	9.00 N	125.30 E
Agustín Codazzi	290	10.02 N	73.14 W
Agutaya	202	11.09 N	120.56 E
Agutaya Island I	202	11.09 N	120.58 E
Ağva	172	41.09 N	29.50 E
Ahaggar ⛰	214	23.00 N	6.30 E
Ahaggar, Tassili des ⛰	222	20.20 N	4.40 E
Ahaggar, Tassili du ⛰[1]	214	21.00 N	6.00 E
Aha Hills ⛰[2]	224	19.45 S	21.10 E
Ahar	208	38.28 N	47.04 E
Ahaura ≃	230	42.21 S	171.32 E
Ahaus	178	52.04 N	7.00 E
Ahfir	168	34.57 N	2.17 W
Ahimanawa Range ⛰	230	39.03 S	176.30 E
Ahipara Bay C	230	35.10 S	173.08 E
Ahırlı	172	38.37 N	26.31 E
Ahklun Mountains ⛰	236	59.15 N	161.00 W
Ahlem	178	52.23 N	9.40 E
Ahlen	178	51.46 N	7.53 E
Ahmadābād	206	23.02 N	72.35 E
Ahmadpur East	206	29.09 N	71.16 E
Ahmar Mountains ⛰	214	9.15 N	41.00 E
Ahmetli	172	38.31 N	27.57 E
Ahmic Lake ⊜	244	45.37 N	79.42 W
Ahome	278	25.55 N	109.11 W
Ahoskie	246	36.17 N	76.59 W
Ahrensburg	178	53.40 N	10.14 E
Ahrweiler	164	50.32 N	7.05 E
Ahtanum	270	46.34 N	120.37 W
Ähtävänjoki ≃	160	63.38 N	22.48 E
Ahtopol	172	42.06 N	27.57 E
Ahuacatlán	278	21.03 N	104.29 W
Ahuachapán	280	13.55 N	89.51 W
Ahumada	258	32.30 N	115.30 W
Ahun	166	46.05 N	2.05 E
Ahuriri ≃	230	44.31 S	170.12 E
Ahvāz	208	31.19 N	48.42 E
Ahvenanmaa (Åland) II	160	60.15 N	20.00 E
Ahwahnee	272	37.23 N	119.44 W
Aḥwar	214	13.31 N	46.42 E
Aialik, Cape ➤	236	59.42 N	149.31 W
Aiapuá	290	4.29 S	62.04 W
Aiapuá, Lago ⊜	290	4.27 S	62.08 W
Aibihu ⊜	190	44.55 N	82.55 E
Aibonito	284m	18.08 N	66.16 W
Aichach	164	48.28 N	11.08 E
Aichi □[5]	192	35.00 N	137.15 E
Aiea	275c	21.23 N	157.56 W
Aigen im Mühlkreis	164	48.39 N	13.58 E
Aigle	166	46.19 N	6.58 E
Aigle, Lac à l' ⊜	240	51.12 N	65.25 W
Aigre	166	45.54 N	0.01 E
Aiguá	294	34.12 S	54.45 W
Aiguebelle, Réserve(Aiguebelle Reserve) ♠	244	48.33 N	78.45 W
Aigueperse	166	46.01 N	3.12 E
Aiguilles	166	44.47 N	6.52 E
Aigurande-sur-Bouzanne	166	46.26 N	1.50 E
Aihun	190	50.13 N	127.33 E
Aija	292	9.45 S	77.35 W
Aikawa	192	38.02 N	138.15 E
Aiken	246	33.34 N	81.43 W
Ailaoshan ⛰	200	24.08 N	101.25 E
Ailigandí	290	9.13 N	78.04 W
Ailsa Craig	244	43.08 N	81.33 W
Ailsa Craig I	162	55.16 N	5.07 W
Aim	186	58.50 N	134.12 E
Aimenguan)(	196	31.24 N	115.22 E
Aimogasta	294	28.30 S	66.49 W
Aimorés	296	19.30 S	41.04 W
Aimorés, Serra dos ⛰	296	19.00 S	41.00 W
Ain □[5]	180	46.10 N	5.20 E
Ain ≃	166	45.48 N	5.10 E
Aïn Arnat	168	36.07 N	5.21 E
Aïn Azel	168	35.49 N	5.31 E
Ainaži	160	57.52 N	24.21 E
Aïn Benian	168	36.45 N	2.51 E
Aïn Berda	170	36.40 N	7.37 E
Aïn Bessem	168	36.17 N	3.41 E
Aïn Defla	168	36.16 N	1.58 E
Aïn Djelloula	170	35.48 N	9.51 E
Aïn Draham	170	36.47 N	8.42 E
Aïn el Hadjel	168	35.34 N	3.56 E
Aïn el Khebira	168	36.22 N	5.31 E
Aïn Oulmène	168	35.55 N	5.17 E
Aïn Oussera	168	35.24 N	2.54 E
Ainslie, Lake ⊜	240	46.08 N	61.12 W
Ainsworth	252	42.33 N	99.52 W
Aïn Tagrout	168	36.08 N	5.05 E
Aïn Tedelès	168	36.00 N	0.21 E
Aïn Témouchent	168	35.16 N	1.04 W
Aïn Touta	168	35.26 N	5.59 E
Aioi	192	34.48 N	134.28 E
Aipe	290	3.13 N	75.15 W
Aiquara	296	14.07 S	39.52 W
Aiquile	292	18.10 S	65.10 W
Aïr ⛰	222	18.00 N	8.30 E
Airabu, Pulau I	200	2.46 N	106.14 E
Airão	290	1.56 S	61.22 W
Airdrie	238	51.18 N	114.02 W
Aire	166	43.42 N	0.16 W
Aire ≃	166	49.19 N	4.49 E
Aires	162	50.38 N	2.24 E
Aire-sur-la-Lys	176	50.38 N	2.24 E
Air Force Island I	232	67.55 N	74.10 W
Airola	184	41.04 N	14.33 E
Airolo	166	46.32 N	8.37 E
Airvault	166	46.50 N	0.08 W
Aisch ≃	164	49.46 N	11.01 E
Aishihik	236	61.35 N	137.30 W
Aishihik Lake ⊜	236	61.25 N	137.06 W
Aisne □[5]	176	49.30 N	3.30 E
Aisne ≃, Bel.	164	50.23 N	5.31 E
Aisne ≃, Fr.	166	49.26 N	2.50 E
Aitana Λ	168	38.44 N	0.16 W
Aitape	198	3.08 S	142.21 E
Aitch	266	40.23 N	78.10 W
Aitkin	244	46.32 N	93.43 W
Aitolía Kai Akarnanía □[5]	172	38.30 N	21.30 E
Aitolikón	172	38.27 N	21.22 E
Aït-Youssef-ou-Ali	168	35.13 N	3.55 W
Aiud	172	46.19 N	23.44 E
Aiuruoca	296	21.58 S	44.36 W
Aix-en-Provence	182	43.32 N	5.26 E
Aix-la-Chapelle → Aachen	164	50.47 N	6.05 E
Aix-les-Bains	182	45.42 N	5.55 E
Aiyansh	238	55.17 N	129.03 W
Aíyina	172	37.44 N	23.27 E
Aíyina I	172	37.46 N	23.26 E
Aiyínion	172	40.30 N	22.33 E
Aíyion	172	38.15 N	22.05 E
Aizhou I	196	22.04 N	114.00 E
Aizu-bange	192	37.34 N	139.49 E
Aizu-wakamatsu	192	37.30 N	139.56 E
Ajaccio	170	41.55 N	8.44 E
Ajaguz	186	47.56 N	80.23 E
Ajan	186	56.27 N	138.10 E
Ajan ≃	186	56.27 N	138.10 E
Ajax	264	43.51 N	79.02 W
Ajdābiyah	214	30.48 N	20.14 E
Ajdovščina	170	45.53 N	13.53 E
Ajigasawa	192	40.47 N	140.12 E
Ajka	164	47.07 N	17.34 E
Ajkino	160	62.15 N	49.56 E
'Ajlūn	210	32.20 N	35.45 E
Ajlune	256	46.31 N	122.26 W
'Ajmah, Jabal al- ⛰	220	29.12 N	34.02 E
Ajmer	206	26.27 N	74.40 E
Ajo	254	32.22 N	112.52 W
Ajo, Cabo de ➤	168	43.31 N	3.35 W
Ajon, Ostrov I	186	69.50 N	168.40 E
Ajoya	278	24.04 N	106.22 W
Ajtos	172	42.42 N	27.15 E
Aju, Kepulauan II	198	0.28 N	131.03 E
Ajusco	258	31.35 N	116.25 W
Ajuterique	280	14.20 N	87.43 W
Ajuy	202	11.10 N	123.01 E
Ajuy Bay C	202	11.08 N	123.03 E
Ak ≃	212	37.50 N	28.15 E
Aka ≃	192	38.54 N	139.50 E
Akaba Dağı Λ	212	40.12 N	40.51 E
Akabira	192a	43.34 N	142.03 E
Akademii, Zaliv C	186	54.15 N	138.05 E
Akagi-san Λ	192	36.33 N	139.11 E
Akaishi-sammyaku ⛰	192	35.18 N	138.07 E
Akaka Falls ♠	275d	19.52 N	155.09 W
Akan	192a	43.06 N	144.10 E
Akan-kokuritsu-kōen ♠	192a	43.30 N	144.15 E
Akaroa Harbour C	230	43.50 S	172.55 E
'Akasha East	214	21.05 N	30.43 E
Akashi	192	34.38 N	134.59 E
Akbou	168	36.28 N	4.32 E
Akçaova, Tür.	172	37.30 N	28.02 E
Akçaova, Tür.	172	41.03 N	29.57 E
Akçay ≃	212	37.20 N	30.50 E
Akdağ Λ, Tür.	212	39.15 N	35.45 E
Akdağ Λ, Tür.	212	36.32 N	29.34 E
Akdağ Λ, Tür.	212	39.29 N	41.54 E
Akeley	244	47.00 N	94.44 W
Aken	164	51.51 N	12.02 E
Akershus □[6]	160	60.00 N	11.10 E
Akesu	190	41.10 N	80.20 E
Aketi	214	2.44 N	23.46 E
Ak Göl ⊜	212	38.58 N	31.48 E
Akhaía □[5]	172	38.00 N	22.00 E
Akharnaí	172	38.05 N	23.44 E
Akhḍar, Wādī al- V	208	27.59 N	36.36 E
Akhelóös ≃	172	38.36 N	21.14 E
Akhiok	236	56.57 N	154.10 W
Akhisar	212	38.55 N	27.51 E
Akhmīm	220	26.34 N	31.44 E
Aki	192	33.30 N	133.54 E
Akiachak	236	60.55 N	161.27 W
Akiak	236	60.55 N	161.12 W
Akimiski Island I	232	53.00 N	81.20 W
Akita	192	39.43 N	140.07 E
Akita-heiya ≚	192	39.45 N	140.10 E
Akjoujt	214	19.45 N	14.23 W
Akkani	236	65.30 N	171.10 W
Akkeshi	192a	43.02 N	144.51 E
'Akko (Acre)	210	32.55 N	35.04 E
Akkol', S.S.S.R.	186	43.25 N	70.47 E
Akkol', S.S.S.R.	186	45.02 N	75.40 E
Akköy	172	37.29 N	27.15 E
Aklan □[4]	202	11.40 N	122.20 E
Aklavik	236	68.12 N	135.00 W
'aklé 'âouâna •[1]	222	18.00 N	5.30 W
Akō	192	34.45 N	134.24 E
Akobo ≃	220	7.48 N	33.03 E
Akordat	214	15.35 N	37.54 E
Akosombo Dam •[6]	222	6.16 N	0.03 E
Akpatok Island I	232	60.25 N	68.00 W
Akranes	160a	64.18 N	22.02 W
Akrítas, Ákra ➤	172	36.43 N	21.54 E
Akron, Ala., U.S.	248	32.53 N	87.51 W
Akron, Colo., U.S.	252	40.10 N	103.13 W
Akron, Ind., U.S.	268	41.02 N	86.01 W
Akron, Iowa, U.S.	252	42.49 N	96.33 W
Akron, N.Y., U.S.	264	43.01 N	78.30 W
Akron, Ohio, U.S.	266	41.05 N	81.31 W
Akron, Pa., U.S.	262	40.09 N	76.12 W
Aksaray	212	38.23 N	34.03 E
Aksarka	186	66.36 N	67.46 E
Akşehir	212	38.21 N	31.25 E
Akşehir Gölü ⊜	212	38.30 N	31.28 E
Aksu ≃	212	37.36 N	36.46 E
Aksuat	186	47.48 N	82.50 E
Aksubajevo	160	54.52 N	50.50 E
Aksum	214	14.08 N	38.48 E
Aktogaj	186	46.57 N	79.40 E
Akt'ubinsk	158	50.17 N	57.10 E
Aku	222	6.42 N	7.20 E
Akune	192	32.01 N	130.11 E
Akun Island I	236	54.12 N	165.35 W
Akure	222	7.15 N	5.12 E
Akureyri	160a	65.44 N	18.08 W
Akuseki-shima I	193b	29.27 N	129.37 E
Akutan	236	54.08 N	165.46 W
Akutan Island I	236	54.10 N	165.55 W
Akutan Pass U	236	54.00 N	166.10 W
Akvirah	172	40.54 N	29.30 E
Akwatia	222	6.04 N	0.49 W
Akwawa Λ[2]	222	6.27 N	0.25 W
Akyab → Sittwe	200	20.09 N	92.54 E
Akžar	186	47.35 N	83.42 E
Ål	160	60.38 N	8.34 E
Alabama	264	43.06 N	78.23 W
Alabama □[3]	234	32.50 N	87.00 W
Alabama ≃	248	31.08 N	87.57 W
Alabama Port	248	30.22 N	88.08 W
Alabaster	248	33.15 N	86.49 W
Alabat Island I	202	14.06 N	122.02 E
Alaçalı	172	41.11 N	29.27 E
Alaçam Dağları ⛰	212	39.20 N	28.32 E
Alaçatı	172	38.16 N	26.23 E
Alachua	246	29.47 N	82.30 W
Aladağ Λ	212	37.44 N	35.09 E
Ala Dağları ⛰	212	37.55 N	35.13 E
Aladža-Džamija ✝[1]	172	43.31 N	18.47 E
Aladža manastir ✝[1]	172	43.17 N	28.01 E
Alagir	158	43.03 N	44.14 E
Alagoa	296	22.10 S	44.38 W
Alagoa Grande	286	7.03 S	35.38 W
Alagoinhas	296	12.07 S	38.26 W
Alagón	168	41.46 N	1.07 W
Alagón ≃	168	39.44 N	6.53 W
Alah ≃	202	6.42 N	124.35 E
Alahärmä	160	63.14 N	22.51 E
Alajõe	160	59.01 N	27.26 E
Alajskij Chrebet ⛰	186	39.45 N	72.00 E
Alajuela	280	10.01 N	84.13 W
Alajuela □[4]	280	10.30 N	84.30 W
Alakanuk	236	62.41 N	164.37 W
Alakol', Ozero ⊜	186	46.10 N	81.45 E
Alakurtti	160	66.57 N	30.18 E
Alalakeiki Channel U	275d	20.35 N	156.30 W
Al-'Alamayn	220	30.49 N	28.57 E
Al-'Amādīyah	208	37.06 N	43.29 E
Alamagan I	198	17.36 N	145.50 E
Al-'Amārah	208	31.50 N	47.09 E
Al-'Amārah □[4]	208	32.00 N	47.00 E
Alameda, Esp.	168	37.12 N	4.39 W
Alameda, Calif., U.S.	272	37.46 N	122.16 W
Alameda, N. Mex., U.S.	254	35.11 N	106.37 W
Alameda □[6]	272	37.35 N	121.55 W
Alamein → Al-'Alamayn	220	30.49 N	28.57 E
Alamillo	254	31.02 N	110.35 W
Alaminos	202	16.10 N	119.59 E
Alamo, Calif., U.S.	272	37.51 N	122.02 W
Alamo, Ga., U.S.	246	32.09 N	82.47 W
Alamo, Mich., U.S.	268	42.22 N	85.43 W
Alamo, Nev., U.S.	258	37.22 N	115.10 W
Alamo, Tenn., U.S.	248	35.47 N	89.07 W
Alamo ≃	258	33.14 N	115.39 W
Álamo de San Felipe, Cerro Λ	278	30.41 N	112.35 W
Alamogordo	254	32.54 N	105.57 W
Alamogordo Reservoir ⊜[1]	250	34.38 N	104.25 W
Alamo Heights	250	29.28 N	98.28 W
Alamor	290	4.02 S	80.02 W
Alamos, Méx.	250	26.25 N	100.25 W
Alamos, Méx.	278	27.01 N	108.56 W
Alamosa	254	37.28 N	105.52 W
Alamosa ≃	254	33.20 N	107.21 W
Alanäs	160	64.10 N	15.42 E
Alangalang	202	11.12 N	124.50 E
Alanje	280	8.20 N	82.40 W
Alanson	244	45.27 N	84.47 W
Alanya	158	36.33 N	32.01 E
Alaotra, Lac ⊜	225b	17.30 S	48.30 E
Alapaha	246	31.23 N	83.13 W
Alapaha ≃	246	30.26 N	83.06 W
Alapajevsk	158	57.52 N	61.42 E
Al-'Aqabah	210	29.31 N	35.00 E
Al-'Aqabah Landing Ground ⊠	210	29.32 N	34.59 E
Al 'araj ☷	220	28.56 N	26.24 E
Alarcón	168	39.33 N	2.05 W
Alarcón, Embalse de ⊜[1]	168	39.36 N	2.10 W
Al-'Arīsh	210	31.08 N	33.48 E
Al-'Arīsh Airfield ⊠	210	31.04 N	33.50 E
Al-'Armah ⛰[1]	208	25.30 N	46.30 E
Al-Arz •[3]	212	34.14 N	36.03 E
Alas, Lae ≃	200	3.05 N	97.54 E
Alaşehir	172	38.21 N	28.32 E
Alashanyouqi	190	40.02 N	103.33 E
Alash Higuito ≃	280	14.43 N	88.40 W
Al-'Āṣimah □[8]	210	31.45 N	36.30 E
Alaska □[3]	236	62.00 N	153.00 W
Alaska, Gulf of C	236	58.00 N	146.00 W
Alaska Peninsula ➤[1]	236	57.00 N	158.00 W
Alaska Range ⛰	236	62.30 N	150.00 W
Al-'Assāfīyah ▾[4]	208	28.21 N	39.08 E
Alassio	182	44.00 N	8.10 E
Al-'Athāmīn ⛰	208	30.22 N	43.40 E
Alatna ≃	236	66.34 N	152.34 W
Alatri	184	41.43 N	13.21 E
Al-'Aṭrūn	214	18.11 N	26.36 E
Alatyr'	160	54.51 N	46.36 E
Alatyr' ≃	160	54.52 N	46.36 E
Alausí	290	2.12 S	78.50 W
Alava □[4]	168	42.50 N	2.45 W
Alavus	160	62.35 N	23.37 E
Al-'Ayn ▾[4]	220	16.36 N	29.19 E
Alayor	168	39.56 N	4.08 E
Al-'Ayyināt ⛰[1]	220	22.08 N	32.45 E
Al-'Azīzīyah	214	32.32 N	13.01 E
Alba, It.	182	44.42 N	8.02 E
Alba, Mich., U.S.	244	44.59 N	84.58 W
Alba, Tex., U.S.	250	32.48 N	95.38 W
Albacete	168	38.59 N	1.51 W
Al-Badārī	220	26.59 N	31.25 E
Alba de Tormes	168	40.49 N	5.31 W
Al-Baḥrayn •[1]	220	28.40 N	26.32 E
Albaida	168	38.51 N	0.31 W
Alba-Iulia	172	46.04 N	23.35 E
Al-Balqā □[8]	210	31.50 N	35.40 E
Al-Bālū'ah ⊜	212	35.55 N	36.28 E
Al-Balyanā	220	26.14 N	32.00 E
Alban	166	43.54 N	2.28 E
Albanel, Lac ⊜	232	51.09 N	73.00 W
Albania □[1], Eur.	158	41.00 N	20.00 E
Albano Laziale	184	41.44 N	12.39 E
Albany, Austl.	226	35.02 S	117.53 E
Albany, Calif., U.S.	272	37.53 N	122.18 W
Albany, Ga., U.S.	246	31.35 N	84.10 W
Albany, Ind., U.S.	268	40.18 N	85.14 W
Albany, Ky., U.S.	248	36.42 N	85.08 W
Albany, Minn., U.S.	244	45.38 N	94.34 W
Albany, Mo., U.S.	248	40.15 N	94.20 W
Albany, N.Y., U.S.	261	42.39 N	73.45 W
Albany, Ohio, U.S.	242	39.14 N	82.12 W
Albany, Oreg., U.S.	256	44.38 N	123.06 W
Albany, Tex., U.S.	250	32.44 N	99.18 W
Albany, Wis., U.S.	244	42.43 N	89.26 W
Albany □[6]	261	42.39 N	73.45 W
Albany ≃	232	52.17 N	81.31 W
Albardón	294	31.26 S	68.30 W
Albarracín	168	40.25 N	1.26 W
Al-Baṣrah (Basra)	208	30.30 N	47.47 E
Al-Baṣrah □[4]	208	30.30 N	47.47 E
Al-Bāṭinah •[1]	208	23.45 N	57.20 E
Albatross Cordillera ✢[3]	148	62.00 S	155.00 W
Albatross Point ➤	230	38.07 S	174.41 E
Al-Bawīṭī	214	28.21 N	28.52 E
Albay □[4]	202	13.00 N	123.40 E
Al-Bayḍā' □[4]	220	32.30 N	21.30 E
Albay Gulf C	202	13.10 N	123.53 E
Albemarle	246	35.21 N	80.12 W
Albemarle Sound U	246	36.03 N	76.12 W
Albenga	182	44.03 N	8.13 E
Albens	166	45.47 N	5.57 E
Alberche ≃	168	39.58 N	4.46 W
Alberdi	294	26.10 S	58.09 W
Alberene	246	37.53 N	78.37 W
Albergaria-a-Velha	168	40.42 N	8.29 W
Alberhill	274	33.44 N	117.23 W
Alberique	168	39.07 N	0.31 W
Alberni	270	49.16 N	124.49 W
Alberobello	170	40.47 N	17.15 E
Albert	176	50.00 N	2.39 E
Albert, Lake ⊜, Afr.	218	1.40 N	31.00 E
Albert, Lake ⊜, Austl.	228	35.38 S	139.17 E
Alberta	248	32.14 N	87.25 W
Alberta □[3]	232	54.00 N	113.00 W
Alberta, Mount Λ	238	52.18 N	117.28 W
Albert Canyon	238	51.08 N	117.52 W
Albert City	252	42.47 N	94.57 W
Albert Edward Bay C	232	69.32 N	103.00 W
Alberti	294	35.01 S	60.16 W
Albertirsa	164	47.15 N	19.38 E
Albert Lea	244	43.39 N	93.22 W
Albert Nile ≃	214	3.36 N	32.02 E
Alberton, P.E.I., Can.	240	46.49 N	64.04 W
Alberton, Mont., U.S.	256	47.00 N	114.29 W
Albert Town	285q	18.17 N	77.33 W
Albertville, Fr.	182	45.41 N	6.23 E
Albertville, Ala., U.S.	248	34.16 N	86.12 W
Albertville → Kalemi,zaïre	218	5.56 S	29.12 E
Albi	166	43.56 N	2.09 E
Albia, Iowa, U.S.	244	41.02 N	92.48 W
Albia, N.Y., U.S.	261	42.43 N	73.39 W
Albin	252	41.25 N	104.06 W
Albina	286	5.30 N	54.03 W
Albino	182	45.46 N	9.47 E
Albion, B.C., Can.	270	49.11 N	122.33 W
Albion, Calif., U.S.	258	39.13 N	123.46 W
Albion, Idaho, U.S.	256	42.25 N	113.35 W
Albion, Ill., U.S.	248	38.23 N	88.04 W
Albion, Ind., U.S.	268	41.24 N	85.25 W
Albion, Iowa, U.S.	244	42.07 N	92.59 W
Albion, Mich., U.S.	268	42.15 N	84.45 W
Albion, Nebr., U.S.	252	41.42 N	98.00 W
Albion, N.Y., U.S.	264	43.15 N	78.12 W
Albion, Pa., U.S.	266	41.53 N	80.22 W
Albion, R.I., U.S.	261	41.57 N	71.27 W
Albion, Tex., U.S.	250	27.45 N	98.05 W
Albion, Wis., U.S.	268	42.53 N	89.04 W
Al-Biqā' □[4]	210	34.00 N	36.00 E
Al-Biqā' V	212	33.50 N	35.45 E
Al-Bīrah	210	31.54 N	35.13 E
Al-Bishrī •[1]	212	35.26 N	39.32 E
Albissola Superiore	182	44.20 N	8.31 E
Alblasserdam	178	51.52 N	4.40 E
Albo, Monte Λ	170	40.29 N	9.33 E
Albocácer	168	40.21 N	0.02 E
Alborán, Isla de I	168	35.58 N	3.02 W
Ålborg	160	57.03 N	9.56 E
Alborz, Reshteh-ye Kūhhā-ye ⛰	208	36.00 N	53.00 E
Albreda	238	52.38 N	119.09 W
Albuera	202	10.55 N	124.42 E
Albufeira	168	37.05 N	8.15 W
Ālbū Gharz, Sabkhat ⊜	212	34.45 N	41.15 E
Al-Buḥayrah al-Murrah al-Kubrā ⊜	220	30.20 N	32.23 E
Albuñol	168	36.47 N	3.12 W
Albuquerque, Bra.	292	19.23 S	57.26 W
Albuquerque, N. Mex., U.S.	254	35.05 N	106.40 W
Albuquerque, Cayos de II	280	12.10 N	81.50 W
Alburg	242	44.59 N	73.18 W
Alburquerque	168	39.13 N	7.00 W
Alburtis	262	40.31 N	75.36 W
Albury	228	36.05 S	146.55 E
Al-Busayṭah ≚	208	29.30 N	38.45 E
Al-Buṭanah •[1]	220	15.00 N	34.40 E
Alca	292	15.10 S	72.46 W
Alcácer do Sal	168	38.22 N	8.30 W
Alcains	168	39.55 N	7.27 W
Alcala	202	17.54 N	121.39 E
Alcalá de Guadaira	168	37.20 N	5.50 W
Alcalá de Henares	168	40.29 N	3.22 W
Alcalá la Real	168	37.28 N	3.56 W
Alcalde	254	36.05 N	106.03 W
Alcamo	170	37.59 N	12.58 E
Alcanadre ≃	168	41.37 N	0.12 W
Alcanar	168	40.33 N	0.29 E
Alcañices	168	41.42 N	6.21 W
Alcañiz	168	41.03 N	0.08 W
Alcântara, Bra.	286	2.24 S	44.24 W
Alcántara, Esp.	168	39.43 N	6.53 W
Alcantara, Pil.	202	12.16 N	122.03 E
Alcantarilla	168	37.58 N	1.13 W
Alcantilado	296	16.23 S	53.31 W
Alcaraz	168	38.40 N	2.29 W
Alcarrache ≃	168	38.16 N	7.24 W
Alcaudete	168	37.36 N	4.05 W
Alcázar de San Juan	168	39.24 N	3.12 W
Alcester	252	43.01 N	96.38 W
Alcira (Gigena), Arg.	294	32.45 S	64.20 W
Alcira, Esp.	168	39.09 N	0.26 W
Alcoa	246	35.48 N	83.59 W
Alcobaça, Bra.	296	17.30 S	39.13 W
Alcobaça, Port.	168	39.33 N	8.59 W
Alcobendas	168	40.32 N	3.38 W
Alcolea del Piuar	168	41.02 N	2.28 W
Alconchel	168	38.31 N	7.04 W
Alcorn College	248	31.52 N	91.09 W
Alcorta	294	33.32 S	61.08 W
Alcoutim	168	37.28 N	7.28 W
Alcova Reservoir ⊜[1]	254	42.32 N	106.45 W
Alcove	261	42.28 N	73.55 W
Alcoy	168	38.42 N	0.28 W
Alcoy, Nevado Λ	292	11.17 S	76.30 W
Alcubierre	168	41.48 N	0.27 W
Alcudia	168	39.52 N	3.07 E
Alcudia, Bahía de C	168	39.48 N	3.13 E
Aldabra Islands I[1]	218	9.25 S	46.22 E
Aldama, Méx.	278	22.55 N	98.04 W
Aldama, Méx.	278	28.51 N	105.54 W
Aldan	186	58.37 N	125.24 E
Aldan ≃	186	63.28 N	129.35 E
Aldanskoje Nagorje ⛰[1]	186	57.00 N	127.00 E
Aldeburgh	162	52.09 N	1.35 E
Aldeia Nova de Santo Bent	168	37.55 N	7.25 W
Alden, Ill., U.S.	268	42.27 N	88.31 W
Alden, Iowa, U.S.	244	42.31 N	93.23 W
Alden, Mich., U.S.	244	44.53 N	85.17 W
Alden, Minn., U.S.	244	43.40 N	93.34 W
Alden, N.Y., U.S.	264	42.54 N	78.30 W
Alden Center	264	42.55 N	78.32 W
Aldergrove	270	49.04 N	122.28 W
Alderley	268	43.13 N	88.27 W
Alderney I	162	49.43 N	2.12 W
Aldershot	174	51.15 N	0.47 W
Alderson	246	37.43 N	80.39 W
Alderton	270	47.10 N	122.14 W
Alderwood Manor	270	47.49 N	122.17 W
Aldridge	174	52.36 N	1.55 W
Aledo	244	41.12 N	90.45 W
Aleg	214	17.03 N	13.55 W
Alegre	296	20.46 S	41.32 W
Alegrete	294	29.46 S	55.46 W
Alegros Mountain Λ	254	34.09 N	108.11 W
Alejandro Roca	294	33.20 S	63.43 W
Alejandro Selkirk, Isla(Isla Más Afuera) I	288	33.45 S	80.46 W
Alejo Ledesma	294	33.38 S	62.40 W
Alejsk	186	52.58 N	82.45 E
Aleknagik	236	59.17 N	158.38 W
Aleknagik, Lake ⊜	236	59.20 N	158.45 W
Aleksandrija	158	48.40 N	33.07 E
Aleksandrov	160	56.24 N	38.43 E
Aleksandrov Gaj	158	50.09 N	48.34 E
Aleksandrovka	160	52.36 N	50.37 E
Aleksandrovsk	158	48.35 N	39.12 E
Aleksandrovskoje	186	60.26 N	77.50 E
Aleksandrovsk-Sachalinskij	186	50.54 N	142.10 E
Aleksandrów Kujawski	164	52.52 N	18.42 E
Aleksandrów Łódzki	164	51.49 N	19.19 E
Aleksejevka	158	50.37 N	38.42 E
Aleksejevsk	186	57.50 N	108.23 E
Aleksin	160	54.31 N	37.05 E
Aleksinac	172	43.32 N	21.43 E
Alemania, Arg.	294	25.35 S	65.40 W
Alemania, Chile	294	25.10 S	69.55 W
Além Paraíba	296	21.52 S	42.41 W
Alençon	176	48.26 N	0.05 E
Alenquer	286	1.56 S	54.46 W
Alenuihaha Channel U	275d	20.26 N	156.00 W
Aleppo → Ḥalab	212	36.12 N	37.10 E
Aléria	170	42.05 N	9.30 E
Alert Bay	238	50.35 N	126.55 W
Alès	182	44.08 N	4.05 E
Aleşd	172	47.04 N	22.24 E
Alessandria	182	44.54 N	8.37 E
Alessandria □[4]	182	44.49 N	8.42 E
Alessano	170	39.53 N	18.20 E
Ålestrup	160	56.42 N	9.30 E
Ålesund	160	62.28 N	6.09 E
Aletai	190	47.52 N	88.07 E
Aleutian Basin ✢[1]	148	57.00 N	179.00 E
Aleutian Islands II	236	52.00 N	176.00 W
Aleutian Range ⛰	236	59.00 N	155.00 W
Aleutian Trench ✢[1]	148	52.00 N	170.00 W
Aleutka	186	45.57 N	150.10 E
Alevina, Mys ➤	186	58.50 N	151.20 E
Alex	250	34.55 N	97.47 W
Alexander, Man., Can.	252	49.50 N	100.17 W
Alexander, N. Dak., U.S.	252	47.51 N	103.39 W
Alexander, N.Y., U.S.	264	42.54 N	78.16 W
Alexander Archipelago II	236	56.30 N	134.00 W
Alexander Bay	218	28.40 S	16.30 E
Alexander City	248	32.56 N	85.57 W
Alexander Indian Reserve •[4]	238	53.09 N	113.58 W
Alexander Island I	148	71.00 S	70.00 W
Alexandra	230	45.20 S	169.23 E
Alexandra Falls L	232	60.29 N	116.18 W
Alexandretta → İskenderun	212	36.37 N	36.07 E
Alexandretta, Gulf of → İskenderun Körfezi C	212	36.30 N	35.40 E
Alexandria, B.C., Can.	238	52.38 N	122.27 W
Alexandria, Ont., Can.	260	45.19 N	74.38 W
Alexandria → Al-Iskandarīyah,miṣr	220	31.12 N	29.54 E
Alexandria, Rom.	172	43.58 N	25.20 E
Alexandria, Ind., U.S.	268	40.16 N	85.41 W
Alexandria, Ky., U.S.	242	38.58 N	84.23 W
Alexandria, La., U.S.	248	31.18 N	92.27 W
Alexandria, Minn., U.S.	252	45.53 N	95.22 W
Alexandria, Mo., U.S.	248	40.27 N	91.28 W
Alexandria, Nebr., U.S.	252	40.15 N	97.23 W
Alexandria, Ohio, U.S.	266	40.05 N	82.37 W
Alexandria, Pa., U.S.	266	40.34 N	78.06 W
Alexandria, S. Dak., U.S.	252	43.39 N	97.47 W
Alexandria, Tenn., U.S.	248	36.05 N	86.02 W
Alexandria, Va., U.S.	262	38.48 N	77.03 W
Alexandria Bay	264	44.20 N	75.55 W
Alexandrina, Lake ⊜	228	35.26 S	139.10 E
Alexandroúpolis	172	40.50 N	25.52 E
Alexis	244	41.04 N	90.33 W
Alexis Creek	238	52.05 N	123.17 W
Alexis Indian Reserve •[4]	238	53.46 N	114.30 W
Al-Fallūjah	208	33.20 N	43.46 E
Alfambra	168	40.33 N	1.02 W
Alfarata	262	40.39 N	77.27 W
Alfaro, Ec.	290	2.12 S	79.50 W
Alfaro, Esp.	168	42.11 N	1.45 W
Alfarrás	168	41.49 N	0.35 E
Al-Fāshir	220	13.38 N	25.21 E
Al-Fashn	220	28.49 N	30.54 E
Alfatar	172	43.57 N	27.17 E
Al-Fayyūm	220	29.19 N	30.50 E
Alfeld	178	51.59 N	9.50 E
Alfenas	296	21.25 S	45.57 W
Alfiós ≃	172	37.40 N	21.33 E
Alfonsine	184	44.30 N	12.03 E
Alfred, Ont., Can.	260	45.34 N	74.53 W
Alfred, Maine, U.S.	242	43.29 N	70.43 W
Alfred, N.Y., U.S.	266	42.15 N	77.47 W
Alfred National Park ♠	228	37.35 S	149.20 E
Alfredo Chaves	296	20.38 S	40.45 W
Alfreton	174	53.06 N	1.23 W
Alga	158	49.46 N	57.20 E
Ålgård	160	58.46 N	5.51 E
Algarrobal	294	28.08 S	70.39 W
Algarrobo, Arg.	294	38.52 S	63.10 W
Algarrobo, Chile	294	28.43 S	71.03 W
Algarrobo, Chile	294	33.22 S	71.40 W
Algarrobo del Águila	294	36.26 S	67.09 W
Algarrobo Verde	294	31.45 S	68.18 W
Algarve □[9]	168	37.10 N	8.15 W
Algeciras, Col.	290	2.35 N	75.18 W
Algeciras, Esp.	168	36.08 N	5.30 W
Algemesí	168	39.11 N	0.26 W
Alger (Algiers), Alg.	168	36.42 N	3.08 E
Alger, Ohio, U.S.	268	40.42 N	83.51 W
Alger, Golfe d' C	168	36.50 N	3.15 E
Algeria □[1]	214	28.00 N	3.00 E
Al-Ghāb ⊜	212	35.30 N	36.18 E
Al-Ghayḍah	204	16.12 N	52.15 E
Alghero	170	40.34 N	8.19 E
Al-Ghubbah I	208	24.18 N	53.18 E
Al-Ghurdaqah	220	27.14 N	33.50 E
Algiers → Alger	168	36.42 N	3.08 E
Alginet	168	39.16 N	0.28 W
Algoabaai C	224	33.50 S	25.50 E
Algodón ≃	290	2.20 S	71.55 W
Algodones	254	35.23 N	106.29 W
Algoma	244	44.36 N	87.27 W
Algoma Mills	244	46.10 N	82.50 W
Algona, Iowa, U.S.	244	43.04 N	94.14 W
Algona, Wash., U.S.	270	47.17 N	122.15 W
Algonac	266	42.37 N	82.32 W
Algonquin	268	42.10 N	88.18 W
Algonquin Provincial Park ♠	244	45.27 N	78.26 W
Algood	248	36.12 N	85.27 W
Algorta	294	32.25 S	57.23 W
Al-Ḥadīthah	208	34.07 N	42.23 E
Al-Ḥajarah •[1]	208	30.00 N	44.00 E
Al-Ḥajar al-Gharbī ⛰	208	24.22 N	56.17 E
Al-Ḥajar ash-Sharqī ⛰	208	23.00 N	59.00 E
Al-Ḥamād ≚	208	32.00 N	39.30 E
Alhama de Granada	168	37.00 N	3.59 W
Alhama de Murcia	168	37.51 N	1.25 W
Al-Hamal •[1]	208	23.30 N	49.45 E
Alhambra	274	34.06 N	118.08 W
Al-Ḥamrā' •[1]	208	22.40 N	55.05 E
Al-Ḥarīq	208	23.37 N	46.31 E
Al-Ḥarrah •[9]	208	31.00 N	38.30 E
Al-Harūj al-Aswad ⛰[2]	214	27.00 N	17.10 E
Al-Ḥasakah	212	36.29 N	40.45 E
Al-Ḥasakah □[8]	212	36.30 N	41.00 E
Al-Ḥassānī I	208	24.58 N	37.05 E
Alhaurín el Grande	168	36.38 N	4.41 W
Al-Ḥawrah	214	13.49 N	47.37 E
Al-ḍ8hayy	204	32.10 N	46.03 E
Al-Ḥijāz •[1]	208	24.30 N	38.30 E
Al-Ḥillah	208	32.29 N	44.25 E
Al-Ḥillah □[4]	208	32.40 N	44.35 E
Al-Hoceima	168	35.15 N	3.55 W
Al-Hoceima, Baie du C	168	35.20 N	3.50 W
Alhucemas, Islas de (Spain) II	168	35.13 N	3.53 W
Al-Ḥudaydah	204	14.48 N	42.57 E
Al-Ḥufrah •[1]	208	28.40 N	38.30 E
Al-Hufūf	208	25.22 N	49.34 E
Al-Ḥulwah	214	23.27 N	46.47 E
Al-Ḥuṣayḥiṣah	220	14.44 N	33.18 E
'Ālī, Sadd al- (Aswān High Dam) •[6]	220	23.58 N	32.52 E
Alía	168	39.27 N	5.13 W
Aliaga	168	40.40 N	0.42 W
Aliağaçiftliği	172	38.48 N	26.59 E
Aliákmon ≃	172	40.30 N	22.36 E
Aliaksin, Cape ➤	236	55.30 N	160.43 W
Ali-Bajramly	208	39.56 N	48.56 E
Alibej, Ozero ⊜	172	45.48 N	30.02 E
Alibey Adası I	212	39.20 N	26.38 E
Alibijaban Island I	202	13.20 N	122.43 E
Alibori ≃	222	11.56 N	3.17 E
Alibunar	172	45.05 N	20.58 E
Alicante	168	38.21 N	0.29 W
Alice	250	27.45 N	98.04 W
Alice, Punta ➤	170	39.24 N	17.10 E
Alice Arm	238	55.29 N	129.29 W
Alicedale	218	33.18 S	26.05 E
Alice Springs	226	23.42 S	133.53 E
Alice Town	282	25.44 N	79.17 W
Aliceville	248	33.08 N	88.09 W
Alicia, Pil.	202	7.30 N	122.56 E
Alicia, Pil.	202	16.45 N	121.42 E
Alicudi, Isola I	170	38.33 N	14.21 E
Alignements de Carnac ⊥	166	47.35 N	3.05 W
Alīgūdarz	208	33.24 N	49.41 E
Alijos, Escollos II[1]	278	24.57 N	115.44 W
Alikovo	160	55.45 N	46.45 E
Alima ≃	218	1.36 S	16.36 E
Alimodian	202	10.48 N	122.25 E
Alingsås	160	57.56 N	12.31 E
Alip Mountains ⛰	202	6.40 N	125.05 E
Aliquippa	266	40.37 N	80.15 W
Al-'Irq	214	29.02 N	21.33 E
Aliseda	168	39.26 N	6.41 W
Al-Iskandarīyah (Alexandria)	220	31.12 N	29.54 E
Al-Ismā'īlīyah	220	30.35 N	32.16 E
Al-Istiwā'īyah □[4]	220	5.00 N	31.00 E
Alistráti	172	41.04 N	23.57 E
Alitak, Cape ➤	236	56.51 N	154.21 W
Alitak Bay C	236	57.00 N	154.05 W
Alivérion	172	38.24 N	24.02 E
Aliwal North	224	30.45 S	26.45 E
Alix	238	52.24 N	113.11 W
Al-Jabal al-Akhḍar ⛰	208	23.15 N	57.20 E
Al-Jabal ash-Sharqī ⛰	210	33.35 N	36.00 E
Al-Jafr ≚	208	30.16 N	36.13 E
Al-Jāfūrah •[2]	208	24.14 N	50.00 E
Al-Jaghbūb	214	29.45 N	24.31 E
Al-Janūb □[4]	210	33.20 N	35.30 E
Al-Jawf, Ar. Sa.	208	29.50 N	39.52 E
Al-Jawf, Lībiya	220	24.11 N	23.19 E
Al-Jaylī	214	16.01 N	32.36 E
Al-Jazīrah •[1]	220	14.25 N	33.00 E
Aljezur	168	37.19 N	8.48 W
Al-Jīzah	220	30.01 N	31.13 E
al-Jīzah, Ahrāmāt ⊥	220	29.59 N	31.08 E
Al-Julaydah ▾[4]	208	29.03 N	45.38 E
Al-Junaynah	220	13.27 N	22.27 E
Aljustrel	168	37.52 N	8.10 W
Alkali Lake	238	51.47 N	122.14 W
Alkali Lake ⊜, Nev., U.S.	258	41.42 N	119.50 W
Alkali Lake ⊜, Oreg., U.S.	256	43.10 N	120.02 W
Al-Karak	210	31.11 N	35.42 E
Al-Karak □[8]	210	31.03 N	35.44 E
Al-Karnak	220	25.43 N	32.39 E
Al-Kāẓimīyah	208	33.22 N	44.20 E
Al-Khābūr ≃	208	35.08 N	40.26 E
Al-Khābūrah	204	23.59 N	57.08 E
Al-Khalīl (Hebron)	210	31.32 N	35.06 E
Al-Khalīl □[8]	210	31.30 N	35.05 E
Al-Khandaq	214	18.36 N	30.34 E
Al-Khārijah	220	25.26 N	30.33 E
Al-Khatam •[1]	208	24.16 N	55.10 E
Al-Khubar	214	26.17 N	50.12 E
Al-Khums	214	32.39 N	14.16 E
Al-Khunfah •[1]	208	28.10 N	39.30 E
Al-Khurṭūm (Khartoum)	220	15.36 N	32.32 E
Al-Khurṭūm □[4]	220	15.45 N	32.30 E
Al-Khurṭūm Baḥrī	220	15.38 N	32.33 E
Alkmaar	178	52.37 N	4.44 E
Al-Kufrah (Cufra) •[1]	220	24.20 N	23.15 E
Al-Kūt □[4]	208	32.45 N	45.25 E
Al-Kuwayt	208	29.20 N	47.59 E
Allacapan	202	18.15 N	121.34 E
Allach-Jun'	186	61.08 N	138.03 E
Al-Lādhiqīyah (Latakia)	212	35.31 N	35.47 E
Al-Lādhiqīyah □[8]	212	35.10 N	36.10 E
Allagash ≃	240	47.05 N	69.02 W
Allahābād	206	25.27 N	81.50 E
Allahüekber Dağları ⛰	212	40.35 N	42.32 E
Allakaket	236	66.34 N	152.41 W
Allanche	166	45.14 N	2.56 E
Allanmyo	200	19.22 N	95.13 E
'Allāq, Bi'r ▾[4]	214	31.05 N	11.42 E
'Allāqī, Wādī al- V	220	23.07 N	32.47 E
Allard, Lac ⊜, Qué., Can.	240	50.34 N	63.29 W
Allard, Lac ⊜, Qué., Can.	244	47.19 N	78.49 W
Allardt	248	36.23 N	84.53 W
Allariz	168	42.11 N	7.48 W
Allatoona Reservoir ⊜[1]	246	34.08 N	84.38 W
Allauch	182	43.20 N	5.29 E
Allegan	268	42.32 N	85.51 W
Allegan □[6]	268	42.35 N	85.53 W
Allegany	266	42.06 N	78.30 W
Allegany □[6]	266	42.13 N	78.02 W
Allegany State Park ♠	242	42.04 N	78.44 W
Alleghany	272	39.28 N	120.51 W
Allegheny □[6]	266	40.26 N	79.59 W
Allegheny ≃	242	40.27 N	80.00 W
Allegheny Mountains ⛰	242	38.30 N	80.00 W
Allegheny Plateau ⛰[1]	242	41.30 N	78.00 W
Allegheny Reservoir ⊜[1]	242	42.00 N	78.56 W
Allen, Arg.	294	38.58 S	67.50 W
Allen, Pil.	202	12.30 N	124.17 E
Allen, Md., U.S.	262	38.17 N	75.42 W
Allen, Mich., U.S.	268	41.57 N	84.46 W
Allen, Nebr., U.S.	252	42.25 N	96.51 W
Allen, Okla., U.S.	250	34.53 N	96.25 W
Allen, Pa., U.S.	262	40.10 N	77.05 W
Allen, S. Dak., U.S.	252	43.17 N	101.55 W
Allen, Tex., U.S.	250	33.06 N	96.40 W
Allen, Wash., U.S.	270	48.31 N	122.23 W
Allen □[6], Ind., U.S.	268	41.04 N	85.09 W
Allen □[6], Ohio, U.S.	268	40.46 N	84.06 W
Allen, Lough ⊜	162	54.08 N	8.08 W
Allen, Mount Λ, N.Z.	230	47.05 S	167.48 E
Allen, Mount Λ, Alaska, U.S.	236	62.14 N	142.13 W
Allenby Bridge •[5]	210	31.52 N	35.52 E
Allendale, Ill., U.S.	248	38.32 N	87.43 W
Allendale, Mich., U.S.	268	42.58 N	85.57 W
Allendale, S.C., U.S.	246	33.06 N	81.18 W
Allende	278	25.17 N	100.01 W
Allendorf	178	51.16 N	9.58 E
Allen Grove	268	42.35 N	88.41 W
Allen Park	268	42.15 N	83.13 W
Allenport, Pa., U.S.	266	40.20 N	77.53 W
Allenport, Pa., U.S.	266	40.06 N	79.51 W
Allenstein → Olsztyn	164	53.48 N	20.29 E
Allensville	266	40.32 N	77.49 W
Allenton, Mich., U.S.	266	42.55 N	82.57 W
Allenton, R.I., U.S.	261	41.32 N	71.29 W
Allentown, N.J., U.S.	262	40.11 N	74.35 W
Allentown, N.Y., U.S.	266	42.05 N	78.04 W
Allentown, Ohio, U.S.	268	40.46 N	84.12 W
Allentown, Pa., U.S.	262	40.36 N	75.29 W
Allentsteig	164	48.42 N	15.20 E
Allenwood	262	40.09 N	74.06 W
Aller ≃	164	52.57 N	9.11 E
Allerton	244	40.42 N	93.22 W
Allevard	166	45.24 N	6.04 E
Allgäuer Alpen ⛰	166	47.20 N	10.25 E
Alliance, Alta., Can.	238	52.26 N	111.47 W
Alliance, Nebr., U.S.	252	42.06 N	102.52 W
Alliance, Ohio, U.S.	266	40.55 N	81.06 W
Al-Lidām	214	20.29 N	44.50 E
Allier □[5]	166	46.25 N	3.00 E
Allier ≃	166	46.58 N	3.04 E
Alligator ≃	246	35.58 N	75.58 W
Alligator Pond	285q	17.52 N	77.34 W
Allinge	160	55.16 N	14.49 E
Allison	244	42.45 N	92.48 W
Allison Harbour	238	51.03 N	127.30 W
Allisonia	246	36.56 N	80.44 W
Allison Park	266	40.34 N	79.57 W
Alliston	264	44.09 N	79.52 W
Al-Līth	214	20.09 N	40.16 E
Alloa	162	56.07 N	3.49 W
Allos	166	44.14 N	6.38 W
Allouez	244	44.29 N	88.01 W
Alloway	262	39.34 N	75.22 W
Allport	266	40.58 N	78.12 W
All Saints	284c	17.03 N	61.48 W
Allschwil	180	47.33 N	7.33 E
Al-Luḥayyah	204	15.42 N	42.42 E
Allumette Lake ⊜	244	45.53 N	77.13 W
Allumettes, Île aux I	242	45.52 N	77.05 W
Allview Estates	262	39.12 N	76.51 W
Allyn	270	47.23 N	122.50 W
Alma, Qué., Can.	240	48.32 N	71.40 W
Alma, Ark., U.S.	248	35.29 N	94.13 W
Alma, Colo., U.S.	254	39.17 N	106.04 W
Alma, Ga., U.S.	246	31.33 N	82.28 W
Alma, Kans., U.S.	252	39.01 N	96.17 W
Alma, Mich., U.S.	244	43.23 N	84.39 W
Alma, Nebr., U.S.	252	40.06 N	99.22 W
Alma, N.Y., U.S.	266	42.01 N	78.03 W
Alma, Wis., U.S.	244	44.20 N	91.55 W

Symbols in the index entries are identified on page 360.

Name	Page	Lat°′	Long°′
Alma-Ata	186	43.15 N	76.57 E
Alma Center	244	44.26 N	90.55 W
Almada	168	38.41 N	9.09 W
Almadén	168	38.46 N	4.50 W
Almadén de la Plata	168	37.52 N	6.04 W
Al-Madīnah (Medina)	208	24.28 N	39.36 E
Al-Mafraq	210	32.21 N	36.12 E
Almafuerte	294	32.15 S	64.15 W
Al-Maghrah ⊜	220	30.15 N	28.56 E
Almagro	168	38.53 N	3.43 W
Almagro Island I	202	11.56 N	124.18 E
Al-Maḥallah al-Kubrā	220	30.58 N	31.10 E
Alma Hill ∧[2]	242	42.03 N	78.01 W
Almajului, Munţii ⛰	172	44.43 N	22.12 E
Almalyk	186	40.50 N	69.38 E
Al-Manāmah	208	26.13 N	50.35 E
Al-Manāṣif ◂[1]	212	35.13 N	40.54 E
Almanor, Lake ⊜	258	40.15 N	121.08 W
Almansa	168	38.52 N	1.05 W
Al-Manshāh	220	26.28 N	31.48 E
Al-Manṣūrah	220	31.03 N	31.23 E
Almanza	168	42.39 N	5.02 W
Al-Manzilah	220	31.09 N	31.56 E
Almanzor, Pico de ∧	168	40.15 N	5.18 W
Almanzora ≃	168	37.14 N	1.46 W
Al-Marāghah	220	26.42 N	31.36 E
Al-Marj	214	32.30 N	20.54 E
Almas, Pico das ∧	296	13.33 S	41.56 W
Al-Maṣīrah I	204	20.25 N	58.50 E
Al-Maṭarīyah	220	31.11 N	32.02 E
Al-Mawṣil (Mosul)	208	36.20 N	43.08 E
Al-Mawṣil □[4]	208	36.10 N	42.35 E
Almazán	168	41.29 N	2.32 W
Almazora	168	39.57 N	0.03 W
Almeida	168	40.43 N	6.54 W
Almeirim	168	39.12 N	8.38 W
Almejas, Bahía C	278	24.25 N	111.40 W
Almelo	178	52.21 N	6.39 E
Almena	252	39.54 N	99.43 W
Almenar	168	41.48 N	2.34 W
Almenara	296	16.11 S	40.42 W
Almenar de Soria	168	41.41 N	2.12 W
Almendralejo	168	38.41 N	6.24 W
Almería	168	36.50 N	2.27 W
Almería, Golfo de C	168	36.46 N	2.30 W
Al'metjevsk	160	54.53 N	52.20 E
Al'mež	160	60.03 N	48.03 E
Almina, Punta ≻	168	35.53 N	5.15 W
Al-Minṭaqah ash-Sharqīyah ◂[1]	208	28.00 N	48.00 E
Al-Minyā	220	28.06 N	30.45 E
Almira	256	47.43 N	118.56 W
Almirante	280	9.17 N	82.23 W
Almirante, Bahía de C	280	9.18 N	82.18 W
Almirante Latorre	294	29.38 S	70.58 W
Almirós	172	39.11 N	22.46 E
Almiroú, Kólpos C	172	35.23 N	24.20 E
Almo	256	42.06 N	113.38 W
Almodôvar	168	37.31 N	8.04 W
Almodóvar del Campo	168	38.43 N	4.10 W
Almolonga	280	14.49 N	91.30 W
Almond, N.Y., U.S.	266	42.19 N	77.44 W
Almond, Wis., U.S.	244	44.16 N	89.24 W
Almonesson	262	39.49 N	75.06 W
Almont	266	42.55 N	83.03 W
Almonte, Ont., Can.	264	45.14 N	76.12 W
Almonte, Esp.	168	37.15 N	6.31 W
Almonte ≃	168	39.42 N	6.28 W
Al-Mubarraz	208	25.55 N	49.36 E
Almudébar	168	42.03 N	0.35 W
Al-Muglad	220	11.02 N	27.44 E
Al-Muḥarraq	208	26.16 N	50.37 E
Al-Mukallā	204	14.32 N	49.08 E
Al-Mukhā	204	13.19 N	43.15 E
Almuñécar	168	36.43 N	3.41 W
Al-Muwaqqar ⊥	210	31.49 N	36.06 E
Al-Muwayliḥ	214	27.41 N	35.27 E
Alnwick	162	55.25 N	1.42 W
Aloândia	296	17.43 S	49.29 W
Aloha	270	45.29 N	122.52 W
Alónnisos	172	39.08 N	23.50 E
Alor, Pulau I	198	8.15 S	124.45 E
Álora	168	36.48 N	4.42 W
Alor Setar	200	6.07 N	100.22 E
Alosno	168	37.33 N	7.07 W
Alost → Aalst	176	50.56 N	4.02 E
Alpachiri	294	37.20 S	63.47 W
Alpaugh	272	35.53 N	119.29 W
Alpena, Ark., U.S.	248	36.17 N	93.18 W
Alpena, Mich., U.S.	244	45.04 N	83.26 W
Alpena, S. Dak., U.S.	252	44.11 N	98.22 W
Alpes Maritimes □[5]	166	44.00 N	7.10 E
Alpha, Austl.	226	23.39 S	146.38 E
Alpha, Ill., U.S.	244	41.12 N	90.23 W
Alpha, Mich., U.S.	244	46.02 N	88.22 W
Alpha, N.J., U.S.	262	40.40 N	75.09 W
Alpharetta	246	34.04 N	84.18 W
Alphen aan den Rijn	178	52.07 N	4.40 E
Alphonse Island I	218	7.00 S	52.45 E
Alpiarça	168	39.15 N	8.35 W
Alpignano	182	45.06 N	7.31 E
Alpilles ⛰[2]	166	43.45 N	4.50 E
Alpine, Ariz., U.S.	254	33.51 N	109.09 W
Alpine, Calif., U.S.	258	32.50 N	116.47 W
Alpine, Tex., U.S.	250	30.22 N	103.40 W
Alpine □[6]	272	38.41 N	119.47 W
Alpinópolis	296	20.52 S	46.23 W
Alportel	168	37.09 N	7.53 W
Alps ⛰	158	46.25 N	10.00 E
Al-Qaḍārif	220	14.02 N	35.24 E
Al-Qāhirah (Cairo)	220	30.03 N	31.15 E
Al-Qā'īyah ▾[4]	208	26.27 N	45.35 E
Al-Qāmishlī	212	37.02 N	41.14 E
Al-Qaryah ash-Sharqīyah	214	30.24 N	13.36 E
Al-Qaṣr	214	25.42 N	28.53 E
Al-Qaṭīf	208	26.33 N	50.00 E
Al-Qaṭrūn	214	24.56 N	14.38 E
Al-Qayṣūmah	214	28.16 N	46.03 E
Al-Quds □[8]	210	31.45 N	35.20 E
Alquízar	284p	22.48 N	82.35 W
Al-Qunayṭirah	210	33.07 N	35.49 E
Al-Qunayṭirah □[8]	210	33.00 N	35.50 E
Al-Qunfudhah	214	19.08 N	41.05 E
Al-Qurnah	208	31.00 N	47.26 E
Al-Quṣayr	214	26.06 N	34.19 E
Al-Qūṣīyah	220	27.26 N	30.49 E
Al-Quṭayfah	210	33.44 N	36.36 E
Alright, Île I	240	47.25 N	61.45 W
Alsace □[9]	180	48.30 N	7.30 E
Alsace ◂[1]	164	48.30 N	7.30 E
Alsager	174	53.06 N	2.17 W
Alsasua	168	42.54 N	2.10 W
Alsea	256	44.23 N	123.36 W
Alsea ≃	256	44.26 N	124.05 W
Alsek ≃	236	59.10 N	138.10 W
Alsen	252	48.38 N	98.42 W
Alsfeld	164	50.45 N	9.16 E
Alsina	294	33.54 S	59.20 W
Alsunga	160	56.59 N	21.34 E
Alta, Nor.	160	69.55 N	23.12 E
Alta, Calif., U.S.	272	39.12 N	120.49 W
Alta, Iowa, U.S.	252	42.40 N	95.18 W
Alta, Mount ∧	230	44.28 S	168.57 E
Altadena	274	34.12 N	118.08 W
Alta Gracia, Arg.	294	31.40 S	64.26 W
Alta Gracia, Nic.	280	11.34 N	85.35 W
Altagracia, Ven.	290	10.43 N	71.32 W
Altagracia de Orituco	290	9.52 N	66.23 W
Alta Hill	272	39.14 N	121.04 W
Al Tahoe	272	38.57 N	119.59 W
Altai ⛰	190	48.00 N	90.00 E
Altaj (Jesönbulag)	190	46.25 N	96.20 E
Alta Loma	274	34.07 N	117.36 W
Altamaha ≃	246	31.19 N	81.17 W
Altamira, Bra.	286	3.12 S	52.12 W
Altamira, Chile	294	25.47 S	69.51 W
Altamira, C.R.	280	10.30 N	84.23 W
Altamira, Las Cuevas de •[5]	168	43.18 N	4.08 W
Altamirano	250	25.55 N	97.47 W
Altamont, Ill., U.S.	248	39.04 N	88.46 W
Altamont, Kans., U.S.	252	37.12 N	95.18 W
Altamont, Oreg., U.S.	256	42.12 N	121.44 W
Altamont, Tenn., U.S.	248	35.26 N	85.43 W
Altamura	170	40.50 N	16.33 E
Altamura, Isla I	278	24.55 N	108.13 W
Altar	278	30.43 N	111.44 W
Altar, Desierto de ◂[2]	278	31.50 N	114.15 W
Altar Wash ∨	254	32.05 N	111.19 W
Altata	278	24.38 N	107.55 W
Alta Verapaz □[5]	280	15.40 N	90.00 W
Altavilla Irpina	184	41.00 N	14.47 E
Altaville	272	38.05 N	120.33 W
Alta Vista, Kans., U.S.	252	38.52 N	96.29 W
Altavista, Va., U.S.	246	37.06 N	79.17 W
Altdorf	180	46.53 N	8.39 E
Alteelva ≃	160	69.58 N	23.23 E
Altena	178	51.17 N	7.40 E
Altenberge	178	52.03 N	7.27 E
Altenburg	164	50.59 N	12.26 E
Altendorf	178	51.25 N	7.06 E
Altenesch	178	53.08 N	8.37 E
Altengamme ◂[8]	178	53.25 N	10.16 E
Altentreptow	164	53.42 N	13.14 E
Alter do Chão	168	39.12 N	7.40 W
Altha	246	30.34 N	85.08 W
Altheimer	248	34.19 N	91.51 W
Althofen	164	46.54 N	14.27 E
Altinópolis	296	21.02 S	47.23 W
Altiplano ⛰[1]	292	18.00 S	68.00 W
Altkirch	166	47.37 N	7.15 E
Altlünen	178	51.38 N	7.31 E
Altmar	264	43.31 N	76.00 W
Altmark □[9]	164	52.40 N	11.20 E
Altmühl ≃	164	48.55 N	11.52 E
Alto, Mich., U.S.	268	42.51 N	85.23 W
Alto, Tex., U.S.	250	31.39 N	95.04 W
Alto, Cerro ∧	292	6.38 S	78.15 W
Alto Alentejo □[9]	168	38.50 N	7.40 W
Alto Araguaia	296	17.19 S	53.12 W
Alto Cedro	284p	20.31 N	75.58 W
Alto Coité	296	15.47 S	54.20 W
Alto del Carmen	294	28.46 S	70.30 W
Alto Garças	296	16.56 S	53.32 W
Altomünster	164	48.28 N	11.58 E
Alton, Ont., Can.	264	43.52 N	80.04 W
Alton, Eng., U.K.	174	51.09 N	0.59 W
Alton, Ill., U.S.	248	38.54 N	90.10 W
Alton, Iowa, U.S.	252	42.59 N	96.01 W
Alton, Kans., U.S.	252	39.28 N	98.57 W
Alton, Mo., U.S.	248	36.42 N	91.24 W
Alton, N.H., U.S.	242	43.27 N	71.13 W
Alton, N.Y., U.S.	264	43.13 N	76.59 W
Alton, R.I., U.S.	261	41.26 N	71.43 W
Altona	252	49.06 N	97.33 W
Altona ◂[8]	178	53.32 N	9.56 E
Altoona, Ala., U.S.	248	34.02 N	86.20 W
Altoona, Iowa, U.S.	244	41.39 N	93.28 W
Altoona, Kans., U.S.	252	37.32 N	95.40 W
Altoona, Pa., U.S.	266	40.30 N	78.24 W
Altoona, Wash., U.S.	270	46.16 N	123.39 W
Altoona, Wis., U.S.	244	44.48 N	91.26 W
Alto Paraguai	292	14.30 S	56.31 W
Alto Paraná □[5]	294	25.00 S	54.50 W
Alto Parnaíba	286	9.06 S	45.57 W
Alto Purus ≃	292	9.57 S	70.58 W
Alto Rio Doce	296	21.02 S	43.25 W
Alto Río Senguerr	288	45.02 S	70.50 W
Alto Sucuriu	296	19.19 S	52.47 W
Altötting	164	48.13 N	12.40 E
Altstätten	180	47.23 N	9.33 E
Altunoluk	172	39.34 N	26.44 E
Altunova	172	39.13 N	26.47 E
Alturas	258	41.29 N	120.32 W
Altus, Ark., U.S.	248	35.27 N	93.46 W
Altus, Okla., U.S.	250	34.38 N	99.20 W
Altus Air Force Base ▪	250	34.40 N	99.16 W
Altus Reservoir ⊜[1]	250	34.56 N	99.18 W
Al-'Ubaylah	214	21.59 N	50.57 E
Al-Ubayyiḍ	220	13.11 N	30.13 E
Alubijid	202	8.35 N	124.29 E
Al-Uḍayyah	214	12.03 N	28.17 E
Alūksne	160	57.25 N	27.03 E
'Alula	214	11.58 N	50.48 E
Alum Bank	266	40.14 N	78.34 W
Aluminé, Lago ⊜	294	38.55 S	71.08 W
Alum Rock	272	37.23 N	121.50 W
Alunda	160	60.04 N	18.05 E
Al-'Uqaylah	214	30.16 N	19.12 E
Al-Uqṣur (Luxor)	220	25.41 N	32.39 E
Al-'Urayq •[8]	208	29.10 N	39.15 E
Al-'Urayq ◂[1]	208	24.47 N	42.55 E
Al-'Uṭayshān ▾[4]	220	16.25 N	34.30 E
Al-'Uwaynidhīyah I	208	26.37 N	36.05 E
Alva, Ky., U.S.	246	36.44 N	83.25 W
Alva, Okla., U.S.	250	36.48 N	98.40 W
Alva ≃	168	40.18 N	8.15 W
Alvada	266	41.03 N	83.24 W
Alvaiázere	168	39.49 N	8.23 W
Alvarado, Méx.	278	18.46 N	95.46 W
Alvarado, Tex., U.S.	250	32.24 N	97.13 W
Alvarães	290	3.12 S	64.50 W
Álvaro Obregón, Presa ⊜[1]	278	27.55 N	109.52 W
Alvaton	246	33.10 N	84.35 W
Älvdalen	160	61.14 N	14.02 E
Alvear	294	29.06 S	56.30 W
Alverca	168	38.54 N	9.02 W
Alverda	266	40.38 N	78.52 W
Alverton	266	40.08 N	79.35 W
Alvesta	160	56.54 N	14.33 E
Alvin, Ill., U.S.	268	40.19 N	87.37 W
Alvin, Tex., U.S.	250	29.25 N	95.15 W
Alvinópolis	296	20.06 S	43.03 W
Alvinston	266	42.49 N	81.52 W
Alviso	272	37.26 N	121.58 W
Alvito	168	38.15 N	7.59 W
Älvkarleby	160	60.34 N	17.27 E
Alvord	250	33.22 N	97.42 W
Alvord Lake ⊜	256	42.23 N	118.36 W
Alvordton	268	41.40 N	84.26 W
Älvsborgs Län □[6]	160	58.00 N	12.30 E
Älvsbyn	160	65.39 N	20.59 E
Al-Wāḥāt ad-Dākhilah ▾[4]	220	25.30 N	29.05 E
Al-Wāḥāt al-Baḥrīyah ▾[4]	220	28.15 N	28.57 E
Al-Wāḥat al-Farāfirah ▾[4]	220	27.15 N	28.10 E
Al-Wāḥāt al-Khārijah ▾[4]	220	25.20 N	30.35 E
Al-Wajh	208	26.15 N	36.26 E
Alwar	206	27.46 N	76.37 E
Al-Wāsiṭah	220	29.20 N	31.12 E
Al-Widyān ⛰[1]	208	31.15 N	41.00 E
Alytus	164	54.24 N	24.03 E
Alzamaj	186	55.33 N	98.39 E
Alzano Lombardo	182	45.44 N	9.43 E
Alzey	164	49.45 N	8.07 E
Amab, Khawr ∨	220	17.08 N	34.51 E
Amacuro ≃	290	8.32 N	60.28 W
Amadi	214	5.31 N	30.20 E
Amadjuak Lake ⊜	232	65.00 N	71.00 W
Amador □[6]	272	38.21 N	120.46 W
Amador City	272	38.25 N	120.56 W
Amagansett	261	40.58 N	72.08 W
Amagasaki	192	34.43 N	135.25 E
Amagi	192	33.25 N	130.39 E
Amagunze	222	6.20 N	7.40 E
Amaichá del Valle	294	26.33 S	65.55 W
Amajac ≃	278	21.15 N	98.46 W
Amak Island I	236	55.25 N	163.07 W
Amakusa-nada ▾[2]	192	32.35 N	130.05 E
Amakusa-shimo-jima I	192	32.20 N	130.05 E
Amakusa-shotō II	192	32.20 N	130.15 E
Åmål	160	59.03 N	12.42 E
Amalfi, Col.	290	6.55 N	75.04 W
Amalfi, It.	184	40.38 N	14.36 E
Amaliás	172	37.49 N	21.23 E
Amalner	206	21.03 N	75.03 E
Amambahag Point ≻	202	11.40 N	124.30 E
Amambaí	296	23.05 S	55.13 W
Amambay □[5]	294	23.00 S	56.00 W
Amambay, Cordillera de ⛰	294	23.10 S	55.30 W
Amami-Ō-shima I	193b	28.15 N	129.20 E
Amami-shotō II	193b	28.16 N	129.21 E
Amana	244	41.48 N	91.52 W
Amana ≃, Ven.	282	9.45 N	62.39 W
Amanã, Lago ⊜	290	2.35 S	64.40 W
Amanavení, Brazo ≃[1]	290	3.43 N	68.58 W
Amanda	242	39.39 N	82.45 W
Amantea	170	39.08 N	16.05 E
Amapá	286	2.03 N	50.48 W
Amapala	280	13.17 N	87.40 W
Amapala, Punta ≻	280	13.10 N	87.55 W
Amarante	286	6.14 S	42.50 W
Amarapura	200	21.54 N	96.03 E
Amărăstii-de-Jos	172	43.59 N	24.04 E
Amareleja	168	38.12 N	7.14 W
Amares	168	41.38 N	8.21 W
Amarete (Charazani)	292	15.14 S	68.58 W
Amargosa, Bra.	296	13.02 S	39.36 W
Amargosa, Calif., U.S.	258	36.18 N	116.25 W
Amargosa ≃	258	36.13 N	116.48 W
Amargosa Range ⛰	258	36.30 N	116.45 W
Amarillo	250	35.13 N	101.49 W
Amaro Leite	296	13.58 S	49.09 W
Amarume	192	38.50 N	139.55 E
Amasa	244	46.14 N	88.27 W
Amasya	212	40.39 N	35.51 E
Amataurá	290	3.29 S	68.06 W
Amatenango de la Frontera	280	15.26 N	92.07 W
Amatignak Island I	237a	51.15 N	179.08 W
Amatique, Bahía de C	280	15.55 N	88.45 W
Amatitlán	280	14.29 N	90.37 W
Amatitlán, Lago de ⊜	280	14.28 N	90.33 W
Amatrice	170	42.38 N	13.17 E
Amatsu-kominato	192	35.07 N	140.10 E
Amawalk	261	41.17 N	73.46 W
Amazon (Solimões) (Amazonas) ≃	286	0.05 S	50.00 W
Amazonas □[3], Bra.	290	4.00 S	64.00 W
Amazonas □[3], Bra.	292	5.00 S	63.00 W
Amazonas □[5], Col.	290	1.00 S	72.00 W
Amazonas □[5], Perú	292	5.00 S	78.00 W
Amazonas □[8]	290	3.30 N	66.00 W
Ambalavao	218	21.50 S	46.56 E
Ambalema	290	4.47 N	74.46 W
Ambanja	218	13.41 S	48.27 E
Ambar	292	10.40 S	77.16 W
Ambarčik	186	69.39 N	162.20 E
Ambarnyj	160	65.56 N	33.43 E
Ambaro, Baie d' C	225b	13.23 S	48.38 E
Ambato	290	1.15 S	78.37 W
Ambatolampy	225b	19.23 S	47.25 E
Ambatondrazaka	225b	17.50 S	48.25 E
Ambelau, Pulau I	198	3.51 S	127.12 E
Ámbelos, Ákra ≻	172	39.56 N	23.55 E
Amberg, B.R.D.	164	49.27 N	11.52 E
Amberg, Wis., U.S.	244	45.30 N	88.00 W
Ambérieu-en-Bugey	180	45.57 N	5.21 E
Amberson	266	40.10 N	77.41 W
Ambert	182	45.33 N	3.45 E
Ambia	268	40.30 N	87.31 W
Ambil	202	13.49 N	120.19 E
Ambil Island I	202	13.48 N	120.18 E
Ambilobe	218	13.12 S	49.04 E
Amble	162	55.20 N	1.34 E
Ambler, Alaska, U.S.	236	67.05 N	157.52 W
Ambler, Pa., U.S.	262	40.09 N	75.13 W
Ambo	292	10.08 S	76.10 W
Ambodifototra	218	16.59 S	49.52 E
Amboise	176	47.25 N	0.59 E
Ambon	198	3.43 S	128.12 E
Ambon, Pulau I	198	3.40 S	128.10 E
Ambositra	225b	20.31 S	47.15 E
Ambovombe	218	25.11 S	46.05 E
Amboy, Ill., U.S.	244	41.44 N	89.20 W
Amboy, Ind., U.S.	268	40.36 N	85.56 W
Amboy, Minn., U.S.	244	43.59 N	94.10 W
Amboy, Wash., U.S.	270	45.55 N	122.27 W
Ambre, Cap d' ≻	225b	11.57 S	49.17 E
Ambre, Montagne d' ∧	225b	12.30 S	49.10 E
Ambridge	266	40.36 N	80.14 W
Ambridge Heights	266	40.36 N	80.13 W
Ambrières	166	48.24 N	0.38 W
Ambriz	218	7.50 S	13.06 E
Ambrizete	218	7.14 S	12.52 E
Ambrose	252	48.57 N	103.29 W
Ambrosia Lake	254	35.26 N	107.54 W
Ambuklao Dam ◂[6]	202	16.28 N	120.45 E
Ambulong Island I	202	12.13 N	121.01 E
Ambunti	198	4.14 S	142.50 E
Amburayan Nabunge ≃	202	16.55 N	120.25 E
Amchitka Island I	237a	51.30 N	179.00 E
Amchitka Pass ⊔	237a	51.30 N	179.30 W
Amderma	186	69.45 N	61.39 E
Ameagle	242	37.57 N	81.25 W
Ameca	278	20.33 N	104.02 W
Amecameca [de Juárez]	278	19.07 N	98.46 W
Ameghino	294	34.50 S	62.30 W
Ameland I	164	53.25 N	5.45 E
Amelia	184	42.33 N	12.25 E
Amelia Court House	246	37.21 N	77.59 W
Amelia Island I	246	30.37 N	81.27 W
Amenia	261	41.51 N	73.33 W
Americana	296	22.45 S	47.20 W
American Falls	256	42.47 N	112.51 W
American Falls Reservoir ⊜[1]	256	43.00 N	113.00 W
American Fork	254	40.23 N	111.48 W
American Highland ⛰[1]	148	72.30 S	78.00 E
American Samoa □[2]	148	14.20 S	170.00 W
Americus, Ga., U.S.	246	32.04 N	84.14 W
Americus, Kans., U.S.	252	38.30 N	96.16 W
Amerique, Sierra de ⛰	280	12.15 N	85.18 W
Amern	178	51.14 N	6.15 E
Amersfoort	178	52.09 N	5.24 E
Amersham	174	51.40 N	0.38 W
Amery	244	45.19 N	92.22 W
Amery Ice Shelf ◹	148	69.30 S	72.00 E
Ames	244	42.02 N	93.37 W
Amesbury, Eng., U.K.	174	51.10 N	1.45 W
Amesbury, Mass., U.S.	261	42.51 N	70.56 W
Amet Sound ⊔	240	45.47 N	63.13 W
Amfíkleia	172	38.38 N	22.35 E
Amfilokhía	172	38.51 N	21.10 E
Ámfissa	172	38.31 N	22.24 E
Amga	186	60.53 N	132.00 E
Amga ≃	186	62.38 N	134.32 E
Amguema	236	66.58 N	179.16 W
Amguema ≃	236	68.10 N	177.40 W
Amgun' ≃	186	52.56 N	139.40 E
Amherst, N.S., Can.	240	45.49 N	64.14 W
Amherst, Mass., U.S.	261	42.23 N	72.31 W
Amherst, N.H., U.S.	261	42.52 N	71.38 W
Amherst, N.Y., U.S.	264	42.58 N	78.48 W
Amherst, Ohio, U.S.	266	41.24 N	82.14 W
Amherst, Tex., U.S.	250	34.01 N	102.25 W
Amherst, Va., U.S.	246	37.35 N	79.03 W
Amherst, Wis., U.S.	244	44.27 N	89.17 W
Amherst, Île I	240	47.15 N	62.57 W
Amherstburg	266	42.06 N	83.06 W
Amherstdale	242	37.47 N	81.49 W
Amherst Island I	244	44.08 N	76.45 W
Amherstview	264	44.13 N	76.38 W
Amidon	252	46.29 N	103.19 W
Amiens	176	49.54 N	2.18 E
Amik Gölü ⊜	212	36.22 N	36.17 E
Aminga	294	28.50 S	66.56 W
Amino	192	35.41 N	135.02 E
Amirante Islands II	218	6.00 S	53.10 E
Amisk	238	52.33 N	111.04 W
Amistad Dam ◂[6]	250	29.25 N	101.06 W
Amistad National Recreation Area ♠	250	29.32 N	101.12 W
Amistad Reservoir ⊜[1]	250	29.34 N	101.15 W
Amite	248	30.44 N	90.30 W
Amite ≃	248	30.12 N	90.35 W
Amity, Ark., U.S.	248	34.16 N	93.28 W
Amity, Ohio, U.S.	266	40.03 N	83.17 W
Amity, Oreg., U.S.	270	45.07 N	123.12 W
Åmli	160	58.47 N	8.30 E
Amlia Island I	236	52.06 N	173.30 W
Amlwch	162	53.25 N	4.20 W
'Ammān	210	31.57 N	35.56 E
Amman Airport ⊠	210	35.57 N	35.58 E
Ammanford	174	51.45 N	0.35 W
Ämmänsaari	160	64.53 N	28.55 E
Ammarnäs	160	65.56 N	16.09 E
Ammeloe	178	52.05 N	6.47 E
Ammerman Mountain ∧	236	68.21 N	141.03 W
Ammókhostos (Famagusta)	212	35.07 N	33.57 E
Ammókhostou, Kólpos C	212	35.10 N	34.00 E
Ammon	256	43.30 N	111.57 W
Ammonoosuc ≃	242	44.10 N	72.02 W
Amnok-kang (Yalujiang) ≃	194	39.55 N	124.22 E
Amo ≃	206	27.02 N	89.14 E
Amohe ≃	200	22.58 N	101.44 E
Āmol	208	36.23 N	52.20 E
Amolar	292	18.01 S	57.30 W
Amorgós	172	36.50 N	25.54 E
Amorgós I	172	36.50 N	25.59 E
Amorinópolis	296	16.36 S	51.08 W
Amory	248	33.59 N	88.29 W
Amos	244	48.34 N	78.07 W
Åmot	160	59.35 N	8.00 E
Amoy → Xiamen	196	24.28 N	118.07 E
Ampanihy	218	24.42 S	44.45 E
Ampaoid, Mount ∧	202	7.55 N	125.40 E
Amparo	296	22.42 S	46.45 W
Ampasilava, Baie d' C	225b	21.16 S	43.43 E
Ampasindava, Baie d' C	225b	13.16 S	48.43 E
Ampezzo	170	46.25 N	12.48 E
Amphitrite Group II	198	17.00 N	112.25 E
Amposta	168	40.43 N	0.35 E
Amqui	240	48.28 N	67.26 W
Amrāvati	206	20.56 N	77.47 E
Amriswil	180	47.33 N	9.18 E
Amritsar	206	31.38 N	74.53 E
Amroha	206	28.54 N	78.38 E
Amrum I	164	54.39 N	8.21 E
Amsden	266	41.13 N	83.20 W
Amstelveen	178	52.18 N	4.51 E
Amsterdam, Ned.	178	52.22 N	4.54 E
Amsterdam, Ga., U.S.	246	30.43 N	84.26 W
Amsterdam, N.Y., U.S.	242	42.57 N	74.11 W
Amsterdam, Ohio, U.S.	266	40.28 N	80.55 W
Amsterdam, Île I	148	37.52 S	77.32 E
Amsterdam-Naturaliste Ridge ✧[3]	148	30.00 S	90.00 E
Amstetten	164	48.07 N	14.53 E
Amston	261	41.38 N	72.21 W
Am Timan	214	11.02 N	20.17 E
Amubri	280	9.31 N	82.56 W
Amu Darya (Amudarja) ≃	186	43.40 N	59.01 E
Amukta Island I	236	52.29 N	171.15 W
Amukta Pass ⊔	236	52.25 N	172.00 W
Amundsen Gulf C	232	71.00 N	124.00 W
Amundsen Sea ▾[2]	148	72.30 S	112.00 W
Amungen ⊜	160	61.09 N	15.39 E
Amuntai	198	2.26 S	115.15 E
Amur (Heilongjiang) ≃	186	52.56 N	141.10 E
'Amūr, Wādī ∨	220	18.56 N	33.34 E
Amurrio	168	43.04 N	3.00 W
Amutag	202	12.23 N	123.16 E
Amvrakikós Kólpos C	172	39.00 N	21.00 E
Amwom, Khawr ∨	220	7.50 N	31.13 E
Anabar ≃	186	73.08 N	113.36 E
'Anabtā	210	32.18 N	35.07 E
Anaco	290	9.27 N	64.28 W
Anacoco	248	31.15 N	93.20 W
Anacoco, Bayou ≃	248	30.52 N	93.34 W
Anaconda	256	46.08 N	112.57 W
Anaconda Range ⛰	256	45.55 N	113.30 W
Anacortes	270	48.30 N	122.37 W
Anacuao, Mount ∧	202	16.15 N	121.53 E
Anadarko	250	35.04 N	98.15 W
Anadyr'	236	64.45 N	177.29 E
Anadyr' ≃	186	64.55 N	176.05 E
Anadyrskaja Nizmennost' ≚	236	65.30 N	176.00 E
Anadyrskij Liman C	236	64.30 N	177.45 E
Anadyrskij Zaliv C	236	64.00 N	179.00 W
Anadyrskoje Ploskogorje ⛰[1]	236	67.00 N	174.00 E
Anáfi I	172	36.21 N	25.50 E
Anagekumuhu ⊜	206	37.33 N	89.15 E
Anagni	184	41.44 N	13.09 E
'Ānah	208	34.28 N	41.56 E
Anaheim	274	33.51 N	117.57 W
Anahim Lake	238	52.28 N	125.18 W
Anahola	275b	22.09 N	159.19 W
Anáhuac, Méx.	250	25.48 N	97.45 W
Anahuac, Tex., U.S.	250	29.46 N	94.41 W
Anaktuvuk ≃	236	69.32 N	151.30 W
Anaktuvuk Pass	236	68.10 N	151.50 W
Analalava	218	14.38 S	47.45 E
Analamaitso, Plateau d' ⛰[1]	225b	16.15 S	48.15 E
Anamã	290	3.35 S	61.22 W
Anamã, Lago ⊜	290	3.32 S	61.35 W
Ana María, Cayos II	284p	21.29 N	78.46 W
Ana María, Golfo de C	284p	21.20 N	78.45 W
Anamas Dağı ∧	212	37.47 N	31.13 E
Anambas, Kepulauan II	200	3.00 N	106.00 E
Anamizu	192	37.14 N	136.54 E
Anamoose	252	47.53 N	100.15 W
Anamosa	244	42.07 N	91.17 W
Anamur	158	36.06 N	32.50 E
Anamur Burnu ≻	212	36.03 N	32.48 E
Anan	192	33.55 N	134.39 E
Ānand	206	22.34 N	72.57 E
Anao-aon	202	9.47 N	125.25 E
Anápolis	296	16.20 S	48.58 W
Añasco	284m	18.17 N	67.08 W
Anastácio	296	21.31 S	54.08 W
Anastasia Island I	246	29.48 N	81.16 W
Anatahan I	198	16.22 N	145.40 E
Añatuya	294	28.30 S	62.50 W
Anaurilândia	296	22.03 S	52.45 W
Anavelona ∧	225b	22.37 S	44.10 E
Anavilhanas, Arquipélago das II	290	2.42 S	60.45 W
Anawalt	246	37.15 N	81.26 W
'Anayzah, Jabal ⛰	208	32.12 N	39.18 E
Anbanjing	190	23.57 N	100.55 E
Ancash □[5]	292	9.30 S	77.45 W
Ancaster	264	43.12 N	80.00 W
Ancasti	294	28.49 S	65.30 W
Ancasti, Sierra de ⛰	294	29.00 S	65.40 W
Ancenis	166	47.22 N	1.11 W
Anchor	268	40.34 N	88.32 W
Anchorage	236	61.13 N	149.53 W
Anchor Bay Gardens	266	42.39 N	82.46 W
Anchorena	294	35.41 S	65.27 W
Anchor Point	236	59.46 N	151.52 W
Anchor Point ≻	236	59.47 N	151.52 W
Anchorville	266	42.42 N	82.41 W
Anchuras	168	39.29 N	4.50 W
Ancienne-Lorette	260	46.48 N	71.23 W
Anclitas, Cayo I	284p	20.48 N	78.54 W
Ancón	292	11.47 S	77.11 W
Ancona	184	43.38 N	13.30 E
Ancona □[4]	184	43.33 N	13.10 E
Ancón de Sardinas, Bahía de C	290	1.30 N	79.00 W
Ancoraimes	292	15.54 S	68.58 W
Ancram	261	42.03 N	73.38 W
Ancud	288	41.52 S	73.50 W
Ancud, Golfo de C	288	42.00 S	73.00 W
Ancy-le-Franc	166	47.46 N	4.10 E
Anda, Pil.	202	16.17 N	119.57 E
Anda, Zhg.	190	46.24 N	125.19 E
Andacollo, Arg.	294	37.10 S	70.40 W
Andacollo, Chile	294	30.14 S	71.06 W
Andahuaylas	292	13.40 S	73.25 W
Andalgalá	294	27.36 S	66.20 W
Andalucía □[9]	168	37.36 N	4.30 W
Andalusia	248	31.19 N	86.29 W
Andaman Basin ✧[1]	148	10.00 N	95.00 E
Andaman Islands II	200	12.00 N	93.00 E
Andaman Sea ▾[2]	200	10.00 N	95.00 E
Andamarca, Bol.	292	18.49 S	67.31 W
Andamarca, Perú	292	11.45 S	74.50 W
Andao I	196	22.37 N	114.57 E
Andapa	218	14.39 S	49.39 E
Andaraí	296	12.48 S	41.20 W
Andarax ≃	168	36.48 N	2.26 W
Andaray	292	15.52 S	72.48 W
Andelot	166	48.15 N	5.18 E
Andenes	160	69.16 N	16.08 E
Andenne	164	50.29 N	5.06 E
Anderlecht	176	50.50 N	4.18 E
Anderlues	176	50.24 N	4.16 E
Andermatt	166	46.38 N	8.36 E
Andernach	166	50.26 N	7.24 E
Anderson, Ala., U.S.	248	34.50 N	87.16 W
Anderson, Alaska, U.S.	236	64.21 N	149.10 W
Anderson, Calif., U.S.	258	40.27 N	122.18 W
Anderson, Ind., U.S.	248	40.10 N	85.41 W
Anderson, Mo., U.S.	248	36.39 N	94.27 W
Anderson, S.C., U.S.	246	34.31 N	82.39 W
Anderson, Tex., U.S.	250	30.29 N	95.59 W
Anderson ≃	236	69.43 N	128.58 W
Anderson Dam	256	43.30 N	115.30 W
Anderson Lake ⊜	238	50.41 N	122.07 W
Anderson Ranch Reservoir ⊜[1]	256	43.25 N	115.20 W
Andes	290	5.40 N	75.53 W
Andes ⛰	148	30.00 S	70.00 W
Andes, Lake ⊜	252	43.11 N	98.27 W
Andfjorden ⊔	160	69.10 N	16.20 E
Andikíthira I	172	35.52 N	23.18 E
Andīmeshk	208	32.27 N	48.21 E
Andižan	186	40.45 N	72.22 E
Andkhūi	206	36.56 N	65.05 E
Andoas	290	2.55 S	76.25 W
Andomskij Pogost	160	61.14 N	36.36 E
Andong, Taehan	194	36.35 N	128.44 E
Andong (Antung), Zhg.	194	40.08 N	124.20 E
Andorra	168	42.30 N	1.31 E
Andorra □[1]	158	42.30 N	1.30 E
Andover, Eng., U.K.	174	51.13 N	1.28 W
Andover, Conn., U.S.	261	41.44 N	72.23 W
Andover, Maine, U.S.	242	44.38 N	70.45 W
Andover, Mass., U.S.	261	42.39 N	71.08 W
Andover, N.Y., U.S.	266	42.09 N	77.48 W
Andover, Ohio, U.S.	266	41.36 N	80.34 W
Andover, S. Dak., U.S.	252	45.25 N	97.54 W
Andøya I	160	69.08 N	15.54 E
Andradina	296	20.54 S	51.23 W
Andramaimba, Baie C	225b	12.15 S	48.50 E
Andreafsky ≃	236	52.02 N	163.16 W
Andreanof Islands II	236	52.00 N	176.00 W
Andreapol'	160	56.39 N	32.15 E
Andreas	262	40.45 N	75.48 W
Andrew	238	53.53 N	112.21 W
Andrew Gordon Bay C	232	64.23 N	75.30 W
Andrews, Ind., U.S.	268	40.52 N	85.36 W
Andrews, Mich., U.S.	268	41.57 N	86.22 W
Andrews, N.C., U.S.	246	35.12 N	83.49 W
Andrews, S.C., U.S.	246	33.27 N	79.34 W
Andrews, Tex., U.S.	250	32.19 N	102.33 W
Andrews Air Force Base ▪	262	38.48 N	76.52 W
Andria	170	41.13 N	16.18 E
Andriamena	218	17.26 S	47.30 E
Andrijevica	172	42.44 N	19.46 E
Androka	218	25.02 S	44.05 E
Andronovskoje	160	60.39 N	34.46 E
Ándros	172	37.50 N	24.57 E
Ándros I	172	37.45 N	24.42 E
Androscoggin ≃	242	43.55 N	69.55 W
Andros Island I	282	24.25 N	78.00 W
Andros Town	282	24.43 N	77.47 W
Andrychów	164	49.52 N	19.21 E
Anducha'nakechi ⊜	206	32.00 N	91.15 E
Andújar	168	38.03 N	4.04 W
Anduo	190	32.18 N	91.04 E
Anduze	166	44.03 N	3.59 E
Anécho	222	6.14 N	1.36 E
Anegada I	282	18.45 N	64.22 W
Anegada Passage ⊔	282	18.15 N	63.45 W
Anegam	254	32.23 N	112.02 W
Añelo	294	38.20 S	68.45 W
Anepahan Peak ∧	202	9.37 N	118.26 E
Aneta	252	47.41 N	97.59 W
Aneto, Pico de ∧	168	42.38 N	0.40 E
Añez	292	17.19 S	63.43 W
Anfengying	200	24.59 N	102.18 E
Angamos, Punta ≻	294	23.01 S	70.32 W
Ang'angxi	190	47.09 N	123.48 E
Angara ≃	186	58.06 N	93.00 E
Angarsk	186	52.34 N	103.54 E
Angastaco	294	25.38 S	66.11 W
Angat	202	14.55 N	121.01 E
Angathonísi I	212	37.28 N	27.00 E
Angatuba	296	23.29 S	48.25 W
Angaur I	198	6.54 N	134.09 E
Ånge	158	62.31 N	15.37 E
Ángel, Cerro ∧	278	22.49 N	102.34 W
Ángel, Salto(Angel Falls) ⌊	290	5.57 N	62.30 W
Angel Albino Corzo	280	15.55 N	92.43 W
Ángel de la Guarda, Isla I	278	29.20 N	113.25 W
Angeles	202	15.09 N	120.35 E
Angeles, Sierra de los ⛰	278	23.30 N	99.33 W
Angel Falls → Ángel, Salto ⌊	290	5.57 N	62.30 W
Ängelholm	160	56.15 N	12.51 E
Angelica	266	42.18 N	78.01 W
Angeln ◂[1]	164	54.43 N	9.50 E
Angels Camp	272	38.04 N	120.32 W
Ångermanälven ≃	160	62.48 N	17.56 E
Angermünde	164	53.01 N	14.00 E
Angers	166	47.28 N	0.33 W
Angerville	166	48.19 N	2.00 E
Angical	296	12.00 S	44.42 W
Angicos	286	5.40 S	36.36 W
Angier	246	35.31 N	78.44 W
Angijak Island I	232	65.40 N	62.15 W
Angikuni Lake ⊜	232	62.13 N	99.50 W
Angkor, Ruines d' ⊥	200	13.25 N	103.52 E
Anglais, Baie des C	240	49.15 N	68.07 W
Anglalinghu ⊜	206	31.40 N	83.00 E
Angle Inlet	252	49.21 N	95.04 W
Anglem, Mount ∧	230	46.44 S	167.55 E
Anglesey □[6]	174	53.18 N	4.20 W
Angleton	250	29.10 N	95.26 W
Anglona ◂[1]	170	40.50 N	8.45 E
Angmagssalik	232	65.36 N	37.41 W
Angol	294	37.48 S	72.43 W
Angola, Ind., U.S.	268	41.38 N	85.00 W
Angola, N.Y., U.S.	266	42.38	79.02 W
Angola □[2]	218	12.30 S	18.30 E
Angola Lake Shore	266	42.37 N	79.05 W
Angoon	236	57.30 N	134.35 W
Angora → Ankara	212	39.56 N	32.52 E
Angoram	198	4.04 S	144.04 E
Angostura	278	25.22 N	108.11 W
Angostura Reservoir ⊜[1]	252	43.18 N	103.27 W
Angoulême	166	45.39 N	0.09 E
Angoumois □[9]	166	45.30 N	0.05 W
Angra dos Reis	296	23.00 S	44.18 W
Angren	186	41.01 N	70.12 E
Angri	184	40.44 N	14.34 E
Angualasto	294	30.05 S	69.12 W
Anguilla	248	32.58 N	90.50 W
Anguilla I	282	18.15 N	63.05 W
Anguilla Cays II	282	23.35 N	79.32 W
Anguille, Cape ≻	240	47.55 N	59.25 W
Angus	264	44.19 N	79.53 W
Angus □[6]	162	56.45 N	2.55 W
Angwin	272	38.34 N	122.26 W
Anhanguera	296	18.19 S	48.14 W
Anholt I	160	56.42 N	11.34 E
Anhui □[4]	196	32.00 N	117.00 E
Aniak	236	61.35 N	159.33 W
Aniak ≃	236	61.34 N	159.30 W
Aniche	176	50.20 N	3.15 E
Anicuns	296	16.28 S	49.58 W
Anié ≃	222	7.40 N	1.18 E
Anie, Pic d' ∧	166	42.57 N	0.43 W
Animas	254	31.57 N	108.48 W
Animas ≃	254	36.43 N	108.13 W
Ánimas, Cerro de las ∧	294	34.46 S	55.19 W
Animas Peak ∧	254	31.35 N	108.47 W
Animas Valley ∨	254	32.05 N	108.50 W
Anina	172	45.05 N	21.51 E
Anita, Iowa, U.S.	252	41.27 N	94.46 W
Anita, Pa., U.S.	266	41.00 N	78.58 W
Aniva, Zaliv C	186	46.16 N	142.48 E
Anjiang	190	27.11 N	110.04 E
Anjigomi Lake ⊜	244	47.51 N	84.34 W
Anjou	260	45.36 N	73.33 W
Anjou □[9]	176	47.20 N	0.30 W
Anjouan I	225a	12.15 S	44.25 E
Anju	194	39.36 N	125.40 E
Anjudin	160	62.33 N	58.12 E
Ankang	190	32.31 N	109.19 E
Ankara	212	39.56 N	32.52 E
Ankara ≃	212	39.51 N	31.55 E
Ankaratra ⛰	225b	19.25 S	47.12 E
Ankaroaka ∧	225b	17.48 S	48.32 E
Ankarsrum	160	57.42 N	16.19 E
Ankavandra	218	18.46 S	45.18 E
Ankazoabo	218	22.18 S	44.31 E
Ankazobe	218	18.21 S	47.07 E
Ankeny	244	41.44 N	93.36 W
Anking → Anqing	196	30.31 N	117.02 E
Anklam	164	53.51 N	13.41 E
Ankober	214	9.30 N	39.44 E
Anlinhu ⊜	194	41.13 N	114.32 E
Anlong	200	25.02 N	105.31 E
Anlu	190	31.17 N	113.40 E
Ann, Cape ≻	148	66.10 S	51.22 E
Anna, Ill., U.S.	248	37.28 N	89.15 W
Anna, Ohio, U.S.	268	40.24 N	84.10 W
Anna, Tex., U.S.	250	33.21 N	96.33 W
Annaba (Bône)	170	36.54 N	7.46 E
Annaba □[5]	170	35.30 N	8.00 E
Annaberg-Buchholz	164	50.35 N	13.00 E
An-Nabk	208	34.01 N	36.44 E
An-Nabqīyah I	208	26.44 N	36.01 E
An-Nafūd ◂[2]	208	28.30 N	41.00 E
An-Najaf	208	31.59 N	44.20 E
Annalee Heights	262	38.52 N	77.11 W
Annamitique, Chaîne ⛰	200	17.00 N	106.00 E
Annan	162	54.59 N	3.16 W
Annandale, Minn., U.S.	244	45.16 N	94.08 W
Annandale, N.J., U.S.	262	40.39 N	74.53 W
Annandale, Va., U.S.	262	38.50 N	77.12 W
Annandale-on-Hudson	261	42.01 N	73.54 W
Anna Paulowna	178	52.52 N	4.50 E
Annapolis	262	38.59 N	76.30 W
Annapolis Basin C	240	44.39 N	65.42 W
Annapolis Royal	240	44.45 N	65.31 W
Annapurna ∧	206	28.34 N	83.50 E
An-Naqīrah ▾[4]	208	27.53 N	48.15 E
Ann Arbor	268	42.18 N	83.45 W
An-Nāṣirīyah	208	31.02 N	46.16 E
An-Nāṣirīyah □[4]	208	31.00 N	46.15 E
Anne Arundel □[6]	262	38.59 N	76.30 W
Annecy	180	45.54 N	6.07 E
Annecy, Lac d' ⊜	166	45.51 N	6.11 E
Annemasse	180	46.12 N	6.15 E
Annenkov Island I	288	54.29 S	37.05 W
Annenskij Most	160	60.45 N	37.10 E
Annette	236	55.03 N	131.34 W
Annette Island I	236	55.10 N	131.28 W
Annezin	176	50.32 N	2.37 E
An-nhon	198	13.53 N	109.06 E
Annieopsquotch Mountains ⛰	240	48.20 N	57.30 W
An-Nīl al-Azraq □[4]	220	13.00 N	33.00 E
Anniston	248	33.40 N	85.50 W
Annobón I	218	1.25 S	5.36 E
Annonay	166	45.14 N	4.40 E
Annopol	164	50.54 N	21.52 E
Annotto Bay	285q	18.15 N	76.45 W
An-Nuhūd	220	12.42 N	28.26 E
An-Nu'mān I	208	27.08 N	35.46 E
Ann'val'kal', Mys ≻	236	65.36 N	180.40 E
Annville, Ky., U.S.	246	37.19 N	83.58 W
Annville, Pa., U.S.	262	40.19 N	76.31 W
Anoka	244	45.11 N	93.23 W
Anori, Bra.	290	3.47 S	61.38 W
Anorí, Col.	290	7.05 N	75.08 W
Anqing	196	30.31 N	117.02 E
Anrath	178	51.17 N	6.28 E
Ansbach	164	49.17 N	10.34 E
Anse-Bertrand	285o	16.29 N	61.31 W
Anse-d'Hainault	282	18.30 N	74.27 W
Anse La Raye	285f	13.57 N	61.03 W
Anselmo	252	41.37 N	99.52 W
Anserma	290	5.13 N	75.48 W
Ansermanuevo	290	4.48 N	75.59 W
Anshan	194	41.08 N	122.59 E
Anshanhu ⊜	196	32.57 N	118.03 E
Anshun	200	26.19 N	105.50 E
Ansina	294	31.54 S	55.28 W
Ansley, La., U.S.	248	32.24 N	92.42 W
Ansley, Nebr., U.S.	252	41.18 N	99.23 W
Anson, Maine, U.S.	242	44.48 N	69.53 W
Anson, Tex., U.S.	250	32.45 N	99.54 W
Ansongo	214	15.40 N	0.30 E
Ansonia, Conn., U.S.	261	41.20 N	73.05 W
Ansonia, Ohio, U.S.	268	40.13 N	84.38 W
Ansonville, Ont., Can.	244	48.45 N	80.41 W
Ansonville, N.C., U.S.	246	35.06 N	80.07 W
Ansonville, Pa., U.S.	266	40.51 N	78.34 W
Ansted	242	38.08 N	81.06 W
Anta	292	13.29 S	72.08 W
Anta, Cachoeira ⌊	296	13.06 S	48.09 W
Anta, Cachoeira da ⌊	292	7.29 S	61.51 W
Antabamba	292	14.25 S	72.55 W
Antakya (Antioch)	212	36.14 N	36.07 E
Antalaha	225b	14.53 S	50.16 E
Antalovcy	164	48.38 N	22.31 E
Antalya	212	36.53 N	30.42 E
Antalya, Gulf of → Antalya Körfezi C	212	36.30 N	31.00 E
Antalya Körfezi C	212	36.30 N	31.00 E
Antarctica •[1]	148	90.00 S	0.00
Antarctic Peninsula ≻[1]	148	69.30 S	65.00 W
Antas, Rio das ≃	294	29.04 S	51.21 W
Antela, Laguna de ⊜	168	42.07 N	7.41 W
Antelope Acres	274	34.44 N	118.19 W
Antelope Peak ∧	258	41.19 N	114.58 W
Antelope Reservoir ⊜[1]	256	42.54 N	117.13 W
Antelope Wash ∨	258	39.33 N	116.17 W
Antequera, Bol.	292	18.29 S	66.53 W
Antequera, Esp.	168	37.01 N	4.33 W
Antequera, Para.	294	24.08 S	57.07 W
Antero Reservoir ⊜[1]	254	39.00 N	105.55 W
Anthon	252	42.23 N	95.52 W
Anthony, Fla., U.S.	246	29.18 N	82.07 W
Anthony, Kans., U.S.	252	37.09 N	98.02 W
Anthony, R.I., U.S.	261	41.42 N	71.32 W
Anthony, Tex., U.S.	278	32.00 N	106.36 W
Antibes	182	43.35 N	7.07 E
Anticosti, Île I	240	49.30 N	63.00 W
Antietam National Battlefield Site	242	39.24 N	77.47 W
Antifer, Cap d' ≻	166	49.41 N	0.10 E
Antigo	244	45.09 N	89.09 W
Antigonish	240	45.35 N	61.55 W
Antigua □[1]	276	17.03 N	61.48 W
Antigua Guatemala	280	14.34 N	90.44 W
Antiguo Morelos	278	22.33 N	99.05 W
Anti-Lebanon → Al-Jabal ash-Sharqī ⛰	210	33.35 N	36.00 E

Symbols in the index entries are identified on page 360.

Name	Page	Lat°′	Long°′
Antilla, Arg.	294	26.07 S	64.36 W
Antilla, Cuba	284p	20.50 N	75.45 W
Antimony	254	38.07 N	111.55 W
Antioch → Antakya, Tür.	212	36.14 N	36.07 E
Antioch, Calif., U.S.	272	38.01 N	121.49 W
Antioch, Ill., U.S.	268	42.29 N	88.06 W
Antioquia	290	6.33 N	75.50 W
Antioquia □[5]	290	7.00 N	75.30 W
Antipino	160	59.01 N	55.10 E
Antipolo	202	14.35 N	121.10 E
Antique □[4]	202	11.00 N	121.45 E
Antler ≃	252	49.08 N	101.00 W
Antlers	250	34.14 N	95.37 W
Antofagasta	294	23.39 S	70.24 W
Antofagasta □[4]	294	23.30 S	69.00 W
Antofagasta de la Sierra	294	26.05 S	67.20 W
Antofalla, Salar de ≚	294	25.40 S	67.45 W
Antofalla, Volcán ∧[1]	294	25.33 S	67.56 W
Antolana ∧	225b	17.04 S	48.09 E
Antón, Pan.	280	8.21 N	80.14 W
Anton, Tex., U.S.	250	33.49 N	102.10 W
Anton Chico	254	35.12 N	105.09 W
Antongil, Baie d' C	225b	15.45 S	49.50 E
Antonina	294	25.27 S	48.43 W
Antonio Amaro	278	24.16 N	104.01 W
António Enes	218	16.14 S	39.54 E
Antônio João	296	23.15 S	55.31 W
Antônio Prado	294	28.51 S	51.17 W
Antonito	254	37.05 N	106.00 W
Antón Lizardo, Punta de ≻	278	19.03 N	95.58 W
Antony	176	48.45 N	2.18 E
Antrain	166	48.27 N	1.29 W
Antrim, N. Ire., U.K.	162	54.43 N	6.13 W
Antrim, Ohio, U.S.	266	40.06 N	81.23 W
Antrim □[6]	162	54.55 N	6.10 W
Antrim, Mountains of ⋀	162	55.00 N	6.10 W
Antrodoco	170	42.25 N	13.05 E
Antropovo	160	58.26 N	43.00 E
Antsirabe	225b	19.51 S	47.02 E
Antsohihy	218	14.52 S	47.59 E
Anttis	160	67.16 N	22.52 E
Antung → Andong	194	40.08 N	124.20 E
Antwerp → Antwerpen, Bel.	176	51.13 N	4.25 E
Antwerp, N.Y., U.S.	264	44.12 N	75.37 W
Antwerp, Ohio, U.S.	268	41.11 N	84.45 W
Antwerpen (Anvers)	176	51.13 N	4.25 E
Antwerpen □[4]	176	51.10 N	4.50 E
An Uaimh (Navan)	162	53.39 N	6.41 W
An'ujsk	186	68.18 N	161.38 E
Anujskij Chrebet ⋀	186	51.30 N	84.55 E
Anuradhapura	204	8.21 N	80.23 E
Anvers → Antwerpen	176	51.13 N	4.25 E
Anvik	236	62.40 N	160.12 W
Anvik ≃	236	62.39 N	160.14 W
Anvil Peak ∧	237a	52.00 N	179.35 E
Anvil Range ⋀	236	62.30 N	133.50 W
Anxi	190	40.32 N	95.51 E
Anyang	194	36.06 N	114.21 E
Anyanghe ≃	194	36.01 N	114.46 E
Anzaldo	292	17.50 S	65.55 W
Anžero-Sudžensk	186	56.07 N	86.00 E
Anzin	176	50.22 N	3.30 E
Anzio	184	41.27 N	12.37 E
Anzoátegui □[3]	290	9.00 N	64.30 W
Anžu, Ostrova II	186	75.30 N	143.00 E
Aoga-shima I	190	32.28 N	139.46 E
Aoíz	168	42.47 N	1.22 W
Aoji	194	42.31 N	130.23 E
Aomar	168	36.30 N	3.46 E
Aomori	192	40.49 N	140.45 E
Aóös (Vijosë) ≃	172	40.37 N	19.20 E
Aôral, Phnum ∧	200	12.02 N	104.10 E
Aorangi Mountains ⋀	230	41.28 S	175.20 E
Aorere ≃	230	40.40 S	172.40 E
Aoshan I	196	29.56 N	122.14 E
Aosta	182	45.44 N	7.20 E
Aosta, Val d' ∨	166	45.46 N	7.25 E
Aoudaghost ⊥	222	17.25 N	10.40 W
Aoudour, Oued ≃	168	35.02 N	5.02 W
Aouk, Bahr ≃	214	8.51 N	18.53 E
Aoukâr ⇀[1]	222	18.00 N	9.30 W
Aoulef	214	26.55 N	1.02 E
Aoya	192	35.31 N	133.59 E
Aozou	214	21.49 N	17.25 E
Apa ≃	294	22.06 S	58.00 W
Apache	250	34.54 N	98.22 W
Apache Lake ◎[1]	254	33.36 N	111.16 W
Apache Peak ∧	254	31.49 N	110.25 W
Apalachee Bay C	246	30.00 N	84.13 W
Apalachicola	246	29.44 N	84.59 W
Apalachicola ≃	246	29.44 N	84.59 W
Apalachicola Bay C	246	29.40 N	85.00 W
Apanás, Lago de ◎	280	13.10 N	86.00 W
Apaporis ≃	290	1.23 S	69.25 W
Aparados da Serra, Parque Nacional dos ♠	294	29.30 S	50.32 W
Aparecida de Goiás	296	14.57 S	49.47 W
Aparri	202	18.22 N	121.38 E
Apaseo el Grande	278	20.33 N	100.41 W
Apastovo	160	55.11 N	48.30 E
Apatin	172	45.40 N	18.59 E
Apatity	160	67.34 N	33.18 E
Apatzingán	276	19.05 N	102.21 W
Apatzingán [de la Constitución]	278	19.05 N	102.21 W
Apaxtla [de Castrejón]	278	18.09 N	99.52 W
Apeldoorn	178	52.13 N	5.58 E
Apen	178	53.13 N	7.48 E
Apenes	270	49.16 N	124.41 W
Apex	246	35.44 N	78.51 W
Apex Mountain ∧	236	62.28 N	138.04 W
Apgar	256	48.32 N	114.00 W
Api ∧	206	30.01 N	80.56 E
Apía	290	5.05 N	75.58 W
Apiacá	296	21.08 S	41.34 W
Apiacás, Serra dos ⋀[1]	292	10.15 S	57.15 W
Apiaí	294	24.31 S	48.50 W
Apidiá ≃	292	11.39 S	61.11 W
Apishapa ≃	252	38.08 N	103.57 W
Apizaco	278	19.25 N	98.09 W
Apizaloya	278	24.50 N	102.15 W
Aplao	292	16.07 S	72.25 W
Apo, Mount ∧	202	7.00 N	125.16 E
Apodaca	250	25.46 N	100.12 W
Apo East Pass)(	202	12.50 N	120.40 E
Apolda	164	51.01 N	11.31 E
Apolinario Saravia	294	24.25 S	64.02 W
Apollo	266	40.35 N	79.34 W
Apolo	292	14.43 S	68.31 W
Apón ≃	290	10.06 N	72.23 W
Aponguao ≃	290	4.48 N	61.36 W
Apopa	280	13.48 N	89.11 W
Apopka, Lake ◎	246	28.37 N	81.38 W
Aporé	296	18.58 S	52.01 W
Aporé ≃	296	19.27 S	50.57 W
Apo Reef ✢[2]	202	12.40 N	120.30 E
Apostle Islands II	244	46.50 N	90.30 W
Apóstoles	294	27.55 S	55.45 W
Apostolovo	158	47.39 N	33.44 E
Apozolco	278	21.22 N	104.00 W
Appalachia	246	36.54 N	82.47 W
Appalachian Mountains ⋀	234	41.00 N	77.00 W
Appen	178	53.40 N	9.44 E
Apennines → Appennino ⋀	170	43.00 N	13.00 E
Appennino ⋀	170	43.00 N	13.00 E
Appennino Abruzzese ⋀	170	42.00 N	14.00 E
Appennino Calabrese ⋀	170	39.00 N	16.30 E
Appennino Ligure ⋀	170	44.30 N	9.00 E
Appennino Lucano ⋀	170	40.30 N	16.00 E
Appennino Napoletano ⋀	170	41.30 N	15.00 E
Appennino Tosco-Emiliano ⋀	170	44.00 N	11.30 E
Appennino Umbro-Marchigiano ⋀	170	43.00 N	13.00 E
Appenweier	164	48.32 N	7.58 E
Appenzell	180	47.20 N	9.25 E
Appenzell-Ausser Rhoden □[3]	180	47.22 N	9.28 E
Appiano (Eppan)	170	46.28 N	11.15 E
Appingedam	178	53.18 N	6.52 E
Apple ≃, U.S.	244	42.11 N	90.14 W
Appleby	162	54.36 N	2.29 W
Apple Creek	266	40.45 N	81.50 W
Applegate	272	39.06 N	120.59 W
Apple Hill	260	45.13 N	74.46 W
Apple Orchard Mountain ∧	246	37.31 N	79.31 W
Appleton, Minn., U.S.	252	45.12 N	96.01 W
Appleton, Wash., U.S.	270	45.49 N	121.16 W
Appleton, Wis., U.S.	244	44.16 N	88.25 W
Appleton City	248	38.11 N	94.02 W
Apple Valley	274	34.32 N	117.14 W
Applewold	266	40.47 N	79.36 W
Appling	246	33.33 N	82.19 W
Appomattox	246	37.21 N	78.50 W
Appomattox ≃	246	37.18 N	77.18 W
Appomattox Court House National Historical Park ♠	246	37.16 N	78.52 W
Aprelevka	160	55.33 N	37.04 E
Apricena	184	41.47 N	15.27 E
Aprilia	184	41.36 N	12.39 E
Apšeronskij Poluostrov ≻[1]	208	40.30 N	50.00 E
Apsley	264	44.45 N	78.06 W
Apt	182	43.53 N	5.24 E
Aptos	272	36.59 N	121.54 W
Apuaú	290	2.25 S	60.53 W
Apucarana	296	23.33 S	51.29 W
Apulia Station	264	42.49 N	76.05 W
Apure □[3]	290	7.10 N	68.50 W
Apure ≃	290	7.37 N	66.25 W
Apurímac □[5]	292	14.00 S	73.00 W
Apurímac ≃	292	12.17 S	73.56 W
Apurito	290	7.56 N	68.27 W
Apuseni, Munţii ⋀	172	46.30 N	22.30 E
Aqaba, Gulf of C	208	29.00 N	34.40 E
'Aqīq, Khalīj C	220	18.20 N	38.10 E
'Aqīq, Wādī al- ∨	208	24.17 N	40.10 E
Aqţţārah, Munkhafaḍ al- ≗[7]	220	30.00 N	27.30 E
Aquarius Plateau ⋀[1]	254	38.05 N	111.40 W
Aquasco	262	38.35 N	76.43 W
Aquebogue	261	40.57 N	72.37 W
Aquibi, Cachoeira ⌊	292	11.08 S	55.22 W
Aquidauana	292	20.28 S	55.48 W
Aquila	278	18.36 N	103.30 W
Aquiles Serdán	278	28.36 N	105.53 W
Aquilla, Ohio, U.S.	266	41.34 N	81.09 W
Aquilla, Tex., U.S.	250	31.51 N	97.13 W
Aquin	282	18.16 N	73.24 W
Aquio ≃	290	2.42 N	67.34 W
Ara ≃, Esp.	168	42.25 N	0.09 E
Ara ≃, Nihon	192	35.39 N	139.51 E
'Ar'a, Wādī ∨	208	31.23 N	42.26 E
Arab	248	34.19 N	86.29 W
'Arab, Baḩr al- ≃	220	9.02 N	29.28 E
'Arab, Khalīj al- C	220	30.55 N	29.05 E
'Arab, Shaţţ al- ≃	208	29.57 N	48.34 E
'Arabah, Wādī ∨	220	29.07 N	32.39 E
'Arabah, Wādī al- ∨	210	30.10 N	35.10 E
Arabelo	290	4.55 N	64.13 W
Arabi	248	29.57 N	90.02 W
Arabian Basin ✢[1]	148	10.00 N	65.00 E
Arabian Peninsula ≻[1]	148	25.00 N	45.00 E
Arabian Sea ▼[2]	204	15.00 N	65.00 E
Aracá ≃	290	0.25 S	62.55 W
Aracaju	286	10.55 S	37.04 W
Aracataca	290	10.36 N	74.12 W
Aracati	286	4.34 S	37.46 W
Araçatuba	296	21.12 S	50.25 W
Araceli	202	10.34 N	119.59 E
Aracena	168	37.53 N	6.33 W
Aracruz	296	19.49 S	40.16 W
Araçuaí	296	16.52 S	42.04 W
Araçuaí ≃	296	16.46 S	42.02 W
Arad	172	46.11 N	21.20 E
Arada	280	14.48 N	88.18 W
Arafura Sea ▼[2]	148	9.00 S	133.00 E
Aragac, Gora ∧	208	40.32 N	44.14 E
Aragarças	296	15.55 S	52.15 W
Arago, Cape ≻	256	43.18 N	124.25 W
Aragoiânia	296	16.57 S	49.30 W
Aragon	246	34.03 N	85.03 W
Aragón □[9]	168	41.00 N	1.00 W
Aragón ≃	168	42.13 N	1.44 W
Aragona	170	37.24 N	13.37 E
Aragua □[3]	290	10.00 N	67.10 W
Araguacema	286	8.50 S	49.34 W
Araguaçu	296	12.49 S	49.51 W
Aragua de Barcelona	290	9.28 N	64.49 W
Aragua de Maturín	290	9.58 N	63.29 W
Araguaia ≃	296	5.21 S	48.41 W
Araguaia, Parque Nacional do ♠	296	12.00 S	50.20 W
Araguainha	296	16.49 S	53.05 W
Araguao, Caño ≃[1]	290	9.15 N	60.50 W
Araguari	296	18.38 S	48.11 W
Araguari ≃, Bra.	286	1.15 N	49.55 W
Araguari ≃, Bra.	296	18.21 S	48.40 W
Araguatins	286	5.38 S	48.07 W
Arai	192	37.01 N	138.15 E
Arak, Alg.	214	25.18 N	3.45 E
Arāk, Īrān	208	34.05 N	49.41 E
Arakamčečen, Ostrov I	236	64.45 N	172.30 W
Arakan □[8]	200	19.00 N	94.15 E
Arakan Yoma ⋀	200	19.00 N	94.40 E
Arákhova	172	38.29 N	22.35 E
Árakhthos ≃	172	39.01 N	21.03 E
Araks (Aras) ≃	158	40.01 N	48.28 E
Aral Sea → Aral'skoje More ▼[2]	186	45.00 N	60.00 E
Aral'sk	186	46.48 N	61.40 E
Aral'skoje More ▼[2]	186	45.00 N	60.00 E
Aramac	226	22.59 S	145.14 E
Aramari	296	12.04 S	38.30 W
Arambaza	290	2.04 S	73.06 W
Aramberri	278	24.06 N	99.49 W
Aramil'	158	56.46 N	60.50 E
Arampampa	292	17.55 S	66.04 W
Ārān	208	34.04 N	51.29 E
Arana, Sierra ⋀	168	37.20 N	3.30 W
Aranda de Duero	168	41.41 N	3.41 W
Arandas	278	20.42 N	102.21 W
Aranđelovac	172	44.18 N	20.44 E
Arani	292	17.34 S	65.46 W
Aran Island I	162	54.58 N	8.33 W
Aran Islands II	162	53.07 N	9.43 W
Aranjuez	168	40.02 N	3.36 W
Aransas Pass	250	27.54 N	97.09 W
Arantes, Ribeirão ≃	296	19.17 S	50.32 W
Aranyaprathet	200	13.42 N	102.32 E
Aranzazu	290	5.16 N	75.30 W
Arao	192	33.00 N	130.28 E
Araouane	214	18.54 N	3.33 W
Arapa, Lago ◎	292	15.11 S	70.00 W
Arapaho	250	35.34 N	98.57 W
Arapahoe	252	40.18 N	99.54 W
Arapawa Island I	230	41.11 S	174.17 E
Arapey	294	30.58 S	57.32 W
Arapiraca	286	9.45 S	36.39 W
Arapongas	296	23.23 S	51.27 W
Arapoti	296	24.08 S	49.50 W
Araquari	294	26.23 S	48.43 W
Araquil ≃	168	42.48 N	1.45 W
Araranguá	294	28.56 S	49.29 W
Araraquara	296	21.47 S	48.10 W
Araras	296	22.22 S	47.23 W
Araras, Serra das ⋀[2]	294	25.10 S	52.00 W
Ararat	228	37.17 S	142.56 E
Ararat, Mount → Büyük Ağrı Dağı ∧	208	39.42 N	44.18 E
Araruva	296	23.45 S	51.19 W
Aras (Araks) ≃	158	40.01 N	48.28 E
Aratiba	294	27.24 S	52.19 W
Aratuípe	296	13.05 S	39.00 W
Arauca	290	7.05 N	70.45 W
Arauca □[5]	290	6.40 N	71.00 W
Arauca ≃	290	7.24 N	66.35 W
Araucária	294	25.35 S	49.25 W
Arauco	294	37.15 S	73.19 W
Arauco □[4]	294	37.50 S	73.15 W
Arauco, Bahía de C	294	37.11 S	73.25 W
Araújos	296	19.56 S	45.04 W
Arauquita	290	7.02 N	71.25 W
Araure	290	9.34 N	69.13 W
Arāvalli Range ⋀	206	25.00 N	73.30 E
Araviana ≃	168	41.41 N	2.07 W
Arawata ≃	230	44.00 S	168.40 E
Araxá	296	19.35 S	46.55 W
Araya	290	10.34 N	64.15 W
Arayat	202	15.09 N	120.46 E
Arayat, Mount ∧	202	15.12 N	120.45 E
Arba ≃	168	41.52 N	1.18 W
Arbagia ⇀[1]	170	40.00 N	9.10 E
Arba Minch	214	6.02 N	37.40 E
Arbaoua	168	34.54 N	5.56 W
Arbaž	160	57.41 N	48.18 E
Arboga	160	59.24 N	15.50 E
Arbois	166	46.54 N	5.46 E
Arboledas	294	36.50 S	61.30 W
Arboles	254	37.01 N	107.24 W
Arboletes	290	8.51 N	76.26 W
Arbon	180	47.31 N	9.26 E
Arborea	170	39.47 N	8.34 E
Arborea ⇀[1]	170	39.55 N	8.50 E
Arbroath	162	56.34 N	2.35 W
Arbuckle	272	39.01 N	122.03 W
Arbuckle, Lake ◎	246	27.41 N	81.24 W
Arbuckle Mountains ⋀	250	34.25 N	97.20 W
Arbuckle National Recreation Area ♠	250	34.24 N	97.07 W
Arbury Hills	268	41.33 N	87.51 W
Arc ≃	166	43.31 N	5.07 E
Arc, Bayou des ≃	248	35.00 N	91.30 W
Arcachon	166	44.37 N	1.12 W
Arcachon, Bassin d' C	166	44.40 N	1.10 W
Arcade, Calif., U.S.	272	34.02 N	118.15 W
Arcade, N.Y., U.S.	266	42.32 N	78.25 W
Arcadia, Calif., U.S.	274	34.08 N	118.01 W
Arcadia, Fla., U.S.	246	27.14 N	81.52 W
Arcadia, Ind., U.S.	248	40.11 N	86.01 W
Arcadia, Iowa, U.S.	252	42.05 N	95.03 W
Arcadia, Kans., U.S.	252	37.38 N	94.37 W
Arcadia, La., U.S.	248	32.33 N	92.55 W
Arcadia, Mich., U.S.	244	44.30 N	86.14 W
Arcadia, Nebr., U.S.	252	41.25 N	99.07 W
Arcadia, Ohio, U.S.	268	41.07 N	83.31 W
Arcadia, Pa., U.S.	266	40.47 N	78.51 W
Arcadia, S.C., U.S.	246	34.57 N	82.00 W
Arcadia, Wis., U.S.	244	44.15 N	91.30 W
Arcângelo	296	21.18 S	44.19 W
Arcanum	242	39.59 N	84.33 W
Arcata	258	40.52 N	124.05 W
Arcatao	280	14.05 N	88.45 W
Arce	170	41.35 N	13.34 E
Arcelia	278	18.17 N	100.16 W
Arcevia	170	43.30 N	12.56 E
Archangel → Archangel'sk	160	64.34 N	40.32 E
Archangel'sk	160	64.34 N	40.32 E
Archbold	268	41.31 N	84.18 W
Archdale	246	35.56 N	79.57 W
Archenu, Jabal ∧	220	22.13 N	24.41 E
Archer	246	29.32 N	82.31 W
Archer City	250	33.36 N	98.38 W
Arches National Monument ♠	254	38.42 N	109.45 W
Archiac	166	45.31 N	0.18 W
Archibald Makin National Park ♠	228	35.50 S	140.25 E
Archidona	168	37.05 N	4.23 W
Archipiélago de Colón □[4]	290a	0.30 S	90.30 W
Archipovka	160	56.38 N	41.14 E
Archipovo	160	66.26 N	45.52 E
Arcidosso	170	42.52 N	11.33 E
Arcisate	182	45.54 N	8.52 E
Arcis-sur-Aube	166	48.32 N	4.08 E
Arco, It.	170	45.55 N	10.53 E
Arco, Ga., U.S.	246	31.10 N	81.30 W
Arco, Idaho, U.S.	256	43.38 N	113.18 W
Arco de Baúlhe	168	41.29 N	7.58 W
Arcola, Sask., Can.	252	49.37 N	102.30 W
Arcola, Ill., U.S.	248	39.41 N	88.19 W
Arcola, Ind., U.S.	268	41.06 N	85.18 W
Arcola, Miss., U.S.	248	33.16 N	90.53 W
Arcos	296	20.17 S	45.32 W
Arcos de la Frontera	168	36.45 N	5.48 W
Arcoverde	286	8.25 S	37.04 W
Arctic Bay	232	73.02 N	85.11 W
Arctic Ocean ▼[1]	148	85.00 N	170.00 E
Arctic Red ≃	236	67.27 N	133.46 W
Arctic Red River	236	67.27 N	133.46 W
Arctic Village	236	68.08 N	145.19 W
Arḍ, Ra's al- ≻	208	29.21 N	48.05 E
Arda ≃	172	41.39 N	26.29 E
Ardabīl	208	38.15 N	48.18 E
Ardahan	158	41.07 N	42.41 E
Ardakān	208	32.19 N	53.59 E
Årdalstangen	160	61.14 N	7.43 E
Arḍ aṣ-Ṣawwān ≚	208	30.45 N	37.15 E
Ardatov	160	55.15 N	43.06 E
Ardèche □[5]	182	44.40 N	4.20 E
Ardee	162	53.52 N	6.33 W
Arden, Calif., U.S.	272	38.36 N	121.23 W
Arden, Del., U.S.	262	39.48 N	75.29 W
Arden, Mount ∧	228	32.09 S	137.59 E
Ardennes □[5]	176	49.40 N	4.40 E
Ardennes ⇀[1]	164	50.10 N	5.45 E
Ardhéa	172	40.59 N	22.03 E
Ardila ≃	168	38.12 N	7.28 W
Ardill	252	49.53 N	105.49 W
Ardino	172	41.35 N	25.08 E
Ardlussa	162	56.02 N	5.47 W
Ardmore, Ala., U.S.	248	34.59 N	86.52 W
Ardmore, Ind., U.S.	268	41.42 N	86.19 W
Ardmore, Okla., U.S.	250	34.10 N	97.08 W
Ardmore, Pa., U.S.	262	40.01 N	75.18 W
Ardooie	176	50.59 N	3.12 E
Arduan Island I	220	19.55 N	30.22 E
Åre	160	63.24 N	13.04 E
Areado	296	21.21 S	46.09 W
Arecibo	284m	18.28 N	66.43 W
Areguá	294	25.18 S	57.25 W
Areia, Ribeirão da ≃	296	16.07 S	45.52 W
Areia Branca	286	4.56 S	37.07 W
Arena de la Ventana, Punta ≻	278	24.04 N	109.52 W
Arena Island I	202	9.13 N	120.44 E
Arenal, C.R.	280	10.29 N	84.53 W
Arenal, P.R.	284m	17.59 N	66.19 W
Arenal, Laguna de ◎	280	10.32 N	84.55 W
Arenal, Punta del ≻	285r	10.03 N	61.56 W
Arenal, Volcán ∧[1]	280	10.28 N	84.44 W
Arenápolis	292	14.26 S	56.49 W
Arenas, Punta ≻	292	21.39 S	70.10 W
Arenas, Punta de ≻	290	10.29 N	64.14 W
Arenas de San Pedro	168	40.12 N	5.05 W
Arendal	160	58.27 N	8.48 E
Arendonk	178	51.19 N	5.05 E
Arendtsville	262	39.55 N	77.18 W
Arenillas	290	3.33 S	80.04 W
Arenys de Mar	168	41.35 N	2.33 E
Arenzano	182	44.24 N	8.41 E
Areq, Sebkha bou C	168	35.10 N	2.45 W
Arequipa	292	16.24 S	71.33 W
Arequipa □[5]	292	16.00 S	72.50 W
Arequito	294	33.10 S	61.29 W
Arès	166	44.46 N	1.08 W
Arévalo	168	41.04 N	4.43 W
Arezzo	184	43.25 N	11.53 E
Arezzo □[4]	184	43.32 N	11.50 E
'Arfa, Wādī ∨	220	30.13 N	36.40 E
Arga ≃	168	42.18 N	1.47 W
Argamasilla de Alba	168	39.07 N	3.06 W
Arganda	168	40.18 N	3.26 W
Argao	202	9.53 N	123.35 E
Argelès-Gazost	166	43.01 N	0.06 E
Argelès-sur-Mer	166	42.33 N	3.01 E
Argens ≃	166	43.24 N	6.44 E
Argent, Côte d' ≗[2]	168	43.30 N	1.30 W
Argenta, It.	184	44.37 N	11.50 E
Argenta, Ill., U.S.	248	39.59 N	88.49 W
Argentan	166	48.45 N	0.01 W
Argentat	166	45.06 N	1.56 E
Argentera	170	44.24 N	6.57 E
Argentera, Cima di ∧	170	44.10 N	7.18 E
Argenteuil	176	48.57 N	2.15 E
Argenteuil □[6]	260	45.50 N	74.25 W
Argentia	240	47.18 N	53.59 W
Argentina □[1]	288	34.00 S	64.00 W
Argentine Basin ✢[1]	148	45.00 S	45.00 W
Argentino, Lago ◎	288	50.15 S	72.25 W
Argenton-Château	166	46.59 N	0.27 W
Argenton-sur-Creuse	166	46.35 N	1.31 E
Argentré	166	48.05 N	0.39 W
Arghandāb ≃	206	31.35 N	64.20 E
Arghastān ≃	206	31.22 N	65.15 E
Argirita	296	21.37 S	42.50 W
Argo Island I	220	19.25 N	30.27 E
Argolikós Kólpos C	172	37.33 N	22.45 E
Argolís □[5]	172	37.40 N	22.50 E
Argonia	252	37.16 N	97.46 W
Argonne	244	45.40 N	88.53 W
Argonne ⇀[1]	166	49.30 N	5.00 E
Árgos, Ellás	172	37.39 N	22.44 E
Argos, Ind., U.S.	268	41.14 N	86.15 W
Árgos Orestikón	172	40.28 N	21.16 E
Argostólion	172	38.10 N	20.30 E
Arguello, Point ≻	258	34.35 N	120.39 W
Argun' (Eergu'nahe) ≃	186	53.20 N	121.28 E
Argungu	222	12.45 N	4.31 E
Argyle	252	48.20 N	96.49 W
Argyll □[6]	162	56.18 N	5.15 W
Århus	160	56.09 N	10.13 E
Ariake-wan C	192	31.28 N	131.08 E
Ariana	170	36.52 N	10.12 E
Ariano Irpino	184	41.09 N	15.05 E
Ariano nel Polesine	170	44.56 N	12.07 E
Arias	294	33.40 S	62.25 W
Ariaú	290	3.11 S	57.14 W
Arica, Chile	292	18.29 S	70.20 W
Arica, Col.	290	2.08 S	71.47 W
Ariccia	184	41.43 N	12.40 E
Arichat	240	45.31 N	61.01 W
Arichuna	290	7.42 N	67.08 W
Arida	192	34.05 N	135.07 E
Ariège □[5]	166	43.00 N	1.30 E
Ariel	270	45.57 N	122.34 W
Arīḥā (Jericho)	210	31.52 N	35.27 E
Arikaree ≃	252	40.01 N	101.56 W
Arikawa	192	32.59 N	129.07 E
Arima	285r	10.38 N	61.17 W
Aringay	202	16.26 N	120.21 E
Arinos ≃	292	10.25 S	58.20 W
Arinthod	166	46.23 N	5.34 E
Ario de Rosales	278	19.12 N	101.43 W
Ariporo ≃	290	6.03 N	69.54 W
Aripuanã	292	9.10 S	60.38 W
Aripuanã ≃	292	5.07 S	60.24 W
Ariquemes	292	9.56 S	63.04 W
'Arīsh, Wādī al- ∨	220	31.09 N	33.49 E
Arismendi	290	8.29 N	68.22 W
Arista, Méx.	278	15.56 N	93.48 W
Arista, Méx.	278	22.39 N	100.50 W
Aristazabal Island I	238	52.30 N	129.05 W
Aritao	202	16.17 N	121.02 E
Ariton	248	31.36 N	85.43 W
Arizaro, Salar de ≚	294	24.40 S	67.55 W
Arizona	294	35.49 S	65.20 W
Arizona □[3]	234	34.00 N	112.00 W
Arizpe	278	30.20 N	110.10 W
Arja	160	57.30 N	46.00 E
Årjäng	160	59.23 N	12.08 E
Arjeplog	160	66.00 N	17.58 E
Arjona, Col.	290	10.15 N	75.21 W
Arjona, Esp.	168	37.56 N	4.03 W
Arka	186	60.03 N	142.12 E
Arkadelphia	248	34.07 N	93.04 W
Arkadhía □[5]	172	37.35 N	22.18 E
Arkalyk	186	50.13 N	66.50 E
Arkansas □[3]	234	34.50 N	93.40 W
Arkansas ≃	234	33.48 N	91.04 W
Arkansas City, Ark., U.S.	248	33.36 N	91.12 W
Arkansas City, Kans., U.S.	252	37.04 N	97.02 W
Arkansas Post National Memorial ⊥	248	33.55 N	91.26 W
Arkhángellos	172	36.12 N	28.08 E
Árki I	212	37.22 N	26.45 E
Arklow	162	52.48 N	6.09 W
Arkport	266	42.24 N	77.42 W
Arktičeskogo Instituta, Ostrova II	186	75.20 N	81.55 E
Arkul'	160	57.17 N	50.03 E
Arkwright	261	41.43 N	71.33 W
Arlanc	166	45.25 N	3.44 E
Arlee	256	47.10 N	114.05 W
Arles	182	43.40 N	4.38 E
Arlesheim	180	47.30 N	7.37 E
Arlington, Fla., U.S.	246	30.20 N	81.36 W
Arlington, Ga., U.S.	246	31.27 N	84.44 W
Arlington, Iowa, U.S.	244	42.45 N	91.40 W
Arlington, Kans., U.S.	252	37.54 N	98.11 W
Arlington, Ky., U.S.	248	36.47 N	89.01 W
Arlington, Mass., U.S.	261	42.25 N	71.09 W
Arlington, Minn., U.S.	244	44.36 N	94.05 W
Arlington, Nebr., U.S.	252	41.27 N	96.21 W
Arlington, N.Y., U.S.	261	41.42 N	73.54 W
Arlington, Ohio, U.S.	268	40.54 N	83.39 W
Arlington, Oreg., U.S.	256	45.16 N	120.13 W
Arlington, S. Dak., U.S.	252	44.22 N	97.08 W
Arlington, Tenn., U.S.	248	35.18 N	89.40 W
Arlington, Tex., U.S.	250	32.44 N	97.07 W
Arlington, Vt., U.S.	242	43.05 N	73.09 W
Arlington, Va., U.S.	262	38.52 N	77.05 W
Arlington, Wash., U.S.	270	48.12 N	122.08 W
Arlington Heights	268	42.05 N	87.59 W
Arlon	164	49.41 N	5.49 E
Arluno	182	45.30 N	8.56 E
Arly, Parc National d' ♠	222	11.35 N	1.15 E
Arma	252	37.33 N	94.42 W
Armada	266	42.51 N	82.53 W
Armagh, N. Ire., U.K.	162	54.21 N	6.39 W
Armagh, Pa., U.S.	266	40.27 N	79.02 W
Armagh □[6]	162	54.18 N	6.35 W
Armagnac ⇀[1]	166	43.45 N	0.10 E
Arm'anskaja Sovetskaja Socialističeskaja Respublika □[3]	186	40.00 N	45.00 E
Armant	220	25.37 N	32.32 E
Armavir	158	45.00 N	41.08 E
Armazém	294	28.16 S	49.01 W
Armbrust	266	40.13 N	79.33 W
Armenia	290	4.31 N	75.41 W
Armenian Soviet Socialist Republic → Arm'anskaja Sovetskaja Socialističeskaja	186	40.00 N	43.00 E
Armeniş	172	45.12 N	22.19 E
Armenistís	172	37.36 N	26.08 E
Armentières	176	50.41 N	2.53 E
Armería	278	18.56 N	103.58 W
Armero	290	4.58 N	74.54 W
Armidale	228	30.31 S	151.39 E
Armijo	254	35.03 N	106.41 W
Armit Lake ◎	232	64.10 N	91.32 W
Armona	272	36.19 N	119.42 W
Armor	264	42.44 N	78.48 W
Armour	252	43.19 N	98.21 W
Armstrong, Arg.	294	32.50 S	61.35 W
Armstrong, B.C., Can.	238	50.27 N	119.12 W
Armstrong, Ill., U.S.	268	40.18 N	87.53 W
Armstrong, Iowa, U.S.	252	43.24 N	94.29 W
Armstrong, Mo., U.S.	248	39.16 N	92.42 W
Armstrong, Tex., U.S.	250	26.55 N	97.47 W
Armstrong □[6]	266	40.49 N	79.32 W
Armstrong, Mount ∧	236	63.12 N	133.16 W
Armstrong Station	232	50.18 N	89.02 W
Armutlu	172	40.31 N	28.50 E
Arnaía	172	40.29 N	23.35 E
Arnarfjörđur C[2]	160a	65.45 N	23.40 W
Arnaud ≃	232	59.59 N	70.00 W
Arnaudville	248	30.24 N	91.56 W
Arnay-le-Duc	166	47.08 N	4.29 E
Arnedo	168	42.13 N	2.06 W
Årnes	160	60.09 N	11.28 E
Arnett	250	36.08 N	99.46 W
Arnhem	178	51.59 N	5.55 E
Arnhem Land ⇀[1]	226	13.10 S	134.30 E
Árnissa	172	40.48 N	21.50 E
Arno ≃	170	43.41 N	10.17 E
Arnold, B.C., Can.	270	49.08 N	122.03 W
Arnold, Calif., U.S.	272	38.15 N	120.21 W
Arnold, Minn., U.S.	244	46.53 N	92.05 W
Arnold, Mo., U.S.	248	38.26 N	90.23 W
Arnold, Nebr., U.S.	252	41.26 N	100.12 W
Arnold, Pa., U.S.	266	40.35 N	79.45 W
Arnolds Park	252	43.22 N	95.08 W
Arnoldstein	164	46.33 N	13.43 E
Arnoútis, Akrotírion ≻	212	35.06 N	32.15 E
Arnoya ≃	168	42.15 N	8.09 W
Arnprior	264	45.26 N	76.21 W
Arnsberg	178	51.24 N	8.03 E
Arnsberg □[5]	178	51.20 N	8.00 E
Arnstadt	164	50.50 N	10.57 E
Aroa	290	10.26 N	68.54 W
Aroab	218	26.47 S	19.40 E
Arolsen	178	51.23 N	9.01 E
Aroma Park	268	41.05 N	87.48 W
Aromas	272	36.53 N	121.39 W
Arona	182	45.46 N	8.34 E
Aropuk Lake ◎	236	61.12 N	163.50 W
Aroroy	202	12.31 N	123.24 E
Arosa	166	46.47 N	9.41 E
Arosa, Isla de I	168	42.34 N	8.53 W
Arosa, Ría de C[1]	168	42.28 N	8.57 W
Arowhana ∧	230	38.07 S	177.52 E
Arp	250	32.13 N	95.04 W
Arpajon	176	48.35 N	2.15 E
Arpino	170	41.39 N	13.36 E
Arpoador, Ponta do ≻	294	24.25 S	47.00 W
Arquata Scrivia	182	44.41 N	8.53 E
Arque	292	17.48 S	66.23 W
Arques	176	50.44 N	2.17 E
Ar-Rab' al-Khālī ⇀[2]	214	20.00 N	51.00 E
Arraga	294	28.04 S	64.14 W
Arrah	206	25.33 N	84.40 E
Ar-Rahad	220	12.43 N	30.39 E
Arraial do Cabo	296	22.58 S	42.01 W
Arraias	296	12.56 S	46.57 W
Ar-Ramādī	208	33.25 N	43.17 E
Ar-Ramādī □[4]	208	33.30 N	43.00 E
Ar-Ramthā	210	32.34 N	36.00 E
Ar-Rank	214	11.45 N	32.48 E
Ar-Raqqah	208	35.56 N	39.01 E
Ar-Raqqah □[8]	212	36.00 N	39.00 E
Arras	176	50.17 N	2.47 E
Ar-Ra's al-Abyaḍ ≻	208	23.32 N	38.32 E
Arrats ≃	166	44.06 N	0.52 E
Arrecife	214	28.57 N	13.32 W
Arrecifes	294	34.05 S	60.05 W
Arrée, Monts d' ⋀	166	48.26 N	3.55 W
Arrey	254	32.51 N	107.19 W
Arriaga	278	16.14 N	93.54 W
Arriba	252	39.17 N	103.17 W
Ar-Riyāḍ (Riyadh)	208	24.38 N	46.43 E
Arroio Grande	294	32.14 S	53.05 W
Arronches	168	39.07 N	7.17 W
Arros ≃	166	43.40 N	0.02 W
Arroux ≃	166	46.29 N	3.58 E
Arrow Dam ⇀[6]	238	49.20 N	117.49 W
Arrowhead Village	262	40.04 N	74.07 W
Arrow Lake ◎	244	48.08 N	90.18 W
Arrowrock Reservoir ◎[1]	256	43.36 N	115.51 W
Arrowsmith	268	40.27 N	88.38 W
Arrowsmith, Mount ∧, Austl.	228	30.09 S	141.50 E
Arrowsmith, Mount ∧, N.Z.	230	43.21 S	170.59 E
Arrowsmith Bay C	232	68.00 N	95.15 W
Arrowsmith Range ⋀	230	43.23 S	170.56 E
Arrowwood	238	50.44 N	113.09 W
Arroyito	294	31.26 S	63.05 W
Arroyo	284m	17.58 N	66.04 W
Arroyo de la Luz	168	39.29 N	6.35 W
Arroyo Grande	258	35.07 N	120.34 W
Arroyo Hondo	254	36.32 N	105.40 W
Arroyos y Esteros	294	25.04 S	57.06 W
Ar-Rukhaymīyah ▼[4]	208	29.14 N	45.35 E
Ar-Ruqayyah ⊥	210	32.47 N	37.05 E
Ar-Ruṣāfah ⊥	212	35.37 N	38.45 E
Ar-Ruṣayriṣ	214	11.51 N	34.23 E
Ar-Ruṭbah	204	33.02 N	40.17 E
Arsenjev	186	44.10 N	133.15 E
Arsıyan Dağı ∧	212	41.24 N	42.30 E
Arsk	160	56.06 N	49.54 E
Ars-on-Ré	166	46.12 N	1.31 W
Árta, Ellás	172	39.09 N	20.59 E
Artá, Esp.	168	39.42 N	3.21 E
Arteaga	278	18.28 N	102.25 W
Arteche	202	12.17 N	125.22 E
Artemisa	284p	22.49 N	82.46 W
Artemón	172	36.59 N	24.43 E
Artenay	166	48.05 N	1.53 E
Artesia, Colo., U.S.	254	40.15 N	109.01 W
Artesia, Miss., U.S.	248	33.25 N	88.39 W
Artesia, N. Mex., U.S.	250	32.51 N	104.24 W
Artesian	252	44.00 N	97.55 W
Arthabaska	260	46.02 N	71.55 W
Arthabaska □[6]	260	46.05 N	72.00 W
Arthur, Ont., Can.	264	43.50 N	80.32 W
Arthur, Ill., U.S.	248	39.43 N	88.28 W
Arthur, Nebr., U.S.	252	41.35 N	101.41 W
K2 → Godwin Austen ∧	206	33.53 N	76.30 E
Arthur, N. Dak., U.S.	252	47.06 N	97.13 W
Arthur, Tenn., U.S.	246	36.33 N	83.40 W
Arthur ≃	228	41.03 S	144.40 E
Arthur Fiord C[2]	232	76.33 N	93.11 W
Arthur's Pass)(	230	42.54 S	171.34 E
Arthur's Pass National Park ♠	230	42.50 S	171.40 E
Arthurs Town	282	24.38 N	75.42 W
Artibonite ≃	282	19.15 N	72.46 W
Artigas	294	30.24 S	56.28 W
Artillery Lake ◎	232	63.09 N	107.52 W
Artois □[9]	176	50.30 N	2.30 E
Art'om	186	43.22 N	132.13 E
Art'omovsk	186	54.21 N	93.26 E
Art'omovskij, S.S.S.R.	158	57.21 N	61.54 E
Art'omovskij, S.S.S.R.	186	58.12 N	114.45 E
Artur de Paiva	218	14.28 S	16.20 E
Artvin	158	41.11 N	41.49 E
Artyk	186	64.12 N	145.06 E
Aru, Kepulauan II	198	6.00 S	134.30 E
Aru, Tandjung ≻	198	2.10 S	116.34 E
Arua	214	3.01 N	30.55 E
Aruanã	296	14.54 S	51.05 W
Aruba I	285s	12.30 N	69.58 W
Aru Basin ✢[1]	148	5.30 S	133.30 E
Arun ≃	162	50.48 N	0.33 W
Arundel	260	45.58 N	74.37 W
Arusha	218	3.22 S	36.41 E
Aruwimi ≃	214	1.13 N	23.36 E
Arvada	254	39.50 N	105.05 W
Arvajcheer	190	46.15 N	102.45 E
Arvida	240	48.26 N	71.11 W
Arvidsjaur	160	65.35 N	19.07 E
Arvika	160	59.39 N	12.36 E
Arvin	274	35.12 N	118.50 W
Arvonia	246	37.41 N	78.20 W
Àrvorezinha	294	28.53 S	52.10 W
Arys'	186	42.26 N	68.48 E
Arzachena	170	41.05 N	9.22 E
Arzamas	160	55.23 N	43.50 E
Arzano	184	40.55 N	14.16 E
Arzew	168	35.50 N	0.23 W
Arzew, Golfe d' C	168	35.50 N	0.10 W
Arzew, Salines d' ◎	168	35.40 N	0.15 W
Arzignano	170	45.31 N	11.20 E
Arzúa	168	42.56 N	8.09 W
Aš, Česko.	164	50.10 N	12.10 E
Ås, Nor.	160	59.40 N	10.48 E
Aša	158	55.00 N	57.16 E
Asahi	192	35.43 N	140.39 E
Asahi ≃	192	34.36 N	133.58 E
Asahi-dake ∧	192a	43.40 N	142.51 E
Asahikawa	192a	43.46 N	142.22 E
Asahi-sanchi ⋀	192	38.25 N	139.50 E
Asamankese	222	5.52 N	0.42 W
Asama-yama ∧	192	36.24 N	138.31 E
Asan-man C	194	36.56 N	126.51 E
Asansol	206	23.41 N	86.58 E
Åsarna	160	62.39 N	14.21 E
Asbesberge ⋀	224	28.55 S	23.15 E
Asbest	158	57.00 N	61.30 E
Asbestos	260	45.46 N	71.57 W
Asbury Park	262	40.13 N	74.01 W
Ascensión, Méx.	278	24.20 N	99.55 W
Ascensión, Méx.	278	31.06 N	107.59 W
Ascension I	148	7.57 S	14.22 W
Ascensión, Bahía de la C	278	19.38 N	87.35 W
Aŝchabad, S.S.S.R.	186		
	208	37.57 N	58.23 E
Aschach an der Donau	170	48.22 N	14.02 E
Aschaffenburg	164	49.59 N	9.09 E
Ascheberg	178	51.47 N	7.37 E
Aschendorf	178	53.04 N	7.22 E
Aschersleben	164	51.45 N	11.27 E
Asciano	170	43.14 N	11.33 E
Ascoli Piceno	184	42.51 N	13.34 E
Ascoli Piceno □[4]	184	43.01 N	13.34 E
Ascoli Satriano	184	41.12 N	15.34 E
Ascona	166	46.09 N	8.46 E
Ascope	292	7.45 S	79.05 W
Ascotán	294	21.44 S	68.18 W
Aseb	214	13.00 N	42.45 E
Åseda	160	57.10 N	15.20 E
Asela	214	7.59 N	39.08 E
Åsele	160	64.10 N	17.20 E
Åsen	160	63.36 N	11.03 E
Asenovgrad	172	42.01 N	24.52 E
Ashanti □[4]	222	6.45 N	1.30 W
Ashaway	261	41.25 N	71.47 W
Ashbourne	174	53.02 N	1.44 W
Ashburn	246	31.43 N	83.39 W
Ashburnham	261	42.38 N	71.55 W
Ashburton	230	43.54 S	171.45 E
Ashburton ≃	230	44.03 S	171.48 E
Ashby	261	42.41 N	71.49 W
Ashby-de-la-Zouch	174	52.46 N	1.28 W
Ashcroft	238	50.43 N	121.17 W
Ashdod	210	31.48 N	34.39 E
Ashdod ⊥	210	31.45 N	34.40 E
Ashdown	248	33.41 N	94.08 W
Asheboro	246	35.42 N	79.49 W
Asherton	250	28.27 N	99.46 W
Asheville	246	35.34 N	82.33 W
Ashfield	261	42.32 N	72.48 W
Ashford, Eng., U.K.	174	51.08 N	0.53 E
Ashford, Ala., U.S.	248	31.11 N	85.14 W
Ashford, Wash., U.S.	270	46.46 N	122.02 W
Ash Fork	254	35.13 N	112.29 W
Ash Grove	248	37.19 N	93.35 W
Ashibe	192	33.48 N	129.46 E
Ashibetsu	192a	43.31 N	142.11 E
Ashikaga	192	36.20 N	139.27 E
Ashio	192	36.38 N	139.27 E
Ashippun	268	43.14 N	88.31 W
Ashiyoro	192a	43.15 N	143.30 E
Ashizuri-zaki ≻	192	32.44 N	133.01 E
Ashkhabad → Aŝchabad	208	37.57 N	58.23 E
Ashkum	268	40.53 N	87.57 W
Ashland, Ala., U.S.	248	33.16 N	85.50 W
Ashland, Ill., U.S.	248	34.53 N	90.01 W
Ashland, Kans., U.S.	252	37.11 N	99.46 W
Ashland, Ky., U.S.	242	38.28 N	82.38 W
Ashland, Maine, U.S.	240	46.38 N	68.24 W
Ashland, Mass., U.S.	261	42.16 N	71.28 W
Ashland, Miss., U.S.	248	34.50 N	89.11 W
Ashland, Mo., U.S.	248	38.47 N	92.16 W
Ashland, Mont., U.S.	256	45.35 N	106.16 W
Ashland, Nebr., U.S.	252	41.03 N	96.22 W
Ashland, N.H., U.S.	242	43.42 N	71.38 W
Ashland, Ohio, U.S.	266	40.52 N	82.19 W
Ashland, Oreg., U.S.	256	42.12 N	122.42 W
Ashland, Pa., U.S.	242	40.47 N	76.21 W
Ashland, Va., U.S.	262	37.45 N	77.29 W
Ashland, Wis., U.S.	244	46.35 N	90.53 W
Ashland □[6]	266	40.52 N	82.19 W
Ashland, Mount ∧	256	42.05 N	122.43 W
Ashland City	248	36.16 N	87.04 W
Ashley, Ill., U.S.	248	38.20 N	89.11 W
Ashley, Ind., U.S.	268	41.32 N	85.04 W
Ashley, Mich., U.S.	244	43.11 N	84.29 W
Ashley, N. Dak., U.S.	252	46.02 N	99.22 W
Ashley, Ohio, U.S.	266	40.25 N	82.57 W
Ashley ≃	230	43.17 S	172.44 E
Ashley Falls	261	42.03 N	73.20 W
Ashmore	248	39.32 N	88.01 W
Ashmore Reef ✢[2]	226	12.14 S	123.05 E
Ashmūn	220	30.18 N	30.58 E
Ashqelon	210	31.39 N	34.35 E
Ash-Shabb ▼[4]	220	22.19 N	29.46 E
Ash-Shallāl al-Khāmis (Fifth Cataract) ⌊	220	18.23 N	33.47 E
Ash-Shallāl ar-Rābi' (Fourth Cataract) ⌊	220	18.47 N	32.03 E
Ash-Shallāl as-Sablūkah (Sixth Cataract) ⌊	220	16.20 N	32.42 E
Ash-Shallāl ath-Thālith (Third Cataract) ⌊	220	19.49 N	30.19 E
Ash-Shamāl □[4]	212	34.30 N	36.00 E
Ash-Shamālīyah □[4]	220	19.00 N	30.00 E
Ash-Shaqrā'	208	25.15 N	45.15 E
Ash-Shāriqah	208	25.22 N	55.23 E
Ash-Sharmah ▼[4]	208	28.01 N	35.18 E
Ash-Sharqāṭ	208	35.27 N	43.16 E
Ash-Shaṭrah	208	31.25 N	46.10 E
Ash-Shiḥr	214	14.44 N	49.35 E
Ashtabula	266	41.52 N	80.48 W
Ashtabula □[6]	266	41.44 N	80.46 W
Ashtabula, Lake ◎[1]	252	47.11 N	97.58 W
Ashtead	174	51.19 N	0.18 W
Ashton, Idaho, U.S.	256	44.04 N	111.27 W
Ashton, Ill., U.S.	244	41.52 N	89.13 W
Ashton, Iowa, U.S.	252	43.19 N	95.47 W
Ashton, Md., U.S.	262	39.09 N	77.00 W
Ashton, Nebr., U.S.	252	41.15 N	98.48 W
Ashton, R.I., U.S.	261	41.56 N	71.26 W
Ashuanipi Lake ◎	232	52.35 N	66.10 W
Ashville, Ala., U.S.	248	33.50 N	86.15 W
Ashville, N.Y., U.S.	266	42.06 N	79.23 W
Ashville, Ohio, U.S.	242	39.43 N	82.57 W
Ashville, Pa., U.S.	266	40.34 N	78.33 W
Ashwaubenon	244	44.29 N	88.03 W
Asia ≗[1]	148	50.00 N	100.00 E
Asia, Kepulauan II	198	1.03 N	131.18 E
Asiago	170	45.52 N	11.30 E
Asia Minor ⇀[1]	158	38.00 N	35.00 E
Asid Gulf C	202	12.08 N	123.30 E
Asilah	168	35.32 N	6.00 W
Asinara, Golfo dell' C	170	41.00 N	8.30 E
Asinara, Isola I	170	41.05 N	8.18 E
Asino	186	57.00 N	86.09 E
'Asīr ⇀[1]	214	19.00 N	42.00 E
Asir, Ras (Cape Guardafui) ≻, Som.	214	11.48 N	51.22 E
Askersund	160	58.53 N	14.54 E
Askham	218	26.59 S	20.47 E
Askja ∧[1]	160a	65.00 N	16.48 W
Askvoll	160	61.21 N	5.04 E
Aslanapa	172	39.13 N	29.52 E
Asmera	214	15.20 N	38.53 E
Åsnen ◎	160	56.38 N	14.42 E
Asnières [-sur-Seine]	176	48.55 N	2.17 E
Aso ≃	170	43.06 N	13.51 E
Aso-kokuritsu-kōen ♠	192	33.00 N	131.07 E

Symbols in the index entries are identified on page 360.

Name	Page	Lat°'	Long°'
Asola	170	45.13 N	10.24 E
Asomante	284m	18.23 N	66.36 W
Asosa	214	10.03 N	34.32 E
Aso-san ∧	192	32.53 N	131.06 E
Asoteriba, Jabal ∧	220	21.51 N	36.30 E
Asotin	256	46.20 N	117.03 W
Aspang Markt	164	47.33 N	16.06 E
Aspe	168	38.21 N	0.46 W
Aspeas	262	39.59 N	77.13 W
Aspen	254	39.11 N	106.49 W
Aspen Butte ∧	256	42.19 N	122.05 W
Aspen Lake ⊜	256	42.18 N	122.00 W
Aspermont	250	33.08 N	100.14 W
Aspid, Mount ∧	236	53.30 N	167.33 W
Aspiring, Mount ∧	230	44.23 S	168.44 E
Aspres-sur-Buëch	166	44.31 N	5.45 E
Aspromonte ⋀	170	38.10 N	15.55 E
Aspropótamos ≃	172	40.52 N	21.41 E
Aspy Bay C	240	46.55 N	60.25 W
'Assâba ⋀[1]	222	16.00 N	12.00 W
Aş-Şabyā	214	17.09 N	42.37 E
Aş-Şaff	220	29.34 N	31.17 E
Aş-Şaḥrā'al-Gharbīyah (Western Desert) ◄[2]	220	27.00 N	27.00 E
Aş-Şaḥrā'al-Lībīyah ◄[2]	214	24.00 N	25.00 E
Aş-Şaḥrā' ash-Sharqīyah (Eastern Desert) ◄[2]	220	28.00 N	32.00 E
Assaí	296	23.22 S	50.49 W
As-Sallūm	214	31.34 N	25.09 E
As-Salţ	210	32.02 N	35.43 E
Assam □[3]	206	26.00 N	92.00 E
As-Samāwah	208	31.18 N	45.17 E
Assateague Island I	242	38.05 N	75.10 W
Assateague Island National Seashore ♠	242	38.18 N	75.19 W
Asse	176	50.55 N	4.12 E
Assebroek	176	51.12 N	3.16 E
Assen	178	52.59 N	6.34 E
Assendelft	178	52.27 N	4.45 E
Assenede	176	51.14 N	3.45 E
Assens	160	55.16 N	9.55 E
Asseria ⊥	170	44.02 N	15.39 E
Assiniboia	252	49.38 N	105.59 W
Assiniboine ≃	252	49.53 N	97.08 W
Assiniboine, Mount ∧	238	50.52 N	115.39 W
Assinica, Lac ⊜	232	50.30 N	75.15 W
Assis	296	22.40 S	50.25 W
Assisi	184	43.04 N	12.37 E
Assonet	261	41.48 N	71.04 W
As-Subū' ⊥	220	22.45 N	32.34 E
As-Sulaymānīyah, Ar. Sa.	214	24.09 N	46.19 E
As-Sulaymānīyah, 'Irāq	208	35.33 N	45.26 E
As-Sulaymānīyah □[4]	208	35.40 N	45.30 E
As-Sulayyil	204	20.27 N	45.34 E
Aş-Şummān ◄[1]	208	25.00 N	47.00 E
Assumption, Ill., U.S.	248	39.31 N	89.03 W
Assumption, Ohio, U.S.	268	41.40 N	83.54 W
Assumption Island I	218	9.45 S	46.30 E
As-Suwaydā'	210	32.42 N	36.34 E
As-Suwaydā' □[8]	210	32.45 N	36.45 E
As-Suways (Suez)	220	29.58 N	32.33 E
Astaffort	166	44.04 N	0.40 E
Astakós	172	38.32 N	21.05 E
Āstārā, Īrān	208	38.26 N	48.52 E
Astara, S.S.S.R.	158	38.28 N	48.52 E
Asten	178	51.24 N	5.45 E
Asti	182	44.54 N	8.12 E
Asti □[4]	182	44.55 N	8.10 E
Astica	294	30.56 S	67.23 W
Astillero	168	43.24 N	3.49 W
Astipálaia I	172	36.35 N	26.25 E
Astola Island I	206	25.07 N	63.51 E
Astolfo Dutra	296	21.19 S	42.52 W
Astorga, Bra.	296	23.13 S	51.40 W
Astorga, Esp.	168	42.27 N	6.03 W
Astorga, Pil.	202	6.54 N	125.27 E
Astoria, Ill., U.S.	248	40.14 N	90.21 W
Astoria, Oreg., U.S.	270	46.11 N	123.50 W
Astove Island I	218	10.06 S	47.45 E
Astrachan'	158	46.21 N	48.03 E
Astrakhan → Astrachan'	158	46.21 N	48.03 E
Astudillo	168	42.12 N	4.18 W
Asturias	202	10.34 N	123.43 E
Asturias □[9]	168	43.20 N	6.00 W
Asunción	294	25.16 S	57.40 W
Asunción, Bahía C	278	27.05 N	114.10 W
Asunción, Cerro de la ∧	278	24.15 N	99.56 W
Asuncion Island I	198	19.40 N	145.24 E
Asunción Mita	280	14.20 N	89.43 W
Asunga, Wādī ∨	220	13.21 N	22.17 E
Aswān	220	24.05 N	32.53 E
Aswān High Dam ◄[6]	214	24.05 N	32.53 E
Asyūţ	220	27.11 N	31.11 E
Asyūţī, Wādī al- ∨	220	27.11 N	31.16 E
Aszód	164	47.39 N	19.31 E
Atacama □[4]	294	27.30 S	70.00 W
Atacama, Desierto de ◄[2]	294	22.30 S	69.15 W
Atacama, Puna de ⋀[1]	294	25.00 S	68.00 W
Atacama, Salar de ≍	294	23.30 S	68.15 W
Atacama Trench ÷[1]	148	21.00 S	72.00 W
Ataco	290	3.35 N	75.23 W
Atacora, Chaîne de l' ⋀	222	10.45 N	1.30 E
Atakora □[5]	222	10.00 N	1.35 E
Atakora, Réserve d' ◄[4]	222	11.30 N	2.10 E
Atakpamé	222	7.32 N	1.08 E
Atalándi	172	38.39 N	23.00 E
Atalaya, Pan.	280	8.02 N	80.58 W
Atalaya, Perú	292	10.45 S	73.50 W
Atalaya, Cerro ∧	292	12.37 S	71.53 W
Atami	192	35.05 N	139.04 E
Atar	222	20.31 N	13.03 W
Atascadero	272	35.29 N	120.40 W
Atasta	278	18.37 N	92.06 W
Atasu	186	48.42 N	71.38 E
Ataúro, Ilha de I	198	8.15 S	125.33 E
Atbara ('Aţbarah) ≃	220	17.40 N	33.56 E
'Aţbarah	214	17.42 N	33.59 E
'Aţbarah (Atbara) ≃	220	17.40 N	33.56 E
Atbasar	186	51.48 N	68.20 E
Atchafalaya Bay C	248	29.25 N	91.20 W
Atchison	252	39.34 N	95.07 W
Atco	262	39.46 N	74.53 W
Ateca	168	41.20 N	1.47 W
Atenas	280	9.58 N	84.23 W
Atenguillo	278	20.25 N	104.31 W
Atglen	262	39.57 N	75.58 W
Ath	176	50.38 N	3.47 E
Athabasca	238	54.43 N	113.17 W
Athabasca ≃	238	58.40 N	110.50 W
Athabasca, Lake ⊜	232	59.07 N	110.00 W
Athalmer	238	50.32 N	116.02 W
Athboy	162	53.37 N	6.55 W
Athena	256	45.49 N	118.30 W
Athenry	162	53.18 N	8.45 W
Athens, Ont., Can.	264	44.38 N	75.57 W
Athens → Athínai, Ellás	172	37.58 N	23.43 E
Athens, Ala., U.S.	248	34.48 N	86.58 W
Athens, Ga., U.S.	246	33.57 N	83.23 W
Athens, Ill., U.S.	248	39.58 N	89.44 W
Athens, La., U.S.	248	32.39 N	93.01 W
Athens, Maine, U.S.	242	44.55 N	69.41 W
Athens, Mich., U.S.	268	42.05 N	85.14 W
Athens, N.Y., U.S.	261	42.16 N	73.49 W
Athens, Ohio, U.S.	242	39.20 N	82.06 W
Athens, Pa., U.S.	242	41.57 N	76.31 W
Athens, Tenn., U.S.	246	35.27 N	84.36 W
Athens, Tex., U.S.	250	32.12 N	95.51 W
Athens, W. Va., U.S.	246	37.25 N	81.01 W
Athens, Wis., U.S.	244	45.02 N	90.05 W
Atherley	264	44.36 N	79.22 W
Atherton, Austl.	228	17.16 S	145.29 E
Atherton, Calif., U.S.	272	37.28 N	122.12 W
Athínai (Athens)	172	37.58 N	23.43 E
Athlone	162	53.25 N	7.56 W
Athol	261	42.36 N	72.14 W
Athol Springs	264	42.46 N	78.52 W
Áthos ∧	172	40.09 N	24.19 E
Athy	162	53.00 N	7.00 W
Ati	214	13.13 N	18.20 E
Atico	292	16.12 S	73.37 W
Aticonipi, Lac ⊜	240	51.52 N	59.22 W
Atienza	168	41.12 N	2.52 W
Atikokan	244	48.45 N	91.37 W
Atikonak Lake ⊜	232	52.40 N	64.30 W
Atil	254	30.50 N	111.35 W
Atimonan	202	14.00 N	121.55 E
Atiquizaya	280	13.58 N	89.46 W
Atitlán, Lago de ⊜	280	14.41 N	91.12 W
Atitlán, Volcán ∧[1]	280	14.35 N	91.11 W
Atka, S.S.S.R.	186	60.50 N	151.48 E
Atka, Alaska, U.S.	236	52.12 N	174.12 W
Atka Island I	236	52.15 N	174.30 W
Atkarsk	158	51.52 N	45.00 E
Atkins	248	35.14 N	92.56 W
Atkinson, Ga., U.S.	246	31.13 N	81.51 W
Atkinson, Ill., U.S.	244	41.25 N	90.01 W
Atkinson, Nebr., U.S.	252	42.32 N	98.59 W
Atkinson, N.H., U.S.	261	42.51 N	71.10 W
Atkinson, N.C., U.S.	246	34.28 N	78.06 W
Atlacomulco [de Fabela]	278	19.48 N	99.53 W
Atlanta, Ga., U.S.	246	33.45 N	84.23 W
Atlanta, Idaho, U.S.	256	43.48 N	115.08 W
Atlanta, Ill., U.S.	248	40.16 N	89.14 W
Atlanta, Mich., U.S.	244	45.00 N	84.09 W
Atlanta, Mo., U.S.	248	39.54 N	92.29 W
Atlanta, Tex., U.S.	248	33.07 N	94.10 W
Atlantic, Iowa, U.S.	252	41.24 N	95.01 W
Atlantic, N.C., U.S.	246	34.54 N	76.20 W
Atlantic, Pa., U.S.	266	41.30 N	80.21 W
Atlantic, Va., U.S.	262	37.54 N	75.30 W
Atlantic □[6]	262	39.27 N	74.44 W
Atlantic City	262	39.22 N	74.26 W
Atlantic Highlands	262	40.25 N	74.03 W
Atlantic-Indian Basin ÷[1]	148	60.00 S	15.00 E
Atlantic Indian Ridge ÷[3]	148	54.00 S	20.00 E
Atlántico □[5]	290	10.45 N	45.00 W
Atlantic Ocean ⊤[1]	148	0.00	25.00 W
Atlantic Peak ∧	254	42.37 N	108.55 W
Atlántida	294	34.46 S	55.45 W
Atlántida □[5]	280	15.30 N	87.00 W
Atlantique □[5]	222	6.35 N	2.15 E
Atlas	262	40.48 N	76.26 W
Atlasburg	266	40.20 N	80.23 W
Atlas Mountains ⋀	214	33.00 N	2.00 W
Atlasova, Ostrov I	186	50.53 N	155.27 E
Atlas Saharien ⋀	214	33.25 N	1.20 E
Atlas Tellien ⋀	214	35.00 N	3.00 E
Atlin	236	59.35 N	133.42 W
Atlin Lake ⊜	236	59.20 N	133.45 W
Atmore	248	31.02 N	87.29 W
Atna Peak ∧	238	53.57 N	128.03 W
Atna Range ⋀	238	55.25 N	127.00 W
Atnarko ≃	238	52.22 N	126.04 W
Atocha	292	20.56 S	66.14 W
Atoka	250	34.23 N	96.08 W
Atomic City	256	43.27 N	112.49 W
Atotonilco, Méx.	250	26.02 N	104.37 W
Atotonilco, Méx.	278	24.15 N	102.45 W
Atotonilco, Cerro ⋀	250	26.08 N	104.38 W
Atotonilco el Alto	278	20.33 N	102.31 W
Atoyac de Alvarez	278	17.12 N	100.26 W
Atrak (Atrek) ≃	208	37.28 N	53.57 E
Atrek (Atrak) ≃	208	37.28 N	53.57 E
Atri	184	42.35 N	13.58 E
Atripalda	184	40.55 N	14.50 E
Atrisco	254	34.59 N	106.41 W
Atsugi	192	35.27 N	139.22 E
Atsumi, Nihon	192	34.37 N	137.07 E
Atsumi, Nihon	192	38.37 N	139.35 E
Atsumi-hantō ≻[1]	192	34.39 N	137.15 E
Aţ-Ţafīlah	210	30.50 N	35.37 E
Aţ-Ţā'if	214	21.16 N	40.24 E
Attalla	248	34.01 N	86.05 W
Attáviros ∧	212	36.10 N	27.45 E
Attawapiskat	232	52.55 N	82.26 W
Attawapiskat Lake ⊜	232	52.18 N	87.54 W
Attawaugan	261	41.52 N	71.53 W
Aţ-Ţawīl ⋀	208	29.20 N	39.35 E
At-Taysīyah ≍	208	28.00 N	44.00 E
Attendorn	178	51.07 N	7.54 E
Attersee	164	47.55 N	13.33 E
Attersee ⊜	164	47.52 N	13.33 E
Attica, Ind., U.S.	268	40.17 N	87.15 W
Attica, Kans., U.S.	252	37.15 N	98.13 W
Attica, N.Y., U.S.	264	42.52 N	78.17 W
Attica, Ohio, U.S.	266	41.04 N	82.53 W
Attigny	166	49.29 N	4.35 E
Attikí □[5]	172	38.00 N	23.30 E
Attikí ◄[1]	172	38.00 N	23.30 E
Attleboro	261	41.56 N	71.17 W
Attnang	164	48.01 N	13.43 E
Attopeu	200	14.48 N	106.50 E
Attow, Ben ∧	162	57.14 N	5.17 W
Attu	237a	52.56 N	174.45 E
Attu Island I	237a	52.55 N	173.00 E
Atucha	294	33.58 S	59.17 W
Atuntagui	290	0.20 N	78.13 W
At'urjevo	160	54.21 N	43.19 E
Åtvidaberg	160	58.12 N	16.00 E
Atwater, Calif., U.S.	272	37.21 N	120.36 W
Atwater, Minn., U.S.	252	45.08 N	94.47 W
Atwater, Ohio, U.S.	266	41.01 N	81.10 W
Atwood, Ont., Can.	264	43.40 N	81.01 W
Atwood, Ill., U.S.	248	39.48 N	88.28 W
Atwood, Ind., U.S.	268	41.16 N	85.59 W
Atwood, Kans., U.S.	252	39.48 N	101.03 W
Atwood, Tenn., U.S.	248	35.59 N	88.41 W
Auasberge ⋀	224	22.45 S	17.22 E
Auati Paraná ≃[1]	290	1.51 S	65.37 W
Auau Channel U	275d	20.51 N	156.45 W
Aubagne	182	43.17 N	5.34 E
Aube □[5]	176	48.15 N	4.05 E
Aube ≃	166	48.34 N	3.43 E
Aubenas	182	44.37 N	4.23 E
Auberive	166	47.47 N	5.03 E
Auberry	272	37.05 N	119.29 W
Aubervilliers	176	48.55 N	2.23 E
Aubigny-en-Artois	162	50.21 N	2.35 E
Aubigny-sur-Nère	166	47.29 N	2.26 E
Aubin	166	44.32 N	2.14 E
Aubinadong ≃	244	46.51 N	83.22 W
Aubrac, Monts d' ⋀	166	44.40 N	3.00 E
Aubry Lake ⊜	236	67.23 N	126.30 W
Auburn, Ala., U.S.	248	32.36 N	85.29 W
Auburn, Calif., U.S.	272	38.54 N	121.04 W
Auburn, Ill., U.S.	248	39.36 N	89.45 W
Auburn, Ind., U.S.	268	41.22 N	85.04 W
Auburn, Ky., U.S.	248	36.52 N	86.43 W
Auburn, Maine, U.S.	242	44.06 N	70.14 W
Auburn, Mass., U.S.	261	42.12 N	71.50 W
Auburn, Mich., U.S.	244	43.36 N	84.04 W
Auburn, Nebr., U.S.	252	40.23 N	95.51 W
Auburn, N.Y., U.S.	264	42.56 N	76.34 W
Auburn, Pa., U.S.	262	40.36 N	76.06 W
Auburn, Wash., U.S.	270	47.18 N	122.13 W
Auburn ≃	228	25.38 S	151.12 E
Auburn Heights	268	42.41 N	83.15 W
Auburn Range ⋀	228	25.10 S	150.30 E
Aubusson	166	45.57 N	2.11 E
Auca Mahuída	294	37.53 S	68.31 W
Auca Mahuida, Sierra ⋀	294	37.45 S	69.00 W
Aucará	292	14.17 S	74.06 W
Auce	160	56.28 N	22.53 E
Auch	166	43.39 N	0.35 E
Auchel	176	50.30 N	2.28 E
Auchterarder	162	56.18 N	3.43 W
Auchtermuchty	162	56.17 N	3.15 W
Auckland	230	36.53 S	174.45 E
Aude □[5]	166	43.05 N	2.30 E
Audenge	166	44.41 N	1.31 W
Auderghem	176	50.49 N	4.26 E
Auderville	162	49.43 N	1.56 W
Audierne	166	48.01 N	4.32 W
Audincourt	180	47.29 N	6.50 E
Audubon, Iowa, U.S.	252	41.43 N	94.55 W
Audubon, N.J., U.S.	262	39.54 N	75.04 W
Aue	164	50.35 N	12.42 E
Auerbach	164	50.41 N	12.54 E
Augathella	228	25.48 S	146.35 E
Auglaize □[6]	268	40.34 N	84.12 W
Auglaize ≃	242	41.17 N	84.21 W
Augrabies Falls National Park ♠	224	28.35 S	20.19 E
Augrabiesvalle ᒐ	224	28.35 S	20.19 E
Au Gres	244	44.03 N	83.42 W
Au Gres ≃	244	44.02 N	83.40 W
Augsburg	180	48.23 N	10.53 E
Augusta, Austl.	226	34.19 S	115.10 E
Augusta, It.	170	37.13 N	15.13 E
Augusta, Ark., U.S.	248	35.17 N	91.22 W
Augusta, Ga., U.S.	246	33.29 N	81.57 W
Augusta, Ill., U.S.	248	40.14 N	90.57 W
Augusta, Kans., U.S.	252	37.41 N	96.58 W
Augusta, Ky., U.S.	242	38.46 N	84.00 W
Augusta, Maine, U.S.	242	44.19 N	69.47 W
Augusta, Mich., U.S.	268	42.20 N	85.21 W
Augusta, Mont., U.S.	256	47.30 N	112.24 W
Augusta, Ohio, U.S.	266	40.41 N	81.01 W
Augusta, Wis., U.S.	244	44.41 N	91.07 W
Augusta, Golfo di C	170	37.10 N	15.20 E
Augustdorf	178	51.53 N	8.43 E
Augustine Island I	236	59.22 N	153.28 W
Augustines, Lac des ⊜	244	47.32 N	76.05 W
Augustów	164	53.51 N	22.59 E
Augustowski, Kanał ≌	164	53.54 N	23.26 E
Auiia, Ribeirão ≃	296	12.09 S	53.20 W
Aulander	246	36.14 N	77.06 W
Aulendorf	180	47.57 N	9.38 E
Aulís ⊥	172	38.27 N	23.35 E
Aulitiving Island I	232	69.32 N	67.50 W
Aulla	170	44.12 N	9.58 E
Aulnay-de-Saintonge	166	46.01 N	0.21 W
Aulnay-sous-Bois	176	48.57 N	2.31 E
Aulne ≃	166	48.17 N	4.16 W
Aulneau Peninsula ≻[1]	252	49.23 N	94.29 W
Ault	166	50.06 N	1.27 E
Aultman	266	40.34 N	79.16 W
Aumale	166	49.46 N	1.45 E
Aumont-Aubrac	166	44.43 N	3.17 E
Aumühle	178	53.31 N	10.19 E
Auneau	166	48.27 N	1.46 E
Auob ≃	224	26.25 S	20.35 E
Aur, Pulau I	200	2.27 N	104.31 E
Auray	166	47.40 N	2.59 W
Aure	160	63.16 N	8.32 E
Aurelius	268	42.31 N	84.31 W
Aurich	178	53.28 N	7.29 E
Aurich □[6]	178	53.20 N	7.20 E
Auriflama	296	20.41 S	50.34 W
Aurilândia	296	16.44 S	50.28 W
Aurillac	166	44.56 N	2.26 E
Aurine, Alpi (Zillertaler Alpen) ⋀	164	47.00 N	11.55 E
Auronzo di Cadore	170	46.33 N	12.26 E
Aurora, Ont., Can.	264	44.00 N	79.28 W
Aurora, Pil.	202	13.21 N	122.31 E
Aurora, Alaska, U.S.	236	64.51 N	147.46 W
Aurora, Colo., U.S.	254	39.44 N	104.52 W
Aurora, Ill., U.S.	268	42.46 N	88.19 W
Aurora, Ind., U.S.	248	39.04 N	84.54 W
Aurora, Maine, U.S.	240	44.51 N	68.20 W
Aurora, Minn., U.S.	244	47.31 N	92.14 W
Aurora, Mo., U.S.	248	36.58 N	93.43 W
Aurora, Nebr., U.S.	252	40.52 N	98.00 W
Aurora, N.C., U.S.	246	35.18 N	76.47 W
Aurora, N.Y., U.S.	264	42.46 N	76.42 W
Aurora, Ohio, U.S.	266	41.19 N	81.21 W
Aurora, Oreg., U.S.	270	45.14 N	122.45 W
Aurora, Utah, U.S.	254	38.55 N	111.56 W
Aurora, W. Va., U.S.	242	39.19 N	79.33 W
Aurukun Mission	226	13.19 S	141.45 E
Aus	218	26.40 S	16.15 E
Ausable ≃, Ont., Can.	244	43.19 N	81.46 W
Au Sable ≃, Mich., U.S.	244	44.25 N	83.20 W
Au Sable Forks	242	44.27 N	73.41 W
Au Sable Point ≻	244	44.20 N	83.20 W
Ausangate, Nevado ∧	292	13.47 S	71.13 W
Auschwitz → Oświęcim	164	50.03 N	19.12 E
Aussig → Ústí nad Labem	164	50.40 N	14.02 E
Aust-Agder □[6]	160	58.50 N	8.00 E
Austerlitz	261	42.19 N	73.28 W
Austin, Man., Can.	252	49.57 N	98.56 W
Austin, Ind., U.S.	248	38.45 N	85.48 W
Austin, Minn., U.S.	244	43.40 N	92.59 W
Austin, Nev., U.S.	258	39.30 N	117.04 W
Austin, Pa., U.S.	266	41.38 N	78.05 W
Austin, Tex., U.S.	250	30.16 N	97.45 W
Austinburg	266	41.46 N	80.51 W
Austin Channel U	232	75.35 N	103.25 W
Austintown	266	41.06 N	80.46 W
Austinville	246	36.51 N	80.55 W
Austonio	250	31.11 N	95.38 W
Australia □[1]	226	25.00 S	135.00 E
Australia Mountain ∧	236	63.36 N	138.08 W
Australian Alps ⋀	228	37.00 S	148.00 E
Australian-Antarctic Rise ÷[3]	148	50.00 S	130.00 E
Australian Capital Territory □[8]	228	35.30 S	149.00 E
Austral Seamount Chain ÷[3]	148	24.00 S	150.00 W
Austria □[1]	158	47.20 N	13.20 E
Austvågøya I	160	68.20 N	14.36 E
Autazes	290	3.35 S	59.08 W
Authie ≃	166	50.21 N	1.38 E
Autlán de Navarro	278	19.46 N	104.22 W
Autun	166	46.57 N	4.18 E
Auvergne □[9]	166	45.25 N	2.30 E
Auvézère ≃	166	45.12 N	0.51 E
Aux Barques, Pointe ≻	244	44.04 N	82.58 W
Auxerre	176	47.48 N	3.34 E
Auxier	246	37.44 N	82.46 W
Auxi-le-Château	166	50.14 N	2.07 E
Auxonne	166	47.12 N	5.23 E
Auxvasse	248	39.01 N	91.54 W
Auyán-Tepuí ∧	290	5.55 N	62.32 W
Auzances	166	46.02 N	2.30 E
Ava, Ill., U.S.	248	37.53 N	89.30 W
Ava, Mo., U.S.	248	36.57 N	92.40 W
Avaí	296	22.08 S	49.22 W
Avala ⊥	172	44.45 N	20.35 E
Avallon	176	47.29 N	3.54 E
Avalon, Calif., U.S.	274	33.49 N	118.16 W
Avalon, N.J., U.S.	262	39.06 N	74.43 W
Avalon, Pa., U.S.	266	40.30 N	80.04 W
Avalon, Wis., U.S.	268	42.38 N	88.52 W
Avalon Peninsula ≻[1]	240	47.30 N	53.30 W
Avant	250	36.29 N	96.04 W
Avaré	296	23.05 S	48.55 W
Avatanak Island I	236	54.03 N	165.19 W
'Avdat ⊥	210	30.38 N	34.46 E
Ave ≃	168	41.20 N	8.45 W
Avegadje ∧	222	7.14 N	0.38 E
Aveiro	168	40.38 N	8.39 W
Aveiro, Ria de ≃[1]	168	40.38 N	8.44 W
Avelgem	176	50.46 N	3.26 E
Avella, It.	184	40.58 N	14.36 E
Avella, Pa., U.S.	266	40.17 N	80.28 W
Avellaneda, Arg.	294	34.40 S	58.20 W
Avellaneda, Arg.	294	29.07 S	59.40 W
Avellino	184	40.54 N	14.47 E
Avellino □[4]	184	40.57 N	15.00 E
Avenal	272	36.00 N	120.08 W
Aven Armand •[5]	166	44.15 N	3.22 E
Avenue	262	38.17 N	76.45 W
Avenwedde	178	51.55 N	8.27 E
Averill Park	261	42.38 N	73.33 W
Aversa	184	40.58 N	14.12 E
Avery, Idaho, U.S.	256	47.15 N	115.49 W
Avery, Tex., U.S.	248	33.33 N	94.47 W
Avery Island	248	29.55 N	91.55 W
Aves, Islas de II	290	12.00 N	67.30 W
Avesnes	166	50.07 N	3.56 E
Avesnes-sur-Helpe	176	50.07 N	3.56 E
Avesta	160	60.09 N	16.12 E
Aveyron □[5]	166	44.15 N	2.40 E
Aveyron ≃	166	44.05 N	1.16 E
Avezzano	184	42.02 N	13.25 E
Aviemore	162	57.12 N	3.50 W
Avigliana	182	45.05 N	7.23 E
Avigliano	170	40.44 N	15.44 E
Avignon	182	43.57 N	4.49 E
Ávila	168	40.39 N	4.42 W
Avila, Parque Nacional el ♠	290	10.35 N	66.48 W
Ávila, Sierra de ⋀	168	40.35 N	5.08 W
Avila Beach	272	35.11 N	120.44 W
Avilés	168	43.33 N	5.55 W
Avilla	268	41.22 N	85.14 W
Avion	176	50.24 N	2.50 E
Avis	242	41.11 N	77.19 W
Aviz	168	39.03 N	7.53 W
Avlan Gölü ⊜	212	36.34 N	29.57 E
Avoca, Iowa, U.S.	252	41.29 N	95.20 W
Avoca, N.Y., U.S.	242	42.25 N	77.25 W
Avola, B.C., Can.	238	51.47 N	119.19 W
Avola, It.	170	36.54 N	15.09 E
Avon, Fr.	176	48.24 N	2.43 E
Avon, Conn., U.S.	261	41.49 N	72.50 W
Avon, Ill., U.S.	244	40.40 N	90.26 W
Avon, Mass., U.S.	261	42.08 N	71.02 W
Avon, Mont., U.S.	256	46.36 N	112.36 W
Avon, N.C., U.S.	246	35.21 N	75.30 W
Avon, N.Y., U.S.	264	42.55 N	77.45 W
Avon, Ohio, U.S.	266	41.27 N	82.01 W
Avon, Pa., U.S.	262	40.22 N	76.23 W
Avon, S. Dak., U.S.	252	43.00 N	98.04 W
Avon ≃, N.S., Can.	240	45.10 N	64.15 W
Avon ≃, Eng., U.K.	162	50.43 N	1.46 W
Avon by the Sea	262	40.12 N	74.01 W
Avondale, Ariz., U.S.	254	33.26 N	112.21 W
Avondale, Colo., U.S.	252	38.14 N	104.21 W
Avondale, La., U.S.	248	29.55 N	90.11 W
Avondale, Ohio, U.S.	266	40.53 N	81.26 W
Avon Downs	226	20.05 S	137.30 E
Avon Lake	266	41.30 N	82.01 W
Avonmore, Ont., Can.	260	45.10 N	74.58 W
Avonmore, Pa., U.S.	266	40.32 N	79.28 W
Avon Park	246	27.36 N	81.31 W
Avranches	166	48.41 N	1.22 W
Avre ≃	166	49.53 N	2.20 E
Avşar Adası I	212	40.30 N	27.30 E
Awaji	192	34.35 N	135.01 E
Awaji-shima I	192	34.21 N	134.51 E
Awara	192	36.13 N	136.12 E
Awarua Bay C	230	44.28 S	168.04 E
Awarua Point ≻	230	44.15 S	168.03 E
Awasan Bay C	202	9.55 N	125.35 E
Awash	214	8.59 N	40.10 E
Awash ≃	220	11.45 N	41.05 E
Awa-shima I	192	38.27 N	139.14 E
Awaso	214	6.14 N	2.16 W
Awatere ≃	230	41.37 S	174.10 E
Awbārī	214	26.35 N	12.46 E
Awe, Loch ⊜	162	56.15 N	5.15 W
Awjilah	214	29.09 N	21.15 E
Awka	222	6.12 N	7.05 E
Awuna ≃	236	69.04 N	155.30 W
Axarfjörður C	160a	66.15 N	16.45 W
Axat	166	42.48 N	2.14 E
Axel	178	51.16 N	3.55 E
Axim	214	4.52 N	2.14 W
Axinim	290	4.02 S	59.22 W
Axiós (Vardar) ≃	172	40.31 N	22.43 E
Ax-les-Thermes	166	42.43 N	1.50 E
Axminster	174	50.47 N	3.00 W
Axtell, Kans., U.S.	252	39.52 N	96.15 W
Axtell, Nebr., U.S.	252	40.29 N	99.08 W
Ayabaca	290	4.39 S	79.40 W
Ayabe	192	35.18 N	135.15 E
Ayacucho, Arg.	294	37.10 S	58.30 W
Ayacucho, Bol.	292	17.51 S	63.20 W
Ayacucho, Perú	292	13.07 S	74.13 W
Ayacucho □[5]	292	14.00 S	74.00 W
Ayamonte	168	37.13 N	7.24 W
Ayapel	290	8.19 N	75.09 W
Ayarza, Laguna de ⊜	280	14.25 N	90.07 W
Ayaviri	292	14.52 S	70.35 W
Ayden	246	35.25 N	77.20 W
Aydın	212	37.51 N	27.51 E
Aydın □[4]	172	37.45 N	28.00 E
Aydın Dağları ⋀	212	38.00 N	28.00 E
Ayer	261	42.34 N	71.35 W
Ayers Cliff	260	45.10 N	72.03 W
Ayersville	268	41.14 N	84.17 W
Aygues ≃	166	44.07 N	4.43 E
Ayía Marína	172	37.09 N	26.52 E
Áyion Óros □[8]	172	40.15 N	24.15 E
Áyion Óros ◄[1]	172	40.15 N	24.15 E
Áyios Andréas, Akrotírion ≻	212	35.40 N	34.35 E
Áyios Kírikos	172	37.37 N	26.14 E
Áyios Nikólaos	172	35.11 N	25.42 E
Aylesbury	174	51.50 N	0.50 W
Aylmer, Mount ∧	238	51.19 N	115.26 W
Aylmer East, Ont., Can.	264	42.46 N	80.59 W
Aylmer East, Qué., Can.	242	45.24 N	75.52 W
Aylmer Lake ⊜	232	64.05 N	108.30 W
Aylmer Sound U	240	50.30 N	59.32 W
Aylmer West	264	42.46 N	80.59 W
'Ayn Dār	214	25.59 N	49.23 E
Aynor	246	34.00 N	79.12 W
Ayo	292	15.40 S	72.18 W
Ayo Ayo	292	17.05 S	68.00 W
Ayoquezco	278	16.41 N	96.50 W
Ayora	168	39.04 N	1.03 W
'Ayoûn el 'Atroûs	214	16.40 N	9.37 W
Ayr, Austl.	228	19.35 S	147.24 E
Ayr, Ont., Can.	264	43.17 N	80.27 W
Ayr, Scot., U.K.	162	55.28 N	4.38 W
Ayr □[6]	162	55.25 N	4.25 W
Ayre, Point of ≻	162	54.26 N	4.22 W
Ayrolle, Étang de l' ⊜	166	43.05 N	3.03 E
Ayton	264	44.03 N	80.56 W
Ayun ≃	200	13.24 N	108.28 E
Ayuñgon	202	9.51 N	123.08 E
Ayutla	278	20.07 N	104.22 W
Ayutla [de los Libres]	278	16.54 N	99.13 W
Ayvacık, Tür.	172	40.04 N	27.43 E
Ayvacık, Tür.	172	39.36 N	26.24 E
Ayvalık	172	39.18 N	26.41 E
Azacualpa, Hond.	280	14.27 N	86.09 W
Azacualpa, Hond.	280	15.19 N	88.33 W
Azaila	168	41.17 N	0.29 W
Azalea Park	246	28.30 N	81.15 W
Azambuja	168	39.04 N	8.52 W
Azángaro	292	14.55 S	70.13 W
Azaouâd ◄[1]	222	19.00 N	3.00 W
Azaouak, Vallée de l' ∨	222	15.30 N	3.18 E
Azar ∨	222	16.02 N	4.04 E
Azare	222	11.40 N	10.11 E
Azay-le-Rideau	166	47.16 N	0.28 E
Azazga	168	36.48 N	4.30 E
Azbāgh, Kūh-e ∧	208	26.37 N	59.58 E
Azeffoun	168	36.51 N	4.25 E
Azerbaidzhan Soviet Socialist Republic → Azerbajdžanskaja Sovetskaja	186	40.30 N	47.30 E
Azerbajdžanskaja Sovetskaja Socialističeskaja Respublika □[3]	186	40.30 N	47.30 E
Azogues	290	2.44 S	78.50 W
Azores → Açores II	148	38.30 N	28.00 W
Azores-Gibraltar Ridge ÷[3]	148	38.00 N	19.00 W
Azores Plateau ÷[3]	148	38.30 N	30.00 W
Azov	158	47.07 N	39.25 E
Azov, Sea of → Azovskoje More ⊤[2]	158	46.00 N	36.00 E
Azovskoje More ⊤[2]	158	46.00 N	36.00 E
Azpeitia	168	43.11 N	2.16 W
Azraq, Wādī al- ∨	220	10.33 N	28.40 E
Aztec	254	36.49 N	107.59 W
Aztec Peak ∧	254	33.48 N	110.55 W
Aztec Ruins National Monument ♠	254	36.51 N	108.10 W
Azua	282	18.27 N	70.44 W
Azuaga	168	38.16 N	5.41 W
Azuay □[4]	290	3.00 S	79.00 W
Azucena	294	37.30 S	59.18 W
Azuer ≃	168	39.08 N	3.36 W
Azuero, Península de ≻[1]	290	7.40 N	80.30 W
Azuga	172	45.27 N	25.33 E
Azul	294	36.45 S	59.50 W
Azul, Cerro ∧, C.R.	280	9.55 N	85.18 W
Azul, Cerro ∧, Ec.	290a	0.54 S	91.21 W
Azul, Cerro ∧, Hond.	280	14.32 N	88.23 W
Azul, Cordillera ⋀	292	9.00 S	76.00 W
Azul, Serra ⋀[1]	296	14.50 S	54.50 W
'Azūm, Wādī (Bahr Azoum) ∨	220	12.00 N	21.40 E
Azur, Côte d' •[2]	166	43.30 N	7.00 E
Azurduy	292	19.59 S	64.29 W
Azure Lake ⊜	238	52.23 N	120.00 W
Azusa	274	34.08 N	117.55 W
Az-Zabdānī	210	33.43 N	36.05 E
Az-Zahrān	208	26.18 N	50.08 E
Az-Zaqāzīq	220	30.35 N	31.31 E
Az-Zarqā'	210	32.04 N	36.05 E
Az-Zāwiyah	214	32.45 N	12.44 E
Azzel Matti, Sebkha ≍	214	25.55 N	0.56 E
Az-Zilfī	214	26.18 N	44.48 E
Az-Zubayr	208	30.23 N	47.43 E
Azzurra, Grotta •[5]	184	40.35 N	14.14 E
B			
Ba ≃	200	13.05 N	109.18 E
Baao	202	13.27 N	123.22 E
Baar	180	47.12 N	8.32 E
Baarn	178	52.13 N	5.16 E
Baasrode	176	51.02 N	4.10 E
Baba	290	1.47 S	79.40 W
Bāba, Koh-i- ⋀	206	34.40 N	67.20 E
Baba Burnu ≻	212	39.29 N	26.04 E
Babadag, Rom.	172	44.54 N	28.43 E
Babadağ, Tür.	172	37.48 N	28.52 E
Babaeski	172	41.26 N	27.06 E
Babahoyo	290	1.49 S	79.31 W
Babajevo	160	59.23 N	35.56 E
Babar, Kepulauan II	198	7.50 S	129.45 E
Babar, Pulau I	198	7.55 S	129.45 E
Bābayn, Jabal ∧	220	22.38 N	25.00 E
Babb	238	48.51 N	113.26 W
Babbitt, Minn., U.S.	244	47.43 N	91.57 W
Babbitt, Nev., U.S.	258	38.39 N	118.37 W
B'abdā	210	33.50 N	35.32 E
Babel, Mont de ∧	240	51.27 N	68.41 W
Babelthuap I	198	7.30 N	134.36 E
Babi, Pulau I	200	2.05 N	96.39 E
Babia, Arroyo de la ≃	250	28.25 N	101.45 W
Babilônia ≃	296	17.10 S	53.05 W
Babimost (Bomst)	164	52.10 N	15.51 E
Babina Greda	172	45.07 N	18.33 E
Babine	238	55.19 N	126.37 W
Babine ≃	238	55.42 N	127.40 W
Babine Lake ⊜	238	54.45 N	126.00 W
Babine Range ⋀	238	55.00 N	126.25 W
Babo	198	2.33 S	133.25 E
Bābol	208	36.34 N	52.42 E
Bābol Sar	208	36.43 N	52.39 E
Babonā ≃	292	6.35 S	66.27 W
Baboquivari Mountains ⋀	254	31.45 N	111.35 W
Baboquivari Peak ∧	254	31.46 N	111.35 W
Babor, Djebel ∧	168	36.34 N	5.27 E
Baborów (Bauerwitz)	164	50.09 N	17.59 E
Bab-Taza	168	35.03 N	5.14 W
Babuškin	186	51.41 N	105.54 E
Babuyan	202	10.00 N	118.54 E
Babuyan Channel U	202	18.40 N	121.30 E
Babuyan Island I	202	19.32 N	121.57 E
Babuyan Islands II	202	19.10 N	121.40 E
Babylon	242	40.42 N	73.20 W
Babylon ⊥	208	32.33 N	44.24 E
Bacabal	286	4.14 S	44.47 W
Bacacay	202	13.18 N	123.47 E
Bacalar, Laguna de ⊜	278	18.45 N	88.16 W
Bacao	202	10.27 N	119.48 E
Bacarra	202	18.15 N	120.37 E
Bacău	172	46.34 N	26.55 E
Baccalieu Island I	240	48.08 N	52.48 W
Bac-can	200	22.08 N	105.49 E
Baccarat	180	48.27 N	6.45 E
Bacchus Marsh	228	37.41 S	144.27 E
Bacerac	278	30.18 N	108.50 W
Bac-giang	200	21.16 N	106.11 E
Bachaquero	290	9.56 N	71.08 W
Bacharden	208	38.26 N	57.25 E
Bachardok	186	38.46 N	58.30 E
Bachawan	202	12.28 N	122.06 E
Bachíniva	278	28.45 N	107.15 W
Bachta	186	62.28 N	89.00 E
Bachu	190	39.50 N	78.20 E
Back ≃	232	67.15 N	95.15 W
Bačka ◄[1]	172	45.50 N	19.30 E
Bačka Palanka	172	45.15 N	19.24 E
Bačka Topola	172	45.49 N	19.38 E
Backbone Ranges ⋀	236	63.30 N	129.00 W
Bački Petrovac	172	45.22 N	19.35 E
Backnang	164	48.56 N	9.25 E
Backstairs Passage U	228	35.42 S	138.05 E
Backwater Draw ∨	250	33.35 N	101.50 W
Bac-ninh	200	21.11 N	106.03 E
Baco, Mount ∧	202	12.55 N	121.08 E
Bacoachi	278	30.38 N	109.56 W
Bacoli	184	40.48 N	14.05 E
Bacolod	202	10.40 N	122.57 E
Bacon	202	13.03 N	124.03 E
Baconton	246	31.23 N	84.10 W
Bacoor	202	14.28 N	120.56 E
Bácsalmás	172	46.08 N	19.20 E
Bács-Kiskun □[6]	164	46.30 N	19.25 E
Bacuag	202	9.37 N	125.38 E
Bacuit Bay C	202	11.08 N	119.15 E
Bácum	278	27.33 N	110.05 W
Bacungan	202	9.56 N	118.42 E
Bačurka	160	68.32 N	56.57 E
Bacuyangan	202	9.39 N	122.27 E
Bad ≃, Mich., U.S.	244	43.18 N	84.06 W
Bad ≃, S. Dak., U.S.	252	44.22 N	100.22 W
Bad ≃, Wis., U.S.	244	46.38 N	90.40 W
Badajós, Lago ⊜	290	3.15 S	62.47 W
Badajoz	168	38.53 N	6.58 W
Badak, Gunung ∧	200	4.03 N	97.48 E
Badakhshān □[4]	206	36.45 N	72.00 E
Badalona	168	41.27 N	2.15 E
Badanah	208	30.59 N	41.02 E
Badas, Kepulauan II	200	0.35 N	107.06 E
Bad Aussee	164	47.36 N	13.47 E
Bad Axe	244	43.48 N	83.00 W
Bad Bergzabern	164	49.07 N	8.00 E
Bad Blankenburg	164	50.41 N	11.16 E
Bad Bramstedt	178	53.55 N	9.53 E
Baddeck	240	46.07 N	60.48 W
Baddo ≃	206	27.59 N	64.21 E
Bad Doberan	164	54.06 N	11.53 E
Bad Driburg	178	51.44 N	9.01 E
Bad Dürkheim	164	49.28 N	8.10 E
Bad Dürrenberg	164	51.18 N	12.04 E
Bad Dürrheim	180	48.01 N	8.32 E
Bad Ems	164	50.20 N	7.43 E
Baden, Ont., Can.	264	43.24 N	80.39 W
Baden, Öst.	164	48.00 N	16.14 E
Baden, Schw.	180	47.29 N	8.18 E
Baden, Pa., U.S.	266	40.38 N	80.14 W
Baden-Baden	164	48.46 N	8.14 E
Badenweiler	164	47.48 N	7.40 E
Baden-Württemberg □[3]	180	48.30 N	9.00 E
Bad Freienwalde	164	52.47 N	14.01 E
Bad Gandersheim	178	51.52 N	10.01 E
Badgastein	164	47.07 N	13.08 E
Badger, Newf., Can.	240	48.58 N	56.03 W
Badger, Minn., U.S.	252	48.47 N	96.01 W
Bādghis □[4]	206	35.00 N	63.45 E
Bad Godesberg	164	50.41 N	7.10 E
Bad Hall	164	48.02 N	14.13 E
Bad Harzburg	164	51.53 N	10.33 E
Bad Hersfeld	164	50.52 N	9.42 E
Badhoevedorp	178	52.21 N	4.46 E
Bad Homburg vor der Höhe	164	50.13 N	8.37 E
Bad Honnef	164	50.39 N	7.13 E
Badinko ≃	222	13.42 N	9.35 W
Badin Lake ⊜[1]	246	35.27 N	80.06 W
Badiraguato	278	25.22 N	107.31 W
Bad Ischl	164	47.43 N	13.37 E
Bad Kissingen	164	50.12 N	10.04 E
Bad Kreuznach	164	49.52 N	7.51 E
Badlands ⋀	252	46.45 N	103.30 W
Badlands ⋀[2]	252	43.30 N	102.20 W
Badlands National Monument ♠	252	43.47 N	102.15 W
Bad Langensalza	164	51.06 N	10.38 E
Bad Lauterberg	178	51.38 N	10.28 E
Bad Leonfelden	164	48.33 N	14.19 E
Bad Liebenwerda	164	51.31 N	13.23 E
Bad Lippspringe	178	51.46 N	8.49 E
Bad Mergentheim	164	49.30 N	9.46 E
Bad Münder	178	52.12 N	9.27 E
Bad Muskau	164	51.32 N	14.43 E
Bad Nauheim	164	50.22 N	8.44 E
Bad Nenndorf	178	52.20 N	9.22 E
Bad Neustadt an der Saale	164	50.19 N	10.13 E
Bad Oeynhausen	178	52.12 N	8.48 E
Bad Oldesloe	178	53.48 N	10.22 E
Bad Orb	164	50.14 N	9.20 E
Bad Pyrmont	178	51.59 N	9.15 E
Bad Ragaz	166	47.00 N	9.30 E
Bad Reichenhall	164	47.43 N	12.52 E
Badreïna ⊤[4]	222	17.44 N	11.05 W
Bad River Indian Reservation ◄[4]	244	46.33 N	90.40 W
Bad Sachsa	164	51.36 N	10.32 E
Bad Salzdetfurth	178	52.03 N	10.01 E
Bad Salzuflen	178	52.05 N	8.44 E
Bad Salzungen	164	50.48 N	10.13 E
Bad Sankt Leonhard im Lavanttal	164	46.58 N	14.48 E
Bad Schwalbach	164	50.08 N	8.04 E
Bad Schwartau	164	53.55 N	10.40 E
Bad Segeberg	178	53.56 N	10.17 E
Bad Sooden-Allendorf	178	51.16 N	9.58 E
Bad Tölz	164	47.46 N	11.34 E
Bad Vöslau	164	47.57 N	16.16 E
Bad Waldsee	180	47.55 N	9.45 E
Bad Wildungen	178	51.07 N	9.07 E
Bad Wörishofen	180	48.00 N	10.36 E
Bad Zwischenahn	178	53.11 N	8.00 E
Baena	168	37.37 N	4.19 W
Baependi	296	21.57 S	44.53 W
Báez	284p	22.13 N	79.45 W
Baeza, Ec.	290	0.27 S	77.53 W
Baeza, Esp.	168	37.59 N	3.28 W
Baezaeko ≃	238	53.09 N	123.48 W
Bafa Gölü ⊜	212	37.30 N	27.25 E
Bafatá	214	12.10 N	14.40 W
Baffin Basin ÷[1]	148	73.00 N	68.00 W
Baffin Bay C, N.A.	148	73.00 N	66.00 W
Baffin Bay C, Tex., U.S.	250	27.15 N	97.33 W
Baffin Island I	232	68.00 N	70.00 W
Bafing ≃	222	13.49 N	10.50 W
Bafoulabé	214	13.48 N	10.50 W
Bafra	212	41.34 N	35.56 E
Bafra Burnu ≻	212	41.44 N	35.58 E
Bafwasende	218	1.05 N	27.16 E
Bagabag	202	16.37 N	121.15 E
Bagac	202	14.36 N	120.23 E
Bagacay Point ≻	202	8.58 N	124.46 E
Bagac Bay C	202	14.34 N	120.20 E
Bagaces	280	10.31 N	85.15 W
Bagahak, Gunong ∧	202	5.03 N	118.44 E
Bagahu ⊜	186	46.57 N	87.27 E
Bagamanoc	202	13.57 N	124.17 E
Bagamoyo	218	6.26 S	38.54 E
Bagañga	202	7.34 N	126.33 E
Bagansiapi-api	200	2.09 N	100.48 E
Bağarası	172	37.42 N	27.33 E
Bagbe ≃	222	8.42 N	11.15 W
Bagdad, Ariz., U.S.	254	34.34 N	113.11 W
Bagdad, Fla., U.S.	248	30.36 N	87.02 W
Bagdad, Ky., U.S.	248	38.16 N	85.04 W
Bagdarin	186	54.26 N	113.36 E
Bagé	294	31.20 S	54.06 W
Baggao	202	17.56 N	121.46 E
Baggeryd	160	57.30 N	14.07 E
Baggs	254	41.02 N	107.39 W
Baghdād	208	33.21 N	44.25 E
Baghdād □[4]	208	34.00 N	43.46 E
Bagheria	170	38.05 N	13.30 E
Bāghlān	206	36.14 N	68.46 E
Bāghlān □[4]	206	35.45 N	69.00 E
Bağırpaşa Dağı ∧	212	39.30 N	40.06 E
Bagley	252	47.31 N	95.24 W
Bagn	160	60.49 N	9.34 E
Bagnacavallo	184	44.25 N	12.00 E
Bagnara Cálabra	170	38.18 N	15.49 E
Bagnères-de-Bigorre	166	43.04 N	0.09 E
Bagnères-de-Luchon	166	42.47 N	0.36 E
Bagni di Lucca	184	44.01 N	10.35 E
Bagno a Ripoli	184	43.45 N	11.19 E
Bagno di Romagna	170	43.50 N	11.57 E
Bagnols-sur-Cèze	182	44.10 N	4.37 E
Bago ≃	202	10.30 N	122.50 E
Bagoé ≃	222	12.36 N	6.34 W
Bagolino	170	45.49 N	10.28 E
Bagot □[6]	260	45.40 N	72.45 W
Bagotville	240	48.21 N	70.53 W
Bagrationovsk (Preussisch Eylau)	164	54.23 N	20.39 E
Bagua	292	5.35 S	78.22 W
Baguio	202	16.25 N	120.36 E
Bagur, Cabo ≻	168	41.57 N	3.14 E
Bagzane, Monts ⋀	222	17.43 N	8.45 E
Bahamas □[2]	276	24.15 N	76.00 W
Bahār	208	34.54 N	48.26 E
Bahāwalnagar	206	29.59 N	73.16 E
Bahāwalpur	206	29.24 N	71.41 E
Bahi	202	13.53 N	123.38 E
Bahía → Salvador	296	12.59 S	38.31 W
Bahia □[3]	296	12.00 S	42.00 W
Bahía, Islas de la II	280	16.20 N	86.30 W
Bahía Blanca	294	38.44 S	62.16 W
Bahía de Caráquez	290	0.36 S	80.25 W
Bahía Honda	284p	22.54 N	83.10 W
Bahia Honda Point ≻	202	9.25 N	118.08 E
Bahía Kino	278	28.50 N	111.55 W
Bahía Negra	292	20.15 S	58.12 W
Bahir Dar	214	11.35 N	37.28 E
Bahoruco, Sierra de ∧	282	18.20 N	71.35 W
Bahraich	206	27.36 N	81.36 E
Bahrain □[1]	204	26.00 N	50.30 E
Baḥr al-Ghazāl □[4]	220	8.00 N	28.00 E
Baḥrānī, Ḥālat al- I	208	24.22 N	54.15 E
Baia-de-Aramă	172	45.00 N	22.49 E
Baia-Mare	172	47.40 N	23.35 E
Baia Sprie	172	47.40 N	23.42 E
Bai-bung, Mui ≻	200	8.36 N	104.43 E
Baicaoling ⋀	200	26.10 N	101.20 E
Baicheng	190	41.46 N	81.52 E
Baidoa	214	3.04 N	43.48 E
Baie-Comeau	240	49.13 N	68.10 W
Baie-des-ha! Ha!	240	50.56 N	58.58 W
Baie-de-Shawinigan	260	46.34 N	72.45 W
Baie-d'Urfé	260	45.25 N	73.55 W
Baie-Johan-Beetz	240	50.17 N	62.48 W
Baie-Mahault	285o	16.16 N	61.35 W
Baiersbronn	180	48.30 N	8.22 E
Baies, Lac des ⊜	244	47.18 N	77.40 W
Baie-Saint-Claire	240	49.53 N	64.29 W
Baie-Saint-Paul	240	47.27 N	70.30 W
Baie-Trinité	240	49.24 N	67.19 W
Baie Verte	240	49.56 N	56.11 W
Baieville	260	46.08 N	72.43 W
Baigneux-les-Juifs	166	47.36 N	4.38 E
Baihe ≃	194	40.22 N	116.19 E
Baihu ⊜, Zhg.	196	31.16 N	117.30 E
Bailadores	290	8.15 N	71.50 W
Baile Átha Cliath → Dublin	162	53.20 N	6.15 W
Băile Govora	172	45.05 N	24.06 E
Băile Herculane	172	44.54 N	22.25 E
Bailén	168	38.06 N	3.46 W
Băile Olănești	172	45.11 N	24.16 E
Băile Slănic	172	46.13 N	26.26 E
Băilești	172	44.02 N	23.21 E
Bailey	246	35.47 N	78.07 W

Symbols in the index entries are identified on page 360.

Name	Page	Lat°′	Long°′
Bailey Lakes	266	40.57 N	82.21 W
Bailleul	176	50.44 N	2.44 E
Baillie ≃	232	65.10 N	104.24 W
Baillieborough	162	53.55 N	6.58 W
Baillie-Hamilton Island I	232	75.53 N	94.35 W
Baillie Islands II	232	70.33 N	128.10 W
Baillies Bacolet	285k	12.02 N	61.41 W
Baillif	285o	16.01 N	61.45 W
Bailuhe ≃	196	32.25 N	115.34 E
Bailuhu ⊜	196	30.03 N	113.06 E
Bainbridge, Ga., U.S.	246	30.54 N	84.34 W
Bainbridge, N.Y., U.S.	242	42.18 N	75.29 W
Bainbridge, Ohio, U.S.	242	39.14 N	83.16 W
Bainbridge, Pa., U.S.	262	40.05 N	76.40 W
Bain-de-Bretagne	166	47.50 N	1.41 W
Baing	226	10.14 S	120.34 E
Bains-les-Bains	166	48.00 N	6.16 E
Bainville	252	48.08 N	104.13 W
Bair	262	39.54 N	76.50 W
Baird	250	32.24 N	99.24 W
Bairdford	266	40.38 N	79.53 W
Baird Inlet C	236	60.45 N	164.00 W
Baird Mountains ⛰	236	67.35 N	161.30 W
Baird Peninsula ≻[1]	232	69.00 N	75.15 W
Baire	284p	20.19 N	76.20 W
Bairnsdale	228	37.50 S	147.38 E
Bairoil	254	42.15 N	107.33 W
Bais, Fr.	166	48.15 N	0.22 W
Bais, Pil.	202	9.35 N	123.07 E
Baise	200	23.57 N	106.26 E
Baisha	200	19.17 N	109.27 E
Baishuijiang	190	33.29 N	106.01 E
Baïsse ≃	166	44.07 N	0.17 E
Baixa Grande	296	11.57 S	40.11 W
Baixo Alentejo □[9]	168	37.55 N	8.10 W
Baiyangdian ⊜	194	38.51 N	116.01 E
Baiyanshan ∧	196	26.05 N	118.25 E
Baiyinchang	190	36.47 N	104.07 E
Baiyunebo	190	41.58 N	110.02 E
Baja	164	46.11 N	18.57 E
Baja, Punta ≻, Méx.	278	29.56 N	115.49 W
Baja, Punta ≻, Méx.	278	28.25 N	111.42 W
Baja California	254	32.18 N	115.12 W
Baja California □[3]	278	30.00 N	115.00 W
Baja California ≻[1]	278	27.30 N	113.00 W
Baja California Seamount Province	148	26.00 N	124.00 W
Baja California Sur □[8]	278	26.00 N	112.00 W
Bajada del Agrio	294	38.24 S	70.02 W
Baján	250	26.32 N	101.15 W
Bajanaul	186	50.47 N	75.42 E
Bajanchongor	190	46.10 N	100.45 E
Bajánsenye	164	46.48 N	16.23 E
Baja Verapaz □[5]	280	15.05 N	90.20 W
Bajdarackaja Guba C	186	69.00 N	67.30 E
Bajiachaidamuhu ⊜	206	37.30 N	95.12 E
Bajimba, Mount ∧	228	29.18 S	152.07 E
Bajina Bašta	172	43.58 N	19.34 E
Bajinghe ≃	200	23.42 N	100.22 E
Bajkal, Ozero ⊜	186	53.00 N	107.40 E
Bajkal'skoje	186	55.21 N	109.12 E
Bajkit	186	61.41 N	96.25 E
Bajkonyr	186	47.50 N	66.03 E
Bajmak	158	52.36 N	58.19 E
Bajmok	172	45.58 N	19.25 E
Bajos de Haina	282	18.25 N	70.01 W
Bajram-Ali	208	37.37 N	62.10 E
Bajsun	186	38.14 N	67.12 E
Bakel	214	14.54 N	12.27 W
Baker, Fla., U.S.	248	30.48 N	86.40 W
Baker, Idaho, U.S.	256	45.06 N	113.44 W
Baker, La., U.S.	248	30.35 N	91.10 W
Baker, Mont., U.S.	252	46.22 N	104.17 W
Baker, Oreg., U.S.	256	44.47 N	117.50 W
Baker, Mount ∧	256	48.47 N	121.49 W
Baker Butte ∧	254	34.27 N	111.22 W
Baker Island I	236	55.20 N	133.36 W
Baker Lake	232	64.15 N	96.00 W
Baker Lake ⊜	232	64.10 N	95.30 W
Bakersfield, Calif., U.S.	274	35.23 N	119.01 W
Bakersfield, Tex., U.S.	250	30.53 N	102.12 W
Bakerstown	266	40.39 N	79.56 W
Bakersville, N.C., U.S.	246	36.01 N	82.09 W
Bakersville, Ohio, U.S.	266	40.21 N	81.39 W
Bakhtegān, Daryācheh-ye ⊜	208	29.20 N	54.05 E
Bakhtīarī va Chahār Maḥāll □[8]	208	32.00 N	51.00 E
Bakır ≃	212	38.55 N	27.00 E
Bakırköy	172	40.59 N	28.52 E
Bakkafjörður	160a	66.04 N	14.45 W
Bakkaflói C	160a	66.10 N	14.45 W
Bakkagerði	160a	65.32 N	13.48 W
Bako	214	5.50 N	36.40 E
Bakony ⛰, Magy.	164	46.55 N	17.40 E
Bakony ⛰, Magy.	170	47.05 N	17.45 E
Bakoye ≃	222	13.49 N	10.50 W
Baku	208	40.23 N	49.51 E
Bakulin Point ≻	202	8.31 N	126.20 E
Bakung, Pulau I	200	0.04 N	104.27 E
Bakwanga → Mbuji-Mayi	218	6.09 S	23.38 E
Bala, Ont., Can.	264	45.01 N	79.37 W
Bala, Wales, U.K.	162	52.54 N	3.35 E
Bala, Cerros de ⛰	292	14.20 S	67.50 W
Balabac	202	7.59 N	117.03 E
Balabac Island I	202	7.55 N	117.00 E
Balabac Strait Џ	198	7.35 N	117.00 E
Ba'labakk (Baalbek)	208	34.00 N	36.12 E
Balaban Dağları ⛰	212	40.28 N	39.15 E
Balachna	160	56.30 N	43.36 E
Balaci	172	44.21 N	24.55 E
Balad'ok	186	53.41 N	133.07 E
Balagne ◂[1]	170	42.30 N	8.50 E
Balaguer	168	41.47 N	0.49 E
Balakovo	158	52.02 N	47.47 E
Balallan	162	58.05 N	6.35 W
Balamban	202	10.30 N	123.42 E
Balambangan, Pulau I	202	7.15 N	116.55 E
Bāla Murghāb	208	35.34 N	63.20 E
Balanga	202	14.41 N	120.32 E
Balangiga	202	11.07 N	125.23 E
Balanguingui Island I	202	6.02 N	121.42 E
Balao ≃	290	2.54 S	79.50 W
Balasore	206	21.29 N	86.56 E
Balašov	158	51.32 N	43.08 E
Balassagyarmat	164	48.05 N	19.18 E
Balatan	202	13.20 N	123.10 E
Balaton	252	44.14 N	95.52 W
Balaton ⊜	164	46.50 N	17.45 E
Balayan	202	13.56 N	120.44 E
Balayan Bay C	202	13.50 N	120.50 E
Balazote	168	38.53 N	2.08 W
Balazote ≃	168	38.59 N	2.05 W
Balbieriškis	164	54.32 N	23.52 E
Balboa	280	8.57 N	79.34 W
Balboa Heights	280	8.57 N	79.34 W
Balbriggan	162	53.37 N	6.11 W
Balcarce	294	37.52 S	58.15 W
Bălceşti	172	44.37 N	23.56 E
Balchaš	186	46.49 N	74.59 E
Balchaš, Ozero ⊜	186	46.00 N	74.00 E
Balčik	172	43.25 N	28.10 E
Balclutha	230	46.15 S	169.43 E
Balcones Escarpment ⍛[4]	250	29.30 N	99.15 W
Balcosna	294	27.54 S	65.43 W
Balde	294	33.21 S	66.38 W
Bald Eagle	266	40.42 N	78.12 W
Baldim	296	19.17 S	43.57 W
Bald Knob	248	35.19 N	91.34 W
Bald Knob ∧	246	37.56 N	79.51 W
Bald Mountain ∧, Colo., U.S.	254	40.45 N	105.41 W
Bald Mountain ∧, N.J., U.S.	242	41.07 N	74.12 W
Bald Mountain ∧, Oreg., U.S.	256	44.36 N	117.53 W
Bald Mountain ∧, Oreg., U.S.	256	43.16 N	121.21 W
Baldock	174	51.59 N	0.12 W
Baldock Lake ⊜	232	56.33 N	97.57 W
Baldur	252	49.23 N	99.15 W
Baldwin, Fla., U.S.	246	30.18 N	81.59 W
Baldwin, La., U.S.	248	29.51 N	91.33 W
Baldwin, Mich., U.S.	244	43.54 N	85.51 W
Baldwin, N. Dak., U.S.	252	47.02 N	100.45 W
Baldwin, Wis., U.S.	244	44.58 N	92.22 W
Baldwin City	252	38.47 N	95.11 W
Baldwin Park	274	34.06 N	117.58 W
Baldwin Peninsula ≻[1]	236	66.44 N	162.15 W
Baldwinsville	264	43.09 N	76.20 W
Baldwinville	261	42.36 N	72.05 W
Baldwyn	248	34.31 N	88.38 W
Baldy Mountain ∧, B.C., Can.	238	51.28 N	120.02 W
Baldy Mountain ∧, Mont., U.S.	256	48.09 N	109.39 W
Baldy Mountain ∧, N. Mex., U.S.	254	36.38 N	105.13 W
Baldy Peak ∧	254	33.55 N	109.35 W
Bâle → Basel, Schw.	180	47.33 N	7.35 E
Baleares □[4]	168	39.30 N	3.00 E
Baleares, Islas II	168	39.30 N	3.00 E
Balearic Islands → Baleares, Islas II	168	39.30 N	3.00 E
Baleia, Ponta da ≻	296	17.40 S	39.07 W
Baleine, Rivière à la ≃	232	58.20 N	67.40 W
Balej	186	51.36 N	116.38 E
Balen	178	51.10 N	5.09 E
Baleno	202	12.29 N	123.30 E
Baler	202	15.46 N	121.34 E
Baler Bay C	202	15.50 N	121.37 E
Balesin Island I	202	14.25 N	122.03 E
Balestrand	160	61.12 N	6.32 E
Balezino	160	57.58 N	53.00 E
Balfate	280	15.48 N	86.25 W
Balfour	246	35.21 N	82.28 W
Bali, Laut (Bali Sea) ⊤[2]	198	7.45 S	115.30 E
Bali, Selat Џ	198	8.18 S	114.25 E
Bali Sea → Bali, Laut ⊤[2]	198	7.45 S	115.30 E
Baliangao	202	8.39 N	123.36 E
Balibago	202	13.37 N	121.18 E
Balicuatro Islands II	202	12.37 N	124.23 E
Balicuatro Point ≻	202	12.35 N	124.16 E
Balıkesir	212	39.39 N	27.53 E
Balıkesir □[4]	172	39.45 N	28.00 E
Balikpapan	198	1.17 S	116.50 E
Balikun	190	43.50 N	93.30 E
Balimbing	202	5.05 N	119.58 E
Balimo	198	8.03 S	142.56 E
Balin	190	48.19 N	122.19 E
Balindong (Watu)	202	7.55 N	124.13 E
Balingasag	202	8.45 N	124.47 E
Balingen	180	48.16 N	8.51 E
Balintang Channel Џ	198	20.00 N	122.00 E
Balinzuoqi	190	44.00 N	119.00 E
Baliuag	202	14.57 N	120.54 E
Baliungan Island I	202	5.10 N	120.12 E
Baliza	296	16.15 S	52.25 W
Balkan Mountains → Stara Planina ⛰	172	43.15 N	25.00 E
Balkh	208	36.44 N	66.47 E
Balkh □[4]	206	36.30 N	67.00 E
Balkhash, Lake → Balchaš, Ozero ⊜	186	46.00 N	74.00 E
Ballachulish	162	56.40 N	5.10 W
Ballangen	160	68.20 N	16.50 E
Ballantine	256	45.57 N	108.09 W
Ballarat	228	37.34 S	143.52 E
Ballard Vale	261	42.38 N	71.10 W
Ballater	162	57.03 N	3.03 W
Ballenas, Bahía de C	278	26.45 N	113.25 W
Ballenas, Canal de Џ	278	29.10 N	113.30 W
Ballenita, Punta ≻	294	25.46 S	70.44 W
Balleny Islands II	148	66.35 S	162.50 E
Balleroy	166	49.11 N	0.50 W
Ballesteros, Arg.	294	32.33 S	63.00 W
Ballesteros, Pil.	202	18.25 N	121.31 E
Ball Ground	246	34.21 N	84.23 W
Ballı	172	40.50 N	27.03 E
Ballia	206	25.45 N	84.20 E
Ballico	272	37.27 N	120.42 W
Ballina, Austl.	228	28.52 S	153.33 E
Ballina, Eire	162	54.07 N	9.09 W
Ballina, Eire	162	52.49 N	8.26 W
Ballinasloe	162	53.20 N	8.13 W
Ballinger	250	31.44 N	99.57 W
Ballinrobe	162	53.37 N	9.13 W
Ballinskelligs Bay C	162	51.50 N	10.15 W
Ballon	162	48.10 N	0.14 E
Ballouville	261	41.52 N	71.52 W
Balls Pyramid I	226	31.45 S	159.15 E
Ballston	270	45.04 N	123.15 W
Ballston Spa	242	43.00 N	73.51 W
Ballville	266	41.20 N	83.09 W
Bally	262	40.24 N	75.35 W
Ballybunion	162	52.31 N	9.40 W
Ballycastle	162	55.12 N	6.15 W
Ballyhaunis	162	53.46 N	8.46 W
Ballymena	162	54.52 N	6.17 W
Ballymoney	162	55.04 N	6.31 W
Ballymote	162	54.06 N	8.31 W
Ballyshannon	162	54.30 N	8.11 W
Balmaceda	288	45.55 S	71.41 W
Balmoral	162	57.20 N	3.15 W
Balmoral Castle ♠	162	57.02 N	3.15 W
Balmorhea	250	30.59 N	103.45 W
Balnearia	294	31.00 S	62.40 W
Balogoje	160	57.54 N	34.02 E
Balonne ≃	228	28.47 S	147.56 E
Balovale	218	13.33 S	23.06 E
Balranald	226	34.38 S	143.33 E
Balş	172	44.21 N	24.06 E
Balsam Lake	244	45.27 N	92.27 W
Balsam Lake ⊜	244	44.35 N	78.50 W
Bálsamo	296	20.27 S	53.57 W
Balsas	286	7.31 S	46.02 W
Balsas ≃, Méx.	278	17.55 N	102.10 W
Balsas ≃, Pan.	290	8.13 N	77.58 W
Balsthal	180	47.19 N	7.42 E
Balta	158	47.55 N	29.37 E
Baltanás	168	41.56 N	4.15 W
Baltasar Brum	294	30.44 S	57.19 W
Baltasi	160	56.21 N	50.12 E
Baltic, Conn., U.S.	261	41.37 N	72.05 W
Baltic, Ohio, U.S.	266	40.27 N	81.42 W
Baltic Bay C	244	48.22 N	83.43 W
Baltic Sea ⊤[2]	160	57.00 N	19.00 E
Baltijsk, S.S.S.R.	158	54.39 N	19.55 E
Baltijsk (Pillau), S.S.S.R.	164	54.39 N	19.55 E
Baltijskaja Kosa ≻[2]	164	54.25 N	19.35 E
Balṭīm	220	31.33 N	31.05 E
Baltimore, Eire	162	51.29 N	9.22 W
Baltimore, Md., U.S.	262	39.17 N	76.37 W
Baltimore, Ohio, U.S.	242	39.51 N	82.36 W
Baltimore □[6]	262	39.24 N	76.36 W
Baltra, Isla I	290a	0.26 S	90.16 W
Baluarte, Río del ≃	278	22.48 N	106.02 W
Balūchestān va Sīstān □[4]	208	28.30 N	60.30 E
Baluchistan ◂[1]	208	28.00 N	63.00 E
Balud	202	12.02 N	123.12 E
Balukbaluk Island I	202	6.42 N	121.41 E
Balut Island I	202	5.25 N	125.13 E
Balvi	160	57.08 N	27.17 E
Balya	172	39.45 N	27.35 E
Balygyčan	186	63.56 N	154.12 E
Balykši	158	47.05 N	51.54 E
Balzac	238	51.10 N	114.01 W
Balzar	290	1.22 S	79.54 W
Bam	208	29.06 N	58.21 E
Bama	200	24.21 N	107.08 E
Bamako	222	12.39 N	8.00 W
Bamako □[4]	222	13.00 N	8.00 W
Bamba	214	17.02 N	1.24 W
Bambamarca	292	6.36 S	78.32 W
Bamban	202	15.17 N	120.34 E
Bambang	202	16.23 N	121.06 E
Bambannan Island I	202	5.38 N	120.16 E
Bambari	214	5.45 N	20.40 E
Bamberg, B.R.D.	164	49.53 N	10.53 E
Bamberg, S.C., U.S.	246	33.17 N	81.02 W
Bamber Lake	262	39.54 N	74.19 W
Bamberton	270	48.35 N	123.31 W
Bambetoka, Baie de C	225b	15.50 S	46.17 E
Bamboesberg ⛰	224	31.30 S	26.10 E
Bambuí	296	20.01 S	45.58 W
Bamenda	222	5.56 N	10.10 E
Bamfield	238	48.50 N	125.08 W
Bāmiān	204	34.51 N	67.48 E
Bāmiān □[4]	206	34.45 N	67.15 E
Bamianshan ∧	196	26.02 N	113.40 E
Bampūr	214	27.12 N	60.27 E
Bampūr ≃	208	27.18 N	59.06 E
Baná	280	13.48 N	85.47 W
Baña, Punta de la ≻	168	40.34 N	0.38 E
Banāder va Jazāyer-e Khalīj-e Fārs □[4]	208	28.00 N	52.00 E
Banāder va Jazāyer-e 'Ommān □[4]	208	27.00 N	56.00 E
Banagher	162	53.11 N	7.59 W
Banago	202	7.30 N	124.07 E
Banahao, Mount ∧	202	14.04 N	121.29 E
Banalia	218	1.33 N	25.20 E
Banamba	222	13.33 N	7.27 W
Banana	218	6.01 S	12.24 E
Banana Islands II	222	8.07 N	13.13 W
Bananal	296	22.41 S	44.19 W
Bananal, Ilha do I	296	11.30 S	50.15 W
Banana River C	246	28.25 N	80.38 W
Banarlı	172	41.04 N	27.20 E
Banās, Ra's ≻	220	23.54 N	35.48 E
Banat ◂[1]	172	45.20 N	19.35 E
Banate Bay C	202	10.57 N	122.48 E
Banay, Mount ∧	202	13.42 N	121.10 E
Banaz	172	38.46 N	29.46 E
Banbridge	162	54.21 N	6.16 W
Banbury	174	52.04 N	1.20 W
Bancalan Island I	202	8.06 N	117.06 E
Banchory	162	57.30 N	2.30 W
Banco, Punta ≻	280	8.22 N	83.09 W
Bancroft, Ont., Can.	264	45.03 N	77.51 W
Bancroft, Idaho, U.S.	256	42.43 N	111.53 W
Bancroft, Iowa, U.S.	244	43.18 N	94.13 W
Bancroft, Mich., U.S.	268	42.53 N	84.04 W
Bancroft, Nebr., U.S.	252	42.00 N	96.34 W
Bancroft → Chililabombwe, Zam.	218	12.18 S	27.43 E
Bānda	206	25.29 N	80.21 E
Banda, Kepulauan II	198	4.34 S	129.55 E
Banda, Laut ⊤[2]	198	5.00 S	128.00 E
Banda Atjeh (Kutaradja)	200	5.34 N	95.20 E
Banda del Río Salí	294	26.50 S	65.10 W
Banda di Dentro ◂[1]	170	42.00 N	9.20 E
Banda di Fuori ◂[1]	170	42.00 N	8.55 E
Bandai-asahi-kokuritsu-kōen ♠	192	38.16 N	139.57 E
Bandai-san ∧	192	37.36 N	140.04 E
Bandama ≃	222	5.10 N	5.00 W
Bandar 'Abbās	208	27.11 N	56.17 E
Bandar-e Lengeh	208	26.33 N	54.53 E
Bandar-e Ma'shūr	208	30.33 N	49.12 E
Bandar-e Pahlavī	208	37.28 N	49.27 E
Bandar-e Shāh	208	36.56 N	54.06 E
Bandar-e Shāhpūr	208	30.25 N	49.05 E
Bandar Maharani	200	2.02 N	102.34 E
Bandar Seri Begawan	198	4.56 N	114.55 E
Banda Sea → Banda, Laut ⊤[2]	198	5.00 S	128.00 E
Bande	168	42.02 N	7.58 W
Banded Peak ∧	254	37.06 N	106.38 W
Bandeira, Pico da ∧	296	20.26 S	41.47 W
Bandeira do Colônia	296	15.07 S	40.06 W
Bandeirante	296	13.41 S	50.48 W
Bandeirantes, Bra.	296	23.06 S	50.21 W
Bandeirantes, Bra.	296	19.53 S	54.23 W
Bandeirantes, Ilha dos I	296	23.22 S	53.50 W
Bandelier National Monument ♠	254	35.45 N	106.20 W
Band-e Nīlāq, Kūh-e ∧	208	26.37 N	59.49 E
Bandera, Arg.	294	28.53 S	62.16 W
Bandera, Tex., U.S.	250	29.44 N	99.04 W
Bandera, Alto de la ∧	282	18.50 N	70.35 W
Bandera Bajada	294	27.16 S	63.31 W
Banderas	254	31.01 N	105.35 W
Banderas, Bahía de C	278	20.40 N	105.25 W
Bandiantaolehai	190	41.41 N	104.06 E
Band-i-Baian ⛰	206	34.22 N	65.20 E
Bandırma	212	40.20 N	27.58 E
Bandırma Körfezi C	212	40.25 N	28.00 E
Band-i-Turkistān ⛰, Afg.	206	35.28 N	64.15 E
Band-i-Turkistān ⛰, Afg.	208	35.02 N	64.00 E
Bandjarmasin	198	3.20 S	114.35 E
Bandon, Eire	162	51.45 N	8.45 W
Bandon, Oreg., U.S.	256	43.07 N	124.25 W
Ban Don, Ao C	200	9.20 N	99.25 E
Bandundu	218	3.18 S	17.20 E
Bandung	198	6.54 S	107.36 E
Băneasa	172	44.04 N	27.42 E
Banes	284p	20.58 N	75.43 W
Banff, Alta., Can.	238	51.10 N	115.34 W
Banff, Scot., U.K.	162	57.40 N	2.33 W
Banff □[6]	162	57.24 N	3.10 W
Banff National Park ♠	238	51.38 N	116.22 W
Bang ≃	200	19.53 N	101.08 E
Banga	202	11.38 N	122.20 E
Bañgad	202	12.10 N	123.24 E
Bangall	261	41.53 N	73.42 W
Bangassou	214	4.50 N	23.07 E
Bangbu	196	32.58 N	117.24 E
Banggai	198	1.34 S	123.30 E
Banggai, Kepulauan II	198	1.30 S	123.15 E
Banggi, Pulau I	202	7.17 N	117.12 E
Banghāzī	214	32.07 N	20.04 E
Bang Hieng ≃	200	16.02 N	105.14 E
Bangka, Selat Џ	198	2.20 S	105.45 E
Bangkalan	198	7.02 S	112.44 E
Bangkaru, Pulau I	200	2.04 N	97.07 E
Bangkok → Krung Thep	200	13.45 N	100.31 E
Bangladesh □[1]	204	24.00 N	90.00 E
Bangmashan ⛰	200	23.42 N	99.44 E
Bang Mun Nak	200	16.02 N	100.23 E
Bangon	202	13.44 N	122.50 E
Bangor, N. Ire., U.K.	162	54.40 N	5.40 W
Bangor, Wales, U.K.	162	53.13 N	4.08 W
Bangor, Calif., U.S.	272	39.23 N	121.24 W
Bangor, Maine, U.S.	242	44.49 N	68.47 W
Bangor, Mich., U.S.	268	42.18 N	86.07 W
Bangor, Pa., U.S.	242	40.52 N	75.13 W
Bangs	250	31.43 N	99.08 W
Bangs, Mount ∧	254	36.48 N	113.51 W
Bangued	202	17.36 N	120.37 E
Bangui, Centraf.	214	4.22 N	18.35 E
Bangui, Pil.	202	18.32 N	120.46 E
Bangui Bay C	202	18.36 N	120.43 E
Bangweulu, Lake ⊜	218	11.05 S	29.45 E
Banhā	220	30.28 N	31.11 E
Bani, Pil.	202	16.11 N	119.52 E
Baní, Rep. Dom.	282	18.17 N	70.20 W
Bani ≃	222	14.30 N	4.12 W
Banie (Bahn)	164	53.08 N	14.38 E
Banihāl Pass)(	206	33.30 N	75.13 E
Banī Mazār	220	28.30 N	30.48 E
Banī Suwayf	220	29.05 N	31.05 E
Banjak, Kepulauan II	200	2.10 N	97.15 E
Banja Luka	170	44.46 N	17.11 E
Banjuwangi	226	8.12 S	114.21 E
Banks, Ala., U.S.	248	31.44 N	85.50 W
Banks, Miss., U.S.	248	34.50 N	90.14 W
Banks, Oreg., U.S.	270	45.37 N	123.07 W
Banks, Point ≻	236	58.36 N	152.18 W
Banks Island I, B.C., Can.	238	53.25 N	130.10 W
Banks Island I, N.W. Ter., Can.	232	73.15 N	121.30 W
Banks Lake ⊜[1]	256	47.45 N	119.15 W
Banks Peninsula ≻[1]	230	43.45 S	172.55 E
Banks Strait Џ	228	40.40 S	148.07 E
Bānkura	206	23.14 N	87.04 E
Ban-me-thuot	200	12.40 N	108.03 E
Bann ≃	162	55.10 N	6.46 W
Ban Na San	200	8.53 N	99.17 E
Banning	274	33.56 N	116.52 W
Banningville → Bandundu	218	3.18 S	17.20 E
Bannock	266	40.06 N	80.59 W
Bannock Peak ∧	256	42.36 N	112.42 W
Bannu	206	32.59 N	70.36 E
Bañolas	168	42.07 N	2.46 E
Banon	166	44.02 N	5.38 E
Baños, Ec.	290	1.24 S	78.25 W
Baños, Perú	292	10.05 S	76.42 W
Baños de Cerrato	168	41.55 N	4.28 W
Bánovce nad Bebravou	164	48.43 N	18.14 E
Ban Pak Phraek	200	8.13 N	100.13 E
Ban Phak Phang	200	16.06 N	101.48 E
Ban Pong	200	13.50 N	99.55 E
Banská Bystrica	164	48.44 N	19.07 E
Banská Stiavnika	164	48.28 N	18.56 E
Bansko	172	41.50 N	23.29 E
Banstead	174	51.19 N	0.12 W
Banta	272	37.45 N	121.22 W
Bantam	261	41.44 N	73.14 W
Bantayan	202	11.10 N	123.43 E
Bantayan Island I	202	11.13 N	123.54 E
Bantigui Point ≻	202	13.32 N	121.28 E
Banton (Jones)	202	12.57 N	122.05 E
Banton Island I	202	12.56 N	122.04 E
Bantry	162	51.41 N	9.27 W
Bantry Bay C	162	51.38 N	9.48 W
Banzare Coast ⍛[2]	148	67.00 S	127.00 E
Baode	190	39.06 N	111.11 E
Baoding (Qingyuan)	194	38.52 N	115.29 E
Baofeng	196	33.55 N	113.02 E
Bao-ha	200	22.11 N	104.21 E
Baoji	190	34.22 N	107.14 E
Baon	202	6.47 N	126.05 E
Baoshan	200	25.09 N	99.09 E
Baoting	200	18.42 N	109.45 E
Baotou	190	40.40 N	109.59 E
Baoulé ≃, Afr.	222	12.36 N	6.34 W
Baoulé ≃, Mali	222	13.33 N	9.54 W
Baoying	196	33.16 N	119.20 E
Baoyinghu ⊜	196	33.05 N	119.10 E
Bapaume	166	50.06 N	2.51 E
Bapchule	254	33.12 N	111.50 W
Baptiste Lake ⊜	244	45.07 N	78.02 W
Baptistown	262	40.31 N	75.00 W
Bāqa al Gharbīya	210	32.25 N	35.03 E
Ba'qūbah	208	33.45 N	44.38 E
Baquedano	294	23.20 S	69.51 W
Bar	172	42.05 N	19.05 E
Barabinsk	186	55.21 N	78.21 E
Barabinskaja Step' ⩧	186	55.00 N	79.00 E
Baraboo	244	43.28 N	89.45 W
Baraboo Range ⛰[2]	244	43.25 N	89.40 W
Baracaldo	168	43.18 N	2.59 W
Barachois-de-Malbaie	240	48.39 N	64.18 W
Barachois Pond Provincial Park ♠	240	48.26 N	58.14 W
Baracoa, Cuba	284p	20.21 N	74.30 W
Baracoa, Hond.	280	15.43 N	87.52 W
Baradero	294	33.50 S	59.30 W
Baraga	244	46.47 N	88.30 W
Baraguá	284p	21.41 N	78.38 W
Baraka, Khawr(Barka) V	220	18.13 N	37.35 E
Baranagar	206	22.38 N	88.22 E
Barang, Dasht-i- ◂[2]	208	32.10 N	61.30 E
Barania Góra ∧	164	49.37 N	19.00 E
Baranoa	290	10.48 N	74.55 W
Barano d'Ischia	184	40.42 N	13.55 E
Baranof	236	57.05 N	134.50 W
Baranof Island I	236	57.00 N	135.00 W
Baranoviči	158	53.08 N	26.02 E
Baranów Sandomierski	164	50.30 N	21.33 E
Baranya □[6]	164	46.05 N	18.15 E
Barão de Bom Jardim	296	12.17 S	38.36 W
Barão de Cocais	296	19.56 S	43.28 W
Barão de Melgaço	292	16.13 S	55.58 W
Baraoltului, Munţii ⛰	172	46.15 N	25.45 E
Baraque de Fraiture ∧	164	50.15 N	5.44 E
Baras	202	13.40 N	124.22 E
Baraški	160	65.40 N	52.10 E
Baratang Island I	200	12.15 N	92.45 E
Barataria	248	29.44 N	90.08 W
Barataria Bay C	248	29.22 N	89.57 W
Barat Daja, Kepulauan II	198	7.25 S	128.00 E
Baraya	290	3.10 N	75.04 W
Barba, Volcán ∧[1]	280	10.09 N	84.05 W
Barbacena	296	21.14 S	43.46 W
Barbacoas	290	1.41 N	78.09 W
Barbadillo del Mercado	168	42.02 N	3.21 W
Barbados □[1]	276	13.10 N	59.32 W
Barbar	220	18.01 N	33.59 E
Bárbara	290	0.53 S	72.30 W
Barbareta, Isla I	280	16.26 N	86.10 W
Barbaros	172	40.54 N	27.27 E
Barbas, Cabo ≻	214	22.18 N	16.41 W
Barbastro	168	42.02 N	0.08 E
Barbate	168	36.12 N	5.55 W
Barberena	280	14.18 N	90.22 W
Barberton, S. Afr.	224	25.48 S	31.03 E
Barberton, Ohio, U.S.	266	41.01 N	81.36 W
Barbezieux	166	45.28 N	0.09 W
Barbosa, Col.	290	5.57 N	73.37 W
Barbosa, Col.	290	6.26 N	75.20 W
Barboursville	242	38.24 N	82.18 W
Barbourville	246	36.52 N	83.53 W
Barbuda I	282	17.38 N	61.48 W
Barby	164	51.58 N	11.53 E
Barca	164	48.41 N	21.16 E
Barcaldine	228	23.33 S	145.17 E
Barcarrota	168	38.31 N	6.51 W
Barce → Al-Marj	214	32.30 N	20.54 E
Barcellona Pozzo di Gotto	170	38.09 N	15.13 E
Barcelona, Esp.	168	41.23 N	2.11 E
Barcelona, Méx.	278	26.12 N	103.25 W
Barcelona, Pil.	202	12.52 N	124.08 E
Barcelona, Ven.	290	10.08 N	64.42 W
Barceloneta	284m	18.27 N	66.32 W
Barcelos, Bra.	290	0.58 S	62.57 W
Barcelos, Port.	168	41.32 N	8.37 W
Barcin	164	52.52 N	17.57 E
Barclay	262	39.08 N	75.51 W
Barcoo ≃	228	25.30 S	142.50 E
Barcs	164	45.58 N	17.28 E
Barczewo (Wartenburg)	164	53.50 N	20.42 E
Barda	208	40.23 N	47.08 E
Barda del Medio	294	38.15 S	68.11 W
Bardaï	214	21.22 N	16.59 E
Bardawīl, Sabkhat al- ⩸	220	31.10 N	33.10 E
Bardejov	164	49.18 N	21.16 E
Bardera	214	2.21 N	42.20 E
Bardi	170	44.38 N	9.44 E
Bardīyah	214	31.46 N	25.06 E
Bardonecchia	170	45.05 N	6.42 E
Bardoux, Lac ⊜	240	51.09 N	67.50 W
Bardstown	248	37.49 N	85.28 W
Bardswell Group II	238	52.10 N	128.20 W
Bardu	160	68.52 N	18.15 E
Bardufoss	160	69.04 N	18.30 E
Bardwell	248	36.52 N	89.01 W
Barei, Wādī V	220	13.27 N	23.57 E
Bareilly	206	28.20 N	79.25 E
Barendrecht	178	51.51 N	4.32 E
Barentin	176	49.33 N	0.57 E
Barents Sea ⊤[2]	148	74.00 N	36.00 E
Barents Trough ⊹[1]	148	74.00 N	28.00 E
Baresville	262	39.48 N	76.57 W
Barfleur	166	49.40 N	1.15 W
Barfleur, Pointe de ≻	166	49.42 N	1.16 W
Bargaintown	262	39.22 N	70.35 W
Bargas	168	39.56 N	4.03 W
Barge	170	44.43 N	7.20 E
Bargoed	174	51.43 N	3.15 W
Bargteheide	178	53.44 N	10.16 E
Bar Harbor	242	44.23 N	68.13 W
Bari	170	41.07 N	16.52 E
Barichara	290	6.38 N	73.14 W
Barīdī, Ra's ≻	208	24.17 N	37.31 E
Barigua, Salina de ⩸	285s	12.08 N	69.59 W
Barika	168	35.23 N	5.17 E
Barilla Draw V	250	31.21 N	103.23 W
Barillas	280	15.48 N	91.18 W
Bariloche → San Carlos de Bariloche	288	41.08 S	71.15 W
Barīm I	214	12.40 N	43.25 E
Barima ≃	290	8.35 N	60.25 W
Barinas, P.R.	284m	18.01 N	66.51 W
Barinas, Ven.	290	8.38 N	70.12 W
Barinas □[3]	290	8.10 N	69.50 W
Baring	270	47.46 N	121.29 W
Baring Cape ≻	232	70.05 N	117.20 W
Baring Channel Џ	232	73.48 N	98.50 W
Barinitas	290	8.45 N	70.25 W
Bariri	296	22.04 S	48.44 W
Bārīs	214	24.40 N	30.36 E
Barisāl	206	22.42 N	90.22 E
Barisan, Pegunungan ⛰	198	3.00 S	102.15 E
Barit Island I	202	18.53 N	121.15 E
Barito ≃	198	3.32 S	114.29 E
Barjac	166	44.18 N	4.21 E
Barjols	166	43.33 N	6.00 E
Barka (Khawr Baraka) ≃	220	18.13 N	37.35 E
Barker	264	43.20 N	78.33 W
Barkerville	238	53.04 N	121.31 W
Barkerville Historical Park ⊥	238	53.04 N	121.30 W
Barkeyville	266	41.12 N	79.58 W
Barking ◂[8]	174	51.33 N	0.06 E
Bark Lake ⊜, Ont., Can.	244	46.54 N	82.28 W
Bark Lake ⊜, Ont., Can.	244	45.27 N	77.51 W
Barkley, Lake ⊜[1]	248	36.40 N	87.55 W
Barkley Sound Џ	238	48.53 N	125.20 W
Barkly East	218	3.58 S	27.33 E
Barksdale	250	29.44 N	100.02 W
Bar-le-Duc	166	48.47 N	5.10 E
Barlee Range ⛰	226	23.35 S	116.00 E
Barletta	170	41.19 N	16.17 E
Barlin	176	50.27 N	2.37 E
Barlinek	164	53.00 N	15.12 E
Barlow	248	37.03 N	89.03 W
Barmer	206	25.45 N	71.23 E
Barmouth	162	52.43 N	4.03 W
Barmstedt	178	53.47 N	9.46 E
Barnard	252	39.11 N	98.03 W
Barnard Castle	162	54.33 N	1.55 E
Barnaul	186	53.22 N	83.45 E
Barn Bluff ∧	228	41.43 S	145.56 E
Barnegat	262	39.45 N	74.13 W
Barnegat Bay C	242	39.52 N	74.07 W
Barnegat Light	262	39.46 N	74.06 W
Barnesboro	266	40.40 N	78.47 W
Barnes Corners	264	43.49 N	75.49 W
Barnesville, Ga., U.S.	246	33.04 N	84.09 W
Barnesville, Minn., U.S.	252	46.39 N	96.25 W
Barnesville, Ohio, U.S.	242	39.59 N	81.11 W
Barnet ◂[8]	174	51.40 N	0.13 W
Barnetts	262	37.22 N	77.09 W
Barneveld	178	52.08 N	5.35 E
Barnhart	250	31.08 N	101.10 W
Barnhill	266	40.27 N	81.21 W
Barnsdall	250	36.34 N	96.10 W
Barnsley	162	53.34 N	1.28 W
Barnstable	261	41.42 N	70.18 W
Barnstable □[6]	261	41.42 N	70.18 W
Barnstaple	174	51.05 N	4.04 W
Barnwell, Alta., Can.	238	49.46 N	112.15 W
Barnwell, S.C., U.S.	246	33.15 N	81.23 W
Baro ≃	214	8.26 N	33.13 E
Barobo	202	8.32 N	126.07 E
Baroda, Bhārat	206	25.30 N	76.40 E
Baroda, Mich., U.S.	268	41.57 N	86.29 W
Barometer ∧	230	41.50 S	173.39 E
Baronissi	184	40.44 N	14.45 E
Barons	238	50.00 N	113.05 W
Barotac Nuevo	202	10.54 N	122.42 E
Barotac Viejo	202	11.03 N	122.51 E
Barotseland □[9]	218	16.00 S	24.00 E
Barqah (Cyrenaica) ◂[1]	214	31.00 N	22.30 E
Barquisimeto	290	10.04 N	69.19 W
Barra	286	11.05 S	43.10 W
Barra I	162	57.00 N	7.30 W
Barra, Ponta da ≻	224	23.45 S	35.30 E
Barracão	294	26.15 S	53.38 W
Barracão do Barreto	292	8.48 S	58.24 W
Barrackville	242	39.30 N	80.10 W
Barra da Estiva	296	13.38 S	41.19 W
Barra do Bugres	292	15.05 S	57.11 W
Barra do Corda	286	5.30 S	45.15 W
Barra do Garças	296	15.53 S	52.15 W
Barra do Mendes	296	11.43 S	42.04 W
Barra do Piraí	296	22.28 S	43.49 W
Barra do Ribeiro	294	30.18 S	51.18 W
Barra Falsa, Ponta da ≻	224	22.55 S	35.37 E
Barrafranca	170	37.23 N	14.13 E
Barra Head ≻	162	56.46 N	7.36 W
Barra Mansa	296	22.32 S	44.11 W
Barranca, Perú	292	10.42 S	77.45 W
Barranca, Perú	292	4.50 S	76.40 W
Barrancabermeja	290	7.03 N	73.52 W
Barranca del Cobre, Parque Nacional ♠	278	27.15 N	107.41 W
Barrancas, Chile	294	33.27 S	70.46 W
Barrancas, Col.	290	10.57 N	72.50 W
Barrancas, Ven.	290	8.42 N	62.11 W
Barrancas, Ven.	290	8.46 N	70.06 W
Barranco Azul	250	29.21 N	104.17 W
Barranco de Guadalupe	250	30.02 N	104.44 W
Barranco do Velho	168	37.14 N	7.56 W
Barrancos	168	38.08 N	6.59 W
Barranqueras	294	27.30 S	58.55 W
Barranquilla	290	10.59 N	74.48 W
Barranquitas	284m	18.11 N	66.18 W
Barras	286	4.15 S	42.18 W
Barrax	168	39.03 N	2.12 W
Barraza	294	30.38 S	71.26 W
Barre, Mass., U.S.	261	42.26 N	72.06 W
Barre, Vt., U.S.	242	44.12 N	72.30 W
Barreal	294	31.38 S	69.28 W
Barre des Écrins ∧	166	44.55 N	6.21 E
Barree	266	40.35 N	78.06 W
Barreiras	296	12.08 S	45.00 W
Barreirinha	290	2.47 S	57.03 W
Barreiro	168	38.40 N	9.04 W
Barreiros	286	8.49 S	35.12 W
Barrême	166	43.57 N	6.22 E
Barren ≃	248	37.11 N	86.37 W
Barren, Îles II	225b	18.25 S	43.40 E
Barren Islands II	236	58.55 N	152.15 W
Barren River Reservoir ⊜[1]	248	36.45 N	86.02 W
Barre Plains	261	42.23 N	72.07 W
Barretos	296	20.33 S	48.33 W
Barrhead	238	54.08 N	114.24 W
Barrie	264	44.24 N	79.40 W
Barriefield	264	44.14 N	76.28 W
Barrie Island I	244	45.55 N	82.40 W
Barrier, Cape ≻	230	36.21 S	175.31 E
Barrington, N.S., Can.	240	43.34 N	65.34 W
Barrington, Ill., U.S.	268	42.09 N	88.08 W
Barrington, R.I., U.S.	261	41.44 N	71.18 W
Barrington Tops ∧	228	32.00 S	151.28 E
Barrita Vieja	280	13.55 N	95.46 W
Barro Alto	296	15.04 S	48.58 W
Barron	244	45.24 N	91.51 W
Barrouallie	285h	13.14 N	61.17 W
Barrow, Arg.	294	38.19 S	60.14 W
Barrow, Alaska, U.S.	236	71.17 N	156.47 W
Barrow, Point ≻	236	71.23 N	156.30 W
Barrow Creek	226	21.33 S	133.53 E
Barrow in Furness	162	54.07 N	3.14 W
Barrow Strait Џ	232	74.21 N	94.10 W
Barrowsville	261	41.57 N	71.12 W
Barry, Wales, U.K.	174	51.24 N	3.18 W
Barry, Ill., U.S.	248	39.42 N	91.02 W
Barry □[6]	268	42.35 N	85.18 W
Barrys Bay	264	45.29 N	77.41 W
Barryton	244	43.45 N	85.09 W
Barrytown	261	41.60 N	73.56 W
Barsinghausen	178	52.18 N	9.27 E
Barssel	178	53.10 N	7.44 E
Barstow, Calif., U.S.	274	34.54 N	117.01 W
Barstow, Tex., U.S.	250	31.28 N	103.24 W
Bar-sur-Aube	166	48.14 N	4.43 E
Bar-sur-Seine	166	48.07 N	4.22 E
Bart	262	39.56 N	76.05 W
Bartang	186	38.05 N	71.51 E
Bartazuga, Jabal ∧	220	21.44 N	33.33 E
Barter Island I	236	70.08 N	143.35 W
Barth	164	54.22 N	12.43 E
Barthelemy, Col)(	200	19.26 N	104.06 E
Bartholomew, Bayou ≃	248	32.43 N	92.04 W
Bartica	290	6.24 N	58.37 W
Bartle Frere ∧	228	17.23 S	145.49 E
Bartlesville	250	36.45 N	95.59 W
Bartlett, Ill., U.S.	268	42.05 N	88.11 W
Bartlett, Nebr., U.S.	252	41.53 N	98.33 W
Bartlett, N.H., U.S.	242	44.05 N	71.17 W
Bartlett, Tenn., U.S.	248	35.12 N	89.52 W
Bartlett, Tex., U.S.	250	30.48 N	97.26 W
Bartlett Cove	236	58.27 N	135.55 W
Bartlett Reservoir ⊜[1]	254	33.52 N	111.37 W
Bartlett's Harbour	240	50.57 N	56.59 W
Bartley	252	40.15 N	100.18 W
Bartolomé de las Casas	294	25.25 S	59.35 W
Bartolomeu Dias	218	21.10 S	35.09 E
Barton, Ohio, U.S.	266	40.06 N	80.51 W
Barton, Vt., U.S.	242	44.45 N	72.11 W
Barton-upon-Humber	162	53.41 N	0.27 W
Bartonville	244	40.39 N	89.39 W
Bartoszyce (Bartenstein)	164	54.16 N	20.49 E
Bartow, Fla., U.S.	246	27.54 N	81.50 W
Bartow, Ga., U.S.	246	32.53 N	82.29 W
Barugo	202	11.29 N	124.44 E
Bāruni	206	25.29 N	85.59 E
Baruun Urt	190	46.40 N	113.12 E
Barvas	162	58.22 N	6.32 W
Barwāh	206	22.16 N	76.03 E
Barwice (Bärwalde)	164	53.45 N	16.22 E
Barwick	246	30.54 N	83.44 W
Barwon ≃	228	30.00 S	148.05 E
Barycz ≃	164	51.42 N	16.15 E
Barykova, Mys ≻	236	63.02 N	179.29 E
Baryš	160	53.39 N	47.08 E
Basail	294	27.52 S	59.18 W
Basalt	254	39.22 N	107.02 W
Basalt ≃	228	19.38 S	145.52 E
Basankusu	218	1.14 N	19.48 E
Basarabi	172	44.10 N	28.24 E
Basatongwulashan ∧	206	33.05 N	91.30 E
Basauri	168	43.01 N	2.24 W
Basavilbaso	294	32.20 S	58.52 W
Basco	198	20.27 N	121.58 E
Bascom	266	41.08 N	83.17 W
Bascuñán, Cabo ≻	294	28.51 S	71.30 W
Basel (Bâle)	180	47.33 N	7.35 E
Basella	168	42.01 N	1.18 E
Basel-Landschaft □[3]	180	47.30 N	7.50 E
Basel-Stadt □[3]	180	47.38 N	7.40 E
Basey	202	11.17 N	125.04 E
Bashākerd, Kūhhā-ye ⛰	208	26.42 N	58.35 E
Bashaw	238	52.35 N	112.58 W
Bashi Channel Џ	198	22.00 N	121.00 E
Basiad Bay C	202	14.12 N	122.18 E
Basilan → Isabela	202	6.42 N	121.58 E
Basilan Island I	202	6.35 N	122.00 E
Basilan Peak ∧	202	6.33 N	122.03 E
Basilan Strait Џ	202	6.49 N	122.05 E
Basildon	174	51.35 N	0.25 E
Basile	248	30.29 N	92.36 W
Basilicata □[4]	170	40.30 N	16.10 E
Basílio	294	31.53 S	53.01 W
Basin, Mont., U.S.	256	46.16 N	112.16 W
Basin, Wyo., U.S.	256	44.23 N	108.02 W
Basingstoke	174	51.15 N	1.05 W
Basīrhāt	206	22.39 N	88.52 E
Basīt, Ra's al- ≻	212	35.51 N	35.48 E
Baška	170	44.58 N	14.46 E
Baskahegan Lake ⊜	242	45.30 N	67.48 W
Baskatong, Réservoir ⊜[1]	244	46.50 N	75.50 W
Basoko	218	1.14 N	23.36 E
Basom	264	43.04 N	78.24 W
Basora, Punt ≻	285s	12.25 N	69.52 W
Basque Provinces → Vascongadas □[9]	168	43.00 N	2.45 W
Basra → Al-Baṣrah	208	30.30 N	47.47 E
Bas-Rhin □[5]	166	48.35 N	7.40 E
Bassano	238	50.47 N	112.28 W
Bassano del Grappa	170	45.46 N	11.44 E
Bassari	222	9.15 N	0.47 E
Bassas da India ⊹[2]	218	21.25 S	39.42 E
Bassein	200	16.47 N	94.44 E
Bassein ≃[1]	200	15.56 N	94.18 E
Basse-Pointe	284e	14.52 N	61.07 W
Basses-Alpes □[5]	182	44.10 N	6.00 E
Basses-Pyrénées □[5]	166	43.15 N	0.50 W
Basse-Terre, Guad.	285o	16.00 N	61.44 W
Basseterre, St. K.-N.-A.	282	17.18 N	62.43 W
Basse Terre, Trin.	285r	10.08 N	61.18 W
Basse-Terre I	282	16.10 N	61.40 W
Bassett, Nebr., U.S.	252	42.35 N	99.32 W
Bassett, Va., U.S.	246	36.46 N	79.59 W
Bassfield	248	31.30 N	89.44 W
Bassin Des Aghlabites ⊥	170	35.43 N	10.10 E
Bass Lake, Calif., U.S.	272	37.19 N	119.33 W
Bass Lake, Ind., U.S.	268	41.12 N	86.36 W
Bass River	240	45.25 N	63.47 W
Bass Strait Џ	228	39.20 S	145.30 E
Bassum	178	52.51 N	8.43 E
Basswood Lake ⊜	244	48.06 N	91.40 W
Båstad	160	56.26 N	12.51 E
Bastelica	170	42.00 N	9.02 E
Basti	206	26.47 N	82.42 E
Bastia, Fr.	166	42.42 N	9.27 E
Bastia, It.	184	43.04 N	12.33 E
Bastian	246	37.09 N	81.09 W
Bastimentos	280	9.20 N	82.16 W
Bastimentos, Isla I	280	9.19 N	82.07 W
Bastogne	164	50.00 N	5.43 E
Bastrop, La., U.S.	248	32.47 N	91.55 W
Bastrop, Tex., U.S.	250	30.07 N	97.19 W
Bastuträsk	160	64.47 N	20.02 E
Basu, Tandjung ≻	200	0.21 S	103.48 E
Bata	218	1.51 N	9.45 E
Bataan □[4]	202	14.40 N	120.25 E
Bataan, Mount ∧	202	14.31 N	120.28 E
Bataan Peninsula ≻[1]	202	14.38 N	120.30 E
Batabanó, Golfo de C	284p	22.15 N	82.30 W
Batac	202	18.03 N	120.34 E
Batad	202	11.26 N	123.06 E
Batagaj	186	67.38 N	134.38 E
Batagaj-Alyta	186	67.48 N	130.25 E
Batag Island I	202	12.38 N	125.04 E
Bataguaçu	296	21.42 S	52.22 W
Bataiporã	296	22.20 S	53.17 W
Batajsk	158	47.10 N	39.44 E
Batak	172	41.57 N	24.13 E
Batak, Jazovir ⊜[1]	172	41.57 N	24.13 E
Batāla	206	31.48 N	75.13 E
Batalha	168	39.39 N	8.50 W
Batam, Pulau I	200	1.05 N	104.03 E
Batamaj	186	63.31 N	129.27 E
Batan	202	11.35 N	122.30 E
Batanes □[4]	202	20.30 N	121.50 E
Batang	190	30.02 N	99.02 E
Batangan, Mui ≻	200	15.14 N	108.56 E
Batangas	202	13.45 N	121.03 E
Batangas □[4]	202	13.50 N	121.00 E
Batangas Bay C	202	13.43 N	121.00 E

Symbols in the index entries are identified on page 360.

Name	Page	Lat°′	Long°′
Batan Island I, Pil.	198	20.25 N	121.57 E
Batan Island I, Pil.	202	13.15 N	124.00 E
Batan Islands II	198	20.35 N	121.55 E
Batanta, Pulau I	198	0.50 S	130.40 E
Batas Island I	202	11.09 N	119.35 E
Bátaszék	164	46.12 N	18.44 E
Batatais	296	20.53 S	47.37 W
Batavia, Arg.	294	34.47 S	65.41 W
Batavia, Ill., U.S.	268	41.51 N	88.19 W
Batavia, Iowa, U.S.	244	41.00 N	92.10 W
Batavia, Mich., U.S.	268	41.55 N	85.06 W
Batavia, N.Y., U.S.	264	43.00 N	78.11 W
Batavia, Ohio, U.S.	242	39.05 N	84.11 W
Batawa	264	44.10 N	77.36 W
Batbatan Island I	202	11.28 N	121.55 E
Batchawana Mountain ∧	244	47.04 N	84.24 W
Bătdâmbăng	200	13.06 N	103.12 E
Bateckij	160	58.39 N	30.19 E
Batemans Bay	228	35.43 S	150.11 E
Batepito	278	30.49 N	109.12 W
Batesburg	246	33.54 N	81.33 W
Batesville, Ark., U.S.	248	35.46 N	91.39 W
Batesville, Ind., U.S.	248	39.18 N	85.13 W
Batesville, Miss., U.S.	248	34.18 N	90.00 W
Batesville, Tex., U.S.	250	28.57 N	99.37 W
Bath, Ont., Can.	264	44.11 N	76.47 W
Bath, Eng., U.K.	174	51.23 N	2.22 W
Bath, Maine, U.S.	242	43.55 N	69.49 W
Bath, Mich., U.S.	268	42.49 N	84.27 W
Bath, N.Y., U.S.	242	42.20 N	77.19 W
Bath, Ohio, U.S.	266	41.11 N	81.38 W
Bath, Pa., U.S.	262	40.44 N	75.24 W
Bath, S.C., U.S.	246	33.31 N	81.51 W
Bathgate, Scot., U.K.	162	55.55 N	3.39 W
Bathgate, N. Dak., U.S.	252	48.53 N	97.29 W
Bathsheba	285g	13.13 N	59.31 W
Bathurst, Austl.	228	33.25 S	149.35 E
Bathurst, N.B., Can.	240	47.36 N	65.39 W
Bathurst, Gam.	222	13.28 N	16.39 W
Bathurst, Cape ≻	232	70.35 N	128.00 W
Bathurst Inlet	232	66.50 N	108.01 W
Bathurst Inlet C	232	68.10 N	108.50 W
Bathurst Island I	232	76.00 N	100.30 W
Bāṭin, Wādī al- ∨	208	29.35 N	47.00 E
Batina	172	45.51 N	18.51 E
Batjan, Pulau I	198	0.35 S	127.30 E
Batman	212	37.52 N	41.07 E
Batna	168	35.34 N	6.15 E
Bato	202	10.20 N	124.47 E
Bato, Lake ⊜	202	13.20 N	123.21 E
Baton Rouge	248	30.23 N	91.11 W
Batorampon Point ≻	202	7.06 N	121.53 E
Batouri	214	4.26 N	14.22 E
Batovi	296	15.53 S	53.24 W
Batovi ≃	296	11.56 S	53.36 W
Batson	250	30.15 N	94.37 W
Batticaloa	204	7.43 N	81.42 E
Battin	270	45.29 N	122.34 W
Battle ≃	232	52.42 N	108.15 W
Battle Creek, Iowa, U.S.	252	42.19 N	95.36 W
Battle Creek, Mich., U.S.	268	42.19 N	85.11 W
Battle Creek, Nebr., U.S.	252	42.00 N	97.36 W
Battle Ground, Ind., U.S.	268	40.31 N	86.50 W
Battle Ground, Wash., U.S.	270	45.47 N	122.32 W
Battle Harbour	232	52.17 N	55.35 W
Battle Lake	252	46.17 N	95.43 W
Battlement Mesa ∧	254	39.20 N	108.00 W
Battle Mountain	258	40.38 N	116.56 W
Battle Mountain ∧	254	41.02 N	107.16 W
Battonya	164	46.17 N	21.01 E
Batu ∧	214	6.55 N	39.46 E
Batu, Kepulauan II	200	0.18 S	98.28 E
Batuan	202	12.25 N	123.47 E
Batu Brinchang, Gunong ∧	200	4.30 N	101.24 E
Batuc	278	29.15 N	109.44 W
Batumi	212	41.38 N	41.38 E
Batu Pahat	200	1.50 N	102.56 E
Batura ∧	206	36.31 N	74.30 E
Baturadja	198	4.08 S	104.10 E
Baturité	286	4.20 S	38.53 W
Batusangkar	200	0.27 S	100.35 E
Bat Yam	210	32.02 N	34.44 E
Bauang	202	16.32 N	120.20 E
Baubau	198	5.28 S	122.38 E
Bauchi	222	10.19 N	9.50 E
Baud	166	47.52 N	3.01 W
Baudette	244	48.43 N	94.36 W
Baudó, Serranía de ⋀⋀	290	6.00 N	77.05 W
Baudouinville	218	7.04 S	29.46 E
Baudour	176	50.29 N	3.49 E
Baugé	166	47.33 N	0.06 W
Baúl, Cerro ∧	278	17.38 N	100.18 W
Bauld, Cape ≻	240	51.38 N	55.25 W
Baumann, Pic ∧	222	6.52 N	0.46 E
Baume-les-Dames	166	47.21 N	6.22 E
Baunei	170	40.02 N	9.40 E
Baures	292	13.35 S	63.35 W
Bauru	296	22.19 S	49.04 W
Baús	296	18.19 S	53.10 W
Bauska	160	56.24 N	24.14 E
Bauta	284p	22.59 N	82.33 W
Bautzen	164	51.11 N	14.26 E
Bauxite	248	34.33 N	92.30 W
Bavaria → Bayern □[9]	164	48.30 N	11.30 E
Baviaanskloofberge ⋀⋀	224	33.35 S	24.10 E
Bavispe	278	30.24 N	108.50 W
Bawean, Pulau I	198	5.46 S	112.40 E
Bawku	222	11.05 N	0.14 W
Baxian	194	39.06 N	116.23 E
Baxley	246	31.47 N	82.21 W
Baxter, Iowa, U.S.	244	41.49 N	93.09 W
Baxter, Minn., U.S.	244	46.20 N	94.16 W
Baxter, Tenn., U.S.	248	36.09 N	85.38 W
Baxter Springs	252	37.02 N	94.44 W
Baxter State Park ♠	242	46.00 N	68.58 W
Baxterville	248	31.06 N	89.36 W
Bay	248	35.45 N	90.34 W
Bay, Laguna de ⊜	202	14.20 N	121.11 E
Bayag	202	18.16 N	121.02 E
Bayambang	202	15.49 N	120.27 E
Bayamo	284p	20.23 N	76.39 W
Bayamón	284m	18.24 N	66.09 W
Bayang	202	7.47 N	124.12 E
Bayanhaote	190	38.50 N	105.41 E
Bayard, Fla., U.S.	246	30.09 N	81.31 W
Bayard, Iowa, U.S.	252	41.51 N	94.33 W
Bayard, Nebr., U.S.	252	41.45 N	103.20 W
Bayard, N. Mex., U.S.	254	32.46 N	108.08 W
Bayard, W. Va., U.S.	242	39.16 N	79.22 W
Bayawan	202	9.22 N	122.48 E
Baybay	202	10.41 N	124.48 E
Bayberry	264	43.08 N	76.13 W
Bayboro	246	35.09 N	76.46 W
Bay Bulls	240	47.19 N	52.49 W
Bay Center	270	46.38 N	123.57 W
Bay City, Mich., U.S.	244	43.36 N	83.53 W
Bay City, Oreg., U.S.	270	45.31 N	123.53 W
Bay City, Tex., U.S.	250	28.59 N	95.58 W
Bay de Verde	240	48.05 N	52.54 W
Bayern □[3]	164	49.00 N	11.30 E
Bayern □[9]	164	48.30 N	11.30 E
Bayeux	166	49.16 N	0.42 W
Bayfield, Colo., U.S.	254	37.14 N	107.36 W
Bayfield, Wis., U.S.	244	46.49 N	90.49 W
Bayfield, Île I	240	51.12 N	58.23 W
Bayfield Ridge ∧	244	46.45 N	91.25 W
Bay Head	262	40.04 N	74.03 W
Bayındır	172	38.13 N	27.40 E
Baykonur → Bajkonyr	186	47.50 N	66.03 E
Bay L'Argent	240	47.33 N	54.53 W
Bayley Point ≻	228	16.56 S	139.02 E
Bay Minette	248	30.53 N	87.47 W
Baynesville	262	38.09 N	76.53 W
Baynūnah ◂[1]	208	23.50 N	52.45 E
Bayo	168	43.09 N	8.58 W
Bayombong	202	16.29 N	121.09 E
Bayon	166	48.29 N	6.19 E
Bayona	168	42.07 N	8.51 W
Bayonne, Fr.	166	43.29 N	1.29 W
Bayonne, N.J., U.S.	262	40.41 N	74.07 W
Bayou Bodcau Reservoir ≃[1]	278	32.45 N	93.30 W
Bayou La Batre	248	30.24 N	88.15 W
Bayovar	292	5.50 S	81.03 W
Bay Port, Mich., U.S.	244	43.51 N	83.23 W
Bayport, Minn., U.S.	244	45.01 N	92.47 W
Bayramiç	172	39.48 N	26.37 E
Bayreuth	164	49.57 N	11.35 E
Bay Ridge	262	38.56 N	76.28 W
Bayrischzell	164	47.40 N	12.00 E
Bay Roberts	240	47.36 N	53.16 W
Bayrūt (Beirut)	210	33.53 N	35.30 E
Bayrūt □[4]	210	33.56 N	35.30 E
Bays, Lake of ⊜	244	45.15 N	79.04 W
Bay Saint Louis	248	30.19 N	89.20 W
Bayshore, Calif., U.S.	272	37.42 N	122.25 W
Bay Shore, N.Y., U.S.	242	40.44 N	73.15 W
Bayside, Ont., Can.	264	44.07 N	77.30 W
Bayside, Wis., U.S.	268	43.11 N	87.54 W
Bay Springs	248	31.53 N	89.17 W
Bayt ad-Din ⊥	210	33.41 N	35.34 E
Bayt al-Faqīh	204	14.32 N	43.20 E
Bayt Jālā	210	31.43 N	35.11 E
Bayt Laḥm (Bethlehem)	210	31.43 N	35.12 E
Baytown	250	29.44 N	94.58 W
Bayt Sāḥūr	210	31.42 N	35.13 E
Bayuan ≃	202	9.20 N	122.48 E
Bay View, N.Y., U.S.	264	42.47 N	78.51 W
Bay View, Ohio, U.S.	266	41.28 N	82.50 W
Bay Village	266	41.29 N	81.55 W
Bayville, N.J., U.S.	262	39.55 N	74.09 W
Bayville, N.Y., U.S.	261	40.54 N	73.33 W
Baywood Park	272	35.20 N	120.50 W
Bayyūḍah ▾[4]	220	17.32 N	32.07 E
Baza	168	37.29 N	2.46 W
Baza, Sierra de ⋀⋀	168	37.15 N	2.45 W
Bazaruto, Ilha do I	224	21.40 S	35.28 E
Bazas	166	44.26 N	0.13 W
Bazetta	266	41.20 N	80.47 W
Baziège	166	43.27 N	1.37 E
Bazine	252	38.27 N	99.42 W
Bazmān, Kūh-e ∧	208	28.04 N	60.01 E
Beach, Ill., U.S.	268	42.26 N	87.50 W
Beach, N. Dak., U.S.	252	46.55 N	103.52 W
Beach City	266	40.39 N	81.35 W
Beach Haven	262	39.34 N	74.14 W
Beach Haven Terrace	262	39.36 N	74.14 W
Beachville	264	43.05 N	80.49 W
Beachwood, N.J., U.S.	262	39.56 N	74.12 W
Beachwood, Ohio, U.S.	266	41.34 N	81.28 W
Beachy Head ≻	162	50.44 N	0.16 E
Beacon	261	41.30 N	73.58 W
Beacon Falls	261	41.27 N	73.04 W
Beacon Hill	270	46.08 N	122.57 W
Beaconsfield, Austl.	226	41.12 S	146.48 E
Beaconsfield, Qué., Can.	260	45.26 N	73.51 W
Beaconsfield, Eng., U.K.	174	51.37 N	0.39 W
Beadle Lake	268	42.18 N	85.12 W
Beagle Bank ⁂[4]	226	15.20 S	123.29 E
Bealanana	218	14.33 S	48.44 E
Beale, Cape ≻	238	48.44 N	125.20 W
Beallsville	266	40.04 N	80.01 W
Beampingaratra ⋀⋀	225b	24.30 S	46.50 E
Beamsville	264	43.10 N	79.29 W
Bear ≃	254	41.30 N	112.08 W
Bear, Mount ∧	236	61.17 N	141.09 W
Bear Bay C	232	75.47 N	87.00 W
Bear Brook State Park ♠	242	43.05 N	71.26 W
Bear Cave Mountain ∧	248	36.41 N	92.26 W
Bearden, Ark., U.S.	248	33.43 N	92.37 W
Bearden, Tenn., U.S.	246	35.56 N	84.00 W
Beardmore	232	49.36 N	87.57 W
Beardstown, Ill., U.S.	248	40.01 N	90.26 W
Beardstown, Ind., U.S.	268	41.08 N	86.36 W
Bear Island I	162	51.40 N	9.48 W
Bear Lake, B.C., Can.	238	56.11 N	126.51 W
Bear Lake, Pa., U.S.	266	41.60 N	79.30 W
Bear Lake ⊜, Alta., Can.	238	55.16 N	119.00 W
Bear Lake ⊜, B.C., Can.	238	56.06 N	126.45 W
Bear Lake ⊜, U.S.	254	42.00 N	111.20 W
Bear Mountain ∧, Ky., U.S.	246	37.32 N	84.16 W
Bear Mountain ∧, Oreg., U.S.	256	43.51 N	122.53 W
Béarn ◂[1]	166	43.20 N	0.45 W
Bearpaw Mountains ⋀⋀	256	48.15 N	109.30 W
Bear River	240	44.34 N	65.39 W
Bear Springs	270	45.07 N	121.35 W
Bear Tooth Pass)(	256	44.58 N	109.28 W
Beartooth Range ⋀⋀	256	45.00 N	109.30 W
Beasain	168	43.03 N	2.11 W
Beas de Segura	168	38.15 N	2.53 W
Beata, Cabo ≻	282	17.35 N	71.25 W
Beata, Isla I	282	17.34 N	71.31 W
Beaton	238	50.44 N	117.44 W
Beatrice, Ala., U.S.	248	31.38 N	87.19 W
Beatrice, Nebr., U.S.	252	40.16 N	96.44 W
Beattie	252	39.52 N	96.25 W
Beatton ≃	238	56.10 N	120.25 W
Beatty	258	36.54 N	116.46 W
Beattyville	246	37.35 N	83.42 W
Beaucaire	182	43.48 N	4.38 E
Beauce ◂[1]	166	48.22 N	1.50 E
Beauceville-Est	242	46.12 N	70.46 W
Beauchêne, Lac ⊜	244	46.37 N	78.50 W
Beaudesert	228	27.59 S	153.00 E
Beaudry, Lac ⊜	244	47.44 N	78.56 W
Beaufort, Malay.	198	5.22 N	115.38 E
Beaufort, N.C., U.S.	246	34.43 N	76.40 W
Beaufort, S.C., U.S.	246	32.26 N	80.40 W
Beaufort ⊥	210	33.19 N	35.32 E
Beaufort Sea ▾[2]	148	73.00 N	140.00 W
Beaufort West	224	32.18 S	22.36 E
Beaugency	166	47.47 N	1.38 E
Beauharnois	260	45.19 N	73.52 W
Beauharnois □[6]	260	45.15 N	74.00 W
Beaujolais, Monts du ⋀⋀	166	46.00 N	4.30 E
Beauly	162	57.29 N	4.29 W
Beauly ≃	162	57.29 N	4.29 W
Beaumaris	162	53.16 N	4.05 W
Beaumetz-lès-Loges	162	50.14 N	2.39 E
Beaumont, Newf., Can.	240	49.34 N	55.36 W
Beaumont, Fr.	166	48.13 N	0.08 E
Beaumont, Calif., U.S.	274	33.56 N	116.58 W
Beaumont, Miss., U.S.	248	31.11 N	88.55 W
Beaumont, Tex., U.S.	248	30.05 N	94.06 W
Beaumont Hague	166	49.40 N	1.51 W
Beaumont Hill ∧[2]	228	31.33 S	145.13 E
Beaumont-sur-Oise	176	49.08 N	2.17 E
Beaumont-sur-Sarthe	166	48.13 N	0.08 E
Beaune	180	47.02 N	4.50 E
Beaune-la-Rolande	166	48.04 N	2.26 E
Beauport	260	46.52 N	71.11 W
Beaupré	240	47.03 N	70.53 W
Beaupréau	166	47.12 N	1.00 W
Beaurepaire-d'Isère	166	45.20 N	5.03 E
Beaurivage	260	46.25 N	71.14 W
Beauséjour	232	50.04 N	96.33 W
Beausoleil	182	43.45 N	7.26 E
Beauvais	176	49.26 N	2.05 E
Beauville	166	44.17 N	0.52 E
Beauvoir-sur-Mer	166	46.55 N	2.02 W
Beauvoir-sur-Niort	166	46.11 N	0.28 W
Beaux Arts	270	47.35 N	122.11 W
Beaver, Alaska, U.S.	236	66.22 N	147.24 W
Beaver, Okla., U.S.	250	36.49 N	100.31 W
Beaver, Oreg., U.S.	270	45.17 N	123.49 W
Beaver, Pa., U.S.	266	40.42 N	80.18 W
Beaver, Utah, U.S.	254	38.17 N	112.38 W
Beaver, Wash., U.S.	270	48.03 N	124.19 W
Beaver, W. Va., U.S.	246	37.45 N	81.09 W
Beaver □[6]	266	40.40 N	80.25 W
Beaver ≃, Can.	232	59.43 N	124.16 W
Beaver ≃, Can.	232	55.25 N	107.45 W
Beaver ≃, U.S.	242	40.40 N	80.18 W
Beaver ≃, N.Y., U.S.	242	43.54 N	75.30 W
Beaver ≃, Utah, U.S.	254	39.10 N	112.57 W
Beaver City	252	40.08 N	99.50 W
Beaver Creek, Yukon, Can.	236	62.22 N	140.52 W
Beavercreek, Oreg., U.S.	270	45.17 N	122.32 W
Beaver Crossing	252	40.47 N	97.17 W
Beaverdale	266	40.19 N	78.42 W
Beaverdam, Ohio, U.S.	268	40.50 N	83.59 W
Beaverdell	238	49.26 N	119.05 W
Beaver Falls, N.Y., U.S.	264	43.53 N	75.26 W
Beaver Falls, Pa., U.S.	266	40.46 N	80.19 W
Beaverhead ≃	256	45.31 N	112.21 W
Beaverhead Mountains ⋀⋀	256	45.00 N	113.20 W
Beaverhill Lake ⊜	238	53.27 N	112.32 W
Beaverhouse Lake ⊜	244	48.32 N	92.05 W
Beaver Island I	244	45.40 N	85.31 W
Beaver Lake ⊜	238	54.43 N	111.50 W
Beaver Lake Indian Reserve ◂[4]	238	54.39 N	111.54 W
Beaverlodge	238	55.13 N	119.26 W
Beaver Meadow	264	42.40 N	75.41 W
Beaver Mountains ⋀⋀	236	62.54 N	156.58 W
Beaver Reservoir ⊜[1]	248	36.20 N	93.55 W
Beaver Springs	262	40.45 N	77.13 W
Beaverton, Ont., Can.	264	44.26 N	79.09 W
Beaverton, Mich., U.S.	244	43.53 N	84.29 W
Beaverton, Oreg., U.S.	270	45.29 N	122.48 W
Beaverville	268	40.57 N	87.39 W
Beāwar	206	26.06 N	74.20 E
Beazley	294	33.45 S	66.40 W
Bebedouro	296	20.56 S	48.28 W
Becal	278	20.27 N	90.02 W
Bécancour	260	46.20 N	72.26 W
Beccaria	266	40.46 N	78.27 W
Beccles	174	52.28 N	1.34 E
Bečej	172	45.37 N	20.03 E
Beceni	172	45.23 N	26.46 E
Becerreá	168	42.51 N	7.10 W
Becerro, Cayos II	280	15.57 N	83.15 W
Béchar	214	31.37 N	2.13 W
Becharof Lake ⊜	236	58.00 N	156.30 W
Bechater	170	37.18 N	9.45 E
Bechetu	172	43.46 N	23.58 E
Bechevin Bay C	236	55.00 N	163.27 W
Bechtelsville	262	40.22 N	75.38 W
Bechuanaland ◂[1]	224	27.30 S	22.30 E
Bechyně	164	49.18 N	14.29 E
Becket	261	42.20 N	73.05 W
Beckley	242	37.46 N	81.13 W
Beckum	178	51.45 N	8.02 E
Beckville	248	32.14 N	94.27 W
Becky Peak ∧	258	39.58 N	114.36 W
Beclean	172	47.11 N	24.10 E
Bedale	162	54.17 N	1.35 W
Bédarieux	166	43.37 N	3.09 E
Bedele	214	8.33 N	36.23 E
Bedeque Bay C	240	46.22 N	63.53 W
Bedford, Qué., Can.	260	44.43 N	63.40 W
Bedford, Eng., U.K.	174	52.08 N	0.29 W
Bedford, Ind., U.S.	248	38.52 N	86.29 W
Bedford, Iowa, U.S.	252	40.40 N	94.44 W
Bedford, Ky., U.S.	248	38.36 N	85.19 W
Bedford, Mass., U.S.	261	42.29 N	71.17 W
Bedford, Mich., U.S.	268	42.23 N	85.14 W
Bedford, N.Y., U.S.	261	41.12 N	73.39 W
Bedford, Ohio, U.S.	266	41.23 N	81.32 W
Bedford, Pa., U.S.	242	40.01 N	78.30 W
Bedford, Va., U.S.	246	37.20 N	79.31 W
Bedford, Wyo., U.S.	254	42.54 N	110.56 W
Bedford □[6]	266	40.09 N	78.30 W
Bedford Hills	261	41.14 N	73.42 W
Bedfordshire □[6]	174	52.05 N	0.30 W
Bedias	250	30.46 N	95.57 W
Bedlington	162	55.08 N	1.35 W
Bedminster	262	40.26 N	75.11 W
Bedworth	174	52.28 N	1.29 W
Beebe, Qué., Can.	260	45.01 N	72.09 W
Beebe, Ark., U.S.	248	35.04 N	91.53 W
Beechbottom	266	40.14 N	80.39 W
Beech Creek	248	37.11 N	87.03 W
Beechcrest	266	41.05 N	81.20 W
Beecher	268	41.21 N	87.38 W
Beech Fork ≃	248	37.46 N	85.41 W
Beech Grove	248	39.43 N	86.03 W
Beechwood	268	46.09 N	88.46 W
Beechworth	228	36.22 S	146.41 E
Beecroft Head ≻	228	35.01 S	150.51 E
Beelitz	164	52.14 N	12.58 E
Beemer	252	41.56 N	96.48 W
Bee Ridge	246	27.16 N	82.31 W
Beernem	176	51.09 N	3.20 E
Beerse	178	51.19 N	4.52 E
Beersheba → Be'er Sheva'	210	31.15 N	34.47 E
Beersheba Springs	248	35.28 N	85.39 W
Be'er Sheva'(Beersheba)	210	31.15 N	34.47 E
Be'er Sheva', Sede-Tek'ufa ⊠	210	31.16 N	34.43 E
Beeskow	164	52.10 N	14.14 E
Beeston	174	52.56 N	1.12 W
Beeton	264	44.05 N	79.47 W
Beetz, Lac ⊜	240	50.34 N	62.43 W
Beeville	250	28.24 N	97.45 W
Befale	218	0.28 N	20.58 E
Befandriana	218	15.16 S	48.32 E
Bega	228	36.40 S	149.50 E
Beggs	250	35.45 N	96.04 W
Begi	214	9.16 N	34.33 E
Bègles	166	44.47 N	0.34 W
Begoml'	160	54.44 N	28.04 E
Begoro	222	6.23 N	0.23 W
Behbehān	208	30.35 N	50.14 E
Behm Canal ⋓	236	55.41 N	131.35 W
Behshahr	208	36.43 N	53.34 E
Beian	190	48.15 N	126.30 E
Beida → Zāwiyat al-Bayḍā'	214	32.46 N	21.43 E
Beïda, Chott el ⊜	168	36.00 N	5.50 E
Beiguanshan I	196	27.10 N	120.32 E
Beihai (Pakhoi)	200	21.29 N	109.05 E
Beijian I	196	21.53 N	114.02 E
Beijing (Peking)	194	39.55 N	116.25 E
Beijing Shih □[7]	194	40.15 N	116.30 E
Beijishan I	196	27.38 N	121.12 E
Beiliu	200	22.42 N	110.22 E
Beilongshan I	196	27.40 N	120.58 E
Beipiao	194	41.49 N	120.46 E
Beira	224	19.49 S	34.52 E
Beira Alta □[9]	168	40.40 N	7.35 W
Beira Baixa □[9]	168	39.45 N	7.30 W
Beira Litoral □[9]	168	40.15 N	8.25 W
Beirut → Bayrūt	210	33.53 N	35.30 E
Beirut International Airport ⊠	210	33.49 N	35.30 E
Beiseker	238	51.23 N	113.32 W
Beitbridge	218	22.13 S	30.00 E
Beiuş	172	46.40 N	22.21 E
Beiyandangshan ∧	196	28.22 N	121.00 E
Beizhen	194	41.36 N	121.47 E
Beja, Port.	168	38.01 N	7.52 W
Béja, Tun.	170	36.44 N	9.11 E
Béja □[8]	170	36.35 N	9.20 E
Bejaïa (Bougie)	168	36.45 N	5.05 E
Béjar	168	40.23 N	5.46 W
Bejestān	204	34.31 N	58.10 E
Bejucal	284p	22.56 N	82.23 W
Bejuco	280	8.35 N	79.55 W
Bejuma	290	10.11 N	68.16 W
Bekabad	186	40.13 N	69.14 E
Bekdaš	186	41.34 N	52.32 E
Békés	164	46.46 N	21.08 E
Békés □[6]	164	46.46 N	21.08 E
Békéscsaba	164	46.41 N	21.06 E
Bekilli	172	38.14 N	29.26 E
Bekily	218	24.13 S	45.19 E
Bekkai	192a	43.23 N	145.17 E
Bekkaria	170	35.23 N	8.15 E
Bekwai	222	6.27 N	1.35 W
Bela	204	26.14 N	66.19 E
Bélâbre	166	46.33 N	1.09 E
Bela Crkva	172	44.54 N	21.26 E
Belaga	198	2.42 N	113.47 E
Bel Air	262	39.32 N	76.21 W
Bel Aire Estates	261	41.23 N	72.00 W
Belaja, Gora ∧	236	65.50 N	174.40 E
Belaja Cerkov'	158	49.49 N	30.07 E
Belaja Cholunica	160	58.50 N	50.48 E
Bel'aka, Kosa ≻[2]	236	67.05 N	174.30 W
Belalcázar	168	38.34 N	5.10 W
Bel Alton	262	38.28 N	76.59 W
Bela Palanka	172	43.13 N	22.19 E
Bela Vista, Bra.	294	22.06 S	56.31 W
Bela Vista, Moç.	218	26.20 S	32.40 E
Bela Vista de Goiás	296	16.58 S	48.57 W
Bela Vista do Paráiso	296	23.00 S	51.12 W
Belawan	198	3.47 N	98.41 E
Belcamp	262	39.28 N	76.14 W
Bełchatów	164	51.22 N	19.21 E
Belcher	248	32.45 N	93.50 W
Belcher Islands II	232	56.20 N	79.30 W
Belchertown	261	42.17 N	72.24 W
Belchite	168	41.18 N	0.45 W
Belcourt	252	48.50 N	99.45 W
Bel'cy	158	47.46 N	27.56 E
Belding	268	43.06 N	85.14 W
Belebej	158	54.07 N	54.07 E
Belecke	178	51.29 N	8.20 E
Beled Weyne	214	4.47 N	45.12 E
Belém	286	1.27 S	48.29 W
Belén, Arg.	294	27.40 S	67.05 W
Belén, Chile	292	18.29 S	69.31 W
Belén, Col.	290	6.00 N	72.55 W
Belén, Col.	290	1.26 N	75.56 W
Belén, Nic.	280	11.30 N	85.53 W
Belén, Para.	294	23.30 S	57.06 W
Belen, N. Mex., U.S.	254	34.40 N	106.46 W
Belén, Ur.	294	30.47 S	57.47 W
Belén de Escobar	294	34.22 S	58.48 W
Belene	172	43.39 N	25.07 E
Belfair	270	47.27 N	122.50 W
Belfast, S. Afr.	218	25.43 S	30.03 E
Belfast, N. Ire., U.K.	162	54.35 N	5.55 W
Belfast, Maine, U.S.	242	44.27 N	69.01 W
Belfast, N.Y., U.S.	266	42.21 N	78.07 W
Belfast Lough C	162	54.40 N	5.50 W
Belfield	252	46.53 N	103.12 W
Belfort	180	47.38 N	6.52 E
Belfort □[8]	180	47.38 N	6.55 E
Belfry, Ky., U.S.	246	37.37 N	82.16 W
Belfry, Mont., U.S.	256	45.09 N	109.01 W
Belgioioso	182	45.10 N	9.19 E
Belgium □[1]	158	50.50 N	4.00 E
Belgodere	170	42.35 N	9.01 E
Belgorod	158	50.36 N	36.35 E
Belgorod-Dnestrovskij	158	46.12 N	30.20 E
Belgrade → Beograd, Jugo.	172	44.50 N	20.30 E
Belgrade, Minn., U.S.	252	45.27 N	95.00 W
Belgrade, Mont., U.S.	256	45.47 N	111.11 W
Belgrade, Nebr., U.S.	252	41.28 N	98.04 W
Belhaven	246	35.33 N	76.37 W
Beli Drim ≃	172	42.06 N	20.25 E
Beli Manastir	172	45.46 N	18.36 E
Belin	166	44.30 N	0.47 W
Belington	242	39.01 N	79.56 W
Belize	278	17.30 N	88.12 W
Belize ≃	278	17.32 N	88.14 W
Belize Inlet C	238	51.08 N	127.15 W
Belkis (Aspendos) ⊥	212	37.08 N	31.12 E
Belknap Crater ▲[6]	256	44.17 N	121.50 W
Belkofski	236	55.05 N	162.02 W
Bell ≃, Qué., Can.	232	49.50 N	77.45 W
Bell ≃, Yukon, Can.	236	67.17 N	137.46 W
Bella Bella	238	52.09 N	128.07 W
Bellac	166	46.07 N	1.02 E
Bella Coola	238	52.22 N	126.46 W
Bella Coola ≃	238	52.22 N	126.43 W
Bella Flor	292	11.09 S	67.49 W
Bellagio	170	45.59 N	9.15 E
Bellaire, Mich., U.S.	244	44.59 N	85.13 W
Bellaire, Ohio, U.S.	242	40.02 N	80.45 W
Bellaire, Tex., U.S.	250	29.43 N	95.03 W
Bellamy, Ala., U.S.	248	32.22 N	88.08 W
Bellamy, Va., U.S.	262	37.24 N	76.34 W
Bellaria	184	44.09 N	12.28 E
Bella Unión	294	30.15 S	57.35 W
Bella Vista, Arg.	294	28.30 S	59.00 W
Bella Vista, Arg.	294	27.02 S	65.19 W
Bella Vista, Para.	294	22.08 S	56.31 W
Bellavista, Perú	292	4.54 S	80.42 W
Bellavista, Perú	292	6.58 S	76.32 W
Belle, Mo., U.S.	248	38.17 N	91.43 W
Belle, W. Va., U.S.	242	38.14 N	81.32 W
Belle Bay C	240	47.36 N	55.18 W
Belle Center	268	40.31 N	83.45 W
Belledonne, Chaîne de ⋀⋀	166	45.18 N	6.08 E
Belle Farm Estates	262	39.23 N	76.45 W
Bellefontaine, Mart.	284e	14.40 N	61.10 W
Bellefontaine, Miss., U.S.	248	33.39 N	89.19 W
Bellefontaine, Ohio, U.S.	268	40.22 N	83.46 W
Bellefonte, Del., U.S.	262	39.46 N	75.30 W
Bellefonte, Pa., U.S.	266	40.55 N	77.46 W
Belle Fourche	252	44.40 N	103.51 W
Belle Fourche ≃	252	44.26 N	102.19 W
Belle Fourche Reservoir ⊜[1]	252	44.44 N	103.42 W
Bellegarde	180	46.06 N	5.49 E
Belle Glade	246	26.41 N	80.40 W
Bellegrove	262	40.22 N	76.33 W
Belle Haven	262	37.33 N	75.49 W
Belle Île I	166	47.20 N	3.10 W
Belle Isle	246	28.27 N	81.21 W
Belle Isle I	232	51.55 N	55.20 W
Belle Isle, Strait of ⋓	240	51.35 N	56.30 W
Belleisle Bay C	240	45.35 N	65.55 W
Bellême	166	48.22 N	0.34 E
Belle Mead	262	40.28 N	74.40 W
Belle Meade	248	36.07 N	86.52 W
Belleoram	240	47.31 N	55.25 W
Belleplain	262	39.11 N	74.46 W
Belle Plaine, Iowa, U.S.	244	41.54 N	92.17 W
Belle Plaine, Kans., U.S.	252	37.24 N	97.17 W
Belle Plaine, Minn., U.S.	244	44.37 N	93.46 W
Belle River	266	42.18 N	82.43 W
Belle Vernon	266	40.07 N	79.50 W
Belleview, Fla., U.S.	246	29.04 N	82.03 W
Belleview, Tenn., U.S.	248	36.04 N	86.56 W
Belle View, Va., U.S.	262	38.47 N	77.03 W
Belleville, Ont., Can.	264	44.10 N	77.23 W
Belleville, Ill., U.S.	248	38.31 N	90.00 W
Belleville, Kans., U.S.	252	39.49 N	97.38 W
Belleville, Mich., U.S.	268	42.12 N	83.29 W
Belleville, N.J., U.S.	262	40.48 N	74.09 W
Belleville, N.Y., U.S.	264	43.47 N	76.07 W
Belleville, Pa., U.S.	266	40.36 N	77.43 W
Belleville, R.I., U.S.	261	41.34 N	71.29 W
Belleville, Wis., U.S.	268	42.52 N	89.32 W
Belleville-sur-Saône	166	46.06 N	4.45 E
Bellevue, Alta., Can.	238	49.35 N	114.22 W
Bellevue, Idaho, U.S.	256	43.28 N	114.16 W
Bellevue, Iowa, U.S.	244	42.16 N	90.26 W
Bellevue, Md., U.S.	262	38.42 N	76.11 W
Bellevue, Mich., U.S.	268	42.27 N	85.01 W
Bellevue, Nebr., U.S.	252	41.09 N	95.54 W
Bellevue, Ohio, U.S.	266	41.17 N	82.50 W
Bellevue, Pa., U.S.	266	40.30 N	80.03 W
Bellevue, Tex., U.S.	250	33.38 N	98.01 W
Bellevue, Wash., U.S.	270	47.37 N	122.12 W
Bell Ewart	264	44.16 N	79.33 W
Belley	182	45.46 N	5.41 E
Bellflower, Calif., U.S.	274	33.53 N	118.07 W
Bellflower, Ill., U.S.	268	40.20 N	88.32 W
Bell Gardens	274	33.58 N	118.09 W
Bellingham, Eng., U.K.	162	55.09 N	2.16 W
Bellingham, Mass., U.S.	261	42.05 N	71.28 W
Bellingham, Minn., U.S.	252	45.08 N	96.17 W
Bellingham, Wash., U.S.	270	48.46 N	122.29 W
Bellingshausen Sea ▾[2]	148	71.00 S	85.00 W
Bellinzago Novarese	182	45.34 N	8.38 E
Bellinzona	180	46.11 N	9.02 E
Bell Island I, Newf., Can.	240	50.44 N	55.35 W
Bell Island I, Newf., Can.	240	47.36 N	52.58 W
Bell Island Hot Springs	238	55.56 N	131.34 W
Bellmawr	262	39.51 N	75.06 W
Bellmead	250	31.35 N	97.06 W
Bell Mountain	274	34.35 N	117.15 W
Bello	290	6.20 N	75.33 W
Bellona	264	42.46 N	77.01 W
Bellona Plateau ⁂[3]	148	21.00 S	160.00 E
Bellone, Cap ≻	225b	16.14 S	49.51 E
Bellot Strait ⋓	232	71.58 N	94.45 W
Bellows Falls	242	43.08 N	72.27 W
Bell Peninsula ≻[1]	232	63.50 N	82.00 W
Bells, Tenn., U.S.	248	35.43 N	89.05 W
Bells, Tex., U.S.	250	33.37 N	96.25 W
Bells Corners	264	45.19 N	75.50 W
Belltown	262	38.45 N	75.11 W
Belluno	170	46.09 N	12.13 E
Bell Ville, Arg.	294	32.40 S	62.40 W
Bellville, S. Afr.	224	33.53 S	18.36 E
Bellville, Ohio, U.S.	266	40.37 N	82.31 W
Bellville, Tex., U.S.	250	29.57 N	96.16 W
Bellwood, Nebr., U.S.	252	41.21 N	97.14 W
Bellwood, Pa., U.S.	266	40.36 N	78.20 W
Belly ≃	238	49.46 N	113.02 W
Belmar	262	40.11 N	74.01 W
Bélmez	168	38.16 N	5.12 W
Belmond	244	42.51 N	93.37 W
Belmont, Man., Can.	252	49.24 N	99.27 W
Belmont, Ont., Can.	264	42.53 N	81.05 W
Belmont, Calif., U.S.	272	37.31 N	122.17 W
Belmont, Miss., U.S.	248	34.31 N	88.13 W
Belmont, N.H., U.S.	242	43.27 N	71.29 W
Belmont, N.Y., U.S.	266	42.13 N	78.02 W
Belmont, Pa., U.S.	266	40.17 N	78.53 W
Belmont, Wis., U.S.	244	42.44 N	90.20 W
Belmont □[6]	266	40.05 N	80.54 W
Belmonte, Bra.	296	15.51 S	38.54 W
Belmonte, Esp.	168	43.10 N	6.05 W
Belmonte, Esp.	168	39.34 N	2.42 W
Belmonte, Port.	168	40.21 N	7.21 W
Belmont Park	266	41.10 N	80.39 W
Belmopan	278	17.15 N	88.47 W
Belmore	268	41.09 N	83.56 W
Belmullet	162	54.14 N	10.00 W
Belo	218	19.42 S	44.33 E
Beloeil	260	45.34 N	73.12 W
Belogorsk	186	45.03 N	34.36 E
Belogradčik	172	43.38 N	22.41 E
Belo Horizonte	296	19.55 S	43.56 W
Beloit, Kans., U.S.	252	39.28 N	98.06 W
Beloit, Ohio, U.S.	266	40.56 N	80.60 W
Beloit, Wis., U.S.	268	42.31 N	89.02 W
Beloje, Ozero ⊜	160	60.11 N	37.37 E
Beloje More (White Sea) ▾[2], S.S.S.R.	158	65.30 N	38.00 E
Beloje More ▾[2], S.S.S.R.	160	66.00 N	40.00 E
Belomorsk	160	64.32 N	34.48 E
Belomorsko-Baltijskij Kanal ☰	160	62.48 N	34.48 E
Belorado	168	42.25 N	3.11 W
Belorečensk	158	44.46 N	39.52 E
Beloreck	158	53.58 N	58.24 E
Belorusskaja Sovetskaja Socialističeskaja Respublika □[3]	186		
Beloščelje	160	64.52 N	46.56 E
Belot, Lac ⊜	236	66.55 N	126.18 W
Bel'ov	158	53.48 N	36.08 E
Belo Vale	296	20.25 S	44.01 W
Belovo	186	54.25 N	86.18 E
Beloz'orsk	160	60.02 N	37.48 E
Belpasso	170	37.35 N	14.59 E
Belper	174	53.01 N	1.29 W
Belpre	242	39.17 N	81.34 W
Belsano	266	40.31 N	78.52 W
Belsele	176	51.09 N	4.05 E
Belspring	246	37.11 N	80.36 W
Belt	256	47.23 N	110.55 W
Belted Range ⋀⋀	258	37.25 N	116.10 W
Belton, Mo., U.S.	248	38.49 N	94.32 W
Belton, S.C., U.S.	246	34.31 N	82.30 W
Belton, Tex., U.S.	250	31.04 N	97.28 W
Beltrán	294	27.50 S	64.04 W
Belucha, Gora ∧	186	49.48 N	86.40 E
Beluran	202	5.54 N	117.34 E
Belušje	160	66.54 N	47.31 E
Belvedere	272	37.52 N	122.28 W
Belvedere Marittimo	170	39.47 N	15.52 E
Belvès	166	44.47 N	1.00 E
Belvidere, Del., U.S.	262	39.43 N	75.37 W
Belvidere, Ill., U.S.	268	42.15 N	88.50 W
Belvidere, N.J., U.S.	242	40.49 N	75.05 W
Belview	252	44.36 N	95.20 W
Belvís de la Jara	168	39.45 N	4.57 W
Belvoir ⊥	210	32.36 N	35.31 E
Belyando ≃	228	21.38 S	146.50 E
Belyj	160	55.50 N	32.56 E
Belyj, Ostrov I	186	73.10 N	70.45 E
Belyj Jar	186	53.57 N	48.58 E
Belz	166	47.41 N	3.10 W
Bełżec	164	50.24 N	23.26 E
Belzig	164	52.08 N	12.35 E
Belzoni	248	33.11 N	90.29 W
Bełżyce	164	51.11 N	22.18 E
Bemaraha, Plateau du ⋀⋀[1]	225b	20.00 S	45.15 E
Bembézar ≃	168	37.45 N	5.13 W
Bement	248	39.55 N	88.34 W
Bemidji	244	47.29 N	94.53 W
Bemis, Tenn., U.S.	248	35.35 N	88.49 W
Bemis, W. Va., U.S.	242	38.49 N	79.44 W
Bemus Point	266	42.09 N	79.24 W
Benāb	208	37.20 N	46.04 E
Benabarre	168	42.07 N	0.29 E
Bena-Dibele	218	4.07 S	22.50 E
Benalla	228	36.33 S	145.59 E
Benamejí	168	37.16 N	4.32 W
Benares → Vārānasi	000	25.20 N	83.00 E
Benavente, Esp.	168	42.00 N	5.41 W
Benavente, Port.	168	38.59 N	8.48 W
Benavides	250	27.36 N	98.25 W
Ben Avon	266	40.31 N	80.05 W
Ben Badis	168	34.57 N	0.55 W
Benbecula I	162	57.27 N	7.20 W
Ben Bolt	250	27.39 N	98.05 W
Benbonyathe Hill ∧	228	30.24 S	139.11 E
Benbrook Lake ⊜[1]	250	32.38 N	97.27 W
Bencha, Khao Phanom ∧	200	8.15 N	98.58 E
Ben-Chicao, Col de)(	168	36.12 N	2.45 E
Bencubbin	226	30.48 S	117.52 E
Bend	256	44.03 N	121.19 W
Bendale	246	34.00 N	81.03 W
Bendeleben, Mount ∧	236	65.10 N	164.03 W
Bendersville	262	39.59 N	77.15 W
Bendery	158	46.48 N	29.29 E
Bendigo	228	36.46 S	144.17 E
Bendorf	164	50.25 N	7.34 E
Bēne	160	56.29 N	23.04 E
Bene Beraq	210	32.06 N	34.51 E
Benedict	262	38.31 N	76.41 W
Benedito Leite	286	7.13 S	44.34 W
Benešov	164	49.47 N	14.43 E
Bénévent-l'Abbaye	166	46.07 N	1.38 E
Benevento	184	41.08 N	14.45 E
Benevento □[4]	184	41.15 N	14.17 E
Benezett	266	41.19 N	78.23 W
Benfeld	166	48.22 N	7.36 E
Bengal, Bay of C	204	15.00 N	90.00 W
Benghazi → Banghāzī	214	32.07 N	20.04 E
Bengkajang	200	0.50 N	109.29 E
Bengkalis	200	1.28 N	102.07 E
Bengkalis, Pulau I	200	1.30 N	102.15 E
Bengkulu	198	3.48 S	102.16 E
Bengough	252	49.24 N	105.08 W
Bengtsfors	160	59.02 N	12.13 E
Benguela	218	12.35 S	13.25 E
Benguérua, Ilha I	224	21.58 S	35.28 E
Benguet □[4]	202	16.30 N	120.40 E
Bengut, Cap ≻	168	36.58 N	3.50 E
Benham	246	36.58 N	82.57 W
Beni	218	0.30 N	29.28 E
Beni ≃	292	10.23 S	65.24 W
Béni Abbès	214	30.05 N	2.05 W
Benicarló	168	40.25 N	0.26 E
Benicia	272	38.03 N	122.09 W
Benicito ≃	292	11.32 S	65.47 W
Benidorm	168	38.32 N	0.08 W
Beni-Mellal	214	32.22 N	6.29 W
Benin, Bight of C[3]	222	5.30 N	3.00 E
Benin City	222	6.19 N	5.41 E
Benisa	168	38.34 N	0.03 E
Beni Saf	168	35.17 N	1.15 W
Benito Juárez, Parque Nacional ♠	278	17.07 N	96.43 W
Benito Juárez, Presa ⊜[1]	278	16.27 N	95.30 W
Benjamin	250	33.35 N	99.48 W
Benjamin Constant	290	4.22 S	70.02 W
Benjamín Hill	278	30.10 N	111.10 W
Benjamín Zorrilla	294	38.42 S	65.28 W
Benkelman	252	40.03 N	101.32 W
Benkovac	170	44.02 N	15.37 E
Benld	248	39.06 N	89.48 W
Ben Lomond, Ark., U.S.	248	33.50 N	94.07 W
Ben Lomond, Calif., U.S.	272	37.05 N	122.05 W
Ben Mehidi	170	36.46 N	7.54 E
Benndale	248	30.52 N	88.48 W
Bennekom	178	52.00 N	5.40 E
Bennet	252	40.41 N	96.30 W
Bennettsville	246	34.37 N	79.41 W
Bennington, Kans., U.S.	252	39.02 N	97.36 W
Bennington, Vt., U.S.	242	42.53 N	73.12 W
Bennington □[6]	261	42.50 N	73.08 W
Ben-ohau Range ⋀⋀	230	44.07 S	169.57 E
Benoit	248	33.39 N	91.01 W
Benom, Gunong ∧	200	3.49 N	102.04 E
Benoni	224	26.19 S	28.27 E
Bénoué (Benue) ≃	214	7.48 N	6.46 E
Benque Viejo	278	17.05 N	89.08 W
Benrath ◂[8]	178	51.10 N	6.51 E
Bensenville	268	41.57 N	87.57 W
Bensheim	164	49.41 N	8.37 E
Bensley Village	262	37.26 N	77.26 W
Benson, Ariz., U.S.	254	31.58 N	110.18 W
Benson, Md., U.S.	262	39.31 N	76.23 W
Benson, Minn., U.S.	252	45.19 N	95.36 W
Benson, N.C., U.S.	246	35.23 N	78.33 W
Benson, Pa., U.S.	266	40.13 N	78.55 W
Bentheim, B.R.D.	178	52.17 N	7.10 E
Bentheim, Mich., U.S.	268	42.42 N	85.55 W
Bentinck Island I, Austl.	228	17.04 S	139.30 E
Bentinck Island I, Mya.	200	11.45 N	98.03 E
Bentley	238	52.28 N	114.04 W
Bentleyville	266	40.07 N	80.01 W
Bento Gonçalves	294	29.10 S	51.31 W
Benton, Ark., U.S.	248	34.34 N	92.35 W
Benton, Ill., U.S.	248	38.00 N	88.55 W
Benton, Ind., U.S.	268	41.31 N	85.46 W
Benton, La., U.S.	248	32.42 N	93.44 W
Benton, Miss., U.S.	248	32.50 N	90.15 W
Benton, Mo., U.S.	248	37.06 N	89.34 W
Benton, Ohio, U.S.	266	40.36 N	81.51 W
Benton, Pa., U.S.	242	41.12 N	76.23 W
Benton, Tenn., U.S.	246	35.10 N	84.39 W
Benton, Wis., U.S.	244	42.34 N	90.23 W
Benton □[6]	268	40.37 N	87.19 W
Benton City	256	46.16 N	119.29 W
Bentong	200	3.32 N	101.57 E
Benton Harbor	268	42.06 N	86.27 W
Benton Heights	268	42.07 N	86.24 W
Bentonia	248	32.38 N	90.22 W
Benton Ridge	268	41.00 N	83.48 W
Bentonville	248	36.22 N	94.13 W
Bent's Old Fort National Historic Site ⊥	252	38.05 N	103.28 W
Benua, Pulau I	200	0.56 N	107.27 E
Benue (Bénoué) ≃	214	7.48 N	6.46 E
Benue-Plateau □[3]	222	8.00 N	9.00 E
Ben Wheeler	250	32.27 N	95.42 W
Benxi (Penhsi)	194	41.18 N	123.45 E
Beograd (Belgrade)	172	44.50 N	20.30 E
Beowawe	258	40.35 N	116.29 W
Beppu	192	33.17 N	131.30 E
Bequia I	282	13.01 N	61.13 W
Berat	172	40.42 N	19.57 E
Berbera	214	10.25 N	45.02 E
Berbérati	214	4.16 N	15.47 E
Berbería, Cabo ≻	168	38.38 N	1.23 E
Berceto	170	44.31 N	9.59 E
Berchem	176	51.12 N	4.26 E
Berchem-Sainte-Agathe	176	50.52 N	4.17 E
Berchtesgaden	164	47.38 N	13.01 E
Berck-Plage	166	50.24 N	1.34 E
Berck-sur-Mer, Fr.	176	50.24 N	1.36 E
Berclair	250	28.32 N	97.36 W
Berd'ansk	158	46.45 N	36.49 E
Berdičev	158	49.54 N	28.36 E
Berdigest'ach	186	62.06 N	126.40 E
Berdsk	186	54.47 N	83.02 E
Berea, Ky., U.S.	246	37.34 N	84.17 W
Berea, Ohio, U.S.	266	41.22 N	81.52 W
Berea, Tex., U.S.	248	32.48 N	94.24 W
Berekua	284d	15.14 N	61.19 W
Berekum	222	7.27 N	2.37 W
Berens River	232	52.22 N	97.02 W
Beresford	252	43.05 N	96.47 W
Bereşti	172	46.06 N	27.53 E
Beretăul (Berettyó) ≃	172	46.59 N	21.07 E
Berettyó (Beretăul) ≃	172	46.59 N	21.07 E
Berettyóújfalu	164	47.14 N	21.32 E
Berezajka	160	57.59 N	33.54 E
Bereznik	160	62.51 N	42.40 E
Berezniki	158	59.24 N	56.46 E
Berg	160	69.26 N	17.15 E
Berga	168	42.06 N	1.51 E
Bergama	212	39.07 N	27.11 E
Bergamo	182	45.41 N	9.43 E
Bergamo □[4]	182	45.50 N	9.48 E
Bergantín	290	10.01 N	64.22 W
Bergby	160	60.56 N	17.02 E
Bergedorf ◂[8]	178	53.29 N	10.13 E
Bergeijk	178	51.19 N	5.22 E
Bergen, B.R.D.	178	52.48 N	9.58 E
Bergen, Ned.	178	52.40 N	4.41 E
Bergen, Nor.	160	60.23 N	5.20 E
Bergen, N.Y., U.S.	264	43.05 N	77.57 W
Bergen op Zoom	178	51.30 N	4.17 E
Bergen / Rügen	164	54.25 N	13.26 E
Bergerac	166	44.51 N	0.29 E
Bergheim	166	50.55 N	6.38 E
Bergholtz	264	43.06 N	78.53 W
Bergholz	266	40.31 N	80.53 W
Bergisch	164	51.09 N	7.15 E
Bergisch Gladbach	164	50.59 N	7.07 E
Bergkamen	178	51.38 N	7.38 E

Symbols in the index entries are identified on page 360.

Name	Page	Lat°′	Long°′
Bergkvara	160	56.23 N	16.05 E
Bergland	244	46.35 N	89.34 W
Bergoo	242	38.29 N	80.18 W
Bergos	172	40.14 N	26.36 E
Bergsjö	160	61.59 N	17.04 E
Berguent	214	34.03 N	2.02 W
Bergues	166	50.58 N	2.26 E
Berhala, Selat ⊔	200	0.48 S	104.25 E
Berhampore	206	24.06 N	88.15 E
Beri	202	12.41 N	124.22 E
Beringa, Ostrov I	186	55.00 N	165.15 E
Bering Glacier ⌂	236	60.15 N	143.30 W
Beringovskij, S.S.S.R.	186		
	236	63.03 N	179.19 E
Bering Sea ⊤[2]	148	60.00 N	175.00 W
Bering Strait ⊔	236	65.30 N	169.00 W
Berino	254	32.04 N	106.37 W
Berja	168	36.51 N	2.57 W
Berkåk	160	62.50 N	10.00 E
Berkane	168	34.59 N	2.20 W
Berkeley, Calif., U.S.	272	37.57 N	122.18 W
Berkeley, R.I., U.S.	261	41.56 N	71.25 W
Berkeley Heights	262	40.41 N	74.27 W
Berkeley Springs	242	39.38 N	78.14 W
Berkhamsted	174	51.46 N	0.35 W
Berkley, Mass., U.S.	261	41.51 N	71.05 W
Berkley, Mich., U.S.	266	42.31 N	83.10 W
Berkner Island I	148	79.30 S	49.30 W
Berks □[6]	262	40.20 N	75.50 W
Berkshire	261	42.30 N	73.12 W
Berkshire □[6], Eng., U.K.	174	51.30 N	1.20 W
Berkshire □[6], Mass., U.S.	261	42.27 N	73.15 W
Berkshire Hills ⋀[2]	242	42.20 N	73.10 W
Berlaar	178	51.07 N	4.39 E
Berlaimont	166	50.12 N	3.49 E
Berland ≃	238	54.01 N	116.50 W
Berlanga de Duero	168	41.28 N	2.51 W
Berleburg	178	51.03 N	8.23 E
Berlenga, Ilha I	168	39.25 N	9.30 W
Berlevåg	160	70.51 N	29.06 E
Berlin, B.R.D.	164	52.31 N	13.24 E
Berlin, Conn., U.S.	261	41.37 N	72.45 W
Berlin, Md., U.S.	262	38.20 N	75.13 W
Berlin, Mass., U.S.	261	42.23 N	71.38 W
Berlin, N.H., U.S.	242	44.29 N	71.10 W
Berlin, N.J., U.S.	262	39.48 N	74.57 W
Berlin, N.Y., U.S.	261	42.42 N	73.23 W
Berlin, Ohio, U.S.	266	40.34 N	81.48 W
Berlin, Pa., U.S.	242	39.55 N	78.57 W
Berlin, Wis., U.S.	244	43.58 N	88.55 W
Berlin, East → Ost-Berlin	164	52.30 N	13.25 E
Berlin, West → West-Berlin	164	52.30 N	13.20 E
Berlin Center	266	41.01 N	80.57 W
Berlinguet Inlet C	232	71.10 N	85.35 W
Berlin Heights	266	41.20 N	82.30 W
Bermejillo	278	25.53 N	103.37 W
Bermejo	294	31.37 S	67.39 W
Bermejo ≃, Arg.	294	32.13 S	67.33 W
Bermejo ≃, S.A.	294	26.51 S	58.23 W
Bermejo, Paso de)(	294	32.50 S	70.05 W
Bermen, Lac ⊜	232	53.30 N	69.00 W
Bermeo	168	43.26 N	2.43 W
Bermillo de Sayago	168	41.22 N	6.06 W
Bermuda □[2]	276	30.20 N	64.45 W
Bermuda Islands II	148	32.20 N	64.45 W
Bermuda Rise ⊹[3]	148	33.00 N	65.00 W
Bern (Berne)	180	46.57 N	7.26 E
Bern (Berne) □[3]	180	46.45 N	7.40 E
Bernalda	170	40.24 N	16.41 E
Bernard Island I	232	73.40 N	124.20 W
Bernardston	261	42.40 N	72.33 W
Bernardsville	262	40.43 N	74.34 W
Bernasconi	294	37.55 S	63.45 W
Bernau bei Berlin	164	52.40 N	13.35 E
Bernaville	162	50.08 N	2.10 E
Bernay	176	49.06 N	0.36 E
Bernburg	164	51.48 N	11.44 E
Berndorf	164	47.57 N	16.08 E
Berne, B.R.D.	178	53.11 N	8.29 E
Berne → Bern, Schw.	180	46.57 N	7.26 E
Berne, Ind., U.S.	268	40.39 N	84.57 W
Berneray I	162	57.43 N	7.15 W
Bernhards Bay	264	43.15 N	75.56 W
Bernice	248	32.49 N	92.39 W
Bernie	248	36.40 N	89.58 W
Bernier Bay C	232	71.00 N	87.30 W
Bernina, Piz ∧	166	46.21 N	9.51 E
Bernkastel-Kues	164	49.55 N	7.04 E
Bernsdorf	164	51.22 N	14.04 E
Bernville	262	40.26 N	76.07 W
Beromünster	166	47.12 N	8.11 E
Berón de Astrada	294	27.35 S	57.32 W
Beroroha	218	21.41 S	45.10 E
Ber'ostovica	164	53.07 N	23.58 E
Beroun	164	49.58 N	14.04 E
Berounka ≃	164	50.00 N	14.24 E
Berovo	172	41.42 N	22.51 E
Ber'ozovka	160	65.00 N	56.26 E
Ber'ozovo	158	63.56 N	65.02 E
Berre, Étang de C	166	43.27 N	5.08 E
Berre-l'Étang	182	43.28 N	5.11 E
Berrien □[6]	268	41.59 N	86.30 W
Berrien Springs	268	41.57 N	86.20 W
Berrouaghia	168	36.09 N	2.55 E
Berrugosa Point ≻	202	10.23 N	125.34 E
Berry	248	33.39 N	87.36 W
Berry □[9]	176	47.20 N	2.10 E
Berry, Canal du ≖	166	47.04 N	3.02 E
Berry Islands II	282	25.40 N	77.50 W
Berrysburg	262	40.36 N	76.49 W
Berryville, Ark., U.S.	248	36.22 N	93.34 W
Berryville, Va., U.S.	242	39.09 N	77.59 W
Bersenbrück	164	52.33 N	7.56 E
Bersimis 2 Dam ⊸[6]	240	49.22 N	69.47 W
Bersimis Indian Reserve ⊸[4]	240	49.05 N	68.37 W
Bersut	160	55.32 N	50.54 E
Berté, Lac ⊜	240	50.47 N	68.30 W
Bertha	252	46.16 N	95.04 W
Berthier □[6]	260	46.30 N	73.45 W
Berthierville	260	46.05 N	73.11 W
Berthold	252	48.19 N	101.44 W
Berthoud	254	40.18 N	105.05 W
Berthoud Pass)(	254	39.45 N	105.45 W
Bertinoro	170	44.09 N	12.08 E
Bertoua	214	4.35 N	13.41 E
Bertram	250	30.45 N	98.03 W
Bertrand, Mich., U.S.	268	41.46 N	86.16 W
Bertrand, Nebr., U.S.	252	40.32 N	99.38 W
Beruri	290	3.54 S	61.22 W
Berville	266	42.55 N	82.53 W
Berwick, N.S., Can.	240	45.03 N	64.44 W
Berwick, La., U.S.	248	29.42 N	91.13 W
Berwick, Maine, U.S.	242	43.16 N	70.51 W
Berwick, Pa., U.S.	242	41.03 N	76.15 W
Berwick □[6]	162	55.46 N	2.30 W
Berwick-upon-Tweed	162	55.46 N	2.00 W
Berwyn, Ill., U.S.	268	41.50 N	87.47 W
Berwyn, Pa., U.S.	262	40.03 N	75.27 W
Besalampy	218	16.45 S	44.30 E
Besana in Brianza	182	45.42 N	9.17 E
Besançon	180	47.15 N	6.02 E
Besar, Gunong ∧	200	2.30 N	103.10 E
Besbes	170	36.42 N	7.59 E
Bešenkoviči	160	55.03 N	29.27 E
Beskid Mountains ⋀	164	49.40 N	20.00 E
Beslan	158	43.12 N	44.33 E
Besozzo	182	45.51 N	8.39 E
Bessèges	182	44.17 N	4.06 E
Bessemer, Ala., U.S.	248	33.25 N	86.57 W
Bessemer, Mich., U.S.	244	46.27 N	89.24 W
Bessemer, Pa., U.S.	266	40.59 N	80.30 W
Bessemer City	246	35.17 N	81.17 W
Best	164	51.31 N	5.24 E
Best'ach	186	61.52 N	129.55 E
Bestobe	186	52.30 N	73.05 E
Bestuževo	160	61.37 N	43.58 E
Betanzos, Bol.	292	19.34 S	65.27 W
Betanzos, Esp.	168	43.17 N	8.12 W
Betanzos, Ría de C[1]	168	43.23 N	8.15 W
Bétaré Oya	214	5.36 N	14.05 E
Bétera	168	39.35 N	0.27 W
Bethal	224	26.27 S	29.28 E
Bethanien	218	26.32 S	17.11 E
Bethanien □[5]	224	26.30 S	17.00 E
Bethany, Conn., U.S.	261	41.26 N	73.01 W
Bethany, Ill., U.S.	248	39.39 N	88.44 W
Bethany, Mo., U.S.	248	40.16 N	94.02 W
Bethany, N.Y., U.S.	264	42.55 N	78.08 W
Bethany, Okla., U.S.	250	35.31 N	97.38 W
Bethany, W. Va., U.S.	266	40.12 N	80.33 W
Bethel, Alaska, U.S.	236	60.48 N	161.46 W
Bethel, Conn., U.S.	261	41.22 N	73.25 W
Bethel, Del., U.S.	262	38.34 N	75.37 W
Bethel, Maine, U.S.	242	44.25 N	70.48 W
Bethel, N.C., U.S.	246	35.48 N	77.22 W
Bethel, Ohio, U.S.	242	38.58 N	84.05 W
Bethel, Pa., U.S.	262	40.28 N	76.18 W
Bethel, Wash., U.S.	270	47.32 N	122.38 W
Bethlehem → Bayt Laḥm, Urd.	210	31.43 N	35.12 E
Bethel Island	272	38.01 N	121.39 W
Bethel Park	266	40.18 N	80.02 W
Bethelsdorp	224	33.52 S	25.34 E
Bethel Springs	248	35.14 N	88.36 W
Bethesda, Md., U.S.	262	38.59 N	77.06 W
Bethesda, Ohio, U.S.	242	40.01 N	81.04 W
Bethlehem, S. Afr.	224	28.15 S	28.15 E
Bethlehem, Conn., U.S.	261	41.38 N	73.13 W
Bethlehem, Pa., U.S.	242	40.37 N	75.25 W
Bethlehem, W. Va., U.S.	242	40.02 N	80.40 W
Bethlehem Center	261	42.40 N	73.42 W
Bethoncourt	180	47.32 N	6.48 E
Béthune, Fr.	176	50.32 N	2.38 E
Bethune, S.C., U.S.	246	34.25 N	80.21 W
Béticos, Sistema ⋀	168	37.00 N	4.00 W
Betijoque	290	9.23 N	70.44 W
Betioky	218	23.42 S	44.22 E
Betong	200	5.45 N	101.05 E
Betpak-Dala ⊸[2]	186	46.00 N	70.00 E
Betroka	218	23.16 S	46.06 E
Bet Sh'ean	210	32.30 N	35.30 E
Bet Shemesh	210	31.45 N	35.00 E
Betsiamites	240	48.56 N	68.38 W
Betsiamites, Pointe ≻	240	48.57 N	68.36 W
Betsiboka ≃	225b	16.03 S	46.36 E
Betsie Point ≻	244	44.42 N	86.16 W
Betsy Layne	246	37.33 N	82.38 W
Bette ∧	214	22.00 N	19.12 E
Bettendorf	244	41.32 N	90.30 W
Betterton	262	39.52 N	76.04 W
Bettiah	206	26.48 N	84.30 E
Bettles Field	236	66.55 N	151.30 W
Bettsville	266	41.15 N	83.14 W
Betuwe ⊸[1]	164	51.55 N	5.30 E
Betzdorf	164	50.47 N	7.53 E
Beulah, Colo., U.S.	254	38.05 N	104.59 W
Beulah, Mich., U.S.	244	44.38 N	86.06 W
Beulah, Miss., U.S.	248	33.42 N	90.59 W
Beulah, N. Dak., U.S.	252	47.16 N	101.47 W
Beulah Beach	266	41.25 N	82.22 W
Beulah Reservoir ⊜[1]	256	43.56 N	118.09 W
Beulaville	246	34.55 N	77.46 W
Beuthen → Bytom	164	50.22 N	18.54 E
Bevensen	178	53.05 N	10.34 E
Beveren	176	51.13 N	4.15 E
Beverley, Austl.	226	36.02 S	116.56 E
Beverley, Eng., U.K.	162	53.52 N	0.26 W
Beverlo	178	51.05 N	5.12 E
Beverly, Mass., U.S.	261	42.33 N	70.53 W
Beverly, N.J., U.S.	262	40.04 N	74.55 W
Beverly, Ohio, U.S.	242	39.33 N	81.38 W
Beverly Hills, Calif., U.S.	274	34.03 N	118.26 W
Beverly Hills, Mich., U.S.	268	42.32 N	83.15 W
Beverly Hills, Va., U.S.	262	37.36 N	77.34 W
Beverly Lake ⊜	232	64.36 N	100.30 W
Beverly Shores	268	41.41 N	86.59 W
Beverungen	164	51.39 N	9.22 E
Beverwijk	178	52.28 N	4.40 E
Bevier	248	39.45 N	92.34 W
Bewdley, Ont., Can.	264	44.05 N	78.19 W
Bewdley, Eng., U.K.	174	52.22 N	2.19 W
Bexar	248	34.11 N	88.09 W
Bexhill	174	50.50 N	0.29 E
Bexley	242	39.58 N	82.56 W
Bexley ⊸[8]	174	51.26 N	0.10 E
Beyazköy	172	41.21 N	27.42 E
Beyçayırı	172	40.15 N	26.55 E
Beyce	172	39.54 N	29.00 E
Bey Dağları ⋀	212	36.40 N	30.15 E
Beykoz	172	41.08 N	29.05 E
Beyla □[4]	222	8.55 N	8.25 W
Beypazarı	158	40.10 N	31.56 E
Beyşehir Gölü ⊜	212	37.40 N	31.30 E
Bezau	164	47.23 N	9.54 E
Bezavona ∧	225b	15.02 S	49.52 E
Bežeck	160	57.47 N	36.39 E
Bezenčuk	160	52.59 N	49.26 E
Béziers	166	43.21 N	3.15 E
Bezwada → Vijayawāda	204	16.31 N	80.37 E
Bhāgalpur	206	25.15 N	86.58 E
Bhaktapur	206	27.42 N	85.27 E
Bhamo	190	24.16 N	97.14 E
Bharatpur	206	27.26 N	77.30 E
Bhatinda	206	30.13 N	74.56 E
Bhātpāra	206	22.52 N	88.24 E
Bhaunagar	206	21.47 N	72.09 E
Bhilai	206	21.11 N	81.20 E
Bhīlwāra	206	25.21 N	74.40 E
Bhiwāni	206	28.48 N	76.08 E
Bhopāl	206	23.15 N	77.25 E
Bhubaneswar	206	20.15 N	85.50 E
Bhuj	206	23.17 N	69.41 E
Bhusāwal	206	21.03 N	75.46 E
Bhutan □[1]	204	27.30 N	90.30 E
Bia, Phou ∧	200	18.59 N	103.10 E
Biafra, Bight of C[3]	214	4.00 N	8.00 E
Biała (Züls)	164	50.23 N	17.40 E
Biała ≃	164	50.03 N	20.55 E
Biała Piska (Gehlenburg)	164	53.37 N	22.04 E
Biała Podlaska	164	52.02 N	23.06 E
Biała Rawska	164	51.49 N	20.29 E
Białobrzegi	164	51.40 N	20.57 E
Białogard (Belgard)	164	54.01 N	16.00 E
Biały Bor (Baldenburg)	164	53.54 N	16.51 E
Białystok	164	53.09 N	23.09 E
Biankouma □[5]	222	7.45 N	7.30 W
Biaro, Pulau I	198	2.05 N	125.20 E
Biarritz	166	43.29 N	1.34 W
Biasca	166	46.22 N	8.58 E
Biassono	182	45.37 N	9.16 E
Bibā	220	28.55 N	30.59 E
Bibai	192a	43.19 N	141.52 E
Bibban, Khawr ∨	220	11.00 N	32.41 E
Bibb City	246	32.30 N	84.59 W
Bibbiena	184	43.42 N	11.49 E
Biberach an der Riss	180	48.06 N	9.47 E
Bible Grove	248	38.52 N	88.27 W
Biblián	290	2.42 S	78.52 W
Bic	240	48.22 N	68.42 W
Bicas	296	21.43 S	43.04 W
Bicaz	172	46.54 N	26.05 E
Bicester	174	51.54 N	1.09 W
Bičevinka	160	59.44 N	37.40 E
Biche, Lac la ⊜	238	54.50 N	112.03 W
Bickle Knob ∧	242	38.56 N	79.44 W
Bicknell, Ind., U.S.	248	38.47 N	87.19 W
Bicknell, Utah, U.S.	254	38.20 N	111.33 W
Bicol ≃	202	13.44 N	123.08 E
Bicske	164	47.29 N	18.37 E
Bida	222	9.05 N	6.01 E
Biddeford	242	43.30 N	70.26 W
Biddle	252	45.11 N	105.21 W
Biddulph	174	53.08 N	2.10 W
Bideford	174	51.01 N	4.13 W
Bidwell	242	38.55 N	82.18 W
Bidwell, Mount ∧	258	41.58 N	120.10 W
Bieber	258	41.07 N	121.08 W
Biebrza ≃	164	53.37 N	22.56 E
Biecz	164	49.44 N	21.14 E
Biedenkopf	164	50.55 N	8.32 E
Biei	192a	43.35 N	142.28 E
Biel (Bienne)	180	47.10 N	7.12 E
Bielawa (Langenbielau)	164	50.41 N	16.38 E
Bielefeld	178	52.01 N	8.31 E
Biele Karpaty ⋀	164	49.00 N	18.00 E
Bieler Lake ⊜	232	70.20 N	73.00 W
Bieler See ⊜	166	47.05 N	7.10 E
Biella	182	45.34 N	8.03 E
Bielsk	164	52.40 N	19.49 E
Bielsko-Biała	164	49.49 N	19.02 E
Bielsk Podlaski	164	52.47 N	23.12 E
Bienfait	252	49.08 N	102.47 W
Bien-hoa	200	10.59 N	106.49 E
Bienne → Biel	180	47.10 N	7.12 E
Bienville	248	32.21 N	92.59 W
Bienville, Lac ⊜	232	55.05 N	72.45 W
Bierné	162	47.49 N	0.32 W
Bieruń Stary	164	50.06 N	19.06 E
Bierutów (Bernstadt)	164	51.08 N	17.32 E
Bietigheim	164	48.58 N	9.07 E
Bifuka	192a	44.29 N	142.21 E
Big ≃	248	38.28 N	90.37 W
Biga	172	40.13 N	27.14 E
Bigadiç	172	39.23 N	28.08 E
Big A Mountain ∧	246	37.03 N	82.02 W
Big Bald ∧	246	34.45 N	84.19 W
Big Bald Mountain ∧	240	47.12 N	66.25 W
Big Baldy ∧	256	44.47 N	115.13 W
Big Baldy Mountain ∧	256	46.58 N	110.37 W
Big Bar Creek	238	51.12 N	122.06 W
Big Basin Redwoods State Park ♦	258	37.09 N	122.17 W
Big Bay	244	46.49 N	87.44 W
Big Bay De Noc C	244	45.46 N	86.43 W
Big Bear City	274	34.16 N	116.51 W
Big Bear Lake	274	34.15 N	116.53 W
Big Beaver, Sask., Can.	252	49.08 N	105.10 W
Big Beaver, Pa., U.S.	266	40.50 N	80.20 W
Big Belt Mountains ⋀	256	46.40 N	111.25 W
Big Bend	268	42.53 N	88.12 W
Big Bend National Park ♦	250	29.12 N	103.12 W
Big Bend Reservoir ⊜[1]	238	52.57 N	115.37 W
Big Blue ≃	252	39.11 N	96.32 W
Big Canyon ∨	250	30.05 N	101.55 W
Big Chino Wash ∨	254	34.52 N	112.28 W
Big Clifty	248	37.33 N	86.09 W
Big Creek, B.C., Can.	238	51.44 N	123.03 W
Big Creek, Calif., U.S.	272	37.12 N	119.09 W
Big Creek Peak ∧	256	44.28 N	113.32 W
Big Cypress Indian Reservation ⊸[4]	246	26.14 N	80.49 W
Big Cypress Swamp ≋	246	26.10 N	81.38 W
Big Delta	236	64.09 N	145.50 W
Big Diomede Island → Ratmanova, Ostrov I	236	65.46 N	169.02 W
Big Duke Lake ⊜[1]	246	35.35 N	80.55 W
Big Eau Pleine ≃	244	44.48 N	90.00 W
Big Falls	244	48.12 N	93.48 W
Bigflat	248	36.00 N	92.24 W
Bigfork, Minn., U.S.	244	47.45 N	93.39 W
Bigfork, Mont., U.S.	256	48.04 N	114.04 W
Big Frog Mountain ∧	246	35.00 N	84.32 W
Biggar, Sask., Can.	232	52.04 N	108.00 W
Biggar, Scot., U.K.	162	55.38 N	3.32 W
Biggers	248	36.20 N	90.48 W
Biggin Hill ⊸[8]	174	51.18 N	0.04 E
Biggleswade	174	52.05 N	0.17 W
Biggs, Calif., U.S.	272	39.25 N	121.43 W
Biggs, Oreg., U.S.	270	45.40 N	120.50 W
Big Hole National Battlefield ⊥	256	45.35 N	113.35 W
Bighorn ≃	256	46.09 N	107.28 W
Big Horn Basin ⊻[1]	256	44.15 N	108.10 W
Bighorn Canyon National Recreation Area ♦	256	45.00 N	108.15 W
Bighorn Mountains ⋀	256	44.00 N	107.30 W
Big Island	246	37.32 N	79.22 W
Big Island I, N.W. Ter., Can.	232	62.43 N	70.43 W
Big Island I, Ont., Can.	252	49.10 N	94.40 W
Big Knob ∧	246	36.40 N	82.31 W
Big Koniuji Island I	236	55.06 N	159.33 W
Big Lake, Alaska, U.S.	236	61.33 N	149.52 W
Big Lake, Minn., U.S.	244	45.20 N	93.45 W
Big Lake, Tex., U.S.	250	31.12 N	101.28 W
Big Lake, Wash., U.S.	270	48.24 N	122.14 W
Big Lake ⊜	240	45.10 N	67.40 W
Bigler	266	40.59 N	78.19 W
Biglerville	262	39.56 N	77.15 W
Big Lookout Mountain ∧	256	44.37 N	117.17 W
Big Maumelle Lake ⊜[1]	248	34.55 N	92.40 W
Big Monon Ditch ≖	248	40.52 N	86.46 W
Big Mountain ∧	236	56.53 N	131.31 W
Bignasco	166	46.20 N	8.36 E
Bigosovo	160	55.49 N	27.43 E
Big Pine	258	37.10 N	118.17 W
Big Pine Mountain ∧	258	34.42 N	119.39 W
Big Piney	254	42.32 N	110.07 W
Bigpoint	248	30.35 N	88.29 W
Big Prairie	266	40.40 N	82.06 W
Big Quill Lake ⊜	232	51.55 N	104.22 W
Big Rapids	244	43.42 N	85.29 W
Big Run	266	40.58 N	78.53 W
Big Sable Point ≻	244	44.03 N	86.31 W
Big Salmon Range ⋀	236	60.20 N	132.40 W
Big Sand Lake ⊜	232	57.45 N	99.42 W
Big Sandy, Mont., U.S.	256	48.11 N	110.07 W
Big Sandy, Tenn., U.S.	248	36.15 N	88.05 W
Big Sandy, Tex., U.S.	250	32.35 N	95.07 W
Big Sandy ≃, U.S.	242	31.20 N	81.20 W
Big Sandy ≃, Tenn., U.S.	248	36.15 N	88.06 W
Big Sandy Reservoir ⊜[1]	254	42.16 N	109.26 W
Bigsby Island I	252	49.04 N	94.35 W
Big Sheep Mountain ∧	256	47.03 N	105.43 W
Big Sioux ≃	252	42.30 N	96.25 W
Big Slough ≃	246	30.56 N	84.33 W
Big Smoky Valley ∨	258	38.30 N	117.15 W
Big Snowy Mountains ⋀	256	46.50 N	109.30 W
Big Southern Butte ∧	256	43.23 N	113.01 W
Big Spring	250	32.15 N	101.28 W
Big Springs	252	41.04 N	102.05 W
Big Spring State Park ♦	248	36.53 N	91.02 W
Big Spruce Knob ∧	242	38.16 N	80.12 W
Big Squaw Mountain ∧	242	45.30 N	69.45 W
Big Stone City	252	45.18 N	96.28 W
Big Stone Gap	246	36.52 N	82.47 W
Big Stone Lake ⊜	252	45.25 N	96.40 W
Big Sur	272	36.15 N	121.48 W
Big Tancook Island I	240	44.27 N	64.10 W
Big Timber	256	45.50 N	109.57 W
Big Tree	264	42.46 N	78.49 W
Biguaçu	294	27.30 S	48.40 W
Big Valley	238	52.02 N	112.46 W
Big Wells	250	28.34 N	99.34 W
Big White Mountain ∧	238	49.42 N	118.58 W
Bihać	170	44.49 N	15.52 E
Bihar	206	25.12 N	85.33 E
Bihār □[3]	206	25.00 N	86.00 E
Biharamulo	218	2.38 S	31.20 E
Bihoro	192a	43.49 N	144.07 E
Bijagós, Arquipélago dos II	222	11.25 N	16.20 W
Bījār	208	35.52 N	47.36 E
Bijeljina	172	44.45 N	19.13 E
Bijelo Polje	172	43.02 N	19.44 E
Bijiang	200	26.30 N	98.55 E
Bijie	190	27.18 N	105.20 E
Bijou	258	38.57 N	119.58 W
Bijsk	186	52.34 N	85.15 E
Bīkaner	206	28.01 N	73.18 E
Bikin	186	46.48 N	134.16 E
Bikoro	218	0.45 S	18.07 E
Bilaa Point ≻	202	9.50 N	125.26 E
Bilac	296	21.24 S	50.28 W
Bilāspur	206	22.05 N	82.08 E
Bilatan Island I	202	5.00 N	120.00 E
Bilauktaung Range ⋀	200	13.00 N	99.00 E
Bilbao	168	43.15 N	2.58 W
Bilbilis ⊥	168	41.25 N	1.39 W
Bileća	172	42.53 N	18.26 E
Bilecik	172	40.09 N	29.59 E
Biłgoraj	164	50.34 N	22.43 E
Bilican Dağları ⋀	212	38.58 N	42.10 E
Bílina	164	50.35 N	13.45 E
Biliran Island I	202	11.35 N	124.30 E
Biliran Strait ⊔	202	11.30 N	124.25 E
Billerica	261	42.34 N	71.16 W
Billericay	174	51.38 N	0.25 E
Billiatt National Park ♦	228	35.00 S	140.30 E
Billings, Mo., U.S.	248	37.04 N	93.33 W
Billings, Mont., U.S.	256	45.47 N	118.27 W
Billings, Okla., U.S.	250	36.32 N	97.27 W
Billom	166	45.44 N	3.21 E
Bill Williams Mountain ∧	254	35.17 N	112.12 W
Billy Chinook, Lake ⊜[1]	256	44.33 N	121.20 W
Billy-Montigny	176	50.25 N	2.52 E
Bilma	214	18.41 N	12.56 E
Biloela	228	24.24 S	150.30 E
Bilo Gora ⋀	170	46.06 N	16.46 E
Biloxi	248	30.24 N	88.53 W
Biloxi ≃	248	30.26 N	89.00 W
Bilpa Morea Claypan ⊻	228	25.00 S	140.00 E
Bilston	174	52.34 N	2.04 W
Bilthoven	178	52.07 N	5.17 E
Biltmore Forest	246	35.32 N	82.32 W
Bilugyun Island I	200	16.24 N	97.32 E
Bilwascarma	280	14.41 N	83.53 W
Bimini Islands II	282	25.42 N	79.25 W
Binalbagan	202	10.12 N	122.51 E
Binalbagan ≃	202	10.12 N	122.50 E
Binalonan	202	16.03 N	120.36 E
Binangonan	202	14.28 N	121.11 E
Binboğadağı ∧	212	38.21 N	36.32 E
Binche	176	50.24 N	4.10 E
Bindal	160	65.06 N	12.30 E
Bindjai	200	3.36 N	98.30 E
Bindura	218	17.19 S	31.20 E
Binéfar	168	41.51 N	0.18 E
Binford	252	47.34 N	98.21 W
Binga	202	10.45 N	119.20 E
Binga, Monte ∧	224	19.45 S	33.04 E
Bingay Point ≻	202	13.04 N	124.11 E
Bingen, B.R.D.	164	48.07 N	9.16 E
Bingen, Wash., U.S.	270	45.43 N	121.28 W
Binger	250	35.18 N	98.21 W
Bingham	242	45.03 N	69.53 W
Binghamton	242	42.08 N	75.54 W
Bingöl	208	38.53 N	40.29 E
Bingöl Dağları ⋀	212	39.20 N	41.20 E
Binhai (Dongkan)	196	34.03 N	119.51 E
Binigsian Point ≻	202	9.51 N	122.23 E
Binit Point ≻	202	9.06 N	125.16 E
Binningen	180	47.32 N	7.34 E
Binongko, Pulau I	198	5.57 S	124.02 E
Bintan, Pulau I	200	1.05 N	104.30 E
Bintimani ∧	222	9.13 N	11.07 W
Bint Jubayl	210	33.07 N	35.26 E
Bintulu	198	3.13 N	113.04 E
Binxian	190	35.00 N	108.08 E
Binyang	200	23.18 N	108.46 E
Binzert (Bizerte)	214	37.17 N	9.52 E
Bío-Bío □[4]	294	37.45 S	72.00 W
Bío-Bío ≃	294	36.49 S	73.10 W
Bio Gorge ∨	222	8.20 N	2.20 W
Biograd	170	43.56 N	15.27 E
Biola	272	36.48 N	120.01 W
Bippus	268	40.57 N	85.37 W
Birao	214	10.17 N	22.47 E
Birātnagar	206	26.18 N	87.17 E
Bir Behar Chergui	170	35.48 N	7.48 E
Bîrca	172	43.58 N	23.37 E
Birch Bay	270	48.55 N	122.45 W
Birch Island	238	51.36 N	119.55 W
Bir Chouhada	168	35.53 N	6.18 E
Birch Run	244	43.15 N	83.48 W
Birch Tree	248	37.00 N	91.30 W
Birchwood, Alaska, U.S.	236	61.28 N	149.22 W
Birchwood, Wis., U.S.	244	45.40 N	91.33 W
Birchwood Park	262	40.06 N	74.09 W
Birchy Bay	240	49.21 N	54.44 W
Bird City	252	39.45 N	101.32 W
Bird Island	252	44.46 N	94.54 W
Bird Island I	288	54.00 S	38.05 W
Bird Islet I	226	22.10 S	155.28 E
Birdsall	266	42.23 N	77.55 W
Birdsboro	262	40.16 N	75.48 W
Birds Landing	272	38.08 N	121.52 W
Birdsville	226	25.54 S	139.22 E
Birdum	226	15.39 S	133.13 E
Bireuen	198	5.12 N	96.42 E
Bīrganj	190	27.01 N	84.54 E
Bir Ghbalou	168	36.16 N	3.35 E
Birigui	296	21.18 S	50.19 W
Biri Island I	202	12.40 N	124.23 E
Biril'ussy	186	57.07 N	90.32 E
Bīrjand	208	32.53 N	59.13 E
Birkeland	160	58.20 N	8.14 E
Birken	238	50.29 N	122.36 W
Birkenfeld	164	49.39 N	7.10 E
Birkenfield	270	46.00 N	123.20 W
Birkenhead, N.Z.	230	36.49 S	174.44 E
Birkenhead, Eng., U.K.	162	53.24 N	3.02 W
Birkerød	160	55.50 N	12.26 E
Birkfeld	164	47.21 N	15.42 E
Bîrlad	172	46.14 N	27.40 E
Birmingham, Eng., U.K.	174	52.30 N	1.50 W
Birmingham, Ala., U.S.	248	33.31 N	86.49 W
Birmingham, Iowa, U.S.	244	40.53 N	91.57 W
Birmingham, Mich., U.S.	268	42.33 N	83.15 W
Birmingham, Ohio, U.S.	266	41.20 N	82.21 W
Birmingham, Pa., U.S.	266	40.38 N	78.13 W
Bir Mogreïn	214	25.14 N	11.35 W
Birnamwood	244	44.56 N	89.13 W
Birnin Kebbi	222	12.32 N	4.12 E
Birni Nkonni	214	13.48 N	5.15 E
Birobidžan	186	48.48 N	132.57 E
Birr	162	53.05 N	7.54 W
Bi'r Safājah	214	26.44 N	33.56 E
Birsk	158	55.25 N	55.32 E
Birzebbuga	170	35.49 N	14.32 E
Bisa, Pulau I	198	1.15 S	127.28 E
Bisaccia	184	41.01 N	15.22 E
Bisbee, Ariz., U.S.	254	31.27 N	109.55 W
Bisbee, N. Dak., U.S.	252	48.37 N	99.23 W
Biscarosse	166	44.24 N	1.10 W
Biscarosse, Étang de C	166	44.20 N	1.10 E
Biscay, Bay of C	158	44.00 N	4.00 W
Biscayne Bay C	246	25.33 N	80.15 W
Bisceglie	170	41.14 N	16.31 E
Bischheim	180	48.37 N	7.45 E
Bischofshofen	164	47.25 N	13.13 E
Bischofswerda	164	51.07 N	14.10 E
Biscoe, Ark., U.S.	248	34.49 N	91.24 W
Biscoe, N.C., U.S.	246	35.22 N	79.47 W
Biscucuy	290	9.22 N	69.59 W
Bishārah, Ma'ṭan ⊤[4]	220	22.58 N	22.39 E
Bishop, Calif., U.S.	258	37.22 N	118.24 W
Bishop, Tex., U.S.	250	27.35 N	97.48 W
Bishop Auckland	162	54.40 N	1.40 W
Bishop's Falls	240	49.01 N	55.30 W
Bishops Head	262	38.16 N	76.05 W
Bishop's Stortford	174	51.53 N	0.09 E
Bishopton	260	45.35 N	71.34 W
Bishopville, Md., U.S.	262	38.22 N	75.12 W
Bishopville, S.C., U.S.	246	34.13 N	80.20 W
Biskotasi Lake ⊜	244	47.18 N	82.05 W
Biskra	214	34.50 N	5.52 E
Biskupiec (Bischofsburg)	164	53.52 N	20.27 E
Bislig	202	8.13 N	126.19 E
Bislig Bay C	202	8.17 N	126.23 E
Bismarck, Ill., U.S.	268	40.16 N	87.37 W
Bismarck, Mo., U.S.	248	37.46 N	90.38 W
Bismarck, N. Dak., U.S.	252	46.48 N	100.47 W
Bismarck Archipelago II	148	5.00 S	150.00 E
Bison	252	45.31 N	102.28 W
Bison Peak ∧	254	39.14 N	105.30 W
Bissa, Djebel ∧	168	36.28 N	1.28 E
Bissau	222	11.51 N	15.35 W
Bissett	232	51.02 N	95.40 W
Bistcho Lake ⊜	232	59.40 N	118.40 W
Bistineau, Lake ⊜[1]	248	32.25 N	93.22 W
Bistreţu	172	43.54 N	23.30 E
Bistriţa	172	47.08 N	24.30 E
Bistriţa ≃	172	46.30 N	26.57 E
Bisztynek (Bischofstein)	164	54.06 N	20.55 E
Bitadton	202	11.30 N	122.05 E
Bitam	218	2.05 N	11.29 E
Bitburg	164	49.58 N	6.31 E
Bitche	166	49.03 N	7.26 E
Bitlis	212	38.22 N	42.06 E
Bitola	172	41.01 N	21.20 E
Bitonto	170	41.06 N	16.42 E
Bitterfeld	164	51.37 N	12.20 E
Bitterfontein	218	31.00 S	18.32 E
Bitterness, Mount ∧	230	44.45 S	170.18 E
Bitterroot Range ⋀	256	47.06 N	115.10 W
Bitti	170	40.29 N	9.23 E
Bitung	198	1.27 N	125.11 E
Bituruna	294	26.10 S	51.34 W
Bivalve	262	38.18 N	75.54 W
Bivins	248	33.01 N	94.12 W
Biwabik	244	47.32 N	92.23 W
Biwa-ko ⊜	192	35.15 N	136.05 E
Bixby	250	35.57 N	95.53 W
Biyang	196	32.44 N	113.20 E
Biysk → Bijsk	186	52.34 N	85.15 E
Bizen	192	34.44 N	134.09 E
Bizerte	170	37.17 N	9.52 E
Bizerte □[8]	170	37.10 N	9.50 E
Bizerte, Lac de ⊜	170	37.12 N	9.52 E
Bjala	172	43.27 N	25.44 E
Bjala Slatina	172	43.28 N	23.56 E
Bjargtangar ≻	160a	65.31 N	24.32 W
Bjärnum	160	56.17 N	13.42 E
Bjelovar	170	45.54 N	16.51 E
Björna	160	63.34 N	18.33 E
Björneborg → Pori, Suomi	160	61.29 N	21.47 E
Bjurholm	160	63.56 N	19.13 E
Blace	172	43.17 N	21.18 E
Black (Lixianjiang) (Da) ≃, As.	200	21.15 N	105.20 E
Black ≃	248	35.38 N	91.19 W
Blackall	228	24.25 S	145.28 E
Black Bay C	244	48.40 N	88.30 W
Blackberry Heights	268	41.45 N	88.23 W
Blackburn	162	53.45 N	2.29 W
Blackburn, Mount ∧	236	61.44 N	143.26 W
Black Butte ∧	256	44.54 N	111.51 W
Black Butte Reservoir ⊜[1]	258	39.45 N	122.20 W
Black Buttes	256	41.33 N	108.42 W
Black Canyon of the Gunnison National Monument ♦	254	38.32 N	107.42 W
Black Creek, B.C., Can.	238	49.50 N	125.08 W
Black Creek, N.Y., U.S.	266	42.17 N	78.14 W
Black Cypress Bayou ≃	248	32.42 N	93.55 W
Black Diamond, Alta., Can.	238	50.42 N	114.14 W
Black Diamond, Wash., U.S.	270	47.18 N	122.00 W
Blackduck	244	47.44 N	94.33 W
Black Eagle	256	47.31 N	111.17 W
Blackfalds	238	52.23 N	113.47 W
Blackfeet Indian Reservation ⊸[4]	256	48.40 N	113.00 W
Blackfoot, Idaho, U.S.	256	43.11 N	112.20 W
Blackfoot, Mont., U.S.	238	48.34 N	112.52 W
Blackfoot Indian Reserve ⊸[4]	238	50.45 N	113.00 W
Blackfoot River Reservoir ⊜[1]	256	42.55 N	111.35 W
Blackford □[6]	268	40.27 N	85.22 W
Black Forest → Schwarzwald ⋀	180	48.00 N	8.15 E
Blackhall Mountain ∧	254	41.02 N	106.41 W
Blackhead Bay C	240	48.34 N	53.15 W
Black Hills ⋀	252	44.00 N	104.00 W
Black Horse	266	41.09 N	81.18 W
Black Lake	260	46.03 N	71.21 W
Black Lake ⊜, Sask., Can.	232	59.10 N	105.20 W
Black Lake ⊜, Mich., U.S.	244	45.28 N	84.15 W
Black Lake ⊜, N.Y., U.S.	242	44.31 N	75.35 W
Black Lick	266	40.28 N	79.12 W
Black Mesa ∧, Ariz., U.S.	254	36.35 N	110.20 W
Black Mesa ∧, Okla., U.S.	250	36.57 N	102.59 W
Blackmore, Mount ∧	256	45.27 N	111.01 W
Black Mountain	246	35.37 N	82.19 W
Black Mountain ∧, Ariz., U.S.	254	32.46 N	110.57 W
Black Mountain ∧, Calif., U.S.	258	35.24 N	120.21 W
Black Mountain ∧, Idaho, U.S.	256	46.53 N	115.33 W
Black Mountain ∧, Ky., U.S.	246	36.54 N	82.54 W
Black Mountain ∧, Mont., U.S.	256	46.44 N	112.31 W
Black Mountain ∧, Oreg., U.S.	256	45.13 N	119.17 W
Black Mountain ∧, Wyo., U.S.	256	44.45 N	107.22 W
Black Mountains ⋀	254	35.30 N	114.30 W
Black Oak	268	41.35 N	87.25 W
Black Peak ∧	254	34.22 N	114.13 W
Black Pine Peak ∧	256	42.08 N	113.08 W
Black Point	272	38.07 N	122.31 W
Black Point ≻	236	57.00 N	153.18 W
Blackpool	162	53.50 N	3.03 W
Black Range ⋀	254	33.20 N	107.50 W
Black River, Jam.	285q	18.00 N	77.50 W
Black River, N.Y., U.S.	264	44.01 N	75.48 W
Black River Bay C	285q	18.00 N	77.51 W
Black River Falls	244	44.23 N	90.52 W
Black Rock	248	36.06 N	91.06 W
Black Rock II[1]	288	53.39 S	41.48 W
Black Rock Desert ⊸[2]	258	41.10 N	119.00 W
Blacksburg, S.C., U.S.	246	35.07 N	81.31 W
Blacksburg, Va., U.S.	246	37.14 N	80.25 W
Black Sea ⊤[2]	158	43.00 N	35.00 E
Blacks Fork ≃	254	41.24 N	109.38 W
Blacks Harbour	240	45.03 N	66.47 W
Blackshear	246	31.18 N	82.14 W
Blackshear, Lake ⊜[1]	246	31.56 N	83.56 W
Blacksod Bay C	162	54.08 N	10.00 W
Blackstone, Mass., U.S.	261	42.01 N	71.30 W
Blackstone, Va., U.S.	246	37.04 N	78.00 W
Blackstone ≃, Alta., Can.	238	52.50 N	116.07 W
Blackstone ≃, Yukon, Can.	236	65.51 N	137.12 W
Blackville	246	33.22 N	81.16 W
Black Volta (Volta Noire) ≃	222	8.41 N	1.33 W
Black Warrior ≃	248	32.32 N	87.51 W
Blackwater ≃	248	30.36 N	87.02 W
Blackwater Lake ⊜	236	64.00 N	123.05 W
Blackwell, Okla., U.S.	250	36.48 N	97.17 W
Blackwell, Tex., U.S.	250	32.05 N	100.19 W
Bladenboro	246	34.33 N	78.48 W
Bladensburg	266	40.17 N	82.17 W
Blades	262	38.38 N	75.36 W
Blaenavon	174	51.48 N	3.05 W
Bláfell ∧	160a	64.32 N	19.53 W
Blagaj	170	43.15 N	17.50 E
Blagodarnoje	158	45.06 N	43.27 E
Blagoevgrad	172	42.01 N	23.06 E
Blagoveščensk	186	50.17 N	127.32 E
Blain, Fr.	166	47.29 N	1.46 W
Blain, Pa., U.S.	262	40.20 N	77.31 W
Blaina	174	51.46 N	3.10 W
Blain City	266	40.40 N	78.34 W
Blaine, Minn., U.S.	244	45.11 N	93.14 W
Blaine, Wash., U.S.	270	48.59 N	122.44 W
Blaineys	270	48.53 N	123.47 W
Blair, Ont., Can.	264	43.23 N	80.23 W
Blair, Nebr., U.S.	252	41.33 N	96.08 W
Blair, Okla., U.S.	250	34.47 N	99.20 W
Blair, Wis., U.S.	244	44.18 N	91.14 W
Blair □[6]	266	40.30 N	78.25 W
Blair Athol	226	22.42 S	147.33 E
Blairgowrie	162	56.36 N	3.21 W
Blairmore	238	49.36 N	114.26 W
Blairs Mills	266	40.17 N	77.43 W
Blairstown	244	41.55 N	92.05 W
Blairsville, Ga., U.S.	246	34.53 N	83.58 W
Blairsville, Pa., U.S.	266	40.26 N	79.16 W
Blaj	172	46.11 N	23.55 E
Blakely	246	31.23 N	84.56 W
Blakes	262	37.30 N	76.22 W
Blakesburg	244	40.58 N	92.38 W
Blakeslee	268	41.31 N	84.44 W
Blake Terrace ⊹[4]	148	31.00 N	79.00 W
Blalock Island I	256	45.53 N	119.41 W
Blanc, Cap ≻, Afr.	214	20.46 N	17.03 E
Blanc, Cap ≻, Tun.	170	37.20 N	9.51 E
Blanc, Mont (Monte Bianco) ∧	166	45.50 N	6.52 E
Blanca	254	37.27 N	105.31 W
Blanca, Bahía C	294	38.55 S	62.10 W
Blanca, Cordillera ⋀	292	9.00 S	77.30 W
Blanca, Isla I	292	9.07 S	78.38 W
Blanca, Punta ≻	280	10.58 N	85.54 W
Blanca, Sierra ∧	254	31.15 N	105.26 W
Blanca Peak ∧	254	37.35 N	105.29 W
Blanchard, Okla., U.S.	250	35.08 N	97.39 W
Blanchard, Wash., U.S.	270	48.36 N	122.26 W
Blanchardville	244	42.49 N	89.52 W
Blanche ≃	244	47.34 N	79.32 W
Blanche, Lake ⊜	228	29.15 S	139.39 E
Blanchester	242	39.17 N	83.55 W
Blanchisseuse	285r	10.47 N	61.18 W
Blanco	250	30.06 N	98.25 W
Blanco ≃, Arg.	294	31.54 S	69.42 W
Blanco ≃, Bol.	292	12.30 S	64.18 W
Blanco ≃, Perú	292	5.33 S	73.53 W
Blanco ≃, Tex., U.S.	250	29.51 N	97.55 W
Blanco, Cabo ≻	280	9.33 N	85.06 W
Blanco, Canyon ∨	254	35.20 N	105.05 W
Blanco, Cape ≻	256	42.50 N	124.34 W
Blanco, Rio ≃	254	37.07 N	107.03 W
Blanc-Sablon	240	51.26 N	57.08 W
Bland, Mo., U.S.	248	38.18 N	91.38 W
Bland, Va., U.S.	246	37.06 N	81.07 W
Blanda ≃	160a	65.39 N	20.18 W
Blandburg	266	40.41 N	78.25 W
Blandford	261	42.11 N	72.56 W
Blandford Forum	162	50.52 N	2.11 W
Blanding	254	37.37 N	109.29 W
Blandinsville	244	40.33 N	90.52 W
Blandon	262	40.26 N	75.53 W
Blanes	168	41.41 N	2.48 E
Blangkedjeren	200	3.58 N	97.19 E
Blangy-sur-Bresle	166	49.56 N	1.38 E
Blankenberge	176	51.19 N	3.08 E
Blankenburg	164	51.48 N	10.58 E
Blankenese ⊸[8]	178	53.33 N	9.48 E
Blankenheim	164	50.26 N	6.39 E
Blanket	250	31.49 N	98.47 W
Blanquefort	166	44.53 N	0.39 W
Blansko	164	49.22 N	16.39 E
Blantyre	218	15.47 S	35.00 E
Blaricum	178	52.16 N	5.15 E
Blarney Castle ♦	162	51.56 N	8.34 W
Blasdell	264	42.47 N	78.49 W
Błaszki	164	51.39 N	18.27 E
Blatná	164	49.26 N	13.53 E
Blatnica	172	43.42 N	28.31 E
Blaubeuren	180	48.24 N	9.47 E
Blaufelden	164	49.18 N	9.58 E
Blaye-et-Sainte-Luce	166	45.08 N	0.39 W
Błażowa	164	49.54 N	22.05 E
Bled	170	46.22 N	14.06 E
Bledsoe	250	33.38 N	103.01 W
Bleiburg	164	46.35 N	14.48 E
Blekinge Län □[6]	160	56.20 N	15.20 E
Blende	252	38.15 N	104.35 W
Blenheim, Ont., Can.	266	42.20 N	82.00 W
Blenheim, N.Z.	230	41.31 S	173.57 E
Bléré	166	47.20 N	1.00 E
Blerick	178	51.23 N	6.10 E
Blessing	250	28.52 N	96.13 W
Bletchley	174	52.00 N	0.46 W
Bletterans	166	46.45 N	5.27 E
Bleus, Monts ⋀	214	4.31 S	21.02 E
Blewett	250	29.11 N	100.01 W
Blewett Falls Lake ⊜[1]	246	35.03 N	79.54 W
Blida	168	36.30 N	2.49 E
Bligh Sound ⊔	230	44.46 S	167.30 E
Blik, Mount ∧	202	6.57 N	124.15 E
Blind River	244	46.10 N	82.58 W
Bliss	266	42.35 N	78.15 W
Blissfield, Mich., U.S.	268	41.50 N	83.52 W
Blissfield, Ohio, U.S.	266	40.24 N	81.58 W
Blitar	226	8.06 S	112.10 E
Block Island	261	41.10 N	71.34 W
Blockton	252	40.37 N	94.29 W
Bloedel	238	50.07 N	125.23 W
Bloemendaal	178	52.24 N	4.37 E
Bloemfontein	224	29.12 S	26.07 E
Bloemhof	218	27.38 S	25.32 E
Blois	176	47.35 N	1.20 E
Blokhus	160	57.15 N	9.35 E
Blomberg	178	51.56 N	9.05 E
Blönduós	160a	65.39 N	20.15 W
Błonie	164	52.12 N	20.37 E
Blood Indian Reserve ⊸[4]	238	49.30 N	113.10 W
Blood Mountain ∧	246	34.44 N	83.56 W
Bloodvein ≃	232	51.45 N	96.44 W
Bloody Foreland ≻	162	55.09 N	8.17 W
Bloomdale	268	41.10 N	83.33 W
Bloomer	244	45.07 N	91.29 W
Bloomfield, Ont., Can.	264	43.59 N	77.14 W
Bloomfield, Conn., U.S.	261	41.50 N	72.44 W
Bloomfield, Ind., U.S.	248	39.01 N	86.56 W
Bloomfield, Iowa, U.S.	244	40.45 N	92.25 W
Bloomfield, Ky., U.S.	248	37.55 N	85.19 W
Bloomfield, Mo., U.S.	248	36.53 N	89.56 W
Bloomfield, Nebr., U.S.	252	42.36 N	97.39 W

Symbols in the index entries are identified on page 360.

Name	Page	Lat°′	Long°′
Bloomfield, N.J., U.S.	262	40.48 N	74.12 E
Bloomfield, N. Mex., U.S.	254	36.43 N	107.59 W
Bloomfield, Ohio, U.S.	266	40.03 N	81.44 W
Bloomfield, Vt., U.S.	242	44.55 N	71.38 W
Bloomfield Hills	268	42.35 N	83.15 W
Bloomfield Village	268	42.33 N	83.15 W
Bloomingdale, Ill., U.S.	268	41.58 N	88.05 W
Bloomingdale, Mich., U.S.	268	42.23 N	85.57 W
Bloomingdale, Ohio, U.S.	266	40.21 N	80.49 W
Blooming Glen	262	40.22 N	75.15 W
Blooming Grove	250	32.06 N	96.43 W
Blooming Prairie	244	43.52 N	93.03 W
Bloomington, Calif., U.S.	274	34.04 N	117.24 W
Bloomington, Ill., U.S.	268	40.29 N	89.00 W
Bloomington, Ind., U.S.	248	39.10 N	86.32 W
Bloomington, Minn., U.S.	244	44.50 N	93.17 W
Bloomington, Tex., U.S.	250	28.39 N	96.54 W
Bloomington, Wis., U.S.	244	42.53 N	90.55 W
Blooming Valley	266	41.40 N	80.03 W
Bloomsburg	242	41.00 N	76.27 W
Bloomsbury	262	40.39 N	75.05 W
Bloomville	266	41.03 N	83.01 W
Bloserville	262	40.12 N	77.24 W
Blossburg	242	41.41 N	77.04 W
Blossom	250	33.40 N	95.23 W
Blossom Hill	262	40.05 N	76.19 W
Blouberg ▲	224	23.01 S	28.59 E
Blouin, Lac ⊜	244	48.10 N	77.45 W
Blountstown	246	30.27 N	85.03 W
Blountsville	248	34.05 N	86.35 W
Blovice	164	49.35 N	13.33 E
Blowering Reservoir ⊜[1]	228	35.30 S	148.15 E
Blowing Rock	246	36.08 N	81.41 W
Bloxom	262	37.50 N	75.38 W
Bludenz	180	47.09 N	9.49 E
Blue Bell	262	40.09 N	75.16 W
Blue Buck Knob ▲[2]	248	36.57 N	92.07 W
Bluecreek	238	48.19 N	117.49 W
Blue Cypress Lake ⊜	246	27.44 N	80.45 W
Blue Earth	244	43.38 N	94.06 W
Blue Earth ≃	244	44.09 N	94.02 W
Bluefield, Va., U.S.	246	37.15 N	81.17 W
Bluefield, W. Va., U.S.	246	37.16 N	81.13 W
Bluefields	280	12.00 N	83.45 W
Bluefields, Laguna de C	280	12.00 N	83.44 W
Bluefields Bay C	285q	18.11 N	78.04 W
Blue Grotto → Azzurra, Grotta •[5]	184	40.35 N	14.14 E
Blue Hill, Maine, U.S.	242	44.25 N	68.36 W
Blue Hill, Nebr., U.S.	252	40.20 N	98.27 W
Blue Hill Bay C	242	44.15 N	68.30 W
Blue Hills	261	41.47 N	72.42 W
Blue Hills of Couteau ⛰[2]	240	47.59 N	57.43 W
Blue Hills Upland ⛰[1]	252	38.50 N	100.10 W
Blue Island	268	41.40 N	87.41 W
Blue Jay	274	34.15 N	117.13 W
Blue Mesa Reservoir ⊜[1]	254	38.27 N	107.10 W
Blue Mound, Ill., U.S.	248	39.42 N	89.07 W
Blue Mound, Kans., U.S.	252	38.05 N	95.00 W
Blue Mountain	248	34.40 N	89.02 W
Blue Mountain ▲, N.B., Can.	240	47.49 N	66.19 W
Blue Mountain ▲, Newf., Can.	240	50.24 N	57.10 W
Blue Mountain ▲, Ark., U.S.	248	34.41 N	94.03 W
Blue Mountain ▲, Mont., U.S.	252	47.16 N	104.10 W
Blue Mountain ▲, N.H., U.S.	242	44.47 N	71.28 W
Blue Mountain ▲, Pa., U.S.	242	40.15 N	77.30 W
Blue Mountain ▲[2]	244	48.15 N	80.07 W
Blue Mountain Peak ▲	285q	18.03 N	76.35 W
Blue Mountains ⛰, Jam.	285q	18.06 N	76.40 W
Blue Mountains ⛰, Maine, U.S.	242	44.50 N	70.35 W
Blue Mountains ⛰, Oreg., U.S.	256	44.35 N	118.25 W
Blue Nile (Al-Baḥr al-Azraq) (Abay) ≃	220	15.38 N	32.31 E
Bluenose Lake ⊜	232	68.30 N	119.35 W
Blue Rapids	252	39.41 N	96.39 W
Blue Ridge, Alta., Can.	238	54.08 N	115.22 W
Blue Ridge, Ga., U.S.	246	34.52 N	84.20 W
Blue Ridge, Ill., U.S.	268	40.17 N	88.29 W
Blue Ridge, Va., U.S.	246	37.22 N	79.49 W
Blue Ridge ⛰	234	37.00 N	82.00 W
Blue Ridge Summit	262	39.43 N	77.28 W
Blue River	238	52.05 N	119.17 W
Bluesky	238	56.04 N	118.14 W
Blue Springs	252	40.09 N	96.40 W
Bluestack ▲	162	54.45 N	8.05 W
Bluestone ≃	246	37.34 N	80.59 W
Bluestone Reservoir ⊜[1]	246	37.30 N	80.50 W
Bluewater	254	35.15 N	107.59 W
Bluff, N.Z.	230	46.36 S	168.20 E
Bluff, Utah, U.S.	254	37.17 N	109.33 W
Bluff Cape ≻	200	18.00 N	94.26 E
Bluff City	246	36.28 N	82.16 W
Bluff Dale	250	32.21 N	98.01 W
Bluff Park	248	33.27 N	86.47 W
Bluffs	248	39.45 N	90.32 W
Bluffton, Ind., U.S.	268	40.44 N	85.11 W
Bluffton, Ohio, U.S.	268	40.54 N	83.54 W
Bluffton, S.C., U.S.	246	32.14 N	80.52 W
Blumberg	180	47.50 N	8.31 E
Blumenau	294	26.56 S	49.03 W
Blunt	252	44.31 N	99.59 W
Bly	256	42.24 N	121.02 W
Blying Sound ⋓	236	59.50 N	149.15 W
Blyth, Ont., Can.	244	43.44 N	81.26 W
Blyth, Eng., U.K.	162	55.07 N	1.30 W
Blythe	258	33.37 N	114.36 W
Blythedale	266	40.15 N	79.48 W
Blytheswood	266	42.07 N	82.36 W
Blytheville	248	35.56 N	89.55 W
Blytheville Air Force Base ■	248	35.57 N	89.57 W
Bø, Nor.	160	68.37 N	14.33 E
Bo, S.L.	222	7.56 N	11.21 W
Boac	202	13.27 N	121.50 E
Boaco	280	12.27 N	85.43 W
Boaco □[5]	280	12.30 N	85.30 W
Boa Esperança	296	21.05 S	45.34 W
Boalsburg	266	40.46 N	77.48 W
Boa Nova	296	14.22 S	40.10 W
Board Camp Mountain ▲	258	40.42 N	123.43 W
Boardman	266	41.02 N	80.40 W
Boardman ≃	244	44.46 N	85.38 W
Boat Basin	238	49.29 N	126.25 W
Boa Vista, Bra.	290	2.49 N	60.40 W
Boa Vista, Bra.	294	26.17 S	48.50 W
Boa Vista I	222a	16.05 N	22.50 W
Boa Vista do Ramos	290	3.08 S	58.05 W
Boavita	290	6.20 N	72.35 W
Boayan Island I	202	10.34 N	119.10 E
Boaz	248	34.12 N	86.10 W
Bobai	200	22.12 N	109.52 E
Bobbio	170	44.46 N	9.23 E
Bobcaygeon	264	44.33 N	78.33 W
Bobigny	176	48.54 N	2.27 E
Bobingen	180	48.16 N	10.50 E
Böblingen	180	48.41 N	9.01 E
Bobo Dioulasso	222	11.12 N	4.18 W
Bobolice (Bublitz)	164	53.57 N	16.36 E
Bobon	202	12.32 N	124.34 E
Bobonaza ≃	290	2.36 S	76.38 W
Boboye, Dallol ∨	222	14.00 N	3.00 E
Bóbr ≃	164	52.04 N	15.04 E
Bobrujsk	158	53.09 N	29.14 E
Bobs Lake ⊜	244	44.40 N	76.35 W
Bobtown	242	39.46 N	79.59 W
Bobures	290	9.15 N	71.11 W
Boby, Pic ▲	225b	22.12 S	46.55 E
Boca Brava, Isla I	280	8.12 N	82.17 W
Boca Chica	284m	17.59 N	66.32 W
Boca del Monte	280	8.22 N	82.08 W
Boca del Pozo	290	11.00 N	64.23 W
Boca de Quadra ⋓	238	55.08 N	130.50 W
Bôca do Acre	292	8.45 S	67.23 W
Boca Grande	246	26.45 N	82.16 W
Bocaiúva	296	17.07 S	43.49 W
Boca Raton	246	26.21 N	80.05 W
Bocas del Toro	280	9.22 N	82.14 W
Bocas del Toro □[4]	280	8.50 N	82.10 W
Bocas del Toro, Archipiélago de II	280	9.17 N	82.10 W
Bocay	280	14.19 N	85.16 W
Bocay ≃	280	14.18 N	85.16 W
Bochnia	164	49.58 N	20.26 E
Bocholt, Bel.	178	51.10 N	5.35 E
Bocholt, B.R.D.	178	51.50 N	6.36 E
Bochum	178	51.28 N	7.13 E
Bockhorn	178	53.23 N	8.01 E
Bockum-Hövel	178	51.42 N	7.46 E
Bocognano	170	42.05 N	9.03 E
Boconó	290	9.15 N	70.16 W
Bodajbo	186	57.51 N	114.10 E
Bode	252	42.52 N	94.17 W
Bodegraven	178	52.05 N	4.45 E
Bodele ⤝[1]	214	16.30 N	16.30 E
Boden	160	65.50 N	21.42 E
Bodensee ⊜	180	47.35 N	9.25 E
Bodine, Mount ▲	238	55.37 N	125.49 W
Bodmin	162	50.29 N	4.43 W
Bodmin Moor ⤝[3]	162	50.33 N	4.33 W
Bodø	160	67.17 N	14.23 E
Bodoquena, Serra da ⛰[1]	292	21.00 S	56.50 W
Bodrum	172	37.02 N	27.26 E
Bodrum (Halicarnassus) ⊥	212	37.03 N	27.23 E
Bodzentyn	164	50.56 N	20.57 E
Boende	218	0.13 S	20.52 E
Boën-sur-Lignon	166	45.44 N	3.59 E
Boeo, Capo ≻	170	37.48 N	12.26 E
Boerne	250	29.47 N	98.44 W
Boesmans ≃	224	33.42 S	26.39 E
Boffa □[4]	222	10.20 N	14.00 W
Bōfu → Hōfu	192	34.03 N	131.34 E
Bogale	200	16.17 N	95.24 E
Bogalusa	248	30.47 N	89.52 W
Bogan ≃	228	32.45 S	148.08 E
Bogata	250	33.28 N	95.13 W
Bogeduoshanmai ⛰	190	43.30 N	89.45 E
Bogen	164	48.55 N	12.43 E
Bogenfels	218	27.23 S	15.22 E
Boger City	246	35.29 N	81.13 W
Bognes	160	68.10 N	16.00 E
Bognor Regis	174	50.47 N	0.41 W
Bogo	202	11.03 N	124.00 E
Bogo Bay C	202	11.05 N	124.00 E
Bogomila	172	41.36 N	21.28 E
Bogong, Mount ▲	228	35.31 S	148.23 E
Bogor	198	6.35 S	106.47 E
Bogorodick	158	53.46 N	38.08 E
Bogorodsk, S.S.S.R.	160	56.06 N	43.31 E
Bogorodsk, S.S.S.R.	160	62.16 N	52.28 E
Bogorodskoje	160	57.51 N	50.45 E
Bogotá	290	4.36 N	74.05 W
Bogotá ≃	290	4.18 N	74.48 W
Bogotol	186	56.12 N	89.33 E
Bogovarovo	160	58.59 N	47.01 E
Bogra	204	24.51 N	89.22 E
Bogučany	186	58.23 N	97.29 E
Bogué	214	16.35 N	14.16 W
Bogue Chitto ≃	248	30.35 N	89.49 W
Bogušovsk	160	54.51 N	30.13 E
Boguszów (Gottesberg)	164	50.46 N	16.12 E
Bohai C	194	38.30 N	120.00 E
Bohain-en-Vermandois	176	49.59 N	3.27 E
Bohaiwan C	194	38.40 N	118.20 E
Bohannon	262	37.24 N	76.22 W
Bohelebung	202	6.32 N	122.12 E
Bohemia → Čechy □[9]	164	49.50 N	14.00 E
Bohemian Forest → Böhmer Wald ⛰	164	49.00 N	13.00 E
Bohinjska Bistrica	170	46.17 N	13.57 E
Böhmerwald ⛰	164	49.00 N	13.00 E
Bohners Lake	268	42.37 N	88.17 W
Bohol □[4]	202	9.50 N	124.10 E
Bohol I	202	9.50 N	124.10 E
Bohol Strait ⋓	202	9.50 N	123.40 E
Bohon	202	18.30 N	120.35 E
Boiaçu	290	0.27 S	61.46 W
Boiano	184	41.29 N	14.29 E
Boiestown	240	46.27 N	66.25 W
Boigu I	226	9.16 S	142.12 E
Boiling Springs, N.C., U.S.	246	35.16 N	81.40 W
Boiling Springs, Pa., U.S.	262	40.09 N	77.08 W
Boipeba, Ilha de I	296	13.39 S	38.55 W
Boiro	168	42.39 N	8.54 W
Bois, Lac des ⊜	236	66.40 N	125.15 W
Bois, Ribeirão dos ≃	296	20.12 S	53.07 W
Bois, Rio dos ≃	296	18.35 S	50.02 W
Bois Blanc Island I	244	45.45 N	84.28 W
Bois Brule ≃	244	46.45 N	91.37 W
Boischatel	260	46.54 N	71.08 W
Bois-des-Filion	260	45.40 N	73.46 W
Bois de Sioux ≃	252	46.16 N	96.36 W
Bois du Roi ▲	166	47.00 N	4.02 E
Boise	256	43.37 N	116.13 W
Boise ≃	256	43.49 N	117.01 W
Boise City	250	36.44 N	102.31 W
Bois-Guillaume	176	49.28 N	1.08 E
Boissevain	252	49.14 N	100.03 W
Boissy-Saint-Léger	162	48.45 N	2.31 E
Boizenburg	164	53.22 N	10.43 E
Bojadła (Boyadel)	164	51.57 N	15.50 E
Bojador, Cabo ≻	214	26.08 N	14.30 W
Bojayá ≃	290	6.35 N	76.54 W
Bojeador, Cape ≻	202	18.30 N	120.34 E
Bojelebung	202	6.32 N	122.12 E
Bojnūrd	208	37.28 N	57.19 E
Bojuru	294	31.38 S	51.26 W
Bokchito	250	34.01 N	96.09 W
Boké	214	10.56 N	14.18 W
Boké □[4]	222	11.00 N	14.20 W
Boketu	190	48.46 N	121.57 E
Bokhara ≃	228	29.55 S	146.42 E
Boknafjorden C[2]	160	59.10 N	5.35 E
Bokod	202	16.30 N	120.50 E
Boksburg	224	26.12 S	28.14 E
Boksitogorsk	160	59.28 N	33.51 E
Bokungu	218	0.41 S	22.19 E
Bol	170	43.16 N	16.40 E
Bolama	214	11.35 N	15.28 W
Bolān ≃	206	28.38 N	67.42 E
Bolanda, Jabal ▲	220	7.44 N	25.28 E
Bolands	284c	17.02 N	61.53 W
Bolaños, Río de ≃	278	21.14 N	104.08 W
Bolaños de Calatrava	168	38.54 N	3.40 W
Bolān Pass)(	206	29.45 N	67.35 E
Bolayır	172	40.31 N	26.45 E
Bolbec	176	49.34 N	0.29 E
Boles	248	34.47 N	94.03 W
Bolesławiec (Bunzlau)	164	51.16 N	15.34 E
Boleszkowice (Fürstenfelde)	164	52.44 N	14.36 E
Boley	250	35.29 N	96.29 W
Bolgatanga	222	10.46 N	0.52 W
Boli	190	45.46 N	130.35 E
Boliden	160	64.52 N	20.23 E
Boligee	248	32.45 N	88.02 W
Bolinao	202	16.23 N	119.54 E
Bolinas	272	37.54 N	122.42 W
Bolívar, Arg.	294	36.14 S	61.07 W
Bolívar, Col.	290	5.50 N	76.01 W
Bolívar, Col.	290	4.21 N	76.10 W
Bolívar, Col.	290	1.50 N	76.58 W
Bolívar, Perú	292	7.18 S	77.48 W
Bolivar, Mo., U.S.	248	37.37 N	93.25 W
Bolivar, N.Y., U.S.	266	42.04 N	78.14 W
Bolivar, Ohio, U.S.	266	40.39 N	81.27 W
Bolivar, Pa., U.S.	266	40.23 N	79.10 W
Bolivar, Tenn., U.S.	248	35.16 N	88.59 W
Bolívar □[3]	290	6.20 N	63.30 W
Bolívar □[4]	290	1.15 S	79.05 W
Bolívar □[5]	290	9.00 N	74.40 W
Bolívar, Cerro ▲	290	7.28 N	63.25 W
Bolívar, Pico (La Columna) ▲	290	8.30 N	71.02 W
Bolivar Peninsula ≻[1]	250	29.27 N	94.39 W
Bolivar Run	266	41.59 N	78.39 W
Bolivia □[1]	286	17.00 S	65.00 W
Boljarovo	172	42.09 N	26.49 E
Boljoon	202	9.38 N	123.29 E
Bolkar Dağları ⛰	212	37.15 N	34.20 E
Bollate	182	45.33 N	9.07 E
Bollène	166	44.17 N	4.45 E
Bolles Harbor	268	41.51 N	83.24 W
Bolling	248	31.43 N	86.42 W
Bollnäs	160	61.21 N	16.25 E
Bollullos par del Condado	168	37.20 N	6.32 W
Bolmen ⊜	160	56.55 N	13.40 E
Bolobo	218	2.10 S	16.14 E
Bologna	170	44.29 N	11.20 E
Bologna □[4]	184	44.28 N	11.26 E
Bolognesi	292	6.35 S	73.15 W
Bologoje	158	57.54 N	34.02 E
Bolomba	218	0.29 N	19.12 E
Bolonchén de Rejón	278	20.00 N	89.49 W
Bolondrón	284p	22.46 N	81.27 W
Bolotnoje	186	55.41 N	84.23 E
Bolovens, Plateau des ⛰[1]	200	15.20 N	106.20 E
Bol'šaja Atn'a	160	56.15 N	49.27 E
Bol'šaja Balachn'a ≃	186	73.37 N	107.05 E
Bol'šaja Ber'ostovica	164	53.11 N	24.01 E
Bol'šaja Çheta ≃	186	69.33 N	84.15 E
Bol'šaja Čuja ≃	186	58.56 N	112.13 E
Bol'šaja Glušica	160	52.24 N	50.28 E
Bol'šaja Golova, Porog ⌊	160	62.49 N	41.48 E
Bol'šaja Kuonamka ≃	186	70.45 N	113.24 E
Bol'šaja Murta	186	56.55 N	93.07 E
Bol'saja Osinovaja ≃	236	66.30 N	174.00 E
Bol'šaja Vys' ≃	172	48.45 N	30.54 E
Bolsa Knolls	272	36.44 N	121.38 W
Bol'šakovo [Kreuzingen]	164	54.53 N	21.40 E
Bol'šelig	160	62.07 N	52.25 E
Bolsena	170	42.39 N	11.59 E
Bolsena, Lago di ⊜	170	42.36 N	11.56 E
Bol'šereck	186	52.25 N	156.24 E
Bol'ševik	186	62.44 N	147.30 E
Bol'ševik, Ostrov I	186	78.40 N	102.30 E
Bol'šezemel'skaja Tunora ⤝[1]	160	67.30 N	56.00 E
Bol'šije Kajbicy	160	55.25 N	48.13 E
Bol'sije Tarchany	160	54.42 N	48.34 E
Bol'šoj An'uj ≃	186	68.30 N	160.49 E
Bol'šoj Balchan, Chrebet ⛰	208	39.40 N	54.30 E
Bol'šoj Begičev, Ostrov I	186	74.20 N	112.30 E
Bol'šoj Jenisej ≃	186	51.43 N	94.26 E
Bol'šoj Kavkaz ⛰	158	43.30 N	45.00 E
Bol'šoj Kujal'nik ≃	172	46.46 N	30.36 E
Bol'šoj Kymenej ▲	236	66.34 N	172.32 W
Bol'šoj L'achovskij, Ostrov I	186	73.35 N	142.00 E
Bol'soj Matacing ▲	236	66.28 N	179.25 W
Bol'šoj Uzen' ≃, S.S.S.R.	158		
	186	48.50 N	49.40 E
Bolsward	178	53.03 N	5.31 E
Boltaña	168	42.27 N	0.04 E
Bolton, Ont., Can.	264	43.53 N	79.44 W
Bolton, Eng., U.K.	162	53.35 N	2.26 W
Bolton, Conn., U.S.	261	41.48 N	72.28 W
Bolton, Miss., U.S.	248	32.21 N	90.28 W
Bolton, N.C., U.S.	246	34.20 N	78.25 W
Bolton Center	261	41.45 N	72.25 W
Bolu	212	40.44 N	31.37 E
Bolvadin	212	38.42 N	31.04 E
Bóly	164	45.58 N	18.32 E
Bolzano	170	46.31 N	11.22 E
Bolzano □[4]	180	46.43 N	11.30 E
Boma	218	5.51 S	13.03 E
Bomarton	250	33.30 N	99.26 W
Bombala	226	36.54 S	149.14 E
Bombarral	168	39.16 N	9.09 W
Bombay	260	44.54 N	74.34 W
Bom Despacho	296	19.43 S	45.15 W
Bom Jardim de Goiás	296	16.17 S	52.07 W
Bom Jesus da Lapa	296	13.15 S	43.25 W
Bømlafjorden C[2]	160	59.39 N	5.20 E
Bomnak	186	54.46 N	128.51 E
Bom Retiro	294	27.48 S	49.31 W
Bom Retiro do Sul	294	29.37 S	51.56 W
Bom Sucesso, Bra.	292	15.43 S	56.07 W
Bom Sucesso, Bra.	296	23.42 S	51.45 W
Bom Sucesso, Ribeirão ≃	296	18.07 S	50.09 W
Bomu (Mbomou) ≃	214	4.08 N	22.26 E
Bon, Cap ≻	170	37.05 N	11.03 E
Boná, Isla I	280	8.32 N	79.36 W
Bon Air	262	37.32 N	77.34 W
Bon Aire	266	40.54 N	79.55 W
Bonaire I	285s	12.10 N	68.15 W
Bonampak ⊥	278	16.43 N	91.05 W
Bonanza, Nic.	280	13.57 N	84.32 W
Bonanza, Oreg., U.S.	256	42.12 N	121.24 W
Bonanza, Utah, U.S.	254	40.01 N	109.11 W
Bonao	282	18.56 N	70.25 W
Bonaparte	244	40.42 N	91.48 W
Bonaparte ≃	238	50.46 N	121.17 W
Bonaparte, Mount ▲	256	48.45 N	119.08 W
Bonaparte Archipelago II	226	14.17 S	125.18 E
Bonaparte Lake ⊜	238	51.16 N	120.35 W
Bonarbridge	162	57.53 N	4.21 W
Bonarcado	170	40.04 N	8.38 E
Bonasila Dome ▲	236	62.19 N	160.30 W
Bonasse	285r	10.05 N	61.52 W
Bonaventure	240	48.03 N	65.29 W
Bonaventure ≃	240	48.02 N	65.26 W
Bonaventure, Île I	240	48.30 N	64.12 W
Bonavista	240	48.39 N	53.07 W
Bonavista, Cape ≻	240	48.42 N	53.05 W
Bonavista Bay C	240	48.45 N	53.20 W
Bonawon	202	9.08 N	122.55 E
Bonbonon Point ≻	202	9.03 N	123.06 E
Bond	248	30.54 N	89.10 W
Bondeno	170	44.53 N	11.25 E
Bondo	214	3.49 N	23.40 E
Bondoc Peninsula ≻[1]	202	13.26 N	122.35 E
Bondoukou	222	8.02 N	2.48 W
Bondoukou □[5]	222	8.45 N	3.30 W
Bondsville	261	42.13 N	72.21 W
Bonduel	244	44.44 N	88.27 W
Bond'užskij	160	55.54 N	52.20 E
Bône → Annaba, Alg.	170	36.54 N	7.46 E
Bone, Teluk C	198	4.00 S	120.40 E
Bönen	178	51.36 N	7.44 E
Bonesteel	252	43.04 N	98.57 W
Bonete, Cerro ▲	294	27.51 S	68.48 W
Bonfinópolis	296	16.38 S	48.58 W
Bong □[6]	222	7.00 N	9.30 W
Bongabon, Pil.	202	15.38 N	121.11 E
Bongabon, Pil.	202	12.45 N	121.30 E
Bongabon ≃	202	12.40 N	121.33 E
Bongandanga	218	1.30 N	21.03 E
Bongao Island I	202	5.01 N	119.45 E
Bonggaw	202	5.02 N	119.46 E
Bongo Island I	202	7.20 N	124.02 E
Bongor	214	10.17 N	15.22 E
Bong Range ⛰	222	6.50 N	10.00 W
Bonham	250	33.35 N	96.11 W
Bonhomme, Pic ▲	282	19.05 N	72.15 W
Bonifacio, Fr.	170	41.23 N	9.10 E
Bonifacio, Pil.	202	8.03 N	123.36 E
Bonifacio, Strait of ⋓	170	41.20 N	9.15 E
Bonifati, Capo ≻	170	39.35 N	15.52 E
Bonifay	248	30.48 N	85.41 W
Bonilla Island I	238	53.29 N	130.36 W
Bonin Islands → Ogasawara-guntō II	148	27.00 N	142.10 E
Bonita	248	32.55 N	91.40 W
Bonita Springs	246	26.21 N	81.47 W
Bonito	292	21.08 S	56.28 W
Bonito ≃	296	16.31 S	51.23 W
Bonito, Pico ▲	280	15.38 N	86.55 W
Bonn	164	50.44 N	7.05 E
Bonneauville	262	39.46 N	77.10 W
Bonne Bay C	240	49.33 N	57.55 W
Bonnechere ≃	244	45.31 N	76.33 W
Bonne Doone	246	35.06 N	78.58 W
Bonner	256	46.52 N	113.52 W
Bonners Ferry	256	48.41 N	116.18 W
Bonnétable	166	48.11 N	0.26 E
Bonne Terre	248	37.55 N	90.33 W
Bonnet Plume ≃	236	65.55 N	134.58 W
Bonneval	166	48.11 N	1.24 E
Bonneville, Fr.	166	46.05 N	6.25 E
Bonneville, Oreg., U.S.	270	45.38 N	121.57 W
Bonneville Peak ▲	256	42.46 N	112.08 W
Bonneville Salt Flats ⌣	254	40.45 N	113.52 W
Bonney Lake	270	47.10 N	122.11 W
Bonnie Rock	226	30.32 S	118.21 E
Bonny	214	4.27 N	7.10 E
Bonny ≃[1]	222	4.20 N	7.10 E
Bonny Blue	246	36.49 N	83.04 W
Bonnyville	238	54.16 N	110.44 W
Bono, It.	170	40.25 N	9.02 E
Bono, Ohio, U.S.	266	41.38 N	83.16 W
Bonorva	170	40.25 N	8.45 E
Bonsall	274	33.17 N	117.13 W
Bon Secour	248	30.19 N	87.44 W
Bonsecours	166	49.26 N	1.08 E
Bonshaw	240	46.12 N	63.21 W
Bonthain	198	5.32 S	119.56 E
Bonthe	214	7.32 N	12.30 W
Bontoc	202	17.06 N	120.58 E
Bon Wier	248	30.44 N	93.39 W
Bonyhád	164	46.19 N	18.32 E
Boogardie	226	28.02 S	117.47 E
Booischot	178	51.03 N	4.46 E
Book Cliffs •[4]	254	39.20 N	109.00 W
Booker	250	36.27 N	100.32 W
Booker T. Washington National Monument ♠	246	37.01 N	79.45 W
Boom	176	51.05 N	4.22 E
Boomer	242	38.09 N	81.17 W
Boonah	226	28.00 S	152.41 E
Boone, Iowa, U.S.	244	42.04 N	93.53 W
Boone, N.C., U.S.	246	36.13 N	81.41 W
Boone □[6]	268	42.15 N	88.50 W
Boone ≃	244	42.19 N	93.56 W
Boone Draw ∨	250	33.51 N	103.42 W
Boone Grove	268	41.21 N	87.08 W
Boone Mill	246	37.07 N	79.57 W
Boone Reservoir ⊜[1]	246	36.25 N	82.25 W
Booneville, Ark., U.S.	248	35.08 N	93.55 W
Booneville, Ky., U.S.	246	37.29 N	83.40 W
Booneville, Miss., U.S.	248	34.39 N	88.34 W
Boonsboro	242	39.30 N	77.39 W
Boon Terrace	266	40.15 N	80.12 W
Boonville, Calif., U.S.	258	39.00 N	123.22 W
Boonville, Ind., U.S.	248	38.03 N	87.16 W
Boonville, Mo., U.S.	248	38.58 N	92.44 W
Boonville, N.Y., U.S.	264	43.29 N	75.20 W
Boopi ≃	292	15.41 S	67.15 W
Bootahnie Indian Reserve ⤝[4]	238	50.24 N	121.31 W
Booth	248	32.30 N	86.41 W
Boothbay Harbor	242	43.51 N	69.38 W
Boothia, Gulf of C	232	71.00 N	91.00 W
Boothia Peninsula ≻[1]	232	70.30 N	95.00 W
Booth Lake ⊜	244	46.45 N	78.34 W
Booué	218	0.06 S	11.56 E
Boquerón	280	8.30 N	82.40 W
Boquerón □[5]	294	21.30 S	60.00 W
Boquete	280	8.46 N	82.27 W
Boquilla, Presa de la ⊜[1]	278	27.30 N	105.30 W
Boquilla del Refugio	250	25.33 N	102.28 W
Boquillas del Carmen	278	29.17 N	102.53 W
Bor, Česko.	164	49.43 N	12.47 E
Bor, Jugo.	172	44.05 N	22.07 E
Bor, S.S.S.R.	160	63.00 N	42.38 E
Bor, S.S.S.R.	160	56.22 N	44.05 E
Bor, Sūd.	214	6.12 N	31.33 E
Bor, Tür.	158	37.54 N	34.34 E
Borah Peak ▲	256	44.08 N	113.48 W
Borama	214	9.58 N	43.07 E
Borås	160	57.43 N	12.55 E
Borāzjān	208	29.16 N	51.12 E
Borba, Bra.	290	4.24 S	59.35 W
Borba, Port.	168	38.48 N	7.27 W
Borborema	296	21.37 S	49.04 W
Borcea ≃	172	44.40 N	27.53 E
Borculo	268	42.53 N	86.01 W
Borda, Cape ≻	228	35.45 S	136.34 E
Bordeaux	166	44.50 N	0.34 W
Borden Lake ⊜	244	47.50 N	83.18 W
Borden Peninsula ≻[1]	232	73.00 N	83.00 W
Bordentown	262	40.09 N	74.42 W
Bordertown	226	36.19 S	140.47 E
Bordesholm	164	54.11 N	10.01 E
Borđeyri	160a	65.15 N	21.10 W
Bordighera	182	43.46 N	7.39 E
Bordj Baniou	168	35.25 N	4.20 E
Bordj Bou Arreridj	168	36.02 N	4.49 E
Bordj Bounaama	168	35.51 N	1.36 E
Bordj Menaïel	168	36.44 N	3.45 E
Borecaia ≃	296	13.51 S	51.38 W
Borehamwood	174	51.40 N	0.16 W
Borek	164	51.55 N	17.14 E
Borgå (Porvoo)	160	60.24 N	25.40 E
Borgarnes	160a	64.35 N	21.53 W
Borger	250	35.39 N	101.24 W
Borgerhout	176	51.13 N	4.26 E
Borgholm	160	56.53 N	16.39 E
Borghorst	178	52.07 N	7.23 E
Borgne, Lake C	248	30.05 N	89.40 W
Borgo	170	46.03 N	11.27 E
Borgo a Mazzano	184	43.59 N	10.33 E
Borgomanero	182	45.42 N	8.28 E
Borgonovo Val Tidone	182	45.01 N	9.26 E
Borgorose	184	42.11 N	13.13 E
Borgo San Dalmazzo	182	44.20 N	7.30 E
Borgo San Lorenzo	184	43.57 N	11.23 E
Borgosesia	182	45.43 N	8.16 E
Borgou □[5]	222	10.30 N	2.50 E
Borgo Val di Taro	170	44.29 N	9.46 E
Boring, Md., U.S.	262	39.31 N	76.49 W
Boring, Oreg., U.S.	270	45.26 N	122.23 W
Borisoglebsk	158	51.23 N	42.06 E
Borisov	158	54.15 N	28.30 E
Borja, Esp.	168	41.50 N	1.32 W
Borja, Perú	290	4.25 S	77.40 W
Borjas Blancas	168	41.31 N	0.52 E
Bork	178	51.40 N	7.30 E
Borken	178	51.51 N	6.51 E
Borkou-Ennedi-Tibesti □[5]	220	18.15 N	18.50 E
Borkoviči	160	55.40 N	28.20 E
Borkum	178	53.35 N	6.40 E
Borlänge	160	60.29 N	15.25 E
Borlu	172	38.44 N	28.27 E
Bormes	166	43.09 N	6.20 E
Bormio	170	46.28 N	10.22 E
Borna	164	51.19 N	13.11 E
Borne	178	52.18 N	6.45 E
Borneo (Kalimantan) I	198	0.30 N	114.00 E
Bornholm I	160	55.10 N	15.00 E
Bornova	212	38.27 N	27.14 E
Boro ≃	220	8.52 N	26.11 E
Borocay Island I	202	11.58 N	121.55 E
Borogoncy	186	62.42 N	131.08 E
Boron	274	35.00 N	117.39 W
Boronga Islands II	200	19.58 N	93.06 E
Borongan	202	11.37 N	125.26 E
Borovan	172	43.26 N	23.45 E
Boroviči	160	58.24 N	33.55 E
Borovl'anka	186	52.38 N	84.29 E
Borovoj	160	59.55 N	51.38 E
Borovskaja	160	60.46 N	41.06 E
Borrachudo ≃	296	18.12 S	45.16 W
Borrazópolis	296	23.56 S	51.36 W
Borroloola	226	16.04 S	136.17 E
Borș	172	47.07 N	21.49 E
Borșa	172	46.56 N	23.40 E
Borșa ≃	172	46.55 N	23.47 E
Borščovočnyj Chrebet ⛰	186	52.00 N	117.00 E
Borskoje	160	53.02 N	51.43 E
Borsod-Abaúj-Zemplén □[6]	164	48.15 N	21.00 E
Borth	162	52.29 N	4.03 W
Bort-les-Orgues	166	45.24 N	2.30 E
Boruca	280	9.00 N	83.20 W
Borūjen	208	31.59 N	51.18 E
Borūjerd	208	33.54 N	48.46 E
Borz'a	186	50.38 N	115.38 E
Borzyszkowy	164	54.03 N	17.22 E
Bosa	170	40.18 N	8.30 E
Bosanska Dubica	170	45.11 N	16.49 E
Bosanska Gradiška	170	45.09 N	17.15 E
Bosanska Krupa	170	44.53 N	16.10 E
Bosanski Novi	170	45.03 N	16.23 E
Bosanski Petrovac	172	44.33 N	16.22 E
Bosanski Šamac	172	45.03 N	18.28 E
Bosansko Grahovo	170	44.11 N	15.52 E
Bosaso	214	11.13 N	49.08 E
Boscobel	244	43.08 N	90.42 W
Boscotrecase	184	40.46 N	14.28 E
Bosencheve, Parque Nacional ♠	278	19.36 N	100.15 W
Boshan	194	36.29 N	117.50 E
Bosilegrad	172	42.29 N	22.28 E
Bositenghu ⊜	190	42.00 N	87.00 E
Boskoop	178	52.04 N	4.35 E
Boskovice	164	49.29 N	16.40 E
Bosna ≃	172	45.04 N	18.29 E
Bosna i Hercegovina □[3]	172	44.15 N	17.50 E
Bosnik	198	1.10 S	136.14 E
Bōsō-hantō ≻[1]	192	35.18 N	140.10 E
Bosporus → İstanbul Boğazı ⋓	212	41.00 N	29.00 E
Bossangoa	214	6.29 N	17.27 E
Bossembélé	214	5.16 N	17.39 E
Bossier City	248	32.31 N	93.43 W
Bosso, Dallol ∨	222	12.25 N	2.50 E
Boston, Pil.	202	7.52 N	126.22 E
Boston, Eng., U.K.	174	52.59 N	0.01 W
Boston, Ga., U.S.	246	30.47 N	83.47 W
Boston, Mass., U.S.	261	42.21 N	71.04 W
Boston, N.Y., U.S.	266	42.38 N	78.44 W
Boston Bar	238	49.52 N	121.26 W
Boston Corners	261	42.03 N	73.31 W
Boston Harbor	270	47.08 N	122.54 W
Boston Heights	266	41.16 N	81.30 W
Boston Mill	266	41.16 N	81.34 W
Boston Mountains ⛰	248	35.50 N	93.20 W
Bosumtwi, Lake ⊜	222	6.30 N	1.25 W
Boswell, Ind., U.S.	268	40.31 N	87.23 W
Boswell, Okla., U.S.	250	34.02 N	95.52 W
Boswell, Pa., U.S.	266	40.10 N	79.02 W
Boswell Bay	236	60.24 N	146.08 W
Bosworth	248	39.28 N	93.20 W
Botanamo ≃	290	7.01 N	61.14 W
Botany Bay C	228	33.59 S	151.12 E
Botas, Ribeirão das ≃	296	20.26 S	53.43 W
Bottenviken (Perämeri) C	160	64.30 N	23.00 E
Boteti ≃	224	20.08 S	23.23 E
Botev ▲	172	42.43 N	24.55 E
Botevgrad	172	42.54 N	23.47 E
Bothell	270	47.46 N	122.12 W
Bothnia, Gulf of C	160	63.00 N	20.00 E
Bothwell	266	42.38 N	81.52 W
Boticas	168	41.41 N	7.40 W
Botkins	268	40.28 N	84.11 W
Botolan	202	15.18 N	120.01 E
Botoșani	172	47.45 N	26.40 E
Botrange ▲	164	50.30 N	6.08 E
Botsford	261	41.22 N	73.15 W
Botswana □[1]	218	22.00 S	24.00 E
Botte Donato ▲	170	39.17 N	16.26 E
Bottenhavet (Selkämeri) C	160	62.00 N	20.00 E
Bottineau	252	48.50 N	100.27 W
Bottrop	178	51.31 N	6.55 E
Botucatu	296	22.52 S	48.26 W
Botwood	240	49.08 N	55.21 W
Bouaflé	214	6.59 N	5.45 W
Bouaflé □[5]	222	7.15 N	5.45 W
Bouaké	222	7.41 N	5.02 W
Bouaké □[5]	222	7.15 N	5.00 W
Bouar	214	5.57 N	15.36 E
Bou Arada	170	36.20 N	9.38 E
Bouaye	166	47.09 N	1.42 W
Bouchegouf	170	36.28 N	7.45 E
Boucher ≃	240	49.10 N	69.05 W
Boucher, Lac ⊜	240	51.06 N	59.32 W
Boucherville	260	45.37 N	73.27 W
Bouches-du-Rhône □[5]	182	43.30 N	5.00 E
Boucle du Baoulé, Parc National de la ♠	222	13.50 N	9.00 W
Boû Djébéh ▾[4]	222	18.33 N	2.45 W
Boudouaou	168	36.44 N	3.24 E
Boufarik	168	36.37 N	2.52 E
Bou Ficha	170	36.18 N	10.29 E
Bougaa	168	36.21 N	5.05 E
Bougaroun, Cap ≻	168	37.10 N	6.30 E
Boughzoul	168	35.42 N	2.52 E
Bougie → Bejaïa	168	36.45 N	5.05 E
Bougouni	214	11.25 N	7.29 W
Bougouriba ≃	222	10.42 N	2.56 W
Bou Hadjar, Alg.	170	36.30 N	8.07 E
Bou Hadjar, Tun.	170	35.42 N	10.48 E
Bou Hamed	168	35.25 N	5.00 W
Bou Hellal, Jbel ▲	168	35.09 N	5.10 W
Bouillante	285o	16.06 N	61.45 W
Bouillon	164	49.48 N	5.04 E
Bouïra	168	36.23 N	3.54 E
Bou Ismail	168	36.40 N	2.44 E
Bouka ≃	222	11.00 N	10.50 W
Bou Kadir	168	36.04 N	1.08 E
Bou Khadra	170	35.46 N	8.02 E
Boularderie Island I	240	46.15 N	60.30 W
Boulay-Moselle	166	49.11 N	6.30 E
Boulder, Austl.	226	30.47 S	121.29 E
Boulder, Colo., U.S.	254	40.01 N	105.17 W
Boulder, Mont., U.S.	256	46.14 N	112.07 W
Boulder ≃, Mont., U.S.	256	45.52 N	111.57 W
Boulder ≃, Mont., U.S.	256	45.51 N	109.55 W
Boulder City	258	35.59 N	114.50 W
Boulder Creek	272	37.07 N	122.07 W
Boulder Hill	268	41.42 N	88.21 W
Boulevard	278	32.40 N	116.16 W
Bouli ≃	222	13.15 N	0.03 E
Boulia	226	22.54 S	139.54 E
Boulogne-Billancourt	176	48.50 N	2.15 E
Boulogne-sur-Gesse	168	43.18 N	0.39 E
Boulogne-sur-Mer	176	50.43 N	1.37 E
Boulogue	166	43.18 N	0.39 E
Bouloire	162	47.58 N	0.33 E
Boû Maya ▾[4]	222	18.17 N	8.07 W
Bou Médfaa	168	36.22 N	2.28 E
Bouna	214	9.16 N	3.00 W
Bouna, Park National de ♠	222	9.00 N	3.30 W
Boundary	236	64.04 N	141.06 W
Boundary Peak ▲	258	37.51 N	118.21 W
Boundary Ranges ⛰	236	59.00 N	134.00 W
Bound Brook	262	40.34 N	74.32 W
Boundiali □[5]	222	9.50 N	6.30 W
Boung ≃	200	15.51 N	107.51 E
Bountiful	254	40.53 N	111.53 W
Bounty Basin ⤳[1]	148	46.30 S	170.00 E
Bourbeuse ≃	248	38.24 N	90.53 W
Bourbon, Ind., U.S.	268	41.18 N	86.07 W
Bourbon, Mo., U.S.	248	38.09 N	91.15 W
Bourbon-Lancy	166	46.38 N	3.46 E
Bourbonnais	268	41.09 N	87.53 W
Bourbonnais □[9]	166	46.20 N	3.00 E
Bourbonne-les-Bains	166	47.57 N	5.45 E
Bourem	214	16.57 N	0.21 W
Bourg	248	29.34 N	90.36 W
Bourganeuf	166	45.57 N	1.46 E
Bourg-de-Péage	182	45.02 N	5.03 E
Bourg-en-Bresse	180	46.12 N	5.13 E
Bourges	166	47.05 N	2.24 E
Bourget	260	45.26 N	75.09 W
Bourget, Lac du ⊜	166	45.44 N	5.52 E
Bourg-Lastic	166	45.39 N	2.33 E
Bourg-les-Valence	182	44.57 N	4.53 E
Bourgneuf-en-Retz	166	47.02 N	1.57 W
Bourgogne □[9]	166	47.00 N	4.30 E
Bourgogne, Canal de ≍	166	47.58 N	3.30 E
Bourgoin	182	45.35 N	5.17 E
Bourg-Saint-Andéol	166	44.22 N	4.39 E
Bourg-Saint-Maurice	166	45.37 N	6.46 E
Bourgtheroulde	162	49.18 N	0.53 E
Bourgueil	166	47.17 N	0.10 E
Bou Rjeïmat ▾[4]	222	19.04 N	15.08 W
Bourke	228	30.05 S	145.56 E
Bourlamaque	244	48.05 N	77.47 W
Bourne	174	52.46 N	0.23 W
Bournemouth	174	50.43 N	1.54 W
Bou Roumane, Djebel ▲	170	35.20 N	8.13 W
Bourtanger Moor ⤝[3]	164	53.00 N	7.15 E
Bou Saâda	168	35.11 N	4.09 E
Bouse	254	33.56 N	114.00 W
Bouse Wash ∨	254	34.02 N	114.20 W
Boussac-Ville	166	46.21 N	2.13 E
Bousso	214	10.29 N	16.43 E
Boussu	176	50.26 N	3.48 E
Bouteldja	170	36.47 N	8.13 E
Boutilimit	214	17.33 N	14.42 W
Bou Zajar	168	35.35 N	1.09 W
Bøvågen	160	60.40 N	4.58 E
Bovalino Marina	170	38.09 N	16.11 E
Bovec	170	46.20 N	13.33 E
Bøverdal	160	61.43 N	8.21 E
Boves	182	44.19 N	7.33 E
Bovey	244	47.17 N	93.25 W
Bovill	256	46.51 N	116.24 W
Bovina	250	34.31 N	102.53 W
Bovino	184	41.15 N	15.20 E
Bovril	294	31.22 S	59.25 W
Bow	270	48.31 N	122.21 W
Bow ≃	238	49.56 N	111.42 W
Bowbells	252	48.48 N	102.15 W
Bowden	238	51.55 N	114.02 W
Bowdle	252	45.27 N	99.39 W
Bowdoin, Lake ⊜	256	48.24 N	108.41 W
Bowdon, Ga., U.S.	246	33.32 N	85.15 W
Bowdon, N. Dak., U.S.	252	47.28 N	99.43 W
Boweiershankou)(	206	33.14 N	84.58 E
Bowen, Arg.	294	35.02 S	67.32 W
Bowen, Austl.	228	20.01 S	148.15 E
Bowen, Ill., U.S.	248	40.14 N	91.04 W
Bowen ≃	228	20.24 S	147.21 E
Bowers	262	39.04 N	75.24 W
Bowerston	266	40.26 N	81.11 W
Bowie, Ariz., U.S.	254	32.19 N	109.29 W
Bowie, Md., U.S.	262	39.00 N	76.47 W
Bowie, Tex., U.S.	250	33.34 N	97.51 W
Bowling Green, Fla., U.S.	246	27.38 N	81.50 W
Bowling Green, Ky., U.S.	248	37.00 N	86.27 W
Bowling Green, Mo., U.S.	248	39.20 N	91.12 W
Bowling Green, Ohio, U.S.	268	41.22 N	83.39 W
Bowling Green, Va., U.S.	262	38.03 N	77.21 W
Bowling Green, Cape ≻	228	19.19 S	145.25 E
Bowman, Calif., U.S.	272	38.57 N	121.03 W
Bowman, Ga., U.S.	246	34.12 N	83.02 W
Bowman, N. Dak., U.S.	252	46.11 N	103.24 W
Bowman, S.C., U.S.	246	33.21 N	80.41 W
Bowman, Mount ▲	238	51.10 N	121.55 W
Bowman Bay C	232	65.30 N	73.40 W
Bowman-Haley Reservoir ⊜[1]	252	46.00 N	103.20 W
Bowmansdale	262	40.10 N	76.59 W
Bowmanstown	262	40.48 N	75.40 W
Bowmansville, N.Y., U.S.	264	42.56 N	78.41 W
Bowmansville, Pa., U.S.	262	40.10 N	76.04 W
Bowmanville	264	43.55 N	78.41 W
Bowmore	162	55.45 N	6.17 W
Bowral	228	34.28 S	150.25 E
Bowron ≃	238	54.04 N	121.48 W
Bowron Lake Porvincial Park ♠	238	53.10 N	121.06 W
Box Elder	256	48.19 N	110.01 W
Boxey	240	47.25 N	55.34 W
Boxey Point ≻	240	47.24 N	55.35 W
Boxford	261	42.40 N	70.60 W
Boxholm	160	58.12 N	15.03 E
Boxian	196	33.53 N	115.45 E
Boxmeer	178	51.39 N	5.57 E
Boxtel	178	51.35 N	5.20 E
Boyacá □[5]	290	5.30 N	72.30 W
Boyalık	172	41.15 N	28.37 E
Boyce	248	31.23 N	92.40 W
Boyceville	244	45.03 N	92.02 W
Boyd, Minn., U.S.	252	44.51 N	95.54 W
Boyd, Tex., U.S.	250	33.05 N	97.34 W
Boyd ≃	228	29.51 S	152.35 E
Boyd's Cove	240	49.27 N	54.39 W
Boydton	246	36.40 N	78.24 W
Boyer ≃	252	41.28 N	95.55 W
Boyer Aḥmadī-ye Sardsīr va Kohkīlūyeh □[4]	208	30.40 N	50.42 E
Boyers	266	41.06 N	79.54 W
Boyertown	262	40.20 N	75.38 W
Boyes Hot Springs	272	38.19 N	122.29 W
Boykins	262	36.35 N	77.12 W
Boyle, Alta., Can.	238	54.35 N	112.49 W
Boyle, Eire	162	53.58 N	8.18 W
Boyle, Miss., U.S.	248	33.42 N	90.50 W
Boylston, Ala., U.S.	248	32.26 N	86.17 W
Boylston, Mass., U.S.	261	42.21 N	71.44 W
Boyne ≃, Austl.	228	23.56 S	151.21 E
Boyne ≃, Ont., Can.	244	44.10 N	7.94 W
Boyne ≃, Eire	162	53.43 N	6.15 W
Boyne City	244	45.13 N	85.01 W
Boynton	250	35.39 N	95.39 W
Boynton Beach	246	26.32 N	80.03 W
Boysen Reservoir ⊜[1]	254	43.19 N	108.11 W
Boys Ranch	250	35.32 N	102.15 W
Boyuibe	292	20.25 S	63.17 W
Bozburun	172	36.41 N	28.04 E
Boz Burun ≻	212	40.24 N	26.54 E
Bozcaada	172	39.50 N	26.04 E
Bozca Ada I	212	39.49 N	26.03 E
Boz Dağ ▲, Tür.	212	37.18 N	29.12 E
Boz Dağ ▲, Tür.	212	38.19 N	28.08 E
Boz Dağlar ⛰	212	38.20 N	27.45 E
Bozdoğan	172	37.40 N	28.19 E
Bozel	166	45.27 N	6.39 E
Bozeman	256	45.41 N	111.02 W
Bozen → Bolzano	170	46.31 N	11.22 E
Bozhen	194	38.07 N	116.32 E
Bozkurt	172	37.49 N	29.37 E
Bozman	262	38.46 N	76.16 W
Bozoum	214	6.19 N	16.23 E
Bozovici	172	44.55 N	21.59 E
Bra	182	44.42 N	7.51 E
Brabant □[4]	176	50.45 N	4.30 E
Brač, Otok I	170	43.20 N	16.40 E

Symbols in the index entries are identified on page 360.

Name	Page	Lat°′	Long°′
Bracciano	184	42.06 N	12.10 E
Bracebridge	264	45.02 N	79.19 W
Braceville	268	41.14 N	88.16 W
Brach	214	27.32 N	14.16 E
Bracieux	166	47.33 N	1.33 E
Bracigovo	172	42.01 N	24.22 E
Bräcke	160	62.43 N	15.27 E
Brackendale	238	49.46 N	123.09 W
Brackenridge	266	40.37 N	79.44 W
Brackettville	250	29.19 N	100.24 W
Brački Kanal Џ	170	43.24 N	16.40 E
Brackley	162	52.02 N	1.09 W
Bracknell	174	51.26 N	0.45 W
Brackwede	178	51.59 N	8.31 E
Braço do Norte	294	28.17 S	49.11 W
Braço Norte ≃	292	10.09 S	55.13 W
Brad	172	46.08 N	22.47 E
Bradano ≃	170	40.23 N	16.51 E
Braddock	266	40.25 N	79.50 W
Braddock Heights, Md., U.S.	262	39.25 N	77.30 W
Braddock Heights, N.Y., U.S.	264	43.19 N	77.42 W
Bradenton	246	27.29 N	82.34 W
Bradenville	266	40.19 N	79.20 W
Bradford, Ont., Can.	264	44.07 N	79.34 W
Bradford, Eng., U.K.	162	53.48 N	1.45 W
Bradford, Ark., U.S.	248	35.25 N	91.27 W
Bradford, Ill., U.S.	244	41.11 N	89.39 W
Bradford, Ohio, U.S.	242	40.08 N	84.26 W
Bradford, Pa., U.S.	266	41.58 N	78.39 W
Bradford, R.I., U.S.	261	41.24 N	71.45 W
Bradford, Tenn., U.S.	248	36.05 N	88.51 W
Bradford, Vt., U.S.	242	43.59 N	72.09 W
Bradford-on-Avon	174	51.20 N	2.15 W
Bradfordwoods	266	40.38 N	80.05 W
Bradley, Ala., U.S.	248	31.02 N	86.43 W
Bradley, Ark., U.S.	248	33.06 N	93.39 W
Bradley, Calif., U.S.	272	35.52 N	120.48 W
Bradley, Fla., U.S.	246	27.48 N	81.59 W
Bradley, Ill., U.S.	268	41.09 N	87.52 W
Bradley, Mich., U.S.	268	42.38 N	85.39 W
Bradley, S. Dak., U.S.	252	45.05 N	97.39 W
Bradley Beach	262	40.12 N	74.01 W
Bradleyville	261	41.31 N	73.05 W
Bradner, B.C., Can.	270	49.06 N	122.25 W
Bradner, Ohio, U.S.	266	41.20 N	83.26 W
Bradore Bay	240	51.28 N	57.14 W
Bradshaw, Md., U.S.	262	39.25 N	76.23 W
Bradshaw, Nebr., U.S.	252	40.53 N	97.45 W
Bradshaw, W. Va., U.S.	246	37.21 N	81.49 W
Brady, Mont., U.S.	256	48.02 N	111.51 W
Brady, Nebr., U.S.	252	41.01 N	100.22 W
Brady, Tex., U.S.	250	31.08 N	99.20 W
Brady Lake	266	41.09 N	81.19 W
Brady Mountains ⋀[2]	250	31.20 N	99.40 W
Braeside	264	45.28 N	76.24 W
Braga	168	41.33 N	8.26 W
Bragado	294	35.10 S	60.30 W
Bragança, Bra.	286	1.03 S	46.46 W
Bragança, Port.	168	41.49 N	6.45 W
Bragança Paulista	296	22.57 S	46.34 W
Braham	244	45.41 N	93.28 W
Brāhmanbāria	206	23.59 N	91.07 E
Brāhmani ≃	206	20.45 N	87.00 E
Brahmaputra (Yaluzangbujiang) ≃	206	24.02 N	90.59 E
Braidwood	268	41.16 N	88.13 W
Brăila	172	45.16 N	27.58 E
Brăilei, Balta ☰	172	45.00 N	28.00 E
Brainard, Nebr., U.S.	252	41.11 N	97.00 W
Brainard, N.Y., U.S.	261	42.30 N	73.31 W
Braine-l'Alleud	176	50.41 N	4.22 E
Braine-le-Comte	176	50.36 N	4.08 E
Brainerd	244	46.21 N	94.12 W
Braintree, Eng., U.K.	174	51.53 N	0.32 E
Braintree, Mass., U.S.	261	42.13 N	71.00 W
Brak ≃	224	29.35 S	22.55 E
Brake, B.R.D.	178	53.19 N	8.28 E
Brake, B.R.D.	178	52.04 N	8.35 E
Brakel	178	51.43 N	9.10 E
Brakpan	224	26.13 S	28.20 E
Bralorne	238	50.47 N	122.49 W
Bramalea	264	43.44 N	79.43 W
Braman	250	36.55 N	97.20 W
Bramfeld ↵[8]	178	53.37 N	10.04 E
Brampton	264	43.41 N	79.46 W
Bramsche	178	52.24 N	7.58 E
Bran, Pasul)(	172	45.26 N	25.17 E
Brancaleone Marina	170	37.58 N	16.06 E
Branch	240	46.53 N	53.57 W
Branch □[6]	268	41.55 N	85.03 W
Branch Dale	262	40.41 N	76.20 W
Branchville, Conn., U.S.	261	41.16 N	73.27 W
Branchville, S.C., U.S.	246	33.15 N	80.49 W
Branchville, Va., U.S.	262	36.34 N	77.15 W
Branco	290	1.24 S	61.51 W
Branco ≃	290	1.24 S	61.51 W
Branco, Ilhéu I	222a	16.39 N	24.41 W
Brandamore	262	40.03 N	75.50 W
Brandaris ∧[2]	285s	12.17 N	68.24 W
Brandberg ∧	224	21.10 S	14.33 E
Brandbu	160	60.28 N	10.30 E
Brandenburg	164	52.24 N	12.32 E
Brandenburg □[9]	164	52.00 N	13.30 E
Brand-Erbisdorf	164	50.52 N	13.19 E
Brandizzo	182	45.11 N	7.51 E
Brandon, Man., Can.	252	49.50 N	99.57 W
Brandon, Fla., U.S.	246	27.56 N	82.17 W
Brandon, Miss., U.S.	248	32.16 N	89.59 W
Brandon, Vt., U.S.	242	43.48 N	73.05 W
Brandon, Wis., U.S.	244	43.44 N	88.47 W
Brandon Bay C	162	52.15 N	10.05 W
Brandon Mountain ∧	162	52.14 N	10.15 W
Brandvlei	218	30.25 S	20.30 E
Brandy Camp	266	41.19 N	78.41 W
Brandy Peak ∧	256	42.36 N	123.53 W
Brandýs nad Labem	164	50.10 N	14.41 E
Branford, Conn., U.S.	261	41.17 N	72.49 W
Branford, Fla., U.S.	246	29.58 N	82.56 W
Braniewo (Braunsberg)	164	54.24 N	19.50 E
Brannica ⋀	212	41.59 N	26.16 E
Branquinho ≃	292	5.45 S	71.27 W
Brańsk, Pol.	164	52.45 N	22.51 E
Br'ansk, S.S.S.R.	158	53.15 N	34.22 E
Branson, Colo., U.S.	252	37.01 N	103.53 W
Branson, Mo., U.S.	248	36.39 N	93.13 W
Brant	266	42.35 N	79.01 W
Brant □[6]	264	43.10 N	80.20 W
Brantford	264	43.08 N	80.16 W
Brant Lake	242	43.41 N	73.45 W
Brantley	248	31.35 N	86.22 W
Brantôme	166	45.22 N	0.39 E
Brantville	240	47.22 N	64.58 W
Bras d'Or Lake ⊜	240	45.52 N	60.50 W
Brasilânia	296	16.01 S	49.32 W
Brasiléia	292	11.00 S	68.44 W
Brasília, Bra.	296	16.12 S	44.26 W
Brasília, Bra.	296	15.47 S	47.55 W
Brasília, Lago de ⊜	296	15.48 S	47.50 W
Braslav	160	55.38 N	27.02 E
Brașov	172	45.39 N	25.37 E
Brass Castle	262	40.47 N	74.58 W
Brasschaat	176	51.17 N	4.27 E
Brassey Range ⋀	202	4.54 N	117.30 E
Brasstown Bald ∧	246	34.52 N	83.48 W
Břasy	164	49.50 N	13.35 E
Bratca	172	46.56 N	22.37 E
Brateș, Lacul ⊜	172	45.30 N	28.05 E
Bratislava	164	48.09 N	17.07 E
Bratsk	186	56.05 N	101.48 E
Bratskoje Vodochranilišče ⊜[1]	186	56.10 N	102.10 E
Brattleboro	242	42.51 N	72.34 W
Braúnas	296	19.04 S	42.43 W
Braunau [am Inn]	164	48.15 N	13.02 E
Braunlage	164	51.44 N	10.37 E
Braunsberg → Braniewo	164	54.24 N	19.50 E
Braunschweig	178	52.16 N	10.31 E
Braunschweig □[6]	178	52.10 N	10.40 E
Brava	214	1.05 N	44.02 E
Brava I	222a	14.52 N	24.43 W
Brava, Costa ⍛[2]	168	41.45 N	3.04 E
Brava, Punta ≻	294	34.56 S	56.10 W
Brave	242	39.44 N	80.16 W
Bravo, Cerro ∧, Bol.	292	17.40 S	64.35 W
Bravo, Cerro ∧, Perú	292	5.31 S	79.16 W
Bravo del Norte (Rio Grande) ≃	234	25.57 N	97.09 W
Brawley	258	32.59 N	115.31 W
Brawley Peaks ⋀	258	38.15 N	118.55 W
Brawly Wash V	254	32.34 N	111.26 W
Bray, Bel.	166	50.26 N	4.06 E
Bray, Eire	162	53.12 N	6.06 W
Bray Island I	232	69.20 N	76.45 W
Braymer	248	39.35 N	93.48 W
Bray [sur-Seine]	166	48.25 N	3.14 E
Brazeau ≃	238	52.55 N	115.15 W
Brazeau, Mount ∧	238	52.33 N	117.21 W
Brazil	248	39.32 N	87.08 W
Brazil □[1]	286	9.00 S	53.00 W
Brazil Basin ⇝[1]	148	15.00 S	26.00 W
Brazoria	250	29.03 N	95.34 W
Brazos ≃	250	28.53 N	95.23 W
Brazos, Clear Fork ≃	250	33.01 N	98.40 W
Brazos, Double Mountain Fork ≃	250	33.15 N	100.00 W
Brazos, Salt Fork ≃	250	33.15 N	100.00 W
Brazzaville	218	4.16 S	15.17 E
Brčko	172	44.53 N	18.48 E
Brda ≃	164	53.07 N	18.08 E
Brea	274	33.55 N	117.54 W
Breakenridge, Mount ∧	238	49.43 N	121.56 W
Breaksea Sound Џ	230	45.35 S	166.39 E
Bream Bay C	230	35.55 S	174.30 E
Bream Head ≻	230	35.51 S	174.35 E
Bream Tail ≻	230	36.03 S	174.35 E
Brea Pozo	294	28.15 S	63.57 W
Breaux Bridge	248	30.16 N	91.54 W
Breaza	172	45.11 N	25.40 E
Brécey	166	48.44 N	1.10 W
Brechin	162	56.44 N	2.40 W
Brecht	178	51.21 N	4.38 E
Breckenridge, Colo., U.S.	254	39.29 N	106.03 W
Breckenridge, Mich., U.S.	244	43.24 N	84.29 W
Breckenridge, Minn., U.S.	252	46.16 N	96.35 W
Breckenridge, Tex., U.S.	250	32.45 N	98.54 W
Breckerfeld	178	51.16 N	7.28 E
Brecknock → Brecon	174	51.57 N	3.24 W
Brecknockshire □[6]	174	52.00 N	3.25 W
Břeclav	164	48.46 N	16.53 E
Brecon	174	51.57 N	3.24 W
Breda, Ned.	178	51.35 N	4.46 E
Breda, Iowa, U.S.	252	42.11 N	94.59 W
Bredasdorp	218	34.32 S	20.02 E
Bredene	176	51.14 N	2.58 E
Bree	178	51.08 N	5.36 E
Breë ≃	224	34.24 S	20.50 E
Breedsville	268	42.21 N	86.08 W
Breese	248	38.36 N	89.32 W
Bregalnica ≃	172	41.43 N	22.09 E
Bregenz	180	47.30 N	9.46 E
Bregovo	172	44.09 N	22.39 E
Breguzzo	170	46.00 N	10.42 E
Bréhal	166	48.54 N	1.31 W
Breiđafjörđur C	160a	65.15 N	23.15 W
Breid Bay C	148	70.15 S	24.15 E
Breil-sur-Roya	166	43.56 N	7.30 E
Breinizer	266	40.24 N	79.16 W
Breisach	180	48.01 N	7.40 E
Brejo	286	3.41 S	42.47 W
Brejões	296	13.06 S	39.48 W
Brejtovo	160	58.18 N	37.52 E
Brekstad	160	63.41 N	9.41 E
Bremen, B.R.D.	178	53.04 N	8.49 E
Bremen, Ga., U.S.	246	33.43 N	85.09 W
Bremen, Ind., U.S.	268	41.27 N	86.09 W
Bremen, Ky., U.S.	248	37.22 N	87.13 W
Bremen, Ohio, U.S.	242	39.42 N	82.26 W
Bremen □[3]	178	53.05 N	8.50 E
Bremerhaven	178	53.33 N	8.34 E
Bremerton	270	47.34 N	122.38 W
Bremerton East	270	47.35 N	122.38 W
Bremervörde	178	53.29 N	9.08 E
Bremner ≃	244	48.41 N	85.31 W
Bremond	250	31.10 N	96.41 W
Brem River	238	50.26 N	124.39 W
Brenes	168	37.33 N	5.52 W
Brenne ↵[1]	166	46.45 N	1.10 E
Brenner Pass)(	164	47.00 N	11.30 E
Breno	170	45.57 N	10.18 E
Brent, Ala., U.S.	248	32.56 N	87.10 W
Brent, Fla., U.S.	248	30.27 N	87.15 W
Brent ↵[8]	174	51.34 N	0.17 W
Brenta ≃	170	45.11 N	12.18 E
Brentwood, Eng., U.K.	174	51.38 N	0.18 E
Brentwood, Calif., U.S.	272	37.56 N	121.42 W
Brentwood, Md., U.S.	262	38.56 N	76.57 W
Brentwood, N.Y., U.S.	242	40.47 N	73.14 W
Brentwood, Pa., U.S.	266	40.22 N	79.59 W
Brentwood Bay	270	48.35 N	123.28 W
Brentwood Estates	266	40.25 N	80.45 W
Brentwood Lake	266	41.19 N	82.05 W
Brescia	170	45.33 N	13.15 E
Brescia □[4]	182	45.38 N	10.18 E
Breslau, Ont., Can.	264	43.28 N	80.25 W
Breslau → Wrocław, Pol.	164	51.06 N	17.00 E
Bressanone (Brixen)	170	46.43 N	11.39 E
Bressay I	162	60.08 N	1.05 W
Bresse ↵[1]	166	46.30 N	5.15 E
Bressler	262	40.14 N	76.49 W
Bressuire	166	46.51 N	0.30 W
Brest, Blg.	172	43.38 N	24.35 E
Brest, Fr.	166	48.24 N	4.29 W
Brest, S.S.S.R.	164	52.06 N	23.42 E
Brestanica	170	45.59 N	15.29 E
Bretagne □[9]	166	48.00 N	3.00 W
Bretenoux	166	44.55 N	1.50 E
Breteuil	166	49.39 N	2.18 E
Breteuil-sur-Iton	166	48.50 N	0.55 E
Breteuil-sur-Noye	166	49.38 N	2.18 E
Brétigny-sur-Orge	176	48.37 N	2.19 E
Breton	238	53.07 N	114.28 W
Bretón, Canal de Џ	284p	21.10 N	79.30 W
Breton, Pertuis Џ	166	46.25 N	1.20 W
Breton Sound Џ	248	29.30 N	89.30 W
Breton Woods	262	40.03 N	74.07 W
Brett, Cape ≻	230	35.11 S	174.20 E
Bretten	164	49.02 N	8.42 E
Bretteville	162	49.03 N	0.20 W
Bretton Woods	268	42.44 N	84.33 W
Bretueil-sur-Iton	166	48.50 N	0.55 E
Breu ≃	290	3.29 S	66.20 W
Breueh, Pulau I	200	5.41 N	95.05 E
Breuil-Cervinia	170	45.56 N	7.38 E
Breukelen	178	52.10 N	5.00 E
Brevard	246	35.09 N	82.44 W
Breves	286	1.40 S	50.29 W
Brevig Mission	236	65.20 N	166.29 W
Brevoort Island I	232	63.30 N	64.20 W
Brewarrina	228	29.57 S	146.52 E
Brewer	242	44.48 N	68.46 W
Brewerton	264	43.14 N	76.08 W
Brewster, Kans., U.S.	252	39.22 N	101.23 W
Brewster, Mass., U.S.	261	41.46 N	70.05 W
Brewster, Minn., U.S.	252	43.42 N	95.28 W
Brewster, Nebr., U.S.	252	41.56 N	99.52 W
Brewster, N.Y., U.S.	261	41.24 N	73.37 W
Brewster, Ohio, U.S.	266	40.43 N	81.36 W
Brewster, Wash., U.S.	256	48.06 N	119.47 W
Brewster, Lake ⊜	228	33.28 S	146.00 E
Brewster, Mount ∧	230	44.04 S	169.27 E
Brewton	248	31.07 N	87.04 W
Breyell (Senne II)	178	51.18 N	6.15 E
Brežice	170	45.54 N	15.36 E
Březniče	164	49.33 N	13.57 E
Breznik	172	42.44 N	22.54 E
Brezno	164	48.50 N	19.39 E
Bria	214	6.32 N	21.59 E
Brian Boru Peak ∧	238	55.05 N	127.35 W
Briançon	182	44.54 N	6.39 E
Brian Head ∧	254	37.41 N	112.50 W
Brianza □[9]	182	45.40 N	9.10 E
Briarcliff Manor	261	41.09 N	73.50 W
Briare	166	47.38 N	2.44 E
Briarwood Beach	266	41.06 N	81.54 W
Bricelyn	244	43.34 N	93.49 W
Brices Cross Roads National Battlefield Site ⊥	248	34.31 N	88.41 W
Briceville	246	36.11 N	84.11 W
Brickaville	218	18.49 S	49.04 E
Brick Town	262	40.04 N	74.08 W
Briçonnet, Lac ⊜	240	51.20 N	60.11 W
Bricquebec	166	49.28 N	1.38 W
Bridal Veil	270	45.33 N	122.11 W
Bridge ≃	238	50.45 N	121.55 W
Bridgeboro	262	40.02 N	74.57 W
Bridge City	248	30.01 N	93.51 W
Bridgehampton	261	40.56 N	72.18 W
Bridge Lake	238	51.29 N	120.43 W
Bridgend	174	51.31 N	3.35 W
Bridgenorth	264	44.23 N	78.23 W
Bridge Point ≻	282	25.35 N	76.42 W
Bridgeport, Ont., Can.	264	43.29 N	80.29 W
Bridgeport, Ala., U.S.	248	34.57 N	85.43 W
Bridgeport, Calif., U.S.	272	38.10 N	119.13 W
Bridgeport, Conn., U.S.	261	41.11 N	73.11 W
Bridgeport, Ill., U.S.	248	38.43 N	87.46 W
Bridgeport, Mich., U.S.	244	43.22 N	83.53 W
Bridgeport, Nebr., U.S.	252	41.40 N	103.06 W
Bridgeport, N.Y., U.S.	264	43.09 N	75.58 W
Bridgeport, Ohio, U.S.	266	40.04 N	80.45 W
Bridgeport, Tex., U.S.	250	33.13 N	97.45 W
Bridgeport, Wash., U.S.	256	48.00 N	119.40 W
Bridgeport, W. Va., U.S.	242	39.17 N	80.15 W
Bridger	256	45.18 N	108.55 W
Bridge River Indian Reserve ↵[4]	238	50.45 N	122.00 W
Bridger Peak ∧	254	41.12 N	107.02 W
Bridgeton	262	39.26 N	75.14 W
Bridgetown, Austl.	226	33.57 S	116.08 E
Bridgetown, Barb.	285g	13.06 N	59.37 W
Bridgetown, N.S., Can.	240	44.51 N	65.18 W
Bridgeville, Del., U.S.	262	38.45 N	75.36 W
Bridgeville, Pa., U.S.	266	40.22 N	80.07 W
Bridgewater, N.S., Can.	240	44.23 N	64.31 W
Bridgewater, Conn., U.S.	261	41.32 N	73.22 W
Bridgewater, Maine, U.S.	240	46.25 N	67.51 W
Bridgewater, Mass., U.S.	261	41.59 N	70.58 W
Bridgewater, S. Dak., U.S.	252	43.33 N	97.30 W
Bridgewater, Va., U.S.	242	38.18 N	78.59 W
Bridgman	268	41.57 N	86.33 W
Bridgnorth	174	52.33 N	2.25 W
Bridgwater	174	51.08 N	3.00 W
Bridgwater Bay C	162	51.16 N	3.12 W
Bridlington	162	54.05 N	0.12 W
Bridlington Bay C	162	54.04 N	0.08 W
Bridport	174	50.44 N	2.46 W
Brie ↵[1]	166	48.40 N	3.20 E
Briec	162	48.06 N	4.00 W
Brieg → Brzeg	164	50.52 N	17.27 E
Brielle	262	40.07 N	74.03 W
Brienne-le-Château	166	48.24 N	4.32 E
Brienz	166	46.46 N	8.03 E
Brienzer See ⊜	166	46.43 N	7.57 E
Brier Hill	264	44.32 N	75.40 W
Brierley Hill	174	52.29 N	2.07 W
Briey	166	49.15 N	5.56 E
Brig	166	46.19 N	8.00 E
Brigantine	262	39.24 N	74.22 W
Brig Bay	240	51.04 N	56.51 W
Brigden	266	42.49 N	82.17 W
Briggs	250	30.53 N	97.56 W
Brigham City	254	41.31 N	112.01 W
Brightlingsea	174	51.49 N	1.02 E
Brighton, Ont., Can.	264	44.02 N	77.44 W
Brighton, Eng., U.K.	174	50.50 N	0.08 W
Brighton, Colo., U.S.	254	39.59 N	104.49 W
Brighton, Fla., U.S.	210	28.52 N	82.20 W
Brighton, Ill., U.S.	248	39.02 N	90.08 W
Brighton, Iowa, U.S.	244	41.10 N	91.49 W
Brighton, Mich., U.S.	268	42.32 N	83.47 W
Brighton, N.Y., U.S.	264	43.08 N	77.34 W
Brighton Indian Reservation ↵[4]	246	27.04 N	81.05 W
Brightwood	270	45.23 N	122.01 W
Brignoles	182	43.24 N	6.04 E
Brigus	240	47.32 N	53.13 W
Brihuega	168	40.48 N	2.52 W
Brikama	214	13.15 N	16.39 W
Brilhante ≃	296	21.58 S	54.18 W
Brilliant, B.C., Can.	238	49.19 N	117.38 W
Brilliant, Ala., U.S.	248	34.01 N	87.46 W
Brilliant, Ohio, U.S.	266	40.16 N	80.38 W
Brillion	244	44.11 N	88.04 W
Brilon	178	51.24 N	8.34 E
Brimfield, Ind., U.S.	268	41.27 N	85.24 W
Brimfield, Mass., U.S.	261	42.07 N	72.12 W
Brimfield, Ohio, U.S.	266	41.06 N	81.21 W
Brindisi	170	40.38 N	17.56 E
Brinje	170	45.00 N	15.08 E
Brinkhaven	266	40.28 N	82.12 W
Brinkley	248	34.53 N	91.12 W
Brinnon	270	47.41 N	122.54 W
Brion, Île de I	240	47.47 N	61.29 W
Brionne	162	49.12 N	0.43 E
Brioso, Ribeirão ≃	296	20.21 S	52.05 W
Brioude	166	45.18 N	3.23 E
Briouze	166	48.42 N	0.22 W
Brisbane, Austl.	228	27.28 S	153.02 E
Brisbane, Calif., U.S.	272	37.41 N	122.24 W
Brisbane Water National Park ♠	228	33.30 S	151.15 E
Brisbin	266	40.50 N	78.21 W
Brisighella	184	44.13 N	11.46 E
Bristol, Eng., U.K.	174	51.27 N	2.35 W
Bristol, Conn., U.S.	261	41.41 N	72.57 W
Bristol, Fla., U.S.	246	30.26 N	84.58 W
Bristol, Ill., U.S.	268	41.39 N	88.27 W
Bristol, Ind., U.S.	268	41.43 N	85.49 W
Bristol, N.H., U.S.	242	43.36 N	71.45 W
Bristol, Pa., U.S.	262	40.06 N	74.52 W
Bristol, R.I., U.S.	261	41.40 N	71.16 W
Bristol, S. Dak., U.S.	252	45.21 N	97.45 W
Bristol, Tenn., U.S.	246	36.36 N	82.11 W
Bristol, Vt., U.S.	242	44.08 N	73.05 W
Bristol, Va., U.S.	246	36.36 N	82.11 W
Bristol, Wis., U.S.	268	42.34 N	88.03 W
Bristol □[6], Mass., U.S.	261	41.54 N	71.06 W
Bristol □[6], R.I., U.S.	261	41.42 N	71.18 W
Bristol Bay C	236	58.00 N	159.00 W
Bristol Center	264	42.49 N	77.23 W
Bristol Channel Џ	162	51.20 N	4.00 W
Bristol Lake ⊜	258	34.28 N	115.41 W
Bristolville	266	41.23 N	80.52 W
Bristow	250	35.50 N	96.23 W
Britânia	296	15.14 S	51.09 W
Britannia Beach	238	49.38 N	123.12 W
British Columbia □[3]	232	54.00 N	125.00 W
British Honduras □[2]	276	17.15 N	88.45 W
British Indian Ocean Territory □[2]	218	10.00 S	50.00 E
British Isles II	148	54.00 N	4.00 W
British Mountains ⋀	236	69.00 N	140.00 W
British Solomon Islands □[2]	226	8.00 S	159.00 E
British Virgin Islands □[2]	284m	18.30 N	64.30 W
Brits	224	25.42 S	27.45 E
Britstown	218	30.37 S	23.30 E
Britt	244	43.06 N	93.48 W
Brittany → Bretagne □[9]	166	48.00 N	3.00 W
Brittingham	250	25.45 N	103.24 W
Britton, Mich., U.S.	268	41.59 N	83.50 W
Britton, S. Dak., U.S.	252	45.48 N	97.45 W
Brive-la-Gaillarde	166	45.10 N	1.32 E
Briviesca	168	42.33 N	3.19 W
Brixham	174	50.24 N	3.30 W
Brno	164	49.12 N	16.37 E
Broa, Ensenada de la C	284p	22.35 N	82.00 W
Broach	206	21.42 N	72.58 E
Broad ≃, U.S.	246	34.00 N	81.04 W
Broad ≃, Ga., U.S.	246	33.59 N	82.39 W
Broadalbin	242	43.03 N	74.12 W
Broadback ≃	232	51.20 N	78.50 W
Broad Bay C	162	58.15 N	6.15 W
Broad Brook	261	41.55 N	72.33 W
Broaddus	248	31.18 N	94.16 W
Broadford	162	57.14 N	5.54 W
Broad Haven C	162	54.18 N	9.55 W
Broad Law ∧	162	55.30 N	3.22 W
Broad Pass)(	236	63.18 N	149.09 W
Broad Sound Џ	228	22.10 S	149.45 E
Broad Sound Channel Џ	228	22.05 S	150.20 E
Broadstairs	174	51.22 N	1.27 E
Broad Top	266	40.12 N	78.08 W
Broadus	252	45.27 N	105.25 W
Broadview	268	41.52 N	87.51 W
Broadview Heights	266	41.19 N	81.41 W
Broadwater	252	41.36 N	102.51 W
Broadway, Ohio, U.S.	266	40.21 N	83.25 W
Broadway, Va., U.S.	242	38.38 N	78.46 W
Brocēni	160	56.42 N	22.35 E
Brochet	232	57.53 N	101.40 W
Brochet, Lac au ⊜	240	49.40 N	69.36 W
Brock	252	40.29 N	95.58 W
Brockport, N.Y., U.S.	264	43.13 N	77.56 W
Brockport, Pa., U.S.	266	41.16 N	78.44 W
Brocks Beach	264	44.27 N	80.06 W
Brockton, Mass., U.S.	261	42.05 N	71.01 W
Brockton, Mont., U.S.	252	48.09 N	104.55 W
Brockton, Pa., U.S.	262	40.45 N	76.04 W
Brockville	264	44.35 N	75.41 W
Brockway	266	41.15 N	78.47 W
Brocton	266	42.23 N	79.27 W
Brod	172	41.31 N	21.12 E
Broderick	272	38.35 N	121.31 W
Brodeur Peninsula ≻[1]	232	73.00 N	88.00 W
Brodhead, Ky., U.S.	246	37.24 N	84.25 W
Brodhead, Wis., U.S.	244	42.37 N	89.22 W
Brodick	162	55.35 N	5.09 W
Brodnax	246	36.42 N	78.02 W
Brodnica	164	53.16 N	19.23 E
Brody (Pförten)	164	51.45 N	14.45 E
Brogan	256	44.15 N	117.31 W
Broglie	166	49.01 N	0.32 E
Brok	164	52.43 N	21.52 E
Broken Arrow	250	36.03 N	95.48 W
Broken Bay C	228	33.34 S	151.18 E
Broken Bow, Nebr., U.S.	252	41.24 N	99.38 W
Broken Bow, Okla., U.S.	248	34.02 N	94.44 W
Broken Hill, Austl.	228	31.57 S	141.27 E
Broken Hill → Kabwe, Zam.	218	14.27 S	28.27 E
Brokopondo	286	5.03 N	54.59 W
Bromberg → Bydgoszcz	164	53.08 N	18.00 E
Brome	260	45.12 N	72.35 W
Brome □[6]	260	45.10 N	72.30 W
Bromley ↵[8]	174	51.24 N	0.02 E
Bromptonville	260	45.28 N	71.57 W
Bromsgrove	174	52.20 N	2.03 W
Bron	182	45.44 N	4.55 E
Bronevskaja	160	61.43 N	39.10 E
Brong-Ahafo □[4]	222	7.45 N	1.30 W
Broni	182	45.04 N	9.16 E
Bronlund Peak ∧	232	57.26 N	126.38 W
Brønnøysund	160	65.30 N	12.10 E
Bronson, Fla., U.S.	246	29.27 N	82.38 W
Bronson, Kans., U.S.	252	37.54 N	95.04 W
Bronson, Mich., U.S.	268	41.52 N	85.12 W
Bronson, Tex., U.S.	248	31.21 N	94.01 W
Bronte, It.	170	37.48 N	14.50 E
Bronte, Tex., U.S.	250	31.53 N	100.18 W
Bronwood	246	31.50 N	84.22 W
Bronx □[6]	261	40.49 N	73.52 W
Brooch, Lac ⊜	240	50.45 N	67.55 W
Brook	268	40.52 N	87.22 W
Brookdale	272	37.06 N	122.06 W
Brooke	262	38.23 N	77.23 W
Brooke □[6]	266	40.18 N	80.33 W
Brookeland	248	31.09 N	94.00 W
Brooker	246	29.53 N	82.20 W
Brooke's Point	202	8.46 N	117.50 E
Brookfield, N.S., Can.	240	45.15 N	63.17 W
Brookfield, Conn., U.S.	261	41.29 N	73.25 W
Brookfield, Ill., U.S.	268	41.49 N	87.51 W
Brookfield, Mass., U.S.	261	42.13 N	72.06 W
Brookfield, Mich., U.S.	268	42.27 N	84.47 W
Brookfield, Mo., U.S.	248	39.47 N	93.04 W
Brookfield, N.Y., U.S.	264	42.49 N	75.19 W
Brookfield, Ohio, U.S.	266	41.14 N	80.34 W
Brookfield, Wis., U.S.	268	43.04 N	88.09 W
Brookfield Center	261	41.28 N	73.23 W
Brookford	246	35.42 N	81.21 W
Brookhaven	248	31.35 N	90.26 W
Brookings, Oreg., U.S.	256	42.03 N	124.17 W
Brookings, S. Dak., U.S.	252	44.19 N	96.48 W
Brooklands	266	42.38 N	83.06 W
Brooklet	246	32.23 N	81.40 W
Brooklin	264	43.57 N	78.57 W
Brookline, Mass., U.S.	261	42.21 N	71.07 W
Brookline, Mich., U.S.	268	42.13 N	84.31 W
Brookline, N.H., U.S.	261	42.44 N	71.40 W
Brooklyn, N.S., Can.	240	44.03 N	64.42 W
Brooklyn, Conn., U.S.	261	41.47 N	71.57 W
Brooklyn, Iowa, U.S.	244	41.44 N	92.27 W
Brooklyn, Mich., U.S.	268	42.06 N	84.15 W
Brooklyn, Miss., U.S.	248	31.03 N	89.11 W
Brooklyn, Ohio, U.S.	266	41.25 N	81.49 W
Brooklyn, Wash., U.S.	270	46.47 N	123.31 W
Brooklyn, Wis., U.S.	268	42.51 N	89.22 W
Brooklyn Center	244	45.05 N	93.20 W
Brookmere	238	49.49 N	120.53 W
Brookneal	246	37.03 N	78.57 W
Brook Park	266	41.24 N	81.48 W
Brookport	248	37.08 N	88.38 W
Brooks, Alta., Can.	238	50.35 N	111.53 W
Brooks, Calif., U.S.	272	38.45 N	122.09 W
Brooks, Maine, U.S.	242	44.33 N	69.07 W
Brooks, Oreg., U.S.	270	45.03 N	122.58 W
Brooks, Mount ∧	236	63.11 N	150.40 W
Brooks Bay C	238	50.13 N	127.55 W
Brookshire	250	29.47 N	95.57 W
Brookside	266	42.08 N	80.00 W
Brooks Mountain ∧	236	65.33 N	167.09 W
Brooks Range ⋀	236	68.00 N	154.00 W
Brookston	268	40.36 N	86.52 W
Brooksvale	261	41.29 N	72.59 W
Brooksville, Fla., U.S.	246	28.33 N	82.23 W
Brooksville, Ky., U.S.	242	38.41 N	84.04 W
Brooksville, Miss., U.S.	248	33.14 N	88.35 W
Brookton	226	32.22 S	117.01 E
Brookview	261	42.32 N	73.43 W
Brookville, Ind., U.S.	248	39.25 N	85.01 W
Brookville, Mass., U.S.	261	42.08 N	71.01 W
Brookville, Pa., U.S.	266	41.09 N	79.05 W
Broomall	262	39.59 N	75.22 W
Broome	226	17.58 S	122.14 E
Broomes Island	262	38.25 N	76.33 W
Broomfield	254	39.56 N	105.04 W
Broons	166	48.19 N	2.16 W
Brooten	252	45.30 N	95.07 W
Brora	162	58.01 N	3.51 W
Brora ≃	162	58.01 N	3.51 W
Brossac	166	45.20 N	0.03 W
Brossard	260	45.26 N	73.29 W
Brotas de Macaúbas	296	12.00 S	42.38 W
Broto	168	42.36 N	0.06 W
Brou	166	48.13 N	1.11 E
Brougham	264	43.55 N	79.06 W
Broughton, Ill., U.S.	248	37.56 N	88.27 W
Broughton, Pa., U.S.	266	40.21 N	79.59 W
Broughton Island I	232	67.35 N	63.50 W
Broughty Ferry	162	56.28 N	2.53 W
Broumov	164	50.35 N	16.20 E
Broussard	248	30.09 N	91.58 W
Browerville	252	46.05 N	94.52 W
Brown City	244	43.13 N	82.59 W
Brown County State Park ♠	248	39.09 N	86.14 W
Brown Deer	268	43.10 N	87.59 W
Browne Bay C	232	73.08 N	97.30 W
Brownfield	250	33.11 N	102.16 W
Brownhills	174	52.39 N	1.55 W
Browning, Ill., U.S.	248	40.08 N	90.22 W
Browning, Mo., U.S.	248	40.02 N	93.10 W
Browning, Mont., U.S.	256	48.34 N	113.01 W
Browning Entrance C	238	53.41 N	130.30 W
Brown Lake ⊜	232	65.55 N	91.15 W
Brownlee	256	44.50 N	116.55 W
Brownlee Dam ↵[6]	256	44.51 N	116.49 W
Brownlee Park	268	42.18 N	85.05 W
Brownlee Reservoir ⊜[1]	256	44.40 N	117.05 W
Brown Mountain ∧	258	35.41 N	117.01 W
Brownsburg, Qué., Can.	260	45.41 N	74.24 W
Brownsburg, Ind., U.S.	248	39.51 N	86.24 W
Brownsdale	244	43.44 N	92.52 W
Brownsmead	270	46.13 N	123.32 W
Browns Mills	262	39.58 N	74.34 W
Browns Point	270	47.18 N	122.21 W
Browns Town, Jam.	285q	18.24 N	77.22 W
Brownstown, Ill., U.S.	248	39.00 N	88.57 W
Brownstown, Ind., U.S.	248	38.53 N	86.03 W
Brownstown, Pa., U.S.	262	40.08 N	76.13 W
Brownstown, Pa., U.S.	266	40.18 N	78.55 W
Browns Valley, Calif., U.S.	272	39.15 N	121.23 W
Browns Valley, Minn., U.S.	252	45.36 N	96.50 W
Brownsville, Ont., Can.	264	42.52 N	80.50 W
Brownsville, Calif., U.S.	272	39.28 N	121.16 W
Brownsville, Ky., U.S.	248	37.12 N	86.16 W
Brownsville, La., U.S.	248	32.30 N	92.10 W
Brownsville, Oreg., U.S.	256	44.24 N	122.59 W
Brownsville, Pa., U.S.	242	40.01 N	79.53 W
Brownsville, Tenn., U.S.	248	35.36 N	89.15 W
Brownsville, Tex., U.S.	250	25.54 N	97.30 W
Brownton	244	44.44 N	94.21 W
Brownvale	238	56.08 N	117.53 W
Brownville, Ala., U.S.	248	33.24 N	87.52 W
Brownville, Maine, U.S.	242	45.18 N	69.02 W
Brownville, N.Y., U.S.	264	40.40 N	73.55 W
Brownville Junction	242	45.21 N	69.03 W
Brownwood	250	31.43 N	98.59 W
Brownwood Reservoir ⊜[1]	250	31.51 N	99.02 W
Browse Island I	226	14.07 S	123.33 E
Broxton	246	31.38 N	82.53 W
Brozas	168	39.37 N	6.46 W
Bruay-en-Artois	176	50.29 N	2.33 E
Bruay-sur-l'Escaut	176	50.23 N	3.32 E
Bruce, Miss., U.S.	248	33.59 N	89.21 W
Bruce, S. Dak., U.S.	252	44.26 N	96.54 W
Bruce, Wis., U.S.	244	45.28 N	91.20 W
Bruce □[6]	264	44.30 N	81.15 W
Bruce Mines	244	46.18 N	83.48 W
Bruce Peninsula ≻[1]	244	44.50 N	81.20 W
Bruchsal	164	49.07 N	8.35 E
Bruck	164	47.17 N	12.49 E
Bruck an der Leitha	164	47.57 N	16.44 E
Bruck an der Mur	164	47.25 N	15.16 E
Brückenau	164	50.18 N	9.47 E
Bruderheim	238	53.47 N	112.56 W
Bruges → Brugge	176	51.13 N	3.14 E
Brugg	180	47.29 N	8.12 E
Brugge, Bel.	164	51.13 N	3.14 E
Brugge (Bruges), Bel.	176	51.13 N	3.14 E
Brüggen	178	51.14 N	6.11 E
Brugherio	182	45.33 N	9.18 E
Brühl	164	50.48 N	6.54 E
Bruin	266	41.04 N	79.44 W
Bruin Point ∧	254	39.39 N	110.22 W
Bruja, Cerro ∧	280	9.28 N	79.33 W
Brujo, Cerro ∧	280	10.08 N	85.38 W
Brule	252	41.06 N	101.53 W
Brule ≃	244	45.57 N	88.12 W
Brûle, Lac ⊜	232	52.15 N	63.30 W
Brumadinho	296	20.08 S	44.13 W
Brumado	296	14.13 S	41.40 W
Brumath	166	48.44 N	7.43 E
Brummen	178	52.05 N	6.09 E
Brumunddal	160	60.53 N	10.56 E
Brundidge	248	31.43 N	85.49 W
Bruneau	256	42.53 N	115.48 W
Bruneau ≃	256	42.57 N	115.58 W
Brunei → Bandar Seri Begawan	198	4.56 N	114.55 E
Brunei □[1]	198	4.50 N	114.55 E
Brunette Island I	240	47.16 N	55.54 W
Brunico (Bruneck)	170	46.48 N	11.56 E
Brunkeberg	160	59.26 N	8.29 E
Brünn → Brno, Česko.	164	49.12 N	16.37 E
Brunn am Gebirge	164	48.07 N	16.17 E
Brunner	230	42.26 S	171.19 E
Brunner, Lake ⊜	230	42.37 S	171.27 E
Brunnerville	262	40.11 N	76.17 W
Brunoy	176	48.42 N	2.30 E
Brunsbüttelkoog	178	53.54 N	9.08 E
Brunson	246	32.56 N	81.11 W
Brunswick → Braunschweig, B.R.D.	178	52.16 N	10.31 E
Brunswick, Ga., U.S.	246	31.10 N	81.29 W
Brunswick, Maine, U.S.	242	43.55 N	69.58 W
Brunswick, Md., U.S.	262	39.19 N	77.37 W
Brunswick, Mo., U.S.	248	39.26 N	93.08 W
Brunswick, Ohio, U.S.	266	41.14 N	81.50 W
Brunswick Lake ⊜	244	49.00 N	83.23 W
Brunswick Naval Air Station ■	242	43.54 N	69.56 W
Bruntál	164	49.59 N	17.28 E
Brus, Laguna de C	280	15.50 N	84.35 W
Brush	252	40.15 N	103.37 W
Brush Valley	266	40.32 N	79.04 W
Brus Laguna	280	15.47 N	84.35 W
Brusque	294	27.06 S	48.56 W
Brussels → Bruxelles, Bel.	176	50.50 N	4.20 E
Brussels, Ont., Can.	264	43.44 N	81.15 W
Brusy	164	53.53 N	17.45 E
Brüx → Most	164	50.32 N	13.39 E
Bruxelles (Brussels) (Brussel)	176	50.50 N	4.20 E
Bruyères	166	48.12 N	6.43 E
Bruzual	290	8.03 N	69.19 W
Brwinów	164	52.09 N	20.43 E
Bryan, Ohio, U.S.	268	41.28 N	84.33 W
Bryan, Tex., U.S.	250	30.40 N	96.22 W
Bryansk → Br'ansk	158	53.15 N	34.22 E
Bryans Road	262	38.38 N	77.04 W
Bryant, Ind., U.S.	268	40.32 N	84.58 W
Bryant, S. Dak., U.S.	252	44.35 N	97.28 W
Bryant Mountain ∧	242	42.28 N	72.58 W
Bryantville	261	42.03 N	70.51 W
Bryce Canyon National Park ♠	254	37.29 N	112.12 W
Brykalansk	160	65.30 N	54.12 E
Brynmawr, Wales, U.K.	174	51.49 N	3.11 W
Bryn Mawr, Calif., U.S.	274	34.03 N	117.14 W
Bryn Mawr, Pa., U.S.	262	40.01 N	75.19 W
Bryson, Qué., Can.	242	45.41 N	76.37 W
Bryson, Tex., U.S.	250	33.10 N	98.23 W
Bryson City	246	35.26 N	83.27 W
Bryte	272	38.36 N	121.33 W
Brza Palanka	172	44.28 N	22.27 E
Brzeg (Brieg)	164	50.52 N	17.27 E
Brześć Kujawski	164	52.37 N	18.55 E
Brześć Nad Bugiem → Brest	164	52.06 N	23.42 E
Brzesko	164	49.59 N	20.36 E
Brzeszcze	164	49.59 N	19.08 E
Brzeziny	164	51.48 N	19.46 E
Brzozów	164	49.42 N	22.02 E
Buad Island I	202	11.40 N	124.51 E
Bua Yai	198	15.34 N	102.24 E
Buayan	202	6.06 N	125.15 E
Buayan ≃	202	6.06 N	125.14 E
Bubaque	214	11.17 N	15.50 W
Būbiyān I	208	29.47 N	48.10 E
Bubuan Island I, Pil.	202	6.12 N	120.58 E
Bubuan Island I, Pil.	202	6.21 N	121.58 E
Bubus (Buket Bubut), Bukit ∧	200	6.12 N	101.06 E
Bubut, Buket(Bukit Bubus) ∧	200	6.12 N	101.06 E
Bubye ≃	224	22.20 S	31.07 E
Bucaramanga	290	7.08 N	73.09 W
Bucas Grande Island I	202	9.40 N	125.57 E
Buccaneer Archipelago II	226	16.17 S	123.20 E
Buccino	170	40.37 N	15.23 E
Buchanan, Liber.	222	5.57 N	10.02 W
Buchanan, Ga., U.S.	246	33.48 N	85.11 W
Buchanan, Mich., U.S.	268	41.50 N	86.22 W
Buchanan, Va., U.S.	246	37.32 N	79.41 W
Buchanan, Lake ⊜	228	21.28 S	145.52 E
Buchanan Lake ⊜[1]	250	30.48 N	98.25 W
Buchan Gulf C	232	71.47 N	74.16 W
Buchan Ness ≻	162	57.32 N	1.48 W
Buchans	240	48.49 N	56.52 W
Buchara	208	39.48 N	64.25 E
Buchardo	294	34.44 S	63.30 W
Bucharest → București	172	44.26 N	26.06 E
Buchen	164	49.32 N	9.17 E
Buchholz	178	53.20 N	9.52 E
Buchloe	180	48.02 N	10.44 E
Buchs, Schw.	180	47.10 N	9.28 E
Buchs, Schw.	180	47.23 N	8.04 E
Buchy	166	49.35 N	1.22 E
Buckatunna	248	31.27 N	88.32 W
Buck Creek	268	40.29 N	86.46 W
Bückeburg	178	52.16 N	9.02 E
Buckeye	254	33.22 N	112.35 W
Buckeye Lake	242	39.56 N	82.29 W
Buckeye Lake ⊜[1]	242	39.55 N	82.30 W
Buckeystown	262	39.20 N	77.26 W
Buckhannon	242	38.59 N	80.14 W
Buckhaven	162	56.11 N	3.03 W
Buckholts	250	30.52 N	97.08 W
Buckhorn ≃	236	66.13 N	161.10 W
Buckie	162	57.40 N	2.58 W
Buckingham, Qué., Can.	242	45.35 N	75.25 W
Buckingham, Pa., U.S.	262	40.18 N	75.01 W
Buckingham, Va., U.S.	246	37.32 N	78.37 W
Buckinghamshire □[6]	174	51.45 N	0.48 W
Buck Lake ⊜	238	53.00 N	114.45 W
Buckland, Alaska, U.S.	236	66.16 N	161.20 W
Buckland, Mass., U.S.	261	42.36 N	72.48 W
Buckland, Ohio, U.S.	268	40.37 N	84.16 W
Buckley, Wales, U.K.	174	53.09 N	3.04 W
Buckley, Ill., U.S.	268	40.36 N	88.02 W
Buckley, Wash., U.S.	270	47.10 N	122.02 W
Buckley ≃	228	20.22 S	137.57 E
Bucklin, Kans., U.S.	252	37.33 N	99.38 W
Bucklin, Mo., U.S.	248	39.47 N	92.53 W
Buck Mountain ∧, Va., U.S.	246	36.40 N	81.15 W
Buck Mountain ∧, Wash., U.S.	256	48.26 N	119.50 W
Bucknell Manor	262	38.46 N	77.04 W
Buckow	164	52.34 N	14.04 E
Bucks □[6]	262	40.19 N	75.08 W
Buckskin Gulch V	254	37.01 N	111.52 W
Bucksport	242	44.34 N	68.48 W
Bucoda	270	46.48 N	122.52 W
Buctouche	240	46.28 N	64.43 W
București	172	44.26 N	26.06 E
Bucutua Island I	202	6.09 N	121.49 E
Bucyrus	266	40.48 N	82.58 W
Buda	244	41.20 N	89.41 W
Budapest	164	47.30 N	19.05 E
Búđardalur	160a	65.10 N	21.42 W
Budaun	206	28.03 N	79.07 E
Budduso	170	40.35 N	9.16 E
Bude, Eng., U.K.	162	50.50 N	4.33 W
Bude, Miss., U.S.	248	31.28 N	90.51 W
Bude Bay C	162	50.50 N	4.37 W
Budelikesihu ⊜	206	33.00 N	86.25 E
Büderich	178	51.15 N	6.41 E
Budești	172	44.14 N	26.28 E
Büdingen	164	50.17 N	9.07 E
Búđir	160a	64.56 N	13.58 W
Budišov nad Budišovka	164	49.47 N	17.38 E
Budogošč'	160	59.17 N	32.27 E
Budweis → České Budějovice	164	48.59 N	14.28 E
Budžak ⋀[1]	172	46.10 N	29.00 E
Buea	214	4.09 N	9.14 E
Buena	262	39.31 N	74.56 W
Buena Esperanza	294	34.46 S	65.16 W
Buena Park	274	33.52 N	118.00 W
Buenaventura, Col.	290	3.53 N	77.04 W
Buenaventura, Méx.	278	29.51 N	107.29 W
Buena Vista, Bol.	292	17.27 S	63.40 W
Buena Vista, Guat.	280	13.49 N	90.19 W
Buena Vista, Méx.	258	32.32 N	116.44 W
Buena Vista, Para.	294	25.55 S	55.34 W
Buenavista, Pil.	202	8.59 N	125.25 E
Buenavista, Pil.	202	10.04 N	118.49 E
Buenavista, Pil.	202	13.15 N	121.57 E

Symbols in the index entries are identified on page 360.

Name	Page	Lat°′	Long°′
Buenavista, Pil.	202	13.44 N	122.28 E
Buenavista, Pil.	202	7.15 N	122.16 E
Buena Vista, Colo., U.S.	254	38.50 N	106.08 W
Buena Vista, Ga., U.S.	246	32.19 N	84.31 W
Buena Vista, Miss., U.S.	248	33.47 N	88.56 W
Buena Vista, Pa., U.S.	266	40.17 N	79.48 W
Buena Vista, Va., U.S.	246	37.44 N	79.21 W
Buenavista, Bahía de C	284p	22.30 N	79.10 W
Buenavista, Cerro ∧	280	9.33 N	83.45 W
Buena Vista, Cordillera de ⋀	290	10.40 N	70.10 W
Buena Vista Lake ⊜	258	35.11 N	119.17 W
Buen Día	250	26.21 N	104.32 W
Buendia, Embalse de ⊜[1]	168	40.25 N	2.43 W
Buenolândia	296	15.48 S	50.17 W
Buenópolis	296	17.54 S	44.11 W
Buenos Aires, Arg.	294	34.36 S	58.27 W
Buenos Aires, Col.	290	3.02 N	76.38 W
Buenos Aires, C.R.	280	9.10 N	83.20 W
Buenos Aires □[4]	294	36.00 S	60.00 W
Buerarema	296	14.57 S	39.19 W
Buerhanbudashan ⋀	206	36.00 N	96.00 E
Buerjin	190	47.43 N	86.53 E
Buesaco	290	1.23 N	77.09 W
Buey ≃	284p	20.28 N	77.06 W
Bufa, Cerro ∧	278	20.44 N	104.50 W
Buffalo, Ind., U.S.	268	40.53 N	86.45 W
Buffalo, Iowa, U.S.	244	41.27 N	90.43 W
Buffalo, Kans., U.S.	252	37.42 N	95.42 W
Buffalo, Minn., U.S.	244	45.10 N	93.53 W
Buffalo, Mo., U.S.	248	37.39 N	93.06 W
Buffalo, N.Y., U.S.	264	42.54 N	78.53 W
Buffalo, Ohio, U.S.	242	39.55 N	81.31 W
Buffalo, Okla., U.S.	250	36.50 N	99.38 W
Buffalo, S.C., U.S.	246	34.43 N	81.41 W
Buffalo, S. Dak., U.S.	252	45.35 N	103.33 W
Buffalo, Tex., U.S.	250	31.28 N	96.04 W
Buffalo, Wyo., U.S.	256	44.21 N	106.42 W
Buffalo ≃, Ark., U.S.	248	36.10 N	92.26 W
Buffalo ≃, Minn., U.S.	252	47.06 N	96.49 W
Buffalo ≃, Tenn., U.S.	248	36.00 N	87.50 W
Buffalo, Mount ∧	228	36.47 S	146.47 E
Buffalo Bill Recreation Area ♠	256	44.29 N	109.11 W
Buffalo Bill Reservoir ⊜[1]	256	44.29 N	109.13 W
Buffalo Center	244	43.23 N	93.57 W
Buffalo Lake	252	44.44 N	94.37 W
Buffalo Lake ⊜, Alta., Can.	238	52.27 N	112.54 W
Buffalo Lake ⊜, N.W. Ter., Can.	232	60.10 N	115.30 W
Buffels ≃	224	33.45 S	21.11 E
Buford	246	34.07 N	84.00 W
Bug ≃	158	52.31 N	21.05 E
Buga	290	3.54 N	76.17 W
Bugalagrande	290	4.11 N	76.09 W
Bugallon	202	15.57 N	120.13 E
Buganga	218	0.03 S	31.59 E
Bugasong	202	11.03 N	122.04 E
Bugeat	166	45.35 N	1.59 E
Buggenhout	176	51.01 N	4.12 E
Buggs Island Lake ⊜[1]	246	36.35 N	70.28 W
Buğlan Geçidi)(	212	38.56 N	41.10 E
Bugni Point ≻	202	12.36 N	123.14 E
Bugojno	170	44.03 N	17.27 E
Bugøynes	160	69.54 N	29.28 E
Bugrino	160	68.48 N	49.09 E
Bugsanga ≃	202	12.26 N	121.00 E
Bugsuk Island I	202	8.15 N	117.18 E
Buguey	202	18.18 N	121.50 E
Bugul'ma	160	54.33 N	52.48 E
Buguruslan	158	53.39 N	52.26 E
Buhamanggenai-shankou)(	206	34.00 N	92.43 E
Buhi	202	13.25 N	123.30 E
Buhi, Lake ⊜	202	13.27 N	123.30 E
Bühl, B.R.D.	180	48.42 N	8.08 E
Buhl, Idaho, U.S.	256	42.36 N	114.46 W
Buhl, Minn., U.S.	244	47.30 N	92.47 W
Buhler	252	38.08 N	97.46 W
Bühlertal	180	48.42 N	8.10 E
Buhuşi	172	46.43 N	26.41 E
Buiksloot ⬩[8]	178	52.24 N	4.55 E
Builth Wells	162	52.09 N	3.24 W
Buin	294	33.44 S	70.45 W
Buinsk, S.S.S.R.	160	54.57 N	48.17 E
Buinsk, S.S.S.R.	160	55.12 N	47.03 E
Buir Nuur ⊜	190	47.48 N	117.42 E
Buj	160	58.30 N	41.30 E
Bujaki	160	59.03 N	48.40 E
Bujalance	168	37.54 N	4.22 W
Bujaraloz	168	41.30 N	0.09 W
Buje	170	45.24 N	13.40 E
Bujnaksk	158	42.49 N	47.07 E
Bujor	172	45.52 N	27.27 E
Bujumbura	218	3.23 S	29.22 E
Buk	164	52.22 N	16.31 E
Bukačača	186	52.59 N	116.55 E
Bukama	218	9.12 S	25.51 E
Bukavu	218	2.30 S	28.52 E
Bukechi ⊜	206	31.30 N	91.05 E
Bukhara → Buchara	208	39.48 N	64.25 E
Bukidnon □[4]	202	8.00 N	125.00 E
Bukittinggi	200	0.19 S	100.22 E
Bükk ⋀	164	48.05 N	20.30 E
Bukoba	218	1.20 S	31.49 E
Bukovica ⬩[1]	170	44.10 N	15.40 E
Bukovina ⬩[1]	172	48.00 N	25.30 E
Būl, Kūh-e ∧	208	30.48 N	52.45 E
Bula	198	3.06 S	130.30 E
Bulacan □[4]	202	15.00 N	121.05 E
Bulacaue Point ≻	202	11.36 N	123.10 E
Bülach	180	47.31 N	8.32 E
Bulalacao	202	12.20 N	121.21 E
Bulalacao Island I	202	11.45 N	120.10 E
Bulan, Pil.	202	12.40 N	123.52 E
Bulan, Ky., U.S.	246	37.18 N	83.10 W
Bulandshahr	206	28.24 N	77.51 E
Bulan Island I	202	6.08 N	121.50 E
Bulaquit Point ≻	202	11.17 N	124.03 E
Bulawayo	224	20.09 S	28.36 E
Bulbul, Wādī ∨	220	10.59 N	24.33 E
Buldan	172	38.03 N	28.51 E
Buldibuyo	292	8.07 S	77.22 W
Buldir Island I	237a	52.21 N	175.54 E
Buldon	202	7.33 N	124.25 E
Buleleng	226	8.06 S	115.05 E
Bulgan, Mong.	190	48.52 N	103.34 E
Bulgan, Mong.	190	46.53 N	91.05 E
Bulgaria □[1]	158	43.00 N	25.00 E
Bulger	266	40.23 N	80.20 W
Buliluyan	202	8.20 N	117.12 E
Buliluyan, Cape ≻	202	8.20 N	117.10 E
Bulkeley	285g	13.07 N	59.32 W
Bulkley ≃	238	55.13 N	127.40 W
Bulkley Ranges ⋀	238	54.30 N	127.30 W
Bull ≃	238	49.28 N	115.26 W
Bullaque ≃	168	38.59 N	4.17 W
Bullard	250	32.08 N	95.19 W
Bulla Regia ⊥	170	36.34 N	8.46 E
Bullas	168	38.03 N	1.40 W
Bull Bay C	246	32.59 N	79.33 W
Bulle	180	46.37 N	7.04 E
Bullen Baai C	285s	12.11 N	69.04 W
Buller ≃	230	41.44 S	171.36 E
Buller, Mount ∧	228	37.09 S	146.26 E
Bullfinch	226	30.59 S	119.06 E
Bull Harbour	238	50.54 N	127.55 W
Bullhead	252	45.46 N	101.05 W
Bull Lake Reservoir ⊜[1]	254	43.11 N	109.07 W
Bull Mountain ∧	256	46.05 N	112.04 W
Bull Mountains ⋀	256	46.05 N	109.00 W
Bullock	246	36.30 N	78.33 W
Bulloo ≃	228	28.43 S	142.30 E
Bulloo Lake ⊜	228	28.43 S	142.25 E
Bulloo River Overflow ≚	228	28.50 S	142.40 E
Bullrun Rock ∧	256	44.21 N	118.17 W
Bullsgap	246	36.15 N	83.05 W
Bull Shoals Dam ⬩[6]	248	36.20 N	92.33 W
Bull Shoals Lake ⊜[1]	248	36.30 N	92.50 W
Bully-les-Mines	176	50.26 N	2.43 E
Bulnes	294	36.44 S	72.18 W
Bulok Gölü ⊜	212	38.32 N	32.55 E
Buluan	202	6.44 N	124.47 E
Buluan ≃	202	7.00 N	124.34 E
Buluan, Lake ⊜	202	6.39 N	124.50 E
Bulukumba	198	5.33 S	120.11 E
Buluntuohai ⊜	190	47.15 N	87.20 E
Bulusan	202	12.45 N	124.08 E
Bulusan Volcano ∧[1]	202	12.46 N	124.03 E
Bumba	218	2.11 N	22.28 E
Bumuhu ⊜	206	31.15 N	91.10 E
Buna	248	30.26 N	93.58 W
Bunawan	202	8.11 N	125.56 E
Bunbah, Khalīj C	220	32.20 N	23.10 E
Bunbury	226	33.19 S	115.38 E
Bunceton	248	38.47 N	92.48 W
Buncrana	162	55.08 N	7.27 W
Bundaberg	228	24.52 S	152.21 E
Bundarra ≃	228	29.54 S	150.59 E
Bünde	178	52.12 N	8.35 E
Bundoran	162	54.28 N	8.17 W
Bunga ≃, Nig.	222	11.23 N	9.56 E
Bunga ≃, Pil.	202	6.40 N	124.35 E
Bungay	162	52.28 N	1.26 E
Bungo-suidō Ʊ	192	33.00 N	132.13 E
Bungo-takada	192	33.33 N	131.27 E
Bunia	218	1.34 N	30.15 E
Bunker	248	37.27 N	91.13 W
Bunker Group II	228	23.48 S	152.20 E
Bunker Hill, Ill., U.S.	248	39.03 N	89.57 W
Bunker Hill, Ind., U.S.	268	40.40 N	86.06 W
Bunker Hill, Oreg., U.S.	256	43.21 N	124.12 W
Bunker Hill ∧	258	39.15 N	117.08 W
Bunkie	248	30.57 N	92.11 W
Bunnell	246	29.28 N	81.15 W
Buñol	168	39.25 N	0.47 W
Bunola	266	40.14 N	79.56 W
Buntay Point ≻	202	11.18 N	123.54 E
Buntok	198	1.42 S	114.48 E
Bununu Dass	222	10.00 N	9.31 E
Buolkalach	186	72.56 N	119.50 E
Buor-Chaja, Guba C	186	71.30 N	131.00 E
Buor-Chaja, Mys ≻	186	71.56 N	132.40 E
Buqayq	214	25.26 N	49.40 E
Bura	218	1.06 S	39.57 E
Burak Sulaymān (Solomon's Pools) ⊥	210	31.41 N	35.11 E
Buraly	160	55.04 N	52.52 E
Buranhém ≃	296	16.27 S	39.04 W
Burao	214	9.30 N	45.30 E
Buras	248	29.21 N	89.32 W
Burauen	202	10.59 N	124.53 E
Buraydah	208	26.20 N	43.59 E
Burbank, Calif., U.S.	272	37.19 N	121.55 W
Burbank, Calif., U.S.	274	34.12 N	118.18 W
Burbank, Ohio, U.S.	266	40.59 N	81.59 W
Burdekin ≃	228	19.39 S	147.30 E
Burdekin Falls L	228	20.39 S	147.09 E
Burden	252	37.19 N	96.45 W
Burdeos	202	14.51 N	121.58 E
Burdeos Bay C	202	14.43 N	122.08 E
Burdett, Alta., Can.	238	49.50 N	111.32 W
Burdett, Kans., U.S.	252	38.12 N	99.32 W
Burdur	212	37.43 N	30.17 E
Burdur Gölü ⊜	212	37.44 N	30.12 E
Burdwān	206	23.14 N	87.52 E
Bureinskij Chrebet ⋀	186	50.35 N	133.35 E
Bureja ≃	186	49.25 N	129.35 E
Büren	178	51.33 N	8.33 E
Burfjord	160	69.56 N	22.00 E
Burford	264	43.06 N	80.26 W
Burg	164	54.26 N	11.12 E
Burgas	172	42.30 N	27.28 E
Burgas □[4]	212	42.10 N	27.30 E
Burgaski zaliv C	172	42.30 N	27.33 E
Burgau	180	48.26 N	10.25 E
Bur Gavo	218	1.10 S	41.50 E
Burgaw	246	34.33 N	77.56 W
Burg bei Magdeburg	164	52.16 N	11.51 E
Burgdorf, B.R.D.	178	52.27 N	10.00 E
Burgdorf, Schw.	180	47.04 N	7.37 E
Burgenland □[3]	164	47.30 N	16.20 E
Burgeo	240	47.36 N	57.34 W
Burgersdorp	224	31.00 S	26.20 E
Burgess	262	37.53 N	76.21 W
Burgess Hill	174	50.57 N	0.07 W
Burgessville	264	43.01 N	80.39 W
Burgettstown	266	40.23 N	80.23 W
Burghausen	164	48.09 N	12.49 E
Burghead	162	57.42 N	3.30 W
Burghill	266	41.22 N	80.34 W
Burghūth, Sabkhat al- ⊜	212	34.58 N	41.06 E
Burgin	248	37.45 N	84.46 W
Burglengenfeld	164	49.13 N	12.03 E
Burgoon	266	41.16 N	83.15 W
Burgos, Esp.	168	42.21 N	3.42 W
Burgos, Méx.	278	24.57 N	98.47 W
Burgos, Pil.	202	16.04 N	119.52 E
Burgos, Pil.	202	15.30 N	120.24 E
Burgos □[4]	168	42.20 N	3.40 W
Burgstädt	164	50.55 N	12.49 E
Burgsteinfurt	178	52.08 N	7.20 E
Burgsvik	160	57.03 N	18.16 E
Burgundy → Bourgogne □[9]	166	47.00 N	4.30 E
Burhaniye, Tür.	172	37.57 N	28.45 E
Burhaniye, Tür.	172	39.30 N	26.58 E
Burhānpur	206	21.19 N	76.14 E
Buri	296	23.48 S	48.35 W
Burias Island I	202	12.55 N	123.05 E
Burias Pass Ʊ	202	13.00 N	123.15 E
Burica, Pico ∧	280	8.22 N	83.00 W
Burica, Punta ≻	280	8.03 N	82.51 W
Burien	270	47.27 N	122.21 W
Burila Mare	172	44.27 N	22.34 E
Burin	240	47.02 N	55.10 W
Burin Peninsula ≻[1]	240	47.00 N	55.40 W
Buriram	200	14.59 N	103.08 E
Buritama	296	21.03 S	50.08 W
Buriti	296	16.27 S	53.27 W
Buriti ≃	292	12.50 S	58.28 W
Buriti Alegre	296	18.09 S	49.03 W
Buritizeiro	296	17.21 S	44.58 W
Burjasot	168	39.31 N	0.25 W
Burkburnett	250	34.06 N	98.34 W
Burke	252	43.11 N	99.18 W
Burke ≃	228	23.12 S	139.33 E
Burke Channel Ʊ	238	52.07 N	127.38 W
Burkesville	248	36.48 N	85.22 W
Burket	268	41.09 N	85.58 W
Burketown	228	17.44 S	139.22 E
Burkettsville	268	40.21 N	84.39 W
Burleigh	262	39.03 N	74.51 W
Burleigh Falls	264	44.34 N	78.13 W
Burleson	250	32.33 N	97.19 W
Burley, Idaho, U.S.	256	42.32 N	113.48 W
Burley, Wash., U.S.	270	47.25 N	122.38 W
Burlingame, Calif., U.S.	272	37.35 N	122.22 W
Burlingame, Kans., U.S.	252	38.45 N	95.50 W
Burlington, Newf., Can.	240	49.45 N	56.02 W
Burlington, Ont., Can.	264	43.19 N	79.47 W
Burlington, Colo., U.S.	252	39.18 N	102.16 W
Burlington, Conn., U.S.	261	41.46 N	72.58 W
Burlington, Ill., U.S.	268	42.03 N	88.33 W
Burlington, Ind., U.S.	268	40.29 N	86.24 W
Burlington, Iowa, U.S.	244	40.49 N	91.14 W
Burlington, Kans., U.S.	252	38.12 N	95.45 W
Burlington, Ky., U.S.	242	39.02 N	84.43 W
Burlington, Maine, U.S.	242	45.12 N	68.26 W
Burlington, Mass., U.S.	261	42.30 N	71.12 W
Burlington, Mich., U.S.	268	42.06 N	85.05 W
Burlington, N.J., U.S.	262	40.04 N	74.49 W
Burlington, N.C., U.S.	246	36.04 N	79.26 W
Burlington, N. Dak., U.S.	252	48.17 N	101.26 W
Burlington, Vt., U.S.	242	44.29 N	73.13 W
Burlington, Wash., U.S.	270	48.28 N	122.20 W
Burlington, Wis., U.S.	268	42.41 N	88.17 W
Burlington, Wyo., U.S.	256	44.27 N	108.26 W
Burlington □[6]	262	39.50 N	74.47 W
Burlington Beach	268	41.30 N	87.03 W
Burlington Junction	248	40.27 N	95.04 W
Burma □[1]	198	22.00 N	98.00 E
Burnaby	238	49.15 N	122.57 W
Burnaby Island I	238	52.24 N	131.20 W
Burnas, Ozero ⊜	172	45.52 N	30.08 E
Burnet	250	30.46 N	98.14 W
Burnett ≃	228	24.46 S	152.25 E
Burnett Bay C	232	73.53 N	124.00 W
Burnettsville	268	40.46 N	86.36 W
Burney	258	40.53 N	121.40 W
Burnham	262	40.38 N	77.34 W
Burnham-on-Sea	174	51.15 N	3.00 W
Burnie	228	41.04 S	145.54 E
Burnips	268	42.44 N	85.50 W
Burnley	162	53.48 N	2.14 W
Burns, Kans., U.S.	252	38.05 N	96.53 W
Burns, Oreg., U.S.	256	43.35 N	119.03 W
Burns, Tenn., U.S.	248	36.03 N	87.19 W
Burns, Wyo., U.S.	252	41.11 N	104.21 W
Burns Flat	250	35.21 N	99.10 W
Burnside, Ky., U.S.	246	36.59 N	84.36 W
Burnside, Pa., U.S.	266	40.49 N	78.47 W
Burnside ≃	232	66.51 N	108.04 W
Burns Lake	238	54.14 N	125.46 W
Burnsville, Ala., U.S.	248	32.28 N	86.53 W
Burnsville, Miss., U.S.	248	34.51 N	88.19 W
Burnsville, N.C., U.S.	246	35.55 N	82.18 W
Burnsville, W. Va., U.S.	242	38.51 N	80.40 W
Burnt Cabins	266	40.05 N	77.54 W
Burnt Island	240	47.35 N	58.50 W
Burntwood ≃	232	56.08 N	96.30 W
Burra	228	33.40 S	138.56 E
Burragorang, Lake ⊜	228	33.58 S	150.25 E
Burra Voe	162	60.32 N	1.28 W
Burray I	162	58.51 N	2.48 W
Burrel, Shq.	172	41.37 N	20.00 E
Burrel, Calif., U.S.	272	36.30 N	119.59 W
Burriana	168	39.53 N	0.05 W
Burrinjuck Reservoir ⊜[1]	228	35.00 S	148.45 E
Burro, Serranías del ⋀	278	28.50 N	101.35 W
Burr Oak, Ind., U.S.	268	41.15 N	86.25 W
Burr Oak, Kans., U.S.	252	39.52 N	98.18 W
Burr Oak, Mich., U.S.	268	41.51 N	85.19 W
Burro-Burro ≃	290	4.50 N	58.50 W
Burrows	268	40.41 N	86.30 W
Burrton	252	38.02 N	97.41 W
Burruyacú	294	26.30 S	64.45 W
Burrwood	248	28.58 N	89.22 W
Burry Port	174	51.42 N	4.15 W
Bursa	212	40.11 N	29.04 E
Bursa □[4]	172	40.10 N	29.00 E
Būr Safājah	220	26.44 N	33.56 E
Būr Sa'īd (Port Said)	220	31.16 N	32.18 E
Burscheid	178	51.05 N	7.06 E
Burslem	174	53.02 N	2.12 W
Būr Sūdān (Port Sudan)	220	19.37 N	37.14 E
Burt, Iowa, U.S.	244	43.12 N	94.14 W
Burt, N.Y., U.S.	264	43.19 N	78.43 W
Burt Lake ⊜	244	45.27 N	84.40 W
Burton, B.C., Can.	238	49.59 N	117.54 W
Burton, Ohio, U.S.	266	41.28 N	81.09 W
Burton, Tex., U.S.	250	30.11 N	96.36 W
Burton, Wash., U.S.	270	47.23 N	122.28 W
Burton, Lake ⊜[1]	246	34.50 N	83.33 W
Burtonsville	262	39.07 N	76.56 W
Burton upon Trent	174	52.49 N	1.36 W
Buru I	198	3.24 S	126.40 E
Buruanga	202	11.51 N	121.53 E
Burullus, Buḥayrat al- ⊜	220	31.30 N	30.50 E
Burundi □[1]	218	3.15 S	30.00 E
Burwash	244	46.19 N	80.48 W
Burwash Landing	236	61.21 N	139.00 W
Burwell	252	41.47 N	99.08 W
Burwick	162	58.44 N	2.57 W
Bury, Qué., Can.	260	45.29 N	71.30 W
Bury, Eng., U.K.	162	53.36 N	2.17 W
Bury Saint Edmunds	174	52.15 N	0.43 E
Burzil Pass)(	206	34.55 N	75.05 E
Busa, Mount ∧	202	6.07 N	124.41 E
Busalla	170	44.34 N	8.57 E
Busambra, Rocca ∧	170	37.51 N	13.24 E
Busby	256	45.32 N	106.58 W
Busca	170	44.31 N	7.29 E
Bush ≃	246	34.08 N	81.36 W
Būshehr	208	28.59 N	50.50 E
Bushey	174	51.39 N	0.22 W
Bushimaie ≃	218	6.02 S	23.45 E
Bushiribana	285s	12.33 N	69.58 W
Bushland	250	35.11 N	102.04 W
Bush Lot	290	6.10 N	57.18 W
Bushman Land □[9], S. Afr.	224	29.00 S	18.30 E
Bushman Land □[9], S. Afr.	218	29.15 S	20.00 E
Bushnell, Fla., U.S.	246	28.40 N	82.07 W
Bushnell, Ill., U.S.	244	40.33 N	90.30 W
Bushton	252	38.31 N	98.24 W
Bushy Head Mountain ∧	248	36.02 N	94.35 W
Buskerud □[6]	160	60.25 N	9.12 E
Busko Zdrój	164	50.28 N	20.44 E
Busovača	170	44.06 N	17.53 E
Busselton	226	33.39 S	115.20 E
Busseri ≃	220	7.41 N	28.03 E
Bussey	244	41.12 N	92.53 W
Bussoleno	182	45.08 N	7.09 E
Bussum	178	52.16 N	5.10 E
Bustamante	278	26.33 N	100.30 W
Buşteni	172	45.25 N	25.32 E
Busti	266	42.02 N	79.17 W
Busto Arsizio	182	45.37 N	8.51 E
Busto Garolfo	182	45.33 N	8.53 E
Busuanga	202	12.09 N	119.55 E
Busuanga Island I	202	12.05 N	120.05 E
Busu-Djanoa	218	1.43 N	21.23 E
Büsum	164	54.08 N	8.51 E
Bū Sunbul, Jabal ∧[2]	220	23.10 N	22.21 E
Buta	214	2.48 N	24.44 E
Butag	202	12.38 N	123.56 E
Butan	172	43.39 N	23.45 E
Buta Ranquil	294	37.04 S	69.50 W
Butare	218	2.36 S	29.44 E
Butauanan Island I	202	14.07 N	123.19 E
Butehaqi	190	48.02 N	122.43 E
Bute Inlet C	238	50.37 N	124.53 W
Butera	170	37.11 N	14.11 E
Butere	218	0.13 N	34.30 E
Buteshire □[6]	162	55.40 N	5.10 W
Buthroton ⊥	172	39.46 N	20.00 E
Butiá	294	30.07 S	51.58 W
Butig Mountains ⋀	202	7.38 N	124.17 E
Butler, Ala., U.S.	248	32.05 N	88.13 W
Butler, Ga., U.S.	246	32.34 N	84.14 W
Butler, Ind., U.S.	268	41.26 N	84.52 W
Butler, Mo., U.S.	248	38.16 N	94.20 W
Butler, Ohio, U.S.	266	40.35 N	82.26 W
Butler, Okla., U.S.	250	35.38 N	99.11 W
Butler, Pa., U.S.	266	40.52 N	79.54 W
Butler, Tenn., U.S.	246	36.20 N	82.00 W
Butler, Wis., U.S.	268	43.06 N	88.05 W
Butler □[6]	266	40.52 N	79.54 W
Butte, Mont., U.S.	256	46.00 N	112.32 W
Butte, Nebr., U.S.	252	42.58 N	98.51 W
Butte □[6]	272	39.27 N	121.30 W
Butte City, Calif., U.S.	272	39.28 N	121.59 W
Butte City, Idaho, U.S.	256	43.36 N	113.15 W
Butte Falls	256	42.33 N	122.34 W
Butte Mountains ⋀	258	39.50 N	115.05 W
Butterfield	252	43.58 N	94.48 W
Butternut	244	46.01 N	90.30 W
Butterworth	200	5.24 N	100.24 E
Büttgen	178	51.12 N	6.36 E
Buttle Lake ⊜	238	49.46 N	125.36 W
Butt of Lewis ≻	162	58.31 N	6.15 W
Button Islands II	232	60.35 N	64.45 W
Buttonwillow	272	35.24 N	119.28 W
Butuan	202	8.57 N	125.33 E
Butuan Bay C	202	9.03 N	125.22 E
Butung, Pulau I	198	5.00 S	122.55 E
Buturlino	160	55.34 N	44.55 E
Butzbach	164	50.26 N	8.40 E
Bützow	164	53.50 N	11.59 E
Butztown	262	40.39 N	75.22 W
Buxtehude	178	53.28 N	9.41 E
Buxton, Guy.	290	6.48 N	58.02 W
Buxton, Eng., U.K.	162	53.15 N	1.55 W
Buxton, N.C., U.S.	246	35.16 N	75.32 W
Buxton, N. Dak., U.S.	252	47.36 N	97.06 W
Buxton, Oreg., U.S.	270	45.41 N	123.12 W
Buxton, Mount ∧	238	51.35 N	127.55 W
Buxy	166	46.43 N	4.41 E
Büyükada	172	40.52 N	29.07 E
Büyük Ağrı Dağı ∧	208	39.42 N	44.18 E
Büyükçekmece	172	41.01 N	28.34 E
Buyuk Doğanca	172	41.11 N	26.25 E
Büyükkale	172	38.01 N	27.34 E
Büyükkarıştıran	172	41.18 N	27.32 E
Büyükkemikli Burnu ≻	212	40.18 N	26.14 E
Büyük Menderes ≃	212	37.28 N	27.10 E
Buzançais	166	46.53 N	1.25 E
Buzancy	166	49.25 N	4.57 E
Buzău	172	45.09 N	26.49 E
Buzăul	172	45.26 N	27.44 E
Buzăului, Munții ⋀	172	45.35 N	26.10 E
Buzen	192	33.40 N	131.18 E
Búzi ≃	224	19.50 S	34.43 E
Buziaş	172	45.39 N	21.36 E
Búzios, Cabo dos ≻	296	22.44 S	41.53 W
Buzuluk	158	52.47 N	52.15 E
Buzzards Bay	261	41.45 N	70.37 W
Byam Channel Ʊ	232	75.20 N	105.20 W
Byam Martin Channel Ʊ	232	75.45 N	104.00 W
Byam Martin Island I	232	75.15 N	104.00 W
Bychawa	164	51.01 N	22.32 E
Byczyna (Pitschen)	164	51.07 N	18.11 E
Bydalen	160	63.06 N	13.47 E
Bydgoski, Kanał ≊	164	53.08 N	17.36 E
Bydgoszcz	164	53.08 N	18.00 E
Byelorussian Soviet Socialist Republic → Belorusskaja Sovetskaja Socialističeskaja	186	53.30 N	28.00 E
Byers, Kans., U.S.	250	37.47 N	98.52 W
Byers, Tex., U.S.	250	34.04 N	98.11 W
Byesville	242	39.58 N	81.32 W
Byfield	261	42.46 N	70.57 W
Byhalia	248	34.52 N	89.41 W
Byk ≃	172	46.55 N	29.28 E
Bykle	160	59.21 N	7.20 E
Bylas	254	33.08 N	110.07 W
Bylnice	164	49.04 N	18.01 E
Bylot Island I	232	73.13 N	78.34 W
Byng Inlet	244	45.46 N	80.33 W
Bynum, Mont., U.S.	238	47.59 N	112.19 W
Bynum, N.C., U.S.	246	35.47 N	79.08 W
Byram	248	32.16 N	90.14 W
Byrd, Lac ⊜	244	47.02 N	76.56 W
Byrd Land ⬩[1]	148	80.00 S	120.00 W
Byrdstown	248	36.34 N	85.08 W
Byrnedale	266	41.17 N	78.30 W
Byron, Calif., U.S.	272	37.52 N	121.38 W
Byron, Ga., U.S.	246	32.39 N	83.46 W
Byron, Ill., U.S.	244	42.08 N	89.15 W
Byron, Mich., U.S.	268	42.49 N	83.57 W
Byron, N.Y., U.S.	264	43.05 N	78.04 W
Byron, Wyo., U.S.	256	44.48 N	108.30 W
Byron, Cape ≻	228	28.39 S	153.38 E
Byron, Isla I	288	47.45 S	75.11 W
Byron Center	268	42.49 N	85.42 W
Byrranga, Gory ⋀	186	75.00 N	104.00 E
Bystřice	164	49.45 N	14.41 E
Bystřice pod Hostýnem	164	49.24 N	17.40 E
Bystrzyca ≃	164	51.13 N	16.54 E
Bystrzyca Kłodzka (Habelschwerdt)	164	50.18 N	16.38 E
Bytantaj ≃	186	68.46 N	134.20 E
Bytča	164	49.14 N	18.36 E
Bytom (Beuthen), Pol.	158	0.00	0.00
Bytom, Pol.	164	50.22 N	18.54 E
Bytów (Bütow)	164	54.11 N	17.30 E
Byxelkrok	160	57.20 N	17.00 E
Bzura ≃	164	52.23 N	20.09 E
C			
Ca ≃, As.	198	18.46 N	105.47 E
Ca ≃, Viet. N.	200	18.46 N	105.47 E
Caacupé	294	25.23 S	57.09 W
Caaguazú	294	25.26 S	56.02 W
Caaguazú □[5]	294	25.00 S	55.45 W
Caamaño Sound Ʊ	238	52.49 N	129.28 W
Caapiranga	290	3.18 S	61.13 W
Caapucú	294	26.13 S	57.12 W
Caazapá	294	26.09 S	56.24 W
Caazapá □[5]	294	26.10 S	56.00 W
Cabadbaran	202	9.07 N	125.31 E
Cabadiangan Plateau ⋀[1]	202	9.45 N	122.35 E
Cabagan	202	17.25 N	121.46 E
Cabaiguán	284p	22.05 N	79.30 W
Cabalete Island I	202	14.17 N	121.50 E
Cabalian	202	10.16 N	125.10 E
Cabaliana, Lago ⊜	290	3.20 S	60.50 W
Cabalian Bay C	202	10.14 N	125.10 E
Cabalian Point ≻	202	12.06 N	122.01 E
Caballería, Cabo de ≻	168	40.05 N	4.05 E
Caballo, Caño ≃[1]	290	8.00 N	66.45 W
Caballocoha	290	3.53 S	70.30 W
Caballones, Cayo I	284p	20.52 N	79.00 W
Caballo Reservoir ⊜[1]	254	32.58 N	107.18 W
Cabana	292	8.25 S	78.05 W
Cabanaconde	292	15.38 S	71.58 W
Cabañas	284p	22.58 N	82.55 W
Cabanatuan	202	15.29 N	120.58 E
Cabangan	202	15.10 N	120.03 E
Cabano	240	47.41 N	68.54 W
Cabarruyan Island I	202	16.18 N	119.58 E
Cabaun Island I	202	12.33 N	124.30 E
Cabeceiras	296	15.48 S	46.59 W
Cabecera de Dupí	280	8.24 N	81.40 W
Cabedelo	286	6.58 S	34.50 W
Cabeleira ≃	296	17.58 S	50.20 W
Cabellera, Sierra de la ⋀	254	30.55 N	109.05 W
Cabery	268	41.00 N	88.12 W
Cabeza, Arrecife ⊹[2]	278	19.04 N	95.51 W
Cabeza de Lagarto, Punta ≻	292	10.07 S	78.11 W
Cabeza del Buey	168	38.43 N	5.13 W
Cabezas	292	18.46 S	63.24 W
Cabiao	202	15.15 N	120.51 E
Cabildo, Arg.	294	38.30 S	61.55 W
Cabildo, Chile	294	32.26 S	71.05 W
Cabimas	290	10.23 N	71.28 W
Cabinda	218	5.33 S	12.12 E
Cabinda □[5]	218	5.00 S	12.30 E
Cabinet Mountains ⋀	256	48.08 N	115.46 W
Cabingaan Island I	202	5.40 N	121.03 E
Cabin John	262	38.58 N	77.09 W
Cable	244	46.13 N	91.17 W
Cabo	286	8.17 S	35.02 W
Cabo Blanco	288	47.15 S	65.45 W
Cabo Frio	296	22.53 S	42.01 W
Cabo Gracias a Dios	280	14.59 N	83.11 W
Cabonga, Réservoir ⊜[1]	244	47.25 N	76.35 W
Cabool	248	37.07 N	92.06 W
Caborca	278	30.37 N	112.06 W
Cabo Rojo	284m	18.05 N	67.09 W
Cabot, Ark., U.S.	248	34.58 N	92.01 W
Cabot, Pa., U.S.	266	40.46 N	79.46 W
Cabot, Mount ∧	242	44.31 N	71.24 W
Cabot Head ≻	244	45.14 N	81.17 W
Cabot Strait Ʊ	240	47.20 N	59.30 W
Cabourg	166	49.17 N	0.08 W
Cabo Verde	296	21.28 S	46.24 W
Cabo Verde, Arquipélago de II	148	16.00 N	24.00 W
Cabra	168	37.28 N	4.27 W
Cabra Island I	202	13.53 N	120.02 E
Cabral	282	18.15 N	71.13 W
Cabras	170	39.56 N	8.32 E
Cabrera I	168	39.09 N	2.56 E
Cabrera Baja, Sierra de la ⋀	168	42.12 N	6.40 W
Cabriel ≃	168	39.14 N	1.03 W
Cabrillo National Monument ♠	258	32.41 N	117.15 W
Cabrobó	286	8.31 S	39.19 W
Cabruta	290	7.38 N	66.15 W
Cabucan Island I	202	6.09 N	120.54 E
Cabucgayan	202	11.29 N	124.32 E
Cabugao	202	17.48 N	120.27 E
Cabulauan Island I	202	11.23 N	120.06 E
Cabure	290	11.08 N	69.38 W
Cabusilan Mountains ⋀	202	15.05 N	120.22 E
Cabuya	280	9.36 N	85.06 W
Cabuyal	280	10.40 N	85.40 W
Cabuyaro	290	4.18 N	72.49 W
Caçador	294	26.47 S	51.00 W
Cacahoatán	280	14.59 N	92.10 W
Čačak	172	43.53 N	20.21 E
Cacaoui, Lac ⊜	240	50.54 N	66.58 W
Caçapava	296	23.06 S	45.42 W
Caçapava do Sul	294	30.30 S	53.30 W
Cacapon ≃	242	39.37 N	78.16 W
Caccamo	170	37.56 N	13.40 E
Caccia, Capo ≻	170	40.34 N	8.09 E
Cacequi	294	29.53 S	54.49 W
Cáceres, Bra.	292	16.04 S	57.41 W
Cáceres, Col.	290	7.35 N	75.20 W
Cáceres, Esp.	168	39.29 N	6.22 W
Cacharí	294	36.23 S	59.29 W
Cache	250	34.38 N	98.38 W
Cache ≃, Ark., U.S.	248	34.42 N	91.20 W
Cache ≃, Ill., U.S.	248	37.04 N	89.10 W
Cache Creek	238	50.48 N	121.19 W
Cache la Poudre ≃	254	40.25 N	104.36 W
Cache Mountain ∧	236	65.31 N	147.20 W
Cache Peak ∧	256	42.11 N	113.40 W
Cacheu C[1]	222	12.10 N	16.21 W
Cachi	294	25.10 S	66.15 W
Cachimbo, Serra do ⋀	292	8.30 S	55.50 W
Cachoeira	296	12.36 S	38.58 W
Cachoeira Alta	296	18.48 S	50.58 W
Cachoeira de Goiás	296	16.44 S	50.38 W
Cachoeira do Sul	294	30.02 S	52.54 W
Cachoeira Paulista	296	22.40 S	45.01 W
Cachoeiras de Macacu	296	22.28 S	42.39 W
Cachoeiro de Itapemirim	296	20.51 S	41.06 W
Cachos, Punta ≻	294	27.39 S	71.02 W
Cachuela Esperanza	292	10.32 S	65.38 W
Cachuma Reservoir ⊜[1]	258	34.35 N	119.55 W
Căciulaţi	172	44.38 N	26.10 E
Cacnipa Island I	202	10.30 N	119.03 E
Cacocum	284p	20.44 N	76.23 W
Cacólo	218	10.07 S	19.17 E
Caconda	218	13.43 S	15.06 E
Cacra	292	12.50 S	75.46 W
Cactus Flat ≚	258	37.45 N	116.45 W
Cactus Peak ∧	258	37.47 N	116.53 W
Caçu	296	18.37 S	51.04 W
Caculé	296	14.30 S	42.13 W
Caçumba, Ilha I	296	17.46 S	39.17 W
Cadambanauan Island I	202	10.40 N	119.35 E
Čadan	186	51.17 N	91.35 E
Cadaqués	168	42.17 N	3.17 E
Čadca	164	49.26 N	18.48 E
Caddo, Okla., U.S.	250	34.07 N	96.16 W
Caddo, Tex., U.S.	250	32.38 N	98.40 W
Caddo ≃	248	34.10 N	93.03 W
Caddo Lake ⊜[1]	248	32.42 N	94.01 W
Caddo Mills	250	33.04 N	96.14 W
Cadena, Cerro ∧	250	25.50 N	104.05 W
Cadereyta Jiménez	278	25.36 N	100.00 W
Cadig Mountains ⋀	202	14.05 N	122.35 E
Cadillac, Fr.	166	44.38 N	0.19 W
Cadillac, Mich., U.S.	244	44.15 N	85.24 W
Cádiz, Esp.	168	36.32 N	6.18 W
Cadiz, Pil.	202	10.58 N	123.19 E
Cadiz, Ohio, U.S.	266	40.16 N	81.00 W
Cádiz, Bahía de C	168	36.32 N	6.16 W
Cádiz, Golfo de C	168	36.50 N	7.10 W
Cadiz Lake ⊜	258	34.18 N	115.24 W
Cadlao Island I	202	11.14 N	119.20 E
Čadobec ≃	186	58.40 N	98.50 E
Cadogan	266	40.45 N	79.35 W
Cadomin	238	53.02 N	117.20 W
Cadott	244	44.57 N	91.09 W
Caduruan Point ≻	202	11.43 N	124.04 E
Cadwell	246	32.20 N	83.03 W
Caen	166	49.11 N	0.21 W
Caerleon	174	51.37 N	2.57 W
Caernarvon	174	53.08 N	4.16 W
Caernarvon Bay C	162	53.05 N	4.30 W
Caernarvonshire □[6]	174	53.03 N	4.05 W
Caerphilly	174	51.35 N	3.14 W
Caetanópolis	296	19.18 S	44.24 W
Caeté	296	19.54 S	43.40 W
Caetité	296	14.04 S	42.29 W
Cafayate	294	26.06 S	65.57 W
Cafelândia do Leste Matogrossense	296	16.40 S	53.25 W
Cagayan □[4]	202	18.10 N	125.50 E
Cagayan ≃	202	18.25 N	121.40 E
Cagayancillo	202	9.34 N	121.12 E
Cagayan de Oro	202	8.29 N	124.39 E
Cagayan de Sulu	202	6.59 N	118.32 E
Cagayan Island I	202	9.37 N	121.12 E
Cagayan Islands II	202	9.40 N	121.25 E
Cagayan Sulu Island I	202	7.00 N	118.28 E
Čagda	186	58.45 N	130.37 E
Çağış	172	39.30 N	28.01 E
Cagli	184	43.33 N	12.39 E
Cagliari	170	39.13 N	9.06 E
Cagliari, Golfo di C	170	39.05 N	9.10 E
Cagnano Varano	184	41.49 N	15.47 E
Cagnes-sur-Mer	182	43.40 N	7.09 E
Čagoda	160	59.10 N	35.17 E
Cagraray Island I	202	13.16 N	123.53 E
Cagua	290	10.11 N	67.27 W
Caguán ≃	290	0.08 S	74.18 W
Caguas	284m	18.14 N	66.02 W
Cagwait	202	8.55 N	126.18 E
Cahaba ≃	248	32.20 N	87.05 W
Cahabón	280	15.34 N	89.49 W
Cahabón ≃	280	15.25 N	89.36 W
Caha Mountains ⋀	162	51.45 N	9.45 W
Caher	162	52.21 N	7.56 W
Cahirciveen	162	51.57 N	10.13 W
Cahore Point ≻	162	52.34 N	6.11 W
Cahors	166	44.27 N	1.26 E
Cahuinari ≃	290	1.21 S	70.44 W
Cahuita, Punta ≻	280	9.44 N	82.48 W
Caia ≃	168	38.50 N	7.05 W
Caiabis, Serra dos ⋀[1]	292	11.30 S	56.30 W
Caiapó ≃	296	15.49 S	51.53 W
Caiapó, Serra ⋀	296	17.00 S	52.00 W
Caiapônia	296	16.57 S	51.49 W
Caibarién	284p	22.31 N	79.28 W
Cai-bau, Dao I	200	21.10 N	107.27 E
Caibiran	202	11.34 N	124.35 E
Caiçara, Bra.	296	15.34 S	50.12 W
Caicara, Ven.	290	7.37 N	66.10 W
Caiçara ≃, Bra.	290	3.11 S	64.49 W
Caicara ≃, Ven.	290	7.44 N	69.04 W
Caicara de Maturín	290	9.49 N	63.36 W
Caicedonia	290	4.20 N	75.50 W
Caicó	286	6.27 S	37.06 W
Caicos Islands II	282	21.50 N	71.50 W
Caicos Passage Ʊ	282	22.15 N	72.40 W
Cailloma	292	15.12 S	71.44 W
Caillou Bay C	248	29.06 N	90.56 W
Caima Bay C	202	13.42 N	122.49 E
Caimán, Laguna ⊜	290	3.38 N	69.30 W
Caimanera	284p	19.59 N	75.09 W
Caiman Point ≻	202	15.55 N	119.47 E
Caina	292	10.12 S	76.25 W
Cains ≃	240	46.40 N	65.47 W
Cainsville	248	40.26 N	93.47 W
Cairnbrook	266	40.07 N	78.49 W
Cairngorm Mountains ⋀	162	57.06 N	3.30 W
Cairn Mountain ∧	236	61.10 N	155.20 W
Cairns	228	16.55 S	145.46 E
Cairo → Al-Qāhirah, Miṣr	220	30.03 N	31.15 E
Cairo, Ga., U.S.	246	30.53 N	84.12 W
Cairo, Ill., U.S.	248	37.00 N	89.11 W
Cairo, Nebr., U.S.	252	41.00 N	98.36 W
Cairo, N.Y., U.S.	261	42.18 N	74.00 W
Cairo, Ohio, U.S.	268	40.50 N	84.05 W
Cairo, W. Va., U.S.	242	39.13 N	81.09 W
Cairo Montenotte	182	44.24 N	8.16 E
Cairu	296	13.30 S	39.03 W
Caithness □[6]	162	58.25 N	3.25 W
Caiundo	218	15.46 S	17.28 E
Caixa, Rio da ≃	296	13.02 S	42.17 W
Caiyu I	196	22.39 N	115.30 E
Caiza	292	20.02 S	65.40 W
Cajabamba, Ec.	290	1.42 S	78.45 W
Cajabamba, Perú	292	7.38 S	78.04 W
Cajacay	292	10.10 S	77.30 W
Cajamarca	292	7.10 S	78.31 W
Cajamarca □[5]	292	6.15 S	78.50 W
Cajarc	166	44.29 N	1.50 E
Cajatambo	292	10.30 S	77.02 W
Cajàzeiras	286	6.54 S	38.34 W
Čajek	186	41.56 N	74.30 E
Čajkovskij	158	56.40 N	54.10 E
Čajniče	172	43.33 N	19.04 E
Cajones, Cayos II	280	16.04 N	83.10 W
Cajon Summit)(	258	34.21 N	117.27 W
Cajuru	296	21.17 S	47.18 W
Çakırgöl Dağı ∧	212	40.34 N	39.42 E
Çakmak Dağı ∧	212	39.46 N	42.12 E
Čakovec	170	46.23 N	16.26 E
Cala, Embalse de ⊜[1]	168	37.50 N	6.00 W
Calabanga	202	13.42 N	123.12 E
Calabar	222	4.57 N	8.19 E
Calabogie	264	45.18 N	76.43 W
Calabozo	290	8.56 N	67.26 W
Calabozo, Ensenada de C	290	11.30 N	71.45 W
Calabria □[4]	170	39.00 N	16.30 E
Calabugdong Island I	202	11.07 N	119.41 E
Calaca	202	13.55 N	120.49 E
Calacuccia	170	42.20 N	9.03 E
Caladang, Mount ∧	202	14.49 N	121.21 E
Calafat	172	43.59 N	22.28 E
Calafate	288	50.20 S	72.16 W
Calagnaan Island I	202	11.29 N	123.13 E
Calaguas Islands II	202	14.25 N	122.56 E
Calahorra	168	42.18 N	1.58 W
Calais, Fr.	176	50.57 N	1.50 E
Calais, Maine, U.S.	242	45.11 N	67.17 W
Calalaste, Sierra de ⋀	294	25.30 S	67.30 W
Calama, Bra.	292	8.03 S	62.53 W
Calama, Chile	294	22.28 S	68.56 W
Calamar, Col.	290	1.58 N	72.32 W
Calamar, Col.	290	10.15 N	74.55 W
Calamarca	292	16.55 S	68.09 W
Calamba, Pil.	202	10.11 N	123.17 E
Calamba, Pil.	202	14.13 N	121.10 E
Calamba, Pil.	202	8.32 N	123.38 E
Calamian Group II	202	12.00 N	120.10 E
Calamocha	168	40.55 N	1.18 W
Calamus ≃	252	41.48 N	99.09 W
Calañas	168	37.39 N	6.53 W
Calanda	168	40.56 N	0.14 W
Calandagan Island I	202	10.40 N	119.55 E
Calangianus	170	40.56 N	9.12 E
Calapan	202	13.25 N	121.11 E
Calape	202	9.53 N	123.52 E
Calapooya Mountains ⋀	256	43.30 N	122.50 W
Călăraşi	172	44.11 N	27.20 E
Cala Ratjada	168	39.42 N	3.25 E
Calarcá	290	4.31 N	75.38 W
Calatafimi	170	37.55 N	12.52 E
Calatagan	202	13.50 N	120.38 E
Calatayud	168	41.21 N	1.38 W
Calau	164	51.45 N	13.56 E
Calauan	202	14.09 N	121.19 E
Calauit Island I	202	12.18 N	119.54 E
Calaveras □[6]	272	38.12 N	120.41 W
Calavite, Cape ≻	202	13.26 N	120.18 E
Calavite, Mount ∧	202	13.29 N	120.24 E
Calavite Passage Ʊ	202	13.33 N	120.20 E
Calayan	202	19.16 N	121.28 E
Calayan Island I	202	19.20 N	121.25 E
Calbayog	202	12.04 N	124.36 E
Calbe	164	51.54 N	11.46 E
Calbiga	202	11.38 N	125.01 E
Calca	292	13.20 S	71.57 W
Calcasieu ≃	248	30.05 N	93.20 W
Calcasieu Lake ⊜	248	29.50 N	93.17 W
Calceta	290	0.51 S	80.10 W
Calcha	292	21.06 S	67.31 W
Calcium	264	44.01 N	75.51 W
Calçoene	286	2.30 N	50.57 W
Calcutta, Bhārat	206	22.34 N	88.20 E
Calcutta, Ohio, U.S.	266	40.41 N	80.34 W
Caldaro (Kaltern)	170	46.25 N	11.14 E
Caldas, Bra.	296	21.56 S	46.23 W
Caldas, Col.	290	6.05 N	75.38 W
Caldas □[5]	290	5.15 N	75.30 W
Caldas da Rainha	168	39.24 N	9.08 W
Caldas de Reyes	168	42.36 N	8.38 W
Caldas Novas	296	17.45 S	48.38 W
Caldeirão, Serra do ⋀	168	37.42 N	8.21 W
Caldera	294	27.04 S	70.50 W
Caldera, Punta ≻	280	9.54 N	84.43 W
Caldwell, Idaho, U.S.	256	43.40 N	116.41 W
Caldwell, Kans., U.S.	252	37.02 N	97.37 W
Caldwell, Ohio, U.S.	242	39.45 N	81.31 W
Caldwell, Tex., U.S.	250	30.32 N	96.42 W
Caledon	264	43.52 N	80.00 W
Caledon ≃	224	30.31 S	26.05 E
Caledon East	264	43.52 N	79.52 W
Caledonia, Br. Hond.	278	18.14 N	88.29 W
Caledonia, N.S., Can.	240	44.22 N	65.02 W
Caledonia, Ont., Can.	264	43.04 N	79.56 W
Caledonia, Ill., U.S.	268	42.22 N	88.53 W
Caledonia, Mich., U.S.	268	42.47 N	85.31 W
Caledonia, Minn., U.S.	244	43.38 N	91.29 W
Caledonia, Miss., U.S.	248	33.39 N	88.20 W
Caledonia, N.Y., U.S.	264	42.58 N	77.51 W
Caledonia, Ohio, U.S.	266	40.38 N	82.58 W
Caledonia, Pa., U.S.	266	41.17 N	78.27 W
Caledonian Canal ≊	162	57.20 N	4.30 W
Calella	168	41.37 N	2.40 E
Calera	248	33.06 N	86.45 W
Caleta, Punta ≻	284p	20.03 N	74.18 W
Caleufú	294	35.36 S	64.33 W
Calexico	258	32.40 N	115.30 W
Calf of Man I	162	54.03 N	4.48 W
Calgary	238	51.03 N	114.05 W
Calhan	252	39.02 N	104.18 W
Calhoun, Ala., U.S.	248	32.03 N	86.33 W
Calhoun, Ga., U.S.	246	34.30 N	84.57 W
Calhoun, Ky., U.S.	248	37.32 N	87.16 W
Calhoun, Mo., U.S.	248	38.28 N	93.37 W

Symbols in the index entries are identified on page 360.

Name	Page	Lat°′	Long°′
Calhoun, Tenn., U.S.	246	35.17 N	84.45 W
Calhoun □[6]	268	42.14 N	85.00 W
Calhoun City	248	33.51 N	89.19 W
Calhoun Falls	246	34.06 N	82.36 W
Cali, Col.	290	3.27 N	76.31 W
Çalı, Tür.	172	40.10 N	28.54 E
Calian Point ➤	202	6.06 N	125.42 E
Calicoan Island I	202	11.00 N	125.48 E
Calico Rock	248	36.07 N	92.09 W
Calicut	204	11.16 N	75.48 E
Caliente, Calif., U.S.	274	35.17 N	118.38 W
Caliente, Nev., U.S.	258	37.37 N	114.31 W
Califon	262	40.43 N	74.50 W
California, Mo., U.S.	248	38.38 N	92.34 W
California, Pa., U.S.	266	40.04 N	79.53 W
California □[3]	234	37.30 N	119.30 W
California, Golfo de C	278	28.00 N	112.00 W
California City	274	35.08 N	117.58 W
Calilegua	294	23.47 S	64.46 W
Călimănești	172	45.14 N	24.20 E
Călimanului, Munții ⋀	172	47.07 N	25.03 E
Calimesa	274	34.00 N	117.03 W
Calingasta	294	31.19 S	69.26 W
Calinog	202	11.07 N	122.32 E
Calintaan	202	12.35 N	120.56 E
Calion	248	33.20 N	92.32 W
Calipatria	258	33.08 N	115.31 W
Calispell Peak Λ	256	48.26 N	117.30 W
Calistoga	272	38.35 N	122.35 W
Calitri	170	40.54 N	15.27 E
Calixtlahuaca ⊥	278	19.20 N	99.42 W
Callabonna, Lake ⊜	228	29.45 S	140.04 E
Callac	166	48.24 N	3.26 W
Callaghan, Mount Λ	258	39.42 N	116.57 W
Callahan	246	30.34 N	81.49 W
Callan	162	52.33 N	7.23 W
Callander, Ont., Can.	244	46.13 N	79.23 W
Callander, Scot., U.K.	162	56.15 N	4.14 W
Callang	202	17.02 N	121.37 E
Callanmarca	292	12.49 S	74.38 W
Callao, Perú	292	12.02 S	77.05 W
Callao, Va., U.S.	262	37.58 N	76.34 W
Callaway	252	41.17 N	99.56 W
Callensburg	266	41.08 N	79.33 W
Callery	266	40.45 N	80.02 W
Calliaqua	285h	13.08 N	61.12 W
Calliham	250	28.29 N	98.21 W
Calling Lake	238	55.15 N	113.12 W
Calling Lake ⊜	238	55.13 N	113.15 W
Callosa de Ensarriá	168	38.39 N	0.07 W
Callosa de Segura	168	38.08 N	0.52 W
Calmar, Alta., Can.	238	53.16 N	113.49 W
Calmar, Iowa, U.S.	244	43.11 N	91.52 W
Călmățui ≃	172	44.50 N	27.50 E
Calm Lake ⊜	244	48.46 N	92.04 W
Čal'mny-Varre	160	67.10 N	37.33 E
Čalna	160	61.55 N	34.01 E
Calne	174	51.27 N	2.00 W
Calobre	280	8.15 N	80.50 W
Calolbon	202	13.36 N	124.06 E
Calolziocorte	182	45.48 N	9.26 E
Calonne-Ricouart	176	50.29 N	2.29 E
Caloosahatchee ≃	246	26.31 N	82.01 W
Calpe	168	38.39 N	0.03 E
Caltagirone	170	37.14 N	14.31 E
Caltanissetta	170	37.29 N	14.04 E
Çaltılıbük	172	39.57 N	28.36 E
Calubian	202	11.26 N	124.25 E
Călugăreni	172	44.07 N	26.01 E
Caluire-et-Cuire	182	45.48 N	4.51 E
Calumet, Mich., U.S.	244	47.14 N	88.27 W
Calumet, Minn., U.S.	244	47.19 N	93.17 W
Calumet, Pa., U.S.	266	40.13 N	79.28 W
Calumet City	268	41.37 N	87.31 W
Calunda	218	12.06 S	23.23 E
Calusa Island I	202	9.38 N	121.01 E
Caluso	182	45.18 N	7.53 E
Caluya Island I	202	11.56 N	121.34 E
Calvados □[5]	176	49.10 N	0.30 W
Calvary	246	30.44 N	84.21 W
Calvert, Ala., U.S.	248	31.09 N	88.01 W
Calvert, Tex., U.S.	250	30.59 N	96.40 W
Calvert □[6]	262	38.33 N	76.35 W
Calvert Island I	238	51.35 N	128.00 W
Calverton	261	40.55 N	72.45 W
Calvi	166	42.34 N	8.45 E
Calvillo	278	21.51 N	102.43 W
Calvin, La., U.S.	248	31.58 N	92.47 W
Calvin, N. Dak., U.S.	252	48.51 N	98.56 W
Calvin, Okla., U.S.	250	34.58 N	96.15 W
Calvin, Pa., U.S.	266	40.20 N	78.02 W
Calvinia	218	31.25 S	19.45 E
Calw	180	48.43 N	8.44 E
Calwa	272	36.42 N	119.46 W
Calypso	246	35.09 N	78.06 W
Calzada	292	6.05 S	77.05 W
Camabatela	218	8.11 S	15.22 E
Camaçari	296	12.41 S	38.18 W
Camachigama, Lac ⊜	244	47.50 N	76.19 W
Camacho	278	24.25 N	102.18 W
Camacosni	280	14.57 N	85.08 W
Camaguán	290	8.06 N	67.36 W
Camagüey	284p	21.23 N	77.55 W
Camagüey □[4]	284p	21.30 N	78.10 W
Camagüey, Archipiélago de II	284p	22.18 N	78.00 W
Camaiore	170	43.56 N	10.18 E
Camajuaní	284p	22.28 N	79.44 W
Camamu	296	13.57 S	39.07 W
Camaná	292	16.36 S	72.40 W
Camanche	244	41.47 N	90.15 W
Camanche Reservoir ⊜[1]	258	38.13 N	120.58 W
Camandag Island I	202	11.58 N	124.25 E
Camano Island	270	48.10 N	122.38 W
Camapuã	296	19.30 S	54.05 W
Camaquã	294	30.51 S	51.49 W
Camaquã ≃	294	31.17 S	51.47 W
Camará	290	3.55 S	62.44 W
Camarat, Cap ➤	166	43.12 N	6.41 E
Camarès	166	43.49 N	2.53 E
Camargo	292	20.39 S	65.13 W
Camargue □[9]	166	43.34 N	4.34 E
Camarillo	274	34.13 N	119.02 W
Camarillo Heights	274	34.14 N	119.02 W
Camarines Norte □[4]	202	14.10 N	122.40 E
Camarines Sur □[4]	202	13.35 N	123.20 E
Camarón, Cabo ➤	280	16.00 N	85.04 W
Camarón, Punta ➤	168	36.45 N	6.25 W
Camaronero, Laguna C	278	23.00 N	106.07 W
Camarones	288	44.45 S	65.40 W
Camas, Esp.	168	37.24 N	6.02 W
Camas, Wash., U.S.	270	45.35 N	122.24 W
Cambados	168	42.30 N	8.48 W
Cambará	296	23.03 S	50.05 W
Çambar Dağı Λ	212	40.21 N	42.26 E
Cambay	206	22.19 N	72.37 E
Cambay, Gulf of C	206	21.30 N	72.30 E
Camberley	174	51.21 N	0.45 W
Cambodia □[1]	198	13.00 N	105.00 E
Camboriú	294	27.01 S	48.38 W
Camboriú, Ponta do ➤	294	25.10 S	47.55 W
Camborne	162	50.12 N	5.19 W
Cambrai	176	50.10 N	3.14 E
Cambria, Calif., U.S.	272	35.34 N	121.05 W
Cambria, Ind., U.S.	268	40.22 N	86.33 W
Cambria, Mich., U.S.	268	41.49 N	84.40 W
Cambria, Wis., U.S.	244	43.33 N	89.06 W
Cambria □[6]	266	40.29 N	79.16 W
Cambria Ice Field ⊠	238	55.55 N	129.30 W
Cambrian Mountains ⋀	162	52.35 N	3.35 W
Cambrian Park	272	37.16 N	121.56 W
Cambridge, N.Z.	230	37.53 S	175.28 E
Cambridge, Eng., U.K.	174	52.13 N	0.08 E
Cambridge, Idaho, U.S.	256	44.34 N	116.41 W
Cambridge, Ill., U.S.	244	41.18 N	90.12 W
Cambridge, Iowa, U.S.	244	41.54 N	93.32 W
Cambridge, Md., U.S.	262	38.34 N	76.04 W
Cambridge, Mass., U.S.	261	42.22 N	71.06 W
Cambridge, Minn., U.S.	244	45.31 N	93.14 W
Cambridge, Nebr., U.S.	252	40.17 N	100.10 W
Cambridge, N.Y., U.S.	242	43.02 N	73.23 W
Cambridge, Ohio, U.S.	242	40.02 N	81.35 W
Cambridge, Wis., U.S.	268	43.00 N	89.01 W
Cambridge Bay	232	69.03 N	105.05 W
Cambridge City	248	39.49 N	85.10 W
Cambridge Fiord C[2]	232	71.20 N	74.44 W
Cambridgeshire and Isle of Ely □[6]	174	52.20 N	0.10 E
Cambridge Springs	266	41.48 N	80.04 W
Cambrils	168	41.04 N	1.03 E
Cambuci	296	21.34 S	41.55 W
Cambuí	296	22.37 S	46.04 W
Camden, Austl.	228	34.03 S	150.42 E
Camden, Ala., U.S.	248	31.59 N	87.17 W
Camden, Ark., U.S.	248	33.35 N	92.50 W
Camden, Del., U.S.	262	39.07 N	75.33 W
Camden, Ind., U.S.	268	40.37 N	86.32 W
Camden, Maine, U.S.	242	44.12 N	69.04 W
Camden, Mich., U.S.	268	41.45 N	84.46 W
Camden, Miss., U.S.	248	32.42 N	89.50 W
Camden, N.J., U.S.	262	39.57 N	75.07 W
Camden, N.C., U.S.	246	36.20 N	76.10 W
Camden, N.Y., U.S.	264	43.02 N	75.45 W
Camden, Ohio, U.S.	242	39.38 N	84.39 W
Camden, S.C., U.S.	246	34.16 N	80.36 W
Camden, Tenn., U.S.	248	36.04 N	88.06 W
Camden, Tex., U.S.	250	30.55 N	94.44 W
Camden □[6], N.J., U.S.	262	39.57 N	75.07 W
Camden □[6], N.C., U.S.	262	36.28 N	76.21 W
Camden ➛[8]	174	51.33 N	0.10 W
Camden Bay C	236	70.00 N	145.00 W
Camdenton	248	38.00 N	92.45 W
Camelback Mountain Λ	236	62.33 N	157.20 W
Camels Back Λ	230	36.58 S	175.35 E
Camels Hump Λ	242	44.19 N	72.53 W
Cameri	182	45.30 N	8.39 E
Camerino	184	43.08 N	13.04 E
Cameron, La., U.S.	248	29.48 N	93.19 W
Cameron, Mo., U.S.	248	39.44 N	94.14 W
Cameron, Pa., U.S.	266	41.27 N	78.10 W
Cameron, S.C., U.S.	246	33.33 N	80.43 W
Cameron, Tex., U.S.	250	30.51 N	96.59 W
Cameron, W. Va., U.S.	242	39.50 N	80.34 W
Cameron, Wis., U.S.	244	45.25 N	91.44 W
Cameron □[6]	266	41.31 N	78.14 W
Cameron Highlands	200	4.25 N	101.23 E
Cameron Hills ⋀[2]	232	59.48 N	118.00 W
Cameron Mountains ⋀	230	45.54 S	167.00 E
Cameroon □[1]	214	6.00 N	12.00 E
Camerota	170	40.02 N	15.23 E
Cameroun, Mont Λ	222	4.12 N	9.11 E
Cameroun Occidental □[4]	222	5.30 N	9.30 E
Cameroun Oriental □[4]	222	6.00 N	13.00 E
Cametá	286	2.15 S	49.30 W
Camiguin □[4]	202	9.15 N	124.40 E
Camiguin Island I, Pil.	202	18.54 N	121.55 E
Camiguin Island I, Pil.	202	9.10 N	124.43 E
Camiling	202	15.42 N	120.24 E
Camilla	246	31.14 N	84.12 W
Camillus	264	43.02 N	76.19 W
Camiña	292	19.18 S	69.26 W
Caminha	168	41.52 N	8.50 W
Camino	272	38.44 N	120.41 W
Camiranga	286	1.48 S	46.17 W
Camiri	292	20.03 S	63.31 W
Camisea ≃	292	11.46 S	73.02 W
Çamlıca	172	40.46 N	26.39 E
Camoapa	280	12.25 N	85.31 W
Camocim	286	2.54 S	40.50 W
Camogli	182	44.21 N	9.09 E
Camooweal	228	19.55 S	138.07 E
Camorta Island I	200	8.10 N	93.30 E
Camotes Islands II	202	10.40 N	124.22 E
Camotes Sea ▼[2]	202	10.30 N	124.20 E
Campagna	170	40.40 N	15.08 E
Campaign	248	35.46 N	85.38 W
Campamento	280	14.33 N	86.42 W
Campamento Alianza	292	20.46 S	69.42 W
Campana	294	34.10 S	58.57 W
Campana, Isla I	288	48.25 S	75.20 W
Campanario	168	38.52 N	5.37 W
Campanario, Cerro de Λ	292	5.58 S	77.33 W
Campania □[4]	184	41.00 N	14.30 E
Campaspe ≃	228	21.00 S	146.24 E
Campbell, Calif., U.S.	272	37.17 N	121.57 W
Campbell, Mo., U.S.	248	36.30 N	90.04 W
Campbell, Nebr., U.S.	252	40.18 N	98.44 W
Campbell, Ohio, U.S.	266	41.05 N	80.36 W
Campbell, Cape ➤	230	41.44 S	174.16 E
Campbellford	264	44.18 N	77.48 W
Campbell Hill Λ[2]	242	40.22 N	83.43 W
Campbell Island	238	52.10 N	128.09 W
Campbell Lake ⊜	238	50.01 N	125.27 W
Campbell Range ⋀	236	61.08 N	129.45 W
Campbell Rise ✣[3]	148	56.00 S	165.00 E
Campbell River	238	50.01 N	125.15 W
Campbells Bay	242	45.44 N	76.36 W
Campbellsport	244	43.36 N	88.17 W
Campbellsville	248	37.21 N	85.20 W
Campbellton, N.B., Can.	240	48.00 N	66.40 W
Campbellton, Newf., Can.	240	49.17 N	54.56 W
Campbellton, P.E.I., Can.	240	46.47 N	64.18 W
Campbellton, Fla., U.S.	246	30.57 N	85.24 W
Campbelltown, Austl.	228	34.04 S	150.49 E
Campbelltown, Pa., U.S.	262	40.17 N	76.35 W
Campbellville	264	43.29 N	79.59 W
Campbeltown	162	55.26 N	5.36 W
Camp Borden ■	244	44.17 N	79.55 W
Camp Douglas	244	43.55 N	90.16 W
Campeche	278	19.51 N	90.32 W
Campeche, Bahía de C	278	20.00 N	94.00 W
Campechuela	284p	20.14 N	77.17 W
Camperdown	228	38.14 S	143.09 E
Cam-pha	200	21.07 N	107.19 E
Camp Hill, Ala., U.S.	248	32.43 N	85.39 W
Camp Hill, Pa., U.S.	242	40.14 N	76.55 W
Camp Howard Ridge Λ	256	45.43 N	116.25 W
Campi Bisenzio	184	43.49 N	11.08 E
Campidano ➛[1]	170	39.30 N	8.50 E
Campiglia Marittima	184	43.03 N	10.37 E
Campillo de Llerena	168	38.30 N	5.50 W
Campillos	168	37.03 N	4.51 W
Campina Grande	286	7.13 S	35.53 W
Campinas	296	22.54 S	47.05 W
Campina Verde	296	19.31 S	49.28 W
Camp Lake	268	42.32 N	88.09 W
Camp Lejeune ■	246	34.40 N	77.21 W
Campli	184	42.43 N	13.41 E
Camp Meaford Tank Range ■	244	44.41 N	80.45 W
Campo	252	37.06 N	102.35 W
Campoalegre	290	2.41 N	75.20 W
Campo Alegre de Goiás	296	17.39 S	47.45 W
Campobasso	184	41.34 N	14.39 E
Campobasso □[4]	184	41.38 N	14.35 E
Campobello di Licata	170	37.15 N	13.55 E
Campobello di Mazara	170	37.38 N	12.45 E
Campobello Island I	240	44.53 N	66.55 W
Campo Belo	296	20.53 S	45.16 W
Campo de Criptana	168	39.24 N	3.07 W
Campo de la Cruz	290	10.23 N	74.53 W
Campo Erê	294	26.23 S	53.03 W
Campo Florido	296	19.47 S	48.35 W
Campo Gallo	294	26.35 S	62.50 W
Campo Grande, Arg.	294	27.18 S	54.57 W
Campo Grande, Bra.	296	20.27 S	54.37 W
Campo Largo, Arg.	294	26.45 S	60.55 W
Campo Largo, Bra.	294	25.26 S	49.32 W
Campo Maior	286	4.49 S	42.10 W
Campo Major	168	39.01 N	7.04 W
Campo Mourão	296	24.03 S	52.22 W
Campo Nôvo	294	27.42 S	53.48 W
Campo Quijano	294	24.54 S	65.40 W
Camporredondo	292	6.08 S	78.25 W
Campos	296	21.45 S	41.18 W
Campos Altos	296	19.41 S	46.10 W
Campo Santo	294	24.42 S	65.06 W
Campos Belos	296	13.03 S	46.53 W
Campos do Jordão	296	22.44 S	45.35 W
Campos Gerais	296	21.14 S	45.46 W
Campos Novos	294	27.24 S	51.12 W
Campo Tures (Sand in Taufers)	170	46.55 N	11.57 E
Campoyo Point ➤	202	9.40 N	123.08 E
Camp Pendleton Marine Corps Base ■	258	33.19 N	117.18 W
Camp Point	248	40.03 N	91.04 W
Camps-en-Amiénois	162	49.52 N	1.58 E
Camp Springs	262	38.48 N	76.55 W
Campti	248	31.54 N	93.07 W
Campton	246	37.44 N	83.33 W
Camptonville	272	39.27 N	121.03 W
Campuya ≃	290	1.40 S	73.30 W
Camp Verde	254	34.34 N	111.51 W
Camp Wood	250	29.40 N	100.01 W
Cam-ranh, Vinh C	200	11.53 N	109.10 E
Camrose	238	53.01 N	112.50 W
Camu ≃	290	1.15 N	57.09 W
Camuy	284m	18.29 N	66.51 W
Çan	172	40.02 N	27.03 E
Čaňa	164	48.37 N	21.18 E
Canaan, Conn., U.S.	261	42.02 N	73.20 W
Canaan, N.Y., U.S.	261	42.25 N	73.27 W
Canaan, Vt., U.S.	242	45.00 N	71.32 W
Cana Brava ≃, Bra.	296	12.12 S	48.40 W
Cana Brava ≃, Bra.	296	13.11 S	48.11 W
Canaçarí, Lago ⊜	290	2.57 S	58.15 W
Canachí	278	24.04 N	107.05 W
Canada □[1]	232	60.00 N	95.00 W
Canada Bay C	240	50.43 N	56.10 W
Cañada de Gómez	294	32.49 S	61.25 W
Cañada Honda	294	32.00 S	68.33 W
Canadian	250	35.55 N	100.23 W
Canadian ≃	250	35.27 N	95.03 W
Canahuan Islands II	202	11.49 N	124.41 E
Canaima, Parque Nacional ♠	290	4.27 N	62.00 W
Canajoharie	242	42.54 N	74.35 W
Çanakkale	212	40.09 N	26.24 E
Çanakkale □[4]	172	40.05 N	26.50 E
Çanakkale Boğazı Ų	212	40.15 N	26.25 E
Canal Flats	238	50.09 N	115.48 W
Canal Fulton	266	40.54 N	81.36 W
Canal Point	246	26.52 N	80.38 W
Canals	294	33.34 S	62.53 W
Canal Winchester	242	39.51 N	82.48 W
Canal Zone □[2]	276	9.10 N	79.48 W
Canan	266	40.28 N	78.26 W
Canandaigua	264	42.54 N	77.17 W
Cananea	278	30.57 N	110.18 W
Cananéia	294	25.01 S	47.57 W
Cananguchal	290	0.51 N	75.47 W
Canápolis	296	18.44 S	49.13 W
Cañar	290	2.33 S	78.56 W
Cañar □[4]	290	2.30 S	79.00 W
Canarias, Islas II	148	28.00 N	15.30 W
Canaries	285f	13.55 N	61.04 W
Canarreos, Archipiélago de los II	284p	21.50 N	82.30 W
Canary Basin ✣[1]	148	27.00 N	25.00 W
Canary Islands → Canarias, Islas II	148	28.00 N	15.30 W
Cañas	280	10.25 N	85.07 W
Canaseraga	266	42.28 N	77.47 W
Cañasgordas	290	6.45 N	76.01 W
Canastota	264	43.10 N	75.45 W
Canastra, Serra da ⋀[2]	296	20.00 S	46.20 W
Canatlán	278	24.31 N	104.47 W
Cañaveras	168	40.22 N	2.24 W
Canavese ➛[1]	182	45.20 N	7.40 E
Canavieiras	296	15.39 S	38.57 W
Cañazas	280	8.25 N	81.10 W
Cañazas, Serranía de ⋀	290	8.54 N	78.30 W
Canberra	228	35.17 S	149.08 E
Canby, Calif., U.S.	258	41.27 N	120.52 W
Canby, Minn., U.S.	252	44.43 N	96.16 W
Canby, Oreg., U.S.	270	45.16 N	122.42 W
Cancajanang, Mount Λ	202	11.02 N	124.49 E
Cancale	166	48.41 N	1.51 W
Canchaque	292	5.18 S	79.35 W
Canche ≃	166	50.31 N	1.39 E
Canchyuaya, Cerros de ⋀	292	7.10 S	74.30 W
Cancon	166	44.32 N	0.38 E
Cancuén ≃	280	16.00 N	89.58 W
Cancún, Punta ➤	278	21.08 N	86.45 W
Candarave	292	17.15 S	70.13 W
Çandarlı	172	38.56 N	26.56 E
Çandarlı Körfezi C	212	38.52 N	26.55 E
Candás	168	43.35 N	5.46 W
Candé	166	47.34 N	1.02 W
Candeias, Bra.	296	20.47 S	45.16 W
Candeias, Bra.	296	12.40 S	38.33 W
Candeias ≃	292	8.39 S	63.31 W
Candela	278	26.50 N	100.40 W
Candela, Río de ≃	278	27.16 N	100.18 W
Candelaria, Arg.	294	27.28 S	55.44 W
Candelaria, Arg.	294	32.04 S	65.50 W
Candelária, Bra.	294	29.40 S	52.48 W
Candelaria, Col.	290	3.25 N	76.20 W
Candelaria, Cuba	284p	22.44 N	82.58 W
Candelaria, Pil.	202	15.38 N	119.56 E
Candelaria ≃	278	18.32 N	91.15 W
Candelaria, Cerro Λ	278	23.25 N	103.43 W
Candeleda	168	40.09 N	5.14 W
Candia → Iráklion	172	35.20 N	25.09 E
Candiac	260	45.23 N	73.33 W
Cándido Aguilar	278	25.30 N	98.02 W
Cândido de Abreu	294	24.35 S	51.20 W
Candijay	202	9.49 N	124.30 E
Candle	236	65.55 N	161.56 W
Candlewood, Lake ⊜	242	41.32 N	73.27 W
Candlewood Isle	261	41.29 N	73.27 W
Candlewood Knolls	261	41.29 N	73.28 W
Candlewood Shores	261	41.29 N	73.26 W
Cando	252	48.32 N	99.12 W
Candon	202	17.12 N	120.27 E
Candor, N.C., U.S.	246	35.18 N	79.45 W
Candor, N.Y., U.S.	242	42.14 N	76.21 W
Cane ≃	246	36.00 N	82.16 W
Canea → Khaniá	172	35.31 N	24.02 E
Canela	294	29.22 S	50.50 W
Canelles, Embalse de ⊜[1]	168	42.10 N	0.30 E
Canelli	182	44.43 N	8.17 E
Canelones	294	34.32 S	56.17 W
Cañete, Chile	294	37.48 S	73.24 W
Cañete, Esp.	168	40.03 N	1.35 W
Cañete, Perú	292	13.08 S	76.28 W
Cañete ≃	292	13.10 S	76.24 W
Caney	252	37.01 N	95.56 W
Caney ≃	250	36.20 N	95.42 W
Canfield, Ark., U.S.	248	33.11 N	93.38 W
Canfield, Ohio, U.S.	266	41.06 N	80.46 W
Canfranc	168	42.43 N	0.31 W
Cangallo	292	13.35 S	74.08 W
Cangas, Bra.	292	16.05 S	56.33 W
Cangas, Esp.	168	42.16 N	8.47 W
Cangas de Narcea	168	43.11 N	6.33 W
Cangas de Onís	168	43.21 N	5.07 W
Cangombe	218	14.24 S	19.59 E
Cangreja, Cerros de ⋀	280	15.35 N	86.55 W
Canguçu	294	31.24 S	52.41 W
Cangyuan	200	23.12 N	99.16 E
Cangzhou	194	38.19 N	116.51 E
Caniapiscau ≃	232	57.40 N	69.30 W
Caniapiscau, Lac ⊜	232	54.15 N	69.50 W
Canicanian	202	14.46 N	122.01 E
Canicattì	170	37.21 N	13.51 E
Canigao Channel Ų	202	10.08 N	124.42 E
Canigou, Mont Λ	168	42.31 N	2.27 E
Canim Lake	238	51.46 N	120.54 W
Canim Lake ⊜	238	51.52 N	120.45 W
Canim Lake Indian Reserve ➛[4]	238	51.47 N	121.00 W
Canimo Island I	202	14.07 N	123.04 E
Canipaan	202	8.35 N	117.16 E
Canipo Island I	202	10.59 N	120.57 E
Canisteo	266	42.16 N	77.36 W
Canisteo ≃	242	42.07 N	77.08 W
Canistota	252	43.36 N	97.18 W
Cañitas	278	23.36 N	102.43 W
Canjáyar	168	37.00 N	2.44 W
Çankırı	212	40.36 N	33.37 E
Canlaon	202	10.24 N	123.12 E
Canlaon Volcano Λ[1]	202	10.24 N	123.08 E
Canmore	238	51.05 N	115.21 W
Canna I	162	57.03 N	6.33 W
Cannel City	246	37.47 N	83.17 W
Cannelton	248	37.55 N	86.45 W
Cannes	182	43.33 N	7.01 E
Cannifton	264	44.12 N	77.23 W
Canning	240	45.09 N	64.25 W
Cannington	264	44.21 N	79.02 W
Cannock	174	52.42 N	2.09 W
Cannon ≃	244	44.35 N	92.33 W
Cannonball ≃	252	46.26 N	100.38 W
Cannon Beach	270	45.55 N	123.57 W
Cannondale	261	41.08 N	73.16 W
Cannon Falls	244	44.31 N	92.54 W
Caño, Isla del I	280	8.43 N	83.53 W
Canoas	294	29.56 S	51.11 W
Canoe	238	50.45 N	119.13 W
Canoe ≃	238	52.09 N	118.27 W
Canoe Creek Indian Reserve ➛[4]	238	51.32 N	122.15 W
Canoinhas	294	26.10 S	50.24 W
Canol	236	65.14 N	126.56 W
Canon	246	34.21 N	83.07 W
Canoncito Indian Reservation ➛[4]	254	35.15 N	107.00 W
Canon City	254	38.27 N	105.14 W
Caño Negro	280	10.54 N	84.44 W
Canonsburg	266	40.16 N	80.11 W
Canoochee ≃	246	31.59 N	81.18 W
Canora	232	51.37 N	102.26 W
Canosa di Puglia	170	41.13 N	16.04 E
Canossa ⊥	170	44.35 N	10.27 E
Canouan I	282	12.43 N	61.20 W
Canova	252	43.53 N	97.30 W
Canova Beach	246	28.08 N	80.34 W
Canso	240	45.20 N	61.00 W
Canso, Strait of Ų	240	45.37 N	61.25 W
Canta	292	11.29 S	76.37 W
Cantábrica, Cordillera ⋀	168	43.00 N	5.00 W
Cantagalo	296	21.58 S	42.22 W
Cantagalo, Cachoeira ↳	292	7.18 S	54.52 W
Cantal □[5]	166	45.05 N	2.45 E
Cantal ⋀	166	45.10 N	2.40 E
Cantalejo	168	41.15 N	3.55 W
Čantal'vejergyn ≃	236	67.38 N	179.22 W
Cantanhede	168	40.21 N	8.36 W
Cantaura	290	9.19 N	64.21 W
Canteleu	176	49.27 N	1.02 E
Canterbury, N.B., Can.	240	45.53 N	67.29 W
Canterbury, Eng., U.K.	174	51.17 N	1.05 E
Canterbury □[9]	230	44.20 S	171.20 E
Canterbury Bight C[3]	230	44.20 S	172.00 E
Canterbury Plains ≚	230	44.00 S	171.20 E
Canterbury Station	242	45.53 N	67.29 W
Can-tho	200	10.02 N	105.47 E
Cantil	274	35.18 N	117.58 W
Cantiles, Cayo I	284p	21.35 N	82.01 W
Canton, Conn., U.S.	261	41.49 N	72.54 W
Canton, Ga., U.S.	246	34.14 N	84.29 W
Canton, Ill., U.S.	244	40.33 N	90.02 W
Canton, Kans., U.S.	252	38.23 N	97.26 W
Canton, Maine, U.S.	242	44.28 N	70.19 W
Canton, Mass., U.S.	261	42.09 N	71.09 W
Canton, Minn., U.S.	244	43.32 N	91.56 W
Canton, Miss., U.S.	248	32.37 N	90.02 W
Canton, N.J., U.S.	262	39.28 N	75.25 W
Canton, N.C., U.S.	246	35.32 N	82.50 W
Canton, N.Y., U.S.	242	44.36 N	75.10 W
Canton, Ohio, U.S.	266	40.48 N	81.22 W
Canton, Okla., U.S.	250	36.03 N	98.35 W
Canton, Pa., U.S.	242	41.39 N	76.51 W
Canton, S. Dak., U.S.	252	43.18 N	96.35 W
Canton, Tex., U.S.	250	32.33 N	95.52 W
Canton → Guangzhou, Zhg.	196	23.06 N	113.16 E
Cantonment	248	30.38 N	87.19 W
Canton Reservoir ⊜[1]	250	36.08 N	98.36 W
Cantù	182	45.44 N	9.08 E
Cantu ≃	294	24.46 S	52.54 W
Cantua Creek	272	36.30 N	120.19 W
Cantwell	236	63.23 N	148.57 W
Cañuelas	294	35.03 S	58.44 W
Canumã	290	4.02 S	59.04 W
Canutama	292	6.32 S	64.20 W
Canutillo	254	31.55 N	106.36 W
Canvey	174	51.32 N	0.36 E
Čany, Ozero ⊜	186	54.50 N	77.30 E
Cany-Barville	166	49.47 N	0.38 E
Canyon, Yukon, Can.	236	60.52 N	137.02 W
Canyon, Calif., U.S.	272	37.49 N	122.09 W
Canyon, Tex., U.S.	250	34.59 N	101.55 W
Canyon City	256	44.23 N	118.57 W
Canyon Creek	238	54.22 N	115.05 W
Canyon de Chelly National Monument ♠	254	36.01 N	109.26 W
Canyon Ferry Lake ⊜[1]	256	46.33 N	111.37 W
Canyon Lake ⊜[1]	250	29.52 N	98.16 W
Canyonlands National Park ♠	254	38.10 N	110.00 W
Canyonville	256	42.56 N	123.17 W
Cao-bang	198	22.40 N	106.15 E
Cao'ejiang ≃	196	30.06 N	120.46 E
Caohe ≃	194	40.29 N	124.08 E
Caonao ≃	284p	22.04 N	78.05 W
Caorle	170	45.36 N	12.53 E
Caoxian	194	34.53 N	115.33 E
Cap, Pointe du ➤	282	14.07 N	60.57 W
Capac	244	43.01 N	82.56 W
Čapajevsk	160	52.58 N	49.41 E
Capalonga	202	14.20 N	122.30 E
Capanaparo ≃	290	7.01 N	67.07 W
Capanema	294	25.40 S	53.48 W
Capannori	184	43.50 N	10.34 E
Capão Bonito	296	24.01 S	48.20 W
Capão Doce, Morro do Λ	294	26.43 S	51.25 W
Capaotigamau, Lac ⊜	240	50.16 N	68.15 W
Capas	202	15.20 N	120.35 E
Capatárida	290	11.11 N	70.37 W
Căpățînei, Culmea ⋀	172	45.20 N	24.00 E
Cap-Chat	240	48.02 N	65.20 W
Cap-de-la-Madeleine	260	46.22 N	72.32 W
Cape ≃	228	20.49 S	146.51 E
Cape Barren Island I	228	40.25 S	148.12 E
Cape Basin ✣[1]	148	35.00 S	5.00 E
Cape Breton Highlands National Park ♠	240	46.45 N	60.45 W
Cape Breton Island I	240	46.00 N	60.30 W
Cape Broyle	240	47.05 N	52.57 W
Cape Canaveral	246	28.24 N	80.37 W
Cape Charles	262	37.16 N	76.01 W
Cape Coast	222	5.05 N	1.15 W
Cape Cod National Seashore ♠	242	41.56 N	70.06 W
Cape Dorset	232	64.14 N	76.32 W
Cape Elizabeth	242	43.34 N	70.12 W
Cape Fear ≃	246	33.53 N	78.00 W
Cape Girardeau	248	37.19 N	89.32 W
Cape Hatteras National Seashore ♠	246	35.30 N	76.35 W
Cape La Hune	240	47.33 N	56.53 W
Capelinha	296	17.42 S	42.31 W
Cape Lisburne	236	68.52 N	166.05 W
Capelle aan de IJssel	178	51.55 N	4.35 E
Cape May	262	38.56 N	74.55 W
Cape May □[6]	262	38.56 N	74.55 W
Cape May Court House	262	39.05 N	74.50 W
Cape May Point	262	38.56 N	74.58 W
Cape of Good Hope (Kaap) □[4]	224	31.00 S	23.00 E
Cape Pole	236	55.58 N	133.48 W
Cape Porpoise	242	43.22 N	70.26 W
Cape Rise ✣[3]	148	41.00 S	13.00 E
Capernaum ⊥	210	32.57 N	35.55 E
Cape Romanzof	236	61.49 N	165.56 W
Cape Sable Island I	240	43.25 N	65.37 W
Capesterre, Guad.	285o	16.03 N	61.34 W
Capesterre, Guad.	285o	15.54 N	61.13 W
Cape Tormentine	240	46.08 N	63.47 W
Cape Town (Kaapstad)	224	33.55 S	18.22 E
Cape Verde Basin ✣[1]	148	14.00 N	33.00 W
Cape Verde Islands □[2]	214	16.00 N	24.00 W
Cape Verde Terrace ✣[3]	148	18.00 N	20.00 W
Capeville	262	37.12 N	75.57 W
Cape Vincent	264	44.08 N	76.20 W
Cape Yakataga	236	60.04 N	142.26 W
Cap-Haïtien	282	19.45 N	72.15 W
Capiibarý ≃	294	24.06 S	56.26 W
Capilla de Farruco	294	32.53 S	55.25 W
Capilla del Monte	294	30.50 S	64.32 W
Capinas Point ➤	202	11.04 N	125.13 E
Capinópolis	296	18.41 S	49.35 W
Capinota	292	17.43 S	66.14 W
Capinzal	294	27.20 S	51.36 W
Capinzal, Cachoeira ↳	292	8.42 S	58.18 W
Capira	280	8.45 N	79.54 W
Cap Island I	202	5.58 N	120.07 E
Capistrano Beach	274	33.27 N	117.40 W
Capistrello	184	41.57 N	13.23 E
Capitachouane ≃	244	47.40 N	76.47 W
Capitan	254	33.35 N	105.35 W
Capitanata ➛[1]	170	41.25 N	15.30 E
Capitán Bado	294	23.16 S	55.32 W
Capitán Bermúdez	294	32.50 S	60.40 W
Capitán Meza	294	26.55 S	55.15 W
Capitan Peak Λ	254	33.36 N	105.16 W
Capitán Sarmiento	294	34.10 S	59.50 W
Capitão, Igarapé ≃	292	5.58 S	64.48 W
Capitão Noronha, Ribeirão ≃	296	13.19 S	54.36 W
Capitari	290	0.59 N	61.24 W
Capitola	272	36.59 N	121.57 W
Capitol Heights	262	38.53 N	76.55 W
Capitol Park	262	39.08 N	75.30 W
Capitol Peak Λ	258	41.50 N	117.18 W
Capitol Reef National Monument ♠	254	38.11 N	111.20 W
Capitol View	246	33.57 N	80.56 W
Capivara, Lago ⊜	290	3.40 S	59.28 W
Capivari	296	23.00 S	47.31 W
Capiz → Roxas	202	11.35 N	122.45 E
Capiz □[4]	202	11.30 N	122.30 E
Caplan	240	48.06 N	65.41 W
Čaplino	236	64.25 N	172.15 W
Čapljina	170	43.07 N	17.42 E
Cap Mountain Λ	236	63.25 N	123.29 W
Capnoyan Island I	202	10.44 N	120.54 E
Capoti-an, Mount Λ	202	11.45 N	125.15 E
Capotoan, Mount Λ	202	12.09 N	124.56 E
Cap-Pelé	240	46.13 N	64.18 W
Capraia	170	43.03 N	9.50 E
Capraia, Isola di I	170	43.02 N	9.49 E
Caprara, Punta ➤	170	41.07 N	8.19 E
Caprarola	184	42.19 N	12.14 E
Capreol	244	46.43 N	80.56 W
Capri	184	40.33 N	14.14 E
Capricorn, Cape ➤	228	23.30 S	151.13 E
Capricorn Group II	228	23.28 S	152.00 E
Caprivi Strip □[9], S.W. Afr.	218	23.00 S	17.59 E
Caprivi Strip (Caprivizipfel) □[9], S.W. Afr.	224	23.00 S	17.59 E
Capron, Ill., U.S.	268	42.24 N	88.44 W
Capron, Va., U.S.	262	36.42 N	77.11 W
Cap-Santé	260	46.40 N	71.47 W
Cap-St.-Jacques → Vung-tau	200	10.21 N	107.04 E
Captain Cook	275d	19.30 N	155.55 W
Captains Flat	228	35.35 S	149.27 E
Captieux	166	44.18 N	0.16 W
Capua	184	41.06 N	14.12 E
Capul	202	12.25 N	124.11 E
Capulín, Río del ≃	250	27.31 N	101.33 W
Capulin Mountain National Monument ♠	250	36.48 N	103.55 W
Capul Island I	202	12.25 N	124.10 E
Caquetá □[8]	290	1.00 N	74.00 W
Caquetá (Japurá) ≃	290	3.08 S	64.46 W
Caquiaviri	292	17.03 S	68.38 W
Čara	186	56.54 N	118.12 E
Čara ≃	186	60.22 N	120.50 E
Carabao Island I	202	12.04 N	121.56 E
Carabaya, Cordillera de ⋀	292	14.00 S	70.00 W
Carabobo □[3]	290	10.10 N	68.05 W
Caracal	172	44.07 N	24.21 E
Caracaraí	290	1.50 N	61.08 W
Caracas	290	10.30 N	66.56 W
Carache	290	9.38 N	70.14 W
Caracol	294	22.01 S	57.02 W
Caracollo	292	17.39 S	67.10 W
Caraga	202	7.19 N	126.33 E
Caraga ≃	202	7.20 N	126.33 E
Caraghnan Mountain Λ	228	31.20 S	149.03 E
Caraguatatuba	296	23.37 S	45.25 W
Caraguatay	294	25.14 S	56.52 W
Caraí	296	17.12 S	41.42 W
Caraigres, Cerro Λ	280	9.43 N	84.08 W
Caramay	202	10.10 N	119.14 E
Caramiñas	168	43.09 N	9.15 W
Caramoan	202	13.46 N	123.53 E
Caramoan Peninsula ➤[1]	202	13.50 N	123.40 E
Caramoran	202	13.59 N	124.08 E
Caranavi	292	15.46 S	67.36 W
Carandaí	296	20.57 S	43.48 W
Carandaiti	292	20.45 S	63.04 W
Carangola	296	20.44 S	42.02 W
Caransebeș	172	45.25 N	22.13 E
Caraparaná ≃	290	1.45 S	73.13 W
Caraparí	292	21.49 S	63.46 W
Carapeguá	294	25.48 S	57.14 W
Carapó	296	22.38 S	54.48 W
Carappee Hill Λ[2]	228	33.26 S	136.16 E
Caraquet	240	47.48 N	64.57 W
Carare ≃	290	6.48 N	74.06 W
Carata, Laguna C	280	13.57 N	83.29 W
Caratasca, Laguna de C	280	15.20 N	83.50 W
Carate Brianza	182	45.41 N	9.14 E
Caratinga	296	19.47 S	42.08 W
Carauari	290	4.52 S	66.54 W
Caravaca	168	38.06 N	1.51 W
Caravaggio	182	45.30 N	9.38 E
Caravela, Ilha I	222	11.30 N	16.20 W
Caravelas	296	17.45 S	39.15 W
Caravelí	292	15.47 S	73.37 W
Caraway	248	35.46 N	90.19 W
Carayaó	294	25.10 S	56.26 W
Caraybamba	292	14.24 S	73.09 W
Caraz	292	9.03 S	77.45 W
Caràzinho	294	28.18 S	52.48 W
Carazo □[5]	280	11.45 N	86.15 W
Carballino	168	42.26 N	8.04 W
Carballo	168	43.13 N	8.41 W
Carberry	252	49.52 N	99.20 W
Carbó	278	29.42 N	110.58 W
Carbon, Alta., Can.	238	51.29 N	113.09 W
Carbon, Tex., U.S.	250	32.16 N	98.50 W
Carbon, Cap ➤	168	36.49 N	5.04 E
Carbonado	270	47.05 N	122.03 W
Carbonara, Capo ➤	170	39.06 N	9.31 E
Carbon-Blanc	166	44.53 N	0.31 W
Carbondale, Colo., U.S.	254	39.24 N	107.13 W
Carbondale, Ill., U.S.	248	37.44 N	89.13 W
Carbondale, Kans., U.S.	252	38.49 N	95.41 W
Carbondale, Pa., U.S.	242	41.35 N	75.30 W
Carbonear	240	47.45 N	53.14 W
Carboneras	168	39.53 N	1.48 W
Carbon Hill	248	33.48 N	87.32 W
Carbonia	170	39.11 N	8.32 E
Carbonin	170	46.37 N	12.13 E
Carcagente	168	39.08 N	0.27 W
Carcajou ≃	236	65.37 N	128.43 W
Carcans, Étang de C	166	45.08 N	1.08 W
Carcar	202	10.06 N	123.38 E
Carcarañá	294	32.52 S	61.09 W
Carcarañá ≃	294	32.27 S	60.48 W
Carcar Point ➤	202	10.05 N	123.40 E
Carcassonne	166	43.13 N	2.21 E
Carcastillo	168	42.23 N	1.26 W
Carchi □[4]	290	0.45 N	78.00 W
Carcross	236	60.10 N	134.42 W
Cárdenas, Cuba	284p	23.05 N	81.10 W
Cárdenas, Méx.	278	22.00 N	99.40 W
Cárdenas, Méx.	278	17.59 N	93.22 W
Cárdenas, Nic.	280	11.12 N	85.31 W
Cárdenas, Bahía de C	284p	23.05 N	81.09 W
Çardi	172	39.41 N	29.10 E
Cardiel, Lago ⊜	288	48.55 S	71.10 W
Cardiff, Wales, U.K.	174	51.29 N	3.13 W
Cardiff, Md., U.S.	262	39.42 N	76.20 W
Cardiff, N.J., U.S.	262	39.25 N	74.36 W
Cardiff-by-the-Sea	274	33.01 N	117.17 W
Cardigan, P.E.I., Can.	240	46.14 N	62.37 W
Cardigan, Wales, U.K.	162	52.06 N	4.40 W
Cardigan Bay C	240	46.10 N	62.30 W
Cardiganshire □[6]	174	52.15 N	4.00 W
Cardinal	264	44.47 N	75.23 W
Cardinal Heights	264	45.27 N	75.37 W
Cardinal Lake	266	41.37 N	80.54 W
Cardinal Lake ⊜	238	56.14 N	117.44 W
Cardington	266	40.30 N	82.53 W
Cardito	184	40.57 N	14.18 E
Cardón, Punta ➤	290	11.37 N	70.14 W
Cardona	294	33.53 S	57.23 W
Cardoner ≃	168	41.41 N	1.51 E
Cardoso	296	20.04 S	49.54 W
Cardozo	294	32.38 S	56.21 W
Cardston	238	49.12 N	113.18 W
Cardwell	248	36.03 N	90.17 W
Cardwell Mountain Λ	248	35.41 N	85.41 W
Čardžou	208	39.06 N	63.34 E
Čardžou □[4]	208	38.51 N	63.34 E
Carei	172	47.42 N	22.28 E
Careiro	290	3.12 S	59.45 W
Careiro, Ilha do I	290	3.10 S	59.44 W
Carén	294	30.51 S	70.47 W
Carencro	248	30.19 N	92.03 W
Carentan	166	49.18 N	1.14 W
Cares ≃	168	43.19 N	4.36 W
Caretta	246	37.20 N	81.41 W
Carey, Ohio, U.S.	266	40.57 N	83.23 W
Carey, Tex., U.S.	250	34.28 N	100.20 W
Carhaix-Plouguer	166	48.17 N	3.35 W
Carhuamayo	292	10.51 S	76.04 W
Carhuanca	292	13.45 S	73.47 W
Carhuaz	292	9.10 S	77.40 W
Carhué	294	37.11 S	62.45 W
Cariacica	296	20.16 S	40.25 W
Cariaco	290	10.29 N	63.33 W
Cariaco, Golfo de C	290	10.30 N	64.00 W
Cariamanga	290	4.20 S	79.35 W
Cariati	170	39.30 N	16.56 E
Caribana, Punta ➤	290	8.37 N	76.52 W
Caribbean Sea ▼[2]	276	15.00 N	73.00 W
Cariboo ≃	238	52.40 N	121.40 W
Cariboo Mountains ⋀	238	53.00 N	121.00 W
Caribou	240	46.52 N	68.01 W
Caribou ≃	232	59.20 N	94.44 W
Caribou Mountain Λ, Idaho, U.S.	256	43.06 N	111.18 W
Caribou Mountain Λ, Maine, U.S.	242	45.26 N	70.38 W
Caribou Mountains ⋀	232	59.12 N	115.40 W
Caribou Range ⋀	256	43.05 N	111.15 W
Carichic	278	27.56 N	107.03 W
Caridad	202	10.50 N	124.45 E
Carigara	202	11.18 N	124.41 E
Carigara Bay C	202	11.25 N	124.40 E
Carignan	166	49.38 N	5.10 E
Carignano	182	44.55 N	7.40 E
Cariñena	168	41.20 N	1.13 W
Carinhanha	296	14.18 S	43.47 W
Carinhanha ≃	296	14.20 S	43.47 W
Carini	170	38.08 N	13.11 E
Carinola	184	41.11 N	13.58 E
Caripe	290	10.12 N	63.29 W
Caripito	290	10.08 N	63.06 W
Carlentini	170	37.16 N	15.02 E
Carles	202	11.35 N	123.08 E
Carlet	168	39.14 N	0.31 W
Carleton, Mich., U.S.	268	42.04 N	83.23 W
Carleton, Nebr., U.S.	252	40.18 N	97.41 W
Carleton □[6]	264	45.15 N	75.45 W
Carleton, Mount Λ	240	47.23 N	66.53 W
Carleton Place	264	45.08 N	76.09 W
Carletonville	224	26.23 S	27.22 E
Carlin	258	40.43 N	116.07 W
Carlinville	248	39.17 N	89.53 W
Carlisle, Ont., Can.	264	43.23 N	79.59 W
Carlisle, Eng., U.K.	162	54.54 N	2.25 W
Carlisle, Ark., U.S.	248	34.47 N	91.45 W
Carlisle, Iowa, U.S.	244	41.30 N	93.29 W
Carlisle, Ky., U.S.	242	38.19 N	84.02 W
Carlisle, Pa., U.S.	262	40.12 N	77.12 W
Carlisle Gardens	264	43.11 N	78.39 W
Carlisle Island I	236	52.52 N	170.02 W
Carlisle Springs	262	40.16 N	77.10 W
Carl Junction	248	37.11 N	94.34 W
Carloforte	170	39.08 N	8.18 E
Carlópolis	296	23.25 S	49.41 W
Carlos Barbosa	294	29.18 S	51.30 W
Carlos Casares	294	35.37 S	61.22 W
Carlos Chagas	296	17.43 S	40.45 W
Carlos Pellegrini	294	32.02 S	61.45 W
Carlos Reyles	294	33.03 S	56.29 W
Carlos Tejedor	294	35.23 S	62.25 W
Carlow	162	52.50 N	6.55 W
Carlow □[6]	162	52.50 N	7.00 W
Carloway	162	58.17 N	6.48 W
Carlsbad → Karlovy Vary, Česko.	164	50.11 N	12.52 E
Carlsbad, Calif., U.S.	274	33.10 N	117.21 W
Carlsbad, N. Mex., U.S.	250	32.25 N	104.14 W
Carlsbad, Tex., U.S.	250	31.36 N	100.38 W
Carlsbad Caverns National Park ♠	250	32.08 N	104.35 W
Carlsberg Ridge ✣[3]	148	4.00 N	65.00 E
Carlsborg	270	48.05 N	123.10 W
Carlton, Eng., U.K.	174	52.58 N	1.05 W
Carlton, Minn., U.S.	244	46.40 N	92.25 W
Carlton, Oreg., U.S.	270	45.18 N	123.11 W
Carlton, Tex., U.S.	250	31.55 N	98.10 W
Carlyle, Sask., Can.	252	49.38 N	102.16 W
Carlyle, Ill., U.S.	248	38.37 N	89.22 W
Carlyle Reservoir ⊜[1]	248	38.40 N	89.18 W
Carmacks	236	62.05 N	136.18 W
Carmagnola	182	44.51 N	7.43 E
Carman	252	49.32 N	98.00 W
Carmangay	238	50.08 N	113.07 W

Symbols in the index entries are identified on page 360.

Name	Page	Lat°′	Long°′
Carman Hill ∧[2]	242	41.54 N	77.58 W
Carmanville	240	49.24 N	54.17 W
Carmarthen	174	51.52 N	4.19 W
Carmarthenshire □[6]	174	51.52 N	4.15 W
Carmaux	166	44.03 N	2.09 E
Carmel, Calif., U.S.	272	36.33 N	121.55 W
Carmel, Ind., U.S.	248	39.59 N	86.08 W
Carmel, N.J., U.S.	262	39.26 N	75.06 W
Carmel, N.Y., U.S.	261	41.26 N	73.41 W
Carmel Highlands	272	36.30 N	121.56 W
Carmel Hills	272	36.32 N	121.53 W
Carmelo	294	34.00 S	58.17 W
Carmel Point	272	36.31 N	122.55 W
Carmel Valley	272	36.29 N	121.43 W
Carmel Woods	272	36.34 N	121.54 W
Carmen, Pil.	202	9.50 N	124.12 E
Carmen, Pil.	202	10.35 N	124.01 E
Carmen, Pil.	202	8.59 N	125.20 E
Carmen, Pil.	202	12.37 N	122.07 E
Carmen, Okla., U.S.	250	36.35 N	98.28 W
Carmen, Ur.	294	33.15 S	56.01 W
Carmen, Isla I	278	25.55 N	111.10 W
Carmen, Isla del I	278	18.42 N	91.40 W
Carmen, Laguna del C	278	18.17 N	93.48 W
Carmen, Río del ≃, Chile	294	28.45 S	70.30 W
Carmen, Río del ≃, Méx.	278	30.42 N	106.29 W
Carmen Alto	294	23.11 S	69.40 W
Carmen de Apicalá	290	4.09 N	74.44 W
Carmen de Areco	294	34.20 S	59.50 W
Carmen de Patagones	288	40.48 S	63.00 W
Carmichael	272	38.38 N	121.19 W
Carmichael Point ≻	282	21.11 N	73.23 W
Carmine	250	30.09 N	96.41 W
Carmo	296	21.56 S	42.37 W
Carmo do Paranaíba	296	18.59 S	46.21 W
Carmo do Rio Verde	296	15.21 S	49.42 W
Carmona, Ang.	218	7.37 S	15.03 E
Carmona, Esp.	168	37.28 N	5.38 W
Carmona, Pil.	202	14.19 N	121.03 E
Carmópolis de Minas	296	20.33 S	44.38 W
Carnarvon, Austl.	226	24.53 S	113.40 E
Carnarvon, S. Afr.	218	30.56 S	22.08 E
Carnarvon Gorge National Park ♠	228	25.00 S	148.15 E
Carnasa Island I	202	11.31 N	124.05 E
Carnation	270	47.39 N	121.55 W
Carndonagh	162	55.15 N	7.15 W
Carnduff	252	49.10 N	101.50 W
Carnegie, N.Y., U.S.	264	42.45 N	78.51 W
Carnegie, Okla., U.S.	250	35.06 N	98.36 W
Carnegie, Pa., U.S.	266	40.24 N	80.06 W
Carnelian Bay	272	39.14 N	120.05 W
Carneys Point	262	39.43 N	75.28 W
Carniche, Alpi ⛰	170	46.40 N	13.00 E
Car Nicobar Island I	200	9.10 N	92.45 E
Carnot	266	40.31 N	80.13 W
Carnot, Cape ≻	228	34.57 S	135.38 E
Carnoustie	162	56.30 N	2.44 W
Carnsore Point ≻	162	52.10 N	6.22 W
Carnwath ≃	236	68.26 N	128.52 W
Caro	244	43.29 N	83.24 W
Carol City	246	25.56 N	80.16 W
Caroleen	246	35.17 N	81.48 W
Carolina, Bra.	286	7.20 S	47.28 W
Carolina, Col.	290	6.43 N	75.17 W
Carolina, El Sal.	280	13.51 N	88.19 W
Carolina, P.R.	284m	18.23 N	65.57 W
Carolina, R.I., U.S.	261	41.28 N	71.40 W
Carolina Beach	246	34.02 N	77.54 W
Caroline □[6], Md., U.S.	262	38.53 N	75.50 W
Caroline □[6], Va., U.S.	262	38.00 N	77.20 W
Caroline Islands II	198	8.00 N	147.00 E
Caroline-New Guinea Ridge ⟡[3]	148	4.00 N	141.30 E
Caroline Peak ∧	230	45.56 S	167.13 E
Caron, Lac ⊜	244	48.00 N	78.55 W
Čaronda	160	60.34 N	38.59 E
Caroní ≃	290	8.21 N	62.43 W
Carora	290	10.11 N	70.05 W
Carouge	180	46.11 N	6.09 E
Carp	264	45.21 N	76.02 W
Carpathian Mountains ⛰	158	48.00 N	24.00 E
Carpații Meridionali ⛰	172	45.30 N	24.15 E
Carpenter	252	41.03 N	104.22 W
Carpenter Lake ⊜	238	51.00 N	122.55 W
Carpentersville	268	42.07 N	88.17 W
Carpentras	182	44.03 N	5.03 E
Carpi	170	44.47 N	10.53 E
Carpineto Romano	184	41.36 N	13.05 E
Carpino	184	41.51 N	15.51 E
Carpinteria	258	34.24 N	119.31 W
Carpio	252	48.27 N	101.43 W
Carp Lake ⊜	238	54.45 N	123.20 W
Carquefou	166	47.18 N	1.30 W
Carrabelle	246	29.51 N	84.40 W
Carrancas	296	21.30 S	44.39 W
Carranglan	202	15.58 N	121.04 E
Carrantuohill ∧	162	52.00 N	9.45 W
Carranza, Cabo ≻	294	35.36 S	72.38 W
Carrao ≃	290	6.17 N	62.51 W
Carrara	170	44.05 N	10.06 E
Carrascal	202	9.22 N	125.56 E
Carrboro	246	35.54 N	79.04 W
Carreria	294	21.59 S	58.35 W
Carreta, Punta ≻	292	14.12 S	76.17 W
Carriacou I	282	12.25 N	61.30 W
Carrickfergus	162	54.43 N	5.49 W
Carrickmacross	162	53.58 N	6.43 W
Carrick on Shannon	162	53.57 N	8.05 W
Carrick on Suir	162	52.21 N	7.25 W
Carriere	248	30.32 N	89.39 W
Carrière, Lac ⊜	244	47.15 N	77.12 W
Carriers Mills	248	37.41 N	88.38 W
Carrillo, C.R.	280	9.52 N	85.30 W
Carrillo, Méx.	278	26.54 N	103.55 W
Carrington	252	47.27 N	99.08 W
Carrión ≃	168	41.53 N	4.32 W
Carrión de los Condes	168	42.20 N	4.36 W
Carrizal, Cerro ∧	250	26.45 N	100.35 W
Carrizal Bajo	294	28.05 S	71.10 W
Carrizo	168	42.35 N	5.50 W
Carrizo Mountains ⛰	254	36.35 N	109.00 W
Carrizo Springs	250	28.31 N	99.52 W
Carrizozo	254	33.38 N	105.53 W
Carroll, Iowa, U.S.	252	42.04 N	94.52 W
Carroll, Nebr., U.S.	252	42.17 N	97.17 W
Carroll □[6], Ind., U.S.	268	40.36 N	86.41 W
Carroll □[6], Md., U.S.	262	39.35 N	77.00 W
Carroll □[6], Ohio, U.S.	266	40.34 N	81.05 W
Carrollton, Ala., U.S.	248	33.16 N	88.05 W
Carrollton, Ga., U.S.	246	33.35 N	85.05 W
Carrollton, Ill., U.S.	248	39.18 N	90.24 W
Carrollton, Ky., U.S.	248	38.41 N	85.11 W
Carrollton, Mich., U.S.	244	43.27 N	83.54 W
Carrollton, Miss., U.S.	248	33.30 N	89.55 W
Carrollton, Mo., U.S.	248	39.22 N	93.30 W
Carrollton, Ohio, U.S.	266	40.34 N	81.05 W
Carrollton, Tex., U.S.	250	32.57 N	96.54 W
Carrollton Manor	262	39.05 N	76.35 W
Carrolltown	266	40.36 N	78.43 W
Carrols	270	46.05 N	122.52 W
Carrot ≃	232	53.50 N	101.17 W
Carrouges	162	48.34 N	0.09 W
Carrowmore Lake ⊜	162	54.12 N	9.47 W
Carrsville	262	36.43 N	76.50 W
Carrville	248	32.33 N	85.52 W
Carry Falls Reservoir ⊜[1]	242	44.25 N	74.45 W
Çarşamba	212	41.12 N	36.44 E
Carseland	238	50.51 N	113.28 W
Čarsk	186	49.35 N	81.05 E
Carsoli	184	42.06 N	13.05 E
Carson, Calif., U.S.	274	33.50 N	118.16 W
Carson, N. Dak., U.S.	252	46.25 N	101.34 W
Carson, Va., U.S.	262	37.02 N	77.24 W
Carson, Wash., U.S.	270	45.44 N	121.49 W
Carson ≃	258	39.45 N	118.40 W
Carson City, Mich., U.S.	244	43.11 N	84.51 W
Carson City, Nev., U.S.	272	39.10 N	119.46 W
Carson Lake ⊜	258	39.19 N	118.43 W
Carson Range ⛰	258	39.15 N	120.20 W
Carson Sink ⊜	258	39.45 N	118.30 W
Carstairs	238	51.34 N	114.06 W
Carstensz-Toppen → Djaja, Puntjak ∧	198	4.05 S	137.11 E
Cartagena, Chile	294	33.33 S	71.37 W
Cartagena, Col.	290	10.25 N	75.32 W
Cartagena, Esp.	168	37.36 N	0.59 W
Cartago, Col.	290	4.45 N	75.55 W
Cartago, C.R.	280	9.52 N	83.55 W
Cartago □[4]	280	9.50 N	83.45 W
Cartaxo	168	39.09 N	8.47 W
Cartaya	168	37.17 N	7.09 W
Carter	250	35.13 N	99.30 W
Carteret, Fr.	166	49.23 N	1.47 W
Carteret, N.J., U.S.	262	40.35 N	74.13 W
Carter Lake	252	41.18 N	95.54 W
Carter Mountain ∧	256	44.12 N	109.25 W
Carters Reservoir ⊜[1]	246	34.35 N	84.35 W
Cartersville	246	34.10 N	84.48 W
Carterton	230	41.02 S	175.32 E
Carterville	248	37.46 N	89.05 W
Carthage, Tun.	170	36.51 N	10.21 E
Carthage, Ark., U.S.	248	34.04 N	92.33 W
Carthage, Ill., U.S.	244	40.25 N	91.08 W
Carthage, Ind., U.S.	248	39.44 N	85.34 W
Carthage, Miss., U.S.	248	32.46 N	89.32 W
Carthage, Mo., U.S.	248	37.11 N	94.19 W
Carthage, N.C., U.S.	246	35.21 N	79.25 W
Carthage, N.Y., U.S.	264	43.59 N	75.37 W
Carthage, S. Dak., U.S.	252	44.10 N	97.43 W
Carthage, Tenn., U.S.	248	36.15 N	85.57 W
Carthage, Tex., U.S.	248	32.09 N	94.20 W
Carthage ⊥	170	36.52 N	10.20 E
Cartier Island I	226	12.32 S	123.32 E
Cartwright, Man., Can.	252	49.06 N	99.20 W
Cartwright, Newf., Can.	232	53.50 N	56.45 W
Caruaru	286	8.17 S	35.58 W
Carumas	292	16.40 S	70.45 W
Carúpano	290	10.40 N	63.14 W
Caruray	202	10.20 N	119.00 E
Carutapera	286	1.13 S	46.01 W
Caruthers	272	36.32 N	119.50 W
Caruthersville	248	36.11 N	89.39 W
Carver	261	41.53 N	70.46 W
Carversville	262	40.23 N	75.04 W
Carvin	176	50.29 N	2.58 E
Carvoeiro	290	1.24 S	61.59 W
Carvoeiro, Cabo ≻	168	39.21 N	9.24 W
Cary, Ill., U.S.	268	42.13 N	88.15 W
Cary, Miss., U.S.	248	32.49 N	90.56 W
Cary, N.C., U.S.	246	35.47 N	78.46 W
Caryville, Fla., U.S.	248	30.46 N	85.49 W
Caryville, Tenn., U.S.	246	36.18 N	84.14 W
Casablanca (Dar-el-Beida)	214	33.39 N	7.35 W
Casa Branca	296	21.46 S	47.04 W
Casacalenda	170	41.44 N	14.51 E
Casa Grande	254	32.53 N	111.45 W
Casa Grande Ruins National Monument ♠	254	32.50 N	111.32 W
Casalbordino	170	42.09 N	14.35 E
Casal di Principe	184	41.00 N	14.08 E
Casale Monferrato	182	45.08 N	8.27 E
Casalnuovo di Napoli	184	40.55 N	14.20 E
Casalpusterlengo	182	45.11 N	9.39 E
Casamance ≃	222	12.33 N	16.46 W
Casamicciola Terme	184	40.45 N	13.54 E
Casanare ≃	290	6.02 N	69.51 W
Casanay	290	10.30 N	63.25 W
Casarano	170	40.00 N	18.10 E
Casar de Cáceres	168	39.34 N	6.25 W
Casas Adobes	254	32.19 N	110.59 W
Casas Ibáñez	168	39.17 N	1.28 W
Casasimarro	168	39.22 N	2.02 W
Casavieja	168	40.17 N	4.46 W
Casbas	294	36.46 S	62.31 W
Casca	294	28.34 S	51.59 W
Casca, Rio da ≃	292	14.52 S	55.52 W
Cascade, B.C., Can.	238	49.01 N	118.13 W
Cascade, Idaho, U.S.	256	44.31 N	116.02 W
Cascade, Iowa, U.S.	244	42.18 N	91.01 W
Cascade, Mich., U.S.	268	42.55 N	85.30 W
Cascade, Mont., U.S.	256	47.16 N	111.42 W
Cascade, Wis., U.S.	244	43.40 N	88.00 W
Cascade ≃	230	44.01 S	168.22 E
Cascade Locks	270	45.40 N	121.54 W
Cascade Point ≻	230	44.00 S	168.22 E
Cascade Range ⛰	234	49.00 N	120.00 W
Cascade Reservoir ⊜[1]	256	44.35 N	116.06 W
Cascais	168	38.42 N	9.25 W
Cascalho Rico	296	18.34 S	47.52 W
Cascapédia ≃	240	48.12 N	65.54 W
Cascavel	294	24.57 S	53.28 W
Cascina	184	43.41 N	10.33 E
Casco Bay C	242	43.40 N	70.00 W
Cascumpeque Bay C	240	46.45 N	64.03 W
Casella	268	40.25 N	84.34 W
Caselle Torinese	182	45.10 N	7.39 E
Casemero Palma	280	16.20 N	88.47 W
Casentino ∨	170	43.40 N	11.50 E
Case-Pilote	284e	14.38 N	61.08 W
Caserta	184	41.04 N	14.20 E
Caserta □[4]	184	41.14 N	14.10 E
Caseville	244	43.56 N	83.16 W
Casey, Ill., U.S.	248	39.18 N	87.59 W
Casey, Iowa, U.S.	252	41.31 N	94.32 W
Casey, Mount ∧	256	48.26 N	116.42 W
Cashel	162	52.31 N	7.53 W
Cashiers	246	35.06 N	83.06 W
Cashmere	256	47.31 N	120.28 W
Cashton	244	43.43 N	90.47 W
Cashtown	262	39.53 N	77.22 W
Casigua (El Cubo)	290	8.46 N	72.30 W
Casiguran, Pil.	202	16.17 N	122.07 E
Casiguran, Pil.	202	12.53 N	124.00 E
Casiguran Sound ⩊	202	16.10 N	122.00 E
Casilda, Arg.	294	33.03 S	61.10 W
Casilda, Cuba	284p	21.46 N	79.59 W
Casimcea	172	44.43 N	28.23 E
Casimiro de Abreu	296	22.29 S	42.12 W
Casino	228	28.52 S	153.03 E
Casiquiare, Brazo ≃	290	2.01 N	67.07 W
Casita	254	31.00 N	110.53 W
Casitas Springs	274	34.22 N	119.18 W
Čáslav	164	49.54 N	15.23 E
Casma	292	9.28 S	78.19 W
Čašniki	160	54.52 N	29.08 E
Časnočor, Gora ∧	160	67.45 N	33.25 E
Casogoran Bay C	202	10.46 N	125.47 E
Casoli	170	42.07 N	14.18 E
Casoria	184	40.54 N	14.17 E
Časovo	160	62.01 N	50.36 E
Caspe	168	41.14 N	0.02 W
Casper	254	42.51 N	106.19 W
Caspian	244	46.03 N	88.38 W
Caspian Sea ▾[2]	186	42.00 N	50.30 E
Cass	242	38.24 N	79.55 W
Cass □[6], Ind., U.S.	268	40.45 N	86.21 W
Cass □[6], Mich., U.S.	268	41.55 N	86.01 W
Cassadaga	266	42.21 N	79.19 W
Cassagnes-Bégonhès	166	44.10 N	2.32 E
Cassai (Kasai) ≃	218	3.06 S	16.57 E
Cassandra	266	40.24 N	78.38 W
Cassano d'Adda	182	45.32 N	9.31 E
Cassano Magnago	182	45.41 N	8.50 E
Cass City	244	43.36 N	83.10 W
Cassel	162	50.48 N	2.29 E
Casselman	260	45.19 N	75.05 W
Casselton	252	46.54 N	97.13 W
Cássia	296	20.36 S	46.56 W
Cassiar	236	59.16 N	129.40 W
Cassiar Mountains ⛰	232	59.00 N	129.00 W
Cassidy	270	49.04 N	123.53 W
Cassilândia	296	19.09 S	51.45 W
Cassinga	218	15.08 S	16.05 E
Cassino, Bra.	294	32.11 S	52.10 W
Cassino, It.	184	41.30 N	13.49 E
Cass Lake	244	47.23 N	94.36 W
Cass Lake ⊜	244	47.25 N	94.32 W
Cassolnovo	182	45.22 N	8.48 E
Cassopolis	268	41.55 N	86.01 W
Cassununga	296	16.03 S	53.38 W
Cassville, Ind., U.S.	268	40.33 N	86.08 W
Cassville, Mo., U.S.	248	36.41 N	93.52 W
Cassville, Pa., U.S.	266	40.18 N	78.02 W
Cassville, Wis., U.S.	244	42.43 N	90.59 W
Castaic	274	34.30 N	118.37 W
Castalia	266	41.24 N	82.48 W
Castanheira de Pêra	168	40.00 N	8.13 W
Castaños	250	26.47 N	101.25 W
Castañones, Punta ≻	280	12.28 N	87.12 W
Castano Primo	182	45.33 N	8.47 E
Casteggio	182	45.00 N	9.07 E
Castelbuono	170	37.56 N	14.06 E
Castel del Piano	170	42.53 N	11.32 E
Castelfidardo	184	43.28 N	13.33 E
Castelfiorentino	184	43.36 N	10.58 E
Castelfranco Veneto	170	45.40 N	11.55 E
Casteljaloux	166	44.19 N	0.05 E
Castellamare del Golfo	170	38.01 N	12.53 E
Castellammare, Golfo di C	170	38.10 N	12.55 E
Castellammare di Stabia	184	40.42 N	14.29 E
Castellamonte	182	45.23 N	7.42 E
Castellana Grotte	170	40.53 N	17.11 E
Castellane	166	43.51 N	6.31 E
Castellaneta	170	40.37 N	16.57 E
Castellanza	182	45.37 N	8.54 E
Castell'Arquato	170	44.51 N	9.52 E
Castellazzo Bormida	182	44.51 N	8.34 E
Castelleone	182	45.18 N	9.46 E
Castelli	294	36.07 S	57.50 W
Castellón □[4]	168	40.10 N	0.10 W
Castellón de la Plana	168	39.59 N	0.02 W
Castellote	168	40.48 N	0.19 W
Castelmassa	170	45.01 N	11.18 E
Castelmoron-sur-Lot	166	44.24 N	0.30 E
Castelnaudary	166	43.19 N	1.57 E
Castelnau-Montratier	166	44.16 N	1.21 E
Castelnovo ne'Monti	170	44.26 N	10.24 E
Castelnuovo di Garfagnana	170	44.06 N	10.24 E
Castelnuovo Scrivia	182	44.59 N	8.53 E
Castelo	296	20.36 S	41.12 W
Castelo Branco	168	39.49 N	7.30 W
Castel San Giorgio	184	40.47 N	14.42 E
Castel San Giovanni	182	45.04 N	9.26 E
Castel San Pietro Terme	184	44.24 N	11.35 E
Castelsardo	170	40.55 N	8.42 E
Castelsarrasin	166	44.02 N	1.06 E
Casteltermini	170	37.32 N	13.39 E
Castelvetrano	170	37.41 N	12.47 E
Castets	166	43.53 N	1.09 W
Castiglione del Lago	184	43.07 N	12.03 E
Castiglione della Pescaia	170	42.46 N	10.53 E
Castiglione Olona	182	45.46 N	8.52 E
Castiglion Fiorentino	170	43.20 N	11.55 E
Castile	266	42.38 N	78.03 W
Castilho	296	20.52 S	51.29 W
Castilla	292	5.12 S	80.38 W
Castilla, Playa de •[2]	168	37.00 N	6.33 W
Castilla, Punta ≻	280	16.01 N	86.02 W
Castilla la Nueva □[9]	168	40.00 N	3.45 W
Castilla la Vieja □[9]	168	41.30 N	4.00 W
Castillo, Pampa del ≚	288	45.58 S	68.24 W
Castillo de San Felipe ⊥	280	15.39 N	89.01 W
Castillo de San Marcos National Monument ♠	246	29.44 N	81.20 W
Castillo Incasico de Ingapirca ⊥	290	2.34 S	78.50 W
Castillon-la-Bataille	166	44.51 N	0.03 W
Castillos	294	34.12 S	53.50 W
Castillos, Laguna de ⊜	294	34.20 S	53.54 W
Castine	242	44.23 N	68.48 W
Castlebar	162	53.52 N	9.17 W
Castleberry	248	31.17 N	87.02 W
Castleblayney	162	54.07 N	6.44 W
Castle Bruce	284d	15.26 N	61.16 W
Castle Cape ≻	236	56.15 N	158.06 W
Castlecliff	230	39.57 S	174.59 E
Castle Dale	254	39.13 N	111.01 W
Castle Dome Peak ∧	254	33.05 N	114.08 W
Castle Douglas	162	54.57 N	3.56 W
Castlegar	238	49.19 N	117.40 W
Castle Hills, Del., U.S.	262	39.41 N	75.34 W
Castle Hills, Tex., U.S.	250	29.32 N	98.31 W
Castleisland	162	52.14 N	9.27 W
Castlemaine	228	37.04 S	144.13 E
Castle Mountain ∧	236	64.32 N	135.25 W
Castle Park	274	32.37 N	117.04 W
Castle Peak ∧	254	39.00 N	106.55 W
Castlereagh	162	53.46 N	8.29 W
Castlereagh ≃	228	30.12 S	147.32 E
Castle Rock, Colo., U.S.	254	39.22 N	104.51 W
Castle Rock, Wash., U.S.	270	46.17 N	122.54 W
Castle Rock ∧, Oreg., U.S.	256	44.02 N	118.11 W
Castle Rock ∧, Va., U.S.	246	37.57 N	78.44 W
Castle Rock Butte ∧	252	45.00 N	103.27 W
Castle Rock Flowage ⊜[1]	244	43.56 N	89.58 W
Castleton	242	43.37 N	73.11 W
Castleton-on-hudson	261	42.32 N	73.45 W
Castletown, I. of Man	162	54.04 N	4.40 W
Castletown, Scot., U.K.	162	58.35 N	3.23 W
Castletown Berehaven	162	51.39 N	9.55 W
Castlewood, S. Dak., U.S.	252	44.43 N	97.02 W
Castlewood, Va., U.S.	246	36.54 N	82.17 W
Castor	238	52.13 N	111.53 W
Castor ≃	248	36.51 N	89.44 W
Castor, Bayou ≃	248	31.47 N	92.22 W
Castorland	264	43.53 N	75.31 W
Castres	166	43.36 N	2.15 E
Castricum	178	52.33 N	4.39 E
Castries	285f	14.01 N	61.00 W
Castro, Bra.	294	24.47 S	50.00 W
Castro, Chile	288	42.29 S	73.46 W
Castro Barros	294	30.35 S	65.44 W
Castro Daire	168	40.54 N	7.56 W
Castro del Río	168	37.41 N	4.28 W
Castrojeriz	168	42.17 N	4.08 W
Castro Marim	168	37.13 N	7.26 W
Castronuño	168	41.23 N	5.16 W
Castropol	168	43.32 N	7.02 W
Castrop-Rauxel	178	51.34 N	7.18 E
Castro Urdiales	168	43.23 N	3.13 W
Castro Valley	272	37.42 N	122.04 W
Castro Verde	168	37.42 N	8.05 W
Castrovillari	170	39.49 N	16.13 E
Castroville, Calif., U.S.	272	36.46 N	121.45 W
Castroville, Tex., U.S.	250	29.21 N	98.53 W
Castrovirreyna	292	13.20 S	75.18 W
Castuera	168	38.43 N	5.33 W
Casupá	294	34.07 S	55.39 W
Caswell Sound ⩊	230	45.00 S	167.08 E
Catacamas	280	14.54 N	85.56 W
Catacaos	292	5.15 S	80.42 W
Catacocha	290	4.04 S	79.38 W
Cataguases	296	21.24 S	42.41 W
Catahoula Lake ⊜	248	31.30 N	92.06 W
Catalaban Island I	202	11.52 N	125.25 E
Catalão	296	18.10 S	47.57 W
Çatalca	172	41.09 N	28.27 E
Catalina, Newf., Can.	240	48.31 N	53.05 W
Catalina, Chile	294	25.13 S	69.43 W
Catalonia → Cataluña □[9]	168	42.00 N	2.00 E
Cataluña □[9]	168	42.00 N	2.00 E
Catamarca	294	28.30 S	65.45 W
Catamarca □[4]	294	27.00 S	67.00 W
Catamayo	290	3.59 S	79.21 W
Catamayo ≃	290	4.18 S	80.09 W
Catanauan	202	13.36 N	122.19 E
Catanduanes □[4]	202	13.47 N	124.16 E
Catanduanes Island I	202	13.45 N	124.15 E
Catanduva	296	21.08 S	48.58 W
Catania	170	37.30 N	15.06 E
Catania, Golfo di C	170	37.25 N	15.15 E
Cataño	284m	18.27 N	66.07 W
Catanzaro	170	38.54 N	16.36 E
Catarama	290	1.35 S	79.28 W
Cataraqui	264	44.16 N	76.32 W
Cataricahua	292	18.14 S	66.49 W
Catarina	250	28.21 N	99.37 W
Catarman, Pil.	202	9.07 N	124.40 E
Catarman, Pil.	202	12.30 N	124.38 E
Catarman ≃	202	12.30 N	124.39 E
Catarroja	168	39.24 N	0.24 W
Catasauqua	262	40.39 N	75.29 W
Catastrophe, Cape ≻	228	34.59 S	136.00 E
Catawba ≃	246	34.36 N	80.54 W
Catawba, Lake ⊜[1]	246	35.07 N	81.02 W
Catawba Dam ◄[6]	246	34.57 N	81.04 W
Catawba Island	266	41.35 N	82.50 W
Catbalogan	202	11.47 N	124.53 E
Catchabutan, Punta ≻	280	15.50 N	86.32 W
Cateel	202	7.48 N	126.27 E
Cateel Bay C	202	7.53 N	126.27 E
Caterham	174	51.17 N	0.04 W
Catete	218	9.06 S	13.43 E
Cathcart	218	31.18 S	27.09 E
Cathedral City	258	33.47 N	116.28 W
Cathedral Mountain ∧	250	30.10 N	103.40 W
Catherines Peak ∧	285q	18.04 N	76.43 W
Cathey's Valley	272	37.25 N	121.51 W
Cathlamet	270	46.12 N	123.23 W
Cat Island I, Ba.	282	24.30 N	75.30 W
Cat Island I, Miss., U.S.	248	30.13 N	89.06 W
Catlettsburg	242	38.25 N	82.36 W
Catlin	248	40.04 N	87.42 W
Catlins ≃	230	46.29 S	169.43 E
Catnip Mountain ∧	258	41.52 N	119.23 W
Cato	264	43.10 N	76.34 W
Catoche, Cabo ≻	278	21.36 N	87.07 W
Cato Island I	228	23.15 S	155.32 E
Catonsville	262	39.16 N	76.44 W
Catoosa	250	36.11 N	95.45 W
Catorce	278	23.42 N	100.54 W
Catriló	294	36.23 S	63.24 W
Catrimani	290	0.27 N	61.41 W
Catskill	261	42.13 N	73.52 W
Catskill Mountains ⛰	242	42.10 N	74.30 W
Catt, Mount ∧	238	54.21 N	128.47 W
Cattaraugus	266	42.20 N	78.52 W
Cattaraugus □[6]	266	42.15 N	78.45 W
Cattolica	184	43.58 N	12.44 E
Catu	296	12.21 S	38.23 W
Catubig	202	12.24 N	125.03 E
Catus	166	44.34 N	1.20 E
Čatyrtaš	186	40.55 N	76.26 E
Cau ≃	200	21.07 N	106.18 E
Cauayan, Pil.	202	16.56 N	121.46 E
Cauayan, Pil.	202	9.58 N	122.37 E
Cauca □[5]	290	2.30 N	76.50 W
Cauca ≃	290	8.54 N	74.28 W
Caucasia	290	8.00 N	75.12 W
Caucasus → Bol'šoj Kavkaz ⛰	158	42.30 N	45.00 E
Caudebec-lés-Elbeuf	176	49.17 N	1.02 E
Caudry	176	50.08 N	3.25 E
Caughdenoy	264	43.16 N	76.12 W
Cauitan, Mount ∧	202	17.15 N	121.00 E
Cauit Point ≻	202	12.16 N	122.38 E
Caulonia	170	38.23 N	16.25 E
Caúngula	218	8.25 S	18.40 E
Čaunskaja Guba C	186	69.20 N	170.00 E
Cauquenes	294	35.58 S	72.21 W
Caura ≃	290	7.38 N	64.53 W
Causapscal	240	48.22 N	67.14 W
Caussade	166	44.10 N	1.32 E
Cautín □[4]	294	39.00 S	72.30 W
Caution, Cape ≻	238	51.10 N	127.47 W
Cauto ≃	284p	20.33 N	77.15 W
Caux, Pays de ◄[1]	166	49.40 N	0.40 E
Cava de'Tirreni	184	40.42 N	14.42 E
Cávado ≃	168	41.32 N	8.48 W
Cavaillon	182	43.50 N	5.02 E
Cavalaire-sur-Mer	166	43.10 N	6.32 E
Cavalcante	296	13.48 S	47.30 W
Cavalese	170	46.17 N	11.27 E
Cavalheiro	296	17.15 S	48.02 W
Cavalier	252	48.48 N	97.37 W
Cavalla (Cavally) ≃	222	4.22 N	7.32 W
Cavalli Islands II	230	35.00 S	173.46 E
Cavally (Cavalla) ≃	222	4.22 N	7.32 W
Cavan	162	54.00 N	7.21 W
Cavan □[6]	162	53.55 N	7.30 W
Čavan'ga	160	66.06 N	37.47 E
Cavarzere	170	45.08 N	12.05 E
Çavdır	172	37.09 N	29.42 E
Cave	184	41.49 N	12.56 E
Cave City, Ark., U.S.	248	35.57 N	91.33 W
Cave City, Ky., U.S.	248	37.08 N	85.58 W
Caveiras ≃	294	27.35 S	50.56 W
Cave Springs	246	34.07 N	85.20 W
Cavili Island I	202	9.07 N	120.50 E
Cavite	202	14.29 N	120.55 E
Cavite □[4]	202	14.15 N	120.50 E
Cavour	182	44.47 N	7.22 E
Cavour, Canale ⩸	170	45.11 N	7.54 E
Cavtat	172	42.35 N	18.13 E
Çavuşcu Gölü ⊜	212	38.25 N	31.53 E
Cawatose Lake ⊜	244	47.20 N	77.07 W
Cawayan	202	11.56 N	123.46 E
Cawit Point ≻	202	9.20 N	126.11 E
Cawker City	252	39.30 N	98.26 W
Cawnpore → Kānpur	206	26.28 N	80.20 E
Cawood	246	36.47 N	83.14 W
Cawston	238	49.11 N	119.45 W
Caxambu	296	21.59 S	44.56 W
Caxias	286	4.50 S	43.21 W
Caxias do Sul	294	29.10 S	51.11 W
Caxito	218	8.33 S	13.36 E
Cayambe	290	0.03 N	78.08 W
Cayambe ∧[1]	290	0.02 N	77.59 W
Cayapoñga	202	5.48 N	125.33 E
Cayce	246	33.59 N	81.04 W
Caycuse	270	48.53 N	124.22 W
Cayenne	286	4.56 N	52.20 W
Cayey	284m	18.07 N	66.10 W
Caylus	166	44.14 N	1.46 E
Cayman Brac I	282	19.43 N	79.49 W
Cayman Islands □[2]	276	19.30 N	80.30 W
Cayman Trench ⟡[1]	148	19.00 N	80.00 W
Cayo Agua, Isla I	280	9.10 N	82.02 W
Cay Sal Bank ⟡[4]	282	23.45 N	80.00 W
Cayucos	272	35.27 N	120.54 W
Cayuga, Ont., Can.	264	42.56 N	79.51 W
Cayuga, Ind., U.S.	248	39.57 N	87.28 W
Cayuga, N. Dak., U.S.	252	46.04 N	97.23 W
Cayuga, N.Y., U.S.	264	42.55 N	76.44 W
Cayuga, Tex., U.S.	250	31.57 N	95.57 W
Cayuga □[6]	264	42.56 N	76.34 W
Cayuga Lake ⊜	242	42.45 N	76.45 W
Cazalla de la Sierra	168	37.56 N	5.45 W
Căzănești	172	44.37 N	27.01 E
Cazaux, Étang de C	166	44.30 N	1.10 W
Cazenovia	264	42.56 N	75.51 W
Cazères	166	43.13 N	1.05 E
Cazin	170	44.58 N	15.57 E
Čazma	170	45.45 N	16.37 E
Cazombo	218	11.54 S	22.52 E
Cazones, Ensenada de C	284p	22.06 N	81.32 W
Cazones, Golfo de C	284p	21.50 N	81.10 W
Cazorla, Esp.	168	37.55 N	3.00 W
Cazorla, Ven.	290	8.01 N	67.00 W
Cazorla, Sierra de ⛰	168	37.55 N	2.55 W
Ccapi	292	13.51 S	72.05 W
Cchinvali	158	42.13 N	43.56 E
Cea ≃	168	42.00 N	5.36 W
Ceanannus Mór	162	53.44 N	6.53 W
Ceará-Mirim	286	5.38 S	35.26 W
Cébaco, Isla I	290	7.33 N	81.09 W
Ceballos	278	26.32 N	104.09 W
Čeboksary	160	56.09 N	47.15 E
Cebollar	294	29.06 S	66.34 W
Cebollatí	294	33.16 S	53.47 W
Cebollín	278	25.47 N	106.10 W
Cebollita Peak ∧	254	34.43 N	107.51 W
Cebreros	168	40.27 N	4.28 W
Čebsara	160	59.12 N	38.50 E
Cebu	202	10.18 N	123.54 E
Cebu □[4]	202	10.20 N	123.45 E
Cebu I	202	10.15 N	123.40 E
Ceccano	184	41.34 N	13.20 E
Ceceda	250	26.04 N	103.25 W
Čečeno-Ingušskaja Avtonomnaja Sovetskaja Socialističeskaja Respublika □[3]	186	43.15 N	45.40 E
Cecerleg	190	48.55 N	101.09 E
Čechov	160	55.09 N	37.27 E
Čechtice	164	49.37 N	15.03 E
Čechy □[9]	164	49.50 N	14.00 E
Cecil, Ga., U.S.	246	31.05 N	83.11 W
Cecil, Ohio, U.S.	268	41.13 N	84.35 W
Cecil, Pa., U.S.	266	40.20 N	80.11 W
Cecil □[6]	262	39.36 N	75.50 W
Cecilia	248	37.40 N	85.57 W
Cecilio Báez	294	25.03 S	56.19 W
Cecilton	262	39.24 N	75.52 W
Cecina	184	43.19 N	10.31 E
Cecita, Lago di ⊜	170	39.24 N	16.30 E
Cedar ≃, Mich., U.S.	244	43.53 N	84.29 W
Cedar ≃, Nebr., U.S.	252	41.22 N	97.57 W
Cedar ≃, N.Y., U.S.	242	43.51 N	74.11 W
Cedar Bayou ≃	248	29.41 N	94.56 W
Cedar Bluff Reservoir ⊜[1]	252	38.47 N	99.47 W
Cedar Bluffs	252	41.24 N	96.37 W
Cedar Breaks National Monument ♠	254	37.29 N	112.53 W
Cedar Brook	262	39.43 N	74.54 W
Cedarburg	244	43.17 N	87.59 W
Cedar City, Mo., U.S.	248	38.36 N	92.11 W
Cedar City, Utah, U.S.	254	37.41 N	113.04 W
Cedar Creek Reservoir ⊜[1]	250	32.20 N	96.10 W
Cedaredge	254	38.54 N	107.56 W
Cedar Falls	244	42.32 N	92.27 W
Cedar Grove, N.J., U.S.	262	40.51 N	74.14 W
Cedar Grove, W. Va., U.S.	242	38.13 N	81.26 W
Cedar Grove, Wis., U.S.	244	43.33 N	87.45 W
Cedar Hill, N.Y., U.S.	261	42.33 N	73.47 W
Cedar Hill, Tenn., U.S.	248	36.33 N	87.01 W
Cedar Hills, Fla., U.S.	246	30.16 N	81.45 W
Cedar Hills, Oreg., U.S.	270	45.31 N	122.46 W
Cedarhurst	262	39.07 N	76.41 W
Cedar Key	246	29.08 N	83.02 W
Cedar Lake	268	41.22 N	87.26 W
Cedar Lake ⊜, Ont., Can.	244	46.02 N	78.30 W
Cedar Lake ⊜, Tex., U.S.	250	32.49 N	102.17 W
Cedar Lake ⊜[1]	232	53.10 N	100.00 W
Cedar Mountain ∧	258	41.36 N	120.16 W
Cedar Park	268	42.42 N	88.14 W
Cedar Point	268	41.16 N	89.08 W
Cedar Rapids, Iowa, U.S.	244	41.59 N	91.40 W
Cedar Rapids, Nebr., U.S.	252	41.34 N	98.09 W
Cedar Ridge	272	39.12 N	121.01 W
Cedar River	244	45.28 N	87.16 W
Cedar Springs, Ont., Can.	266	42.17 N	82.02 W
Cedar Springs, Mich., U.S.	244	43.13 N	85.33 W
Cedartown	246	34.01 N	85.15 W
Cedarvale, B.C., Can.	238	55.01 N	128.20 W
Cedar Vale, Kans., U.S.	252	37.06 N	96.30 W
Cedarville, Calif., U.S.	258	41.32 N	120.10 W
Cedarville, Ind., U.S.	268	40.12 N	85.01 W
Cedarville, Mass., U.S.	261	41.49 N	70.32 W
Cedarville, Mich., U.S.	244	46.00 N	84.22 W
Cedarville, N.J., U.S.	242	39.20 N	75.12 W
Cedar Wash ∨	254	35.53 N	111.25 W
Cedarwood Park	262	40.03 N	74.08 W
Cedeira	168	43.39 N	8.03 W
Cedros, Hond.	280	14.35 N	87.08 W
Cedros, Méx.	278	24.41 N	101.47 W
Cedros, Isla I	278	28.10 N	115.15 W
Ceduna	226	32.07 S	133.40 E
Cedynia (Zehden)	164	52.50 N	14.14 E
Ceepeecee	238	49.52 N	126.43 W
Cefalonia → Kefallinía I	172	38.15 N	20.35 E
Cefalù	170	38.02 N	14.01 E
Cega ≃	168	41.33 N	4.46 W
Čegdomyn	186	51.07 N	133.05 E
Čegitun'	236	66.34 N	171.06 W
Cegléd	164	47.10 N	19.48 E
Ceglie Messapico	170	40.39 N	17.31 E
Cehegín	168	38.06 N	1.48 W
Ceheng	200	25.10 N	105.48 E
Cehu-Silvaniei	172	47.25 N	23.11 E
Ceiba	284m	18.16 N	65.39 W
Čekšino	160	59.39 N	40.33 E
Čekujevo	160	63.34 N	38.56 E
Cela	218	11.25 S	15.07 E
Čel'abinsk	158	55.10 N	61.24 E
Čelákovice	164	50.10 N	14.46 E
Celano	184	42.05 N	13.33 E
Celanova	168	42.09 N	7.58 W
Celaque, Montaña de ⛰	280	14.32 N	88.43 W
Celaya	278	20.31 N	100.37 W
Celebes → Sulawesi I	198	2.00 S	121.00 E
Celebes Basin ⟡[1]	148	4.00 N	122.00 E
Celebes Sea ▾[2]	198	3.00 N	122.00 E
Čeleken, S.S.S.R.	158		
	208	39.26 N	53.07 E
Celendín	292	6.52 S	78.10 W
Celeste	250	33.18 N	96.12 W
Celestún	278	20.52 N	90.24 W
Celica	290	4.07 S	79.59 W
Celina, Ohio, U.S.	268	40.33 N	84.34 W
Celina, Tenn., U.S.	248	36.33 N	85.30 W
Celina, Tex., U.S.	250	33.19 N	96.47 W
Celinograd	186	51.10 N	71.30 E
Celje	170	46.14 N	15.16 E
Čelkar	158	47.50 N	59.36 E
Celldömölk	164	47.16 N	17.09 E
Celle	178	52.37 N	10.05 E
Čelmozero	160	64.18 N	31.48 E
Celorico da Beira	168	40.38 N	7.23 W
Celoron	266	42.06 N	79.17 W
Čel'uskin, Mys ≻	186	77.45 N	104.20 E
Cement City	268	42.04 N	84.20 W
Cementon, N.Y., U.S.	261	42.09 N	73.55 W
Cementon, Pa., U.S.	262	40.41 N	75.30 W
Čemerno)(	172	43.14 N	18.37 E
Cenajo, Embalse del ⊜[1]	168	38.25 N	2.00 W
Cenepa ≃	290	4.40 S	78.10 W
Ceno ≃	170	44.41 N	10.05 E
Cenovo	172	43.32 N	25.39 E
Centenario	294	38.48 S	68.08 W
Centenário do Sul	296	22.48 S	51.37 W
Centennial Mountains ⛰	256	44.35 N	111.55 W
Centennial Wash ∨	254	33.14 N	112.46 W
Center, Colo., U.S.	254	37.45 N	106.06 W
Center, Ind., U.S.	268	40.26 N	86.04 W
Center, Mo., U.S.	248	39.30 N	91.32 W
Center, Nebr., U.S.	252	42.37 N	97.53 W
Center, N. Dak., U.S.	252	47.07 N	101.18 W
Center, Tex., U.S.	248	31.48 N	94.11 W
Centerbrook	261	41.21 N	72.25 W
Center Brunswick	261	42.45 N	73.37 W
Centerburg	266	40.18 N	82.42 W
Center City	244	45.24 N	92.49 W
Center Cross	262	37.48 N	76.47 W
Centereach	261	40.51 N	73.06 W
Center Hill	246	28.38 N	82.03 W
Center Hill Lake ⊜[1]	248	36.00 N	85.45 W
Center Line	266	42.29 N	83.03 W
Center Moriches	242	40.48 N	72.48 W
Center Mountain ∧	256	45.06 N	115.13 W
Center Point, Ala., U.S.	248	33.38 N	86.41 W
Center Point, Iowa, U.S.	244	42.11 N	91.46 W
Center Point, Tex., U.S.	250	29.57 N	99.02 W
Centerport	262	40.29 N	76.01 W
Center Square	262	40.10 N	75.18 W
Center Valley	262	40.32 N	75.24 W
Centerville, Ind., U.S.	248	39.49 N	85.00 W
Centerville, Iowa, U.S.	244	40.43 N	92.52 W
Centerville, Mass., U.S.	261	41.39 N	70.21 W
Centerville, Mo., U.S.	248	37.26 N	90.58 W
Centerville, N.Y., U.S.	266	42.29 N	78.15 W
Centerville, Pa., U.S.	266	41.44 N	79.46 W
Centerville, S. Dak., U.S.	252	43.07 N	96.58 W
Centerville, Tenn., U.S.	248	35.47 N	87.28 W
Centerville, Tex., U.S.	250	31.16 N	95.59 W
Centerville, Utah, U.S.	254	40.55 N	111.52 W
Centerville, Wash., U.S.	270	45.45 N	120.54 W
Centinela	250	28.47 N	100.34 W
Centinela, Cerro del ∧	278	19.13 N	104.17 W
Cento	170	44.43 N	11.17 E
Central, Alaska, U.S.	236	65.34 N	144.48 W
Central, Ariz., U.S.	254	32.52 N	109.48 W
Central, N. Mex., U.S.	254	32.46 N	108.09 W
Central, S.C., U.S.	246	34.44 N	82.47 W
Central □[4]	222	5.30 N	1.00 W
Central □[5], Bots.	224	21.30 S	26.00 E
Central □[5], Para.	294	25.30 S	57.30 W
Central, Cordillera ⛰, Bol.	292	18.30 S	64.55 W
Central, Cordillera ⛰, Col.	290	5.00 N	75.00 W
Central, Cordillera ⛰, C.R.	280	10.10 N	84.05 W
Central, Cordillera ⛰, Perú	292	8.00 S	77.00 W
Central, Cordillera ⛰, Pil.	202	17.30 N	121.00 E
Central, Cordillera ⛰, P.R.	282	18.08 N	66.35 W
Central, Cordillera ⛰, Rep. Dom.	282	19.15 N	71.00 W
Central, Massif ⛰	166	45.00 N	3.10 E
Central, Planalto ⛰[1]	286	18.00 S	47.00 W
Central African Republic □[1]	214	7.00 N	21.00 E
Central Aguirre	284m	17.57 N	66.13 W
Central Avenue Park	266	41.40 N	83.42 W
Central Basin ⟡[1]	148	10.00 S	80.00 E
Central Brāhui Range ⛰	206	29.20 N	66.55 E
Central City, Ill., U.S.	248	41.14 N	88.16 W
Central City, Iowa, U.S.	244	42.12 N	91.31 W
Central City, Ky., U.S.	248	37.18 N	87.07 W
Central City, Nebr., U.S.	252	41.07 N	98.00 W
Central City, Pa., U.S.	266	40.06 N	78.48 W
Central Falls	261	41.54 N	71.23 W
Central Heights	254	32.25 N	110.48 W
Centralia, Ill., U.S.	248	38.31 N	89.08 W
Centralia, Kans., U.S.	252	39.44 N	96.08 W
Centralia, Mo., U.S.	248	39.13 N	92.08 W
Centralia, Wash., U.S.	270	46.43 N	122.58 W
Centralia Draw ∨	250	31.27 N	101.16 W
Centralina	296	18.34 S	49.13 W
Central Lake	244	45.04 N	85.16 W
Central Makrān Range ⛰	206	26.40 N	64.30 E
Central'nyje Karakumy ◄[2]	208	39.00 N	60.00 E
Central Park	270	46.58 N	123.41 W
Central Point, Oreg., U.S.	256	42.23 N	122.57 W
Central Point, Va., U.S.	262	37.58 N	77.08 W
Central Range ⛰	224	29.35 S	28.35 E
Central Square	264	43.17 N	76.09 W
Central Utah Canal ⩸	254	39.35 N	112.12 W
Central Valley	258	40.41 N	122.22 W
Central Village	261	41.43 N	71.54 W
Centre	248	34.09 N	85.40 W
Centre □[5]	222	13.00 N	1.00 W
Centre □[6]	262	40.55 N	77.47 W
Centre, Canal du ⩸	166	46.27 N	4.07 E
Centre Hall	266	40.51 N	77.41 W
Centre Island I	230	46.27 S	167.51 E
Centre Peak ∧	238	55.41 N	126.26 W
Centreville, Ala., U.S.	248	32.56 N	87.08 W
Centreville, Md., U.S.	262	39.03 N	76.04 W
Centreville, Mich., U.S.	268	41.55 N	85.32 W
Centreville, Miss., U.S.	248	31.05 N	91.04 W
Centreville, Va., U.S.	262	38.50 N	77.26 W
Centro Puntas	284m	18.22 N	67.16 W
Century, Fla., U.S.	248	30.58 N	87.16 W
Century, W. Va., U.S.	242	39.06 N	80.11 W
Čepca ≃	160	58.36 N	50.04 E
Čepelare	172	41.44 N	24.41 E
Ceram → Seram I	198	3.00 S	129.00 E
Ceram Sea → Seram, Laut ▾[2]	198	2.30 S	128.00 E
Cerano	182	45.25 N	8.47 E
Čerčany	164	49.51 N	14.43 E
Čerchov ∧	164	49.23 N	12.47 E
Cercola	184	40.51 N	14.21 E
Čerdakly	160	54.23 N	48.51 E
Cerdas	292	20.48 S	66.29 W
Čerdyn'	160	60.23 N	56.24 E
Cereales	294	36.49 S	63.50 W
Čeremchovo	186	53.09 N	103.05 E
Čeremušskij	160	61.16 N	47.12 E
Čerepanovo	186	54.13 N	83.22 E
Čerepovec	160	59.08 N	37.54 E
Ceres, Arg.	294	29.50 S	61.55 W
Ceres, Bra.	296	15.17 S	49.35 W
Ceres, Calif., U.S.	272	37.35 N	120.57 W
Ceres, N.Y., U.S.	266	42.00 N	78.16 W
Ceresco, Mich., U.S.	268	42.16 N	85.04 W
Ceresco, Nebr., U.S.	252	41.03 N	96.39 W
Ceresole Reale	170	45.26 N	7.15 E
Céret	166	42.29 N	2.45 E

Symbols in the index entries are identified on page 360.

Name	Page	Lat°′	Long°′
Ceretê	290	8.53 N	75.48 W
Čerevkovo	160	61.46 N	45.12 E
Cerf Island I	218	9.32 S	50.59 E
Cerignola	170	41.16 N	15.54 E
Cérilly	166	46.37 N	2.49 E
Cerisiers	166	48.08 N	3.29 E
Čerkassy	158	49.26 N	32.04 E
Čerkessk	158	44.14 N	42.04 E
Çerkezköy	172	41.17 N	28.00 E
Cerknica	170	45.48 N	14.22 E
Cerkovišče	160	55.54 N	30.51 E
Čerlak	186	54.09 N	74.48 E
Cermei	172	46.33 N	21.51 E
Cerna, Jugo.	172	45.11 N	18.49 E
Cerna, Rom.	172	45.04 N	28.18 E
Čern'achovsk (Insterburg)	164	54.38 N	21.49 E
Černá horá ∧	164	48.58 N	13.48 E
Cernăuţi → Černovcy	172	48.18 N	25.56 E
Cernavodă	172	44.21 N	28.01 E
Cernay	180	47.49 N	7.10 E
Cernei, Munţii ⛰	172	45.02 N	22.31 E
Černigov	158	51.30 N	31.18 E
Černi vrăh ∧	172	42.34 N	23.17 E
Cernobbio	182	45.50 N	9.04 E
Černogorsk	186	53.49 N	91.18 E
Černovcy	172	48.18 N	25.56 E
Černovskoje	160	58.42 N	47.23 E
Cernusco sul Naviglio	182	45.31 N	9.19 E
Černyševa, Kr'až ⛰	160	66.30 N	59.00 E
Černyševskij	186	63.00 N	112.15 E
Čer'omošč ≃	172	48.23 N	25.37 E
Çerovodë	172	40.30 N	20.13 E
Cerralvo	278	26.06 N	99.37 W
Cerralvo, Isla I	278	24.17 N	109.52 W
Cërrik	172	41.02 N	19.57 E
Cerrillos, Arg.	294	24.55 S	65.29 W
Cerrillos, N. Mex., U.S.	254	35.26 N	106.08 W
Cerritos	278	22.26 N	100.17 W
Cerro Azul, Arg.	294	27.33 S	55.29 W
Cêrro Azul, Bra.	294	24.50 S	49.15 W
Cerro Azul, Méx.	278	21.12 N	97.44 W
Cerro Azul, Perú	292	13.03 S	76.30 W
Cerro Chato	294	33.06 S	55.08 W
Cerro Colorado	294	33.52 S	55.33 W
Cerro de las Mesas ⊥	278	18.47 N	96.05 W
Cerro de Pasco	292	10.41 S	76.16 W
Cerro Gordo	248	39.53 N	88.44 W
Cêrro Largo	294	28.09 S	54.45 W
Cerro Moreno	294	23.26 S	70.26 W
Cerro Prieto	258	32.27 N	115.17 W
Cerro Vera	294	33.11 S	57.28 W
Čerskij	186	68.45 N	161.45 E
Čerskogo, Chrebet ⛰	186	52.00 N	114.00 E
Certaldo	184	43.33 N	11.02 E
Cervantes	202	16.59 N	120.44 E
Cervati, Monte ∧	170	40.17 N	15.29 E
Červen brjag	172	43.16 N	24.06 E
Červený Kostelec	164	50.29 N	16.06 E
Cervera	168	41.40 N	1.17 E
Cervera del Río Alhama	168	42.01 N	1.57 W
Cervera de Pisuerga	168	42.52 N	4.30 W
Cerveteri	184	42.00 N	12.06 E
Cervia	184	44.15 N	12.22 E
Cervialto, Monte ∧	170	40.47 N	15.08 E
Cervignano del Friuli	170	45.49 N	13.20 E
Cervinara	184	41.01 N	14.37 E
Cervione	170	42.20 N	9.31 E
Cervo	168	43.40 N	7.25 W
Červonograd	158	50.24 N	24.14 E
Cesano Maderno	182	45.38 N	9.08 E
Cesena	184	44.08 N	12.15 E
Cesenatico	184	44.12 N	12.24 E
Cēsis	160	57.18 N	25.15 E
Česká Kamenice	164	50.47 N	14.26 E
Česká Lípa	164	50.42 N	14.32 E
Česká Třebová	164	49.54 N	16.27 E
České Budějovice	164	48.59 N	14.28 E
Českomoravská vrchovina ⛰[1]	164	49.20 N	15.30 E
Český Brod	164	50.02 N	14.58 E
Český Krumlov	164	48.49 N	14.19 E
Český les ⛰	164	49.40 N	12.40 E
Český Těšín	164	49.45 N	18.37 E
Çeşme	172	38.18 N	26.19 E
Céspedes	284p	21.35 N	78.17 W
Češskaja Guba C	160	67.30 N	46.30 E
Cessnock	228	32.50 S	151.21 E
Cestos ≃	222	5.40 N	9.10 W
Cesvaine	160	56.58 N	26.19 E
Cetate	172	44.06 N	23.03 E
Cetina ≃	170	43.26 N	16.42 E
Cetinje	172	42.23 N	18.55 E
Četlasskij Kamen', Gora ∧[2]	160	64.22 N	50.45 E
Cetronia	262	40.35 N	75.31 W
Ceuta	168	35.53 N	5.19 W
Ceva	170	44.23 N	8.02 E
Cévennes ◆[1]	182	44.00 N	3.30 E
Ceyhan	212	37.04 N	35.47 E
Ceyhan ≃	212	36.45 N	35.42 E
Ceylon, Sask., Can.	252	49.28 N	104.36 W
Ceylon, Minn., U.S.	252	43.32 N	94.38 W
Ceylon □[1]	204	7.00 N	81.00 E
Chaatl Island I	238	53.00 N	132.25 W
Chabanais	166	45.52 N	0.43 E
Chabaricha	160	65.50 N	52.16 E
Chabarovo	186	69.39 N	60.24 E
Chabarovsk	186	48.27 N	135.06 E
Chabás	294	33.15 S	61.20 W
Chabeuil	166	44.54 N	5.01 E
Chablais ◆[1]	166	46.18 N	6.39 E
Chablis	166	47.49 N	3.48 E
Chabro, Oued ≃	170	35.49 N	7.53 E
Chacabuco	294	34.38 S	60.29 W
Chacaltaya, Nevado ∧	292	16.20 S	68.08 W
Chacayán	292	10.22 S	76.30 W
Chachani, Nevado ∧	292	16.12 S	71.32 W
Chachapoyas	292	6.10 S	77.50 W
Chachas	292	15.30 S	72.15 W
Chachoengsao	200	13.42 N	101.06 E
Chaco □[4]	294	26.25 S	60.30 W
Chaco ≃	254	36.46 N	108.39 W
Chaco Austral ◆[1]	294	26.30 S	61.30 W
Chaco Boreal ◆[1]	294	23.00 S	60.00 W
Chaco Canyon National Monument ♠	254	36.06 N	108.00 W
Chaco Central ◆[1]	294	25.00 S	59.45 W
Chacon, Cape >	236	54.42 N	132.00 W
Chacorão, Cachoeira do L	292	6.32 S	58.12 W
Chad □[1]	214	15.00 N	19.00 E
Chad, Lake(Lac Tchad) ⊜	214	13.20 N	14.00 E
Chadbourn	246	34.19 N	78.50 W
Chadileuvú ≃	294	37.46 S	66.00 W
Chadron	252	42.50 N	103.02 W
Chadwick	244	42.01 N	89.53 W
Chadžibejskij Liman ⊜	172	46.39 N	30.33 E
Chaem ≃	200	18.10 N	98.40 E
Chafarinas, Islas (Spain) II	168	35.11 N	2.26 W
Chaffee	248	37.11 N	89.40 W
Chaffins	261	42.21 N	71.51 W
Chafurray	290	3.10 N	73.14 W
Chāgai Hills ⛰	208	29.30 N	64.15 E
Chagang Do □[4]	194	40.50 N	126.30 E
Chagny	166	46.55 N	4.45 E
Chagos Archipelago II	148	6.00 S	72.00 E
Chagrin Falls	266	41.26 N	81.24 W
Chagrin Falls Park	266	41.21 N	81.32 W
Chaguanas	285r	10.31 N	61.25 W
Chaguaramas	290	9.20 N	66.16 W
Chaguaya	292	21.49 S	64.50 W
Chahal	280	15.45 N	89.34 W
Chahanhu ⊜	194	41.23 N	113.55 E
Chahār Burjak	214	31.00 N	60.00 E
Chāh Bahār	204	25.18 N	60.37 E
Chāh Gheybī, Hāmūn-e ☷	208	28.06 N	60.50 E
Chaidamupendi ≚[1]	206	37.00 N	95.00 E
Chaillé-les-Marais	166	46.24 N	1.01 W
Chaîne Annamitique ⛰	200	17.00 N	106.00 E
Chaiyaphum	198	15.48 N	102.02 E
Chajarí	294	30.45 S	57.59 W
Chajpudyrskaja Guba C	160	68.30 N	59.30 E
Chajul	280	15.30 N	91.02 W
Chakachamna Lake ⊜	236	61.13 N	152.35 W
Chake Chake	218	5.15 S	39.46 E
Chakhānsūr □[4]	208	30.30 N	62.00 E
Chala	292	15.53 S	74.18 W
Chalais	166	45.16 N	0.02 E
Chalap Dalān ⛰	206	33.45 N	64.45 E
Chalatenango	280	14.03 N	88.56 W
Chalchuapa	280	13.59 N	89.41 W
Chalcis → Khalkís	172	38.28 N	23.36 E
Chaleur Bay C	240	48.00 N	65.45 W
Chalfont	262	40.17 N	75.13 W
Chalhuanca	292	14.20 S	73.10 W
Chalk Draw V	250	29.36 N	103.15 W
Chalk River	244	46.01 N	77.27 W
Chalkyitsik	236	66.39 N	143.43 W
Challans	166	46.51 N	1.53 W
Challapata	292	18.54 S	66.47 W
Challenge	272	39.29 N	121.13 W
Challis	256	44.30 N	114.14 W
Challviri, Salar de ≚	292	22.32 S	67.34 W
Chal'mer-Ju	160	67.58 N	64.50 E
Chalmers	268	40.40 N	86.52 W
Chalmette	248	29.56 N	89.58 W
Chalonnes-sur-Loire	166	47.21 N	0.46 W
Châlons-sur-Marne	176	48.57 N	4.22 E
Chalon-sur-Saône	180	46.47 N	4.51 E
Chalosse ◆[1]	166	43.45 N	0.30 W
Chalturin	160	58.33 N	48.50 E
Chaluolehu ⊜	206	34.00 N	81.45 E
Châlus, Fr.	166	45.39 N	0.59 E
Chālūs, Īrān	208	36.38 N	51.26 E
Cham, B.R.D.	164	49.13 N	12.41 E
Cham, Schw.	180	47.11 N	8.28 E
Chama	254	36.54 N	106.35 W
Chama, Rio ≃	254	36.03 N	106.05 W
Chamá, Sierra de ⛰	280	15.35 N	90.20 W
Chamaicó	294	35.05 S	64.55 W
Chaman	208	30.55 N	66.22 E
Chamao, Khao ∧	200	12.58 N	101.45 E
Chambas	284p	22.12 N	78.55 W
Chambas ≃	284p	22.24 N	78.54 W
Chamberlain	252	43.49 N	99.20 W
Chamberlain Lake ⊜	240	46.17 N	69.20 W
Chamberlin, Mount ∧	236	69.16 N	144.55 W
Chambers, Ariz., U.S.	254	35.11 N	109.26 W
Chambers, Nebr., U.S.	252	42.12 N	98.45 W
Chambersburg	262	39.56 N	77.39 W
Chambers Island I	244	45.11 N	87.12 W
Chambéry	182	45.34 N	5.56 E
Chambi, Djebel ∧	214	35.11 N	8.42 E
Chambira ≃, Perú	290	3.52 S	73.42 W
Chambira ≃, Perú	290	4.30 S	74.45 W
Chamblee	246	33.54 N	84.18 W
Chambley-Bussières	166	49.03 N	5.54 E
Chambly	176	49.10 N	2.15 E
Chambly □[6]	260	45.30 N	73.20 W
Chambon-sur-Voueize	166	46.11 N	2.25 E
Chambord, Château de ⊥	166	47.37 N	1.31 E
Chamdo → Changdu	190	31.11 N	97.15 E
Chame	280	8.35 N	79.50 W
Chame, Punta >	280	8.38 N	79.42 W
Chamela, Bahía C	278	19.33 N	105.07 W
Chamelecón	280	15.24 N	88.01 W
Chamelecón ≃	280	15.54 N	87.48 W
Chamical (Gobernador Gordillo)	294	30.22 S	66.19 W
Chamois	248	38.41 N	91.46 W
Chamonix-Mont-Blanc	180	45.55 N	6.52 E
Champagne	236	60.47 N	136.29 W
Champagne □[9]	166	49.00 N	4.30 E
Champagne Castle ∧	224	29.06 S	29.20 E
Champagnole	180	46.45 N	5.55 E
Champaign	248	40.07 N	88.14 W
Champaign □[6], Ill., U.S.	268	40.07 N	88.12 W
Champaign □[6], Ohio, U.S.	268	40.07 N	83.45 W
Champaquí, Cerro ∧	294	31.58 S	64.56 W
Champassak	200	14.53 N	105.52 E
Champdeniers	166	46.29 N	0.24 W
Champdoré, Lac ⊜	232	55.55 N	65.50 W
Champeix	166	45.36 N	3.08 E
Champerico	280	14.18 N	91.55 W
Champéry	166	46.10 N	6.52 E
Champigny	260	46.47 N	71.23 W
Champion, Alta., Can.	238	50.14 N	113.09 W
Champion, Mich., U.S.	244	46.31 N	87.58 W
Champion, Ohio, U.S.	266	41.17 N	80.51 W
Champion, Pa., U.S.	266	40.05 N	79.21 W
Champlain	260	44.59 N	73.27 W
Champlain □[6]	260	46.45 N	72.35 W
Champlain, Lake ⊜	242	44.45 N	73.15 W
Champlitte-et-le-Prélot	166	47.37 N	5.31 E
Champotón	278	19.21 N	90.43 W
Chamusca	168	39.21 N	8.29 W
Chañar	294	30.33 S	65.58 W
Chañaral	294	26.21 S	70.37 W
Chañaral, Isla I	294	29.02 S	71.35 W
Chancay	292	11.32 S	77.25 W
Chancay ≃	292	11.37 S	77.16 W
Chance	262	38.11 N	75.56 W
Chanch	190	51.30 N	100.40 E
Chan Chan ⊥	292	8.10 S	79.00 W
Chanchelulla Peak ∧	258	40.28 N	122.59 W
Chanco	294	35.44 S	72.32 W
Chandalar	236	67.30 N	148.30 W
Chandalar ≃	236	66.36 N	145.48 W
Chandeleur Islands II	248	29.48 N	88.51 W
Chandeleur Sound ⨆	248	29.55 N	89.10 W
Chandīgarh	206	30.44 N	76.47 E
Chandler, Qué., Can.	240	48.21 N	64.41 W
Chandler, Ariz., U.S.	254	33.18 N	111.50 W
Chandler, Ind., U.S.	248	38.03 N	87.22 W
Chandler, Okla., U.S.	250	35.42 N	96.53 W
Chandler, Tex., U.S.	250	32.18 N	95.29 W
Chandler ≃	236	69.27 N	151.30 W
Chandler Lake ⊜	236	68.15 N	152.43 W
Chandlers Valley	266	41.56 N	79.18 W
Chandlerville	248	40.03 N	90.09 W
Chandless ≃	292	9.08 S	69.51 W
Chandos Lake ⊜	244	44.49 N	78.00 W
Chāndpur, Bngl.	204	22.08 N	91.55 E
Chāndpur, Pāk.	190	23.13 N	90.39 E
Chandyga	186	62.40 N	135.36 E
Chang, Ko I	200	12.05 N	102.20 E
Changajn Nuruu ⛰	190	47.30 N	100.00 E
Changane ≃	224	24.43 S	33.32 E
Changbaishan ⛰	194	42.05 N	128.00 E
Changcheng (Great Wall) ⊥	194	40.30 N	117.00 E
Changchiak'ou → Zhangjiakou	194	40.50 N	114.53 E
Changchou → Zhangzhou	196	24.33 N	117.39 E
Changchow → Changzhou	196	31.47 N	119.57 E
Changchun	190	43.53 N	125.19 E
Changde	190	28.55 N	111.38 E
Changdu	190	31.11 N	97.15 E
Change Islands	240	49.40 N	54.24 W
Changgi-got >	194	36.05 N	129.34 E
Ch'anghsü Shan I	196	26.14 N	119.58 E
Changhu ⊜	196	30.15 N	112.35 E
Changhua	196	24.05 N	120.32 E
Changji	190	44.01 N	87.19 E
Changjiang, Zhg.	196	25.52 N	116.20 E
Changjiang, Zhg.	200	19.17 N	109.02 E
Changjiang (Yangtze) ≃	190	31.48 N	121.10 E
Changli	194	39.43 N	119.11 E
Changning	200	24.55 N	99.35 E
Changokurt	158	61.58 N	64.18 E
Changsan-got >	194	38.08 N	124.39 E
Changsha	196	28.11 N	113.01 E
Changshanjiang ≃	196	28.57 N	118.50 E
Changshanqundao II	194	39.00 N	122.45 E
Changshu	196	31.39 N	120.45 E
Changsŏn-gang ≃	194	39.15 N	126.02 E
Changuinola ≃	280	9.28 N	82.28 W
Changxi ≃	196	26.53 N	119.41 E
Changxingdao I	194	39.34 N	121.23 E
Changzhi	190	36.11 N	113.08 E
Changzhou (Changchow)	196	31.47 N	119.57 E
Chanka, Ozero (Xingkathu) ⊜	190	45.00 N	132.24 E
Channahon	268	41.26 N	88.14 W
Channel Islands II, Eur.	162	49.20 N	2.20 W
Channel Islands II, Calif., U.S.	258	34.00 N	120.00 W
Channel Islands National Monument ♠	258	34.00 N	119.26 W
Channel Lake	268	42.29 N	88.08 W
Channel-Port-aux-Basques	240	47.35 N	59.11 W
Channelview	250	29.46 N	95.07 W
Channing, Mich., U.S.	244	46.09 N	88.05 W
Channing, Tex., U.S.	250	35.41 N	102.20 W
Chantada	168	42.37 N	7.46 W
Chantajskoje, Ozero ⊜	186	68.20 N	91.00 E
Chanthaburi	200	12.37 N	102.09 E
Chantilly	176	49.12 N	2.28 E
Chantonnay	166	46.41 N	1.03 W
Chantrey Inlet C	232	67.48 N	96.20 W
Chanty-Mansijsk	186	61.00 N	69.06 E
Chanute	252	37.41 N	95.27 W
Chanute Air Force Base ■	248	40.18 N	88.09 W
Chao, Isla I	292	8.46 S	78.48 W
Chaoan	196	23.41 N	116.38 E
Chaobaixinhe ≃	194	39.37 N	117.26 E
Chaohu ⊜	196	31.31 N	117.33 E
Chao Phraya ≃	200	13.32 N	100.36 E
Chaoyang	194	41.35 N	120.28 E
Chapada dos Guimarães	292	15.26 S	55.45 W
Chapala	278	20.18 N	103.12 W
Chapala, Lago de ⊜	278	20.15 N	103.00 W
Chaparé ≃	292	15.58 S	64.42 W
Chaparra	284p	21.10 N	76.29 W
Chaparra, Bahía de C	284p	21.12 N	76.32 W
Chaparral	290	3.43 N	75.28 W
Chapčeranga	186	49.42 N	112.24 E
Chapecó	294	27.06 S	52.36 W
Chapecó ≃	294	27.06 S	53.01 W
Chapel Hill, N.C., U.S.	246	35.55 N	79.04 W
Chapel Hill, Tenn., U.S.	248	35.38 N	86.41 W
Chapelton	285q	18.05 N	77.16 W
Chapicuy	294	31.39 S	57.54 W
Chapimarca	292	13.58 S	73.04 W
Chapin	248	39.46 N	90.24 W
Chaplain ≃	248	37.50 N	85.11 W
Chapleau	244	47.50 N	83.24 W
Chapleau ≃	244	48.29 N	82.57 W
Chaplin	261	41.48 N	72.08 W
Chapman, Kans., U.S.	252	38.58 N	97.01 W
Chapman, Nebr., U.S.	252	41.02 N	98.09 W
Chapman, Pa., U.S.	262	40.46 N	75.24 W
Chapman ≃	224	22.19 S	20.00 E
Chapman, Cape >	232	69.12 N	88.59 W
Chapman, Mount ∧	238	51.50 N	118.20 W
Chapmanville	242	37.58 N	82.01 W
Chapo	250	29.17 N	104.20 W
Chappell	252	41.06 N	102.28 W
Chappell Hill	250	30.09 N	96.16 W
Chāpra	206	23.31 N	88.33 E
Chapultepec, Méx.	254	32.22 N	115.05 W
Chapultepec, Méx.	258	31.50 N	116.38 W
Chapultepec ∧	278	23.27 N	103.04 W
Chaqui	292	19.36 S	65.32 W
Chaquiago	294	27.33 S	66.20 W
Charadai	294	27.40 S	59.55 W
Charagua	292	19.48 S	63.13 W
Charalá	290	6.17 N	73.10 W
Charaña	292	17.36 S	69.28 W
Charapán	278	19.41 N	102.06 W
Charata	294	27.15 S	61.15 W
Charbala	186	64.07 N	120.19 E
Charcana	292	15.13 S	73.05 W
Charcas	278	23.08 N	101.07 W
Charco Azul, Bahía de C	280	8.10 N	82.42 W
Charco Hondo	284m	18.25 N	66.43 W
Charcos de Figueroa	278	27.45 N	102.11 W
Charcos de Risa	278	26.15 N	103.10 W
Chard	174	50.53 N	2.58 W
Chardon	266	41.35 N	81.12 W
Chardzhou → Čardžou	208	39.06 N	63.34 E
Charente □[5]	166	45.40 N	0.10 E
Charente ≃	166	45.57 N	1.05 W
Charente-Maritime □[5]	166	45.30 N	0.45 W
Charenton-du-Cher	166	46.44 N	2.38 E
Chari ≃	214	12.58 N	14.31 E
Chārikār	204	35.02 N	69.11 E
Charing Cross	266	42.20 N	82.06 W
Chariton	244	41.01 N	93.19 W
Chariton ≃	248	39.19 N	92.57 W
Charitonovo	160	61.27 N	47.28 E
Charity	290	7.24 N	58.36 W
Char'kov	158	50.00 N	36.15 E
Charlemagne	260	45.43 N	73.29 W
Charlemont	261	42.38 N	72.52 W
Charleroi, Bel.	176	50.25 N	4.26 E
Charleroi, Pa., U.S.	266	40.09 N	79.57 W
Charles □[6]	262	38.32 N	76.59 W
Charlesbourg	260	46.52 N	71.16 W
Charles City, Iowa, U.S.	244	43.04 N	92.40 W
Charles City, Va., U.S.	262	37.20 N	77.04 W
Charles City □[6]	262	37.20 N	77.02 W
Charles Island I	232	62.40 N	74.15 W
Charles Mound ∧[2]	244	42.30 N	90.14 W
Charles Sound ⨆	230	45.03 S	167.05 E
Charleston, Ark., U.S.	248	35.18 N	94.02 W
Charleston, Ill., U.S.	248	39.30 N	88.10 W
Charleston, Miss., U.S.	248	34.00 N	90.04 W
Charleston, Mo., U.S.	248	36.55 N	89.21 W
Charleston, S.C., U.S.	246	32.48 N	79.57 W
Charleston, W. Va., U.S.	242	38.21 N	81.38 W
Charleston Heights	246	32.51 N	80.00 W
Charleston Peak ∧	258	36.16 N	115.42 W
Charlestown, St. K.-N.-A.	282	17.08 N	62.37 W
Charlestown, Ind., U.S.	248	38.27 N	85.40 W
Charlestown, N.H., U.S.	242	43.14 N	72.26 W
Charlestown, R.I., U.S.	261	41.23 N	71.45 W
Charles Town, W. Va., U.S.	242	39.17 N	77.52 W
Charlesville	218	5.27 S	20.58 E
Charleville	228	26.24 S	146.15 E
Charleville-Mézières	166	49.46 N	4.43 E
Charlevoix	244	45.19 N	85.16 W
Charlevoix, Lake ⊜	244	45.15 N	85.08 W
Charley ≃	236	65.20 N	142.49 W
Charlie Lake	238	56.16 N	120.57 W
Charlieu	166	46.10 N	4.10 E
Charlotte, Mich., U.S.	268	42.36 N	84.50 W
Charlotte, N.C., U.S.	246	35.14 N	80.50 W
Charlotte, Tenn., U.S.	248	36.11 N	87.24 W
Charlotte, Tex., U.S.	250	28.52 N	98.43 W
Charlotte Amalie	284m	18.21 N	64.56 W
Charlotte Court House	246	37.03 N	78.39 W
Charlotte Harbor C	246	26.45 N	82.12 W
Charlotte Lake ⊜	238	52.11 N	125.20 W
Charlottenberg	160	59.53 N	12.17 E
Charlottesville	246	38.02 N	78.29 W
Charlottetown, P.E.I., Can.	240	46.14 N	63.08 W
Charlotte Town (Gouyave), Gren.	285k	12.10 N	61.44 W
Charlovka	160	68.47 N	37.15 E
Charlton	261	42.08 N	71.58 W
Charlton City	261	42.09 N	71.58 W
Charlton Island I	232	52.00 N	79.30 W
Charlton Kings	174	51.53 N	2.03 W
Charlu	160	61.48 N	30.52 E
Charm	266	40.30 N	81.47 W
Charmes	166	48.22 N	6.17 E
Charny	260	46.43 N	71.16 W
Charolles	166	46.26 N	4.17 E
Charovsk	160	59.59 N	40.11 E
Charroux	166	46.09 N	0.24 E
Chārsadda	206	34.09 N	71.44 E
Charter Oak	252	42.04 N	95.35 W
Charters Towers	228	20.05 S	146.16 E
Chartley	261	41.57 N	71.14 W
Chartres	176	48.27 N	1.30 E
Char Us Nuur ⊜	190	48.00 N	92.10 E
Charutajuvom	160	66.49 N	59.30 E
Chasavjurt	158	43.15 N	46.37 E
Chascomús	294	35.35 S	58.00 W
Chase, B.C., Can.	238	50.49 N	119.41 W
Chase, Alaska, U.S.	236	62.27 N	150.07 W
Chase, Kans., U.S.	252	38.21 N	98.21 W
Chase, Md., U.S.	262	39.22 N	76.22 W
Chase, Mount ∧	242	46.07 N	68.29 W
Chase City	246	36.48 N	78.28 W
Chase Lake	264	43.46 N	75.19 W
Chase River	270	49.08 N	123.55 W
Chashui ≃	196	31.44 N	113.11 E
Chaska	244	44.47 N	93.35 W
Chaslands Mistake >	230	46.38 S	169.22 E
Chassignolle, Lac ⊜	244	48.20 N	78.20 W
Chastang	248	31.02 N	88.02 W
Chasuta	292	6.32 S	76.07 W
Chatanbulag	190	43.11 N	109.10 E
Chatanga	186	71.58 N	102.30 E
Chatanga ≃	186	72.55 N	106.00 E
Chatangskij Zaliv C	186	73.30 N	109.00 E
Chatanika	236	65.07 N	147.31 W
Chatanika ≃	236	65.04 N	149.18 W
Chateaubelair	285h	13.17 N	61.15 W
Châteaubriant	166	47.43 N	1.23 W
Château-Chinon	166	47.04 N	3.56 E
Château d'Oex	166	46.28 N	7.08 E
Château-du-Loir	166	47.42 N	0.25 E
Châteaudun	176	48.05 N	1.20 E
Chateaugay	260	44.56 N	74.05 W
Château-Gontier	166	47.50 N	0.42 W
Châteauguay	260	45.23 N	73.45 W
Châteauguay □[6]	260	45.15 N	73.45 W
Châteauguay (Chateaugay) ≃	260	45.24 N	73.45 W
Châteauguay-Centre	260	45.22 N	73.45 W
Château-Landon	166	48.09 N	2.42 E
Château-la-Vallière	166	47.33 N	0.19 E
Châteaulin	166	48.12 N	4.05 W
Châteaumeillant	166	46.34 N	2.12 E
Châteauneuf	166	43.23 N	5.10 E
Châteauneuf-de-Randon	166	44.39 N	3.40 E
Châteauneuf-en-Thymerais	166	48.35 N	1.15 E
Châteauneuf-sur-Charente	166	45.36 N	0.03 W
Châteauneuf-sur-Loire	166	47.52 N	2.14 E
Châteauneuf-sur-Sarthe	166	47.41 N	0.30 W
Châteaurenard-Provence	182	43.53 N	4.51 E
Château-Renault	166	47.35 N	0.55 E
Château-Richer	240	47.00 N	71.01 W
Châteauroux	166	46.49 N	1.42 E
Château-Salins	166	48.49 N	6.30 E
Château-Thierry	176	49.03 N	3.24 E
Châtelet	176	50.24 N	4.31 E
Châtelineau	176	50.25 N	4.31 E
Châtellerault	166	46.49 N	0.33 E
Châtel-sur-Moselle	166	48.18 N	6.24 E
Châtelus-Malvaleix	166	46.18 N	2.01 E
Chatfield, Minn., U.S.	244	43.51 N	92.11 W
Chatfield, Ohio, U.S.	266	40.57 N	82.56 W
Chatgal	190	50.26 N	100.07 E
Chatham, N.B., Can.	240	47.02 N	65.28 W
Chatham, Ont., Can.	266	42.24 N	82.11 W
Chatham, Eng., U.K.	174	51.23 N	0.32 E
Chatham, Ill., U.S.	248	39.40 N	89.42 W
Chatham, La., U.S.	248	32.19 N	92.27 W
Chatham, Mass., U.S.	261	41.41 N	69.58 W
Chatham, N.J., U.S.	262	40.44 N	74.23 W
Chatham, N.Y., U.S.	261	42.22 N	73.36 W
Chatham, Ohio, U.S.	266	41.06 N	82.01 W
Chatham, Pa., U.S.	262	39.51 N	75.49 W
Chatham, Va., U.S.	246	36.50 N	79.24 W
Chatham, Wyo., U.S.	254	43.52 N	108.10 W
Chatham Head	240	47.00 N	65.33 W
Chatham Rise ✣[3]	148	43.30 S	178.00 W
Chatham Sound ⨆	238	54.32 N	130.35 W
Chatham Strait ⨆	236	57.30 N	134.45 W
Châtillon	170	45.45 N	7.37 E
Châtillon-Coligny	166	47.50 N	2.51 E
Châtillon-en-Bazois	166	47.03 N	3.49 E
Châtillon-sur-Chalaronne	166	46.07 N	4.58 E
Châtillon-sur-Indre	166	46.59 N	1.11 E
Châtillon-sur-Seine	180	47.51 N	4.33 E
Chatom	248	31.28 N	88.16 W
Chatsquot Mountain ∧	238	53.08 N	127.30 W
Chatsworth, Ont., Can.	264	44.27 N	80.54 W
Chatsworth, Ga., U.S.	246	34.46 N	84.46 W
Chatsworth, Ill., U.S.	268	40.45 N	88.18 W
Chatsworth, N.J., U.S.	262	39.46 N	74.33 W
Chattahoochee	246	30.42 N	84.51 W
Chattahoochee ≃	246	30.52 N	84.57 W
Chattanooga, Ohio, U.S.	268	40.38 N	84.47 W
Chattanooga, Tenn., U.S.	248	35.03 N	85.19 W
Chattaroy	242	37.42 N	82.17 W
Chatteris	174	52.27 N	0.03 E
Chatwood	262	39.58 N	75.35 W
Chatyrka	186	62.03 N	175.15 E
Chaudes-Aigues	166	44.51 N	3.00 E
Chauekuktuli, Lake ⊜	236	60.03 N	158.45 W
Chauk	200	20.54 N	94.50 E
Chaullay	292	13.01 S	72.37 W
Chaumont, Fr.	180	48.07 N	5.08 E
Chaumont, N.Y., U.S.	264	44.04 N	76.08 W
Chaumont-en-Vexin	166	49.16 N	1.53 E
Chaumont-Porcien	166	49.39 N	4.15 E
Chauncey	242	39.24 N	82.08 W
Chauny	176	49.37 N	3.13 E
Chau-phu	200	10.42 N	105.06 E
Chaussin	166	46.58 N	5.25 E
Chautauqua	266	42.14 N	79.28 W
Chautauqua □[6]	266	42.15 N	79.30 W
Chautauqua Lake ⊜	242	42.12 N	79.27 W
Chauvigny	166	46.34 N	0.39 E
Chavanges	166	48.31 N	4.34 E
Chavannes, Lac ⊜	244	46.51 N	77.10 W
Chavarría	294	28.57 S	58.34 W
Chaves	168	41.44 N	7.28 W
Chaviña	292	14.59 S	73.51 W
Cháviva	290	4.22 N	72.20 W
Chay ≃	200	21.39 N	105.12 E
Chayanta	292	18.27 S	66.30 W
Chazy	242	44.53 N	73.26 W
Chbar ≃	200	13.22 N	107.04 E
Cheaha Mountain ∧	248	33.30 N	85.47 W
Cheakamus Indian Reserve ◆[4]	238	49.48 N	123.11 W
Cheam View	270	49.15 N	121.41 W
Cheb	164	50.01 N	12.25 E
Chebanse	268	41.00 N	87.54 W
Chebogue Point >	240	43.45 N	66.07 W
Cheboygan	244	45.39 N	84.29 W
Chech, Erg ◆[2]	214	25.00 N	2.15 W
Chechaouèn	168	35.10 N	5.16 W
Chech'on	194	37.08 N	128.12 E
Chęciny	164	50.48 N	20.28 E
Checleset Bay C	238	50.03 N	127.40 W
Checotah	250	35.28 N	95.31 W
Chedabucto Bay C	240	45.23 N	61.10 W
Cheddar	162	51.17 N	2.46 W
Cheduba Island I	200	18.48 N	93.38 E
Cheduba Strait ⨆	200	18.56 N	93.45 E
Cheektowaga	264	42.55 N	78.46 W
Cheerchenghe ≃	206	39.25 N	88.20 E
Chef-Boutonne	166	46.07 N	0.04 W
Chefoo → Yantai	194	37.33 N	121.20 E
Chefornak	236	60.13 N	164.12 W
Chehalis	270	46.40 N	122.58 W
Cheiron, Montagne du ∧	166	43.49 N	6.58 E
Cheju	190	33.31 N	126.32 E
Cheju-do I	190	33.20 N	126.30 E
Chekiang → Zhejiang □[4]	196	29.00 N	120.00 E
Chelan	256	47.51 N	120.01 W
Chelan □[6]	270	47.56 N	120.52 W
Chelan, Lake ⊜	256	48.05 N	120.30 W
Chelforó	294	39.05 S	66.30 W
Chelghoum el Aïd	168	36.10 N	6.08 E
Chélia, Djebel ∧	214	35.19 N	6.42 E
Chéliff, Oued ≃	168	36.01 N	0.07 E
Chelles	176	48.53 N	2.36 E
Chełm	164	51.10 N	23.28 E
Chełmno	164	53.22 N	18.26 E
Chelmsford, Ont., Can.	244	46.35 N	81.12 W
Chelmsford, Eng., U.K.	174	51.44 N	0.28 E
Chelmsford, Mass., U.S.	261	42.36 N	71.21 W
Chełmża	164	53.12 N	18.37 E
Chelsea, Iowa, U.S.	244	41.55 N	92.24 W
Chelsea, Mass., U.S.	261	42.24 N	71.02 W
Chelsea, Mich., U.S.	268	42.19 N	84.01 W
Chelsea, Okla., U.S.	250	36.32 N	95.26 W
Chelsea, Vt., U.S.	242	43.59 N	72.27 W
Chelsea Estates	262	39.41 N	75.36 W
Chelsea Park	270	47.28 N	122.21 W
Cheltenham, Eng., U.K.	174	51.54 N	2.04 W
Cheltenham, Md., U.S.	262	38.44 N	76.50 W
Cheltenham, Pa., U.S.	262	40.04 N	75.08 W
Chelva	168	39.45 N	0.59 W
Chelyabinsk → Čel'abinsk	158	55.10 N	61.24 E
Chelyan	242	38.12 N	81.30 W
Chemainus	238	48.55 N	123.43 W
Chemax	278	20.39 N	87.56 W
Chemillé	166	47.13 N	0.44 W
Chemnitz → Karl-Marx-Stadt	164	50.50 N	12.55 E
Chemult	256	43.13 N	121.47 W
Chemung	268	42.25 N	88.40 W
Chemung ≃	244	41.55 N	76.31 W
Chemung Lake ⊜	244	44.25 N	78.22 W
Chena ≃	236	64.48 N	147.55 W
Chenāb ≃	206	29.23 N	71.02 E
Chenachane	214	26.04 N	4.15 E
Chenango □[6]	264	42.32 N	75.31 W
Chenango Bridge	242	42.10 N	75.52 W
Chenderoh Lake ⊜	200	4.58 N	100.57 E
Chêne-Bourg	180	46.12 N	6.12 E
Chenequa	268	43.07 N	88.23 W
Chénéville	260	45.53 N	75.03 W
Cheney, Kans., U.S.	252	37.38 N	97.47 W
Cheney, Wash., U.S.	256	47.29 N	117.34 W
Cheney Reservoir ⊜[1]	252	37.45 N	97.50 W
Cheneys Point	266	42.08 N	79.24 W
Cheneyville	248	31.01 N	92.17 W
Chengchow → Zhengzhou	190	34.48 N	113.39 E
Chengde	194	40.58 N	117.53 E
Chengdu	190	30.39 N	104.04 E
Chengjiang	200	24.45 N	102.54 E
Chengmai	200	19.48 N	110.02 E
Chengshanjiao >	190	37.23 N	122.39 E
Chengtu → Chengdu	190	30.39 N	104.04 E
Chengxihu ⊜	196	32.24 N	116.15 E
Chenhu ⊜	196	30.29 N	113.22 E
Chenil, Lac ⊜	240	51.52 N	59.40 W
Chenoa	268	40.45 N	88.43 W
Chenôve	180	47.17 N	5.00 E
Chenoweth	270	45.37 N	121.13 W
Chepachet	261	41.55 N	71.40 W
Chepén	292	7.15 S	79.25 W
Chepes	294	31.21 S	66.40 W
Chépica	294	34.44 S	71.17 W
Chepo	290	9.11 N	79.06 W
Chepstow	174	51.39 N	2.41 W
Cher □[5]	166	47.05 N	2.30 E
Cher ≃	166	47.21 N	0.29 E
Cheraw	246	34.42 N	79.53 W
Cherbourg	166	49.39 N	1.39 W
Cherchell	168	36.35 N	2.16 E
Cheremkhovo → Čeremchovo	186	53.09 N	103.05 E
Cherepovets → Čerepovec	160	59.08 N	37.54 E
Chergui, Chott ech ⊜	214	34.15 N	0.30 E
Cheribon → Tjirebon	198	6.44 S	108.34 E
Cherita, Sebkret ech ⊜	170	35.21 N	10.19 E
Cheriton	262	37.17 N	75.58 W
Cherkassy → Čerkassy	158	49.26 N	32.04 E
Chernigov → Černigov	158	51.30 N	31.18 E
Chernofski	236	53.24 N	167.33 W
Cherokee, Ala., U.S.	248	34.46 N	87.58 W
Cherokee, Iowa, U.S.	252	42.45 N	95.33 W
Cherokee, Kans., U.S.	252	37.21 N	94.49 W
Cherokee, Okla., U.S.	250	36.45 N	98.21 W
Cherokee, Tex., U.S.	250	30.59 N	98.43 W
Cherokee Dam ◆[6]	246	36.12 N	83.35 W
Cherokee Indian Reservation ◆[4]	246	35.25 N	83.24 W
Cherokee Lake ⊜[1]	246	36.16 N	83.20 W
Cherokee Plains ≚	248	37.00 N	95.15 W
Cherokee Point >	246	26.20 N	77.03 W
Cherokee Ranch	262	40.25 N	75.55 W
Cherokees, Lake O' The ⊜[1]	250	36.39 N	94.49 W
Cherokee Sound	282	26.17 N	77.02 W
Cherquenco	294	38.41 S	72.00 W
Cherry Creek, B.C., Can.	270	49.17 N	124.47 W
Cherry Creek, N.Y., U.S.	266	42.18 N	79.06 W
Cherry Grove	270	45.27 N	123.15 W
Cherry Hill	262	39.55 N	75.01 W
Cherryland	272	37.41 N	122.06 W
Cherryplain	261	42.38 N	73.22 W
Cherryvale	252	37.16 N	95.33 W
Cherry Valley, Ark., U.S.	248	35.24 N	90.45 W
Cherry Valley, Calif., U.S.	274	33.57 N	116.53 W
Cherry Valley, Ill., U.S.	268	42.13 N	88.59 W
Cherry Valley, Mass., U.S.	261	42.15 N	71.52 W
Cherry Valley, Pa., U.S.	266	41.10 N	79.48 W
Cherryville, N.C., U.S.	246	35.23 N	81.23 W
Cherryville, Pa., U.S.	262	40.45 N	75.33 W
Cherson	158	46.38 N	32.35 E
Chertsey	174	51.24 N	0.30 W
Chesaning	244	43.11 N	84.07 W
Chesapeake	262	36.43 N	76.15 W
Chesapeake Bay C	234	38.40 N	76.25 W
Chesapeake Bay Bridge-Tunnel ◆[5]	246	37.00 N	76.02 W
Chesapeake Beach	262	38.41 N	76.32 W
Chesapeake City	262	39.32 N	75.49 W
Chesaw	238	48.57 N	119.03 W
Chesham	174	51.43 N	0.38 W
Cheshire, Conn., U.S.	261	41.30 N	72.54 W
Cheshire, Mass., U.S.	261	42.34 N	73.10 W
Cheshire, N.Y., U.S.	264	42.49 N	77.20 W
Cheshire □[6], Eng., U.K.	174	53.23 N	2.30 W
Cheshire □[6], N.H., U.S.	261	42.50 N	72.15 W
Cheshunt	174	51.43 N	0.02 W
Cheslatta Lake ⊜	238	53.44 N	125.18 W
Chesley	264	44.17 N	81.05 W
Chesnee	246	35.09 N	81.52 W
Chester, Eng., U.K.	162	53.12 N	2.54 W
Chester, Calif., U.S.	258	40.19 N	121.14 W
Chester, Conn., U.S.	261	41.24 N	72.27 W
Chester, Ill., U.S.	248	37.55 N	89.49 W
Chester, Md., U.S.	262	38.58 N	76.17 W
Chester, Mass., U.S.	261	42.17 N	72.59 W
Chester, Mont., U.S.	256	48.31 N	110.58 W
Chester, Nebr., U.S.	252	40.01 N	97.37 W
Chester, N.J., U.S.	262	40.47 N	74.42 W
Chester, Okla., U.S.	250	36.13 N	98.55 W
Chester, Pa., U.S.	262	39.51 N	75.21 W
Chester, S.C., U.S.	246	34.43 N	81.12 W
Chester, Tex., U.S.	248	30.55 N	94.36 W
Chester, Vt., U.S.	242	43.16 N	72.36 W
Chester, Va., U.S.	262	37.21 N	77.27 W
Chester, W. Va., U.S.	266	40.37 N	80.34 W
Chester □[6]	262	39.58 N	75.36 W
Chester Basin	240	44.34 N	64.19 W
Chesterfield, Eng., U.K.	162	53.15 N	1.25 W
Chesterfield, Conn., U.S.	261	41.24 N	72.11 W
Chesterfield, Mass., U.S.	261	42.24 N	72.50 W
Chesterfield, S.C., U.S.	246	34.44 N	80.05 W
Chesterfield, Va., U.S.	246	37.23 N	77.31 W
Chesterfield □[6]	262	37.20 N	77.25 W
Chesterfield, Île I	218	16.20 S	43.58 E
Chesterfield, Îles II	226	19.30 S	158.00 E
Chesterfield Inlet	232	63.21 N	90.42 W
Chesterfield Inlet C	232	63.25 N	90.45 W
Chesterhill, Ohio, U.S.	242	39.29 N	81.52 W
Chester Hill, Pa., U.S.	266	40.53 N	78.14 W
Chesterland	266	41.31 N	81.21 W
Chester-le-Street	162	54.52 N	1.34 W
Chesterton	268	41.37 N	87.04 W
Chesterton Range ⛰	228	25.30 S	147.27 E
Chestertown	262	39.13 N	76.04 W
Chesterville, Ont., Can.	264	45.06 N	75.14 W
Chesterville, Ohio, U.S.	266	40.29 N	82.41 W
Chestnut Hill	261	41.40 N	72.16 W
Chest Peak ∧	230	43.06 S	172.01 E
Chest Springs	266	40.35 N	78.37 W
Chesuncook Lake ⊜	242	46.00 N	69.20 W
Cheswick	266	40.32 N	79.47 W
Cheswold	262	39.13 N	75.35 W
Cheta ≃	186	71.54 N	102.06 E
Chetaïbi	170	37.03 N	7.23 E
Chetco ≃	256	42.03 N	124.16 W
Chetek	244	45.19 N	91.39 W
Chéticamp	240	46.38 N	61.01 W
Chetopa	252	37.02 N	95.05 W
Chetumal Bay C	278	18.35 N	88.07 W
Chetwynd	238	55.42 N	121.40 W
Chevak	236	61.39 N	165.17 W
Cheval-Blanc, Montagne du ⛰	166	44.07 N	6.26 E
Cheval Blanc, Pointe du >	282	19.41 N	73.27 W
Cheviot	242	39.11 N	84.35 W
Cheviot Range ⛰	228	25.20 S	143.40 E
Chevy Chase Heights	266	40.36 N	79.08 W
Chewaucan ≃	256	42.30 N	120.18 W
Chew Bahir (Lake Stefanie) ⊜	214	4.40 N	36.50 E
Chewelah	256	48.17 N	117.43 W
Chewton	266	40.53 N	80.20 W
Cheyenne, Okla., U.S.	250	35.37 N	99.40 W
Cheyenne, Wyo., U.S.	254	41.08 N	104.49 W
Cheyenne ≃	252	44.40 N	101.15 W
Cheyenne River Indian Reservation ◆[4]	252	45.05 N	101.20 W
Cheyenne Wells	252	38.51 N	102.11 W
Chezhou	196	25.48 N	112.59 E
Chhâk Kâmpóng Saôm C	200	10.50 N	103.32 E
Chhay Arêng ≃	200	11.31 N	103.25 E
Chhindwāra	206	22.04 N	78.56 E
Chhlong ≃	200	12.15 N	106.00 E
Ch'hsing Yen I	196	21.44 N	120.50 E
Chi ≃	200	15.13 N	104.45 E
Chía	290	4.52 N	74.04 W
Chiai	196	23.29 N	120.27 E
Chiamussu → Jiamusi	190	46.50 N	130.21 E
Chianciano Terme	170	43.03 N	11.50 E
Chiang Khan	200	17.50 N	101.39 E
Chiang Mai	200	18.46 N	98.58 E
Chiang Rai	200	19.54 N	99.50 E
Chianti □[4]	184	43.22 N	11.23 E
Chianti, Monti del ⛰	170	43.32 N	11.25 E
Chiapa	292	19.32 S	69.13 W
Chiapa de Corzo	278	16.42 N	93.00 W
Chiapas □[3]	278	16.30 N	92.30 W
Chiaramonte Gulfi	170	37.01 N	14.43 E
Chiaravalle	184	43.36 N	13.19 E
Chiaravalle Centrale	170	38.41 N	16.25 E
Chiari	182	45.32 N	9.56 E
Chiasso	166	45.50 N	9.01 E
Chiautla de Tapia	278	18.17 N	98.36 W
Chiavari	182	44.19 N	9.19 E
Chiavenna	170	46.19 N	9.24 E
Chiba	192	35.36 N	140.07 E
Chibiribira Falls L	224	21.14 S	32.20 E
Chibougamau	232	49.53 N	74.21 W
Chibuto	218	24.44 S	33.33 E
Chibuzhangchuhu ⊜	206	33.25 N	90.15 E
Chicago	268	41.53 N	87.38 W
Chicago Heights	268	41.30 N	87.38 W
Chicago Park	272	39.09 N	120.58 W
Chicago Ridge	268	41.42 N	87.47 W
Chicama ≃	292	7.56 S	79.15 W
Chicapa ≃	218	6.26 S	20.47 E
Chic-Chocs, Réserve des(Chic-Chocs Reserve) ♠	240	49.05 N	65.42 W
Chichagof Island I	236	57.30 N	135.30 W
Chichas, Cordillera de ⛰	292	20.30 S	66.30 W
Chichén Itzá	278	20.40 N	88.34 W
Chichén Itzá ⊥	278	20.40 N	88.35 W
Chichester	174	50.50 N	0.48 W
Chichibu	192	35.59 N	139.05 E
Chichibu-tama-kokuritsu-kōen ♠	192	35.52 N	139.00 E
Chichica	280	8.22 N	81.40 W
Chichicastenango	280	14.56 N	91.07 W

Symbols in the index entries are identified on page 360.

Name	Page	Lat°′	Long°′
Chichigalpa	280	12.34 N	87.02 W
Chichimilá	278	20.37 N	88.13 W
Chichiriviche	290	10.56 N	68.16 W
Chickaloon	236	61.48 N	148.28 W
Chickamauga	246	34.52 N	85.18 W
Chickamauga Lake ⊜[1]	248	35.22 N	85.02 W
Chickamin ≃	238	55.47 N	130.58 W
Chickasaw, Ala., U.S.	248	30.46 N	88.05 W
Chickasaw, Ohio, U.S.	268	40.26 N	84.30 W
Chickasaw Bogue ≃	248	32.17 N	87.55 W
Chickasawhay ≃	248	31.00 N	88.45 W
Chickasha	250	35.02 N	97.58 W
Chicken	236	64.04 N	141.56 W
Chiclana de la Frontera	168	36.25 N	6.08 W
Chiclayo	292	6.46 S	79.50 W
Chico, Calif., U.S.	258	39.44 N	121.50 W
Chico, Tex., U.S.	250	33.18 N	97.48 W
Chico, Wash., U.S.	270	47.37 N	122.43 W
Chico ≃, Arg.	288	50.00 S	68.30 W
Chico ≃, Arg.	288	43.50 S	66.25 W
Chico ≃, Pan.	280	8.20 N	80.29 W
Chico ≃, Pil.	202	17.55 N	121.35 E
Chicoa	218	15.37 S	32.24 E
Chicobi, Lac ⊜	244	48.52 N	78.30 W
Chicomuselo	278	15.46 N	92.16 W
Chicopee, Ga., U.S.	246	34.16 N	83.51 W
Chicopee, Mass., U.S.	261	42.10 N	72.36 W
Chicora	266	40.57 N	79.45 W
Chicorato	278	26.02 N	107.54 W
Chicouimi, Réserve de(Chicoutimi Reserve) ♠	240	48.30 N	70.15 W
Chicoutimi	240	48.26 N	71.04 W
Chicoutimi ≃	240	48.27 N	71.04 W
Chicxulub	278	21.08 N	89.31 W
Chidester	248	33.42 N	93.01 W
Chidley, Cape ≻	232	60.23 N	64.26 W
Chiefland	246	29.29 N	82.52 W
Chiemsee ⊜	164	47.54 N	12.29 E
Chien, Bayou du ≃	248	36.35 N	89.11 W
Chieri	182	45.01 N	7.49 E
Chieti	184	42.21 N	14.10 E
Chieti □[4]	184	42.07 N	14.21 E
Chifeng	194	42.18 N	119.00 E
Chigasaki	192	35.19 N	139.24 E
Chiginagak, Mount ∧	236	57.08 N	156.59 W
Chigmit Mountains ⛰	236	60.00 N	153.00 W
Chignahuapan	278	19.50 N	98.02 W
Chignecto, Cape ≻	240	45.20 N	64.57 W
Chignecto Bay C	240	45.35 N	64.45 W
Chignik	236	56.18 N	158.23 W
Chignik Bay C	236	56.22 N	158.15 W
Chignik Lagoon	236	56.14 N	158.44 W
Chignik Lake	236	56.20 N	158.29 W
Chigorodó	290	7.41 N	76.42 W
Chigwell	174	51.38 N	0.05 E
Chihli, Gulf of → Bohai C	194	38.30 N	120.00 E
Chihuahua	278	28.38 N	106.05 W
Chihuxi ≃	196	26.38 N	117.24 E
Chii-san ∧	194	35.20 N	127.44 E
Chiitola	160	61.16 N	29.38 E
Chikaskia ≃	250	36.37 N	97.15 W
Chikindzonot	278	20.20 N	88.29 W
Chikrêng ≃	200	12.51 N	104.14 E
Chikugo ≃	192	33.09 N	130.21 E
Chikuma ≃	192	36.59 N	138.35 E
Chikuminuk Lake ⊜	236	60.14 N	159.00 W
Chilako ≃	238	53.54 N	122.59 W
Chilanko Forks	238	52.06 N	124.10 W
Chilapa de Alvarez	278	17.36 N	99.10 W
Chilās	204	35.25 N	74.05 E
Chilca	292	12.30 S	76.45 W
Chilca, Cordillera de ⛰	292	15.30 S	71.50 W
Chilca, Punta ≻	292	12.31 S	76.47 W
Chilco Lake Indian Reserve ⇝[4]	238	51.25 N	124.07 W
Chilcotin ≃	238	51.45 N	122.24 W
Childers	226	25.14 S	152.17 E
Childersburg	248	33.16 N	86.21 W
Childress	250	34.25 N	100.13 W
Chile	294	25.09 S	69.54 W
Chile □[1]	288	30.00 S	71.00 W
Chile Chico	288	46.33 S	71.44 W
Chilecito, Arg.	294	29.10 S	67.30 W
Chilecito, Arg.	294	33.53 S	69.03 W
Chile Rise ✧[3]	148	40.00 S	90.00 W
Chilete	292	7.14 S	78.51 W
Chilhowie	246	36.48 N	81.41 W
Chili	268	40.52 N	86.02 W
Chili ≃	292	16.25 S	71.35 W
Chilia, Braţul ≃[1]	172	45.18 N	29.40 E
Chili Center	264	43.06 N	77.44 W
Chililabombwe (Bancroft)	218	12.18 S	27.43 E
Chilin → Jilin	190	43.51 N	126.33 E
Chilka Lake ⊜	206	19.45 N	85.25 E
Chilkat Pass)(	236	59.43 N	136.35 W
Chilko ≃	238	52.08 N	123.30 W
Chilko Lake ⊜	238	51.20 N	124.05 W
Chillagoe	226	17.09 S	144.32 E
Chillán	294	36.36 S	72.07 W
Chillar	294	37.19 S	59.59 W
Chillicothe, Ill., U.S.	244	40.55 N	89.29 W
Chillicothe, Mo., U.S.	248	39.48 N	93.33 W
Chillicothe, Ohio, U.S.	242	39.20 N	82.59 W
Chillicothe, Tex., U.S.	250	34.10 N	99.31 W
Chilliwack	238	49.10 N	121.57 W
Chilloa, Ciénaga ⊜	290	9.10 N	74.05 W
Chillón ≃	292	11.57 S	77.09 W
Chillon ⊥	166	46.25 N	6.56 E
Chillum	262	38.58 N	76.59 W
Chilmark	261	41.21 N	70.45 W
Chiloane, Ilha I	224	20.40 S	34.55 E
Chiloé, Isla de I	288	42.30 S	73.55 W
Chilok	186	51.21 N	110.28 E
Chilok ≃	186	51.19 N	106.59 E
Chilón	278	17.14 N	92.25 W
Chiloquin	256	42.35 N	121.52 W
Chilpancingo [de los Bravos]	278	17.33 N	99.30 W
Chilton	244	44.02 N	88.10 W
Chiluage	218	9.30 S	21.47 E
Chilung	196	25.08 N	121.44 E
Chilwa, Lake ⊜	218	15.12 S	35.50 E
Chimaltenango	280	14.40 N	90.49 W
Chimaltenango □[5]	280	14.40 N	90.55 W
Chimán	290	8.45 N	78.40 W
Chimayo	254	36.00 N	105.56 W
Chimbarongo	294	34.42 S	71.03 W
Chimbas	294	31.28 S	68.30 W
Chimborazo □[4]	290	2.00 S	78.40 W
Chimborazo ∧[1]	290	1.28 S	78.48 W
Chimbote	292	9.05 S	78.36 W
Chimbote, Bahía de C	292	9.07 S	78.35 W
Chimichagua	290	9.15 N	73.49 W
Chimkent → Čimkent	186	42.18 N	69.36 E
Chimney Rock National Historic Site ♠	252	41.39 N	103.20 W
Chimpay	294	39.10 S	66.09 W
Chin □[8]	200	22.00 N	93.30 E
China	278	25.42 N	99.14 W
China □[1]	190	33.00 N	105.00 E
Chinácota	290	7.37 N	72.36 W
China Grove	246	35.34 N	80.35 W
China Lake ⊜	258	35.46 N	117.39 W
Chinameca	280	13.30 N	88.21 W
Chinan → Jinan	194	36.40 N	116.57 E
Chinandega	280	12.37 N	87.09 W
Chinandega □[5]	280	12.45 N	87.05 W
Chinati Peak ∧	250	29.57 N	104.29 W
Chincha, Islas de II	292	13.39 S	76.24 W
Chincha Alta	292	13.27 S	76.08 W
Chinchaga ≃	232	58.50 N	118.20 W
Chincheros	292	13.33 S	73.50 W
Chinchilla, Austl.	228	26.45 S	150.38 E
Chinchilla, Esp.	168	38.55 N	1.55 W
Chinchiná	290	4.58 N	75.36 W
Chinchón	168	40.08 N	3.25 W
Chinchorro, Banco ✧[4]	278	18.35 N	87.20 W
Chincolco	294	32.13 S	70.50 W
Chincoteague	262	37.56 N	75.23 W
Chinde	224	18.37 S	36.24 E
Chin-do I	194	34.25 N	126.15 E
Chindwin ≃	200	21.26 N	95.15 E
Chinese Camp	272	37.52 N	120.26 W
Chingola	218	12.32 S	27.52 E
Ch'ingtao → Qingdao	194	36.06 N	120.19 E
Chingtechen → Jingdezhen	196	29.16 N	117.11 E
Chinguetti	214	20.27 N	12.22 W
Chinhae	194	35.09 N	128.40 E
Chin Hills ⛰[2]	198	22.30 N	93.30 E
Chiniak, Cape ≻	236	57.36 N	152.08 W
Chiniot	206	31.43 N	72.59 E
Chinitna Point ≻	236	59.43 N	153.02 W
Chinitos	278	25.01 N	107.54 W
Chinju	194	35.11 N	128.05 E
Chinkiang → Zhenjiang	196	32.13 N	119.26 E
Chinko ≃	220	4.50 N	23.53 E
Chin Lakes ⊜	238	49.37 N	112.13 W
Chinle	254	36.09 N	109.33 W
Chinmen Tao I	196	24.27 N	118.23 E
Chinnampo → Namp'o	194	38.45 N	125.23 E
Chino	274	34.01 N	117.42 W
Chinon	176	47.10 N	0.15 E
Chinook, Mont., U.S.	256	48.35 N	109.14 W
Chinook, Wash., U.S.	270	46.16 N	123.57 W
Chinook Cove	238	51.14 N	120.10 W
Chino Valley	254	34.45 N	112.27 W
Chinowths Corner	272	36.20 N	119.19 W
Chinquapin	246	34.50 N	77.49 W
Chinsali	218	10.34 S	32.03 E
Chinú	290	9.06 N	75.24 W
Chinwangtao → Qinhuangdao	194	39.56 N	119.36 E
Chioggia	170	45.13 N	12.17 E
Chios → Khíos	172	38.22 N	26.08 E
Chios → Khíos I	172	38.22 N	26.00 E
Chipao	292	14.17 S	73.56 W
Chipei Tao I	196	23.42 N	119.35 E
Chip Lake ⊜	238	53.40 N	115.20 W
Chipley	248	30.47 N	85.32 W
Chipman	240	46.11 N	65.53 W
Chipola ≃	246	30.01 N	85.05 W
Chippawa	264	43.04 N	79.03 W
Chippenham	174	51.28 N	2.07 W
Chippewa ≃, Mich., U.S.	244	43.35 N	84.17 W
Chippewa ≃, Minn., U.S.	252	44.56 N	95.44 W
Chippewa ≃, Wis., U.S.	244	44.25 N	92.10 W
Chippewa Falls	244	44.56 N	91.24 W
Chippewa Lake	266	41.04 N	81.54 W
Chippewa Lake ⊜	244	45.56 N	91.13 W
Chipping Norton	162	51.56 N	1.32 W
Chiquián	292	10.07 S	77.10 W
Chiquimula	280	14.48 N	89.33 W
Chiquimula □[5]	280	14.40 N	89.25 W
Chiquimulilla	280	14.05 N	90.23 W
Chiquinata, Bahía C	292	20.20 S	70.10 W
Chiquinquirá	290	5.37 N	73.50 W
Chiquintirca	292	13.06 S	73.41 W
Chiquitos, Llanos de ≚	292	18.00 S	61.30 W
Chira ≃	290	4.54 S	81.08 W
Chira, Isla de I	280	10.06 N	85.09 W
Chireno	248	31.30 N	94.21 W
Chirfa	214	20.57 N	12.21 E
Chiriaco (Imaza) ≃	292	5.09 S	78.19 W
Chiricahua Mountains ⛰	254	31.50 N	109.15 W
Chiricahua National Monument ♠	254	32.02 N	109.19 W
Chiricahua Peak ∧	254	31.52 N	109.20 W
Chiriguaná	290	9.22 N	73.36 W
Chirikof Island I	236	55.50 N	155.35 W
Chirilagua	280	13.13 N	88.08 W
Chirinos	292	5.15 S	78.52 W
Chiriquí	280	8.22 N	82.19 W
Chiriquí □[4]	280	8.30 N	82.00 W
Chiriquí ≃	280	8.18 N	82.25 W
Chiriquí, Golfo de C	280	8.00 N	82.20 W
Chiriquí, Laguna de C	280	9.02 N	82.00 W
Chiriquí, Volcán de(Volcán Barú) ∧[1]	280	8.49 N	82.32 W
Chiriquí Grande	280	8.57 N	82.07 W
Chiriquí Viejo ≃	280	8.19 N	82.42 W
Chiromo	218	16.33 S	35.08 E
Chirote, Isla I	280	8.14 N	82.21 W
Chirripó ≃	280	10.41 N	83.41 W
Chirripó, Cerro ∧	280	9.29 N	83.29 W
Chisago City	244	45.22 N	92.53 W
Chisana	236	62.09 N	142.10 W
Chiscas	290	6.33 N	72.29 W
Chisec	280	15.49 N	90.17 W
Chisholm, Ala., U.S.	248	32.25 N	86.15 W
Chisholm, Maine, U.S.	242	44.29 N	70.12 W
Chisholm, Minn., U.S.	244	47.29 N	92.53 W
Chisholm Mills	238	54.55 N	114.08 W
Chişineu-Criş	172	46.31 N	21.31 E
Chisone ≃	170	44.49 N	7.25 E
Chisos Mountains ⛰	250	29.15 N	103.20 W
Chistochina	236	62.34 N	144.40 W
Chistyakovo → Torez	000	48.01 N	38.37 E
Chita, Col.	290	6.11 N	72.28 W
Chitado	218	17.20 S	13.54 E
Chitagá	290	7.09 N	72.40 W
Chita-hantō ≻[1]	192	34.50 N	136.53 E
Chitembo	218	13.34 S	16.40 E
Chitina	236	61.31 N	144.27 W
Chitina ≃	236	61.30 N	144.28 W
Chitipa	218	9.43 S	33.15 E
Chitose	192a	42.49 N	141.39 E
Chitoushan I	196	27.40 N	120.50 E
Chitrāl	204	35.51 N	71.47 E
Chitré	280	7.58 N	80.26 W
Chittagong	206	22.20 N	91.50 E
Chittenango Falls	264	42.59 N	75.50 W
Chíuchíu	294	22.21 S	68.39 W
Chiumbe ≃	218	7.00 S	21.12 E
Chiusi	184	43.01 N	11.57 E
Chiuta, Lake ⊜	218	14.55 S	35.50 E
Chiva, Esp.	168	39.28 N	0.43 W
Chiva, S.S.S.R.	186	41.24 N	60.22 E
Chivacoa	290	10.10 N	68.54 W
Chivasso	182	45.11 N	7.53 E
Chivato, Punta ≻	278	27.05 N	111.59 W
Chivay	292	15.40 S	71.35 W
Chivilcoy	294	34.52 S	60.02 W
Chixoy (Negro) ≃	280	16.05 N	90.26 W
Chizu	192	35.16 N	134.14 E
Chkalov → Orenburg	158	51.54 N	55.06 E
Chloride	254	35.25 N	114.19 W
Chmel'nickij	158	49.25 N	27.00 E
Chmielnik	164	50.37 N	20.46 E
Chŏâm Khsant	198	14.13 N	104.56 E
Choapa ≃	294	31.38 S	71.34 W
Choapan	278	17.20 N	95.57 W
Chobe □[5]	224	18.30 S	25.00 E
Chobe (Linyanti) ≃	224	17.50 S	25.05 E
Chobeju	160	64.53 N	60.10 E
Chobe National Park ♠	224	18.45 S	24.15 E
Choceň	164	50.00 N	16.13 E
Chochis, Cerro ∧	292	18.10 S	59.53 W
Chocianów (Kotzenau)	164	51.25 N	15.55 E
Chociwel (Freienwalde in Pommern)	164	53.28 N	15.19 E
Chocó □[5]	290	6.00 N	77.00 W
Chocolate Mountains ⛰	254	33.25 N	114.10 W
Chocontá	290	5.09 N	73.41 W
Chocope	292	7.47 S	79.12 W
Choctaw	248	32.13 N	88.06 W
Choctawhatchee Bay C	248	30.25 N	86.21 W
Choctaw Indian Reservation ⇝[4]	248	32.49 N	89.14 W
Chodecz	164	52.24 N	19.01 E
Chodovaricha	160	68.57 N	53.40 E
Chodžejli	186	42.48 N	59.25 E
Chodzież	164	52.59 N	16.56 E
Choele-Choel	294	39.15 S	65.30 W
Choiseul	285f	13.47 N	61.03 W
Choiseul I	226	7.00 S	157.00 E
Choix	278	26.43 N	108.17 W
Chojna (Königsberg)	164	52.58 N	14.28 E
Chojnice	164	53.42 N	17.34 E
Chojnów (Haynau)	164	51.17 N	15.56 E
Chōkai-zan ∧	192	39.06 N	140.03 E
Chokio	252	45.34 N	96.10 W
Cholame	272	35.43 N	120.18 W
Cholet	166	47.04 N	0.53 W
Chŏlla Namdo □[4]	194	34.45 N	127.00 E
Chŏlla Pukdo □[4]	194	35.45 N	127.15 E
Cholm	160	57.09 N	31.11 E
Cholmogorskaja	160	63.49 N	40.39 E
Cholmogory	160	64.15 N	41.40 E
Cholmsk	186	47.03 N	142.03 E
Cholm-Žirkovskij	160	55.31 N	33.29 E
Cholo	218	16.10 S	35.10 E
Choloma	280	15.34 N	87.56 W
Cholopeniči	160	54.31 N	28.58 E
Cholula [de Rivadabia]	278	19.04 N	98.18 W
Choluteca	280	13.18 N	87.12 W
Choluteca □[5]	280	13.20 N	87.10 W
Choluteca ≃	280	13.05 N	87.20 W
Choma	218	16.48 S	26.59 E
Chomo Lhāri ∧	204	27.50 N	89.15 E
Chomutov	164	50.28 N	13.26 E
Ch'ŏnan	194	36.48 N	127.09 E
Chon Buri	200	13.22 N	100.59 E
Chone	290	0.41 S	80.06 W
Chone ≃	290	0.35 S	80.25 W
Ch'ŏngch'ŏn-gang ≃	194	39.35 N	125.28 E
Ch'ŏngjin	194	41.47 N	129.50 E
Chŏngju, C.M.I.K.	194	39.41 N	125.13 E
Ch'ŏngju, Taehan	194	36.39 N	127.31 E
Chongmingdao I	196	31.36 N	121.33 E
Chongos Bajo	292	12.09 S	75.16 W
Chongoyape	292	6.35 S	79.25 W
Chŏngp'yŏng-chŏsuji ⊜	194	37.40 N	127.30 E
Chongqing, Zhg.	190	29.39 N	106.34 E
Chongqing, Zhg.	190	30.39 N	103.41 E
Chŏngŭp	194	35.36 N	126.51 E
Chongxi ≃	196	27.12 N	118.13 E
Chongzuo	190	22.21 N	107.26 E
Chŏnju	194	35.49 N	127.08 E
Chontales □[5]	280	12.05 N	85.10 W
Chonuu	186	66.27 N	143.06 E
Cho Oyu ∧	206	28.06 N	86.39 E
Chopim ≃	294	25.35 S	53.05 W
Chopinzinho	294	25.51 S	52.30 W
Chop'or ≃	158	49.36 N	42.19 E
Chor ≃	186	47.48 N	134.43 E
Chorcha, Cerro ∧	280	8.38 N	82.08 W
Chorejver	160	67.25 N	58.03 E
Chorges	166	44.33 N	6.17 E
Choro ≃	292	16.25 S	64.35 W
Chorog	186	37.31 N	71.33 E
Chorolque, Cerro ∧	292	20.56 S	66.01 W
Choros, Cabo ≻	294	29.15 S	71.28 W
Choros, Isla I	294	29.16 S	71.33 W
Choroszcz	164	53.09 N	22.59 E
Chorreras, Cerro ∧	278	26.02 N	106.24 W
Ch'ŏrwŏn	190	38.16 N	127.12 E
Chorzele	164	53.16 N	20.55 E
Chorzów	164	50.19 N	18.57 E
Chosedachard	160	67.02 N	59.22 E
Chosen	246	26.42 N	80.41 W
Chōshi	192	35.44 N	140.50 E
Choshui Ch'i ≃	196	24.03 N	120.23 E
Chosica	292	11.57 S	76.42 W
Chos Malal	294	37.20 S	70.15 W
Choszczno (Arnswalde)	164	53.10 N	15.26 E
Chota	292	6.33 S	78.39 W
Choteau	256	47.49 N	112.11 W
Chotěboř	164	49.43 N	15.40 E
Chotla, Cerro de ∧	278	17.55 N	101.31 W
Chouteau	250	36.11 N	95.21 W
Chovd	190	48.01 N	91.39 E
Chovd ≃	190	48.06 N	92.11 E
Chövsgöl Nuur ⊜	190	51.00 N	100.30 E
Chowan ≃	246	36.00 N	76.40 W
Chowchilla	272	37.07 N	120.16 W
Chown, Mount ∧	238	53.24 N	119.22 W
Choya	294	28.29 S	64.52 W
Chrisman	248	39.48 N	87.41 W
Christchurch, N.Z.	230	43.42 S	172.38 E
Christchurch, Eng., U.K.	174	50.44 N	1.45 W
Christian ≃	236	66.36 N	145.49 W
Christian, Cape ≻	232	70.31 N	68.18 W
Christiana, Jam.	285q	18.10 N	77.29 W
Christiana, Pa., U.S.	262	39.57 N	76.00 W
Christian Island I	244	44.50 N	80.10 W
Christiansburg	246	37.08 N	80.24 W
Christian Sound ⊔	236	55.56 N	134.40 W
Christiansted	285n	17.45 N	64.42 W
Christie, Mount ∧	236	63.02 N	129.40 W
Christie Bay C	232	62.32 N	111.10 W
Christina ≃	238	56.40 N	111.03 W
Christina Lake ⊜, Alta., Can.	238	55.38 N	110.55 W
Christina Lake ⊜, B.C., Can.	238	49.05 N	118.14 W
Christmas Island □[2]	198	10.30 S	105.40 E
Christmas Lake ⊜	256	43.18 N	120.36 W
Christmas Mountain ∧	236	64.34 N	160.34 W
Christoforovo	160	60.53 N	47.13 E
Christopher	248	37.58 N	89.03 W
Christoval	250	31.12 N	100.30 W
Chroma ≃	186	71.36 N	144.49 E
Chromtau	158	50.17 N	58.27 E
Chrudim	164	49.57 N	15.48 E
Chrysler	248	31.18 N	87.42 W
Chrzanów	164	50.09 N	19.24 E
Chu ≃	198	19.53 N	105.45 E
Chuacús, Sierra de ⛰	280	15.05 N	90.45 W
Chualar	272	36.34 N	121.31 W
Chuanyanghe ≃	196	33.46 N	119.51 E
Chuathbaluk	236	61.40 N	159.15 W
Chubbuck	256	42.55 N	112.28 W
Chūbu-sangaku-kokuritsu-kōen ♠	192	36.30 N	137.41 E
Chuchi Lake ⊜	238	55.10 N	124.33 W
Chu Chua	238	51.21 N	120.10 W
Chuchuwayha Indian Reserve ⇝[4]	238	49.21 N	120.06 W
Chuckatuck	262	36.52 N	76.35 W
Chucuito	292	15.55 S	69.55 W
Chucunaque ≃	290	8.12 N	77.45 W
Chugach Islands II	236	59.06 N	151.42 W
Chugach Mountains ⛰	236	61.00 N	145.00 W
Chugiak	236	61.25 N	149.30 W
Chuginadak Island I	236	52.49 N	169.50 W
Chūgoku-sanchi ⛰	192	34.58 N	132.57 E
Chugwater	254	41.46 N	104.49 W
Chuhuichupa	278	29.38 N	108.22 W
Chuí	294	33.41 S	53.27 W
Chuius Mountain ∧	238	54.51 N	124.30 W
Chukai	200	4.14 N	103.24 E
Chukchi Sea ⊤[2]	236	69.00 N	171.00 W
Chukehu ⊜	206	31.40 N	88.00 E
Chula	248	39.55 N	93.29 W
Chulakeaganhe ≃	206	36.35 N	92.20 E
Chula Vista	274	32.39 N	117.05 W
Chulga ≃	160	64.20 N	61.00 E
Chulucanas	292	5.06 S	80.10 W
Chulumani	292	16.24 S	67.31 W
Chuma	292	15.24 S	68.56 W
Chumaerhe ≃	206	34.39 N	95.00 E
Chumbicha	294	28.50 S	66.18 W
Chumphon	200	10.32 N	99.13 E
Chumpi	292	15.04 S	73.46 W
Chum Saeng	200	15.55 N	100.15 E
Chunchi	290	2.17 S	78.55 W
Ch'unch'ŏn	194	37.52 N	127.43 E
Chunchula	248	30.55 N	88.12 W
Ch'ungch'ŏng Namdo □[4]	194	36.30 N	127.00 E
Ch'ungch'ŏng Pukdo □[4]	194	36.45 N	128.00 E
Ch'ungju	194	36.58 N	127.58 E
Chungking → Chongqing	190	29.39 N	106.34 E
Chungyang Shanmo ⛰	196	23.30 N	121.00 E
Chunhuás	278	19.12 N	88.55 W
Chuntuquí	278	17.31 N	90.09 W
Chuŏr Phnum Krâvanh ⛰	200	12.00 N	103.15 E
Chupaca	292	12.05 S	75.10 W
Chupadera Arroyo ∨	254	33.47 N	106.37 W
Chupadero, Cerro ∧	254	31.05 N	111.37 W
Chupaderos	278	23.50 N	102.20 W
Chupara Point ≻	285r	10.50 N	61.22 W
Chuquibamba	292	15.50 S	72.37 W
Chuquibambilla	292	14.07 S	72.41 W
Chuquicamata	294	22.19 S	68.56 W
Chuquisaca □[5]	292	20.00 S	64.20 W
Chur	180	46.51 N	9.32 E
Churcampa	292	12.41 S	74.22 W
Church Hill	262	39.08 N	75.59 W
Churchill, Man., Can.	232	58.46 N	94.10 W
Churchill, Ohio, U.S.	266	41.09 N	80.39 W
Churchill ≃, Can.	232	58.47 N	94.12 W
Churchill ≃, Newf., Can.	232	53.30 N	60.10 W
Churchill, Cape ≻	232	58.46 N	93.12 W
Churchill, Mount ∧, B.C., Can.	238	49.58 N	123.51 W
Churchill, Mount ∧, Alaska, U.S.	236	61.25 N	141.43 W
Churchill Falls ↳	232	53.35 N	64.27 W
Churchill Lake ⊜	232	55.55 N	108.20 W
Church of the Nativity ✝[1]	210	31.43 N	35.12 E
Church Point	248	30.24 N	92.13 W
Church Rock	254	35.46 N	108.35 W
Churchton	262	38.48 N	76.32 W
Churchtown	262	40.08 N	75.58 W
Church View	262	37.41 N	76.41 W
Churchville, Ont., Can.	264	43.38 N	79.45 W
Churchville, Md., U.S.	262	39.34 N	76.15 W
Churchville, N.Y., U.S.	264	43.06 N	77.53 W
Churdan	252	42.09 N	94.29 W
Churia Range ⛰	206	27.40 N	83.40 E
Churu	206	28.18 N	74.58 E
Churubusco, Ind., U.S.	268	41.14 N	85.19 W
Churubusco, N.Y., U.S.	260	44.57 N	73.56 W
Churuguara	290	10.49 N	69.32 W
Chushui ≃	196	26.02 N	113.09 E
Chuska Mountains ⛰	254	36.15 N	108.50 W
Chuska Peak ∧	254	35.53 N	108.50 W
Chust	158	48.10 N	23.18 E
Chutag	186	49.23 N	102.43 E
Chute-à-Blondeau	260	45.35 N	74.29 W
Chute-Panet	260	46.51 N	71.52 W
Chuxian	196	32.19 N	118.17 E
Chuxiong	200	25.02 N	101.30 E
Chuy	294	33.41 S	53.27 W
Chužir	186	53.11 N	107.20 E
Chvalynsk	158	52.30 N	48.07 E
Chvojnaja	160	58.54 N	34.32 E
Chyrov	164	49.33 N	22.49 E
Ciales	284m	18.20 N	66.28 W
Cianorte	296	23.37 S	52.37 W
Cibecue	254	34.03 N	110.29 W
Cibuta	254	31.04 N	110.54 W
Ćićarija ⛰	170	45.30 N	13.54 E
Cicciano	184	40.58 N	14.32 E
Cicero, Ill., U.S.	268	41.51 N	87.45 W
Cicero, Ind., U.S.	248	40.08 N	86.01 W
Cicero, N.Y., U.S.	264	43.10 N	76.07 W
Čichačovo	160	57.17 N	29.54 E
Cidacos ≃	168	42.21 N	1.38 W
Cidra	284m	18.11 N	66.10 W
Ciechanów	164	52.53 N	20.38 E
Ciechanowiec	164	52.42 N	22.31 E
Ciechocinek	164	52.52 N	18.49 E
Ciego de Avila	284p	21.51 N	78.46 W
Ciempozuelos	168	40.10 N	3.37 W
Ciénaga	290	11.01 N	74.15 W
Ciénaga de Oro	290	8.53 N	75.37 W
Ciénega de Flores	250	25.57 N	100.11 W
Cienfuegos	284p	22.09 N	80.27 W
Cienfuegos, Bahzzia de C	284p	22.06 N	80.28 W
Cieplice Śląskie Zdrój	164	50.52 N	15.41 E
Čierna [Nad Tisou]	164	48.25 N	22.05 E
Čierny Balog	164	48.45 N	19.40 E
Cíes, Islas II	168	42.13 N	8.54 W
Cieszanów	164	50.16 N	23.08 E
Cieszyn	164	49.45 N	18.38 E
Cieza	168	38.14 N	1.25 W
Cifuentes, Cuba	284p	22.39 N	80.03 W
Cifuentes, Esp.	168	40.47 N	2.37 W
Čiganak	186	51.47 N	43.18 E
Cihangir	172	40.03 N	29.07 E
Cihe ≃	196	33.27 N	115.31 E
Čiili	186	44.10 N	66.45 E
Cijara, Embalse de ⊜[1]	168	39.18 N	4.52 W
Čikoj ≃	186	51.02 N	106.39 E
Cilento ⇝[1]	170	40.15 N	15.10 E
Čilik	186	43.36 N	78.15 E
Cilleruelu de Bezana	168	42.58 N	3.51 W
Cil'ma ≃	160	65.27 N	52.06 E
Cimarron, Kans., U.S.	252	37.48 N	100.21 W
Cimarron, N. Mex., U.S.	254	36.31 N	104.55 W
Cimarron ≃	250	36.10 N	96.17 W
Čimbaj	186	42.57 N	59.47 E
Čimčinej, Gora ∧[2]	236	63.37 N	178.04 E
Cimitile	184	40.56 N	14.31 E
Čimkent	186	42.18 N	69.36 E
Ciml'anskoje Vodochranilišče ⊜[1]	158	48.00 N	43.00 E
Cimone, Monte ∧	170	44.12 N	10.42 E
Cîmpeni	172	46.22 N	23.03 E
Cîmpia Turzii	172	46.33 N	23.54 E
Cîmpina	172	45.08 N	25.44 E
Cîmpulung	172	45.16 N	25.03 E
Cîmpulung Moldovenesc	172	47.31 N	25.34 E
Činadijevo	172	48.30 N	22.50 E
Çınarcık	172	40.39 N	29.06 E
Cinaruco ≃	290	6.41 N	67.07 W
Cinca ≃	168	41.26 N	0.21 E
Cincer ∧	170	43.54 N	17.04 E
Cincinnati, Iowa, U.S.	244	40.38 N	92.56 W
Cincinnati, Ohio, U.S.	242	39.06 N	84.31 W
Cinco Balas, Cayos II	284p	21.06 N	79.20 W
Cinco de Mayo	250	25.46 N	104.19 W
Cinco Pinos	280	13.11 N	86.54 W
Cinco Saltos	294	38.50 S	68.04 W
Çine	172	37.36 N	28.04 E
Cinebar	270	46.36 N	122.32 W
Cinema	238	53.11 N	122.30 W
Ciney	164	50.18 N	5.06 E
Cingoli	170	43.22 N	13.13 E
Činja-Voryk	160	63.13 N	52.38 E
Cinqueterre □[9]	182	44.10 N	9.45 E
Cintalapa [de Figueroa]	278	16.44 N	93.43 W
Cinto, Mont ∧	170	42.23 N	8.56 E
Cintra → Sintra	168	38.48 N	9.23 W
Cinzas, Rio das ≃	296	22.56 S	50.32 W
Ciocăneşti	172	44.12 N	27.04 E
Čiovo, Otok I	170	43.30 N	16.20 E
Cipa ≃	186	55.23 N	115.55 E
Cipolândia	296	20.08 S	55.24 W
Cipolletti	294	38.56 S	67.59 W
Circeo, Parco Nazionale del ♠	170	41.17 N	13.05 E
Čirčik	186	41.29 N	69.35 E
Circle, Alaska, U.S.	236	65.50 N	144.04 W
Circle, Mont., U.S.	256	47.25 N	105.35 W
Circle Hot Springs	236	65.28 N	144.39 W
Circleville, Ohio, U.S.	242	39.36 N	82.57 W
Circleville, Utah, U.S.	254	38.10 N	112.16 W
Cirencester	174	51.44 N	1.59 W
Cirey-sur-Vezouze	166	48.35 N	6.57 E
Ciriè	182	45.14 N	7.36 E
Ciriquiri ≃	292	8.05 S	65.18 W
Cirk, Gora ∧	236	64.33 N	175.25 E
Cîrlibaba	172	47.35 N	25.07 E
Cirò Marina	170	39.22 N	17.08 E
Čirpan	172	42.12 N	25.20 E
Cirque, Cerro ∧	292	17.22 S	69.22 W
Cisco	250	32.23 N	98.59 W
Cislago	182	45.39 N	8.58 E
Cisnădie	172	45.43 N	24.09 E
Cisne	248	38.31 N	88.26 W
Cisneros	290	6.33 N	75.04 W
Cissna Park	268	40.34 N	87.54 W
Cisterna di Latina	184	41.35 N	12.49 E
Cistierna	168	42.48 N	5.07 W
Čistopol'	160	55.21 N	50.37 E
Čita	186	52.03 N	113.30 E
Citac, Nevado ∧	292	12.50 S	75.15 W
Citlaltépetl, Volcán ∧[1]	278	19.01 N	97.16 W
Citra	246	29.25 N	82.06 W
Citronelle	248	31.06 N	88.14 W
Citrus Heights	272	38.42 N	121.17 W
Cittadella	170	45.39 N	11.47 E
Città del Vaticano (Vatican City) □[1]	184	41.45 N	12.27 E
Città di Castello	184	43.27 N	12.14 E
Cittanova	170	38.21 N	16.05 E
City of Refuge National Historical Park ♠	275d	19.25 N	155.54 W
City Point	246	28.24 N	80.45 W
City View	246	34.51 N	82.26 W
Ciucaş ∧	172	45.31 N	25.55 E
Ciudad	278	23.44 N	105.42 W
Ciudad Acuña	278	29.18 N	100.55 W
Ciudad Allende	278	28.20 N	100.51 W
Ciudad Altamirano	278	18.20 N	100.40 W
Ciudad Anáhuac	278	27.14 N	100.09 W
Ciudad Barrios	280	13.46 N	88.16 W
Ciudad Bolívar	290	8.08 N	63.33 W
Ciudad Bolivia	290	8.21 N	70.34 W
Ciudad Camargo, Méx.	278	27.40 N	105.10 W
Ciudad Camargo, Méx.	278	26.19 N	98.50 W
Ciudad Chetumal	278	18.30 N	88.18 W
Ciudad Darío	280	12.42 N	86.08 W
Ciudad de Guayana → Santo Tomé de Guayana	290	8.22 N	62.40 W
Ciudad del Carmen	278	18.38 N	91.50 W
Ciudad del Maíz	278	22.24 N	99.36 W
Ciudad de México (Mexico City)	278	19.24 N	99.09 W
Ciudad de Valles	278	21.59 N	99.01 W
Ciudad de Villaldama	278	26.30 N	100.26 W
Ciudadela	168	40.02 N	3.50 E
Ciudad Guerrero	278	28.33 N	107.30 W
Ciudad Guzmán	278	19.41 N	103.29 W
Ciudad Hidalgo, Méx.	278	19.41 N	100.34 W
Ciudad Hidalgo, Méx.	280	14.41 N	92.09 W
Ciudad Ixtepec	278	16.34 N	95.06 W
Ciudad Jiménez	278	27.08 N	104.55 W
Ciudad Juárez	278	31.44 N	106.29 W
Ciudad Lerdo	250	25.32 N	103.32 W
Ciudad Madero	278	22.16 N	97.50 W
Ciudad Mante	278	22.44 N	98.57 W
Ciudad Manuel Doblado	278	20.44 N	101.56 W
Ciudad Melchor Múzquiz	278	27.53 N	101.31 W
Ciudad Mier	278	26.26 N	99.09 W
Ciudad Miguel Alemán	278	26.23 N	99.01 W
Ciudad Obregón	278	27.29 N	109.56 W
Ciudad Ojeda (Lagunillas)	290	10.12 N	71.19 W
Ciudad Piar	290	7.27 N	63.19 W
Ciudad Real	168	38.59 N	3.56 W
Ciudad Rodrigo	168	40.36 N	6.32 W
Ciudad Tecún Umán	280	14.40 N	92.09 W
Ciudad Trujillo → Santo Domingo	282	18.28 N	69.54 W
Ciudad Victoria, Méx.	258	32.20 N	115.06 W
Ciudad Victoria, Méx.	278	23.44 N	99.08 W
Ciudad Vieja	280	14.31 N	90.46 W
Ciurana ≃	168	41.08 N	0.39 E
Civa Burnu ≻	212	41.22 N	36.35 E
Cividale del Friuli	170	46.06 N	13.25 E
Civil'sk	160	55.53 N	47.29 E
Civita Castellana	184	42.17 N	12.25 E
Civitanova Marche	184	43.18 N	13.44 E
Civitavecchia	184	42.06 N	11.48 E
Civray	166	46.09 N	0.18 E
Çivril	172	38.18 N	29.45 E
Čiža	160	67.06 N	44.19 E
Cizre	208	37.20 N	42.12 E
C.J. Strike Reservoir ⊜[1]	256	42.57 N	115.53 W
Čkalovsk	160	56.46 N	43.16 E
Clackamas	270	45.25 N	122.34 W
Clackamas □[6]	270	45.10 N	122.16 W
Clackamas ≃	256	45.22 N	122.36 W
Clackamas Heights	270	45.23 N	122.34 W
Clackmannan □[6]	162	56.10 N	3.47 W
Clacton-on-Sea	174	51.48 N	1.09 E
Claflin	252	38.31 N	98.32 W
Claiborne	248	31.32 N	87.31 W
Clain ≃	166	46.47 N	0.32 E
Claire, Lake ⊜	232	58.30 N	112.00 W
Clairemont	250	33.10 N	100.45 W
Clair Engle Lake ⊜[1]	258	40.52 N	122.43 W
Clair Haven	266	42.34 N	82.47 W
Clairmont	238	55.16 N	118.47 W
Clairton	266	40.18 N	79.53 W
Clairvaux-les-Lacs	166	46.34 N	5.45 E
Clallam □[6]	270	48.10 N	123.49 W
Clallam Bay	270	48.15 N	124.16 W
Clam ≃, Mich., U.S.	244	44.05 N	85.00 W
Clam ≃, Wis., U.S.	244	45.57 N	92.33 W
Clamecy	166	47.27 N	3.31 E
Clam Gulch	236	60.15 N	151.22 W
Clan Alpine Mountains ⛰	258	39.40 N	117.55 W
Clandonald	238	53.34 N	110.44 W
Clanton	248	32.50 N	86.38 W
Clanwilliam	218	32.11 S	18.54 E
Clapperton Island I	244	46.02 N	82.13 W
Clapp Farm	266	41.24 N	79.32 W
Clara, Eire	162	53.20 N	7.36 W
Clara, Miss., U.S.	248	31.35 N	88.42 W
Clara ≃	228	18.30 S	141.18 E
Clara City	252	44.57 N	95.22 W
Clara Island I	200	10.54 N	97.55 E
Claraz	294	37.54 S	59.17 W
Clare	244	43.49 N	84.46 W
Clare □[6]	162	52.50 N	9.00 W
Clare ≃	162	53.20 N	9.03 W
Clare Island I	162	53.48 N	10.00 W
Claremont, Ont., Can.	264	43.58 N	79.07 W
Claremont, Calif., U.S.	274	34.06 N	117.43 W
Claremont, N.H., U.S.	242	43.23 N	72.20 W
Claremont, S. Dak., U.S.	252	45.40 N	98.01 W
Claremont, Va., U.S.	262	37.14 N	76.58 W
Claremont ∧	258	39.53 N	120.57 W
Claremore	250	36.19 N	95.36 W
Claremorris	162	53.44 N	9.00 W
Clarence, Ill., U.S.	268	40.28 N	87.58 W
Clarence, Iowa, U.S.	244	41.53 N	91.04 W
Clarence, Mo., U.S.	248	39.44 N	92.16 W
Clarence, N.Y., U.S.	264	42.59 N	78.35 W
Clarence, Pa., U.S.	266	41.03 N	77.56 W
Clarence ≃, Austl.	228	29.25 S	153.22 E
Clarence ≃, N.Z.	230	42.10 S	173.56 E
Clarence, Port C	236	65.15 N	166.40 W
Clarence Center	264	43.00 N	78.35 W
Clarence Strait ⊔	236	55.25 N	132.00 W
Clarence Town	282	23.06 N	74.59 W
Clarenceville	260	45.04 N	73.15 W
Clarendon, Ark., U.S.	248	34.42 N	91.18 W
Clarendon, N.Y., U.S.	264	43.11 N	78.04 W
Clarendon, Pa., U.S.	266	41.47 N	79.06 W
Clarendon, Tex., U.S.	250	34.56 N	100.53 W
Clarendon Lake ⊜	244	44.50 N	76.58 W
Clarenville	240	48.10 N	53.58 W
Claresholm	238	50.02 N	113.35 W
Claridge	266	40.22 N	79.37 W
Clarin	202	9.57 N	124.01 E
Clarinda	252	40.44 N	95.02 W
Clarines	290	9.56 N	65.10 W
Clarington	266	41.20 N	79.07 W
Clarion, Iowa, U.S.	244	42.44 N	93.44 W
Clarion, Pa., U.S.	266	41.13 N	79.24 W
Clarion □[6]	266	41.13 N	79.24 W
Clarion ≃	242	41.07 N	79.41 W
Clarión, Isla I	278	18.22 N	114.44 W
Clarion Fracture Zone ✧	148	19.00 N	122.00 W
Clarissa	252	46.08 N	94.57 W
Clark, Ohio, U.S.	266	40.27 N	81.54 W
Clark, Pa., U.S.	266	41.17 N	80.26 W
Clark, S. Dak., U.S.	252	44.53 N	97.44 W
Clark □[6]	270	45.48 N	122.31 W
Clark, Lake ⊜	236	60.15 N	154.15 W
Clark, Mount ∧	236	64.25 N	124.12 W
Clark, Point ≻	244	44.04 N	81.45 W
Clark Air Base ■	202	15.11 N	120.33 E
Clark Canyon Reservoir ⊜[1]	256	44.58 N	112.51 W
Clarkdale	254	34.46 N	112.03 W
Clarke ≃	228	19.12 S	145.30 E
Clarke City	240	50.12 N	66.38 W
Clarke Island I	228	40.33 S	148.10 E
Clarke Range ⛰	228	20.50 S	148.33 E
Clarkfield	252	44.48 N	95.48 W
Clark Fork	256	48.08 N	116.11 W
Clark Fork ≃	256	48.09 N	116.15 W
Clark Hill Reservoir ⊜[1]	246	33.50 N	82.20 W
Clarklake	268	42.04 N	84.21 W
Clark Mills	264	43.06 N	75.22 W
Clark Mountain ∧	258	35.32 N	115.35 W
Clarks, La., U.S.	248	32.02 N	92.08 W
Clarks, Nebr., U.S.	252	41.13 N	97.50 W
Clarksburg, Ont., Can.	264	44.43 N	80.27 W
Clarksburg, Calif., U.S.	272	38.25 N	121.32 W
Clarksburg, Md., U.S.	262	39.14 N	77.17 W
Clarksburg, N.J., U.S.	262	40.12 N	74.27 W
Clarksburg, W. Va., U.S.	242	39.17 N	80.21 W
Clarksdale	248	34.12 N	90.34 W
Clark's Harbour	240	43.26 N	65.38 W
Clarks Hill	268	40.15 N	86.43 W
Clarks Mills	266	41.24 N	80.11 W
Clarkson	248	37.30 N	86.13 W
Clarks Point	236	58.51 N	158.30 W
Clarks Summit	242	41.30 N	75.42 W
Clarkston	268	42.44 N	83.25 W
Clark's Town	285q	18.25 N	77.34 W
Clarksville, Ark., U.S.	248	35.28 N	93.28 W
Clarksville, Del., U.S.	262	38.33 N	75.09 W
Clarksville, Ga., U.S.	246	34.37 N	83.31 W
Clarksville, Ind., U.S.	248	38.17 N	85.45 W
Clarksville, Iowa, U.S.	244	42.47 N	92.40 W
Clarksville, Md., U.S.	262	39.13 N	76.57 W
Clarksville, Mich., U.S.	268	42.50 N	85.15 W
Clarksville, N.Y., U.S.	261	42.35 N	73.58 W
Clarksville, Tenn., U.S.	248	36.32 N	87.21 W
Clarksville, Tex., U.S.	250	33.37 N	95.03 W
Clarksville, Va., U.S.	246	36.37 N	78.34 W
Clarkton, Mo., U.S.	248	36.27 N	89.58 W
Clarkton, N.C., U.S.	246	34.29 N	78.39 W
Claro, Ribeirão ≃	296	17.37 S	46.47 W
Clatskanie	270	46.06 N	123.12 W
Clatskanie ≃	256	46.08 N	123.14 W
Clatsop □[6]	270	46.01 N	123.41 W
Claude	250	35.07 N	101.22 W
Clausthal-Zellerfeld	178	51.48 N	10.20 E
Claver	202	9.34 N	125.43 E
Claverack	261	42.13 N	73.44 W
Claveria, Pil.	202	12.54 N	123.15 E
Claveria, Pil.	202	8.37 N	124.54 E
Claveria, Pil.	202	18.37 N	121.05 E
Clavos, Laguna de ⊜	250	27.40 N	104.50 W
Clawit, Mount ∧	202	16.58 N	120.59 E
Clawson	268	42.32 N	83.09 W
Claxton	246	32.10 N	81.55 W
Clay, Ky., U.S.	248	37.29 N	87.49 W
Clay, Tex., U.S.	250	30.23 N	96.21 W
Clay, W. Va., U.S.	242	38.28 N	81.05 W
Clay Center, Kans., U.S.	252	39.23 N	97.08 W
Clay Center, Nebr., U.S.	252	40.32 N	98.03 W
Clay Center, Ohio, U.S.	266	41.34 N	83.22 W
Clay City, Ill., U.S.	248	38.41 N	88.21 W
Clay City, Ind., U.S.	248	39.17 N	87.07 W
Clay City, Ky., U.S.	246	37.52 N	83.55 W
Clay Cross	174	53.10 N	1.24 W
Clayhole Wash ∨	254	36.59 N	113.17 W
Clayhurst	238	56.15 N	120.01 W
Claymont	262	39.48 N	75.28 W
Clayoquot Sound ⊔	238	49.11 N	126.08 W
Claypool, Ariz., U.S.	254	33.25 N	110.51 W
Claypool, Ind., U.S.	268	41.08 N	85.53 W
Claysburg	266	40.18 N	78.27 W
Clay Springs	254	34.22 N	110.18 W
Claysville	266	40.07 N	80.25 W
Clayton, Ala., U.S.	248	31.53 N	85.27 W
Clayton, Calif., U.S.	272	37.57 N	121.56 W
Clayton, Del., U.S.	262	39.17 N	75.38 W
Clayton, Ga., U.S.	246	34.53 N	83.23 W
Clayton, Idaho, U.S.	256	44.16 N	114.24 W
Clayton, Ill., U.S.	248	40.02 N	90.57 W
Clayton, Mich., U.S.	268	41.52 N	84.14 W
Clayton, Mo., U.S.	248	38.39 N	90.20 W
Clayton, N.J., U.S.	262	39.39 N	75.06 W
Clayton, N. Mex., U.S.	250	36.27 N	103.11 W
Clayton, N.C., U.S.	246	35.39 N	78.28 W
Clayton, N.Y., U.S.	264	44.14 N	76.05 W
Clayton, Okla., U.S.	250	34.35 N	95.21 W
Clayton, Wash., U.S.	238	48.00 N	117.33 W
Clayton ≃	228	29.06 S	138.05 E
Claytonia	266	41.00 N	79.58 W
Claytonville	268	40.34 N	87.49 W
Clear ≃	238	56.11 N	119.42 W
Clear, Cape ≻	236	59.48 N	147.54 W
Clear, Lake ⊜	244	45.25 N	77.12 W
Clearbrook, B.C., Can.	270	49.08 N	122.26 W
Clearbrook, Minn., U.S.	252	47.42 N	95.26 W
Clearfield, Iowa, U.S.	252	40.48 N	94.29 W
Clearfield, Pa., U.S.	266	41.02 N	78.27 W
Clearfield, Utah, U.S.	254	41.07 N	112.01 W

Symbols in the index entries are identified on page 360.

Name	Page	Lat°′	Long°′
Clearfield □[6]	266	41.02 N	78.27 W
Clear Island I	162	51.26 N	9.30 W
Clear Lake, Iowa, U.S.	244	43.08 N	93.23 W
Clear Lake, S. Dak., U.S.	252	44.45 N	96.41 W
Clearlake, Wash., U.S.	270	48.28 N	122.14 W
Clear Lake, Wis., U.S.	244	45.15 N	92.16 W
Clear Lake ⊜[1], Calif., U.S.	258	39.02 N	122.50 W
Clear Lake ⊜[1], La., U.S.	248	31.55 N	93.05 W
Clearlake Highlands	272	38.57 N	122.38 W
Clearlake Oaks	272	39.07 N	122.40 W
Clearlake Park	272	38.58 N	122.39 W
Clear Lake Reservoir ⊜[1]	258	41.52 N	121.08 W
Clearmont	256	44.38 N	106.23 W
Clear Run	266	41.08 N	78.45 W
Clear Site	236	64.19 N	149.11 W
Clearview, Wash., U.S.	270	47.45 N	122.06 W
Clearview, W. Va., U.S.	266	40.09 N	80.41 W
Clearwater, B.C., Can.	238	51.38 N	120.02 W
Clearwater, Man., Can.	252	49.08 N	99.01 W
Clearwater, Fla., U.S.	246	27.58 N	82.48 W
Clearwater, Kans., U.S.	252	37.30 N	97.30 W
Clearwater, Nebr., U.S.	252	42.10 N	98.11 W
Clearwater ≃, Can.	232	56.44 N	111.25 W
Clearwater ≃, Alta., Can.	238	52.23 N	114.50 W
Clearwater ≃, B.C., Can.	238	51.42 N	120.00 W
Clearwater ≃, Idaho, U.S.	256	46.25 N	117.02 W
Clearwater ≃, Minn., U.S.	252	47.54 N	96.16 W
Clearwater ≃, Mont., U.S.	256	46.58 N	113.23 W
Clearwater Lake ⊜	238	52.15 N	120.13 W
Clearwater Mountains ⋏	256	46.00 N	115.30 W
Clebit	250	34.21 N	94.52 W
Cleburne	250	32.21 N	97.23 W
Cle Elum	270	47.12 N	120.56 W
Cleethorpes	162	53.34 N	0.02 W
Clefmont	164	48.06 N	5.31 E
Clelles	166	44.50 N	5.37 E
Clementsport	240	44.40 N	65.37 W
Clemson	246	34.41 N	82.50 W
Clendenin	242	38.29 N	81.21 W
Clendening Reservoir ⊜[1]	242	40.16 N	81.13 W
Cleona	262	40.20 N	76.29 W
Cleopatra Needle ∧	202	10.08 N	119.00 E
Clerke Rocks II[1]	288	55.01 S	34.41 W
Clermont, Austl.	228	22.49 S	147.39 E
Clermont, Qué., Can.	240	47.42 N	70.14 W
Clermont, Fr.	176	49.23 N	2.24 E
Clermont, Fla., U.S.	246	28.33 N	81.46 W
Clermont, Pa., U.S.	266	41.41 N	78.29 W
Clermont-en-Argonne	166	49.06 N	5.04 E
Clermont-Ferrand	166	45.47 N	3.05 E
Clermont Harbor	248	30.16 N	89.25 W
Cles	170	46.22 N	11.02 E
Clevedon	174	51.27 N	2.51 W
Cleveland, Ala., U.S.	248	33.59 N	86.35 W
Cleveland, Ga., U.S.	246	34.36 N	83.46 W
Cleveland, Miss., U.S.	248	33.45 N	90.50 W
Cleveland, N.C., U.S.	246	35.44 N	80.40 W
Cleveland, N.Y., U.S.	264	43.14 N	75.53 W
Cleveland, Ohio, U.S.	266	41.30 N	81.41 W
Cleveland, Okla., U.S.	250	36.19 N	96.28 W
Cleveland, Tenn., U.S.	248	35.10 N	84.53 W
Cleveland, Tex., U.S.	250	30.21 N	95.05 W
Cleveland, Va., U.S.	246	36.57 N	82.09 W
Cleveland, Cape ≻	228	19.11 S	147.01 E
Cleveland, Mount ∧, Austl.	228	41.25 S	145.23 E
Cleveland, Mount ∧, Mont., U.S.	256	48.56 N	113.51 W
Cleveland Heights	266	41.30 N	81.34 W
Clevelândia	294	26.24 S	52.21 W
Cleveland Peninsula ≻[1]	238	55.45 N	132.00 W
Cleversburg	262	40.02 N	77.28 W
Cleves → Kleve, B.R.D.	178	51.48 N	6.09 E
Clew Bay C	162	53.50 N	9.50 W
Clewiston	246	26.45 N	80.56 W
Clichy	176	48.54 N	2.18 E
Clifden	162	53.29 N	10.01 W
Cliffdell	270	46.44 N	120.42 W
Clifford	264	43.58 N	80.58 W
Cliffside	246	35.14 N	81.46 W
Clifton, Ariz., U.S.	254	33.03 N	109.18 W
Clifton, Ill., U.S.	268	40.56 N	87.56 W
Clifton, Kans., U.S.	252	39.34 N	97.17 W
Clifton, N.Y., U.S.	264	43.03 N	77.49 W
Clifton, Oreg., U.S.	270	46.12 N	123.27 W
Clifton, Tenn., U.S.	248	35.23 N	88.01 W
Clifton, Tex., U.S.	250	31.47 N	97.35 W
Clifton Forge	246	37.49 N	79.49 W
Clifton Point ≻	246	25.01 N	77.34 W
Clifton Springs	264	42.58 N	77.08 W
Climax, Sask., Can.	256	49.13 N	108.23 W
Climax, Colo., U.S.	254	39.22 N	106.11 W
Climax, Ga., U.S.	246	30.53 N	84.26 W
Climax, Mich., U.S.	268	42.14 N	85.20 W
Climax, Pa., U.S.	266	40.59 N	79.23 W
Clinch ≃	246	35.53 N	84.29 W
Clinchco	246	37.10 N	82.22 W
Clingmans Dome ∧	246	35.35 N	83.30 W
Clint	254	31.35 N	106.14 W
Clinton, B.C., Can.	238	51.05 N	121.35 W
Clinton, Ont., Can.	244	43.37 N	81.32 W
Clinton, Ala., U.S.	248	32.55 N	87.60 W
Clinton, Ark., U.S.	248	35.36 N	92.28 W
Clinton, Conn., U.S.	261	41.17 N	72.32 W
Clinton, Ill., U.S.	248	40.09 N	88.57 W
Clinton, Ind., U.S.	248	39.40 N	87.24 W
Clinton, Iowa, U.S.	244	41.51 N	90.12 W
Clinton, Ky., U.S.	248	36.40 N	89.02 W
Clinton, La., U.S.	248	30.52 N	91.01 W
Clinton, Maine, U.S.	242	44.38 N	69.30 W
Clinton, Md., U.S.	262	38.46 N	76.54 W
Clinton, Mass., U.S.	261	42.25 N	71.41 W
Clinton, Mich., U.S.	268	42.04 N	83.58 W
Clinton, Minn., U.S.	252	45.28 N	96.26 W
Clinton, Miss., U.S.	248	32.20 N	90.20 W
Clinton, Mo., U.S.	248	38.22 N	93.46 W
Clinton, N.J., U.S.	262	40.38 N	74.55 W
Clinton, N.C., U.S.	246	35.00 N	78.20 W
Clinton, N.Y., U.S.	264	43.03 N	75.23 W
Clinton, Ohio, U.S.	266	40.56 N	81.42 W
Clinton, Okla., U.S.	250	35.31 N	98.59 W
Clinton, Pa., U.S.	266	40.29 N	80.18 W
Clinton, S.C., U.S.	246	34.29 N	81.53 W
Clinton, Tenn., U.S.	246	36.06 N	84.08 W
Clinton, Wash., U.S.	270	47.59 N	122.22 W
Clinton, Wis., U.S.	268	42.34 N	88.52 W
Clinton □[6], Ind., U.S.	268	40.17 N	86.31 W
Clinton □[6], Mich., U.S.	268	42.56 N	84.36 W
Clinton □[6], N.Y., U.S.	260	44.57 N	73.42 W
Clinton □[6], Pa., U.S.	266	41.08 N	71.26 W
Clinton, Cape ≻	228	22.32 S	150.47 E
Clinton-Colden Lake ⊜	232	63.58 N	107.27 W
Clinton Park	261	42.36 N	73.43 W
Clintonville, Pa., U.S.	266	41.12 N	79.53 W
Clintonville, Wis., U.S.	244	44.37 N	88.46 W
Clintwood	246	37.09 N	82.27 W
Clio, Ala., U.S.	248	31.43 N	85.36 W
Clio, Mich., U.S.	244	43.11 N	83.44 W
Clio, S.C., U.S.	246	34.35 N	79.33 W
Clipperton I	276	10.17 N	109.13 W
Clipperton Fracture Zone ⟡	148	10.00 N	112.00 W
Clisson	166	47.05 N	1.17 W
Cliza	292	17.36 S	65.56 W
Clodomira	294	27.35 S	64.10 W
Cloe	266	40.56 N	78.56 W
Cloete	250	27.55 N	101.10 W
Clogher Head ≻	162	53.48 N	6.12 W
Clonakilty	162	51.37 N	8.54 W
Clonakilty Bay C	162	51.35 N	8.50 W
Cloncurry	228	20.42 S	140.30 E
Cloncurry ≃	228	18.37 S	140.40 E
Clondalkin	162	53.19 N	6.24 W
Clonmel	162	52.21 N	7.42 W
Clo-oose	238	48.40 N	124.49 W
Cloppenburg	178	52.50 N	8.02 E
Cloquet	244	46.43 N	92.28 W
Cloquet ≃	244	46.52 N	92.35 W
Clorinda	294	25.20 S	57.40 W
Cloudcroft	254	32.58 N	105.45 W
Cloud Peak ∧	256	44.25 N	107.10 W
Cloudy Bay C	230	41.26 S	174.06 E
Cloudy Mountain ∧	236	63.11 N	156.05 W
Clover	246	35.07 N	81.14 W
Clover Bank	264	42.45 N	78.53 W
Cloverdale, B.C., Can.	270	49.06 N	122.44 W
Cloverdale, Ala., U.S.	248	34.56 N	87.46 W
Cloverdale, Calif., U.S.	258	38.48 N	123.01 W
Cloverdale, Ind., U.S.	248	39.31 N	86.48 W
Cloverdale, Mich., U.S.	268	42.32 N	85.23 W
Cloverdale, Ohio, U.S.	268	41.01 N	84.18 W
Cloverdale, Oreg., U.S.	270	45.12 N	123.53 W
Clover Pass	236	55.28 N	131.47 W
Cloverport	248	37.50 N	86.38 W
Cloverville	268	43.11 N	86.10 W
Clovis, Calif., U.S.	272	36.49 N	119.42 W
Clovis, N. Mex., U.S.	250	34.24 N	103.12 W
Cluj	172	46.47 N	23.36 E
Clune	266	40.34 N	79.18 W
Cluny	166	46.26 N	4.39 E
Cluses	166	46.04 N	6.36 E
Clusone	170	45.53 N	9.57 E
Clute	250	29.01 N	95.24 W
Clutha ≃	230	46.20 S	169.49 E
Clyde, Alta., Can.	238	54.09 N	113.39 W
Clyde, N.W. Ter., Can.	232	70.25 N	68.30 W
Clyde, Calif., U.S.	272	38.02 N	122.02 W
Clyde, Kans., U.S.	252	39.36 N	97.24 W
Clyde, N.Y., U.S.	264	43.05 N	76.52 W
Clyde, Ohio, U.S.	266	41.18 N	82.59 W
Clyde, Tex., U.S.	250	32.24 N	99.30 W
Clyde ≃, N.S., Can.	240	43.35 N	65.25 W
Clyde ≃, Ont., Can.	244	44.58 N	76.22 W
Clyde ≃, Scot., U.K.	162	55.56 N	4.29 W
Clyde ≃, Vt., U.S.	242	44.56 N	72.12 W
Clyde, Firth of C[1]	162	55.42 N	5.00 W
Clyde Lake ⊜	238	55.18 N	111.28 W
Clyde No.3	266	39.59 N	80.03 W
Clyde Park	256	45.53 N	110.36 W
Clymer, N.Y., U.S.	266	42.03 N	79.35 W
Clymer, Pa., U.S.	266	40.40 N	79.01 W
Ćmielów	164	50.53 N	21.31 E
Cna ≃	160	54.32 N	42.05 E
Coa ≃	168	41.05 N	7.06 W
Coachella	258	33.41 N	116.10 W
Coachella Canal ≊	258	33.34 N	116.00 W
Coacoyole	278	24.31 N	106.34 W
Coahoma	250	32.18 N	101.18 W
Coahuila	254	32.12 N	114.59 W
Coahuila □[3]	278	27.20 N	102.00 W
Coal ≃	236	59.39 N	126.57 W
Coalburg	266	41.11 N	80.36 W
Coal City	268	41.17 N	88.17 W
Coalcomán de Matamoros	278	18.47 N	103.09 W
Coal Creek	236	65.22 N	143.10 W
Coaldale	238	49.43 N	112.37 W
Coal Fork	242	38.19 N	81.32 W
Coalgate	250	34.32 N	96.13 W
Coal Grove	242	38.30 N	82.39 W
Coal Harbour	238	50.36 N	127.35 W
Coal Hill	248	35.26 N	93.40 W
Coalhurst	238	49.45 N	112.56 W
Coalinga	272	36.09 N	120.21 W
Coal Island I	230	46.07 S	166.37 E
Coalmont	238	49.31 N	120.41 W
Coalport	266	40.45 N	78.32 W
Coal River	236	59.45 N	126.55 W
Coalspur	238	53.11 N	117.01 W
Coaltown	266	41.02 N	80.20 W
Coal Valley ∨	258	38.56 N	115.25 W
Coalville, Eng., U.K.	174	52.44 S	1.20 W
Coalville, Utah, U.S.	254	40.55 N	111.24 W
Coamo	284m	18.05 N	66.22 W
Coan, Cerro ∧	292	7.26 S	78.43 W
Coaraci	296	14.38 S	39.32 W
Coari	290	4.05 S	63.08 W
Coari ≃	290	4.30 S	63.33 W
Coari, Lago de ⊜	290	4.15 S	63.22 W
Coarsegold	272	37.16 N	119.42 W
Coast Mountains ⋏	232	55.00 N	129.00 W
Coast Ranges ⋏	234	41.00 N	123.30 W
Coatán ≃	280	14.48 N	92.30 W
Coatbridge	162	55.52 N	4.01 W
Coatepeque	280	14.42 N	91.52 W
Coatepeque, Lago de ⊜	280	13.52 N	89.33 W
Coatesville	262	39.59 N	75.49 W
Coatiçaba	296	13.59 S	46.31 W
Coaticook	260	45.08 N	71.48 W
Coats Island I	232	62.30 N	83.00 W
Coats Land ⬩[1]	148	77.00 S	28.00 W
Coatzacoalcos	278	18.09 N	94.25 W
Coayllo	292	12.42 S	76.29 W
Cobá ⊥	278	20.36 N	87.35 W
Cobadin	172	44.04 N	28.13 E
Cobalt, Ont., Can.	244	47.24 N	79.41 W
Cobalt, Conn., U.S.	261	41.34 N	72.34 W
Cobán	280	15.29 N	90.19 W
Cobar	228	31.30 S	145.49 E
Cobb	272	38.49 N	122.43 W
Cobberas, Mount ∧	228	36.52 S	148.10 E
Cobb Island	262	38.16 N	76.51 W
Cobble Hill	270	48.41 N	123.36 W
Cobb Seamount ⟡[3]	148	46.45 N	130.50 W
Cobden, Ont., Can.	244	45.38 N	76.53 W
Cobden, Ill., U.S.	248	37.32 N	89.15 W
Cobequid Bay C	240	45.21 N	63.45 W
Cobequid Mountains ⋏	240	45.30 N	63.30 W
Cobh	162	51.51 N	8.17 W
Cobham ≃	232	53.15 N	93.58 W
Cobija, Bol.	292	11.02 S	68.44 W
Cobija, Chile	294	22.33 S	70.16 W
Cobleskill	242	42.41 N	74.29 W
Coboconk	264	44.39 N	78.48 W
Coboto, Cerro ∧	254	31.32 N	112.05 W
Cobourg	264	43.58 N	78.10 W
Cobquecura	294	36.08 S	72.47 W
Cobre ≃	280	8.02 N	81.18 W
Cobres, Ribeira de ≃	168	37.50 N	7.52 W
Cóbuè	218	12.04 S	34.50 E
Coburg	164	50.15 N	10.58 E
Coburg Island I	232	76.00 N	79.25 W
Coburn Mountain ∧	242	45.28 N	70.06 W
Cobuya ≃	290	2.20 S	70.50 W
Coca ≃	290	0.29 S	76.58 W
Coca, Punta ≻	280	12.28 N	83.29 W
Cocachacra	292	17.05 S	71.46 W
Cocentaina	168	38.45 N	0.26 W
Cochabamba	292	17.24 S	66.09 W
Cochabamba □[5]	292	17.30 S	65.40 W
Cochagual	294	31.54 S	68.23 W
Coche, Isla I	290	10.45 N	63.55 W
Cochem	164	50.11 N	7.09 E
Cochinos, Bahzzia de(Bay of Pigs) C	284p	22.07 N	81.10 W
Cochinos, Cayos II	280	16.00 N	86.30 W
Cochise Head ∧	254	32.03 N	109.18 W
Cochituate	261	42.19 N	71.22 W
Cochran	246	32.23 N	83.21 W
Cochrane, Alta., Can.	238	51.11 N	114.28 W
Cochrane, Ont., Can.	232	49.04 N	81.01 W
Cochrane, Wis., U.S.	244	44.14 N	91.50 W
Cochrane ≃	232	57.52 N	101.38 W
Cochrane, Lago (Lago Puyerredón) ⊜	288	47.20 S	72.00 W
Cochranton	266	41.31 N	80.03 W
Cochranville	262	39.53 N	75.55 W
Cockburn Island I	244	45.55 N	83.22 W
Cockermouth	162	54.40 N	3.21 W
Cockeysville	262	39.29 N	76.39 W
Cockpit Country ⬩[1]	285q	18.18 N	77.43 W
Coclé □[4]	280	8.30 N	80.15 W
Coclé del Norte ≃	280	9.03 N	80.35 W
Coco ≃	280	15.00 N	83.08 W
Coco, Cayo I	284p	22.30 N	78.28 W
Coco, Isla del I	276	5.32 N	87.04 W
Cocoa	246	28.21 N	80.44 W
Cocoa Beach	246	28.19 N	80.36 W
Coco Channel ⩌	200	13.45 N	93.00 E
Cocodrie Lake ⊜[1]	248	30.58 N	92.25 W
Coco Islands II	200	14.05 N	93.18 E
Coconino Plateau ⋏[1]	254	36.00 N	112.35 W
Cocorocuma, Cayos ⟡[2]	280	15.45 N	83.00 W
Côcos	296	14.10 S	44.33 W
Côcos, Vereda de ≃	296	12.44 S	44.48 W
Cocos Bay C	285r	10.30 N	61.00 W
Cocos Islands II	148	12.10 S	96.55 W
Cocos Ridge ⟡[3]	148	5.30 N	87.30 W
Cocuiza ≃	290	10.59 N	71.17 W
Cocula	278	20.23 N	103.50 W
Cod, Cape ≻	234	41.42 N	70.15 W
Codăești	172	46.52 N	27.46 E
Codajás	290	3.50 S	62.05 W
Codera, Cabo ≻	290	10.35 N	66.05 W
Codesa	238	55.45 N	118.04 W
Codfish Island I	230	46.47 S	167.38 E
Codigoro	184	44.49 N	12.08 E
Cod Island I	232	57.45 N	61.50 W
Codlea	172	45.42 N	25.27 E
Codó	286	4.29 S	43.53 W
Codogno	182	45.09 N	9.42 E
Codorus	262	39.48 N	76.52 W
Codpa	292	18.50 S	69.44 W
Codroipo	170	45.58 N	12.59 E
Codroy	240	47.52 N	59.23 W
Codroy Pond	240	48.04 N	58.52 W
Cody, Nebr., U.S.	252	42.56 N	101.15 W
Cody, Wyo., U.S.	256	44.32 N	109.03 W
Coeburn	246	36.57 N	82.28 W
Coelemu	294	36.29 S	72.42 W
Coen	226	13.56 S	143.12 E
Coesfeld	178	51.56 N	7.10 E
Coetivy Island I	218	7.08 S	56.16 E
Coeur d'Alene	256	47.41 N	116.46 W
Coeur d'Alene ≃	256	47.45 N	116.00 W
Coeur d'Alene Indian Reservation ⬩[4]	256	47.18 N	116.45 W
Coeur d'Alene Lake ⊜[1]	256	47.32 N	116.48 W
Coeur d'Alene Mountains ⋏	256	47.20 N	116.35 W
Coevorden	178	52.40 N	6.45 E
Coeymans	261	42.28 N	73.48 W
Coffeen	248	39.05 N	89.24 W
Coffeeville	248	33.59 N	89.40 W
Coffeyville	252	37.02 N	95.37 W
Coffin, Île I	240	47.34 N	61.30 W
Coffs Harbour	228	30.18 S	153.08 E
Cofradía	280	15.24 N	88.09 W
Cofre de Perote, Parque Nacional ♠	278	19.32 N	97.10 W
Cofrentes	168	39.14 N	1.04 W
Coggon	244	42.17 N	91.32 W
Coglians, Monte ∧	164	46.37 N	12.53 E
Cognac	166	45.42 N	0.20 W
Cogoleto	182	44.23 N	8.39 E
Cogolin	166	43.15 N	6.32 E
Cogolludo	168	40.57 N	3.05 W
Cogswell	252	46.07 N	97.47 W
Cogtong Bay C	202	9.50 N	124.32 E
Cohasset	261	42.14 N	70.48 W
Cohenga ≃	292	10.18 S	73.59 W
Cohoctah	268	42.46 N	83.57 W
Cohocton ≃	242	42.09 N	77.05 W
Cohoe	236	60.23 N	151.18 W
Cohoes	261	42.46 N	73.42 W
Cohoni	292	16.44 S	67.51 W
Coiba, Isla de I	290	7.23 N	81.48 W
Coig (Coyle) ≃	288	51.00 S	69.10 W
Coimbra, Bra.	292	19.55 S	57.47 W
Coimbra, Bra.	296	20.52 S	42.48 W
Coimbra, Port.	168	40.12 N	8.25 W
Coín, Esp.	168	36.40 N	4.45 W
Coin, Iowa, U.S.	252	40.40 N	95.14 W
Coipasa, Lago de ⊜	292	19.12 S	68.07 W
Coipasa, Salar de ⩡	292	19.26 S	68.09 W
Čojbalsan	190	48.34 N	114.50 E
Cojedes	290	9.37 N	68.55 W
Cojedes □[3]	290	9.20 N	68.20 W
Cojedes ≃	290	8.34 N	68.05 W
Cojutepeque	280	13.43 N	88.56 W
Cokato	244	45.05 N	94.11 W
Cokeburg	266	40.06 N	80.04 W
Cokeville	254	42.05 N	110.57 W
Čokurdach	186	70.38 N	147.55 E
Colac	228	38.20 S	143.35 E
Colalao del Valle	294	26.22 S	65.56 W
Colapsin Point ≻	202	6.38 N	125.25 E
Colares	168	38.48 N	9.27 W
Colatina	296	19.32 S	40.37 W
Colbeck, Cape ≻	148	77.06 S	157.48 W
Colbert	250	33.51 N	96.30 W
Colborne, Ont., Can.	264	42.51 N	80.19 W
Colborne, Ont., Can.	264	44.00 N	77.53 W
Colbún	294	35.42 S	71.25 W
Colburn	268	40.31 N	86.43 W
Colby, Kans., U.S.	252	39.24 N	101.03 W
Colby, Wis., U.S.	244	44.55 N	90.19 W
Colca	292	12.20 S	75.15 W
Colca ≃	292	15.49 S	72.24 W
Colcamar	292	6.21 S	77.55 W
Colcapirhua	292	17.25 S	66.15 W
Colchagua □[4]	294	34.30 S	71.15 W
Colchester, Ont., Can.	266	41.59 N	82.56 W
Colchester, Eng., U.K.	174	51.54 N	0.54 E
Colchester, Conn., U.S.	261	41.34 N	72.20 W
Colchester, Ill., U.S.	244	40.25 N	90.48 W
Cold Bay	236	55.11 N	162.30 W
Cold Bay C	236	55.13 N	162.33 W
Colden	266	42.39 N	78.41 W
Cold Spring, Minn., U.S.	244	45.27 N	94.26 W
Cold Spring, N.J., U.S.	262	38.59 N	74.57 W
Cold Spring, N.Y., U.S.	261	41.25 N	73.57 W
Coldspring, Tex., U.S.	250	30.36 N	95.08 W
Coldsprings, Ont., Can.	264	44.17 N	78.18 W
Cold Springs, N.Y., U.S.	264	43.08 N	76.15 W
Coldstream	162	55.39 N	2.15 W
Coldwater, Ont., Can.	264	44.42 N	79.40 W
Coldwater, Kans., U.S.	252	37.16 N	99.19 W
Coldwater, Mich., U.S.	268	41.57 N	85.00 W
Coldwater, Miss., U.S.	248	34.41 N	89.59 W
Coldwater, Ohio, U.S.	268	40.29 N	84.38 W
Coldwater Indian Reserve ⬩[4]	238	50.04 N	120.48 W
Colebrook, N.H., U.S.	242	44.54 N	71.30 W
Colebrook, Ohio, U.S.	266	41.32 N	80.46 W
Cole Camp	248	38.28 N	93.12 W
Coleen ≃	236	67.05 N	142.31 W
Coleman, Alta., Can.	238	49.38 N	114.30 W
Coleman, Fla., U.S.	246	28.48 N	82.04 W
Coleman, Md., U.S.	262	39.21 N	76.05 W
Coleman, Mich., U.S.	244	43.46 N	84.35 W
Coleman, Tex., U.S.	250	31.50 N	99.26 W
Coleman, Wis., U.S.	244	45.04 N	88.02 W
Çölemerik	208	37.34 N	43.45 E
Colerain	266	40.07 N	80.49 W
Coleraine, N. Ire., U.K.	162	55.08 N	6.40 W
Coleraine, Minn., U.S.	244	47.17 N	93.27 W
Coleridge	252	42.30 N	97.13 W
Coleridge, Lake ⊜	230	43.18 S	171.30 E
Coles	248	31.17 N	91.03 W
Colesberg	218	30.45 S	25.05 E
Coles Point	262	38.09 N	76.38 W
Coleville	272	38.33 N	119.30 W
Colfax, Calif., U.S.	272	39.06 N	120.57 W
Colfax, Ill., U.S.	268	40.34 N	88.37 W
Colfax, Ind., U.S.	248	40.12 N	86.40 W
Colfax, Iowa, U.S.	244	41.41 N	93.14 W
Colfax, La., U.S.	248	31.31 N	92.42 W
Colfax, Wash., U.S.	256	46.53 N	117.22 W
Colfax, Wis., U.S.	244	45.00 N	91.44 W
Colgate	268	43.12 N	88.12 W
Colhué Huapi, Lago ⊜	288	45.30 S	68.48 W
Colico	170	46.08 N	9.22 E
Colima, Méx.	254	32.25 N	115.05 W
Colima, Méx.	278	19.14 N	103.43 W
Colima, Nevado de ∧	278	19.33 N	103.38 W
Colimes ≃	290	1.32 S	80.00 W
Colina	294	33.12 S	70.41 W
Colinas	296	14.12 S	48.03 W
Colinet	240	47.13 N	53.33 W
Colinton	238	54.37 N	113.15 W
Coll I	162	56.40 N	6.35 W
Collamer	264	43.06 N	76.04 W
Collbran	254	39.14 N	107.57 W
Colle di Val d'Elsa	184	43.25 N	11.07 E
Colleferro	184	41.44 N	12.59 E
College	236	64.51 N	147.47 W
College City	272	39.00 N	122.00 W
Collegedale	248	35.04 N	85.03 W
College Heights	248	33.35 N	91.49 W
College Park, Ga., U.S.	246	33.39 N	84.27 W
College Park, Md., U.S.	262	39.00 N	76.55 W
College Place	256	46.03 N	118.23 W
College Station	250	30.37 N	96.21 W
Collegeville, Ind., U.S.	268	40.56 N	87.09 W
Collegeville, Minn., U.S.	244	45.36 N	94.22 W
Collegeville, Pa., U.S.	262	40.11 N	75.27 W
Collegno	182	45.05 N	7.34 E
Collesalvetti	184	43.35 N	10.28 E
Colleymount	238	54.01 N	126.09 W
Colleyville	250	32.53 N	97.09 W
Collie	226	33.21 S	116.09 E
Collier Bay C	226	16.10 S	124.15 E
Colliers	266	40.22 N	80.33 W
Collierville	248	35.03 N	89.40 W
Collingdale	262	39.55 N	75.17 W
Collingwood	264	44.29 N	80.13 W
Collins, Ga., U.S.	246	32.11 N	82.07 W
Collins, Iowa, U.S.	244	41.54 N	93.18 W
Collins, Miss., U.S.	248	31.39 N	89.33 W
Collins, N.Y., U.S.	266	42.30 N	78.55 W
Collins ≃	248	35.48 N	85.37 W
Collins, Mount ∧[2]	244	47.51 N	80.59 W
Collins Bay	264	44.15 N	76.36 W
Collinsburg	266	40.13 N	79.46 W
Collins Center	266	42.30 N	78.51 W
Collins Park	262	39.41 N	75.33 W
Collinston	248	32.41 N	91.52 W
Collinsville, Austl.	226	20.34 S	147.51 E
Collinsville, Ala., U.S.	248	34.16 N	85.52 W
Collinsville, Conn., U.S.	261	41.49 N	72.55 W
Collinsville, Miss., U.S.	248	32.30 N	88.51 W
Collinsville, Okla., U.S.	250	36.22 N	95.51 W
Collinwood	248	35.10 N	87.44 W
Collipulli	294	37.57 S	72.26 W
Collooney	162	54.11 N	8.29 W
Colma	272	37.41 N	122.28 W
Colman	252	43.59 N	96.49 W
Colmar	180	48.05 N	7.22 E
Colmars	166	41.11 N	6.38 E
Colmenar	168	36.54 N	4.20 W
Colmenar de Oreja	168	40.06 N	3.23 W
Colmenar Viejo	168	40.40 N	3.46 W
Colmeneros	278	18.06 N	101.40 W
Colmesneil	248	30.54 N	94.25 W
Colnett, Cabo ≻	278	31.00 N	116.20 W
Colo	244	42.01 N	93.19 W
Colo ≃	228	33.26 S	150.53 E
Cologne → Köln, B.R.D.	164	50.56 N	6.59 E
Cologne, Minn., U.S.	244	44.47 N	93.46 W
Cologne, N.J., U.S.	262	39.30 N	74.37 W
Cologno al Serio	182	45.37 N	9.42 E
Cololo, Nevado ∧	292	14.53 S	69.06 W
Coloma, Calif., U.S.	272	38.48 N	120.53 W
Coloma, Mich., U.S.	268	42.11 N	86.19 W
Coloma, Wis., U.S.	244	44.02 N	89.31 W
Coloma, Ensenada de C	284p	22.13 N	83.34 W
Colomb-Béchar → Béchar	214	31.37 N	2.13 W
Colombes	176	48.55 N	2.15 E
Colombey-les-Belles	166	48.32 N	5.54 E
Colombia, Col.	290	3.24 N	74.49 W
Colombia, Méx.	250	27.42 N	99.45 W
Colombia □[1]	286	4.00 N	72.00 W
Colombian Basin ⟡[1]	148	13.00 N	75.00 W
Colombo, Bra.	294	25.17 S	49.14 W
Colombo, Sih.	204	6.56 N	79.51 E
Colome	252	43.15 N	99.43 W
Colón, Arg.	294	33.55 S	61.05 W
Colón, Arg.	294	32.15 S	58.10 W
Colón, Cuba	284p	22.43 N	80.54 W
Colón, Pan.	280	9.22 N	79.54 W
Colon, Mich., U.S.	268	41.57 N	85.19 W
Colón, Ur.	294	33.53 S	54.43 W
Colón □[4]	280	9.00 N	80.20 W
Colón □[5]	280	15.20 N	84.30 W
Colón, Archipiélago de □[2]	290a	1.00 N	90.00 W
Colón, Archipiélago de II	290a	0.30 S	90.30 W
Colón, Isla I	280	9.24 N	82.16 W
Colón, Montañas de ⋏	280	14.55 N	84.45 W
Colonet	258	31.05 N	116.10 W
Colonia	262	40.35 N	74.18 W
Colônia ≃	296	15.11 S	39.45 W
Colonia Agrícola Turén	290	9.15 N	69.05 W
Colonia Alvear Oeste	294	35.01 S	67.40 W
Colonia Anáhuac	278	28.25 N	106.40 W
Colonia Benjamín Aceval	294	24.58 S	57.34 W
Colonia Caroya	294	31.03 S	64.05 W
Colonia del Sacramento	294	34.28 S	57.51 W
Colonia Dora	294	28.40 S	63.00 W
Colonia Elisa	294	26.51 S	59.31 W
Colonia Guadalupe	258	32.04 N	116.37 W
Colonia José Mármol	294	26.59 S	60.44 W
Colonial Acres	262	39.31 N	76.20 W
Colonia Las Heras	288	46.33 S	68.57 W
Colonia Lavalleja	294	31.06 S	57.01 W
Colonial Beach	262	38.15 N	76.58 W
Colonial Crest	262	40.20 N	76.50 W
Colonial Heights	262	37.15 N	77.25 W
Colonial National Historical Park ♠	246	37.12 N	76.45 W
Colonial Park	262	40.18 N	76.49 W
Colonial Village, Ill., U.S.	268	41.03 N	88.02 W
Colonial Village, N.Y., U.S.	264	43.08 N	78.58 W
Colonia Morelos	254	30.50 N	109.10 W
Colonia Progreso	258	32.35 N	115.37 W
Colonia Providencia	284m	17.59 N	66.00 W
Colonias Unidas	294	26.42 S	59.38 W
Colonia Vicente Guerrero	278	30.45 N	116.00 W
Colonia Villafañe	294	26.08 S	59.07 W
Colonie	261	42.43 N	73.50 W
Colonne, Capo ≻	170	39.02 N	17.11 E
Colonsay I	162	56.05 N	6.10 W
Colony	252	38.04 N	95.22 W
Colora	262	39.40 N	76.06 W
Coloradas, Lomas ⋏[2]	288	43.55 S	67.20 W
Colorado, C.R.	280	10.46 N	83.35 W
Colorado, Hond.	280	15.47 N	87.19 W
Colorado, Alaska, U.S.	236	63.09 N	149.26 W
Colorado □[3]	234	39.30 N	105.30 W
Colorado ≃, Arg.	294	39.50 S	62.08 W
Colorado ≃, Bra.	292	13.03 S	62.20 W
Colorado ≃, N.A.	254	31.45 N	114.40 W
Colorado ≃, Tex., U.S.	250	28.36 N	95.58 W
Colorado, Arroyo ∨	254	34.58 N	107.13 W
Colorado, Cerro ∧	278	31.32 N	115.31 W
Colorado City, Ariz., U.S.	254	36.58 N	112.58 W
Colorado City, Tex., U.S.	250	32.24 N	100.52 W
Colorado de Abajo	250	26.28 N	99.54 W
Colorado Desert ⬩[2]	258	33.15 N	115.15 W
Colorado National Monument ♠	254	39.04 N	108.25 W
Colorado Plateau ⋏[1]	254	36.30 N	108.00 W
Colorado River Indian Reservation ⬩[4]	254	34.00 N	114.25 W
Colorado Springs	254	38.50 N	104.49 W
Colotepec ≃	278	15.47 N	97.03 W
Colotlán	278	22.06 N	103.16 W
Colquechaca	292	18.40 S	66.01 W
Colquencha	292	17.00 S	68.17 W
Colquiri	292	17.25 S	67.08 W
Colquitt	246	31.10 N	84.44 W
Colstrip	256	45.53 N	106.38 W
Colt	248	35.08 N	90.49 W
Colta	292	15.10 S	73.18 W
Coltauco	294	34.18 S	71.06 W
Colton, Calif., U.S.	274	34.04 N	117.20 W
Colton, Ohio, U.S.	268	41.28 N	83.57 W
Colton, Oreg., U.S.	270	45.10 N	12.26 W
Colton, S. Dak., U.S.	252	43.47 N	96.56 W
Coltons Point	262	38.14 N	76.45 W
Colts Neck	262	40.17 N	74.11 W
Coltsville Center	266	41.05 N	80.34 W
Columbia, Ala., U.S.	246	31.18 N	85.07 W
Columbia, Calif., U.S.	272	38.02 N	120.24 W
Columbia, Conn., U.S.	261	41.42 N	72.18 W
Columbia, Ill., U.S.	248	38.27 N	90.12 W
Columbia, Ky., U.S.	248	37.06 N	85.18 W
Columbia, La., U.S.	248	32.06 N	92.05 W
Columbia, Md., U.S.	262	39.13 N	76.52 W
Columbia, Miss., U.S.	248	31.15 N	89.56 W
Columbia, Mo., U.S.	248	38.57 N	92.20 W
Columbia, N.C., U.S.	246	35.55 N	76.15 W
Columbia, Pa., U.S.	262	40.02 N	76.30 W
Columbia, S.C., U.S.	246	34.00 N	81.03 W
Columbia, Tenn., U.S.	248	35.37 N	87.02 W
Columbia □[6], N.Y., U.S.	261	42.15 N	73.47 W
Columbia □[6], Oreg., U.S.	270	45.57 N	123.03 W
Columbia ≃	232	46.15 N	124.05 W
Columbia, Mount ∧	238	52.09 N	117.25 W
Columbia Basin ⩡[1]	256	46.45 N	119.05 W
Columbia City, Ind., U.S.	268	41.10 N	85.29 W
Columbia City, Oreg., U.S.	270	45.55 N	122.51 W
Columbia Falls, Maine, U.S.	242	44.39 N	67.44 W
Columbia Falls, Mont., U.S.	256	48.23 N	114.11 W
Columbia Heights	270	46.09 N	122.58 W
Columbia Icefield ⩍	238	52.10 N	117.30 W
Columbia Lake ⊜	238	50.15 N	115.57 W
Columbia Lake Indian Reserve ⬩[4]	238	50.25 N	115.57 W
Columbia Mountains ⋏	238	51.30 N	118.30 W
Columbiana, Ala., U.S.	248	33.11 N	86.36 W
Columbiana, Ohio, U.S.	266	40.53 N	80.42 W
Columbiana □[6]	266	40.47 N	80.46 W
Columbia Park	272	38.01 N	121.52 W
Columbia Plateau ⋏[1]	256	44.00 N	117.30 W
Columbia Road Reservoir ⊜[1]	252	45.45 N	98.15 W
Columbia Station	266	41.20 N	81.57 W
Columbiaville, Mich., U.S.	244	43.09 N	83.25 W
Columbiaville, N.Y., U.S.	261	42.19 N	73.45 W
Columbine, Cape ≻	224	32.47 S	18.52 E
Columbretes, Islas II	168	39.52 N	0.40 E
Columbus, Ga., U.S.	246	32.29 N	84.59 W
Columbus, Ind., U.S.	248	39.13 N	85.55 W
Columbus, Kans., U.S.	252	37.10 N	94.50 W
Columbus, Ky., U.S.	248	36.46 N	89.06 W
Columbus, Miss., U.S.	248	33.30 N	88.25 W
Columbus, Mont., U.S.	256	45.38 N	109.15 W
Columbus, Nebr., U.S.	252	41.25 N	97.22 W
Columbus, N.J., U.S.	262	40.04 N	74.43 W
Columbus, N. Mex., U.S.	254	31.50 N	107.38 W
Columbus, N.C., U.S.	246	35.15 N	82.12 W
Columbus, N. Dak., U.S.	252	48.54 N	102.47 W
Columbus, Ohio, U.S.	266	39.57 N	83.00 W
Columbus, Pa., U.S.	266	41.56 N	79.35 W
Columbus, Tex., U.S.	250	29.42 N	96.33 W
Columbus, Wis., U.S.	244	43.21 N	89.01 W
Columbus Grove	268	40.55 N	84.04 W
Columbus Junction	244	41.17 N	91.22 W
Columbus Point ≻, Ba.	282	24.08 N	75.16 W
Columbus Point ≻, Trin.	285r	11.08 N	60.47 W
Columbus Salt Marsh ☷	258	38.04 N	117.58 W
Coluna	296	18.14 S	42.50 W
Colusa	272	39.13 N	122.01 W
Colusa □[6]	272	39.13 N	122.01 W
Colver	266	40.33 N	78.47 W
Colville	256	48.33 N	117.54 W
Colville ≃, Alaska, U.S.	236	70.25 N	150.30 W
Colville ≃, Wash., U.S.	256	48.37 N	118.05 W
Colville, Cape ≻	230	36.28 S	175.21 E
Colville Indian Reservation ⬩[4]	256	48.15 N	119.00 W
Colville Lake ⊜	236	67.10 N	126.00 W
Colwood	270	48.26 N	123.29 W
Colwyn Bay	162	53.18 N	3.43 W
Comacchio	184	44.42 N	12.11 E
Comacchio, Valli di C	166	44.38 N	12.06 E
Comala	278	19.19 N	103.45 W
Comalapa, Guat.	280	14.44 N	90.53 W
Comalapa, Nic.	280	12.18 N	85.30 W
Comalcalco	278	18.16 N	93.13 W
Comales	278	26.10 N	98.56 W
Comanche, Okla., U.S.	250	34.22 N	97.58 W
Comanche, Tex., U.S.	250	31.54 N	98.36 W
Comandante Fontana	294	25.20 S	59.41 W
Comandante Leal	294	30.54 S	65.48 W
Comandante Nicanor Otamendi	294	38.10 S	57.50 W
Comănești	172	46.25 N	26.26 E
Comarapa	292	17.54 S	64.29 W
Comas	292	11.43 S	75.03 W
Comayagua	280	14.25 N	87.37 W
Comayagua □[5]	280	14.30 N	87.40 W
Comayagua, Montañas de ⋏	280	14.23 N	87.26 W
Combahee ≃	246	32.30 N	80.31 W
Combarbalá	294	31.11 S	71.02 W
Combeaufontaine	166	47.43 N	5.53 E
Comber	266	42.14 N	82.33 W
Combermere Bay C	200	19.37 N	93.34 E
Combourg	166	48.25 N	1.45 W
Combronde	166	45.59 N	3.05 E
Combs	248	35.50 N	93.50 W
Comb Wash ∨	254	37.13 N	109.42 W
Come by Chance	240	47.51 N	53.58 W
Comemoração ≃	292	11.45 S	60.56 W
Comendador Gomes	296	19.41 S	49.05 W
Comer	246	34.04 N	83.08 W
Comercinho	296	16.19 S	41.47 W
Comerío	284m	18.13 N	66.14 W
Comet ≃	228	23.34 S	148.32 E
Comfort, N.C., U.S.	246	35.00 N	77.30 W
Comfort, Tex., U.S.	250	29.58 N	98.49 W
Comfort, Cape ≻	232	65.08 N	83.21 W
Comfrey	252	44.07 N	94.54 W
Comilla	206	23.28 N	91.10 E
Comines	176	50.46 N	3.01 E
Comino I	170	36.00 N	14.20 E
Comino, Capo ≻	170	40.31 N	9.50 E
Comiso	170	36.56 N	14.37 E
Comitán	280	16.15 N	92.08 W
Comitán [de Domínguez]	278	16.15 N	92.08 W
Comloșu Mare	172	45.54 N	20.38 E
Commack	261	40.51 N	73.18 W
Commentry	166	46.17 N	2.44 E
Commerce, Ga., U.S.	246	34.12 N	83.28 W
Commerce, Mich., U.S.	268	42.34 N	83.30 W
Commerce, Okla., U.S.	250	36.56 N	94.53 W
Commerce, Tex., U.S.	250	33.15 N	95.54 W
Commerce City	254	39.49 N	104.55 W
Commercy	166	48.45 N	5.35 E
Comminges ⬩[1]	166	43.15 N	0.45 E
Committee Bay C	232	68.30 N	86.30 W
Commodore	266	40.43 N	78.57 W
Community Center	274	34.16 N	118.44 W
Como, It.	182	45.47 N	9.05 E
Como, Miss., U.S.	248	34.31 N	90.03 W
Como, N.C., U.S.	262	36.30 N	77.00 W
Como, Tex., U.S.	250	33.03 N	95.28 W
Como, Wis., U.S.	268	42.37 N	88.28 W
Como □[4]	182	45.59 N	9.13 E
Como, Lago di ⊜	170	46.00 N	9.20 E
Comodoro Py	294	35.20 S	60.30 W
Comodoro Rivadavia	288	45.50 S	67.30 W
Como Lake ⊜	244	47.55 N	83.30 W
Comondú	278	26.03 N	111.46 W
Comores, Archipel des II	148	12.10 S	44.15 E
Comoro Islands □[2]	218	12.10 S	44.15 E
Comox	238	49.40 N	124.55 W
Compiègne	176	49.25 N	2.50 E
Compostela, Méx.	278	21.15 N	104.53 W
Compostela, Pil.	202	7.40 N	126.02 E
Comprida, Ilha I	294	24.50 S	47.42 W
Comps[-sur-Artuby]	166	43.43 N	6.30 E
Compton, Calif., U.S.	274	33.54 N	118.13 W
Compton, Ill., U.S.	268	41.42 N	89.05 W
Compton □[6]	260	45.20 N	71.25 W
Comstock, Mich., U.S.	268	42.16 N	85.31 W
Comstock, Nebr., U.S.	252	41.33 N	99.14 W
Comstock, Tex., U.S.	250	29.41 N	101.11 W
Comstock Park	268	43.02 N	85.40 W
Con ≃	200	19.04 N	105.00 E
Čona ≃	186	62.54 N	111.06 E
Conakry	222	9.31 N	13.43 W
Conambo ≃	290	2.07 S	76.03 W
Conasauga ≃	246	34.33 N	84.55 W
Concarán	294	32.32 S	65.15 W
Concarneau	166	47.52 N	3.55 W
Conceição	292	7.24 S	58.05 W
Conceição ≃	296	12.24 S	46.57 W
Conceição, Cachoeira da ⅃	292	9.34 S	64.22 W
Conceição da Aparecida	296	21.06 S	46.12 W
Conceição da Barra	296	18.35 S	39.45 W
Conceição das Alagoas	296	19.55 S	48.23 W
Conceição de Ipanema	296	19.55 S	41.41 W
Conceição do Almeida	296	12.48 S	39.12 W
Conceição do Araguaia	286	8.15 S	49.17 W
Conceição do Mato Dentro	296	19.01 S	43.25 W
Conceição do Maú	290	3.35 N	59.53 W
Conceição do Norte	296	12.13 S	47.18 W
Concepción, Arg.	294	27.20 S	65.36 W
Concepción, Arg.	294	28.24 S	57.53 W
Concepción, Bol.	292	16.15 S	62.04 W
Concepción, Bol.	292	11.29 S	66.42 W
Concepción, Chile	294	36.50 S	73.03 W
Concepción, Col.	290	6.46 N	72.42 W
Concepción, Guat.	280	15.37 N	91.41 W
Concepción, Pan.	280	8.31 N	82.38 W
Concepción, Para.	294	23.25 S	57.17 W
Concepción, Perú	292	11.54 S	75.19 W
Concepcion, Pil.	202	11.13 N	123.06 E
Concepcion, Pil.	202	15.20 N	120.39 E
Concepcion, Pil.	202	12.24 N	122.06 E
Concepcion, Pil.	202	10.42 N	123.03 E
Concepción □[4]	294	37.00 S	72.30 W
Concepción □[5]	294	23.00 S	57.00 W
Concepción, Bahía C	278	26.40 N	111.50 W
Concepción, Laguna ⊜	292	17.29 S	61.25 W
Concepción, Río de la ≃	278	30.32 N	112.59 W
Concepción, Volcán ∧[1]	280	11.33 N	85.37 W
Concepcion Bay C	202	11.20 N	123.16 E
Concepción de Ataco	280	13.52 N	89.51 W
Concepción de la Sierra	294	28.00 S	55.31 W
Concepcíon del Oro	278	24.38 N	101.25 W
Concepción del Uruguay	294	32.30 S	58.14 W
Concepción Quezaltepeque	280	14.06 N	88.58 W
Conception, Point ≻	258	34.27 N	120.27 W
Conception Bay C, Newf., Can.	240	47.45 N	53.00 W
Conception Bay C, S.W. Afr.	224	23.53 S	14.28 E
Conchagua	280	13.19 N	87.52 W
Conchagua, Volcán de ∧[1]	280	13.16 N	87.51 W
Conchas ≃	250	35.23 N	104.18 W
Conchas Dam	250	35.22 N	104.11 W
Conchas Reservoir ⊜[1]	250	35.25 N	104.14 W
Conche	240	50.53 N	55.54 W
Conches	166	48.51 N	2.43 E
Conches-en-Ouche	166	48.58 N	0.56 E
Conchi	294	22.02 S	68.38 W
Concho	254	34.28 N	109.36 W
Conchos ≃, Méx.	278	25.09 N	98.35 W

Symbols in the index entries are identified on page 360.

Name	Page	Lat°′	Long°′
Conchos ≃, Méx.	278	29.32 N	104.25 W
Concón	294	32.55 S	71.31 W
Conconongon Point ➤	202	12.14 N	120.13 E
Conconully	238	48.34 N	119.45 W
Concord, Ont., Can.	264	43.48 N	79.29 W
Concord, Calif., U.S.	272	37.59 N	122.02 W
Concord, Ga., U.S.	246	33.05 N	84.26 W
Concord, Mass., U.S.	261	42.27 N	71.21 W
Concord, Mich., U.S.	268	42.10 N	84.38 W
Concord, N.H., U.S.	242	43.12 N	71.32 W
Concord, N.C., U.S.	246	35.25 N	80.35 W
Concord, Pa., U.S.	266	40.15 N	77.42 W
Concord, Tenn., U.S.	246	35.52 N	84.08 W
Concordia, Arg.	294	31.24 S	58.02 W
Concórdia, Bra.	290	4.35 S	66.35 W
Concórdia, Bra.	294	27.14 S	52.01 W
Concordia, Méx.	278	25.47 N	103.07 W
Concordia, Méx.	278	23.17 N	106.04 W
Concordia, Kans., U.S.	252	39.34 N	97.39 W
Concordia, Mo., U.S.	248	38.59 N	93.34 W
Concorezzo	182	45.35 N	9.20 E
Concrete	270	48.32 N	121.45 W
Condat-en-Féniers	166	45.21 N	2.46 E
Conde, Bra.	296	11.49 S	37.37 W
Condé, Fr.	166	48.51 N	0.33 W
Conde, S. Dak., U.S.	252	45.09 N	98.06 W
Condega	280	13.21 N	86.25 W
Condega, Punta ➤	280	13.06 N	87.25 W
Condeúba	296	14.53 S	41.59 W
Condobolin	228	33.05 S	147.09 E
Condom	166	43.58 N	0.22 E
Condon	256	45.14 N	120.11 W
Condoto, Col.	290	5.06 N	76.37 W
Condoto, Perú	290	4.30 S	74.55 W
Condroz □[9]	166	50.25 N	5.00 E
Cone	250	33.48 N	101.23 W
Conecuh ≃	248	30.58 N	87.14 W
Conegliano	170	45.53 N	12.18 E
Conejos, Méx.	250	26.14 N	103.53 W
Conejos, Colo., U.S.	254	37.05 N	106.01 W
Conejos ≃	254	37.18 N	105.44 W
Conemaugh	266	40.24 N	78.52 W
Cone Mountain ∧	236	66.12 N	156.03 W
Conestoga	262	39.57 N	76.21 W
Conestogo	264	43.32 N	80.30 W
Conesus	264	42.43 N	77.41 W
Conesville	266	40.11 N	81.54 W
Conflans-Sainte-Honorine	176	48.59 N	2.06 E
Confluence	242	39.49 N	79.21 W
Confolens	166	46.01 N	0.41 E
Confusion Bay C	240	49.58 N	55.47 W
Confuso ≃	294	25.09 S	57.34 W
Congamond	261	42.01 N	72.46 W
Congaree ≃	246	33.45 N	80.37 W
Conger	244	43.37 N	93.32 W
Congers	261	41.09 N	74.11 W
Conghua	196	23.32 N	113.32 E
Congjiang	200	25.41 N	108.47 E
Congleton	174	53.10 N	2.13 W
Congo □[1]	218	1.00 S	15.00 E
Congo, Democratic Republic of the → Zaire □[1]	218	0.00	25.00 E
Congo (Zaire) (Zaïre) ≃	218	6.04 S	12.24 E
Congonhinhas	296	23.33 S	50.33 W
Congress, Sask., Can.	252	49.46 N	106.00 W
Congress, Ohio, U.S.	266	40.55 N	82.03 W
Coniston	244	46.29 N	80.51 W
Conitaca	278	24.10 N	106.43 W
Conjeeveram → Kānchipuram	204	12.50 N	79.43 E
Conjuror Bay C	232	65.45 N	118.07 W
Conklin	238	55.38 N	111.05 W
Conklingville Dam ◄[6]	242	43.17 N	74.02 W
Çonlu	172	40.13 N	28.06 E
Conn, Lough ⊜	162	54.04 N	9.20 W
Conneaut	266	41.57 N	80.34 W
Conneaut Lake	266	41.36 N	80.19 W
Conneaut Lake Park	266	41.38 N	80.19 W
Conneautville	266	41.36 N	80.18 W
Connecticut □[3]	234	41.45 N	72.45 W
Connecticut ≃	242	41.17 N	72.21 W
Connell	256	46.40 N	118.52 W
Connell, Mount ∧	238	49.18 N	115.38 W
Connellsville	242	40.01 N	79.35 W
Connelly	261	41.55 N	73.59 W
Conner	202	17.48 N	121.19 E
Connersville	248	39.39 N	85.08 W
Conning Towers	261	41.22 N	72.05 W
Conn Lake ⊜	232	70.34 N	73.30 W
Connoquenessing	266	40.49 N	80.59 W
Connors Range ⋀	228	21.40 S	149.10 E
Cononaco ≃	290	1.32 S	75.35 W
Conover	246	35.42 N	81.12 W
Conowingo	262	39.40 N	76.09 W
Conquista	296	19.56 S	47.33 W
Conrad, Iowa, U.S.	244	42.14 N	92.52 W
Conrad, Mont., U.S.	256	48.10 N	111.57 W
Conroe	250	30.19 N	95.27 W
Consecon	264	44.00 N	77.31 W
Conselheiro Lafaiete	296	20.40 S	43.48 W
Conselheiro Pena	296	19.10 S	41.30 W
Conselice	184	44.31 N	11.49 E
Consett	162	54.51 N	1.49 W
Conshohocken	262	40.05 N	75.18 W
Consolación del Norte	284p	22.45 N	83.33 W
Consolación del Sur	284p	22.30 N	83.31 W
Con Son II	200	8.43 N	106.36 E
Constable	260	44.56 N	74.18 W
Constableville	264	43.34 N	75.26 W
Constance → Konstanz	180	47.40 N	9.10 E
Constance, Lake → Bodensee ⊜	180	47.35 N	9.25 E
Constanța	172	44.11 N	28.39 E
Constantia	264	43.15 N	76.00 W
Constantina	168	37.52 N	5.37 W
Constantine, Alg.	214	36.25 N	6.43 E
Constantine, Mich., U.S.	268	41.50 N	85.40 W
Constantine □[8]	170	36.25 N	6.42 E
Constantine, Cape ➤	236	58.25 N	158.50 W
Constantinople → İstanbul	212	41.01 N	28.58 E
Constânzia	168	39.28 N	8.20 W
Constitución, Chile	294	35.20 S	72.25 W
Constitución, Ur.	294	31.05 S	57.50 W
Consuegra	168	39.28 N	3.36 W
Consul	256	49.21 N	109.30 W
Contamana	292	75.02 S	7.15 W
Contas, Rio de ≃	296	14.17 S	39.01 W
Contee	262	39.05 N	76.52 W
Contendas do Sincorá	296	13.45 S	41.02 W
Contes	166	43.49 N	7.19 E
Continental	268	41.06 N	84.16 W
Continental Peak ∧	254	42.16 N	108.43 W
Contoocook ≃	242	43.27 N	71.35 W
Contraalmirante Cordero	294	38.45 S	68.05 W
Contra Costa □[6]	272	37.55 N	121.55 W
Contramaestre	284p	20.19 N	76.13 W
Contramaestre ≃	284p	20.32 N	76.19 W
Contratación	290	6.18 N	73.29 W
Contrecoeur	260	45.52 N	73.14 W
Contreras, Embalse de ⊜[1]	168	39.32 N	1.30 W
Contres	166	47.25 N	1.26 E
Controller Bay C	236	60.07 N	144.15 W
Contumaza	292	7.22 S	78.49 W
Contwoyto Lake ⊜	232	65.42 N	110.50 W
Conty	166	49.44 N	2.09 E
Convención	290	8.28 N	73.21 W
Convent	248	30.06 N	90.50 W
Convento	280	9.21 N	83.30 W
Conversano	170	40.58 N	17.08 E
Converse	268	40.35 N	85.52 W
Convoy	268	40.55 N	84.42 W
Conway, Wales, U.K.	162	53.17 N	3.50 W
Conway, Ark., U.S.	248	35.05 N	92.26 W
Conway, Mass., U.S.	261	42.31 N	72.42 W
Conway, Miss., U.S.	248	32.51 N	89.36 W
Conway, Mo., U.S.	248	37.30 N	92.49 W
Conway, N.H., U.S.	242	43.59 N	71.07 W
Conway, N.C., U.S.	246	36.26 N	77.20 W
Conway, Pa., U.S.	266	40.40 N	80.14 W
Conway, S.C., U.S.	246	33.50 N	79.03 W
Conway, Wash., U.S.	270	48.21 N	122.21 W
Conway, Cape ➤	228	20.32 S	148.56 E
Conway, Lake ⊜[1]	248	35.00 N	92.25 W
Conway Springs	252	37.24 N	97.39 W
Conway Station	240	46.40 N	63.59 W
Conyers	246	33.40 N	84.01 W
Cooch Behār	206	26.20 N	89.27 E
Coogoon ≃	228	27.19 S	148.50 E
Cook, Ind., U.S.	268	41.22 N	87.26 W
Cook, Minn., U.S.	244	47.51 N	92.41 W
Cook, Nebr., U.S.	252	40.31 N	96.10 W
Cook, Wash., U.S.	270	45.43 N	121.40 W
Cook □[6]	268	41.53 N	87.38 W
Cook, Cape ➤	238	50.08 N	127.55 W
Cook, Mount ∧	230	43.36 S	170.08 E
Cookeville	248	36.10 N	85.31 W
Cookham	174	51.34 N	0.43 W
Cooking Lake ⊜	238	53.25 N	113.02 W
Cook Inlet C	236	60.30 N	152.00 W
Cook Islands II	148	20.00 S	158.00 W
Cooksburg	266	41.20 N	79.12 W
Cook's Harbour	240	51.36 N	55.52 W
Cookshire	260	45.25 N	71.38 W
Cooks Mills	244	46.24 N	79.28 W
Cooks Peak ∧	254	32.32 N	107.44 W
Cookstown, Ont., Can.	264	44.11 N	79.42 W
Cookstown, N. Ire., U.K.	162	54.39 N	6.45 W
Cook Strait U	230	41.14 S	174.30 E
Cooksville, Ill., U.S.	268	40.33 N	88.43 W
Cooksville, Md., U.S.	262	39.19 N	77.01 W
Cooksville, Wis., U.S.	268	42.50 N	89.14 W
Cooktown	226	15.28 S	145.15 E
Cooleemee	246	35.49 N	80.33 W
Coolgardie	226	30.57 S	121.10 E
Coolidge, Ariz., U.S.	254	32.59 N	111.31 W
Coolidge, Ga., U.S.	246	31.01 N	83.52 W
Coolidge, Tex., U.S.	250	31.45 N	96.39 W
Coolidge, Mount ∧	252	43.44 N	103.29 W
Coolidge Dam ◄[6]	254	33.00 N	110.20 W
Coolin	256	48.28 N	116.51 W
Coolspring	266	41.02 N	79.05 W
Cooma	228	36.14 S	149.08 E
Coonamble	228	30.57 S	148.23 E
Coon Rapids, Iowa, U.S.	252	41.52 N	94.41 W
Coon Rapids, Minn., U.S.	244	45.09 N	93.18 W
Coon Valley	244	43.42 N	91.01 W
Cooper, Ala., U.S.	248	32.46 N	86.33 W
Cooper, Tex., U.S.	250	33.23 N	95.35 W
Cooper ≃	246	32.50 N	79.56 W
Cooper Center	268	42.23 N	85.37 W
Cooper Lake ⊜	254	41.37 N	105.50 W
Cooper Landing	236	61.57 N	145.18 W
Cooper Mountain ∧	236	60.23 N	149.51 W
Coopersburg	262	40.31 N	75.23 W
Cooperstown, N. Dak., U.S.	252	47.27 N	98.07 W
Cooperstown, N.Y., U.S.	242	42.42 N	74.56 W
Cooperstown, Pa., U.S.	266	41.30 N	79.52 W
Coopersville	268	43.04 N	85.57 W
Coos □[6]	260	45.04 N	71.20 W
Coosa ≃	248	32.30 N	86.16 W
Coosawhatchie ≃	246	32.32 N	80.52 W
Coos Bay	256	43.22 N	124.13 W
Coos Bay C	256	43.23 N	124.16 W
Cootamundra	228	34.39 S	148.02 E
Cootehill	162	54.04 N	7.05 W
Čop	164	48.26 N	22.10 E
Copacabana, Arg.	294	28.15 S	67.29 W
Copacabana, Bol.	292	16.10 S	69.05 W
Copainalá	278	17.05 N	93.12 W
Copake	261	42.06 N	73.33 W
Copake Falls	261	42.07 N	73.31 W
Copalis Beach	270	47.07 N	124.10 W
Copalquín	278	25.29 N	107.00 W
Copán, Hond.	280	14.50 N	89.09 W
Copan, Okla., U.S.	250	36.54 N	95.56 W
Copán □[5]	280	14.50 N	89.00 W
Copán ⊥	280	14.50 N	89.09 W
Copano Bay C	250	28.05 N	97.05 W
Copatana	290	2.48 S	67.04 W
Cope	252	39.40 N	102.51 W
Copeá, Paraná ≃[1]	290	3.52 S	63.20 W
Copeland	246	25.57 N	81.22 W
Copenhagen → København, Dan.	160	55.40 N	12.35 E
Copenhagen, N.Y., U.S.	264	43.54 N	75.41 W
Copertino	170	40.16 N	18.03 E
Copetonas	294	38.45 S	60.25 W
Copiapó	294	27.22 S	70.20 W
Copiapó ≃	294	27.19 S	70.56 W
Coplay	262	40.44 N	75.29 W
Copley, Austl.	226	30.32 S	138.25 E
Copley, Ohio, U.S.	266	41.06 N	81.39 W
Copoas, Mount ∧	202	10.48 N	119.17 E
Coporito	290	8.56 N	62.00 W
Copparo	170	44.54 N	11.49 E
Copper ≃	236	60.30 N	144.50 W
Copperas Cove	250	31.08 N	97.54 W
Copper Butte ∧	256	48.42 N	118.28 W
Copper Center	236	61.58 N	145.19 W
Copper Cliff	244	46.28 N	81.04 W
Copper Harbor	244	47.27 N	87.53 W
Coppermine	232	67.50 N	115.05 W
Coppermine ≃	232	67.49 N	115.04 W
Coppermine Point ➤	244	46.59 N	84.47 W
Copper Mountain	238	49.20 N	120.33 W
Copper Mountain ∧, Alaska, U.S.	236	55.14 N	132.36 W
Copper Mountain ∧, Wyo., U.S.	254	43.27 N	107.57 W
Copperopolis	272	37.59 N	120.38 W
Copton Point ➤	202	10.00 N	123.22 E
Copulhué, Paso de)(	294	37.35 S	71.08 W
Coquí	284m	17.59 N	66.14 W
Coquilhatville → Mbandaka	218	0.04 N	18.16 E
Coquille	256	43.11 N	124.11 W
Coquille ≃	256	43.07 N	124.26 W
Coquimbana	294	28.21 S	70.56 W
Coquimbo	294	29.58 S	71.21 W
Coquimbo □[4]	294	31.00 S	71.00 W
Corabia	172	43.46 N	24.30 E
Coração de Jesus	296	16.42 S	44.22 W
Coração de Maria	296	12.14 S	38.45 W
Coracora	292	15.02 S	73.48 W
Çorak Gölü ⊜	212	37.40 N	29.46 E
Coral	266	40.30 N	79.11 W
Coralaque ≃	292	16.26 S	70.45 W
Coral Bay C	202	8.28 N	117.20 E
Coral Gables	246	25.45 N	80.16 W
Coral Harbour	232	64.08 N	83.10 W
Coral Sea ⊤•[2]	226	20.00 S	158.00 E
Coral Sea Basin ⊹[1]	148	14.00 S	152.00 E
Coral Sea Plateau ⊹[3]	148	17.00 S	149.00 E
Coralville	244	41.40 N	91.35 W
Coralville Reservoir ⊜[1]	244	41.47 N	91.48 W
Coram, Mont., U.S.	256	48.36 N	114.02 W
Coram, N.Y., U.S.	261	40.52 N	73.00 W
Corantijn (Courantyne) ≃	290	5.55 N	57.05 W
Coraopolis	266	40.31 N	80.10 W
Corato	170	41.09 N	16.25 E
Corbeil-Essonnes	176	48.36 N	2.29 E
Corbett	270	45.32 N	122.17 W
Corbetta	182	45.28 N	8.55 E
Corbières ⋀	166	42.55 N	2.38 E
Corbigny	166	47.15 N	3.40 E
Corbin	246	36.57 N	84.05 W
Corbones ≃	168	37.36 N	5.39 W
Corbu	172	44.33 N	24.24 E
Corby	174	52.29 N	0.40 W
Córcega	284m	18.19 N	67.15 W
Corcoran	272	36.06 N	119.33 W
Corcovado, Golfo C	288	43.30 S	73.20 W
Corcovado, Volcán ∧[1]	288	43.12 S	72.48 W
Corcubión	168	42.57 N	9.11 W
Cordeiro	296	22.02 S	42.22 W
Cordele	246	31.58 N	83.47 W
Cordell	250	35.17 N	98.59 W
Cordell Hull Reservoir ⊜[1]	248	36.25 N	85.40 W
Corder	248	39.06 N	93.38 W
Cordes	166	44.04 N	1.57 E
Cordillera □[5]	294	25.15 S	57.00 W
Cordisburgo	296	19.07 S	44.21 W
Córdoba, Arg.	294	31.25 S	64.10 W
Córdoba, Esp.	168	37.53 N	4.46 W
Córdoba, Méx.	278	18.53 N	96.56 W
Córdoba □[4]	294	32.00 S	64.00 W
Córdoba □[5]	290	8.20 N	75.40 W
Cordon	202	16.41 N	121.28 E
Cordova → Córdoba, Esp.	168	37.53 N	4.46 W
Córdova, Perú	292	14.04 S	75.10 W
Cordova, Ala., U.S.	248	33.46 N	87.11 W
Cordova, Alaska, U.S.	236	60.33 N	145.46 W
Cordova, Ill., U.S.	244	41.41 N	90.19 W
Cordova, Md., U.S.	262	38.52 N	76.00 W
Cordova Bay C	236	54.55 N	132.35 W
Cordova Peak ∧	236	60.51 N	145.16 W
Cordu, Munții ⋀	172	46.30 N	22.20 E
Corerepe	278	25.40 N	108.40 W
Corfu → Kérkira, Ellás	172	39.36 N	19.56 E
Corfu, N.Y., U.S.	264	42.58 N	78.24 W
Corfu → Kérkira I	172	39.40 N	19.42 E
Cori	184	41.39 N	12.55 E
Coria	168	39.59 N	6.32 W
Coria del Río	168	37.16 N	6.03 W
Coribe	296	13.50 S	44.28 W
Corigliano Calabro	170	39.36 N	16.31 E
Coringa Islets II	228	16.58 S	149.58 E
Corinna	242	44.55 N	69.16 W
Corinne, Utah, U.S.	254	41.35 N	112.07 W
Corinne, W. Va., U.S.	246	37.34 N	81.22 W
Corinth → Kórinthos, Ellás	172	37.56 N	22.56 E
Corinth, Miss., U.S.	248	34.56 N	88.31 W
Corinth, N.Y., U.S.	242	43.15 N	73.49 W
Corinth, Gulf of → Korinthiakós Kólpos C	172	38.19 N	22.04 E
Corinto, Bra.	296	18.21 S	44.27 W
Corinto, El Sal.	280	13.49 N	87.58 W
Corinto, Nic.	280	12.29 N	87.12 W
Coripata	292	16.18 S	67.36 W
Corire	292	16.14 S	72.29 W
Coris	292	9.50 S	77.44 W
Corixa Grande ≃	286	17.31 S	57.52 W
Corixao ≃	292	18.22 S	57.23 W
Cork	162	51.54 N	8.28 W
Cork □[6]	162	52.00 N	8.30 W
Cork Harbour C	162	51.45 N	8.15 W
Corlay	166	48.19 N	3.03 W
Corleone	170	37.49 N	13.18 E
Corleto Perticara	170	40.23 N	16.03 E
Çorlu	212	41.09 N	27.48 E
Cormeilles	166	49.15 N	0.23 E
Cormeilles-en-Parisis	176	48.59 N	2.12 E
Cormons	170	45.58 N	13.28 E
Čormoz	158	58.53 N	56.08 E
Čornaja	160	68.35 N	56.30 E
Čornaja Cholunica	160	58.51 N	51.42 E
Čornaja Sloboda	160	60.48 N	37.46 E
Cornelia	246	34.31 N	83.32 W
Cornélio Procópio	296	23.08 S	50.39 W
Cornelius, N.C., U.S.	246	35.29 N	80.52 W
Cornelius, Oreg., U.S.	270	45.31 N	123.04 W
Cornelius Grinnell Bay C	232	63.20 N	64.50 W
Cornell, Calif., U.S.	274	34.08 N	118.47 W
Cornell, Ill., U.S.	268	40.59 N	88.44 W
Cornell, Wis., U.S.	244	45.10 N	91.09 W
Corner Brook	240	48.57 N	57.57 W
Cornfield	254	35.39 N	109.41 W
Corning, Ark., U.S.	248	36.24 N	90.35 W
Corning, Calif., U.S.	258	39.56 N	122.11 W
Corning, Iowa, U.S.	252	40.59 N	94.44 W
Corning, Kans., U.S.	252	39.39 N	96.02 W
Corning, N.Y., U.S.	242	42.09 N	77.04 W
Corning, Ohio, U.S.	242	39.36 N	82.05 W
Cornish	242	43.48 N	70.48 W
Corn Islands II	280	12.15 N	83.00 W
Corno Grande ∧	170	42.28 N	13.34 E
Cornucopia	256	45.00 N	117.12 W
Cornwall, Ont., Can.	260	45.02 N	74.44 W
Cornwall, Pa., U.S.	262	40.14 N	76.31 W
Cornwall □[6]	174	50.30 N	4.40 W
Cornwall Bridge	261	41.49 N	73.22 W
Cornwallis Island I	232	75.15 N	94.30 W
Čornyj Mys	160	68.20 N	38.37 E
Coro	290	11.25 N	69.41 W
Coro, Golfete de C	285s	11.30 N	69.55 W
Coroaci	296	18.35 S	42.17 W
Čoroch (Çoruh) ≃	212	41.36 N	41.35 E
Corocoro	292	17.12 S	68.29 W
Corocoro Island I	290	8.30 N	60.10 W
Coroico	292	16.10 S	67.44 W
Coroico ≃	292	15.27 S	67.50 W
Coromandel	296	18.28 S	47.13 W
Coromandel Peninsula ➤[1]	230	37.00 S	175.40 E
Coromandel Range ⋀	230	37.00 S	175.40 E
Coron	202	12.00 N	120.12 E
Corona, Calif., U.S.	274	33.52 N	117.34 W
Corona, N. Mex., U.S.	254	34.15 N	105.36 W
Corona Del Mar	274	33.36 N	117.52 W
Coronado, Méx.	278	22.55 N	100.56 W
Coronado, Calif., U.S.	274	32.41 N	117.11 W
Coronado, Bahía de C	280	9.00 N	83.50 W
Coronado, Sierra ⋀	278	23.05 N	100.56 W
Coronado National Memorial ▲	254	31.10 N	110.29 W
Coronation	238	52.05 N	111.27 W
Coronation Gulf C	232	68.25 N	110.00 W
Coronation Island I	236	55.52 N	134.15 W
Coron Bay C	202	11.55 N	120.10 E
Coronda	294	31.55 S	60.55 W
Coronel	294	37.01 S	73.08 W
Coronel Bogado	294	27.11 S	56.18 W
Coronel Brandsen	294	35.10 S	58.15 W
Coronel Dorrego	294	38.45 S	61.17 W
Coronel Du Graty	294	27.41 S	60.56 W
Coronel Eugenio del Busto	294	38.57 S	64.15 W
Coronel Fabriciano	296	19.31 S	42.38 W
Coronel Moldes	294	25.17 S	65.29 W
Coronel Murta	296	16.37 S	42.11 W
Coronel Oviedo	294	25.25 S	56.27 W
Coronel Ponce	296	15.34 S	55.01 W
Coronel Pringles	294	38.00 S	61.20 W
Coronel Suárez	294	37.25 S	61.56 W
Coronel Vidal	294	37.27 S	57.44 W
Coronel Vivida	294	25.58 S	52.34 W
Corongo	292	8.30 S	77.53 W
Coronie □[5]	290	5.55 N	56.20 W
Coron Island I	202	11.55 N	120.14 E
Coropuna, Nevado ∧	292	15.30 S	72.41 W
Corozal, Br. Hond.	278	18.24 N	88.24 W
Corozal, Col.	290	9.19 N	75.18 W
Corozal, Hond.	280	15.48 N	86.43 W
Corozal, P.R.	284m	18.21 N	66.17 W
Corps	166	44.49 N	5.57 E
Corpus	294	27.08 S	55.30 W
Corpus Christi	250	27.48 N	97.24 W
Corpus Christi, Lake ⊜[1]	250	28.10 N	97.53 W
Corpus Christi Bay C	250	27.48 N	97.20 W
Corpus Christi Naval Air Station ■	250	27.42 N	97.16 W
Corque	292	18.21 S	67.42 W
Corquín	280	14.34 N	88.52 W
Corral	288	39.52 S	73.26 W
Corral de Almaguer	168	39.46 N	3.11 W
Corral de Bustos	294	33.20 S	62.10 W
Corralillo	284p	22.59 N	80.35 W
Corralitos, Méx.	250	26.57 N	104.39 W
Corralitos, Calif., U.S.	272	36.59 N	121.48 W
Correctionville	252	42.28 N	95.47 W
Correggio	170	44.46 N	10.47 E
Corregidor Island I	202	14.23 N	120.35 E
Córrego do Ouro	296	16.18 S	50.32 W
Córrego Rico	296	15.14 S	47.48 W
Corrente ≃, Bra.	296	13.08 S	43.28 W
Corrente ≃, Bra.	296	19.19 S	50.50 W
Corrente Grande ≃	296	19.02 S	42.09 W
Correntes ≃	296	17.38 S	55.08 W
Correntes, Cabo das ➤	224	24.11 S	35.34 E
Correnti, Isola delle I	170	36.38 N	15.05 E
Correntina	296	13.20 S	44.39 W
Corrèze □[5]	166	45.20 N	1.50 E
Corrib, Lough ⊜	162	53.05 N	9.10 W
Corrientes	294	27.30 S	58.50 W
Corrientes □[4]	294	29.00 S	58.00 W
Corrientes ≃, Arg.	294	30.21 S	59.33 W
Corrientes ≃, S.A.	290	3.43 S	74.35 W
Corrientes, Cabo ➤, Arg.	294	38.02 S	57.31 W
Corrientes, Cabo ➤, Col.	290	5.30 N	77.34 W
Corrientes, Cabo ➤, Cuba	284p	21.45 N	84.31 W
Corrientes, Cabo ➤, Méx.	278	20.25 N	105.42 W
Corrientes, Ensenada de C	284p	21.50 N	84.35 W
Corrigan	248	30.59 N	94.50 W
Corry	266	41.56 N	73.39 W
Corse □[5]	170	42.00 N	9.00 E
Corse I	170	42.00 N	9.00 E
Corse, Cap ➤	170	43.00 N	9.25 E
Corsica, Pa., U.S.	266	41.10 N	79.12 W
Corsica, S. Dak., U.S.	252	43.25 N	98.24 W
Corsica → Corse I	170	42.00 N	9.00 E
Corsicana	250	32.06 N	96.28 W
Corsico	182	45.26 N	9.07 E
Cort Adalaer, Kap ➤	232	62.00 N	42.00 W
Cortaderas	294	32.30 S	65.01 W
Cortazar	278	20.29 N	100.56 W
Corte	170	42.18 N	9.08 E
Cortegana	168	37.55 N	6.49 W
Corte Madera	272	37.55 N	122.31 W
Cortemilia	170	44.35 N	8.12 E
Cortes	202	9.16 N	126.11 E
Cortés □[5]	280	15.30 N	88.00 W
Cortés, Ensenada de C	284p	22.05 N	83.50 W
Cortez	254	37.21 N	108.35 W
Cortez Mountains ⋀	258	40.20 N	116.20 W
Cortina d'Ampezzo	170	46.32 N	12.08 E
Cortland, Ill., U.S.	268	41.55 N	88.41 W
Cortland, Nebr., U.S.	252	40.30 N	96.42 W
Cortland, N.Y., U.S.	242	42.36 N	76.11 W
Cortland, Ohio, U.S.	266	41.20 N	80.44 W
Cortland □[6]	264	42.36 N	76.11 W
Cortona	184	43.16 N	11.59 E
Corubal (Koliba) ≃	222	11.57 N	15.06 W
Coruche	168	38.57 N	8.31 W
Çorum	212	40.33 N	34.58 E
Çorum □[4]	208	40.05 N	34.30 E
Corumbá	292	19.01 S	57.39 W
Corumbá ≃	296	18.19 S	48.55 W
Corumbá de Goiás	296	15.55 S	48.48 W
Corumbaíba	296	18.09 S	48.34 W
Corumbataí ≃	294	23.55 S	51.57 W
Corumbaú, Ponta de ➤	296	16.53 S	39.06 W
Corumbiara Antigo ≃	292	13.13 S	62.06 W
Corumo ≃	290	6.49 N	60.52 W
Corund	172	46.28 N	25.11 E
Corunna, Ont., Can.	266	42.53 N	82.26 W
Corunna, Ind., U.S.	268	41.26 N	85.09 W
Corunna, Mich., U.S.	268	42.59 N	84.07 W
Coruripe	286	10.08 S	36.10 W
Corvallis, Mont., U.S.	256	46.19 N	114.07 W
Corvallis, Oreg., U.S.	256	44.34 N	123.16 W
Corwin, Cape ➤	236	59.54 N	165.41 W
Corwith	244	42.59 N	93.57 W
Corydon, Ind., U.S.	248	38.13 N	86.07 W
Corydon, Iowa, U.S.	244	40.45 N	93.19 W
Corydon, Ky., U.S.	248	37.44 N	87.43 W
Coryville	266	41.53 N	78.24 W
Corzu	172	44.28 N	23.10 E
Corzuela	294	27.00 S	60.58 W
Cos → Kos I	172	36.50 N	27.10 E
Cosamaloapan [de Carpio]	278	18.22 N	95.48 W
Cosapa	292	18.11 S	68.40 W
Coseley	174	52.33 N	2.06 W
Cosenza	170	39.17 N	16.15 E
Coshocton	266	40.16 N	81.51 W
Coshocton □[6]	266	40.16 N	81.51 W
Cosigüina, Punta ➤	280	12.53 N	87.42 W
Cosigüina, Volcán ∧[1]	280	12.58 N	87.35 W
Cosmoledo II	218	9.43 S	47.35 E
Cosmoledo Group II	218	9.43 S	47.35 E
Cosmopolis	270	46.57 N	123.46 W
Cosmorama	296	20.28 S	49.47 W
Cosne-sur-Loire	176	47.24 N	2.55 E
Cospán	292	7.23 S	78.35 W
Cosquín	294	31.25 S	64.25 W
Cossato	182	45.34 N	8.10 E
Cossatot ≃	248	33.48 N	94.09 W
Cossé-le-Vivien	162	47.57 N	0.55 W
Čošskaja Guba C	160	67.30 N	46.30 E
Cosson ≃	166	47.30 N	1.15 E
Costa Mesa	274	33.39 N	117.55 W
Costa Rica	278	28.55 N	111.36 W
Costa Rica □[1]	276	10.00 N	84.00 W
Costello	266	41.36 N	78.03 W
Costermansville → Bukavu	218	2.30 S	28.52 E
Costești	172	44.40 N	24.53 E
Costiera, Catena ⋀	170	39.20 N	16.05 E
Costilla	254	36.59 N	105.32 W
Coswig	164	51.53 N	12.26 E
Cotabambas	292	13.45 S	72.20 W
Cotabato	202	7.14 N	124.15 E
Cotabato □[4]	202	6.40 N	124.45 E
Cotacajes ≃	292	16.00 S	67.01 W
Cotagaita	292	20.50 S	65.41 W
Cotagaita ≃	292	21.01 S	65.23 W
Cotahuasi	292	15.12 S	72.50 W
Cotati	272	38.20 N	122.42 W
Coteau-Landing	260	45.16 N	74.14 W
Coteau-Station	260	45.17 N	74.14 W
Coteaux	282	18.12 N	74.02 W
Côte-d'Or □[5]	166	47.30 N	4.50 E
Côte-d'Or ◄[1]	164	47.30 N	4.50 E
Cotegipe	296	12.02 S	44.15 W
Cotentin ➤[1]	166	49.30 N	1.30 W
Côtes-du-Nord □[5]	166	48.25 N	2.40 W
Coti ≃	292	8.36 S	65.33 W
Cotija de la Paz	278	19.49 N	102.43 W
Cotingo ≃	290	3.55 N	60.30 W
Cotmeana ≃	172	44.24 N	24.45 E
Cotoca	292	17.49 S	63.03 W
Cotonou	222	6.21 N	2.26 E
Cotopaxi □[4]	290	0.55 S	78.55 W
Cotopaxi ∧[1]	290	0.40 S	78.26 W
Cotorra, Isla I	285r	10.02 N	62.16 W
Cotovêlo, Cachoeira do ↳	292	7.08 S	58.43 W
Cotswold Hills ⋀[2]	162	51.45 N	2.10 W
Cottage Grove, Oreg., U.S.	256	43.48 N	123.03 W
Cottage Grove, Wis., U.S.	268	43.05 N	89.12 W
Cottageville	246	32.56 N	80.29 W
Cottam	266	42.08 N	82.45 W
Cottbus	164	51.45 N	14.19 E
Cottel Island I	240	48.51 N	53.42 W
Cotter	248	36.16 N	92.32 W
Cottiennes, Alpes(Alpi Cozie) ⋀	170	44.45 N	7.00 E
Cottondale, Ala., U.S.	248	33.11 N	87.27 W
Cottondale, Fla., U.S.	246	30.48 N	85.23 W
Cotton Plant	248	35.00 N	91.15 W
Cottonport	248	30.59 N	92.03 W
Cotton Valley	248	32.49 N	93.25 W
Cottonwood, Ariz., U.S.	254	34.45 N	112.01 W
Cottonwood, Calif., U.S.	258	40.23 N	122.17 W
Cottonwood, Idaho, U.S.	256	46.03 N	116.21 W
Cottonwood, Minn., U.S.	252	44.37 N	95.41 W
Cottonwood ≃, Kans., U.S.	252	38.23 N	96.03 W
Cottonwood ≃, Minn., U.S.	252	44.17 N	94.25 W
Cottonwood Falls	252	38.22 N	96.32 W
Cottonwood Wash ∨	254	36.19 N	113.59 W
Cotuhé ≃	290	2.53 S	69.44 W
Cotuí	282	19.03 N	70.09 W
Cotuit	261	41.37 N	70.26 W
Cotulla	250	28.26 N	99.14 W
Coubre, Pointe de la ➤	166	45.41 N	1.13 W
Couchiching, Lake ⊜	244	44.40 N	79.23 W
Coudekerque-Branche	176	51.02 N	2.24 E
Coudersport	266	41.46 N	78.01 W
Coudres, Île aux I	240	47.24 N	70.22 W
Couer d'Alene Indian Reservation ◄[4]	256	47.18 N	116.45 W
Couesnon ≃	162	48.37 N	1.31 W
Couffo ≃	222	6.35 N	1.59 E
Cougar	270	46.03 N	122.18 W
Cougar Reservoir ⊜[1]	256	44.06 N	122.12 W
Couhé	166	46.18 N	0.11 E
Couillet	176	50.23 N	4.27 E
Coulee City	256	47.37 N	119.17 W
Coulee Dam	256	47.58 N	118.59 W
Coulee Dam National Recreation Area ▲	256	47.48 N	119.45 W
Coulihaut	284d	15.30 N	61.29 W
Coulommiers	176	48.49 N	3.05 E
Coulonge ≃	244	45.51 N	76.45 W
Coulonge-Est ≃	244	46.06 N	76.43 W
Coulterville, Calif., U.S.	272	37.43 N	120.12 W
Coulterville, Ill., U.S.	248	38.11 N	89.36 W
Council	256	44.44 N	116.26 W
Council Bluffs	252	41.16 N	95.52 W
Council Grove	252	38.40 N	96.29 W
Council Grove Reservoir ⊜[1]	252	38.42 N	96.31 W
Country Club Subdivision	268	42.15 N	83.39 W
Country Homes	256	47.45 N	117.24 W
Coupar Angus	162	56.33 N	3.17 W
Coupeville	270	48.13 N	122.41 W
Coupon	266	40.32 N	78.31 W
Courantyne (Corantijn) ≃	290	5.55 N	57.05 W
Courbevoie	176	48.54 N	2.15 E
Courcelles	176	50.28 N	4.22 E
Courcelles-les-Lens	176	50.25 N	3.01 E
Courchevel	166	45.25 N	6.38 E
Courçon-d'Aunis	166	46.15 N	0.49 W
Courpière	166	45.45 N	3.33 E
Courseulles	162	49.20 N	0.27 W
Courson-les-Carrières	166	47.36 N	3.30 E
Courtalain	162	48.05 N	1.09 E
Courtenay	238	49.41 N	125.00 W
Courtice	264	43.55 N	78.46 W
Courtland, Ont., Can.	264	42.51 N	80.38 W
Courtland, Ala., U.S.	248	34.40 N	87.18 W
Courtland, Calif., U.S.	272	38.20 N	121.34 W
Courtland, Va., U.S.	262	36.43 N	77.04 W
Courtrai → Kortrijk	176	50.50 N	3.16 E
Courtright	266	42.49 N	82.28 W
Court-Saint-Étienne	176	50.39 N	4.34 E
Courville	260	46.53 N	71.09 W
Coushatta	248	32.00 N	93.21 W
Coutances	166	49.03 N	1.26 W
Couto de Magalhães ≃	296	13.37 S	53.09 W
Coutras	166	45.02 N	0.08 W
Coutts	238	49.00 N	111.57 W
Couture, Lac ⊜	232	60.10 N	75.20 W
Covasna	172	45.51 N	26.11 E
Cove	256	45.18 N	117.49 W
Cove Island I	244	45.17 N	81.44 W
Covelo	258	39.48 N	123.15 W
Coventry, Eng., U.K.	174	52.25 N	1.30 W
Coventry, Conn., U.S.	261	41.48 N	72.23 W
Coventry, Ohio, U.S.	266	41.00 N	81.32 W
Coventry, R.I., U.S.	261	41.41 N	71.34 W
Cove Point	262	38.23 N	76.24 W
Covered Wells	254	32.10 N	112.08 W
Covert	268	42.17 N	86.16 W
Covilhã	168	40.17 N	7.30 W
Covina	274	34.05 N	117.53 W
Covington, Ind., U.S.	248	40.09 N	87.24 W
Covington, Ky., U.S.	242	39.05 N	84.30 W
Covington, La., U.S.	248	30.29 N	90.06 W
Covington, Ohio, U.S.	242	40.07 N	84.21 W
Covington, Okla., U.S.	250	36.18 N	97.35 W
Covington, Tenn., U.S.	248	35.34 N	89.38 W
Covington, Va., U.S.	246	37.47 N	79.59 W
Covunco, Arroyo ≃	294	38.28 S	69.32 W
Cow ≃	244	47.23 N	83.59 W
Cowal, Lake ⊜	228	33.35 S	147.25 E
Cowan	248	35.10 N	86.01 W
Cowansville, Qué., Can.	260	45.12 N	72.45 W
Cowansville, Pa., U.S.	266	40.53 N	79.36 W
Coward	246	33.58 N	79.45 W
Cowden	248	39.15 N	88.52 W
Cowdenbeath	162	56.07 N	3.21 W
Cowell	228	33.41 S	136.55 E
Cowen	242	38.25 N	80.34 W
Cowen, Mount ∧	256	45.23 N	110.29 W
Cowes	174	50.45 N	1.18 W
Coweta	250	35.57 N	95.39 W
Cow Head	240	49.55 N	57.49 W
Cowichan Bay	238	48.44 N	123.40 W
Cowichan Lake ⊜	238	48.54 N	124.20 W
Cowlesville	264	42.51 N	78.28 W
Cowley, Alta., Can.	238	49.34 N	114.05 W
Cowley, Eng., U.K.	174	51.43 N	1.12 W
Cowley, Wyo., U.S.	256	44.53 N	108.28 W
Cowlitz □[6]	270	46.07 N	122.43 W
Cowpasture ≃	242	37.48 N	79.45 W
Cowpens	246	35.01 N	81.48 W
Cowpens National Battlefield Site ⊥	246	35.06 N	81.46 W
Cowra	228	33.50 S	148.41 E
Coxá ≃	296	14.16 S	44.11 W
Coxim	296	18.30 S	54.45 W
Coxim ≃	296	18.34 S	54.46 W
Coxipi, Lac ⊜	240	51.32 N	58.23 W
Coxipó da Ponte	292	15.38 S	56.04 W
Coxsackie	261	42.21 N	73.48 W
Cox's Bāzār	204	21.26 N	91.59 E
Cox's Cove	240	49.07 N	58.04 W
Coyame	278	29.28 N	105.06 W
Coyanosa Draw ∨	250	31.18 N	103.06 W
Coya Sur	294	22.25 S	69.38 W
Coyhaique	288	45.34 S	72.04 W
Coyote	272	37.13 N	121.44 W
Coyote ≃	278	30.48 N	112.35 W
Coyote, Punta ➤	280	9.46 N	85.30 W
Coyote Lake ⊜	258	35.04 N	116.45 W
Coyote Wash ∨	254	32.40 N	114.08 W
Coyuca de Benítez	278	17.02 N	100.04 W
Coyuca de Catalán	278	18.20 N	100.39 W
Cozad	252	40.52 N	99.59 W
Cozes	166	45.35 N	0.50 W
Cozie, Alpi(Alpes Cottiennes) ⋀	170	44.45 N	7.00 E
Cozón	254	31.18 N	112.29 W
Cozumel	278	20.31 N	86.55 W
Cozumel, Isla de I	278	20.25 N	86.55 W
Crab Hill	285g	13.19 N	59.38 W
Crab Orchard, Ky., U.S.	246	37.28 N	84.30 W
Crab Orchard, Tenn., U.S.	246	35.55 N	84.53 W
Crab Orchard Lake ⊜[1]	248	37.43 N	89.05 W
Crabtree	266	40.22 N	79.35 W
Crabtree Mills	260	45.58 N	73.28 W
Cradle Mountain National Park ▲	228	42.00 S	146.00 E
Cradock	224	32.08 S	25.36 E
Crafton	266	40.26 N	80.04 W
Craig, B.C., Can.	270	49.18 N	124.15 W
Craig, Alaska, U.S.	236	55.29 N	133.09 W
Craig, Colo., U.S.	254	40.31 N	107.33 W
Craig, Mo., U.S.	248	40.11 N	95.23 W
Craig, Nebr., U.S.	252	41.47 N	96.22 W
Craig Air Force Base ■	248	32.21 N	86.59 W
Craig Beach	266	41.07 N	81.01 W
Craigellachie	238	50.59 N	118.43 W
Craigmont	256	46.15 N	116.28 W
Craigmyle	238	51.40 N	112.15 W
Craignure	162	56.28 N	5.42 W
Craigsville, Pa., U.S.	266	40.51 N	79.39 W
Craigsville, Va., U.S.	246	38.05 N	79.23 W
Craigville	268	40.47 N	85.06 W
Crailsheim	164	49.08 N	10.04 E
Craiova	172	44.19 N	23.48 E
Craley	262	39.57 N	76.31 W
Cranberry	266	41.21 N	79.43 W
Cranberry Lake ⊜	242	44.10 N	74.50 W
Cranbrook	238	49.31 N	115.46 W
Crandon	244	45.34 N	88.54 W
Crane, Ind., U.S.	248	38.54 N	86.54 W
Crane, Mo., U.S.	248	36.54 N	93.34 W
Crane, Oreg., U.S.	256	43.25 N	118.35 W
Crane, Tex., U.S.	250	31.24 N	102.21 W
Crane Creek Reservoir ⊜[1]	256	44.22 N	116.35 W
Crane Mountain ∧	256	42.04 N	120.13 W
Cranesville	266	41.54 N	80.21 W
Cranford	262	40.39 N	74.19 W
Cranston	261	41.47 N	71.26 W
Craon	166	47.51 N	0.57 W
Craonne	166	49.27 N	3.47 E
Craponne	166	45.20 N	3.51 E
Craryville	261	42.11 N	73.35 W
Crasna	172	45.36 N	26.08 E
Crasna (Kraszna) ≃	172	48.09 N	22.20 E
Crater Lake ⊜	256	42.56 N	122.06 W
Crater Lake National Park ▲	256	42.49 N	122.08 W
Craters of the Moon National Monument ▲	256	43.20 N	113.35 W
Cratéus	286	5.10 S	40.40 W
Crato	286	7.14 S	39.23 W
Crau □[9]	182	43.36 N	4.50 E
Crauford, Cape ➤	232	73.43 N	84.50 W
Cravari ≃	292	12.06 S	58.03 W
Cravo Norte	290	6.18 N	70.12 W
Cravo Norte ≃	290	6.18 N	70.12 W
Cravo Sur ≃	290	4.42 N	71.36 W
Crawford, Colo., U.S.	254	38.42 N	107.37 W
Crawford, Miss., U.S.	248	33.18 N	88.37 W
Crawford, Nebr., U.S.	252	42.41 N	103.25 W
Crawford, Tex., U.S.	250	31.32 N	97.27 W
Crawford □[6], Ohio, U.S.	266	40.48 N	82.58 W
Crawford □[6], Pa., U.S.	266	41.39 N	80.10 W
Crawford Bay	238	49.42 N	116.48 W
Crawfordsville, Ark., U.S.	248	35.14 N	90.20 W
Crawfordsville, Ind., U.S.	248	40.02 N	86.54 W
Crawfordville, Fla., U.S.	246	30.11 N	84.23 W
Crawfordville, Ga., U.S.	246	33.33 N	82.54 W
Crawley	174	51.07 N	0.12 W
Crazy Mountains ⋀	256	46.08 N	110.20 W
Crazy Peak ∧	256	46.01 N	110.16 W
Creal Springs	248	37.37 N	88.50 W
Crécy-en-Brie	166	48.51 N	2.55 E
Crécy-en-Ponthieu	166	50.15 N	1.53 E
Cree ≃	232	59.00 N	105.47 W
Creede	254	37.51 N	106.56 W
Creedmoor	246	36.07 N	78.41 W
Creekside	266	40.41 N	79.12 W
Creel	278	27.45 N	107.38 W
Cree Lake ⊜	232	57.30 N	106.30 W
Creemore	264	44.19 N	80.06 W
Creighton, Nebr., U.S.	252	42.28 N	97.54 W
Creighton, Pa., U.S.	266	40.35 N	79.47 W
Creighton Mine	244	46.28 N	81.11 W
Creil	176	49.16 N	2.29 E
Crema	182	45.22 N	9.41 E
Crémieu	166	45.43 N	5.15 E
Cremona, Alta., Can.	238	51.33 N	114.29 W
Cremona, It.	170	45.07 N	10.02 E
Cremona □[4]	182	45.14 N	9.56 E
Crenshaw, Miss., U.S.	248	34.30 N	90.12 W
Crenshaw, Pa., U.S.	266	41.15 N	78.46 W
Crepori ≃	292	5.42 S	57.08 W
Crépy-en-Valois	176	49.14 N	2.54 E
Cres	170	44.58 N	14.25 E
Cres, Otok I	170	44.50 N	14.25 E
Cresaptown	242	39.36 N	78.50 W
Crescent, Okla., U.S.	250	35.57 N	97.36 W
Crescent, Oreg., U.S.	256	43.29 N	121.41 W
Crescent Beach	270	49.04 N	122.53 W
Crescent City, Calif., U.S.	258	41.45 N	124.12 W
Crescent City, Fla., U.S.	246	29.26 N	81.30 W
Crescent City, Ill., U.S.	268	40.46 N	87.51 W
Crescent Group II	198	16.31 N	111.38 E
Crescent Lake ⊜, Fla., U.S.	246	29.28 N	81.30 W
Crescent Lake ⊜, Oreg., U.S.	256	43.29 N	121.59 W
Crescent Spur	238	53.35 N	120.41 W
Cresco	244	43.22 N	92.07 W
Crespin	176	50.25 N	3.39 E
Crespo	294	32.02 S	60.20 W
Cresson, Pa., U.S.	266	40.28 N	78.35 W
Cresson, Tex., U.S.	250	32.32 N	97.37 W
Cressona	262	40.38 N	76.12 W
Cressy	272	37.25 N	120.40 W
Crest	166	44.44 N	5.02 E
Crested Butte	254	38.52 N	106.59 W
Crestline, Calif., U.S.	274	34.14 N	117.17 W
Crestline, Ohio, U.S.	266	40.47 N	82.44 W
Crestmont Village	266	40.36 N	80.16 W
Creston, B.C., Can.	238	49.06 N	116.31 W
Creston, Newf., Can.	240	47.09 N	55.12 W
Creston, Calif., U.S.	272	35.31 N	120.31 W
Creston, Ill., U.S.	268	41.56 N	88.58 W
Creston, Iowa, U.S.	252	41.04 N	94.22 W
Creston, Ohio, U.S.	266	40.59 N	81.54 W
Crestone Peak ∧	254	37.58 N	105.36 W
Crestview	248	30.46 N	86.34 W
Crestwood Acres	262	39.26 N	76.15 W
Creswell	256	43.55 N	123.01 W
Creswell Bay C	232	72.35 N	93.25 W
Crete, Ill., U.S.	244	41.27 N	87.38 W
Crete, Nebr., U.S.	252	40.38 N	96.58 W
Crete → Kríti I	172	35.29 N	24.42 E
Crete, Sea of → Kritikón Pélagos ⊤•[2]	172	35.46 N	23.54 E
Créteil	176	48.48 N	2.28 E
Crétéville	170	36.40 N	10.20 E
Creus, Cabo ➤	168	42.19 N	3.19 E
Creuse □[5]	166	46.05 N	2.00 E
Creuse ≃	166	47.00 N	0.34 E

Symbols in the index entries are identified on page 360.

Name	Page	Lat°′	Long°′
Creussen	164	49.51 N	11.37 E
Creve Coeur	244	40.39 N	89.35 W
Crevillente	168	38.15 N	0.48 W
Crewe, Eng., U.K.	174	53.05 N	2.27 W
Crewe, Va., U.S.	246	37.05 N	78.08 W
Crewkerne	162	50.53 N	2.48 W
Cricamola ≃	280	8.58 N	81.55 W
Criciúma	294	28.40 S	49.23 W
Cricket	246	36.11 N	81.12 W
Cridersville	268	40.39 N	84.09 W
Crieff	162	56.23 N	3.52 W
Crikvenica	170	45.11 N	14.42 E
Crillon, Mount ∧	236	58.40 N	137.10 W
Crimea → Krymskij Poluostrov ≻[1]	158	45.00 N	34.00 E
Crimmitschau	164	50.49 N	12.23 E
Crîngeni	172	44.01 N	24.47 E
Cripple Creek	254	38.45 N	105.11 W
Crisfield	262	37.59 N	75.51 W
Criss Creek	238	51.03 N	120.44 W
Crissiumal	294	27.30 S	54.07 W
Cristal, Sierra del ⋀	284p	20.33 N	75.30 W
Cristalândia	286	10.36 S	49.11 W
Cristalina	296	16.45 S	47.36 W
Cristalino ≃	296	12.38 S	50.40 W
Cristianópolis	296	17.13 S	48.45 W
Cristóbal	280	9.20 N	79.55 W
Cristóbal, Punta de ≻	284p	22.11 N	81.50 W
Cristóbal Colón, Pico ∧	290	10.50 N	73.45 W
Cristo Redentor ⊥	294	32.49 S	70.04 W
Cristuru-Secuiesc	172	46.17 N	25.02 E
Crişul Alb ≃	172	46.42 N	21.17 E
Crişul Negru ≃	172	46.42 N	21.16 E
Crişul Repede (Sebes Köröl) ≃	172	46.55 N	20.59 E
Crivitz	244	45.14 N	88.01 W
Crixalândia	296	15.18 S	47.15 W
Crixás	296	14.27 S	49.58 W
Crixás Açu ≃	296	13.19 S	50.36 W
Crixás Mirim ≃	296	13.30 S	50.30 W
Crna ≃	172	41.35 N	21.59 E
Crna Gora ☐[3]	172	42.30 N	19.18 E
Črnomelj	170	45.34 N	15.11 E
Croatia → Hrvatska ☐[3]	170	45.10 N	15.30 E
Crocheron	262	38.15 N	76.03 W
Crocker	248	37.57 N	92.16 W
Crockett, Calif., U.S.	272	38.03 N	122.13 W
Crockett, Tex., U.S.	250	31.19 N	95.28 W
Crocus Hill	282	18.13 N	63.04 W
Crofton, B.C., Can.	270	48.52 N	123.38 W
Crofton, Ky., U.S.	248	37.03 N	87.29 W
Crofton, Nebr., U.S.	252	42.44 N	97.30 W
Croghan	264	43.54 N	75.24 W
Croix	176	50.40 N	3.09 E
Croix, Lac à la ⊜, Qué., Can.	240	48.15 N	67.45 W
Croix, Lac à la ⊜, Qué., Can.	240	51.16 N	70.13 W
Croix, Lac la ⊜	244	48.21 N	92.05 W
Croker, Cape ≻	244	44.58 N	80.59 W
Cromarty	162	57.40 N	4.02 W
Cromer	162	52.56 N	1.18 E
Cromínia	296	17.17 S	49.21 W
Cromwell, Ala., U.S.	248	32.14 N	88.17 W
Cromwell, Conn., U.S.	261	41.36 N	72.39 W
Cromwell, Ind., U.S.	268	41.24 N	85.37 W
Cronin, Mount ∧	238	54.54 N	126.52 W
Crook	252	40.51 N	102.48 W
Crooked ≃, B.C., Can.	238	54.50 N	122.54 W
Crooked ≃, Mo., U.S.	248	39.13 N	93.49 W
Crooked ≃, Oreg., U.S.	256	44.34 N	121.16 W
Crooked Creek	236	61.52 N	158.08 W
Crooked Island I	282	22.45 N	74.12 W
Crooked Island Passage ⊔	282	23.00 N	74.30 W
Crooked Lake, Ind., U.S.	268	41.41 N	85.02 W
Crooked Lake, Mich., U.S.	268	42.29 N	85.25 W
Crooked Lake ⊜, Newf., Can.	240	48.24 N	56.17 W
Crooked Lake ⊜, Fla., U.S.	246	27.48 N	81.35 W
Crooks Inlet C	232	63.03 N	71.00 W
Crookston	252	47.47 N	96.37 W
Crooksville	242	39.46 N	82.06 W
Crosby, Minn., U.S.	244	46.28 N	93.57 W
Crosby, Miss., U.S.	248	31.17 N	91.04 W
Crosby, N. Dak., U.S.	252	48.55 N	103.18 W
Crosby, Pa., U.S.	266	41.45 N	78.24 W
Crosby, Mount ∧	254	43.52 N	109.20 W
Crosbyton	250	33.40 N	101.14 W
Cross ≃	222	4.42 N	8.21 E
Cross, Cape ≻	224	21.49 S	13.57 E
Cross City	246	29.39 N	83.07 W
Crossett	248	33.08 N	91.58 W
Cross Fell ∧	162	54.42 N	2.29 W
Crossfield	238	51.26 N	114.02 W
Cross Lake ⊜, Man., Can.	232	54.45 N	97.30 W
Cross Lake ⊜, Ont., Can.	244	44.55 N	76.48 W
Cross Lake ⊜, Ont., Can.	244	46.53 N	79.57 W
Crossley, Mount ∧	230	42.50 S	172.04 E
Crossman Peak ∧	254	34.32 N	114.07 W
Cross Plains, Tex., U.S.	250	32.08 N	99.11 W
Cross Plains, Wis., U.S.	244	43.07 N	89.39 W
Cross Sound ⊔	236	58.10 N	136.30 W
Crossville, Ill., U.S.	248	38.10 N	88.04 W
Crossville, Tenn., U.S.	248	35.58 N	85.02 W
Croswell	244	43.16 N	82.37 W
Crothersville	248	38.48 N	85.50 W
Croton	266	40.14 N	82.41 W
Crotone	170	39.05 N	17.07 E
Croton Falls	261	41.21 N	73.40 W
Croton-on-hudson	261	41.12 N	73.54 W
Crow ≃	244	45.15 N	93.31 W
Crow Agency	256	45.36 N	107.27 W
Crowborough	174	51.03 N	0.09 E
Crow Creek Indian Reservation ⊸[4]	252	44.11 N	99.30 W
Crowder	250	35.07 N	95.40 W
Crowdy Head ≻	228	31.50 S	152.45 E
Crowe ≃	244	44.22 N	77.46 W
Crowell	250	33.59 N	99.43 W
Crow Indian Reservation ⊸[4]	256	45.27 N	108.00 W
Crow Lake	252	49.12 N	93.57 W
Crowley, Calif., U.S.	272	36.21 N	119.17 W
Crowley, La., U.S.	248	30.13 N	92.22 W
Crowley, Lake ⊜[1]	258	37.37 N	118.44 W
Crowleys Ridge ∧	248	35.45 N	90.45 W
Crown	266	41.23 N	79.16 W
Crown Hill	264	44.26 N	79.39 W
Crown Point	268	41.25 N	87.22 W
Crown Prince Frederick Island I	232	70.02 N	86.50 W
Crow Peak ∧	256	46.18 N	111.54 W
Crows Landing	272	37.24 N	121.04 W
Crowsnest	238	49.38 N	114.41 W
Crows Nest Peak ∧	252	44.03 N	103.58 W
Crow Wing ≃	252	46.19 N	94.20 W
Croydon, Austl.	226	18.12 S	142.14 E
Croydon, Pa., U.S.	262	40.05 N	74.54 W
Croydon ⊸[8]	174	51.23 N	0.06 W
Croydon Peak ∧	242	43.28 N	72.13 W
Croydon Station	238	53.05 N	119.44 W
Crozet	246	38.04 N	78.42 W
Crozet, Îles II	148	46.00 S	52.00 E
Crozon	166	48.15 N	4.29 W
Crucea	172	44.32 N	28.14 E
Crucero	292	14.20 S	70.04 W
Crucero, Cerro ∧	278	21.41 N	104.25 W
Cruces	284p	22.21 N	80.16 W
Crucible	242	39.57 N	79.58 W
Crucilândia	296	20.23 S	44.21 W
Cruger	248	33.14 N	90.14 W
Cruillas	278	24.45 N	98.31 W
Crumlin	264	43.01 N	81.09 W
Crump Lake ⊜	256	42.17 N	119.50 W
Crumpton	262	39.14 N	75.55 W
Crumstown	268	41.38 N	86.25 W
Cruz, Cabo ≻	284p	19.51 N	77.44 W
Cruz, Cayo I	284p	22.15 N	77.49 W
Cruz Alta, Arg.	294	33.00 S	61.50 W
Cruz Alta, Bra.	294	28.39 S	53.36 W
Cruz Bay	284m	18.20 N	64.48 W
Cruz del Eje	294	30.44 S	64.49 W
Cruzeiro	296	22.34 S	44.58 W
Cruzeiro do Oeste	296	23.46 S	53.04 W
Cruzeiro do Sul	292	7.38 S	72.36 W
Cruz Grande	294	29.25 S	71.18 W
Cruzília	296	21.50 S	44.48 W
Cruz Machado	294	26.01 S	51.21 W
Crvenka	172	45.39 N	19.28 E
Crysler	242	45.13 N	75.09 W
Crystal, Minn., U.S.	244	45.00 N	93.25 W
Crystal, N. Dak., U.S.	252	48.36 N	97.40 W
Crystal ≃	254	39.25 N	107.14 W
Crystal Bay	272	39.15 N	120.00 W
Crystal Beach, Ont., Can.	264	42.52 N	79.04 W
Crystal Beach, Fla., U.S.	246	28.06 N	82.47 W
Crystal City, Man., Can.	252	49.09 N	98.56 W
Crystal City, Mo., U.S.	248	38.13 N	90.23 W
Crystal City, Tex., U.S.	250	28.41 N	99.50 W
Crystal Falls	244	46.05 N	88.20 W
Crystal Gardens	268	42.14 N	88.23 W
Crystal Lake, Ill., U.S.	268	42.14 N	88.19 W
Crystal Lake, N.Y., U.S.	266	42.28 N	78.20 W
Crystal Lake ⊜	244	44.40 N	86.10 W
Crystal Lawns	268	41.34 N	88.09 W
Crystal Manor	268	42.14 N	88.17 W
Crystal River	246	28.54 N	82.36 W
Crystal Springs	248	31.59 N	90.21 W
Crystal Vista	268	42.14 N	88.24 W
Csesznek ⊥	164	47.16 N	17.53 E
Csongrád	164	46.43 N	20.09 E
Csongrád ☐[6]	164	46.25 N	20.15 E
Csorna	164	47.37 N	17.16 E
Csurgó	164	46.16 N	17.06 E
Ču	186	43.36 N	73.45 E
Ču ≃	186	45.00 N	67.44 E
Cúa	290	10.10 N	66.54 W
Cuácua ≃	224	17.54 S	36.48 E
Cuadro Nacional	294	34.37 S	68.17 W
Cuajinicuilapa	278	16.28 N	98.25 W
Cuambog	202	7.21 N	125.52 E
Cuando (Kwando) ≃	218	18.27 S	23.32 E
Cuando-Cubango ☐[5]	224	16.00 S	20.00 E
Cuangar	218	17.36 S	18.39 E
Cuango	218	6.17 S	16.41 E
Cuango (Kwango) ≃	218	3.14 S	17.23 E
Cuao ≃	290	4.55 N	67.40 W
Cuaró	294	30.37 S	56.54 W
Cuarto ≃	294	33.28 S	63.04 W
Cuatro Ciénegas [de Carranza]	278	26.59 N	102.05 W
Cuatro Islands II	202	10.30 N	124.30 E
Cuauhtémoc	278	28.25 N	106.52 W
Cuautitlán	278	19.26 N	104.23 W
Cuautitlán [de Romero Rubio]	278	19.40 N	99.11 W
Cuautla	278	18.48 N	98.57 W
Cuba, Port.	168	38.10 N	7.53 W
Cuba, Ala., U.S.	248	32.26 N	88.23 W
Cuba, Ill., U.S.	244	40.30 N	90.12 W
Cuba, Kans., U.S.	252	39.48 N	97.27 W
Cuba, Mo., U.S.	248	38.04 N	91.24 W
Cuba, N. Mex., U.S.	254	36.01 N	107.04 W
Cuba, N.Y., U.S.	266	42.13 N	78.17 W
Cuba ☐[1]	276	21.30 N	80.00 W
Cubabi, Cerro ∧	254	31.43 N	112.50 W
Cubagua, Isla I	290	10.48 N	64.10 W
Cubango (Okavango) ≃	218	18.50 S	22.25 E
Čublas	160	64.44 N	45.00 E
Cucalaya ≃	280	13.34 N	83.40 W
Cucamonga	274	34.06 N	117.35 W
Cuchara, Río de la ≃	278	16.35 N	97.40 W
Cucharas	278	22.52 N	105.19 W
Cucharas ≃	254	37.55 N	104.32 W
Cuchilla Alta, Cerro ∧	280	15.10 N	88.12 W
Cuchilla Águila, Cerro ∧	278	21.27 N	101.03 W
Cuchillo-Có	294	38.20 S	64.37 W
Cuchillo Negro ≃	254	33.08 N	107.14 W
Cuchivero ≃	290	7.40 N	65.57 W
Čuchloma	160	58.45 N	42.41 E
Cuchumatanes, Altos ⋀	280	15.40 N	91.25 W
Cuckfield	174	51.00 N	0.09 W
Čučkovo	160	59.36 N	41.14 E
Cucuí	290	1.12 N	66.50 W
Cucurpe	278	30.20 N	110.43 W
Cúcuta	290	7.54 N	72.31 W
Cudahy	268	42.57 N	87.52 W
Cuddy Mountain ∧	256	44.46 N	116.47 W
Čudovo	160	59.07 N	31.41 E
Čudskoje Ozero (Peipsi Järvi) ⊜	160	58.45 N	27.30 E
Cue	226	27.25 S	117.54 E
Cuéllar	168	41.25 N	4.19 W
Cuemaní ≃	290	0.20 S	73.06 W
Cuenca, Ec.	290	2.53 S	78.59 W
Cuenca, Esp.	168	40.04 N	2.08 W
Cuencamé [de Ceniceros]	278	24.53 N	103.42 W
Cuerámaro	278	20.37 N	101.43 W
Cuernavaca	278	18.55 N	99.15 W
Cuero	250	29.06 N	97.18 W
Cuers	166	43.14 N	6.04 E
Cuervo, Laguna del ⊜	278	29.15 N	105.55 W
Cuervos	278	32.38 N	114.52 W
Cuesmes	176	50.26 N	3.55 E
Cuesta Pass)(	258	35.21 N	120.38 W
Cueto	284p	20.39 N	75.56 W
Cuetzalan [del Progreso]	278	20.02 N	97.31 W
Cuevas, Cerro ∧	292	22.00 S	65.12 W
Cuevas del Almanzora	168	37.18 N	1.53 W
Cuevo	292	20.27 S	63.32 W
Cuevo Canyon ∨	254	32.50 N	105.00 W
Cufra → Al-Kufrah ⊸[1]	220	24.20 N	23.15 E
Cufra (Al-Kufrah) ⊸[1]	220	24.20 N	23.15 E
Cuggiono	182	45.31 N	8.49 E
Cuglieri	170	40.11 N	8.34 E
Cuiabá	292	15.35 S	56.05 W
Cuiari	290	1.30 N	68.11 W
Cuiari ≃	290	1.30 N	68.11 W
Cuicatlán	278	17.48 N	96.58 W
Cuilapa	280	14.17 N	90.18 W
Cuilco	280	15.24 N	91.58 W
Cuilco ≃	280	15.27 N	92.05 W
Cuillin Hills ⋀[2]	162	57.14 N	6.15 W
Cuillin Sound ⊔	162	57.04 N	6.20 W
Cuilo (Kwilu) ≃	218	3.22 S	17.22 E
Cuiseaux	166	46.30 N	5.24 E
Cuíto ≃	218	18.01 S	20.48 E
Cuíto-Cuanavale	218	15.10 S	19.10 E
Cuitzeo, Lago de ⊜	278	19.55 N	101.05 W
Cuiuni ≃	290	0.45 S	63.07 W
Čukotskij, Mys ≻	236	64.14 N	173.10 W
Čukotskij Poluostrov ≻[1]	236	66.00 N	175.00 W
Culaba	202	11.40 N	124.32 E
Culaman	202	5.58 N	125.40 E
Culasi, Pil.	202	11.26 N	122.03 E
Culasi, Pil.	202	10.43 N	125.43 E
Culasian	202	8.51 N	117.29 E
Culasi Point ≻	202	11.35 N	122.42 E
Culbertson, Mont., U.S.	252	48.09 N	104.31 W
Culbertson, Nebr., U.S.	252	40.14 N	100.50 W
Culebra, Bahía de C	280	10.37 N	85.40 W
Culebra, Isla de I	282	18.19 N	65.18 W
Culebra, Sierra de la ⋀	168	41.54 N	6.20 W
Culemborg	178	51.56 N	5.13 E
Culgoa ≃	228	29.56 S	146.20 E
Culiacán	278	24.48 N	107.24 W
Culiacancito	278	24.50 N	107.32 W
Culion	202	11.54 N	120.01 E
Culion Island I	202	11.50 N	120.00 E
Cúllar de Baza	168	37.35 N	2.34 W
Cullen	248	32.58 N	93.27 W
Culleoka	248	35.29 N	86.59 W
Cullera	168	39.10 N	0.15 W
Cullman	248	34.11 N	86.51 W
Cullom	268	40.53 N	88.16 W
Cullowhee	246	35.19 N	83.11 W
Čul'man	186	56.52 N	124.52 E
Culpeper	242	38.28 N	77.53 W
Culpina	292	20.50 S	64.58 W
Cultus Lake	270	49.04 N	121.58 W
Culuene ≃	296	12.56 S	52.51 W
Culver, Ind., U.S.	268	41.13 N	86.25 W
Culver, Oreg., U.S.	256	44.32 N	121.13 W
Culver City	274	34.01 N	118.24 W
Čulym	186	55.06 N	80.58 E
Čulym ≃	186	57.43 N	83.51 E
Čum	160	67.06 N	63.07 E
Cumalı	172	36.42 N	27.27 E
Cumaná	290	10.28 N	64.10 W
Cumanacoa	290	10.15 N	63.55 W
Cumanayagua	284p	22.09 N	80.12 W
Cumaovası	172	38.15 N	27.09 E
Cumari	296	18.16 S	48.11 W
Cumbal	290	0.54 N	77.47 W
Cumbal, Volcán de ∧[1]	290	0.57 N	77.52 W
Cumberland, B.C., Can.	238	49.37 N	125.01 W
Cumberland, Iowa, U.S.	252	41.16 N	94.52 W
Cumberland, Ky., U.S.	246	36.59 N	82.59 W
Cumberland, Md., U.S.	242	39.39 N	78.46 W
Cumberland, R.I., U.S.	261	41.54 N	71.24 W
Cumberland, Va., U.S.	246	37.30 N	78.15 W
Cumberland, Wash., U.S.	270	47.17 N	121.56 W
Cumberland, Wis., U.S.	244	45.32 N	92.01 W
Cumberland ☐[6], Eng., U.K.	162	54.40 N	2.50 W
Cumberland ☐[6], N.J., U.S.	262	39.26 N	75.14 W
Cumberland ☐[6], Pa., U.S.	262	40.12 N	77.12 W
Cumberland ≃	234	37.09 N	88.25 W
Cumberland, Lake ⊜[1]	248	36.57 N	84.55 W
Cumberland City	248	36.23 N	87.38 W
Cumberland Gap)(	246	36.36 N	83.41 W
Cumberland Gap National Historical Park ♠	246	36.36 N	83.40 W
Cumberland Hill	261	41.59 N	71.28 W
Cumberland Island I	246	30.51 N	81.27 W
Cumberland Islands II	228	20.40 S	149.09 E
Cumberland Peninsula ≻[1]	232	66.50 N	64.00 W
Cumberland Plateau ⋀[1]	234	36.00 N	85.00 W
Cumberland Sound ⊔	232	65.10 N	65.30 W
Cumbres de Monterrey, Parque Nacional ♠	278	25.31 N	100.18 W
Cumby	250	33.08 N	95.50 W
Cumeral Nuevo	254	30.54 N	110.51 W
Čumerna ∧	172	42.47 N	25.58 E
Čumikan	186	54.42 N	135.19 E
Cumming	246	34.13 N	84.08 W
Cummington	261	42.27 N	72.54 W
Cummins, Mount ∧	238	52.03 N	118.15 W
Cumnock	162	55.27 N	4.16 W
Cumpas	278	30.02 N	109.48 W
Cumshewa Inlet C	238	53.03 N	131.45 W
Cumuripa	278	28.08 N	109.53 W
Čumyš ≃	186	53.31 N	83.10 E
Čuna ≃	186	57.47 N	95.26 E
Cunani	286	2.52 N	51.06 W
Cunauaru ≃	290	3.10 S	63.01 W
Cunaviche	290	7.22 N	67.25 W
Cunco	294	38.55 S	72.02 W
Cuncumén	294	31.53 S	70.38 W
Cundanama ≃	290	3.30 N	65.06 W
Cundinamarca ☐[5]	290	5.00 N	74.00 W
Cunene ≃	218	17.20 S	11.50 E
Cuneo	182	44.23 N	7.32 E
Cuneo ☐[4]	182	44.31 N	7.34 E
Cung-hau, Cua ≃[1]	200	9.50 N	106.30 E
Cunha	296	23.05 S	44.58 W
Cunha Porã	294	26.54 S	53.09 W
Cunhuã, Igarapé ≃	292	5.46 S	64.36 W
Cunillera, Isla I	168	39.00 N	1.12 E
Cunlhat	166	45.38 N	3.35 E
Cunnamulla	228	28.04 S	145.41 E
Cunningham	252	37.39 N	98.26 W
Čuny	160	59.39 N	36.04 E
Cuorgnè	182	45.23 N	7.39 E
Čupa	160	66.16 N	33.00 E
Cupar	162	56.19 N	3.01 W
Cupertino	272	37.19 N	122.02 W
Cupica, Golfo de C	290	6.35 N	77.25 W
Cupins	296	19.51 S	51.03 W
Ćuprija	172	43.56 N	21.23 E
Cuquenán ≃	290	4.45 N	61.30 W
Čur	160	57.07 N	52.58 E
Curaçao I	285s	12.11 N	69.00 W
Curacautín	294	38.26 S	71.53 W
Curacaví	294	33.24 S	71.09 W
Curacó ≃	294	38.49 S	65.01 W
Curahuara	292	17.40 S	68.02 W
Curanga ≃	292	9.57 S	70.58 W
Curanilahue	294	37.28 S	73.21 W
Curanipe	294	35.50 S	72.38 W
Čurapča	186	62.00 N	132.24 E
Curaray ≃	290	2.20 S	74.05 W
Curcani	172	44.12 N	26.35 E
Curcubăta ∧	172	46.27 N	22.42 E
Curecanti National Recreation Area ♠	254	38.24 N	107.25 W
Curepipe	225c	20.19 S	57.31 E
Curepto	294	35.05 S	72.01 W
Curiapo	290	8.33 N	61.00 W
Curicó	294	34.59 S	71.14 W
Curicuriari ≃	290	0.14 S	66.48 W
Curinhuás ≃	280	12.46 N	83.40 W
Curitiba	294	25.25 S	49.15 W
Curitibanos	294	27.18 S	50.36 W
Curiuaú ≃	290	1.51 S	61.14 W
Curiúva	296	24.02 S	50.27 W
Curlew	238	48.53 N	118.36 W
Currais Novos	286	6.15 S	36.31 W
Curralinho	286	1.48 S	49.47 W
Currant Mountain ∧	258	38.55 N	115.25 W
Current ≃	244	48.27 N	89.11 W
Current Islands II	246	25.22 N	76.49 W
Currie	252	43.59 N	95.40 W
Currituck	246	36.27 N	76.01 W
Currituck ☐[6]	262	36.28 N	76.03 W
Currituck Sound ⊔	246	36.20 N	75.52 W
Curry	236	62.37 N	150.01 W
Curryville	266	40.17 N	78.20 W
Curslack ⊸[8]	178	53.27 N	10.13 E
Curtea-de-Argeş	172	45.08 N	24.41 E
Curtice	266	41.37 N	83.22 W
Curtina	294	32.09 S	56.07 W
Curtis, Esp.	168	43.07 N	8.03 W
Curtis, Ark., U.S.	248	34.00 N	93.06 W
Curtis, Nebr., U.S.	252	40.38 N	100.31 W
Curtis, Port ⊤[3]	228	24.00 S	151.30 E
Curtis Island I	228	23.38 S	151.09 E
Curtis Lake ⊜	232	66.38 N	89.02 W
Curtisville	266	40.37 N	79.50 W
Curuá ≃	292	5.23 S	54.22 W
Curuan	202	7.13 N	122.13 E
Curubandé	280	10.43 N	85.26 W
Curuçá ≃	290	4.27 S	71.23 W
Ćurug	172	45.29 N	20.04 E
Curuguaty	294	24.31 S	55.42 W
Çürüksu ≃	172	37.57 N	28.58 E
Curupira, Sierra de ⋀	290	1.25 N	64.30 W
Curuquetê ≃	292	8.20 S	65.40 W
Cururu ≃	292	7.12 S	58.03 W
Cururu-Açu ≃	292	8.58 S	57.13 W
Cururupu	286	1.50 S	44.52 W
Curutú ≃	290	5.05 N	63.28 W
Curuzú-Cuatiá	294	29.50 S	58.05 W
Curvelo	296	18.45 S	44.25 W
Curwensville	266	40.58 N	78.32 W
Curwood, Mount ∧[2]	244	46.42 N	88.14 W
Cusano Milanino	182	45.33 N	9.11 E
Cusapin	280	9.11 N	81.54 W
Cusco → Cuzco	292	13.31 S	71.59 W
Cushabatay ≃	292	7.12 S	75.17 W
Cushing, Okla., U.S.	250	35.59 N	96.46 W
Cushing, Tex., U.S.	248	31.43 N	94.50 W
Cushman	248	35.53 N	91.45 W
Cusiana ≃	290	4.33 N	71.51 W
Cusick	256	48.20 N	117.18 W
Cusihuiriáchic	278	28.14 N	106.50 W
Čusovoj	158	58.17 N	57.49 E
Cusseta	246	32.18 N	84.47 W
Custar	268	41.17 N	83.51 W
Custer, Mich., U.S.	244	43.58 N	86.14 W
Custer, Mont., U.S.	256	46.08 N	107.33 W
Custer, Okla., U.S.	250	35.40 N	98.53 W
Custer, S. Dak., U.S.	252	43.46 N	103.36 W
Custer, Wash., U.S.	270	48.55 N	122.38 W
Custer Battlefield National Monument ♠	256	45.25 N	107.26 W
Custer City	266	41.54 N	78.39 W
Custer State Park ♠	252	43.43 N	103.23 W
Cut Bank	256	48.38 N	112.20 W
Cutbank ≃	238	54.44 N	118.31 W
Cutervo	292	6.25 S	78.55 W
Cuthbert	246	31.46 N	84.48 W
Cutler, Calif., U.S.	272	36.31 N	119.17 W
Cutler, Maine, U.S.	242	44.40 N	67.12 W
Cutlerville	268	42.51 N	85.40 W
Cutral-Có	294	38.58 S	69.15 W
Cutro	170	39.02 N	16.59 E
Cuttack	206	20.26 N	85.53 E
Cutzamalá ≃	278	18.22 N	100.39 W
Cuvilly	162	49.33 N	2.42 E
Cuvo ≃	218	10.50 S	1.34 E
Cuxhaven	178	53.52 N	8.42 E
Cuyagnateje ≃	284p	22.04 N	83.58 W
Cuyahoga ☐[6]	266	41.30 N	81.41 W
Cuyahoga Falls	266	41.08 N	81.29 W
Cuyama ≃	258	34.54 N	120.18 W
Cuyamaca Peak ∧	258	32.57 N	116.36 W
Cuyamel	280	15.38 N	88.12 W
Cuyapo	202	15.47 N	120.40 E
Cuyk	178	51.44 N	5.52 E
Cuylerville	264	42.47 N	77.52 W
Cuyo	202	10.51 N	121.00 E
Cuyo East Pass ⊔	202	11.20 N	121.30 E
Cuyo Island I	202	10.50 N	121.02 E
Cuyo Islands II	202	10.53 N	121.00 E
Cuyo West Pass ⊔	202	11.25 N	120.25 E
Cuyuni ≃	290	6.23 N	58.41 W
Cuzco	292	13.31 S	71.59 W
Cuzco ☐[5]	292	12.30 S	72.30 W
Cuzcuz	294	31.39 S	71.14 W
Cuzna ≃	168	38.04 N	4.41 W
Cwmbran	174	51.39 N	3.00 W
C.W. McConaughy, Lake ⊜[1]	252	41.15 N	101.50 W
Cyangugu	218	2.29 S	28.54 E
Cybinka	164	52.12 N	14.48 E
Cyclone	266	41.50 N	78.35 W
Cygnet	268	41.14 N	83.39 W
Cynthiana	242	38.23 N	84.18 W
Cypern → Cyprus ☐[1]	158	35.00 N	33.00 E
Cyrenaica → Barqah ⊸[1]	214	31.00 N	22.30 E
Cypress	248	31.36 N	93.02 W
Cypress Bayou ≃	248	35.03 N	91.42 W
Cypress River	252	49.34 N	99.05 W
Cyprus ☐[1]	158	35.00 N	33.00 E
Cyril	250	34.54 N	98.12 W
Cyrus Field Bay C	232	62.50 N	64.55 W
Cythera → Kíthira I	172	36.20 N	22.58 E
Czaplinek (Tempelburg)	164	53.34 N	16.14 E
Czarna Wieś	164	53.19 N	23.16 E
Czarna Woda	164	53.51 N	18.06 E
Czarne (Hammerstein)	164	53.42 N	16.57 E
Czarnków	164	52.55 N	16.34 E
Czechoslovakia ☐[1]	158	49.30 N	17.00 E
Czechowice-Dziedzice	164	49.54 N	19.00 E
Czempiń	164	52.10 N	16.47 E
Czerniejewo	164	52.26 N	17.30 E
Czernowitz → Černovcy	172	48.18 N	25.56 E
Czersk	164	53.48 N	18.00 E
Częstochowa	164	50.49 N	19.06 E
Człopa (Schloppe)	164	53.06 N	16.08 E
Człuchów (Schlochau)	164	53.41 N	17.21 E
Czudec	164	49.57 N	21.50 E
D			
Daan	200	23.19 N	110.34 E
Daanbantayan	202	11.15 N	123.59 E
Dabajuro	290	11.02 N	70.40 W
Dabeiba	290	7.01 N	76.16 W
Dąbie	164	52.06 N	18.49 E
Dabieshan ⋀	196	31.00 N	115.40 E
Dabney	250	29.10 N	100.03 W
Dabola	214	10.45 N	11.07 W
Dabola ☐[4]	222	10.36 N	11.07 W
Dabrowa	164	53.39 N	23.20 E
Dąbrowa Górnicza	164	50.20 N	19.11 E
Dąbrowa Tarnowska	164	50.11 N	21.00 E
Dacca	206	23.43 N	90.25 E
Dachaidan	190	37.53 N	95.07 E
Dachau	164	48.15 N	11.27 E
Dachstein ∧	164	47.28 N	13.35 E
Dačice	164	49.05 N	15.26 E
Dacoma	250	36.40 N	98.34 W
Dadanawa	290	2.50 N	59.30 W
Dade City	246	28.22 N	82.12 W
Dadeville	248	32.50 N	85.46 W
Dadiangas	202	6.08 N	125.11 E
Dādu	204	26.44 N	67.47 E
Daduhe ≃	190	29.33 N	103.45 E
Daerhanmaoming'-anqi	190	41.42 N	110.23 E
Daet	202	14.07 N	122.57 E
Dagana	214	16.31 N	15.30 W
Daggett	274	34.52 N	116.53 W
Dağkızılca	172	38.18 N	27.24 E
Dagsboro	262	38.33 N	75.15 W
Dagu	194	38.59 N	117.41 E
Dagua, Col.	290	3.40 N	76.41 W
Dagua, N.G. Ter.	198	3.25 S	143.20 E
Daguao	284m	18.14 N	65.41 W
Dagupan	202	16.03 N	120.20 E
Dagus Mines	266	41.21 N	78.37 W
Dahl	178	51.18 N	7.31 E
Dahlak Archipelago II	214	15.45 N	40.30 E
Dahlak Kebir Island I	214	15.38 N	40.11 E
Dahlgren, Ill., U.S.	248	38.12 N	88.41 W
Dahlgren, Va., U.S.	262	38.20 N	77.03 W
Dahlonega	246	34.32 N	89.59 W
Dahlonega Plateau ⋀[1]	246	34.10 N	84.20 W
Dahme	164	51.52 N	13.25 E
Dahomey ☐[1]	214	9.30 N	2.15 E
Dahongshan ⋀	196	31.30 N	113.00 E
Dahra	214	29.34 N	17.50 E
Dahra ⋀	168	36.25 N	1.00 E
Daḥy, Nafūd ad- ⊸[2]	214	22.20 N	45.35 E
Daia	172	44.00 N	25.59 E
Daimiel	168	39.04 N	3.37 W
Daingean	162	53.18 N	7.17 W
Daingerfield	248	33.02 N	94.44 W
Daireaux	294	36.37 S	61.45 W
Dairen → Lüda	194	38.53 N	121.35 E
Dai-sen ∧	192	35.22 N	133.33 E
Dai-sen-oki-kokuritsu-kōen ♠	192	35.20 N	133.35 E
Daisetta	250	30.07 N	94.39 W
Daisy	248	35.15 N	85.11 W
Daiyunshan ⋀	196	25.46 N	118.16 E
Dajabón	282	19.34 N	71.43 W
Dajarra	226	21.42 S	139.31 E
Dajiyang ⊔	196	30.54 N	122.18 E
Dakar	222	14.40 N	17.26 W
Dak-gle	198	15.12 N	107.48 E
Dak Lake (Dagat) ⊜	208	32.50 N	61.30 E
Dakota City, Iowa, U.S.	244	42.43 N	94.12 W
Dakota City, Nebr., U.S.	252	42.25 N	96.25 W
Đakovica	172	42.23 N	20.25 E
Đakovo	172	45.19 N	18.25 E
Dalaba ☐[4]	222	10.45 N	12.18 W
Dalaguete	202	9.46 N	123.32 E
Dalälven ≃	160	60.38 N	17.27 E
Dalama	172	37.47 N	28.04 E
Dalaman ≃	212	36.40 N	28.45 E
Dalandzadgad	190	43.35 N	104.30 E
Da-lat	200	11.56 N	108.25 E
Dālbandin	204	28.53 N	64.25 E
Dalbeattie	162	54.56 N	3.49 W
Dalby	228	27.11 S	151.16 E
Dale, Nor.	160	61.22 N	5.25 E
Dale, Ind., U.S.	248	38.10 N	86.59 W
Dale, Pa., U.S.	266	40.18 N	78.54 W
Dale Hollow Lake ⊜[1]	246	36.36 N	85.19 W
Dalesville	260	45.42 N	74.23 W
Daleszyce	164	50.48 N	20.48 E
Daleville	248	40.07 N	85.33 W
Dalhart	250	36.04 N	102.31 W
Dalhousie	240	48.04 N	66.23 W
Dalhousie, Cape ≻	236	70.14 N	129.42 W
Dali	200	25.38 N	100.09 E
Dalías	168	36.49 N	2.52 W
Dalinghe ≃	194	40.56 N	121.43 E
Dalinghekou ≃[1]	194	40.55 N	121.50 E
Dalj	172	45.29 N	18.59 E
Daljā'	220	27.39 N	30.42 E
Dāllah, 'Ayn ⊤[4]	220	27.19 N	27.20 E
Dallas, Ala., U.S.	248	33.50 N	86.40 W
Dallas, Ga., U.S.	246	33.55 N	84.51 W
Dallas, N.C., U.S.	246	35.19 N	81.11 W
Dallas, Oreg., U.S.	256	44.55 N	123.19 W
Dallas, Pa., U.S.	242	41.20 N	75.58 W
Dallas, Tex., U.S.	250	32.47 N	96.48 W
Dallas, Wis., U.S.	244	45.16 N	91.51 W
Dallas Center	244	41.41 N	93.58 W
Dallas City	244	40.38 N	91.10 W
Dallastown	262	39.54 N	76.39 W
Dall Island I	236	54.50 N	132.55 W
Dall Lake ⊜	236	60.18 N	163.35 W
Dalmā' I	208	24.30 N	52.20 E
Dalmatia ☐[9]	170	43.00 N	17.00 E
Dalmacio Vélez Sarsfield	294	32.40 S	63.36 W
Dalmatia, Pa., U.S.	262	40.39 N	76.54 W
Dalmine	182	45.39 N	9.36 E
Daloa	222	6.53 N	6.27 W
Daloa ☐[5]	222	7.00 N	6.45 W
Dalqū	214	20.07 N	30.37 E
Dalroy	238	51.07 N	113.39 W
Dalrymple, Mount ∧	228	21.02 S	148.38 E
Dal'stroja	236	68.19 N	177.39 W
Dalton, Ga., U.S.	246	34.47 N	84.58 W
Dalton, Mass., U.S.	261	42.29 N	73.09 W
Dalton, Nebr., U.S.	252	41.25 N	102.58 W
Dalton, N.Y., U.S.	266	42.32 N	77.57 W
Dalton, Ohio, U.S.	266	40.48 N	81.42 W
Dalton, Pa., U.S.	242	41.32 N	75.45 W
Dalton Gardens	256	47.44 N	116.46 W
Dalupiri Island I, Pil.	202	19.05 N	121.13 E
Dalvík	160a	65.59 N	18.32 W
Dalwallinu	226	30.17 S	116.40 E
Daly Bay C	232	64.00 N	89.40 W
Daly City	272	37.42 N	122.29 W
Daly Waters	226	16.15 S	133.22 E
Damanhūr	220	31.02 N	30.28 E
Damaraland ☐[9]	224	22.34 S	17.06 E
Damariscotta	242	44.02 N	69.32 W
Damascus → Dimashq, Sūrīy.	210	33.30 N	36.18 E
Damascus, Ark., U.S.	248	35.22 N	92.25 W
Damascus, Ga., U.S.	246	31.18 N	84.43 W
Damascus, Md., U.S.	262	39.17 N	77.12 W
Damascus, Ohio, U.S.	266	40.54 N	80.58 W
Damascus, Va., U.S.	246	36.37 N	81.46 W
Damāvand, Qolleh-ye ∧	208	35.56 N	52.08 E
Damba	218	6.41 S	15.08 E
Damergou ⊸[1]	222	15.00 N	8.55 E
Dames Quarter	262	38.11 N	75.54 W
Dāmghān	208	39.09 N	54.22 E
Damianópolis	296	14.33 S	46.10 W
Damiaoshan	200	25.06 N	109.15 E
Dămieneşti	172	46.44 N	26.59 E
Damietta → Dumyāṭ	220	31.25 N	31.48 E
Damietta Mouth → Dumyāṭ, Maṣabb ≃[1]	220	31.32 N	31.51 E
Dammarie-lès-Lys	176	48.31 N	2.39 E
Dammartin-en-Goële	166	49.03 N	2.41 E
Damme	178	52.30 N	8.08 E
Dāmodar ≃	206	23.17 N	88.05 E
Damoh	206	23.50 N	79.27 E
Damolândia	296	16.16 S	49.22 W
Damous	168	36.31 N	1.45 E
Dampar, Tasek ⊜	200	3.02 N	102.43 E
Dampier	226	20.39 S	116.45 E
Dampier, Selat ⊔	198	0.40 S	130.40 E
Dâmri, Chuŏr Phnum ⋀	200	11.00 N	104.05 E
Damuyang C	196	29.20 N	122.06 E
Dan ≃	246	36.42 N	78.45 W
Danakil Plain ≚	214	12.25 N	40.30 E
Danané ☐[5]	222	7.15 N	8.00 W
Da-nang	200	16.04 N	108.13 E
Danao, Pil.	202	10.31 N	124.01 E
Danao, Pil.	202	12.29 N	122.39 E
Dana Point	274	33.29 N	117.44 W
Danboro	262	40.21 N	75.08 W
Danbury, Conn., U.S.	261	41.23 N	73.27 W
Danbury, Iowa, U.S.	252	42.14 N	95.43 W
Danbury, Nebr., U.S.	252	40.03 N	100.24 W
Danbury, N.C., U.S.	246	36.24 N	80.12 W
Danbury, Tex., U.S.	250	29.14 N	95.21 W
Danby Lake ⊜	258	34.14 N	115.07 W
Dandenong	228	37.59 S	145.12 E
Dandridge	246	36.01 N	83.25 W
Dane ☐[6]	268	43.04 N	89.15 W
Danforth, Ill., U.S.	268	40.49 N	87.59 W
Danforth, Maine, U.S.	242	45.40 N	67.52 W
Danforth Hills ⋀	254	40.15 N	108.00 W
Danganqundao II	196	22.00 N	114.14 E
Dan'ganshan I	196	22.03 N	114.16 E
Dangé	166	46.56 N	0.36 E
Danger Point ≻	224	34.40 S	19.17 E
Dangla	214	11.18 N	36.54 E
Dania	246	26.03 N	80.09 W
Daniel	254	42.52 N	110.04 W
Daniel, Serra ⋀[1]	296	13.40 S	54.55 W
Daniel's Harbour	240	50.14 N	57.35 W
Danielson	261	41.48 N	71.53 W
Danielsville, Ga., U.S.	246	34.07 N	83.13 W
Danielsville, Pa., U.S.	262	40.48 N	75.32 W
Danilov	160	58.12 N	40.12 E
Danjo-guntō II	192	32.02 N	128.23 E
Danlí	280	14.00 N	86.35 W
Dannebrog	252	41.07 N	98.33 W
Dannemora	242	44.43 N	73.43 W
Dannenberg	164	53.06 N	11.05 E
Dannevirke	230	40.12 S	176.06 E
Dansville, Mich., U.S.	268	42.34 N	84.18 W
Dansville, N.Y., U.S.	266	42.34 N	77.42 W
Dante, Tenn., U.S.	246	36.02 N	84.00 W
Dante, Va., U.S.	246	36.53 N	82.18 W
Danube ≃	158	45.20 N	29.40 E
Danvers, Ill., U.S.	244	40.32 N	89.11 W
Danvers, Mass., U.S.	261	42.34 N	70.56 W
Danville, Qué., Can.	260	45.47 N	72.01 W
Danville, Ark., U.S.	248	35.03 N	93.24 W
Danville, Calif., U.S.	272	37.49 N	122.00 W
Danville, Ga., U.S.	246	32.37 N	83.15 W
Danville, Ill., U.S.	248	40.08 N	87.37 W
Danville, Ind., U.S.	248	39.46 N	86.32 W
Danville, Ky., U.S.	248	37.39 N	84.46 W
Danville, Pa., U.S.	242	40.57 N	76.37 W
Danville, Vt., U.S.	242	44.25 N	66.09 W
Danville, Va., U.S.	246	36.35 N	79.24 W
Danville, Wash., U.S.	238	48.59 N	118.30 W
Danxian	194	34.48 N	116.03 E
Danyang	196	32.00 N	119.35 E
Danzig → Gdańsk	164	54.23 N	18.40 E
Danzig, Gulf of C	164	54.40 N	19.15 E
Dao	202	10.31 N	121.58 E
Dao ≃	168	40.20 N	8.11 W
Daocheng	190	29.06 N	100.38 E
Daoshui ≃	196	30.44 N	114.39 E
Daoulas	166	48.22 N	4.15 W
Daoxian	200	25.35 N	111.27 E
Dapa	202	9.45 N	126.03 E
Dapango	222	10.52 N	0.12 E
Dapdap	202	14.14 N	122.15 E
Daphne	248	30.36 N	87.54 W
Dapiak, Mount ∧	202	8.15 N	123.28 E
Dapitan	202	8.40 N	123.25 E
Dapitan ≃	202	8.38 N	123.23 E
Dapitan Bay C	202	8.39 N	123.23 E
Daqinghe ≃, Zhg.	194	42.26 N	123.50 E
Daqinghe ≃, Zhg.	194	39.04 N	116.55 E
Daqushan I	196	27.48 N	121.08 E
Dar'ā	210	32.37 N	36.06 E
Dar'ā ☐[8]	210	33.00 N	36.10 E
Dārāb	208	28.45 N	54.34 E
Darabani	172	48.00 N	26.23 E
Daraga	202	11.54 N	123.52 E
Daraj	214	30.09 N	10.26 E
Daram Island I	202	11.38 N	124.47 E
Darāw	220	24.25 N	32.56 E
Dārayyā	210	33.27 N	36.15 E
Dar-Beni-Kriche-Bahri	168	35.30 N	5.20 W
Darbhanga	206	26.10 N	85.56 E
D'Arbonne, Lake ⊜	278	32.40 N	92.25 W
Darbun	248	31.16 N	90.03 W
Darby, Mont., U.S.	256	46.01 N	114.11 W
Darby, Pa., U.S.	262	39.54 N	75.15 W
Darby, Cape ≻	236	64.20 N	162.22 W
Darchan	190	49.28 N	105.56 E
D'Archiac, Mount ∧	230	43.28 S	170.32 E
D'Arcy	238	50.33 N	122.29 W
Darda	172	45.37 N	18.41 E
Dardanelle, Ark., U.S.	248	35.13 N	93.09 W
Dardanelle, Calif., U.S.	272	38.20 N	119.50 W
Dardanelle Reservoir ⊜[1]	248	35.25 N	93.20 W
Dardanelles → Çanakkale Boğazı ⊔	212	40.15 N	26.25 E
Dardara	168	35.08 N	5.15 W
Dare	262	37.10 N	76.26 W
Dar-el-Beida → Casablanca	214	33.39 N	7.35 W
Dar-es-Salaam	218	6.48 S	39.17 E
Darfo	180	45.53 N	10.11 E
Dārfūr ☐[4]	220	13.00 N	25.00 E
Dargan-Ata	186	40.29 N	62.10 E
Dargaville	230	35.56 S	173.52 E
Dari	190	33.55 N	99.54 E
Darıca	172	40.45 N	29.23 E
Darién, Col.	290	3.56 N	76.31 W
Darien, Conn., U.S.	261	41.05 N	73.28 W
Darien, Ga., U.S.	246	31.22 N	81.26 W
Darien, N.Y., U.S.	264	41.43 N	70.37 W
Darien, Wis., U.S.	268	42.36 N	88.42 W
Darién, Cordillera de ⋀	280	12.55 N	85.30 W
Daríen, Serranía del ⋀	290	8.20 N	77.22 W
Darien Center	264	42.54 N	78.23 W
Dariganga	190	45.21 N	113.38 E
Darigayos Point ≻	202	16.50 N	120.20 E
Darjeeling	206	27.02 N	88.16 E
Darke ☐[6]	268	40.06 N	84.38 W
Darlaston	174	52.34 N	2.02 W
Darling	248	34.22 N	90.23 W
Darling ≃	228	34.07 S	141.55 E
Darling, Lake ⊜[1]	252	48.35 N	101.40 W
Darling Downs ⊸[1]	228	27.30 S	150.30 E
Darlingford	252	49.12 N	98.22 W
Darlington, Eng., U.K.	162	54.31 N	1.34 W
Darlington, Md., U.S.	262	39.39 N	76.11 W
Darlington, Pa., U.S.	266	40.49 N	80.26 W
Darlington, S.C., U.S.	246	34.18 N	79.52 W
Darlington, Wis., U.S.	244	42.41 N	90.07 W
Darłowo (Rügenwalde)	164	54.26 N	16.23 E
Darmstadt	164	49.53 N	8.40 E
Darnah	214	32.46 N	22.39 E
Darnah ☐[4]	220	32.30 N	22.45 E
Darnétal	176	49.27 N	1.09 E
Darney	166	48.05 N	6.03 E
Darnley Bay C	236	69.35 N	123.30 W
Daroca	168	41.07 N	1.25 W
Darr ≃	228	23.39 S	143.50 E
Darrah, Mount ∧	238	49.28 N	114.35 W
Darregueira	294	37.40 S	63.10 W
Darreh Gaz	208	37.27 N	59.07 E
Darrington	270	48.15 N	121.36 W
Darrouzett	250	36.27 N	100.20 W
Dartford	174	51.27 N	0.14 E
Dartmoor ⊸[3]	162	50.35 N	4.00 W
Dartmoor National Park ♠	162	50.37 N	3.52 W
Dartmouth, N.S., Can.	240	44.40 N	63.34 W
Dartmouth, Eng., U.K.	174	50.21 N	3.35 W
Dartmouth ≃	240	48.50 N	64.35 W
Dartmouth, Lake ⊜	228	26.04 S	145.18 E
Dartuch, Cabo ≻	168	39.56 N	3.48 E
Daru	198	9.04 S	143.12 E
Daruvar	170	45.36 N	17.13 E
Darvaza	186	40.11 N	58.24 E
Darvel Bay C	202	4.50 N	118.25 E
Darvinskij Zapovednik ⊸[4]	160	58.50 N	37.40 E
Darwin	226	12.28 S	130.50 E
Darwin, Isla I	290a	1.39 N	92.00 W
Darwin, Volcán ∧[1]	290a	0.10 S	91.18 W
Dās I	208	25.09 N	52.53 E
Dashahu ⊜	196	30.11 N	113.46 E
Dash Point	270	47.19 N	122.26 W
Dasht ≃	208	25.10 N	61.40 E
Dashtīārī ≃	208	25.09 N	61.32 E
Dašinčilen	190	47.51 N	104.03 E
Dasol	202	15.59 N	119.52 E
Dasol Bay C	202	15.56 N	119.50 E
Dassalan Island I	202	6.44 N	121.28 E
Dassel	244	45.05 N	94.19 W
Dasseneiland I	224	33.26 S	18.04 E
Dasserat, Lac ⊜	244	48.15 N	79.24 W
Dassow	164	53.50 N	10.59 E
Date	192a	42.27 N	140.51 E
Datong	190	40.08 N	113.13 E
Datonghe ≃	190	36.20 N	102.55 E
Datteln	178	51.40 N	7.23 E
Datu, Tandjung ≻	200	2.06 N	109.39 E
Datu Bay C	200	1.56 N	110.40 E
Datu Piang	202	7.02 N	124.29 E
Daugai	164	54.22 N	24.20 E
Daugava ≃	160	57.04 N	24.03 E
Daugavpils	160	55.53 N	26.32 E
Dauin	202	9.12 N	123.16 E

Symbols in the index entries are identified on page 360.

Name	Page	Lat°′	Long°′
Daule, Ec.	290	1.50 S	79.56 W
Daule, Ec.	290	0.24 N	80.00 W
Daule ≃	290	2.10 S	79.52 W
Daun	164	50.11 N	6.50 E
Daung Kyun I	200	12.14 N	98.05 E
Dauphin, Man., Can.	232	51.09 N	100.03 W
Dauphin, Pa., U.S.	262	40.22 N	76.56 W
Dauphin □[6]	262	40.15 N	76.52 W
Dauphiné □[9]	166	44.50 N	6.00 E
Dauphin Island I	248	30.14 N	88.12 W
Dauphin Lake ⊜	232	51.17 N	99.48 W
D'Auteuil, Lac ⊜	240	50.37 N	61.17 W
Davant	248	29.37 N	89.51 W
Davao	202	7.04 N	125.36 E
Davao ≃	202	7.03 N	125.36 E
Davao del Norte □[4]	202	7.10 N	125.50 E
Davao del Sur □[4]	202	6.15 N	125.40 E
Davao Gulf C	202	6.40 N	125.45 E
Davao Oriental □[4]	202	7.30 N	126.30 E
Daveluyville	260	46.12 N	72.08 W
Davenport, Calif., U.S.	272	37.01 N	122.12 W
Davenport, Fla., U.S.	246	28.10 N	81.36 W
Davenport, Iowa, U.S.	244	41.32 N	90.41 W
Davenport, Nebr., U.S.	252	40.19 N	97.49 W
Davenport, Okla., U.S.	250	35.42 N	96.46 W
Davenport, Wash., U.S.	256	47.39 N	118.09 W
Daventry	174	52.16 N	1.09 W
Davey, Port C	228	43.19 S	145.55 E
David	280	8.25 N	82.27 W
David City	252	41.15 N	97.08 W
Davidson, N.C., U.S.	246	35.30 N	80.51 W
Davidson, Okla., U.S.	250	34.14 N	99.05 W
Davidson Mountains ⋀	236	68.45 N	142.10 W
Davidsville	266	40.14 N	78.56 W
Davila	202	18.27 N	120.34 E
Davinópolis	296	15.58 S	50.08 W
Davis, Calif., U.S.	272	38.33 N	121.44 W
Davis, N.C., U.S.	246	34.48 N	76.28 W
Davis, Okla., U.S.	250	34.30 N	97.03 W
Davis, W. Va., U.S.	242	39.08 N	79.28 W
Davis, Mount ∧	242	39.47 N	79.10 W
Davisboro	246	32.59 N	82.36 W
Davisburg	268	42.45 N	83.33 W
Davis City	244	40.38 N	93.49 W
Davis Cove	240	47.40 N	54.18 W
Davis Dam	254	35.11 N	114.35 W
Davis Lake ⊜	256	43.37 N	121.51 W
Davis Mountains ⋀	250	30.35 N	104.00 W
Davison	268	43.02 N	83.31 W
Davisson Lake ⊜[1]	256	46.30 N	122.20 W
Davis Strait ⋓	232	67.00 N	57.00 W
Davlekanovo	158	54.13 N	55.03 E
Davos	180	46.48 N	9.50 E
Davutlar	172	37.43 N	27.17 E
Davy	246	37.29 N	81.39 W
Dawa (Daua) ≃	214	4.11 N	42.06 E
Dawangjiadao I	194	39.27 N	123.07 E
Dawanshan I	196	21.57 N	113.43 E
Dawenhe ≃	194	35.38 N	116.24 E
Dawley	174	52.40 N	2.28 W
Dawlish	174	50.35 N	3.28 W
Dawn	262	37.50 N	77.22 W
Dawna Range ⋀	200	16.50 N	98.15 E
Dawson, Yukon, Can.	236	64.04 N	139.25 W
Dawson, Ga., U.S.	246	31.47 N	84.26 W
Dawson, Minn., U.S.	252	44.56 N	96.03 W
Dawson, Nebr., U.S.	252	40.08 N	95.50 W
Dawson, Tex., U.S.	250	31.54 N	96.43 W
Dawson ≃	228	23.38 S	149.46 E
Dawson, Isla I	288	54.00 S	70.40 W
Dawson, Mount ∧	238	51.09 N	117.25 W
Dawson Creek	238	55.46 N	120.14 W
Dawson Inlet C	232	61.50 N	93.25 W
Dawson Range ⋀, Austl.	228	24.20 S	149.45 E
Dawson Range ⋀, Yukon, Can.	236	62.40 N	139.00 W
Dawson Ridge	266	40.42 N	80.22 W
Dawson Springs	248	37.10 N	87.41 W
Dawsonville	246	34.25 N	84.07 W
Dax	166	43.43 N	1.03 W
Daxi ≃	196	28.18 N	119.44 E
Daxian	190	31.18 N	107.30 E
Daxiaoqindao I	194	38.18 N	120.48 E
Daxing'anling-shanmai ⋀	190	49.40 N	122.00 E
Daxueshan ⋀	190	30.10 N	101.50 E
Daya	190	25.24 N	114.22 E
Dayanghe ≃	194	39.54 N	123.40 E
Dayaniguas, Ensenada de C	284p	22.18 N	83.14 W
Dayao	200	25.43 N	101.13 E
Daye	190	30.06 N	114.57 E
Dayingjiang ≃	200	24.19 N	97.12 E
Day Island	270	47.15 N	122.33 W
Dayr, Jabal ad- ∧	220	12.27 N	30.42 E
Dayr az-Zawr	212	35.20 N	40.09 E
Dayr az-Zawr □[8]	212	35.30 N	39.00 E
Dayrūṭ	220	27.33 N	30.49 E
Daysland	238	52.52 N	112.15 W
Dayton, Ill., U.S.	268	41.23 N	88.47 W
Dayton, Ind., U.S.	268	40.23 N	86.46 W
Dayton, Iowa, U.S.	244	42.16 N	94.04 W
Dayton, Mich., U.S.	268	41.48 N	86.26 W
Dayton, Nev., U.S.	272	39.14 N	119.36 W
Dayton, Ohio, U.S.	242	39.45 N	84.15 W
Dayton, Oreg., U.S.	270	45.13 N	123.05 W
Dayton, Pa., U.S.	266	40.53 N	79.16 W
Dayton, Tenn., U.S.	248	35.30 N	85.00 W
Dayton, Tex., U.S.	250	30.03 N	94.54 W
Dayton, Va., U.S.	242	38.25 N	78.56 W
Dayton, Wash., U.S.	256	46.19 N	117.59 W
Dayton, Wis., U.S.	268	42.49 N	89.31 W
Dayton, Wyo., U.S.	256	44.53 N	107.16 W
Daytona Beach	246	29.12 N	81.00 W
Dayudao I	196	22.16 N	113.56 E
Dayuling ⋀	196	25.20 N	114.16 E
Dayville, Conn., U.S.	261	41.51 N	71.53 W
Dayville, Oreg., U.S.	256	44.28 N	119.32 W
Dazixi ≃	196	25.45 N	118.27 E
Dazuojiao ≻	196	24.54 N	118.58 E
De Aar	224	30.39 S	24.00 E
Dead ≃	244	46.34 N	87.24 W
Deadhorse	236	70.11 N	148.27 W
Dead Knoll ∧	254	42.24 N	110.29 W
Deadman ≃	238	50.45 N	120.55 W
Deadmans Cay	282	23.14 N	75.14 W
Deadman Wash ∨	254	35.34 N	111.17 W
Dead Sea ⊜	208	31.30 N	35.30 E
Deadwood	252	44.23 N	103.44 W
Deadwood ≃	256	44.05 N	115.40 W
Deadwood Reservoir ⊜[1]	256	44.19 N	115.40 W
Deagan Island I	202	12.14 N	123.51 E
Deakin	226	30.46 S	129.58 E
Deal, Eng., U.K.	174	51.14 N	1.24 E
Deal, N.J., U.S.	262	40.15 N	74.00 W
Deale	262	38.47 N	76.33 W
Deal Island	262	38.09 N	75.56 W
Dean ≃	238	52.50 N	126.57 W
Dean Channel ⋓	238	52.33 N	127.13 W
Deán Funes	294	30.25 S	64.20 W
Deans Dundas Bay C	232	72.15 N	118.25 W
Deanwood	246	31.14 N	82.23 W
Dearborn	268	42.18 N	83.10 W
Dearborn ≃	256	47.07 N	111.55 W
Dearborn Heights	268	42.19 N	83.14 W
Dearg, Beinn ∧	162	57.48 N	4.57 W
Dease ≃	236	59.54 N	128.30 W
Dease Arm C	236	66.52 N	119.37 W
Dease Lake ⊜	236	58.35 N	130.02 W
Dease Strait ⋓	232	68.40 N	108.00 W
Death Valley	258	36.18 N	116.25 W
Death Valley ∨	258	36.30 N	117.00 W
Death Valley National Monument ♠	258	36.30 N	117.00 W
Deatsville	248	32.37 N	86.24 W
Deauville	176	49.22 N	0.04 E
Debar	172	41.31 N	20.30 E
De Bary	246	28.52 N	81.15 W
Debauch Mountain ∧	236	64.31 N	159.52 W
Débé	285r	10.12 N	61.27 W
De Beque	254	39.20 N	108.13 W
De Berry	248	32.18 N	94.10 W
Debesy	160	57.39 N	53.49 E
Dębica	164	50.04 N	21.24 E
De Bilt	178	52.06 N	5.10 E
Dęblin	164	51.35 N	21.50 E
Dębno (Neudamm)	164	52.45 N	14.40 E
Debo, Lac ⊜	222	15.18 N	4.09 W
Deborah, Mount ∧	236	63.38 N	147.15 W
Debrecen	164	47.32 N	21.38 E
Debre Markos	214	10.20 N	37.45 E
Debre Tabor	214	11.50 N	38.05 E
Debrzno (Preussisch Friedland)	164	53.33 N	17.14 E
Decatur, Ala., U.S.	248	34.36 N	86.59 W
Decatur, Ga., U.S.	246	33.46 N	84.18 W
Decatur, Ill., U.S.	248	39.51 N	89.32 W
Decatur, Ind., U.S.	268	40.50 N	84.56 W
Decatur, Mich., U.S.	268	42.17 N	85.58 W
Decatur, Miss., U.S.	248	32.26 N	89.07 W
Decatur, Nebr., U.S.	252	42.00 N	96.15 W
Decatur, Tenn., U.S.	246	35.31 N	84.47 W
Decatur, Tex., U.S.	250	33.14 N	97.35 W
Decaturville	248	35.35 N	88.07 W
Decazeville	166	44.34 N	2.15 E
Decelles, Réservoir ⊜[1]	244	47.40 N	78.08 W
Dechêne, Lac ⊜	240	51.15 N	67.52 W
Decherd	248	35.13 N	86.05 W
Déchy	176	50.21 N	3.07 E
Decimomannu	170	39.19 N	8.58 E
Děčín	164	50.48 N	14.13 E
Decize	166	46.50 N	3.27 E
Decker Lake	238	54.17 N	125.50 W
Deckers Point	266	40.46 N	78.59 W
Deckerville	244	43.32 N	82.44 W
Decorah	244	43.18 N	91.48 W
Decs	164	46.17 N	18.46 E
Deda	172	46.57 N	24.53 E
Dedegöl Dağı ∧	212	37.39 N	31.17 E
Dedeköy	172	37.58 N	29.36 E
Dedemsvaart	178	52.36 N	6.28 E
Dedham	261	42.15 N	71.10 W
Dédougou	214	12.28 N	3.28 W
Dedoviči	160	57.32 N	29.56 E
Dee ≃, U.K.	162	51.20 N	4.00 W
Dee ≃, Scot., U.K.	162	57.08 N	2.04 W
Deedsville	268	40.55 N	86.06 W
Deep ≃	246	35.36 N	79.03 W
Deep River, Ont., Can.	244	46.06 N	77.30 W
Deep River, Conn., U.S.	261	41.23 N	72.26 W
Deep River, Iowa, U.S.	244	41.35 N	92.22 W
Deep River, Wash., U.S.	270	46.21 N	123.41 W
Deepwater, Mo., U.S.	248	38.16 N	93.47 W
Deep Water, N.J., U.S.	262	39.41 N	75.29 W
Deer	248	35.50 N	93.12 W
Deer ≃	242	44.55 N	74.43 W
Deer Creek, Ind., U.S.	268	40.37 N	86.23 W
Deer Creek, Minn., U.S.	252	46.24 N	95.19 W
Deer Creek Canyon ∨	252	40.28 N	100.00 W
Deerfield, Ill., U.S.	268	42.10 N	87.51 W
Deerfield, Ind., U.S.	268	40.17 N	84.59 W
Deerfield, Kans., U.S.	252	37.59 N	101.08 W
Deerfield, Mass., U.S.	261	42.33 N	72.36 W
Deerfield, Mich., U.S.	268	41.53 N	83.47 W
Deerfield, Ohio, U.S.	266	41.02 N	81.03 W
Deerfield, Wis., U.S.	268	43.03 N	89.05 W
Deerfield Beach	246	26.19 N	80.06 W
Deerfield Street	262	39.31 N	75.14 W
Deer Harbor	270	48.37 N	123.00 W
Deering	236	66.05 N	162.43 W
Deer Island I, N.B., Can.	240	45.00 N	66.57 W
Deer Island I, Alaska, U.S.	236	54.53 N	162.25 W
Deer Isle	242	44.13 N	68.41 W
Deer Isle I	240	44.10 N	68.40 W
Deer Lake, Newf., Can.	240	49.10 N	57.25 W
Deer Lake, Pa., U.S.	262	40.37 N	76.03 W
Deer Lake ⊜	240	49.07 N	57.35 W
Deerlijk	176	50.51 N	3.21 E
Deer Lodge	256	46.24 N	112.44 W
Deer Mountain ∧	242	45.01 N	70.56 W
Deer Park, Ala., U.S.	248	31.13 N	88.19 W
Deer Park, Wash., U.S.	256	47.57 N	117.28 W
Deerpass Bay C	232	65.56 N	122.25 W
Deer Pond ⊜	240	48.30 N	54.45 W
Deer River, Minn., U.S.	244	47.20 N	93.48 W
Deer River, N.Y., U.S.	264	43.56 N	75.36 W
Deersville	266	40.19 N	81.11 W
Deer Trail	252	39.37 N	104.02 W
Deerwood	244	46.28 N	93.54 W
Deferiet	264	44.02 N	75.41 W
Defiance, Iowa, U.S.	252	41.49 N	95.20 W
Defiance, Ohio, U.S.	268	41.17 N	84.22 W
Defiance, Pa., U.S.	266	40.10 N	78.14 W
Defiance □[6]	268	41.19 N	84.30 W
Defiance, Mount ∧	256	45.38 N	121.43 W
Defiance Plateau ⋀[1]	254	35.40 N	109.20 W
De Forest	244	43.15 N	89.20 W
De Funiak Springs	248	30.43 N	86.07 W
Dege	190	31.50 N	98.40 E
Degebe, Ribeira de ≃	168	38.13 N	7.29 W
Degeberga	160	55.50 N	14.05 E
Degeh-Bur	214	8.14 N	43.35 E
Degerfors	160	59.14 N	14.26 E
Deggendorf	164	48.51 N	12.59 E
Değirmendere	172	38.07 N	27.09 E
De Graff	268	40.19 N	83.55 W
De Gray Reservoir ⊜[1]	248	34.15 N	93.15 W
Degt'arsk	158	56.42 N	60.06 E
Dehiwala-Mount Lavinia	204	6.51 N	79.52 E
Dehkhvāreqān	208	37.45 N	45.59 E
Deh Kord	208	33.49 N	48.53 E
Dehra Dūn	206	30.20 N	78.02 E
Dehri	206	24.53 N	84.14 E
Dehui	190	44.34 N	125.43 E
Deinze	176	50.59 N	3.32 E
Dej	172	47.09 N	23.43 E
Deje	160	59.36 N	13.28 E
Dejnau	186	39.15 N	63.11 E
Deka ≃	224	18.05 S	26.44 E
De Kalb, Ill., U.S.	268	41.56 N	88.45 W
De Kalb, Miss., U.S.	248	32.46 N	88.39 W
De Kalb, Tex., U.S.	248	33.31 N	94.37 W
De Kalb □[6], Ill., U.S.	268	41.59 N	88.41 W
De Kalb □[6], Ind., U.S.	268	41.22 N	85.04 W
De Kalb Junction	264	44.30 N	75.16 W
Dekese	218	3.27 S	21.24 E
De La Blache, Lac ⊜	240	50.05 N	69.29 W
Delafield	268	43.04 N	88.24 W
Delami Mayal, Jabal ∧	220	11.38 N	30.23 E
De Lancey	266	40.59 N	78.58 W
Delanco	262	40.03 N	74.57 W
De Land	246	29.02 N	81.18 W
Delano, Calif., U.S.	272	35.41 N	119.15 W
Delano, Minn., U.S.	244	45.02 N	93.47 W
Delano Peak ∧	254	38.22 N	112.23 W
Delarof Islands II	237a	51.30 N	178.45 W
Delavan, Ill., U.S.	248	40.22 N	89.33 W
Delavan, Wis., U.S.	268	42.38 N	88.39 W
Delaware, Ont., Can.	266	42.55 N	81.25 W
Delaware, Ohio, U.S.	266	40.18 N	83.04 W
Delaware, Okla., U.S.	250	36.47 N	95.38 W
Delaware □[6], Ind., U.S.	268	40.18 N	85.23 W
Delaware □[6], Ohio, U.S.	266	40.18 N	83.04 W
Delaware □[6], Pa., U.S.	262	39.55 N	75.23 W
Delaware □[3]	234	39.10 N	75.30 W
Delaware ≃, U.S.	242	39.20 N	75.25 W
Delaware ≃, Kans., U.S.	252	39.03 N	95.24 W
Delaware Bay C	242	39.05 N	75.15 W
Delaware City	262	39.34 N	75.36 W
Delaware Mountains ⋀	250	31.35 N	104.40 W
Delaware Park	262	40.43 N	75.11 W
Delbrück	178	51.46 N	8.33 E
Delburne	238	52.12 N	113.14 W
Del Campillo	294	34.22 S	64.30 W
Del City	250	35.27 N	97.27 W
Del Dios	274	33.04 N	117.08 W
Delémont	180	47.22 N	7.21 E
De Leon	250	32.07 N	98.32 W
De Leon Springs	246	29.07 N	81.21 W
Delevan	266	42.29 N	78.29 W
Delfinópolis	296	20.20 S	46.51 W
Delft	178	52.00 N	4.21 E
Delfzijl	178	53.19 N	6.46 E
Del Gallego	202	13.56 N	122.36 E
Del Haven	262	39.03 N	74.56 W
Delhi, Bhārat	206	28.37 N	77.12 E
Delhi, Ont., Can.	264	42.51 N	80.30 W
Delhi, Calif., U.S.	272	37.26 N	120.46 W
Delhi, Iowa, U.S.	244	42.26 N	91.20 W
Delhi, La., U.S.	248	32.27 N	91.30 W
Delhi, N.Y., U.S.	242	42.17 N	74.55 W
Delia	238	51.38 N	112.23 W
Deliblato	172	44.50 N	21.03 E
Delices	284d	15.17 N	61.16 W
Deliceto	184	41.13 N	15.23 E
Delicias, Cuba	284p	21.11 N	76.34 W
Delicias, Méx.	278	28.13 N	105.28 W
Delicias, Laguna ⊜	278	28.10 N	105.40 W
Delight	248	34.02 N	93.30 W
Delightful	266	41.18 N	80.57 W
Delıklıkaya ≻	212	41.12 N	30.20 E
Delingha	190	37.14 N	97.11 E
Delitua	200	3.29 N	98.41 E
Delitzsch	164	51.31 N	12.20 E
Delkern	274	35.21 N	119.01 W
Dell City	254	31.56 N	105.12 W
Delle	180	47.30 N	7.00 E
Dellenbough, Mount ∧	254	36.07 N	113.32 W
Dell Rapids	252	43.50 N	96.43 W
Dellroy	266	40.33 N	81.12 W
Dellys	168	36.50 N	3.55 E
Del Macho, Arroyo ∨	250	33.36 N	104.28 W
Del Mar, Calif., U.S.	274	32.58 N	117.16 W
Delmar, Del., U.S.	262	38.27 N	75.34 W
Delmar, Iowa, U.S.	244	42.00 N	90.37 W
Delmar, Md., U.S.	262	38.27 N	75.34 W
Del Mar Heights	272	35.26 N	120.52 W
Delmenhorst	178	53.03 N	8.38 E
Delmont, N.J., U.S.	262	39.13 N	74.57 W
Delmont, Pa., U.S.	266	40.25 N	79.34 W
Delmont, S. Dak., U.S.	252	43.16 N	98.10 W
Del Monte Heights	272	36.36 N	121.50 W
Del Monte Park	272	36.36 N	121.56 W
Delnice	170	45.24 N	14.48 E
Del Norte	254	37.41 N	106.21 W
De-Longa, Ostrova II	186	76.30 N	153.00 E
De Long Mountains ⋀	236	68.20 N	162.00 W
Deloraine	252	49.12 N	100.29 W
Delorme, Lac ⊜	232	54.40 N	69.50 W
Deloro	264	44.31 N	77.37 W
Delos → Dhílos ⊥	172	37.26 N	25.16 E
Delphi	268	40.36 N	86.41 W
Delphi → Dhelfoí ⊥	172	38.30 N	22.29 E
Delphi Falls	264	42.53 N	75.55 W
Delphos, Kans., U.S.	252	39.16 N	97.46 W
Delphos, Ohio, U.S.	268	40.50 N	84.20 W
Delray Beach	246	26.28 N	80.04 W
Del Rey	272	36.40 N	119.36 W
Del Rey Oaks	272	36.36 N	121.50 W
Del Rio	250	29.22 N	100.54 W
Del Rosa	274	34.08 N	117.15 W
Delson	260	45.23 N	73.33 W
Delta, Ont., Can.	264	44.37 N	76.08 W
Delta, Méx.	254	32.22 N	115.12 W
Delta, Colo., U.S.	254	38.44 N	108.04 W
Delta, Mo., U.S.	248	37.12 N	89.44 W
Delta, Ohio, U.S.	268	41.34 N	84.00 W
Delta, Pa., U.S.	262	39.44 N	76.19 W
Delta, Utah, U.S.	254	39.21 N	112.35 W
Delta ≃	236	64.09 N	146.18 W
Delta Amacuro □[8]	290	8.30 N	61.30 W
Delta City	248	33.04 N	90.48 W
Delta Junction	236	64.02 N	145.41 W
Delta Peak ∧	236	56.39 N	129.34 W
Deltaville	262	37.33 N	76.20 W
Delton	268	42.30 N	85.24 W
Del Valle	250	30.12 N	97.40 W
Delvinë	172	39.57 N	20.06 E
Demarcation Point ≻	236	69.40 N	141.15 W
Demavend, Mount → Damāvand, Qolleh-ye ∧	208	35.56 N	52.08 E
Demba	218	5.30 S	22.16 E
Dembidolo	214	8.30 N	34.48 E
Demerara ≃	290	6.50 N	58.10 W
Demidov	160	55.16 N	31.31 E
Deming, N. Mex., U.S.	254	32.16 N	107.45 W
Deming, Wash., U.S.	270	48.49 N	122.13 W
Demini ≃	290	0.46 S	62.56 W
Demirci	172	39.03 N	28.40 E
Demircidere	172	37.33 N	27.50 E
Demirciköy	172	38.05 N	29.24 E
Demir Kapija ∨	172	41.24 N	22.15 E
Demirköy	172	41.49 N	27.45 E
Demirtaş	172	40.16 N	29.06 E
Demjanka ≃	158	59.34 N	69.17 E
Demjanovo	160	60.22 N	47.03 E
Demjansk	160	57.38 N	32.28 E
Demjanskoje	158	59.36 N	69.18 E
Demmin	164	53.54 N	13.02 E
Demmitt	238	55.26 N	119.54 W
Demonte	170	44.19 N	7.17 E
De Montigny, Lac ⊜	244	48.10 N	77.53 W
Demopolis	248	32.31 N	87.50 W
Demorest	246	34.31 N	83.32 W
Demotte	268	41.12 N	87.12 W
Dempo, Gunung ∧	198	4.02 S	103.09 E
Demre ⊥	212	36.15 N	29.54 E
Demta	198	2.20 S	140.08 E
Denain	176	50.20 N	3.23 E
Denair	272	37.32 N	120.47 W
Denali	236	63.11 N	147.28 W
Denau	186	38.16 N	67.54 E
Denbigh, Ont., Can.	264	45.08 N	77.16 W
Denbigh, Wales, U.K.	162	53.11 N	3.25 W
Denbigh, Cape ≻	236	64.23 N	161.31 W
Denbighshire □[6]	174	53.05 N	3.20 W
Den Burg	164	53.03 N	4.48 E
Dender (Dendre) ≃	176	51.02 N	4.06 E
Denderleeuw	176	50.53 N	4.04 E
Dendermonde	176	51.02 N	4.07 E
Dendron	262	37.03 N	76.56 W
Denham	268	41.09 N	86.43 W
Denham, Mount ∧	285q	18.13 N	77.32 W
Denham Island I	228	16.43 S	139.09 E
Denham Range ⋀	228	21.55 S	147.46 E
Denham Springs	248	30.29 N	90.57 W
Den Helder	178	52.54 N	4.45 E
Denia	168	38.51 N	0.07 E
Deniliquin	228	35.32 S	144.58 E
Denison, Iowa, U.S.	252	42.01 N	95.21 W
Denison, Tex., U.S.	250	33.45 N	96.33 W
Denison, Mount ∧	236	58.25 N	154.27 W
Denison Dam ⊸[6]	250	33.36 N	96.18 W
Denisovka	160	66.14 N	55.20 E
Denizli	212	37.46 N	29.06 E
Denizli □[4]	172	37.30 N	29.00 E
Denkendorf	180	48.41 N	9.19 E
Denmark, Austl.	226	34.57 S	117.21 E
Denmark, S.C., U.S.	246	33.19 N	81.09 W
Denmark, Wis., U.S.	244	44.21 N	87.50 W
Denmark □[1]	158	56.00 N	10.00 E
Denmark Bay C	232	70.33 N	103.20 W
Denmark Strait ⋓	148	67.00 N	25.00 W
Dennery	285f	13.55 N	60.54 W
Dennis	261	41.44 N	70.12 W
Dennison	266	40.24 N	81.19 W
Dennis Port	261	41.39 N	70.08 W
Dennisville	262	39.12 N	74.49 W
Denpasar	226	8.39 S	115.13 E
Denton, Md., U.S.	262	38.53 N	75.50 W
Denton, Mont., U.S.	256	47.19 N	109.57 W
Denton, Tex., U.S.	250	33.13 N	97.08 W
D'Entrecasteaux Islands II	226	9.30 S	150.40 E
Denver, Colo., U.S.	254	39.43 N	105.01 W
Denver, Ind., U.S.	268	40.52 N	86.05 W
Denver, Iowa, U.S.	244	42.40 N	92.20 W
Denver, Pa., U.S.	262	40.14 N	76.08 W
Denver City	250	32.58 N	102.50 W
Denzlingen	180	48.04 N	7.52 E
Deogarh ∧	206	23.31 N	82.15 E
Deogarh Hills ⋀[2]	206	23.35 N	82.30 E
Deosai Mountains ⋀	206	35.10 N	75.20 E
De Panne	176	51.06 N	2.35 E
Departure Bay	270	49.12 N	123.58 W
Depauville	264	44.08 N	76.04 W
De Pere	244	44.27 N	88.04 W
Depew, N.Y., U.S.	264	42.54 N	78.42 W
Depew, Okla., U.S.	250	35.48 N	96.31 W
Depoe Bay	256	44.49 N	124.04 W
Deport	250	33.32 N	95.19 W
Deposit	242	42.04 N	75.25 W
Depósito	290	3.12 N	60.35 W
Depue	244	41.19 N	89.19 W
Deqin	190	28.38 N	98.52 E
De Queen	248	34.02 N	94.21 W
De Quincy	248	30.27 N	93.26 W
Derac	282	19.41 N	71.48 W
Dera Ghāzi Khān	206	30.03 N	70.38 E
Dera Ismāīl Khān	206	31.50 N	70.54 E
Derbent	158	42.03 N	48.18 E
Derby, Austl.	226	17.18 S	123.38 E
Derby, Eng., U.K.	174	52.55 N	1.29 W
Derby, Conn., U.S.	261	41.19 N	73.05 W
Derby, Kans., U.S.	252	37.33 N	97.16 W
Derby, Maine, U.S.	242	45.14 N	68.59 W
Derby, N.Y., U.S.	264	42.41 N	78.58 W
Derby Acres	272	35.15 N	119.35 W
Derby Center	260	44.57 N	72.08 W
Derby Line	242	45.00 N	72.06 W
Derbyshire □[6]	174	53.00 N	1.33 W
Derecho ≃	290	2.38 S	69.54 W
Derecske	164	47.21 N	21.34 E
Dereköy	172	41.56 N	27.21 E
Derev'anka	160	61.34 N	34.27 E
Derg, Lough ⊜	162	53.00 N	8.20 W
De Ridder	248	30.51 N	93.17 W
Derita	246	35.18 N	80.48 W
Dermott	248	33.32 N	91.26 W
Dernieres, Isles II	248	29.02 N	90.47 W
Deroche	270	49.11 N	122.04 W
Déroute, Passage de la ⋓	162	49.12 N	1.51 W
Derrame	250	26.19 N	104.23 W
Derrick City	266	41.58 N	78.34 W
Derry → Londonderry, N. Ire., U.K.	162	55.00 N	7.19 W
Derry, N.H., U.S.	242	42.53 N	71.19 W
Derry, Pa., U.S.	266	40.20 N	79.18 W
De Ruyter	264	42.46 N	75.53 W
Derval	166	47.40 N	1.40 W
Derventa	172	44.58 N	17.55 E
Derwent	238	53.39 N	110.58 W
Derwent ≃	228	43.03 S	147.22 E
Deržavinskij	186	51.03 N	66.19 E
Desaguadero ≃, Arg.	294	34.13 S	66.47 W
Desaguadero ≃, Bol.	292	18.24 S	67.05 W
Des Allemands	248	29.50 N	90.28 W
Des Arc	248	34.58 N	91.30 W
Descabezado Grande, Volcán ∧[1]	294	35.36 S	70.45 W
Descanso, Bra.	294	26.50 S	53.35 W
Descanso, Calif., U.S.	258	32.51 N	116.37 W
Descanso, Punta ≻	258	32.15 N	117.00 W
Deschaillons	260	46.33 N	72.07 W
Deschambault	260	46.39 N	71.56 W
Deschambault Lake ⊜	232	54.40 N	103.35 W
Deschênes	242	45.32 N	75.49 W
Deschutes ≃	256	45.38 N	120.54 W
Deschutes-Umatilla Plateau ⋀[1]	256	45.00 N	119.40 W
Dese	214	11.05 N	39.41 E
Desengaño, Punta ≻	288	49.15 S	67.35 W
Desenzano del Garda	170	45.28 N	10.32 E
Deseret Peak ∧	254	40.28 N	112.38 W
Deseronto	264	44.12 N	77.03 W
Désert ≃	244	46.27 N	76.02 W
Désert, Lac ⊜	244	46.35 N	76.17 W
Desert Peak ∧	254	41.11 N	113.22 W
Desert Valley ∨	258	41.15 N	118.20 W
Desert View Highland	274	34.37 N	118.13 W
Deshaies	285o	16.18 N	61.48 W
Deshler, Nebr., U.S.	252	40.08 N	97.44 W
Deshler, Ohio, U.S.	268	41.12 N	83.54 W
Deshon Manor	266	40.52 N	79.57 W
Desiderio Tello	294	31.13 S	66.19 W
Desio	182	45.37 N	9.13 E
Des Lacs ≃	252	48.17 N	101.25 W
Desmarais	238	55.56 N	113.49 W
De Smet	252	44.23 N	97.33 W
De Smet, Lake ⊜[1]	256	44.29 N	106.45 W
Des Moines, Iowa, U.S.	244	41.35 N	93.37 W
Des Moines, N. Mex., U.S.	250	36.46 N	103.50 W
Des Moines, Wash., U.S.	270	47.24 N	122.19 W
Des Moines ≃	244	40.22 N	91.26 W
Desmoronado, Cerro ∧	278	20.21 N	104.59 W
Desna ≃	158	50.33 N	30.32 E
Desolación, Isla I	288	53.00 S	74.10 W
Desolation Point ≻	202	10.28 N	125.29 E
De Soto, Ill., U.S.	248	37.49 N	89.14 W
De Soto, Kans., U.S.	252	38.59 N	94.58 W
De Soto, Mo., U.S.	248	38.08 N	90.33 W
De Soto National Memorial ⊥	246	27.31 N	82.40 W
Despatch	224	33.46 S	25.30 E
Despeñaperros, Desfiladero de)(	168	38.24 N	3.30 W
Des Plaines	268	42.02 N	87.54 W
Despotovac	172	44.05 N	21.33 E
Despujols	202	12.31 N	121.59 E
Desroches, Île I	218	5.41 S	53.41 E
Desruisseaux	285f	13.47 N	60.56 W
Dessau	164	51.50 N	12.14 E
Dessel	178	51.14 N	5.07 E
Destacado Island I	202	12.16 N	124.06 E
Destelbergen	176	51.03 N	3.48 E
Destin	248	30.24 N	86.30 W
Destruction Bay	236	61.15 N	138.48 W
Desvres	176	50.40 N	1.50 E
Deta	172	45.24 N	21.13 E
Detmold	178	51.56 N	8.52 E
Detmold □[6]	178	51.48 N	8.00 E
De Tour	244	46.00 N	83.53 W
Detour, Point ≻	244	45.36 N	86.37 W
Detrital Wash ∨	254	36.02 N	114.28 W
Detroit, Mich., U.S.	268	42.20 N	83.03 W
Detroit, Oreg., U.S.	256	44.44 N	122.09 W
Detroit, Tex., U.S.	250	33.40 N	95.16 W
Detroit ≃	244	42.06 N	83.08 W
Detroit Beach	268	41.55 N	83.20 W
Detroit Lakes	252	46.49 N	95.51 W
Detroit Reservoir ⊜[1]	256	44.42 N	122.10 W
Dettifoss ⌊	160a	65.50 N	16.20 W
Detva	164	48.31 N	19.28 E
Deurne, Bel.	176	51.13 N	4.28 E
Deurne, Ned.	178	51.28 N	5.47 E
Deutsche Bucht C	164	54.30 N	7.30 E
Deutsch Eylau → Iława	164	53.37 N	19.33 E
Deutschlandsberg	164	46.49 N	15.13 E
Deux-Montagnes	260	45.33 N	73.53 W
Deux-Montagnes □[6]	260	45.35 N	74.05 W
Deux-Sèvres □[5]	166	46.30 N	0.20 W
Deva	172	45.53 N	22.55 E
De Valls Bluff	248	34.47 N	91.28 W
Dev'atiny	160	60.56 N	36.46 E
Dévaványa	164	47.02 N	20.58 E
Devecikonağı	172	39.55 N	28.34 E
Devecser	164	47.06 N	17.26 E
Deve Dağı ∧	212	40.34 N	41.21 E
Deventer	178	52.15 N	6.10 E
Devët Skal ∧	164	49.40 N	16.02 E
De View, Bayou ≃	248	34.48 N	91.18 W
Déville-lès-Rouen	176	49.28 N	1.02 E
Devil River Peak ∧	230	40.58 S	172.39 E
Devils ≃	250	29.39 N	100.58 W
Devil's Island → Diable, Île du I	286	5.18 N	52.35 W
Devils Lake	252	48.07 N	98.59 W
Devils Lake ⊜	252	48.01 N	98.52 W
Devils Paw ∧	236	58.44 N	133.50 W
Devils Postpile National Monument ♠	258	37.40 N	119.05 W
Devils Tower National Monument ♠	252	44.31 N	104.57 W
Devin	172	41.45 N	24.24 E
Devine, B.C., Can.	238	50.32 N	122.30 W
Devine, Tex., U.S.	250	29.08 N	98.54 W
Devizes	174	51.22 N	1.59 W
Devoll ≃	172	40.49 N	19.51 E
Devon	238	53.22 N	113.44 W
Devon □[6]	174	50.45 N	3.50 W
Devon Island I	232	75.00 N	87.00 W
Devon Park	268	40.15 N	85.25 W
Devonport, Austl.	228	41.11 S	146.21 E
Devonport, N.Z.	230	36.49 S	174.48 E
Devonport, Eng., U.K.	174	50.22 N	4.10 W
Devore	274	34.13 N	117.25 W
Devoto	294	31.25 S	62.20 W
Devres ≃	212	41.06 N	34.25 E
Devure ≃	224	19.50 S	31.45 E
Dewa-kyūryō ⋀[2]	192	39.05 N	140.10 E
Dewās	206	22.57 N	76.04 E
Dewdney	238	49.10 N	122.12 W
Dewey, P.R.	284m	18.18 N	65.18 W
Dewey, Ill., U.S.	268	40.19 N	88.17 W
Dewey, Okla., U.S.	250	36.48 N	95.56 W
Deweyville	248	30.18 N	93.45 W
De Witt, Ark., U.S.	248	34.18 N	91.20 W
De Witt, Iowa, U.S.	244	41.49 N	90.33 W
DeWitt, Mich., U.S.	268	42.51 N	84.34 W
De Witt, Nebr., U.S.	252	40.24 N	96.55 W
De Witt, N.Y., U.S.	264	43.02 N	76.04 W
De Witt □[6]	268	40.12 N	88.55 W
Dewittville	266	42.14 N	79.27 W
Dewsbury	162	53.42 N	1.37 W
Dexter, Kans., U.S.	252	37.11 N	96.43 W
Dexter, Maine, U.S.	242	45.01 N	69.18 W
Dexter, Mich., U.S.	268	42.20 N	83.53 W
Dexter, Mo., U.S.	248	36.48 N	89.57 W
Dexter, N. Mex., U.S.	250	33.12 N	104.22 W
Dexter, N.Y., U.S.	264	44.01 N	76.03 W
Dexterity Fiord C[2]	232	71.11 N	73.03 W
Dez ≃	208	31.39 N	48.52 E
Dezadeash Lake ⊜	236	60.28 N	136.58 W
Dezfūl	208	32.23 N	48.24 E
Dezhou	194	37.27 N	116.18 E
Dežneva, Mys ≻	236	66.06 N	169.45 W
Dháfni	172	37.48 N	22.01 E
Dhahran → Aẓ-Ẓahrān	208	26.18 N	50.08 E
Dhamār	204	14.46 N	44.23 E
Dhānbād	206	23.47 N	86.26 E
Dhangarhi	190	28.41 N	80.38 E
D'hanis	250	29.20 N	99.17 W
Dhaulāgiri ∧	206	28.42 N	83.31 E
Dhebar Lake ⊜	206	24.20 N	74.00 E
Dhelfoí ⊥	172	38.30 N	22.29 E
Dhërmiu ⊍[1]	172	40.08 N	19.42 E
Dheskáti	172	39.55 N	21.49 E
Dhidhimótikhon	172	41.21 N	26.30 E
Dhíkti ⋀	172	35.08 N	25.22 E
Dhílos ⊥	172	37.26 N	25.16 E
Dhimitsána	172	37.37 N	22.03 E
Dhodhekánisos II	172	36.30 N	27.00 E
Dhodhekánisos II	172	36.35 N	27.10 E
Dhodhóni ⊥	172	39.34 N	20.47 E
Dhorāji	206	21.44 N	70.26 E
Dhoxáton	172	41.05 N	24.14 E
Dhule	206	20.54 N	74.47 E
Diable, Île du I	286	5.18 N	52.35 W
Diablo, Calif., U.S.	272	37.50 N	121.58 W
Diablo, Wash., U.S.	270	48.43 N	121.09 W
Diablo, Canyon ∨	254	35.18 N	110.59 W
Diablo, Mount ∧	258	37.53 N	121.55 W
Diablo, Sierra del ⋀	250	27.20 N	104.05 W
Diablo Plateau ⋀[1]	254	31.30 N	105.30 W
Diablo Range ⋀	258	37.00 N	121.20 W
Diagonal	252	40.48 N	94.20 W
Diaka ≃[1]	222	15.13 N	4.14 W
Diamante	294	32.05 S	60.35 W
Diamante ≃	294	34.31 S	66.56 W
Diamantina	296	18.15 S	43.36 W
Diamantina ≃	228	26.45 S	139.10 E
Diamantino	292	14.25 S	56.27 W
Diamond, Ill., U.S.	268	41.17 N	88.15 W
Diamond, Mo., U.S.	248	37.00 N	94.19 W
Diamond, Ohio, U.S.	266	41.06 N	81.01 W
Diamond Bar	274	33.58 N	117.51 W
Diamond Hill	261	41.59 N	71.25 W
Diamond Islets II	228	17.25 S	150.58 E
Diamond Lake	268	42.15 N	88.00 W
Diamond Lake ⊜	256	43.10 N	122.09 W
Diamond Peak ∧, Idaho, U.S.	256	44.09 N	113.05 W
Diamond Peak ∧, Oreg., U.S.	256	43.33 N	122.09 W
Diamond Peak ∧, Wash., U.S.	256	46.07 N	117.32 W
Diamond Springs	272	38.42 N	120.49 W
Diamondville	254	41.47 N	110.32 W
Diana, Baie C	232	60.50 N	69.50 W
Dianbai (Shuidong)	200	21.33 N	111.16 E
Dianchi ⊜	200	24.50 N	102.42 E
Dianópolis	286	11.38 S	46.50 W
Diavolitsion	172	37.18 N	21.58 E
Diavolo, Mount ∧	200	12.40 N	92.55 E
Dibaya	218	6.30 S	22.57 E
Dibble Iceberg Tongue ⊓	148	65.40 S	135.10 E
D'Iberville	248	30.26 N	88.54 W
D'Iberville, Lac ⊜	232	55.55 N	73.15 W
Diboll	248	31.11 N	94.47 W
Dibrugarh	206	27.29 N	94.55 E
Dibs, Bi'r ⊤[4]	220	22.12 N	29.32 E
Dickens	250	33.37 N	100.50 W
Dickerson	262	39.13 N	77.25 W
Dickinson, N. Dak., U.S.	252	46.53 N	102.47 W
Dickinson, Pa., U.S.	262	40.07 N	77.20 W
Dickinson, Tex., U.S.	250	29.28 N	95.03 W
Dickson	248	36.05 N	87.23 W
Diculom	202	7.54 N	122.14 E
Didbiran	186	51.58 N	139.20 E
Didcot	174	51.37 N	1.15 W
Didim (Didyma) ⊥	212	37.22 N	27.19 E
Didsbury	238	51.40 N	114.08 W
Die	166	44.45 N	5.22 E
Die Berg ∧	224	25.12 S	30.09 E
Dieburg	164	49.54 N	8.50 E
Dieciocho de Julio	294	33.41 S	53.33 W
Dieciocho de Marzo	278	25.38 N	97.50 W
Diego de Almagro, Isla I	288	51.25 S	75.10 W
Diego de Ocampo, Pico ∧	282	19.36 N	70.45 W
Diégo-Suarez	225b	12.16 S	49.17 E
Diégo-Suarez □[4]	225b	13.30 S	49.10 E
Diemen	178	52.20 N	4.58 E
Dien-bien-phu	198	21.23 N	103.01 E
Diepholz	178	52.35 N	8.21 E
Dieppe, N.B., Can.	240	46.06 N	64.45 W
Dieppe, Fr.	176	49.56 N	1.05 E
Dieren	178	52.03 N	6.06 E
Dierks	248	34.07 N	94.01 W
Diest	164	50.59 N	5.03 E
Dietikon	180	47.24 N	8.24 E
Dietrich	256	42.55 N	114.16 W
Dieu, Mui ≻	200	12.53 N	109.28 E
Dieulefit	166	44.31 N	5.04 E
Dieuze	166	48.49 N	6.43 E
Dif	214	1.00 N	41.00 E
Differdange	164	49.32 N	5.52 E
Diffun	202	16.34 N	121.33 E
Digboi	206	27.23 N	95.38 E
Digby	240	44.37 N	65.46 W
Digby Neck ≻[1]	240	44.30 N	66.10 W
Digges Islands II	232	62.35 N	77.50 W
Dighton, Kans., U.S.	252	38.29 N	100.28 W
Dighton, Mass., U.S.	261	41.49 N	71.07 W
Di Giorgio	274	35.15 N	118.51 W
Digne	182	44.06 N	6.14 E
Digoin	166	46.29 N	3.59 E
Digos	202	6.45 N	125.23 E
Dijag	160	65.48 N	57.39 E
Dijohan Point ≻	202	16.18 N	122.14 E
Dijon	180	47.19 N	5.01 E
Dike	244	42.28 N	92.38 W
Dikhil	214	11.06 N	42.22 E
Dikili	172	39.04 N	26.53 E
Dikomu Di Kai ∧	224	24.58 S	24.31 E
Diksmuide (Dixmude)	166	51.02 N	2.52 E
Dikson	186	73.30 N	80.35 E
Dikwa	214	12.02 N	13.56 E
Dilbeek	176	50.51 N	4.16 E
Dile Point ≻	202	17.34 N	120.20 E
Dili	198	8.33 S	125.35 E
Diligent Strait ⋓	200	12.10 N	92.55 E
Dill City	250	35.17 N	99.08 W
Dillenburg	164	50.44 N	8.17 E
Diller	252	40.07 N	96.56 W
Dilley, Oreg., U.S.	270	45.29 N	123.07 W
Dilley, Tex., U.S.	250	28.40 N	99.10 W
Dilling	220	12.03 N	29.39 E
Dillingen an der Donau	180	48.34 N	10.29 E
Dillingham	236	59.02 N	158.29 W
Dillon, Colo., U.S.	254	39.37 N	106.04 W
Dillon, Mont., U.S.	256	45.13 N	112.38 W
Dillon, S.C., U.S.	246	34.25 N	79.22 W
Dillon Cone ∧	230	42.16 S	173.13 E
Dillon Reservoir ⊜[1], Colo., U.S.	254	39.35 N	106.02 W
Dillon Reservoir ⊜[1], Ohio, U.S.	242	40.02 N	82.10 W
Dillonvale	266	40.12 N	80.47 W
Dillsburg	262	40.07 N	77.02 W
Dilltown	266	40.29 N	79.00 W
Dillwyn	246	37.32 N	78.27 W
Dilolo	218	10.42 S	22.20 E
Dilworth	252	46.53 N	96.42 W
Dimasalang	202	12.12 N	123.51 E
Dimashq (Damascus)	210	33.30 N	36.18 E
Dimashq □[8]	212	34.00 N	36.45 E
Dimasse, Ras ≻	170	35.37 N	11.03 E
Dimataling	202	7.32 N	123.22 E
Dimbokro	222	6.39 N	4.42 W
Dimbokro □[5]	222	6.45 N	4.15 W
Dîmbovița ≃	172	44.14 N	26.27 E
Dime Box	250	30.21 N	96.50 W
Dimetoka	172	40.16 N	27.17 E
Dimitrovgrad, Blg.	172	42.03 N	25.36 E
Dimitrovgrad, Jugo.	172	43.01 N	22.47 E
Dimlang ∧	214	8.24 N	11.47 E
Dimmitt	250	34.33 N	102.19 W
Dimona	210	31.03 N	35.01 E
Dimondale	268	42.39 N	84.39 W
Dinagat	202	9.57 N	125.35 E
Dinagat Island I	202	10.10 N	125.35 E
Dinagat Sound ⋓	202	10.05 N	125.50 E
Dinahican Point ≻	202	14.42 N	121.45 E
Dinājpur	206	25.38 N	88.38 E
Dinalupihan	202	14.52 N	120.28 E
Dinamita	250	25.43 N	103.38 W
Dinan	166	48.27 N	2.02 W
Dinant	164	50.16 N	4.55 E
Dinara ⋀	170	43.50 N	16.35 E
Dinard	166	48.38 N	2.04 W
Dinaric Alps → Dinara ⋀	170	43.50 N	16.35 E
Dinas	202	7.37 N	123.20 E
Dindar, Nahr ad- (Dinder) ≃	220	14.06 N	33.40 E
Dindar National Park ♠	220	12.40 N	35.20 E
Dinder (Nahr ad-Dindar) ≃	220	14.06 N	33.40 E
Dingalan Bay C	202	15.15 N	121.25 E
Dingan	200	19.44 N	110.21 E
Dingelstädt	178	51.18 N	10.19 E
Dingle	162	52.08 N	10.15 W
Dingle Bay C	162	52.05 N	10.15 W
Dingnanshui ≃	196	24.28 N	115.26 E
Dingolfing	164	48.38 N	12.31 E
Dingqing	190	31.32 N	95.27 E
Dingras	202	18.06 N	120.42 E
Dingri	190	28.35 N	86.38 E
Dingshan	196	31.17 N	119.50 E
Dinguiraye □[4]	222	11.30 N	10.55 W
Dingwall, N.S., Can.	240	46.54 N	60.28 W
Dingwall, Scot., U.K.	162	57.35 N	4.29 W
Dingxi	190	35.38 N	104.29 E
Dingxian	194	38.32 N	114.59 E
Dingzigang C	194	36.37 N	120.50 E
Dinh, Mui ≻	200	11.22 N	109.01 E
Dinh-lap	200	21.33 N	107.06 E
Dinkelsbühl	164	49.04 N	10.19 E
Dinklage	178	52.40 N	8.07 E
Dinnebito Wash ∨	254	35.29 N	111.14 W
Dinosaur National Monument ♠	254	40.32 N	108.58 W
Dinslaken	178	51.34 N	6.44 E
Dinsmore	246	30.26 N	81.46 W
Dinuba	272	36.32 N	119.23 W
Dinwiddie	262	37.05 N	77.35 W
Dinwiddie □[6]	262	37.10 N	77.20 W
Diois □[9]	182	44.40 N	5.20 E
Diomede	236	65.47 N	169.00 W
Dion ≃	222	10.12 N	8.39 W
Dionísio	296	19.49 S	42.45 W
Dionísio Cerqueira	294	26.15 S	53.38 W
Dionne, Lac ⊜	240	49.36 N	67.53 W
Diorama	296	16.21 S	51.14 W
Diourbel	222	14.40 N	16.15 W
Diourbel □[4]	222	15.30 N	15.30 W
Dipaculao	202	15.51 N	121.32 E
Dipolog	202	8.36 N	123.20 E
Dippoldiswalde	164	50.54 N	13.40 E
Dīr	204	35.12 N	71.53 E
Dirah, Djebel ∧	168	36.05 N	3.38 E
Dire Dawa	214	9.37 N	41.52 E
Diriamba	280	11.53 N	86.15 W
Dirico	218	17.58 S	20.47 E
Diriomo	280	11.52 N	86.03 W
Dirranbandi	226	28.35 S	148.14 E
Dirty Devil ≃	254	37.53 N	110.24 W
Disappointment, Cape ≻, Falk. Is.	288	54.53 S	36.07 W
Disappointment, Cape ≻, Wash., U.S.	256	46.18 N	124.03 W
Disaster Bay C	228	37.17 S	150.00 E
Disco, Ind., U.S.	268	41.00 N	85.57 W
Disco, Mich., U.S.	266	42.41 N	83.02 W
Discovery Bay C, Austl.	228	38.12 S	141.07 E
Discovery Bay C, Jam.	285q	18.25 N	77.25 W
Discovery Passage ⋓	238	50.00 N	125.15 W
Discovery Tablemount ⊹[3]	148	42.00 S	0.05 E
Disentis	166	46.43 N	8.51 E
Dishman	256	47.39 N	117.17 W
Dishnā	220	26.07 N	32.28 E
Dishna ≃	236	63.37 N	157.18 W
Disko I	232	69.50 N	53.30 W
Disko Bugt C	232	69.15 N	52.00 W
Dismal ≃	252	41.50 N	100.05 W
Dismal Lakes ⊜	232	67.26 N	117.07 W
Dismal Swamp ☷	246	36.40 N	76.27 W
Disna	160	55.33 N	28.10 E
Disney	250	36.29 N	95.01 W
Disputanta	262	37.08 N	77.14 W
Disraëli	260	45.54 N	71.21 W
Diss	162	42.23 N	1.06 E
Dissimieux, Lac ⊜	240	49.51 N	69.48 W
Distant	266	40.59 N	79.22 W
Disteghil Sar ∧	206	36.22 N	75.12 E

Symbols in the index entries are identified on page 360.

Name	Page	Lat°′	Long°′
District of Columbia □[3]	234	38.54 N	77.01 W
Distrito Federal □[5], Bra.	296	15.45 S	47.45 W
Distrito Federal □[5], Ven.	290	10.30 N	66.55 W
Disūq	220	31.08 N	30.39 E
Dithmarschen ◂[1]	164	54.10 N	9.15 E
Dit Island I	202	11.15 N	120.56 E
Diuata Mountains ⋀	202	9.10 N	125.47 E
Diuata Point ›	202	9.05 N	125.12 E
Divalá	280	8.22 N	82.42 W
Divernon	248	39.34 N	89.39 W
Dives ≃	162	49.19 N	0.05 W
Dividing Creek	262	39.16 N	75.06 W
Divilican Bay C	202	17.23 N	122.20 E
Divino	296	20.37 S	42.09 W
Divino de Virginópolis	296	18.48 S	42.38 W
Divinópolis	296	20.09 S	44.54 W
Divion	176	50.28 N	2.30 E
Divisões, Serra das ⋀[2]	296	17.00 S	51.00 W
Divisor, Serra do(Cordillera Ultraoriental) ⋀[1]	292	8.20 S	73.30 W
Divnoje	158	45.55 N	43.22 E
Divo □[5]	222	5.40 N	5.30 W
Divôr ≃	168	38.59 N	8.29 W
Dix	252	41.14 N	103.29 W
Dix ≃	246	37.49 N	84.43 W
Dixfield	242	44.32 N	70.27 W
Dix Hills	261	40.49 N	73.22 W
Dixie	248	31.08 N	86.44 W
Dixie Valley V	258	39.50 N	117.55 W
Dix-Milles, Lac ⊜	244	46.47 N	77.45 W
Dixon, Calif., U.S.	272	38.27 N	121.49 W
Dixon, Ill., U.S.	244	41.50 N	89.29 W
Dixon, Ky., U.S.	248	37.31 N	87.41 W
Dixon, Mo., U.S.	248	37.60 N	92.06 W
Dixon, N. Mex., U.S.	254	36.12 N	105.53 W
Dixon, Ohio, U.S.	268	40.57 N	84.48 W
Dixon Entrance ⊔	236	54.25 N	132.30 W
Dixons Mills	248	32.04 N	87.47 W
Dixonville	266	40.43 N	79.01 W
Dixville	260	45.04 N	71.46 W
Diyālā □[4]	208	34.00 N	45.00 E
Diyālā ≃	208	33.14 N	44.31 E
Diyarbakır	212	37.55 N	40.14 E
Dja ≃	214	2.02 N	15.12 E
Djabung, Tandjung ›	200	1.01 S	104.22 E
Djailolo	198	1.05 N	127.30 E
Djaja, Puntjak Λ	198	4.05 S	137.11 E
Djajapura	198	2.32 S	140.42 E
Djakarta	198	6.10 S	106.48 E
Djambala	218	2.33 S	14.45 E
Djambi → Telanaipura	198	1.36 S	103.37 E
Djambi □[4]	200	1.30 S	103.00 E
Djamboaje ≃	200	5.16 N	97.29 E
Djanet	214	24.28 N	9.36 E
Djawa I	198	7.30 S	110.00 E
Djawa, Laut (Java Sea) ▾[2]	198	5.00 S	110.00 E
Djedi, Oued V	214	34.28 N	6.05 E
Djelfa	214	34.30 N	3.20 E
Djemadja, Pulau I	200	2.55 N	105.45 E
Djember	226	8.10 S	113.42 E
Djemila ⊥	168	36.25 N	5.44 E
Djénné	214	13.54 N	4.33 W
Djerba, Île de I	214	33.48 N	10.54 E
Djerem ≃	214	5.20 N	13.24 E
Djibouti	214	11.36 N	43.09 E
Djidjelli	168	36.52 N	5.50 E
Djombang	198	7.33 S	112.14 E
Djouab	168	36.08 N	3.25 E
Djougou	214	9.42 N	1.40 E
Djúpivogur	160a	64.40 N	14.10 W
Djurås	160	60.33 N	15.08 E
Dmitrija Lapteva, Proliv ⊔	186	73.00 N	142.00 E
Dmitrov	160	56.21 N	37.31 E
Dnepr ≃	158	46.30 N	32.18 E
Dneprodzeržinsk	158	48.30 N	34.37 E
Dnepropetrovsk	158	48.27 N	34.59 E
Dneprovskoje	160	55.40 N	33.55 E
Dnestr ≃	158	46.18 N	30.17 E
Dnestrovskij Liman ⊜	172	46.15 N	30.17 E
Dnieper → Dnepr ≃	000	46.30 N	32.18 E
Dniester → Dnestr ≃	158	46.18 N	30.17 E
Dno	160	57.50 N	29.59 E
Do, Lac ⊜	222	15.54 N	2.45 W
Doaktown	240	46.33 N	66.08 W
Doany	218	14.22 S	49.31 E
Doba	214	8.39 N	16.51 E
Dobbiaco (Toblach)	170	46.44 N	12.14 E
Dobbie, Mount Λ	228	23.19 S	137.39 E
Dobbins	272	39.22 N	121.12 W
Dobbs Ferry	261	41.01 N	73.52 W
Dobbyn	226	19.48 S	140.00 E
Dobczyce	164	49.54 N	20.06 E
Döbeln	164	51.07 N	13.07 E
Doberai, Djazirah ›[1]	198	1.30 S	132.30 E
Dobiegniew (Woldenburg)	164	52.59 N	15.47 E
Dobo	198	5.46 S	134.13 E
Doboj	172	44.44 N	18.06 E
Dobra (Daber), Pol.	164	53.35 N	15.18 E
Dobra, Pol.	164	51.54 N	18.37 E
Dobra ≃	170	45.33 N	15.31 E
Dobr'anka	158	52.04 N	31.11 E
Dobre Miasto (Guttstadt)	164	53.59 N	20.25 E
Dobříš	164	49.47 N	14.11 E
Dobrodzień (Guttentag)	164	50.44 N	18.27 E
Dobromil'	164	49.34 N	22.47 E
Dobroteasa	172	44.47 N	24.23 E
Dobrudžansko plato ⋀[1]	172	43.32 N	27.50 E
Dobruška	164	50.17 N	16.10 E
Dobrzany (Jakobshagen)	164	53.22 N	15.25 E
Dobrzyń nad Wisłą	164	52.38 N	19.20 E
Dobšiná	164	48.49 N	20.23 E
Dobson	246	36.24 N	80.43 W
Doce ≃, Bra.	296	19.37 S	39.49 W
Doce ≃, Bra.	296	18.28 S	51.05 W
Doce de Octubre	250	25.38 N	97.47 W
Doce Leguas, Cayos de las II	284p	20.55 N	79.05 W
Dockton	270	47.22 N	122.28 W
Doctor Arroyo	278	23.40 N	100.11 W
Doctor Coss	250	25.55 N	99.11 W
Doctor González	278	25.52 N	99.57 W
Doddridge	248	33.06 N	93.54 W
Doddsville	248	33.39 N	90.31 W
Dodecanese → Dhodhekánisos II	172	36.30 N	27.00 E
Dodge	252	41.43 N	96.52 W
Dodge □[6]	268	43.14 N	88.40 W
Dodge Center	244	44.02 N	92.51 W
Dodge City	252	37.45 N	100.01 W
Dodgeville	244	42.58 N	90.08 W
Dodman Point ›	162	50.13 N	4.48 W
Dodola	214	7.02 N	39.07 E
Dodoma	218	6.11 S	35.45 E
Dodson, La., U.S.	248	32.05 N	92.39 W
Dodson, Mont., U.S.	256	48.24 N	108.15 W
Dodson, Tex., U.S.	250	34.46 N	100.02 W
Dodurga	172	39.48 N	29.55 E
Doe River	238	56.00 N	120.05 W
Doerun	246	31.19 N	83.55 W
Doesburg	178	52.01 N	6.09 E
Doetinchem	178	51.58 N	6.17 E
Dog ≃	244	48.51 N	89.37 W
Doğanbey, Tür.	172	37.37 N	27.11 E
Doğanbey, Tür.	172	38.04 N	26.53 E
Dog Creek	238	51.35 N	122.15 W
Dog Lake ⊜, Ont., Can.	244	48.46 N	89.32 W
Dog Lake ⊜, Ont., Can.	244	48.18 N	84.10 W
Dōgo II	192	36.15 N	133.16 E
Dogondoutchi	214	13.38 N	4.02 E
Doha → Ad-Dawḥah	208	25.17 N	51.32 E
Dohinog ≃	202	8.31 N	123.10 E
Doiran, Lake ⊜	172	41.13 N	22.44 E
Dois de Novembro, Cachoeira L	292	8.52 S	62.16 W
Dokka	160	60.50 N	10.05 E
Dokkum	178	53.19 N	6.00 E
Doksy	164	50.35 N	14.38 E
Dolak, Pulau I	198	7.50 S	138.30 E
Doland	252	44.54 N	98.06 W
Dolbeau	232	48.53 N	72.14 W
Dol-de-Bretagne	166	48.33 N	1.45 W
Dole	180	47.06 N	5.30 E
Dolega	280	8.33 N	82.26 W
Dolenjsko ◂[1]	170	45.55 N	15.10 E
Dolgellau	162	52.44 N	3.53 W
Dolgeville	242	43.06 N	74.46 W
Dolgij, Ostrov I	160	69.15 N	59.04 E
Dolgoi Island I	236	55.10 N	161.45 W
Dolgoščelje	160	66.03 N	43.24 E
Dolianova	170	39.23 N	9.11 E
Dolinsk	186	47.21 N	142.48 E
Dolisie	218	4.12 S	12.41 E
Dollard (Dollart) C	178	53.17 N	7.10 E
Dollard-des-Ormeaux	260	45.30 N	73.49 W
Dollarhide	250	32.09 N	103.03 W
Dolni Dâbnik	172	43.24 N	24.26 E
Dolni Lom	172	43.31 N	22.47 E
Dolný Kubín	164	49.12 N	19.17 E
Dolo	214	4.13 N	42.08 E
Dolomites → Dolomiti ⋀	170	46.25 N	11.50 E
Dolomiti ⋀	170	46.25 N	11.50 E
Dolores, Arg.	294	36.19 S	57.40 W
Dolores, Col.	290	3.33 N	74.54 W
Dolores, Esp.	168	38.08 N	0.46 W
Dolores, Guat.	278	16.31 N	89.25 W
Dolores, Méx.	250	26.20 N	101.29 W
Dolores, Méx.	278	28.53 N	108.27 W
Dolores, Colo., U.S.	254	37.28 N	108.30 W
Dolores, Ur.	294	33.33 S	58.13 W
Dolores, Ven.	290	8.18 N	69.34 W
Dolores ≃, Pil.	202	12.01 N	125.29 E
Dolores ≃, U.S.	254	38.49 N	109.17 W
Dolores Hidalgo	278	21.10 N	100.56 W
Dolphin and Union Strait ⊔	232	69.05 N	114.45 W
Dolphin Head Λ	285q	18.22 N	78.10 W
Dolsk	164	52.00 N	17.03 E
Dolton	268	41.39 N	87.37 W
Domažlice	164	49.27 N	12.56 E
Dombarovskij	158	50.46 N	59.32 E
Dombås	160	62.05 N	9.08 E
Dombasle-sur-Meurthe	180	48.38 N	6.21 E
Dombes ◂[1]	166	46.00 N	5.03 E
Dombóvár	164	46.23 N	18.08 E
Dombrád	164	48.14 N	21.56 E
Dom Cavati	296	19.23 S	42.06 W
Dome Creek	238	53.44 N	121.01 W
Dome of the Rock, The (Mosque of Omar) ℣[1]	210	31.47 N	35.13 E
Dome Peak Λ	202	5.37 N	125.20 E
Domeyko	294	28.57 S	70.54 W
Domeyko, Cordillera ⋀	294	24.30 S	69.00 W
Domfront	166	48.36 N	0.39 W
Domiciano Ribeiro	296	16.56 S	47.46 W
Domingos Martins	296	20.22 S	40.40 W
Dominica □[2]	276	15.30 N	61.20 W
Dominica Channel ⊔	282	15.10 N	61.15 W
Dominical	280	9.13 N	83.51 W
Dominical, Punta ›	280	9.13 N	83.50 W
Dominican Republic □[1]	276	19.00 N	70.40 W
Dominion	240	46.13 N	60.01 W
Dominion, Cape ›	232	66.13 N	74.28 W
Dominion City	252	49.08 N	97.09 W
Dom Joaquim	296	18.57 S	43.16 W
Domnești	172	44.25 N	25.27 E
Dom Noi ≃	200	15.18 N	105.30 E
Domo	214	7.54 N	46.52 E
Domodedovo	158	55.26 N	37.46 E
Domodossola	170	46.07 N	8.17 E
Dom Pedrito	294	30.59 S	54.40 W
Dompierre-sur-Besbre	166	46.31 N	3.41 E
Dom Silvério	296	20.09 S	42.58 W
Domuyo, Volcán Λ[1]	294	36.37 S	70.28 W
Dom Yai ≃	200	15.19 N	105.10 E
Domžale	170	46.08 N	14.36 E
Don ≃, S.S.S.R.	186	47.04 N	39.18 E
Don ≃, Scot., U.K.	162	57.10 N	2.04 W
Dona Ana	254	32.23 N	106.49 W
Donadeu	294	26.44 S	62.43 W
Donaghadee	162	54.39 N	5.33 W
Donalda	238	52.35 N	112.34 W
Donaldson, Ark., U.S.	248	34.14 N	92.55 W
Donaldson, Ind., U.S.	268	41.22 N	86.27 W
Donaldson, Pa., U.S.	262	40.38 N	76.24 W
Donaldsonville	248	30.06 N	90.59 W
Donalsonville	246	31.03 N	84.53 W
Donaueschingen	180	47.57 N	8.29 E
Donauwörth	164	48.43 N	10.46 E
Don Benito	168	38.57 N	5.52 W
Doncaster, Ont., Can.	264	43.48 N	79.25 W
Doncaster, Eng., U.K.	162	53.32 N	1.07 W
Dondo, Ang.	218	9.38 S	14.25 E
Dondo, Moç.	218	19.36 S	34.44 E
Dondra Head ›	204	5.55 N	80.35 E
Done ≃	200	15.07 N	105.47 E
Doneck	158	48.00 N	37.48 E
Donegal, Eire	162	54.39 N	8.07 W
Donegal, Pa., U.S.	266	40.07 N	79.23 W
Donegal □[6]	162	54.50 N	8.00 W
Donegal Bay C	162	54.30 N	8.30 W
Donelson	248	36.10 N	86.40 W
Donetsk → Doneck	158	48.00 N	37.48 E
Donga ≃	222	8.19 N	9.58 E
Dongan	200	26.17 N	111.07 E
Dongao I	196	22.01 N	113.43 E
Dongara	226	29.15 S	114.56 E
Dongchuan	200	26.10 N	103.01 E
Dongen	178	51.37 N	4.56 E
Dongfang (Basuo)	200	19.05 N	108.39 E
Dongfeng	194	42.40 N	125.28 E
Donggala	198	0.40 S	119.44 E
Donggongshan ⋀	196	27.36 N	119.26 E
Dongguan	196	23.03 N	113.46 E
Dongguayu I	196	27.38 N	121.07 E
Donghai (Haizhou)	194	34.34 N	119.11 E
Donghaidao I	200	21.02 N	110.25 E
Dong-hoi	200	17.29 N	106.36 E
Donghu ⊜	206	32.10 N	84.40 E
Dongjiadao I	196	25.19 N	119.46 E
Dongjiang ≃	196	23.06 N	114.00 E
Dongjidao I	196	28.43 N	121.55 E
Dongjinghe ≃	196	30.31 N	112.50 E
Dong-nai ≃	200	10.45 N	106.48 E
Dongola → Dunqulah	220	19.10 N	30.29 E
Dongon Point ›	202	12.43 N	120.47 E
Dongpinghu ⊜	194	36.00 N	116.12 E
Dongqi ≃	196	25.00 N	118.27 E
Dongshan	196	23.46 N	117.31 E
Dongshaqundao I	190	20.42 N	116.43 E
Dongtai	196	32.51 N	120.20 E
Dongtinghu ⊜	196	29.20 N	112.54 E
Dongtoushan I	196	27.50 N	121.08 E
Dongwenhe ≃	194	35.28 N	118.32 E
Dongxi ≃, Zhg.	196	27.02 N	118.18 E
Dongxi ≃, Zhg.	196	24.36 N	117.37 E
Dongxiangdao I	196	25.36 N	119.48 E
Dongyang	190	29.16 N	120.14 E
Donie	250	31.29 N	96.13 W
Doniphan, Mo., U.S.	248	36.37 N	90.50 W
Doniphan, Nebr., U.S.	252	40.46 N	98.22 W
Don Islands II	202	11.03 N	123.38 E
Donja Stubica	170	45.59 N	15.58 E
Donjek ≃	236	62.35 N	140.00 W
Donji Vakuf	170	44.09 N	17.25 E
Don Martín	250	27.32 N	100.37 W
Don Matías	290	6.30 N	75.22 W
Donnacona	260	46.40 N	71.47 W
Donnelly, Alta., Can.	238	55.44 N	117.06 W
Donnelly, Alaska, U.S.	236	63.41 N	145.53 W
Donnelly, Idaho, U.S.	256	44.44 N	116.05 W
Donner	248	29.42 N	90.58 W
Donner Pass)(	258	39.19 N	120.20 W
Donner und Blitzen ≃	256	43.17 N	118.49 W
Donora	266	40.11 N	79.52 W
Donovan	268	40.53 N	87.37 W
Don Peninsula ›[1]	238	52.30 N	128.10 W
Donsol	202	12.54 N	123.35 E
Donzdorf	180	48.41 N	9.48 E
Doon, Ont., Can.	264	43.23 N	80.26 W
Doon, Iowa, U.S.	252	43.17 N	96.14 W
Doonerak, Mount Λ	236	67.56 N	150.37 W
Doorn	178	52.03 N	5.21 E
Door Peninsula ›[1]	244	44.55 N	87.20 W
Dora	248	33.44 N	87.05 W
Dorado	284m	18.28 N	66.15 W
Doraville	246	33.54 N	84.17 W
Dorchester, N.B., Can.	240	45.54 N	64.31 W
Dorchester, Ont., Can.	264	42.59 N	81.04 W
Dorchester, Eng., U.K.	174	50.43 N	2.26 W
Dorchester, Nebr., U.S.	252	40.39 N	97.07 W
Dorchester, N.J., U.S.	262	39.17 N	74.58 W
Dorchester, Wis., U.S.	244	45.00 N	90.20 W
Dorchester □[6]	262	38.34 N	76.04 W
Dorchester, Cape ›	232	65.29 N	77.30 W
Dorchester Crossing	240	46.10 N	64.34 W
Dordogne □[5]	166	45.10 N	0.45 E
Dordogne ≃	166	45.02 N	0.35 W
Dordrecht	178	51.49 N	4.40 E
Dore, Monts ⋀	166	45.30 N	2.45 E
Doré Lake ⊜	232	54.46 N	107.17 W
Dorena	256	43.47 N	122.55 W
Dorena Reservoir ⊜[1]	256	43.46 N	122.55 W
Dores do Indaiá	296	19.27 S	45.36 W
Dorfen	164	48.17 N	12.08 E
Dorgali	170	40.17 N	9.35 E
Dori	214	14.02 N	0.02 W
Dorion-Vaudreuil	260	45.23 N	74.01 W
Dorking	174	51.14 N	0.20 W
Dormagen	178	51.05 N	6.50 E
Dormans	166	49.04 N	3.38 E
Dormont	266	40.24 N	80.03 W
Dornbirn	180	47.25 N	9.44 E
Dornoch	162	57.52 N	4.02 W
Dornoch Firth C[2]	162	57.52 N	4.02 W
Dornsife	262	40.45 N	76.47 W
Dorog	164	47.43 N	18.44 E
Dorogobuž	160	54.55 N	33.18 E
Dorohoi	172	47.57 N	26.24 E
Dorotea	160	64.16 N	16.24 E
Dorothy	262	39.24 N	74.49 W
Dorr	268	42.43 N	85.43 W
Dorrance	252	38.51 N	98.35 W
Dorris	258	41.58 N	121.55 W
Dorset	266	41.41 N	80.40 W
Dorset □[6]	174	50.47 N	2.20 W
Dorset Peak Λ	242	43.19 N	73.02 W
Dorsten	178	51.39 N	6.58 E
Dortmund	178	51.31 N	7.28 E
Dortmund-Ems-Kanal ≅	164	51.32 N	7.27 E
Dorton	246	37.17 N	82.35 W
Doruma	214	4.44 N	27.42 E
Dorval	260	45.26 N	73.44 W
Dosatuj	186	50.23 N	118.38 E
Dos Bahías, Cabo ›	288	44.55 S	65.32 W
Dos Bocas	284m	18.20 N	66.40 W
Dos Hermanas	168	37.17 N	5.55 W
Dos Palos	272	36.59 N	120.37 W
Dos Reyes, Punta ›	294	24.33 S	70.35 W
Dosso	222	13.03 N	3.12 E
Dosso □[5]	222	13.00 N	3.00 E
Dossor	158	47.32 N	53.01 E
Doster	268	42.27 N	85.33 W
Doswell	262	37.52 N	77.27 W
Dothan	248	31.13 N	85.24 W
Doting Cove	240	49.27 N	53.57 W
Dot Klish Wash V	254	36.09 N	111.00 W
Dot Lake	236	63.40 N	194.04 W
Dotnuva	160	55.21 N	23.54 E
Doty	270	46.38 N	123.17 W
Douai	176	50.22 N	3.04 E
Douala	222	4.03 N	9.42 E
Douarnenez	166	48.06 N	4.20 W
Double, Lac ⊜	240	50.46 N	70.14 W
Double Cone Λ	230	45.04 S	168.48 E
Double Island Point ›	228	25.56 S	153.11 E
Double Point ›	228	17.39 S	146.09 E
Double Springs	248	34.09 N	87.24 W
Doubletop Peak Λ	254	43.21 N	110.17 W
Doubs □[5]	180	47.10 N	6.25 E
Doubs ≃	166	46.54 N	5.02 E
Doubtful Sound ⊔	230	45.16 S	166.51 E
Doubtless Bay C	230	34.55 S	173.27 E
Douchy-les-Mines	176	50.18 N	3.23 E
Doudeville	166	49.43 N	0.48 E
Doué ≃[1]	222	16.38 N	15.02 W
Douentza	214	15.00 N	2.57 W
Dougga ⊥	170	36.25 N	9.13 E
Doughboy Bay C	230	47.02 S	167.40 E
Douglas, Ont., Can.	264	45.31 N	76.56 W
Douglas, I. of Man	162	54.09 N	4.28 W
Douglas, Alaska, U.S.	236	58.16 N	134.22 W
Douglas, Ariz., U.S.	254	31.21 N	109.33 W
Douglas, Ga., U.S.	246	31.31 N	82.51 W
Douglas, Mich., U.S.	268	42.38 N	86.12 W
Douglas, N. Dak., U.S.	252	47.51 N	101.30 W
Douglas, Wyo., U.S.	254	42.45 N	105.24 W
Douglas □[6]	272	38.55 N	119.39 W
Douglas, Cape ›	236	58.52 N	153.18 W
Douglas, Mount Λ	236	58.52 N	153.31 W
Douglas Channel ⊔	238	53.30 N	129.12 W
Douglas Lake	238	50.10 N	120.12 W
Douglas Lake ⊜[1]	246	36.00 N	83.22 W
Douglas Lake Indian Reserve ◂[4]	238	50.10 N	120.49 W
Douglass, Kans., U.S.	252	37.31 N	97.01 W
Douglass, Tex., U.S.	248	31.40 N	94.53 W
Douglas Station	252	49.53 N	99.46 W
Douglassville	262	40.15 N	75.44 W
Douglasville	246	33.45 N	84.45 W
Douhe ≃	194	39.13 N	118.03 E
Doulaincourt	166	48.19 N	5.12 E
Doulevant-le-Château	166	48.23 N	4.55 E
Doullens	176	50.09 N	2.21 E
Dour	176	50.24 N	3.47 E
Dourada, Serra ⋀[1]	296	13.10 S	48.45 W
Dourado ≃	296	21.22 S	49.41 W
Dourados	296	22.13 S	54.48 W
Dourados ≃	296	21.58 S	54.18 W
Dourados, Serra dos ⋀[1]	296	23.30 S	53.30 W
Dourdan	166	48.32 N	2.01 E
Dourdou ≃	166	44.00 N	2.41 E
Douro (Duero) ≃	168	41.08 N	8.40 W
Douro Litoral □[9]	168	41.05 N	8.20 W
Dousman	268	43.01 N	88.28 W
Douvres	166	49.17 N	0.23 W
Douze ≃	166	43.54 N	0.30 W
Dove Creek	254	37.46 N	108.54 W
Dover, Eng., U.K.	174	51.08 N	1.19 E
Dover, Ark., U.S.	248	35.24 N	93.07 W
Dover, Del., U.S.	262	39.10 N	75.32 W
Dover, Idaho, U.S.	256	48.15 N	116.36 W
Dover, N.H., U.S.	242	43.12 N	70.56 W
Dover, N.J., U.S.	242	40.53 N	74.34 W
Dover, N.C., U.S.	246	35.13 N	77.26 W
Dover, Ohio, U.S.	266	40.32 N	81.29 W
Dover, Okla., U.S.	250	35.59 N	97.55 W
Dover, Pa., U.S.	262	40.00 N	76.51 W
Dover, Tenn., U.S.	248	36.29 N	87.50 W
Dover, Strait of(Pas de Calais) ⊔	162	51.00 N	1.30 E
Dover Air Force Base ■	242	39.08 N	75.28 W
Dover-Foxcroft	242	45.11 N	69.13 W
Dover Plains	261	41.44 N	73.35 W
Dowagiac	268	41.59 N	86.06 W
Dow City	252	41.56 N	95.30 W
Dowell	262	38.21 N	76.27 W
Dowling Lake ⊜	238	51.44 N	112.00 W
Down □[6]	162	54.24 N	5.55 W
Downers Grove	268	41.48 N	88.01 W
Downey, Calif., U.S.	274	33.56 N	118.08 W
Downey, Idaho, U.S.	256	42.26 N	112.07 W
Downham Market	162	52.36 N	0.23 E
Downieville	272	39.34 N	120.50 W
Downing	248	40.29 N	92.22 W
Downingtown	262	40.00 N	75.42 W
Downpatrick	162	54.20 N	5.43 W
Downpatrick Head ›	162	54.20 N	9.20 W
Downs, Ill., U.S.	268	40.24 N	88.52 W
Downs, Kans., U.S.	252	39.30 N	98.33 W
Downs Mountain Λ	254	43.18 N	109.40 W
Downsville	242	42.05 N	75.00 W
Downton, Mount Λ	238	52.42 N	124.51 W
Downton Lake ⊜	238	50.51 N	123.00 W
Dow Rūd	208	33.28 N	49.04 E
Dows	244	42.39 N	93.30 W
Doyles	240	47.47 N	59.10 W
Doylesburg	266	40.13 N	77.42 W
Doylestown, Ohio, U.S.	266	40.58 N	81.42 W
Doylestown, Pa., U.S.	262	40.19 N	75.08 W
Doyline	248	32.32 N	93.25 W
Dozier	248	31.30 N	86.28 W
Dozois, Réservoir ⊜[1]	244	47.30 N	77.00 W
Drâa, Oued V	214	28.43 N	11.09 W
Dracena	296	21.32 S	51.29 W
Drachten	178	53.06 N	6.05 E
Dračie Jaskyně •[5]	164	49.05 N	19.35 E
Dracut	261	42.40 N	71.18 W
Dra el Mizan	168	36.32 N	3.50 E
Dragalina	172	44.26 N	27.20 E
Drăgănești-Olt	172	44.10 N	24.32 E
Drăgănești-Vlașca	172	44.06 N	25.36 E
Drăgășani	172	44.40 N	24.16 E
Dragerton	254	39.33 N	110.25 W
Drag Lake ⊜	244	45.05 N	78.24 W
Dragonera I	168	39.35 N	2.19 E
Dragons Mouth ⊔	285r	10.45 N	61.46 W
Dragoon	254	32.02 N	110.02 W
Draguignan	182	43.32 N	6.28 E
Drain	256	43.40 N	123.19 W
Drake	252	47.55 N	100.23 W
Drakensberg ⋀	224	27.00 S	30.00 E
Drake Passage ⊔	148	58.00 S	70.00 W
Drake Peak Λ	256	42.19 N	120.07 W
Drakesboro	248	37.13 N	87.03 W
Drakes Branch	246	37.00 N	78.36 W
Dráma	172	41.09 N	24.08 E
Drammen	160	59.44 N	10.15 E
Drancy	176	48.56 N	2.27 E
Drang ≃	200	13.19 N	107.21 E
Drangajökull ⊠	160a	66.11 N	22.15 W
Dranov, Ostrovul I	172	44.52 N	29.15 E
Draper, N.C., U.S.	246	36.31 N	79.41 W
Draper, Utah, U.S.	254	40.32 N	111.52 W
Drau (Drava) (Dráva) ≃	170	45.33 N	18.55 E
Drava (Drau) (Dráva) ≃	170	45.33 N	18.55 E
Draveil	176	48.41 N	2.25 E
Dravinja ≃	170	46.22 N	15.57 E
Dravograd	170	46.35 N	15.02 E
Drawa ≃	164	52.52 N	15.59 E
Drawno (Neuwedell)	164	53.13 N	15.45 E
Drawsko Pomorskie (Dramburg)	164	53.32 N	15.48 E
Drayton, Ont., Can.	264	43.46 N	80.40 W
Drayton, N. Dak., U.S.	252	48.38 N	97.11 W
Drayton, S.C., U.S.	246	34.58 N	81.54 W
Drayton Plains	268	42.41 N	83.23 W
Drayton Valley	238	53.13 N	114.59 W
Dréan	170	36.41 N	7.46 E
Drenovec	172	43.42 N	22.59 E
Drenthe □[4]	178	52.45 N	6.30 E
Dresden, Ont., Can.	266	42.35 N	82.11 W
Dresden, D.D.R.	164	51.03 N	13.44 E
Dresden, N.Y., U.S.	264	42.41 N	76.58 W
Dresden, Ohio, U.S.	266	40.07 N	82.01 W
Dresden, Tenn., U.S.	248	36.18 N	88.42 W
Dreux	176	48.44 N	1.22 E
Drew	248	33.49 N	90.32 W
Drewryville	262	36.43 N	77.18 W
Drews Reservoir ⊜[1]	256	42.10 N	120.40 W
Drezdenko (Driesen)	164	52.51 N	15.50 E
Driebergen	178	52.03 N	5.16 E
Drienov	164	48.53 N	21.17 E
Driffield	162	54.00 N	0.27 E
Driftpile ≃	238	55.23 N	115.40 W
Drift Pile River Indian Reserve ◂[4]	238	55.18 N	115.45 W
Driftwood	266	41.20 N	78.08 W
Driftwood ≃, B.C., Can.	238	55.43 N	126.15 W
Driftwood ≃, Ind., U.S.	248	39.12 N	85.56 W
Driggs	256	43.44 N	111.14 W
Drin ≃	172	41.17 N	20.02 E
Drina ≃	172	44.53 N	19.21 E
Drinit, Pellg i C	172	41.45 N	19.28 E
Driscoll	250	27.40 N	97.45 W
Driskill Mountain Λ[2]	248	32.25 N	92.54 W
Driver	262	36.49 N	76.30 W
Drjanovo	172	42.58 N	25.27 E
Drniš	170	43.51 N	16.09 E
Drochtersen	178	53.42 N	9.23 E
Drogheda	162	53.43 N	6.21 W
Drogobyč	158	49.21 N	23.30 E
Drohiczyn	164	52.24 N	22.41 E
Droichead Nua	162	53.11 N	6.48 W
Droitwich	174	52.16 N	2.09 W
Drôme □[5]	182	44.35 N	5.10 E
Dronero	170	44.28 N	7.22 E
Drongen	176	51.03 N	3.40 E
Dronne ≃	166	45.02 N	0.09 W
Droué	166	48.02 N	1.05 E
Drožžanoje	160	54.44 N	47.34 E
Dr. Petru Groza	172	46.32 N	22.28 E
Drum, Mount Λ	236	62.07 N	144.35 W
Drumbo	264	43.14 N	80.33 W
Drumheller	238	51.28 N	112.42 W
Drummond, Mont., U.S.	256	46.40 N	113.09 W
Drummond, Wis., U.S.	244	46.20 N	91.15 W
Drummond □[6]	260	45.50 N	72.20 W
Drummond, Mount Λ	228	18.47 S	137.30 E
Drummond Island I	244	46.00 N	83.40 W
Drummond Range ⋀	228	23.30 S	147.15 E
Drummondville	260	45.53 N	72.30 W
Drumright	250	35.59 N	96.36 W
Drunen	178	51.42 N	5.08 E
Druskininkai	164	54.01 N	23.58 E
Družba	186	45.15 N	82.26 E
Družina	186	68.14 N	145.18 E
Drvar	170	44.22 N	16.24 E
Drwęca ≃	164	53.00 N	18.42 E
Dry Bay C	236	59.08 N	138.25 W
Dry Cimarron ≃	250	36.54 N	102.59 W
Dry Creek Mountain Λ	258	41.22 N	116.22 W
Dryden, Ont., Can.	232	49.47 N	92.50 W
Dryden, N.Y., U.S.	242	42.29 N	76.18 W
Dryden, Tex., U.S.	250	30.03 N	102.07 W
Dryden, Wash., U.S.	270	47.33 N	120.34 W
Dry Devils ≃	250	29.47 N	100.59 W
Dry Frio ≃	250	29.17 N	99.39 W
Dry Lake ⊜	252	48.15 N	98.58 W
Dry Prong	248	31.35 N	92.32 W
Dry Ridge	242	38.41 N	84.35 W
Dry Run	266	40.10 N	77.45 W
Dry Tortugas II	246	24.38 N	82.55 W
Drzewica	164	51.27 N	20.28 E
Dschang	214	5.27 N	10.04 E
Duan	200	24.06 N	108.10 E
Duarte	274	34.08 N	117.58 W
Duarte, Pico Λ	282	19.00 N	71.00 W
Duartina	296	22.24 S	49.25 W
Dubach	248	32.42 N	92.39 W
Dubawnt ≃	232	64.33 N	100.06 W
Dubawnt Lake ⊜	232	63.08 N	101.30 W
Dubayy	208	25.18 N	55.18 E
Dubbo	228	32.15 S	148.36 E
Dübendorf	180	47.25 N	8.38 E
Duberger	260	46.54 N	71.20 W
Dubh Artach ✧[2]	162	56.08 N	6.42 W
Dubica	170	45.11 N	16.48 E
Dublin, Ont., Can.	264	43.31 N	81.17 W
Dublin (Baile Átha Cliath), Eire	162	53.20 N	6.15 W
Dublin, Calif., U.S.	272	37.42 N	121.56 W
Dublin, Ga., U.S.	246	32.32 N	82.54 W
Dublin, Md., U.S.	262	39.39 N	76.15 W
Dublin, Ohio, U.S.	266	40.06 N	83.07 W
Dublin, Pa., U.S.	262	40.22 N	75.12 W
Dublin, Tex., U.S.	250	32.05 N	98.21 W
Dublin, Va., U.S.	246	37.06 N	80.41 W
Dublin □[6]	162	53.20 N	6.15 W
Dubna	160	56.44 N	37.10 E
Dubňany	164	48.55 N	17.06 E
Dubnica	164	48.58 N	18.09 E
Dubois, Idaho, U.S.	256	44.10 N	112.14 W
Dubois, Ind., U.S.	248	38.27 N	86.48 W
Du Bois, Nebr., U.S.	252	40.02 N	96.04 W
Du Bois, Pa., U.S.	266	41.07 N	78.46 W
Dubois, Wyo., U.S.	254	43.33 N	109.38 W
Dubovka	158	49.03 N	44.50 E
Dubréka	214	9.48 N	13.31 W
Dubreka □[4]	222	10.00 N	13.40 W
Dubrovnik	172	42.38 N	18.07 E
Dubuque	244	42.30 N	90.41 W
Dubuque Hills ⋀[2]	244	42.15 N	90.00 W
Duchcov	164	50.37 N	13.45 E
Duchesne	254	40.10 N	110.24 W
Duchesne ≃	254	40.05 N	109.41 W
Duchess	226	21.22 S	139.52 E
Duchovščina	160	55.12 N	32.25 E
Duck ≃	248	36.02 N	87.52 W
Duck Hill	248	33.38 N	89.43 W
Duck Lake	268	42.24 N	84.47 W
Ducktown	246	35.03 N	84.23 W
Duck Valley Indian Reservation ◂[4]	258	42.00 N	116.10 W
Duclair	166	49.29 N	0.53 E
Ducos	284e	14.34 N	60.58 W
Du Couedic, Cape ›	228	36.04 S	136.42 E
Duda ≃	290	2.33 N	74.02 W
Dudelange	164	49.28 N	6.05 E
Duderstadt	178	51.31 N	10.16 E
Dudinka	186	69.25 N	86.15 E
Dudley, Eng., U.K.	174	52.30 N	2.05 W
Dudley, Mass., U.S.	261	42.03 N	71.56 W
Dudley, Pa., U.S.	266	40.12 N	78.10 W
Dudweiler	164	49.17 N	7.02 E
Duerna ≃	168	42.19 N	5.54 W
Duero (Douro) ≃	168	41.08 N	8.40 W
Due West	246	34.20 N	82.23 W
Dufault, Lac ⊜	244	48.18 N	79.00 W
Duffel	176	51.06 N	4.31 E
Dufferin □[6]	264	44.05 N	80.15 W
Duffer Peak Λ	258	41.40 N	118.44 W
Dufourspitze Λ	170	45.55 N	7.52 E
Dufur	270	45.27 N	121.08 W
Duga Resa	170	45.27 N	15.30 E
Dugdemona ≃	248	31.47 N	92.22 W
Dugger	248	39.04 N	87.16 W
Dugi Otok I	170	44.00 N	15.04 E
Du Gué ≃	232	57.25 N	70.45 W
Duida, Cerro Λ	290	3.25 N	65.40 W
Duisburg	178	51.25 N	6.46 E
Duitama	290	5.50 N	73.02 W
Dujiadao I	194	36.44 N	121.27 E
Duke	250	34.40 N	99.34 W
Duke Island I	236	54.56 N	131.20 W
Duke Islands II	228	21.58 S	150.09 E
Duke of York Bay C	232	65.25 N	84.50 W
Dukes □[6]	261	41.23 N	70.31 W
Duk Fadiat	214	7.45 N	31.25 E
Dukhān	208	25.25 N	50.48 E
Dukla	164	49.34 N	21.41 E
Dulag	202	10.57 N	125.02 E
Dulan	190	36.16 N	98.28 E
Dulayb, Khawr V	220	11.45 N	32.47 E
Dulce	254	36.56 N	107.00 W
Dulce ≃	294	30.32 S	62.33 W
Dulce, Golfo C	280	8.36 N	83.15 W
Dulce Nombre de Culmí	280	15.09 N	85.37 W
Dul'durga	186	50.41 N	113.36 E
Dulgalach ≃	186	67.44 N	133.12 E
Duljo Point ›	202	9.35 N	123.43 E
Dülken	178	51.15 N	6.20 E
Dülmen	178	51.51 N	7.16 E
Dulovo	172	43.49 N	27.09 E
Duluquin Point ›	202	7.44 N	122.05 E
Duluth, Ga., U.S.	246	34.00 N	84.09 W
Duluth, Minn., U.S.	244	46.47 N	92.06 W
Dūmā	210	33.35 N	36.24 E
Dumaguete	202	9.18 N	123.18 E
Dumalag	202	11.18 N	122.37 E
Dumalinao	202	7.49 N	123.23 E
Dumali Point ›	202	13.08 N	121.33 E
Dumanjug	202	10.04 N	123.26 E
Dumanquilas Bay C	202	7.37 N	123.05 E
Dumaran Channel ⊔	202	10.32 N	119.43 E
Dumaran Island I	202	10.33 N	119.50 E
Dumaresq ≃	228	28.40 S	150.28 E
Dumaring	198	1.36 N	118.12 E
Dumas, Ark., U.S.	248	33.53 N	91.29 W
Dumas, Tex., U.S.	250	35.52 N	101.58 W
Dumbarton	162	55.57 N	4.35 W
Dumbier Λ	164	48.57 N	19.37 E
Dumbrăveni	172	46.14 N	24.35 E
Dumfries, Scot., U.K.	162	55.04 N	3.37 W
Dumfries, Va., U.S.	262	38.34 N	77.20 W
Dumfries □[6]	162	55.12 N	3.30 W
Dumlupınar	172	38.52 N	30.00 E
Dumoine ≃	244	46.13 N	77.50 W
Dumoine, Lac ⊜	244	46.52 N	77.52 W
Dumont, Iowa, U.S.	244	42.45 N	92.58 W
Dumont, Tex., U.S.	250	33.49 N	100.31 W
Dumont, Lac ⊜	244	46.04 N	76.28 W
Dumyāṭ	220	31.25 N	31.48 E
Dumyāṭ, Maṣabb ≃[1]	220	31.32 N	31.51 E
Dunaföldvár	164	46.48 N	18.55 E
Dunaharaszti	164	47.21 N	19.25 E
Dunaj, Ostrova II	186	73.52 N	124.29 E
Dunajec ≃	164	50.15 N	20.44 E
Dunajská Streda	164	48.01 N	17.35 E
Dunakeszi	164	47.38 N	19.08 E
Dunărea Veche ≃	172	45.17 N	28.02 E
Dunas	294	31.45 S	52.17 W
Dunaújváros	164	46.58 N	18.57 E
Dunavățu	172	44.59 N	29.13 E
Duna-völgyi-főcsatorna ≅	164	46.12 N	18.56 E
Dunbar	242	38.22 N	81.45 W
Dunbarton □[6]	162	56.04 N	4.42 W
Dunblane	162	56.12 N	3.59 W
Duncan, B.C., Can.	238	48.47 N	123.42 W
Duncan, Ariz., U.S.	254	32.43 N	109.06 W
Duncan, Miss., U.S.	248	34.03 N	90.45 W
Duncan, Okla., U.S.	250	34.30 N	97.57 W
Duncan ≃	238	50.11 N	116.57 W
Duncan Lake ⊜	238	50.20 N	117.00 W
Duncannon	262	40.23 N	77.02 W
Duncan Passage ⊔	200	11.05 N	92.45 E
Duncans	285q	18.28 N	77.32 W
Duncansby Head ›	162	58.39 N	3.01 W
Duncansville	266	40.25 N	78.26 W
Dundaga	160	57.31 N	22.21 E
Dundalk, Ont., Can.	264	44.10 N	80.24 W
Dundalk, Eire	162	54.01 N	6.25 W
Dundalk, Md., U.S.	262	39.15 N	76.31 W
Dundalk Bay C	162	53.57 N	6.17 W
Dundas, Ont., Can.	264	43.16 N	79.58 W
Dundas, Minn., U.S.	244	44.26 N	93.12 W
Dundas □[6]	264	45.00 N	75.20 W
Dundas Island I	238	54.33 N	130.55 W
Dundas Peninsula ›[1]	232	74.50 N	111.30 W
Dundee, S. Afr.	224	28.12 S	30.16 E
Dundee, Scot., U.K.	162	56.28 N	3.00 W
Dundee, Fla., U.S.	246	28.07 N	81.37 W
Dundee, Ill., U.S.	268	42.06 N	88.17 W
Dundee, Mich., U.S.	268	41.57 N	83.40 W
Dundee, Miss., U.S.	248	34.32 N	90.27 W
Dundee, N.Y., U.S.	242	42.31 N	76.59 W
Dundee, Ohio, U.S.	266	40.35 N	81.37 W
Dundee, Oreg., U.S.	270	45.17 N	123.01 W
Dundrum Bay C	162	54.13 N	5.45 W
Dunedin, N.Z.	230	45.53 S	170.30 E
Dunedin, Fla., U.S.	246	28.00 N	82.47 W
Dunfermline	162	56.04 N	3.29 W
Dung ≃	200	11.12 N	107.15 E
Du Ngae, Khao Λ	200	15.13 N	98.44 E
Dungannon, N. Ire., U.K.	162	54.31 N	6.46 W
Dungannon, Va., U.S.	246	36.50 N	82.28 W
Dungarvan	162	52.05 N	7.37 W
Dungarvan Harbour C	162	52.10 N	7.35 W
Dungeness ›	162	50.55 N	0.58 E
Dunham	260	45.08 N	72.48 W
Dunhe ≃	196	30.27 N	114.11 E
Dunhua	190	43.21 N	128.13 E
Dunhuang	190	40.12 N	94.41 E
Dunkerque	176	51.03 N	2.22 E
Dunkirk, Ind., U.S.	268	40.23 N	85.13 W
Dunkirk, N.Y., U.S.	266	42.29 N	79.20 W
Dunkirk, Ohio, U.S.	268	40.48 N	83.39 W
Dunkwa	222	5.58 N	1.46 W
Dún Laoghaire	162	53.17 N	6.08 W
Dunlap, Ind., U.S.	268	41.36 N	85.50 W
Dunlap, Iowa, U.S.	252	41.51 N	95.36 W
Dunlap, Tenn., U.S.	248	35.23 N	85.23 W
Dunlap Acres	274	34.03 N	117.06 W
Dun-le-Palestel	166	46.17 N	1.48 E
Dunlo	266	40.18 N	78.43 W
Dunmore	242	41.25 N	75.38 W
Dunmore Town	282	25.30 N	76.39 W
Dunn	246	35.19 N	78.37 W
Dunnellon	246	29.03 N	82.28 W
Dunnet Head ›	162	58.39 N	3.23 W
Dunnigan	272	38.53 N	121.58 W
Dunning	252	41.50 N	100.06 W
Dunns Bridge	268	41.13 N	86.59 W
Dunnville	264	42.54 N	79.36 W
Dunoon	162	55.57 N	4.56 W
Dunqul ▾[4]	220	23.26 N	31.37 E
Dunqulah	220	19.10 N	30.29 E
Dunqunāb, Khalīj C	220	21.05 N	37.08 E
Dunrea	252	49.25 N	99.44 W
Duns	162	55.47 N	2.20 W
Dunseith	252	48.50 N	100.02 W
Dunsmuir	258	41.13 N	122.16 W
Dunstable, Eng., U.K.	174	51.53 N	0.32 W
Dunstable, Mass., U.S.	261	42.40 N	71.29 W
Dunstan Mountains ⋀	230	44.55 S	169.30 E
Dunster	238	53.08 N	119.50 W
Dun-sur-Auron	166	46.53 N	2.34 E
Dun-sur-Meuse	166	49.23 N	5.11 E
Dunville	240	47.16 N	53.54 W
Duobe ≃	222	5.45 N	8.00 W
Duolun	190	33.25 N	93.54 E
Duomaer	190	34.15 N	79.45 E
Duomula	190	34.07 N	82.30 E
Du Page □[6]	268	41.52 N	88.06 W
Du Page ≃	244	41.25 N	88.14 W
Dupangling ⋀	200	25.32 N	111.11 E
Duparquet, Lac ⊜	244	48.28 N	79.15 W
Dupax	202	16.17 N	121.05 E
Dupont, Ohio, U.S.	268	41.03 N	84.18 W
Dupont, S.C., U.S.	246	32.47 N	80.03 W
Du Pont, Wash., U.S.	270	47.06 N	122.38 W
Dupree	252	45.03 N	101.36 W
Dupuyer	238	48.11 N	112.30 W
Duque de Caxias	296	22.47 S	43.18 W
Duque de York, Isla I	288	50.37 S	75.25 W
Duquesne	266	40.21 N	79.51 W
DuQuoin	248	38.01 N	89.14 W
Durack Range ⋀	226	17.00 S	128.00 E
Durak	172	39.42 N	28.17 E
Duran	254	34.28 N	105.24 W
Durance ≃	166	44.35 N	5.10 E
Durand, Ill., U.S.	244	42.26 N	89.20 W
Durand, Mich., U.S.	268	42.55 N	83.59 W
Durand, Wis., U.S.	244	44.38 N	91.58 W
Durango, Esp.	168	43.10 N	2.37 W
Durango, Méx.	278	24.02 N	104.40 W
Durango, Colo., U.S.	254	37.16 N	107.53 W
Durant, Iowa, U.S.	244	41.36 N	90.54 W
Durant, Miss., U.S.	248	33.04 N	89.51 W
Durant, Okla., U.S.	250	33.60 N	96.23 W
Duras	166	44.41 N	0.11 E
Duraton ≃	168	41.37 N	4.07 W
Durazno	294	33.22 S	56.31 W
Durazzo → Durrës	172	41.19 N	19.26 E
Durban	224	29.55 S	30.56 E
Durbe	160	56.35 N	21.21 E
Durbin	242	38.33 N	79.50 W
Đurđevac	170	46.03 N	17.04 E
Düren	164	50.48 N	6.28 E
Durg	206	21.11 N	81.17 E
Durham, Ont., Can.	264	44.10 N	80.49 W
Durham, Eng., U.K.	162	54.47 N	1.34 W
Durham, Calif., U.S.	258	39.44 N	121.48 W
Durham, Conn., U.S.	261	41.29 N	72.41 W
Durham, N.H., U.S.	242	43.08 N	70.56 W
Durham, N.C., U.S.	246	35.59 N	78.54 W
Durham, Oreg., U.S.	270	45.25 N	122.46 W
Durham □[6], Ont., Can.	264	44.05 N	78.35 W
Durham □[6], Eng., U.K.	162	54.45 N	1.45 W
Durhamville	264	43.07 N	75.40 W
Durmitor ⋀	172	43.08 N	19.01 E
Durness	162	58.33 N	4.45 W
Dürnkrut	164	48.28 N	16.51 E
Durón	168	40.38 N	2.43 W
Durrell	240	49.42 N	54.44 W
Durrës	172	41.19 N	19.26 E
Dursey Head ›	162	51.35 N	10.14 W
Dursley	174	51.42 N	2.21 W
Dursunbey	172	39.35 N	28.38 E
D'Urville Island I	230	40.50 S	173.50 E
Dušanbe	186	38.35 N	68.48 E
Dušekan	186	60.39 N	109.03 E
Dushan	200	25.53 N	107.30 E
Dushanhu ⊜	194	35.06 N	116.52 E
Dushanzi	190	44.20 N	84.51 E
Dushore	242	41.31 N	76.24 W
Dusky Sound ⊔	230	45.47 S	166.29 E
Duson	248	30.12 N	92.11 W
Düsseldorf	178	51.12 N	6.47 E
Düsseldorf □[5]	178	51.15 N	7.00 E
Dutaliutexingsishan ⋀	206	34.15 N	87.00 E
Dutchess □[6]	261	41.42 N	73.56 W
Dutch Harbor	236	53.53 N	166.32 W
Dutch John	254	40.55 N	109.24 W
Dutchman Draw V	254	37.00 N	113.29 W
Dutovo	160	63.47 N	56.35 E
Dutton, Ont., Can.	266	42.39 N	81.30 W
Dutton, Mich., U.S.	268	42.50 N	85.35 W
Dutton, Mont., U.S.	256	47.51 N	111.43 W
Dutton ≃	228	20:45 S	143.12 E
Dutton, Mount Λ, Alaska, U.S.	236	55.10 N	162.15 W
Dutton, Mount Λ, Utah, U.S.	254	38.01 N	112.13 W
Duval, Lac ⊜	242	46.19 N	76.55 W
Duvall	270	47.44 N	121.59 W
Duvno	170	43.43 N	17.14 E
Duwamish	270	47.32 N	122.19 W
Duxbury	261	42.02 N	70.40 W
Duyagan Point ›	202	12.36 N	121.34 E
Duyun	200	26.12 N	107.31 E
Duzce	212	40.50 N	31.10 E
Dve Mogili	172	43.36 N	25.52 E
Dvinsk → Daugavpils	160	55.53 N	26.32 E
Dvinskaja Guba C	160	65.00 N	39.45 E
Dvoriši	160	58.12 N	35.13 E
Dvugorbaja, Gora Λ	236	68.30 N	179.20 E
Dvůr Králové nad Labem	164	50.26 N	15.48 E
Dwight	268	41.05 N	88.26 W
Dyer, Ind., U.S.	268	41.30 N	87.31 W

Symbols in the index entries are identified on page 360.

Name	Page	Lat°′	Long°′
Dyer, Tenn., U.S.	248	36.04 N	88.59 W
Dyer, Cape ≻	232	66.37 N	61.18 W
Dyer Bay C	244	45.10 N	81.18 W
Dyersburg	248	36.03 N	89.23 W
Dyersville	244	42.29 N	91.08 W
Dyje (Thaya) ≃	164	48.37 N	16.56 E
Dynów	164	49.49 N	22.14 E
Dysart, Iowa, U.S.	244	42.10 N	92.18 W
Dysart, Pa., U.S.	266	40.36 N	78.31 W
Džalal-Abad	186	40.56 N	73.00 E
Džalinda	186	53.29 N	123.54 E
Džambejty	158	50.16 N	52.35 E
Džambul	186	42.54 N	71.22 E
Džankoj	158	45.43 N	34.24 E
Džanybek	158	49.25 N	46.51 E
Dzaoudzi	225a	12.47 S	45.17 E
Džardžan	186	68.43 N	124.02 E
Dzaudzhikau → Ordžonikidze	158	43.03 N	44.40 E
Dzavchan ≃	190	48.54 N	93.23 E
Dželinda	186	70.08 N	114.00 E
Dzemul	278	21.12 N	89.18 W
Dženretlen, Mys ≻	236	67.07 N	173.45 W
Dzeržinsk	160	56.15 N	43.24 E
Dzeržinskoje	186	45.50 N	81.07 E
Džetygara	158	52.11 N	61.12 E
Džezkazgan	186	47.47 N	67.46 E
Działdowo	164	53.15 N	20.10 E
Działoszyce	164	50.22 N	20.21 E
Dzibalchén	278	19.31 N	89.45 W
Dzibilchaltun ⊥	278	21.05 N	89.36 W
Dzierzgoń (Christburg)	164	53.56 N	19.21 E
Dzierżoniów (Reichenbach)	164	50.44 N	16.39 E
Dzilam González	278	21.17 N	88.56 W
Dzitás	278	20.51 N	88.31 W
Dzitbalché	278	20.19 N	90.03 W
Dziwnów (Dievenow)	164	54.03 N	14.45 E
Džizak	186	40.06 N	67.50 E
Džugdžur, Chrebet ⛰	186	58.00 N	136.00 E
Džul'fa	158	38.58 N	45.38 E
Dzungarian Basin → Zhuangaerpendi ⌣[1]	190	45.00 N	88.00 E
Džungarskij Alatau, Chrebet ⛰	186	45.00 N	80.00 E
Džusaly	186	45.28 N	64.05 E
Dzüüncharaa	190	48.52 N	106.28 E
Dzuunmod	190	47.45 N	106.58 E
E			
Eads	252	38.29 N	102.47 W
Eagar	254	34.06 N	109.11 W
Eagle, Alaska, U.S.	236	64.46 N	141.16 W
Eagle, Colo., U.S.	254	39.39 N	106.50 W
Eagle, N.Y., U.S.	266	42.33 N	78.18 W
Eagle, Wis., U.S.	268	42.53 N	88.28 W
Eagle ≃, Newf., Can.	232	53.35 N	57.25 W
Eagle ≃, Yukon, Can.	236	67.20 N	137.10 W
Eagle ≃, Colo., U.S.	254	39.39 N	107.04 W
Eagle Bay	238	50.56 N	119.12 W
Eagle Bend	252	44.10 N	93.53 W
Eagle Butte	252	45.00 N	101.14 W
Eagle Creek	270	45.21 N	122.21 W
Eagledale	270	47.37 N	122.32 W
Eagle Grove	244	42.40 N	93.54 W
Eagle Harbor	264	43.15 N	78.15 W
Eagle Lake, Maine, U.S.	240	47.02 N	68.36 W
Eagle Lake, Mich., U.S.	268	41.48 N	86.02 W
Eagle Lake, Tex., U.S.	250	29.35 N	96.20 W
Eagle Lake ⊜, B.C., Can.	238	51.55 N	124.25 W
Eagle Lake ⊜, Calif., U.S.	258	40.39 N	120.44 W
Eagle Mountain ∧[2]	244	47.54 N	90.33 W
Eagle Nest Butte ∧	252	43.27 N	101.39 W
Eagle Pass	250	28.43 N	100.30 W
Eagle Peak ∧	258	41.17 N	120.12 W
Eagle River, Alaska, U.S.	236	61.19 N	149.34 W
Eagle River, Mich., U.S.	244	47.24 N	88.18 W
Eagle River, Wis., U.S.	244	45.55 N	89.15 W
Eagle Rock, Pa., U.S.	266	41.27 N	79.35 W
Eagle Rock, Va., U.S.	246	37.38 N	79.48 W
Eaglesham	238	55.47 N	117.53 W
Eagle Village	236	64.47 N	141.07 W
Eagleville	261	41.47 N	72.17 W
Ealing ⊸[8]	174	51.31 N	0.20 W
Earle	248	35.16 N	90.28 W
Earlham	248	41.30 N	94.07 W
Earlimart	272	35.53 N	119.16 W
Earlington	248	37.16 N	87.30 W
Earl Park	268	40.42 N	87.25 W
Earlton	261	42.21 N	73.54 W
Earlville, Ill., U.S.	268	41.35 N	88.55 W
Earlville, N.Y., U.S.	264	42.44 N	75.33 W
Earlville, Pa., U.S.	262	40.19 N	75.44 W
Early	252	42.28 N	95.09 W
Earnshaw, Mount ∧	230	44.38 S	168.24 E
Earth	250	34.14 N	102.24 W
Easley	246	34.50 N	82.36 W
East ≃, Colo., U.S.	254	38.40 N	106.51 W
East Alliance	266	40.55 N	81.04 W
East Alton	248	38.53 N	90.06 W
East Amherst	264	43.01 N	78.42 W
East Angus	260	45.29 N	71.40 W
East Aurora	264	42.46 N	78.37 W
East Avon	264	42.55 N	77.42 W
East Bank	248	29.55 N	90.12 W
East Bay C, Fla., U.S.	246	30.05 N	85.32 W
East Bay C, Tex., U.S.	250	29.30 N	94.35 W
East Bend	246	36.13 N	80.31 W
East Berbice □[5]	290	5.00 N	57.58 W
East Berlin, Conn., U.S.	261	41.37 N	72.43 W
East Berlin, Pa., U.S.	262	39.56 N	76.59 W
East Bernard	250	29.32 N	96.04 W
East Bernstadt	246	37.11 N	84.07 W
East Bethany	264	42.56 N	78.06 W
East Blackstone	261	42.02 N	71.31 W
East Bloomfield	264	42.54 N	77.26 W
Eastbourne	174	50.46 N	0.17 E
East Brady	266	40.59 N	79.37 W
East Braintree	252	49.37 N	95.38 W
East Brewster	261	41.46 N	70.04 W
East Brewton	248	31.05 N	87.04 W
East Bridgewater	261	42.02 N	70.58 W
East Brookfield	261	42.14 N	72.03 W
East Brooklyn	261	41.48 N	71.54 W
East Brunswick	262	40.25 N	74.23 W
East Butler	266	40.53 N	79.51 W
East Butte ∧	256	48.52 N	111.09 W
East Caicos I	282	21.40 N	71.32 W
East Canaan	261	42.01 N	73.17 W
East Canton	266	40.47 N	81.17 W
East Cape ≻, N.Z.	230	37.41 S	178.33 E
East Cape ≻, Fla., U.S.	246	25.07 N	81.05 W
East Carlisle	266	41.19 N	82.05 W
East Caroline Basin ✢[1]	148	3.00 N	147.00 E
East-Central □[3]	222	6.00 N	7.30 E
East Channel ≃[1]	236	69.20 N	134.00 W
East Chatham	261	42.25 N	73.32 W
East Chelmsford	261	42.36 N	71.18 W
Eastchester	261	40.57 N	73.49 W
East Chicago	268	41.38 N	87.27 W
East China Sea ▾[2]	190	30.00 N	126.00 E
East Claridon	266	41.32 N	81.07 W
East Cleveland	266	41.32 N	81.35 W
East Coast Bays	230	36.45 S	174.46 E
East Concord	266	42.33 N	78.38 W
East Corinth	242	45.00 N	69.01 W
East Cote Blanche Bay C	248	29.35 N	91.40 W
East Coulée	238	51.20 N	112.19 W
East Crozet Basin ✢[1]	148	40.00 S	60.00 E
East Demerara □[5]	290	6.20 N	58.00 W
East Dennis	261	41.45 N	70.10 W
East Dereham	174	52.41 N	0.56 E
East Detroit	266	42.28 N	82.56 W
East Douglas	261	42.04 N	71.43 W
East Dublin	246	32.32 N	82.52 W
East Dubuque	244	42.30 N	90.39 W
East Dundee	268	42.06 N	88.16 W
East Ely	258	39.15 N	114.53 W
East End	284m	18.21 N	64.40 W
East End Point ≻	246	25.03 N	77.15 W
Easter Island → Pascua, Isla de I	148	27.07 S	109.22 W
Eastern □[4], Ghana	222	6.30 N	0.30 W
Eastern □[4], S.L.	222	8.15 N	11.00 W
Eastern Caprivi Strip □[5]	224	17.45 S	24.00 E
Eastern Channel → Tsushima-kaikyō ⊔	192	34.00 N	129.00 E
Eastern Desert → Aṣ-Ṣaḥrā' ash-Sharqīyah ⊸[2]	220	28.00 N	32.00 E
Eastern Sayans → Vostočnyj Sajan ⛰	186	53.00 N	97.00 E
East Falkland I	288	51.45 S	58.50 W
East Falmouth	261	41.35 N	70.34 W
East Fayetteville	246	35.05 N	78.51 W
East Flat Rock	246	35.17 N	82.32 W
Eastford	261	41.54 N	72.05 W
East Freedom	266	40.21 N	78.26 W
East Freetown	261	41.46 N	70.58 W
East Frisian Islands → Ostfriesische Inseln II	178	53.44 N	7.25 E
East Gaffney	246	35.05 N	81.42 W
East Gary	268	41.34 N	87.15 W
Eastgate	270	47.34 N	122.08 W
East Glacier Park	256	48.27 N	113.13 W
East Grand Forks	252	47.56 N	97.01 W
East Grand Rapids	268	42.56 N	85.35 W
East Greenbush	261	42.35 N	73.42 W
East Greenville, Ohio, U.S.	266	40.48 N	81.36 W
East Greenville, Pa., U.S.	262	40.24 N	75.30 W
East Greenwich	261	41.40 N	71.27 W
East Grinstead	174	51.08 N	0.01 W
East Haddam	261	41.27 N	72.28 W
Eastham	261	41.50 N	69.58 W
East Hampton, Conn., U.S.	261	41.35 N	72.31 W
Easthampton, Mass., U.S.	261	42.16 N	72.40 W
East Hampton, N.Y., U.S.	261	40.58 N	72.11 W
East Hartford	261	41.46 N	72.39 W
East Hartland	261	42.00 N	72.55 W
East Harwich	261	41.43 N	70.02 W
East Haven	261	41.17 N	72.52 W
East Helena	256	46.35 N	111.56 W
East Hickory	266	41.35 N	79.24 W
East-Indian Ridge ✢[3]	148	15.00 S	88.00 E
East Jordan	244	45.10 N	85.07 W
East Kelowna	238	49.51 N	119.25 W
East Kilbride	162	55.46 N	4.10 W
East Kildonan	252	49.55 N	97.05 W
East Killingly	261	41.51 N	71.49 W
East Kingston	261	41.57 N	73.58 W
Eastlake, Mich., U.S.	244	44.15 N	86.18 W
Eastlake, Ohio, U.S.	266	41.34 N	81.35 W
Eastland	250	32.24 N	98.49 W
East Lansing	268	42.44 N	84.29 W
East Laurinburg	246	34.46 N	79.27 W
Eastlawn	268	42.15 N	83.35 W
Eastleigh	174	50.58 N	1.22 W
East Liberty	268	40.20 N	83.35 W
East Liverpool	266	40.38 N	80.35 W
East London (Oos-Londen)	224	33.00 S	27.55 E
East Longmeadow	261	42.04 N	72.31 W
East Los Angeles	274	34.01 N	118.09 W
East Lothian □[6]	162	55.56 N	2.40 W
East Lyme	261	41.22 N	72.13 W
East Lynn	268	40.28 N	87.48 W
East Lynn Reservoir ⊜[1]	242	38.05 N	82.20 W
East Machias	242	44.44 N	67.24 W
Eastmain	232	52.15 N	78.30 W
Eastmain ≃	232	52.20 N	78.30 W
Eastman, Qué., Can.	260	45.18 N	72.19 W
Eastman, Ga., U.S.	246	32.12 N	83.11 W
East Marion	246	35.42 N	81.59 W
East Meadowview	268	41.08 N	87.52 W
East Millbury	261	42.13 N	71.45 W
East Millcreek	254	40.43 N	111.51 W
East Millinocket	242	45.37 N	68.35 W
East Moline	244	41.31 N	90.25 W
East Naples	246	26.08 N	81.46 W
East Nassau	261	42.30 N	73.30 W
East New Market	262	38.36 N	75.56 W
East Nishnabotna ≃	252	40.39 N	95.37 W
East Norriton	262	40.09 N	75.18 W
East Northfield	261	42.43 N	72.27 W
East Northport	261	40.52 N	73.19 W
East Norwich	261	40.50 N	73.32 W
East Novaya Zemlya Trough ✢[1]	148	74.00 N	60.00 E
East Olympia	270	46.58 N	122.50 W
Easton, Calif., U.S.	272	36.39 N	119.47 W
Easton, Conn., U.S.	261	41.15 N	73.18 W
Easton, Md., U.S.	262	38.46 N	76.04 W
Easton, Pa., U.S.	262	40.42 N	75.12 W
Easton, Wash., U.S.	270	47.14 N	121.11 W
East Orange	262	40.46 N	74.13 W
East Orleans	261	41.47 N	69.58 W
East Otto	266	42.23 N	78.45 W
Eastover	246	33.52 N	80.41 W
East Palatka	246	29.40 N	81.35 W
East Palestine	266	40.50 N	80.33 W
East Palo Alto	272	37.27 N	122.07 W
East Peak ∧	202	11.13 N	119.29 E
East Pembroke	264	42.59 N	78.18 W
East Peoria	244	40.40 N	89.34 W
East Pepperell	261	42.40 N	71.34 W
East Petersburg	262	40.06 N	76.21 W
East Pine	238	55.43 N	121.13 W
East Point	246	33.40 N	84.27 W
East Point ≻	240	46.27 N	61.58 W
Eastport, Newf., Can.	240	48.39 N	53.45 W
Eastport, Idaho, U.S.	256	48.59 N	116.11 W
Eastport, Maine, U.S.	242	44.54 N	67.00 W
Eastport, N.Y., U.S.	261	40.49 N	72.44 W
East Prairie	248	36.47 N	89.23 W
East Prospect	262	39.58 N	76.31 W
East Providence	261	41.49 N	71.23 W
East Pryor Mountain ∧	256	45.11 N	108.20 W
East Quogue	261	40.51 N	72.35 W
East Rainelle	242	37.58 N	80.46 W
East Randolph	266	42.10 N	78.57 W
East Retford	162	53.19 N	0.56 W
East Richmond	272	37.57 N	122.19 W
East Rochester, N.Y., U.S.	264	43.07 N	77.29 W
East Rochester, Ohio, U.S.	266	40.45 N	81.02 W
East Rochester, Pa., U.S.	266	40.42 N	80.14 W
East Rockingham	246	34.57 N	79.45 W
East Rockwood	268	42.03 N	83.13 W
East Saint Louis	248	38.38 N	96.08 W
East Salem	262	40.37 N	77.14 W
East Sandwich	261	41.45 N	70.27 W
East Schodack	261	42.34 N	73.38 W
East Scotia Basin ✢[1]	148	57.00 S	35.00 W
East Setauket	261	40.57 N	73.06 W
East Smethport	266	41.49 N	78.26 W
East Somerset	246	37.06 N	84.35 W
East Sooke	270	48.22 N	123.43 W
Eastsound	270	48.42 N	122.55 W
East Sparta	266	40.40 N	81.21 W
East Spencer	246	35.41 N	80.26 W
East Springfield, Ohio, U.S.	266	40.27 N	80.52 W
East Springfield, Pa., U.S.	266	41.57 N	80.28 W
East Stroudsburg	242	41.00 N	75.11 W
East Sullivan	242	44.30 N	68.09 W
East Syracuse	264	43.07 N	76.05 W
East Tawas	244	44.17 N	83.29 W
East Templeton	261	42.34 N	78.02 W
East Thompson	261	42.00 N	71.48 W
East Troy	268	42.47 N	88.24 W
East Tulare	272	36.12 N	119.20 W
Eastvale	266	40.46 N	80.19 W
East Vandergrift	266	40.36 N	79.34 W
Eastview	264	45.26 N	75.40 W
Eastville	262	37.21 N	75.57 W
East Walker ≃	258	38.53 N	119.10 W
East Walpole	261	42.10 N	71.13 W
East Wareham	261	41.46 N	70.40 W
East Washington	266	40.10 N	80.14 W
East Waterford	262	40.22 N	77.36 W
East Wenatchee	256	47.25 N	120.16 W
East Williamson	264	43.14 N	77.09 W
East Wilmington	246	34.13 N	77.53 W
Eastwood, Eng., U.K.	174	53.01 N	1.18 W
Eastwood, Mich., U.S.	268	42.19 N	85.32 W
East York, Ont., Can.	264	43.41 N	79.20 W
East York, Pa., U.S.	262	39.58 N	76.43 W
Eaton, Colo., U.S.	254	40.32 N	104.42 W
Eaton, Ind., U.S.	268	40.21 N	85.21 W
Eaton, N.Y., U.S.	264	42.51 N	75.37 W
Eaton, Ohio, U.S.	248	39.45 N	84.38 W
Eaton Estates	266	41.19 N	81.59 W
Eaton Rapids	268	42.36 N	84.39 W
Eatonton	246	33.20 N	83.23 W
Eatontown	262	40.18 N	74.07 W
Eatonville	270	46.52 N	122.16 W
Eau, Cap de l' ≻	168	35.10 N	2.25 W
Eau Claire, Mich., U.S.	268	41.59 N	86.18 W
Eau Claire, Pa., U.S.	266	41.08 N	79.48 W
Eau Claire, Wis., U.S.	244	44.49 N	91.31 W
Eau Claire ≃, Wis., U.S.	244	44.49 N	91.31 W
Eau Claire ≃, Wis., U.S.	244	44.55 N	89.37 W
Eau-Claire, Lac à l' ⊜	232	56.10 N	74.30 W
Eau Gallie	246	28.08 N	80.38 W
Eauripik I[1]	198	6.42 N	143.03 E
Eauze	166	43.52 N	0.06 E
Ebanito	250	25.55 N	97.35 W
Ebano	278	22.13 N	98.22 W
Ebba Ksour	170	35.57 N	8.50 E
Ebbw Vale	174	51.47 N	3.12 W
Eben Junction	244	46.21 N	86.58 W
Ebenrode → Nesterov	164	54.38 N	22.34 E
Ebensburg	266	40.29 N	78.44 W
Ebensee	164	47.48 N	13.46 E
Eberbach	164	49.28 N	8.59 E
Eber Gölü ⊜	212	38.38 N	31.12 E
Ebermannstadt	164	49.23 N	11.13 E
Ebern	164	50.05 N	10.47 E
Eberndorf	164	46.35 N	14.38 E
Ebersbach	164	51.00 N	14.35 E
Ebersberg	164	48.05 N	11.58 E
Eberstein	164	46.48 N	14.34 E
Eberswalde	164	52.50 N	13.49 E
Ebetsu	192a	43.07 N	141.34 E
Ebingen	180	48.13 N	9.01 E
Ebola ≃	214	3.20 N	20.57 E
Eboli	170	40.37 N	15.04 E
Ebolowa	214	2.54 N	11.09 E
Ébrié, Lagune C	222	5.14 N	4.26 W
Ebro ≃	168	40.43 N	0.54 E
Ebro, Delta del ≚[2]	168	40.43 N	0.54 E
Ebro, Pantano del ⊜[1]	168	43.00 N	3.58 W
Ecaussinnes-d'Enghien	176	50.34 N	4.10 E
Eccles	246	37.47 N	81.16 W
Eceabat	172	40.11 N	26.21 E
Echague	202	16.42 N	121.40 E
Echaporã	296	22.26 S	50.12 W
Echigo-sammyaku ⛰	192	37.50 N	139.50 E
Echo	252	44.37 N	95.25 W
Echt	178	51.06 N	5.52 E
Echterdingen	180	48.41 N	9.10 E
Echuca	228	36.08 S	144.46 E
Écija	168	37.32 N	5.05 W
Eckernförde	164	54.28 N	9.50 E
Eckert	254	38.51 N	107.58 W
Eckville	238	52.21 N	114.22 W
Eclipse	262	36.55 N	76.30 W
Eclipse Sound ⊔	232	72.38 N	79.00 W
Ečmiadzin	158	40.10 N	44.18 E
Écommoy	166	47.50 N	0.16 E
Economy	266	40.39 N	80.14 W
Écorce, Lac de l' ⊜[1]	244	47.05 N	76.25 W
Ecorse	268	42.15 N	83.09 W
Écouen	166	49.01 N	2.23 E
Ecru	248	34.21 N	89.01 W
Ecstall ≃	238	54.09 N	129.56 W
Ecuador □[1]	286	2.00 S	77.30 W
Écueillé	166	47.05 N	1.21 E
Ecum Secum	240	44.58 N	62.08 W
Ed	160	58.55 N	11.55 E
Edam	164	52.31 N	5.03 E
Eday I	162	59.11 N	2.47 W
Eddrachillis Bay C	162	58.19 N	5.15 W
Eddystone	262	39.51 N	75.21 W
Eddystone Point ≻	228	41.00 S	148.21 E
Eddyville, Ill., U.S.	248	37.30 N	88.35 W
Eddyville, Iowa, U.S.	244	41.09 N	92.38 W
Eddyville, Ky., U.S.	248	37.03 N	88.04 W
Ede, Ned.	178	52.03 N	5.40 E
Ede, Nig.	222	7.44 N	4.27 E
Edéa	214	3.48 N	10.08 E
Edegem	178	51.09 N	4.27 E
Edéia	296	17.18 S	49.55 W
Edelény	164	48.18 N	20.49 E
Eden, Austl.	226	37.04 S	149.54 E
Eden, Mich., U.S.	268	42.32 N	84.26 W
Eden, Miss., U.S.	248	32.59 N	90.20 W
Eden, N.Y., U.S.	266	42.39 N	78.54 W
Eden, Tex., U.S.	250	31.13 N	99.51 W
Eden, Wyo., U.S.	254	42.03 N	109.26 W
Eden ≃	162	54.57 N	3.01 W
Edendale	224	29.39 S	30.18 E
Edenderry	162	53.21 N	7.35 W
Eden Mills	264	43.35 N	80.09 W
Edenton	246	36.04 N	76.39 W
Eden Valley	244	45.19 N	94.33 W
Eder ≃	164	51.13 N	9.27 E
Edessa → Édhessa	172	40.48 N	22.03 E
Edewecht	178	53.07 N	8.02 E
Edgar, Nebr., U.S.	252	40.22 N	97.58 W
Edgar, Wis., U.S.	244	44.55 N	90.00 W
Edgard	248	30.03 N	90.34 W
Edgartown	261	41.23 N	70.31 W
Edgefield	246	33.47 N	81.56 W
Edgeley	252	46.22 N	98.43 W
Edgemere	262	39.14 N	76.27 W
Edgemont, Calif., U.S.	274	33.53 N	117.18 W
Edgemont, S. Dak., U.S.	252	43.18 N	103.50 W
Edgemont Park	268	42.44 N	84.36 W
Edge Mountain ∧	236	58.12 N	152.06 W
Edgerton, Ind., U.S.	268	41.05 N	84.49 W
Edgerton, Minn., U.S.	252	43.53 N	96.08 W
Edgerton, Ohio, U.S.	268	41.27 N	84.45 W
Edgerton, Wis., U.S.	268	42.50 N	89.04 W
Edgerton, Wyo., U.S.	254	43.25 N	106.15 W
Edgewater, Ala., U.S.	248	33.32 N	86.57 W
Edgewater, Fla., U.S.	246	29.00 N	80.54 W
Edgewood, B.C., Can.	238	49.47 N	118.08 W
Edgewood, Ill., U.S.	248	38.55 N	88.40 W
Edgewood, Ind., U.S.	248	39.41 N	86.09 W
Edgewood, Iowa, U.S.	244	42.39 N	91.24 W
Edgewood, Md., U.S.	242	39.25 N	76.18 W
Edgewood, Ohio, U.S.	266	41.52 N	80.46 W
Edgewood, Tex., U.S.	250	32.42 N	95.53 W
Edgeworth	266	40.33 N	80.11 W
Édhessa	172	40.48 N	22.03 E
Edina, Minn., U.S.	244	44.55 N	93.20 W
Edina, Mo., U.S.	248	40.10 N	92.11 W
Edinboro	266	41.52 N	80.08 W
Edinburg, Ill., U.S.	248	39.39 N	89.23 W
Edinburg, Ind., U.S.	248	39.21 N	85.58 W
Edinburg, Miss., U.S.	248	32.48 N	89.20 W
Edinburg, N. Dak., U.S.	252	48.30 N	97.52 W
Edinburg, Ohio, U.S.	266	41.06 N	81.09 W
Edinburg, Pa., U.S.	266	41.01 N	80.26 W
Edinburg, Tex., U.S.	250	26.18 N	98.10 W
Edinburg, Va., U.S.	242	38.49 N	78.34 W
Edinburgh	162	55.57 N	3.13 W
Edinburgh Channel ⊔	280	14.42 N	82.40 W
Edincik	172	40.20 N	27.51 E
Edirne	212	41.40 N	26.34 E
Edirne □[4]	172	41.15 N	26.40 E
Edison, Ga., U.S.	246	31.33 N	84.44 W
Edison, N.J., U.S.	262	40.31 N	74.24 W
Edison, Ohio, U.S.	266	40.33 N	82.52 W
Edison, Pa., U.S.	262	40.17 N	75.07 W
Edison Station	270	48.33 N	122.27 W
Edisto ≃	246	32.39 N	80.24 W
Edith, Mount ∧	256	46.26 N	111.11 W
Edjeleh	214	27.38 N	9.50 E
Edmond	250	35.39 N	97.29 W
Edmonds	270	47.48 N	122.22 W
Edmondson Acres	274	35.14 N	118.49 W
Edmonton, Alta., Can.	238	53.33 N	113.28 W
Edmonton, Ky., U.S.	248	36.59 N	85.37 W
Edmore, Mich., U.S.	244	43.25 N	85.03 W
Edmore, N. Dak., U.S.	252	48.25 N	98.27 W
Edmundston	240	47.22 N	68.20 W
Edna, Kans., U.S.	252	37.04 N	95.22 W
Edna, Tex., U.S.	250	28.59 N	96.39 W
Edna Bay	236	55.57 N	133.40 W
Ednor	262	39.09 N	76.59 W
Edolo	170	46.11 N	10.20 E
Edon	268	41.33 N	84.46 W
Edough, Massif de l' ⛰	170	36.55 N	7.35 E
Edremit	212	39.35 N	27.01 E
Edremit Körfezi C	212	39.30 N	26.45 E
Edrengijn Nuruu ⛰	190	44.15 N	97.45 E
Edsbro	160	59.54 N	18.29 E
Edsbruk	160	58.02 N	16.28 E
Edsbyn	160	61.23 N	15.49 E
Edson	238	53.35 N	116.26 W
Edson Butte ∧	256	42.52 N	124.20 W
Eduardo Castex	294	35.55 S	64.20 W
Eduni, Mount ∧	236	64.15 N	128.04 W
Edward, Lake ⊜	218	0.25 S	29.30 E
Edward Island I	244	48.24 N	88.36 W
Edwards, Calif., U.S.	274	34.54 N	117.53 W
Edwards, Miss., U.S.	248	32.20 N	90.36 W
Edwards, N.Y., U.S.	264	44.20 N	75.15 W
Edwards ≃	244	41.09 N	90.59 W
Edwards Air Force Base ■	258	34.54 N	117.52 W
Edwardsburg	268	41.48 N	86.05 W
Edwards Butte ∧	256	45.23 N	123.41 W
Edwards Plateau ⛰[1]	250	31.20 N	101.00 W
Edwardsville	248	38.49 N	89.58 W
Edward VII Peninsula ≻[1]	148	77.40 S	155.00 W
Edziza Peak ∧	236	57.40 N	130.36 W
Eek	236	60.12 N	162.15 W
Eek ≃	236	60.12 N	162.15 W
Eeklo	176	51.11 N	3.34 E
Eel ≃, Calif., U.S.	258	40.40 N	124.20 W
Eel ≃, Ind., U.S.	244	40.45 N	86.22 W
Eel ≃, Ind., U.S.	248	39.07 N	86.57 W
Eergu'nahe (Argun') ≃	186	53.20 N	121.28 E
Eferding	164	48.18 N	14.02 E
Effiakuma	222	5.06 N	1.39 W
Effigy Mounds National Monument ♣	244	43.06 N	91.13 W
Effingham, Ill., U.S.	248	39.07 N	88.33 W
Effingham, Kans., U.S.	252	39.31 N	95.24 W
Eforie	172	44.00 N	28.19 E
Egadi, Isole I	170	37.56 N	12.16 E
Egaña	294	36.57 S	59.06 W
Egan Range ⛰	258	39.00 N	115.00 W
Eganville	244	45.32 N	77.06 W
Egede og Rothes Fjord C[2]	232	66.00 N	38.00 W
Egedesminde	232	68.42 N	52.45 W
Egegik	236	58.13 N	157.22 W
Egelston	268	43.14 N	86.10 W
Eger → Cheb, Česko.	164	50.01 N	12.25 E
Eger, Magy.	164	47.54 N	20.23 E
Egeria Mountain ∧	238	53.55 N	130.22 W
Egersund	160	58.27 N	6.00 E
Eggenburg	164	48.39 N	15.50 E
Eggenfelden	164	48.25 N	12.46 E
Egg Harbor City	262	39.32 N	74.39 W
Egham	174	51.26 N	0.34 W
Egilsstaðir	160a	65.16 N	14.18 W
Égletons	166	45.24 N	2.03 E
Egmont, Cape ≻, N.Z.	230	39.16 S	173.45 E
Egmont, Mount ∧	230	39.18 S	174.03 E
Egmont Bay C	240	46.35 N	64.12 W
Egmont National Park ♣	230	39.15 S	174.05 E
Egremont	238	54.02 N	113.08 W
Eğridir Gölü ⊜	212	38.02 N	30.53 E
Eğriköy	172	38.44 N	27.21 E
Egvekinot	236	66.19 N	179.10 W
Egypt, Mass., U.S.	261	42.13 N	70.46 W
Egypt, Pa., U.S.	262	40.41 N	75.32 W
Egypt □[1]	214	27.00 N	30.00 E
Egypt, Lake of ⊜[1]	248	37.35 N	88.55 W
Eha-Amufu	222	6.40 N	7.46 E
Ehime □[5]	192	33.40 N	132.50 E
Ehingen	180	48.17 N	9.43 E
Ehrenberg	254	33.36 N	114.31 W
Ehrenfeld	266	40.22 N	78.47 W
Ehrhardt	246	33.06 N	81.01 W
Ei	192	31.12 N	130.30 E
Éibar	168	43.11 N	2.28 W
Eibiswald	164	46.41 N	15.15 E
Eichstätt	164	48.54 N	11.12 E
Eidelstedt ⊸[8]	178	53.36 N	9.53 E
Eidenau	266	40.48 N	80.06 W
Eidsvoll	160	60.19 N	11.14 E
Eifel ⛰	164	50.15 N	6.45 E
Eigg I	162	56.54 N	6.10 W
Eights Coast ≗[2]	148	73.30 S	93.00 W
Eightyfour	266	40.11 N	80.08 W
Eil	214	8.00 N	49.51 E
Eildon, Lake ⊜[1]	228	37.11 S	145.55 E
Eileen	268	41.17 N	88.15 W
Eilenburg	164	51.27 N	12.37 E
Eina	160	60.38 N	10.36 E
Einasleigh	226	18.31 S	144.05 E
Einasleigh ≃	228	17.30 S	142.17 E
Einbeck	178	51.49 N	9.52 E
Eindhoven	178	51.26 N	5.28 E
Einsiedeln	166	47.08 N	8.45 E
Eire → Ireland □[1]	158	53.00 N	8.00 W
Eiru ≃	292	6.42 S	69.52 W
Eirunepé	292	6.40 S	69.52 W
Eiseb ≃	224	20.26 S	20.05 E
Eisenach	164	50.59 N	10.19 E
Eisenberg	164	50.58 N	11.53 E
Eisenerz	164	47.33 N	14.53 E
Eisenerzer Alpen ⛰	164	47.28 N	14.45 E
Eisenhower, Mount ∧	238	51.18 N	115.55 W
Eisenhüttenstadt	164	52.10 N	14.39 E
Eisenkappel	172	46.29 N	14.36 E
Eisenstadt	164	47.51 N	16.32 E
Eisfeld	164	50.26 N	10.54 E
Eisleben	164	51.31 N	11.32 E
Eislingen	180	48.42 N	9.42 E
Eitorf	164	50.46 N	7.26 E
Ejea de los Caballeros	168	42.08 N	1.08 W
Ejido	290	8.33 N	71.14 W
Ejigbo	222	7.55 N	4.19 E
Ejinaqi	190	41.50 N	100.50 E
Ejutla de Crespo	278	16.34 N	96.44 W
Ekalaka	252	45.53 N	104.33 W
Ekaterinburg → Sverdlovsk	158	56.51 N	60.36 E
Ekaterinodar → Krasnodar	158	45.02 N	39.00 E
Ekaterinoslav → Dnepropetrovsk	158	48.27 N	34.59 E
Ekenäs (Taamisaari)	160	59.58 N	23.26 E
Ekeren	176	51.17 N	4.25 E
Ekhínos	172	41.17 N	24.59 E
Ekiatap ≃	236	68.46 N	179.00 W
Ekiatapskij Chrebet ⛰	236	69.00 N	177.00 E
Ekibastuz	186	51.42 N	75.22 E
Ekimčan	186	53.04 N	132.58 E
Ekitykskij Chrebet ⛰	236	67.45 N	179.00 E
Ekka Island I	232	66.18 N	122.25 W
Ekonda	186	65.47 N	105.17 E
Eksjö	160	57.40 N	14.57 E
Ekuk	236	58.49 N	158.34 W
Ekwok	236	59.22 N	157.30 W
El- → Ad-, Al-, An-, Ar-, As-, Ash-, At-, Az-			
El Aaiún	214	27.09 N	13.12 W
El Adelanto	280	14.10 N	89.50 W
El Affroun	168	36.30 N	2.38 E
El Aguilar	294	23.15 S	65.40 W
Elaía	172	39.35 N	20.20 E
Elaine	248	34.18 N	90.51 W
El Alamein → Al-'Alamayn	220	30.49 N	28.57 E
El Álamo, Méx.	250	27.32 N	100.52 W
El Alamo, Méx.	250	26.29 N	99.46 W
El Álamo, Méx.	258	31.34 N	116.02 W
El Alia	170	37.10 N	10.03 E
El Alto	290	4.15 S	81.14 W
El Amparo de Apure	290	7.06 N	70.45 W
Elands ≃	224	25.10 S	29.10 E
El Angel	290	0.37 N	77.56 W
Elanul ≃	172	46.07 N	28.04 E
El Aouinet	170	35.52 N	7.54 E
El Arahal	168	37.16 N	5.33 W
El Arba	168	36.37 N	3.13 E
El Arco	278	28.00 N	113.25 W
El Aroussa	170	36.22 N	9.28 E
El Asnam (Orléansville)	168	36.10 N	1.20 E
Elassón	172	39.54 N	22.11 E
Elat	210	29.33 N	34.56 E
Elat, Gulf of → Aqaba, Gulf of C	208	29.00 N	33.40 E
El Avión	278	24.08 N	106.59 W
Elâzığ	212	38.41 N	39.14 E
Elba, Ala., U.S.	248	31.25 N	86.04 W
Elba, N.Y., U.S.	264	43.05 N	78.11 W
Elba, Isola d' I	170	42.46 N	10.17 E
El Banco	290	9.00 N	73.58 W
El Barco de Avila	168	40.21 N	5.31 W
El Barco de Valdeorras	168	42.25 N	6.59 W
El Barreal	254	31.17 N	107.10 W
Elbasan	172	41.06 N	20.05 E
El Baúl	290	8.57 N	68.17 W
El Bayito	250	27.33 N	99.31 W
Elbe	270	46.45 N	121.49 W
Elbe (Labe) ≃	164	53.50 N	9.00 E
Elbe-Havel-Kanal Ξ	164	52.24 N	12.23 E
Elbe-Lübeck-Kanal Ξ	164	53.49 N	10.38 E
El Beni □[5]	292	14.00 S	65.30 W
Elbert	252	39.13 N	104.32 W
Elbert, Mount ∧	254	39.07 N	106.27 W
Elberta, Ala., U.S.	248	30.25 N	87.42 W
Elberta, Mich., U.S.	244	44.37 N	86.14 W
Elberton	246	34.07 N	82.52 W
Elbeuf	176	49.17 N	1.00 E
Elbing → Elbląg	164	54.10 N	19.25 E
Elbląg (Elbing)	164	54.10 N	19.25 E
Elbląski, Kanał Ξ	164	53.43 N	19.53 E
El Bluff	280	11.59 N	83.40 W
El Bonillo	168	38.57 N	2.32 W
El Bordo	290	2.06 N	76.58 W
El-Borj	168	35.43 N	5.40 W
Elbow ≃	238	51.03 N	114.02 W
Elbow Lake	252	45.59 N	95.58 W
Elbridge	264	43.02 N	76.27 W
El'brus, Gora ∧	158	43.21 N	42.26 E
Elbrus, Mount → El'brus, Gora ∧	158	43.21 N	42.26 E
Elbsandsteingebirge ⛰	164	50.55 N	14.10 E
El Burgo de Osma	168	41.35 N	3.04 W
Elburn	268	41.54 N	88.28 W
Elburz Mountains → Alborz, Reshteh-ye Kūhhā-ye ⛰	208	36.00 N	53.00 E
El Caburé	294	26.02 S	62.22 W
El Cajon	274	32.48 N	116.58 W
El Callao	290	7.21 N	61.49 W
El Calvario	290	4.22 N	73.40 W
El Calverio	290	8.59 N	67.00 W
El Camarón	280	12.48 N	85.28 W
El Campamento	284m	18.22 N	66.28 W
El Campo	250	29.12 N	96.16 W
El Capitan ∧	256	46.01 N	114.23 W
El Carmen, Arg.	294	24.24 S	65.15 W
El Carmen, Bol.	292	18.49 S	58.33 W
El Carmen, Col.	290	8.30 N	73.27 W
El Carmen, Nic.	280	11.59 N	86.31 W
El Carmen, Perú	292	13.28 S	76.04 W
El Carmen de Bolívar	290	9.43 N	75.08 W
El Carricito	278	28.24 N	103.23 W
El Carril	294	25.05 S	65.29 W
El Carrizo	278	29.58 N	105.16 W
El Casco	250	25.34 N	104.35 W
El Castillo	280	11.01 N	84.25 W
El Cedral	280	16.26 N	90.03 W
El Cedrito	278	29.11 N	101.59 W
El Centinela	258	32.38 N	115.40 W
El Centro	258	32.48 N	115.34 W
El Cerrito, Col.	290	3.42 N	76.19 W
El Cerrito, Calif., U.S.	272	37.55 N	122.18 W
El Cerro	292	17.31 S	61.34 W
El Cerro del Aripo ∧	285r	10.44 N	61.15 W
El Cesar □[5]	290	9.00 N	73.40 W
El Charco Largo	278	24.10 N	97.58 W
Elche	168	38.15 N	0.42 W
Elche de la Sierra	168	38.27 N	2.03 W
El Chimborazo, Cerro ∧	280	13.05 N	85.58 W
Elcho	244	45.26 N	89.11 W
El Cholar	294	37.27 S	70.38 W
El Chorrillo	294	33.17 S	66.16 W
El Ciprés	258	31.50 N	116.38 W
El Cobre	284p	20.03 N	75.57 W
El Cocuy	290	6.25 N	72.27 W
El Colorado	294	26.20 S	59.20 W
El Cóndor, Cerro ∧	294	26.39 S	68.24 W
El Congo	280	13.54 N	89.30 W
El Consuelo	278	31.02 N	111.53 W
El Corazón	290	1.12 S	79.06 W
El Corpus	280	13.16 N	87.03 W
El Coto	284m	18.28 N	66.44 W
El Coyote	254	30.50 N	112.40 W
El Cozón	278	31.18 N	112.29 W
El Cristo	284p	20.07 N	75.45 W
El Cuco	280	13.10 N	88.07 W
El Cuervo Grande	250	30.19 N	105.01 W
Elda	168	38.29 N	0.47 W
El Dátil	278	30.07 N	112.15 W
Eldersville	266	40.21 N	80.29 W
Elderton	266	40.42 N	79.21 W
El Descanso	258	32.12 N	116.55 W
El Desemboque, Méx.	278	29.30 N	112.27 W
El Desemboque, Méx.	278	30.30 N	112.59 W
El'dikan	186	60.48 N	135.11 E
El Diviso	290	1.22 N	78.14 W
El Djouf ⊸[2]	214	20.30 N	8.00 W
Eldon, Iowa, U.S.	244	40.55 N	92.13 W
Eldon, Mo., U.S.	248	38.21 N	92.35 W
Eldora	244	42.19 N	93.26 W
Eldorado, Arg.	294	26.26 S	54.40 W
Eldorado, Bra.	294	24.32 S	48.06 W
Eldorado, Méx.	278	24.17 N	107.21 W
El Dorado, Ark., U.S.	248	33.13 N	92.40 W
El Dorado, Calif., U.S.	272	38.41 N	120.51 W
Eldorado, Ill., U.S.	248	37.49 N	88.26 W
El Dorado, Kans., U.S.	252	37.49 N	96.52 W
Eldorado, Okla., U.S.	250	34.28 N	99.39 W
Eldorado, Tex., U.S.	250	30.52 N	100.36 W
El Dorado, Ven.	290	6.44 N	61.38 W
El Dorado □[6]	272	38.43 N	120.48 W
Eldorado Hills	272	38.37 N	120.27 W
El Dorado Springs	248	37.52 N	94.01 W
Eldoret	218	0.31 N	35.17 E
Eldred	266	41.57 N	78.23 W
Eldridge, Mount ∧	236	64.46 N	141.48 W
Eldridge Park	262	40.16 N	74.45 W
Eleanor	242	38.32 N	81.56 W
Electra	250	34.02 N	98.55 W
Eleele	275b	21.55 N	159.35 W
Elefantes, Rio dos(Olifants) ≃	224	24.10 S	32.40 E
Elei, Wādī ∨	220	22.04 N	34.27 E
Eleja	160	56.26 N	23.42 E
Elektrostal'	158	55.47 N	38.28 E
Elena	172	42.56 N	25.53 E
El Encanto, Col.	290	1.37 S	73.14 W
El Encanto, Guat.	278	17.17 N	89.34 W
Elephant Butte Reservoir ⊜[1]	254	33.19 N	107.10 W
Elephant Mountain ∧	242	44.46 N	70.46 W
El Estor	280	15.32 N	89.21 W
El Eulma	168	36.08 N	5.40 E
Eleusis → Elevsís	172	38.02 N	23.32 E
Eleuthera I	282	25.15 N	76.20 W
Eleuthera Point ≻	282	24.40 N	76.11 W
Eleva	244	44.35 N	91.28 W
Eleven Point ≃	248	36.09 N	91.05 W
Elevsís	172	38.02 N	23.32 E
Elevtheroúpolis	172	40.55 N	24.16 E
El Fahs	170	36.22 N	9.55 E
El Faro	284m	18.00 N	66.47 W
El Ferrol del Caudillo	168	43.29 N	8.14 W
Elfin Cove	236	58.12 N	136.20 W
Elfrida	254	31.41 N	109.41 W
El Fuerte	278	26.25 N	108.39 W
El Galpón	294	25.24 S	64.39 W
El Garrobo	280	13.35 N	85.29 W
Elgin, Ont., Can.	264	44.36 N	76.13 W
Elgin, Scot., U.K.	162	57.39 N	3.20 W
Elgin, Ill., U.S.	268	42.02 N	88.17 W
Elgin, Iowa, U.S.	244	42.57 N	91.38 W
Elgin, Minn., U.S.	244	44.08 N	92.15 W
Elgin, Nebr., U.S.	252	41.59 N	98.05 W
Elgin, N. Dak., U.S.	252	46.24 N	101.51 W
Elgin, Ohio, U.S.	268	40.44 N	84.28 W
Elgin, Oreg., U.S.	256	45.34 N	117.55 W
Elgin, Pa., U.S.	266	41.54 N	79.45 W
Elgin, Tex., U.S.	250	30.21 N	97.22 W
Elgin □[6]	266	42.42 N	81.15 W
El Gogorrón, Parque Nacional ♣	278	21.48 N	100.48 W
El Goléa	214	30.30 N	2.50 E
El Golfete ⊜	280	15.45 N	88.54 W
El Golfo de Santa Clara	278	31.34 N	114.19 W
Elgon, Mount ∧	218	1.08 N	34.33 E
Elgoras, Gora ∧	160	68.06 N	31.30 E
El Granada	272	37.30 N	122.28 W
El Guaje	278	27.52 N	103.18 W
El Guamo	290	10.02 N	74.59 W
El Guapo	290	10.09 N	65.58 W
El Guayabo	290	8.37 N	72.20 W
El Hadjar	170	36.48 N	7.45 E
El Hank ≗[4]	214	24.30 N	7.00 W
El Haouaria	170	37.03 N	11.02 E
Elhovo	172	42.10 N	26.34 E
El Huecu	294	37.35 S	70.37 W
Elia	282	20.59 N	77.26 W
Elías Piña	282	18.53 N	71.42 W
Eliasville	250	32.57 N	98.46 W
Elida, N. Mex., U.S.	250	33.57 N	103.39 W
Elida, Ohio, U.S.	268	40.47 N	84.12 W
Elim	236	64.37 N	162.15 W
Elinghu ⊜	190	34.50 N	97.35 E
Elin Pelin	172	42.40 N	23.36 E
Eliot	242	43.09 N	70.48 W
Élisabethville → Lubumbashi, Zaïre	218	11.40 S	27.28 E
Elisenvaara	160	61.25 N	29.46 E
Elista	158	46.16 N	44.14 E
Elizabeth, Austl.	228	34.43 S	138.40 E
Elizabeth, Colo., U.S.	254	39.22 N	104.36 W
Elizabeth, Ill., U.S.	244	42.19 N	90.13 W
Elizabeth, La., U.S.	248	30.52 N	92.48 W
Elizabeth, N.J., U.S.	262	40.40 N	74.11 W
Elizabeth, Pa., U.S.	266	40.16 N	79.53 W
Elizabeth, W. Va., U.S.	242	39.04 N	81.24 W
Elizabeth Bay C	224	27.04 S	15.11 E
Elizabeth City	246	36.18 N	76.14 W
Elizabeth Reef ✢[2]	226	29.56 S	159.04 E
Elizabethton	246	36.21 N	82.13 W
Elizabethtown, Ill., U.S.	248	37.27 N	88.18 W
Elizabethtown, Ky., U.S.	248	37.42 N	85.52 W
Elizabethtown, N.C., U.S.	246	34.38 N	78.37 W
Elizabethtown, N.Y., U.S.	242	44.13 N	73.36 W
Elizabethtown, Pa., U.S.	262	40.09 N	76.36 W
Elizabethville	262	40.33 N	76.49 W
Elizaville	261	42.03 N	73.48 W
El-Jadida	214	33.16 N	8.30 W
El Jaralito	278	26.07 N	104.10 W
El-Jebha	168	35.13 N	4.38 W
El Jem	170	35.18 N	10.43 E
El Jícaro	280	13.42 N	86.08 W
Ełk (Lyck), Pol.	164	53.50 N	22.22 E
Elk, Wyo., U.S.	254	43.47 N	110.33 W
Elk □[6]	266	41.26 N	78.43 W
Elk ≃, Alta., Can.	238	52.55 N	115.40 W
Elk ≃, B.C., Can.	238	49.10 N	115.14 W
Ełk ≃, Pol.	164	53.31 N	22.47 E
Elk ≃, Colo., U.S.	254	40.29 N	106.58 W
Elk ≃, Kans., U.S.	252	37.15 N	95.41 W
Elk ≃, Minn., U.S.	244	45.18 N	93.34 W
Elk ≃, Mo., U.S.	248	36.38 N	94.38 W
Elk ≃, W. Va., U.S.	242	38.21 N	81.38 W
Elk ≃, Wis., U.S.	244	45.42 N	90.37 W
Elkader	244	42.51 N	91.24 W
El Kairouan	170	35.41 N	10.07 E
El Kala	170	36.50 N	8.30 E
El Kasserine	214	35.11 N	8.48 E
Elk City	250	35.25 N	99.25 W
Elk City Reservoir ⊜[1]	252	37.25 N	95.55 W
Elk Creek	258	39.36 N	122.32 W
El Kef	170	36.11 N	8.43 E
El Kef □[8]	170	36.00 N	9.00 E
El Kerma	168	35.36 N	0.35 W
Elk Grove	272	38.25 N	121.22 W
Elkhart, Ind., U.S.	268	41.41 N	85.58 W
Elkhart, Kans., U.S.	252	37.00 N	101.54 W
Elkhart, Tex., U.S.	250	31.38 N	95.35 W
Elkhart □[6]	268	41.35 N	85.50 W
Elkhart ≃	248	41.41 N	85.58 W
Elkhart Lake	244	43.50 N	88.01 W
Elkhead Mountains ⛰	254	40.50 N	107.05 W
Elkhorn, Man., Can.	252	49.58 N	101.14 W
Elk Horn, Iowa, U.S.	252	41.36 N	95.03 W
Elkhorn, Wis., U.S.	268	42.40 N	88.33 W
Elkhorn ≃	252	41.07 N	96.19 W
Elkhorn City	246	37.18 N	82.21 W
Elkhorn Peaks ⛰	256	43.22 N	111.06 W
Elkin	246	36.16 N	80.51 W
Elkins	242	38.55 N	79.51 W
Elkins Park	262	40.05 N	75.08 W
Elk Island National Park ♣	238	53.37 N	112.45 W
Elkland	242	41.59 N	77.21 W
Elk Mills	262	39.39 N	75.50 W
Elk Mountain	254	41.41 N	106.25 W

Symbols in the index entries are identified on page 360.

Name	Page	Lat°′	Long°′
Elk Mountain ∧	254	41.38 N	106.32 W
Elko, B.C., Can.	238	49.18 N	115.07 W
Elko, Nev., U.S.	258	40.50 N	115.46 W
El Kouif	170	35.29 N	8.19 E
Elk Peak ∧	256	46.27 N	110.46 W
Elk Point, Alta., Can.	238	53.34 N	110.54 W
Elk Point, S. Dak., U.S.	252	42.41 N	96.41 W
Elk Rapids	244	44.54 N	85.25 W
El Krib	170	36.19 N	9.09 E
Elkridge	262	39.13 N	76.42 W
Elk River, Idaho, U.S.	256	46.47 N	116.11 W
Elk River, Minn., U.S.	244	45.18 N	93.35 W
El Kseur	168	36.46 N	4.49 E
Elkton, Ky., U.S.	248	36.49 N	87.09 W
Elkton, Md., U.S.	262	39.36 N	75.50 W
Elkton, Mich., U.S.	244	43.49 N	83.11 W
Elkton, Ohio, U.S.	266	40.46 N	80.42 W
Elkton, S. Dak., U.S.	252	44.14 N	96.29 W
Elkton, Va., U.S.	242	38.25 N	78.38 W
Elk Valley	246	36.28 N	84.17 W
Elkville	248	37.55 N	89.14 W
Ellamore	242	38.56 N	80.06 W
Ellaville	246	32.15 N	84.18 W
Ellen, Mount ∧	254	38.07 N	110.49 W
Ellendale, Del., U.S.	262	38.47 N	75.25 W
Ellendale, Minn., U.S.	244	43.52 N	93.18 W
Ellendale, N. Dak., U.S.	252	46.06 N	98.32 W
Ellensburg	256	47.00 N	120.32 W
Ellenton	246	31.11 N	83.35 W
Ellenville	242	41.43 N	74.28 W
Ellerbee	246	35.04 N	79.46 W
Ellès	170	35.57 N	9.06 E
Ellesmere	162	52.54 N	2.54 W
Ellesmere, Lake ⊜	230	43.47 S	172.28 E
Ellettsville	248	39.14 N	86.37 W
Ellice ≃	232	68.02 N	103.26 W
Ellice Island I	232	69.05 N	135.45 W
Ellice Islands II	148	8.00 S	178.00 E
Ellicott City	262	39.16 N	76.48 W
Ellicottville	266	42.17 N	78.40 W
Ellijay	246	34.42 N	84.28 W
El Limón, Méx.	278	24.16 N	107.04 W
El Limón, Nic.	280	12.45 N	86.44 W
Ellington, Conn., U.S.	261	41.54 N	72.28 W
Ellington, Mo., U.S.	248	37.14 N	90.58 W
Ellington, N.Y., U.S.	266	42.13 N	79.07 W
Ellinwood	252	38.21 N	98.35 W
Elliot	218	31.18 S	27.50 E
Elliot, Mount ∧	228	19.29 S	146.58 E
Elliot Lake	244	46.23 N	82.39 W
Elliott, Ill., U.S.	268	40.28 N	88.16 W
Elliott, Iowa, U.S.	252	41.09 N	95.10 W
Elliott Key I	246	25.27 N	80.11 W
Ellis	252	38.56 N	99.34 W
Ellisburg	264	43.44 N	76.08 W
Ellisport	270	47.25 N	122.26 W
Elliston, Austl.	226	33.39 S	134.55 E
Elliston, Newf., Can.	240	48.38 N	53.03 W
Elliston, Mont., U.S.	256	46.33 N	112.26 W
Ellisville	248	31.36 N	89.12 W
Ellon	162	57.22 N	2.05 W
Elloree	246	33.32 N	80.34 W
Ellport	266	40.52 N	80.16 W
Ellsinore	248	36.56 N	90.45 W
Ellsworth, Ill., U.S.	268	40.27 N	88.43 W
Ellsworth, Kans., U.S.	252	38.44 N	98.14 W
Ellsworth, Maine, U.S.	242	44.33 N	68.26 W
Ellsworth, Mich., U.S.	244	45.10 N	85.15 W
Ellsworth, Minn., U.S.	252	43.31 N	96.01 W
Ellsworth, Pa., U.S.	266	40.07 N	80.01 W
Ellsworth, Wis., U.S.	244	44.44 N	92.29 W
Ellsworth Air Force Base ■	252	44.08 N	103.05 W
El Lucero	250	25.53 N	103.25 W
Ellwangen	164	48.57 N	10.07 E
Ellwood City	266	40.50 N	80.17 W
Elm	166	46.55 N	9.11 E
Elm ≃, U.S.	252	45.36 N	98.19 W
Elm ≃, N. Dak., U.S.	252	47.15 N	96.50 W
Elma, Iowa, U.S.	244	43.15 N	92.26 W
Elma, N.Y., U.S.	264	42.51 N	78.38 W
Elma, Wash., U.S.	270	47.00 N	123.25 W
Elma Dağı ∧	212	39.49 N	33.00 E
El Mahdia	170	35.30 N	11.04 E
El Malah	168	35.24 N	1.05 W
Elmalı	172	36.44 N	29.56 E
El Manchón	280	14.23 N	92.02 W
El Maneadero	278	31.45 N	116.35 W
El Manteco	290	7.27 N	62.32 W
El Marqués	250	26.39 N	101.20 W
Elm City	246	35.48 N	77.52 W
Elm Creek, Man., Can.	252	49.41 N	98.00 W
Elm Creek, Nebr., U.S.	252	40.43 N	99.22 W
El Médano	278	24.25 N	111.30 W
Elmer	262	39.36 N	75.10 W
Elm Grove	268	43.03 N	88.04 W
Elmhurst	268	41.53 N	87.56 W
El Milia	168	36.48 N	6.14 E
El Mimbre	250	25.40 N	102.20 W
El Minao	284m	18.22 N	66.05 W
Elmira, Ont., Can.	264	43.36 N	80.33 W
Elmira, P.E.I., Can.	240	46.27 N	62.04 W
Elmira, Calif., U.S.	272	38.21 N	121.55 W
Elmira, N.Y., U.S.	242	42.06 N	76.49 W
El Mirage	254	33.36 N	112.19 W
Elmira Heights	242	42.08 N	76.49 W
Elmo	238	47.50 N	114.21 W
El Modeno	274	33.47 N	117.49 W
El Moknine	170	35.38 N	10.54 E
El Molinillo	168	39.28 N	4.13 W
Elmont	262	37.43 N	77.30 W
El Monte, Chile	294	33.41 S	71.01 W
El Monte, Calif., U.S.	272	37.59 N	122.00 W
El Monte, Calif., U.S.	274	34.04 N	118.02 W
Elmora	266	40.36 N	78.45 W
El Moral	250	28.51 N	100.39 W
Elmore, Minn., U.S.	244	43.30 N	94.05 W
Elmore, Ohio, U.S.	266	41.29 N	83.18 W
Elmore City	250	34.37 N	97.24 W
El Morro National Monument ♠	254	35.05 N	108.22 W
El Mreyyé ↲	222	19.30 N	7.00 W
Elmsdale	240	44.58 N	63.30 W
Elmsford	261	41.03 N	73.49 W
Elmshorn	178	53.45 N	9.39 E
El Mulato	250	29.22 N	104.10 W
Elmvale	264	44.35 N	79.52 W
Elmwood, Ont., Can.	264	44.14 N	81.03 W
Elmwood, Ill., U.S.	244	40.47 N	89.58 W
Elmwood, Nebr., U.S.	252	40.50 N	96.18 W
Elmwood, Wis., U.S.	244	44.47 N	92.09 W
Elmwood Park	268	41.55 N	87.49 W
El Naranjo	294	25.43 S	65.00 W
Elne	166	42.36 N	2.58 E
El Negrito	280	15.16 N	87.41 W
El Nevado, Cerro ∧	290	3.59 N	74.04 W
El Nido, Pil.	202	11.11 N	119.23 E
El Nido, Calif., U.S.	272	37.08 N	120.29 W
El Nihuil	294	34.52 S	68.38 W
Elnora, Alta., Can.	238	51.59 N	113.12 W
Elnora, Ind., U.S.	248	38.53 N	87.05 W
Eloise	246	28.00 N	81.44 W
Elora, Ont., Can.	264	43.41 N	80.26 W
Elora, Tenn., U.S.	248	35.01 N	86.21 W
Elorn ≃	162	48.27 N	4.16 W
El Oro □[4]	290	3.30 S	79.50 W
Elortondo	294	33.45 S	61.35 W
Elorza	290	7.03 N	69.31 W
El Oso	290	4.59 N	65.25 W
El Oued	214	33.20 N	6.58 E
Eloy	254	32.45 N	111.33 W
El Pacayal	278	15.37 N	92.02 W
El Palmar, Bol.	292	21.54 S	63.39 W
El Palmar, Ven.	290	7.58 N	61.53 W
El Palqui	294	30.45 S	70.59 W
El Pao, Ven.	290	8.01 N	62.38 W
El Pao, Ven.	290	9.38 N	68.08 W
El Paradero	290	10.38 N	69.32 W
El Paraíso	280	13.51 N	86.34 W
El Paraíso □[5]	280	14.10 N	86.30 W
El Paso, Nic.	280	12.06 N	85.54 W
El Paso, Ill., U.S.	268	40.44 N	89.01 W
El Paso, Tex., U.S.	254	31.45 N	106.29 W
El Pato	290	2.50 N	74.48 W
El Peñuelo	278	24.34 N	100.46 W
El Perú	290	7.19 N	61.49 W
El Petén □[5]	280	16.15 N	89.50 W
El Pilar	290	10.32 N	63.09 W
El Piñón	290	10.24 N	74.50 W
El Pintado	294	24.38 S	61.26 W
El Piquete	294	24.15 S	64.40 W
El Platanillo	278	18.28 N	101.52 W
El Plomo	254	31.15 N	112.04 W
El Polvorín	284m	18.26 N	66.17 W
El Portal	272	37.41 N	119.47 W
El Porvenir, Méx.	250	27.33 N	104.57 W
El Porvenir, Méx.	258	32.05 N	116.38 W
El Porvenir, Méx.	278	31.15 N	105.51 W
El Potosí	278	24.51 N	100.19 W
El Potosí, Parque Nacional ♠	278	22.00 N	99.58 W
El Potrero	250	26.23 N	100.27 W
El Potro, Cerro ∧	294	28.24 S	69.39 W
El Progreso, Ec.	290a	0.54 S	89.33 W
El Progreso, Guat.	280	14.51 N	90.04 W
El Progreso, Guat.	280	14.21 N	89.51 W
El Progreso, Hond.	280	15.21 N	87.49 W
El Progreso □[5]	280	14.50 N	90.00 W
El Puente Arzobispo	168	39.48 N	5.10 W
El Puerto de Santa María	168	36.36 N	6.13 W
El Puesto	294	27.58 S	67.38 W
El Quebrachal	294	25.17 S	64.04 W
El Quelite	278	23.32 N	106.28 W
Elqui ≃	294	29.54 S	71.17 W
El Quiché □[5]	280	15.30 N	90.55 W
Elrama	266	40.15 N	79.56 W
El Rastro	290	9.03 N	67.27 W
El Real	290	8.07 N	77.43 W
El Remolino	250	28.44 N	101.07 W
El Reno	250	35.32 N	97.57 W
El Rio	274	34.14 N	119.10 W
El Rito	254	36.21 N	106.11 W
El Rito ≃	254	36.12 N	106.14 W
Elroy	244	43.45 N	90.16 W
Elsa, Yukon, Can.	236	63.55 N	135.28 W
Elsa, Tex., U.S.	250	26.18 N	97.59 W
El Sahuaro	254	31.05 N	112.55 W
El Salto	278	23.47 N	105.22 W
El Salvador	202	8.34 N	124.32 E
El Salvador □[1]	276	13.50 N	88.55 W
El Samán de Apure	290	7.55 N	68.44 W
El Santo	284p	22.42 N	79.41 W
El Sauce	280	12.53 N	86.32 W
El Sauz	278	29.02 N	106.16 W
El Sauzal	278	31.54 N	116.41 W
Elsberry	248	39.10 N	90.47 W
El Segundo	274	33.55 N	118.24 W
El Seibo	282	18.46 N	69.02 W
Elsen	178	51.44 N	8.39 E
Elsfleth	178	53.14 N	8.28 E
Elsie, Mich., U.S.	268	43.05 N	84.23 W
Elsie, Oreg., U.S.	270	45.52 N	123.35 W
Elsinore → Helsingør, Dan.	160	56.02 N	12.37 E
Elsinore, Calif., U.S.	274	33.40 N	117.20 W
Elsinore, Utah, U.S.	254	38.41 N	112.09 W
Elsinore, Lake ⊜[1]	258	33.39 N	117.21 W
Elsmere, Del., U.S.	262	39.44 N	75.36 W
Elsmere, N.Y., U.S.	261	42.38 N	73.49 W
El Sobrante	272	37.58 N	122.19 W
El Socorro	290	8.59 N	65.44 W
El Sombrero	290	9.23 N	67.03 W
Elspe	178	51.09 N	8.04 E
Elst	178	51.55 N	5.50 E
Elsterwerda	164	51.28 N	13.31 E
Elston	268	40.22 N	86.55 W
El Sueco	278	29.54 N	106.24 W
El Tajín ⊥	278	20.27 N	97.23 W
El Tamarindo	280	13.11 N	87.54 W
El Tambo	290	1.26 N	77.23 W
El Tanque	250	26.28 N	99.38 W
El Tarf	170	36.45 N	8.20 E
El Teleño ∧	168	42.21 N	6.23 W
Eltham	230	39.26 S	174.18 E
El Tigre, Col.	290	2.28 N	68.15 W
El Tigre, Ven.	290	8.55 N	64.15 W
El Tisey, Cerro ∧	280	12.59 N	86.22 W
Eltmann	164	49.58 N	10.40 E
El Toco	294	22.05 S	69.35 W
El Tocuyo	290	9.47 N	69.48 W
El Tofo	294	29.27 S	71.15 W
Elton, La., U.S.	248	30.29 N	92.42 W
Elton, Pa., U.S.	266	40.17 N	78.48 W
El Toro	274	33.38 N	117.42 W
El Toro, Cerro ∧	278	20.40 N	100.43 W
El Tránsito, Chile	294	28.52 S	70.17 W
El Tránsito, El Sal.	280	13.22 N	88.21 W
El Trapiche	290	3.03 N	77.33 W
El Trébol	294	32.20 S	61.40 W
El Triunfo, Hond.	280	15.46 N	87.26 W
El Triunfo, Hond.	280	13.06 N	87.00 W
El Triunfo, Méx.	278	23.47 N	110.08 W
El Tunal	294	24.50 S	65.43 W
El Turbio	288	51.41 S	72.05 W
El Valle	280	8.36 N	80.08 W
Elvas	168	38.53 N	7.10 W
Elven	166	47.44 N	2.35 W
El Verano	272	38.18 N	122.29 W
Elverta	272	38.43 N	121.28 W
Elverum	160	60.53 N	11.34 E
El Viejo	280	12.38 N	87.11 W
El Vigía	290	8.38 N	71.39 W
Elvira	294	35.15 S	59.30 W
Elvira Island I	232	73.35 N	108.00 W
El Volcán, Arg.	294	33.15 S	66.12 W
El Volcán, Chile	294	33.49 S	70.11 W
Elwood, Ill., U.S.	268	41.24 N	88.07 W
Elwood, Ind., U.S.	268	40.17 N	85.50 W
Elwood, Kans., U.S.	252	39.45 N	94.52 W
Elwood, Nebr., U.S.	252	40.36 N	99.52 W
Elwood, N.J., U.S.	262	39.35 N	74.43 W
Elwood, N.Y., U.S.	261	40.51 N	73.20 W
Ely, Eng., U.K.	174	52.24 N	0.16 E
Ely, Minn., U.S.	244	47.54 N	91.51 W
Ely, Nev., U.S.	258	39.15 N	114.53 W
El Yagual	290	7.29 N	68.25 W
El Yopal	290	5.21 N	72.23 W
Elyria	266	41.22 N	82.06 W
El Zapote de Calabacillas	278	25.42 N	106.32 W
Elze	178	52.07 N	9.44 E
Emba	158	48.50 N	58.08 E
Emba ≃	186	46.38 N	53.14 E
Embarcación	294	23.15 S	64.10 W
Embarras ≃	238	53.27 N	116.37 W
Embarrass	244	44.40 N	88.42 W
Embarrass ≃, Ill., U.S.	248	38.39 N	87.37 W
Embarrass ≃, Minn., U.S.	244	47.24 N	92.25 W
Embarrass ≃, Wis., U.S.	244	44.23 N	88.45 W
Embetsu	192a	44.44 N	141.47 E
Embid	168	40.58 N	1.43 W
Embira ≃	292	7.19 S	70.15 W
Embreeville	246	36.11 N	82.28 W
Embro	264	43.09 N	80.54 W
Embrun, Ont., Can.	264	45.16 N	75.17 W
Embrun, Fr.	166	44.34 N	6.30 E
Emden, B.R.D.	178	53.22 N	7.12 E
Emden, Ill., U.S.	248	40.18 N	89.29 W
Emeigh	266	40.42 N	78.47 W
Emelle	248	32.44 N	88.19 W
Emerado	252	47.55 N	97.22 W
Emerald	228	23.32 S	148.10 E
Emerald Lake	272	37.28 N	122.16 W
Emero ≃	292	13.19 S	67.17 W
Emerson, Man., Can.	252	49.00 N	97.12 W
Emerson, Ark., U.S.	248	33.06 N	93.11 W
Emerson, Ga., U.S.	246	34.08 N	84.45 W
Emerson, Iowa, U.S.	252	41.01 N	95.24 W
Emerson, Nebr., U.S.	252	42.17 N	96.44 W
Emery, S. Dak., U.S.	252	43.36 N	97.37 W
Emery, Utah, U.S.	254	38.55 N	111.15 W
Emeryville, Ont., Can.	266	42.18 N	82.45 W
Emeryville, Calif., U.S.	272	37.50 N	122.17 W
Emet	172	39.20 N	29.15 E
Emigrant Gap	272	39.19 N	120.38 W
Emigsville	262	40.01 N	76.44 W
Emiliano Zapata	278	17.45 N	91.46 W
Emilia-Romagna □[4]	184	44.35 N	11.00 E
Emine, nos ≻	172	42.42 N	27.51 E
Eminence, Ky., U.S.	248	38.22 N	85.11 W
Eminence, Mo., U.S.	248	37.09 N	91.22 W
Emiralem	172	38.36 N	27.09 E
Emir Dağları ⋀	212	38.50 N	31.15 E
Emlembe ∧	224	25.57 S	31.11 E
Emlenton	266	41.11 N	79.43 W
Emmaus	262	40.32 N	75.30 W
Emmeloord	178	52.43 N	5.45 E
Emmen	178	52.47 N	7.00 E
Emmenbrücke	180	47.04 N	8.17 E
Emmendingen	180	48.07 N	7.50 E
Emmer-Compascuum	178	52.48 N	7.02 E
Emmerich	178	51.50 N	6.15 E
Emmet	248	33.44 N	93.28 W
Emmetsburg	252	43.07 N	94.41 W
Emmett, Idaho, U.S.	256	43.52 N	116.30 W
Emmett, Mich., U.S.	266	42.59 N	82.46 W
Emmitsburg	262	39.42 N	77.20 W
Emmonak	236	62.46 N	164.30 W
Emo	244	48.38 N	93.50 W
Emőd	164	47.56 N	20.49 E
Emory	250	32.52 N	95.46 W
Emory ≃	246	35.56 N	84.29 W
Emory Peak ∧	250	29.13 N	103.17 W
Emory University	246	33.48 N	84.19 W
Empalme	278	27.58 N	110.51 W
Empangeni	218	28.51 S	31.48 E
Empedrado, Arg.	294	27.55 S	58.45 W
Empedrado, Chile	294	35.36 S	72.17 W
Empelde	178	52.20 N	9.40 E
Emperor Seamount Chain ⩫[3]	148	45.00 N	170.00 E
Empire, Calif., U.S.	272	37.38 N	120.54 W
Empire, Nev., U.S.	272	40.37 N	119.21 W
Empire, Ohio, U.S.	266	40.31 N	80.37 W
Empire, Oreg., U.S.	256	43.23 N	124.17 W
Empoli	184	43.43 N	10.57 E
Emporia, Kans., U.S.	252	38.24 N	96.11 W
Emporia, Va., U.S.	262	36.41 N	77.32 W
Emporium	266	41.31 N	78.14 W
Ems ≃	164	51.09 N	9.26 E
Emsdetten	178	52.10 N	7.31 E
Emstek	178	52.50 N	8.09 E
Emsworth	266	40.30 N	80.04 W
Emukae	192	33.18 N	129.38 E
En (Inn) ≃	166	48.35 N	13.28 E
Enard Bay C	162	58.06 N	5.20 W
Encampment	254	41.12 N	106.47 W
Encampment ≃	254	41.18 N	106.43 W
Encantado	294	29.15 S	51.53 W
Encanto, Cape ≻	202	15.44 N	121.36 E
Encarnación	294	27.20 S	55.54 W
Enchilayas	254	30.50 N	112.50 W
Encinal	250	28.02 N	99.21 W
Encinas	250	25.40 N	101.08 W
Encinitas	274	33.03 N	117.17 W
Encino, N. Mex., U.S.	254	34.39 N	105.28 W
Encino, Tex., U.S.	250	26.57 N	98.08 W
Encontrados	290	9.03 N	72.14 W
Encounter Bay C	228	35.35 S	138.44 E
Encrucijada	284p	22.37 N	79.52 W
Encruzilhada	296	15.31 S	40.54 W
Encruzilhada do Sul	294	30.32 S	52.31 W
Encs	164	48.20 N	21.08 E
Endako	238	54.05 N	125.02 W
Endako ≃	238	54.05 N	124.55 W
Endau	200	2.40 N	103.37 E
Ende	198	8.50 S	121.39 E
Endeavor, Pa., U.S.	266	41.35 N	79.23 W
Endeavor, Wis., U.S.	244	43.43 N	89.29 W
Enderby	238	50.33 N	119.08 W
Enderby Land ↲	148	67.30 S	53.00 E
Enderlin	252	46.37 N	97.36 W
Endicott, N.Y., U.S.	242	42.06 N	76.03 W
Endicott, Wash., U.S.	256	46.56 N	117.41 W
Endicott Mountains ⋀	236	67.50 N	152.00 W
Endimari ≃	292	8.46 S	66.07 W
Ene ≃	292	11.10 S	74.18 W
Enez	172	40.44 N	26.04 E
Enfidha	170	36.07 N	10.23 E
Enfield, Conn., U.S.	261	41.58 N	72.36 W
Enfield, N.H., U.S.	242	43.34 N	71.57 W
Enfield, N.C., U.S.	246	36.11 N	77.47 W
Enfield, Va., U.S.	262	37.43 N	77.12 W
Enfield ↲[8]	174	51.40 N	0.05 W
Engaño, Cabo ≻	282	18.40 N	68.20 W
Engaru	192a	44.03 N	143.31 E
Engelhard	246	35.31 N	76.02 W
Engel's	158	51.30 N	46.07 E
Engenho	292	15.10 S	56.25 W
Enger	178	52.08 N	8.34 E
Enggano, Pulau I	198	5.24 S	102.16 E
Enghien (Les-Bains)	176	48.58 N	2.19 E
Engizek Dağı ∧	212	37.50 N	37.10 E
England	248	34.33 N	91.58 W
England □[8]	174	52.30 N	1.30 W
Englee	240	50.44 N	56.06 W
Englefield, Cape ≻	232	69.51 N	85.39 W
Englehart	244	47.49 N	79.52 W
Englehart ≃	244	47.51 N	79.50 W
Englewood, B.C., Can.	238	50.33 N	126.53 W
Englewood, Colo., U.S.	254	39.39 N	104.59 W
Englewood, Fla., U.S.	246	26.58 N	82.21 W
Englewood, Kans., U.S.	252	37.02 N	100.01 W
Englewood, Tenn., U.S.	246	35.26 N	84.29 W
English	248	38.20 N	86.28 W
English ≃, Ont., Can.	232	50.12 N	95.00 W
English ≃, N.A.	242	45.13 N	73.50 W
English ≃, Iowa, U.S.	244	41.29 N	91.30 W
English Bay	236	59.22 N	151.55 W
English Bāzār	206	25.00 N	88.09 E
English Channel (La Manche) ⋃	162	50.20 N	1.00 W
English Coast ⩫[2]	148	73.45 S	73.00 W
English Harbour West	240	47.28 N	55.30 W
Englishtown	262	40.18 N	74.22 W
Enguera	168	38.59 N	0.41 W
Engure	160	57.10 N	23.13 E
Enhaut	262	40.14 N	76.50 W
Enid, Miss., U.S.	248	34.07 N	89.56 W
Enid, Okla., U.S.	250	36.19 N	97.48 W
Enid Lake ⊜[1]	248	34.10 N	89.50 W
Enilda	238	55.25 N	116.18 W
Eningen	180	48.29 N	9.16 E
Eniwa	192a	42.45 N	141.33 E
Enka	246	35.32 N	82.38 W
Enkhuizen	178	52.42 N	5.17 E
Enköping	160	59.38 N	17.04 E
Enmedio	250	29.04 N	103.29 W
Enmelen	236	65.01 N	175.54 W
Enmore	290	6.45 N	57.59 W
Enna	170	37.34 N	14.17 E
Ennadai Lake ⊜	232	60.53 N	101.15 W
Enndja, Oued ≃	168	36.31 N	6.15 E
Ennedi ⋀[1]	220	17.15 N	22.00 E
Ennepetal	178	51.18 N	7.22 E
Ennigerloh	178	51.50 N	8.02 E
Ennigloh	178	52.12 N	8.34 E
Ennis, Eire	162	52.50 N	8.59 W
Ennis, Mont., U.S.	256	45.21 N	111.44 W
Ennis, Tex., U.S.	250	32.20 N	96.38 W
Enniscorthy	162	52.30 N	6.34 W
Enniskillen	162	54.21 N	7.38 W
Ennis Lake ⊜[1]	256	45.26 N	111.41 W
Ennistymon	162	52.57 N	9.13 W
Enns	164	48.13 N	14.29 E
Enns ≃	164	48.14 N	14.32 E
Enochs	250	33.52 N	102.46 W
Enola	262	40.17 N	76.56 W
Enon	242	39.53 N	83.56 W
Enontekiö	160	68.23 N	23.38 E
Enon Valley	266	40.51 N	80.28 W
Enoree ≃	246	34.26 N	81.25 W
Enosburg Falls	242	44.55 N	72.48 W
Enragé, Point ≻	240	44.16 N	64.15 W
Enrile	202	17.34 N	121.42 E
Enrique Urien	294	27.10 S	60.30 W
Enriquillo	282	17.54 N	71.14 W
Enriquillo, Lago ⊜	282	18.30 N	71.37 W
Enschede	178	52.12 N	6.53 E
Ensenada, Arg.	294	34.51 S	57.55 W
Ensenada, Méx.	278	31.52 N	116.37 W
Ensenada, P.R.	284m	17.58 N	66.56 W
Enshi	190	30.17 N	109.19 E
Enshū-nada ⩫[2]	192	34.27 N	137.38 E
Ensign	244	45.54 N	86.52 W
Entebbe	218	0.04 N	32.28 E
Entenbühl ∧	164	49.46 N	12.24 E
Enterprise, Guy.	290	6.50 N	58.25 W
Enterprise, Ala., U.S.	248	31.19 N	85.51 W
Enterprise, Calif., U.S.	258	39.32 N	121.22 W
Enterprise, Kans., U.S.	252	38.54 N	97.07 W
Enterprise, Miss., U.S.	248	32.10 N	88.49 W
Enterprise, Oreg., U.S.	256	45.25 N	117.17 W
Enterprise, Utah, U.S.	254	37.34 N	113.43 W
Entiat ≃	256	47.40 N	120.14 W
Entiat, Lake ⊜	256	47.40 N	120.12 W
Entinas, Punta de las ≻	168	36.41 N	2.46 W
Entraygues	166	44.39 N	2.34 E
Entrée, Île de l' I	240	47.16 N	61.40 W
Entrepeñas, Embalse de ⊜[1]	168	40.34 N	2.42 W
Entre Ríos, Bol.	292	21.32 S	64.12 W
Entre Rios, Bra.	296	11.56 S	38.05 W
Entre-Rios, Moç.	218	14.57 S	37.20 E
Entre Ríos □[4]	294	32.00 S	59.20 W
Entre Ríos, Cordillera ⋀	280	14.00 N	86.00 W
Entre Rios de Minas	296	20.41 S	44.04 W
Entriken	266	40.20 N	78.12 W
Entroncamento	168	39.28 N	8.28 W
Entwistle	238	53.36 N	115.00 W
Enugu	222	6.27 N	7.27 E
Enumclaw	270	47.12 N	121.59 W
Enurmino	236	66.57 N	171.49 W
Envalira, Port d')(	168	42.35 N	1.45 E
Envermeu	166	49.54 N	1.16 E
Envigado	290	6.10 N	75.35 W
Envira	292	7.18 S	70.13 W
Enys, Mount ∧	230	43.14 S	171.38 E
Enza ≃	170	44.54 N	10.31 E
Eo ≃	168	43.28 N	7.03 W
Eola	270	44.55 N	123.07 W
Eolia	248	39.14 N	91.01 W
Eolie, Isole II	170	38.30 N	15.00 E
Epanomí	172	40.26 N	22.56 E
Epazote, Cerro ∧	278	24.35 N	105.07 W
Epe, B.R.D.	178	52.11 N	7.02 E
Epe, Ned.	178	52.21 N	6.00 E
Epe, Nig.	222	6.37 N	3.59 E
Epecuén, Lago ⊜	294	37.09 S	62.52 W
Épernay	176	49.03 N	3.57 E
Epes	248	32.42 N	88.07 W
Ephesus ⊥	212	37.55 N	27.17 E
Ephraim	254	39.22 N	111.35 W
Ephrata, Pa., U.S.	262	40.11 N	76.10 W
Ephrata, Wash., U.S.	256	47.19 N	119.33 W
Épila	168	41.36 N	1.17 W
Épinal	180	48.11 N	6.27 E
Episkopís, Kólpos C	212	34.38 N	32.50 E
Epping, Eng., U.K.	174	51.43 N	0.07 E
Epping, N.H., U.S.	242	43.02 N	71.04 W
Epsom	174	51.20 N	0.16 W
Epte ≃	166	49.04 N	1.37 E
Épuisay	162	47.54 N	0.56 E
Epukiro	218	21.41 S	19.08 E
Epukiro ≃	224	20.45 S	21.05 E
Equality	248	37.44 N	88.20 W
Equatorial Guinea □[1]	214	2.00 N	9.00 E
Eraclea	170	45.35 N	12.40 E
Eran Bay C	202	9.05 N	117.43 E
Erath	248	29.58 N	92.02 W
Erba	182	45.48 N	9.15 E
Erba, Jabal ∧, Sūd.	220	19.04 N	36.46 E
Erba, Jabal ∧, Sūd.	220	20.45 N	36.50 E
Erbach	164	49.40 N	8.59 E
Erbeskope ∧	166	49.44 N	7.05 E
Erciyas Dağı ∧	212	38.32 N	35.28 E
Érd	164	47.23 N	18.56 E
Erdaobaihe ≃	194	42.34 N	128.08 E
Erdek	172	40.24 N	27.48 E
Erdene	190	44.40 N	111.05 E
Erdevik	172	45.07 N	19.25 E
Erding	164	48.18 N	11.54 E
Erebato ≃	290	5.54 N	64.16 W
Erechim	294	27.38 S	52.17 W
Ereğli	212	37.31 N	34.04 E
Erei, Monti ⋀	170	37.20 N	14.20 E
Erenas	202	12.25 N	124.19 E
Erenköy	172	40.00 N	26.20 E
Erepecu, Lago do ⊜	290	1.20 S	56.35 W
Eresma ≃	168	41.26 N	4.45 W
Eressós	172	39.18 N	25.51 E
Erfoud	214	31.28 N	4.10 W
Erft ≃	164	51.11 N	6.44 E
Erfurt	164	50.58 N	11.01 E
Erfurt □[6]	178	51.10 N	10.45 E
Ergene ≃	212	41.01 N	26.22 E
Erges (Erjas) ≃	168	39.40 N	7.01 W
Ērgli	160	56.54 N	25.38 E
Erguvejem ≃	236	65.20 N	176.00 W
Erhai ⊜	200	25.48 N	100.11 E
Érherhi, Ahzar ∨	222	14.56 N	3.24 E
Eria ≃	168	42.03 N	5.44 W
Erial	262	39.46 N	75.01 W
Erice	170	38.02 N	12.36 E
Ericeira	168	38.59 N	9.25 W
Erichsen Lake ⊜	232	70.38 N	80.21 W
Ericht, Loch ⊜	162	56.50 N	4.25 W
Erick	250	35.13 N	99.52 W
Erickson	238	49.05 N	116.28 W
Ericson	252	41.47 N	98.41 W
Erie, Colo., U.S.	254	40.03 N	105.03 W
Erie, Ill., U.S.	244	41.39 N	90.05 W
Erie, Kans., U.S.	252	37.34 N	95.15 W
Erie, Mich., U.S.	268	41.48 N	83.30 W
Erie	266	42.08 N	80.04 W
Erie □[6], N.Y., U.S.	264	42.54 N	78.53 W
Erie □[6], Ohio, U.S.	266	41.27 N	82.42 W
Erie □[6], Pa., U.S.	266	42.08 N	80.04 W
Erie, Lake ⊜	244	42.15 N	81.00 W
Erieau	266	42.16 N	81.56 W
Erie Beach, Ont., Can.	264	42.53 N	78.57 W
Erie Beach, Ont., Can.	266	42.16 N	82.00 W
Erie Canal → New York State Barge Canal ☰	242	43.05 N	78.43 W
Erigavo	214	10.37 N	47.24 E
Erímanthos ∧	172	37.59 N	21.51 E
Erimo-misaki ≻	192a	41.55 N	143.15 E
Erin	264	43.45 N	80.07 W
Eriskay I	162	57.04 N	7.13 W
Erithraí	172	38.13 N	23.19 E
Eritrea □[9]	214	15.20 N	39.00 E
Erivan → Jerevan	208	40.11 N	44.30 E
Erjas (Erges) ≃	168	39.40 N	7.01 W
Erkelenz	178	51.05 N	6.19 E
Erkner	164	52.25 N	13.45 E
Erkrath	178	51.13 N	6.55 E
Erlands Point	270	47.36 N	122.42 W
Erlangen	164	49.36 N	11.01 E
Erlian	190	43.46 N	112.05 E
Erling, Lake ⊜[1]	248	33.05 N	93.35 W
Erma	262	38.59 N	74.54 W
Ermelo, Ned.	178	52.17 N	5.37 E
Ermelo, S. Afr.	224	26.34 S	29.58 E
Ermineskin Indian Reserve ⩫[4]	238	52.52 N	113.30 W
Ermont	176	48.59 N	2.16 E
Ermoúpolis	172	37.26 N	24.56 E
Erne, Lough ⊜	162	54.10 N	7.30 W
Ernée	166	48.18 N	0.56 W
Ernest	266	40.41 N	79.10 W
Ernest Sound ⋃	238	55.52 N	132.10 W
Eromanga	226	26.40 S	143.16 E
Erongoberge ⋀	224	21.45 S	15.37 E
Errigal ∧	162	55.02 N	8.07 W
Errington	270	49.17 N	124.22 W
Erris Head ≻	162	54.19 N	10.00 W
Errol	242	44.47 N	71.08 W
Errol Heights	270	45.29 N	122.33 W
Ersekë	172	40.20 N	20.41 E
Erskine	252	47.40 N	96.00 W
Erskine Inlet C	232	76.15 N	102.20 W
Erstein	180	48.26 N	7.40 E
Ertai	190	46.07 N	90.06 E
Ertuğrul	172	39.34 N	27.43 E
Erval	294	32.02 S	53.24 W
Erval d'Oeste	294	27.13 S	51.34 W
Erving	261	42.36 N	72.24 W
Ervy-le-Châtel	166	48.02 N	3.55 E
Erwin, N.C., U.S.	246	35.20 N	78.41 W
Erwin, Tenn., U.S.	246	36.09 N	82.25 W
Erwitte	178	51.37 N	8.20 E
Erzgebirge (Krušné hory) ⋀	164	50.30 N	13.10 E
Erzhou I	196	22.00 N	114.11 E
Erzin	186	50.15 N	95.10 E
Erzincan	212	39.44 N	39.29 E
Erzurum	212	39.55 N	41.17 E
Esan-saki ≻	192a	41.49 N	141.11 E
Esashi, Nihon	192	41.52 N	140.07 E
Esashi, Nihon	192	39.12 N	141.09 E
Esashi, Nihon	192a	44.56 N	142.35 E
Esbjerg	160	55.28 N	8.27 E
Esca ≃	168	42.37 N	1.03 W
Escalante, Pil.	202	10.50 N	123.33 E
Escalante, Utah, U.S.	254	37.47 N	111.36 W
Escalante ≃, Utah, U.S.	254	37.17 N	110.53 W
Escalante ≃, Ven.	290	9.15 N	71.50 W
Escalante Desert ⩫[2]	254	37.50 N	113.30 W
Escalón, Méx.	278	26.45 N	104.20 W
Escalon, Calif., U.S.	272	37.48 N	121.00 W
Escalona	168	40.10 N	4.24 W
Escambia ≃	248	30.32 N	87.11 W
Escanaba	244	45.45 N	87.04 W
Escanaba ≃	244	45.47 N	87.04 W
Escandón, El Puerto de)(	168	40.17 N	1.00 W
Escárcega de Matamoros	278	18.37 N	90.43 W
Escarpada Point ≻	202	18.31 N	122.13 E
Escarpado Peak ∧	202	8.36 N	117.22 E
Escatawpa ≃	248	30.25 N	88.35 W
Escaudain	176	50.20 N	3.21 E
Escaut (Schelde)	176	51.22 N	4.15 E
Eschach	180	47.44 N	9.36 E
Eschscholtz Bay C	236	66.18 N	161.25 W
Esch-sur-Alzette	164	49.30 N	5.59 E
Eschwege	178	51.11 N	10.04 E
Eschweiler	164	50.49 N	6.16 E
Escobal	280	9.10 N	80.00 W
Escobas	250	27.04 N	99.01 W
Escobedo	250	27.13 N	101.21 W
Escocesa, Bahía C	282	19.20 N	69.40 W
Escoheag	261	41.35 N	71.32 W
Escondido, Bra.	296	17.05 S	39.31 W
Escondido, Calif., U.S.	274	33.07 N	117.05 W
Escondido ≃, Méx.	250	28.40 N	100.30 W
Escondido ≃, Nic.	280	12.10 N	83.42 W
Escondido Draw ∨	250	30.51 N	102.33 W
Escravos ≃[1]	222	5.35 N	5.10 E
Escudo de Veraguas, Isla I	280	9.06 N	81.32 W
Escuinapa [de Hidalgo]	278	22.51 N	105.48 W
Escuintla, Guat.	280	14.18 N	90.47 W
Escuintla, Méx.	278	15.20 N	92.38 W
Escuintla □[5]	280	14.10 N	91.00 W
Escuminac, Point ≻	240	47.04 N	64.46 W
Ésera ≃	168	42.06 N	0.15 E
Eşfahān (Isfahan)	208	32.40 N	51.38 E
Eşfahān □[4]	208	32.30 N	53.00 E
Esfí ≃	280	8.25 N	82.17 W
Esgueva ≃	168	41.40 N	4.43 W
Eshan	200	24.11 N	102.22 E
Esher	174	51.23 N	0.22 W
Eshowe	218	28.58 S	31.29 E
Esk ≃	230	43.06 S	171.57 E
Eskdale	242	38.05 N	81.27 W
Eskifjördur	160a	65.04 N	13.59 W
Eskilstuna	160	59.22 N	16.30 E
Eskimo Lakes ⊜	236	69.15 N	132.17 W
Eskimo Point	232	61.07 N	94.03 W
Eskişehir	212	39.46 N	30.32 E
Eskridge	252	38.52 N	96.06 W
Esla ≃	168	41.29 N	6.03 W
Eşme	172	38.24 N	28.59 E
Esmeralda, Cuba	284p	21.51 N	78.07 W
Esmeralda, Méx.	250	25.40 N	103.30 W
Esmeralda, Ven.	290	3.10 N	65.33 W
Esmeralda, Isla I	288	48.55 S	75.25 W
Esmeraldas	290	0.59 N	79.42 W
Esmeraldas □[4]	290	0.40 N	79.30 W
Esmeraldas ≃	290	0.58 N	79.38 W
Esmond, N. Dak., U.S.	252	48.02 N	99.46 W
Esmond, R.I., U.S.	261	41.53 N	71.30 W
Esnagi Lake ⊜	244	48.38 N	84.32 W
Espada, Punta ≻	290	12.00 N	71.08 W
Espalion	166	44.31 N	2.46 E
Espanola, Ont., Can.	244	46.15 N	81.46 W
Espanola, N. Mex., U.S.	254	36.06 N	106.02 W
Española, Isla I	290a	1.25 S	89.42 W
Esparta	280	9.59 N	84.40 W
Esparto	272	38.42 N	122.01 W
Espejo	168	37.41 N	4.33 W
Espelkamp	178	52.25 N	8.36 E
Espenberg, Cape ≻	236	66.33 N	163.36 W
Espera Feliz	296	20.39 S	41.55 W
Esperança	290	4.24 S	69.52 W
Esperance	226	33.51 S	121.53 E
Esperanza, Arg.	294	31.30 S	60.55 W
Esperanza, Méx.	254	31.18 N	105.59 W
Esperanza, Méx.	278	27.35 N	109.56 W
Esperanza, Pil.	202	11.44 N	124.02 E
Esperanza, Pil.	202	8.42 N	125.36 E
Esperanza, P.R.	284m	18.06 N	65.28 W
Esperanza, Sierra de la ⋀	280	15.40 N	85.45 W
Esperanza Inlet C	238	49.48 N	127.10 W
Espichel, Cabo de ≻	168	38.25 N	9.13 W
Espinal	290	4.09 N	74.53 W
Espinazo	250	26.16 N	101.06 W
Espinhaço, Serra do ⋀	296	17.30 S	43.30 W
Espinho	168	41.00 N	8.39 W
Espinillo	294	24.58 S	58.34 W
Espino	290	8.34 N	66.01 W
Espinosa	296	14.56 S	42.50 W
Espírito Santo □[3]	296	19.30 S	40.30 W
Espíritu Santo, Bahía del C	278	19.20 N	87.35 W
Espíritu Santo, Isla del I	278	24.30 N	110.20 W
Espita	278	21.01 N	88.19 W
Esplanada	296	11.47 S	37.57 W
Espoir, Bay d' C	240	47.50 N	55.51 W
Espoo (Esbo)	160	60.13 N	24.40 E
Esposende	168	41.32 N	8.47 W
Espumoso	294	28.44 S	52.51 W
Espungabera	218	20.29 S	32.48 E
Espyville Station	266	41.36 N	80.29 W
Esquatzel Coulee ∨	256	46.17 N	119.07 W
Esquel	288	42.55 S	71.20 W
Esquimalt	238	48.26 N	123.24 W
Esquina	294	30.00 S	59.30 W
Esquina Negra	294	35.03 S	58.04 W
Esquipulas, Guat.	280	14.34 N	89.21 W
Esquipulas, Nic.	280	12.37 N	85.49 W
Esquiú	294	29.23 S	65.18 W
Essaouira	214	31.30 N	9.47 W
Essen, Bel.	176	51.28 N	4.28 E
Essen, B.R.D.	178	52.43 N	7.57 E
Essen, B.R.D.	178	51.28 N	7.01 E
Essequibo □[5]	290	7.00 N	59.00 W
Essequibo ≃	290	6.50 N	58.30 W
Essequibo Islands □[5]	290	6.55 N	58.55 W
Es Sers	170	36.04 N	9.02 E
Essex, Ont., Can.	266	42.10 N	82.49 W
Essex, Conn., U.S.	261	41.21 N	72.24 W
Essex, Ill., U.S.	268	41.11 N	88.11 W
Essex, Iowa, U.S.	252	40.50 N	95.18 W
Essex, Md., U.S.	262	39.18 N	76.29 W
Essex, Mass., U.S.	261	42.38 N	70.47 W
Essex, Mo., U.S.	248	36.49 N	95.52 W
Essex, Mont., U.S.	238	48.17 N	113.37 W
Essex □[6], Ont., Can.	266	42.10 N	82.50 W
Essex □[6], Eng., U.K.	174	51.48 N	0.40 E
Essex □[6], Mass., U.S.	261	42.31 N	70.55 W
Essex □[6], N.J., U.S.	262	40.48 N	74.12 W
Essex □[6], Vt., U.S.	260	44.57 N	71.43 W
Essex □[6], Va., U.S.	262	37.55 N	76.55 W
Essex Junction	242	44.29 N	73.07 W
Essexville	244	43.37 N	83.50 W
Esslingen	164	48.45 N	9.16 E
Es Smala es Souassi	170	35.21 N	10.33 E
Essonne □[5]	176	48.36 N	2.20 E
Essoyes	166	48.04 N	4.32 E
Es-Suki	220	13.20 N	33.54 E
Est □[5]	222	12.00 N	1.00 E
Est, Cap ≻	225b	15.16 S	50.29 E
Est, Île de l' I	240	47.38 N	61.28 W
Est, Pointe de l' ≻	240	49.08 N	61.41 W
Estacada	270	45.17 N	122.20 W
Estaca de Bares, Punta de la ≻	168	43.46 N	7.42 W
Estacado, Llano ⩫	250	33.30 N	102.40 W
Eşţahbānāt	208	29.08 N	54.04 E
Estância, Bra.	286	11.16 S	37.26 W
Estancia, Pil.	202	11.28 N	123.09 E
Estancia, N. Mex., U.S.	254	34.45 N	106.04 W
Estanislao del Campo	294	25.03 S	60.06 W
Estanzuelas	280	13.38 N	88.30 W
Estarreja	168	40.45 N	8.34 W
Estats, Pique d' ∧	166	42.40 N	1.24 E
Estcourt	224	29.01 S	29.52 E
Este	170	45.14 N	11.39 E
Esteio	294	29.51 S	51.10 W
Estelí	280	13.05 N	86.23 W
Estelí □[5]	280	13.10 N	86.20 W
Estella	168	42.40 N	2.02 W
Estelline, S. Dak., U.S.	252	44.35 N	96.54 W
Estelline, Tex., U.S.	250	34.33 N	100.26 W
Estell Manor	262	39.23 N	74.48 W
Estepa	168	37.18 N	4.54 W
Estepona	168	36.26 N	5.08 W
Ester	236	64.51 N	148.01 W
Esternay	166	48.44 N	3.34 E
Esteros	294	26.37 S	63.39 W
Estes Park	254	40.23 N	105.31 W
Este Sudeste, Cayos del II	280	12.25 N	81.28 W
Estevan	252	49.07 N	103.05 W
Estevan Group II	238	53.05 N	129.40 W
Estevan Point	238	49.23 N	126.33 W
Esther Island I	236	60.50 N	148.05 W
Estherville	252	43.24 N	94.50 W
Estill	246	32.45 N	81.14 W
Estissac	166	48.16 N	3.49 E
Eston	232	51.10 N	108.46 W
Estrées-Saint-Denis	166	49.26 N	2.39 E
Estrêla	294	29.29 S	51.58 W
Estrela ∧	168	40.19 N	7.37 W
Estrela, Serra da ⋀	168	40.20 N	7.38 W
Estrêla do Indaiá	296	19.31 S	45.47 W
Estrêla do Leste	296	16.17 S	53.34 W
Estrêla do Norte	296	13.49 S	49.04 W
Estrêla do Sul	296	18.46 S	47.42 W
Estrella, Punta ≻	278	30.55 N	114.43 W
Estremadura □[9]	168	39.15 N	9.10 W
Estremoz	168	38.51 N	7.35 W
Esztergom	164	47.48 N	18.45 E
Étables	166	48.38 N	2.50 W
Étain	166	49.13 N	5.38 E
Étampes	176	48.26 N	2.09 E
Etamunbanie, Lake ⊜	228	26.15 S	139.44 E
Étaples	176	50.31 N	1.39 E
Etāwah	206	25.33 N	76.22 E
Etchemin ≃	240	46.45 N	71.14 W
Etchojoa	278	26.55 N	109.38 W
Etchoropo	278	26.41 N	109.40 W
Eten	292	6.55 S	79.50 W
Ethan	252	43.33 N	103.59 W
Ethel	248	33.07 N	89.34 W
Ethel Lake ⊜	236	63.21 N	136.00 W
Ethiopia □[1]	214	9.00 N	41.00 E
Ethridge, Mont., U.S.	238	48.34 N	112.07 W
Ethridge, Tenn., U.S.	248	35.19 N	87.18 W
Etili	172	39.59 N	26.54 E
Etiwanda	274	34.08 N	117.31 W
Etjo ∧	224	21.09 S	16.30 E
Etna, Calif., U.S.	258	41.27 N	122.54 W
Etna, Pa., U.S.	266	40.30 N	79.57 W
Etna, Wyo., U.S.	254	43.02 N	111.00 W
Etna, Monte ∧[1]	170	37.46 N	15.00 E
Etna Green	268	41.17 N	86.03 W
Etobicoke	264	43.39 N	79.34 W
Etolin Island I	236	56.08 N	132.26 W
Etolin Strait ⋃	236	60.20 N	165.15 W
Eton	174	51.31 N	0.37 W
Etosha National Park ⩫[4]	224	18.45 S	15.00 E
Etoshapan ⩫	224	18.45 S	16.15 E
Etowah	246	35.20 N	84.32 W
Etowah ≃	246	34.15 N	85.11 W
Étretat	166	49.42 N	0.12 E
'Etsion-Gever ⊥	210	29.32 N	34.59 E
Ettelbruck	164	49.52 N	6.05 E
Etten	178	51.34 N	4.38 E
Etterbeek	176	50.50 N	4.23 E
Etters	262	40.09 N	76.45 W
Ettlingen	164	48.56 N	8.24 E
Ettrick	262	37.14 N	77.25 W
Etzatlán	278	20.46 N	104.05 W
Etzikom Coulee ≃	238	49.25 N	111.10 W
Etzná-Tixmucuy ⊥	278	19.35 N	90.13 W
Eu	176	50.03 N	1.25 E
Euboea → Évvoia I	172	38.34 N	23.50 E
Eucalyptus Hills	274	32.56 N	116.56 W
Euchiniko ≃	238	53.20 N	123.50 W
Eucla	226	31.43 S	128.52 E
Euclid, Ohio, U.S.	266	41.34 N	81.32 W
Euclid, Pa., U.S.	266	41.00 N	79.56 W
Euclid Center	268	42.08 N	86.24 W
Euclid Heights	248	34.29 N	93.02 W
Eucumbene, Lake ⊜	228	36.05 S	148.45 E
Eudistes, Lac des ⊜	240	50.30 N	65.15 W
Eudora, Ark., U.S.	248	33.07 N	91.16 W
Eudora, Kans., U.S.	252	38.57 N	95.06 W
Eufaula, Ala., U.S.	248	31.54 N	85.09 W
Eufaula, Okla., U.S.	250	35.17 N	95.35 W
Eufaula, Lake ⊜[1]	246	31.45 N	85.10 W
Eufaula Reservoir ⊜[1]	250	35.17 N	95.31 W
Eugene	256	44.02 N	123.05 W
Eugenia, Punta ≻	278	27.50 N	115.03 W
Eugenio Bustos	294	33.45 S	69.03 W
Eugênio Penzo	294	22.13 S	55.53 W
Eugenópolis	296	18.12 S	49.44 W
Eume ≃	168	43.25 N	8.08 W
Eungela National Park ♠	228	21.00 S	148.30 E
Eunice, La., U.S.	248	30.30 N	92.25 W
Eunice, N. Mex., U.S.	250	32.26 N	103.09 W
Eupen	164	50.38 N	6.02 E
Euphrates (Fırat) (Al-Furāt) ≃	208	31.00 N	47.25 E
Eupora	248	33.32 N	89.16 W
Eure	262	36.26 N	76.51 W
Eure □[5]	176	49.10 N	1.00 E
Eure-et-Loir □[5]	176	48.30 N	1.30 E
Eureka, Alaska, U.S.	236	65.11 N	150.13 W
Eureka, Calif., U.S.	258	40.47 N	124.09 W
Eureka, Ill., U.S.	244	40.43 N	89.16 W

Symbols in the index entries are identified on page 360.

Name	Page	Lat°′	Long°′
Eureka, Kans., U.S.	252	37.49 N	96.17 W
Eureka, Mont., U.S.	256	48.53 N	115.03 W
Eureka, Nev., U.S.	258	39.31 N	115.58 W
Eureka, Pa., U.S.	266	40.15 N	78.46 W
Eureka, S. Dak., U.S.	252	45.46 N	99.38 W
Eureka, Utah, U.S.	254	39.57 N	112.07 W
Eureka Springs	248	36.24 N	93.44 W
Euroa	228	36.45 S	145.35 E
Europa, Île	218	22.20 S	40.22 E
Europa, Picos de	168	43.12 N	4.48 W
Europa Point	168	36.10 N	5.22 W
Europe	148	50.00 N	28.00 E
Europoort	164	51.58 N	4.00 E
Euskirchen	166	50.39 N	6.47 E
Eustace	250	32.18 N	96.01 W
Eustis, Fla., U.S.	246	28.51 N	81.41 W
Eustis, Nebr., U.S.	252	40.40 N	100.02 W
Eustis, Lake	246	28.50 N	81.44 W
Eutaw	248	32.50 N	87.53 W
Eutin	164	54.08 N	10.37 E
Eutsuk Lake	238	53.20 N	126.44 W
Eva, Bra.	290	3.00 S	59.18 W
Eva, Ala., U.S.	248	34.20 N	86.46 W
Evadale	248	30.21 N	94.04 W
Evans, Lac	232	50.50 N	77.00 W
Evans, Mount	254	39.35 N	105.38 W
Evansburg	238	53.36 N	115.01 W
Evans Center	264	42.39 N	79.02 W
Evans City	266	40.45 N	80.03 W
Evansdale	244	42.30 N	92.17 W
Evans Head	228	29.07 S	153.26 E
Evans Mills	264	44.05 N	75.48 W
Evansport	268	41.25 N	84.24 W
Evans Strait	232	63.15 N	82.00 W
Evanston, Ill., U.S.	268	42.03 N	87.42 W
Evanston, Wyo., U.S.	254	41.16 N	110.58 W
Evansville, Ill., U.S.	248	38.05 N	89.56 W
Evansville, Ind., U.S.	248	37.58 N	87.35 W
Evansville, Wis., U.S.	268	42.47 N	89.18 W
Evansville, Wyo., U.S.	254	42.52 N	106.16 W
Evant	250	31.29 N	98.09 W
Evart	244	43.54 N	85.08 W
Evarts	246	36.52 N	83.12 W
Evaton	224	26.31 S	27.54 E
Eveleth	244	47.28 N	92.32 W
Evening Shade	248	36.04 N	91.37 W
Evensk	186	61.57 N	159.14 E
Everard, Cape	228	37.48 S	149.17 E
Everard, Mount	238	51.05 N	125.45 W
Everest	252	39.41 N	95.26 W
Everest, Mount(Zhumulangmafeng)	206	27.59 N	86.56 E
Everett, Ont., Can.	264	44.11 N	79.57 W
Everett, Mass., U.S.	261	42.24 N	71.03 W
Everett, Pa., U.S.	242	40.01 N	78.23 W
Everett, Wash., U.S.	270	47.59 N	122.13 W
Everett, Mount	242	42.06 N	73.25 W
Everett Mountains	232	62.45 N	67.12 W
Evergem	176	51.07 N	3.42 E
Everglades	246	25.52 N	81.23 W
Everglades National Park	246	25.27 N	80.53 W
Evergreen, Ala., U.S.	248	31.26 N	86.57 W
Evergreen, Calif., U.S.	258	35.54 N	120.26 W
Evergreen Park, Ill., U.S.	268	41.43 N	87.42 W
Evergreen Park, Mich., U.S.	268	43.04 N	86.10 W
Everly	252	43.10 N	95.20 W
Everson, Pa., U.S.	266	40.06 N	79.35 W
Everson, Wash., U.S.	270	48.55 N	122.21 W
Evesham	174	52.06 N	1.56 W
Évian-les-Bains	166	46.23 N	6.35 E
Evijärvi	160	63.22 N	23.29 E
Evisa	170	42.15 N	8.47 E
Evje	160	58.36 N	7.51 E
Évora	168	38.34 N	7.54 W
Évreux	176	49.01 N	1.09 E
Evritanía	172	38.50 N	21.40 E
Évros	172	41.00 N	26.00 E
Évros (Marica) (Meriç)	172	40.52 N	26.12 E
Evrótas	172	36.48 N	22.40 E
Évry	166	48.38 N	2.27 E
Évvoia	172	38.34 N	23.50 E
Évvois	172	38.30 N	24.00 E
Ewa	275c	21.21 N	158.02 W
Ewa Beach	275c	21.20 N	158.04 W
Ewarton	285q	18.11 N	77.05 W
Ewell	262	37.59 N	76.02 W
Ewen	244	46.32 N	89.17 W
Ewing, Nebr., U.S.	252	42.16 N	98.21 W
Ewing, Va., U.S.	246	36.38 N	83.26 W
Ewing, Mount	228	22.58 S	137.14 E
Ewo	218	0.53 S	14.49 E
Exaltación	292	13.16 S	65.15 W
Excelsior Mountain	258	38.02 N	119.18 W
Excelsior Springs	248	39.20 N	94.13 W
Excursion Inlet	236	58.25 N	135.27 W
Exe	162	50.37 N	3.25 W
Executive Committee Range	148	76.50 S	126.00 W
Exeter, Ont., Can.	244	43.21 N	81.29 W
Exeter, Eng., U.K.	174	50.43 N	3.31 W
Exeter, Calif., U.S.	272	36.18 N	119.09 W
Exeter, Nebr., U.S.	252	40.39 N	97.27 W
Exeter, N.H., U.S.	242	42.59 N	70.57 W
Exeter, R.I., U.S.	261	41.35 N	71.32 W
Exeter	242	43.02 N	70.55 W
Exeter Sound	232	66.14 N	62.00 W
Exira	252	41.35 N	94.52 W
Exmoor National Park	162	51.12 N	3.46 W
Exmore	262	37.32 N	75.50 W
Exmouth	174	50.37 N	3.25 W
Expedition Range	228	24.30 S	149.05 E
Experiment	246	33.16 N	84.17 W
Exploits	240	49.05 N	55.20 W
Exploits, Bay of	240	49.24 N	55.00 W
Export	266	40.25 N	79.37 W
Exshaw	238	51.03 N	115.09 W
Extension	270	49.06 N	123.57 W
Exton	262	40.02 N	75.37 W
Extrema	296	22.51 S	46.19 W
Extremadura	168	39.00 N	6.00 W
Exuma Sound	282	24.00 N	76.00 W
Eyak	236	60.32 N	145.36 W
Eyasi, Lake	218	3.40 S	35.05 E
Eye	162	52.19 N	1.09 E
Eyemouth	162	55.52 N	2.06 W
Eye Peninsula	162	58.13 N	6.05 W
Eyjafjördur	160a	65.54 N	18.15 W
Eylar Mountain	258	37.28 N	121.33 W
Eymet	166	44.40 N	0.24 E
Eymoutiers	166	45.44 N	1.44 E
Eynihal	172	36.14 N	29.59 E
Eyota	244	43.59 N	92.14 W
Eyrarbakki	160a	63.53 N	21.05 W
Eyre	226	32.15 S	126.18 E
Eyre (South), Lake, Austl.	228	29.30 S	137.20 E
Eyre (North), Lake, Austl.	228	28.40 S	137.10 E
Eyre Mountains	230	45.20 S	168.25 E
Eyre Peninsula	228	34.00 S	135.45 E
Ezeriş	172	45.24 N	21.53 E
Ezine	172	39.47 N	26.20 E
Ežva	160	61.47 N	50.40 E

F

Name	Page	Lat°′	Long°′
Fabens	254	31.30 N	106.10 W
Faber Lake	232	63.56 N	117.15 W
Fabius	264	42.50 N	75.59 W
Fåborg	160	55.06 N	10.15 E
Fábrega, Cerro	280	9.07 N	82.52 W
Fabriano	184	43.20 N	12.54 E
Fabrica	202	10.54 N	123.23 E
Facatativá	290	4.49 N	74.22 W
Faches-Thumesnil	176	50.35 N	3.04 E
Factoryville	242	41.34 N	75.47 W
Fada	214	17.14 N	21.33 E
Fada Ngourma	222	12.04 N	0.21 E
Fadd	164	46.28 N	18.50 E
Faddejevskij, Ostrov	186	75.30 N	144.00 E
Faenza	184	44.17 N	11.53 E
Faeroe Islands	158	62.00 N	7.00 W
Fafe	168	41.27 N	8.10 W
Fafen	214	6.07 N	44.20 E
Faga	222	13.15 N	0.55 E
Făgăraş	172	45.51 N	24.58 E
Făgăraşului, Munţii	172	45.35 N	25.00 E
Fagernes	160	60.59 N	9.15 E
Fagersta	160	60.00 N	15.47 E
Făget	172	45.51 N	22.10 E
Fagnano Olona	182	45.40 N	8.52 E
Faguibine, Lac	222	16.45 N	3.54 W
Fagurhólsmýri	160a	63.54 N	16.38 W
Fairbank	244	42.38 N	92.03 W
Fairbanks, Alaska, U.S.	236	64.51 N	147.43 W
Fairbanks, La., U.S.	248	32.39 N	92.02 W
Fair Bluff	246	34.19 N	79.02 W
Fairburn	246	33.34 N	84.35 W
Fairbury, Ill., U.S.	268	40.45 N	88.31 W
Fairbury, Nebr., U.S.	252	40.08 N	97.11 W
Fairchance	242	39.49 N	79.45 W
Fairchild	244	44.36 N	90.58 W
Fairchild Air Force Base	256	47.38 N	117.38 W
Fairdale	268	42.06 N	88.56 W
Faire	202	17.53 N	121.34 E
Fairfax, Ala., U.S.	248	32.48 N	85.11 W
Fairfax, Calif., U.S.	272	38.00 N	122.35 W
Fairfax, Ind., U.S.	268	41.04 N	85.06 W
Fairfax, Minn., U.S.	252	44.32 N	94.31 W
Fairfax, Okla., U.S.	250	36.34 N	96.42 W
Fairfax, S.C., U.S.	246	33.01 N	81.18 W
Fairfax, S. Dak., U.S.	252	43.02 N	98.54 W
Fairfax, Vt., U.S.	242	44.40 N	73.01 W
Fairfax, Va., U.S.	262	38.51 N	77.18 W
Fairfax	262	38.45 N	77.15 W
Fairfield, Ala., U.S.	248	33.29 N	86.55 W
Fairfield, Calif., U.S.	272	38.15 N	122.03 W
Fairfield, Conn., U.S.	261	41.09 N	73.15 W
Fairfield, Idaho, U.S.	256	43.21 N	114.48 W
Fairfield, Ill., U.S.	248	38.23 N	88.22 W
Fairfield, Iowa, U.S.	244	40.56 N	91.57 W
Fairfield, Maine, U.S.	242	44.35 N	69.36 W
Fairfield, Mont., U.S.	256	47.37 N	111.59 W
Fairfield, Nebr., U.S.	252	40.26 N	98.06 W
Fairfield, Ohio, U.S.	242	39.20 N	84.33 W
Fairfield, Pa., U.S.	266	39.47 N	77.22 W
Fairfield, Tex., U.S.	250	31.44 N	96.10 W
Fairfield	261	41.11 N	73.11 W
Fairgrove	244	43.31 N	83.33 W
Fairhaven, Mass., U.S.	261	41.39 N	70.54 W
Fair Haven, Mich., U.S.	266	42.41 N	82.39 W
Fair Haven, N.J., U.S.	262	40.23 N	74.03 W
Fair Haven, N.Y., U.S.	264	43.19 N	76.42 W
Fair Haven, Vt., U.S.	242	43.36 N	73.16 W
Fair Head	162	55.13 N	6.09 W
Fairhope, Ala., U.S.	248	30.31 N	87.54 W
Fairhope, Ohio, U.S.	266	40.51 N	81.19 W
Fairhope, Pa., U.S.	266	40.07 N	79.50 W
Fair Isle	162	59.30 N	1.40 W
Fairland, Ind., U.S.	248	39.35 N	85.52 W
Fairland, Okla., U.S.	250	36.45 N	94.51 W
Fairlawn	266	41.08 N	81.36 W
Fairless Hills	262	40.11 N	74.50 W
Fairlie	230	44.06 S	170.50 E
Fairmont, Minn., U.S.	252	43.39 N	94.28 W
Fairmont, Nebr., U.S.	252	40.38 N	97.35 W
Fairmont, N.C., U.S.	246	34.30 N	79.07 W
Fairmont, Wash., U.S.	270	48.54 N	122.16 W
Fairmont, W. Va., U.S.	242	39.29 N	80.09 W
Fairmont Hot Springs	238	50.19 N	115.53 W
Fairmount, Ga., U.S.	246	34.26 N	84.42 W
Fairmount, Ill., U.S.	248	40.03 N	87.56 W
Fairmount, Ind., U.S.	268	40.25 N	85.39 W
Fairmount, N. Dak., U.S.	252	46.03 N	96.36 W
Fairmount, N.Y., U.S.	264	43.04 N	76.15 W
Fairmount City	266	41.01 N	79.19 W
Fairmount Heights	262	38.54 N	76.55 W
Fairness Point	232	63.24 N	72.05 W
Fair Oaks, Calif., U.S.	272	37.58 N	121.12 W
Fair Oaks, Calif., U.S.	272	38.39 N	121.16 W
Fair Oaks, Ga., U.S.	246	33.55 N	84.32 W
Fair Oaks, Ind., U.S.	268	41.05 N	87.16 W
Fair Plain	268	42.05 N	86.28 W
Fairplay	254	39.19 N	105.60 W
Fairpoint	266	40.07 N	80.56 W
Fairport	264	43.06 N	77.27 W
Fairport Harbor	266	41.45 N	81.17 W
Fairton	262	39.23 N	75.13 W
Fairview, Alta., Can.	238	56.04 N	118.23 W
Fairview, Ga., U.S.	246	34.58 N	85.16 W
Fairview, Ill., U.S.	244	40.38 N	90.10 W
Fairview, Ind., U.S.	268	40.18 N	85.11 W
Fairview, Kans., U.S.	252	39.50 N	95.44 W
Fairview, Md., U.S.	262	39.09 N	76.29 W
Fairview, Mich., U.S.	244	44.44 N	84.03 W
Fairview, Mont., U.S.	252	47.51 N	104.03 W
Fairview, N.Y., U.S.	261	41.44 N	73.56 W
Fairview, Ohio, U.S.	266	40.03 N	81.14 W
Fairview, Okla., U.S.	250	36.16 N	98.29 W
Fairview, Oreg., U.S.	270	45.32 N	122.26 W
Fairview, Pa., U.S.	266	41.01 N	79.44 W
Fairview, Pa., U.S.	266	42.03 N	80.13 W
Fairview, Tenn., U.S.	248	35.59 N	87.07 W
Fairview, Utah, U.S.	254	39.38 N	111.26 W
Fairview, W. Va., U.S.	242	39.36 N	80.15 W
Fairview Park, Ind., U.S.	248	39.41 N	87.25 W
Fairview Park, Ohio, U.S.	266	41.27 N	81.51 W
Fairview Peak, Nev., U.S.	258	39.14 N	118.08 W
Fairview Peak, Oreg., U.S.	256	43.35 N	122.39 W
Fairweather, Cape	232	58.45 N	137.55 W
Fairweather, Mount	236	58.54 N	137.32 W
Fais	198	9.46 N	140.31 E
Faison	246	35.07 N	78.08 W
Faistós	172	35.01 N	24.48 E
Faith	252	45.02 N	102.02 W
Faiyum → Al-Fayyūm	220	29.19 N	30.50 E
Faizābād, Afg.	206	37.06 N	70.34 E
Faizābād, Bhārat	206	26.47 N	82.08 E
Fajardo	284m	18.20 N	65.39 W
Fajr, Wādī	208	30.06 N	38.18 E
Fakel	160	57.38 N	53.02 E
Fakenham	162	52.50 N	0.51 E
Fakfak	198	2.55 S	132.18 E
Faku	194	42.30 N	123.24 E
Falaise	166	48.54 N	0.12 W
Falam	200	22.55 N	93.40 E
Fălciu	172	46.18 N	28.08 E
Falcón	290	11.00 N	69.50 W
Falcon, Cap	168	35.45 N	1.00 W
Falcon, Cape	256	45.46 N	123.59 W
Falconara Marittima	184	43.37 N	13.24 E
Falconbridge	244	46.35 N	80.48 W
Falconer	266	42.07 N	79.12 W
Falcon Reservoir	250	26.37 N	99.11 W
Falconwood	264	43.00 N	78.57 W
Falémé	222	14.46 N	12.14 W
Falfurrias	250	27.14 N	98.09 W
Falher	238	55.44 N	117.12 W
Falkenberg, D.D.R.	164	51.35 N	13.14 E
Falkenberg, Sve.	160	56.54 N	12.28 E
Falkensee	164	52.33 N	13.04 E
Falkenstein, B.R.D.	164	49.06 N	12.30 E
Falkenstein, D.D.R.	164	50.29 N	12.22 E
Falkirk	162	56.00 N	3.48 W
Falkland	238	50.30 N	119.33 W
Falkland Islands (Islas Malvinas)	288	51.45 S	59.00 W
Falkland Rise	148	52.00 S	50.00 W
Falkland Sound	288	51.45 S	59.25 W
Falköping	160	58.10 N	13.31 E
Fall	252	37.24 N	95.40 W
Fallbrook	274	33.23 N	117.15 W
Fall City	270	47.34 N	121.53 W
Fall Creek	244	44.46 N	91.17 W
Fallen Leaf	272	38.53 N	120.04 W
Fallentimber	266	40.41 N	78.30 W
Fallersleben	164	52.25 N	10.43 E
Falling	246	37.01 N	78.55 W
Fallingbostel	178	52.52 N	9.41 E
Falling Water	248	36.02 N	85.47 W
Fallon, Mont., U.S.	252	46.50 N	105.07 W
Fallon, Nev., U.S.	258	39.28 N	118.47 W
Fall River, Kans., U.S.	252	37.36 N	96.02 W
Fall River, Mass., U.S.	261	41.43 N	71.08 W
Fall River, Wis., U.S.	244	43.23 N	89.03 W
Fall River Mills	258	41.00 N	121.26 W
Fall River Reservoir	252	37.42 N	96.08 W
Falls Church	262	38.53 N	77.11 W
Falls City, Nebr., U.S.	252	40.03 N	95.36 W
Falls City, Oreg., U.S.	256	44.52 N	123.26 W
Falls Creek	266	41.09 N	78.48 W
Fallsington	262	40.12 N	74.48 W
Fallston	262	39.31 N	76.25 W
Falls Village	261	41.57 N	73.22 W
Falmouth, Jam.	285q	18.30 N	77.40 W
Falmouth, Eng., U.K.	174	50.08 N	5.04 W
Falmouth, Ky., U.S.	242	38.40 N	84.20 W
Falmouth, Maine, U.S.	242	43.39 N	70.16 W
Falmouth, Mass., U.S.	261	41.34 N	70.38 W
Falmouth, Va., U.S.	262	38.19 N	77.28 W
Falmouth Heights	261	41.33 N	70.36 W
Falsa Chipana, Punta	292	21.20 S	70.06 W
False Pass	236	54.52 N	163.24 W
Falset	168	41.08 N	0.49 E
Falso, Cabo, Hond.	280	15.12 N	83.21 W
Falso, Cabo, Rep. Dom.	282	17.45 N	71.40 W
Falster	164	54.48 N	11.58 E
Fălticeni	172	47.28 N	26.18 E
Falun	160	60.36 N	15.38 E
Famagusta → Ammókhostos	212	35.07 N	33.57 E
Famaillá	294	27.05 S	65.25 W
Famatina	294	28.58 S	67.30 W
Famatina, Nevado de	294	29.00 S	67.51 W
Famenne	166	50.10 N	5.15 E
Fanado	296	17.10 S	42.40 W
Fancher	264	43.15 N	66.06 W
Fancy	285h	13.22 N	61.11 W
Fangak	214	9.04 N	30.53 E
Fangcheng	196	33.16 N	112.59 E
Fanghe	194	35.05 N	118.24 E
Fannettsburg	266	40.04 N	77.50 W
Fannrem	160	63.16 N	9.50 E
Fanny, Mount	256	45.20 N	117.41 W
Fanny Bay	238	49.30 N	124.50 W
Fano	184	43.50 N	13.01 E
Fan-si-pan	200	22.15 N	103.46 E
Faraday, Mount	228	24.55 S	147.17 E
Faraday Seamount Group	148	49.30 N	28.00 W
Faradje	214	3.44 N	29.43 E
Farafangana	225b	22.49 S	47.50 E
Farah	208	32.21 N	62.07 E
Farah	208	33.00 N	62.30 E
Farah	206	31.30 N	61.30 E
Farā'id, Jabal al-	220	23.31 N	35.20 E
Fara in Sabina	184	42.12 N	12.43 E
Farallon de Medinilla	198	16.01 N	146.04 E
Farallon de Pajaros	198	20.32 N	144.54 E
Faranah	214	10.02 N	10.44 W
Faranah	222	10.00 N	10.50 W
Farasān, Jazā'ir	214	16.48 N	41.54 E
Faraulep	198	8.36 N	144.33 E
Farcăul	172	47.56 N	24.27 E
Fardes	168	37.35 N	3.00 W
Fareham	174	50.51 N	1.10 W
Farewell	236	62.31 N	153.53 W
Farewell, Cape	230	40.30 S	172.41 E
Farewell Spit	230	40.31 S	172.50 E
Fargo	252	46.52 N	96.48 W
Faribault	244	44.18 N	93.16 W
Faribault, Lac	232	59.00 N	71.55 W
Farīdpur	204	23.38 N	89.46 E
Farilhao Point	224	22.15 S	14.15 E
Farilhões, Ilhas	168	39.28 N	9.34 W
Farina	248	38.50 N	88.46 W
Faringdon	174	51.40 N	1.35 W
Fāriskūr	220	31.20 N	31.43 E
Färjestaden	160	56.39 N	16.27 E
Farley	244	42.27 N	91.00 W
Farmer City	268	40.15 N	88.39 W
Farmersburg	248	39.15 N	87.23 W
Farmers Fork	262	38.02 N	76.45 W
Farmersville, Calif., U.S.	272	36.18 N	119.12 W
Farmersville, Ill., U.S.	248	39.26 N	89.39 W
Farmersville, Pa., U.S.	262	40.08 N	76.10 W
Farmersville, Tex., U.S.	250	33.10 N	96.22 W
Farmersville Station	266	42.26 N	78.22 W
Farmerville	248	32.47 N	92.24 W
Farmingdale	262	40.12 N	74.10 W
Farmington, Calif., U.S.	272	37.56 N	120.59 W
Farmington, Conn., U.S.	261	41.43 N	72.50 W
Farmington, Del., U.S.	262	38.52 N	75.35 W
Farmington, Ill., U.S.	244	40.42 N	90.00 W
Farmington, Iowa, U.S.	244	40.38 N	91.44 W
Farmington, Maine, U.S.	242	44.40 N	70.09 W
Farmington, Mich., U.S.	268	42.28 N	83.22 W
Farmington, Minn., U.S.	244	44.38 N	93.08 W
Farmington, Mo., U.S.	248	37.47 N	90.25 W
Farmington, Mont., U.S.	238	47.54 N	112.11 W
Farmington, N.H., U.S.	242	43.24 N	71.04 W
Farmington, N. Mex., U.S.	254	36.44 N	108.12 W
Farmington, Utah, U.S.	254	40.59 N	111.53 W
Farmingville	261	40.39 N	73.02 W
Far Mountain	238	52.46 N	125.17 W
Farmville, N.C., U.S.	246	35.36 N	77.35 W
Farmville, Va., U.S.	246	37.18 N	78.24 W
Farnam	252	40.42 N	100.13 W
Farnborough	174	51.17 N	0.46 W
Farne Islands	162	55.38 N	1.38 W
Farnham, Qué., Can.	260	45.17 N	72.59 W
Farnham, Eng., U.K.	174	51.13 N	0.49 W
Farnham, Va., U.S.	262	37.53 N	76.38 W
Farnham, Mount	238	50.29 N	116.30 W
Farnhamville	252	42.17 N	94.24 W
Faro, Bra.	290	2.11 S	56.44 W
Faro, Port.	168	37.01 N	7.56 W
Faro	214	9.21 N	12.55 E
Faro, Punta	290	11.06 N	74.50 W
Faro, Punta del	170	38.17 N	15.39 E
Fårön	160	57.56 N	19.08 E
Fårösund	160	57.52 N	19.03 E
Farquhar Group	218	10.10 S	51.10 E
Farragut	252	40.43 N	95.29 W
Farrell	266	41.13 N	80.30 W
Farrukhābād	206	27.24 N	79.35 E
Fārs	208	29.00 N	53.00 E
Fársala	172	39.18 N	22.23 E
Farsund	160	58.05 N	6.48 E
Fartak, Ra's	204	15.38 N	52.15 E
Farvel, Kap	232	59.45 N	44.00 W
Farwell, Mich., U.S.	244	43.50 N	84.52 W
Farwell, Tex., U.S.	250	34.23 N	103.02 W
Faryab	206	36.00 N	65.00 E
Fasā	208	28.56 N	53.42 E
Fasano	170	40.50 N	17.22 E
Fastnet Rock	162	51.24 N	9.35 W
Fatala	222	10.13 N	14.00 W
Fátima, Bra.	296	16.11 S	54.58 W
Fátima, Port.	168	39.37 N	8.39 W
Fatshan → Foshan	196	23.03 N	113.09 E
Faucilles, Monts	166	48.07 N	6.16 E
Faulkton	252	45.02 N	99.08 W
Faulquemont	166	49.03 N	6.36 E
Fauquembergues	162	50.36 N	2.05 E
Fauquier	238	49.53 N	118.05 W
Fauquier	262	38.35 N	77.35 W
Făurei	172	45.06 N	27.09 E
Fauske	160	67.15 N	15.24 E
Faust	238	55.19 N	115.38 W
Favara	170	37.19 N	13.40 E
Faverges	166	45.45 N	6.18 E
Faversham	174	51.20 N	0.53 E
Favignana, Isola	170	37.56 N	12.19 E
Fawcett	238	54.32 N	114.05 W
Fawcett Lake	238	55.19 N	113.57 W
Fawn	232	55.22 N	88.20 W
Fawn Grove	262	39.44 N	76.27 W
Fawnie Nose	238	53.16 N	125.08 W
Fawnie Range	238	53.10 N	125.00 W
Faxaflói	160a	64.25 N	23.00 W
Faxälven	160	63.13 N	17.13 E
Faxinal	296	23.59 S	51.22 W
Faxinal do Soturno	294	29.37 S	53.26 W
Fayence	166	43.37 N	6.41 E
Fayette, Ala., U.S.	248	33.42 N	87.50 W
Fayette, Iowa, U.S.	244	42.51 N	91.48 W
Fayette, Miss., U.S.	248	31.42 N	91.04 W
Fayette, Mo., U.S.	248	39.09 N	92.41 W
Fayette, N.Y., U.S.	264	42.49 N	76.49 W
Fayette, Ohio, U.S.	268	41.40 N	84.20 W
Fayette	266	40.05 N	79.39 W
Fayette City	266	40.06 N	79.50 W
Fayetteville, Ark., U.S.	248	36.04 N	94.10 W
Fayetteville, Ga., U.S.	246	33.27 N	84.27 W
Fayetteville, N.C., U.S.	246	35.03 N	78.54 W
Fayetteville, N.Y., U.S.	264	43.02 N	76.00 W
Fayetteville, Pa., U.S.	262	39.55 N	77.33 W
Fayetteville, Tenn., U.S.	248	35.09 N	86.35 W
Fayetteville, W. Va., U.S.	242	38.03 N	81.06 W
Faylakah	208	29.25 N	48.22 E
Fayl-Billot	166	47.47 N	5.36 E
Fayville	261	42.18 N	71.31 W
Fazenda de Cima	292	15.56 S	56.37 W
Fazenda Nova	296	16.11 S	50.48 W
Fazzān (Fezzan)	214	26.00 N	14.00 E
Fdérik	214	22.41 N	12.43 W
Feale	162	52.28 N	9.40 W
Fear, Cape	246	33.50 N	77.58 W
Feasterville	262	40.09 N	75.00 W
Feather	258	38.47 N	121.36 W
Feather Falls	258	39.38 N	121.16 W
Feathertop, Mount	228	36.54 S	147.08 E
Fécamp	176	49.45 N	0.22 E
Fedala → Mohammedia	214	33.44 N	7.24 W
Federación	294	31.00 S	57.55 W
Federal	294	30.55 S	58.45 W
Federalsburg	262	38.42 N	75.47 W
Federal Way	270	47.20 N	122.20 W
Federaun	164	46.35 N	13.49 E
Fedosejevskaja	160	62.07 N	40.42 E
Feeding Hills	261	42.04 N	72.41 W
Fehmarn	164	54.28 N	11.08 E
Fehmarn Belt	164	54.35 N	11.15 E
Feia, Lagoa	296	22.00 S	41.20 W
Feihuanghekou	196	34.16 N	120.18 E
Feijó	292	8.09 S	70.21 W
Feilding	230	40.13 S	175.34 E
Feio	296	21.03 S	51.47 W
Feira	218	15.37 S	30.25 E
Feira de Santana	296	12.15 S	38.57 W
Feistritz	164	47.01 N	16.08 E
Feiyunjiang	196	27.48 N	120.36 E
Fejér	164	47.10 N	18.35 E
Felanitx	168	39.28 N	3.08 E
Felda	246	26.33 N	81.26 W
Feldbach	164	46.57 N	15.54 E
Feldkirch	180	47.14 N	9.36 E
Feldkirchen in Kärnten	164	46.43 N	14.05 E
Feliciano	284m	18.28 N	67.08 W
Felipe Carrillo Puerto	278	19.35 N	88.03 W
Felix, Cape	232	69.54 N	97.50 W
Felix, Rio	250	33.08 N	104.19 W
Félix Gómez	278	29.50 N	111.30 W
Felixlândia	296	18.47 S	44.55 W
Felixstowe	174	51.58 N	1.20 E
Félix U. Gómez	278	30.35 N	105.50 W
Fellbach	164	48.48 N	9.15 E
Felletin	166	45.53 N	2.10 E
Fellows	272	35.11 N	119.32 W
Fellsburg	266	40.11 N	79.49 W
Fellsmere	246	27.46 N	80.36 W
Felton, Calif., U.S.	272	37.03 N	122.04 W
Felton, Del., U.S.	262	39.01 N	75.35 W
Felton, Pa., U.S.	262	39.51 N	76.34 W
Feltre	170	46.01 N	11.54 E
Felts Mills	264	44.01 N	75.46 W
Femeas, Rio das	296	12.27 S	45.12 W
Femund	160	62.12 N	11.52 E
Femundsenden	160	61.55 N	11.55 E
Fenelon Falls	264	44.32 N	78.45 W
Fenelton	266	40.52 N	79.44 W
Fener Burnu	212	41.07 N	39.25 E
Fenérgyarmat	164	47.58 N	22.32 E
Fénérive	218	17.22 S	49.25 E
Fengcheng, Zhg.	194	40.28 N	124.00 E
Fengcheng, Zhg.	196	28.10 N	115.46 E
Fengdu	190	29.58 N	107.41 E
Fengfeng	190	36.28 N	114.14 E
Fengling	196	28.14 N	118.29 E
Fengmingdao	194	39.24 N	121.22 E
Fengyang	190	32.52 N	117.34 E
Fengzhen	190	40.24 N	113.09 E
Fenhe	190	37.19 N	112.05 E
Fenholloway	246	29.59 N	83.47 W
Fenimore Pass	236	52.00 N	175.35 W
Fennimore	244	42.59 N	90.39 W
Fennville	268	42.36 N	86.06 W
Feno, Cap de	170	41.57 N	8.36 E
Fenton	268	42.48 N	83.42 W
Fentress	250	29.45 N	97.47 W
Fenwick, Ont., Can.	264	43.01 N	79.22 W
Fenwick, W. Va., U.S.	242	38.14 N	80.35 W
Fenyang	190	37.18 N	111.41 E
Feodosija	158	45.02 N	35.23 E
Ferdig	238	48.45 N	111.46 W
Ferdinand	248	38.14 N	86.52 W
Ferdows	208	34.00 N	58.09 E
Fère-Champenoise	166	48.45 N	3.59 E
Fère-en-Tardenois	166	49.12 N	3.31 E
Ferentino	184	41.42 N	13.15 E
Fergana	186	40.23 N	71.46 E
Fergus	264	43.42 N	80.22 W
Fergus Falls	252	46.17 N	96.04 W
Ferguson, B.C., Can.	238	50.41 N	117.28 W
Ferguson, Ky., U.S.	246	37.03 N	84.36 W
Ferkéssédougou	222	9.30 N	4.50 W
Ferlach	164	46.31 N	14.18 E
Ferlo	222	0.15 N	0.14 W
Ferlo, Vallée du	222	15.42 N	15.30 W
Fermanagh	162	54.20 N	7.45 W
Fermo	184	43.09 N	13.43 E
Fermoselle	168	41.19 N	6.23 W
Fermoy	162	52.08 N	8.16 W
Fernández	294	27.55 S	63.54 W
Fernández Leal	254	30.51 N	108.17 W
Fernandina, Isla	290a	0.25 S	91.30 W
Fernandina Beach	246	30.40 N	81.27 W
Fernando de la Mora	294	25.19 S	57.36 W
Fernandópolis	296	20.16 S	50.14 W
Fernando Póo, Afr.	222	3.30 N	8.42 E
Fernando Póo, Gui. Ecu.	222	3.30 N	8.42 E
Fernán-Núñez	168	37.40 N	4.43 W
Ferndale, Calif., U.S.	258	40.35 N	124.16 W
Ferndale, Md., U.S.	262	39.11 N	76.38 W
Ferndale, Mich., U.S.	268	42.28 N	83.08 W
Ferndale, Pa., U.S.	262	40.32 N	75.11 W
Ferndale, Pa., U.S.	266	40.18 N	78.55 W
Ferndale, Wash., U.S.	270	48.51 N	122.36 W
Fernie	238	49.30 N	115.03 W
Fernley	258	39.36 N	119.15 W
Fern Park	246	28.41 N	81.20 W
Fern Ridge Reservoir	256	44.05 N	123.18 W
Fernway	266	40.41 N	80.07 W
Fernwood, Idaho, U.S.	256	47.07 N	116.23 W
Fernwood, Miss., U.S.	248	31.12 N	90.23 W
Ferrandina	170	40.29 N	16.28 E
Ferrara	170	44.50 N	11.35 E
Ferrara	184	44.48 N	11.50 E
Ferrat, Cap	168	35.55 N	0.30 W
Ferrato, Capo	170	39.18 N	9.38 E
Ferreira do Alentejo	168	38.03 N	8.07 W
Ferreñafe	292	6.35 S	79.45 W
Ferret, Cap	166	44.37 N	1.15 W
Ferreyra	294	31.28 S	64.07 W
Ferriday	248	31.38 N	91.33 W
Ferrière-la-Grande	176	50.15 N	4.00 E
Ferrières	166	48.05 N	2.47 E
Ferris, Ont., Can.	244	46.18 N	79.28 W
Ferris, Tex., U.S.	250	32.32 N	96.40 W
Ferro	296	12.27 S	54.31 W
Ferrol → El Ferrol del Caudillo	168	43.29 N	8.14 W
Ferrol, Península de	292	9.10 S	78.35 W
Ferron	254	39.05 N	111.08 W
Ferros	296	19.14 S	43.02 W
Ferryland	240	47.02 N	52.53 W
Ferrysburg	268	43.05 N	86.11 W
Ferryville → Menzel Bourguiba	170	37.10 N	9.48 E
Fertile	252	47.32 N	96.17 W
Fertő (Neusiedler See)	164	47.50 N	16.46 E
Fertöd	164	47.37 N	16.53 E
Fès	214	34.05 N	4.57 W
Feshi	218	6.07 S	18.10 E
Fessenden	252	47.39 N	99.38 W
Festus	248	38.13 N	90.24 W
Feteşti	172	44.23 N	27.50 E
Fethiye	172	36.37 N	29.07 E
Fethiye Körfezi	212	36.40 N	29.00 E
Fetisovo	158	42.46 N	52.38 E
Fetlar	162	60.37 N	0.52 W
Fetzara	170	36.44 N	7.37 E
Fetzara, Lac	170	36.47 N	7.30 E
Feucht	164	49.22 N	11.13 E
Feuchtwangen	164	49.10 N	10.20 E
Feuilles, Inlet aux	232	58.50 N	69.30 W
Feuilles, Rivière aux	232	58.45 N	70.00 W
Feura Bush	261	42.35 N	73.53 W
Feurs	182	45.45 N	4.14 E
Fez → Fès	214	34.05 N	4.57 W
Ffestiniog	174	52.58 N	3.55 W
Fiambalá	294	27.45 S	67.36 W
Fianarantsoa	225b	21.26 S	47.05 E
Fianarantsoa	225b	22.00 S	47.00 E
Fichtelberg	164	50.26 N	12.57 E
Fichtelgebirge	164	50.26 N	12.57 E
Ficksburg	224	28.57 S	27.50 E
Fiddletown	272	38.30 N	120.46 W
Fidenza	170	44.52 N	10.03 E
Fiditi	222	7.45 N	3.53 E
Field	238	51.24 N	116.29 W
Fieldale	246	36.42 N	79.57 W
Fier	172	40.43 N	19.34 E
Fiesch	166	46.20 N	8.10 E
Fiesole	184	43.48 N	11.17 E
Fife	270	47.14 N	122.22 W
Fife	162	56.13 N	3.02 W
Fife Lake, Sask., Can.	252	49.12 N	105.43 W
Fife Lake, Mich., U.S.	244	44.35 N	85.21 W
Fife Lake	252	49.14 N	105.53 W
Fife Ness	162	56.17 N	2.36 W
Fifield	244	45.53 N	90.25 W
Fifth Cataract → Ash-Shallāl al-Khāmis	220	18.23 N	33.47 E
Figeac	166	44.37 N	2.02 E
Fig Garden	272	36.48 N	119.47 W
Figline Valdarno	184	43.37 N	11.28 E
Figueira, Cachoeira	292	9.49 S	58.13 W
Figueira da Foz	168	40.09 N	8.52 W
Figueras	168	42.16 N	2.58 E
Figuig	214	32.10 N	1.15 W
Fiherenana	225b	23.19 S	43.37 E
Fiji	148	18.00 S	175.00 E
Fiji Islands	148	18.00 S	175.00 E
Filadelfia, C.R.	280	10.26 N	85.34 W
Filadelfia, It.	170	38.48 N	16.18 E
Fil'akovo	164	48.17 N	19.51 E
Filchner Ice Shelf	148	79.00 S	40.00 W
Filey	162	54.12 N	0.17 W
Filí	172	38.10 N	23.40 E
Filiaşi	172	44.33 N	23.31 E
Filiatrá	172	37.10 N	21.35 E
Filicudi, Isola	170	38.35 N	14.34 E
Fílippoi	172	41.00 N	24.16 E
Fillaoussene, Djebel	168	35.00 N	1.45 W
Fillmore, Sask., Can.	252	49.50 N	103.25 W
Fillmore, Calif., U.S.	274	34.24 N	118.55 W
Fillmore, N.Y., U.S.	266	42.28 N	78.07 W
Fillmore, Utah, U.S.	254	38.58 N	112.20 W
Filton	174	51.31 N	2.35 W
Fimi	218	3.01 S	16.58 E
Fina, Réserve de	222	12.50 N	8.30 W
Finale Emilia	170	44.50 N	11.17 E
Finale Ligure	182	44.10 N	8.20 E
Finca El Rey, Parque Nacional	294	25.00 S	64.40 W
Fincastle	246	37.30 N	79.53 W
Finch	260	45.11 N	75.07 W
Findlay, Ill., U.S.	248	39.31 N	88.45 W
Findlay, Ohio, U.S.	268	41.02 N	83.39 W
Findlay, Mount	238	50.04 N	116.28 W
Findley Lake	266	42.07 N	79.44 W
Finesville	262	40.36 N	75.10 W
Fingal, Ont., Can.	266	42.43 N	81.19 W
Fingal, N. Dak., U.S.	252	46.46 N	97.47 W
Fingoè	218	15.12 S	31.50 E
Finike	172	36.18 N	30.09 E
Finike Körfezi	212	36.17 N	30.16 E
Finistère	166	48.20 N	4.00 W
Finisterre	250	25.59 N	103.15 W
Finisterre, Cabo	168	42.53 N	9.16 W
Finke	226	25.34 S	134.35 E
Finke	228	26.20 S	136.00 E
Finkenwerder	178	53.31 N	9.52 E
Finksburg	262	39.30 N	76.54 W
Finland	158	64.00 N	26.00 E
Finland, Gulf of	160	60.00 N	27.00 E
Finlay	232	57.00 N	125.05 W
Finley, N. Dak., U.S.	252	47.31 N	97.50 W
Finley, Okla., U.S.	250	34.20 N	95.30 W
Finleyville, Pa., U.S.	266	40.15 N	80.00 W
Finleyville, Pa., U.S.	266	40.09 N	78.11 W
Finmoore	238	53.59 N	123.37 W
Finn	162	54.50 N	7.29 W
Finnegan	238	51.07 N	112.05 W
Finnie Bay	232	65.13 N	77.30 W
Finnmark	160	70.00 N	25.00 E
Finn Mountain	236	60.37 N	157.11 W
Finnsnes	160	69.14 N	17.59 E
Finse	160	60.36 N	7.30 E
Finspång	160	58.43 N	15.47 E
Finsterwalde	164	51.38 N	13.42 E
Fiora	170	42.20 N	11.34 E
Fiordland National Park	230	45.30 S	167.20 E
Fiorenzuola d'Arda	170	44.56 N	9.55 E
Fiq	210	32.47 N	35.42 E
Firavitoba	290	5.40 N	73.00 W
Fircrest	270	47.14 N	123.31 W
Fire	244	48.52 N	83.21 W
Firebaugh	272	36.52 N	120.27 W
Fire Island National Seashore	242	40.38 N	73.08 W
Firenze (Florence)	184	43.46 N	11.15 E
Firenze	184	43.50 N	11.20 E
Firenzuola	170	44.07 N	11.23 E
Firmat	294	33.25 S	61.30 W
Firminópolis	296	16.40 S	50.19 W
Firminy	182	45.23 N	4.18 E
Firovo	160	57.29 N	33.40 E
Fīrozābād	206	27.09 N	78.24 E
Fīrozpur	206	30.55 N	74.38 E
First Broad	246	35.11 N	81.37 W
First Cataract	220	24.01 N	32.52 E
Firth	252	40.33 N	96.37 W
Firth	236	69.32 N	139.22 W
Fischbacher Alpen	164	47.28 N	15.30 E
Fish, S.W. Afr.	224	28.07 S	17.45 E
Fish, Ala., U.S.	248	30.25 N	87.50 W
Fish Camp	272	37.29 N	119.38 W
Fisher, Ark., U.S.	248	35.30 N	90.58 W
Fisher, Ill., U.S.	268	40.19 N	88.21 W
Fisher, La., U.S.	248	31.30 N	93.28 W
Fisher, Pa., U.S.	266	41.16 N	79.15 W
Fisher	238	48.22 N	115.19 W
Fisher Channel	238	52.10 N	127.42 W
Fisher Peak	246	36.33 N	80.50 W
Fishers	264	43.00 N	77.28 W
Fishers Peak	252	37.06 N	104.28 W
Fisher Strait	232	63.15 N	83.30 W
Fishertown	266	40.08 N	78.35 W
Fishguard	162	51.59 N	4.59 W
Fishing Creek	262	38.20 N	76.14 W
Fishkill	261	41.32 N	73.53 W
Fish Lake	268	41.34 N	86.33 W
Fisk	248	36.47 N	90.12 W
Fiskárdho	172	38.27 N	20.35 E
Fiskdale	261	42.07 N	72.07 W
Fismes	166	49.18 N	3.41 E
Fitchburg	261	42.35 N	71.48 W
Fitchville	261	41.34 N	72.09 W
Fitzcarrald	292	11.45 S	72.25 W
Fitzgerald	246	31.43 N	83.15 W
Fitz Hugh Sound	238	51.40 N	127.57 W
Fitz Roy	288	47.00 S	67.15 W
Fitzroy	228	23.32 S	150.52 E
Fitzroy, Monte(Cerro Chaltel)	288	49.17 S	73.05 W
Fitzroy Crossing	226	18.11 S	125.35 E
Fitzwilliam	261	42.47 N	72.08 W
Fitzwilliam Island	244	45.30 N	81.45 W
Fiuggi	184	41.48 N	13.13 E
Fiume → Rijeka	170	45.20 N	14.27 E
Fiumicino	170	41.46 N	12.14 E
Fiumicino	184	41.46 N	12.14 E
Five Islands	240	45.25 N	64.02 W
Five Points, Calif., U.S.	272	36.26 N	120.06 W
Five Points, N. Mex., U.S.	254	35.04 N	106.41 W
Five Points, Pa., U.S.	266	40.34 N	80.15 W
Fivizzano	170	44.14 N	10.08 E
Fizi	218	4.18 S	28.57 E
Fjällåsen	160	67.29 N	20.10 E
Flagler	252	39.18 N	103.04 W
Flagler Beach	246	29.29 N	81.07 W
Flagstaff	254	35.12 N	111.39 W
Flagstaff Lake	240	45.10 N	70.15 W
Flagtown	262	40.31 N	74.41 W
Flåm	160	60.50 N	7.07 E
Flambeau	244	45.18 N	91.15 W
Flambeau Flowage	244	46.05 N	90.11 W
Flamborough Head	162	54.07 N	0.04 W
Fläming	164	52.00 N	12.30 E
Flaming Gorge National Recreation Area	254	41.30 N	109.30 W
Flaming Gorge Reservoir	254	41.15 N	109.30 W
Flanagan	268	40.53 N	88.52 W
Flanders, Ont., Can.	244	48.44 N	92.05 W
Flanders, N.Y., U.S.	261	40.49 N	72.36 W
Flanders (Flandre) (Vlaanderen)	176	51.00 N	3.00 E
Flandes	290	4.18 N	74.49 W
Flandreau	252	44.03 N	96.36 W
Flasher	252	46.27 N	101.14 W
Flat, Alaska, U.S.	236	62.27 N	158.01 W
Flat, Tex., U.S.	250	31.19 N	97.38 W
Flat	236	61.33 N	125.18 W
Flat, Mich., U.S.	244	42.56 N	85.20 W
Flat, N.C., U.S.	246	36.05 N	78.49 W
Flat Bay	240	48.24 N	58.35 W
Flatey	160a	65.19 N	23.07 W
Flateyri	160a	65.59 N	23.42 W
Flathead	256	47.22 N	114.47 W
Flathead, South Fork	256	48.23 N	114.04 W
Flathead Indian Reservation	256	47.30 N	114.25 W
Flathead Lake	256	47.52 N	114.08 W
Flat Island	225c	19.52 S	57.40 E
Flat Lake	238	54.39 N	112.55 W
Flat Lick	246	36.50 N	83.46 W
Flatonia	250	29.47 N	97.06 W
Flat River, P.E.I., Can.	240	46.01 N	62.52 W
Flat River, Mo., U.S.	248	37.51 N	90.31 W
Flat Rock, Ala., U.S.	248	34.46 N	85.42 W
Flat Rock, Ill., U.S.	248	38.54 N	87.40 W
Flat Rock, Mich., U.S.	268	42.06 N	83.18 W
Flat Rock, Ohio, U.S.	266	41.14 N	82.52 W
Flattery, Cape	256	48.23 N	124.43 W
Flat Tops	254	40.00 N	107.10 W
Flatts	284a	32.19 N	64.44 W
Flatwood	248	32.09 N	87.31 W
Flatwoods	242	38.31 N	82.43 W
Flawil	180	47.24 N	9.12 E
Flaxman Island	236	70.13 N	146.00 W
Flaxton	252	48.54 N	102.24 W
Flaxville	252	48.49 N	105.10 W
Flechas Point	202	10.23 N	119.32 E
Fleet	174	51.16 N	0.50 W
Fleetwood, Eng., U.K.	162	53.56 N	3.01 W
Fleetwood, Pa., U.S.	262	40.27 N	75.49 W
Flekkefjord	160	58.17 N	6.41 E
Fleming, Colo., U.S.	252	40.41 N	102.50 W
Fleming, Pa., U.S.	266	40.55 N	77.52 W
Flemingsburg	242	36.25 N	83.44 W
Flemington	262	40.31 N	74.52 W
Flen	160	59.04 N	16.35 E
Flensburg	164	54.47 N	9.26 E
Flers	166	48.45 N	0.34 W
Flesherton	264	44.16 N	80.33 W
Fletcher, Ont., Can.	266	42.18 N	82.18 W
Fletcher, N.C., U.S.	246	35.26 N	82.30 W
Fletcher, Okla., U.S.	250	34.52 N	98.17 W
Fletcher Pond	244	44.58 N	83.52 W
Fleurance	166	43.50 N	0.40 E
Fleur-de-Lys	240	50.06 N	56.08 W
Fleury-les-Aubrais	176	47.56 N	1.55 E
Fleury-sur-Andelle	166	49.22 N	1.21 E
Fleuve	222	16.00 N	14.30 W
Flinders	228	17.36 S	140.36 E
Flinders Chase	228	35.54 S	136.40 E
Flinders Island	228	40.00 S	148.00 E
Flinders Reefs	228	17.37 S	148.31 E
Flin Flon	232	54.46 N	101.53 W
Flint, Wales, U.K.	162	53.15 N	3.07 W
Flint, Mich., U.S.	268	43.01 N	83.41 W

Symbols in the index entries are identified on page 360.

Name	Page	Lat°′	Long°′
Flint ≃, Ga., U.S.	246	30.52 N	84.38 W
Flint ≃, Mich., U.S.	244	43.21 N	84.03 W
Flint Creek Range ⋀	256	46.20 N	113.05 W
Flint Hills ⋀[2]	252	38.50 N	100.00 W
Flint Lake ⊜	232	69.10 N	74.20 W
Flinton	266	40.43 N	78.31 W
Flintridge	274	34.11 N	118.11 W
Flintshire □[6]	174	53.10 N	3.10 W
Flintville	248	34.59 N	86.25 W
Flisa	160	60.34 N	12.06 E
Flize	166	49.42 N	4.46 E
Flomaton	248	31.00 N	87.16 W
Flomot	250	34.14 N	100.59 W
Floodwood	244	46.55 N	92.56 W
Flora, Nor.	160	61.36 N	5.00 E
Flora, Ill., U.S.	248	38.40 N	88.29 W
Flora, Ind., U.S.	268	40.33 N	86.31 W
Flora, Miss., U.S.	248	32.33 N	90.19 W
Florac	166	44.19 N	3.36 E
Florala	248	31.00 N	86.20 W
Floral City	246	28.45 N	82.18 W
Floral Park	256	45.57 N	112.26 W
Flora Vista	254	36.48 N	108.02 W
Flor de Chile	294	25.19 S	69.50 W
Florence → Firenze, It.	184	43.46 N	11.15 E
Florence, Ala., U.S.	248	34.49 N	87.40 W
Florence, Ariz., U.S.	254	33.02 N	111.23 W
Florence, Calif., U.S.	274	33.58 N	118.15 W
Florence, Colo., U.S.	254	38.23 N	105.08 W
Florence, Kans., U.S.	252	38.15 N	96.56 W
Florence, Miss., U.S.	248	32.10 N	90.07 W
Florence, Oreg., U.S.	256	43.58 N	124.07 W
Florence, Pa., U.S.	266	40.26 N	80.26 W
Florence, S.C., U.S.	246	34.12 N	79.46 W
Florence, Tex., U.S.	250	30.51 N	97.48 W
Florence, Wis., U.S.	244	45.56 N	88.07 W
Florencia	290	1.36 N	75.36 W
Florencio Sánchez	294	33.53 S	57.24 W
Florenville	164	49.42 N	5.18 E
Flores	286	7.51 S	37.59 W
Flores I	226	8.30 S	121.00 E
Flores, Cachoeira das ∟	296	14.19 S	53.32 W
Flores, Laut (Flores Sea) ⏉[2]	198	8.00 S	120.00 E
Flores da Cunha	294	29.02 S	51.11 W
Flores Island I	238	49.20 N	126.10 W
Flores Sea → Flores, Laut ⏉[2]	198	8.00 S	120.00 E
Floresta Azul	296	14.51 S	39.41 W
Florestina	296	18.29 S	48.01 W
Floresville	250	29.08 N	98.10 W
Florham Park	262	40.47 N	74.23 W
Floriano	286	6.47 S	43.01 W
Floriano Peixoto	292	9.03 S	67.24 W
Florianópolis	294	27.35 S	48.34 W
Florida, Col.	290	3.21 N	76.15 W
Florida, Cuba	284p	21.32 N	78.14 W
Florida, Hond.	280	15.01 N	88.50 W
Florida, P.R.	284m	18.22 N	66.34 W
Florida, P.R.	284m	18.14 N	65.47 W
Florida, Ohio, U.S.	268	41.20 N	84.12 W
Florida, Ur.	294	34.06 S	56.13 W
Florida □[3]	234	28.00 N	82.00 W
Florida ≃	254	37.03 N	107.52 W
Florida, Straits of ⋃	282	24.00 N	81.00 W
Florida Bay C	246	25.00 N	80.45 W
Floridablanca	290	7.04 N	73.06 W
Florida City	246	25.27 N	80.29 W
Florida Keys II	246	24.45 N	81.00 W
Floridia	170	37.04 N	15.10 E
Florido ≃	278	27.43 N	105.10 W
Florien	248	31.27 N	93.27 W
Florin	272	38.30 N	121.24 W
Flórina	172	40.47 N	21.24 E
Florissant	248	38.48 N	90.20 W
Floriston	272	39.24 N	120.01 W
Flossmoor	268	41.33 N	87.40 W
Flower's Cove	240	51.18 N	56.44 W
Flowery Branch	246	34.11 N	83.55 W
Floyd, N. Mex., U.S.	250	34.13 N	103.35 W
Floyd, Va., U.S.	246	36.55 N	80.19 W
Floyd ≃	252	42.29 N	96.23 W
Floydada	250	33.59 N	101.20 W
Flumen ≃	168	41.43 N	0.09 W
Flumendosa ≃	170	39.26 N	9.38 E
Fluminimaggiore	170	39.26 N	8.30 E
Flushing → Vlissingen, Ned.	178	51.26 N	3.35 E
Flushing, Mich., U.S.	268	43.04 N	83.51 W
Flushing, Ohio, U.S.	266	40.09 N	81.04 W
Fluvanna, N.Y., U.S.	266	42.07 N	79.18 W
Fluvanna, Tex., U.S.	250	32.53 N	101.09 W
Fluvia ≃	168	42.12 N	3.07 E
Fly ≃	198	7.45 S	141.45 E
Foča, Jugo.	172	43.31 N	18.46 E
Foça, Tür.	172	38.39 N	26.46 E
Focşani	172	45.41 N	27.11 E
Fodda, Oued ≃	168	35.14 N	1.28 E
F'odorovka	160	53.28 N	49.38 E
Foeni	172	45.30 N	20.53 E
Fogang (Shijiao)	196	23.52 N	113.32 E
Fogelsville	262	40.35 N	75.38 W
Foggia	184	41.27 N	15.34 E
Foggia □[4]	184	41.30 N	15.30 E
Foggy Island Bay C	236	70.15 N	147.30 W
Fogo	240	49.43 N	54.17 W
Fogo I	222a	14.55 N	24.25 W
Fogo, Cape ≻	240	49.39 N	54.00 W
Fogo Island I	240	49.40 N	54.13 W
Fohnsdorf	164	47.13 N	14.41 E
Föhr I	164	54.43 N	8.30 E
Foia ∧	168	37.19 N	8.36 W
Foins, Lac aux ⊜	244	47.04 N	78.10 W
Foix	166	42.58 N	1.36 E
Foix ⇀[1]	166	43.00 N	1.40 E
Fojnica	170	43.58 N	17.54 E
Fokino	158	53.27 N	34.24 E
Fokís □[5]	172	38.30 N	22.30 E
Foley, Ala., U.S.	248	30.25 N	87.41 W
Foley, Minn., U.S.	244	45.40 N	93.55 W
Foleyet	244	48.16 N	82.30 W
Foley Island I	232	68.35 N	75.10 W
Folgares	218	14.54 S	15.08 E
Foligno	184	42.57 N	12.42 E
Folkestone	174	51.05 N	1.11 E
Folkston	246	30.50 N	82.01 W
Follansbee	266	40.20 N	80.36 W
Folldal	160	62.08 N	10.03 E
Follett	250	36.26 N	100.08 W
Föllinge	160	63.40 N	14.37 E
Follonica	184	42.55 N	10.45 E
Follonica, Golfo di C	170	42.54 N	10.43 E
Folsom, Calif., U.S.	272	38.41 N	121.15 W
Folsom, La., U.S.	248	30.38 N	90.11 W
Folsom, N.J., U.S.	262	39.38 N	74.51 W
Folsom, N. Mex., U.S.	250	36.51 N	103.55 W
Fombell	266	40.49 N	80.12 W
Fomento	284p	22.06 N	79.43 W
Fominskaja	160	61.17 N	48.40 E
Fominskoje, S.S.S.R.	160	59.43 N	42.05 E
Fominskoje, S.S.S.R.	160	58.59 N	39.06 E
Fonda, Iowa, U.S.	252	42.35 N	94.51 W
Fonda, N.Y., U.S.	242	42.57 N	74.22 W
Fond du Lac, Sask., Can.	232	59.19 N	107.10 W
Fond du Lac, Wis., U.S.	244	43.47 N	88.27 W
Fond du Lac ≃	232	59.17 N	106.00 W
Fond du Lac Indian Reservation ⇀[4]	244	46.45 N	92.37 W
Fondi	184	41.21 N	13.25 E
Fondouk el Aouareb	170	35.34 N	9.46 E
Fondovegas	168	42.57 N	6.36 W
Fonni	170	40.07 N	9.15 E
Fonsagrada	168	43.08 N	7.04 W
Fonseca	290	10.54 N	72.51 W
Fonseca, Golfo de C	280	13.08 N	87.40 W
Fontaine	182	45.11 N	5.40 E
Fontainebleau	176	48.24 N	2.42 E
Fontana, Arg.	294	27.25 S	59.02 W
Fontana, Calif., U.S.	274	34.06 N	117.26 W
Fontana, Wis., U.S.	268	42.33 N	88.35 W
Fontana Lake ⊜[1]	246	35.26 N	83.38 W
Fontanelle	252	41.17 N	94.34 W
Fontarabie, Lac ⊜	240	51.10 N	66.25 W
Fontas ≃	232	58.20 N	121.50 W
Fonte Boa	290	2.32 S	66.01 W
Fontenay-le-Comte	166	46.28 N	0.48 W
Fontenelle	240	48.52 N	64.52 W
Fontenelle Reservoir ⊜[1]	254	42.05 N	110.06 W
Fonthill	264	43.02 N	79.17 W
Fontibón	290	4.40 N	74.09 W
Fontur ≻	160a	66.23 N	14.30 W
Fonyód	172	46.44 N	17.34 E
Foochow → Fuzhou	196	26.06 N	119.17 E
Foothill Farms	272	38.40 N	121.21 W
Foothills	238	53.04 N	116.48 W
Footville	268	42.40 N	89.12 W
Foraker, Mount ∧	236	62.56 N	151.26 W
Forbach, B.R.D.	164	48.41 N	8.21 E
Forbach, Fr.	166	49.11 N	6.54 E
Forbes	228	33.23 S	148.01 E
Forbes, Mount ∧	238	51.52 N	116.56 W
Forbes Road	266	40.21 N	79.32 W
Forbestown	272	39.31 N	121.16 W
Forcados ≃[1]	222	5.25 N	5.19 E
Force	266	41.15 N	78.30 W
Forchheim	164	49.43 N	11.04 E
Ford	252	37.38 N	99.45 W
Ford □[6]	268	40.27 N	88.06 W
Ford ≃	244	45.40 N	87.09 W
Ford City, Calif., U.S.	272	35.09 N	119.27 W
Ford City, Pa., U.S.	266	40.46 N	79.32 W
Ford Cliff	266	40.45 N	79.32 W
Førde	160	61.27 N	5.52 E
Ford Lake ⊜	258	33.38 N	115.00 W
Fords Prairie	270	46.47 N	123.05 W
Fordsville	248	37.38 N	86.43 W
Fordville	252	48.13 N	97.47 W
Fordyce	248	33.49 N	92.25 W
Forécariah □[4]	222	9.30 N	13.15 W
Forel, Mont ∧	232	67.00 N	37.00 W
Foreman	248	33.43 N	94.24 W
Foremost	256	49.29 N	111.25 W
Foresman	268	40.52 N	87.18 W
Forest, Bel.	176	50.48 N	4.19 E
Forest, Ont., Can.	244	43.06 N	82.00 W
Forest, Ind., U.S.	268	40.22 N	86.20 W
Forest, Miss., U.S.	248	32.22 N	89.28 W
Forest, Ohio, U.S.	268	40.48 N	83.31 W
Forest □[6]	266	41.29 N	79.27 W
Forest ≃	252	48.21 N	97.09 W
Forest Acres	246	34.01 N	80.58 W
Forestburg	238	52.35 N	112.04 W
Forest City, Iowa, U.S.	244	43.16 N	93.39 W
Forest City, N.C., U.S.	246	35.20 N	81.52 W
Forest City, Pa., U.S.	242	41.39 N	75.28 W
Forest Grove, B.C., Can.	238	51.46 N	121.06 W
Forest Grove, Oreg., U.S.	270	45.31 N	123.07 W
Foresthill, Calif., U.S.	272	39.01 N	120.49 W
Forest Hill, Md., U.S.	262	39.35 N	76.23 W
Forest Home	248	31.52 N	86.50 W
Forestier Peninsula ≻[1]	228	42.57 S	147.55 E
Forest Lake, Ill., U.S.	268	42.13 N	88.03 W
Forest Lake, Minn., U.S.	244	45.17 N	92.59 W
Forest Park	246	33.37 N	84.22 W
Forestville, Qué., Can.	240	48.45 N	69.06 W
Forestville, N.Y., U.S.	266	42.26 N	79.10 W
Forestville, Pa., U.S.	266	41.06 N	80.00 W
Forestville, Wis., U.S.	244	44.41 N	87.29 W
Forez, Monts du ⋀	166	45.35 N	3.48 E
Forfar	162	56.38 N	2.54 W
Forgan	250	36.54 N	100.32 W
Forges-les-Eaux	162	49.37 N	1.33 E
Forge Village	261	42.35 N	71.29 W
Forggensee ⊜	164	47.36 N	10.44 E
Fork	262	39.28 N	76.27 W
Forked Deer ≃	248	35.56 N	89.35 W
Forked River	262	39.51 N	74.12 W
Forks	270	47.57 N	124.23 W
Forlì □[4]	184	44.05 N	12.02 E
Forlimpopoli	184	44.11 N	12.07 E
Forman	252	46.07 N	97.38 W
Formby Point ≻	162	53.33 N	3.06 W
Formentera I	168	38.42 N	1.28 E
Formentor, Cabo de ≻	168	39.58 N	3.12 E
Formerie	166	49.39 N	1.44 E
Formia	184	41.15 N	13.37 E
Formiga	296	20.27 S	45.25 W
Formosa, Arg.	294	26.10 S	58.11 W
Formosa, Bra.	296	15.32 S	47.20 W
Formosa □[4]	294	25.00 S	60.00 W
Formosa, Serra ⋀[1]	296	12.00 S	55.00 W
Formosa Strait ⋃	196	24.00 N	119.00 E
Forney	250	32.45 N	96.28 W
Fornovo di Taro	170	44.42 N	10.06 E
Forres, Arg.	294	27.53 S	63.59 W
Forres, Scot., U.K.	162	57.37 N	3.38 W
Forrest, Austl.	226	30.51 S	128.06 E
Forrest, Ill., U.S.	268	40.45 N	88.25 W
Forrest City	248	35.01 N	90.47 W
Forrester Island I	236	54.48 N	133.32 W
Forreston	244	42.08 N	89.35 W
Forsan	250	32.07 N	101.22 W
Forsayth	228	18.35 S	143.36 E
Forst	164	51.44 N	14.39 E
Forsyth, Ga., U.S.	246	33.02 N	83.56 W
Forsyth, Mo., U.S.	248	36.41 N	93.06 W
Forsyth, Mont., U.S.	256	46.16 N	106.41 W
Forsyth Island I	228	16.50 S	139.06 E
Forsyth Range ⋀	228	22.45 S	143.15 E
Fort Adams	248	31.05 N	91.33 W
Fort Albany	232	52.15 N	81.37 W
Fortaleza	286	3.43 S	38.30 W
Fortaleza de Santa Teresa ♠	294	33.59 S	53.32 W
Fortaleza do Ituxi	292	7.29 S	66.20 W
Fort Amherst National Historic Park ♠	240	46.15 N	63.06 W
Fort Anne National Historic Park ♠	240	44.44 N	65.26 W
Fort Apache Indian Reservation ⇀[4]	254	34.01 N	110.28 W
Fort-Archambault	214	9.09 N	18.23 E
Fort Assiniboine	238	54.20 N	114.46 W
Fort Atkinson	268	42.56 N	88.50 W
Fort Augustus	162	57.09 N	4.41 W
Fort Bayard → Zhanjiang	200	21.16 N	110.28 E
Fort Beaufort	224	32.46 S	26.40 E
Fort Beauséjour National Historic Park ♠	240	45.53 N	64.10 W
Fort Belknap Indian Reservation ⇀[4]	256	48.16 N	108.38 W
Fort Benning ■	246	32.22 N	84.50 W
Fort Benton	256	47.49 N	110.40 W
Fort Berthold Indian Reservation ⇀[4]	252	47.40 N	102.25 W
Fort Bidwell	258	41.52 N	120.09 W
Fort Bragg	258	39.26 N	123.48 W
Fort Bragg ■	246	35.09 N	78.59 W
Fort Branch	248	38.15 N	87.35 W
Fort Bridger	254	41.19 N	110.23 W
Fort Campbell ■	248	36.39 N	87.29 W
Fort Caroline National Memorial ⊥	246	30.20 N	81.30 W
Fort Carson ■	254	38.44 N	104.48 W
Fort Chambly National Historic Park ♠	242	45.27 N	73.17 W
Fort-Chimo	232	58.10 N	68.30 W
Fort Chipewyan	232	58.42 N	111.08 W
Fort Clatsop National Memorial ⊥	256	40.08 N	123.54 W
Fort Cobb	250	35.06 N	98.26 W
Fort Cobb Reservoir ⊜[1]	250	35.12 N	98.29 W
Fort Collins	254	40.35 N	105.05 W
Fort-Coulonge	242	45.51 N	76.44 W
Fort Covington	260	44.59 N	74.30 W
Fort-Dauphin	225b	25.02 S	47.00 E
Fort Davis, Ala., U.S.	248	32.15 N	85.43 W
Fort Davis, Tex., U.S.	250	30.35 N	103.54 W
Fort Davis National Historic Site ⊥	250	30.33 N	103.53 W
Fort Defiance	254	35.45 N	109.05 W
Fort-de-France	284e	14.36 N	61.05 W
Fort Deposit	248	31.59 N	86.35 W
Fort Dix ■	242	40.00 N	74.33 W
Fort Dodge	244	42.30 N	94.10 W
Fort Donelson National Military Park ♠	248	36.26 N	87.49 W
Fort Duchesne	254	40.17 N	109.52 W
Forteau	240	51.27 N	56.57 W
Forte dei Marmi	170	43.57 N	10.10 E
Fort Edward	242	43.16 N	73.35 W
Fort Erie	264	42.54 N	78.56 W
Fortezza (Franzensfeste)	170	46.47 N	11.37 E
Fort Fairfield	240	46.46 N	67.50 W
Fort Fitzgerald	232	59.53 N	111.37 W
Fort Frances	244	48.36 N	93.24 W
Fort Franklin	236	65.11 N	123.46 W
Fort Fraser	238	54.04 N	124.33 W
Fort Frederica National Monument ♠	246	31.12 N	81.26 W
Fort Gaines	246	31.37 N	85.03 W
Fort Garland	254	37.26 N	105.26 W
Fort Gay	242	38.07 N	82.36 W
Fort-George	232	53.50 N	79.00 W
Fort Gibson	250	35.48 N	95.15 W
Fort Gibson Reservoir ⊜[1]	250	36.00 N	95.18 W
Fort Good Hope	236	66.15 N	128.38 W
Fort Gordon ■	246	33.25 N	82.11 W
Forth, Firth of C[1]	162	56.05 N	2.55 W
Fort Hall Indian Reservation ⇀[4]	256	43.10 N	112.10 W
Fort Hood ■	250	31.08 N	97.46 W
Fort Howard	262	39.12 N	76.27 W
Fort Huachuca ■	254	31.33 N	110.20 W
Fortierville	260	46.28 N	72.03 W
Fortin, Lac ⊜	240	50.50 N	67.45 W
Fortín Ayacucho	292	19.58 S	59.47 W
Fortín Coronel Eugenio Garay	292	20.31 S	62.08 W
Fortine	238	48.46 N	114.54 W
Fortín Florida	292	20.45 S	59.17 W
Fortín Garrapatal	292	21.27 S	61.30 W
Fortín Ingavi	292	19.55 S	60.47 W
Fortín Paredes (Coroneles Sánchez)	292	19.20 S	59.58 W
Fortín Teniente Montanía	294	22.04 S	59.57 W
Fortín Uno	294	38.50 S	65.18 W
Fort Jackson ■	246	34.01 N	80.57 W
Fort Jefferson National Monument ♠	246	24.40 N	82.51 W
Fort Jennings	268	40.54 N	84.18 W
Fort Jones	258	41.36 N	122.51 W
Fort Kent	240	47.15 N	68.36 W
Fort Klamath	256	42.42 N	122.00 W
Fort Knox ■	248	37.54 N	85.57 W
Fort-Lamy	214	12.07 N	15.03 E
Fort Langley	270	49.10 N	122.35 W
Fort Laramie	254	42.13 N	104.31 W
Fort Laramie National Historic Site ♠	254	42.09 N	104.41 W
Fort Lauderdale	246	26.07 N	80.08 W
Fort Leavenworth ■	252	39.21 N	94.55 W
Fort Lennox National Historic Park ♠	242	45.06 N	73.16 W
Fort Leonard Wood ■	248	37.45 N	92.07 W
Fort Lewis ■	256	47.05 N	122.37 W
Fort Liard	232	60.15 N	123.28 W
Fort Littleton	266	40.04 N	77.58 W
Fort Loramie	268	40.21 N	84.22 W
Fort Loudoun Reservoir ⊜[1]	246	35.45 N	84.10 W
Fort Lupton	254	40.05 N	104.49 W
Fort Macleod	238	49.43 N	113.25 W
Fort Madison	244	40.38 N	91.27 W
Fort Matanzas National Monument ♠	246	29.40 N	81.18 W
Fort McClellan ■	248	34.43 N	85.47 W
Fort McDowell Indian Reservation ⇀[4]	254	33.38 N	111.41 W
Fort McMurray	232	56.44 N	111.23 W
Fort McPherson	236	67.27 N	134.53 W
Fort Meade	246	27.45 N	81.48 W
Fort Meade ■	262	39.05 N	76.50 W
Fort Mill	246	35.01 N	80.57 W
Fort Mohave Indian Reservation ⇀[4]	254	34.55 N	114.35 W
Fort Morgan	252	40.15 N	103.48 W
Fort Myers	246	26.37 N	81.54 W
Fort Myers Beach	246	26.27 N	81.57 W
Fort Necessity National Battlefield ⊥	242	39.47 N	79.39 W
Fort Nelson	232	58.49 N	122.39 W
Fort Nelson ≃	232	59.30 N	124.00 W
Fort Norman	236	64.54 N	125.34 W
Fort Ogden	246	27.05 N	81.57 W
Fort Ord ■	272	36.40 N	121.48 W
Fort Payne	248	34.27 N	85.43 W
Fort Peck	256	48.01 N	106.27 W
Fort Peck Indian Reservation ⇀[4]	256	48.22 N	105.40 W
Fort Peck Reservoir ⊜[1]	256	47.45 N	106.50 W
Fort Pierce	246	27.27 N	80.20 W
Fort Pierre	252	44.21 N	100.22 W
Fort Plain	242	42.56 N	74.38 W
Fort Polk ■	248	31.04 N	93.11 W
Fort Portal	218	0.40 N	30.17 E
Fort Providence	232	61.21 N	117.39 W
Fort Pulaski National Monument ♠	246	32.01 N	80.59 W
Fort Qu'Appelle	232	50.56 N	103.09 W
Fort Raleigh National Historic Site ⊥	246	35.55 N	75.40 W
Fort Recovery	268	40.25 N	84.47 W
Fort Reliance	232	62.42 N	109.08 W
Fort Resolution	232	61.10 N	113.40 W
Fortress Mountain ∧	256	44.20 N	109.47 W
Fortress of Louisburg National Historic Park ♠	240	45.56 N	59.57 W
Fort Riley ■	252	39.04 N	96.47 W
Fortrose	162	57.34 N	4.09 W
Fort Rosebery → Mansa	218	11.12 S	28.53 E
Fort-Rousset	218	0.29 S	15.55 E
Fort Saint James	238	54.26 N	124.15 W
Fort Saint John	238	56.15 N	120.51 W
Fort Sandeman	204	31.20 N	69.27 E
Fort Saskatchewan	238	53.43 N	113.13 W
Fort Scott	252	37.50 N	94.42 W
Fort Şeneca	266	41.13 N	83.10 W
Fort-Ševčenko	158	44.31 N	50.16 E
Fort Severn	232	56.00 N	87.38 W
Fort Shawnee	268	40.42 N	84.07 W
Fort Simpson	232	61.52 N	121.23 W
Fort Smith, N.W. Ter., Can.	232	60.00 N	111.53 W
Fort Smith, Ark., U.S.	248	35.23 N	94.25 W
Fort Steele	238	49.37 N	115.38 W
Fort Stewart ■	246	31.52 N	81.37 W
Fort Stockton	250	30.53 N	102.53 W
Fort Sumner	250	34.28 N	104.15 W
Fort Sumter National Monument ♠	246	32.44 N	79.46 W
Fort Supply	250	36.35 N	99.35 W
Fort Thomas	254	33.02 N	109.58 W
Fort Thompson	252	44.03 N	99.26 W
Fort Totten Indian Reservation ⇀[4]	252	47.53 N	98.50 W
Fort Towson	250	34.01 N	95.16 W
Fortuna, Arg.	294	35.08 S	65.24 W
Fortuna, Calif., U.S.	258	40.36 N	124.09 W
Fortuna, Río de la ≃	292	16.36 S	58.46 W
Fortuna Ledge (Marshall)	236	61.53 N	162.05 W
Fortune	240	47.04 N	55.51 W
Fortune Bay C	240	47.25 N	55.25 W
Fortune Harbour	240	49.28 N	55.20 W
Fort Union National Monument ♠	254	35.55 N	105.07 W
Fort Valley	246	32.33 N	83.53 W
Fort Vancouver National Historic Site ♠	256	45.38 N	122.37 W
Fort Vermilion	232	58.24 N	116.00 W
Fort Victoria	224	20.05 S	30.50 E
Fortville	248	39.56 N	85.51 W
Fort Walton Beach	248	30.25 N	86.36 W
Fort Washakie	254	43.00 N	108.53 W
Fort Washington	262	40.09 N	75.13 W
Fort Washington Forest	262	38.43 N	76.59 W
Fort Wayne	268	41.04 N	85.09 W
Fort Wellington	290	6.30 N	57.30 W
Fort Wellington National Historic Park ♠	242	44.44 N	75.31 W
Fort White	246	29.55 N	82.43 W
Fort William	162	56.49 N	5.07 W
Fort William → Thunder Bay, Ont., Can.	244	48.23 N	89.15 W
Fort Worth	250	32.45 N	97.20 W
Fort Yates	252	46.05 N	100.38 W
Fort Yukon	236	66.34 N	145.17 W
Fort Yuma Indian Reservation ⇀[4]	258	32.50 N	114.38 W
Forūr, Jazīreh-ye I	208	26.17 N	54.32 E
Foshan	196	23.03 N	113.09 E
Fossano	182	44.33 N	7.43 E
Fossil	256	45.00 N	120.13 W
Fossombrone	184	43.41 N	12.48 E
Fosston	252	47.35 N	95.45 W
Foster, Austl.	226	38.39 S	146.12 E
Foster, Qué., Can.	260	45.17 N	72.30 W
Foster, R.I., U.S.	261	41.47 N	71.44 W
Foster ≃	232	55.47 N	105.49 W
Foster, Mount ∧	236	59.48 N	135.29 W
Foster Brook	266	41.59 N	78.37 W
Foster Park	274	34.21 N	119.18 W
Fosters	248	33.06 N	87.41 W
Foster Village	275c	21.22 N	157.56 W
Fostoria	266	41.09 N	83.25 W
Fouesnant	166	47.54 N	4.01 W
Fougamou	218	1.13 S	10.36 E
Fougères	166	48.21 N	1.12 W
Fouke	248	33.16 N	93.53 W
Foula I	162	60.10 N	2.05 W
Foul Bay C	220	23.30 N	35.39 E
Foulness Island I	162	51.36 N	0.55 E
Foulwind, Cape ≻	230	41.45 S	171.28 E
Foumban	214	5.43 N	10.55 E
Foumbouni	218	11.50 S	43.30 E
Fountain	252	38.41 N	104.42 W
Fountain □[6]	268	40.17 N	87.13 W
Fountain City	244	44.08 N	91.43 W
Fountain Green	254	39.38 N	111.38 W
Fountain Hill	262	40.36 N	75.24 W
Fountain Inn	246	34.42 N	82.12 W
Fountain Park	268	41.50 N	84.32 W
Fountain Peak ∧	258	34.57 N	115.32 W
Fountain Place	248	30.31 N	91.09 W
Fountain Valley	274	33.43 N	117.57 W
Fouquières-lès Béthune	176	50.31 N	2.37 E
Four Buttes	256	48.48 N	105.37 W
Fourche la Fave ≃	248	34.58 N	92.35 W
Fourche Maline ≃	250	34.55 N	94.55 W
Fourchu	240	45.43 N	60.15 W
Four Corners	270	44.56 N	123.02 W
Four Hole Swamp ≃	246	33.03 N	80.24 W
Fourmies	176	50.00 N	4.03 E
Four Mountains, Islands of the II	236	52.50 N	170.00 W
Fournaise, Piton de la ∧	225c	21.14 S	55.43 E
Fournier, Lac ⊜	240	51.32 N	65.25 W
Fournière, Lac ⊜	244	48.04 N	78.04 W
Foúrnoi I	212	37.34 N	26.30 E
Four Oaks	246	35.27 N	78.26 W
Fours	166	46.49 N	3.43 E
Fourth Cataract → Ash-Shallāl ar-Rābi' ∟	220	18.47 N	32.03 E
Foustown	262	40.00 N	76.46 W
Fouta Djallon ⇀[1]	222	11.30 N	12.30 W
Foveaux Strait ⋃	230	46.40 S	168.10 E
Fowey	162	50.20 N	4.38 W
Fowler, Calif., U.S.	272	36.38 N	119.41 W
Fowler, Colo., U.S.	252	38.08 N	104.01 W
Fowler, Ind., U.S.	268	40.37 N	87.19 W
Fowler, Kans., U.S.	252	37.23 N	100.12 W
Fowler, Mich., U.S.	268	43.00 N	84.44 W
Fowler, Ohio, U.S.	266	41.19 N	80.40 W
Fowlerton	250	28.28 N	98.48 W
Fowlerville	268	42.40 N	84.04 W
Fox ≃, U.S.	248	40.18 N	91.30 W
Fox ≃, Ill., U.S.	248	38.32 N	88.08 W
Fox ≃, Wis., U.S.	244	44.32 N	88.01 W
Fox, Cape ≻	238	54.47 N	130.51 W
Fox Bay	240	49.17 N	61.50 W
Foxboro, Ont., Can.	264	44.15 N	77.26 W
Foxboro, Mass., U.S.	261	42.04 N	71.16 W
Foxburg	266	41.09 N	79.41 W
Foxe Basin C	232	68.25 N	77.00 W
Foxe Channel ⋃	232	64.30 N	80.00 W
Foxe Peninsula ≻[1]	232	65.00 N	76.00 W
Fox Harbour	240	47.19 N	53.55 W
Fox Islands II	236	54.00 N	168.00 W
Fox Lake, Ill., U.S.	268	42.24 N	88.11 W
Fox Lake, Wis., U.S.	244	43.34 N	88.55 W
Fox Mountain ∧	236	61.55 N	133.22 W
Foxpark	254	41.05 N	106.09 W
Fox Point	268	43.09 N	87.54 W
Fox River Estates	268	41.58 N	88.20 W
Fox River Grove	268	42.12 N	88.13 W
Foxwells	262	37.38 N	76.18 W
Foxworth	248	31.14 N	89.52 W
Foyle, Lough ⊜	162	55.07 N	7.08 W
Foynes	162	52.37 N	9.06 W
Foz do Cunene	218	17.16 S	11.50 E
Foz do Iguaçu	294	25.33 S	54.35 W
Foz do Jordão	292	9.23 S	71.56 W
Foz Giraldo	168	40.00 N	7.43 W
Frackville	262	40.47 N	76.14 W
Frade, Rio do ≃	296	16.41 S	39.06 W
Fraga, Arg.	294	33.30 S	65.48 W
Fraga, Esp.	168	41.31 N	0.21 E
Fragoso, Cayo I	284p	22.42 N	79.25 W
Fragua, Sierra de la ⋀	250	26.41 N	102.13 W
Fraile Muerto	294	32.31 S	54.32 W
Frailes, Laguna de los ⊜	250	27.14 N	103.16 W
Fraïn, Chott el ⊜	168	36.00 N	5.30 E
Frameries	176	50.24 N	3.54 E
Framingham	261	42.17 N	71.25 W
Frampol	164	50.41 N	22.40 E
Franca	296	20.32 S	47.24 W
Francavilla al Mare	184	42.25 N	14.17 E
Francavilla Fontana	170	40.31 N	17.35 E
France □[1]	158	46.00 N	2.00 E
Frances ≃	236	60.12 N	129.02 W
Francés, Cabo ≻	284p	21.54 N	84.02 W
Francés, Punta ≻	284p	21.38 N	83.12 W
Frances Lake ⊜	236	61.25 N	129.30 W
Francés Viejo, Cabo ≻	282	19.40 N	70.00 W
Francesville	268	40.59 N	86.53 W
Franceville	218	1.38 S	13.35 E
Franche-Comté □[9]	180	47.00 N	6.00 E
Francia	294	32.33 S	56.37 W
Francisca, Punta ≻	278	21.34 N	87.21 W
Francis Case, Lake ⊜[1]	252	43.15 N	99.00 W
Francisco Beltrão	294	26.05 S	53.04 W
Francisco de Orellana	290	0.28 S	76.58 W
Francisco González Villarreal	278	25.22 N	97.53 W
Francisco Horta Barbosa ≃	296	14.50 S	52.34 W
Francisco I. Madero, Méx.	278	25.45 N	103.21 W
Francisco I. Madero, Méx.	278	24.32 N	104.22 W
Francisco Morazán □[5]	280	14.15 N	87.15 W
Francisco Sá	296	16.28 S	43.30 W
Francisco Zarco	258	32.06 N	116.30 W
Francistown	224	21.11 S	27.32 E
Francofonte	170	37.13 N	14.53 E
François	240	47.34 N	56.44 W
François, Lacs à ⊜	240	51.40 N	65.50 W
François Lake	238	54.04 N	125.44 W
François Lake ⊜	238	54.00 N	125.40 W
Franconia	262	38.47 N	77.08 W
Franeker	178	53.11 N	5.32 E
Frangy	166	46.01 N	5.56 E
Frankel City	250	32.23 N	102.47 W
Frankenberg	164	50.54 N	13.01 E
Frankenberg-Eder	178	51.03 N	8.48 E
Frankenmuth	244	43.20 N	83.44 W
Frankfield	285q	18.09 N	77.22 W
Frankford, Ont., Can.	264	44.12 N	77.36 W
Frankford, Del., U.S.	262	38.31 N	75.14 W
Frankford, Mo., U.S.	248	39.29 N	91.19 W
Frankfort, Ill., U.S.	268	41.30 N	87.51 W
Frankfort, Ind., U.S.	268	40.17 N	86.31 W
Frankfort, Kans., U.S.	252	39.42 N	96.25 W
Frankfort, Ky., U.S.	248	38.12 N	84.52 W
Frankfort, Maine, U.S.	242	44.36 N	68.53 W
Frankfort, Mich., U.S.	244	44.38 N	86.14 W
Frankfort, N.Y., U.S.	242	43.02 N	75.04 W
Frankfort, Ohio, U.S.	242	39.24 N	83.11 W
Frankfort, S. Dak., U.S.	252	44.53 N	98.18 W
Frankfort Springs	266	40.30 N	80.25 W
Frankfurt am Main	164	50.07 N	8.40 E
Frankfurt an der Oder	162	52.20 N	14.33 E
Fränkische Alb ⋀	164	49.00 N	11.30 E
Franklin, Ariz., U.S.	254	32.42 N	109.05 W
Franklin, Ga., U.S.	246	33.17 N	85.08 W
Franklin, Idaho, U.S.	256	40.31 N	111.48 W
Franklin, Ill., U.S.	248	39.37 N	90.03 W
Franklin, Ind., U.S.	248	39.29 N	86.03 W
Franklin, Ky., U.S.	248	36.43 N	86.35 W
Franklin, La., U.S.	248	29.48 N	91.30 W
Franklin, Maine, U.S.	242	44.32 N	68.09 W
Franklin, Mass., U.S.	261	42.05 N	71.24 W
Franklin, Mich., U.S.	268	42.31 N	83.18 W
Franklin, Minn., U.S.	252	44.32 N	94.53 W
Franklin, Nebr., U.S.	252	40.06 N	98.57 W
Franklin, N.H., U.S.	242	43.27 N	71.39 W
Franklin, N.J., U.S.	242	41.07 N	74.35 W
Franklin, N.C., U.S.	246	35.11 N	83.23 W
Franklin, Ohio, U.S.	242	39.34 N	84.18 W
Franklin, Pa., U.S.	266	40.20 N	78.53 W
Franklin, Pa., U.S.	266	41.24 N	79.50 W
Franklin, Tenn., U.S.	248	35.55 N	86.52 W
Franklin, Tex., U.S.	250	31.02 N	96.29 W
Franklin, Vt., U.S.	260	44.59 N	72.55 W
Franklin, Va., U.S.	262	36.41 N	76.55 W
Franklin, W. Va., U.S.	242	38.39 N	79.20 W
Franklin, Wis., U.S.	268	42.54 N	88.03 W
Franklin □[5]	232	72.00 N	100.00 W
Franklin □[6], Mass., U.S.	261	42.36 N	72.36 W
Franklin □[6], N.Y., U.S.	260	44.57 N	74.18 W
Franklin □[6], Ohio, U.S.	266	39.57 N	83.00 W
Franklin □[6], Pa., U.S.	262	39.56 N	77.40 W
Franklin □[6], Vt., U.S.	260	44.57 N	72.52 W
Franklin, Point ≻	236	70.54 N	158.48 W
Franklin Bay C	236	68.45 N	125.35 W
Franklin D. Roosevelt Lake ⊜[1]	256	48.20 N	118.10 W
Franklin Grove	244	41.50 N	89.18 W
Franklin Harbour C	228	33.42 S	136.56 E
Franklin Lake ⊜, N.W. Ter., Can.	232	66.56 N	96.03 W
Franklin Lake ⊜, Nev., U.S.	258	40.24 N	115.12 W
Franklin Mountains ⋀, N.W. Ter., Can.	232	63.15 N	123.30 W
Franklin Mountains ⋀, N.Z.	230	44.55 S	167.45 E
Franklin Park, Ill., U.S.	268	41.56 N	87.49 W
Franklin Park, N.Y., U.S.	264	43.05 N	76.05 W
Franklin River	270	49.06 N	124.49 W
Franklin Springs	264	43.02 N	75.24 W
Franklin Strait ⋃	232	72.00 N	96.00 W
Franklinton, La., U.S.	248	30.51 N	90.09 W
Franklinton, N.C., U.S.	246	36.06 N	78.27 W
Franklintown	262	40.05 N	77.02 W
Franklinville, N.J., U.S.	262	39.37 N	75.05 W
Franklinville, N.C., U.S.	246	35.45 N	79.42 W
Franklinville, N.Y., U.S.	266	42.20 N	78.28 W
Franks Peak ∧	256	43.58 N	109.20 W
Frankston	250	32.03 N	95.30 W
Franksville	268	42.46 N	87.55 W
Frankton	268	40.13 N	85.46 W
Frankville	248	31.39 N	88.09 W
Franz Josef Land → Zeml'a Franca-Iosifa II	148	81.00 N	55.00 E
Frascati	184	41.48 N	12.41 E
Fraser, Colo., U.S.	254	39.57 N	105.49 W
Fraser, Mich., U.S.	266	42.32 N	82.57 W
Fraser ≃, B.C., Can.	238	49.09 N	123.12 W
Fraser ≃, Newf., Can.	232	56.35 N	61.55 W
Fraser ≃, Colo., U.S.	254	40.06 N	105.58 W
Fraserburgh	162	57.42 N	2.00 W
Fraser Island I	228	25.15 S	153.10 E
Fraser Lake	238	54.04 N	124.51 W
Fraser Lake ⊜	238	54.05 N	124.35 W
Fraser Mills	270	49.14 N	122.52 W
Fraser Plateau ⋀[1]	238	51.30 N	122.00 W
Frattamaggiore	184	40.57 N	14.16 E
Frauenfeld	180	47.34 N	8.54 E
Fray Bentos	294	33.08 S	58.18 W
Fray Marcos	294	34.11 S	55.44 W
Frazee	252	46.44 N	95.42 W
Frazer, Mont., U.S.	256	48.03 N	106.02 W
Frazer, Pa., U.S.	262	40.02 N	75.33 W
Frazeysburg	266	40.07 N	82.07 W
Frazier Park	274	34.49 N	118.56 W
Frechilla	168	42.08 N	4.50 W
Frederic	244	45.40 N	92.28 W
Frederica	262	39.01 N	75.28 W
Fredericia	160	55.35 N	9.46 E
Frederick, Md., U.S.	262	39.25 N	77.25 W
Frederick, Okla., U.S.	250	34.23 N	99.01 W
Frederick, S. Dak., U.S.	252	45.50 N	98.30 W
Frederick □[6]	262	39.25 N	77.25 W
Frederick House ≃	244	49.19 N	81.16 W
Frederick House Lake ⊜	244	48.40 N	80.55 W
Frederick Reef ✢[2]	228	20.58 S	154.23 E
Fredericksburg, Iowa, U.S.	244	42.58 N	92.12 W
Fredericksburg, Ohio, U.S.	266	40.41 N	81.52 W
Fredericksburg, Pa., U.S.	266	40.27 N	76.26 W
Fredericksburg, Tex., U.S.	250	30.17 N	98.52 W
Fredericksburg, Va., U.S.	262	38.18 N	77.29 W
Fredericksburg and Spotsylvania County Battlefields Memorial National Military Park	262	38.15 N	77.36 W
Frederick Sound ⋃	236	57.00 N	133.00 W
Fredericktown, Mo., U.S.	248	37.33 N	90.18 W
Fredericktown, Ohio, U.S.	266	40.29 N	82.33 W
Frederico Westphalen	294	27.22 S	53.24 W
Fredericton	240	45.58 N	66.39 W
Fredericton Junction	240	45.40 N	66.37 W
Frederik Hendrik Island → Dolak, Pulau I	198	7.50 S	138.30 E
Frederikshåb	232	62.00 N	49.43 W
Frederikshavn	160	57.26 N	10.32 E
Frederiksted	285n	17.43 N	64.53 W
Frederik Willem IV Vallen ∟	290	3.30 N	57.40 W
Fredonia, Col.	290	5.55 N	75.41 W
Fredonia, Ariz., U.S.	254	36.57 N	112.32 W
Fredonia, Kans., U.S.	252	37.32 N	95.49 W
Fredonia, N. Dak., U.S.	252	46.20 N	99.06 W
Fredonia, N.Y., U.S.	266	42.27 N	79.20 W
Fredonia, Pa., U.S.	266	41.20 N	80.14 W
Fredrika	160	64.05 N	18.24 E
Fredriksberg	160	60.08 N	14.23 E
Fredrikstad	160	59.13 N	10.57 E
Freeburg, Ill., U.S.	248	38.26 N	89.55 W
Freeburg, Mo., U.S.	248	38.19 N	91.55 W
Freeburg, Pa., U.S.	262	40.46 N	76.57 W
Freedom, Calif., U.S.	272	36.55 N	121.48 W
Freedom, Pa., U.S.	266	40.41 N	80.15 W
Freehold	262	40.16 N	74.17 W
Freeland, Mich., U.S.	244	43.32 N	84.07 W
Freeland, Pa., U.S.	242	41.01 N	75.47 W
Freeland, Wash., U.S.	270	48.01 N	122.32 W
Freeland Park	268	40.37 N	87.30 W
Freel Peak ∧	258	38.52 N	119.54 W
Freels, Cape ≻	240	49.15 N	53.28 W
Freeman	252	43.21 N	97.26 W
Freeman ≃	238	54.20 N	114.47 W
Freeport, Ba.	282	26.30 N	78.45 W
Freeport, N.S., Can.	240	44.17 N	66.19 W
Freeport, Ont., Can.	264	43.25 N	80.25 W
Freeport, Fla., U.S.	248	30.30 N	86.08 W
Freeport, Ill., U.S.	244	42.17 N	89.36 W
Freeport, Maine, U.S.	242	43.51 N	70.06 W
Freeport, Mich., U.S.	268	42.45 N	85.19 W
Freeport, Minn., U.S.	252	45.40 N	94.42 W
Freeport, N.Y., U.S.	242	43.09 N	73.35 W
Freeport, Ohio, U.S.	266	40.13 N	81.16 W
Freeport, Pa., U.S.	242	40.40 N	79.41 W
Freeport, Tex., U.S.	250	28.58 N	95.22 W
Freer	250	27.53 N	98.37 W
Freetown, Antig.	284c	17.03 N	61.42 W
Freetown, S.L.	222	8.30 N	13.15 W
Freetown, N.Y., U.S.	261	40.58 N	72.11 W
Freewood Acres	262	40.10 N	74.15 W
Freezeout Lake ⊜	256	47.40 N	112.03 W
Fregenal de la Sierra	168	38.10 N	6.39 W
Fregene ⇀[8]	184	41.51 N	12.12 E
Freiberg	164	50.54 N	13.20 E
Freiburg im Breisgau	180	47.59 N	7.51 E
Freirina	294	28.30 S	71.06 W
Freising	164	48.23 N	11.44 E
Freistadt	164	48.31 N	14.31 E
Freital	164	51.00 N	13.39 E
Fréjus	182	43.26 N	6.44 E
Fremantle	226	32.03 S	115.45 E
Fremont, Calif., U.S.	272	37.34 N	122.01 W
Fremont, Ind., U.S.	268	41.44 N	84.56 W
Fremont, Iowa, U.S.	244	41.13 N	92.26 W
Fremont, Mich., U.S.	244	43.28 N	85.57 W
Fremont, Nebr., U.S.	252	41.26 N	96.30 W
Fremont, N.C., U.S.	246	35.33 N	77.58 W
Fremont, Ohio, U.S.	266	41.21 N	83.07 W
Fremont, Wis., U.S.	244	44.16 N	88.52 W
Fremont ≃	254	38.24 N	110.42 W
Fremont Island I	254	41.09 N	112.20 W
Fremont Lake ⊜	254	42.57 N	109.49 W
French ≃	244	45.56 N	80.54 W
French Broad ≃	246	35.57 N	83.51 W
Frenchburg	246	37.57 N	83.37 W
French Camp	272	37.53 N	121.16 W
French Guiana □[2]	286	4.00 N	53.00 W
French Island I	228	38.21 S	145.21 E
French Lick	248	38.33 N	86.37 W
Frenchman Bay C	242	44.25 N	68.10 W
Frenchman Flat ≚	258	36.50 N	115.55 W
Frenchman Lake ⊜	258	36.48 N	116.56 W
Frenchmans Cap ∧	228	42.16 S	145.50 E
French Polynesia □[2]	148	17.00 S	158.00 W
French Southern and Antarctic Territories □[2]	148	49.30 S	69.30 E
Frenchtown	262	40.32 N	75.04 W
Frenštát pod Radhoštěm	164	49.33 N	18.14 E
Freshfield, Mount ∧	238	51.44 N	116.57 W
Fresne-Saint-Mamès	166	47.33 N	5.52 E
Fresnes-en-Woëvre	166	49.08 N	5.39 E
Fresnes-sur-Escaut	176	50.26 N	3.35 E
Fresnillo	278	23.10 N	102.53 W
Fresno, Col.	290	5.09 N	75.01 W
Fresno, Calif., U.S.	272	36.45 N	119.45 W
Fresno, Ohio, U.S.	266	40.20 N	81.44 W
Fresno □[6]	272	36.38 N	119.45 W
Fresno Reservoir ⊜[1]	256	48.41 N	109.57 W
Freu, Cabo del ≻	168	39.45 N	3.27 E
Freudenstadt	180	48.28 N	8.25 E
Frewsburg	266	42.03 N	79.10 W
Freycinet Peninsula ≻[1]	228	42.13 S	148.18 E
Freyre	294	31.10 S	62.05 W
Fria □[4]	222	10.30 N	13.40 W
Fria, Cape ≻	218	18.30 S	12.01 E
Friant	272	36.59 N	119.43 W
Friars Point	248	34.22 N	90.38 W
Frías, Arg.	294	28.40 S	65.10 W
Frías, Perú	292	4.55 S	79.57 W
Fribourg (Freiburg)	180	46.48 N	7.09 E
Fribourg (Freiburg) □[3]	180	46.45 N	7.05 E
Friday Harbor	270	48.32 N	123.01 W
Fridley	244	45.06 N	93.15 W
Friedberg, B.R.D.	180	48.21 N	10.58 E
Friedberg, Öst.	164	47.27 N	16.03 E
Friedens	266	40.03 N	78.59 W
Friedensburg	262	40.36 N	76.14 W
Friedland	164	53.40 N	13.33 E
Friedrichshafen	180	47.39 N	9.28 E
Friedrichsort	164	54.24 N	10.11 E
Friedrichstadt	164	54.22 N	9.05 E
Friend, Nebr., U.S.	252	40.38 N	97.17 W
Friend, Oreg., U.S.	270	45.21 N	121.16 W
Friendship, N.Y., U.S.	266	42.12 N	78.08 W
Friendship, Tenn., U.S.	248	35.55 N	89.14 W
Friendship, Wis., U.S.	244	43.58 N	89.49 W
Fries	246	36.43 N	80.59 W
Friesach	164	46.57 N	14.24 E
Friesland □[4]	178	53.03 N	5.45 E
Friesoythe	178	53.01 N	7.51 E
Frignano	184	41.00 N	14.10 E
Frío ≃, N.A.	280	11.07 N	84.46 W
Frio ≃, Tex., U.S.	250	28.30 N	98.10 W
Frio, Cabo ≻	296	22.53 S	42.00 W
Frio Draw ∨	250	34.50 N	102.19 W
Friona	250	34.38 N	102.43 W
Frisco, Pa., U.S.	266	40.51 N	80.16 W
Frisco, Tex., U.S.	250	33.09 N	96.49 W
Frisco City	248	31.26 N	87.24 W
Frisian Islands II	158	53.35 N	6.40 E
Fritch	250	35.38 N	101.36 W
Fritzlar	178	51.08 N	9.16 E
Friuli-Venezia-Giulia □[4]	170	46.00 N	13.00 E
Frobisher	252	49.12 N	102.26 W

Symbols in the index entries are identified on page 360.

Name	Page	Lat°′	Long°′
Frobisher Bay	232	63.44 N	68.28 W
Frobisher Bay C	232	62.30 N	66.00 W
Frobisher Lake ⊜	232	56.25 N	108.20 W
Frohnleiten	164	47.16 N	15.20 E
Froid	252	48.20 N	104.30 W
Frolovo	158	49.47 N	43.39 E
Fromberg	256	45.23 N	108.54 W
Frome	174	51.14 N	2.20 W
Frome, Lake ⊜	228	30.48 S	139.48 E
Fröndenberg	178	51.28 N	7.46 E
Frontenac □[6], Ont., Can.	264	44.40 N	76.45 W
Frontenac □[6], Qué., Can.	260	45.42 N	71.15 W
Frontera	278	18.32 N	92.38 W
Frontera, Punta ›	278	18.36 N	92.42 W
Fronteras	254	30.56 N	109.31 W
Frontier, Sask., Can.	256	49.12 N	108.34 W
Frontier, Mich., U.S.	268	41.47 N	84.36 W
Frontier, Wyo., U.S.	254	41.49 N	110.32 W
Frontignan	182	43.27 N	3.45 E
Frontino	290	6.46 N	76.08 W
Frontino, Páramo Λ	290	6.28 N	76.04 W
Front Range ⛰	254	39.45 N	105.45 W
Front Royal	242	38.55 N	78.11 W
Frosinone	184	41.38 N	13.19 E
Frosinone □[4]	184	41.37 N	13.27 E
Frösön	160	63.11 N	14.32 E
Frost	250	32.05 N	96.48 W
Frostburg	242	39.39 N	78.56 W
Frostproof	246	27.44 N	81.32 W
Frövi	160	59.28 N	15.22 E
Fruges	166	50.31 N	2.08 E
Fruita	254	39.09 N	108.44 W
Fruitdale	248	31.20 N	88.25 W
Fruithurst	248	33.44 N	85.25 W
Fruitland	262	38.19 N	75.37 W
Fruitport	268	43.07 N	86.09 W
Fruitridge	272	38.31 N	121.27 W
Fruitvale, B.C., Can.	238	49.07 N	117.33 W
Fruitvale, Calif., U.S.	272	37.47 N	122.13 W
Fruitville	246	27.20 N	82.30 W
Frumușița	172	45.40 N	28.04 E
Frunze	186	42.54 N	74.36 E
Frutal	296	20.02 S	48.55 W
Frutigen	180	46.35 N	7.39 E
Fryburg	266	41.21 N	79.26 W
Fry Canyon	254	37.38 N	110.08 W
Frýdek-Místek	164	49.41 N	18.22 E
Frýdlant	164	50.56 N	15.05 E
Fryeburg	242	44.01 N	70.59 W
Fryingpan ≃	254	39.22 N	107.02 W
Fthiótis □[5]	172	38.45 N	22.30 E
Fucecchio	184	43.44 N	10.48 E
Fuchū	192	34.34 N	133.14 E
Fuchunjiang ≃	196	30.10 N	120.09 E
Fuencaliente	168	38.24 N	4.18 W
Fuensalida	168	40.03 N	4.12 W
Fuensanta, Embalse de la ⊜[1]	168	38.23 N	2.13 W
Fuente	250	28.40 N	100.32 W
Fuente de Cantos	168	38.15 N	6.18 W
Fuente de Oro	290	3.28 N	73.37 W
Fuente-Obejuna	168	38.16 N	5.25 W
Fuentesaúco	168	41.14 N	5.30 W
Fuentes de Ebro	168	41.31 N	0.38 W
Fuerte ≃	278	25.50 N	109.25 W
Fuerte Olimpo	292	21.02 S	57.54 W
Fufeng	190	34.20 N	107.51 E
Fuga Island I	202	18.53 N	121.22 E
Fugama, Wādī V	220	14.43 N	24.36 E
Fugløysund ⋓	160	70.12 N	20.20 E
Fugong	200	27.09 N	98.52 E
Fuji	192	35.09 N	138.39 E
Fuji ≃	192	35.07 N	138.38 E
Fuji, Mount → Fuji-san Λ[1]	192	35.22 N	138.44 E
Fujian □[4]	196	26.00 N	118.00 E
Fujieda	192	34.52 N	138.16 E
Fuji-hakone-izu-kokuritsu-kōen ♣	192	35.21 N	138.44 E
Fujin	190	47.14 N	132.00 E
Fujinomiya	192	35.12 N	138.38 E
Fuji-san (Fujiyama) Λ[1]	192	35.22 N	138.44 E
Fujisawa	192	35.21 N	139.29 E
Fuji-yoshida	192	35.38 N	138.42 E
Fukagawa	192a	43.43 N	142.03 E
Fukaya	192	36.12 N	139.17 E
Fukien → Fujian □[4]	196	26.00 N	118.00 E
Fukuchiyama	192	35.18 N	135.07 E
Fukue	192	32.41 N	128.50 E
Fukuei Chiao ›	196	25.19 N	121.34 E
Fukue-shima I	192	32.40 N	128.45 E
Fukui	192	36.04 N	136.13 E
Fukuoka, Nihon	192	40.16 N	141.18 E
Fukuoka, Nihon	192	33.35 N	130.24 E
Fukuroi	192	34.45 N	137.55 E
Fukushima, Nihon	192	37.45 N	140.28 E
Fukushima, Nihon	192a	41.29 N	140.15 E
Fukuyama	192	34.29 N	133.22 E
Fulaerji	190	47.13 N	123.39 E
Fulda, B.R.D.	164	50.33 N	9.41 E
Fulda, Minn., U.S.	252	43.52 N	95.36 W
Fulda ≃	164	51.25 N	9.39 E
Fulford Harbor	270	48.46 N	123.27 W
Fuling	190	29.42 N	107.21 E
Fullarton ≃	228	20.15 S	141.10 E
Fullerton, Calif., U.S.	274	33.52 N	117.55 W
Fullerton, Nebr., U.S.	252	41.22 N	97.58 W
Fullerton, Pa., U.S.	262	40.38 N	75.28 W
Fulpmes	164	47.10 N	11.21 E
Fulton, Ala., U.S.	248	31.47 N	87.43 W
Fulton, Ark., U.S.	248	33.37 N	93.49 W
Fulton, Ill., U.S.	244	41.52 N	90.11 W
Fulton, Ind., U.S.	268	40.57 N	86.16 W
Fulton, Kans., U.S.	252	38.01 N	94.43 W
Fulton, Ky., U.S.	248	36.30 N	88.53 W
Fulton, Md., U.S.	262	39.09 N	76.56 W
Fulton, Mich., U.S.	268	42.06 N	85.22 W
Fulton, Miss., U.S.	248	34.16 N	88.31 W
Fulton, Mo., U.S.	248	38.52 N	91.57 W
Fulton, N.Y., U.S.	264	43.19 N	76.25 W
Fulton, Ohio, U.S.	266	40.28 N	82.50 W
Fulton, Tex., U.S.	250	28.04 N	97.02 W
Fulton □[6], Ind., U.S.	268	41.04 N	86.13 W
Fulton □[6], Ohio, U.S.	268	41.33 N	84.09 W
Fulton □[6], Pa., U.S.	266	40.06 N	78.04 W
Fulton ≃	238	54.48 N	126.07 W
Fultondale	248	33.36 N	86.48 W
Fumay	166	49.59 N	4.42 E
Fumel	166	44.29 N	0.57 E
Fumin	200	25.16 N	102.26 E
Funabashi	192	35.42 N	139.59 E
Funan	190	22.32 N	107.56 E
Funchal	214	32.38 N	16.54 W
Fundación	290	10.31 N	74.11 W
Fundão, Bra.	296	19.55 S	40.24 W
Fundão, Port.	168	40.08 N	7.30 W
Fundición de Avalos	278	28.35 N	106.00 W
Fundy, Bay of C	240	45.00 N	66.00 W
Fundy National Park ♣	240	45.38 N	65.00 W
Funhalouro	218	23.03 S	34.25 E
Funiushan ⛰	196	33.40 N	112.30 E
Funk Island I	240	49.46 N	53.10 W
Funtua	222	11.31 N	7.17 E
Fuquay Springs	246	35.35 N	78.48 W
Fúquene, Laguna de ⊜	290	5.28 N	73.45 W
Furano	192a	43.21 N	142.24 E
Furculești	172	43.52 N	25.09 E
Furlong	262	40.18 N	75.05 W
Furmanov	160	57.15 N	41.07 E
Furnas, Represa de ⊜[1]	296	20.45 S	46.00 W
Furneaux Group II	228	40.10 S	148.05 E
Furongshan Λ	196	27.30 N	115.52 E
Fürstenau	178	52.31 N	7.40 E
Fürstenberg/Havel	164	53.11 N	13.08 E
Fürstenfeld	164	47.03 N	16.05 E
Fürstenfeldbruck	164	48.10 N	11.15 E
Fürstenwalde	164	52.21 N	14.04 E
Fürth	164	49.28 N	10.59 E
Furth im Wald	164	49.18 N	12.51 E
Furtwangen	180	48.03 N	8.12 E
Furudal	160	61.10 N	15.08 E
Furukawa	192	38.34 N	140.58 E
Fury and Hecla Strait ⋓	232	69.56 N	84.00 W
Fusagasugá	290	4.21 N	74.22 W
Fushui ≃	196	29.52 N	115.28 E
Fushun	194	41.52 N	123.53 E
Füssen	180	47.34 N	10.42 E
Fuste, Picacho del Λ	250	27.37 N	102.47 W
Futunxi ≃	196	26.51 N	117.46 E
Fuwah	220	31.12 N	30.33 E
Fuxian	194	39.37 N	122.01 E
Fuxianhu ⊜	200	24.30 N	102.55 E
Fuxin	194	42.08 N	121.45 E
Fuxinshi	194	42.03 N	121.46 E
Fuyang	196	32.52 N	115.42 E
Fuyanghe ≃	194	38.14 N	116.05 E
Fuyaoshan I	196	26.57 N	120.21 E
Fuyu	190	45.10 N	124.50 E
Fuyuan	200	25.39 N	104.12 E
Fuzhong	200	24.28 N	111.22 E
Fuzhou, Zhg.	196	28.01 N	116.20 E
Fuzhou (Foochow), Zhg.	196	26.06 N	119.17 E
Fuzhouwan C	194	39.18 N	121.35 E
Fyn I	160	55.20 N	10.30 E
Fyne, Loch C	162	56.30 N	5.20 W
G			
Gabaldon	202	15.28 N	121.19 E
Gabare	172	43.19 N	23.55 E
Gabarouse	240	45.50 N	60.09 W
Gabarus Bay C	240	45.51 N	60.07 W
Gabas ≃	166	43.46 N	0.42 W
Gabbs	258	38.52 N	117.55 W
Gabby Heights	266	40.09 N	80.15 W
Gabela	218	10.48 S	14.20 E
Gabès	214	33.53 N	10.07 E
Gabès, Golfe de C	214	34.00 N	10.25 E
Gabiarra	296	16.15 S	39.41 W
Gąbin	164	52.25 N	19.44 E
Gable Mountain Λ	238	54.30 N	121.40 W
Gablonz → Jablonec nad Nisou	164	50.44 N	15.10 E
Gabon □[1]	218	1.00 S	11.45 E
Gaborone	224	24.45 S	25.55 E
Gabriel Strait ⋓	232	61.45 N	65.30 W
Gabriel y Galan, Embalse ⊜[1]	168	40.15 N	6.15 W
Gabriola	270	49.12 N	123.50 W
Gabrovo	172	42.52 N	25.19 E
Gacé	166	48.48 N	0.18 E
Gachetá	290	4.49 N	73.36 W
Gach Sārān	204	30.12 N	50.47 E
Gackle	252	46.38 N	99.09 W
Gacko	172	43.10 N	18.32 E
Gäddede	160	64.30 N	14.09 E
Gadderbaum	178	52.00 N	8.31 E
Gádor	168	36.57 N	2.29 W
Gádor, Sierra de ⛰	168	36.54 N	2.47 W
Gadsden, Ala., U.S.	248	34.02 N	86.02 W
Gadsden, Ariz., U.S.	254	32.33 N	108.47 W
Găești	172	44.43 N	25.19 E
Gaeta	184	41.12 N	13.35 E
Gaferut I	198	9.14 N	145.23 E
Gaffney	246	35.05 N	81.39 W
Gafour	170	36.18 N	9.19 E
Gafsa	214	34.25 N	8.48 E
Gagarin	160	55.33 N	35.00 E
Gage	250	36.19 N	99.45 W
Gagetown	240	45.47 N	66.09 W
Gaggenau	164	48.48 N	8.19 E
Gaggiano	182	45.24 N	9.02 E
Gagino	160	55.14 N	45.02 E
Gagliano del Capo	170	39.50 N	18.22 E
Gagnoa	222	6.08 N	5.56 W
Gagnoa □[5]	222	6.15 N	5.40 W
Gagnon	232	51.55 N	68.10 W
Gago Coutinho	218	14.08 S	21.25 E
Gagra	158	43.20 N	40.15 E
Gaiab ≃	224	28.31 S	19.35 E
Gail	250	32.46 N	101.27 W
Gail ≃	164	46.36 N	13.53 E
Gaillac	166	43.54 N	1.55 E
Gaillard, Lac ⊜	240	50.06 N	68.47 W
Gaillefontaine	162	49.39 N	1.37 E
Gaillon	166	49.10 N	1.20 E
Gainesboro	248	36.21 N	85.39 W
Gainesville, Fla., U.S.	246	29.40 N	82.20 W
Gainesville, Ga., U.S.	246	34.18 N	83.50 W
Gainesville, Mo., U.S.	248	36.36 N	92.26 W
Gainesville, N.Y., U.S.	266	42.39 N	78.08 W
Gainesville, Tex., U.S.	250	33.37 N	97.08 W
Gainsborough, Sask., Can.	252	49.10 N	101.26 W
Gainsborough, Eng., U.K.	162	53.24 N	0.46 W
Gaiping	194	40.24 N	122.22 E
Gairdner, Lake ⊜	228	31.35 S	136.00 E
Gaital, Cerro Λ	280	8.37 N	80.07 W
Gaither	262	39.21 N	77.01 W
Gaithersburg	262	39.09 N	77.12 W
Gaj	170	45.29 N	17.02 E
Gajny	160	60.15 N	54.15 E
Gajutino	160	58.42 N	38.32 E
Gakarosa Λ	224	27.50 S	23.38 E
Gakona	236	62.18 N	145.18 W
Gakugsa	160	61.34 N	36.26 E
Galahad	238	52.31 N	111.56 W
Galán, Cerro Λ	294	25.55 S	66.52 W
Galana ≃	218	3.09 S	40.08 E
Galanta	164	48.12 N	17.43 E
Galapagos Islands → Colón, Archipiélago de II	290a	0.30 S	90.30 W
Galaroza	168	37.55 N	6.42 W
Galas ≃	200	5.31 N	102.12 E
Galashiels	162	55.37 N	2.49 W
Galați	172	45.26 N	28.03 E
Galatia	248	37.51 N	88.37 W
Galatina	170	40.10 N	18.10 E
Galax	246	36.40 N	80.56 W
Galaxídhion	172	38.22 N	22.23 E
Gale, Lac ⊜	244	46.46 N	76.51 W
Galeana, Méx.	278	24.50 N	100.04 W
Galeana, Méx.	278	30.07 N	107.38 W
Galela	198	1.50 N	127.50 E
Galena, Alaska, U.S.	236	64.44 N	156.57 W
Galena, Ill., U.S.	244	42.25 N	90.26 W
Galena, Kans., U.S.	252	37.04 N	94.38 W
Galena, Md., U.S.	262	39.20 N	75.55 W
Galena, Mo., U.S.	248	36.48 N	93.28 W
Galena, Ohio, U.S.	266	40.13 N	82.53 W
Galena Park	250	29.44 N	95.14 W
Galeota Point ›	285r	10.08 N	61.00 W
Galera ≃	292	14.25 S	60.07 W
Galera, Punta ›, Chile	288	39.59 S	73.43 W
Galera, Punta ›, Ec.	290	0.49 N	80.03 W
Galera Point ›	285r	10.49 N	60.55 W
Galesburg, Ill., U.S.	244	40.57 N	90.22 W
Galesburg, Mich., U.S.	268	42.14 N	85.25 W
Gales Creek	270	45.39 N	123.13 W
Gales Ferry	261	41.26 N	72.05 W
Galesville, Md., U.S.	262	38.50 N	76.31 W
Galesville, Wis., U.S.	244	44.05 N	91.21 W
Galeton	266	41.44 N	77.39 W
Galeville	264	43.05 N	76.11 W
Galheirão ≃	296	12.23 S	45.05 W
Galheiros	296	13.18 S	46.25 W
Galiano	270	48.52 N	123.21 W
Galiano Island I	238	48.56 N	123.29 W
Galič	160	58.23 N	42.21 E
Galicia □[9], Esp.	168	43.00 N	8.00 W
Galicia (Galicja) □[9], Eur.	164	49.50 N	21.00 E
Galičsko-Čuchlomskaja Vozvyšennosť ⛰[2]	160	58.25 N	42.20 E
Galien	268	41.48 N	86.30 W
Galilee	261	41.23 N	71.30 W
Galilee → HaGalil ⬩[1]	210	32.55 N	35.18 E
Galilee, Lake ⊜	228	22.21 S	145.48 E
Galilee, Sea of → Kinneret, Yam ⊜	210	32.49 N	35.36 E
Galiléia	296	19.00 S	41.33 W
Galina Point ›	285q	18.23 N	76.52 W
Galion	266	40.44 N	82.47 W
Galite, Canal de la ⋓	170	37.20 N	9.00 E
Galiuro Mountains ⛰	254	32.40 N	110.20 W
Galka'yo	214	6.49 N	47.23 E
Gallarate	182	45.40 N	8.47 E
Gallatin, Mo., U.S.	248	39.55 N	93.58 W
Gallatin, Tenn., U.S.	248	36.24 N	86.27 W
Gallatin ≃	256	45.56 N	111.29 W
Gallatin Range ⛰	256	45.15 N	111.05 W
Galle	204	6.02 N	80.13 E
Gállego ≃	168	41.39 N	0.51 W
Gallegos Canyon V	254	36.41 N	108.07 W
Galliate	182	45.29 N	8.42 E
Gallinas ≃	250	35.10 N	104.55 W
Gallinas, Punta ›	290	12.25 N	71.40 W
Gallipoli, It.	170	40.03 N	17.58 E
Gallipoli → Gelibolu, Tür.	212	40.24 N	26.40 E
Gallipoli Peninsula → Gelibolu Yarımadası ›[1]	212	40.20 N	26.30 E
Gallipolis	242	38.49 N	82.12 W
Gallitzin	266	40.29 N	78.33 W
Gällivare	160	67.07 N	20.45 E
Gallo, Capo ›	170	38.13 N	13.19 E
Gallo Arroyo V	254	33.55 N	105.00 W
Galloo Island I	242	43.54 N	76.25 W
Gallup	254	35.32 N	108.44 W
Gallur	168	41.52 N	1.19 W
Gallura ⬩[1]	170	41.05 N	9.15 E
Galluzzo ⬩[8]	184	43.44 N	11.13 E
Galston	162	55.36 N	4.24 W
Galt, Ont., Can.	264	43.22 N	80.19 W
Galt, Calif., U.S.	272	38.15 N	121.18 W
Galtür	164	46.58 N	10.11 E
Galty Mountains ⛰	162	52.25 N	8.10 W
Galva, Ill., U.S.	244	41.10 N	90.03 W
Galva, Iowa, U.S.	252	42.30 N	95.25 W
Galvarino	294	38.24 S	72.47 W
Galveston, Ind., U.S.	268	40.35 N	86.11 W
Galveston, Tex., U.S.	250	29.18 N	94.48 W
Galveston Bay C	250	29.36 N	94.57 W
Galveston Island I	250	29.13 N	94.55 W
Gálvez	294	32.02 S	61.15 W
Galvin	270	46.45 N	123.02 W
Galway	162	53.16 N	9.03 W
Galway □[6]	162	53.20 N	9.00 W
Galway Bay C	162	53.10 N	9.15 W
Gam ≃	200	21.55 N	105.12 E
Gamaches	162	49.59 N	1.33 E
Gamagōri	192	34.50 N	137.14 E
Gamaliel	248	36.38 N	85.48 W
Gamarra	290	8.20 N	73.45 W
Gamay	202	12.23 N	125.18 E
Gamay Bay C	202	12.20 N	125.20 E
Gambela	214	8.18 N	34.37 E
Gambell	236	63.46 N	171.46 W
Gamber	262	39.28 N	76.56 W
Gambia □[1]	214	13.25 N	16.00 W
Gambia (Gambie) ≃	222	13.28 N	16.34 W
Gambie (Gambia) ≃	222	13.28 N	16.34 W
Gambier	266	40.23 N	82.24 W
Gambo	240	48.46 N	54.14 W
Gamboa	280	9.05 N	79.40 W
Gambolò	182	45.15 N	8.51 E
Gamboma	218	1.53 S	15.51 E
Gamka ≃, S. Afr.	224	33.18 S	21.39 E
Gamka ≃, S.W. Afr.	224	28.15 S	17.26 E
Gamleby	160	57.54 N	16.24 E
Gamtoos ≃	224	33.58 S	25.01 E
Ganado, Ariz., U.S.	254	35.43 N	109.33 W
Ganado, Tex., U.S.	250	29.02 N	96.31 W
Ganano ≃	202	16.45 N	121.42 E
Gananoque	264	44.20 N	76.10 W
Ganassi	202	7.49 N	124.06 E
Gand → Gent	176	51.03 N	3.43 E
Gandak ≃	206	25.40 N	85.13 E
Gander	240	48.57 N	54.34 W
Gander ≃	240	49.15 N	54.30 W
Gander Bay	240	49.15 N	54.29 W
Gander Bay C	240	49.25 N	54.28 W
Ganderkesee	178	53.02 N	8.32 E
Gander Lake ⊜	240	48.55 N	54.40 W
Gandesa	168	41.03 N	0.26 E
Gandhi Sagar Reservoir ⊜[1]	206	24.18 N	75.21 E
Gandi	222	12.55 N	5.49 E
Gandi, Wādī V	220	11.23 N	24.31 E
Gandía	168	38.58 N	0.11 W
Gandino	182	45.49 N	9.54 E
Gandu	296	13.45 S	39.30 W
Gangaw	198	22.11 N	94.07 E
Gangaw Range ⛰	200	24.50 N	96.40 E
Gangdisishan Λ	206	31.29 N	80.45 E
Gangdisishanmai ⛰	206	29.30 N	87.00 E
Ganges, B.C., Can.	238	48.51 N	123.30 W
Ganges, Fr.	166	43.56 N	3.42 E
Ganges (Ganga) (Padma) ≃	206	23.22 N	90.32 E
Ganges, Mouths of the ≃[1]	206	22.00 N	89.00 E
Gangi	170	37.49 N	14.13 E
Ganglasishan ⛰	206	31.00 N	82.50 E
Ganglingshan ⛰	206	32.00 N	83.00 E
Gang Ranch	238	51.33 N	122.20 W
Gangtok	190	27.20 N	88.37 E
Gangu	190	34.38 N	105.27 E
Ganjiang ≃	196	29.12 N	116.00 E
Ganlanshan Λ	206	29.54 N	90.02 E
Gannat	166	46.06 N	3.12 E
Gannett Peak Λ	254	43.10 N	109.40 W
Gannvalley	252	44.02 N	98.59 W
Ganongga I	226	8.05 S	156.35 E
Ganos Dağı Λ	212	40.47 N	27.16 E
Gänserndorf	164	48.20 N	16.43 E
Ganshoren	176	50.52 N	4.18 E
Ganso Azul	292	8.45 S	74.43 W
Gansu □[4]	190	37.00 N	103.00 E
Gantheaume, Cape ›	228	36.05 S	137.27 E
Gantt	248	31.25 N	86.29 W
Gantung, Mount Λ	202	8.58 N	117.49 E
Ganzhou	196	25.54 N	114.55 E
Ganzi	190	31.40 N	100.01 E
Gao	222	16.16 N	0.03 W
Gao □[4]	222	18.15 N	1.00 W
Gaokeng	196	27.40 N	113.58 E
Gaolandao I	196	21.55 N	113.15 E
Gaona	294	25.12 S	64.05 W
Gaoual □[4]	222	11.45 N	13.12 W
Gaoyou	196	32.47 N	119.27 E
Gaoyouhu ⊜	196	32.50 N	119.20 E
Gaozhou	200	21.55 N	110.50 E
Gap, Fr.	182	44.34 N	6.05 E
Gap, Pa., U.S.	262	39.59 N	76.01 W
Gapan	202	15.19 N	120.57 E
Garachiné	290	8.05 N	78.20 W
Garachiné, Punta ›	290	8.08 N	78.27 W
Garagoa	290	5.05 N	73.21 W
Garanhuns	286	8.54 S	36.29 W
Garbagnate	182	45.34 N	9.04 E
Garber	250	36.26 N	97.35 W
Garberville	258	40.06 N	123.48 W
Garbsen	178	52.25 N	9.34 E
Garça	296	22.14 S	49.37 W
Garças, Rio das ≃	296	15.54 S	52.16 W
Garches	176	48.51 N	2.11 E
Garchitorena	202	13.55 N	123.40 E
García	278	29.59 N	108.20 W
Garcia Hernandez	202	9.37 N	124.18 E
Garcias, Bra.	296	20.34 S	52.13 W
Garcias, Méx.	250	27.17 N	99.30 W
Gard □[5]	182	44.00 N	4.00 E
Gard, Pont du ⬩[5]	166	43.56 N	4.36 E
Garda	170	45.34 N	10.42 E
Garda, Lago di ⊜	170	45.40 N	10.41 E
Gardanne	182	43.27 N	5.28 E
Garde, Lac la ⊜	244	46.46 N	78.14 W
Gardelegen	164	52.31 N	11.23 E
Garden ≃	244	46.32 N	84.09 W
Gardena	274	33.53 N	118.18 W
Garden City, Ga., U.S.	246	32.06 N	81.09 W
Garden City, Kans., U.S.	252	37.58 N	100.53 W
Garden City, Mich., U.S.	268	42.20 N	83.20 W
Garden City, Mo., U.S.	248	38.34 N	94.12 W
Garden City, Tex., U.S.	250	31.52 N	101.29 W
Gardendale	248	33.39 N	86.49 W
Garden Farms	272	35.24 N	120.07 W
Garden Grove, Calif., U.S.	274	33.46 N	117.57 W
Garden Grove, Iowa, U.S.	244	40.50 N	93.36 W
Garden Home	270	45.26 N	122.47 W
Garden Island I	244	45.49 N	85.30 W
Garden Plain	252	37.39 N	97.41 W
Garden Prairie	268	42.15 N	88.44 W
Garden Reach	206	22.33 N	88.17 E
Gardenton	252	49.05 N	96.40 W
Garden Valley	272	38.51 N	120.51 W
Gardenville	262	40.22 N	75.07 W
Gardey	294	37.17 S	59.22 W
Gardez	206	33.36 N	69.06 E
Gardiner, Maine, U.S.	242	44.14 N	69.46 W
Gardiner, Mont., U.S.	256	45.02 N	110.42 W
Gardiner, Oreg., U.S.	256	43.44 N	124.07 W
Gardiner, Wash., U.S.	270	48.03 N	122.55 W
Gardiners Bay C	242	41.08 N	72.10 W
Gardner, Colo., U.S.	254	37.47 N	105.10 W
Gardner, Ill., U.S.	268	41.11 N	88.18 W
Gardner, Kans., U.S.	252	38.49 N	94.56 W
Gardner, Mass., U.S.	261	42.34 N	71.59 W
Gardner Canal C	238	53.28 N	128.15 W
Gardnerville	272	38.56 N	119.45 W
Gardo	214	9.30 N	49.03 E
Gardone Val Trompia	170	45.41 N	10.11 E
Gareloi Island I	237a	51.47 N	178.48 W
Garešnica	170	45.39 N	16.49 E
Garessio	170	44.12 N	8.02 E
Garfield, Kans., U.S.	252	38.05 N	99.14 W
Garfield, N. Mex., U.S.	254	32.46 N	107.16 W
Garfield, Wash., U.S.	256	47.01 N	117.09 W
Garfield Heights	266	41.26 N	81.37 W
Garfield Mountain Λ	256	44.31 N	112.38 W
Garfield Peak Λ	254	42.47 N	107.18 W
Gargaliánoi	172	37.04 N	21.39 E
Gargano, Testa del ›	170	41.49 N	16.12 E
Gargantua, Cape ›	244	47.36 N	85.02 W
Garibaldi, Bra.	294	29.15 S	51.32 W
Garibaldi, B.C., Can.	238	49.58 N	123.09 W
Garibaldi, Oreg., U.S.	270	45.34 N	123.55 W
Garibaldi, Mount Λ	238	49.51 N	123.01 W
Garies	218	30.30 S	18.00 E
Gariglione, Monte Λ	170	39.09 N	16.41 E
Garissa	218	0.28 S	39.38 E
Garita Palmera	280	13.44 N	90.05 W
Garland, Ala., U.S.	248	31.33 N	86.49 W
Garland, Pa., U.S.	266	41.49 N	79.27 W
Garland, Tex., U.S.	250	32.54 N	96.39 W
Garland, Utah, U.S.	254	41.45 N	112.10 W
Garlasco	182	45.12 N	8.55 E
Garliava	160	54.49 N	23.52 E
Garlin	166	43.34 N	0.15 W
Garm	186	39.02 N	70.22 E
Garmisch-Partenkirchen	164	47.29 N	11.05 E
Garnavillo	244	42.52 N	91.14 W
Garner, Iowa, U.S.	244	43.06 N	93.36 W
Garner, N.C., U.S.	246	35.43 N	78.37 W
Garnet Bay C	232	65.17 N	75.15 W
Garnet Range ⛰	256	46.45 N	113.15 W
Garnett	252	38.17 N	95.14 W
Garnish	240	47.14 N	55.22 W
Garonne ≃	166	45.02 N	0.36 W
Garou, Lac ⊜	222	16.04 N	2.45 W
Garoua	214	9.18 N	13.24 E
Garrel	178	52.57 N	8.01 E
Garretson	252	43.43 N	96.30 W
Garrett, Ind., U.S.	268	41.21 N	85.08 W
Garrett, Ky., U.S.	246	37.29 N	82.50 W
Garrett Park	262	39.02 N	77.06 W
Garrettsville	266	41.17 N	81.06 W
Garrison, Md., U.S.	262	39.24 N	76.45 W
Garrison, Mont., U.S.	256	46.31 N	112.57 W
Garrison, N. Dak., U.S.	252	47.40 N	101.25 W
Garrison, Tex., U.S.	248	31.49 N	94.29 W
Garrovillas	168	39.43 N	6.33 W
Garry Bay C	232	68.55 N	85.05 W
Garry Lake ⊜	232	66.00 N	100.00 W
Garsen	218	2.16 S	40.07 E
Garson	244	46.34 N	80.52 W
Garstedt	178	53.41 N	9.58 E
Gartempe ≃	166	46.48 N	0.50 E
Garthby Station (Beaulac)	260	45.50 N	71.23 W
Garut	198	7.13 S	107.54 E
Garvie Mountains ⛰	230	45.27 S	168.55 E
Garwin	244	42.06 N	92.40 W
Garwolin	164	51.54 N	21.37 E
Garwood	250	29.27 N	96.24 W
Gary, Ind., U.S.	268	41.36 N	87.20 W
Gary, S. Dak., U.S.	252	44.48 N	96.27 W
Gary, Tex., U.S.	248	32.07 N	94.22 W
Garysburg	262	36.27 N	77.33 W
Garza	294	28.09 S	63.33 W
Garza Ayala	250	26.29 N	100.02 W
Garza-Little Elm Reservoir ⊜[1]	250	33.08 N	97.00 W
Garzón, Col.	290	2.12 N	75.38 W
Garzón, Ur.	294	34.36 S	54.33 W
Gasan	202	13.19 N	121.51 E
Gasan-Kuli	158	37.27 N	53.59 E
Gas City	268	40.29 N	85.37 W
Gasconade ≃	248	38.40 N	91.33 W
Gasconade, Osage Fork ≃	248	37.45 N	92.26 W
Gash (Nahr al-Qāsh) ≃	220	16.48 N	35.51 E
Gashaka	214	7.21 N	11.27 E
Gaspar	294	26.56 S	48.58 W
Gasparilla Island I	246	26.46 N	82.16 W
Gaspé	240	48.50 N	64.29 W
Gaspé, Baie de ≃	240	48.45 N	64.15 W
Gaspé, Cap ›	240	48.45 N	64.09 W
Gaspé, Détroit de ⋓	240	49.25 N	64.25 W
Gaspé, Péninsule de ›[1]	240	48.30 N	65.00 W
Gaspereau Lake ⊜	240	44.57 N	64.34 W
Gasport	264	43.12 N	78.35 W
Gas-san Λ	192	38.32 N	140.01 E
Gassaway	242	38.40 N	80.47 W
Gassino Torinese	182	45.08 N	7.49 E
Gaston, Ind., U.S.	268	40.19 N	85.30 W
Gaston, N.C., U.S.	246	36.30 N	77.38 W
Gaston, Oreg., U.S.	270	45.26 N	123.08 W
Gaston, Lake ⊜[1]	246	36.35 N	78.00 W
Gastonia	246	35.16 N	81.11 W
Gastoúni	172	37.51 N	21.16 E
Gastre	288	42.17 S	69.15 W
Gata, Cabo de ›	168	36.43 N	2.12 W
Gata, Sierra de ⛰	168	40.14 N	6.45 W
Gătaia	172	45.26 N	21.26 E
Gátas, Akrotírion ›	212	34.32 N	33.01 E
Gatčina	160	59.34 N	30.08 E
Gate	250	36.51 N	100.04 W
Gate City	246	36.38 N	82.35 W
Gatehouse of Fleet	162	54.53 N	4.11 W
Gates, N.C., U.S.	262	36.30 N	76.46 W
Gates, N.Y., U.S.	264	43.09 N	77.41 W
Gates □[6]	262	36.28 N	76.43 W
Gateshead	162	54.58 N	1.37 W
Gateshead Island I	232	70.22 N	100.27 W
Gatesville, N.C., U.S.	246	36.19 N	76.45 W
Gatesville, Tex., U.S.	250	31.26 N	97.45 W
Gateway	254	38.41 N	108.59 W
Gâtine, Hauteurs de ⛰[2]	166	46.40 N	0.50 W
Gatineau	264	45.29 N	75.39 W
Gatineau □[6]	264	46.30 N	76.00 W
Gatineau ≃	242	45.27 N	75.40 W
Gatliff	246	36.41 N	84.01 W
Gatlinburg	246	35.43 N	83.31 W
Gatooma	224	18.21 S	29.55 E
Gattinara	182	45.37 N	8.22 E
Gatun Lake ⊜[1]	280	9.10 N	79.55 W
Gaucín	168	36.31 N	5.19 W
Gaud-i-Zirreh ⩸	214	29.50 N	62.00 E
Gaud-i-Zirreh ⊜	208	29.50 N	62.00 E
Gauer Lake ⊜	232	57.00 N	97.50 W
Gauhāti	206	26.10 N	91.45 E
Gauri Sankar Λ	206	27.57 N	86.21 E
Gauja ≃	160	57.09 N	24.16 E
Gauley ≃	242	38.10 N	81.12 W
Gauley Bridge	242	38.10 N	81.11 W
Gaurama	294	27.34 S	52.03 W
Gauri Sankar Λ	206	27.57 N	86.21 E
Gause	250	30.47 N	96.43 W
Gauting	164	48.04 N	11.23 E
Gavá	168	41.18 N	2.01 E
Gávdhos I	214	34.50 N	24.06 E
Gave d'Aspe ≃	166	43.12 N	0.36 W
Gavião ≃	296	14.06 S	41.01 W
Gavirate	182	45.50 N	8.43 E
Gāvkhūnī, Bāṭlāq-e ≋	208	32.06 N	52.52 E
Gävle	160	60.40 N	17.10 E
Gävleborgs Län □[6]	160	61.30 N	16.15 E
Gavorrano	184	42.55 N	10.54 E
Gavriila, Guba C	236	62.25 N	179.15 E
Gavrilov-Jam	160	57.18 N	39.51 E
Gávrion	172	37.52 N	24.46 E
Gawler	228	34.37 S	138.44 E
Gay	244	47.13 N	88.10 W
Gaya, Bhārat	206	24.48 N	85.03 E
Gaya, Nig.	222	11.53 N	9.02 E
Gay Head	261	41.21 N	70.49 W
Gaylord, Mich., U.S.	244	45.02 N	84.40 W
Gaylord, Minn., U.S.	244	44.33 N	94.13 W
Gaylordsville	261	41.39 N	73.29 W
Gayndah	226	25.37 S	151.36 E
Gays Mills	244	43.19 N	90.51 W
Gaza → Ghazzah	210	31.30 N	34.28 E
Gaza □[5]	224	23.30 S	32.45 E
Gaza Strip □[9]	210	31.25 N	34.20 E
Gazelle Basin ⊹[1]	148	32.00 S	170.00 E
Gaziantep	212	37.05 N	37.22 E
Gazzaniga	182	45.48 N	9.50 E
Gbanka	222	7.00 N	9.29 W
Gboko	222	7.20 N	8.57 E
Gbongan	222	7.29 N	4.21 E
Gdańsk (Danzig)	164	54.23 N	18.40 E
Gdov	160	58.44 N	27.48 E
Gdyel	168	35.48 N	0.26 W
Gdynia	164	54.32 N	18.33 E
Gearhart	270	46.01 N	123.55 W
Gearhart Mountain Λ	256	42.30 N	120.53 W
Gearhartville	266	40.53 N	78.15 W
Geary, N.B., Can.	240	45.46 N	66.29 W
Geary, Okla., U.S.	250	35.38 N	98.19 W
Geauga □[6]	266	41.35 N	81.12 W
Gêba ≃	222	11.46 N	15.36 W
Gebe, Pulau I	198	0.05 S	129.20 E
Gebeler	172	39.26 N	29.00 E
Gebo	254	43.47 N	108.13 W
Gebze	172	40.48 N	29.25 E
Geddes	252	43.15 N	98.42 W
Gedera	210	31.48 N	34.46 E
Gediz	172	39.02 N	29.25 E
Gediz ≃	212	38.35 N	26.48 E
Gedser	164	54.35 N	11.57 E
Geel	178	51.10 N	5.00 E
Geelong	228	38.08 S	144.21 E
Geer	190	31.44 N	80.21 E
Ge'ermu	190	36.23 N	94.50 E
Geesthacht	178	53.26 N	10.22 E
Geeveston	226	43.10 S	146.55 E
Gehrden	178	52.18 N	9.36 E
Geiger	248	32.52 N	88.18 W
Geigertown	262	40.13 N	75.50 W
Geikie ≃	232	57.45 N	103.52 W
Geilo	160	60.31 N	8.12 E
Geisenfeld	164	48.41 N	11.37 E
Geislingen an der Steige	180	48.36 N	9.50 E
Geistown	266	40.17 N	78.52 W
Geisweid	164	50.55 N	8.01 E
Geita	218	2.52 S	32.10 E
Geithain	164	51.03 N	12.41 E
Gejinhe ≃	194	38.12 N	117.46 E
Gejiu (Kokiu)	200	23.22 N	103.06 E
Geka, Mys ›	236	64.26 N	178.10 E
Gela	170	37.03 N	14.15 E
Gela, Golfo di C	170	37.00 N	14.10 E
Gelai Λ[1]	218	2.33 S	36.05 E
Gelang, Tanjong ›	200	3.58 N	103.26 E
Gelderland □[4]	178	52.10 N	5.50 E
Geldern	178	51.31 N	6.20 E
Geldrop	178	51.25 N	5.33 E
Geleen	164	50.58 N	5.52 E
Gelenbe	172	39.10 N	27.50 E
Gelibolu	172	40.24 N	26.40 E
Gelibolu Yarımadası ›[1]	212	40.20 N	26.30 E
Gelidonya Burnu ›	212	36.13 N	30.25 E
Gélise ≃	166	44.11 N	0.17 E
Gelsenkirchen	178	51.31 N	7.07 E
Geluwe	176	50.48 N	3.04 E
Gem Beach	266	41.35 N	82.50 W
Gembloux	164	50.34 N	4.41 E
Gemena	214	3.15 N	19.46 E
Gemengchi ⊜	206	31.15 N	89.15 E
Gemert	178	51.34 N	5.40 E
Gemlik	172	40.26 N	29.09 E
Gemlik Körfezi C	212	40.25 N	28.55 E
Gemona del Friuli	170	46.16 N	13.09 E
Gemu Gofa □[4]	220	4.45 N	37.00 E
Gemünden	164	50.03 N	9.41 E
Gemuzhakechi ⊜	206	33.47 N	85.30 E
Genale ≃	214	5.43 N	40.53 E
Gençay	166	46.23 N	0.24 E
General Acha	294	37.20 S	64.35 W
General Alvear, Arg.	294	36.00 S	60.00 W
General Alvear, Arg.	294	34.59 S	67.42 W
General Aquino	294	24.26 S	56.42 W
General Arenales	294	34.20 S	61.15 W
General Artigas	294	26.53 S	56.17 W
General Belgrano	294	35.45 S	58.30 W
General Bravo	278	25.48 N	99.10 W
General Cabrera	294	32.49 S	63.52 W
General Câmara	294	29.54 S	51.46 W
General Campos	294	31.30 S	58.25 W
General Carneiro	296	15.42 S	52.45 W
General Cepeda	278	25.23 N	101.27 W
General Conesa	294	36.30 S	57.19 W
General Daniel Cerri	294	38.42 S	62.24 W
General Enrique Martínez	294	33.12 S	53.48 W
General Enrique Mosconi	294	22.36 S	63.49 W
General Escobedo, Méx.	250	25.49 N	100.20 W
General Escobedo, Méx.	278	25.30 N	105.15 W
General Eugenio A. Garay	294	25.55 S	56.11 W
General Galarza	294	32.45 S	59.25 W
General Guido	294	36.40 S	57.45 W
General Gutiérrez	294	32.58 S	68.45 W
General Island I	202	9.25 N	126.00 E
General José de San Martín	294	26.35 S	59.20 W
General Juan Madariaga	294	37.00 S	57.05 W
General La Madrid	294	37.15 S	61.16 W
General Lavalle	294	36.22 S	56.55 W
General Levalle	294	34.00 S	63.55 W
General Luna, Pil.	202	9.47 N	126.09 E
General Luna, Pil.	202	13.41 N	122.10 E
General MacArthur (Pambuhan Sur)	202	11.15 N	125.32 E
General Machado	218	12.03 S	17.30 E
General Manuel Belgrano, Cerro Λ	294	29.02 S	67.51 W
General Martín Miguel de Güemes	294	24.40 S	65.00 W
General O'Brien	294	34.54 S	60.46 W
General Paz, Arg.	294	27.45 S	57.40 W
General Paz, Arg.	294	35.32 S	58.18 W
General Pico	294	35.38 S	63.46 W
General Pinedo	294	27.20 S	61.20 W
General Pinto	294	34.45 S	61.54 W
General Pizarro	294	24.13 S	64.01 W
General Plaza (Limón)	290	2.58 S	78.25 W
General Roca	294	39.02 S	67.33 W
General Rojo	294	33.29 S	60.17 W
General Rondon	294	24.34 S	54.04 W
General Saavedra	292	17.15 S	63.10 W
General San Martín, Arg.	294	34.35 S	58.30 W
General San Martín, Arg.	294	38.00 S	63.35 W
General Santos (Dadiangas)	202	6.08 N	125.11 E
General Terán	278	25.16 N	99.41 W
General Tinio	202	15.21 N	121.03 E
General Toševo	172	43.42 N	28.02 E
General Treviño	250	26.14 N	99.29 W
General Vargas	294	29.42 S	54.40 W
General Viamonte (Los Toldos)	294	35.00 S	61.05 W
General Villegas	294	35.02 S	63.02 W
General Zuazua	250	25.54 N	100.07 W
Genesee, Idaho, U.S.	256	46.33 N	116.56 W
Genesee, Mich., U.S.	242	43.07 N	83.37 W
Genesee, Pa., U.S.	266	41.59 N	77.52 W
Genesee, Wis., U.S.	268	42.58 N	88.21 W
Genesee □[6], Mich., U.S.	268	42.56 N	83.41 W
Genesee □[6], N.Y., U.S.	264	43.00 N	78.11 W
Genesee ≃	244	43.16 N	77.36 W
Geneseo, Ill., U.S.	244	41.27 N	90.09 W
Geneseo, Kans., U.S.	252	38.31 N	98.09 W
Geneseo, N.Y., U.S.	264	42.48 N	77.49 W
Geneva → Genève, Schw.	180	46.12 N	6.09 E
Geneva, Ala., U.S.	248	31.02 N	85.52 W
Geneva, Ill., U.S.	268	41.53 N	88.18 W
Geneva, Ind., U.S.	268	40.36 N	84.58 W
Geneva, Nebr., U.S.	252	40.32 N	97.36 W
Geneva, N.Y., U.S.	264	42.52 N	76.59 W
Geneva, Ohio, U.S.	266	41.48 N	80.57 W
Geneva, Pa., U.S.	266	41.35 N	80.14 W
Geneva, Wash., U.S.	270	48.45 N	122.24 W
Geneva, Lake ⊜	166	46.25 N	6.30 E
Geneva-on-the-lake	266	41.52 N	80.57 W
Genève (Geneva)	180	46.12 N	6.09 E
Genève □[3]	180	46.15 N	6.10 E
Genevia	248	34.43 N	92.13 W
Genévriers, Île des I	240	51.15 N	58.30 W
Gengenbach	180	48.24 N	8.01 E
Gengma	200	23.34 N	99.06 E
Genil ≃	168	37.42 N	5.19 W
Genk	164	50.58 N	5.30 E
Genkai-nada ▾[2]	192	34.00 N	130.00 E
Genkanyj, Chrebet ⛰	236	66.15 N	172.20 W
Genlis	164	47.14 N	5.13 E
Gennargentu, Monti del ⛰	170	39.59 N	9.19 E
Gennes	166	47.20 N	0.14 W
Genoa → Genova, It.	182	44.25 N	8.57 E
Genoa, Ill., U.S.	268	42.06 N	88.42 W
Genoa, Nebr., U.S.	252	41.27 N	97.44 W
Genoa, Nev., U.S.	272	39.00 N	119.51 W
Genoa, N.Y., U.S.	264	42.40 N	76.32 W
Genoa, Ohio, U.S.	266	40.48 N	81.28 W
Genoa, Ohio, U.S.	266	41.31 N	83.22 W
Genoa, Wis., U.S.	244	43.35 N	91.13 W
Genoa City	268	42.30 N	88.20 W
Genova (Genoa)	182	44.25 N	8.57 E
Genova □[4]	182	44.30 N	9.04 E
Genova, Golfo di C	170	44.10 N	8.55 E
Genovesa, Isla I	290a	0.20 N	89.58 W
Genrijetty, Ostrov I	186	77.06 N	156.30 E
Gens de Terre ≃	244	46.53 N	76.00 W
Gent (Gand)	176	51.03 N	3.43 E
Gentbrugge	176	51.03 N	3.45 E
Genthin	164	52.24 N	12.09 E
Gentilly	260	46.24 N	72.19 W
Gentioux	166	45.47 N	1.59 E
Genval	176	50.43 N	4.29 E
Genzano di Roma	184	41.42 N	12.41 E
Geokčaj	208	40.39 N	47.44 E
George, S. Afr.	224	33.58 S	22.24 E
George, Iowa, U.S.	252	43.21 N	96.00 W
George ≃	232	58.30 N	66.00 W
George, Cape ›	240	45.53 N	61.53 W
George, Lake ⊜, Austl.	228	35.05 S	149.25 E
George, Lake ⊜, N.A.	244	46.28 N	84.10 W
George, Lake ⊜, Ug.	218	0.02 N	30.12 E
George, Lake ⊜, Fla., U.S.	246	29.17 N	81.36 W
George, Lake ⊜, N.Y., U.S.	242	43.35 N	73.35 W
George Bay C	240	45.50 N	61.45 W
George River	232	58.35 N	65.59 W
George Sound ⋓	230	44.51 S	167.21 E
Georges Run	266	40.21 N	80.37 W
George Town, Austl.	228	41.06 S	146.50 E
Georgetown, Ont., Can.	264	43.39 N	79.55 W
Georgetown, P.E.I., Can.	240	46.11 N	62.32 W
Georgetown, Cay. Is.	282	19.18 N	81.23 W
Georgetown, Gam.	214	13.30 N	14.47 W
Georgetown, Guy.	290	6.48 N	58.10 W
George Town → Pinang, Malay.	200	5.24 N	100.19 E
Georgetown, St. Vin.	285h	13.16 N	61.08 W
Georgetown, Calif., U.S.	272	38.54 N	120.50 W
Georgetown, Conn., U.S.	261	41.16 N	73.26 W
Georgetown, Del., U.S.	262	38.42 N	75.23 W
Georgetown, Fla., U.S.	246	29.23 N	81.38 W
Georgetown, Ga., U.S.	246	31.53 N	85.06 W
Georgetown, Idaho, U.S.	256	42.29 N	111.22 W
Georgetown, Ill., U.S.	248	39.59 N	87.38 W
Georgetown, Ky., U.S.	242	38.13 N	84.33 W
Georgetown, La., U.S.	248	31.46 N	92.23 W
Georgetown, Mass., U.S.	261	42.43 N	71.00 W
Georgetown, Miss., U.S.	248	31.52 N	90.10 W
Georgetown, N.Y., U.S.	264	42.46 N	75.44 W
Georgetown, Ohio, U.S.	242	38.52 N	83.54 W
Georgetown, Pa., U.S.	266	40.39 N	80.30 W
Georgetown, S.C., U.S.	246	33.23 N	79.17 W
Georgetown, Tex., U.S.	250	30.38 N	97.41 W
Georgetown Lake ⊜	256	46.11 N	113.17 W
George V Coast ⬩[2]	148	68.30 S	147.30 E
George Washington Carver National Monument ♣	248	37.00 N	94.19 W
George West	250	28.20 N	98.07 W
Georgia □[3]	234	32.50 N	83.15 W
Georgia, Strait of ⋓	238	49.20 N	124.00 W
Georgiana	248	31.33 N	86.44 W
Georgian Bay C	244	45.15 N	80.50 W
Georgian Bay Islands National Park ♣	244	44.54 N	79.52 W
Georgian Soviet Socialist Republic → Gruzinskaja Sovetskaja Socialističeskaja	186	42.00 N	44.00 E
Georgijevsk	158	44.09 N	43.28 E
Georgina ≃	228	23.30 S	139.47 E
Georgiu-Dež (Liski)	158	50.59 N	39.30 E
Georgsmarienhütte	178	52.12 N	8.02 E
Gera	164	50.52 N	12.04 E

Symbols in the index entries are identified on page 360.

Name	Page	Lat°′	Long°′
Geraardsbergen	176	50.46 N	3.52 E
Gerais, Chapada dos ⛰[1]	296	17.40 S	45.20 W
Geral, Serra ⛰	296	14.00 S	41.00 W
Geral, Serra ⌓[4]	294	26.30 S	50.30 W
Gerald	248	38.24 N	91.20 W
Geral de Goiás, Serra ⌓[4]	296	13.00 S	46.15 W
Geraldine, N.Z.	230	44.05 S	171.14 E
Geraldine, Mont., U.S.	256	47.36 N	110.16 W
Geral do Paranã, Serra ⛰[2]	296	14.45 S	47.30 W
Geraldton, Austl.	226	28.46 S	114.36 E
Geraldton, Ont., Can.	232	49.44 N	86.57 W
Gérardmer	180	48.04 N	6.53 E
Gerasa ⊥	210	32.17 N	35.53 E
Gerber	258	40.03 N	122.09 W
Gerber Reservoir ⊜[1]	256	42.12 N	121.06 W
Gerdine, Mount ∧	236	61.35 N	152.26 W
Gérgal	168	37.07 N	2.33 W
Gering	252	41.50 N	103.40 W
Gerlachovský štít ∧	164	49.12 N	20.08 E
Germaine Bank ✧[4]	148	5.05 N	107.35 W
Germán	278	25.10 N	98.54 W
Germania	266	41.39 N	77.40 W
Germano	266	40.25 N	80.57 W
Germansen, Mount ∧	238	55.37 N	124.50 W
Germansen Lake ⊜	238	55.41 N	124.53 W
Germansen Landing	238	55.47 N	124.43 W
Germansville	262	40.42 N	75.42 W
Germantown, Ill., U.S.	248	38.33 N	89.32 W
Germantown, N.Y., U.S.	261	42.08 N	73.54 W
Germantown, Tenn., U.S.	248	35.05 N	89.49 W
Germantown, Wis., U.S.	268	43.14 N	88.06 W
Germany, East □[1]	158	52.00 N	12.30 E
Germany, West □[1]	158	51.00 N	9.00 E
Germencik	172	37.51 N	27.37 E
Germfask	244	46.15 N	85.55 W
Germiston	224	26.15 S	28.05 E
Gero	192	35.48 N	137.14 E
Gerolzhofen	164	49.54 N	10.21 E
Gerona, Esp.	168	41.59 N	2.49 E
Gerona, Pil.	202	15.36 N	120.36 E
Gerrei ⇐[1]	170	39.28 N	9.20 E
Gerry	266	42.12 N	79.15 W
Gers □[5]	166	43.40 N	0.30 E
Gers ≃	166	44.09 N	0.39 E
Gerstetten	180	48.37 N	10.01 E
Gersthofen	180	48.25 N	10.53 E
Gervais	270	45.07 N	122.54 W
Gesäuse V	164	47.35 N	14.40 E
Gescher	178	51.57 N	6.59 E
Geseke	178	51.38 N	8.31 E
Geser	198	3.53 S	130.54 E
Geta	160	60.23 N	19.50 E
Getafe	168	40.18 N	3.43 W
Gethsémani	240	50.13 N	60.40 W
Gettysburg, Pa., U.S.	262	39.50 N	77.14 W
Gettysburg, S. Dak., U.S.	252	45.01 N	99.57 W
Gettysburg National Military Park ♠	242	39.49 N	77.15 W
Getulina	296	21.49 S	49.55 W
Getulio	202	10.44 N	122.40 E
Getúlio Vargas	294	27.50 S	52.16 W
Getz Ice Shelf ⊡	148	75.00 S	129.00 W
Getzville	264	43.01 N	78.46 W
Gevelsberg	178	51.19 N	7.20 E
Gevgelija	172	41.08 N	22.30 E
Gévora ≃	168	38.53 N	6.57 W
Gex	166	46.20 N	6.04 E
Geyikli	172	39.48 N	26.12 E
Geyser	256	47.16 N	110.30 W
Geyser, Banc du ✧[2]	218	12.25 S	46.25 E
Geyserville	258	38.42 N	122.54 W
Gez Gölü ⊜	212	38.35 N	33.06 E
Gezihu ⊜	206	38.10 N	90.42 E
Ghāghara ≃	206	25.45 N	84.40 E
Ghallah, Wādī al- V	220	10.25 N	27.32 E
Ghana □[1]	214	8.00 N	2.00 W
Ghanzi	218	21.38 S	21.45 E
Ghanzi □[5]	224	22.00 S	23.00 E
Ghardaïa	214	32.31 N	3.37 E
Ghardimaou	170	36.26 N	8.27 E
Gharyān	214	32.10 N	13.01 E
Ghāt	214	24.58 N	10.11 E
Ghazāl, Bahr al- ≃	220	9.31 N	30.25 E
Ghazal, Bahr el ≃	214	13.01 N	15.28 E
Ghazaouet	168	35.06 N	1.51 W
Ghāziābād	206	28.40 N	77.26 E
Ghāzīpur	206	25.35 N	83.35 E
Ghazni	206	33.34 N	68.26 E
Ghazni □[4]	206	33.00 N	68.00 E
Ghazzah (Gaza)	210	31.30 N	34.28 E
Ghedi	170	45.24 N	10.16 E
Ghent → Gent, Bel.	176	51.03 N	3.43 E
Ghent, N.Y., U.S.	261	42.20 N	73.37 W
Ghent, Ohio, U.S.	266	41.09 N	81.38 W
Gheorghe Gheorghiu-Dej	172	46.14 N	26.22 E
Gheorgheni	172	46.43 N	25.36 E
Gherla	172	47.02 N	23.55 E
Ghīn, Tall ∧	208	32.39 N	36.43 E
Ghisonáccia	170	42.00 N	9.25 E
Ghlin	176	50.28 N	3.53 E
Ghor □[4]	206	34.00 N	65.00 E
Ghudāmis	214	30.08 N	9.30 E
Ghuriān	208	34.20 N	61.26 E
Gia-dinh	200	10.49 N	106.42 E
Giang ≃	200	17.40 N	106.30 E
Giant Mountain ∧	242	44.10 N	73.44 W
Giant's Castle ∧	224	29.20 S	29.30 E
Giant's Causeway ♠	162	55.14 N	6.30 W
Giants Neck	261	41.18 N	72.11 W
Giarre	170	37.43 N	15.11 E
Giaveno	182	45.02 N	7.21 E
Gibara	284p	21.07 N	76.08 W
Gibbon, Minn., U.S.	244	44.32 N	94.31 W
Gibbon, Nebr., U.S.	252	40.45 N	98.51 W
Gibbons	238	53.50 N	113.20 W
Gibbonsville	256	45.33 N	113.55 W
Gibbstown	262	39.50 N	75.17 W
Gibeon	218	25.09 S	17.43 E
Gibeon □[5]	224	25.00 S	19.00 E
Gibraleón	168	37.23 N	6.58 W
Gibraltar, Gib.	168	36.09 N	5.21 W
Gibraltar, Mich., U.S.	268	42.06 N	83.12 W
Gibraltar, Pa., U.S.	262	40.17 N	75.52 W
Gibraltar □[2]	158	36.11 N	5.22 W
Gibraltar, Strait of(Estrecho de Gibraltar) ⩌	168	35.57 N	5.36 W
Gibsland	248	32.33 N	93.03 W
Gibson	246	33.14 N	82.36 W
Gibsonburg	266	41.23 N	83.19 W
Gibson City	268	40.28 N	88.22 W
Gibsonia	266	40.38 N	79.59 W
Gibsons	238	49.24 N	123.30 W
Gidajevo	160	59.57 N	52.22 E
Giddings	250	30.11 N	96.56 W
Gideon	248	36.27 N	89.55 W
Gien	176	47.42 N	2.38 E
Giengen	180	48.37 N	10.14 E
Giessen	164	50.35 N	8.40 E
Giffard	260	46.51 N	71.12 W
Gifford, Fla., U.S.	246	27.41 N	80.25 W
Gifford, Ill., U.S.	268	40.18 N	88.01 W
Gifford, Ind., U.S.	268	41.06 N	87.01 W
Gifford, Pa., U.S.	266	41.51 N	78.36 W
Gifford ≃	232	70.21 N	83.05 W
Gifhorn	178	52.29 N	10.33 E
Gifu	192	35.25 N	136.45 E
Giganta, Cerro ∧	278	26.09 N	111.36 W
Giganta, Sierra de la ⛰	278	25.30 N	111.15 W
Gigante	290	2.23 N	75.33 W
Gigante Islands II	202	11.35 N	123.20 E
Gigatangan Island I	202	11.35 N	124.18 E
Gigen	172	43.42 N	24.29 E
Gigha Island I	162	55.41 N	5.44 W
Gig Harbor	270	47.20 N	122.35 W
Giglio, Isola del I	170	42.21 N	10.54 E
Gigmoto	202	13.47 N	124.23 E
Gigüela ≃	168	39.08 N	3.44 W
Gijón	168	43.32 N	5.40 W
Gila ≃	254	32.43 N	114.33 W
Gila Bend	254	32.57 N	112.43 W
Gila Bend Mountains ⛰	254	33.10 N	113.10 W
Gila Cliff Dwellings National Monument ♠	254	33.02 N	108.16 W
Gila Mountains ⛰, Ariz., U.S.	254	33.05 N	109.50 W
Gila Mountains ⛰, Ariz., U.S.	254	32.30 N	114.20 W
Gīlān □[4]	208	37.00 N	49.00 E
Gila River Indian Reservation ⇐[4]	254	33.12 N	112.00 W
Gilbert, La., U.S.	248	32.03 N	91.39 W
Gilbert, Minn., U.S.	244	47.29 N	92.28 W
Gilbert ≃	228	16.35 S	141.15 E
Gilbert, Mount ∧	238	50.51 N	124.20 W
Gilbert Islands II	148	0.30 S	174.00 E
Gilbertown	248	31.53 N	88.19 W
Gilbert Seamount ✧[3]	148	52.50 N	150.05 W
Gilbertsville	262	40.19 N	75.37 W
Gilbertville	261	42.19 N	72.12 W
Gilboa	268	41.01 N	83.55 W
Gilbués	286	9.50 S	45.21 W
Gildford	256	48.34 N	110.18 W
Gilead	268	41.48 N	85.09 W
Gilford Island I	238	50.45 N	126.25 W
Gilford Park	262	39.58 N	74.08 W
Gilgandra	226	31.42 S	148.39 E
Gilgit	204	35.55 N	74.20 E
Gilgit □[8]	206	36.00 N	74.00 E
Gilgit ≃	206	35.47 N	74.35 E
Gil Island I	238	53.13 N	129.15 W
Gillam	232	56.21 N	94.43 W
Gilles, Lake ⊜	228	32.50 S	136.45 E
Gillespie	248	39.07 N	89.49 W
Gillespie Point ≻	230	43.24 S	169.50 E
Gillett, Ark., U.S.	248	34.07 N	91.22 W
Gillett, Wis., U.S.	244	44.54 N	88.18 W
Gillette	252	44.18 N	105.30 W
Gillian, Lake ⊜	232	69.32 N	75.23 W
Gillingham	174	51.24 N	0.33 E
Gilman, Conn., U.S.	261	41.34 N	72.16 W
Gilman, Ill., U.S.	268	40.46 N	87.59 W
Gilman, Iowa, U.S.	244	41.53 N	92.47 W
Gilman, Mont., U.S.	238	47.31 N	112.21 W
Gilman, Wis., U.S.	244	45.10 N	90.48 W
Gilman Hot Springs	274	33.50 N	116.59 W
Gilmer	250	32.44 N	94.57 W
Gilmer Park	268	41.36 N	86.15 W
Gilmore City	252	42.44 N	94.27 W
Gilo ≃	214	8.10 N	33.15 E
Gilroy	272	37.00 N	121.34 W
Giltner	252	40.47 N	98.09 W
Gil'uj ≃	186	53.58 N	127.30 E
Gimborn	178	51.03 N	7.28 E
Gimie, Mount ∧	282	13.51 N	61.00 W
Gimli	232	50.38 N	96.59 W
Gimoly	160	63.03 N	32.19 E
Gimone ≃	166	44.00 N	1.06 E
Gimont	166	43.38 N	0.53 E
Gingell	268	42.43 N	83.17 W
Gingoog	202	8.50 N	125.07 E
Gingoog Bay C	202	8.55 N	125.05 E
Ginir	214	7.07 N	40.46 E
Ginosa	170	40.34 N	16.46 E
Ginowan	193b	26.17 N	127.46 E
Ginter	266	40.46 N	78.23 W
Ginzo de Limia	168	42.03 N	7.43 W
Gioia del Colle	170	40.48 N	16.56 E
Gioia Tauro	170	38.26 N	15.54 E
Gioiosa Ionica	170	38.20 N	16.18 E
Giporlos	202	11.07 N	125.27 E
Gipsy	266	40.48 N	78.53 W
Giraltovce	164	49.07 N	21.31 E
Girard, Ill., U.S.	248	39.27 N	89.47 W
Girard, Kans., U.S.	252	37.31 N	94.51 W
Girard, Mich., U.S.	268	42.02 N	85.00 W
Girard, Ohio, U.S.	266	41.10 N	80.42 W
Girard, Pa., U.S.	266	42.00 N	80.19 W
Girard, Tex., U.S.	250	33.22 N	100.40 W
Girardot	290	4.18 N	74.48 W
Girardville	262	40.47 N	76.17 W
Girbovu	172	44.44 N	23.21 E
Girdletree	262	38.06 N	75.24 W
Girdwood	236	60.57 N	149.10 W
Giresnn	212	40.55 N	38.24 E
Giresun □[4]	208	40.15 N	38.25 E
Girgenti → Agrigento	170	37.18 N	13.35 E
Gir Hills ⛰[2]	206	21.10 N	70.50 E
Girifalco	170	38.49 N	16.25 E
Girishk	208	31.50 N	64.35 E
Giromagny	166	47.45 N	6.50 E
Girón	290	3.10 S	79.08 W
Gironde □[5]	166	44.45 N	0.35 W
Gironde C[1]	166	45.20 N	0.45 W
Girou ≃	166	43.46 N	1.23 E
Girouxville	238	55.45 N	117.20 W
Giruá	294	28.02 S	54.21 W
Girvan	162	55.15 N	4.51 W
Girvas	160	62.30 N	33.40 E
Girvas, Vodopad ↲	160	62.27 N	33.40 E
Girwa ≃	206	28.15 N	81.05 E
Gisborne	230	38.40 S	178.02 E
Gisborne Lake ⊜	240	47.48 N	54.50 W
Giscome	238	54.04 N	122.22 W
Gisenyi	218	1.42 S	29.15 E
Gislaved	160	57.18 N	13.32 E
Gisors	176	49.17 N	1.47 E
Gistel	176	51.10 N	2.57 E
Gitega	218	3.26 S	29.56 E
Giugliano in Campania	184	40.56 N	14.12 E
Giulianova	184	42.45 N	13.57 E
Giurgiu	172	43.53 N	25.57 E
Giussano	182	45.42 N	9.14 E
Giv'atayim	210	32.04 N	34.49 E
Give	160	55.51 N	9.15 E
Givet	166	50.08 N	4.50 E
Givors	182	45.35 N	4.46 E
Givry	166	46.47 N	4.45 E
Giyon	214	8.30 N	38.00 E
Giza → Al-Jīzah	220	30.01 N	31.13 E
Giždavan	208	40.06 N	64.41 E
Gižiga	186	62.03 N	160.30 E
Gižiginskaja Guba C	186	61.30 N	158.00 E
Gizo	226	8.07 S	156.52 E
Giżycko (Lötzen)	164	54.03 N	21.47 E
Gjirokastër	172	40.05 N	20.10 E
Gjoa Haven	232	68.38 N	95.57 W
Gjuesevo	172	42.14 N	22.28 E
Gjuhëzës, Kep i ≻	172	40.25 N	19.18 E
Glace Bay	240	46.12 N	59.57 W
Glacier, B.C., Can.	238	51.16 N	117.31 W
Glacier, Wash., U.S.	270	48.53 N	121.57 W
Glacier Bay C	236	58.40 N	136.00 W
Glacier Bay National Monument ♠	236	58.45 N	136.30 W
Glacier National Park ♠, B.C., Can.	238	51.15 N	117.35 W
Glacier National Park ♠, Mont., U.S.	256	48.35 N	113.40 W
Glacier Peak ∧	256	48.07 N	121.07 W
Gladbach → Mönchengladbach	000	51.12 N	6.28 E
Gladbeck	178	51.34 N	6.59 E
Gladbrook	244	42.11 N	92.43 W
Glade Spring	246	36.47 N	81.47 W
Gladewater	248	32.33 N	94.56 W
Gladstone, Austl.	228	23.51 S	151.16 E
Gladstone, Mich., U.S.	244	45.50 N	87.03 W
Gladstone, Mo., U.S.	248	39.13 N	94.34 W
Gladstone, N.J., U.S.	262	40.43 N	74.40 W
Gladstone, Oreg., U.S.	270	45.23 N	122.36 W
Gladwin	244	43.59 N	84.29 W
Gladys Lake ⊜	236	59.55 N	132.55 W
Gláma ∧	160a	65.47 N	23.00 W
Glåma ≃	160	59.12 N	10.57 E
Glamoč	170	44.03 N	16.51 E
Glamorganshire □[6]	174	51.35 N	3.35 W
Glan	202	5.50 N	125.12 E
Glan ≃	202	5.50 N	125.12 E
Glandorf	268	41.07 N	84.05 W
Glanerbrug	178	52.13 N	6.58 E
Glarner Alpen ⛰	166	46.55 N	9.00 E
Glarus	180	47.02 N	9.04 E
Glarus □[3]	180	47.00 N	9.03 E
Glasco, Kans., U.S.	252	39.22 N	97.50 W
Glasco, N.Y., U.S.	261	42.03 N	73.57 W
Glasgow, Scot., U.K.	162	55.53 N	4.15 W
Glasgow, Ky., U.S.	248	37.00 N	85.55 W
Glasgow, Mo., U.S.	248	39.14 N	92.50 W
Glasgow, Mont., U.S.	256	48.12 N	106.38 W
Glasgow, Pa., U.S.	266	40.42 N	78.27 W
Glasgow, Va., U.S.	246	37.38 N	79.27 W
Glas Maol ∧	162	56.52 N	3.22 W
Glassboro	262	39.42 N	75.07 W
Glass Mountains ⛰	250	30.25 N	103.15 W
Glassport	266	40.19 N	79.54 W
Glastonbury, Eng., U.K.	174	51.06 N	2.43 W
Glastonbury, Conn., U.S.	261	41.43 N	72.37 W
Glatz → Kłodzko	164	50.27 N	16.39 E
Glauchau	164	50.49 N	12.32 E
Glazier	250	36.01 N	100.16 W
Glazov	160	58.09 N	52.40 E
Gleason	248	36.13 N	88.37 W
Gleed	270	46.40 N	120.37 W
Gle Hulu Masen ∧	200	5.03 N	95.40 E
Gleichen	238	50.52 N	113.03 W
Gleinalpe ⛰	164	47.15 N	15.03 E
Gleisdorf	164	47.06 N	15.44 E
Gleiwitz → Gliwice	164	50.17 N	18.40 E
Glen Allen	262	37.40 N	77.30 W
Glen Alpine	246	35.44 N	81.47 W
Glenarden	262	38.56 N	76.52 W
Glen Avon Heights	274	34.01 N	117.29 W
Glenboro	252	49.32 N	99.15 W
Glenbrook Heights	272	39.15 N	121.02 W
Glenburn	252	48.31 N	101.13 W
Glen Burnie	262	39.10 N	76.37 W
Glen Burnie Park	262	39.09 N	76.38 W
Glen Campbell	266	40.49 N	78.50 W
Glen Canyon	254	37.05 N	111.41 W
Glen Canyon V	254	37.10 N	110.50 W
Glen Canyon National Recreation Area ♠	254	37.00 N	111.20 W
Glencoe, Ont., Can.	266	42.45 N	81.43 W
Glencoe, S. Afr.	224	28.12 S	30.07 E
Glencoe, Ala., U.S.	248	33.57 N	85.56 W
Glencoe, Ill., U.S.	268	42.08 N	87.45 W
Glencoe, Md., U.S.	262	39.33 N	76.38 W
Glencoe, Minn., U.S.	244	44.46 N	94.09 W
Glen Cove	261	40.52 N	73.37 W
Glendale, Ariz., U.S.	254	33.32 N	112.11 W
Glendale, Calif., U.S.	274	34.10 N	118.17 W
Glendale, Mass., U.S.	261	42.17 N	73.21 W
Glendale, Oreg., U.S.	256	42.44 N	123.26 W
Glendale, R.I., U.S.	261	41.58 N	71.38 W
Glendale, Utah, U.S.	254	37.19 N	112.36 W
Glendale, Wis., U.S.	268	43.07 N	87.57 W
Glendive	252	47.06 N	104.43 W
Glendo	254	42.30 N	105.02 W
Glendon, Alta., Can.	238	54.15 N	111.10 W
Glendon, Pa., U.S.	262	40.40 N	75.14 W
Glendora	274	34.08 N	117.52 W
Glendo Reservoir ⊜[1]	254	42.31 N	104.58 W
Glendoveer	270	45.32 N	122.30 W
Glen Elder	252	39.30 N	98.18 W
Glenelg ≃	228	38.03 S	141.00 E
Glen Ellen	272	38.22 N	122.31 W
Glenfield	264	43.43 N	75.24 W
Glen Flora	250	29.21 N	96.12 W
Glen Gardner	262	40.42 N	74.56 W
Glengarriff	162	51.45 N	9.33 W
Glengarry □[6]	260	45.15 N	74.40 W
Glenham	261	41.31 N	73.56 W
Glen Hills	262	39.04 N	77.12 W
Glen Innes	228	29.44 S	151.44 E
Glen Lake	270	48.26 N	123.31 W
Glen Lyon	242	41.10 N	76.05 W
Glen Miller	264	44.08 N	77.35 W
Glenmont, N.Y., U.S.	261	42.36 N	73.46 W
Glenmont, Ohio, U.S.	266	40.31 N	82.06 W
Glenmoor	266	40.40 N	80.37 W
Glen Moore, Pa., U.S.	262	40.03 N	76.18 W
Glenmoore, Pa., U.S.	262	40.05 N	75.46 W
Glenmora	248	30.59 N	92.35 W
Glenn, Calif., U.S.	272	39.31 N	122.01 W
Glenn, Mich., U.S.	268	42.31 N	86.14 W
Glenn □[6]	272	39.29 N	122.18 W
Glennallen	236	62.07 N	145.33 W
Glenns Ferry	256	42.57 N	115.18 W
Glennville	246	31.56 N	81.56 W
Glenoma	256	46.31 N	122.09 W
Glen Park	264	44.00 N	75.57 W
Glen Richey	266	40.57 N	78.29 W
Glen Robertson	260	45.21 N	74.30 W
Glen Rock, Pa., U.S.	262	39.48 N	76.44 W
Glenrock, Wyo., U.S.	254	42.52 N	105.52 W
Glen Rose	250	32.14 N	97.45 W
Glen Ross	264	44.16 N	77.36 W
Glenroy ≃	230	42.00 S	172.20 E
Glens Falls	242	43.19 N	73.39 W
Glenshaw	266	40.31 N	79.57 W
Glenside, N.J., U.S.	262	39.40 N	75.29 W
Glenside, Pa., U.S.	262	40.06 N	75.09 W
Glenties	162	54.47 N	8.17 W
Glen Ullin	252	46.49 N	101.50 W
Glenview	268	42.04 N	87.48 W
Glenville, Minn., U.S.	244	43.34 N	93.17 W
Glenville, Pa., U.S.	262	39.46 N	76.49 W
Glenville, W. Va., U.S.	242	38.56 N	80.50 W
Glen White	246	37.44 N	81.17 W
Glenwillard	266	40.34 N	80.13 W
Glen Williams	264	43.40 N	79.55 W
Glenwillow	266	41.22 N	81.28 W
Glenwood, N.B., Can.	240	48.59 N	54.52 W
Glenwood, Ala., U.S.	248	31.40 N	86.10 W
Glenwood, Ark., U.S.	248	34.20 N	93.33 W
Glenwood, Ga., U.S.	246	32.11 N	82.40 W
Glenwood, Iowa, U.S.	252	41.03 N	95.45 W
Glenwood, Minn., U.S.	252	45.39 N	95.23 W
Glenwood, N. Mex., U.S.	254	33.19 N	108.53 W
Glenwood, N.Y., U.S.	266	42.37 N	78.39 W
Glenwood, Oreg., U.S.	270	45.39 N	123.16 W
Glenwood, Utah, U.S.	254	38.46 N	111.59 W
Glenwood, Va., U.S.	246	36.35 N	79.22 W
Glenwood, Wash., U.S.	270	46.01 N	121.17 W
Glenwood City	244	45.04 N	92.10 W
Glenwood Springs	254	39.33 N	107.19 W
Glenwoodville	238	49.22 N	113.21 W
Glidden, Iowa, U.S.	252	42.04 N	94.44 W
Glidden, Wis., U.S.	244	46.09 N	90.34 W
Glide	256	43.18 N	123.06 W
Glífa	172	38.57 N	22.58 E
Glina	170	45.20 N	16.16 E
Glina ≃	170	45.26 N	16.07 E
Glinde	178	53.32 N	10.13 E
Glittertinden ∧	160	61.39 N	8.33 E
Gliwice (Gleiwitz)	164	50.17 N	18.40 E
Gliwicki, Kanał ≌	164	50.22 N	18.05 E
Globe	254	33.24 N	110.47 W
Glodeanu-Siliştea	172	44.50 N	26.48 E
Gloggnitz	164	47.40 N	15.57 E
Głogów (Glogau)	164	51.40 N	16.05 E
Głogówek (Oberglogau)	164	50.22 N	17.51 E
Głogów Małopolski	164	50.10 N	21.58 E
Glommersträsk	160	65.16 N	19.38 E
Gloria, Sierra de la ⛰	250	26.45 N	101.10 W
Gloria Glens Park	266	41.03 N	81.54 W
Glorieta	254	35.35 N	105.46 W
Glorieuses, Îles II	218	11.30 S	47.20 E
Gloster, La., U.S.	248	32.12 N	93.49 W
Gloster, Miss., U.S.	248	31.12 N	91.01 W
Glotovka	160	53.57 N	46.42 E
Glotovo	160	63.30 N	49.23 E
Gloucester, Eng., U.K.	174	51.53 N	2.14 W
Gloucester, Mass., U.S.	261	42.41 N	70.39 W
Gloucester, Va., U.S.	262	37.25 N	76.32 W
Gloucester □[6], N.J., U.S.	262	39.50 N	75.10 W
Gloucester □[6], Va., U.S.	262	37.25 N	76.30 W
Gloucester Island I	228	20.01 S	148.27 E
Gloucester Point	262	37.16 N	76.30 W
Gloucestershire □[6]	174	51.47 N	2.15 W
Glouster	242	39.30 N	82.05 W
Glover	248	37.29 N	90.42 W
Glover Island I	240	48.44 N	57.45 W
Glover Reef ✧[2]	278	16.47 N	87.45 W
Gloversville	242	43.03 N	74.20 W
Glovertown	240	48.41 N	54.02 W
Gloverville	246	33.32 N	81.50 W
Głowno	164	51.58 N	19.44 E
Głubczyce (Leobschütz)	164	50.13 N	17.49 E
Głuchołazy (Ziegenhals)	164	50.20 N	17.22 E
Glücksburg	164	54.50 N	9.33 E
Glückstadt	178	53.47 N	9.25 E
Glyndon, Md., U.S.	262	39.29 N	76.49 W
Glyndon, Minn., U.S.	252	46.52 N	96.35 W
Gmünd	164	48.47 N	15.00 E
Gmunden	164	47.55 N	13.48 E
Gnadenhutten	266	40.22 N	81.26 W
Gnarp	160	62.03 N	17.16 E
Gnesen → Gniezno	164	52.31 N	17.37 E
Gniew	164	53.51 N	18.49 E
Gniewkowo	164	52.54 N	18.25 E
Gniezno	164	52.31 N	17.37 E
Gnjilane	172	42.28 N	21.58 E
Gnoien	164	53.58 N	12.42 E
Gnowangerup	226	33.56 S	117.59 E
Gō ≃	192	35.02 N	132.13 E
Goa	202	13.42 N	123.29 E
Goalen Head ≻	228	36.40 S	150.05 E
Goangoa ≃	220	5.48 N	25.09 E
Goascorán	280	13.36 N	87.45 W
Goascorán ≃	280	13.25 N	87.48 W
Goat Mountain ∧	256	47.21 N	113.21 W
Goba	214	7.02 N	40.00 E
Gobabis	224	22.30 S	18.58 E
Gobabis □[5]	224	22.00 S	19.00 E
Göbel	172	40.00 N	28.09 E
Gobernador Gregores	288	48.46 S	70.15 W
Gobernador Ingenierovalentín Virasoro	294	28.02 S	56.00 W
Gobernador Juan E. Martínez	294	28.55 S	58.56 W
Gobernador Racedo	294	31.35 S	60.05 W
Gobi ⇐[2]	190	43.00 N	105.00 E
Gobles	268	42.21 N	85.53 W
Goçbeyli	172	39.13 N	27.25 E
Goce Delčev	172	41.34 N	23.44 E
Goch	178	51.41 N	6.10 E
Go-cong	198	10.22 N	106.40 E
Gođafoss ↲	160a	65.40 N	17.30 W
Godalming	174	51.11 N	0.37 W
Godbout	240	49.19 N	67.37 W
Goderich	244	43.45 N	81.43 W
Goderville	166	49.39 N	0.22 E
Godfrey	248	38.57 N	90.11 W
Godhavn	232	69.15 N	53.33 W
Godhra	206	22.46 N	73.36 E
Gödöllő	172	47.36 N	19.22 E
Godoy Cruz	294	32.55 S	68.50 W
Gods ≃	232	56.22 N	92.51 W
Gods Lake ⊜	232	54.45 N	94.00 W
Gods Mercy, Bay of C	232	63.30 N	86.10 W
Godthåb	232	64.11 N	51.44 W
Godwin Austen (K2) ∧	206	35.53 N	76.30 E
Goéland, Lac au ⊜	232	49.47 N	76.41 W
Goes	178	51.30 N	3.54 E
Goff	252	39.40 N	95.56 W
Goff Creek ≃	250	36.43 N	101.29 W
Goffstown	242	43.01 N	71.36 W
Gogama	244	47.40 N	81.43 W
Gogebic, Lake ⊜	244	46.30 N	89.35 W
Gogebic Range ⛰[2]	244	46.45 N	89.25 W
Göggingen	180	48.20 N	10.52 E
Gogolin	164	50.30 N	18.02 E
Gohfeld	178	52.12 N	8.45 E
Goiana	286	7.33 S	34.59 W
Goianápolis	296	16.30 S	49.01 W
Goiandira	296	18.08 S	48.06 W
Goianésia	296	15.18 S	49.07 W
Goiânia	296	16.40 S	49.16 W
Goianira	296	16.30 S	49.26 W
Goiás	296	15.56 S	50.08 W
Goiás □[3]	296	12.00 S	48.00 W
Goiatuba	296	18.01 S	49.22 W
Goio-Erê	294	24.12 S	53.01 W
Goio-Erê ≃	294	24.14 S	53.21 W
Goirle	178	51.32 N	5.04 E
Góis	168	40.09 N	8.07 W
Goito	170	45.15 N	10.40 E
Gojō	192	34.21 N	135.42 E
Gojōme	192	39.56 N	140.07 E
Gokase ≃	192	32.35 N	131.42 E
Gökçen	172	38.07 N	27.53 E
Göksu ≃, Tür.	212	37.37 N	35.35 E
Göksu ≃, Tür.	212	36.20 N	34.05 E
Göktepe	172	37.15 N	28.36 E
Gol	160	60.42 N	8.57 E
Gol, Khawr V	220	6.55 N	30.16 E
Golāghāt	200	26.30 N	94.00 E
Gołańcz	164	52.57 N	17.18 E
Gol'čicha	186	71.43 N	83.36 E
Golconda, Ill., U.S.	248	37.22 N	88.29 W
Golconda, Nev., U.S.	258	40.57 N	117.30 W
Gölcuk, Tür.	172	39.18 N	27.59 E
Gölcük, Tür.	172	40.44 N	29.48 E
Gołdap (Goldap)	164	54.19 N	22.19 E
Gold Bar	270	47.51 N	121.42 W
Gold Beach	256	42.25 N	124.25 W
Goldbey	180	48.12 N	6.26 E
Goldboro	240	45.11 N	61.39 W
Gold Bridge	238	50.51 N	122.50 W
Southport, Austl.	228	27.58 S	153.25 E
Gold Coast ⌓[2]	222	5.20 N	0.45 W
Gold Creek	236	62.46 N	149.41 W
Golden, B.C., Can.	238	51.18 N	116.58 W
Golden, Colo., U.S.	254	39.46 N	105.13 W
Golden, Ill., U.S.	248	40.07 N	91.01 W
Golden Bay C	230	40.40 S	172.50 E
Golden City	248	37.24 N	94.05 W
Goldendale	270	45.49 N	120.50 W
Golden Gate Highlands National Park ♠	224	28.30 S	28.40 E
Golden Hinde ∧	238	49.40 N	125.45 W
Golden Lake ⊜	244	45.35 N	77.20 W
Golden Meadow	248	29.23 N	90.16 W
Goldfield, Iowa, U.S.	244	42.44 N	93.55 W
Goldfield, Nev., U.S.	258	37.42 N	117.14 W
Goldonna	248	32.01 N	92.54 W
Goldpan Peak ∧	236	61.12 N	153.22 W
Gold River	238	49.41 N	126.08 W
Gold Run	272	39.10 N	120.52 W
Goldsboro, Md., U.S.	262	39.02 N	75.47 W
Goldsboro, N.C., U.S.	246	35.23 N	77.59 W
Goldsmith, Ind., U.S.	268	40.17 N	86.09 W
Goldsmith, Tex., U.S.	250	31.59 N	102.40 W
Goldston	246	35.36 N	79.20 W
Goldthwaite	250	31.27 N	98.34 W
Golec-In'aptuk, Gora ∧	186	56.22 N	110.11 E
Golec-Skalistyj, Gora ∧	186	56.24 N	119.12 E
Goleniów (Gollnow)	164	53.36 N	14.50 E
Goleta	258	34.27 N	119.50 W
Goleta, Cerro ∧	278	18.38 N	100.04 W
Golfcrest	266	41.57 N	83.22 W
Golfito	280	8.38 N	83.11 W
Golf View	262	39.43 N	75.28 W
Goliad	250	28.40 N	97.23 W
Golicyno	160	53.38 N	44.07 E
Golina	164	52.16 N	18.05 E
Goljama Kamčija ≃	172	43.03 N	27.29 E
Goljam Perelik ∧	172	41.36 N	24.34 E
Gölmarmara	172	38.42 N	27.56 E
Golo ≃	166	42.31 N	9.32 E
Golodnaja Guba, Ozero ⊜	160	67.52 N	52.48 E
Golovin	236	64.33 N	163.02 W
Golpāyegān	208	33.27 N	50.18 E
Golspie	162	57.58 N	3.58 W
Golub-Dobrzyń	164	53.08 N	19.02 E
Golva	252	46.44 N	103.51 W
Golyšmanovo	158	56.23 N	68.23 E
Goma	218	1.41 S	29.14 E
Gomas, Sierra de ⛰	250	26.20 N	100.28 W
Gomati ≃	206	25.32 N	83.11 E
Gombe ≃	218	4.38 S	31.40 E
Gomel'	158	52.25 N	31.00 E
Gomer	268	40.51 N	84.11 W
Gómez Farías	278	29.18 N	107.40 W
Gómez Palacio	278	25.34 N	103.30 W
Gómez Plata	290	6.41 N	75.12 W
Gonābād	204	34.20 N	58.42 E
Gonaïves	282	19.30 N	72.40 W
Gonam	186	57.21 N	131.12 E
Gonam ≃	186	57.21 N	131.14 E
Gonâve, Golfe de la C	282	19.20 N	73.15 W
Gonâve, Île de la I	282	18.45 N	73.00 W
Gonbad-e Kāvūs	208	37.17 N	55.17 E
Gonda	206	27.08 N	81.58 E
Gondal	206	21.58 N	70.48 E
Gonder	214	12.40 N	37.30 E
Gondia	206	21.27 N	80.12 E
Gondomar	168	41.09 N	8.32 W
Gondrecourt-le-Château	166	48.31 N	5.30 E
Gönen	172	40.06 N	27.39 E
Gonesse	176	48.59 N	2.27 E
Gongbujiangda	190	30.01 N	93.08 E
Gongcheng	200	24.49 N	110.46 E
Gonggashan ∧	190	29.35 N	101.51 E
Gonggeershan ∧	206	38.37 N	75.20 E
Gongogi	296	14.19 S	39.29 W
Gongshui ≃	196	26.00 N	115.22 E
Gongxian	190	34.48 N	113.03 E
Goñi	294	33.31 S	56.24 W
Goniądz	164	53.30 N	22.45 E
Gonnesa	170	39.15 N	8.28 E
Gōnoura	192	33.45 N	129.41 E
Gonzaga, It.	170	44.57 N	10.49 E
Gonzaga, Pil.	202	18.16 N	122.00 E
Gonzales, Calif., U.S.	272	36.31 N	121.32 W
Gonzales, La., U.S.	248	30.14 N	90.55 W
Gonzales, Tex., U.S.	250	29.30 N	97.27 W
González Chaves	294	38.02 S	60.05 W
González Moreno	294	35.33 S	63.20 W
González Ortega	258	32.40 N	115.23 W
Gonzanamá	290	4.15 S	79.27 W
Goochland	246	37.41 N	77.53 W
Goode, Mount ∧	236	61.20 N	148.02 W
Goodells	266	42.59 N	82.40 W
Goodenough, Mount ∧	236	67.56 N	135.31 W
Gooderham	264	44.54 N	78.23 W
Good Hope, Cape of ≻	224	34.24 S	18.30 E
Goodhope Bay C	236	66.10 N	163.45 W
Good Hope Mountain ∧	238	51.09 N	124.10 W
Goodhue	244	44.24 N	92.37 W
Gooding	256	42.56 N	114.43 W
Goodison	266	42.44 N	83.10 W
Goodland, Fla., U.S.	246	25.55 N	81.39 W
Goodland, Ind., U.S.	268	40.46 N	87.18 W
Goodland, Kans., U.S.	252	39.21 N	101.43 W
Goodlands	252	49.05 N	100.35 W
Goodlettsville	248	36.19 N	86.43 W
Goodman, Miss., U.S.	248	32.58 N	89.55 W
Goodman, Wis., U.S.	244	45.38 N	88.21 W
Goodnews Bay	236	59.07 N	161.35 W
Goodnight	250	35.02 N	101.11 W
Goodrich, Mich., U.S.	268	42.55 N	83.30 W
Goodrich, N. Dak., U.S.	252	47.28 N	100.08 W
Goodrich, Tex., U.S.	250	30.36 N	94.57 W
Good Thunder	244	44.00 N	94.04 W
Goodview	244	44.04 N	91.41 W
Goodville	262	40.08 N	76.00 W
Goodwater	248	33.04 N	86.03 W
Goodwell	250	36.36 N	101.38 W
Goodwood	264	44.02 N	79.12 W
Goodyear	254	33.26 N	112.21 W
Goole	162	53.42 N	0.52 W
Goondiwindi	228	28.32 S	150.19 E
Goor	178	52.14 N	6.35 E
Goose ≃, Alta., Can.	238	54.58 N	117.11 W
Goose ≃, N. Dak., U.S.	252	47.28 N	96.52 W
Goose Bay	232	53.19 N	60.24 W
Goose Island I	238	51.55 N	128.25 W
Goose Lake ⊜	258	41.57 N	120.25 W
Goose Prairie	270	46.54 N	121.15 W
Göppingen	180	48.42 N	9.40 E
Góra (Guhrau)	164	51.40 N	16.33 E
Góra Kalwaria	164	51.59 N	21.12 E
Gorakhpur	206	26.45 N	83.22 E
Goražde	172	43.40 N	18.56 E
Gorčucha	160	57.43 N	43.43 E
Gorda, Punta ≻, Chile	292	19.18 S	70.18 W
Gorda, Punta ≻, C.R.	280	10.31 N	85.50 W
Gorda, Punta ≻, Cuba	284p	21.05 N	75.39 W
Gorda, Punta ≻, Cuba	284p	22.24 N	82.10 W
Gorda, Punta ≻, Nic.	280	14.20 N	83.12 W
Gorda, Punta ≻, Nic.	280	11.26 N	83.48 W
Gorda, Punta ≻, Rep. Dom.	282	19.00 N	69.00 W
Gördes	172	38.54 N	28.18 E
Gordil	214	9.44 N	21.35 E
Gordium ⊥	212	39.41 N	32.01 E
Gordo	248	33.19 N	87.54 W
Gordon, Ga., U.S.	246	32.53 N	83.20 W
Gordon, Nebr., U.S.	252	42.48 N	102.12 W
Gordon, Pa., U.S.	262	40.45 N	76.21 W
Gordon, Wis., U.S.	244	46.15 N	91.48 W
Gordon ≃	228	42.25 S	145.31 E
Gordon Downs	226	18.44 S	128.35 E
Gordon Heights	261	40.51 N	72.58 W
Gordon Horne Peak ∧	238	51.46 N	118.50 W
Gordon River	270	48.47 N	124.21 W
Gordonsville	242	38.08 N	78.11 W
Gore, N.S., Can.	240	45.07 N	63.43 W
Gore, N.Z.	230	46.06 S	168.56 E
Gore, Yai.	214	8.08 N	35.33 E
Gore Bay	244	45.55 N	82.28 W
Goree	250	33.28 N	99.31 W
Göreme ⊥	212	38.26 N	34.54 E
Gore Mountain ∧	242	44.55 N	71.48 W
Gorenjsko ⇐[1]	170	46.10 N	14.20 E
Gore Point ≻, Austl.	228	17.38 S	139.56 E
Gore Point ≻, Alaska, U.S.	236	59.12 N	151.00 W
Goreville	248	37.33 N	88.58 W
Gorgān	208	36.50 N	54.29 E
Gorgany ⛰	172	48.30 N	24.00 E
Gorgol Blanc ≃	222	16.14 N	12.58 W
Gorgol Noir ≃	222	16.13 N	12.58 W
Gorgona, Isla I	290	2.59 N	78.12 W
Gorgonzola	182	45.32 N	9.24 E
Gorgor	292	10.32 S	77.02 W
Gorgota	172	44.47 N	26.05 E
Gorgova	172	45.11 N	29.10 E
Gorham, Maine, U.S.	242	43.41 N	70.26 W
Gorham, N.H., U.S.	242	44.23 N	71.10 W
Gorham, N.Y., U.S.	264	42.48 N	77.08 W
Gori	158	41.58 N	44.07 E
Goricy	160	57.09 N	36.44 E
Gorin	248	40.22 N	92.01 W
Gorinchem	178	51.50 N	5.00 E
Goris	208	39.31 N	46.23 E
Gorizia	170	45.57 N	13.38 E
Gorjani	172	45.24 N	18.21 E
Gorki → Gor'kij, S.S.S.R.	160	56.20 N	44.00 E
Gor'kij (Gorky)	160	56.20 N	44.00 E
Gor'kovskoje Vodochranilišče ⊜[1]	160	57.00 N	43.10 E
Gorlice	164	49.40 N	21.10 E
Görlitz	164	53.24 N	13.54 E
Gorlovka	158	48.18 N	38.03 E
Gorman, Calif., U.S.	274	34.48 N	118.51 W
Gorman, Tex., U.S.	250	32.12 N	98.41 W
Gorn'ackij	160	67.32 N	64.03 E
Gornaorjahovica	172	43.07 N	25.41 E
Gornja Radgona	170	46.41 N	16.00 E
Gornji Grad	170	46.18 N	14.49 E
Gornji Milanovac	172	44.01 N	20.27 E
Gornji Vakuf	170	43.56 N	17.35 E
Gorno-Altajsk	186	51.58 N	85.58 E
Gorno-Čujskij	186	59.12 N	112.25 E
Gornozavodsk	186	46.34 N	141.49 E
Gornyj Tikič ≃	172	48.47 N	30.53 E
Gorodec	160	56.38 N	43.30 E
Gorodišče	160	53.17 N	45.42 E
Gorodok	160	55.28 N	29.59 E
Goroka	198	6.05 S	145.25 E
Gorongosa ≃	224	20.30 S	34.40 E
Gorongosa, Parque Nacional da ♠	224	18.45 S	34.15 E
Gorongosa, Serra da ∧	224	18.30 S	34.03 E
Gorontalo	198	0.33 N	123.03 E
Górowo Iławeckie (Landsberg in Ostpreussen)	164	54.17 N	20.30 E
Gorron	162	48.25 N	0.49 W
Gorst	270	47.32 N	122.42 W
Gort	162	53.04 N	8.50 W
Görukle	172	40.14 N	28.50 E
Gorul, Muntele ∧	172	45.48 N	26.25 E
Gorutuba ≃	296	14.57 S	43.33 W
Gory	162	52.40 N	6.18 W
Górzno	164	53.13 N	19.38 E
Gorzów Śląski (Landsberg in Oberschlesien)	164	51.02 N	18.24 E
Gorzów Wielkopolski (Landsberg an der Warthe)	164	52.44 N	15.15 E
Gosainthan ∧	206	28.22 N	85.50 E
Gose	192	34.27 N	135.44 E
Gosen	192	37.44 N	139.11 E
Gosford	228	33.26 S	151.21 E
Goshen, N.S., Can.	240	45.23 N	61.59 W
Goshen, Calif., U.S.	272	36.21 N	119.25 W
Goshen, Conn., U.S.	261	41.50 N	73.14 W
Goshen, Ind., U.S.	268	41.35 N	85.50 W
Goshen, Mass., U.S.	261	42.27 N	72.48 W
Goshen, N.J., U.S.	262	39.08 N	74.51 W
Goshen, N.Y., U.S.	242	41.24 N	74.20 W
Goshogawara	192	40.48 N	140.27 E
Goshute Indian Reservation ⇐[4]	254	39.53 N	114.08 W
Goshute Lake ⊜	258	40.08 N	114.38 W
Goslar	178	51.54 N	10.25 E
Gospić	170	44.33 N	15.23 E
Gosport, Eng., U.K.	174	50.48 N	1.08 W
Gosport, Ind., U.S.	248	39.21 N	86.40 W
Gossau	180	47.25 N	9.15 E
Gostivar	172	41.47 N	20.24 E
Gostyń	164	51.53 N	17.00 E
Gostynin	164	52.26 N	19.29 E
Göta älv ≃	160	57.42 N	11.52 E
Gotebo	250	35.04 N	98.53 W
Göteborg (Gothenburg)	160	57.43 N	11.58 E
Göteborgs Och Bohus län □[6]	160	58.30 N	11.30 E
Gotemba	192	35.18 N	138.56 E
Gotha	164	50.57 N	10.41 E
Goyania → Goiânia	296	16.40 S	49.16 W
Gothenburg, Nebr., U.S.	252	40.56 N	100.09 W
Gotland I	160	57.30 N	18.33 E
Gotlands Län □[6]	160	57.30 N	18.30 E
Gotō-rettō II	192	32.50 N	129.00 E
Gotska Sandön I	160	58.23 N	19.16 E
Gōtsu	192	35.00 N	132.14 E
Göttingen	178	51.32 N	9.55 E
Gottmadingen	180	47.44 N	8.47 E
Gottwaldov	164	49.13 N	17.41 E
Götzis	180	47.20 N	9.38 E
Gouala ≃	222	10.14 N	8.38 W
Gouarec	162	48.13 N	3.11 W
Gouda	178	52.01 N	4.43 E
Goudge	294	34.41 S	68.07 W
Goufi, Djebel el ∧	168	36.58 N	6.27 E
Gough Island I	148	40.20 S	10.00 W
Gough Lake ⊜	238	52.02 N	112.28 W
Gouin, Réservoir ⊜[1]	232	48.35 N	74.50 W
Goulais ≃	244	46.43 N	84.27 W
Goulburn	228	34.45 S	149.43 E
Gould	248	33.59 N	91.34 W
Gould City	244	46.06 N	85.42 W
Gould Park	266	40.04 N	82.53 W
Goulds	246	25.33 N	80.23 W
Goumbati ∧[2]	222	13.08 N	12.06 W
Gouménissa	172	40.57 N	22.27 E
Goundam	214	16.25 N	3.40 W
Gouraya	168	36.34 N	1.55 E
Gourbeyre	285o	16.00 N	61.42 W
Gourdon	166	44.44 N	1.23 E
Gouré	214	13.58 N	10.18 E
Gourin	166	48.08 N	3.36 W
Gourlay Lake ⊜	244	48.52 N	84.54 W
Gournay-en-Bray	166	49.29 N	1.44 E
Goussainville	176	49.01 N	2.28 E
Gouvêa	296	18.27 S	43.44 W
Gouverneur	264	44.20 N	75.28 W
Gove	252	38.58 N	100.29 W
Govenlock	256	49.15 N	109.48 W
Goverla, Gora ∧	172	48.10 N	24.32 E
Governador Valadares	296	18.51 S	41.56 W
Government Camp	270	45.18 N	21.45 W
Governor Generoso	202	6.39 N	126.05 E
Governors Harbour	282	25.10 N	76.14 W
Govind Sāgar ⊜[1]	206	31.20 N	76.45 E
Gowanda	266	42.28 N	78.56 W
Gowan Range ⛰	228	25.00 S	145.00 E
Gowen City	262	40.45 N	76.32 W
Gowrie	252	42.17 N	94.17 W
Goya	294	29.10 S	59.20 W
Goyave	285o	16.08 N	61.34 W
Goyelle, Lac ⊜	240	50.46 N	60.45 W
Gozdnica (Freiwaldau)	164	51.26 N	15.06 E
Gozo I	170	36.03 N	14.15 E
Graaff-Reinet	224	32.14 S	24.32 E
Grabow	164	53.16 N	11.34 E
Grabowiec	164	50.50 N	23.33 E
Grabów nad Prosną	164	51.31 N	18.06 E
Gračac	170	44.18 N	15.51 E
Gračanica	172	44.42 N	18.19 E
Graçay	166	47.08 N	1.51 E
Grace	256	42.35 N	111.44 W
Gracefield	242	46.06 N	76.03 W
Graceham	262	39.37 N	77.24 W
Graceton	266	40.30 N	79.10 W
Graceville, Fla., U.S.	246	30.58 N	85.31 W
Graceville, Minn., U.S.	252	45.34 N	96.26 W
Gracewood	246	33.22 N	82.02 W
Gracias	280	14.35 N	88.35 W
Gracias a Dios □[5]	280	15.10 N	84.20 W
Gracias a Dios, Cabo ≻	280	15.00 N	83.08 W
Gradačac	172	44.53 N	18.26 E
Gradaús	286	7.43 S	51.11 W
Grado, Esp.	168	43.23 N	6.04 W
Grado, It.	170	45.40 N	13.23 E
Grady, Ark., U.S.	248	34.05 N	91.42 W

Symbols in the index entries are identified on page 360.

Name	Page	Lat°′	Long°′
Grady, N. Mex., U.S.	250	34.49 N	103.19 W
Graettinger	252	43.14 N	94.45 W
Grafenau	164	48.52 N	13.25 E
Gräfenhainichen	164	51.44 N	12.27 E
Grafing	164	48.02 N	11.59 E
Graford	250	32.56 N	98.14 W
Grafton, Austl.	228	29.41 S	152.56 E
Grafton, Ont., Can.	264	44.00 N	78.01 W
Grafton, Ill., U.S.	248	38.58 N	90.26 W
Grafton, Mass., U.S.	261	42.12 N	71.41 W
Grafton, N. Dak., U.S.	252	48.25 N	97.25 W
Grafton, N.Y., U.S.	261	42.46 N	73.27 W
Grafton, Ohio, U.S.	266	41.16 N	82.04 W
Grafton, W. Va., U.S.	242	39.20 N	80.01 W
Grafton, Wis., U.S.	244	43.19 N	87.56 W
Grafton, Cape ≻	228	16.52 S	145.55 E
Gragnano	184	40.41 N	14.31 E
Graham, Ky., U.S.	248	37.15 N	87.17 W
Graham, N.C., U.S.	246	36.05 N	79.25 W
Graham, Tex., U.S.	250	33.06 N	98.35 W
Graham, Wash., U.S.	270	47.03 N	122.15 W
Graham, Mount ∧	254	32.42 N	109.52 W
Graham Island I	238	53.40 N	132.30 W
Graham Lake ⊜	240	44.40 N	68.25 W
Graham Moore, Cape ≻	232	72.52 N	76.04 W
Graham Moore Bay C	232	75.26 N	101.25 W
Grahamstown	224	33.19 S	26.31 E
Graie, Alpi (Alpes Grées) ⋀	182	45.30 N	7.10 E
Graíko, Akrotírion ≻	212	34.48 N	33.37 E
Grain Coast ◂[2]	222	5.00 N	9.00 W
Grainfield	252	39.07 N	100.28 W
Grajaú	286	5.49 S	46.08 W
Grajewo	164	53.39 N	22.27 E
Gramada	172	43.50 N	22.39 E
Gramado	294	29.24 S	50.54 W
Gramalote	290	7.53 N	72.48 W
Gramat	166	44.47 N	1.43 E
Grambling	248	32.32 N	92.43 W
Gramilla	294	27.18 S	64.37 W
Grammichele	170	37.13 N	14.38 E
Grampian	266	40.58 N	78.37 W
Grampian Mountains ⋀	162	56.45 N	4.00 W
Gramsh	172	40.52 N	20.11 E
Granada, Col.	290	3.34 N	73.45 W
Granada, Esp.	168	37.13 N	3.41 W
Granada, Nic.	280	11.56 N	85.57 W
Granada, Pil.	202	10.39 N	123.05 E
Granada, Colo., U.S.	252	38.04 N	102.19 W
Granada, Minn., U.S.	244	43.42 N	94.21 W
Granada □[5]	280	11.50 N	86.00 W
Granadella	168	41.21 N	0.40 E
Granard	162	53.47 N	7.30 W
Granbury	250	32.27 N	97.47 W
Granby, Qué., Can.	260	45.24 N	72.43 W
Granby, Colo., U.S.	254	40.05 N	105.56 W
Granby, Conn., U.S.	261	41.57 N	72.47 W
Granby, Mo., U.S.	248	36.55 N	94.15 W
Granby ≃	238	49.03 N	118.25 W
Granby, Lake ⊜[1]	254	40.09 N	105.50 W
Gran Chaco ≚	288	23.00 S	60.00 W
Grand ≃, Ont., Can.	244	42.51 N	79.34 W
Grand ≃, U.S.	248	39.23 N	93.06 W
Grand ≃, N. Dak., U.S.	252	45.40 N	100.38 W
Grand ≃, S. Dak., U.S.	252	45.40 N	100.32 W
Grand ≃, Wis., U.S.	244	43.45 N	89.16 W
Grand, Lac ⊜	244	47.10 N	76.56 W
Grandas de Salime	168	43.13 N	6.52 W
Grand Bahama I	282	26.40 N	78.20 W
Grand Ballon ∧	166	47.55 N	7.08 E
Grand Bank	240	47.06 N	55.47 W
Grand Banks ✧[4]	148	47.00 N	52.00 W
Grand Bassa □[6]	222	6.00 N	9.30 W
Grand-Bassam	222	5.12 N	3.44 W
Grand Bay, N.B., Can.	240	45.18 N	66.12 W
Grand Bay, Ala., U.S.	248	30.29 N	88.21 W
Grand Bend	244	43.15 N	81.45 W
Grand Blanc	268	42.56 N	83.38 W
Grand-Bourg	285o	15.53 N	61.19 W
Grand-Bruit	240	47.41 N	58.13 W
Grand Caicos I	282	21.45 N	71.45 W
Grand-Calumet, Île du I	242	45.44 N	76.41 W
Grand Canal → Yunhe Ξ, Zhg.	190	32.12 N	119.31 E
Grand Cane	248	32.05 N	93.49 W
Grand Cañon du Verdon ♠	166	43.47 N	6.27 E
Grand Canyon	254	36.03 N	112.09 W
Grand Canyon ∨	254	36.10 N	112.45 W
Grand Canyon National Monument ♠	254	36.15 N	112.58 W
Grand Canyon National Park ♠	254	36.07 N	112.30 W
Grand Cape Mount □[6]	222	7.00 N	11.00 W
Grand Cayman I	282	19.20 N	81.15 W
Grand Cess	214	4.36 N	8.10 W
Grand Champ	162	47.46 N	2.51 W
Grand-Charmont	180	47.32 N	6.50 E
Grand Chenier	248	29.46 N	92.58 W
Grand Coulee	256	47.56 N	119.00 W
Grand Coulee Dam ◂[6]	256	47.57 N	118.59 W
Grand-Couronne	176	49.21 N	1.00 E
Grande ≃, Arg.	294	24.12 S	64.42 W
Grande ≃, Arg.	294	36.52 S	69.45 W
Grande ≃, Bol.	292	15.51 S	64.39 W
Grande ≃, Bra.	296	19.52 S	50.20 W
Grande ≃, Bra.	296	11.45 S	44.50 W
Grande ≃, Qué., Can.	240	48.23 N	64.32 W
Grande ≃, Chile	294	30.35 S	71.11 W
Grande ≃, Esp.	168	39.07 N	0.44 W
Grande ≃, Pan.	280	8.18 N	80.24 W
Grande ≃, Perú	292	15.00 S	75.27 W
Grande, Arroyo ≃	294	33.08 S	57.09 W
Grande, Boca ≃[1]	290	8.38 N	60.30 W
Grande, Cayo I	284p	20.59 N	79.09 W
Grande, Cuchilla ∧	294	33.15 S	55.07 W
Grande, Ilha I, Bra.	296	23.45 S	54.03 W
Grande, Ilha I, Bra.	296	23.09 S	44.14 W
Grande, Ponta ≻	296	16.22 S	39.01 W
Grande, Punta ≻	294	25.06 S	70.30 W
Grande, Rio (Bravo del Norte) ≃	234	25.57 N	97.09 W
Grande, Sierra ⋀, Arg.	294	31.30 S	65.00 W
Grande, Sierra ⋀, Méx.	250	29.35 N	104.55 W
Grande-Anse, N.B., Can.	240	47.48 N	65.11 W
Grande Anse, Guad.	285o	16.18 N	61.04 W
Grande Cayemite I	282	18.35 N	73.45 W
Grande-Chartreuse ⩔[1]	166	45.22 N	5.50 E
Grande Comore I	225a	11.35 S	43.20 E
Grande da Botija, Ilha I	290	3.58 S	62.53 W
Grande de Lipez ≃	292	20.47 S	67.14 W
Grande de Manacapuru, Lago ⊜	290	3.04 S	61.25 W
Grande de Matagalpa ≃	280	12.54 N	83.32 W
Grande de San Miguel ≃	280	13.14 N	88.22 W
Grande de Santa Marta, Ciénaga C	290	10.50 N	74.25 W
Grande de Santiago, Río ≃	278	21.36 N	105.26 W
Grande de Tarija ≃	292	22.53 S	64.21 W
Grande de Térraba ≃	280	9.00 N	83.40 W
Grande do Gurupá, Ilha I	286	1.00 S	51.30 W
Grand-Entrée	240	47.35 N	61.30 W
Grande-Prairie	238	55.10 N	118.48 W
Grand Erg de Bilma ◂[2]	214	18.30 N	14.00 E
Grand Erg Occidental ◂[2]	214	30.30 N	0.30 E
Grand Erg Oriental ◂[2]	214	30.30 N	7.00 E
Grande-Rivière	240	48.24 N	64.30 W
Grande Ronde ≃	256	46.05 N	116.59 W
Grandes, Salinas ≚	294	29.37 S	64.56 W
Grandes-Piles	260	46.41 N	72.44 W
Grand-Étang	240	46.33 N	61.02 W
Grande-Terre I	282	16.20 N	61.25 W
Grand Falls, N.B., Can.	240	46.55 N	67.45 W
Grand Falls, Newf., Can.	240	48.56 N	55.40 W
Grandfalls, Tex., U.S.	250	31.20 N	102.51 W
Grandfather Mountain ∧	246	36.07 N	81.48 W
Grandfield	250	34.13 N	98.41 W
Grand Forks, B.C., Can.	238	49.02 N	118.27 W
Grand Forks, N. Dak., U.S.	252	47.55 N	97.03 W
Grand Gedeh □[6]	222	6.00 N	8.00 W
Grandglaise	248	35.29 N	91.23 W
Grandgousie Hill ∧[2]	244	47.35 N	84.56 W
Grand Haven	268	43.04 N	86.13 W
Grand Hers ≃	166	43.47 N	1.20 E
Grandiči	164	53.43 N	23.49 E
Grandin, Lac ⊜	232	63.59 N	119.00 W
Grand Island, Nebr., U.S.	252	40.55 N	98.21 W
Grand Island, N.Y., U.S.	264	43.01 N	78.58 W
Grand Island I	244	46.30 N	86.40 W
Grand Isle	248	29.14 N	90.00 W
Grand Isle □[6]	260	44.57 N	73.17 W
Grand Junction, Colo., U.S.	254	39.05 N	108.33 W
Grand Junction, Iowa, U.S.	252	42.02 N	94.14 W
Grand Junction, Mich., U.S.	268	42.24 N	86.04 W
Grand Junction, Tenn., U.S.	248	35.03 N	89.10 W
Grand lac du Nord ⊜	240	50.54 N	67.07 W
Grand lac Germain ⊜	240	51.12 N	66.40 W
Grand lac Victoria ⊜	244	47.40 N	77.30 W
Grand Lake	254	40.15 N	105.49 W
Grand Lake ⊜, N.B., Can.	240	45.42 N	66.05 W
Grand Lake ⊜, Newf., Can.	240	49.00 N	57.25 W
Grand Lake ⊜, N.A.	240	45.43 N	67.50 W
Grand Lake ⊜, La., U.S.	248	29.55 N	92.47 W
Grand Lake ⊜, Maine, U.S.	242	45.15 N	67.50 W
Grand Lake ⊜, Mich., U.S.	244	45.18 N	83.30 W
Grand Ledge	268	42.45 N	84.45 W
Grand-Lieu, Lac de ⊜	166	47.06 N	1.40 W
Grand Manan I	240	44.40 N	66.50 W
Grand Manan Channel Џ	240	44.45 N	66.52 W
Grand Marais, Mich., U.S.	244	46.40 N	85.59 W
Grand Marais, Minn., U.S.	244	47.45 N	90.20 W
Grand Meadow	244	43.42 N	92.34 W
Grand'Mère	260	46.37 N	72.41 W
Grand Mesa ∧	254	39.00 N	108.00 W
Grandmesnil, Lac ⊜	240	51.19 N	67.35 W
Grândola	168	38.10 N	8.34 W
Grand-Pabos, Riviére du ≃	240	48.20 N	64.40 W
Grand Portage	244	47.58 N	89.41 W
Grand Portage Indian Reservation ◂[4]	244	47.55 N	89.45 W
Grand Portage National Monument ♠	244	48.02 N	89.57 W
Grand Prairie	250	32.45 N	96.59 W
Grand Pré National Historic Park ♠	240	45.08 N	64.18 W
Grand Rapids, Man., Can.	232	53.08 N	99.20 W
Grand Rapids, Mich., U.S.	268	42.58 N	85.40 W
Grand Rapids, Minn., U.S.	244	47.14 N	93.31 W
Grand Rapids, Ohio, U.S.	268	41.25 N	83.52 W
Grand Ridge	268	41.14 N	88.50 W
Grandrieu	166	44.47 N	3.38 E
Grand River	266	41.44 N	81.17 W
Grand' Rivière	284e	14.52 N	61.11 W
Grand rivière de la Baleine ≃	232	55.15 N	77.45 W
Grand Ronde	270	45.04 N	123.37 W
Grand Roy	285k	12.08 N	61.45 W
Grand-Saint-Bernard, Col du)(	180	45.50 N	7.10 E
Grand Saline	250	32.41 N	95.43 W
Grand Terrace	274	34.03 N	117.20 W
Grand Teton ∧	254	43.44 N	110.48 W
Grand Teton National Park ♠	254	43.30 N	43.57 W
Grand Tower	248	37.38 N	89.30 W
Grand Traverse Bay C	244	45.02 N	85.30 W
Grand Turk	282	21.28 N	71.08 W
Grand Valley, Ont., Can.	264	43.54 N	80.19 W
Grand Valley, Colo., U.S.	254	39.27 N	108.03 W
Grand Valley, Pa., U.S.	266	41.43 N	79.32 W
Grandview, Man., Can.	232	51.10 N	100.45 W
Grandview, Mo., U.S.	248	38.53 N	94.32 W
Grandview, Ohio, U.S.	242	39.31 N	81.05 W
Grandview, Tex., U.S.	250	32.16 N	97.11 W
Grandview, Wash., U.S.	256	46.15 N	119.54 W
Grandview, Wis., U.S.	244	46.22 N	91.06 W
Grandview Beach	268	41.50 N	83.24 W
Grandview Heights	262	40.03 N	76.17 W
Grandview Homes	268	40.44 N	84.04 W
Grandville	268	42.54 N	85.46 W
Grand Wash Cliffs ◂[4]	254	36.30 N	113.40 W
Grandyle	264	43.00 N	78.57 W
Grañén	168	41.56 N	0.22 W
Graneros	294	34.04 S	70.44 W
Grangärde	160	60.16 N	14.59 E
Granger, Tex., U.S.	250	30.43 N	97.27 W
Granger, Utah, U.S.	254	40.42 N	111.57 W
Granger, Wash., U.S.	256	46.21 N	120.11 W
Granger, Wyo., U.S.	254	41.35 N	109.58 W
Grangeville, Idaho, U.S.	256	45.56 N	116.07 W
Grangeville, Pa., U.S.	262	39.47 N	76.58 W
Gran Guardia	294	25.52 S	58.54 W
Granite	250	34.58 N	99.23 W
Granite City	248	38.42 N	90.09 W
Granite Falls, Minn., U.S.	252	44.49 N	95.33 W
Granite Falls, N.C., U.S.	246	35.48 N	81.26 W
Granite Falls, Wash., U.S.	270	48.05 N	121.58 W
Granite Lake ⊜	240	48.10 N	57.00 W
Granite Mountain ∧, Alaska, U.S.	236	65.26 N	161.14 W
Granite Mountain ∧, Alaska, U.S.	238	55.30 N	132.35 W
Granite Pass)(	256	44.38 N	107.30 W
Granite Peak ∧, Mont., U.S.	256	45.10 N	109.48 W
Granite Peak ∧, Mont., U.S.	256	45.34 N	112.02 W
Granite Peak ∧, Nev., U.S.	258	41.40 N	117.35 W
Granite Peak ∧, Nev., U.S.	258	40.48 N	119.25 W
Granite Range ⋀	258	41.00 N	119.35 W
Graniteville, Mass., U.S.	261	42.36 N	71.28 W
Graniteville, S.C., U.S.	246	33.34 N	81.48 W
Graniteville, Vt., U.S.	242	44.08 N	72.29 W
Granitola, Capo ≻	170	37.33 N	12.40 E
Granki	160	54.51 N	31.27 E
Gränna	160	58.01 N	14.28 E
Granollers	168	41.37 N	2.18 E
Gran Pajonal ⋀	292	10.50 S	74.20 W
Gran Pampa Salada ≚	292	20.35 S	67.15 W
Gran Paradiso ∧	170	45.32 N	7.16 E
Gran Paradiso, Parco del ♠	170	45.34 N	7.18 E
Gran Piedra ∧	284p	19.59 N	75.36 W
Gran Quivira National Monument ♠	254	34.05 N	106.14 W
Gransee	164	53.00 N	13.09 E
Grant, Fla., U.S.	246	27.56 N	80.32 W
Grant, Mich., U.S.	244	43.20 N	85.49 W
Grant, Nebr., U.S.	252	40.50 N	101.56 W
Grant □[6]	268	40.33 N	85.40 W
Grant ≃	244	42.40 N	90.45 W
Grant, Mount ∧	258	38.34 N	118.48 W
Grant City	248	40.29 N	94.25 W
Grantham, Eng., U.K.	174	52.55 N	0.39 W
Grantham, Pa., U.S.	262	40.09 N	77.00 W
Grantown on Spey	162	57.20 N	3.58 W
Grant Park	268	41.14 N	87.39 W
Grant Point ≻[1]	232	68.19 N	98.53 W
Grant Range ⋀	258	38.25 N	115.30 W
Grants	254	35.09 N	107.52 W
Grantsburg	244	45.47 N	92.41 W
Grants Pass	256	42.26 N	123.19 W
Grant-Suttie Bay C	232	69.47 N	77.15 W
Grantsville, Utah, U.S.	254	40.36 N	112.28 W
Grantsville, W. Va., U.S.	242	38.55 N	81.06 W
Grantville, Ga., U.S.	246	33.14 N	84.50 W
Grantville, Pa., U.S.	262	40.23 N	76.39 W
Granum	238	49.52 N	113.30 W
Granville, Fr.	166	48.50 N	1.36 W
Granville, Ill., U.S.	244	41.16 N	89.14 W
Granville, Mass., U.S.	261	42.04 N	72.52 W
Granville, N. Dak., U.S.	252	48.16 N	100.47 W
Granville, N.Y., U.S.	242	43.24 N	73.16 W
Granville, Ohio, U.S.	266	40.04 N	82.31 W
Granville, Pa., U.S.	262	40.33 N	77.38 W
Granville, W. Va., U.S.	242	39.39 N	79.59 W
Granville Lake ⊜	232	56.18 N	100.30 W
Granvin	160	60.33 N	6.43 E
Grão Mogol	296	16.34 S	42.54 W
Grapeland	250	31.29 N	95.29 W
Grapeview	270	47.20 N	122.50 W
Grapeville	266	40.19 N	79.36 W
Grapevine Peak ∧	258	36.57 N	117.09 W
Grarem	168	36.31 N	6.19 E
Gras, Lac de ⊜	232	64.30 N	110.30 W
Grasonville	262	38.57 N	76.13 W
Grass ≃, Man., Can.	232	56.03 N	96.33 W
Grass ≃, N.Y., U.S.	242	44.59 N	74.46 W
Grassano	170	40.38 N	16.18 E
Grass Cay I	280	16.07 N	88.15 W
Grass Creek	256	43.56 N	108.39 W
Grasse	182	43.40 N	6.55 E
Grassflat	266	41.00 N	78.07 W
Grass Lake	268	42.15 N	84.13 W
Grassrange	256	47.01 N	108.48 W
Grass Valley, Calif., U.S.	272	39.13 N	121.04 W
Grass Valley, Oreg., U.S.	270	45.22 N	120.47 W
Grassy ≃	244	48.42 N	81.27 W
Grassy Lake	238	49.49 N	111.43 W
Grassy Plains	238	53.57 N	125.54 W
Gråsten	164	54.55 N	9.36 E
Grates Point ≻	240	48.09 N	52.57 W
Gratz	262	40.37 N	76.43 W
Graubünden (Grischun) □[3]	180	46.45 N	9.30 E
Graudenz → Grudziądz	164	53.29 N	18.45 E
Gravatá	286	8.12 S	35.34 W
Gravata ≃	296	16.53 S	42.10 W
Gravelbourg	232	49.53 N	106.34 W
Gravelines	166	50.59 N	2.07 E
Gravell Point ≻	232	67.10 N	76.43 W
Gravenhurst	264	44.55 N	79.22 W
Grave Peak ∧	256	46.24 N	114.44 W
Gravesend	174	51.27 N	0.24 E
Gravette	248	36.26 N	94.27 W
Gravina in Puglia	170	40.49 N	16.25 E
Gravina Island I	238	55.17 N	131.45 W
Gray, Fr.	180	47.27 N	5.35 E
Gray, Ga., U.S.	246	33.01 N	83.32 W
Gray, Ky., U.S.	246	36.57 N	84.00 W
Gray, Maine, U.S.	242	43.53 N	70.20 W
Gray, Pa., U.S.	266	40.08 N	79.05 W
Grayback Mountain ∧, Alaska, U.S.	236	57.08 N	153.54 W
Grayback Mountain ∧, Oreg., U.S.	256	42.07 N	123.18 W
Grayland	270	46.48 N	124.06 W
Grayling, Alaska, U.S.	236	62.57 N	160.03 W
Grayling, Mich., U.S.	244	44.40 N	84.43 W
Grays Harbor □[6]	270	47.09 N	123.45 W
Grayslake	268	42.21 N	88.03 W
Grays Lake ⊜	256	43.04 N	111.26 W
Grays Lake Outlet ≃	256	43.22 N	111.46 W
Grayson, Ala., U.S.	248	34.15 N	87.24 W
Grayson, Ky., U.S.	242	38.20 N	82.57 W
Grays Peak ∧	254	39.37 N	105.45 W
Grays River	270	46.21 N	123.37 W
Grays Thurrock	174	51.29 N	0.20 E
Graysville	248	35.27 N	85.05 W
Graytown	266	41.33 N	83.16 W
Grayville	248	38.16 N	87.59 W
Graz	164	47.05 N	15.27 E
Grazalema	168	36.46 N	5.22 W
Gr'azi	158	52.29 N	39.57 E
Gr'azovec	160	58.53 N	40.14 E
Grdelica	172	42.54 N	22.04 E
Greaca, Lacul ⊜	172	44.05 N	26.23 E
Great Abaco I	282	26.25 N	77.10 W
Great Artesian Basin ◂[1]	228	25.00 S	143.00 E
Great Bahama Bank ✧[4]	282	23.15 N	78.00 W
Great Barrier Island I	230	36.11 S	175.25 E
Great Barrier Reef ✧[2]	228	18.00 S	146.50 E
Great Barrington	261	42.12 N	73.22 W
Great Basin ≚[1]	234	40.00 N	117.00 W
Great Bear ≃	236	64.54 N	125.35 W
Great Bear Lake ⊜	232	66.00 N	120.00 W
Great Beaver Lake ⊜	238	54.25 N	123.45 W
Great Bend, Kans., U.S.	252	38.22 N	98.46 W
Great Bend, N.Y., U.S.	264	44.02 N	75.43 W
Great Bitter Lake → Al-Buḥayrah al-Murrah al-Kubrā ⊜	220	30.20 N	32.23 E
Great Blasket Island I	162	52.05 N	10.32 W
Great Burnt Lake ⊜	240	48.20 N	56.13 W
Great Central Lake ⊜	238	49.27 N	125.12 W
Great Channel Џ	200	6.25 N	94.20 E
Great Chazy ≃	242	44.56 N	73.23 W
Great Cloche Island I	244	46.01 N	81.52 W
Great Coco Island I	200	14.05 N	93.24 E
Great Dividing Range ⋀	228	25.00 S	147.00 E
Great Duck Island I	244	45.40 N	82.58 W
Great Dunmow	162	51.53 N	0.22 E
Greater Antilles II	282	20.00 N	74.00 W
Greater Khingan Mountains → Daxing'anling-shanmai ⋀	190	49.40 N	122.00 E
Greater Leech Lake Indian Reservation ◂[4]	244	47.30 N	94.27 W
Greater Sunda Islands II	198	2.00 S	110.00 E
Great Exuma I	282	23.30 N	75.50 W
Great Falls, Mont., U.S.	256	47.30 N	111.17 W
Great Falls, S.C., U.S.	246	34.34 N	80.54 W
Great Guana Cay I	282	24.00 N	76.20 W
Great Himalaya Range ⋀	206	29.00 N	83.00 E
Greathouse Peak ∧	256	46.46 N	109.21 W
Great Inagua I	282	21.02 N	73.20 W
Great Indian Desert (Thar Desert) ◂[2]	206	28.00 N	72.00 E
Great Island I	230	46.00 S	166.34 E
Great Karroo ⋀[1]	224	32.25 S	22.40 E
Great Lake ⊜	228	41.52 S	146.45 E
Great Lakes Naval Training Center ■	268	42.18 N	87.50 W
Great Malvern (Malvern)	174	52.07 N	2.19 W
Great Mercury Island I	230	36.37 S	175.48 E
Great Meteor Seamount ✧[3]	148	30.00 N	28.30 W
Great Miami ≃	242	39.06 N	84.49 W
Great Mills	262	38.14 N	76.30 W
Great Namaland □[9]	224	25.00 S	17.00 E
Great Nicobar I	200	7.00 N	93.50 E
Great Palm Island I	228	18.43 S	146.37 E
Great Plain of the Koukdjuak ≚	232	66.00 N	73.00 W
Great Plains ≚	148	42.00 N	100.00 W
Great Plains Reservoir ⊜[1]	252	38.19 N	102.44 W
Great Pubnico Lake ⊜	240	43.42 N	65.43 W
Great Ruaha ≃	218	7.56 S	37.52 E
Great Sacandaga Lake ⊜	242	43.08 N	74.10 W
Great Saint Bernard Pass → Grand-Saint-Bernard, Col du)(	180	45.50 N	7.10 E
Great Saint Bernard Tunnel ◂[5]	170	45.50 N	7.10 E
Great Sale Cay I	246	27.00 N	78.15 W
Great Salt Lake ⊜	254	41.10 N	112.30 W
Great Salt Lake Desert ◂[2]	254	40.40 N	113.30 W
Great Salt Plains Reservoir ⊜[1]	250	36.44 N	98.12 W
Great Sand Dunes National Monument ♠	254	37.43 N	105.36 W
Great Sandy Desert ◂[2]	256	43.35 N	120.15 W
Great Santa Cruz Island I	202	6.52 N	122.04 E
Great Scarcies (Kolenté) ≃	222	8.55 N	13.08 W
Great Sitkin Island I	236	52.03 N	176.07 W
Great Slave Lake ⊜	232	61.30 N	114.00 W
Great Smoky Mountains ⋀	246	35.35 N	83.30 W
Great Smoky Mountains National Park ♠	246	35.39 N	83.30 W
Great Tenasserim ≃	200	12.24 N	98.37 E
Great Tsau ∧	224	21.14 S	22.45 E
Great Valley	266	42.13 N	78.38 W
Great Whale River	232	55.20 N	76.50 W
Great Yarmouth	174	52.37 N	1.44 E
Great Zab (Büyükzap) (Az-Zāb al-Kabīr) ≃	208	36.00 N	43.21 E
Gréboun, Mont ∧	222	20.00 N	8.35 E
Grecia	280	10.05 N	84.18 W
Greco	294	32.48 S	57.03 W
Gredos, Sierra de ⋀	168	40.18 N	5.05 W
Greece	264	43.14 N	77.38 W
Greece □[1]	158	39.00 N	22.00 E
Greeley, Colo., U.S.	254	40.25 N	104.42 W
Greeley, Kans., U.S.	252	38.22 N	95.08 W
Greeley, Nebr., U.S.	252	41.33 N	98.32 W
Greeleyville	246	33.35 N	79.58 W
Green □[6]	268	42.48 N	89.25 W
Green ≃, N.B., Can.	240	47.18 N	68.09 W
Green ≃, U.S.	254	38.11 N	109.53 W
Green ≃, Ill., U.S.	244	41.28 N	90.23 W
Green ≃, Ky., U.S.	248	37.55 N	87.30 W
Green ≃, N. Dak., U.S.	252	46.52 N	102.35 W
Green ≃, Wash., U.S.	256	46.20 N	122.34 W
Green ≃, Wash., U.S.	256	47.33 N	122.20 W
Greenacres, Calif., U.S.	272	35.23 N	119.07 W
Greenacres, Wash., U.S.	256	47.39 N	117.06 W
Greenbackville	262	38.01 N	75.23 W
Greenbank	270	48.06 N	122.34 W
Green Bay	244	44.30 N	88.01 W
Green Bay C, Newf., Can.	240	49.43 N	55.58 W
Green Bay C, U.S.	244	45.00 N	87.30 W
Greenbrae	272	37.57 N	122.31 W
Greenbrier, Ark., U.S.	248	35.14 N	92.23 W
Greenbrier, Tenn., U.S.	248	36.27 N	86.49 W
Greenburg	248	30.51 N	90.40 W
Greenbush, Mass., U.S.	261	42.11 N	70.45 W
Greenbush, Minn., U.S.	252	48.42 N	96.11 W
Greenbush, Va., U.S.	262	37.45 N	75.41 W
Green Camp	266	40.32 N	83.13 W
Green Cape ≻	228	37.15 S	150.03 E
Greencastle, Ind., U.S.	248	39.38 N	86.52 W
Greencastle, Pa., U.S.	242	39.47 N	77.44 W
Green City	248	40.16 N	92.57 W
Green Cove Springs	246	30.00 N	81.41 W
Green Creek	262	39.03 N	74.54 W
Greencrest Park	266	41.23 N	80.24 W
Greendale	248	39.07 N	84.52 W
Greene, Iowa, U.S.	244	42.54 N	92.48 W
Greene, Maine, U.S.	242	44.11 N	70.08 W
Greene, N.Y., U.S.	242	42.20 N	75.46 W
Greene, R.I., U.S.	261	41.41 N	71.44 W
Greeneville	246	36.10 N	82.50 W
Greenfield, Calif., U.S.	272	36.19 N	121.15 W
Greenfield, Ill., U.S.	248	39.21 N	90.12 W
Greenfield, Iowa, U.S.	252	41.18 N	94.28 W
Greenfield, Mass., U.S.	261	42.36 N	72.36 W
Greenfield, Mo., U.S.	248	37.25 N	93.51 W
Greenfield, Ohio, U.S.	242	39.21 N	83.23 W
Greenfield, Tenn., U.S.	248	36.09 N	88.48 W
Greenfield, Wis., U.S.	268	42.58 N	88.02 W
Greenford	266	40.57 N	80.48 W
Green Forest	248	36.20 N	93.26 W
Green Harbor	261	42.05 N	70.39 W
Greenhorn ≃	254	38.08 N	104.38 W
Greenhurst	266	42.07 N	79.19 W
Green Island, N.Z.	230	45.54 S	170.26 E
Green Island, N.Y., U.S.	261	42.45 N	73.41 W
Green Island Bay C	202	10.15 N	119.25 E
Green Knob ∧	242	38.54 N	79.26 W
Green Lake	244	43.51 N	88.57 W
Green Lake ⊜, B.C., Can.	238	51.24 N	121.15 W
Green Lake ⊜, Wis., U.S.	244	43.41 N	88.57 W
Greenland	244	46.46 N	89.06 W
Greenland □[2]	232	71.00 N	40.00 W
Greenland-Iceland Rise ✧[3]	148	66.00 N	30.00 W
Greenland Sea ▼[2]	148	77.00 N	1.00 W
Green Lane	262	40.20 N	75.28 W
Greenlay	260	45.34 N	72.01 W
Greenleaf	252	39.44 N	96.59 W
Greenmount	262	39.38 N	76.52 W
Green Mountain Reservoir ⊜[1]	254	39.52 N	106.17 W
Green Mountains ⋀	242	43.45 N	72.45 W
Green Mountain Village	254	39.41 N	105.05 W
Greenock	162	55.57 N	4.45 W
Greenore Point ≻	162	52.15 N	6.18 W
Greenough, Mount ∧	236	69.10 N	141.35 W
Green Park	262	40.23 N	77.19 W
Green Peter Reservoir ⊜[1]	256	44.28 N	122.30 W
Green Pond	246	32.44 N	80.37 W
Greenport	261	41.06 N	72.22 W
Green River, Utah, U.S.	254	38.59 N	110.10 W
Green River, Wyo., U.S.	254	41.32 N	109.28 W
Green River Reservoir ⊜[1]	248	37.15 N	85.15 W
Greensboro, Ala., U.S.	248	32.42 N	87.36 W
Greensboro, Fla., U.S.	246	30.34 N	84.45 W
Greensboro, Ga., U.S.	246	33.35 N	83.11 W
Greensboro, Md., U.S.	242	38.59 N	75.48 W
Greensboro, N.C., U.S.	246	36.04 N	79.47 W
Greensburg, Ind., U.S.	248	39.20 N	85.29 W
Greensburg, Kans., U.S.	252	37.36 N	99.18 W
Greensburg, Ky., U.S.	248	37.16 N	85.30 W
Greensburg, Ohio, U.S.	266	40.56 N	81.28 W
Greensburg, Pa., U.S.	266	40.18 N	79.33 W
Greens Peak ∧	254	34.05 N	109.33 W
Greenspond	240	49.04 N	53.34 W
Green Springs	266	41.15 N	83.03 W
Greenstone	262	39.45 N	77.27 W
Greensville □[6]	262	36.40 N	77.30 W
Green Swamp ☷	246	34.10 N	78.20 W
Greentown, Ind., U.S.	268	40.29 N	85.58 W
Greentown, Ohio, U.S.	266	40.56 N	81.28 W
Greenup, Ill., U.S.	248	39.15 N	88.10 W
Greenup, Ky., U.S.	242	38.34 N	82.50 W
Green Valley, Ont., Can.	260	45.16 N	74.36 W
Green Valley, Ill., U.S.	244	40.24 N	89.38 W
Greenview	248	40.05 N	89.44 W
Greenvillage	262	40.00 N	77.36 W
Greenville, Liber.	222	5.01 N	9.03 W
Greenville, Ala., U.S.	248	31.50 N	86.38 W
Greenville, Calif., U.S.	258	40.08 N	120.57 W
Greenville, Fla., U.S.	246	30.28 N	83.38 W
Greenville, Ill., U.S.	248	38.53 N	89.25 W
Greenville, Ky., U.S.	248	37.12 N	87.11 W
Greenville, Maine, U.S.	242	45.28 N	69.35 W
Greenville, Mich., U.S.	244	43.11 N	85.15 W
Greenville, Miss., U.S.	248	33.25 N	91.05 W
Greenville, Mo., U.S.	248	37.08 N	90.27 W
Greenville, N.H., U.S.	242	42.46 N	71.49 W
Greenville, N.C., U.S.	246	35.37 N	77.23 W
Greenville, N.Y., U.S.	261	42.25 N	74.01 W
Greenville, Ohio, U.S.	242	40.06 N	84.38 W
Greenville, Pa., U.S.	266	41.24 N	80.23 W
Greenville, R.I., U.S.	261	41.52 N	71.33 W
Greenville, S.C., U.S.	246	34.51 N	82.23 W
Greenville, Tex., U.S.	250	33.08 N	96.07 W
Greenwater Lake ⊜	244	48.34 N	90.26 W
Greenwich, Conn., U.S.	261	41.01 N	73.38 W
Greenwich, N.J., U.S.	262	39.24 N	75.21 W
Greenwich, N.Y., U.S.	242	43.05 N	73.30 W
Greenwich, Ohio, U.S.	266	41.02 N	82.31 W
Greenwich ◂[8]	174	51.28 N	0.02 E
Greenwood, B.C., Can.	238	49.05 N	118.41 W
Greenwood, Ark., U.S.	248	35.13 N	94.15 W
Greenwood, Calif., U.S.	272	38.54 N	120.55 W
Greenwood, Del., U.S.	262	38.49 N	75.35 W
Greenwood, Ind., U.S.	248	39.37 N	86.07 W
Greenwood, Miss., U.S.	248	33.31 N	90.11 W
Greenwood, Nebr., U.S.	252	40.58 N	96.27 W
Greenwood, N.Y., U.S.	266	42.08 N	77.39 W
Greenwood, Pa., U.S.	266	40.32 N	78.21 W
Greenwood, S.C., U.S.	246	34.12 N	82.10 W
Greenwood, Wis., U.S.	244	44.46 N	90.36 W
Greenwood, Lake ⊜[1]	246	34.15 N	82.02 W
Greer, Ohio, U.S.	266	40.31 N	82.13 W
Greer, S.C., U.S.	246	34.56 N	82.14 W
Greers Ferry Reservoir ⊜[1]	248	35.30 N	92.10 W
Greeson, Lake ⊜[1]	248	34.10 N	93.45 W
Grefrath	178	51.20 N	6.20 E
Gregório ≃	292	6.50 S	70.46 W
Gregory, Mich., U.S.	244	42.28 N	84.05 W
Gregory, S. Dak., U.S.	252	43.14 N	99.26 W
Gregory, Tex., U.S.	250	27.55 N	97.17 W
Gregory ≃	228	17.53 S	139.17 E
Gregory, Lake ⊜	228	28.55 S	139.00 E
Gregory Range ⋀	228	19.00 S	143.05 E
Greifswald	164	54.05 N	13.23 E
Greifswalder Bodden C	164	54.15 N	13.35 E
Grein	164	48.14 N	14.51 E
Greiz	164	50.39 N	12.12 E
Grem'ačinsk	158	58.34 N	57.51 E
Gremeč ⋀	170	44.40 N	16.30 E
Gremicha	160	68.03 N	39.27 E
Grenå	160	56.25 N	10.53 E
Grenada	248	33.47 N	89.55 W
Grenada □[2]	276	12.07 N	61.40 W
Grenada Reservoir ⊜[1]	248	33.50 N	89.40 W
Grenadine Islands II	282	12.40 N	61.15 W
Grenay	176	50.27 N	2.44 E
Grenchen	180	47.11 N	7.24 E
Grenell	264	44.16 N	76.04 W
Grenfell	228	33.54 S	148.10 E
Grenoble	182	45.10 N	5.43 E
Grenola	252	37.21 N	96.27 W
Grenora	252	48.37 N	103.56 W
Grenville, Qué., Can.	260	45.38 N	74.36 W
Grenville, Gren.	285k	12.07 N	61.37 W
Grenville □[6]	264	44.50 N	75.40 W
Grenville Bay	260	45.39 N	74.37 W
Grenville Channel Џ	238	53.40 N	129.40 W
Gréoux-les-Bains	166	43.45 N	5.53 E
Gresham	270	45.30 N	122.26 W
Gresham Park	246	33.42 N	84.19 W
Gresik	198	7.09 S	112.38 E
Gressitt	262	37.29 N	76.43 W
Gresten	164	48.00 N	15.02 E
Gretna, Man., Can.	252	49.02 N	97.35 W
Gretna, La., U.S.	248	29.55 N	90.03 W
Gretna, Va., U.S.	246	36.57 N	79.22 W
Greve	184	43.35 N	11.19 E
Greven	178	52.05 N	7.36 E
Grevená	172	40.05 N	21.25 E
Grevenbroich	178	51.05 N	6.35 E
Grevenbrück	178	51.08 N	8.01 E
Grevesmühlen	164	53.51 N	11.10 E
Greville Bay C	240	45.22 N	64.38 W
Grey □[6]	264	44.20 N	80.45 W
Grey ≃, Newf., Can.	240	47.38 N	57.05 W
Grey ≃, N.Z.	230	42.27 S	171.12 E
Grey, Point ≻, B.C., Can.	270	49.16 N	123.16 W
Greybull	256	44.30 N	108.03 W
Greybull ≃	256	44.28 N	108.03 W
Grey Eagle	244	45.50 N	94.45 W
Grey Islands II	240	50.50 N	55.37 W
Greylock, Mount ∧	242	42.38 N	73.10 W
Greymouth	230	42.27 S	171.12 E
Grey Range ⋀	228	27.00 S	143.35 E
Greys ≃	254	43.10 N	111.00 W
Greytown	224	29.07 S	30.30 E
Grez-en-Bouère	162	47.53 N	0.31 W
Gribanovskij	158	51.27 N	41.58 E
Gribbel Island I	238	53.25 N	129.00 W
Gridley, Calif., U.S.	272	39.22 N	121.42 W
Gridley, Ill., U.S.	268	40.45 N	88.53 W
Gridley, Kans., U.S.	252	38.06 N	95.53 W
Griesbach	164	48.28 N	13.11 E
Griesheim	164	49.50 N	8.34 E
Griffin, Sask., Can.	252	49.40 N	103.26 W
Griffin, Ga., U.S.	246	33.15 N	84.16 W
Griffin, Lake ⊜	246	28.52 N	81.51 W
Griffith, Austl.	228	34.17 S	146.03 E
Griffith, Ind., U.S.	268	41.32 N	87.25 W
Griffith Island I	232	74.35 N	95.30 W
Grifton	246	35.23 N	77.26 W
Griggsville	248	39.42 N	90.43 W
Grignan	166	44.25 N	4.54 E
Grignols	166	44.23 N	0.03 W
Grigny	182	45.37 N	4.47 E
Grijalva ≃	278	18.36 N	92.39 W
Grik	200	5.24 N	101.07 E
Grim, Cape ≻	228	40.41 S	144.41 E
Grimbergen	176	50.56 N	4.23 E
Grimes, Calif., U.S.	272	39.04 N	121.54 W
Grimes, Iowa, U.S.	248	41.41 N	93.47 W
Grimma	164	51.14 N	12.43 E
Grimmen	164	54.07 N	13.02 E
Grimsby, Ont., Can.	264	43.12 N	79.34 W
Grimsby, Eng., U.K.	162	53.35 N	0.05 W
Grimsby Beach	264	43.12 N	79.32 W
Grímsey I	160a	66.34 N	18.00 W
Grimshaw	238	56.11 N	117.36 W
Grímsstadir	160a	65.40 N	16.01 W
Grimstad	160	58.20 N	8.36 E
Grimstead	262	37.30 N	76.18 W
Grindavík	160a	63.52 N	22.27 W
Grindelwald	166	46.37 N	8.02 E
Grindstone Island (Cap-aux-Meules)	240	47.23 N	61.52 W
Gringo	266	40.34 N	80.16 W
Grinnell	244	41.45 N	92.43 W
Grinnell Peninsula ≻[1]	232	76.40 N	95.00 W
Grintavec ∧	170	46.21 N	14.32 E
Griqualand East ◂[1]	224	30.30 S	29.00 E
Griqualand West ◂[1]	224	28.30 S	23.00 E
Grisdale	270	47.22 N	123.37 W
Gris-Nez, Cap ≻	166	50.52 N	1.35 E
Griswold, Man., Can.	252	49.45 N	100.25 W
Griswold, Iowa, U.S.	252	41.14 N	95.08 W
Griswoldville	261	42.39 N	72.49 W
Grizzly Bear Mountains ⋀	232	65.22 N	121.00 W
Grizzly Flats	272	38.38 N	120.31 W
Grizzly Mountain ∧, Idaho, U.S.	256	47.43 N	116.06 W
Grizzly Mountain ∧, Oreg., U.S.	256	44.26 N	120.57 W
Grizzly Mountain ∧, Wash., U.S.	256	48.25 N	118.30 W
Groais Island I	240	50.57 N	55.35 W
Grodków (Grottkau)	164	50.43 N	17.22 E
Grodno	164	53.41 N	23.50 E
Grodno □[4]	160	54.45 N	26.00 E
Grodzisk Mazowiecki	164	52.07 N	20.37 E
Grodzisk Wielkopolski	164	52.14 N	16.22 E
Groen ≃	224	30.40 S	23.17 E
Groenlo	178	52.03 N	6.38 E
Groesbeck	250	31.31 N	96.32 W
Groesbeek	178	51.47 N	5.55 E
Grofa, Gora ∧	172	48.37 N	23.56 E
Groix	166	47.38 N	3.28 W
Groix, Île de I	166	47.38 N	3.27 W
Grójec	164	51.52 N	20.52 E
Grombalia	170	36.36 N	10.30 E
Gronau, B.R.D.	178	52.13 N	7.00 E
Gronau, B.R.D.	178	52.05 N	9.46 E
Grondines	260	46.36 N	72.02 W
Grong	160	64.28 N	12.18 E
Groningen	178	53.13 N	6.33 E
Groningen □[4]	178	53.15 N	6.45 E
Groom	250	35.12 N	101.06 W
Groom Lake ⊜	258	37.15 N	115.48 W
Groot ≃, S. Afr.	224	33.45 S	24.36 E
Groot ≃, S. Afr.	224	33.54 S	21.39 E
Groot-Berg ≃	224	32.47 S	18.08 E
Grootfontein	224	19.32 S	18.05 E
Grootfontein □[5]	224	19.00 S	20.00 E
Groot-Karasberge ⋀	224	27.20 S	18.40 E
Groot-Kei ≃	224	32.41 S	28.22 E
Groot Laagte ≃	224	20.37 S	21.37 E
Groot Letaba ≃	224	23.58 S	31.50 E
Groot Shingwidzi (Singuédeze) ≃	224	23.53 S	32.17 E
Groot-Swartberge ⋀	224	32.22 S	22.20 E
Groot-Vis ≃	224	33.30 S	27.08 E
Grootvloer ⊜	224	30.00 S	20.40 E
Gröpelingen ◂[8]	178	53.07 N	8.46 E
Gropeni	172	45.04 N	27.53 E
Gros Islet	285f	14.05 N	60.58 W
Gros-Morne	284e	14.43 N	61.01 W
Gros Morne ∧	240	49.36 N	57.48 W
Grosse Ile	268	42.08 N	83.09 W
Grosse Île I	240	47.37 N	61.31 W
Grossenhain	164	51.17 N	13.31 E
Grossenkneten	178	52.56 N	8.16 E
Grosse Pointe	266	42.24 N	82.55 W
Grosse Pointe Farms	266	42.25 N	82.53 W
Grosse Pointe Park	266	42.23 N	82.56 W
Grosse Pointe Shores	266	42.26 N	82.53 W
Grosse Pointe Woods	266	42.27 N	82.55 W
Grosser Arber ∧	164	49.07 N	13.07 E
Grosser Beerberg ∧	164	50.37 N	10.44 E
Grosser Feldberg ∧	164	50.14 N	8.26 E
Grosser Priel ∧	164	47.43 N	14.04 E
Grosser Rachel ∧	164	48.59 N	13.24 E
Grosseto	184	42.46 N	11.08 E
Grosseto □[4]	184	42.50 N	11.15 E
Gross-Gerau	164	49.55 N	8.29 E
Grosshansdorf	178	53.40 N	10.17 E
Grossmont	274	32.47 N	116.59 W
Grossräschen	164	51.35 N	14.00 E
Gross Reken	178	51.50 N	7.02 E
Grosvenor, Lake ⊜	236	58.40 N	155.15 W
Grosvenor Dale	261	41.58 N	71.54 W
Gros Ventre ≃	254	43.33 N	110.46 W
Groswater Bay C	232	54.20 N	57.30 W
Groton, Conn., U.S.	261	41.19 N	72.12 W
Groton, Mass., U.S.	261	42.37 N	71.34 W
Groton, N.Y., U.S.	242	42.35 N	76.22 W
Groton, S. Dak., U.S.	252	45.27 N	98.06 W
Grottaferrata	184	41.47 N	12.40 E
Grottaglie	170	40.32 N	17.26 E
Grottaminarda	170	41.04 N	15.02 E
Grottammare	170	42.59 N	13.52 E
Grottoes	242	38.16 N	78.56 W
Grouard Mission	238	55.31 N	116.09 W
Groundbirch	238	55.47 N	120.55 W
Groundhog ≃	244	49.43 N	81.58 W
Grouse Creek	254	41.42 N	113.53 W
Grouse Creek Mountain ∧	256	44.22 N	113.54 W
Grove, Esp.	168	42.30 N	8.52 W
Grove, Okla., U.S.	250	36.36 N	94.46 W
Grove City, Minn., U.S.	252	45.09 N	94.41 W
Grove City, Ohio, U.S.	242	39.53 N	83.06 W
Grove City, Pa., U.S.	266	41.10 N	80.05 W
Grove Hill	248	31.42 N	87.47 W

Symbols in the index entries are identified on page 360.

Name	Page	Lat°'	Long°'
Groveland, Calif., U.S.	272	37.50 N	120.14 W
Groveland, Fla., U.S.	246	28.34 N	81.51 W
Groveland, Mass., U.S.	261	42.46 N	71.02 W
Groveland, N.Y., U.S.	264	42.40 N	77.46 W
Grover City	258	35.07 N	120.37 W
Grover Hill	268	41.01 N	84.29 W
Groves	248	29.57 N	93.55 W
Groveton, N.H., U.S.	242	44.36 N	71.31 W
Groveton, Tex., U.S.	250	31.03 N	95.08 W
Grovetown	246	33.27 N	82.12 W
Groveville	262	40.11 N	74.40 W
Growler Peak ▲	254	32.24 N	113.07 W
Growler Wash ∨	254	32.35 N	113.30 W
Groznyj	158	43.20 N	45.42 E
Grubišno Polje	170	45.42 N	17.10 E
Grudovo	172	42.21 N	27.10 E
Grudziądz	164	53.29 N	18.45 E
Gruesa, Punta ≻	292	20.22 S	70.11 W
Gruetli	248	35.22 N	85.40 W
Grugliasco	182	45.04 N	7.35 E
Gruia	172	44.16 N	22.42 E
Grulla	250	26.16 N	98.39 W
Grumo Appula	170	41.01 N	16.43 E
Grünau im Almtal	164	47.51 N	13.57 E
Grünberg → Zielona Góra, Pol.	164	51.56 N	15.31 E
Grundy	246	37.17 N	82.06 W
Grundy □[6]	268	41.22 N	88.26 W
Grundy Center	244	42.22 N	92.47 W
Grunthal	252	49.25 N	96.52 W
Grušino	160	59.27 N	44.09 E
Gruver	250	36.16 N	101.24 W
Gruzinskaja Sovetskaja Socialističeskaja Respublika □[3]	186	42.00 N	44.00 E
Grybów	164	49.38 N	20.56 E
Gryfice (Greifenberg)	164	53.56 N	15.12 E
Gryfino (Greifenhagen)	164	53.12 N	14.30 E
Gstaad	166	47.11 N	7.24 E
Guabito	280	9.30 N	82.37 W
Guacanayabo, Golfo de C	284p	20.30 N	77.35 W
Guacara	290	10.14 N	67.53 W
Guacarí	290	3.46 N	76.20 W
Guacayá ≃	290	0.36 S	70.30 W
Gu Achi	254	32.20 N	112.02 W
Guachiría ≃	290	5.27 N	70.36 W
Guachochic	278	26.51 N	107.05 W
Guaçuí	296	20.46 S	41.41 W
Guadajira ≃	168	38.52 N	6.41 W
Guadajoz ≃	168	37.50 N	4.51 W
Guadalajara, Esp.	168	40.38 N	3.10 W
Guadalajara, Méx.	278	20.40 N	103.20 W
Guadalamar ≃	168	38.05 N	3.06 W
Guadalaviar ≃	168	40.21 N	1.08 W
Guadalcanal	168	38.06 N	5.49 W
Guadalcanal I	226	9.32 S	160.12 E
Guadalén ≃	168	38.05 N	3.32 W
Guadalén, Embalse del ⊜[1]	168	38.25 N	3.15 W
Guadalete ≃	168	36.35 N	6.13 W
Guadalhorce ≃	168	36.41 N	4.27 W
Guadalmena ≃	168	38.19 N	2.56 W
Guadalmez ≃	168	38.46 N	5.04 W
Guadalope ≃	168	41.15 N	0.03 W
Guadalquivir ≃	168	36.47 N	6.22 W
Guadalupe, Bol.	292	18.33 S	64.05 W
Guadalupe, Col.	290	2.01 N	75.45 W
Guadalupe, C.R.	280	9.57 N	84.03 W
Guadalupe, Méx.	250	28.09 N	100.36 W
Guadalupe, Méx.	278	25.41 N	100.15 W
Guadalupe, Méx.	278	22.45 N	102.31 W
Guadalupe, Méx.	278	16.16 N	91.27 W
Guadalupe, Perú	292	7.12 S	79.30 W
Guadalupe, Calif., U.S.	258	34.58 N	120.34 W
Guadalupe ≃, Méx.	258	32.05 N	116.53 W
Guadalupe ≃, Tex., U.S.	250	28.30 N	96.53 W
Guadalupe, Isla de I	234	29.00 N	118.16 W
Guadalupe, Sierra de ⛰	168	39.26 N	5.25 W
Guadalupe [Bravos]	278	31.23 N	106.07 W
Guadalupe Garzarón	278	24.35 N	101.15 W
Guadalupe Mountains ⛰	250	32.20 N	105.00 W
Guadalupe Peak ▲	250	31.50 N	104.52 W
Guadalupe Victoria, Méx.	250	27.47 N	101.04 W
Guadalupe Victoria, Méx.	278	24.27 N	104.07 W
Guadalupita	254	36.08 N	105.14 W
Guadarrama ≃	168	39.53 N	4.10 W
Guadarrama, Puerto de)(	168	40.43 N	4.10 W
Guadarrama, Sierra de ⛰	168	40.55 N	4.00 W
Guadazaón ≃	168	39.42 N	1.36 W
Guadeloupe □[2]	276	16.15 N	61.35 W
Guadeloupe Passage ⋃	282	16.40 N	61.50 W
Guadiana ≃	168	37.14 N	7.22 W
Guadiana, Bahía de C	284p	22.04 N	84.25 W
Guadiana Menor ≃	168	37.56 N	3.15 W
Guadiaro ≃	168	36.17 N	5.17 W
Guadiela ≃	168	40.22 N	2.49 W
Guadix	168	37.18 N	3.08 W
Guafo, Isla I	288	43.35 S	74.50 W
Guagua	202	14.58 N	120.38 E
Guaíba	294	30.06 S	51.19 W
Guaíba C[1]	294	30.15 S	51.12 W
Guaimaca	280	14.32 N	86.51 W
Guáimaro	284p	21.03 N	77.21 W
Guaimbé-Piriú ≃	294	22.55 S	55.03 W
Guainía □[5]	290	2.30 N	69.00 W
Guainía ≃	290	2.01 N	67.07 W
Guaiquinima, Cerro ▲	290	5.49 N	63.40 W
Guaíra, Bra.	294	24.04 S	54.15 W
Guaíra, Bra.	296	20.19 S	48.18 W
Guairá □[5]	294	25.45 S	56.30 W
Guairá, Salto del(Salto das Sete Quedas) L	294	24.02 S	54.16 W
Guáitara ≃	290	1.34 N	77.27 W
Guajaba, Cayo I	284p	21.50 N	77.30 W
Guajará Mirim	292	10.48 S	65.22 W
Gualaca	280	8.32 N	82.17 W
Gualaceo	290	2.54 S	78.47 W
Gualán	280	15.08 N	89.22 W
Gualaquiza	290	3.24 S	78.33 W
Gualdo Tadino	184	43.14 N	12.47 E
Gualeguay	294	33.10 S	59.20 W
Gualeguay ≃	294	33.18 S	59.38 W
Gualeguaychú	294	33.00 S	58.30 W
Gualicho, Salina ≍	288	40.25 S	65.20 W
Guamá ≃	284p	22.11 N	83.40 W
Guamal, Col.	290	3.52 N	73.44 W
Guamal, Col.	290	9.09 N	74.14 W
Guaminí	294	37.02 S	62.36 W
Guamo	290	4.02 N	74.58 W
Guamo Embarcadero	284p	20.37 N	76.58 W
Guamote	290	1.56 S	78.43 W
Guampí, Sierra de ⛰	290	6.00 N	65.35 W
Guampú ≃	280	14.59 N	85.03 W
Guamúchil	278	25.28 N	108.06 W
Guamués ≃	290	0.32 N	76.33 W
Gu'an	194	39.26 N	116.18 E
Guanabacoa	284p	23.07 N	82.18 W
Guanábana	284m	18.01 N	67.07 W
Guanacaste □[4]	280	10.30 N	85.15 W
Guanacaste, Cordillera de ⛰	280	10.45 N	85.05 W
Guanacaure, Cerro ▲	280	13.14 N	87.04 W
Guanaceví	278	25.56 N	105.57 W
Guanahacabibes, Golfo de C	284p	22.08 N	84.35 W
Guanahacabibes, Península de ≻[1]	284p	21.55 N	84.40 W
Guanaja	280	16.27 N	85.54 W
Guanaja, Isla de I	280	16.28 N	85.54 W
Guanajay	284p	22.55 N	82.42 W
Guanajuato	278	21.01 N	101.15 W
Guanambi	296	14.13 S	42.47 W
Guañape, Isla I	292	8.34 S	78.58 W
Guanare	290	9.03 N	69.45 W
Guanare ≃	290	8.13 N	67.46 W
Guanare Viejo ≃	290	8.19 N	68.10 W
Guanarito	290	8.42 N	69.12 W
Guanay	292	15.28 S	67.52 W
Guandacol	294	29.30 S	68.35 W
Guane	284p	22.12 N	84.05 W
Guang'an	190	30.28 N	106.39 E
Guangdong □[4]	190	23.00 N	113.00 E
Guanghua	190	32.25 N	111.36 E
Guangludao I	194	39.09 N	122.21 E
Guangnan	190	24.10 N	105.06 E
Guangxi Zhuang Zizhiqu □[4]	190	24.00 N	109.00 E
Guangyuan	190	32.23 N	105.58 E
Guangzhou (Canton)	196	23.06 N	113.16 E
Guanhe ≃, Zhg.	194	34.29 N	119.49 E
Guanhe ≃, Zhg.	196	32.16 N	115.42 E
Guanhekou ≃[1]	196	34.29 N	119.50 E
Guánica	284m	17.58 N	66.55 W
Guanipa ≃	290	9.56 N	62.26 W
Guanling	200	25.57 N	105.29 E
Guano	290	1.35 S	78.38 W
Guanpata	280	15.01 N	85.02 W
Guanshan I	196	27.21 N	120.36 E
Guanta	290	10.14 N	64.36 W
Guantánamo	284p	20.08 N	75.12 W
Guantánamo ≃	284p	19.58 N	75.10 W
Guantánamo, Bahía de C	284p	20.00 N	75.07 W
Guantanamo Bay Naval Station ■	284p	19.55 N	75.10 W
Guantingshuiku ⊜[1]	194	40.20 N	115.38 E
Guanxian	190	31.00 N	103.40 E
Guapí	290	2.36 N	77.54 W
Guapiara	296	24.10 S	48.32 W
Guápiles	280	10.13 N	83.46 W
Guapó	296	16.49 S	49.32 W
Guapo Bay C	285r	10.13 N	61.40 W
Guaporé	294	28.51 S	51.54 W
Guaporé ≃, Bra.	294	29.10 S	51.54 W
Guaporé (Iténez) ≃, S.A.	292	11.55 S	65.04 W
Guaqui	292	16.35 S	68.51 W
Guará ≃	296	12.59 S	44.49 W
Guara, Sierra de ⛰	168	42.17 N	0.10 W
Guarabira	286	6.51 S	35.29 W
Guarabo	284m	18.16 N	65.58 W
Guaraçaí	296	21.02 S	51.11 W
Guaracha ≃	292	5.48 S	74.23 W
Guaraci, Bra.	296	20.29 S	48.57 W
Guaraci, Bra.	296	22.57 S	51.40 W
Guaraciama	296	17.03 S	43.41 W
Guaraguara, Punta ≻	285r	10.31 N	62.19 W
Guaramirim	294	26.27 S	49.00 W
Guaranda	290	1.36 S	79.00 W
Guaraniaçu	294	25.06 S	52.52 W
Guarani das Missões	294	28.08 S	54.34 W
Guarapari	296	20.40 S	40.30 W
Guarapuava	294	25.23 S	51.27 W
Guaraqueçaba	294	25.17 S	48.21 W
Guararé	290	7.50 N	80.18 W
Guaratinguetá	296	22.49 S	45.13 W
Guaratuba	294	25.54 S	48.34 W
Guarda	168	40.32 N	7.16 W
Guardado de Abajo	250	26.22 N	98.57 W
Guardafui, Cape → Asir, Ras ≻	214	11.48 N	51.22 E
Guardavalle	170	38.30 N	16.30 E
Guardia Escolta	294	29.00 S	62.08 W
Guardiagrele	184	42.11 N	14.13 E
Guardia Sanframondi	184	41.15 N	14.36 E
Guardiato ≃	168	38.20 N	5.22 W
Guardo	168	42.47 N	4.50 W
Guardunha, Serra da ⛰	168	40.05 N	7.31 W
Guareí ≃	296	22.40 S	53.34 W
Guareim (Quaraí) ≃	294	30.12 S	57.36 W
Guareña	168	38.51 N	6.06 W
Guareña ≃	168	41.29 N	5.23 W
Guarenas	290	10.28 N	66.37 W
Guaribe ≃, Bra.	292	7.41 S	60.18 W
Guaribe ≃, Ven.	290	9.53 N	65.11 W
Guarichapo ≃	290	7.27 N	62.03 W
Guarico	290	9.32 N	69.48 W
Guárico □[3]	290	8.40 N	66.35 W
Guárico ≃	290	7.55 N	67.23 W
Guárico, Embalse de ⊜[1]	290	9.05 N	67.25 W
Guarico, Punta ≻	284p	20.37 N	74.44 W
Guarizama	280	14.55 N	86.20 W
Guarulhos	296	23.28 S	46.32 W
Guarunta, Laguna ⊜	280	15.22 N	84.11 W
Guarus	296	21:44 S	41.20 W
Guasare ≃	290	11.03 N	72.02 W
Guasave	278	25.34 N	108.27 W
Guascama, Punta ≻	290	2.32 N	78.24 W
Guasdualito	290	7.15 N	70.44 W
Guasipati	290	7.28 N	61.54 W
Guastalla	170	44.55 N	10.39 E
Guatajiagua	280	13.40 N	88.13 W
Guatemala	280	14.38 N	90.31 W
Guatemala □[5]	280	14.40 N	90.30 W
Guatemala □[1]	276	15.30 N	90.15 W
Guateque	290	5.00 N	73.28 W
Guatimozín	294	33.30 S	62.20 W
Guatire	290	10.28 N	66.32 W
Guatopo, Parque Nacional ♠	290	10.05 N	66.25 W
Guatraché	294	37.40 S	63.32 W
Guaviare ≃	290	4.03 N	67.44 W
Guavio ≃	290	4.44 N	73.03 W
Guaxupé	296	21.18 S	46.42 W
Guayabal, Cuba	284p	20.42 N	77.36 W
Guayabal, Ven.	290	8.00 N	67.24 W
Guayabero ≃	290	2.36 N	72.47 W
Guayabo	278	26.00 N	107.26 W
Guayacán	294	29.58 S	71.22 W
Guayaguayare	285r	10.08 N	61.02 W
Guayama	284m	17.59 N	66.07 W
Guayambre ≃	280	14.26 N	85.58 W
Guayanilla	284m	18.01 N	66.47 W
Guayape	280	14.45 N	86.52 W
Guayape ≃	280	14.26 N	85.58 W
Guayapo ≃	290	4.30 N	67.35 W
Guayaquil	290	2.10 S	79.50 W
Guayaquil, Golfo de C	290	3.00 S	80.30 W
Guayas □[4]	290	2.00 S	80.00 W
Guayas ≃, Col.	290	1.23 N	74.50 W
Guayas ≃, Ec.	290	2.36 S	79.52 W
Guaycora	278	28.50 N	109.21 W
Guaymallén	294	32.54 S	68.47 W
Guaymas	278	27.56 N	110.54 W
Guaymoreto, Laguna de C	280	15.58 N	85.55 W
Guaynabo	284m	18.22 N	66.07 W
Guayquiraró ≃	294	30.25 S	59.36 W
Guayuriba ≃	290	3.55 N	73.05 W
Guazacapán	280	14.04 N	90.25 W
Guazapares	278	27.22 N	108.15 W
Guazárachic	278	26.57 N	106.43 W
Gubacha	158	58.52 N	57.36 E
Gubat	202	12.55 N	124.07 E
Gubbio	184	43.21 N	12.35 E
Gubin	164	51.56 N	14.45 E
Gubkin	158	51.18 N	37.32 E
Gúdar, Sierra de ⛰	168	40.27 N	0.42 W
Gudermes	158	43.20 N	46.08 E
Guebwiller (Gebweiler)	180	47.55 N	7.12 E
Guecho	168	43.22 N	3.01 W
Guéckédou □[4]	222	8.40 N	10.15 W
Guéguen, Lac ⊜	244	48.06 N	77.15 W
Güejar ≃	290	2.55 N	73.14 W
Guelma	170	36.28 N	7.26 E
Guelph	264	43.33 N	80.15 W
Guéméné-sur-Scorff	166	48.04 N	3.12 W
Guer	162	47.54 N	2.07 W
Güera	214	20.48 N	17.08 W
Guérande	166	47.20 N	2.26 W
Güere ≃	290	9.50 N	65.08 W
Guéret	166	46.10 N	1.52 E
Guerla Mandatashan ▲	206	30.26 N	81.20 E
Guerneville	258	38.30 N	123.00 W
Guernica y Luno	168	43.19 N	2.41 W
Guernsey, Ohio, U.S.	266	40.11 N	81.36 W
Guernsey, Wyo., U.S.	254	42.16 N	104.45 W
Guernsey □[6]	266	40.08 N	81.30 W
Guernsey □[2]	158	49.28 N	2.35 W
Guernsey I	166	49.27 N	2.35 W
Guernsey Reservoir ⊜[1]	254	42.19 N	104.48 W
Guerra	250	26.53 N	98.54 W
Guerrero	250	28.20 N	100.23 W
Guerrero □[3]	278	17.40 N	100.00 W
Gueydan	248	30.02 N	92.30 W
Guga	186	52.43 N	137.35 E
Guge ▲	214	6.10 N	37.26 E
Guglionesi	184	41.55 N	14.55 E
Guguan I	198	17.19 N	145.51 E
Guia	292	15.22 S	56.14 W
Guia Lopes	296	20.15 S	46.22 W
Guia Lopes da Laguna	292	21.26 S	56.07 W
Guiana Basin •-[1]	148	10.00 N	50.00 W
Guibes	218	26.41 S	16.42 E
Güicán	290	6.28 N	72.25 W
Guichen	166	47.58 N	1.48 W
Guichón	294	32.21 S	57.12 W
Guide	190	36.03 N	101.28 E
Guide Rock	252	40.04 N	98.20 W
Guiding	200	26.28 N	107.07 E
Guidonia	184	42.01 N	12.45 E
Guiers, Lac de ⊜	222	16.12 N	15.50 W
Guiglo □[5]	222	6.20 N	7.45 W
Guihulngan	202	10.07 N	123.16 E
Güija, Lago de ⊜	280	14.16 N	89.31 W
Guijalo	202	13.44 N	123.52 E
Guijuelo	168	40.33 N	5.40 W
Guildford	174	51.14 N	0.35 W
Guildhall	242	44.34 N	71.34 W
Guilford, Conn., U.S.	261	41.17 N	72.41 W
Guilford, Maine, U.S.	242	45.14 N	69.29 W
Guilford College	246	36.05 N	79.53 W
Guilford Courthouse National Military Park ♠	246	36.01 N	79.45 W
Guilin (Kweilin)	200	25.11 N	110.09 E
Guillaumes	166	44.05 N	6.51 E
Guillestre	166	44.40 N	6.39 E
Guilvinec	166	47.47 N	4.17 W
Guimarães	168	41.27 N	8.18 W
Guimaras Island I	202	10.35 N	122.37 E
Guimaras Strait ⋃	202	10.46 N	122.50 E
Guimba	202	15.40 N	120.46 E
Guimbal	202	10.40 N	122.20 E
Guimuzhang ▲	196	24.40 N	116.48 E
Guin	248	33.58 N	87.55 W
Güina	280	14.04 N	85.22 W
Guinayangan	202	13.54 N	122.27 E
Guinda	272	38.50 N	122.12 W
Guindulman	202	9.46 N	124.30 E
Guindulman Bay C	202	9.42 N	124.30 E
Guinea □[1]	214	11.00 N	10.00 W
Guinea, Gulf of C	214	2.00 N	2.30 E
Guinea Basin •-[1]	148	3.00 S	0.30 W
Guinea Rise •-[3]	148	3.00 S	0.30 W
Guinecourt, Lac ⊜	240	50.55 N	69.16 W
Güines, Cuba	284p	22.50 N	82.02 W
Guînes, Fr.	166	50.52 N	1.52 E
Guingamp	166	48.33 N	3.11 W
Guinobatan	202	13.11 N	123.36 E
Güinope	280	13.51 N	86.55 W
Guintacan Island I	202	11.18 N	123.54 E
Guintinguintin, Mount ▲	202	12.25 N	122.24 E
Guiones, Punta ≻	280	9.54 N	85.41 W
Guiong	202	6.25 N	122.01 E
Guiping	200	23.20 N	110.09 E
Guipúzcoa	168	43.10 N	2.10 W
Güira de Melena	284p	22.48 N	82.30 W
Guiratinga	296	16.21 S	53.45 W
Güiria	290	10.34 N	62.18 W
Guiricema	296	21.00 S	42.43 W
Guise	176	49.54 N	3.38 E
Guishui ≃	196	28.27 N	112.47 E
Guisijan	202	11.05 N	122.03 E
Güisisil, Cerro ▲	280	12.37 N	86.13 W
Guitinua Island I	202	14.25 N	122.58 E
Guitiriz	168	43.11 N	7.54 W
Guitres	166	45.03 N	0.11 W
Guiuan	202	11.02 N	125.44 E
Guixian	200	23.06 N	109.39 E
Guiyang (Kweiyang)	200	26.35 N	106.43 E
Güiza ≃	290	1.22 N	78.36 W
Guizhou □[4]	190	27.00 N	107.00 E
Gujarat □[3]	206	22.00 N	72.00 E
Gujrānwāla	206	32.26 N	74.33 E
Gujrāt	206	32.34 N	74.05 E
Gul'ajevskije Koški, Ostrova II	160	68.55 N	55.10 E
Gulangyu I	196	24.28 N	118.04 E
Gulbene	160	57.11 N	26.45 E
Gulf Hammock	246	29.15 N	82.43 W
Gulf of Alaska Seamount Province	148	55.00 N	144.00 W
Gulfport, Fla., U.S.	246	27.44 N	82.43 W
Gulfport, Miss., U.S.	248	30.22 N	89.06 W
Gulf Shores	248	30.17 N	87.41 W
Gulistan	186	40.30 N	68.46 E
Guljanci	172	43.38 N	24.42 E
Gulkana	236	62.16 N	145.23 W
Gullfoss L	160a	64.24 N	20.08 W
Gull Lake	232	50.08 N	108.27 W
Gull Lake ⊜	238	52.35 N	114.00 W
Güllü Dağı ▲	212	41.21 N	42.10 E
Güllük	172	37.14 N	27.36 E
Gülpınar	172	39.32 N	26.07 E
Gulu	214	2.47 N	32.18 E
Gumaca	202	13.55 N	122.06 E
Gumahang	202	12.35 N	122.16 E
Gumal ≃	206	31.56 N	70.22 E
Gumbinnen → Gusev	164	54.36 N	22.12 E
Gumel	222	12.39 N	9.22 E
Gumma □[5]	192	36.30 N	139.00 E
Gummersbach	164	51.02 N	7.34 E
Gummi	222	12.09 N	5.09 E
Gümüşhane	208	40.27 N	39.29 E
Gundagai	226	35.04 S	148.07 E
Güney	172	38.09 N	29.05 E
Gungu	218	5.44 S	19.19 E
Gunisao ≃	232	53.54 N	97.58 W
Gunnar	232	59.23 N	108.53 W
Gunnarn	160	65.00 N	17.40 E
Gunnbjørns Fjeld ▲	148	68.55 N	29.53 W
Gunnedah	228	30.59 S	150.15 E
Gunnison, Colo., U.S.	254	38.33 N	106.56 W
Gunnison, Utah, U.S.	254	39.09 N	111.49 W
Gunnison ≃	254	39.03 N	108.35 W
Guntersville	248	34.21 N	86.18 W
Guntersville Lake ⊜[1]	248	34.45 N	86.03 W
Guntramsdorf	164	48.03 N	16.19 E
Gunungsitoli	200	1.17 N	97.37 E
Günzburg	180	48.27 N	10.16 E
Gunzenhausen	164	49.07 N	10.45 E
Guohe ≃	196	32.57 N	117.14 E
Gu Oidak Wash ∨	254	31.57 N	112.21 W
Gura	160	57.18 N	51.25 E
Gura, Wādī ∨	220	17.28 N	35.10 E
Gurahonț	172	46.16 N	22.21 E
Gura Humorului	172	47.33 N	25.48 E
Gurara ≃	222	8.12 N	6.41 E
Gurdon	248	33.55 N	93.09 W
Güre	172	38.39 N	29.10 E
Gurgei, Jabal ▲	220	13.50 N	24.19 E
Gurghiului, Munții ⛰	172	46.41 N	25.12 E
Gurjev	158	47.07 N	51.56 E
Gurjevsk	186	54.17 N	85.56 E
Gurjevsk [Neuhausen]	164	54.47 N	20.38 E
Gurk ≃	170	46.36 N	14.31 E
Gurkha	190	28.01 N	84.38 E
Gurla Mandhata → Guerla Mandatashan ▲	206	30.26 N	81.20 E
Gurnee	268	42.22 N	87.55 W
Gürsu	172	40.13 N	29.12 E
Gurupá	286	1.25 S	51.39 W
Gurupi	286	11.43 S	49.04 W
Guru Sikhar ▲	206	24.45 N	72.45 E
Gurvan Sajchan Uul ⛰	190	43.50 N	103.30 E
Gusau	222	12.12 N	6.40 E
Gus'-Chrustal'nyj	160	55.37 N	40.40 E
Gusev	160	54.36 N	22.12 E
Gusev [Gumbinnen]	164	54.36 N	22.12 E
Gushan ▲	196	26.05 N	119.22 E
Gushi	196	32.12 N	115.41 E
Gushikawa	193b	26.21 N	127.52 E
Gusi	202	6.07 N	117.09 E
Gusinoozersk	186	51.17 N	106.30 E
Guspini	170	39.32 N	8.38 E
Güssing	164	47.04 N	16.20 E
Gustav Holm, Kap ≻	232	67.00 N	34.00 W
Gustavus	236	58.25 N	135.44 W
Gustine, Calif., U.S.	272	37.16 N	121.00 W
Gustine, Tex., U.S.	250	31.51 N	98.24 W
Gustorf	178	51.04 N	6.34 E
Güstrow	164	53.48 N	12.10 E
Gütersloh	178	51.54 N	8.23 E
Guthrie, Ky., U.S.	248	36.39 N	87.10 W
Guthrie, Okla., U.S.	250	35.53 N	97.25 W
Guthrie, Tex., U.S.	250	33.37 N	100.19 W
Guthrie Center	252	41.41 N	94.30 W
Gutian	190	26.36 N	118.46 E
Gutianxi ≃	196	26.22 N	118.42 E
Gutiérrez	292	19.25 S	63.34 W
Gutiérrez Zamora	278	20.27 N	97.05 W
Guttenberg	244	42.47 N	91.06 W
Guyana □[1]	286	5.00 N	59.00 W
Guyenne □[9]	166	44.30 N	1.00 E
Guymon	250	36.41 N	101.29 W
Guyot, Mount ▲	246	35.42 N	83.15 W
Guysborough	240	45.23 N	61.30 W
Guys Mills	266	41.38 N	79.59 W
Guyton	246	32.20 N	81.24 W
Guyuan	190	35.58 N	106.45 E
Guzar	186	38.36 N	66.15 E
Güzelbahçe	172	38.21 N	26.54 E
Guzmán	278	31.13 N	107.27 W
Guzmán, Laguna de ⊜	278	31.25 N	107.25 W
Gvardejsk (Tapiau)	164	54.39 N	21.05 E
Gwadabawa	222	13.20 N	5.15 E
Gwādar	208	25.07 N	62.19 E
Gwai	218	19.15 S	27.42 E
Gwai ≃	224	17.59 S	26.52 E
Gwalior	206	26.13 N	78.10 E
Gwanda	224	20.57 S	29.01 E
Gwātar Bay C	208	25.04 N	61.36 E
Gwda ≃	164	53.04 N	16.44 E
Gweebarra Bay C	162	54.52 N	8.20 W
Gweedore	162	55.03 N	8.14 W
Gwelo	224	19.27 S	29.49 E
Gwelo ≃	224	18.45 S	28.36 E
Gwinn	244	46.17 N	87.26 W
Gwydir ≃	228	29.27 S	149.48 E
Gwynn	262	37.30 N	76.17 W
Gyda	186	70.52 N	78.30 E
Gydanskaja Guba C	186	71.20 N	76.30 E
Gydanskij Poluostrov ≻[1]	186	70.50 N	79.00 E
Gy [les-Nonains]	166	47.24 N	5.49 E
Gympie	228	26.11 S	152.40 E
Gyoma	164	46.56 N	20.50 E
Gyöngyös	164	47.47 N	19.56 E
Győr	164	47.42 N	17.38 E
Győr-Sopron □[6]	164	47.35 N	17.15 E
Gypsum, Colo., U.S.	254	39.39 N	106.57 W
Gypsum, Kans., U.S.	252	38.42 N	97.26 W
Gypsum, Ohio, U.S.	266	41.30 N	82.52 W
Gypsum Hills ⛰[2]	250	36.25 N	99.20 W
Gypsum Point ≻	232	61.53 N	114.35 W
Gyula	164	46.39 N	21.17 E
H			
Haag in Oberbayern	164	48.10 N	12.11 E
Haaksbergen	178	52.09 N	6.44 E
Haaltert	176	50.54 N	4.00 E
Haan	178	51.11 N	7.00 E
Haapajärvi	160	63.45 N	25.20 E
Haapamäki	160	62.15 N	24.28 E
Haapsalu	160	58.56 N	23.33 E
Haar	164	48.06 N	11.44 E
Haarlem	178	52.23 N	4.38 E
Haast ≃	230	43.50 S	169.02 E
Haast Pass)(	230	44.07 S	169.21 E
Hab ≃	206	24.53 N	66.41 E
Ḥabbānīyah, Hawr al- ⊜	208	33.17 N	43.29 E
Habersham	246	34.36 N	83.34 W
Habob, Wādī ∨	220	18.07 N	35.01 E
Haboro	192a	44.22 N	141.42 E
Hache, Lac la ⊜	238	51.50 N	121.30 W
Hachef, Oued ≃	168	35.32 N	5.52 W
Hachijō-jima I	190	33.05 N	139.48 E
Hachiman	192	35.45 N	136.57 E
Hachinohe	192	40.30 N	141.29 E
Hachiōji	192	35.39 N	139.20 E
Hachita	254	31.55 N	108.19 W
Hacienda Heights	274	33.58 N	117.58 W
Hacienda Miravalles	280	10.41 N	85.14 W
Hackberry, Ariz., U.S.	254	35.22 N	113.44 W
Hackberry, La., U.S.	248	29.59 N	93.21 W
Hackensack	242	40.53 N	74.03 W
Hackett	248	35.11 N	94.25 W
Hackettstown	242	40.51 N	74.50 W
Hackleburg	248	34.17 N	87.50 W
Hackney •-[8]	174	51.33 N	0.03 W
Hack Point	262	39.28 N	75.53 W
Haçlı Gölü ⊜	212	39.00 N	42.18 E
Haçreş Dağları ⛰	212	38.38 N	41.37 E
Ḥadāribah, Ra's al- ≻	220	22.04 N	36.54 E
HaDarom □[5]	210	31.05 N	34.50 E
Ḥadd, Ra's al- ≻	204	22.32 N	59.48 E
Haddam, Conn., U.S.	261	41.29 N	72.31 W
Haddam, Kans., U.S.	252	39.51 N	97.18 W
Haddington	162	55.58 N	2.47 W
Haddock	246	33.02 N	83.26 W
Haddonfield	262	39.54 N	75.02 W
Haddon Heights	262	39.52 N	75.02 W
Hadejia	222	12.30 N	9.59 E
Hadejia ≃	214	12.50 N	10.51 E
Hadera	210	32.26 N	34.55 E
Haderslev	160	55.15 N	9.30 E
Hadīyah	214	25.34 N	38.41 E
Hadjout	168	36.31 N	2.25 E
Hadley, Mass., U.S.	261	42.21 N	72.35 W
Hadley, Pa., U.S.	266	41.25 N	80.14 W
Hadley Bay C	232	72.30 N	107.45 W
Hadlock	256	48.02 N	122.46 W
Hadlyme	261	41.25 N	72.25 W
Ha-dong	200	20.58 N	105.46 E
Ḥaḍramawt •-[1]	214	15.00 N	50.00 E
Hadrian's Wall ⊥	162	54.59 N	2.26 W
Hadsund	160	56.43 N	10.07 E
Ḥadūr Shu'ayb ▲	204	15.20 N	43.55 E
Haeju	194	38.02 N	125.42 E
Haena	275b	22.14 N	159.34 W
Haerbin	190	45.45 N	126.41 E
Haffouz	170	35.38 N	9.41 E
Ḥafīra, Qā' al- ≍	208	31.05 N	36.13 E
Ḥafīt, Jabal ▲	208	24.03 N	55.46 E
Hafnarfjörður	160a	64.03 N	21.56 W
Haft Gel	204	31.27 N	49.27 E
Hafun, Ras ≻	214	10.27 N	51.26 E
HaGalil •-[1]	210	32.55 N	35.18 E
Hagan	246	32.09 N	81.56 W
Hagar Shores	268	42.13 N	86.22 W
Hagemeister Island I	236	58.40 N	161.00 W
Hagen	178	51.22 N	7.28 E
Hagenow	164	53.26 N	11.11 E
Hagensborg	238	52.23 N	126.33 W
Hagerman, Idaho, U.S.	256	42.49 N	114.54 W
Hagerman, N. Mex., U.S.	250	33.07 N	104.20 W
Hagerstown, Ind., U.S.	248	39.55 N	85.10 W
Hagerstown, Md., U.S.	242	39.39 N	77.43 W
Hagersville	264	42.58 N	80.03 W
Hagetmau	166	43.40 N	0.35 W
Hagfors	160	60.02 N	13.42 E
Haggin, Mount ▲	256	46.05 N	113.05 W
Hagi	192	34.24 N	131.25 E
Ha-giang	200	22.50 N	104.59 E
Hagondange	166	49.15 N	6.10 E
Hags Head ≻	162	52.57 N	9.30 W
Hague	252	46.02 N	99.59 W
Hague, Cap de la ≻	166	49.43 N	1.57 W
Haguenau	166	48.49 N	7.47 E
Hagues Peak ▲	254	40.29 N	105.38 W
Hahira	246	30.57 N	83.22 W
Haho ≃	222	6.17 N	1.23 E
Haian	196	32.34 N	120.28 E
Haianshan ⛰	196	22.40 N	114.20 E
Haian Shanmo ⛰	196	23.25 N	121.25 E
Haicheng	194	40.52 N	122.45 E
Haïdra	170	35.34 N	8.27 E
Hai-duong	200	20.56 N	106.19 E
Haifa → Hefa	210	32.49 N	35.00 E
Haifa, Bay of → Hefa, Mifraz C	210	32.52 N	35.02 E
Haig	226	31.01 S	126.05 E
Haig, Mount ▲	238	49.17 N	114.29 W
Haigler	252	40.01 N	101.56 W
Haikang (Leizhou)	200	20.56 N	110.04 E
Haikou	200	20.06 N	110.21 E
Haiku	275a	20.55 N	156.20 W
Ḥā'il	208	27.33 N	41.42 E
Hailaer	190	49.12 N	119.42 E
Hailaerhe ≃	190	49.35 N	117.55 E
Hailesboro	264	44.18 N	75.27 W
Hailey	256	43.31 N	114.19 W
Haillicourt	176	50.28 N	2.35 E
Hailun	190	47.28 N	126.58 E
Hailuoto I	160	65.02 N	24.42 E
Haimen, Zhg.	196	23.14 N	116.38 E
Haimen, Zhg.	196	28.41 N	121.27 E
Haimenwan C	196	23.09 N	116.34 E
Hainan → Hainandao I	200	19.00 N	109.30 E
Hainandao I	200	19.00 N	109.30 E
Hainaut □[4]	176	50.30 N	3.50 E
Hainburg an der Donau	164	48.09 N	16.57 E
Haines, Alaska, U.S.	236	59.15 N	135.25 W
Haines, Oreg., U.S.	256	44.55 N	117.56 W
Haines City	246	28.07 N	81.37 W
Haines Junction	236	60.45 N	137.30 W
Hainesport	262	39.59 N	74.50 W
Hainfeld	164	48.02 N	15.46 E
Haining	196	30.25 N	120.32 E
Hai-phong	200	20.52 N	106.41 E
Haitandao I	196	25.33 N	119.48 E
Haitanxia ⋃	196	25.27 N	119.38 E
Haiyangdao I	194	39.02 N	123.14 E
Hajdú-Bihar □[6]	164	47.25 N	21.30 E
Hajdúböszörmény	164	47.41 N	21.30 E
Hajdúnánás	164	47.51 N	21.26 E
Hajdúszoboszló	164	47.27 N	21.24 E
Hajeb el Aïoun	170	35.24 N	9.33 E
Hajiki-saki ≻	192	38.19 N	138.31 E
Hajnówka	164	52.45 N	23.36 E
Hakataramea ≃	230	44.43 S	170.29 E
Hakken-san ▲	192	34.10 N	135.54 E
Hakkōda-san ▲	192	40.40 N	140.53 E
Hako-dake ▲	192a	44.40 N	142.25 E
Hakodate	192a	41.45 N	140.43 E
Hakone-yama ▲	192	35.14 N	139.02 E
Hakskeenpan ⊜	224	26.48 S	20.12 E
Hakui	192	36.53 N	136.47 E
Haku-san-kokuritsu-kōen ♠	192	36.12 N	136.47 E
Ḥalab (Aleppo)	212	36.12 N	37.10 E
Ḥalab □[8]	212	36.00 N	37.00 E
Halachó	278	20.29 N	90.05 W
Ḥalā'ib	214	22.13 N	36.38 E
Halaula	275d	20.14 N	155.46 W
Halawa, Cape ≻	275d	21.10 N	156.43 W
Halawa Heights	275c	21.23 N	157.55 W
Halberstadt	164	51.54 N	11.02 E
Halbrite	252	49.20 N	103.32 W
Halcon, Mount ▲	202	13.15 N	121.00 E
Halden	160	59.09 N	11.23 E
Haldensleben	164	52.18 N	11.26 E
Haldimand □[6]	264	42.57 N	79.50 W
Hale	248	39.36 N	93.20 W
Haleakala National Park ♠	275d	20.44 N	156.13 W
Hale Center	250	34.04 N	101.51 W
Haleiwa	275c	21.35 N	158.07 W
Halenkov	164	49.19 N	18.08 E
Hales Corners	268	42.56 N	88.03 W
Halesite	261	40.52 N	73.25 W
Halesowen	174	52.26 N	2.05 W
Halethorpe	242	39.15 N	76.41 W
Haleyville	248	34.14 N	87.37 W
Halfaya Pass → Ḥalfāyah, Naqb al-)(	220	31.30 N	25.11 E
Ḥalfāyah, Naqb al- (Halfaya Pass))(	220	31.30 N	25.11 E
Halfmoon Bay, B.C., Can.	238	49.31 N	123.54 W
Half Moon Bay, Calif., U.S.	272	37.28 N	122.26 W
Halfway, Md., U.S.	242	39.37 N	77.46 W
Halfway, Oreg., U.S.	256	44.53 N	117.07 W
Halfway ≃	232	56.10 N	121.35 W
Haliburton	264	45.03 N	78.03 W
Haliburton □[6]	264	44.10 N	78.30 W
Halifax, N.S., Can.	240	44.39 N	63.36 W
Halifax, Eng., U.K.	162	53.44 N	1.52 W
Halifax, Mass., U.S.	261	41.59 N	70.52 W
Halifax, N.C., U.S.	246	36.20 N	77.35 W
Halifax, Pa., U.S.	262	40.28 N	76.56 W
Halifax, Va., U.S.	246	36.46 N	78.56 W
Halifax Bay C	228	18.50 S	146.30 E
Halifax Citadel National Historic Park ♠	240	44.40 N	63.36 W
Halifax Harbour C	240	44.35 N	63.31 W
Haliimaile	275a	20.52 N	156.20 W
Halīl ≃	208	27.28 N	58.44 E
Halkett, Cape ≻	236	70.49 N	152.12 W
Halkirk	162	58.30 N	3.30 W
Hall	264	42.48 N	77.04 W
Hallam Peak ▲	238	52.11 N	118.46 W
Hallandale	246	25.59 N	80.09 W
Hallands Län □[6]	160	56.45 N	13.00 E
Halla-san ▲	190	33.22 N	126.32 E
Halle, Bel.	176	50.44 N	4.13 E
Halle, B.R.D.	178	52.04 N	8.22 E
Halle, D.D.R.	164	51.29 N	11.58 E
Hällefors	160	59.47 N	14.30 E
Hallein	164	47.41 N	13.06 E
Hallettsville	250	29.27 N	96.56 W
Halliday	252	47.21 N	102.20 W
Halligen II	164	54.35 N	8.35 E
Hall Island I	236	60.40 N	173.05 W
Hall Lake ⊜	232	68.41 N	82.17 W
Hall Mountain ▲	256	48.49 N	117.15 W
Hällnäs	160	64.19 N	19.38 E
Hallock	252	48.47 N	96.57 W
Hallowell	242	44.17 N	69.48 W
Hall Peninsula ≻[1]	232	63.30 N	66.00 W
Halls	248	35.53 N	89.24 W
Hallsberg	160	59.04 N	15.07 E
Halls Creek	226	18.13 S	127.40 E
Hallstahammar	160	59.37 N	16.13 E
Hallstatt	164	47.33 N	13.39 E
Hallstavik	160	60.03 N	18.36 E
Hallstead	242	41.58 N	75.45 W
Hall Summit	248	32.11 N	93.18 W
Hallsville	248	32.30 N	94.34 W
Halluin	176	50.47 N	3.08 E
Hallwood	262	37.53 N	75.35 W
Halmahera I	198	1.00 N	128.00 E
Halmahera, Laut ⚲[2]	198	1.00 S	129.00 E
Halmahera Sea → Halmahera, Laut ⚲[2]	198	1.00 S	129.00 E
Halmstad	160	56.39 N	12.50 E
Halsey, Nebr., U.S.	252	41.54 N	100.16 W
Halsey, Oreg., U.S.	256	44.23 N	123.07 W
Halsey Harbor C	202	11.45 N	119.57 E
Hälsingborg	160	56.03 N	12.42 E
Halstad	252	47.21 N	96.50 W
Halstead, Eng., U.K.	174	51.57 N	0.38 E
Halstead, Kans., U.S.	252	38.00 N	97.30 W
Halstenbek	178	53.38 N	9.50 E
Halteman Village	268	40.14 N	85.24 W
Haltern	178	51.46 N	7.10 E
Haltiatunturi ▲	160	69.18 N	21.16 E
Haltom City	250	32.48 N	97.16 W
Halton □[6]	264	43.30 N	79.53 W
Haltwhistle	162	54.58 N	2.27 W
Halver	178	51.11 N	7.30 E
Halvorson, Mount ▲	238	53.15 N	120.33 W
Hamaca ≃	280	14.13 N	85.14 W
Hamada	192	34.53 N	132.05 E
Hamadān	208	34.48 N	48.30 E
Hamadān □[8]	208	35.00 N	48.40 E
Ḥamāh	212	35.08 N	36.45 E
Ḥamāh □[8]	212	35.10 N	37.00 E
Hamamatsu	192	34.42 N	137.44 E
Hamanaka	192a	43.05 N	145.10 E
Hamana-ko ⊜	192	34.45 N	137.34 E
Hamar	160	60.48 N	11.06 E
Ḥamāṭah, Jabal ▲	220	24.12 N	35.00 E
Hama-tombetsu	192a	45.07 N	142.23 E
Hambaek-san ▲	194	37.09 N	128.55 E
Hambridge National Park ♠	228	33.25 S	136.00 E
Hamburg, B.R.D.	178	53.33 N	9.59 E
Hamburg, Ark., U.S.	248	33.14 N	91.48 W
Hamburg, Conn., U.S.	261	41.23 N	72.21 W
Hamburg, Iowa, U.S.	252	40.36 N	95.39 W
Hamburg, Mich., U.S.	268	42.27 N	83.48 W
Hamburg, N.J., U.S.	242	41.09 N	74.35 W
Hamburg, N.Y., U.S.	264	42.43 N	78.50 W
Hamburg, Pa., U.S.	262	40.34 N	75.59 W
Hamburg □[3]	178	53.35 N	10.00 E
Ḥamḍ, Wādī al- ∨	208	25.54 N	36.38 E
Hamdamao, Dasht-i- •-[2]	208	34.30 N	61.40 E
Hamden, Conn., U.S.	261	41.21 N	72.56 W
Hamden, Ohio, U.S.	242	39.10 N	82.32 W
Hämeen lääni □[4]	160	61.30 N	24.30 E
Hämeenlinna	160	61.00 N	24.27 E
Hameln	178	52.06 N	9.21 E
HaMerkaz □[5]	210	32.15 N	34.55 E
Hamgyŏng Namdo □[4]	194	40.00 N	127.30 E
Hamgyŏng-pukdo □[4]	194	41.45 N	129.50 E
Hamgyŏng-sanmaek ⛰	194	41.50 N	128.30 E
Hamhŭng	194	39.54 N	127.32 E
Hami	190	42.47 N	93.32 E
Hamidiye	172	41.09 N	26.40 E
Hamiguitan, Mount ▲	202	6.45 N	126.11 E
Hamilton, Austl.	228	37.45 S	142.02 E
Hamilton, Ber.	284a	32.17 N	64.46 W
Hamilton, Ont., Can.	264	43.15 N	79.51 W
Hamilton, N.Z.	230	37.47 S	175.17 E
Hamilton, Scot., U.K.	162	55.47 N	4.03 W
Hamilton, Ala., U.S.	248	34.09 N	88.06 W
Hamilton, Alaska, U.S.	236	62.54 N	163.53 W
Hamilton, Ga., U.S.	246	32.45 N	84.53 W
Hamilton, Ill., U.S.	244	40.24 N	91.21 W
Hamilton, Ind., U.S.	268	41.32 N	84.55 W
Hamilton, Kans., U.S.	252	37.59 N	96.10 W
Hamilton, Mass., U.S.	261	42.37 N	70.52 W
Hamilton, Mich., U.S.	268	42.41 N	86.00 W
Hamilton, Mo., U.S.	248	39.45 N	94.01 W
Hamilton, Mont., U.S.	256	46.15 N	114.09 W
Hamilton, N.C., U.S.	246	35.57 N	77.12 W
Hamilton, N.Y., U.S.	264	42.50 N	75.33 W
Hamilton, Ohio, U.S.	242	39.26 N	84.30 W
Hamilton, R.I., U.S.	261	41.33 N	71.26 W
Hamilton, Tex., U.S.	250	31.42 N	98.07 W
Hamilton, Wash., U.S.	270	48.31 N	121.59 W
Hamilton ≃	228	23.30 S	139.47 E
Hamilton, Lake ⊜[1]	248	34.30 N	93.05 W
Hamilton, Mount ▲, Alaska, U.S.	236	61.10 N	159.46 W
Hamilton, Mount ▲, Calif., U.S.	258	37.21 N	121.38 W
Hamilton, Mount ▲, Nev., U.S.	258	39.14 N	115.32 W
Hamilton Acres	236	64.51 N	147.40 W
Hamilton City	258	39.45 N	122.01 W
Hamilton Creek Indian Reserve •-[4]	238	50.11 N	120.30 W
Hamilton Dome	254	43.46 N	108.34 W
Hamilton Inlet C	232	54.00 N	57.30 W
Hamilton Mountain ▲	242	43.25 N	74.22 W
Hamilton Park, Ind., U.S.	268	40.17 N	85.19 W
Hamilton Park, Pa., U.S.	262	40.02 N	76.20 W
Hamilton Sound ⋃	240	49.30 N	54.30 W
Ḥamīm, Wādī al- ∨	220	30.10 N	21.32 E
Hamina	160	60.34 N	27.12 E
Ḥamir, Wādī ∨	208	31.37 N	42.12 E
Hamler	268	41.14 N	84.02 W
Hamlet, Ind., U.S.	268	41.23 N	86.35 W
Hamlet, N.C., U.S.	246	34.53 N	79.42 W
Hamlet, Mount ▲	236	68.47 N	165.57 W
Hamlin, N.Y., U.S.	264	43.18 N	77.55 W
Hamlin, Tex., U.S.	250	32.53 N	100.08 W
Hamlin, W. Va., U.S.	242	38.17 N	82.06 W
Hamlin Lake ⊜	244	44.03 N	86.27 W
Hamlin Valley Wash ∨	254	38.53 N	114.01 W
Hamm, B.R.D.	178	51.41 N	7.49 E
Hamm, B.R.D.	178	51.43 N	7.10 E
Hammamet	170	36.24 N	10.37 E
Hammamet, Golfe de C	170	36.05 N	10.40 E
Hammam Lif	170	36.44 N	10.20 E
Ḥammār, Hawr al- ⊜	208	30.50 N	47.10 E
Hamme	176	51.06 N	4.08 E
Hammelburg	164	50.07 N	9.53 E
Hammerdal	160	63.36 N	15.21 E
Hammerfest	160	70.40 N	23.42 E
Hammersmith •-[8]	174	51.30 N	0.14 W
Hammon	250	35.38 N	99.23 W
Hammond, Ind., U.S.	268	41.36 N	87.30 W
Hammond, La., U.S.	248	30.30 N	90.28 W
Hammond, N.Y., U.S.	264	44.27 N	75.42 W
Hammond, Oreg., U.S.	270	46.12 N	123.57 W
Hammond, Wis., U.S.	244	44.59 N	92.26 W
Hammondsport	242	42.25 N	77.13 W
Hammondsville	266	40.33 N	80.43 W
Hammonton	262	39.38 N	74.48 W
Hamningberg	160	70.31 N	30.29 E
Ham-Nord	260	45.54 N	71.39 W
Hamont	178	51.15 N	5.33 E
Hamoyet, Jabal ▲	220	17.33 N	38.00 E
Hampden, Newf., Can.	240	49.33 N	56.52 W
Hampden, Maine, U.S.	242	44.45 N	68.50 W
Hampden, Mass., U.S.	261	42.04 N	72.25 W
Hampden, N. Dak., U.S.	252	48.32 N	98.40 W
Hampden □[6]	261	42.07 N	72.36 W
Hampshire	268	42.06 N	88.32 W
Hampshire □[6], Eng., U.K.	174	51.05 N	1.15 W
Hampshire □[6], Mass., U.S.	261	42.19 N	72.38 W
Hampstead	246	34.22 N	77.49 W
Hampton, N.B., Can.	240	45.32 N	65.51 W
Hampton, Ont., Can.	264	43.58 N	78.45 W
Hampton, Ark., U.S.	248	33.32 N	92.28 W
Hampton, Conn., U.S.	261	41.47 N	72.03 W
Hampton, Fla., U.S.	246	29.52 N	82.07 W
Hampton, Ga., U.S.	246	33.23 N	84.17 W
Hampton, Iowa, U.S.	244	42.45 N	93.12 W
Hampton, Nebr., U.S.	252	40.53 N	97.53 W
Hampton, N.H., U.S.	242	42.56 N	70.50 W
Hampton, N.J., U.S.	262	40.42 N	74.58 W
Hampton, Pa., U.S.	262	39.56 N	77.04 W
Hampton, S.C., U.S.	246	32.52 N	81.07 W
Hampton, Va., U.S.	262	37.01 N	76.22 W

Symbols in the index entries are identified on page 360.

Name	Page	Lat°′	Long°′
Hampton Bays	261	40.53 N	72.31 W
Hampton Butte ∧	256	43.46 N	120.17 W
Hamra	160	61.39 N	15.00 E
Hamra, Saguia el ∨	214	27.15 N	13.21 W
Hams Fork ≃	254	41.35 N	109.59 W
Ham-Sud	260	45.46 N	71.36 W
Ham-tan	200	10.40 N	107.45 E
Hamtramck	268	42.24 N	83.03 W
Han, Nong ⊜	200	17.10 N	104.05 E
Hana	275a	20.45 N	155.59 W
Hanábana ≃	284p	22.20 N	81.01 W
Hanahan	246	32.55 N	80.00 W
Hanalei	275b	22.07 N	159.30 W
Hanamaki	192	39.23 N	141.07 E
Hanamaulu	275b	21.59 N	159.22 W
Hanang ∧	218	4.26 S	35.24 E
Hanapepe	275b	21.55 N	159.35 W
Hanau	164	50.08 N	8.55 E
Hanawa	192	40.11 N	140.47 E
Hanbury ≃	232	63.37 N	104.33 W
Hanceville, B.C., Can.	238	51.55 N	123.03 W
Hanceville, Ala., U.S.	248	34.04 N	86.46 W
Hancheng	190	35.29 N	110.25 E
Hancock, Md., U.S.	242	39.42 N	78.11 W
Hancock, Mich., U.S.	244	47.07 N	88.35 W
Hancock, Minn., U.S.	252	45.30 N	95.48 W
Hancock, N.Y., U.S.	242	41.57 N	75.17 W
Hancock, Wis., U.S.	244	44.08 N	89.31 W
Hancock □[6], Ohio, U.S.	268	41.02 N	83.39 W
Hancock □[6], W. Va., U.S.	266	40.30 N	80.33 W
Hancock, Lake ⊜	246	27.58 N	81.50 W
Hancocks Bridge	262	39.31 N	75.28 W
Handa	192	34.53 N	136.56 E
Handan	194	36.37 N	114.29 E
Handig Point ≻	202	10.48 N	125.42 E
Handlová	164	48.44 N	18.46 E
Hando	214	10.39 N	51.08 E
Handsboro	248	30.25 N	89.02 W
Handsworth	252	49.48 N	103.00 W
HaNegev ◆[1]	208	30.45 N	34.50 E
Haney	238	49.13 N	122.36 W
Hanford	272	36.20 N	119.39 W
Han-gang ≃	194	37.45 N	126.11 E
Hangchow → Hangzhou	196	30.15 N	120.10 E
Hangchow Bay → Hangzhouwan C	196	30.20 N	121.00 E
Hangjinhouqi	190	40.41 N	106.59 E
Hangjinqi	190	39.59 N	108.57 E
Hangklip, Kaap ≻	224	34.26 S	18.48 E
Hangö (Hanko)	160	59.50 N	22.57 E
Hangu	194	39.15 N	117.47 E
Hangzhou (Hangchow)	196	30.15 N	120.10 E
Hangzhouwan C	196	30.20 N	121.00 E
Hanjiang	196	25.30 N	119.06 E
Hanjiang ≃	196	23.41 N	116.38 E
Hankinson	252	46.04 N	96.54 W
Hankow → Wuhan	196	30.36 N	114.17 E
Hanmer	244	46.30 N	80.56 W
Hanna, Alta., Can.	238	51.38 N	111.54 W
Hanna, Ind., U.S.	268	41.25 N	86.47 W
Hanna, Okla., U.S.	250	35.12 N	95.53 W
Hanna, Wyo., U.S.	254	41.52 N	106.34 W
Hanna City	244	40.42 N	89.48 W
Hannaford	252	47.19 N	98.11 W
Hannah	252	48.58 N	98.42 W
Hannah Bay C	232	51.05 N	79.45 W
Hannastown	266	40.21 N	79.30 W
Hannibal, Mo., U.S.	248	39.42 N	91.22 W
Hannibal, N.Y., U.S.	264	43.19 N	76.35 W
Hannover	178	52.24 N	9.44 E
Hannover □[6]	178	52.30 N	9.00 E
Ha-noi	200	21.02 N	105.51 E
Hanover → Hannover, B.R.D.	178	52.24 N	9.44 E
Hanover, Ont., Can.	264	44.09 N	81.02 W
Hanover, Conn., U.S.	261	41.38 N	72.04 W
Hanover, Ill., U.S.	244	42.15 N	90.17 W
Hanover, Ind., U.S.	248	38.43 N	85.28 W
Hanover, Kans., U.S.	252	39.54 N	96.53 W
Hanover, Mass., U.S.	261	42.07 N	70.49 W
Hanover, Mich., U.S.	268	42.06 N	84.33 W
Hanover, N.H., U.S.	242	43.42 N	72.18 W
Hanover, Ohio, U.S.	266	40.04 N	82.15 W
Hanover, Pa., U.S.	262	39.48 N	76.59 W
Hanover, Va., U.S.	262	37.46 N	77.22 W
Hanover, Wis., U.S.	268	42.38 N	89.10 W
Hanover □[6]	262	37.42 N	77.20 W
Hanover Park	268	42.00 N	88.09 W
Hanoverton	266	40.45 N	80.56 W
Hansard	238	54.05 N	121.52 W
Hanshui ≃	196	30.35 N	114.17 E
Hanska	252	44.09 N	94.30 W
Hanson	261	42.05 N	70.53 W
Hanstholm	160	57.07 N	8.38 E
Hansville	270	47.55 N	122.33 W
Hantamsberg ⋀	224	31.22 S	19.45 E
Hant's Harbour	240	48.01 N	53.16 W
Hantsport	240	45.04 N	64.11 W
Hantzsch ≃	232	67.32 N	72.25 W
Hanušovce nad Topľou	164	49.02 N	21.30 E
Hanušovice	164	50.05 N	16.55 E
Hanzhong	190	32.59 N	107.11 E
Haoxi ≃	196	28.27 N	119.56 E
Haparanda	160	65.50 N	24.10 E
Hapeville	246	33.40 N	84.24 W
Happy	250	34.45 N	101.52 W
Happy Camp	258	41.48 N	123.22 W
Happy Jack	254	34.45 N	111.11 W
Hāpur	206	28.44 N	77.46 E
Haquira	292	14.14 S	72.12 W
Haranomachi	192	37.38 N	140.58 E
Harar → Harer	214	9.18 N	42.08 E
Ḥarash, Bi'r al- ⊤[4]	220	25.30 N	22.12 E
Harbert	268	41.52 N	86.38 W
Harbeson	262	38.43 N	75.17 W
Harbin → Haerbin	190	45.45 N	126.41 E
Harbor	256	42.03 N	124.15 W
Harbor Beach	244	43.51 N	82.39 W
Harborcreek	266	42.10 N	79.57 W
Harbor Side	274	32.37 N	117.05 W
Harbor Springs	244	45.26 N	84.59 W
Harborton	262	37.40 N	75.50 W
Harbor View	266	41.42 N	83.27 W
Harbour Breton	240	47.29 N	55.48 W
Harbour Buffett	240	47.32 N	54.05 W
Harbour Deep	240	50.22 N	56.27 W
Harbour Grace	240	47.42 N	53.13 W
Harbourville	240	45.09 N	64.49 W
Harburg ◆[8]	178	53.28 N	9.59 E
Harcuvar Mountains ⋀	254	34.00 N	113.30 W
Hard	180	47.29 N	9.41 E
Hardangerfjorden C[2]	160	60.10 N	6.00 E
Hardeeville	246	32.17 N	81.05 W
Hardenberg	164	52.34 N	6.37 E
Harderwijk	178	52.21 N	5.36 E
Hardesty	250	36.37 N	101.12 W
Hardin, Ill., U.S.	248	39.09 N	90.37 W
Hardin, Mont., U.S.	256	45.44 N	107.37 W
Hardin, Tex., U.S.	250	30.09 N	94.44 W
Hardin □[6]	268	40.39 N	83.36 W
Harding, S. Afr.	218	30.34 S	29.58 E
Harding, Ill., U.S.	268	41.31 N	88.51 W
Harding, Lake ⊜[1]	246	32.40 N	85.06 W
Harding Lakes	262	39.27 N	74.45 W
Hardinsburg	248	37.47 N	86.28 W
Hardisty	238	52.40 N	111.18 W
Hardisty Lake ⊜	232	64.30 N	117.45 W
Hardtner	252	37.01 N	98.39 W
Hardwār	206	29.52 N	78.10 E
Hardwick, Ga., U.S.	246	33.09 N	83.13 W
Hardwick, Mass., U.S.	261	42.21 N	72.12 W
Hardwick, Vt., U.S.	242	44.30 N	72.22 W
Hardwicke Island I	238	50.30 N	125.30 W
Hardwood Ridge ∧	242	41.15 N	75.23 W
Hardy, Ark., U.S.	248	36.19 N	91.29 W
Hardy, Nebr., U.S.	252	40.01 N	97.56 W
Hardy Bay C	232	75.02 N	115.16 W
Hare Bay	240	48.51 N	54.01 W
Hare Bay C	240	51.18 N	55.50 W
Hare Indian ≃	232	66.18 N	128.38 W
Harelbeke	176	50.51 N	3.18 E
Haren, B.R.D.	178	52.47 N	7.14 E
Haren, Ned.	178	53.10 N	6.35 E
Hareøen I	232	70.25 N	54.50 W
Harer	214	9.18 N	42.08 E
Harford □[6]	262	39.32 N	76.21 W
Hargeysa	214	9.30 N	44.03 E
Harī ≃, Afg.	208	34.20 N	64.30 E
Harī (Tedžen) (Harīrūd) ≃, As.	208	37.24 N	60.38 E
Hari ≃, Indon.	200	1.16 S	104.05 E
Ḥarim, Jabal al- ∧	208	23.58 N	56.14 E
Haringey ◆[8]	174	51.35 N	0.07 W
Harkers Island	246	34.42 N	76.34 W
Harkin Bay C	232	64.52 N	78.18 W
Harksheide	178	53.43 N	10.00 E
Harlan, Ind., U.S.	268	41.12 N	84.55 W
Harlan, Iowa, U.S.	252	41.39 N	95.19 W
Harlan, Ky., U.S.	246	36.51 N	83.19 W
Harlan County Reservoir ⊜[1]	252	40.04 N	99.16 W
Harlem, Fla., U.S.	246	26.44 N	80.58 W
Harlem, Ga., U.S.	246	33.25 N	82.19 W
Harlem, Mont., U.S.	256	48.32 N	108.47 W
Harlem Springs	266	40.31 N	81.02 W
Harleysville	262	40.17 N	75.23 W
Harlingen, Ned.	178	53.10 N	5.24 E
Harlingen, Tex., U.S.	250	26.11 N	97.42 W
Harlow	174	51.47 N	0.08 E
Harlowton	256	46.26 N	109.50 W
Harman	242	38.55 N	79.32 W
Harmånger	160	61.56 N	17.13 E
Harmanli	172	41.56 N	25.54 E
Harmonsburg	266	41.40 N	80.19 W
Harmony, Calif., U.S.	272	35.35 N	121.01 W
Harmony, Ind., U.S.	248	39.32 N	87.04 W
Harmony, Maine, U.S.	242	44.58 N	69.33 W
Harmony, Minn., U.S.	244	43.33 N	92.01 W
Harmony, Pa., U.S.	266	40.48 N	80.06 W
Harmony, R.I., U.S.	261	41.53 N	71.36 W
Harnes	176	50.27 N	2.54 E
Harney, Lake ⊜	246	28.45 N	81.03 W
Harney Basin ⊻[1]	256	43.15 N	120.40 W
Harney Lake ⊜	256	43.14 N	119.07 W
Harney Peak ∧	252	44.00 N	103.30 W
Härnösand	160	62.38 N	17.56 E
Haro	168	42.35 N	2.51 W
Harpenden	174	51.49 N	0.22 W
Harper, Liber.	222	4.25 N	7.43 W
Harper, Kans., U.S.	252	37.17 N	98.01 W
Harper, Tex., U.S.	250	30.18 N	99.15 W
Harper, Wash., U.S.	270	47.31 N	122.46 W
Harper, Mount ∧	236	64.14 N	143.50 W
Harpers Ferry National Historical Park ♠	242	39.13 N	77.45 W
Harper Woods	266	42.24 N	82.55 W
Harpster	266	40.44 N	83.15 W
Harquahala Mountain ∧	254	33.49 N	113.21 W
Harrell	248	33.31 N	92.24 W
Harricana ≃	232	51.15 N	79.45 W
Harriman	246	35.56 N	84.33 W
Harrington, Del., U.S.	262	38.56 N	75.35 W
Harrington, Maine, U.S.	242	44.37 N	67.49 W
Harrington, Wash., U.S.	256	47.29 N	118.15 W
Harris, Minn., U.S.	244	45.35 N	92.59 W
Harris, R.I., U.S.	261	41.44 N	71.32 W
Harris I	162	57.53 N	6.55 W
Harris, Lake ⊜	246	28.46 N	81.49 W
Harris, Sound of ⊔	162	57.45 N	7.08 W
Harrisburg, Ark., U.S.	248	35.34 N	90.43 W
Harrisburg, Ill., U.S.	248	37.44 N	88.33 W
Harrisburg, Nebr., U.S.	252	41.33 N	103.44 W
Harrisburg, Oreg., U.S.	256	44.16 N	123.10 W
Harrisburg, Pa., U.S.	262	40.16 N	76.52 W
Harris Hill	264	42.58 N	78.40 W
Harrismith	224	28.18 S	29.03 E
Harris Mountains ⋀	230	44.40 S	168.50 E
Harrison, Ark., U.S.	248	36.14 N	93.07 W
Harrison, Idaho, U.S.	256	47.27 N	116.47 W
Harrison, Ill., U.S.	268	42.25 N	89.11 W
Harrison, Mich., U.S.	244	44.01 N	84.48 W
Harrison, Nebr., U.S.	252	42.41 N	103.53 W
Harrison, N.Y., U.S.	261	40.58 N	73.43 W
Harrison □[6]	266	40.16 N	81.05 W
Harrison, Cape ≻	232	54.55 N	57.55 W
Harrison Bay C	236	70.30 N	151.30 W
Harrisonburg, La., U.S.	248	31.46 N	91.49 W
Harrisonburg, Va., U.S.	242	36.34 N	78.58 W
Harrison Hot Springs	270	49.18 N	121.47 W
Harrison Islands II	232	69.13 N	90.30 W
Harrison Lake ⊜	238	49.30 N	121.50 W
Harrison Mills	270	49.14 N	121.57 W
Harrison Valley	266	41.57 N	77.39 W
Harrisonville	248	38.39 N	94.21 W
Harriston, Ont., Can.	264	43.54 N	80.53 W
Harriston, Miss., U.S.	248	31.44 N	91.02 W
Harrisville, Mich., U.S.	244	44.39 N	83.17 W
Harrisville, N.Y., U.S.	264	44.09 N	75.19 W
Harrisville, Ohio, U.S.	266	40.11 N	80.53 W
Harrisville, Pa., U.S.	266	41.08 N	80.01 W
Harrisville, R.I., U.S.	261	41.58 N	71.41 W
Harrisville, W. Va., U.S.	242	39.13 N	81.03 W
Harrod	268	40.43 N	83.55 W
Harrodsburg	248	37.46 N	84.51 W
Harrogate	162	54.00 N	1.33 W
Harrold	250	34.05 N	99.02 W
Harrow	266	42.02 N	82.55 W
Harrow ◆[8]	174	51.35 N	0.21 W
Harrowsmith	264	44.24 N	76.40 W
Harsens Island	266	42.34 N	82.34 W
Harsewinkel	178	51.58 N	8.13 E
Harşit ≃	212	41.01 N	38.52 E
Harstad	160	68.46 N	16.30 E
Hart, Mich., U.S.	244	43.42 N	86.22 W
Hart, Tex., U.S.	250	34.23 N	102.07 W
Hart ≃	236	65.51 N	136.22 W
Hart, Lake ⊜	228	31.08 S	136.24 E
Hartbees ≃	224	28.45 S	20.32 E
Hartberg	164	47.17 N	15.59 E
Hartfield	262	37.33 N	76.27 W
Hartford, Ala., U.S.	248	31.06 N	85.42 W
Hartford, Ark., U.S.	248	35.01 N	94.23 W
Hartford, Conn., U.S.	261	41.46 N	72.41 W
Hartford, Kans., U.S.	252	38.18 N	95.58 W
Hartford, Ky., U.S.	248	37.27 N	86.55 W
Hartford, Mich., U.S.	268	42.12 N	86.10 W
Hartford, Ohio, U.S.	266	41.19 N	80.34 W
Hartford, S. Dak., U.S.	252	43.37 N	96.57 W
Hartford, Wis., U.S.	244	43.19 N	88.22 W
Hartford □[6]	261	41.46 N	72.41 W
Hartford City	268	40.27 N	85.22 W
Hartington	252	42.37 N	97.16 W
Hart Lake ⊜	256	42.24 N	119.51 W
Hartland, N.B., Can.	240	46.18 N	67.32 W
Hartland, Ill., U.S.	268	42.22 N	88.31 W
Hartland, Maine, U.S.	242	44.53 N	69.27 W
Hartland, Mich., U.S.	268	42.39 N	83.45 W
Hartland, N.Y., U.S.	264	43.14 N	78.35 W
Hartland, Wis., U.S.	268	43.06 N	88.21 W
Hartlepool	162	54.42 N	1.11 W
Hartley, Rh.	224	18.10 S	30.14 E
Hartley, Iowa, U.S.	252	43.11 N	95.29 W
Hartley, Tex., U.S.	250	35.53 N	102.24 W
Hartley Bay	238	53.25 N	129.15 W
Hart Lot	264	43.01 N	76.28 W
Hartly	262	39.10 N	75.43 W
Hartney	252	49.28 N	100.30 W
Hartola	160	61.35 N	26.01 E
Harts ≃	224	28.24 S	24.17 E
Hartsdale	261	41.01 N	73.48 W
Hartselle	248	34.27 N	86.56 W
Hartshorne	250	34.51 N	95.34 W
Hartstown	266	41.33 N	80.23 W
Hartsville, S.C., U.S.	246	34.23 N	80.04 W
Hartsville, Tenn., U.S.	248	36.24 N	86.10 W
Hartville, Mo., U.S.	248	37.15 N	92.31 W
Hartville, Ohio, U.S.	266	40.58 N	81.20 W
Hartwell	246	34.21 N	82.56 W
Hartwell Reservoir ⊜[1]	246	34.30 N	82.55 W
Hartz Mountain's National Park ♠	228	43.15 S	146.50 E
Harvard, Ill., U.S.	268	42.25 N	88.37 W
Harvard, Mass., U.S.	261	42.30 N	71.35 W
Harvard, Nebr., U.S.	252	40.37 N	98.06 W
Harvey, N.B., Can.	240	45.43 N	64.43 W
Harvey, Ill., U.S.	268	41.37 N	87.39 W
Harvey, La., U.S.	248	29.54 N	90.05 W
Harvey, N. Dak., U.S.	252	47.47 N	99.56 W
Harwich, Eng., U.K.	174	51.57 N	1.17 E
Harwich, Mass., U.S.	261	41.41 N	70.01 W
Harwich Port	261	41.40 N	70.05 W
Harwinton	261	41.46 N	73.04 W
Haryana □[3]	206	29.20 N	76.20 E
Harz ⋀	164	51.45 N	10.30 E
Harz, Naturpark ♠	164	51.44 N	10.30 E
Ḥaṣā, Bi'r al- ⊤[4]	220	22.58 N	35.40 E
Hasaki	192	35.44 N	140.50 E
Hasan Dağı ∧	212	38.08 N	34.12 E
Ḥāṣbānī, Nahr al- ≃	210	33.11 N	35.37 E
Hasdo ≃	206	21.43 N	82.44 E
Hase ≃	164	52.41 N	7.18 E
Haselünne	178	52.40 N	7.29 E
Hasenkamp	294	31.30 S	59.50 W
Hashima	192	35.19 N	136.42 E
Hashimoto	192	34.19 N	135.37 E
Haskell, Okla., U.S.	250	35.50 N	95.40 W
Haskell, Tex., U.S.	250	33.10 N	99.44 W
Haskins	268	41.28 N	83.42 W
Haskovo	172	41.56 N	25.33 E
Hasköy	172	41.38 N	26.41 E
Haslach	180	48.16 N	8.06 E
Haslemere	174	51.06 N	0.43 W
Haslett	268	42.45 N	84.19 W
Ḥasmat 'Umar, Bi'r ⊤[4]	220	21.46 N	34.00 E
Ḥaṣṣ, Jabal al- ∧[2]	212	35.52 N	37.22 E
Hassayampa ≃	254	33.20 N	112.43 W
Hasseïra ⋀[1]	222	17.28 N	11.41 W
Hasselt	164	50.56 N	5.20 E
Hassfurt	164	50.02 N	10.31 E
Hassi el Ghella	168	35.28 N	1.03 W
Hassi Mamèche	168	35.52 N	0.04 E
Hassi Messaoud	214	31.43 N	5.59 E
Hassi R'Mel	214	32.35 N	3.24 E
Hassi Zehana	168	35.01 N	0.53 W
Hässleholm	160	56.09 N	13.46 E
Hasslinghausen	178	51.20 N	7.17 E
Hasson Heights	266	41.26 N	79.41 W
Hastings, Barb.	285g	13.04 N	59.35 W
Hastings, Ont., Can.	264	44.18 N	77.57 W
Hastings, N.Z.	230	39.38 S	176.51 E
Hastings, Eng., U.K.	174	50.51 N	0.36 E
Hastings, Fla., U.S.	246	29.40 N	81.30 W
Hastings, Mich., U.S.	268	42.39 N	85.17 W
Hastings, Minn., U.S.	244	44.44 N	92.51 W
Hastings, Nebr., U.S.	252	40.35 N	98.23 W
Hastings, N.Y., U.S.	264	43.22 N	76.09 W
Hastings, Pa., U.S.	266	40.40 N	78.42 W
Hastings □[6]	264	44.45 N	77.40 W
Hasty	252	38.07 N	102.58 W
Haswell	252	38.27 N	103.09 W
Hatay □[4]	212	36.30 N	36.15 E
Hatboro	262	40.11 N	75.06 W
Hatch, N. Mex., U.S.	254	32.40 N	107.09 W
Hatch, Utah, U.S.	254	37.39 N	112.26 W
Hatchet Lake	240	44.35 N	63.40 W
Hatchie ≃	248	35.35 N	89.53 W
Hatchville	261	41.38 N	70.34 W
Hatch Wash ∨	254	38.32 N	109.36 W
Haţeg	172	45.37 N	22.57 E
Hatfield, Eng., U.K.	174	51.46 N	0.13 W
Hatfield, Ark., U.S.	248	34.29 N	94.23 W
Hatfield, Mass., U.S.	261	42.22 N	72.36 W
Hathaway Mead	270	45.27 N	123.47 W
Hathaway Pines	272	38.07 N	120.28 W
Hathob, Oued el ∨	170	35.23 N	9.32 E
Hāthras	206	27.36 N	78.03 E
Ha-tien	198	10.23 N	104.29 E
Hatillo	284m	18.29 N	66.49 W
Ha-tinh	200	18.20 N	105.54 E
Hato	285s	12.12 N	68.57 W
Hato, Bocht van C	285s	12.13 N	68.58 W
Hato del Volcán	280	8.47 N	82.37 W
Hato Mayor [del Rey]	282	18.46 N	69.15 W
Hato Rey	284m	18.25 N	66.03 W
Hattah Lakes National Park ♠	228	34.40 S	142.30 E
Hattem	178	52.28 N	6.04 E
Hatten	178	53.02 N	8.22 E
Hatteras	246	35.13 N	75.42 W
Hatteras, Cape ≻	246	35.13 N	75.32 W
Hatteras Island I	246	35.25 N	75.30 W
Hattingen	178	51.23 N	7.10 E
Hatton, Ala., U.S.	248	32.06 N	86.35 W
Hatton, N. Dak., U.S.	252	47.38 N	97.27 W
Hatton Fields	272	36.33 N	121.54 W
Hatvan	164	47.40 N	19.41 E
Hat Yai	200	7.01 N	100.27 E
Hatzic	270	49.09 N	122.15 W
Hau	178	51.45 N	6.10 E
Haubourdin	176	50.36 N	2.59 E
Haubstadt	248	38.12 N	87.34 W
Hauge	160	58.18 N	6.15 E
Haugesund	160	59.25 N	5.18 E
Haugsdorf	164	48.42 N	16.05 E
Hauhungaroa Range ⋀	230	38.50 S	175.34 E
Haukeligrend	160	59.45 N	7.31 E
Haukivesi ⊜	160	62.06 N	28.28 E
Haukivuori	160	62.01 N	27.13 E
Haunstetten	180	48.18 N	10.54 E
Hauppauge	261	40.49 N	73.12 W
Hauraki Gulf C	230	36.33 S	175.05 E
Hauroko, Lake ⊜	230	46.00 S	167.19 E
Hausach	164	48.17 N	8.10 E
Hausruck ⋀	166	48.07 N	13.35 E
Haut, Isle au I	242	44.03 N	68.38 W
Haut-Bassins □[5]	222	12.30 N	2.30 W
Haute-Garonne □[5]	166	43.25 N	1.30 E
Haute-Loire □[5]	166	45.05 N	3.50 E
Haute-Marne □[5]	180	48.05 N	5.10 E
Hauterive	240	49.11 N	68.16 W
Hautes-Alpes □[5]	182	44.40 N	6.30 E
Haute-Saône □[5]	180	47.40 N	6.10 E
Haute-Savoie □[5]	166	46.00 N	6.20 E
Hautes Fagnes ⋀	164	50.30 N	6.05 E
Hautes-Pyrénées □[5]	166	43.00 N	0.10 E
Haute-Vienne □[5]	166	45.50 N	1.15 E
Haut-Mbomou □[5]	220	6.00 N	26.00 E
Hautmont	176	50.15 N	3.56 E
Haut-Rhin □[5]	180	47.53 N	7.13 E
Hauts-de-Seine □[5]	166	48.50 N	2.11 E
Hauts Plateaux ⋀[1]	214	34.00 N	0.00
Hauula	275c	21.37 N	157.55 W
Havana → La Habana, Cuba	284p	23.08 N	82.22 W
Havana, Ark., U.S.	248	35.07 N	93.32 W
Havana, Fla., U.S.	246	30.38 N	84.25 W
Havana, Ill., U.S.	248	40.18 N	90.04 W
Havana, N. Dak., U.S.	252	45.57 N	97.37 W
Havant	162	50.51 N	0.29 W
Havasu Lake ⊜[1]	254	34.30 N	114.20 W
Havelberg	164	52.50 N	12.04 E
Havelock, Ont., Can.	264	44.26 N	77.53 W
Havelock, N.C., U.S.	246	34.53 N	76.54 W
Havelock I	200	12.00 N	93.00 E
Havelock North	230	39.40 S	176.53 E
Havelse	178	52.24 N	9.36 E
Haven, Eng., U.K.	174	50.51 N	0.59 W
Haven, Kans., U.S.	252	37.54 N	97.47 W
Haverfordwest	174	51.49 N	4.58 W
Haverhill, Eng., U.K.	174	52.05 N	0.26 E
Haverhill, Mass., U.S.	261	42.47 N	71.05 W
Havering ◆[8]	174	51.34 N	0.14 E
Haverstraw	242	41.12 N	73.58 W
Havertown	262	39.59 N	75.18 W
Haviland, Kans., U.S.	252	37.37 N	99.06 W
Haviland, Ohio, U.S.	268	41.01 N	84.35 W
Havířov	164	49.47 N	18.27 E
Havlíčkův Brod	164	49.36 N	15.35 E
Havran	172	39.33 N	27.06 E
Havré, Bel.	176	50.28 N	4.02 E
Havre → Le Havre, Fr.	176	49.30 N	0.08 E
Havre, Mont., U.S.	256	48.33 N	109.41 W
Havre-Aubert	240	47.14 N	61.50 W
Havre de Grace	242	39.33 N	76.06 W
Havre-Saint-Pierre	240	50.15 N	63.36 W
Havsa	172	41.33 N	26.49 E
Haw ≃	246	35.36 N	79.03 W
Hawaii □[3]	275d	20.00 N	157.45 W
Hawaii I	275d	19.30 N	155.30 W
Hawaiian Islands II	148	24.00 N	167.00 W
Hawaii Volcanoes National Park ♠	275d	19.23 N	155.17 W
Hawarden	252	43.00 N	96.29 W
Ḥawashīyah, Wādī ∨	220	28.31 N	32.58 E
Hawea, Lake ⊜	230	44.31 S	169.17 E
Hawera	230	39.35 S	174.17 E
Hawesville	248	37.54 N	86.45 W
Hawi	275d	20.14 N	155.50 W
Hawick	162	55.25 N	2.47 W
Hawkdun Range ⋀	230	44.45 S	170.00 E
Hawke, Cape ≻	228	32.13 S	152.34 E
Hawke Bay C	230	39.20 S	177.30 E
Hawker	226	31.53 S	138.25 E
Hawkesbury	260	45.36 N	74.37 W
Hawkesbury Island I	238	53.38 N	129.00 W
Hawkeye	244	42.56 N	91.57 W
Hawkins, Tex., U.S.	250	32.35 N	95.12 W
Hawkins, Wis., U.S.	244	45.31 N	90.43 W
Hawkins Island I	236	60.30 N	146.00 W
Hawkinsville	246	32.17 N	83.28 W
Hawk Junction	244	48.05 N	84.34 W
Hawk Lake	252	49.48 N	93.59 W
Haw Knob ∧	246	35.19 N	84.02 W
Hawk Run	266	40.55 N	78.13 W
Hawksbill ∧	242	38.33 N	78.23 W
Hawksbill Creek C	246	26.40 N	78.45 W
Hawks Nest Point ≻	282	24.09 N	75.32 W
Hawley, Minn., U.S.	252	46.53 N	96.19 W
Hawley, Pa., U.S.	242	41.28 N	75.11 W
Hawleyville	261	41.26 N	73.21 W
Ḥawrān, Wādī ∨	208	33.58 N	42.34 E
Hawthorn	266	41.01 N	79.17 W
Hawthorne, Calif., U.S.	274	33.55 N	118.21 W
Hawthorne, Fla., U.S.	246	29.36 N	82.05 W
Hawthorne, Nev., U.S.	258	38.32 N	118.38 W
Hawthorne, N.Y., U.S.	261	41.07 N	73.48 W
Haxtun	252	40.39 N	102.38 W
Hay	228	34.30 S	144.51 E
Hay ≃, Austl.	228	25.14 S	138.00 E
Hay ≃, Can.	232	60.51 N	115.44 W
Hay ≃, Wis., U.S.	244	44.59 N	91.51 W
Hay, Cape ≻	232	74.25 N	113.00 W
Hay, Mount ∧	236	59.15 N	137.37 W
Hayachine-san ∧	192	39.34 N	141.29 E
Hayange	166	49.20 N	6.03 E
Haybān, Jabal ∧	220	11.15 N	30.31 E
Hayden, Ariz., U.S.	254	33.00 N	110.47 W
Hayden, Colo., U.S.	254	40.30 N	107.16 W
Hayden Peak ∧	256	42.59 N	116.39 W
Haydenville, Mass., U.S.	261	42.22 N	72.42 W
Haydenville, Ohio, U.S.	242	39.29 N	82.20 W
Hayes ≃, Man., Can.	232	57.03 N	92.09 W
Hayes ≃, N.W. Ter., Can.	232	67.18 N	95.02 W
Hayes, Mount ∧	236	63.37 N	146.43 W
Hayes Center	252	40.31 N	101.01 W
Hayesville, N.C., U.S.	246	35.03 N	83.49 W
Hayesville, Ohio, U.S.	266	40.46 N	82.16 W
Hayesville, Oreg., U.S.	270	44.59 N	122.58 W
Hayfield	244	43.53 N	92.51 W
Hayford Peak ∧	258	36.40 N	115.11 W
Hayfork	258	40.33 N	123.11 W
Hayfork Bally ∧	258	40.39 N	123.13 W
Hay Lakes	238	53.13 N	113.03 W
Haynes	248	34.53 N	90.47 W
Haynesville, La., U.S.	248	32.58 N	93.08 W
Haynesville, Va., U.S.	262	37.57 N	76.40 W
Hayneville	248	32.06 N	86.35 W
Hayrabolu	172	41.12 N	27.06 E
Hay River	232	60.51 N	115.40 W
Hays, Alta., Can.	238	50.06 N	111.48 W
Hays, Kans., U.S.	252	38.53 N	99.20 W
Hays, Mont., U.S.	256	48.03 N	108.43 W
Hay Springs	252	42.41 N	102.41 W
Haystack Mountain ∧	258	41.39 N	115.38 W
Haystack Peak ∧	254	39.50 N	113.55 W
Haysville	252	37.34 N	97.21 W
Hayti, Mo., U.S.	248	36.14 N	89.44 W
Hayti, Pa., U.S.	262	39.59 N	75.51 W
Hayti, S. Dak., U.S.	252	44.40 N	97.12 W
Hayward, Calif., U.S.	272	37.40 N	122.05 W
Hayward, Wis., U.S.	244	46.01 N	91.29 W
Haywards Heath	174	51.00 N	0.06 W
HaZafon □[5]	210	32.50 N	35.20 E
Hazard	246	37.15 N	83.12 W
Hazardville	261	41.59 N	72.33 W
Hazar Gölü ⊜	212	38.30 N	39.25 E
Hazāribāgh	206	23.59 N	85.21 E
Hazebrouck	176	50.43 N	2.32 E
Hazel ≃	242	38.33 N	77.51 W
Hazel Dell	270	45.39 N	122.41 W
Hazel Green	244	42.32 N	90.26 W
Hazel Hurst	266	41.42 N	78.35 W
Hazel Park	268	42.29 N	83.06 W
Hazelton, B.C., Can.	238	55.15 N	127.40 W
Hazelton, Idaho, U.S.	256	42.41 N	114.08 W
Hazelton, N. Dak., U.S.	252	46.29 N	100.17 W
Hazelton Mountains ⋀	238	55.00 N	128.00 W
Hazelton Peak ∧	256	44.06 N	107.03 W
Hazelwood	246	35.28 N	83.00 W
Hazen, Ark., U.S.	248	34.47 N	91.35 W
Hazen, Nev., U.S.	272	39.04 N	119.03 W
Hazen, N. Dak., U.S.	252	47.18 N	101.38 W
Hazen, Pa., U.S.	266	41.12 N	78.58 W
Hazen Bay C	236	61.00 N	165.10 W
Hazlehurst	246	31.52 N	82.36 W
Hazlet	262	40.26 N	74.13 W
Hazleton, Iowa, U.S.	244	42.37 N	91.54 W
Hazleton, Pa., U.S.	242	40.58 N	75.59 W
Hazor	210	32.59 N	35.33 E
Head Bay d'Espoir	240	47.56 N	55.45 W
Headington	174	51.45 N	1.13 W
Headland	248	31.21 N	85.20 W
Headley, Mount ∧	256	47.44 N	115.15 W
Healdsburg	258	38.37 N	122.52 W
Healdton	250	34.14 N	97.29 W
Healy, Alaska, U.S.	236	63.52 N	148.58 W
Healy, Kans., U.S.	252	38.36 N	100.37 W
Healy, Mount ∧	236	63.46 N	149.01 W
Heanor	174	53.01 N	1.22 W
Hearne	250	30.53 N	96.36 W
Hearst	232	49.41 N	83.40 W
Heart ≃, Alta., Can.	238	56.14 N	117.17 W
Heart ≃, N. Dak., U.S.	252	46.47 N	100.51 W
Heart Lake ⊜	238	55.02 N	111.30 W
Heart Lake Indian Reserve ◆[4]	238	55.02 N	111.30 W
Heart's Content	240	47.52 N	53.22 W
Heath, Mass., U.S.	261	42.40 N	72.49 W
Heath, Ohio, U.S.	266	39.58 N	82.29 W
Heath, Pointe ≻	240	49.05 N	61.45 W
Heath Springs	246	34.36 N	80.40 W
Heathsville	262	37.55 N	76.28 W
Heavener	248	34.53 N	94.36 W
Hebaodao I	196	21.52 N	113.09 E
Hebbronville	250	27.18 N	98.41 W
Hebei □[4]	194	38.00 N	116.00 E
Heber, Ariz., U.S.	254	34.26 N	110.36 W
Heber, Calif., U.S.	258	32.44 N	115.32 W
Heber, Utah, U.S.	254	40.30 N	111.25 W
Heber Springs	248	35.30 N	92.02 W
Hebgen Lake ⊜[1]	256	44.47 N	111.14 W
Hebi	190	35.59 N	114.11 E
Hebo	270	45.14 N	123.52 W
Hebrides II	162	57.00 N	6.30 W
Hebrides, Sea of the ⊤[2]	162	57.00 N	7.00 W
Hebron → Al-Khalīl, Urd.	210	31.32 N	35.06 E
Hebron, Conn., U.S.	261	41.39 N	72.22 W
Hebron, Ill., U.S.	268	42.28 N	88.26 W
Hebron, Ind., U.S.	268	41.19 N	87.12 W
Hebron, Md., U.S.	242	38.25 N	75.41 W
Hebron, Nebr., U.S.	252	40.10 N	97.35 W
Hebron, N. Dak., U.S.	252	46.54 N	102.03 W
Hebron, Pa., U.S.	262	40.21 N	76.24 W
Hebron, Wis., U.S.	268	42.56 N	88.42 W
Hecate Strait ⊔	238	53.00 N	131.00 W
Hecelchakán	278	20.10 N	90.08 W
Heceta Island I	236	55.45 N	133.35 W
Hechi	200	24.51 N	107.59 E
Hechiceros	250	28.33 N	103.38 W
Hechingen	180	48.21 N	8.58 E
Hechuan	190	30.00 N	106.16 E
Hecla	252	45.53 N	98.09 W
Hectanooga	240	44.06 N	66.02 W
Hector	252	44.45 N	94.43 W
Hector ∧	230	40.57 S	175.16 E
Hédé, Fr.	166	48.18 N	1.48 W
Hede, Sve.	160	62.25 N	13.30 E
Hedemora	160	60.17 N	15.59 E
He Devil ∧	256	45.21 N	116.33 W
Hedley, B.C., Can.	238	49.21 N	120.04 W
Hedley, Tex., U.S.	250	34.52 N	100.39 W
Hedmark □[6]	160	61.30 N	11.45 E
Hedrick	244	41.11 N	92.19 W
Heemskerk	178	52.31 N	4.40 E
Heemstede	178	52.21 N	4.37 E
Heepen	178	52.01 N	8.35 E
Heerenveen	178	52.57 N	5.55 E
Heeren-Werve	178	51.35 N	7.43 E
Heerlen	166	50.54 N	5.59 E
Heessen	178	51.42 N	7.50 E
Hefa (Haifa)	210	32.49 N	35.00 E
Hefa □[5]	210	32.40 N	35.00 E
Hefa, Mifraz C	210	32.52 N	35.02 E
Hefei	196	31.51 N	117.17 E
Heflin	248	33.39 N	85.35 W
Hegang	190	47.24 N	130.17 E
Hegins	262	40.39 N	76.30 W
Heguaizi	190	39.39 N	106.41 E
Heho	198	20.43 N	96.49 E
Heide	164	54.12 N	9.06 E
Heidelberg, B.R.D.	164	49.25 N	8.43 E
Heidelberg, Ont., Can.	264	43.31 N	80.37 W
Heidelberg, S. Afr.	224	26.32 S	28.18 E
Heidelberg, Miss., U.S.	248	31.53 N	88.59 W
Heiden, Port C	236	56.55 N	158.45 W
Heidenheim an der Brenz	180	48.40 N	10.08 E
Heidenreichstein	164	48.52 N	15.07 E
Heidlersburg	262	39.57 N	77.09 W
Heihe	190	31.34 N	92.00 E
Heihe ≃	194	40.44 N	116.27 E
Heilbron	224	27.21 S	27.58 E
Heilbronn	164	49.08 N	9.13 E
Heiligenblut	164	47.02 N	12.50 E
Heiligenhafen	164	54.22 N	10.58 E
Heiligenhaus	178	51.19 N	6.59 E
Heiligenstadt	178	51.23 N	10.09 E
Heilongjiang □[4]	190	48.00 N	128.00 E
Heiloo	178	52.36 N	4.43 E
Heilungkiang → Heilongjiang □[4]	190	48.00 N	128.00 E
Heilwood	266	40.37 N	78.55 W
Heinävesi	160	62.26 N	28.36 E
Heinola	160	61.13 N	26.02 E
Heinsberg	178	51.03 N	6.05 E
Heishan	194	41.41 N	122.07 E
Heisler	238	52.41 N	112.13 W
Heislerville	262	39.15 N	75.07 W
Heist-aan-Zee	176	51.21 N	3.15 E
Heist-op-den-Berg	178	51.05 N	4.43 E
Hejaz → Al-Ḥijāz ◆[1]	208	24.30 N	38.30 E
Hekla ∧[1]	160a	64.00 N	19.39 W
Hekou	200	22.38 N	103.56 E
Hekura-jima I	192	37.51 N	136.55 E
Hel	164	54.37 N	18.48 E
Helbra	164	51.33 N	11.29 E
Helen, Mount ∧	228	21.34 S	141.13 E
Helena, Ark., U.S.	248	34.32 N	90.35 W
Helena, Mont., U.S.	256	46.36 N	112.01 W
Helena, N.Y., U.S.	260	44.55 N	74.44 W
Helena, Ohio, U.S.	266	41.21 N	83.18 W
Helena, Okla., U.S.	250	36.33 N	98.16 W
Helendale	274	34.45 N	117.18 W
Helen Island I	198	2.58 N	131.49 E
Helensburgh	162	56.01 N	4.44 W
Helensville	230	36.41 S	174.27 E
Helenville	268	43.01 N	88.41 W
Helenwood	246	36.26 N	84.32 W
Helfenstein	262	40.45 N	76.27 W
Helgoland I	164	54.12 N	7.53 E
Helgoländer Bucht C	164	54.10 N	8.04 E
Hellam	262	40.00 N	76.36 W
Ḥelleh ≃	208	29.10 N	50.40 E
Hellemmes-Lille	176	50.37 N	3.07 E
Hellertown	262	40.35 N	75.21 W
Hellesylt	160	62.05 N	6.54 E
Hellín	168	38.31 N	1.41 W
Hells Canyon ∨	256	45.20 N	116.45 W
Hells Gate ♠	238	49.47 N	121.27 W
Hell-Ville	225b	13.25 S	48.16 E
Helm	272	36.32 N	120.06 W
Helmand □[4]	206	31.00 N	64.00 E
Helmand ≃	208	31.12 N	61.34 E
Helmcken Falls L	238	51.57 N	120.11 W
Helmond	178	51.29 N	5.40 E
Helmsdale	162	58.07 N	3.40 W
Helmstedt	164	52.13 N	11.00 E
Helmville	256	46.52 N	112.58 W
Helper	254	39.41 N	110.51 W
Helsingborg → Hälsingborg	160	56.03 N	12.42 E
Helsingfors → Helsinki	160	60.10 N	24.58 E
Helsingør (Elsinore)	160	56.02 N	12.37 E
Helsinki (Helsingfors)	160	60.10 N	24.58 E
Helska, Mierzeja ≻[2]	164	54.45 N	18.39 E
Helston	162	50.05 N	5.16 W
Helvecia	294	31.06 S	60.05 W
Hemau	164	49.03 N	11.47 E
Hemel Hempstead	174	51.46 N	0.28 W
Hemelingen ◆[8]	178	53.03 N	8.53 E
Hemer	178	51.23 N	7.46 E
Hemet	274	33.45 N	116.58 W
Hemford	240	44.30 N	64.47 W
Hemiksem	176	51.09 N	4.21 E
Hemingford	252	42.19 N	103.04 W
Hemingway	246	33.45 N	79.27 W
Hemlock	264	42.48 N	77.36 W
Hemmingen-Westerfeld	178	52.19 N	9.45 E
Hemphill	248	31.20 N	93.51 W
Hempstead	250	30.06 N	96.05 W
Hemse	160	57.14 N	18.22 E
Hemsedal	160	60.52 N	8.34 E
Henan □[4]	190	34.00 N	114.00 E
Hen And Chickens Islands II	230	35.55 S	174.43 E
Henares ≃	168	40.24 N	3.30 W
Henderson, Arg.	294	36.20 S	61.42 W
Henderson, N.Z.	230	36.53 S	174.38 E
Henderson, Ky., U.S.	248	37.50 N	87.35 W
Henderson, Minn., U.S.	244	44.31 N	93.55 W
Henderson, Nebr., U.S.	252	40.47 N	97.49 W
Henderson, Nev., U.S.	258	36.02 N	114.59 W
Henderson, N.C., U.S.	246	36.20 N	78.25 W
Henderson, N.Y., U.S.	264	43.51 N	76.11 W
Henderson, Tenn., U.S.	248	35.27 N	88.38 W
Henderson, Tex., U.S.	248	32.09 N	94.48 W
Hendersonville, N.C., U.S.	246	35.19 N	82.28 W
Hendersonville, Pa., U.S.	266	40.18 N	80.09 W
Hendersonville, Tenn., U.S.	248	36.18 N	86.37 W
Hendorābī, Jazīreh-ye I	208	26.40 N	53.37 E
Hendricks, Minn., U.S.	252	44.30 N	96.25 W
Hendricks, W. Va., U.S.	242	39.05 N	79.38 W
Hendrysburg	266	40.04 N	81.10 W
Henefer	254	41.01 N	111.30 W
Hengām, Jazīreh-ye I	208	26.39 N	55.53 E
Hengelo	178	52.15 N	6.45 E
Hengoed	174	51.39 N	3.10 W
Hengshan	196	27.15 N	112.51 E
Hengxian	200	22.42 N	109.13 E
Hengyang	190	26.51 N	112.30 E
Hénin-Liétard	176	50.25 N	2.56 E
Henley-on-Thames	174	51.32 N	0.56 W
Henlopen, Cape ≻	242	38.48 N	75.05 W
Hennaya	168	34.58 N	1.22 W
Hennebont	166	47.48 N	3.17 W
Hennef	164	50.46 N	7.16 E
Hennen	178	51.27 N	7.39 E
Hennepin	244	41.15 N	89.21 W
Hennessey	250	36.06 N	97.54 W
Hennigsdorf	164	52.38 N	13.12 E
Henniker	242	43.11 N	71.49 W
Henning, Ill., U.S.	268	40.18 N	87.42 W
Henning, Minn., U.S.	252	46.19 N	95.27 W
Henning, Tenn., U.S.	248	35.41 N	89.34 W
Henrico □[6]	262	37.30 N	77.20 W
Henrietta, N.Y., U.S.	264	43.03 N	77.37 W
Henrietta, Tex., U.S.	250	33.49 N	98.12 W
Henrietta Maria, Cape ≻	232	55.09 N	82.20 W
Henrique de Carvalho	218	9.39 S	20.24 E
Henry, Ill., U.S.	244	41.47 N	89.41 W
Henry, S. Dak., U.S.	252	44.53 N	97.28 W
Henry □[6]	268	41.20 N	84.04 W
Henry, Cap ≻	240	49.48 N	64.23 W
Henry, Mount ∧	256	48.53 N	115.31 W
Henryetta	250	35.27 N	95.59 W
Henry Kater, Cape ≻	232	69.05 N	66.44 W
Henry Mountains ⋀	254	37.55 N	110.50 W
Henry Pittier, Parque Nacional ♠	290	10.25 N	67.43 W
Henrys Bend	266	41.28 N	79.37 W
Henrys Fork ≃	254	41.00 N	109.39 W
Henryville	260	45.08 N	73.12 W
Hensall	244	43.26 N	81.30 W
Henshaw, Lake ⊜[1]	258	33.15 N	116.45 W
Hensley	248	34.30 N	92.12 W
Henzada	200	17.38 N	95.28 E
Hephzibah	246	33.19 N	82.06 W
Heppenheim	164	49.39 N	8.38 E
Heppner	256	45.21 N	119.33 W
Hepu (Lianzhou)	200	21.39 N	109.11 E
Hepworth	264	44.37 N	81.09 W
Heqing	200	26.30 N	100.20 E
Héradsflói C	160a	65.45 N	14.10 W
Herāt	208	34.20 N	62.07 E
Herāt □[4]	208	34.30 N	62.00 E
Hérault □[5]	166	43.40 N	3.30 E
Hérault ≃	166	43.17 N	3.26 E
Herbede	178	51.25 N	7.16 E
Herbert ≃	228	18.32 S	146.17 E
Herbert Hoover National Historic Site ⊥	244	41.38 N	91.23 W
Herbert Island I	236	52.45 N	170.10 W
Herbert Peak ∧	230	43.41 S	172.44 E
Herbignac	166	47.27 N	2.19 W
Herblay	176	49.00 N	2.10 E
Herborn	164	50.40 N	8.17 E
Herbrechtingen	180	48.37 N	10.10 E
Hercegnovi	172	42.27 N	18.32 E
Herculaneum	248	38.16 N	90.23 W
Hercules	272	38.01 N	122.17 W
Herdecke	178	51.24 N	7.26 E
Herđubreid ∧	160a	65.13 N	16.18 W
Heredia	280	10.00 N	84.07 W
Heredia □[4]	280	10.30 N	84.00 W
Hereford, Eng., U.K.	174	52.04 N	2.43 W
Hereford, Ariz., U.S.	254	31.26 N	110.06 W
Hereford, Md., U.S.	262	39.35 N	76.40 W
Hereford, Tex., U.S.	250	34.49 N	102.24 W
Herefordshire □[6]	174	52.05 N	2.45 W
Hereke	172	40.48 N	29.39 E
Herencia	168	39.21 N	3.22 W
Herentals	178	51.11 N	4.50 E
Herford	178	52.06 N	8.40 E
Hergla	170	36.02 N	10.31 E
Héricourt	180	47.35 N	6.45 E
Héricourt-en-Caux	162	49.42 N	0.42 E
Herington	252	38.40 N	96.57 W
Herisau	180	47.23 N	9.17 E
Herkimer	242	43.02 N	74.59 W
Herleshausen	164	51.00 N	10.09 E
Herlong	258	40.09 N	120.08 W
Hermagor	164	46.37 N	13.22 E
Herman, Minn., U.S.	252	45.49 N	96.08 W
Herman, Nebr., U.S.	252	41.40 N	96.13 W
Herman, Pa., U.S.	266	40.50 N	79.49 W
Hermana Mayor Island I	202	15.48 N	119.48 E
Hermanas	250	27.13 N	101.14 W
Hermann	248	38.42 N	91.27 W
Hermannsdenkmal ⊥	164	51.55 N	8.50 E
Hermano Peak ∧	254	37.13 N	108.48 W
Hermansville	244	45.42 N	87.37 W
Hermanus	218	34.25 S	19.16 E
Hermanville	248	31.58 N	90.50 W
Herminie	266	40.16 N	79.43 W
Hermiston	256	45.51 N	119.17 W
Hermitage, Newf., Can.	240	47.34 N	55.56 W
Hermitage, Ark., U.S.	248	33.27 N	92.10 W
Hermitage, Mo., U.S.	248	37.56 N	93.19 W
Hermitage Bay C	240	47.35 N	56.05 W
Hermleigh	250	32.38 N	100.46 W
Hermon	264	44.28 N	75.14 W
Hermon, Mount → Shaykh, Jabal ash- ∧	210	33.26 N	35.51 E
Hermosa Beach	274	33.52 N	118.24 W
Hermosillo, Méx.	254	32.30 N	114.59 W
Hermosillo, Méx.	278	29.04 N	110.58 W
Hermoso, Cerro ∧	290	1.10 S	78.12 W
Hernád (Hornád) ≃	164	47.56 N	21.08 E
Hernandarias	294	25.22 S	54.45 W
Hernando, Arg.	294	32.26 S	63.45 W
Hernando, Fla., U.S.	246	28.54 N	82.22 W
Hernando, Miss., U.S.	248	34.49 N	89.59 W
Hernani	202	11.19 N	125.37 E
Herndon, Calif., U.S.	272	36.49 N	119.54 W
Herndon, Kans., U.S.	252	39.55 N	100.47 W
Herndon, Pa., U.S.	262	40.43 N	76.51 W
Herndon, Va., U.S.	262	38.58 N	77.23 W
Herne	178	51.32 N	7.13 E
Herne Bay	174	51.23 N	1.08 E
Herning	160	56.08 N	8.59 E
Heron Lake	252	43.47 N	95.19 W
Herowābād	208	37.37 N	48.32 E
Herradura	294	26.29 S	58.19 W
Herreid	252	45.50 N	100.04 W
Herrenberg	180	48.35 N	8.52 E
Herrera	294	28.30 S	63.04 W
Herrera □[4]	280	7.54 N	80.38 W
Herrera del Duque	168	39.10 N	5.03 W
Herrera de Pisuerga	168	42.36 N	4.20 W
Herreras	278	25.10 N	105.31 W
Herrick Grove	264	44.04 N	76.12 W
Herrin	248	37.48 N	89.02 W
Herring Cove, N.S., Can.	240	44.34 N	63.34 W

Symbols in the index entries are identified on page 360.

Name	Page	Lat°′	Long°′
Herring Cove, Alaska, U.S.	236	55.21 N	131.41 W
Herringen	178	51.40 N	7.44 E
Hersbruck	164	49.30 N	11.26 E
Herschel Island I	236	69.35 N	139.05 W
Herscher	268	41.03 N	88.06 W
Herselt	178	51.03 N	4.53 E
Hershey, Nebr., U.S.	252	41.10 N	101.00 W
Hershey, Pa., U.S.	262	40.17 N	76.39 W
Herstal	164	50.40 N	5.38 E
Herten	178	51.35 N	7.07 E
Hertford, Eng., U.K.	174	51.48 N	0.05 W
Hertford, N.C., U.S.	246	36.11 N	76.28 W
Hertford □[6]	262	36.28 N	77.01 W
Hertfordshire □[6]	174	51.50 N	0.10 W
Hervás	168	40.16 N	5.51 W
Hervey Bay C	228	25.00 S	153.00 E
Herzberg	164	51.41 N	13.14 E
Herzberg am Harz	178	51.39 N	10.20 E
Herzebrock	178	51.53 N	8.14 E
Herzliyya	210	32.10 N	34.50 E
Herzogenburg	164	48.17 N	15.42 E
Hesdin	166	50.22 N	2.02 E
Hespeler	264	43.26 N	80.19 W
Hesperia, Calif., U.S.	274	34.25 N	117.18 W
Hesperia, Mich., U.S.	244	43.34 N	86.04 W
Hesperus Mountain ∧	254	37.27 N	108.05 W
Hess ≃	236	63.34 N	133.57 W
Hessen □[3]	164	50.30 N	9.15 E
Hessen Cassal	268	41.00 N	85.05 W
Hessisch Lichtenau	178	51.12 N	9.43 E
Hesston, Kans., U.S.	252	38.08 N	97.26 W
Hesston, Pa., U.S.	266	40.26 N	78.07 W
Het ≃	200	20.49 N	104.01 E
Hetian	190	37.08 N	79.54 E
Hetianhe ≃	190	40.30 N	80.45 E
Het Loo, Paleis ♜	164	52.14 N	5.56 E
Hetouxi ≃	196	23.58 N	117.24 E
Hettinger	252	46.00 N	102.39 W
Hettstedt	164	51.38 N	11.30 E
Heuchin	162	50.28 N	2.16 E
Heule	176	50.50 N	3.14 E
Heusden	176	51.02 N	5.16 E
Heuvelton	264	44.37 N	75.25 W
Hève, Cap de la ➤	162	49.31 N	0.04 E
Heves	164	47.36 N	20.17 E
Heves □[6]	164	47.50 N	20.15 E
Hewlett	262	37.55 N	77.35 W
Hexian	190	24.15 N	111.43 E
Heyburn	256	42.34 N	113.46 W
Heyrieux	166	45.38 N	5.03 E
Heysham	162	54.02 N	2.54 W
Heyworth	268	40.19 N	88.59 W
Heze	194	35.17 N	115.27 E
Hialeah	246	25.49 N	80.17 W
Hiawassee	246	34.58 N	83.46 W
Hiawatha, Kans., U.S.	252	39.51 N	95.32 W
Hiawatha, Utah, U.S.	254	39.29 N	111.01 W
Hibaiyo	202	10.16 N	123.19 E
Hibbing	244	47.25 N	92.56 W
Hibbs, Point ➤	228	42.38 S	145.15 E
Hibernia Reef ✧[2]	226	12.00 S	123.23 E
Hibuson Island I	202	10.26 N	125.29 E
Hickman, Calif., U.S.	272	37.37 N	120.45 W
Hickman, Ky., U.S.	248	36.34 N	89.11 W
Hickman, Nebr., U.S.	252	40.37 N	96.38 W
Hickman's Harbour	240	48.06 N	53.44 W
Hickory, Miss., U.S.	248	32.19 N	89.01 W
Hickory, N.C., U.S.	246	35.44 N	81.21 W
Hickory, Pa., U.S.	266	40.18 N	80.18 W
Hickory Corners	268	42.27 N	85.22 W
Hickory Hills	268	41.43 N	87.49 W
Hicksville	268	41.18 N	84.46 W
Hico	250	31.59 N	98.02 W
Hidaka-sammyaku ⋀	192a	42.35 N	142.45 E
Hidalgo, Méx.	278	23.10 N	103.13 W
Hidalgo, Méx.	278	25.59 N	100.27 W
Hidalgo, Méx.	278	27.47 N	99.52 W
Hidalgo, Méx.	278	24.15 N	99.26 W
Hidalgo □[3]	278	20.30 N	99.00 W
Hidalgo, Presa @[1]	278	26.30 N	108.35 W
Hidalgo del Parral	278	26.56 N	105.40 W
Hida-sammyaku ⋀	192	36.25 N	137.40 E
Hidden Hills	274	34.09 N	118.43 W
Hidrolândia	296	16.58 S	49.14 W
Hidrolina	296	14.37 S	49.25 W
Hieflau	164	47.36 N	14.44 E
Higashiichiki	192	31.40 N	130.20 E
Higashine	192	38.26 N	140.24 E
Higashiōsaka	192	34.39 N	135.35 E
Higbee	248	39.19 N	92.31 W
Higganum	261	41.30 N	72.34 W
Higgins	250	36.07 N	100.02 W
Higgins Lake @	244	44.30 N	84.45 W
Higginsville	248	39.04 N	93.43 W
High Bar Indian Reserve •[4]	238	51.06 N	122.00 W
High Bridge	262	40.40 N	74.54 W
Highgate	266	42.30 N	81.49 W
Highgate Center	260	44.58 N	73.03 W
Highgate Springs	260	44.58 N	72.59 W
Highgrove	274	34.01 N	117.20 W
High Island I	244	45.42 N	85.40 W
High Knob ∧	242	39.08 N	78.26 W
Highland, Calif., U.S.	274	34.08 N	117.12 W
Highland, Ill., U.S.	248	38.44 N	89.41 W
Highland, Ind., U.S.	268	41.33 N	87.27 W
Highland, Kans., U.S.	252	39.52 N	95.16 W
Highland, Md., U.S.	262	39.11 N	76.57 W
Highland, N.Y., U.S.	261	41.43 N	73.58 W
Highland Falls	261	41.22 N	73.58 W
Highland Heights	266	41.32 N	81.29 W
Highland Home	248	31.57 N	86.19 W
Highland Park, Ill., U.S.	268	42.11 N	87.48 W
Highland Park, Mich., U.S.	268	42.24 N	83.06 W
Highland Park, Tex., U.S.	250	32.50 N	96.48 W
Highland Peak ∧	258	38.33 N	119.45 W
Highlands, N.J., U.S.	262	40.24 N	73.59 W
Highlands, N.C., U.S.	246	35.03 N	83.12 W
Highlands, Tex., U.S.	250	29.49 N	95.04 W
Highland Springs	262	37.33 N	77.20 W
Highmore	252	44.31 N	99.27 W
High Peak ∧	202	15.30 N	120.07 E
High Plains ≚	234	38.30 N	103.00 W
High Point	246	35.58 N	80.01 W
High Point ∧	242	41.19 N	74.40 W
High Prairie	238	55.26 N	116.29 W
High River	238	50.35 N	113.52 W
High Rock	246	26.36 N	76.18 W
High Rock ∧	242	39.33 N	79.06 W
High Rock Lake @[1]	246	35.40 N	80.17 W
High Spire	262	40.13 N	76.48 W
High Springs	246	29.50 N	82.36 W
Hightstown	262	40.16 N	74.31 W
Highwater	260	45.01 N	72.26 W
Highway City	272	36.49 N	119.54 W
Highwood, Ill., U.S.	268	42.13 N	87.48 W
Highwood, Mont., U.S.	256	47.35 N	110.47 W
Highwood ≃	238	50.49 N	113.47 W
Highwood Baldy ∧	256	47.27 N	110.37 W
Highwood Mountains ⋀	256	47.25 N	110.30 W
High Wycombe	174	51.38 N	0.46 W
Higuera de Zaragozao	278	25.59 N	109.16 W
Higuera Gorda	278	22.04 N	104.29 W
Higueras	250	25.58 N	100.01 W
Higüero, Punta ➤	282	18.22 N	67.16 W
Higuerote	290	10.29 N	66.06 W
Higüey	282	18.37 N	68.42 W
Hiiumaa I	160	58.52 N	22.40 E
Híjar	168	41.10 N	0.27 W
Ḥijāz, Jabal al- ⋀	214	19.45 N	41.55 E
Hikari	192	33.58 N	131.56 E
Hikone	192	35.15 N	136.15 E
Hikurangi ∧	230	38.21 S	176.52 E
Hilaban Island I	202	11.57 N	125.34 E
Hilbert	244	44.09 N	88.10 W
Hildburghausen	164	50.25 N	10.44 E
Hilden	178	51.10 N	6.56 E
Hildesheim	178	52.09 N	9.57 E
Hildesheim □[6]	178	51.40 N	10.00 E
Hildreth	252	40.20 N	99.03 W
Hillaby, Mount ∧	282	13.12 N	59.35 W
Hill Bank	278	17.35 N	88.42 W
Hill City, Kans., U.S.	252	39.22 N	99.51 W
Hill City, Minn., U.S.	244	46.59 N	93.36 W
Hill City, S. Dak., U.S.	252	43.56 N	103.35 W
Hillcrest	268	41.57 N	89.04 W
Hillcrest Center	274	35.23 N	118.57 W
Hillcrest Mines	238	49.34 N	114.23 W
Hillcrest Orchard	268	41.51 N	83.29 W
Hillcrest Park	272	38.07 N	122.16 W
Hillegom	178	52.18 N	4.35 E
Hillerød	160	55.56 N	12.19 E
Hilliard, Fla., U.S.	246	30.41 N	81.55 W
Hilliard, Ohio, U.S.	266	40.02 N	83.10 W
Hilliards	266	41.05 N	79.50 W
Hillingdon •[8]	174	51.32 N	0.27 W
Hillisburg	268	40.17 N	86.20 W
Hill Island Lake @	232	60.29 N	109.50 W
Hillister	248	30.40 N	94.23 W
Hillman	244	45.04 N	83.54 W
Hills	252	43.32 N	96.21 W
Hills and Dales	266	39.42 N	84.13 W
Hillsboro, Ill., U.S.	248	39.09 N	89.29 W
Hillsboro, Kans., U.S.	252	38.21 N	97.12 W
Hillsboro, Md., U.S.	262	38.55 N	75.50 W
Hillsboro, Mo., U.S.	248	38.14 N	90.34 W
Hillsboro, N.H., U.S.	242	43.07 N	71.54 W
Hillsboro, N. Mex., U.S.	254	32.55 N	107.34 W
Hillsboro, N.C., U.S.	246	36.05 N	79.07 W
Hillsboro, N. Dak., U.S.	252	47.26 N	97.03 W
Hillsboro, Ohio, U.S.	242	39.12 N	83.37 W
Hillsboro, Oreg., U.S.	270	45.31 N	122.59 W
Hillsboro, Tex., U.S.	250	32.01 N	97.08 W
Hillsboro, Wis., U.S.	244	43.39 N	90.21 W
Hillsboro Canal ☰	246	26.19 N	80.05 W
Hillsborough, N.B., Can.	240	45.56 N	64.39 W
Hillsborough, Calif., U.S.	272	37.34 N	122.20 W
Hillsborough □[6]	261	42.49 N	71.41 W
Hillsborough ≃	246	27.56 N	82.27 W
Hillsborough, Cape ➤	228	20.54 S	149.03 E
Hillsborough Bay C	240	46.10 N	63.05 W
Hillsburgh	264	43.47 N	80.09 W
Hills Creek Reservoir @[1]	256	43.40 N	122.26 W
Hillsdale, Mich., U.S.	268	41.55 N	84.38 W
Hillsdale, N.Y., U.S.	261	42.11 N	73.31 W
Hillsdale, Pa., U.S.	266	40.45 N	78.53 W
Hillsdale □[6]	268	41.53 N	84.36 W
Hills Flat	272	39.14 N	121.03 W
Hillside Gardens	268	42.16 N	84.27 W
Hillside Lake	261	41.36 N	73.50 W
Hillston	226	33.29 S	145.32 E
Hillsville, Pa., U.S.	266	41.01 N	80.30 W
Hillsville, Va., U.S.	246	36.46 N	80.44 W
Hilltop	262	39.49 N	75.04 W
Hilltown	262	40.20 N	75.14 W
Hilmar	272	37.25 N	120.51 W
Hilo	275d	19.43 N	155.05 W
Hilo Bay C	275d	19.44 N	155.05 W
Hilonghilong, Mount ∧	202	9.05 N	125.42 E
Hilongos	202	10.23 N	124.45 E
Hilton, N.Y., U.S.	264	43.17 N	77.48 W
Hilton, Pa., U.S.	262	40.00 N	76.49 W
Hilton Head Island	246	32.13 N	80.45 W
Hilton Head Island I	246	32.12 N	80.45 W
Hiltrup	178	51.54 N	7.38 E
Hilts	258	41.59 N	122.37 W
Hilversum	178	52.14 N	5.10 E
Hima	246	37.07 N	83.47 W
Himachal Pradesh □[8]	206	32.00 N	77.00 E
Himalayas ⋀	206	28.00 N	84.00 E
Himamaylan	202	10.06 N	122.52 E
Himarë	172	40.07 N	19.44 E
Himeji	192	34.49 N	134.42 E
Himi	192	36.51 N	136.59 E
Himmelsthür	178	52.09 N	9.55 E
Ḥimṣ (Homs)	212	34.44 N	36.43 E
Ḥimṣ □[8]	212	34.15 N	38.00 E
Ḥimṣ, Baḥrat @[1]	212	34.39 N	36.34 E
Hinabangan	202	11.42 N	125.04 E
Hinatuan	202	8.22 N	126.22 E
Hinatuan Island I	202	9.47 N	125.42 E
Hinatuan Passage Ц	202	9.35 N	125.55 E
Hinche	282	19.09 N	72.01 W
Hinchinbrook Entrance Ц	236	60.25 N	146.50 W
Hinchinbrook Island I, Austl.	228	18.23 S	146.17 E
Hinchinbrook Island I, Alaska, U.S.	236	60.22 N	146.30 W
Hinckley, Eng., U.K.	174	52.33 N	1.21 W
Hinckley, Ill., U.S.	268	41.46 N	88.38 W
Hinckley, Minn., U.S.	244	46.01 N	92.56 W
Hinckley, Ohio, U.S.	266	41.14 N	81.45 W
Hinckley, Utah, U.S.	254	39.20 N	112.40 W
Hincks, Murlong, and Nicholls National Park ♠	228	33.50 S	136.00 E
Hindang	202	10.26 N	124.44 E
Hindenburg → Zabrze	164	50.18 N	18.46 E
Hindman	246	37.20 N	82.59 W
Hindmarsh, Lake @	228	36.03 S	141.55 E
Hinds Lake @	240	48.57 N	57.00 W
Hindu Kush ⋀	206	36.00 N	71.30 E
Hines	256	43.34 N	119.05 W
Hines Creek	238	56.15 N	118.36 W
Hinesville	246	31.51 N	81.36 W
Hingal ≃	208	25.30 N	65.30 E
Hingatungan	202	10.35 N	125.11 E
Hingham	261	42.14 N	70.53 W
Hingol ≃	206	25.23 N	65.28 E
Hinigaran	202	10.17 N	122.51 E
Hinkley	274	34.56 N	117.12 W
Hinnøya I	160	68.30 N	16.00 E
Hino ≃	192	35.27 N	133.23 E
Hinoba-an	202	9.35 N	122.28 E
Hinojosa del Duque	168	38.30 N	5.09 W
Hinokage	192	32.39 N	131.24 E
Hinsdale, Ill., U.S.	268	41.48 N	87.56 W
Hinsdale, Mass., U.S.	261	42.26 N	73.08 W
Hinsdale, Mont., U.S.	256	48.24 N	107.05 W
Hinsdale, N.H., U.S.	242	42.47 N	72.29 W
Hinsdale, N.Y., U.S.	266	42.10 N	78.23 W
Hinterrhein ≃	166	46.32 N	9.12 E
Hinton, Alta., Can.	238	53.25 N	117.34 W
Hinton, Okla., U.S.	250	35.28 N	98.21 W
Hinton, W. Va., U.S.	246	37.41 N	80.53 W
Hinundayan	202	10.21 N	125.15 E
Hipólito	278	25.41 N	101.26 W
Hipólito Yrigoyen	294	32.55 S	66.20 W
Hirado	192	33.22 N	129.33 E
Hirado-shima I	192	33.20 N	129.30 E
Hiraizumi	192	38.59 N	141.07 E
Hirākud @[1]	206	21.31 N	83.52 E
Hiram, Maine, U.S.	242	43.53 N	70.49 W
Hiram, Ohio, U.S.	266	41.19 N	81.09 W
Hirata	192	35.26 N	132.49 E
Hiratsuka	192	35.19 N	139.21 E
Hirfanlı Barajı •[6]	212	39.18 N	33.29 E
Hîrlău	172	47.25 N	26.54 E
Hiroo	192a	42.17 N	143.19 E
Hirosaki	192	40.35 N	140.28 E
Hiroshima	192	34.24 N	132.27 E
Hirson	176	49.55 N	4.05 E
Hîrșova	172	44.41 N	27.57 E
Hirtshals	160	57.35 N	9.58 E
Hisār	206	29.09 N	75.44 E
Hisār, Koh-i- ⋀	206	34.45 N	66.35 E
Ḥismā ≚	208	29.00 N	35.40 E
Hispaniola I	282	19.00 N	71.00 W
Hita	192	33.19 N	130.56 E
Hitachi	192	36.36 N	140.39 E
Hitachi-ōta	192	36.32 N	140.31 E
Hitchcock	250	29.21 N	95.01 W
Hitchin	174	51.57 N	0.17 W
Hitchins	242	38.17 N	82.55 W
Hitoyoshi	192	32.13 N	130.45 E
Hiuchiga-take ∧	192	36.57 N	139.17 E
Hi Vista	274	34.44 N	117.47 W
Hiwannee	248	31.43 N	88.48 W
Hiwasa	192	33.44 N	134.25 E
Hiwassee ≃	246	35.19 N	84.47 W
Hiwassee Reservoir @[1]	246	35.10 N	84.05 W
Hixon	238	53.27 N	122.36 W
Hixson	246	35.09 N	85.14 W
Hjälmaren @	160	59.15 N	15.45 E
Hjelmelandsvågen	160	59.14 N	6.11 E
Hjo	160	58.18 N	14.17 E
Hjørring	160	57.28 N	9.59 E
Hjort Basin ✧[1]	148	59.00 S	158.00 E
Hlinsko	164	49.45 N	15.55 E
Hlohovec	164	48.50 N	17.35 E
Hluboká nad Vltavou	164	49.03 N	14.27 E
Hlučín	164	49.54 N	18.12 E
Hnilec ≃	164	48.53 N	21.01 E
Ho	222	6.35 N	0.30 E
Hoa-binh	200	20.50 N	105.20 E
Hoagland	268	40.57 N	85.00 W
Hoanib ≃	224	19.27 S	12.46 E
Hoare Bay C	232	65.20 N	62.30 W
Hoarusib ≃	224	19.03 S	12.36 E
Hoback ≃	254	43.19 N	110.44 W
Hobart, Austl.	228	42.53 S	147.19 E
Hobart, Ind., U.S.	268	41.32 N	87.15 W
Hobart, Okla., U.S.	250	35.01 N	99.06 W
Hobart, Wash., U.S.	270	47.25 N	121.58 W
Hobbs, Ind., U.S.	268	40.17 N	85.57 W
Hobbs, N. Mex., U.S.	250	32.42 N	103.08 W
Hobe Sound	246	27.04 N	80.08 W
Hobgood	246	36.02 N	77.24 W
Hobo	290	2.35 N	75.27 W
Hoboken, Bel.	176	51.10 N	4.21 E
Hoboken, N.J., U.S.	242	40.45 N	74.03 W
Hobra Bet She'arim ⊥	210	32.42 N	35.08 E
Hobson, Mont., U.S.	256	47.00 N	109.52 W
Hobson, Va., U.S.	262	36.54 N	76.31 W
Hobson Lake @	238	52.30 N	120.20 W
Hocalı	172	38.41 N	27.41 E
Hochandochtla Mountain ∧	236	65.32 N	154.50 W
Hochdahl	178	51.13 N	6.56 E
Hochgolling ∧	164	47.16 N	13.45 E
Hochneukirch	178	51.06 N	6.26 E
Hochschwab ⋀	164	47.36 N	15.05 E
Höchst	166	49.48 N	8.59 E
Höchstadt an der Aisch	164	49.42 N	10.44 E
Hochtaunus, Naturpark ♠	166	50.20 N	8.20 E
Hockenheim	164	49.19 N	8.33 E
Hocking ≃	242	39.12 N	81.45 W
Hoddesdon	174	51.46 N	0.01 W
Hodeida → Al-Ḥudaydah	204	14.48 N	42.57 E
Hodge	248	32.17 N	92.43 W
Hodgenville	248	37.34 N	85.44 W
Hodges Hill ∧[2]	240	49.04 N	55.53 W
Hodh •[1]	222	16.10 N	8.40 W
Hod HaSharon	210	32.09 N	34.53 E
Hódmezővásárhely	164	46.25 N	20.20 E
Hodna, Chott el @	168	35.30 N	4.45 E
Hodna, Monts du ⋀	168	35.50 N	4.50 E
Hodna, Plaine du ≚	168	35.38 N	4.30 E
Hodonín	164	48.51 N	17.08 E
Hodzana ≃	236	66.15 N	147.48 W
Hoehne	252	37.17 N	104.23 W
Hoek van Holland	178	51.59 N	4.09 E
Hoeryŏng	194	42.27 N	129.44 E
Hof, B.R.D.	164	50.18 N	11.55 E
Hof, Ísland	160a	64.34 N	14.39 W
Hofei → Hefei	196	31.51 N	117.17 E
Hoffman	252	45.50 N	95.48 W
Hoffman Estates	268	42.03 N	88.05 W
Hofgeismar	178	51.30 N	9.22 E
Hofheim i Ufr	164	50.08 N	10.31 E
Höfn	160a	64.17 N	15.10 W
Hofors	160	60.33 N	16.17 E
Hofsjökull ⩛	160a	64.48 N	18.50 W
Hōfu	192	34.03 N	131.34 E
Hofuf → Al-Hufūf	208	25.22 N	49.34 E
Höganäs	160	56.12 N	12.33 E
Hogan Lake @	244	45.52 N	78.30 W
Hogansburg	260	44.59 N	74.40 W
Hogansville	246	33.11 N	84.55 W
Hogarth, Mount ∧[2]	228	21.48 S	136.58 E
Hogatza ≃	236	66.00 N	155.29 W
Hogback Mountain ∧, Mont., U.S.	256	44.54 N	112.07 W
Hogback Mountain ∧, S.C., U.S.	246	35.10 N	82.17 W
Hogeland	256	48.51 N	108.40 W
Hoggar → Ahaggar ⋀	214	23.00 N	6.30 E
Hog Island I	244	45.48 N	85.22 W
Hog Point ➤	202	5.18 N	119.15 E
Högsby	160	57.10 N	16.02 E
Hohe Acht ∧	164	50.23 N	7.00 E
Hohenau	294	27.05 S	55.45 W
Hohenau an der March	164	48.36 N	16.55 E
Hohenems	180	47.22 N	9.41 E
Hohenlimburg	178	51.21 N	7.35 E
Hohen-Neuendorf	164	52.40 N	13.16 E
Hohensalza → Inowrocław	164	52.48 N	18.15 E
Hohenthurn	164	46.33 N	13.40 E
Hohenwald	248	35.33 N	87.33 W
Hohoe	222	7.09 N	0.28 E
Hōhoku	192	34.17 N	130.57 E
Hoholitna ≃	236	61.31 N	157.00 W
Hoi-an	200	15.52 N	108.19 E
Hoisington	252	38.31 N	98.47 W
Hojāi	200	26.00 N	92.51 E
Hōjō	192	33.58 N	132.46 E
Hokah	244	43.45 N	91.21 W
Hokendauqua	262	40.39 N	75.29 W
Hokes Bluff	248	33.59 N	85.52 W
Hokianga Harbour C	230	35.25 S	173.24 E
Hokitika	230	42.43 S	170.58 E
Hokkaidō □[5]	192a	44.00 N	143.00 E
Holberg	238	50.31 N	128.01 W
Holbrook, Ariz., U.S.	254	34.54 N	110.10 W
Holbrook, Mass., U.S.	261	42.09 N	71.01 W
Holbrook, Nebr., U.S.	252	40.18 N	100.01 W
Holcomb, Ill., U.S.	268	42.04 N	89.06 W
Holcomb, N.Y., U.S.	264	42.54 N	77.25 W
Holden, Alta., Can.	238	53.14 N	112.14 W
Holden, Mass., U.S.	261	42.21 N	71.52 W
Holden, Mo., U.S.	248	38.43 N	94.01 W
Holden, Utah, U.S.	254	39.06 N	112.16 W
Holden, W. Va., U.S.	242	37.50 N	82.04 W
Holden Village	270	48.12 N	120.47 W
Holdenville	250	35.05 N	96.24 W
Holder	246	28.58 N	82.25 W
Holdingford	244	45.44 N	94.26 W
Holdrege	252	40.26 N	99.22 W
Hole in the Mountain Peak ∧	258	40.55 N	115.05 W
Holešov	164	49.20 N	17.35 E
Holetown	285g	13.11 N	59.39 W
Holgate	268	41.15 N	84.08 W
Holguín	284p	20.53 N	76.15 W
Holič	164	48.49 N	17.10 E
Holice	164	50.04 N	15.59 E
Holiday Hills	268	42.18 N	88.13 W
Holitna ≃	236	61.40 N	157.12 W
Höljes	160	60.54 N	12.36 E
Hollabrunn	164	48.34 N	16.05 E
Holladay	254	40.40 N	111.49 W
Hollam's Bird Island I	224	24.45 S	14.34 E
Holland → Netherlands □[1]	158	52.15 N	5.30 E
Holland, Man., Can.	252	49.32 N	98.55 W
Holland, Mich., U.S.	268	42.47 N	86.07 W
Holland, N.Y., U.S.	266	42.38 N	78.33 W
Holland, Ohio, U.S.	268	41.37 N	83.43 W
Holland, Tex., U.S.	250	30.53 N	97.24 W
Holland, Va., U.S.	262	36.41 N	76.47 W
Holland □[6]	174	52.53 N	0.05 W
Holland □[9]	178	52.20 N	4.45 E
Hollandale	248	33.10 N	90.58 W
Hollandia → Djajapura	198	2.32 S	140.42 E
Holland Landing	264	44.06 N	79.29 W
Holland-on-Sea	174	51.48 N	1.13 E
Höllental V	164	47.41 N	15.43 E
Holley	264	43.14 N	78.02 W
Holliday	250	33.49 N	98.42 W
Hollidaysburg	266	40.26 N	78.23 W
Hollis, N.H., U.S.	261	42.44 N	71.35 W
Hollis, Okla., U.S.	250	34.41 N	99.55 W
Hollister	272	36.51 N	121.24 W
Holliston	261	42.12 N	71.26 W
Holloway	266	40.10 N	81.08 W
Hollow Rock	248	36.02 N	88.16 W
Hollowville	261	42.12 N	73.42 W
Hollsopple	266	40.13 N	78.56 W
Holly, Colo., U.S.	252	38.03 N	102.07 W
Holly, Mich., U.S.	268	42.48 N	83.38 W
Holly, Wash., U.S.	270	47.34 N	122.58 W
Holly Grove	248	34.36 N	91.12 W
Holly Hill, Fla., U.S.	246	29.14 N	81.02 W
Holly Hill, S.C., U.S.	246	33.19 N	80.25 W
Holly Park	262	39.53 N	74.10 W
Holly Ridge	248	32.28 N	91.38 W
Holly Springs	248	34.41 N	89.26 W
Hollywood, Fla., U.S.	246	26.00 N	80.09 W
Hollywood, Md., U.S.	262	38.21 N	76.34 W
Hollywood •[8]	274	34.06 N	118.21 W
Holman Island	232	70.43 N	117.43 W
Hólmavík	160a	65.43 N	21.43 W
Holmdel	262	40.21 N	74.11 W
Holmen	244	43.58 N	91.15 W
Holmes	261	41.31 N	73.39 W
Holmes □[6]	266	40.33 N	81.55 W
Holmes, Mount ∧	256	44.49 N	110.51 W
Holmestrand	160	59.29 N	10.18 E
Holmesville	266	40.38 N	81.55 W
Holmia	290	4.59 N	59.40 W
Holmsjön @	160	62.41 N	16.33 E
Holmsund	160	63.42 N	20.21 E
Holod	172	46.47 N	22.08 E
Holoit, Punta ➤	278	21.35 N	88.10 W
Holon	210	32.01 N	34.46 E
Holstebro	160	56.21 N	8.38 E
Holstein	252	42.29 N	95.33 W
Holsteinsborg	232	66.55 N	53.40 W
Holston ≃	246	35.57 N	83.51 W
Holston High Knob ∧	246	36.27 N	82.05 W
Holsworthy	162	50.49 N	4.21 W
Holt, Ala., U.S.	248	33.15 N	87.29 W
Holt, Calif., U.S.	272	37.56 N	121.26 W
Holt, Fla., U.S.	248	30.43 N	86.45 W
Holt, Mich., U.S.	268	42.39 N	84.31 W
Holter Lake @[1]	256	46.55 N	111.57 W
Holton	252	39.28 N	95.44 W
Holtville	258	32.49 N	115.23 W
Holtwood	262	39.50 N	76.19 W
Holy Cross	236	62.12 N	159.47 W
Holy Cross Mountain ∧	238	53.47 N	120.47 W
Holyhead	162	53.19 N	4.38 W
Holy Island I	162	55.41 N	1.48 W
Holyoke, Colo., U.S.	252	40.35 N	102.18 W
Holyoke, Mass., U.S.	261	42.12 N	72.37 W
Holyrood	252	38.35 N	98.25 W
Holy Sepulchre, The Church of the ♜[1]	210	31.46 N	35.14 E
Holýšov	164	49.36 N	13.05 E
Holzen	178	51.26 N	7.31 E
Holzgerlingen	180	48.38 N	9.00 E
Holzhausen	178	52.13 N	8.01 E
Holzheim	178	51.09 N	6.39 E
Holzkirchen	164	47.52 N	11.42 E
Holzminden	178	51.50 N	9.27 E
Holzwickede	178	51.30 N	7.36 E
Homalin	190	24.52 N	94.55 E
Homathko ≃	238	50.55 N	124.50 W
Homathko Snowfield ⩛	238	51.05 N	124.30 W
Homāyunshahr	208	32.41 N	51.31 E
Homberg	178	51.28 N	6.38 E
Hombori Tondo ∧	222	15.16 N	1.40 W
Hombre Muerto, Salar de ≚	294	25.20 S	67.05 W
Homburg → Bad Homburg vor der Höhe, B.R.D.	164	50.13 N	8.37 E
Homburg, B.R.D.	164	49.19 N	7.20 E
Home, Pa., U.S.	266	40.44 N	79.06 W
Home, Wash., U.S.	270	47.17 N	122.46 W
Homeacre	266	40.51 N	79.55 W
Home Bay C	232	68.45 N	67.10 W
Home Corner	268	40.32 N	85.40 W
Homedale, Idaho, U.S.	256	43.37 N	116.56 W
Homedale, Ohio, U.S.	266	40.04 N	83.02 W
Home Gardens	274	33.53 N	117.30 W
Home Hill	228	19.40 S	147.25 E
Homer, Alaska, U.S.	236	59.39 N	151.33 W
Homer, Ga., U.S.	246	34.20 N	83.30 W
Homer, La., U.S.	248	32.48 N	93.04 W
Homer, Mich., U.S.	268	42.09 N	84.49 W
Homer, Nebr., U.S.	252	42.19 N	96.29 W
Homer, N.Y., U.S.	264	42.38 N	76.11 W
Homer, Ohio, U.S.	266	40.15 N	82.31 W
Homer City	266	40.32 N	79.10 W
Homer Tunnel •[5]	230	44.45 S	168.00 E
Homerville, Ga., U.S.	246	31.02 N	82.45 W
Homerville, Ohio, U.S.	266	41.02 N	82.08 W
Homer Youngs Peak ∧	256	45.19 N	113.41 W
Homestead, Fla., U.S.	246	25.29 N	80.29 W
Homestead, Pa., U.S.	266	40.24 N	79.54 W
Homestead National Monument of America ♠	252	40.14 N	96.54 W
Homewood, Ala., U.S.	248	33.29 N	86.48 W
Homewood, Ill., U.S.	268	41.34 N	87.40 W
Homeworth	266	40.50 N	81.04 W
Hominy	250	36.25 N	96.24 W
Hommura	192	34.22 N	139.15 E
Homochitto ≃	248	31.09 N	91.31 W
Homonhon Island I	202	10.45 N	125.43 E
Homosassa	246	28.47 N	82.37 W
Homs → Al-Khums, Lībīya	214	32.39 N	14.16 E
Homs → Ḥimṣ, Sūrīy	212	34.44 N	36.43 E
Honaker	246	37.01 N	81.59 W
Honan → Henan □[4]	190	34.00 N	114.00 E
Honaz	172	37.45 N	29.17 E
Honbetsu	192a	43.07 N	143.37 E
Honda	290	5.12 N	74.45 W
Honda, Bahía C, Col.	290	12.23 N	71.46 W
Honda, Bahía C, Cuba	284p	22.57 N	83.10 W
Honda Bay C	202	9.50 N	118.53 E
Hon-dien, Nui ∧	200	11.35 N	108.40 E
Hondo, Alta., Can.	238	55.04 N	114.02 W
Hondo, Nihon	192	32.27 N	130.12 E
Hondo, N. Mex., U.S.	254	33.23 N	105.16 W
Hondo, Tex., U.S.	250	29.21 N	99.09 W
Hondo ≃	278	18.29 N	88.19 W
Hondo, Rio ≃	250	33.22 N	104.24 W
Hondsrug ⋀[2]	164	52.50 N	6.50 E
Honduras □[1]	276	15.00 N	86.30 W
Honduras, Cabo de ➤	280	16.00 N	85.55 W
Honduras, Gulf of C	276	16.10 N	87.50 W
Honea Path	246	34.27 N	82.24 W
Hønefoss	160	60.10 N	10.18 E
Honeoye	264	42.47 N	77.31 W
Honeoye Falls	264	42.57 N	77.36 W
Honesdale	242	41.34 N	75.16 W
Honey Brook	262	40.06 N	75.55 W
Honey Creek	268	42.45 N	88.19 W
Honey Grove	250	33.35 N	95.55 W
Honey Lake @	258	40.16 N	120.19 W
Honeymoon Bay	238	48.49 N	124.10 W
Honeyville	254	41.38 N	112.04 W
Honfleur	176	49.25 N	0.14 E
Hon-gai	200	20.57 N	107.05 E
Hongdong	190	36.19 N	111.39 E
Honge ≃	196	32.25 N	115.35 E
Honghaiwan C	196	22.40 N	115.10 E
Honghe	200	23.23 N	102.35 E
Honghu	196	29.48 N	113.27 E
Honghu @	196	29.52 N	113.23 E
Hongjiang	190	27.00 N	109.51 E
Hong Kong □[2]	190	25.15 N	114.10 E
Hong Kong I	196	22.15 N	114.11 E
Hongliuyuan	190	41.04 N	95.26 E
Hongshuihe ≃	200	23.24 N	110.12 E
Hongtuzhang ∧	196	23.46 N	115.56 E
Hongzehu @	196	33.16 N	118.34 E
Honiara	226	9.27 S	159.57 E
Honiton	162	50.48 N	3.13 W
Honjō, Nihon	192	39.23 N	140.03 E
Honjō, Nihon	192	36.14 N	139.11 E
Honningsvåg	160	70.59 N	25.50 E
Honokaa	275d	20.05 N	155.28 W
Honokahua	275a	21.00 N	156.39 W
Honokawai	275a	20.57 N	156.41 W
Honolulu	275c	21.19 N	157.52 W
Honolulu □[6]	275c	21.19 N	157.52 W
Honomu	275d	19.52 N	155.07 W
Honouliuli	275c	21.22 N	158.02 W
Honshū I	192	36.00 N	138.00 E
Honuapo Bay C	275d	19.05 N	155.33 W
Hood	272	38.22 N	121.31 W
Hood ≃	232	67.26 N	108.53 W
Hood, Mount ∧	256	45.23 N	121.41 W
Hoodoo Peak ∧	256	48.15 N	120.19 W
Hood River	270	45.43 N	121.31 W
Hood River □[6]	270	45.30 N	121.40 W
Hoodsport	270	47.24 N	123.09 W
Hoods Range ⋀	228	28.35 S	144.30 E
Hoogeveen	178	52.43 N	6.29 E
Hoogezand	178	53.09 N	6.47 E
Hooghly ≃	206	21.56 N	88.04 E
Hoogvliet	178	51.52 N	4.21 E
Hooker	250	36.52 N	101.13 W
Hook Head ➤	162	52.07 N	6.55 W
Hook Island I	228	20.08 S	148.55 E
Hook Point ➤	228	25.48 S	153.05 E
Hooks	248	33.28 N	94.15 W
Hoolehua	275a	21.10 N	157.06 W
Hoonah	236	58.07 N	135.26 W
Hoopa	258	41.03 N	123.40 W
Hoopa Valley Indian Reservation •[4]	258	41.08 N	123.40 W
Hooper	252	41.37 N	96.33 W
Hooper Bay	236	61.31 N	166.06 W
Hoopersville	262	38.16 N	76.11 W
Hoopeston	268	40.28 N	87.40 W
Hooping Harbour	240	50.37 N	56.17 W
Hoople	252	48.32 N	97.38 W
Hoorn	178	52.38 N	5.04 E
Hoosick Falls	242	42.54 N	73.21 W
Hoover Dam •[6]	254	36.00 N	114.27 W
Hooversville	266	40.09 N	78.55 W
Hope, B.C., Can.	238	49.23 N	121.26 W
Hope, Alaska, U.S.	236	60.55 N	149.38 W
Hope, Ark., U.S.	248	33.40 N	93.36 W
Hope, Ind., U.S.	248	39.18 N	85.46 W
Hope, N. Mex., U.S.	250	32.49 N	104.44 W
Hope, N. Dak., U.S.	252	47.19 N	97.43 W
Hope, R.I., U.S.	261	41.44 N	71.34 W
Hope, Ben ∧	162	58.24 N	4.36 W
Hope, Point ➤	236	68.21 N	166.50 W
Hopedale, Newf., Can.	232	55.50 N	60.10 W
Hopedale, Ill., U.S.	248	40.25 N	89.25 W
Hopedale, La., U.S.	248	29.51 N	89.41 W
Hopedale, Mass., U.S.	261	42.08 N	71.33 W
Hopedale, Ohio, U.S.	266	40.20 N	80.54 W
Hope Farm	261	41.44 N	73.40 W
Hopeh → Hebei □[4]	194	38.00 N	116.00 E
Hope Island I	238	50.55 N	127.53 W
Hopeland	262	40.14 N	76.16 W
Hopelchén	278	19.46 N	89.51 W
Hope Mills	246	34.59 N	78.57 W
Hope Mountains ⋀	232	54.20 N	62.50 W
Hopes Advance, Baie C	232	59.25 N	69.40 W
Hopes Advance, Cap ➤	232	61.05 N	69.35 W
Hopetoun	226	33.57 S	120.07 E
Hopetown	218	29.34 S	24.03 E
Hope Valley	261	41.30 N	71.43 W
Hopewell, N.J., U.S.	262	40.23 N	74.46 W
Hopewell, Pa., U.S.	266	40.08 N	78.16 W
Hopewell, Va., U.S.	262	37.18 N	77.17 W
Hopewell Islands II	232	58.25 N	78.00 W
Hopewell Junction	261	41.35 N	73.48 W
Hopewell Village National Historic Site ⊥	242	40.12 N	75.46 W
Hopi Buttes ∧	254	35.20 N	110.15 W
Hopi Indian Reservation •[4]	254	36.00 N	110.35 W
Hopkins, Mich., U.S.	268	42.37 N	85.45 W
Hopkins, Mo., U.S.	248	40.33 N	94.49 W
Hopkinsville	248	36.52 N	87.29 W
Hopkinton, Iowa, U.S.	244	42.21 N	91.15 W
Hopkinton, Mass., U.S.	261	42.13 N	71.31 W
Hopkinton, R.I., U.S.	261	41.28 N	71.47 W
Hopland	258	38.58 N	123.07 W
Hoppo → Hepu	200	21.39 N	109.11 E
Hopwood, Mount ∧	228	21.49 S	144.26 E
Hoquiam	270	46.59 N	123.53 W
Horace Mountain ∧	236	67.40 N	149.06 W
Horatio	248	33.56 N	94.21 W
Horazdovice	164	49.20 N	13.43 E
Horb	164	48.26 N	8.41 E
Horconcitos	280	8.20 N	82.10 W
Hordaland □[6]	160	60.15 N	6.30 E
Horezu	172	45.08 N	23.59 E
Horgen	180	47.15 N	8.36 E
Hořice	164	50.22 N	15.38 E
Horicon	244	43.27 N	88.38 W
Horizon Tablemount ✧[3]	148	19.30 N	169.00 W
Horizontina	294	27.37 S	54.19 W
Horley	174	51.11 N	0.11 W
Hormigueros	284m	18.09 N	67.08 W
Hormoz, Jazīreh-ye I	208	27.04 N	56.28 E
Hormuz, Strait of Ц	208	26.34 N	56.15 E
Horn, B.R.D.	178	51.52 N	8.56 E
Horn, Öst.	164	48.40 N	15.40 E
Horn •[8]	178	53.38 N	10.05 E
Horn ➤	160a	66.28 N	22.28 W
Horn ≃	232	61.30 N	118.01 W
Hornaday ≃	236	69.22 N	123.50 W
Hornafjörður C	160a	64.17 N	15.16 W
Hornavan @	160	66.10 N	17.30 E
Hornbeak	248	36.20 N	89.18 W
Hornbeck	248	31.20 N	93.24 W
Hornby Bay C	232	66.35 N	117.50 W
Horn, Cape → Hornos, Cabo de ➤	288	56.00 S	67.16 W
Horncastle	162	53.13 N	0.07 W
Hornell	266	42.19 N	77.40 W
Hornepayne	232	49.13 N	84.47 W
Hornerstown	262	40.06 N	74.31 W
Horní Počernice	164	50.06 N	14.38 E
Horn Island I	248	30.13 N	88.38 W
Horní Slavkov	164	50.07 N	12.46 E
Hornitos	272	37.30 N	120.14 W
Horn Lake	248	34.58 N	90.02 W
Horn Mountains ⋀	232	62.20 N	120.15 W
Hornos, Cabo de(Cape Horn) ➤	288	56.00 S	67.16 W
Hornsbyville	262	37.12 N	76.28 W
Hornsea	162	53.55 N	0.10 W
Horntown	262	37.58 N	75.28 W
Hornu	176	50.26 N	3.49 E
Horoizumi	192a	42.01 N	143.09 E
Horoshiri-dake ∧	192a	42.43 N	142.41 E
Hořovice	164	49.50 N	13.54 E
Horqueta	294	23.24 S	56.53 W
Horseback Knob ∧[2]	242	39.14 N	83.06 W
Horse Cave	248	37.11 N	85.54 W
Horse Creek	254	41.25 N	105.11 W
Horsefly	238	52.20 N	121.24 W
Horsefly Lake @	238	52.25 N	121.00 W
Horse Head Lake @	252	47.02 N	99.47 W
Horseheads	242	42.10 N	76.50 W
Horse Heaven Hills ⋀[2]	256	46.10 N	119.45 W
Horse Islands II	240	50.13 N	55.45 W
Horsens	160	55.52 N	9.52 E
Horse Shoe Bend	256	43.55 N	116.12 W
Horseshoe Bend National Military Park ♠	248	33.00 N	85.46 W
Horse Shoe Reef ✧[2]	282	18.35 N	64.15 W
Horsham, Austl.	226	36.43 S	142.13 E
Horsham, Eng., U.K.	174	51.04 N	0.21 W
Horsham, Pa., U.S.	262	40.11 N	75.06 W
Horšovský Týn	164	49.32 N	12.56 E
Horsunlu	172	37.55 N	28.36 E
Horten	160	59.25 N	10.30 E
Hortobágy □[9], Magy.	164	47.35 N	21.00 E
Hortobágy □[9], Magy.	172	47.40 N	21.10 E
Horton, Kans., U.S.	252	39.40 N	95.32 W
Horton, Mich., U.S.	268	42.09 N	84.31 W
Horton ≃	236	70.00 N	126.53 W
Horton, Réserve(Horton Reserve) •[4]	240	48.07 N	68.10 W
Horton Lake @	232	67.30 N	122.28 W
Hortonville	244	44.20 N	88.38 W
Horvot Meẓada (Masada) ⊥	210	31.19 N	35.21 E
Horvot Qesari (Cæsarea) ⊥	210	32.30 N	34.53 E
Horvot Shivta (Subeita) ⊥	210	30.53 N	34.38 E
Horw	180	47.01 N	8.18 E
Horwood Lake @	244	48.03 N	82.20 W
Horzum	172	37.10 N	29.30 E
Hosaina	214	7.38 N	37.52 E
Hösbach	164	50.00 N	9.12 E
Hosére Vokré ∧	214	8.20 N	13.15 E
Hosford	246	30.23 N	84.48 W
Hoshiarpur	206	28.35 N	77.22 E
Hosmer, B.C., Can.	238	49.35 N	114.57 W
Hosmer, S. Dak., U.S.	252	45.34 N	99.28 W
Hospers	252	43.04 N	95.54 W
Hospital de Orbigo	168	42.28 N	5.53 W
Hospitalet	168	41.22 N	2.08 E
Hossegor	166	43.40 N	1.27 W
Hosston	248	32.53 N	93.53 W
Hosta Butte ∧	254	35.35 N	108.12 W
Hoste, Isla I	288	55.10 S	69.00 W
Hostetter	266	40.16 N	79.24 W
Hotaka-dake ∧	192	36.17 N	137.39 E
Hotarele	172	44.10 N	26.22 E
Hotchkiss	254	38.48 N	107.43 W
Hotchkissville	261	41.46 N	73.13 W
Hot Creek Range ⋀	258	38.30 N	116.25 W
Hotevilla	254	35.56 N	110.41 W
Hotham Inlet C	236	66.45 N	162.00 W
Hotham Peak ∧	236	66.48 N	160.42 W
Hoting	160	64.07 N	16.10 E
Hot Springs, Mont., U.S.	256	47.37 N	114.40 W
Hot Springs, N.C., U.S.	246	35.54 N	82.50 W
Hot Springs, S. Dak., U.S.	252	43.26 N	103.29 W
Hot Springs, Va., U.S.	246	38.00 N	79.50 W
Hot Springs National Park	248	34.30 N	93.03 W
Hot Springs Peak ∧, Calif., U.S.	258	40.22 N	120.07 W
Hot Springs Peak ∧, Nev., U.S.	258	41.22 N	117.26 W
Hot Sulphur Springs	254	40.04 N	106.06 W
Hottah Lake @	232	65.04 N	118.29 W
Hottentot Bay C	224	26.05 S	14.58 E
Houdain	176	50.27 N	2.32 E
Houdan	166	48.47 N	1.36 E
Houdeng-Aimeries	176	50.29 N	4.08 E
Houeillès	166	44.12 N	0.02 E
Houei Sai	198	20.18 N	100.26 E
Houghton, Mich., U.S.	244	47.06 N	88.34 W
Houghton, N.Y., U.S.	266	42.25 N	78.10 W
Houghton, Wash., U.S.	270	47.40 N	122.12 W
Houghton Lake	244	44.18 N	84.45 W
Houghton Lake @	244	44.20 N	84.45 W
Houghton Reservoir @[1]	252	45.50 N	98.10 W
Hou Hoi Wan C	196	22.28 N	113.56 E
Houlka	248	34.02 N	89.01 W
Houlton	242	46.08 N	67.51 W
Houma, La., U.S.	248	29.36 N	90.43 W
Houma, Zhg.	190	35.40 N	111.29 E
Hounslow •[8]	174	51.29 N	0.22 W
Houplines	176	50.42 N	2.55 E
Housatonic	261	42.16 N	73.22 W
House	250	34.39 N	103.54 W
Houserville	266	40.50 N	77.50 W
Houston, B.C., Can.	238	54.24 N	126.38 W
Houston, Del., U.S.	262	38.55 N	75.30 W
Houston, Minn., U.S.	244	43.45 N	91.34 W
Houston, Miss., U.S.	248	33.54 N	89.00 W
Houston, Mo., U.S.	248	37.22 N	91.58 W
Houston, Ohio, U.S.	268	40.15 N	84.20 W
Houston, Pa., U.S.	266	40.15 N	80.13 W
Houston, Tex., U.S.	250	29.46 N	95.22 W
Houston ≃	248	30.16 N	93.13 W
Houston, Lake @[1]	250	29.58 N	95.07 W
Hout ≃	224	23.04 S	29.36 E
Houtman Rocks II[1]	226	28.35 S	113.45 E
Houtzdale	266	40.49 N	78.21 W
Hove	174	50.49 N	0.10 W
Hövelhof	178	51.49 N	8.40 E
Hoven	252	45.15 N	99.47 W
Hovenweep National Monument ♠	254	37.24 N	108.59 W
Hovmantorp	160	56.47 N	15.08 E
Howa (Wādī Howar), Ouadi V	220	17.30 N	27.08 E
Howar, Wādī(Ouadi Howa) V	220	17.30 N	27.08 E
Howard, Kans., U.S.	252	37.28 N	96.16 W
Howard, Ohio, U.S.	266	40.25 N	82.20 W
Howard, Pa., U.S.	266	41.01 N	77.40 W
Howard, S. Dak., U.S.	252	44.01 N	97.32 W
Howard, Wis., U.S.	244	44.33 N	88.04 W
Howard □[6], Ind., U.S.	268	40.29 N	86.08 W
Howard □[6], Md., U.S.	262	39.16 N	76.48 W
Howard City	244	43.24 N	85.28 W
Howard Lake	244	45.04 N	94.04 W
Howard Pass)(	236	68.13 N	156.55 W
Howard Prairie Reservoir @[1]	256	42.15 N	122.20 W
Howe	268	41.43 N	85.25 W
Howe, Cape ➤	228	37.31 S	149.59 E
Howe Island I	244	44.17 N	76.15 W
Howell	268	42.36 N	83.55 W
Howells	252	41.43 N	97.00 W
Howe Sound Ц	238	49.22 N	123.18 W
Howick, Qué., Can.	260	45.11 N	73.51 W
Howick, N.Z.	230	36.54 S	174.56 E
Howitt, Mount ∧	228	37.10 S	146.40 E
Howland	242	45.14 N	68.40 W
Howley	240	49.10 N	57.07 W
Howley, Mount ∧	240	48.17 N	58.26 W
Howrah	206	22.35 N	88.20 E
Howse Peak ∧	238	51.49 N	116.41 W
Howser	238	50.18 N	116.57 W
Howson Peak ∧	238	54.25 N	127.44 W
Hoxie, Ark., U.S.	248	36.03 N	90.58 W
Hoxie, Kans., U.S.	252	39.21 N	100.26 W
Höxter	178	51.46 N	9.23 E
Hoy I	162	58.52 N	3.18 W
Høyanger	160	61.13 N	6.05 E
Hoyerswerda	164	51.26 N	14.14 E
Hoyleton	248	38.27 N	89.16 W
Hoyos	168	40.10 N	6.43 W
Hoyran Gölü @	212	38.12 N	30.50 E
Hoyt Lakes	244	47.31 N	92.08 W

Symbols in the index entries are identified on page 360.

Name	Page	Lat°′	Long°′
Hoytville	268	42.45 N	84.53 W
Hradec Králové	164	50.12 N	15.50 E
Hrádek nad Nisou	164	50.48 N	14.51 E
Hranice	164	49.33 N	17.44 E
Hriňová	164	48.36 N	19.31 E
Hron ≃	164	47.49 N	18.45 E
Hronov	164	50.29 N	16.12 E
Hrubieszów	164	50.49 N	23.55 E
Hrubý Jeseník ⛰	164	50.00 N	17.20 E
Hrvatska □[3]	170	45.10 N	15.30 E
Hsian → Xi'an	190	34.15 N	108.52 E
Hsiaohungt'ou Hsü I	196	21.57 N	121.35 E
Hsichi Hsü I	196	23.15 N	119.37 E
Hsich'üan Tao I	196	25.59 N	119.57 E
Hsilo Ch'i ≃	196	23.47 N	120.15 E
Hsinchu	196	24.48 N	120.58 E
Hsinkao Shan Λ	196	23.28 N	120.57 E
Hsipaw	198	22.37 N	97.18 E
Hsip'ing Hsü I	196	23.14 N	119.36 E
Hsiukuluan Ch'i ≃	196	23.28 N	121.29 E
Hsüehweng Shan Λ	196	24.24 N	121.12 E
Huab ≃	224	20.52 S	13.25 E
Huacaña	292	14.04 S	74.03 W
Huacapistea ≃	292	9.46 S	72.44 W
Huacaraje	292	13.33 S	63.45 W
Huacaybamba	292	9.00 S	76.49 W
Huachacalla	292	18.45 S	68.17 W
Huachi, Lago ⊜	292	14.11 S	63.30 W
Huacho	292	11.07 S	77.37 W
Huachón	292	10.37 S	75.57 W
Huachos	292	13.05 S	75.31 W
Huachuca City	254	31.34 N	110.21 W
Huaco	294	30.08 S	68.29 W
Huacrachuco	292	8.40 S	77.05 W
Huadian	190	42.58 N	126.43 E
Huadingshan Λ	196	29.15 N	121.05 E
Huagaruancha, Cerro Λ	292	10.32 S	75.56 W
Hua Hin	200	12.34 N	99.58 E
Hua Hsü I	196	23.24 N	119.20 E
Huahua ≃	280	13.54 N	83.27 W
Huaian	196	33.32 N	119.10 E
Huaide	190	43.32 N	124.50 E
Huaihe ≃, Zhg.	194	37.28 N	114.55 E
Huaihe ≃, Zhg.	196	32.58 N	118.17 E
Huailai	194	40.23 N	115.33 E
Huaillati	292	13.56 S	72.30 W
Huaillay	292	11.01 S	76.25 W
Huainan	196	32.40 N	117.00 E
Huairou	194	40.19 N	116.37 E
Huaiyang	196	33.44 N	114.53 E
Huaiyin	196	33.35 N	119.02 E
Huaiyuan	196	32.57 N	117.12 E
Huaiyushan ⛰	196	28.50 N	117.50 E
Huajiaodao I	194	39.26 N	121.17 E
Huajuapan de León	278	17.48 N	97.46 W
Hualahuises	278	24.53 N	99.41 W
Hualalai Λ[1]	275d	19.42 N	155.52 W
Hualañé	294	34.59 S	71.49 W
Hualapai Indian Reservation ➛[4]	254	35.38 N	113.30 W
Hualapai Mountains ⛰	254	34.50 N	113.55 W
Hualapai Peak Λ	254	35.04 N	113.55 W
Hualfín	294	27.15 S	66.50 W
Hualgayoc	292	6.46 S	78.37 W
Hualien	196	23.58 N	121.36 E
Hualien Ch'i ≃	196	23.57 N	121.36 E
Hualla	292	13.45 S	73.55 W
Huallaga ≃	292	5.07 S	75.30 W
Huallanca, Perú	292	9.50 S	76.56 W
Huallanca, Perú	292	8.50 S	77.50 W
Huamachuco	292	7.50 S	78.05 W
Huamanquiquia	292	13.42 S	74.14 W
Huambo	292	15.44 S	72.08 W
Huambo ≃	292	7.02 S	77.08 W
Huambos	292	6.24 S	78.58 W
Huameishan Λ	196	25.28 N	113.58 E
Huamuxtitlán	278	17.49 N	98.34 W
Huancabamba, Perú	292	10.26 S	75.30 W
Huancabamba, Perú	292	5.14 S	79.28 W
Huancané	292	15.10 S	69.45 W
Huancapi	292	13.35 S	74.05 W
Huancarama	292	13.38 S	73.05 W
Huancarqui	292	16.07 S	72.28 W
Huancavelica	292	12.46 S	75.02 W
Huancavelica □[5]	292	13.00 S	75.00 W
Huancayo	292	12.04 S	75.14 W
Huanchaca	292	20.20 S	66.39 W
Huanchaca, Serranía de ⛰	292	14.30 S	60.39 W
Huando	292	12.33 S	74.56 W
Huangchuan	196	32.09 N	115.03 E
Huangdao I	196	27.58 N	121.06 E
Huangdayang ∪	196	30.03 N	122.26 E
Huanggaihu ⊜	196	29.44 N	113.23 E
Huanggang	190	30.27 N	114.52 E
Huanghe (Hwang Ho) ≃, Zhg.	194	37.32 N	118.19 E
Huanghe ≃, Zhg.	196	32.19 N	115.02 E
Huangjiadao I	194	36.43 N	121.37 E
Huangjiangshui ≃	196	22.54 N	115.18 E
Huangling	190	35.41 N	109.09 E
Huangnixi ≃	196	24.48 N	116.31 E
Huangshi	196	30.13 N	115.05 E
Huangtanghu ⊜	196	30.00 N	114.12 E
Huanguelén	294	37.04 S	61.57 W
Huangyan	196	28.39 N	121.15 E
Huangyuan	190	36.42 N	101.25 E
Huangzeshan I	196	30.31 N	122.16 E
Huangzeyang ∪	196	30.36 N	122.28 E
Huani, Laguna C	280	14.50 N	83.17 W
Huaning	200	24.14 N	102.56 E
Huanjiang (Sien)	200	24.54 N	108.21 E
Huanshui ≃	196	30.40 N	114.05 E
Huanta	292	12.55 S	74.20 W
Huantar	292	9.20 S	77.15 W
Huánuco	292	9.55 S	76.14 W
Huánuco □[5]	292	9.55 S	76.14 W
Huanuni	292	18.16 S	66.51 W
Huanzo, Cordillera de ⛰	292	14.35 S	73.20 W
Huapí, Montañas de ⛰	280	12.30 N	85.00 W
Huap'ing Hsü I	196	25.24 N	121.58 E
Huara	292	19.59 S	69.47 W
Huaral	292	11.32 S	77.13 W
Huaraz	292	9.32 S	77.32 W
Huari, Bol.	292	19.00 S	66.48 W
Huari, Perú	292	9.14 S	77.14 W
Huariaca	292	10.30 S	76.10 W
Huaribamba	292	12.13 S	74.57 W
Huarina	292	16.12 S	68.38 W
Huarmey	292	10.04 S	78.10 W
Huarochirí	292	12.09 S	76.15 W
Huarocondo	292	13.26 S	72.14 W
Huásabas	278	29.47 N	109.18 W
Huasaga ≃	290	3.42 S	76.26 W
Huasamota	278	22.30 N	104.30 W
Huascarán, Nevado Λ	292	9.07 S	77.37 W
Huasco	294	28.28 S	71.14 W
Huasco ≃	294	28.27 S	71.13 W
Huashishan ⛰	196	24.24 N	113.38 E
Huaspuc ≃	280	14.34 N	84.26 W
Huatabampo	278	26.50 N	109.38 W
Huatunas, Laguna ⊜	292	13.06 S	66.15 W
Huauchinango	278	20.11 N	98.03 W
Huaunta	280	13.30 N	83.32 W
Huaunta, Laguna C	280	13.38 N	83.35 W
Huaura	292	11.06 S	77.38 W
Huaura ≃	292	11.06 S	77.37 W
Huautla de Jiménez	278	18.08 N	96.51 W
Huaxian	190	23.22 N	113.12 E
Huayna Potosí, Nevado Λ	292	16.16 S	68.11 W
Huaytará	292	13.30 S	75.19 W
Huayuri, Pampa de ⚌	292	14.30 S	75.30 W
Huazhou	200	21.40 N	110.33 E
Hubbard, Iowa, U.S.	244	42.18 N	93.18 W
Hubbard, Ohio, U.S.	266	41.10 N	80.34 W
Hubbard, Oreg., U.S.	270	45.11 N	122.48 W
Hubbard, Tex., U.S.	250	31.51 N	96.48 W
Hubbard Creek Reservoir ⊜[1]	250	32.45 N	99.00 W
Hubbard Lake ⊜	244	44.49 N	83.34 W
Hubbards	240	44.38 N	64.04 W
Hubbardston	261	42.29 N	72.01 W
Hubbell	244	47.11 N	88.26 W
Hubei □[4]	190	31.00 N	112.00 E
Huberdeau	242	45.59 N	74.38 W
Hückelhoven	178	51.03 N	6.13 E
Hückeswagen	178	51.08 N	7.20 E
Huckleberry Mountain Λ	256	43.51 N	122.19 W
Hucknall	174	53.02 N	1.11 W
Huddersfield	162	53.39 N	1.47 W
Huddinge	160	59.14 N	17.59 E
Hude	178	53.07 N	8.27 E
Hudiksvall	160	61.44 N	17.07 E
Hudson, Qué., Can.	260	45.27 N	74.09 W
Hudson, Fla., U.S.	246	28.22 N	82.42 W
Hudson, Ill., U.S.	268	40.36 N	88.59 W
Hudson, Ind., U.S.	268	41.32 N	85.05 W
Hudson, Iowa, U.S.	244	42.24 N	92.28 W
Hudson, Md., U.S.	262	38.35 N	76.15 W
Hudson, Mass., U.S.	261	42.24 N	71.35 W
Hudson, Mich., U.S.	268	41.51 N	84.21 W
Hudson, N.H., U.S.	242	42.46 N	71.26 W
Hudson, N.C., U.S.	246	35.51 N	81.30 W
Hudson, N.Y., U.S.	261	42.15 N	73.47 W
Hudson, Ohio, U.S.	266	41.15 N	81.26 W
Hudson, S. Dak., U.S.	252	43.08 N	96.27 W
Hudson, Wis., U.S.	244	44.53 N	92.45 W
Hudson, Wyo., U.S.	254	42.54 N	108.35 W
Hudson ≃, U.S.	242	40.42 N	74.02 W
Hudson ≃, Ga., U.S.	246	34.14 N	83.10 W
Hudson, Lake ⊜[1]	250	36.20 N	95.05 W
Hudson Bay	232	52.52 N	102.25 W
Hudson Bay C	232	60.00 N	86.00 W
Hudson Falls	242	43.18 N	73.35 W
Hudson Heights	260	45.27 N	74.08 W
Hudson Hope	238	56.02 N	121.55 W
Hudson Lake	268	41.43 N	86.32 W
Hudson Strait ∪	232	62.30 N	72.00 W
Hudsonville	268	42.52 N	85.52 W
Hue	200	16.28 N	107.36 E
Huebra ≃	168	41.02 N	6.48 W
Huedin	172	46.52 N	23.02 E
Huehuetán	280	15.01 N	92.22 W
Huehuetenango	280	15.20 N	91.28 W
Huehuetenango □[5]	280	15.40 N	91.35 W
Huejutla [de Reyes]	278	21.08 N	98.25 W
Huelgoat	166	48.22 N	3.45 W
Huelma	168	37.39 N	3.27 W
Huelva	168	37.16 N	6.57 W
Huelva, Río de ≃	168	37.27 N	6.00 W
Huenque ≃	292	16.12 S	69.43 W
Huentelauquén	294	31.35 S	71.32 W
Huércal-Overa	168	37.23 N	1.57 W
Huerfano ≃	252	38.14 N	104.15 W
Huerta, Sierra de la ⛰	294	31.00 S	67.30 W
Huerva ≃	168	41.39 N	0.52 W
Huesca	168	42.08 N	0.25 W
Huesca □[4]	166	42.08 N	0.25 W
Huéscar	168	37.49 N	2.32 W
Huetamo de Núñez	278	18.35 N	100.53 W
Huete	168	40.08 N	2.41 W
Hueytown	248	33.27 N	86.59 W
Hugh Butler Lake ⊜[1]	252	40.22 N	100.42 W
Hughenden	228	20.51 S	144.12 E
Hughes, Alaska, U.S.	236	66.03 N	154.16 W
Hughes, Ark., U.S.	248	34.57 N	90.28 W
Hughes Springs	248	33.05 N	94.38 W
Hughesville	242	41.14 N	76.44 W
Hughson	272	37.36 N	120.52 W
Hugo, Colo., U.S.	252	39.08 N	103.28 W
Hugo, Okla., U.S.	250	34.01 N	95.31 W
Hugoton	252	37.11 N	101.21 W
Huhehaote	190	40.51 N	111.40 E
Huhehot → Huhehaote	190	40.51 N	111.40 E
Huiarau Range ⛰	230	38.41 S	176.54 E
Huib-Hochplato ⛰[1]	224	27.00 S	16.45 E
Huibieyang ∪	196	30.08 N	121.44 E
Huichapan	278	20.23 N	99.39 W
Hŭich'ŏn	190	40.10 N	126.17 E
Huicungo	292	7.17 S	76.48 W
Huidong	200	26.41 N	102.36 E
Huijihe ≃	194	33.53 N	115.36 E
Huila □[5]	290	2.30 N	75.45 W
Huila, Nevado del Λ	290	3.00 N	76.00 W
Huili	200	26.43 N	102.10 E
Huillapima	294	28.44 S	66.00 W
Huilotas, Sierra de las ⛰	250	28.12 N	102.04 W
Huimin	190	37.29 N	117.29 E
Huinan	194	42.40 N	126.00 E
Huinca Renancó	294	34.50 S	64.25 W
Huisachal	250	26.47 N	101.07 W
Huishui	200	26.07 N	106.24 E
Huisne ≃	166	47.59 N	0.11 E
Huissen	178	51.57 N	5.56 E
Huittinen (Lauttakylä)	160	61.11 N	22.42 E
Huitzuco [de los Figueroa]	278	18.18 N	99.21 W
Huixtla	278	15.09 N	92.28 W
Huiyang (Huizhou)	196	23.05 N	114.24 E
Huizache	278	22.55 N	100.25 W
Huize	200	26.27 N	103.09 E
Huizen	178	52.17 N	5.14 E
Hukayyim, Bi'r al- ⊸[4]	220	31.36 N	23.29 E
Hŭksan-chedo II	194	34.30 N	125.20 E
Hulahula ≃	236	70.00 N	144.01 W
Hulan	190	46.00 N	126.38 E
Hulbert, Mich., U.S.	244	46.21 N	85.09 W
Hulbert, Okla., U.S.	248	35.56 N	95.09 W
Hulberton	264	43.15 N	78.04 W
Huldange Λ	164	50.10 N	6.01 E
Hulett	252	44.41 N	104.36 W
Hulín	164	49.19 N	17.28 E
Huliuhe ≃	194	40.10 N	114.33 E
Hull, Qué., Can.	264	45.26 N	75.43 W
Hull → Kingston upon Hull, Eng., U.K.	162	53.45 N	0.20 W
Hull, Ill., U.S.	248	39.43 N	91.13 W
Hull, Iowa, U.S.	252	43.11 N	96.08 W
Hull, Mass., U.S.	261	42.17 N	70.53 W
Hull, Tex., U.S.	250	30.09 N	94.39 W
Hull □[6]	264	45.40 N	75.35 W
Hulot, Lac ⊜	240	50.14 N	69.18 W
Hüls	178	51.22 N	6.30 E
Hülscheid	178	51.16 N	7.34 E
Hulst	178	51.17 N	4.03 E
Hultsfred	160	57.29 N	15.20 E
Hulunchi ⊜	190	49.01 N	117.32 E
Hulwān	220	29.51 N	31.20 E
Huma	190	51.43 N	126.38 E
Humacao	284m	18.09 N	65.50 W
Humahuaca	294	23.12 S	65.25 W
Humaitá, Bra.	292	7.31 S	63.02 W
Humaitá, Para.	294	27.03 S	58.33 W
Humaitá ≃	292	8.16 S	72.44 W
Humansdorp	218	34.02 S	24.46 E
Humansville	248	37.48 N	93.35 W
Humara, Jabal al- Λ	220	16.16 N	30.59 E
Humbe	218	16.40 S	14.55 E
Humbe, Serra do ⛰	218	12.13 S	15.25 E
Humbermouth	240	48.58 N	57.55 W
Humberto Primo	294	30.50 S	61.20 W
Humbird	244	44.32 N	90.53 W
Humboldt, Sask., Can.	232	52.12 N	105.07 W
Humboldt, Ariz., U.S.	254	34.30 N	112.14 W
Humboldt, Ill., U.S.	248	39.36 N	88.19 W
Humboldt, Iowa, U.S.	244	42.43 N	94.13 W
Humboldt, Kans., U.S.	252	37.49 N	95.26 W
Humboldt, Nebr., U.S.	252	40.10 N	95.57 W
Humboldt, S. Dak., U.S.	252	43.39 N	97.04 W
Humboldt, Tenn., U.S.	248	35.49 N	88.55 W
Humboldt ≃	258	40.02 N	118.31 W
Humboldt Bay C	258	40.47 N	124.11 W
Humboldt Lake ⊜	258	39.58 N	118.38 W
Humboldt Mountains ⛰	230	44.44 S	168.15 E
Humboldt Salt Marsh ☷	258	39.50 N	117.55 W
Hume, Calif., U.S.	258	36.47 N	118.55 W
Hume, N.Y., U.S.	266	42.29 N	78.08 W
Hume, Lake ⊜[1]	228	36.06 S	147.05 E
Humen C[1]	196	22.44 N	113.40 E
Humenné	164	48.56 N	21.55 E
Humeston	244	40.52 N	93.30 W
Hummelstown	262	40.16 N	76.43 W
Humphrey, Ark., U.S.	248	34.25 N	91.42 W
Humphrey, Nebr., U.S.	252	41.41 N	97.29 W
Humphreys, Mount Λ	258	37.17 N	118.40 W
Humphreys Peak Λ	254	35.20 N	111.40 W
Humpolec	164	49.32 N	15.22 E
Humppila	160	60.56 N	23.22 E
Humptulips	270	47.14 N	123.57 W
Humuya ≃	280	15.13 N	87.57 W
Húnaflói C	160a	65.50 N	20.50 W
Hunan □[4]	196	28.00 N	111.00 E
Hunchun	190	42.54 N	130.22 E
Hundred	242	39.41 N	80.28 W
Hundred Island National Park ♠	202	16.13 N	120.01 E
Hundred Islands II	202	16.12 N	120.02 E
Hunedoara	172	45.45 N	22.54 E
Hünfeld	164	50.40 N	9.46 E
Hungary □[1]	158	47.00 N	20.00 E
Hungerford	250	29.24 N	96.05 W
Hungf'ou Hsü I	196	22.03 N	121.33 E
Hŭngnam	194	39.50 N	127.38 E
Hungry Horse	238	48.23 N	114.04 W
Hungry Horse Reservoir ⊜[1]	256	48.15 N	113.50 W
Hung-yen	200	20.39 N	106.04 E
Hunhe ≃	194	41.01 N	122.27 E
Huningue	166	47.36 N	7.35 E
Hunjiang	190	41.56 N	126.29 E
Hunkurāb, Ra's ≻	220	24.34 N	35.10 E
Hunsberge	218	27.45 S	17.12 E
Hunsberge ⛰, S.W. Afr.	224	27.45 S	17.12 E
Hunsrück ⛰	164	49.50 N	6.40 E
Hunstanton	162	52.57 N	0.30 E
Hunter	252	47.12 N	97.13 W
Hunter ≃, Austl.	228	32.50 S	151.42 E
Hunter ≃, N.Z.	230	44.41 S	169.11 E
Hunter, Mount Λ	236	62.57 N	151.05 W
Hunterdon □[6]	262	40.31 N	74.52 W
Hunter Island I, Austl.	228	40.32 S	144.45 E
Hunter Island I, B.C., Can.	238	51.55 N	128.05 W
Hunter Island Ridge ⩲[3]	148	21.30 S	175.00 E
Hunter Mountain Λ	242	42.10 N	74.14 W
Hunter Mountains ⛰	230	45.40 S	167.25 E
Hunters	238	48.07 N	118.12 W
Hunters Bay C	200	19.57 N	93.19 E
Hunters River	240	46.21 N	63.21 W
Hunters Run	262	40.05 N	77.11 W
Huntersville	246	35.25 N	80.50 W
Hunters Wash V	254	36.17 N	108.34 W
Huntertown	268	41.14 N	85.10 W
Huntingburg	248	38.18 N	86.57 W
Huntingdon, B.C., Can.	270	49.00 N	122.16 W
Huntingdon, Qué., Can.	260	45.05 N	74.11 W
Huntingdon, Eng., U.K.	174	52.20 N	0.12 W
Huntingdon, Pa., U.S.	266	40.29 N	78.01 W
Huntingdon, Tenn., U.S.	248	36.00 N	88.26 W
Huntingdon □[6], Qué., Can.	260	45.05 N	74.00 W
Huntingdon □[6], Pa., U.S.	266	40.29 N	78.01 W
Huntingdon and Peterborough □[6]	174	52.25 N	0.17 W
Hunting Island State Park ♠	246	32.20 N	80.30 W
Huntington, Ind., U.S.	268	40.53 N	85.30 W
Huntington, Mass., U.S.	261	42.14 N	72.53 W
Huntington, N.Y., U.S.	261	40.51 N	73.25 W
Huntington, Oreg., U.S.	256	44.21 N	117.16 W
Huntington, Tex., U.S.	248	31.17 N	94.34 W
Huntington, Utah, U.S.	254	39.20 N	110.58 W
Huntington, W. Va., U.S.	242	38.25 N	82.26 W
Huntington □[6]	268	40.53 N	85.30 W
Huntington Beach	274	33.39 N	118.01 W
Huntington Lake	272	37.15 N	119.14 W
Huntington Park	274	33.59 N	118.13 W
Huntington Reservoir ⊜[1]	244	40.50 N	85.25 W
Huntington Station	261	40.51 N	73.25 W
Huntingtown	262	38.37 N	76.37 W
Huntingville	260	45.20 N	71.51 W
Huntley, Ill., U.S.	268	42.10 N	88.26 W
Huntley, Mont., U.S.	256	45.54 N	108.19 W
Huntly, N.Z.	230	37.33 S	175.10 E
Huntly, Scot., U.K.	162	57.27 N	2.47 W
Hunt Mountain Λ	256	44.44 N	107.45 W
Huntsburg	266	41.32 N	81.03 W
Hunts Point	270	47.39 N	122.14 W
Huntsville, Ont., Can.	264	45.20 N	79.13 W
Huntsville, Ala., U.S.	248	34.44 N	86.35 W
Huntsville, Ark., U.S.	248	36.05 N	93.44 W
Huntsville, Mo., U.S.	248	39.26 N	92.33 W
Huntsville, Ohio, U.S.	268	40.26 N	83.49 W
Huntsville, Tenn., U.S.	246	36.25 N	84.29 W
Huntsville, Tex., U.S.	250	30.43 N	95.33 W
Huntsville, Utah, U.S.	254	41.16 N	111.46 W
Hunucmá	278	21.01 N	89.52 W
Hünxe	178	51.38 N	6.46 E
Hunyani ≃	218	15.37 S	30.39 E
Huoerpahu ⊜	206	34.32 N	81.03 E
Huonville	226	43.01 S	147.02 E
Huoshao Tao I	196	22.40 N	121.30 E
Huotongxi ≃	196	26.50 N	119.32 E
Huoxi ≃	196	25.20 N	117.21 E
Hupeh → Hubei □[4]	190	31.00 N	112.00 E
Hurao	190	45.46 N	132.59 E
Hurd, Cape ≻	244	45.13 N	81.44 W
Huriel	166	46.23 N	2.29 E
Hurley, Miss., U.S.	248	30.40 N	88.30 W
Hurley, N. Mex., U.S.	254	32.42 N	108.08 W
Hurley, S. Dak., U.S.	252	43.17 N	97.05 W
Hurley, Wis., U.S.	244	46.28 N	90.08 W
Hurlock	242	38.38 N	75.52 W
Huron, Calif., U.S.	272	36.12 N	120.06 W
Huron, Ohio, U.S.	266	41.24 N	82.33 W
Huron, S. Dak., U.S.	252	44.22 N	98.13 W
Huron □[6], Ont., Can.	264	43.45 N	81.10 W
Huron □[6], Ohio, U.S.	266	41.15 N	82.37 W
Huron, Lake ⊜	244	44.30 N	82.15 W
Huron Gardens	268	42.38 N	83.20 W
Huron Mountains ⛰[2]	244	46.45 N	87.45 W
Hurricane, Alaska, U.S.	236	62.59 N	149.38 W
Hurricane, Utah, U.S.	254	37.11 N	113.17 W
Hurricane, W. Va., U.S.	242	38.26 N	82.01 W
Hurtado ≃	294	30.35 S	71.11 W
Hürth	164	50.52 N	6.51 E
Hurtsboro	248	32.14 N	85.25 W
Hurunui ≃	230	42.54 S	173.18 E
Húsavík	160a	66.04 N	17.18 W
Husem	270	45.49 N	121.29 W
Huşi	172	46.40 N	28.04 E
Huskerville	252	40.52 N	96.47 W
Huskvarna	160	57.48 N	14.16 E
Huslia	236	65.42 N	156.25 W
Hussar	238	51.03 N	112.41 W
Hustisford	244	43.21 N	88.36 W
Hustontown	266	40.03 N	78.02 W
Husum	164	54.28 N	9.03 E
Hutanopan	198	0.41 N	99.42 E
Hutaym, Ḥarrat ⚉[9]	208	26.15 N	40.20 E
Hutchinson, Kans., U.S.	252	38.05 N	97.56 W
Hutchinson, Minn., U.S.	244	44.54 N	94.22 W
Hutchinson, Pa., U.S.	266	40.13 N	79.44 W
Hutchinson Island I	246	27.25 N	80.17 W
Hutch Mountain Λ	254	34.47 N	111.22 W
Hutouxi ≃	196	25.57 N	118.02 E
Hutsonville	248	39.07 N	87.39 W
Hutte Sauvage, Lac de la ⊜	232	56.25 N	64.50 W
Huttig	248	33.02 N	92.11 W
Hutto	250	30.33 N	97.33 W
Hutton, Mount Λ	228	25.51 S	148.20 E
Huttonsville	264	43.38 N	79.48 W
Hutuohe ≃	194	38.14 N	116.05 E
Huxford	248	31.13 N	87.28 W
Huxley	238	51.56 N	113.14 W
Huy	164	50.31 N	5.14 E
Huzhou	196	30.52 N	120.06 E
Hvannadalshnúkur Λ	160a	64.01 N	16.41 W
Hvar	170	43.10 N	16.27 E
Hvar, Otok I	170	43.09 N	16.45 E
Hvarski Kanal ∪	170	43.15 N	16.37 E
Hveragerði	160a	64.03 N	21.10 W
Hvolsvöllur	160a	63.45 N	20.10 W
Hwach'ŏn-chŏsuji ⊜	194	38.07 N	127.52 E
Hwaining → Anqing	196	30.31 N	117.02 E
Hwanghae Namdo □[4]	194	38.15 N	125.30 E
Hwanghae Pukdo □[4]	194	38.30 N	126.25 E
Hwang Ho → Huanghe ≃	190	37.32 N	118.19 E
Hyak	270	47.24 N	121.24 W
Hyannis, Mass., U.S.	261	41.39 N	70.17 W
Hyannis, Nebr., U.S.	252	41.59 N	101.44 W
Hyannis Port	261	41.38 N	70.18 W
Hyattville	256	44.15 N	107.36 W
Hybart	248	31.50 N	87.23 W
Hybla Valley	262	38.45 N	77.05 W
Hydaburg	236	55.12 N	132.49 W
Hyde	266	41.00 N	78.28 W
Hyden, Austl.	226	32.27 S	118.53 E
Hyden, Ky., U.S.	246	37.10 N	83.22 W
Hyde Park, Guy.	290	6.30 N	58.16 W
Hyde Park, N.Y., U.S.	261	41.47 N	73.56 W
Hyde Park, Vt., U.S.	242	44.36 N	72.37 W
Hyder	236	55.55 N	130.01 W
Hyderābād	206	25.22 N	68.22 E
Hydetown	266	41.40 N	79.44 W
Hydra → Ídhra I	172	37.20 N	23.32 E
Hydraulic	238	52.36 N	121.42 W
Hyères	182	43.07 N	6.07 E
Hyères, Îles d' II	168	43.00 N	6.20 E
Hyesan	194	41.23 N	128.12 E
Hyland ≃	236	59.50 N	128.10 W
Hymera	248	39.11 N	87.18 W
Hyndman	242	39.49 N	78.44 W
Hyndman Peak Λ	256	43.50 N	114.10 W
Hyōgo □[5]	192	35.12 N	134.51 E
Hyrum	254	41.38 N	111.51 W
Hysham	256	46.18 N	107.14 W
Hythe, Alta., Can.	238	55.20 N	119.33 W
Hythe, Eng., U.K.	174	51.05 N	1.05 E
Hyūga	192	32.25 N	131.38 E
Hyūga-nada ⊸[2]	192	32.00 N	131.35 E
Hyvinkää	160	60.38 N	24.52 E
I			
I □[4]	222	17.00 N	7.15 W
Iacanga	296	21.54 S	49.01 W
Iaciara	296	14.09 S	46.40 W
Iaco (Yaco) ≃	292	9.03 S	68.34 W
Iaçu	296	12.45 S	40.13 W
Iaeger	246	37.28 N	81.49 W
Ialomița ≃	172	44.42 N	27.51 E
Ialomiței, Balta ☷	172	44.30 N	28.00 E
Iamonia, Lake ⊜	246	30.38 N	84.14 W
Iapó ≃	294	24.30 S	50.24 W
Iapu	296	19.26 S	42.13 W
Iași	172	47.10 N	27.35 E
Iatt, Lake ⊜[1]	248	31.35 N	92.40 W
Iauaretê	290	0.36 N	69.12 W
Iazu	172	44.44 N	27.25 E
Iba	202	15.20 N	119.59 E
Ibadan	222	7.17 N	3.30 E
Ibagué	290	4.27 N	75.14 W
Ibaiti	296	23.50 S	50.10 W
Ibajay	202	11.49 N	122.10 E
Ibajay ≃	202	11.50 N	122.10 E
Ibănești	172	48.04 N	26.22 E
Ibar ≃	172	43.43 N	20.45 E
Ibaraki □[5]	192	36.30 N	140.30 E
Ibarra	290	0.21 N	78.07 W
Ibarreta	294	25.15 S	59.51 W
Ibb	204	14.01 N	44.10 E
Ibba ≃	220	7.09 N	28.41 E
Ibbenbüren	178	52.16 N	7.43 E
Iberia, Mo., U.S.	248	38.05 N	92.18 W
Iberia, Ohio, U.S.	266	40.40 N	82.51 W
Iberian Basin ⩲[1]	148	40.00 N	16.00 W
Iberian Peninsula ≻[1]	148	40.00 N	5.00 W
Ibérico, Sistema ⛰	168	41.00 N	2.30 W
Iberville	260	45.19 N	73.14 W
Iberville □[6]	260	45.15 N	73.10 W
Ibiá	296	19.29 S	46.32 W
Ibicaraí	296	14.51 S	39.36 W
Ibicuí	296	14.51 S	39.59 W
Ibicuí ≃	294	29.25 S	56.47 W
Ibicuí da Armada ≃	294	30.16 S	54.54 W
Ibicuy	294	33.45 S	59.13 W
Ibiquera	296	12.38 S	40.57 W
Ibiraci	296	20.28 S	47.08 W
Ibiraçu	296	19.50 S	40.22 W
Ibirama	294	27.04 S	49.31 W
Ibirapuã	296	17.39 S	40.07 W
Ibirapuitã ≃	294	29.22 S	55.57 W
Ibirataia	296	14.04 S	39.38 W
Ibirubá	294	28.38 S	53.06 W
Ibitiara	296	12.39 S	42.13 W
Ibitinga	296	21.45 S	48.49 W
Ibiza	168	38.54 N	1.26 E
Ibiza I	168	39.00 N	1.25 E
Iblei, Monti ⛰	170	37.10 N	14.50 E
Ibn Hāni', Ra's ≻	212	35.35 N	35.43 E
Ibo	218	12.20 S	40.35 E
Ibor ≃	168	39.49 N	5.33 W
Ibotirama	296	12.11 S	43.13 W
Iboundji, Mont Λ	218	1.08 S	11.48 E
Ibrah, Wādī V	220	10.36 N	24.58 E
Ibresi	160	55.18 N	47.03 E
'Ibrī	208	23.14 N	56.30 E
İbriktepe	172	41.00 N	26.30 E
Ibshawāy	220	29.22 N	30.41 E
Ibusuki	192	31.16 N	130.39 E
Ica	292	14.04 S	75.42 W
Ica □[5]	292	14.20 S	75.30 W
Ica ≃, Perú	292	14.53 S	75.33 W
Içá (Putumayo) ≃, S.A.	290	3.07 S	67.58 W
Icabarú ≃	290	4.45 N	62.15 W
Icadambanauan Island I	202	10.27 N	122.41 E
Icamaquã ≃	294	28.34 S	56.00 W
Icamole	250	25.55 N	100.43 W
Içana	290	0.21 N	67.19 W
Içana (Isana) ≃	290	0.26 N	67.19 W
Icaño, Arg.	294	28.55 S	65.19 W
Icaño, Arg.	294	28.42 S	62.50 W
Icayché	278	18.05 N	89.10 W
Iceberg Pass)(	254	40.25 N	105.45 W
İçel □[4]	212	36.45 N	34.00 E
Iceland □[1]	158	65.00 N	18.00 W
Icém	296	20.21 S	49.12 W
Ice Mountain Λ	238	54.25 N	121.08 W
Ichang → Yichang	190	30.42 N	111.11 E
Ichihara	192	35.31 N	140.05 E
Ichikawa	192	35.44 N	139.55 E
Ichilo ≃	292	15.57 S	64.42 W
Ichinohe	192	40.13 N	141.17 E
Ichinomiya, Nihon	192	35.18 N	136.48 E
Ichinomiya, Nihon	192	32.57 N	131.07 E
Ichinoseki	192	38.55 N	141.08 E
Ichkeul, Garaet ⊜	170	37.10 N	9.40 E
Ichoca	292	17.12 S	67.17 W
Ichtegem	176	51.06 N	3.00 E
Ickesburg	262	40.27 N	77.21 W
Icó	286	6.24 S	38.51 W
Iconha	296	20.48 S	40.48 W
Icoraci	286	1.18 S	48.28 W
Icy Bay C	236	60.00 N	141.15 W
Icy Cape ≻	236	70.20 N	161.52 W
Icy Strait ∪	236	58.18 N	135.30 W
Ida	268	41.55 N	83.34 W
Ida, Mount Λ	285q	17.58 N	77.43 W
Idabel	248	33.54 N	94.50 W
Ida Grove	252	42.21 N	95.28 W
Idah	222	7.07 N	6.43 E
Idaho □[3]	234	45.00 N	115.00 W
Idaho City	256	43.50 N	115.50 W
Idaho Falls	256	43.30 N	112.02 W
Idaho Springs	252	39.45 N	105.31 W
Idalou	250	33.40 N	101.41 W
Idanha-a-Nova	168	39.55 N	7.14 W
Idar-Oberstein	164	49.42 N	7.19 E
Idaville, Ind., U.S.	268	40.46 N	86.39 W
Idaville, Oreg., U.S.	270	45.31 N	123.53 W
Idel'	160	64.08 N	34.14 E
Iderijn ≃	190	49.16 N	100.41 E
Idfū	220	24.58 N	32.52 E
Ídhi Óros Λ	172	35.18 N	24.43 E
Ídhra	172	37.20 N	23.29 E
Ídhra I	172	37.20 N	23.32 E
Idi	200	4.55 N	97.47 E
Idio	202	11.38 N	122.06 E
Idiofa	218	5.02 S	19.36 E
Iditarod ≃	236	63.02 N	158.58 W
Idlib	212	35.55 N	36.38 E
Idlib □[8]	212	35.50 N	36.40 E
Ídolo, Isla del I	278	21.25 N	97.27 W
Idre	160	61.52 N	12.43 E
Idria	272	36.25 N	120.40 W
Idrica	160	56.21 N	28.53 E
Idrija	170	46.00 N	14.01 E
Iduburojo, Isla I	290	9.05 N	60.42 W
Idutywa	218	32.02 S	28.16 E
Idyllwild	258	33.45 N	116.43 W
Idylside	268	41.31 N	88.07 W
Iepê	296	22.40 S	51.05 W
Ieper (Ypres)	176	50.51 N	2.53 E
Ierápetra	172	35.00 N	25.45 E
Ierissós	172	40.24 N	23.52 E
Iesi	184	43.31 N	13.14 E
Iesolo	170	45.32 N	12.38 E
Ifalik I[1]	198	7.15 N	144.27 E
Ife	222	7.30 N	4.30 E
Iferouâne	214	19.04 N	8.24 E
Ifni □[9]	214	29.00 N	10.00 W
Iforas, Adrar des ⛰	222	20.00 N	2.00 E
Ifugao □[4]	202	16.45 N	121.15 E
Igal	164	46.31 N	17.55 E
Igaporã	296	13.46 S	42.43 W
Igara Paraná ≃	290	2.09 S	71.47 W
Igarka	186	67.28 N	86.35 E
Igarra	222	7.18 N	6.07 E
Igatimí	294	24.05 S	55.30 W
Igbo-Ora	222	7.26 N	3.17 E
Igbor	222	7.27 N	8.34 E
Igel'vejem ≃	236	65.40 N	172.50 W
Ighil Izane	168	35.44 N	0.30 E
Igiugig	236	59.20 N	155.55 W
Iglau → Jihlava	164	49.24 N	15.36 E
Iglesia	294	30.22 S	69.15 W
Iglesias	170	39.19 N	8.32 E
Iglesiente ➛[1]	170	39.20 N	8.40 E
Igloo	252	43.12 N	103.51 W
Igloolik	232	69.24 N	81.49 W
Ignacio, Calif., U.S.	272	38.05 N	122.32 W
Ignacio, Colo., U.S.	254	37.07 N	107.38 W
Ignacio Zaragoza	278	29.35 N	107.30 W
Ignatovka	160	53.57 N	47.38 E
İğneada	172	41.52 N	27.58 E
İğneada Burnu ≻	212	41.54 N	28.03 E
Igoumenítsa	172	39.30 N	20.16 E
Igra	160	57.33 N	53.04 E
Iguaçu ≃	294	25.36 S	54.36 W
Iguaçu, Saltos do (Iguassu Falls) ᒐ	294	25.41 S	54.26 W
Iguaí	296	14.45 S	40.04 W
Iguala	278	18.21 N	99.32 W
Igualada	168	41.35 N	1.38 E
Iguana ≃	290	7.54 N	65.46 W
Iguana, Sierra de la ⛰	250	26.40 N	100.20 W
Iguape	294	24.43 S	47.33 W
Iguaraçu	296	23.11 S	51.50 W
Iguassu Falls → Iguaçu, Saltos do ᒐ	294	25.41 N	54.26 W
Iguatemi	296	23.40 S	54.34 W
Iguatemi ≃	296	23.55 S	54.10 W
Iguatu	286	6.22 S	39.18 W
Iguazú (Iguaçu), Parque Nacional ♠	294	25.35 S	54.20 W
Iguéla	218	1.55 S	9.19 E
Iguidi, Erg ⚉[8]	214	26.35 N	5.40 W
Iguig	202	17.45 N	121.44 E
Igvak, Cape ≻	236	57.26 N	156.00 W
Igžej	186	53.59 N	103.10 E
Iheya-shima I	193b	27.00 N	127.56 E
Ihiala	222	5.51 N	6.51 E
Ihosy	218	22.24 S	46.08 E
Ihosy ≃	225b	21.58 S	43.38 E
Ihotry, Lac ⊜	225b	21.56 S	43.41 E
Ihringshausen	178	51.21 N	9.31 E
Ihtiman	172	42.26 N	23.49 E
II □[4]	222	16.30 N	10.00 W
Iida	192	35.31 N	137.50 E
III □[4]	222	16.15 N	11.45 W
Iijoki ≃	160	65.20 N	25.17 E
Iisalmi	160	63.34 N	27.11 E
Iiyama	192	36.51 N	138.22 E
Iizuka	192	33.38 N	130.41 E
Ijebu-Igbo	222	6.56 N	4.01 E
Ijebu-Ode	222	6.50 N	3.56 E
IJmuiden	178	52.27 N	4.36 E
IJser (Yser) ≃	176	51.09 N	2.43 E
IJsselmeer (Zuiderzee) ⊸[2]	178	52.45 N	5.25 E
IJsselstein	178	52.02 N	5.03 E
Ijuí	294	28.23 S	53.55 W
Ijuí ≃	294	27.58 S	55.20 W
Ika	186	59.18 N	106.12 E
Ikahavo, Plateau de l' ⛰[1]	225b	17.25 S	45.50 E
Ikare	222	7.32 N	5.45 E
Ikaría I	172	37.41 N	26.20 E
Ikatan	236	54.45 N	163.19 W
Ikawhenua Range ⛰	230	39.20 S	176.56 E
Ikeda, Nihon	192	34.01 N	133.48 E
Ikeda, Nihon	192a	42.55 N	143.27 E
Ikela	218	1.11 S	23.16 E
Ikepa ≃	225b	17.01 S	46.45 E
Ikerre	222	7.31 N	5.14 E
Iki I	192	33.47 N	129.43 E
Ikire	222	7.23 N	4.12 E
Ikirun	222	7.55 N	4.41 E
Ikolik, Cape ≻	236	57.17 N	154.48 W
Ikorodu	222	6.37 N	3.31 E
Ikot Ekpene	222	5.12 N	7.40 E
Ikpikpuk ≃	236	70.50 N	154.25 W
Ikti, Cape ≻	236	56.00 N	158.30 W
Ikuktlitlig Mountain Λ	236	59.16 N	161.27 W
Ikuno	192	35.10 N	134.48 E
Ila	222	8.01 N	4.55 E
Ilabaya	292	17.25 S	70.31 W
Ilacaon Point ≻	202	11.00 N	123.11 E
Ilagan	202	17.09 N	121.53 E
Ilagan ≃	202	17.06 N	121.53 E
Ilan	196	24.45 N	121.44 E
Ilan Ch'uan ≃	196	24.42 N	121.48 E
Ilanskij	186	56.14 N	96.03 E
Ilanz	166	46.46 N	9.12 E
Ilaro	222	6.53 N	3.03 E
Iława (Deutsch Eylau)	164	53.37 N	19.33 E
Ilbenge	186	62.49 N	124.24 E
Île-à-la-Crosse	232	55.27 N	107.53 W
Île-à-la-Crosse, Lac ⊜	232	55.40 N	107.45 W
Ilebo	218	4.19 S	20.35 E
Île-de-France □[9]	176	49.00 N	2.20 E
Île de la Camargue □[9]	182	43.34 N	4.34 E
Ilek ≃	186	51.30 N	53.20 E
Île-Perrot	260	45.21 N	73.54 W
Ilesha	222	7.38 N	4.45 E
Ilevskij Pogost	160	60.41 N	43.46 E
Ileza	160	60.43 N	43.54 E
Ilfracombe, Austl.	226	23.30 S	144.30 E
Ilfracombe, Eng., U.K.	174	51.13 N	4.08 W
İlgaz Dağları ⛰	212	41.00 N	33.35 E
Ilhabela	296	23.47 S	45.21 W
Ilha Grande	290	0.27 S	65.02 W
Ilha Grande, Baía da C	296	23.09 S	44.30 W
Ilhas, Cachoeira das ᒐ	290	1.03 S	57.33 W
Ilhavo	168	40.36 N	8.40 W
Ilhéus	296	14.49 S	39.02 W
Ili	186	43.53 N	77.12 E
Ili ≃	190	45.24 N	74.02 E
Ilia	172	45.56 N	22.39 E
Ilía □[5]	172	37.50 N	21.30 E
Iliamna	236	59.45 N	154.54 W
Iliamna Lake ⊜	236	59.30 N	155.00 W
Ilian, Mount Λ	202	10.25 N	119.32 E
Ilıca	172	39.52 N	27.46 E
Ilicínea	296	20.56 S	45.50 W
Iliff	252	40.45 N	103.04 W
Iligan	202	8.14 N	124.14 E
Iligan Bay C	202	8.20 N	124.00 E
Ilijan	202	13.38 N	121.04 E
Ilimsk	186	56.46 N	103.52 E
Ilin	202	12.15 N	121.02 E
Ilin Island I	202	12.14 N	121.05 E
Ilinta ≃	225b	25.02 S	44.05 E
Ilion	242	43.01 N	75.02 W
Ilio Point ≻	275d	21.13 N	157.15 W
Ilirska Bistrica	170	45.34 N	14.15 E
Iljinskij, S.S.S.R.	160	58.35 N	55.41 E
Iljinskij, S.S.S.R.	186	47.58 N	142.12 E
Iljinskoje	160	61.02 N	32.41 E
Iljinsko-Podomskoje	160	61.08 N	47.56 E
Ilkeston	174	52.59 N	1.18 W
Ilkley	162	53.55 N	1.50 W
Illampu, Nevado Λ	292	15.50 S	68.34 W
Illana Bay C	202	7.35 N	123.45 E
Illapel	294	31.38 S	71.10 W
Illapel ≃	294	31.37 S	71.09 W
Ille-et-Vilaine □[5]	166	48.10 N	1.30 W
Illéla	214	14.28 N	5.15 E
Iller ≃	164	48.23 N	9.58 E
Illertissen	180	48.13 N	10.06 E
Illescas, Esp.	168	40.07 N	3.50 W
Illescas, Méx.	278	23.13 N	102.07 W
Illiers	166	48.18 N	1.15 E
Illimani, Nevado Λ	292	16.39 S	67.48 W
Illimo	292	6.28 S	79.52 W
Illinois □[3]	234	40.00 N	89.00 W
Illinois ≃, Ill., U.S.	244	38.58 N	90.27 W
Illinois ≃, Oreg., U.S.	256	42.33 N	124.03 W
Illinois Peak Λ	256	47.02 N	115.04 W
Illiopolis	248	39.51 N	89.15 W
Illiwa ≃	290	3.55 N	58.45 W
Illizi	214	26.29 N	8.28 E
Illkirch-Graffenstaden	180	48.32 N	7.43 E
Il'men', Ozero ⊜	160	58.17 N	31.20 E
Ilmenau	164	50.41 N	10.55 E
Ilo	292	17.38 S	71.20 W
Ilobasco	280	13.51 N	88.51 W
Iloc Island I	202	11.17 N	119.40 E
Ilocos Norte □[4]	202	18.10 N	120.45 E
Ilocos Sur □[4]	202	17.05 N	120.35 E
Ilog ≃	202	10.00 N	122.45 E
Iloilo	202	10.43 N	122.33 E
Iloilo □[4]	202	11.00 N	122.35 E
Iloilo Strait ∪	202	10.40 N	122.35 E
Ilomantsi	160	62.44 N	22.34 E
Ilopango, Lago de ⊜	280	13.41 N	89.03 W
Ilora	222	7.45 N	3.50 E
Ilorin	222	8.30 N	4.32 E
Iłowa (Halbau)	164	51.30 N	15.12 E
Il'pyrskij	186	59.56 N	164.10 E
Ilwaco	270	46.19 N	124.03 W
Ilwaki	198	7.56 S	126.26 E
Iłża	164	51.11 N	21.14 E
Imabari	192	34.03 N	133.00 E
Imaichi	192	36.43 N	139.41 E
Imaloto ≃	225b	23.27 S	45.13 E
Iman	186	45.55 N	133.43 E
Imandra, Ozero ⊜	160	67.30 N	33.00 E
Imari	192	33.16 N	129.53 E
Imaruí	294	28.21 S	48.49 W
Imaruí, Lagoa C	294	28.21 S	48.52 W
Imathía □[5]	172	40.30 N	22.20 E
Imatra	160	61.10 N	28.46 E
Imbābah	220	30.04 N	31.13 E
Imbabura □[4]	290	0.22 N	78.25 W
Imbituba	294	28.14 S	48.40 W
Imbituva	294	25.12 S	50.35 W
Imboden	248	36.12 N	91.10 W
Imeni Babuškina	160	59.45 N	43.07 E
Imeni Kirova	186	46.27 N	77.13 E
Imeni Moskvy, Kanal ☲	160	56.43 N	37.08 E
Imeni Stepana Razina	160	54.54 N	44.18 E
Imeni Žel'abova	160	58.57 N	36.36 E
Imi	214	6.28 N	42.18 E
Imías	284p	20.04 N	74.38 W
Imilac	294	24.14 S	68.53 W
Imjin-gang ≃	194	37.47 N	126.40 E
Imlay	258	40.39 N	118.09 W
Imlay City	244	43.02 N	83.05 W
Imlaystown	262	40.10 N	74.31 W
Imler	266	40.12 N	78.31 W
Immenstadt	180	47.33 N	10.13 E
Immingham	162	53.37 N	0.12 W
Immokalee	246	26.25 N	81.25 W
Imnaha	256	45.34 N	116.50 W
Imnaha ≃	256	45.49 N	116.46 W
Imo ≃	222	4.36 N	7.35 E
Imola	184	44.21 N	11.42 E
Imotski	170	43.27 N	17.13 E
Impasugong	202	8.19 N	125.00 E
Impenekuim, Gora Λ	236	65.42 N	176.30 E
Imperatriz	286	5.32 S	47.29 W
Imperia	182	43.53 N	8.03 E
Imperia □[4]	182	43.58 N	7.47 E
Imperial, Perú	292	13.04 S	76.21 W
Imperial, Calif., U.S.	258	32.51 N	115.34 W
Imperial, Nebr., U.S.	252	40.31 N	101.39 W
Imperial, Pa., U.S.	266	40.27 N	80.15 W
Imperial, Tex., U.S.	250	31.16 N	102.41 W
Imperial Beach	274	32.35 N	117.08 W
Imperial de Aragón, Canal ☲	168	42.02 N	1.33 W
Imperial Mills	238	55.00 N	111.44 W
Imperial Valley V	258	32.50 N	115.30 W
Impfondo	218	1.37 N	18.04 E
Imphāl	206	24.48 N	93.56 E
Impilachti	160	61.40 N	31.04 E
İmralı I	212	40.32 N	28.32 E
İmroz	172	40.11 N	25.55 E
İmroz Adası I	212	40.10 N	25.50 E
Imst	180	47.14 N	10.44 E
Imuris	278	30.47 N	110.52 W
Imuruan Bay C	202	10.37 N	119.15 E
Imuruk Basin ⊜	236	65.06 N	165.36 W
Imuruk Lake ⊜	236	65.36 N	163.10 W
Ina, Nihon	192	35.50 N	137.57 E
In'a, S.S.S.R.	186	59.24 N	144.48 E
Ina, Ill., U.S.	248	38.09 N	88.54 W
In'a ≃	186	54.59 N	82.59 E
Inagawan	202	9.33 N	118.40 E
Inambari ≃	292	12.41 S	69.40 W
In Aménas	214	28.05 N	9.30 E
Inanwatan	198	2.01 S	132.07 E
Iñapari	292	10.56 S	69.45 W
Inari	160	68.54 N	27.01 E
Inari ⊜	160	69.00 N	28.00 E
Inarigda	186	63.14 N	107.27 E
Inauini ≃	292	8.30 S	67.24 W
Inawasiro-ko ⊜	192	37.29 N	140.06 E

Symbols in the index entries are identified on page 360.

Name	Page	Lat°′	Long°′
Inca	168	39.43 N	2.54 E
Inca de Oro	294	26.45 S	69.54 W
Incaguasi	294	29.13 S	71.03 W
İncekum Burnu ≻	212	36.13 N	33.58 E
Inchcape (Bell Rock II[1]	162	56.55 N	2.50 W
Inchelium	238	48.18 N	118.12 W
Inch'ŏn	194	37.28 N	126.38 E
İncirliova	172	37.50 N	27.43 E
Incomati (Komati) ≃	224	25.46 S	32.43 E
Inčoun	236	66.18 N	170.17 W
Incudine, Mont l' ∧	170	41.51 N	9.12 E
Incy	160	65.48 N	40.26 E
Indaiá ≃	296	18.27 S	45.22 W
Indaiá Grande ≃	296	19.31 S	52.29 W
Indalsälven ≃	160	62.31 N	17.27 E
Indanan	202	5.58 N	120.58 E
Indawgyi In ⊜	200	25.10 N	96.19 E
Indé	278	25.54 N	105.13 W
Independence, Calif., U.S.	258	36.48 N	118.12 W
Independence, Ind., U.S.	268	40.20 N	87.10 W
Independence, Iowa, U.S.	244	42.28 N	91.54 W
Independence, Kans., U.S.	252	37.13 N	95.42 W
Independence, Ky., U.S.	242	38.57 N	84.32 W
Independence, La., U.S.	248	30.38 N	90.30 W
Independence, Mo., U.S.	248	39.05 N	94.24 W
Independence, Oreg., U.S.	256	44.51 N	123.11 W
Independence, Pa., U.S.	266	40.15 N	80.31 W
Independence, Va., U.S.	246	36.37 N	81.09 W
Independence, Wis., U.S.	244	44.21 N	91.25 W
Independence ≃	242	43.45 N	75.20 W
Independence Hill	268	41.29 N	87.20 W
Independence Mountains ⋀	258	41.15 N	116.05 W
Independencia	292	17.07 S	66.53 W
Independencia, Isla I	292	14.17 S	76.12 W
Independența	172	43.58 N	28.05 E
Inderborskij	158	48.33 N	51.44 E
Index	270	47.50 N	121.33 W
India □[1]	204	20.00 N	80.00 E
Indialantic	246	28.05 N	80.34 W
Indian ≃, Mich., U.S.	244	45.59 N	86.15 W
Indian ≃, N.Y., U.S.	242	43.58 N	75.17 W
Indiana	266	40.37 N	79.09 W
Indiana □[6]	266	40.37 N	79.09 W
Indiana □[3]	234	40.00 N	86.15 W
Indianapolis	248	39.46 N	86.09 W
Indian Bayou ≃	248	34.14 N	91.52 W
Indian Brook	240	46.23 N	60.32 W
Indian Church	278	17.45 N	88.40 W
Indian Grave Mountain ∧[2]	246	32.59 N	84.21 W
Indian Head	232	50.32 N	103.40 W
Indian Lake, Mich., U.S.	268	41.59 N	86.12 W
Indian Lake, N.Y., U.S.	242	43.47 N	74.16 W
Indian Lake ⊜, Ont., Can.	244	47.08 N	82.08 W
Indian Lake ⊜, Mich., U.S.	244	45.59 N	86.20 W
Indian Neck	261	41.15 N	72.46 W
Indian Ocean ▾[1]	148	10.00 S	70.00 E
Indianola, Iowa, U.S.	244	41.22 N	93.34 W
Indianola, Miss., U.S.	248	33.27 N	90.39 W
Indianola, Nebr., U.S.	252	40.14 N	100.25 W
Indianola, Wash., U.S.	270	47.45 N	122.31 W
Indianópolis	296	19.02 S	47.55 W
Indian Peak ∧, Utah, U.S.	254	38.16 N	113.53 W
Indian Peak ∧, Wyo., U.S.	256	44.47 N	109.51 W
Indian River	244	45.25 N	84.37 W
Indian River C	246	28.00 N	80.34 W
Indian Springs	258	36.34 N	115.40 W
Indiantown	246	27.01 N	80.28 W
Indian Village	264	42.57 N	76.10 W
Indiaporã	296	19.57 S	50.17 W
Indiera Alta	284m	18.09 N	66.53 W
Indiga	160	67.41 N	49.00 E
Indigirka ≃	186	70.48 N	148.54 E
Inđija	172	45.03 N	20.05 E
Indio	258	33.43 N	116.13 W
Indio ≃, Nic.	280	11.00 N	83.46 W
Indio ≃, Pan.	280	9.11 N	80.11 W
Indios, Canal de los ⊔	284p	21.55 N	83.16 W
Indispensable Reefs ✣[2]	226	12.40 S	160.25 E
Indochina •[1]	148	16.00 N	107.00 E
Indom	160	64.36 N	55.22 E
Indonesia □[1]	198	5.00 S	120.00 E
Indore	206	22.43 N	75.52 E
Indragiri ≃	200	0.22 S	103.26 E
Indre □[5]	166	46.45 N	1.30 E
Indre ≃	166	47.16 N	0.19 E
Indre-et-Loire □[5]	166	47.15 N	0.45 E
Induno Olona	182	45.52 N	8.51 E
Indura	164	53.27 N	23.53 E
Indus	252	48.37 N	93.50 W
Indus ≃	206	24.20 N	67.47 E
Industry, Ill., U.S.	248	40.20 N	90.36 W
Industry, Pa., U.S.	266	40.39 N	80.25 W
Industry, Tex., U.S.	250	29.58 N	96.30 W
İnece	172	41.41 N	27.04 E
İnecik	172	40.56 N	27.16 E
İnegöl	212	40.05 N	29.31 E
İnekollar	172	39.33 N	28.56 E
Ineu	172	46.26 N	21.49 E
Inez, Ky., U.S.	246	37.52 N	82.32 W
Inez, Tex., U.S.	250	28.54 N	96.47 W
Infanta, Pil.	202	14.45 N	121.39 E
Infanta, Pil.	202	15.50 N	119.54 E
Infante, Kaap ≻	224	34.29	20.51 E
Infantes	168	38.44 N	3.01 W
Inferior, Laguna C	278	16.20 N	94.40 W
Infiernillo, Canal del ⊔	278	29.10 N	112.12 W
Infiernillo, Presa del ⊜[1]	278	18.35 N	101.45 W
Infiesto	168	43.21 N	5.22 W
Ing ≃	200	20.13 N	100.27 E
Ingaí ≃	296	21.23 S	44.52 W
I-n-Gall	214	16.47 N	6.56 E
Ingalls Park	268	41.32 N	88.03 W
Ingelheim	164	49.59 N	8.05 E
Ingelmunster	176	50.55 N	3.15 E
Ingende	218	0.15 S	18.57 E
Ingeniero Luiggi	294	35.25 S	64.29 W
Ingeniero Luis A. Huergo	294	39.05 S	67.14 W
Ingeniero White	294	38.47 S	62.16 W
Ingenio, Río del ≃	292	14.38 S	75.15 W
Ingenio La Esperanza	294	24.15 S	64.51 W
Ingenio Santa Ana	294	27.25 S	65.35 W
Ingersoll	264	43.02 N	80.53 W
Ingham	228	18.39 S	146.10 E
Ingham □[6]	268	42.37 N	84.22 W
Ingleside, Ont., Can.	260	45.00 N	75.00 W
Ingleside, Ill., U.S.	268	42.23 N	88.09 W
Ingleside, Tex., U.S.	250	27.53 N	97.13 W
Inglewood, Ont., Can.	264	43.47 N	79.56 W
Inglewood, N.Z.	230	39.09 S	174.12 E
Inglewood, Calif., U.S.	274	33.58 N	118.21 W
Inglewood, Tenn., U.S.	248	36.12 N	86.46 W
Ingolstadt	164	48.46 N	11.27 E
Ingomar, Mont., U.S.	256	46.35 N	107.23 W
Ingomar, Pa., U.S.	266	40.35 N	80.05 W
Ingonish	240	46.42 N	60.22 W
Ingornachoix Bay C	240	50.38 N	57.20 W
Ingram	250	30.04 N	99.14 W
In Guezzam	214	19.32 N	5.42 E
Ingwiller	166	48.52 N	7.29 E
Inhaca, Ilha da I	224	26.03 S	32.57 E
Inhambane	224	23.51 S	35.29 E
Inhambane □[5]	224	23.00 S	34.30 E
Inhambane, Baía de C	224	23.58 S	35.51 E
Inhambupe	296	11.47 S	38.21 W
Inhaminga	218	18.24 S	35.00 E
Inhapim	296	19.33 S	42.07 W
Inharrime	218	24.29 S	35.01 E
Inharrime ≃	224	24.29 S	35.01 E
Inhaúma	296	19.29 S	44.22 W
Inhobi ≃	296	23.45 S	54.40 W
Inhumas	296	16.22 S	49.30 W
Iniesta	168	39.26 N	1.45 W
Inimutaba	296	18.45 S	44.22 W
Ining → Yining	190	43.55 N	81.14 E
Inírida ≃	290	3.55 N	67.52 W
Inishbofin I	162	53.37 N	10.15 W
Inisheer I	162	53.02 N	9.26 W
Inishmaan I	162	53.05 N	9.32 W
Inishmore I	162	53.07 N	9.45 W
Inishturk I	162	53.43 N	10.08 W
Initao	202	8.30 N	124.18 E
Injasuti ∧	224	29.09 S	29.23 E
Injune	226	25.51 S	148.34 E
Inkster, Mich., U.S.	268	42.17 N	83.17 W
Inkster, N. Dak., U.S.	252	48.09 N	97.39 W
Inland Kaikoura Range ⋀	230	42.00 S	173.38 E
Inland Lake ⊜	236	66.27 N	159.47 W
Inland Sea → Seto-naikai ▾[2]	192	34.20 N	133.30 E
Inle Lake ⊜	200	20.32 N	96.55 E
Inmaculadita	278	29.55 N	111.48 W
Inman	246	35.03 N	82.05 W
Inman Mills	246	35.02 N	82.06 W
Inn (En) ≃	166	48.35 N	13.28 E
Innamincka	226	27.45 S	140.44 E
Inner Hebrides II	162	57.00 N	6.45 W
Innerkip	264	43.13 N	80.42 W
Inner Mongolia → Neimenggu Zizhiqu □[4]	190	43.00 N	115.00 E
Inner Sound ⊔	162	57.30 N	5.55 W
Innisfail, Austl.	228	17.32 S	146.02 E
Innisfail, Alta., Can.	238	52.02 N	113.57 W
Innisfree	238	53.22 N	111.32 W
Innoko ≃	236	62.14 N	159.45 W
Innoshima	192	34.20 N	133.10 E
Innsbruck	164	47.16 N	11.24 E
Innviertel •[1]	166	48.10 N	13.15 E
Ino, Nihon	192	33.33 N	133.26 E
Ino, Va., U.S.	262	37.46 N	76.48 W
Inocência	296	19.47 S	51.48 W
Inola	250	36.09 N	95.31 W
Inongo	218	1.57 S	18.16 E
Inowrocław	164	52.48 N	18.15 E
In Salah	214	27.12 N	2.28 E
Insar	160	53.52 N	44.21 E
Insch	162	57.21 N	2.37 W
Insein	200	16.53 N	96.07 E
Ińsko (Nörenberg)	164	53.27 N	15.33 E
Inspiration	254	33.25 N	110.53 W
Insterburg → Černachovsk	164	54.38 N	21.49 E
Inta	160	66.02 N	60.08 E
I-n-Tebezas ▾[4]	222	17.49 N	1.53 E
Intendente Alvear	294	35.15 S	63.35 W
Intercourse	262	40.02 N	76.06 W
Interlaken, Schw.	166	46.41 N	7.51 E
Interlaken, Mass., U.S.	261	42.19 N	73.20 W
Interlaken, N.J., U.S.	262	40.14 N	74.01 W
Interlândia	296	16.12 S	49.02 W
International Falls	244	48.36 N	93.25 W
International Peace Garden ↟	252	49.00 N	100.07 W
Interstate Park ↟	244	45.23 N	92.40 W
Inthanon, Doi ∧	200	18.38 N	98.30 E
Intibucá	280	14.16 N	88.10 W
Intibucá □[5]	280	14.20 N	88.15 W
Intipucá	280	13.12 N	88.04 W
Intiyaco	294	28.40 S	60.05 W
Intracoastal Waterway ≡, U.S.	246	33.40 N	79.00 W
Intracoastal Waterway ≡, U.S.	250	28.45 N	95.40 W
Intutu	290	3.32 S	74.48 W
Inubō-saki ≻	192	35.42 N	140.53 E
Inuvik	236	68.25 N	133.30 W
Inuya ≃	292	10.40 S	73.29 W
Inveraray	162	56.13 N	5.05 W
Inverbervie	162	56.51 N	2.17 W
Invercargill	230	46.25 S	168.27 E
Inverell	228	29.47 S	151.07 E
Invergordon	162	57.42 N	4.10 W
Invermere	238	50.30 N	116.02 W
Inverness, N.S., Can.	240	46.14 N	61.18 W
Inverness, Qué., Can.	260	46.16 N	71.31 W
Inverness, Scot., U.K.	162	57.27 N	4.15 W
Inverness, Calif., U.S.	258	38.06 N	122.51 W
Inverness, Fla., U.S.	246	28.51 N	82.20 W
Inverness, Ill., U.S.	268	42.07 N	88.05 W
Inverness, Miss., U.S.	248	33.21 N	90.35 W
Inverness □[6]	162	57.07 N	4.35 W
Inveruno	182	45.31 N	8.51 E
Inverurie	162	57.17 N	2.23 W
Investigator Strait ⊔	228	35.25 S	137.10 E
Inwood, Ont., Can.	266	42.49 N	81.59 W
Inwood, Ind., U.S.	268	41.19 N	86.12 W
Inwood, Iowa, U.S.	252	43.18 N	96.26 W
Inyanga Mountains ⋀	224	18.00 S	33.00 E
Inyangani ∧	224	18.20 S	32.50 E
Inyan Kara Mountain ∧	252	44.13 N	104.21 W
Inyo, Mount ∧	258	36.44 N	117.59 W
Inyokern	258	35.39 N	117.49 W
Inyo Mountains ⋀	258	36.40 N	118.10 W
Inza	160	53.51 N	46.21 E
Inzago	182	45.32 N	9.29 E
Inzana Lake ⊜	238	54.58 N	124.40 W
Ioanna, Gora ∧	236	64.50 N	178.08 E
Ioánnina	172	39.40 N	20.50 E
Ioco	270	49.18 N	122.52 W
Iō-jima I	193b	30.48 N	130.18 E
Iokanga	160	68.00 N	39.37 E
Iokanga ≃	160	68.00 N	39.43 E
Iola, Kans., U.S.	252	37.55 N	95.24 W
Iola, Wis., U.S.	244	44.36 N	89.08 W
Iolotan', S.S.S.R.	186		
	208	37.18 N	62.21 E
Iona	240	45.58 N	60.48 W
Iona I	162	56.19 N	6.25 W
Ionaivo ≃	225b	22.56 S	46.54 E
Ione, Calif., U.S.	272	38.21 N	120.56 W
Ione, Oreg., U.S.	256	45.30 N	119.50 W
Ione, Wash., U.S.	256	48.45 N	117.25 W
Ionia, Mich., U.S.	268	42.59 N	85.04 W
Ionia, N.Y., U.S.	264	42.56 N	77.30 W
Ionia □[6]	268	42.56 N	85.04 W
Ionian Islands → Iónioi Nísoi II	172	38.30 N	20.30 E
Ionian Sea ▾[2]	158	39.00 N	19.00 E
Iónioi Nísoi II	172	38.30 N	20.30 E
Ionivejem ≃	236	66.12 N	174.00 W
Iony, Ostrov I	186	56.26 N	143.25 E
Íos	172	36.44 N	25.17 E
Íos I	172	36.42 N	25.24 E
Iosegun ≃	238	54.44 N	117.11 W
Iosegun Lake	238	54.29 N	116.50 W
Iowa	248	30.14 N	93.01 W
Iowa □[3]	234	42.15 N	93.15 W
Iowa ≃	244	41.10 N	91.02 W
Iowa City	244	41.40 N	91.32 W
Iowa Falls	244	42.31 N	93.16 W
Iowa Park	250	33.57 N	98.40 W
Ipameri	296	17.43 S	48.09 W
Ipat	160	66.13 N	56.33 E
Ipatinga	296	19.30 S	42.32 W
Ipava	248	40.21 N	90.19 W
Ípeiros •[1]	172	39.40 N	20.50 E
Ipel' ≃	164	47.49 N	18.52 E
Iperu	222	6.52 N	3.38 E
Iphigenia Bay C	236	55.40 N	133.55 W
Ipiales	290	0.50 N	77.37 W
Ipiaú	296	14.08 S	39.44 W
Ipil	202	7.47 N	122.33 E
Ipin → Yibin	190	28.47 N	104.38 E
Ipirá	296	12.10 S	39.44 W
Ipiranga, Bra.	290	3.12 S	66.01 W
Ipiranga, Bra.	294	25.01 S	50.35 W
Ipitá	292	19.20 S	63.32 W
Ipixuna ≃, Bra.	292	7.11 S	71.51 W
Ipixuna ≃, Bra.	292	5.45 S	63.02 W
Ipixuna ≃, Bra.	292	6.16 S	61.52 W
İpkaiye	172	40.12 N	27.06 E
Ipoh	200	4.35 N	101.04 E
Iporã, Bra.	296	23.59 S	53.37 W
Iporá, Bra.	296	16.28 S	51.07 W
İpsala	172	40.55 N	26.23 E
Ipswich, Austl.	228	27.36 S	152.46 E
Ipswich, Eng., U.K.	174	52.04 N	1.10 E
Ipswich, Mass., U.S.	261	42.41 N	70.50 W
Ipswich, S. Dak., U.S.	252	45.27 N	99.02 W
Ipu	286	4.20 S	40.42 W
Ipupiara	296	11.49 S	42.37 W
Iquique	292	20.13 S	70.10 W
Iquitos	290	3.50 S	73.15 W
Ira	250	32.35 N	101.00 W
Iraan, Pil.	202	9.04 N	117.42 E
Iraan, Tex., U.S.	250	30.54 N	101.54 W
Iraí	294	27.11 S	53.15 W
Irajol'	160	64.27 N	55.08 E
Iráklion	172	35.20 N	25.09 E
Irala	294	25.54 S	54.43 W
Iran (Īrān) □[1]	204	32.00 N	53.00 E
Iran Mountains ⋀	198	2.05 N	114.55 E
Īrānshahr	204	27.13 N	60.41 E
Irapa	290	10.34 N	62.35 W
Irapuato	278	20.41 N	101.28 W
Iraq □[1]	204	33.00 N	44.00 E
Irará	296	12.02 S	38.46 W
Irati	294	25.27 S	50.39 W
Irati ≃	168	42.35 N	1.16 W
Irazú, Volcán ∧[1]	280	9.59 N	83.51 W
Irbid	210	32.33 N	35.51 E
Irbid □[8]	210	32.27 N	35.51 E
Irbīl	208	36.11 N	44.01 E
Irbīl □[4]	208	36.10 N	44.00 E
Irbit	158	57.41 N	63.03 E
Irdning	164	47.33 N	14.01 E
Iregua ≃	168	42.27 N	2.24 W
Ireland □[1]	158	53.00 N	8.00 W
Irene	252	43.05 N	97.10 W
Ireng (Maú) ≃	290	3.33 N	59.51 W
Ireton	252	42.58 N	96.19 W
Irgiz	158	48.37 N	61.16 E
Iri	194	35.56 N	126.57 E
Iriga	202	13.25 N	123.25 E
Irîgui •[1]	222	16.43 N	5.30 W
Iringa	218	7.46 S	35.42 E
Iriona	280	15.57 N	85.11 W
Iriri ≃	286	3.52 S	52.37 W
Irish, Mount ∧	258	37.38 N	115.24 W
Irish Sea ▾[2]	162	53.30 N	5.20 W
Irkutsk	186	52.16 N	104.20 E
Irma	238	52.55 N	111.14 W
Iroise C	166	48.15 N	4.55 W
Iron Belt	244	46.25 N	90.19 W
Iron Bridge	244	46.17 N	83.14 W
Iron City	248	35.01 N	87.35 W
Irondale, Ala., U.S.	248	33.32 N	86.42 W
Irondale, Mo., U.S.	248	37.50 N	90.41 W
Irondale, Ohio, U.S.	266	40.34 N	80.44 W
Irondequoit	264	43.12 N	77.36 W
Iron Gate V	172	44.41 N	22.31 E
Iron Knob	228	32.44 S	137.08 E
Iron Mountain	244	45.49 N	88.04 W
Iron Mountain ∧	254	33.27 N	111.10 W
Iron Mountains ⋀	246	36.30 N	81.50 W
Iron Range	226	12.42 S	143.18 E
Iron River, Mich., U.S.	244	46.05 N	88.39 W
Iron River, Wis., U.S.	244	46.34 N	91.24 W
Iron Springs	262	39.46 N	77.25 W
Ironstone Kopje ∧	224	25.08 S	24.05 E
Ironton, Minn., U.S.	244	46.28 N	93.59 W
Ironton, Mo., U.S.	248	37.36 N	90.38 W
Ironton, Ohio, U.S.	242	38.31 N	82.40 W
Ironwood	244	46.27 N	90.10 W
Iroquois, Ont., Can.	264	44.51 N	75.19 W
Iroquois, Ill., U.S.	268	40.50 N	87.35 W
Iroquois, S. Dak., U.S.	252	44.22 N	97.51 W
Iroquois □[6]	268	40.47 N	87.44 W
Iroquois ≃	244	41.05 N	87.49 W
Iroquois Falls	244	48.46 N	80.41 W
Irosin	202	12.42 N	124.02 E
Irō-zaki ≻	192	34.36 N	138.51 E
Irrawaddy □[8]	200	17.00 N	95.00 E
Irrawaddy ≃	200	15.50 N	95.06 E
Irricana	238	51.19 N	113.37 W
Irrigon	256	45.54 N	119.30 W
Irsina	170	40.45 N	16.15 E
Irthlingborough	174	52.20 N	0.37 W
Irtyš ≃	186	61.04 N	68.52 E
Irtysh → Irtyš ≃	186	61.04 N	68.52 E
Irtyšsk	186	53.21 N	75.27 E
Irumu	218	1.27 N	29.52 E
Irún	168	43.21 N	1.47 W
Irupana	292	16.28 S	67.28 W
Irurzun	168	42.55 N	1.50 W
Irvine, Scot., U.K.	162	55.37 N	4.40 W
Irvine, Calif., U.S.	274	33.41 N	117.46 W
Irvine, Ky., U.S.	246	37.42 N	83.58 W
Irvine, Pa., U.S.	266	41.50 N	79.17 W
Irvines Landing	238	49.38 N	124.03 W
Irvinestown	162	54.29 N	7.38 W
Irving, Ill., U.S.	248	39.12 N	89.24 W
Irving, N.Y., U.S.	266	42.34 N	79.07 W
Irving, Tex., U.S.	250	32.49 N	96.56 W
Irvington, Ky., U.S.	248	37.53 N	86.17 W
Irvington, N.J., U.S.	262	40.44 N	74.14 W
Irvington, Va., U.S.	262	37.40 N	76.25 W
Irvona	266	40.46 N	78.33 W
Irwinton	246	32.49 N	83.10 W
Irwŏl-san ∧	194	36.50 N	129.06 E
Is, Jabal ∧	220	21.49 N	35.39 E
Isa	222	13.14 N	6.24 E
Isaac ≃	228	22.52 S	149.20 E
Isaac Lake ⊜	238	53.10 N	120.50 W
Isaba	168	42.52 N	0.55 W
Isabel, Pil.	202	10.56 N	124.26 E
Isabel, S. Dak., U.S.	252	45.24 N	101.26 W
Isabel, Bahía C	290a	0.38 S	91.27 W
Isabela, Pil.	202	10.12 N	122.59 E
Isabela (Basilan), Pil.	202	6.42 N	121.58 E
Isabela, P.R.	284m	18.30 N	67.01 W
Isabela □[4]	202	17.00 N	122.00 E
Isabela, Cabo ≻	282	20.00 N	71.00 W
Isabela, Canal ⊔	290a	0.20 S	90.55 W
Isabela, Isla I, Ec.	290a	0.30 S	91.06 W
Isabela, Isla I, Méx.	278	21.51 N	105.55 W
Isabella, Cordillera ⋀	280	13.45 N	85.15 W
Isabella Reservoir ⊜[1]	258	35.40 N	118.26 W
Isabelle ≃	244	47.50 N	91.41 W
Isabel Segunda	284m	18.09 N	65.27 W
Isábena ≃	168	42.11 N	0.21 E
Isaccea	172	45.16 N	28.28 E
Ísafjarđardjúp C[2]	160a	66.10 N	23.00 W
Ísafjörđur	160a	66.08 N	23.13 W
Isahaya	192	32.50 N	130.03 E
Isajgino	160	57.46 N	46.51 E
Isak	200	4.27 N	96.53 E
Isakly	160	54.08 N	51.32 E
Isalnița	172	44.24 N	23.44 E
Isalo, Parc National de l' ↟	225b	22.45 S	45.15 E
Isana (Içana) ≃	290	0.26 N	67.19 W
Isanti	244	45.29 N	93.15 W
Isar ≃	164	48.49 N	12.58 E
Isara	222	6.59 N	3.41 E
Isarog, Mount ∧	202	13.40 N	123.23 E
Ischia	184	40.44 N	13.57 E
Ischitella	184	41.54 N	15.54 E
Ischodnaja, Gora ∧	236	64.50 N	173.26 W
Ischua	266	42.15 N	78.24 W
Iscuandé ≃	290	2.38 N	78.04 W
Ise (Uji-yamada)	192	34.29 N	136.42 E
Iselin, N.J., U.S.	262	40.34 N	74.19 W
Iselin, Pa., U.S.	266	40.34 N	79.24 W
Iseo, Lago d' ⊜	170	45.43 N	10.04 E
Isère □[5]	182	45.10 N	5.50 E
Iserlohn	178	51.22 N	7.41 E
Isernia	184	41.36 N	14.14 E
Isesaki	192	36.19 N	139.12 E
Ise-shima-kokuritsu-kōen ↟	192	34.23 N	136.48 E
Iset' ≃	186	56.36 N	66.24 E
Ise-wan C	192	34.43 N	136.43 E
Iseyin	222	7.58 N	3.36 E
Isfahan → Eşfahān	208	32.40 N	51.38 E
Isherton	290	2.20 N	59.25 W
Ishikari-dake ∧	192a	44.33 N	143.02 E
Ishikari-heiya ⩦	192a	43.15 N	141.23 E
Ishikari-wan C	192a	43.25 N	141.01 E
Ishikawa	193b	26.25 N	127.50 E
Ishikawa □[5]	192	36.45 N	136.45 E
Ishinomaki	192	38.25 N	141.18 E
Ishioka	192	36.11 N	140.16 E
Ishizuchi-san ∧	192	33.46 N	133.07 E
Ishpeming	244	46.30 N	87.40 W
Isiboro ≃	292	15.28 S	65.05 W
Isigny	166	49.19 N	1.06 W
Işıklı	172	38.19 N	29.51 E
Isil'-Kul'	186	54.55 N	71.16 E
Išim	186	56.09 N	69.27 E
Išim ≃	186	57.45 N	71.12 E
Išimbaj	158	53.28 N	56.02 E
Išimskaja Step' ⩦	186	55.00 N	70.00 E
Isiolo	218	0.21 N	37.35 E
Isiro	214	2.47 N	27.37 E
Iskabad Canal ≡	208	37.10 N	66.10 E
Iskâr ≃	172	43.44 N	24.27 E
Iskâr, Jazovir ⊜[1]	172	43.23 N	27.29 E
Iskaten', Chrebet ⋀	236	66.30 N	179.00 W
İskenderun	212	36.37 N	36.07 E
İskenderun Körfezi C	212	36.30 N	35.40 E
Iskitim	186	54.38 N	83.18 E
Iskut ≃	236	56.42 N	131.45 W
Isla	278	18.01 N	95.30 W
Isla Cristina	168	37.12 N	7.19 W
Isla de Maipo	294	33.45 S	70.54 W
Islāmābād	206	33.42 N	73.10 E
Isla Mujeres	278	21.12 N	86.43 W
Island	248	37.27 N	87.09 W
Island □[6]	270	48.07 N	122.36 W
Island Bay C	202	9.07 N	118.12 E
Island Falls	242	46.00 N	68.16 W
Island Heights	262	39.57 N	74.09 W
Island Lagoon ⊜	228	31.30 S	136.40 E
Island Lake	268	42.17 N	88.12 W
Island Lake ⊜	232	53.47 N	94.25 W
Island Park, Idaho, U.S.	256	44.24 N	111.19 W
Island Park, R.I., U.S.	261	41.37 N	71.14 W
Island Park Reservoir ⊜[1]	256	44.25 N	111.29 W
Island Pond	242	44.49 N	71.53 W
Island Pond ⊜	240	48.25 N	56.23 W
Islands, Bay of C, Newf., Can.	240	49.10 N	58.15 W
Islands, Bay Of C, N.Z.	230	35.14 S	174.08 E
Isla Patrulla	294	32.59 S	54.35 W
Islas de la Bahía □[5]	280	16.20 N	86.30 W
Isla Verde	294	33.15 S	62.24 W
Isla Vista	258	34.25 N	119.53 W
Islay I	162	55.46 N	6.10 W
Islay, Punta ≻	292	17.03 S	72.08 W
Isle	244	46.08 N	93.29 W
Isle ≃	166	44.55 N	0.15 W
Isle-aux-Morts	240	47.35 N	58.59 W
Isle of Hope	246	31.58 N	81.05 W
Isle of Man □[2]	158	54.15 N	4.30 W
Isle of Palms	246	32.47 N	79.48 W
Isle of Wight	262	36.54 N	76.43 W
Isle of Wight □[6]	262	36.50 N	76.42 W
Isle Royale National Park ↟	244	48.00 N	89.00 W
Isle Saint George	266	41.43 N	82.49 W
Islesboro Island I	242	44.20 N	68.53 W
Isleta	254	34.55 N	106.42 W
Isleta Indian Reservation •[4]	254	34.55 N	106.45 W
Isleton	272	38.10 N	121.37 W
Islets-Caribou	240	49.30 N	67.16 W
Islington	261	42.13 N	71.11 W
Islington •[8]	174	51.34 N	0.06 W
Islón	294	29.54 S	71.12 W
Ismael Cortinas	294	33.58 S	57.06 W
Ismailia → Al-Ismā'īlīyah	220	30.35 N	32.16 E
İsmailli	172	38.56 N	27.13 E
Ismaning	164	48.14 N	11.41 E
Isnā	220	25.18 N	32.33 E
Isny	180	47.41 N	10.02 E
Isola	248	33.16 N	90.36 W
Isola della Scala	170	45.16 N	11.00 E
Isola del Liri	184	41.41 N	13.34 E
Isola di Capo Rizzuto	170	38.58 N	17.06 E
Isola Farnese •[8]	184	42.01 N	12.23 E
İsparta	212	37.46 N	30.33 E
Isperih	172	43.43 N	26.50 E
Ispica	170	36.46 N	14.55 E
Israel □[1]	204	31.40 N	34.50 E
Israel ≃	242	44.29 N	71.35 W
Issa	160	53.52 N	44.51 E
Issano	290	5.49 N	59.26 W
Issaquah	270	47.32 N	122.02 W
Issen, Oued ≃	168	36.52 N	3.48 E
Isser, Oued ≃	168	35.08 N	1.28 W
Issigeac	166	44.44 N	0.36 E
Issoire	166	45.33 N	3.15 E
Issoudun	166	46.57 N	2.00 E
Is-sur-Tille	166	47.31 N	5.06 E
Issyk-Kul', Ozero ⊜	186	42.25 N	77.15 E
İstanbul	212	41.01 N	28.58 E
İstanbul □[4]	172	41.25 N	29.00 E
İstanbul Boğazı ⊔	212	41.00 N	29.00 E
Istiaía	172	38.57 N	23.09 E
Istmina	290	5.10 N	76.39 W
Isto, Mount ∧	236	69.12 N	143.48 W
Istok	172	42.47 N	20.29 E
Istokpoga, Lake ⊜	246	27.22 N	81.17 W
Istoro Nāl ∧	204	36.23 N	71.54 E
Istra	160	55.55 N	36.52 E
Istra ≻[1]	170	45.15 N	14.00 E
İstranca Dağları ⋀	212	41.50 N	27.30 E
Istres	182	43.31 N	4.59 E
Itá	294	25.29 S	57.21 W
Itabaiana, Bra.	286	7.20 S	35.20 W
Itabaiana, Bra.	286	10.41 S	37.26 W
Itabapoana	296	21.18 S	40.58 W
Itaberá	296	23.51 S	49.09 W
Itaberaba	296	12.32 S	40.18 W
Itaberaí	296	16.02 S	49.48 W
Itabira	296	19.37 S	43.13 W
Itabuna	296	14.48 S	39.16 W
Itacambiruçu ≃	296	16.44 S	42.45 W
Itacaré	296	14.18 S	39.00 W
Itacoatiara	290	3.08 S	58.25 W
Itacuaí ≃	290	4.20 S	70.12 W
Itacurubí del Rosario	294	24.29 S	56.41 W
Itaetê	296	12.59 S	40.58 W
Itagi	296	14.10 S	40.01 W
Itaguaçu	296	19.48 S	40.51 W
Itaguaí	296	22.52 S	43.47 W
Itaguajé	296	22.37 S	51.59 W
Itaguara	296	20.23 S	44.29 W
Itaguari ≃	296	14.11 S	44.40 W
Itaguaru	296	15.44 S	49.37 W
Itagüí	290	6.10 N	75.36 W
Itaguira	296	15.09 S	39.44 W
Itaí	296	23.24 S	49.06 W
Itá-Ibaté	294	27.26 S	57.20 W
Itaimbey ≃	294	24.46 S	54.24 W
Itaiópolis	294	26.20 S	49.56 W
Itaituba	286	4.17 S	55.59 W
Itaja	296	19.07 S	51.37 W
Itajaí	294	26.53 S	48.39 W
Itajaí do Norte ≃	294	27.05 S	49.30 W
Itajaí do Sul ≃	294	27.12 S	49.39 W
Itajubá	296	22.26 S	45.27 W
Itajuípe	296	14.41 S	39.22 W
Itakyry	294	24.56 S	55.13 W
Italica ⊥	168	37.30 N	6.05 W
Italy	250	32.11 N	96.53 W
Italy □[1]	158	42.50 N	12.50 E
Itamarandiba	296	17.51 S	42.51 W
Itamarandiba ≃	296	17.18 S	42.48 W
Itamari	296	13.47 S	39.37 W
Itambacuri	296	18.01 S	41.42 W
Itambé	296	15.15 S	40.37 W
Itami	192	34.46 N	135.25 E
Itanhaém	296	24.11 S	46.47 W
Itanhauã ≃	290	4.45 S	63.48 W
Itanhém	296	17.09 S	40.20 W
Itanhém ≃	296	17.32 S	39.12 W
Itanhomi	296	19.10 S	41.52 W
Itaobim	296	16.34 S	41.30 W
Itapaci	296	14.57 S	49.34 W
Itapagipe	296	19.54 S	49.22 W
Itaparaná ≃	292	5.47 S	63.03 W
Itaparica, Ilha de I	296	13.00 S	38.42 W
Itapaya	292	17.34 S	66.21 W
Itapé	296	14.54 S	39.26 W
Itapebi	296	15.56 S	39.32 W
Itapecerica	296	20.28 S	45.07 W
Itapecuru-Mirim	286	3.24 S	44.20 W
Itapemirim	296	21.01 S	40.50 W
Itaperina, Pointe ≻	225b	24.59 S	47.06 E
Itaperuna	296	21.12 S	41.54 W
Itapetinga	296	15.15 S	40.15 W
Itapetininga	296	23.36 S	48.03 W
Itapetininga ≃	294	23.35 S	48.27 W
Itapeva	296	23.58 S	48.52 W
Itapi ≃	290	0.47 S	57.16 W
Itapicuru ≃, Bra.	286	2.52 S	44.12 W
Itapira	296	22.26 S	46.50 W
Itapiranga, Bra.	290	2.45 S	58.01 W
Itapiranga, Bra.	294	27.08 S	53.43 W
Itapirapuã	296	15.52 S	50.36 W
Itapitanga	296	14.26 S	39.34 W
Itápolis	296	21.35 S	48.46 W
Itaporã	296	22.01 S	54.54 W
Itaporanga	296	23.42 S	49.29 W
Itapúa □[5]	294	26.50 S	55.50 W
Itapuranga	296	15.35 S	49.59 W
Itaquara	296	13.27 S	39.57 W
Itaquari	296	20.20 S	40.22 W
Itaqui	294	29.08 S	56.33 W
Itarantim	296	15.39 S	40.03 W
Itararé	296	24.07 S	49.20 W
Itararé ≃	296	23.10 S	49.42 W
Itarumã	296	18.42 S	51.25 W
Itasca	250	32.10 N	97.09 W
Itata ≃	294	36.23 S	72.52 W
Itatí	294	27.17 S	58.15 W
Itatiaia, Parque Nacional do ↟	296	22.28 S	44.37 W
Itatiba	296	23.00 S	46.51 W
Itatinga	296	23.07 S	48.36 W
Itauçu	296	16.13 S	49.37 W
Itaúna	296	20.04 S	44.34 W
Itaúnas ≃	296	18.25 S	39.42 W
Itbayat Island I	198	20.45 N	121.50 E
Itchen Lake ⊜	232	65.33 N	112.50 W
Ité ≃	290	7.00 N	74.15 W
Itéa	172	38.26 N	22.24 E
Iténez (Guaporé) ≃	292	11.55 S	65.04 W
Ithaca, Mich., U.S.	244	43.18 N	84.36 W
Ithaca, N.Y., U.S.	242	42.27 N	76.30 W
Itháki	172	38.23 N	20.42 E
Itháki I	172	38.24 N	20.42 E
Itinga	296	16.36 S	41.47 W
Itinga ≃	296	16.35 S	41.45 W
Itiquira	296	17.12 S	54.07 W
Itiquira ≃	296	17.18 S	56.44 W
Itirapina	296	22.15 S	47.49 W
Itiruçu	296	13.31 S	40.09 W
Itkillik ≃	236	70.08 N	150.57 W
Itō	192	34.58 N	139.05 E
Itoigawa	192	37.02 N	137.51 E
Itomamo, Lac ⊜	240	49.11 N	70.19 W
Itonamas ≃	292	12.28 S	64.24 W
Itororó	296	15.07 S	40.06 W
Itri	184	41.17 N	13.32 E
Itsuki	192	32.24 N	130.50 E
Itsuwa	192	32.30 N	130.10 E
Itta Bena	248	33.30 N	90.20 W
Ittiri	170	40.36 N	8.33 E
Ittygran, Ostrov I	236	64.36 N	172.40 W
Itu	296	23.16 S	47.19 W
Itu ≃	294	29.25 S	55.51 W
Ituaçu	296	13.49 S	41.18 W
Ituango	290	7.04 N	75.45 W
Ituberá	296	13.44 S	39.09 W
Itucumã ≃	292	6.59 S	69.48 W
Itueta	296	19.23 S	41.11 W
Ituí ≃	290	4.38 S	70.19 W
Ituim ≃	294	28.35 S	51.20 W
Ituiutaba	296	18.58 S	49.28 W
Itumbiara	296	18.25 S	49.13 W
Ituporanga	294	27.25 S	49.36 W
Iturama	296	19.44 S	50.11 W
Iturbe	294	26.01 S	56.30 W
Iturbide	278	19.40 N	89.37 W
Iturup, Ostrov (Etorofu-tō) I	192a	44.54 N	147.30 E
Ituverava	296	20.20 S	47.47 W
Ituxi ≃	292	7.18 S	64.51 W
Ituzaingó	294	27.35 S	56.40 W
Itzehoe	178	53.55 N	9.31 E
I'udkovo	160	54.36 N	34.43 E
Iuka	248	34.49 N	88.11 W
Iul'tin	236	67.50 N	178.48 W
Iul'tin, Gora ∧	236	67.50 N	178.25 W
Iúna	296	20.21 S	41.32 W
IV □[4]	222	15.45 N	13.00 W
Iva	246	34.19 N	82.40 W
Ivačovo	160	60.32 N	36.22 E
Ivaí ≃	296	23.18 S	53.42 W
Ivaiporã	294	24.15 S	51.45 W
Ivajlovgrad	172	41.32 N	26.08 E
Ivakoany, Massif de l' ⋀	225b	23.50 S	46.25 E
Ivalo	160	68.42 N	27.30 E
Ivalojoki ≃	160	68.43 N	27.36 E
Ivančice	164	49.06 N	16.23 E
Ivanec	170	46.13 N	16.08 E
Ivangorod	160	59.24 N	28.10 E
Ivangrad	172	42.50 N	19.52 E
Ivanhoe, Austl.	226	32.54 S	144.18 E
Ivanhoe, Calif., U.S.	272	36.23 N	119.13 W
Ivanhoe, Minn., U.S.	252	44.28 N	96.15 W
Ivanhoe, Va., U.S.	246	36.50 N	80.58 W
Ivanhoe ≃	244	48.40 N	82.11 W
Ivanhoe Lake ⊜	244	48.05 N	82.38 W
Ivanić Grad	170	45.42 N	16.24 E
Ivanjica	172	43.35 N	20.14 E
Ivan'kovskoje Vodochranilišče ⊜[1]	160	56.37 N	36.32 E
Ivanof Bay	236	55.54 N	159.29 W
Ivano-Frankovsk	158	48.55 N	24.43 E
Ivanovo	160	57.00 N	40.59 E
Ivanovskaja	160	60.48 N	55.52 E
Ivatuba	296	23.37 S	52.13 W
Ivdel'	158	60.42 N	60.24 E
Ivinheima ≃	296	23.14 S	53.42 W
Ivo	292	20.27 S	63.26 W
Ivón ≃	292	11.06 S	66.08 W
Ivor	262	36.54 N	76.54 W
Ivory Coast □[1]	214	8.00 N	5.00 W
Ivory Coast •[2]	222	5.10 N	5.00 W
Ivoryton	261	41.21 N	72.27 W
Ivrea	182	45.28 N	7.52 E
İvrindi	172	39.34 N	27.29 E
Ivry-sur-Seine	176	48.49 N	2.23 E
Ivugivik	232	62.25 N	77.54 W
Ivywild	252	39.49 N	104.51 W
Iwaizumi	192	39.50 N	141.48 E
Iwaki (Taira)	192	37.03 N	140.55 E
Iwaki-san ∧	192	40.39 N	140.18 E
Iwakuni	192	34.09 N	132.11 E
Iwami	192	35.35 N	134.20 E
Iwamizawa	192a	43.12 N	141.46 E
Iwanai	192a	42.58 N	140.30 E
Iwanuma	192	38.06 N	140.52 E
Iwata	192	34.42 N	137.48 E
Iwate □[5]	192	39.37 N	141.22 E
Iwate-san ∧	192	39.51 N	141.00 E
Iwo	222	7.38 N	4.11 E
Ixcán ≃	280	16.07 N	91.05 W
Ixchiguán	280	15.12 N	91.53 W
Ixelles	176	50.50 N	4.22 E
Ixiamas	292	13.45 S	68.09 W
Iximché ⊥	280	14.44 N	90.59 W
Ixmiquilpan	278	20.29 N	99.14 W
Ixonia	268	43.09 N	88.36 W
Ixtacihuatl ∧[1]	278	19.11 N	98.39 W
Ixtapan de la Sal	278	18.50 N	99.41 W
Ixtlán de Juárez	278	17.20 N	96.29 W
Ixtlán del Río	278	21.02 N	104.22 W
Iyo	192	33.46 N	132.42 E
Iyo-mishima	192	33.58 N	133.33 E
Iyo-nada ▾[2]	192	33.40 N	132.20 E
Iza ≃	172	47.54 N	23.57 E
Izabal	280	15.24 N	89.08 W
Izabal □[5]	280	15.30 N	89.00 W
Izabal, Lago de ⊜	280	15.30 N	89.10 W
Izalco	280	13.45 N	89.40 W
Izapa ⊥	278	14.55 N	92.10 W
Izberbaš	158	42.33 N	47.52 E
Izbica (Giesebitz), Pol.	164	54.42 N	17.26 E
Izbica, Pol.	164	50.54 N	23.09 E
Izd'oškovo	160	55.08 N	33.37 E
Izegem	176	50.55 N	3.12 E
Izena-shima I	193b	26.56 N	127.56 E
Iževsk	160	56.51 N	53.14 E
Izieux	182	45.28 N	4.30 E
Ižma	160	65.02 N	53.55 E
Ižma ≃	160	65.19 N	52.54 E
Izmail	158	45.21 N	28.50 E
İzmir	212	38.25 N	27.09 E
İzmir □[4]	172	38.15 N	27.30 E
İzmir Körfezi C	212	38.30 N	26.50 E
İzmit (Kocaeli)	212	40.46 N	29.55 E
İzmit Körfezi C	212	40.45 N	29.35 E
Iznajar, Embalse de ⊜[1]	168	37.15 N	4.30 W
Iznalloz	168	37.23 N	3.31 W
İznik	172	40.26 N	29.43 E
İznik Gölü ⊜	212	40.26 N	29.30 E
Izozog, Bañados de ☷	292	18.48 S	62.10 W
Izra'	210	32.51 N	36.15 E
Izsák	164	46.48 N	19.22 E
Iztapa	280	13.56 N	90.43 W
Izúcar de Matamoros	278	18.36 N	98.28 W
Izu-hantō ≻[1]	192	34.45 N	139.00 E
Izuhara	192	34.12 N	129.17 E
Iz'um	158	49.12 N	37.19 E
Izumi, Nihon	192	32.05 N	130.22 E
Izumi, Nihon	192	34.29 N	135.26 E
Izumo	192	35.22 N	132.46 E
Izu-shotō II	192	32.00 N	140.00 E
Izvestij CIK, Ostrova II	186	75.55 N	82.30 E
J			
Jabal Abyad Plateau ⋀[1]	220	19.00 N	29.00 E
Jabal al-Awliyā'	214	15.14 N	32.30 E
Jabal Lubnān □[4]	210	33.50 N	35.40 E
Jabalón ≃	168	38.53 N	4.05 W
Jabalpur	206	23.10 N	79.57 E
Jabbūl, Sabkhat al- ⊜	212	36.03 N	37.39 E
Jabjabah, Wādī V	220	22.37 N	33.17 E
Jablah	208	35.21 N	35.55 E
Jablanac	170	44.42 N	14.54 E
Jablanica ≃	172	43.07 N	21.57 E
Jablonec nad Nisou	164	50.44 N	15.10 E
Jablonica	164	48.37 N	17.25 E
Jabłonka	164	49.29 N	19.41 E
Jablonovyj Chrebet (Yablonovy Range) ⋀	186	53.30 N	115.00 E
Jabłonowo	164	53.24 N	19.09 E
Jablunkov	164	49.35 N	18.47 E
Jaboatão	286	8.07 S	35.01 W
Jaboncillos	278	28.57 N	102.39 W
Jabonga	202	9.20 N	125.31 E
Jaborandi	296	20.40 S	48.25 W
Jaboticabal	296	21.16 S	48.19 W
Jabrat Sa'īd ▾[4]	220	16.06 N	31.50 E
Jabrīn ▾[4]	208	23.17 N	48.58 E
Jaca	168	42.34 N	0.33 W
Jacala de Ledesma	278	21.01 N	99.11 W
Jacaleapa	280	14.00 N	86.40 W
Jacaltenango	280	15.40 N	91.44 W
Jacaraci	296	14.51 S	42.26 W
Jacaré ≃, Bra.	292	5.49 S	63.35 W
Jacaré ≃, Bra.	296	13.50 S	40.42 W
Jacaré Guaçu ≃	296	21.50 S	48.56 W
Jacareí	296	23.19 S	45.58 W
Jacaré Pepira ≃	296	21.54 S	48.52 W
Jacarèzinho	296	23.09 S	49.59 W
Jáchal	294	30.15 S	68.45 W
Jáchal ≃	294	30.47 S	68.14 W
Jaciara	296	15.59 S	54.57 W
Jacinto	296	16.10 S	40.17 W
Jacinto Aráuz	294	38.05 S	63.26 W
Jacinto City	250	29.46 N	95.16 W
Jacinto Machado	294	29.00 S	49.46 W
Jaci Paraná	292	9.15 S	64.23 W
Jaciparaná ≃	292	9.22 S	64.22 W
Jackman	242	45.38 N	70.16 W
Jackman Station	242	45.37 N	70.15 W
Jack Mountain ∧, Mont., U.S.	256	46.21 N	112.18 W
Jack Mountain ∧, Wash., U.S.	256	48.47 N	120.57 W
Jacksboro, Tenn., U.S.	246	36.20 N	84.11 W
Jacksboro, Tex., U.S.	250	33.13 N	98.10 W
Jackson, Ala., U.S.	248	31.31 N	87.53 W
Jackson, Calif., U.S.	272	38.21 N	120.46 W
Jackson, Ga., U.S.	246	33.18 N	83.58 W
Jackson, Ky., U.S.	246	37.33 N	83.23 W
Jackson, La., U.S.	248	30.50 N	91.13 W
Jackson, Mich., U.S.	268	42.15 N	84.24 W
Jackson, Minn., U.S.	252	43.37 N	95.01 W
Jackson, Miss., U.S.	248	32.18 N	90.12 W
Jackson, Mo., U.S.	248	37.23 N	89.40 W
Jackson, N.J., U.S.	262	40.06 N	74.23 W
Jackson, N.C., U.S.	246	36.23 N	77.25 W
Jackson, Ohio, U.S.	242	39.03 N	82.39 W
Jackson, S.C., U.S.	246	33.20 N	81.47 W
Jackson, Tenn., U.S.	248	35.37 N	88.49 W
Jackson, Wyo., U.S.	254	43.29 N	110.38 W
Jackson □[6]	268	42.15 N	84.24 W
Jackson ≃	242	37.47 N	79.46 W
Jackson, Cape ≻	230	41.00 S	174.13 E
Jackson, Lake ⊜	246	30.30 N	84.17 W
Jackson, Port C	228	33.50 S	151.16 E
Jackson Bay C	230	43.57 S	168.43 E
Jackson Center, Ohio, U.S.	268	40.27 N	84.02 W
Jackson Center, Pa., U.S.	266	41.16 N	80.09 W
Jackson Head ≻	230	43.58 S	168.37 E
Jackson Lake ⊜[1], Ga., U.S.	246	33.22 N	83.52 W
Jackson Lake ⊜[1], Wyo., U.S.	254	43.55 N	110.40 W
Jackson Mountain ∧	242	44.46 N	70.32 W
Jackson's Arm	240	49.52 N	56.47 W
Jacksonville, Ala., U.S.	248	33.49 N	85.46 W
Jacksonville, Ark., U.S.	248	34.52 N	92.07 W
Jacksonville, Fla., U.S.	246	30.20 N	81.40 W
Jacksonville, Ill., U.S.	248	39.44 N	90.14 W
Jacksonville, N.C., U.S.	246	34.45 N	77.26 W
Jacksonville, Oreg., U.S.	256	42.19 N	122.57 W
Jacksonville, Tex., U.S.	250	31.58 N	95.17 W
Jacksonville, Vt., U.S.	261	42.47 N	72.49 W
Jacksonville Beach	246	30.18 N	81.24 W
Jacks Reef	264	43.06 N	76.25 W

Symbols in the index entries are identified on page 360.

Name	Page	Lat°′	Long°′
Jacmel	282	18.14 N	72.32 W
Jacob	218	4.11 S	13.17 E
Jacobābād	206	28.17 N	68.26 E
Jacobina	286	11.11 S	40.31 W
Jacobus	262	39.53 N	76.43 W
Jacques, Lac à ⊜	236	66.10 N	127.25 W
Jacques-Cartier	260	45.31 N	73.28 W
Jacques-Cartier, Mont Λ	240	48.59 N	65.57 W
Jacques-Cartier, Passage de ⋓	240	50.00 N	63.00 W
Jacquet River	240	47.55 N	66.00 W
Jacuba ≃	296	18.25 S	52.28 W
Jacuí ≃	294	30.02 S	51.15 W
Jacuípe	296	12.29 S	38.38 W
Jacuípe ≃	296	12.30 S	39.05 W
Jacumba	258	32.37 N	116.11 W
Jacupiranga	294	24.42 S	48.00 W
Jadal ⬩[1]	222	19.00 N	4.15 E
Jaddi, Rās ≻	206	25.14 N	63.31 E
Jadito Wash V	254	35.22 N	110.50 W
Jadotville → Likasi	218	10.59 S	26.44 E
Jadraque	168	40.55 N	2.55 W
Jadrin	160	55.56 N	46.12 E
Jaén, Esp.	168	37.46 N	3.47 W
Jaén, Perú	292	5.21 S	78.28 W
Jaffa, Cape ≻	228	36.58 S	139.40 E
Jaffa, Tel Aviv- → Tel Aviv-Yafo	210	32.03 N	34.46 E
Jaffna	204	9.40 N	80.00 E
Jaffrey	242	42.50 N	72.04 W
Jafjaf aṣ-Ṣaghīr ⛰[2]	220	20.50 N	21.35 E
Jagādhri	206	30.10 N	77.18 E
Jagersfontein	218	29.44 S	25.29 E
Jagged Mountain Λ	236	58.38 N	162.02 W
Jagodnoje	186	62.33 N	149.40 E
Jagst ≃	164	49.14 N	9.11 E
Jaguaquara	296	13.32 S	39.58 W
Jaguarão	294	32.34 S	53.23 W
Jaguarão (Yaguarón) ≃	294	32.39 S	53.12 W
Jaguari	294	29.30 S	54.41 W
Jaguari ≃, Bra.	294	29.42 S	55.07 W
Jaguari ≃, Bra.	296	22.41 S	47.17 W
Jaguariaíva	294	24.15 S	49.42 W
Jaguaripe	296	13.06 S	38.53 W
Jaguaruna	294	28.36 S	49.02 W
Jagüé	294	28.39 S	68.24 W
Jagüey Grande	284p	22.32 N	81.08 W
Jahorina ⛰	172	43.42 N	18.35 E
Jahrom	208	28.31 N	53.33 E
Jaipur	206	26.56 N	75.50 E
Jaja	186	56.12 N	86.26 E
Jajce	170	44.21 N	17.16 E
Jakarta → Djakarta	198	6.10 S	106.48 E
Jakdūl ⊜	220	17.39 N	32.59 E
Jake Creek Mountain Λ	258	41.13 N	116.54 W
Jakkonen	160	66.33 N	29.52 E
Jakobshavn	232	69.13 N	51.06 W
Jakobstad (Pietarsaari)	160	63.40 N	22.42 E
Jakša	160	61.48 N	56.49 E
Jakšur-Bodja	160	57.11 N	53.09 E
Jakutsk	186	62.13 N	129.49 E
Jal	250	32.07 N	103.12 W
Jalajala	202	14.21 N	121.19 E
Jalālābād	206	34.26 N	70.25 E
Jalán ≃	280	14.42 N	86.11 W
Jalapa, Guat.	280	14.38 N	89.59 W
Jalapa, Nic.	280	13.55 N	86.09 W
Jalapa □[5]	280	14.35 N	89.55 W
Jalapa Enríquez	278	19.32 N	96.55 W
Jalaud ≃	202	10.45 N	122.40 E
Jālgaon	206	21.01 N	75.34 E
Jalisco □[3]	278	20.20 N	103.40 W
Jallas ≃	168	42.54 N	9.08 W
Jallieu	182	45.35 N	5.16 E
Jalón ≃	168	41.47 N	1.04 W
Jalostotitlán	278	21.12 N	102.28 W
Jalpa	278	21.38 N	102.58 W
Jalpaiguri	206	26.32 N	88.44 E
Jalpan	278	21.14 N	99.29 W
Jalpug ≃	172	45.41 N	28.35 E
Jalta	158	46.58 N	37.16 E
Jalta	158	44.30 N	34.10 E
Jaltepec ≃	278	17.26 N	94.59 W
Jalutorovsk	158	56.40 N	66.18 E
Jamaare ≃	222	12.06 N	10.14 E
Jamaica	284p	20.12 N	75.09 W
Jamaica □[1]	276	18.15 S	77.30 W
Jamaica Channel ⋓	282	18.00 N	75.30 W
Jamal, Poluostrov ≻[1]	186	70.00 N	70.00 E
Jamalo-Neneckij Nacionalnyj Okrug □[8]	160	66.30 N	64.00 E
Jamālpur	206	25.25 N	86.40 E
Jamame	218	0.04 N	42.46 E
Jamanari ≃	290	2.58 S	68.53 W
Jamantau, Gora Λ	186	54.15 N	58.06 E
Jamanxim ≃	292	4.43 S	56.18 W
Jamari ≃	292	8.27 S	63.30 W
Jamari, Lago ⊜	290	1.26 S	56.35 W
Jamarovka	186	50.38 N	110.16 E
Jambelí, Canal de ⋓	290	3.00 S	80.00 W
Jambes	164	50.28 N	4.52 E
Jambol	172	42.29 N	26.30 E
Jambol □[4]	212	42.10 N	26.30 E
Jamdena, Pulau I	198	7.36 S	131.25 E
James ≃, Austl.	228	20.36 S	137.41 E
James ≃, Alta., Can.	238	51.55 N	114.34 W
James ≃, U.S.	252	42.52 N	97.18 W
James ≃, Mo., U.S.	248	36.45 N	93.30 W
James ≃, Va., U.S.	246	36.57 N	76.26 W
James, Lake ⊜[1]	246	35.45 N	81.55 W
James Bay C	232	53.30 N	80.30 W
Jamesburg	262	40.21 N	74.26 W
James City, N.C., U.S.	246	35.05 N	77.02 W
James City, Pa., U.S.	266	41.37 N	78.50 W
James City □[6]	262	37.17 N	76.48 W
James Craik	294	32.10 S	63.30 W
James Creek	266	40.23 N	78.10 W
James Island	270	48.37 N	123.22 W
James Point ≻	246	25.22 N	76.25 W
Jamesport	248	39.58 N	93.48 W
James Ross, Cape ≻	232	74.40 N	114.25 W
James Ross Strait ⋓	232	69.40 N	95.30 W
Jamestown, Austl.	228	33.12 S	138.36 E
Jamestown, Calif., U.S.	272	37.57 N	120.25 W
Jamestown, Kans., U.S.	252	39.36 N	97.52 W
Jamestown, Ky., U.S.	248	36.59 N	85.04 W
Jamestown, N.C., U.S.	246	35.59 N	79.56 W
Jamestown, N. Dak., U.S.	252	46.54 N	98.42 W
Jamestown, N.Y., U.S.	266	42.06 N	79.14 W
Jamestown, Ohio, U.S.	242	39.39 N	83.44 W
Jamestown, Pa., U.S.	266	41.29 N	80.27 W
Jamestown, R.I., U.S.	261	41.30 N	71.22 W
Jamestown, Tenn., U.S.	248	36.26 N	84.57 W
Jamestown, Va., U.S.	262	37.12 N	76.46 W
Jamestown Reservoir ⊜[1]	252	47.15 N	98.40 W
Jamesville, N.Y., U.S.	264	42.59 N	76.04 W
Jamesville, Va., U.S.	262	37.31 N	75.56 W
Jamiltepec	278	16.17 N	97.49 W
Jaminauá ≃	292	9.20 S	70.59 W
Jamison	262	40.16 N	75.05 W
Jamm	160	58.26 N	28.03 E
Jammu	206	32.44 N	74.52 E
Jammu and Kashmīr □[8]	206	34.00 N	76.00 E
Jamnagar	206	22.28 N	70.05 E
Jämsä	160	61.52 N	25.12 E
Jamshedpur	206	22.48 N	86.11 E
Jamsk	186	59.35 N	154.10 E
Jämtlands Län □[6]	160	63.00 N	14.40 E
Jamuna ≃	206	23.51 N	89.45 E
Jamundí	290	3.15 N	76.32 W
Jana ≃	186	71.31 N	136.32 E
Janauacá, Lago ⊜	290	3.28 S	60.17 W
Janaúba	296	15.48 S	43.19 W
Janda, Laguna de la ⊜	168	36.15 N	5.51 W
Jandaia	296	17.06 S	50.07 W
Jandaia do Sul	296	23.36 S	51.39 W
Jandiatuba ≃	290	3.28 S	68.42 W
Jandrakinot	236	64.54 N	172.32 W
Jándula ≃	168	38.03 N	4.06 W
Jándula, Embalse del ⊜[1]	168	38.30 N	4.00 W
Jane Peak Λ	230	45.20 S	168.19 E
Janesville, Minn., U.S.	244	44.07 N	93.42 W
Janesville, Wis., U.S.	268	42.41 N	89.01 W
Jangarej	160	68.46 N	61.25 E
Jangel'urta, Gora Λ[2]	160	67.33 N	38.02 E
Jangijul'	186	41.07 N	69.03 E
Janikowo	164	52.45 N	18.07 E
Janīn	210	32.28 N	35.18 E
Janisjarvi, Ozero ⊜	160	61.59 N	30.57 E
Janiuay	202	10.57 N	122.30 E
Janja	172	44.40 N	19.15 E
Janjina	170	42.56 N	17.26 E
Jan Mayen I	148	71.00 N	8.20 W
Janos	278	30.54 N	108.10 W
Janos, Río de ≃	278	30.56 N	108.08 W
Jánoshalma	164	46.18 N	19.20 E
Jánosháza	164	47.08 N	17.10 E
Janoviči	160	55.17 N	30.42 E
Janowiec Wielkopolski	164	52.46 N	17.31 E
Janów Lubelski	164	50.43 N	22.24 E
Janskij	186	68.28 N	134.48 E
Janskij Zaliv C	186	71.50 N	136.00 E
Jantarnyj [Palmnicken]	164	54.52 N	19.57 E
Januária	296	15.29 S	44.22 W
Janzé	166	47.58 N	1.30 W
Japan □[1]	190	36.00 N	138.00 E
Japan, Sea of ▼[2]	190	40.00 N	135.00 E
Japan Basin ✢[1]	148	40.00 N	135.00 E
Japen, Pulau I	198	1.45 S	136.15 E
Japiim	292	7.37 S	72.54 W
Japtiksal'a	186	69.21 N	72.32 E
Japurá	290	1.48 S	66.30 W
Japurá (Caquetá) ≃	290	3.08 S	64.46 W
Jaqué	290	7.45 N	78.15 W
Jaqui	292	15.28 S	74.27 W
Jar	160	58.15 N	52.06 E
Jaraguá	296	15.45 S	49.20 W
Jaraguá do Sul	294	26.29 S	49.04 W
Jaraicejo	168	39.40 N	5.49 W
Jaráiz	168	40.04 N	5.45 W
Jarales	254	34.37 N	106.46 W
Jarama ≃	168	40.02 N	3.39 W
Jarandilla	168	40.08 N	5.39 W
Jaransk	160	57.19 N	47.54 E
Jarash	210	32.17 N	35.53 E
Jarbah, Wāḥat ▼[4]	220	29.21 N	25.20 E
Jarbidge ≃	256	42.19 N	115.39 W
Jarcevo	160	55.04 N	32.41 E
Jardim	292	21.28 S	56.09 W
Jardín América	294	27.03 S	55.14 W
Jardines de la Reina II	284p	20.45 N	78.50 W
Jardinópolis	296	21.02 S	47.46 W
Jarega	160	63.27 N	53.26 E
Jarenga	160	62.43 N	49.30 E
Jarensk	160	62.11 N	49.02 E
Jargeau	166	47.52 N	2.07 E
Jari ≃, Bra.	286	1.09 S	51.54 W
Jari ≃, Bra.	292	5.07 S	62.21 W
Jari, Lago ⊜	290	5.00 S	62.19 W
Jarita	250	25.40 N	97.41 W
Jarmen	164	53.55 N	13.20 E
Jarnac	166	45.41 N	0.10 W
Jaro	202	11.11 N	124.46 E
Jarocin	164	51.59 N	17.31 E
Jaroměř	164	50.21 N	15.55 E
Jaroslavl'	160	57.37 N	39.52 E
Jarosław	164	50.02 N	22.42 E
Jarratt	262	36.48 N	77.28 W
Jarrettsville	262	39.36 N	76.29 W
Jar-Sale	186	66.50 N	70.50 E
Jaru	292	10.26 S	62.27 W
Jaru ≃	292	10.05 S	61.59 W
Jaruco	284p	23.03 N	82.01 W
Järva-Jaani	160	59.02 N	25.53 E
Järvakandi	160	58.47 N	24.49 E
Järvenpää	160	60.28 N	25.06 E
Jarvie	238	54.27 N	113.59 W
Jarville-la-Malgrange	180	48.40 N	6.13 E
Jarvis	264	42.53 N	80.06 W
Jarvisburg	246	36.09 N	75.52 W
Järvsö	160	61.43 N	16.10 E
Jasaan	202	8.39 N	124.45 E
Jaša Tomić	172	45.27 N	20.51 E
Jasień (Gassen)	164	51.46 N	15.01 E
Jašil'kul', Ozero ⊜	206	37.45 N	72.55 E
Jāsk	204	25.38 N	57.46 E
Jasło	164	49.45 N	21.29 E
Jasnogorsk	160	54.29 N	37.42 E
Jasnyj	186	53.17 N	127.59 E
Jason Islands II	288	51.00 S	61.00 W
Jasonville	248	39.10 N	87.12 W
Jasper, Alta., Can.	238	52.53 N	118.05 W
Jasper, Ala., U.S.	248	33.50 N	87.17 W
Jasper, Ark., U.S.	248	36.00 N	93.11 W
Jasper, Fla., U.S.	246	30.31 N	82.57 W
Jasper, Ga., U.S.	246	34.28 N	84.26 W
Jasper, Ind., U.S.	248	38.24 N	86.56 W
Jasper, Mich., U.S.	268	41.48 N	84.02 W
Jasper, Minn., U.S.	252	43.51 N	96.24 W
Jasper, Mo., U.S.	248	37.20 N	94.18 W
Jasper, Tenn., U.S.	248	35.04 N	85.38 W
Jasper, Tex., U.S.	248	30.55 N	94.01 W
Jasper □[6]	268	40.57 N	87.09 W
Jasper Lake ⊜	238	53.07 N	118.00 W
Jasper National Park ♠	238	52.53 N	118.03 W
Jastarnia	164	54.43 N	18.40 E
Jastrebac ⛰	172	43.23 N	21.30 E
Jastrebarsko	170	45.40 N	15.39 E
Jastrowie (Jastrow)	164	53.26 N	16.49 E
Jászapáti	164	47.22 N	20.09 E
Jászberény	164	47.30 N	19.55 E
Jat, Uad el V	214	26.45 N	13.03 W
Jataí	296	17.53 S	51.43 W
Jatapu ≃	290	2.13 S	58.17 W
Jatate ≃	280	16.15 N	91.17 W
Jatibonico	284p	21.56 N	79.10 W
Jatibonico del Sur ≃	284p	21.33 N	79.10 W
Játiva	168	38.59 N	0.31 W
Jatobá ≃	296	12.23 S	54.07 W
Jaú	296	22.18 S	48.33 W
Jaú ≃	290	1.54 S	61.26 W
Jauaperi ≃	290	1.26 S	61.35 W
Jauja	292	11.46 S	75.28 W
Jaúna ≃	292	6.24 S	59.57 W
Jaungulbene	160	57.04 N	26.36 E
Jaunjelgava	160	56.37 N	25.05 E
Jaunpur	206	25.45 N	82.42 E
Jaupaci	296	16.18 S	50.54 W
Jauquara ≃	292	15.06 S	57.06 W
Jauru ≃, Bra.	292	16.22 S	57.46 W
Jauru ≃, Bra.	296	18.40 S	54.36 W
Java	252	45.30 N	99.53 W
Java → Djawa I	198	7.30 S	110.00 E
Java Center	266	42.39 N	78.23 W
Javalambre Λ	168	40.06 N	1.03 W
Javari (Yavarí) ≃	286	4.21 S	70.02 W
Javas	160	54.26 N	42.51 E
Java Sea → Djawa, Laut ▼[2]	198	5.00 S	110.00 E
Java Trench ✢[1]	148	10.00 S	110.00 E
Java Village	266	42.40 N	78.26 W
Jávea	168	38.47 N	0.10 E
Javor ⛰	172	44.05 N	19.05 E
Javorie Λ	164	48.27 N	19.18 E
Javorník	164	50.23 N	17.00 E
Javorníky ⛰	164	49.20 N	18.20 E
Javorová skála Λ	164	49.31 N	14.30 E
Javr ≃	160	68.09 N	30.06 E
Jävre	160	65.09 N	21.59 E
Jawbar	210	33.31 N	36.19 E
Jawor (Jauer)	164	51.03 N	16.11 E
Jaworzno	164	50.13 N	19.15 E
Jay, Fla., U.S.	248	30.57 N	87.09 W
Jay, Okla., U.S.	250	36.25 N	94.48 W
Jay □[6]	268	40.26 N	84.59 W
Jayanca	292	6.24 S	79.50 W
Jaynes	254	32.16 N	111.01 W
Jay Peak Λ	242	44.55 N	72.32 W
Jayton	250	33.15 N	100.34 W
Jayuya	284m	18.13 N	66.36 W
Jazevec	160	65.43 N	46.30 E
Jažma	160	66.56 N	44.29 E
Jaz Mūriān, Hāmūn-e ☰	208	27.20 N	58.55 E
Jazykovo	160	54.18 N	47.24 E
J B Thomas, Lake ⊜[1]	250	32.35 N	101.10 W
Jdiouia	168	35.57 N	0.50 E
Jeanerette	248	29.55 N	91.40 W
Jeannette	266	40.20 N	79.35 W
Jebala ⛰	168	35.25 N	5.30 W
Jebba	214	9.08 N	4.50 E
Jebel	172	45.33 N	21.14 E
Jebel Abiod	170	36.58 N	9.05 E
Jeberos	292	5.15 S	76.10 W
Jebibina	170	36.07 N	10.06 E
Jedburgh	162	55.29 N	2.34 W
Jędrzejów	164	50.39 N	20.18 E
Jedwabne	164	53.17 N	22.19 E
Jeffers	252	44.03 N	95.12 W
Jefferson, Ga., U.S.	246	34.07 N	83.35 W
Jefferson, Ind., U.S.	268	40.17 N	86.36 W
Jefferson, Iowa, U.S.	252	42.01 N	94.23 W
Jefferson, La., U.S.	248	29.58 N	90.10 W
Jefferson, Md., U.S.	262	39.22 N	77.32 W
Jefferson, Mass., U.S.	261	42.22 N	71.53 W
Jefferson, N.C., U.S.	246	36.26 N	81.28 W
Jefferson, N.Y., U.S.	261	42.14 N	73.54 W
Jefferson, Ohio, U.S.	266	41.44 N	80.46 W
Jefferson, Oreg., U.S.	256	44.43 N	123.01 W
Jefferson, S.C., U.S.	246	34.39 N	80.23 W
Jefferson, S. Dak., U.S.	252	42.36 N	96.34 W
Jefferson, Tex., U.S.	248	32.46 N	94.21 W
Jefferson, Wis., U.S.	268	43.00 N	88.48 W
Jefferson □[6], N.Y., U.S.	264	43.59 N	75.55 W
Jefferson □[6], Ohio, U.S.	266	40.22 N	80.37 W
Jefferson □[6], Pa., U.S.	266	41.09 N	79.05 W
Jefferson □[6], Wash., U.S.	270	47.50 N	122.36 W
Jefferson □[6], Wis., U.S.	268	43.02 N	88.46 W
Jefferson ≃	256	45.56 N	111.30 W
Jefferson, Mount Λ, Idaho, U.S.	256	44.34 N	111.30 W
Jefferson, Mount Λ, Nev., U.S.	258	38.46 N	116.55 W
Jefferson, Mount Λ, Oreg., U.S.	256	44.40 N	121.47 W
Jefferson City, Mo., U.S.	248	38.34 N	92.10 W
Jefferson City, Tenn., U.S.	246	36.07 N	83.30 W
Jeffersonton	242	38.38 N	77.55 W
Jeffersontown	248	38.12 N	85.35 W
Jeffersonville, Ga., U.S.	246	32.41 N	83.20 W
Jeffersonville, Ind., U.S.	248	38.17 N	85.44 W
Jeffersonville, Ohio, U.S.	242	39.39 N	83.34 W
Jeffrey City	254	42.29 N	107.49 W
Jefimovskij	160	59.30 N	34.40 E
Jefremov	158	53.09 N	38.07 E
Jega	222	12.15 N	4.23 E
Jegorjevsk	160	55.23 N	39.02 E
Jeguitinhonha	296	16.26 S	41.00 W
Jehol → Chengde	194	40.58 N	117.53 E
Jejsk	158	46.42 N	38.16 E
Jejui Guazú ≃	294	24.13 S	57.09 W
Jēkabpils	160	56.29 N	25.51 E
Jekateriny, Proliv ⋓	186	53.53 N	140.25 E
Jekyll Island I	246	31.04 N	81.25 W
Jelabuga	160	55.47 N	52.04 E
Jelancy	186	52.49 N	106.25 E
Jelchovka	160	53.51 N	50.18 E
Jel'cy	160	56.40 N	33.51 E
Jelec	158	52.37 N	38.30 E
Jeleckij	160	67.03 N	64.10 E
Jelenia Góra (Hirschberg)	164	50.55 N	15.46 E
Jelgava	160	56.39 N	23.42 E
Jelizarovo	160	58.33 N	44.50 E
Jelizavely, Mys ≻	186	54.24 N	142.42 E
Jellico	246	36.35 N	84.08 W
Jelloway	266	40.33 N	82.18 W
Jelm Mountain Λ	254	41.06 N	105.58 W
Jel'n'a	160	54.35 N	33.11 E
Jeloguj ≃	186	63.13 N	87.45 E
Jelšava	164	48.39 N	20.14 E
Jemanželinsk	158	54.45 N	61.20 E
Jemappes	176	50.27 N	3.53 E
Jembongan, Pulau I	202	6.40 N	117.27 E
Jemca	160	63.04 N	40.20 E
Jemca ≃	160	63.15 N	41.20 E
Jemel'stan	160	61.13 N	52.29 E
Jemez ≃	254	35.22 N	106.31 W
Jemez Springs	254	35.46 N	106.42 W
Jemmal	170	35.37 N	10.46 E
Jemnice	164	49.01 N	15.35 E
Jemniště ⊥	164	49.45 N	14.48 E
Jena, D.D.R.	164	50.56 N	11.35 E
Jena, La., U.S.	248	31.41 N	92.08 W
Jenašimskij Polkan, Gora Λ	186	59.50 N	92.52 E
Jenbach	164	47.24 N	11.47 E
Jendouba (Souk el Arba)	170	36.30 N	8.47 E
Jendouba □[8]	170	36.30 N	8.45 E
Jenera	268	40.54 N	83.44 W
Jenisej ≃	186	71.50 N	82.40 E
Jenisejsk	186	58.27 N	92.10 E
Jenisejskij Kr'až ⛰	186	59.00 N	93.00 E
Jenisejskij Zaliv C	186	72.30 N	80.00 E
Jenison	268	42.54 N	85.47 W
Jenkinsville	246	34.16 N	81.17 W
Jenkintown	262	40.06 N	75.08 W
Jenks	250	36.01 N	95.58 W
Jenners	266	40.09 N	79.03 W
Jennersdorf	164	46.57 N	16.08 E
Jennerstown	266	40.10 N	79.04 W
Jennings, Fla., U.S.	246	30.36 N	83.06 W
Jennings, Kans., U.S.	252	39.41 N	100.18 W
Jennings, La., U.S.	248	30.13 N	92.39 W
Jennings Lodge	270	45.24 N	122.38 W
Jensen	254	40.22 N	109.17 W
Jensen Beach	246	27.15 N	80.14 W
Jens Munk Island I	232	69.42 N	79.30 W
Jepač	160	66.58 N	61.22 E
Jepelacio	292	6.09 S	76.55 W
Jeptha Knob Λ	248	38.11 N	85.07 W
Jequeri	296	20.27 S	42.40 W
Jequetepeque ≃	292	7.21 S	79.37 W
Jequié	296	13.51 S	40.05 W
Jequitaí	296	17.15 S	44.28 W
Jequitinhonha ≃	296	15.51 S	38.53 W
Jerachtur	160	54.43 N	41.09 E
Jerada	214	34.17 N	2.13 W
Jeradou	170	36.15 N	10.23 E
Jerbogačon	186	61.16 N	108.00 E
Jercevo	160	60.48 N	40.05 E
Jerécuaro	278	20.09 N	100.31 W
Jérémie	282	18.39 N	74.08 W
Jeremoabo	286	10.04 S	38.21 W
Jerevan	208	40.11 N	44.30 E
Jerez de García Salinas	278	22.39 N	103.00 W
Jerez de la Frontera	168	36.41 N	6.08 W
Jerez de los Caballeros	168	38.19 N	6.46 W
Jergeni ⛰[2]	158	47.00 N	44.00 E
Jericho → Arīḥā, Urd.	210	31.52 N	35.27 E
Jericó	290	5.47 N	75.47 W
Jerid, Chott ☰	214	33.42 N	8.26 E
Jerimoth Hill Λ[2]	242	41.52 N	71.47 W
Jermica	160	66.56 N	52.15 E
Jeroaquara	296	15.23 S	50.25 W
Jerofej Pavlovič	186	53.58 N	122.01 E
Jerome, Ariz., U.S.	254	34.45 N	112.07 W
Jerome, Idaho, U.S.	256	42.43 N	114.31 W
Jerome, Mich., U.S.	268	42.01 N	84.28 W
Jerome, Pa., U.S.	266	40.13 N	78.59 W
Jeromesville	266	40.48 N	82.12 W
Jerônimo Monteiro	296	20.47 S	41.24 W
Jeropol	186	65.15 N	168.40 E
Jerry City	268	41.15 N	83.36 W
Jersey	266	40.03 N	82.46 W
Jersey □[2]	158	49.15 N	2.10 W
Jersey City	262	40.44 N	74.02 W
Jersey Mountain Λ	256	45.29 N	115.34 W
Jersey Shore	242	41.12 N	77.16 W
Jerseyville	248	39.07 N	90.20 W
Jeršov	158	51.20 N	48.17 E
Jerte ≃	168	39.58 N	6.17 W
Jertom	160	63.32 N	47.48 E
Jerusalem → Yerushalayim	210	31.46 N	35.13 E
Jerusalim (Talusan)	202	7.26 N	122.49 E
Jervis, Cape ≻	228	35.38 S	138.06 E
Jervis Bay C	228	35.05 S	150.44 E
Jervis Inlet C	238	49.46 N	124.10 W
Jerykly	160	55.11 N	51.26 E
Jesenice, Česko.	164	50.04 N	13.29 E
Jesenice, Jugo.	170	46.26 N	14.04 E
Jesi → Iesi	184	43.31 N	13.14 E
Jesil'	186	51.58 N	66.24 E
Jessej	186	68.29 N	102.10 E
Jesselton → Kota Kinabalu	198	5.58 N	116.04 E
Jessen	164	51.47 N	12.58 E
Jessentuki	158	44.03 N	42.51 E
Jessore	206	23.10 N	89.13 E
Jessup	242	41.28 N	75.34 W
Jessup, Lake ⊜	246	28.43 N	81.14 W
Jesup, Ga., U.S.	246	31.36 N	81.53 W
Jesup, Iowa, U.S.	244	42.29 N	92.04 W
Jesús	294	27.03 S	55.47 W
Jesús Carranza, Méx.	250	31.30 N	106.12 W
Jesús Carranza, Méx.	278	17.26 N	95.02 W
Jesús de Otoro	280	14.26 N	87.59 W
Jesús María, Arg.	294	31.00 S	64.05 W
Jesús María, Méx.	278	25.06 N	107.28 W
Jesús María, Nic.	280	11.38 N	84.45 W
Jet	250	36.40 N	98.11 W
Jeta, Ilha de I	222	11.53 N	16.15 W
Jetafe	202	10.09 N	124.09 E
Jetmore	252	38.03 N	99.54 W
Jette	176	50.52 N	4.20 E
Jeumont	176	50.18 N	4.06 E
Jeune Landing	238	50.27 N	127.30 W
Jever	178	53.34 N	7.54 E
Jevíčko	164	49.38 N	16.43 E
Jevišovka ≃	164	48.48 N	16.28 E
Jevlach, S.S.S.R.	158		
	208	40.36 N	47.09 E
Jevlaš'ovo	160	53.07 N	46.51 E
Jevpatorija	158	45.12 N	33.22 E
Jewel Cave National Monument ♠	252	43.42 N	103.50 W
Jewell, Iowa, U.S.	244	42.20 N	93.39 W
Jewell, Kans., U.S.	252	39.40 N	98.10 W
Jewell, N.Y., U.S.	264	43.13 N	75.48 W
Jewell, Ohio, U.S.	268	41.20 N	84.17 W
Jewell, Oreg., U.S.	270	45.56 N	123.30 W
Jewell Ridge	246	37.11 N	81.48 W
Jewett, Ill., U.S.	248	39.13 N	88.15 W
Jewett, Ohio, U.S.	266	40.22 N	81.00 W
Jewett, Tex., U.S.	250	31.22 N	96.09 W
Jewett City	261	41.36 N	71.59 W
Jezerce Λ	172	42.26 N	19.49 E
Jezerišče	160	55.50 N	29.59 E
Jeziorany (Seeburg)	164	53.58 N	20.46 E
Jezreel, Valley of → Yizre'el, 'emeq V	210	32.32 N	35.24 E
Jhang Maghiāna	206	31.16 N	72.19 E
Jhānsi	206	25.27 N	78.35 E
Jhelum	206	32.56 N	73.44 E
Jhelum ≃	206	31.12 N	72.08 E
Jiabong	202	11.46 N	124.57 E
Jiading	196	31.23 N	121.15 E
Jiali	190	30.47 N	93.24 E
Jialingjiang ≃	190	30.02 N	106.18 E
Jiamusi	190	46.50 N	130.21 E
Ji'an	196	27.07 N	114.58 E
Jianchuan	200	26.34 N	99.53 E
Jiangcheng	200	22.40 N	101.48 E
Jiangda	190	31.27 N	98.15 E
Jiangjin	190	29.17 N	106.15 E
Jiangkou	190	23.31 N	110.17 E
Jiangmen	196	22.35 N	113.05 E
Jiangshan'gang ≃	196	28.57 N	118.50 E
Jiangsu □[4]	190	33.00 N	120.00 E
Jiangxi □[4]	196	28.00 N	116.00 E
Jiangyan	196	32.31 N	120.09 E
Jiangyin	196	31.54 N	120.16 E
Jiangzi	190	28.57 N	89.35 E
Jianou	196	27.03 N	118.19 E
Jianshui	200	23.38 N	102.49 E
Jianxi ≃	196	26.38 N	118.12 E
Jiaohe	190	43.42 N	127.19 E
Jiaotinghu Xuhongqu ⊜[1]	196	32.45 N	114.39 E
Jiaoxian	190	36.18 N	119.58 E
Jiaozuo	190	35.15 N	113.18 E
Jiashan	196	32.47 N	118.00 E
Jiashunhu ⊜	206	34.35 N	86.05 E
Jiawang	194	34.27 N	117.27 E
Jiaxian	196	34.00 N	113.12 E
Jiaxing	196	30.46 N	120.45 E
Jiayunhu ⊜	206	35.02 N	85.40 E
Jiazi	196	22.55 N	116.04 E
Jiaziwan C	196	22.52 N	116.05 E
Jibacoa ≃	284p	20.15 N	77.12 W
Jibão, Serra do Λ	296	14.48 S	45.00 W
Jiboa ≃	280	13.22 N	89.04 W
Jicarilla Apache Indian Reservation ⬩[4]	254	36.40 N	107.00 W
Jícaro ≃	280	13.30 N	86.02 W
Jicarón, Isla I	290	7.10 N	81.50 W
Jicatuyo ≃	280	15.00 N	88.16 W
Jičín	164	50.26 N	15.21 E
Jidda → Juddah	204	21.30 N	39.12 E
Jiedihe ≃	194	38.36 N	117.33 E
Jieshiwan C	196	22.46 N	115.40 E
Jieshou	196	33.18 N	115.20 E
Jieyang	196	23.35 N	116.21 E
Jifjāfah, Bi'r ▼[4]	220	30.27 N	33.11 E
Jiftūn, Jazā'ir II	220	27.13 N	33.56 E
Jiguaní	284p	20.22 N	76.26 W
Jigüey, Bahía de C	284p	22.07 N	78.06 W
Jihlava	164	49.24 N	15.36 E
Jihočeský □[4]	164	49.05 N	14.30 E
Jihomoravský □[4]	164	49.10 N	16.40 E
Jijia ≃	172	46.54 N	28.05 E
Jijiga	214	9.22 N	42.47 E
Jijona	168	38.32 N	0.30 W
Jilemutu	190	52.14 N	120.47 E
Jilib	218	0.28 N	42.50 E
Jilin	190	43.51 N	126.33 E
Jilin □[4], Zhg.	190	44.00 N	126.00 E
Jiloca ≃	168	41.21 N	1.39 W
Jima	214	7.36 N	36.50 E
Jimbolia	172	45.47 N	20.43 E
Jimena de la Frontera	168	36.26 N	5.27 W
Jiménez, Méx.	250	25.49 N	103.22 W
Jiménez, Méx.	278	29.02 N	100.41 W
Jimenez, Pil.	202	8.20 N	123.50 E
Jiménez del Teúl	278	23.10 N	104.05 W
Jim Thorpe	242	40.52 N	75.45 W
Jinan (Tsinan)	194	36.40 N	116.57 E
Jincheng	190	35.30 N	112.50 E
Jindřichův Hradec	164	49.09 N	15.00 E
Jingdezhen (Kingtechen)	196	29.16 N	117.11 E
Jingdong	200	24.28 N	100.52 E
Jinggangshan	190	26.36 N	114.05 E
Jinghaigang C	196	23.01 N	116.34 E
Jinghong	200	22.01 N	100.49 E
Jingjiang	196	32.01 N	120.15 E
Jingxi	200	23.08 N	106.29 E
Jingxian	190	37.42 N	116.16 E
Jinhua	196	29.07 N	119.39 E
Jinhuajiang ≃	196	29.06 N	119.39 E
Jining	194	35.25 N	116.36 E
Jinja	218	0.26 N	33.12 E
Jinjiang ≃, Zhg.	196	28.24 N	115.49 E
Jinjiang ≃, Zhg.	196	24.54 N	118.35 E
Jinjiang ≃, Zhg.	196	24.48 N	113.35 E
Jinning (Jiukunyang)	200	24.41 N	102.35 E
Jinotega	280	13.06 N	86.00 W
Jinotega □[5]	280	14.00 N	85.25 W
Jinotepe	280	11.51 N	86.12 W
Jinping	200	26.38 N	109.03 E
Jinshi	190	29.33 N	111.50 E
Jinshui ≃	196	32.05 N	112.25 E
Jintotolo Channel ⋓	202	11.45 N	123.10 E
Jintotolo Island I	202	11.51 N	123.08 E
Jinxi	194	40.45 N	120.50 E
Jinxi ≃	196	26.51 N	117.46 E
Jinxian	194	39.04 N	121.40 E
Jinzhonghe ≃	194	39.08 N	117.42 E
Jinzhou (Chinchou)	194	41.07 N	121.08 E
Jinzū ≃	192	36.46 N	137.13 E
Jiparaná ≃	292	8.03 S	62.52 W
Jipengqundao II	196	21.52 N	114.00 E
Jipijapa	290	1.20 S	80.35 W
Jiquilisco	280	13.19 N	88.35 W
Jiquilisco, Bahía de C	280	13.14 N	88.34 W
Jiquiriçá	296	13.14 S	39.36 W
Jiquiriçá ≃	296	13.12 S	38.57 W
Jirjā	220	26.20 N	31.53 E
Jirkov	164	50.30 N	13.27 E
Jisr ash-Shughūr	208	35.48 N	36.19 E
Jitai	190	44.01 N	89.28 E
Jitaúna	296	14.01 S	39.57 W
Jiugongshan Λ	196	29.26 N	114.42 E
Jiuhuanghekou ≃[1]	194	38.15 N	118.05 E
Jiujiang	196	29.44 N	115.59 E
Jiul ≃	172	43.47 N	23.48 E
Jiulianshan ⛰	196	24.40 N	114.46 E
Jiulingshan ⛰	196	28.46 N	114.45 E
Jiulongxi ≃	196	25.59 N	117.18 E
Jiumangya	190	37.40 N	91.50 E
Jiupengxi ≃	196	25.00 N	117.32 E
Jiuquan	190	39.45 N	98.34 E
Jiutai	190	44.08 N	125.50 E
Jixi	190	45.17 N	130.59 E
Jixian	194	35.26 N	114.05 E
Jizera ≃	164	50.10 N	14.43 E
Jizl, Wādī al- V	208	25.38 N	38.21 E
Joaçaba	294	27.10 S	51.30 W
Joaíma	296	16.39 S	41.02 W
Joanésia	296	19.12 S	42.40 W
Joanna	246	34.25 N	81.49 W
João Belo	218	25.02 S	33.34 E
João de Tiba ≃	296	16.16 S	39.01 W
João Neiva	296	19.45 S	40.24 W
João Pessoa	286	7.07 S	34.52 W
João Pinheiro	296	17.45 S	46.10 W
Joaquim Távora	296	23.30 S	49.58 W
Joaquin	248	31.58 N	94.03 W
Joaquín V. González	294	25.05 S	64.11 W
Jobabo	284p	20.54 N	77.17 W
Jobo Point ≻	202	8.41 N	126.20 E
Jobos	284m	17.58 N	66.10 W
Job Peak Λ	258	39.35 N	118.14 W
Jobson (Vera)	294	29.30 S	60.10 W
Jocko ≃	256	47.20 N	114.17 W
Jocolí	294	32.36 S	68.40 W
Jocón	280	15.17 N	86.58 W
Jocoro	280	13.37 N	88.01 W
Jocotán	280	14.49 N	89.23 W
Jocotán ≃	280	14.52 N	89.28 W
Jocuixtita	278	24.15 N	106.16 W
Jódar	168	37.50 N	3.21 W
Jodhpur	206	26.17 N	73.01 E
Joe Batt's Arm	240	49.44 N	54.10 W
Joensuu	160	62.36 N	29.46 E
Joffre, Mount Λ	238	50.32 N	115.13 W
Jõgeva	160	58.45 N	26.24 E
Joggins	240	45.42 N	64.27 W
Jogjakarta	226	7.48 S	110.22 E
Jōhana	192	36.31 N	136.57 E
Johannesburg, S. Afr.	224	26.15 S	28.00 E
Johannesburg, Calif., U.S.	274	35.22 N	117.38 W
Johanngeorgenstadt	164	50.26 N	12.43 E
Johar	214	2.48 N	45.33 E
Jōhen	192	32.57 N	132.35 E
John ≃	236	66.55 N	151.35 W
John Day	256	44.25 N	118.57 W
John Day ≃	256	45.44 N	120.39 W
John Fitzgerald Kennedy Space Center ⚲[3]	246	28.40 N	80.40 W
John Martin Reservoir ⊜[1]	252	38.05 N	103.02 W
John o'groats	162	58.38 N	3.05 W
Johnson, Kans., U.S.	252	37.34 N	101.45 W
Johnson, Nebr., U.S.	252	40.24 N	96.01 W
Johnson, Vt., U.S.	242	44.38 N	72.41 W
Johnsonburg, N.Y., U.S.	264	42.44 N	78.18 W
Johnsonburg, Pa., U.S.	266	41.29 N	78.41 W
Johnson City, N.Y., U.S.	242	42.07 N	75.57 W
Johnson City, Tenn., U.S.	246	36.19 N	82.21 W
Johnson City, Tex., U.S.	250	30.17 N	98.25 W
Johnson Creek	268	43.05 N	88.47 W
Johnsondale	258	35.58 N	118.32 W
Johnsons Crossing	236	60.29 N	133.16 W
Johnsonville	246	33.49 N	79.27 W
Johnston, R.I., U.S.	261	41.50 N	71.30 W
Johnston, S.C., U.S.	246	33.50 N	81.48 W
Johnston City	248	37.49 N	88.56 W
Johnstone Strait ⋓	238	50.25 N	126.00 W
Johnston Island I	148	16.45 N	169.32 W
Johnstown, Colo., U.S.	254	40.20 N	104.54 W
Johnstown, N.Y., U.S.	242	43.00 N	74.22 W
Johnstown, Ohio, U.S.	266	40.09 N	82.41 W
Johnstown, Pa., U.S.	266	40.20 N	78.55 W
Johnstown Center	268	42.42 N	88.50 W
Johore □[3]	200	2.00 N	103.30 E
Johore Bahru	200	1.27 N	103.45 E
Joigny	176	47.59 N	3.24 E
Joiner	248	35.31 N	90.09 W
Joinvile	294	26.18 S	48.50 W
Joinville	166	48.27 N	5.08 E
Jokioinen	160	60.49 N	23.28 E
Jokkmokk	160	66.37 N	19.50 E
Jökulsá á Brú ≃	160a	65.41 N	14.13 W
Joliet, Ill., U.S.	268	41.32 N	88.05 W
Joliet, Mont., U.S.	256	45.29 N	108.58 W
Joliett	262	40.37 N	76.27 W
Joliette	260	46.01 N	73.26 W
Joliette □[6]	260	46.25 N	74.00 W
Jöllenbeck	178	52.11 N	8.45 E
Jolo	202	6.03 N	121.00 E
Jolo Group II	202	5.55 N	121.10 E
Jolo Island I	202	6.00 N	121.10 E
Jomalig Island I	202	14.42 N	122.23 E
Jones, Pil.	202	16.33 N	121.42 E
Jones, Mich., U.S.	268	41.54 N	85.48 W
Jones, Okla., U.S.	250	35.34 N	97.17 W
Jonesboro, Ark., U.S.	248	35.50 N	90.42 W
Jonesboro, Ga., U.S.	246	33.32 N	84.21 W
Jonesboro, Ill., U.S.	248	37.27 N	89.16 W
Jonesboro, Ind., U.S.	268	40.29 N	85.38 W
Jonesboro, La., U.S.	248	32.15 N	92.43 W
Jonesboro, Maine, U.S.	242	44.40 N	67.35 W
Jonesboro, Tenn., U.S.	246	36.18 N	82.28 W
Jonesburg	248	38.51 N	91.18 W
Jones Mill	248	34.27 N	92.50 W
Jones Mills	266	40.05 N	79.21 W
Jonesport	242	44.32 N	67.36 W
Jones Sound ⋓	232	76.00 N	85.00 W
Jonestown	248	34.14 N	90.28 W
Jonesville, La., U.S.	248	31.38 N	91.49 W
Jonesville, Mich., U.S.	268	41.59 N	84.40 W
Jonesville, N.C., U.S.	246	36.15 N	80.51 W
Jonesville, S.C., U.S.	246	34.50 N	81.41 W
Jonesville, Va., U.S.	246	36.41 N	83.07 W
Jong ≃	222	7.32 N	12.23 W
Jönköping	160	57.47 N	14.11 E
Jonquière	240	48.25 N	71.15 W
Jonuta	278	18.05 N	92.08 W
Jonzac	166	45.27 N	0.26 W
Joplin, Mo., U.S.	248	37.06 N	94.31 W
Joplin, Mont., U.S.	256	48.34 N	110.46 W
Joppa	248	37.12 N	88.51 W
Jordan, Ont., Can.	264	43.09 N	79.23 W
Jordan, Pil.	202	10.40 N	122.35 E
Jordan, Minn., U.S.	244	44.40 N	93.37 W
Jordan, Mont., U.S.	256	47.19 N	106.55 W
Jordan, N.Y., U.S.	264	43.04 N	76.28 W
Jordan □[1]	204	31.00 N	36.00 E
Jordan ≃, Utah, U.S.	254	40.49 N	112.08 W
Jordan (Al-Urdunn) (HaYarden) ≃, As.	210	31.46 N	35.33 E
Jordan Bay C	240	43.45 N	65.12 W
Jordânia	296	15.54 S	40.11 W
Jordanów	164	49.40 N	19.50 E
Jordan Valley	256	42.58 N	117.03 W
Jordão ≃	294	25.46 S	52.07 W
Jorhāt	206	26.46 N	94.13 E
Jörn	160	65.04 N	20.02 E
Jornado del Muerto ⬩[2]	254	33.20 N	106.50 W
Joroinen	160	62.11 N	27.50 E
Jos	222	9.55 N	8.53 E
Jose Abad Santos	202	5.38 N	125.27 E
José Batlle y Ordóñez	294	33.28 S	55.07 W
José Bonifácio	296	21.03 S	49.41 W
José de San Martín	288	44.04 S	70.26 W
Josellandia	292	16.32 S	56.12 W
José María Blanco (Tres Lomas)	294	36.27 S	62.51 W
Jose Panganiban	202	14.17 N	122.41 E
José Pedro ≃	296	19.32 S	41.25 W
José Pedro Varela	294	33.27 S	54.32 W
Joseph	256	45.21 N	117.14 W
Joseph, Lac ⊜	232	52.45 N	65.15 W
Joseph, Lake ⊜	244	45.14 N	79.45 W
Joseph City	254	34.57 N	110.20 W
Josephine	266	40.29 N	79.11 W
Jōshin'etsu-kōgen - kokuritsu-kōen ♠	192	36.46 N	138.40 E
Joshua	250	32.28 N	97.23 W
Joshua Tree	258	34.08 N	116.19 W
Joshua Tree National Monument ♠	258	33.55 N	116.00 W
Joškar-Ola	160	56.38 N	47.52 E
Jos Plateau ⛰[1]	222	9.30 N	9.00 E
Josselin	166	47.57 N	2.33 W
Jostedalsbreen ⛆	160	61.40 N	7.00 E
Joué-lès-Tours	176	47.21 N	0.40 E
Jourdanton	250	28.55 N	98.33 W
Joure	178	52.57 N	5.47 E
Joutsa	160	61.44 N	26.07 E
Joutsijärvi	160	66.40 N	28.00 E
Jovellanos	284p	22.48 N	81.12 W
Jovellar	202	13.04 N	123.36 E
Joviânia	296	17.49 S	49.30 W
Jovita	294	34.32 S	63.57 W
Jowzjan □[4]	206	36.30 N	66.00 E
Joy, Mount Λ	236	63.46 N	132.55 W
Joyuda	284m	18.07 N	67.11 W
Józefów	164	52.09 N	21.12 E
Juagdan	202	9.59 N	124.34 E
Juami ≃	290	1.45 S	67.30 W
Juana Díaz	284m	18.03 N	66.31 W
Juan Aldama	278	24.19 N	103.21 W
Juan B. Arruabarrena	294	30.25 S	58.15 W
Juan de Fuca, Strait of ⋓	238	48.18 N	124.00 W
Juan de Garay	294	38.33 S	64.41 W
Juan de Mena	294	24.55 S	56.44 W
Juan de Nova, Île I	218	17.03 S	42.45 E
Juan E. Barra	294	37.50 S	60.30 W
Juan Eugenio	278	25.10 N	103.20 W
Juan Fernández, Islas II	288	33.00 S	80.00 W
Juangriego	290	11.05 N	63.57 W
Juan Gualberto Gómez	284p	22.52 N	81.33 W
Juan Guerra	292	6.39 S	76.20 W
Juanita	270	47.42 N	122.13 W
Juan Jorba	294	33.37 S	65.16 W
Juan José Castelli	294	25.37 S	60.57 W
Juanjuí	292	7.10 S	76.45 W
Juan L. Lacaze	294	34.26 S	57.27 W
Juan N. Fernández	294	38.01 S	59.16 W
Juan Perez Sound ⋓	238	52.30 N	131.18 W
Juan Viñas	280	9.54 N	83.45 W
Juárez, Arg.	294	37.41 S	59.49 W
Juárez, Méx.	278	27.37 N	100.44 W
Juárez → Ciudad Juárez, Méx.	278	31.44 N	106.29 W
Juárez, Sierra de ⛰	278	32.00 N	115.45 W
Juatinga, Ponta de ≻	296	23.17 S	44.30 W
Juàzeiro	286	9.25 S	40.30 W
Juàzeiro do Norte	286	7.12 S	39.20 W
Jūbā	214	4.51 N	31.37 E
Juba ≃, Afr.	218	0.12 S	42.40 E
Juba ≃, Bra.	292	14.59 S	57.44 W
Jūbāl, Maḍīq (Strait of Jubal) ⋓, Miṣr	220	27.40 N	33.55 E
Jubal, Strait of → Jūbāl, Maḍīq ⋓	220	27.40 N	33.55 E
Jubbulpore → Jabalpur	206	23.10 N	79.57 E
Jubilee Lake ⊜	240	48.04 N	55.11 W
Jubones ≃	290	3.13 S	79.57 W
Júcar	168	39.09 N	0.14 W
Juçara	296	15.53 S	50.51 W
Júcaro	284p	21.37 N	78.51 W
Jüchen	178	51.06 N	6.30 E
Juchipila	278	21.25 N	103.07 W
Juchitán	276	16.26 N	95.01 W
Juchitán [de Zaragoza]	278	16.26 N	95.01 W
Juchnov	160	54.45 N	35.14 E
Jucu ≃	296	20.24 S	40.19 W
Jucuapa	280	13.31 N	88.24 W
Jucurucu ≃	296	17.21 S	39.13 W
Judas, Punta ≻	280	9.31 N	84.32 W
Juddah (Jidda)	204	21.30 N	39.12 E
Jude Island I	240	47.15 N	54.59 W
Judenburg	164	47.10 N	14.40 E
Judío, Rambla del ≃	168	38.15 N	1.27 W
Judique	240	45.52 N	61.30 W
Judith ≃	256	47.44 N	109.38 W
Judith Gap	256	46.41 N	109.45 W
Judith Mountains ⛰	256	47.12 N	109.15 W
Judith Peak Λ	256	47.13 N	109.13 W
Judoma ≃	186	59.08 N	135.06 E
Judson	246	34.50 N	82.27 W
Judsonia	248	35.16 N	91.38 W
Jueshui ≃	196	31.42 N	113.20 E
Jufari ≃	290	1.13 S	62.00 W
Jug ≃	160	60.45 N	46.20 E
Jugon	166	48.25 N	2.20 W
Jugorskij Šar, Proliv ⋓	186	69.45 N	60.35 E
Juhe ≃	194	39.45 N	117.35 E
Juhuadao I	194	40.29 N	120.47 E
Juigalpa	280	12.05 N	85.24 W
Juillac	166	45.19 N	1.19 E
Juiná ≃	292	12.36 S	58.57 W
Juiz de Fora	296	21.45 S	43.20 W
Jujuy → San Salvador de Jujuy	294	24.10 S	65.20 W
Jujuy □[4]	294	23.00 S	66.00 W
Jukagirskoje Ploskogorje ⛰[1]	186	66.00 N	155.00 E
Jukamenskoje	160	57.53 N	52.15 E
Jukao → Rugao	196	32.25 N	120.36 E

Symbols in the index entries are identified on page 360.

Name	Page	Lat°′	Long°′
Juksejevo	160	59.52 N	54.19 E
Jukte	186	63.23 N	105.41 E
Jula ≃	160	63.49 N	44.44 E
Julesburg	252	40.59 N	102.16 W
Juli	292	16.12 S	69.29 W
Juliaca	292	15.30 S	70.08 W
Julia Creek	228	20.39 S	141.45 E
Julian	266	40.52 N	77.56 W
Julian Alps ⛰	170	46.00 N	14.00 E
Julianatop ∧	290	3.40 N	56.30 W
Julianehåb	232	60.43 N	46.01 W
Jülich	164	50.55 N	6.21 E
Julimes	278	28.25 N	105.27 W
Júlio de Castilhos	294	29.14 S	53.41 W
Jullundur	206	31.20 N	75.35 E
Juma	160	65.07 N	33.16 E
Juma ≃	290	4.57 S	64.31 W
Jumahe ≃	194	39.14 N	115.45 E
Jumay, Volcán ∧[1]	280	14.42 N	90.00 W
Jumbilla	292	5.51 S	77.46 W
Jumbo	218	0.12 S	42.38 E
Jumbo Peak ∧	258	36.12 N	114.11 W
Jumentos Cays II	282	23.00 N	75.50 W
Jumet	176	50.26 N	4.25 E
Jumilla	168	38.29 N	1.17 W
Jump ≃	244	45.17 N	91.05 W
Junāgadh	206	21.31 N	70.27 E
Junaynah, Ra's al- ∧	220	29.01 N	33.58 E
Juncos	284m	18.14 N	65.55 W
Junction, Tex., U.S.	250	30.29 N	99.46 W
Junction, Utah, U.S.	254	38.14 N	112.13 W
Junction City, Ark., U.S.	248	33.01 N	92.43 W
Junction City, Kans., U.S.	252	39.02 N	96.50 W
Junction City, Ky., U.S.	248	37.35 N	84.48 W
Junction City, Oreg., U.S.	256	44.13 N	123.12 W
Junction City, Wash., U.S.	270	46.58 N	123.46 W
Jundiaí	296	23.11 S	46.52 W
Jundiaí do Sul	296	23.27 S	50.17 W
Juneau, Alaska, U.S.	236	58.20 N	134.27 W
Juneau, Wis., U.S.	244	43.24 N	88.42 W
Junee	228	34.52 S	147.35 E
June Lake	258	37.47 N	119.04 W
Juniata	252	40.36 N	98.30 W
Juniata □[6]	262	40.34 N	77.24 W
Juniata ≃	242	40.24 N	77.01 W
Juniata Terrace	262	40.35 N	77.34 W
Junín, Arg.	294	34.35 S	60.58 W
Junín, Ec.	290	0.56 S	80.13 W
Junín, Perú	292	11.12 S	76.00 W
Junín □[5]	292	11.30 S	75.00 W
Junín, Lago de ⊜	292	11.00 S	76.09 W
Junín de los Andes	288	39.55 S	71.05 W
Junior	242	38.59 N	79.57 W
Juniper	240	46.33 N	67.13 W
Juniville	166	49.24 N	4.23 E
Junqueirópolis	296	21.32 S	51.26 W
Junsele	160	63.41 N	16.54 E
Junxian	190	32.42 N	111.13 E
Juparanã, Lagoa ⊜	296	19.35 S	40.18 W
Jupiá	296	20.47 S	51.39 W
Jupiter	246	26.56 N	80.06 W
Jupiter ≃	240	49.29 N	63.32 W
Juquiá	294	24.19 S	47.38 W
Jur, Česko.	164	48.15 N	17.13 E
Jur, S.S.S.R.	186	59.52 N	137.39 E
Jur ≃	220	8.39 N	29.18 E
Jura □[5]	180	46.50 N	5.50 E
Jura ⛰	166	46.45 N	6.30 E
Jura I	162	56.00 N	5.50 W
Jura, Sound of ⊔	162	55.55 N	5.22 W
Juramento	296	16.50 S	43.35 W
Jurbarkas	160	55.05 N	22.48 E
Jurenino	160	59.24 N	42.47 E
Jurga	186	55.42 N	84.51 E
Jurino	160	56.18 N	46.18 E
Jurja	160	59.03 N	49.14 E
Jurjevec	160	57.18 N	43.06 E
Jurla	160	59.17 N	54.19 E
Jūrmala	160	56.58 N	23.42 E
Jurty	186	56.03 N	97.37 E
Juruá	290	3.27 S	66.03 W
Juruá ≃	286	2.37 S	65.44 W
Juruá Mirim ≃	292	8.08 S	72.48 W
Juruàzinho ≃	292	6.01 S	69.30 W
Juruena ≃	292	7.20 S	58.03 W
Jurupari ≃	292	7.45 S	70.10 W
Jur'uzan'	158	54.52 N	58.26 E
Juscelândia	296	15.20 S	51.19 W
Jusepín	290	9.45 N	63.31 W
Jushui ≃	196	30.38 N	114.51 E
Juskatla	238	53.37 N	132.18 W
Juškovo	160	59.46 N	45.11 E
Juškozero	160	64.44 N	32.06 E
Jussey	166	47.49 N	5.54 E
Justiniano Posse	294	32.53 S	62.40 W
Justino Solari	294	29.23 S	58.12 W
Justo Daract	294	33.52 S	65.11 W
Justus	266	40.42 N	81.35 W
Jus'va	160	58.56 N	54.57 E
Jutaí	292	5.11 S	68.54 W
Jutaí ≃	290	2.43 S	66.57 W
Jüterbog	164	51.59 N	13.04 E
Juti	296	22.52 S	54.37 W
Jutiapa	280	14.17 N	89.54 W
Jutiapa □[5]	280	14.10 N	89.50 W
Juticalpa	280	14.42 N	86.15 W
Jutiquile	280	14.45 N	86.08 W
Jutland → Jylland ≻[1]	160	56.00 N	9.15 E
Jutrosin	164	51.40 N	17.10 E
Juvisy-sur-Orge	176	48.41 N	2.23 E
Juwara	204	18.55 N	57.17 E
Juža	160	56.35 N	42.01 E
Juzihe ≃	194	40.18 N	123.35 E
Južno-Aličurskij Chrebet ⛰	206	37.30 N	73.20 E
Južno-Jenisejskij	186	58.48 N	94.39 E
Južno-Sachalinsk	186	46.58 N	142.42 E
Južno-Ural'sk	158	54.26 N	61.15 E
Južnyj Bug ≃	172	46.59 N	31.58 E
Jwayyā	210	33.14 N	35.19 E
Jylland ≻[1]	160	56.00 N	9.15 E
Jyväskylä	160	62.14 N	25.44 E
K			
Ka ≃	222	11.40 N	4.10 E
Kaaawa	275c	21.33 N	157.51 W
Kaachka	186	37.21 N	59.36 E
Kaala ∧	275d	21.31 N	158.09 W
Kaalaea	275c	21.28 N	157.51 W
Kaalualu Bay C	275d	18.58 N	155.37 W
Kaap Plato ⛰[1]	224	28.20 S	23.57 E
Kaarst	178	51.14 N	6.37 E
Kaatoan, Mount ∧	202	8.07 N	124.55 E
Kaatsheuvel	178	51.40 N	5.02 E
Kaba, Goulbin V	222	13.42 N	6.19 E
Kabacan	202	7.05 N	124.50 E
Kabacan ≃	202	7.08 N	124.53 E
Kabaena, Pulau I	198	5.15 S	121.55 E
Kabah ⊥	278	20.07 N	89.29 W
Kabale	218	1.15 S	29.59 E
Kabalo	218	6.03 S	26.55 E
Kabambare	218	4.42 S	27.43 E
Kabankalan	202	9.59 N	122.49 E
Kabardino-Balkarskaja Avtonomnaja Sovetskaja Socialističeskaja Respublika □[8]	186	43.30 N	43.30 E
Kabasalan	202	7.47 N	122.44 E
Kabayan	202	16.37 N	120.50 E
Kabba	222	7.50 N	6.03 E
Kåbdalis	160	66.10 N	20.00 E
Kabd aṣ-Ṣārim ⇜[1]	212	34.34 N	39.33 E
Kabd Warqah ⇜[1]	212	34.20 N	39.37 E
Kabe	192	34.31 N	132.31 E
Kabenung Lake ⊜	244	48.16 N	85.00 W
Kabetogama Lake ⊜	244	48.28 N	92.59 W
Kabhegy ∧	164	46.58 N	17.30 E
Kabinakagami Lake ⊜	244	48.54 N	84.25 W
Kabinda	218	6.08 S	24.29 E
Kabīr Kūh ⛰	208	33.25 N	46.45 E
Kabompo ≃	218	14.10 S	23.11 E
Kabongo	218	7.19 S	25.35 E
Kābul	206	34.30 N	69.11 E
Kābul □[4]	206	34.30 N	69.00 E
Kābul ≃	206	33.55 N	72.14 E
Kaburuang, Pulau I	198	3.48 N	126.48 E
Kabwe (Broken Hill)	218	14.27 S	28.27 E
Kabylie ⇜[1]	168	36.30 N	4.30 E
Kačanik	172	42.13 N	21.14 E
Kachemak Bay C	236	59.35 N	151.30 W
Kachin □[3]	200	26.00 N	97.30 E
Kachovskoje Vodochranilišče ⊜[1]	158	47.25 N	34.10 E
K'achta	186	50.26 N	106.25 E
Kaçkar Dağı ∧	212	40.50 N	41.10 E
Kačug	186	53.58 N	105.52 E
Kadaň	164	50.20 N	13.15 E
Kadanai ≃	206	31.22 N	65.45 E
Kadan Kyun I	200	12.30 N	98.22 E
Kade	214	6.05 N	0.50 W
Kadeï ≃	214	3.31 N	16.05 E
Kadena	193b	26.22 N	127.45 E
Kadhimain → Al-Kāẓimīyah	208	33.22 N	44.20 E
Kadijevka	158	48.34 N	38.40 E
Kadıköy	172	40.46 N	26.46 E
Kadina	228	33.58 S	137.43 E
Kading ≃	200	18.19 N	104.00 E
Kairouan → El Kairouan	170	35.41 N	10.07 E
Kadja, Ouadi (Wādī Kaja) V	220	12.02 N	22.28 E
Kadogawa	192	32.28 N	131.39 E
Kadoka	252	43.50 N	101.31 W
Kadom	160	54.34 N	42.30 E
Kaduna	222	10.33 N	7.27 E
Kaduna ≃	222	8.45 N	5.45 E
Kāduqlī	220	11.01 N	29.43 E
Kadyj	160	57.47 N	43.11 E
Kadykčan	186	63.02 N	146.50 E
Kadžerom	160	64.41 N	55.54 E
Kaédi	222	16.09 N	13.30 W
Kaegudeck Lake ⊜	240	48.07 N	55.11 W
Kaena Point ≻	275d	21.35 N	158.17 W
Kaesŏng	194	37.59 N	126.33 E
Kaesŏng □[4]	194	38.00 N	126.30 E
Kafan	208	39.13 N	46.24 E
Kafia Kingi	214	9.16 N	24.25 E
Kafirévs, Ákra ≻	172	38.09 N	24.36 E
Kafirnigan ≃	206	36.58 N	68.02 E
Kafr ad-Dawwār	220	31.08 N	30.07 E
Kafr ash-Shaykh	220	31.07 N	30.56 E
Kafu ≃	218	1.08 N	31.05 E
Kafue ≃	218	15.56 S	28.55 E
Kaga	192	36.18 N	136.18 E
Kagalaska Island I	236	51.47 N	176.23 W
Kagamigahara	192	35.24 N	136.54 E
Kagamil Island I	236	53.00 N	169.43 W
Kagan	208	39.43 N	64.33 E
Kagawa □[5]	192	31.25 N	134.00 E
Kagawong Lake ⊜	244	45.49 N	82.18 W
Kagera ≃	218	0.57 S	31.47 E
Kagoshima	192	31.36 N	130.33 E
Kagoshima □[5]	193b	31.10 N	130.30 E
Kagoshima-wan C	192	31.25 N	130.38 E
Kagul	158	45.54 N	28.11 E
Kahajan ≃	198	3.20 S	114.04 E
Kahaluu	275c	21.28 N	157.50 W
Kahama	218	3.50 S	32.36 E
Kahemba	218	7.17 S	19.00 E
Kahiu Point C	275d	21.13 N	156.58 W
Kahler Asten ∧	164	51.11 N	8.29 E
Kahoka	248	40.25 N	91.43 W
Kahoolawe I	275d	20.33 N	156.37 W
Kahoué, Mont ∧	222	7.06 N	7.15 W
Kahuku	275c	21.41 N	157.57 W
Kahuku Point ≻	275d	21.43 N	157.59 W
Kahului	275a	20.54 N	156.28 W
Kahului Bay C	275d	20.54 N	156.28 W
Kahurangi Point ≻	230	40.46 S	172.13 E
Kai, Kepulauan II	198	5.35 S	132.45 E
Kaia, Wādī V	220	11.31 N	24.15 E
Kaiai, Jabal ∧	220	19.54 N	36.48 E
Kaiapoi	230	43.23 S	172.39 E
Kaibab Indian Reservation ⇜[4]	254	36.55 N	112.40 W
Kaibab Plateau ⛰[1]	254	36.30 N	112.15 W
Kai Besar I	198	5.35 S	133.00 E
Kaibito Plateau ⛰[1]	254	36.40 N	111.20 W
Kaieteur Fall L	290	5.10 N	59.35 W
Kaifeng	194	34.51 N	114.21 E
Kai Ketjil I	198	5.45 S	132.40 E
Kaikohe	230	35.25 S	173.48 E
Kaikoura	230	42.24 S	173.41 E
Kaikoura Peninsula ≻[1]	230	42.25 S	173.42 E
Kaili	200	26.22 N	108.01 E
Kailu	190	43.36 N	121.14 E
Kailua	275c	21.24 N	157.44 W
Kailua Kona	275d	19.39 N	155.59 W
Kaimana	198	3.39 S	133.45 E
Kaimanawa Mountains ⛰	230	39.14 S	175.55 E
Kaimon-dake ∧	192	31.11 N	130.32 E
Kainan	192	34.09 N	135.12 E
Kainji Lake ⊜[1]	222	10.30 N	4.35 E
Kaipara Harbour C	230	36.23 S	174.43 E
Kaiparowits Plateau ⛰[1]	254	37.20 N	111.15 W
Kairouan □[8]	170	35.30 N	9.55 E
Kaiserslautern	164	49.26 N	7.46 E
Kaitaia	230	35.07 S	173.15 E
Kaitangata	230	46.17 S	169.51 E
Kaituma ≃	290	8.10 N	59.43 W
Kaiwi Channel ⊔	275d	21.15 N	157.30 W
Kaiyuan, Zhg.	194	42.37 N	124.04 E
Kaiyuan, Zhg.	200	23.44 N	103.11 E
Kaiyuh Mountains ⛰	236	64.00 N	158.00 W
Kaj ≃	206	32.54 N	65.30 E
Kajaani	160	64.14 N	27.41 E
Kajan ≃	198	2.55 N	117.35 E
Kajang	200	2.59 N	101.47 E
Kajiki	192	31.44 N	130.40 E
Kajnar	186	49.12 N	77.25 E
Kajnupil'gyn, Laguna C	236	63.30 N	178.50 E
Kajuagung	198	3.24 S	104.50 E
Kakagi Lake ⊜	252	49.13 N	93.52 W
Kakamas	218	28.45 S	20.33 E
Kakanui Mountains ⛰	230	45.05 S	170.23 E
Kaka Point ≻	275d	20.31 N	156.33 W
Kake, Nihon	192	34.36 N	132.19 E
Kake, Alaska, U.S.	236	56.58 N	133.46 W
Kakegawa	192	34.46 N	138.01 E
Kakhonak	236	59.26 N	154.51 W
Kakisa Lake ⊜	232	60.55 N	117.40 W
Kakizaki	192	37.15 N	138.25 E
Kako ≃	290	5.45 N	60.33 W
Kakogawa	192	34.46 N	134.51 E
Kaktovik	236	70.08 N	143.37 W
Kakuda	192	37.58 N	140.47 E
Kakunodate	192	39.35 N	140.34 E
Kakwa ≃	238	54.36 N	118.28 W
Kalaa Jerda	170	35.40 N	8.36 E
Kalaa Kebira	170	35.52 N	10.32 E
Kalaa Srira	170	35.49 N	10.33 E
Kalabahi	198	8.13 S	124.31 E
Kalabáka	172	39.42 N	21.43 E
Kalabo	218	14.57 S	22.40 E
Kalač	158	50.25 N	41.01 E
Kalačinsk	186	55.03 N	74.34 E
Kalač-na-Donu	158	48.43 N	43.31 E
Kaladan ≃	200	20.09 N	92.57 E
Kaladar	264	44.39 N	77.07 W
Kalae	275a	21.10 N	157.00 W
Ka Lae ≻	275d	18.55 N	155.41 W
Kalaeerqisihe ≃	190	47.52 N	84.50 E
Kalahari Desert ⇜[2]	224	24.00 S	21.30 E
Kalahari Gemsbok National Park ♠	224	25.30 S	20.30 E
Kalaheo	275b	21.56 N	159.32 W
Kalai-Mor	208	35.39 N	62.33 E
Kalajoki	160	64.15 N	23.57 E
Kalakan	186	55.08 N	116.45 E
Kalakashihe ≃	206	37.00 N	79.45 E
Kalām	204	35.28 N	72.35 E
Kalama	270	46.01 N	122.51 W
Kalámai	172	37.04 N	22.07 E
Kalamaki	172	36.15 N	29.24 E
Kalamalka Lake ⊜	238	50.09 N	119.22 W
Kalamaria	172	40.35 N	22.58 E
Kalamazoo	268	42.17 N	85.32 W
Kalamazoo □[6]	268	42.14 N	85.32 W
Kalamo	268	42.32 N	85.01 W
Kalampáka	172	39.42 N	21.39 E
Kalamulunshankou)(	206	36.17 N	87.06 E
Kalao, Pulau I	198	7.18 S	120.58 E
Kalaong	202	6.04 N	124.28 E
Kalaotoa, Pulau I	198	7.22 S	121.47 E
Kalapana	275d	19.22 N	154.58 W
Kalasin	200	16.29 N	103.31 E
Kalašnikovo	160	57.17 N	35.13 E
Kalāt	204	29.02 N	66.35 E
Kalāt □[8]	208	28.00 N	66.45 E
Kalāt-i-Ghilzai	208	32.08 N	66.52 E
Kalatungan Mountain ∧	202	7.58 N	124.47 E
Kalaupapa	275a	21.11 N	156.59 W
Kalavárdha	172	36.20 N	27.57 E
Kalávrita	172	38.01 N	22.06 E
Kal'azin	160	57.15 N	37.52 E
Kalb, Ra's al- ≻	214	14.02 N	48.40 E
Kaldenkirchen	178	51.19 N	6.12 E
Kale	172	37.26 N	28.51 E
Kaleden	238	49.23 N	119.35 W
Kalegauk Island I	200	15.32 N	97.40 E
Kaleindaung ≃	200	18.50 N	94.00 E
Kalemi (Albertville)	218	5.56 S	29.12 E
Kalety (Schützenbruch)	164	50.34 N	18.54 E
Kalevala	160	65.13 N	31.08 E
Kalewa	198	23.12 N	94.17 E
Kálfafell	160a	63.58 N	17.40 W
Kalgačicha	160	63.20 N	36.44 E
Kalgan → Zhangjiakou	194	40.50 N	114.53 E
Kalgin Island I	236	60.28 N	151.55 W
Kalgoorlie	226	30.45 S	121.28 E
Kāli ≃	206	29.25 N	80.15 E
Kaliakra, nos ≻	172	43.21 N	28.27 E
Kalibo	202	11.43 N	122.22 E
Kalida	268	40.59 N	84.12 W
Kalima	218	2.34 S	26.37 E
Kálimnos	172	36.57 N	26.59 E
Kálimnos I	172	37.00 N	27.00 E
Kalinga-Apayao □[4]	202	17.50 N	121.10 E
Kalinin	160	56.52 N	35.55 E
Kaliningrad, S.S.S.R.	158	55.55 N	37.49 E
Kaliningrad (Königsberg), S.S.S.R.	164	54.43 N	20.30 E
Kalinovik	172	43.31 N	18.26 E
Kalispell	256	48.12 N	114.19 W
Kalisz	164	51.46 N	18.06 E
Kalisz Pomorski (Kallies)	164	53.19 N	15.54 E
Kalixälven ≃	160	65.50 N	23.11 E
Kalkaska	244	44.44 N	85.11 W
Kallaste	160	58.39 N	27.09 E
Kallavesi ⊜	160	62.50 N	27.45 E
Kallsjön ⊜	160	63.37 N	13.00 E
Kalmar	160	56.40 N	16.22 E
Kalmarsund ⊔	160	56.40 N	16.25 E
Kalmthout	176	51.23 N	4.28 E
Kalničko Gorje ⛰	170	46.10 N	16.30 E
Kalocsa	164	46.32 N	18.59 E
Kalofer	172	42.37 N	24.59 E
Kalohi Channel ⊔	275d	21.00 N	156.56 W
Kaloli Point ≻	275d	19.38 N	154.57 W
Kalomo	218	17.02 S	26.30 E
Kalona	244	41.29 N	91.43 W
Kalone Peak ∧	238	52.38 N	126.37 W
Kalpákion	172	39.55 N	20.20 E
Kalskag	236	61.30 N	160.23 W
Kaltag	236	64.20 N	158.44 W
Kaltan	186	53.30 N	87.17 E
Kaltenkirchen	178	53.50 N	9.58 E
Kaluga	160	54.31 N	36.16 E
Kalumba, Mount ∧	228	31.49 S	146.22 E
Kalundborg	160	55.41 N	11.06 E
Kałuszyn	164	52.13 N	21.49 E
Kalvarija	164	54.21 N	23.14 E
Kalwang	164	47.26 N	14.46 E
Kalwaria Zebrzydowska	164	49.52 N	19.41 E
Kama ≃	160	55.45 N	52.00 E
Kamae	192	32.48 N	131.56 E
Kamaishi	192	39.16 N	141.53 E
Kamakou ∧	275d	21.07 N	156.52 W
Kamakura	192	35.19 N	139.33 E
Kamālia	206	30.44 N	72.39 E
Kaman ≃	200	14.48 N	106.51 E
Kamaniskeg Lake ⊜	244	45.25 N	77.42 W
Kamarān I	214	15.21 N	42.34 E
Kamaran, Hadjer ∧	220	12.41 N	21.46 E
Kamarang ≃	290	5.53 N	60.35 W
Kamas	254	40.38 N	111.17 W
Kamay	250	33.51 N	98.48 W
Kambarka	158	56.17 N	54.12 E
Kamčatka ≃	186	56.15 N	162.30 E
Kamčatka, Poluostrov ≻[1]	186	56.00 N	160.00 E
Kamčija ≃	172	43.02 N	27.53 E
Kameda, Nihon	192	37.52 N	139.07 E
Kameda, Nihon	192a	41.48 N	140.36 E
Kamen	178	51.35 N	7.40 E
Kamenec	164	52.24 N	23.49 E
Kamenec-Podol'skij	172	48.41 N	26.36 E
Kamenjak, Rt ≻	170	44.46 N	13.55 E
Kamenka, S.S.S.R.	158	53.13 N	44.03 E
Kamenka, S.S.S.R.	160	65.54 N	44.05 E
Kamen'-na-Obi	186	53.47 N	81.20 E
Kamennogorsk	160	60.58 N	29.07 E
Kamennougol'naja Gr'ada ⛰	160	65.30 N	51.00 E
Kamenskoje	186	62.30 N	166.12 E
Kamensk-Ural'skij	158	56.28 N	61.54 E
Kamenz	164	51.16 N	14.06 E
Kāmet ∧	206	30.54 N	79.37 E
Kamiah	256	46.14 N	116.02 W
Kamiak Butte ∧	256	46.52 N	117.10 W
Kamień Krajeński	164	53.33 N	17.32 E
Kamienna ≃	164	51.06 N	21.47 E
Kamień Pomorski (Cammin)	164	53.58 N	14.46 E
Kamieńsk	164	51.12 N	19.30 E
Kamiere, Lake ⊜	230	42.49 S	171.09 E
Kamiiso	192a	41.49 N	140.39 E
Kamikawa	192a	43.49 N	142.45 E
Kamilukuak Lake ⊜	232	62.22 N	101.40 W
Kamina	218	8.44 S	25.00 E
Kaminak Lake ⊜	232	62.10 N	95.00 W
Kaminaljuyú ⊥	280	14.39 N	90.32 W
Kaminokuni	192a	41.48 N	140.06 E
Kaminoyama	192	38.09 N	140.17 E
Kaminuriak Lake ⊜	232	63.00 N	95.40 W
Kamioka	192	36.16 N	137.18 E
Kámiros ⊥	172	36.19 N	27.57 E
Kamishak Bay C	236	59.15 N	153.45 W
Kamisunagawa	192a	43.30 N	142.00 E
Kamitsushima	192	34.50 N	129.28 E
Kamloops	238	50.40 N	120.20 W
Kamloops Indian Reserve ⇜[4]	238	50.42 N	120.20 W
Kamloops Lake ⊜	238	50.43 N	120.33 W
Kammuri-yama ∧	192	34.28 N	132.05 E
Kamnik	170	46.13 N	14.37 E
Kamo, Nihon	192	37.39 N	139.03 E
Kamo, S.S.S.R.	208	40.22 N	45.08 E
Kamoa Mountains ⛰	290	1.30 N	59.00 W
Kamojima	192	34.04 N	134.21 E
Kampala	218	0.19 N	32.25 E
Kampar	200	4.17 N	101.08 E
Kampar ≃	200	0.32 N	103.08 E
Kampar-kanan ≃	200	0.16 N	101.41 E
Kampar-kiri ≃	200	0.16 N	101.41 E
Kampen	178	52.33 N	5.54 E
Kampeska, Lake ⊜	252	44.55 N	97.12 W
Kamphaeng, Khao ∧	200	14.40 N	99.15 E
Kamphaeng Phet	200	16.26 N	99.33 E
Kamp-Lintfort	178	51.30 N	6.31 E
Kâmpóng Cham	200	12.00 N	105.27 E
Kâmpóng Chhnăng	200	12.15 N	104.40 E
Kâmpóng Thum	200	12.42 N	104.52 E
Kâmpôt	200	10.37 N	104.11 E
Kampsville	248	39.18 N	90.37 W
Kamrau, Teluk C	198	3.30 S	133.36 E
Kamsack	232	51.34 N	101.54 W
Kamskij	160	60.04 N	53.13 E
Kamskoje Ustje	160	55.13 N	49.16 E
Kamskoje Vodochranilišče ⊜[1]	160	58.52 N	56.15 E
Kamuela (Waimea)	275d	20.01 N	155.41 W
Kamui-misaki ≻	192a	43.20 N	140.21 E
Kámuk, Cerro ∧	280	9.16 N	83.01 W
Kamyšin	158	50.06 N	45.24 E
Kamyšlov	158	56.52 N	62.43 E
Kan ≃	200	13.32 N	105.58 E
Kana ≃	224	18.30 S	27.22 E
Kanaaupscow ≃	232	53.40 N	77.10 W
Kanab	254	37.03 N	112.32 W
Kanaga Island I	236	51.45 N	177.10 W
Kanaga Volcano ∧[1]	236	51.50 N	177.09 W
Kanagawa □[5]	192	35.30 N	139.30 E
Kanairiktok ≃	232	55.05 N	60.20 W
Kanā'is, Ra's al- ≻	220	31.15 N	27.51 E
Kananaskis ≃	238	51.05 N	115.03 W
Kananga (Luluabourg)	218	5.54 S	22.25 E
Kanarraville	254	37.32 N	113.11 W
Kanaš	160	55.31 N	47.30 E
Kanava	160	61.07 N	54.58 E
Kanawha	244	42.56 N	93.48 W
Kanawha ≃	242	38.50 N	82.08 W
Kanazawa	192	36.34 N	136.39 E
Kanbe	200	16.42 N	96.01 E
Kančalan ≃	236	65.08 N	176.25 E
Kanchanaburi	200	14.02 N	99.33 E
Kānchenjunga ∧	206	27.42 N	88.09 E
Kānchipuram	204	12.50 N	79.43 E
Kanchow → Ganzhou	196	25.54 N	114.55 E
Kańczuga	164	49.59 N	22.24 E
Kanda	192	33.47 N	130.59 E
Kandagač	158	49.28 N	57.25 E
Kandahār	206	31.32 N	65.30 E
Kandahār □[4]	206	31.00 N	65.45 E
Kandalakša	160	67.09 N	32.21 E
Kandalakšskaja Guba C	160	66.55 N	32.45 E
Kandangan	198	2.47 S	115.16 E
Kandel	164	49.05 N	8.11 E
Kandi	214	11.08 N	2.56 E
Kandik ≃	236	65.24 N	142.34 W
Kandy	204	7.18 N	80.38 E
Kane, Ill., U.S.	248	39.11 N	90.21 W
Kane, Pa., U.S.	266	41.40 N	78.49 W
Kane □[6]	268	41.53 N	88.18 W
Kanektok ≃	236	59.45 N	161.55 W
Kanemi	202	6.55 N	123.58 E
Kanenmyvejem ≃	236	66.04 N	178.40 W
Kaneohe	275c	21.25 N	157.48 W
Kaneohe Bay C	275d	21.28 N	157.49 W
Kangalassy	186	62.23 N	129.59 E
Kangar	200	6.26 N	100.12 E
Kangaroo Island I	228	35.50 S	137.06 E
Kangaroo Range National Park ♠	228	29.35 S	152.10 E
Kangding	190	30.03 N	102.02 E
Kangean, Kepulauan II	198	6.55 S	115.30 E
Kangen ≃	220	6.47 N	33.09 E
Kanggye	194	40.58 N	126.34 E
Kanghwa-do I	194	37.40 N	126.27 E
Kanghwa-man C	194	37.20 N	126.35 E
Kangnŭng	194	37.45 N	128.54 E
Kango	218	0.09 N	10.08 E
Kangwŏn Do □[4], C.M.I.K.	194	38.45 N	127.35 E
Kangwŏn Do □[4], Taehan	194	37.45 N	128.15 E
Kanhar ≃	206	24.28 N	83.09 E
Kaniama	218	7.31 S	24.11 E
Kanin, Poluostrov ≻[1]	160	68.00 N	45.00 E
Kanin Kamen' ∧	160	68.18 N	45.00 E
Kanin Nos	160	68.39 N	43.14 E
Kanin Nos, Mys ≻	160	68.39 N	43.16 E
Kanjiža	172	46.04 N	20.04 E
Kankakee	268	41.07 N	87.52 W
Kankakee □[6]	268	41.07 N	87.52 W
Kankakee ≃	248	41.23 N	88.16 W
Kankan	222	10.23 N	9.18 W
Kankan □[4]	222	10.10 N	9.15 W
Kankunskij	186	57.37 N	126.08 E
Kanmaw Kyun I	200	11.40 N	98.28 E
Kannapolis	246	35.30 N	80.37 W
Kannonkoski	160	62.58 N	25.15 E
Kannus	160	63.54 N	23.54 E
Kano	222	12.00 N	8.30 E
Kano □[3]	222	11.45 N	9.00 E
Kanon, Punt ≻	285s	12.02 N	68.45 W
Kanonji	192	34.07 N	133.39 E
Kanopolis	252	38.43 N	98.09 W
Kanopolis Reservoir ⊜[1]	252	38.38 N	98.00 W
Kanorado	252	39.20 N	102.02 W
Kanosh	254	38.48 N	112.26 W
Kan'ovka	160	67.08 N	39.40 E
Kanowna	226	30.36 S	121.36 E
Kanoya	192	31.23 N	130.51 E
Kānpur	206	26.28 N	80.20 E
Kansas, Ill., U.S.	248	39.33 N	87.56 W
Kansas, Ohio, U.S.	266	41.15 N	83.17 W
Kansas □[3]	234	38.45 N	98.15 W
Kansas ≃	252	39.07 N	94.36 W
Kansas City, Kans., U.S.	252	39.07 N	94.39 W
Kansas City, Mo., U.S.	248	39.05 N	94.35 W
Kansk	186	56.13 N	95.41 E
Kansu → Gansu □[4]	190	37.00 N	103.00 E
Kant	186	42.55 N	74.55 E
Kantang	198	7.23 N	99.32 E
Kantishna ≃	236	64.45 N	149.58 W
Kantner	266	40.06 N	78.56 W
Kantō-heiya ⩧	192	36.00 N	139.30 E
Kantō-sammyaku ⛰	192	35.50 N	138.50 E
Kantunilkín	278	21.06 N	87.29 W
Kanturk	162	52.10 N	8.55 W
Kanuku Mountains ⛰	290	3.12 N	59.30 W
Kanuma	192	36.33 N	139.44 E
Kanuti ≃	236	66.26 N	153.02 W
Kanye	224	24.59 S	25.19 E
Kanygtokynmankyn, Laguna C	236	69.20 N	178.45 E
Kanzanavolok	160	62.23 N	36.58 E
Kaohsiung	196	22.38 N	120.17 E
Kaohsiung Ch'uan C	196	22.37 N	120.12 E
Kaohsiunghsien	196	22.38 N	120.21 E
Kaokoveld ⛰[1]	224	21.00 S	14.20 E
Kaolack	222	14.09 N	16.04 W
Kapaa	275b	22.05 N	159.19 W
Kapalong	202	7.30 N	125.40 E
Kapanga	218	8.21 S	22.35 E
Kapangan	202	16.35 N	120.35 E
Kapaonik ⛰	172	43.20 N	20.50 E
Kapatagan	202	7.52 N	123.43 E
Kapellen, Bel.	176	51.19 N	4.26 E
Kapellen, B.R.D.	178	51.25 N	6.35 E
Kapfenberg	164	47.26 N	15.18 E
Kapıdağı Yarımadası ≻[1]	212	40.28 N	27.50 E
Kāpīsā □[4]	206	34.45 N	69.30 E
Kapiskau ≃	232	52.47 N	81.55 W
Kapit	198	2.02 N	112.54 E
Kapiti Island I	230	40.51 S	174.55 E
Kapka, Massif du ⛰	220	15.07 N	21.45 E
Kaplan	248	30.00 N	92.17 W
Kaplice	164	48.45 N	14.30 E
Kapos ≃	164	46.44 N	18.30 E
Kaposvár	164	46.22 N	17.47 E
Kapowsin	270	46.59 N	122.13 W
Kappeln	164	54.40 N	9.56 E
Kaprun	164	47.16 N	12.46 E
Kapsukas	164	54.33 N	23.21 E
Kaptol	172	45.26 N	17.44 E
Kapuas ≃	198	0.25 S	109.04 E
Kapuskasing	232	49.25 N	82.26 W
Kapuskasing ≃	234	49.49 N	82.00 W
Kapuskasing Lake ⊜	244	48.30 N	82.55 W
Kapuvár	164	47.36 N	17.02 E
Kara	186	69.14 N	65.00 E
Kara ≃	222	10.01 N	0.25 E
Karaaul	186	48.57 N	79.15 E
Kara-Balty	186	42.50 N	73.52 E
Karabaš	158	55.29 N	60.14 E
Karabiğa	172	40.24 N	27.18 E
Karabil', Vozvyšennost' ⛰[1]	208	36.25 N	64.00 E
Kara-Bogaz-Gol, Zaliv C	186	41.00 N	53.15 E
Karabük	212	41.12 N	32.37 E
Karabula	186	58.08 N	97.23 E
Karacabey	172	40.13 N	28.21 E
Karacadağ	172	41.57 N	27.40 E
Karaca Dağ ∧	212	37.40 N	39.50 E
Karacaköy	172	41.24 N	28.22 E
Karacasu	172	37.43 N	28.37 E
Karāchi	206	24.52 N	67.03 E
Karāchi □[8]	208	25.40 N	65.00 E
Karagaj	160	58.16 N	54.56 E
Karaganda	186	49.50 N	73.10 E
Karaginskij Zaliv C	186	58.50 N	164.00 E
Karagölü ⊜	212	36.42 N	29.50 E
Karagoš, Gora ∧	186	51.44 N	89.24 E
Karahallı	172	38.20 N	29.32 E
Karaj	208	35.48 N	50.59 E
Karakelong, Pulau I	198	4.15 N	126.48 E
Karakoram Range ⛰	206	35.30 N	77.00 E
Karakoro ≃	222	14.43 N	12.03 W
Karaköse	208	39.44 N	43.03 E
Karakul'	186	39.32 N	63.50 E
Karakumskij Kanal ☰	208	37.35 N	61.50 E
Karakumy ⇜[2]	186	39.00 N	60.00 E
Karamai → Kelamayi	190	45.37 N	84.53 E
Karaman, Tür.	172	37.05 N	29.20 E
Karaman, Tür.	212	37.11 N	33.14 E
Karamanlı	172	37.22 N	29.49 E
Karamea ≃	230	41.15 S	172.06 E
Karamea Bight C[3]	230	41.20 S	171.50 E
Karamıkbataklığı ☷	212	38.25 N	30.50 E
Karamursel	172	40.42 N	29.36 E
Karamyševo	160	57.45 N	28.45 E
Karanti	172	40.15 N	27.07 E
Karasburg	218	28.00 S	18.43 E
Karasjok	160	69.27 N	25.30 E
Karasuk	186	53.44 N	78.02 E
Karatau	186	43.10 N	70.28 E
Karatau, Chrebet ⛰	186	43.50 N	68.30 E
Karatepe ⊥	212	37.17 N	36.13 E
Karaton	158	46.25 N	53.30 E
Karatsu	192	33.26 N	129.58 E
Karaul	186	70.06 N	83.08 E
Karavanke (Karawanken) ⛰	170	46.30 N	14.25 E
Karavás	172	36.21 N	22.57 E
Karawanken (Karavanke) ⛰	170	46.30 N	14.25 E
Karažal	186	48.02 N	70.49 E
Kara Sea → Karskoje More ⊤[2]	186	76.00 N	80.00 E
Karbalā'	208	32.36 N	44.02 E
Karbalā' □[4]	208	32.15 N	43.07 E
Kårböle	160	61.59 N	15.19 E
Karcag	164	47.19 N	20.56 E
Karczew	164	52.06 N	21.15 E
Kardhámaina	172	36.47 N	27.09 E
Kardhítsa	172	39.21 N	21.55 E
Kärdla	160	59.00 N	22.45 E
Kârdžali	172	41.39 N	25.22 E
Kareeberge ⛰	224	30.53 S	21.57 E
Karepino	160	61.02 N	57.02 E
Karesuando	160	68.25 N	22.30 E
Kargali	160	55.12 N	50.54 E
Karganaj	236	65.21 N	175.25 E
Kargapazari Dağları ⛰	212	40.07 N	41.35 E
Kargasok	186	59.07 N	80.53 E
Kargopol'	160	61.30 N	38.58 E
Karhula	160	60.31 N	26.57 E
Kariaí	172	40.16 N	24.15 E
Kariba	224	16.30 S	28.45 E
Kariba, Lake ⊜[1]	218	17.00 S	28.00 E
Karibib	218	21.58 S	15.51 E
Karibib □[5]	224	22.20 S	16.00 E
Kariega ≃	224	33.03 S	23.28 E
Karigasniemi	160	69.24 N	25.50 E
Karikari, Cape ≻	230	34.48 S	173.24 E
Karimata, Kepulauan II	198	1.25 S	109.05 E
Karimata, Selat (Karimata Strait) ⊔	198	2.05 S	108.40 E
Karimundjawa, Kepulauan II	198	5.50 S	110.25 E
Karin	214	10.51 N	45.45 E
Karis (Karjaa)	160	60.05 N	23.40 E
Káristos	172	38.00 N	24.24 E
Kariya	192	34.59 N	136.59 E
Karjepolje	160	65.34 N	43.40 E
Karkabet	214	16.13 N	37.30 E
Karkaralinsk	186	49.23 N	75.21 E
Karkheh ≃	208	31.46 N	47.55 E
Karlino (Körlin)	164	54.03 N	15.51 E
Karl-Marx-Stadt (Chemnitz)	164	50.50 N	12.55 E
Karl-Marx-Stadt □[5]	166	50.45 N	12.45 E
Karlobag	170	44.32 N	15.05 E
Karlovac	170	45.29 N	15.34 E
Karlovo	172	42.38 N	24.48 E
Karlovy Vary	164	50.11 N	12.52 E
Karlsbad → Karlovy Vary	164	50.11 N	12.52 E
Karlsborg	160	65.48 N	23.17 E
Karlshamn	160	56.10 N	14.51 E
Karlskoga	160	59.20 N	14.31 E
Karlskrona	160	56.10 N	15.35 E
Karlsruhe	164	49.03 N	8.24 E
Karlstad, Sve.	160	59.22 N	13.30 E
Karlstad, Minn., U.S.	252	48.35 N	96.31 W
Karlstadt	164	49.57 N	9.45 E
Karluk	236	57.34 N	154.28 W
Karnack	248	32.40 N	94.10 W
Karnak → Al-Karnak, Miṣr	220	25.43 N	32.39 E
Karnak, Ill., U.S.	248	37.18 N	88.58 W
Karnāl	206	29.41 N	76.59 E
Karnāla Pass)(	206	33.50 N	68.11 E
Karnaphuli Reservoir ⊜[1]	206	22.30 N	92.20 E
Karnes City	250	28.53 N	97.54 W
Karnobat	172	42.39 N	26.59 E
Karns City	266	40.59 N	79.44 W
Kärnten □[3]	164	46.50 N	13.50 E
Karomatan	202	7.46 N	123.44 E
Karonga	218	9.56 S	33.56 E
Kárpathos I	172	35.40 N	27.10 E
Karpenísion	172	38.55 N	21.40 E
Karpinsk	158	59.45 N	60.01 E
Karpogory	160	64.00 N	44.24 E
Karpovo	160	60.02 N	36.43 E
Karrats Fjord C[2]	232	71.20 N	54.00 W
Kars	208	40.36 N	43.05 E
Kars □[4]	212	40.30 N	42.45 E
Karsakpaj	186	47.49 N	66.41 E
Kärsämäki	160	63.58 N	25.46 E
Kārsava	160	56.47 N	27.40 E
Karši	208	38.53 N	65.48 E
Karsin	164	53.54 N	17.56 E
Karšinskaja Step' ⩧	208	39.10 N	65.00 E
Karskije Vorota, Proliv ⊔	186	70.30 N	58.00 E
Karskoje More (Kara Sea) ⊤[2]	186	76.00 N	80.00 E
Karsun	160	54.11 N	46.59 E
Kartajol'	160	64.32 N	53.14 E
Kartal	172	40.53 N	29.10 E
Kartala ∧	225a	11.45 S	43.22 E
Kartaly	186	53.03 N	60.40 E
Karthaus	266	41.07 N	78.07 W
Kartuzy	164	54.20 N	18.12 E
Karufa	198	3.50 S	133.26 E
Karumai	192	40.19 N	141.28 E
Kārūn ≃	208	30.25 N	48.12 E
Karungi	160	66.03 N	23.57 E
Karviná	164	49.50 N	18.30 E
Karymskoje	186	51.37 N	114.21 E
Kaş	172	36.12 N	29.38 E
Kasaan	236	55.32 N	132.24 W
Kasai (Cassai) ≃	218	3.06 S	16.57 E
Kasaji	218	10.22 S	23.27 E
Kasama, Nihon	192	36.23 N	140.16 E
Kasama, Zam.	218	10.13 S	31.12 E
Kasan	208	39.02 N	65.35 E
Kasanga	218	8.28 S	31.09 E
Kasaoka	192	34.30 N	133.30 E
Kasba Lake ⊜	232	60.18 N	102.07 W
Kaşçiftliği	172	36.36 N	29.45 E
Kaseda	192	31.25 N	130.19 E
Kasempa	218	13.27 S	25.50 E
Kasenga	218	10.22 S	28.38 E
Kasese, Ug.	218	0.10 N	30.05 E
Kasese, Zaïre	218	1.38 S	27.07 E
Kashabowie Lake ⊜	244	48.42 N	90.25 W
Kāshān	208	33.59 N	51.29 E
Kashegelok	236	60.50 N	157.50 W
Kashgar → Kashi	190	39.29 N	75.59 E
Kashi (Kashgar)	190	39.29 N	75.59 E
Kashihara	192	34.27 N	135.46 E
Kashima	192	33.07 N	130.06 E
Kashima-nada ⊤[2]	192	36.15 N	140.45 E
Kashiwa	192	35.52 N	139.59 E
Kashiwazaki	192	37.22 N	138.33 E
Kāshmar	208	35.12 N	58.27 E
Kashunuk ≃	236	61.18 N	165.36 W
Kasigluk	236	60.52 N	162.32 W
Kasilof	236	60.23 N	151.18 W
Kasimov	160	54.56 N	41.24 E
Kašin	160	57.21 N	37.37 E
Kašira	160	54.51 N	38.10 E
Kasiruta, Pulau I	198	0.25 S	127.12 E
Kaskaskia ≃	248	37.59 N	89.56 W
Kaskattama ≃	232	57.03 N	90.07 W
Kaskö (Kaskinen)	160	62.23 N	21.13 E
Kasli	158	55.53 N	60.46 E
Kaslo	238	49.55 N	116.55 W
Kasongo	218	4.27 S	26.40 E
Kasongo-Lunda	218	6.28 S	16.49 E
Kásos I	172	35.22 N	26.56 E
Kasota	244	44.18 N	93.57 W
Kaspijsk	158	42.52 N	47.38 E
Kaspijskij	158	45.22 N	47.24 E
Kasr, Ra's ≻	220	18.02 N	38.35 E
Kassalā	220	15.28 N	36.24 E
Kassalā □[4]	220	18.00 N	36.00 E
Kassándra ≻[1]	172	40.06 N	23.22 E
Kassel	178	51.19 N	9.29 E
Kassel □[5]	178	51.10 N	9.20 E
Kasserine → El Kasserine	214	35.11 N	8.48 E
Kasserine □[8]	170	35.30 N	8.45 E
Kassikaityu ≃	290	1.50 N	58.35 W
Kassîr, Sabkhat al- ⊜	212	35.03 N	41.07 E
Kasson	244	44.03 N	92.45 W
Kastamonu	212	41.22 N	33.47 E
Kastanéai	172	41.38 N	26.28 E
Kastéllion Erétrie	172	35.30 N	23.38 E
Kastellórizon I	212	36.08 N	29.34 E
Kastl	164	49.22 N	11.42 E
Kastoría	172	40.31 N	21.15 E
Kastorías, Límni ⊜	172	40.30 N	21.17 E
Kástron	172	39.52 N	25.04 E
Kasugai	192	35.14 N	136.58 E
Kasumi	192	35.38 N	134.38 E
Kasumiga-ura ⊜	192	36.00 N	140.25 E
Kasūr	206	31.07 N	74.27 E
Kaszuby □[9]	164	54.10 N	18.15 E
Kaszuby ⇜[1]	164	54.10 N	18.15 E
Katahdin, Mount ∧	242	45.55 N	68.55 W
Katalla	236	60.12 N	144.31 W
Katanga ≃	186	58.18 N	104.10 E
Katanglad Mountains ⛰	202	8.08 N	124.55 E
Katanning	226	33.42 S	117.33 E
Katāwāz	204	32.47 N	68.30 E
Katchall Island I	200	7.55 N	93.25 E
Kateel ≃	236	65.28 N	157.35 W
Kateríni	172	40.16 N	22.30 E
Kater Point ≻	232	67.44 N	109.04 W
Kates Needle ∧	236	57.03 N	132.03 W
Katha	190	24.11 N	96.21 E
Katherine	226	14.28 S	132.16 E
Kāthiāwār ≻[1]	204	22.00 N	71.00 E
Katiola	222	8.08 N	5.06 W
Katiola □[5]	222	8.30 N	4.45 W
Katipunan	202	8.31 N	123.17 E
Katmai, Mount ∧	236	58.17 N	154.56 W
Katmai National Monument ♠	236	58.30 N	155.00 W
Kātmāndu	206	27.42 N	85.20 E
Káto Akhaïa	172	38.09 N	21.32 E
Katonah	261	41.16 N	73.41 W
Katoomba	228	33.42 S	150.18 E
Katoúna	172	38.47 N	21.07 E
Katowice	164	50.16 N	19.00 E
Katrīnah, Jabal ∧	220	28.31 N	33.57 E
Katrineholm	160	59.00 N	16.12 E
Katsina	222	13.00 N	7.32 E
Katsina Ala ≃	222	7.45 N	9.05 E
Katsuta	192	36.24 N	140.30 E
Katsuura	192	35.08 N	140.18 E
Katsuyama, Nihon	192	36.03 N	136.30 E
Katsuyama, Nihon	192	35.05 N	133.41 E
Kattakurgan	186	39.55 N	66.15 E
Kattaviá	172	35.57 N	27.46 E
Kattegat ⊔	160	57.00 N	11.00 E
Kattonghu ⊜	206	35.30 N	92.00 E
Katul, Jabal ∧	220	14.16 N	29.23 E
Katun' ≃	186	52.25 N	85.05 E
Katunino	160	58.01 N	45.39 E
Katwijk aan de Rijn	178	52.11 N	4.26 E
Katwijk aan Zee	178	52.13 N	4.24 E
Kąty Wrocławskie (Kanth)	164	51.02 N	16.46 E
Katzenbuckel ∧	164	49.28 N	9.02 E
Kauai □[6]	275b	21.59 N	159.22 W
Kauai Channel ⊔	275d	21.45 N	158.50 W
Kau Desert ⇜[2]	275d	19.21 N	155.19 W
Kaufbeuren	180	47.53 N	10.37 E
Kaufman	250	32.35 N	96.19 W
Kauiki Head ≻	275d	20.45 N	155.59 W
Kaukauna	244	44.17 N	88.17 W
Kaukauveld ⛰[1]	224	22.00 S	20.30 E
Kaula Island I	275d	21.45 N	160.30 W
Kauliranta	160	66.27 N	23.41 E
Kaumakani	275b	21.06 N	157.02 W
Kaumalapau	275a	20.47 N	156.59 W
Kaunakakai	275a	21.06 N	157.01 W
Kaunas	160	54.54 N	23.54 E
Kaura Namoda	222	12.35 N	6.35 E
Kaustinen	160	63.32 N	23.42 E
Kauswagan	202	8.10 N	124.05 E
Kautokeino	160	69.00 N	23.02 E
Kauttua	160	61.06 N	22.10 E
Kau-ye Kyun I	200	11.01 N	98.32 E
Kavača	186	60.16 N	169.51 E
Kavacık	172	39.40 N	28.30 E
Kavadarci	172	41.26 N	22.00 E
Kavajë	172	41.11 N	19.33 E
Kavakköy	172	40.13 N	27.46 E
Kavaklıdere	172	37.26 N	28.22 E
Kavalerovo	186	44.15 N	135.04 E
Kavála	172	40.56 N	24.25 E
Kavarna	172	43.25 N	28.20 E
Kavīr, Dasht-e ⇜[2]	208	34.40 N	54.30 E
Kaw	250	36.46 N	96.50 W
Kawagama Lake ⊜	244	45.18 N	78.45 W
Kawagoe	192	35.55 N	139.29 E
Kawaguchi	192	35.48 N	139.43 E
Kawaihae Bay C	275d	20.02 N	155.50 W
Kawaihoa Point ≻	275d	21.47 N	160.12 W
Kawaikini ∧	275d	22.05 N	159.29 W
Kawailoa	275c	21.36 N	158.05 W
Kawailoa Beach	275c	21.37 N	158.05 W
Kawamata	192	37.39 N	140.36 E
Kawambwa	218	9.47 S	29.05 E
Kawanoe	192	34.01 N	133.34 E
Kawartha Park	264	44.32 N	78.12 W
Kawasaki	192	35.32 N	139.43 E
Kawatana	192	33.04 N	129.52 E
Kawau Island I	230	36.25 S	174.52 E
Kawayan	202	11.41 N	124.21 E
Kaweka ∧	230	39.17 S	176.23 E
Kaweka Range ⛰	230	39.17 S	176.19 E
Kawerau	230	38.03 S	176.43 E
Kawhia Harbour C	230	38.05 S	174.49 E
Kawich Peak ∧	258	37.58 N	116.27 W
Kawich Range ⛰	258	37.40 N	116.30 W
Kawm Umbū	220	24.28 N	32.57 E
Kawnipi Lake ⊜	244	48.24 N	91.14 W
Kawthule □[3]	200	17.30 N	97.45 E

Symbols in the index entries are identified on page 360.

Name	Page	Lat°′	Long°′
Kayah □[3]	200	19.15 N	97.30 E
Kayak Island I	236	59.52 N	144.30 W
Kayan	200	16.54 N	96.34 E
Kayangel Islands II	198	8.04 N	134.43 E
Kayapa	202	16.21 N	120.53 E
Kaya-san Λ	194	35.49 N	128.07 E
Kaycee	254	43.43 N	106.38 W
Kayes, Congo	218	4.25 S	11.41 E
Kayes, Mali	222	14.27 N	11.26 W
Kayes □[4]	222	14.00 N	11.00 W
Kaymakçı	172	38.10 N	28.08 E
Kay Point ≻	236	69.18 N	138.22 W
Kayseri	212	38.43 N	35.30 E
Kaysville	254	41.02 N	111.56 W
Kazachskaja Sovetskaja Socialističeskaja Respublika □[3]	186	48.00 N	68.00 E
Kazachskij Melkosopočnik ⛰[2]	186	49.00 N	72.00 E
Kažačinskoje	186	57.49 N	93.17 E
Kazačje	186	70.44 N	136.13 E
Kazakh Soviet Socialist Republic → Kazachskaja Sovetskaja Socialističeskaja	186	48.00 N	68.00 E
Kazalinsk	186	45.46 N	62.07 E
Kazan'	160	55.49 N	49.08 E
Kazan ≃	232	64.02 N	95.30 W
Kazandžik	208	39.16 N	55.32 E
Kazanlâk	172	42.38 N	25.21 E
Kazbek, Gora Λ	158	42.42 N	44.31 E
Kaz Dağı Λ	212	39.42 N	26.50 E
Kāzerūn	208	29.37 N	51.38 E
Kažim	160	60.20 N	51.30 E
Kazi-Magomed	208	40.03 N	48.56 E
Kazimierza Wielka	164	50.16 N	20.30 E
Kazimierz Dolny	164	51.20 N	21.58 E
Kazincbarcika	164	48.16 N	20.37 E
Kazungula	218	17.45 S	25.20 E
Kazym ≃	186	63.54 N	65.50 E
Kazymskaja Kul'tbaza	186	63.40 N	67.14 E
Kazyr ≃	186	53.47 N	92.53 E
Kazzī, Qārat Λ[2]	220	21.26 N	24.30 E
Kbely	164	50.07 N	14.32 E
Kcynia	164	53.00 N	17.30 E
Kdyně	164	49.23 N	13.02 E
Kéa	172	37.38 N	24.21 E
Kéa I	172	37.34 N	24.22 E
Keaau	275d	19.37 N	155.02 W
Keahole Point ≻	275d	19.44 N	156.03 W
Kealaikahiki Channel ⊔	275d	20.37 N	156.50 W
Kealaikahiki Point ≻	275d	20.32 N	156.42 W
Kealakekua Bay C	275d	19.28 N	155.56 W
Kealia	275b	22.06 N	159.19 W
Keams Canyon	254	35.49 N	110.12 W
Keanae	275a	20.52 N	156.09 W
Keanapapa Point ≻	275d	20.54 N	157.04 W
Keansburg	262	40.27 N	74.08 W
Kearney, Mo., U.S.	248	39.22 N	94.22 W
Kearney, Nebr., U.S.	252	40.42 N	99.05 W
Kearney, Pa., U.S.	266	40.08 N	78.12 W
Kearns	254	40.39 N	111.59 W
Kearny, Ariz., U.S.	254	33.03 N	110.55 W
Kearny, N.J., U.S.	262	40.46 N	74.09 W
Kébir, Oued el ≃	168	36.50 N	6.07 E
Kebnekaise Λ	160	67.53 N	18.33 E
Kebri Dehar	214	6.47 N	44.17 E
Kecel, Jersey	172	46.32 N	19.16 E
Kecel, Magy.	164	46.32 N	19.16 E
Kech ≃	208	26.00 N	62.44 E
Kechika ≃	236	59.36 N	127.05 W
Kecksburg	266	40.11 N	79.28 W
Kecskemét	164	46.54 N	19.42 E
Kedah □[3]	200	6.00 N	100.40 E
Kėdainiai	158	55.17 N	24.00 E
Kedgwick	240	47.39 N	67.21 W
Kédhron	172	39.13 N	22.03 E
Kediri	226	7.49 S	112.01 E
Kedon	186	64.08 N	159.14 E
Kédougou	214	12.33 N	12.11 W
Kedrasju	160	64.36 N	60.24 E
Kedvavom	160	64.15 N	53.27 E
Kędzierzyn (Heydebreck)	164	50.20 N	18.12 E
Keefers	238	50.02 N	121.33 W
Keego Harbor	268	42.37 N	83.21 W
Keele ≃	236	64.24 N	124.50 W
Keele Peak Λ	236	63.26 N	130.19 W
Keels	240	48.36 N	53.24 W
Keelung → Chilung	196	25.08 N	121.44 E
Keene, Ont., Can.	264	44.15 N	78.10 W
Keene, Calif., U.S.	274	35.13 N	118.33 W
Keene, Ky., U.S.	246	37.57 N	84.38 W
Keene, N.H., U.S.	242	42.56 N	72.17 W
Keene, Ohio, U.S.	266	40.21 N	81.52 W
Keene, Tex., U.S.	250	32.24 N	97.20 W
Keenesburg	254	40.07 N	104.31 W
Keeney Knob Λ	246	37.47 N	80.42 W
Keeper Hill Λ[2]	162	52.45 N	8.16 W
Keeseville	242	44.30 N	73.29 W
Keetmanshoop	224	26.36 S	18.08 E
Keetmanshoop □[5]	224	26.30 S	19.00 E
Keewatin, Ont., Can.	252	49.46 N	94.34 W
Keewatin, Minn., U.S.	244	47.24 N	93.05 W
Keewatin □[5]	232	65.00 N	95.00 W
Kefallinía I	172	38.15 N	20.35 E
Kéfalos	172	36.45 N	27.00 E
Kefar Sava	210	32.10 N	34.54 E
Keffi	222	8.51 N	7.52 E
Keflavík	160a	64.02 N	22.36 W
Kega	160	65.10 N	36.54 E
Ke-ga, Mui ≻	200	10.42 N	107.59 E
Kégashka, Lac ⊜	240	50.20 N	61.25 W
Kegaska	240	50.12 N	61.17 W
Keglo, Baie C	232	59.10 N	65.50 W
Keg River	232	57.48 N	117.52 W
Kehiwin Indian Reserve ◆[4]	238	54.07 N	110.48 W
Kehl	180	48.35 N	7.50 E
Kehra	160	59.20 N	25.20 E
Ke-hsi Mānsām	198	21.56 N	97.50 E
Keighley	162	53.52 N	1.54 W
Keijō → Sŏul	194	37.33 N	126.58 E
Keila	160	59.18 N	24.25 E
Keiser	248	35.41 N	90.06 W
Keith	162	57.32 N	2.57 W
Keith Arm C	236	65.20 N	122.15 W
Keithley Creek	238	52.45 N	121.24 W
Keithsburg	244	41.06 N	90.56 W
Keizer	270	44.57 N	123.01 W
Kejimkujik National Park ♠	240	44.21 N	65.18 W
Kejni, Gora Λ	236	64.30 N	174.54 W
Kejvy ⛰	160	67.35 N	38.00 E
Kekaha	275b	21.58 N	159.43 W
Kékek ≃	244	48.26 N	75.47 W
Kekertaluk Island I	232	68.10 N	66.30 W
Kékes Λ	164	47.55 N	20.02 E
Kekeshili	190	35.11 N	93.35 E
Kekexilishanmai ⛰	206	35.20 N	90.00 E
Kekurnoi, Cape ≻	236	57.44 N	155.15 W
Kelafo	214	5.40 N	44.20 E
Kelai ≃	198	2.10 N	117.29 E
Kelalihu ⊜	206	34.36 N	87.16 E
Kelamayi	190	45.37 N	84.53 E
Kelang	200	3.02 N	101.28 E
Kelantan □[3]	200	5.20 N	102.00 E
Kelantan ≃	200	6.11 N	102.15 E
Kelasa, Selat ⊔	198	2.40 S	107.15 E
Kelbia, Sebkra ⊜	170	35.51 N	10.16 E
Kelenken', Gora Λ	236	66.07 N	170.52 W
Keles	172	39.55 N	29.14 E
Keleti-főcsatorna ⩧	164	48.01 N	21.20 E
Kelheim	164	48.55 N	11.52 E
Kelibia	170	36.51 N	11.06 E
Keliyahe ≃	206	39.00 N	81.40 E
Kelkit ≃	212	40.46 N	36.32 E
Kellen	178	51.48 N	6.10 E
Keller, Va., U.S.	262	37.37 N	75.46 W
Keller, Wash., U.S.	238	48.05 N	118.41 W
Kellerberrin	226	31.38 S	117.43 E
Keller Lake ⊜	232	64.00 N	121.30 W
Kellerton	248	40.43 N	94.03 W
Kellett, Cape ≻	232	71.59 N	125.34 W
Kellettville	266	41.33 N	79.16 W
Kelleys Island	266	41.36 N	82.42 W
Kellinghusen	178	53.57 N	9.43 E
Kellogg, Idaho, U.S.	256	47.32 N	116.07 W
Kellogg, Iowa, U.S.	244	41.43 N	92.54 W
Kellogg, Minn., U.S.	244	44.18 N	91.59 W
Kelloggsville	266	41.52 N	80.36 W
Kelloselkä	160	66.56 N	28.50 E
Kelly Lake ⊜	236	65.30 N	126.10 W
Kellyville	250	35.57 N	96.13 W
Kélo	214	9.19 N	15.48 E
Kelolokan	198	1.08 N	117.54 E
Kelottijärvi	160	68.31 N	22.04 E
Kelowna	238	49.53 N	119.29 W
Kelsey Bay	238	50.24 N	125.57 W
Kelseyville	258	38.59 N	122.50 W
Kelso, Scot., U.K.	162	55.36 N	2.25 W
Kelso, Wash., U.S.	270	46.09 N	122.54 W
Keltie Inlet C	232	64.28 N	73.28 W
Keltys	248	31.22 N	94.45 W
Kelvin Seamount ⟡[3]	148	39.00 N	64.00 W
Kem'	160	64.57 N	34.36 E
Kem' ≃	160	64.57 N	34.41 E
Kemah	250	29.32 N	95.01 W
Kemalpaşa	172	38.25 N	27.26 E
Kemano	238	53.34 N	127.56 W
Kemblesville	262	39.45 N	75.50 W
Kemer	172	36.38 N	29.21 E
Kemer Barajı ◆[6]	212	37.34 N	28.31 E
Kemerovo	186	55.20 N	86.05 E
Kemi	160	65.49 N	24.32 E
Kemijärvi	160	66.40 N	27.25 E
Kemijärvi ⊜	160	66.36 N	27.24 E
Kemijoki ≃	160	65.47 N	24.30 E
Keml'a	160	54.42 N	45.15 E
Kemmerer	254	41.48 N	110.32 W
Kemnath	164	49.52 N	11.54 E
Kemp	250	32.26 N	96.14 W
Kemp, Lake ⊜[1]	250	33.45 N	99.13 W
Kempen	178	51.22 N	6.25 E
Kempen □[9]	178	51.10 N	5.20 E
Kempner	250	31.05 N	98.00 W
Kemps Bay	282	24.02 N	77.33 W
Kempsey	228	31.05 S	152.50 E
Kempston	174	52.07 N	0.30 W
Kempt, Lac ⊜	232	47.25 N	74.15 W
Kempten (Allgäu)	180	47.43 N	10.19 E
Kempton, Ill., U.S.	268	40.56 N	88.14 W
Kempton, Ind., U.S.	268	40.17 N	86.14 W
Kemptville	264	45.01 N	75.38 W
Kemul, Kong Λ	198	1.52 N	116.11 E
Ken ≃	206	25.46 N	80.31 E
Kena ≃	160	62.05 N	39.06 E
Kenadsa	214	31.48 N	2.26 W
Kenai	236	60.33 N	151.15 W
Kenai Mountains ⛰	236	60.00 N	150.00 W
Kenai Peninsula ≻[1]	236	60.10 N	150.00 W
Kenansville, Fla., U.S.	246	27.53 N	80.59 W
Kenansville, N.C., U.S.	246	34.58 N	77.58 W
Kenbridge	246	36.58 N	78.08 W
Kendal	162	54.20 N	2.45 W
Kendal, Mount Λ	230	41.22 S	172.24 E
Kendall, Fla., U.S.	246	25.41 N	80.19 W
Kendall, Mich., U.S.	268	42.22 N	85.49 W
Kendall, N.Y., U.S.	264	43.20 N	78.02 W
Kendall, Wis., U.S.	244	43.48 N	90.21 W
Kendall □[6]	268	41.38 N	88.27 W
Kendall, Cape ≻	232	63.36 N	87.09 W
Kendall Park	262	40.25 N	74.34 W
Kendallville	268	41.27 N	85.16 W
Kendari	198	3.57 S	122.35 E
Kendrick, Fla., U.S.	246	29.22 N	82.12 W
Kendrick, Idaho, U.S.	256	46.37 N	116.39 W
Kenedy	250	28.49 N	97.51 W
Kenema	222	7.52 N	11.12 W
Kenesaw	252	40.37 N	98.39 W
Kenge	218	4.52 S	16.59 E
Kēng Tung	198	21.17 N	99.36 E
Kenhardt	218	29.19 S	21.12 E
Kenhorst	262	40.18 N	75.57 W
Kenilworth, Eng., U.K.	174	52.21 N	1.34 W
Kenilworth, Pa., U.S.	262	40.14 N	75.38 W
Kenitra	214	34.16 N	6.40 W
Kenly	246	35.36 N	78.07 W
Kenmare, Eire	162	51.53 N	9.35 W
Kenmare, N. Dak., U.S.	252	48.40 N	102.05 W
Kenmore, N.Y., U.S.	264	42.58 N	78.53 W
Kenmore, Wash., U.S.	270	47.46 N	122.14 W
Kennard, Nebr., U.S.	252	41.28 N	96.12 W
Kennard, Pa., U.S.	266	41.28 N	80.20 W
Kennard, Tex., U.S.	250	31.22 N	95.11 W
Kennebec	252	43.54 N	99.52 W
Kennebec ≃	242	44.00 N	69.50 W
Kennebecasis Bay C	240	45.25 N	66.00 W
Kennebunk	242	43.23 N	70.33 W
Kennedy, Ala., U.S.	248	33.35 N	87.59 W
Kennedy, N.Y., U.S.	266	42.10 N	79.06 W
Kennedy, Cape ≻	246	28.27 N	80.32 W
Kennedy, Mount Λ, B.C., Can.	238	50.49 N	125.33 W
Kennedy, Mount Λ, Yukon, Can.	236	60.30 N	139.00 W
Kennedy Entrance ⊔	236	59.00 N	152.00 W
Kennedy Lake ⊜	238	49.05 N	125.40 W
Kennedy Peak Λ	200	23.19 N	93.45 E
Kennedyville	262	39.18 N	76.00 W
Kenner	248	29.59 N	90.15 W
Kennerdell	266	41.16 N	79.51 W
Kennetcook	240	45.11 N	63.44 W
Kennett	248	36.14 N	90.03 W
Kennett Square	262	39.51 N	75.43 W
Kennewick	256	46.12 N	119.07 W
Kenn Reefs ⟡[2]	226	21.12 S	155.46 E
Kennydale	270	47.31 N	122.12 W
Kénogami	240	48.26 N	71.14 W
Kenogami ≃	232	51.06 N	84.28 W
Kenogamissi Lake ⊜	244	48.15 N	81.31 W
Keno Hill	236	63.55 N	135.18 W
Kenora	252	49.47 N	94.29 W
Kenosha	268	42.35 N	87.49 W
Kenosha □[6]	268	42.06 N	88.04 W
Kenova	242	38.24 N	82.35 W
Kenozero, Ozero ⊜	160	62.03 N	38.14 E
Kensal	252	47.18 N	98.44 W
Kensington, P.E.I., Can.	240	46.26 N	63.38 W
Kensington, Calif., U.S.	272	37.54 N	122.16 W
Kensington, Conn., U.S.	261	41.38 N	72.46 W
Kensington, Kans., U.S.	252	39.46 N	99.02 W
Kensington, Ohio, U.S.	266	40.44 N	80.57 W
Kensington Park	246	27.22 N	82.31 W
Kent, Ala., U.S.	248	32.37 N	85.57 W
Kent, Conn., U.S.	261	41.43 N	73.29 W
Kent, N.Y., U.S.	264	43.20 N	78.08 W
Kent, Ohio, U.S.	266	41.09 N	81.22 W
Kent, Oreg., U.S.	270	45.12 N	120.42 W
Kent, Tex., U.S.	250	31.04 N	104.13 W
Kent, Wash., U.S.	270	47.23 N	122.14 W
Kent □[6], Ont., Can.	266	42.25 N	82.10 W
Kent □[6], Eng., U.K.	174	51.15 N	0.40 E
Kent □[6], Del., U.S.	262	39.10 N	75.32 W
Kent □[6], Md., U.S.	262	39.13 N	76.04 W
Kent □[6], Mich., U.S.	268	42.56 N	85.33 W
Kent □[6], R.I., U.S.	261	41.40 N	71.38 W
Kent Acres	262	39.08 N	75.31 W
Kentau	186	43.36 N	68.36 E
Kent Bay C	232	69.59 N	96.02 W
Kent Bridge	266	42.31 N	82.04 W
Kentfield	272	37.57 N	122.33 W
Kent Group II	228	39.27 S	147.20 E
Kentland	268	40.46 N	87.27 W
Kenton, Del., U.S.	262	39.14 N	75.40 W
Kenton, Mich., U.S.	244	46.28 N	88.54 W
Kenton, Ohio, U.S.	268	40.39 N	83.36 W
Kenton, Tenn., U.S.	248	36.12 N	89.01 W
Kent Peninsula ≻[1]	232	68.30 N	107.00 W
Kentucky □[3]	234	37.30 N	85.15 W
Kentucky ≃	246	38.41 N	85.11 W
Kentucky Lake ⊜[1]	248	36.25 N	88.05 W
Kentville	240	45.05 N	64.30 W
Kentwood, La., U.S.	248	30.56 N	90.31 W
Kentwood, Mich., U.S.	268	42.53 N	85.35 W
Kenwood	272	38.25 N	122.33 W
Kenya □[1]	218	1.00 N	38.00 E
Kenya, Mount Λ	218	0.10 S	37.20 E
Kenyon, Minn., U.S.	244	44.16 N	92.59 W
Kenyon, R.I., U.S.	261	41.27 N	71.38 W
Keokea	275a	20.24 N	156.21 W
Keokuk	244	40.24 N	91.24 W
Keo Neua, Col de)(	200	18.23 N	105.09 E
Keosauqua	244	40.44 N	91.58 W
Keota, Iowa, U.S.	244	41.21 N	91.57 W
Keota, Okla., U.S.	250	35.15 N	94.55 W
Kepi	198	6.34 S	139.20 E
Kępice (Hammermühle)	164	54.15 N	16.52 E
Kepina	160	65.24 N	41.50 E
Kępno	164	51.17 N	17.59 E
Keppel Bay C	228	23.21 S	150.55 E
Kepsut	172	39.41 N	28.09 E
Kerang	228	35.44 S	143.55 E
Keratéa	172	37.48 N	23.59 E
Kerava	160	60.24 N	25.07 E
Kerby	256	42.12 N	123.39 W
Kerč'	158	45.22 N	36.27 E
Kerčemja	160	61.28 N	53.50 E
Kerčevskij	160	59.55 N	56.17 E
Kerec, Mys ≻	160	65.20 N	39.40 E
Keremeos	238	49.12 N	119.50 W
Kerempe Burnu ≻	212	42.01 N	33.21 E
Keren	214	15.46 N	38.28 E
Kerens	250	32.08 N	96.14 W
Keret'	160	66.16 N	33.34 E
Keret', Ozero ⊜	160	65.55 N	32.56 E
Kerga	160	62.39 N	46.00 E
Kerguélen, Îles II	148	49.15 S	69.10 E
Kerguelen-Gaussberg Ridge ⟡[3]	148	55.00 S	75.00 E
Kericho	218	0.22 S	35.17 E
Kerintji, Gunung Λ	198	1.42 S	101.16 E
Keríon	172	37.40 N	20.48 E
Kerkenna, Îles II	214	34.44 N	11.12 E
Kerkhoven	252	45.12 N	95.19 W
Kerki, S.S.S.R.	160	63.43 N	54.05 E
Kerki	208	37.50 N	65.12 E
Kérkira (Corfu)	172	39.36 N	19.56 E
Kérkira I	172	39.40 N	19.42 E
Kerkrade, B.R.D.	164	50.52 N	6.04 E
Kerkrade, Ned.	164	50.52 N	6.04 E
Kérkyra I	172	39.40 N	19.42 E
Kermadec Ridge ⟡[3]	148	31.00 S	177.30 W
Kermadec Trench ⟡[1]	148	30.30 S	176.00 W
Kermān, Īrān	208	30.17 N	57.05 E
Kerman, Calif., U.S.	272	36.43 N	120.04 W
Kermān □[4]	208	29.00 N	57.30 E
Kermānshāh	208	34.19 N	47.04 E
Kermānshāhān □[4]	208	34.30 N	47.00 E
Kerme Körfezi C	212	36.50 N	28.00 E
Kermit	250	31.51 N	103.06 W
Kermode, Mount Λ	238	52.57 N	131.51 W
Kern □[6]	274	35.20 N	118.55 W
Kern ≃	258	35.13 N	119.17 W
Kern City	274	35.18 N	119.05 W
Kernersville	246	36.07 N	80.04 W
Kernville	258	35.43 N	118.26 W
Keros	160	60.44 N	52.50 E
Kérouané □[4]	222	9.10 N	8.50 W
Kerpe Burnu ≻	212	41.10 N	30.11 E
Kerr	266	41.03 N	78.25 W
Kerre ≃	220	5.19 N	25.40 E
Kerrera I	162	56.24 N	5.33 W
Kerrobert	232	51.55 N	109.08 W
Kerr Reservoir ⊜[1]	246	36.35 N	70.28 W
Kerrtown	266	41.38 N	80.10 W
Kerrville	250	30.03 N	99.08 W
Kerry □[6]	162	52.10 N	9.30 W
Kerry Head ≻	162	52.25 N	9.57 W
Kersey	266	41.22 N	78.36 W
Kershaw	246	34.33 N	80.35 W
Kersley	238	52.49 N	122.25 W
Kert, Oued ≃	168	35.15 N	3.15 W
Kerulen (Cherlen) (Kelulunhe) ≃	190	48.48 N	117.00 E
Kesagami Lake ⊜	232	50.23 N	80.15 W
Keşan	212	40.51 N	26.37 E
Kesennuma	192	38.54 N	141.35 E
Keshena	244	44.52 N	88.38 W
Keşiş Dağları ⛰	212	39.50 N	39.45 E
Keski-Suomen lääni □[4]	160	62.30 N	25.30 E
Keskozero	160	61.24 N	33.12 E
Keskuvejem, Gora Λ	236	66.12 N	177.40 W
Kesova Gora	160	57.35 N	37.17 E
Kesra	170	35.49 N	9.22 E
Kestel Gölü ⊜	212	37.26 N	30.28 E
Kesten'ga	160	65.55 N	31.47 E
Kestep	172	36.27 N	29.16 E
Kesteven □[8]	174	52.57 N	0.30 W
Keswick, Ont., Can.	264	44.15 N	79.28 W
Keswick, Eng., U.K.	162	54.37 N	3.08 W
Keszthely	164	46.46 N	17.15 E
Ket' ≃	186	58.55 N	81.32 E
Keta	222	5.55 N	1.00 E
Keta, Ozero ⊜	186	68.44 N	90.00 E
Keta Lagoon C	222	5.54 N	0.56 E
Ketama	168	34.50 N	4.37 W
Ketapang	198	1.52 S	109.59 E
Ketchikan	236	55.21 N	131.35 W
Ketchum	256	43.41 N	114.22 W
Kete Krachi	214	7.46 N	0.03 W
Ketoj, Ostrov I	186	47.20 N	152.28 E
Kétou	222	7.22 N	2.36 E
Kętrzyn (Rastenburg)	164	54.06 N	21.23 E
Kettering, Eng., U.K.	174	52.24 N	0.44 W
Kettering, Ohio, U.S.	242	39.41 N	84.10 W
Kettle ≃, N.A.	238	48.42 N	118.07 W
Kettle ≃, Minn., U.S.	244	45.52 N	46.45 W
Kettle Falls	256	48.36 N	118.03 W
Kettleman City	272	36.06 N	119.58 W
Kettle River Range ⛰	256	48.30 N	118.40 W
Kettlersville	268	40.22 N	84.16 W
Kettwig	178	51.22 N	6.56 E
Kęty	164	49.53 N	19.13 E
Keudepasi	200	4.18 N	95.56 E
Keudeteunom	200	4.27 N	95.48 E
Keuka Lake ⊜	242	42.27 N	77.10 W
Keukenhof ♠	164	52.16 N	4.33 E
Keuruu	160	62.16 N	24.42 E
Kevelaer	178	51.35 N	6.15 E
Kevin	256	48.45 N	111.58 W
Kew	282	21.54 N	72.02 W
Kewanee	244	41.14 N	89.56 W
Kewanna	268	41.01 N	86.25 W
Kewaunee	244	44.27 N	87.30 W
Keweenaw Bay C	244	46.56 N	88.23 W
Keweenaw Peninsula ≻[1]	244	47.12 N	88.25 W
Keweenaw Point ≻	244	47.30 N	87.50 W
Keyangkeershan Λ	206	31.20 N	87.13 E
Keya Paha ≃	252	42.54 N	99.00 W
Keyes, Calif., U.S.	272	37.33 N	120.54 W
Keyes, Okla., U.S.	250	36.49 N	102.15 W
Keyhole Reservoir ⊜[1]	252	44.21 N	104.51 W
Key Largo	246	25.04 N	80.28 W
Key Largo I	246	25.16 N	80.19 W
Keynsham	174	51.26 N	2.30 W
Keyport	270	47.42 N	122.38 W
Keystone, Ind., U.S.	268	40.36 N	85.16 W
Keystone, Iowa, U.S.	244	42.00 N	92.12 W
Keystone, S. Dak., U.S.	252	43.54 N	103.25 W
Keystone, W. Va., U.S.	246	37.25 N	81.27 W
Keystone Heights	246	29.47 N	82.01 W
Keystone Peak Λ	254	31.53 N	111.13 W
Keystone Reservoir ⊜[1]	250	36.15 N	96.25 W
Keysville	246	37.04 N	78.29 W
Keytesville	248	39.26 N	92.56 W
Key West	246	24.33 N	81.48 W
Kez	160	57.53 N	53.43 E
Kežma	186	58.59 N	101.09 E
Kežmarok	164	49.08 N	20.25 E
Kgalagadi □[5]	224	25.00 S	22.00 E
Kgatleng □[5]	224	24.28 S	26.05 E
Kgun Lake ⊜	236	61.32 N	163.45 W
Khābūr, Nahr al- ≃	212	35.08 N	40.26 E
Khadari, Wādī al- ∨	220	10.29 N	26.15 E
Khadaungnge Taung Λ	200	18.57 N	94.37 E
Khadi	204	18.34 N	73.52 E
Khadra	168	36.15 N	0.35 E
Khairpur	206	27.32 N	68.46 E
Kha Khaeng ≃	200	14.55 N	99.10 E
Khakhea	218	24.51 S	23.20 E
Khālidī, Khirbat al- ⊥	210	29.39 N	35.14 E
Khálki I	212	36.17 N	27.35 E
Khalkidhikí □[5]	172	40.25 N	23.27 E
Khalkidhikí □[9]	172	40.25 N	23.27 E
Khalkís	172	38.28 N	23.36 E
Khan ≃	224	22.37 S	14.56 E
Khānābād	206	36.41 N	69.05 E
Khānaqīn	208	34.21 N	45.22 E
Khandwa	206	21.50 N	76.20 E
Khānewāl	206	30.18 N	71.56 E
Khanh-hung	200	9.36 N	105.58 E
Khaniá	172	35.31 N	24.02 E
Khaníon, Kólpos C	172	35.34 N	23.48 E
Khānpur	204	28.39 N	70.39 E
Khanty-Mansiysk → Chanty-Mansijsk	186	61.00 N	69.06 E
Khān Yūnis	210	31.21 N	34.19 E
Kharagpur	206	22.20 N	87.19 E
Kharāyij, Sabkhat al- ⊜	212	35.40 N	37.20 E
Kharīṭ, Wādī al- ∨	220	24.26 N	33.03 E
Khārk, Jazīreh-ye I	208	29.15 N	50.20 E
Kharkov → Char'kov	158	50.00 N	36.15 E
Khartoum → Al-Khurṭūm	220	15.36 N	32.32 E
Khartoum North → Al-Khurṭūm Baḥrī	220	15.38 N	32.33 E
Khāsh ≃	208	31.15 N	62.05 E
Khash Desert ◆[2]	208	31.40 N	62.25 E
Khashm al-Qirbah	220	14.58 N	35.55 E
Khashm al-Qirbah, Khazzān ⊜[1]	220	14.40 N	35.55 E
Khasi Hills ⛰[2]	204	25.45 N	91.30 E
Khaskovo → Haskovo	172	41.56 N	25.33 E
Khaybar	208	25.42 N	39.31 E
Khaybar, Ḥarrat ⩮[9]	208	25.30 N	39.45 E
Khayung ≃	200	15.14 N	104.50 E
Khemis el Khechna	168	36.39 N	3.20 E
Khemis Miliana	168	36.16 N	2.13 E
Kherrata	168	36.31 N	5.26 E
Khersan ≃	208	31.33 N	50.22 E
Kherson → Cherson	158	46.38 N	32.35 E
Khíos	172	38.22 N	26.08 E
Khíos I	172	38.22 N	26.00 E
Khiva → Chiva	186	41.24 N	60.22 E
Khoai, Hon I	200	8.26 N	104.48 E
Khomas Highland ⛰[1]	224	22.30 S	16.30 E
Khong	200	14.07 N	105.51 E
Khong Sédone	200	15.34 N	105.49 E
Khon Kaen	200	16.26 N	102.50 E
Khóra	172	37.04 N	21.43 E
Khorāsān □[4]	208	35.00 N	58.00 E
Khóra Sfakíon	172	35.12 N	24.09 E
Khorramābād	208	33.30 N	48.20 E
Khorramshahr	208	30.25 N	48.11 E
Khouribga	214	32.54 N	6.57 W
Khrisokhoús, Kólpos C	212	35.05 N	32.20 E
Khrisoúpolis	172	40.58 N	24.42 E
Khuff ⊤[4]	208	24.57 N	44.42 E
Khulna	206	22.48 N	89.33 E
Khun Tan, Doi Λ	200	18.30 N	99.20 E
Khūryān Mūryān II	204	17.30 N	56.00 E
Khuzdār	204	27.48 N	66.37 E
Khūzestān □[4]	208	31.00 N	49.00 E
Khvoy	208	38.33 N	44.58 E
Khwae Noi ≃	200	14.00 N	99.33 E
Khwāja Muhammad, Koh-i- ⛰	206	36.00 N	70.00 E
Khyber Pass)(	206	34.05 N	71.10 E
Kiamba	202	5.59 N	124.37 E
Kiamichi ≃	250	33.57 N	95.14 W
Kiana	236	66.59 N	160.25 W
Kiangarow, Mount Λ	228	26.49 S	151.33 E
Kiangsi → Jiangxi □[4]	196	28.00 N	116.00 E
Kiangsu → Jiangsu □[4]	190	33.00 N	120.00 E
Kiantajärvi ⊜	160	65.03 N	29.07 E
Kibangou	218	3.27 S	12.21 E
Kibāsī	208	30.34 N	47.50 E
Kibawe	202	7.34 N	125.00 E
Kibbie	268	42.25 N	86.12 W
Kibombo	218	3.54 S	25.55 E
Kibondo	218	3.35 S	30.42 E
Kibre Mengist	214	5.52 N	39.00 E
Kičevo	172	41.31 N	20.57 E
Kichčik	186	53.24 N	156.03 E
Kickapoo ≃	244	43.05 N	90.53 W
Kicking Horse Pass)(	238	51.27 N	116.18 W
Kičmengskij Gorodok	160	59.59 N	45.48 E
Kidal	214	18.26 N	1.24 E
Kidapawan	202	7.01 N	125.03 E
Kidderminster	174	52.23 N	2.14 W
Kidira	214	14.28 N	12.13 W
Kidnappers, Cape ≻	230	39.39 S	177.05 E
Kidron	266	40.44 N	81.45 W
Kidsgrove	174	53.06 N	2.15 W
Kidwelly	162	51.45 N	4.18 W
Kiefersfelden	164	47.37 N	12.11 E
Kiel, B.R.D.	164	54.20 N	10.08 E
Kiel, Wis., U.S.	244	43.55 N	88.02 W
Kiel Canal → Nord-Ostsee-Kanal ⩧	164	53.53 N	9.08 E
Kielce	164	50.52 N	20.37 E
Kieler Bucht C	164	54.35 N	10.35 E
Kierspe	178	51.08 N	7.35 E
Kiester	244	43.32 N	93.42 W
Kietrz (Katscher)	164	50.05 N	18.01 E
Kiev → Kijev	158	50.26 N	30.31 E
Kiffa	214	16.37 N	11.24 W
Kifisiá	172	38.04 N	23.48 E
Kigali	218	1.57 S	30.04 E
Kigoma	218	4.52 S	29.38 E
Kigun, Cape ≻	236	52.00 N	175.21 W
Kihei	275a	20.47 N	156.28 W
Kihniö	160	62.12 N	23.11 E
Kiholo Bay C	275d	19.52 N	155.56 W
Kii-hantō ≻[1]	192	34.00 N	135.45 E
Kii-sanchi ⛰	192	34.00 N	135.50 E
Kii-suidō ⊔	192	33.55 N	134.55 E
Kijev	158	50.26 N	30.31 E
Kijkašor	160	60.46 N	49.24 E
Kikai-shima I	193b	28.19 N	129.59 E
Kikerk Lake ⊜	232	67.20 N	113.20 W
Kikinda	172	45.50 N	20.28 E
Kikládhes II	172	37.30 N	25.00 E
Kikori	198	7.35 S	144.16 E
Kikuchi	192	32.59 N	130.45 E
Kikwit	218	5.02 S	18.49 E
Kil	160	59.30 N	13.19 E
Kilambé, Cerro Λ	280	13.36 N	85.39 W
Kilauea	275b	22.13 N	159.25 W
Kilauea Crater ⩮[6]	275d	19.25 N	155.17 W
Kilauea Point ≻	275d	22.14 N	159.24 W
Kilbourne	266	40.20 N	82.58 W
Kilbrannan Sound ⊔	162	55.40 N	5.25 W
Kilbuck Mountains ⛰	236	60.30 N	159.45 W
Kilchberg	180	47.19 N	8.33 E
Kilcoy	226	26.57 S	152.33 E
Kildare (Saint-Ambroise-de-Kildare), Qué., Can.	260	46.05 N	73.32 W
Kildare, Eire	162	53.10 N	6.55 W
Kildare □[6]	162	53.15 N	6.45 W
Kildare, Cape ≻	240	46.52 N	63.58 W
Kil'dinstroj	160	68.48 N	33.06 E
Kildonan	238	49.00 N	125.00 W
Kilgard	270	49.03 N	122.12 W
Kilgore, Ohio, U.S.	266	40.28 N	81.00 W
Kilgore, Tex., U.S.	248	32.23 N	94.53 W
Kilimanjaro Λ	218	3.04 S	37.22 E
Kılınç	172	40.38 N	29.23 E
Kılınç Tepesi Λ	212	40.32 N	38.10 E
Kilindoni	218	7.55 S	39.39 E
Kilingi-Nõmme	160	58.09 N	24.58 E
Kilis	212	36.44 N	37.05 E
Kilkee	162	52.41 N	9.38 W
Kilkenny	162	52.39 N	7.15 W
Kilkenny □[6]	162	52.40 N	7.20 W
Kilkieran Bay C	162	53.15 N	9.45 W
Kilkís	172	41.00 N	22.53 E
Killala	162	54.13 N	9.13 W
Killala Bay C	162	54.15 N	9.10 W
Killaloe	162	52.48 N	8.27 W
Killaloe Station	244	45.33 N	77.25 W
Killam	238	52.47 N	111.51 W
Killarney, Man., Can.	252	49.12 N	99.42 W
Killarney, Ont., Can.	244	45.58 N	81.31 W
Killarney, Eire	162	52.03 N	9.30 W
Killarney, Lakes of ⊜	162	52.01 N	9.30 W
Kill Buck, N.Y., U.S.	266	42.10 N	78.41 W
Killbuck, Ohio, U.S.	266	40.30 N	81.59 W
Killdeer	252	47.22 N	102.45 W
Killeen	250	31.08 N	97.44 W
Killen	248	34.52 N	87.32 W
Killian	246	34.08 N	80.57 W
Killik ≃	236	69.00 N	153.58 W
Killington Mountain Λ	242	43.36 N	72.49 W
Killingworth	261	41.21 N	72.30 W
Killíni	172	37.55 N	21.09 E
Killíni Λ	172	37.57 N	22.23 E
Killorglin	162	52.06 N	9.47 W
Killybegs	162	54.38 N	8.27 W
Kilmarnock, Scot., U.K.	162	55.36 N	4.30 W
Kilmarnock, Va., U.S.	262	37.43 N	76.23 W
Kil'mez'	160	57.01 N	51.22 E
Kilmichael	248	33.27 N	89.34 W
Kilombero ≃	218	8.31 S	37.22 E
Kilómetro Cincuenta	278	19.45 N	88.45 W
Kilomines	218	1.48 N	30.14 E
Kilosa	218	6.50 S	36.59 E
Kilpisjärvi	160	69.03 N	20.48 E
Kilrush	162	52.39 N	9.30 W
Kilwa	218	9.18 S	28.25 E
Kilwa Kisiwani	218	8.58 S	39.30 E
Kilwa Kivinje	218	8.45 S	39.24 E
Kim	252	37.15 N	103.21 W
Kim ≃	214	5.28 N	11.07 E
Kimba	228	33.09 S	136.25 E
Kimball, Minn., U.S.	244	45.19 N	94.18 W
Kimball, Nebr., U.S.	252	41.14 N	103.40 W
Kimball, S. Dak., U.S.	252	43.45 N	98.57 W
Kimball, Mount Λ	236	63.14 N	144.39 W
Kimberley, B.C., Can.	238	49.41 N	115.59 W
Kimberley, S. Afr.	224	28.43 S	24.46 E
Kimberley Plateau ⛰[1]	226	17.00 S	127.00 E
Kimberly, Idaho, U.S.	256	42.32 N	114.22 W
Kimberly, Wis., U.S.	244	44.17 N	88.20 W
Kimberton	262	40.08 N	75.34 W
Kimbolton	266	40.09 N	81.34 W
Kimch'aek (Sŏngjin)	194	40.41 N	129.12 E
Kimch'ŏn	194	36.07 N	128.05 E
Kimenola Wash ∨	254	36.07 N	108.11 W
Kími	172	38.37 N	24.06 E
Kimito (Kemiö)	160	60.10 N	22.45 E
Kimiwan Lake ⊜	238	55.45 N	116.54 W
Kimmell	268	41.24 N	85.33 W
Kimovsk	158	53.58 N	38.32 E
Kimpō-zan Λ	192	35.53 N	138.38 E
Kimry	160	56.52 N	37.21 E
Kimsquit	238	52.49 N	126.58 W
Kinabalian, Mount Λ	202	8.15 N	125.25 E
Kinabatangan ≃	202	5.42 N	118.23 E
Kinangaly Λ	225b	19.12 S	45.40 E
Kinapusan Island I	202	5.07 N	120.40 E
Kínaros I	212	36.59 N	26.17 E
Kinbasket Lake ⊜	238	51.58 N	118.03 W
Kincaid	248	39.35 N	89.25 W
Kincaid, Lake ⊜[1]	248	39.35 N	89.30 W
Kincardine	244	44.11 N	81.38 W
Kincardine □[6]	162	56.56 N	2.28 W
Kincolith	238	55.00 N	129.57 W
Kindberg	164	47.31 N	15.27 E
Kinde	244	43.56 N	83.00 W
Kinder	248	30.29 N	92.51 W
Kinderhook, Mich., U.S.	268	41.48 N	85.00 W
Kinderhook, N.Y., U.S.	261	42.24 N	73.42 W
Kindersley	232	51.27 N	109.10 W
Kindia	222	10.04 N	12.51 W
Kindia □[4]	222	10.00 N	12.45 W
Kindred	252	46.39 N	97.01 W
Kindu-Port-Empain	218	2.57 S	25.56 E
Kinel'	160	53.14 N	50.39 E
Kineo, Mount Λ	242	45.42 N	69.44 W
Kinešma	160	57.26 N	42.09 E
King	246	36.17 N	80.22 W
King □[6]	270	47.26 N	121.48 W
King, Mount Λ	228	25.10 S	147.31 E
King and Queen □[6]	262	37.42 N	76.50 W
King and Queen Court House	262	37.40 N	76.53 W
Kingaroy	228	26.33 S	151.50 E
King City, Ont., Can.	264	43.56 N	79.32 W
King City, Calif., U.S.	272	36.13 N	121.08 W
King City, Mo., U.S.	248	40.03 N	94.31 W
Kingcome Inlet C	238	50.50 N	126.10 W
King Cove	236	55.04 N	162.19 W
Kingersheim	180	47.48 N	7.20 E
King Ferry	264	42.40 N	76.37 W
Kingfield	242	44.57 N	70.09 W
Kingfisher	250	35.52 N	97.56 W
King George	262	38.16 N	77.11 W
King George □[6]	262	38.15 N	77.10 W
King George, Mount Λ	238	50.35 N	115.24 W
King George Islands II	232	57.20 N	78.25 W
King Hill	256	43.00 N	115.12 W
King Island I, Austl.	228	39.50 S	144.00 E
King Island I, B.C., Can.	238	52.12 N	127.42 W
King Island I, Alaska, U.S.	236	64.58 N	168.05 W
Kingissepp	160	58.15 N	22.28 E
King Lake National Park ♠	228	37.35 S	145.25 E
King Lear Peak Λ	258	41.12 N	118.34 W
King Leopold Ranges ⛰	226	17.30 S	125.45 E
Kingman, Ariz., U.S.	254	35.12 N	114.04 W
Kingman, Kans., U.S.	252	37.39 N	98.07 W
Kingman, Maine, U.S.	242	45.33 N	68.12 W
King Mountain Λ, B.C., Can.	236	58.17 N	128.54 W
King Mountain Λ, Oreg., U.S.	256	42.42 N	123.14 W
King Mountain Λ, Oreg., U.S.	256	43.49 N	118.52 W
King of Prussia	262	40.05 N	75.23 W
Kings □[6], Calif., U.S.	272	36.20 N	119.39 W
Kings □[6], N.Y., U.S.	262	40.42 N	74.00 W
Kings ≃, Ark., U.S.	248	36.29 N	93.35 W
Kings ≃, Calif., U.S.	258	36.03 N	119.49 W
Kings ≃, Nev., U.S.	258	41.31 N	118.08 W
King Salmon	236	58.14 N	157.24 W
King Salmon ≃	236	58.15 N	157.30 W
Kings Beach	272	39.14 N	120.01 W
Kingsbridge	162	50.17 N	3.46 W
Kingsburg	272	36.31 N	119.33 W
Kingsbury	268	41.31 N	86.42 W
Kings Canyon National Park ♠	258	36.48 N	118.30 W
Kingsford	244	45.48 N	88.04 W
Kingsford Heights	268	41.29 N	86.42 W
Kingsgate	238	49.00 N	116.11 W
Kingshill	285n	17.44 N	64.48 W
Kingsland, Ark., U.S.	248	33.52 N	92.18 W
Kingsland, Ga., U.S.	246	30.48 N	81.41 W
Kingsland, Va., U.S.	262	37.24 N	77.26 W
Kingsley, Iowa, U.S.	252	42.35 N	95.58 W
Kingsley, Mich., U.S.	244	44.35 N	85.32 W
King's Lynn	174	52.45 N	0.24 E
Kings Mountain	246	35.15 N	81.20 W
Kings Mountain National Military Park ♠	246	35.07 N	81.33 W
King Solomon's Mines ⊥	210	29.45 N	34.56 E
Kings Park	261	40.53 N	73.16 W
Kings Peak Λ, Calif., U.S.	258	40.10 N	124.08 W
Kings Peak Λ, Utah, U.S.	254	40.46 N	110.22 W
King's Point	240	49.35 N	56.11 W
Kingsport	246	36.32 N	82.33 W
Kingston, Austl.	226	36.50 S	139.51 E
Kingston, N.S., Can.	240	44.59 N	64.57 W
Kingston, Ont., Can.	264	44.14 N	76.30 W
Kingston, Jam.	285q	18.00 N	76.50 W
Kingston, Ga., U.S.	246	34.15 N	84.57 W
Kingston, Ill., U.S.	268	42.06 N	88.46 W
Kingston, Mass., U.S.	261	41.59 N	70.43 W
Kingston, Mo., U.S.	248	39.39 N	94.02 W
Kingston, N.Y., U.S.	261	41.56 N	74.00 W
Kingston, Ohio, U.S.	242	39.28 N	82.55 W
Kingston, Okla., U.S.	250	34.00 N	96.43 W
Kingston, Pa., U.S.	242	41.16 N	75.54 W
Kingston, R.I., U.S.	261	41.29 N	71.31 W
Kingston, Tenn., U.S.	246	35.52 N	84.31 W
Kingston, Wash., U.S.	270	47.48 N	122.30 W
Kingston ◆[8]	174	51.25 N	0.19 W
Kingston Mills	264	44.17 N	76.27 W
Kingston upon Hull	162	53.45 N	0.20 W
Kingstown	285h	13.09 N	61.14 W
Kingstree	246	33.40 N	79.50 W
Kings Valley	256	44.42 N	123.26 W
Kingsville, Ont., Can.	266	42.02 N	82.45 W
Kingsville, Ohio, U.S.	266	41.53 N	80.41 W
Kingsville, Tex., U.S.	250	27.31 N	97.52 W
Kingswood	174	51.27 N	2.22 W
Kingtechen → Jingdezhen	196	29.16 N	117.11 E
King William	262	37.41 N	77.01 W
King William □[6]	262	37.42 N	77.05 W
King William Island I	232	69.00 N	97.30 W
King William's Town	224	32.51 S	27.22 E
Kingwood	242	39.28 N	79.41 W
Kinhwa → Jinhua	196	29.07 N	119.39 E
Kınık	172	39.05 N	27.23 E
Kinkony, Lac ⊜	225b	16.08 S	45.50 E
Kinmount	264	44.47 N	78.39 W
Kinmundy	248	38.46 N	88.51 W
Kinna	160	57.30 N	12.41 E
Kinnaird	238	49.17 N	117.39 W
Kinnairds Head Of	162	57.42 N	2.00 W
Kinneret, Yam ⊜	210	32.49 N	35.36 E
Kino ≃	192	34.13 N	135.09 E
Kino, Bahía C	278	28.48 N	112.00 W
Kinogitan	202	8.59 N	124.48 E
Kinojevis ≃	244	47.55 N	78.40 W
Kinosaki	192	35.37 N	134.49 E
Kinpoku-san Λ	192	38.05 N	138.22 E
Kinross	162	56.13 N	3.27 W
Kinross □[6]	162	56.10 N	3.30 W
Kinsale, Eire	162	51.42 N	8.32 W
Kinsale, Va., U.S.	262	38.02 N	76.35 W
Kinsarvik	160	60.23 N	6.43 E
Kinsey	256	46.34 N	105.40 W
Kinshasa (Léopoldville)	218	4.18 S	15.18 E
Kinsley	252	37.55 N	99.25 W
Kinsman, Ill., U.S.	268	41.11 N	88.34 W
Kinsman, Ohio, U.S.	266	41.27 N	80.36 W
Kinston	246	35.16 N	77.35 W
Kintyre ≻[1]	162	55.32 N	5.35 W
Kinuseo Falls ⌊	238	54.47 N	121.12 W
Kinuso	238	55.20 N	115.25 W
Kinyeti Λ	214	4.50 N	31.00 E
Kinzua	256	44.59 N	120.03 W
Kioshkokwi Lake ⊜	244	46.05 N	78.52 W
Kiowa, Colo., U.S.	252	39.21 N	104.28 W
Kiowa, Kans., U.S.	252	37.01 N	98.29 W
Kiowa, Okla., U.S.	250	34.43 N	95.54 W
Kiparissía	172	37.14 N	21.40 E
Kiparissiakós Kólpos C	172	37.37 N	21.24 E
Kipawa ≃	244	47.03 N	79.23 W
Kipawa, Lac ⊜	244	46.55 N	79.00 W
Kipembawe	218	7.39 S	33.24 E
Kipengere Range ⛰	218	9.10 S	34.15 E
Kipijevo	160	65.40 N	54.23 E
Kipili	218	7.26 S	30.36 E
Kipini	218	2.32 S	40.31 E
Kipnuk	236	59.56 N	164.03 W
Kipton	266	41.16 N	82.18 W
Kipushi	218	11.46 N	27.14 E
Kir'a	160	55.04 N	46.53 E
Kiraz	172	38.13 N	28.13 E
Kirazlı	172	40.02 N	26.41 E
Kirbyville	248	30.40 N	93.54 W
Kırcasalih	172	41.23 N	26.48 E
Kirchbach in Steiermark	164	46.54 N	15.44 E
Kirchberg	164	49.12 N	9.58 E
Kirchdorf an der Krems	164	47.56 N	14.14 E
Kirchheim	164	48.10 N	10.30 E
Kirchheimbolanden	164	49.40 N	8.00 E
Kirchheim unter Teck	180	48.39 N	9.27 E
Kirchhellen	178	51.36 N	6.55 E
Kirchhundem	178	51.05 N	8.05 E
Kirchmöser	164	52.22 N	12.25 E
Kirchschlag in der Buckligen Welt	164	47.31 N	16.18 E
Kirchwerder ◆[8]	178	53.25 N	10.11 E
Kirchweyhe	178	52.59 N	8.52 E
Kireç	172	39.33 N	28.22 E
Kirenga ≃	186	57.47 N	108.07 E
Kirensk	186	57.46 N	108.08 E
Kirghiz Soviet Socialist Republic → Kirgizskaja Sovetskaja Socialističeskaja	186	41.30 N	75.00 E
Kirgizskaja Sovetskaja Socialističeskaja Respublika □[3]	186	41.30 N	75.00 E
Kirgizskij Chrebet ⛰	186	42.30 N	74.00 E
Kiri	218	1.27 S	19.00 E
Kırıkhan	212	36.32 N	36.19 E
Kırıkkale	212	39.50 N	33.31 E
Kirillov	160	59.52 N	38.23 E
Kirillovo	160	57.07 N	45.27 E
Kirin → Jilin	190	43.51 N	126.33 E
Kirin → Jilin □[4]	190	44.00 N	126.00 E
Kirishima-yaku-kokuritsu-kōen ♠, Nihon	192	31.55 N	130.51 E
Kirishima-yaku-kokuritsu-kōen ♠, Nihon	193b	31.12 N	130.31 E
Kirishima-yama Λ	192	31.56 N	130.52 E
Kiriši	160	59.27 N	32.02 E
Kırkağaç	172	39.06 N	27.40 E
Kirkby in Ashfield	174	53.06 N	1.15 W
Kirkcaldy	162	56.07 N	3.10 W
Kirkcudbright	162	54.50 N	4.03 W
Kirkcudbright □[6]	162	55.02 N	4.05 W
Kirkee → Khadki	204	18.34 N	73.52 E
Kirkenes	160	69.40 N	30.03 E
Kirkjubæjarklaustur	160a	63.47 N	18.04 W
Kirkland, Ill., U.S.	268	42.06 N	88.51 W
Kirkland, Tex., U.S.	250	34.23 N	100.04 W
Kirkland, Wash., U.S.	270	47.41 N	122.12 W
Kirkland Lake	244	48.09 N	80.02 W
Kırklareli	212	41.44 N	27.12 E
Kırklareli □[4]	172	41.40 N	27.30 E
Kirklin	248	40.12 N	86.22 W
Kirkliston Range ⛰	230	44.30 S	170.32 E

Symbols in the index entries are identified on page 360.

Name	Page	Lat°′	Long°′
Kirkpatrick, Mount ∧	148	84.20 S	166.19 E
Kirkpatrick Lake ◎	238	51.52 N	111.18 W
Kirksville	248	40.12 N	92.35 W
Kirkūk	208	35.28 N	44.28 E
Kirkūk □[4]	208	35.00 N	44.35 E
Kirkville	264	43.05 N	75.57 W
Kirkwall	162	58.59 N	2.58 W
Kirkwood, S. Afr.	218	33.24 S	25.26 E
Kirkwood, Del., U.S.	262	39.34 N	75.42 W
Kirkwood, Ill., U.S.	244	40.52 N	90.45 W
Kirkwood, Mo., U.S.	248	38.35 N	90.24 W
Kirn	164	49.47 N	7.28 E
Kirov	160	58.38 N	49.42 E
Kirova, Zaliv C	208	39.09 N	49.03 E
Kirovabad	208	40.40 N	46.22 E
Kirovakan	158	40.48 N	44.30 E
Kirovgrad	158	57.26 N	60.04 E
Kirovo-Čepeck	160	58.33 N	50.01 E
Kirovograd	158	48.30 N	32.18 E
Kirovograd □[4]	172	48.10 N	30.20 E
Kirovsk, S.S.S.R.	160	67.37 N	33.35 E
Kirovsk, S.S.S.R.	160	59.52 N	31.00 E
Kirovsk, S.S.S.R.	186	37.42 N	60.23 E
Kirovskij, S.S.S.R.	186	54.18 N	155.47 E
Kirovskij, S.S.S.R.	186	44.52 N	78.12 E
Kirriemuir	162	56.41 N	3.01 W
Kirs	160	59.21 N	52.14 E
Kirsanov	158	52.38 N	42.43 E
Kırşehir	212	39.09 N	34.10 E
Kīrthar Range ⋀	206	27.00 N	67.10 E
Kirtland, N. Mex., U.S.	254	36.44 N	108.21 W
Kirtland, Ohio, U.S.	266	41.34 N	81.18 W
Kirtland Hills	266	41.37 N	81.24 W
Kiruna	160	67.51 N	20.16 E
Kirwin	252	39.40 N	99.07 W
Kirwin Reservoir ◎[1]	252	39.39 N	99.50 W
Kiryū	192	36.24 N	139.20 E
Kiržač	160	56.09 N	38.52 E
Kisa	160	57.59 N	15.37 E
Kisakata	192	39.13 N	139.54 E
Kisangani (Stanleyville)	218	0.30 N	25.12 E
Kisar, Pulau I	198	8.05 S	127.10 E
Kisaralik ≃	236	60.51 N	161.16 W
Kisarazu	192	35.23 N	139.55 E
Kisbér	164	47.30 N	18.02 E
Kisbey	252	49.38 N	102.41 W
Kisel'ovsk	186	54.00 N	86.39 E
Kishb, Ḥarrat al- •[9]	208	23.00 N	41.25 E
Kishinev → Kišin'ov	158	47.00 N	28.50 E
Kishiwada	192	34.28 N	135.22 E
Kishwaukee ≃	244	42.11 N	89.08 W
Kisii	218	0.41 S	34.46 E
Kišin'ov	158	47.00 N	28.50 E
Kiska Island I	237a	52.00 N	178.30 E
Kiskatinaw ≃	238	56.06 N	120.08 W
Kiska Volcano ∧[1]	237a	52.07 N	177.36 E
Kiskőrös	164	46.38 N	19.17 E
Kiskunfélegyháza	164	46.43 N	19.52 E
Kiskunhalas	164	46.26 N	19.30 E
Kiskunmajsa	164	46.30 N	19.45 E
Kislovodsk	158	43.55 N	42.44 E
Kismayu	218	0.23 S	42.30 E
Kiso ≃	192	35.02 N	136.45 E
Kiso-sammyaku ⋀	192	35.43 N	137.50 E
Kispal ∨	170	47.30 N	17.15 E
Kispiox	238	55.21 N	127.41 W
Kispiox ≃	238	55.16 N	127.41 W
Kispiox Mountain ∧	238	55.25 N	127.57 W
Kissidougou	214	9.11 N	10.06 W
Kissidougou □[4]	222	9.15 N	9.55 W
Kissimmee	246	28.18 N	81.24 W
Kissimmee ≃	246	27.10 N	80.53 W
Kissimmee, Lake ◎	246	27.55 N	81.16 W
Kississing Lake ◎	232	55.10 N	101.20 W
Kissū, Jabal ∧	220	21.35 N	25.09 E
Kistanje	170	43.59 N	15.58 E
Kistler	266	40.22 N	77.51 W
Kisújszállás	164	47.13 N	20.46 E
Kisuki	192	35.17 N	132.54 E
Kisumu	218	0.06 S	34.45 E
Kisvárda	164	48.13 N	22.05 E
Kita	214	13.03 N	9.29 W
Kita-daitō-jima I	190	25.57 N	131.18 E
Kitaibaraki	192	36.48 N	140.45 E
Kitakami	192	39.18 N	141.07 E
Kitakami ≃	192	38.25 N	141.19 E
Kitakami-sanchi ⋀	192	39.30 N	141.30 E
Kitakata	192	37.39 N	139.52 E
Kitakyūshū	192	33.53 N	130.50 E
Kitale	218	1.01 N	35.00 E
Kitami	192a	43.48 N	143.54 E
Kitami-sanchi ⋀	192a	44.22 N	142.43 E
Kit Carson, Calif., U.S.	272	38.41 N	120.07 W
Kit Carson, Colo., U.S.	252	38.46 N	102.48 W
Kitchener	264	43.27 N	80.29 W
Kitega → Gitega	218	3.26 S	29.56 E
Kíthira	172	36.09 N	23.00 E
Kíthira I	172	36.20 N	22.58 E
Kíthnos	172	37.26 N	24.26 E
Kíthnos I	172	37.25 N	24.28 E
Kitimat	238	54.03 N	128.33 W
Kitimat ≃	238	54.06 N	128.38 W
Kitimat Ranges ⋀	238	53.30 N	128.50 W
Kitinen ≃	160	67.08 N	27.29 E
Kitíou, Akrotírion ≻	212	34.48 N	33.37 E
Kitlope ≃	238	53.10 N	127.45 W
Kitlope Lake ◎	238	53.07 N	127.47 W
Kitsap □[6]	270	47.41 N	122.44 W
Kitsuki	192	33.25 N	131.37 E
Kittanning	266	40.49 N	79.32 W
Kittery	242	43.05 N	70.45 W
Kittery Point	242	43.05 N	70.41 W
Kittilä	160	67.40 N	24.54 E
Kittitas	256	46.59 N	120.25 W
Kittitas □[6]	270	47.13 N	121.01 W
Kitui	218	1.22 S	38.01 E
Kitwanga	238	55.06 N	128.03 W
Kitwangar Indian Reserve ◆[4]	238	55.06 N	128.04 W
Kitwe	218	12.49 S	28.13 E
Kitzbühel	164	47.27 N	12.23 E
Kitzbühler Alpen ⋀	164	47.20 N	12.20 E
Kitzingen	164	49.44 N	10.09 E
Kiukiang → Jiujiang	196	29.44 N	115.59 E
Kiuruvesi	160	63.39 N	26.37 E
Kivač, Vodopad ↳	160	62.16 N	33.59 E
Kivak	236	64.16 N	172.57 W
Kivalina	236	67.59 N	164.33 W
Kiviõli	160	59.21 N	26.57 E
Kivu, Lac ◎	218	2.00 S	29.10 E
Kiwalik	236	66.02 N	161.50 W
Kiwanis Lake	266	41.28 N	81.09 W
Kizel	158	59.03 N	57.40 E
Kizil ≃, Tür.	212	39.30 N	36.15 E
Kızıl ≃, Tür.	212	41.44 N	35.58 E
Kızıl Adalar II	212	40.52 N	29.05 E
Kızılcabölük	172	37.37 N	29.01 E
Kızıldağ ∧	212	36.25 N	32.42 E
Kızılhisar	172	37.33 N	29.18 E
Kızkalesi ⊥	212	36.28 N	34.04 E
Kizl'ar	158	43.50 N	46.40 E
Kiz'oma	160	61.08 N	44.50 E
Kizyl-Arvat	208	38.58 N	56.15 E
Kizyl-Atrek	158	37.36 N	54.46 E
Kjustendil	172	42.17 N	22.41 E
Klabat, Gunung ∧	198	1.28 N	125.02 E
Kladanj	172	44.13 N	18.41 E
Kladno	164	50.08 N	14.05 E
Kladovo	172	44.37 N	22.37 E
Klagan	202	5.59 N	117.26 E
Klagenfurt	164	46.38 N	14.18 E
Klagetoh	254	35.30 N	109.32 W
Klahoose Indian Reserve ◆[4]	238	50.31 N	124.19 W
Klaipėda (Memel)	160	55.43 N	21.07 E
Klamath	258	41.32 N	124.02 W
Klamath ≃	258	41.33 N	124.04 W
Klamath Falls	256	42.13 N	121.46 W
Klamath Marsh ☷	256	42.54 N	121.44 W
Klamath Mountains ⋀	258	41.40 N	123.20 W
Klang → Kelang, Malay.	200	3.02 N	101.28 E
Klarälven ≃	158	59.23 N	13.32 E
Klatovy	164	49.24 N	13.18 E
Klatt Road	236	61.05 N	149.48 W
Klawer	218	31.44 S	18.36 E
Klawock	236	55.33 N	133.06 W
Klazienaveen	178	52.44 N	7.00 E
Kl'az'ma ≃	160	56.10 N	42.58 E
Kłecko	164	52.38 N	17.26 E
Kleczew	164	52.23 N	18.10 E
Kleena Kleene	238	51.58 N	124.59 W
Klein	256	46.24 N	108.32 W
Klein Bonaire I	285s	12.10 N	68.18 W
Klein Curaçao I	285s	12.00 N	68.40 W
Kleinfeltersville	262	40.18 N	76.15 W
Klekovača ∧	170	44.26 N	16.31 E
Klemme	244	43.01 N	93.36 W
Klemtu	238	52.36 N	128.31 W
Klerksdorp	224	26.58 S	26.39 E
Klet' ∧	164	48.52 N	14.17 E
Kleve	178	51.48 N	6.09 E
Klickitat	270	45.49 N	121.09 W
Klickitat □[6]	270	45.50 N	121.07 W
Klimovsk	160	55.22 N	37.32 E
Klimpfjäll	160	65.04 N	14.52 E
Klin	160	56.20 N	36.44 E
Klinaklini ≃	238	51.05 N	125.36 W
Klincy	158	52.47 N	32.14 E
Kling	202	5.58 N	124.42 E
Klingenthal	164	50.21 N	12.28 E
Klingerstown	262	40.40 N	76.41 W
Klinghardtsberge ∧	224	27.18 S	15.48 E
Klínovec ∧	164	50.24 N	12.58 E
Klintehamn	160	57.24 N	18.12 E
Klip ≃	224	27.20 S	27.10 E
Klipplaat	218	33.02 S	24.21 E
Klisura	172	42.42 N	24.27 E
Ključ	170	44.32 N	16.47 E
Kłobuck	164	50.55 N	18.57 E
Kłodawa	164	52.16 N	18.55 E
Kłodzko (Glatz)	164	50.27 N	16.39 E
Kłomnice	164	50.56 N	19.21 E
Klondike	268	40.29 N	86.57 W
Klondike □[9]	232	63.30 N	139.00 W
Klondike ≃	236	64.05 N	139.26 W
Klosterneuburg	164	48.18 N	16.20 E
Klosters	166	46.54 N	9.53 E
Klosterwappen ∧	164	47.46 N	15.48 E
Kloten	180	47.27 N	8.35 E
Klotz, Lac ◎	232	60.30 N	73.30 W
Klötze	164	52.38 N	11.10 E
Klouto	214	6.57 N	0.34 E
Kluane Lake ◎	236	61.15 N	138.40 W
Kluang	200	2.01 N	103.19 E
Kl'učevaja	160	65.16 N	41.32 E
Kl'učevskaja Sopka, Vulkan ∧[1]	186	56.04 N	160.38 E
Kl'uči	186	56.18 N	160.51 E
Kluczbork (Kreuzburg)	164	50.59 N	18.13 E
Klukwan	236	59.24 N	135.54 W
Klüppelberg	178	51.06 N	7.28 E
Klutina Lake ◎	236	61.37 N	146.55 W
Knapp	244	44.57 N	92.05 W
Knapp Creek	266	42.00 N	78.30 W
Knäred	160	56.32 N	13.19 E
Knaresborough	162	54.00 N	1.27 W
Knee Lake ◎	232	55.03 N	94.40 W
Kneža	172	43.30 N	24.05 E
Knić	172	43.55 N	20.43 E
Knickerbocker	250	31.16 N	100.38 W
Knife ≃	252	47.20 N	101.23 W
Knight Inlet C	238	50.41 N	125.40 W
Knight Island I	236	60.20 N	147.45 W
Knighton	162	52.21 N	3.03 W
Knightsen	272	37.58 N	121.40 W
Knights Landing	272	38.48 N	121.43 W
Knightstown	248	39.48 N	85.32 W
Knik Arm C	236	61.25 N	149.45 W
Knin	170	44.02 N	16.12 E
Knippa	250	29.18 N	99.38 W
Knittelfeld	164	47.14 N	14.50 E
Knjaževac	172	43.34 N	22.16 E
Knob Noster	248	38.46 N	93.33 W
Knob Peak ∧	202	12.28 N	121.21 E
Knokke	176	51.21 N	3.17 E
Knollwood	261	41.17 N	72.13 W
Knollwood Park	268	42.14 N	84.22 W
Knossos ⊥	172	35.20 N	25.10 E
Knotts Island	262	36.01 N	75.55 W
Knowlesville	264	43.14 N	78.19 W
Knowlton	260	45.13 N	72.31 W
Knox, Ind., U.S.	268	41.18 N	86.37 W
Knox, Pa., U.S.	266	41.14 N	79.32 W
Knox □[6]	266	40.23 N	82.29 W
Knox, Cape ≻	238	54.11 N	133.04 W
Knoxboro	264	42.58 N	75.36 W
Knox City, Mo., U.S.	248	40.09 N	92.01 W
Knox City, Tex., U.S.	250	33.25 N	99.49 W
Knox Coast •[2]	148	66.30 S	105.00 E
Knox Dale	266	41.05 N	79.02 W
Knoxville, Ark., U.S.	248	35.23 N	93.22 W
Knoxville, Ga., U.S.	246	32.44 N	84.01 W
Knoxville, Ill., U.S.	244	40.55 N	90.17 W
Knoxville, Iowa, U.S.	244	41.19 N	93.06 W
Knoxville, Tenn., U.S.	246	35.58 N	83.56 W
Knysna	224	34.02 S	23.02 E
Knyszyn	164	53.19 N	22.55 E
Kob'aj	186	63.34 N	126.30 E
Kobarid	170	46.15 N	13.35 E
Kobar Sink •[7]	214	14.00 N	40.30 E
Kobayashi	192	31.59 N	130.59 E
Kōbe	192	34.41 N	135.10 E
København (Copenhagen)	160	55.40 N	12.35 E
Koblenz	164	50.21 N	7.35 E
Kobona	160	60.01 N	31.36 E
Koboža	160	58.49 N	35.01 E
Kobra	160	60.03 N	50.44 E
Kobroor, Pulau I	198	6.12 S	134.32 E
Kobuk	236	66.54 N	156.52 W
Kobuk ≃	236	66.45 N	161.00 W
Kobylin	164	51.43 N	17.13 E
Kobyl'nik	160	54.56 N	26.41 E
Köca ≃	212	36.16 N	29.15 E
Kocaeli → İzmit	212	40.46 N	29.55 E
Kocaeli □[4]	212	40.55 N	29.55 E
Kočani	172	41.55 N	22.25 E
Koçarlı	172	37.45 N	27.42 E
Kočečum ≃	186	64.17 N	100.10 E
Kočevje	170	45.38 N	14.52 E
Kočevo	160	59.36 N	54.18 E
Kocher ≃	164	49.14 N	9.12 E
Kōchi	192	33.33 N	133.33 E
Koch Island I	232	69.38 N	78.15 W
Koch Peak ∧	256	45.02 N	111.28 W
Kock	164	51.39 N	22.27 E
Kočmes	160	66.12 N	60.44 E
Kodačdikost	160	63.11 N	55.49 E
Kodari	190	27.56 N	85.56 E
Kodiak	236	57.48 N	152.23 W
Kodiak Island I	236	57.30 N	153.30 W
Kodino	160	63.43 N	39.41 E
Kodo, Jabal ∧	220	12.26 N	23.38 E
Kodok	214	9.53 N	32.07 E
Kodry ∧[2]	172	47.10 N	28.25 E
Kodyma ≃	172	48.01 N	30.48 E
Koekelare	176	51.05 N	2.58 E
Koersel	178	51.04 N	5.16 E
Koes	218	25.59 S	19.08 E
Kofa Mountains ⋀	254	33.20 N	114.00 W
Köflach	164	47.04 N	15.05 E
Koforidua	222	6.03 N	0.17 W
Kōfu	192	35.39 N	138.35 E
Koga	192	36.11 N	139.43 E
Kogaluk ≃, Newf., Can.	232	56.12 N	61.45 W
Kogâluk ≃, Qué., Can.	232	59.35 N	77.30 W
Køge	160	55.27 N	12.11 E
Køge Bugt C	232	65.00 N	40.30 W
Kogil'nik ≃	172	45.51 N	29.38 E
Kogon ≃	222	11.09 N	14.42 W
Kohala Mountains ⋀	275d	20.05 N	155.45 W
Kohāt	206	33.35 N	71.26 E
Kohila	160	59.10 N	24.45 E
Kohīma	200	25.40 N	94.06 E
Kohler	244	43.44 N	87.46 W
Kohnāk Khole ∧	206	32.48 N	68.45 E
Kohtla-Järve	160	59.24 N	27.15 E
Koide	192	37.13 N	138.57 E
Koidern	236	61.58 N	140.25 W
Kojā ≃	208	25.34 N	61.13 E
Kojda	160	66.23 N	42.31 E
Kŏje-do I	194	34.52 N	128.37 E
Kojetín	164	49.21 N	17.18 E
Kojgorodok	160	60.26 N	50.58 E
Ko-jima I	192a	41.22 N	139.48 E
Kojnatchyn, Ozero ◎	236	65.20 N	180.00 E
Kok ≃	200	20.14 N	100.09 E
Kokand	186	40.33 N	70.57 E
Kokava nad Rimavicou	164	48.34 N	19.50 E
Kokčetav	186	53.17 N	69.25 E
Kokcha ≃	206	37.10 N	69.25 E
Kokemäki	160	61.15 N	22.21 E
Kokkola (Gamlakarleby)	160	63.50 N	23.07 E
Kokolik ≃	236	69.46 N	165.00 W
Kokomo, Haw., U.S.	275a	20.53 N	156.19 W
Kokomo, Ind., U.S.	268	40.29 N	86.08 W
Kokomo, Miss., U.S.	248	31.12 N	90.00 W
Kokonau	198	4.43 S	136.25 E
Koko Nor → Qinghai ◎	190	36.50 N	100.20 E
Kokonselkä ◎	160	61.45 N	28.50 E
Kokrines	236	64.56 N	154.42 W
Kokrines Hills ⋀[2]	236	65.15 N	154.00 W
Kokšaalatau, Chrebet ⋀	186	41.00 N	78.00 E
Koksijde	176	51.06 N	2.39 E
Koksilah	270	48.40 N	123.38 W
Koksoak ≃	232	58.30 N	68.10 W
Kokstad	224	30.32 S	29.29 E
Kokubu	192	31.44 N	130.46 E
Kol ≃	208	27.59 N	55.47 E
Kola	160	68.53 N	33.01 E
Kola ≃	160	68.53 N	33.02 E
Kola Peninsula → Kol'skij Poluostrov ≻[1]	160	67.30 N	37.00 E
Kola, Pulau I	198	5.30 S	134.35 E
Kolāchi ≃	206	27.08 N	67.02 E
Kolaka	198	4.03 S	121.36 E
Kolambugan	202	8.07 N	123.54 E
Kolari	160	67.20 N	23.48 E
Kolarovgrad → Šumen	172	43.16 N	26.55 E
Kolárovo	164	47.52 N	18.02 E
Kolašin	172	42.39 N	19.31 E
Kolberg → Kołobrzeg	164	54.12 N	15.33 E
Kolbio	218	1.10 S	41.15 E
Kolbuszowa	164	50.15 N	21.47 E
Kol'čugino	160	56.18 N	39.23 E
Kolda	222	12.53 N	14.57 W
Kolding	160	55.31 N	9.29 E
Koléa	168	36.38 N	2.46 E
Kolenté (Great Scarcies) ≃	222	8.55 N	13.08 W
Kolgujev, Ostrov I	160	69.05 N	49.15 E
Kolho	160	62.08 N	24.31 E
Koli, Jabal ∧	220	14.05 N	25.31 E
Koliba (Corubal) ≃	222	11.57 N	15.06 W
Koliganek	236	59.48 N	157.25 W
Kolimbine ≃	222	15.00 N	11.00 W
Kolín	164	50.01 N	15.13 E
Kolka	160	57.45 N	22.35 E
Kolmogorovo	186	59.15 N	91.20 E
Köln (Cologne)	164	50.56 N	6.59 E
Kolno	164	53.25 N	21.56 E
Koło	164	52.12 N	18.38 E
Koloa	275b	21.55 N	159.28 W
Kołobrzeg (Kolberg)	164	54.12 N	15.33 E
Kologriv	160	58.51 N	44.17 E
Kolombangara I	226	8.00 S	157.05 E
Kolomna	160	55.05 N	38.49 E
Kolomyja	158	48.32 N	25.04 E
Kolpaševo	186	58.20 N	82.50 E
Kolpino	160	59.45 N	30.36 E
Kol'skij Poluostrov ≻[1]	160	67.30 N	37.00 E
Kol'učinskaja Guba C	236	66.40 N	174.30 W
Koluszki	164	51.44 N	19.49 E
Kolva ≃	160	65.55 N	57.15 E
Kolvereid	160	64.51 N	11.32 E
Kolwezi	218	10.43 S	25.28 E
Kolyma ≃	186	69.30 N	161.00 E
Kolymskaja	186	68.44 N	158.44 E
Kolymskaja Nizmennost' ☷	186	68.30 N	154.00 E
Kom ∧	172	43.10 N	23.03 E
Komadugu Yobe ≃	214	13.43 N	13.20 E
Komagane	192	35.43 N	137.55 E
Komaga-take ∧	192a	42.04 N	140.41 E
Komandorskije Ostrova II	186	55.00 N	167.00 E
Komandorski Village	272	37.43 N	121.54 W
Komarniki	164	49.00 N	23.04 E
Komárno	164	47.45 N	18.09 E
Komárom	164	47.44 N	18.08 E
Komárom □[6]	164	47.40 N	18.15 E
Komati (Incomati) ≃	224	25.46 S	32.43 E
Komatipoort	218	25.25 S	31.55 E
Komatsu	192	36.24 N	136.27 E
Komatsushima	192	34.00 N	134.35 E
Komering ≃	198	2.59 S	104.50 E
Komi-Perm'ackij Nacional'nyj Okrug □[8]	160	60.00 N	54.30 E
Komló	164	46.12 N	18.16 E
Kommunarsk	158	48.30 N	38.47 E
Kommunizma, Pik ∧	186	38.57 N	72.01 E
Komodo, Pulau I	198	8.36 S	119.30 E
Komoé ≃	222	5.12 N	3.44 W
Komoro	192	36.19 N	138.26 E
Komotau → Chomutov	164	50.28 N	13.26 E
Komotiní	172	41.08 N	25.25 E
Komovi ⋀	172	42.40 N	19.40 E
Kompasberg ∧	224	31.45 S	24.32 E
Komsberg ⋀	224	32.40 S	20.50 E
Komsomolec	158	53.45 N	62.02 E
Komsomolec, Zaliv C	186	45.30 N	52.45 E
Komsomol'sk	160	57.02 N	40.21 E
Komsomol'skij, S.S.S.R.	160	67.35 N	63.47 E
Komsomol'skij, S.S.S.R.	160	54.27 N	45.49 E
Komsomol'sk-na-Amure	186	50.35 N	137.02 E
Kona Coast •[2]	275d	19.25 N	155.55 W
Konakovo	160	56.42 N	36.46 E
Konakpınar	172	39.26 N	27.53 E
Konarhā □[4]	206	35.15 N	71.00 E
Konawa	250	34.58 N	96.45 W
Konda	158	61.20 N	63.58 E
Konda ≃	158	60.40 N	69.46 E
Kondega	160	60.14 N	33.30 E
Kondiaronk, Lac ◎	244	46.56 N	76.45 W
Kondoa	218	4.54 S	35.47 E
Kondopoga	160	62.12 N	34.17 E
Kondrovo	160	54.48 N	35.56 E
Konecbor	160	64.52 N	57.44 E
Konergino	236	65.54 N	178.50 W
Kông, Kaôh I	200	11.20 N	103.00 E
Kongakut ≃	236	69.48 N	141.50 W
Kongiganak	236	59.58 N	162.45 W
Kongju	194	36.27 N	127.07 E
Kongmoon → Jiangmen	196	22.35 N	113.05 E
Kongolo	218	5.23 S	27.00 E
Kongquehe ≃	190	40.40 N	90.10 E
Kongsberg	160	59.39 N	9.39 E
Kongsvinger	160	60.12 N	12.00 E
Kongsvoll	160	62.18 N	9.37 E
Kongtongdao I	194	37.33 N	121.27 E
Konice	164	49.35 N	16.53 E
Koniecpol	164	50.48 N	19.41 E
Königgrätz → Hradec Králové	164	50.12 N	15.50 E
Königsberg → Kalingrad, S.S.S.R.	164	54.43 N	20.30 E
Königsbrunn	180	48.16 N	10.53 E
Königssee ◎	164	47.36 N	12.59 E
Königswinter	164	50.40 N	7.11 E
Königs Wusterhausen	164	52.18 N	13.37 E
Konin	164	52.13 N	18.16 E
Konispol	172	39.39 N	20.10 E
Kónitsa	172	40.02 N	20.45 E
Köniz	180	46.56 N	7.25 E
Konjic	172	43.39 N	17.57 E
Könkämäälv ≃	160	68.29 N	22.17 E
Konkiep ≃	224	28.03 S	17.21 E
Konkouré ≃	222	9.58 N	13.42 W
Konnarock	246	36.40 N	81.38 W
Konongo	222	6.37 N	1.11 W
Konoša	160	60.58 N	40.15 E
Kōnosu	192	36.03 N	139.31 E
Konotop	158	51.14 N	33.12 E
Kon'ovo	160	62.08 N	39.16 E
Konpienga ≃	222	10.52 N	0.51 E
Konsen-daichi ⋀	192a	63.25 N	144.52 E
Końskie	164	51.12 N	20.26 E
Konstantinovka, S.S.S.R.	158	48.32 N	37.43 E
Konstantinovka, S.S.S.R.	160	56.41 N	50.53 E
Konstantynów Łódzki	164	51.45 N	19.20 E
Konstanz	180	47.40 N	9.10 E
Kontagora	222	10.24 N	5.28 E
Kontich	176	51.08 N	4.27 E
Kontiomäki	160	64.21 N	28.09 E
Kontum	200	14.21 N	108.00 E
Konus, Gora ∧	236	67.34 N	178.10 E
Konya	212	37.52 N	32.31 E
Konz	164	49.42 N	6.34 E
Konza	218	1.45 S	37.07 E
Konžakovskij Kamen', Gora ∧	186	59.38 N	59.08 E
Koocanusa, Lake ◎[1]	238	49.00 N	115.10 W
Koog aan de Zaan	178	52.27 N	4.49 E
Koolau Range ⋀	275d	21.35 N	158.00 W
Koontz Lake	268	41.25 N	86.29 W
Koosharem	254	38.31 N	111.53 W
Kooskia	256	46.09 N	115.59 W
Kootenai (Kootenay) ≃	238	49.15 N	117.39 W
Kootenay Indian Reserve ◆[4]	238	49.37 N	115.45 W
Kootenay Lake ◎	238	49.35 N	116.50 W
Kootenay National Park ♠	238	51.00 N	116.00 W
Kópasker	160a	66.20 N	16.24 W
Kópavogur	160a	64.06 N	21.50 W
Kopdağı Geçidi)(	212	40.03 N	40.33 E
Kopejsk	158	55.07 N	61.37 E
Koper	170	45.33 N	13.44 E
Kopervik	160	59.17 N	5.18 E
Köping	160	59.31 N	16.00 E
Koplik	172	42.13 N	19.26 E
Koppang	160	61.34 N	11.04 E
Koppány ≃	164	46.35 N	18.26 E
Kopparbergs Län □[6]	160	61.00 N	14.30 E
Koppeh Dāgh ⋀	208	37.50 N	58.00 E
Koppel	266	40.50 N	80.20 W
Koprivnica	170	46.10 N	16.50 E
Köprü ≃	212	36.49 N	31.10 E
Köprüören	172	39.30 N	29.47 E
Kopylovo	160	60.35 N	45.02 E
Korab ⋀	172	41.47 N	20.34 E
Koralpe ⋀	164	46.50 N	14.58 E
Koraraika, Baie de C	225b	17.45 S	43.57 E
Korarou, Lac ◎	222	15.15 N	3.16 W
Korat → Nakhon Ratchasima	200	14.57 N	102.09 E
Kor'atskoje Nagorje ⋀	186	62.30 N	172.00 E
Kor'ažma	160	61.18 N	47.06 E
Korba	170	36.35 N	10.52 E
Korbach	178	51.16 N	8.52 E
Korbous	170	36.49 N	10.35 E
Korçë	172	40.37 N	20.46 E
Korčula	170	42.58 N	17.08 E
Korčula, Otok I	170	42.57 N	16.50 E
Korčulanski Kanal ⋓	170	43.03 N	16.40 E
Kordestān □[4]	208	35.30 N	47.00 E
Kord Kūy	208	36.48 N	54.07 E
Korea, North □[1]	190	40.00 N	127.00 E
Korea, South □[1]	190	36.30 N	128.00 E
Korea Bay C	194	39.00 N	124.00 E
Korea Strait ⋓	190	34.00 N	129.00 E
Korelakša	160	65.33 N	32.22 E
Korf	186	60.19 N	165.50 E
Korfovskij	186	48.14 N	135.02 E
Korhogo	222	9.27 N	5.38 W
Korhogo □[5]	222	9.30 N	5.45 W
Korinthía (Corinthia) □[5]	172	37.50 N	22.50 E
Korinthiakós Kólpos C	172	38.19 N	22.04 E
Kórinthos (Corinth)	172	37.56 N	22.56 E
Korínthou, Dhiórix ☲	172	37.57 N	22.56 E
Kőrishegy ∧	164	47.18 N	17.45 E
Kōriyama	192	37.24 N	140.23 E
Korkino	158	54.54 N	61.23 E
Korliki	186	61.31 N	82.22 E
Kormakítis, Akrotírion ≻	212	35.24 N	33.55 E
Körmend	164	47.01 N	16.37 E
Kornat, Otok I	170	43.50 N	15.16 E
Korner	238	48.59 N	112.15 W
Korneuburg	164	48.21 N	16.20 E
Kórnik	164	52.17 N	17.04 E
Köroglu Tepesi ∧	212	40.31 N	31.53 E
Korogwe	218	5.09 S	38.29 E
Koronadal	202	6.12 N	125.01 E
Koróni	172	36.48 N	21.56 E
Korónia, Límni ◎	172	40.41 N	23.05 E
Koronowo	164	53.19 N	17.57 E
Koropí	172	37.54 N	23.53 E
Koror	198	7.20 N	134.29 E
Körös ≃	164	46.43 N	20.12 E
Korosten'	158	50.57 N	28.39 E
Koro Toro	214	16.05 N	18.30 E
Korovin Island I	236	55.25 N	160.15 W
Korovin Volcano ∧[1]	236	52.22 N	174.10 W
Korpela	160	66.15 N	30.01 E
Korpilahti	160	62.01 N	25.33 E
Korsakov	186	46.38 N	142.46 E
Korschenbroich	178	51.11 N	6.31 E
Korsnäs	160	62.47 N	21.12 E
Korso	160	60.21 N	25.06 E
Korsør	160	55.20 N	11.09 E
Korsze (Korschen)	164	54.10 N	21.09 E
Kortemark	176	51.02 N	3.02 E
Kortkeros	160	61.49 N	51.28 E
Kortrijk (Courtrai)	176	50.50 N	3.16 E
Korucu	172	39.28 N	27.22 E
Kos	172	36.53 N	27.18 E
Kos I	172	36.50 N	27.10 E
Kosa	160	59.56 N	54.55 E
Kosa ≃	160	60.11 N	55.10 E
Kosa ⊥	222	15.50 N	7.00 W
Koš-Agač	186	50.00 N	88.40 E
Kosai	192	34.43 N	137.33 E
Kosaka	192	40.19 N	140.44 E
Kosa-Meečkyn, Ostrov I	236	65.26 N	178.00 W
Kosčagyl	158	46.51 N	53.48 E
Kościan	164	52.06 N	16.38 E
Kościerzyna	164	54.08 N	18.00 E
Kosciusko	248	32.58 N	89.35 W
Kosciusko □[6]	268	41.14 N	85.51 W
Kosciusko, Mount ∧	228	36.27 S	148.16 E
Kösdağı ∧	212	40.59 N	34.25 E
Koshikijima-rettō II	192	31.45 N	129.49 E
Koshkonong	248	36.36 N	91.39 W
Kōshoku	192	36.38 N	138.06 E
Kosi, Lake ◎	224	26.55 S	32.52 E
Košice	164	48.43 N	21.15 E
Kosju	160	65.38 N	59.03 E
Kosju ≃	160	66.18 N	59.53 E
Kosjuvom	160	66.17 N	59.50 E
Köşk	172	37.51 N	28.03 E
Koskaecodde Lake ◎	240	48.00 N	55.20 W
Koskenkylä	160	60.30 N	25.56 E
Koski	160	60.39 N	23.09 E
Koskullskulle	160	67.12 N	20.50 E
Koslan	160	63.28 N	48.52 E
Köslin → Koszalin	164	54.12 N	16.09 E
Kosogor	160	57.07 N	47.34 E
Kosovska Mitrovica	172	42.53 N	20.52 E
Kosse	250	31.18 N	96.38 W
Kossuth	266	41.17 N	79.35 W
Kostajnica	170	45.14 N	16.33 E
Kostelec nad Orlicí	164	50.07 N	16.13 E
Kostenec	172	42.16 N	23.49 E
Kostroma	160	57.46 N	40.55 E
Kostroma ≃	160	57.47 N	40.55 E
Kostrzyn (Küstrin), Pol.	164	52.37 N	14.39 E
Kostrzyn, Pol.	164	52.25 N	17.14 E
Koszalin (Köslin), Pol.	164	54.12 N	16.09 E
Kőszeg	164	47.23 N	16.33 E
Koszyce	164	50.11 N	20.35 E
Kota	206	25.11 N	75.50 E
Kotabaru	198	3.14 S	116.13 E
Kota Bharu	200	6.07 N	102.15 E
Kotabumi	198	4.50 S	104.54 E
Kotadabok	198	0.30 S	104.33 E
Kota Kinabalu (Jesselton)	198	5.58 N	116.04 E
Kotamobagu	198	0.46 N	124.19 E
Kotari ⋀	170	44.05 N	15.30 E
Kota Tinggi	200	1.44 N	103.53 E
Kotcho Lake ◎	232	59.05 N	121.10 W
Kotel	172	42.53 N	26.27 E
Kotel'nič	160	58.18 N	48.20 E
Kotel'nikovo	158	58.18 N	48.20 E
Kotel'nyj, Ostrov I	186	75.45 N	138.44 E
Köthen	164	51.45 N	11.58 E
Kotka	160	60.28 N	26.55 E
Kotkino	160	67.02 N	51.03 E
Kotlas	160	61.16 N	46.35 E
Kotlenski prohod)(	172	42.53 N	26.27 E
Kotlik	236	63.02 N	163.33 W
Kotly	160	59.36 N	28.45 E
Kotohira	192	34.11 N	133.49 E
Kotor	172	42.25 N	18.46 E
Kotoriba	170	46.21 N	16.49 E
Kotor Varoš	170	44.37 N	17.23 E
Kotovsk	158	47.45 N	29.32 E
Kötschach	164	46.40 N	13.00 E
Kotto ≃	214	4.14 N	22.02 E
Kotuj ≃	186	71.55 N	102.05 E
Kotzebue	236	66.53 N	162.39 W
Kotzebue Sound ⋓	236	66.20 N	163.00 W
Kötzting	164	49.11 N	12.52 E
Kouchibouguac Bay C	240	46.50 N	64.50 W
Koudougou	222	12.15 N	2.22 W
Kougaberge ⋀	224	33.40 S	23.50 E
Kougarok Mountain ∧	236	65.41 N	165.13 W
Koukdjuak ≃	232	66.45 N	73.09 W
Koula-Moutou	218	1.08 S	12.29 E
Koulikoro	214	12.53 N	7.33 W
Koulountou ≃	222	13.15 N	13.37 W
Koumbisaleh ⊥	222	15.55 N	8.05 W
Koumi	192	36.05 N	138.29 E
Koumra	214	8.55 N	17.33 E
Kounda Ko ≃	222	12.13 N	11.03 W
Koundara □[4]	222	12.25 N	13.10 W
Koundian ⊥	222	13.10 N	10.41 W
Kounradskij	186	46.59 N	75.00 E
Kountze	248	30.23 N	94.19 W
Koupé, Mont ∧	222	4.47 N	9.43 E
Kouroussa	214	10.39 N	9.53 W
Kouroussa □[4]	222	10.40 N	9.55 W
Koussi, Emi ∧	214	19.50 N	18.30 E
Koutiala	214	12.23 N	5.28 W
Kouts	268	41.19 N	87.02 W
Kouvola	160	60.52 N	26.42 E
Kouya ≃	222	10.09 N	9.45 W
Kovarskas	160	55.26 N	24.55 E
Kovdor	160	67.34 N	30.22 E
Kovdozero, Ozero ◎	160	66.47 N	32.00 E
Kovel'	158	51.14 N	24.41 E
Kovin	172	44.45 N	20.59 E
Kovno → Kaunas	160	54.54 N	23.54 E
Kovrov	160	56.22 N	41.18 E
Kovylkino	160	54.02 N	43.56 E
Kovža	160	61.09 N	38.58 E
Kowal	164	52.32 N	19.09 E
Kowalewo Pomorskie	164	53.10 N	18.53 E
Kowary (Schmiedeberg)	164	50.49 N	15.51 E
Kowloon (Jiulong)	196	22.18 N	114.10 E
Köyceğiz Gölü ◎	212	36.55 N	28.40 E
Koyuk	236	64.56 N	161.08 W
Koyuk ≃	236	64.55 N	161.12 W
Koyukuk	236	64.53 N	157.43 W
Koyukuk ≃	236	64.56 N	157.30 W
Koyuneli	172	39.50 N	27.15 E
Koza, Nihon	193b	26.20 N	127.50 E
Koža, S.S.S.R.	160	57.47 N	48.57 E
Kō-zaki ≻	192	34.05 N	129.13 E
Kozan	212	37.27 N	35.49 E
Kozáni	172	40.18 N	21.47 E
Kozarac	170	44.58 N	16.51 E
Kozara Planina ⋀	170	45.00 N	16.50 E
Kozdinga	160	63.43 N	47.32 E
Kozhikode → Calicut	204	11.16 N	75.48 E
Koziegłowy	164	50.36 N	19.09 E
Kozienice	164	51.35 N	21.33 E
Kožim	160	65.48 N	59.28 E
Kožimiz, Gora ∧	160	63.12 N	58.48 E
Koźle (Cosel)	164	50.20 N	18.08 E
Kozlov Bereg	160	58.57 N	27.44 E
Koźmin	164	51.50 N	17.28 E
Koz'mino	160	61.56 N	48.19 E
Koz'modemjansk	160	56.20 N	46.36 E
Koz'mogorodskoje	160	65.32 N	44.55 E
Kożpos'olok	160	63.10 N	38.06 E
Kożuchów (Freistadt)	164	51.45 N	15.35 E
Kōzu-shima I	192	34.13 N	139.10 E
Kožva	160	65.07 N	56.57 E
Kpandu	222	7.00 N	0.18 E
Kra, Isthmus of •[3]	200	10.20 N	99.00 E
Kraai ≃	224	30.40 S	26.45 E
Kra Buri	198	10.24 N	98.47 E
Krâchéh	200	12.29 N	106.01 E
Kragerø	160	58.52 N	9.25 E
Kragujevac	172	44.01 N	20.55 E
Krajenka (Krojanke)	164	53.19 N	17.00 E
Krajina ◆[1]	170	44.50 N	16.30 E
Krakovec	164	49.57 N	23.07 E
Kraków	164	50.03 N	19.58 E
Kralendijk	285s	12.10 N	68.17 W
Kraljevica	170	45.16 N	14.34 E
Kraljevo	172	43.43 N	20.41 E
Kralovice	164	49.59 N	13.29 E
Kralupy nad Vltavou	164	50.11 N	14.18 E
Kramatorsk	158	48.43 N	37.32 E
Kramer	268	40.20 N	87.17 W
Kramfors	160	62.56 N	17.47 E
Kranenburg	178	51.47 N	6.03 E
Krångede	160	63.09 N	16.05 E
Kranídhion	172	37.22 N	23.10 E
Kranj	170	46.15 N	14.21 E
Krapina	170	46.10 N	15.52 E
Krapkowice (Krappitz)	164	50.29 N	17.56 E
Krasavino	160	60.58 N	46.26 E
Krasieo ≃	200	14.48 N	100.07 E
Krasino	186	70.45 N	54.27 E
Kraslice	164	50.18 N	12.31 E
Krasnaja Gorbatka	160	55.52 N	41.46 E
Krasnaja Jaranga	236	65.40 N	172.50 W
Krasneno	236	64.38 N	174.48 E
Kraśnik	164	50.56 N	22.13 E
Kraśnik Fabryczny	164	50.58 N	22.12 E
Krasnoarmejskij	186	69.35 N	172.00 E
Krasnoarmejskoje	160	52.44 N	50.02 E
Krasnoborsk	160	61.34 N	45.53 E
Krasnobród	164	50.33 N	23.13 E
Krasnodar	158	45.02 N	39.00 E
Krasnogorsk	186	55.05 N	37.20 E
Krasnogorskij	160	56.09 N	48.20 E
Krasnojarsk	186	56.01 N	92.50 E
Krasnoje	160	59.12 N	47.49 E
Krasnokamsk	158	58.04 N	55.48 E
Krasnolesje [Hardteck]	164	54.24 N	22.23 E
Krasnoščelje	160	67.21 N	37.02 E
Krasnosel'kup	186	65.41 N	82.28 E
Krasnosielc	164	53.03 N	21.10 E
Krasnoslobodsk	158	48.42 N	44.34 E
Krasnoturjinsk	158	59.46 N	60.12 E
Krasnoufimsk	158	56.37 N	57.46 E
Krasnoural'sk	158	58.21 N	60.03 E
Krasnovišersk	160	60.23 N	56.59 E
Krasnovodsk	208	40.00 N	53.00 E
Krasnovodskij Poluostrov ≻[1]	208	40.30 N	53.15 E
Krasnovodskij Zaliv C	208	39.55 N	53.15 E
Krasnozatonskij	160	61.41 N	50.58 E
Krasnoznamensk [Haselberg]	164	54.57 N	22.30 E
Krasnoznamenskij	186	51.03 N	69.30 E
Krasnoz'orskoje	186	53.59 N	79.14 E
Krasnyj	160	54.34 N	31.26 E
Krasnyj Cholm	160	58.03 N	37.07 E
Krasnyje Baki	160	57.08 N	45.10 E
Krasnyj Gul'aj	160	54.01 N	48.22 E
Krasnyj Kut	158	50.57 N	46.58 E
Krasnyj Luč	160	57.04 N	30.05 E
Krasnystaw	164	50.59 N	23.10 E
Kraszna (Crasna) ≃	172	48.09 N	22.20 E
Kratovo	172	42.05 N	22.11 E
Kravaře	164	49.56 N	18.01 E
Krbava ◆[1]	170	44.40 N	15.35 E
Krebs	250	34.56 N	95.43 W
Krečetovo	160	60.56 N	38.30 E
Kredidja, Lalla ∧	168	36.27 N	4.15 E
Krefeld	178	51.20 N	6.34 E
Kremenčug	158	49.04 N	33.25 E
Kremenčugskoje Vodochranilišče ◎[1]	158	49.20 N	32.30 E
Kremmling	254	40.03 N	106.24 W
Kremnica	164	48.43 N	18.54 E
Krems an der Donau	164	48.25 N	15.36 E
Kremsmünster	164	48.03 N	14.08 E
Krenitzin Islands II	236	54.08 N	166.00 W
Kreole	248	30.24 N	88.30 W
Krepoljin	172	44.26 N	21.35 E
Kress	250	34.22 N	101.45 W
Kressbronn	180	47.35 N	9.36 E
Kresta, Zaliv C	236	66.00 N	180.00 E
Krestcy	160	58.23 N	39.00 E
Krest-Major	186	67.37 N	144.45 E
Krestovaja Guba	186	74.07 N	55.33 E
Kretinga	160	55.53 N	21.13 E
Kreuz (an der Ostbahn) → Krzyż	164	52.54 N	16.01 E
Kreuzlingen	180	47.39 N	9.11 E
Kría Vrísi	172	40.41 N	22.18 E
Kribi	214	2.57 N	9.55 E
Kriens	180	47.02 N	8.17 E
Krigujgun, Mys ≻	236	65.30 N	171.05 W
Kriljon, Mys ⋓	192a	45.53 N	142.05 E
Křimice	164	49.46 N	13.15 E
Krimml	164	47.13 N	12.11 E
Krimpen aan de IJssel	178	51.54 N	4.35 E
Krymskij Poluostrov ≻[1]	158	45.00 N	34.00 E
Krishnanagar	206	23.24 N	88.30 E
Kristdala	160	57.24 N	16.11 E
Kristiansand	160	58.10 N	8.00 E
Kristianstad	160	56.02 N	14.08 E
Kristiansund	160	63.07 N	7.45 E
Kristineberg	160	65.04 N	18.35 E
Kristinehamn	160	59.20 N	14.07 E
Kristinestad	158	62.17 N	21.23 E
Kríti I	172	35.29 N	24.42 E
Kritikón Pélagos ▾[2]	172	35.46 N	23.54 E
Krivaja ≃	172	44.27 N	18.09 E
Kriva Palanka	172	42.12 N	22.20 E
Kriviči	160	54.43 N	27.17 E
Krivodol	172	43.23 N	23.29 E
Krivoj Rog	158	47.55 N	33.21 E
Križevci	170	46.02 N	16.33 E
Krk, Otok I	170	45.05 N	14.35 E
Krn ∧	166	46.16 N	13.40 E
Krnov	164	50.05 N	17.41 E
Krobia	164	51.47 N	16.58 E
Kroken	160	65.22 N	14.20 E
Krokodil ≃	224	24.12 S	26.52 E
Krokowo	164	54.48 N	18.11 E
Królewska Huta → Chorzów	164	50.19 N	18.57 E
Kroměříž	164	49.18 N	17.24 E
Krommenie	178	52.29 N	4.45 E
Krompachy	164	48.56 N	20.52 E
Kronach	164	50.14 N	11.20 E
Krong-bolah ≃	200	13.58 N	107.40 E
Krŏng Kêb	200	10.30 N	104.19 E
Krŏng Khémôreăh Phumĭnt	200	11.37 N	102.59 E
Krŏng Preăh Seihanŭ	200	10.38 N	103.30 E
Kronobergs Län □[6]	160	56.40 N	14.40 E
Kronockij Zaliv C	186	54.12 N	160.36 E
Kronoki	186	54.36 N	161.10 E
Kronštadt	160	59.59 N	29.45 E
Kroonstad	224	27.46 S	27.12 E
Kropotkin	158	45.26 N	40.34 E
Krościenko	164	49.27 N	20.26 E
Krośniewice	164	52.16 N	19.10 E
Krosno	164	49.42 N	21.46 E
Krosno Odrzańskie (Crossen)	164	52.04 N	15.05 E
Krotoszyn	164	51.42 N	17.26 E
Krotz Springs	248	30.32 N	91.45 W
Krs, Vrh ∧	172	44.13 N	22.14 E
Krško	170	45.58 N	15.29 E
Kruger National Park ♠	224	24.00 S	31.40 E
Krugersdorp	224	26.05 S	27.35 E
Krui	198	5.11 S	103.56 E
Krujë	172	41.30 N	19.48 E
Kr'ukovo	186	66.30 N	159.31 E
Krulevščina	160	55.02 N	27.45 E
Krumbach [Schwaben]	164	48.14 N	10.22 E
Krumovgrad	172	41.28 N	25.39 E
Krumroy	266	39.58 N	81.24 W
Krung Thep (Bangkok)	200	13.45 N	100.31 E
Krupinská vrchovina ⋀	164	48.23 N	19.15 E
Krupka	164	50.43 N	13.46 E
Kruså	160	54.50 N	9.25 E
Krusenstern, Cape ≻	236	67.07 N	163.43 W
Kruševac	172	43.35 N	21.20 E
Kruševo	172	41.22 N	21.14 E
Krušné hory (Erzgebirge) ⋀	164	50.30 N	13.15 E
Kruszwica	164	52.41 N	18.19 E
Krutaja	160	63.02 N	54.38 E
Krutcy	160	57.10 N	29.23 E
Kruzenšterna, Proliv ⋓	186	48.30 N	153.50 E
Kruzof Island I	236	57.10 N	135.40 W
Krymskij Poluostov ≻[1]	186	45.00 N	34.00 E
Krynica	164	49.25 N	20.56 E
Krzepice	164	50.58 N	18.44 E
Krzeszowice	164	50.09 N	19.39 E
Krzna ≃	164	52.08 N	23.31 E
Krzywiń	164	51.58 N	16.49 E
Krzyż (Kreuz[an der Ostbahn])	164	52.54 N	16.01 E
Ksar el Boukhari	168	35.51 N	2.52 E
Ksar-el-Kebir	168	35.01 N	5.54 W
Ksar-es-Seghir	168	35.50 N	5.32 W
Ksar-es-Souk	214	31.58 N	4.25 W
Ksar Hellal	170	35.39 N	10.54 E
Ksenjevka	186	53.34 N	118.44 E
Ksenofontova	160	60.58 N	56.12 E
Książ Wielkopolski	164	52.05 N	17.14 E
Ksour Essaf	170	35.25 N	11.00 E
Kstovo	160	56.11 N	44.11 E
Kuaijishan ⋀	196	29.32 N	120.30 E
Kuala Dungun	200	4.47 N	103.26 E
Kuala Kangsar	200	4.47 N	100.56 E
Kualakapuas	198	2.59 S	114.21 E
Kuala Krai	200	5.31 N	102.13 E
Kuala Kubu Bharu	200	3.34 N	101.39 E
Kuala Lipis	200	4.09 N	102.02 E
Kuala Lumpur	200	3.09 N	101.43 E
Kuala Nerang	200	6.15 N	100.36 E

Symbols in the index entries are identified on page 360.

Name	Page	Lat°′	Long°′
Kuala Pilah	200	2.45 N	102.17 E
Kualapuu	275a	21.09 N	157.01 W
Kuala Selangor	200	3.20 N	101.16 E
Kuala Trengganu	200	5.19 N	103.09 E
Kualu ≃	200	2.45 N	100.00 E
Kuamut	202	5.09 N	117.28 E
Kuamut ≃	202	5.13 N	117.32 E
Kuan Shan ∧	196	23.14 N	120.54 E
Kuantan	200	3.50 N	103.20 E
Kuantan, Batang ≃	200	0.22 S	103.26 E
Kuba	158	41.22 N	48.31 E
Kuban' ≃	186	45.20 N	37.30 E
Kubenskoje	160	59.26 N	39.40 E
Kubenskoje, Ozero ⊜	160	59.40 N	39.25 E
Kubokawa	192	33.12 N	133.08 E
Kubrat	172	43.48 N	26.30 E
Kučema	160	65.37 N	42.28 E
Kučevo	172	44.27 N	21.44 E
Kuche	190	41.43 N	82.54 E
Kuching	200	1.32 N	110.19 E
Kuchinoerabu-jima I	193b	30.28 N	130.12 E
Kuchino-shima I	193b	29.57 N	129.57 E
Küçükbahce	172	38.33 N	26.24 E
Küçükkuyu	172	39.32 N	26.36 E
Kučurgan ≃	172	46.43 N	29.53 E
Kudamatsu	192	34.00 N	131.52 E
Kudat	198	6.53 N	116.46 E
Kūdī, Qārat ⛰[2]	220	23.30 N	23.52 E
Kudus	198	6.48 S	110.50 E
Kudymkar	160	59.01 N	54.37 E
Kueishan Tao I	196	24.50 N	121.56 E
Kuekvun' ≃	236	69.14 N	179.25 E
Kuerle	190	41.44 N	86.09 E
Kufrinja	210	32.17 N	35.42 E
Kufstein	164	47.35 N	12.10 E
Kugaluk ≃	236	69.10 N	131.00 W
Kugmallit Bay C	236	69.33 N	133.25 W
Kühlungsborn	164	54.09 N	11.43 E
Kuhmo	160	64.08 N	29.31 E
Kuhmoinen	160	61.34 N	25.11 E
Kūhrān, Kūh-e ∧	208	26.46 N	58.12 E
Kuiseb ≃	224	22.59 S	14.31 E
Kuiu Island I	236	57.45 N	134.10 W
Kuivaniemi	160	65.35 N	25.11 E
Kuivastu	160	58.35 N	23.22 E
Kuja, S.S.S.R.	160	65.05 N	40.06 E
Kuja, S.S.S.R.	160	67.46 N	53.10 E
Kujasovo	160	56.21 N	53.07 E
Kujawy ⤶[1]	164	52.45 N	18.30 E
Kujbyšev, S.S.S.R.	160	53.12 N	50.09 E
Kujbyšev, S.S.S.R.	160	54.57 N	49.05 E
Kujbyševskij Zaton	160	55.09 N	49.12 E
Kujbyševskoje Vodochranilišče ⊜[1]	160	53.40 N	49.00 E
Kujbyshevskij	186	37.52 N	68.44 E
Kuji	192	40.11 N	141.46 E
Kuji ≃	192	36.29 N	140.37 E
Kujūkuri-hama ⛱[2]	192	35.45 N	140.30 E
Kujū-san ∧	192	33.05 N	131.15 E
Kujvikej, Gora ∧	236	67.05 N	173.12 E
Kuk ≃	236	70.36 N	160.00 W
Kukaklek Lake ⊜	236	59.09 N	155.20 W
Kukawa	214	12.56 N	13.35 E
Kukës	172	42.05 N	20.24 E
Kukmor	160	56.13 N	50.54 E
Kükong → Shaoguan, Zhg.	196	24.50 N	113.37 E
Kukpowruk ≃	236	69.35 N	163.00 W
Kukpuk ≃	236	68.23 N	166.20 W
Kukuj	160	59.21 N	32.33 E
Kula, Blg.	172	43.53 N	22.31 E
Kula, Jugo.	172	45.36 N	19.32 E
Kula, Tür.	172	38.32 N	28.40 E
Kula, Haw., U.S.	275a	20.46 N	156.20 W
Kul'ab	206	37.55 N	69.46 E
Kula Kangri ∧	206	28.14 N	90.37 E
Kulassein Island I	202	6.25 N	120.40 E
Kuldīga	160	56.58 N	21.59 E
Kuldja → Yining	190	43.55 N	81.14 E
Kulebaki	160	55.24 N	42.32 E
Kulen Vakuf	170	44.34 N	16.06 E
Kulik Lake ⊜	236	68.55 N	155.00 W
Kulim	200	5.22 N	100.34 E
Kulm	252	46.24 N	98.57 W
Kulmbach	164	50.06 N	11.27 E
Kuloj, S.S.S.R.	160	64.58 N	43.28 E
Kuloj, S.S.S.R.	160	61.02 N	42.29 E
Kulpawn ≃	222	10.21 N	1.05 W
Kulpmont	262	40.48 N	76.28 W
Kul'sary	158	46.59 N	54.01 E
Kültepe ⊥	212	38.44 N	35.34 E
Kuluha, Jabal ∧	220	15.31 N	23.25 E
Kulundinskaja Step' ≚	186	53.00 N	79.00 E
Kulundinskoje, Ozero ⊜	186	53.00 N	79.36 E
Kulunqi	190	42.44 N	121.40 E
Kuma ≃, Nihon	192	32.30 N	130.34 E
Kuma ≃, S.S.S.R.	186	44.56 N	47.00 E
Kumagaya	192	36.08 N	139.23 E
Kumaishi	192a	42.08 N	139.59 E
Kumalarang	202	7.44 N	123.08 E
Kumamoto	192	32.48 N	130.43 E
Kumano	192	33.54 N	136.05 E
Kumano ≃	192	33.44 N	136.01 E
Kumano-nada ▾[2]	192	33.47 N	136.20 E
Kumanovo	172	42.08 N	21.43 E
Kumasi	222	6.41 N	1.35 W
Kumba	214	4.38 N	9.25 E
Kum-Dag	208	39.16 N	54.35 E
Kumeny	160	58.07 N	49.56 E
Kumertau	158	52.46 N	55.47 E
Kume-shima I	193b	26.20 N	126.47 E
Kŭmgang-san ∧	194	38.35 N	128.10 E
Kumla	160	59.08 N	15.08 E
Kumo	214	10.03 N	11.13 E
Kumon Range ⛰	200	26.30 N	97.15 E
Kumora	186	55.53 N	111.13 E
Kumukahi, Cape ≻	275d	19.31 N	154.49 W
Kunar ≃	206	34.26 N	70.32 E
Kunašir, Ostrov (Kunashiri-tō) I	192a	44.10 N	146.00 E
Kunda	160	59.29 N	26.32 E
Kundar ≃	206	31.56 N	69.19 E
Kundur, Pulau I	200	0.45 N	103.26 E
Kundūz	204	37.47 N	68.50 E
Kundūz ☐[4]	206	36.45 N	68.30 E
Kundūz ≃	206	37.02 N	68.15 E
Kunes	160	70.21 N	26.31 E
Kungälv	160	57.52 N	11.58 E
Kungchuling → Huaide	190	43.32 N	124.50 E
Kunghit Island I	238	52.06 N	131.04 W
Kungrad	186	43.06 N	58.54 E
Kungsbacka	160	57.29 N	12.04 E
Kungur	158	57.25 N	56.57 E
Kunhegyes	164	47.22 N	20.38 E
Kunia	275c	21.29 N	158.07 W
Kunisaki	192	33.33 N	131.45 E
Kunisaki-hantō ≻[1]	192	33.30 N	131.40 E
Kunkle	268	41.38 N	84.30 W
Kunlunshanmai ⛰	206	36.30 N	88.00 E
Kunming	200	25.05 N	102.40 E
Kunovice	164	49.03 N	17.29 E
Kunsan	194	35.58 N	126.41 E
Kunshan	196	31.23 N	120.57 E
Kunszentmárton	164	46.51 N	20.18 E
Kununurra	226	15.47 S	128.44 E
Künzelsau	164	49.16 N	9.41 E
Kuocangshan ⛰	196	28.30 N	118.46 E
Kuolajarvi	160	66.58 N	29.12 E
Kuopio	160	62.54 N	27.41 E
Kuopion lääni ☐[4]	160	63.00 N	27.30 E
Kupa ≃	170	45.28 N	16.24 E
Kupang	226	10.10 S	123.35 E
Kup'ansk	158	49.42 N	37.38 E
Kupanskoje	160	56.51 N	38.43 E
Kuparuk ≃	236	70.25 N	148.55 W
Kupino	186	54.22 N	77.18 E
Küplü	172	41.07 N	26.21 E
Kupol, Gora ∧	236	68.38 N	174.45 E
Kupreanof Island I	236	56.50 N	133.30 W
Kupreanof Point ≻	236	55.34 N	159.35 W
Kupres	170	44.00 N	17.17 E
Kura ≃	208	39.24 N	49.24 E
Kuramā', Ḥarrat ⛱[9]	208	24.30 N	40.15 E
Kurashiki	192	34.35 N	133.46 E
Kuraymah	220	18.33 N	31.51 E
Kurayoshi	192	35.26 N	133.49 E
Kurbağa Gölü ⊜	212	38.21 N	35.17 E
K'urdamir	208	40.21 N	48.08 E
Kurdufān ☐[4]	220	13.00 N	30.00 E
Kure	192	34.14 N	132.34 E
Kurejka ≃	186	66.30 N	87.12 E
Kurenalus	160	65.21 N	26.59 E
Kurgan	158	55.26 N	65.18 E
Kurgan-T'ube	206	37.50 N	68.48 E
Kuria Muria Islands → Khūryān Mūryān II	204	17.30 N	56.00 E
Kurikka	160	62.37 N	22.25 E
Kuril Islands → Kuril'skije Ostrova II	186	46.10 N	152.00 E
Kuril'sk	186	45.14 N	147.53 E
Kuril'skije Ostrova II	186	46.10 N	152.00 E
Kuril Strait → Pervyj Kuril'skij Proliv ⋃	186	50.50 N	156.36 E
Kuril Trench ⊹[1]	148	47.00 N	155.00 E
Kuřim	164	49.18 N	16.32 E
Ku-ring-gai Chase ♠	228	33.38 S	151.15 E
Kurinskaja Kosa ≻[2]	208	39.03 N	49.13 E
Kuriyama	192a	43.03 N	141.47 E
Kurja	160	61.42 N	57.09 E
Kurjanovskaja	160	60.19 N	41.33 E
Kurmuk	214	10.33 N	34.17 E
Kurobe	192	36.51 N	137.26 E
Kuroishi	192	40.38 N	140.36 E
Kuro-shima I	193b	30.50 N	129.57 E
Kurovskoje	160	55.34 N	38.55 E
Kuršėnai	160	56.00 N	22.56 E
Kursk	158	51.42 N	36.12 E
Kuršumlija	172	43.08 N	21.17 E
Kūrtī	214	18.07 N	31.33 E
Kurtistown	275d	19.36 N	155.04 W
Kurtköy	172	39.04 N	30.07 E
Kuru ≃	220	9.08 N	26.57 E
Kuruca Geçidi)(	212	38.58 N	40.16 E
Kuruman	218	27.28 S	23.28 E
Kuruman ≃	224	26.56 S	20.39 E
Kuruman Heuwells ⛰[2]	224	27.40 S	23.25 E
Kurume	192	33.19 N	130.31 E
Kurumkan	186	54.18 N	110.18 E
Kurunegala	204	7.29 N	80.22 E
Kurur, Jabal ∧	220	20.31 N	31.32 E
Kuryŏng-gang ≃	194	39.43 N	125.47 E
Kusa	158	55.20 N	59.29 E
Kuşadası	172	37.51 N	27.15 E
Kuşadası Körfezi C	212	37.50 N	27.08 E
Kusathu ⊜	206	35.43 N	92.45 E
Kusawa Lake ⊜	236	60.20 N	136.15 W
Kusaybah, Bi'r ▾[4]	220	22.41 N	29.55 E
Kusel	164	49.32 N	7.24 E
Kushikino	192	31.44 N	130.16 E
Kushima	192	31.29 N	131.14 E
Kushimoto	192	33.28 N	135.47 E
Kushiro	192a	42.58 N	144.23 E
Kushtia	204	23.55 N	89.07 E
Kushui	190	42.11 N	94.25 E
Kusiyāra ≃	206	24.36 N	91.44 E
Kuška	208	35.16 N	62.20 E
Kuška ≃	208	36.00 N	62.40 E
Kuskokwim ≃	236	60.17 N	162.27 W
Kuskokwim Bay C	236	59.45 N	162.25 W
Kuskokwim Mountains ⛰	236	62.30 N	156.00 W
Kuškušara	160	64.58 N	40.21 E
Kušmurun	158	52.27 N	64.36 E
Kussharo-ko ⊜	192a	43.38 N	144.21 E
Küssnacht	180	47.05 N	8.27 E
Kustanaj	158	53.10 N	63.35 E
Kūstī	220	13.10 N	32.40 E
Küstrin → Kostrzyn	164	52.37 N	14.39 E
Kusu	192	33.16 N	131.09 E
K'us'ur	186	70.39 N	127.15 E
Kušva	158	58.18 N	59.45 E
Kut, Ko I	200	11.40 N	102.35 E
Kütahya	212	39.25 N	29.59 E
Kutaisi	158	42.15 N	42.40 E
Kūt al-Imāra	208	32.25 N	45.49 E
Kutaradja → Banda Atjeh	200	5.34 N	95.20 E
Kutch, Gulf of C	206	22.30 N	69.30 E
Kutchan	192a	42.54 N	140.45 E
Kutcharo-ko ⊜	192a	45.09 N	142.19 E
K'utdligssat	232	70.04 N	53.01 W
Kutina	170	45.35 N	16.46 E
Kutná Hora	164	49.57 N	15.16 E
Kutno	164	52.15 N	19.23 E
Kuttawa	248	37.04 N	88.06 W
Kuttura	160	68.24 N	26.28 E
Kuttusvaara	160	67.46 N	28.50 E
Kutu	218	2.44 S	18.09 E
Kutubdia Island I	206	21.50 N	91.52 E
Kutum	220	14.12 N	24.40 E
Kúty	164	48.40 N	17.03 E
Kutztown	242	40.31 N	75.47 W
Kuurne	176	50.51 N	3.17 E
Kuusamo	160	65.58 N	29.11 E
Kuusankoski	160	60.54 N	26.38 E
Kuvandyk	158	51.28 N	57.21 E
Kuvet ≃	236	69.14 N	175.00 E
Kuvšinovo	160	57.02 N	34.10 E
Kuwait ☐[1]	204	29.30 N	47.45 E
Kuwait Bay → Kuwayt, Khalīj al- C	208	29.30 N	48.00 E
Kuwana	192	35.04 N	136.42 E
Kuwayt, Khalīj al- C	208	29.30 N	48.00 E
Kuybyshev → Kujbyšev	160	53.12 N	50.09 E
Kuyucak	172	37.55 N	28.28 E
Kuyuwini ≃	290	2.15 N	58.10 W
Kuyuyukak, Cape ≻	236	56.54 N	156.50 W
Kuzaranda	160	62.22 N	35.37 E
Kužener	160	56.48 N	48.56 E
Kuženkino	160	57.44 N	33.59 E
Kuzitrin ≃	236	65.10 N	165.28 W
Kuz'movka	186	62.19 N	92.02 E
Kuzneck	160	53.07 N	46.36 E
Kuzneckij Alatau ⛰	186	54.45 N	88.00 E
Kuznecovka	160	56.18 N	28.33 E
Kuzomen', S.S.S.R.	160	64.17 N	42.53 E
Kuzomen', S.S.S.R.	160	66.17 N	36.54 E
Kuzovatovo	160	53.33 N	47.41 E
Kuzuryū ≃	192	36.13 N	136.08 E
Kvænangen C[2]	160	70.05 N	21.13 E
Kvaløy I	160	69.40 N	18.30 E
Kvaløya I	160	70.37 N	23.52 E
Kvam	160	61.40 N	9.42 E
Kvarner C	170	44.45 N	14.15 E
Kvarnerić ⋃	170	44.45 N	14.35 E
Kvenna ≃	160	60.01 N	7.56 E
Kverkfjöll ∧	160a	64.43 N	16.38 W
Kvichak Bay C	236	58.48 N	157.30 W
Kvikkjokk	160	66.55 N	17.50 E
Kwahu Plateau ⛰[1]	222	6.30 N	0.30 W
Kwakoegron	286	5.12 N	55.22 W
Kwamisa ∧	222	7.08 N	1.53 W
Kwando (Cuando) ≃	218	18.27 N	23.32 E
Kwangchow → Guangzhou	196	23.06 N	113.16 E
Kwangju	194	35.09 N	126.54 E
Kwango (Cuango) ≃	218	3.14 S	17.23 E
Kwangsi Chuang Autonomous Region → Guangxi Zhuang Zizhiqu ☐[4]	190	24.00 N	109.00 E
Kwangtung → Guangdong ☐[4]	190	23.00 N	113.00 E
Kwanmo-bong ∧	194	41.42 N	129.13 E
Kwanto Plain → Kantō-heiya ≚	192	36.00 N	139.30 E
Kwara ☐[3]	222	9.00 N	4.30 E
Kweichow → Guizhou ☐[4]	190	27.00 N	107.00 E
Kweilin → Guilin	200	25.11 N	110.09 E
Kweisui → Huhehaote	190	40.51 N	111.40 E
Kweiyang → Guiyang	200	26.35 N	106.43 E
Kweneng ☐[5]	224	24.00 S	24.00 E
Kwenge ≃	218	4.50 S	18.42 E
Kwethluk	236	60.49 N	161.27 W
Kwethluk ≃	236	60.46 N	161.26 W
Kwidzyn	164	53.45 N	18.56 E
Kwigillingok	236	59.51 N	163.08 W
Kwiguk	236	62.45 N	164.28 W
Kwilu (Cuilo) ≃	218	3.22 S	17.22 E
Kwisa ≃	164	51.35 N	15.25 E
Kwitaro ≃	290	3.20 N	58.45 W
Kyabram	228	36.19 S	145.03 E
Kyaiklat	200	16.26 N	95.44 E
Kyaikto	200	17.18 N	97.01 E
Kyaukpyu	200	19.05 N	93.52 E
Kyauktaw	198	20.51 N	92.59 E
Kybartai	164	54.39 N	22.45 E
Kyburz	272	38.47 N	120.18 W
Kyebang-san ∧	194	37.43 N	128.29 E
Kyjov	164	49.01 N	17.08 E
Kyle, S. Dak., U.S.	252	43.26 N	102.10 W
Kyle, Tex., U.S.	250	29.59 N	97.53 W
Kyle, Lake ⊜[1]	224	20.14 S	31.00 E
Kyle Dam Game Reserve ⤶[4]	224	20.14 S	31.00 E
Kyle of Lochalsh	162	57.17 N	5.43 W
Kylertown	266	41.00 N	78.10 W
Kymen lääni ☐[4]	160	61.00 N	28.00 E
Kymynejvejem ≃	236	67.26 N	175.28 W
Kynlyn	262	39.45 N	75.39 W
Kynšperk nad Ohří	164	50.04 N	12.32 E
Kyoga, Lake ⊜	214	1.30 N	33.00 E
Kyōga-saki ≻	192	35.46 N	135.13 E
Kyogle	228	28.37 S	153.00 E
Kyom ≃	220	8.58 N	28.13 E
Kyŏnggi Do ☐[4]	194	37.30 N	127.15 E
Kyŏnggi-man C	194	37.25 N	126.00 E
Kyŏngju	194	35.51 N	129.14 E
Kyŏngsang Namdo ☐[4]	194	35.15 N	128.30 E
Kyŏngsang Pukdo ☐[4]	194	36.15 N	128.45 E
Kyōto	192	35.00 N	135.45 E
Kyren	186	51.41 N	102.08 E
Kyritz	164	52.56 N	12.23 E
Kyrönjoki ≃	160	63.14 N	21.45 E
Kyrta	160	64.04 N	57.42 E
Kyštovka	186	56.33 N	76.38 E
Kyštym	158	55.42 N	60.34 E
Kysucké Nové Mesto	164	49.19 N	18.47 E
Kyte ≃	248	42.00 N	89.19 W
Kyungyi I	200	15.04 N	97.44 E
Kyuquot	238	50.02 N	127.23 W
Kyuquot Sound ⋃	238	50.05 N	127.15 W
Kyūroku-jima I	192	40.32 N	139.29 E
Kyūshū I	192	33.00 N	131.00 E
Kyūshū-sanchi ⛰	192	32.35 N	131.17 E
Kyyjärvi	160	63.02 N	24.34 E
Kyzyl	186	51.42 N	94.27 E
Kyzyl-Kija	186	40.16 N	72.08 E
Kyzylkum ⤶[2]	186	42.00 N	64.00 E
Kzyl-Orda	186	44.48 N	65.28 E
Kzyltu	186	53.38 N	72.20 E
L			
Laa an der Thaya	164	48.43 N	16.23 E
La Aguja, Cabo de ≻	290	11.18 N	74.11 W
La Albuera	168	38.43 N	6.49 W
La Albufera ⊜	168	39.20 N	0.22 W
La Alcarria ⤶[1]	168	40.30 N	2.45 W
La Algaba	168	37.28 N	6.01 W
La Almarcha	168	39.41 N	2.22 W
La Almunia de Doña Godina	168	41.29 N	1.22 W
La Arena	280	7.57 N	80.27 W
La Asunción	290	11.02 N	63.53 W
Laatzen	178	52.19 N	9.47 E
Laau Point ≻	275d	21.06 N	157.19 W
La Azufrosa	250	28.14 N	100.50 W
La Babia	278	28.34 N	102.04 W
L'Abacou, Pointe ≻	282	18.01 N	73.47 W
Labadieville	248	29.50 N	90.57 W
Laban	262	37.24 N	76.17 W
La Banda	294	27.44 S	64.15 W
La Bandera	250	25.59 N	98.58 W
La Bañeza	168	42.18 N	5.54 W
La Barca	278	20.17 N	102.34 W
La Barge	254	42.16 N	110.12 W
Labason	202	8.04 N	122.31 E
La Bassée	176	50.32 N	2.48 E
Labastide-Murat	166	44.39 N	1.34 E
La Baule	166	47.17 N	2.24 W
Labé	222	11.19 N	12.17 W
Labé ☐[4]	222	11.23 N	12.07 W
Labe (Elbe) ≃	164	53.50 N	9.00 E
Labelle, Qué., Can.	260	46.17 N	74.45 W
La Belle, Fla., U.S.	246	26.46 N	81.26 W
La Belle, Mo., U.S.	248	40.07 N	91.55 W
Labelle ☐[6]	260	46.20 N	75.00 W
Laberge, Lake ⊜	236	61.11 N	135.12 W
Laberinto de las Doce Leguas I	284p	20.35 N	78.30 W
La Biche ≃	238	55.01 N	112.44 W
Labin	170	45.05 N	14.07 E
Labinsk	158	44.38 N	40.44 E
Labis	200	2.23 N	103.02 E
La Bisbal	168	41.57 N	3.03 E
Łabiszyn	164	52.57 N	17.55 E
La Blanquilla I	290	11.51 N	64.37 W
Labná ⊥	278	20.11 N	89.34 W
Labo	202	14.09 N	122.50 E
Labo ≃	202	14.12 N	122.57 E
Labo, Mount ∧	202	14.01 N	122.47 E
Laboe	164	54.24 N	10.15 E
Laboratory	266	40.09 N	80.13 W
Laborde	294	33.09 S	62.51 W
Laborec ≃	164	48.31 N	21.54 E
Laborie	285f	13.45 N	61.00 W
Labouheyre	166	44.13 N	0.55 W
Laboulaye	294	34.05 S	63.25 W
La Bouverie	176	50.24 N	3.52 E
Labrador ⤶[1]	232	54.00 N	62.00 W
Labrador Basin ⊹[1]	148	54.00 N	47.00 W
Labrador City	232	52.57 N	66.54 W
Labrador Sea ▾[2]	232	57.00 N	53.00 W
Lábrea, Bra.	292	7.16 S	64.47 W
La Brea, Trin.	285r	10.15 N	61.37 W
Labrède	166	44.41 N	0.31 W
Labrit	166	44.07 N	0.33 W
La Broquerie	252	49.28 N	96.27 W
Labuchongshan ⛰	206	30.30 N	85.00 E
Labuha	198	0.37 S	127.29 E
Labuk ≃	202	5.54 N	117.30 E
Labuk Bay C	202	6.07 N	117.46 E
Laburnum Manor	262	37.34 N	77.26 W
Labutta	200	16.09 N	94.46 E
Labytnangi	186	66.39 N	66.21 E
Lač	160	63.18 N	54.28 E
Lača, Ozero ⊜	160	61.20 N	38.48 E
La Cadena	250	25.53 N	104.12 W
La Cal ≃	292	17.27 S	58.15 W
Lac-à-la-Tortue	260	46.36 N	72.39 W
La Calera	294	32.47 S	71.12 W
Lac Allard	240	50.38 N	63.28 W
La Campana	168	37.34 N	5.26 W
La Campiña ⤶[1]	168	37.45 N	4.45 W
La Canada	274	34.12 N	118.12 W
Lacanau	166	44.59 N	1.05 W
Lacanau, Étang de C	166	44.58 N	1.07 E
La Candelaria, Arg.	294	26.05 S	65.05 W
La Candelaria, Méx.	254	31.07 N	106.29 W
La Cãniza	168	42.13 N	8.16 W
La Canourgue	166	44.26 N	3.13 E
Lacantum ≃	278	16.36 N	90.40 W
La Capelle-en-Thiérache	166	49.58 N	3.55 E
Lacapelle-Marival	166	44.44 N	1.54 E
La Carlota, Arg.	294	33.25 S	63.18 W
La Carlota, Pil.	202	10.26 N	122.55 E
Lacarne	266	41.31 N	83.03 W
La Carolina	168	38.15 N	3.37 W
La Castellana	202	10.21 N	123.01 E
Lacaune	166	43.43 N	2.42 E
La Cavalerie	166	44.00 N	3.10 E
Lac-Bellemare	260	46.34 N	73.26 W
Lacchiarella	182	45.19 N	9.08 E
Lac Courte Oreilles Indian Reservation ⤶[4]	244	45.55 N	91.19 W
Lac du Flambeau	244	45.58 N	89.53 W
Lac du Flambeau Indian Reservation ⤶[4]	244	45.59 N	89.53 W
Lacedonia	184	41.03 N	15.25 E
La Ceiba, Hond.	280	15.47 N	86.50 W
La Ceiba, Ven.	290	9.28 N	71.04 W
La Center, Ky., U.S.	248	37.04 N	88.58 W
La Center, Wash., U.S.	270	45.52 N	122.40 W
Lacepede Bay C	228	36.47 S	139.45 E
Lac-Etchemin	240	46.24 N	70.30 W
Lacey	270	47.07 N	122.49 W
Lac-Frontière	240	46.42 N	70.00 W
La Chaise-Dieu	166	45.19 N	3.42 E
La Chambre	166	45.22 N	6.18 E
La Chapelle-d'Angillon	166	47.22 N	2.26 E
La Charité[-sur-Loire]	166	47.11 N	3.01 E
La Chartre-sur-le-Loir	166	47.44 N	0.35 E
La Châtaigneraie	166	46.39 N	0.44 W
La Châtre	166	46.35 N	1.59 E
La Chaux-de-Fonds	180	47.06 N	6.50 E
Lachay, Punta ≻	292	11.17 S	77.44 W
Lachdenpochja	160	61.31 N	30.08 E
Lachine	260	45.26 N	73.40 W
Lachkaltsap Indian Reserve ⤶[4]	238	55.03 N	129.34 W
Lachlan ≃	228	34.21 S	143.57 E
La Chorrera, Col.	290	0.44 S	73.01 W
La Chorrera, Pan.	280	8.53 N	79.47 W
L'achovskije Ostrova II	186	73.30 N	141.00 E
Lachute	260	45.39 N	74.21 W
La Ciénaga	294	27.30 S	66.58 W
La Cinta Creek ≃	250	35.24 N	104.06 W
La Ciotat	182	43.10 N	5.36 E
La Citadelle ⊥	282	19.35 N	72.13 W
La Ciudad, Parque Nacional ♠	278	23.55 N	105.35 W
Lackawanna	264	42.49 N	78.50 W
Lackawanna ≃	242	41.21 N	75.47 W
Lackey	262	37.14 N	76.33 W
Lackland Air Force Base ■	250	29.27 N	98.37 W
Lackoje	160	58.05 N	38.08 E
Lac La Belle	268	43.09 N	88.32 W
Lacla Biche	238	54.46 N	111.58 W
Lac la Hache	238	51.49 N	121.28 W
La Clayette	166	46.18 N	4.19 E
Laclede, Idaho, U.S.	238	49.58 N	116.45 W
Laclede, Mo., U.S.	248	39.47 N	93.10 W
La Clotilde	294	27.08 S	60.40 W
Lac-Masson	260	46.02 N	74.03 W
Lac-Mégantic	242	45.36 N	70.53 W
Lacob ti-duyong, Mount ∧	202	17.35 N	121.09 E
La Cocha	294	27.45 S	65.35 W
La Cocha, Laguna de ⊜	290	1.05 N	77.09 W
Lacolle	260	45.05 N	73.23 W
La Colorada	278	28.41 N	110.25 W
Lacombe	238	52.28 N	113.44 W
Lacon	244	41.02 N	89.24 W
Lacona, Iowa, U.S.	244	41.12 N	93.23 W
Lacona, N.Y., U.S.	264	43.39 N	76.04 W
La Concepción, Ven.	290	10.25 N	71.41 W
La Concepción, Ven.	290	10.38 N	71.50 W
La Concordia	278	16.05 N	92.38 W
Laconia	242	43.31 N	71.29 W
La Conner	270	48.23 N	122.30 W
La Consulta	294	33.45 S	69.06 W
Lacoochee	246	28.28 N	82.10 W
La Coruña	168	43.22 N	8.23 W
Lacosta Island I	246	26.41 N	82.15 W
La Coste	250	29.19 N	98.49 W
La Courtine	166	45.42 N	2.16 E
Lac qui Parle ≃	252	45.01 N	95.53 W
Lacre Punt ≻	285s	12.02 N	68.15 W
La Crescent	244	43.50 N	91.19 W
La Crescenta	274	34.12 N	118.12 W
La Croft	266	40.39 N	80.35 W
La Crosse, Ind., U.S.	268	41.19 N	86.53 W
La Crosse, Kans., U.S.	252	38.32 N	99.18 W
La Crosse, Va., U.S.	246	36.42 N	78.06 W
Lacrosse, Wash., U.S.	256	46.49 N	117.53 W
La Crosse, Wis., U.S.	244	43.49 N	91.15 W
La Crosse ≃	244	43.49 N	91.16 W
La Cruz, Arg.	294	29.10 S	56.35 W
La Cruz, Col.	290	1.35 N	76.58 W
La Cruz, C.R.	280	11.04 N	85.39 W
La Cruz, Méx.	250	28.33 N	100.48 W
La Cruz, Ur.	294	33.56 S	56.15 W
La Cruz de Río Grande	280	13.04 N	84.15 W
Lac-Saguay	260	46.30 N	75.09 W
La Cuesta, C.R.	280	8.30 N	82.50 W
La Cuesta, P.R.	284m	18.25 N	66.49 W
La Cumbre	294	31.00 S	64.30 W
La Cygne	252	38.21 N	94.46 W
Ladainha	296	17.39 S	41.44 W
Ladākh ⤶[1]	204	34.45 N	76.30 E
Ladākh Range ⛰	206	34.00 N	78.00 E
Ladário	292	19.01 S	57.35 W
Ladd	244	41.23 N	89.13 W
Laddicea ⊥	212	37.56 N	29.02 E
Laddonia	248	39.15 N	91.39 W
La Digue I	218	4.21 S	55.50 E
L'adiny	160	61.33 N	38.20 E
Ladispoli	170	41.56 N	12.05 E
Lādīz	204	28.56 N	61.19 E
Ladner	238	49.05 N	123.05 W
Ladoga	248	39.55 N	86.48 W
Ladoga, Lake → Ladožskoje Ozero ⊜	160	61.00 N	31.30 E
Ladonia	250	33.25 N	95.57 W
La Dorada	290	5.27 N	74.40 W
La Dormida	294	33.20 S	67.56 W
L'adova ≃	172	48.28 N	27.37 E
Ladožskoje Ozero ⊜	160	61.00 N	31.30 E
Ladue ≃	236	63.09 N	140.25 W
Laduškin [Ludwigsort]	164	54.36 N	20.11 E
Ladva	160	61.21 N	34.34 E
Ladva-Vetka	160	61.21 N	34.27 E
Ladvozero	160	65.00 N	29.50 E
L'ady	160	58.38 N	28.47 E
Lady Ann Strait ⋃	232	75.40 N	79.50 W
Ladybrand	224	29.19 S	27.25 E
Lady Elliot Island I	228	24.07 S	152.42 E
Lady Evelyn Lake ⊜	244	47.20 N	80.10 W
Ladysmith, B.C., Can.	238	48.58 N	123.49 W
Ladysmith, S. Afr.	224	28.34 S	29.45 E
Ladysmith, Wis., U.S.	244	45.28 N	91.12 W
Laem, Khao ∧	200	14.27 N	101.34 E
La Encantada	294	27.05 S	65.14 W
La Encantada, Cerro de ∧	278	31.00 N	115.24 W
La Escondida, Arg.	294	27.05 S	59.28 W
La Escondida, Méx.	250	26.17 N	99.46 W
La Escondida, Méx.	278	25.40 N	98.18 W
La Esmeralda, Méx.	278	27.17 N	103.39 W
La Esmeralda, Para.	294	22.13 S	62.38 W
Læsø I	160	57.16 N	11.01 E
La Esperanza, Cuba	284p	22.46 N	83.44 W
La Esperanza, Cuba	284p	22.27 N	80.06 W
La Esperanza, Hond.	280	14.15 N	88.10 W
La Esperanza, Méx.	250	26.46 N	104.00 W
La Esperanza, Méx.	254	32.06 N	114.47 W
La Esperanza, P.R.	284m	18.22 N	66.07 W
La Estrada	168	42.41 N	8.29 W
La Estrella, Bol.	292	16.30 S	63.45 W
La Estrella, Chile	294	34.12 S	71.40 W
La Estrella, Col.	290	6.10 N	75.39 W
La Falda	294	31.05 S	64.30 W
La Farge	244	43.35 N	90.38 W
La Fargeville	264	44.12 N	75.58 W
Lafayette, Ala., U.S.	248	32.54 N	85.24 W
Lafayette, Calif., U.S.	272	37.54 N	122.07 W
Lafayette, Colo., U.S.	252	39.60 N	105.05 W
La Fayette, Ga., U.S.	246	34.42 N	85.17 W
Lafayette, Ind., U.S.	268	40.25 N	86.53 W
Lafayette, La., U.S.	248	30.14 N	92.01 W
Lafayette, Minn., U.S.	244	44.27 N	94.24 W
La Fayette, N.Y., U.S.	264	42.54 N	76.06 W
La Fayette, Ohio, U.S.	268	40.46 N	83.57 W
Lafayette, Oreg., U.S.	270	45.15 N	123.07 W
La Fayette, R.I., U.S.	261	41.34 N	71.29 W
Lafayette, Tenn., U.S.	248	36.32 N	86.01 W
La Fayette, Tex., U.S.	248	32.54 N	94.51 W
Lafayette, Mount ∧	242	44.10 N	71.38 W
La Fère	166	49.40 N	3.22 E
La Feria	250	26.09 N	97.50 W
La Ferté-Bernard	176	48.11 N	0.40 E
La Ferté-Gaucher	166	48.47 N	3.18 E
La Ferté-Macé	166	48.36 N	0.22 W
La Ferté-Saint-Aubin	166	47.43 N	1.56 E
La Ferté-Vidame	162	48.37 N	0.55 E
Lafferty	266	40.07 N	81.01 W
Lafia	222	8.30 N	8.30 E
Lafiagi	222	8.52 N	5.25 E
Laflamme ≃	244	48.56 N	77.18 W
La Flèche	166	47.42 N	0.05 W
La Flor	280	11.30 N	84.21 W
La Florida	278	16.33 N	90.27 W
Lafnitz ≃	164	46.57 N	16.16 E
La Follette	246	36.23 N	84.07 W
Lafontaine, Qué., Can.	260	45.47 N	74.01 W
La Fontaine, Ind., U.S.	268	40.40 N	85.43 W
La Forteleza, Río de ≃	292	10.40 S	77.51 W
La Fortuna	280	10.30 N	84.35 W
Lafourche, Bayou ≃, La., U.S.	248	32.06 N	91.58 W
Lafourche, Bayou ≃, La., U.S.	248	29.05 N	90.14 W
La Fragua	294	26.07 S	64.20 W
La Francia	294	31.25 S	62.38 W
La Fregeneda	168	40.59 N	6.52 W
La Fría	290	8.13 N	72.15 W
La Fuente de San Esteban	168	40.48 N	6.15 W
La Gacilly	162	47.46 N	2.09 W
La Galite I	170	37.32 N	8.56 E
La Gallareta	294	29.35 S	60.24 W
La Gallega	168	41.54 N	3.16 W
Lagan ≃	160	56.33 N	12.56 E
Lagarto	280	10.07 N	84.56 W
Lagawe	202	16.45 N	121.10 E
Lagay	202	14.06 N	122.13 E
Lagayan	202	17.43 N	120.42 E
Lage, B.R.D.	178	51.59 N	8.48 E
Lage, Esp.	168	43.13 N	9.00 W
Lagechi ⊜	206	30.42 N	81.16 E
Lågen ≃	160	59.03 N	10.05 E
Laghmān ☐[4]	206	35.00 N	70.15 E
Laghouat	214	33.50 N	2.59 E
La Gloria, Col.	290	8.37 N	73.48 W
La Gloria, Méx.	250	25.56 N	99.13 W
La Gloria, Bahía C	284p	21.50 N	77.40 W
Lagna ≃	200	11.12 N	107.16 E
Lagny, Fr.	166	49.37 N	2.55 E
Lagny, Fr.	176	48.52 N	2.43 E
Lagoa da Prata	296	20.01 S	45.33 W
Lagoa Dourada	296	20.55 S	44.05 W
Lagoa Formosa	296	18.47 S	46.24 W
Lagoa Santa	296	19.38 S	43.53 W
Lagoa Vermelha	294	28.13 S	51.32 W
Lagolândia	296	15.37 S	49.02 W
La Gomera	280	14.05 N	91.03 W
Lagonegro	170	40.07 N	15.46 E
Lagonglong	202	8.48 N	124.47 E
Lagonoy	202	13.43 N	123.30 E
Lagonoy Gulf C	202	13.30 N	124.00 E
Lagos, Nig.	222	6.27 N	3.24 E
Lagos, Port.	168	37.06 N	8.40 W
Lagos ☐[8]	222	6.30 N	3.30 E
Lagos de Moreno	278	21.21 N	101.55 W
La Goulette	170	36.49 N	10.18 E
La Grand'Combe	182	44.13 N	4.02 E
La Grande	256	45.20 N	118.05 W
La Grande-Rivière ≃	232	53.50 N	79.00 W
La Grange, Austl.	226	18.41 S	121.45 E
LaGrange, Calif., U.S.	272	37.40 N	120.28 W
La Grange, Ga., U.S.	246	33.02 N	85.02 W
La Grange, Ill., U.S.	268	41.49 N	87.55 W
Lagrange, Ind., U.S.	268	41.39 N	85.25 W
La Grange, Ky., U.S.	248	38.24 N	85.23 W
La Grange, Maine, U.S.	242	45.10 N	68.51 W
La Grange, Mo., U.S.	248	40.03 N	91.35 W
La Grange, N.C., U.S.	246	35.19 N	77.47 W
Lagrange, Ohio, U.S.	266	41.14 N	82.07 W
La Grange, Tex., U.S.	250	29.54 N	96.52 W
Lagrange, Wyo., U.S.	252	41.38 N	104.10 W
Lagrange ☐[6]	268	41.39 N	85.25 W
Lagrangeville	261	41.39 N	73.46 W
La Gran Sabana ≚	290	5.30 N	61.30 W
La Grave	166	45.03 N	6.18 E
La Grita	290	8.08 N	71.59 W
Lagro	268	40.50 N	85.44 W
La Guadeloupe (Saint Evariste)	242	45.58 N	70.56 W
La Guaira	290	10.36 N	66.56 W
La Guajira ☐[5]	290	11.30 N	72.30 W
La Guajira, Península de ≻[1]	290	12.00 N	71.40 W
La Guardia, Arg.	294	29.34 S	65.27 W
La Guardia, Bol.	292	17.54 S	63.20 W
Laguardia, Esp.	168	42.33 N	2.35 W
La Guardia, Esp.	168	41.54 N	8.53 W
La Gudiña	168	42.04 N	7.08 W
La Guerche-de-Bretagne	166	47.56 N	1.14 W
La Guerche-sur-l'Aubois	166	46.57 N	2.57 E
Laguiole	166	44.41 N	2.51 E
Laguna, Bra.	294	28.29 S	48.47 W
Laguna, N. Mex., U.S.	254	35.02 N	107.23 W
Laguna ☐[4]	202	14.10 N	121.20 E
Laguna Beach	274	33.33 N	117.51 W
Laguna Blanca	284p	20.27 N	76.07 W
Laguna Carapã	296	22.27 S	55.01 W
Laguna de Jaco	278	27.50 N	104.00 W
Laguna Indian Reservation ⤶[4]	254	35.00 N	107.20 W
Laguna Larga	294	31.50 S	63.50 W
Laguna Limpia	294	26.30 S	59.42 W
Lagunas	292	5.15 S	75.45 W
Lagunillas, Bol.	292	19.38 S	63.43 W
Lagunillas, Ven.	290	8.31 N	71.24 W
Lagunillás, Lago ⊜	292	15.43 S	70.43 W
Laguntara C	280	15.12 N	83.30 W
La Habana (Havana)	284p	23.08 N	82.22 W
La Habana ☐[4]	284p	22.45 N	82.10 W
La Habana, Bahía de C	284p	23.08 N	82.20 W
La Habra	274	33.56 N	117.57 W
Lahad Datu	202	5.03 N	118.19 E
Lahaina	275a	20.52 N	156.41 W
La Harpe, Ill., U.S.	244	40.35 N	90.58 W
La Harpe, Kans., U.S.	252	37.55 N	95.18 W
Lahaska	262	40.21 N	75.02 W
Lahat	198	3.48 S	103.32 E
La Have ≃	240	44.14 N	64.20 W
La Have Islands II	240	44.12 N	64.23 W
La Haye Descartes	166	46.58 N	0.42 E
La Haye-du-Puits	166	49.18 N	1.33 W
La Higuera	294	29.30 S	71.17 W
Laḥij	214	13.02 N	44.54 E
Lāhījān	208	37.12 N	50.01 E
Laholm	160	56.31 N	13.02 E
La Honda	272	37.19 N	122.16 W
Lahontan Reservoir ⊜[1]	258	39.24 N	119.07 W
Lahore	206	31.35 N	74.18 E
La Horqueta	290	3.06 N	72.50 W
Lahr	180	48.20 N	7.52 E
Lahti	160	60.58 N	25.40 E
La Huaca	292	4.55 S	80.55 W
La Huacana	278	18.58 N	101.49 W
Lahuy Island I	202	13.57 N	123.50 E
Laibach → Ljubljana	170	46.03 N	14.31 E
Laichingen	180	48.29 N	9.41 E
Laichow Bay → Laizhouwan C	194	37.36 N	119.30 E
Laie	275c	21.39 N	157.56 W
L'Aigle	176	48.45 N	0.38 E
Laignes	166	47.50 N	4.22 E
Laihia	160	62.58 N	22.01 E
Lainate	182	45.34 N	9.02 E
La Independencia, Bahía de C	292	14.15 S	76.13 W
Laindon	174	51.34 N	0.26 E
Laingsburg, S. Afr.	218	33.11 S	20.51 E
Laingsburg, Mich., U.S.	268	42.54 N	84.21 W
Lainioälven ≃	160	67.22 N	23.39 E
Lairg	162	58.01 N	4.25 W
Lais, Indon.	198	3.32 S	102.03 E
Lais, Pil.	202	6.20 N	125.39 E
La Isabela	284p	22.57 N	80.01 W
Laissac	166	44.23 N	2.49 E
Laisvall	160	66.05 N	17.10 E
Laitila	160	60.53 N	21.41 E
Laiwui	198	1.22 S	127.40 E
Laiya	202	13.40 N	121.24 E
Laiyang	194	36.58 N	120.44 E
Laizhouwan C	194	37.36 N	119.30 E
Laja ≃	160	66.20 N	56.16 E
Laja, Laguna de la ⊜	294	37.21 S	71.19 W
Laja, Río de la ≃	278	20.55 N	100.46 W
Laja, Salto del ᒪ	294	37.22 S	72.25 W
La Jalca	292	6.30 S	77.40 W
La Jara	254	37.16 N	105.58 W
La Jara ⤶[1]	168	39.42 N	4.54 W
La Jarita	278	28.03 N	103.20 W
La Jarrie	166	46.08 N	1.00 W
Lajas	284m	18.03 N	67.04 W
La Javie	166	44.10 N	6.21 E
Laje	296	13.10 S	39.25 W
Lajeado	294	29.27 S	51.58 W
Lajes	294	27.48 S	50.19 W
Lajinha	296	20.09 S	41.37 W
Lajitas	250	29.16 N	103.48 W
La Jolla ⤶[8]	274	32.51 N	117.16 W
La Jose	266	40.50 N	78.41 W
Lajosmizse	164	47.02 N	19.34 E
La Joya, Méx.	250	26.26 N	101.08 W
La Joya, Méx.	278	32.08 N	114.01 W
La Joya, Perú	292	16.43 S	71.52 W
Lajta (Leitha) ≃	164	47.54 N	17.17 E
La Junta, Méx.	278	28.28 N	107.20 W
La Junta, Colo., U.S.	252	37.59 N	103.33 W
Lake, Miss., U.S.	248	32.21 N	89.20 W
Lake, N.Y., U.S.	266	42.26 N	78.29 W
Lake ☐[6], Calif., U.S.	272	39.01 N	122.33 W
Lake ☐[6], Ill., U.S.	268	42.22 N	87.50 W
Lake ☐[6], Ind., U.S.	268	41.25 N	87.22 W
Lake ☐[6], Ohio, U.S.	266	41.43 N	81.15 W
Lake Alfred	246	28.05 N	81.44 W
Lake Alpine	272	38.28 N	120.00 W
Lake Andes	252	43.09 N	98.32 W
Lake Arrowhead	274	34.15 N	117.12 W
Lake Arthur, La., U.S.	248	30.05 N	92.41 W
Lake Arthur, N. Mex., U.S.	250	33.00 N	104.22 W
Lake Benton	252	44.16 N	96.17 W
Lake Beseck	261	41.30 N	72.14 W
Lake Bluff	268	42.16 N	87.50 W
Lake Butler	246	30.01 N	82.20 W
Lake Cargelligo	226	33.18 S	146.23 E
Lake Carmel	261	41.27 N	73.40 W
Lake Charles	248	30.13 N	93.12 W
Lake Chelan National Recreation Area ♠	238	48.22 N	120.12 W
Lake City, Ark., U.S.	248	35.49 N	90.26 W
Lake City, Colo., U.S.	254	38.02 N	107.19 W
Lake City, Fla., U.S.	246	30.12 N	82.38 W
Lake City, Iowa, U.S.	252	42.16 N	94.44 W
Lake City, Mich., U.S.	244	44.20 N	85.13 W
Lake City, Minn., U.S.	244	44.27 N	92.16 W
Lake City, Pa., U.S.	266	42.01 N	80.21 W
Lake City, S.C., U.S.	246	33.52 N	79.45 W
Lake City, Tenn., U.S.	246	36.13 N	84.09 W
Lake Como	264	42.41 N	76.18 W
Lake Cowichan	238	48.50 N	124.03 W
Lake Crescent	270	48.06 N	123.50 W
Lake Crystal	244	44.06 N	94.13 W
Lake Dalecarlia	268	41.20 N	87.24 W
Lake Dallas	250	33.07 N	97.02 W
Lake Delton	244	43.35 N	89.47 W
Lake District National Park ♠	162	54.30 N	3.05 W
Lake Eliza	268	41.26 N	87.10 W
Lake Errock	270	49.13 N	122.02 W
Lakefield, Ont., Can.	264	44.26 N	78.16 W
Lakefield, Minn., U.S.	252	43.41 N	95.10 W
Lake Forest, Fla., U.S.	246	30.24 N	81.41 W
Lake Forest, Ill., U.S.	268	42.15 N	87.50 W
Lake Forest Park	270	47.45 N	122.17 W
Lake Geneva	268	42.36 N	88.26 W
Lake George	242	43.26 N	73.43 W
Lake Harbor	246	26.42 N	80.48 W
Lake Harbour	232	62.51 N	69.53 W
Lake Hattie Reservoir ⊜[1]	254	41.15 N	105.55 W
Lake Havasu City	254	34.27 N	114.22 W
Lake Helen	246	28.59 N	81.14 W
Lake Hills, Ind., U.S.	268	41.28 N	87.27 W
Lake Hills, Wash., U.S.	270	47.36 N	122.08 W
Lake Hopatcong	242	40.55 N	74.39 W
Lake Hughes	274	34.40 N	118.26 W
Lakehurst	262	40.01 N	74.19 W
Lake in the Hills	268	42.11 N	88.20 W
Lake Jackson	250	29.02 N	95.27 W
Lake James	268	41.42 N	85.03 W
Lake Katrine	261	41.59 N	73.59 W
Lakeland, Fla., U.S.	246	28.03 N	81.57 W
Lakeland, Ga., U.S.	246	31.02 N	83.04 W
Lakeland, Mich., U.S.	268	42.28 N	83.51 W
Lakeland, N.Y., U.S.	264	43.06 N	76.15 W
Lakeland Park	268	42.21 N	88.17 W
Lakeland Village	274	33.39 N	117.22 W
Lake Linden	244	47.11 N	88.26 W
Lakeline	266	41.35 N	81.28 W
Lake Louise, Alta., Can.	238	51.26 N	116.11 W
Lake Louise, Wash., U.S.	270	47.05 N	122.36 W
Lake Lucerne	266	41.24 N	81.21 W
Lake Manawa	252	41.12 N	95.55 W
Lake Mead National Recreation Area ♠	254	36.00 N	114.30 W
Lake Mills, Iowa, U.S.	244	43.25 N	93.32 W
Lake Mills, Wis., U.S.	268	43.05 N	88.55 W
Lake Milton	266	41.06 N	80.58 W
Lake Minchumina	236	63.53 N	152.19 W
Lake Mohawk	242	41.01 N	74.39 W
Lakemont	266	40.31 N	78.23 W
Lakemoor	268	42.20 N	88.12 W
Lakemore	266	41.01 N	81.25 W
Lake Nepessing	268	43.02 N	83.22 W
Lake Norden	252	44.35 N	97.13 W
Lake Odessa	268	42.47 N	85.08 W
Lake of the Woods	268	41.26 N	86.14 W
Lake Orion	268	42.47 N	83.14 W
Lake Orion Heights	268	42.46 N	83.18 W
Lake Oswego	270	45.26 N	122.39 W
Lake Ozark	248	38.12 N	92.38 W
Lake Park, Fla., U.S.	246	26.49 N	80.04 W
Lake Park, Iowa, U.S.	252	43.27 N	95.19 W
Lake Park, Minn., U.S.	252	46.53 N	96.06 W
Lake Pine	262	39.52 N	74.51 W

Symbols in the index entries are identified on page 360.

Name	Page	Lat°′	Long°′
Lake Placid, Fla., U.S.	246	27.18 N	81.22 W
Lake Placid, N.Y., U.S.	242	44.17 N	73.59 W
Lake Pleasant	242	43.28 N	74.25 W
Lakeport, Calif., U.S.	258	39.03 N	122.55 W
Lakeport, Mich., U.S.	244	43.07 N	82.30 W
Lakeport, N.Y., U.S.	264	43.09 N	75.52 W
Lake Preston	252	44.22 N	97.23 W
Lake Providence	248	32.48 N	91.11 W
Lake Riviera	262	40.03 N	74.10 W
Lake Ronkonkoma	261	40.49 N	73.07 W
Lake Sawyer	270	47.20 N	122.03 W
Lake Serene	270	47.50 N	122.22 W
Lakeshore, Calif., U.S.	272	37.15 N	119.12 W
Lake Shore, Fla., U.S.	246	30.17 N	81.43 W
Lakeside, N.S., Can.	240	44.38 N	63.41 W
Lakeside, Ariz., U.S.	254	34.09 N	109.58 W
Lakeside, Calif., U.S.	274	32.52 N	116.55 W
Lakeside, Conn., U.S.	261	41.26 N	73.16 W
Lakeside, Conn., U.S.	261	41.41 N	73.15 W
Lakeside, Mich., U.S.	268	41.51 N	86.40 W
Lakeside, Mont., U.S.	256	48.01 N	114.13 W
Lakeside, Ohio, U.S.	266	41.32 N	82.45 W
Lakeside, Va., U.S.	262	37.37 N	77.28 W
Lakes National Park ♦	228	38.05 S	147.40 E
Lake Stevens	270	48.01 N	122.04 W
Laketon	268	40.58 N	85.50 W
Laketown	254	41.49 N	111.19 W
Lakeview, Ont., Can.	244	43.35 N	79.34 W
Lakeview, Calif., U.S.	274	33.50 N	117.07 W
Lakeview, Ga., U.S.	246	34.59 N	85.16 W
Lake View, Iowa, U.S.	252	42.18 N	95.03 W
Lakeview, Mich., U.S.	268	42.18 N	85.11 W
Lake View, N.Y., U.S.	264	42.43 N	78.56 W
Lakeview, Ohio, U.S.	268	40.29 N	83.56 W
Lakeview, Oreg., U.S.	256	42.11 N	120.21 W
Lake View, S.C., U.S.	246	34.21 N	79.10 W
Lakeview, Tex., U.S.	248	29.55 N	93.54 W
Lakeview, Tex., U.S.	250	34.40 N	100.42 W
Lakeview, Wash., U.S.	270	47.10 N	122.30 W
Lakeview Mountain ∧	238	49.03 N	120.09 W
Lake Village, Ark., U.S.	248	33.20 N	91.17 W
Lake Village, Ind., U.S.	268	41.08 N	87.27 W
Lakeville, Conn., U.S.	261	41.58 N	73.27 W
Lakeville, Ind., U.S.	268	41.31 N	86.16 W
Lakeville, Mich., U.S.	266	42.49 N	83.09 W
Lakeville, Minn., U.S.	244	44.39 N	93.14 W
Lakeville, N.Y., U.S.	264	42.50 N	77.42 W
Lakeville, Ohio, U.S.	266	40.40 N	82.07 W
Lake Wales	246	27.54 N	81.35 W
Lake Wilson	252	43.59 N	95.57 W
Lakewood, Calif., U.S.	274	33.50 N	118.08 W
Lakewood, Colo., U.S.	254	39.44 N	105.06 W
Lakewood, Ill., U.S.	268	39.19 N	88.54 W
Lakewood, Mich., U.S.	268	42.18 N	85.31 W
Lakewood, N.J., U.S.	262	40.06 N	74.13 W
Lakewood, N.Y., U.S.	266	42.06 N	79.20 W
Lakewood, Ohio, U.S.	266	41.29 N	81.48 W
Lakewood, Wash., U.S.	270	48.09 N	122.12 W
Lakewood, Wis., U.S.	244	45.18 N	88.31 W
Lakewood Center	270	47.10 N	122.31 W
Lakewood Park	252	48.04 N	98.56 W
Lakewood Shores	268	41.17 N	88.10 W
Lake Worth	246	26.37 N	80.03 W
Lake Worth Village	250	32.49 N	97.27 W
Lake Zurich	268	42.12 N	88.06 W
Lakhdaria	168	36.34 N	3.35 E
Lakhish ⊥	210	31.33 N	34.51 E
Lakin	252	37.56 N	101.15 W
Lakinskij	160	56.01 N	39.57 E
Lakonía □[5]	172	37.00 N	22.45 E
Lakonikós Kólpos C	172	36.25 N	22.37 E
Lakota, Iowa, U.S.	244	43.23 N	94.06 W
Lakota, N. Dak., U.S.	252	48.02 N	98.21 W
Laksefjorden C[2]	160	70.58 N	27.00 E
Lakselv	160	70.04 N	24.56 E
Lākshām	198	23.14 N	91.08 E
Lala	202	7.59 N	123.45 E
La Lajilla	278	26.47 N	99.37 W
Lâlapaşa	172	41.50 N	26.44 E
Lalbenque	166	44.20 N	1.33 E
Lāleh Zār, Kūh-e ∧	208	29.24 N	56.46 E
La Leona	250	25.52 N	101.05 W
La Leonesa	294	27.05 S	58.40 W
Lalibela	214	12.02 N	39.02 E
La Libertad, El Sal.	280	13.29 N	89.19 W
La Libertad, Guat.	278	16.47 N	90.07 W
La Libertad, Hond.	280	14.43 N	87.36 W
La Libertad, Méx.	278	29.55 N	112.43 W
La Libertad, Nic.	280	12.15 N	85.10 W
La Libertad □[5]	292	8.00 S	78.30 W
La Ligua	294	32.27 S	71.14 W
La Lima	280	15.24 N	87.56 W
Lalín	168	42.39 N	8.07 W
Lalinde	166	44.51 N	0.44 E
La Línea	168	36.10 N	5.19 W
Lalitpur	206	27.41 N	85.20 E
La Loche	232	56.29 N	109.27 W
La Loupe	166	48.28 N	1.01 E
La Louvière	176	50.28 N	4.11 E
Lal'sk	160	60.44 N	47.34 E
La Luz	250	25.52 N	97.37 W
Lama, Ozero ⊜	186	69.30 N	90.30 E
La Maddalena	170	41.13 N	9.24 E
La Madeleine	176	50.39 N	3.04 E
La Madrid, Arg.	294	27.40 S	65.15 W
Lamadrid, Méx.	250	27.05 N	101.50 W
Lama-Kara	222	9.33 N	1.12 E
La Malbaie	240	47.39 N	70.10 W
Lamaline	240	46.52 N	55.48 W
La Mancha	278	24.52 N	102.47 W
La Mancha ⌐	168	39.05 N	3.00 W
La Manche (English Channel) Ш	162	50.20 N	1.00 W
Lamandau ≃	198	2.42 S	111.34 E
La Mansión	280	10.06 N	85.22 W
Lamar, Colo., U.S.	252	38.05 N	102.37 W
Lamar, Mo., U.S.	248	37.29 N	94.17 W
Lamar, S.C., U.S.	246	34.10 N	80.04 W
Lamar ≃	256	44.56 N	110.24 W
Lamarche	166	48.04 N	5.47 E
La Mariscala	294	34.03 S	54.47 W
La Maroma	250	28.34 N	100.45 W
Lamarque	294	39.24 S	65.40 W
La Marsa	170	36.53 N	10.20 E
Lamas	292	6.25 S	76.30 W
La Masica	280	15.37 N	87.07 W
Lamastre	166	44.59 N	4.35 E
La Maya	284p	20.10 N	75.39 W
Lamballe	166	48.28 N	2.31 W
Lambaréné	218	0.42 S	10.13 E
Lambari ≃	296	19.30 S	45.00 W
Lambayeque	292	6.42 S	79.55 W
Lambayeque □[5]	292	6.20 S	80.00 W
Lambayeque, Río de ≃	292	6.43 S	80.02 W
Lambay Island I	162	53.29 N	6.01 W
Lambersart	176	50.39 N	3.02 E
Lambert, Miss., U.S.	248	34.12 N	90.24 W
Lambert, Mont., U.S.	252	47.41 N	104.37 W
Lambert Glacier ⊼	148	71.00 S	70.00 E
Lamberton	252	44.14 N	95.16 W
Lambert's Bay	218	32.05 S	18.17 E
Lambertville, Mich., U.S.	268	41.46 N	83.35 W
Lambertville, N.J., U.S.	262	40.22 N	74.57 W
Lambeth	266	42.54 N	81.18 W
Lambeth ⌐[8]	174	51.30 N	0.07 W
Lambrama	292	13.52 S	72.46 W
Lambton □[6]	266	42.45 N	82.15 W
Lambton, Cape ≻	232	71.05 N	123.10 W
Lambunao	202	11.03 N	122.28 E
L'amca	160	64.27 N	37.04 E
Lame Deer	256	45.37 N	106.40 W
Lamego	168	41.06 N	7.49 W
La Mendieta	294	24.19 S	64.55 W
L'amen'ga	160	59.51 N	44.31 E
Lamentin	285o	16.16 N	61.38 W
Lamèque	240	47.47 N	64.38 W
La Merced, Arg.	294	24.59 S	65.28 W
La Merced, Arg.	294	28.10 S	65.40 W
La Merced, Perú	292	11.03 S	75.20 W
La Mesa, Pan.	280	8.07 N	81.10 W
La Mesa, Calif., U.S.	274	32.46 N	117.01 W
La Mesa, N. Mex., U.S.	254	32.07 N	106.42 W
Lamesa, Tex., U.S.	250	32.44 N	101.57 W
La Mesa, Cerro ∧	278	26.59 N	113.43 W
Lamía	172	38.54 N	22.26 E
L'amin ≃	186	61.18 N	71.48 E
Lamine ≃	248	38.59 N	92.51 W
La Minerve	260	46.15 N	74.56 W
Lamington National Park ♦	228	28.15 S	153.12 E
Laminusa	202	5.33 N	120.55 E
La Mirada	274	33.54 N	118.01 W
La Misión	258	32.05 N	116.50 W
Lamitan	202	6.40 N	122.08 E
Lammerlaw Top ∧	230	45.40 S	169.38 E
Lammi	160	61.05 N	25.01 E
Lamming Mills	238	53.22 N	120.18 W
La Moille, Ill., U.S.	244	41.32 N	89.17 W
Lamoille, Nev., U.S.	258	40.44 N	115.29 W
Lamoille ≃	242	44.35 N	73.10 W
La Moine ≃	248	39.59 N	90.31 W
Lamon Bay C	202	14.33 N	121.50 E
Lamoni	244	40.37 N	93.56 W
Lamont, Alta., Can.	238	53.46 N	112.48 W
Lamont, Calif., U.S.	274	35.15 N	118.55 W
Lamont, Iowa, U.S.	244	42.36 N	91.39 W
Lamont, Okla., U.S.	250	36.41 N	97.33 W
La Monte	248	38.46 N	93.25 W
La Morita, Méx.	250	26.17 N	99.11 W
La Morita, Méx.	278	28.30 N	104.28 W
La Mothe, Réservoir ⊜[1]	240	48.46 N	71.10 W
La Mothe-Achard	166	46.37 N	1.40 W
La Mothe-Saint-Héraye	166	46.22 N	0.07 W
La Motte, Lac ⊜	244	48.25 N	78.02 W
Lamotte-Beuvron	166	47.36 N	2.01 E
La Motte-Chalançon	166	44.29 N	5.23 E
La Motte-du-Caire	166	44.21 N	6.02 E
La Moure	252	46.21 N	98.18 W
Lampa	292	15.22 S	70.22 W
Lampang	200	18.16 N	99.34 E
Lampasas	250	31.04 N	98.11 W
Lampasas ≃	250	30.59 N	97.24 W
Lampazos	276	27.01 N	100.31 W
Lampazos de Naranjo	278	27.01 N	100.31 W
Lampedusa I	170	35.31 N	12.35 E
Lampertheim	164	49.35 N	8.28 E
Lampeter, Wales, U.K.	162	52.07 N	4.05 W
Lampeter, Pa., U.S.	262	39.58 N	76.14 W
Lamphun	200	18.35 N	99.00 E
Lampman	252	49.23 N	102.45 W
Lamu	218	2.16 S	40.54 E
Lamud	292	6.10 S	77.57 W
La Mure	182	44.54 N	5.47 E
Lamy	254	35.29 N	105.53 W
Lan, Loi ∧	200	19.40 N	97.55 E
Lana	170	46.37 N	11.09 E
Lanai I	275d	20.50 N	156.55 W
Lanai City	275a	20.50 N	156.55 W
Lanaihale ∧	275d	20.49 N	156.52 W
Lanalhue, Lago ⊜	294	37.55 S	73.18 W
Lanao, Lake ⊜	202	7.52 N	124.15 E
Lanao del Norte □[4]	202	8.00 N	124.00 E
Lanao del Sur □[4]	202	7.58 N	124.03 E
Lanark, Ont., Can.	264	45.01 N	76.22 W
Lanark, Scot., U.K.	162	55.41 N	3.46 W
Lanark, Ill., U.S.	244	42.06 N	89.50 W
Lanark, Pa., U.S.	262	40.33 N	75.26 W
Lanark □[6], Ont., Can.	264	45.05 N	76.20 W
Lanark □[6], Scot., U.K.	162	55.37 N	3.50 W
La Nava de Ricomalillo	168	39.39 N	4.59 W
Lanbi Kyun I	200	10.50 N	98.15 E
Lanboyan Point ≻	202	8.18 N	122.56 E
Lancang	200	23.00 N	100.02 E
Lancashire □[6]	162	53.45 N	2.30 W
Lancaster, N.B., Can.	240	45.15 N	66.06 W
Lancaster, Ont., Can.	242	45.15 N	74.30 W
Lancaster, Eng., U.K.	162	54.03 N	2.48 W
Lancaster, Calif., U.S.	274	34.42 N	118.08 W
Lancaster, Ky., U.S.	246	37.37 N	84.35 W
Lancaster, Mass., U.S.	261	42.28 N	71.41 W
Lancaster, Minn., U.S.	252	48.52 N	96.48 W
Lancaster, Mo., U.S.	248	40.31 N	92.32 W
Lancaster, N.H., U.S.	242	44.29 N	71.34 W
Lancaster, N.Y., U.S.	264	42.54 N	78.40 W
Lancaster, Ohio, U.S.	242	39.43 N	82.36 W
Lancaster, Pa., U.S.	262	40.02 N	76.19 W
Lancaster, S.C., U.S.	246	34.43 N	80.46 W
Lancaster, Tex., U.S.	250	32.36 N	96.46 W
Lancaster, Va., U.S.	262	37.46 N	76.28 W
Lancaster, Wis., U.S.	244	42.51 N	90.43 W
Lancaster □[6], Pa., U.S.	262	40.02 N	76.19 W
Lancaster □[6], Va., U.S.	262	37.45 N	76.30 W
Lancaster Mills	246	34.42 N	80.16 W
Lancaster Sound Ш	232	74.13 N	84.00 W
Lance Creek	254	43.02 N	104.39 W
Lanchow → Lanzhou	190	36.03 N	103.41 E
Lanciano	184	42.14 N	14.23 E
Lancing, Eng., U.K.	174	50.50 N	0.19 W
Lancing, Tenn., U.S.	246	36.13 N	84.39 W
Lancones	290	4.30 S	80.30 W
Łańcut	164	50.05 N	22.13 E
Lancy	180	46.11 N	6.07 E
Landang Gua	202	6.58 N	122.15 E
Landau	164	49.12 N	8.07 E
Landau an der Isar	164	48.40 N	12.43 E
Land Between the Lakes Recreation Area ♦	248	36.55 N	88.05 W
Landeck	180	47.08 N	10.34 E
Landenberg	262	39.47 N	75.46 W
Lander	254	42.50 N	108.44 W
Landerneau	166	48.27 N	4.15 W
Landes □[5]	166	44.20 N	1.00 W
Landete	168	39.54 N	1.22 W
Landingville	262	40.38 N	76.07 W
Landis	246	35.33 N	80.37 W
Landisburg	262	40.20 N	77.18 W
Landisville	262	40.06 N	76.25 W
Landivisiau	166	48.31 N	4.04 W
Lando	246	34.43 N	81.01 W
Land O'lakes	244	46.10 N	89.13 W
Landquart	166	46.58 N	9.33 E
Landrum	246	35.11 N	82.11 W
Landsberg am Lech	180	48.05 N	10.55 E
Landsberg an der Warthe → Gorzów Wielkopolski	164	52.44 N	15.15 E
Land's End ≻	162	50.03 N	5.44 W
Landshut	164	48.33 N	12.09 E
Landskrona	160	55.52 N	12.50 E
Landsmeer	178	52.26 N	4.52 E
Landstuhl	164	49.25 N	7.34 E
Landusky	256	47.54 N	108.37 W
La Negra	294	23.45 S	70.19 W
Lanesboro, Mass., U.S.	261	42.31 N	73.14 W
Lanesboro, Minn., U.S.	244	43.43 N	91.59 W
Lanesville, Conn., U.S.	261	41.33 N	73.25 W
Lanesville, Va., U.S.	262	37.37 N	76.59 W
Lanett	248	32.57 N	85.12 W
Lanexa	262	37.24 N	76.55 W
Lanezi Lake ⊜	238	53.03 N	120.56 W
Lang	252	49.56 N	104.23 W
Langadhás	172	40.45 N	23.04 E
Langádhia	172	37.41 N	22.02 E
Langano, Lake ⊜	214	7.35 N	38.48 E
Langara Island I	238	54.14 N	133.00 W
Langarūd	208	37.11 N	50.10 E
L'angasovo	160	58.32 N	49.30 E
Långban	160	59.51 N	14.15 E
Langbank	252	50.05 N	102.20 W
Lang Bay	238	49.47 N	124.21 W
Langchuhe (Sutlej) ≃	206	29.23 N	71.02 E
Langdale	248	32.44 N	85.11 W
Langdon	252	48.46 N	98.22 W
Langdondale	266	40.08 N	78.15 W
Langeac	166	45.06 N	3.30 E
Langeais	166	47.20 N	0.24 E
Langeberg ⋀	224	34.00 S	20.40 E
Langeland I	164	55.00 N	10.50 E
Langeloth	266	40.23 N	80.24 W
Langelsheim	178	51.56 N	10.19 E
Langen	178	53.36 N	8.35 E
Langenau	180	48.30 N	10.07 E
Langenfeld, B.R.D.	178	51.07 N	6.56 E
Längenfeld, Öst.	164	47.04 N	10.58 E
Langenhagen	178	52.27 N	9.44 E
Langenthal	180	47.13 N	7.47 E
Langford, B.C., Can.	270	48.27 N	123.30 W
Langford, N.Y., U.S.	266	42.35 N	78.51 W
Langford, S. Dak., U.S.	252	45.36 N	97.50 W
Langhe □[9]	182	44.30 N	8.00 E
Langholm	162	55.09 N	3.00 W
Langhorne	262	40.10 N	74.55 W
Langjishan I	196	28.32 N	121.36 E
Lang Ka, Doi ∧	200	19.00 N	99.22 E
Langkawi, Pulau I	200	6.22 N	99.50 E
Langlade I	240	46.50 N	56.20 W
Langley, B.C., Can.	238	49.06 N	122.39 W
Langley, S.C., U.S.	246	33.31 N	81.50 W
Langley, Wash., U.S.	270	48.02 N	122.25 W
Langlo ≃	228	26.26 S	146.05 E
Langlois	256	42.56 N	124.27 W
Långnäs	160	60.03 N	22.28 E
Langnau	180	46.57 N	7.47 E
Langogne	166	44.43 N	3.51 E
Langon	166	44.33 N	0.15 W
Langøya I	160	68.44 N	14.50 E
Langres	180	47.52 N	5.20 E
Langsa	200	4.28 N	97.58 E
Langsa, Teluk C	200	4.35 N	98.02 E
Lang-son	200	21.50 N	106.44 E
Langstaff	264	43.50 N	79.25 W
Langton	264	42.45 N	80.35 W
Langtry	250	29.48 N	101.34 W
Langue	280	13.37 N	87.39 W
Languedoc □[9]	166	44.00 N	4.00 E
L'Anguille ≃	248	34.44 N	90.40 W
Langui y Layo, Lago de ⊜	292	14.30 S	71.14 W
Langzhong	190	31.35 N	105.59 E
Lanhil Island I	202	6.46 N	122.22 E
Lanibga, Mount ∧	202	10.27 N	123.50 E
Länkipohja	160	61.44 N	24.48 E
Lank-Latum	178	51.18 N	6.41 E
Lannemezan	166	43.08 N	0.23 E
Lannilis	166	48.34 N	4.31 W
Lannion	166	48.44 N	3.28 W
Lannon	268	43.09 N	88.10 W
L'Annonciation	260	46.25 N	74.52 W
Lanoka Harbor	262	39.52 N	74.10 W
Lanoraie	260	45.57 N	73.13 W
Lanping	200	26.29 N	99.23 E
Lanquín	280	15.34 N	89.58 W
Lansdale	262	40.15 N	75.17 W
Lansdowne, Ont., Can.	264	44.24 N	76.01 W
Lansdowne, Pa., U.S.	262	39.56 N	75.17 W
L'Anse, Mich., U.S.	244	46.45 N	88.27 W
Lanse, Pa., U.S.	266	40.59 N	78.08 W
L'Anse-à-Valleau	240	49.05 N	64.33 W
L'Anse Indian Reservation ⌐[4]	244	46.48 N	88.22 W
Lansford	252	48.38 N	101.23 W
Lansing, Ill., U.S.	268	41.35 N	87.32 W
Lansing, Iowa, U.S.	244	43.22 N	91.13 W
Lansing, Mich., U.S.	268	42.43 N	84.34 W
Lansing, Ohio, U.S.	266	40.04 N	80.47 W
Lanškroun	164	49.55 N	16.37 E
Lanslebourg	166	45.17 N	6.52 E
Lantana	246	26.35 N	80.03 W
Lan Tao I	196	22.17 N	113.59 E
Lanta Yai, Ko I	200	7.35 N	99.05 E
Lantzville	270	49.15 N	124.05 W
Lanusei	170	39.52 N	9.34 E
Lanuza	202	9.14 N	126.03 E
Lanuza Bay C	202	9.19 N	126.04 E
Lanxi	196	29.12 N	119.28 E
Lanzhou	190	36.03 N	103.41 E
Lanzo Torinese	182	45.16 N	7.28 E
Lao ≃	200	19.59 N	99.59 E
Laoag	202	18.12 N	120.36 E
Laoag ≃	202	18.12 N	120.30 E
Laoang	202	12.34 N	125.00 E
Laoang Island I	202	12.35 N	125.02 E
Laobieshan ⋀	200	23.49 N	99.11 E
Lao-cai	200	22.30 N	103.57 E
Laodaohe ≃	196	28.16 N	112.58 E
Laohokow → Guanghua	190	32.25 N	111.36 E
Laoighis □[6]	162	53.00 N	7.30 W
Laon	176	49.34 N	3.40 E
Laona	244	45.34 N	88.40 W
La Orchila I	290	11.48 N	66.09 W
La Oroya	292	11.32 S	75.54 W
Laos □[1]	198	18.00 N	105.00 E
Laoshanwan C	194	36.24 N	122.45 E
Laotto	268	41.17 N	85.12 W
Laou, Oued ≃	168	35.29 N	5.04 W
Laowangpo Xuhongqu ⊜[1]	196	33.28 N	114.00 E
Laozhouwan C	194	36.00 N	120.30 E
Lapa	294	25.45 S	49.42 W
Lapac Island I	202	5.32 N	120.47 E
Lapaine	170	36.23 N	7.31 E
Lapalisse	166	46.15 N	3.38 E
La Palma, Col.	290	5.22 N	74.24 W
La Palma, El Sal.	280	14.19 N	89.11 W
La Palma, Méx.	250	26.53 N	99.24 W
La Palma, Pan.	290	8.25 N	78.07 W
La Palma, Pan.	290	7.41 N	80.13 W
La Palma del Condado	168	37.23 N	6.33 W
La Palmita	250	25.57 N	99.18 W
La Paloma	294	34.40 S	54.10 W
La Pampa □[4]	294	37.00 S	66.00 W
La Paragua	290	6.50 N	63.20 W
Laparan Island I	202	5.55 N	119.58 E
Laptev Sea → Laptevych, More ▾[2]	186	76.00 N	126.00 E
La Patrie	260	45.24 N	71.15 W
La Paz, Arg.	294	33.28 S	67.34 W
La Paz, Arg.	294	30.45 S	59.38 W
La Paz, Bol.	292	16.30 S	68.09 W
La Paz, Col.	290	10.23 N	73.10 W
La Paz, Hond.	280	14.16 N	87.40 W
La Paz, Méx.	250	25.58 N	98.03 W
La Paz, Méx.	278	23.41 N	100.43 W
La Paz, Méx.	278	24.10 N	110.18 W
La Paz, Pil.	202	8.19 N	125.43 E
Lapaz, Ind., U.S.	268	41.28 N	86.18 W
La Paz, Ur.	294	34.46 S	56.15 W
La Paz □[5], Bol.	292	15.30 S	68.00 W
La Paz □[5], Hond.	280	14.15 N	87.50 W
La Paz, Bahía de C	278	24.15 N	110.30 W
La Paz, Río de ≃	292	16.27 S	67.19 W
La Paz Centro	280	12.20 N	86.41 W
La Pedrera	290	1.18 S	69.43 W
Lapeer	268	43.03 N	83.19 W
Lapeer □[6]	268	42.59 N	85.20 W
La Perouse Strait (Sōya-kaikyō) Ш	192a	45.45 N	142.00 E
La Pesca	278	23.46 N	97.47 W
La Piedad [Cavadas]	278	20.21 N	102.00 W
La Piedra	280	9.29 N	83.40 W
La Pine	256	43.40 N	121.30 W
Lapinin Island I	202	10.05 N	124.34 E
Lapin Lääni □[4]	160	68.00 N	27.00 E
Lapinlahti	160	63.22 N	27.24 E
La Pintada	280	8.40 N	80.30 W
La Plaine	284d	15.20 N	61.15 W
Lapland ⌐[1]	160	68.00 N	25.00 E
Laplandija	160	68.16 N	33.19 E
Laplandskij Zapovednik ⌐[4]	160	67.50 N	32.10 E
La Plata, Arg.	294	34.55 S	57.57 W
La Plata, Col.	290	2.23 N	75.53 W
La Plata, Md., U.S.	242	38.32 N	76.59 W
La Plata, Mo., U.S.	248	40.02 N	92.29 W
La Plata ≃	254	36.54 N	108.15 W
La Plata, Isla I	290	1.16 S	81.06 W
La Plata Peak ∧	254	39.02 N	106.28 W
La Pocatière	240	47.21 N	70.02 W
La Poile Bay C	240	47.38 N	58.20 W
Lapominka	160	64.48 N	40.28 E
Laporte, Colo., U.S.	254	40.38 N	105.08 W
La Porte, Ind., U.S.	268	41.36 N	86.43 W
Laporte, Ohio, U.S.	266	41.20 N	82.07 W
Laporte, Pa., U.S.	242	41.25 N	76.30 W
La Porte □[6]	268	41.36 N	86.43 W
La Porte City	244	42.19 N	92.12 W
La Potherie, Lac ⊜	232	58.45 N	72.20 W
Lappajärvi ⊜	160	63.08 N	23.40 E
Lappeenranta	160	61.04 N	28.11 E
Lappfjärd (Lapväärtti)	160	62.15 N	21.32 E
Laprairie	260	45.25 N	73.29 W
Laprairie □[6]	260	45.20 N	73.35 W
La Presa	274	32.48 N	117.01 W
Laprida, Arg.	294	37.30 S	60.50 W
Laprida, Arg.	294	28.23 S	64.33 W
La Providence	260	45.38 N	72.55 W
La Pryor	250	28.57 N	99.51 W
Lâpseki	172	40.20 N	26.41 E
Laptevych, More (Laptev Sea) ▾[2]	186	76.00 N	126.00 E
Lapua	160	62.57 N	23.00 E
La Puebla	168	39.46 N	3.01 E
La Puebla de Cazalla	168	37.14 N	5.19 W
La Puebla de Montalbán	168	39.52 N	4.21 W
La Puente	274	34.01 N	117.57 W
La Puerta	294	28.10 S	65.48 W
Lapu-Lapu (Opon)	202	10.19 N	123.57 E
La Puntilla ≻	290	2.11 S	81.01 W
La Purísima	278	26.10 N	112.04 W
Lăpuş	172	47.30 N	24.01 E
La Push	270	47.55 N	124.38 W
Lapuyan	202	7.36 N	123.12 E
Lapwai	256	46.24 N	116.48 W
Łapy	164	53.00 N	22.53 E
La Quemada ⊥	278	22.27 N	102.45 W
La Quiaca	294	22.05 S	65.36 W
L'Aquila	184	42.22 N	13.22 E
L'Aquila □[4]	184	42.05 N	13.40 E
Lār	208	27.41 N	54.17 E
Lara □[3]	290	10.10 N	69.50 W
Laracha	168	43.15 N	8.35 W
Larache	168	35.12 N	6.10 W
Laragne	166	44.19 N	5.49 E
Laramate	292	14.16 S	74.52 W
La Rambla	168	37.36 N	4.44 W
Laramie	254	41.19 N	105.35 W
Laramie ≃	254	42.12 N	104.32 W
Laramie Mountains ⋀	254	42.00 N	105.40 W
Laramie Peak ∧	254	42.17 N	105.27 W
Laranjaí ≃	296	23.12 S	53.45 W
Laranjal	296	21.22 S	42.28 W
Laranjeiras do Sul	294	25.25 S	52.25 W
Larantuka	198	8.21 S	122.59 E
Laraos	292	12.18 S	75.46 W
Larap	202	14.18 N	122.39 E
Larat, Pulau I	198	7.10 S	131.50 E
La Raya, Abra)(	292	14.35 S	70.59 W
L'Arbaa Naït Irathen	168	36.38 N	4.12 E
L'Arbresle	166	45.50 N	4.37 E
Lärbro	160	57.47 N	18.47 E
Larbut, Jazīrat I	220	18.47 N	37.33 E
Larch ≃	232	57.40 N	69.30 W
Larche, Col de)(	166	44.25 N	6.53 E
Larchmont	261	40.55 N	73.44 W
Larchwood	252	43.27 N	96.26 W
Lardeau	238	50.09 N	116.57 W
Larder Lake ⊜	244	48.05 N	79.36 W
L'Ardoise	240	45.37 N	60.45 W
Laredo, Esp.	168	43.24 N	3.25 W
Laredo, Mo., U.S.	248	40.02 N	93.27 W
Laredo, Tex., U.S.	250	27.31 N	99.30 W
Laredo Sound Ш	238	52.32 N	128.53 W
La Reforma	278	25.06 N	108.05 W
Laren	178	52.15 N	5.14 E
Larena	202	9.15 N	123.35 E
La Réole	166	44.35 N	0.02 W
Lares, Perú	292	13.04 S	72.05 W
Lares, P.R.	284m	18.18 N	66.53 W
Largeau	214	17.55 N	19.07 E
L'Argentière-la-Bessée	166	44.47 N	6.33 E
Largo	246	27.55 N	82.47 W
Largo, Canyon ∨	254	36.40 N	107.43 W
Largo, Cayo I	284p	21.38 N	81.28 W
Largs	162	55.48 N	4.52 W
Lari	292	15.41 S	71.48 W
Lari ≃	280	9.33 N	82.56 W
Lariang ≃	198	1.25 S	119.17 E
La Ricamarie	182	45.24 N	4.22 E
Larimer	266	40.21 N	79.44 W
Larimore	252	47.54 N	97.38 W
Larino	170	41.48 N	14.54 E
La Rioja, Arg.	294	29.25 S	66.50 W
La Rioja, Cuba	284p	20.46 N	76.36 W
La Rioja	294	29.30 S	67.00 W
La Rioja ⌐[1]	168	42.20 N	0.22 W
Lárisa	172	39.38 N	22.25 E
Larjak	186	61.16 N	80.15 E
Lārkāna	206	27.33 N	68.13 E
Lark Harbour	240	49.06 N	58.22 W
Larkspur	272	37.56 N	122.32 W
Larnaca → Lárnax	212	34.47 N	33.38 E
Lárnakos, Kólpos C	212	34.55 N	33.45 E
Lárnax (Larnaca)	212	34.47 N	33.38 E
Larne	162	54.51 N	5.49 W
Larned	252	38.11 N	99.06 W
La Robla	168	42.48 N	5.37 W
La Roca de la Sierra	168	39.07 N	6.41 W
La Roche Bernard	166	47.31 N	2.18 W
La Roche-Derrien	162	48.45 N	3.16 W
La Rochefoucauld	166	45.45 N	0.23 E
La Rochelle	166	46.10 N	1.10 W
La Roche-sur-Yon	166	46.40 N	1.26 W
La Roda	168	39.13 N	2.09 W
La Romana	282	18.25 N	68.58 W
La Ronge	232	55.06 N	105.17 W
Laroquebrou	166	44.58 N	2.11 E
Larose	248	29.35 N	90.23 W
La Rosita	250	28.24 N	101.43 W
Larraldeña	250	26.29 N	100.10 W
Larreynaga	280	12.40 N	86.34 W
Larry's River	240	45.13 N	61.23 W
Larsen Bay	236	57.33 N	154.04 W
Larsen Ice Shelf ⊼	148	68.30 S	62.30 W
La Rubia	294	30.05 S	61.50 W
La Rue	266	40.35 N	83.23 W
La Rumorosa	258	32.34 N	116.06 W
Laruns	166	42.59 N	0.25 W
Larvik	160	59.04 N	10.00 E
Larwill	268	41.11 N	85.38 W
Larzac, Causse du ⋀[1]	166	44.00 N	3.15 E
Lasa (Lhasa)	206	29.40 N	91.09 E
La Sabana	294	27.52 S	59.58 W
La Sagra ∧	168	37.57 N	2.34 W
La Sal	254	38.19 N	109.15 W
La Salle, Ont., Can.	266	42.14 N	83.06 W
La Salle, Qué., Can.	260	45.26 N	73.39 W
La Salle, Colo., U.S.	254	40.21 N	104.42 W
La Salle, Ill., U.S.	268	41.20 N	89.06 W
La Salle □[6]	268	41.21 N	88.51 W
La Salle Gardens	268	42.39 N	83.21 W
La Sal Mountains ⋀	254	38.30 N	109.10 W
Las Animas	252	38.04 N	103.13 W
Las Ánimas, Punta ≻	278	28.50 N	113.15 W
Las Anod	214	8.26 N	47.24 E
Las Arenas	284m	18.02 N	67.09 W
La Sarre	244	48.48 N	79.12 W
La Sarre ≃	244	48.42 N	79.15 W
Las Arrias	294	30.22 S	63.38 W
La Sauceda	250	28.26 N	100.38 W
Las Bárdenas ⋀[1]	168	42.10 N	1.25 W
Las Blancas	250	25.42 N	97.35 W
Las Bonitas	290	7.52 N	65.40 W
Las Breñas	294	27.05 S	61.05 W
Las Cabezas de San Juan	168	36.59 N	5.56 W
Las Cabras	294	34.18 S	71.19 W
Lascano	294	33.40 S	54.12 W
Las Casitas, Cerro ∧	278	23.32 N	109.59 W
Las Casuarinas	294	31.45 S	68.15 W
Las Catitas	294	33.18 S	68.03 W
Las Cejas	294	26.53 S	64.45 W
L'Ascension	260	46.38 N	74.50 W
Las Choapas	278	17.55 N	94.05 W
Las Chorreras	278	28.50 N	105.18 W
La Scie	240	49.57 N	55.36 W
Las Colimas	278	25.21 N	98.40 W
Las Cruces, Méx.	250	28.44 N	104.19 W
Las Cruces, Méx.	278	29.26 N	107.24 W
Las Cruces, N. Mex., U.S.	254	32.23 N	106.29 W
Las Cruces, Cerro ∧	280	8.48 N	83.01 W
Las Cuevas	278	29.38 N	101.19 W
Las Delicias	278	15.58 N	91.50 W
La Selle, Pic ∧	282	18.22 N	72.00 W
La Selva Beach	272	36.55 N	121.51 W
La Serena	294	29.54 S	71.16 W
La Serena ⌐[1]	168	38.45 N	5.30 W
Las Escobas	278	30.33 N	115.56 W
La Seyne-sur-Mer	182	43.06 N	5.53 E
Las Flores, Arg.	294	36.02 S	59.07 W
Las Flores, Arg.	294	30.21 S	69.15 W
Las Flores, P.R.	284m	18.03 N	66.22 W
Las Garcitas	294	26.36 S	59.50 W
Las Guayabas	278	24.00 N	97.45 W
Las Heras	294	32.50 S	68.50 W
Lashio	198	22.56 N	97.45 E
Lasia, Pulau I	200	2.12 N	96.39 E
La Sierra, Montaña ⋀	280	14.04 N	87.54 W
Las Iglesias	250	27.35 N	101.21 W
La Sila ⋀	170	39.15 N	16.30 E
Łasin	164	53.32 N	19.05 E
Las Juntas	280	10.16 N	85.00 W
Łask	164	51.36 N	19.07 E
Łaskarzew Osada	164	51.48 N	21.35 E
L'askel'a	160	61.45 N	30.59 E
Laško	170	46.09 N	15.14 E
Las Lajas, Arg.	294	38.30 S	70.23 W
Las Lajas, Pan.	280	8.15 N	81.52 W
Las Lajitas	294	24.41 S	64.15 W
Las Lomas	290	4.36 S	80.15 W
Las Lomitas	294	24.43 S	60.35 W
Lašma	160	54.56 N	41.09 E
Las Malvinas	294	34.51 S	68.15 W
Las Mareas	284m	17.56 N	66.09 W
Las Margaritas	278	16.19 N	91.59 W
Las Marianas	294	35.04 S	59.30 W
Las Marías	284m	18.15 N	67.00 W
Las Marismas ☷	168	37.00 N	6.15 W
Las Mercedes	290	9.07 N	66.24 W
Las Minas, Cerro ∧	280	14.33 N	88.39 W
Las Navas	202	12.21 N	125.02 E
Las Nieves	278	26.24 N	105.22 W
La Solana	168	38.56 N	3.14 W
Las Ovejas	294	37.01 S	70.45 W
Las Palmas, Arg.	294	27.05 S	58.40 W
Las Palmas, Pan.	280	8.08 N	81.28 W
Las Palmas, P.R.	284m	17.59 N	66.02 W
Las Palmas de Gran Canaria	214	28.06 N	15.24 W
Las Palomas	278	31.44 N	107.37 W
La Spezia	182	44.07 N	9.50 E
La Spezia □[4]	182	44.13 N	9.40 E
Las Piedras, Bol.	292	11.06 S	66.10 W
Las Piedras, P.R.	284m	18.11 N	65.52 W
Las Piedras, Ur.	294	34.44 S	56.13 W
Las Piedras, Río de ≃	292	12.37 S	69.10 W
Las Piñas	284m	18.15 N	65.55 W
Las Pirquitas	294	28.17 S	65.40 W
Las Plumas	288	43.40 S	67.15 W
Lasqueti Island I	238	49.29 N	124.17 W
Las Ramas	290	1.50 S	79.48 W
Las Rosas, Arg.	294	32.30 S	61.34 W
Las Rosas, Méx.	278	16.24 N	92.23 W
Las Salinas de Zipaquirá ∪[1]	290	5.04 N	73.56 W
Lassance	296	17.54 S	44.34 W
Lassay	166	48.26 N	0.30 W
Lassen Peak ∧[1]	258	40.29 N	121.31 W
Lassen Volcanic National Park ♦	258	40.30 N	121.19 W
L'Assomption	260	45.50 N	73.25 W
L'Assomption □[6]	260	45.48 N	73.35 W
Las Tablas	290	7.47 N	80.17 W
Las Termas	294	27.30 S	64.50 W
Las Tinajas	294	27.28 S	62.56 W
Last Mountain Lake ⊜	232	51.05 N	105.10 W
Las Tórtolas, Cerro ∧	294	29.56 S	69.54 W
Las Toscas	294	28.21 S	59.15 W
Lastoursville	218	0.49 S	12.42 E
Lastovo, Otok I	170	42.45 N	16.53 E
Lastovski Kanal Ш	170	42.50 N	16.59 E
Lastra a Signa	184	43.46 N	11.06 E
Las Tres Vírgenes, Volcán ∧[1]	278	27.28 N	112.35 W
Lastrup	178	52.48 N	7.52 E
Las Tunas Grandes, Laguna ⊜	294	36.00 S	62.25 W
La Suze	166	47.54 N	0.02 E
Las Varas, Méx.	278	29.29 N	108.01 W
Las Varas, Méx.	278	21.10 N	105.10 W
Las Varillas	294	31.50 S	62.44 W
Las Vegas, Hond.	280	14.49 N	88.06 W
Las Vegas, P.R.	284m	18.11 N	67.02 W
Las Vegas, Nev., U.S.	258	36.11 N	115.08 W
Las Vegas, N. Mex., U.S.	254	35.36 N	105.13 W
Las Vegas, Ven.	290	9.35 N	68.37 W
Las Villas □[4]	284p	22.15 N	80.00 W
La Tabatière	240	50.50 N	58.57 W
Latacunga	290	0.56 S	78.37 W
La Tagua	290	0.03 S	74.40 W
Latakia → Al-Lādhiqīyah	212	35.31 N	35.47 E
La Tasajera	280	13.16 N	88.52 W
Laterrière	240	48.19 N	71.07 W
La Teste-de-Buch	166	44.38 N	1.09 W
Latham	261	42.45 N	73.46 W
Lathrop, Calif., U.S.	272	37.49 N	121.16 W
Lathrop, Mo., U.S.	248	39.33 N	94.20 W
Latian, Mount ∧	202	6.13 N	125.29 E
Latimer	244	42.46 N	93.22 W
Latina	184	41.28 N	12.52 E
Latina □[4]	184	41.27 N	13.06 E
Latisana	170	45.47 N	13.00 E
Latjuga	160	64.16 N	48.46 E
La Toma	294	33.04 S	65.35 W
Laton	272	36.26 N	119.41 W
Latorica ≃	164	48.28 N	21.50 E
Latornell ≃	238	54.58 N	118.00 W
La Tortuga, Isla I	290	10.56 N	65.20 W
Latouche Island I	236	60.00 N	147.55 W
La Tour-d'Auvergne	166	45.32 N	2.41 E
La Tour-de-Peilz	180	46.27 N	6.49 E
La Tour-du-Pin	166	45.34 N	5.27 E
Latowicz	164	52.02 N	21.48 E
La Tremblade	166	45.46 N	1.08 W
La Trimouille	166	46.28 N	1.02 E
La Trinidad, Arg.	294	27.25 S	65.30 W
La Trinidad, Nic.	280	12.55 N	86.21 W
La Trinidad, Pil.	202	16.26 N	120.35 E
La Trinidad de Orichuna	290	7.07 N	69.45 W
La Trinité	284e	14.44 N	60.58 W
Latrobe	266	40.19 N	79.23 W
Latronico	170	40.05 N	16.01 E
Latta	246	34.21 N	79.26 W
Lattasburg	266	40.53 N	82.06 W
Latty	268	41.05 N	84.35 W
La Tuque	232	47.27 N	72.47 W
Latvian Soviet Socialist Republic → Latvijskaja Sovetskaja Socialističeskaja	186	57.00 N	25.00 E
Latvijskaja Sovetskaja Socialističeskaja Respublika □[3]	186	57.00 N	25.00 E
Lauca ≃	292	19.09 S	68.10 W
Lauchhammer	164	51.30 N	13.47 E
Lauder	162	55.43 N	2.45 W
Lauderdale	248	32.31 N	88.31 W
Lauenburg	178	53.22 N	10.33 E
Lauenburgische Seen, Naturpark ♦	164	53.38 N	10.45 E
Lauf an der Pegnitz	164	49.30 N	11.17 E
Laufen	164	47.56 N	12.55 E
Laughlin Peak ∧	250	36.38 N	104.12 W
Laughlintown	266	40.13 N	79.12 W
Lauingen	180	48.34 N	10.25 E
Laukaa	160	62.25 N	25.57 E
Launceston, Austl.	228	41.26 S	147.08 E
Launceston, Eng., U.K.	162	50.38 N	4.21 W
La Unión, Chile	288	40.17 S	73.05 W
La Unión, Col.	290	1.36 N	77.09 W
La Unión, El Sal.	280	13.20 N	87.51 W
La Unión, Esp.	168	37.37 N	0.52 W
La Unión, Méx.	278	17.58 N	101.49 W
La Unión, Perú	292	9.43 S	76.45 W
La Unión, Perú	292	5.20 S	80.45 W
La Union, Pil.	202	6.42 N	126.05 E
La Union, N. Mex., U.S.	254	31.57 N	106.39 W
La Unión, Ven.	290	8.13 N	67.46 W
La Union □[4]	202	16.35 N	120.25 E
La Unión de Coto	280	8.36 N	83.03 W
Laupheim	180	48.14 N	9.52 E
Laur	202	15.35 N	121.11 E
Laura	226	15.34 S	144.28 E
La Urbana	290	7.08 N	66.56 W
Laureana di Borrello	170	38.30 N	16.05 E
Laurel, Del., U.S.	262	38.33 N	75.34 W
Laurel, Fla., U.S.	246	27.08 N	82.27 W
Laurel, Ind., U.S.	248	39.30 N	85.11 W
Laurel, Md., U.S.	242	39.06 N	76.51 W
Laurel, Miss., U.S.	248	31.42 N	89.08 W
Laurel, Mont., U.S.	256	45.40 N	108.46 W
Laurel, Nebr., U.S.	252	42.26 N	97.06 W
Laurel, Va., U.S.	262	37.38 N	77.31 W
Laurel, Wash., U.S.	270	45.57 N	121.23 W
Laurel ≃	246	36.57 N	84.18 W
Laurel Bay	246	32.27 N	80.48 W
Laureldale, N.J., U.S.	262	39.30 N	74.41 W
Laureldale, Pa., U.S.	262	40.23 N	75.55 W
Laureles	294	31.22 S	55.51 W
Laurelville, Ohio, U.S.	242	39.28 N	82.44 W
Laurelville, Pa., U.S.	266	40.09 N	79.29 W
Laurencekirk	162	56.50 N	2.29 W
Laurens, Iowa, U.S.	252	42.51 N	94.51 W
Laurens, S.C., U.S.	246	34.30 N	82.01 W
Laurentian Highlands ⋀[1]	148	50.00 N	70.00 W
Laurentides	260	45.51 N	73.45 W
Lauria	170	40.02 N	15.50 E
Laurier	260	46.33 N	71.38 W
Laurière	166	46.05 N	1.28 E
Laurierville	260	46.18 N	71.39 W
Laurinburg	246	34.47 N	79.27 W
Lauritsala	160	61.04 N	28.16 E
Laurium	244	47.14 N	88.26 W
Lauro, Monte ∧	170	37.08 N	14.47 E
Lauro Müller	294	28.24 S	49.23 W
Laurys Station	262	40.43 N	75.32 W
Lausanne	180	46.31 N	6.38 E
Laut, Pulau I	200	4.43 N	107.59 E
Lauta	164	51.27 N	14.04 E
Lautaro	294	38.31 S	72.27 W
Lauter	164	50.33 N	12.44 E
Lauterbach	164	50.38 N	9.24 E
Lauterbrunnen	166	46.36 N	7.55 E
Laut Ketjil, Kepulauan II	198	4.50 S	115.45 E
Lau Trough ✣[1]	148	20.00 S	177.00 W
Lauwe	176	50.48 N	3.11 E
Lauzerte	166	44.15 N	1.08 E
Lauzon	260	46.50 N	71.10 W
Lauzun	166	44.38 N	0.28 E
Lava (Łyna) ≃	164	54.37 N	21.14 E
Lava, Nosy I	225b	14.33 S	47.36 E
Lava Beds National Monument ♦	258	41.42 N	121.30 W
Lavaca ≃	250	28.50 N	96.36 W
Lavaca Bay C	250	28.35 N	96.35 W
Lavagna	182	44.18 N	9.20 E
Lava Hot Springs	256	42.37 N	112.01 W
Lavaisse	294	33.50 S	65.26 W
Laval, Qué., Can.	260	45.33 N	73.44 W
Laval, Fr.	166	48.04 N	0.46 W
Lavalle, Arg.	294	29.02 S	59.09 W
Lavalle, Arg.	294	28.12 S	65.07 W
Lavallette	262	39.58 N	74.04 W
Lavalley	254	37.06 N	105.22 W
Lavaltrie	260	45.53 N	73.17 W
Lavant ≃	164	46.38 N	14.57 E
Lavanttal ∨	164	46.45 N	14.50 E
Lavapié, Punta ≻	294	37.09 S	73.35 W
Lavardac	166	44.11 N	0.18 E
Lāvar Meydān ☷	208	30.20 N	54.30 E
Lavassaare	160	58.31 N	24.22 E
Lava Tudo ≃	294	28.26 S	50.25 W
La Vecilla	168	42.51 N	5.24 W
Laveen	254	33.22 N	112.10 W
La Vega	282	19.13 N	70.31 W
La Vega ⌐[1]	168	37.10 N	3.50 W
Lavela, S.S.S.R.	160	63.38 N	45.31 E
La Vela, Ven.	290	11.27 N	69.34 W
La Vela, Cabo de ≻	290	12.15 N	72.10 W
Lavelanet	166	42.56 N	1.51 E
Lavelle	262	40.46 N	76.22 W
Lavello	170	41.03 N	15.48 E
La Venada	250	25.50 N	97.30 W
Laveno	180	45.55 N	8.37 E
La Venta ⊥	278	18.08 N	94.03 W
La Ventura	278	24.38 N	100.54 W
La Vera ⌐[1]	168	40.20 N	5.30 W
La Verde	294	27.08 S	59.23 W
Laverne	250	36.43 N	99.54 W
La Vernia	250	29.21 N	98.07 W
Laverton	226	28.38 S	122.25 E
La Veta	254	37.31 N	105.00 W
Lavezares	202	12.32 N	124.20 E
Lavia	160	61.36 N	22.36 E
Lavic Lake ⊜	258	34.40 N	116.21 W
La Victoria	290	10.14 N	67.20 W
Lavieille, Lake ⊜	244	45.51 N	78.14 W
La Vieja, Punta ≻	294	35.36 S	72.38 W
Lavik	160	61.06 N	5.30 E
La Villa ≃	280	8.00 N	80.24 W
Lavillette	240	47.16 N	65.18 W
La Viña, Arg.	294	25.28 S	65.35 W
Lavina, Mont., U.S.	256	46.18 N	108.56 W
La Virginia	290	4.54 N	75.53 W
Lavit	166	43.58 N	0.55 E
La Volla	258	32.51 N	117.16 W
Lavonia	246	34.26 N	83.06 W
La Voulte-sur-Rhône	166	44.48 N	4.47 E
Lavras	296	21.14 S	45.00 W
Lavras do Sul	294	30.49 S	53.55 W
Lavre ≃	168	38.49 N	8.40 W
Lavrentija	236	65.35 N	171.00 E
Lavrentija, Zaliv C	236	65.40 N	171.15 W
Lávrion	172	37.44 N	24.04 E
Lavumisa	218	27.20 S	31.55 E
Lawa	202	6.12 N	125.42 E
Lawai	275b	21.55 N	159.31 W
Lawdar	214	13.53 N	45.52 E
Lawernce □[6]	266	41.00 N	80.20 W
Lawers, Ben ∧	162	56.33 N	4.15 W
Lawler	244	43.04 N	92.09 W
Lawn, Newf., Can.	240	46.56 N	55.33 W

Symbols in the index entries are identified on page 360.

Name	Page	Lat°′	Long°′
Lawn, Pa., U.S.	262	40.13 N	76.32 W
Lawn, Tex., U.S.	250	32.08 N	99.49 W
Lawn Bay C	240	46.53 N	55.35 W
Lawndale, Calif., U.S.	274	33.54 N	118.21 W
Lawndale, N.C., U.S.	246	35.25 N	81.34 W
Lawrence, Ind., U.S.	248	39.50 N	86.02 W
Lawrence, Kans., U.S.	252	38.58 N	95.14 W
Lawrence, Mass., U.S.	261	42.42 N	71.09 W
Lawrence, Mich., U.S.	268	42.13 N	86.03 W
Lawrence, Nebr., U.S.	252	40.17 N	98.16 W
Lawrenceburg, Ind., U.S.	248	39.06 N	84.51 W
Lawrenceburg, Ky., U.S.	248	38.02 N	84.54 W
Lawrenceburg, Tenn., U.S.	248	35.15 N	87.20 W
Lawrence Park	266	42.09 N	80.01 W
Lawrenceville, Ill., U.S.	248	38.44 N	87.41 W
Lawrenceville, N.J., U.S.	262	40.18 N	74.44 W
Lawrenceville, Va., U.S.	246	36.45 N	77.51 W
Lawson	248	39.26 N	94.12 W
Lawtey	246	30.03 N	82.04 W
Lawton, Mich., U.S.	268	42.10 N	85.50 W
Lawton, N. Dak., U.S.	252	48.18 N	98.22 W
Lawton, Okla., U.S.	250	34.37 N	98.25 W
Lawz, Jabal al- ▲	208	28.40 N	35.18 E
Laxå	160	58.59 N	14.37 E
Laxou	180	48.41 N	6.09 E
Layhill	262	39.05 N	77.03 W
Layou	285h	13.12 N	61.17 W
Layton	254	41.04 N	111.58 W
Laytonville	258	39.41 N	123.29 W
La Zarca	278	25.50 N	104.44 W
Lazarev	186	52.13 N	141.32 E
Lazaro Cárdenas	250	25.23 N	103.10 W
Lazdijai	164	54.14 N	23.31 E
Lazi	202	9.08 N	123.38 E
Lazio □⁴	184	42.00 N	12.30 E
Leachville	248	35.56 N	90.15 W
Leacock	262	40.05 N	76.12 W
Lead	252	44.21 N	103.46 W
Leader	232	50.53 N	109.31 W
Lead Hill ▲²	248	37.06 N	92.38 W
Leadore	256	44.41 N	113.21 W
Leadville	254	39.15 N	106.20 W
Leadwood	248	37.52 N	90.36 W
Leaf ≃, Minn., U.S.	252	46.29 N	94.53 W
Leaf ≃, Miss., U.S.	248	31.00 N	88.45 W
League City	250	29.31 N	95.05 W
Leakesville	248	31.09 N	88.33 W
Leakey	250	29.44 N	99.46 W
Leaksville	246	36.29 N	79.53 W
Lealman	246	27.50 N	82.41 W
Leamington	266	42.03 N	82.36 W
Leamington Spa	162	52.18 N	1.31 W
Leán ≃	280	15.49 N	87.19 W
Leandro N. Alem	294	27.36 S	55.19 W
Leane, Lough ⊜	162	52.05 N	9.35 W
Leary	246	31.29 N	84.31 W
Leatherhead	174	51.18 N	0.20 W
Leatherman Peak ▲	256	44.05 N	113.44 W
Leatherwood	246	37.02 N	83.11 W
Leavenworth, Kans., U.S.	252	39.19 N	94.55 W
Leavenworth, Wash., U.S.	270	47.36 N	120.40 W
Leavittsburg	266	41.14 N	80.53 W
Leawood	252	37.03 N	94.31 W
Łeba (Leba)	164	54.47 N	17.33 E
Łeba ≃	164	54.47 N	17.33 E
Lebak	202	6.37 N	124.03 E
Lebam	270	46.34 N	123.33 W
Lebanon, Conn., U.S.	261	41.38 N	72.13 W
Lebanon, Ind., U.S.	248	40.03 N	86.28 W
Lebanon, Kans., U.S.	252	39.49 N	98.33 W
Lebanon, Ky., U.S.	248	37.34 N	85.15 W
Lebanon, Mo., U.S.	248	37.41 N	92.40 W
Lebanon, N.H., U.S.	242	43.38 N	72.15 W
Lebanon, N.J., U.S.	262	40.39 N	74.50 W
Lebanon, N.Y., U.S.	248	42.47 N	75.39 W
Lebanon, Ohio, U.S.	242	39.26 N	84.13 W
Lebanon, Oreg., U.S.	256	44.32 N	122.54 W
Lebanon, Pa., U.S.	262	40.20 N	76.25 W
Lebanon, S. Dak., U.S.	252	45.04 N	99.46 W
Lebanon, Tenn., U.S.	248	36.12 N	86.18 W
Lebanon, Va., U.S.	246	36.54 N	82.05 W
Lebanon □¹	206	34.00 N	36.00 E
Lebanon □¹	204	34.00 N	36.00 E
Lebanon Junction	248	37.50 N	85.44 W
Lebanon Mountains → Lubnān, Jabal ▲	210	34.00 N	36.00 E
Lebanon Springs	261	42.29 N	73.23 W
Leb'ažje, S.S.S.R.	160	57.25 N	49.32 E
Leb'ažje, S.S.S.R.	186	51.28 N	77.46 E
Lebbeke	176	51.00 N	4.08 E
Lebec	274	34.50 N	118.52 W
Lebedino	160	55.14 N	49.50 E
Lebesby	160	70.34 N	26.59 E
Le Blanc	166	46.38 N	1.04 E
Lebo	252	38.25 N	95.51 W
Lebombo Mountains ▲²	224	25.15 S	32.00 E
Lebon Régis	294	26.56 S	50.42 W
Lębork (Lauenburg)	164	54.33 N	17.44 E
Le Bourg-d'Oisans	166	45.03 N	6.02 E
Lebrija	168	36.55 N	6.04 W
Lebrija ≃	290	8.08 N	73.47 W
Łebsko, Jezioro C	164	54.44 N	17.24 E
Lebu	294	37.37 S	73.39 W
Le Bugue	166	44.55 N	0.56 E
Le Cannet	182	43.34 N	7.01 E
Le Carbet	284e	14.43 N	61.11 W
Le Cateau	176	50.06 N	3.33 E
Lecce	170	40.23 N	18.11 E
Lecco	182	45.51 N	9.23 E
Le Center	244	44.24 N	93.44 W
Lech ≃	164	48.44 N	10.56 E
Le Chambon-Feugerolles	182	45.24 N	4.19 E
Le-Château-d'Oleron	166	45.53 N	1.11 W
Le Chatelet-en-Berry	166	46.39 N	2.17 E
Le Chesne	166	49.31 N	4.46 E
Le Cheylard	166	44.45 N	4.25 E
Lechiguanas, Islas de las II	294	33.26 S	59.42 W
Lechiguiri, Cerro ▲	278	16.43 N	95.30 W
Lechta	160	60.49 N	48.28 E
Lechtaler Alpen ▲	164	47.15 N	10.30 E
Le Claire	244	41.36 N	90.21 W
l'Ecole	176	48.48 N	2.04 E
Lecompte	248	31.05 N	92.24 W
Le Conquet	166	48.22 N	4.46 W
Lecontes Mills	266	41.05 N	78.17 W
Le Creusot	180	46.48 N	4.26 E
Le Croisic	166	47.18 N	2.31 W
Łęczna	164	51.19 N	22.52 E
Łęczyca	164	52.04 N	19.13 E
Led'anaja, Gora ▲	186	49.28 N	142.45 E
Ledbury	162	52.02 N	2.25 W
Lede	176	50.58 N	3.58 E
Ledesma	168	41.05 N	6.00 W
Le Diamant	284e	14.29 N	61.02 W
Ledkovo	160	67.14 N	50.33 E
Ledong	200	18.45 N	109.12 E
Le Donjon	166	46.21 N	3.48 E
Le Dorat	166	46.13 N	1.05 E
Le Doré, Lac ⊜	240	51.16 N	61.23 W
Ledu	190	36.32 N	102.25 E
Leduc	238	53.16 N	113.33 W
Lędyczek (Landeck in Westpreussen)	164	53.33 N	16.58 E
Lee, Ill., U.S.	268	41.48 N	88.56 W
Lee, Mass., U.S.	261	42.19 N	73.15 W
Lee □⁶	268	41.50 N	89.29 W
Lee Center	268	41.45 N	89.17 W
Leechburg	266	40.38 N	79.36 W
Leech Lake ⊜	244	47.09 N	94.23 W
Leechtown	270	48.30 N	123.42 W
Leedey	250	35.52 N	99.21 W
Leeds, Eng., U.K.	162	53.50 N	1.35 W
Leeds, Ala., U.S.	248	33.33 N	86.33 W
Leeds, N. Dak., U.S.	252	48.17 N	99.27 W
Leeds, N.Y., U.S.	261	42.15 N	73.54 W
Leeds □⁶	264	44.35 N	76.00 W
Leeds Point	262	39.30 N	74.26 W
Leek	174	53.06 N	2.01 W
Leelanau, Lake ⊜	244	44.55 N	85.43 W
Leeper	266	41.22 N	79.18 W
Leer	178	53.14 N	7.26 E
Leerdam	178	51.54 N	5.05 E
Lées ≃	166	43.38 N	0.14 W
Leesburg, Fla., U.S.	246	28.49 N	81.53 W
Leesburg, Ga., U.S.	246	31.44 N	84.10 W
Leesburg, Ind., U.S.	268	41.20 N	85.51 W
Leesburg, N.J., U.S.	262	39.15 N	74.59 W
Leesburg, Va., U.S.	262	39.07 N	77.34 W
Leesport	262	40.27 N	75.58 W
Lees Summit	248	38.55 N	94.23 W
Leeste	178	52.59 N	8.49 E
Leesville, Ill., U.S.	268	41.01 N	87.33 W
Leesville, La., U.S.	248	31.08 N	93.16 W
Leesville, Ohio, U.S.	266	40.27 N	81.13 W
Leesville, Tex., U.S.	250	29.24 N	97.45 W
Leesville Lake ⊜¹	246	37.05 N	79.25 W
Leesville Reservoir ⊜¹	242	40.30 N	81.10 W
Leeton	228	34.33 S	146.24 E
Leetonia	266	40.53 N	80.45 W
Leetsdale	266	40.34 N	80.13 W
Leeuwarden	178	53.12 N	5.46 E
Lee Vining	272	37.58 N	119.07 W
Leeward Islands II	282	17.00 N	62.00 W
Le Faouët	166	48.02 N	3.29 W
Le Feuvre Inlet C	232	72.20 N	96.40 W
Leforest	176	50.26 N	3.04 E
Lefors	250	35.26 N	100.48 W
Le François	284e	14.37 N	60.54 W
Lefroy	264	44.16 N	79.34 W
Legal	238	53.57 N	113.35 W
Legazpi	202	13.08 N	123.44 E
Légé	166	46.53 N	1.36 W
Legges Tor ▲	228	41.32 S	147.40 E
Leggett	258	39.52 N	123.43 W
Legion	250	30.07 N	99.07 W
Legionowo	164	52.25 N	20.56 E
Legnago	182	45.36 N	8.54 E
Legnica (Liegnitz)	164	51.13 N	16.09 E
Le Gosier	285o	16.12 N	61.30 W
Le Grand	272	37.14 N	120.15 W
Le Grand-Fougeray	166	47.44 N	1.44 W
Le Grand-Lucé	166	47.52 N	0.28 E
Le Grand-Quevilly	176	49.25 N	1.02 E
Le Grau-du-Roi	166	43.32 N	4.08 E
Le Guelta	168	36.22 N	0.50 E
Le Havre	176	49.30 N	0.08 E
Lehčevo	172	43.32 N	23.32 E
Lehi	254	40.24 N	111.51 W
Lehigh, Iowa, U.S.	244	42.22 N	94.03 W
Lehigh, Okla., U.S.	250	34.28 N	96.13 W
Lehigh □⁶	262	40.36 N	75.29 W
Lehigh Acres	246	26.36 N	81.39 W
Lehighton	242	40.49 N	75.45 W
Lehman Caves National Monument ♦	254	39.01 N	114.14 W
Lehr	252	46.17 N	99.21 W
Lehrte	178	52.22 N	9.59 E
Lehua Island I	275d	22.01 N	160.06 W
Lehututu	218	23.58 S	21.51 E
Leibnitz	164	46.48 N	15.32 E
Leicester, Eng., U.K.	174	52.38 N	1.05 W
Leicester, Mass., U.S.	261	42.15 N	71.55 W
Leicester, N.Y., U.S.	264	42.46 N	77.54 W
Leicestershire □⁶	174	52.40 N	1.10 W
Leichhardt Range ▲	228	20.40 S	147.25 E
Leichhardt ≃	228	17.35 S	139.48 E
Leichhardt Falls ⚟	228	18.14 S	139.53 E
Leichlingen	178	51.06 N	7.01 E
Leiden	178	52.09 N	4.30 E
Leiderdorp	178	52.09 N	4.32 E
Leidschendam	178	52.05 N	4.24 E
Leie (Lys) ≃	166	51.03 N	3.43 E
Leigh	252	41.42 N	97.14 W
Leigh Creek	228	30.28 S	138.25 E
Leighton	248	34.42 N	87.32 W
Leighton Buzzard	174	51.55 N	0.40 W
Leikanger	160	61.10 N	6.52 E
Leinfelden	180	48.41 N	9.08 E
Leinster, Mount ▲	162	52.37 N	6.44 W
Leipalingis	164	54.05 N	23.51 E
Leipheim	180	48.27 N	10.13 E
Leipsic, Del., U.S.	262	39.14 N	75.31 W
Leipsic, Ohio, U.S.	268	41.06 N	83.59 W
Leipzig	164	51.19 N	12.20 E
Leiria	168	39.45 N	8.48 W
Leishui ≃	196	26.54 N	112.39 E
Leitchfield	248	37.29 N	86.18 W
Leiters Ford	268	41.07 N	86.23 W
Leitha (Lajta) ≃	164	47.54 N	17.17 E
Leitrim	162	54.00 N	8.04 W
Leitrim □⁶	162	54.20 N	8.20 W
Leiva	290	5.38 N	73.34 W
Leiyang	196	26.24 N	112.51 E
Leizhoubandao ⊱¹	200	21.15 N	110.09 E
Lejía, Cerro ▲	294	23.33 S	67.46 W
Lekhainá	172	37.56 N	21.17 E
Leksvik	160	63.40 N	10.37 E
Le Lamentin	284e	14.37 N	61.01 W
Leland, Ill., U.S.	268	41.37 N	88.48 W
Leland, Mich., U.S.	244	45.01 N	85.45 W
Leland, Miss., U.S.	248	33.24 N	90.54 W
Leleiwi Point ⊱	275d	19.44 N	155.00 W
Leleque	288	42.24 S	71.04 W
Lelia Lake	250	34.54 N	100.46 W
Le Lion-d'Angers	166	47.38 N	0.43 W
Lelishan ▲	206	33.26 N	81.42 E
Le Locle	180	47.03 N	6.45 E
Le Lorrain	284e	14.50 N	61.04 W
Le Lude	166	47.39 N	0.09 E
Le Madonie ▲	170	37.50 N	14.00 E
Le Maire, Estrecho de 𝔘	288	54.50 S	65.00 W
Le Mans	176	48.00 N	0.12 E
Le Marin	284e	14.28 N	60.53 W
Le Mars	252	42.47 N	96.10 W
Lemay, Lac ⊜	240	50.35 N	68.25 W
Le Mayet-de-Montagne	166	46.05 N	3.40 E
Lembeek	176	50.43 N	4.13 E
Lemberg ▲	180	48.09 N	8.45 E
Leme	296	22.12 S	47.24 W
Le Merlerault	166	48.42 N	0.18 E
Lemery	202	13.53 N	120.55 E
Lemesós (Limassol)	212	34.40 N	33.03 E
Lemeta	236	64.52 N	147.44 W
Lemgo	178	52.02 N	8.54 E
Lemhi ≃	256	45.12 N	113.53 W
Lemhi Pass ⅹ	256	44.58 N	113.27 W
Lemhi Range ▲	256	44.30 N	113.25 W
Lemieux Islands II	232	64.30 N	64.40 W
Leming	250	29.04 N	98.29 W
Lemitar	254	34.09 N	106.55 W
Lemmenjoen Kansallispuisto ♦	160	68.40 N	26.00 E
Lemmon	252	45.56 N	102.10 W
Lemmon, Mount ▲	254	32.26 N	110.47 W
Lemnos → Límnos I	172	39.54 N	25.21 E
Lemoine, Lac ⊜	244	48.02 N	78.00 W
Le Monastier	166	45.56 N	4.00 E
Lemoncove	258	36.23 N	119.01 W
Lemon Grove	274	32.44 N	117.02 W
Lemont, Ill., U.S.	268	41.40 N	88.00 W
Lemont, Pa., U.S.	266	40.49 N	77.49 W
Lemont Furnace	266	39.55 N	79.40 W
Le Mont Saint-Michel 𝔙¹	166	48.38 N	1.32 W
Lemoore	272	36.18 N	119.47 W
Le Moule	285o	16.20 N	61.21 W
Lemoyne, Ohio, U.S.	266	41.30 N	83.38 W
Lemoyne, Pa., U.S.	262	40.15 N	76.54 W
Le Moyne, Lac ⊜	232	57.00 N	68.20 W
Lempa ≃	280	13.15 N	88.50 W
Lempira □⁵	280	14.15 N	88.35 W
Lemro ≃	200	20.25 N	93.20 E
Lemukutan, Pulau I	200	0.45 N	108.43 E
Le Murge ▲¹	170	40.52 N	16.42 E
Lemva ≃	160	66.30 N	61.48 E
Lena, Ill., U.S.	244	42.23 N	89.50 W
Lena, Wis., U.S.	244	44.57 N	88.03 W
Lena ≃	186	72.25 N	126.40 E
Lenart	170	46.35 N	15.50 E
Lenawee □⁶	268	41.53 N	84.04 W
Lencloître	166	46.49 N	0.20 E
Lençóis	296	12.34 S	41.23 W
Lendery	160	63.26 N	31.03 E
Lendinara	170	45.05 N	11.36 E
Lendringsen	178	51.24 N	7.49 E
Le Neubourg	162	49.09 N	0.55 E
Lengerich	178	52.11 N	7.50 E
Lenggries	164	47.41 N	11.34 E
Lenghu	190	38.30 N	93.15 E
Lengshuitan	200	26.14 N	111.29 E
Lengua de Vaca, Punta ⊱	294	30.14 S	71.38 W
Lenhartsville	262	40.34 N	75.53 W
Lenhovda	160	57.00 N	15.17 E
Lenina, Pik ▲	186	39.20 N	72.55 E
Leninabad	186	40.17 N	69.37 E
Leninakan	158	40.48 N	43.50 E
Leningrad	160	59.55 N	30.15 E
Leninogorsk	160	54.36 N	52.30 E
Leninsk	186	40.38 N	72.15 E
Leninskij	160	54.18 N	37.28 E
Leninsk-Kuzneckij	186	54.38 N	86.10 E
Leninskoje	160	58.19 N	47.06 E
Lenk	166	46.28 N	7.27 E
Lenkerville	262	40.32 N	76.58 W
Lenkoran'	208	38.45 N	48.50 E
Lenkorap ▲⁸	178	51.12 N	7.15 E
Lennox, Calif., U.S.	274	33.56 N	118.21 W
Lennox, S. Dak., U.S.	252	43.21 N	96.53 W
Lennox, Isla I	288	55.18 S	66.50 W
Lennox and Addington □⁶	264	44.30 N	77.00 W
Lennoxville	260	45.22 N	71.51 W
Lenoir	246	35.55 N	81.32 W
Lenoir City	246	35.48 N	84.16 W
Lenora	166	48.56 N	13.48 E
Lenox, Ga., U.S.	246	31.16 N	83.28 W
Lenox, Iowa, U.S.	250	40.53 N	94.34 W
Lenox, Mass., U.S.	261	42.22 N	73.17 W
Lenox, Tenn., U.S.	248	36.05 N	89.30 W
Lenox Dale	261	42.20 N	73.15 W
Lens	176	50.26 N	2.50 E
Lensk	186	61.00 N	114.50 E
Lenti	164	46.37 N	16.33 E
Lentini	170	37.17 N	15.00 E
Lentua ⊜	160	64.14 N	29.36 E
Lenwood	274	34.53 N	117.07 W
Lenya ≃	200	11.40 N	98.43 E
Lenzburg	180	47.23 N	8.11 E
Léo, Hi. Vol.	214	11.06 N	2.06 W
Leo, Ind., U.S.	268	41.13 N	85.01 W
Leoben	164	47.23 N	15.06 E
Léogâne	282	18.31 N	72.38 W
Leola, Ark., U.S.	248	34.10 N	92.35 W
Leola, Pa., U.S.	262	40.05 N	76.11 W
Leola, S. Dak., U.S.	252	45.43 N	98.56 W
Leominster, Eng., U.K.	174	52.14 N	2.45 W
Leominster, Mass., U.S.	261	42.32 N	71.45 W
León, Esp.	168	42.36 N	5.34 W
León, Fr.	166	43.53 N	1.18 W
León, Nic.	280	12.26 N	86.54 W
Leon, Pil.	202	10.47 N	122.23 E
Leon, Iowa, U.S.	244	40.44 N	93.45 W
Leon, Kans., U.S.	252	37.42 N	96.46 W
Leon, N.Y., U.S.	266	42.18 N	79.01 W
León □⁹	168	42.00 N	6.00 W
León □⁴	278	21.10 N	101.42 W
Leon ≃	250	30.59 N	97.24 W
León, Arroyo V	254	35.35 N	107.31 W
León, Montañas de ▲	168	42.30 N	6.18 W
Leona ≃	250	28.45 N	99.11 W
Leona, Punta ⊱	288	9.42 N	84.40 W
Leonard, Mich., U.S.	266	42.52 N	83.09 W
Leonard, N. Dak., U.S.	252	46.39 N	97.15 W
Leonard, Tex., U.S.	250	33.23 N	96.15 W
Leonardsburg	266	40.21 N	82.59 W
Leonardtown	262	38.17 N	76.38 W
Leonardville	252	39.22 N	96.51 W
Leonessa	170	42.34 N	12.58 E
Leonforte	170	37.39 N	14.24 E
Leonidas	266	42.01 N	85.21 W
Leonidhion	172	37.10 N	22.52 E
Leonora	228	28.53 S	121.20 E
León Guzmán	250	25.31 N	103.34 W
Leonicha	160	59.37 N	38.51 E
Leonidas	168	39.45 N	8.48 W
Leon Rougés	294	27.30 S	65.37 W
Leonville	248	30.29 N	91.59 W
Leopold and Astrid Coast ⌇²	148	67.10 S	84.10 E
Léopold II, Lac ⊜	218	2.00 S	18.20 E
Leopoldina	296	21.32 S	42.38 W
Leopoldo de Bulhões	296	16.37 S	48.46 W
Leopoldsburg	178	51.07 N	5.15 E
Léopoldville → Kinshasa	218	4.18 S	15.18 E
Leoti	252	38.29 N	101.21 W
Le Palais	166	47.21 N	3.09 W
Lepanto, C.R.	280	9.57 N	85.02 W
Lepanto → Návpaktos, Ellás	172	38.23 N	21.50 E
Lepanto, Ark., U.S.	248	35.36 N	90.20 W
Lepe	168	37.15 N	7.12 W
Le Péage-de-Roussillon	182	45.22 N	4.48 E
Lepel'	160	54.53 N	28.42 E
Le Pellerin	166	47.12 N	1.45 W
Le Petit-Quevilly	176	49.26 N	1.02 E
Leping	196	28.57 N	117.05 E
L'Epiphanie	260	45.51 N	73.29 W
Le Pont-de-Beauvoisin	166	45.32 N	5.40 E
Lepontine, Alpi ▲	166	46.25 N	8.40 E
Le Portel	225c	20.55 S	55.18 E
Le Port	176	50.42 N	1.38 E
Lepreau, Point ⊱	240	45.04 N	66.27 W
Le Prêcheur	284e	14.48 N	61.14 W
Lepsy	186	46.15 N	78.55 E
Le Puy	182	45.02 N	3.53 E
Lequeitio	168	43.22 N	2.30 W
Lérabá ≃	222	9.42 N	5.11 W
Lercara Friddi	170	37.45 N	13.36 E
Lere	222	9.43 N	9.21 E
Lerga, Merdia C	168	34.50 N	6.15 W
Lerici	170	44.04 N	9.55 E
Lérida, Col.	290	0.10 N	70.42 W
Lérida, Esp.	168	41.37 N	0.37 E
Lerma	168	42.02 N	3.45 W
Lerma ≃	278	20.13 N	102.46 W
Le Robert	284e	14.41 N	60.57 W
Léros I	172	37.08 N	26.52 E
Leroux Wash V	254	34.54 N	110.12 W
LeRoy, Ill., U.S.	268	40.21 N	88.46 W
Le Roy, Kans., U.S.	252	38.05 N	95.38 W
Le Roy, Minn., U.S.	244	43.31 N	92.30 W
Le Roy, N.Y., U.S.	264	42.59 N	77.59 W
Leroy, Ohio, U.S.	266	41.06 N	81.55 W
Lerwick	162	60.09 N	1.09 W
Léry	260	45.20 N	73.49 W
Les Abymes	285o	16.16 N	61.31 W
Le Saint-Esprit	284e	14.34 N	60.57 W
Les Aix-d'Angillon	166	47.12 N	2.34 E
Les Andelys	176	49.15 N	1.25 E
Les Anses-d'Arlets	284e	14.29 N	61.05 W
Les Avalloirs ▲²	166	48.28 N	0.07 W
Lesbos → Lésvos I	172	39.10 N	26.20 E
Les Cayes	282	18.12 N	73.45 W
Les Échelles	166	45.26 N	5.45 E
Les Écureuils	260	46.39 N	71.43 W
Le Sel	166	47.53 N	1.36 W
Les Essarts	166	46.46 N	1.14 W
Leshan	190	29.34 N	103.45 E
Les Herbiers	166	46.52 N	1.01 W
Leshui ≃	196	26.54 N	113.12 E
Lesina	184	41.52 N	15.21 E
Lesjöfors	160	59.59 N	14.11 E
Lesko	164	49.29 N	22.21 E
Leskovac	172	42.59 N	21.57 E
Leslie, Ark., U.S.	248	35.50 N	92.34 W
Leslie, Ga., U.S.	246	31.57 N	84.05 W
Leslie, Mich., U.S.	268	42.27 N	84.26 W
Leslie, W. Va., U.S.	242	38.03 N	80.43 W
Leśna (Marklissa)	164	51.02 N	15.16 E
Lesna ≃	164	52.10 N	23.33 E
Lesneven	162	48.34 N	4.19 W
Lešnica	172	44.39 N	19.19 E
Lesnoj	160	59.48 N	52.08 E
Lesnoje	160	58.17 N	35.32 E
Lesný ▲	164	50.02 N	12.37 E
Lesnyje Po'any	160	58.58 N	52.26 E
Lesogorskij	160	61.02 N	28.53 E
Lesotho □¹	218	29.30 S	28.30 E
Lesozavodsk	186	45.28 N	133.27 E
Lesozavodskij	160	66.44 N	32.49 E
Lesparre-Médoc	166	45.18 N	0.56 W
Les Pieux	166	49.31 N	1.48 W
Les Riceys	166	47.59 N	4.22 E
Les Sables-d'Olonne	166	46.30 N	1.47 W
Les Saintes-Maries	166	43.27 N	4.26 E
Les Saules	260	46.48 N	71.17 W
Lessay	166	49.13 N	1.32 W
Lesser Antilles II	282	15.00 N	61.00 W
Lesser Khingan Mountains → Xiaoxing'anling-shanmai ▲	190	50.00 N	126.25 E
Lesser Slave ≃	238	55.10 N	114.03 W
Lesser Slave Lake ⊜	238	55.25 N	115.30 W
Lesser Sunda Islands II	198	9.00 S	120.00 E
Lessines (Lessen)	176	50.43 N	3.50 E
Lester	270	47.12 N	121.29 W
Lestijoki ≃	160	64.04 N	23.38 E
Le Sueur	244	44.27 N	93.54 W
Le Sueur ≃	244	44.07 N	94.03 W
Lešukonskoje	160	64.54 N	45.40 E
Les Vans	166	44.24 N	4.08 E
Lésvos I	172	39.10 N	26.20 E
Leszno	164	51.51 N	16.35 E
Letcher	252	43.54 N	98.08 W
Letchworth	174	51.58 N	0.14 W
Letea, Ostrovul I	172	45.20 N	29.20 E
Le Teil	182	44.33 N	4.41 E
Letenye	164	46.26 N	16.43 E
Lethbridge, Alta., Can.	238	49.42 N	112.50 W
Lethbridge, Newf., Can.	240	48.21 N	53.50 W
Lethem	290	3.20 N	59.50 W
Le Thillot	166	47.53 N	6.46 E
Leti, Kepulauan II	198	8.12 S	127.41 E
Letiahau ≃	224	21.16 S	24.00 E
Leticia	290	4.09 S	69.57 W
Letka	160	59.36 N	49.22 E
Letmathe	178	51.22 N	7.37 E
Letn'aja Zolotica	160	64.57 N	36.50 E
Letnerečenskij	160	64.18 N	34.29 E
Letpadan	200	17.47 N	95.45 E
Le Trayas	166	43.28 N	6.55 E
Le Tréport	176	50.04 N	1.22 E
Letsôk-aw Kyun I	200	11.37 N	98.15 E
Letter	178	52.24 N	9.38 E
Letterkenny	162	54.57 N	7.44 W
Lettsworth	248	30.56 N	91.42 W
Leu	172	44.11 N	24.00 E
Leucadia	274	33.04 N	117.18 W
Leuk	166	46.19 N	7.38 E
Leuna	164	51.19 N	12.01 E
Leuser, Gunung ▲	200	3.44 N	97.10 E
Leutkirch	180	47.49 N	10.01 E
Leuven (Louvain)	176	50.53 N	4.42 E
Leuze	176	50.36 N	3.36 E
Levack	244	46.38 N	81.23 W
Levádheia	172	38.25 N	22.54 E
Levan	254	39.33 N	111.52 W
Levanger	158	63.45 N	11.18 E
Levante, Riviera di ⌇²	170	45.15 N	9.30 E
Levanto	170	44.10 N	9.38 E
Levanzo, Isola di I	170	38.00 N	12.20 E
Le Vauclin	284e	14.33 N	60.51 W
Leveaux Mountain ▲²	244	47.37 N	90.47 W
Leveland	250	33.35 N	102.23 W
Levelock	236	59.07 N	156.52 W
Level Park	268	42.22 N	85.18 W
Levering	242	45.38 N	84.47 W
Leverkusen	164	51.03 N	6.59 E
Leverville	218	4.50 S	18.44 E
Levice	164	48.13 N	18.37 E
Levie	170	41.42 N	9.07 E
Levier	166	46.57 N	6.08 E
Le Vigan	166	43.59 N	3.35 E
Levin	230	40.37 S	175.17 E
Lévis	260	46.48 N	71.11 W
Lévis □⁶	260	46.40 N	71.15 W
Levitha I	212	37.00 N	26.28 E
Levittown	262	40.09 N	74.50 W
Lévka Óri ▲	172	35.18 N	24.01 E
Levkás	172	38.50 N	20.41 E
Levkás I	172	38.39 N	20.27 E
Levkímmi	172	39.25 N	20.04 E
Levkosía (Nicosia)	212	35.11 N	33.21 E
Levoča	164	49.02 N	20.36 E
Levroux	166	46.59 N	1.37 E
Levski	172	43.22 N	25.08 E
Lewellen	252	41.20 N	102.09 W
Lewer ≃	224	25.30 S	17.45 E
Lewes, Eng., U.K.	174	50.52 N	0.01 E
Lewes, Del., U.S.	262	38.47 N	75.08 W
Lewin Brzeski (Löwen)	164	50.46 N	17.37 E
Lewis, Iowa, U.S.	252	41.18 N	95.05 W
Lewis, Kans., U.S.	252	37.56 N	99.15 W
Lewis □⁶, N.Y., U.S.	264	43.47 N	75.29 W
Lewis □⁶, Wash., U.S.	270	46.35 N	122.22 W
Lewis I	162	58.10 N	6.40 W
Lewis, Mount ▲	258	40.24 N	116.51 W
Lewis and Clark Lake ⊜¹	252	42.50 N	97.45 W
Lewisberry	262	40.08 N	76.52 W
Lewisburg, Ky., U.S.	248	36.59 N	86.57 W
Lewisburg, Pa., U.S.	242	40.58 N	76.53 W
Lewisburg, Tenn., U.S.	248	35.27 N	86.48 W
Lewisburg, W. Va., U.S.	242	37.48 N	80.27 W
Lewis Center	266	40.12 N	83.01 W
Lewisetta	262	38.01 N	76.28 W
Lewisham ▲⁸	174	51.27 N	0.01 E
Lewis Hills ▲²	240	48.48 N	58.30 W
Lewis Isle of I	158	58.10 N	6.40 W
Lewis Pass ⅹ	230	42.23 S	172.24 E
Lewisport	248	37.56 N	86.54 W
Lewisporte	240	49.15 N	55.03 W
Lewis Range ▲	256	48.30 N	113.15 W
Lewis Run	266	41.52 N	78.40 W
Lewis Smith Lake ⊜¹	248	34.05 N	87.07 W
Lewiston, Calif., U.S.	258	40.43 N	122.48 W
Lewiston, Idaho, U.S.	256	46.25 N	117.01 W
Lewiston, Maine, U.S.	242	44.06 N	70.13 W
Lewiston, Mich., U.S.	244	44.53 N	84.18 W
Lewiston, Minn., U.S.	244	44.00 N	91.49 W
Lewiston, N.Y., U.S.	264	43.10 N	79.03 W
Lewiston, Utah, U.S.	254	41.58 N	111.52 W
Lewiston Orchards	256	46.23 N	116.59 W
Lewistown, Ill., U.S.	248	40.24 N	90.09 W
Lewistown, Md., U.S.	262	39.32 N	77.25 W
Lewistown, Mo., U.S.	248	40.05 N	91.49 W
Lewistown, Mont., U.S.	256	47.04 N	109.26 W
Lewistown, Ohio, U.S.	268	40.25 N	83.53 W
Lewistown, Pa., U.S.	262	40.36 N	77.31 W
Lewisville, N.B., Can.	240	45.06 N	64.46 W
Lewisville, Ark., U.S.	248	33.22 N	93.35 W
Lewisville, Pa., U.S.	262	39.43 N	75.53 W
Lewisville, Tex., U.S.	250	33.03 N	96.60 W
Lexa	248	34.36 N	90.45 W
Lexington, Ga., U.S.	246	33.52 N	83.07 W
Lexington, Ill., U.S.	268	40.39 N	88.47 W
Lexington, Ky., U.S.	246	38.03 N	84.30 W
Lexington, Mass., U.S.	261	42.27 N	71.14 W
Lexington, Mich., U.S.	244	43.16 N	82.32 W
Lexington, Miss., U.S.	248	33.07 N	90.03 W
Lexington, Mo., U.S.	248	39.11 N	93.52 W
Lexington, Nebr., U.S.	252	40.47 N	99.45 W
Lexington, N.C., U.S.	246	35.49 N	80.15 W
Lexington, Ohio, U.S.	266	40.41 N	82.35 W
Lexington, Okla., U.S.	250	35.01 N	97.20 W
Lexington, Oreg., U.S.	256	45.27 N	119.41 W
Lexington, S.C., U.S.	246	33.59 N	81.14 W
Lexington, Tenn., U.S.	248	35.39 N	88.24 W
Lexington, Tex., U.S.	250	30.25 N	97.01 W
Lexington, Va., U.S.	246	37.47 N	79.27 W
Lexington Park	242	38.16 N	76.27 W
Leyne	172	37.22 N	28.02 E
Leyre ≃	166	44.39 N	1.01 W
Leyte	202	11.23 N	124.29 E
Leyte I	202	10.50 N	124.55 E
Leyte Gulf C	202	10.55 N	124.50 E
Leyte Gulf C	202	10.40 N	125.25 E
Leżajsk	164	50.16 N	22.24 E
Lezama	290	9.43 N	66.24 W
Lezhë	172	41.47 N	19.39 E
L'gov	158	51.43 N	35.17 E
Lhasa → Lasa	206	29.40 N	91.09 E
L'Hillil	168	35.41 N	0.19 E
Lhokseumawe	200	5.29 N	95.15 E
Lhokseumawe	200	5.10 N	97.08 E
Lhoksukon	200	5.03 N	97.19 E
Lhut ≃	214	10.25 N	51.05 E
Li ≃	200	18.25 N	98.45 E
Lianga	202	8.38 N	126.06 E
Lianga Bay C	202	8.36 N	126.10 E
Liangshan ▲, Zhg.	200	23.45 N	99.45 E
Liangshan ▲, Zhg.	200	24.05 N	99.02 E
Liangzihu ⊜	196	30.16 N	114.34 E
Lianjiang	200	21.38 N	110.17 E
Lianjiang ≃, Zhg.	196	25.46 N	115.38 E
Lianjiang ≃, Zhg.	196	24.02 N	113.18 E
Lianjiang ≃, Zhg.	196	23.16 N	116.32 E
Lianshui ≃	196	25.07 N	116.24 E
Lianxian	196	24.44 N	112.21 E
Lianyun'gang	190	34.36 N	119.13 E
Lianyunshan ▲	196	28.32 N	113.50 E
Liaocheng	196	36.30 N	115.59 E
Liaodongbandao ⊱¹	194	40.00 N	122.20 E
Liaodongwan C	194	40.30 N	121.30 E
Liaohe ≃	194	40.40 N	122.09 E
Liaoning □⁴	194	41.00 N	123.00 E
Liaoshui ≃	196	29.11 N	116.00 E
Liaotung, Gulf of → Liaodongwan C	194	40.30 N	121.30 E
Liaotung Peninsula → Liaodongbandao ⊱¹	194	40.00 N	122.20 E
Liaoyang	194	41.17 N	123.11 E
Liaoyuan	190	42.54 N	125.07 E
Liapádhes	172	39.40 N	19.44 E
Liard ≃	232	61.52 N	121.18 W
Libano	290	4.55 N	75.04 W
Libby	256	48.23 N	115.33 W
Libenge	218	3.39 N	18.38 E
Liberal, Kans., U.S.	252	37.02 N	100.55 W
Liberal, Mo., U.S.	248	37.34 N	94.31 W
Liberdade	296	22.01 S	44.19 W
Liberec	164	50.46 N	15.03 E
Liberia	280	10.38 N	85.27 W
Liberia □¹	214	6.00 N	10.00 W
Libertad	284c	17.02 N	61.47 W
Libertad, Ur.	294	34.38 S	56.39 W
Libertad, Ven.	290	9.23 N	68.44 W
Libertad, Ven.	290	8.20 N	69.37 W
Libertador	290	30.12 S	59.23 W
Libertador General San Martín (Ledesma), Arg.	294	23.50 S	64.45 W
Libyan Plateau → Aḍ-Ḍiffah ▲¹	220	30.30 N	25.30 E
Libertador General San Martín	294	26.48 S	55.02 W
Liberty, Ind., U.S.	248	39.38 N	84.56 W
Liberty, Ky., U.S.	248	37.19 N	84.56 W
Liberty, Miss., U.S.	248	31.09 N	90.48 W
Liberty, Mo., U.S.	248	39.15 N	94.25 W
Liberty, Nebr., U.S.	252	40.05 N	96.29 W
Liberty, N.C., U.S.	246	35.51 N	79.34 W
Liberty, N.Y., U.S.	262	41.48 N	74.45 W
Liberty, S.C., U.S.	246	34.48 N	82.42 W
Liberty, Tex., U.S.	250	30.03 N	94.47 W
Liberty Center, Ind., U.S.	268	40.42 N	85.17 W
Liberty Center, Ohio, U.S.	268	41.27 N	84.07 W
Liberty Farms	272	38.19 N	121.42 W
Liberty Hill	250	30.40 N	97.55 W
Liberty Mills	268	41.02 N	85.44 W
Liberty Plain	261	42.11 N	70.53 W
Libertyville	268	42.17 N	87.57 W
Libo	200	25.28 N	107.53 E
Libog	202	8.20 N	124.44 E
Libourne	166	44.55 N	0.14 W
Libramont	176	49.55 N	5.23 E
Library	266	40.18 N	80.02 W
Librazhd	172	41.11 N	20.19 E
Libres	278	19.28 N	97.41 W
Libreville	218	0.23 N	9.27 E
Librobo Point ⊱	202	11.25 N	119.26 E
Libucan Island I	202	11.54 N	124.38 E
Libya □¹	214	27.00 N	17.00 E
Libyan Desert → Aṣ-Ṣaḥrā' al-Lībīyah ⌇²	214	24.00 N	25.00 E
Licantén	294	34.59 S	72.00 W
Licata	170	37.05 N	13.56 E
Lich	164	50.33 N	8.50 E
Lichfield	174	52.42 N	1.48 W
Lichitiseni	172	46.23 N	27.17 E
Lichoslavl'	160	57.07 N	35.28 E
Lichtenburg	224	26.08 S	26.08 E
Lichtenfels	164	50.09 N	11.04 E
Lichtenstein	164	50.45 N	12.37 E
Lichtenvoorde	178	51.59 N	6.34 E
Lichtervelde	176	51.02 N	3.09 E
Lickershamn	160	57.50 N	18.31 E
Licking	248	37.30 N	91.51 W
Licking □⁶	266	40.10 N	82.30 W
Licking ≃	242	39.06 N	84.30 W
Lickingville	266	41.22 N	79.22 W
Ličko Polje ⚟	170	44.35 N	15.25 E
Lida	158	53.53 N	25.18 E
Liddon Gulf C	232	75.03 N	113.00 W
Liden	160	62.42 N	16.48 E
Lidgerwood	252	46.05 N	97.09 W
Lidice	180	50.08 N	14.12 E
Lidköping	160	58.30 N	13.10 E
Lido di Ostia	170	41.44 N	12.14 E
Lidzbark	164	53.17 N	19.49 E
Lidzbark Warmiński (Heilsberg)	164	54.09 N	20.35 E
Liebenhausen	178	51.03 N	7.40 E
Liechtenstein □¹	158	47.09 N	9.35 E
Liedekerke	176	50.52 N	4.05 E
Liège	176	50.38 N	5.34 E
Liegnitz → Legnica	164	51.13 N	16.09 E
Lieksa	160	63.19 N	30.01 E
Lienen	178	52.09 N	7.58 E
Lienz	164	46.50 N	12.47 E
Liepāja	160	56.31 N	21.01 E
Lier (Lierre)	176	51.08 N	4.34 E
Liesborn	178	51.43 N	8.15 E
Liestal	180	47.29 N	7.44 E
Liesti	172	45.37 N	27.32 E
Liévin	176	50.25 N	2.46 E
Lièvre, Rivière du ≃	242	45.35 N	75.53 W
Liezen	164	47.35 N	14.15 E
Lifford	162	54.50 N	7.29 W
Liffré	162	48.13 N	1.30 W
Ligao, Pil.	202	13.14 N	123.32 E
Ligao, Pil.	202	6.17 N	124.09 E
Lightfoot	262	37.20 N	76.45 W
Lighthouse Point	246	26.17 N	80.07 W
Lighthouse Point ⊱, Fla., U.S.	246	29.54 N	84.21 W
Lighthouse Point ⊱, Mich., U.S.	244	45.13 N	85.32 W
Lighthouse Reef ⚘²	278	17.20 N	87.32 W
Lightsville	268	40.18 N	84.42 W
Lignières	166	46.45 N	2.11 E
Lignite	252	48.53 N	102.34 W
Ligny-en-Barrois	180	48.41 N	5.20 E
Ligonier, Ind., U.S.	268	41.28 N	85.35 W
Ligonier, Pa., U.S.	266	40.15 N	79.14 W
Ligueil	166	47.03 N	0.49 E
Ligui	278	25.43 N	111.16 W
Liguria □⁴	182	44.30 N	8.50 E
Ligurian Sea ⚘²	170	43.30 N	9.00 E
Lihou Reefs ⚘²	228	17.25 S	151.40 E
Lihue	275b	21.59 N	159.22 W
Lijiang	190	26.57 N	100.15 E
Lijiang ≃	196	24.16 N	115.12 E
Lik ≃	200	18.33 N	102.31 E
Likasi (Jadotville)	218	10.59 S	26.44 E
Likely	238	52.37 N	121.34 W
Liknes	160	58.19 N	6.59 E
Likouala ≃	218	0.50 S	17.11 E
Lila, Cerro ▲	294	23.48 S	68.23 W
Lilbourn	248	36.35 N	89.37 W
L'Île-Bouchard	166	47.07 N	0.25 E
L'Île-Rousse	166	42.38 N	8.56 E
Lilienfeld	164	48.03 N	15.36 E
Lilienthal	178	53.08 N	8.55 E
Liling	196	27.40 N	113.30 E
Lilio	202	14.08 N	121.26 E
Lillafüred ♦	172	48.07 N	20.38 E
Lille	176	50.38 N	3.04 E
Lille Bælt 𝔘	164	55.20 N	9.45 E
Lillebonne	176	49.31 N	0.33 E
Lillehammer	160	61.08 N	10.30 E
Lillers	176	50.34 N	2.29 E
Lillesand	160	58.15 N	8.24 E
Lillestrøm	160	59.57 N	11.05 E
Lillhärdal	160	61.51 N	14.04 E
Lillington	246	35.24 N	78.49 W
Lillo	168	39.43 N	3.18 W
Lillooet	238	50.42 N	121.56 W
Lillooet ≃	238	49.45 N	122.08 W
Lillooet Lake ⊜	238	50.13 N	122.29 W
Lilly	266	40.25 N	78.33 W
Liloan	202	10.09 N	125.07 E
Lilongwe	218	13.59 S	33.44 E
Lilo Viejo	294	26.56 S	62.58 W
Liloy	202	8.08 N	122.40 E
Lily	246	37.02 N	84.17 W
Lilydale, Austl.	228	41.15 S	147.13 E
Lily Dale, N.Y., U.S.	266	42.21 N	79.19 W
Lima, Para.	294	23.54 S	56.20 W
Lima, Perú	292	12.03 S	77.03 W
Lima, Mont., U.S.	256	44.38 N	112.36 W
Lima, N.Y., U.S.	264	42.54 N	77.37 W
Lima, Ohio, U.S.	268	40.46 N	84.06 W
Lima □⁵	292	12.00 S	76.35 W
Lima (Limia) ≃	168	41.41 N	8.50 W
Lima Center	268	42.47 N	88.49 W
Limache	294	33.01 S	71.16 W
Limanowa	164	49.43 N	20.26 E
Lima Nueva	280	15.23 N	87.56 W
Lima Reservoir ⊜¹	256	44.38 N	112.17 W
Limari ≃	294	30.44 S	71.43 W
Limasawa Island I	202	9.56 N	125.04 E
Limassol → Lemesós	212	34.40 N	33.03 E
Limavady	162	55.03 N	6.57 W
Limaville	266	40.59 N	81.09 W
Limay, Fr.	176	49.00 N	1.44 E
Limay, Pil.	202	14.34 N	120.36 E
Limay ≃	294	39.00 S	68.00 W
Limay Mahuida	294	37.11 S	66.40 W
Limbang	198	4.45 N	115.00 E
Limbani	292	14.08 S	69.40 W
Limbara, Monte ▲	170	40.51 N	9.11 E
Limbaži	160	57.31 N	24.42 E
Limbiate	182	45.36 N	9.07 E
Limburg □⁴, Bel.	178	51.00 N	5.30 E
Limburg □⁴, Ned.	178	51.14 N	5.50 E
Limburg an der Lahn	164	50.23 N	8.04 E
Limeira	296	22.34 S	47.24 W
Limerick, Sask., Can.	252	49.40 N	106.15 W
Limerick, Eire	162	52.40 N	8.38 W
Limerick □⁶	162	52.30 N	9.00 W
Limerock	261	41.55 N	71.28 W
Lime Springs	244	43.27 N	92.17 W
Limestone, Maine, U.S.	240	46.55 N	67.50 W
Limestone, N.Y., U.S.	266	42.02 N	78.38 W
Limestone, Pa., U.S.	266	41.08 N	79.20 W
Lime Village	236	61.21 N	155.28 W
Limfjorden 𝔘	160	56.55 N	9.10 E
Limia (Lima) ≃	168	41.41 N	8.50 W
Liminka	160	64.49 N	25.24 E
Límin Vathéos	172	37.45 N	27.00 E
Limmared	160	57.32 N	13.21 E
Límnos I	172	39.54 N	25.21 E
Limoeiro	286	7.52 S	35.27 W
Limoges, Ont., Can.	260	45.20 N	75.15 W
Limoges, Fr.	166	45.50 N	1.16 E
Limogne	166	44.24 N	1.46 E
Limón, C.R.	280	10.00 N	83.02 W
Limón, Hond.	280	15.52 N	85.33 W
Limon, Colo., U.S.	252	39.16 N	103.41 W
Limón □⁴	280	10.00 N	83.15 W
Limonar	284p	22.57 N	81.24 W
Limón de Ramos	278	24.55 N	107.08 W
Limone Piemonte	170	44.12 N	7.34 E
Limours	176	48.39 N	2.05 E
Limousins, Plateau du ⚟	166	45.30 N	1.15 E
Limoux	166	43.04 N	2.14 E
Limpopo ≃	224	25.15 S	33.30 E
Limuling ▲	200	19.10 N	109.30 E
Linachamari	160	69.40 N	31.26 E
Linao Bay C	202	6.25 N	124.00 E
Linapacan Island I	202	11.29 N	119.47 E
Linapacan Strait 𝔘	202	11.35 N	119.50 E
Linares, Chile	294	35.51 S	71.36 W
Linares, Col.	290	1.23 N	77.31 W
Linares, Esp.	168	38.05 N	3.38 W
Linares, Méx.	278	24.52 N	99.34 W
Linares □⁴	294	36.00 S	71.35 W
Linariá	172	38.50 N	24.32 E
Linatchyrvavaam ≃	236	67.18 N	175.20 W
Lincang	200	23.45 N	102.20 E
Linch	254	43.37 N	106.12 W
Lincoln, Arg.	294	34.55 S	61.30 W
Lincoln, Eng., U.K.	162	53.14 N	0.33 W
Lincoln, Ark., U.S.	248	35.57 N	94.25 W
Lincoln, Calif., U.S.	272	38.54 N	121.17 W
Lincoln, Del., U.S.	262	38.52 N	75.25 W
Lincoln, Ill., U.S.	248	40.09 N	89.22 W
Lincoln, Ind., U.S.	268	40.37 N	86.12 W
Lincoln, Kans., U.S.	252	39.02 N	98.09 W
Lincoln, Maine, U.S.	242	45.22 N	68.30 W
Lincoln, Mass., U.S.	261	42.26 N	71.18 W
Lincoln, Mich., U.S.	244	44.41 N	83.25 W
Lincoln, Mo., U.S.	248	38.23 N	93.20 W
Lincoln, Mont., U.S.	256	46.58 N	112.41 W
Lincoln, Nebr., U.S.	252	40.48 N	96.42 W
Lincoln, N.H., U.S.	242	44.03 N	71.40 W
Lincoln, Pa., U.S.	262	40.18 N	76.20 W
Lincoln, R.I., U.S.	261	41.54 N	71.25 W
Lincoln □⁶, Ont., Can.	264	43.05 N	79.34 W
Lincoln □⁶, Oreg., U.S.	270	44.39 N	123.52 W
Lincoln, Mount ▲	254	39.21 N	106.07 W
Lincoln Acres	274	32.40 N	117.04 W
Lincoln Boyhood National Memorial ⊥	248	38.10 N	86.58 W
Lincoln City	270	44.59 N	123.59 W
Lincolndale	261	41.19 N	73.43 W

Symbols in the index entries are identified on page 360.

Name Page Lat°′ Long°′

Lincoln Heights 266 40.47 N 82.30 W
Lincoln National Park ♠ 228 34.50 S 135.35 E
Lincoln Park, Ga., U.S. 246 32.52 N 84.19 W
Lincoln Park, Mich., U.S. 268 42.14 N 83.09 W
Lincoln Park, N.Y., U.S. 261 41.57 N 74.00 W
Lincolnshire 268 42.11 N 87.54 W
Lincolnshire □[6] 174 52.55 N 0.22 W
Lincolnton, Ga., U.S. 246 33.48 N 82.28 W
Lincolnton, N.C., U.S. 246 35.29 N 81.14 W
Lincoln University 262 39.48 N 75.55 W
Lincoln Village 272 38.01 N 121.19 W
Lincolnville 266 41.47 N 79.51 W
Lincolnwood 268 42.00 N 87.46 W
Lincroft 262 40.20 N 74.07 W
Lind 256 46.58 N 118.37 W
Linda 272 39.08 N 121.34 W
Lindale, Ga., U.S. 246 34.11 N 85.11 W
Lindale, Tex., U.S. 250 32.31 N 95.25 W
Lindau 180 47.33 N 9.41 E
Linde ≃ 186 64.57 N 124.36 E
Linden, Ala., U.S. 248 32.18 N 87.47 W
Linden, Calif., U.S. 272 38.01 N 121.05 W
Linden, Mich., U.S. 268 42.49 N 83.47 W
Linden, N.J., U.S. 262 40.38 N 74.15 W
Linden, Tenn., U.S. 248 35.37 N 87.50 W
Linden, Tex., U.S. 248 33.01 N 94.22 W
Lindenberg im Allgäu 180 47.36 N 9.53 E
Lindenhurst 268 42.25 N 88.02 W
Linden Park 268 40.13 N 85.23 W
Lindenwold 262 39.49 N 74.59 W
Lindenwood 268 42.03 N 89.02 W
Líndhos 172 36.06 N 28.04 E
Líndhos ⊥ 172 36.06 N 28.05 E
Lindi 218 10.00 S 39.43 E
Lindis Pass)(230 44.42 S 169.29 E
Lindlar 164 51.01 N 7.23 E
Lind National Park ♠ 228 37.35 S 149.05 E
Lindon 252 39.44 N 103.24 W
Lindsay, Ont., Can. 264 45.05 N 81.23 W
Lindsay, Calif., U.S. 258 36.12 N 119.05 W
Lindsay, Nebr., U.S. 252 41.42 N 97.42 W
Lindsay, Okla., U.S. 250 34.50 N 97.38 W
Lindsborg 252 38.35 N 97.40 W
Lindsey 266 41.25 N 83.13 W
Lindsey □[8] 174 53.23 N 0.20 W
Lindstrom 244 45.23 N 92.52 W
Lineboro 262 39.43 N 76.51 W
Line Islands II 148 0.05 N 157.00 W
Line Lexington 262 40.17 N 75.16 W
Linesville 266 41.39 N 80.26 W
Lineville, Ala., U.S. 248 33.19 N 85.45 W
Lineville, Iowa, U.S. 244 40.35 N 93.32 W
Linfen 190 36.05 N 111.32 E
Linfield 262 40.13 N 75.34 W
Lingao 200 20.00 N 109.40 E
Lingayen 202 16.01 N 120.14 E
Lingayen Gulf C 202 16.10 N 120.15 E
Lingbo 160 61.03 N 16.41 E
Lingen 178 52.31 N 7.19 E
Lingga, Kepulauan II 198 0.10 S 104.35 E
Lingga, Pulau I 200 0.12 S 104.35 E
Lingig 202 8.02 N 126.24 E
Lingle 254 42.08 N 104.21 W
Linglestown 262 40.21 N 76.48 W
Lingling 200 26.11 N 111.29 E
Lingolsheim 180 48.34 N 7.41 E
Lingshan 200 22.28 N 109.17 E
Lingshui 200 18.31 N 110.03 E
Linguère 214 15.24 N 15.07 W
Linh, Ngoc Λ 200 15.05 N 108.00 E
Linhai 196 28.51 N 121.07 E
Linhares 296 19.25 S 40.04 W
Linhe 190 40.51 N 107.30 E
Linjiang 194 41.49 N 126.54 E
Linköping 160 58.25 N 15.37 E
Linkou 190 45.15 N 130.16 E
Linkuva 160 56.05 N 23.59 E
Linkwood 262 38.32 N 75.57 W
Linlithgow 162 55.59 N 3.37 W
Linn, Kans., U.S. 252 39.41 N 97.05 W
Linn, Mo., U.S. 248 38.29 N 91.51 W
Linnansaaren Kansallispuisto ♠ 160 62.07 N 28.31 E
Linnell 272 36.21 N 119.11 W
Linneus 248 39.53 N 93.11 W
Linn Grove 268 40.39 N 85.02 W
Linnhe, Loch C 162 56.37 N 5.25 W
Linosa, Isola di I 170 35.52 N 12.52 E
Linqing 194 36.53 N 115.41 E
Linru 196 34.11 N 112.49 E
Lins 296 21.40 S 49.45 W
Linstead 285q 18.08 N 77.02 W
Linta ≃ 225b 25.02 S 44.05 E
Lintao 190 35.27 N 103.46 E
Linthal 166 46.55 N 9.00 E
Linton, Ind., U.S. 248 39.02 N 87.10 W
Linton, Ky., U.S. 248 36.41 N 87.55 W
Linton, N. Dak., U.S. 252 46.16 N 100.14 W
Lintorf 178 51.20 N 6.49 E
Linville 246 36.04 N 81.52 W
Linwood, Mass., U.S. 261 42.06 N 71.39 W
Linwood, N.J., U.S. 262 39.21 N 74.34 W
Linworth 266 40.06 N 83.04 W
Linxi 190 43.30 N 118.00 E
Linxia 190 35.34 N 103.08 E
Linyi 194 35.04 N 118.22 E
Linyü → Shanhaiguan 194 40.01 N 119.44 E
Linz 164 48.18 N 14.18 E
Lion, Golfe du C 166 43.00 N 4.00 E
Lionel Town 285q 17.48 N 77.14 W
Lion's Head 264 44.59 N 81.15 W
Liozno 160 55.02 N 30.48 E
Lipa 202 13.57 N 121.10 E
Lipan 250 32.31 N 98.03 W
Lipany 164 49.10 N 20.58 E
Lipari 170 38.28 N 14.57 E
Lipari, Isola I 170 38.30 N 14.57 E
Lipeck 158 52.37 N 39.35 E
Lipez, Cordillera de ⋀ 292 21.40 S 66.35 W
Lipiany 164 53.00 N 14.59 E
Lipin Bor 160 60.16 N 37.57 E
Liping 200 26.17 N 109.00 E
Lipník nad Bečvou 164 49.31 N 17.35 E
Lipno 164 52.51 N 19.10 E
Lipoa Point ➤ 275d 21.02 N 156.38 W
Lipova 172 46.05 N 21.40 E
Lippstadt 178 51.40 N 8.19 E
Lipscomb 250 36.14 N 100.16 W
Lipsko 164 51.09 N 21.39 E
Lipsós I 212 37.20 N 26.45 E
Liptovská Teplička 164 48.59 N 20.06 E
Liptovský Mikuláš 164 49.06 N 19.37 E
Liptrap, Cape ➤ 228 38.54 S 145.55 E
Lipu 200 24.25 N 110.29 E
Lira 214 2.15 N 32.54 E
Lircay 292 12.59 S 74.42 W
Liria 168 39.38 N 0.36 W
Lisa, Punta ➤ 280 8.01 N 80.22 W
Lisala 214 2.09 N 21.31 E
Lisboa (Lisbon) 168 38.43 N 9.08 W
Lisbon → Lisboa, Port. 168 38.43 N 9.08 W
Lisbon, Ill., U.S. 268 41.29 N 88.29 W
Lisbon, Maine, U.S. 242 44.02 N 70.06 W
Lisbon, Md., U.S. 262 39.20 N 77.04 W
Lisbon, N.H., U.S. 242 44.13 N 71.55 W
Lisbon, N. Dak., U.S. 252 46.27 N 97.41 W
Lisbon, Ohio, U.S. 266 40.47 N 80.46 W
Lisbon Falls 242 44.03 N 70.03 W
Lisburn 162 54.31 N 6.03 W
Lisburne, Cape ➤ 236 68.52 N 166.14 W
Liscannor Bay C 162 52.55 N 9.25 W
Liscia ≃ 170 41.11 N 9.19 E
Lishehe ≃ 200 24.18 N 101.32 E
Lishui 196 28.27 N 119.54 E
Lisičansk 158 48.55 N 38.26 E
Lisieux, Sask., Can. 252 49.17 N 105.59 W
Lisieux, Fr. 176 49.09 N 0.14 E
Liski → Georgiu-Dež 158 50.59 N 39.30 E
L'Isle, Fr. 176 49.07 N 2.14 E
Lisle, Ill., U.S. 268 41.48 N 88.05 W
l'Isle-en-Dodon 166 43.23 N 0.51 E
L'Isle Jourdain 166 46.14 N 0.41 E
L'Isle-sur-le-Doubs 166 47.27 N 6.35 E
Lisman 248 32.05 N 88.17 W
Lismore, Austl. 228 28.48 S 153.17 E
Lismore, N.S., Can. 240 45.42 N 62.16 W
Lismore Island I 162 56.30 N 5.30 W
Lišov 164 49.01 N 14.37 E
Lisse 178 52.15 N 4.33 E
Lissone 182 45.37 N 9.14 E
Lištica 170 43.23 N 17.36 E
Listowel, Ont., Can. 264 43.44 N 80.57 W
Listowel, Eire 162 52.27 N 9.29 W
Lit 160 63.19 N 14.49 E
Litang, Malay. 202 5.24 N 118.28 E
Litang, Zhg. 190 29.59 N 100.19 E
Litang, Zhg. 190 23.11 N 109.05 E
Litanghe ≃ 190 28.04 N 101.30 E
Litchfield, Conn., U.S. 261 41.45 N 73.11 W
Litchfield, Ill., U.S. 248 39.11 N 89.39 W
Litchfield, Mich., U.S. 268 42.03 N 84.46 W
Litchfield, Minn., U.S. 244 45.08 N 94.31 W
Litchfield, Nebr., U.S. 252 41.09 N 99.09 W
Litchfield, Ohio, U.S. 266 41.10 N 82.02 W
Litchfield □[6] 261 41.45 N 73.11 W
Litchfield Park 254 33.30 N 112.22 W
Litchville 252 46.39 N 98.11 W
Lithgow 228 33.29 S 150.09 E
Líthinon, Ákra ➤ 172 34.55 N 24.44 E
Lithonia 246 33.43 N 84.06 W
Lithuanian Soviet Socialist Republic → Litovskaja Sovetskaja Socialističeskaja 186 56.00 N 24.00 E
Litija 170 46.03 N 14.50 E
Lititz 262 40.09 N 76.18 W
Litókhoron 172 40.06 N 22.30 E
Litoměřice 164 50.35 N 14.09 E
Litomyšl 164 49.52 N 16.19 E
Litovel 164 49.42 N 17.05 E
Litovko 186 49.15 N 135.11 E
Litovskaja Sovetskaja Socialističeskaja Respublik □[3] 186 56.00 N 24.00 E
Littau 180 47.03 N 8.16 E
Little ≃, U.S. 248 33.37 N 93.52 W
Little ≃, Ala., U.S. 248 34.16 N 85.40 W
Little ≃, Ala., U.S. 248 31.18 N 87.46 W
Little ≃, Fla., U.S. 246 30.28 N 84.32 W
Little ≃, Ga., U.S. 246 33.39 N 82.32 W
Little ≃, Ga., U.S. 246 30.51 N 83.21 W
Little ≃, Ky., U.S. 248 36.51 N 87.58 W
Little ≃, N.C., U.S. 246 35.15 N 78.42 W
Little ≃, N.C., U.S. 246 35.21 N 78.02 W
Little ≃, Okla., U.S. 250 35.00 N 96.25 W
Little ≃, S.C., U.S. 246 34.10 N 81.11 W
Little ≃, S.C., U.S. 246 34.11 N 81.45 W
Little ≃, S.C., U.S. 246 33.56 N 82.25 W
Little ≃, Tenn., U.S. 246 35.51 N 83.57 W
Little ≃, Va., U.S. 246 37.05 N 80.32 W
Little Abaco Island I 282 26.54 N 77.42 W
Little Andaman I 200 10.40 N 92.30 E
Little Arkansas ≃ 252 37.43 N 97.22 W
Little Barrier Island I 230 36.12 S 175.05 E
Little Bay Island 240 49.39 N 55.47 W
Little Bear ≃ 254 41.42 N 111.57 W
Little Belt Mountains ⋀ 256 46.45 N 110.35 W
Little Bighorn ≃ 256 45.44 N 107.34 W
Little Bitterroot ≃ 256 47.30 N 114.19 W
Little Black ≃ 248 36.25 N 90.45 W
Little Blackfoot ≃ 256 46.31 N 112.48 W
Little Blue ≃ 252 39.41 N 96.40 W
Little Bow ≃ 238 49.53 N 112.29 W
Little Bow Lake ⊜ 238 50.12 N 112.41 W
Little Buffalo ≃ 232 61.00 N 113.46 W
Little Cacapon ≃ 242 39.31 N 78.30 W
Little Catalina 240 48.33 N 53.03 W
Little Cayman I 282 19.41 N 80.03 W
Little Cedar ≃ 244 42.57 N 92.31 W
Little Chute 244 44.17 N 88.16 W
Little Coco Island I 200 14.00 N 93.13 E
Little Colorado ≃ 254 36.11 N 111.48 W
Little Compton 261 41.30 N 71.10 W
Little Cooley 266 41.44 N 79.53 W
Little Cottonwood ≃ 252 44.15 N 94.20 W
Little Creek 262 39.10 N 75.27 W
Little Current 244 45.58 N 81.56 W
Little Current ≃ 232 50.57 N 84.36 W
Little Cypress Bayou ≃ 248 32.41 N 94.15 W
Little Deschutes ≃ 256 43.51 N 121.27 W
Little Diomede Island I 236 65.45 N 168.57 W
Little Eau Pleine ≃ 244 44.40 N 89.41 W
Little Falls 244 45.59 N 94.21 W
Littlefield 250 33.55 N 102.20 W
Littlefork 244 48.24 N 93.33 W
Little Fork ≃ 244 48.31 N 93.35 W
Little Fort 238 51.25 N 120.12 W
Little Genesee 266 42.02 N 78.13 W
Littlehampton 174 50.48 N 0.33 W
Little Harbour Deep 240 50.11 N 56.30 W
Little Hope 266 42.06 N 79.49 W
Little Humboldt ≃ 258 41.00 N 117.43 W
Little Inagua I 282 21.30 N 73.00 W
Little Kanawha ≃ 242 39.16 N 81.34 W
Little Karroo ⋀[1] 224 33.45 S 21.30 E
Little Koniuji Island I 236 55.01 N 159.26 W
Little Lake ⊜ 248 29.30 N 90.10 W
Little Laramie ≃ 254 41.28 N 105.44 W
Little London 285q 18.15 N 78.13 W
Little Lost ≃ 256 43.46 N 112.58 W
Little Lun ≃ 202 6.02 N 125.17 E
Little Minch ⋃ 162 57.35 N 6.45 W
Little Missouri ≃, U.S. 252 47.30 N 102.25 W
Little Missouri ≃, Ark., U.S. 248 33.49 N 92.54 W
Little Muddy ≃, Ill., U.S. 248 37.50 N 89.11 W
Little Muddy ≃, N. Dak., U.S. 252 48.12 N 103.36 W
Little Namaqualand □[9] 224 29.00 S 17.00 E
Little Nemaha ≃ 252 40.19 N 95.40 W
Little Niangua ≃ 248 38.04 N 92.54 W
Little Nicobar I 200 7.20 N 93.40 E
Little Ohoopee ≃ 246 32.27 N 82.24 W
Little Osage ≃ 248 38.02 N 94.14 W
Little Owyhee ≃ 256 42.28 N 117.15 W
Little Pee Dee ≃ 246 33.42 N 79.11 W
Little Pic ≃ 244 48.48 N 86.37 W
Little Platte ≃ 248 39.24 N 94.41 W
Little Popo Aggie ≃ 254 42.54 N 108.35 W
Little Powder ≃ 252 45.28 N 105.20 W
Little Rann of Kutch ≚ 206 23.30 N 71.15 E
Little Red ≃ 248 35.11 N 91.27 W
Little Red Deer ≃ 238 52.04 N 114.09 W
Little River 252 38.24 N 98.01 W
Little Rock, Ark., U.S. 248 34.44 N 92.15 W
Littlerock, Calif., U.S. 274 34.31 N 117.59 W
Little Rock, Ill., U.S. 268 41.43 N 88.34 W
Littlerock, Wash., U.S. 270 46.54 N 123.01 W
Little Rock ≃ 252 43.16 N 96.15 W
Little Rockies ⋀ 256 47.50 N 108.10 W
Little Sable Point ➤ 244 43.38 N 86.32 W
Little Sac ≃ 248 37.39 N 93.46 W
Little Saint Bernard Pass)(170 45.41 N 6.53 E
Little Salkehatchie ≃ 246 32.37 N 80.53 W
Little Salmon ≃ 256 45.25 N 116.19 W
Little Salt Lake ⊜ 254 37.55 N 112.53 W
Little Sandy ≃ 242 38.30 N 82.50 W
Little Scarcies ≃ 222 8.51 N 13.09 W
Little Sioux ≃ 252 41.49 N 96.04 W
Little Sioux, West Fork ≃ 252 42.04 N 96.00 W
Little Sitkin Island I 237a 51.55 N 178.30 E
Little Smoky ≃ 238 55.42 N 117.38 W
Little Snake ≃ 254 40.27 N 108.26 W
Littlestown 262 39.45 N 77.05 W
Little Tallapoosa ≃ 246 33.18 N 85.34 W
Little Tanaga Island I 236 51.48 N 176.10 W
Little Tennessee ≃ 246 35.47 N 84.15 W
Little Tobago I 285r 11.18 N 12.30 W
Littleton, Colo., U.S. 254 39.37 N 105.01 W
Littleton, Mass., U.S. 261 42.32 N 71.31 W
Littleton, N.H., U.S. 242 44.18 N 71.46 W
Littleton, N.C., U.S. 246 36.26 N 77.54 W
Littleton, W. Va., U.S. 242 39.42 N 80.31 W
Littleton Common 261 42.32 N 71.28 W
Little Traverse Bay C 244 45.24 N 85.03 W
Little Valley 266 42.15 N 78.48 W
Little Wabash ≃ 248 37.54 N 88.05 W
Little Washita ≃ 250 34.58 N 97.51 W
Little Wichita ≃ 250 33.54 N 97.59 W
Little Wind ≃ 254 42.57 N 108.29 W
Little Wolf ≃ 244 44.23 N 88.48 W
Little Wood ≃ 256 42.57 N 114.21 W
Little York 264 42.42 N 76.10 W
Little Zab (Zāb-e Kūchek) (Az-Zāb aṣ-Ṣaghīr) ≃ 208 35.12 N 43.25 E
Litvínov 164 50.37 N 13.36 E
Liuan 196 31.44 N 116.31 E
Liucheng 200 24.32 N 109.21 E
Liuch'iu Hsü I 196 22.20 N 120.22 E
Liuchonghe ≃ 190 29.40 N 107.25 E
Liuchow → Liuzhou 200 24.22 N 109.32 E
Liucura 294 38.39 S 71.05 W
Liuguhe ≃ 194 40.22 N 120.26 E
Liuhe 196 32.22 N 118.49 E
Liuhe ≃, Zhg. 194 40.38 N 118.09 E
Liuhe ≃, Zhg. 194 42.45 N 126.04 E
Liuhengdao I 196 29.43 N 122.08 E
Liukedao I 196 22.34 N 114.52 E
Liuku 200 25.48 N 98.52 E
Liushishan Λ 206 36.15 N 82.05 E
Liuxihe ≃ 196 23.22 N 112.54 E
Liuyanghe ≃ 196 28.13 N 112.58 E
Liuzhou 200 24.22 N 109.32 E
Livada 172 47.52 N 23.07 E
Livanátai 172 38.42 N 23.03 E
Livanjsko Polje ≚ 170 43.55 N 16.45 E
Livarot 166 49.01 N 0.09 E
Lively, Ont., Can. 244 46.26 N 81.09 W
Lively, Va., U.S. 262 37.47 N 76.31 W
Livengood 236 65.32 N 148.33 W
Live Oak, Calif., U.S. 272 39.17 N 121.40 W
Live Oak, Fla., U.S. 246 30.18 N 82.59 W
Livermore, Calif., U.S. 272 37.41 N 121.46 W
Livermore, Iowa, U.S. 244 42.52 N 94.10 W
Livermore, Ky., U.S. 248 37.29 N 87.08 W
Livermore Falls 242 44.28 N 70.11 W
Liverpool, N.S., Can. 240 44.02 N 64.43 W
Liverpool, Eng., U.K. 162 53.25 N 2.55 W
Liverpool, Ind., U.S. 268 41.34 N 87.18 W
Liverpool, N.Y., U.S. 264 43.06 N 76.13 W
Liverpool, Pa., U.S. 262 40.34 N 77.00 W
Liverpool, Cape ➤ 232 73.38 N 78.06 W
Liverpool Bay C, N.W. Ter., Can. 236 69.45 N 130.00 W
Liverpool Bay C, N.S., Can. 240 44.02 N 64.41 W
Liverpool Heights 264 43.07 N 76.13 W
Liverpool Range ⋀ 228 31.40 S 150.30 E
Livigno 170 46.32 N 10.04 E
Lívingston, Guat. 280 15.50 N 88.45 W
Livingston, Ala., U.S. 248 32.35 N 88.11 W
Livingston, Calif., U.S. 272 37.23 N 120.43 W
Livingston, Ill., U.S. 248 38.58 N 89.46 W
Livingston, Ky., U.S. 246 37.18 N 84.13 W
Livingston, La., U.S. 248 30.30 N 90.45 W
Livingston, Mont., U.S. 256 45.40 N 110.34 W
Livingston, N.J., U.S. 262 40.48 N 74.19 W
Livingston, N.Y., U.S. 261 42.09 N 73.47 W
Livingston, Tenn., U.S. 248 36.23 N 85.19 W
Livingston, Tex., U.S. 250 30.43 N 94.56 W
Livingston, Wis., U.S. 244 42.54 N 90.26 W
Livingston □[6], Ill., U.S. 268 40.53 N 88.38 W
Livingston □[6], Mich., U.S. 268 42.38 N 83.50 W
Livingston □[6], N.Y., U.S. 264 42.48 N 77.49 W
Livingston, Chutes de ⌊ 218 4.50 S 14.30 E
Livingstone 224 17.50 S 25.53 E
Livingstone Falls → Livingstone, Chutes de ⌊ 218 4.50 S 14.30 E
Livingstone Mountains ⋀ 230 45.08 S 168.05 E
Livingstonia 218 10.36 S 34.07 E
Livingston Manor 242 41.54 N 74.50 W
Livno 170 43.50 N 17.01 E
Livojoki ≃ 160 65.24 N 26.48 E
Livonia, La., U.S. 248 30.33 N 91.33 W
Livonia, Mich., U.S. 268 42.25 N 83.23 W
Livonia, N.Y., U.S. 264 42.49 N 77.40 W
Livonia Center 264 42.49 N 77.38 W
Livorno (Leghorn) 184 43.33 N 10.19 E
Livorno □[4] 184 43.14 N 10.35 E
Livramento do Brumado 296 13.39 S 41.50 W
Liwale 218 9.46 S 37.56 E
Lixi 190 29.15 N 114.46 E
Lixoúrion 172 38.12 N 20.26 E
Lixus ⊥ 168 35.16 N 6.13 W
Liyang 196 31.26 N 119.29 E
Lizard Head Peak Λ 254 42.47 N 109.11 W
Lizard Point ➤ 162 49.56 N 5.13 W
Ljubija 170 44.56 N 16.37 E
Ljubimec 172 41.50 N 26.05 E
Ljubinje 172 42.57 N 18.05 E
Ljubljana 170 46.03 N 14.31 E
Ljubovija 172 44.11 N 19.22 E
Ljubuški 170 43.12 N 17.33 E
Ljugarn 160 57.19 N 18.42 E
Ljungan ≃ 160 62.19 N 17.23 E
Ljungaverk 160 62.29 N 16.03 E
Ljungby 160 56.50 N 13.56 E
Ljusdal 160 61.50 N 16.05 E
Ljusnan ≃ 160 61.12 N 17.08 E
Ljutomer 170 46.31 N 16.12 E
Llaima, Volcán Λ[1] 294 38.43 S 71.43 W
Llallagua 292 18.25 S 66.38 W
Llancañelo, Salina ≚ 294 35.36 S 69.11 W
Llandaff 174 51.30 N 3.14 W
Llandovery 162 51.59 N 3.48 W
Llandrindod Wells 162 52.15 N 3.23 W
Llandudno 162 53.19 N 3.49 W
Llanelli 174 51.42 N 4.10 W
Llanes 168 43.25 N 4.45 W
Llanfyllin 162 52.46 N 3.17 W
Llangefni 162 53.16 N 4.18 W
Llangollen, Wales, U.K. 162 52.58 N 3.10 W
Llangollen, Del., U.S. 262 39.39 N 75.37 W
Llanidloes 162 52.27 N 3.32 W
Llano 250 30.45 N 98.41 W
Llano ≃ 250 30.35 N 98.25 W
Llano Colorado 258 31.38 N 115.55 W
Llanos ≚ 290 5.00 N 70.00 W
Llanquera 292 18.06 S 67.47 W
Llansá 168 42.22 N 3.09 E
Llanta 294 26.20 S 69.49 W
Llantrisant 174 51.33 N 3.23 W
Llanwrtyd Wells 162 52.07 N 3.38 W
Llata 292 9.23 S 76.45 W
Llentrisca, Cabo de ➤ 168 38.51 N 1.14 E
Llera 278 23.19 N 99.01 W
Llerena 168 38.14 N 6.01 W
Lleulleu, Lago ⊜ 294 38.09 S 73.20 W
Llica 292 19.52 S 68.16 W
Llico 294 34.46 S 72.05 W
Llobregat ≃ 168 41.19 N 2.09 E
Llo-Lleo 294 33.37 S 71.37 W
Llorente 202 11.24 N 125.32 E
Llorente ≃ 202 11.25 N 125.32 E
Lloydell 266 40.19 N 78.42 W
Lloyd Harbor 261 40.54 N 73.28 W
Lloydminster 232 53.17 N 110.00 W
Lloyds ≃ 240 48.33 N 57.13 W
Lluchmayor 168 39.29 N 2.54 E
Llullaillaco, Volcán Λ[1] 294 24.43 S 68.33 W
Llusco 292 14.21 S 72.07 W
Lo ≃ 200 21.18 N 105.25 E
Loa 254 38.24 N 111.38 W
Loa ≃ 292 21.26 S 70.04 W
Loami 248 39.40 N 89.51 W
Loanda 296 22.54 S 53.10 W
Loange (Luangue) ≃ 218 4.17 S 20.02 E
Loano 182 44.08 N 8.15 E
Loay 202 9.36 N 124.01 E
Loban 160 65.44 N 45.25 E
Lobatse 218 25.11 S 25.40 E
Löbau 164 51.05 N 14.40 E
Lobaye ≃ 214 3.41 N 18.35 E
Lobberich 178 51.18 N 6.16 E
Lobenstein 164 50.26 N 11.38 E
Lobería 294 38.07 S 58.47 W
Łobez (Labes) 164 53.39 N 15.36 E
Lobito 218 12.20 S 13.34 E
Lobitos 290 4.27 S 81.15 W
Lobo, Pil. 202 13.39 N 121.13 E
Lobo, Tex., U.S. 250 30.52 N 104.48 W
Lobo ≃ 222 6.02 N 6.47 W
Lobos 294 35.10 S 59.05 W
Lobos, Cabo ➤, Chile 292 18.47 S 70.21 W
Lobos, Cabo ➤, Méx. 278 29.55 N 112.45 W
Lobos, Estero de C 278 27.20 N 110.32 W
Lobos, Punta ➤ 292 21.01 S 70.11 W
Lobos de Afuera, Islas II 292 6.57 S 80.42 W
Lobos de Tierra, Isla I 292 6.27 S 80.52 W
Lobskoje 160 62.45 N 35.16 E
Lobstick Lake ⊜ 232 54.00 N 64.50 W
Łobżenica 164 53.16 N 17.15 E
Locarno 180 46.10 N 8.48 E
Locate Triulzi 182 45.21 N 9.13 E
Lochaline 162 56.32 N 5.47 W
Lochboisdale 162 57.09 N 7.19 W
Lochem 178 52.09 N 6.25 E
Loches 166 47.08 N 1.00 E
Lochgilphead 162 56.03 N 5.26 W
Lochinver 162 58.09 N 5.15 W
Lochmaben 162 55.08 N 3.27 W
Lochristi 176 51.06 N 3.50 E
Lochsa ≃ 256 46.08 N 115.36 W
Locke, Calif., U.S. 272 38.15 N 121.31 W
Locke, Ind., U.S. 268 41.28 N 86.00 W
Locke, N.Y., U.S. 264 42.40 N 76.26 W
Lockeford 272 38.10 N 121.09 W
Lockeport 240 43.42 N 65.07 W
Lockerbie 162 55.07 N 3.22 W
Lockesburg 248 33.58 N 94.10 W
Lockhart 250 29.53 N 97.41 W
Lock Haven 242 41.08 N 77.27 W
Lockington 268 40.12 N 84.13 W
Lockney 250 34.07 N 101.27 W
Löcknitz 164 53.27 N 14.12 E
Lockport, Ill., U.S. 268 41.36 N 88.03 W
Lockport, La., U.S. 248 29.39 N 90.32 W
Lockport, N.Y., U.S. 264 43.10 N 78.42 W
Locksley Park 264 42.45 N 78.52 W
Lockwood, Calif., U.S. 272 35.56 N 121.05 W
Lockwood, Mo., U.S. 248 37.23 N 93.57 W
Lockwood, Ohio, U.S. 266 41.28 N 80.51 W
Lockwood Corners 266 41.00 N 81.34 W
Locminé 162 47.53 N 2.50 W
Loc-ninh 198 11.50 N 106.35 E
Locri 170 38.14 N 16.16 E
Locroja 292 12.41 S 74.26 W
Locsin 202 13.09 N 123.43 E
Locumba 292 17.37 S 70.44 W
Locumba ≃ 292 17.54 S 70.58 W
Locust 262 40.24 N 74.01 W
Locustdale 262 40.47 N 76.22 W
Locust Grove 250 36.12 N 95.10 W
Locust Valley 261 40.53 N 73.36 W
Lod (Lydda) 210 31.57 N 34.54 E
Loda 268 40.31 N 88.04 W
Lodejnoje Polje 160 60.44 N 33.30 E
Lodève 166 43.43 N 3.19 E
Lodge Grass 256 45.19 N 107.22 W
Lodgepole, Alta., Can. 238 53.06 N 115.19 W
Lodgepole, Nebr., U.S. 252 41.09 N 102.38 W
Lodi, It. 182 45.19 N 9.30 E
Lodi, Calif., U.S. 272 38.08 N 121.16 W
Lodi, Ohio, U.S. 266 41.03 N 82.01 W
Lodi, Wis., U.S. 244 43.19 N 89.32 W
Lodja 218 3.29 S 23.26 E
Lodosa 168 42.25 N 2.05 W
Lodwar 214 3.07 N 35.36 E
Łódź 164 51.46 N 19.30 E
Loei 200 17.32 N 101.34 E
Loei ≃ 200 17.50 N 101.35 E
Lofer 164 47.35 N 12.41 E
Loffa □[6] 222 7.40 N 10.00 W
Loffa ≃ 222 6.36 N 11.08 W
Lofoten II 160 68.30 N 15.00 E
Loga 178 53.14 N 7.29 E
Logan, Iowa, U.S. 252 41.39 N 95.47 W
Logan, Kans., U.S. 252 39.40 N 99.34 W
Logan, N. Mex., U.S. 250 35.22 N 103.25 W
Logan, Ohio, U.S. 242 39.32 N 82.25 W
Logan, Utah, U.S. 254 41.44 N 111.50 W
Logan, W. Va., U.S. 242 37.51 N 81.59 W
Logan □[6] 268 40.22 N 83.46 W
Logan ≃, Alta., Can. 238 55.09 N 111.42 W
Logan ≃, Utah, U.S. 254 41.44 N 111.57 W
Logan, Mount Λ 236 60.34 N 140.24 W
Logandale 258 36.36 N 114.29 W
Logan Martin Lake ⊜[1] 248 33.40 N 86.15 W
Logan Mountains ⋀ 236 61.30 N 129.00 W
Logan Pass)(256 48.41 N 113.44 W
Logansport, Ind., U.S. 268 40.45 N 86.21 W
Logansport, La., U.S. 248 31.58 N 93.58 W
Loganville, Ga., U.S. 246 33.50 N 83.54 W
Loganville, Pa., U.S. 262 39.52 N 76.42 W
Logar □[4] 206 33.50 N 69.00 E
Logduz 160 60.00 N 44.41 E
Logone ≃ 214 12.06 N 15.02 E
Logroño 168 42.28 N 2.27 W
Logroño □[4] 166 42.28 N 2.27 W
Logrosán 168 39.20 N 5.29 W
Løgstør 160 56.58 N 9.15 E
Logudoro ◆[1] 170 40.38 N 8.38 E
Lohfelden 178 51.16 N 9.32 E
Lohiniva 160 67.10 N 24.58 E
Lohja 160 60.15 N 24.05 E
Lohne, B.R.D. 178 52.42 N 8.12 E
Löhne, B.R.D. 178 52.11 N 8.41 E
Lohr 164 50.00 N 9.34 E
Lohrville 252 42.17 N 94.33 W
Loi, Phou Λ 200 20.16 N 103.12 E
Loibl Pass)(170 46.26 N 14.16 E
Loi-kaw 200 19.41 N 97.13 E
Loimaa 160 60.51 N 23.03 E
Loir ≃ 166 47.33 N 0.32 W
Loire □[5] 166 45.30 N 4.00 E
Loire ≃ 166 47.16 N 2.11 W
Loire-Atlantique □[5] 166 47.20 N 1.35 W
Loiret □[5] 176 47.55 N 2.20 E
Loir-et-Cher □[5] 176 47.30 N 1.30 E
Loïs, Lake ⊜ 244 48.34 N 78.44 W
Loitz 164 53.58 N 13.07 E
Loíza 284m 18.23 N 65.54 W
Loíza Aldea 284m 18.26 N 65.53 W
Loja, Ec. 290 4.00 S 79.13 W
Loja, Esp. 168 37.10 N 4.09 W
Lojga 160 61.05 N 44.37 E
Lojno 160 59.44 N 52.39 E
Lokan ≃ 202 5.25 N 117.44 E
Lokan Allasalue ⊜[1] 160 67.55 N 27.40 E
Lokandu 218 2.31 S 25.47 E
Lokbatan 208 40.20 N 49.43 E
Løken 160 59.48 N 11.29 E
Lokeren 176 51.06 N 4.00 E
Loket 164 50.09 N 12.43 E
Lokka 160 67.49 N 27.44 E
Lokn'a 160 56.50 N 30.09 E
Lokoja 222 7.47 N 6.45 E
Lokolama 218 2.34 S 19.53 E
Lokoro ≃ 218 1.43 S 18.23 E
Loks Land I 232 62.26 N 64.38 W
Lol ≃ 220 9.13 N 28.59 E
Lola, Mount Λ 258 39.26 N 120.22 W
Loliondo 218 2.03 S 35.37 E
Lolita 250 28.50 N 96.32 W
Lolland I 164 54.46 N 11.30 E
Lolo 256 46.45 N 114.05 W
Lolo Pass)(256 46.38 N 114.35 W
Lolotique 280 13.33 N 88.21 W
Lolworth Range ⋀ 228 20.20 S 145.15 E
Lom, Blg. 172 43.49 N 23.14 E
Lom, Nor. 160 61.50 N 8.33 E
Lom, S.S.S.R. 160 57.54 N 39.12 E
Loma Blanca 254 31.35 N 106.17 W
Loma Linda 274 34.04 N 117.16 W
Loma Mansa Λ 222 9.13 N 11.07 W
Lomami ≃ 218 0.46 N 24.16 E
Loma Mountains ⋀ 222 9.10 N 11.07 W
Lomas 292 15.32 S 74.50 W
Lomas de Monreal 254 31.17 N 110.56 W
Lomas de Zamora 294 34.46 S 58.24 W
Lomax 244 40.41 N 91.04 W
Łomazy 164 51.55 N 23.10 E
Lomazzo 182 45.42 N 9.02 E
Lombard 268 41.53 N 88.01 W
Lombardia □[4] 182 45.40 N 9.30 E
Lomblen, Pulau I 198 8.25 S 123.30 E
Lombok I 226 8.45 S 116.30 E
Lomé 222 6.08 N 1.13 E
Lomela 218 2.18 S 23.17 E
Lomela ≃ 218 0.14 S 20.42 E
Lomellina □[9] 182 45.15 N 8.45 E
Lometa 250 31.13 N 98.24 W
Lomi 160 67.05 N 16.09 E
Lomira 244 43.35 N 88.27 W
Lo Miranda 294 34.11 S 70.54 W
Lomita 274 33.48 N 118.19 W
Lomme 176 50.39 N 2.59 E
Lommel 178 51.14 N 5.18 E
Lomnice nad Popelkou 164 50.32 N 15.22 E
Lomond 238 50.21 N 112.39 W
Lomond, Loch ⊜, N.S., Can. 240 45.46 N 60.35 W
Lomond, Loch ⊜, Ont., Can. 244 48.26 N 89.19 W
Lomond, Loch ⊜, Scot., U.K. 162 56.08 N 4.38 W
Lomonosov 160 59.55 N 29.46 E
Lomonosovskij 186 52.50 N 66.28 E
Lomovoje 160 64.01 N 40.40 E
Lompoc 258 34.38 N 120.27 W
Lom Sak 200 16.47 N 101.12 E
Łomża 164 53.11 N 22.05 E
Lonaconing 242 39.34 N 78.59 W
Lonate Pozzolo 182 45.36 N 8.45 E
Loncoche 288 39.22 S 72.38 W
Loncopué 294 38.04 S 70.37 W
Londerzeel 176 51.00 N 4.18 E
Londinières 166 49.50 N 1.24 E
London, Ont., Can. 264 42.59 N 81.14 W
London, Eng., U.K. 174 51.30 N 0.10 W
London, Calif., U.S. 272 36.30 N 119.25 W
London, Ky., U.S. 246 37.08 N 84.05 W
London, Ohio, U.S. 242 39.53 N 83.27 W
London, Tex., U.S. 250 30.41 N 99.35 W
London, Wis., U.S. 268 43.03 N 89.01 W
Londonderry, N.S., Can. 240 45.29 N 63.36 W
Londonderry, N. Ire., U.K. 162 55.00 N 7.19 W
Londonderry, N.H., U.S. 261 42.51 N 71.22 W
Londonderry, Ohio, U.S. 266 39.16 N 82.47 W
Londonderry □[6] 162 54.50 N 7.10 W
Londonderry, Isla I 288 55.03 S 70.40 W
Londres 294 27.45 S 67.10 W
Londrina 296 23.18 S 51.09 W
Lone Mountain Λ, Nev., U.S. 258 38.02 N 117.29 W
Lone Mountain Λ, S. Dak., U.S. 252 45.23 N 103.44 W
Lone Oak, Ky., U.S. 248 37.02 N 88.40 W
Lone Oak, Tex., U.S. 250 33.01 N 95.57 W
Lone Pine 258 36.36 N 118.04 W
Lone Rock 244 43.11 N 90.12 W
Lone Star 248 32.55 N 94.43 W
Lone Tree 244 41.29 N 91.26 W
Lone Wolf 250 34.59 N 99.15 W
Longa ≃ 218 10.15 S 13.30 E
Longa, Proliv ⋃ 186 70.20 N 178.00 E
Longarone 170 46.16 N 12.18 E
Longasy 160 61.58 N 35.09 E
Longaví 294 35.58 S 71.41 W
Long Barn 272 38.05 N 120.08 W
Long Bay C, Jam. 285q 17.50 N 77.25 W
Long Bay C, U.S. 246 33.35 N 78.45 W
Long Beach, Calif., U.S. 274 33.46 N 118.11 W
Long Beach, Ind., U.S. 268 41.44 N 86.52 W
Long Beach, Miss., U.S. 248 30.22 N 89.07 W
Long Beach, N.Y., U.S. 242 40.35 N 73.41 W
Long Beach, Wash., U.S. 270 46.21 N 124.03 W
Longboat Key 246 27.24 N 82.39 W
Long Branch, Ont., Can. 264 43.35 N 79.32 W
Long Branch, N.J., U.S. 262 40.18 N 74.00 W
Longbranch, Wash., U.S. 270 47.13 N 122.46 W
Longchang 190 29.21 N 105.17 E
Long Creek 256 44.43 N 119.06 W
Long Eaton 174 52.54 N 1.15 W
Longeau 166 47.46 N 5.18 E
Longford 162 53.44 N 7.47 W
Longford □[6] 162 53.40 N 7.40 W
Long Green 262 39.28 N 76.31 W
Long Harbour 240 47.26 N 53.49 W
Long Harbour C 240 47.44 N 55.01 W
Longhurst 246 36.25 N 78.58 W
Long Island I, Austl. 228 22.09 S 149.54 E
Long Island I, Ba. 282 23.10 N 75.10 W
Long Island I, Newf., Can. 240 47.35 N 54.05 W
Long Island I, N.W. Ter., Can. 232 54.50 N 79.20 W
Long Island I, N.S., Can. 240 44.20 N 66.15 W
Long Island I, N.Z. 230 47.14 S 167.24 E
Long Island I, Alaska, U.S. 238 54.54 N 132.45 W
Long Island I, N.Y., U.S. 242 40.50 N 73.00 W
Long Island Sound ⋃ 242 41.05 N 72.58 W
Longitudinal, Valle V 294 36.00 S 72.00 W
Longjiang 190 47.19 N 123.12 E
Longjiang ≃, Zhg. 196 23.26 N 114.38 E
Longjiang ≃, Zhg. 196 22.59 N 116.18 E
Longjie Λ 200 25.15 N 98.25 E
Longjumeau 176 48.42 N 2.18 E
Longkou 190 37.38 N 120.18 E
Long Lake, Mich., U.S. 244 44.25 N 83.52 W
Long Lake, N.Y., U.S. 242 43.58 N 74.25 W
Long Lake ⊜, Mich., U.S. 244 45.12 N 83.30 W
Long Lake ⊜, N. Dak., U.S. 252 46.43 N 100.07 W
Long Lake ⊜, N.Y., U.S. 242 44.04 N 74.20 W
Longlangshan ⋀ 200 21.50 N 100.30 E
Longleaf 248 31.00 N 92.34 W
Long Leaf Park 246 34.12 N 77.56 W
Longli 200 26.26 N 106.58 E
Longling 200 24.39 N 98.40 E
Longmeadow 261 42.03 N 72.34 W
Longmire 270 46.45 N 121.49 W
Longmont 254 40.10 N 105.06 W
Longnawan 198 1.54 N 114.53 E
Longny 162 48.32 N 0.45 E
Long Pine 252 42.32 N 99.42 W
Long Point ➤, Newf., Can. 240 48.48 N 58.46 W
Long Point ➤, Pil. 202 9.39 N 118.20 E
Long Point ➤[1] 244 42.34 N 80.15 W
Long Point Bay C 244 42.40 N 80.14 W
Longport 262 39.19 N 74.32 W
Long Prairie 252 45.59 N 94.52 W
Long Prairie ≃ 252 46.20 N 94.36 W
Longquan 190 28.04 N 119.07 E
Long Range Mountains ⋀ 240 50.00 N 57.00 W
Longreach 228 23.26 S 144.15 E
Long Sault 242 45.02 N 74.53 W
Longsheng 200 25.42 N 110.01 E
Longs Peak Λ 254 40.15 N 105.37 W
Long Tom ≃ 256 44.23 N 123.15 W
Longton, Eng., U.K. 174 53.00 N 2.09 W
Longton, Kans., U.S. 252 37.23 N 96.05 W
Longué 166 47.23 N 0.06 W
Longueau 176 49.52 N 2.21 E
Longueuil 260 45.33 N 73.30 W
Longuyon 166 49.26 N 5.36 E
Long Valley 262 40.47 N 74.47 W
Longview, Alta., Can. 238 50.32 N 114.14 W
Longview, N.C., U.S. 246 35.44 N 81.23 W
Longview, Tex., U.S. 248 32.30 N 94.44 W
Longview, Wash., U.S. 270 46.08 N 122.57 W
Longwood Park 246 34.55 N 79.42 W
Longworth 238 53.55 N 121.28 W
Longwy 166 49.31 N 5.46 E
Longxi 190 34.56 N 104.47 E
Longxi ≃ 196 26.24 N 118.26 E
Long-xuyen 200 10.23 N 105.25 E
Longzhou 200 22.22 N 106.52 E
Lonigo 170 45.23 N 11.23 E
Löningen 178 52.44 N 7.46 E
Lonja ≃ 170 45.27 N 16.41 E
Lonoke 248 34.47 N 91.54 W
Lønsdal 160 66.44 N 15.28 E
Lonsdale 244 44.29 N 93.25 W
Lons-le-Saunier 180 46.40 N 5.33 E
Lontra, Ribeirão ≃ 296 21.28 S 53.37 W
Looc 202 12.16 N 121.59 E
Looe 162 50.20 N 4.30 W
Loogootee 248 38.41 N 86.55 W
Lookout, Cape ➤, N.C., U.S. 246 34.35 N 76.32 W
Lookout, Cape ➤, Oreg., U.S. 256 45.20 N 124.00 W
Lookout Mountain Λ, U.S. 248 34.25 N 85.40 W
Lookout Mountain Λ, Oreg., U.S. 256 44.20 N 120.22 W
Lookout Pass)(256 47.27 N 115.42 W
Lookout Point Reservoir ⊜[1] 256 43.52 N 122.40 W
Lookout Ridge ⋀ 236 69.07 N 158.36 W
Loomis, Calif., U.S. 272 38.49 N 121.12 W
Loomis, Nebr., U.S. 252 40.29 N 99.31 W
Loomis, Wash., U.S. 238 48.49 N 119.38 W
Loon 202 9.48 N 123.47 E
Loon op Zand 164 51.38 N 5.04 E
Loop 250 32.55 N 102.25 W
Loop Head ➤ 162 52.34 N 9.56 W
Loos 176 50.37 N 3.01 E
Loosduinen ◆[8] 178 52.04 N 4.13 E
Lop ≃ 200 13.17 N 107.41 E
Lopatina, Gora Λ 186 50.52 N 143.10 E
Lopatka, Mys ➤ 186 50.52 N 156.40 E
Lop Buri 200 14.48 N 100.37 E
Lopez 270 48.31 N 122.54 W
Lopez, Cap ➤ 218 0.37 S 8.43 E
Lopez Bay C 202 14.00 N 122.00 E
López Collada 278 31.45 N 113.55 W
Lop Nor → Luobubo ⊜ 190 40.20 N 90.15 E
Lopšen'ga 160 64.58 N 37.41 E
Lopt'uga 160 63.16 N 47.56 E
Łopuszno 164 50.57 N 20.15 E
Lora ≃, Afg. 206 31.32 N 66.32 E
Lora ≃, Ven. 290 9.25 N 72.25 W
Lora, Hāmūn-i- ⊜ 208 29.20 N 64.50 E
Lora del Río 168 37.39 N 5.32 W
Lorain, Ohio, U.S. 266 41.28 N 82.10 W
Lorain, Pa., U.S. 266 40.18 N 78.54 W
Lorain □[6] 266 41.22 N 82.06 W
Loraine, Calif., U.S. 274 35.19 N 118.25 W
Loraine, Tex., U.S. 250 32.25 N 100.43 W
Lorca 168 37.40 N 1.42 W
Lord Howe Island I 226 31.33 S 159.05 E
Lord Howe Rise ✢[3] 148 29.00 S 162.30 E
Lord Mayor Bay C 232 69.44 N 92.00 W
Lordsburg 254 32.21 N 108.43 W
Lordstown 266 41.09 N 80.53 W
Loreauville 248 30.03 N 91.44 W
Loree Estates 272 37.19 N 122.01 W
Loreley ♠ 166 50.08 N 7.44 E
Lorena 296 22.44 S 45.08 W
Lorenzo 250 33.40 N 101.32 W
Lorenzo Geyres (Queguay) 294 32.05 S 57.55 W
Lorestān □[8] 208 33.30 N 48.30 E
Loreto, Arg. 294 27.46 S 57.17 W
Loreto, Bol. 292 15.13 S 64.40 W
Loreto, Bra. 286 7.05 S 45.09 W
Loreto, Col. 290 3.48 S 70.15 W
Loreto, It. 184 43.26 N 13.36 E
Loreto, Méx. 278 26.01 N 111.21 W
Loreto, Méx. 278 22.16 N 101.58 W
Loreto, Para. 294 23.16 S 57.11 W
Loreto, Pil. 202 8.12 N 125.45 E
Loreto, Pil. 202 10.21 N 125.34 E
Loreto □[5] 292 5.00 S 75.00 W
Lorette 252 49.44 N 96.52 W
Loretteville 260 46.51 N 71.21 W
Loretto, Pa., U.S. 266 40.31 N 78.38 W
Loretto, Tenn., U.S. 248 35.05 N 87.26 W
Lorica 290 9.14 N 75.49 W
Lorient 166 47.45 N 3.22 W
L'Orignal 260 45.37 N 74.42 W
Lorimor 248 41.07 N 94.03 W
Loring 256 48.47 N 107.52 W
Lorino 236 65.30 N 171.43 W
Loriol-du-Comtat 166 44.45 N 4.49 E
Loris 246 34.04 N 78.53 W
Lorman 248 31.49 N 91.03 W
Lormes 166 47.17 N 3.49 E
Lorn, Firth of C[2] 162 56.20 N 5.40 W
Lorne 240 47.53 N 66.08 W
Lörrach 180 47.37 N 7.40 E
Lorraine □[9] 166 49.00 N 6.00 E
Lorris 166 47.53 N 2.31 E
Los, Îles de II 222 9.30 N 13.48 W
Losada ≃ 290 2.12 N 73.55 W
Los Alamos, Méx. 278 28.40 N 103.30 W
Los Alamos, N. Mex., U.S. 254 35.53 N 106.19 W
Los Aldamas 278 26.03 N 99.11 W
Los Altos, Méx. 250 26.14 N 98.28 W
Los Altos, Calif., U.S. 272 37.23 N 122.06 W
Los Altos Hills 272 37.21 N 122.08 W
Los Amates 280 15.16 N 89.06 W
Los Andes 294 32.50 S 70.37 W
Los Ángeles, Chile 294 37.28 S 72.21 W
Los Angeles, Méx. 250 25.55 N 98.05 W
Los Ángeles, Nic. 280 13.14 N 85.47 W
Los Angeles, Calif., U.S. 274 34.03 N 118.15 W
Los Angeles □[6] 274 34.20 N 118.10 W
Los Angeles Aqueduct ⊼[1] 258 35.22 N 118.05 W
Los Arabos 284p 22.44 N 80.43 W
Los Arados 250 25.53 N 97.35 W
Los Arroyos, Lago de ⊜ 292 12.38 S 65.00 W
Los Banos 272 37.04 N 120.51 W
Los Berros 294 31.57 S 68.40 W
Los Blancos 294 23.40 S 62.35 W
Los Burros 278 25.03 N 110.50 W
Los Cerrillos 294 31.59 S 65.30 W

Symbols in the index entries are identified on page 360.

Name	Page	Lat°′	Long°′
Los Chacos	292	14.33 S	62.11 W
Los Chiles	280	11.02 N	84.43 W
Los Conquistadores	294	30.35 S	58.28 W
Los Ebanos, Méx.	278	24.40 N	97.45 W
Los Ebanos, Tex., U.S.	250	26.14 N	98.34 W
Los Encuentros	280	12.39 N	85.12 W
Los Esclavos ≃	280	13.51 N	90.19 W
Los Frentones	294	26.25 S	61.10 W
Los Fresnos, Méx.	250	30.20 N	104.50 W
Los Fresnos, Tex., U.S.	250	26.04 N	97.29 W
Los Garzas	250	26.23 N	99.46 W
Los Gatos	272	37.14 N	121.59 W
Los Guerras	250	26.25 N	99.05 W
Los Hermanos, Islas II	290	11.45 N	64.25 W
Los Herreras	250	25.55 N	99.24 W
Łosice	164	52.14 N	22.43 E
Lošinj, Otok I	170	44.36 N	14.24 E
Losinoborskaja	186	58.27 N	89.28 E
Los Juríes	294	28.30 S	62.10 W
Los Lagos	288	39.51 S	72.50 W
Los Llanos	284m	18.03 N	66.24 W
Los López	250	26.15 N	99.05 W
Los Lunas	254	34.48 N	106.44 W
Los Mármoles, Parque Nacional ♠	278	20.55 N	99.12 W
Los Médanos, Istmo de •[3]	285s	11.35 N	69.45 W
Los Mochis	278	25.45 N	108.57 W
Los Molinos	258	40.03 N	122.06 W
Los Navalmorales	168	39.43 N	4.38 W
Los Nietos	274	33.58 N	118.04 W
Los Nogales	250	26.16 N	99.43 W
Los Osos	272	35.19 N	120.50 W
Los Palacios, Arg.	294	29.22 S	68.11 W
Los Palacios, Cuba	284p	22.35 N	83.15 W
Los Palacios y Villafranca	168	37.10 N	5.56 W
Los Pinos ≃	254	36.56 N	107.36 W
Los Pozos	294	26.32 S	70.20 W
Los Quirquinchos	294	33.20 S	61.40 W
Los Rábanos	284m	18.11 N	66.50 W
Los Ramones	250	25.42 N	99.37 W
Los Remotos	250	26.12 N	100.45 W
Los Reyes [de Salgado]	278	19.35 N	102.29 W
Los Ríos □[4]	290	1.30 S	79.25 W
Los Roques, Islas II	290	11.50 N	66.45 W
Los Santos	290	7.55 N	80.25 W
Los Santos de Maimona	168	38.27 N	6.23 W
Los Sauces	294	37.58 S	72.50 W
Losse ≃	166	44.07 N	0.17 E
Losser	178	52.15 N	7.00 E
Los Serranos	274	33.59 N	117.42 W
Lossiemouth	162	57.43 N	3.18 W
Lost ≃, U.S.	256	41.56 N	121.30 W
Lost ≃, Ind., U.S.	248	38.33 N	86.49 W
Lost ≃, Minn., U.S.	252	47.51 N	96.02 W
Lost ≃, W. Va., U.S.	242	39.05 N	78.36 W
Lostant	268	41.09 N	89.04 W
Los Taques	290	11.50 N	70.16 W
Lost Draw ∨	250	32.58 N	102.02 W
Los Telares	294	29.00 S	63.27 W
Los Teques	290	10.21 N	67.02 W
Los Testigos, Islas II	290	11.22 N	63.06 W
Lost Hills	258	35.37 N	119.41 W
Lostine ≃	256	45.33 N	117.29 W
Lost Nation	244	41.58 N	90.49 W
Los Torres	280	13.25 N	85.48 W
Los Tres Palos	278	24.33 N	98.18 W
Lost River Range ∧∧	256	44.10 N	113.35 W
Lost Trail Pass)(	256	45.41 N	113.57 W
Los Vidrios	278	32.01 N	113.28 W
Los Vilos	294	31.55 S	71.31 W
Los Yébenes	168	39.34 N	3.53 W
Lot □[5]	166	44.35 N	1.40 E
Lot ≃	166	44.18 N	0.20 E
Lota	294	37.05 S	73.10 W
Lotbinière □[6]	260	46.30 N	71.40 W
Lot-et-Garonne □[5]	166	44.20 N	0.20 E
Lothair	246	37.15 N	83.10 W
Lothringen → Lorraine □[9]	166	49.00 N	6.00 E
Lotošino	160	56.14 N	35.38 E
Lotsane ≃	224	22.41 S	28.11 E
Lott	250	31.12 N	97.02 W
Lotta ≃	160	68.36 N	31.06 E
Lottivue	266	42.40 N	83.46 W
Lotung	190	24.41 N	121.46 E
Louang Prabang	200	19.52 N	102.08 E
L'Ouarsenis, Massif de ∧∧	168	35.40 N	1.50 E
Louchi	160	66.04 N	33.00 E
Loudéac	166	48.10 N	2.45 W
Loudon	246	35.44 N	84.20 W
Loudonville, N.Y., U.S.	261	42.42 N	73.47 W
Loudonville, Ohio, U.S.	266	40.38 N	82.14 W
Loudoun □[6]	262	39.05 N	77.30 W
Loudun	166	47.01 N	0.05 E
Loué	166	48.00 N	0.09 W
Louga	222	15.37 N	16.13 W
Louge	294	36.57 S	61.40 W
Louge ≃	166	43.27 N	1.20 E
Loughborough	174	52.47 N	1.11 W
Loughrea	162	53.12 N	8.34 W
Loughros More Bay C	162	54.47 N	8.35 W
Louhans	166	46.38 N	5.13 E
Louin	248	31.59 N	89.16 W
Louisa, Ky., U.S.	246	38.07 N	82.36 W
Louisa, Va., U.S.	246	38.01 N	78.01 W
Louis Bull Indian Reserve ◂[4]	238	52.53 N	113.31 W
Louisburg, N.S., Can.	240	45.55 N	59.58 W
Louisburg, Kans., U.S.	252	38.37 N	94.41 W
Louisburg, N.C., U.S.	246	36.06 N	78.18 W
Louisdale	240	45.36 N	61.04 W
Louise, Miss., U.S.	248	32.59 N	90.35 W
Louise, Tex., U.S.	250	29.06 N	96.25 W
Louise, Lake ⊜	236	62.20 N	146.30 W
Louise Island I	238	52.58 N	131.50 W
Louiseville	260	46.16 N	72.57 W
Louisiade Archipelago II	226	11.00 S	153.00 E
Louisiana	248	39.27 N	91.03 W
Louisiana □[3]	234	31.15 N	92.30 W
Louis Trichardt	224	23.01 S	29.43 E
Louisville, Ont., Can.	266	42.28 N	82.07 W
Louisville, Ala., U.S.	248	31.47 N	85.33 W
Louisville, Colo., U.S.	254	39.59 N	105.08 W
Louisville, Ga., U.S.	246	33.00 N	82.24 W
Louisville, Ill., U.S.	248	38.46 N	88.30 W
Louisville, Ky., U.S.	248	38.16 N	85.45 W
Louisville, Miss., U.S.	248	33.07 N	89.03 W
Louisville, Nebr., U.S.	252	41.00 N	96.10 W
Louisville, Ohio, U.S.	266	40.50 N	81.16 W
Louisville Ridge ⊹[3]	148	31.30 S	173.30 W
Louis XIV, Pointe ≻	232	54.35 N	79.50 W
Loukos, Oued ≃	168	34.58 N	5.52 W
Loulé	168	37.08 N	8.02 W
Louny	164	50.19 N	13.46 E
Loup ≃	252	41.24 N	97.19 W
Loup City	252	41.17 N	98.58 W
Lourches	176	50.19 N	3.21 E
Lourdes, Newf., Can.	240	48.39 N	59.00 W
Lourdes, Fr.	166	43.06 N	0.03 W
Lourenço Marques	224	25.58 S	32.35 E
Lourenço Marques □[5]	224	26.00 S	32.25 E
Lourenço Marques, Baie de C	218	25.48 S	32.51 E
Loures	168	38.50 N	9.10 W
Lourinhã	168	39.14 N	9.19 W
Lourosa	168	40.19 N	7.56 W
Lousã	168	40.07 N	8.15 W
Louth, Eire	162	53.37 N	6.53 W
Louth, Eng., U.K.	162	53.22 N	0.01 W
Louth □[6]	162	53.55 N	6.30 W
Louth Bay C	228	34.34 S	136.02 E
Loutrá Aidhipsoúx	172	38.51 N	23.02 E
Loutre, Bayou de ≃	248	32.41 N	92.08 W
Louvain → Leuven	164	50.53 N	4.42 E
Louviers, Fr.	176	49.13 N	1.10 E
Louviers, Colo., U.S.	254	39.28 N	105.01 W
Louvigné-du-Désert	166	48.29 N	1.08 W
Louvroil	176	50.16 N	3.58 E
Lóvago ≃	280	11.48 N	85.16 W
Lövånger	160	64.22 N	21.18 E
Lovat' ≃	160	58.14 N	31.28 E
Loveč	172	43.08 N	24.43 E
Lovelady	250	31.08 N	95.27 W
Loveland	254	40.24 N	105.05 W
Lovell	256	44.50 N	108.24 W
Lovelock	258	40.11 N	118.28 W
Lovely	246	37.50 N	82.24 W
Lovere	170	45.49 N	10.04 E
Loves Park	268	42.19 N	89.03 W
Lovilia	244	41.08 N	92.55 W
Loving, N. Mex., U.S.	250	32.17 N	104.06 W
Loving, Tex., U.S.	250	33.16 N	98.31 W
Lovingston	246	37.46 N	78.52 W
Lovington, Ill., U.S.	248	39.43 N	88.38 W
Lovington, N. Mex., U.S.	250	32.57 N	103.21 W
Lovosice	164	50.31 N	14.03 E
Lovozero	160	68.00 N	35.00 E
Lövstabruk	160	60.24 N	17.53 E
Low	242	45.49 N	75.57 W
Low, Cape ≻	232	63.07 N	85.18 W
Lowden	244	41.52 N	90.56 W
Lowell, Ind., U.S.	268	41.18 N	87.25 W
Lowell, Mass., U.S.	261	42.39 N	71.18 W
Lowell, Mich., U.S.	268	42.56 N	85.20 W
Lowell, Oreg., U.S.	256	43.55 N	122.47 W
Lowell, Lake ⊜[1]	256	43.33 N	116.40 W
Lowellville	266	41.02 N	80.32 W
Löwenberg	164	52.54 N	13.08 E
Lower Alkali Lake ⊜	258	41.15 N	120.02 W
Lower Arrow Lake ⊜	238	49.40 N	118.08 W
Lower Brule Indian Reservation ◂[4]	252	44.05 N	99.44 W
Lower Burrell	266	40.35 N	79.44 W
Lower Hutt	230	41.13 S	174.55 E
Lower Kalskag	236	61.31 N	160.22 W
Lower Klamath Lake ⊜	258	41.55 N	121.42 W
Lower Lake	272	38.55 N	122.36 W
Lower Paia	275a	20.55 N	156.23 W
Lower Post	232	59.55 N	128.30 W
Lower Red Lake ⊜	252	48.00 N	94.50 W
Lower Red Rock Lake ⊜	256	44.38 N	111.51 W
Lower Ugashik Lake ⊜	236	57.30 N	156.56 W
Lower West Pubnico	240	43.38 N	65.48 W
Lower Woods Harbour	240	43.31 N	65.44 W
Lowestoft	174	52.29 N	1.45 E
Łowicz	164	52.07 N	19.56 E
Lowman	256	44.05 N	115.37 W
Lowmoor	246	37.47 N	79.53 W
Low Rocky Point ≻	228	43.00 S	145.30 E
Lowry City	248	38.08 N	93.44 W
Lowville, N.Y., U.S.	264	43.47 N	75.29 W
Lowville, Pa., U.S.	266	42.01 N	79.49 W
Loxley	248	30.37 N	87.45 W
Loxton	228	34.27 S	140.35 E
Loyal	244	44.44 N	90.30 W
Loyalhanna	266	40.19 N	79.21 W
Loyalton	258	39.41 N	120.14 W
Loyalty Islands → Loyauté, Îles II	148	21.00 S	167.00 E
Loyang → Luoyang	000	34.41 N	112.28 E
Loyauté, Îles II	148	21.00 S	167.00 E
Loysburg	266	40.10 N	78.23 W
Loysville	262	40.22 N	77.21 W
Lozère □[5]	166	44.30 N	3.30 E
Lozère, Mont ∧	166	44.25 N	3.45 E
Loznica	172	44.32 N	19.13 E
Lozoyuela	168	40.55 N	3.37 W
Lua Makika •[6]	275d	20.34 N	156.34 W
Luana Point ≻	285q	18.02 N	77.52 W
Luanda	218	8.48 S	13.14 E
Luando ≃	218	10.19 S	16.40 E
Luang ≃	200	18.00 N	103.05 E
Luang, Khao ∧	200	8.30 N	99.45 E
Luang, Thale C	200	7.40 N	100.15 E
Luang Chiang Dao, Doi ∧	200	19.22 N	98.52 E
Luang Praban Range ∧∧	200	18.30 N	101.15 E
Luang Prabang → Louang Prabang	200	19.52 N	102.08 E
Luangue (Loange) ≃	218	4.17 S	20.02 E
Luanguinga ≃	218	15.11 S	22.56 E
Luangwa ≃	218	15.40 N	30.25 E
Luanhe ≃	194	40.32 N	118.15 E
Luanshya	218	13.08 S	28.24 E
Luán Toro	294	36.10 S	65.07 W
Luapula ≃	218	9.26 S	28.33 E
Luarca	168	43.32 N	6.32 W
Lubaantum ⊥	278	16.18 N	88.58 W
Lubaczów	164	50.10 N	23.07 E
Lubań (Lauban), Pol.	164	51.08 N	15.18 E
L'uban', S.S.S.R.	160	59.21 N	31.13 E
Lubang	202	13.52 N	120.07 E
Lubang Island I	202	13.45 N	120.10 E
Lubang Islands II	202	13.45 N	120.15 E
Lub'any	160	56.02 N	51.24 E
Lubartów	164	51.28 N	22.46 E
Lubawa	164	53.30 N	19.45 E
Lübbecke	178	52.18 N	8.36 E
Lübben	164	51.56 N	13.53 E
Lübbenau	164	51.52 N	13.57 E
Lubbock	250	33.35 N	101.51 W
Lubec	242	44.52 N	66.59 W
Lübeck	178	53.52 N	10.40 E
Lubefu	218	4.43 S	24.25 E
Lubelska, Wyżyna ∧∧[2]	164	51.00 N	23.00 E
L'ubercy	160	55.41 N	37.53 E
Lubéron, Montagne du ∧∧	166	43.48 N	5.22 E
Lubersac	166	45.27 N	1.24 E
Lubic Island I	202	10.58 N	120.43 E
Lubień Kujawski	164	52.25 N	19.10 E
Lubin (Lüben)	164	51.24 N	16.13 E
Lublin	164	51.15 N	22.35 E
Lubliniec	164	50.40 N	18.41 E
Lubnān, Jabal(Lebanon Mountains) ∧∧	210	34.00 N	36.00 E
Lubny	158	50.01 N	33.00 E
Lubomierz (Liebenthal)	164	51.01 N	15.30 E
Luboń	164	52.23 N	16.54 E
L'ubotin	158	49.57 N	35.57 E
Lubraniec	164	52.33 N	18.50 E
Lubsko (Sommerfeld)	164	51.46 N	14.59 E
Lübtheen	164	53.18 N	11.04 E
Lubuagan	202	17.21 N	121.10 E
Lubudi	218	6.51 S	21.18 E
Lubudi ≃	218	9.13 S	25.38 E
Lubuklinggau	198	3.18 S	102.52 E
Lubuksikaping	200	0.08 N	100.10 E
Lubumbashi (Élisabethville)	218	11.40 S	27.28 E
Lubutu	218	0.44 S	26.35 E
L'ubytino	160	58.49 N	33.23 E
Lübz	164	53.27 N	12.01 E
Lucan	244	43.11 N	81.24 W
Lucanas	292	14.37 S	74.14 W
Lucania ◂[1]	170	40.30 N	16.00 E
Lucania, Mount ∧	236	61.01 N	140.28 W
L'uca-Ongokton, Gora ∧	186	67.52 N	106.24 E
Lucas, Iowa, U.S.	244	41.02 N	93.28 W
Lucas, Kans., U.S.	252	39.04 N	98.32 W
Lucas, Ohio, U.S.	266	40.42 N	82.25 W
Lucas □[6]	266	41.39 N	83.32 W
Lucas González	294	32.25 S	59.33 W
Lucasville	242	38.53 N	82.60 W
Lucban	202	14.07 N	121.33 E
Lucca	184	43.50 N	10.29 E
Lucca □[4]	184	44.02 N	10.27 E
Lucea	285q	18.25 N	78.10 W
Luce Bay C	162	54.47 N	4.50 W
Lucedale	248	30.55 N	88.35 W
Lucena, Esp.	168	37.24 N	4.29 W
Lucena, Pil.	202	13.56 N	121.37 E
Lucena del Cid	168	40.08 N	0.17 W
Lucenay-l'Évêque	166	47.05 N	4.15 E
Luc-en-Diois	166	44.37 N	5.27 E
Lučenec	164	48.20 N	19.40 E
Lucera	184	41.30 N	15.20 E
Lucerne → Luzern, Schw.	180	47.03 N	8.18 E
Lucerne, Calif., U.S.	258	39.06 N	122.48 W
Lucerne, Ind., U.S.	268	40.52 N	86.24 W
Lucernemines	266	40.34 N	79.09 W
Lucerne Valley	274	34.27 N	116.57 W
Lucero	254	30.49 N	106.30 W
Lucero, Lake ⊜	254	32.42 N	106.25 W
Luchena ≃	168	37.44 N	1.50 W
Luchiang	196	24.04 N	120.26 E
Luchovicy	160	54.59 N	39.03 E
Lüchow	164	52.58 N	11.10 E
Lucie ≃	290	3.35 N	57.38 W
Lucinda	266	41.19 N	79.22 W
Lucipara, Kepulauan II	198	5.30 S	127.33 E
Lucira	218	13.51 S	12.31 E
Luciyu I	196	25.07 N	119.22 E
Luck, S.S.S.R.	158	50.44 N	25.20 E
Luck, Wis., U.S.	244	45.34 N	92.28 W
Luckau	164	51.51 N	13.43 E
Luckenwalde	164	52.05 N	13.10 E
Luckey	266	41.27 N	83.29 W
Luckiamute ≃	256	44.45 N	123.09 W
Lucknow, Bhārat	206	26.50 N	80.52 E
Lucknow, Ont., Can.	244	43.57 N	81.31 W
Lucknow, Pa., U.S.	262	40.20 N	76.54 W
Lucky Peak Reservoir ⊜[1]	256	43.33 N	116.00 W
Luçon	166	46.27 N	1.10 W
Lüda (Dairen)	194	38.53 N	121.35 E
Luda Kamčija ≃	172	43.03 N	27.29 E
Ludao I	194	39.44 N	123.45 E
Ludbreg	170	46.15 N	16.37 E
Lüdenscheid	178	51.13 N	7.38 E
Lüderitz	224	26.38 S	15.10 E
Lüderitz □[5]	224	26.30 S	15.45 E
Ludhiāna	206	30.55 N	75.51 E
Lüdinghausen	178	51.46 N	7.26 E
Ludington	244	43.57 N	86.27 W
Ludingtonville	261	41.29 N	73.39 W
L'udinovo	158	53.52 N	34.27 E
Ludlam	246	25.44 N	80.18 W
Ludlow, Eng., U.K.	174	52.22 N	2.43 W
Ludlow, Colo., U.S.	252	37.20 N	104.35 W
Ludlow, Ill., U.S.	268	40.23 N	88.08 W
Ludlow, Mass., U.S.	261	42.10 N	72.29 W
Ludlow, Pa., U.S.	266	41.44 N	78.57 W
Ludlow, Vt., U.S.	242	43.24 N	72.42 W
Ludowici	246	31.43 N	81.45 W
Luduș	172	46.29 N	24.05 E
Ludvika	160	60.09 N	15.11 E
Ludwigsburg	164	48.53 N	9.11 E
Ludwigsfelde	164	52.17 N	13.16 E
Ludwigshafen	164	49.29 N	8.26 E
Ludwigslust	164	53.19 N	11.30 E
Luebo	218	5.21 S	21.25 E
Lueders	250	32.48 N	99.37 W
Luena	218	9.27 S	25.47 E
Luena ≃	218	12.31 S	22.34 E
Luepa	290	5.43 N	61.31 W
Lufeng, Zhg.	196	22.57 N	115.38 E
Lufeng, Zhg.	200	25.07 N	102.07 E
Lufkin	248	31.20 N	94.44 W
Luga	160	58.44 N	29.52 E
Luga ≃	160	59.40 N	28.18 E
Lugano	180	46.01 N	8.58 E
Lugano, Lago di ⊜	170	46.00 N	9.00 E
Lugansk → Vorošilovgrad	158	48.34 N	39.20 E
Lugareño	284p	21.33 N	77.28 W
Lügde	178	51.57 N	9.15 E
Lugh Ganane	214	3.56 N	42.32 E
Lugnaquillia Mountain ∧	162	52.58 N	6.27 W
Lugo, Esp.	168	43.00 N	7.34 W
Lugo, It.	184	44.25 N	11.54 E
Lugoj	172	45.41 N	21.54 E
Lugus Island I	202	5.41 N	120.50 E
Luilaka ≃	218	0.52 S	20.12 E
Luing I	162	56.13 N	5.39 W
Luino	170	46.00 N	8.44 E
Luirojoki ≃	160	67.08 N	27.29 E
Luís Alves	294	26.44 S	48.57 W
Luis Beltrán	294	39.19 S	65.46 W
Luis D'Abreu (Calchaquí)	294	29.54 S	60.18 W
Luishia	218	11.10 S	27.02 E
Luisiânia	296	21.41 S	50.17 W
Luiza	218	7.12 S	22.25 E
Luján, Arg.	294	32.22 S	65.56 W
Luján, Arg.	294	33.05 S	68.55 W
Lujiang ≃	196	27.02 N	115.03 E
Lukanga Swamp ☷	218	14.25 S	27.45 E
Lukenie ≃	218	2.44 S	18.09 E
Lukeville	254	31.53 N	112.49 W
Lukojanov	160	55.02 N	44.30 E
Lukolela	218	1.03 S	17.12 E
Lukovit	172	43.12 N	24.10 E
Łuków	164	51.56 N	22.23 E
Lukulu	218	14.25 S	23.12 E
Lula	248	34.27 N	90.29 W
Luleå	160	65.34 N	22.10 E
Luleälven ≃	160	65.35 N	22.03 E
Lüleburgaz	212	41.24 N	27.21 E
Lules	294	26.55 S	65.20 W
Luliang	200	25.05 N	103.36 E
Luling	250	29.41 N	97.39 W
Lulonga ≃	218	0.42 N	18.23 E
Lulua ≃	218	5.02 S	21.07 E
Luluabourg → Kananga	218	5.54 S	22.25 E
Lulu Island I	238	55.28 N	133.30 W
Lumban	202	14.18 N	121.27 E
Lumber ≃	246	34.12 N	79.10 W
Lumber City	246	31.56 N	82.41 W
Lumberport	242	39.23 N	80.21 W
Lumberton, Miss., U.S.	248	31.00 N	89.27 W
Lumberton, N.J., U.S.	262	39.58 N	74.48 W
Lumberton, N.C., U.S.	246	34.37 N	79.00 W
Lumbovka	160	67.44 N	40.30 E
Lumbrales	168	40.56 N	6.43 W
Lumbres	166	50.42 N	2.08 E
Lumby	238	50.15 N	118.58 W
Lumding	206	25.46 N	93.10 E
Lumerau ≃	202	5.21 N	118.53 E
Luminárias	296	21.30 S	44.54 W
Lumintao ≃	202	12.43 N	120.55 E
Lummi Island	270	48.42 N	122.40 W
Lumpkin	246	32.03 N	84.48 W
Lumsden	240	49.19 N	53.37 W
Lumuhu ⊜	206	33.45 N	79.30 E
Lumut	200	4.13 N	100.39 E
Lumut, Tandjung ≻	198	3.50 S	105.57 E
Luna, Pil.	202	18.18 N	121.21 E
Luna, Pil.	202	16.51 N	120.23 E
Luna ≃, Bra.	290	4.32 S	60.41 W
Luna ≃, Esp.	168	41.58 N	5.40 W
Luna Pier	268	41.48 N	83.27 W
Lund, B.C., Can.	238	49.58 N	124.44 W
Lund, Sve.	160	55.42 N	13.11 E
Lund, Nev., U.S.	258	38.52 N	115.00 W
Lundale	242	37.48 N	81.45 W
Lundazi	218	12.19 S	33.13 E
Lundi ≃	224	21.43 S	32.34 E
Lüneberg	160	53.15 N	10.23 E
Lüneburg	178	53.15 N	10.23 E
Lüneburg □[6]	178	53.00 N	10.15 E
Lüneburger Heide, Naturpark ♠	164	51.37 N	7.31 E
Lunel	166	43.41 N	4.08 E
Lünen	178	51.36 N	7.32 E
Lunenburg, N.S., Can.	240	44.23 N	64.19 W
Lunenburg, Mass., U.S.	261	42.36 N	71.44 W
Lunenburg, Va., U.S.	246	36.58 N	78.16 W
Lunéville	180	48.36 N	6.30 E
Lunga ≃	218	14.34 S	26.25 E
Lungch'i → Zhangzhou	196	24.33 N	117.39 E
Lungi	214	8.38 N	13.13 W
Lungué-Bungo ≃	218	14.19 S	23.14 E
Lūni ≃	206	24.40 N	71.15 E
Lunino	160	53.35 N	45.14 E
Lunnaja, Gora ∧	236	68.14 N	174.20 E
Lunsar	222	8.41 N	12.32 W
Luobubo (Lop Nor) ⊜	190	40.20 N	90.15 E
Luoding	200	22.47 N	111.31 E
Luofushan ∧∧	196	23.28 N	114.10 E
Luogosanto	170	41.02 N	9.12 E
Luohanshan ∧	196	25.51 N	119.13 E
Luohe	196	33.35 N	114.01 E
Luohe ≃	190	34.42 N	110.15 E
Luolong	190	30.45 N	96.09 E
Luoping	200	24.59 N	104.21 E
Luosuojiang ≃	200	21.51 N	101.13 E
Luoyang	190	34.41 N	112.28 E
Lupao	202	15.53 N	120.54 E
Łupawa (Lupow)	164	54.26 N	17.24 E
Lupeni	172	45.22 N	23.13 E
Lupon	202	6.54 N	125.59 E
Luqu	190	34.41 N	102.22 E
Luque	168	37.33 N	4.16 W
Luquillo	284m	18.22 N	65.43 W
Luray	242	38.40 N	78.28 W
Lure	180	47.41 N	6.30 E
Luremo	218	8.31 S	17.50 E
Lurgan	162	54.28 N	6.20 W
Luribay	292	17.06 S	67.39 W
Lurín	292	12.17 S	76.52 W
Lúrio	218	13.35 S	40.30 E
Lúrio ≃	218	13.35 S	40.32 E
Lusaka	218	15.25 S	28.17 E
Lusambo	218	4.58 S	23.27 E
Luscar	238	53.04 N	117.24 W
Luserna San Giovanni	182	44.48 N	7.15 E
Lushan	190	30.15 N	102.58 E
Lushan ∧	196	29.31 N	115.58 E
Lushnje	172	40.56 N	19.42 E
Lushoto	218	4.47 S	38.17 E
Lushui ≃	196	27.04 N	115.00 E
Lüshun (Port Arthur)	194	38.47 N	121.13 E
Lusignan	166	46.26 N	0.07 E
Lusk	254	42.46 N	104.27 W
Luso	218	11.47 S	19.52 E
Luspebryggan	160	67.01 N	19.51 E
Lussac-les-Châteaux	166	46.24 N	0.44 E
Lustenau	180	47.26 N	9.39 E
Luster	160	61.26 N	7.24 E
Lūt, Dasht-e •[2]	208	33.00 N	57.00 E
Lü-ta → Lüda	194	38.53 N	121.35 E
Lutao	202	10.00 N	124.04 E
Lutcher	248	30.02 N	90.42 W
Lutesville	248	37.18 N	89.59 W
Luther, Mich., U.S.	244	44.02 N	85.41 W
Luther, Okla., U.S.	250	35.40 N	97.12 W
Luther Lake ⊜	244	43.55 N	80.26 W
Luthersburg	266	41.03 N	78.43 W
Luton	174	51.53 N	0.25 W
Lutong	198	4.32 N	114.00 E
Luttrell	246	36.12 N	83.44 W
Lutz	246	28.09 N	82.28 W
Lützow	164	53.40 N	11.11 E
Lützow-Holm Bay C	148	69.10 S	37.30 E
Luverne, Ala., U.S.	248	31.43 N	86.16 W
Lu Verne, Iowa, U.S.	244	42.55 N	94.05 W
Luverne, Minn., U.S.	252	43.39 N	96.13 W
Luvuvhu ≃	224	22.40 S	30.55 E
Luwegu ≃	218	8.31 S	37.23 E
Luwuk	198	0.56 S	122.47 E
Luxana Bay C	238	52.03 N	131.00 W
Luxembourg	164	49.36 N	6.09 E
Luxembourg □[1]	158	49.45 N	6.05 E
Luxemburg	244	44.32 N	87.42 W
Luxeuil-les-Bains	180	47.49 N	6.23 E
Luxi (Mangshi)	200	24.20 N	98.25 E
Luxi ≃	196	28.11 N	116.48 E
Luxor → Al-Uqṣur, Miṣr	220	25.41 N	32.39 E
Luxor, Pa., U.S.	266	40.20 N	79.28 W
Luxora	248	35.45 N	89.56 W
Luy ≃	166	43.39 N	1.08 W
Luy de Béarn ≃	168	43.38 N	0.47 W
Luy de France ≃	166	43.38 N	0.47 W
Luz	296	19.48 S	45.40 W
Luza, S.S.S.R.	160	60.39 N	47.10 E
Luza, S.S.S.R.	160	62.42 N	37.06 E
Luzarches	166	49.07 N	2.25 E
Luzern	180	47.03 N	8.18 E
Luzern □[3]	180	47.05 N	8.05 E
Luzhai	200	24.31 N	109.50 E
Luzhou	190	28.54 N	105.27 E
Luziânia	296	16.15 S	47.56 W
Luzon	280	9.25 N	82.32 W
Luzon I	202	16.00 N	121.00 E
Luzon Strait ⋓	198	20.30 N	121.00 E
Luzy	166	46.48 N	3.58 E
L'vov	158	49.50 N	24.00 E
Lwów → L'vov	158	49.50 N	24.00 E
Lwówek	164	52.28 N	16.10 E
Lwówek Śląski (Löwenberg)	164	51.07 N	15.35 E
Lyall, Mount ∧	230	45.17 S	167.34 E
Lyallpur	206	31.25 N	73.05 E
Lybster	162	58.18 N	3.18 W
Lycaonia □[9]	212	37.50 N	33.15 E
Lycia □[9]	212	36.20 N	30.00 E
Lyčkovo	160	57.55 N	32.24 E
Lycksele	160	64.36 N	18.40 E
Lydd	162	50.57 N	0.55 E
Lydda → Lod	210	31.57 N	34.54 E
Lydenburg	224	25.10 S	30.29 E
Lydia □[9]	212	38.40 N	27.30 E
Lydia Mills	246	34.28 N	81.55 W
Lydick	268	41.42 N	86.22 W
Lyell, Mount ∧	238	51.57 N	117.06 W
Lyell Island I	238	52.40 N	131.30 W
Lyerly	248	34.20 N	85.27 W
Lyford	250	26.24 N	97.48 W
Lykens	262	40.34 N	76.43 W
Lyle, Minn., U.S.	244	43.30 N	92.57 W
Lyle, Wash., U.S.	270	45.42 N	121.17 W
Lyles	248	35.55 N	87.21 W
Lyman, Nebr., U.S.	252	41.55 N	104.02 W
Lyman, S.C., U.S.	246	34.56 N	82.09 W
Lyman, Wash., U.S.	270	48.31 N	122.04 W
Lyman, Wyo., U.S.	254	41.20 N	110.18 W
Lyme	261	41.19 N	72.10 W
Lyme Bay C	162	50.38 N	3.00 W
Lyme Regis	162	50.44 N	2.57 W
Lymington	174	50.46 N	1.33 W
Lyn	264	44.35 N	75.47 W
Łyna (Lava) ≃	164	54.37 N	21.14 E
Lynch, Ky., U.S.	246	36.58 N	82.55 W
Lynch, Nebr., U.S.	252	42.50 N	98.28 W
Lynchburg, Ohio, U.S.	242	39.14 N	83.48 W
Lynchburg, S.C., U.S.	246	34.04 N	80.04 W
Lynchburg, Tenn., U.S.	248	35.17 N	86.22 W
Lynchburg, Va., U.S.	246	37.24 N	79.10 W
Lynches ≃	246	33.50 N	79.22 W
Lynch Lake ⊜	242	46.25 N	77.05 W
Lynchville	266	41.26 N	78.34 W
Lynd ≃	228	16.28 S	143.18 E
Lynden, Ont., Can.	264	43.14 N	80.09 W
Lynden, Wash., U.S.	270	48.57 N	122.27 W
Lyndhurst	266	41.31 N	81.30 W
Lyndon, Kans., U.S.	252	38.36 N	95.41 W
Lyndon, Ky., U.S.	248	38.16 N	85.34 W
Lyndonville, N.Y., U.S.	264	43.19 N	78.23 W
Lyndonville, Vt., U.S.	242	44.32 N	72.01 W
Lyndora	266	40.51 N	79.55 W
Lyngdal	160	58.08 N	7.05 E
Lyngen	160	69.34 N	20.10 E
Lynher Reef ⊹[2]	226	15.27 S	121.55 E
Lynn, Ala., U.S.	248	34.03 N	87.33 W
Lynn, Ind., U.S.	248	40.03 N	84.56 W
Lynn, Mass., U.S.	261	42.28 N	70.57 W
Lynn Canal C	236	58.50 N	135.15 W
Lynndyl	254	39.31 N	112.22 W
Lynnfield	261	42.32 N	71.03 W
Lynn Gardens	246	36.35 N	82.34 W
Lynn Haven	248	30.15 N	85.39 W
Lynn Lake	232	56.51 N	101.03 W
Lynnville	244	41.35 N	92.47 W
Lynnwood, Pa., U.S.	266	40.07 N	79.51 W
Lynnwood, Wash., U.S.	270	47.49 N	122.19 W
Lynton	162	51.15 N	3.50 W
Lynwood	274	33.55 N	118.12 W
Lynx Lake ⊜	232	62.25 N	106.15 W
Lyon	182	45.45 N	4.51 E
Lyon □[6]	272	39.00 N	119.15 W
Lyon Inlet C	232	66.32 N	83.53 W
Lyon Mountain	242	44.43 N	73.55 W
Lyon Mountain ∧	242	44.43 N	73.52 W
Lyonnais □[9]	182	45.45 N	4.30 E
Lyonnais, Monts du ∧∧	166	45.40 N	4.30 E
Lyons, Colo., U.S.	254	40.13 N	105.16 W
Lyons, Ga., U.S.	246	32.12 N	82.19 W
Lyons, Ill., U.S.	268	41.49 N	87.50 W
Lyons, Ind., U.S.	248	38.59 N	87.05 W
Lyons, Kans., U.S.	252	38.21 N	98.12 W
Lyons, Mich., U.S.	268	42.59 N	84.57 W
Lyons, Nebr., U.S.	252	41.56 N	96.28 W
Lyons, N.Y., U.S.	264	43.04 N	77.00 W
Lyons, Ohio, U.S.	268	41.42 N	84.04 W
Lyons, Wis., U.S.	268	42.39 N	88.21 W
Lyons Falls	264	43.37 N	75.22 W
Lyons Plains	261	41.13 N	73.21 W
Lyon Station	262	40.28 N	75.45 W
Lys (Leie) ≃	166	50.39 N	2.24 E
Lysá pod Makytou	164	49.12 N	18.13 E
Lysekil	160	58.16 N	11.26 E
Łysica ∧	164	50.54 N	20.55 E
Lyskovo	160	56.04 N	45.02 E
Lyss	180	47.04 N	7.18 E
Lyster Station	260	46.22 N	71.32 W
Lys'va	158	58.07 N	57.47 E
Lytham	162	53.45 N	2.57 W
Lytle	250	29.14 N	98.48 W
Lyttelton	230	43.35 S	172.43 E
Lytton	238	50.14 N	121.34 W
M			
Ma ≃	200	19.47 N	105.56 E
Maad, Djebel bou ∧	168	36.28 N	2.13 E
Maâdid, Djebel ∧	168	35.52 N	4.46 E
Maalaea Bay C	275d	20.47 N	156.29 W
Ma'ān	210	30.12 N	35.44 E
Ma'ān □[8]	210	30.20 N	36.30 E
Maanshan	196	31.42 N	118.30 E
Ma-ao	202	10.29 N	122.59 E
Maardu	160	59.28 N	25.02 E
Ma'arrat an-Nu'mān	208	35.38 N	36.40 E
Maarssen	178	52.08 N	5.08 E
Maas (Meuse) ≃	164	51.49 N	5.01 E
Maaseik	178	51.06 N	5.48 E
Maasin	202	10.08 N	124.50 E
Maasniel	178	51.13 N	6.01 E
Maassluis	178	51.55 N	4.15 E
Maastricht	164	50.52 N	5.43 E
Ma-ayon ≃	202	11.25 N	122.45 E
Mababe Depression •[7]	224	18.50 S	24.15 E
Mabaho, Mount ∧	202	9.15 N	125.42 E
Mabana	270	48.06 N	122.25 W
Mabank	250	32.22 N	96.06 W
Mabaruma	290	8.10 N	59.50 W
Mabay	284p	20.16 N	76.40 W
Mabel Lake ⊜	238	50.35 N	118.44 W
Maben	248	33.33 N	89.05 W
Mabeul	170	36.27 N	10.46 E
Mablethorpe	162	53.21 N	0.15 E
Mableton	246	33.49 N	84.35 W
Mabole ≃	222	9.01 N	12.44 W
Mabou	240	46.05 N	61.22 W
Mača	186	59.54 N	117.35 E
Macabu ≃	296	21.59 S	41.28 W
Macachín	294	37.09 S	63.40 W
McAdam	240	45.36 N	67.20 W
McAdoo	242	40.54 N	76.01 W
Macaé	296	22.23 S	41.47 W
Macajalar Bay C	202	8.35 N	124.38 E
Macajuba	296	12.09 S	40.22 W
Macalaya	202	12.53 N	123.46 E
Macalelon	202	13.45 N	122.08 E
McAlester	250	34.56 N	95.46 W
Macalister	238	52.27 N	122.24 W
Macalister ≃	228	38.02 S	146.59 E
McAlister, Mount ∧	228	34.27 S	149.45 E
McAlisterville	262	40.38 N	77.16 W
McAllen	250	26.12 N	98.15 W
McAlmont	248	34.49 N	92.10 W
McAlpine	262	39.16 N	76.50 W
MacAlpine Lake ⊜	232	66.40 N	103.15 W
McAlveys Fort	266	40.39 N	77.50 W
Macamic, Lac ⊜	244	48.46 N	79.00 W
Macao → Macau □[2]	190	22.10 N	113.33 E
Macão	168	39.33 N	8.00 W
Macapá	286	0.02 N	51.03 W
Macará	290	4.23 S	79.57 W
Macarani	296	15.33 S	40.24 W
Macarena, Serranía de la ∧∧	290	2.45 N	73.55 W
Macareo, Caño ≃[1]	290	9.47 N	61.37 W
MacArthur	202	10.50 N	125.00 E
McArthur	242	39.15 N	82.29 W
Macaruma ≃	290	7.37 N	61.48 W
Macas	290	2.19 S	78.07 W
Macassar → Makasar	198	5.07 S	119.24 E
Macau, Bra.	286	5.07 S	36.38 W
Macau (Aomen), Macau	196	22.14 N	113.35 E
Macau □[2]	190	22.10 N	113.33 E
Macau, Ilha I	224	20.55 S	35.05 E
Macauã ≃	292	9.13 S	68.44 W
Macaúbas	296	13.02 S	42.42 W
Macaya ≃	290	0.59 N	72.20 W
Macaya, Pic de ∧	282	18.25 N	74.00 W
McBain	244	44.12 N	85.13 W
McBee	246	34.28 N	80.15 W
McBride	238	53.18 N	120.10 W
McCall	256	44.55 N	116.06 W
McCall Creek	248	31.31 N	90.42 W
McCallum	240	47.38 N	56.15 W
McCamey	250	31.08 N	102.13 W
McCammon	256	42.39 N	112.12 W
Mccarthy	236	61.26 N	142.55 W
McCauley Island I	238	53.40 N	130.15 W
McCaysville	246	34.59 N	84.23 W
McChesneytown	266	40.19 N	79.22 W
McClean Mountain ∧	240	47.07 N	68.50 W
McCleary	270	47.03 N	123.16 W
McClellanville	246	33.05 N	79.28 W
Macclenny	246	30.18 N	82.07 W
Macclesfield	162	53.16 N	2.07 W
McClintock, Mount ∧	148	80.13 S	157.26 E
McCloud	258	41.15 N	122.08 W
McCloud ≃	258	40.46 N	122.18 W
McClure, Ill., U.S.	248	37.19 N	89.26 W
McClure, Ohio, U.S.	268	41.22 N	83.57 W
McClure, Pa., U.S.	242	40.42 N	77.19 W
McClusky	252	47.29 N	100.27 W
McColl	246	34.40 N	79.33 W
McComas	246	37.23 N	81.17 W
McComb, Miss., U.S.	248	31.14 N	90.27 W
McComb, Ohio, U.S.	268	41.06 N	83.48 W
McConnell Range ∧∧	236	64.00 N	123.50 W
McConnellsburg	242	39.56 N	77.59 W
McConnellstown	266	40.27 N	78.05 W
McConnellsville	264	43.16 N	75.42 W
McConnelsville	242	39.39 N	81.51 W
McCook	252	40.12 N	100.38 W
McCormick	246	33.55 N	82.17 W
McCoy	270	45.03 N	123.13 W
McCrory	248	35.16 N	91.12 W
McCullom Lake	268	42.22 N	88.18 W
McCullough Mountain ∧	258	35.36 N	115.11 W
McCune	252	37.21 N	95.01 W
McCurtain	250	35.09 N	94.58 W
McCutchenville	266	40.59 N	83.16 W
McDade	250	30.17 N	97.15 W
McDavid	248	30.52 N	87.19 W
McDermitt	258	41.59 N	117.36 W
McDermott	242	38.50 N	83.04 W
Macdhui, Ben ∧, Afr.	224	30.39 S	27.58 E
Macdhui, Ben ∧, Scot., U.K.	162	57.04 N	3.40 W
McDonald	252	39.47 N	101.22 W
McDonald, Lake ⊜	256	48.35 N	113.55 W
MacDonald Pass)(	256	46.34 N	112.18 W
Macdonald Range ∧∧	238	49.12 N	114.46 W
McDonough	246	33.27 N	84.09 W
McDougall, Mount ∧	254	42.54 N	110.36 W
McDowell Peak ∧	254	33.40 N	111.50 W
Macduff	162	57.40 N	2.29 W
Macedo de Cavaleiros	168	41.32 N	6.58 W
Macedon	264	43.04 N	77.18 W
Macedonia, Conn., U.S.	261	41.47 N	73.30 W
Macedonia, Ohio, U.S.	266	41.19 N	81.31 W
Macedonia → Makedonija □[3]	172	41.50 N	22.00 E
Macedonia □[9]	172	41.00 N	23.00 E
Maceió	286	9.40 S	35.43 W
Mcensk	158	53.17 N	36.35 E
Macenta	214	8.33 N	9.28 W
Macenta □[4]	222	8.30 N	9.25 W
Maceo	290	6.33 N	74.47 W
Macerata	184	43.18 N	13.27 E
Macerata □[4]	184	43.12 N	13.10 E
McEwen	248	36.06 N	87.38 W
McFadden	254	41.39 N	106.08 W
McFarland, Calif., U.S.	272	35.41 N	119.14 W
McFarland, Wis., U.S.	268	43.01 N	89.17 W
MacFarlane ≃	232	59.12 N	107.58 W
Macfarlane, Lake ⊜	228	31.55 S	136.42 E
Macfarlane, Mount ∧	230	43.56 S	169.23 E
McGehee	248	33.38 N	91.24 W
McGill	258	39.23 N	114.47 W
McGillivray Lake ⊜	242	46.04 N	77.06 W
McGovern	266	40.14 N	80.13 W
Mcgrann	266	40.47 N	79.31 W
Mcgrath	236	62.58 N	155.38 W
McGraw	242	42.36 N	76.06 W
MacGregor	252	49.57 N	98.49 W
McGregor, Ont., Can.	266	42.09 N	82.58 W
McGregor, Iowa, U.S.	244	43.01 N	91.11 W
McGregor, Tex., U.S.	250	31.26 N	97.24 W
McGregor ≃	238	54.11 N	122.00 W
McGregor Lake ⊜	238	50.31 N	112.53 W
McGregor Range ∧∧	228	26.40 S	142.45 E
McGuffey	268	40.42 N	83.47 W
McGuire, Mount ∧	256	45.10 N	114.36 W
McGuire Air Force Base ■	262	40.02 N	74.35 W
Macha	292	18.49 S	66.05 W
Machacamarca	292	18.10 S	67.02 W
Machachi	290	0.30 S	78.34 W
Machačkala	158	42.58 N	47.30 E
Machadinho ≃	292	9.00 S	61.52 W
Machado	296	21.41 S	45.56 W
Machærus ⊥	210	31.34 N	35.38 E
Machagai	294	26.56 S	60.05 W
Machala	290	3.16 S	79.58 W
Machalí	294	34.11 S	70.40 W
Machangjianhe ≃	194	39.00 N	117.40 E
Machattie, Lake ⊜	228	24.50 S	139.48 E
Machecoul	166	47.00 N	1.50 W
Machelen	176	50.55 N	4.26 E
McHenry, Ill., U.S.	268	42.21 N	88.16 W
McHenry, Miss., U.S.	248	30.42 N	89.08 W
Mc Henry □[6]	268	42.19 N	88.27 W
Machias, Maine, U.S.	242	44.43 N	67.28 W
Machias, N.Y., U.S.	266	42.25 N	78.30 W
Machias ≃	242	44.43 N	67.22 W
Machias Bay C	240	44.40 N	67.20 W
Machichaco, Cabo ≻	168	43.27 N	2.45 W
Mchinji	218	13.41 S	32.55 E
Machiques	290	10.04 N	72.34 W
Machroha	170	36.21 N	7.51 E
Machupicchu	292	13.08 S	72.32 W
Machu Picchu ⊥	292	13.10 S	72.35 W
Machupo ≃	292	12.34 S	64.25 W
Machynlleth	162	52.35 N	3.51 W
Maciá	294	32.11 S	59.25 W
Măcin	172	45.15 N	28.08 E
Macina ◂[1]	222	14.30 N	5.00 W
McIntosh, Ala., U.S.	248	31.16 N	88.02 W
McIntosh, Ill., U.S.	268	42.03 N	88.23 W
McIntosh, Minn., U.S.	252	47.38 N	95.53 W
McIntosh, S. Dak., U.S.	252	45.55 N	101.21 W
McIntyre	266	40.34 N	79.18 W
Macintyre ≃, Austl.	228	28.38 S	150.47 E
Macintyre ≃, Austl.	228	30.00 S	148.05 E
McIntyre Bay C	238	54.05 N	131.55 W
Mackay, Austl.	228	21.09 S	149.11 E
Mackay, Idaho, U.S.	256	43.55 N	113.37 W
MacKay Lake ⊜	232	63.55 N	110.25 W
McKean	266	41.59 N	80.09 W
McKean □[6]	266	41.49 N	78.27 W
McKeand ≃	232	65.26 N	68.10 W
McKee	246	37.25 N	84.01 W
Mckee City	262	39.26 N	74.37 W
McKeesport	266	40.21 N	79.52 W
McKees Rocks	266	40.28 N	80.10 W
Mckenna	270	46.56 N	122.33 W
Mackenzie	290	6.00 N	58.17 W
McKenzie, Ala., U.S.	248	31.33 N	86.43 W
McKenzie, Tenn., U.S.	248	36.08 N	88.31 W
Mackenzie □[5]	236	65.00 N	115.00 W
Mackenzie ≃	232	69.15 N	134.08 W
McKenzie ≃	256	44.07 N	123.06 W
MacKenzie Bay C, Ant.	148	68.20 S	71.15 E
Mackenzie Bay C, Can.	236	69.00 N	136.30 W
McKenzie Bridge	256	44.05 N	123.04 W
Mackenzie Mountains ∧∧	236	64.00 N	130.00 W
Mckerrow, Lake ⊜	230	44.26 S	168.03 E
Mackinac, Straits of ⋓	244	45.49 N	84.42 W
Mackinac Bridge ◂[5]	244	45.50 N	84.45 W
Mackinac Island	244	45.51 N	84.37 W
Mackinac Island I	244	45.51 N	84.38 W
Mackinaw	244	40.32 N	89.21 W
Mackinaw ≃	244	40.33 N	89.44 W
Mackinaw City	244	45.47 N	84.44 W
McKinlay ≃	228	20.50 S	141.28 E
McKinley	242	44.16 N	68.19 W
McKinley, Mount ∧	236	63.30 N	151.00 W
Mc Kinley Park	236	63.44 N	148.54 W
McKinleyville, Calif., U.S.	258	40.57 N	124.06 W
McKinleyville, W. Va., U.S.	266	40.15 N	80.36 W
McKinney, Ky., U.S.	246	37.27 N	84.46 W
McKinney, Tex., U.S.	250	33.12 N	96.37 W
Mackinnon Road	218	3.44 S	39.03 E
McKittrick	272	35.18 N	119.37 W
McKittrick Summit ∧	258	35.18 N	119.46 W
McKnightstown	262	39.52 N	77.20 W
Mckownville	261	42.41 N	73.50 W
Macksville	252	37.58 N	98.58 W
McLaughlin	252	45.49 N	100.49 W
McLaurin	248	31.10 N	89.13 W
Maclean	226	29.28 S	153.13 E
McLean, Ill., U.S.	248	40.19 N	89.10 W
McLean, Tex., U.S.	250	35.14 N	100.36 W
McLean, Va., U.S.	262	38.56 N	77.11 W
Mc Lean □[6]	268	40.29 N	88.45 W
McLeansboro	248	38.06 N	88.32 W
Maclear	218	31.02 S	28.23 E
Macleay ≃	228	30.52 S	153.01 E
McLennan	238	55.42 N	116.54 W
McLeod ≃	238	54.08 N	115.42 W
McLeod Bay C	232	62.53 N	110.00 W
McLeod Lake	238	54.59 N	123.02 W

Symbols in the index entries are identified on page 360.

Name	Page	Lat°′	Long°′
McLoughlin, Mount ∧	256	42.27 N	122.19 W
McLoughlin Bay C	232	67.50 N	99.00 W
Maclovio Herrera	278	29.05 N	105.08 W
McLure	238	51.03 N	120.14 W
McMasterville	260	45.33 N	73.13 W
MacMillan ≃	236	62.52 N	135.55 W
McMillan, Lake ⊜[1]	250	32.40 N	104.20 W
McMinnville, Oreg., U.S.	270	45.13 N	123.12 W
McMinnville, Tenn., U.S.	248	35.41 N	85.46 W
McMurdo Sound ⊔	148	77.30 S	165.00 E
McMurray	266	40.17 N	80.05 W
McNary	254	34.04 N	109.51 W
McNary Reservoir ⊜[1]	256	46.07 N	119.58 W
McNeil	248	33.21 N	93.13 W
McNeil, Mount ∧	238	54.35 N	130.14 W
McNeill	248	30.40 N	89.38 W
Macocha ∨	164	49.23 N	16.45 E
Macolla, Punta ≻	285s	12.06 N	70.13 W
Macomb	244	40.27 N	90.40 W
Macomb □[6]	266	42.40 N	82.54 W
Macomer	170	40.16 N	8.46 E
Mâcon, Fr.	180	46.18 N	4.50 E
Macon, Ga., U.S.	246	32.50 N	83.38 W
Macon, Ill., U.S.	248	39.43 N	89.00 W
Macon, Miss., U.S.	248	33.07 N	88.34 W
Macon, Mo., U.S.	248	39.44 N	92.28 W
Macon, Bayou ≃	248	31.55 N	91.33 W
Mâconnais, Monts du ⋀	166	46.18 N	4.45 E
Macorís, Cabo ≻	282	19.50 N	70.25 W
McPherson	252	38.22 N	97.40 W
McPherson Range ⋀	228	28.20 S	153.00 E
Macquarie ≃, Austl.	228	41.44 S	147.08 E
Macquarie ≃, Austl.	228	30.07 S	147.24 E
Macquarie, Lake ⊜	228	33.05 S	151.35 E
Macquarie Harbour C	228	42.19 S	145.23 E
Macquarie Marshes ≚	228	30.50 S	147.32 E
Macquarie Rise ⟡[3]	148	55.00 S	150.00 E
McQueeney	250	29.35 N	98.02 W
McRae, Ark., U.S.	248	35.07 N	91.49 W
McRae, Ga., U.S.	246	32.04 N	82.53 W
McRoberts	246	37.12 N	82.40 W
Mac Robertson Coast ●[2]	148	68.10 S	65.00 E
Macrohon	202	10.05 N	124.57 E
Macroom	162	51.54 N	8.57 W
Mcsherrystown	262	39.48 N	77.02 W
Mactan Island I	202	10.18 N	123.58 E
MacTier	264	45.08 N	79.47 W
Macuapanim, Ilhas II	290	2.35 S	65.28 W
Macuelizo	280	15.18 N	88.31 W
Macujer	290	0.24 N	73.07 W
Maculabo Island I	202	14.23 N	122.50 E
Macuma ≃	290	2.44 S	77.24 W
Macungie	262	40.31 N	75.34 W
Macuro	290	10.39 N	61.56 W
Macusani	292	14.04 S	70.29 W
Macuspana	278	17.46 N	92.36 W
McVeigh	246	37.32 N	82.15 W
McVeytown	266	40.30 N	77.44 W
McVille	252	47.46 N	98.11 W
McWilliams	248	31.50 N	87.06 W
Macy	268	40.58 N	86.08 W
Mad ≃, Ont., Can.	244	44.25 N	79.54 W
Mad ≃, Calif., U.S.	258	40.57 N	124.07 W
Mad ≃, Ohio, U.S.	242	39.46 N	84.11 W
Mad ≃, Vt., U.S.	242	44.18 N	72.41 W
Mada ≃	222	7.59 N	7.55 E
Ma'dabā	210	31.43 N	35.47 E
Madagascar I	225b	20.00 S	47.00 E
Madagascar Basin ⟡[1]	148	34.00 S	38.00 E
Madagascar Plateau ⟡[3]	148	32.00 S	44.00 E
Madame Island I	240	45.33 N	61.02 W
Madan	172	41.30 N	24.57 E
Madawaska, Ont., Can.	264	45.30 N	77.59 W
Madawaska, Maine, U.S.	240	47.21 N	68.20 W
Madawaska ≃	244	45.27 N	76.21 W
Maddalena, Isola I	170	41.13 N	9.24 E
Maddaloni	184	41.02 N	14.23 E
Maddela	202	16.21 N	121.41 E
Madden Lake ⊜[1]	280	9.15 N	79.34 W
Maddock	252	47.58 N	99.32 W
Made	178	51.41 N	4.46 E
Madeira I	214	32.44 N	17.00 W
Madeira ≃	286	3.22 S	58.45 W
Madeira, Arquipélago da II	148	32.40 N	16.45 W
Madeirinha ≃	292	8.31 S	60.46 W
Madeirinha, Paraná ≃[1]	290	3.25 S	58.51 W
Madeleine, Îles de la II	240	47.20 N	61.50 W
Madeleine-Centre	240	49.15 N	65.21 W
Mädelgabel ∧	166	47.18 N	10.18 E
Madelia	244	44.03 N	94.25 W
Madera, Méx.	278	29.12 N	108.07 W
Madera, Calif., U.S.	272	36.57 N	120.03 W
Madera, Pa., U.S.	266	40.50 N	78.26 W
Madera □[6]	272	37.15 N	119.45 W
Madera, Volcán ∧[1]	280	11.27 N	85.31 W
Madhya Pradesh □[4]	206	23.00 N	79.00 E
Madidi ≃	292	12.32 S	66.52 W
Madill	250	34.06 N	96.46 W
Madimba	218	4.58 S	15.08 E
Madīnat ash-Sha'b	204	12.50 N	44.56 E
Madingou	218	4.09 S	13.34 E
Madison, Ala., U.S.	248	34.42 N	86.45 W
Madison, Calif., U.S.	272	38.41 N	121.58 W
Madison, Conn., U.S.	261	41.17 N	72.36 W
Madison, Fla., U.S.	246	30.28 N	83.25 W
Madison, Ga., U.S.	246	33.36 N	83.28 W
Madison, Ind., U.S.	248	38.44 N	85.23 W
Madison, Kans., U.S.	252	38.08 N	96.08 W
Madison, Maine, U.S.	240	44.48 N	69.53 W
Madison, Md., U.S.	262	38.31 N	76.13 W
Madison, Minn., U.S.	252	45.01 N	96.11 W
Madison, Miss., U.S.	248	32.28 N	90.07 W
Madison, Nebr., U.S.	252	41.50 N	97.27 W
Madison, N.J., U.S.	262	40.46 N	74.25 W
Madison, N.C., U.S.	246	36.23 N	79.58 W
Madison, N.Y., U.S.	264	42.54 N	75.31 W
Madison, Ohio, U.S.	266	41.46 N	81.03 W
Madison, S. Dak., U.S.	252	44.00 N	97.07 W
Madison, Tenn., U.S.	248	36.16 N	86.42 W
Madison, Va., U.S.	242	38.23 N	78.15 W
Madison, W. Va., U.S.	242	38.04 N	81.49 W
Madison, Wis., U.S.	268	43.05 N	89.22 W
Madison □[6], Ind., U.S.	268	40.10 N	85.41 W
Madison □[6], N.Y., U.S.	264	43.05 N	75.42 W
Madison □[6], Ohio, U.S.	266	39.53 N	83.27 W
Madison ≃	256	45.56 N	111.30 W
Madisonburg	266	40.51 N	81.55 W
Madison Heights, Mich., U.S.	266	42.30 N	83.06 W
Madison Heights, Va., U.S.	246	37.25 N	79.08 W
Madison-on-the-lake	266	41.42 N	81.24 W
Madison Range ⋀	256	45.15 N	111.20 W
Madisonville, Ky., U.S.	248	37.20 N	87.30 W
Madisonville, La., U.S.	248	30.24 N	90.09 W
Madisonville, Tenn., U.S.	246	35.31 N	84.22 W
Madisonville, Tex., U.S.	250	30.57 N	95.55 W
Madiun	226	7.37 S	111.31 E
Madjene	198	3.33 S	118.57 E
Madoc	264	44.30 N	77.28 W
Mado Gashi	218	0.44 S	39.10 E
Madonna di Campiglio	170	46.14 N	10.49 E
Madras	256	44.38 N	121.08 W
Madre, Laguna C, Méx.	278	25.00 N	97.40 W
Madre, Laguna C, Tex., U.S.	250	27.00 N	97.35 W
Madre, Sierra ⋀	202	17.15 N	122.00 E
Madre de Deus	296	12.44 S	38.37 W
Madre de Dios □[5]	292	12.00 S	70.15 W
Madre de Dios ≃	292	10.59 S	66.08 W
Madre de Dios, Isla I	288	50.15 S	75.10 W
Madre del Sur, Sierra ⋀	278	17.00 N	100.00 W
Madre Occidental, Sierra ⋀	278	25.00 N	105.00 W
Madre Oriental, Sierra ⋀	278	22.00 N	99.30 W
Madre Vieja ≃	280	14.00 N	91.26 W
Madrid, Col.	290	4.44 N	74.16 W
Madrid, Esp.	168	40.24 N	3.41 W
Madrid, Pil.	202	9.16 N	125.57 E
Madrid, Ala., U.S.	248	31.01 N	85.24 W
Madrid, Iowa, U.S.	244	41.53 N	93.49 W
Madrid, Nebr., U.S.	252	40.51 N	101.33 W
Madrid, Punta ≻	292	19.01 S	70.19 W
Madridejos, Esp.	168	39.28 N	3.32 W
Madridejos, Pil.	202	9.46 N	123.21 E
Madrigalejo	168	39.09 N	5.37 W
Madriz □[5]	280	13.30 N	86.30 W
Madroñera	168	39.26 N	5.46 W
Madruga	284p	22.55 N	81.51 W
Maducang Island I	202	10.43 N	120.40 E
Maduo	190	34.53 N	98.24 E
Madura I	198	7.00 S	113.20 E
Madyan ◂[1]	208	27.40 N	35.35 E
Maeander Reef ⟡[2]	202	8.06 N	119.18 E
Maebaru	192	33.33 N	130.12 E
Maebashi	192	36.23 N	139.04 E
Mae Hong Son	198	19.16 N	97.56 E
Mae Klong ≃	200	13.21 N	100.00 E
Maershan ∧	200	26.18 N	100.20 E
Mae Sariang	198	18.10 N	97.59 E
Maeser	254	40.28 N	109.32 W
Mae Sot	200	16.40 N	98.35 E
Maesteg	174	51.37 N	3.40 W
Maestra, Sierra ⋀	284p	20.00 N	76.45 W
Maestre de Campo Island I	202	12.54 N	121.43 E
Maestu	168	42.44 N	2.27 W
Maevarano ≃	225b	14.35 S	47.58 E
Maevatanana	218	16.56 S	46.49 E
Mafeking	224	25.53 S	25.39 E
Maffra	228	37.53 S	147.59 E
Mafia Island I	218	7.50 S	39.50 E
Mafou ≃	222	10.32 N	10.08 W
Mafra, Bra.	294	26.07 S	49.49 W
Mafra, Port.	168	38.56 N	9.20 W
Magadan	186	59.34 N	150.48 E
Magadi	218	1.54 S	36.17 E
Magaguadavic Lake ⊜	240	45.43 N	67.12 W
Magallanes → Punta Arenas, Chile	288	53.09 S	70.55 W
Magallanes, Pil.	202	12.50 N	123.50 E
Magallanes, Estrecho de ⊔	288	54.00 S	71.00 W
Magangué	290	9.14 N	74.45 W
Maganoy ≃	202	6.55 N	124.30 E
Magat ≃	202	17.02 N	121.50 E
Magazine Mountain ∧	248	35.10 N	93.38 W
Magdagači	186	53.27 N	125.48 E
Magdalena, Arg.	294	35.04 S	57.32 W
Magdalena, Bol.	292	13.20 S	64.08 W
Magdalena, Méx.	278	20.55 N	103.57 W
Magdalena, Méx.	278	30.38 N	110.57 W
Magdalena, Perú	292	6.41 S	77.50 W
Magdalena, N. Mex., U.S.	254	34.07 N	107.14 W
Magdalena □[5]	290	10.00 N	74.00 W
Magdalena ≃, Col.	290	11.06 N	74.51 W
Magdalena ≃, Méx.	278	30.40 N	112.25 W
Magdalena, Bahía C	278	24.40 N	112.00 W
Magdalena, Isla I	288	44.42 S	73.10 W
Magdalena, Punta ≻	290	3.56 N	77.21 W
Magdeburg	164	52.07 N	11.38 E
Magderburger Börde ≚	164	52.00 N	11.30 E
Magdiwang	202	12.30 N	122.31 E
Magé	296	22.39 S	43.02 W
Magee	248	31.52 N	89.44 W
Magelang	226	7.28 S	110.13 E
Magellan, Strait of → Magallanes, Estrecho de ⊔	288	54.00 S	71.00 W
Magenta	182	45.28 N	8.53 E
Magerøy I	160	71.03 N	25.45 E
Maggiorasca, Monte ∧	170	44.33 N	9.26 E
Maggiore, Lago ⊜	170	46.00 N	8.40 E
Maghāghah	220	28.39 N	30.50 E
Magic Reservoir ⊜[1]	256	43.17 N	114.23 W
Magina ∧	168	37.43 N	3.28 W
Magiolobo Bay C	202	11.06 N	125.18 E
Magione	170	43.08 N	12.12 E
Maglaj	172	44.33 N	18.06 E
Maglie	170	40.07 N	18.19 E
Magna	254	40.42 N	112.06 W
Magnetawan ≃	244	45.46 N	80.37 W
Magnetic Island I	228	19.08 S	146.50 E
Magnetic Springs	266	40.21 N	83.16 W
Magnisía □[5]	172	39.10 N	23.30 E
Magnitogorsk	158	53.27 N	59.04 E
Magnolia, Ark., U.S.	248	33.16 N	93.14 W
Magnolia, Del., U.S.	262	39.04 N	75.29 W
Magnolia, Md., U.S.	262	39.24 N	76.19 W
Magnolia, Minn., U.S.	252	43.39 N	96.05 W
Magnolia, Miss., U.S.	248	31.09 N	90.28 W
Magnolia, N.C., U.S.	246	34.54 N	78.03 W
Magnolia, Ohio, U.S.	266	40.39 N	81.18 W
Magnolia, Tex., U.S.	250	30.13 N	95.45 W
Magny-en-Vexin	166	49.09 N	1.47 E
Magog	260	45.16 N	72.09 W
Magpie	240	50.19 N	64.30 W
Magpie ≃, Ont., Can.	244	47.56 N	84.50 W
Magpie ≃, Qué., Can.	240	50.18 N	64.28 W
Magpie, Lac ⊜	240	50.55 N	64.39 W
Magrath	238	49.25 N	112.52 W
Magro ≃	168	39.11 N	0.25 W
Magruder Mountain ∧	258	37.25 N	117.33 W
Magsaysay (Linugos)	202	9.01 N	125.10 E
Magsingal	202	17.41 N	120.25 E
Maguarinho, Cabo ≻	286	0.18 S	48.22 W
Magueyes	278	25.44 N	97.47 W
Maguse Lake ⊜	232	61.40 N	95.10 W
Magwe	200	20.09 N	94.55 E
Magwe □[8]	200	23.00 N	95.00 E
Mahābād	208	36.45 N	45.43 E
Mahābhārat Lekh ⋀	206	27.40 N	84.30 E
Mahabo	218	20.23 S	44.40 E
Mahāded Hills ⋀[2]	206	22.10 N	78.30 E
Mahaffey	266	40.53 N	78.44 W
Mahaicony	290	6.36 N	57.48 W
Mahajamba ≃	225b	15.33 S	47.08 E
Mahajamba, Baie de la C	225b	15.24 S	47.05 E
Mahajilo ≃	225b	19.42 S	45.22 E
Mahakam ≃	198	0.35 S	117.17 E
Mahalatswe	224	23.05 S	26.51 E
Mahānadi ≃	204	20.00 N	86.25 E
Mahanay Island I	202	10.11 N	124.13 E
Mahanoro	218	19.54 S	48.48 E
Mahanoy City	262	40.49 N	76.08 W
Mahārāshtra □[4]	206	19.00 N	76.00 E
Mahārlū, Daryācheh-ye ⊜	208	29.25 N	52.50 E
Maha Sarakham	200	16.12 N	103.16 E
Mahates	290	10.14 N	75.12 W
Maḩaţţat 'aqabat al-Ḩijāzīyah	210	29.44 N	35.52 E
Maḩaţţat Ḩaraḑ	214	24.08 N	49.05 E
Maḩaţţat Jurf ad-Darāwīsh	210	30.42 N	35.52 E
Mahaut	284d	15.21 N	61.25 W
Mahavavy ≃, Malg.	225b	15.57 S	45.54 E
Mahavavy ≃, Malg.	225b	13.00 S	48.55 E
Maḩbas, Wādī al- ∨	220	15.50 N	29.45 E
Mahd adh-Dhahab	214	23.30 N	40.52 E
Mahébourg	225c	20.24 S	57.42 E
Mahé Island I	218	4.40 S	55.28 E
Mahendraganj	206	25.20 N	89.45 E
Mahenge	218	8.41 S	36.43 E
Mahi ≃	206	22.15 N	73.00 E
Mahia Peninsula ≻[1]	230	39.10 S	177.54 E
Mahinerangi, Lake ⊜	230	45.51 S	170.03 E
Mahinog	202	9.09 N	124.47 E
Mahnomen	252	47.19 N	96.01 W
Mahogany Mountain ∧	256	43.14 N	117.16 W
Mahomet	268	40.12 N	88.24 W
Mahón	168	39.53 N	4.15 E
Mahone Bay	240	44.27 N	64.23 W
Mahone Bay C	240	44.30 N	64.15 W
Mahoning □[6]	266	41.06 N	80.39 W
Mahony Lake ⊜	236	65.30 N	125.20 W
Mahood Falls	238	51.50 N	120.39 W
Mahood Lake ⊜	238	51.55 N	120.24 W
Mahopac	261	41.22 N	73.45 W
Mahopac Falls	261	41.22 N	71.46 W
Mahora	168	39.13 N	1.44 W
Mahtomedi	244	45.04 N	92.57 W
Maia	168	41.14 N	8.37 W
Maicao	290	11.23 N	72.13 W
Maîche	166	47.15 N	6.48 E
Maici ≃	292	6.30 S	61.43 W
Maiden	246	35.35 N	81.13 W
Maidenhead	174	51.32 N	0.44 W
Maidstone, Ont., Can.	266	42.13 N	82.53 W
Maidstone, Eng., U.K.	174	51.17 N	0.32 E
Maiduguri	214	11.51 N	13.10 E
Maignelay	166	49.33 N	2.31 E
Maigneley	162	49.33 N	2.31 E
Maigo	202	8.10 N	123.57 E
Maijoma	250	28.55 N	104.21 W
Maikala Range ⋀	206	22.00 N	81.00 E
Maikoor, Pulau I	198	6.15 S	134.15 E
Maili	275c	21.25 N	158.11 W
Maillezais	166	46.22 N	0.44 W
Maimāna	206	35.55 N	64.38 E
Maimbung	202	5.56 N	121.02 E
Main ≃	164	50.00 N	8.18 E
Mainart ≃	296	20.27 S	43.17 W
Main Barrier Range ⋀	228	31.25 S	141.25 E
Mainburg	164	48.38 N	11.47 E
Main Channel ⊔	244	45.22 N	81.50 W
Maine □[9]	166	48.15 N	0.05 W
Maine □[3]	234	45.15 N	69.15 W
Maine-et-Loire □[5]	166	47.25 N	0.30 W
Mainhardt	164	49.04 N	9.33 E
Mainit	202	9.31 N	125.31 E
Mainit, Lake ⊜	202	9.27 N	125.30 E
Mainland I, Scot., U.K.	162	60.20 N	1.22 W
Mainland I, Scot., U.K.	162	59.00 N	3.10 W
Maintenon	166	48.35 N	1.35 E
Maintirano	218	18.03 S	44.01 E
Main Topsail ∧	240	49.08 N	56.33 W
Mainz	164	50.01 N	8.16 E
Maio I	222a	15.15 N	23.10 W
Maiori	184	40.39 N	14.38 E
Maipo ≃	294	33.37 S	71.39 W
Maipo, Volcán ∧[1]	294	34.10 S	69.50 W
Maipú, Arg.	294	36.52 S	57.54 W
Maipú, Arg.	294	33.00 S	68.47 W
Maipú, Chile	294	33.31 S	70.46 W
Maiquetía	290	10.36 N	66.57 W
Mairipotaba	296	17.18 S	49.28 W
Maisí, Cabo ≻	284p	20.17 N	74.09 W
Maiskhāl Island I	206	21.36 N	91.56 E
Maisons-Laffitte	176	48.57 N	2.09 E
Maitengwe ≃	224	19.59 S	26.26 E
Maitland, Austl.	228	32.44 S	151.33 E
Maitland, N.S., Can.	240	45.19 N	63.30 W
Maitland, Ont., Can.	264	44.38 N	75.37 W
Maitland, Mo., U.S.	248	40.12 N	95.05 W
Maitland ≃	244	43.45 N	81.43 W
Maíz ≃	280	11.18 N	83.52 W
Maizuru	192	35.27 N	135.20 E
Maja ≃	186	54.31 N	134.41 E
Majagua	284p	21.55 N	79.00 W
Majagual	290	8.33 N	74.38 W
Majari ≃	290	3.29 N	60.58 W
Majenica	268	40.46 N	85.27 W
Majes, Río de ≃	292	16.40 S	72.44 W
Majevica ⋀	172	44.30 N	18.55 E
Maji	214	6.11 N	35.38 E
Majiahe ≃	194	38.09 N	117.53 E
Majinxi ≃	196	29.00 N	118.21 E
Majja	186	61.44 N	130.18 E
Majkain	186	51.27 N	75.52 E
Majkop	158	44.35 N	40.07 E
Majkor	160	59.01 N	55.54 E
Majnic, Ozero ⊜	236	63.15 N	176.40 E
Majno-Gytkino	236	63.36 N	176.30 E
Majno-Pyl'gino, S.S.S.R.	186		
	236	62.32 N	177.02 E
Majorca → Mallorca I	168	39.30 N	3.00 E
Majrūr, Wādī ∨	220	15.44 N	26.26 E
Majskij	186	52.18 N	129.38 E
Majskoje	186	50.55 N	78.15 E
Majunga	225b	15.43 S	46.19 E
Majunga □[4]	225b	17.00 S	46.00 E
Makabana	218	2.48 S	12.29 E
Makadasa ≃	202	7.13 N	124.15 E
Makaha	275c	21.28 N	158.13 W
Makah Indian Reservation ◂[4]	256	48.20 N	124.41 W
Makahuena Point ≻	275d	21.52 N	159.27 W
Makale	198	3.06 S	119.51 E
Makallé	294	27.12 S	59.21 W
Makālu ∧	206	27.54 N	87.06 E
Makapuu Head ≻	275d	21.19 N	157.39 W
Makar-Ib	160	63.39 N	49.24 E
Makaricha	160	66.15 N	58.20 E
Makarjev	160	57.52 N	43.48 E
Makarov	186	50.28 N	29.49 E
Makarska	170	43.18 N	17.02 E
Makasar	198	5.07 S	119.24 E
Makasar, Selat (Makassar Strait) ⊔	198	2.00 S	117.30 E
Makassar Strait → Makasar, Selat ⊔	198	2.00 S	117.30 E
Makat	158	47.39 N	53.19 E
Makawao	275a	20.52 N	156.19 W
Makaweli	275b	21.55 N	159.38 W
Makay, Massif du ⋀	225b	21.15 S	45.15 E
Makaza)(	172	41.16 N	25.26 E
Makedonija □[3]	172	41.50 N	22.00 E
Makehahu ⊜	206	35.00 N	83.03 E
Makejevka	158	48.02 N	37.58 E
Makemie Park	262	37.55 N	75.34 W
Makena	275a	20.39 N	156.27 W
Makeni	222	8.53 N	12.03 W
Makgadikgadi Pans ≚	224	20.45 S	25.30 E
Makhachkala → Machačkala	000	42.58 N	47.30 E
Maki	192	37.45 N	138.53 E
Makilala	202	6.55 N	125.05 E
Makindu	218	2.17 S	37.49 E
Makinsk	186	52.37 N	70.26 E
M'akit	186	61.24 N	152.09 E
Makkah (Mecca)	214	21.27 N	39.49 E
Maklakovo	186	58.16 N	92.29 E
Makó	164	46.13 N	20.29 E
Makobe Lake ⊜	244	47.27 N	80.25 W
Makokou	218	0.34 N	12.52 E
Makorako ∧	230	39.09 S	176.02 E
Makoua	218	0.01 N	15.39 E
Makov	164	49.23 N	18.30 E
Maków Mazowiecki	164	52.52 N	21.06 E
Maków Podhalański	164	49.44 N	19.41 E
M'aksa	160	58.54 N	38.12 E
Maksaticha	160	57.48 N	35.53 E
Makthar	170	35.51 N	9.12 E
Makumbi	218	5.51 S	20.41 E
Makurazaki	192	31.16 N	130.19 E
Makurdi	222	7.45 N	8.32 E
Makushin Volcano ∧[1]	236	53.53 N	166.50 W
Makwassie	218	27.26 S	26.00 E
Mala	292	12.40 S	76.38 W
Mala, Punta ≻, C.R.	280	9.02 N	83.38 W
Mala, Punta ≻, Pan.	290	7.28 N	80.02 W
Mala, Río de ≃	292	12.42 S	76.41 W
Malabang	202	7.36 N	124.04 E
Malabon	202	14.39 N	120.57 E
Malabrigo Point ≻	202	13.36 N	121.25 E
Malabuyoc	202	9.39 N	123.20 E
Malacacheta	296	17.50 S	42.05 W
Malacca	200	2.11 N	102.16 E
Malacca □[3]	200	2.15 N	102.15 E
Malacca, Strait of ⊔	200	2.30 N	101.20 E
Malacky	164	48.27 N	17.00 E
Malad City	256	42.12 N	112.15 W
Málaga, Col.	290	6.42 N	72.44 W
Málaga, Esp.	168	36.43 N	4.25 W
Malaga, Calif., U.S.	272	36.42 N	119.46 W
Malaga, N.J., U.S.	262	39.34 N	75.02 W
Malaga, N. Mex., U.S.	250	32.14 N	104.04 W
Malagash	240	45.46 N	63.23 W
Malagasy Republic □[1]	218	19.00 S	46.00 E
Malago ≃	202	10.55 N	123.02 E
Malagón	168	39.10 N	3.51 W
Malagón ≃	168	37.35 N	7.29 W
Malagrotta ◂[8]	184	41.53 N	12.20 E
Malahat	270	48.32 N	123.34 W
Malaimbandy	218	20.20 S	45.36 E
Malaja Kuril'skaja Gr'ada (Habomai-shotō) II	192a	43.30 N	146.10 E
Malaja Pera	160	64.11 N	54.47 E
Malaja Višera	160	58.51 N	32.14 E
Malaka, Lintasan ⊔	200	5.40 N	95.25 E
Malakāl	220	9.31 N	31.39 E
Mala Kapela ⋀	170	44.50 N	15.30 E
Malakoff	250	32.10 N	96.01 W
Malalag	202	6.36 N	125.23 E
Malamaui Island I	202	6.44 N	121.57 E
Malambunga	202	9.02 N	117.38 E
Malampaya Sound ⊔	202	10.50 N	119.20 E
Malān, Rās ≻	208	25.18 N	65.11 E
Malanao Island I	202	9.27 N	118.48 E
Malanas ≃	202	17.40 N	120.42 E
Malang	226	7.59 S	112.37 E
Malangas	202	7.37 N	123.01 E
Malanipa Island I	202	6.52 N	122.18 E
Malanje	218	9.32 S	16.20 E
Malanut Bay C	202	9.18 N	118.00 E
Malanville	214	11.52 N	3.23 E
Malanzán	294	30.49 S	66.37 W
Mała Panew ≃	164	50.44 N	17.52 E
Malapantao, Mount ∧	202	9.53 N	122.49 E
Malapascua Island I	202	11.20 N	124.07 E
Mälaren ⊜	158	59.30 N	17.12 E
Malargüe	294	35.30 S	69.35 W
Malartic	244	48.08 N	78.08 W
Malartic, Lac ⊜	244	48.15 N	78.05 W
Malasiqui	202	15.55 N	120.24 E
Malaspina Glacier ⊿	236	59.50 N	140.30 W
Malaspina Strait ⊔	238	49.44 N	124.20 W
Malåträsk	160	65.11 N	18.44 E
Malatya	212	38.21 N	38.19 E
Malaucène	166	44.10 N	5.08 E
Malawali, Pulau I	202	7.03 N	117.18 E
Malawi □[1]	218	12.00 S	34.30 E
Malawi, Lake → Nyasa, Lake ⊜	218	12.00 S	34.30 E
Malayal	202	7.12 N	121.56 E
Malaybalay	202	8.09 N	125.05 E
Malāyer	208	34.17 N	48.50 E
Malay Peninsula ≻[1]	200	6.00 N	102.00 E
Malay Reef ⟡[2]	228	17.59 S	149.18 E
Malaysia □[1]	198	3.00 N	103.00 E
Malazán, Sierra de ⋀	294	30.50 S	66.20 W
Malazgirt	208	39.09 N	42.31 E
Mal Baie C	240	48.35 N	64.16 W
Malbaie ≃	240	47.40 N	70.05 W
Malbork (Marienburg)	164	54.02 N	19.01 E
Malbrán	294	29.21 S	62.27 W
Malchin	164	53.44 N	12.46 E
Malchow	164	53.28 N	12.25 E
Malcolm	226	28.56 S	121.30 E
Malcom	244	41.43 N	92.33 W
Malczyce (Maltsch)	164	51.14 N	16.29 E
Maldegem, Bel.	176	51.13 N	3.27 E
Maldegem, Ned.	164	51.13 N	3.27 E
Malden, Mass., U.S.	261	42.26 N	71.04 W
Malden, Mo., U.S.	248	36.34 N	89.57 W
Malden Bridge	261	42.28 N	73.35 W
Malden-on-hudson	261	42.06 N	73.56 W
Maldive Islands II	148	5.00 N	73.00 E
Maldon	174	51.45 N	0.40 E
Maldonado	294	34.54 S	54.57 W
Male	170	46.21 N	10.55 E
Maléa, Ákra ≻	172	36.26 N	23.12 E
Maleit, Lake ⊜	220	7.55 N	28.35 E
Malen'ga	160	63.50 N	36.25 E
Malente	164	54.10 N	10.33 E
Malesherbes	166	48.18 N	2.25 E
Malestroit	166	47.49 N	2.23 W
Malha Wells	214	15.08 N	26.12 E
Malheur ≃	256	44.03 N	116.59 W
Malheur Lake ⊜	256	43.20 N	118.45 W
Mali □[4]	222	12.05 N	12.05 W
Mali □[1]	214	17.00 N	4.00 W
Mali ≃	200	25.43 N	97.29 E
Malibu	274	34.02 N	118.42 W
Maligay Bay C	202	7.28 N	123.13 E
Maligne ≃	238	52.56 N	118.02 W
Maligne Lake ⊜	238	52.40 N	117.31 W
Malik, Wādī al- ∨	220	18.02 N	30.58 E
Mali Kyun I	200	13.06 N	98.16 E
Malimono	202	9.34 N	125.25 E
Malin	256	42.01 N	121.24 W
Malinalco ⊥	278	18.57 N	99.30 W
Malinaltepec	278	17.03 N	98.40 W
Malinau	198	3.35 N	116.38 E
Malindang, Mount ∧	202	8.13 N	123.40 E
Malindi	218	3.13 S	40.07 E
Malines → Mechelen	176	51.02 N	4.28 E
Malingguan)(	194	37.20 N	114.00 E
Malin Head ≻	162	55.23 N	7.24 W
Malinta	268	41.19 N	84.02 W
Mali Rajinac ∧	170	44.48 N	15.02 E
Malita	202	6.25 N	125.36 E
Malitbog	202	10.10 N	125.00 E
Maljamar	250	32.51 N	103.46 W
Malka	186	53.20 N	157.30 E
Malkara	172	40.53 N	26.54 E
Malko Târnovo	172	41.59 N	27.32 E
Mallacoota National Park ▲	228	37.30 S	149.50 E
Mallaig, Alta., Can.	238	54.13 N	111.22 W
Mallaig, Scot., U.K.	162	57.00 N	5.50 W
Mallawī	220	27.44 N	30.50 E
Malleco □[4]	294	38.10 S	72.20 W
Mallersdorf	164	48.47 N	12.16 E
Mallery Lake ⊜	232	63.55 N	98.25 W
Malles Venosta (Mals)	170	46.41 N	10.32 E
Mallet	294	25.55 S	50.50 W
Mallig	202	17.10 N	121.40 E
Malligasta	294	29.11 S	67.24 W
Mallnitz	164	46.59 N	13.10 E
Mallorca I	168	39.30 N	3.00 E
Mallorytown	264	44.29 N	75.53 W
Mallow	162	52.08 N	8.39 W
Mallwood	268	42.51 N	89.02 W
Malm	160	64.04 N	11.13 E
Malmberget	160	67.10 N	20.40 E
Malmedy	164	50.25 N	6.02 E
Malmesbury	224	33.28 S	18.44 E
Malmö	160	55.36 N	13.00 E
Malmöhus Län □[6]	160	55.45 N	13.30 E
Malmyž	160	56.31 N	50.41 E
Malna	202	8.08 N	124.27 E
Malnate	182	45.48 N	8.53 E
Maloja	166	46.24 N	9.41 E
Malojaroslavec	158	55.01 N	36.28 E
Malo-les-Bains	176	51.03 N	2.24 E
Malolos	202	14.51 N	120.49 E
Maloma ≃	160	58.20 N	48.28 E
Malone, Fla., U.S.	246	30.57 N	85.10 W
Malone, N.Y., U.S.	242	44.51 N	74.17 W
Malone, Wash., U.S.	270	46.58 N	123.20 W
Malonga	218	10.24 S	23.10 E
Małopolska ◂[1]	164	50.30 N	20.30 E
Malošujka	160	63.45 N	37.22 E
Malott	238	48.17 N	119.42 W
Małowice (Mallwitz)	164	51.34 N	15.27 E
Måløy	160	61.56 N	5.07 E
Malozemel'skaja Tundra ◂[1]	160	67.50 N	51.00 E
Malpaisillo	280	12.35 N	86.41 W
Malpartida de Plasencia	168	39.59 N	6.02 W
Malpaso, Presa de ⊜[1]	278	17.10 N	93.40 W
Malpelo, Isla de I	286	3.59 N	81.35 W
Malpeque Bay C	240	46.30 N	63.47 W
Målselv ≃	160	69.14 N	18.30 E
Malta, Ill., U.S.	268	41.56 N	88.52 W
Malta, Mont., U.S.	256	48.21 N	107.52 W
Malta, Ohio, U.S.	242	39.39 N	81.52 W
Malta □[1]	158	35.50 N	14.35 E
Malta I	170	35.53 N	14.27 E
Maltahöhe	218	24.50 S	17.00 E
Maltahöhe □[5]	224	25.00 S	16.30 E
Malte Brun, Mount ∧	230	43.33 S	170.18 E
Maltepe	172	40.02 N	27.58 E
Malton, Ont., Can.	264	43.42 N	79.38 W
Malton, Eng., U.K.	162	54.08 N	0.48 W
Malu	172	44.15 N	23.51 E
Maluku II	198	2.00 S	128.00 E
Maluku, Laut ⊤[2]	198	0.30 S	125.00 E
Malung	160	60.40 N	13.44 E
Maluso	202	6.33 N	121.53 E
Malvern, Ark., U.S.	248	34.22 N	92.49 W
Malvern, Iowa, U.S.	252	41.00 N	95.35 W
Malvern, Ohio, U.S.	266	40.41 N	81.11 W
Malvinas	294	29.36 S	58.59 W
Malý Dunaj ≃	164	48.08 N	17.09 E
Malyje Karmakuly	186	72.23 N	52.44 E
Malyj Kavkaz ⋀	158	41.00 N	44.35 E
Malyj L'achovskij, Ostrov I	186	74.07 N	140.36 E
Malyj Tajmyr, Ostrov I	186	78.08 N	107.12 E
Malyj Uzen' ≃	186	48.50 N	49.39 E
Malzéville	180	48.43 N	6.12 E
Mama	186	58.18 N	112.54 E
Mamadyš	160	55.44 N	51.25 E
Mamaia	172	44.15 N	28.19 E
Mamara	292	14.14 S	72.35 W
Mamaroneck	261	40.57 N	73.44 W
Mambaí	296	14.28 S	46.07 W
Mambajao	202	9.15 N	124.43 E
Mambajao, Mount ∧	202	9.10 N	124.43 E
Mambalot	202	8.51 N	117.55 E
Mamberamo ≃	198	1.26 S	137.53 E
Mambéré ≃	214	3.31 N	16.03 E
Mamburao	202	13.13 N	120.35 E
Mambusao ≃	202	11.25 N	122.45 E
Ma-Me-O Beach	238	52.58 N	113.59 W
Mamers	166	48.21 N	0.23 E
Mamfe	214	5.46 N	9.17 E
Mamiá, Lago ⊜	290	4.15 S	63.03 W
Mamie	246	36.08 N	75.50 W
Mamiña	292	20.05 S	69.14 W
Mammola	170	38.22 N	16.15 E
Mammoth, Ariz., U.S.	254	32.43 N	110.38 W
Mammoth, Pa., U.S.	266	40.12 N	79.28 W
Mammoth, W. Va., U.S.	242	38.16 N	81.22 W
Mammoth Cave National Park ▲	248	37.08 N	86.13 W
Mammoth Lakes	258	37.38 N	118.58 W
Mammoth Spring	248	36.30 N	91.33 W
Mamonovo [Heiligenbeil]	164	54.28 N	19.57 E
Mamoré ≃	292	10.23 S	65.53 W
Mamori, Lago ⊜	290	3.38 S	60.07 W
Mamoriá ≃	292	7.30 S	66.21 W
Mamoriàzinho ≃	292	7.27 S	65.18 W
Mamoritanas ≃	290	1.39 S	67.22 W
Mamou, Guin.	214	10.23 N	12.05 W
Mamou, La., U.S.	248	30.38 N	92.25 W
Mamou □[4]	222	10.30 N	12.00 W
Mampikony	218	16.06 S	47.38 E
Mamry, Jezioro ⊜	164	54.08 N	21.42 E
Mamulique	250	26.08 N	100.20 W
Mamuru ≃	290	2.42 S	56.44 W
Mamykovo	160	54.38 N	50.37 E
Mamyl'	160	61.57 N	56.41 E
Man, C. Iv.	222	7.24 N	7.33 W
Man, W. Va., U.S.	246	37.45 N	81.53 W
Man □[5]	222	7.15 N	7.30 W
Man, Isle of → Isle of Man □[2]	158	54.15 N	4.30 W
Mana	275b	22.02 N	159.46 W
Mana ≃	286	5.45 N	53.55 W
Manabí □[4]	290	0.40 S	80.05 W
Manabique, Punta de ≻	280	15.56 N	88.37 W
Manacá ≃	290	2.52 S	61.50 W
Manacacías ≃	290	4.23 N	72.04 W
Manacapuru	290	3.18 S	60.37 W
Manacor	168	39.34 N	3.12 E
Manado	198	1.29 N	124.51 E
Managua	280	12.09 N	86.17 W
Managua □[5]	280	12.00 N	86.25 W
Managua, Lago de ⊜	280	12.18 N	86.20 W
Manahawkin	262	39.42 N	74.16 W
Manahiki I[1]	148	10.24 S	161.01 W
Manakalampona ∧	225b	15.23 S	48.50 E
Manakara	225b	22.08 S	48.01 E
Manakau ∧	230	42.14 S	173.37 E
Manam I	198	4.05 S	145.05 E
Manama → Al-Manāmah	208	26.13 N	50.35 E
Manambaroa ≃	225b	17.41 S	44.04 E
Manambolo ≃	225b	19.18 S	44.24 E
Mánamo, Caño ≃[1]	290	9.55 N	62.16 W
Manamoc Island I	202	11.18 N	120.40 E
Mananantanana ≃	225b	21.25 S	45.33 E
Mananao	202	13.30 N	120.34 E
Mananara	218	16.10 S	49.46 E
Mananara ≃	225b	23.21 S	47.42 E
Mananjary	225b	21.13 S	48.20 E
Manaoag	202	16.02 N	120.29 E
Manapiare ≃	290	5.04 N	66.30 W
Manapire ≃	290	7.42 N	66.07 W
Manapla	202	10.58 N	123.07 E
Manapouri, Lake ⊜	230	45.32 S	167.31 E
Manaquiri, Lago ⊜	290	3.29 S	60.31 W
Manās ≃	206	26.12 N	90.40 E
Ma'nasaluowochi ⊜	206	30.42 N	81.27 E
Ma'nasi	190	44.18 N	86.13 E
Manāslu ∧	206	28.33 N	84.35 E
Manasquan	262	40.07 N	74.03 W
Manassa	254	37.11 N	105.56 W
Manassas	262	38.45 N	77.28 W
Manassas National Battlefield Park ▲	242	38.48 N	77.34 W
Manassas Park	262	38.47 N	77.28 W
Maná-Tará, Cerro ∧	290	10.06 N	72.52 W
Manatawny	262	40.17 N	75.41 W
Manatee ≃	246	27.32 N	82.38 W
Manatí, Col.	290	10.27 N	74.58 W
Manatí, Cuba	284p	21.19 N	76.56 W
Manatí, P.R.	284m	18.26 N	66.29 W
Manatí ≃	284p	21.40 N	79.50 W
Manaul	202	12.27 N	121.25 E
Manaus	290	3.08 S	60.01 W
Manawa	244	44.28 N	88.55 W
Manawatu ≃	230	40.28 S	175.13 E
Manay	202	7.12 N	126.32 E
Mancelona	244	44.54 N	85.04 W
Mancha Real	168	37.47 N	3.37 W
Manchaug	261	42.06 N	71.45 W
Manche □[5]	166	49.00 N	1.10 W
Manchester, Eng., U.K.	162	53.30 N	2.15 W
Manchester, Conn., U.S.	261	41.47 N	72.31 W
Manchester, Ga., U.S.	246	32.51 N	84.37 W
Manchester, Iowa, U.S.	244	42.29 N	91.27 W
Manchester, Ky., U.S.	246	37.09 N	83.46 W
Manchester, Mass., U.S.	261	42.34 N	70.46 W
Manchester, Mich., U.S.	268	42.09 N	84.02 W
Manchester, N.H., U.S.	242	42.59 N	71.28 W
Manchester, N.Y., U.S.	264	42.58 N	77.14 W
Manchester, Ohio, U.S.	242	38.41 N	83.36 W
Manchester, Pa., U.S.	262	40.04 N	76.43 W
Manchester, Tenn., U.S.	248	35.29 N	86.05 W
Manchester, Vt., U.S.	242	43.10 N	73.05 W
Manchester, Wash., U.S.	270	47.33 N	122.33 W
Manchester Bridge	261	41.41 N	73.52 W
Manchioneal	285q	18.02 N	76.17 W
Manchouli → Manzhouli	190	49.35 N	117.22 E
Manchuria ◂[1]	190	47.00 N	125.00 E
Manciano	184	42.35 N	11.31 E
Mancornado, Isla I	280	11.10 N	85.01 W
Mancos	254	37.21 N	108.18 W
Mand ≃	208	28.11 N	51.17 E
Manda	218	10.28 S	34.35 E
Manda, Jabal ∧	220	8.39 N	24.27 E
Mandabe	218	21.03 S	44.55 E
Mandaguaçu	296	23.20 S	52.05 W
Mandaguari	296	23.32 S	51.42 W
Mandal	160	58.02 N	7.27 E
Mandal, Jibāl ∧[2]	220	12.09 N	29.31 E
Mandala, Puntjak ∧	198	4.40 S	140.16 E
Mandalay	200	22.00 N	96.05 E
Mandalay □[5]	200	22.00 N	96.00 E
Mandale	268	41.01 N	84.20 W
Mandalgov'	190	45.45 N	106.20 E
Mandalī	208	33.45 N	45.32 E
Mandalya Körfezi C	212	37.12 N	27.20 E
Mandan	252	46.50 N	100.54 W
Mandara Mountains ⋀	214	10.45 N	13.40 E
Mandas	170	39.39 N	9.08 E
Mandasor	206	24.04 N	75.04 E
Mandaue	202	10.20 N	123.56 E
Mandeb, Bab el- ⊔	214	12.40 N	43.20 E
Mandello del Lario	180	45.54 N	9.19 E
Manderson	256	44.16 N	107.58 W
Mandeure	180	47.27 N	6.48 E
Mandeville, Qué., Can.	260	46.21 N	73.21 W
Mandeville, Jam.	285q	18.02 N	77.30 W
Mandeville, La., U.S.	248	30.22 N	90.04 W
Mandimba	218	14.21 S	35.39 E
Mandinga	290	9.32 N	79.04 W
Mandioli, Pulau I	198	0.44 S	127.14 E
Mandioré, Lagoa ⊜	292	18.08 S	57.33 W
Mandrare ≃	225b	25.10 S	46.27 E
Mandritsara	218	15.50 S	48.49 E
Manduri	296	23.01 S	49.19 W
Manduria	170	40.24 N	17.38 E
Māndvi	206	22.50 N	69.22 E
Maneadero ≃	284p	21.36 N	78.50 W
Máneora	290	4.06 S	81.05 W
Manerbio	170	45.21 N	10.08 E
Manfalūţ	214	27.19 N	30.58 E
Manfredonia	184	41.38 N	15.55 E
Manga	296	14.46 S	43.56 W
Mangagoy	202	8.11 N	126.21 E
Mangahao ≃	230	40.23 S	175.50 E
Mangakino	230	38.22 S	175.47 E
Mangalia	172	43.50 N	28.10 E
Mangatarem	202	15.47 N	120.18 E
Mangaweka ∧	230	39.49 S	176.05 E
Mangcao Point ≻	202	11.01 N	123.54 E
Mangchang	190	25.08 N	107.31 E
Mangham	248	32.19 N	91.47 W
Mangin Range ⋀	200	24.20 N	95.42 E
Mangkalihat, Tandjung ≻	198	1.02 N	118.59 E
Manglares, Cabo ≻	290	1.36 N	79.02 W
Mangoche	218	14.28 S	35.16 E
Mangoky ≃, Malg.	225b	23.27 S	45.13 E
Mangoky ≃, Malg.	225b	21.29 S	43.41 E
Mangole, Pulau I	198	1.53 S	125.50 E
Mangoro ≃	225b	20.00 S	48.45 E
Mangotsfield	174	51.28 N	2.28 W
Mangrove Cay I	282	24.10 N	77.45 W
Mangualde	168	40.36 N	7.46 W
Mangueira, Lagoa C	294	33.06 S	52.48 W
Mangueirinha	294	25.57 S	52.09 W
Manguito	284p	22.35 N	80.55 W
Mangulile	280	15.03 N	86.49 W
Mangum	250	34.53 N	99.30 W
Mangya	190	37.40 N	90.50 E
Manhã	296	12.43 S	46.24 W
Manhattan, Ill., U.S.	268	41.25 N	87.59 W
Manhattan, Kans., U.S.	252	39.11 N	96.35 W
Manhattan, Mont., U.S.	256	45.52 N	111.20 W
Manhattan Beach	274	33.54 N	118.24 W
Manheim	262	40.10 N	76.24 W
Manhuaçu	296	20.15 S	42.02 W
Manhuaçu ≃	296	19.30 S	41.06 W
Manhumirim	296	20.22 S	41.57 W
Maní	284m	18.15 N	67.10 W
Mania ≃	225b	19.42 S	45.22 E
Maniago	170	46.10 N	12.43 E
Maniamba	218	12.43 S	35.00 E
Manica e Sofala □[5]	224	19.00 S	34.00 E
Manicahan	202	7.01 N	122.12 E
Manicaland □[4]	224	19.30 S	32.15 E
Manicani Island I	202	11.00 N	125.38 E
Manicaragua	284p	22.09 N	79.58 W
Manicoré	292	5.49 S	61.17 W
Manicoré ≃	292	5.51 S	61.19 W
Manicouagane ≃	240	49.15 N	68.20 W
Manicouagane, Lac ⊜[1]	240	51.30 N	68.19 W
Maniguin Island I	202	11.36 N	121.42 E
Manila, Pil.	202	14.35 N	120.59 E
Manila, Ark., U.S.	248	35.53 N	90.10 W
Manila, Utah, U.S.	254	40.59 N	109.43 W
Manila Bay C	202	14.35 N	120.45 E
Manily	186	62.29 N	165.36 E
Manindjau, Danau ⊜	200	0.20 S	100.11 E
Maningory ≃	225b	17.13 S	49.28 E
Manipa, Selat ⊔	198	3.20 S	127.23 E
Manipur □[8]	206	25.00 N	94.00 E
Manisa	212	38.36 N	27.26 E
Manisa □[4]	172	38.50 N	28.10 E
Manistee	244	44.15 N	86.19 W
Manistee ≃	244	44.15 N	86.21 W
Manistique	244	45.57 N	86.15 W
Manistique ≃	244	45.57 N	86.15 W
Manistique Lake ⊜	244	46.15 N	85.45 W
Manito	248	40.25 N	89.47 W
Manitoba □[3]	232	54.00 N	97.00 W
Manitoba, Lake ⊜	232	51.00 N	98.45 W
Manitou	252	49.15 N	98.31 W
Manitou, Lac ⊜, Qué., Can.	240	50.52 N	65.17 W
Manitou, Lac ⊜, Qué., Can.	240	50.29 N	63.53 W
Manitou Beach	268	41.58 N	84.19 W
Manitou Lake ⊜	244	45.48 N	82.00 W
Manitoulin Island I	244	45.45 N	82.30 W
Manitou Springs	254	38.52 N	104.55 W
Manitowaning	244	45.45 N	81.49 W
Manitowik Lake ⊜	244	48.10 N	84.24 W
Manitowish Waters	244	46.09 N	89.53 W
Manitowoc	244	44.06 N	87.40 W
Manitowoc ≃	244	44.05 N	87.39 W
Maniwaki	242	46.23 N	75.58 W
Manizales	290	5.05 N	75.32 W
Manja	218	21.26 S	44.20 E
Manjacaze	218	24.44 S	33.53 E
Manjimup	226	34.14 S	116.09 E
Manjuyod	202	9.41 N	123.09 E
Mankato, Kans., U.S.	252	39.47 N	98.12 W
Mankato, Minn., U.S.	244	44.10 N	94.01 W
Mankoya	218	14.47 S	24.48 E
Manley Hot Springs	236	65.00 N	150.37 W
Manlius	264	43.01 N	75.59 W
Manlléu	168	42.00 N	2.17 E
Manly	244	43.17 N	93.12 W
Manna	198	4.27 S	102.55 E

Symbols in the index entries are identified on page 360.

Name	Page	Lat°′	Long°′
Mannar, Gulf of C	204	8.30 N	79.00 E
Männedorf	180	47.15 N	8.42 E
Mannheim	164	49.29 N	8.29 E
Manning, N. Dak., U.S.	252	47.14 N	102.47 W
Manning, S.C., U.S.	246	33.42 N	80.13 W
Mannington	242	39.32 N	80.20 W
Mannsville	264	43.43 N	76.04 W
Mannu ≃	170	40.50 N	8.23 E
Mannville	238	53.20 N	111.10 W
Mano ≃	222	6.56 N	11.31 W
Manoa	292	9.40 S	65.27 W
Manokotak	236	58.40 N	159.09 W
Manokwari	198	0.52 S	134.05 E
Manolo Fortich (Maluko)	202	8.25 N	124.57 E
Manomet	261	41.55 N	70.34 W
Manono	218	7.18 S	27.25 E
Manor, Sask., Can.	252	49.36 N	102.05 W
Manor, Pa., U.S.	266	40.20 N	79.40 W
Manor, Tex., U.S.	250	30.20 N	97.33 W
Manorhamilton	162	54.18 N	8.10 W
Manor Hill	266	40.38 N	77.55 W
Manorville	266	40.48 N	79.31 W
Manosque	182	43.50 N	5.47 E
Manotick	264	45.15 N	75.37 W
Manouane ≃	240	49.29 N	71.13 W
Manouane, Lac ⊜	240	50.40 N	70.45 W
Manouanis ≃	240	50.37 N	70.18 W
Manouanis, Lac ⊜	240	50.51 N	70.17 W
Manouba	170	36.50 N	10.06 E
Manresa	168	41.44 N	1.50 E
Mansa	218	11.12 S	28.53 E
Mansalay	202	12.31 N	121.26 E
Manseau	260	46.22 N	72.00 W
Mansel Island I	232	62.00 N	79.50 W
Mansfield, Eng., U.K.	174	53.09 N	1.11 W
Mansfield, Ark., U.S.	248	35.04 N	94.13 W
Mansfield, Ga., U.S.	246	33.31 N	83.44 W
Mansfield, Ill., U.S.	268	40.13 N	88.31 W
Mansfield, La., U.S.	248	32.02 N	93.43 W
Mansfield, Mass., U.S.	261	42.02 N	71.13 W
Mansfield, Mo., U.S.	248	37.06 N	92.35 W
Mansfield, Ohio, U.S.	266	40.46 N	82.31 W
Mansfield, Pa., U.S.	242	41.48 N	77.05 W
Mansfield, Tex., U.S.	250	32.34 N	97.09 W
Mansfield, Mount ∧	242	44.33 N	72.49 W
Mansfield Center	261	41.50 N	72.16 W
Mansfield Woodhouse	174	53.11 N	1.12 W
Mansle	166	45.53 N	0.11 E
Manso ≃, Bra.	296	14.42 S	56.16 W
Manso ≃, Bra.	296	13.18 S	46.51 W
Manson, Iowa, U.S.	252	42.32 N	94.32 W
Manson, Wash., U.S.	238	47.53 N	120.09 W
Manson ≃	238	55.42 N	123.47 W
Mansonville	260	45.03 N	72.24 W
Mansura → Al-Manşūrah, Mişr	220	31.03 N	31.23 E
Mansura, La., U.S.	248	31.04 N	92.03 W
Manta	290	0.57 S	80.44 W
Manta, Bahía de C	290	0.54 S	80.44 W
Mantabuan Island I	202	5.01 N	120.13 E
Mantalingajan, Mount ∧	202	8.50 N	117.40 E
Mantalingajan Range ⋀	202	8.50 N	117.43 E
Mantangule Island I	202	8.10 N	117.10 E
Mantaro ≃	292	12.15 S	73.58 W
Manteca	272	37.48 N	121.13 W
Mantecal	290	7.33 N	69.09 W
Mantekamuhu ⊜	206	34.30 N	89.15 E
Manteno	268	41.14 N	88.12 W
Manteo	246	35.55 N	75.40 W
Mantes-la-Jolie	176	48.59 N	1.43 E
Manti	254	39.16 N	111.38 W
Manticao	202	8.23 N	124.16 E
Mantiqueira, Serra da ⋀	296	22.00 S	44.45 W
Manton	244	44.24 N	85.24 W
Mantorville	244	44.05 N	92.45 W
Mantos Blancos	294	23.25 S	70.05 W
Mantova	170	45.09 N	10.48 E
Mantua, Cuba	284p	22.17 N	84.17 W
Mantua → Mantova, It.	170	45.09 N	10.48 E
Mantua, N.J., U.S.	262	39.48 N	75.10 W
Mantua, Ohio, U.S.	266	41.17 N	81.14 W
Mantua ≃	284p	22.08 N	84.21 W
Manturovo	160	58.20 N	44.46 E
Mäntyharju	160	61.25 N	26.53 E
Mäntyluoto	160	61.35 N	21.29 E
Manu	292	12.25 S	70.51 W
Manu ≃	292	12.16 S	70.55 W
Manu Chico ≃	292	11.41 S	71.48 W
Manuel	278	22.44 N	98.19 W
Manuel Benavides	278	29.05 N	103.55 W
Manuel Derqui	294	27.51 S	58.47 W
Manuel Ribas	294	24.31 S	51.39 W
Manuel Urbano	292	8.53 S	69.18 W
Manuherikia ≃	230	45.16 S	169.24 E
Manui, Pulau I	198	3.35 S	123.08 E
Manukan	202	8.31 N	123.06 E
Manukau	230	37.02 S	174.54 E
Manukau Harbour C	230	37.01 S	174.44 E
Manupari ≃	292	11.50 S	67.16 W
Manurimi ≃	292	11.42 S	67.16 W
Manuripi ≃	292	11.07 S	67.36 W
Manvel	252	48.04 N	97.10 W
Manville, N.J., U.S.	262	40.32 N	74.36 W
Manville, R.I., U.S.	261	41.58 N	71.28 W
Manville, Wyo., U.S.	254	42.47 N	104.37 W
Many	248	31.34 N	93.29 W
Manyara, Lake ⊜	218	3.35 S	35.50 E
Manyas Gölü ⊜	212	40.10 N	27.57 E
Manyberries	256	49.24 N	110.42 W
Manyč ≃	186	47.15 N	40.00 E
Manyoni	218	5.45 S	34.50 E
Manzanares	168	39.00 N	3.22 W
Manzanares ≃	168	40.19 N	3.32 W
Manzanillo, Cuba	284p	20.21 N	77.07 W
Manzanillo, Méx.	278	19.03 N	104.20 W
Manzanillo, Punta ≻, Pan.	280	9.36 N	79.31 W
Manzanillo, Punta ≻, Ven.	285s	11.32 N	69.17 W
Manzanillo Bay ≃	282	19.40 N	71.45 W
Manzanita, Oreg., U.S.	270	45.43 N	123.56 W
Manzanita, Wash., U.S.	270	47.42 N	122.33 W
Manzano	254	34.39 N	106.21 W
Manzanola	252	38.06 N	103.52 W
Manzano Peak ∧	254	34.35 N	106.26 W
Manzhouli	190	49.35 N	117.22 E
Manzilah, Buḥayrat al- ⊜	208	31.15 N	32.00 E
Manzini	224	26.30 S	31.25 E
Mao	214	14.07 N	15.19 E
Mao Hsü I	196	23.19 N	119.19 E
Maoming	190	21.55 N	110.52 E
Maouri, Dallol V	222	12.05 N	3.32 E
Mapastepec	278	15.26 N	92.54 W
Mapi	198	7.07 S	139.23 E
Mapia, Kepulauan II	198	0.50 N	134.20 E
Mapimí	278	25.49 N	103.51 W
Mapimí, Bolsón de ◆[2]	278	27.30 N	103.15 W
Mapimí, Bufa de ∧	250	25.48 N	103.48 W
Mapire	290	7.45 N	64.42 W
Mapiri	292	15.15 S	68.10 W
Mapiri ≃	292	9.52 S	66.21 W
Mapiripán, Laguna ⊜	290	2.58 N	71.45 W
Mapixari, Ilha I	290	2.10 S	65.08 W
Maple	264	43.51 N	79.31 W
Maple ≃, Iowa, U.S.	252	42.00 N	95.59 W
Maple ≃, Mich., U.S.	244	42.59 N	84.57 W
Maple ≃, Minn., U.S.	244	44.05 N	94.00 W
Maple ≃, N. Dak., U.S.	252	46.56 N	96.55 W
Maple Bay	270	48.49 N	123.36 W
Maple Bluff	268	43.07 N	89.22 W
Maple Creek	232	49.55 N	109.27 W
Maple Falls	270	48.56 N	122.05 W
Maple Grove, Ont., Can.	264	43.55 N	78.44 W
Maple Grove, Qué., Can.	260	45.19 N	73.51 W
Maple Heights	266	41.25 N	81.34 W
Maple Lake	244	45.14 N	94.00 W
Maple Lane	268	41.45 N	86.14 W
Maple Mount	248	37.42 N	87.26 W
Maple Park	268	41.55 N	88.36 W
Maples	268	41.01 N	84.58 W
Maple Shade	262	39.57 N	75.00 W
Maple Springs	266	42.12 N	79.25 W
Maplesville	248	32.47 N	86.52 W
Mapleton, Iowa, U.S.	252	42.10 N	95.47 W
Mapleton, Minn., U.S.	244	43.56 N	93.57 W
Mapleton, Oreg., U.S.	256	44.02 N	123.52 W
Mapleton, Utah, U.S.	254	40.08 N	111.36 W
Mapleton Depot	266	40.24 N	77.57 W
Maple Valley	270	47.25 N	122.03 W
Mapleville	261	41.57 N	71.39 W
Maplewood, La., U.S.	248	30.15 N	93.16 W
Maplewood, Ohio, U.S.	268	40.23 N	84.02 W
Maplewood, Wash., U.S.	270	47.30 N	122.07 W
Mapuera ≃	290	1.05 S	57.02 W
Mapulau ≃	290	1.23 N	63.24 W
Maputo (Great Usutu) ≃	224	26.11 S	32.42 E
Maqueda	168	40.04 N	4.22 W
Maqueda Bay C	202	11.40 N	124.57 E
Maqueda Channel ⊔	202	13.50 N	124.05 E
Maquela do Zombo	218	6.03 S	15.07 E
Maquereau, Pointe au ≻	240	48.12 N	64.46 W
Maquiling, Mount ∧	202	14.08 N	121.11 E
Maquinchao	288	41.15 S	68.44 W
Maquoketa	244	42.04 N	90.40 W
Maquoketa ≃	244	42.11 N	90.19 W
Mar, Serra do ≗[4]	296	25.00 S	48.00 W
Mara	292	14.06 S	72.07 W
Mara ≃	218	1.31 S	33.56 E
Maraã	290	1.50 S	65.22 W
Marabá	286	5.21 S	49.07 W
Marabut	202	11.08 N	125.12 E
Maracá, Ilha de I	290	3.25 N	61.40 W
Maracaí	296	22.36 S	50.39 W
Maracaí, Lago de ⊜	290	1.28 S	65.44 W
Maracaibo	290	10.40 N	71.37 W
Maracaibo, Lago de ⊜	290	9.50 N	71.30 W
Maracajá ≃	296	12.21 S	51.00 W
Maracaju	296	21.38 S	55.09 W
Maracaju, Serra de ⋀[2]	296	23.57 S	55.01 W
Maracanã ≃	292	8.22 S	59.41 W
Maracás	296	13.26 S	40.27 W
Maracay	290	10.15 N	67.36 W
Marādah	214	29.14 N	19.13 E
Maradi	222	13.29 N	7.06 E
Maradi □[5]	222	14.00 N	7.00 E
Marāghah, Sabkhat al- ⊜	212	35.39 N	37.39 E
Marāgheh	208	37.23 N	46.13 E
Maragogipe	296	12.46 S	38.55 W
Marāḩ, Jabal al- ⋀	212	34.52 N	38.06 E
Marahuaca, Cerro ∧	290	3.34 N	65.27 W
Marajó, Baía de C	286	1.00 S	48.30 W
Marajó, Ilha de I	286	1.00 N	49.30 W
Maralal	218	1.06 N	36.42 E
Maralinga	226	29.45 S	131.35 E
Maramag	202	7.46 N	125.00 E
Marambaia, Ilha da I	296	23.04 S	43.58 W
Marampa	214	8.41 N	12.28 W
Maramureşului, Munţii ⋀	172	47.50 N	24.45 E
Maran	200	3.35 N	102.46 E
Mārān, Koh-i- ∧	206	29.26 N	66.49 E
Marana	254	32.27 N	111.13 W
Maranchón	168	41.03 N	2.12 W
Marand	208	38.26 N	45.46 E
Marandellas	224	18.10 S	31.36 E
Marang	200	5.12 N	103.11 E
Marangani	292	14.25 S	71.15 W
Marangas	202	8.40 N	117.38 E
Maranguape	286	3.53 S	38.40 W
Maranhão ≃	296	14.34 S	49.02 W
Maranhão, Cachoeira ∟	292	4.49 S	56.18 W
Maranoa ≃	228	27.50 S	148.37 E
Marano di Napoli	184	40.54 N	14.11 E
Marañón ≃	292	4.30 S	73.35 W
Marans	166	46.19 N	1.00 W
Marapanim	286	0.42 S	47.42 W
Marapi ≃	290	0.37 N	55.58 W
Marari ≃	290	0.53 N	64.25 W
Mararoa ≃	230	45.37 S	167.41 E
Maras, Perú	292	13.20 S	72.10 W
Maraş, Tür.	212	37.36 N	36.55 E
Marasany	160	57.27 N	54.25 E
Maraş Dağları ⋀	212	37.40 N	37.00 E
Mărăşeşti	172	45.52 N	27.14 E
Maratea	170	39.59 N	15.45 E
Marathon, Ont., Can.	244	48.40 N	86.25 W
Marathón, Ellás	172	38.10 N	23.58 E
Marathon, N.Y., U.S.	242	42.26 N	76.02 W
Marathon, Tex., U.S.	250	30.12 N	103.15 W
Marathon, Wis., U.S.	244	44.56 N	89.50 W
Marau, Bra.	294	28.27 S	52.12 W
Maraú, Bra.	296	14.06 S	39.00 W
Marauiá ≃	290	0.23 S	65.13 W
Maravilha	294	26.47 S	53.09 W
Maravillas	278	27.22 N	104.29 W
Mara Vista	261	41.33 N	70.34 W
Marav Lake ⊜	206	29.04 N	69.18 E
Marawi, Pil.	202	8.01 N	124.19 E
Marawī, Sūd.	214	18.29 N	31.49 E
Marayes	294	31.29 S	67.22 W
Marbella	168	36.31 N	4.53 W
Marble, Minn., U.S.	244	47.19 N	93.18 W
Marble, N.C., U.S.	246	35.10 N	83.55 W
Marble, Pa., U.S.	266	41.20 N	79.26 W
Marble Bar	226	21.11 S	119.44 E
Marble Canyon V	254	36.30 N	111.50 W
Marble Falls	250	30.34 N	98.17 W
Marble Hall	218	24.57 S	29.13 E
Marblehead, Mass., U.S.	261	42.30 N	70.51 W
Marblehead, Ohio, U.S.	266	41.32 N	82.44 W
Marble Hill	248	37.18 N	89.58 W
Marblemount	270	48.32 N	121.26 W
Marble Rock	244	42.58 N	92.52 W
Marbleton	260	45.38 N	71.35 W
Marburg an der Drau → Maribor	170	46.33 N	15.39 E
Marburg an der Lahn	164	50.49 N	8.46 E
Marcaconga	292	13.58 S	71.37 W
Marcal ≃	164	47.41 N	17.32 E
Marcala	280	14.07 N	88.00 W
Marcali	164	46.35 N	17.25 E
Marcaria	170	45.07 N	10.32 E
Marceau, Lac ⊜	240	51.25 N	66.41 W
Marceline	248	39.43 N	92.57 W
Marcelino Ramos	294	27.28 S	51.54 W
Marcellus, Mich., U.S.	268	42.03 N	85.49 W
Marcellus, N.Y., U.S.	264	42.59 N	76.20 W
Marcellus Falls	264	43.00 N	76.20 W
March	174	52.33 N	0.06 E
March (Morava) ≃	164	48.10 N	16.59 E
Marcha	186	61.49 N	122.20 E
Marcha ≃	186	61.49 N	122.20 E
Marchand	266	40.51 N	79.02 W
Marche □[4]	184	43.30 N	13.15 E
Marche □[9]	166	46.05 N	2.10 E
Marche-en-Famenne	164	50.12 N	5.20 E
Marchegg	164	48.17 N	16.55 E
Marchena	168	37.20 N	5.24 W
Marchena, Isla I	290a	0.21 N	90.29 W
Marchesa Bay C	202	6.35 N	117.40 E
Marchienne-au-Pont	176	50.24 N	4.23 E
Mar Chiquita, Laguna C	294	37.40 S	57.23 W
Mar Chiquita, Laguna ⊜	294	30.42 S	62.36 W
Marcianise	184	41.02 N	14.17 E
Marcigny	166	46.17 N	4.02 E
Marcillac-Vallon	166	44.29 N	2.28 E
Marcola	256	44.10 N	122.52 W
Marcolino, Igarapé ≃	292	11.03 S	58.35 W
Marcona	292	15.10 S	75.00 W
Marcos Juárez	294	32.42 S	62.05 W
Marcos Paz	294	34.49 S	58.51 W
Marcq-en-Baroeul	176	50.40 N	3.05 E
Marcus	252	42.50 N	95.48 W
Marcus Baker, Mount ∧	236	61.26 N	147.45 W
Marcus Hook	262	39.49 N	75.25 W
Marcus-Necker Ridge ⟡[3]	148	20.00 N	179.00 E
Marcus Island → Minami-Tori-shima I	148	24.18 N	153.58 E
Marcy, Mount ∧	242	44.07 N	73.56 W
Mardān	206	34.12 N	72.02 E
Mardela Springs	262	38.28 N	75.45 W
Mar del Plata	294	38.01 S	57.35 W
Mardi, Hadjer ∧	220	14.49 N	22.04 E
Mardin	212	37.18 N	40.44 E
Maree, Loch ⊜	162	57.40 N	5.30 W
Mareeba	228	17.00 S	145.26 E
Mareg	214	3.47 N	47.18 E
Maremma ◆[1]	170	42.30 N	11.30 E
Marengo, Ill., U.S.	268	42.15 N	88.37 W
Marengo, Ind., U.S.	248	38.22 N	86.21 W
Marengo, Iowa, U.S.	244	41.48 N	92.04 W
Marengo, Mich., U.S.	268	42.17 N	84.51 W
Marengo, Ohio, U.S.	266	40.24 N	82.49 W
Marenisco	244	46.23 N	90.30 W
Marennes	166	45.50 N	1.06 W
Marettimo, Isola I	170	37.58 N	12.04 E
Mareuil-sur-Belle	166	45.28 N	0.28 E
Marevo	160	57.19 N	32.05 E
Marfa	250	30.18 N	104.01 W
Marfrance	242	38.04 N	80.41 W
Marganec	158	47.38 N	34.40 E
Margaree	240	46.24 N	61.05 W
Margaree Harbour	240	46.26 N	61.07 W
Margaret Bay	238	51.20 N	127.29 W
Margarettsville	262	36.32 N	77.21 W
Margaretville	242	42.09 N	74.39 W
Margarita, Isla I	290	9.15 N	74.30 W
Margarita, Isla de I	290	11.00 N	64.00 W
Margarita Belén	294	27.15 S	58.58 W
Margate, Eng., U.K.	174	51.24 N	1.24 E
Margate, Fla., U.S.	246	26.18 N	80.12 W
Margate City	262	39.20 N	74.31 W
Margecany	164	48.54 N	21.01 E
Margelan → Margilan	186	40.28 N	71.44 E
Margeride, Monts de la ⋀	166	44.50 N	3.30 E
Margherita di Savoia	170	41.23 N	16.09 E
Margherita Peak	218	0.22 N	29.51 E
Marghita	172	47.21 N	22.21 E
Margilan	186	40.28 N	71.44 E
Margny-lès-Compiègne	176	49.26 N	2.49 E
Margo, Dasht-i- ◆[2]	208	30.40 N	62.30 E
Margonin	164	52.59 N	17.05 E
Margos	292	10.05 S	76.29 W
Margosatubig	202	7.35 N	123.10 E
Margua ≃	290	7.03 N	72.05 W
Marguerite Bay C	148	68.30 S	68.30 W
Mari ≃	292	7.05 S	64.34 W
Maria	202	9.12 N	123.39 E
María Cleofas, Isla I	278	21.16 N	106.14 W
María Elena	294	22.21 S	69.40 W
Maria Gail	164	46.36 N	13.52 E
María Grande	294	31.40 S	59.55 W
María Ignacia (Vela)	294	37.24 S	59.29 W
Maria Island I	228	42.39 S	148.04 E
María la Baja	290	9.59 N	75.17 W
María Madre, Isla I	278	21.35 N	106.33 W
María Magdalena, Isla I	278	21.25 N	106.24 W
Mariana	296	20.23 S	43.25 W
Mariana Basin ⟡[1]	148	12.00 N	154.00 E
Mariana Islands II	198	16.00 N	145.30 E
Marianao	284p	23.05 N	82.26 W
Mariana Ridge ⟡[3]	148	17.00 N	146.00 E
Mariana Trench ⟡[1]	148	16.00 N	148.00 E
Mariāni	200	26.39 N	94.19 E
Marian Lake ⊜	232	63.00 N	116.10 W
Marianna, Ark., U.S.	248	34.46 N	90.46 W
Marianna, Fla., U.S.	246	30.47 N	85.14 W
Mariano Comense	182	45.42 N	9.11 E
Mariano Machado	218	13.02 S	14.40 E
Mariano Moreno	294	38.45 S	70.02 W
Mariánské Lázně (Marienbad)	164	49.59 N	12.43 E
Marias ≃	256	47.56 N	110.30 W
Marias Pass)(	256	48.19 N	113.21 W
Maria Stein	268	40.24 N	84.28 W
María Teresa	294	34.00 S	61.55 W
Mariato, Punta ≻	290	7.11 N	80.53 W
Maria Van Diemen, Cape ≻	230	34.28 S	172.39 E
Mariazell	164	47.47 N	15.19 E
Maribo	164	54.46 N	11.31 E
Maribojoc Bay C	202	9.40 N	123.48 E
Maribor	170	46.33 N	15.39 E
Marica, Blg.	172	42.02 N	25.50 E
Maricá, Bra.	296	22.55 S	42.49 W
Marica (Évros) (Meriç) ≃	172	40.52 N	26.12 E
Maricaban Island I	202	13.39 N	120.54 E
Maricao	284m	18.11 N	66.59 W
Marico ≃	224	24.12 S	26.52 E
Maricopa, Ariz., U.S.	254	33.04 N	112.03 W
Maricopa, Calif., U.S.	258	35.03 N	119.24 W
Maricopa Indian Reservation ◆[4]	254	33.02 N	112.05 W
Maricunga, Salar de ≚	294	26.55 S	69.05 W
Maridagao ≃	202	7.06 N	124.44 E
Marié ≃	290	0.27 S	66.26 W
Mariec	160	56.32 N	49.50 E
Marie-Galante I	282	15.56 N	61.16 W
Mariehamn	160	60.06 N	19.57 E
Mariel	284p	22.59 N	82.45 W
Marienbad → Mariánské Lázně	164	49.59 N	12.43 E
Marienburg → Malbork	164	54.02 N	19.01 E
Marienheide	178	51.05 N	7.32 E
Mariental	218	24.36 S	17.59 E
Marienville	266	41.28 N	79.07 W
Maries ≃	248	38.30 N	92.01 W
Mariestad	160	58.43 N	13.51 E
Marieta ≃	290	5.02 N	66.38 W
Marietta, Fla., U.S.	246	30.19 N	81.47 W
Marietta, Ga., U.S.	246	33.57 N	84.33 W
Marietta, Minn., U.S.	252	45.01 N	96.25 W
Marietta, Ohio, U.S.	242	39.25 N	81.27 W
Marietta, Okla., U.S.	250	33.56 N	97.07 W
Marietta, Pa., U.S.	262	40.04 N	76.35 W
Marietta, Wash., U.S.	270	48.47 N	122.36 W
Marieville	260	45.26 N	73.10 W
Mariga ≃	222	9.40 N	5.55 E
Marigliano	184	40.56 N	14.27 E
Marignane	182	43.25 N	5.13 E
Marigot, Dom.	284d	15.32 N	61.18 W
Marigot, Guad.	282	18.04 N	63.06 W
Marihatag	202	8.48 N	126.17 E
Mariinsk	186	56.13 N	87.45 E
Marília	296	22.13 S	49.56 W
Marilla	264	42.50 N	78.33 W
Marimari ≃	290	3.58 S	58.49 W
Marimba	218	8.28 S	17.08 E
Marín, Esp.	168	42.23 N	8.42 W
Marín, Méx.	278	25.52 N	100.03 W
Marin □[6]	272	38.03 N	122.33 W
Marina	272	36.41 N	121.48 W
Marina di Gioiosa Ionica	170	38.18 N	16.20 E
Marina di Ravenna	170	44.29 N	12.17 E
Marina Fall ∟	290	5.25 N	59.30 W
Marin City	272	37.52 N	122.31 W
Marinduque □[4]	202	13.25 N	121.55 E
Marinduque Island I	202	13.25 N	122.00 E
Marine City	266	42.43 N	82.30 W
Marinette	244	45.06 N	87.38 W
Maringá	296	23.25 S	51.55 W
Maringa ≃	218	1.14 N	19.48 E
Maringouin	248	30.29 N	91.31 W
Marinha Grande	168	39.45 N	8.56 W
Marino	184	41.46 N	12.39 E
Marinskij Posad	160	56.07 N	47.43 E
Marinwood	272	38.02 N	122.32 W
Marion, Ala., U.S.	248	32.32 N	87.26 W
Marion, Ark., U.S.	248	35.13 N	90.12 W
Marion, Conn., U.S.	261	41.34 N	72.56 W
Marion, Ill., U.S.	248	37.44 N	88.56 W
Marion, Ind., U.S.	268	40.33 N	85.40 W
Marion, Iowa, U.S.	244	42.02 N	91.36 W
Marion, Kans., U.S.	252	38.21 N	97.01 W
Marion, Ky., U.S.	248	37.20 N	88.05 W
Marion, La., U.S.	248	32.54 N	92.15 W
Marion, Mass., U.S.	261	41.42 N	70.46 W
Marion, Mich., U.S.	244	44.06 N	85.09 W
Marion, Miss., U.S.	248	32.25 N	88.39 W
Marion, N.C., U.S.	246	35.41 N	82.01 W
Marion, N. Dak., U.S.	252	46.37 N	98.20 W
Marion, N.Y., U.S.	264	43.08 N	77.11 W
Marion, Ohio, U.S.	266	40.35 N	83.08 W
Marion, S.C., U.S.	246	34.11 N	79.24 W
Marion, S. Dak., U.S.	252	43.25 N	97.16 W
Marion, Va., U.S.	246	36.50 N	81.31 W
Marion, Wis., U.S.	244	44.21 N	89.05 W
Marion □[6], Ohio, U.S.	266	40.35 N	83.08 W
Marion □[6], Oreg., U.S.	270	45.06 N	122.47 W
Marion, Lake ⊜	246	28.05 N	81.32 W
Marion, Lake ⊜[1]	246	33.30 N	80.25 W
Marion Bay C	228	42.48 S	147.55 E
Marion Center	266	40.46 N	79.03 W
Marion Hill	266	40.44 N	80.18 W
Marion Junction	248	32.26 N	87.14 W
Marion Reef ⟡[2]	228	19.10 S	152.17 E
Marion Station	262	38.02 N	75.46 W
Marionville	248	37.00 N	93.38 W
Mariópolis	294	26.20 S	52.33 W
Maripa	290	7.26 N	65.09 W
Maripipi Island I	202	11.48 N	124.19 E
Mariposa	272	37.29 N	119.58 W
Mariposa □[6]	272	37.29 N	119.58 W
Mariquita	290	5.12 N	74.54 W
Mariscal Estigarribia	294	22.02 S	60.38 W
Marissa	248	38.15 N	89.45 W
Maritime Alps ⋀	166	44.15 N	7.10 E
Mari-Turek	160	56.47 N	49.36 E
Mariupol' → Ždanov	158	47.06 N	37.33 E
Mariusa, Caño ≃[1]	290	9.43 N	61.26 W
Mariusa, Isla I	285r	9.39 N	61.19 W
Mariveles	202	14.26 N	120.29 E
Märjamaa	160	58.54 N	24.26 E
Marka	214	1.47 N	44.52 E
Markaryd	160	56.26 N	13.36 E
Markdale	264	44.19 N	80.39 W
Markdorf	180	47.43 N	9.23 E
Marked Tree	248	35.32 N	90.25 W
Markerwaard ◆[1]	164	52.33 N	5.15 E
Markesan	244	43.42 N	88.59 W
Market Drayton	174	52.54 N	2.29 W
Market Harborough	174	52.29 N	0.55 W
Market Weighton	162	53.52 N	0.40 W
Markham, Ont., Can.	264	43.52 N	79.16 W
Markham, Ill., U.S.	268	41.36 N	87.42 W
Markham, Tex., U.S.	250	28.57 N	96.04 W
Markham, Mount ∧	148	82.51 S	161.21 E
Markham Bay C	232	63.30 N	71.48 W
Markle	268	40.50 N	85.20 W
Markleeville	272	38.41 N	119.47 W
Markovo	186	64.40 N	170.25 E
Marks, S.S.S.R.	158	51.42 N	46.46 E
Marks, Miss., U.S.	248	34.16 N	90.16 W
Marksville	248	31.08 N	92.04 W
Marktheidenfeld	164	49.50 N	9.36 E
Marktoberdorf	180	47.47 N	10.37 E
Marktredwitz	164	50.00 N	12.06 E
Marl	178	51.38 N	7.05 E
Marlboro, Alta., Can.	238	53.33 N	116.45 W
Marlboro, Conn., U.S.	261	41.38 N	72.28 W
Marlboro, Mass., U.S.	261	42.21 N	71.33 W
Marlboro, N.H., U.S.	242	42.54 N	72.12 W
Marlboro, N.J., U.S.	262	40.19 N	74.15 W
Marlboro, N.Y., U.S.	261	41.36 N	73.58 W
Marlboro, Ohio, U.S.	266	40.53 N	81.12 W
Marlborough, Guy.	290	7.29 N	58.38 W
Marlborough, Eng., U.K.	174	51.26 N	1.43 W
Marlborough □[9]	230	41.40 S	173.45 E
Marlene Village	270	45.32 N	122.49 W
Marles-les-Mines	176	50.30 N	2.31 E
Marlette	244	43.20 N	83.05 W
Marlin	250	31.18 N	96.53 W
Marlow, Eng., U.K.	174	51.35 N	0.48 W
Marlow, Okla., U.S.	250	34.39 N	97.57 W
Marlton	262	39.54 N	74.55 W
Marly-le-Roi	176	48.52 N	2.05 E
Marmaduke	248	36.11 N	90.23 W
Marmande	166	44.30 N	0.10 E
Marmara, Sea of → Marmara Denizi ⊤[2]	212	40.40 N	28.15 E
Marmara Adası I	212	40.38 N	27.37 E
Marmara Denizi ⊤[2]	212	40.40 N	28.15 E
Marmaraereğlisi	172	40.58 N	27.57 E
Marmara Gölü ⊜	212	38.37 N	28.02 E
Marmaris	172	36.51 N	28.16 E
Marmarth	252	46.18 N	103.54 W
Marmaton ≃	248	38.00 N	94.19 W
Marmelada ≃	296	19.01 S	45.08 W
Marmelos	292	6.08 S	61.50 W
Marmelos, Rio dos ≃	292	6.06 S	61.46 W
Marmet	242	38.15 N	81.04 W
Marmion Lake ⊜[1]	244	48.54 N	91.30 W
Marmora, Ont., Can.	264	44.29 N	77.41 W
Marmora, N.J., U.S.	262	39.16 N	74.39 W
Marmora, Punta la ∧	170	39.59 N	9.19 E
Marmot Bay C	236	58.00 N	152.20 W
Marmot Island I	236	58.13 N	151.51 W
Marnay	166	47.17 N	5.46 E
Marne, B.R.D.	178	53.57 N	9.00 E
Marne, Mich., U.S.	268	43.02 N	85.50 W
Marne □[5]	166	48.55 N	4.10 E
Marne ≃	166	48.49 N	2.24 E
Marne au Rhin, Canal de la ≊	166	48.35 N	7.47 E
Maroa, Ill., U.S.	248	40.02 N	88.57 W
Maroa, Ven.	290	2.43 N	67.33 W
Maroantsetra	218	15.26 S	49.44 E
Maromme	176	49.28 N	1.02 E
Maromokotro ∧	225b	14.01 S	48.59 E
Maros (Mureşul) ≃	172	46.15 N	20.13 E
Maroua	214	10.36 N	14.20 E
Marovoay	225b	16.06 S	46.39 E
Marowijne (Maroni) ≃	286	5.45 N	53.58 W
Marquam	270	45.04 N	122.41 W
Marquand	248	37.26 N	90.10 W
Marquesas Islands → Marquises, Îles II	148	9.00 S	139.30 W
Marquesas Keys II	246	24.34 N	82.08 W
Marquette, Kans., U.S.	252	38.33 N	97.50 W
Marquette, Mich., U.S.	244	46.33 N	87.24 W
Marquina	168	43.16 N	2.30 W
Marquis	285k	12.06 N	61.37 W
Marquise	166	50.49 N	1.42 E
Marquises, Îles II	148	9.00 S	139.30 W
Marrabios, Cordillera de los ⋀	280	12.35 N	86.50 W
Marradi	170	44.04 N	11.37 E
Marrah, Jabal ∧	220	14.04 N	24.21 E
Marra Hills ⋀[2]	220	6.05 N	27.33 E
Marrakech	214	31.38 N	8.00 W
Marree	226	29.39 S	138.04 E
Marrero	248	29.54 N	90.07 W
Marromeu	218	18.20 S	35.56 E
Mars	266	40.42 N	80.06 W
Marsabit	214	2.20 N	37.59 E
Marsala	170	37.48 N	12.26 E
Marsberg	164	48.24 N	12.15 E
Marsciano	184	42.54 N	12.20 E
Marseille	182	43.18 N	5.24 E
Marseille-en-Beauvaisis	166	49.35 N	1.57 E
Marseilles, Ill., U.S.	268	41.20 N	88.43 W
Marseilles, Ohio, U.S.	266	40.42 N	83.23 W
Marsfjället ∧	160	65.05 N	15.28 E
Marshall, Liber.	214	6.10 N	10.23 W
Marshall, Ark., U.S.	248	35.55 N	92.38 W
Marshall, Ill., U.S.	248	39.23 N	87.42 W
Marshall, Mich., U.S.	268	42.16 N	84.58 W
Marshall, Minn., U.S.	252	44.27 N	95.47 W
Marshall, Mo., U.S.	248	39.07 N	93.12 W
Marshall, N.C., U.S.	246	35.48 N	82.41 W
Marshall, Tex., U.S.	248	32.33 N	94.23 W
Marshall, Va., U.S.	242	38.52 N	77.52 W
Marshall, Wis., U.S.	268	43.10 N	89.04 W
Marshall □[6], Ill., U.S.	268	41.02 N	89.24 W
Marshall □[6], Ind., U.S.	268	41.21 N	86.19 W
Marshallberg	246	34.44 N	76.31 W
Marshall Hall	262	38.41 N	77.06 W
Marshall Islands II	148	9.00 N	168.00 E
Marshall Northeast	248	32.34 N	94.20 W
Marshallton	262	39.45 N	75.39 W
Marshalltown	244	42.03 N	92.55 W
Marshallville, Ga., U.S.	246	32.27 N	89.56 W
Marshallville, Ohio, U.S.	266	40.54 N	81.44 W
Marshfield, Mass., U.S.	261	42.07 N	70.43 W
Marshfield, Mo., U.S.	248	37.15 N	92.54 W
Marshfield, Wis., U.S.	244	44.40 N	90.10 W
Marshfield Hills	261	42.09 N	70.44 W
Marsh Harbour	282	26.33 N	77.03 W
Mars Hill, Maine, U.S.	240	46.31 N	67.52 W
Mars Hill, N.C., U.S.	246	35.47 N	82.29 W
Marsh Island I	248	29.35 N	91.53 W
Marsh Lake ⊜	236	60.25 N	134.18 W
Marsh Peak ∧	254	40.43 N	109.50 W
Marshville	246	34.59 N	80.26 W
Marsing	256	43.33 N	116.48 W
Märsta	160	59.37 N	17.51 E
Marsteller	266	40.39 N	78.47 W
Marstons Mills	261	41.39 N	70.25 W
Mart	250	31.33 N	96.50 W
Martaban	198	16.32 N	97.37 E
Martaban, Gulf of C	200	16.30 N	97.00 E
Martapura	198	3.25 S	114.51 E
Martel, Fr.	166	44.56 N	1.37 E
Martel, Ohio, U.S.	266	40.40 N	82.55 W
Marten Lake ⊜	244	46.42 N	79.41 W
Marten Mountain ∧	238	55.28 N	114.43 W
Martha Lake	270	47.51 N	122.20 W
Martí, Cuba	284p	22.57 N	80.55 W
Martí, Cuba	284p	21.09 N	77.27 W
Martigny	180	46.06 N	7.04 E
Martigues	182	43.24 N	5.03 E
Martil	168	35.37 N	5.17 W
Martin, Česko.	164	49.05 N	18.55 E
Martin, Ky., U.S.	246	37.34 N	82.45 W
Martin, Mich., U.S.	268	42.37 N	85.39 W
Martin, N. Dak., U.S.	252	47.50 N	100.07 W
Martin, Ohio, U.S.	266	41.33 N	83.20 W
Martin, S. Dak., U.S.	252	43.10 N	101.44 W
Martin, Tenn., U.S.	248	36.21 N	88.51 W
Martín ≃	168	41.18 N	0.19 W
Martina Franca	170	40.42 N	17.21 E
Martindale	250	29.50 N	97.51 W
Martinengo	182	45.34 N	9.46 E
Mărtineşti	172	45.30 N	27.18 E
Martinez	272	37.55 N	121.55 W
Martínez de la Torre	278	20.04 N	97.03 W
Martinho Campos	296	19.20 S	45.13 W
Martinique □[2]	276	14.40 N	61.00 W
Martin Lake ⊜[1]	248	32.50 N	85.55 W
Martinniemi	160	65.13 N	25.18 E
Martin Point ≻	236	70.08 N	143.16 W
Martinsberg	164	48.22 N	15.09 E
Martinsburg, N.Y., U.S.	264	43.44 N	75.28 W
Martinsburg, Ohio, U.S.	266	40.16 N	82.21 W
Martinsburg, Pa., U.S.	266	40.19 N	78.20 W
Martinsburg, W. Va., U.S.	242	39.27 N	77.58 W
Martins Creek	262	40.47 N	75.11 W
Martinsdale	256	46.28 N	110.19 W
Martins Ferry	266	40.06 N	80.44 W
Martinsville, Ill., U.S.	248	39.20 N	87.53 W
Martinsville, Ind., U.S.	248	39.26 N	86.25 W
Martinsville, Va., U.S.	246	36.41 N	79.52 W
Martinton	268	40.55 N	87.44 W
Martintown	260	45.09 N	74.42 W
Martin Vaz, Ilhas II	288	20.30 S	28.51 W
Marton	230	40.04 S	175.22 E
Martos	168	37.43 N	3.58 W
Martre, Lac la ⊜	232	63.15 N	116.55 W
Martti	160	67.28 N	28.28 E
Marudi	198	4.11 N	114.19 E
Marugame	192	34.17 N	133.47 E
Maruia ≃	230	41.47 S	172.13 E
Maruoka	192	36.09 N	136.16 E
Marv Dasht	208	29.50 N	52.40 E
Marvejols	166	44.33 N	3.18 E
Marvell	248	34.33 N	90.55 W
Marvine, Mount ∧	254	38.40 N	111.39 W
Marwood	266	40.48 N	79.47 W
Mary	208	37.36 N	61.50 E
Mary □[4]	208	37.36 N	61.50 E
Mary, Lake ⊜	228	23.07 S	150.35 E
Maryborough, Austl.	228	37.03 S	143.45 E
Maryborough, Austl.	228	25.32 S	152.42 E
Mary D	262	40.45 N	76.04 W
Marydel	262	39.07 N	75.45 W
Maryfield	252	49.48 N	101.32 W
Maryhill	270	45.41 N	120.49 W
Mary Kathleen	228	20.49 S	140.02 E
Maryknoll	261	41.11 N	73.50 W
Maryland □[6]	222	4.40 N	8.00 W
Maryland □[3]	234	39.00 N	76.45 W
Maryland Line	262	39.43 N	76.40 W
Maryneal	250	32.14 N	100.27 W
Maryport	162	54.43 N	3.30 W
Marys ≃, Ill., U.S.	248	37.53 N	89.47 W
Marys ≃, Nev., U.S.	258	41.04 N	115.16 W
Mary's Igloo	236	65.09 N	165.04 W
Marys Peak ∧	256	44.30 N	123.33 W
Marystown	240	47.11 N	55.10 W
Marysvale	254	38.27 N	112.11 W
Marysville, B.C., Can.	238	49.38 N	115.57 W
Marysville, N.B., Can.	240	45.59 N	66.35 W
Marysville, Calif., U.S.	272	39.09 N	121.35 W
Marysville, Kans., U.S.	252	39.51 N	96.39 W
Marysville, Mich., U.S.	266	42.54 N	82.29 W
Marysville, Ohio, U.S.	266	40.14 N	83.22 W
Marysville, Pa., U.S.	262	40.20 N	76.56 W
Marysville, Wash., U.S.	270	48.03 N	122.11 W
Maryville, Mo., U.S.	248	40.21 N	94.52 W
Maryville, Tenn., U.S.	246	35.46 N	83.58 W
Marywood	268	41.48 N	88.18 W
Marzagão	296	17.59 S	48.39 W
Marzo, Punta ≻	290	6.50 N	77.42 W
Marzūq	214	25.55 N	13.55 E
Masachapa	280	11.47 N	86.31 W
Más Afuera, Isla → Alejandro Selkirk, Isla I	288	33.45 S	80.46 W
Masagua	280	14.12 N	90.51 W
Masaguisi	202	12.41 N	121.32 E
Masai Steppe ⋀[1]	218	4.45 S	37.00 E
Masaka	218	0.20 S	31.44 E
Masalembo-besar, Pulau I	198	5.34 S	114.26 E
Masan	194	35.11 N	128.32 E
Masapelid Island I	202	9.42 N	125.40 E
Masasi	218	10.43 S	38.48 E
Masatepe	280	11.55 N	86.09 W
Más a Tierra, Isla → Róbinson Crusoe, Isla I	288	33.38 S	78.52 W
Masaya	280	11.59 N	86.06 W
Masaya □[5]	280	12.00 N	86.10 W
Masbate	202	12.22 N	123.37 E
Masbate □[4]	202	12.20 N	123.30 E
Masbate Island I	202	12.10 N	123.30 E
Masbate Pass ⊔	202	12.30 N	123.35 E
Mascara	214	35.45 N	0.01 E
Mascarene Basin ⟡[1]	148	27.00 S	55.00 E
Mascarene Islands II	225c	21.00 S	57.00 E
Mascasín	294	31.24 S	66.59 W
Mascot	246	36.04 N	83.44 W
Mascota	278	20.32 N	104.49 W
Mascouche	260	45.52 N	73.35 W
Mascoutah	248	38.29 N	89.48 W
Masefield	256	49.09 N	107.48 W
Maseru	224	29.28 S	27.30 E
Mashaba Mountains ⋀	224	18.45 S	30.32 E
Mashābih I	208	25.37 N	36.29 E
Mashan	200	23.50 N	108.16 E
Masherbrum ∧	206	35.38 N	76.18 E
Mashhad	208	36.18 N	59.36 E
Mashike	192a	43.51 N	141.31 E
Mashiko	192	36.28 N	140.06 E
Māshkel, Hāmūn-i- ⊜	206	28.15 N	63.00 E
Mashonaland South □[4]	224	18.15 S	30.45 E
Mashpee	261	41.39 N	70.29 W
Mashra'ar-Raqq	214	8.25 N	29.16 E
Mashū-ko ⊜	192a	43.35 N	144.32 E
Masi Manimba	218	4.46 S	17.55 E
Masindi	214	1.41 N	31.43 E
Masinloc	202	15.32 N	119.57 E
Maşīrah, Khalīj al- C	204	20.10 N	58.15 E
Masisea	292	8.35 S	74.20 W
Masjed Soleymān	208	31.58 N	49.18 E
Mask, Lough ⊜	162	53.35 N	9.20 W
Maskinongé □[6]	260	46.35 N	73.30 W
Masoala, Cap ≻	225b	15.59 S	50.13 E
Masoala, Presqu'île ≻[1]	225b	15.40 S	50.12 E
Mason, Mich., U.S.	268	42.35 N	84.26 W
Mason, Ohio, U.S.	242	39.17 N	84.19 W
Mason, Tenn., U.S.	248	35.25 N	89.33 W
Mason, Tex., U.S.	250	30.45 N	99.14 W
Mason, W. Va., U.S.	242	39.01 N	82.01 W
Mason □[6]	270	47.20 N	123.09 W
Mason Bay C	230	46.55 S	167.42 E
Mason City, Ill., U.S.	248	40.12 N	89.42 W
Mason City, Iowa, U.S.	244	43.09 N	93.12 W
Mason City, Nebr., U.S.	252	41.13 N	99.18 W
Mason Creek	238	55.40 N	124.29 W
Masontown	242	39.51 N	79.54 W
Masoura	168	36.05 N	4.28 E
Masparro, Punta ≻	290	10.40 N	66.15 W
Masqaṭ (Muscat)	208	23.37 N	58.35 E
Massa	170	44.01 N	10.09 E
Massachusetts □[3]	234	42.15 N	71.50 W
Massacre Lake ⊜	258	41.39 N	119.35 W
Massafra	170	40.35 N	17.07 E
Massa Lombarda	184	44.27 N	11.49 E
Massa Lubrense	184	40.36 N	14.20 E
Massa Marittima	184	43.03 N	10.53 E
Massangena	218	21.32 S	32.57 E
Massarosa	184	43.52 N	10.20 E
Massaua → Mesewa	214	15.38 N	39.28 E
Massen	178	51.32 N	7.38 E
Massena, Iowa, U.S.	252	41.15 N	94.46 W
Massena, N.Y., U.S.	260	44.56 N	74.54 W
Massenya	214	11.24 N	16.10 E
Masset	238	54.02 N	132.09 W
Masset Inlet C	238	53.42 N	132.20 W
Masseube	166	43.26 N	0.35 E
Massey	244	46.12 N	82.05 W
Massiac	166	45.15 N	3.12 E
Massif Central → Central, Massif ⋀	166	45.00 N	3.10 E
Massillon	266	40.48 N	81.32 W
Massinga	218	23.20 S	35.25 E
Massive, Mount ∧	254	39.12 N	106.28 W
Maštaga	208	40.32 N	50.00 E
Masterson	250	35.38 N	101.58 W
Masterton	230	40.57 S	175.39 E
Mastic Point	246	25.03 N	77.57 W
Mastung	204	29.48 N	66.51 E
Masuda	192	34.40 N	131.51 E
Masury	266	41.13 N	80.33 W
Maszewo	164	53.29 N	15.02 E
Mat ≃	172	41.39 N	19.34 E
Matabeleland ◆[1]	224	19.30 S	28.00 E
Matabeleland North □[4]	224	19.00 S	27.15 E
Matabeleland South □[4]	224	21.00 S	29.15 E
Matabuena	168	41.10 N	3.40 W
Matachel ≃	168	38.50 N	6.17 W
Matachewan	244	47.56 N	80.39 W
Mata de São João	296	12.31 S	38.17 W
Matadi	218	5.49 S	13.27 E
Matador	250	34.01 N	100.49 W
Matagalpa	280	12.53 N	85.57 W
Matagalpa □[5]	280	13.00 N	85.30 W
Matag-ob	202	11.07 N	124.29 E
Matagorda	250	28.41 N	95.58 W
Matagorda Bay C	250	28.35 N	96.20 W
Matagorda Island I	250	28.15 N	96.30 W
Matagorda Peninsula ≻[1]	250	28.32 N	96.07 W
Matak, Pulau I	200	3.18 N	106.16 E
Matakana Island I	230	37.34 S	176.05 E
Matakitaki ≃	230	41.47 S	172.18 E
Matam	214	15.40 N	13.15 W
Matama, Cerro ∧	280	9.48 N	83.14 W
Matamata	230	37.49 S	175.46 E
Matamoras	242	41.22 N	74.42 W
Matamoros	278	25.53 N	97.30 W
Matamoros de la Laguna	278	25.32 N	103.15 W
Matandu ≃	218	8.45 S	39.19 E
Matane	240	48.51 N	67.32 W
Matane, Réserve(Matane Reserve) ◆[4]	240	48.47 N	67.22 W
Matanuska ≃	236	61.30 N	149.15 W
Matanzas, Cuba	284p	23.03 N	81.35 W
Matanzas, Méx.	278	21.37 N	101.38 W
Matanzas □[4]	284p	22.40 N	81.10 W
Matanzas, Bahía de C	284p	23.08 N	81.30 W
Matão	296	16.13 S	49.12 W
Mata Ortiz	278	30.08 N	108.03 W
Matapalo, Cabo ≻	280	8.22 N	83.18 W
Matape ≃	278	28.18 N	110.40 W
Matapédia	240	47.58 N	66.56 W
Matapédia, Lac ⊜	240	48.33 N	67.32 W
Mataquito ≃	294	34.59 S	72.12 W
Matará, Perú	292	7.10 S	78.15 W
Matara, Sīh.	204	5.56 N	80.33 E
Mataram	226	8.35 S	116.07 E
Matarani	292	16.58 S	72.07 W
Matarca	290	0.30 S	72.38 W
Matarinao Bay C	202	11.14 N	125.37 E
Mataró	168	41.32 N	2.27 E
Matarraña ≃	168	41.14 N	0.22 E
Matatiele	218	30.24 S	28.43 E
Matatindoc Point ≻	202	9.43 N	122.23 E
Matauré ≃, Bra.	292	5.30 S	60.45 W
Mataura ≃, N.Z.	230	46.34 S	168.47 E
Matawan	262	40.25 N	74.14 W
Matchi-Manitou, Lac ⊜	244	48.00 N	77.03 W
Mateare	280	12.14 N	86.26 W
Matehuala	278	23.39 N	100.39 W
Mateira	296	18.54 S	50.30 W
Mateke Hills ⋀[2]	224	21.48 S	31.00 E
Matelica	170	43.15 N	13.00 E
Matera	170	40.40 N	16.37 E
Materborn	178	51.46 N	6.06 E
Mátészalka	164	47.57 N	22.19 E
Mateur	170	37.03 N	9.40 E

Symbols in the index entries are identified on page 360.

Name	Page	Lat°′	Long°′
Matewan	246	37.37 N	82.10 W
Matfield	261	42.02 N	71.00 W
Matha	166	45.52 N	0.19 W
Mather, Man., Can.	252	49.06 N	99.07 W
Mather, Calif., U.S.	272	37.53 N	119.52 W
Mather, Pa., U.S.	242	39.56 N	80.05 W
Matheson	244	48.32 N	80.28 W
Mathews	262	37.26 N	76.19 W
Mathews □[6]	262	37.25 N	76.20 W
Mathis	250	28.06 N	97.50 W
Mathon Chaung ≃	200	18.32 N	94.55 E
Mathura	206	27.30 N	77.41 E
Mati	202	6.57 N	126.13 E
Maṭī, Sabkhat ⊜	208	23.51 N	52.00 E
Matias Barbosa	296	21.53 S	43.20 W
Matías Romero	278	16.53 N	95.02 W
Maticora ≃	290	11.03 N	71.09 W
Matignon	166	48.36 N	2.18 W
Matiguás	280	12.53 N	85.26 W
Matinenda Lake ⊜	244	46.22 N	82.57 W
Matinicus Island I	240	43.54 N	68.55 W
Matipó	296	20.17 S	42.21 W
Matipó ≃	296	19.53 S	42.33 W
Matiyure ≃	290	7.36 N	67.39 W
Matlock, Eng., U.K.	174	53.08 N	1.32 W
Matlock, Wash., U.S.	270	47.14 N	123.25 W
Matnog	202	12.36 N	124.05 E
Mato ≃	290	7.09 N	65.07 W
Mato, Cerro ∧	290	7.15 N	65.14 W
Matoaca	262	37.14 N	77.29 W
Matočkin Šar	186	73.16 N	56.27 E
Mato Grosso, Bra.	286		
	292	15.00 S	59.57 W
Mato Grosso □[3]	296	16.00 S	56.00 W
Mato Grosso, Planalto do ⋏[1]	296	15.30 S	56.00 W
Matonipi ≃	240	51.22 N	69.46 W
Matopo Hills ⋏[2]	224	20.36 S	28.28 E
Matopos National Park ♠	224	20.33 S	28.20 E
Matos ≃	292	14.07 S	65.25 W
Matoury	286	4.51 N	52.21 W
Mato Verde	296	15.23 S	42.52 W
Matozinhos, Bra.	296	19.35 S	44.07 W
Matozinhos, Port.	168	41.11 N	8.42 W
Matra ⋏	164	47.55 N	20.00 E
Maṭraḥ	208	23.38 N	58.34 E
Matrei in Osttirol	164	47.00 N	12.32 E
Maṭrūḥ	220	31.21 N	27.14 E
Matsiatra ≃	225b	21.25 S	45.33 E
Matsqui	270	49.12 N	122.25 W
Matsu → Matsu Shan I	196	26.09 N	119.56 E
Matsudo	192	35.47 N	139.54 E
Matsue	192	35.28 N	133.04 E
Matsumae	192a	41.26 N	140.07 E
Matsumoto	192	36.14 N	137.58 E
Matsu Shan I	196	26.09 N	119.56 E
Matsushima	192	38.22 N	141.04 E
Matsutō	192	36.31 N	136.34 E
Matsuura	192	33.22 N	129.42 E
Matsuyama	192	33.50 N	132.45 E
Matsuzaka	192	34.34 N	136.32 E
Mattagami ≃	244	50.43 N	81.29 W
Mattagami Heights	244	48.29 N	81.22 W
Mattagami Lake ⊜	244	47.54 N	81.35 W
Mattamuskeet, Lake ⊜	246	35.30 N	76.11 W
Mattapoisett	261	41.40 N	70.49 W
Mattaponi	262	37.32 N	76.46 W
Mattawa, Ont., Can.	244	46.19 N	78.42 W
Mattawa, Wash., U.S.	256	46.44 N	119.54 W
Mattawa ≃	244	46.19 N	78.43 W
Mattawamkeag	242	45.31 N	68.21 W
Mattawamkeag ≃	242	45.30 N	68.24 W
Mattawan	268	42.12 N	85.47 W
Mattawana	266	40.30 N	77.44 W
Matterhorn ∧, Eur.	166	45.59 N	7.43 E
Matterhorn ∧, Nev., U.S.	258	41.49 N	115.23 W
Mattersburg	164	47.44 N	16.25 E
Matteson	268	41.30 N	87.40 W
Matthews	268	40.23 N	85.30 W
Matthews Mountain ∧	248	37.29 N	90.21 W
Matthews Ridge	290	7.30 N	60.10 W
Matthew Town	282	20.57 N	73.40 W
Mattighofen	164	48.06 N	13.09 E
Mattituck	261	40.59 N	72.32 W
Mattole ≃	258	40.18 N	124.21 W
Mattoon, Ill., U.S.	248	39.29 N	88.22 W
Mattoon, Wis., U.S.	244	45.01 N	89.02 W
Mattydale	264	43.06 N	76.09 W
Matucana	292	11.50 S	76.25 W
Matunuck	261	41.23 N	71.32 W
Matuog	202	9.55 N	123.09 E
Matura Bay C	285r	10.38 N	61.01 W
Maturín	290	9.45 N	63.11 W
Maturino	160	59.06 N	37.55 E
Matutina	296	19.13 S	45.58 W
Matutum, Mount ∧	202	6.22 N	125.04 E
Maú (Ireng) ≃	290	3.33 N	59.51 W
Maúa	218	13.51 S	37.10 E
Mauban	202	14.12 N	121.44 E
Maubeuge	176	50.17 N	3.58 E
Ma-ubin	200	16.44 N	95.39 E
Maud, Okla., U.S.	250	35.08 N	96.46 W
Maud, Tex., U.S.	248	33.20 N	94.21 W
Maués	290	3.24 S	57.42 W
Maués Açu ≃	290	3.22 S	57.44 W
Maug ≃	202	8.20 N	125.53 E
Mauger, Île I	240	51.04 N	58.45 W
Maug Islands II	198	20.01 N	145.13 E
Maui □[6]	275a	20.53 N	156.30 W
Maui I	275d	20.45 N	156.15 W
Mauldin	246	34.47 N	82.19 W
Maule □[4]	294	35.45 S	72.15 W
Maule ≃	294	35.19 S	72.25 W
Maule, Laguna del ⊜	294	36.04 S	70.30 W
Mauléon	166	46.56 N	0.45 W
Maumee	266	41.34 N	83.39 W
Maumee ≃	242	41.42 N	83.28 W
Maumere	198	8.37 S	122.14 E
Maun	218	20.00 S	23.25 E
Maunabo	284m	18.01 N	65.54 W
Mauna Kea ∧[1]	275d	19.50 N	155.28 W
Maunaloa	275a	21.08 N	157.13 W
Mauna Loa ∧[1]	275d	19.29 N	155.36 W
Maunath Bhanjan	206	25.57 N	83.34 E
Maunoir, Lac ⊜	236	67.30 N	125.00 W
Maupin	270	45.11 N	121.05 W
Maure-de-Bretagne	166	47.54 N	1.59 W
Maurepas, Lake ⊜	248	30.15 N	90.30 W
Maures, Massif des ⋏	166	43.16 N	6.23 E
Mauri ≃	292	17.18 S	68.41 W
Mauriac	166	45.13 N	2.20 E
Mauricetown	262	39.17 N	74.58 W
Mauritania □[1]	214	20.00 N	12.00 W
Mauritius □[2]	218	20.17 S	57.33 E
Mauritius I	225c	20.17 S	57.33 E
Mauron	166	48.05 N	2.18 W
Maurs-du-Cantal	166	44.43 N	2.11 E
Maury Channel ⊔	232	75.44 N	94.40 W
Mauston	244	43.48 N	90.05 W
Mauterndorf	164	47.08 N	13.40 E
Mauthausen	164	48.14 N	14.32 E
Mauvais Coulee ∨	252	48.21 N	99.06 W
Mauvezin	166	43.44 N	0.55 E
Mauzé-sur-le-Mignon	166	46.12 N	0.40 W
Mavá ≃	290	0.44 N	69.30 W
Mavaca ≃	290	2.31 N	65.11 W
Maverick Canal ☲	250	28.25 N	100.18 W
Mavinga	218	15.50 S	20.21 E
Mavora, Mount ∧	230	45.02 S	168.08 E
Mawangkanlishan ∧	206	34.19 N	80.03 E
Maw-daung Pass)(	200	11.47 N	99.39 E
Mawlaik	200	23.38 N	94.24 E
Maw Taung ∧	200	11.39 N	99.35 E
Max	252	47.49 N	101.18 W
Maxatawny	262	40.33 N	75.41 W
Maxcanú	278	20.35 N	89.59 W
Maxéville	180	48.43 N	6.10 E
Maxie	248	30.59 N	89.18 W
Maximo	266	40.53 N	81.11 W
Maxixe	218	23.51 S	35.21 E
Maxton	246	34.44 N	79.21 W
Maxville	260	45.17 N	74.51 W
Maxwell, Calif., U.S.	272	39.17 N	122.11 W
Maxwell, Iowa, U.S.	244	41.53 N	93.24 W
Maxwell, Nebr., U.S.	252	41.05 N	100.31 W
Maxwell, N. Mex., U.S.	250	36.32 N	104.33 W
Maxwell Bay C	232	74.35 N	89.00 W
May	250	31.59 N	98.55 W
May ≃	238	55.43 N	111.22 W
May, Cape ≻	242	38.58 N	74.55 W
May, Mount ∧	238	54.02 N	119.58 W
Mayaguana I	282	22.21 N	73.00 W
Mayaguana Passage ⊔	282	22.25 N	73.30 W
Mayagüez	284m	18.12 N	67.09 W
Mayajigua	284p	22.14 N	79.04 W
Mayales, Punta ≻	280	11.52 N	85.28 W
Maya Mountains ⋏	278	16.40 N	88.50 W
Mayantoc	202	15.37 N	120.23 E
Mayapan ⊥	278	20.38 N	89.27 W
Mayarí	284p	20.40 N	75.41 W
Mayarí Arriba	284p	20.25 N	75.32 W
Mayaro Bay C	285r	10.15 N	60.58 W
Maybee	268	42.00 N	83.31 W
Maybell	254	40.31 N	108.05 W
Maybeury	246	37.22 N	81.22 W
Maybole	162	55.21 N	4.41 W
Maydolong	202	11.30 N	125.30 E
Mayen	164	50.19 N	7.13 E
Mayenne	166	48.18 N	0.37 W
Mayenne □[5]	166	48.05 N	0.40 W
Mayenne ≃	166	47.30 N	0.33 W
Mayer	254	34.24 N	112.14 W
Mayersville	248	32.54 N	91.03 W
Mayerthorpe	238	53.57 N	115.08 W
Mayfield, Ky., U.S.	248	36.44 N	88.38 W
Mayfield, Utah, U.S.	254	39.07 N	111.42 W
Mayfield Heights	266	41.31 N	81.27 W
Mayfield Reservoir ⊜[1]	256	46.30 N	122.30 W
Mayhill	254	32.53 N	105.29 W
May Inlet C	232	76.15 N	100.45 W
Maymyo	200	22.02 N	96.28 E
Maynard, Iowa, U.S.	244	42.46 N	91.53 W
Maynard, Mass., U.S.	261	42.30 N	71.33 W
Maynard, Ohio, U.S.	266	40.07 N	80.53 W
Maynardville	246	36.15 N	83.48 W
Mayne	270-	48.51 N	123.18 W
Mayne ≃	228	23.34 S	141.18 E
Maynooth	162	53.23 N	6.35 W
Mayo, Yukon, Can.	236	63.35 N	135.54 W
Mayo, Fla., U.S.	246	30.03 N	83.10 W
Mayo □[6]	162	53.50 N	9.30 W
Mayo ≃, Col.	290	1.40 N	77.21 W
Mayo ≃, Méx.	278	26.45 N	109.47 W
Mayo ≃, Perú	292	6.38 S	76.15 W
Mayo Bay C	202	6.55 N	126.22 E
Mayodan	246	36.25 N	79.58 W
Mayo Lake ⊜	236	63.46 N	135.10 W
Mayon Volcano ∧[1]	202	13.15 N	123.42 E
Mayor, Puig ∧	168	39.48 N	2.48 E
Mayor Buratovich	294	39.16 S	62.40 W
Mayor Island I	230	37.17 S	176.15 E
Mayotte I	225a	12.50 S	45.10 E
Mayoyao	202	16.49 N	121.13 E
May Pen	285q	17.58 N	77.14 W
Mayport	266	41.02 N	79.15 W
Mayraira Point ≻	202	18.40 N	120.50 E
Mayrán, Laguna de ⩦	250	25.50 N	102.35 W
Mayrhofen	164	47.10 N	11.52 E
Mays Landing	262	39.27 N	74.44 W
Maysville, Ky., U.S.	242	38.39 N	83.46 W
Maysville, Mo., U.S.	248	39.48 N	94.35 W
Maysville, N.C., U.S.	246	34.59 N	77.14 W
Maysville, Okla., U.S.	250	34.49 N	97.24 W
Maytiguid Island I	202	11.03 N	119.36 E
Maytown	262	40.04 N	76.35 W
Mayumba	218	3.25 S	10.39 E
Mayville, Mich., U.S.	244	43.20 N	83.21 W
Mayville, N. Dak., U.S.	252	47.30 N	97.19 W
Mayville, N.Y., U.S.	266	42.15 N	79.30 W
Mayville, Wis., U.S.	244	43.30 N	88.33 W
Maywood, Ill., U.S.	268	41.53 N	87.51 W
Maywood, Nebr., U.S.	252	40.39 N	100.37 W
Maywood, N.Y., U.S.	261	42.42 N	73.52 W
Maza	294	36.48 S	63.20 W
Mazabuka	218	15.51 S	27.46 E
Mazagan → El-Jadida	214	33.16 N	8.30 W
Mazagão	286	0.07 S	51.17 W
Ma'zah, Jabal ∧	212	35.51 N	40.38 E
Mazamet	166	43.30 N	2.24 E
Mazán ≃	290	3.30 S	73.10 W
Māzandarān □[4]	208	36.30 N	53.30 E
Mazara del Vallo	170	37.39 N	12.36 E
Mazār-i-Sharīf	206	36.41 N	67.00 E
Mazarrón	168	37.36 N	1.19 W
Mazarrón, Golfo de C	168	37.30 N	1.18 W
Mazaruni ≃	290	6.25 N	58.35 W
Mazaruni-Potaro □[5]	290	6.00 N	60.00 W
Mazatenango	280	14.32 N	91.30 W
Mazatlán	278	23.13 N	106.25 W
Mazatzal Mountains ⋏	254	34.00 N	111.55 W
Mazatzal Peak ∧	254	34.03 N	111.28 W
Mažeikiai	160	56.19 N	22.20 E
Mazenod	252	49.53 N	106.14 W
Mazeppa	244	44.17 N	92.32 W
Maẓhūr, Khubb al- ⊸[8]	208	27.45 N	43.55 E
Mazoe ≃	218	16.32 S	33.25 E
Mazomanie	244	43.11 N	89.48 W
Mazon	268	41.14 N	88.25 W
Mazowsze ◆[1]	164	52.30 N	20.40 E
Mazury □[9]	164	53.45 N	21.00 E
Mazury ◆[1]	164	53.45 N	21.00 E
Mbabane	224	26.18 S	31.06 E
Mbaïki	214	3.53 N	18.00 E
Mbala	218	8.50 S	31.22 E
Mbale	218	1.05 N	34.10 E
Mbalmayo	214	3.31 N	11.30 E
Mbamba Bay	218	11.17 S	34.46 E
Mbandaka (Coquilhatville)	218	0.04 N	18.16 E
Mbanza-Ngungu	218	5.15 S	14.52 E
Mbarara	218	0.37 S	30.39 E
Mbari ≃	214	4.34 N	22.43 E
Mberubu	222	6.10 N	7.38 E
Mbeya	218	8.54 S	33.27 E
Mbeya ∧	218	8.50 S	33.22 E
Mbinda	218	2.00 S	12.55 E
Mbomou (Bomu) ≃	214	4.08 N	22.26 E
Mbour	222	14.24 N	16.58 W
Mbout	214	16.02 N	12.35 W
Mbuji-Mayi (Bakwanga)	218	6.09 S	23.38 E
Mburucuyá	294	28.02 S	58.15 W
Mbuyapey	294	26.12 S	56.50 W
Mc → Mac			
M'Chedillah	168	36.21 N	4.16 E
M'Clintock Channel ⊔	232	71.00 N	101.00 W
M'Clure, Cape ≻	232	74.35 N	121.08 W
M'Clure Strait ⊔	232	74.30 N	116.00 W
M'Daourouch	170	36.05 N	7.49 E
Mead, Lake ⊜[1]	254	36.05 N	114.25 W
Meade, Kans., U.S.	252	37.17 N	100.20 W
Meade, Mich., U.S.	266	42.43 N	82.52 W
Meade ≃	236	70.50 N	156.25 W
Meaden Peak ∧	254	40.46 N	107.03 W
Meade Peak ∧	256	42.30 N	111.15 W
Meadow, Tex., U.S.	250	33.20 N	102.12 W
Meadow, Utah, U.S.	254	38.53 N	112.24 W
Meadowbrook	268	41.03 N	85.03 W
Meadow Lands	266	40.15 N	80.13 W
Meadowvale	264	43.37 N	79.43 W
Meadow Valley Wash ∨	258	36.39 N	114.35 W
Meadowview	246	36.46 N	81.52 W
Meadow Vista	272	39.06 N	121.01 W
Meadville, Miss., U.S.	248	31.28 N	90.54 W
Meadville, Mo., U.S.	248	39.47 N	93.18 W
Meadville, Pa., U.S.	266	41.38 N	80.09 W
Meaford	264	44.36 N	80.35 W
Meaghers Grant	240	44.55 N	63.15 W
Me-akan-dake ∧	192a	43.23 N	144.01 E
Meakerville	236	60.32 N	145.00 W
Mealhada	168	40.22 N	8.27 W
Méan	164	50.22 N	5.20 E
Meander River	232	59.02 N	117.42 W
Meath □[6]	162	53.35 N	6.40 W
Meaux	176	48.57 N	2.52 E
Mebane	246	36.06 N	79.16 W
Mécatina, Cap ≻	240	50.45 N	59.01 W
Mecaya ≃	290	0.29 N	75.11 W
Mecca	266	41.24 N	80.45 W
Mechanic Falls	242	44.07 N	70.24 W
Mechanicsburg, Ohio, U.S.	242	40.04 N	83.34 W
Mechanicsburg, Pa., U.S.	242	40.13 N	77.01 W
Mechanicstown	266	40.37 N	80.57 W
Mechanicsville, Iowa, U.S.	244	41.54 N	91.15 W
Mechanicsville, Md., U.S.	262	38.26 N	76.44 W
Mechanicsville, Va., U.S.	246	37.36 N	77.22 W
Mechanicville	242	42.54 N	73.42 W
Mechelen (Malines)	176	51.02 N	4.28 E
Mechita	294	35.04 S	60.24 W
Mechra-Saf-Saf	168	34.52 N	2.36 W
Mechren'ga	160	61.46 N	40.57 E
Mechrenga ≃	160	63.15 N	41.20 E
Mecidiye, Tür.	172	38.53 N	27.42 E
Mecidiye, Tür.	172	40.38 N	26.32 E
Mečigmen	236	65.28 N	172.05 W
Mečigmeskij Zaliv C	236	65.25 N	172.00 W
Meckenbeuren	180	47.42 N	9.34 E
Mecklenburg □[9]	164	53.30 N	13.00 E
Mecoacán, Laguna C	278	18.22 N	93.09 W
Mecsek ⋏	164	46.15 N	18.05 E
Meda, It.	182	45.40 N	9.09 E
Meda, Port.	168	40.58 N	7.16 W
Medan	200	3.35 N	98.40 E
Médanos	294	38.50 S	62.42 W
Medanosa, Punta ≻	288	48.08 S	65.58 W
Medaryville	268	41.05 N	86.55 W
Mede	182	45.06 N	8.44 E
Médéa	168	36.12 N	2.50 E
Medeiros Neto	296	17.20 S	40.14 W
Medellín, Col.	290	6.15 N	75.35 W
Medellin, Pil.	202	11.08 N	123.58 E
Médenine	214	32.21 N	10.30 E
Medfield	261	42.11 N	71.18 W
Medford, Mass., U.S.	261	42.25 N	71.07 W
Medford, N.J., U.S.	262	39.54 N	74.49 W
Medford, Okla., U.S.	250	36.48 N	97.44 W
Medford, Oreg., U.S.	256	42.19 N	122.52 W
Medford, Wis., U.S.	244	45.09 N	90.20 W
Medfra	236	63.06 N	154.44 W
Medgidia	172	44.15 N	28.16 E
Media	262	39.54 N	75.23 W
Media Agua	294	31.59 S	68.24 W
Media Luna, Arrecife de la ⌇[2]	280	15.14 N	82.39 W
Mediapolis	244	41.00 N	91.10 W
Mediaș	172	46.10 N	24.21 E
Medical Lake	256	47.34 N	117.41 W
Medicina	184	44.28 N	11.38 E
Medicine Bow	254	41.54 N	106.12 W
Medicine Bow ≃	254	42.00 N	106.40 W
Medicine Bow Mountains ⋏	254	41.10 N	106.25 W
Medicine Bow Peak ∧	254	41.21 N	106.19 W
Medicine Hat	232	50.03 N	110.40 W
Medicine Lake	252	48.30 N	104.30 W
Medicine Lake ⊜	252	48.28 N	104.24 W
Medicine Lodge	252	37.17 N	98.35 W
Medicine Lodge ≃	250	36.49 N	98.20 W
Medina → Al-Madīnah, Ar. Sa.	208	24.28 N	39.36 E
Medina, Bra.	296	16.15 S	41.29 W
Medina, Pil.	202	8.54 N	125.01 E
Medina, N. Dak., U.S.	252	46.54 N	99.18 W
Medina, N.Y., U.S.	264	43.13 N	78.23 W
Medina, Ohio, U.S.	266	41.08 N	81.52 W
Medina, Tex., U.S.	250	29.48 N	99.15 W
Medina, Wash., U.S.	270	47.37 N	122.14 W
Medina □[6]	266	41.08 N	81.52 W
Medina ≃	250	29.12 N	98.20 W
Medinaceli	168	41.10 N	2.26 W
Medina del Campo	168	41.18 N	4.55 W
Medina de Ríoseco	168	41.53 N	5.02 W
Medina Sidonia	168	36.27 N	5.55 W
Medininkai	160	54.32 N	25.40 E
Mediterranean Sea ⊤[2]	148	35.00 N	20.00 E
Medjana	168	36.08 N	4.41 E
Medjerda, Monts de la ⋏	170	36.35 N	8.15 E
Medjerda, Oued ≃	170	37.07 N	10.13 E
Medkovec	172	43.37 N	23.10 E
Mednogorsk	158	51.24 N	57.37 E
Mednyj, Ostrov I	186	54.45 N	167.35 E
Médoc ◆[1]	166	45.20 N	1.00 W
Medora, Ind., U.S.	248	38.49 N	86.10 W
Medora, N. Dak., U.S.	252	46.55 N	103.31 W
Médouneu	218	0.57 N	10.47 E
Meductic	240	46.00 N	67.29 W
Medveđa	172	42.50 N	21.35 E
Medvedica ≃	158	49.35 N	42.41 E
Medvedok	160	57.23 N	50.05 E
Medvežjegorsk	160	62.55 N	34.23 E
Medvežskaja	160	64.57 N	57.34 E
Medway, Maine, U.S.	242	45.37 N	68.35 W
Medway, Mass., U.S.	261	42.08 N	71.24 W
Medway ≃, N.S., Can.	240	44.08 N	64.36 W
Medway ≃, Eng., U.K.	162	51.27 N	0.44 E
Medyn'	160	54.58 N	35.52 E
Medynskij Zavorot, Mys ≻	160	68.58 N	59.17 E
Medzilaborce	164	49.16 N	21.55 E
Meekatharra	226	26.36 S	118.29 E
Meeker, Colo., U.S.	254	40.02 N	107.55 W
Meeker, Ohio, U.S.	266	40.39 N	83.18 W
Meeks Bay	272	39.02 N	120.08 W
Meelpaeg Lake ⊜	240	48.16 N	56.35 W
Meerane	164	50.51 N	12.28 E
Meerbeke	176	50.50 N	4.02 E
Meerhout	178	51.08 N	5.05 E
Meersburg	164	47.41 N	9.16 E
Meerut	206	29.00 N	77.43 E
Meeteetse	256	44.09 N	108.52 W
Mega	214	4.07 N	38.16 E
Mega, Pulau I	198	3.55 S	100.55 E
Megálo Khorío	172	36.27 N	27.21 E
Megalópolis	172	37.24 N	22.08 E
Mégantic □[6]	260	46.10 N	71.30 W
Mégantic, Lac ⊜	242	45.30 N	70.55 W
Mégara	172	38.01 N	23.21 E
Megargel	250	33.27 N	98.56 W
Megasini ∧	206	21.38 N	86.20 E
Meghalaya □[3]	206	25.30 N	91.15 E
Meghna ≃	204	22.50 N	90.50 E
Mégiscane ≃	244	48.30 N	77.10 W
Mégiscane, Lac ⊜	244	48.30 N	76.04 W
Megra	160	66.09 N	41.37 E
Mehadia	172	44.55 N	22.22 E
Meherrin ≃	246	36.26 N	76.57 W
Mehun-sur-Yérve	176	47.09 N	2.13 E
Meia Ponte ≃	296	18.32 S	49.36 W
Meigs	246	31.04 N	83.06 W
Meihekou	194	42.27 N	125.33 E
Meijiang ≃, Zhg.	196	24.24 N	116.34 E
Meijiang ≃, Zhg.	196	26.00 N	115.23 E
Meiktila	200	20.52 N	95.52 E
Meilen	180	47.16 N	8.38 E
Meiners Oaks	274	34.30 N	119.17 W
Meinerzhagen	178	51.06 N	7.38 E
Meiningen	164	50.34 N	10.25 E
Meio, Rio do ≃	296	17.47 S	39.47 W
Meiringen	166	46.43 N	8.12 E
Meissen	164	51.10 N	13.28 E
Meiss Lake ⊜	258	41.52 N	122.04 W
Meixian	196	24.21 N	116.08 E
Meizhoudao I	196	25.06 N	119.07 E
Meizhouwan C	196	25.06 N	119.00 E
Mejez el Bab	170	36.39 N	9.37 E
Mejillones	294	23.06 S	70.27 W
Mejillones del Sur, Bahía de C	294	23.03 S	70.27 W
Mejocote ≃	280	14.43 N	88.39 W
Mekambo	218	1.01 N	13.56 E
Mekele	214	13.33 N	39.30 E
Mekerra, Oued ≃	168	35.00 N	0.45 W
Mekerrhane, Sebkha ⩦	214	26.19 N	1.20 E
Meknès	214	33.53 N	5.37 W
Mekong ≃	200	10.33 N	105.24 E
Mekoryuk	236	60.23 N	166.12 W
Mékrou ≃	222	12.24 N	2.49 E
Melado ≃	294	35.43 S	71.05 W
Melanesia II	148	13.00 S	164.00 E
Melawi ≃	198	0.05 S	111.29 E
Melbern	268	41.28 N	84.39 W
Melbourne, Austl.	228	37.49 S	144.58 E
Melbourne, Ont., Can.	266	42.49 N	81.33 W
Melbourne, Ark., U.S.	248	36.04 N	91.54 W
Melbourne, Fla., U.S.	246	28.05 N	80.37 W
Melbourne, Iowa, U.S.	244	41.57 N	93.06 W
Melbourne Island I	232	68.30 N	104.45 W
Melby	162	60.18 N	1.39 W
Melcher	244	41.13 N	93.14 W
Melchor Ocampo	250	26.03 N	99.33 W
Melcroft	266	40.03 N	79.24 W
Meldola	184	44.07 N	12.05 E
Meldorf	164	54.05 N	9.05 E
Meldrum Bay	244	45.56 N	83.07 W
Meldrum Creek	238	52.07 N	122.20 W
Melegnano	182	45.21 N	9.19 E
Melekess	160	54.14 N	49.39 E
Melena del Sur	284p	22.47 N	82.09 W
Melendiz Dağı ∧	212	38.07 N	34.25 E
Melenki	160	55.20 N	41.38 E
Meleuz	158	52.58 N	55.55 E
Melfa	262	37.39 N	75.45 W
Melfi, It.	170	40.59 N	15.40 E
Melfi, Tchad	214	11.04 N	17.56 E
Melfort	232	52.52 N	104.36 W
Melgaço	168	42.07 N	8.16 W
Melgar	290	4.12 N	74.39 W
Melhus	160	63.17 N	10.16 E
Meli ≃	222	8.17 N	10.41 W
Meligalás	172	37.13 N	21.59 E
Melilla	168	35.19 N	2.58 W
Melincué	294	33.39 S	61.28 W
Melipilla	294	33.42 S	71.13 W
Melita	252	49.16 N	101.00 W
Melito di Porto Salvo	170	37.56 N	15.47 E
Melitopol'	158	46.50 N	35.22 E
Melívoia	172	39.45 N	22.48 E
Melk	164	48.14 N	15.20 E
Melksham	174	51.23 N	2.09 W
Mellansel	160	63.26 N	18.19 E
Melle	178	52.12 N	8.20 E
Mellègue, Oued ≃	170	36.32 N	8.51 E
Mellen	244	46.20 N	90.40 W
Mellenville	261	42.15 N	73.40 W
Mellerud	160	58.42 N	12.28 E
Melle-sur-Béronne	166	46.13 N	0.09 W
Mellette	252	45.09 N	98.30 W
Mellid	168	42.55 N	8.00 W
Mellish Reef ⌇[2]	226	17.25 S	155.50 E
Melmore	266	41.02 N	83.07 W
Mělník	164	50.20 N	14.29 E
Melo	294	32.22 S	54.11 W
Melo, Ilha de I	222	11.02 N	15.13 W
Melocheville	260	45.19 N	73.56 W
Melos → Mílos I	172	36.41 N	24.15 E
Melozitna ≃	236	64.46 N	155.29 W
Melrhir, Chott ⊜	214	34.17 N	6.24 E
Melrose, Scot., U.K.	162	55.36 N	2.44 W
Melrose, Mass., U.S.	261	42.27 N	71.04 W
Melrose, Minn., U.S.	252	45.40 N	94.49 W
Melrose, N. Mex., U.S.	250	34.26 N	103.38 W
Melrose, N.Y., U.S.	261	42.50 N	73.37 W
Melrose, Ohio, U.S.	268	41.05 N	84.25 W
Melrose, Wis., U.S.	244	44.08 N	91.01 W
Melrose Park, Ill., U.S.	268	41.54 N	87.51 W
Melrose Park, N.Y., U.S.	264	42.54 N	76.32 W
Melstone	256	46.36 N	107.52 W
Melsungen	178	51.08 N	9.32 E
Melta, Mount ∧	202	5.41 N	117.20 E
Meltaus	160	66.54 N	25.22 E
Melton Hill Reservoir ⊜[1]	246	36.00 N	84.15 W
Melton Mowbray	174	52.46 N	0.53 W
Melúa	290	3.55 N	72.50 W
Melun	176	48.32 N	2.40 E
Melvern	252	38.30 N	95.38 W
Melvich	162	58.33 N	3.55 W
Melville, Sask., Can.	232	50.55 N	102.48 W
Melville, La., U.S.	248	30.42 N	91.45 W
Melville, Cape ≻	202	7.48 N	117.00 E
Melville, Lake ⊜	232	53.45 N	59.30 W
Melville Hills ⋏[2]	232	69.20 N	122.00 W
Melville Island I	232	75.15 N	110.00 W
Melville Peninsula ≻[1]	232	68.00 N	84.00 W
Melville Sound ⊔	232	68.05 N	107.30 W
Melvin, Ill., U.S.	268	40.34 N	88.15 W
Melvin, Tex., U.S.	250	31.13 N	99.35 W
Melvin, Lough ⊜	162	54.26 N	8.10 W
Melvindale	266	42.17 N	83.11 W
Mélykút	164	46.13 N	19.24 E
Melzo	182	45.30 N	9.25 E
Memel → Klaipėda	160	55.43 N	21.07 E
Memel → Nemunas ≃	158	55.18 N	21.23 E
Memewin Lake ⊜	244	46.29 N	78.42 W
Memmingen	180	47.59 N	10.11 E
Memo ≃	290	9.16 N	66.40 W
Mempawah	200	0.22 N	108.58 E
Memphis, Fla., U.S.	246	27.32 N	82.34 W
Memphis, Mich., U.S.	266	42.54 N	82.46 W
Memphis, Mo., U.S.	248	40.28 N	92.10 W
Memphis, Tenn., U.S.	248	35.08 N	90.03 W
Memphis, Tex., U.S.	250	34.44 N	100.32 W
Mena	248	34.35 N	94.15 W
Menahga	252	46.45 N	95.06 W
Menai Bridge	162	53.14 N	4.10 W
Ménaka	214	15.55 N	2.24 E
Menarandra ≃	225b	25.17 S	44.30 E
Menard	250	30.55 N	99.47 W
Menasha	244	44.13 N	88.26 W
Mendarik, Pulau I	200	1.18 N	107.02 E
Mendawai ≃	198	3.17 S	113.21 E
Mende	166	44.30 N	3.30 E
Menden	178	51.26 N	7.47 E
Mendenhall	248	31.58 N	89.52 W
Mendenhall, Cape ≻	236	59.51 N	166.15 W
Mendes	296	22.32 S	43.44 W
Méndez	290	2.43 S	78.19 W
Mendez-Nuñez	202	14.08 N	120.54 E
Mendi, Papua	198	6.10 S	143.40 E
Mendi, Yai.	214	9.50 N	35.06 E
Mendocino	258	39.19 N	123.48 W
Mendocino, Cape ≻	258	40.25 N	124.25 W
Mendocino Seascarp ⌇[4]	148	41.00 N	140.00 W
Mendon, Mass., U.S.	261	42.06 N	71.33 W
Mendon, Mich., U.S.	268	42.00 N	85.27 W
Mendon, N.Y., U.S.	264	43.00 N	77.34 W
Mendon, Ohio, U.S.	268	40.40 N	84.31 W
Mendota, Calif., U.S.	272	36.45 N	120.23 W
Mendota, Ill., U.S.	268	41.33 N	89.07 W
Mendoza, Arg.	294	32.54 S	68.50 W
Mendoza, Perú	292	6.17 S	77.17 W
Mendoza □[4]	294	34.40 S	68.30 W
Mendrisio	180	45.52 N	8.59 E
Ménéac	162	48.09 N	2.28 W
Mene de Mauroa	290	10.43 N	71.01 W
Mene Grande	290	9.49 N	70.56 W
Menemen	172	38.36 N	27.04 E
Menen	176	50.48 N	3.07 E
Mengcheng	190	33.17 N	116.33 E
Mengen	180	48.03 N	9.20 E
Menges Mills	262	39.52 N	76.54 W
Menggala	198	4.28 S	105.17 E
Menghai	200	22.00 N	100.26 E
Menglian	200	22.20 N	99.38 E
Mengzhi	200	24.10 N	99.46 E
Mengzi	200	23.22 N	103.20 E
Menihek Lakes ⊜	232	54.00 N	66.35 W
Menindee	228	32.24 S	142.26 E
Menindee Lake ⊜	228	32.21 S	142.20 E
Menlo	270	46.38 N	123.39 W
Menlo Park	272	37.28 N	122.13 W
Mennighüffen	178	52.13 N	8.43 E
Menno	252	43.14 N	97.34 W
Meno	250	36.24 N	98.11 W
Menominee	244	45.06 N	87.37 W
Menominee ≃	244	45.05 N	87.36 W
Menomonee Falls	268	43.11 N	88.07 W
Menomonie	244	44.53 N	91.55 W
Menor, Mar C	168	37.43 N	0.48 W
Menorca I	168	40.00 N	4.00 E
Mens	166	44.49 N	5.45 E
Mentana	184	42.02 N	12.38 E
Mentasta Lake	236	62.55 N	143.45 W
Mentasta Mountains ⋏	236	62.40 N	143.07 W
Mentawai, Kepulauan II	198	2.00 S	99.30 E
Mentawi, Selat ⊔	200	1.56 S	100.12 E
Menti	170	37.36 N	12.58 E
Menton	182	43.47 N	7.30 E
Mentone, Calif., U.S.	274	34.05 N	117.08 W
Mentone, Ind., U.S.	268	41.10 N	86.02 W
Mentone, Tex., U.S.	250	31.42 N	103.36 W
Mentor	266	41.40 N	81.20 W
Mentor-on-the-lake	266	41.43 N	81.21 W
Mentzdam ◆[6]	224	33.10 S	25.09 E
Menzel Bourguiba	170	37.10 N	9.48 E
Menzel Bou Zelfa	170	36.41 N	10.36 E
Menzelinsk	160	55.43 N	53.08 E
Menzel Jemil	170	37.14 N	9.55 E
Menzel Temime	170	36.47 N	10.59 E
Menzies	226	29.41 S	121.02 E
Meob Bay C	224	24.25 S	14.34 E
Meoqui	278	28.17 N	105.29 W
Mepisckaro, Gora ∧	212	41.50 N	42.40 E
Meppel	178	52.42 N	6.11 E
Meppen	178	52.41 N	7.17 E
Mequon	268	43.13 N	87.58 W
Mer	166	47.42 N	1.30 E
Merambéllou, Kólpos C	172	35.14 N	25.47 E
Meramec ≃	248	38.23 N	90.21 W
Merasheen	240	47.25 N	54.21 W
Merasheen Island I	240	47.30 N	54.15 W
Merate	182	45.42 N	9.25 E
Merauke	198	8.28 S	140.20 E
Mercaderes	290	1.47 N	77.10 W
Mercato San Severino	184	40.47 N	14.46 E
Merced	272	37.18 N	120.29 W
Merced □[6]	272	37.18 N	120.29 W
Mercedario, Cerro ∧	294	31.58 S	70.07 W
Mercedes, Arg.	294	29.10 S	58.02 W
Mercedes, Arg.	294	34.40 S	59.25 W
Mercedes, Arg.	294	33.40 S	65.30 W
Mercedes, Pil.	202	14.06 N	123.00 E
Mercedes, Tex., U.S.	250	26.09 N	97.55 W
Mercedes, Ur.	294	33.16 S	58.01 W
Mercer, Mo., U.S.	248	40.31 N	93.32 W
Mercer, Ohio, U.S.	268	40.40 N	84.35 W
Mercer, Pa., U.S.	266	41.14 N	80.15 W
Mercer, Wis., U.S.	244	46.10 N	90.04 W
Mercer □[6], N.J., U.S.	262	40.13 N	74.45 W
Mercer □[6], Ohio, U.S.	268	40.33 N	84.34 W
Mercer □[6], Pa., U.S.	266	41.14 N	80.15 W
Mercer Island	270	47.35 N	122.15 W
Mercersburg	242	39.50 N	77.54 W
Mercerville	262	40.14 N	74.41 W
Merchants Bay C	232	67.10 N	62.50 W
Merchtem	176	50.58 N	4.14 E
Mercoal	238	53.10 N	117.05 W
Mercury	258	36.40 N	115.59 W
Mercury Island II	230	36.38 S	175.52 E
Mercy Bay C	232	74.05 N	119.00 W
Meredith	242	43.39 N	71.30 W
Meredith, Lake ⊜[1]	250	35.36 N	101.42 W
Meredosia	248	39.50 N	90.34 W
Merelbeke	176	51.00 N	3.45 E
Merevari ≃	290	4.28 N	63.57 W
Mergaïeb, Djebel ∧	168	36.22 N	2.50 E
Mergui (Myeik)	200	12.26 N	98.36 E
Mergui Archipelago II	200	12.00 N	98.00 E
Meriç (Marica) (Évros) ≃	172	40.52 N	26.12 E
Méricourt	176	50.24 N	2.52 E
Mérida, Esp.	168	38.55 N	6.20 W
Mérida, Méx.	278	20.58 N	89.37 W
Merida, Pil.	202	10.55 N	124.32 E
Mérida, Ven.	290	8.36 N	71.08 W
Mérida □[3]	290	8.30 N	71.10 W
Mérida, Cordillera de ⋏	290	8.40 N	71.00 W
Meriden	261	41.32 N	72.48 W
Meridian, Calif., U.S.	272	39.09 N	121.55 W
Meridian, Ga., U.S.	246	31.27 N	81.23 W
Meridian, Idaho, U.S.	256	43.37 N	116.24 W
Meridian, Miss., U.S.	248	32.22 N	88.42 W
Meridian, N.Y., U.S.	264	43.10 N	76.32 W
Meridian, Pa., U.S.	266	40.51 N	79.58 W
Meridian, Tex., U.S.	250	31.55 N	97.39 W
Mérignac	166	44.50 N	0.42 W
Merigold	248	33.50 N	90.50 W
Merikarvia	160	61.51 N	21.30 E
Merín, Laguna (Lagoa Mirim) C	294	32.45 S	52.50 W
Merino	252	40.29 N	103.21 W
Merinos	294	32.24 S	56.54 W
Merionethshire □[6]	174	52.48 N	3.45 W
Merir I	198	4.19 N	132.19 E
Merivale Gardens	264	45.19 N	75.44 W
Merkel	250	32.28 N	100.01 W
Merkendorf	164	49.12 N	10.42 E
Merkinė	164	54.10 N	24.10 E
Merksem	176	51.15 N	4.27 E
Merlin, Ont., Can.	266	42.14 N	82.14 W
Merlin, Oreg., U.S.	256	42.31 N	123.25 W
Merlo	294	32.21 S	65.02 W
Merna	252	41.29 N	99.46 W
Mernye	164	46.30 N	17.50 E
Meron, Hare ∧	208	32.58 N	35.25 E
Merouana	168	35.38 N	5.55 E
Merredin	226	31.29 S	118.16 E
Merrick ∧	162	55.08 N	4.29 W
Merrickville	264	44.55 N	75.50 W
Merrill, Iowa, U.S.	252	42.43 N	96.15 W
Merrill, Mich., U.S.	244	43.25 N	84.20 W
Merrill, Oreg., U.S.	256	42.01 N	121.36 W
Merrill, Wis., U.S.	244	45.11 N	89.41 W
Merrillan	244	44.27 N	90.50 W
Merrillville	268	41.30 N	87.15 W
Merrimac	261	42.50 N	71.00 W
Merriman	252	42.55 N	101.42 W
Merritt, B.C., Can.	238	50.07 N	120.47 W
Merritt, Wash., U.S.	270	47.47 N	120.51 W
Merritt Island	246	28.21 N	80.42 W
Merritt Reservoir ⊜[1]	252	42.35 N	100.55 W
Mer Rouge	248	32.47 N	91.48 W
Merrow	261	41.49 N	72.19 W
Merryville	248	30.45 N	93.33 W
Merseburg	164	51.21 N	11.59 E
Mers el Kébir	168	35.45 N	0.43 W
Mersey ≃, Austl.	228	41.10 S	146.22 E
Mersey ≃, N.S., Can.	240	44.02 N	64.43 W
Mersin	212	36.48 N	34.38 E
Mersing	200	2.26 N	103.51 E
Merthyr Tydfil	174	51.46 N	3.23 W
Mértola	168	37.38 N	7.40 W
Merton	268	43.09 N	88.18 W
Merton ◆[8]	174	51.25 N	0.12 W
Mertzon	250	31.16 N	100.49 W
Mertztown	262	40.30 N	75.40 W
Méru, Fr.	176	49.14 N	2.08 E
Meru, Kenya	218	0.03 N	37.39 E
Merv → Mary	208	37.36 N	61.50 E
Merville	176	50.38 N	2.38 E
Méry	164	48.30 N	3.53 E
Merzifon	212	40.53 N	35.29 E
Merzig	164	49.27 N	6.36 E
Mesa	254	33.25 N	111.50 W
Mesa ≃	168	41.15 N	1.48 W
Mesabi Range ⋏[2]	244	47.30 N	92.50 W
Mesachie Lake	270	48.49 N	124.07 W
Mesagne	170	40.33 N	17.49 E
Mesa Peak ∧	254	37.55 N	106.38 W
Mesarás, Kólpos C	172	34.58 N	24.36 E
Mesa Verde National Park ♠	254	37.13 N	108.30 W
Mescalero	254	33.09 N	105.46 W
Mescalero Indian Reservation ◆[4]	254	33.12 N	105.40 W
Meschede	178	51.20 N	8.17 E
Meschetskij Chrebet ⋏	212	41.48 N	42.30 E
Mescit Dağı ∧	212	40.22 N	41.11 E
Meščura	160	63.20 N	50.52 E
Mesewa (Massaua)	214	15.38 N	39.28 E
Mesgouez, Lac ⊜	232	51.25 N	75.00 W
Meshed → Mashhad	208	36.18 N	59.36 E
Mesick	244	44.24 N	85.43 W
Mesilinka ≃	238	56.09 N	124.28 W
Mesilla	254	32.16 N	106.48 W
Mesilla Park	254	32.17 N	106.46 W
Meskiana	170	35.39 N	7.41 E
Meskiana, Oued ≃	170	35.49 N	7.53 E
Meslay-du-Maine	166	47.57 N	0.33 W
Mesocco	166	46.23 N	9.14 E
Mesola	184	44.55 N	12.14 E
Mesolóngion	172	38.21 N	21.17 E
Mesopotamia	266	41.27 N	80.57 W
Mesopotamia ◆[1]	208	34.00 N	44.00 E
Mesquita	296	19.13 S	42.35 W
Mesquite, Nev., U.S.	258	36.48 N	114.04 W
Mesquite, Tex., U.S.	250	32.46 N	96.36 W
Mesquite Flat ⩦	258	36.40 N	117.10 W
Messent National Park ♠	228	36.05 S	139.50 E
Messina, It.	170	38.11 N	15.33 E
Messina, S. Afr.	224	22.23 S	30.00 E
Messina, Stretto di ⊔	170	38.15 N	15.35 E
Messíni	172	37.04 N	22.00 E
Messíni ⊥	172	37.11 N	21.57 E
Messinía □[5]	172	37.20 N	22.50 E
Messiniakós Kólpos C	172	36.58 N	22.00 E
Messkirch	164	47.59 N	9.07 E
Messojacha ≃	186	67.52 N	77.27 E
Mesta (Néstos) ≃	172	40.41 N	24.44 E
Mestre	170	45.29 N	12.15 E
Mestre, Espigão ⋏[1]	296	12.30 S	46.10 W
Mesum	178	52.13 N	7.29 E
Meszah Peak ∧	236	58.28 N	131.26 W
Meta	184	40.39 N	14.24 E
Meta □[5]	290	3.30 N	73.00 W
Meta ≃	290	6.12 N	67.28 W
Metairie	248	29.59 N	90.09 W
Metaline Falls	256	48.52 N	117.22 W
Metallifere, Colline ⋏	170	43.15 N	11.00 E
Metamora, Ill., U.S.	244	40.47 N	89.22 W
Metamora, Ohio, U.S.	268	41.43 N	83.55 W
Metán	294	25.30 S	65.00 W
Metapán	280	14.20 N	89.27 W
Meta Pond ⊜	240	48.13 N	54.55 W
Metcalfe	264	45.14 N	75.28 W
Metchosin	270	48.22 N	123.33 W
Meteghan	240	44.11 N	66.10 W
Methóni	172	36.50 N	21.43 E
Methow	238	48.08 N	120.00 W
Methow ≃	256	48.03 N	119.53 W
Methuen	261	42.44 N	71.11 W
Methven	230	43.28 S	171.38 E
Metković	170	43.03 N	17.39 E
Metlakatla, B.C., Can.	238	54.20 N	130.27 W
Metlakatla, Alaska, U.S.	236	55.08 N	131.35 W
Metlatonoc	278	17.11 N	98.20 W
Metlika	170	45.39 N	15.19 E
Metmahu ⊜	206	34.15 N	82.20 E
Meto, Bayou ≃	248	34.05 N	91.26 W
Metolius ≃	256	44.36 N	121.17 W
Metropolis	248	37.09 N	88.44 W
Metropolitan	244	45.60 N	87.53 W
Métsovon	172	39.46 N	21.11 E
Metter	246	32.24 N	82.03 W
Mettingen	178	52.18 N	7.46 E
Mettmann	178	51.15 N	6.58 E
Metuchen	262	40.33 N	74.22 W
Metz	166	49.08 N	6.10 E
Metzger	270	45.26 N	122.44 W
Metzingen	180	48.32 N	9.17 E
Meu ≃	162	48.02 N	1.47 W
Meulaboh	198	4.09 N	96.07 E
Meulan	166	49.01 N	1.54 E
Meulebeke	176	50.57 N	3.17 E
Meules, Île aux I	240	47.23 N	61.54 W
Meurthe ≃	166	48.47 N	6.09 E
Meurthe-et-Moselle □[5]	166	48.35 N	6.10 E
Meuse □[5]	180	49.00 N	5.30 E
Meuse (Maas) ≃	164	51.49 N	5.01 E
Meuselwitz	164	51.02 N	12.17 E
Mexcala	278	17.56 N	99.37 W
Mexia	250	31.41 N	96.29 W
Mexicali	278	32.40 N	115.29 W
Mexican Basin ⌇[1]	148	25.00 N	91.00 W
Mexican Hat	254	37.09 N	109.52 W
Mexico (México) □[1]	276	23.00 N	102.00 W
Mexico, Ind., U.S.	268	40.49 N	86.07 W
Mexico, Maine, U.S.	242	44.34 N	70.33 W
Mexico, Mo., U.S.	248	39.10 N	91.53 W
Mexico, N.Y., U.S.	264	43.28 N	76.14 W
Mexico, Pa., U.S.	262	40.32 N	77.21 W
México □[3]	278	19.20 N	99.45 W
Mexico, Gulf of C	276	25.00 N	90.00 W
Mexico Bay C	242	43.31 N	76.17 W
Mexico City → Ciudad de México	278	19.24 N	99.09 W
Meximieux	166	45.54 N	5.12 E
Meycauayan	202	14.44 N	120.57 E
Meydān-e Gel ⩦	208	29.04 N	54.50 E
Meyers Chuck	236	55.44 N	132.12 W
Meyersdale	242	39.45 N	79.05 W
Meyers Lake	266	40.52 N	81.24 W
Meymac	166	45.32 N	2.09 E
Meyrargues	166	43.38 N	5.32 E
Meyrin	180	46.14 N	6.05 E
Meyrueis	166	44.10 N	3.26 E
Mezapa	280	15.33 N	87.23 W
Mezdra	172	43.09 N	23.42 E
Meždurečensk	186	53.42 N	88.03 E
Mèze	166	43.25 N	3.36 E
Mézel	166	43.59 N	6.12 E
Mezen'	160	65.50 N	44.13 E
Mezen' ≃	160	66.11 N	43.59 E
Mézenc, Mont ∧	166	44.55 N	4.11 E
Mezenskaja Guba C	160	66.40 N	43.45 E
Meziadin Lake ⊜	238	56.04 N	129.18 W
Mézières-en-Brenne	166	46.49 N	1.13 E
Mézin	166	44.03 N	0.16 E
Mezőberény	164	46.50 N	21.02 E
Mezőcsát	164	47.49 N	20.55 E
Mezőkovácsháza	164	46.25 N	20.46 E
Mezőkövesd	164	47.50 N	20.34 E
Mezőtúr	164	47.00 N	20.38 E
Mezquital	278	23.29 N	104.23 W
Mezquital ≃	278	22.54 N	104.54 W
Mezzolombardo	170	46.13 N	11.05 E
M'goun, Irhil ∧	214	31.31 N	6.25 W
M'hai, B'nom ∧	200	11.33 N	107.45 E
Mhow	206	22.33 N	75.45 E
Miagao	202	10.38 N	122.14 E
Miahuatlán de Porfirio Díaz	278	16.20 N	96.36 W
Miajadas	168	39.09 N	5.54 W
Miami, Man., Can.	252	49.21 N	98.11 W
Miami, Ariz., U.S.	254	33.24 N	110.52 W
Miami, Fla., U.S.	246	25.46 N	80.12 W
Miami, Ind., U.S.	268	40.37 N	86.06 W
Miami, Okla., U.S.	248	36.53 N	94.53 W
Miami, Tex., U.S.	250	35.42 N	100.38 W
Miami □[6]	268	40.45 N	86.04 W
Miami Beach, Ont., Can.	264	44.13 N	79.29 W

Symbols in the index entries are identified on page 360.

Name	Page	Lat°′	Long°′
Miami Beach, Fla., U.S.	246	25.47 N	80.08 W
Miami Canal ≋	246	25.47 N	80.15 W
Miamisburg	242	39.38 N	84.17 W
Miami Springs	246	25.49 N	80.17 W
Mīāndow Āb	208	36.58 N	46.06 E
Miandrivazo	218	19.31 S	45.28 E
Mīāneh	208	37.26 N	47.42 E
Miang, Phu ▲	200	17.45 N	100.58 E
Miangas, Pulau I	198	5.35 N	126.35 E
Miāni Hōr C	206	25.34 N	66.19 E
Miānwāli	206	32.35 N	71.33 E
Mianyang, Zhg.	190	30.23 N	113.25 E
Mianyang, Zhg.	190	31.30 N	104.49 E
Miaodaoqundao II	194	37.56 N	120.60 E
Miaoli	190	23.45 N	120.15 E
Miaoling ▲▲	200	26.15 N	107.26 E
Miaowan I	196	21.54 N	114.00 E
Miarayon	202	8.04 N	124.50 E
Miass	158	54.59 N	60.06 E
Miasteczko Krajeńskie	164	53.06 N	17.01 E
Miastko (Rummelsburg)	164	54.01 N	17.00 E
Micanopy	246	29.30 N	82.17 W
Mičavičevnik	160	64.14 N	57.58 E
Michaga, Cerro ▲	292	19.28 S	66.32 W
Michajlov	160	54.14 N	39.02 E
Michajlovka	158	50.05 N	43.15 E
Michajlovskij	160	60.05 N	43.29 E
Michalovce	164	48.45 N	21.55 E
Michaud Point >	240	45.34 N	60.40 W
Michel	238	49.43 N	114.49 W
Michel Peak ▲	238	53.35 N	126.26 W
Michelson, Mount ▲	236	69.19 N	144.17 W
Miches	282	18.59 N	69.02 W
Michigamee ≃	244	46.04 N	88.13 W
Michigan	252	48.07 N	98.07 W
Michigan □[3]	234	44.00 N	85.00 W
Michigan, Lake ⊜	244	44.00 N	87.00 W
Michigan Center	268	42.14 N	84.33 W
Michigan City	268	41.43 N	86.54 W
Michigantown	268	40.20 N	86.23 W
Michikamau Lake ⊜	232	54.00 N	64.00 W
Michipicoten Bay C	244	47.55 N	84.56 W
Michipicoten Island I	244	47.45 N	85.45 W
Michninskaja	160	60.26 N	46.14 E
Michoacán	258	32.28 N	115.20 W
Michoacán □[3]	278	19.10 N	101.50 W
Michów	164	51.32 N	22.19 E
Mico ≃	280	12.08 N	84.15 W
Mico, Montañas del ▲▲	280	15.38 N	88.50 W
Mico, Punta >	280	11.36 N	83.38 W
Micoud	285f	13.50 N	60.54 W
Micronesia II	148	11.00 N	159.00 E
Mičurin	172	42.10 N	27.51 E
Mičurinsk	158	52.54 N	40.30 E
Midai, Pulau I	200	3.00 N	107.47 E
Midale	252	49.22 N	103.27 W
Midar	168	34.58 N	3.30 W
Mid-Atlantic Ridge ✣[3]	148	0.00	25.00 W
Middelburg, Ned.	178	51.30 N	3.37 E
Middelburg, S. Afr.	224	25.47 S	29.28 E
Middelharnis	164	51.45 N	4.11 E
Middle ≃, B.C., Can.	238	54.50 N	125.08 W
Middle ≃, Minn., U.S.	252	48.22 N	97.04 W
Middle Alkali Lake ⊜	258	41.28 N	120.04 W
Middle America Trench ✣[1]	148	15.00 N	95.00 W
Middle Andaman I	200	12.30 N	92.53 E
Middle Bass	266	41.41 N	82.50 W
Middle Bay	240	51.28 N	57.29 W
Middleboro	261	41.49 N	70.55 W
Middlebourne	242	39.30 N	80.54 W
Middlebranch	266	40.54 N	81.20 W
Middlebro	252	49.01 N	95.21 W
Middle Brook	240	48.45 N	54.15 W
Middleburg, Md., U.S.	262	39.36 N	77.16 W
Middleburg, N.Y., U.S.	242	42.36 N	74.20 W
Middleburg, Ohio, U.S.	268	40.18 N	83.35 W
Middleburg, Pa., U.S.	262	40.47 N	77.03 W
Middleburg, Va., U.S.	242	38.58 N	77.44 W
Middlebury, Conn., U.S.	261	41.32 N	73.07 W
Middlebury, Ind., U.S.	268	41.41 N	85.42 W
Middlebury, Vt., U.S.	242	44.01 N	73.10 W
Middle Channel ≃[1]	236	69.05 N	136.00 W
Middle Concho ≃	250	31.27 N	100.25 W
Middle Fabius ≃	248	39.58 N	91.35 W
Middlefield, Conn., U.S.	261	41.31 N	72.43 W
Middlefield, Ohio, U.S.	266	41.28 N	81.05 W
Middle Haddam	261	41.33 N	72.33 W
Middle Hope	261	41.34 N	74.01 W
Middle Island	261	40.53 N	72.56 W
Middle Loup ≃	252	41.17 N	98.23 W
Middle Musquodoboit	240	45.03 N	63.09 W
Middle Pease ≃	250	34.15 N	100.07 W
Middle Point	268	40.51 N	84.27 W
Middleport, N.Y., U.S.	264	43.13 N	78.29 W
Middleport, Ohio, U.S.	242	39.00 N	82.03 W
Middleport, Pa., U.S.	262	40.44 N	76.05 W
Middle Raccoon ≃	252	41.34 N	94.12 W
Middle River	262	39.19 N	76.27 W
Middlesboro	246	36.36 N	83.43 W
Middlesbrough (Teesside)	162	54.35 N	1.14 W
Middlesex, Br. Hond.	278	17.02 N	88.31 W
Middlesex, N.J., U.S.	262	40.34 N	74.31 W
Middlesex, N.C., U.S.	246	35.47 N	78.12 W
Middlesex, N.Y., U.S.	264	42.42 N	77.16 W
Middlesex □[6], Ont., Can.	264	43.00 N	81.08 W
Middlesex □[6], Conn., U.S.	261	41.33 N	72.39 W
Middlesex □[6], Mass., U.S.	261	42.22 N	71.06 W
Middlesex □[6], N.J., U.S.	262	40.29 N	74.27 W
Middlesex □[6], Va., U.S.	262	37.40 N	76.35 W
Middle Stewiacke	240	45.13 N	63.08 W
Middleton, N.S., Can.	240	44.57 N	65.04 W
Middleton, Mass., U.S.	261	42.36 N	71.01 W
Middleton, Mich., U.S.	244	43.11 N	84.43 W
Middleton, Tenn., U.S.	248	35.04 N	88.54 W
Middleton, Wis., U.S.	268	43.06 N	89.30 W
Middleton ≃	228	22.35 S	141.51 E
Middleton Island I	236	59.25 N	146.25 W
Middleton Reef ✣[2]	226	29.28 S	159.06 E
Middletown, Calif., U.S.	272	38.45 N	122.37 W
Middletown, Conn., U.S.	261	41.33 N	72.39 W
Middletown, Del., U.S.	262	39.25 N	75.47 W
Middletown, Ill., U.S.	248	40.11 N	89.35 W
Middletown, Ind., U.S.	248	40.03 N	85.32 W
Middletown, Ky., U.S.	248	38.15 N	85.32 W
Middletown, Md., U.S.	242	39.27 N	77.33 W
Middletown, N.Y., U.S.	242	41.27 N	74.25 W
Middletown, Ohio, U.S.	242	39.29 N	84.25 W
Middletown, Pa., U.S.	242	40.12 N	76.44 W
Middletown, R.I., U.S.	261	41.32 N	71.17 W
Middletown, Va., U.S.	242	39.02 N	78.17 W
Middleville	268	42.43 N	85.28 W
Middlewich	174	53.11 N	2.27 W
Midgic	240	45.59 N	64.18 W
Midhurst	264	44.27 N	79.44 W
Midi, Canal du ≋	166	43.26 N	1.58 E
Midi de Bigorre, Pic du ▲	166	42.56 N	0.08 E
Mid-Indian Ridge ✣[3]	148	20.00 S	67.00 E
Midland, Ont., Can.	264	44.45 N	79.53 W
Midland, Calif., U.S.	258	33.52 N	114.48 W
Midland, Mich., U.S.	244	43.37 N	84.14 W
Midland, N.C., U.S.	246	35.14 N	80.30 W
Midland, Pa., U.S.	266	40.38 N	80.27 W
Midland, Pa., U.S.	266	40.15 N	80.13 W
Midland, S. Dak., U.S.	252	44.04 N	101.10 W
Midland, Tex., U.S.	250	32.00 N	102.05 W
Midland, Wash., U.S.	270	47.10 N	122.24 W
Midland Park	268	42.23 N	85.22 W
Midlands □[4]	224	19.00 S	29.45 E
Midleton	162	51.55 N	8.10 W
Midlothian, Ill., U.S.	268	41.38 N	87.42 W
Midlothian, Tex., U.S.	250	32.29 N	97.00 W
Midlothian □[6]	162	55.50 N	3.15 W
Midnapore, Bhārat	206	22.25 N	87.20 E
Midnapore, Alta., Can.	238	50.55 N	114.05 W
Midongy Sud	218	23.35 S	47.01 E
Midpines	272	37.33 N	119.56 W
Midsayap	202	7.12 N	124.32 E
Midvale, Idaho, U.S.	256	44.28 N	116.44 W
Midvale, Ohio, U.S.	266	40.26 N	81.23 W
Midvale, Utah, U.S.	254	40.37 N	111.54 W
Midville	246	32.49 N	88.14 W
Midway, Ala., U.S.	248	32.05 N	85.31 W
Midway, Ky., U.S.	242	38.09 N	84.41 W
Midway, Pa., U.S.	266	40.22 N	80.18 W
Midway, Tex., U.S.	250	31.02 N	95.45 W
Midway, Utah, U.S.	254	40.31 N	111.28 W
Midway Islands II	148	28.13 N	177.26 W
Midway Park	246	34.43 N	77.21 W
Midwest	254	43.25 N	106.16 W
Midwest City	250	35.27 N	97.24 W
Mid-Western □[3]	222	6.00 N	6.00 E
Midye	172	41.38 N	28.05 E
Midžor (Midžur) ▲	172	43.23 N	22.42 E
Mie	192	32.58 N	131.35 E
Mie □[5]	192	34.30 N	136.30 E
Miechów	164	50.23 N	20.01 E
Międzybórz (Neumittelwalde)	164	51.24 N	17.40 E
Międzychód (Mitteldorf)	164	52.28 N	15.55 E
Międzylesie (Mittwalde)	164	50.10 N	16.40 E
Międzyrzec Podlaski	164	52.00 N	22.47 E
Międzyrzecz (Meseritz)	164	52.28 N	15.35 E
Międzyzdroje (Misdroy)	164	53.55 N	14.28 E
Miejska Górka	164	51.40 N	16.58 E
Miélan	166	43.26 N	0.19 E
Mielec	164	50.18 N	21.25 E
Mielno (Gross Möllen)	164	54.16 N	16.01 E
Mienhua Hsü I	196	25.29 N	122.06 E
Miercurea-Ciuc	172	46.22 N	25.42 E
Mieres	168	43.15 N	5.46 W
Mieroszów (Friedland)	164	50.41 N	16.10 E
Miersig	172	46.53 N	21.51 E
Mier y Noriega	278	23.25 N	100.07 W
Miesbach	164	47.47 N	11.50 E
Mieszkowice (Bärwalde)	164	52.46 N	14.30 E
Mifflin, Ohio, U.S.	266	40.47 N	82.22 W
Mifflin, Pa., U.S.	262	40.34 N	77.24 W
Mifflin □[6]	266	40.40 N	77.33 W
Mifflinburg	242	40.55 N	77.03 W
Mifflintown	262	40.34 N	77.24 W
Migdal Ha'Emeq	210	32.41 N	35.14 E
Migennes	176	47.58 N	3.31 E
Mıgırtepe ▲	212	36.50 N	36.22 E
Miguel Alemán, Presa ⊜[1]	278	18.13 N	96.32 W
Miguel Auza	278	24.18 N	103.25 W
Miguel de la Borda	280	9.05 N	80.20 W
Miguelópolis	296	20.12 S	48.03 W
Miguel Riglos	294	36.50 S	63.42 W
Mihăești	172	45.07 N	25.00 E
Mihai Viteazu	172	44.39 N	28.41 E
Mihajlovgrad	172	43.25 N	23.13 E
Mihara	192	34.24 N	133.05 E
Mihara-yama ▲	192	34.43 N	139.23 E
Mihe ≃	194	37.12 N	119.10 E
Mijares ≃	168	39.55 N	0.01 W
Mikame	192	33.25 N	132.27 E
Mikasa	192a	43.20 N	141.40 E
Mikínai ⊥	172	37.44 N	22.45 E
Mikindani	218	10.17 S	40.07 E
Mikkeli	160	61.41 N	27.15 E
Mikkelin lääni □[4]	160	62.00 N	27.30 E
Mikkwa ≃	232	58.25 N	114.45 W
Mikołajki (Nikolaiken)	164	53.49 N	21.36 E
Mikolów	164	50.11 N	18.55 E
Míkonos	172	37.26 N	25.20 E
Míkonos I	172	37.29 N	25.25 E
Mikre	172	43.02 N	24.31 E
Mikrí Préspa, Límni ⊜	172	40.46 N	21.04 E
Mikstat	164	51.32 N	17.59 E
Mikulkin, Mys >	160	67.48 N	46.40 E
Mikulov	164	48.49 N	16.39 E
Mikumi	218	7.24 S	36.59 E
Mikun'	160	62.21 N	50.06 E
Mikuni	192	36.13 N	136.09 E
Mikuni-sammyaku ▲▲	192	36.50 N	138.40 E
Mikura-jima I	192	33.52 N	139.36 E
Mila	168	36.27 N	6.16 E
Milaca	244	45.45 N	93.39 W
Milagro, Arg.	294	31.00 S	66.00 W
Milagro, Ec.	290	2.07 S	79.36 W
Milagros	202	12.13 N	123.30 E
Milan, Ga., U.S.	246	32.01 N	83.04 W
Milan, Ind., U.S.	248	39.07 N	85.08 W
Milan → Milano, It.	182	45.28 N	9.12 E
Milan, Mich., U.S.	268	42.05 N	83.40 W
Milan, Minn., U.S.	252	45.07 N	95.55 W
Milan, Mo., U.S.	248	40.12 N	93.07 W
Milan, N. Mex., U.S.	254	35.09 N	107.54 W
Milan, Ohio, U.S.	266	41.18 N	82.36 W
Milan, Tenn., U.S.	248	35.55 N	88.46 W
Milano (Milan), It.	182	45.28 N	9.12 E
Milano, Tex., U.S.	250	30.43 N	96.52 W
Milano □[4]	182	45.30 N	9.30 E
Milanówek	164	52.08 N	20.40 E
Milâs	172	37.19 N	27.47 E
Milazzo	170	38.14 N	15.15 E
Milbank	252	45.13 N	96.38 W
Milbanke Sound U	238	52.18 N	128.33 W
Milbridge	242	44.32 N	67.53 W
Milbuk	202	6.10 N	124.16 E
Milburn	250	34.14 N	96.33 W
Mildenhall	174	52.21 N	0.30 E
Mildmay	264	44.03 N	81.07 W
Mildura	228	34.12 S	142.09 E
Mile	200	24.26 N	103.26 E
Miléai	172	39.20 N	23.09 E
100 Mile House, B.C., Can.	238	51.39 N	121.18 W
150 Mile House, B.C., Can.	238	52.07 N	122.56 W
70 Mile House, B.C., Can.	238	51.18 N	121.24 W
Miles, Austl.	226	26.40 S	150.11 E
Miles, Tex., U.S.	250	31.36 N	100.11 W
Milesburg	266	40.56 N	77.47 W
Miles City	256	46.25 N	105.51 W
Mile Seven Hundred Thirty Three	236	60.03 N	131.07 W
Milestone	252	50.00 N	104.30 W
Milevsko	164	49.27 N	14.22 E
Milford, Conn., U.S.	261	41.13 N	73.04 W
Milford, Del., U.S.	262	38.55 N	75.25 W
Milford, Ill., U.S.	268	40.38 N	87.42 W
Milford, Ind., U.S.	268	41.25 N	85.51 W
Milford, Iowa, U.S.	252	43.20 N	95.09 W
Milford, Maine, U.S.	242	44.57 N	68.39 W
Milford, Mass., U.S.	261	42.08 N	71.32 W
Milford, Mich., U.S.	268	42.35 N	83.36 W
Milford, Nebr., U.S.	252	40.47 N	97.03 W
Milford, N.H., U.S.	242	42.50 N	71.39 W
Milford, N.J., U.S.	262	40.34 N	75.06 W
Milford, Pa., U.S.	242	41.19 N	74.48 W
Milford, Utah, U.S.	254	38.24 N	113.01 W
Milford, Va., U.S.	262	38.01 N	77.22 W
Milford Center	242	40.11 N	83.26 W
Milford Haven	174	51.40 N	5.02 W
Milford Reservoir ⊜[1]	252	39.15 N	97.00 W
Milford Sound U	230	44.34 S	167.48 E
Milford Station	240	45.03 N	63.26 W
Mil'guvejem ≃	236	68.22 N	171.30 E
Milḥ, Baḥr al- ⊜	208	32.40 N	43.35 E
Milḥ, Ra's al- >	220	32.19 N	23.08 E
Milḥat Ashqar ⊜	208	35.18 N	41.55 E
Miliana	168	36.15 N	2.15 E
Miliane, Oued ≃	170	36.46 N	10.18 E
Milicz (Militsch)	164	51.32 N	17.17 E
Milk ≃	256	48.05 N	106.15 W
Mil'kovo	186	54.43 N	158.37 E
Milk River	238	49.09 N	112.05 W
Milk River Ridge ▲	238	49.15 N	112.30 W
Milk River Ridge Reservoir ⊜[1]	238	49.15 N	112.17 W
Millard	252	41.13 N	96.07 W
Millau	166	44.06 N	3.05 E
Mill Bay	270	48.39 N	123.34 W
Millboro	246	37.59 N	79.36 W
Millbrae	272	37.36 N	122.24 W
Millbrook, Ont., Can.	264	44.09 N	78.27 W
Millbrook, N.Y., U.S.	261	41.47 N	73.42 W
Millbury, Mass., U.S.	261	42.11 N	71.46 W
Millbury, Ohio, U.S.	266	41.34 N	83.25 W
Mill City	256	44.45 N	122.29 W
Mill Creek, Pa., U.S.	266	40.26 N	77.56 W
Mill Creek, W. Va., U.S.	242	38.44 N	79.58 W
Milldale	261	41.34 N	72.53 W
Milledgeville, Ga., U.S.	246	33.04 N	83.14 W
Milledgeville, Ill., U.S.	244	41.58 N	89.46 W
Mille Lacs, Lac des ⊜	244	48.50 N	90.30 W
Mille Lacs Lake ⊜	244	46.15 N	93.40 W
Millen	246	32.48 N	81.57 W
Miller, Ala., U.S.	248	32.09 N	87.47 W
Miller, Mo., U.S.	248	37.13 N	93.50 W
Miller, S. Dak., U.S.	252	44.31 N	98.59 W
Miller, Mount ▲	236	60.25 N	142.23 W
Miller City	268	41.06 N	84.08 W
Miller House	236	65.32 N	145.11 W
Millerovo	158	48.55 N	40.25 E
Miller Peak ▲	254	31.23 N	110.17 W
Miller Place	261	40.58 N	73.00 W
Millersburg, Ind., U.S.	268	41.32 N	85.42 W
Millersburg, Ky., U.S.	242	38.18 N	84.10 W
Millersburg, Mich., U.S.	244	45.20 N	84.04 W
Millersburg, Ohio, U.S.	266	40.33 N	81.55 W
Millersburg, Pa., U.S.	262	40.33 N	76.58 W
Millers Falls	261	42.35 N	72.30 W
Millers Ferry	248	32.06 N	87.22 W
Millersport	242	39.54 N	82.32 W
Millersview	250	31.25 N	99.45 W
Millersville, Ohio, U.S.	266	41.19 N	83.17 W
Millersville, Pa., U.S.	262	40.00 N	76.22 W
Millerton	261	41.57 N	73.31 W
Millertown	240	48.49 N	56.32 W
Millertown Junction	240	49.01 N	56.20 W
Millet	238	53.06 N	113.28 W
Millett, Mich., U.S.	268	42.42 N	84.38 W
Millett, Tex., U.S.	250	28.35 N	99.12 W
Millevaches, Plateau de ▲▲[1]	166	45.30 N	2.10 E
Mill Grove	268	40.25 N	85.17 W
Mill Hall	242	41.06 N	77.29 W
Millicent	228	37.36 S	140.22 E
Milligan, Fla., U.S.	248	30.45 N	86.38 W
Milligan, Nebr., U.S.	252	40.30 N	97.23 W
Millington, Ill., U.S.	268	41.34 N	88.36 W
Millington, Md., U.S.	262	39.16 N	75.50 W
Millington, Mich., U.S.	244	43.17 N	83.32 W
Millington, N.J., U.S.	262	40.40 N	74.31 W
Millington, Tenn., U.S.	248	35.21 N	89.54 W
Millinocket	242	45.39 N	68.43 W
Millis	261	42.10 N	71.22 W
Mill Island I	232	64.00 N	78.00 W
Millport, Scot., U.K.	162	55.46 N	4.55 W
Millport, Ala., U.S.	248	33.34 N	88.05 W
Millport, Pa., U.S.	266	41.55 N	78.07 W
Mill River	261	42.07 N	73.16 W
Millry	248	31.33 N	88.19 W
Mills	266	41.57 N	77.41 W
Millsboro	262	38.36 N	75.17 W
Mills Lake ⊜	232	61.30 N	118.10 W
Millstatt	164	46.48 N	13.35 E
Millstream	270	48.30 N	123.31 W
Milltown, Mont., U.S.	256	46.53 N	113.52 W
Milltown, N.J., U.S.	262	40.27 N	74.27 W
Milltown, Wis., U.S.	244	45.32 N	92.30 W
Milltown Malbay	162	52.52 N	9.23 W
Mill Valley	272	37.54 N	122.32 W
Millville, Mass., U.S.	261	42.02 N	71.35 W
Millville, N.J., U.S.	262	39.24 N	75.02 W
Millwood, N.Y., U.S.	261	41.11 N	73.48 W
Millwood, Va., U.S.	242	39.04 N	78.02 W
Millwood Reservoir ⊜[1]	248	33.45 N	94.00 W
Milmay	262	39.26 N	74.52 W
Milner	270	49.20 N	122.42 W
Milnor	252	46.16 N	97.27 W
Milo, Alta., Can.	238	50.34 N	112.53 W
Milo, Iowa, U.S.	244	41.17 N	93.27 W
Milo, Maine, U.S.	242	45.15 N	68.59 W
Milo ≃	222	11.04 N	9.14 W
Mílos	172	36.45 N	24.27 E
Mílos I	172	36.41 N	24.15 E
Miłosław	164	52.13 N	17.29 E
Milparinka	228	29.44 S	141.53 E
Milpitas	272	37.26 N	121.54 W
Milroy, Ind., U.S.	248	39.30 N	85.28 W
Milroy, Pa., U.S.	262	40.43 N	77.35 W
Miltenberg	164	49.42 N	9.15 E
Milton, Ont., Can.	244	43.31 N	79.53 W
Milton, N.Z.	230	46.07 S	169.58 E
Milton, Del., U.S.	262	38.47 N	75.19 W
Milton, Fla., U.S.	248	30.38 N	87.03 W
Milton, Iowa, U.S.	244	40.41 N	92.10 W
Milton, Mass., U.S.	261	42.15 N	71.05 W
Milton, N. Dak., U.S.	252	48.38 N	98.03 W
Milton, N.Y., U.S.	261	41.39 N	73.57 W
Milton, Pa., U.S.	242	41.01 N	76.51 W
Milton, Vt., U.S.	242	44.38 N	73.07 W
Milton, Wash., U.S.	270	47.15 N	122.19 W
Milton, W. Va., U.S.	242	38.26 N	82.08 W
Milton, Wis., U.S.	268	42.47 N	88.56 W
Milton-freewater	256	45.56 N	118.23 W
Miltonvale	252	39.21 N	97.27 W
Milton West	264	43.31 N	79.53 W
Mil'utke, Gora ▲	236	65.42 N	178.03 W
Milverton	264	43.34 N	80.55 W
Milwaukee	268	43.02 N	87.55 W
Milwaukee □[6]	268	43.02 N	87.58 W
Milwaukee ≃	244	43.02 N	87.54 W
Milwaukie	270	45.27 N	122.38 W
Mimbres ≃	254	32.13 N	107.28 W
Mimbres Mountains ▲▲	254	32.45 N	107.45 W
Mimi ≃	192	32.20 N	131.37 E
Mimico	244	43.37 N	79.30 W
Mimizan	166	44.12 N	1.14 W
Mimmaya	192	41.12 N	140.26 E
Mimoň	164	50.40 N	14.30 E
Mimoso, Bra.	292	16.17 S	55.48 W
Mimoso, Bra.	296	15.10 S	48.05 W
Mimoso do Sul	296	21.04 S	41.22 W
Mims	246	28.40 N	80.51 W
Mina, Méx.	250	26.01 N	100.32 W
Mina, Nev., U.S.	258	38.24 N	118.07 W
Mina, Oued ≃	168	35.47 N	0.30 E
Mīnā' al-Aḥmadī	208	29.04 N	48.08 E
Minahasa >[1]	198	1.00 N	124.35 E
Minakuchi	192	34.58 N	136.10 E
Minam ≃	256	45.37 N	117.43 W
Minamata	192	32.13 N	130.24 E
Minami-alps-kokuritsu-kōen ♣	192	35.40 N	138.13 E
Minami-Daitō-jima I	190	25.50 N	131.15 E
Minami-Tori-shima I	148	24.18 N	153.58 E
Mina Pirquitas	294	22.41 S	66.30 W
Minas, Cuba	284p	21.29 N	77.37 W
Minas, Ur.	294	34.23 S	55.14 W
Minas, Sierra de las ▲▲	280	15.10 N	89.40 W
Minas Basin C	240	45.20 N	64.00 W
Minas Channel U	240	45.15 N	64.45 W
Minas de Barroterán	278	27.30 N	101.20 W
Minas de Corrales	294	31.35 S	55.28 W
Minas de Matahambre	284p	22.35 N	83.57 W
Minas de Oro	280	14.46 N	87.20 W
Minas Gerais □[3]	296	18.00 S	44.00 W
Minas Novas	296	17.15 S	42.36 W
Mînăstirea	172	44.13 N	26.54 E
Minatare	252	41.48 N	103.30 W
Minatitlán	278	17.59 N	94.31 W
Minchumina, Lake ⊜	236	63.52 N	152.15 W
Minco	250	35.19 N	97.57 W
Minčol ▲	164	49.15 N	20.59 E
Mindanao I	202	7.30 N	125.00 E
Mindanao ≃	202	7.07 N	124.24 E
Mindanao Sea ≈[2]	202	9.10 N	124.20 E
Mindanao Trench ✣[1]	148	9.00 N	127.00 E
Mindelheim	180	48.03 N	10.29 E
Mindelo	214	16.53 N	25.00 W
Mindemoya	244	45.44 N	82.10 W
Minden, B.R.D.	178	52.17 N	8.55 E
Minden, Ont., Can.	264	44.55 N	78.43 W
Minden, La., U.S.	248	32.37 N	93.17 W
Minden, Nebr., U.S.	252	40.30 N	98.57 W
Minden, Nev., U.S.	272	38.57 N	119.45 W
Minden, W. Va., U.S.	242	37.59 N	81.07 W
Minden City	244	43.40 N	82.47 W
Mindenmines	248	37.28 N	94.35 W
Mindoro I	202	13.00 N	121.10 E
Mindoro Occidental □[4]	202	13.00 N	121.00 E
Mindoro Oriental □[4]	202	13.00 N	121.20 E
Mindoro Strait U	202	12.30 N	120.30 E
Mine	192	34.10 N	131.13 E
Mine Centre	244	48.45 N	92.37 W
Minehead	174	51.13 N	3.29 W
Mineiros	296	17.34 S	52.34 W
Mineola	250	32.40 N	95.29 W
Mineral, Tex., U.S.	250	28.33 N	97.54 W
Mineral, Wash., U.S.	270	46.43 N	122.11 W
Mineral City	266	40.36 N	81.25 W
Mineral Mountains ▲▲	254	38.30 N	112.45 W
Mineral'nyje Vody	158	44.12 N	43.08 E
Mineral Point, Pa., U.S.	266	40.23 N	78.50 W
Mineral Point, Wis., U.S.	244	42.52 N	90.11 W
Mineral Ridge	266	41.08 N	80.46 W
Mineral Springs, Ark., U.S.	248	33.53 N	93.55 W
Mineral Springs, Pa., U.S.	266	41.00 N	78.22 W
Mineral Wells	250	32.48 N	98.07 W
Minersville, Pa., U.S.	262	40.41 N	76.16 W
Minersville, Utah, U.S.	254	38.13 N	112.55 W
Minerva	266	40.44 N	81.06 W
Minerva Park	266	40.04 N	83.00 W
Minervino Murge	170	41.05 N	16.05 E
Minetto	264	43.24 N	76.29 W
Mineville	242	44.05 N	73.31 W
Minfeng	190	37.05 N	82.40 E
Mingan	240	50.18 N	64.02 W
Mingan, Îles de II	240	50.10 N	63.30 W
Mingan Mountains ▲▲	202	15.35 N	121.25 E
Mingečaur	158	40.45 N	47.03 E
Minglanilla	168	39.32 N	1.36 W
Mingo	268	40.13 N	83.38 W
Mingo Junction	266	40.19 N	80.37 W
Mingo Lake ⊜	232	64.35 N	72.10 W
Mingorría	168	40.45 N	4.40 W
Mingoville	266	40.56 N	77.39 W
Mingulay I	162	56.50 N	7.40 W
Minho □[9]	168	41.40 N	8.30 W
Minho (Miño) ≃	168	41.52 N	8.51 W
Minićevo	172	43.41 N	22.18 E
Minier	248	40.26 N	89.19 W
Minilulan Point >	202	9.08 N	123.42 E
Miniota	252	50.08 N	101.00 W
Minirodo, Baie de C	225b	25.10 S	44.15 E
Minisinakwa Lake ⊜	244	47.40 N	81.43 W
Minjar	158	55.04 N	57.33 E
Minjiang ≃	196	26.05 N	119.32 E
Minjiangkou ≃[1]	196	26.06 N	119.40 E
Minle	190	38.27 N	100.56 E
Minna	222	9.37 N	6.33 E
Minneapolis, Kans., U.S.	252	39.08 N	97.42 W
Minneapolis, Minn., U.S.	244	44.59 N	93.13 W
Minnedosa	232	50.14 N	99.51 W
Minnehaha	270	45.39 N	122.37 W
Minneola	252	37.26 N	100.01 W
Minneota	252	44.58 N	93.12 W
Minnesota □[3]	234	46.00 N	94.15 W
Minnesota ≃	244	44.54 N	93.10 W
Minnesota Lake	244	43.51 N	93.50 W
Minnewanka, Lake ⊜	238	51.15 N	115.20 W
Minnewaukan	252	48.04 N	99.15 W
Mino	192	35.32 N	136.55 E
Miño (Minho) ≃	168	41.52 N	8.51 W
Minoa	264	43.04 N	76.00 W
Minocqua	244	45.52 N	89.43 W
Mino-mikawa-kōgen ▲▲[1]	192	35.11 N	137.23 E
Minong	244	46.06 N	91.49 W
Minonk	268	40.54 N	89.02 W
Minooka	268	41.27 N	88.16 W
Minorca → Menorca I	168	40.00 N	4.00 E
Minot	252	48.14 N	101.18 W
Minsk	158	53.54 N	27.34 E
Minsk □[4]	160	54.30 N	28.00 E
Mińsk Mazowiecki	164	52.11 N	21.34 E
Minster	268	40.24 N	84.23 W
Mintaka Pass)(	206	36.58 N	74.54 E
Mint Canyon	274	34.26 N	118.25 W
Minto, N.B., Can.	240	46.05 N	66.05 W
Minto, Yukon, Can.	236	62.34 N	136.51 W
Minto, Alaska, U.S.	236	64.53 N	149.11 W
Minto, N. Dak., U.S.	252	48.17 N	97.15 W
Minto, Lac ⊜	232	57.15 N	74.50 W
Minto Inlet C	232	71.20 N	117.00 W
Minton	252	49.05 N	105.35 W
Minturn	254	39.35 N	106.26 W
Minturno	184	41.15 N	13.45 E
Minūf	220	30.28 N	30.56 E
Minusinsk	186	53.43 N	91.42 E
Minxian	190	34.22 N	104.08 E
Minya → Al-Minyā	220	28.06 N	30.45 E
Minya Konka → Gonggashan ▲	190	29.35 N	101.51 E
Mio	244	44.39 N	84.08 W
Mionica	172	44.15 N	20.05 E
Miquelon I	240	47.03 N	56.20 W
Mira, It.	170	45.26 N	12.08 E
Mira, Port.	168	40.26 N	8.44 W
Mira ≃, N.S., Can.	240	46.03 N	60.00 W
Mira ≃, Col.	290	1.36 N	79.01 W
Mira ≃, Port.	168	37.43 N	8.47 W
Mira Bay C	240	46.02 N	59.56 W
Miracema do Norte	286	9.33 S	48.24 W
Mirador	286	6.22 S	44.22 W
Miradouro	296	20.53 S	42.21 W
Miraflores, Arg.	294	28.36 S	65.54 W
Miraflores, Col.	290	5.12 N	73.12 W
Miraflores, Col.	290	1.25 N	72.13 W
Mīrah, Wādī al- V	208	32.26 N	41.42 E
Miraleste	274	33.46 N	118.19 W
Mira Loma	274	34.01 N	117.31 W
Miramar, Arg.	294	38.16 S	57.52 W
Miramar, Arg.	294	30.58 S	62.40 W
Miramar, C.R.	280	10.06 N	84.44 W
Miramar, Laguna ⊜	280	16.23 N	91.16 W
Miramas	166	43.35 N	5.00 E
Mirambeau	166	45.23 N	0.34 W
Miramichi Bay C	240	47.08 N	65.08 W
Mira Monte	274	36.42 N	119.03 W
Miranda, Bra.	292	20.14 S	56.22 W
Miranda, Col.	290	3.15 N	76.14 W
Miranda, Calif., U.S.	258	40.14 N	123.49 W
Miranda □[3]	290	10.15 N	66.25 W
Miranda ≃	292	19.25 S	57.20 W
Miranda de Ebro	168	42.41 N	2.57 W
Miranda do Douro	168	41.30 N	6.16 W
Mirande	166	43.31 N	0.25 E
Mirandela	168	41.29 N	7.11 W
Mirando City	250	27.26 N	99.00 W
Mirandola	170	44.53 N	11.04 E
Mirante do Paranapanema	296	22.17 S	51.54 W
Mirapuxi ≃	296	13.06 S	51.10 W
Miravalles, Volcán ▲[1]	280	10.45 N	85.10 W
Miravete, Puerto de)(	168	39.43 N	5.43 W
Mirbāṭ	204	17.00 N	54.45 E
Mirebeau-sur-Bèze	166	47.24 N	5.19 E
Mirecourt	180	48.18 N	6.08 E
Mireny	172	46.58 N	29.04 E
Miri	198	4.23 N	113.59 E
Mirim, Lagoa (Laguna Merín) C	294	32.45 S	52.50 W
Miriñay ≃	294	30.10 S	57.38 W
Miriti	292	6.15 S	59.00 W
Miritiparaná ≃	290	1.11 S	70.02 W
Mirnyj, S.S.S.R.	160	53.30 N	50.18 E
Mirnyj, S.S.S.R.	186	62.33 N	113.53 E
Mironeasa	172	46.58 N	27.25 E
Miroslav	164	48.57 N	16.18 E
Mirosławiec (Märkisch Friedland)	164	53.21 N	16.05 E
Mirow	164	53.16 N	12.49 E
Mīrpur	204	33.11 N	73.47 E
Mīrpur Khās	206	25.32 N	69.00 E
Mirranponga Pangunna Lake ⊜	228	25.56 S	137.42 E
Mirror	238	52.28 N	113.07 W
Mirs Bay C	196	22.30 N	114.24 E
Mirtóön Pélagos ≈[2]	172	36.51 N	23.18 E
Miryang	194	35.31 N	128.44 E
Mirzāpur	206	25.09 N	82.35 E
Misāḥah, Bi'r ≈[4]	220	22.12 N	27.57 E
Mi-saki >	193b	30.50 N	131.04 E
Misamis Occidental □[4]	202	8.20 N	123.42 E
Misamis Oriental □[4]	202	8.45 N	125.00 E
Misantla	278	19.56 N	96.50 W
Misasa	192	35.24 N	133.54 E
Misawa	192	40.41 N	141.24 E
Misburg	178	52.23 N	9.51 E
Miscou Centre	240	47.57 N	64.34 W
Miscou Island I	240	47.57 N	64.33 W
Miscou Point >	240	48.03 N	64.32 W
Misema ≃	244	47.54 N	79.53 W
Misenheimer	246	35.29 N	80.17 W
Mish'āb, Ra's al- >	208	28.12 N	48.39 E
Mishan	190	45.33 N	131.52 E
Mishaua ≃	292	11.12 S	72.58 W
Mishawaka	268	41.40 N	86.11 W
Misheguk Mountain ▲	236	68.15 N	161.03 W
Mishibishu Lake ⊜	244	48.05 N	85.25 W
Mishicot	244	44.14 N	87.38 W
Mishima	192	35.07 N	138.55 E
Mi-shima I	192	34.46 N	131.09 E
Mishmi Hills ▲▲[2]	206	29.00 N	96.00 E
Mishui ≃, Zhg.	196	28.50 N	113.06 E
Mishui ≃, Zhg.	196	27.09 N	112.51 E
Misilmeri	170	38.01 N	13.27 E
Misima Island I	226	10.40 S	152.45 E
Misiones □[4]	294	27.00 S	54.40 W
Misiones □[5]	294	27.00 S	57.00 W
Misión San Francisco de Laishí	294	26.15 S	58.35 W
Miskito Channel U	280	14.25 N	83.05 W
Miskitos, Cayos II	280	14.23 N	82.46 W
Miskitos Reef ✣[2]	280	14.28 N	82.42 W
Miskolc	164	48.06 N	20.47 E
Mislivna ▲	164	48.40 N	14.44 E
Mismār, Jabal ▲	220	18.06 N	35.42 E
Misool, Pulau I	198	1.52 S	130.10 E
Misquamicut	261	41.20 N	71.49 W
Misrātah	214	32.23 N	15.06 E
Misserghin	168	35.37 N	0.45 W
Missinaibi ≃	244	50.44 N	81.29 W
Missinaibi Lake ⊜	244	48.23 N	83.40 W
Mission, Kans., U.S.	248	39.03 N	94.38 W
Mission, S. Dak., U.S.	252	43.18 N	100.40 W
Mission, Tex., U.S.	250	26.13 N	98.20 W
Mission City	238	49.08 N	122.18 W
Mission Range ▲▲	256	47.30 N	113.55 W
Missisquoi □[6]	260	45.10 N	72.55 W
Mississagi ≃	244	46.10 N	83.01 W
Mississauga	264	43.35 N	79.37 W
Mississinewa ≃	268	40.46 N	86.02 W
Mississippi □[3]	234	32.50 N	89.30 W
Mississippi ≃, Ont., Can.	244	45.26 N	76.16 W
Mississippi ≃, U.S.	234	29.00 N	89.15 W
Mississippi City	248	30.24 N	89.01 W
Mississippi Delta ⩦[2]	248	29.10 N	89.15 W
Mississippi Lake ⊜	244	45.05 N	76.12 W
Mississippi Sound U	248	30.15 N	88.40 W
Missolonghi → Mesolóngion	172	38.21 N	21.17 E
Missoula	256	46.52 N	114.01 W
Missouri □[3]	234	38.30 N	93.30 W
Missouri ≃	234	38.50 N	90.08 W
Missouri, Coteau du ▲▲[2]	252	46.00 N	99.30 W
Missouri Buttes ▲	252	44.37 N	104.47 W
Missouri Valley	252	41.33 N	95.53 W
Mistaken, Point >	240	46.38 N	53.10 W
Mistanipisipou ≃	240	51.31 N	61.51 W
Mistassibi ≃	232	48.53 N	72.14 W
Mistassibi-Nord-Est ≃	240	49.50 N	71.56 W
Mistassini, Lac ⊜	232	51.15 N	73.10 W
Mistelbach an der Zaya	164	48.34 N	16.35 E
Misterbianco	170	37.31 N	15.01 E
Misteriosa Bank ✣[4]	282	18.52 N	83.50 W
Misti, Volcán ▲[1]	292	16.17 S	71.24 W
Mistrás ⊥	172	37.04 N	22.21 E
Mistretta	170	37.56 N	14.22 E
Misumi, Nihon	192	32.37 N	130.27 E
Misumi, Nihon	192	34.46 N	131.58 E
Mita, Punta de >	278	20.47 N	105.33 W
Mitchell, Austl.	228	26.29 S	147.58 E
Mitchell, Ont., Can.	264	43.28 N	81.12 W
Mitchell, Ind., U.S.	248	38.44 N	86.28 W
Mitchell, Nebr., U.S.	252	41.57 N	103.48 W
Mitchell, Oreg., U.S.	256	44.34 N	120.09 W
Mitchell, S. Dak., U.S.	252	43.43 N	104.01 W
Mitchell ≃, Austl.	228	29.21 S	152.32 E
Mitchell ≃, Austl.	228	37.53 S	147.41 E
Mitchell, Lake ⊜[1]	248	32.50 N	86.30 W
Mitchell, Mount ▲	246	35.46 N	82.16 W
Mitchell Corners	264	43.57 N	78.48 W
Mitchell Lake ⊜	238	52.53 N	120.36 W
Mitchellville	244	41.40 N	93.22 W
Mitcheltown	162	52.16 N	8.16 W
Mīt Ghamr	220	30.43 N	31.16 E
Míthimna	172	39.22 N	26.10 E
Mitidja ⩦	168	36.45 N	3.00 E
Mitilíni	172	39.06 N	26.32 E
Mitiwanga	266	41.22 N	82.27 W
Mitkof Island I	236	56.45 N	132.50 W
Mitla ⊥	278	16.55 N	96.17 W
Mito	192	36.22 N	140.28 E
Mitre ▲	230	40.48 S	175.29 E
Mitre Peak ▲	230	44.38 S	167.50 E
Mitrofania Island I	236	55.51 N	158.49 W
Mitrofanovo	160	63.13 N	56.00 E
Mitsio, Nosy I	225b	12.54 S	48.36 E
Mitsuke	192	37.32 N	138.56 E
Mittellandkanal ≋	164	52.16 N	11.41 E
Mittenwald	164	47.27 N	11.15 E
Mittersill	164	47.16 N	12.29 E
Mittweida	164	50.59 N	12.59 E
Mitú	290	1.08 N	70.03 W
Mitwaba	218	8.38 S	27.20 E
Mitzic	218	0.47 N	11.34 E
Miura	192	35.08 N	139.37 E
Miura-hantō >[1]	192	35.15 N	139.39 E
Mixco Viejo ⊥	280	14.53 N	90.39 W
Mixian	196	34.31 N	113.22 E
Miya ≃	192	34.32 N	136.44 E
Miyagi □[5]	192	38.22 N	140.52 E
Miyāh, Wādī al- V	220	25.00 N	33.23 E
Miyajima	192	34.18 N	132.19 E
Miyake-jima I	192	34.05 N	139.32 E
Miyako	192	39.38 N	141.57 E
Miyakonojō	192	31.44 N	131.04 E
Miyama	192	34.06 N	136.14 E
Miyanojō	192	31.54 N	130.27 E
Miyanoura-dake ▲	193b	30.20 N	130.31 E
Miyazaki	192	31.54 N	131.26 E
Miyazu	192	35.32 N	135.11 E
Miyoshi	192	34.48 N	132.51 E
Miyun	190	40.22 N	116.50 E
Mizdah	214	31.26 N	12.59 E
Mize	248	31.52 N	89.34 W
Mizen Head >, Eire	162	55.52 N	6.03 W
Mizen Head >, Eire	162	51.27 N	9.49 W
Mizil	172	45.00 N	26.26 E
Mizpah	262	39.29 N	74.50 W
Mizque	292	17.56 S	65.19 W
Mizukaidō	192	36.01 N	139.59 E
Mizusawa	192	39.08 N	141.08 E
Mjölby	160	58.19 N	15.08 E
Mjøsa ⊜	160	60.40 N	11.00 E
Mkalama	218	4.07 S	34.38 E
Mkomazi ≃	224	30.12 S	30.50 E
Mkuze ≃	224	27.53 S	32.29 E
Mladá Boleslav	164	50.23 N	14.59 E
Mladenovac	172	44.26 N	20.42 E
M'Lang	202	6.55 N	124.53 E
M'Lang	202	6.52 N	124.45 E
Mlava ≃	172	44.45 N	21.13 E
Mława	164	53.06 N	20.23 E
Mljet, Otok I	170	42.45 N	17.30 E
Mljetski Kanal U	170	42.48 N	17.35 E
Mmanford	174	51.48 N	3.59 W
Mníšek pod Brdy	164	49.52 N	14.16 E
Mo	160	66.15 N	14.08 E
Mo ≃	222	8.45 N	0.11 E
Moa ≃, Afr.	222	6.59 N	11.36 W
Moa ≃, Bra.	292	7.39 S	72.41 W
Moa, Pulau I	198	8.10 S	127.56 E
Moab	254	38.35 N	109.33 W
Moaco ≃	292	7.41 S	68.18 W
Moalboal	202	9.56 N	123.23 E
Moanda, Gabon	218	1.34 S	13.11 E
Moanda, Zaïre	218	5.56 S	12.21 E
Moate	162	53.24 N	7.58 W
Mobara	192	35.25 N	140.18 E
Mobaye	214	4.19 N	21.11 E
Mobeetie	250	35.31 N	100.26 W
Moberly	248	39.25 N	92.26 W
Moberly ≃	238	56.12 N	120.55 W
Moberly Lake	238	55.48 N	121.45 W
Mobile, Ala., U.S.	248	30.42 N	88.05 W
Mobile, Ariz., U.S.	254	33.03 N	112.16 W
Mobile ≃	248	30.40 N	88.02 W
Mobile Bay C	248	30.25 N	88.00 W
Mobjack	262	37.23 N	76.21 W
Mobridge	252	45.32 N	100.26 W
Moca, P.R.	284m	18.24 N	67.07 W
Moca, Rep. Dom.	282	19.24 N	70.31 W
Moçambique	218	15.06 S	40.50 E
Moçâmedes	218	15.10 S	12.09 E
Moccasin	272	37.49 N	120.18 W
Mocha → Al-Mukhā	204	13.19 N	43.15 E
Mocha, Isla I	294	38.22 S	73.56 W
Mochudi	224	24.28 S	26.05 E
Mocímboa da Praia	218	11.20 S	40.21 E
Mocksville	246	35.54 N	80.34 W
Moclips	270	47.14 N	124.13 W
Mocó ≃	290	1.49 S	66.48 W
Môco, Serra ▲	218	12.28 S	15.10 E
Mocoa	290	1.09 N	76.37 W
Mococa	296	21.28 S	47.01 W
Mocomoco	292	15.22 S	68.59 W
Mocoretá	294	30.37 S	57.58 W
Mocorito	278	25.29 N	107.55 W
Moctezuma	278	29.48 N	109.42 W
Moctezuma ≃, Méx.	278	21.59 N	98.34 W
Moctezuma ≃, Méx.	278	29.09 N	109.40 W
Mocuba	218	16.50 S	36.59 E
Močurica ≃	172	42.31 N	26.32 E
Modane	170	45.12 N	6.40 E
Modaomen C	196	22.08 N	113.24 E
Modder ≃	224	29.02 S	24.37 E
Modena	170	44.40 N	10.55 E
Modeste, Mount ▲	238	48.37 N	124.06 W
Modesto	272	37.39 N	121.00 W
Modica	170	36.51 N	14.47 E
Modjokerto	198	7.28 S	112.26 E
Mödling	164	48.05 N	16.17 E
Modowi	198	4.05 S	134.39 E
Modra	164	48.21 N	17.17 E
Modřany	164	50.01 N	14.25 E
Modra Špilja ⏏[5]	170	43.00 N	16.02 E
Modriča	172	44.57 N	18.18 E
Moe	228	38.10 S	146.15 E
Moecherville	268	41.44 N	88.17 W
Moeda	296	20.20 S	44.03 W
Moehau ▲	230	36.35 S	175.24 E
Moema	296	19.50 S	45.24 W
Moengo	286	5.37 N	54.24 W
Moenkopi	254	36.07 N	111.13 W
Moenkopi Wash V	254	36.54 N	111.26 W
Moeraki Point >	230	45.22 S	170.51 E
Moerbeke	176	51.10 N	3.56 E
Moers	178	51.27 N	6.37 E
Moffat	162	55.20 N	3.27 W
Moffet Point >	236	55.26 N	162.32 W
Moffit	252	46.41 N	100.18 W
Moga	206	30.48 N	75.10 E
Mogadisho	214	2.01 N	45.20 E
Mogador → Essaouira	214	31.30 N	9.47 W
Mogadore	266	41.03 N	81.24 W
Mogadouro	168	41.20 N	6.39 W
Mogalakwena ≃	224	23.00 S	28.40 E
Mogami ≃	192	38.55 N	139.48 E
Mogaung	200	25.18 N	96.56 E
Mogi das Cruzes	296	23.31 S	46.11 W
Mogielnica	164	51.42 N	20.43 E
Mogi-Guaçu ≃	296	20.53 S	48.10 W
Mogilno	164	52.40 N	17.58 E
Mogil'ov	158	53.54 N	30.21 E
Mogil'ov-Podol'skij	158	48.27 N	27.48 E
Mogi-Mirim	296	22.26 S	46.57 W
Mogincual	218	15.35 S	40.25 E
Moglal, Wādī V	220	19.18 N	34.29 E
Mogliano Veneto	170	45.33 N	12.14 E
Mogoča	186	53.44 N	119.44 E
Mogočin	186	57.43 N	83.34 E
Mogollon Mountains ▲▲	254	33.25 N	108.40 W
Mogollon Rim ⏏[4]	254	32.30 N	111.00 W
Mogotes	290	6.30 N	72.58 W
Mogotes, Punta >	294	38.02 S	57.31 W
Mogotón, Cerro ▲	280	13.45 N	86.26 W
Mograt Island I	220	19.30 N	33.15 E
Moguer	168	37.16 N	6.50 W
Mogzon	186	51.45 N	111.58 E
Mohács	164	45.59 N	18.42 E
Mohaka ≃	230	39.07 S	177.12 E
Mohall	252	48.46 N	101.31 W
Mohammadia	168	35.33 N	0.03 E
Mohammedia	214	33.44 N	7.24 W
Mohave Lake ⊜[1]	258	35.25 N	114.38 W
Mohawk	244	47.18 N	88.26 W
Mohawk ≃	242	42.47 N	73.42 W
Mohawk Mountain ▲	242	41.49 N	73.17 W
Mohe	190	53.29 N	122.19 E
Mohegan	261	41.28 N	72.06 W

Symbols in the index entries are identified on page 360.

Name	Page	Lat°′	Long°′
Mohegan Lake	261	41.19 N	73.51 W
Moheli I	225a	12.15 S	43.45 E
Mohelnice	164	49.46 N	16.55 E
Mohican, Cape ➤	236	60.12 N	167.28 W
Mohicanville Reservoir ⊜[1]	244	40.45 N	82.00 W
Mohinora, Cerro Λ	278	26.06 N	107.04 W
Mohns Ridge ⊹[3]	148	73.00 N	5.00 E
Mohnton	262	40.17 N	75.59 W
Moho ≃	280	16.03 N	88.51 W
Mohrsville	262	40.28 N	75.59 W
Moi	160	58.28 N	6.32 E
Moinești	172	46.28 N	26.29 E
Mointy	186	47.13 N	73.21 E
Moiporá	296	16.34 S	50.42 W
Moira ≃	244	44.09 N	77.23 W
Mõisaküla	160	58.06 N	25.11 E
Moisdon	166	47.37 N	1.22 W
Moisés Ville	294	30.40 S	61.30 W
Moisie	240	50.11 N	66.05 W
Moisie ≃	240	50.13 N	66.02 W
Moisie, Baie C	240	50.16 N	65.55 W
Moisling ◆[8]	178	53.50 N	10.38 E
Moissac	166	44.06 N	1.05 E
Moita	168	38.39 N	8.59 W
Moitaco	290	8.01 N	64.21 W
Mojacar	168	37.08 N	1.51 W
Mojave	274	35.03 N	118.10 W
Mojave ≃	258	35.06 N	116.04 W
Mojave Desert ◆[2]	258	35.00 N	117.00 W
Mojjero ≃	186	68.44 N	103.42 E
Mojo	214	8.38 N	39.07 E
Mojo, Pulau I	198	8.15 S	117.32 E
Mōka	192	36.26 N	140.01 E
Mokapu Peninsula ➤[1]	275d	21.27 N	157.45 W
Mokau ≃	230	38.42 S	174.37 E
Mokelumne Hill	272	38.18 N	120.42 W
Mokena	268	41.32 N	87.53 W
Mokochu, Khao Λ	200	15.57 N	99.00 E
Mokp'o	194	34.48 N	126.22 E
Mokrissèt	168	34.59 N	5.20 W
Mokša ≃	160	54.44 N	41.53 E
Mokuleia	275c	21.35 N	158.09 W
Mol	178	51.11 N	5.06 E
Mola di Bari	170	41.04 N	17.05 E
Molalla	270	45.09 N	122.35 W
Moláoi	172	36.48 N	22.52 E
Molat, Otok I	170	44.15 N	14.49 E
Mold	174	53.10 N	3.08 W
Moldau → Vltava ≃	164	50.21 N	14.30 E
Moldavia □[9]	172	46.30 N	27.00 E
Moldavian Soviet Socialist Republic → Moldavskaja Sovetskaja Socialističeskaja	186	47.00 N	29.00 E
Moldavskaja Sovetskaja Socialističeskaja Respublika □[3]	186	47.00 N	29.00 E
Molde	160	62.44 N	7.11 E
Moldes	294	33.40 S	64.35 W
Moldova-Nouă	172	44.44 N	21.40 E
Moldoveanul Λ	172	45.36 N	24.44 E
Môle, Cap du ➤	282	19.50 N	73.25 W
Molega Lake ⊜	240	44.22 N	64.53 W
Molenbeek-St.-Jean	176	50.51 N	4.19 E
Molepolole	224	24.25 S	25.30 E
Molfetta	170	41.12 N	16.36 E
Molina	294	35.07 S	71.17 W
Molina de Aragón	168	40.51 N	1.53 W
Molina de Segura	168	38.03 N	1.12 W
Moline, Ill., U.S.	244	41.30 N	90.31 W
Moline, Kans., U.S.	252	37.22 N	96.18 W
Moline, Mich., U.S.	268	42.44 N	85.40 W
Molinella	170	44.37 N	11.40 E
Molino	248	30.43 N	87.20 W
Molinos	294	25.25 S	66.19 W
Molíns de Rey	168	41.25 N	2.01 E
Molise □[4]	184	41.35 N	14.30 E
Mollendo	292	17.02 S	72.01 W
Mollepata	292	13.30 S	72.33 W
Moller, Port C	236	55.51 N	160.25 W
Mölln	164	53.37 N	10.41 E
Mollusk	262	37.44 N	76.32 W
Mölndal	160	57.39 N	12.01 E
Molocaboc Island I	202	10.58 N	123.33 E
Molodečno	160	54.19 N	26.49 E
Molodoj Tud	160	56.26 N	33.36 E
Mologa ≃	160	58.50 N	37.11 E
Molokai I	275d	21.07 N	157.00 W
Molokovo	160	58.10 N	36.45 E
Molopo ≃	224	28.30 S	20.13 E
Molotov → Perm'	158	58.00 N	56.15 E
Molotovsk → Severodvinsk	160	64.34 N	39.50 E
Molsheim	166	48.32 N	7.29 E
Molson Lake ⊜	232	54.12 N	96.45 W
Molu, Pulau I	198	6.45 S	131.33 E
Moluccas → Maluku II	198	2.00 S	128.00 E
Molucca Sea → Maluku, Laut ⊤[2]	198	0.30 S	125.00 E
Molundo	202	7.56 N	124.22 E
Moma	218	16.44 S	39.14 E
Moma ≃	186	66.26 N	143.06 E
Mombachito, Cerro Λ	280	12.25 N	85.35 W
Mombacho, Volcán Λ[1]	280	11.50 N	85.58 W
Mombasa	218	4.03 S	39.40 E
Mombetsu	192a	44.21 N	143.22 E
Mombuey	168	42.02 N	6.20 W
Momčilgrad	172	41.32 N	25.25 E
Momence	268	41.10 N	87.40 W
Momotombo, Volcán Λ[1]	280	12.26 N	86.33 W
Mompog Island I	202	13.31 N	122.10 E
Mompog Pass ⊔	202	13.40 N	122.00 E
Mompós	290	9.14 N	74.26 W
Momskij Chrebet ⛰	186	66.00 N	146.00 E
Møn I	164	55.00 N	12.20 E
Mon ≃	200	20.20 N	94.54 E
Mona	254	39.49 N	111.51 W
Mona, Canal de la ⊔	282	18.30 N	67.45 W
Mona, Isla I	282	18.05 N	67.53 W
Mona, Punta ➤	280	9.37 N	82.36 W
Monaca	266	40.41 N	80.17 W
Monach Islands II	162	57.32 N	7.40 W
Monaco	168	43.42 N	7.23 E
Monaco □[1]	158	43.45 N	7.25 E
Monadhliath Mountains ⛰	162	57.15 N	4.10 W
Monadnock, Mount Λ	242	42.52 N	72.07 W
Monagas □[3]	290	9.20 N	63.00 W
Monaghan	162	54.15 N	6.58 W
Monaghan □[6]	162	54.10 N	7.00 W
Monagrillo	280	7.59 N	80.28 W
Monahans	250	31.36 N	102.54 W
Monango	252	46.10 N	98.43 W
Monarch	246	34.43 N	81.35 W
Monarch Mountain Λ	238	51.54 N	125.53 W
Monarch Pass ⟩⟨	254	38.30 N	106.19 W
Monashee Mountains ⛰	238	50.30 N	118.30 W
Monastir	170	35.47 N	10.50 E
Moncada	202	15.44 N	120.34 E
Moncalieri	182	45.00 N	7.41 E
Monção, Bra.	286	3.30 S	45.15 W
Moncão, Port.	168	42.05 N	8.29 W
Monceau-sur-Sambre	176	50.25 N	4.22 E
Mončegorsk	160	67.54 N	32.58 E
Mönchengladbach	178	51.12 N	6.28 E
Monchique	168	37.19 N	8.33 W
Moncks Corner	246	33.12 N	80.01 W
Monclova	278	26.54 N	101.25 W
Moncontour	162	48.21 N	2.39 W
Moncoutant	166	46.43 N	0.35 W
Moncton	240	46.06 N	64.47 W
Mondaí	294	27.05 S	53.25 W
Monday ≃	294	25.33 S	54.41 W
Mondego ≃	168	40.09 N	8.52 W
Mondego, Cabo ➤	168	40.11 N	8.55 W
Mondoñedo	168	43.26 N	7.22 W
Mondoubleau	162	47.59 N	0.54 E
Mondovì, It.	182	44.23 N	7.49 E
Mondovi, Wis., U.S.	244	44.34 N	91.40 W
Mondragon	202	12.31 N	124.45 E
Mondragone	184	41.07 N	13.53 E
Mondsee	164	47.52 N	13.21 E
Monee	268	41.25 N	87.45 W
Monemvasía	172	36.41 N	23.03 E
Monero	254	36.54 N	106.52 W
Monessen	266	40.09 N	79.53 W
Monesterio	168	38.05 N	6.16 W
Monett	248	36.55 N	93.55 W
Monette	248	35.53 N	90.21 W
Monfalcone	170	45.49 N	13.32 E
Monflanquin	166	44.32 N	0.46 E
Monforte	168	39.03 N	7.26 W
Monforte de Lemos	168	42.31 N	7.30 W
Mongaguá	296	24.06 S	46.37 W
Mongala ≃	214	1.53 N	19.46 E
Mongalla	214	5.12 N	31.46 E
Mongaup ≃	242	41.25 N	74.45 W
Mong-cai	200	21.32 N	107.58 E
Möng Hsat	198	20.32 N	99.15 E
Monghyr	206	25.23 N	86.29 E
Môngkôl Bori ≃	200	13.19 N	103.24 E
Mongo, Tchad	214	12.11 N	18.42 E
Mongo, Ind., U.S.	268	41.41 N	85.17 W
Mongo ≃	222	9.34 N	12.11 W
Mongol Altajn Nuruu ⛰	190	47.00 N	92.00 E
Mongolia □[1]	190	47.30 N	104.00 E
Mongpong ≃	202	12.43 N	120.48 E
Mongu	218	15.15 S	23.09 E
Monheim	178	51.05 N	6.52 E
Moniaive	162	55.12 N	3.55 W
Monico	244	45.35 N	89.09 W
Monida Pass ⟩⟨	256	44.33 N	112.18 W
Moninger	266	40.14 N	80.13 W
Moniquirá	290	5.52 N	73.36 W
Mõniste	160	57.35 N	26.33 E
Monistrol-sur-Loire	166	45.17 N	4.10 E
Monkayo	202	7.50 N	126.03 E
Monkey River	280	16.22 N	88.29 W
Mońki	164	53.24 N	22.49 E
Monkton	264	43.35 N	81.05 W
Monmouth, Wales, U.K.	174	51.50 N	2.43 W
Monmouth, Ill., U.S.	244	40.55 N	90.39 W
Monmouth, Ind., U.S.	268	40.52 N	84.57 W
Monmouth, Oreg., U.S.	256	44.51 N	123.14 W
Monmouth □[6]	262	40.16 N	74.17 W
Monmouth Junction	262	40.20 N	74.36 W
Monmouth Mountain Λ	238	51.00 N	123.47 W
Monmouth Peak Λ	256	44.48 N	123.33 W
Monmouthshire □[6]	174	51.43 N	2.57 W
Mono □[5]	222	6.45 N	1.50 E
Mono □[6]	272	38.18 N	119.22 W
Mono ≃	222	6.17 N	1.51 E
Monocacy Station	262	40.16 N	75.46 W
Mono Lake ⊜	258	38.00 N	119.00 W
Monolith	274	35.07 N	118.22 W
Monon	268	40.52 N	86.53 W
Monona, Iowa, U.S.	244	43.03 N	91.23 W
Monona, Wis., U.S.	268	43.04 N	89.20 W
Monongahela	266	40.11 N	79.56 W
Monopoli	170	40.57 N	17.19 E
Monor	164	47.21 N	19.27 E
Monos ⊥	278	18.25 N	89.02 W
Monóvar	168	38.25 N	0.47 W
Monowai, Lake ⊜	230	45.53 S	167.26 E
Monponsett	261	42.01 N	70.51 W
Monreal	168	42.42 N	1.30 W
Monreal del Campo	168	40.47 N	1.21 W
Monreale	170	38.05 N	13.17 E
Monroe, Conn., U.S.	261	41.20 N	73.12 W
Monroe, Ga., U.S.	246	33.47 N	83.43 W
Monroe, Ind., U.S.	268	40.45 N	84.56 W
Monroe, Iowa, U.S.	244	41.31 N	93.06 W
Monroe, La., U.S.	248	32.33 N	92.07 W
Monroe, Mich., U.S.	266	41.55 N	83.24 W
Monroe, Nebr., U.S.	252	41.28 N	97.36 W
Monroe, N.C., U.S.	246	34.59 N	80.33 W
Monroe, N.Y., U.S.	242	41.20 N	74.11 W
Monroe, Oreg., U.S.	256	44.19 N	123.18 W
Monroe, Utah, U.S.	254	38.38 N	112.07 W
Monroe, Va., U.S.	246	37.30 N	79.08 W
Monroe, Wash., U.S.	270	47.51 N	121.58 W
Monroe, Wis., U.S.	244	42.36 N	89.38 W
Monroe □[6], Mich., U.S.	268	41.55 N	83.26 W
Monroe □[6], N.Y., U.S.	264	43.10 N	77.36 W
Monroe, Lake ⊜	246	28.52 N	81.16 W
Monroe Bridge	261	42.43 N	72.57 W
Monroe Center	268	42.06 N	89.00 W
Monroe City, Ind., U.S.	248	38.37 N	87.21 W
Monroe City, Mo., U.S.	248	39.39 N	91.44 W
Monroe Manor	268	41.36 N	86.40 W
Monroe Reservoir ⊜[1]	248	39.05 N	86.25 W
Monroeville, Ala., U.S.	248	31.31 N	87.20 W
Monroeville, Ind., U.S.	268	40.58 N	84.52 W
Monroeville, N.J., U.S.	262	39.38 N	75.10 W
Monroeville, Ohio, U.S.	266	41.15 N	82.42 W
Monroeville, Pa., U.S.	266	40.26 N	79.47 W
Monrovia, Liber.	222	6.18 N	10.47 W
Monrovia, Calif., U.S.	274	34.09 N	118.03 W
Mons (Bergen)	176	50.27 N	3.56 E
Monsarás, Ponta do ➤	296	19.35 S	39.45 W
Monschau	164	50.33 N	6.14 E
Monsefú	292	6.52 S	79.52 W
Monselice	170	45.14 N	11.45 E
Monserrato	170	39.15 N	9.08 E
Monson, Maine, U.S.	242	45.17 N	69.30 W
Monson, Mass., U.S.	261	42.06 N	72.19 W
Monster	178	52.02 N	4.10 E
Mönsterås	160	57.02 N	16.26 E
Monsummano Terme	184	43.52 N	10.49 E
Montabaur	164	50.26 N	7.50 E
Montagnana	170	45.14 N	11.28 E
Montagrier	166	45.16 N	0.29 E
Montagu	218	33.45 S	20.08 E
Montague, P.E.I., Can.	240	46.10 N	62.39 W
Montague, Calif., U.S.	258	41.44 N	122.32 W
Montague, Mass., U.S.	261	42.32 N	72.32 W
Montague, Mich., U.S.	244	43.25 N	86.22 W
Montague, Tex., U.S.	250	33.40 N	97.43 W
Montague, Isla I	278	31.45 N	114.45 W
Montague City	261	42.35 N	72.35 W
Montague Island I	236	60.00 N	147.30 W
Montague Peak Λ	236	60.15 N	147.01 W
Montaigu	166	46.59 N	1.19 W
Montaigut-en-Combraille	166	46.11 N	2.38 E
Montalbán	168	40.50 N	0.48 W
Montalbano di Elicona	170	38.02 N	15.02 E
Montalbano Ionico	170	40.17 N	16.34 E
Montalcino	170	43.03 N	11.29 E
Montalegre	168	41.49 N	7.48 W
Mont Alto	262	39.50 N	77.34 W
Montalto Λ	170	38.10 N	15.55 E
Montalto di Castro	170	42.21 N	11.37 E
Montalto Uffugo	170	39.25 N	16.10 E
Montalvin Manor	272	37.59 N	122.21 W
Montalvo	274	34.15 N	119.12 W
Montana, Schw.	166	46.18 N	7.29 E
Montana, Alaska, U.S.	236	62.05 N	150.04 W
Montana □[3]	234	47.00 N	110.00 W
Montana Indian Reserve ◆[4]	238	52.43 N	113.25 W
Montánchez	168	39.13 N	6.09 W
Montara	272	37.33 N	122.31 W
Montargil	168	39.05 N	8.10 W
Montargis	176	48.00 N	2.45 E
Montataire	176	49.16 N	2.26 E
Montauban	166	44.01 N	1.21 E
Montauban-les-Mines	260	46.49 N	72.21 W
Montauk	261	41.03 N	71.57 W
Montauk Point ➤	242	41.04 N	71.52 W
Monta Vista, Calif., U.S.	272	37.19 N	122.03 W
Monta Vista, Wash., U.S.	270	47.11 N	122.29 W
Montbard	176	47.37 N	4.20 E
Montbarrey	166	47.01 N	5.39 E
Montbéliard	180	47.31 N	6.48 E
Mont Belvieu	250	29.51 N	94.54 W
Montblanch	168	41.22 N	1.10 E
Montbrison	182	45.36 N	4.03 E
Montbron	166	45.40 N	0.30 E
Montcalm □[6]	260	46.20 N	74.20 W
Montceau [-les-Mines]	180	46.40 N	4.22 E
Montcevelles, Lac ⊜	240	51.06 N	60.35 W
Montchanin	180	46.45 N	4.27 E
Montclair, Calif., U.S.	274	34.06 N	117.41 W
Montclair, N.J., U.S.	242	40.49 N	74.13 W
Mont Clare	262	40.08 N	75.30 W
Mont-de-Marsan	166	43.53 N	0.30 W
Montdidier	176	49.39 N	2.34 E
Monte, Castel del ⊥	170	41.05 N	16.15 E
Monte, Lago del ⊜	294	37.00 S	62.52 W
Monteagle	248	35.15 N	85.50 W
Monteagudo	292	19.49 S	63.59 W
Monte Albán ⊥	278	17.02 N	96.45 W
Monte Alegre	286	2.01 S	54.04 W
Monte Alegre ≃	296	17.16 S	50.41 W
Monte Alegre de Goiás	296	13.14 S	47.10 W
Monte Alegre de Minas	296	18.52 S	48.52 W
Monte Azul	296	15.09 S	42.53 W
Monte Azul Paulista	296	20.55 S	48.38 W
Montebello, Qué., Can.	260	45.39 N	74.56 W
Montebello, P.R.	284m	18.22 N	66.31 W
Montebello, Calif., U.S.	274	34.01 N	118.06 W
Montebello Ionico	170	37.59 N	15.45 E
Monte Bello Islands II	226	20.25 S	115.32 E
Monte Buey	294	32.55 S	62.30 W
Montecarlo	294	26.33 S	54.47 W
Monte Carlo	182	43.44 N	7.25 E
Monte Carmelo	296	18.43 S	47.29 W
Monte Caseros	294	30.15 S	57.38 W
Montecassino, Abbazia di ⊕[1]	170	41.29 N	13.48 E
Montecatini Terme	184	43.53 N	10.46 E
Montech	166	43.57 N	1.14 E
Montecillos, Cordillera de ⛰	280	14.25 N	87.51 W
Montecito	258	34.26 N	119.39 W
Monte Comán	294	34.36 S	67.50 W
Monte Creek	238	50.39 N	119.57 W
Montecristi, Ec.	290	1.03 S	80.40 W
Montecristi, Rep. Dom.	282	19.52 N	71.39 W
Monte Cristo	292	14.43 S	61.14 W
Monte Cristo, Cerro Λ	280	14.25 N	89.21 W
Montecristo, Isola di I	170	42.20 N	10.19 E
Monte di Procida	184	40.48 N	14.03 E
Monte Escobedo	278	22.18 N	103.35 W
Montefalco	170	42.54 N	12.39 E
Montefeltro ◆[1]	184	43.50 N	12.30 E
Montefiascone	184	42.32 N	12.02 E
Montefrío	168	37.19 N	4.01 W
Montego Bay	285q	18.30 N	77.55 W
Monte Grande	294	30.06 S	70.31 W
Montegut	248	29.29 N	90.33 W
Monteith, Mount Λ	238	55.45 N	122.30 W
Montejicar	168	37.34 N	3.30 W
Montelíbano	290	8.05 N	75.29 W
Montélimar	182	44.34 N	4.45 E
Monte Lindo ≃	294	23.56 S	57.12 W
Montella	184	40.51 N	15.01 E
Montellano	168	37.00 N	5.34 W
Montello, Nev., U.S.	258	41.16 N	114.12 W
Montello, Wis., U.S.	244	43.48 N	89.20 W
Montelupo Fiorentino	184	43.44 N	11.01 E
Monte Maíz	294	33.20 S	62.37 W
Montemorelos	278	25.12 N	99.49 W
Montemor-o-Novo	168	38.39 N	8.13 W
Montemor o Velho	168	40.10 N	8.41 W
Montemuro Λ[2]	168	38.54 N	9.14 W
Montendre	166	45.17 N	0.24 W
Montenegro	294	29.42 S	51.28 W
Montenero di Bisaccia	184	41.57 N	14.47 E
Monte Pascoal, Parque Nacional de ♠	296	16.54 S	39.24 W
Monte Patria	294	30.42 S	70.58 W
Montepuez	218	12.32 S	40.27 E
Montepulciano	184	43.05 N	11.47 E
Monte Quemado	294	25.50 S	62.50 W
Montereale	184	42.31 N	13.15 E
Montereau-faut-Yonne	176	48.23 N	2.57 E
Monterey, Calif., U.S.	272	36.37 N	121.55 W
Monterey, Ind., U.S.	268	41.09 N	86.29 W
Monterey, Tenn., U.S.	248	36.09 N	85.16 W
Monterey, Va., U.S.	242	38.25 N	79.35 W
Monterey □[6]	272	36.40 N	121.38 W
Monterey Bay C	234	36.45 N	121.55 W
Monterey Park	274	34.04 N	118.07 W
Montería	290	8.46 N	75.53 W
Montero	292	17.20 S	63.15 W
Monteros	294	27.10 S	65.30 W
Monterotondo	184	42.03 N	12.37 E
Monterrey	278	25.40 N	100.19 W
Montesano, It.	170	40.16 N	15.43 E
Montesano, Wash., U.S.	270	46.59 N	123.36 W
Monte Sant'Angelo	184	41.42 N	15.57 E
Monte Santu, Capo di ➤	170	40.05 N	9.44 E
Montesarchio	184	41.04 N	14.38 E
Montes Claros	296	16.43 S	43.52 W
Monte Sereno	272	37.15 N	122.01 W
Montesilvano	184	42.29 N	14.08 E
Montevallo	248	33.06 N	86.52 W
Montevarchi	184	43.31 N	11.34 E
Montevideo, Minn., U.S.	252	44.57 N	95.43 W
Montevideo, Ur.	294	34.53 S	56.11 W
Monte Vista	254	37.35 N	106.09 W
Montezuma, Ga., U.S.	246	32.18 N	84.02 W
Montezuma, Ind., U.S.	248	39.48 N	87.22 W
Montezuma, Iowa, U.S.	244	41.35 N	92.32 W
Montezuma, Kans., U.S.	252	37.36 N	100.27 W
Montezuma, N.Y., U.S.	264	43.00 N	76.42 W
Montezuma, Ohio, U.S.	268	40.29 N	84.33 W
Montezuma Castle National Monument ♠	254	34.30 N	112.00 W
Montfaucon	166	45.10 N	4.18 E
Montfort, Fr.	166	48.08 N	1.58 W
Montfort, Wis., U.S.	244	42.58 N	90.26 W
Montgomery, Wales, U.K.	162	52.33 N	3.03 W
Montgomery, Ala., U.S.	248	32.23 N	86.18 W
Montgomery, Ill., U.S.	268	41.44 N	88.21 W
Montgomery, La., U.S.	248	31.40 N	92.53 W
Montgomery, Mich., U.S.	268	41.47 N	84.48 W
Montgomery, Minn., U.S.	244	44.26 N	93.35 W
Montgomery, Pa., U.S.	242	41.10 N	76.52 W
Montgomery → Sāhīwāl, Pāk.	206	30.40 N	73.06 E
Montgomery, Tex., U.S.	250	30.23 N	95.42 W
Montgomery, W. Va., U.S.	242	38.11 N	81.19 W
Montgomery □[6], Md., U.S.	262	39.05 N	77.09 W
Montgomery □[6], Pa., U.S.	262	40.07 N	75.21 W
Montgomery City	248	38.59 N	91.30 W
Montgomeryshire □[6]	174	52.38 N	3.30 W
Montguyon	166	45.13 N	0.11 W
Monthermé	166	49.53 N	4.44 E
Monthey	180	46.15 N	6.57 E
Monthois	166	49.19 N	4.43 E
Monticello, Ark., U.S.	248	33.38 N	91.47 W
Monticello, Fla., U.S.	246	30.33 N	83.52 W
Monticello, Ga., U.S.	246	33.18 N	83.40 W
Monticello, Ill., U.S.	248	40.01 N	88.34 W
Monticello, Ind., U.S.	268	40.45 N	86.46 W
Monticello, Iowa, U.S.	244	42.15 N	91.12 W
Monticello, Ky., U.S.	248	36.50 N	84.51 W
Monticello, Minn., U.S.	244	45.18 N	93.48 W
Monticello, Miss., U.S.	248	31.33 N	90.07 W
Monticello, Mo., U.S.	248	40.07 N	91.43 W
Monticello, N. Mex., U.S.	254	33.24 N	107.27 W
Monticello, N.Y., U.S.	242	41.39 N	74.42 W
Monticello, Utah, U.S.	254	37.52 N	109.21 W
Monticello, Wis., U.S.	244	42.45 N	89.35 W
Montichiari	170	45.25 N	10.23 E
Montiel, Campo de ≚	168	38.46 N	2.44 W
Montignac	166	45.04 N	1.10 E
Montigny-le-Roi	166	48.00 N	5.30 E
Montigny-sur-Aube	166	47.57 N	4.46 E
Montijo, Esp.	168	38.55 N	6.37 W
Montijo, Pan.	280	8.00 N	81.01 W
Montijo, Port.	168	38.42 N	8.58 W
Montijo, Golfo de C	290	7.35 N	81.08 W
Montilla	168	37.35 N	4.38 W
Montividiu	296	17.24 S	51.14 W
Montividiu ≃	296	17.10 S	50.57 W
Montivilliers	176	49.33 N	0.12 E
Mont-Joli	240	48.35 N	68.11 W
Mont-Laurier	232	46.33 N	75.30 W
Mont-Louis	166	42.31 N	2.07 E
Montluçon	166	46.21 N	2.36 E
Montluel	166	45.51 N	5.03 E
Montmagny	240	46.59 N	70.33 W
Montmédy	166	49.31 N	5.22 E
Montmirail	166	48.06 N	0.48 E
Montmoreau	166	45.24 N	0.08 E
Montmorenci	268	40.28 N	87.02 W
Montmorency, Qué., Can.	260	46.53 N	71.09 W
Montmorency, Fr.	176	49.00 N	2.20 E
Montmorency ≃	240	46.53 N	71.08 W
Montmorillon	166	46.26 N	0.52 E
Montmort	166	48.55 N	3.49 E
Monto	228	24.52 S	151.07 E
Montorio al Vomano	184	42.35 N	13.38 E
Montoro	168	38.01 N	4.23 W
Montour Falls	242	42.21 N	76.51 W
Montoursville	242	41.15 N	76.55 W
Montpelier, Jam.	285q	18.22 N	77.56 W
Montpelier, Idaho, U.S.	256	42.19 N	111.18 W
Montpelier, Ind., U.S.	268	40.33 N	85.17 W
Montpelier, Miss., U.S.	248	33.43 N	88.57 W
Montpelier, Ohio, U.S.	268	41.35 N	84.36 W
Montpelier, Vt., U.S.	242	44.16 N	72.35 W
Montpellier	182	43.36 N	3.53 E
Montpon-sur-l'Isle	166	45.00 N	0.10 E
Montréal, Qué., Can.	260	45.31 N	73.34 W
Montreal, Wis., U.S.	244	46.26 N	90.14 W
Montreal ≃, Ont., Can.	244	47.08 N	79.27 W
Montreal ≃, Ont., Can.	244	47.14 N	84.39 W
Montreal ≃, U.S.	244	46.44 N	90.25 W
Montréal-Est	260	45.38 N	73.29 W
Montreal Lake ⊜	232	54.20 N	105.40 W
Montréal-Nord	260	45.35 N	73.38 W
Montrésor	166	47.09 N	1.12 E
Montreuil-Bellay	166	47.08 N	0.09 W
Montreuil-sous-Bois	176	48.52 N	2.26 E
Montreuil-sur-Mer	166	50.28 N	1.46 E
Montreux	180	46.26 N	6.55 E
Montrevel [-en-Bresse]	166	46.20 N	5.08 E
Montrichard	166	47.21 N	1.11 E
Mont-Rolland	260	45.57 N	74.07 W
Montrose, Scot., U.K.	162	56.43 N	2.29 W
Montrose, Calif., U.S.	274	34.12 N	118.13 W
Montrose, Colo., U.S.	254	38.29 N	107.53 W
Montrose, Iowa, U.S.	244	40.31 N	91.25 W
Montrose, Mich., U.S.	244	43.11 N	83.54 W
Montrose, N.Y., U.S.	261	41.15 N	73.56 W
Montrose, Ohio, U.S.	266	41.08 N	81.37 W
Montrose, Pa., U.S.	242	41.50 N	75.53 W
Montrose, S. Dak., U.S.	252	43.42 N	97.11 W
Montross	262	38.06 N	76.50 W
Monts, Pointe des ➤	240	49.19 N	67.23 W
Mont-Saint-Aignan	162	49.28 N	1.05 E
Mont-Saint-Hilaire	260	45.32 N	73.11 W
Mont-Saint-Michel → Le Mont Saint-Michel ⊕[1]	166	48.38 N	1.32 W
Montserrado □[6]	222	6.40 N	10.40 W
Montserrat □[2]	276	16.45 N	62.12 W
Montserrat, Monasterio de ⊕[1]	168	41.36 N	1.49 E
Montsûrs	162	48.08 N	0.33 W
Montuenga	168	41.03 N	4.37 W
Montvale	246	37.23 N	79.43 W
Montville, Conn., U.S.	261	41.27 N	72.08 W
Montville, Ohio, U.S.	266	41.36 N	81.03 W
Monument, Oreg., U.S.	256	44.49 N	119.25 W
Monument, Pa., U.S.	266	41.07 N	77.42 W
Monument Beach	261	41.43 N	70.37 W
Monument Draw V	250	32.26 N	102.10 W
Monumento	278	29.23 N	111.00 W
Monument Peak Λ, Colo., U.S.	254	39.43 N	107.55 W
Monument Peak Λ, Idaho, U.S.	256	42.07 N	114.14 W
Monument Valley V	254	36.50 N	110.20 W
Monywa	200	22.05 N	95.08 E
Monza	182	45.35 N	9.16 E
Monzen	192	37.17 N	136.46 E
Monzón, Esp.	168	41.55 N	0.12 E
Monzón, Perú	292	9.08 S	76.20 W
Moodie Island I	232	64.37 N	65.30 W
Moodus	261	41.30 N	72.27 W
Moody, Maine, U.S.	242	43.16 N	70.36 W
Moody, Tex., U.S.	250	31.19 N	97.21 W
Mooers	260	44.58 N	73.35 W
Mooi ≃	224	28.45 S	30.34 E
Moon	266	40.31 N	80.14 W
Moonie ≃	228	29.19 S	148.43 E
Moon Run	266	40.30 N	80.14 W
Moonta	228	34.04 S	137.35 E
Moora	226	30.39 S	116.00 E
Moorcroft	252	44.16 N	104.57 W
Moore, Idaho, U.S.	256	43.44 N	113.22 W
Moore, Mont., U.S.	256	46.59 N	109.42 W
Moore, Okla., U.S.	250	35.20 N	97.29 W
Moore, Tex., U.S.	250	29.03 N	99.01 W
Moorefield, Ohio, U.S.	266	40.12 N	81.10 W
Moorefield, W. Va., U.S.	242	39.04 N	78.58 W
Moore Haven	246	26.50 N	81.05 W
Mooreland	250	36.26 N	99.12 W
Moore Reservoir ⊜[1]	242	44.25 N	71.50 W
Moores Creek National Military Park ♠	246	34.24 N	78.08 W
Moorestown	262	39.58 N	74.57 W
Mooresville, Ind., U.S.	248	39.37 N	86.22 W
Mooresville, N.C., U.S.	246	35.35 N	80.48 W
Moorhead, Minn., U.S.	252	46.53 N	96.45 W
Moorhead, Miss., U.S.	248	33.27 N	90.30 W
Mooringsport	248	32.41 N	93.58 W
Moornanyah Lake ⊜	228	33.02 S	143.58 E
Moorpark	274	34.17 N	118.53 W
Moors Island I	282	26.19 N	77.33 W
Moorslede	176	50.53 N	3.04 E
Moosburg	164	48.29 N	11.57 E
Moose Creek	260	45.15 N	74.58 W
Moosehead Lake ⊜	242	45.40 N	69.40 W
Mooseheart	268	41.49 N	88.20 W
Moose Heights	238	53.05 N	122.30 W
Moose Jaw	232	50.23 N	105.32 W
Moose Lake	244	46.26 N	92.45 W
Moose Lake ⊜	238	54.15 N	110.55 W
Mooselookmeguntic Lake ⊜	242	44.53 N	70.48 W
Moose Pass	236	60.29 N	149.22 W
Moosomin	232	50.07 N	101.40 W
Moosonee	232	51.17 N	80.39 W
Moosup	261	41.43 N	71.53 W
Mopanyang ⊔	196	29.32 N	122.16 E
Mopti	222	14.30 N	4.12 W
Mopti □[4]	222	14.40 N	4.15 W
Moquegua	292	17.20 S	70.55 W
Moquegua □[5]	292	16.50 S	70.55 W
Mór	164	47.23 N	18.12 E
Mora, Esp.	168	39.41 N	3.46 W
Mora, Port.	168	38.56 N	8.10 W
Mora, Sve.	160	61.00 N	14.33 E
Mora, Minn., U.S.	244	45.53 N	93.18 W
Mora, N. Mex., U.S.	254	35.58 N	105.20 W
Mora ≃	254	35.44 N	104.23 W
Morada	272	38.01 N	121.15 W
Morādābād	206	28.50 N	78.47 E
Morada Nova de Minas	296	18.37 S	45.22 W
Mora de Rubielos	168	40.15 N	0.45 W
Morado, Cerro Λ	294	22.55 S	65.09 W
Morafenobe	218	17.49 S	44.55 E
Morąg (Mohrungen)	164	53.56 N	19.56 E
Moraga	272	37.50 N	122.08 W
Mórahalom	164	46.13 N	19.54 E
Moral de Calatrava	168	38.50 N	3.35 W
Morales, Guat.	280	15.29 N	88.49 W
Morales, Perú	292	6.28 S	76.28 W
Morales, Laguna de C	278	23.35 N	97.47 W
Moran, Kans., U.S.	252	37.55 N	95.10 W
Moran, Mich., U.S.	244	46.00 N	84.50 W
Moran, Tex., U.S.	250	32.33 N	99.10 W
Morann	266	40.48 N	78.21 W
Morant Bay	285q	17.50 N	76.25 W
Morant Cays II	282	17.22 N	76.00 W
Morant Point ➤	285q	17.55 N	76.10 W
Mor'arovskij Zaton	186	56.45 N	84.41 E
Morás, Cabo ➤	168	43.44 N	7.28 W
Morasverdes	168	40.36 N	6.16 W
Moratalla	168	38.12 N	1.53 W
Morattico	262	37.47 N	76.38 W
Moratuwa	204	6.46 N	79.53 E
Morava □[9]	164	49.20 N	17.00 E
Morava (March) ≃, Eur.	164	48.10 N	16.59 E
Morava ≃, Jugo.	172	44.43 N	21.03 E
Moravia → Morava □[9]	164	49.20 N	17.00 E
Moravia, C.R.	280	9.51 N	83.26 W
Moravia, Iowa, U.S.	244	40.53 N	92.49 W
Moravia, N.Y., U.S.	264	42.43 N	76.25 W
Moravská Třebová	164	49.45 N	16.40 E
Moravské Budějovice	164	49.03 N	15.49 E
Moravský Krumlov	164	49.03 N	16.19 E
Morawhanna	290	8.17 N	59.44 W
Moray □[6]	162	57.32 N	3.25 W
Moraya	292	21.45 S	65.32 W
Moray Firth C[1]	162	57.50 N	3.30 W
Morazán, Guat.	280	14.56 N	90.09 W
Morazán, Hond.	280	15.17 N	87.34 W
Morbegno	170	46.08 N	9.34 E
Morbihan □[5]	166	47.55 N	2.50 W
Morcenx	166	44.02 N	0.55 W
Morden	252	49.11 N	98.05 W
Mordino	160	61.21 N	51.52 E
Mordoğan	172	38.30 N	26.37 E
Mordovskij Zapovednik ◆[4]	160	54.48 N	43.20 E
Mordy	164	52.13 N	22.31 E
More, Ben Λ	162	56.23 N	4.31 W
More Assynt, Ben Λ	162	58.07 N	4.51 W
Moreau ≃	252	45.18 N	100.43 W
Morecambe	162	54.04 N	2.53 W
Moree, Austl.	228	29.28 S	149.51 E
Morée, Fr.	166	47.54 N	1.14 E
Morehead	242	38.11 N	83.25 W
Morehead City	246	34.43 N	76.43 W
Morehouse	248	36.51 N	89.41 W
Moreland, Ga., U.S.	246	33.17 N	84.46 W
Moreland, Ky., U.S.	248	37.30 N	84.49 W
Morelia	278	19.42 N	101.07 W
Morell	240	46.25 N	62.42 W
Morella	168	40.37 N	0.06 W
Morelos, Méx.	250	28.25 N	100.53 W
Morelos, Méx.	278	26.42 N	107.40 W
Morelos □[3]	278	18.45 N	99.00 W
Morena, Serra ⛰	292	9.00 S	58.30 W
Morena, Sierra ⛰	168	38.00 N	5.00 W
Morenci, Ariz., U.S.	254	33.05 N	109.22 W
Morenci, Mich., U.S.	268	41.43 N	84.13 W
Moreni	172	45.00 N	25.39 E
Moreno	274	33.55 N	117.09 W
Moreno, Bahía C	294	23.35 S	70.30 W
Møre og Romsdal □[6]	160	62.40 N	7.50 E
Morere ≃	290	10.14 N	69.57 W
Moreru ≃	292	8.45 S	59.15 W
Moresby Island I	238	52.50 N	131.55 W
Morestel	166	45.40 N	5.28 E
Moreton Island I	228	27.10 S	153.25 E
Moreuil	166	49.46 N	2.29 E
Morey Park	261	42.33 N	73.43 W
Morey Peak Λ	258	38.37 N	116.17 W
Morez	180	46.31 N	6.02 E
Mórfou, Kólpos C	212	35.10 N	32.50 E
Morgan, Ga., U.S.	246	31.32 N	84.36 W
Morgan, Minn., U.S.	252	44.25 N	94.56 W
Morgan, Mont., U.S.	256	49.00 N	107.50 W
Morgan, Tex., U.S.	250	32.01 N	97.37 W
Morgan, Utah, U.S.	254	41.02 N	111.41 W
Morgan City, Ala., U.S.	248	34.28 N	86.34 W
Morgan City, La., U.S.	248	29.42 N	91.12 W
Morganfield	248	37.41 N	87.55 W
Morgan Hill	272	37.08 N	121.39 W
Morganito	290	5.04 N	67.44 W
Morganton	246	35.45 N	81.41 W
Morgantown, Ind., U.S.	248	39.22 N	86.16 W
Morgantown, Ky., U.S.	248	37.14 N	86.41 W
Morgantown, Md., U.S.	262	38.21 N	76.58 W
Morgantown, Miss., U.S.	248	31.19 N	89.55 W
Morgantown, Pa., U.S.	262	40.09 N	75.54 W
Morgantown, W. Va., U.S.	242	39.38 N	79.57 W
Morganville	262	40.23 N	74.15 W
Morganza	248	30.44 N	91.36 W
Morges	180	46.31 N	6.30 E
Morguilla, Punta ➤	294	37.46 S	73.40 W
Mori	192a	42.06 N	140.35 E
Moriah	285r	11.15 N	60.43 W
Moriah, Mount Λ	258	39.17 N	114.12 W
Moriarty	254	34.59 N	106.03 W
Morice ≃	238	54.24 N	126.45 W
Morice Lake ⊜	238	54.00 N	127.37 W
Morichal Largo ≃	290	9.27 N	62.25 W
Moriki	222	12.52 N	6.30 E
Moringen	164	51.42 N	9.52 E
Morino	160	57.54 N	30.22 E
Morinville	238	53.48 N	113.39 W
Morioka	192	39.42 N	141.09 E
Moriyoshi-zan Λ	192	39.58 N	140.33 E
Morki	160	56.25 N	49.01 E
Morkill ≃	238	53.42 N	120.30 W
Morkoka ≃	186	65.10 N	115.52 E
Morlaix	166	48.35 N	3.50 W
Morland	252	39.21 N	100.05 W
Morlanwelz	176	50.27 N	4.14 E
Morley, Mich., U.S.	244	43.29 N	85.27 W
Morley, N.Y., U.S.	264	44.40 N	75.12 W
Mormanno	170	39.53 N	16.00 E
Mormon Lake ⊜	254	34.57 N	111.27 W
Mormon Peak Λ	258	36.57 N	114.30 W
Morne-à-l'Eau	285o	16.21 N	61.31 W
Morne-Rouge	284e	14.46 N	61.08 W
Morningdale	261	42.19 N	71.41 W
Morning Sun	244	41.05 N	91.15 W
Mornington, Isla I	288	49.45 S	75.20 W
Mornington Island I	228	16.33 S	139.24 E
Mornou, Hadjer Λ	220	17.12 N	23.08 E
Moro	270	45.29 N	120.44 W
Moro ≃	222	7.25 N	11.03 W
Morocco	268	40.57 N	87.27 W
Morocco □[1]	214	32.00 N	5.50 W
Morococala	292	18.10 S	66.44 W
Morococala, Cerro Λ	292	18.08 S	66.43 W
Morococha	292	11.40 S	76.10 W
Morogoro	218	6.49 S	37.40 E
Moro Gulf C	202	6.30 N	123.10 E
Moroleón	278	20.08 N	101.12 W
Morombe	218	21.45 S	43.22 E
Morón, Arg.	294	34.39 S	58.37 W
Morón, Cuba	284p	22.06 N	78.38 W
Mörön, Mong.	190	49.38 N	100.10 E
Morón, Ven.	290	10.29 N	68.11 W
Morona ≃	290	4.40 S	77.10 W
Morona-Santiago □[4]	290	2.30 S	78.00 W
Morondava	225b	20.17 S	44.17 E
Morón de Almazán	168	41.25 N	2.25 W
Morón de la Frontera	168	37.08 N	5.27 W
Morones, Cerro Λ	278	21.45 N	103.05 W
Morong	202	14.40 N	120.16 E
Moroni, Comores	225a	11.41 S	43.16 E
Moroni, Utah, U.S.	254	39.32 N	111.35 W
Moros ≃	168	40.03 N	5.31 W
Morošečnoje	186	56.24 N	156.12 E
Morotai I	198	2.20 N	128.25 E
Morovis	284m	18.20 N	66.24 W
Morozovsk	158	48.22 N	41.50 E
Morozovskaja	160	61.10 N	50.18 E
Morpeth, Ont., Can.	266	42.23 N	81.51 W
Morpeth, Eng., U.K.	162	55.10 N	1.41 W
Morral	266	40.41 N	83.13 W
Morretes	294	25.28 S	48.49 W
Morrice	268	42.50 N	84.11 W
Morrill	252	41.58 N	103.56 W
Morrilton	248	35.09 N	92.45 W
Morrin	238	51.40 N	112.47 W
Morrinhos	296	17.44 S	49.07 W
Morrinsville	230	37.39 S	175.32 E
Morris, Man., Can.	252	49.21 N	97.22 W
Morris, Conn., U.S.	261	41.43 N	73.15 W
Morris, Ill., U.S.	268	41.22 N	88.26 W
Morris, Minn., U.S.	252	45.35 N	95.55 W
Morris, Okla., U.S.	250	35.36 N	95.51 W
Morris □[6]	262	40.48 N	74.29 W
Morris ≃	252	49.21 N	97.22 W
Morrisburg	264	44.54 N	75.11 W
Morrisdale	266	40.57 N	78.14 W
Morrison, Arg.	294	32.36 S	62.50 W
Morrison, Ill., U.S.	244	41.49 N	89.58 W
Morrisonville	248	39.25 N	89.27 W
Morristown, Ariz., U.S.	254	33.51 N	112.37 W
Morristown, Ill., U.S.	268	42.10 N	89.03 W
Morristown, Ind., U.S.	248	39.40 N	85.42 W
Morristown, Minn., U.S.	244	44.14 N	93.26 W
Morristown, N.J., U.S.	242	40.48 N	74.29 W
Morristown, N.Y., U.S.	264	44.35 N	75.39 W
Morristown, Ohio, U.S.	266	40.04 N	81.05 W
Morristown, S. Dak., U.S.	252	45.56 N	101.43 W
Morristown, Tenn., U.S.	246	36.13 N	83.18 W
Morrisville, N.Y., U.S.	264	42.54 N	75.39 W
Morrisville, Pa., U.S.	242	40.13 N	74.47 W
Morrisville, Vt., U.S.	242	44.34 N	72.44 W
Morrito	280	11.37 N	85.05 W
Morro	290	2.39 S	80.19 W
Morro, Punta ➤	294	27.07 S	70.57 W
Morro Bay	272	35.22 N	120.51 W
Morro do Chapéu	286	11.33 S	41.09 W
Morro do Pilar	296	19.12 S	43.23 W
Morropón	292	5.15 S	80.00 W
Morrosquillo, Golfo de C	290	9.35 N	75.40 W
Morrow	248	30.50 N	92.05 W
Morrow □[6]	266	40.33 N	82.50 W
Morrow Point Reservoir ⊜[1]	254	38.25 N	107.30 W
Morrumbene	218	23.39 S	35.20 E
Moršansk	158	53.26 N	41.49 E
Morse, La., U.S.	248	30.08 N	92.30 W
Morse, Tex., U.S.	250	36.04 N	101.29 W
Morskaja Masel'ga	160	63.06 N	34.54 E
Morson	252	49.03 N	94.18 W
Morsott	170	35.40 N	8.01 E
Mortagne	166	48.31 N	0.33 E
Mortagne-au-Perche	166	48.31 N	0.33 E
Mortagne-sur-Sèvre	166	47.00 N	0.57 W
Mortain	166	48.39 N	0.56 W
Mortara	182	45.15 N	8.44 E
Morteau	180	47.04 N	6.37 E
Morteros	294	30.40 S	62.00 W
Mortes, Rio das ≃	296	11.45 S	50.44 W
Morton, Ill., U.S.	244	40.37 N	89.28 W
Morton, Minn., U.S.	252	44.33 N	94.59 W
Morton, Miss., U.S.	248	32.21 N	89.40 W
Morton, N.Y., U.S.	264	43.20 N	77.59 W
Morton, Tex., U.S.	250	33.44 N	102.46 W
Morton, Wash., U.S.	270	46.33 N	122.17 W
Mortons Gap	248	37.14 N	87.28 W
Mortsel	176	51.10 N	4.28 E
Morvan ⛰	166	47.05 N	4.00 E
Morven, Ga., U.S.	246	30.56 N	83.30 W
Morven, N.C., U.S.	246	34.52 N	80.01 W
Morven Λ	162	58.13 N	3.42 W
Morvi	206	22.50 N	70.50 E
Morwell	228	38.14 S	146.24 E
Moryń	164	52.49 N	14.13 E
Morzalândia	296	14.47 S	50.35 W
Morzhovoi	236	54.55 N	163.18 W
Moržovec, Ostrov I	160	66.44 N	42.35 E
Moša ≃	160	62.25 N	39.46 E
Mosal'sk	160	54.29 N	34.59 E
Mosbach	164	49.21 N	9.08 E
Moscos Islands II	200	14.00 N	97.45 E
Moscow → Moskva, S.S.S.R.	160	55.45 N	37.35 E
Moscow	256	46.44 N	116.60 W
Moscow → Moskva ≃	160	55.05 N	38.50 E
Mosel □[5]	164	50.22 N	7.36 E
Mosel (Moselle) ≃	166	50.22 N	7.36 E
Moselebe ≃	224	25.03 S	23.13 E
Moselle	248	31.30 N	89.17 W
Moselle □[5]	166	49.00 N	6.30 E
Moselle (Mosel) ≃	164	50.22 N	7.36 E
Moser River	240	44.59 N	62.15 W
Moses Lake	256	47.08 N	119.17 W

Symbols in the index entries are identified on page 360.

Name Page Lat°′ Long°′

Moses Point 236 64.42 N 162.03 W
Mosgiel 230 45.53 S 170.21 E
Moshannon 266 41.02 N 78.00 W
Mosheim 246 36.11 N 82.57 W
Moshi 218 3.21 S 37.20 E
Moshupa 224 24.50 S 25.31 E
Mosier 270 45.41 N 121.24 W
Mosina 164 52.16 N 16.51 E
Mosinee 244 44.47 N 89.43 W
Mosjøen 160 65.50 N 13.10 E
Moskenesøya I 160 67.59 N 13.00 E
Moskva (Moscow) 160 55.45 N 37.35 E
Moskva ≃ 160 55.05 N 38.50 E
Mosonmagyaróvár 164 47.51 N 17.17 E
Mosquera 290 2.30 N 78.29 W
Mosquero 250 35.47 N 103.58 W
Mosquito, Baie C 232 60.45 N 78.00 W
Mosquito, Punta ≻ 290 9.08 N 77.55 W
Mosquitos, Costa de •[2] 280 13.00 N 83.45 W
Mosquitos, Golfo de los C 280 9.00 N 81.20 W
Moss 160 59.26 N 10.42 E
Mossaka 218 1.13 S 16.48 E
Mossâmedes 296 16.07 S 50.11 W
Mossbank 252 49.55 N 105.59 W
Moss Beach 272 37.32 N 122.31 W
Mosselbaai 224 34.11 S 22.08 E
Mossendjo 218 2.57 S 12.44 E
Mössingen 180 48.24 N 9.03 E
Moss Landing 272 36.48 N 121.47 W
Mossleigh 238 50.43 N 113.20 W
Moss Mountain Λ 248 34.50 N 92.40 W
Mossoró 286 5.11 S 37.20 W
Moss Point 248 30.25 N 88.29 W
Mossyrock 270 46.32 N 122.29 W
Most 164 50.32 N 13.39 E
Mostaganem 168 35.51 N 0.07 E
Mostar 170 43.20 N 17.49 E
Mostardas 294 31.06 S 50.57 W
Møsting, Kap ≻ 232 64.00 N 41.00 W
Mostiska 164 49.48 N 23.09 E
Mosul → Al-Mawṣil 208 36.20 N 43.08 E
Mota 214 11.02 N 37.52 E
Mota del Cuervo 168 39.30 N 2.52 W
Mota del Marqués 168 41.38 N 5.10 W
Motagua ≃ 280 15.44 N 88.14 W
Motala 160 58.33 N 15.03 E
Motatán 290 9.24 N 70.36 W
Motherwell 162 55.48 N 4.00 W
Motilla del Palancar 168 39.34 N 1.53 W
Motiong 202 11.47 N 125.00 E
Motiti Island I 230 37.38 S 176.25 E
Motloutse ≃ 224 22.15 S 29.00 E
Motomachi 192 34.45 N 139.21 E
Motozintla de Mendoza 278 15.22 N 92.14 W
Motril 168 36.45 N 3.31 W
Mott 252 46.22 N 102.20 W
Mottola 170 40.38 N 17.03 E
Mottville, Mich., U.S. 268 41.48 N 85.45 W
Mottville, N.Y., U.S. 264 42.59 N 76.27 W
Motu ≃ 230 37.51 S 177.35 E
Motueka 230 41.07 S 173.00 E
Motueka ≃ 230 41.05 S 173.01 E
Motupe 292 6.10 S 79.35 W
Motygino 186 58.11 N 94.40 E
Motyklejka 186 59.26 N 148.38 E
Mouchalagane, Lac ⊜ 240 51.25 N 69.07 W
Mouchoir Bank ✧[4] 282 20.55 N 70.45 W
Mouchoir Passage Ц 282 21.15 N 71.00 W
Moúdhros 172 39.52 N 25.16 E
Mouding 200 25.24 N 101.35 E
Moudjéria 214 17.53 N 12.20 W
Moudon 166 46.40 N 6.48 E
Mouila 218 1.52 S 11.01 E
Moulay-bou-Selham 168 34.53 N 6.15 W
Moulay-Idriss 214 34.02 N 5.27 W
Moulins 166 46.34 N 3.20 E
Moulins-la-Marche 166 48.39 N 0.29 E
Moulmein 200 16.30 N 97.38 E
Moulmeingyun 200 16.23 N 95.16 E
Moulouya, Oued ≃ 168 35.05 N 2.25 W
Moulton, Ala., U.S. 248 34.29 N 87.18 W
Moulton, Iowa, U.S. 244 40.41 N 92.41 W
Moulton, Tex., U.S. 250 29.34 N 97.09 W
Moultrie 246 31.11 N 83.47 W
Moultrie, Lake ⊜[1] 246 33.20 N 80.05 W
Mound City, Ill., U.S. 248 37.05 N 89.10 W
Mound City, Kans., U.S. 252 38.08 N 94.49 W
Mound City, Mo., U.S. 248 40.07 N 95.14 W
Mound City, S. Dak., U.S. 252 45.44 N 100.04 W
Mound City Group National Monument ♠ 242 39.22 N 83.00 W
Moundou 214 8.34 N 16.05 E
Moundridge 252 38.12 N 97.31 W
Mounds, Ill., U.S. 248 37.07 N 89.12 W
Mounds, Okla., U.S. 250 35.53 N 96.04 W
Moundsville 242 39.55 N 80.44 W
Moundville 248 32.59 N 87.38 W
Moungahaumi Λ 230 38.18 S 177.40 E
Mount, Cape ≻ 222 6.47 N 11.20 W
Mount Aetna 262 40.25 N 76.18 W
Mountain 244 45.11 N 88.28 W
Mountain □[4] 202 17.20 N 121.10 E
Mountain ≃ 236 65.41 N 128.50 W
Mountainair 254 34.31 N 106.15 W
Mountain Ash 174 51.42 N 3.24 W
Mountain Brook 248 33.29 N 86.46 W
Mountain City, Ga., U.S. 246 34.55 N 83.23 W
Mountain City, Nev., U.S. 258 41.50 N 115.58 W
Mountain City, Tenn., U.S. 246 36.28 N 81.48 W
Mountain Creek 248 32.43 N 86.29 W
Mountain Grove 248 37.08 N 92.16 W
Mountain Home, Ark., U.S. 248 36.20 N 92.23 W
Mountain Home, Idaho, U.S. 256 43.08 N 115.41 W
Mountain Iron 244 47.32 N 92.37 W
Mountain Lake 252 43.57 N 94.56 W
Mountain Nile (Baḥr al-Jabal) ≃ 214 9.30 N 30.30 E
Mountain Park 238 52.55 N 117.14 W
Mountain Pine 248 34.34 N 93.10 W
Mountain Point 236 55.18 N 131.32 W
Mountain Ranch 272 38.14 N 120.33 W
Mountainside 262 40.40 N 74.21 W
Mountain View, Ark., U.S. 248 35.52 N 92.07 W
Mountain View, Calif., U.S. 272 37.23 N 122.04 W
Mountain View, Mo., U.S. 248 36.59 N 91.42 W
Mountain View, Okla., U.S. 250 35.06 N 98.45 W
Mountain View, Wyo., U.S. 254 42.52 N 106.55 W
Mountain View, Wyo., U.S. 254 41.16 N 110.20 W
Mountain View Acres 274 34.31 N 117.24 W
Mountain Village 236 62.05 N 163.44 W
Mountain Zebra National Park ♠ 224 32.16 S 25.29 E
Mount Airy, Md., U.S. 242 39.23 N 77.09 W
Mount Airy, N.C., U.S. 246 36.31 N 80.37 W
Mount Albert 264 44.08 N 79.19 W
Mount Angel 270 45.04 N 122.48 W
Mount Apo National Park ♠ 202 6.57 N 125.16 E
Mount Arayat National Park ♠ 202 15.13 N 120.46 E
Mount Ayr, Ind., U.S. 268 40.57 N 87.18 W
Mount Ayr, Iowa, U.S. 252 40.43 N 94.14 W
Mount Berry 246 34.17 N 85.11 W
Mount Blanchard 268 40.54 N 83.33 W
Mount Brydges 266 42.54 N 81.29 W
Mount Calm 250 31.45 N 96.53 W
Mount Carmel, Newf., Can. 240 47.09 N 53.29 W
Mount Carmel, Ill., U.S. 248 38.25 N 87.46 W
Mount Carmel, Pa., U.S. 262 40.48 N 76.25 W
Mount Carroll 244 42.06 N 89.58 W
Mount Clare 242 39.13 N 80.21 W
Mount Clemens 266 42.36 N 82.53 W
Mount Cook National Park ♠ 230 43.35 S 170.15 E
Mount Cory 268 40.56 N 83.50 W
Mount Desert Island I 242 44.20 N 68.20 W
Mount Dora 246 28.48 N 81.38 W
Mount Eaton 266 40.42 N 81.42 W
Mount Eden 272 37.38 N 122.06 W
Mount Edgecumbe 236 57.03 N 135.21 W
Mount Enterprise 248 31.55 N 94.41 W
Mount Field National Park ♠ 228 43.10 S 146.45 E
Mount Forest 264 43.59 N 80.44 W
Mount Gambier 228 37.50 S 140.46 E
Mount Gay 242 37.51 N 82.00 W
Mount Gilead, N.C., U.S. 246 35.10 N 79.56 W
Mount Gilead, Ohio, U.S. 266 40.33 N 82.50 W
Mount Hagen 198 5.50 S 144.15 E
Mount Hermon, Calif., U.S. 272 37.03 N 122.04 W
Mount Hermon, Mass., U.S. 261 42.40 N 72.29 W
Mount Holly, Ark., U.S. 248 33.18 N 92.57 W
Mount Holly, N.J., U.S. 262 39.59 N 74.47 W
Mount Holly, N.C., U.S. 246 35.18 N 81.01 W
Mount Holly Springs 262 40.07 N 77.11 W
Mount Hope, Ont., Can. 264 43.09 N 79.55 W
Mount Hope, Kans., U.S. 252 37.52 N 97.40 W
Mount Hope, Ohio, U.S. 266 40.38 N 81.47 W
Mount Hope, W. Va., U.S. 242 37.54 N 81.10 W
Mount Horeb 244 43.00 N 89.44 W
Mount Ida 248 34.34 N 93.38 W
Mount Isa 228 20.44 S 139.30 E
Mount Jackson, Pa., U.S. 266 40.58 N 80.26 W
Mount Jackson, Va., U.S. 242 38.45 N 78.39 W
Mount Jewett 266 41.44 N 78.38 W
Mount Juliet 248 36.12 N 86.31 W
Mount Kisco 261 41.12 N 73.44 W
Mountlake Terrace 270 47.47 N 122.18 W
Mount Lebanon 266 40.23 N 80.03 W
Mount Liberty 266 40.21 N 82.38 W
Mount Marion 261 42.02 N 73.59 W
Mount Maunganui 230 37.38 S 176.11 E
Mount Mayon National Park ♠ 202 13.16 N 123.39 E
Mount McKinley National Park ♠ 236 63.30 N 150.00 W
Mountmellick 162 53.07 N 7.20 W
Mount Morgan 228 23.39 S 150.23 E
Mount Morris, Ill., U.S. 244 42.03 N 89.26 W
Mount Morris, Mich., U.S. 244 43.07 N 83.42 W
Mount Morris, N.Y., U.S. 264 42.44 N 77.53 W
Mount Nimba National Park ♠ 222 7.40 N 8.27 W
Mount Olive, Ill., U.S. 248 39.04 N 89.43 W
Mount Olive, Miss., U.S. 248 31.46 N 89.39 W
Mount Olive, N.C., U.S. 246 35.12 N 78.04 W
Mount Olivet 242 38.32 N 84.02 W
Mount Orab 242 39.02 N 83.56 W
Mount Penn 262 40.20 N 75.54 W
Mount Pleasant, Ont., Can. 264 43.05 N 80.19 W
Mount Pleasant, Iowa, U.S. 244 40.58 N 91.33 W
Mount Pleasant, Mich., U.S. 244 43.35 N 84.47 W
Mount Pleasant, N.C., U.S. 246 35.24 N 80.26 W
Mount Pleasant, Ohio, U.S. 266 40.11 N 80.48 W
Mount Pleasant, Pa., U.S. 266 40.09 N 79.33 W
Mount Pleasant, S.C., U.S. 246 32.47 N 79.52 W
Mount Pleasant, Tenn., U.S. 248 35.32 N 87.13 W
Mount Pleasant, Tex., U.S. 250 33.09 N 94.58 W
Mount Pleasant, Utah, U.S. 254 39.33 N 111.27 W
Mount Pleasant Mills 262 40.43 N 77.01 W
Mount Pocono 242 41.08 N 75.22 W
Mount Prospect 268 42.04 N 87.56 W
Mount Pulaski 248 40.01 N 89.17 W
Mount Rainier National Park ♠ 256 46.52 N 121.43 W
Mount Revelstoke National Park ♠ 238 51.06 N 118.00 W
Mount Roskill 230 36.55 S 174.45 E
Mount-Royal 260 45.31 N 73.39 W
Mount Rushmore National Memorial ⊥ 252 43.50 N 103.24 W
Mount Savage 242 39.42 N 78.53 W
Mounts Bay C 162 50.03 N 5.25 W
Mount Shasta 258 41.19 N 122.19 W
Mount Sterling, Ill., U.S. 248 39.59 N 90.45 W
Mount Sterling, Ky., U.S. 246 38.04 N 83.56 W
Mount Sterling, Ohio, U.S. 242 39.43 N 83.16 W
Mount Stewart 240 46.22 N 62.52 W
Mount Uniacke 240 44.54 N 63.50 W
Mount Union 266 40.23 N 77.53 W
Mount Vernon, Ala., U.S. 248 31.05 N 88.01 W
Mount Vernon, Ga., U.S. 246 32.11 N 82.36 W
Mount Vernon, Ill., U.S. 248 38.19 N 88.55 W
Mount Vernon, Ind., U.S. 248 37.56 N 87.54 W
Mount Vernon, Iowa, U.S. 244 41.55 N 91.23 W
Mount Vernon, Ky., U.S. 246 37.21 N 84.20 W
Mount Vernon, Mo., U.S. 248 37.06 N 93.49 W
Mount Vernon, N.Y., U.S. 261 40.54 N 73.50 W
Mount Vernon, N.Y., U.S. 264 42.45 N 78.53 W
Mount Vernon, Ohio, U.S. 266 40.23 N 82.29 W
Mount Vernon, S. Dak., U.S. 252 43.43 N 104.16 W
Mount Vernon, Tex., U.S. 250 33.11 N 95.13 W
Mount Vernon, Wash., U.S. 270 48.25 N 122.20 W
Mount Victory 268 40.32 N 83.31 W
Mount View 261 41.39 N 71.25 W
Mountville 262 40.02 N 76.26 W
Mount Wellington 230 36.54 S 174.51 E
Mount Willingdon 238 51.45 N 116.15 W
Mount Wolf 262 40.04 N 76.43 W
Moura, Bra. 290 1.27 S 61.38 W
Moura, Port. 168 38.08 N 7.27 W
Mourdi, Dépression du •[7] 220 18.10 N 23.00 E
Mourne Mountains ⋀ 162 54.10 N 6.04 W
Mouscron 176 50.44 N 3.13 E
Moussoro 214 13.39 N 16.29 E
Moutier 180 47.17 N 7.23 E
Moutiers 170 49.14 N 5.58 E
Moutong 198 0.28 N 121.14 E
Mouton Island I 240 43.54 N 64.46 W
Mouzákion 172 39.26 N 21.40 E
Mouzon 166 49.36 N 5.05 E
Móvano 278 26.42 N 103.39 W
Moville, Eire 162 55.11 N 7.03 W
Moville, Iowa, U.S. 252 42.29 N 96.04 W
Moweaqua 248 39.38 N 89.01 W
Moxos, Llanos de ≃ 292 15.00 S 65.00 W
Moy ≃ 162 54.12 N 9.08 W
Moya 292 12.20 S 75.09 W
Moyahua 278 21.16 N 103.10 W
Moyale 214 3.32 N 39.03 E
Moyamba 214 8.10 N 12.26 W
Moyedao I 194 36.55 N 122.32 E
Moyen Atlas ⋀ 214 33.30 N 5.00 W
Moyeuvre-Grande 166 49.15 N 6.02 E
Moyie 238 49.17 N 115.50 W
Moyie ≃ 238 48.42 N 116.11 W
Moyie Springs 256 48.43 N 116.11 W
Moyobamba 292 6.02 S 76.58 W
Moyock 262 36.32 N 76.11 W
Moyogalpa 280 11.32 N 85.42 W
Moyuta, Volcán Λ[1] 280 14.02 N 90.06 W
M'oža ≃ 160 55.27 N 30.43 E
Možajsk 160 55.30 N 36.01 E
Mozambique □[2] 218 18.00 S 36.00 E
Mozambique Channel Ц 218 19.00 S 41.00 E
Mozambique Plateau ✧[3] 148 32.00 S 35.00 E
Mozdok 158 43.44 N 44.38 E
Možga 160 56.27 N 52.13 E
Mozhabong Lake ⊜ 244 46.57 N 82.05 W
Mozuli 160 56.36 N 28.11 E
Mozyr' 158 52.03 N 29.14 E
Mpanda 218 6.22 S 31.02 E
Mpika 218 11.54 S 31.26 E
Mpraeso 214 6.35 N 0.44 W
Mpwapwa 218 6.21 S 36.29 E
Mrągowo (Sensburg) 164 53.52 N 21.19 E
Mrhila, Djebel Λ 170 35.25 N 9.14 E
Mrkonjić Grad 170 44.25 N 17.05 E
Mrkopalj 170 45.19 N 14.51 E
Mrocza 164 53.14 N 17.36 E
Msaken 170 35.44 N 10.35 E
M'Sila 168 35.46 N 4.31 E
Mšinskaja 160 59.01 N 29.57 E
Msta ≃ 160 58.25 N 31.20 E
Mszana Dolna 164 49.42 N 20.05 E
Mszczonów 164 51.58 N 20.31 E
Mtamvuna ≃ 224 31.06 S 30.12 E
Mtilikwe ≃ 224 21.09 S 31.30 E
Mtwara 218 10.16 S 40.11 E
Mu ≃, Mya. 200 21.56 N 95.38 E
Mu ≃, Nihon 192a 42.33 N 141.56 E
Mu, Cerro Λ 290 9.29 N 73.07 W
Muang Khammouan 200 17.24 N 104.48 E
Muang Luong Nam Tha 200 20.57 N 101.25 E
Muang Pakxan 200 18.22 N 103.39 E
Muang Xépôn 198 16.41 N 106.14 E
Muar ≃ 200 2.03 N 102.35 E
Muarasiberut 198 1.36 S 99.11 E
Muaratewe 198 0.57 S 114.53 E
Mubende 218 0.35 N 31.23 E
Mubur, Pulau I 200 3.20 N 106.12 E
Mucajaí ≃ 290 2.25 N 60.52 W
Muchea 226 31.35 S 115.59 E
Mücheln 164 51.18 N 11.48 E
Muchinga Mountains ⋀ 218 12.00 S 31.45 E
Muchtolovo 160 55.27 N 43.13 E
Much Wenlock 174 52.36 N 2.34 W
Muck I 162 56.50 N 6.14 W
Mučkas 160 64.02 N 48.27 E
Mucuchíes 290 8.45 N 70.55 W
Mucugê 296 13.00 S 41.23 W
Mucuim ≃ 292 6.33 S 64.18 W
Muçum 294 29.10 S 51.53 W
Mucupina, Monte Λ 280 15.08 N 86.38 W
Mucuri 296 18.05 S 39.34 W
Mucuri ≃ 296 18.05 S 39.34 W
Mud ≃, Ky., U.S. 248 37.13 N 86.54 W
Mud ≃, W. Va., U.S. 242 38.25 N 82.17 W
Muda ≃ 200 5.33 N 100.22 E
Mudanjiang 190 44.35 N 129.36 E
Mudanya 172 40.22 N 28.52 E
Muddus Nationalpark ♠ 160 67.00 N 20.16 E
Muddy ≃ 258 36.27 N 114.22 W
Muddy Mountains ⋀ 258 36.20 N 114.40 W
Muddy Peak Λ 258 36.18 N 114.42 W
Mudgee 228 32.36 S 149.35 E
Mudjuga 160 63.46 N 39.15 E
Mud Lake ⊜, Idaho, U.S. 256 43.53 N 112.24 W
Mud Lake ⊜, Minn., U.S. 252 48.20 N 95.58 W
Mud Lake ⊜, Nev., U.S. 258 37.52 N 117.04 W
Mudon 200 16.15 N 97.44 E
Mudurnu ≃ 212 40.49 N 30.33 E
Muelle de los Bueyes 280 12.07 N 84.28 W
Muenster 250 33.39 N 97.23 W
Muerto, Mar C 278 16.10 N 94.10 W
Mufulira 218 12.33 S 28.14 E
Mufushan Λ 196 29.02 N 113.54 E
Mufushan ⋀ 196 29.00 N 114.00 E
Mugi 192 33.40 N 134.25 E
Mu Gia Pass (Deo Mu Gia))(200 17.40 N 105.47 E
Muğla 172 37.12 N 28.22 E
Muğla □[4] 172 37.00 N 28.30 E
Mugodžary ⋀[2] 186 49.00 N 58.40 E
Mugron 166 43.45 N 0.45 W
Mūḥ, Sabkhat ⊜ 212 34.30 N 38.20 E
Muḥammad, Ra's ≻ 220 27.44 N 34.15 E
Mühlacker 164 48.57 N 8.50 E
Mühldorf 164 48.15 N 12.32 E
Mühlhausen 178 51.12 N 10.27 E
Mühlviertel •[1] 164 48.25 N 14.10 E
Muhola 160 63.20 N 25.05 E
Muhos 160 64.48 N 25.59 E
Muhu I 160 58.38 N 23.15 E
Muir, Mich., U.S. 268 43.00 N 84.56 W
Muir, Pa., U.S. 262 40.36 N 76.31 W
Muir, Mount Λ 236 61.06 N 148.24 W
Muisne 290 0.36 N 80.02 W
Muja 186 56.24 N 115.39 E
Mujeres, Isla I 278 21.13 N 86.43 W
Mujezerskij 160 63.57 N 31.55 E
Mujnak 186 43.48 N 59.02 E
Mukačevo 164 48.27 N 22.45 E
Mukah 198 2.54 N 112.02 E
Mukalla → Al-Mukallā 204 14.32 N 49.08 E
Mukawwar I 220 20.48 N 37.13 E
Mukden → Shenyang 194 41.48 N 123.27 E
Mukilteo 270 47.57 N 122.18 W
Mukry 186 37.36 N 65.44 E
Mukwonago 268 42.52 N 88.20 W
Mula 168 38.03 N 1.30 W
Mūla ≃ 206 27.57 N 67.36 E
Mulanay 202 13.31 N 122.24 E
Mulanje 218 16.02 S 35.30 E
Mulatos 278 28.39 N 108.51 W
Mulatupo 290 8.56 N 77.46 W
Mulayit Taung Λ 200 16.11 N 98.32 E
Mulberry, Ark., U.S. 248 35.30 N 94.03 W
Mulberry, Fla., U.S. 246 27.54 N 81.59 W
Mulberry, Ind., U.S. 268 40.21 N 86.40 W
Mulberry ≃ 248 35.28 N 94.03 W
Mulberry Mountain Λ 248 35.42 N 92.56 W
Mulchatna ≃ 236 59.39 N 157.08 W
Mulchén 294 37.43 S 72.14 W
Mul'da 160 67.28 N 63.34 E
Muldoon 250 29.49 N 97.04 W
Muldraugh 248 37.56 N 85.59 W
Muldrow 248 35.24 N 94.36 W
Mulegé 278 26.53 N 112.01 W
Muleshoe 250 34.13 N 102.43 W
Mulgrave 240 45.37 N 61.23 W
Mulgrave Hills ⋀[2] 236 67.42 N 163.24 W
Mulhacén Λ 168 37.03 N 3.19 W
Mulhall 250 36.04 N 97.24 W
Mülheim an der Ruhr 178 51.24 N 6.54 E
Mulhouse (Mülhausen) 180 47.45 N 7.20 E
Mulino 270 45.13 N 122.35 W
Mulita ≃ 202 7.18 N 124.50 E
Mull I 162 56.27 N 6.00 W
Mullan 256 47.28 N 115.48 W
Mullen 252 42.03 N 101.01 W
Mullens 246 37.35 N 81.23 W
Muller, Pegunungan ⋀ 198 0.40 N 113.50 E
Mullett Lake ⊜ 244 45.30 N 84.30 W
Mullewa 226 28.33 S 115.31 E
Müllheim 180 47.48 N 7.38 E
Mullica ≃ 242 39.33 N 74.25 W
Mullica Hill 262 39.44 N 75.13 W
Mulligan ≃ 228 25.00 S 138.30 E
Mulliken 268 42.46 N 84.54 W
Mullin 250 31.33 N 98.40 W
Mullingar 162 53.32 N 7.20 W
Mullins 246 34.12 N 79.15 W
Mullinville 252 37.35 N 99.29 W
Mullovka 160 54.13 N 49.25 E
Multān 206 30.11 N 71.29 E
Multé 278 17.41 N 91.24 W
Multnomah □[6] 270 45.30 N 122.22 W
Muluwusuhe ≃ 206 34.40 N 95.00 E
Mulvane 252 37.29 N 97.14 W
Mulyah Mountain Λ 228 30.37 S 144.31 E
Mumbwa 218 14.59 S 27.04 E
Mumcular 172 37.05 N 27.40 E
Mumford, N.Y., U.S. 264 42.59 N 77.52 W
Mumford, Tex., U.S. 250 30.44 N 96.34 W
Mun ≃ 200 15.19 N 105.31 E
Mun, Jabal Λ 220 14.08 N 22.42 E
Muna 278 20.29 N 89.43 W
Muna ≃ 186 67.52 N 123.06 E
Muna, Pulau I 198 5.00 S 122.30 E
Münchberg 164 50.11 N 11.47 E
München (Munich) 164 48.08 N 11.34 E
München-Gladbach → Mönchengladbach 178 51.12 N 6.28 E
Münchenstein 180 47.31 N 7.37 E
Munchique, Cerro Λ 290 2.32 N 76.57 W
Muncie 268 40.11 N 85.23 W
Muncoonie, Lake ⊜ 228 25.20 S 138.30 E
Muncy 242 41.12 N 76.47 W
Mundare 238 53.36 N 112.20 W
Munday 250 33.27 N 99.38 W
Mundelein 268 42.16 N 88.00 W
Münden 178 51.25 N 9.39 E
Mundo ≃ 168 38.19 N 1.40 W
Mundo Novo 296 11.52 S 40.28 W
Munducurus 290 4.47 S 58.16 W
Munera 168 39.02 N 2.28 W
Munford 248 35.27 N 89.47 W
Munfordville 248 37.16 N 85.54 W
Mungbere 214 2.38 N 28.30 E
Mungindi 226 28.58 S 148.59 E
Munhall 266 40.24 N 79.53 W
Munhango 218 12.12 S 18.42 E
Munich → München 164 48.08 N 11.34 E
Muniesa 168 41.02 N 0.48 W
Munising 244 46.25 N 86.40 W
Muniz Freire 296 20.28 S 41.25 W
Munku-Sardyk, Gora Λ 186 51.45 N 100.32 E
Munnsville 264 42.59 N 75.35 W
Muñoz 202 15.43 N 120.54 E
Muñoz ≃ 284p 21.21 N 78.32 W
Munozero 160 67.05 N 34.12 E
Munroe Falls 266 41.08 N 81.26 W
Münsingen, B.R.D. 164 48.25 N 9.29 E
Münsingen, Schw. 180 46.53 N 7.34 E
Munson, Alta., Can. 238 51.34 N 112.45 W
Munson, Pa., U.S. 266 40.57 N 78.10 W
Münster, B.R.D. 178 51.57 N 7.37 E
Munster, B.R.D. 178 52.59 N 10.05 E
Munster, Fr. 166 48.03 N 7.08 E
Munster, Ind., U.S. 268 41.34 N 87.30 W
Münster □[6] 178 51.50 N 7.25 E
Muntelui, Vîrful Λ 172 46.29 N 23.14 E
Muntok 198 2.04 S 105.11 E
Munuscong Lake ⊜ 244 46.10 N 84.08 W
Munzur Silsilesi ⋀ 212 39.30 N 39.10 E
Muong Ngoi 198 20.43 N 102.41 E
Muong Sing 200 21.11 N 101.09 E
Muonio 160 67.57 N 23.42 E
Muoro 170 40.20 N 9.20 E
Muqaddam, Wādī V 220 18.04 N 31.30 E
Muqayshiṭ I 208 24.12 N 53.42 E
Muqsam, Jabal Λ 220 13.38 N 27.42 E
Muqui 296 20.57 S 41.20 W
Mur (Mura) ≃ 164 46.18 N 16.53 E
Muradiye 172 38.39 N 27.21 E
Murafa ≃ 172 48.13 N 28.14 E
Murakami 192 38.14 N 139.29 E
Muráň 164 48.46 N 20.02 E
Muraši 160 59.24 N 48.55 E
Murat 166 45.07 N 2.52 E
Murat ≃ 212 38.52 N 38.48 E
Muratdağı Λ 212 38.55 N 29.43 E
Muratlı 172 41.10 N 27.30 E
Murau 164 47.07 N 14.10 E
Murauaú ≃ 290 0.09 N 60.40 W
Muravera 170 39.25 N 9.35 E
Murayama 192 38.28 N 140.22 E
Murca 168 41.24 N 7.27 W
Murchison 250 32.17 N 95.45 W
Murchison, Mount Λ 230 43.00 S 171.22 E
Murchison Falls Ⳑ 214 2.17 N 31.41 E
Murchison Mountains ⋀ 230 45.13 S 167.30 E
Murcia, Esp. 168 37.59 N 1.07 W
Murcia, Pil. 202 10.36 N 123.02 E
Murcia □[9] 168 38.30 N 1.45 W
Murciélago 280 10.55 N 85.44 W
Murciélagos, Islas II 280 10.52 N 85.57 W
Murcielagos Bay C 202 8.39 N 123.33 E
Mur-de-Barrez 166 44.51 N 2.39 E
Murdo 252 43.53 N 100.43 W
Mureck 172 46.42 N 15.36 E
Mürefte 172 40.40 N 27.14 E
Mureşul (Maros) ≃ 172 46.15 N 20.13 E
Muret 166 43.28 N 1.21 E
Murfreesboro, Ark., U.S. 248 34.04 N 93.41 W
Murfreesboro, N.C., U.S. 246 36.27 N 77.06 W
Murfreesboro, Tenn., U.S. 248 35.51 N 86.23 W
Murgab 186 38.10 N 73.59 E
Murgab (Murghāb) ≃ 208 38.18 N 61.12 E
Murgeni 172 46.12 N 28.01 E
Murghāb (Murgab) ≃ 208 38.18 N 61.12 E
Murgon 226 26.15 S 151.57 E
Murguía 168 42.57 N 2.49 W
Muri 180 46.56 N 7.29 E
Muriaé 296 21.08 S 42.22 W
Muriaé ≃ 296 21.43 S 41.22 W
Murias de Paredes 168 42.51 N 6.11 W
Muriel Lake ⊜ 238 54.10 N 110.40 W
Murih, Pulau I 200 1.54 N 108.38 E
Muritiba 296 12.39 S 38.59 W
Müritz ⊜ 160 53.25 N 12.43 E
Murmansk 160 68.58 N 33.05 E
Murmansk Rise ✧[3] 148 74.00 N 37.00 E
Murmaši 160 68.47 N 32.42 E
Murmino 160 54.36 N 40.03 E
Murnau 164 47.40 N 11.12 E
Muro, Capo di ≻ 170 41.44 N 8.40 E
Muro Lucano 170 40.45 N 15.30 E
Murom 160 55.34 N 42.02 E
Muroran 192a 42.18 N 140.59 E
Muros 168 42.47 N 9.02 W
Muros y Noya, Ría de C[1] 168 42.45 N 9.00 W
Muroto 192 33.18 N 134.09 E
Muroto-zaki ≻ 192 33.15 N 134.11 E
Murowana Goślina 164 52.35 N 17.01 E
Murphy, Idaho, U.S. 256 43.13 N 116.33 W
Murphy, N.C., U.S. 246 35.05 N 84.01 W
Murphy Lake ⊜ 238 52.00 N 121.00 W
Murphys 272 38.08 N 120.28 W
Murphysboro 248 37.46 N 89.20 W
Murrah al-Kubrā, Al-Buḥayrah al-(Great Bitter Lake) ⊜ 220 30.20 N 32.23 E
Murrāt, Ābār ⊤[4] 220 21.03 N 32.55 E
Murray, Iowa, U.S. 244 41.03 N 93.57 W
Murray, Ky., U.S. 248 36.37 N 88.19 W
Murray, Utah, U.S. 254 40.40 N 111.53 W
Murray ≃, Austl. 228 35.22 S 139.22 E
Murray ≃, B.C., Can. 238 55.40 N 121.10 W
Murray, Lake ⊜[1] 246 34.04 N 81.23 W
Murray, Mount Λ 236 60.54 N 128.49 W
Murray Bay → La Malbaie 240 47.39 N 70.10 W
Murray Bridge 228 35.07 S 139.17 E
Murray City 242 39.31 N 82.10 W
Murray Fracture Zone ✧ 148 34.00 N 133.00 W
Murray Harbour 240 46.00 N 62.31 W
Murray Head ≻ 240 46.00 N 62.28 W
Murray Maxwell Bay C 232 70.00 N 80.00 W
Murray River 240 46.01 N 62.37 W
Murraysburg 218 31.58 S 23.47 E
Murrayville, B.C., Can. 270 49.10 N 122.36 W
Murrayville, Ill., U.S. 248 39.35 N 90.15 W
Murree 204 33.54 N 73.24 E
Murrhardt 164 48.59 N 9.34 E
Murrí ≃ 290 6.33 N 76.52 W
Murrieta 274 33.33 N 117.13 W
Murrumbidgee ≃ 228 34.43 S 143.12 E
Murska Sobota 170 46.40 N 16.10 E
Murten 166 46.56 N 7.07 E
Murter, Otok I 170 43.48 N 15.37 E
Murtle Lake ⊜ 238 52.08 N 119.38 W
Murtosa 168 40.44 N 8.38 W
Muru ≃ 292 8.09 S 70.45 W
Murukta 186 67.46 N 102.01 E
Murutinga 290 3.26 S 59.12 W
Murvaul Bayou ≃ 248 32.05 N 94.12 W
Murwāra 206 23.50 N 86.24 E
Murwillumbah 228 28.19 S 153.24 E
Mürzzuschlag 164 47.36 N 15.41 E
Muş 208 38.44 N 41.30 E
Mūsā, Jabal(Mount Sinai) Λ 220 28.32 N 33.59 E
Musala Λ 172 42.11 N 23.34 E
Musala, Pulau I 200 1.40 N 98.30 E
Musan 194 42.14 N 129.13 E
Musandam, Ra's ≻ 208 26.23 N 56.32 E
Musay'īd 214 24.59 N 51.32 E
Muscat → Masqaṭ 208 23.37 N 58.35 E
Muscat and Oman → Oman □[1] 204 22.00 N 58.00 E
Muscatatuck ≃ 248 38.46 N 86.10 W
Muscatine 244 41.25 N 91.03 W
Mus-Chaja, Gora Λ 186 62.35 N 140.50 E
Muscle Shoals 248 34.45 N 87.40 W
Musclow, Mount Λ 238 53.17 N 127.09 W
Muscoda 244 43.11 N 90.27 W
Muscongus Bay C 240 43.55 N 69.20 W
Muscoy 274 34.09 N 117.19 W
Muse 266 40.18 N 80.12 W
Müsgebi 172 37.02 N 27.21 E
Musgrave, Austl. 226 14.47 S 143.30 E
Musgrave, B.C., Can. 270 48.45 N 123.32 W
Musgrave, Mount Λ 230 43.48 S 170.43 E
Musgravetown 240 48.25 N 53.54 W
Mushandike National Park ♠ 224 20.10 S 30.38 E
Mushie 218 3.01 S 16.54 E
Mushin 222 6.32 N 3.22 E
Mushitageshan Λ 206 38.17 N 75.11 E
Mushui ≃ 196 27.00 N 119.41 E
Musi ≃ 198 2.20 S 104.56 E
Musishan Λ 206 36.03 N 80.07 E
Muskeg ≃ 238 54.01 N 119.03 W
Muskego 268 42.54 N 88.08 W
Muskegon 268 43.14 N 86.16 W
Muskegon □[6] 268 43.12 N 86.08 W
Muskegon ≃ 244 43.14 N 86.20 W
Muskegon Heights 268 43.12 N 86.12 W
Muskingum □[6] 266 40.06 N 81.51 W
Muskogee 250 35.45 N 95.22 W
Muskoka □[6] 264 45.05 N 79.03 W
Muskoka, Lake ⊜ 244 45.00 N 79.25 W
Muskrat Lake ⊜ 244 45.40 N 76.55 W
Muskwa ≃ 232 58.45 N 122.35 W
Muskwa Lake ⊜ 238 56.09 N 114.38 W
Musoma 218 1.30 S 33.48 E
Musquanousse, Lac ⊜ 240 50.22 N 61.04 W
Musquaro, Lac ⊜ 240 50.35 N 61.05 W
Musquodoboit Harbour 240 44.47 N 63.09 W
Musselkanaal 178 52.56 N 7.00 E
Musselshell 256 46.31 N 108.06 W
Musselshell ≃ 256 47.21 N 107.58 W
Mussidan 166 45.02 N 0.22 E
Mussomeli 170 37.35 N 13.46 E
Mussuma 218 14.14 S 21.59 E
Mustafakemalpaşa 212 40.02 N 28.24 E
Mustang Island I 250 28.00 N 96.55 W
Mustinka ≃ 252 45.45 N 96.38 W
Musu-dan ≻ 194 40.50 N 129.43 E
Muswellbrook 228 32.16 S 150.53 E
Muszyna 164 49.21 N 20.54 E
Mutá, Ponta do ≻ 296 13.52 S 38.56 W
Mutankiang → Mudanjiang 190 44.35 N 129.36 E
Mutoraj 186 61.20 N 100.30 E
Mutquín 294 28.19 S 66.10 W
Mutsamudu 218 12.09 S 44.25 E
Mutsu 192 41.17 N 141.10 E
Mutsu-wan C 192 41.05 N 140.55 E
Muttenz 180 47.32 N 7.39 E
Mutton Bay 240 50.47 N 59.02 W
Muttra → Mathura 206 27.30 N 77.41 E
Mutuípe 296 13.15 S 39.31 W
Mutum, Bra. 296 15.48 S 54.53 W
Mutum, Bra. 296 19.49 S 41.26 W
Mutum ≃, Bra. 290 4.25 S 68.03 W
Mutum ≃, Bra. 296 20.25 S 52.56 W
Mutunópolis 296 13.40 S 49.15 W
Muxima 218 9.31 S 13.56 E
Muymanu ≃ 292 11.27 S 69.03 W
Muy Muy 280 12.39 N 85.36 W
Muyumba 218 7.15 S 26.59 E
Muzaffarābād 204 34.22 N 73.28 E
Muzaffarnagar 206 29.28 N 77.42 E
Muzaffarpur 206 26.08 N 85.24 E
Muži 186 65.22 N 64.40 E
Muzillac 166 47.33 N 2.29 W
Muzon, Cape ≻ 236 54.41 N 132.44 W
Mwadui 218 3.33 S 33.36 E
Mwanza 218 2.31 S 32.54 E
Mweelrea Λ 162 53.38 N 9.50 W
Mweka 218 4.51 S 21.34 E
Mweru, Lake ⊜ 218 9.00 S 28.45 E
Mwinilunga 218 11.44 S 24.26 E
Myakka ≃ 246 26.56 N 82.11 W
Myanaung 200 18.17 N 95.19 E
Myaungmya 200 16.36 N 94.56 E
Myerstown 262 40.22 N 76.19 W
Myingyan 200 21.28 N 95.23 E
Myinmoletkat Taung Λ 200 13.28 N 98.48 E
Myitkyinā 200 25.23 N 97.24 E
Myittha ≃ 200 23.12 N 94.17 E
Myjava 164 48.45 N 17.34 E
Myjeldino 160 61.46 N 54.48 E
Myla 160 65.25 N 50.48 E
Myllymäki 160 62.32 N 24.17 E
Mymensingh 206 24.45 N 90.24 E
Mynämäki 160 60.40 N 22.00 E
Myohyang-san ⋀ 194 40.02 N 126.17 E
Myohyang-sanmaek ⋀ 194 40.30 N 127.00 E
Myōkō-zan Λ 192 36.52 N 138.07 E
Mýrdalsjökull ⛝ 160a 63.40 N 19.05 W
Myrnam 238 53.40 N 111.14 W
Myrskylä 160 60.40 N 25.51 E
Myrtle Beach 246 33.42 N 78.52 W
Myrtle Creek 256 43.01 N 123.17 W
Myrtle Grove 248 30.25 N 87.18 W
Myrtle Point 256 43.04 N 124.08 W
Mysen 160 59.33 N 11.20 E
Mysia □[9] 212 39.15 N 28.00 E
Myski 186 53.42 N 87.48 E
Myškino 160 57.47 N 38.27 E
Myślenice 164 49.51 N 19.56 E
Myślibórz (Soldin) 164 52.55 N 14.52 E
Mysłowice 164 50.15 N 19.07 E
Mys Šmidta, S.S.S.R. 186 68.56 N 179.26 E
Mys Šmidta, S.S.S.R. 236 68.56 N 179.26 W
Mystic, Conn., U.S. 261 41.21 N 71.58 W
Mystic, Iowa, U.S. 244 40.47 N 92.57 W
Mys Vchodnoj 186 73.53 N 86.43 E
Mysy 160 60.34 N 53.57 E
Mys Želanija 186 76.56 N 68.35 E
Myszków 164 50.36 N 19.20 E
Myszyniec 164 53.24 N 21.21 E
Myt 160 56.48 N 42.21 E
My-tho 200 10.21 N 106.21 E
Mytilene → Mitilíni 172 39.06 N 26.32 E
Mytišči 160 55.55 N 37.46 E
Myton 254 40.12 N 110.04 W
Mývatn ⊜ 160a 65.37 N 16.58 W
Mže ≃ 164 49.46 N 13.24 E
Mzimba 218 11.52 S 33.34 E
Mzuzu 218 11.27 S 33.55 E

N

Naab ≃ 164 49.01 N 12.02 E
Naach, Jbel Λ 168 34.53 N 3.22 W
Naaldwijk 178 52.00 N 4.12 E
Naalehu 275d 19.04 N 155.35 W
Naarden 178 52.17 N 5.09 E
Naas 162 53.13 N 6.39 W
Nabā, Jabal an- Λ 210 31.46 N 35.44 E
Nabadwīp 206 23.25 N 88.22 E
Nabari 192 34.37 N 136.05 E
Nabas 202 11.50 N 122.06 E
Nabburg 164 49.28 N 12.11 E
Nabereżnyje Čelny 160 55.42 N 52.19 E
Nabesna 236 62.22 N 143.00 W
Nabesna ≃ 236 63.03 N 141.52 W
Nabeul 170 36.27 N 10.44 E
Nabeul □[8] 170 36.35 N 10.45 E
Nabileque ≃ 292 20.55 S 57.49 W
Nabire 198 3.22 S 135.26 E
Nabisipi ≃ 240 50.14 N 62.14 W
Nabnasset 261 42.37 N 71.25 W
Nabogame 278 26.14 N 106.57 W
Nabua 202 13.24 N 123.22 E
Nābulus 210 32.13 N 35.15 E
Nābulus □[8] 210 32.18 N 35.17 E
Nabunturan 202 7.38 N 125.58 E
Nacala-Velha 218 14.32 S 40.37 E
Nacaome 280 13.31 N 87.30 W
Naches 270 46.44 N 120.42 W
Naches ≃ 256 46.38 N 120.31 W
Nachičevan' 208 39.13 N 45.24 E
Nachi-katsuura 192 33.30 N 135.55 E
Nachingwea 218 10.23 S 38.46 E
Náchod 164 50.25 N 16.10 E
Nachodka 186 42.48 N 132.52 E
Nachrodt-Wiblingwerde 178 51.19 N 7.37 E
Nacimiento 294 37.30 S 72.45 W
Naco, Méx. 278 31.20 N 109.56 W
Naco, Ariz., U.S. 254 31.20 N 109.57 W
Nacogdoches 248 31.36 N 94.39 W
Nácori Chico 278 29.39 N 109.01 W
Nacozari [de García] 278 30.24 N 109.39 W
Ñacunday 294 26.01 S 54.46 W
Nadadores 250 27.03 N 101.36 W
Nadela 168 42.58 N 7.30 W
Naden Harbour C 238 54.00 N 132.35 W
Nadiād 206 22.42 N 72.52 E
Nadir 284m 18.19 N 64.53 W
Nădlac 172 46.10 N 20.45 E
Nador 168 35.12 N 2.55 W
Nadporožje 160 60.28 N 34.17 E
Nadvoicy 160 63.52 N 34.15 E
Nadym 186 65.35 N 72.42 E
Nadym ≃ 186 66.12 N 72.00 E
Nærbø 160 58.40 N 5.39 E
Næstved 160 55.14 N 11.46 E
Näfels 166 47.06 N 9.04 E
Naga, Pil. 202 13.38 N 123.11 E
Naga, Pil. 202 10.12 N 123.45 E
Nagahama, Nihon 192 35.23 N 136.16 E
Nagahama, Nihon 192 33.36 N 132.29 E
Nagai 192 38.06 N 140.02 E
Nagai Island I 236 55.11 N 159.55 W
Nagaland □[3] 206 26.00 N 95.00 E
Nagano 192 36.39 N 138.11 E
Nagaoka 192 37.27 N 138.51 E
Nagara ≃ 192 35.01 N 136.43 E
Nagarote 280 12.16 N 86.34 W
Nagas 202 13.06 N 123.17 E
Nagasaki 192 32.48 N 129.55 E
Nagashima 192 34.12 N 136.20 E
Nagasin Lake ⊜ 244 47.44 N 83.37 W
Nagato 192 34.21 N 131.10 E
Nagcarlan 202 11.50 N 125.00 E
Nagiba 202 13.42 N 120.54 E
Nagłowice 164 50.41 N 20.06 E
Nago 193b 26.35 N 127.59 E
Nagold 180 48.33 N 8.43 E
Nagornyj 186 55.58 N 124.57 E
Nagorsk 160 59.18 N 50.48 E
Nagoya 192 35.10 N 136.55 E
Nāgpur 206 21.08 N 79.04 E
Nagrom 270 47.13 N 121.36 W
Nagua 282 19.23 N 69.50 W
Naguabo 284m 18.13 N 65.44 W
Naguilian 202 17.01 N 121.50 E
Nagumbuaya Point ≻ 202 13.33 N 124.20 E
Nagyatád 164 46.14 N 17.22 E
Nagybajom 164 46.23 N 17.31 E
Nagyecsed 164 47.42 N 22.19 E
Nagykálló 172 47.53 N 21.51 E
Nagykanizsa 164 46.27 N 17.00 E
Nagykáta 164 47.25 N 19.45 E
Nagykőrös 164 47.02 N 19.43 E
Nagy-Milic Λ 164 48.35 N 21.28 E
Naha 193b 26.13 N 127.40 E
Nahant 261 42.25 N 70.55 W
Nahariya 210 33.00 N 35.05 E
Nahar Ouassel, Oued ≃ 168 35.42 N 2.48 E
Nahāvand 208 34.12 N 48.22 E
Nahcotta 270 46.30 N 124.02 W
Nahe 190 48.28 N 124.52 E
Nahe ≃ 164 49.58 N 7.57 E
Nahma 244 45.50 N 86.40 W
Nahuala, Laguna C 278 16.46 N 99.44 W
Nahualate ≃ 280 14.03 N 91.32 W
Nahuel Huapi, Lago ⊜ 288 41.00 S 71.32 W
Nahuizalco 280 13.46 N 89.45 W
Nahunta 246 31.12 N 81.59 W
Naic 202 14.19 N 120.46 E
Naicá 278 27.53 N 105.31 W
Naidong 190 29.14 N 31.46 E
Naiguatá, Pico Λ 290 10.33 N 66.46 W
Naila 164 50.19 N 11.42 E
Nain, Newf., Can. 232 57.00 N 61.40 W
Nā'īn, Īrān 204 32.52 N 53.05 E
Naipli 172 39.48 N 27.13 E
Naiqiguolehe ≃ 206 35.58 N 95.00 E
Nairn 162 57.35 N 3.53 W
Nairn □[6] 162 57.27 N 3.52 W
Nairobi 218 1.17 S 36.49 E
Naivasha 218 0.43 S 36.26 E
Najac 166 44.17 N 2.00 E
Najafābād 208 32.37 N 51.21 E
Najasa ≃ 284p 20.42 N 77.58 W
Nájera 168 42.25 N 2.44 W
Naj'Ḥammādī 220 26.03 N 32.15 E
Najin 194 42.15 N 130.18 E
Najramdal Uul Λ 190 49.10 N 87.52 E
Najstenjarvi 160 62.16 N 32.38 E
Naju 194 35.03 N 126.43 E
Naka ≃ 192 36.20 N 140.36 E
Nakadōri-shima I 192 32.57 N 129.04 E
Nakajō 192 38.03 N 139.24 E
Nakama 192 33.50 N 130.43 E
Nakaminato 192 36.21 N 140.36 E

Symbols in the index entries are identified on page 360.

Name Page Lat°′ Long°′

Nakamura 192 32.59 N 132.56 E
Nakano 192 36.45 N 138.22 E
Nakano-shima I 193b 29.49 N 129.52 E
Nakanoshima-suidō I 193b 29.44 N 129.49 E
Nakashibetsu 192a 43.33 N 144.59 E
Nakatsu 192 33.34 N 131.13 E
Nakatsugawa 192 35.29 N 137.30 E
Nakehe ≃ 206 31.29 N 93.51 E
Nakhon Nayok 200 14.12 N 101.13 E
Nakhon Pathom 200 13.49 N 100.06 E
Nakhon Phanom 200 17.22 N 104.46 E
Nakhon Ratchasima 200 14.57 N 102.09 E
Nakhon Sawan 200 15.42 N 100.06 E
Nakhon Si Thammarat 200 8.26 N 99.58 E
Nakina 232 50.10 N 86.42 W
Nakło nad Notecią 164 53.08 N 17.35 E
Naknek 236 58.44 N 157.02 W
Naknek Lake ⊜ 236 58.40 N 156.15 W
Nakskov 164 54.50 N 11.09 E
Naktong-gang ≃ 194 35.07 N 128.57 E
Nakuru 218 0.17 S 36.04 E
Nakusimi ≃ 244 49.08 N 82.17 W
Nakusp 238 50.15 N 117.48 W
Nāl ≃ 206 26.02 N 65.19 E
Nalajch 190 47.45 N 107.13 E
Nal'čik 158 43.29 N 43.37 E
Nałęczów 164 51.18 N 22.11 E
Nalón ≃ 168 43.32 N 6.04 W
Nālūt 214 31.52 N 10.59 E
Namak, Daryācheh-ye ⊜ 208 34.45 N 51.36 E
Namak, Kavīr-e ◆2 208 34.30 N 52.40 E
Namakan Lake ⊜ 244 48.27 N 92.35 W
Namangan 186 41.00 N 71.40 E
Namapa 218 13.43 S 39.50 E
Nambour 226 26.38 S 152.58 E
Namcha Barwa → Namuchabawashan ∧ 206 29.38 N 95.04 E
Namdae-ch'ŏn ≃ 194 40.46 N 129.22 E
Nam Dinh 200 20.25 N 106.10 E
Nameigos Lake ⊜ 244 48.46 N 84.43 W
Namekagon ≃ 244 46.05 N 92.06 W
Namerikawa 192 36.46 N 137.20 E
Námestovo 164 49.25 N 19.30 E
Nam-gang ≃ 194 39.03 N 125.52 E
Namhan-gang ≃ 194 37.31 N 127.18 E
Namhkam 190 23.50 N 97.41 E
Namib Desert ◆2 224 23.00 S 15.00 E
Namie 192 37.29 N 141.00 E
Namlea 198 3.18 S 127.06 E
Namnoi, Khao ∧ 200 10.36 N 98.38 E
Namoi ≃ 228 30.00 S 148.07 E
Nampa, Alta., Can. 238 56.02 N 117.08 W
Nampa, Idaho, U.S. 256 43.34 N 116.34 W
Nampicuan 202 15.44 N 120.38 E
Namp'o 194 38.45 N 125.23 E
Namp'ot'ae-san ∧ 194 41.44 N 128.24 E
Nampula 218 15.07 S 39.15 E
Namsen ≃ 160 64.27 N 11.28 E
Namsos 160 64.29 N 11.30 E
Namtu 198 23.05 N 97.24 E
Namu 238 51.49 N 127.52 W
Namuchabawashan ∧ 206 29.38 N 95.04 E
Namuhu ⊜ 206 30.42 N 90.30 E
Namur, Bel. 164 50.28 N 4.52 E
Namur, Qué., Can. 260 45.54 N 74.56 W
Namur □4 176 50.20 N 4.50 E
Namutoni 218 18.49 S 16.55 E
Namwŏn 194 35.25 N 127.21 E
Namysłów (Namslau) 164 51.05 N 17.42 E
Nan 200 18.48 N 100.46 E
Nan ≃ 200 15.42 N 100.11 E
Nanaimo 238 49.10 N 123.56 W
Nanakuli 275c 21.23 N 158.09 W
Nanam 190 41.43 N 129.41 E
Nanango 226 26.40 S 152.00 E
Nanao 192 37.03 N 136.58 E
Nan'aodao I 196 23.26 N 117.03 E
Nanao-wan C 192 37.06 N 137.00 E
Nanatsu-shima II 192 37.36 N 136.53 E
Nanay ≃ 290 3.40 S 73.15 W
Nanchang 196 28.41 N 115.53 E
Nancheng, Zhg. 190 27.35 N 116.40 E
Nancheng → Hanzhong, Zhg. 190 32.59 N 107.11 E
Nanchong 190 30.48 N 106.04 E
Nancowry Island I 200 7.58 N 93.33 E
Nancy, Fr. 180 48.41 N 6.12 E
Nancy, Ky., U.S. 246 37.04 N 84.45 W
Nanda Devi ∧ 206 30.22 N 79.59 E
Nandaime 280 11.46 N 86.03 W
Nandan 192 34.15 N 134.43 E
Nandinghe ≃ 200 23.25 N 98.41 E
N'andoma 160 61.40 N 40.12 E
Nanduhe ≃ 200 20.04 N 110.22 E
Nandurbār 206 21.23 N 74.15 E
Nangalao Island I 202 11.28 N 120.10 E
Nangang C 196 23.30 N 117.00 E
Nānga Parbat ∧ 206 35.14 N 74.35 E
Nangarhār □4 206 34.15 N 70.30 E
Nangariza ≃ 290 3.45 S 78.38 W
Nangō 192 31.30 N 131.30 E
Nanhuta Shan ∧ 196 24.22 N 121.26 E
Nanika Lake ⊜ 238 53.45 N 127.40 W
Nanjemoy 262 38.27 N 77.13 W
Nanjiaohe ≃ 194 36.15 N 120.06 E
Nanjing (Nanking) 196 32.03 N 118.47 E
Nanjishan I 196 27.28 N 121.04 E
Nanjiushan I 196 29.26 N 122.12 E
Nankin 266 40.55 N 82.17 W
Nanking → Nanjing 196 32.03 N 118.47 E
Nankoku 192 33.39 N 133.44 E
Nankou 190 40.14 N 116.07 E
Nanling ⋀, Zhg. 190 25.00 N 112.00 E
Nanling ⋀, Zhg. 196 25.24 N 113.30 E
Nannine 226 26.53 S 118.20 E
Nanning 200 22.48 N 108.20 E
Nanoose Bay 270 49.16 N 124.12 W
Nanpanjiang ≃ 200 25.07 N 106.00 E
Nanping 196 26.38 N 118.10 E
Nanpuxi ≃ 196 27.02 N 118.18 E
Nanridao I 196 25.13 N 119.30 E
Nanruhe ≃ 196 32.43 N 115.01 E
Nansa ≃ 168 43.22 N 4.29 W
Nansei 192 34.22 N 136.41 E
Nansei-shotō (Ryukyu Islands) II 190 26.30 N 128.00 E
Nansemond □6 262 36.43 N 76.40 W
Nanshan → Qilianshanmai ⋀ 190 39.06 N 98.40 E
Nant 166 44.01 N 3.18 E
Nantais, Lac ⊜ 232 60.58 N 74.00 W
Nantai-zan ∧ 192 36.46 N 139.29 E
Nanterre 176 48.53 N 2.12 E
Nantes 166 47.13 N 1.33 W
Nanteuil-le-Haudouin 166 49.08 N 2.48 E
Nanticoke 242 41.12 N 76.00 W
Nanticoke ≃ 242 38.16 N 75.56 W
Nanto 192 34.20 N 136.31 E
Nanton 238 50.21 N 113.46 W
Nantong 196 32.02 N 120.53 E
Nantua 166 46.09 N 5.37 E
Nantucket 261 41.17 N 70.06 W
Nantucket □6 261 41.17 N 70.06 W
Nantucket Island I 242 41.16 N 70.03 W
Nantwich 174 53.04 N 2.32 W
Nanty Glo 266 40.28 N 78.50 W
Nanuque 296 17.50 S 40.21 W
Nanusa, Pulau-pulau II 198 4.42 N 127.06 E
Nanushuk ≃ 236 69.18 N 151.00 W
Nan Wan C 196 21.53 N 120.48 E
Nanxi ≃, Zhg. 196 24.29 N 117.48 E
Nanxi ≃, Zhg. 196 28.15 N 120.43 E
Nanxiang 196 31.17 N 121.18 E
Nanxiong 196 25.10 N 114.20 E
Nanyandangshan ∧ 196 27.36 N 120.04 E
Nanyang 196 33.00 N 112.32 E
Nanyanghu ⊜ 194 35.12 N 116.41 E
Nanyō 192 38.03 N 140.10 E
Nanyuki 218 0.01 N 37.04 E
Nanyunhe (Grand Canal) ⌶ 194 39.08 N 117.09 E
Nao, Cabo de la ⟩ 168 38.44 N 0.14 E
Naococane, Lac ⊜ 232 52.50 N 70.40 W
Naoetsu 192 37.11 N 138.15 E
Não-me-Toque 294 28.28 S 52.49 W
Náousa 172 40.37 N 22.05 E
Naozhoudao I 200 20.57 N 110.34 E
Napa 272 38.18 N 122.17 W
Napa □6 272 38.18 N 122.17 W
Napacao Point ⟩ 202 9.42 N 124.30 E
Napajedla 164 49.10 N 17.31 E
Napakiak 236 60.42 N 161.57 W
Napalkovo 186 70.03 N 73.47 E
Napamute 236 61.33 N 158.42 W
Napanee 264 44.15 N 76.57 W
Napaskiak 236 60.42 N 161.54 W
Napavine 270 46.35 N 122.54 W
Napayauan Island I 202 12.22 N 123.15 E
Napenay 294 26.44 S 60.37 W
Naperville 268 41.47 N 88.09 W
Napétipi ≃ 240 51.27 N 58.05 W
Napier 230 39.29 S 176.54 E
Napierville 260 45.11 N 73.24 W
Napierville □6 260 45.10 N 73.35 W
Napinka 252 49.17 N 100.50 W
Naplate 268 41.20 N 88.54 W
Naples → Napoli, It. 184 40.51 N 14.17 E
Naples, Fla., U.S. 246 26.08 N 81.48 W
Naples, Idaho, U.S. 256 48.34 N 116.24 W
Naples, N.Y., U.S. 242 42.37 N 77.25 W
Naples, Tex., U.S. 248 33.12 N 94.41 W
Napo □4 290 0.30 S 77.00 W
Napo ≃ 290 3.20 S 72.40 W
Napoleon, Mich., U.S. 268 42.10 N 84.15 W
Napoleon, N. Dak., U.S. 252 46.30 N 99.46 W
Napoleon, Ohio, U.S. 268 41.23 N 84.08 W
Napoleonville 248 29.57 N 91.01 W
Napoli (Naples) 184 40.51 N 14.17 E
Napoli □4 184 40.53 N 14.25 E
Nappanee 268 41.27 N 86.00 W
Naquhe ≃ 206 31.15 N 94.37 E
Nara, Mali 214 15.10 N 7.17 W
Nara, Nihon 192 34.41 N 135.50 E
Nāra ≃ 206 24.07 N 69.07 E
Naracoorte 228 36.58 S 140.44 E
Naramata 238 49.36 N 119.35 W
Naranjal 290 2.42 S 79.37 W
Naranjito, Hond. 280 14.57 N 88.41 W
Naranjito, P.R. 284m 18.18 N 66.15 W
Naranjo 280 10.06 N 84.22 W
Naranjo ≃ 280 14.30 N 92.11 W
Naranjo Islands II 202 12.22 N 124.02 E
Narao 192 32.50 N 129.04 E
Narathiwat 200 6.25 N 101.48 E
Nara Visa 250 35.37 N 103.06 W
Nārāyanganj 206 23.37 N 90.30 E
Narberth 162 51.48 N 4.45 W
Narbonne 166 43.11 N 3.00 E
Narcea ≃ 168 43.28 N 6.06 W
Nardò 170 40.11 N 18.02 E
Nare ≃ 290 6.12 N 74.35 W
Narew ≃ 164 52.26 N 20.42 E
Nāri ≃ 206 28.35 N 67.50 E
Nārī, Jabal an- ⋀2 220 24.30 N 22.42 E
Narinda, Baie de C 225b 14.55 S 47.30 E
Nariño □5 290 1.30 N 78.00 W
Narita 192 35.47 N 140.19 E
Narizón, Punta ⟩ 278 27.50 N 110.52 W
Narjan-Mar 160 67.39 N 53.00 E
Narmada ≃ 204 21.35 N 72.35 E
Narni 184 42.31 N 12.31 E
Naro 170 37.17 N 13.48 E
Narodnaja, Gora ∧ 160 65.04 N 60.09 E
Naro-Fominsk 160 55.23 N 36.43 E
Naro Island I 202 11.54 N 123.40 E
Narol 164 50.22 N 23.21 E
Narón 168 43.32 N 8.10 W
Narovčat 160 53.52 N 43.41 E
Narrabri 228 30.19 S 149.47 E
Narragansett 261 41.26 N 71.27 W
Narran ≃ 228 29.45 S 147.20 E
Narrandera 228 34.45 S 146.33 E
Narraway ≃ 238 54.48 N 119.56 W
Narrogin 226 32.56 S 117.10 E
Narromine 228 32.14 S 148.15 E
Narrows, Md., U.S. 262 38.58 N 76.15 W
Narrows, Va., U.S. 246 37.20 N 80.48 W
Narssak 232 60.54 N 46.00 W
Naru 192 32.49 N 128.56 E
Naruko 192 38.44 N 140.43 E
Naruto 192 34.11 N 134.37 E
Narva 160 59.23 N 28.12 E
Narva ≃ 160 59.27 N 28.02 E
Narvacan 202 17.25 N 120.28 E
Narvik 160 68.26 N 17.25 E
Narvskij Zaliv C 160 59.30 N 27.40 E
Naryn 186 41.26 N 75.59 E
Naryn ≃ 190 40.54 N 71.45 E
Narynkol 186 42.43 N 80.12 E
Näsåker 160 63.26 N 16.54 E
Năsăud 172 47.17 N 24.24 E
Nasbinals 166 44.40 N 3.03 E
Naschel 294 32.56 S 65.28 W
Naselle 270 46.22 N 123.49 W
Nash 248 33.27 N 94.08 W
Nashport 266 40.04 N 82.09 W
Nashua, Iowa, U.S. 244 42.57 N 92.32 W
Nashua, Minn., U.S. 252 46.02 N 96.18 W
Nashua, Mont., U.S. 256 48.08 N 106.22 W
Nashua, N.H., U.S. 242 42.46 N 71.27 W
Nashville, Ark., U.S. 248 33.57 N 93.51 W
Nashville, Ga., U.S. 246 31.12 N 83.15 W
Nashville, Ill., U.S. 248 38.21 N 89.23 W
Nashville, Ind., U.S. 248 39.12 N 86.15 W
Nashville, Mich., U.S. 268 42.36 N 85.05 W
Nashville, N.C., U.S. 246 35.58 N 77.58 W
Nashville, Ohio, U.S. 266 40.36 N 82.07 W
Nashville, Tenn., U.S. 248 36.09 N 86.48 W
Nashwaak ≃ 240 45.57 N 66.37 W
Nashwaaksis 240 45.59 N 66.39 W
Nashwauk 244 47.23 N 93.10 W
Našice 172 45.29 N 18.06 E
Nasielsk 164 52.36 N 20.48 E
Näsijärvi ⊜ 160 61.37 N 23.42 E
Nāsir 214 8.36 N 33.04 E
Naskaupi ≃ 232 53.45 N 60.50 W
Naṣrānī, Jabal an- ∧ 212 34.06 N 37.24 E
Nass ≃ 238 55.00 N 129.50 W
Nassau, Ba. 284b 25.05 N 77.21 W
Nassau, N.Y., U.S. 261 42.31 N 73.37 W
Nassau □6 261 40.45 N 73.38 W
Nassawadox 262 37.28 N 75.51 W
Nasser, Lake ⊜1 220 22.40 N 32.00 E
Nassereith 164 47.19 N 10.50 E
Nässjö 160 57.39 N 14.41 E
Nastapoca ≃ 232 56.53 N 76.40 W
Nastapoka Islands II 232 57.00 N 76.50 W
Nasu 192 37.01 N 140.07 E
Nasu-dake ∧ 192 37.07 N 139.58 E
Nasugbu 202 14.04 N 120.38 E
Nasukoin Mountain ∧ 256 48.49 N 114.35 W
Nasva 160 56.35 N 30.10 E
Nat ≃ 244 48.48 N 82.07 W
Nata, Bots. 218 20.12 S 26.12 E
Natá, Pan. 280 8.20 N 80.30 W
Nata ≃ 224 20.14 S 26.10 E
Natagaima 290 3.37 N 75.06 W
Natal, Bra. 286 5.47 S 35.13 W
Natal, B.C., Can. 238 49.44 N 114.50 W
Natal, Indon. 198 0.33 N 99.07 E
Natal □3 224 28.40 S 30.40 E
Natalia 250 29.11 N 98.52 W
Natalkuz Lake ⊜ 238 53.26 N 125.20 W
Natan, Cabo ⟩ 280 11.06 N 85.46 W
Natanes Plateau ⋀1 254 33.35 N 110.15 W
Natash, Wādī ∨ 220 24.25 N 33.26 E
Natashquan 240 50.11 N 61.49 W
Natashquan ≃ 232 50.06 N 61.49 W
Natashquan, Pointe ⟩ 240 50.06 N 61.45 W
Natashquan-Est ≃ 240 51.21 N 61.41 W
Natchez 248 31.34 N 91.23 W
Natchitoches 248 31.46 N 93.05 W
Natick 261 42.17 N 71.21 W
Nation ≃ 238 55.28 N 125.35 W
National City 274 32.40 N 117.06 W
Nation Lakes ⊜ 238 55.10 N 125.00 W
Natipi, Lac ⊜ 240 51.27 N 71.22 W
Native Bay C 232 63.52 N 82.30 W
Natividade 286 11.43 S 47.47 W
Nativity, Church of the v1 210 31.43 N 35.12 E
Natoma 252 39.11 N 99.01 W
Natori 192 38.08 N 140.55 E
Natron, Lake ⊜ 218 2.25 S 36.00 E
Natrona Heights 266 40.38 N 79.44 W
Naṭrūn, Wādī an- ⊻7 220 30.25 N 30.13 E
Nattastunturit ∧ 160 68.12 N 27.20 E
Nattaung ∧ 200 18.48 N 97.02 E
Natukanaoka Pan ≚ 224 18.40 S 15.45 E
Natuna Besar I 198 4.00 N 108.15 E
Natuna Besar, Kepulauan II 200 4.40 N 108.00 E
Natuna Besar, Pulau I 200 4.00 N 108.15 E
Natuna Selatan, Kepulauan II 200 2.45 N 109.00 E
Natural Bridge 264 44.04 N 75.30 W
Natural Bridges National Monument ♠ 254 37.30 N 110.08 W
Naturita 254 38.14 N 108.34 W
Naucelle 166 44.12 N 2.20 E
Nauders 164 46.53 N 10.30 E
Nauen 164 52.36 N 12.52 E
Naugatuck 261 41.30 N 73.04 W
Naughton 244 46.24 N 81.12 W
Naujan 202 13.19 N 121.18 E
Naujan, Lake ⊜ 202 13.10 N 121.21 E
Naukan 236 66.01 N 169.43 W
Naumburg 164 51.09 N 11.48 E
Ñaupe 292 5.35 S 79.50 W
Naustdal 160 61.31 N 5.43 E
Nauta 290 4.30 S 73.40 W
Nautla 278 20.13 N 96.47 W
Nauvoo 244 40.33 N 91.23 W
Nava 278 28.25 N 100.46 W
Nava, Laguna de la ⊜ 168 42.03 N 4.39 W
Nava del Rey 168 41.20 N 5.05 W
Navahermosa 168 39.38 N 4.28 W
Navajo ≃ 254 37.01 N 107.10 W
Navajo Indian Reservation ◆4 254 36.25 N 110.00 W
Navajo Mountain ∧ 254 37.02 N 110.52 W
Navajo National Monument ♠ 254 36.40 N 110.33 W
Navajo Reservoir ⊜1 254 36.55 N 107.30 W
Naval 202 11.34 N 124.35 E
Navalcarnero 168 40.18 N 4.00 W
Navalmoral de la Mata 168 39.54 N 5.32 W
Navalvillar de Pela 168 39.06 N 5.28 W
Navāpur 206 21.10 N 73.48 E
Navarin, Mys ⟩ 236 62.16 N 179.10 E
Navarino, Isla I 288 55.05 S 67.40 W
Navarra □4 168 42.40 N 1.30 W
Navarre 266 40.43 N 81.32 W
Navarro 294 35.00 S 59.10 W
Navarro ≃ 258 39.11 N 123.45 W
Navarro Mills Reservoir ⊜1 250 31.56 N 96.45 W
Navasota 250 30.23 N 96.05 W
Navasota ≃ 250 30.20 N 96.09 W
Navassa 246 34.16 N 77.58 W
Navassa Island I 282 18.24 N 75.01 W
Navia, Arg. 294 34.47 S 66.36 W
Navia, Esp. 168 43.32 N 6.43 W
Navia ≃ 168 43.33 N 6.44 W
Navidad 294 33.57 S 71.50 W
Navidad ≃ 250 28.41 N 96.35 W
Navidad Bank ◆4 282 20.05 N 68.50 W
Naviraí 296 23.08 S 54.13 W
Navoi 186 40.15 N 65.15 E
Navojoa 278 27.06 N 109.26 W
Navolato 278 24.47 N 107.42 W
Návpaktos 172 38.23 N 21.50 E
Návplion 172 37.34 N 22.48 E
Navsāri 206 20.57 N 72.56 E
Navy Yard City 270 47.32 N 122.41 W
Nawābshāh 206 26.15 N 68.25 E
Naxera 262 37.20 N 76.27 W
Náxos 172 37.06 N 25.23 E
Náxos I 172 37.02 N 25.35 E
Nayarit 258 32.20 N 115.19 W
Nayarit □3 278 22.00 N 105.00 W
Naylor 248 36.34 N 90.36 W
Nayoro 192a 44.21 N 142.28 E
Nayyāl, Wādī ∨ 208 28.40 N 39.26 E
Nazaré, Bra. 296 13.02 S 39.00 W
Nazaré, Port. 168 39.36 N 9.04 W
Nazaré da Mata 286 7.44 S 35.14 W
Nazareth 262 40.44 N 75.19 W
Nazareth → Naẕerat, Yis. 210 32.42 N 35.18 E
Nazário 296 16.36 S 49.54 W
Nazarovo 186 56.01 N 90.26 E
Nazas 278 25.14 N 104.08 W
Nazas ≃, Méx. 250 25.35 N 103.25 W
Nazas ≃, Méx. 278 25.35 N 105.00 W
Nazca 292 14.50 S 74.55 W
Naze 193b 28.23 N 129.30 E
N'azepetrovsk 158 56.03 N 59.36 E
Naẕerat (Nazareth) 210 32.42 N 35.18 E
Naẕerat 'Illit 210 32.42 N 35.19 E
Nazija 160 59.50 N 31.35 E
Nazik Gölü ⊜ 212 38.53 N 42.16 E
Nazilli 212 37.55 N 28.21 E
Nazko ≃ 238 53.07 N 123.34 W
Nazwā 208 22.56 N 57.32 E
Nazyvajevsk 186 55.34 N 71.21 E
Ndélé 214 8.24 N 20.39 E
Ndendé 218 2.23 S 11.23 E
Ndjolé 218 0.11 S 10.45 E
Ndola 218 12.58 S 28.38 E
Ndrhamcha, Sebkha de ⊜ 222 18.45 N 15.48 W
Neagh, Lough ⊜ 162 54.38 N 6.24 W
Neah Bay 270 48.22 N 124.37 W
Neajlovul ≃ 172 44.11 N 26.12 E
Néa Páfos 212 34.45 N 32.26 E
Neápolis, Ellás 172 36.30 N 23.04 E
Neápolis, Ellás 172 35.15 N 25.37 E
Néa Psará 172 38.23 N 23.48 E
Near Islands II 237a 52.40 N 173.30 E
Neasons Hill 266 41.37 N 80.08 W
Neath 174 51.40 N 3.48 W
Neavitt 262 38.44 N 76.17 W
Nebaj 280 15.24 N 91.08 W
Nebb ◆1 170 42.40 N 9.10 E
Nebbid ◆1 166 42.40 N 9.20 E
Nebeur 170 36.17 N 8.47 E
Nebit-Dag 208 39.30 N 54.22 E
Nebo, Ill., U.S. 248 39.27 N 90.47 W
Nebo, La., U.S. 248 31.34 N 92.08 W
Nebo, Mount → Nabā, Jabal an- ∧, Urd. 210 31.46 N 35.44 E
Nebo, Mount ∧ 254 39.49 N 111.46 W
Nebolči 160 59.08 N 33.18 E
Nebraska □3 234 41.30 N 100.00 W
Nebraska City 252 40.41 N 95.52 W
Nebrodi ⋀ 170 37.55 N 14.35 E
Necadah 244 44.02 N 90.05 W
Nechako ≃ 238 53.56 N 122.42 W
Nechako Plateau ⋀1 238 54.00 N 124.30 W
Nechako Range ⋀ 238 53.20 N 124.30 W
Nechako Reservoir ⊜1 238 53.25 N 125.10 W
Neche 252 48.59 N 97.33 W
Neches 250 31.52 N 95.30 W
Neches ≃ 250 29.55 N 93.52 W
Nechí 290 8.07 N 74.46 W
Nechí ≃ 290 8.08 N 74.46 W
Nechmeya 170 36.36 N 7.31 E
Neckar ≃ 164 49.31 N 8.26 E
Neckarsulm 164 49.12 N 9.13 E
Necochea 294 38.34 S 58.45 W
Nederbrakel 176 50.48 N 3.46 E
Nederland, Colo., U.S. 254 39.58 N 105.31 W
Nederland, Tex., U.S. 248 29.58 N 93.60 W
Nedre Soppero 160 68.01 N 21.44 E
Nédroma 168 35.01 N 1.45 W
Nedrow 264 42.59 N 76.09 W
Neebish Island I 244 46.16 N 84.09 W
Neede 178 52.08 N 6.36 E
Needham 261 42.17 N 71.14 W
Needham Market 162 52.09 N 1.03 W
Needle Mountain ∧ 256 44.05 N 109.37 W
Needle Range ⋀ 254 38.25 N 113.55 W
Needles 258 34.51 N 114.37 W
Needles Point ⟩ 230 36.02 S 175.25 E
Needmore 242 39.51 N 78.09 W
Needville 250 29.24 N 95.51 W
Neelyton 266 40.10 N 77.50 W
Ñeembucú □5 294 27.00 S 58.00 W
Neemuch 206 24.28 N 74.52 E
Neenah 244 44.11 N 88.28 W
Neepawa 232 50.13 N 99.29 W
Neeroeteren 178 51.05 N 5.42 E
Neerpelt 178 51.13 N 5.25 E
Neffs 262 40.42 N 75.37 W
Neffsville 262 40.06 N 76.18 W
Neftečala 158 39.23 N 49.16 E
Negage 218 7.45 S 15.16 E
Negaunee 244 46.30 N 87.36 W
Negele 214 5.20 N 39.36 E
Negley 266 40.48 N 80.32 W
Negombo 204 7.13 N 79.50 E
Negotin 172 44.14 N 22.32 E
Negra, Cordillera ⋀ 292 9.30 S 77.30 W
Negra, Laguna ⊜ 294 34.03 S 53.40 W
Negra, Punta ⟩, Br. Hond. 278 16.16 N 88.32 W
Negra, Punta ⟩, Perú 292 6.06 S 81.10 W
Negra, Serranía ⋀ 292 13.45 S 60.58 W
Negreira 168 42.54 N 8.44 W
Negrești, Rom. 172 47.52 N 23.25 E
Negrești, Rom. 172 46.50 N 27.27 E
Negri Sembilan □3 200 2.45 N 102.10 E
Negritos 290 4.36 S 81.15 W
Negro ≃, Bol. 292 14.11 S 63.07 W
Negro ≃, Bol. 292 9.49 S 65.42 W
Negro ≃, Bra. 292 5.15 S 70.53 W
Negro ≃, Bra. 294 26.01 S 50.30 W
Negro ≃, Bra. 296 19.13 S 57.17 W
Negro ≃, Col. 290 5.44 N 74.39 W
Negro ≃, N.A. 280 13.02 N 87.18 W
Negro ≃, Para. 294 24.23 S 57.11 W
Negro ≃, S.A. 290 3.06 S 59.52 W
Negro ≃, S.A. 294 33.24 S 58.22 W
Negro ≃, Ven. 290 9.36 N 72.15 W
Negros I 202 10.00 N 123.00 E
Negros Occidental □4 202 10.20 N 123.00 E
Negros Oriental □4 202 9.40 N 123.00 E
Negru-Vodă 172 43.50 N 28.05 E
Neguac 240 47.15 N 65.05 W
Nehalem 270 45.43 N 123.54 W
Nehalem ≃ 256 45.40 N 123.56 W
Nehawka 252 40.50 N 95.59 W
Nehbandān 204 31.32 N 60.02 E
Neheim-Hüsten 178 51.27 N 7.57 E
Neiba 282 18.28 N 71.25 W
Neiba, Bahía de C 282 18.15 N 71.00 W
Neige, Crêt de la ∧ 166 46.16 N 5.56 E
Neiges, Piton des ∧ 225c 21.05 S 55.29 E
Neihart 256 46.56 N 110.44 W
Neiheshui ≃ 196 22.54 N 115.38 E
Neijiang 190 29.35 N 105.03 E
Neillsville 244 44.34 N 90.36 W
Neimenggu Zizhiqu □4 190 43.00 N 115.00 E
Neira 290 5.10 N 75.32 W
Neisse (Nysa Łużycka) (Nisa) ≃ 164 52.04 N 14.46 E
Neiva 290 2.56 N 75.18 W
Neiva ≃ 290 4.35 S 77.50 W
Neizengshan ∧ 196 24.02 N 117.32 E
Neja 160 58.18 N 43.54 E
Nejapa de Madero 278 16.37 N 95.59 W
Nejdek 164 50.17 N 12.42 E
Nekemte 214 9.02 N 36.31 E
Nekhab ⊥ 220 25.10 N 32.48 E
Nekoi, Oued ≃ 168 35.14 N 3.45 W
Nekoosa 244 44.19 N 89.54 W
Neksø 160 55.04 N 15.09 E
Nela ≃ 168 42.48 N 3.23 W
Nelichu ∧ 220 6.08 N 34.25 E
Nelidovo 160 56.13 N 32.46 E
Neligh 252 42.08 N 98.02 W
Nel'kan 186 57.40 N 136.13 E
Nellie 266 40.20 N 82.04 W
Nellingen 180 48.33 N 9.47 E
Nel'ma 186 47.39 N 139.09 E
Nelson, B.C., Can. 238 49.29 N 117.17 W
Nelson, N.Z. 230 41.17 S 173.17 E
Nelson, Nebr., U.S. 252 40.12 N 98.04 W
Nelson □9 230 41.25 S 172.20 E
Nelson ≃ 232 57.04 N 92.30 W
Nelson, Cape ⟩ 228 38.26 S 141.33 E
Nelson Island I 236 60.35 N 164.45 W
Nelson Lakes National Park ♠ 230 41.50 S 172.40 E
Nelson Reservoir ⊜1 256 48.30 N 107.34 W
Nelsonville 242 39.27 N 82.14 W
Nelspruit 224 25.30 S 30.58 E
Néma 214 16.37 N 7.15 W
Néma, Dhar ⊻4 222 16.40 N 7.13 W
Nemacolin 242 39.52 N 79.56 W
Nemadji ≃ 244 46.41 N 92.02 W
Nemaha 252 40.20 N 95.40 W
Nemaha ≃ 252 40.02 N 95.43 W
Neman 160 55.02 N 22.02 E
Neman ≃ 164 55.18 N 21.23 E
Neman [Ragnit] 164 55.02 N 22.02 E
Nembe 222 4.35 N 6.26 E
Nembro 182 45.45 N 9.45 E
Nemegosenda ≃ 244 48.31 N 82.53 W
Nemenčinė 160 54.51 N 25.29 E
Nemira ∧ 172 46.15 N 26.19 E
Nemours 176 48.16 N 2.42 E
Nemrut Gölü ⊜ 212 38.37 N 42.12 E
Nemuna, Bjeshkët e ⋀ 172 42.27 N 19.47 E
Nemunas (Neman) ≃ 158 55.18 N 21.23 E
Nemuro 192a 43.20 N 145.35 E
Nemuro-hantō ⟩1 192a 43.21 N 145.42 E
Nemuro Strait ⋃ 192a 44.00 N 145.20 E
Nenagh 162 52.52 N 8.12 W
Nenana 236 64.34 N 149.07 W
Nenana ≃ 236 64.30 N 149.00 W
Neneckij Nacionalnyj Okrug □8 160 67.30 N 54.00 E
Nentón ≃ 280 15.48 N 91.55 W
Neodesha 252 37.25 N 95.41 W
Neoga 248 39.19 N 88.27 W
Neola, Iowa, U.S. 252 41.27 N 95.37 W
Neola, Utah, U.S. 254 40.26 N 110.02 W
Neon 246 37.12 N 82.43 W
Néon Karlovási 172 37.48 N 26.44 E
Neopit 244 44.59 N 88.50 W
Neosho 248 36.52 N 94.22 W
Neosho ≃ 248 35.48 N 95.18 W
Neosho Falls 252 37.59 N 95.33 W
Neotsu 270 45.00 N 123.59 W
Nepa ≃ 186 59.16 N 108.16 E
Nepal (Nepāl) □1 204 28.00 N 84.00 E
Nepal □1 190 0.00 0.00
Nepālganj 190 28.03 N 81.38 E
Nepeña 292 9.09 S 78.22 W
Nepewassi Lake ⊜ 244 46.20 N 80.40 W
Nephi 254 39.43 N 111.50 W
Nephin ∧ 162 54.01 N 9.22 W
Nepisiguit ≃ 240 47.37 N 65.38 W
Nepisiguit Bay C 240 47.46 N 65.32 W
Nepomuk 164 49.29 N 13.36 E
Neptune, N.J., U.S. 262 40.12 N 74.02 W
Neptune, Ohio, U.S. 268 40.36 N 84.30 W
Neptune Beach 246 30.19 N 81.24 W
Neptune City 262 40.12 N 74.03 W
Nera ≃ 170 42.26 N 12.24 E
Nérac 166 44.08 N 0.20 E
Nerastro, Sarīr ◆2 214 24.20 N 20.37 E
Nerča ≃ 186 51.56 N 116.40 E
Nerčinsk 186 51.58 N 116.35 E
Nerčinskij Zavod 186 51.19 N 119.36 E
Nerechta 160 57.28 N 40.34 E
Nereta 160 56.13 N 25.18 E
Neretva ≃ 170 43.01 N 17.27 E
Neretvica ≃ 172 43.44 N 15.52 E
Neriquinha 218 15.58 S 21.42 E
Nerja 168 36.44 N 3.52 W
Nerka, Lake ⊜ 236 59.30 N 158.45 W
Nérondes 166 47.00 N 2.49 E
Nerópolis 296 16.25 S 49.14 W
Nerva 168 37.42 N 6.32 W
Nerviano 182 45.33 N 8.58 E
Nes, Ned. 164 53.26 N 5.45 E
Nes', S.S.S.R. 160 66.37 N 44.36 E
Nesbyen 160 60.34 N 9.09 E
Nesco 262 39.38 N 74.42 W
Nesebâr 172 42.39 N 27.44 E
Neshaminy 262 40.14 N 75.08 W
Nesher 210 32.45 N 35.03 E
Neshoba 248 32.37 N 89.08 W
Neškan 236 67.03 N 173.01 W
Neškanpil'gun, Laguna C 236 66.57 N 172.45 W
Neskaupstaður 160a 65.10 N 13.43 W
Neskowin 270 45.05 N 123.59 W
Nesle 166 49.46 N 2.55 E
Nesna 160 66.12 N 13.02 E
Nespelem 238 48.10 N 118.59 W
Ness, Loch ⊜ 162 57.15 N 4.30 W
Ness City 252 38.27 N 99.54 W
Nesselrode, Mount ∧ 236 58.58 N 134.18 W
Nesselwang 164 47.37 N 10.30 E
Nesterkovo 160 59.10 N 30.33 E
Nesterov [Ebenrode] 164 54.38 N 22.34 E
Néstos (Mesta) ≃ 172 40.41 N 24.44 E
Nestucca ≃ 256 45.12 N 123.57 W
Nes Ẕiyyona 210 31.55 N 34.48 E
Netanya 210 32.20 N 34.51 E
Netarts 270 45.26 N 123.57 W
Netawaka 248 39.36 N 95.43 W
Netherdale 226 21.08 S 148.32 E
Netherlands □1 158 52.15 N 5.30 E
Netherlands Antilles □2 276 28.00 84.00
Neto ≃ 170 39.13 N 17.08 E
Netolice 164 49.03 N 14.12 E
Nettilling Lake ⊜ 232 66.30 N 70.40 W
Nett Lake Indian Reservation ◆4 244 48.06 N 93.10 W
Nettleton 248 34.05 N 88.44 W
Nettuno 184 41.27 N 12.39 E
Neubeckum 178 51.48 N 8.01 E
Neubrandenburg 164 53.33 N 13.15 E
Neuburg an der Donau 164 48.44 N 11.11 E
Neuchâtel 180 46.59 N 6.56 E
Neuchâtel □3 180 47.00 N 6.55 E
Neuchâtel, Lac de ⊜ 166 46.52 N 6.50 E
Neuenhagen 164 52.32 N 13.41 E
Neuenkirchen 178 52.14 N 7.22 E
Neuenrade 178 51.17 N 7.47 E
Neuerburg 164 50.00 N 6.17 E
Neuf-Brisach 166 48.01 N 7.32 E
Neufchâteau, Bel. 164 49.50 N 5.26 E
Neufchâteau, Fr. 166 48.21 N 5.42 E
Neufchâtel-en-Bray 176 49.44 N 1.27 E
Neugersdorf 164 50.59 N 14.36 E
Neugraben-Fischbek ◆8 178 53.28 N 9.52 E
Neuhausen 180 47.41 N 8.37 E
Neuhausen auf den Fildern 180 48.41 N 9.16 E
Neuillé-Pont-Pierre 166 47.33 N 0.33 E
Neuilly-sur-Seine 176 48.53 N 2.16 E
Neu-Isenburg 164 50.03 N 8.41 E
Neukirchen-Vluyn 178 51.27 N 6.33 E
Neumarkt 164 48.16 N 13.45 E
Neumarkt in der Oberpfalz 164 49.16 N 11.28 E
Neumarkt in Steiermark 164 47.05 N 14.26 E
Neumarkt-Sankt-Veit 164 48.22 N 12.30 E
Neumünster 164 54.04 N 9.59 E
Neun ≃ 200 19.42 N 104.03 E
Neunburg vorm Wald 164 49.21 N 12.24 E
Neunkirchen 164 47.43 N 16.05 E
Neunkirchen / saar 164 47.38 N 9.46 E
Neuquén 294 39.00 S 68.05 W
Neurara 294 24.10 S 68.29 W
Neuruppin 164 52.55 N 12.48 E
Neuse ≃ 246 35.06 N 76.30 W
Neusiedler See (Fertő) ⊜ 164 47.50 N 16.46 E
Neuss 178 51.12 N 6.41 E
Neustadt, B.R.D. 180 47.54 N 8.13 E
Neustadt, Ont., Can. 264 44.05 N 81.00 W
Neustadt, D.D.R. 164 50.44 N 11.44 E
Neustadt ◆8 178 53.04 N 8.47 E
Neustadt am Rübenberge 178 52.30 N 9.28 E
Neustadt an der Waldnaab 164 49.44 N 12.11 E
Neustadt an der Weinstrasse 164 49.21 N 8.08 E
Neustadt bei Coburg 164 50.19 N 11.07 E
Neustadt in Holstein 164 54.06 N 10.48 E
Neustettin → Szczecinek 164 53.43 N 16.42 E
Neustrelitz 164 53.21 N 13.04 E
Neutral Zone □2 204 29.10 N 45.30 E
Neu-Ulm 180 48.23 N 10.01 E
Neuves-Maisons 180 48.37 N 6.06 E
Neuvic-d'Ussel 166 45.23 N 2.16 E
Neuville-de-Poitou 166 46.41 N 0.15 E
Neuville-lès Dieppe 176 49.55 N 1.06 E
Neuville-sur-Saône 166 45.52 N 4.51 E
Neuwied 164 50.25 N 7.27 E
Neu Wulmstorf 178 53.28 N 9.48 E
Nevada, Iowa, U.S. 244 42.01 N 93.27 W
Nevada, Mo., U.S. 248 37.51 N 94.22 W
Nevada, Ohio, U.S. 266 40.49 N 83.08 W
Nevada □6 272 39.16 N 121.01 W
Nevada □3 234 39.00 N 117.00 W
Nevada, Sierra ⋀, Esp. 168 37.05 N 3.10 W
Nevada, Sierra ⋀, Calif., U.S. 258 38.00 N 119.15 W
Nevada City 272 39.16 N 121.01 W
Nevada de Santa Marta, Sierra ⋀ 290 10.50 N 73.40 W
Nevado, Cerro ∧ 294 35.34 S 68.29 W
Nevado, Sierra del ⋀ 294 35.40 S 68.30 W
Nevado de Toluca, Parque Nacional ♠ 278 19.10 N 99.50 W
Nevel' 160 56.02 N 29.55 E
Nevel'sk 186 46.40 N 141.53 E
Never 186 53.58 N 124.05 E
Nevers 166 47.00 N 3.09 E
Nevesinje 172 43.15 N 18.07 E
Neviges 178 51.19 N 7.05 E
Nevinnomyssk 158 44.38 N 41.56 E
Nevis I 282 17.10 N 62.35 W
Nevis, Ben ∧ 162 56.48 N 5.01 W
Nevjansk 158 57.32 N 60.13 E
Nevşehir 212 38.38 N 34.43 E
New ≃, Br. Hond. 278 18.20 N 88.22 W
New ≃, Guy. 290 3.20 N 57.37 W
New ≃, N.A. 258 33.08 N 115.44 W
New ≃, U.S. 246 38.10 N 81.21 W
New ≃, Ariz., U.S. 254 33.31 N 112.18 W
New ≃, Fla., U.S. 246 29.50 N 84.40 W
New ≃, Fla., U.S. 246 29.55 N 82.25 W
New ≃, N.C., U.S. 246 34.32 N 77.20 W
New ≃, S.C., U.S. 246 32.09 N 80.50 W
New ≃, Tenn., U.S. 246 36.25 N 84.38 W
New Albany, Ind., U.S. 248 38.18 N 85.49 W
New Albany, Miss., U.S. 248 34.29 N 89.00 W
New Albany, Ohio, U.S. 266 40.05 N 82.49 W
New Albin 244 43.30 N 91.17 W
New Alexandria, Ohio, U.S. 266 40.17 N 80.40 W
New Alexandria, Pa., U.S. 266 40.24 N 79.25 W
New Almaden 272 37.11 N 121.49 W
New Amsterdam 290 6.17 N 57.36 W
Newark, Ark., U.S. 248 35.42 N 91.27 W
Newark, Calif., U.S. 272 37.32 N 122.02 W
Newark, Del., U.S. 262 39.41 N 75.45 W
Newark, Ill., U.S. 268 41.32 N 88.35 W
Newark, Md., U.S. 262 38.15 N 75.17 W
Newark, N.J., U.S. 262 40.44 N 74.10 W
Newark, N.Y., U.S. 264 43.03 N 77.06 W
Newark, Ohio, U.S. 266 40.04 N 82.24 W
Newark Lake ⊜ 258 39.41 N 115.44 W
Newark upon Trent 174 53.05 N 0.49 W
Newark Valley 242 42.14 N 76.11 W
New Athens, Ill., U.S. 248 38.19 N 89.53 W
New Athens, Ohio, U.S. 266 40.11 N 80.59 W
New Augusta 248 31.12 N 89.02 W
Newaygo 244 43.25 N 85.48 W
New Baden 248 38.32 N 89.42 W
New Baltimore, Mich., U.S. 266 42.41 N 82.44 W
New Baltimore, N.Y., U.S. 261 42.27 N 73.47 W
New Bavaria 268 41.12 N 84.10 W
New Bedford, Mass., U.S. 261 41.38 N 70.56 W
New Bedford, Pa., U.S. 266 41.06 N 80.30 W
Newberg 270 45.18 N 122.58 W
New Berlin, Ill., U.S. 248 39.44 N 89.55 W
New Berlin, N.Y., U.S. 264 42.38 N 75.20 W
New Berlin, Wis., U.S. 268 42.58 N 88.07 W
New Berlinville 262 40.20 N 75.38 W
Newbern, Ala., U.S. 248 32.36 N 87.38 W
New Bern, N.C., U.S. 246 35.07 N 77.03 W
Newberry, Fla., U.S. 246 29.39 N 82.37 W
Newberry, Mich., U.S. 244 46.21 N 85.30 W
Newberry, S.C., U.S. 246 34.17 N 81.37 W
New Bethlehem 266 41.00 N 79.20 W
New Bloomfield 262 40.25 N 77.11 W
New Bloomington 266 40.35 N 83.19 W
Newboro 264 44.39 N 76.19 W
New Boston, Ill., U.S. 244 41.10 N 91.00 W
New Boston, Mich., U.S. 268 42.10 N 83.24 W
New Boston, Ohio, U.S. 242 38.45 N 82.56 W
New Boston, Tex., U.S. 248 33.28 N 94.25 W
New Braintree 261 42.19 N 72.07 W
New Braunfels 250 29.42 N 98.08 W
New Bremen 268 40.26 N 84.23 W
New Brighton, N.Z. 230 43.30 S 172.42 E
New Brighton, Pa., U.S. 266 40.44 N 80.19 W
New Britain, Conn., U.S. 261 41.40 N 72.47 W
New Britain, Pa., U.S. 262 40.18 N 75.11 W
New Brockton 248 31.23 N 85.57 W
Newbrook 238 54.19 N 112.57 W
New Brunswick 262 40.29 N 74.27 W
New Brunswick □3 232 47.00 N 66.00 W
New Buffalo, Mich., U.S. 268 41.47 N 86.45 W
New Buffalo, Pa., U.S. 262 40.27 N 76.58 W
Newburg, Mo., U.S. 248 37.55 N 91.54 W
Newburg, Pa., U.S. 262 40.08 N 77.32 W
Newburg, Pa., U.S. 266 40.31 N 78.25 W
Newburgh, Ont., Can. 264 44.19 N 76.52 W
Newburgh, Ind., U.S. 248 37.57 N 87.24 W
Newburgh, N.Y., U.S. 261 41.30 N 74.01 W
Newbury, Ont., Can. 266 42.41 N 81.48 W
Newbury, Eng., U.K. 174 51.25 N 1.20 W
Newbury, Mass., U.S. 261 42.48 N 70.52 W
Newbury Old Town 261 42.46 N 70.51 W
Newbury Park 274 34.11 N 118.53 W
Newburyport 261 42.49 N 70.53 W
New Caledonia → Nouvelle-Calédonie I 148 21.30 S 165.30 E
New Canaan 261 41.09 N 73.30 W
New Canton 246 37.42 N 78.18 W
New Carlisle, Qué., Can. 240 48.01 N 65.20 W
New Carlisle, Ind., U.S. 268 41.42 N 86.31 W
New Carlisle, Ohio, U.S. 242 39.56 N 84.02 W
Newcastle, Austl. 228 32.56 S 151.46 E
Newcastle, N.B., Can. 240 47.00 N 65.34 W
Newcastle, Ont., Can. 264 43.55 N 78.35 W
Newcastle, S. Afr. 224 27.49 S 29.55 E
Newcastle, Eng., U.K. 158 52.26 N 3.06 W
Newcastle, N. Ire., U.K. 162 54.12 N 5.54 W
Newcastle, Calif., U.S. 272 38.53 N 121.08 W
New Castle, Colo., U.S. 254 39.34 N 107.32 W
New Castle, Del., U.S. 262 39.40 N 75.34 W
New Castle, Ind., U.S. 248 39.55 N 85.22 W
New Castle, Ky., U.S. 248 38.26 N 85.10 W
Newcastle, Maine, U.S. 242 44.02 N 69.33 W
Newcastle, Nebr., U.S. 252 42.39 N 96.53 W
New Castle, Ohio, U.S. 266 40.20 N 82.10 W
New Castle, Pa., U.S. 266 41.00 N 80.20 W
New Castle, Tex., U.S. 250 33.12 N 98.44 W
New Castle, Va., U.S. 246 37.30 N 80.07 W
Newcastle, Wyo., U.S. 252 43.50 N 104.11 W
New Castle □6 262 39.44 N 75.33 W
Newcastle Emlyn 162 52.02 N 4.28 W
Newcastle Mine 238 51.28 N 112.46 W
Newcastle under Lyme 174 53.00 N 2.14 W
Newcastle-upon-Tyne 162 54.59 N 1.35 W
Newcastle Waters 226 17.24 S 133.24 E
Newcastle West 162 52.27 N 9.03 W
New Chicago 268 41.34 N 87.16 W
New Church 262 37.59 N 75.32 W
New City 242 41.09 N 73.59 W
Newcomerstown 266 40.16 N 81.36 W
New Concord 242 40.00 N 81.44 W
New Corydon 268 40.34 N 84.51 W
New Cumberland, Pa., U.S. 242 40.14 N 76.53 W
New Cumberland, W. Va., U.S. 266 40.30 N 80.36 W
New Dayton 238 49.25 N 112.23 W
Newdegate 226 33.06 S 119.01 E
New Delhi 206 28.36 N 77.15 E
New Denver 238 49.59 N 117.22 W
New Derry 266 40.21 N 79.19 W
New Dundee 264 43.21 N 80.31 W
New Eagle 266 40.12 N 79.56 W
New Edinburg 248 33.46 N 92.14 W
New Effington 252 45.51 N 96.55 W
New Egypt 262 40.04 N 74.32 W
Newell, Iowa, U.S. 252 42.36 N 95.00 W
Newell, S. Dak., U.S. 252 44.43 N 103.25 W
Newell, W. Va., U.S. 266 40.36 N 80.36 W
Newell, Lake ⊜ 238 50.25 N 111.56 W
New Ellenton 246 33.24 N 81.42 W
Newellton 248 32.10 N 91.14 W
New Empire 272 40.35 N 119.21 W
New England 252 46.32 N 102.52 W
New England National Park ♠ 228 30.30 S 152.15 E
New England Range ⋀ 228 30.00 S 151.50 E
Newenham, Cape ⟩ 236 58.37 N 162.12 W
New Enterprise 266 40.10 N 78.25 W
Newfane, N.Y., U.S. 264 43.17 N 78.43 W
Newfane, Vt., U.S. 242 42.59 N 72.39 W
Newfield 262 39.33 N 75.01 W
New Florence, Mo., U.S. 248 38.54 N 91.27 W
New Florence, Pa., U.S. 266 40.23 N 79.05 W
Newfound Gap)(246 35.37 N 83.25 W
Newfoundland □3 232 52.00 N 56.00 W
Newfoundland I 240 48.30 N 56.00 W

Symbols in the index entries are identified on page 360.

Name	Page	Lat°′	Long°′
Newfoundland Basin ⊹[1]	148	43.00 N	43.00 W
New Franklin	248	39.01 N	92.44 W
New Freedom	262	39.44 N	76.42 W
New Galilee	266	40.50 N	80.24 W
New Galloway	162	55.05 N	4.10 W
Newgate	238	49.00 N	115.10 W
New Georgia I	226	8.15 S	157.30 E
New Germantown	262	40.18 N	77.34 W
New Germany	240	44.33 N	64.43 W
New Glarus	244	42.49 N	89.38 W
New Glasgow	240	45.35 N	62.39 W
New Gretna	262	39.35 N	74.28 W
New Guinea I	148	5.00 S	140.00 E
New Guinea, Territory of □[2]	198	6.00 S	150.00 E
Newgulf	250	29.16 N	95.54 W
Newhalem	270	48.41 N	121.16 W
Newhalen	236	59.43 N	154.54 W
Newhall	274	34.23 N	118.31 W
Newham ⊸[8]	174	51.32 N	0.03 E
New Hamburg, Ont., Can.	264	43.23 N	80.42 W
New Hamburg, N.Y., U.S.	261	41.35 N	73.57 W
New Hampshire	268	40.33 N	83.57 W
New Hampshire □[3]	234	43.35 N	71.40 W
New Hampton	244	43.03 N	92.19 W
New Harmony	248	38.08 N	87.56 W
New Hartford, Conn., U.S.	261	41.53 N	72.59 W
New Hartford, Iowa, U.S.	244	42.34 N	92.37 W
New Hartford, N.Y., U.S.	264	43.04 N	75.18 W
Newhaven, Eng., U.K.	174	50.47 N	0.03 E
New Haven, Conn., U.S.	261	41.18 N	72.56 W
New Haven, Ill., U.S.	248	37.55 N	88.08 W
New Haven, Ind., U.S.	268	41.04 N	85.01 W
New Haven, Ky., U.S.	248	37.39 N	85.36 W
New Haven, Mich., U.S.	266	42.44 N	82.48 W
New Haven, Mo., U.S.	248	38.37 N	91.13 W
New Haven, N.Y., U.S.	264	43.29 N	76.19 W
New Haven, Ohio, U.S.	266	41.02 N	82.41 W
New Haven, W. Va., U.S.	242	38.59 N	81.58 W
New Haven □[6]	261	41.18 N	72.56 W
New Hazelton	238	55.15 N	127.35 W
New Hebrides II	148	16.00 S	167.00 E
New Hebrides Trench ⊹[1]	148	19.00 S	168.00 E
Newhebron	248	31.44 N	83.58 W
New Hogan Reservoir ⊜[1]	258	38.07 N	120.50 W
New Holland, Ohio, U.S.	242	39.33 N	83.15 W
New Holland, Pa., U.S.	262	40.06 N	76.05 W
New Holstein	244	43.57 N	88.05 W
New Hope, Ala., U.S.	248	34.32 N	86.24 W
New Hope, Pa., U.S.	262	40.22 N	74.57 W
New Hope ≃	246	35.40 N	79.04 W
New Iberia	248	30.00 N	91.49 W
Newington, Ont., Can.	260	45.07 N	75.01 W
Newington, Conn., U.S.	261	41.43 N	72.45 W
New Ipswich	261	42.46 N	71.51 W
New Jersey □[3]	234	40.15 N	74.30 W
New Kensington	266	40.34 N	79.46 W
New Kent	262	37.31 N	76.59 W
New Kent □[6]	262	37.30 N	77.00 W
New Kingstown	262	40.13 N	77.07 W
Newkirk, N. Mex., U.S.	250	35.04 N	104.16 W
Newkirk, Okla., U.S.	250	36.53 N	97.03 W
New Knoxville	268	40.30 N	84.19 W
New Lake ⊜	246	35.38 N	76.20 W
Newland	246	36.05 N	81.56 W
New Lebanon, N.Y., U.S.	261	42.28 N	73.24 W
New Lebanon, Pa., U.S.	266	41.25 N	80.04 W
New Lebanon Center	261	42.28 N	73.25 W
New Leipzig	252	46.22 N	101.57 W
New Lenox	268	41.31 N	87.58 W
New Lexington	242	39.43 N	82.13 W
New Lisbon	244	43.53 N	90.10 W
New Liskeard	244	47.30 N	79.40 W
New London, Conn., U.S.	261	41.21 N	72.07 W
New London, Iowa, U.S.	244	40.55 N	91.24 W
New London, Minn., U.S.	252	45.18 N	94.56 W
New London, Mo., U.S.	248	39.35 N	91.24 W
New London, N.H., U.S.	242	43.25 N	71.59 W
New London, Ohio, U.S.	266	41.05 N	82.24 W
New London, Pa., U.S.	262	39.47 N	75.52 W
New London, Tex., U.S.	248	32.15 N	94.56 W
New London, Wis., U.S.	244	44.23 N	88.45 W
New London □[6]	261	41.21 N	72.07 W
New Lyme	266	41.36 N	80.47 W
New Madrid	248	36.36 N	89.32 W
Newman, Calif., U.S.	272	37.19 N	121.01 W
Newman, Ill., U.S.	248	39.48 N	87.59 W
Newman Grove	252	41.45 N	97.47 W
Newmanstown	262	40.21 N	76.13 W
Newmarket, Ont., Can.	264	44.03 N	79.28 W
Newmarket, Eire	162	52.13 N	9.00 W
Newmarket, Eng., U.K.	174	52.15 N	0.25 E
New Market, Ala., U.S.	248	34.55 N	86.26 W
New Market, Iowa, U.S.	252	40.44 N	94.54 W
New Market, Md., U.S.	262	39.23 N	77.16 W
Newmarket, N.H., U.S.	242	43.05 N	70.56 W
New Market, Va., U.S.	242	38.39 N	78.40 W
New Martinsville	242	39.39 N	80.52 W
New Meadows	256	44.58 N	116.32 W
New Mexico □[3]	234	34.30 N	106.00 W
New Middletown	266	40.58 N	80.34 W
New Milford, Conn., U.S.	261	41.35 N	73.25 W
New Milford, Ill., U.S.	268	42.11 N	89.04 W
New Milford, Ohio, U.S.	266	41.06 N	81.13 W
New Milford, Pa., U.S.	242	41.52 N	75.44 W
New Millport	266	40.54 N	78.32 W
New Munster	268	42.35 N	88.14 W
Newnan	246	33.23 N	84.48 W
Newnans Lake ⊜	246	29.39 N	82.13 W
New Norfolk	228	42.47 S	147.03 E
New Norway	238	52.53 N	112.58 W
New Orleans	248	29.58 N	90.07 W
New Oxford	262	39.52 N	77.04 W
New Paltz	242	41.45 N	74.05 W
New Paris, Ind., U.S.	268	41.30 N	85.50 W
New Paris, Ohio, U.S.	242	39.51 N	84.48 W
New Paris, Pa., U.S.	266	40.06 N	78.39 W
New Philadelphia, Ohio, U.S.	266	40.30 N	81.27 W
New Philadelphia, Pa., U.S.	262	40.43 N	76.07 W
New Pine Creek	256	42.01 N	120.18 W
New Pittsburg	266	40.50 N	82.06 W
New Plymouth, N.Z.	230	39.04 S	174.04 E
New Plymouth, Idaho, U.S.	256	43.58 N	116.49 W
Newport, Qué., Can.	240	48.16 N	64.45 W
New Port, Ned. Ant.	285s	12.03 N	68.49 W
Newport, Eng., U.K.	174	50.42 N	1.18 W
Newport, Eng., U.K.	174	52.47 N	2.22 W
Newport, Scot., U.K.	162	56.27 N	2.56 W
Newport, Wales, U.K.	174	51.35 N	3.00 W
Newport, Ark., U.S.	248	35.37 N	91.17 W
Newport, Del., U.S.	262	39.43 N	75.37 W
Newport, Ind., U.S.	248	39.53 N	87.24 W
Newport, Ky., U.S.	242	39.06 N	84.29 W
Newport, Maine, U.S.	242	44.50 N	69.17 W
Newport, Md., U.S.	262	38.25 N	76.54 W
Newport, Mich., U.S.	268	42.00 N	83.18 W
Newport, N.H., U.S.	242	43.21 N	72.09 W
Newport, N.J., U.S.	262	39.18 N	75.11 W
Newport, Ohio, U.S.	268	39.23 N	81.14 W
Newport, Oreg., U.S.	256	44.38 N	124.03 W
Newport, Pa., U.S.	242	40.29 N	77.08 W
Newport, R.I., U.S.	261	41.13 N	71.18 W
Newport, Tenn., U.S.	246	35.58 N	83.11 W
Newport, Vt., U.S.	242	44.57 N	72.12 W
Newport, Wash., U.S.	256	48.11 N	117.03 W
Newport □[6]	261	41.35 N	71.15 W
Newport Beach	274	33.37 N	117.56 W
Newport Center	260	44.57 N	72.19 W
Newport News	262	37.04 N	76.28 W
Newport Pagnell	174	52.05 N	0.44 W
New Port Richey	246	28.16 N	82.43 W
New Prague	244	44.32 N	93.34 W
New Preston	261	41.40 N	73.21 W
New Providence, Pa., U.S.	262	39.56 N	76.12 W
New Providence, Tenn., U.S.	248	36.32 N	87.23 W
New Providence I	282	25.25 N	78.35 E
Newquay, Eng., U.K.	174	50.25 N	5.05 W
New Quay, Wales, U.K.	162	52.13 N	4.22 W
New Richland	244	43.54 N	93.30 W
New Richmond, Qué., Can.	240	48.10 N	65.52 W
New Richmond, Ohio, U.S.	242	38.57 N	84.17 W
New Richmond, Wis., U.S.	244	45.07 N	92.32 W
New Riegel	266	41.03 N	83.19 W
New Ringgold	262	40.41 N	76.00 W
New Road	240	44.45 N	63.28 W
New Roads	248	30.42 N	91.26 W
New Rochelle	261	40.55 N	73.47 W
New Rockford	252	47.41 N	99.15 W
New Ross, N.S., Can.	240	44.44 N	64.27 W
New Ross, Eire	162	52.24 N	6.56 W
Newry, N. Ire., U.K.	162	54.11 N	6.20 W
Newry, Pa., U.S.	266	40.24 N	78.26 W
Newry, S.C., U.S.	246	34.43 N	82.55 W
New Salem	252	46.51 N	101.25 W
New Schwabenland ⊸[1]	148	72.30 S	1.00 E
New Sharon	244	41.28 N	92.39 W
New Sheffield	266	40.36 N	80.17 W
Newsiedl am See	164	47.57 N	16.51 E
New Smyrna Beach	246	29.02 N	80.56 W
Newsoms	262	36.37 N	77.14 W
New South Wales □[3]	228	33.00 S	146.00 E
New Springfield	266	40.55 N	80.36 W
New Stanton	266	40.13 N	79.37 W
New Stuyahok	236	59.29 N	157.20 W
New Suffolk	261	40.60 N	72.28 W
Newtok	236	60.56 N	164.38 W
Newton, Ala., U.S.	248	31.20 N	85.36 W
Newton, Ga., U.S.	246	31.19 N	84.20 W
Newton, Ill., U.S.	248	38.59 N	88.10 W
Newton, Iowa, U.S.	244	41.42 N	93.03 W
Newton, Kans., U.S.	252	38.03 N	97.21 W
Newton, Mass., U.S.	261	42.21 N	71.11 W
Newton, Miss., U.S.	248	32.19 N	89.10 W
Newton, N.J., U.S.	242	41.03 N	74.45 W
Newton, N.C., U.S.	246	35.40 N	81.13 W
Newton, Tex., U.S.	248	30.51 N	93.46 W
Newton □[6]	268	40.46 N	87.27 W
Newton Abbot	174	50.32 N	3.36 W
Newton Falls, N.Y., U.S.	242	44.13 N	74.59 W
Newton Falls, Ohio, U.S.	266	41.11 N	80.59 W
Newton Hamilton	266	40.24 N	77.51 W
Newton Stewart	162	54.57 N	4.29 W
Newtonville, Ont., Can.	264	43.56 N	78.30 W
Newtonville, N.J., U.S.	262	39.34 N	74.52 W
New Toronto	264	43.36 N	79.30 W
Newtown, Newf., Can.	240	49.15 N	53.33 W
Newtown, Scot., U.K.	162	55.34 N	2.40 W
Newtown, Wales, U.K.	162	52.32 N	3.19 W
Newtown, Conn., U.S.	261	41.25 N	73.19 W
Newtown, Ind., U.S.	268	40.12 N	87.09 W
New Town, N. Dak., U.S.	252	47.59 N	102.30 W
Newtown, Pa., U.S.	262	40.14 N	74.56 W
Newtownabbey	162	54.42 N	5.54 W
Newtownards	162	54.36 N	5.41 W
Newtown Square	262	39.59 N	75.24 W
New Tripoli	262	40.41 N	75.45 W
New Troy	268	41.53 N	86.33 W
New Ulm, Minn., U.S.	244	44.19 N	94.28 W
New Ulm, Tex., U.S.	250	29.53 N	96.29 W
New Vienna	242	39.19 N	83.42 W
Newville, Ind., U.S.	268	41.21 N	84.51 W
Newville, Pa., U.S.	242	40.10 N	77.24 W
New Vineyard	242	44.48 N	70.07 W
New Washington, Pil.	202	11.39 N	122.26 E
New Washington, Ohio, U.S.	266	40.58 N	82.51 W
New Waterford, N.S., Can.	240	46.15 N	60.05 W
New Waterford, Ohio, U.S.	266	40.51 N	80.37 W
New Waverly, Ind., U.S.	268	40.46 N	86.12 W
New Waverly, Tex., U.S.	250	30.32 N	95.29 W
New Westminster	238	49.12 N	122.55 W
New Whiteland	248	39.33 N	86.05 W
New Wilmington	266	41.07 N	80.20 W
New Woodstock	264	42.51 N	75.51 W
New World Island I	240	49.35 N	54.40 W
New York	242	40.43 N	74.01 W
New York □[3]	234	43.00 N	75.00 W
New York Mills, Minn., U.S.	252	46.31 N	95.22 W
New York Mills, N.Y., U.S.	264	43.06 N	75.18 W
New York State Barge Canal ≋	242	43.05 N	78.43 W
New Zealand □[1]	230	41.00 S	174.00 E
New Zealand Plateau ⊹[3]	148	51.00 S	170.00 E
Nexon	166	45.41 N	1.11 E
Nexpa ≃	278	18.05 N	102.46 W
Ney	268	41.23 N	84.32 W
Neyrīz	208	29.12 N	54.19 E
Neyshābūr	208	36.12 N	58.50 E
Nežin	158	51.03 N	31.54 E
Nezperce	256	46.14 N	116.14 W
Nez Perce Indian Reservation ⊸[4]	256	46.20 N	116.30 W
Ngabang	200	0.23 N	109.57 E
Ngami, Lake ⊜	224	20.37 S	22.40 E
Ngamiland □[5]	224	19.09 S	22.47 E
Ngaoundéré	214	7.19 N	13.35 E
Ngaruawahia	230	37.40 S	175.09 E
Ngaruroro ≃	230	39.34 S	176.55 E
Ngat ≃	200	19.09 N	99.01 E
Ngauruhoe ∧	230	39.09 S	175.40 E
Ngaya ∧	220	9.18 N	23.28 E
Ngesi National Park ♠	224	18.40 S	30.28 E
Nggela Group II	226	9.00 S	160.10 E
Nghabe ≃	224	20.22 S	22.58 E
Ngiap ≃	200	18.24 N	103.36 E
Ngoko ≃	218	1.40 N	16.03 E
Ngol-Kedju Hill ∧[2]	222	6.20 N	9.45 E
Nguigmi	214	14.15 N	13.07 E
Ngulu I[1]	198	8.27 N	137.29 E
Ngum ≃	200	18.09 N	103.06 E
Nguru	214	12.52 N	10.27 E
Ngwakets	224	24.45 S	24.00 E
Nhamundá	290	2.14 S	56.43 W
Nhamundá ≃	290	2.12 S	56.41 W
Nhandeara	296	20.40 S	50.02 W
Nha-trang	200	12.15 N	109.11 E
Nhecolândia	292	19.16 S	57.04 W
Niafounké	214	15.56 N	4.00 W
Niagara	244	45.46 N	88.02 W
Niagara □[6]	264	43.10 N	78.42 W
Niagara ≃	244	43.15 N	79.04 W
Niagara Falls, Ont., Can.	264	43.06 N	79.04 W
Niagara Falls, N.Y., U.S.	264	43.06 N	79.02 W
Niagara Falls ↳	264	43.05 N	79.04 W
Niagara-on-the-Lake	264	43.15 N	79.04 W
Niah	198	3.55 N	113.41 E
Niamey	222	13.31 N	2.07 E
Niamey □[5]	222	14.00 N	2.00 E
Niamtougou	222	9.46 N	1.06 E
Niangara	214	3.42 N	27.52 E
Niangay, Lac ⊜	222	15.50 N	3.00 W
Niangua ≃	248	37.58 N	92.48 W
Nianqingtanggula-shanmai ⋀	206	30.00 N	90.00 E
Niantan ≃	222	10.30 N	10.26 W
Niantic, Conn., U.S.	261	41.19 N	72.12 W
Niantic, Ill., U.S.	248	39.51 N	89.10 W
Nias, Pulau I	200	1.05 N	97.30 E
Nica ≃	186	57.29 N	64.33 E
Nicaragua □[1]	276	13.00 N	85.00 W
Nicaragua, Lago de ⊜	280	11.35 N	85.25 W
Nicaro	284p	20.42 N	75.33 W
Nicastro	170	38.59 N	16.20 E
Nice	182	43.42 N	7.15 E
Niceville	248	30.31 N	86.29 W
Nichelino	182	44.59 N	7.38 E
Nichinan	192	31.36 N	131.23 E
Nicholas Channel ⋃	282	23.25 N	80.05 W
Nicholasville	246	37.53 N	84.34 W
Nicholls	246	31.31 N	82.38 W
Nichols Hills	250	35.33 N	97.32 W
Nicholson, Miss., U.S.	248	30.29 N	89.42 W
Nicholson, Pa., U.S.	242	41.38 N	75.47 W
Nicholson ≃	228	17.31 S	139.36 E
Nickerie □[5]	290	4.00 N	57.00 W
Nickerie ≃	290	5.58 N	57.00 W
Nickerson	252	38.08 N	98.05 W
Nicktown	266	40.37 N	78.48 W
Nicobar Basin ⊹[1]	148	5.00 N	92.00 E
Nicobar Islands II	200	8.00 N	93.50 E
Nicola	238	50.10 N	120.40 W
Nicola ≃	238	50.25 N	121.18 W
Nicolae Bălcescu	172	47.34 N	26.52 E
Nicola Lake ⊜	238	50.10 N	120.25 W
Nicola Mameet Indian Reserve ⊸[4]	238	50.11 N	120.49 W
Nicolaus	272	38.54 N	121.35 W
Nicolet	260	46.14 N	72.37 W
Nicolet □[6]	260	46.15 N	72.20 W
Nicollet	244	44.17 N	94.11 W
Nicolls Town	282	25.08 N	78.00 W
Nicosia → Levkosía, Kípros	212	35.11 N	33.21 E
Nicosia, It.	170	37.45 N	14.24 E
Nicotera	170	38.34 N	15.57 E
Nicoya	280	10.09 N	85.27 W
Nicoya, Golfo de C	280	9.47 N	84.48 W
Nicoya, Península de ≻[1]	280	10.00 N	85.25 W
Nida ≃	164	50.18 N	20.52 E
Nidwalden □[3]	180	46.55 N	8.28 E
Nidže (Nítse Óros) ≃	172	40.58 N	21.49 E
Nidzica (Neidenburg)	164	53.22 N	20.26 E
Niebüll	164	54.48 N	8.50 E
Niederbronn-les-Bains	166	48.57 N	7.38 E
Niedere Tauern ⋀	164	47.18 N	14.00 E
Niederkrüchten	178	51.12 N	6.13 E
Niedermarsberg	178	51.28 N	8.50 E
Niederösterreich □[3]	164	48.20 N	15.50 E
Niedersachsen □[3]	178	52.00 N	10.00 E
Niel	176	51.07 N	4.20 E
Niemodlin (Falkenberg)	164	50.39 N	17.37 E
Nienburg	178	52.38 N	9.13 E
Niénokoué, Mont ∧	222	5.26 N	7.10 W
Niepołomice	164	50.03 N	20.13 E
Niéri Ko ≃	222	13.21 N	13.23 W
Niesky	164	51.17 N	14.49 E
Nieszawa	164	52.50 N	18.55 E
Nieuw Amsterdam	286	5.53 N	55.05 W
Nieuwendam ⊸[8]	178	52.23 N	4.53 E
Nieuw Nickerie	290	5.57 N	56.59 W
Nieuwpoort	176	51.08 N	2.45 E
Nievenheim	178	51.07 N	6.46 E
Nieves	278	24.00 N	103.01 W
Nièvre □[5]	166	47.05 N	3.30 E
Niğde	212	37.59 N	34.42 E
Nigel	224	26.30 S	28.28 E
Niger □[1]	214	16.00 N	8.00 E
Niger ≃	222	5.33 N	6.33 E
Niger Delta ≚[2]	222	4.50 N	6.00 E
Nigeria □[1]	214	10.00 N	8.00 E
Nighthawk	238	48.58 N	119.38 W
Nighthawk Lake ⊜	244	48.28 N	81.00 W
Nightmute	236	60.29 N	164.00 W
Nigríta	172	40.55 N	23.30 E
Nihommatsu	192	37.35 N	140.26 E
Nihuil, Embalse de ⊜[1]	294	35.05 S	68.40 W
Niigata	192	37.55 N	139.03 E
Niigata-heiya ≚	192	37.45 N	139.00 E
Niihama	192	33.58 N	133.16 E
Niihau I	275d	21.55 N	160.10 W
Niimi	192	34.59 N	133.28 E
Niinisalo	160	61.50 N	22.29 E
Nii-shima I	192	34.22 N	139.16 E
Niitsu	192	37.48 N	139.07 E
Níjar	168	36.58 N	2.12 W
Nijkerk	178	52.13 N	5.30 E
Nijlen	178	51.10 N	4.39 E
Nijmegen	178	51.50 N	5.50 E
Nijverdal	178	52.22 N	6.27 E
Nike	222	6.26 N	7.29 E
Nikel'	160	69.24 N	30.12 E
Nikishka	236	60.44 N	151.19 W
Nikkō	192	36.45 N	139.37 E
Nikkō-kokuritsu-kōen ♠	192	36.49 N	139.33 E
Nikolai	236	62.58 N	154.09 W
Nikolajev	158	46.58 N	32.00 E
Nikolajevsk-na-Amure	186	53.08 N	140.44 E
Nikol'sk, S.S.S.R.	160	53.45 N	46.05 E
Nikol'sk, S.S.S.R.	160	59.30 N	45.27 E
Nikolski	236	53.15 N	168.22 W
Nikol'skij	160	60.55 N	34.00 E
Nikol'skoje, S.S.S.R.	160	59.23 N	44.36 E
Nikol'skoje, S.S.S.R.	186	55.12 N	166.00 E
Nikopol, Blg.	172	43.42 N	24.54 E
Nikopol', S.S.S.R.	158	47.35 N	34.25 E
Nikšik	172	42.46 N	18.56 E
Nila, Pulau I	198	6.44 S	129.31 E
Niland	258	33.14 N	115.31 W
Nile (Nahr an-Nīl) ≃	220	30.10 N	31.06 E
Niles, Ill., U.S.	268	42.01 N	87.49 W
Niles, Mich., U.S.	268	41.50 N	86.15 W
Niles, Ohio, U.S.	266	41.11 N	80.45 W
Nilgaut, Lac ⊜	244	46.36 N	77.15 W
Nilo Peçanha	296	13.37 S	39.06 W
Nilsiä	160	63.12 N	28.05 E
Nimba □[6]	222	7.40 N	8.50 W
Nimba, Mont ∧	214	7.37 N	8.25 W
Nimba Mountains ⋀	222	7.30 N	8.30 W
Nîmes	182	43.50 N	4.21 E
Nimisila	266	40.56 N	81.34 W
Nimpkish Lake ⊜	238	50.25 N	126.59 W
Nimrod Lake ⊜[1]	248	34.55 N	93.20 W
Nimule	214	3.36 N	32.03 E
Nina Bang Lake ⊜	232	70.51 N	79.07 W
Nin Bay C	202	12.13 N	123.14 E
Nindirí	280	12.00 N	86.08 W
Nine Degree Channel ⋃	204	9.00 N	73.00 E
Ninette	252	49.22 N	99.43 W
Ninety Mile Beach ▲[2], Austl.	228	38.13 S	147.23 E
Ninety Mile Beach ▲[2], N.Z.	230	34.48 S	173.00 E
Ninety Six	246	34.11 N	82.01 W
Nineveh ⊥	208	36.25 N	43.10 E
Ninga	252	49.13 N	99.51 W
Ningbo	196	29.52 N	121.31 E
Ningcheng	190	41.33 N	119.20 E
Ningdu	190	26.31 N	115.58 E
Ningming	200	22.07 N	107.09 E
Ningpo → Ningbo	196	29.52 N	121.31 E
Ningshan	190	33.04 N	108.39 E
Ningsia → Yinchuan	190	38.30 N	106.18 E
Ningsia Hui Autonomous Region → Ningxia Huizu Zizhiqu □[4]	190	37.00 N	106.00 E
Ningwu	190	39.01 N	112.21 E
Ningxia Huizu Zizhiqu □[4]	190	37.00 N	106.00 E
Ningyuan	200	25.37 N	111.46 E
Ninh-binh	200	20.15 N	105.59 E
Ninhue	294	36.24 S	72.24 W
Ninigo Islands II	198	1.15 S	144.15 E
Ninilchik	236	60.03 N	151.41 W
Ninnescah ≃	252	37.20 N	97.10 W
Ninove	176	50.50 N	4.01 E
Nioaque	292	21.08 S	55.48 W
Nioaque ≃	292	20.46 S	56.04 W
Niobe	266	42.01 N	79.27 W
Niobrara	252	42.45 N	98.02 W
Niobrara ≃	252	42.45 N	98.00 W
Nioki	218	2.43 S	17.41 E
Niokolo Koba, Parc National du ♠	222	13.00 N	13.00 W
Niole ⊸[1]	170	42.25 N	9.05 E
Niono	214	14.15 N	6.00 W
Niordenskiold ≃	236	62.05 N	136.18 W
Nioro du Sahel	222	15.15 N	9.35 W
Niort	166	46.19 N	0.27 W
Niota	246	35.31 N	84.33 W
Niout ▼[4]	222	16.03 N	6.52 W
Nipawin	232	53.22 N	104.00 W
Nipe, Bahía de C	284p	20.47 N	75.42 W
Nipe, Sierra de ⋀	284p	20.28 N	75.49 W
Nipigon	244	49.01 N	88.16 W
Nipigon, Lake ⊜	232	49.50 N	88.30 W
Nipigon Bay C	244	48.53 N	87.50 W
Nipisi Lake ⊜	238	55.47 N	114.57 W
Nipissing □[6]	264	45.30 N	78.50 W
Nipissing, Lake ⊜	244	46.17 N	80.00 W
Nipissis, Lac ⊜	240	51.02 N	66.10 W
Nipisso, Lac ⊜	240	50.52 N	65.49 W
Nippers Harbour	240	49.47 N	55.52 W
Niquelândia	296	14.27 S	48.27 W
Niquero	284p	20.03 N	77.35 W
Niquivil	294	30.24 S	68.42 W
Nīr, Jabal an- ⋀[2]	208	24.10 N	43.20 E
Nirasaki	192	35.42 N	138.27 E
Nirgua	290	10.09 N	68.34 W
Niš	172	43.19 N	21.54 E
Nisa	168	39.31 N	7.39 W
Nišava ≃	172	43.22 N	21.46 E
Niscemi	170	37.08 N	14.24 E
Nishinoomote	193b	30.44 N	131.00 E
Nishio	192	34.52 N	137.03 E
Nishiwaki	192	34.59 N	134.58 E
Nísiros I	172	36.35 N	27.10 E
Niskayuna	261	42.46 N	73.50 W
Nisling ≃	236	62.27 N	139.30 W
Nissan ≃	160	56.40 N	12.51 E
Nisser ⊜	160	59.10 N	8.30 E
Nisswa	244	46.31 N	94.17 W
Nisutlin ≃	236	60.10 N	132.30 W
Niterói	296	22.53 S	43.07 W
Nith ≃, Ont., Can.	244	43.12 N	80.22 W
Nith ≃, Scot., U.K.	162	55.00 N	3.35 W
Nithi River	238	54.01 N	125.01 W
Nitinat	270	48.55 N	124.29 W
Nitinat Lake ⊜	238	48.45 N	124.45 W
Nitra	164	48.20 N	18.05 E
Nitra ≃	164	47.46 N	18.10 E
Nitro	242	38.25 N	81.50 W
Niulanjiang ≃	200	27.28 N	103.10 E
Niushandao I	196	25.26 N	119.56 E
Niut, Gunung ∧	200	0.57 N	110.06 E
Niuzhuang	194	40.58 N	122.32 E
Nive ≃, Austl.	228	26.02 S	146.25 E
Nive ≃, Fr.	166	43.30 N	1.29 W
Nivelles (Nijvel)	176	50.36 N	4.20 E
Nivernais □[9]	166	47.00 N	3.30 E
Niverville, Man., Can.	252	49.37 N	97.01 W
Niverville, N.Y., U.S.	261	42.26 N	73.40 W
Nivskij	160	67.16 N	32.23 E
Nixa	248	37.03 N	93.18 W
Nixon, Nev., U.S.	258	39.50 N	119.21 W
Nixon, Pa., U.S.	266	42.32 N	74.53 W
Nixon, Tex., U.S.	250	29.16 N	97.46 W
Niyodo ≃	192	33.27 N	133.29 E
Niža	160	66.20 N	43.16 E
Nižankoviči	164	49.40 N	22.47 E
Nizhny Novgorod → Gor'kij	160	56.20 N	44.00 E
Nizip	212	37.01 N	37.46 E
Nízke Beskydy ⋀	164	49.20 N	21.30 E
Nízke Tatry ⋀	164	48.54 N	19.40 E
Nizký Jeseník	164	50.14 N	17.13 E
Nizn'aja Omra	160	62.46 N	55.46 E
Nižn'aja Peša	160	66.43 N	47.36 E
Nižn'aja Pojma	186	56.11 N	97.13 E
Nižn'aja Tojma	160	62.24 N	44.10 E
Nižn'aja Tunguska ≃	186	65.48 N	88.04 E
Nižn'aja Tura	158	58.37 N	59.49 E
Nižneangarsk	186	55.47 N	109.33 E
Nižneilimsk	186	57.11 N	103.16 E
Nižneje Kujto, Ozero ⊜	160	64.58 N	31.38 E
Nižnekamskij	160	55.32 N	51.58 E
Nižnelemskij	160	64.01 N	56.16 E
Nižneudinsk	186	54.54 N	99.03 E
Nižnij Kuranach	186	58.49 N	125.32 E
Nižnij Odec	160	63.40 N	54.52 E
Nižnij P'andž	186	37.08 N	68.32 E
Nižnij Tagil	158	57.55 N	59.57 E
Nižnij Trojanov Val ⊥	172	45.40 N	28.30 E
Nižnij V'aloz'orskij	160	66.44 N	35.10 E
Nizza Monferrato	182	44.46 N	8.21 E
Njombe	218	9.20 S	34.46 E
Njombe ≃	218	6.56 S	35.06 E
Nkawkaw	222	6.33 N	0.47 W
Nkhata Bay	218	11.33 S	34.18 E
Nkhota Kota	218	12.57 S	34.17 E
Nkongsamba	214	4.57 N	9.56 E
Nmai ≃	200	25.42 N	97.30 E
Nnewi	222	6.00 N	6.59 E
Noākhāli	204	22.51 N	91.06 E
Noank	261	41.19 N	72.01 W
Noatak	236	67.34 N	162.59 W
Noatak ≃	236	67.00 N	162.30 W
Nobel	264	45.25 N	80.06 W
Nobeoka	192	32.35 N	131.40 E
Nōbi-heiya ≚	192	35.15 N	136.45 E
Noble, Ill., U.S.	248	38.42 N	88.13 W
Noble, Okla., U.S.	250	35.08 N	97.24 W
Noble □[6]	268	41.24 N	85.25 W
Noblesville	248	40.03 N	86.01 W
Nobleton	264	43.54 N	79.40 W
Noboribetsu	192a	42.27 N	141.11 E
Nobres	292	14.44 S	56.20 W
Nobsa	290	5.46 N	72.57 W
Nocatee	246	27.09 N	81.53 W
Noce ≃	170	46.09 N	11.04 E
Nocera Inferiore	184	40.44 N	14.38 E
Nocera Superiore	184	40.44 N	14.40 E
Nochixtlán	278	17.28 N	97.14 W
Noci	170	40.48 N	17.08 E
Nocona	250	33.47 N	97.44 W
Nocupétaro	278	18.48 N	101.04 W
Noda	192	35.56 N	139.52 E
Nodaway ≃	248	39.54 N	94.58 W
Nodier, Lac ⊜	244	47.38 N	78.26 W
Nodre Strømfjord C[2]	232	67.50 N	52.00 W
Noel	248	36.33 N	94.29 W
Noetinger	294	32.20 S	62.20 W
Nœux-les-Mines	176	50.29 N	2.40 E
Nogales, Chile	294	32.44 S	71.15 W
Nogales, Méx.	278	31.20 N	110.56 W
Nogales, Ariz., U.S.	254	31.20 N	110.56 W
Nogara	170	45.11 N	11.04 E
Nogaro	166	43.46 N	0.02 W
Nōgata	192	33.44 N	130.44 E
Nogent-le-Rotrou	176	48.19 N	0.50 E
Nogent-sur-Marne	176	48.50 N	2.29 E
Nogent-sur-Oise	176	49.16 N	2.28 E
Nogent-sur-Seine	166	48.29 N	3.30 E
Noginsk	160	55.51 N	38.27 E
Nogoa ≃	228	23.33 S	148.32 E
Nogoyá	294	32.22 S	59.49 W
Nógrád □[6]	164	48.00 N	19.35 E
Noguera Pallarese ≃	168	42.15 N	0.54 E
Noguera Ribagorzana ≃	168	41.40 N	0.43 E
Noheji	192	40.52 N	141.08 E
Noi ≃	200	17.05 N	105.02 E
Noir, Causse ⋀[1]	166	44.10 N	3.15 E
Noire ≃	242	45.55 N	76.56 W
Noires, Montagnes ⋀, Fr.	162	48.09 N	3.40 W
Noires, Montagnes ⋀, Fr.	166	43.28 N	2.18 E
Noirétable	166	45.49 N	3.46 E
Noirmoutier	166	47.00 N	2.14 W
Noirmoutier, Île de I	166	47.00 N	2.15 W
Noisy-le-Sec	176	48.53 N	2.28 E
Nojima-zaki ≻	192	34.56 N	139.53 E
Nokia	160	61.28 N	23.30 E
Nokomis, Fla., U.S.	246	27.07 N	82.27 W
Nokomis, Ill., U.S.	248	39.18 N	89.18 W
Nol	172	45.25 N	19.53 E
Nola	184	40.55 N	14.33 E
Nolichuckey ≃	246	36.07 N	83.14 W
Nolin ≃	248	37.13 N	86.15 W
Nolin Reservoir ⊜[1]	248	37.20 N	86.10 W
Nolinsk	160	57.33 N	49.57 E
Noma Omuramba ≃	224	18.52 S	20.53 E
Nombre de Dios, Méx.	278	28.41 N	106.05 W
Nombre de Dios, Méx.	278	23.51 N	104.14 W
Nombre de Dios, Pan.	280	9.34 N	79.28 W
Nome	236	64.30 N	165.24 W
Nomgon	190	42.57 N	104.55 E
Nominingue	260	46.24 N	75.02 W
Nomozaki	192	32.35 N	129.45 E
Nonacho Lake ⊜	232	61.42 N	109.40 W
Nonancourt	166	48.46 N	1.12 E
Nonburg	160	65.34 N	50.32 E
Nondalton	236	60.03 N	154.49 W
Nongan	190	44.25 N	125.10 E
Nong Khai	200	17.52 N	102.45 E
Nonoai	294	27.21 S	52.47 W
Nonoava	278	27.28 N	106.44 W
Nonoc Island I	202	9.52 N	125.37 E
Nonogasta	294	29.20 S	67.30 W
Nonthaburi	200	13.51 N	100.34 E
Nontron	166	45.32 N	0.40 E
Nonvianuk Lake ⊜	236	59.00 N	155.15 W
Nooksack	270	48.55 N	122.19 W
Nooksack ≃	256	48.46 N	122.35 W
Noonan	252	48.54 N	103.01 W
Noord-Beveland I	164	51.35 N	3.45 E
Noord-Brabant □[4]	178	51.30 N	5.00 E
Noord-Holland □[4]	178	52.40 N	4.50 E
Noordoost Polder ⊸[1]	164	52.42 N	5.45 E
Noordpunt ≻	285s	12.23 N	69.10 W
Noordwijk aan Zee	178	52.14 N	4.26 E
Noordwijk-Binnen	178	52.13 N	4.27 E
Noordwijkerhout	178	52.15 N	4.30 E
Noorvik	236	66.50 N	161.12 W
Nootka Island I	238	49.32 N	126.42 W
Nootka Sound ⋃	238	49.33 N	126.38 W
Nóqui	218	5.51 S	13.25 E
Nora, Sve.	160	59.31 N	15.02 E
Nora, Ind., U.S.	248	39.55 N	86.08 W
Nora Islands II	214	16.02 N	39.58 E
Norala	202	6.28 N	124.38 E
Noralee	238	53.59 N	126.26 W
Noranda	244	48.15 N	79.01 W
Nora Springs	244	43.09 N	93.01 W
Norberto de la Riestra	294	35.15 S	59.46 W
Norborne	248	39.18 N	93.40 W
Norbottens Län □[6]	160	66.00 N	20.00 E
Norcatur	252	39.50 N	100.11 W
Norcia	184	42.48 N	13.05 E
Norco	274	33.56 N	117.33 W
Norcross	246	33.57 N	84.13 W
Nord □[5]	176	50.20 N	3.40 E
Nordegg	238	52.28 N	116.04 W
Nordegg ≃	238	52.53 N	115.18 W
Nordeifel, Naturpark ♠	164	50.40 N	6.20 E
Norden, B.R.D.	178	53.36 N	7.12 E
Norden, Calif., U.S.	272	39.20 N	120.22 W
Nordenham	178	53.29 N	8.28 E
Norderney	178	53.42 N	7.08 E
Nordfjord C[2]	160	61.54 N	5.12 E
Nordfjordeid	160	61.54 N	6.00 E
Nordfold	160	67.46 N	15.12 E
Nordfriesland ⊸[1]	164	54.40 N	8.55 E
Nordhausen	164	51.30 N	10.47 E
Nordheim	250	28.55 N	97.36 W
Nordhorn	178	52.27 N	7.05 E
Nordkapp ≻	160	71.11 N	25.48 E
Nordkjosbotn	160	69.13 N	19.30 E
Nordkynhalvøya ≻[1]	160	70.55 N	27.45 E
Nordland □[6]	160	67.00 N	14.40 E
Nördlingen	164	48.51 N	10.30 E
Nordmaling	160	63.34 N	19.30 E
Nordman	238	48.38 N	116.57 W
Nord-Ostsee-Kanal ≋	164	53.53 N	9.08 E
Nordreisa	160	69.46 N	21.03 E
Nordrhein-Westfalen □[3]	178	51.30 N	7.00 E
Nordstrand I	164	54.30 N	8.53 E
Nord-Trøndelag □[6]	160	64.25 N	12.00 E
Nordvik	186	74.02 N	111.32 E
Nordwalde	178	52.05 N	7.28 E
Nordwürttemberg □[5]	180	49.00 N	9.45 E
Nore	160	60.10 N	9.01 E
Nore ≃	162	52.25 N	6.58 W
Norfield	248	31.25 N	90.28 W
Norfolk, Conn., U.S.	261	41.59 N	73.12 W
Norfolk, Nebr., U.S.	252	42.02 N	97.25 W
Norfolk, Va., U.S.	262	36.40 N	76.14 W
Norfolk □[6], Ont., Can.	264	42.48 N	80.25 W
Norfolk □[6], Eng., U.K.	174	52.35 N	1.00 E
Norfolk □[6], Mass., U.S.	261	42.15 N	71.10 W
Norfolk Island I	148	29.02 S	167.57 E
Norfolk Island Ridge ⊹[3]	148	29.00 S	167.00 E
Norfolk Island Trough ⊹[1]	148	30.00 S	165.00 E
Norfolk Naval Base ■	262	36.57 N	76.18 W
Norfork Lake ⊜[1]	248	36.25 N	92.10 W
Norikura-dake ∧	192	36.06 N	137.33 E
Noril'sk	186	69.20 N	88.06 E
Norische Alpen ⋀	164	46.55 N	14.05 E
Norland	264	44.43 N	78.49 W
Norlina	246	36.27 N	78.12 W
Norma	262	39.29 N	75.05 W
Normal, Ala., U.S.	248	34.47 N	86.34 W
Normal, Ill., U.S.	268	40.31 N	88.59 W
Norman, Ark., U.S.	248	34.27 N	93.41 W
Norman, Okla., U.S.	250	35.13 N	97.26 W
Norman ≃	228	17.28 S	140.49 E
Normandie □[9]	166	49.00 N	0.05 W
Normandie, Collines de ⋀[2]	162	48.50 N	1.00 W
Normandy → Normandie □[9]	166	49.00 N	0.05 W
Normandy Park	270	47.27 N	122.21 W
Normangee	250	31.02 N	96.07 W
Norman Park	246	31.16 N	83.38 W
Normanton	228	17.40 S	141.05 E
Norman Wells	236	65.17 N	126.51 W
Norogachic	278	27.15 N	107.07 W
Norphlet	248	33.19 N	92.40 W
Ñorquincó	288	41.50 S	70.55 W
Norra Kvarken (Merenkurkku) ⋃	160	63.36 N	20.43 E
Norra Storfjället ∧	160	65.52 N	15.18 E
Nørresundby	160	57.04 N	9.55 E
Norridgewock	242	44.43 N	69.48 W
Norris	246	36.12 N	84.04 W
Norris Arm	240	49.05 N	55.16 W
Norris City	248	37.59 N	88.20 W
Norris Lake ⊜[1]	246	36.20 N	83.55 W
Norris Point	240	49.31 N	57.53 W
Norristown	262	40.07 N	75.21 W
Norrköping	160	58.36 N	16.11 E
Norrtälje	160	59.46 N	18.42 E
Norseman	226	32.12 S	121.46 E
Norsjö	160	64.55 N	19.29 E
Norsk	186	52.20 N	129.55 E
Norte, Canal do ⋃	286	0.30 N	50.30 W
Norte, Punta ≻	294	36.17 S	56.46 W
Norte, Serra do ⋀[1]	292	11.20 S	59.00 W
Norte de Santander □[5]	290	8.00 N	73.00 W
Nortelândia	292	14.25 S	56.48 W
North, S.C., U.S.	246	33.37 N	81.06 W
North, Va., U.S.	262	37.27 N	76.25 W
North ≃, Newf., Can.	232	57.30 N	62.05 W
North ≃, Ala., U.S.	248	33.15 N	87.30 W
North ≃, Iowa, U.S.	244	41.31 N	93.27 W
North ≃, Va., U.S.	242	38.18 N	78.49 W
North, Cape ▲[2]	240	47.02 N	60.25 W
North Abington	261	42.08 N	70.57 W
North Adams, Mass., U.S.	261	42.42 N	73.07 W
North Adams, Mich., U.S.	268	41.58 N	84.32 W
Northallerton	162	54.20 N	1.26 W
Northam, Austl.	226	31.39 S	116.40 E
Northam, Eng., U.K.	174	51.02 N	4.12 W
North America ▲[1]	148	45.00 N	100.00 W
North American Basin ⊹[1]	148	31.00 N	62.00 W
North Amherst	261	42.25 N	72.32 W
Northampton, Austl.	226	28.21 S	114.37 E
Northampton, Eng., U.K.	174	52.14 N	0.54 W
Northampton, Mass., U.S.	261	42.19 N	72.38 W
Northampton, N.Y., U.S.	261	40.54 N	72.40 W
Northampton, Pa., U.S.	262	40.41 N	75.30 W
Northampton □[6], N.C., U.S.	262	36.28 N	77.21 W
Northampton □[6], Pa., U.S.	262	40.42 N	75.12 W
Northampton □[6], Va., U.S.	262	37.20 N	75.50 W
Northamptonshire □[6]	174	52.20 N	0.50 W
North Andaman I	200	13.20 N	93.00 E
North Andover	261	42.42 N	71.08 W
North Anna ≃	246	37.48 N	77.25 W
North Anson	242	44.52 N	69.54 W
North Apollo	266	40.35 N	79.34 W
North Atlanta	246	33.51 N	84.21 W
North Attleboro	261	41.59 N	71.20 W
North Augusta	246	33.30 N	81.58 W
North Aulatsivik Island I	232	59.50 N	64.00 W
North Aurora	268	41.48 N	88.20 W
North Balabac Strait ⋃	202	8.07 N	117.06 E
North Baltimore	268	41.11 N	83.41 W
North Battleford	232	52.47 N	108.17 W
North Bay, Ont., Can.	244	46.19 N	79.28 W
North Bay, N.Y., U.S.	264	43.14 N	75.45 W
North Bay, Wis., U.S.	268	42.46 N	87.47 W
North Belle Vernon	266	40.08 N	79.52 W
North Bend, B.C., Can.	238	49.53 N	121.27 W
North Bend, Nebr., U.S.	252	41.28 N	96.47 W
North Bend, Oreg., U.S.	256	43.24 N	124.14 W
North Bend, Pa., U.S.	266	41.21 N	77.42 W
North Bend, Wash., U.S.	270	47.30 N	121.47 W
North Bennington	242	42.56 N	73.15 W
North Berwick, Scot., U.K.	162	56.04 N	2.44 W
North Berwick, Maine, U.S.	242	43.17 N	70.45 W
North Bethlehem	261	42.40 N	73.50 W
North Billerica	261	42.35 N	71.17 W
North Bloomfield	266	41.28 N	80.52 W
North Bonneville	270	45.39 N	121.57 W
Northboro	261	42.19 N	71.39 W
North Bosque ≃	250	31.40 N	97.24 W
North Boston	264	42.41 N	78.47 W
North Branch, Mich., U.S.	244	43.14 N	83.12 W
North Branch, Minn., U.S.	244	45.31 N	92.58 W
North Branch, N.J., U.S.	262	40.36 N	74.41 W
North Branford	261	41.20 N	72.46 W
Northbridge	261	42.09 N	71.39 W
North Bristol	266	41.24 N	80.52 W
North Brook, Ont., Can.	264	44.44 N	77.10 W
Northbrook, Ill., U.S.	268	42.08 N	87.50 W
North Brookfield, Mass., U.S.	261	42.16 N	72.05 W
North Brookfield, N.Y., U.S.	264	42.51 N	75.24 W
North Brunswick	262	40.28 N	74.28 W
North Caicos I	282	21.55 N	71.56 W
North Canadian ≃	250	35.17 N	95.31 W
North Canton, Conn., U.S.	261	41.54 N	72.54 W
North Canton, Ga., U.S.	246	34.15 N	84.29 W
North Canton, Ohio, U.S.	266	40.53 N	81.24 W
North Cape	268	42.47 N	88.05 W
North Cape ≻, N.Z.	230	34.25 S	173.03 E
North Cape → Nordkapp ≻, Nor.	160	71.11 N	25.48 E
North Cape May	262	38.59 N	74.67 W
North Caribou Lake ⊜	232	52.50 N	90.40 W
North Carlsbad	274	33.11 N	117.21 W
North Carolina □[3]	234	35.30 N	80.00 W
North Carver	261	41.55 N	70.48 W
North Cascades National Park ♠	238	48.45 N	121.14 W
North Catasauqua	262	40.40 N	75.29 W
North-Central □[3]	222	11.00 N	7.45 E
North Channel ⋃, Ont., Can.	244	46.02 N	82.50 W
North Channel ⋃, U.K.	162	55.10 N	5.40 W
North Charleroi	266	40.09 N	79.54 W
North Charleston	246	32.53 N	80.00 W
North Chatham	261	42.29 N	73.38 W
North Chelmsford	261	42.38 N	71.23 W
North Chicago	268	42.20 N	87.51 W
North Chili	264	43.06 N	77.45 W
North Chillicothe	248	40.56 N	89.29 W
North City	270	47.30 N	121.47 W
North Clymer	266	42.04 N	79.34 W
North College Hill	242	39.12 N	84.32 W
North Collins	266	42.36 N	78.56 W
North Concho ≃	250	31.27 N	100.25 W
North Conway	242	44.03 N	71.08 W
North Creek	242	43.42 N	73.59 W
North Dakota □[3]	234	47.30 N	100.15 W
North Dartmouth	261	41.38 N	70.59 W
North Dighton	261	41.52 N	71.08 W
North East, Md., U.S.	242	39.36 N	75.56 W
North East, Pa., U.S.	266	42.13 N	79.50 W

Symbols in the index entries are identified on page 360.

Name	Page	Lat°′	Long°′
North East □[5]	224	21.00 S	27.30 E
Northeast Cape	236	63.18 N	168.42 W
Northeast Cape ≻	236	63.17 N	168.45 W
Northeast Cape Fear ≃	246	34.11 N	77.57 W
North-Eastern □[3]	222	11.00 N	12.00 E
North East Frontier Agency □[8]	206	28.00 N	94.00 E
North Eastham	261	41.52 N	69.59 W
Northeast Harbor	242	44.18 N	68.17 W
North Easton	261	42.04 N	71.06 W
Northeast Point ≻, Ba.	282	21.20 N	73.00 W
Northeast Point ≻, Ba.	282	22.42 N	73.50 W
Northeast Providence Channel ⋃	282	25.30 N	77.10 W
North Edwards	274	35.01 N	117.44 W
North Egremont	261	42.12 N	73.26 W
Northeim	178	51.42 N	10.00 E
North English	244	41.31 N	92.05 W
Northern □[4], Ghana	222	9.30 N	1.00 W
Northern □[4], S.L.	222	9.15 N	11.45 W
Northern Arm	240	49.10 N	55.22 W
Northern Cheyenne Indian Reservation ⇀[4]	256	45.31 N	106.45 W
Northern Dvina → Severnaja Dvina ≃	160	64.32 N	40.30 E
Northern Indian Lake ⊜	232	57.20 N	97.20 W
Northern Ireland □[8]	162	54.40 N	6.45 W
Northern Light Lake ⊜	244	48.15 N	90.38 W
Northern Territory □[8]	228	20.00 S	134.00 E
North Evans	264	42.42 N	78.56 W
North Fabius ≃	248	39.54 N	91.30 W
North Fairfield	266	41.06 N	82.37 W
North Falmouth	261	41.39 N	70.37 W
Northfield, B.C., Can.	270	49.11 N	123.59 W
Northfield, Mass., U.S.	261	42.42 N	72.27 W
Northfield, Minn., U.S.	244	44.27 N	93.09 W
Northfield, N.J., U.S.	262	39.22 N	74.33 W
Northfield, Ohio, U.S.	266	41.20 N	81.32 W
Northfield, Vt., U.S.	242	44.09 N	72.40 W
North Fiji Basin ⁓[1]	148	17.00 S	173.00 E
North Fillmore	274	34.24 N	118.56 W
Northfleet	174	51.27 N	0.21 E
North Flinders Ranges ⩕	228	31.00 S	139.00 E
North Fond du Lac	244	43.38 N	88.28 W
Northford	261	41.24 N	72.48 W
North Fork	272	37.14 N	119.31 W
North Fork ≃	248	36.13 N	92.17 W
North Fort Myers	246	26.40 N	81.54 W
North Freedom	244	43.27 N	89.52 W
North Frisian Islands II	160	54.50 N	8.12 E
Northgate	268	43.01 N	85.36 W
North Georgetown	266	40.51 N	80.59 W
North Glanford	264	43.11 N	79.54 W
North Gower	264	45.08 N	75.43 W
North Grafton	261	42.14 N	71.42 W
North Granby	261	41.59 N	72.50 W
North Greece	264	43.15 N	77.44 W
North Grosvenor Dale	261	41.59 N	71.54 W
North Grove	268	40.37 N	85.58 W
North Hadley	261	42.23 N	72.36 W
North Haven	261	41.23 N	72.52 W
North Havre	256	48.36 N	109.41 W
North Hawaiian Seamount Range ⁓[3]	148	29.00 N	163.00 W
North Hero	242	44.49 N	73.18 W
North Highlands	272	38.40 N	121.23 W
North Hornell	266	42.21 N	77.40 W
North Hudson	244	44.59 N	92.46 W
North Industry	266	40.45 N	81.22 W
North Island I	230	39.00 S	176.00 E
North Islet I	202	8.55 N	119.57 E
North Jackson	266	41.06 N	80.52 W
North Java	264	42.41 N	78.20 W
North Judson	268	41.13 N	86.46 W
North Kingstown	261	41.34 N	71.27 W
North Kingsville	266	41.54 N	80.42 W
North Korea → Korea, North □[1]	194	40.00 N	127.00 E
North Laramie ≃	254	42.08 N	104.56 W
North Las Vegas	258	36.12 N	115.07 W
North La Veta Pass)(	254	37.37 N	105.11 W
North Lawrence	266	40.51 N	81.38 W
North Lewisburg	268	40.13 N	83.33 W
North Liberty	268	41.32 N	86.26 W
North Lima	266	40.57 N	80.40 W
North Little Rock	248	34.46 N	92.14 W
North Loma Linda	274	34.02 N	117.05 W
North Loon Mountain ∧	256	45.07 N	115.52 W
North Loup	252	41.30 N	98.46 W
North Loup ≃	252	41.17 N	98.23 W
North Madison	266	41.48 N	81.03 W
North Mamm Peak ∧	254	39.23 N	107.52 W
North Manchester	268	41.00 N	85.46 W
North Manitou Island I	244	45.06 N	86.01 W
North Mankato	244	44.10 N	94.00 W
North Miami	246	25.54 N	80.11 W
North Miami Beach	246	25.56 N	80.09 W
North Middleboro	261	41.53 N	70.55 W
North Minch ⋃	162	58.05 N	5.55 W
North Mount Lofty Ranges ⩕	228	33.50 S	138.30 E
North Muskegon	268	43.15 N	86.17 W
North Myrtle Beach	246	33.48 N	78.42 W
North New River Canal ≍	246	26.05 N	80.12 W
North Ogden	254	41.18 N	112.00 W
North Olmsted	266	41.25 N	81.56 W
Northome	244	47.52 N	94.17 W
North Oxford	261	42.10 N	71.53 W
North Palisade ∧	258	37.06 N	118.31 W
North Palm Beach	246	26.49 N	80.04 W
North Park	268	42.20 N	89.02 W
North Peak ∧	236	62.34 N	162.23 W
North Pease ≃	250	34.15 N	100.07 W
North Perry	266	41.47 N	81.07 W
North Pine Grove	266	41.24 N	79.13 W
North Plainfield	262	40.37 N	74.25 W
North Plains	270	45.36 N	123.00 W
North Platte	252	41.08 N	100.46 W
North Platte ≃	234	41.15 N	100.45 W
North Point, Pa., U.S.	266	40.10 N	78.12 W
North Point, Pa., U.S.	266	40.54 N	79.08 W
North Point ≻, P.E.I., Can.	240	47.05 N	64.00 W
North Point ≻, Mich., U.S.	244	45.02 N	83.16 W
North Pole	236	64.40 N	147.07 W
Northport, Ala., U.S.	248	33.14 N	87.35 W
Northport, Mich., U.S.	244	45.08 N	85.37 W
Northport, N.Y., U.S.	261	40.53 N	73.20 W
Northport, Wash., U.S.	256	48.55 N	117.48 W
North Portal	252	49.00 N	102.33 W
North Powder	256	45.13 N	117.55 W
North Pownal	261	42.48 N	73.16 W
North Prairie	268	42.56 N	88.24 W
North Providence	261	41.50 N	71.25 W
North Puyallup	270	47.12 N	122.17 W
North Raccoon ≃	252	41.32 N	93.58 W
North Ram ≃	238	52.16 N	115.38 W
North Reading	261	42.34 N	71.05 W
North Richland Hills	250	32.51 N	97.12 W
North Ridgeville	266	41.23 N	82.01 W
North Rim	254	36.12 N	112.03 W
North Robinson	266	40.48 N	82.51 W
North Ronaldsay I	162	59.25 N	2.30 W
North Rose	264	43.11 N	76.54 W
North Royalton	266	41.19 N	81.44 W
North Rustico	240	46.27 N	63.19 W
North Salem	266	40.09 N	81.33 W
North Salt Lake	254	40.50 N	111.55 W
North San Juan	272	39.22 N	121.06 W
North Santiam ≃	256	44.41 N	123.00 W
North Saskatchewan ≃	232	53.15 N	105.06 W
North Scituate, Mass., U.S.	261	42.14 N	70.47 W
North Scituate, R.I., U.S.	261	41.50 N	71.35 W
North Sea ▿[2]	158	55.20 N	3.00 E
North Shafter	272	35.31 N	119.18 W
North Shore	268	42.16 N	88.23 W
North Shores	268	41.50 N	83.25 W
North Shoshone Peak ∧	258	39.09 N	117.29 W
North Shreveport	248	32.35 N	93.48 W
North Siberian Lowland → Severo-Sibirskaja Nizmennost' ≚	186	73.00 N	100.00 E
North Skunk ≃	244	41.15 N	92.02 W
North Sound ⋃	162	59.18 N	2.45 W
North Spicer Island I	232	68.30 N	78.55 W
North Spot I	280	16.13 N	88.12 W
North Springfield	266	41.59 N	80.26 W
North Stradbroke Island I	228	27.35 S	153.28 E
North Sulphur ≃	250	33.23 N	95.18 W
North Sunderland	162	55.34 N	1.39 W
North Swansea	261	41.47 N	71.16 W
North Sydney	240	46.13 N	60.15 W
North Syracuse	264	43.08 N	76.08 W
North Taranaki Bight C[3]	230	38.50 S	174.15 E
North Terre Haute	248	39.31 N	87.22 W
North Thompson ≃	238	50.41 N	120.21 W
North Toe ≃	246	36.00 N	82.16 W
North Tokelau Trough ⁓[1]	148	4.00 S	168.00 W
North Tonawanda	264	43.02 N	78.53 W
North Troy	242	45.00 N	72.24 W
North Truro	261	42.02 N	70.06 W
North Turlock	272	37.31 N	120.51 W
North Ubian Island I	202	6.10 N	120.28 E
North Uist I	162	57.37 N	7.22 W
Northumberland	244	40.54 N	76.48 W
Northumberland □[6], Ont., Can.	264	44.10 N	78.00 W
Northumberland □[6], Eng., U.K.	162	55.15 N	2.05 W
Northumberland □[6], Pa., U.S.	262	40.52 N	76.47 W
Northumberland □[6], Va., U.S.	262	37.50 N	76.25 W
Northumberland Islands II	228	21.40 S	150.00 E
Northumberland National Park ♠	162	55.15 N	2.20 W
Northumberland Strait ⋃	240	46.00 N	63.30 W
North Umpqua ≃	256	43.16 N	123.27 W
North Uxbridge	261	42.06 N	71.39 W
North Vancouver	238	49.19 N	123.04 W
North Vandergrift	266	40.37 N	79.34 W
North Vassalboro	242	44.29 N	69.37 W
North Vernon	248	39.00 N	85.38 W
North Vietnam → Vietnam, North □[1]	200	21.00 N	105.00 E
Northville, Mich., U.S.	268	42.26 N	83.29 W
Northville, N.Y., U.S.	242	43.13 N	74.11 W
North Wabasca Lake ≃	238	56.00 N	113.55 W
North Wales	262	40.13 N	75.17 W
North Wales National Park ♠	162	53.00 N	3.57 W
North Walsham	174	52.50 N	1.24 E
North Warren	266	41.38 N	79.09 W
North Washington	266	41.03 N	79.49 W
Northway	236	62.59 N	141.43 W
North Webster	268	41.19 N	85.42 W
North West □[5]	290	7.30 N	59.50 W
Northwest Cape ≻	236	63.46 N	171.45 W
North Westchester	261	41.35 N	72.24 W
Northwest Christmas Island Ridge ⁓[3]	148	6.30 N	159.00 W
North Western	264	43.20 N	75.22 W
North-Western □[3]	222	11.00 N	5.30 E
Northwest Head ≻	202	10.07 N	118.47 E
North West Highlands ⩕[1]	162	57.30 N	5.00 W
Northwest Miramichi ≃	240	46.58 N	65.35 W
North Westport	261	41.41 N	71.07 W
Northwest Providence Channel ⋃	282	26.10 N	78.20 W
North West Rivers	232	53.32 N	60.09 W
Northwest Territories □[8]	232	70.00 N	100.00 W
Northwich	162	53.16 N	2.32 W
North Wichita ≃	250	33.43 N	99.29 W
North Wilbraham	261	42.09 N	72.25 W
North Wildwood	262	39.00 N	74.48 W
North Wilkesboro	246	36.10 N	81.09 W
North Windham, Conn., U.S.	261	41.45 N	72.09 W
North Windham, Maine, U.S.	242	43.50 N	70.26 W
Northwood, Iowa, U.S.	244	43.27 N	93.13 W
Northwood, Mich., U.S.	268	42.19 N	85.38 W
Northwood, N. Dak., U.S.	252	47.44 N	97.34 W
Northwood, Ohio, U.S.	266	41.37 N	83.30 W
North Wyaconda ≃	248	40.25 N	91.52 W
North Yamhill ≃	256	45.13 N	123.08 W
North York, Ont., Can.	264	43.46 N	79.25 W
North York, Pa., U.S.	262	39.59 N	76.44 W
North York Moors National Park ♠	162	54.23 N	0.50 W
North Zulch	250	30.55 N	96.07 W
Norton, N.B., Can.	240	45.38 N	65.42 W
Norton, Kans., U.S.	252	39.50 N	99.53 W
Norton, Mass., U.S.	261	41.58 N	71.11 W
Norton, Ohio, U.S.	266	41.01 N	81.39 W
Norton, Vt., U.S.	260	45.00 N	71.48 W
Norton, Va., U.S.	246	36.56 N	82.38 W
Norton Bay C	236	64.45 N	161.15 W
Norton Shores	268	43.10 N	86.14 W
Norton Sound ⋃	236	63.50 N	164.00 W
Nortonville	252	39.25 N	95.20 W
Nort-sur-Erdre	166	47.26 N	1.30 W
Norval	264	43.39 N	79.51 W
Norvegia, Cape ≻	148	71.25 S	12.18 W
Norvell	268	42.10 N	84.11 W
Norvelt	266	40.12 N	79.32 W
Norwalk, Calif., U.S.	274	33.54 N	118.05 W
Norwalk, Conn., U.S.	261	41.07 N	73.27 W
Norwalk, Iowa, U.S.	244	41.29 N	93.41 W
Norwalk, Ohio, U.S.	266	41.15 N	82.37 W
Norway, Ind., U.S.	268	40.47 N	86.46 W
Norway, Iowa, U.S.	244	41.54 N	91.55 W
Norway, Maine, U.S.	242	44.13 N	70.32 W
Norway, Mich., U.S.	244	45.47 N	87.55 W
Norway □[1]	158	62.00 N	10.00 E
Norway Bay C	232	71.08 N	104.35 W
Norway House	232	53.59 N	97.50 W
Norwegian Basin ⁓[1]	148	70.00 N	5.00 E
Norwegian Sea ▿[2]	148	70.00 N	2.00 E
Norwich, Ont., Can.	264	42.59 N	80.36 W
Norwich, Eng., U.K.	162	52.38 N	1.18 E
Norwich, Conn., U.S.	261	41.32 N	72.05 W
Norwich, Kans., U.S.	252	37.27 N	97.51 W
Norwich, N.Y., U.S.	242	42.32 N	75.31 W
Norwood, Ont., Can.	264	44.23 N	77.59 W
Norwood, Colo., U.S.	254	38.08 N	108.20 W
Norwood, Mass., U.S.	261	42.11 N	71.12 W
Norwood, Minn., U.S.	244	44.46 N	93.55 W
Norwood, N.C., U.S.	246	35.14 N	80.07 W
Norwood, N.Y., U.S.	242	44.45 N	75.00 W
Norwood, Ohio, U.S.	242	39.10 N	84.28 W
Norwood Addition	268	40.13 N	85.24 W
Norwoodville	244	41.39 N	93.33 W
Norzagaray	202	14.54 N	121.03 E
Nosbonsing, Lake ⊜	244	46.12 N	79.13 W
Noshiro	192	40.12 N	140.02 E
Nosovaja	160	68.15 N	54.35 E
Nosovščina	160	62.56 N	37.03 E
Nossa Senhora do Livramento	292	15.48 S	56.22 W
Nossi-Bé I	225b	13.20 S	48.15 E
Nossob (Nossop) ≃	224	26.55 S	20.37 E
Nošul'	160	60.09 N	49.28 E
Nosy Varika	218	20.35 S	48.32 E
Nota ≃	160	68.38 N	31.45 E
Notasulga	248	32.34 N	85.40 W
Notch Hill	238	50.52 N	119.26 W
Notch Peak ∧	254	39.08 N	113.24 W
Noteć ≃	164	52.44 N	15.26 E
Notecka, Puszcza ⇀[3]	164	52.45 N	16.00 E
Notikewin ≃	232	57.15 N	117.05 W
Noto, It.	170	36.53 N	15.05 E
Noto, Nihon	192	37.18 N	137.09 E
Noto, Golfo di C	170	36.50 N	15.15 E
Notodden	160	59.34 N	9.17 E
Noto-hantō ≻[1]	192	37.20 N	137.00 E
Notoro-ko ⊜	192a	44.05 N	144.10 E
Notozero, Ozero ⊜	160	66.28 N	32.05 E
Notranjsko ≚	170	45.45 N	14.30 E
Notre-Dame, N.B., Can.	240	46.19 N	64.43 W
Notre Dame, Ind., U.S.	268	41.42 N	86.14 W
Notre Dame, Monts ⩕	240	48.00 N	69.00 W
Notre Dame Bay C	240	49.45 N	55.15 W
Notre-Dame-de-Lourdes	252	49.32 N	98.33 W
Notre-Dame-de-Pierreville	260	46.37 N	72.52 W
Notre-Dame-du-Laus	242	46.05 N	75.37 W
Notre-Dame-du-Nord	244	47.36 N	79.29 W
Notrees	250	31.55 N	102.45 W
Nottawa	268	41.55 N	85.27 W
Nottawasaga ≃	244	44.32 N	80.01 W
Nottawasaga Bay C	244	44.40 N	80.30 W
Nottaway ≃	232	51.25 N	79.50 W
Nottingham, Eng., U.K.	174	52.58 N	1.10 W
Nottingham, Pa., U.S.	262	39.45 N	76.01 W
Nottingham Island I	232	63.20 N	77.55 W
Nottinghamshire □[6]	174	53.00 N	1.00 W
Nottoway	246	37.08 N	78.05 W
Nottoway ≃	246	36.33 N	76.55 W
Nottuln	178	51.55 N	7.22 E
Notwani ≃	224	23.35 S	26.58 E
Nouadhibou	214	20.54 N	17.04 W
Nouakchott	222	18.06 N	15.57 W
Nouamrhar	214	19.22 N	16.31 W
Noupoort	218	31.10 S	24.57 E
Nouveau-Québec, Cratère du ⌓[6]	232	61.20 N	73.40 W
Nouvelle	240	48.09 N	66.22 W
Nouvelle ≃	240	48.06 N	66.18 W
Nouvelle-Anvers	218	1.36 N	19.07 E
Nouvelle-Calédonie I	148	21.30 S	165.30 E
Nouvelle-France, Cap de ≻	232	62.30 N	73.40 W
Nova	266	41.02 N	82.18 W
Nova, Serra ⩕[1]	292	9.30 S	62.48 W
Nova América	296	15.01 S	49.56 W
Nova Andradina	296	22.10 S	53.15 W
Nova Aurora	296	18.04 S	48.16 W
Nová Baňa	164	48.26 N	18.39 E
Nová Bystřice	164	49.01 N	15.06 E
Nova Caipemba	218	7.26 S	14.38 E
Nova Chaves	218	10.34 S	21.17 E
Nova Cruz	286	6.28 S	35.26 W
Nova Era	296	19.45 S	43.03 W
Nova Esperança	296	25.57 S	53.48 W
Nova Fátima	296	23.29 S	50.33 W
Novafeltria	170	43.53 N	12.17 E
Nova Freixo	218	14.49 S	36.33 E
Nova Friburgo	296	22.16 S	42.32 W
Nova Gaia	218	10.09 S	17.31 E
Nova Gradiska	170	45.16 N	17.23 E
Nova Granada	296	20.29 S	49.19 W
Nova Iguaçu	296	22.45 S	43.27 W
Novaja Kachovka	158	46.45 N	33.23 E
Novaja Kazanka	158	48.57 N	49.36 E
Novaja Ladoga	160	60.05 N	32.16 E
Novaja Sibir', Ostrov I	186	75.00 N	149.00 E
Novaja Zeml'a II	186	74.00 N	57.00 E
Nováky	164	48.43 N	18.34 E
Nova Lima	296	19.59 S	43.51 W
Nova Lisboa	218	12.44 S	15.47 E
Nova Mambone	218	20.59 S	35.01 E
Nova Olinda do Norte	290	3.45 S	59.03 W
Nová Paka	164	50.29 N	15.31 E
Nova Ponte	296	19.08 S	47.41 W
Nova Prata	294	28.47 S	51.36 W
Novar	264	45.27 N	79.15 W
Novara	182	45.28 N	8.38 E
Novara □[4]	182	45.58 N	8.24 E
Nova Resende	296	21.08 S	46.25 W
Nova Roma	296	13.51 S	46.57 W
Nova Scotia □[3]	232	45.00 N	63.00 W
Nova Sofala	218	20.09 S	34.42 E
Novato	272	38.06 N	122.34 W
Nova Varoš	172	43.28 N	19.48 E
Nova Venécia	296	18.43 S	40.24 W
Nova Veneza	294	28.39 S	49.30 W
Nova Vida	292	10.11 S	62.47 W
Nova Vida, Cachoeira ↳	292	9.25 S	63.36 W
Novaya Zemlya Ridge ⁓[3]	148	73.00 N	51.00 E
Nova Zagora	172	42.29 N	26.01 E
Nova Zembla Island I	232	72.10 N	74.50 W
Nové Hrady	164	48.47 N	14.37 E
Novelda	168	38.23 N	0.46 W
Nové Město	164	50.21 N	16.09 E
Nové Město nad Váhom	164	48.46 N	17.49 E
Nové Město na Moravé	164	49.34 N	16.04 E
Nové Zámky	164	47.59 N	18.11 E
Novgorod	160	58.31 N	31.17 E
Novi, Jugo.	170	45.08 N	14.48 E
Novi, Mich., U.S.	268	42.29 N	83.28 W
Novi Bečej	172	45.36 N	20.08 E
Novice	250	31.59 N	99.37 W
Novi di Modena	170	44.54 N	10.54 E
Novigrad, Jugo.	170	44.11 N	15.33 E
Novigrad, Jugo.	170	45.19 N	13.34 E
Novi Ligure	182	44.46 N	8.47 E
Novinger	248	40.19 N	92.42 W
Novi Pazar, Blg.	172	43.21 N	27.12 E
Novi Pazar, Jugo.	172	43.08 N	20.31 E
Novi Sad	172	45.15 N	19.50 E
Novo ≃	292	4.55 S	70.33 W
Nôvo Acôrdo	296	13.10 S	46.48 W
Novoaltajsk	186	53.24 N	83.58 E
Novoanninskij	158	50.32 N	42.41 E
Novo Aripuanã	290	5.08 S	60.22 W
Nôvo Brasil	296	16.11 S	50.38 W
Novočerkassk	158	47.25 N	40.06 E
Nôvo Cruzeiro	296	17.29 S	41.53 W
Novodugino	160	55.38 N	34.18 E
Novograd-Volynskij	158	50.36 N	27.36 E
Nôvo Hamburgo	294	29.41 S	51.08 W
Nôvo Horizonte	296	21.28 S	49.13 W
Novokazalinsk	186	45.50 N	62.10 E
Novokujbyševsk	160	53.07 N	49.58 E
Novokuzneck	186	53.45 N	87.06 E
Novo Mesto	170	45.48 N	15.10 E
Novomoskovsk	158	54.05 N	38.13 E
Novo Redondo	218	11.13 S	13.50 E
Novorossijsk	158	44.45 N	37.45 E
Novorybnoje	186	72.50 N	105.50 E
Novoržev	160	57.02 N	29.20 E
Novošachtinsk	158	47.45 N	39.56 E
Novosibirsk	186	55.02 N	82.55 E
Novosibirskije Ostrova II	186	75.00 N	142.00 E
Novosokol'niki	160	56.21 N	30.10 E
Novostrojevo [Trempen]	164	54.27 N	21.50 E
Novotroick	158	51.12 N	58.20 E
Novouzensk	158	50.28 N	48.08 E
Novov'atsk	160	58.29 N	49.44 E
Novovolynsk	158	50.50 N	24.05 E
Novožilovskaja	160	64.50 N	51.20 E
Novozybkov	158	52.32 N	31.56 E
Novska	170	45.21 N	16.59 E
Nový Bohumín	164	49.56 N	18.20 E
Nový Bor	164	50.45 N	14.33 E
Novyj Bor	160	66.43 N	52.16 E
Novyj Bujan	160	53.41 N	50.04 E
Nový Jičín	164	49.36 N	18.00 E
Novyj Port	186	67.40 N	72.52 E
Nowa Dęba	164	50.26 N	21.46 E
Nowa Ruda (Neurode)	164	50.35 N	16.31 E
Nowa Sól (Neusalz)	164	51.48 N	15.44 E
Nowata	250	36.42 N	95.38 W
Nowe	164	53.40 N	18.43 E
Nowe Miasteczko (Neustädtel)	164	51.42 N	15.45 E
Nowe Miasto Lubawskie	164	53.27 N	19.35 E
Nowe Miasto nad Pilicą	164	51.38 N	20.35 E
Nowe Warpno (Neuwarp)	164	53.44 N	14.38 E
Nowgong	206	26.20 N	92.42 E
Nowitna ≃	236	65.55 N	154.17 W
Nowogard	164	53.40 N	15.08 E
Nowogród	164	53.15 N	21.53 E
Nowogrodziec (Naumburg am Queiss)	164	51.12 N	15.25 E
Nowood ≃	256	44.17 N	107.58 W
Nowra	228	34.53 S	150.36 E
Nowshera	206	34.01 N	71.59 E
Nowy Dwór Gdański (Tiegenhof)	164	54.13 N	19.06 E
Nowy Dwór Mazowiecki	164	52.26 N	20.43 E
Nowy Sącz	164	49.38 N	20.42 E
Nowy Staw (Neuteich)	164	54.09 N	19.00 E
Nowy Targ	164	49.29 N	20.02 E
Nowy Tomyśl	164	52.20 N	16.07 E
Noxapater	248	33.00 N	89.04 W
Noxen	242	41.25 N	76.03 W
Noxon	256	48.01 N	115.47 W
Noxon Reservoir ⊜[1]	256	47.54 N	115.40 W
Noya	168	42.47 N	8.53 W
Noya ≃	168	41.28 N	1.56 E
Noyant	166	47.31 N	0.08 E
Noyes Island I	236	55.30 N	133.40 W
Noyon	176	49.35 N	3.00 E
Nozay	166	47.34 N	1.38 W
Nsanje	218	16.55 S	35.12 E
Nsawam	222	5.50 N	0.20 W
Nsukka	222	6.52 N	7.24 E
Ntakat ▿[4]	222	16.49 N	11.43 W
Ntem ≃	214	2.15 N	9.45 E
Ntwetwe Pan ≚	224	20.50 S	25.15 E
Nuanetsi	218	21.22 S	30.45 E
Nuanetsi ≃	224	22.40 S	31.50 E
Nūbah, Jibāl an- ⩕	220	12.00 N	30.45 E
Nubian Desert ⇀[2]	220	20.30 N	33.00 E
Ñuble □[4]	294	36.35 S	71.50 W
Ñuble ≃	294	36.39 S	72.27 W
Nucet	172	46.28 N	22.35 E
Nucha → Šeki	158	41.12 N	47.12 E
Nuchatlitz Inlet C	238	49.45 N	126.55 W
N'uchča	160	63.27 N	46.28 E
Nucla	254	38.16 N	108.33 W
N'učpas	160	60.51 N	51.18 E
Nucuray ≃	290	5.00 S	75.25 W
Nueces ≃	250	27.50 N	97.30 W
Nueces Plains ≚	250	28.30 N	99.15 W
Nueltin Lake ⊜	232	60.20 N	99.50 W
Nüerhe ≃	194	40.57 N	121.19 E
Nuestra Señora de Talavera	294	25.26 S	63.48 W
Nueva, Isla I	288	55.13 S	66.30 W
Nueva Antioquia	290	6.05 N	69.26 W
Nueva California	294	32.46 S	68.20 W
Nueva Casas Grandes	278	30.25 N	107.55 W
Nueva Ciudad Guerrero	278	26.35 N	99.15 W
Nueva Concepción	280	14.08 N	89.18 W
Nueva Ecija □[4]	202	15.40 N	120.00 E
Nueva Esparta □[3]	290	11.00 N	64.00 W
Nueva Francia	294	28.11 S	64.12 W
Nueva Galia	294	35.07 S	65.16 W
Nueva Germania	294	23.54 S	56.34 W
Nueva Gerona	284p	21.53 N	82.48 W
Nueva Helvecia	294	34.19 S	57.13 W
Nueva Imperial	294	38.44 S	72.57 W
Nueva Italia de Ruiz	278	19.01 N	102.06 W
Nueva Palmira	294	33.53 S	58.25 W
Nueva Paz	284p	22.46 N	81.45 W
Nueva Rosita	278	27.57 N	101.13 W
Nueva San Salvador	280	13.41 N	89.17 W
Nueva Segovia □[5]	280	13.40 N	86.10 W
Nueva Venecia	280	14.03 N	91.33 W
Nueva Vizcaya □[4]	202	16.20 N	121.20 E
Nueve de Julio	294	35.30 S	60.50 W
Nuevitas	284p	21.33 N	77.16 W
Nuevitas, Bahía de C	284p	21.30 N	77.12 W
Nuevo	274	33.48 N	117.09 W
Nuevo, Golfo C	288	42.42 S	64.35 W
Nuevo Berlín	294	32.59 S	58.03 W
Nuevo Camarón	250	27.05 N	99.55 W
Nuevo Chagres	280	9.14 N	80.08 W
Nuevo Laredo	278	27.30 N	99.31 W
Nuevo Léon	258	32.20 N	115.12 W
Nuevo León □[3]	278	25.40 N	100.00 W
Nuevo Mundo, Cerro ∧	292	21.55 S	66.53 W
Nuevo Poblado el Oro	250	26.50 N	101.19 W
Nuevo Primero de Mayo	250	26.01 N	98.02 W
Nuevo Progreso	278	18.38 N	92.18 W
Nuevo Rocafuerte	290	0.56 S	75.24 W
Nuevo Saucillo	250	27.20 N	104.54 W
Nugget Point ≻	230	46.27 S	169.49 E
Nugssuaq ≻[1]	232	71.45 N	53.00 W
Nūh, Rās ≻	208	25.05 N	62.24 E
Nuhūd, Jabal an- ∧	220	14.50 N	29.53 E
Nuits-Saint-Georges	166	47.08 N	4.57 E
N'uja	186	60.32 N	116.14 E
N'uja ≃	186	60.32 N	116.20 E
Nujiang (Salween) ≃	200	16.31 N	97.37 E
N'uk, Ozero ⊜	160	64.27 N	31.45 E
Nuka Island I	236	59.21 N	150.42 W
Nukey Bluff ⌓[4]	228	32.33 S	135.40 E
Nukhaylah ▿[4]	220	19.03 N	26.19 E
N'uksenica	160	60.25 N	44.13 E
Nukus	186	42.50 N	59.29 E
Nulato	236	64.43 N	158.06 W
Nules	168	39.51 N	0.09 W
Nullagine	226	21.53 S	120.06 E
Numancia	202	9.52 N	125.58 E
Numancia ⊥	168	41.48 N	2.25 W
Numata, Nihon	192	36.38 N	139.03 E
Numata, Nihon	192a	43.48 N	141.57 E
Numatinna ≃	220	7.14 N	27.37 E
Numazu	192	35.06 N	138.52 E
Number 5 Mine	266	41.08 N	80.11 W
Numila	275b	21.54 N	159.34 W
Nu Mine	266	40.48 N	79.18 W
Numto	186	63.40 N	71.20 E
Nun ≃[1]	222	4.20 N	6.00 E
Nun'amo	236	65.37 N	170.40 W
Nunapitchuk	236	60.54 N	162.29 W
Nunda	266	42.35 N	77.57 W
Nuneaton	174	52.32 N	1.28 W
Nunez ≃	222	10.36 N	14.40 W
Nunivak Island I	236	60.00 N	166.30 W
Nunjiang	190	49.10 N	125.11 E
Nunkiní	278	20.20 N	90.11 W
Nunkun ∧	206	33.59 N	76.02 E
Nunligran	236	64.48 N	175.24 W
Nunnelly	248	35.52 N	87.28 W
Nunspeet	178	52.23 N	5.46 E
Nuoro	170	40.19 N	9.20 E
Nuqruș, Jabal ∧	220	24.49 N	34.36 E
Nuquí	290	5.42 N	77.17 W
Nura ≃	186	50.30 N	69.59 E
Nuraghe San Antine ⊥	170	40.30 N	8.46 E
Nurallao	170	39.46 N	9.05 E
N'urba	186	63.17 N	118.20 E
Nürburgring ♠	166	50.12 N	7.20 E
Nur Dağları ⩕	212	36.45 N	36.20 E
Nuremberg → Nürnberg, B.R.D.	164	49.27 N	11.04 E
Nuri	278	28.02 N	109.22 W
Nurlat	160	54.26 N	50.46 E
Nurlaty	160	55.37 N	48.18 E
Nürnberg	164	49.27 N	11.04 E
Nurra ⇀[1]	170	40.45 N	8.15 E
Nurri	170	39.42 N	9.14 E
Nurri, Mount ∧	228	31.42 S	146.02 E
Nursery	250	28.56 N	97.06 W
Nürtingen	180	48.38 N	9.20 E
Nuruhak Dağı ∧	212	38.04 N	37.29 E
Nusaybin	208	37.03 N	41.13 E
Nușayrīyah, Jabal an- ⩕	212	35.30 N	36.12 E
Nushagak ≃	236	59.00 N	158.30 W
Nushagak Bay C	236	58.40 N	158.40 W
Nushagak Peninsula ≻[1]	236	58.30 N	159.00 W
Nushan ⩕	200	26.50 N	99.03 E
Nushki	204	29.33 N	66.01 E
Nutauge, Laguna C	236	67.55 N	176.45 W
Nutepelmen, S.S.S.R.	236	65.31 N	178.30 W
Nutepel'men, S.S.S.R.	236	67.26 N	174.56 W
Nutrioso	254	33.57 N	109.13 W
Nuttby Mountain ∧[2]	240	45.33 N	63.13 W
Nutter Fort	242	39.20 N	80.19 W
Nutting Lake	261	42.32 N	71.16 W
Nutzotin Mountains ⩕	236	62.10 N	141.40 W
N'uvčim	160	61.22 N	50.42 E
Nuwara-Eliya	204	6.58 N	80.46 E
Nuweveldberge ⩕	224	32.13 S	21.40 E
Nuyakuk Lake ⊜	236	60.00 N	158.40 W
Nyabing	226	33.32 S	118.09 E
Nyac	236	61.01 N	159.57 W
Nyack	261	41.05 N	73.55 W
Nyakrom	222	5.37 N	0.48 W
Nyala	220	12.03 N	24.53 E
Nyanding, Khawr ∨	220	8.40 N	32.41 E
Nyangui ∧	224	17.53 S	32.44 E
Nyanza	218	2.21 S	29.45 E
Nyasa, Lake ⊜	218	12.00 S	34.30 E
Nyaunglebin	200	17.57 N	96.44 E
Nyazvidzi ≃	224	20.00 S	32.17 E
Nybergsund	160	61.15 N	12.19 E
Nyborg	160	55.19 N	10.48 E
Nybro	160	56.45 N	15.54 E
Nyda	186	66.36 N	72.54 E
Nyeri	218	0.25 S	36.57 E
Nygligan, Mys ≻	236	65.05 N	172.06 W
Nyíradony	164	47.41 N	21.55 E
Nyírbátor	164	47.50 N	22.08 E
Nyíregyháza	164	47.59 N	21.43 E
Nykøbing, Dan.	160	55.55 N	11.41 E
Nykøbing, Dan.	164	54.46 N	11.53 E
Nyköping	160	58.45 N	17.00 E
Nyland Acres	274	34.14 N	119.09 W
Nylstroom	218	24.42 S	28.20 E
Nymboida ≃	228	29.39 S	152.30 E
Nymburk	164	50.11 N	15.03 E
Nynäshamn	160	58.54 N	17.57 E
Nyngan	228	31.34 S	147.11 E
Nyon	180	46.23 N	6.14 E
Nyong ≃	214	3.17 N	9.54 E
Nyons	166	44.22 N	5.08 E
Nyrov	160	60.42 N	56.40 E
Nýrsko	164	49.18 N	13.09 E
Nysa (Neisse)	164	50.29 N	17.20 E
Nysa Kłodzka ≃	164	50.49 N	17.50 E
Nyssa	256	43.53 N	117.00 W
Nytva	160	57.56 N	55.20 E
Nyūdō-zaki ≻	192	40.00 N	139.42 E
Nyūzen	192	36.56 N	137.30 E
Nzérékoré	222	7.45 N	8.49 W
Nzérékoré □[4]	222	7.50 N	8.45 W
Nzheleledam ⇀[6]	224	22.44 S	30.06 E
Nzi ≃	222	5.57 N	4.50 W
Nzo ≃	222	6.16 N	7.03 W
O			
Oacoma	252	43.48 N	99.24 W
Oadby	174	52.36 N	1.04 W
Oahe Reservoir ⊜[1]	252	45.30 N	100.25 W
Oahu I	275d	21.30 N	158.00 W
O-akan-dake ∧	192a	43.27 N	144.10 E
Oak Bay	238	48.27 N	123.18 W
Oak Bluffs	261	41.27 N	70.34 W
Oakboro	246	35.13 N	80.20 W
Oak City, N.C., U.S.	246	35.58 N	77.18 W
Oak City, Utah, U.S.	254	39.22 N	112.20 W
Oak Creek, Colo., U.S.	254	40.16 N	106.57 W
Oak Creek, Wis., U.S.	268	42.53 N	87.55 W
Oakdale, Calif., U.S.	272	37.46 N	120.51 W
Oakdale, Conn., U.S.	261	41.28 N	72.10 W
Oakdale, La., U.S.	248	30.49 N	92.40 W
Oakdale, Mass., U.S.	261	42.23 N	71.48 W
Oakdale, Nebr., U.S.	252	42.04 N	97.58 W
Oakdale, Pa., U.S.	266	40.24 N	80.11 W
Oakdale, Tenn., U.S.	246	35.59 N	84.33 W
Oakengates	174	52.42 N	2.28 W
Oakes	252	46.08 N	98.06 W
Oakesdale	256	47.08 N	117.15 W
Oakfield, Maine, U.S.	242	46.06 N	68.10 W
Oakfield, N.Y., U.S.	264	43.04 N	78.16 W
Oakfield, Ohio, U.S.	266	41.24 N	80.50 W
Oakfield, Wis., U.S.	244	43.41 N	88.34 W
Oakford, Ill., U.S.	248	40.06 N	89.58 W
Oakford, Ind., U.S.	268	40.25 N	86.06 W
Oakford, Pa., U.S.	262	40.09 N	74.58 W
Oak Forest	268	41.36 N	87.45 W
Oak Grove, La., U.S.	248	32.52 N	91.23 W
Oak Grove, Oreg., U.S.	270	45.26 N	122.38 W
Oak Hall	262	37.56 N	75.33 W
Oakham	162	52.40 N	0.43 W
Oak Harbor, Ohio, U.S.	266	41.30 N	83.09 W
Oak Harbor, Wash., U.S.	270	48.18 N	122.39 W
Oak Hill, Fla., U.S.	246	28.52 N	80.51 W
Oak Hill, Mich., U.S.	244	44.13 N	86.19 W
Oak Hill, Ohio, U.S.	242	38.54 N	82.34 W
Oak Hill, Tenn., U.S.	248	36.05 N	86.48 W
Oak Hill, W. Va., U.S.	242	37.59 N	81.09 W
Oakhurst, Calif., U.S.	272	37.19 N	119.40 W
Oakhurst, N.J., U.S.	262	40.16 N	74.01 W
Oakhurst, Tex., U.S.	250	30.44 N	95.19 W
Oak Lake	252	49.47 N	100.38 W
Oak Lake ⊜	252	49.40 N	100.45 W
Oakland, Ont., Can.	266	42.09 N	82.36 W
Oakland, Calif., U.S.	272	37.47 N	122.13 W
Oakland, Ill., U.S.	248	39.39 N	88.02 W
Oakland, Iowa, U.S.	252	41.19 N	95.23 W
Oakland, Maine, U.S.	242	44.33 N	69.43 W
Oakland, Md., U.S.	242	39.25 N	79.24 W
Oakland, Mich., U.S.	268	42.44 N	83.24 W
Oakland, Miss., U.S.	248	34.03 N	89.55 W
Oakland, Nebr., U.S.	252	41.50 N	96.28 W
Oakland, Oreg., U.S.	256	43.25 N	123.18 W
Oakland, Pa., U.S.	266	40.26 N	79.58 W
Oakland □[6]	268	42.40 N	83.23 W
Oakland Beach	266	41.37 N	80.18 W
Oakland City	248	38.20 N	87.21 W
Oakland Park	246	26.12 N	80.07 W
Oak Lawn, Ill., U.S.	268	41.43 N	87.45 W
Oaklawn, Kans., U.S.	252	37.36 N	97.18 W
Oakley, Calif., U.S.	272	37.58 N	121.43 W
Oakley, Idaho, U.S.	256	42.15 N	113.53 W
Oakley, Kans., U.S.	252	39.08 N	100.51 W
Oakley Park	268	42.34 N	83.30 W
Oakman	248	33.37 N	87.23 W
Oakmont, Pa., U.S.	266	40.18 N	78.53 W
Oakmont, Pa., U.S.	266	40.31 N	79.50 W
Oak Park, Ill., U.S.	268	41.53 N	87.48 W
Oak Park, Mich., U.S.	268	42.28 N	83.11 W
Oakridge, Calif., U.S.	272	38.03 N	121.20 W
Oakridge, Oreg., U.S.	256	43.45 N	122.28 W
Oak Ridge, Pa., U.S.	266	41.00 N	79.18 W
Oak Ridge, Tenn., U.S.	246	36.01 N	84.16 W
Oak Ridge Area (Atomic Energy Commission Reservation) Ʋ[3]	246	35.56 N	85.15 W
Oak Ridges	264	43.56 N	79.27 W
Oaktown	248	38.52 N	87.26 W
Oak Valley	262	39.49 N	75.10 W
Oak View	274	34.24 N	119.18 W
Oakview Beach	264	44.29 N	80.03 W
Oakville, Man., Can.	252	49.56 N	97.58 W
Oakville, Ont., Can.	264	43.27 N	79.41 W
Oakville, Conn., U.S.	261	41.36 N	73.05 W
Oakville, Tenn., U.S.	248	35.04 N	89.56 W
Oakville, Wash., U.S.	270	46.50 N	123.14 W
Oakwood, Ont., Can.	264	44.20 N	78.53 W
Oakwood, Ohio, U.S.	242	41.06 N	84.23 W
Oakwood, Ohio, U.S.	266	41.22 N	81.30 W
Oakwood, Tex., U.S.	250	31.35 N	95.51 W
Oakwood Beach	262	39.33 N	75.31 W
Oamaru	230	45.06 S	170.58 E
Oancea	172	45.55 N	28.06 E
Ōarai	192	36.18 N	140.34 E
Oates Coast ⌓[2]	148	70.00 S	160.00 E
Oatman	254	35.02 N	114.23 W
Oaxaca [de Juárez]	278	17.03 N	96.43 W
Ob' ≃	186	66.45 N	69.30 E
Oba ≃	244	48.55 N	84.17 W
Obabika Lake ⊜	244	47.05 N	80.17 W
Oba Lake ⊜	244	48.38 N	84.18 W
Oballos	250	27.27 N	101.23 W
Obama, Nihon	192	35.30 N	135.45 E
Obama, Nihon	192	32.43 N	130.13 E
Oban	162	56.25 N	5.29 W
Obanazawa	192	38.36 N	140.24 E
Oban Hills ⩕[2]	222	5.35 N	8.35 E
Obbia	214	5.20 N	48.38 E
Obed	238	53.33 N	117.12 W
Obed ≃	248	36.04 N	84.39 W
Obeh	208	34.20 N	63.16 E
Oberá	294	27.30 S	55.07 W
Oberdrauburg	164	46.45 N	12.58 E
Ober Ennstal ∨	164	47.28 N	14.10 E
Obergurgl	164	46.52 N	11.01 E
Oberhausen	178	51.28 N	6.50 E
Oberkaufungen	178	51.17 N	9.38 E
Oberkirch	180	48.31 N	8.05 E
Ober-Lahnstein	164	50.18 N	7.37 E
Oberlin, Kans., U.S.	252	39.49 N	100.32 W
Oberlin, La., U.S.	248	30.37 N	92.46 W
Oberlin, Ohio, U.S.	266	41.18 N	82.13 W
Oberlin, Pa., U.S.	262	40.14 N	76.49 W
Obernai	166	48.28 N	7.28 E
Obernbeck	178	52.12 N	8.41 E
Obernburg am Main	164	49.50 N	9.08 E
Oberndorf am Neckar	180	48.18 N	8.34 E
Obernkirchen	178	52.16 N	9.07 E
Oberösterreich □[3]	164	48.15 N	14.00 E
Oberpullendorf	164	47.31 N	16.31 E
Oberriet	180	47.19 N	9.33 E
Oberstdorf	180	47.24 N	10.16 E
Oberursel	164	50.11 N	8.35 E
Obervellach	164	46.56 N	13.12 E
Oberviechtach	164	49.28 N	12.25 E
Oberwart	164	47.17 N	16.13 E
Oberwölz-Stadt	164	47.13 N	14.17 E
Obey ≃	246	36.34 N	85.31 W
Obi, Kepulauan II	198	1.23 S	127.45 E
Obi, Pulau I	198	1.30 S	127.45 E
Óbidos	286	1.55 S	55.31 W
Obihiro	192a	42.55 N	143.12 E
Obilatu, Pulau I	198	1.25 S	127.20 E
Obing	164	48.00 N	12.24 E
Obion	248	36.16 N	89.12 W
Obion ≃	248	35.55 N	89.39 W
Obira	192a	44.00 N	141.35 E
Obispo, Punta ≻	280	15.50 N	87.21 W
Objačevo	160	60.20 N	49.34 E
Oblong	248	39.00 N	87.55 W
Oblučje	186	49.03 N	131.04 E
Obninsk	160	55.05 N	36.37 E
Obnova	172	43.26 N	24.59 E
Obock	214	11.59 N	43.16 E
Oborniki	164	52.39 N	16.51 E
Oboz'orskij	160	63.28 N	40.18 E
Obra ≃	164	52.36 N	15.28 E
Obrenovac	172	44.39 N	20.12 E
O'brien	256	42.04 N	123.42 W
Obrighoven-Lackhausen	178	51.40 N	6.38 E
Obrovac	170	44.12 N	15.41 E
Obščij Syrt ∧	158	52.00 N	51.30 E
Observation Peak ∧	258	40.46 N	120.10 W
Observatory Inlet ⋃	238	55.10 N	129.54 W
Obskaja Guba C	186	69.00 N	73.00 E
Obuasi	222	6.14 N	1.39 W
Obuchova	160	56.06 N	32.22 E
Obvinsk	160	58.29 N	54.51 E
Obwalden □[3]	180	46.50 N	8.14 E
Ocala	246	29.11 N	82.07 W
Ocallí	292	6.10 S	78.17 W
Ocamo ≃	290	2.48 N	65.14 W
Ocampo, Méx.	278	27.20 N	102.21 W
Ocampo, Méx.	278	28.11 N	108.23 W
Ocaña, Col.	290	8.15 N	73.20 W
Ocaña, Esp.	168	39.56 N	3.31 W
Occidental, Cordillera ⩕, Col.	290	5.00 N	76.00 W
Occidental, Cordillera ⩕, Perú	292	14.00 S	74.00 W
Occoquan	262	38.41 N	77.16 W
Ocean □[6]	262	39.58 N	74.12 W
Oceana	246	37.42 N	81.38 W
Ocean Bluff	261	42.06 N	70.39 W
Ocean Cape ≻	232	59.30 N	139.45 W
Ocean City, Md., U.S.	242	38.20 N	75.05 W
Ocean City, N.J., U.S.	262	39.16 N	74.36 W
Ocean City, Wash., U.S.	270	47.04 N	124.10 W
Ocean Falls	238	52.21 N	127.40 W
Ocean Gate	262	39.39 N	74.08 W
Ocean Grove	261	41.44 N	71.12 W
Ocean Lake ⊜[1]	254	43.11 N	108.36 W
Oceano	258	35.06 N	120.37 W
Ocean Park, B.C., Can.	270	49.02 N	122.53 W
Ocean Park, Wash., U.S.	270	46.30 N	124.03 W
Ocean Shores	270	46.58 N	124.09 W
Oceanside	274	33.12 N	117.23 W
Ocean Springs	248	30.25 N	88.50 W
Ocean View, Del., U.S.	262	38.33 N	75.05 W
Ocean View, N.J., U.S.	262	39.10 N	74.44 W
Oceanville	262	39.28 N	74.28 W
Oceanway	246	30.28 N	81.38 W
Oceola	266	40.51 N	83.06 W
Očer	160	57.53 N	54.42 E
Ocha	186	53.34 N	142.56 E
Ocheyedan	252	43.25 N	95.32 W
Ocheyedan ≃	252	43.08 N	95.09 W
Ocheyedan Mound ∧[2]	252	43.25 N	95.33 W
O'chiese Indian Reserve ⇀[4]	238	52.50 N	115.28 W
Ochlocknee	246	30.59 N	84.05 W
Ochlockonee ≃	246	29.58 N	84.21 W
Ochoco Mountains ⩕	256	44.30 N	120.35 W
Ocho Rios	285q	18.25 N	77.07 W
Ochota ≃	186	59.20 N	143.04 E
Ochotsk	186	59.23 N	143.18 E
Ochsenfurt	164	49.40 N	10.03 E
Ochsenwerder ⇀[8]	178	53.28 N	10.05 E
Ochtrup	178	52.13 N	7.11 E
Ocilla	246	31.36 N	83.15 W
Ockelbo	160	60.53 N	16.43 E
Ocmulgee ≃	246	31.58 N	82.32 W
Ocmulgee National Monument ♠	246	32.43 N	83.38 W

Symbols in the index entries are identified on page 360.

Name	Page	Lat°′	Long°′
Ocna Mureş	172	46.23 N	23.51 E
Ocoee	246	28.35 N	81.33 W
Ocoee ≃	246	35.12 N	84.40 W
Ocon, Bahía de C	282	18.23 N	70.40 W
Ocoña	292	16.26 S	73.08 W
Ocoña ≃	292	16.28 S	73.08 W
Oconee ≃	246	31.58 N	82.32 W
Ocongate	292	13.38 S	71.25 W
Oconomowoc	268	43.07 N	88.30 W
Oconto	244	44.43 N	87.52 W
Oconto ≃	244	44.53 N	87.50 W
Oconto Falls	244	44.42 N	88.08 W
Ocós	280	14.31 N	92.11 W
Ocotal	280	13.37 N	86.31 W
Ocotepeque	280	14.24 N	89.13 W
Ocotepeque □[5]	280	14.30 N	89.00 W
Ocotlán	278	20.21 N	102.46 W
Ocotlán de Morelos	278	16.48 N	96.40 W
Ocozingo	278	16.54 N	92.07 W
Ocozocoautla [de Espinosa]	278	16.46 N	93.22 W
Ocracoke	246	35.07 N	75.58 W
Ocracoke Island I	246	35.09 N	75.53 W
Ocresa, Ribeira ≃	168	39.32 N	7.50 W
Ocros	292	10.20 S	77.20 W
Ocú	280	7.53 N	80.48 W
Ocumare del Tuy	290	10.07 N	66.46 W
Ocurí	292	18.50 S	65.50 W
Ocussi	226	9.12 S	124.21 E
Oda, Ghana	214	5.55 N	0.59 W
Ōda, Nihon	192	35.11 N	132.30 E
Oda, Jabal Λ	220	20.21 N	36.39 E
Ōdaigahara-san Λ	192	34.11 N	136.05 E
Odaka	192	37.34 N	141.00 E
Ōdate	192	40.16 N	140.34 E
Odawara	192	35.15 N	139.10 E
Odda	160	60.04 N	6.33 E
Odebolt	252	42.19 N	95.15 W
Odell, Ill., U.S.	268	41.00 N	88.31 W
Odell, Nebr., U.S.	252	40.03 N	96.48 W
Odell, Oreg., U.S.	270	45.38 N	121.32 W
Odell, Tex., U.S.	250	34.21 N	99.25 W
Odell Lake ⊜	256	43.34 N	122.00 W
Odem	250	27.57 N	97.35 W
Odemira	168	37.36 N	8.38 W
Ödemiş	212	38.13 N	27.59 E
Odendaalsrus	224	27.48 S	26.45 E
Odense	160	55.24 N	10.23 E
Odenton	242	39.05 N	76.42 W
Odenwald ⛰	164	49.40 N	9.00 E
Oder (Odra) ≃	164	53.32 N	14.38 E
Oderberg	164	52.52 N	14.02 E
Oderhaff C	164	53.46 N	14.14 E
Oderzo	170	45.47 N	12.29 E
Odessa, Ont., Can.	264	44.17 N	76.43 W
Odessa, S.S.S.R.	158	46.28 N	30.44 E
Odessa, Del., U.S.	262	39.27 N	75.40 W
Odessa, Mo., U.S.	248	39.00 N	93.57 W
Odessa, Tex., U.S.	250	31.51 N	102.22 W
Odessa, Wash., U.S.	256	47.20 N	118.41 W
Odessa □[4]	172	46.00 N	30.00 E
Odesskoje	186	54.13 N	72.58 E
Odib, Wādī V	220	22.38 N	36.06 E
Odiel ≃	168	37.10 N	6.54 W
Odienné	222	9.30 N	7.34 W
Odienné □[5]	222	9.30 N	7.20 W
Odin, Mount Λ	238	50.33 N	118.08 W
Odiongan	202	12.24 N	121.59 E
Odiongan Bay C	202	12.28 N	122.00 E
Odobeşti	172	45.45 N	27.04 E
Odolanów	164	51.35 N	17.39 E
Odon	248	38.51 N	86.59 W
Odonnell	250	32.58 N	101.50 W
Odorhei	172	46.18 N	25.18 E
Odra (Oder) ≃	164	53.33 N	14.38 E
Odry	164	49.39 N	17.50 E
Odrzywół	164	51.32 N	20.33 E
Odum	246	31.40 N	82.02 W
Odžaci	172	45.30 N	19.16 E
Odzi ≃	224	19.45 S	32.24 E
Oebisfelde	164	52.25 N	10.59 E
Oedelem	176	51.10 N	3.20 E
Oedt	178	51.19 N	6.22 E
Oegstgeest	178	52.10 N	4.29 E
Oeiras	286	7.01 S	42.08 W
Oelde	178	51.49 N	8.08 E
Oelsnitz	164	50.24 N	12.10 E
Oelwein	244	42.41 N	91.55 W
Oer-Erkenschwick	178	51.39 N	7.15 E
Oerlinghausen	178	51.57 N	8.39 E
Oesede	178	52.12 N	8.04 E
Oeventrop	178	51.23 N	8.08 E
Ofanto ≃	170	41.22 N	16.13 E
Ofaqim	210	31.19 N	34.37 E
Offa	222	8.09 N	4.44 E
Offaly □[6]	162	53.20 N	7.30 W
Offenbach	164	50.08 N	8.47 E
Offenburg	180	48.28 N	7.57 E
Offida	170	42.56 N	13.41 E
Oficina Vergara	294	22.28 S	69.38 W
Ofotfjorden C[2]	160	68.23 N	16.10 E
Oftringen	180	47.19 N	7.56 E
Ōfunato	192	39.04 N	141.43 E
Oga	192	39.53 N	139.51 E
Oga-hantō ≻[1]	192	39.55 N	139.50 E
Ōgaki	192	35.21 N	136.37 E
Ogallala	252	41.08 N	101.43 W
Ogasawara-guntō II	148	27.00 N	142.10 E
Ogatsu	192	38.41 N	141.28 E
Ogawa	192	32.35 N	130.43 E
Ogawara-ko ⊜	192	40.47 N	141.20 E
Ogbomosho	222	8.08 N	4.15 E
Ogden, Iowa, U.S.	244	42.02 N	94.02 W
Ogden, Kans., U.S.	252	39.07 N	96.43 W
Ogden, Pa., U.S.	262	39.49 N	75.27 W
Ogden, Utah, U.S.	254	41.14 N	111.58 W
Ogden, Mount Λ	236	58.26 N	133.23 W
Ogden Dunes	268	41.38 N	87.12 W
Ogdensburg	264	44.42 N	75.29 W
Ogeechee ≃	246	31.51 N	81.06 W
Ogema	252	49.35 N	104.55 W
Ogilvie	244	45.50 N	93.26 W
Ogilvie ≃	236	65.52 N	137.16 W
Ogilvie Mountains ⛰	236	65.00 N	139.30 W
Oglala	252	43.17 N	102.44 W
Ogle □[6]	268	42.01 N	89.20 W
Oglesby, Ill., U.S.	268	41.18 N	89.04 W
Oglesby, Tex., U.S.	250	31.25 N	97.31 W
Oglethorpe	246	32.18 N	84.04 W
Ogliastra ◆[1]	170	40.00 N	9.30 E
Oglio ≃	170	45.02 N	10.39 E
Ogmore Vale	174	51.38 N	3.31 W
Ognon ≃	166	47.20 N	5.29 E
Ogoja	214	6.40 N	8.48 E
Ogoki ≃	232	51.38 N	85.57 W
Ogooué ≃	218	0.49 S	9.00 E
Ogōri	192	34.06 N	131.24 E
Ogou ≃	222	7.50 N	1.19 E
Ogre	160	56.51 N	24.36 E
Ogrodzieniec	164	50.27 N	19.31 E
Ogulin	170	45.16 N	15.14 E
Oguni	192	38.04 N	139.45 E
Ogunquit	240	43.15 N	70.36 W
Ogurčinskij, Ostrov I	208	38.55 N	53.02 E
Oguta	222	5.44 N	6.44 E
Ogwashi-Uku	222	6.10 N	6.31 E
Ohakune	230	39.25 S	175.25 E
Ohanet	214	28.45 N	8.55 E
Ōhara	192	35.15 N	140.23 E
Ōhata	192a	41.24 N	141.10 E
Ohau, Lake ⊜	230	44.14 S	169.51 E
O'Higgins □[4]	294	34.15 S	70.45 W
O'Higgins, Lago(Lago San Martín) ⊜	288	49.00 S	72.40 W
Ohio	244	41.34 N	89.28 W
Ohio □[6]	266	40.09 N	80.35 W
Ohio □[3]	234	40.15 N	82.45 W
Ohio ≃	234	36.59 N	89.08 W
Ohio City	268	40.46 N	84.37 W
Ohio Peak Λ	254	38.49 N	107.07 W
Ohioville	266	40.41 N	80.30 W
Ohoopee ≃	246	31.54 N	82.07 W
Ohře ≃	164	50.32 N	14.08 E
Ohrid	172	41.07 N	20.47 E
Ohrid, Lake ⊜	172	41.02 N	20.43 E
Öhringen	164	49.12 N	9.29 E
Ohuira, Bahía de C	278	25.40 N	109.00 W
Ōi ≃	192	34.46 N	138.18 E
Oiapoque	286	3.50 N	51.50 W
Oies, Île aux I	240	47.05 N	70.30 W
Oignies	176	50.28 N	2.59 E
Oil Center	250	32.30 N	103.16 W
Oil City, La., U.S.	248	32.45 N	93.58 W
Oil City, Pa., U.S.	266	41.26 N	79.42 W
Oildale	272	35.25 N	119.01 W
Oilmont	238	48.44 N	111.51 W
Oil Springs	266	42.47 N	82.07 W
Oilton, Okla., U.S.	250	36.05 N	96.35 W
Oilton, Tex., U.S.	250	27.33 N	98.59 W
Oise □[5]	176	49.30 N	2.30 E
Oise ≃	166	49.00 N	2.04 E
Oiseaux, Lac des ≡	170	36.48 N	8.00 E
Oisemont	166	49.57 N	1.46 E
Oissel	176	49.20 N	1.06 E
Oisterwijk	178	51.35 N	5.12 E
Oistins	285g	13.04 N	59.32 W
Ōita	192	33.14 N	131.36 E
Oituz, Pasul)(	172	46.03 N	26.23 E
Ojai	274	34.27 N	119.15 W
Ojat' ≃	160	60.31 N	33.00 E
Öje	160	60.49 N	13.51 E
Ojika-hantō ≻[1]	192	38.20 N	141.30 E
Ojinaga	278	29.34 N	104.25 W
Ojiya	192	37.18 N	138.48 E
Ojm'akon	186	63.28 N	142.49 E
Ojocaliente	278	22.34 N	102.15 W
Ojo de la Casa	254	31.23 N	106.32 W
Ojo de Liebre, Laguna C	278	27.50 N	114.20 W
Ojos del Salado, Cerro Λ	294	27.06 S	68.32 W
Oka ≃, S.S.S.R.	160	56.20 N	43.59 E
Oka ≃, S.S.S.R.	186	55.15 N	102.10 E
Okaba	198	8.06 S	139.42 E
Okahandja	218	21.59 S	16.58 E
Okahandja □[5]	224	21.30 S	17.00 E
Okanagan (Okanogan) ≃	238	48.06 N	75.01 W
Okanagan Centre	238	50.03 N	119.27 W
Okanagan Falls	238	49.21 N	119.34 W
Okanagan Indian Reserve ◆[4]	238	50.21 N	119.17 W
Okanagan Lake ⊜	238	50.00 N	119.28 W
Okanagan Landing	238	50.14 N	119.22 W
Okanogan	256	48.22 N	119.35 W
Okanogan □[6]	270	48.39 N	120.41 W
Okanogan Range (Okanagan Range) ⛰	238	49.00 N	120.00 W
Okāra	206	30.49 N	73.27 E
Okarche	250	35.44 N	97.58 W
Okataina, Lake ⊜	230	38.07 S	176.25 E
Okauchee	268	43.07 N	88.26 W
Okaukuejo	218	19.10 S	15.54 E
Okavango (Cubango) ≃	218	18.50 S	22.25 E
Okavango Swamp ≡	224	18.45 S	22.45 E
Ōkawa	192	33.12 N	130.23 E
Okawville	248	38.26 N	89.33 W
Okaya	192	36.03 N	138.03 E
Okayama	192	34.39 N	133.55 E
Okayama-heiya ≚	192	34.35 N	133.51 E
Okazaki	192	34.57 N	137.10 E
Okeechobee	246	27.15 N	80.50 W
Okeechobee, Lake ⊜	246	26.55 N	80.45 W
Okeene	250	36.07 N	98.19 W
Okefenokee Swamp ≡	246	30.42 N	82.20 W
Okehampton	162	50.44 N	4.00 W
Okemah	250	35.26 N	96.19 W
Okemos	268	42.43 N	84.26 W
Okene	222	7.33 N	6.15 E
Oker	178	51.54 N	10.29 E
Okhotsk, Sea of(Ochotskoje More) ▼[2]	186	53.00 N	150.00 E
Okhotsk Basin ⊹[1]	148	52.00 N	150.00 E
Okiep	218	29.39 S	17.53 E
Oki-guntō II	192	36.15 N	133.15 E
Okinawa □[5]	193b	26.31 N	127.59 E
Okinawa-jima I	193b	26.30 N	128.00 E
Okino-Daitō-jima I	190	24.28 N	131.11 E
Okino-Erabu-shima I	193b	27.22 N	128.35 E
Okino-Tori-shima I	190	20.25 N	136.00 E
Oklahoma	266	41.07 N	78.44 W
Oklahoma □[3]	234	35.30 N	98.00 W
Oklahoma City	250	35.28 N	97.32 W
Oklawaha ≃	246	29.28 N	81.41 W
Oklee	252	47.50 N	95.51 W
Okmulgee	250	35.37 N	95.58 W
Oko, Wādī V	220	21.15 N	35.56 E
Okolona, Ark., U.S.	248	34.00 N	93.20 W
Okolona, Ky., U.S.	248	38.08 N	85.41 W
Okolona, Miss., U.S.	248	34.00 N	88.45 W
Okonek (Ratzebuhr)	164	53.33 N	16.50 E
Okotoks	238	50.44 N	113.59 W
Okpara ≃	222	7.40 N	2.35 E
Okrika	222	4.47 N	7.04 E
Okskij Zapovednik ◆[4]	160	54.45 N	40.45 E
Oksovskij	160	62.37 N	39.55 E
Okstinderne Λ	160	65.59 N	14.15 E
Okt'abr'sk	160	53.11 N	48.40 E
Okt'abr'skij, S.S.S.R.	158	54.28 N	53.28 E
Okt'abr'skij, S.S.S.R.	160	58.19 N	44.19 E
Okt'abr'skij, S.S.S.R.	160	59.29 N	48.50 E
Okt'abr'skij, S.S.S.R.	160	61.04 N	43.08 E
Okt'abr'skoje	158	62.28 N	66.03 E
Okt'abr'skoj Revol'ucii, Ostrov I	186	79.30 N	97.00 E
Okucani	170	45.16 N	17.12 E
Ōkuchi	192	32.04 N	130.37 E
Okuku ≃	230	43.15 S	172.28 E
Okulovka	160	58.26 N	33.18 E
Okun'ov Nos	160	66.15 N	52.28 E
Okushiri	192a	42.10 N	139.31 E
Okushiri-tō I	192a	42.10 N	139.27 E
Okutango-hantō ≻[1]	192	35.40 N	135.10 E
Okwa ≃	224	22.30 S	23.00 E
Olá, Pan.	280	8.20 N	80.37 W
Ola, S.S.S.R.	186	59.35 N	151.17 E
Ola, Ark., U.S.	248	35.02 N	93.13 W
Ólafsfjörđur	160a	66.06 N	18.38 W
Olancha	258	36.17 N	118.01 W
Olancha Peak Λ	258	36.16 N	118.07 W
Olanchito	280	15.30 N	86.35 W
Olancho □[5]	280	14.45 N	86.00 W
Öland I	160	56.45 N	16.38 E
Olango Island I	202	10.18 N	124.03 E
Olanta	246	33.58 N	79.56 W
Olar	246	33.11 N	81.11 W
Olary	226	32.17 S	140.19 E
Olascoaga	294	35.14 S	60.37 W
Olathe, Colo., U.S.	254	38.36 N	107.59 W
Olathe, Kans., U.S.	252	38.53 N	94.49 W
Olavarría	294	36.53 S	60.20 W
Oława (Ohlau)	164	50.57 N	17.17 E
Olbia	170	40.55 N	9.29 E
Olca, Volcán Λ[1]	292	20.57 S	68.30 W
Ol'chon, Ostrov I	186	53.09 N	107.24 E
Olcott	264	43.20 N	78.43 W
Old Bahama Channel ⊔	282	22.33 N	78.05 W
Old Bight	282	24.15 N	75.21 W
Oldbury	174	52.30 N	2.00 W
Oldcastle	162	53.46 N	7.10 W
Old Crow	236	67.35 N	139.50 W
Old Crow ≃	236	67.35 N	139.50 W
Oldebroek	164	52.26 N	5.54 E
Olden	250	32.25 N	98.45 W
Oldenburg, B.R.D.	164	54.17 N	10.52 E
Oldenburg, B.R.D.	178	53.08 N	8.13 E
Oldenburg □[6]	178	53.10 N	8.10 E
Oldenburg □[9]	164	53.00 N	8.00 E
Oldenzaal	178	52.19 N	6.56 E
Old Fletton	174	52.33 N	0.15 W
Old Ford Mountain Λ	238	55.05 N	126.30 W
Old Forge, N.Y., U.S.	242	43.43 N	74.58 W
Old Forge, Pa., U.S.	242	41.22 N	75.44 W
Old Fort	266	41.15 N	83.09 W
Old Fort Bay	240	51.26 N	57.50 W
Oldham, Eng., U.K.	162	53.33 N	2.07 W
Oldham, S. Dak., U.S.	252	48.23 N	89.15 W
Oldham Village	261	42.04 N	70.50 W
Old Harbor	236	57.12 N	153.19 W
Old Harbour	285q	17.56 N	77.07 W
Old Head of Kinsale ≻	162	51.36 N	8.32 W
Old Hickory	248	36.16 N	86.39 W
Old Hickory Lake ⊜[1]	248	36.18 N	86.30 W
Old Hometown	248	35.01 N	90.01 W
Old Lyme	261	41.19 N	72.20 W
Oldman ≃	238	49.56 N	111.42 W
Old Man Mountain Λ	240	49.08 N	57.43 W
Oldmeldrum	162	57.20 N	2.20 W
Old Mines	248	38.00 N	90.45 W
Old Mystic	261	41.23 N	71.58 W
Old Orchard Beach	242	43.31 N	70.23 W
Old Perlican	240	48.05 N	52.59 W
Old Road	284c	17.01 N	61.50 W
Olds	238	51.47 N	114.06 W
Old Saybrook	261	41.18 N	72.23 W
Old Speck Mountain Λ	242	44.34 N	70.57 W
Old Tate	218	21.22 S	27.46 E
Old Town, Maine, U.S.	242	44.56 N	68.39 W
Old Town, N.C., U.S.	246	36.09 N	80.18 W
Old Trap	246	36.15 N	76.02 W
Oldwick	262	40.40 N	74.45 W
Old Wives Lake ⊜	232	50.06 N	106.00 W
Old Zoinsville	262	40.29 N	75.31 W
Olean	266	42.05 N	78.26 W
O'Leary Station	240	46.42 N	64.13 W
Olecko (Treuburg)	164	54.03 N	22.30 E
Oleggio	182	45.36 N	8.38 E
Olekma → Ol'okma ≃	186	60.22 N	120.42 E
Olema	160	64.30 N	46.08 E
Olen	178	51.09 N	4.51 E
Olenegorsk	160	68.09 N	33.15 E
Olenica	160	66.29 N	35.20 E
Olenij, Ostrov I	186	72.25 N	77.45 E
Olenino	160	56.12 N	33.29 E
Olen'ok	186	68.33 N	112.18 E
Olen'ok ≃	186	73.00 N	119.55 E
Olen'okskij Zaliv C	186	73.20 N	121.00 E
Ølensjøen	160	59.36 N	5.48 E
Oleopolis	266	41.27 N	79.37 W
Oléron, Île d' I	166	45.56 N	1.15 W
Oleśnica (Oels)	164	51.13 N	17.23 E
Olesno (Preussisch Königsdorf)	164	50.53 N	18.25 E
Olevano Romano	184	41.52 N	13.02 E
Oley	262	40.23 N	75.47 W
Ol'ga, S.S.S.R.	186	43.45 N	135.18 E
Olga, Wash., U.S.	270	48.37 N	122.50 W
Olgiate Comasco	182	45.48 N	8.58 E
Olgiate Olona	182	45.38 N	8.53 E
Ölgij	190	48.56 N	89.57 E
Olhão	168	37.02 N	8.50 W
Ôlho d'Água	296	16.02 S	48.36 W
Oli ≃	222	9.45 N	4.38 E
Olib, Otok I	170	44.22 N	14.48 E
Oliena	170	40.16 N	9.24 E
Olifants (Rio dos Elefantes) ≃, Afr.	224	24.10 S	32.40 E
Olifants ≃, S. Afr.	224	31.42 S	18.12 E
Olifants ≃, S.W. Afr.	224	25.30 S	19.30 E
Olimarao I[1]	198	7.41 N	145.52 E
Olimbía ⊥	172	37.38 N	21.41 E
Ólimbos	172	35.44 N	27.11 E
Ólimbos Λ, Ellás	172	40.05 N	22.21 E
Ólimbos Λ, Kípros	212	34.56 N	32.49 E
Olímpia	296	20.44 S	48.54 W
Olimpo □[5]	292	20.30 S	58.45 W
Olin	244	42.00 N	91.09 W
Olinalá	278	17.50 N	98.51 W
Olinda	286	8.01 S	34.51 W
Olite	168	42.29 N	1.39 W
Oliva, Arg.	294	32.05 S	63.35 W
Oliva, Esp.	168	38.55 N	0.07 W
Oliva de Jerez	168	38.16 N	6.55 W
Olive Branch	248	34.58 N	89.50 W
Olive Hill	242	38.16 N	83.10 W
Olivehurst	272	39.06 N	121.34 W
Oliveira	296	20.41 S	44.49 W
Oliveira dos Brejinhos	296	12.19 S	42.54 W
Oliveira Salazar, Barragem ◆[6]	224	19.08 S	33.00 E
Olivenza	168	38.41 N	7.06 W
Oliver	238	49.11 N	119.33 W
Oliver Springs	246	36.03 N	84.20 W
Olivet, Fr.	176	47.52 N	1.54 E
Olivet, Mich., U.S.	268	42.27 N	84.56 W
Olivet, S. Dak., U.S.	252	43.14 N	97.40 W
Olivia	252	44.46 N	94.59 W
Olivine Range ⛰	230	44.17 S	168.30 E
Olivo	202	10.52 N	123.53 E
Olkusz	164	50.17 N	19.35 E
Olla	248	31.54 N	92.14 W
Ollagüe	292	21.14 S	68.16 W
Ollagüe, Volcán (Volcán Oyahue) Λ[1]	292	21.18 S	68.12 W
Ollantaitambo	292	13.15 S	72.17 W
Olmedillo de Roa	168	41.47 N	3.56 W
Olmedo	168	41.23 N	4.41 W
Olmos	292	5.59 S	79.46 W
Olmos Park	250	29.28 N	98.29 W
Olmsted	266	41.24 N	81.44 W
Olney, Ill., U.S.	248	38.44 N	88.05 W
Olney, Mont., U.S.	238	48.33 N	114.35 W
Olney, Tex., U.S.	250	33.22 N	98.45 W
Oloj ≃	186	66.29 N	159.29 E
Ol'okma ≃	186	60.22 N	120.42 E
Ol'okminsk	186	60.24 N	120.24 E
Olomane ≃	240	50.13 N	60.39 W
Olomega, Laguna ⊜	280	13.18 N	88.03 W
Olomouc	164	49.36 N	17.16 E
Olonec	160	61.00 N	32.57 E
Olongapo	202	14.49 N	120.17 E
Oloron, Gave d' ≃	168	43.33 N	1.05 W
Oloron-Sainte-Marie	166	43.12 N	0.36 W
Olot	168	42.11 N	2.29 E
Olov'annaja, S.S.S.R.	186	50.56 N	115.35 E
Olov'annaja, S.S.S.R.	236	66.10 N	178.59 W
Olpe, B.R.D.	164	51.02 N	7.52 E
Olpe, Kans., U.S.	252	38.16 N	96.10 W
Olsztyn (Allenstein)	164	53.48 N	20.29 E
Olsztynek (Hohenstein)	164	53.36 N	20.17 E
Olt ≃	172	43.43 N	24.51 E
Olta	294	30.37 S	66.16 W
Olten	180	47.21 N	7.54 E
Olteni	172	44.10 N	25.18 E
Olteniţa	172	44.05 N	26.39 E
Olton	250	34.11 N	102.08 W
Oltu ≃	212	40.50 N	41.40 E
Oluan Pi ≻	196	21.54 N	120.51 E
Olustee, Fla., U.S.	246	30.12 N	82.26 W
Olustee, Okla., U.S.	250	34.33 N	99.25 W
Olutanga (Suba Nipa)	202	7.20 N	122.50 E
Olutanga Island I	202	7.22 N	122.51 E
Olutaya Island I	202	11.38 N	122.50 E
Ol'utorskij Zaliv C	186	59.55 N	170.27 E
Olvera	168	36.56 N	5.16 W
Olympia → Olimbía ⊥, Ellás	172	37.38 N	21.41 E
Olympia, Wash., U.S.	270	47.03 N	122.53 W
Olympia Fields	268	41.32 N	87.42 W
Olympic Mountains ⛰	256	47.50 N	123.45 W
Olympic National Park ♠	256	47.48 N	123.30 W
Olympic View	270	47.43 N	122.45 W
Olympus, Mount → Ólimbos Λ, Ellás	172	40.05 N	22.21 E
Olympus, Mount Λ, Ky., U.S.	246	38.03 N	83.39 W
Olympus, Mount Λ, Wash., U.S.	256	47.48 N	123.43 W
Om' ≃	186	54.59 N	73.22 E
Oma	248	31.44 N	90.09 W
Ōmachi	192	36.30 N	137.52 E
Omdurman → Umm Durmān	220	15.38 N	32.30 E
Omae-zaki ≻	192	34.36 N	138.14 E
Ōmagari	192	39.27 N	140.29 E
Omagh	162	54.36 N	7.18 W
Omaguas	290	4.10 S	73.25 W
Omaha	252	41.16 N	95.57 W
Omaha Indian Reservation ◆[4]	252	42.08 N	96.22 W
Omak	256	48.24 N	119.31 W
Omak Lake ⊜	256	48.16 N	119.23 W
Oman □[1]	204	22.00 N	58.00 E
Oman, Gulf of C	204	24.30 N	58.30 E
Omar	246	37.46 N	82.00 W
Omaruru	218	21.28 S	15.56 E
Omaruru ≃	224	22.07 S	14.15 E
Omas	292	12.33 S	76.40 W
Omatako Λ	224	21.07 S	16.43 E
Omate	292	16.40 S	70.58 W
Ōma-zaki ≻	192	41.32 N	140.55 E
Omboué	218	1.34 S	9.15 E
Ombrone ≃	170	42.39 N	11.00 E
Ombutosu Λ	224	21.22 S	16.50 E
Omčak	186	61.38 N	147.55 E
Ōme	192	35.47 N	139.15 E
Omega	246	31.21 N	83.36 W
Omegna	182	45.53 N	8.24 E
Omemee	264	44.18 N	78.33 W
Ömerköy	172	39.48 N	28.03 E
Ömerli	172	41.05 N	29.19 E
Omerville	260	45.17 N	72.07 W
Ometepe, Isla de I	280	11.30 N	85.33 W
Ometepec	278	16.41 N	98.25 W
Ōmi-hachiman	192	35.08 N	136.06 E
Omineca ≃	238	56.05 N	124.30 W
Omineca Mountains ⛰	238	56.00 N	125.00 W
Omišalj	170	45.13 N	14.34 E
Ōmiya	192	35.54 N	139.38 E
Ommaney, Cape ≻	236	56.10 N	134.39 W
Ommanney Bay C	232	73.07 N	100.11 W
Ommen	164	52.32 N	6.25 E
Omoa, Bahía de C	280	15.40 N	88.08 W
Omodeo, Lago ⊜	170	40.08 N	8.55 E
Omoko	222	5.20 N	6.39 E
Omoloj ≃	186	71.10 N	132.08 E
Omolon ≃	186	68.42 N	158.36 E
Omono ≃	192	39.46 N	140.03 E
Omo Ranch	272	38.35 N	120.35 W
Omrel'kaj ≃	236	68.34 N	170.30 E
Omro	244	44.02 N	88.44 W
Omsk	186	55.00 N	73.24 E
Omsukčan	186	62.32 N	155.48 E
Ōmu	192a	44.34 N	142.58 E
Ōmuda → Ōmuta	192	33.02 N	130.27 E
Omul Λ	172	45.26 N	25.26 E
Omulew ≃	164	53.05 N	21.32 E
Ōmura	192	32.54 N	129.57 E
Omuramba Omatako ≃	224	17.59 S	20.30 E
Omurtag	172	43.06 N	26.25 E
Ōmuta	192	33.02 N	130.27 E
Omutninsk	160	58.40 N	52.12 E
Oña, Ec.	290	3.32 S	79.10 W
Ona → Bir'usa ≃, S.S.S.R.	186	57.43 N	95.24 E
Onaga	252	39.29 N	96.10 W
Onagawa	192	38.26 N	141.27 E
Onalaska, Wash., U.S.	270	46.35 N	122.42 W
Onalaska, Wis., U.S.	244	43.53 N	91.14 W
Onamia	244	46.04 N	93.40 W
Onancock	262	37.43 N	75.45 W
Onaping ≃	244	46.37 N	81.18 W
Onaping Lake ⊜	244	46.57 N	81.30 W
Onarga	268	40.43 N	88.01 W
Onatchiway, Lac ⊜	240	49.03 N	71.03 W
Onawa	252	42.02 N	96.06 W
Onaway	244	45.21 N	84.14 W
Oncativo	294	31.55 S	63.45 W
Onda	168	39.58 N	0.15 W
Ondangua	218	17.55 S	16.00 E
Ondas, Rio das ≃	296	12.08 S	45.00 W
Ondava ≃	164	48.27 N	21.48 E
Ondo, Nig.	222	7.04 N	4.47 E
Ondo, Nihon	192	34.11 N	132.32 E
Öndörchaan	190	47.19 N	110.39 E
O'Neals	272	37.08 N	119.42 W
Oneco, Conn., U.S.	261	41.42 N	71.48 W
Oneco, Fla., U.S.	246	27.27 N	82.33 W
Onega	160	63.55 N	38.05 E
Onega ≃	160	63.58 N	37.55 E
Onega, Lake → Onežskoje Ozero ⊜	160	61.30 N	35.45 E
One Hundred and Two ≃	248	39.44 N	94.43 W
One Hundred Fifty Mile House	238	52.07 N	121.56 W
One Hundred Mile House	238	51.39 N	121.18 W
Onehunga	230	36.56 S	174.47 E
Oneida, Ill., U.S.	244	41.04 N	90.13 W
Oneida, Ky., U.S.	246	37.16 N	83.39 W
Oneida, N.Y., U.S.	264	43.06 N	75.39 W
Oneida, Tenn., U.S.	246	36.30 N	84.31 W
Oneida □[6]	264	43.10 N	75.20 W
Oneida Castle	264	43.05 N	75.40 W
Oneida Lake ⊜	242	43.13 N	76.00 W
O'Neill	252	42.27 N	98.39 W
Onekama	244	44.22 N	86.12 W
Onekotan, Ostrov I	186	49.25 N	154.45 E
Onemen, Zaliv C	236	64.45 N	176.35 E
Oneonta, Ala., U.S.	248	33.57 N	86.29 W
Oneonta, N.Y., U.S.	242	42.27 N	75.04 W
Onežskaja Guba C	160	64.20 N	36.30 E
Onežskij Poluostrov ≻[1]	160	64.35 N	38.00 E
Onežskoje Ozero (Lake Onega) ⊜	160	61.30 N	35.45 E
Onida	252	44.42 N	100.04 W
Onilahy ≃	225b	23.34 S	43.45 E
Onistagane, Lac ⊜	240	50.42 N	71.19 W
Onitsha	222	6.09 N	6.47 E
Onley	262	37.41 N	75.43 W
Onnaing	176	50.23 N	3.36 E
Ōno, Nihon	192	35.59 N	136.29 E
Ono, Pa., U.S.	262	40.24 N	76.32 W
Onoda	192	33.59 N	131.11 E
Onomichi	192	34.25 N	133.12 E
Onon ≃	190	51.42 N	115.50 E
Onondaga, Mich., U.S.	268	42.27 N	84.34 W
Onondaga, N.Y., U.S.	264	43.00 N	76.11 W
Onondaga □[6]	264	43.03 N	76.09 W
Onoto	290	9.36 N	65.12 W
Onoville	266	42.02 N	78.58 W
Onoway	238	53.42 N	114.12 W
Ons, Isla de I	168	42.23 N	8.56 W
Onset	261	41.45 N	70.39 W
Onslow	226	21.39 S	115.06 E
Onslow Bay C	246	34.20 N	77.20 W
Onsted	268	42.00 N	84.11 W
Onstmettingen	180	48.17 N	9.00 E
Ontake-san Λ	192	35.53 N	137.29 E
Ontario, Calif., U.S.	274	34.04 N	117.39 W
Ontario, Ind., U.S.	268	41.43 N	85.23 W
Ontario, N.Y., U.S.	264	43.13 N	77.17 W
Ontario, Ohio, U.S.	266	40.46 N	82.39 W
Ontario, Oreg., U.S.	256	44.02 N	116.58 W
Ontario □[6], Ont., Can.	264	44.15 N	79.05 W
Ontario □[6], N.Y., U.S.	264	42.54 N	77.17 W
Ontario □[3]	232	51.00 N	85.00 W
Ontario, Lake ⊜	244	43.45 N	78.00 W
Ontario Center	264	43.14 N	77.19 W
Onteniente	168	38.49 N	0.37 W
Ontonagon	244	46.52 N	89.19 W
Ontonagon ≃	244	46.52 N	89.20 W
Onverwacht	286	5.35 N	55.10 W
Onward	268	40.42 N	86.12 W
Oodnadatta	226	27.33 S	135.28 E
Ooldea	226	30.27 S	131.50 E
Oolitic	248	38.54 N	86.31 W
Oologah Reservoir ⊜[1]	250	36.33 N	95.36 W
Oona River	238	53.57 N	130.18 W
Oostakker	176	51.06 N	3.46 E
Oostburg	244	43.37 N	87.48 W
Oostelijk Flevoland ◆[1]	164	52.30 N	5.45 E
Oostende (Ostende)	176	51.13 N	2.55 E
Oosterbeek	178	52.00 N	5.50 E
Oosterhout	178	51.38 N	4.51 E
Ooster Schelde C	164	51.30 N	4.00 E
Oostkamp	176	51.09 N	3.14 E
Oostrozebeke	176	50.55 N	3.20 E
Oost-Souburg	178	51.27 N	3.35 E
Oost-Vlaanderen □[4]	176	51.00 N	3.45 E
Oost-Vlieland	164	53.17 N	5.04 E
Ootsa Lake	238	53.47 N	126.03 W
Ootsa Lake ⊜	238	53.49 N	126.18 W
Opaka	172	43.27 N	26.10 E
Opala	218	0.37 S	24.21 E
Opalaca, Sierra de ⛰	280	14.30 N	88.20 W
Opal Cliffs	272	36.58 N	121.58 W
Opalenica	164	52.19 N	16.23 E
Oparino	160	59.52 N	48.17 E
Opasatica, Lac ⊜	244	48.05 N	79.18 W
Opatija	170	45.21 N	14.19 E
Opatów	164	50.49 N	21.26 E
Opava	164	49.56 N	17.54 E
Opečenskij Posad	160	58.16 N	34.07 E
Opeepeesway Lake ⊜	244	47.38 N	82.14 W
Opelika	248	32.39 N	85.23 W
Opelousas	248	30.32 N	92.05 W
Open Bay Islands II	230	43.52 S	168.52 E
Opeongo ≃	244	45.30 N	77.57 W
Opeongo Lake ⊜	244	45.42 N	78.23 W
Ophain-Bois-Seigneur-Isaac	176	50.40 N	4.21 E
Opheim	256	48.51 N	106.24 W
Ophir, Alaska, U.S.	236	63.10 N	156.31 W
Ophir, Oreg., U.S.	256	42.34 N	124.23 W
Opihikao	275d	19.26 N	154.53 W
Opinaca ≃	232	52.20 N	78.00 W
Opiscotéo, Lac ⊜	232	53.10 N	68.10 W
Opiscotiche, Lac ⊜	232	53.10 N	67.50 W
Opladen	178	51.04 N	7.00 E
Opobo	222	4.34 N	7.27 E
Opočka	160	56.43 N	28.38 E
Opoczno	164	51.23 N	20.17 E
Opol	202	8.31 N	124.35 E
Opole (Oppeln)	164	50.41 N	17.55 E
Opole Lubelskie	164	51.09 N	21.58 E
Opon	202	10.19 N	123.57 E
Opunono Lake ⊜	224	18.08 S	15.45 E
Oporto → Porto	168	41.11 N	8.36 W
Opotiki	230	38.08 S	177.17 E
Opp	248	31.17 N	86.22 W
Oppdal	160	62.36 N	9.40 E
Oppeln → Opole	164	50.41 N	17.55 E
Oppido Mamertina	170	38.16 N	16.00 E
Oppland □[6]	160	61.10 N	9.40 E
Opportunity, Mont., U.S.	256	46.07 N	112.49 W
Opportunity, Wash., U.S.	256	47.39 N	117.15 W
Opuha ≃	230	44.10 S	171.00 E
Opunake	230	39.27 S	173.52 E
Opwijk	176	50.58 N	4.11 E
Oquawka	244	40.56 N	90.57 W
Oquendo	202	12.08 N	124.32 E
Ora (Auer)	170	46.21 N	11.18 E
Oracle	254	32.37 N	110.46 W
Oradea	172	47.03 N	21.57 E
Öræfajökull ◸	160a	64.03 N	16.38 W
Orahovica	172	45.31 N	17.53 E
Oraibi	254	35.53 N	110.37 W
Oraibi Wash V	254	35.26 N	110.49 W
Oran (Ouahran), Alg.	168	35.43 N	0.43 W
Oran, Mo., U.S.	248	37.05 N	89.39 W
Oran, Sebkra d' ⊜	168	35.30 N	1.00 W
Orange, Austl.	228	33.17 S	149.06 E
Orange, Fr.	182	44.08 N	4.48 E
Orange, Calif., U.S.	274	33.47 N	117.51 W
Orange, Conn., U.S.	261	41.17 N	73.02 W
Orange, Mass., U.S.	261	42.35 N	72.19 W
Orange, N.J., U.S.	262	40.46 N	74.14 W
Orange, Tex., U.S.	248	30.01 N	93.44 W
Orange, Va., U.S.	242	38.15 N	78.07 W
Orange □[6]	274	33.43 N	117.54 W
Orange (Oranje) ≃	224	28.41 S	16.28 E
Orange, Cabo ≻	286	4.24 N	51.33 W
Orangeburg, N.Y., U.S.	261	41.03 N	73.57 W
Orangeburg, S.C., U.S.	246	33.30 N	80.52 W
Orange City, Fla., U.S.	246	28.57 N	81.17 W
Orange City, Iowa, U.S.	252	43.00 N	96.03 W
Orange Cove	272	36.37 N	119.19 W
Orange Free State (Oranje-Vrystaat) □[3]	224	28.30 S	27.00 E
Orange Grove	250	27.58 N	97.56 W
Orange Lake	246	29.25 N	82.13 W
Orange Lake ⊜	246	29.29 N	82.10 W
Orange Park	246	30.10 N	81.42 W
Orangevale	272	38.41 N	121.13 W
Orangeville, Ont., Can.	264	43.55 N	80.06 W
Orangeville, Ohio, U.S.	266	41.20 N	80.31 W
Orangeville, Utah, U.S.	254	39.13 N	111.03 W
Orange Walk	278	18.06 N	88.33 W
Orango, Ilha de I	222	11.10 N	16.08 W
Orani	202	14.48 N	120.32 E
Oranienburg	164	52.45 N	13.14 E
Oranje Gebergte ⛰	286	3.15 N	54.50 W
Oranjemund	218	28.38 S	16.24 E
Oranjestad	285s	12.33 N	70.06 W
Or 'Aqiva	210	32.30 N	34.54 E
Orari ≃	230	44.14 S	171.25 E
Oras	202	12.09 N	125.26 E
Oras ≃	202	13.08 N	125.26 E
Oras Bay C	202	12.07 N	125.30 E
Orăştie	172	45.50 N	23.12 E
Oraşul Stalin → Braşov	172	45.39 N	25.37 E
Oravais (Oravainen)	160	63.18 N	22.23 E
Oraviţa	172	45.02 N	21.41 E
Orb ≃	166	43.15 N	3.18 E
Orbassano	182	45.01 N	7.32 E
Orbe	166	46.43 N	6.32 E
Orbetello	184	42.27 N	11.13 E
Orbieu ≃	166	43.14 N	2.54 E
Orbisonia	266	40.15 N	77.54 W
Orbost	228	37.42 S	148.27 E
Örbyhus	160	60.14 N	17.42 E
Orcas	270	48.36 N	122.57 W
Orce ≃	168	37.44 N	2.28 W
Orcera	168	38.19 N	2.39 W
Orchard	252	42.20 N	98.14 W
Orchard Avenue	256	47.40 N	117.18 W
Orchard Beach	266	42.14 N	79.50 W
Orchard Heights	270	47.32 N	122.41 W
Orchard Homes	256	46.55 N	114.04 W
Orchard Island	268	40.28 N	83.53 W
Orchard Lake	268	42.35 N	83.21 W
Orchard Park	264	42.43 N	78.45 W
Orchards	270	45.40 N	122.34 W
Orchard Valley	254	41.06 N	104.19 W
Orchies	176	50.28 N	3.14 E
Orchon ≃	190	50.21 N	106.05 E
Orcotuna	292	11.56 S	75.20 W
Ord	252	41.36 N	98.56 W
Ord, Mount Λ	226	17.20 S	125.34 E
Órdenes	168	43.04 N	8.24 W
Orderville	254	37.16 N	112.38 W
Ordesa, Parque Nacional de ♠	168	42.39 N	0.02 E
Ord Mountain Λ	258	34.40 N	116.49 W
Ordoqui	294	35.55 S	61.09 W
Ordu	212	41.00 N	37.53 E
Ordway	252	38.13 N	103.46 W
Ordžonikidze	158	43.03 N	44.40 E
Örebro	160	59.17 N	15.13 E
Orechovo-Zujevo	160	55.49 N	38.59 E
Ore City	248	32.48 N	94.43 W
Orefield	262	40.38 N	75.35 W
Oregon, Ill., U.S.	244	42.01 N	89.20 W
Oregon, Mo., U.S.	248	39.59 N	95.09 W
Oregon, Ohio, U.S.	266	41.38 N	83.28 W
Oregon, Wis., U.S.	268	42.56 N	89.23 W
Oregon □[3]	234	44.00 N	121.00 W
Oregon Caves National Monument ♠	256	42.06 N	123.24 W
Oregon City	270	45.21 N	122.36 W
Orel → Or'ol	158	52.59 N	36.05 E
Orellana	292	6.51 S	75.08 W
Orem	254	40.19 N	111.42 W
Orenburg	158	51.54 N	55.06 E
Örencik	172	39.16 N	29.33 E
Orense, Arg.	294	38.40 S	59.45 W
Orense, Esp.	168	42.20 N	7.51 W
Orestes	268	40.16 N	85.44 W
Orestiás	172	41.30 N	26.31 E
Oreti ≃	230	46.28 S	168.18 E
Orfordville	244	42.38 N	89.16 W
Organ Needle Λ	254	32.21 N	106.33 W
Órganos, Sierra de los ⛰	284p	22.25 N	83.55 W
Organ Pipe Cactus National Monument ♠	254	32.00 N	112.55 W
Orgaz	168	39.39 N	3.54 W
Orgelet	166	46.31 N	5.37 E
Orgiva	168	36.54 N	3.25 W
Orhangazi	172	40.30 N	29.18 E
Orhanlar	172	39.54 N	27.37 E
Oria ≃	168	43.17 N	2.08 W
Orica	280	14.41 N	86.56 W
Orick	258	41.17 N	124.04 W
Orient, Iowa, U.S.	252	41.12 N	94.25 W
Orient, N.Y., U.S.	261	41.08 N	72.18 W
Orient, Wash., U.S.	256	48.52 N	118.12 W
Oriental	246	35.02 N	76.42 W
Oriental, Cordillera ⛰, Bol.	292	17.30 S	64.30 W
Oriental, Cordillera ⛰, Col.	290	6.00 N	73.00 W
Oriental, Cordillera ⛰, Perú	292	13.00 S	72.00 W
Oriental de Zapata, Ciénaga ≡	284p	22.10 N	80.50 W
Orientalıă, Poarta)(	172	45.06 N	22.18 E
Oriental Park	266	42.09 N	79.22 W
Oriente	294	38.44 S	60.37 W
Oriente □[4]	284p	20.35 N	76.00 W
Orihuela	168	38.05 N	0.57 W
Orillia	264	44.37 N	79.25 W
Orimattila	160	60.48 N	25.45 E
Orinda	272	37.53 N	122.11 W
Orinduik	290	4.40 N	60.03 W
Orinoco ≃	290	8.37 N	62.15 W
Orinoco, Delta del ≚[2]	290	9.15 N	61.30 W
Oriole	262	38.10 N	75.49 W
Orion, Pil.	202	14.37 N	120.35 E
Orion, Ill., U.S.	244	41.21 N	90.23 W
Oripää	160	60.51 N	22.41 E
Oriskany	264	43.09 N	75.20 W
Oriskany Falls	264	42.56 N	75.28 W
Orissa □[3]	206	20.00 N	84.00 E
Oristano	170	39.54 N	8.35 E
Orituco ≃	290	8.45 N	67.27 W
Orivesi	160	61.41 N	24.21 E
Orivesi ⊜	160	62.16 N	29.24 E
Oriximiná	286	1.45 S	55.52 W
Orizaba	278	18.51 N	97.06 W
Orizaba, Pico de → Citlaltépetl, Volcán Λ[1]	278	19.01 N	97.16 W
Orizona	296	17.03 S	48.18 W
Orjahovo	172	43.45 N	23.57 E
Orjen Λ	172	42.30 N	18.38 E
Örkelljunga	160	56.17 N	13.17 E
Orkney, Sask., Can.	256	49.08 N	107.55 W
Orkney, S. Afr.	224	27.00 S	26.39 E
Orkney □[6]	162	59.00 N	3.00 W
Orkney Islands II	162	59.00 N	3.00 W
Orland, Calif., U.S.	258	39.45 N	122.11 W
Orland, Ind., U.S.	268	41.44 N	85.10 W
Orlândia	296	20.43 S	47.53 W
Orlando	246	28.32 N	81.23 W
Orland Park	268	41.38 N	87.52 W
Orleães	294	28.21 S	49.18 W
Orléanais □[9]	176	47.50 N	2.00 E
Orléans, Ont., Can.	264	45.28 N	75.31 W
Orléans, Fr.	176	47.55 N	1.54 E
Orleans, Calif., U.S.	258	41.18 N	123.32 W
Orleans, Ind., U.S.	248	38.40 N	86.27 W
Orleans, Mass., U.S.	261	41.47 N	70.00 W
Orleans, Nebr., U.S.	252	40.08 N	99.27 W
Orleans, Vt., U.S.	242	44.49 N	72.12 W
Orleans □[6], N.Y., U.S.	264	43.15 N	78.12 W
Orleans □[6], Vt., U.S.	260	44.57 N	72.12 W
Orléans, Canal d' ≍	166	47.54 N	1.55 E
Orléans, Île d' I	240	46.55 N	71.00 W
Orléansville → El Asnam	168	36.10 N	1.20 E
Orlik	186	52.30 N	99.55 E
Orlinda	248	36.37 N	86.43 W
Orlinnaja, Gora Λ	236	62.35 N	178.30 E
Orlová	164	49.50 N	18.24 E
Ormāra	204	25.12 N	64.38 E
Ormāra, Rās ≻	206	25.09 N	64.35 E
Ormiston	252	49.45 N	105.22 W
Ormoc	202	11.00 N	124.37 E
Ormoc Bay C	202	10.55 N	124.36 E
Ormond Beach	246	29.17 N	81.02 W
Ormož	170	46.25 N	16.09 E
Ormsby	266	41.48 N	78.33 W
Ormsby □[6]	272	39.11 N	119.46 W
Ormstown	260	45.07 N	73.59 W
Ornans	166	47.06 N	6.09 E
Orne □[5]	166	48.40 N	0.05 E
Orne ≃	166	48.08 N	0.11 E
Orneta (Wormditt)	164	54.08 N	20.08 E
Örnsköldsvik	160	63.18 N	18.43 E
Oro, Río de ≃	290	9.06 N	72.45 W
Oro, Río del ≃, Méx.	278	18.27 N	100.57 W
Oro, Río del ≃, Méx.	278	25.35 N	105.02 W
Oročen	186	58.28 N	125.26 E
Orocovis	284m	18.14 N	66.23 W
Orocué	290	4.48 N	71.20 W
Orocuina	280	13.26 N	87.06 W
Orofino	256	46.29 N	116.15 W
Oro Grande, Calif., U.S.	274	34.36 N	117.20 W
Orogrande, N. Mex., U.S.	254	32.23 N	106.08 W
Or'ol, S.S.S.R.	158	52.59 N	36.05 E
Or'ol, S.S.S.R.	160	59.21 N	56.35 E
Oromocto	240	45.51 N	66.29 W
Oromocto ≃	240	45.51 N	66.29 W
Oromocto Lake ⊜	240	45.36 N	67.00 W
Oron	222	4.48 N	8.14 E
Oron ◆[7]	210	30.55 N	35.01 E
Oronato ≃	290	7.23 N	62.01 W
Orono, Ont., Can.	264	43.59 N	78.37 W
Orono, Maine, U.S.	242	44.53 N	68.40 W
Oronogue ≃	290	2.45 N	57.25 W
Oronsay I	162	56.01 N	6.14 W
Oroquieta	202	8.29 N	123.48 E
Oroquieta ≃	202	8.28 N	123.50 E
Orosei, Golfo di C	170	40.10 N	9.50 E
Orosháza	164	46.34 N	20.40 E
Orosi	272	36.33 N	119.17 W
Orosi, Volcán Λ[1]	280	10.59 N	85.28 W
Oroszlány	164	47.30 N	18.19 E
Orotina	280	9.54 N	84.31 W
Oroville, Calif., U.S.	272	39.31 N	121.33 W
Oroville, Wash., U.S.	256	48.56 N	119.26 W
Oroville Reservoir ⊜[1]	258	39.32 N	121.25 W
Orrick	248	39.13 N	94.07 W
Orrin	252	48.05 N	100.10 W
Orrs Island	242	43.46 N	69.59 W
Orrtanna	262	39.51 N	77.22 W
Orrville, Ala., U.S.	248	32.18 N	87.15 W
Orrville, Ohio, U.S.	266	40.50 N	81.46 W
Orša	160	54.30 N	30.24 E
Orsainville	260	46.53 N	71.18 W
Orsara di Puglia	184	41.17 N	15.16 E
Orsay	176	48.48 N	2.11 E
Orsières	166	46.02 N	7.09 E
Orsk	158	51.12 N	58.34 E
Orşova	172	44.42 N	22.24 E
Ortaca	172	36.49 N	28.47 E
Ortaklar	172	37.53 N	27.30 E

Symbols in the index entries are identified on page 360.

Name	Page	Lat°′	Long°′
Orta Nova	184	41.19 N	15.42 E
Orte	184	42.27 N	12.23 E
Ortega	290	3.56 N	75.13 W
Ortegal, Cabo ≻	168	43.45 N	7.53 W
Orteguaza ≃	290	0.43 N	75.16 W
Orthez	166	43.29 N	0.46 W
Ortigueira, Bra.	294	24.12 S	50.55 W
Ortigueira, Esp.	168	43.41 N	7.51 W
Orting	270	47.06 N	122.12 W
Ortisei (Sankt Ulrich)	170	46.34 N	11.40 E
Ortiz, Méx.	278	28.17 N	110.43 W
Ortiz, Ven.	290	9.37 N	67.17 W
Ortón ≃	292	10.50 S	66.04 W
Ortona	184	42.21 N	14.24 E
Ortonville, Mich., U.S.	268	42.51 N	83.27 W
Ortonville, Minn., U.S.	252	45.19 N	96.27 W
Orto-Tokoj	186	42.21 N	76.01 E
Oruro	292	17.59 S	67.09 W
Oruro □[5]	292	18.40 S	67.30 W
Orvieto	184	42.43 N	12.07 E
Orvilla	262	40.16 N	75.17 W
Orviston	266	41.06 N	77.45 W
Orvyn, Gora ∧	236	65.14 N	175.20 W
Orwell, N.Y., U.S.	264	43.35 N	76.00 W
Orwell, Ohio, U.S.	266	41.32 N	80.52 W
Orwigsburg	262	40.39 N	76.06 W
Orwin	262	40.35 N	76.31 W
Or Yehuda	210	32.01 N	34.51 E
Orzinuovi	182	45.24 N	9.55 E
Orzyc ≃	164	52.47 N	21.13 E
Orzysz (Arys)	164	53.49 N	21.56 E
Os, Nor.	160	62.30 N	11.12 E
Oš, S.S.S.R.	186	40.33 N	72.48 E
Osa, Península de ≻[1]	280	8.35 N	83.33 W
Osage, Iowa, U.S.	244	43.17 N	92.49 W
Osage, Wyo., U.S.	252	43.59 N	104.25 W
Osage ≃	248	38.35 N	91.57 W
Osage Beach	248	38.09 N	92.37 W
Osage City	252	38.38 N	95.50 W
Osage Plains ≍	250	36.00 N	96.30 W
Ōsaka	192	34.40 N	135.30 E
Ōsaka-wan C	192	34.30 N	135.18 E
Osakis	252	45.52 N	95.09 W
Osâm ≃	172	43.42 N	24.51 E
Osawatomie	252	38.31 N	94.57 W
Osborne	252	39.26 N	98.42 W
Osburn	256	47.30 N	116.00 W
Oscar Peak ∧	238	54.51 N	129.07 W
Oscarville	236	60.43 N	161.46 W
Oscawana Lake	261	41.23 N	73.52 W
Osceola, Ark., U.S.	248	35.42 N	89.58 W
Osceola, Ind., U.S.	268	41.40 N	86.04 W
Osceola, Iowa, U.S.	244	41.02 N	93.46 W
Osceola, Mo., U.S.	248	38.03 N	93.42 W
Osceola, Nebr., U.S.	252	41.11 N	97.33 W
Osceola, Wis., U.S.	244	45.19 N	92.42 W
Osceola Mills	266	40.51 N	78.16 W
Oschatz	164	51.17 N	13.07 E
Oschersleben	164	52.01 N	11.13 E
Oscoda	244	44.26 N	83.20 W
Osečina	172	44.23 N	19.36 E
Osen	160	64.17 N	10.30 E
Osgood, Ind., U.S.	248	39.08 N	85.17 W
Osgood, Ohio, U.S.	268	40.20 N	84.30 W
Osgoode Station	264	45.08 N	75.36 W
Oshamambe	192a	42.30 N	140.22 E
O'Shanassy ≃	228	18.59 S	138.46 E
Oshawa	264	43.54 N	78.51 W
Oshika	192	38.16 N	141.32 E
Ōshima	192	33.03 N	129.33 E
Ō-shima I, Nihon	192	34.43 N	139.23 E
Ō-shima I, Nihon	192	33.28 N	135.50 E
Ō-shima I, Nihon	192a	41.30 N	139.22 E
Oshima-hantō ≻[1]	192a	42.00 N	140.30 E
Oshkosh, Nebr., U.S.	252	41.24 N	102.21 W
Oshkosh, Wis., U.S.	244	44.01 N	88.33 W
Oshogbo	222	7.47 N	4.34 E
Oshtemo	268	42.15 N	85.41 W
Oshtorān Kūh ∧	208	33.20 N	49.16 E
Oshwe	218	3.24 S	19.30 E
Osica de Jos	172	44.15 N	24.17 E
Osiek	164	50.31 N	21.28 E
Osijek	172	45.33 N	18.41 E
Osilinka ≃	238	56.05 N	124.29 W
Osilo	170	40.44 N	8.39 E
Osimo	184	43.29 N	13.29 E
Osinki	160	52.52 N	47.32 E
Osinniki	186	58.03 N	47.02 E
Osinovskij Chrebet ⛰	236	67.10 N	175.00 E
Osintorf	160	54.42 N	30.39 E
Osio Sotto	182	45.36 N	9.35 E
Osipaonica	172	44.33 N	21.04 E
Osipenko → Berd'ansk	158	46.45 N	36.49 E
Oskaloosa, Iowa, U.S.	244	41.18 N	92.39 W
Oskaloosa, Kans., U.S.	252	39.13 N	95.19 W
Oskarshamn	160	57.16 N	16.26 E
Oskarström	160	56.48 N	12.58 E
Oskolkovo	160	67.58 N	53.42 E
Oskū	208	37.55 N	46.06 E
Oslava ≃	164	49.05 N	16.22 E
Ösling □[9]	166	49.55 N	6.00 E
Oslo	160	59.55 N	10.45 E
Oslob	202	9.31 N	123.26 E
Oslofjorden C[2]	160	59.20 N	10.35 E
Osmaneli	172	40.22 N	30.01 E
Osmaniye	212	37.05 N	36.14 E
Osmeña	202	10.11 N	125.31 E
Osminog, Gora ∧	236	67.54 N	176.50 E
Osmond	252	42.22 N	97.36 W
Osmore, Río de ≃	292	17.38 S	71.22 W
Osnabrück	178	52.16 N	8.02 E
Osnabrück □[6]	178	52.30 N	7.40 E
Ośno (Drossen)	164	52.28 N	14.50 E
Oso	270	48.16 N	121.56 W
Osore-san ∧	192	41.18 N	144.05 E
Osório	294	29.54 S	50.16 W
Osório Fonseca	290	3.40 S	58.13 W
Osorno, Chile	288	40.34 S	73.09 W
Osorno, Esp.	168	42.24 N	4.22 W
Osoyoos	238	49.02 N	119.28 W
Osoyoos Indian Reserve ⬩[4]	238	49.08 N	119.30 W
Osoyoos Lake ⊜	238	49.00 N	119.26 W
Osøyra	160	60.11 N	5.28 E
Ospino	290	9.18 N	69.27 W
Oss	178	51.46 N	5.31 E
Ossa, Mount ∧	228	41.54 S	146.01 E
Ossabaw Island I	246	31.47 N	81.06 W
Osse ≃	222	6.10 N	5.20 E
Osseo, Mich., U.S.	268	41.53 N	84.33 W
Osseo, Wis., U.S.	244	44.35 N	91.12 W
Ossian, Ind., U.S.	268	40.53 N	85.10 W
Ossian, Iowa, U.S.	244	43.09 N	91.46 W
Ossining	261	41.10 N	73.52 W
Ossipee	242	43.41 N	71.07 W
Ossokmanuan Lake ⊜	232	53.25 N	65.00 W
Ossora	186	59.20 N	163.13 E
Ošta	160	60.49 N	35.32 E
Ostaboningue, Lac ⊜	244	47.09 N	78.52 W
Ostaškov	160	57.09 N	33.06 E
Ost-Berlin	164	52.30 N	13.25 E
Ostende → Oostende	176	51.13 N	2.55 E
Osterath	178	51.16 N	6.37 E
Osterburg, D.D.R.	164	52.47 N	11.44 E
Osterburg, Pa., U.S.	266	40.16 N	78.31 W
Östergötlands Län □[6]	160	58.25 N	15.45 E
Osterholz-Scharmbeck	178	53.14 N	8.47 E
Ostermundigen	180	46.58 N	7.29 E
Osterode	178	51.43 N	10.14 E
Österreichische Alpen ⛰	164	47.40 N	15.10 E
Östersund	160	63.11 N	14.39 E
Osterville	261	41.38 N	70.22 W
Osterwieck	164	51.58 N	10.42 E
Østfold □[6]	160	59.20 N	11.30 E
Ostfriesische Inseln II	164	53.44 N	7.25 E
Ostfriesland □[9]	178	53.20 N	7.40 E
Östhammar	160	60.16 N	18.22 E
Ostrander	266	40.16 N	83.13 W
Ostrava	164	49.50 N	18.17 E
Ostredok ∧	164	48.55 N	19.04 E
Ostricourt	176	50.27 N	3.02 E
Ostróda (Osterode)	164	53.43 N	19.59 E
Ostrogożsk	158	50.52 N	39.05 E
Ostrołęka	164	53.06 N	21.34 E
Ostroróg	164	52.39 N	16.27 E
Ostrov, Česko.	164	50.17 N	12.57 E
Ostrov, Rom.	172	44.06 N	27.22 E
Ostrov, S.S.S.R.	160	57.20 N	28.22 E
Ostrov ⬩[1]	164	47.55 N	17.35 E
Ostrovec	160	54.37 N	25.57 E
Ostrov-Zalit	160	58.01 N	28.04 E
Ostrów (Wielkopolski)	164	51.39 N	17.49 E
Ostrowiec Świętokrzyski	164	50.57 N	21.23 E
Ostrów Lubelski	164	51.30 N	22.52 E
Ostrów Mazowiecka	164	52.49 N	21.54 E
Ostrów Wielkopolski	164	51.39 N	17.49 E
Ostrzeszów	164	51.25 N	17.57 E
Osttirol ⬩[1]	164	46.55 N	12.30 E
Ostuni	170	40.44 N	17.35 E
Osum ≃	172	40.48 N	19.52 E
Ōsumi-hantō ≻[1]	192	31.20 N	130.55 E
Ōsumi-kaikyō ⩌	192	31.00 N	131.00 E
Ōsumi-shotō II	193b	30.30 N	130.00 E
Osuna	168	37.14 N	5.07 W
Osvaldo Cruz	296	21.47 S	50.50 W
Osveja	160	56.01 N	28.06 E
Ošvor	160	66.58 N	62.53 E
Oswayo	266	41.55 N	78.01 W
Oswegatchie ≃	242	44.42 N	75.30 W
Oswego, Ill., U.S.	268	41.41 N	88.21 W
Oswego, Ind., U.S.	268	41.19 N	85.47 W
Oswego, Kans., U.S.	252	37.10 N	95.06 W
Oswego, N.Y., U.S.	264	43.27 N	76.31 W
Oswego □[6]	264	43.22 N	76.15 W
Oswestry	174	52.52 N	3.04 W
Oświęcim	164	50.03 N	19.12 E
Osyka	248	31.00 N	90.28 W
Ōta	192	36.18 N	139.22 E
Otago □[9]	230	44.45 S	169.10 E
Otago Peninsula ≻[1]	230	45.51 S	170.39 E
Otahuhu	230	36.57 S	174.50 E
Ōtake	192	34.12 N	132.13 E
Otaki	230	40.45 S	175.08 E
Otanmäki	160	64.07 N	27.06 E
Otaru	192a	43.13 N	141.00 E
Otava	160	61.39 N	27.04 E
Otava ≃	164	49.26 N	14.12 E
Otavalo	290	0.14 N	78.16 W
Otavi	218	19.39 S	17.20 E
Ōtawara	192	36.52 N	140.02 E
Otay	274	32.36 N	117.04 W
Oteros ≃	278	26.53 N	108.20 W
Othello	256	46.50 N	119.10 W
Othonoí I	172	39.50 N	19.26 E
Oti ≃	222	8.40 N	0.13 E
Otinapa	278	24.11 N	105.02 W
Otis, Colo., U.S.	252	40.09 N	102.58 W
Otis, Ind., U.S.	268	41.36 N	86.54 W
Otis, Kans., U.S.	252	38.32 N	99.03 W
Otish Mountains ⛰	232	52.45 N	69.15 W
Otjiwarongo	224	20.29 S	16.36 E
Otjiwarongo □[5]	224	21.45 S	17.00 E
Otjosondjou ≃	224	19.30 S	20.04 E
Otju □[5]	224	20.00 S	15.00 E
Otmuchów (Ottmachau)	164	50.28 N	17.10 E
Otočac	170	44.52 N	15.14 E
Oton	202	10.41 N	122.28 E
Otoque, Isla I	280	8.35 N	79.37 W
Otorohanga	230	38.11 S	175.12 E
Otoskwin ≃	232	52.13 N	88.06 W
Otra ≃	160	58.09 N	8.00 E
Otradnyj	160	53.22 N	51.21 E
Otranto	170	40.09 N	18.30 E
Otranto, Strait of ⩌[1]	172	40.00 N	19.00 E
Otrokovice	164	49.13 N	17.31 E
Ötscher ∧	164	47.52 N	15.12 E
Otsego, Mich., U.S.	268	42.27 N	85.42 W
Otsego, Ohio, U.S.	266	40.07 N	81.46 W
Otselic ≃	242	42.20 N	75.58 W
Ōtsu	192	35.00 N	135.52 E
Ōtsuchi	192	39.21 N	141.54 E
Ōtsuki	192	35.36 N	138.57 E
Otta	160	61.46 N	9.32 E
Ottaviano	184	40.51 N	14.28 E
Ottawa, Ont., Can.	264	45.25 N	75.42 W
Ottawa, Ill., U.S.	268	41.21 N	88.51 W
Ottawa, Kans., U.S.	252	38.37 N	95.16 W
Ottawa, Ohio, U.S.	268	41.01 N	84.03 W
Ottawa □[6], Mich., U.S.	268	42.57 N	86.02 W
Ottawa □[6], Ohio, U.S.	266	41.31 N	82.56 W
Ottawa ≃	234	45.20 N	73.58 W
Ottawa Hills	266	41.40 N	83.39 W
Ottawa Islands II	232	59.30 N	80.10 W
Ottenby	160	56.14 N	16.25 E
Otterbein	268	40.29 N	87.06 W
Otterburne	252	49.30 N	97.03 W
Otterburn Park	260	45.33 N	73.13 W
Otter Creek	246	29.19 N	82.48 W
Otter Creek Reservoir ⊜[1]	254	38.12 N	111.59 W
Otter Lake, Qué., Can.	242	45.51 N	76.26 W
Otter Lake, Mich., U.S.	244	43.13 N	83.28 W
Otterndorf	178	53.48 N	8.53 E
Otter River	261	42.36 N	72.03 W
Otter Tail Lake ≃	252	46.16 N	96.36 W
Otterville, Ont., Can.	264	42.55 N	80.36 W
Otterville, Mo., U.S.	248	38.42 N	93.00 W
Öttingen in Bayern	164	48.57 N	10.36 E
Otto	266	42.21 N	78.50 W
Ottobrunn	164	48.04 N	11.40 E
Ottoville	268	40.54 N	84.18 W
Ottumwa	244	41.01 N	92.25 W
Ottweiler	164	49.24 N	7.09 E
Otukpa	222	7.09 N	7.41 E
Otumpa	294	27.20 S	62.14 W
Otuzco	292	7.50 S	78.30 W
Otway, Cape ≻	228	38.52 S	143.31 E
Otwock	164	52.07 N	21.16 E
Ötz	164	47.12 N	10.54 E
Ötztaler Alpen (Alpi Venoste) ⛰	166	46.45 N	10.55 E
Ou ≃	200	20.04 N	102.13 E
Ouachita ≃	248	31.38 N	91.49 W
Ouachita, Lake ⊜[1]	248	34.40 N	93.25 W
Ouachita Mountains ⛰	248	34.40 N	94.25 W
Ouadda	214	8.04 N	22.24 E
Ouadou ∨	222	15.40 N	9.53 W
Ouagadougou	222	12.22 N	1.31 W
Ouahigouya	222	13.35 N	2.25 W
Ouahran → Oran	168	35.43 N	0.43 W
Ouaka ≃	214	4.59 N	19.56 E
Oualâta	214	17.18 N	7.02 W
Oualâta, Dhar ⬩[4]	222	17.48 N	7.24 W
Ouallene	214	24.37 N	1.14 E
Oua-n-Agadez, Irhazer ∨	222	17.28 N	6.26 E
Ouanda Djallé	214	8.54 N	22.48 E
Ouarane ⬩[1]	222	21.00 N	10.30 W
Ouargla	214	31.59 N	5.25 E
Ouarsenis, Djebel ∧	168	35.52 N	1.42 E
Ouarzazate	214	30.57 N	6.50 W
Ouassoulou ≃	222	11.35 N	8.11 W
Oubangui (Ubangi) ≃	214	1.15 N	17.50 E
Ōuchi	192	34.16 N	134.18 E
Oucques	162	47.49 N	1.18 E
Oud-Beijerland	178	51.49 N	4.25 E
Oudenaarde	176	50.51 N	3.36 E
Oudenbosch	178	51.35 N	4.31 E
Oude-Pekela	178	53.04 N	6.58 E
Oudtshoorn	224	33.35 S	22.14 E
Oued Athménia	168	36.15 N	6.17 E
Oued Cheham	170	36.23 N	7.46 E
Oued Fodda	168	36.11 N	1.32 E
Oued Meliz	170	36.27 N	8.34 E
Oued Rhiou	168	35.58 N	0.55 E
Oued Tlélat	168	35.34 N	0.27 W
Oued Zarga	170	36.40 N	9.25 E
Ouémé □[5]	222	7.00 N	2.35 E
Ouémé ≃	222	6.29 N	2.32 E
Ouenza	170	35.57 N	8.04 E
Ouenza, Djebel ∧	170	35.57 N	8.06 E
Ouessant, Île d' I	166	48.28 N	5.05 W
Ouesso	218	1.37 N	16.04 E
Ouest, Pointe ≻	240	49.52 N	64.31 W
Ouezzane	168	34.52 N	5.35 W
Ouham ≃	214	9.18 N	18.14 E
Ouidah	222	6.22 N	2.05 E
Ouistreham	166	49.17 N	0.15 W
Oujda	214	34.41 N	1.45 W
Oujiang ≃	196	28.04 N	120.35 E
Oulainen	160	64.16 N	24.48 E
Oulangan Kansallispuisto ♠	160	66.12 N	29.30 E
Ouled Aglat	168	35.58 N	4.45 E
Oullins	182	45.43 N	4.48 E
Oulu	160	65.01 N	25.28 E
Oulujärvi ⊜	160	64.20 N	27.15 E
Oulujoki ≃	160	65.01 N	25.25 E
Oulun lääni □[4]	160	65.00 N	27.00 E
Oum Chalouba	214	15.48 N	20.46 E
Oum er Rbia, Oued ≃	214	33.19 N	8.21 W
Ounasjoki ≃	160	66.30 N	25.45 E
Ounianga Kébir	214	19.04 N	20.29 E
Ouray	254	38.01 N	107.40 W
Ouray, Mount ∧	254	38.25 N	106.14 W
Ourinhos	296	22.59 S	49.52 W
Ourique	168	37.39 N	8.13 W
Ouro Fino	296	22.17 S	46.22 W
Ouro Prêto	296	20.23 S	43.30 W
Ouro Prêto ≃	292	11.02 S	65.13 W
Ouroufa, Vallée d' ∨	222	14.42 N	7.00 E
Ōu-sammyaku ⛰	192	38.45 N	140.50 E
Oust ≃	166	47.39 N	2.06 W
Outardes, Baie aux C	240	49.02 N	68.32 W
Outardes, Rivière aux ≃	240	49.04 N	68.25 W
Outeniekwaberge ⛰	224	33.53 S	22.35 E
Outer Hebrides II	162	57.50 N	7.32 W
Outer Santa Barbara Passage ⩌	258	33.10 N	118.30 W
Outes	168	42.51 N	8.54 W
Outjo	218	20.08 S	16.08 E
Outlook, Sask., Can.	232	51.30 N	107.03 W
Outlook, Mont., U.S.	252	48.53 N	104.47 W
Outpost Mountain ∧	236	69.08 N	151.12 W
Outreau	176	50.42 N	1.35 E
Outremont	260	45.31 N	73.38 W
Ouvidor	296	18.14 S	47.50 W
Ouyen	228	35.04 S	142.20 E
Ouzinkie	236	57.55 N	152.30 W
Ouzouer-le-Marché	166	47.55 N	1.32 E
Ovada	182	44.38 N	8.38 E
Ovalle	294	30.36 S	71.12 W
Ovamboland □[5]	224	18.00 S	16.00 E
Ovamboland □[9]	224	17.45 S	16.30 E
Ovando, Bahía de C	284p	20.07 N	74.13 W
Ovar	168	40.52 N	8.38 W
Ovejas	290	9.32 N	75.14 W
Overbrook	252	38.47 N	95.33 W
Overflakkee I	164	51.45 N	4.10 E
Overhalla	160	64.30 N	11.57 E
Overijssel □[4]	178	52.25 N	6.30 E
Överkalix	160	66.21 N	22.56 E
Overland Park	252	38.59 N	94.40 W
Overpelt	178	51.13 N	5.25 E
Overton, Nebr., U.S.	252	40.44 N	99.32 W
Overton, Nev., U.S.	258	36.33 N	114.27 W
Overton, Tex., U.S.	250	32.16 N	94.59 W
Overton Arm C	258	36.20 N	114.25 W
Övertorneå	160	66.23 N	23.40 E
Ovett	248	31.29 N	89.02 W
Ovid, Mich., U.S.	268	43.01 N	84.22 W
Ovid, N.Y., U.S.	264	42.41 N	76.49 W
Oviedo	168	43.22 N	5.50 W
Owasco	264	42.51 N	76.28 W
Owase	192	34.04 N	136.12 E
Owasso	250	36.16 N	95.51 W
Owatonna	244	44.05 N	93.14 W
Owego	242	42.06 N	76.16 W
Owen	244	44.57 N	90.33 W
Owen, Mount ∧	230	41.33 S	172.33 E
Owens	246	35.03 N	78.57 W
Owens ≃	258	36.31 N	117.57 W
Owensboro	248	37.46 N	87.07 W
Owens Lake ⊜	258	36.25 N	117.56 W
Owen Sound	264	44.34 N	80.56 W
Owen Sound C	244	44.40 N	80.55 W
Owensville, Ind., U.S.	248	38.16 N	87.41 W
Owensville, Mo., U.S.	248	38.21 N	91.30 W
Owenton, Ky., U.S.	248	38.32 N	84.50 W
Owenton, Va., U.S.	262	37.53 N	77.06 W
Owerri	222	5.29 N	7.02 E
Owikeno Lake ⊜	238	51.41 N	127.00 W
Owings	262	38.43 N	76.36 W
Owingsville	242	38.09 N	83.46 W
Owl ≃, Alta., Can.	238	54.54 N	111.57 W
Owl ≃, Man., Can.	232	57.51 N	92.44 W
Owl Creek Mountains ⛰	254	43.30 N	108.35 W
Owo	222	7.15 N	5.37 E
Owosso	268	43.00 N	84.10 W
Owyhee	258	41.57 N	116.06 W
Owyhee ≃	256	43.46 N	117.02 W
Owyhee, Lake ⊜[1]	256	43.28 N	117.20 W
Oxapampa	292	10.33 S	75.26 W
Oxbow, Sask., Can.	252	49.14 N	102.11 W
Oxbow, N.Y., U.S.	264	44.17 N	75.37 W
Oxelösund	160	58.40 N	17.06 E
Oxford, N.S., Can.	240	45.44 N	63.52 W
Oxford, N.Z.	230	43.18 S	172.11 E
Oxford, Eng., U.K.	174	51.46 N	1.15 W
Oxford, Ala., U.S.	248	33.37 N	85.50 W
Oxford, Conn., U.S.	261	41.20 N	73.07 W
Oxford, Ga., U.S.	246	33.37 N	83.52 W
Oxford, Ind., U.S.	268	40.31 N	87.15 W
Oxford, Iowa, U.S.	244	41.43 N	91.47 W
Oxford, Kans., U.S.	252	37.16 N	97.10 W
Oxford, Maine, U.S.	242	44.08 N	70.30 W
Oxford, Md., U.S.	262	38.42 N	76.10 W
Oxford, Mass., U.S.	261	42.07 N	71.52 W
Oxford, Mich., U.S.	268	42.49 N	83.16 W
Oxford, Miss., U.S.	248	34.22 N	89.32 W
Oxford, Nebr., U.S.	252	40.15 N	99.38 W
Oxford, N.J., U.S.	262	40.48 N	74.60 W
Oxford, N.C., U.S.	246	36.19 N	78.35 W
Oxford, N.Y., U.S.	242	42.27 N	75.36 W
Oxford, Ohio, U.S.	242	39.30 N	84.44 W
Oxford, Pa., U.S.	262	39.47 N	75.59 W
Oxford, Wis., U.S.	244	43.47 N	89.34 W
Oxford □[6]	264	43.08 N	80.50 W
Oxford Junction	244	41.59 N	90.57 W
Oxford Lake ⊜	232	54.51 N	95.37 W
Oxford Peak ∧	256	42.16 N	112.06 W
Oxfordshire □[6]	174	51.50 N	1.15 W
Oxnard	274	34.12 N	119.11 W
Oxnard Beach	274	34.09 N	119.13 W
Oxus → Amu Darya ≃	186	43.40 N	59.01 E
Oyabe	192	36.40 N	136.52 E
Oyahue, Volcán(Volcán Ollagüe) ∧[1]	292	21.18 S	68.12 W
Oyama, B.C., Can.	238	50.07 N	119.22 W
Oyama, Nihon	192	36.18 N	139.48 E
Oyano	192	32.35 N	130.30 E
Oyapock (Oiapoque) ≃	286	4.08 N	51.40 W
Oyem	218	1.37 N	11.35 E
Oyo	222	7.51 N	3.56 E
Ōyodo ≃	192	31.53 N	131.28 E
Oyón	292	10.37 S	76.47 W
Oyonnax	180	46.15 N	5.40 E
Oyotún	292	6.48 S	79.18 W
Oymyakon → Ojm'akon	186	63.28 N	142.49 E
Oyster	262	37.17 N	75.55 W
Oyster Bay	261	40.52 N	73.32 W
Oyster Bay C	228	42.11 S	148.11 E
Oysterville	270	46.33 N	124.02 W
Ozamiz	202	8.09 N	123.51 E
Ozark, Ala., U.S.	248	31.28 N	85.38 W
Ozark, Ark., U.S.	248	35.29 N	93.50 W
Ozark, Mo., U.S.	248	37.01 N	93.12 W
Ozark Escarpment ⬩[4]	248	36.15 N	91.15 W
Ozark Plateau ⛰[1]	248	37.00 N	93.00 W
Ozarks, Lake of the ⊜[1]	248	38.10 N	92.50 W
Ozaukee □[6]	268	44.14 N	88.00 W
Ózd	164	48.14 N	20.18 E
Ozeblin ∧	170	44.35 N	15.53 E
Ozernovskij	186	51.30 N	156.31 E
Ozernyj	236	66.24 N	179.06 W
Ozette Lake ⊜	256	48.06 N	124.38 W
Ozieri	170	40.35 N	9.00 E
Ozimek (Malapane)	164	50.41 N	18.13 E
Ozona	250	30.43 N	101.12 W
Ozorków	164	51.58 N	19.19 E
Oz'orsk [Angerapp]	164	54.25 N	22.01 E
Oz'ory	164	53.43 N	24.11 E
Ōzu, Nihon	192	33.30 N	132.33 E
Ōzu, Nihon	192	32.52 N	130.52 E
Ozubulu	222	5.57 N	6.51 E
Ozuluama	278	21.40 N	97.51 W
P			
Paal	178	51.02 N	5.11 E
Pa-an	200	16.53 N	97.38 E
Paarl	224	33.45 S	18.56 E
Paauilo	275d	20.02 N	155.22 W
Pabbay I	162	57.47 N	7.20 W
Pabellón, Ensenada del C	278	24.25 N	107.35 W
Pabianice	164	51.40 N	19.22 E
Pablo	256	47.36 N	114.07 W
Pābna	206	24.00 N	89.15 E
Pacaás Novos ≃	292	10.51 S	65.20 W
Pacaás Novos, Serra dos ⛰	292	10.45 S	64.15 W
Pacaembu	296	21.34 S	51.17 W
Pacahuaras ≃	292	10.04 S	65.46 W
Pacarán	292	12.50 S	76.03 W
Pacaraos	292	11.12 S	76.42 W
Pacasmayo	292	7.20 S	79.35 W
Pacatu	296	11.57 S	38.58 W
Paccha ≃	292	9.05 S	76.54 W
Pace	248	33.42 N	90.52 W
Pachača	186	60.34 N	169.03 E
Pachacamac	292	12.14 S	77.53 W
Pachacamac ⊥	292	12.14 S	76.52 W
Pacheco	272	37.59 N	122.04 W
Pachino	170	36.42 N	15.06 E
Pachitea ≃	292	8.46 S	74.33 W
Pachiza	292	7.16 S	76.46 W
Pacho	290	5.08 N	74.10 W
Pachuca [de Soto]	278	20.07 N	98.44 W
Pacific, B.C., Can.	238	54.46 N	128.17 W
Pacific, Mo., U.S.	248	38.29 N	90.45 W
Pacific, Wash., U.S.	270	47.16 N	122.15 W
Pacific □[6]	270	46.30 N	123.39 W
Pacifica	272	37.38 N	122.29 W
Pacific Beach	270	47.13 N	124.12 W
Pacific City	270	45.12 N	123.57 W
Pacific Grove	272	36.38 N	121.56 W
Pacific Islands Trust Territory □[2]	198	10.00 N	155.00 E
Pacific Ocean ≂[1]	148	10.00 S	150.00 W
Pacific Ranges ⛰	238	50.45 N	125.30 W
Pacijan Island I	202	10.40 N	124.20 E
Packard Mountain ∧[2]	242	42.28 N	72.21 W
Packwood	270	46.36 N	121.40 W
Pacllón	292	10.17 S	77.05 W
Pacolet ≃	246	34.50 N	81.27 W
Pacolet Mills	246	34.55 N	81.45 W
Pácora, Col.	290	5.31 N	75.27 W
Pacora, Pan.	290	9.05 N	79.20 W
Pacov	164	49.28 N	15.00 E
Pacquet	240	50.00 N	55.50 W
Pacuare ≃	280	10.14 N	83.17 W
Pacuí ≃	296	16.46 S	45.01 W
Pacuneiro ≃	296	13.02 S	53.25 W
Pacy-sur-Eure	166	49.01 N	1.23 E
Paczkow	164	50.27 N	17.00 E
Padada	202	6.42 N	125.22 E
Padada ≃	202	6.41 N	125.23 E
Padamo ≃	290	2.54 N	65.17 W
Padang	200	0.57 S	100.21 E
Padang, Pulau I	200	1.10 N	102.21 E
Padangpandjang	200	0.27 S	100.25 E
Padangsidempuan	200	1.23 N	99.16 E
Padany	160	63.17 N	33.22 E
Padauari ≃	290	0.15 S	64.05 W
Padcaya	292	21.52 S	64.48 W
Paddle ≃	238	54.05 N	114.15 W
Paddle Rairie	232	57.57 N	117.29 W
Paddock Lake	268	42.34 N	88.07 W
Padea	172	44.00 N	23.26 E
Paden City	242	39.36 N	80.56 W
Paderborn	178	51.43 N	8.45 E
Padilla, Bol.	292	19.19 S	64.20 W
Padilla, Méx.	278	24.01 N	98.47 W
Padjelanta Nationalpark ♠	160	67.28 N	16.41 E
Padloping Island I	232	67.07 N	62.35 W
Padova	170	45.25 N	11.53 E
Padre Bernardo	296	15.21 S	48.30 W
Padre Burgos	202	10.02 N	125.01 E
Padre Island I	250	27.00 N	97.15 W
Padre Island National Seashore ♠	250	26.26 N	27.43 W
Padre Paraíso	296	17.06 S	41.31 W
Padrón	168	42.44 N	8.40 W
Padstow	162	50.33 N	4.56 W
Padua → Padova	170	45.25 N	11.53 E
Paduari ≃	290	2.08 S	61.15 W
Paducah, Ky., U.S.	248	37.05 N	88.36 W
Paducah, Tex., U.S.	250	34.01 N	100.18 W
Paektu-san ∧	194	42.00 N	128.03 E
Paestum ⊥	170	40.25 N	15.00 E
Paete	202	14.23 N	121.29 E
Páez ≃	290	2.28 N	75.34 W
Pafúri	218	22.27 S	31.21 E
Pag	170	44.27 N	15.04 E
Pag, Otok I	170	44.30 N	15.00 E
Pagadian	202	7.50 N	123.27 E
Pagadian Bay C	202	7.46 N	123.35 E
Pagai Selatan, Pulau I	198	3.00 S	100.20 E
Pagai Utara, Pulau I	198	2.42 S	100.07 E
Pagalungan	202	7.03 N	124.41 E
Pagan I	198	18.07 N	145.46 E
Pagancillo	294	29.35 S	68.03 W
Pagani	184	40.45 N	14.37 E
Pagasitikós Kólpos C	172	39.15 N	22.51 E
Pagbilao	202	13.58 N	121.41 E
Pagbilao Grande Island I	202	13.55 N	121.46 E
Pagdanan Bay C	202	10.30 N	119.10 E
Page, Ariz., U.S.	254	36.57 N	111.27 W
Page, N. Dak., U.S.	252	47.09 N	97.34 W
Pagėgiai	160	55.09 N	21.54 E
Pageland	246	34.46 N	80.24 W
Paget, Mount ∧	288	54.26 S	36.33 W
Pagoda Peak ∧	254	40.10 N	107.20 W
Pagoda Point ≻	200	15.57 N	94.15 E
Pagosa Springs	254	37.16 N	107.01 W
Pagsangahan	202	13.13 N	122.32 E
Pagsanjan	202	14.16 N	121.27 E
Paguate	254	35.08 N	107.23 W
Pagudpud	202	18.34 N	120.47 E
Pahala	275d	19.12 N	155.29 W
Pahang ≃	200	3.32 N	103.28 E
Pahaska	256	44.30 N	109.58 W
Pahia Point ≻	230	46.20 S	167.41 E
Pahoa	275d	19.28 N	154.51 W
Pahokee	246	26.49 N	80.40 W
Pahsimeroi ≃	256	44.41 N	114.03 W
Pahute Peak ∧	258	41.17 N	119.04 W
Pai ≃	200	19.08 N	97.33 E
Paia	275a	20.54 N	156.22 W
Paicines	272	36.44 N	121.17 W
Paico	292	14.03 S	73.40 W
Paige	250	30.13 N	97.07 W
Paignton	174	50.26 N	3.34 W
Paiguano	294	30.01 S	70.32 W
Paiján	292	7.42 S	79.20 W
Päijänne ⊜	160	61.35 N	25.30 E
Paila ≃	292	16.02 S	64.12 W
Pailitas	290	8.58 N	73.38 W
Pailolo Channel ⩌	275d	21.05 N	156.42 W
Paimboeuf	166	47.17 N	2.02 W
Paimpol	166	48.46 N	3.03 W
Painan	200	1.21 S	100.34 E
Paincourt	266	42.23 N	82.17 W
Painesdale	244	47.02 N	88.41 W
Painesville	266	41.43 N	81.15 W
Pains	296	20.22 S	45.40 W
Paint ≃	244	45.58 N	88.15 W
Painted Desert ⬩[2]	254	36.00 N	111.20 W
Painter	262	37.34 N	75.44 W
Paint Rock	250	31.30 N	99.55 W
Paint Rock ≃	248	34.28 N	86.28 W
Paintsville	246	37.49 N	82.48 W
Paisley, Ont., Can.	264	44.18 N	81.16 W
Paisley, Scot., U.K.	162	55.50 N	4.26 W
Paisley, Oreg., U.S.	256	42.42 N	120.32 W
Paita	292	5.05 S	81.10 W
Paita, Bahía de C	292	5.03 S	81.05 W
Paitan ≃	202	6.30 N	117.30 E
Paitan Bay C	202	6.45 N	117.20 E
Paiva ≃	168	41.04 N	8.16 W
Paj	160	61.13 N	34.24 E
Pajakumbuh	200	0.14 S	100.37 E
Pajala	160	67.11 N	23.29 E
Paján	290	1.34 S	80.25 W
Pajares, Puerto de)(	168	43.00 N	5.46 W
Pajaro	272	36.54 N	121.39 W
Paj-Choj ⛰[2]	186	69.00 N	63.00 E
Pajęczno	164	51.09 N	19.00 E
Pajjer, Gora ∧	186	66.42 N	64.25 E
Pak ≃	200	21.05 N	102.31 E
Pakanbaru	200	0.32 N	101.27 E
Pakaraima Mountains ⛰	290	5.30 N	60.40 W
Pakenham	264	45.20 N	76.17 W
Pakhoi → Beihai	200	21.29 N	109.05 E
Pakistan (Pākistān) □[1]	204	30.00 N	70.00 E
Pākistān, East → Banglasesh □[1]	204	24.00 N	90.00 E
Pākistān, West □[4]	208	30.00 N	70.00 E
Paklay	198	18.12 N	101.25 E
Pakokku	200	21.20 N	95.05 E
Pakość	164	52.49 N	18.05 E
Pak Phanang	200	8.21 N	100.12 E
Pakrac	170	45.26 N	17.12 E
Paks	164	46.39 N	18.53 E
Paksé	200	15.07 N	105.47 E
Paktīā □[4]	206	33.30 N	69.30 E
P'akupur ≃	186	65.00 N	77.48 E
Pala, Tchad	214	9.22 N	14.54 E
Pala, Calif., U.S.	274	33.22 N	117.05 W
Palacios	250	28.42 N	96.13 W
Palagonia	170	37.19 N	14.45 E
Palagruža, Otoci II	170	42.24 N	16.15 E
Palaiá Epídhavros	172	37.38 N	23.09 E
Palaiokhóra	172	35.14 N	23.41 E
Palaiseau	176	48.43 N	2.15 E
Palamás	172	39.28 N	22.05 E
Palamós	168	41.51 N	3.08 E
Palana	186	59.07 N	159.58 E
Palanan, Mount ∧	202	17.02 N	122.17 E
Palanan Bay C	202	17.09 N	122.28 E
Palanan Point ≻	202	17.09 N	122.31 E
Palanas	202	12.09 N	123.55 E
Palandöken Dağları ⛰	212	39.47 N	41.15 E
Palangkaraja	198	2.16 S	113.56 E
Palanguinos	168	42.27 N	5.31 W
Palaoa Point ≻	275d	20.44 N	156.58 W
Palapag	202	12.33 N	125.07 E
Palapye	218	22.37 S	27.06 E
Palasan Island I	202	14.51 N	122.03 E
Palas del Rey	168	42.52 N	7.52 W
Palatine	268	42.07 N	88.03 W
Palatka, S.S.S.R.	186	60.06 N	150.54 E
Palatka, Fla., U.S.	246	29.39 N	81.38 W
Palau	250	27.54 N	101.26 W
Palauig	202	15.26 N	119.54 E
Palaui Island I	202	18.33 N	122.08 E
Palau Islands II	198	7.30 N	134.30 E
Palau-Kyushu Ridge ⌖[3]	148	13.00 N	135.00 E
Pal'avaam ≃	236	68.50 N	170.45 E
Pal'avaamskij Chrebet ⛰	236	68.20 N	177.00 E
Palawan I	202	9.30 N	118.30 E
Palawan Passage ⩌	202	10.30 N	118.20 E
Palayan	202	15.33 N	121.06 E
Palazzolo Acreide	170	37.03 N	14.54 E
Palazzolo sull'Oglio	182	45.36 N	9.53 E
Palazzo San Gervaiso	170	40.56 N	16.00 E
P'albong-san ∧	194	40.16 N	127.57 E
Palca, Bol.	292	16.34 S	67.59 W
Palca, Perú	292	11.20 S	75.32 W
Palcamayo	292	11.16 S	75.46 W
Paldi	270	48.48 N	123.51 W
Paldiski	160	59.20 N	24.06 E
Palembang	198	3.00 S	104.45 E
Palena	170	41.59 N	14.08 E
Palencia	168	42.01 N	4.32 W
Palen Lake ⊜	258	33.46 N	115.12 W
Palenque	278	17.31 N	91.58 W
Palenque ≃	290	1.02 S	79.28 W
Palenque ⊥	278	17.30 N	92.00 W
Palenque, Punta ≻	282	18.13 N	70.10 W
Palenville	261	42.10 N	74.01 W
Palermo, Ont., Can.	264	43.26 N	79.47 W
Palermo, Col.	290	2.54 N	75.26 W
Palermo, It.	170	38.07 N	13.21 E
Palermo, Calif., U.S.	272	39.26 N	121.33 W
Palermo, Ur.	294	33.48 S	55.59 W
Palermo, Golfo di C	170	38.10 N	13.30 E
Palestina, Bra.	296	20.23 S	49.25 W
Palestina, Méx.	250	29.10 N	100.55 W
Palestine, Ill., U.S.	248	39.00 N	87.37 W
Palestine, Tex., U.S.	250	31.46 N	95.38 W
Palestine □[9]	210	32.30 N	35.15 E
Palestrina	184	41.50 N	12.53 E
Paletwa	200	21.18 N	92.51 E
Palgrave Point ≻	224	20.45 S	13.20 E
Pāli	206	25.46 N	73.20 E
Palidoro ⬩[8]	184	41.56 N	12.11 E
Palimbang	202	6.12 N	124.11 E
Palimé	222	6.54 N	0.38 E
Palín	280	14.24 N	90.42 W
Palin, Mount ∧	202	6.21 N	117.08 E
Palinges	166	46.33 N	4.13 E
Palisade, Colo., U.S.	254	39.07 N	108.21 W
Palisade, Nebr., U.S.	252	40.21 N	101.07 W
Palisades	256	43.21 N	111.13 W
Palisades Park	268	42.18 N	86.19 W
Palisades Reservoir ⊜[1]	256	43.15 N	111.05 W
Palit, Kep i ≻	172	41.24 N	19.24 E
Palizada	278	18.15 N	92.05 W
Paljenik ∧	170	44.17 N	17.32 E
Palkino, S.S.S.R.	160	58.15 N	42.56 E
Palkino, S.S.S.R.	160	57.32 N	28.01 E
Palk Strait ⩌	204	10.00 N	79.45 E
Pallasca	292	8.12 S	78.00 W
Pallas-Ounastunturin Kansallispuisto ♠	160	68.06 N	24.00 E
Pallastunturi ∧	160	68.06 N	24.00 E
Palling	238	54.21 N	125.55 W
Palliser, Cape ≻	230	41.36 S	175.17 E
Palliser Bay C	230	41.26 S	175.05 E
Palluau	166	46.48 N	1.37 W
Palma, Bra.	296	21.22 S	42.19 W
Palma, Moç.	218	10.46 S	40.29 E
P'al'ma, S.S.S.R.	160	62.26 N	35.53 E
Palma ≃	296	12.33 S	47.52 W
Palma, Bahía de C	168	39.27 N	2.35 E
Palma, Río de la ≃	284p	23.03 N	80.54 W
Palma, Sierra de la ⛰	250	25.55 N	101.40 W
Palma Campania	184	40.52 N	14.33 E
Palma del Río	168	37.42 N	5.17 W
Palma [de Mallorca]	168	39.34 N	2.39 E
Palma di Montechiaro	170	37.11 N	13.46 E
Palmanova	170	45.54 N	13.19 E
Palmar ≃	290	10.10 N	71.50 W
Palmar Camp	278	16.26 N	88.53 W
Palmar de Sepúlveda	278	25.43 N	107.55 W
Palmar de Varela	290	10.45 N	74.45 W
Palmarejo	284m	18.03 N	67.05 W
Palmares, Bra.	286	8.41 S	35.36 W
Palmares, C.R.	280	10.03 N	84.26 W
Palmares, C.R.	280	9.21 N	83.40 W
Palmares do Sul	294	30.16 S	50.31 W
Palmarito	290	7.37 N	70.10 W
Palmar Sur	280	8.58 N	83.29 W
Palmas	294	26.30 S	52.00 W
Palmas, Cape ≻	222	4.22 N	7.44 W
Palmas, Golfo di C	170	39.00 N	8.30 E
Palmas Bellas	280	9.13 N	80.06 W
Palmas de Monte Alto	296	14.16 S	43.10 W
Palma Soriano	284p	20.13 N	76.00 W
Palm Bay	246	28.02 N	80.35 W
Palm Beach	246	26.42 N	80.02 W
Palmdale, Calif., U.S.	274	34.35 N	118.07 W
Palmdale, Fla., U.S.	246	26.57 N	81.19 W
Palmdale, Pa., U.S.	262	40.18 N	76.37 W
Palmeira	294	25.25 S	50.00 W
Palmeira das Missões	294	27.55 S	53.17 W
Palmeira d'Oeste	296	20.23 S	50.47 W
Palmeira dos Índios	286	9.25 S	36.37 W
Palmeiras	296	12.31 S	41.34 W
Palmeiras ≃, Bra.	296	12.22 S	47.08 W
Palmeiras ≃, Bra.	296	15.25 S	51.10 W
Palmelo	296	17.20 S	48.27 W
Palmer, P.R.	284m	18.22 N	65.46 W
Palmer, Alaska, U.S.	236	61.36 N	149.07 W
Palmer, Mass., U.S.	261	42.09 N	72.20 W
Palmer, Mich., U.S.	244	46.27 N	87.35 W
Palmer, Nebr., U.S.	252	41.13 N	98.15 W
Palmer, Tenn., U.S.	248	35.21 N	85.34 W
Palmer, Tex., U.S.	250	32.26 N	96.40 W
Palmer Heights	262	40.42 N	75.16 W
Palmer Lake	254	39.07 N	104.55 W
Palmer Point ≻	232	74.54 N	108.01 W
Palmers Crossing	248	31.16 N	89.15 W
Palmerston	264	43.50 N	80.51 W
Palmerston, Cape ≻	228	21.32 S	149.29 E
Palmerston North	230	40.21 S	175.37 E
Palmerton	242	40.48 N	75.37 W
Palmetto, Fla., U.S.	246	27.31 N	82.35 W
Palmetto, Ga., U.S.	246	33.31 N	84.40 W
Palmetto, La., U.S.	248	30.43 N	91.55 W
Palmi	170	38.21 N	15.51 E
Palminópolis	296	16.47 S	50.08 W
Palmira, Arg.	294	33.03 S	68.34 W
Palmira, Col.	290	3.32 N	76.16 W
Palmira, Cuba	284p	22.14 N	80.23 W
Palmira, Ec.	290	2.05 S	78.43 W
Palmira, Méx.	250	28.58 N	100.47 W
Palmitas	294	33.31 S	57.49 W
Palmito, Presa ⊜[1]	278	25.35 N	105.02 W
Palmitos	294	27.05 S	53.08 W
Palm Springs	258	33.50 N	116.33 W
Palmyra → Tudmur, Sūrīy.	212	34.33 N	38.17 E
Palmyra, Ill., U.S.	248	39.26 N	90.00 W
Palmyra, Mich., U.S.	268	41.52 N	83.56 W
Palmyra, Mo., U.S.	248	39.48 N	91.31 W
Palmyra, N.J., U.S.	262	40.00 N	75.01 W
Palmyra, N.Y., U.S.	264	43.04 N	77.14 W
Palmyra, Ohio, U.S.	266	41.07 N	81.02 W
Palmyra, Pa., U.S.	262	40.18 N	76.36 W
Palmyra, Va., U.S.	246	37.51 N	78.16 W
Palmyra, Wis., U.S.	268	42.53 N	88.35 W
Palo	202	11.10 N	124.59 E
Palo Alto, Méx.	250	26.32 N	99.45 W
Palo Alto, Calif., U.S.	272	37.27 N	122.09 W
Palo Alto, Pa., U.S.	262	40.41 N	76.11 W
Palo Blanco, Méx.	250	26.45 N	101.32 W
Palo Blanco, P.R.	284m	18.26 N	66.39 W
Palo Flechado Pass)(	254	36.30 N	105.30 W
Paloich	214	10.28 N	32.32 E
Palojoensuu	160	68.17 N	23.05 E
Palomar Mountain ∧	258	33.22 N	116.50 W
Palomar Park	272	37.29 N	122.16 W
Palomas	250	28.43 N	103.45 W
Palomas ≃	254	33.03 N	107.16 W
Palomas, Mesa de ∧	278	28.40 N	103.40 W
Palombara Sabina	184	42.04 N	12.46 E
Palometillas ≃	292	16.36 S	64.18 W
Palompon	202	11.03 N	124.23 E
Palo Negro	290	10.11 N	67.33 W
Palo Pinto	250	32.46 N	98.18 W
Palo Pinto Reservoir ⊜[1]	250	32.38 N	98.18 W
Palopo	198	3.00 S	120.12 E
Palora ≃	290	1.51 S	77.49 W
Palos	284p	22.48 N	81.44 W
Palos, Cabo de ≻	168	37.38 N	0.41 W
Palo Santo	294	25.34 S	59.20 W
Palo Seco	284m	18.28 N	66.09 W
Palos Heights	268	41.40 N	87.48 W
Palos Verdes Estates	274	33.48 N	118.24 W
Palouse	256	46.55 N	117.04 W
Palouse ≃	256	46.35 N	118.13 W
Palpa	292	14.30 S	75.15 W
Palpalá	294	24.15 S	65.15 W
Palu	198	0.53 S	119.51 E
Paluan	202	13.25 N	120.28 E
Paluan Bay C	202	13.23 N	120.26 E
Paluga	160	65.16 N	45.11 E
Pambuhan	202	13.59 N	123.05 E
Pambujan	202	12.34 N	124.56 E
Pambunan ≃	202	12.34 N	124.54 E
Pamekasan	198	7.10 S	113.28 E
Pamel	176	50.50 N	4.04 E
Pamiers	166	43.07 N	1.36 E
Pamir ⛰	186	38.00 N	73.00 E
Pamlico ≃	246	35.20 N	76.30 W
Pamlico Sound ⩌	246	35.20 N	75.55 W
Pampa	250	35.32 N	100.58 W
Pampã ≃	296	17.43 S	40.36 W
Pampa Almirón	294	24.15 S	65.12 W
Pampacolca	292	15.42 S	72.35 W
Pampa del Chañar	294	30.11 S	68.43 W
Pampa del Indio	294	26.03 S	59.55 W
Pampa del Infierno	294	26.30 S	61.10 W
Pampa de los Guanacos	294	26.14 S	61.52 W
Pampa Grande	292	18.05 S	64.06 W
Pampana ≃	222	8.24 N	12.00 W
Pampanga □[4]	202	15.05 N	120.40 E
Pampanga ≃	202	14.46 N	120.40 E
Pampas	292	12.20 S	74.56 W
Pampas ≃	292	13.24 S	73.12 W
Pampas ⬩[1]	294	35.00 S	63.00 W
Pamphylia □[9]	212	37.00 N	31.00 E
Pamplico	246	34.00 N	79.34 W
Pamplona, Col.	290	7.23 N	72.39 W
Pamplona, Esp.	168	42.49 N	1.38 W
Pana	248	39.23 N	89.05 W
Panabá	278	21.17 N	88.16 W
Panabo	202	7.19 N	125.42 E
Panaca	258	37.47 N	114.23 W
Panacachi	292	18.23 S	66.21 W
Panacan	202	9.16 N	118.25 E
Panacea	246	30.02 N	84.23 W
Panache, Lake ⊜	244	46.15 N	81.20 W
Panagjurište	172	42.30 N	24.11 E
Panagtaran Point ≻	202	9.40 N	118.45 E
Panaji	204	15.29 N	73.50 E
Panamá, Bra.	296	18.11 S	49.21 W
Panamá, Pan.	280	8.58 N	79.31 W
Panama, Ill., U.S.	248	39.02 N	89.32 W
Panama, N.Y., U.S.	266	42.05 N	79.29 W
Panama, Okla., U.S.	248	35.10 N	94.40 W
Panamá □[4]	280	8.48 N	79.55 W
Panama (Panamá) □[1]	276	9.00 N	80.00 W
Panama, Bay of C	290	8.50 N	79.20 W
Panama, Gulf of C	290	8.00 N	79.10 W
Panama, Isthmus of ⬩[3]	276	9.20 N	79.30 W
Panama Canal ≡	280	9.00 N	79.37 W
Panama City	248	30.10 N	85.41 W
Panamá Viejo ⊥, C.Z.	280	9.00 N	79.30 W
Panamá Viejo ⊥, Pan.	280	9.00 N	79.30 W
Panambi	294	28.18 S	53.30 W
Panamint Range ⛰	258	36.30 N	117.20 W
Pananaw	202	5.59 N	121.13 E
Panao	292	9.52 S	75.55 W
Panaon Island I	202	10.03 N	125.13 E

Symbols in the index entries are identified on page 360.

Name	Page	Lat°′	Long°′
Panarea, Isola I	170	38.38 N	15.05 E
Panaro ≃	170	44.55 N	11.25 E
Panay I	202	11.10 N	122.30 E
Panay ≃	202	11.35 N	122.48 E
Panay Gulf C	202	10.15 N	122.25 E
Panayía	172	39.56 N	25.20 E
Panay Island I	202	13.58 N	124.20 E
Pancas ≃	296	19.30 S	40.36 W
Pančevo	172	44.52 N	20.39 E
Panciu	172	45.55 N	27.05 E
Pandan, Pil.	202	14.03 N	124.10 E
Pandan, Pil.	202	11.43 N	122.06 E
Pandanan Island I	202	8.16 N	117.13 E
Pandan Bay C	202	11.40 N	122.00 E
Pandarochan Bay C	202	12.12 N	121.10 E
Pan de Azúcar	294	34.48 S	55.14 W
Pan de Azucar Island I	202	11.17 N	123.10 E
Pandėlys	160	56.01 N	25.13 E
Pandjang, Pulau I	200	2.44 N	108.55 E
Pandjang, Selat ⊔	200	0.40 N	103.02 E
Pando	294	34.43 S	55.57 W
Pando □[5]	292	11.20 S	67.40 W
Pando, Cerro ∧	280	8.56 N	82.43 W
Pandora	268	40.57 N	83.58 W
P'andž (Āb-i-Panja) ≃	206	37.06 N	68.20 E
Panevėžys	160	55.44 N	24.21 E
Panfilov	186	44.10 N	80.01 E
Pangala	218	3.19 S	14.34 E
Pangalanes, Canal des ☰	225b	22.40 S	47.50 E
Pangani	218	5.26 S	38.58 E
Pangani ≃	218	5.26 S	38.58 E
Panganiran	202	13.02 N	123.26 E
Pangantocan	202	7.50 N	124.49 E
Panganuran	202	7.24 N	122.03 E
Pangasinan □[4]	202	16.00 N	120.20 E
Pangburn	248	35.15 N	91.51 W
Pangfou → Bangbu	196	32.58 N	117.24 E
Pangi	218	3.11 S	26.38 E
Pangkalanbuun	198	2.41 S	111.37 E
Pangkalpinang	198	2.08 S	106.08 E
Panglao	202	9.35 N	123.48 E
Panglao Island I	202	9.35 N	123.48 E
Pangman	252	49.39 N	104.38 W
Pangnirtung	232	66.08 N	65.44 W
Pangubatan	202	6.57 N	125.47 E
Panguil Bay C	202	8.01 N	123.42 E
Panguiranan	202	12.04 N	123.19 E
Panguitch	254	37.49 N	112.26 W
Pangutaran	202	6.18 N	120.35 E
Pangutaran Group II	202	6.15 N	120.35 E
Pangutaran Island I	202	6.18 N	120.32 E
Pangutaran Passage ⊔	202	6.13 N	120.30 E
Pangyan	202	5.42 N	125.17 E
Panhandle	250	35.21 N	101.23 W
Panhe ≃	196	33.11 N	115.07 E
Paniau ∧	275d	21.57 N	160.05 W
Pānīpat	206	29.25 N	76.59 E
Paniqui	202	15.41 N	120.35 E
Panitian	202	9.05 N	118.05 E
Panjgūr	204	26.58 N	64.06 E
Panjim → Panaji	204	15.29 N	73.50 E
Pankof, Cape ≻	236	54.40 N	163.04 W
Pankratovo	160	59.10 N	43.30 E
Pannonhalma ⌂[1]	164	47.28 N	17.50 E
Panola	248	32.57 N	88.16 W
Panora	252	41.42 N	94.22 W
Panorama	296	21.21 S	51.51 W
Pánormos	172	37.38 N	25.02 E
Panovo	160	59.48 N	46.27 E
Pansic ↳	280	14.30 N	85.15 W
Pantabañgan	202	15.50 N	121.09 E
Pantar, Pulau I	198	8.25 S	124.07 E
Pantelleria	170	36.49 N	11.57 E
Pantelleria I	170	36.47 N	12.00 E
Pantex	250	35.20 N	101.35 W
Panther Lake	264	43.19 N	75.54 W
Pantin	176	48.54 N	2.24 E
Pánuco	278	22.03 N	98.10 W
Pánuco ≃	278	22.16 N	97.47 W
Panukulan	202	14.56 N	121.49 E
Panulcillo	294	30.27 S	71.14 W
Panxian	200	25.50 N	104.36 E
Panyam	222	9.25 N	9.13 E
Panyu	196	22.57 N	113.20 E
Panzós	280	15.24 N	89.40 W
Pao ≃, Thai	200	16.12 N	103.40 E
Pao ≃, Ven.	290	8.33 N	68.01 W
Pao ≃, Ven.	290	8.06 N	64.17 W
Paola, It.	170	39.22 N	16.03 E
Paola, Kans., U.S.	252	38.35 N	94.53 W
Paoli, Ind., U.S.	248	38.33 N	86.28 W
Paoli, Pa., U.S.	262	40.02 N	75.29 W
Paoli, Wis., U.S.	268	42.56 N	89.32 W
Paonia	254	38.52 N	107.36 W
Paotow → Baotou	190	40.40 N	109.59 E
Paoting → Baoding	194	38.52 N	115.29 E
Paôy Pêt	198	13.39 N	102.33 E
P'aozero, Ozero ⊚	160	66.05 N	30.58 E
Pápa	164	47.19 N	17.28 E
Papagaio ≃	290	1.53 S	62.35 W
Papagayo, Golfo del C	280	10.45 N	85.45 W
Papago Indian Reservation ↞[4]	254	32.20 N	112.00 W
Papaikou	275d	19.47 N	155.06 W
Papakura	230	37.04 S	174.57 E
Papantla [de Olarte]	278	20.27 N	97.19 W
Paparoa Range ⛰	230	41.56 S	171.38 E
Papatoetoe	230	36.59 S	174.52 E
Papawai Point ≻	275d	20.47 N	156.33 W
Papa Westray I	162	59.22 N	2.54 W
Papa Yacu, Lago ⊚	292	5.05 S	76.25 W
Papenburg	178	53.05 N	7.23 E
Papendrecht	178	51.50 N	4.40 E
Papey I	160a	64.37 N	14.11 W
Paphos → Néa Páfos	212	34.45 N	32.26 E
Papigochic ≃	278	29.09 N	109.40 W
Papillion	252	41.09 N	96.03 W
Papineau	268	40.58 N	87.43 W
Papineau □[6]	260	45.50 N	75.00 W
Papineauville	260	45.37 N	75.01 W
Paposo	294	25.01 S	70.28 W
Papua □[2]	198	8.00 S	144.00 E
Papudo	294	32.31 S	71.27 W
Papulovo	160	60.34 N	48.00 E
Papun	198	18.04 N	97.27 E
Papunaua ≃	290	2.09 N	70.32 W
Papurí ≃	290	0.36 N	69.11 W
Paquera	280	9.50 N	84.56 W
Paquica, Cabo ≻	294	21.54 S	70.12 W
Pará □[3]	290	4.00 S	53.00 W
Pará ≃, Bra.	286	1.30 S	48.55 W
Pará ≃, Bra.	296	19.13 S	45.07 W
Parabel'	186	58.43 N	81.31 E
Parabiago	182	45.33 N	8.57 E
Paracale	202	14.17 N	122.47 E
Paracari ≃	290	4.36 S	57.47 W
Paracas, Península ≻[1]	292	13.53 S	76.20 W
Paracatu	296	17.13 S	46.52 W
Paracatu ≃, Bra.	296	16.35 S	45.06 W
Paracatu ≃, Bra.	296	16.30 S	45.04 W
Paracel Islands II	198	16.30 N	112.15 E
Paracho [de Verduzco]	278	19.39 N	102.04 W
Paraćin	172	43.52 N	21.24 E
Paraconi	290	3.58 S	58.48 W
Parád	164	47.55 N	20.02 E
Parada, Punta ≻	292	15.22 S	75.11 W
Parada Pucheta	294	29.54 S	57.34 W
Paradas	168	37.18 N	5.30 W
Paradise, Calif., U.S.	258	39.46 N	121.37 W
Paradise, Mont., U.S.	256	47.23 N	114.48 W
Paradise, Pa., U.S.	262	40.01 N	76.08 W
Paradise, Tex., U.S.	250	33.09 N	97.41 W
Paradise Hill	236	62.25 N	160.03 W
Paradise Valley, Ariz., U.S.	254	33.32 N	111.57 W
Paradise Valley, Nev., U.S.	258	41.30 N	117.32 W
Parado ≃	292	10.17 S	55.39 W
Paragonah	254	37.53 N	112.46 W
Paragould	248	36.03 N	90.29 W
Paraguá ≃, Bol.	292	13.34 S	61.53 W
Paragua ≃, Ven.	290	6.55 N	62.55 W
Paraguaçu ≃	296	12.45 S	38.54 W
Paraguaçu Paulista	296	22.25 S	50.34 W
Paraguaipoa	290	11.21 N	71.57 W
Paraguaná, Península de ≻[1]	290	11.55 N	70.00 W
Paraguarí	294	25.38 S	57.09 W
Paraguarí □[5]	294	26.00 S	57.10 W
Paraguay □[1]	288	23.00 S	58.00 W
Paraguay ≃	288	27.18 S	58.38 W
Paraíba do Sul ≃	296	21.37 S	41.03 W
Paraibuna	296	23.23 S	45.39 W
Paraibuna ≃	296	23.22 S	45.40 W
Paraíso, Bra.	296	19.03 S	52.59 W
Paraíso, C.Z.	280	9.03 N	79.38 W
Paraíso, C.R.	280	9.50 N	83.51 W
Paraíso, Méx.	278	18.24 N	93.14 W
Paraíso, Serra do ⛰[1]	296	15.53 S	53.47 W
Paraíso do Norte	296	23.13 S	52.38 W
Paraisópolis	296	22.33 S	45.47 W
Paraitinga ≃	296	23.22 S	45.40 W
Parakou	222	9.21 N	2.37 E
Paramaribo	286	5.50 N	55.10 W
Paramillo ∧	290	7.04 N	75.55 W
Paramirim	296	13.26 S	42.15 W
Paramirim ≃	296	11.34 S	43.18 W
Paramithiá	172	39.28 N	20.30 E
Paramonga	292	10.40 S	77.50 W
Paramount	274	33.53 N	118.09 W
Paramus	242	40.57 N	74.04 W
Paramušir, Ostrov I	186	50.25 N	155.50 E
Paraná, Arg.	294	31.45 S	60.30 W
Paranã, Bra.	296	12.33 S	47.52 W
Paraná □[3]	296	24.00 S	51.00 W
Paranã ≃, Bra.	296	12.30 S	48.14 W
Paraná ≃, S.A.	288	33.43 S	59.15 W
Paranaguá	294	25.31 S	48.30 W
Paranaguá, Baía de C	294	25.29 S	48.33 W
Paranaíba	296	19.40 S	51.11 W
Paranaíba ≃	296	20.07 S	51.05 W
Paranaíta ≃	292	9.28 S	56.43 W
Paranam	286	5.35 N	55.10 W
Paranapanema ≃	296	22.40 S	53.09 W
Paranapiacaba, Serra do ⛰	294	24.20 S	49.00 W
Paranavaí	296	23.04 S	52.28 W
Parang, Pil.	202	7.23 N	124.16 E
Parang, Pil.	202	5.55 N	120.54 E
Parangaba	286	3.45 S	38.33 W
Paranhos	296	23.55 S	55.25 W
Paraopeba	296	19.18 S	44.25 W
Parapara	290	9.44 N	67.18 W
Parapetí ≃	292	18.58 S	62.21 W
Parás, Méx.	250	26.30 N	99.31 W
Paras, Perú	292	13.26 S	74.38 W
Parasan	202	8.05 N	123.33 E
Paratinga	296	12.42 S	43.10 W
Parauari ≃	290	4.36 S	57.47 W
Paraúna	296	17.02 S	50.26 W
Paray-le-Monial	166	46.27 N	4.07 E
Pārbati ≃	206	25.51 N	76.34 E
Parchim	164	53.25 N	11.51 E
Parchment	268	42.19 N	85.33 W
Parczew	164	51.39 N	22.54 E
Pardeeville	244	43.32 N	89.18 W
Pardes Ẕanna	210	32.28 N	34.58 E
Pardo ≃, Bra.	294	29.59 S	52.23 W
Pardo ≃, Bra.	294	21.46 S	52.09 W
Pardo ≃, Bra.	296	15.39 S	38.57 W
Pardo ≃, Bra.	296	15.48 S	44.48 W
Pardo ≃, Bra.	296	20.10 S	48.38 W
Pardo ≃, Bra.	296	22.55 S	49.58 W
Pardubice	164	50.02 N	15.47 E
Parecis	292	14.09 S	56.56 W
Parecis ≃	292	12.56 S	56.43 W
Parecis, Serra dos ⛰	292	13.00 S	60.00 W
Paredes de Nava	168	42.09 N	4.41 W
Paredón	278	25.56 N	100.58 W
Paren'	186	62.28 N	163.05 E
Paren' ≃	186	62.25 N	163.10 E
Parengarenga Harbour C	230	34.31 S	172.57 E
Parent	232	47.55 N	74.37 W
Parent, Lac ⊚	244	48.40 N	77.00 W
Parentis-en-Born	166	44.21 N	1.05 W
Parepare	198	4.01 S	119.38 E
Parera	294	35.08 S	64.32 W
Parfenjevo, S.S.S.R.	160	61.21 N	42.43 E
Parfenjevo, S.S.S.R.	160	58.29 N	43.25 E
Parfino	160	57.58 N	31.41 E
Párga	172	39.17 N	20.23 E
Pargas (Parainen)	160	60.18 N	22.18 E
Parham	284c	17.05 N	61.46 W
Paria ≃	254	36.52 N	111.36 W
Paria, Gulf of C	290	10.20 N	62.00 W
Paria, Península de ≻[1]	285r	10.40 N	62.30 W
Pariaguán	290	8.51 N	64.43 W
Pariaman	200	0.38 S	100.08 E
Pariamanu ≃	292	12.27 S	69.15 W
Paricá, Lago ⊚	290	1.53 S	65.45 W
Parícutin ∧[1]	278	19.28 N	102.15 W
Parida, Isla I	280	8.06 N	82.20 W
Parika	290	6.51 N	58.26 W
Parikkala	160	61.33 N	29.30 E
Parima ≃	290	3.34 N	63.47 W
Parima, Sierra ⛰	290	2.30 N	64.00 W
Pariñas, Punta ≻	290	4.40 S	81.20 W
Parîngul ∧	172	45.22 N	23.33 E
Parintins	290	2.36 S	56.44 W
Pariquera-Açu	294	24.43 S	47.53 W
Paris, Ont., Can.	264	43.12 N	80.23 W
Paris, Fr.	176	48.52 N	2.20 E
Paris, Ark., U.S.	248	35.18 N	93.44 W
Paris, Idaho, U.S.	256	42.14 N	111.24 W
Paris, Ill., U.S.	248	39.36 N	87.42 W
Paris, Ky., U.S.	242	38.13 N	84.14 W
Paris, Maine, U.S.	242	44.16 N	70.30 W
Paris, Mo., U.S.	248	39.29 N	92.00 W
Paris, Ohio, U.S.	266	40.48 N	81.10 W
Paris, Pa., U.S.	266	40.24 N	80.31 W
Paris, Tenn., U.S.	248	36.19 N	88.20 W
Paris, Tex., U.S.	250	33.40 N	95.33 W
Parish	264	43.24 N	76.08 W
Parismina	280	10.12 N	83.38 W
Parismina ≃	280	10.18 N	83.01 W
Parita, Bahía de C	280	8.10 N	80.20 W
Parita, Golfo de C	290	8.10 N	80.20 W
Parit Buntar	200	5.05 N	100.29 E
Park ≃	252	48.28 N	97.09 W
Parkano	160	62.01 N	23.01 E
Park City, Ill., U.S.	268	42.21 N	87.53 W
Park City, Kans., U.S.	252	37.46 N	97.19 W
Park City, Mont., U.S.	256	45.38 N	108.55 W
Park City, Utah, U.S.	254	40.39 N	111.30 W
Parkdale, P.E.I., Can.	240	46.15 N	63.07 W
Parkdale, Oreg., U.S.	270	45.31 N	121.36 W
Parker, Ariz., U.S.	254	34.09 N	114.17 W
Parker, Fla., U.S.	248	30.08 N	85.36 W
Parker, Ind., U.S.	248	40.11 N	85.12 W
Parker, Pa., U.S.	266	41.06 N	79.41 W
Parker, S. Dak., U.S.	252	43.24 N	97.08 W
Parker, Cape ≻	232	75.04 N	79.40 W
Parkerdale	268	41.07 N	85.06 W
Parker Dam	258	34.17 N	114.09 W
Parker Peak ∧	252	43.24 N	103.41 W
Parkersburg, Ill., U.S.	248	38.36 N	88.03 W
Parkersburg, Iowa, U.S.	244	42.35 N	92.47 W
Parkersburg, W. Va., U.S.	242	39.17 N	81.32 W
Parkers Prairie	252	46.09 N	95.20 W
Parker Volcano ∧[1]	202	6.05 N	124.53 E
Parkes	228	33.08 S	148.11 E
Parkesburg	262	39.58 N	75.55 W
Park Falls	244	45.56 N	90.32 W
Park Forest	268	41.28 N	87.38 W
Park Hall	262	38.13 N	76.26 W
Parkhill, Ont., Can.	244	43.09 N	81.41 W
Parkhill, Pa., U.S.	266	40.22 N	78.52 W
Parkin	248	35.16 N	90.34 W
Park Lake	268	42.48 N	84.27 W
Parkland	270	47.09 N	122.26 W
Park Lane	261	41.36 N	73.25 W
Parkman	266	41.22 N	81.04 W
Park Plateau ⛰[1]	254	37.15 N	104.45 W
Park Range ⛰	254	40.00 N	106.30 W
Park Rapids	252	46.55 N	95.04 W
Park Ridge	268	42.01 N	87.50 W
Park River	252	48.24 N	97.45 W
Parkrose	270	45.34 N	122.33 W
Park Shore Resort	268	41.55 N	85.59 W
Parksley	262	37.47 N	75.39 W
Parkston	252	43.24 N	97.59 W
Parksville	238	49.19 N	124.19 W
Parkville, Md., U.S.	262	39.23 N	76.32 W
Parkville, Mo., U.S.	252	39.11 N	94.41 W
Parkway	272	38.30 N	121.27 W
Parlier	272	36.37 N	119.32 W
Parma, It.	170	44.48 N	10.20 E
Parma, Idaho, U.S.	256	43.47 N	116.57 W
Parma, Mich., U.S.	268	42.15 N	84.36 W
Parma, Mo., U.S.	248	36.37 N	89.48 W
Parma, Ohio, U.S.	266	41.22 N	81.43 W
Parma ≃	170	44.56 N	10.26 E
Parma Heights	266	41.23 N	81.45 W
Parnaguá	286	10.13 S	44.38 W
Parnaíba	286	2.54 S	41.47 W
Parnassós ∧	172	38.32 N	22.35 E
Parnell	268	40.14 N	88.42 W
Párnis ∧	172	38.11 N	23.42 E
Parnon ⛰	172	37.18 N	22.35 E
Pärnu	160	58.24 N	24.32 E
Paro	204	27.26 N	89.25 E
Paromaj	186	52.50 N	143.02 E
Paroo ≃	228	31.28 S	143.32 E
Paropamisus ⛰	208	34.40 N	62.50 E
Páros	172	37.04 N	25.08 E
Páros I	172	37.08 N	25.12 E
Parowan	254	37.51 N	112.57 W
Parpaillon ⛰	166	44.30 N	6.40 E
Parr	268	41.02 N	87.13 W
Parral, Chile	294	36.09 S	71.50 W
Parral → Hidalgo del Parral, Méx.	278	26.56 N	105.40 W
Parral, Ohio, U.S.	266	40.33 N	81.30 W
Parramatta	228	33.49 S	151.00 E
Parras de la Fuente	278	25.25 N	102.11 W
Parrish, Ala., U.S.	248	33.44 N	87.17 W
Parrish, Fla., U.S.	246	27.35 N	82.25 W
Parrita	280	9.30 N	84.19 W
Parrsboro	240	45.24 N	64.20 W
Parry, Cape ≻	232	70.08 N	124.24 W
Parry, Mount ∧	238	52.53 N	128.45 W
Parry Bay C	232	68.07 N	82.00 W
Parry Island I	244	45.18 N	80.10 W
Parry Peninsula ≻[1]	236	69.45 N	124.30 W
Parry Sound	264	45.21 N	80.02 W
Parry Sound □[6]	264	45.25 N	79.55 W
Parryville	262	40.49 N	75.40 W
Parsberg	164	49.09 N	11.43 E
Parsęta ≃	164	54.12 N	15.33 E
Parshall	252	47.57 N	102.08 W
Parsnip ≃	238	55.10 N	123.00 W
Parsons, Kans., U.S.	252	37.20 N	95.16 W
Parsons, Tenn., U.S.	248	35.39 N	88.07 W
Parsons, W. Va., U.S.	242	39.06 N	79.41 W
Parsons Pond ⊚	240	50.00 N	57.35 W
Partanna	170	37.43 N	12.53 E
Parthenay	166	46.39 N	0.15 W
Partinico	170	38.03 N	13.07 E
Partizánske	164	48.39 N	18.23 E
Partridge Point ≻	240	50.09 N	56.10 W
Parú ≃	290	4.20 N	66.27 W
Parubcan	202	13.42 N	123.45 E
Paruro	292	13.50 S	71.51 W
Pârvomaj	172	42.06 N	25.13 E
Parwān □[4]	206	35.15 N	69.30 E
Parys	224	27.04 S	27.16 E
Pasacao	202	13.31 N	123.03 E
Pasaco	280	13.59 N	90.12 W
Pasadena, Newf., Can.	240	49.01 N	57.36 W
Pasadena, Calif., U.S.	274	34.09 N	118.09 W
Pasadena, Tex., U.S.	250	29.42 N	95.13 W
Pasado, Cabo ≻	290	0.22 S	80.30 W
Pasai, Pegunungan ⛰	200	4.50 N	97.05 E
Pasaje	290	3.20 S	79.49 W
Pasaje ≃	294	25.39 S	63.56 W
Pa Sak ≃	200	14.11 N	100.40 E
Pasaleng Bay C	202	18.36 N	120.57 E
Paşalimanı Adası I	212	40.28 N	27.37 E
Pasatiempo	272	37.02 N	122.02 W
Pascagama, Lac ⊚	244	48.54 N	75.36 W
Pascagoula	248	30.23 N	88.31 W
Pascagoula ≃	248	30.21 N	88.34 W
Pascalis, Lac ⊚	244	48.15 N	77.25 W
Paşcani	172	47.15 N	26.44 E
Pasco	256	46.14 N	119.06 W
Pasco □[5]	292	10.30 S	75.15 W
Pascoag	261	41.57 N	71.42 W
Pascua, Isla de (Easter Island) I	148	27.07 S	109.22 W
Pas-de-Calais □[5]	176	50.30 N	2.20 E
Pasewalk	164	53.30 N	14.00 E
Pasig	202	14.34 N	121.05 E
P'asina ≃	186	73.50 N	87.10 E
Pasing ↞[8]	164	48.08 N	11.27 E
P'asino, Ozero ⊚	186	69.45 N	87.45 E
P'asinskij Zaliv C	186	74.00 N	86.00 E
Pasión, Río de la ≃	280	16.28 N	90.33 W
Pasir Mas	200	6.02 N	102.07 E
Pasir Puteh	200	5.48 N	102.24 E
Pasłęk (Preussisch Holland)	164	54.05 N	19.39 E
Pasley Bay C	232	70.40 N	96.27 W
Pašman, Otok I	170	43.58 N	15.21 E
Pasmore ≃	228	31.07 S	139.48 E
Pašn'a	160	63.21 N	56.28 E
Pasni	208	25.16 N	63.28 E
Paso de Indios	288	43.50 S	69.06 W
Paso del Cerro	294	31.29 S	55.50 W
Paso de los Libres	294	29.45 S	57.05 W
Paso de los Toros	294	32.49 S	56.31 W
Paso de Patria	294	27.13 S	58.35 W
Paso de San Antonio	250	29.05 N	103.55 W
Paso Hondo	278	15.49 N	92.02 W
Pasorapa	292	18.16 S	64.37 W
Paso Robles	272	35.38 N	120.41 W
Paso Seco	284m	17.59 N	66.23 W
Pašozero	160	60.02 N	34.37 E
Pasquotank □[6]	262	36.26 N	76.26 W
Pasquotank ≃	246	36.10 N	76.03 W
Passadumkeag	242	45.11 N	68.37 W
Passadumkeag Mountain ∧	242	45.10 N	68.20 W
Passagem	296	12.11 S	43.14 W
Passage West	162	51.52 N	8.20 W
Passaic	242	40.51 N	74.08 W
Passamaquoddy Bay C	240	45.06 N	66.59 W
Passau	164	48.35 N	13.28 E
Passero, Capo ≻	170	36.40 N	15.09 E
Pass Island	240	47.29 N	56.11 W
Passo Fundo	294	28.15 S	52.24 W
Passo Fundo ≃	294	27.16 S	52.42 W
Passos	296	20.43 S	46.37 W
Passy ↞[8]	166	48.52 N	2.17 E
Pastaza □[4]	290	2.00 S	77.00 W
Pastaza ≃	290	4.50 S	76.25 W
Pastecho ≃	238	56.07 N	114.15 W
Pastęka ≃	164	54.26 N	19.45 E
Pasteur, Lac ⊚	240	50.15 N	66.57 W
Pastillo	284m	17.59 N	66.29 W
Pasto	290	1.13 N	77.17 W
Pastol Bay C	236	63.07 N	163.15 W
Pastora Peak ∧	254	36.47 N	109.10 W
Pastrana	168	40.25 N	2.55 W
Pasuquin	202	18.20 N	120.37 E
Pasuruan	198	7.38 S	112.54 E
Pasvalys	160	56.04 N	24.24 E
Pásztó	164	47.55 N	19.42 E
Pata	202	5.52 N	121.10 E
Patacamaya	292	17.14 S	67.55 W
Patache, Punta ≻	292	20.49 S	70.13 W
Patagonia	254	31.33 N	110.45 W
Pata Island I	202	5.48 N	121.10 E
Pātan	206	23.51 N	72.06 E
Patapsco	262	39.32 N	76.54 W
Patargān, Daqq-e ☷	208	33.30 N	60.40 E
Pataz	292	7.45 S	77.35 W
Patchogue	242	40.46 N	73.00 W
Patea	230	39.45 S	174.28 E
Patea ≃	230	39.46 S	174.29 E
Paterna	168	39.30 N	0.26 W
Paternion	164	46.43 N	13.38 E
Paternò	170	37.34 N	14.54 E
Pateros	238	48.03 N	119.54 W
Paterson	242	40.55 N	74.10 W
Pathānkot	206	32.17 N	75.40 E
Pathfinder Reservoir ⊚[1]	254	42.30 N	106.50 W
Pati ≃	290	3.41 S	67.37 W
Patía	290	2.04 N	77.04 W
Patía ≃	290	2.13 N	78.40 W
Patiāla	206	30.19 N	76.23 E
P'atigorsk	158	44.03 N	43.04 E
Patikul	202	6.04 N	121.06 E
Patillas	284m	18.00 N	66.01 W
Pătîrlagele	172	45.19 N	26.22 E
Pativilca	292	10.42 S	77.48 W
Pativilca ≃	292	10.43 S	77.47 W
Pātkai Range ⛰	206	27.00 N	96.00 E
Pátmos I	212	37.20 N	26.33 E
Patna	206	21.56 N	87.52 E
Patnanongan Island I	202	14.48 N	122.10 E
Patnoñgon	202	10.55 N	122.00 E
Pato Branco	294	26.13 S	52.40 W
Patoka	248	38.45 N	89.06 W
Patoka ≃	248	38.25 N	87.44 W
Patos	286	7.01 S	37.16 W
Patos, Cachoeira dos ↳	292	9.20 S	60.15 W
Patos, Lagoa dos C	294	31.06 S	51.15 W
Patos, Río de los ≃	294	31.17 S	69.23 W
Patos, Rio dos ≃, Bra.	292	13.33 S	56.29 W
Patos, Rio dos ≃, Bra.	296	14.59 S	48.46 W
Patos de Minas	296	18.35 S	46.32 W
Patquía	294	30.02 S	66.55 W
Pátrai	172	38.15 N	21.44 E
Patraïkós Kólpos C	172	38.14 N	21.15 E
Patreksfjörđur (Vatneyri)	160a	65.38 N	23.57 W
Patricio Lynch, Isla I	288	48.35 S	75.30 W
Patrick Air Force Base ■	246	28.15 N	80.36 W
Patrocínio	296	18.57 S	46.59 W
Patrocínio Paulista	296	20.38 S	47.17 W
Patroon	248	31.38 N	93.59 W
Pattada	170	40.35 N	9.07 E
Pattani	200	6.51 N	101.16 E
Pattani ≃	200	6.53 N	101.16 E
Patten	242	46.01 N	68.27 W
Pattenburg	262	40.38 N	75.01 W
Patterson, Calif., U.S.	272	37.28 N	121.07 W
Patterson, Ga., U.S.	246	31.23 N	82.08 W
Patterson, La., U.S.	248	29.42 N	91.18 W
Patterson, N.Y., U.S.	261	41.31 N	73.36 W
Patterson, Ohio, U.S.	268	40.47 N	83.32 W
Patterson, Mount ∧	236	64.04 N	134.39 W
Patterson Gardens	268	41.56 N	83.25 W
Patterson Heights	266	40.45 N	80.19 W
Patterson Island I	244	48.39 N	87.00 W
Patti	170	38.09 N	14.58 E
Patti, Golfo di C	170	38.12 N	15.05 E
Pattison	248	31.53 N	90.53 W
Patton	266	40.38 N	78.39 W
Pattonsburg	248	40.03 N	94.08 W
Patton Seamount Group ✣[3]	148	55.30 N	149.30 W
Pattullo, Mount ∧	236	56.14 N	129.39 W
Patuca ≃	280	15.50 N	84.18 W
Patuca, Punta ≻	280	15.50 N	84.16 W
Patulul	280	14.25 N	91.10 W
Pat'ung Kuan)(	196	23.30 N	121.01 E
Patutu ∧	230	39.15 S	175.51 E
Pátzcuaro	278	19.31 N	101.36 W
Patzicía	280	14.38 N	90.56 W
Patzún	280	14.41 N	91.01 W
Pau	166	43.18 N	0.22 W
Pau, Gave de ≃	166	43.33 N	1.12 W
Pau Brasil	296	15.27 S	39.39 W
Paucarbamba	292	12.25 S	74.25 W
Paucarpata	292	16.23 S	71.31 W
Paucartambo	292	13.19 S	71.35 W
Pauini	292	7.40 S	66.58 W
Pauini ≃, Bra.	290	1.42 S	62.50 W
Pauini ≃, Bra.	292	7.47 S	67.05 W
Pauk	198	21.27 N	94.27 E
Pauksa Taung ∧	200	19.55 N	94.18 E
Paul	256	42.40 N	113.36 W
Paul, Lac à ⊚	240	49.52 N	70.46 W
Paula Lima	296	21.35 S	43.29 W
Paulaya ≃	280	15.48 N	85.06 W
Paulding, Miss., U.S.	248	32.02 N	89.02 W
Paulding, Ohio, U.S.	268	41.08 N	84.35 W
Paulding □[6]	268	41.08 N	84.35 W
Paulhan	166	43.32 N	3.27 E
Paulicéia	296	21.17 S	51.51 W
Paulina Peak ∧	256	43.41 N	121.15 W
Pauline, Mount ∧	238	53.33 N	119.54 W
Paulistana	286	8.09 S	41.09 W
Paulistas	296	18.25 S	42.52 W
Paullina	252	42.59 N	95.41 W
Paullo	182	45.25 N	9.24 E
Paulo Afonso	286	9.21 S	38.14 W
Paulo de Faria	296	20.02 S	49.24 W
Pauloff Harbor (Pavlof Harbor)	236	54.27 N	162.42 W
Paulsboro	262	39.50 N	75.15 W
Pauls Cross Roads	262	37.52 N	76.53 W
Pauls Valley	250	34.44 N	97.13 W
Paungde	200	18.29 N	95.30 E
Pausa	292	15.16 S	73.22 W
Paute	290	2.47 S	79.50 W
Paute ≃	290	2.46 S	78.16 W
Pauto ≃	290	5.09 N	70.55 W
Pauwela	275a	20.56 N	156.19 W
Pavant Range ⛰	254	39.00 N	112.15 W
Pavia	182	45.10 N	9.10 E
Pavia □[4]	182	45.07 N	9.08 E
Pavilion, B.C., Can.	238	50.52 N	121.50 W
Pavilion, N.Y., U.S.	264	42.53 N	70.81 W
Pavillion	254	43.15 N	108.42 W
Pavilly	166	49.34 N	0.58 E
Pāvilosta	160	56.53 N	21.14 E
Pavino	160	59.07 N	46.07 E
Pavlikeni	172	43.14 N	25.18 E
Pavlodar	186	52.18 N	76.57 E
Pavlof Bay C	236	55.30 N	161.32 W
Pavlof Volcano ∧[1]	236	55.24 N	161.52 W
Pavlovo	158	55.58 N	43.04 E
Pavo	246	30.57 N	83.45 W
Pavón	290	3.37 N	72.15 W
Pavonia	266	40.49 N	82.26 W
Pavullo nel Frignano	170	44.20 N	10.50 E
Pavy	160	58.03 N	29.30 E
Pawan ≃	198	1.51 S	109.57 E
Pawcatuck	261	41.22 N	71.52 W
Paw Creek	246	35.17 N	80.56 W
Pawhuska	250	36.40 N	96.20 W
Pawling	261	41.34 N	73.36 W
Pawnee, Ill., U.S.	248	39.35 N	89.35 W
Pawnee, Okla., U.S.	250	36.20 N	96.48 W
Pawnee ≃	252	38.10 N	99.06 W
Pawnee City	252	40.07 N	96.09 W
Pawnee Rock	252	38.16 N	99.01 W
Pawpaw, Ill., U.S.	268	41.41 N	88.59 W
Paw Paw, Mich., U.S.	268	42.13 N	85.53 W
Paw Paw, W. Va., U.S.	242	39.32 N	78.27 W
Paw Paw Lake	268	42.12 N	86.15 W
Pawtucket	261	41.53 N	71.23 W
Paxoí I	172	39.12 N	20.12 E
Paxson	236	63.02 N	145.30 W
Paxton, Ill., U.S.	268	40.27 N	88.06 W
Paxton, Mass., U.S.	261	42.19 N	71.56 W
Paxton, Nebr., U.S.	252	41.07 N	101.21 W
Paxtonia	262	40.19 N	76.48 W
Paxtonville	262	40.46 N	77.05 W
Paya	280	15.37 N	85.17 W
Payas, Cerro ∧	280	15.45 N	84.56 W
Payerne	180	46.49 N	6.56 E
Payette	256	44.05 N	116.56 W
Payette ≃	256	44.05 N	116.57 W
Payette Lake ⊚[1]	256	44.57 N	116.05 W
Payne	268	41.05 N	84.44 W
Payne, Baie C	232	60.00 N	69.45 W
Payne, Lac ⊚	232	59.30 N	74.00 W
Payne Bay	232	60.00 N	70.01 W
Paynesville	252	45.23 N	94.43 W
Paysandú	294	32.19 S	58.05 W
Payson, Ariz., U.S.	254	34.14 N	111.20 W
Payson, Ill., U.S.	248	39.49 N	73.14 W
Payson, Utah, U.S.	254	40.03 N	111.44 W
Payún, Cerro ∧	294	36.31 S	69.17 W
Paz ≃	280	13.44 N	90.10 W
Pazarcık	172	40.00 N	29.54 E
Pazardžik	172	42.12 N	24.20 E
Pazarköy	172	39.51 N	27.24 E
Pazaryeri	172	38.05 N	28.14 E
Paz de Ariporo	290	5.53 N	71.54 W
Paz de Río	290	5.59 N	72.47 W
P'ažijeva Sel'ga	160	61.29 N	34.29 E
Pazin	170	45.14 N	13.56 E
Pazña	292	18.36 S	66.55 W
Pea ≃	248	31.01 N	85.51 W
Peabody, Kans., U.S.	252	38.10 N	97.07 W
Peabody, Mass., U.S.	261	42.32 N	70.55 W
Peace ≃, Can.	232	59.00 N	111.25 W
Peace ≃, Fla., U.S.	246	26.55 N	82.05 W
Peace Dale	261	41.27 N	71.30 W
Peace River	238	56.14 N	117.17 W
Peach Creek	242	37.53 N	81.59 W
Peachland	238	49.46 N	119.44 W
Peach Springs ↞	254	35.32 N	113.25 W
Peacock Hills ⛰[2]	232	66.05 N	110.45 W
Peak District National Park ♣	162	53.17 N	1.45 W
Peaked Mountain ∧	240	46.34 N	68.49 W
Peak Hill	226	25.38 S	118.43 E
Peäldoaivi ∧	160	69.11 N	26.36 E
Peale, Mount ∧	254	38.26 N	109.14 W
Pearblossom	274	34.30 N	117.55 W
Pearce	254	31.54 N	109.49 W
Peard Bay C	236	70.51 N	159.10 W
Pea Ridge National Military Park ♣	248	36.29 N	94.06 W
Pearisburg	246	37.20 N	80.44 W
Pearl, Ill., U.S.	248	39.28 N	90.38 W
Pearl, Miss., U.S.	248	32.18 N	90.12 W
Pearl ≃	248	30.11 N	89.32 W
Pearland	250	29.34 N	95.17 W
Pearl Bank ✣[4]	202	5.50 N	119.52 E
Pearl Beach	266	42.37 N	82.35 W
Pearl City	275c	21.24 N	157.59 W
Pearl Harbor Naval Station ■	275c	21.21 N	157.57 W
Pearl Peak ∧	258	40.14 N	115.32 W
Pearl River, La., U.S.	248	30.23 N	89.45 W
Pearl River, N.Y., U.S.	242	41.04 N	74.02 W
Pearsall	250	28.53 N	99.06 W
Pearse Island I	238	54.51 N	130.21 W
Pearsoll Peak ∧	256	42.18 N	123.50 W
Pearson	246	31.18 N	82.51 W
Pease ≃	250	34.12 N	99.07 W
Pebane	218	17.10 S	38.08 E
Pebas	290	3.17 S	71.55 W
Pebble Beach	272	36.34 N	121.57 W
Peć	172	42.40 N	20.19 E
Pecan Bayou ≃	250	31.28 N	98.43 W
Pecan Gap	250	33.26 N	95.51 W
Peçanha	296	18.33 S	42.34 W
Peças, Ilha das I	294	25.26 S	48.19 W
Pecatonica	244	42.19 N	89.22 W
Pecatonica ≃	244	42.27 N	89.05 W
Pečenga	160	69.33 N	31.07 E
Pechora → Pečora ≃	160	68.13 N	54.10 E
Pecica	172	46.10 N	21.05 E
Peck	244	43.16 N	82.49 W
Pečora	160	65.10 N	57.11 E
Pečora (Pechora) ≃, S.S.S.R.	160	68.13 N	54.10 E
Pečora ≃, S.S.S.R.	186	66.00 N	52.30 E
Pecoraro, Monte ∧	170	38.32 N	16.20 E
Pečoro-Ilyčskij Zapovednik ↞[4]	160	62.20 N	59.00 E
Pečorskaja Guba C	160	68.40 N	54.45 E
Pečorskoje More ▾[2]	160	70.00 N	54.00 E
Pečory	160	57.49 N	27.36 E
Pecos, N. Mex., U.S.	254	35.29 N	105.41 W
Pecos, Tex., U.S.	250	31.25 N	103.30 W
Pecos ≃	250	29.42 N	101.22 W
Pecos National Monument ♣	254	35.26 N	105.56 W
Pecos Plains ≚	250	33.20 N	104.30 W
Pecquencourt	176	50.23 N	3.13 E
Pécs	164	46.05 N	18.13 E
Pedasí	290	7.32 N	80.03 W
Pedernales, Arg.	294	35.16 S	59.37 W
Pedernales, Rep. Dom.	282	18.02 N	71.44 W
Pedernales, Ven.	290	9.58 N	62.16 W
Pedernales ≃	250	30.26 N	98.04 W
Pedernales, Salar de ≚	294	26.15 S	69.10 W
Pedjantan, Pulau I	200	0.07 N	107.14 E
Pedley	274	33.59 N	117.28 W
Pedra Azul	296	16.01 S	41.16 W
Pedra Grande, Recifes da ✣[2]	296	17.45 S	38.58 W
Pedras	290	2.48 S	57.16 W
Pedras, Rio das ≃	296	12.13 S	45.15 W
Pedras Negras	292	12.51 S	62.54 W
Pedras Salgadas	168	41.32 N	7.36 W
Pedraza	290	10.11 N	74.55 W
Pedregal, Pan.	280	8.22 N	82.27 W
Pedregal, Ven.	290	11.01 N	70.08 W
Pedregulho	296	20.16 S	47.29 W
Pedreiras	286	4.30 S	44.35 W
Pedriceña	278	25.06 N	103.47 W
Pedricktown	262	39.46 N	75.24 W
Pedro Afonso	286	8.59 S	48.11 W
Pedro Bay	236	59.47 N	154.07 W
Pedro Betancourt	284p	22.44 N	81.17 W
Pedro de Valdivia	294	22.36 S	69.40 W
Pedrogão Grande	168	39.55 N	8.09 W
Pedro Gomes	296	18.04 S	54.32 W
Pedro González, Isla I	290	8.22 N	79.07 W
Pedro II	286	4.25 S	41.28 W
Pedro Juan Caballero, Bra.	296	22.34 S	55.37 W
Pedro Juan Caballero, Para.	294	22.34 S	55.37 W
Pedro Leopoldo	296	19.38 S	44.03 W
Pedro Luro	294	39.30 S	62.42 W
Pedro Muñoz	168	39.24 N	2.58 W
Pedro Osório	294	31.51 S	52.45 W
Pedro R. Fernández	294	28.40 S	58.40 W
Peebles, Scot., U.K.	162	55.39 N	3.12 W
Peebles, Ohio, U.S.	242	38.57 N	83.24 W
Peebles □[6]	162	55.37 N	3.15 W
Pee Dee ≃	246	33.21 N	79.16 W
Peekaboo Mountain ∧[2]	242	45.45 N	67.53 W
Peekskill	261	41.17 N	73.55 W
Peel	162	54.13 N	4.40 W
Peel □[6]	264	43.45 N	79.47 W
Peel ≃	236	67.37 N	134.40 W
Peel Channel ≃[1]	236	68.13 N	135.00 W
Pe Ell	270	46.34 N	123.18 W
Peel Point ≻	232	73.22 N	114.35 W
Peel Sound ⊔	232	73.15 N	96.30 W
Peer	178	51.08 N	5.28 E
Peerless	256	48.47 N	105.50 W
Peers	238	53.40 N	116.00 W
Peetz	252	40.58 N	103.07 W
Pefferlaw	264	44.19 N	79.12 W
Pegasus Bay C	230	43.20 S	172.55 E
Pegnitz	164	49.45 N	11.33 E
Pegnitz ≃	164	49.29 N	11.00 E
Pego	168	38.51 N	0.07 W
Pegtymel' ≃	236	69.25 N	174.35 E
Pegtymel'skij Chrebet ⛰	236	68.30 N	175.00 E
Pegu	200	17.20 N	96.29 E
Pegu □[8]	200	17.30 N	96.30 E
Pegu ≃	200	16.47 N	96.13 E
Pegu Yoma ⛰	200	19.00 N	95.50 E
Pegyš	160	63.26 N	50.30 E
Pehčevo	172	41.46 N	22.54 E
Pehlivanköy	172	41.21 N	26.55 E
Pehuajó	294	35.45 S	61.58 W
Peichiang Ch'i ≃	196	23.32 N	120.09 E
Peigan Indian Reserve ↞[4], Alta., Can.	238	49.35 N	113.40 W
Peigan Indian Reserve ↞[4], Alta., Can.	238	49.45 N	113.55 W
Peikang	196	23.35 N	120.19 E
Peinanta Ch'i ≃	196	22.46 N	121.10 E
Peine	178	52.19 N	10.13 E
Peinnechaung I	200	19.59 N	93.04 E
Peip'ing → Beijing	194	39.55 N	116.25 E
Peïra-Cava	170	43.56 N	7.22 E
Peirce, Cape ≻	236	58.35 N	161.47 W
Peissenberg	164	47.48 N	11.04 E
Peiting	180	47.47 N	10.55 E
Peixe	296	12.03 S	48.32 W
Peixe, Rio do ≃, Bra.	296	21.31 S	51.58 W
Peixe, Rio do ≃, Bra.	296	14.06 S	50.51 W
Peixes ≃	292	10.42 S	57.56 W
Peixes, Rio dos ≃	296	15.17 S	52.02 W
Peixian	190	34.21 N	117.59 E
Pekalongan	198	6.53 S	109.40 E
Pekin, Ill., U.S.	244	40.35 N	89.40 W
Pekin, Ind., U.S.	248	38.30 N	86.00 W
Peking → Beijing	194	39.55 N	116.25 E
Pekul'nej, Chrebet ⛰	236	66.00 N	175.00 E
Pelagie, Isole II	170	35.40 N	12.40 E
Pelahatchie	248	32.19 N	89.48 W
Pełczyce (Bernstein)	164	53.03 N	15.18 E
Peleaga, Vîrful ∧	172	45.22 N	22.54 E
Pelechuco	292	14.48 S	69.04 W
Peleduj	186	59.36 N	112.45 E
Pelee Island I	244	41.46 N	82.39 W
Pelee Point ≻	244	41.54 N	82.30 W
Peleliu I	198	7.01 N	134.15 E
Peleng, Pulau I	198	1.20 S	123.10 E
Pelham, Ga., U.S.	246	31.08 N	84.09 W
Pelham, Mass., U.S.	261	42.24 N	72.24 W
Pelham, N.H., U.S.	261	42.44 N	71.19 W
Pelhřimov	164	49.26 N	15.13 E
Pelican	236	57.57 N	136.14 W
Pelican ≃	252	46.17 N	96.08 W
Pelican Cays II	278	16.43 N	88.12 W
Pelican Lake	244	45.30 N	89.10 W
Pelican Lake ⊚, Alta., Can.	238	55.47 N	113.15 W
Pelican Lake ⊚, Man., Can.	252	49.20 N	99.35 W
Pelican Mountain ∧	238	55.35 N	113.40 W
Pelican Rapids	252	46.34 N	96.05 W
Pelileo	290	1.19 S	78.32 W
Pelister ∧	172	41.00 N	21.12 E
Peljekaise Nationalpark ♣	160	66.18 N	16.58 E
Pelješac, Poluotok ≻[1]	170	42.58 N	17.20 E
Pelkosenniemi	160	67.07 N	27.30 E
Pella	244	41.25 N	92.55 W
Pélla □[5]	172	40.50 N	22.00 E
Pélla ⊥	172	40.45 N	22.33 E
Pell City	248	33.35 N	86.17 W
Pellegrini	294	36.15 S	63.10 W
Pellegrini, Lago ⊚	294	38.40 S	68.00 W
Pellegrino, Cozza ∧	170	39.45 N	16.03 E
Pell Lake	268	42.32 N	88.21 W
Pello	160	66.47 N	24.00 E
Pellston	244	45.33 N	84.47 W
Pellworm I	164	54.31 N	8.38 E
Pelly ≃	236	62.47 N	137.19 W
Pelly Bay C	232	68.53 N	89.51 W
Pelly Crossing	236	62.50 N	136.35 W
Pelly Lake ⊚	232	65.59 N	101.12 W
Pelly Mountains ⛰	236	62.00 N	133.00 W
Pelón de Ñado, Cerro ∧	278	20.05 N	99.55 W
Pelopónnisos ↞[1]	172	37.30 N	22.00 E
Peloritani, Monti ⛰	170	38.05 N	15.25 E
Pelotas	294	31.46 S	52.20 W
Pelotas ≃	294	27.28 S	51.55 W
Pelplin	164	53.56 N	18.42 E
Pelusium Bay → Ţīnah, Khalīj aţ- C	220	31.08 N	32.40 E
Pemadumcook Lake ⊚	242	45.40 N	68.55 W
Pematangsiantar	200	2.58 N	99.03 E
Pemba Island I	218	7.31 S	39.25 E
Pemberton, Austl.	226	34.28 S	116.01 E
Pemberton, B.C., Can.	238	50.20 N	122.48 W
Pemberton, N.J., U.S.	262	39.58 N	74.41 W
Pemberton, Ohio, U.S.	268	40.18 N	84.02 W
Pemberton Indian Reserve ↞[4]	238	50.19 N	122.42 W
Pemberville	266	41.25 N	83.28 W
Pembina	252	48.58 N	97.15 W
Pembina ≃, Alta., Can.	238	54.45 N	114.15 W
Pembina ≃, N.A.	252	49.00 N	98.12 W
Pembina Mountains ⛰	252	49.00 N	98.05 W
Pembine	244	45.38 N	87.59 W
Pembrey	174	51.42 N	4.16 W
Pembroke, Ont., Can.	244	45.49 N	77.07 W
Pembroke, Wales, U.K.	174	51.41 N	4.55 W
Pembroke, Ga., U.S.	246	32.08 N	81.37 W
Pembroke, Ky., U.S.	248	36.47 N	87.21 W
Pembroke, Maine, U.S.	242	44.57 N	67.10 W
Pembroke, Mass., U.S.	261	42.04 N	70.49 W
Pembroke, N.C., U.S.	246	34.41 N	79.12 W
Pembroke, N.Y., U.S.	264	43.00 N	78.27 W
Pembroke, Va., U.S.	246	37.19 N	80.38 W
Pembroke, Cape ≻	232	62.56 N	81.55 W
Pembrokeshire □[6]	174	51.52 N	4.52 W
Pembrokeshire Coast National Park ♣	162	51.47 N	5.06 W
Pembuang ≃	198	3.24 S	112.33 E
Pemigewasset ≃	242	43.26 N	71.40 W
Pemuco	294	36.58 S	72.06 W
Pemynoos Indian Reserve ↞[4]	238	50.29 N	121.15 W
Peña Blanca	280	8.28 N	81.40 W
Peña de Francia, Sierra de ⛰	168	40.33 N	6.06 W
Peñafiel, Esp.	168	41.36 N	4.07 W
Penafiel, Port.	168	41.12 N	8.17 W
Peñagolosa ∧	168	40.13 N	0.21 W
Peñalara ∧	168	40.51 N	3.57 W
Peña Negra, Punta ≻	290	4.15 S	81.15 W
Peña Nevada, Cerro ∧	278	23.46 N	99.52 W
Penang → Pinang	200	5.24 N	100.19 E
Penápolis	296	21.24 S	50.04 W
Peñaranda de Bracamonte	168	40.54 N	5.12 W
Pen Argyl	242	40.52 N	75.16 W
Peñarroya Pueblonuevo	168	38.18 N	5.16 W
Penarth	174	51.27 N	3.11 W
Peñas, Cabo de ≻	168	43.39 N	5.51 W
Penas, Golfo de C	288	47.20 S	75.00 W
Peñas, Punta ≻	290	10.40 N	61.40 W
Peñas Blancas, Cerro ∧	280	13.15 N	85.41 W
Penasco	254	36.10 N	105.41 W
Penasco, Rio ≃	250	32.45 N	104.19 W
Penbrook	262	40.17 N	76.51 W
Pencahue	294	35.24 S	71.49 W
Pence	244	46.25 N	90.16 W
Pendembu	214	9.06 N	12.12 W
Pender	252	42.07 N	96.43 W

Symbols in the index entries are identified on page 360.

Name	Page	Lat°′	Long°′
Pendjari ≃	222	10.54 N	0.51 E
Pendjari, Parc National de la ♠	222	11.20 N	1.15 E
Pendleton, Ind., U.S.	248	40.01 N	85.45 W
Pendleton, Oreg., U.S.	256	45.40 N	118.47 W
Pendleton, S.C., U.S.	246	34.39 N	82.47 W
Pend Oreille ≃	256	49.04 N	117.37 W
Pend Oreille, Lake ⊜	238	48.10 N	116.11 W
Pend Oreille, Mount ∧	256	48.25 N	116.10 W
Pend Oreille Lake ⊜	256	48.10 N	116.11 W
Penedo	286	10.17 S	36.36 W
Penedono	168	40.59 N	7.24 W
Penela	168	40.02 N	8.23 W
Penetanguishene	264	44.47 N	79.55 W
Penfield, N.Y., U.S.	264	43.08 N	77.29 W
Penfield, Ohio, U.S.	266	41.10 N	82.08 W
Penfield, Pa., U.S.	266	41.13 N	78.34 W
P'engchia Hsü I	196	25.38 N	122.04 E
P'enghu	198	23.34 N	119.43 E
P'enghu Liehtao II	196	23.30 N	119.30 E
P'enghu Shuitao Ш	196	23.30 N	119.50 E
Pengiki, Pulau I	200	0.15 N	108.03 E
Penglai	190	37.48 N	120.42 E
Pengpu → Bangbu	196	32.58 N	117.24 E
Pengshui	190	29.18 N	108.09 E
Pengwaluoteshan ∧	206	33.30 N	86.35 E
Pengxian	190	31.00 N	103.50 E
Penha	294	26.46 S	48.39 W
Penhold	238	52.08 N	113.52 W
Peniche	168	39.21 N	9.23 W
Peninsula	266	41.14 N	81.33 W
Peñíscola	168	40.21 N	0.25 E
Penitas	250	26.17 N	98.27 W
Penjamillo [de Degollado]	278	20.06 N	101.54 W
Penjamo	278	20.26 N	101.44 W
Penju, Kepulauan II	198	5.22 S	127.46 E
Penki → Benxi	194	41.18 N	123.45 E
Penmarch	166	47.48 N	4.22 W
Penmarch, Pointe de ≻	166	47.48 N	4.22 W
Pennant Point ≻	240	44.26 N	63.39 W
Pennask Lake ⊜	238	50.00 N	120.05 W
Pennask Mountain ∧	238	49.53 N	120.07 W
Penne	184	42.27 N	13.55 E
Penne-d'Agenais	166	44.23 N	0.49 E
Penney Farms	246	29.59 N	81.49 W
Penngrove	272	38.18 N	122.40 W
Penn Hills	266	40.28 N	79.53 W
Pennine, Alpi ⋀	170	46.05 N	7.50 E
Pennington	262	40.19 N	74.48 W
Pennington ≃[1]	222	4.45 N	5.35 E
Pennington Gap	246	36.41 N	83.02 W
Penn Run	266	40.37 N	79.01 W
Pennsboro	242	39.17 N	80.58 W
Pennsburg	262	40.23 N	75.30 W
Penns Grove	262	39.43 N	75.28 W
Pennside	262	40.20 N	75.53 W
Pennsville	262	39.39 N	75.31 W
Pennsylvania □[3]	234	40.45 N	77.30 W
Pennville	268	40.30 N	85.09 W
Penny	238	53.50 N	121.17 W
Penn Yan	264	42.40 N	77.03 W
Penny Highland ⋀[1]	232	67.19 N	66.20 W
Penny Strait Ш	232	76.30 N	97.00 W
Peno	160	56.55 N	32.45 E
Penobscot ≃	240	44.30 N	68.50 W
Penobscot Bay C	242	44.15 N	68.52 W
Penola	226	37.23 S	140.50 E
Peñoles	250	25.39 N	104.30 W
Peñón Blanco	278	24.47 N	104.02 W
Peñón de Ifach ♠	168	38.38 N	0.05 E
Peñón del Rosario, Cerro ∧	278	19.40 N	98.11 W
Penong	226	31.55 S	133.01 E
Penonomé	280	8.31 N	80.21 W
Penrith, Austl.	228	33.45 S	150.42 E
Penrith, Eng., U.K.	162	54.40 N	2.44 W
Penryn, Calif., U.S.	272	38.51 N	121.10 W
Penryn, Pa., U.S.	262	40.12 N	76.22 W
Pensacola	248	30.25 N	87.13 W
Pensacola Bay C	248	30.25 N	87.06 W
Pensaukee ≃	244	44.49 N	87.55 W
Pensilvania	290	5.31 N	75.05 W
Pentagon Mountain ∧	256	47.56 N	113.07 W
Pentecôte, Lac ⊜	240	49.53 N	67.20 W
Penticton	238	49.30 N	119.35 W
Penticton Indian Reserve ◄[4]	238	49.30 N	119.40 W
Pentland	226	20.32 S	145.24 E
Pentland Firth Ш	162	58.44 N	3.13 W
Pentwater	244	43.47 N	86.26 W
Penuba	200	0.20 S	104.28 E
Peñuelas	284m	18.03 N	66.43 W
Penwell	250	31.44 N	102.35 W
Penza	158	53.13 N	45.00 E
Penzance	162	50.07 N	5.33 W
Penzberg	164	47.45 N	11.23 E
Penžina ≃	186	62.28 N	165.18 E
Penžinskaja Guba C	186	61.00 N	162.00 E
Penžinskij Chrebet ⋀	186	62.30 N	167.00 E
People's Democratic Republic of Yemen □[1]	204	15.00 N	48.00 E
Peoria, Ariz., U.S.	254	33.35 N	112.14 W
Peoria, Ill., U.S.	244	40.42 N	89.36 W
Peotone	268	41.20 N	87.47 W
Pepin	244	44.27 N	92.09 W
Pepin, Lake ⊜	244	44.30 N	92.15 W
Pepperell	261	42.40 N	71.35 W
Peqin	172	41.03 N	19.45 E
Pequez	262	39.53 N	76.22 W
Pequop Mountains ⋀	258	40.45 N	114.40 W
Pequot Lakes	244	46.36 N	94.19 W
Perabumulih	198	3.27 S	104.15 E
Perak □[3]	200	5.00 N	101.00 E
Perak ≃	200	3.58 N	100.53 E
Perak, Kuala C	200	4.00 N	100.47 E
Perales de Alfambra	168	40.38 N	1.00 W
Peralillo	294	34.29 S	71.29 W
Peralta	254	34.50 N	106.41 W
Perämeri (Bottenviken) C	160	65.00 N	23.00 E
Percé	240	48.31 N	64.13 W
Perchas	284m	18.19 N	66.59 W
Perche, Collines du ⋀[2]	166	48.25 N	0.40 E
Perchtoldsdorf	164	48.07 N	16.17 E
Percy Islands II	228	21.39 S	150.16 E
Perdido	248	31.00 N	87.37 W
Perdido ≃, Bra.	294	22.10 S	57.33 W
Perdido ≃, U.S.	248	30.29 N	87.26 W
Perdido, Monte ∧	168	42.40 N	0.05 E
Perdido Bay C	248	30.21 N	87.27 W
Perdix	262	40.22 N	76.57 W
Perdizes	296	19.21 S	47.17 W
Perdu, Lac ⊜	240	50.44 N	70.12 W
Perečin	164	48.44 N	22.26 E
Pereira	290	4.49 N	75.43 W
Pereira Barreto	296	20.38 S	51.07 W
Pereira de Eça	218	17.03 S	15.47 E
Perejež'na	160	59.43 N	48.12 E
Pere Marquette ≃	244	43.57 N	86.27 W
Peremyšl'	160	54.16 N	36.10 E
Perene ≃	292	11.09 S	74.14 W
Pereslavl'-Zalesskij	160	56.44 N	38.51 E
Pérez	294	33.00 S	60.45 W
Perg	164	48.15 N	14.37 E
Pergamino	294	33.53 S	60.36 W
Pergine Valsugana	170	46.04 N	11.14 E
Pergola	170	43.34 N	12.50 E
Perham	252	46.36 N	95.34 W
Péribonca ≃	240	48.45 N	72.05 W
Péribonca, Lac ⊜	240	50.07 N	71.15 W
Perico, Arg.	294	24.25 S	65.10 W
Perico, Cuba	284p	22.46 N	81.01 W
Pericos	278	25.03 N	107.42 W
Peridot	254	33.18 N	110.28 W
Périers	166	49.11 N	1.25 W
Périgord □[9]	166	45.20 N	1.00 E
Périgueux	166	45.11 N	0.43 E
Perijá, Sierra de ⋀	290	10.00 N	73.00 W
Perim → Barīm I	214	12.40 N	43.25 E
Periperi de Poções	296	14.39 S	40.29 W
Periprava	172	45.24 N	29.32 E
Perito Moreno	288	46.36 S	70.56 W
Perkam, Tandjung ≻	198	1.28 S	137.24 E
Perkasie	262	40.22 N	75.18 W
Perkins	250	35.58 N	97.02 W
Perkinsfield	264	44.42 N	79.57 W
Perkinston	248	30.47 N	89.08 W
Perkinsville	266	42.32 N	77.38 W
Perlas, Archipiélago de las II	290	8.20 N	79.02 W
Perlas, Laguna de C	280	12.35 N	83.35 W
Perlas, Punta de ≻	280	12.22 N	83.30 W
Perleberg	164	53.04 N	11.51 E
Perlez	172	45.12 N	20.24 E
Perlis □[3]	200	6.30 N	100.15 E
Perm'	158	58.00 N	56.15 E
Permas	160	59.20 N	45.34 E
Përmet	172	40.14 N	20.21 E
Permskaja Oblast' □[4]	160	59.00 N	56.00 E
Pernatty Lagoon ⊜	228	31.31 S	137.14 E
Pernik	172	42.36 N	23.02 E
Péronne	176	49.56 N	2.56 E
Péronnes	176	50.26 N	4.08 E
Perosa Argentina	170	44.58 N	7.10 E
Perote	278	19.34 N	97.14 W
Perotó	292	14.50 S	64.31 W
Perow	238	54.31 N	126.26 W
Perpignan	166	42.41 N	2.53 E
Perrin, Tex., U.S.	250	33.02 N	98.04 W
Perrin, Va., U.S.	262	37.17 N	76.26 W
Perrine	246	25.36 N	80.21 W
Perrineville	262	40.14 N	74.27 W
Perris	274	33.47 N	117.14 W
Perro, Laguna del ⊜	254	34.40 N	105.57 W
Perros, Bahía de C	284p	22.25 N	78.36 W
Perros-Guirec	166	48.49 N	3.27 W
Perry, Fla., U.S.	246	30.07 N	83.35 W
Perry, Ga., U.S.	246	32.27 N	83.44 W
Perry, Iowa, U.S.	244	41.50 N	94.06 W
Perry, Kans., U.S.	252	39.05 N	95.24 W
Perry, Maine, U.S.	242	44.58 N	67.05 W
Perry, Mich., U.S.	268	42.50 N	84.13 W
Perry, Mo., U.S.	248	39.26 N	91.40 W
Perry, N.Y., U.S.	264	42.43 N	78.00 W
Perry, Ohio, U.S.	266	41.46 N	81.09 W
Perry, Okla., U.S.	250	36.17 N	97.17 W
Perry, Utah, U.S.	254	35.18 N	105.22 W
Perry □[6]	262	40.25 N	77.11 W
Perrydale	270	45.03 N	123.16 W
Perry Heights	266	40.48 N	81.24 W
Perryopolis	266	40.05 N	79.45 W
Perry Reservoir ⊜[1]	252	39.20 N	95.30 W
Perrysburg, N.Y., U.S.	266	42.27 N	79.00 W
Perrysburg, Ohio, U.S.	266	41.33 N	83.38 W
Perrysville, Ohio, U.S.	266	40.40 N	82.19 W
Perrysville, Pa., U.S.	266	40.32 N	80.02 W
Perryton	250	36.24 N	100.48 W
Perryville, Alaska, U.S.	236	55.54 N	159.10 W
Perryville, Ark., U.S.	248	35.00 N	92.48 W
Perryville, Mo., U.S.	248	37.43 N	89.52 W
Perryville, N.Y., U.S.	264	43.01 N	75.48 W
Persan	176	49.09 N	2.16 E
Perseverancia	292	14.44 S	62.48 W
Persia	252	41.34 N	95.35 W
Persia → Iran □[1]	204	32.00 N	53.00 E
Persian Gulf C	208	27.00 N	51.00 E
Perstorp	160	56.08 N	13.23 E
Perth, Austl.	226	31.56 S	115.50 E
Perth, N.B., Can.	240	46.44 N	67.42 W
Perth, Ont., Can.	264	44.54 N	76.15 W
Perth, Scot., U.K.	162	56.24 N	3.28 W
Perth □[6], Ont., Can.	264	43.30 N	81.05 W
Perth □[6], Scot., U.K.	162	56.30 N	4.00 W
Perth Amboy	262	40.31 N	74.16 W
Pertuis	166	43.41 N	5.30 E
Peru, Ill., U.S.	268	41.20 N	89.08 W
Peru, Ind., U.S.	268	40.45 N	86.04 W
Peru, Nebr., U.S.	252	40.29 N	95.44 W
Peru, N.Y., U.S.	242	44.35 N	73.32 W
Peru (Perú) □[1]	286	10.00 S	76.00 W
Peruacu ≃	296	15.11 S	44.07 W
Perugia	184	43.08 N	12.22 E
Perugia □[4]	184	43.03 N	12.33 E
Perugorria	294	29.21 S	58.36 W
Peruíbe	294	24.19 S	47.00 W
Peruípe ≃	296	17.43 S	39.16 W
Perušić	170	44.39 N	15.23 E
Péruwelz	176	50.31 N	3.35 E
Pervoje Pole	236	63.05 N	179.19 W
Pervomajsk	160	54.53 N	43.49 E
Pervomajskij	160	64.26 N	40.47 E
Pervoural'sk	158	56.54 N	59.58 E
Pervyj Kuril'skij Proliv Ш	186	50.50 N	156.36 E
Pes'	160	58.55 N	34.19 E
Pes'akov, Ostrov I	160	68.47 N	57.35 E
Pesaro	184	43.54 N	12.55 E
Pesaro e Urbino □[4]	184	43.40 N	12.38 E
Pesca	290	5.33 N	73.03 W
Pescadero	272	37.15 N	122.23 W
Pescadores → P'enghu Liehtao II	196	23.30 N	119.30 E
Pescadores, Punta ≻, Méx.	278	23.42 N	109.42 W
Pescadores, Punta ≻, Perú	292	16.34 S	73.16 W
Pesčanoje	160	62.12 N	35.45 E
Pescara	184	42.28 N	14.13 E
Pescara □[4]	184	42.20 N	13.57 E
Pescia	184	43.54 N	10.41 E
Pescina	184	42.02 N	13.39 E
Pescorocchiano	184	42.12 N	13.09 E
Pesé	280	7.53 N	80.36 W
Peshastin	270	47.34 N	120.36 W
Peshāwar	206	34.01 N	71.33 E
Peshkopi	172	41.41 N	20.26 E
Peshtigo	244	45.03 N	87.45 W
Peshtigo ≃	244	44.58 N	87.40 W
Peskovka	160	59.04 N	52.22 E
Pesmes	166	47.17 N	5.34 E
Peso da Régua	168	41.10 N	7.47 W
Pespire	280	13.35 N	87.22 W
Pesqueira	286	8.22 S	36.42 W
Pesquería	250	25.47 N	100.03 W
Pessac	166	44.48 N	0.38 W
Pest □[6]	164	47.25 N	19.20 E
Peštera	172	42.02 N	24.18 E
Pestovo	160	58.36 N	35.48 E
Petacalco, Bahía de C	278	17.57 N	102.05 W
Petaẕ Tiqwa	210	32.05 N	34.53 E
Petal	248	31.21 N	89.17 W
Petalcingo	278	17.17 N	92.27 W
Petalión, Kólpos C	172	37.59 N	24.02 E
Petaluma	272	38.14 N	122.39 W
Petare	290	10.29 N	66.49 W
Petatlán	278	17.31 N	101.16 W
Petawawa	244	45.54 N	77.17 W
Petawawa ≃	244	45.55 N	77.15 W
Petegem	176	50.58 N	3.32 E
Peteń Itzaø Lago ⊜	278	16.58 N	89.50 W
Peterboro	264	42.58 N	75.41 W
Peterborough, Austl.	228	32.58 S	138.50 E
Peterborough, Ont., Can.	264	44.18 N	78.19 W
Peterborough, Eng., U.K.	174	52.35 N	0.15 W
Peterborough, N.H., U.S.	242	42.53 N	71.57 W
Peterborough □[6]	264	44.33 N	78.15 W
Peterhead	162	57.30 N	1.49 W
Peter Lake ⊜	232	63.08 N	92.48 W
Peterlee	162	54.46 N	1.19 W
Peter Pond Lake ⊜	232	55.55 N	108.44 W
Petersburg, Alaska, U.S.	236	56.50 N	132.59 W
Petersburg, Ill., U.S.	248	40.01 N	89.51 W
Petersburg, Ind., U.S.	248	38.30 N	87.17 W
Petersburg, Mich., U.S.	268	41.54 N	83.43 W
Petersburg, Nebr., U.S.	252	41.51 N	98.05 W
Petersburg, N.J., U.S.	262	39.15 N	74.43 W
Petersburg, N.Y., U.S.	261	42.45 N	73.21 W
Petersburg, Ohio, U.S.	266	40.55 N	80.32 W
Petersburg, Pa., U.S.	266	40.34 N	78.03 W
Petersburg, Tenn., U.S.	248	35.19 N	86.38 W
Petersburg, Tex., U.S.	250	33.52 N	101.36 W
Petersburg, Va., U.S.	262	37.13 N	77.24 W
Petersburg, W. Va., U.S.	242	39.00 N	79.07 W
Petersfield	174	51.00 N	0.56 W
Petersham	261	42.29 N	72.11 W
Peterson	252	42.55 N	95.21 W
Peter the Great Bay → Petra Velikogo, Zaliv C	186	42.40 N	132.00 E
Pétervására	164	48.01 N	20.06 E
Petilia Policastro	170	39.07 N	16.47 E
Pétionville	282	18.31 N	72.17 W
Petit Bois Island I	248	30.12 N	88.26 W
Petit-Bourg	285o	16.12 N	61.36 W
Petit-Canal	285o	16.23 N	61.29 W
Petitcodiac	240	45.56 N	65.10 W
Petitcodiac ≃	240	45.50 N	64.33 W
Petite rivière de la Baleine ≃	232	56.00 N	76.40 W
Petite Rivière Noire, Piton de la ∧	225c	20.24 S	57.24 E
Petite-Synthe	176	51.01 N	2.19 E
Petite-Goâve	282	18.26 N	72.52 W
Petit Jean ≃	248	35.10 N	92.56 W
Petit lac du Nord ⊜	240	50.50 N	67.09 W
Petit lac Témiscamie ⊜	240	51.15 N	72.03 W
Petit-Mécatina, Île du I	240	50.35 N	59.20 W
Petit-Mécatina, Rivière du ≃	232	50.28 N	59.35 W
Petitot ≃	232	60.14 N	123.29 W
Petitsikapau Lake ⊜	232	54.45 N	66.25 W
Petkeljärven Kansallispuisto ♠	160	62.35 N	31.12 E
Petlād	206	22.28 N	72.47 E
Petlalcingo	278	18.05 N	97.54 W
Peto	278	20.08 N	88.55 W
Petone	230	41.15 S	174.47 E
Petorca	294	32.15 S	70.56 W
Petoskey	244	45.22 N	84.57 W
Petra ⊥	210	30.20 N	35.26 E
Petralia Soprana	170	37.47 N	14.06 E
Petra Velikogo, Zaliv C	186	42.40 N	132.00 E
Petre, Point ≻	244	43.50 N	77.09 W
Petrecovo	160	61.18 N	57.07 E
Petrič	172	41.24 N	23.13 E
Petrified Forest National Park ♠	254	34.55 N	109.49 W
Petrila	172	45.27 N	23.25 E
Petrinja	170	45.26 N	16.17 E
Petrodvorec	160	59.53 N	29.54 E
Petrograd → Leningrad	160	59.55 N	30.15 E
Petrokrepost'	160	59.57 N	31.02 E
Petrólea	290	8.30 N	72.35 W
Petroleum	268	40.37 N	85.09 W
Petrolia, Ont., Can.	266	42.52 N	82.09 W
Petrolia, Pa., U.S.	266	41.01 N	79.43 W
Petrolia, Tex., U.S.	250	34.01 N	98.14 W
Petrolina	286	9.24 S	40.30 W
Petrolina de Goiás	296	16.06 S	49.20 W
Petrominsk	160	64.47 N	38.25 E
Petropavlovsk	186	54.54 N	69.06 E
Petropavlovsk-Kamčatskij	186	53.01 N	158.39 E
Petrópolis	296	22.31 S	43.10 W
Petros	246	36.06 N	84.26 W
Petroșeni	172	45.25 N	23.22 E
Petrovac	172	44.22 N	21.27 E
Petrovsk	158	52.19 N	45.23 E
Petrovskij	160	56.39 N	40.19 E
Petrovsk-Zabajkal'skij	186	51.17 N	108.50 E
Petrozavodsk	160	61.47 N	34.20 E
Petrun'	160	66.28 N	60.43 E
Pettenwell Flowage ⊜[1]	244	44.10 N	89.57 W
Pettisville	268	41.32 N	84.14 W
Pettus	250	28.37 N	97.48 W
Petty Harbour	240	47.28 N	52.43 W
Petuchovo	158	55.06 N	67.58 E
Peuerbach	164	48.21 N	13.56 E
Peuetsagoe, Gunung ∧	200	4.53 N	96.20 E
Peumo	294	34.24 S	71.10 W
Peusangan ≃	200	5.16 N	96.50 E
Pevek	186	69.42 N	170.17 E
Pewamo	268	43.00 N	84.51 W
Pewaukee	268	43.05 N	88.16 W
Peykjahlid	160a	65.40 N	16.50 W
Peyruis	166	44.02 N	5.56 E
Peza ≃	160	65.36 N	44.35 E
Pezawa Taung ∧	200	19.33 N	94.31 E
Pézenas	166	43.27 N	3.25 E
Pezinok	164	48.18 N	17.17 E
Pfaffenhofen an der Ilm	164	48.31 N	11.30 E
Pfäffikon	180	47.22 N	8.47 E
Pfälzer Bergland ⋀	166	49.33 N	7.22 E
Pfarrkirchen	164	48.27 N	12.56 E
Pfastatt	180	47.47 N	7.18 E
Pforzheim	164	48.54 N	8.42 E
Pfronten	180	47.34 N	10.33 E
Pfuhl	180	48.24 N	10.02 E
Pfullendorf	180	47.55 N	9.15 E
Pfullingen	180	48.28 N	9.13 E
Pfunds	164	46.58 N	10.33 E
Pfungstadt	164	49.48 N	8.36 E
Phachi ≃	200	13.55 N	99.25 E
Phalanx	266	41.15 N	80.58 W
Phalsbourg	166	48.46 N	7.16 E
Phangan, Ko I	200	9.45 N	100.04 E
Phang Hoei, Khao ∧	200	15.37 N	101.20 E
Phangnga	198	8.28 N	98.32 E
Phaniang ≃	200	16.46 N	102.25 E
Phanom Dongrak, Thiu Khao ⋀	200	14.25 N	103.30 E
Phan-rang	200	11.34 N	108.59 E
Phan-thiet	200	10.56 N	108.06 E
Pharr	250	26.12 N	98.11 W
Phatthalung	200	7.38 N	100.04 E
Phayao	200	19.11 N	99.55 E
Pheba	248	33.35 N	88.57 W
Phelan	274	34.25 N	117.34 W
Phelps, N.Y., U.S.	264	42.57 N	77.03 W
Phelps, Wis., U.S.	244	46.04 N	89.05 W
Phelps Lake ⊜	246	35.46 N	76.27 W
Phenix City	246	32.29 N	85.01 W
Phet Buri	200	13.06 N	99.56 E
Phet Buri ≃	200	13.10 N	99.57 E
Phetchabun, Thiu Khao ⋀	200	16.20 N	100.55 E
Philadelphia, Miss., U.S.	248	32.46 N	89.07 W
Philadelphia, N.Y., U.S.	264	44.09 N	75.43 W
Philadelphia, Pa., U.S.	262	39.57 N	75.07 W
Philadelphia, Tenn., U.S.	246	35.41 N	84.24 W
Philae ⊥	220	24.01 N	32.53 E
Phil Campbell	248	34.21 N	87.42 W
Philip	252	44.02 N	101.40 W
Philipp	248	33.45 N	90.12 W
Philippeville, Bel.	164	50.12 N	4.32 E
Philippi	242	39.09 N	80.02 W
Philippi, Lake ⊜	228	24.22 S	139.00 E
Philippine Basin ⊹[1]	148	18.00 N	133.00 E
Philippines □[1]	198	12.00 N	123.00 E
Philippine Sea ▼[2]	148	20.00 N	135.00 E
Philipsburg, Qué., Can.	260	45.03 N	73.05 W
Philipsburg, Ned. Ant.	282	17.59 N	63.10 W
Philipsburg, Mont., U.S.	256	46.20 N	113.18 W
Philipsburg, Pa., U.S.	266	40.53 N	78.05 W
Philip Smith Mountains ⋀	236	68.30 N	148.00 W
Phillip Island I	228	38.29 S	145.14 E
Phillips, Maine, U.S.	242	44.49 N	70.21 W
Phillips, Tex., U.S.	250	35.42 N	101.22 W
Phillips, Wis., U.S.	244	45.41 N	90.24 W
Phillipsburg, Kans., U.S.	252	39.45 N	99.19 W
Phillipsburg, N.J., U.S.	262	40.42 N	75.12 W
Philmont	261	42.15 N	73.39 W
Philo, Ill., U.S.	248	40.01 N	88.09 W
Philo, Ohio, U.S.	242	39.52 N	81.55 W
Philomath	256	44.32 N	123.22 W
Philpots Island I	232	74.48 N	80.00 W
Phimai	198	15.13 N	102.29 E
Phitsanulok	200	16.49 N	100.15 E
Phnum Pénh	200	11.33 N	104.55 E
Phoenix, Ariz., U.S.	254	33.27 N	112.05 W
Phoenix, Md., U.S.	262	39.31 N	76.37 W
Phoenix, N.Y., U.S.	264	43.14 N	76.18 W
Phoenix, Oreg., U.S.	256	42.17 N	122.49 W
Phoenix Islands II	148	4.00 S	172.00 W
Phoenixville	262	40.08 N	75.31 W
Phon	200	15.50 N	102.35 E
Phong ≃	200	16.27 N	102.57 E
Phong Saly	200	21.41 N	102.06 E
Phrae	200	18.07 N	100.11 E
Phra Nakhon Si Ayutthaya	200	14.21 N	100.33 E
Phra Rop, Khao ∧	200	13.10 N	99.30 E
Phrygia □[9]	212	39.00 N	30.00 E
Phu-cuong	200	10.58 N	106.39 E
Phuket	200	7.54 N	98.24 E
Phuket, Ko I	200	8.00 N	98.22 E
Phu-ly	200	20.32 N	105.56 E
Phum Duang ≃	200	9.10 N	99.20 E
Phumĭ Ângk Tasaôm	200	11.01 N	104.41 E
Phumĭ Béng	200	13.05 N	104.18 E
Phumĭ Chuuk	200	10.50 N	104.28 E
Phumĭ Kâmpŏng Trâbêk	200	13.06 N	105.14 E
Phumĭ Svay Riĕng	198	11.05 N	105.48 E
Phuoc-le	198	10.30 N	107.10 E
Phu-quoc, Dao I	200	10.13 N	104.00 E
Phu-tho	200	21.24 N	105.13 E
Phu-vinh	200	9.56 N	106.20 E
Piacatu	296	21.38 S	50.30 W
Piacenza	182	45.01 N	9.40 E
Piacenza □[4]	182	44.53 N	9.35 E
Piacouadie, Lac ⊜	240	51.18 N	70.54 W
Piako ≃	230	37.12 S	175.30 E
Pialba	226	25.17 S	152.51 E
Pian, Lac ⊜	244	47.49 N	79.07 W
Piana	170	42.14 N	8.38 E
Piana degli Albanesi	170	38.00 N	13.17 E
Pianella	170	42.24 N	14.02 E
Pianezza	182	45.06 N	7.33 E
Pianoro	170	44.22 N	11.20 E
Pianosa, Isola I	170	42.35 N	10.04 E
Piares, Punta ≻	278	16.49 N	99.55 W
Piaseczno	164	52.05 N	21.01 E
Piashti, Lac ⊜	240	50.30 N	62.52 W
Piaski	164	51.08 N	22.51 E
Piat	202	17.48 N	121.29 E
Piatã	296	13.09 S	41.48 W
Piatra-Neamț	172	46.56 N	26.22 E
Piatra Olt	172	44.24 N	24.08 E
Piatt □[6]	268	40.00 N	88.35 W
Piauí ≃	296	16.41 S	41.53 W
Piaus, Rio dos ≃	296	12.27 S	49.32 W
Piave ≃	170	45.32 N	12.44 E
Piaxtla ≃	278	23.42 N	106.49 W
Piazza Armerina	170	37.23 N	14.22 E
Pibor ≃	220	8.26 N	33.13 E
Pibor Post	214	6.48 N	33.08 E
Pibroch	238	54.16 N	113.52 W
Pic ≃	244	48.36 N	86.18 W
Pica	292	20.30 S	69.21 W
Picacho	254	32.43 N	111.30 W
Picanoe ≃	242	46.04 N	76.02 W
Picardie □[9]	176	50.00 N	3.30 E
Picayune	248	30.26 N	89.41 W
Piccadilly	240	48.35 N	58.56 W
Pic de Tio ∧	222	8.52 N	8.54 W
Pichana ≃	290	3.30 S	71.45 W
Pichanal	294	23.20 S	64.15 W
Picher	250	36.59 N	94.50 W
Pichilemu	294	34.23 S	72.02 W
Pichimá	290	4.24 N	77.21 W
Pichi-Mahuída	294	38.50 S	64.57 W
Pichincha □[4]	290	0.10 S	78.40 W
Pichis ≃	292	9.55 S	74.55 W
Pichucalco	278	17.31 N	93.09 W
Pic Island I	244	48.43 N	86.38 W
Pickardville	238	54.03 N	113.53 W
Pickens, Miss., U.S.	248	32.53 N	89.58 W
Pickens, S.C., U.S.	246	34.53 N	82.42 W
Pickens, W. Va., U.S.	242	38.39 N	80.13 W
Pickensville	248	33.14 N	88.16 W
Pickerel ≃	244	45.55 N	80.50 W
Pickering, Ont., Can.	264	43.52 N	79.02 W
Pickering, Eng., U.K.	162	54.14 N	0.46 W
Pickering Beach	264	43.50 N	78.59 W
Pickford	244	46.10 N	84.22 W
Pickle Crow	232	51.30 N	90.04 W
Pickstown	252	43.04 N	98.32 W
Pickton	250	33.02 N	95.24 W
Pickwick Lake ⊜[1]	248	34.55 N	88.10 W
Pico ∧	222a	14.56 N	24.21 W
Pico de Orizaba, Parque Nacional ♠	278	19.05 N	97.16 W
Pico de Tancítaro, Parque Nacional ♠	278	19.27 N	102.22 W
Pico Rivera	274	33.58 N	118.07 W
Picos	286	7.05 S	41.28 W
Picota	292	6.54 S	76.24 W
Picquigny	166	49.57 N	2.09 E
Picton, Ont., Can.	264	44.00 N	77.08 W
Picton, N.Z.	230	41.16 S	174.00 E
Picton, Isla I	288	55.02 S	66.57 W
Pictou	240	45.41 N	62.43 W
Pictou Island I	240	45.50 N	62.34 W
Picture Butte	238	49.53 N	112.47 W
Piedecuesta	290	6.59 N	73.03 W
Pie de Palo, Sierra ⋀	294	31.20 S	68.00 W
Piedicroce	166	42.23 N	9.23 E
Piedimonte d'Alife	184	41.21 N	14.22 E
Piedmont, Ala., U.S.	248	33.55 N	85.37 W
Piedmont, Calif., U.S.	272	37.50 N	122.15 W
Piedmont, Mo., U.S.	248	37.09 N	90.42 W
Piedmont, Ohio, U.S.	266	40.11 N	81.12 W
Piedmont, S.C., U.S.	246	34.42 N	82.28 W
Piedmont, W. Va., U.S.	242	39.28 N	79.02 W
Piedmont Reservoir ⊜[1]	242	40.10 N	81.15 W
Piedra	272	36.47 N	119.25 W
Piedra ≃	254	37.01 N	107.24 W
Piedra, Cerro ∧	294	37.41 S	73.07 W
Piedra Blanca	278	29.05 N	102.19 W
Piedrabuena	168	39.02 N	4.10 W
Piedra del Águila	288	40.02 S	70.04 W
Piedrafita, Puerto de)(	168	42.40 N	7.01 W
Piedrahita	168	40.28 N	5.19 W
Piedra Roja	280	8.38 N	81.48 W
Piedras, Punta ≻, Arg.	294	35.25 S	57.07 W
Piedras, Punta ≻, Ven.	290	10.53 N	64.07 W
Piedras Blancas	294	31.11 S	59.57 W
Piedras Coloradas	294	32.23 S	57.36 W
Piedras de Tunja ♠	290	4.49 N	74.20 W
Piedras Negras, Guat.	278	17.11 N	91.15 W
Piedras Negras, Méx.	278	28.42 N	100.31 W
Piedra Sola	294	32.04 S	56.21 W
Pie Island I	244	48.15 N	89.05 W
Pieksämäki	160	62.18 N	27.08 E
Pielavesi	160	63.14 N	26.45 E
Pielinen ⊜	160	63.15 N	29.40 E
Piemonte □[4]	182	45.00 N	8.00 E
Piendamó	290	2.38 N	76.30 W
Pieniężno (Mehlsack)	164	54.15 N	20.08 E
Pieńsk (Penzig)	164	51.15 N	15.03 E
Pienza	170	43.04 N	11.41 E
Pierce, Colo., U.S.	254	40.38 N	104.45 W
Pierce, Idaho, U.S.	256	46.29 N	115.48 W
Pierce, Nebr., U.S.	252	42.12 N	97.32 W
Pierce □[6]	270	47.04 N	122.07 W
Pierce, Lake ⊜	246	27.58 N	81.31 W
Pierce City	248	36.57 N	94.01 W
Pierceton	268	41.12 N	85.42 W
Piería □[5]	172	40.10 N	22.15 E
Piermont	261	41.03 N	73.55 W
Pierpont, Ohio, U.S.	266	41.45 N	80.34 W
Pierpont, S. Dak., U.S.	252	45.30 N	97.50 W
Pierre	252	44.22 N	100.21 W
Pierre, Bayou ≃, La., U.S.	248	31.51 N	93.06 W
Pierre, Bayou ≃, Miss., U.S.	248	31.55 N	91.11 W
Pierre-Buffière	166	45.42 N	1.21 E
Pierrefonds	260	45.27 N	73.55 W
Pierrepont Manor	264	43.44 N	76.04 W
Pierreville, Qué., Can.	260	46.04 N	72.49 W
Pierreville, Trin.	285r	10.18 N	61.01 W
Pierson	246	29.14 N	81.28 W
Pierz	244	45.59 N	94.06 W
Piešt'any	164	48.36 N	17.50 E
Pietermaritzburg	224	29.37 S	30.16 E
Pietersburg	224	23.54 S	29.25 E
Pie Town	254	34.18 N	108.09 W
Pietrasanta	170	43.57 N	10.14 E
Piet Retief	224	27.01 S	30.50 E
Pietrosu ∧	172	47.08 N	25.11 E
Pietrosul ∧	172	47.36 N	24.38 E
Pieve di Cadore	170	46.26 N	12.22 E
Piffard	264	42.50 N	77.51 W
Pigeon, Mich., U.S.	244	43.50 N	83.16 W
Pigeon, Pa., U.S.	266	41.32 N	79.03 W
Pigeon ≃, N.A.	244	48.00 N	89.34 W
Pigeon ≃, U.S.	246	36.00 N	83.11 W
Pigeon ≃, Mich., U.S.	244	43.56 N	83.17 W
Pigeon ≃, Mich., U.S.	244	45.27 N	84.33 W
Pigeon Cove	261	42.41 N	70.38 W
Pigeon Forge	246	35.47 N	83.33 W
Pigeon Lake ⊜, Alta., Can.	238	53.00 N	114.00 W
Pigeon Lake ⊜, Ont., Can.	244	44.30 N	78.30 W
Pigg ≃	246	37.00 N	79.29 W
Piggott	248	36.23 N	90.11 W
Pigkawagan	202	7.12 N	124.32 E
Pigna	170	43.56 N	7.40 E
Pigüé	294	37.40 S	62.24 W
Pihtipudas	160	63.23 N	25.34 E
Pijijiapan	278	15.42 N	93.14 W
Pijnacker	178	52.02 N	4.27 E
Pijol, Pico ∧	280	15.06 N	87.35 W
Pikal'ovo	160	59.31 N	34.06 E
Pike	266	42.33 N	78.09 W
Pike ≃, Minn., U.S.	244	47.48 N	92.22 W
Pike ≃, Wis., U.S.	244	45.26 N	87.52 W
Pikes Peak ∧	254	38.51 N	105.03 W
Pikes Rock ∧[2]	242	41.56 N	79.24 W
Pikesville	242	39.23 N	76.44 W
Piketberg	218	32.54 S	18.46 E
Piketon	242	39.04 N	83.01 W
Piketown	262	40.23 N	76.45 W
Pikeville, Ky., U.S.	246	37.29 N	82.31 W
Pikeville, Tenn., U.S.	248	35.36 N	85.11 W
Pila, Arg.	294	36.00 S	58.10 W
Piła (Schneidemühl), Pol.	164	53.10 N	16.44 E
Pilanesberg ∧	224	25.14 S	27.04 E
Pilar, Arg.	294	31.25 S	61.16 W
Pilar, Arg.	294	31.41 S	63.55 W
Pilar, Para.	294	26.52 S	58.23 W
Pilar, Pil.	202	9.51 N	126.05 E
Pilar, Pil.	202	11.29 N	122.59 E
Pilar Bay C	202	11.34 N	123.00 E
Pilar de Goiás	296	14.41 S	49.27 W
Pilar do Sul	296	23.49 S	47.42 W
Pilares	250	30.24 N	104.52 W
Pilas Group II	202	6.35 N	121.50 E
Pilas Island I	202	6.39 N	121.37 E
Pilawa	164	51.58 N	21.31 E
Pilaya ≃	292	20.55 S	64.04 W
Pilcomayo ≃	294	25.21 S	57.42 W
Pil'dozero	160	65.43 N	33.28 E
Pilger	252	42.00 N	97.03 W
Pil'gyn	236	69.18 N	179.08 W
Pili	202	13.33 N	123.16 E
Pīlībhīt	206	28.37 N	79.48 E
Pilica ≃	164	51.52 N	21.17 E
Píllaro	290	1.10 S	78.32 W
Pillau → Baltijsk	164	54.39 N	19.55 E
Pilley's Island	240	49.30 N	55.44 W
Pillow	262	40.38 N	76.48 W
Pilón ≃	278	25.22 N	99.32 W
Pílos	172	36.55 N	21.43 E
Pilot Grove	248	38.53 N	92.55 W
Pilot Hill	272	38.50 N	121.02 W
Pilot Knob ∧, Ark., U.S.	248	35.42 N	93.57 W
Pilot Knob ∧, Idaho, U.S.	256	45.54 N	115.42 W
Pilot Mound	252	49.16 N	98.55 W
Pilot Mountain	246	36.23 N	80.28 W
Pilot Peak ∧, Nev., U.S.	258	41.02 N	114.06 W
Pilot Peak ∧, Nev., U.S.	258	38.21 N	117.58 W
Pilot Peak ∧, Wyo., U.S.	256	44.58 N	109.53 W
Pilot Point, Alaska, U.S.	236	57.34 N	157.35 W
Pilot Point, Tex., U.S.	250	33.24 N	96.58 W
Pilot Rock	256	45.29 N	118.50 W
Pilot Station	236	61.56 N	162.54 W
Pilpah Range ⋀	228	20.23 S	138.34 E
Pilsen → Plzeň	164	49.45 N	13.23 E
Pilzno	164	49.59 N	21.17 E
Pim ≃	186	61.18 N	71.57 E
Pima	254	32.54 N	109.50 W
Pimba	226	31.15 S	136.47 E
Pimenta	296	20.28 S	45.48 W
Pimentel	292	6.45 S	79.55 W
Pina, Cuba	284p	22.01 N	78.43 W
Pina, Esp.	168	41.29 N	0.32 W
Pinacanauan ≃	202	17.38 N	121.43 E
Pinacate, Cerro ∧	278	31.47 N	113.30 W
Pinamalayan	202	13.03 N	121.29 E
Pinamungajan	202	10.16 N	123.35 E
Pinang (George Town)	200	5.24 N	100.19 E
Pinang □[3]	200	5.20 N	100.20 E
Pınar	172	37.02 N	27.57 E
Pinar del Río	284p	22.25 N	83.42 W
Pinar del Río □[4]	284p	22.35 N	83.40 W
Pinardville	242	42.59 N	71.33 W
Pınarhisar	172	41.37 N	27.30 E
Pinas, Arg.	294	31.12 S	65.28 W
Piñas, Ec.	290	3.42 S	79.42 W
Piñas, Cerro ∧	280	15.25 N	85.47 W
Pinatubo, Mount ∧	202	15.08 N	120.21 E
Pincher Creek	238	49.29 N	113.57 W
Pinchi Lake ⊜	238	54.35 N	124.20 W
Pinckney	268	42.27 N	83.57 W
Pinckneyville	248	38.05 N	89.23 W
Pinconning	244	43.51 N	83.58 W
Pincourt	260	45.22 N	73.59 W
Pińczów	164	50.32 N	20.35 E
Pindamonhangaba	296	22.55 S	45.28 W
Pindaré-Mirim	240	3.37 S	45.21 W
Píndhos Óros ⋀	172	39.49 N	21.14 E
Pindo ≃	290	2.07 S	76.03 W
Pindus Mountains → Píndhos Óros ⋀	172	39.49 N	21.14 E
Pinduši	160	62.56 N	34.35 E
Pine ≃, B.C., Can.	238	56.08 N	120.41 W
Pine ≃, Mich., U.S.	244	44.26 N	83.21 W
Pine ≃, Mich., U.S.	244	43.35 N	84.08 W
Pine ≃, Mich., U.S.	244	46.03 N	84.40 W
Pine ≃, Wis., U.S.	244	44.08 N	88.54 W
Pine ≃, Wis., U.S.	244	45.50 N	88.08 W
Pine ≃, Wis., U.S.	244	43.12 N	90.18 W
Pine, Cape ≻	240	46.37 N	53.30 W
Pine Apple	248	31.52 N	86.59 W
Pine Beach	260	45.32 N	73.56 W
Pine Bluff	248	34.13 N	92.01 W
Pine Bluffs	252	41.11 N	104.04 W
Pine Bluff Southeast	248	34.12 N	92.00 W
Pine Bush	242	41.37 N	74.18 W
Pine Castle	246	28.28 N	81.22 W
Pine City	244	45.50 N	92.59 W
Pine Creek	226	13.49 S	131.49 E
Pinecrest	262	38.50 N	77.09 W
Pinedale, Calif., U.S.	272	36.50 N	119.48 W
Pinedale, Wyo., U.S.	254	42.52 N	109.52 W
Pine Falls	232	50.35 N	96.15 W
Pinega	160	64.42 N	43.19 E
Pinega ≃	160	64.08 N	41.54 E
Pine Glen	264	45.19 N	75.43 W
Pine Grove, Ont., Can.	264	43.48 N	79.35 W
Pine Grove, Pa., U.S.	262	40.33 N	76.23 W
Pine Grove, W. Va., U.S.	242	39.34 N	80.41 W
Pine Grove Mills	266	40.44 N	77.53 W
Pine Hill, Ala., U.S.	248	31.59 N	87.35 W
Pine Hill, Ky., U.S.	246	37.20 N	84.16 W
Pine Hill, N.J., U.S.	262	39.47 N	74.59 W
Pine Hills	246	28.35 N	81.27 W
Pinehouse Lake ⊜	232	55.32 N	106.35 W
Pinehurst, Ga., U.S.	246	32.12 N	83.46 W
Pinehurst, Idaho, U.S.	256	47.32 N	116.14 W
Pinehurst, Mass., U.S.	261	42.32 N	71.14 W
Pinehurst, N.C., U.S.	246	35.12 N	79.28 W
Pinehurst Lake ⊜	238	54.39 N	111.25 W
Pine Island	244	44.12 N	92.38 W
Pine Island I	246	26.35 N	82.06 W
Pinelake	268	41.38 N	86.45 W
Pineland	248	31.15 N	93.58 W
Pinellas Park	246	27.51 N	82.43 W
Pine Mountain ∧, U.S.	246	36.55 N	83.20 W
Pine Mountain ∧, Calif., U.S.	258	35.41 N	121.05 W
Pine Mountain ∧, Ga., U.S.	246	32.51 N	84.47 W
Pine Mountain ∧, Oreg., U.S.	256	43.47 N	120.54 W
Pine Mountain ∧, Wyo., U.S.	254	41.02 N	109.01 W
Pine Pass)(	238	55.22 N	122.40 W
Pine Plains	261	41.59 N	73.40 W
Pine Point	232	61.01 N	114.15 W
Pine Ridge	252	43.02 N	102.33 W
Pine Ridge ∧	252	42.40 N	103.50 W
Pine Ridge Indian Reservation ◄[4]	252	43.25 N	102.21 W
Pine River	244	46.43 N	94.24 W
Pinerolo	182	44.53 N	7.21 E
Pines, Lake o' the ⊜[1]	248	32.46 N	94.35 W
Pine Swamp Knob ∧	242	39.33 N	79.31 W
Pinetop	254	34.08 N	109.56 W
Pinetops	246	35.46 N	77.38 W
Pinetown	224	29.52 S	30.46 E
Pine Tree Hill ∧	200	3.43 N	101.42 E
Pine Village	268	40.27 N	87.15 W
Pineville, Ky., U.S.	246	36.46 N	83.42 W
Pineville, La., U.S.	248	31.19 N	92.26 W
Pineville, Mo., U.S.	248	36.36 N	94.23 W
Pineville, N.C., U.S.	246	35.05 N	80.53 W
Pineville, Pa., U.S.	262	40.18 N	75.00 W
Pineville, W. Va., U.S.	246	37.35 N	81.32 W
Pinewood	246	33.44 N	80.27 W
Piney	166	48.22 N	4.20 E
Piney ≃	248	35.49 N	87.33 W
Piney Buttes ∧	256	47.30 N	107.00 W
Piney Fork	266	40.15 N	80.50 W
Ping ≃	200	15.40 N	100.09 E
Pingba	200	26.22 N	106.09 E
Pingdu	190	36.47 N	119.54 E
Pinghaiwan C	196	25.10 N	119.20 E
Pingheshui ≃	196	24.25 N	116.36 E
Pinghu	196	30.42 N	121.01 E
Pingjiang	190	28.44 N	113.34 E
Pingjiang ≃	196	25.59 N	115.07 E
Pingle	200	24.37 N	110.40 E
Pingliang	190	35.27 N	107.10 E
Pingquan	190	40.59 N	118.34 E
Pingtoushan I	196	27.59 N	121.11 E
P'ingtung	196	22.40 N	120.29 E
Pingues, Cayos II	284p	20.47 N	78.15 W
Pingüicas, Cerro ∧	278	21.10 N	99.42 W
Pingwu	190	32.29 N	104.37 E
Pingxiang, Zhg.	196	27.38 N	113.50 E
Pingxiang, Zhg.	200	22.09 N	106.43 E
Pingyao	190	37.16 N	112.09 E
Pinhal	296	22.12 S	46.45 W
Pinhal Novo	168	38.38 N	8.55 W
Pinheiro	286	2.31 S	45.05 W
Pinheiro Machado	294	31.34 S	53.23 W
Pinhel	168	40.46 N	7.04 W
Pinhua ≃	292	6.21 S	65.00 W
Pini, Pulau I	200	0.07 N	98.42 E
Pinillos	290	8.55 N	74.28 W
Piniós ≃	172	39.54 N	22.45 E
Pinjarra	226	32.37 S	115.53 E
Pinkstaff	248	38.48 N	87.40 W
Pinnacle ∧, N.Z.	230	41.49 S	173.17 E
Pinnacle ∧, N.Y., U.S.	242	43.13 N	74.23 W
Pinnacle Buttes ∧	254	43.44 N	109.57 W
Pinnacle Island I	236	60.12 N	172.46 W
Pinnacles National Monument ♠	258	36.28 N	121.19 W
Pinnaroo	226	35.16 S	140.55 E
Pinneberg	178	53.40 N	9.47 E
Pino, Sierra del ⋀	250	28.15 N	103.03 W
Pinola	248	31.47 N	90.04 W
Pinole	272	38.00 N	122.17 W
Pinos	278	22.18 N	101.34 W
Pinos, Isla de(Isle of Pines) I	284p	21.40 N	82.50 W
Pinos, Mount ∧	258	34.50 N	119.09 W
Pinos-Puente	168	37.15 N	3.45 W
Pinrang	198	3.48 S	119.38 E
Pins, Pointe aux ≻	244	42.15 N	81.51 W
Pinsk	158	52.07 N	26.04 E
Pinson	248	33.41 N	86.41 W
Pinta, Isla I	290a	0.35 N	90.44 W
Pintado ≃	296	13.33 S	50.16 W
Pintados	292	20.37 S	69.38 W
Pinto	294	29.08 S	62.40 W
Pintos, Sierra de ⋀	254	31.05 N	110.47 W
Pintoyacu ≃	290	3.35 S	73.55 W
Pintuyan	202	9.57 N	125.15 E
Pin'ug	160	60.15 N	47.48 E
Pinukpuk	202	17.35 N	121.22 E
Pinzón, Isla I	290a	0.36 S	90.40 W
Pioche	258	37.56 N	114.27 W
Piombino	184	42.55 N	10.32 E
Pioneer, Calif., U.S.	272	38.25 N	120.33 W
Pioneer, La., U.S.	248	32.44 N	91.26 W
Pioneer, Ohio, U.S.	268	41.41 N	84.33 W
Pioneer Mine	238	50.46 N	122.46 W
Pioneer Mountains ⋀	256	45.40 N	113.00 W
Pionki	164	51.30 N	21.27 E
Piorini ≃	290	3.23 S	63.30 W
Piorini, Lago ⊜	290	3.34 S	63.15 W
Piotrków Trybunalski	164	51.25 N	19.42 E
Pio V. Corpus (Limbujan)	202	11.55 N	124.05 E
Piove di Sacco	170	45.18 N	12.02 E
Piper City	268	40.45 N	88.11 W
Pipe Spring National Monument ♠	254	36.43 N	112.33 W
Pipestone	252	43.58 N	96.19 W
Pipestone ≃	232	52.53 N	89.23 W
Pipestone National Monument ♠	252	44.00 N	96.18 W
Pipinas	294	35.30 S	57.19 W
Pipmouacane, Réservoir ⊜[1]	240	49.35 N	70.30 W
Pipriac	162	47.49 N	1.57 W
Piquete	296	22.36 S	45.11 W

Symbols in the index entries are identified on page 360.

Name	Page	Lat°′	Long°′
Piquiri ≃, Bra.	294	24.03 S	54.14 W
Piquiri ≃, Bra.	296	17.23 S	55.38 W
Piracanjuba	296	17.18 S	49.01 W
Piracanjuba ≃, Bra.	296	17.18 S	48.13 W
Piracanjuba ≃, Bra.	296	18.14 S	48.48 W
Piracicaba	296	22.43 S	47.38 W
Piracicaba ≃	296	22.36 S	48.19 W
Piraeus → Piraiévs	172	37.57 N	23.38 E
Piraí	296	22.38 S	43.54 W
Piraí do Sul	294	24.31 S	49.56 W
Piraiévs (Piraeus)	172	37.57 N	23.38 E
Piraju	296	23.12 S	49.23 W
Pirajuba	296	19.54 S	48.42 W
Pirajuí	296	21.59 S	49.29 W
Pirámide Xochicalco ⊥	278	18.48 N	99.19 W
Piran	170	45.32 N	13.34 E
Pirané	294	25.44 S	59.07 W
Piranga	296	20.41 S	43.18 W
Piranhas	296	16.31 S	51.51 W
Pirapetinga	296	21.39 S	42.21 W
Pirapó ≃	296	22.30 S	52.01 W
Pirapora	296	17.21 S	44.56 W
Piraputanga	296	20.26 S	55.32 W
Piraquara	294	25.26 S	49.04 W
Pirarajá	294	33.44 S	54.45 W
Piraras, Cachoeira de ↳	296	14.02 S	53.25 W
Pirassununga	296	21.59 S	47.25 W
Piratinga ≃	296	15.41 S	46.07 W
Piratini	294	31.27 S	53.06 W
Piratini ≃	294	28.06 S	55.27 W
Piratuba	294	27.27 S	51.48 W
Piratucu ≃	290	1.59 S	56.58 W
Piraube, Lac ⊜	240	50.26 N	71.44 W
Piray ≃	292	16.32 S	63.45 W
Pirdop	172	42.42 N	24.11 E
Pirenópolis	296	15.51 S	48.57 W
Pires do Rio	296	17.18 S	48.17 W
Pírgos	172	37.41 N	21.28 E
Piriápolis	294	34.54 S	55.17 W
Piribebuy	294	25.29 S	57.03 W
Pirin ⋀	172	41.40 N	23.30 E
Píritu, Ven.	290	11.22 N	69.08 W
Píritu, Ven.	290	9.23 N	69.12 W
Pirmasens	164	49.12 N	7.36 E
Pirna	164	50.58 N	13.56 E
Pirón ≃	168	41.23 N	4.31 W
Pirot	172	43.09 N	22.35 E
Pirovano	294	36.31 S	61.34 W
Pīr Panjāl Range ⋀	206	33.37 N	74.32 E
Pirrís ≃	280	9.28 N	84.20 W
Pirtleville	254	31.22 N	109.34 W
Piru, Indon.	198	3.03 S	128.12 E
Piru, Calif., U.S.	274	34.25 N	118.48 W
Pisa	184	43.43 N	10.23 E
Pisa □[4]	184	43.25 N	10.43 E
Pisa ≃	164	53.15 N	21.52 E
Pisa, Mount ∧	230	44.53 S	169.12 E
Pisac ⊥	292	13.25 S	71.53 W
Pisagua	292	19.36 S	70.13 W
Pisam-bong ∧	194	40.41 N	126.34 E
Pisau, Tanjong ≻	202	6.04 N	118.03 E
Pişchia	172	45.55 N	21.20 E
Pisco	292	13.42 S	76.13 W
Pisco ≃	292	13.42 S	76.13 W
Pisco, Bahía de C	292	13.47 S	76.17 W
Pişcolt	172	47.35 N	22.18 E
Písek	164	49.19 N	14.10 E
Pishan	190	37.37 N	78.18 E
Pishan I	196	28.06 N	121.30 E
Pishīn Lora ≃	206	29.09 N	64.55 E
Pisidia □[9]	212	31.30 N	31.00 E
Pisinimo	254	32.02 N	112.19 W
Pišnur	160	57.47 N	47.58 E
Piso, Lake ⊜	222	6.48 N	11.17 W
Pisogne	180	45.48 N	10.06 E
Pisqui ≃	292	7.40 S	75.05 W
Pissos	166	44.19 N	0.47 W
Pistakee	268	42.25 N	88.11 W
Pisticci	170	40.23 N	16.34 E
Pistoia	184	43.55 N	10.54 E
Pistoia □[4]	184	43.58 N	10.50 E
Pistolet Bay C	240	51.32 N	55.50 W
Pistuk Peak ∧	236	59.43 N	159.42 W
Pisuerga ≃	168	41.33 N	4.52 W
Pisz (Johannisburg)	164	53.38 N	21.49 E
Pit ≃	258	40.45 N	122.22 W
Pita □[4]	222	11.00 N	12.45 W
Pital	290	2.16 N	75.49 W
Pitalito	290	1.51 N	76.02 W
Pitanga	294	24.46 S	51.44 W
Pitangueiras	296	21.02 S	48.13 W
Pitangui	296	19.40 S	44.54 W
Piteå	160	65.20 N	21.30 E
Piteälven ≃	160	65.14 N	21.32 E
Pitelino	160	54.34 N	41.49 E
Piteşti	172	44.52 N	24.52 E
Pithiviers	176	48.10 N	2.15 E
Pitigliano	170	42.38 N	11.40 E
Pitiquito	278	30.42 N	112.02 W
Pitk'aranta	160	61.34 N	31.27 E
Pitkas Point	236	62.02 N	163.17 W
Pitlochry	162	56.43 N	3.45 W
Pitman	262	39.44 N	75.08 W
Pitogo	202	10.08 N	124.33 E
Pitomača	170	45.57 N	17.14 E
Pitt Island I	238	53.35 N	129.45 W
Pitt Lake ⊜	238	49.25 N	122.32 W
Pittsboro, Miss., U.S.	248	33.56 N	89.20 W
Pittsboro, N.C., U.S.	246	35.43 N	79.11 W
Pittsburg, Calif., U.S.	272	38.02 N	121.53 W
Pittsburg, Kans., U.S.	252	37.25 N	94.42 W
Pittsburg, N.H., U.S.	260	45.03 N	71.21 W
Pittsburg, Tex., U.S.	250	33.00 N	94.58 W
Pittsburgh, Ind., U.S.	268	40.37 N	86.42 W
Pittsburgh, Pa., U.S.	266	40.26 N	80.00 W
Pittsfield, Ill., U.S.	248	39.36 N	90.48 W
Pittsfield, Maine, U.S.	242	44.47 N	69.23 W
Pittsfield, Mass., U.S.	261	42.27 N	73.15 W
Pittsfield, N.H., U.S.	242	43.18 N	71.19 W
Pittsfield, Pa., U.S.	266	41.50 N	79.23 W
Pittsford, Mich., U.S.	268	41.52 N	84.28 W
Pittsford, N.Y., U.S.	264	43.05 N	77.31 W
Pittston	242	41.19 N	75.47 W
Pittsview	248	32.11 N	85.10 W
Pittsville	262	38.24 N	75.52 W
Pituil	294	28.34 S	67.26 W
Pitumarca	292	13.59 S	71.25 W
Piu, Cerro ∧	280	13.38 N	84.52 W
Pium	286	10.27 S	49.11 W
Piura	292	5.12 S	80.38 W
Piura □[5]	292	5.10 S	80.00 W
Piura ≃	292	5.35 S	80.50 W
Piute Peak ∧	258	35.27 N	118.24 W
Piute Reservoir ⊜[1]	254	38.17 N	112.12 W
Pivan'	186	50.29 N	137.06 E
Pivijay	290	10.28 N	74.37 W
Piwniczna	164	49.27 N	20.42 E
Pixley	272	35.58 N	119.17 W
Piyadin	172	37.01 N	29.58 E
Pizarro	290	4.58 N	77.22 W
Pizzighettone	182	45.11 N	9.47 E
Pizzo	170	38.44 N	16.10 E
Pjalka	160	66.43 N	40.59 E
Placentia, Newf., Can.	240	47.15 N	53.58 W
Placentia, Calif., U.S.	274	33.52 N	117.46 W
Placentia Bay C	240	47.15 N	54.30 W
Placer, Pil.	202	11.52 N	123.55 E
Placer, Pil.	202	9.39 N	125.35 E
Placer □[6]	272	38.54 N	121.04 W
Placerville	272	38.43 N	120.48 W
Placetas	284p	22.19 N	79.40 W
Plácido de Castro	292	10.20 S	67.11 W
Plácido Rosas	294	32.45 S	53.44 W
Placitas	254	35.18 N	106.25 W
Plačkovica ⋀	172	41.45 N	22.35 E
Plai Mat ≃	200	15.23 N	102.47 E
Plain	270	47.46 N	120.39 W
Plain City, Ohio, U.S.	266	40.06 N	83.16 W
Plain City, Utah, U.S.	254	41.18 N	112.06 W
Plain Dealing	248	32.54 N	93.42 W
Plainfield, Conn., U.S.	261	41.41 N	71.55 W
Plainfield, Ill., U.S.	268	41.37 N	88.12 W
Plainfield, Ind., U.S.	248	39.42 N	86.24 W
Plainfield, Mass., U.S.	261	42.31 N	72.55 W
Plainfield, N.J., U.S.	262	40.37 N	74.26 W
Plainfield, Ohio, U.S.	266	40.13 N	81.43 W
Plainfield, Pa., U.S.	262	40.12 N	77.17 W
Plainfield, Wis., U.S.	244	44.13 N	89.30 W
Plainfield Heights	268	43.01 N	85.37 W
Plains, Ga., U.S.	246	32.02 N	84.24 W
Plains, Kans., U.S.	252	37.16 N	100.35 W
Plains, Mont., U.S.	256	47.27 N	114.53 W
Plains, Tex., U.S.	250	33.11 N	102.50 W
Plainsboro	262	40.20 N	74.36 W
Plainview, Calif., U.S.	272	36.08 N	119.08 W
Plainview, Minn., U.S.	244	44.10 N	92.10 W
Plainview, Nebr., U.S.	252	42.21 N	97.47 W
Plainview, Tex., U.S.	250	34.11 N	101.43 W
Plainville, Conn., U.S.	261	41.41 N	72.51 W
Plainville, Ind., U.S.	248	38.48 N	87.09 W
Plainville, Kans., U.S.	252	39.14 N	99.18 W
Plainville, Mass., U.S.	261	42.00 N	71.20 W
Plainville, N.Y., U.S.	264	43.10 N	76.27 W
Plainwell	268	42.27 N	85.38 W
Plaisance, Baie de C	240	47.16 N	61.52 W
Plaistow	242	42.50 N	71.06 W
Plaksino	160	56.11 N	30.42 E
Plamondon	238	54.51 N	112.19 W
Planá	164	49.52 N	12.44 E
Planada	272	37.18 N	120.19 W
Planaltina	296	15.37 S	47.40 W
Planalto	294	27.20 S	53.03 W
Planeta Rica	290	8.25 N	75.36 W
Plankinton	252	43.43 N	98.29 W
Plano, Ill., U.S.	268	41.40 N	88.32 W
Plano, Tex., U.S.	250	33.01 N	96.42 W
Plantagenet	260	45.32 N	75.00 W
Plantation	246	26.05 N	80.14 W
Plant City	246	28.01 N	82.08 W
Plantersville, Ala., U.S.	248	32.40 N	86.55 W
Plantersville, Miss., U.S.	248	34.12 N	88.40 W
Plantsite	254	33.02 N	109.21 W
Plantsville	261	41.35 N	72.54 W
Plaquemine	248	30.17 N	91.14 W
Plaridel, Pil.	202	10.33 N	124.46 E
Plaridel, Pil.	202	8.37 N	123.42 E
Plasencia	168	40.02 N	6.05 W
Plaski	170	45.05 N	15.22 E
Plast	158	54.22 N	60.50 E
Plaster City	278	32.47 N	115.51 W
Plaster Rock	240	46.54 N	67.24 W
Plasy	164	49.56 N	13.24 E
Plata, Río de la C[1]	294	35.00 S	57.00 W
Platani ≃	170	37.23 N	13.16 E
Platea	266	41.57 N	80.20 W
Plateau du Kontum	200	13.55 N	108.05 E
Platinum	236	59.01 N	161.49 W
Plato	290	9.47 N	74.47 W
Platte	252	43.23 N	98.51 W
Platte ≃, U.S.	248	39.16 N	94.50 W
Platte ≃, Minn., U.S.	244	45.47 N	94.17 W
Platte ≃, Nebr., U.S.	252	41.04 N	95.53 W
Platte ≃, Wis., U.S.	244	42.37 N	90.40 W
Platte Center	252	41.32 N	97.29 W
Platte City	248	39.22 N	94.47 W
Platte Island I	218	5.52 S	55.23 E
Platteville, Colo., U.S.	254	40.13 N	104.49 W
Platteville, Wis., U.S.	244	42.44 N	90.29 W
Plattling	164	48.47 N	12.53 E
Platt National Park ♠	250	34.25 N	97.00 W
Plattsburg	248	39.34 N	94.27 W
Plattsburgh	242	44.42 N	73.28 W
Plattsmouth	252	41.01 N	95.53 W
Plattsville	264	43.18 N	80.37 W
Plau	164	53.27 N	12.16 E
Plauen	164	50.30 N	12.08 E
Plav	172	42.36 N	19.56 E
Plaviņas	160	56.37 N	25.43 E
Playa Azul	278	17.59 N	102.24 W
Playa Bonita	280	9.39 N	84.27 W
Playa de Fajardo	284m	18.20 N	65.38 W
Playa de Guayanés	284m	18.04 N	65.49 W
Playa de Guayanilla	284m	18.01 N	66.46 W
Playa de Naguabo	284m	18.12 N	65.43 W
Playa de Ponce	284m	17.59 N	66.37 W
Playa Noriega, Laguna ⊜	278	29.10 N	111.50 W
Playas Lake ⊜	254	31.50 N	108.34 W
Playa Vicente	278	17.50 N	95.49 W
Playgreen Lake ⊜	232	54.00 N	98.10 W
Playon Grande	290	9.30 N	78.20 W
Plaza	252	48.01 N	101.58 W
Plaza de Caisan	280	8.45 N	82.48 W
Plaza Huincul	294	38.57 S	69.12 W
Pleasant, Lake ⊜[1]	254	33.53 N	112.16 W
Pleasant, Mount ∧	246	37.44 N	79.10 W
Pleasant Bay	240	46.49 N	60.48 W
Pleasant Bay C	240	44.30 N	67.45 W
Pleasantdale	261	42.47 N	73.40 W
Pleasant Gap	266	40.52 N	77.45 W
Pleasant Garden	246	35.58 N	79.46 W
Pleasant Grove, Calif., U.S.	272	38.49 N	121.29 W
Pleasant Grove, Utah, U.S.	254	40.22 N	111.44 W
Pleasant Hill, Calif., U.S.	272	37.56 N	122.04 W
Pleasant Hill, Ill., U.S.	248	39.27 N	90.52 W
Pleasant Hill, La., U.S.	248	31.49 N	93.31 W
Pleasant Hill, Mo., U.S.	248	38.47 N	94.16 W
Pleasant Hill, N.C., U.S.	262	36.32 N	77.32 W
Pleasant Hills	266	40.20 N	79.58 W
Pleasant Home	270	45.28 N	122.20 W
Pleasant Lake, Ind., U.S.	268	41.35 N	85.01 W
Pleasant Lake, Mich., U.S.	268	42.23 N	84.22 W
Pleasant Mills	268	40.47 N	84.51 W
Pleasanton, Calif., U.S.	272	37.40 N	121.53 W
Pleasanton, Kans., U.S.	252	38.11 N	94.43 W
Pleasanton, Tex., U.S.	250	28.58 N	98.29 W
Pleasant Plains, Ill., U.S.	248	39.52 N	89.55 W
Pleasant Plains, N.J., U.S.	262	40.00 N	74.13 W
Pleasant Prairie	268	42.33 N	87.57 W
Pleasant Unity	266	40.15 N	79.28 W
Pleasant Valley	261	41.45 N	73.50 W
Pleasantville, Iowa, U.S.	244	41.23 N	93.18 W
Pleasantville, N.J., U.S.	262	39.23 N	74.32 W
Pleasantville, N.Y., U.S.	261	41.08 N	73.48 W
Pleasantville, Pa., U.S.	266	41.36 N	79.35 W
Pleasure Beach	261	41.18 N	72.08 W
Pléaux	166	45.08 N	2.14 E
Pleiku	200	13.58 N	108.01 E
Pleine d'Aleria ◂[1]	170	42.05 N	9.25 E
Plélan-le-Grand	166	48.00 N	2.06 W
Pléneuf	166	48.36 N	2.33 W
Plenty, Bay Of C	230	37.40 S	177.10 E
Plentywood	252	48.47 N	104.34 W
Pleseck	160	62.43 N	40.20 E
Plessisville	260	46.13 N	71.47 W
Pleszew	164	51.54 N	17.48 E
Pleternica	172	45.17 N	17.48 E
Plétipi, Lac ⊜	232	51.45 N	70.08 W
Plettenberg	178	51.13 N	7.52 E
Pleven	172	43.25 N	24.37 E
Plevna	252	46.25 N	104.31 W
Pleyben	162	48.14 N	3.58 W
Plješevica ⋀	170	44.40 N	15.45 E
Pljevlja	172	43.21 N	19.21 E
Ploaghe	170	40.40 N	8.44 E
Ploče	170	43.04 N	17.26 E
Płock	164	52.33 N	19.43 E
Plöckenpass)(	164	46.36 N	12.58 E
Ploërmel	166	47.56 N	2.24 W
Plogastel-Saint-Germain	162	47.59 N	4.16 W
Ploieşti	172	44.56 N	26.02 E
Plomárion	172	38.59 N	26.22 E
Plomb du Cantal ∧	166	45.03 N	2.46 E
Plombières-les-Bains	170	47.58 N	6.29 E
Plomer, Point ≻	228	31.19 S	152.58 E
Plön	164	54.09 N	10.25 E
Płońsk	164	52.38 N	20.23 E
Ploskoš'	160	56.46 N	31.16 E
Plottier	294	38.57 S	68.14 W
Płoty (Plathe)	164	53.49 N	15.16 E
Plouaret	166	48.37 N	3.28 W
Plouay	166	47.55 N	3.20 W
Ploubalay	166	48.35 N	2.09 W
Ploudalmézeau	166	48.32 N	4.39 W
Plouescat	166	48.40 N	4.10 W
Plouguenast	166	48.17 N	2.43 W
Plouha	166	48.41 N	2.56 W
Plovdiv	172	42.09 N	24.45 E
Plover ≃	244	44.29 N	89.35 W
Plover Islands II	236	71.15 N	155.30 W
Plum, Pa., U.S.	266	40.28 N	79.44 W
Plum, Pa., U.S.	266	41.35 N	79.51 W
Plumb	270	46.56 N	122.51 W
Plumerville	248	35.10 N	92.38 W
Plummer	256	47.20 N	116.53 W
Plumsteadville	262	40.23 N	75.09 W
Plumtree	218	20.30 S	27.50 E
Plumville	266	40.48 N	79.11 W
Pl'usa	160	58.26 N	29.21 E
Pluvigner	162	47.46 N	3.01 W
Plymouth, Monts.	282	16.42 N	62.13 W
Plymouth, Trin.	285r	11.13 N	60.47 W
Plymouth, Eng., U.K.	174	50.23 N	4.10 W
Plymouth, Calif., U.S.	272	38.29 N	120.51 W
Plymouth, Conn., U.S.	261	41.40 N	73.03 W
Plymouth, Ill., U.S.	248	40.29 N	90.58 W
Plymouth, Ind., U.S.	268	41.21 N	86.19 W
Plymouth, Mass., U.S.	261	41.58 N	70.41 W
Plymouth, Mich., U.S.	268	42.22 N	83.28 W
Plymouth, Nebr., U.S.	252	40.18 N	97.00 W
Plymouth, N.H., U.S.	242	43.45 N	71.41 W
Plymouth, N.C., U.S.	246	35.52 N	76.43 W
Plymouth, Ohio, U.S.	266	40.59 N	82.40 W
Plymouth, Pa., U.S.	242	41.14 N	75.58 W
Plymouth, Wis., U.S.	244	43.45 N	87.58 W
Plymouth □[6]	261	41.58 N	70.41 W
Plympton, Eng., U.K.	174	50.23 N	4.03 W
Plympton, Mass., U.S.	261	41.57 N	70.49 W
Plymptonville	266	41.03 N	78.28 W
Plymstock	174	50.22 N	4.04 W
Plzeň	164	49.45 N	13.23 E
Pniewy	164	52.31 N	16.15 E
Po ≃	170	44.57 N	12.04 E
Poana ≃	290	0.56 N	57.03 W
Poás, Volcán ∧[1]	280	10.12 N	84.13 W
Pobé	222	6.58 N	2.41 E
Pobeda, Gora ∧	186	65.12 N	146.12 E
Pobedino	186	49.51 N	142.49 E
Pobedy, Pik ∧	186	42.02 N	80.05 E
Poblado Cerro Gordo	284m	18.29 N	66.20 W
Poblado Jacaguas	284m	18.03 N	66.32 W
Poblado Medianía Alta	284m	18.26 N	65.50 W
Poblado Sábalos	284m	18.11 N	67.09 W
Poblado Santana	284m	18.27 N	66.40 W
Pocahontas, Ark., U.S.	248	36.16 N	90.58 W
Pocahontas, Ill., U.S.	248	38.50 N	89.33 W
Pocahontas, Iowa, U.S.	252	42.44 N	94.40 W
Pocasset	261	41.41 N	70.37 W
Pocatalico ≃	242	38.29 N	81.49 W
Pocatello	256	42.52 N	112.27 W
Počegda	160	62.42 N	43.23 E
Počep	158	52.56 N	33.27 E
Pöchlarn	164	48.12 N	15.13 E
Pochutla	278	15.44 N	96.28 W
Pochvistnevo	160	53.38 N	52.08 E
Počinki	160	54.42 N	44.51 E
Pocitos	294	22.05 S	63.44 W
Pocoata	292	18.41 S	66.11 W
Poções	296	14.31 S	40.21 W
Poço Fundo	294	21.48 S	45.58 W
Pocomoke ≃	242	37.58 N	75.39 W
Pocomoke City	242	38.05 N	75.34 W
Pocona	292	17.39 S	65.24 W
Poconé	292	16.15 S	56.37 W
Pocono Mountains ⋀[2]	242	41.10 N	75.20 W
Poços de Caldas	296	21.48 S	46.34 W
Pocrane	296	19.37 S	41.37 W
Pocrí	280	7.40 N	80.07 W
Podčerje	160	63.53 N	57.57 E
Poddębice	164	51.53 N	18.58 E
Poddemjur	160	64.05 N	53.26 E
Poddorje	160	57.28 N	31.07 E
Poděbrady	164	50.08 N	15.07 E
Podensac	166	44.39 N	0.22 W
Podgorica → Titograd	172	42.26 N	19.14 E
Podhale ⋀[2]	164	49.25 N	20.00 E
Podkamennaja Tunguska	186	61.36 N	90.09 E
Podkamennaja Tunguska ≃	186	61.36 N	90.18 E
Podlasie ◂[1]	164	52.20 N	23.00 E
Podol'sk	160	55.26 N	37.33 E
Podol'skaja Vozvyšennost' ⋀[1]	158	49.00 N	27.00 E
Podor	222		
	214	16.40 N	14.57 W
Podora	160	62.22 N	54.19 E
Podosinovec	160	60.17 N	47.04 E
Podporožje	160	60.53 N	34.07 E
Podravina ◂[1]	172	45.40 N	17.40 E
Podravska Slatina	172	45.42 N	17.42 E
Podrezčicha	160	59.22 N	51.28 E
Pod'uga	160	61.06 N	40.53 E
Podujevo	172	42.55 N	21.11 E
Podu-Turcului	172	46.12 N	27.23 E
Poe	268	40.56 N	85.05 W
Poelela, Lagoa ⊜	224	24.38 S	35.00 E
Poestenkill	261	42.41 N	73.34 W
Pofadder	218	29.10 S	19.22 E
Pogamasing Lake ⊜	244	46.57 N	81.50 W
Pogănişul ≃	172	45.41 N	21.22 E
Poggibonsi	184	43.28 N	11.09 E
Poggiomarino	184	40.48 N	14.32 E
Pogoanele	172	44.54 N	27.00 E
Pogoniani	172	40.00 N	20.25 E
Pogradec	172	40.54 N	20.39 E
Pograničnyj	186	46.57 N	45.46 E
Pogromni Volcano ∧[1]	236	54.33 N	164.45 W
Pogruznaja	160	54.14 N	50.29 E
P'ohang	194	36.03 N	129.20 E
Pohjois-Karjalan lääni □[4]	160	63.00 N	30.00 E
Pohořelice	164	48.59 N	16.32 E
Pohorje ⋀	170	46.30 N	15.20 E
Pohue Bay C	275d	19.00 N	155.48 W
Poiana Mare	172	43.55 N	23.04 E
Poinsett, Cape ≻	148	65.42 S	113.18 E
Poinsett, Lake ⊜	252	44.34 N	97.05 W
Point	250	32.56 N	95.52 W
Point Arena	258	38.55 N	123.41 W
Point Au Fer Island I	248	29.15 N	91.15 W
Point Baker	236	56.21 N	133.37 W
Point Chautauqua	266	42.14 N	79.28 W
Point Comfort	250	28.41 N	96.33 W
Pointe-à-la-Frégate	240	49.12 N	64.56 W
Pointe-à-la-Garde	240	48.05 N	66.33 W
Pointe a la Hache	248	29.35 N	89.48 W
Pointe-à-Maurier	240	50.21 N	59.50 W
Pointe-à-Pitre	285o	16.14 N	61.32 W
Pointe-au-Chêne	260	45.39 N	74.45 W
Pointe Aux Peaux Farms	268	41.57 N	83.16 W
Pointe-aux-Trembles	260	45.39 N	73.29 W
Pointe-Claire	260	45.26 N	73.49 W
Point Edward	266	43.00 N	82.24 W
Pointe-Gatineau	264	45.27 N	75.43 W
Pointe-Noire, Congo	218	4.48 S	11.51 E
Pointe-Noire, Guad.	285o	16.14 N	61.47 W
Pointers	262	39.36 N	75.28 W
Point Fortin	285r	10.11 N	61.41 W
Point Hope	236	68.21 N	166.41 W
Point Imperial ∧	254	36.16 N	111.58 W
Point Independence	261	41.44 N	70.39 W
Point Lake ⊜	232	65.15 N	113.04 W
Point Leamington	240	49.20 N	55.24 W
Point Marion	242	39.44 N	79.53 W
Point of Rocks	262	39.17 N	77.32 W
Point Pelee National Park ♠	244	41.57 N	82.30 W
Point Pleasant, N.J., U.S.	262	40.05 N	74.04 W
Point Pleasant, Pa., U.S.	262	40.25 N	75.04 W
Point Pleasant Beach	262	40.05 N	74.03 W
Point Reyes National Seashore ♠	258	38.00 N	122.58 W
Point Roberts	270	48.59 N	123.13 W
Point Sapin	240	46.58 N	64.50 W
Point Whiteshed	236	60.28 N	145.57 W
Poirino	182	44.55 N	7.51 E
Poisson-Blanc, Lac ⊜[1]	242	46.00 N	75.44 W
Poissy	176	48.56 N	2.03 E
Poitiers	166	46.35 N	0.20 E
Poitou □[9]	166	46.20 N	0.30 W
Poix	166	49.47 N	1.59 E
Pojarkovo	186	49.38 N	128.38 E
Pojiang ≃	196	28.57 N	116.39 E
Pojo	292	17.45 S	64.49 W
Pojoaque Valley	254	35.53 N	105.59 W
Pojuca	296	12.21 S	38.20 W
Pojuca ≃	296	12.34 S	38.03 W
Pokhara	190	28.12 N	83.59 E
Pok Liu Chau I	196	22.12 N	114.07 E
Pokrovsk	186	61.29 N	129.06 E
Pokur	186	61.02 N	75.26 E
Pola → Pula, Jugo.	170	44.52 N	13.50 E
Pola, Phil.	202	13.09 N	121.26 E
Pola Bay C	202	13.10 N	121.30 E
Polacca	254	35.50 N	110.23 W
Polacca Wash ∨	254	35.22 N	110.50 W
Pola de Laviana	168	43.15 N	5.34 W
Pola de Lena	168	43.10 N	5.49 W
Pola de Siero	168	43.23 N	5.40 W
Polanco	294	33.54 S	55.09 W
Poland	266	41.01 N	80.37 W
Poland □[1]	158	52.00 N	19.00 E
Polangui	202	13.17 N	123.29 E
Polanów (Pollnow)	164	54.08 N	16.39 E
Pol'arnik	236	67.00 N	179.15 W
Pol'arnyj	160	69.12 N	33.22 E
Pol'arnyj Ural ⋀	160	66.55 N	64.30 E
Polatlı	212	39.36 N	32.09 E
Polcirkeln	160	66.34 N	21.05 E
Polcura	294	37.17 S	71.43 W
Połczyn Zdrój (Bad Polzin)	164	53.46 N	16.06 E
Poldnevica	160	58.37 N	46.38 E
Polebridge	238	48.46 N	114.17 W
Pole Mountain ∧	254	41.14 N	105.23 W
Polesje ◂[1]	186	52.30 N	27.30 E
Polessk	160	54.52 N	21.05 E
Polessk [Labiau]	164	54.52 N	21.05 E
Polevskoj	158	56.26 N	60.11 E
Polgár	164	47.52 N	21.08 E
Policastro, Golfo di C	170	40.00 N	15.30 E
Police (Pölitz)	164	53.33 N	14.35 E
Polička	164	49.43 N	16.16 E
Polidoro ◂[8]	184	41.55 N	12.10 E
Poligny	166	46.50 N	5.43 E
Políkastron	172	41.00 N	22.34 E
Políkhnitos	172	39.05 N	26.11 E
Polillo	202	14.43 N	121.56 E
Polillo Island I	202	14.50 N	121.55 E
Polillo Islands II	202	14.50 N	122.10 E
Polillo Strait ⊔	202	14.50 N	121.45 E
Polistena	170	38.25 N	16.05 E
Políyiros	172	40.23 N	23.27 E
Polk, Nebr., U.S.	252	41.05 N	97.46 W
Polk, Ohio, U.S.	266	40.57 N	82.13 W
Polk, Pa., U.S.	266	41.22 N	79.56 W
Polk □[6]	270	45.00 N	123.23 W
Pol'kino	186	71.10 N	99.13 E
Polkton	246	35.00 N	80.12 W
Polkville	248	32.12 N	89.41 W
Polla	170	40.30 N	15.30 E
Pöllau	164	47.18 N	15.51 E
Pollino, Monte ∧	170	39.55 N	16.11 E
Polloc Harbor C	202	7.22 N	124.13 E
Pollock, La., U.S.	248	31.31 N	92.24 W
Pollock, S. Dak., U.S.	252	45.55 N	100.17 W
Pollock Pines	272	38.46 N	120.34 W
Pollux ∧	230	44.14 S	168.52 E
Polmak	160	70.04 N	28.00 E
Polná	164	49.29 N	15.43 E
Polo, Ill., U.S.	244	41.59 N	89.35 W
Polo, Mo., U.S.	248	39.33 N	94.03 W
Polochic ≃	280	15.26 N	89.20 W
Polock	160	55.31 N	28.46 E
Polom	160	59.13 N	50.50 E
Poloninskij Chrebet ⋀	172	48.40 N	23.20 E
Polonio, Cabo ≻	294	34.24 S	53.46 W
Polonnaruwa	204	7.56 N	81.00 E
Polos	172	41.50 N	27.04 E
Polski Trâmbeš	172	43.22 N	25.38 E
Polson	256	47.41 N	114.09 W
Polsum	178	51.37 N	7.03 E
Poltava	158	49.35 N	34.34 E
Poltimore	242	45.47 N	75.42 W
Põltsamaa	160	58.38 N	25.58 E
Poluj ≃	186	66.31 N	66.33 E
Polunočnoje	158	60.52 N	60.25 E
Polvijärvi	160	62.51 N	29.22 E
Polynesia II	148	4.00 S	156.00 W
Polysajevo	186	54.35 N	86.14 E
Pomabamba	292	8.50 S	77.25 W
Pomacanchi	292	14.02 S	71.35 W
Pomacocha	292	5.52 S	77.55 W
Pomahaka ≃	230	46.08 S	169.34 E
Pomán	294	28.33 S	66.12 W
Pomarance	184	43.18 N	10.52 E
Pomarkku	160	61.42 N	22.00 E
Pomaro	278	18.20 N	103.18 W
Pomata	292	16.18 S	69.20 W
Pombal	168	39.55 N	8.38 W
Pombas, Rio das ≃	292	6.27 S	60.18 W
Pomerania → Pomorze □[9]	164	54.00 N	16.00 E
Pomeranian Bay (Pommersche Bucht) ⊤[2]	164	54.00 N	14.15 E
Pomerene	254	32.01 N	110.17 W
Pomerode	294	26.45 S	49.11 W
Pomeroon ≃	290	7.35 N	58.45 W
Pomeroy, Iowa, U.S.	252	42.33 N	94.41 W
Pomeroy, Ohio, U.S.	242	39.02 N	82.02 W
Pomeroy, Pa., U.S.	262	39.58 N	75.53 W
Pomeroy, Wash., U.S.	256	46.28 N	117.36 W
Pomezia	184	41.40 N	12.30 E
Pomfret, Conn., U.S.	261	41.54 N	71.58 W
Pomfret, Md., U.S.	262	38.35 N	77.02 W
Pomi	172	47.42 N	23.19 E
Pomigliano d'Arco	184	40.54 N	14.23 E
Pomme de Terre ≃, Minn., U.S.	252	45.10 N	96.05 W
Pomme de Terre ≃, Mo., U.S.	248	38.11 N	93.24 W
Pomme de Terre Reservoir ⊜[1]	248	37.51 N	93.19 W
Pomona, Calif., U.S.	274	34.04 N	117.45 W
Pomona, Kans., U.S.	252	38.36 N	95.27 W
Pomona, Mo., U.S.	248	36.52 N	91.55 W
Pomona, N.J., U.S.	262	39.29 N	74.35 W
Pomona Park	246	29.30 N	81.36 W
Pomona Reservoir ⊜[1]	252	38.40 N	95.35 W
Pomorie	172	42.33 N	27.39 E
Pomorze □[9]	164	54.00 N	16.00 E
Pomozdino	160	62.12 N	54.06 E
Pompano Beach	246	26.15 N	80.07 W
Pompei	184	40.45 N	14.30 E
Pompei ⊥	170	40.45 N	14.30 E
Pompéia	296	22.08 S	50.10 W
Pompéu	296	19.12 S	44.59 W
Pompey	264	42.54 N	76.01 W
Pompton Lakes	242	41.00 N	74.17 W
Pomquet	240	45.38 N	61.51 W
Ponazyrevo	160	58.21 N	46.19 E
Ponca	252	42.34 N	96.43 W
Ponca City	250	36.42 N	97.05 W
Ponce	284m	18.01 N	66.37 W
Ponce de Leon	248	30.44 N	85.56 W
Ponce de Leon Inlet C	246	29.04 N	80.55 W
Poncha Pass)(	254	38.25 N	106.05 W
Ponchatoula	248	30.26 N	90.26 W
Pondcreek	250	36.40 N	97.48 W
Ponderay	238	48.18 N	116.32 W
Pond Inlet	232	72.41 N	78.00 W
Pond Inlet C	232	72.46 N	77.00 W
Pond Meadow	261	41.20 N	72.28 W
Pondoland ◂[1]	224	31.00 S	29.30 E
Pondosa, Calif., U.S.	258	41.12 N	121.41 W
Pondosa, Oreg., U.S.	256	45.01 N	117.38 W
Poneas Island I	202	9.55 N	125.56 E
Ponente, Riviera di •[2]	170	44.10 N	8.20 E
Poneto	268	40.39 N	85.13 W
Ponferrada	168	42.33 N	6.35 W
Pongo ≃	220	8.42 N	27.40 E
Pon'goma	160	65.21 N	34.25 E
Ponhook Lake ⊜	240	44.18 N	64.54 W
Poniatowa	164	51.11 N	22.05 E
Poniec	164	51.47 N	16.50 E
Ponoj	160	67.05 N	41.07 E
Ponoj ≃	160	66.59 N	41.17 E
Ponoka	238	52.42 N	113.35 W
Pons, Esp.	168	41.55 N	1.12 E
Pons, Fr.	166	45.35 N	0.33 W
Ponsacco	184	43.37 N	10.38 E
Ponson Island I	202	10.47 N	124.32 E
Ponsul ≃	168	39.40 N	7.31 W
Pont-à-Celles	176	50.30 N	4.21 E
Ponta da Areia	296	17.44 S	39.14 W
Ponta Grossa	294	25.05 S	50.09 W
Pontalina	296	17.31 S	49.27 W
Pont-à-Marcq	166	50.31 N	3.07 E
Pont-à-Mousson	166	48.54 N	6.04 E
Pontão	168	39.55 N	8.22 W
Ponta Porã	296	22.32 S	55.43 W
Pontarlier	180	46.54 N	6.22 E
Pontassieve	184	43.46 N	11.26 E
Pont-Audemer	176	49.21 N	0.31 E
Pontaumur	166	45.52 N	2.40 E
Pont-Aven	166	47.51 N	3.45 W
Pontbriand	260	46.09 N	71.15 W
Pont Canavese	182	45.25 N	7.36 E
Pontchartrain, Lake ⊜	248	30.10 N	90.10 W
Pontchâteau	166	47.26 N	2.05 W
Pont-Croix	166	48.02 N	4.29 W
Pont-d'Ain	166	46.03 N	5.20 E
Pont-de-Salars	166	44.17 N	2.44 E
Pont de Suert	168	42.24 N	0.45 E
Pont-de-Vaux	166	46.26 N	4.56 E
Ponte Alta do Bom Jesus	296	12.06 S	46.29 W
Pontebba	164	46.30 N	13.18 E
Ponte Branca	296	16.27 S	52.40 W
Pontecorvo	184	41.27 N	13.40 E
Ponte da Barca	168	41.48 N	8.25 W
Pontedera	184	43.40 N	10.38 E
Ponte de Sôr	168	39.15 N	8.01 W
Ponte do Lima	168	41.46 N	8.35 W
Ponte Nova	296	20.24 S	42.54 W
Ponte San Pietro	182	45.42 N	9.35 E
Ponte Serrada	294	26.52 S	51.58 W
Pontevedra, Esp.	168	42.26 N	8.38 W
Pontevedra, Pil.	202	10.22 N	122.52 E
Pontevedra, Ría de C[1]	168	42.22 N	8.45 W
Pontgibaud	166	46.50 N	2.51 E
Ponthierville → Ubundi	218	0.21 S	25.29 E
Pontiac, Ill., U.S.	268	40.53 N	88.38 W
Pontiac, Mich., U.S.	268	42.37 N	83.18 W
Pontiac □[6]	264	46.30 N	77.00 W
Pontianak	198	0.02 S	109.20 E
Pontivy	166	48.04 N	2.59 W
Pont-l'Abbé	166	47.52 N	4.13 W
Pont-l'Évêque	166	49.18 N	0.11 E
Pontoise	176	49.03 N	2.06 E
Pontoosuc Lake	261	42.30 N	73.15 W
Pontorson	166	48.33 N	1.31 W
Pontotoc, Miss., U.S.	248	34.15 N	89.00 W
Pontotoc, Tex., U.S.	250	30.54 N	98.59 W
Pontremoli	170	42.22 N	9.53 E
Pontresina	166	46.28 N	9.53 E
Pont-Rouge	260	46.45 N	71.42 W
Pont-Sainte-Maxence	176	49.18 N	2.36 E
Pont-Scorff	162	47.50 N	3.24 W
Pont-sur-Yonne	166	48.17 N	3.12 E
Pontus □[9]	212	40.15 N	38.00 E
Pontvallain	162	47.45 N	0.12 E
Pontycymmer	174	51.37 N	3.34 W
Pontypool	174	51.43 N	3.02 W
Pontypridd	174	51.37 N	3.22 W
Pony	256	45.40 N	111.54 W
Ponza, Isola di I	170	40.54 N	12.57 E
Poole	174	50.43 N	1.59 W
Poole, Mount ∧	228	29.37 S	141.46 E
Pooler	246	32.07 N	81.15 W
Poolesville	262	39.09 N	77.25 W
Pooley Island I	238	52.44 N	128.16 W
Poolville	250	32.58 N	97.52 W
Poona → Pune	204	18.31 N	73.54 E
Poona-Bayabo (Gata)	202	7.51 N	124.22 E
Poopelloe Lake ⊜	228	31.39 S	144.00 E
Poopó	292	18.23 S	66.59 W
Poopó, Lago de ⊜	292	18.45 S	67.07 W
Poor Knights Islands II	230	35.30 S	174.44 E
Popa, Isla I	280	9.11 N	82.06 W
Popayán	290	2.27 N	76.36 W
Pope	248	34.13 N	89.57 W
Poperinge	176	50.51 N	2.43 E
Popeşti-Leordeni	172	44.23 N	26.10 E
Pope Valley	272	38.37 N	122.26 W
Popham Bay C	232	64.10 N	65.10 W
Popigaj	186	71.55 N	110.47 E
Popigaj ≃	186	72.54 N	106.36 E
Popiltah, Lake ⊜	228	33.10 S	141.43 E
Popinci	172	42.25 N	24.17 E
Popkum	270	49.12 N	121.44 W
Poplar, Calif., U.S.	272	36.03 N	119.08 W
Poplar, Mont., U.S.	252	48.07 N	105.12 W
Poplar, Wis., U.S.	244	46.35 N	91.48 W
Poplar ≃, Can.	232	53.00 N	97.18 W
Poplar ≃, N.A.	252	48.05 N	105.11 W
Poplar ≃, Minn., U.S.	252	47.51 N	96.04 W
Poplar Bluff	248	36.45 N	90.24 W
Poplar Grove	268	42.22 N	88.49 W
Poplar Mountain ∧	248	36.43 N	85.03 W
Poplar Point	252	50.04 N	97.57 W
Poplar Ridge	264	42.44 N	76.37 W
Poplar Springs	262	39.21 N	77.06 W
Poplarville	248	30.51 N	89.32 W
Popo Aggie ≃	254	43.01 N	108.21 W
Popocatépetl, Volcán ∧[1]	278	19.02 N	98.38 W
Popof Island I	236	55.17 N	160.25 W
Popokabaka	218	5.42 S	16.35 E
Popoli	184	42.10 N	13.50 E
Popovka	160	60.08 N	39.21 E
Popovo	172	43.21 N	26.13 E
Poppenbüttel ◂[8]	178	53.39 N	10.04 E
Poppi	170	43.43 N	11.46 E
Popple ≃	244	45.50 N	88.21 W
Poprad	164	49.03 N	20.18 E
Poprad ≃	164	49.38 N	20.42 E
Popricani	172	47.18 N	27.31 E
Poptún	280	16.21 N	89.26 W
Poquetanuck	261	41.29 N	72.03 W
Poquonock	261	41.54 N	72.41 W
Poquonock Bridge	261	41.19 N	72.11 W
Poquoson	262	37.07 N	76.21 W
Porāli Nai ≃	206	25.58 N	66.26 E
Porangatu	296	13.26 S	49.10 W
Porbandar	206	21.38 N	69.36 E
Porce ≃	290	7.28 N	74.53 W
Porcher Island I	238	53.57 N	130.30 W
Porchov	160	57.46 N	29.34 E
Porciúncula	296	20.58 S	42.02 W
Porco	292	19.50 S	65.59 W
Porcos, Rio dos ≃	296	12.42 S	45.07 W
Porcuna	168	37.52 N	4.11 W
Porcupine ≃	236	66.35 N	145.15 W
Porcupine Dome ∧	236	65.31 N	145.31 W
Porcupine Mountains ⋀	244	46.40 N	89.40 W
Porcupine Point ≻	236	60.45 N	146.44 W
Pordenone	170	45.57 N	12.39 E
Pordim	172	43.23 N	24.51 E
Poreč	170	45.13 N	13.37 E
Porecatu	296	22.43 S	51.24 W
Porečje, S.S.S.R.	160	55.43 N	35.33 E
Porečje, S.S.S.R.	164	53.55 N	24.07 E
Poreckoje	160	55.12 N	46.20 E
Porelou, Réservoir de ⊜[1]	166	44.15 N	2.45 E
Porez	160	57.40 N	51.10 E
Pori	160	61.29 N	21.47 E
Porirua	230	41.08 S	174.51 E
Porjaguba	160	66.47 N	33.45 E
Porkkala	160	59.59 N	24.26 E
Porlamar	290	10.57 N	63.51 W
Porma ≃	168	42.29 N	5.28 W
Pornic	166	47.07 N	2.06 W
Pornos, Embalse de ⊜[1]	168	36.50 N	5.30 W
Porog	160	63.50 N	38.29 E
Poro Island I	202	10.40 N	124.27 E
Poroma	292	18.29 S	65.30 W
Poronajsk	186	49.14 N	143.04 E
Poroškovo	164	48.41 N	22.45 E
Porosozero	160	62.43 N	32.42 E
Porpoise Bay C	148	66.30 S	128.30 E
Porrentruy	180	47.25 N	7.05 E
Porretta Terme	170	44.09 N	10.59 E
Porsangen C[2]	160	70.58 N	27.00 E
Porsangerhalvøya ≻[1]	160	70.50 N	25.00 E
Porsgrunn	160	59.09 N	9.40 E
Porsuk ≃	212	39.42 N	31.59 E
Portachuelo	292	17.21 S	63.24 W
Port Adelaide	228	34.51 S	138.30 E
Portadown	162	54.26 N	6.27 W
Portage, Alaska, U.S.	236	60.50 N	148.58 W
Portage, Ind., U.S.	268	41.34 N	87.14 W
Portage, Mich., U.S.	268	42.12 N	85.41 W
Portage, Ohio, U.S.	268	41.20 N	83.39 W
Portage, Pa., U.S.	266	40.23 N	78.41 W
Portage, Utah, U.S.	254	41.59 N	112.14 W
Portage, Wis., U.S.	244	43.33 N	89.28 W
Portage □[6]	266	41.09 N	81.15 W
Portage Lakes	266	40.59 N	81.32 W
Portage-la-Prairie	252	49.59 N	98.18 W
Portageville, Mo., U.S.	248	36.26 N	89.42 W
Portageville, N.Y., U.S.	266	42.34 N	78.02 W
Portal, Ga., U.S.	246	32.33 N	81.56 W
Portal, N. Dak., U.S.	252	48.59 N	102.33 W
Port Alberni	238	49.14 N	124.48 W
Portal del Infierno ↳	280	14.22 N	85.38 W
Portalegre	168	39.17 N	7.26 W
Portales	250	34.11 N	103.20 W
Port Alexander	236	56.15 N	134.39 W
Port-Alfred, Qué., Can.	240	48.20 N	70.53 W
Port Alfred, S. Afr.	218	33.36 S	26.55 E
Port Alice	238	50.23 N	127.27 W
Port Allegany	266	41.49 N	78.17 W
Port Allen	248	30.27 N	91.12 W
Port Alma	266	42.11 N	82.15 W
Port Alsworth	236	60.12 N	154.20 W
Port Angeles	270	48.07 N	123.27 W
Port Anson	240	49.32 N	55.50 W
Port Antonio	285q	18.10 N	76.28 W
Port Aransas	250	27.50 N	97.04 W
Portarlington	162	53.10 N	7.11 W
Port Arthur, Austl.	226	43.09 S	147.51 E
Port Arthur → Thunder Bay, Ont., Can.	244	48.23 N	89.15 W
Port Arthur, Tex., U.S.	248	29.55 N	93.55 W
Port Arthur → Lüshun, Zhg.	194	38.47 N	121.13 E
Port Ashton	236	60.04 N	148.01 W
Port Askaig	162	55.51 N	6.07 W
Port Augusta	228	32.30 S	137.46 E
Port-au-Port	240	48.33 N	58.43 W
Port au Port Bay C	240	48.40 N	58.45 W
Port au Port Peninsula ≻[1]	240	48.35 N	59.00 W
Port-au-Prince	282	18.32 N	72.20 W
Port-au-Prince, Baie de C	282	18.40 N	72.30 W
Port Austin	244	44.03 N	83.01 W
Port Barre	248	30.34 N	91.57 W
Port-Bergé	218	15.33 S	47.40 E
Port Blair	200	11.39 N	92.45 E
Port Blakely	270	47.37 N	122.28 W
Port Blandford	240	48.21 N	54.10 W
Port Borden	240	46.15 N	63.42 W
Port-Bouët	214	5.15 N	3.58 W
Port Burwell	264	42.39 N	80.49 W
Port Byron, Ill., U.S.	244	41.36 N	90.20 W
Port Byron, N.Y., U.S.	264	43.02 N	76.38 W
Port Carbon	262	40.42 N	76.10 W
Port Carling	264	45.07 N	79.35 W
Port-Cartier	240	50.01 N	66.53 W
Port Chalmers	230	45.49 S	170.37 E
Port Charlotte	246	26.59 N	82.06 W
Port Chester	261	41.00 N	73.40 W
Port Chicago	272	38.03 N	122.01 W
Port Clements	238	53.42 N	132.11 W
Port Clinton, Ohio, U.S.	266	41.31 N	82.56 W
Port Clinton, Pa., U.S.	262	40.35 N	76.02 W
Port Clyde	242	43.56 N	69.15 W
Port Colborne	264	42.53 N	79.14 W
Port Colden	262	40.46 N	74.57 W
Port Coquitlam	238	49.16 N	122.46 W
Port Costa	272	38.03 N	122.11 W
Port Credit	264	43.33 N	79.35 W
Port-Daniel, Rśerve (Port Daniel Reserve) ◂[4]	240	48.18 N	64.55 W
Port-de-Bouc	182	43.24 N	4.59 E
Port-de-Paix	282	19.57 N	72.50 W
Port Dickson	200	2.32 N	101.48 E
Port Dover	264	42.47 N	80.12 W
Port Edward	238	54.14 N	130.18 W
Port Edwards	244	44.21 N	90.05 W
Portegolpe	280	10.20 N	85.46 W
Porteirinha	296	15.44 S	43.02 W
Portel, Bra.	286	1.57 S	50.49 W
Portel, Port.	168	38.18 N	7.42 W
Port Elgin, N.B., Can.	240	46.03 N	64.05 W
Port Elgin, Ont., Can.	244	44.26 N	81.24 W
Port Elizabeth, St. Vin.	285h	13.03 N	61.13 W
Port Elizabeth, S. Afr.	224	33.58 S	25.40 E
Port Elizabeth, N.J., U.S.	262	39.19 N	74.59 W
Port Ellen	162	55.39 N	6.12 W
Porteña	294	31.01 S	62.02 W
Port-en-Bessin	166	49.21 N	0.45 W
Porter, Ind., U.S.	268	41.37 N	87.04 W
Porter, Maine, U.S.	242	43.48 N	70.56 W
Porter, Okla., U.S.	250	35.52 N	95.31 W

Symbols in the index entries are identified on page 360.

Name	Page	Lat°′	Long°′
Porter, Pa., U.S.	266	40.56 N	79.10 W
Porter, Tex., U.S.	250	30.06 N	95.14 W
Porter, Wash., U.S.	270	46.56 N	123.18 W
Porter □[6]	268	41.28 N	87.04 W
Portersville	266	40.56 N	80.09 W
Porterville, Calif., U.S.	258	36.04 N	119.01 W
Porterville, Miss., U.S.	248	32.41 N	88.28 W
Port Essington	238	54.09 N	129.57 W
Portete, Bahía de C	290	12.12 N	71.56 W
Port Ewen	261	41.54 N	73.59 W
Port Fairy	226	38.23 S	142.14 E
Port Gamble	270	47.51 N	122.35 W
Port-Gentil	218	0.43 S	8.47 E
Port Gibson, Miss., U.S.	248	31.58 N	90.58 W
Port Gibson, N.Y., U.S.	264	43.02 N	77.09 W
Port Graham	236	59.21 N	151.50 W
Port Greville	240	45.24 N	64.33 W
Port Hammond	270	49.13 N	122.39 W
Port Harcourt	222	4.43 N	7.05 E
Port Hardy	238	50.43 N	127.29 W
Port Hawkesbury	240	45.37 N	61.21 W
Porthcawl	174	51.29 N	3.43 W
Port Hedland	226	20.19 S	118.34 E
Port Heiden	236	56.55 N	158.41 W
Port Henry	242	44.03 N	73.28 W
Port Hill	240	46.35 N	63.53 W
Port Honduras C	280	16.13 N	88.42 W
Port Hood	240	46.01 N	61.32 W
Port Hope, Ont., Can.	264	43.57 N	78.18 W
Port Hope, Mich., U.S.	244	43.57 N	82.43 W
Port Hueneme	274	34.09 N	119.12 W
Port Huron	266	42.58 N	82.27 W
Portici	184	40.49 N	14.20 E
Portillo	284p	19.55 N	77.11 W
Portimão	168	37.08 N	8.32 W
Port Isabel	250	26.04 N	97.13 W
Portishead	174	51.30 N	2.46 W
Port Jefferson, N.Y., U.S.	261	40.57 N	73.04 W
Port Jefferson, Ohio, U.S.	268	40.20 N	84.06 W
Port Jefferson Station	261	40.56 N	73.03 W
Port Jervis	242	41.22 N	74.41 W
Port Kembla	228	34.29 S	150.54 E
Port Lambton	266	42.39 N	82.30 W
Portland, Austl.	228	38.21 S	141.36 E
Portland, Ark., U.S.	248	33.14 N	91.30 W
Portland, Conn., U.S.	261	41.34 N	72.38 W
Portland, Ind., U.S.	268	40.26 N	84.59 W
Portland, Maine, U.S.	242	43.39 N	70.17 W
Portland, Mich., U.S.	268	42.52 N	84.54 W
Portland, N. Dak., U.S.	252	47.30 N	97.22 W
Portland, N.Y., U.S.	266	42.23 N	79.28 W
Portland, Oreg., U.S.	270	45.33 N	122.36 W
Portland, Tenn., U.S.	248	36.35 N	86.31 W
Portland, Tex., U.S.	250	27.53 N	97.20 W
Portland, Wis., U.S.	268	43.12 N	88.58 W
Portland, Bill of ≻	162	50.31 N	2.27 W
Portland, Cape ≻	228	40.45 S	147.57 E
Portland Bay C	228	38.19 S	141.47 E
Portland Bight C[3]	285q	17.50 N	77.05 W
Portland Canal ⋓	236	55.10 N	130.08 W
Portland Inlet C	238	54.50 N	130.15 W
Portland Island I	230	39.18 S	177.52 E
Portland Mills	266	41.23 N	78.50 W
Portland Point ≻	285q	17.43 N	77.07 W
Port Laoise	162	53.02 N	7.17 W
Port Lavaca	250	28.37 N	96.38 W
Port Leyden	264	43.35 N	75.21 W
Port Lincoln	228	34.44 S	135.52 E
Port Lions	236	57.52 N	152.53 W
Port Loko	214	8.46 N	12.47 W
Port-Louis, Fr.	166	47.43 N	3.21 W
Port-Louis, Guad.	285o	16.25 N	61.32 W
Port Louis, Maus.	225c	20.10 S	57.30 E
Port Ludlow	270	47.56 N	122.41 W
Port-Lyautey → Kenitra	214	34.16 N	6.40 W
Port Macquarie	228	31.26 S	152.55 E
Portmahomack	162	57.49 N	3.50 W
Port Maitland, N.S., Can.	240	43.59 N	66.09 W
Port Maitland, Ont., Can.	266	42.52 N	79.34 W
Port Maria	285q	18.25 N	76.55 W
Port Matilda	266	40.48 N	78.03 W
Port McNeill	238	50.35 N	127.06 W
Port McNicoll	264	44.45 N	79.49 W
Port Mellon	238	49.32 N	123.29 W
Port-Menier	240	49.49 N	64.20 W
Port Moller	236	55.59 N	160.34 W
Port Moody	238	49.17 N	122.51 W
Port Morant	285q	17.54 N	76.19 W
Port-Morien	240	46.08 N	59.52 W
Port-Mouton	240	43.56 N	64.51 W
Port Murray	262	40.47 N	74.55 W
Port Neches	248	29.59 N	93.58 W
Portneuf	260	46.51 N	71.53 W
Portneuf □[6]	260	46.45 N	72.00 W
Portneuf ≃, Qué., Can.	240	48.37 N	69.05 W
Portneuf ≃, Idaho, U.S.	256	42.58 N	112.35 W
Portneuf, Lac ⊜	240	49.09 N	70.19 W
Portneuf-Station	260	46.52 N	71.53 W
Portneuf-sur-Mer	240	48.36 N	69.06 W
Port Neville	238	50.29 N	126.05 W
Port Nolloth	218	29.17 S	16.51 E
Port Norris	262	39.15 N	75.02 W
Porto	168	41.11 N	8.36 W
Pôrto Acre	292	9.34 S	67.31 W
Pôrto Alegre	294	30.04 S	51.11 W
Porto Alexandre	218	15.49 S	11.53 E
Pôrto Amazonas	294	25.33 S	49.53 W
Porto Amboim	218	10.44 S	13.44 E
Porto Amélia	218	12.58 S	40.30 E
Pôrto Belo, Bra.	294	27.10 S	48.33 W
Portobelo, Pan.	280	9.33 N	79.39 W
Pôrto de Mós	168	39.36 N	8.39 W
Pôrto de Moz	286	1.45 S	52.14 W
Pôrto de Pedras	286	9.10 S	35.17 W
Porto Empedocle	170	37.17 N	13.32 E
Pôrto Esperana	292	19.37 S	57.27 W
Pôrto Esperidião	292	15.51 S	58.28 W
Porto Farina	170	37.10 N	10.12 E
Pôrto Feliz	296	23.13 S	47.32 W
Portoferraio	184	42.49 N	10.19 E
Pôrto Ferreira	296	21.51 S	47.28 W
Port of Spain	285r	10.39 N	61.31 W
Portogruaro	170	45.47 N	12.50 E
Portola	258	39.48 N	120.28 W
Portola Valley	272	37.23 N	122.13 W
Pôrto Lucena	294	27.51 S	55.01 W
Pörtom (Pirttikylä	160	62.42 N	21.37 E
Portomaggiore	170	44.42 N	11.48 E
Pôrto Mendes	294	24.30 S	54.20 W
Pôrto Murtinho	292	21.42 S	57.52 W
Pôrto Nacional	286	10.42 S	48.25 W
Porto-Novo	222	6.29 N	2.37 E
Port Orange	246	29.09 N	80.59 W
Port Orchard	270	47.32 N	122.38 W
Porto Recanati	170	43.26 N	13.40 E
Port Orford	256	42.45 N	124.30 W
Porto San Giorgio	184	43.11 N	13.48 E
Porto Sant'Elpidio	184	43.15 N	13.45 E
Porto Santo I	214	33.04 N	16.20 W
Porto Santo Stefano	170	42.26 N	11.07 E
Pôrto São José	296	22.43 S	53.10 W
Pôrto Seguro	296	16.26 S	39.05 W
Porto Tolle	184	44.56 N	12.22 E
Porto Torres	170	40.50 N	8.23 E
Pôrto União	294	26.15 S	51.05 W
Pôrto Valter	292	8.15 S	72.45 W
Porto-Vecchio	170	41.35 N	9.16 E
Pôrto Velho	292	8.46 S	63.54 W
Portoviejo	290	1.03 S	80.27 W
Port Pegasus C	230	47.13 S	167.41 E
Port Penn	262	39.31 N	75.35 W
Port Perry	264	44.06 N	78.57 W
Port Phillip Bay C	228	38.07 S	144.48 E
Port Pirie	228	33.11 S	138.01 E
Port Radium	232	66.05 N	118.02 W
Portree	162	57.24 N	6.12 W
Port Renfrew	238	48.33 N	124.25 W
Port Republic	262	39.31 N	74.29 W
Port Rexton	240	48.23 N	53.20 W
Port Richey	246	28.16 N	82.44 W
Port Richmond	262	37.33 N	76.49 W
Port Robinson	264	43.02 N	79.13 W
Port Rowan	266	42.37 N	80.28 W
Port Royal, Jam.	285q	17.56 N	76.51 W
Port Royal, Pa., U.S.	262	40.32 N	77.23 W
Port Royal, Va., U.S.	262	38.10 N	77.12 W
Port Royal National Historic Park ♠	240	44.44 N	65.40 W
Portrush	162	55.12 N	6.40 W
Port Said → Būr Sa'īd	220	31.16 N	32.18 E
Port-Sainte-Marie	166	44.15 N	0.24 E
Port Saint Joe	246	29.49 N	85.18 W
Port Saint Johns	218	31.38 S	29.33 E
Port-Saint-Louis	182	43.23 N	4.48 E
Port Saint Lucie	246	27.20 N	80.20 W
Port Saint Servan	240	51.19 N	58.01 W
Port Sanilac	244	43.26 N	82.33 W
Port Saunders	240	50.39 N	57.18 W
Port Shepstone	218	30.46 S	30.22 E
Port Simpson	238	54.33 N	130.25 W
Portslade	174	50.50 N	0.11 W
Portsmouth, Dom.	284d	15.35 N	61.28 W
Portsmouth, Eng., U.K.	162	51.29 N	0.15 E
Portsmouth, Eng., U.K.	174	50.48 N	1.05 W
Portsmouth, N.H., U.S.	242	43.04 N	70.46 W
Portsmouth, Ohio, U.S.	242	38.45 N	82.59 W
Portsmouth, R.I., U.S.	261	41.36 N	71.15 W
Portsmouth, Va., U.S.	262	36.52 N	76.24 W
Portsoy	162	57.41 N	2.41 W
Port Stanley	266	42.40 N	81.13 W
Portstewart	162	55.11 N	6.43 W
Port Sudan → Būr Sūdān	220	19.37 N	37.14 E
Port Sulphur	248	29.29 N	89.42 W
Port Swettenham	200	3.00 N	101.25 E
Port Talbot	174	51.36 N	3.47 W
Porttipahdan tekojärvi ⊜[1]	160	68.08 N	26.40 E
Port Townsend	270	48.07 N	122.46 W
Port Trevorton	262	40.42 N	76.52 W
Portugal □[1]	158	39.30 N	8.00 W
Portugal, Cachoeira ʟ	292	9.55 S	64.16 W
Portugal Cove South	240	46.42 N	53.15 W
Portugalete	168	43.19 N	3.01 W
Portugália	218	7.20 S	20.47 E
Portuguesa □[3]	290	9.10 N	69.15 W
Portuguesa ≃	290	7.57 N	67.32 W
Portuguese Guinea □[2]	214	12.00 N	16.00 W
Portuguese Timor □[2]	198	8.35 S	126.00 E
Portumna	162	53.06 N	8.13 W
Port Union	240	44.30 N	53.05 W
Port-Vendres	166	42.31 N	3.07 E
Portville	266	42.02 N	78.20 W
Port-Vladimir	160	69.25 N	33.06 E
Port Wakefield	236	57.52 N	152.51 W
Port Washington, B.C., Can.	270	48.49 N	123.19 W
Port Washington, N.Y., U.S.	261	40.49 N	73.41 W
Port Washington, Ohio, U.S.	266	40.20 N	81.31 W
Port Washington, Wis., U.S.	244	43.23 N	87.53 W
Port Weld	200	4.49 N	100.38 E
Port Wentworth	246	32.09 N	81.10 W
Port Wing	244	46.47 N	91.23 W
Porum	250	35.22 N	95.16 W
Pôrŭng ≃	200	12.55 N	105.35 E
Porus	285q	18.02 N	77.25 W
Porvenir	288	53.18 S	70.22 W
Porz	164	50.53 N	7.03 E
Porzuna	168	39.09 N	4.09 W
Posada	170	40.38 N	9.43 E
Posada ≃	170	40.39 N	9.45 E
Posadas, Arg.	294	27.25 S	55.50 W
Posadas, Esp.	168	37.48 N	5.06 W
Posavina ◆[1]	172	45.10 N	17.20 E
Poschiavo	166	46.18 N	10.04 E
Pošechonje-Volodarsk	160	58.30 N	39.07 E
Posen → Poznań, Pol.	164	52.25 N	16.55 E
Posen, Mich., U.S.	244	45.16 N	83.42 W
Posets, Pico de ∧	168	42.39 N	0.25 E
Poshan → Boshan	194	36.29 N	117.50 E
Posio	160	66.06 N	28.09 E
Positano	170	40.38 N	14.29 E
Posjet	186	42.39 N	130.50 E
Poso	198	1.23 S	120.44 E
Posooy, Mount ∧	202	17.21 N	120.47 E
Posse	296	14.05 S	46.22 W
Possidhonia ⊥	172	37.40 N	24.00 E
Pössneck	164	50.42 N	11.37 E
Possum Kingdom Reservoir ⊜[1]	250	32.55 N	98.28 W
Post	250	33.12 N	101.23 W
Postavy	160	55.07 N	26.50 E
Poste-Mistassini	232	50.25 N	73.52 W
Post Falls	256	47.43 N	116.57 W
Post Maurice Cortier (Bidon Cinq)	214	22.18 N	1.05 E
Postojna	170	45.47 N	14.13 E
Postojnska Jama ●[7]	170	45.47 N	14.12 E
P'ostraja Dresva	186	61.34 N	156.41 E
Postre Valle	292	18.29 S	63.51 W
Postville	244	43.05 N	91.34 W
Pótam	278	27.36 N	110.23 W
Potaro ≃	290	5.25 N	58.50 W
Potaro Landing	290	5.22 N	59.09 W
Potawatomie Indian Reservation ◆[4]	252	39.20 N	95.50 W
Potchefstroom	224	26.46 S	27.01 E
Poté	296	17.49 S	41.49 W
Poteau	248	35.03 N	94.37 W
Poteau ≃	248	35.23 N	94.26 W
Poteet	250	29.02 N	98.34 W
Potenza	170	40.38 N	15.49 E
Potenza Picena	184	43.22 N	13.37 E
Poteriteri, Lake ⊜	230	46.05 S	167.07 E
Potes	168	43.09 N	4.37 W
Potgietersrus	224	24.15 S	28.55 E
Poth	250	29.04 N	98.05 W
Potholes Reservoir ⊜[1]	256	47.01 N	119.19 W
Poti	212	42.09 N	41.40 E
Potiraguá	296	15.36 S	39.53 W
Potirendaba	296	21.08 S	49.08 W
Potiskum	214	11.43 N	11.05 E
Potlatch	256	46.55 N	116.54 W
Potlatch ≃	256	46.28 N	116.46 W
Poto	292	14.30 S	69.30 W
Po Toi Group II	196	22.11 N	114.16 E
Potol Point ≻	202	11.56 N	121.57 E
Potomac	248	40.18 N	87.48 W
Potomac ≃	242	38.00 N	76.18 W
Potomac Heights	242	38.36 N	77.08 W
Potosí, Bol.	292	19.35 S	65.45 W
Potosi, Mo., U.S.	248	37.56 N	90.47 W
Potosí □[5]	292	20.40 S	67.00 W
Potosí, Cerro ∧	278	24.50 N	100.15 W
Potosí, Laguna de C	278	17.32 N	101.23 W
Pototan	202	10.56 N	122.38 E
Potrerillos, Chile	294	26.26 S	69.29 W
Potrerillos, Hond.	280	15.11 N	87.58 W
Potrerillos Arriba	280	8.40 N	82.30 W
Potrero del Llano	250	29.12 N	104.28 W
Potrero Grande, C.R.	280	9.00 N	83.11 W
Potrero Grande, Méx.	278	24.59 N	106.26 W
Potsdam, D.D.R.	164	52.24 N	13.04 E
Potsdam, N.Y., U.S.	242	44.40 N	74.59 W
Potter	252	41.13 N	103.19 W
Potter □[6]	266	41.47 N	78.01 W
Potter Lake	268	44.07 N	88.06 W
Potters Bar	174	51.42 N	0.11 W
Potters Mills	262	40.48 N	77.32 W
Potterville	268	42.38 N	84.45 W
Potts Camp	248	34.39 N	89.18 W
Pottstown	262	40.15 N	75.38 W
Pottsville	262	40.41 N	76.12 W
Potwin	252	37.56 N	97.01 W
Pouancé	166	47.44 N	1.11 W
Pouce-Coupe	238	55.43 N	120.08 W
Pouce Coupé ≃	238	56.08 N	119.52 W
Pouch Cove	240	47.46 N	52.46 W
Poughkeepsie	261	41.42 N	73.56 W
Poughquag	261	41.37 N	73.41 W
Poulan	246	31.31 N	83.47 W
Poulance	162	47.45 N	1.10 W
Poulaphouca Reservoir ⊜[1]	162	53.08 N	6.31 W
Poulin-de-Courval, Lac ⊜	240	48.52 N	70.27 W
Poullaouen	162	48.20 N	3.39 W
Poulsbo	270	47.44 N	122.39 W
Poulter, Lac ⊜	244	47.05 N	76.44 W
Poultney	242	43.31 N	73.14 W
Pound	246	37.07 N	82.36 W
Pouso Alegre	296	22.13 S	45.56 W
Pouso Redondo	294	27.15 S	49.57 W
Poŭthĭsăt	200	12.35 N	103.55 E
Poŭthĭsăt ≃	200	12.41 N	104.09 E
Pouzauges	166	46.47 N	0.50 W
Považská Bystrica	164	49.08 N	18.27 E
Povenec	160	62.51 N	34.45 E
Poverty Bay C	230	38.43 S	178.00 E
Povlen ⛰	172	43.55 N	19.30 E
Póvoa de Varzim	168	41.23 N	8.46 W
Povorino	158	51.12 N	42.14 E
Povungnituk	232	59.12 N	77.51 W
Povungnituk ≃	232	60.05 N	77.10 W
Powassan	244	46.05 N	79.22 W
Poway	274	32.58 N	117.02 W
Powder ≃, U.S.	234	46.44 N	105.26 W
Powder ≃, Oreg., U.S.	256	44.45 N	117.03 W
Powderly	250	33.49 N	95.31 W
Powder River Pass)(	256	44.09 N	107.04 W
Powell, Ohio, U.S.	266	40.09 N	83.05 W
Powell, Wyo., U.S.	256	44.45 N	108.46 W
Powell ≃	246	36.29 N	83.42 W
Powell, Lake ⊜[1]	254	37.25 N	110.45 W
Powell, Mount ∧	254	39.46 N	106.20 W
Powell Creek	226	18.05 S	133.40 E
Powellhurst	270	45.31 N	122.11 W
Powell Lake ⊜	238	50.11 N	124.24 W
Powell River	238	49.52 N	124.33 W
Powells Valley	262	40.26 N	76.56 W
Powellton	242	38.05 N	81.19 W
Powers, Mich., U.S.	244	45.39 N	87.32 W
Powers, Oreg., U.S.	256	42.53 N	124.04 W
Powers Lake, N. Dak., U.S.	252	48.34 N	102.39 W
Powers Lake, Wis., U.S.	268	42.33 N	88.17 W
Powhatan, Ark., U.S.	248	36.05 N	91.07 W
Powhatan, La., U.S.	248	31.52 N	93.12 W
Powhatan, Va., U.S.	246	37.29 N	77.55 W
Powhatan Point	242	39.52 N	80.49 W
Pownal	261	42.46 N	73.14 W
Poxoreu	296	15.50 S	54.23 W
Poyang	196	28.59 N	116.40 E
Poyanghu ⊜	196	29.00 N	116.25 E
Poyen	248	34.19 N	92.38 W
Poygan, Lake ⊜	244	44.19 N	88.50 W
Poynette	244	43.24 N	89.24 W
Poza Grande	278	25.50 N	112.05 W
Požarevac	172	44.37 N	21.11 E
Poza Rica de Hidalgo	278	20.33 N	97.27 W
Požega	172	43.50 N	20.02 E
Poznań	164	52.25 N	16.55 E
Pozo Alcón	168	37.42 N	2.56 W
Pozo Almonte	292	20.16 S	69.48 W
Pozoblanco	168	38.22 N	4.51 W
Pozo-Cañada	168	38.48 N	1.45 W
Pozo del Molle	294	32.01 S	62.58 W
Pozo del Tigre	294	24.54 S	60.19 W
Pozo Hondo	294	27.10 S	67.30 W
Pozuelo de Alarcón	168	40.26 N	3.49 W
Pozuelos	290	10.11 N	64.39 W
Pozuelos, Laguna de ⊜	294	22.22 S	66.00 W
Pozuzo	292	10.05 S	75.35 W
Pozuzo ≃	292	9.50 S	74.56 W
Požva	160	59.05 N	56.05 E
Pozzallo	170	36.43 N	14.52 E
Pozzuoli	184	40.49 N	14.07 E
Pra ≃	222	5.01 N	1.37 W
Prabuty (Riesenburg)	164	53.46 N	19.10 E
Prachatice	164	49.01 N	14.00 E
Prachin Buri	200	14.03 N	101.25 E
Prachuap Khiri Khan	198	11.48 N	99.47 E
Pradera	290	3.25 N	76.15 W
Prades	166	42.37 N	2.26 E
Prado	296	17.21 S	39.13 W
Prados	296	21.03 S	44.05 W
Prague → Praha, Česko.	164	50.05 N	14.26 E
Prague, Nebr., U.S.	252	41.19 N	96.48 W
Prague, Okla., U.S.	250	35.29 N	96.41 W
Praha (Prague)	164	50.05 N	14.26 E
Praha ∧	164	49.40 N	13.49 E
Prahova ≃	172	44.43 N	26.27 E
Praia	222a	14.55 N	23.31 W
Praia Grande	294	29.12 S	49.57 W
Prainha	292	7.16 S	60.23 W
Prairie ≃, Minn., U.S.	244	47.18 N	93.29 W
Prairie ≃, Wis., U.S.	244	45.10 N	89.42 W
Prairie City, Iowa, U.S.	244	41.36 N	93.14 W
Prairie City, Oreg., U.S.	256	44.28 N	118.43 W
Prairie du Chien	244	43.03 N	91.09 W
Prairie du Sac	244	43.17 N	89.43 W
Prairie Grove	248	35.59 N	94.19 W
Prairies, Coteau des ⛰[2]	252	44.30 N	96.45 W
Prairie View	250	30.04 N	96.00 W
Prairie Village	252	39.01 N	94.38 W
Praja	198	8.42 S	116.17 E
Pran Buri ≃	200	12.25 N	100.00 E
Praslin, Lac ⊜	240	50.05 N	69.49 W
Praslin Island I	218	4.19 S	55.44 E
Prasonísi, Ákra ≻	212	35.42 N	27.46 E
Praszka	164	51.04 N	18.26 E
Prata	296	19.18 S	48.55 W
Prata, Rio da ≃, Bra.	296	17.28 S	46.35 W
Prata, Rio da ≃, Bra.	296	18.49 S	49.54 W
Prata, Rio da ≃, Bra.	296	18.50 S	52.11 W
Pratápolis	296	20.45 S	46.52 W
Pratas Island → Dongshaqundao I	190	20.42 N	116.43 E
Prat del Llobregat	168	41.20 N	2.06 E
Pratinha	296	19.46 S	46.24 W
Prato	184	43.53 N	11.06 E
Pratola Peligna	184	42.06 N	13.52 E
Pratt	252	37.39 N	98.44 W
Pratteln	180	47.31 N	7.42 E
Prattsburg	242	42.32 N	77.17 E
Prattville, Ala., U.S.	248	32.28 N	86.29 W
Prattville, Okla., U.S.	250	36.07 N	96.07 W
Pratudão ≃	296	13.56 S	44.55 W
Pravia	168	43.29 N	6.07 W
Pr'aža	160	61.42 N	33.35 E
Preajba	172	44.24 N	25.20 E
Preble, Ind., U.S.	268	40.50 N	85.01 W
Preble, N.Y., U.S.	264	42.44 N	76.09 W
Prečistoje, S.S.S.R.	160	55.31 N	32.22 E
Prečistoje, S.S.S.R.	160	58.27 N	40.19 E
Predazzo	170	46.19 N	11.36 E
Predeal	172	45.30 N	25.35 E
Predeşti	172	44.21 N	23.36 E
Predlitz	164	47.04 N	13.55 E
Pré-en-Pail	166	48.27 N	0.12 W
Preetz	164	54.14 N	10.16 E
Pregarten	164	48.21 N	14.22 E
Pregol'a ≃	160	54.41 N	20.22 E
Pregonero	290	8.01 N	71.46 W
Preili	160	56.18 N	26.43 E
Preko	170	44.05 N	15.11 E
Přelouč	164	50.02 N	15.34 E
Prémery	166	47.10 N	3.20 E
Premnitz	164	52.32 N	12.19 E
Prémont, Qué., Can.	260	46.21 N	73.04 W
Premont, Tex., U.S.	250	27.22 N	98.08 W
Premuda, Otok I	170	44.20 N	14.37 E
Prendergast Point	266	42.11 N	79.26 W
Prentice	244	45.33 N	90.17 W
Prentiss	248	31.36 N	89.52 W
Prenzlau	164	53.19 N	13.52 E
Preparis Island I	200	14.52 N	93.41 E
Preparis North Channel ⋓	200	15.27 N	94.05 E
Preparis South Channel ⋓	200	14.40 N	94.00 E
Přerov	164	49.27 N	17.27 E
Pré-Saint-Didier	166	45.46 N	6.59 E
Prescott, Ont., Can.	264	44.43 N	75.31 W
Prescott, Ariz., U.S.	254	34.33 N	112.28 W
Prescott, Ark., U.S.	248	33.48 N	93.23 W
Prescott, Oreg., U.S.	270	46.03 N	122.54 W
Prescott, Wis., U.S.	244	44.45 N	92.48 W
Prescott □[6]	260	45.30 N	74.45 W
Prescott Island I	232	73.01 N	96.50 W
Preševo	172	42.18 N	21.39 E
Presho	252	43.54 N	100.04 W
Presidencia de la Plaza	294	27.02 S	59.50 W
Presidencia Roca	294	26.08 S	59.36 W
Presidencia Roque Sáenz Peña	294	26.50 S	60.30 W
Presidente Epitácio	296	21.46 S	52.06 W
Presidente Getúlio	294	27.03 S	49.37 W
Presidente Hayes □[5]	294	24.00 S	59.00 W
Presidente Olegário	296	18.25 S	46.25 W
Presidente Prudente	296	22.07 S	51.22 W
Presidente Venceslau	296	21.52 S	51.50 W
President Roxas	202	11.25 N	122.58 E
Presidio	250	29.33 N	104.23 W
Presidio ■	272	37.48 N	122.28 W
Presidio, Río del ≃	278	23.05 N	106.17 W
Prešov	164	49.00 N	21.15 E
Prespa, Lake ⊜	172	40.55 N	21.00 E
Prespuntal ≃	290	10.08 N	64.39 W
Presque Isle	240	46.41 N	68.01 W
Presque Isle ≃	244	46.43 N	89.59 W
Pressburg → Bratislava	164	48.09 N	17.07 E
Prestea	222	5.27 N	2.08 W
Přeštice	164	49.34 N	13.20 E
Presto	292	18.55 S	64.56 W
Preston, Ont., Can.	264	43.23 N	80.21 W
Preston, Cuba	284p	20.46 N	75.39 W
Preston, Eng., U.K.	162	53.46 N	2.42 W
Preston, Ga., U.S.	246	31.59 N	84.37 W
Preston, Idaho, U.S.	256	42.06 N	111.53 W
Preston, Iowa, U.S.	244	42.03 N	90.24 W
Preston, Kans., U.S.	252	37.46 N	98.33 W
Preston, Md., U.S.	262	38.43 N	75.54 W
Preston, Minn., U.S.	244	43.40 N	92.05 W
Preston, Wash., U.S.	270	47.31 N	121.56 W
Preston Heights	268	41.28 N	88.08 W
Preston Peak ∧	258	41.50 N	123.37 W
Prestonsburg	246	37.40 N	82.46 W
Preststranda	160	59.06 N	9.04 E
Prestville	238	55.45 N	118.06 W
Prestwick	162	55.30 N	4.37 W
Pretoria	224	25.45 S	28.10 E
Pretty Prairie	252	37.47 N	98.01 W
Préveza	172	38.57 N	20.44 E
Prey Vêng	200	11.29 N	105.19 E
Pribilof Islands II	236	57.00 N	170.00 W
Priboj	172	43.35 N	19.31 E
Příbor	164	49.39 N	18.10 E
Příbram	164	49.42 N	14.01 E
Price, Tex., U.S.	248	32.08 N	94.57 W
Price, Utah, U.S.	254	39.36 N	110.48 W
Price ≃	254	39.10 N	110.06 W
Price, Cape ≻	200	13.35 N	93.05 E
Price Island I	238	52.23 N	128.36 W
Prichard	248	30.44 N	88.07 W
Pričornomorskaja Nizmennost' ⚍	172	47.00 N	33.00 E
Priddy	250	31.40 N	98.31 W
Priego	168	40.27 N	2.18 W
Priego de Córdoba	168	37.26 N	4.11 W
Priekulė, S.S.S.R.	160	55.33 N	21.19 E
Priekule, S.S.S.R.	160	56.26 N	21.35 E
Prien	164	47.51 N	12.20 E
Prieska	218	29.40 S	22.42 E
Priest ≃	238	48.11 N	116.53 W
Priest Lake ⊜	256	48.34 N	116.52 W
Priestley, Mount ∧	238	55.13 N	128.53 W
Priest Rapids Reservoir ⊜[1]	256	46.45 N	119.55 W
Priest River	256	48.11 N	116.55 W
Prieta, Peña ∧	168	43.01 N	4.44 W
Prieto Diaz	202	13.03 N	124.12 E
Prievidza	164	48.47 N	18.37 E
Prijedor	170	44.59 N	16.43 E
Prijepolje	172	43.23 N	19.39 E
Prijutovo	158	53.54 N	53.56 E
Prikaspijskaja Nizmennost' ⚍	158	48.00 N	52.00 E
Prikumsk	158	44.46 N	44.09 E
Prilep	172	41.20 N	21.33 E
Prilly	180	46.32 N	6.36 E
Priluki	158	50.36 N	32.24 E
Primeiro de Maio	296	22.48 S	51.01 W
Primera	250	26.14 N	97.43 W
Primero de Mayo	250	27.12 N	101.15 W
Primghar	252	43.05 N	95.38 W
Primorje	160	54.57 N	20.02 E
Primorje [Warnicken]	164	54.57 N	20.02 E
Primorsk, S.S.S.R.	160	60.22 N	28.36 E
Primorsk, S.S.S.R.	164	54.44 N	20.01 E
Primorsk, S.S.S.R.	208	40.13 N	49.33 E
Primorsk [Fischhausen]	164	54.44 N	20.01 E
Primorsko	172	42.16 N	27.46 E
Primrose Lake ⊜	232	54.55 N	109.45 W
Prince Albert, Ont., Can.	264	44.05 N	78.58 W
Prince Albert, Sask., Can.	232	53.12 N	105.46 W
Prince Albert Sound ⋓	232	70.25 N	115.00 W
Prince Charles Island I	232	67.50 N	76.00 W
Prince-de-Galles, Cap ≻	232	61.35 N	71.35 W
Prince Edward □[6]	264	44.00 N	77.15 W
Prince Edward Island □[3]	232	46.20 N	63.20 W
Prince Edward Island National Park ♠	240	46.31 N	63.26 W
Prince Frederick	242	38.33 N	76.35 W
Prince George, B.C., Can.	238	53.55 N	122.45 W
Prince George, Va., U.S.	262	37.13 N	77.17 W
Prince George □[6]	262	37.13 N	77.10 W
Prince Georges □[6]	262	38.49 N	76.45 W
Prince Kemal el Din's Monument ⊥	220	22.51 N	25.48 E
Prince Leopold Island I	232	74.02 N	89.55 W
Prince of Wales, Cape ≻	236	65.40 N	168.05 W
Prince of Wales Island I, N.W. Ter., Can.	232	72.40 N	99.00 W
Prince of Wales Island I, Alaska, U.S.	236	55.47 N	132.50 W
Prince of Wales Strait ⋓	232	73.00 N	117.00 W
Prince Olav Coast ●[2]	148	68.30 S	42.30 E
Prince Patrick Island I	148	76.45 N	119.30 W
Prince Regent Inlet C	232	73.00 N	90.30 W
Prince Rupert	238	54.19 N	130.19 W
Princesa, Puerto C	202	9.45 N	118.43 E
Princess Anne	242	38.12 N	75.41 W
Princess Astrid Coast ●[2]	148	70.45 S	12.30 E
Princess Martha Coast ●[2]	148	72.00 S	7.30 W
Princess Ragnhild Coast ●[2]	148	70.15 S	27.30 E
Princess Royal Channel ⋓	238	53.10 N	128.37 W
Princess Royal Island I	238	52.57 N	128.49 W
Princes Town	285r	10.16 N	61.23 W
Princeton, B.C., Can.	238	49.27 N	120.31 W
Princeton, Newf., Can.	240	48.21 N	53.32 W
Princeton, Ont., Can.	264	43.10 N	80.32 W
Princeton, Calif., U.S.	272	39.24 N	122.01 W
Princeton, Ill., U.S.	244	41.23 N	89.28 W
Princeton, Ind., U.S.	248	38.21 N	87.34 W
Princeton, Iowa, U.S.	244	41.40 N	90.20 W
Princeton, Ky., U.S.	248	37.07 N	87.53 W
Princeton, Maine, U.S.	242	45.13 N	67.34 W
Princeton, Mich., U.S.	244	46.17 N	87.29 W
Princeton, Minn., U.S.	244	45.34 N	93.35 W
Princeton, Mo., U.S.	248	40.24 N	93.35 W
Princeton, N.J., U.S.	262	40.21 N	74.40 W
Princeton, N.C., U.S.	246	35.28 N	78.10 W
Princeton, W. Va., U.S.	246	37.22 N	81.06 W
Princeton, Wis., U.S.	244	43.51 N	89.08 W
Princeton Junction	262	40.19 N	74.37 W
Princeville, Qué., Can.	260	46.10 N	71.53 W
Princeville, Ill., U.S.	244	40.45 N	89.45 W
Princeville, N.C., U.S.	246	35.53 N	77.82 W
Prince William □[6]	262	38.42 N	77.27 W
Prince William Sound ⋓	236	60.40 N	147.00 W
Príncipe I	214	1.37 N	7.25 E
Principe Channel ⋓	238	53.28 N	130.00 W
Príncipe da Beira	292	12.25 S	64.25 W
Prineville	256	44.18 N	120.51 W
Prineville Reservoir ⊜[1]	256	44.08 N	120.42 W
Prineville Southeast	256	44.17 N	120.53 W
Prinzapolca	280	13.20 N	83.35 W
Prinzapolca ≃	280	13.23 N	83.36 W
Prior, Cabo ≻	168	43.34 N	8.19 W
Prioz'orsk	160	61.02 N	30.04 E
Prip'at' ≃	158	51.21 N	30.09 E
Pripet → Prip'at' ≃	158	51.21 N	30.09 E
Pripol'arnyj Ural ⛰	160	65.00 N	60.00 E
Priština	172	42.39 N	21.10 E
Pritchett	252	37.22 N	102.52 W
Pritzwalk	164	53.09 N	12.10 E
Privas	182	44.44 N	4.36 E
Priverno	184	41.28 N	13.11 E
Privodino	160	61.05 N	46.28 E
Privolžje	160	52.52 N	48.37 E
Privolžskaja Vozvyšennost' ⛰[1]	160	52.00 N	46.00 E
Privolžskij	158	51.24 N	46.02 E
Prizren	172	42.12 N	20.44 E
Prizzi	170	37.43 N	13.26 E
Prnjavor	170	44.52 N	17.40 E
Probolinggo	198	7.45 S	113.13 E
Probstzella	164	50.32 N	11.22 E
Prochladnyj	158	43.46 N	44.00 E
Prochowice (Parchwitz)	164	51.17 N	16.22 E
Procida	184	40.46 N	14.02 E
Procter	238	49.37 N	116.57 W
Proctor, Minn., U.S.	244	46.45 N	92.13 W
Proctor, Vt., U.S.	242	43.40 N	73.02 W
Proctor Reservoir ⊜[1]	250	32.02 N	98.32 W
Proença-a-Nova	168	39.45 N	7.55 W
Progreso, Méx.	250	27.28 N	100.59 W
Progreso, Méx.	278	21.17 N	89.40 W
Progreso, Ur.	294	34.40 S	56.13 W
Progress, Oreg., U.S.	270	45.28 N	122.47 W
Progress, Pa., U.S.	262	40.08 N	76.34 W
Project City	258	40.41 N	122.21 W
Prokopjevsk	186	53.53 N	86.45 E
Prokuplje	172	43.14 N	21.36 E
Prokuševo	160	59.55 N	34.56 E
Prome → Pyè	200	18.49 N	95.13 E
Promissão	296	21.32 S	49.52 W
Promyšlennyj	160	67.35 N	63.55 E
Pronsk	160	54.07 N	39.37 E
Prophestown	244	41.40 N	89.56 W
Prophet ≃	232	58.45 N	122.45 W
Propriá	286	10.13 S	36.51 W
Propriano	170	41.40 N	8.55 E
Proserpine	228	20.24 S	148.34 E
Proskurov → Chmel'nickij	158	49.25 N	27.00 E
Prosna ≃	164	52.10 N	17.39 E
Prosotsáni	172	41.10 N	23.59 E
Prospect, Conn., U.S.	261	41.30 N	72.59 W
Prospect, Ohio, U.S.	266	40.27 N	83.11 W
Prospect, Pa., U.S.	266	40.54 N	80.03 W
Prospect Park	266	41.31 N	78.13 W
Prosperidad	202	8.37 N	125.53 E
Prosser	256	46.12 N	119.46 W
Prostějov	164	49.29 N	17.07 E
Prostki (Prostken)	164	53.43 N	22.26 E
Proszowice	164	50.12 N	20.18 E
Protection	252	37.12 N	99.29 W
Protville	170	36.54 N	10.01 E
Proulxville	260	46.40 N	72.30 W
Provadija	172	43.11 N	27.26 E
Provence □[9]	182	44.00 N	6.00 E
Providence, Ky., U.S.	248	37.24 N	87.39 W
Providence, R.I., U.S.	261	41.50 N	71.25 W
Providence, Tenn., U.S.	248	36.05 N	86.42 W
Providence, Utah, U.S.	254	41.43 N	111.49 W
Providence □[6]	261	41.52 N	71.36 W
Providence, Cape ≻	230	46.01 S	166.28 E
Providence Forge	262	37.27 N	77.02 W
Providence Island I	218	9.14 S	51.02 E
Providencia	250	27.06 N	103.32 W
Providencia, Isla de I	280	13.21 N	81.22 W
Providência, Serra da ⛰[1]	292	10.30 S	61.25 W
Providenciales I	282	21.49 N	72.15 W
Providenija	236	64.23 N	173.18 W
Providenija, Buchta C	236	64.30 N	173.20 W
Provincetown	261	42.03 N	70.11 W
Provins	176	48.33 N	3.18 E
Provo	254	40.14 N	111.39 W
Provo ≃	254	40.14 N	111.44 W
Prozor	170	43.49 N	17.37 E
Pruden	246	36.35 N	83.54 W
Prudentópolis	294	25.12 S	50.57 W
Prudhoe Bay C	236	70.20 N	148.20 W
Prudhoe Island I	228	21.19 S	149.40 E
Prudnik (Neustadt in Oberschlesien)	164	50.19 N	17.34 E
Prüm	164	50.12 N	6.25 E
Prunedale	272	36.47 N	121.40 W
Pruszków	164	52.11 N	20.48 E
Prutul (Prut) ≃	172	45.27 N	28.12 E
Prutz	164	47.05 N	10.40 E
Prydz Bay C	148	69.00 S	76.00 E
Pryor, Mont., U.S.	256	45.26 N	108.32 W
Pryor, Okla., U.S.	250	36.19 N	95.19 W
Pryor Creek ≃	256	45.54 N	108.19 W
Przasnysz	164	53.01 N	20.55 E
Przedbórz	164	51.06 N	19.53 E
Przemków (Primkenau)	164	51.32 N	15.48 E
Przemyśl	164	49.47 N	22.47 E
Prževal'sk	186	42.29 N	78.24 E
Przeworsk	164	50.05 N	22.29 E
Przysucha	164	51.22 N	20.38 E
Psakhná	172	38.35 N	23.38 E
Psará	172	38.46 N	25.36 E
Psará I	172	38.35 N	25.37 E
Psárion	172	37.20 N	21.51 E
Pskov	160	57.50 N	28.20 E
Pskovskoje Ozero ⊜	160	58.00 N	28.00 E
Pszczyna	164	49.59 N	18.57 E
Pszów	164	50.03 N	18.24 E
Ptolemaís	172	40.31 N	21.41 E
Ptuj	170	46.25 N	15.52 E
Puán	294	37.30 S	62.45 W
Pubnico	240	43.42 N	65.47 W
Pucabi ≃	290	1.06 S	66.20 W
Pucacuro ≃	290	3.20 S	74.58 W
Pucallpa	292	8.20 S	74.30 W
Pucará	292	18.43 S	64.11 W
Pucarani	292	16.23 S	68.30 W
Puce	266	42.18 N	82.47 W
Pučevejem ≃	236	68.48 N	170.30 E
Pučež	160	56.59 N	43.11 E
Pucheng	196	27.55 N	118.31 E
Púchov	164	49.08 N	18.20 E
Pucioasa	172	45.04 N	25.26 E
Pucio Point ≻	202	11.45 N	121.52 E
Pučišća	170	43.21 N	16.44 E
Puck	164	54.44 N	18.27 E
Puckett	248	32.05 N	89.47 W
Pudding ≃	256	45.18 N	122.43 W
Pudem	160	58.18 N	52.10 E
Puding	200	26.21 N	105.40 E
Pudož	160	61.48 N	36.32 E
Puduhe ≃	200	26.19 N	102.45 E
Puebla de Alcocer	168	38.59 N	5.15 W
Puebla de Don Fadrique	168	37.58 N	2.26 W
Puebla de Don Rodrigo	168	39.05 N	4.37 W
Puebla de Sanabria	168	42.03 N	6.38 W
Puebla de Trives	168	42.20 N	7.15 W
Puebla [de Zaragoza]	278	19.03 N	98.12 W
Pueblito de Ponce	284m	18.26 N	66.58 W
Pueblo	254	38.16 N	104.37 W
Pueblo, Rio ≃	254	36.12 N	105.45 W
Pueblo Colorado Wash ∨	254	35.05 N	110.22 W
Pueblo Hundido	294	26.23 S	70.03 W
Pueblo Ledesma	294	23.50 S	64.45 W
Pueblo Mountain ∧	256	42.06 N	118.39 W
Pueblonuevo, Col.	290	8.31 N	75.15 W
Pueblo Nuevo, Nic.	280	13.22 N	86.31 W
Pueblo Nuevo, Perú	292	4.53 S	81.05 W
Pueblo Nuevo, P.R.	284m	18.28 N	66.51 W
Pueblo Nuevo, Ven.	290	11.58 N	69.55 W
Pueblo Nuevo Comaltitlán	280	15.13 N	92.35 W
Puebloviejo, Ec.	290	1.34 S	79.30 W
Pueblo Viejo, Méx.	278	17.24 N	93.47 W
Pueblo Viejo, Laguna de C	278	22.10 N	97.53 W
Puelches	294	38.09 S	65.58 W
Puente Alto	294	33.37 S	70.35 W
Puenteáreas	168	42.11 N	8.30 W
Puente Caldelas	168	42.23 N	8.30 W
Puentedeume	168	43.24 N	8.10 W
Puente-Genil	168	37.23 N	4.47 W
Puente la Reina	168	42.40 N	1.49 W
Puente Negro	250	27.55 N	101.01 W
Puente Nuevo, Embalse de ⊜[1]	168	38.00 N	5.00 W
Pueo Point ≻	275d	21.54 N	160.04 W
Puerco ≃	254	34.22 N	107.50 W
Puertas Verdes	250	25.55 N	97.35 W
Puerto Acosta	292	15.32 S	69.15 W
Puerto Adela	294	24.33 S	54.22 W
Puerto Aisén	288	45.24 S	72.42 W
Puerto Alegre	292	13.53 S	61.36 W
Puerto Alfonso	290	2.11 S	71.01 W
Puerto Ángel	278	15.40 N	96.29 W
Puerto Armuelles	280	8.18 N	82.52 W
Puerto Asís	290	0.30 N	76.31 W
Puerto Ayacucho	290	5.40 N	67.35 W
Puerto Baquerizo Moreno	290a	0.54 S	89.36 W
Puerto Barrios	280	15.43 N	88.36 W
Puerto Belgrano	294	38.54 S	62.05 W
Puerto Bermejo	294	26.56 S	58.30 W
Puerto Bermúdez	292	10.17 S	74.57 W
Puerto Berrío	290	6.29 N	74.24 W
Puerto Bolívar	290	3.16 S	79.59 W
Puerto Boyacá	290	5.45 N	74.39 W
Puerto Cabello	290	10.28 N	68.01 W
Puerto Cabezas	280	14.02 N	83.24 W
Puerto Carreño	290	6.12 N	67.22 W
Puerto Casado	294	22.20 S	57.55 W
Puerto Castilla	280	16.01 N	86.01 W
Puerto Chicama	292	7.42 S	79.27 W
Puertocito Indian Reservation ◆[4]	254	34.30 N	107.30 W
Puerto Colombia	290	10.59 N	74.58 W
Puerto Cortés, C.R.	280	8.58 N	83.32 W
Puerto Cortés, Hond.	280	15.48 N	87.56 W
Puerto Cumarebo	290	11.29 N	69.21 W
Puerto de Lajas, Cerro ∧	278	28.58 N	107.15 W
Puerto Delicia	294	26.12 S	54.37 W
Puerto de Nutrias	290	8.05 N	69.18 W
Puerto de Pollensa	168	39.55 N	3.05 E
Puerto de San José	280	13.55 N	90.49 W
Puerto de San Juan	292	15.20 S	75.09 W
Puerto Deseado	288	47.45 S	65.55 W
Puerto El Triunfo	280	13.17 N	88.33 W
Puerto Escondido	278	15.50 N	97.10 W
Puerto Esperanza	294	26.01 S	54.39 W
Puerto Estrella	290	12.21 N	71.19 W
Puerto Fonciere	294	22.29 S	57.48 W
Puerto Galera	202	13.30 N	120.57 E
Puerto Guaraní	292	21.18 S	57.55 W
Puerto Heath	292	12.30 S	68.40 W
Puerto Iguazú	294	25.40 S	54.25 W
Puerto Jiménez	280	8.33 N	83.19 W
Puerto Juárez	278	21.11 N	86.49 W
Puerto la Cruz	290	10.13 N	64.38 W
Puerto Leda	292	20.41 S	58.02 W
Puerto Leguízamo	290	0.12 S	74.46 W
Puerto Libertad	294	25.58 S	54.35 W
Puerto Limón	290	3.23 N	73.30 W
Puertollano	168	38.41 N	4.07 W
Puerto Lobos	288	42.01 S	65.04 W
Puerto López	290	4.05 N	72.58 W
Puerto Madryn	288	42.46 S	65.02 W
Puerto Maldonado	292	12.36 S	69.11 W
Puerto Manatí	284p	21.22 N	76.50 W
Puerto Mihanovich	292	20.52 S	57.59 W
Puerto Montt	288	41.28 S	72.57 W
Puerto Morazán	280	12.50 N	87.11 W
Puerto Morelos	278	20.50 N	86.52 W
Puerto Nariño	290	4.56 N	67.48 W
Puerto Natales	288	51.44 S	72.31 W
Puerto Ordaz	290	8.16 N	62.44 W
Puerto Padilla	292	10.15 S	71.39 W
Puerto Padre	284p	21.12 N	76.36 W
Puerto Páez	290	6.13 N	67.28 W
Puerto Palmer, Pico ∧	250	27.08 N	101.47 W
Puerto Pelón	280	14.22 N	85.53 W
Puerto Peñasco	278	31.20 N	113.33 W
Puerto Pilón	280	9.22 N	79.50 W
Puerto Pinasco	294	22.43 S	57.50 W
Puerto Pirámides	288	42.35 S	64.15 W
Puerto Piray	294	26.27 S	54.43 W
Puerto Píritu	290	10.04 N	65.03 W
Puerto Plata	282	19.48 N	70.41 W
Puerto Portillo	292	9.45 S	72.42 W
Puerto Potrero	280	10.28 N	85.47 W
Puerto Princesa, Pil.	202	9.44 N	118.44 E
Puerto Princesa, Pil.	202	10.06 N	125.29 E
Puerto Real, Esp.	168	36.32 N	6.11 W
Puerto Real, P.R.	284m	18.05 N	67.11 W
Puerto Reyes	290	0.59 S	73.17 W
Puerto Rico, Bol.	292	11.05 S	67.38 W
Puerto Rico, Col.	290	1.54 N	75.10 W
Puerto Rico □[2]	276	18.15 N	66.30 W
Puerto Rondón	290	6.17 N	71.06 W
Puerto Saavedra	294	38.47 S	73.24 W
Puerto Salgar	290	5.28 N	74.39 W
Puerto Sastre	294	22.06 S	57.59 W
Puerto Siles	292	12.48 S	65.05 W
Puerto Somoza	280	12.12 N	86.46 W
Puerto Suárez	292	18.57 S	57.51 W
Puerto Sucre	292	10.48 S	65.23 W

Symbols in the index entries are identified on page 360.

Name	Page	Lat°′	Long°′
Puerto Supe	292	10.48 S	77.45 W
Puerto Tejada	290	3.14 N	76.24 W
Puerto Toledo	290	0.59 S	74.09 W
Puerto Umbría	290	0.52 N	76.33 W
Puerto Vallarta	278	20.37 N	105.15 W
Puerto Varas	288	41.19 S	72.59 W
Puerto Victoria, Arg.	294	26.18 S	54.39 W
Puerto Victoria, Perú	292	9.55 S	74.75 W
Puerto Viejo, C.R.	280	10.26 N	83.59 W
Puerto Viejo, C.R.	280	9.39 N	82.45 W
Puerto Villamizar	290	8.19 N	72.26 W
Puerto Wilches	290	7.21 N	73.54 W
Puerto Ybapobó	294	23.42 S	57.12 W
Pueyrredón, Lago(Lago Cochrane) ≚	288	47.20 S	72.00 W
Pugačov	158	52.01 N	48.50 E
Puget, Cape ≻	236	59.52 N	148.26 W
Puget-Théniers	170	43.57 N	6.54 E
Pughtown	266	40.32 N	80.34 W
Puglia □[4]	184	41.15 N	16.15 E
Pugwash	240	45.51 N	63.40 W
Puhi	275b	21.58 N	159.24 W
Puhos	160	62.05 N	29.54 E
Puiești	172	46.25 N	27.33 E
Puigcerdá	168	42.26 N	1.56 E
Puigmal ∧	168	42.23 N	2.07 E
Puinahua, Canal de ≃[1]	292	5.09 S	74.07 W
Pujada Bay C	202	6.50 N	126.15 E
Pujilí	290	0.57 S	78.41 W
Pukaki, Lake ⊜	230	44.06 S	170.10 E
Pukalani	275a	20.51 N	156.20 W
Pukaskwa ≃	244	48.00 N	85.53 W
Pukch'ŏng	194	40.15 N	128.20 E
Pukë	172	42.03 N	19.54 E
Pukeashun Mountain ∧	238	51.12 N	119.14 W
Pukekohe	230	37.12 S	174.54 E
Puketeraki Range ⋀	230	43.00 S	172.07 E
Puketoi Range ⋀	230	40.30 S	176.05 E
Pukhan-gang ≃	194	37.31 N	127.18 E
Pukoo	275c	21.04 N	156.48 W
Pukou	196	32.07 N	118.43 E
Puksoozero	160	62.38 N	40.36 E
Puksubaek-san ∧	194	40.42 N	127.44 E
Puktae-ch'ŏn ≃	194	40.28 N	129.00 E
Pula	170	44.52 N	13.50 E
Pulacayo	292	20.25 S	66.41 W
Pulanduta Point ≻	202	11.54 N	123.10 E
Pulangi ≃	202	7.18 N	124.50 E
Pulanzong	190	30.16 N	81.14 E
Pulaski, Ind., U.S.	268	40.59 N	86.40 W
Pulaski, Mich., U.S.	268	42.07 N	84.40 W
Pulaski, N.Y., U.S.	264	43.34 N	76.08 W
Pulaski, Ohio, U.S.	268	41.30 N	84.26 W
Pulaski, Pa., U.S.	266	41.07 N	80.26 W
Pulaski, Tenn., U.S.	248	35.12 N	87.02 W
Pulaski, Va., U.S.	246	37.03 N	80.47 W
Pulaski, Wis., U.S.	244	44.41 N	88.14 W
Pulaski □[6]	268	41.03 N	86.36 W
Puławy	164	51.25 N	21.57 E
Pulkkila	160	64.16 N	25.52 E
Pullman, Mich., U.S.	268	42.29 N	86.05 W
Pullman, Wash., U.S.	256	46.44 N	117.10 W
Pullo	292	15.10 S	73.48 W
Pully	180	46.31 N	6.39 E
Pulo Anna I	198	4.40 N	131.58 E
Pulog, Mount ∧	202	16.35 N	120.54 E
Pulon'ga	160	66.17 N	40.02 E
Púlpito, Punta ≻	278	26.31 N	111.28 W
Pulsano	170	40.23 N	17.22 E
Pultneyville	264	43.17 N	77.11 W
Pułtusk	164	52.43 N	21.05 E
Pülümür Geçidi)(	212	39.31 N	39.54 E
Pulupandan	202	10.31 N	122.48 E
Pumpkin Buttes ∧	254	43.44 N	105.54 W
Pumpkin Center	274	35.18 N	119.05 W
Puna	292	19.46 S	65.28 W
Puná, Isla I	290	2.50 S	80.08 W
Punakha	204	27.37 N	89.51 E
Punaluu	275c	21.35 N	157.53 W
Punata	292	17.32 S	65.50 W
Punchaw	238	53.28 N	123.13 W
Pundaguitan	202	6.22 N	126.10 E
Pune	204	18.31 N	73.54 E
Pungești	172	46.42 N	27.20 E
Pungo ≃	246	35.23 N	76.33 W
Púngoè ≃	224	19.50 S	34.48 E
Punia	218	1.28 S	26.27 E
Punitaqui	294	30.50 S	71.16 W
Punjabi Suba □[3]	206	31.00 N	75.30 E
Puno	292	15.50 S	70.02 W
Puno □[5]	292	15.00 S	70.00 W
Punta, Cerro de ∧	282	18.10 N	66.35 W
Punta Alegre	284p	22.23 N	78.49 W
Punta Alta	294	38.53 S	62.04 W
Punta Arenas	288	53.09 S	70.55 W
Punta Banda, Cabo ≻	278	31.45 N	116.45 W
Punta Cardón	290	11.38 N	70.14 W
Punta de Bombón	292	17.10 S	71.48 W
Punta de Díaz	294	28.03 S	70.37 W
Punta del Cobre	294	27.30 S	70.16 W
Punta del Este	294	34.58 S	54.57 W
Punta Delgada	288	42.43 S	63.38 W
Punta de los Llanos	294	30.19 S	66.33 W
Punta de Mata	290	9.43 N	63.38 W
Punta de Piedras	290	10.54 N	64.06 W
Punta Flecha	202	7.23 N	123.25 E
Punta Gorda, Br. Hond.	278	16.07 N	88.48 W
Punta Gorda, Nic.	280	11.31 N	83.47 W
Punta Gorda, Fla., U.S.	246	26.56 N	82.03 W
Punta Moreno	292	7.36 S	78.54 W
Punta Negra, Salar de ≚	294	24.35 S	69.00 W
Punta Piedra, Sierra ⋀	280	15.21 N	85.16 W
Punta Porá	294	25.05 S	58.30 W
Punta Prieta	278	28.58 N	114.17 W
Puntarenas	280	9.58 N	84.50 W
Puntarenas □[4]	280	9.00 N	83.15 W
Punta Santiago	284m	18.10 N	65.45 W
Puntas del Sauce	294	33.51 S	57.01 W
Punto Fijo	290	11.42 N	70.13 W
Puntzi Lake ⊜	238	52.12 N	124.02 W
Punxsutawney	266	40.57 N	78.59 W
Puolanka	160	64.52 N	27.40 E
Puolo Point ≻	275d	21.54 N	159.36 W
Pupuña ≃	290	2.12 S	70.53 W
Puqi	190	29.43 N	113.53 E
Puquio	292	14.43 S	74.17 W
Pur ≃	186	67.31 N	77.55 E
Puracé, Volcán ∧[1]	290	2.21 N	76.23 W
Purcell	250	35.01 N	97.22 W
Purcell Mountains ⋀	238	50.00 N	116.30 W
Purcellville	242	39.08 N	77.43 W
Purchena	168	37.21 N	2.22 W
Purdy	248	36.49 N	93.55 W
Pureora, Mount ∧	230	38.33 S	175.38 E
Purgatoire ≃	252	38.04 N	103.10 W
Purgatoire Peak ∧	254	37.04 N	105.13 W
Puri	206	19.48 N	85.50 E
Purial, Sierra de ⋀	284p	20.12 N	74.42 W
Purian Point ≻	200	15.50 N	94.24 E
Purificación, Col.	290	3.51 N	74.55 W
Purificación, Méx.	278	19.43 N	104.38 W
Purificación ≃	278	23.58 N	98.42 W
Purísima, Méx.	250	29.09 N	100.46 W
Purísima, Méx.	278	25.25 N	105.26 W
Purísima, Sierra de la ⋀	250	26.28 N	101.45 W
Purkersdorf	164	48.12 N	16.11 E
Purley	250	33.05 N	95.16 W
Purmerend	178	52.31 N	4.57 E
Purnea	206	25.47 N	87.31 E
Puronga	160	60.09 N	40.54 E
Puruê ≃	290	1.40 S	68.08 W
Purūlia	206	23.20 N	86.22 E
Puruni ≃	290	6.01 N	59.10 W
Purus (Purús) ≃	288	3.42 S	61.28 W
Puruvesi ⊜	160	61.50 N	29.27 E
Purvis	248	31.09 N	89.25 W
Purwakarta	198	6.34 S	107.26 E
Purwokerto	198	7.25 S	109.14 E
Pusan	194	35.06 N	129.03 E
Pusan □[8]	194	35.10 N	129.05 E
Pusat Gajo, Pegunungan ⋀	200	4.15 N	97.05 E
Pusgo Point ≻	202	13.31 N	122.38 E
Pushthrough	240	47.38 N	56.11 W
Puškin	160	59.43 N	30.25 E
Puškino	160	56.01 N	37.51 E
Puškinskije Gory	160	57.01 N	28.54 E
Puskwaskau ≃	238	55.29 N	118.10 W
Püspökladány	164	47.19 N	21.07 E
Pustoška	160	56.20 N	29.22 E
Pustozersk	160	67.33 N	52.27 E
Puszczykowo	164	52.17 N	16.52 E
Putaendo	294	32.38 S	70.44 W
Putao	190	27.21 N	97.24 E
Putaruru	230	38.03 S	175.47 E
Put'atino	160	54.10 N	41.07 E
Putian	196	25.28 N	119.02 E
Putina	292	14.55 S	69.55 W
Put-in-Bay	266	41.39 N	82.49 W
Puting, Tandjung ≻	198	3.31 S	111.46 E
Putnam, Conn., U.S.	261	41.55 N	71.55 W
Putnam, Tex., U.S.	250	32.22 N	99.12 W
Putnam □[6], N.Y., U.S.	261	41.26 N	73.41 W
Putnam □[6], Ohio, U.S.	268	41.01 N	84.03 W
Putnam Lake	261	41.28 N	73.35 W
Putnam Valley	261	41.20 N	73.52 W
Putney, Ga., U.S.	246	31.29 N	84.07 W
Putney, Vt., U.S.	242	42.59 N	72.31 W
Putneyville	266	40.57 N	79.19 W
Putorana, Plato ⋀[1]	186	69.00 N	95.00 E
Putre	292	18.12 S	69.35 W
Puttalam	204	8.02 N	79.49 E
Putte	178	51.04 N	4.38 E
Putten	178	52.15 N	5.36 E
Puttgarden	164	54.30 N	11.13 E
Putú	294	35.13 S	72.17 W
Putumayo □[8]	290	0.30 N	76.00 W
Putumayo (Içá) ≃	290	3.07 S	67.58 W
Putu Range ⋀	222	5.30 N	8.10 W
Puukolii	275a	20.56 N	156.41 W
Puu Kukui ∧	275d	20.52 N	156.35 W
Puulavesi ⊜	160	61.50 N	26.42 E
Puumala	160	61.32 N	28.11 E
Puunene	275a	20.52 N	156.28 W
Puurs	176	51.05 N	4.17 E
Puuwai	275b	21.54 N	160.12 W
Puxico	248	36.57 N	90.10 W
Puyallup	270	47.11 N	122.18 W
Puyang	194	35.43 N	115.01 E
Puyanga ≃	290	3.52 S	80.12 W
Puyangjiang ≃	196	30.05 N	120.11 E
Puyca	292	15.04 S	72.42 W
Puy-de-Dôme □[5]	166	45.45 N	3.05 E
Puy de Dôme ∧	166	45.47 N	2.58 E
Puy de Sancy ∧	166	45.32 N	2.49 E
Puylaurens	166	43.34 N	2.01 E
Puy L'Evêque	166	44.30 N	1.08 E
Puymorens, Col de)(	166	42.30 N	1.50 E
Puyo	290	1.28 S	77.59 W
Puysegur Point ≻	230	46.09 S	166.37 E
Pūzak, Hāmūn-i- ⊜	208	31.30 N	61.30 E
Pweto	218	8.28 S	28.54 E
Pwllheli	162	52.53 N	4.25 W
Pyamalaw ≃[1]	200	15.49 N	94.42 E
Pyapon	200	16.17 N	95.41 E
Pyatigorsk → P'atigorsk	158	44.03 N	43.04 E
Pyčas	160	56.29 N	52.28 E
Pyè (Prome)	200	18.49 N	95.13 E
Pye Islands II	236	59.22 N	150.25 W
Pyhähäkin Kansallis Puisto ♠	160	62.52 N	25.30 E
Pyhäjoki	160	64.28 N	24.14 E
Pyhäjoki ≃	160	64.28 N	24.13 E
Pyhäselkä	160	62.26 N	29.58 E
Pyhäselkä ⊜	160	62.26 N	29.58 E
Pyhätunturi ∧	160	67.01 N	27.09 E
Pyhätunturin Kansallispuisto ♠	160	67.01 N	27.10 E
Pyinmana	200	19.44 N	96.13 E
Pylos → Pílos	172	36.55 N	21.43 E
Pymatuning Reservoir ⊜[1]	242	41.37 N	80.30 W
Pyngopil'gyn, Laguna C	236	67.24 N	175.10 W
P'yŏngan Namdo □[4]	194	39.20 N	126.00 E
P'yŏngan-pukdo □[4]	194	40.10 N	125.20 E
P'yŏngyang	194	39.01 N	125.45 E
P'yŏngyang □[4]	194	39.05 N	125.50 E
Pyote	250	31.32 N	103.08 W
Pyramid Lake ⊜	258	40.00 N	119.35 W
Pyramid Lake Indian Reservation ⊸[4]	258	40.20 N	119.35 W
Pyramid Peak ∧	254	43.27 N	110.28 W
Pyramids ⊥	220	29.53 N	31.13 E
Pyrenees ⋀	168	42.40 N	1.00 E
Pyrénées-Orientales □[5]	166	42.30 N	2.20 E
Pyre Peak ∧	236	52.20 N	172.31 W
Pyrgos → Pírgos	172	37.41 N	21.28 E
Pyrkanajan, Gora ∧	236	69.14 N	175.50 E
Pyrmont	268	40.28 N	86.41 W
Pyrzyce (Pyritz)	164	53.10 N	14.55 E
Pysht	270	48.12 N	124.07 W
Pyskowice (Peiskretscham)	164	50.24 N	18.38 E
Pytalovo	160	57.04 N	27.56 E
Pythonga, Lac ⊜	242	46.23 N	76.26 W
Pyu	200	18.29 N	96.26 E
Pyzdry	164	52.11 N	17.41 E

Q

Name	Page	Lat°′	Long°′
Qala-i-Kāng	208	31.07 N	61.58 E
Qala Nau	208	34.58 N	63.04 E
Qala Qausi	204	34.28 N	65.02 E
Qal'at Bīshah	214	20.01 N	42.36 E
Qallābāt	214	12.58 N	36.09 E
Qalqilīya	210	32.11 N	34.58 E
Qalyūb	220	30.11 N	31.12 E
Qamar, Ghubbat al- C	204	16.00 N	52.30 E
Qānā	210	33.13 N	35.18 E
Qandala	214	11.23 N	49.53 E
Qareh Sū ≃	208	39.27 N	47.24 E
Qarrit, Qaf' e)(	172	40.29 N	20.40 E
Qārūn, Birkat ⊜	220	29.28 N	30.40 E
Qāsh, Nahr al-(Gash) ≃	220	16.48 N	35.51 E
Qaṣr al-Burayqah	214	30.25 N	19.34 E
Qaṣr al-Farāfirah	214	27.03 N	27.58 E
Qaṣr Banī Walīd	214	31.45 N	14.01 E
Qaṭanā	210	33.26 N	36.05 E
Qatar (Qaṭar) □[1]	204	25.00 N	51.10 E
Qattara Depression → Aqṭṭārah, Munkhafaḍ al- •[7]	220	30.00 N	27.30 E
Qaṭṭārah, Munkhafaḍ al-(Qattara Depression) •[7]	220	30.00 N	27.30 E
Qāyen	204	33.44 N	59.11 E
Qazvīn	208	36.16 N	50.00 E
Qeqertag I	232	•71.55 N	55.30 W
Qeshm	208	26.58 N	56.16 E
Qeshm I	208	26.45 N	55.45 E
Qeys, Jazīreh-ye I	208	26.32 N	53.56 E
Qezel Owzan ≃	208	36.45 N	49.22 E
Qiemo	190	38.08 N	85.32 E
Qijiang	190	29.02 N	106.39 E
Qilaguganishan ∧	206	28.46 N	87.38 E
Qilianshanmai ⋀	190	39.06 N	98.40 E
Qilinhu ⊜	206	31.50 N	89.00 E
Qinā	220	26.10 N	32.43 E
Qinā, Wādī V	220	26.12 N	32.44 E
Qingcao'ai)(	196	27.40 N	119.34 E
Qingdao (Tsingtao)	194	36.06 N	120.19 E
Qinghai □[4]	190	36.00 N	96.00 E
Qinghai ⊜	190	36.50 N	100.20 E
Qinghuashui ≃	196	25.00 N	114.00 E
Qingjiang	196	28.05 N	115.29 E
Qinglong	200	25.50 N	105.10 E
Qinglonghe ≃	194	39.35 N	117.46 E
Qingshuilangshan ⋀	200	26.15 N	99.35 E
Qingtang	190	24.14 N	113.51 E
Qingyang	190	36.06 N	107.47 E
Qingyihu ⊜	194	34.22 N	118.54 E
Qingyuan	196	23.43 N	113.01 E
Qingzhen	200	26.29 N	106.22 E
Qinhuangdao (Chinwangtao)	194	39.56 N	119.36 E
Qinjiang ≃, Zhg.	196	23.58 N	115.47 E
Qinjiang ≃, Zhg.	196	26.16 N	115.52 E
Qinlingshanmai ⋀	190	34.00 N	108.00 E
Qinxian (Qinzhou)	200	21.59 N	108.36 E
Qionghai (Jiaji)	200	19.20 N	110.30 E
Qionglai	190	30.25 N	103.27 E
Qiongzhou haixia ⋃	200	20.10 N	110.15 E
Qiqihaer (Tsitsihar)	190	47.19 N	123.55 E
Qiryat Ata	210	32.47 N	35.06 E
Qiryat Bialik	210	32.50 N	35.05 E
Qiryat Gat	210	31.36 N	34.47 E
Qiryat Malakhi	210	31.44 N	34.45 E
Qiryat Motzkin	210	32.49 N	35.03 E
Qiryat Ono	210	32.04 N	34.52 E
Qiryat Shemona	210	33.12 N	35.35 E
Qiryat Tiv'on	210	32.43 N	35.08 E
Qiryat Yam	210	32.51 N	35.04 E
Qishn	214	15.26 N	51.40 E
Qishui ≃	196	30.09 N	115.20 E
Qiubei	200	24.07 N	104.12 E
Qiyang	200	26.29 N	111.43 E
Qīzān	214	16.54 N	42.29 E
Qom	208	34.39 N	50.54 E
Quadra Island I	238	50.08 N	125.16 W
Quadros, Lagoa dos C	294	29.42 S	50.05 W
Quail Valley	274	33.43 N	117.15 W
Quakenbrück	178	52.40 N	7.57 E
Quaker Hill, Conn., U.S.	261	41.24 N	72.07 W
Quaker Hill, N.Y., U.S.	261	41.35 N	73.33 W
Quakertown, N.J., U.S.	262	40.34 N	74.57 W
Quakertown, Pa., U.S.	262	40.26 N	75.21 W
Qualicum Beach	238	49.21 N	124.27 W
Quanah	250	34.18 N	99.44 W
Quang-ngai	200	15.07 N	108.48 E
Quang-tri	200	16.45 N	107.13 E
Quan-long (Ca-mau)	200	9.11 N	105.08 E
Quantico, Md., U.S.	262	38.23 N	75.44 W
Quantico, Va., U.S.	262	38.31 N	77.17 W
Quanzhou	196	24.54 N	118.35 E
Quanzhougang C	196	24.52 N	118.37 E
Qu'Appelle ≃	232	50.25 N	101.20 W
Quaraí	294	30.23 S	56.27 W
Quaraí (Guareim) ≃	294	30.12 S	57.36 W
Quaregnon	176	50.26 N	3.51 E
Quarrata	184	43.51 N	10.58 E
Quarryville, Conn., U.S.	261	41.32 N	72.42 W
Quarryville, Pa., U.S.	262	39.54 N	76.10 W
Quartu Sant'Elena	170	39.14 N	9.11 E
Quartz Hill	274	34.39 N	118.13 W
Quartz Lake ⊜	232	70.55 N	80.33 W
Quartz Mountain ∧	256	43.10 N	122.40 W
Quartzsite	254	33.40 N	114.13 W
Quatá	296	22.16 S	50.42 W
Quatsino Sound ⋃	238	50.25 N	127.55 W
Qūchān	208	37.06 N	58.30 E
Queanbeyan	228	35.21 S	149.14 E
Québec	260	46.49 N	71.13 W
Québec □[6]	260	46.50 N	71.20 W
Quebec (Québec) □[3]	232	52.00 N	72.00 W
Quebeck	248	35.49 N	85.34 W
Quebra-Anzol ≃	296	19.09 S	47.38 W
Quebracho	294	31.57 S	57.53 W
Quebrada Seca	284m	18.14 N	65.40 W
Quebradillas	284m	18.29 N	66.56 W
Quecreek	266	40.06 N	79.05 W
Quedlinburg	164	51.48 N	11.09 E
Queen	266	40.16 N	78.31 W
Queen Anne	262	38.55 N	75.57 W
Queen Annes □[6]	262	39.03 N	76.04 W
Queen Bess, Mount ∧	238	51.16 N	124.34 W
Queen Charlotte	238	53.16 N	132.05 W
Queen Charlotte Islands II	238	53.00 N	132.00 W
Queen Charlotte Mountains ⋀	238	53.00 N	132.00 W
Queen Charlotte Sound ⋃	238	51.30 N	129.30 W
Queen Charlotte Strait ⋃	238	50.50 N	127.25 W
Queen City, Mo., U.S.	248	40.25 N	92.34 W
Queen City, Tex., U.S.	248	33.09 N	94.09 W
Queen Mary Coast •[2]	148	67.00 S	96.00 E
Queen Maud Gulf C	232	68.25 N	102.30 W
Queen Maud Land ⊸[1]	148	72.30 S	12.00 E
Queen Maud Mountains ⋀	148	86.00 S	160.00 W
Queens Channel II	232	76.11 N	96.00 W
Queens Channel ⋃	226	14.46 S	129.24 E
Queensland □[3]	228	22.00 S	145.00 E
Queensport	240	45.20 N	61.16 W
Queens Sound ⋃	238	51.55 N	128.11 W
Queenston	264	43.10 N	79.03 W
Queenstown, Austl.	226	42.05 S	145.33 E
Queenstown → Cobh, Eire	162	51.51 N	8.17 W
Queenstown, Guy.	290	7.12 N	58.30 W
Queenstown, N.Z.	230	45.02 S	168.40 E
Queenstown, S. Afr.	224	31.52 S	26.52 E
Queenstown, Md., U.S.	262	38.59 N	76.09 W
Queensville	264	44.08 N	79.28 W
Queets	270	47.32 N	124.20 W
Queguay Grande ≃	294	32.09 S	58.09 W
Queimadinhas	296	13.03 S	40.45 W
Queimados	296	22.42 S	43.34 W
Quelimane	218	17.53 S	36.51 E
Quelle	178	52.00 N	8.29 E
Quelpart Island → Cheju-do I	190	33.20 N	126.30 E
Quemado, N. Mex., U.S.	254	34.20 N	108.30 W
Quemado, Tex., U.S.	250	28.56 N	100.38 W
Quemado de Güines	284p	22.48 N	80.15 W
Quemoy → Chinmen Tao I	196	24.27 N	118.23 E
Quemú Quemú	294	36.05 S	63.35 W
Quentin	262	40.17 N	76.26 W
Quepos	280	9.27 N	84.09 W
Que Que	224	18.55 S	29.49 E
Quequén	294	38.34 S	58.42 W
Quercy □[9]	166	44.30 N	1.25 E
Querecotillo	292	4.51 S	80.40 W
Querência do Norte	296	23.00 S	53.28 W
Querétaro	278	20.36 N	100.23 W
Querobabi	278	30.03 N	111.01 W
Querobamba	292	13.51 S	73.51 W
Quesada, C.R.	280	10.19 N	84.26 W
Quesada, Esp.	168	37.51 N	3.04 W
Quesnel	238	52.59 N	122.30 W
Quesnel ≃	238	53.00 N	122.30 W
Quesnel Lake ⊜	238	52.32 N	121.05 W
Questa	254	36.42 N	105.36 W
Questembert	166	47.40 N	2.27 W
Quetena	292	22.10 S	67.25 W
Quetico Lake ⊜	244	48.34 N	91.52 W
Quetta	206	30.12 N	67.00 E
Quetta □[8]	208	30.15 N	68.30 E
Quettehou	166	49.36 N	1.18 W
Quevedo	290	1.02 S	79.29 W
Quezaltenango	280	14.50 N	91.31 W
Quezaltenango □[5]	280	14.45 N	91.40 W
Quezaltepeque, El Sal.	280	13.50 N	89.17 W
Quezaltepeque, Guat.	280	14.38 N	89.27 W
Quezon, Pil.	202	15.34 N	120.49 E
Quezon, Pil.	202	14.00 N	122.10 E
Quezon □[4]	202	13.58 N	122.02 E
Quezon City	202	14.38 N	121.00 E
Quezon National Park ♠	202	14.01 N	121.51 E
Qufu	190	35.36 N	117.02 E
Quiabaya	292	15.37 S	68.46 W
Quibdó	290	5.42 N	76.40 W
Quiberon	166	47.29 N	3.07 W
Quíbor	290	9.56 N	69.37 W
Quiches	292	8.23 S	77.26 W
Quickborn	178	53.44 N	9.53 E
Quidapil Point ≻	202	6.49 N	123.56 E
Quidnessett	261	41.39 N	71.26 W
Quidnick	261	41.42 N	71.33 W
Quiévrain	176	50.24 N	3.41 E
Quiindy	294	25.58 S	57.16 W
Quijos ≃	290	0.14 S	77.43 W
Quijotosa Wash V	254	32.56 N	112.46 W
Quilá	278	24.23 N	107.13 W
Quilalí	280	13.32 N	86.00 W
Quilatés, Cap ≻	168	35.20 N	3.45 W
Quilcene	270	47.49 N	122.53 W
Quilimarí	294	32.07 S	71.30 W
Quilino	294	30.15 S	64.31 W
Quillabamba	292	12.48 S	72.40 W
Quillacas	292	19.14 S	66.58 W
Quillacollo	292	17.26 S	66.17 W
Quillagua	292	21.39 S	69.33 W
Quillan	166	42.52 N	2.11 E
Quillota	294	32.53 S	71.16 W
Quilpie	226	26.37 S	144.15 E
Quilpué	294	33.03 S	71.27 W
Quimarí, Alto de ∧	290	8.07 N	76.23 W
Quimbaya	290	4.38 N	75.47 W
Quimby	252	42.38 N	95.38 W
Quime	292	17.02 S	67.15 W
Quimilí	294	27.40 S	62.30 W
Quimper	166	48.00 N	4.06 W
Quimperlé	166	47.52 N	3.33 W
Quimpitirique	292	12.24 S	73.46 W
Quinalasag Island I	202	13.57 N	123.48 E
Quinault	270	47.28 N	123.50 W
Quinault Indian Reservation ⊸[4]	256	47.24 N	124.10 W
Quincemil	292	13.15 S	70.40 W
Quinches	292	12.16 S	76.07 W
Quincy, Calif., U.S.	258	39.56 N	120.57 W
Quincy, Ill., U.S.	248	39.56 N	91.23 W
Quincy, Mass., U.S.	261	42.15 N	71.01 W
Quincy, Mich., U.S.	268	41.57 N	84.53 W
Quincy, Ohio, U.S.	268	40.18 N	83.58 W
Quincy, Oreg., U.S.	270	46.04 N	123.05 W
Quincy, Pa., U.S.	262	39.48 N	77.35 W
Quincy, Wash., U.S.	256	47.14 N	119.51 W
Quincy Hills ⋀[2]	248	39.55 N	91.15 W
Quindío □[5]	290	5.20 N	75.40 W
Quinebaug	261	42.01 N	71.57 W
Quines	294	32.14 S	65.48 W
Quinga	218	15.49 S	40.15 E
Quinhagak	236	59.45 N	161.43 W
Qui-nhon	200	13.46 N	109.14 E
Quiniluban Group II	202	11.25 N	120.50 E
Quiniluban Island I	202	11.36 N	120.50 E
Quinlan	250	32.55 N	96.08 W
Quinn ≃	258	39.55 N	119.00 W
Quintanar de la Orden	168	39.34 N	3.03 W
Quintana Roo □[8]	278	18.45 N	88.10 W
Quinte, Bay of C	244	44.07 N	77.15 W
Quinter	252	39.04 N	100.14 W
Quintero	294	32.47 S	71.32 W
Quintin	166	48.24 N	2.55 W
Quinto	168	41.25 N	0.29 W
Quinton, N.J., U.S.	262	39.33 N	75.25 E
Quinton, Okla., U.S.	250	35.07 N	95.22 W
Quinze, Lac des ⊜	244	47.30 N	79.00 W
Quipar ≃	168	38.14 N	1.36 W
Quipit ≃	202	8.05 N	122.28 E
Quirauk Mountain ∧	242	39.42 N	77.31 W
Quiriguá ⊥	280	15.18 N	89.07 W
Quirihue	294	36.17 S	72.32 W
Quirinópolis	296	18.32 S	50.30 W
Quiriquire	290	9.59 N	63.13 W
Quirke Lake ⊜	244	46.28 N	82.33 W
Quiroga, Esp.	168	42.29 N	7.16 W
Quiroga, Méx.	278	19.40 N	101.32 W
Quirós	294	28.57 S	65.07 W
Quirpon Island I	240	51.35 N	55.25 W
Quiruvilca	292	8.01 S	78.19 W
Quissanga	218	12.25 S	40.29 E
Quitaque	250	34.22 N	101.04 W
Quita Sueño Bank ⊹[4]	280	14.20 N	81.09 W
Quitéria ≃	296	20.16 S	51.08 W
Quitilipi	294	26.53 S	60.15 W
Quitman, Ga., U.S.	246	30.47 N	83.33 W
Quitman, Miss., U.S.	248	32.03 N	88.43 W
Quitman, Tex., U.S.	250	32.48 N	95.27 W
Quito	290	0.13 S	78.30 W
Quivilla	292	9.30 S	76.40 W
Quixadá	286	4.58 S	39.01 W
Quixito ≃	290	4.29 S	70.18 W
Qujing	200	25.32 N	103.41 E
Qul'ān, Jazā'ir II	208	24.22 N	35.23 E
Qulay'ah, Ra's al- ≻	208	28.53 N	48.18 E
Qulin	248	36.36 N	90.15 W
Qulūd, Jabal ∧[2]	220	11.41 N	29.31 E
Qumalai	190	34.35 N	95.27 E
Qumrān, Khirbat ⊥	210	31.44 N	35.28 E
Qunayfidhah, Nafūd •[8]	208	24.45 N	45.30 E
Quoich ≃	232	64.00 N	93.30 W
Quoin Point ≻	224	34.46 S	19.37 E
Quorn	228	32.21 S	138.03 E
Qurayyāt, Al- □[4]	210	31.28 N	37.05 E
Qūṣ	220	25.55 N	32.45 E
Qushan I	196	30.27 N	122.20 E
Quthing	218	30.30 S	27.36 E
Quxian	196	28.58 N	118.52 E
Quyon	242	45.31 N	76.14 W
Quyquyhó	294	26.14 S	57.01 W

R

Name	Page	Lat°′	Long°′
Raab (Rába) ≃	164	47.42 N	17.38 E
Raahe	160	64.41 N	24.29 E
Raalte	178	52.24 N	6.16 E
Raamsdonk	178	51.42 N	4.56 E
Ra'ananna	210	32.11 N	34.52 E
Raasay I	162	57.25 N	6.04 W
Rab	170	44.46 N	14.46 E
Rab, Otok I	170	44.47 N	14.45 E
Raba	198	8.27 S	118.46 E
Rába (Raab) ≃, Eur.	164	47.42 N	17.38 E
Raba ≃, Pol.	164	50.09 N	20.30 E
Rabaçal ≃	168	41.30 N	7.12 W
Rábade	168	43.07 N	7.37 W
Rabat, Magreb	214	34.02 N	6.51 W
Rabat, Malta	170	35.52 N	14.25 E
Rabbit Ears Pass)(	254	40.24 N	106.37 W
Rabbit Lake ⊜, Ont., Can.	244	47.00 N	79.37 W
Rabbit Lake ⊜, Qué., Can.	244	47.30 N	78.22 W
Rābigh	208	22.48 N	39.01 E
Rabinal	280	15.06 N	90.27 W
Rabka	164	49.36 N	19.56 E
Rabočeostrovsk	160	64.02 N	34.46 E
Rabun Bald ∧	246	34.58 N	83.18 W
Răcari	172	44.38 N	25.45 E
Racconigi	182	44.46 N	7.46 E
Raccoon ≃	244	41.35 N	93.37 W
Race, Cape ≻	240	46.40 N	53.10 W
Raceland	248	29.48 N	90.40 W
Rach-gia	200	10.00 N	105.04 E
Rach-gia, Vinh C	200	10.00 N	105.00 E
Raciąż	164	52.47 N	20.06 E
Racibórz (Ratibor)	164	50.06 N	18.13 E
Racine, Pa., U.S.	266	40.49 N	80.20 W
Racine, Wis., U.S.	268	42.43 N	87.48 W
Racine □[6]	268	42.45 N	88.05 W
Ráckeve	164	47.10 N	18.56 E
Raco	244	46.22 N	84.43 W
Radama, Îles II	225b	14.00 S	47.47 E
Radama, Presqu'île ≻[1]	225b	14.16 S	47.53 E
Rădăuți	172	47.51 N	25.55 E
Radbuza ≃	164	49.46 N	13.24 E
Radcliff	248	37.51 N	85.57 W
Radeberg	164	51.07 N	13.55 E
Radebeul	164	51.06 N	13.40 E
Radeče	170	46.04 N	15.11 E
Radevormwald	178	51.12 N	7.21 E
Radford	246	37.08 N	80.34 W
Rădinești	172	44.48 N	23.46 E
Radium Hot Springs	238	50.38 N	116.03 W
Radix, Point ≻	285r	10.20 N	61.00 W
Radja, Udjung ≻	200	3.43 N	96.32 E
Radkersburg	172	46.41 N	15.59 E
Radnevo	172	42.18 N	25.56 E
Radnice	164	49.51 N	13.37 E
Radnor	266	40.23 N	83.09 W
Radnor □[6]	174	52.17 N	3.20 W
Radolfzell	180	47.44 N	8.58 E
Radom	164	51.25 N	21.10 E
Radomir	172	42.33 N	22.58 E
Radomka ≃	164	51.43 N	21.26 E
Radomsko	164	51.05 N	19.25 E
Radomyśl Wielki	164	50.12 N	21.16 E
Radotin	164	50.00 N	14.22 E
Radoviš	172	41.38 N	22.28 E
Radovljica	170	46.21 N	14.11 E
Radstadt	164	47.23 N	13.27 E
Radviliškis	160	55.50 N	23.31 E
Radville	252	49.27 N	104.17 W
Raḍwā, Jabal ∧	208	24.34 N	38.18 E
Radway	238	54.04 N	112.57 W
Radymno	164	49.57 N	22.48 E
Radziejów	164	52.38 N	18.32 E
Radzyń Chełmiński	164	53.24 N	18.56 E
Radzyń Podlaski	164	51.48 N	22.38 E
Rae	232	62.50 N	116.03 W
Rae ≃	232	67.55 N	115.30 W
Raeford	246	34.59 N	79.14 W
Rae Isthmus •[3]	232	66.55 N	86.10 W
Rae Strait ⋃	232	68.45 N	95.00 W
Rafael, Cachoeira do ⌊	292	10.25 S	63.15 W
Rafaela	294	31.17 S	61.30 W
Rafaḥ	210	31.18 N	34.15 E
Raffadali	170	37.24 N	13.33 E
Rafḥā'	214	29.42 N	43.30 E
Rafsanjān	208	30.24 N	56.01 E
Raft ≃	256	42.37 N	113.15 W
Raft River Mountains ⋀	254	41.55 N	113.25 W
Raft Swamp ≃	246	34.38 N	79.03 W
Raga	214	8.28 N	25.41 E
Ragang, Mount ∧	202	7.41 N	124.30 E
Ragay	202	13.49 N	122.47 E
Ragay Gulf C	202	13.40 N	122.40 E
Ragged Island I	282	22.20 N	75.40 W
Ragged Top Mountain ∧	254	41.27 N	105.20 W
Ragland	248	33.45 N	86.09 W
Ragusa, It.	170	36.55 N	14.44 E
Ragusa → Dubrovnik, Jugo.	172	42.38 N	18.07 E
Raḥā, Ḥarrat ar- •[9]	220	27.40 N	36.35 E
Rahad (Nahr ar-Rahad) ≃	220	14.28 N	33.31 E
Rahaṭ, Ḥarrat •[9]	220	22.20 N	40.05 E
Rahīmyār Khān	206	28.25 N	70.18 E
Rahlstedt ⊸[8]	178	53.36 N	10.09 E
Rahouia	168	35.32 N	1.01 E
Rahway	262	40.37 N	74.17 W
Raiford	246	30.04 N	82.14 W
Railroad	262	39.46 N	76.42 W
Rail Road Flat	272	38.20 N	120.30 W
Railroad Valley V	258	38.25 N	115.40 W
Rainbow	274	33.24 N	117.10 W
Rainbow Bridge National Monument ♠	254	36.58 N	110.56 W
Rainbow City	280	9.20 N	79.55 W
Rainbow Falls ⌊	238	52.23 N	119.59 W
Rainbow Shores	264	43.37 N	76.12 W
Rainelle	242	37.58 N	80.47 W
Rainham	174	51.23 N	0.36 E
Rainham ⊸[8]	174	51.31 N	0.11 E
Rainier, Oreg., U.S.	270	46.06 N	122.56 W
Rainier, Wash., U.S.	270	46.53 N	122.41 W
Rainier, Mount ∧	256	46.52 N	121.46 W
Rainy ≃, N.A.	244	48.50 N	94.41 W
Rainy ≃, Mich., U.S.	244	45.27 N	84.13 W
Rainy Lake ⊜	232	48.42 N	93.10 W
Rainy River	244	48.43 N	94.29 W
Raipur	206	21.14 N	81.38 E
Raisin	272	36.36 N	119.54 W
Raismes	176	50.23 N	3.29 E
Raiti	280	14.38 N	85.08 W
Rajajooseppi	160	68.28 N	28.21 E
Rājasthān □[4]	206	27.00 N	74.00 E
Rājasthān Canal ≂	206	31.10 N	75.00 E
Rajčichinsk	186	49.46 N	129.25 E
Rajgród	164	53.44 N	22.42 E
Rajka	164	48.02 N	17.11 E
Rājkot	206	22.18 N	70.47 E
Rāj-Nāndgaon	206	21.06 N	81.03 E
Rājshāhi	206	24.22 N	88.36 E
Rakaia ≃	230	43.54 S	172.12 E
Rakamaz	164	48.08 N	21.30 E
Rakaposhi ∧	206	36.09 N	74.28 E
Rakhshān ≃	206	27.10 N	63.25 E
Rakoniewice	164	52.10 N	16.16 E
Rakovník	164	50.05 N	13.43 E
Rakovski	172	42.18 N	24.58 E
Råkvåg	160	63.46 N	10.05 E
Rakvere	160	59.22 N	26.20 E
Raleigh, Newf., Can.	240	51.34 N	55.44 W
Raleigh, Miss., U.S.	248	32.02 N	89.30 W
Raleigh, N.C., U.S.	246	35.47 N	78.39 W
Raleigh Hills	270	45.29 N	122.46 W
Ralls	250	33.41 N	101.23 W
Ralston, Nebr., U.S.	252	41.12 N	96.03 W
Ralston, Pa., U.S.	242	41.31 N	76.57 W
Ram ≃	238	52.23 N	115.25 W
Rama	280	12.09 N	84.15 W
Rama ≃	280	12.08 N	84.15 W
Ramacca	170	37.23 N	14.42 E
Ramah	254	35.08 N	108.30 W
Ramales de la Victoria	168	43.15 N	3.27 W
Ramalho, Serra do ⋀	296	13.45 S	44.00 W
Rām Allāh	210	31.54 N	35.12 E
Ramallo	294	33.28 S	60.02 W
Ramanetaka, Baie C	225b	14.13 S	47.52 E
Ramat Gan	210	32.05 N	34.48 E
Ramat HaSharon	210	32.07 N	34.50 E
Rambervillers	180	48.21 N	6.38 E
Rambleton Acres	262	39.39 N	75.38 W
Rambouillet	176	48.39 N	1.50 E
Ramea	240	47.31 N	57.25 W
Ramea Islands II	240	47.31 N	57.21 W
Ramenje	160	60.17 N	43.46 E
Ramer	248	32.03 N	86.13 W
Rameški	160	57.21 N	36.03 E
Ramey	266	40.48 N	78.24 W
Ramingstein	164	47.04 N	13.50 E
Ramírez, Méx.	250	27.20 N	100.58 W
Ramírez, Méx.	250	25.57 N	97.46 W
Ramiriquí	290	5.24 N	73.20 W
Ramla	210	31.50 N	34.52 E
Ramlo ∧	214	13.20 N	41.45 E
Ramm, Jabal ∧	220	29.36 N	35.24 E
Ramona, Calif., U.S.	274	33.08 N	116.52 W
Ramona, Okla., U.S.	250	36.32 N	95.55 W
Ramona, S. Dak., U.S.	252	44.07 N	97.13 W
Ramos	278	22.50 N	101.55 W
Ramos ≃[1]	222	5.08 N	5.22 E
Ramos Arizpe	278	25.33 N	100.58 W
Ramos Island I	202	8.06 N	117.01 E
Rampart	236	65.30 N	150.10 W
Ramparts ≃	236	66.11 N	129.03 W
Rāmpur	206	28.48 N	79.03 E
Ramree Island I	200	19.06 N	93.48 E
Ramsay	244	46.33 N	90.00 W
Ramsele	160	63.33 N	16.29 E
Ramseur	246	35.44 N	79.39 W
Ramsey, I. of Man	162	54.20 N	4.21 W
Ramsey, Eng., U.K.	174	52.27 N	0.07 W
Ramsey, Ill., U.S.	248	39.08 N	89.06 W
Ramsey Bay C	162	54.20 N	4.20 W
Ramsey Lake ⊜	244	47.15 N	82.16 W
Ramsgate	174	51.20 N	1.25 E
Ramshorn Peak ∧	256	45.09 N	111.06 W
Ramsjö	160	62.11 N	15.39 E
Ramygala	160	55.31 N	24.18 E
Ranau	198	5.57 N	116.40 E
Ranburne	248	33.31 N	85.21 W
Rancagua	294	34.10 S	70.45 W
Rance ≃	162	48.31 N	1.59 W
Rancharia	296	22.15 S	50.55 W
Rancheria	236	60.05 N	130.40 W
Ranchería ≃	290	11.34 N	72.54 W
Rancheria Rock ∧	256	44.53 N	120.08 W
Ranches of Taos	254	36.22 N	105.37 W
Ranchester	256	44.54 N	107.16 W
Rānchī	206	23.22 N	85.19 E
Ranchillos	294	26.57 S	65.03 W
Rancho Cordova	272	38.36 N	121.17 W
Rancho Del Mar	272	38.10 N	122.15 W
Rancho Nuevo, Méx.	250	26.22 N	99.54 W
Rancho Nuevo, Méx.	250	28.18 N	101.02 W
Rancho Rinconado	272	37.18 N	122.01 W
Rancho Santa Fe	274	33.01 N	117.12 W
Rancho Veloz	284p	22.53 N	80.23 W
Ranchuelo	284p	22.23 N	80.09 W
Rancocas	262	40.01 N	74.52 W
Rancul	294	35.04 S	64.41 W
Randan	166	46.01 N	3.21 E
Randazzo	170	37.53 N	14.57 E
Randers	160	56.28 N	10.03 E
Randfontein	224	26.11 S	27.42 E
Randle	270	46.32 N	121.57 W
Randleman	246	35.49 N	79.48 W
Randlett	250	34.11 N	98.28 W
Randolph, Ariz., U.S.	254	32.55 N	111.31 W
Randolph, Maine, U.S.	242	44.19 N	69.46 W
Randolph, Mass., U.S.	261	42.10 N	71.03 W
Randolph, Nebr., U.S.	252	42.23 N	97.21 W
Randolph, N.Y., U.S.	266	42.10 N	78.59 W
Randolph, Ohio, U.S.	266	41.02 N	81.15 W
Randolph, Utah, U.S.	254	41.40 N	111.11 W
Randolph, Vt., U.S.	242	43.55 N	72.40 W
Randolph, Wis., U.S.	244	43.35 N	89.00 W
Randolph □[6]	268	40.10 N	85.00 W
Random Island I	240	48.08 N	53.45 W
Random Lake	244	43.33 N	87.57 W
Randsburg	274	35.22 N	117.39 W
Randsfjorden ⊜	160	60.25 N	10.24 E
Rāngāmāti	204	22.38 N	92.12 E
Rangaunu Bay C	230	34.57 S	173.17 E
Range Indian Reserve ⊸[4]	238	49.09 N	119.50 W
Rangeley	242	44.58 N	70.39 W
Rangeley Lake ⊜	240	44.55 N	70.43 W
Rangely	254	40.05 N	108.48 W
Ranger	250	32.28 N	98.41 W
Ranger Lake ⊜	244	46.54 N	83.35 W
Rangiora	230	43.18 S	172.35 E
Rangitaiki ≃	230	37.54 S	176.53 E
Rangitata ≃	230	44.11 S	171.30 E
Rangitikei ≃	230	40.18 S	175.14 E
Rangitoto Range ⋀	230	38.26 S	175.34 E
Rangoon	200	16.47 N	96.10 E
Rangoon ≃	200	16.29 N	26.21 E
Rangpur	206	30.31 N	71.34 E
Rangsang, Pulau I	200	1.01 N	102.54 E
Ranguana Cay I	280	16.19 N	88.10 W
Ranguana Entrance ⋃	280	16.16 N	88.12 W
Ranken ≃	228	20.31 S	137.36 E
Ranken Store	226	19.35 S	136.55 E
Rankin, Ill., U.S.	268	40.28 N	87.54 W
Rankin, Tex., U.S.	250	31.13 N	101.56 W
Rankin Inlet	232	62.45 N	92.10 W
Rankweil	180	47.17 N	9.39 E
Ranlo	246	35.17 N	81.07 W
Rannoch, Loch ⊜	162	56.41 N	4.20 W
Rann of Kutch ≚	206	24.00 N	70.00 E
Ranobe ≃	225b	17.10 S	44.08 E
Ranshaw	262	40.47 N	76.31 W
Ransiki	198	1.30 S	134.10 E
Ransom, Ill., U.S.	268	41.09 N	88.39 W
Ransom, Kans., U.S.	252	38.38 N	99.56 W
Ransomville	264	43.14 N	78.55 W
Ranson	242	39.18 N	77.52 W
Rantauprapat	200	2.06 N	99.50 E
Rantekombola, Bulu ∧	198	3.21 S	120.01 E
Rantoul	268	40.19 N	88.09 W
Raon-l'Étape	180	48.24 N	6.51 E
Raoping	196	23.43 N	117.01 E
Raoyanghe ≃	194	41.11 N	122.02 E
Rapa, Ponta do ≻	294	27.22 S	48.26 W
Rapallo	182	44.21 N	9.14 E
Rapel ≃	294	33.55 S	71.51 W
Rapelje	256	45.58 N	109.16 W
Rapelli	294	26.24 S	64.30 W
Rapid ≃, Mich., U.S.	244	45.55 N	86.58 W
Rapid ≃, Minn., U.S.	244	48.42 N	94.26 W
Rapidan ≃	242	38.22 N	77.37 W
Rapid City, Mich., U.S.	244	44.50 N	85.17 W
Rapid City, S. Dak., U.S.	252	44.05 N	103.14 W
Räpina	160	58.06 N	27.27 E
Rapperswil	180	47.14 N	8.50 E
Rāpti ≃	206	26.17 N	83.41 E
Rápulo ≃	292	13.43 S	65.32 W
Rapu-Rapu	202	13.11 N	124.08 E
Rapu-Rapu Island I	202	13.12 N	124.08 E
Rardin	248	39.36 N	88.06 W
Raritan	262	40.34 N	74.38 W
Rasa Island I	202	9.13 N	118.26 E
Ras Dashen ∧	214	13.10 N	38.26 E
Ras Djebel	170	37.13 N	10.09 E
Ras el Aïoum	170	35.30 N	8.18 E
Ras el Oued	168	35.57 N	5.03 E
Rashīd	220	31.24 N	30.25 E
Rashīd, Maṣabb ≃[1]	220	31.30 N	30.20 E
Rasht	208	37.16 N	49.36 E
Raška	172	43.17 N	20.37 E
Rasm al-Arwām, Sabkhat ⊜	212	35.53 N	37.40 E
Raso, Ilhéu I	222a	16.37 N	24.36 W
Raspberry Peak ∧	248	34.23 N	94.01 W
Rasskazovo	158	52.40 N	41.53 E
Rasšua, Ostrov I	186	47.45 N	153.01 E
Rastatt	164	48.51 N	8.12 E
Rastede	178	53.15 N	8.11 E
Rastegai'sa ∧	160	70.00 N	26.18 E
Rastu	172	43.53 N	23.17 E
Rasu, Monte ∧	170	40.25 N	9.00 E
Răsvani	172	44.25 N	26.53 E
Rat ≃	252	49.35 N	97.08 W
Rätansbyn	160	62.29 N	14.32 E
Rat Buri	200	13.32 N	99.49 E
Rathbun Reservoir ⊜[1]	244	40.54 N	93.05 W
Rathdrum, Eire	162	52.56 N	6.13 W
Rathdrum, Idaho, U.S.	256	47.49 N	116.54 W
Ratheim	178	51.04 N	6.10 E
Rathenow	164	52.36 N	12.20 E
Rathkeale	162	52.32 N	8.56 W
Rathlin Island I	162	55.18 N	6.13 W
Rath Luirc (Charleville)	162	52.21 N	8.41 W
Rathwell	252	49.40 N	98.32 W
Ratibor → Racibórz	164	50.06 N	18.13 E
Ratingen	178	51.18 N	6.51 E
Rat Island I	237a	51.55 N	178.20 E
Rat Islands II	237a	52.00 N	178.00 E
Ratlām	206	23.28 N	75.00 E
Ratmanova, Ostrov I	236	65.46 N	169.02 W
Ratnapura	204	6.41 N	80.24 E
Raton	250	36.54 N	104.24 W
Rattlesnake Hills ⋀[2]	254	42.45 N	107.10 W
Rattling Brook	240	49.38 N	56.10 W
Rättvik	160	60.53 N	15.06 E
Ratz, Mount ∧	236	57.23 N	132.19 W
Ratzeburg	164	53.42 N	10.46 E
Raub, Malay.	200	3.50 N	101.52 E
Raub, Ind., U.S.	268	40.44 N	87.29 W
Raubsville	262	40.38 N	75.12 W
Rauch	294	36.47 S	59.05 W
Raufarhöfn	160a	66.30 N	15.57 W
Raukumara Range ⋀	230	37.56 S	177.56 E
Raul Soares	296	20.05 S	42.22 W
Rauma	160	61.08 N	21.30 E
Rauma ≃	158	62.33 N	7.43 E
Raupal'an	236	65.28 N	171.59 W
Raurkela	206	22.14 N	84.54 E
Rausu	192a	44.01 N	145.12 E
Ravanusa	170	37.16 N	13.58 E
Ravelo	292	18.48 S	65.32 W
Ravena	261	42.29 N	73.49 W

Symbols in the index entries are identified on page 360.

Name	Page	Lat°′	Long°′
Ravenna, It.	184	44.25 N	12.12 E
Ravenna, Ky., U.S.	246	37.41 N	83.57 W
Ravenna, Mich., U.S.	268	43.11 N	85.56 W
Ravenna, Nebr., U.S.	252	41.02 N	98.55 W
Ravenna, Ohio, U.S.	266	41.09 N	81.15 W
Ravenna □[4]	184	44.25 N	11.59 E
Ravensburg	180	47.47 N	9.37 E
Ravensdale	270	47.21 N	121.59 W
Ravenshoe	226	17.37 S	145.29 E
Ravensthorpe	226	33.35 S	120.02 E
Ravenswood, Mich., U.S.	268	42.45 N	84.36 W
Ravenswood, W. Va., U.S.	242	38.57 N	81.46 W
Rāvi ≃	206	30.35 N	71.48 E
Ravine	262	40.34 N	76.24 W
Ravna Gora	170	45.23 N	14.57 E
Rāwalpindi	206	33.36 N	73.04 E
Rawa Mazowiecka	164	51.46 N	20.16 E
Rawḍah ⊜	212	35.15 N	41.05 E
Rawḍah, Wādī ar- ∨	212	34.22 N	37.21 E
Rawdon	260	46.03 N	73.43 W
Rawhide Lake ⊜	244	46.39 N	82.37 W
Rawicz	164	51.37 N	16.52 E
Rawlinna	226	31.01 S	125.20 E
Rawlins	254	41.47 N	107.14 W
Rawson, Arg.	294	34.40 S	60.02 W
Rawson, Ohio, U.S.	268	40.57 N	83.47 W
Ray, Ariz., U.S.	254	33.11 N	111.00 W
Ray, Ind., U.S.	268	41.45 N	84.53 W
Ray, N. Dak., U.S.	252	48.21 N	103.10 W
Ray, Cape ≻	240	47.40 N	59.18 W
Rayland	266	40.11 N	80.41 W
Rayleigh	174	51.36 N	0.36 E
Raymond, Alta., Can.	238	49.27 N	112.39 W
Raymond, Calif., U.S.	272	37.13 N	119.54 W
Raymond, Ga., U.S.	246	33.20 N	84.43 W
Raymond, Ill., U.S.	248	39.19 N	89.34 W
Raymond, Minn., U.S.	252	45.01 N	95.14 W
Raymond, Miss., U.S.	248	32.15 N	90.25 W
Raymond, Ohio, U.S.	268	40.20 N	83.28 W
Raymond, Wash., U.S.	270	46.41 N	123.44 W
Raymondville	250	26.29 N	97.47 W
Ray Mountains ⛰	236	65.45 N	151.30 W
Rayne	248	30.14 N	92.16 W
Raynham	261	41.57 N	71.04 W
Rayón	278	29.43 N	110.35 W
Rayones	278	25.01 N	100.05 W
Rayong	200	12.43 N	101.20 E
Rayrah ▾[4]	220	15.21 N	34.41 E
Raytown	248	39.00 N	94.28 W
Rayville	248	32.28 N	91.45 W
Rayyikhah I	208	26.12 N	36.21 E
Raz, Pointe du ≻	166	48.02 N	4.44 W
R'azan'	160	54.38 N	39.44 E
Ražanj	172	43.40 N	21.33 E
Războeni	172	47.05 N	26.32 E
Razdan	208	40.30 N	44.46 E
Razelm, Lacul ⊜	172	44.54 N	28.57 E
Razgrad	172	43.32 N	26.31 E
Razlog	172	41.53 N	23.28 E
Razorback Mountain ∧	238	51.35 N	124.42 W
R'ažsk	158	53.43 N	40.04 E
Ré, Île de I	166	46.12 N	1.25 W
Reading, Eng., U.K.	174	51.28 N	0.59 W
Reading, Ill., U.S.	268	41.05 N	88.51 W
Reading, Kans., U.S.	252	38.31 N	95.58 W
Reading, Mass., U.S.	261	42.31 N	71.07 W
Reading, Mich., U.S.	268	41.50 N	84.45 W
Reading, Ohio, U.S.	242	39.14 N	84.27 W
Reading, Pa., U.S.	262	40.20 N	75.56 W
Readlyn	244	42.42 N	92.13 W
Readsboro	261	42.46 N	72.57 W
Readstown	244	43.27 N	90.45 W
Real	202	14.40 N	121.36 E
Real, Cordillera ⛰	292	17.00 S	67.10 W
Real Corona ≃	290	7.33 N	64.06 W
Real del Castillo	278	31.58 N	116.19 W
Real del Padre	294	34.50 S	67.46 W
Realicó	294	35.02 S	64.16 W
Realitos	250	27.27 N	98.32 W
Réalmont	166	43.47 N	2.12 E
Reamstown	262	40.13 N	76.08 W
Reardan	256	47.40 N	117.53 W
Reata	278	26.08 N	101.05 W
Reay	162	58.33 N	3.47 W
Rebeida, Wādī ∨	220	20.45 N	34.06 E
Rebiana ▾[4]	220	24.15 N	22.00 E
Rebiana Sand Sea → Nerastro, Sarīr ◂[2]	214	24.20 N	20.37 E
Rebojo, Cachoeira do ↳	292	9.13 S	58.38 W
Reboly	160	63.50 N	30.47 E
Rebouças	294	25.36 S	50.42 W
Rebun-jima I	192a	45.23 N	141.02 E
Recalde	294	36.39 S	61.05 W
Recanati	184	43.24 N	13.32 E
Rečica	158	52.22 N	26.48 E
Recife	286	8.03 S	34.54 W
Recinto	294	36.48 S	71.44 W
Recke	178	52.22 N	7.43 E
Recklinghausen	178	51.36 N	7.13 E
Reconquista	294	29.10 S	59.40 W
Recreio, Bra.	292	8.11 S	58.14 W
Recreio, Bra.	296	21.32 S	42.28 W
Recreo	294	29.20 S	65.04 W
Rector	248	36.16 N	90.17 W
Recuay	292	9.43 S	77.28 W
Recz (Reetz in der Neumark)	164	53.16 N	15.33 E
Red (Hong) (Yuanjiang) ≃, As.	200	20.17 N	106.34 E
Red ≃, N.A.	234	50.24 N	96.48 W
Red ≃, U.S.	234	31.00 N	91.40 W
Red ≃, U.S.	248	36.32 N	87.22 W
Red ≃, Idaho, U.S.	256	45.48 N	115.28 W
Red ≃, Ky., U.S.	246	37.51 N	84.05 W
Red ≃, N. Mex., U.S.	254	36.39 N	105.42 W
Red ≃, Wis., U.S.	244	44.49 N	88.38 W
Reda	164	54.37 N	18.21 E
Redang, Pulau I	200	5.47 N	103.00 E
Red Bank, N.J., U.S.	242	40.21 N	74.03 W
Red Bank, Tenn., U.S.	248	35.07 N	85.17 W
Red Banks	248	34.50 N	89.34 W
Red Bay, Newf., Can.	240	51.44 N	56.25 W
Red Bay, Ala., U.S.	248	34.27 N	88.09 W
Redbay, Fla., U.S.	248	30.35 N	85.57 W
Redbird	266	41.48 N	81.06 W
Red Bird ≃	246	37.16 N	83.38 W
Red Bluff	258	40.11 N	122.15 W
Red Bluff Reservoir ⊜[1]	250	31.57 N	103.56 W
Red Boiling Springs	248	36.32 N	85.51 W
Redbridge ◂[8]	174	51.34 N	0.05 E
Red Bud	248	38.13 N	89.59 W
Red Canyon ∨	252	43.18 N	103.49 W
Redcar	162	54.37 N	1.04 W
Red Cedar ≃	244	44.42 N	91.53 W
Red Cedar Lake ⊜	244	46.45 N	79.54 W
Redcliff, Rh.	224	19.02 S	29.50 E
Redcliff, Colo., U.S.	254	39.31 N	106.22 W
Redcliffe	228	27.14 S	153.07 E
Red Cliff Indian Reservation ◂[4]	244	46.50 N	90.47 W
Red Cliffs	228	34.19 S	142.11 E
Red Cloud	252	40.05 N	98.32 W
Red Creek	264	43.15 N	76.43 W
Red Deer	238	52.16 N	113.48 W
Red Deer ≃, Can.	232	52.53 N	101.01 W
Red Deer ≃, Can.	232	50.56 N	109.54 W
Red Deer Lake ⊜, Alta., Can.	238	52.43 N	113.02 W
Red Deer Lake ⊜, Man., Can.	232	52.56 N	101.20 W
Red Devil	236	61.46 N	157.18 W
Reddick	268	41.06 N	88.15 W
Redding, Calif., U.S.	258	40.35 N	122.24 W
Redding, Conn., U.S.	261	41.18 N	73.23 W
Redding Ridge	261	41.19 N	73.21 W
Redditch	174	52.19 N	1.56 W
Redeye ≃	252	46.26 N	94.49 W
Redfield, Iowa, U.S.	252	41.35 N	94.12 W
Redfield, N.Y., U.S.	264	43.32 N	75.49 W
Redfield, S. Dak., U.S.	252	44.53 N	98.31 W
Redfish Lake ⊜	256	44.07 N	114.56 W
Redford	250	29.47 N	104.10 W
Redford Heights	268	42.25 N	83.16 W
Redhead	285r	10.47 N	60.57 W
Redhill, Eng., U.K.	174	51.14 N	0.11 W
Red Hill, Pa., U.S.	262	40.22 N	75.29 W
Red Hill ∧	230	41.38 S	173.04 E
Red Hook	261	41.55 N	73.53 W
Red Indian Lake ⊜	240	48.40 N	56.50 W
Red Island I	240	47.23 N	54.11 W
Redkey	268	40.21 N	85.09 W
Red Lake	232	51.03 N	93.49 W
Red Lake ⊜, Ont., Can.	232	51.01 N	94.05 W
Red Lake ⊜, Ariz., U.S.	254	35.40 N	114.04 W
Red Lake ⊜, S. Dak., U.S.	252	43.44 N	99.13 W
Red Lake ≃	252	47.55 N	97.01 W
Red Lake Falls	252	47.53 N	96.16 W
Red Lake Indian Reservation ◂[4]	244	48.05 N	95.05 W
Redlands	274	34.03 N	117.11 W
Red Level	248	31.24 N	86.36 W
Red Lick	248	31.48 N	90.59 W
Red Lion	242	39.54 N	76.36 W
Red Lodge	256	45.11 N	109.15 W
Red Mill	260	46.24 N	72.28 W
Redmond, Oreg., U.S.	256	44.17 N	121.11 W
Redmond, Utah, U.S.	254	39.00 N	111.52 W
Redmond, Wash., U.S.	270	47.40 N	122.07 W
Redmond Reservoir ⊜[1]	252	38.18 N	95.55 W
Red Mountain	258	34.48 N	117.40 W
Red Mountain ∧, Calif., U.S.	258	41.35 N	123.06 W
Red Mountain ∧, Mont., U.S.	256	47.07 N	112.44 W
Red Mountain Pass)(	254	37.54 N	107.43 W
Red Oak, Iowa, U.S.	252	41.01 N	95.14 W
Red Oak, Okla., U.S.	250	34.57 N	95.05 W
Red Oaks Mill	261	41.40 N	73.53 W
Redon	166	47.39 N	2.05 W
Redonda I	282	16.55 N	62.19 W
Redonda, Isla I	285r	9.52 N	61.35 W
Redonda Islands II	238	50.13 N	124.48 W
Redondela	168	42.17 N	8.36 W
Redondo, Port.	168	38.39 N	7.33 W
Redondo, Wash., U.S.	270	47.21 N	122.19 W
Redondo, Mount ∧	202	10.21 N	125.38 E
Redondo Beach	274	33.51 N	118.23 W
Redoubt Volcano ∧[1]	236	60.29 N	152.45 W
Red Pass	238	52.59 N	118.59 W
Red River Valley ∨	252	47.30 N	96.55 W
Red Rock, B.C., Can.	238	53.39 N	122.41 W
Red Rock, Ont., Can.	244	48.58 N	88.15 W
Red Rock ≃	256	44.59 N	112.52 W
Red Rock, Lake ⊜[1]	244	41.30 N	93.20 W
Redruth	162	50.13 N	5.14 W
Red Sea ▾[2]	214	25.00 N	35.00 E
Red Springs	246	34.49 N	79.11 W
Redstone	238	52.08 N	123.42 W
Redstone ≃, N.W. Ter., Can.	236	64.17 N	124.33 W
Redstone ≃, Ont., Can.	244	48.27 N	81.03 W
Redstone Lake ⊜	244	45.11 N	78.32 W
Redvers	252	49.33 N	101.39 W
Redwater	238	53.57 N	113.06 W
Redwater ≃, U.S.	252	44.40 N	103.51 W
Redwater ≃, Mont., U.S.	252	48.03 N	105.13 W
Redwillow ≃	238	55.04 N	119.21 W
Red Wing	244	44.34 N	92.31 W
Redwood	264	44.18 N	75.48 W
Redwood ≃	252	44.34 N	95.05 W
Redwood City	272	37.29 N	122.13 W
Redwood Estates	272	37.10 N	121.59 W
Redwood Falls	252	44.32 N	95.07 W
Redwood Valley	258	39.16 N	123.12 W
Ree, Lough ⊜	162	53.35 N	8.00 W
Reed City	244	43.53 N	85.31 W
Reeder	252	46.06 N	102.57 W
Reedley	272	36.36 N	119.27 W
Reedsburg, Ohio, U.S.	266	40.49 N	82.07 W
Reedsburg, Wis., U.S.	244	43.32 N	90.00 W
Reeds Peak ∧	254	33.09 N	107.51 W
Reedsport	256	43.42 N	124.06 W
Reedsville, Pa., U.S.	262	40.40 N	77.36 W
Reedsville, Wis., U.S.	244	44.09 N	87.57 W
Reedurban	266	40.47 N	81.22 W
Reedville	262	37.51 N	76.17 W
Reefton	230	42.07 S	171.52 E
Reelfoot Lake ⊜	248	36.25 N	89.22 W
Rees	178	51.45 N	6.23 E
Reese	244	43.27 N	83.42 W
Reese ≃	258	40.39 N	116.54 W
Reese Village	250	33.36 N	102.01 W
Reeseville	244	43.18 N	88.51 W
Refaa, Djebel ∧	168	35.34 N	5.53 E
Reform	248	33.23 N	88.01 W
Refton	262	39.57 N	76.14 W
Refuge Cove	238	50.07 N	124.50 W
Refugio	250	28.18 N	97.17 W
Refugio, Cerro del ∧	278	22.19 N	104.15 W
Refugio Island I	202	10.28 N	123.26 E
Rega ≃	164	54.10 N	15.18 E
Regaïa	168	35.38 N	5.46 W
Regen	164	48.59 N	13.07 E
Regen ≃	164	49.01 N	12.06 E
Regensburg	164	49.01 N	12.06 E
Regent	252	46.25 N	102.33 W
Reggane	214	26.42 N	0.10 E
Reggello	170	43.41 N	11.32 E
Reggio di Calabria	170	38.07 N	15.39 E
Reggio nell'Emilia	170	44.43 N	10.36 E
Reghin	172	46.47 N	24.32 E
Regina, Sask., Can.	232	50.25 N	104.39 W
Régina, Guy. fr.	286	4.19 N	52.08 W
Registān ◂[2]	208	30.30 N	65.00 E
Registro	294	24.30 S	47.50 W
Registro do Araguaia	296	15.44 S	51.50 W
Regla	284p	23.08 N	82.20 W
Regnéville	166	49.01 N	1.33 W
Regozero	160	65.28 N	31.10 E
Reguengos de Monsaraz	168	38.25 N	7.32 W
Rehau	164	50.15 N	12.02 E
Rehe ≃	194	40.54 N	117.55 E
Rehme	178	52.12 N	8.49 E
Rehoboth	218	23.18 S	17.03 E
Rehoboth □[5]	224	23.30 S	17.30 E
Rehoboth Beach	262	38.43 N	75.05 W
Rehoboth Seamount ⊹[3]	148	37.35 N	59.55 W
Reẕovot	210	31.53 N	34.48 E
Reichenbach	164	50.37 N	12.18 E
Reichenberg → Liberec	164	50.46 N	15.03 E
Reid, Mount ∧	236	55.42 N	131.15 W
Reidsville, Ga., U.S.	246	32.06 N	82.07 W
Reidsville, N.C., U.S.	246	36.21 N	79.40 W
Reiffton	262	40.19 N	75.53 W
Reigate	174	51.14 N	0.13 W
Reihoku	192	32.31 N	130.02 E
Reims	176	49.15 N	4.02 E
Reinach, Schw.	180	47.15 N	8.11 E
Reinach, Schw.	180	47.30 N	7.35 E
Reinbeck	244	42.19 N	92.36 W
Reinbek	178	53.31 N	10.14 E
Reindeer Lake ⊜	232	57.15 N	102.40 W
Reindeer Station	236	68.42 N	134.06 W
Reinerton	262	40.36 N	76.34 W
Reinfeld	178	53.49 N	10.28 E
Reinga, Cape ≻	230	34.26 S	172.40 E
Reinosa	168	43.00 N	4.08 W
Reisaelva ≃	160	69.48 N	21.00 E
Reisterstown	242	39.28 N	76.50 W
Rejowiec Fabryczny	164	51.08 N	23.13 E
Reliance	254	41.40 N	109.12 W
Rellingen	178	53.39 N	9.49 E
Remada	214	32.19 N	10.24 E
Remagen	166	50.34 N	7.13 E
Remanso	286	9.41 S	42.04 W
Remchi	168	35.04 N	1.26 W
Remecó	294	37.37 S	63.40 W
Remedios, Col.	290	7.02 N	74.41 W
Remedios, Cuba	284p	22.30 N	79.33 W
Remedios, Pan.	280	8.15 N	81.50 W
Remedios, Punta ≻	280	13.31 N	89.50 W
Remer	244	47.03 N	93.55 W
Rémigny, Lac ⊜	244	47.50 N	79.10 W
Reminderville	266	41.20 N	81.23 W
Remington, Ind., U.S.	268	40.46 N	87.09 W
Remington, Va., U.S.	242	38.32 N	77.49 W
Remiremont	180	48.01 N	6.35 E
Remoulins	166	43.56 N	4.34 E
Rempang, Pulau I	200	0.51 N	104.10 E
Remscheid	178	51.11 N	7.11 E
Remsen	252	42.49 N	95.58 W
Remus	244	43.36 N	85.09 W
Rena	160	61.08 N	11.22 E
Rena Point ≻	202	16.10 N	119.45 E
Renascença	290	3.50 S	66.21 W
Renata	238	49.26 N	118.06 W
Rencontre East	240	47.38 N	55.13 W
Rende	170	39.19 N	16.11 E
Rend Lake ⊜[1]	248	38.05 N	88.58 W
Rendova I	226	8.33 S	157.17 E
Rendsburg	164	54.18 N	9.40 E
Renens	180	46.32 N	6.35 E
Renews	240	46.56 N	52.56 W
Renfrew, Ont., Can.	264	45.28 N	76.41 W
Renfrew, Pa., U.S.	266	40.46 N	79.58 W
Renfrew □[6], Ont., Can.	264	45.25 N	77.05 W
Renfrew □[6], Scot., U.K.	162	55.50 N	4.34 W
Rengat	198	0.24 S	102.33 E
Rengo	294	34.25 S	70.52 W
Renick	242	38.00 N	80.22 W
Renkum	178	51.58 N	5.45 E
Renmark	228	34.11 S	140.45 E
Renminshenliqu ≋	194	35.10 N	113.55 E
Rennell Island I	226	11.40 S	160.10 E
Rennes	166	48.05 N	1.41 W
Rennie	252	49.51 N	95.33 W
Reno, Nev., U.S.	272	39.31 N	119.48 W
Reno, Pa., U.S.	266	41.25 N	79.45 W
Reno Beach	266	41.40 N	83.15 W
Reno Hill ∧	254	42.35 N	106.03 W
Renous	240	46.49 N	65.48 W
Renous ≃	240	46.50 N	65.50 W
Renovo	266	41.20 N	77.38 W
Rensjön	160	68.05 N	19.49 E
Rensselaer, Ind., U.S.	268	40.57 N	87.09 W
Rensselaer, N.Y., U.S.	261	42.39 N	73.44 W
Rensselaer □[6]	261	42.43 N	73.40 W
Rensselaer Falls	264	44.35 N	75.19 W
Rentería	168	43.19 N	1.54 W
Renton	270	47.30 N	122.11 W
Renville	252	44.48 N	95.13 W
Renwick	244	42.50 N	93.59 W
Reo	198	8.19 S	120.30 E
Répce ≃	164	47.41 N	17.03 E
Repentigny	260	45.45 N	73.26 W
Repetek	186	38.34 N	63.11 E
Repton	248	31.25 N	87.14 W
Republic, Kans., U.S.	252	39.55 N	97.49 W
Republic, Mich., U.S.	244	46.22 N	87.59 W
Republic, Mo., U.S.	248	37.07 N	93.29 W
Republic, Ohio, U.S.	266	41.08 N	83.01 W
Republic, Wash., U.S.	256	48.39 N	118.44 W
Republican ≃	252	39.03 N	96.48 W
Republican, South Fork ≃	252	40.03 N	101.31 W
Repueblo de Oriente	250	25.51 N	99.39 W
Repulse Bay	232	66.32 N	86.15 W
Repulse Bay C	228	20.36 S	148.43 E
Repvåg	160	70.42 N	25.35 E
Requena, Esp.	168	39.29 N	1.06 W
Requena, Perú	292	5.00 S	73.50 W
Réquista	166	44.02 N	2.32 E
Reşadiye	172	36.45 N	27.40 E
Reşadiye Yarımadası ≻[1]	212	36.40 N	27.45 E
Resang, Tanjong ≻	200	2.35 N	103.51 E
Rescue	262	36.59 N	76.34 W
Resen	172	41.05 N	21.00 E
Reserva	294	24.38 S	50.52 W
Reserve, La., U.S.	248	30.04 N	90.34 W
Reserve, N. Mex., U.S.	254	33.43 N	108.45 W
Resia, Passo di)(	166	46.50 N	10.30 E
Resina	184	40.48 N	14.21 E
Resistencia	294	27.30 S	58.59 W
Reşiţa	172	45.17 N	21.53 E
Resko (Regenwalde)	164	53.47 N	15.25 E
Resolute	232	74.41 N	94.54 W
Resolution Island I, N.W. Ter., Can.	232	61.30 N	65.00 W
Resolution Island I, N.Z.	230	45.40 S	166.38 E
Rešoty	160	57.09 N	28.30 E
Resplendor	296	19.20 S	41.15 W
Resthaven	268	41.16 N	88.09 W
Restigouche ≃	240	48.04 N	66.20 W
Restinga	168	35.42 N	5.23 W
Restinga Sêca	294	29.49 S	53.23 W
Reston, Man., Can.	252	49.35 N	101.02 W
Reston, Va., U.S.	262	38.58 N	77.21 W
Restoule Lake ⊜	244	46.03 N	79.47 W
Restrepo, Col.	290	4.15 N	73.33 W
Restrepo, Col.	290	3.48 N	76.31 W
Resülhınzır ≻	212	36.22 N	35.45 E
Retalhuleu	280	14.32 N	91.41 W
Retalhuleu □[5]	280	14.20 N	91.50 W
Retamosa	294	33.35 S	54.44 W
Rethel	176	49.31 N	4.22 E
Réthimnon	172	35.22 N	24.29 E
Retie	178	51.16 N	5.04 E
Retiers	162	47.55 N	1.23 W
Retsof	264	42.50 N	77.53 W
Reunion (Réunion) □[2]	218	21.06 S	55.36 E
Reus	168	41.09 N	1.07 E
Reuss ≃	166	47.28 N	8.14 E
Reut ≃	172	47.15 N	29.09 E
Reutlingen	180	48.29 N	9.11 E
Reval → Tallinn	160	59.25 N	24.45 E
Revda	160	67.55 N	34.30 E
Revelstoke	238	50.59 N	118.12 W
Reventazón	292	6.10 S	80.58 W
Reventazón ≃	280	10.19 N	83.20 W
Revere, Mass., U.S.	261	42.24 N	71.01 W
Revere, Pa., U.S.	262	40.31 N	75.10 W
Reviga	172	44.42 N	27.06 E
Revigny-sur-Ornain	166	48.50 N	4.59 E
Revilla del Campo	168	42.13 N	3.32 W
Revillagigedo, Islas de II	278	19.00 N	111.30 W
Revillagigedo Channel ⋓	238	55.10 N	131.13 W
Revillagigedo Island I	236	55.35 N	131.23 W
Revillo	252	45.01 N	96.34 W
Revin	166	49.56 N	4.38 E
Revloc	266	40.29 N	78.46 W
Revol'ucii, Pik ∧	206	38.31 N	72.21 E
Revuè ≃	224	19.49 S	34.00 E
Revuelto ≃	250	35.22 N	103.23 W
Rew	266	41.54 N	78.32 W
Rewa	206	24.32 N	81.17 E
Rewāri	206	28.12 N	76.37 E
Rexburg	256	43.49 N	111.47 W
Rexford, Kans., U.S.	252	39.28 N	100.45 W
Rexford, Mont., U.S.	256	48.53 N	115.13 W
Rexton, N.B., Can.	240	46.39 N	64.52 W
Rexton, Mich., U.S.	244	46.10 N	85.14 W
Rexville	266	42.05 N	77.40 W
Rey	208	35.35 N	51.25 E
Rey, Isla del I	290	8.22 N	78.52 W
Rey, Laguna del ⊜	278	27.02 N	103.25 W
Reyes	292	14.19 S	67.23 W
Reyes, Point ≻	258	38.00 N	123.01 W
Reykjanes ≻[1]	160a	63.49 N	22.43 W
Reykjanes Ridge ⊹[3]	148	60.00 N	28.00 W
Reykjavík	160a	64.09 N	21.51 W
Reynaldo Cullen	294	31.15 S	60.40 W
Reynolds, Ga., U.S.	246	32.34 N	84.06 W
Reynolds, Ind., U.S.	268	40.45 N	86.52 W
Reynolds, N. Dak., U.S.	252	47.40 N	97.07 W
Reynoldsville	266	41.06 N	78.53 W
Reynosa	278	26.07 N	98.18 W
Rež	158	57.23 N	61.24 E
Reza, Gora(Kūh-e Rīzeh) ∧	208	37.47 N	58.05 E
Reẕā'īyeh	208	37.33 N	45.04 E
Reẕā'īyeh, Daryācheh-ye ⊜	208	37.40 N	45.30 E
Rēzekne	160	56.30 N	27.19 E
Rezovo	172	41.59 N	28.02 E
Rezovska (Rezve) ≃	212	41.59 N	28.01 E
Rhaetian Alps ⛰	166	46.30 N	10.00 E
Rhame	252	46.14 N	103.39 W
Rhätikon ⛰	170	47.03 N	9.40 E
Rheda	178	51.51 N	8.17 E
Rhede	178	51.50 N	6.11 E
Rheden	178	52.01 N	6.02 E
Rheems	262	40.08 N	76.34 W
Rheem Valley	272	37.52 N	122.07 W
Rheims → Reims	176	49.15 N	4.02 E
Rheinberg	178	51.33 N	6.35 E
Rheinbischofsheim	180	48.39 N	7.55 E
Rheine	178	52.17 N	7.26 E
Rheinfelden, B.R.D.	180	47.33 N	7.47 E
Rheinfelden, Schw.	180	47.33 N	7.48 E
Rheinhausen	178	51.24 N	6.44 E
Rheinkamp	178	51.30 N	6.37 E
Rheinland-Pfalz □[3]	164	50.00 N	7.00 E
Rhenen	178	51.57 N	5.34 E
Rheydt	178	51.10 N	6.25 E
Rhine	246	31.59 N	83.12 W
Rhine (Rijn) (Rhein) (Rhin) ≃	164	51.52 N	6.02 E
Rhinebeck	261	41.56 N	73.55 W
Rhinecliff	261	41.55 N	73.57 W
Rhinelander	244	45.38 N	89.25 W
Rhinns Point ≻	162	55.40 N	6.30 W
Rhiou, Oued ≃	168	36.00 N	0.55 E
Rhis, Oued ≃	168	35.14 N	3.57 W
Rho	182	45.32 N	9.02 E
Rhode Island □[3]	234	41.40 N	71.30 W
Rhode Island Sound ⋓	242	41.25 N	71.25 W
Rhodes → Ródhos, Ellás	172	36.26 N	28.13 E
Rhodes → Ródhos I	172	36.10 N	28.00 E
Rhodesia □[1]	218	20.00 S	30.00 E
Rhodes Inyanga National Park ♠	224	18.12 S	32.45 E
Rhodes Peak ∧	256	46.41 N	114.47 W
Rhodes Salt Marsh ≡	258	38.17 N	118.06 W
Rhodes' Tomb ⊥	224	20.30 S	28.30 E
Rhododendron	270	45.20 N	121.55 W
Rhodope Mountains ⛰	172	41.30 N	24.30 E
Rhomara ◂[1]	168	35.15 N	5.00 W
Rhondda	174	51.40 N	3.27 W
Rhône □[5]	166	46.00 N	4.30 E
Rhône ≃	166	43.20 N	4.50 E
Rhône au Rhin, Canal du ≋	166	47.06 N	5.19 E
Rhue ≃	166	45.23 N	2.29 E
Rhum I	162	57.00 N	6.20 W
Rhyl	162	53.19 N	3.29 W
Rhymney	174	51.46 N	3.18 W
Riachão	286	7.22 S	46.37 W
Riacho de Santana	296	13.37 S	42.57 W
Rialma	296	15.18 S	49.34 W
Rialto	274	34.06 N	117.22 W
Rianápolis	296	15.29 S	49.28 W
Riaño	168	42.58 N	5.01 W
Riánsares ≃	168	39.32 N	3.18 W
Riau, Kepulauan II	200	1.00 N	104.30 E
Riaza	168	41.17 N	3.28 W
Riaza ≃	168	41.42 N	3.55 W
Ribadavia	168	42.17 N	8.08 W
Ribadeo	168	43.32 N	7.02 W
Ribadesella	168	43.28 N	5.04 W
Ribagorza ◂[1]	168	42.15 N	0.30 E
Ribas do Rio Pardo	296	20.27 S	53.46 W
Ribatejo □[9]	168	39.15 N	8.30 W
Ribeauvillé	170	48.12 N	7.19 E
Ribeira, Bra.	294	24.40 S	49.01 W
Ribeira, Esp.	168	42.33 N	9.00 W
Ribeira de Iguape ≃	294	24.40 S	47.24 W
Ribeirão do Pinhal	296	23.24 S	50.18 W
Ribeirão Prêto	296	21.10 S	47.48 W
Ribeirao Vermelho	296	21.11 S	45.03 W
Ribeirãozinho	296	16.27 S	52.35 W
Ribemont	166	49.48 N	3.28 E
Ribera	170	37.30 N	13.16 E
Ribérac	166	45.15 N	0.20 E
Riberalta	292	10.59 S	66.06 W
Rib Lake	244	45.20 N	90.12 W
Ribnica	170	45.44 N	14.44 E
Ribnitz-Damgarten	164	54.15 N	12.28 E
Ricardo	250	27.25 N	97.51 W
Ricardo Flores Magón	278	29.58 N	106.58 W
Ricaurte	290	1.13 N	77.59 W
Riccarton	230	43.40 S	172.22 E
Riccia	170	41.29 N	14.50 E
Riccione	184	43.59 N	12.39 E
Rice	250	32.15 N	96.30 W
Rice Lake	244	45.30 N	91.44 W
Rice Lake ⊜, Ont., Can.	244	47.42 N	82.08 W
Rice Lake ⊜, Ont., Can.	244	44.08 N	78.13 W
Riceville, Iowa, U.S.	244	43.22 N	92.33 W
Riceville, Pa., U.S.	266	41.47 N	79.48 W
Riceville, Tenn., U.S.	246	35.23 N	84.42 W
Richard Collinson Inlet C	232	72.45 N	113.45 W
Richards	250	30.32 N	95.51 W
Richard's Bay C	224	28.50 S	32.02 E
Richard's Harbour	240	47.36 N	56.25 W
Richards Island I	236	69.20 N	134.30 W
Richardson, Tex., U.S.	250	32.57 N	96.44 W
Richardson, Wash., U.S.	270	48.27 N	122.54 W
Richardson ≃	232	58.30 N	111.30 W
Richardson Lakes ⊜	242	44.50 N	70.52 W
Richardson Mountains ⛰, Can.	236	67.15 N	136.30 W
Richardson Mountains ⛰, N.Z.	230	44.45 S	168.33 E
Richardsville	266	41.14 N	79.01 W
Richardton	252	46.53 N	102.19 W
Richboro	262	40.13 N	75.01 W
Richburg	266	42.05 N	78.09 W
Riche, Pointe ≻	240	50.42 N	57.25 W
Richelieu	166	47.01 N	0.19 E
Richelieu □[6]	260	45.55 N	73.00 W
Richer	252	49.39 N	96.28 W
Richey	252	47.39 N	105.04 W
Richfield, Idaho, U.S.	256	43.03 N	114.09 W
Richfield, Kans., U.S.	252	37.16 N	101.47 W
Richfield, Minn., U.S.	244	44.53 N	93.17 W
Richfield, Pa., U.S.	262	40.41 N	77.07 W
Richfield, Utah, U.S.	254	38.46 N	112.05 W
Richfield Springs	242	42.51 N	74.59 W
Richford	242	45.00 N	72.40 W
Richgrove	272	35.48 N	119.07 W
Rich Hill	248	38.06 N	94.22 W
Richibucto	240	46.41 N	64.52 W
Richland, Ga., U.S.	246	32.06 N	84.39 W
Richland, Mich., U.S.	268	42.22 N	85.31 W
Richland, Mo., U.S.	248	37.51 N	92.26 W
Richland, Mont., U.S.	256	48.49 N	106.03 W
Richland, N.J., U.S.	262	39.30 N	74.52 W
Richland, N.Y., U.S.	264	43.34 N	76.03 W
Richland, Pa., U.S.	262	40.21 N	76.16 W
Richland, Tex., U.S.	250	31.56 N	96.26 W
Richland, Wash., U.S.	256	46.17 N	119.18 W
Richland □[6]	266	40.46 N	82.31 W
Richland Center	244	43.20 N	90.23 W
Richlands, N.C., U.S.	246	34.54 N	77.34 W
Richlands, Va., U.S.	246	37.06 N	81.48 W
Richland Springs	250	31.16 N	98.57 W
Richmond, Austl.	228	20.44 S	143.08 E
Richmond, Austl.	228	33.36 S	150.46 E
Richmond, B.C., Can.	238	49.09 N	123.06 W
Richmond, Ont., Can.	264	45.11 N	75.50 W
Richmond, Qué., Can.	260	45.40 N	72.08 W
Richmond, N.Z.	230	41.20 S	173.11 E
Richmond, Eng., U.K.	162	54.24 N	1.44 W
Richmond, Calif., U.S.	272	37.57 N	122.22 W
Richmond, Ill., U.S.	268	42.28 N	88.18 W
Richmond, Ind., U.S.	248	39.50 N	84.54 W
Richmond, Kans., U.S.	252	38.24 N	95.15 W
Richmond, Ky., U.S.	246	37.45 N	84.18 W
Richmond, Maine, U.S.	242	44.05 N	69.48 W
Richmond, Mass., U.S.	261	42.23 N	73.22 W
Richmond, Mich., U.S.	266	42.49 N	82.45 W
Richmond, Minn., U.S.	244	45.27 N	94.31 W
Richmond, Mo., U.S.	248	39.17 N	93.58 W
Richmond, Ohio, U.S.	266	40.26 N	80.46 W
Richmond, Tex., U.S.	250	29.35 N	95.46 W
Richmond, Utah, U.S.	254	41.55 N	111.48 W
Richmond, Vt., U.S.	242	44.24 N	72.59 W
Richmond, Va., U.S.	262	37.30 N	77.28 W
Richmond □[6], Qué., Can.	260	45.40 N	72.00 W
Richmond □[6], N.Y., U.S.	262	40.38 N	74.05 W
Richmond □[6], Va., U.S.	262	37.32 N	77.28 W
Richmond ◂[8]	174	51.28 N	0.18 W
Richmond, Golfe de C	232	56.15 N	76.20 W
Richmond, Mount ∧	230	41.28 S	173.24 E
Richmond Beach	270	47.46 N	122.23 W
Richmond Heights, Fla., U.S.	246	25.58 N	80.22 W
Richmond Heights, Ohio, U.S.	266	41.33 N	81.29 W
Richmond Highlands	270	47.46 N	122.22 W
Richmond Hill, Ont., Can.	264	43.52 N	79.27 W
Richmond Hill, Ga., U.S.	246	31.56 N	81.18 W
Richmond Range ⛰	230	41.30 S	173.15 E
Richmondville	242	42.38 N	74.34 W
Rich Square	246	36.16 N	77.17 W
Richterswil	180	47.13 N	8.42 E
Richton	248	31.16 N	88.56 W
Richvale, Ont., Can.	264	43.51 N	79.26 W
Richvale, Calif., U.S.	272	39.30 N	121.45 W
Richville, N.Y., U.S.	264	44.25 N	75.23 E
Richville, Ohio, U.S.	266	40.45 N	81.27 W
Richwood, Ohio, U.S.	266	40.26 N	83.18 W
Richwood, W. Va., U.S.	242	38.14 N	80.32 W
Rickmansworth	174	51.39 N	0.29 W
Rico	254	37.41 N	108.02 W
Ricoa ≃	285s	11.30 N	69.12 W
Ridderkerk	178	51.52 N	4.36 E
Riddle	256	42.57 N	123.22 W
Riddle Mountain ∧	256	43.07 N	118.30 W
Riddlesburg	266	40.10 N	78.15 W
Rideau Lake ⊜	244	44.45 N	76.14 W
Ridge	261	40.54 N	72.53 W
Ridgecrest, Calif., U.S.	258	35.38 N	117.36 W
Ridgecrest, Wash., U.S.	270	47.45 N	122.21 W
Ridge Farm	248	39.54 N	87.39 W
Ridgefield, Conn., U.S.	261	41.17 N	73.30 W
Ridgefield, Wash., U.S.	270	45.49 N	122.45 W
Ridgeland	246	32.29 N	80.59 W
Ridgely	248	36.16 N	89.29 W
Ridgetown	266	42.26 N	81.54 W
Ridgeville, Man., Can.	252	49.02 N	96.58 W
Ridgeville, Ont., Can.	264	43.02 N	79.19 W
Ridgeville, Ind., U.S.	268	40.18 N	85.02 W
Ridgeville, Md., U.S.	262	39.22 N	77.10 W
Ridgeville, S.C., U.S.	246	33.06 N	80.19 W
Ridgeville Corners	268	41.26 N	84.16 W
Ridgeway, Ont., Can.	264	42.53 N	79.03 W
Ridgeway, Mich., U.S.	268	41.59 N	83.52 W
Ridgeway, Mo., U.S.	248	40.23 N	93.56 W
Ridgeway, N.J., U.S.	262	40.02 N	74.17 W
Ridgeway, Ohio, U.S.	268	40.31 N	83.34 W
Ridgeway, Wis., U.S.	244	43.01 N	90.01 W
Ridgewood	268	41.33 N	88.03 W
Ridgway, Colo., U.S.	254	38.09 N	107.46 W
Ridgway, Ill., U.S.	248	37.48 N	88.16 W
Ridgway, Pa., U.S.	266	41.26 N	78.44 W
Riding, East □[8]	162	53.55 N	0.40 W
Riding, North □[8]	162	54.20 N	1.15 W
Riding, West □[8]	162	53.50 N	1.35 W
Ridotta Capuzzo	214	31.35 N	25.03 E
Ried im Innkreis	164	48.13 N	13.30 E
Riedisheim	180	47.45 N	7.22 E
Riedlingen	180	48.09 N	9.28 E
Riegelsville	262	40.36 N	75.12 W
Riehen	180	47.35 N	7.39 E
Rielasingen	180	47.44 N	8.50 E
Rienzi	248	34.46 N	88.38 W
Riesa	164	51.18 N	13.17 E
Riesco, Isla I	288	52.55 S	72.40 W
Riesi	170	37.17 N	14.05 E
Riet ≃	224	29.00 S	23.54 E
Rietavas	160	55.44 N	21.56 E
Rietberg	178	51.47 N	8.25 E
Rieti	184	42.24 N	12.51 E
Rieti □[4]	184	42.18 N	12.52 E
Rif ⛰	168	35.00 N	4.00 W
Rifle	254	39.32 N	107.47 W
Rifle ≃	244	44.00 N	83.45 W
Rifstangi ≻	160a	66.35 N	16.10 W
Rift Valley ∨	148	3.00 S	29.00 E
Rīga, S.S.S.R.	160	56.57 N	24.06 E
Riga, Mich., U.S.	268	41.49 N	83.50 W
Riga, Gulf of → Rižskij Zaliv C	160	57.30 N	23.35 E
Rigaud	260	45.29 N	74.18 W
Rigby	256	43.40 N	111.55 W
Riggins	256	45.25 N	116.19 W
Rigi ⛰	166	47.05 N	8.30 E
Rigolet	232	54.20 N	58.35 W
Riguldi	160	59.08 N	23.33 E
Rīḥ, Jazīrat ar- ≻[1]	220	18.10 N	38.27 E
Riihimäki	160	60.45 N	24.46 E
Rijeka	170	45.20 N	14.27 E
Rijen	178	51.35 N	4.55 E
Rijkevorsel	178	51.21 N	4.46 E
Rijnsburg	178	52.12 N	4.27 E
Rijssen	178	52.18 N	6.30 E
Rijswijk	178	52.04 N	4.20 E
Rikeze	206	29.17 N	88.53 E
Riksgränsen	160	68.24 N	18.12 E
Rikuchūkaigan-kokuritsu-kōen ♠	192	39.25 N	141.57 E
Rikujō-jieitai-asahikawa-chūtonchi ■	192a	43.49 N	142.25 E
Rikujō-jieitai-chitose-chūtonchi ■	192a	42.46 N	141.40 E
Rikujō-jieitai-kengun-chūtonchi ■	192	32.46 N	130.45 E
Rikujō-jieitai-sōmahara-chūtonchi ■	192	36.26 N	139.58 E
Rikuzen-takata	192	39.01 N	141.38 E
Rila ⛰	172	42.08 N	23.33 E
Riley	252	39.18 N	96.50 W
Rillito	254	32.25 N	111.09 W
Rillton	266	40.17 N	79.44 W
Rima ≃	222	13.04 N	5.10 E
Rímac ≃	292	12.02 S	77.09 W
Rimachi, Lago ⊜	290	4.25 S	76.45 W
Rimavská Sobota	164	48.23 N	20.02 E
Rimbey	238	52.38 N	114.14 W
Rimbo	160	59.45 N	18.22 E
Rimersburg	266	41.02 N	79.30 W
Rimini	184	44.04 N	12.34 E
Rîmna ≃	172	45.39 N	27.19 E
Rîmnicu-Sărat	172	45.23 N	27.03 E
Rîmnicu-Vîlcea	172	45.06 N	24.22 E
Rimouski	240	48.27 N	68.32 W
Rimouski ≃	240	48.26 N	68.32 W
Rincón, C.R.	280	8.42 N	83.29 W
Rincon, Ned. Ant.	285s	12.15 N	68.20 W
Rincón, P.R.	284m	18.20 N	67.15 W
Rincon, Ga., U.S.	246	32.18 N	81.14 W
Rincon, N. Mex., U.S.	254	32.40 N	107.04 W
Rinconada, Arg.	294	22.26 S	66.10 W
Rinconada, Méx.	250	25.42 N	100.43 W
Rincón del Ocote, Cerro ∧	280	13.36 N	87.10 W
Rincón de Romos	278	22.14 N	102.18 W
Rincon Valley	272	38.28 N	122.39 W
Rindal	160	63.03 N	9.13 E
Ringebu	160	61.31 N	10.10 E
Ringgold, Ga., U.S.	246	34.55 N	85.07 W
Ringgold, La., U.S.	248	32.20 N	93.17 W
Ringgold, Pa., U.S.	266	41.00 N	79.10 W
Ringkøbing	160	56.05 N	8.15 E
Ringling	250	34.10 N	97.36 W
Ringoes	262	40.26 N	74.52 W
Ringsted	252	43.18 N	94.31 W
Ringvassøy I	160	69.55 N	19.15 E
Rinteln	178	52.11 N	9.04 E
Rintja, Pulau I	198	8.41 S	119.42 E
Rio	244	43.27 N	89.14 W
Río Ariguaisa	290	9.35 N	72.40 W
Rio Azul	294	25.43 S	50.47 W
Río Balsas	278	17.59 N	99.47 W
Riobamba	290	1.40 S	78.38 W
Río Benito	218	1.35 N	9.37 E
Río Blanco	294	32.55 S	70.19 W
Rio Branco, Bra.	292	9.58 S	67.48 W
Río Branco, Ur.	294	32.34 S	53.25 W
Río Bravo, Méx.	250	28.17 N	100.55 W
Río Bravo, Méx.	278	25.59 N	98.06 W
Rio Brilhante	296	21.48 S	54.33 W
Río Caribe	290	10.42 N	63.07 W
Rio Casca	296	20.13 S	42.39 W
Río Cauto	284p	20.33 N	76.55 W
Río Ceballos	294	31.11 S	64.20 W
Rio Claro, Bra.	296	22.24 S	47.33 W
Rio Claro, Trin.	285r	10.18 N	61.11 W
Río Colorado	294	39.01 S	64.05 W
Río Cuarto	294	33.08 S	64.20 W
Rio das Antas	294	26.55 S	51.04 W
Rio das Flores	296	22.10 S	43.35 W
Rio de Contas	296	13.36 S	41.48 W
Rio de Janeiro	296	22.54 S	43.15 W
Rio de Janeiro □[3]	296	22.00 S	42.30 W
Río de Jesús	280	7.55 N	81.05 W
Rio Dell	258	40.30 N	124.07 W
Rio-del-Rey C[1]	222	4.31 N	8.45 E
Río de Oro	290	8.17 N	73.23 W
Rio d'Oeste	294	27.12 S	49.48 W
Rio do Prado	296	16.35 S	40.34 W
Rio do Sul	294	27.13 S	49.39 W
Rio Espera	296	20.51 S	43.29 W
Rio Fortuna	294	28.06 S	49.07 W
Río Gallegos	288	51.37 S	69.10 W
Río Grande, Arg.	288	53.50 S	67.40 W
Rio Grande, Bra.	294	32.02 S	52.05 W
Río Grande, Méx.	278	23.50 N	103.02 W
Río Grande, Nic.	280	12.54 N	83.33 W
Río Grande, Pan.	280	8.33 N	81.20 W
Río Grande, P.R.	284m	18.23 N	65.50 W
Rio Grande, N.J., U.S.	262	39.01 N	74.53 W
Rio Grande City	250	26.23 N	98.49 W
Rio Grande do Sul □[3]	294	30.00 S	54.00 W
Rio Grande Ridge ⊹[3]	148	48.00 S	39.00 W
Ríohacha	290	11.33 N	72.55 W
Río Hato	280	8.22 N	80.10 W
Rio Hondo	250	26.14 N	97.35 W
Rioja	292	6.03 S	77.05 W
Río Jueyes	284m	18.01 N	66.20 W
Río Lagartos	278	21.36 N	88.10 W
Riolândia	296	19.59 S	49.40 W
Rio Largo	286	9.29 S	35.51 W
Rio Linda	272	38.41 N	121.27 W
Riom	166	45.54 N	3.07 E
Río Mayo	288	45.40 S	70.15 W
Río Mulato	292	19.42 S	66.47 W
Rio Muni □[2]	214	1.35 N	10.30 E
Riondel	238	49.46 N	116.52 W
Rio Negrinho	294	26.15 S	49.31 W
Rio Negro, Bra.	294	26.06 S	49.48 W
Rio Negro, Bra.	296	19.27 S	54.58 W
Rionegro, Col.	290	7.16 N	73.09 W
Rionegro, Col.	290	6.09 N	75.22 W
Río Negro □[4]	294	40.00 S	67.00 W
Río Negro, Embalse del ⊜[1]	294	32.45 S	56.00 W
Rio Negro, Pantanal do ≡	292	19.00 S	56.00 W
Rionero in Vulture	170	40.56 N	15.41 E
Rio Novo	296	21.29 S	43.08 W
Rio Novo do Sul	296	20.52 S	40.56 W
Riópar	168	38.30 N	2.27 W
Rio Pardo	294	29.59 S	52.22 W
Rio Pardo de Minas	296	15.37 S	42.33 W
Río Piedras, Arg.	294	25.18 S	64.55 W
Río Piedras, P.R.	284m	18.24 N	66.03 W
Río Pilcomayo, Parque Nacional ♠	294	25.10 S	58.00 W
Rio Piracicaba	296	19.55 S	43.11 W
Rio Pomba	296	21.17 S	43.11 W
Rio Prêto	296	22.06 S	43.50 W
Río San Juan □[5]	280	11.10 N	84.30 W
Río Seco	292	21.02 S	70.10 W
Río Segundo	294	31.40 S	63.58 W
Ríosucio, Col.	290	7.27 N	77.07 W
Ríosucio, Col.	290	5.25 N	75.42 W
Río Tercero	294	32.10 S	64.05 W
Rio Tinto, Bra.	286	6.48 S	35.05 W
Ríotinto, Esp.	168	37.40 N	6.39 W
Rio Tuba	202	8.30 N	117.25 E
Rio Verde, Bra.	296	17.43 S	50.56 W
Ríoverde, Méx.	278	21.56 N	99.59 W
Rio Verde de Mato Grosso	296	18.56 S	54.52 W
Rio Vermelho	296	18.18 S	43.00 W
Rio Vista	272	38.10 N	121.42 W
Rioz	166	47.25 N	6.04 E
Riozinho ≃	290	2.55 S	67.07 W
Ripatransone	170	43.00 N	13.46 E
Ripley, Eng., U.K.	174	53.03 N	1.24 W
Ripley, Ind., U.S.	268	41.06 N	86.39 W
Ripley, Miss., U.S.	248	34.44 N	88.57 W
Ripley, N.Y., U.S.	266	42.16 N	79.43 W
Ripley, Ohio, U.S.	242	38.45 N	83.51 W
Ripley, Tenn., U.S.	248	35.45 N	89.32 W
Ripley, W. Va., U.S.	242	38.49 N	81.43 W
Ripoll	168	42.12 N	2.12 E
Ripon, Qué., Can.	260	45.47 N	75.06 W
Ripon, Eng., U.K.	162	54.08 N	1.31 W
Ripon, Calif., U.S.	272	37.44 N	121.07 W
Ripon, Wis., U.S.	244	43.51 N	88.50 W
Riposto	170	37.45 N	15.12 E
Ririe	256	43.38 N	111.46 W

Symbols in the index entries are identified on page 360.

Name	Page	Lat°′	Long°′
Risaralda □[5]	290	5.00 N	76.10 W
Risbäck	160	64.42 N	15.32 E
Risca	174	51.37 N	3.07 W
Risción, Punta de la ≻	278	25.03 N	108.20 W
Riscle	166	43.40 N	0.05 W
Rishikesh	206	30.07 N	78.42 E
Rishiri-suidō ⋃	192a	45.10 N	141.25 E
Rishiri-tō I	192a	45.11 N	141.15 E
Rishiri-zan Λ	192a	45.11 N	141.15 E
Rishon leẔiyyon	210	31.58 N	34.48 E
Rising	261	42.14 N	73.21 W
Rising Star	250	32.06 N	98.58 W
Rising Sun, Ind., U.S.	248	38.57 N	84.51 W
Rising Sun, Md., U.S.	242	39.42 N	76.04 W
Risingsun, Ohio, U.S.	266	41.16 N	83.25 W
Risle ≃	166	49.26 N	0.23 E
Rîşnov	172	45.36 N	25.28 E
Rison, Ark., U.S.	248	33.58 N	92.11 W
Rison, Md., U.S.	262	38.33 N	77.11 W
Risør	160	58.43 N	9.14 E
Ris-Orangis	176	48.39 N	2.25 E
Ristijärvi	160	64.44 N	28.24 E
Ristna	160	58.56 N	22.05 E
Ritter, Mount Λ	258	37.42 N	119.12 W
Ritterhude	178	53.11 N	8.45 E
Rittman	266	40.58 N	81.47 W
Ritzville	256	47.08 N	118.23 W
Riva	170	45.53 N	10.50 E
Rivadavia, Arg.	294	33.10 S	68.28 W
Rivadavia, Arg.	294	31.30 S	68.35 W
Rivadavia, Arg.	294	35.29 S	62.59 W
Rivadavia, Arg.	294	24.11 S	62.53 W
Rivadavia, Chile	294	29.58 S	70.34 W
Rivanna ≃	246	37.45 N	78.10 W
Rivare	268	40.49 N	84.50 W
Rivarolo Canavese	182	45.19 N	7.43 E
Rivas	280	11.26 N	85.51 W
Rivas □[5]	280	11.25 N	85.50 W
Rive-de-Gier	182	45.32 N	4.37 E
Rivera, Arg.	294	37.10 S	63.15 W
Rivera, Col.	290	2.47 N	75.15 W
Rivera, Ur.	294	30.54 S	55.31 W
Riverbank	272	37.44 N	120.56 W
River Cess	214	5.28 N	9.32 W
Riverdale, Calif., U.S.	272	36.26 N	119.52 W
Riverdale, N. Dak., U.S.	252	47.30 N	101.22 W
Riverdale, Oreg., U.S.	270	45.27 N	122.41 W
River Drive Park	264	44.08 N	79.31 W
River Falls, Ala., U.S.	248	31.21 N	86.33 W
River Falls, Wis., U.S.	244	44.52 N	92.38 W
Rivergaro	170	44.55 N	9.36 E
River Haven	268	41.05 N	85.02 W
Riverhead	261	40.55 N	72.40 W
River Hébert	240	45.42 N	64.23 W
River Hills	268	43.12 N	87.57 W
Riverina ◂[1]	228	35.30 S	145.30 E
River John	240	45.45 N	63.03 W
River Jordan	238	48.25 N	124.03 W
Riverland Terrace	246	32.47 N	80.02 W
Riverlea	266	40.05 N	83.02 W
River of Ponds	240	50.32 N	57.27 W
River Pines, Calif., U.S.	272	38.33 N	120.45 W
River Pines, Mass., U.S.	261	42.34 N	71.17 W
River Plaza	262	40.21 N	74.05 W
River Rouge	268	42.16 N	83.08 W
Rivers	252	50.02 N	100.12 W
Rivers □[3]	222	4.30 N	6.30 E
Rivers, Lake of the ⊜	252	49.45 N	105.45 W
Riverside, Calif., U.S.	274	33.59 N	117.22 W
Riverside, Iowa, U.S.	244	41.29 N	91.35 W
Riverside, Mich., U.S.	268	42.17 N	84.29 W
Riverside, Mich., U.S.	268	42.11 N	86.23 W
Riverside, N.J., U.S.	262	40.02 N	74.58 W
Riverside, Tex., U.S.	250	30.57 N	95.24 W
Riverside, Wash., U.S.	238	48.30 N	119.31 W
Riverside □[6]	274	33.45 N	117.10 W
Rivers Inlet	238	51.41 N	127.15 W
Rivers Inlet C	238	51.39 N	127.30 W
Riverton, Ill., U.S.	248	39.51 N	89.33 W
Riverton, Nebr., U.S.	252	40.05 N	98.46 W
Riverton, N.J., U.S.	262	40.01 N	75.01 W
Riverton, Utah, U.S.	254	40.31 N	111.56 W
Riverton, Va., U.S.	242	38.57 N	78.12 W
Riverton, Wyo., U.S.	254	43.02 N	108.23 W
Riverton Heights	270	47.28 N	122.17 W
River View, Ala., U.S.	248	32.47 N	85.09 W
Riverview, Fla., U.S.	246	27.52 N	82.20 W
Riverview, Mich., U.S.	268	42.11 N	83.10 W
Rives	248	36.21 N	89.04 W
Rivesaltes	166	42.46 N	2.52 E
Rives Junction	268	42.23 N	84.28 W
Rivesville	242	39.32 N	80.07 W
Riviera	250	27.18 N	97.49 W
Riviera Beach	246	26.47 N	80.04 W
Rivière-à-Claude	240	49.13 N	65.56 W
Rivière-au-Renard	240	49.01 N	64.25 W
Rivière-au-Tonnerre	240	50.17 N	64.46 W
Rivière-Bleue	240	47.26 N	69.03 W
Rivière-Bois-Clair	260	46.34 N	71.50 W
Rivière-de-la-Chaloupe	240	49.05 N	62.33 W
Rivière-du-Loup	240	47.50 N	69.32 W
Rivière-du-Moulin	240	48.26 N	71.02 W
Rivière du Rempart	225c	20.06 S	57.41 E
Rivière-Matane	240	48.39 N	67.20 W
Rivière-Pentecôte	240	49.47 N	67.10 W
Rivière-Pilote	284e	14.29 N	60.54 W
Rivière-Salée	284e	14.32 N	60.59 W
Rivière-Trois-Pistoles	240	48.07 N	69.10 W
Rivoli	182	45.04 N	7.31 E
Rivoli Bay C	228	37.32 S	140.04 E
Rixford	266	41.55 N	78.30 W
Riyadh → Ar-Riyāḍ	208	24.38 N	46.43 E
Rīz	208	32.23 N	51.20 E
Rizal	202	15.43 N	121.06 E
Rizal □[4]	202	14.35 N	121.50 E
Rize	212	41.02 N	40.31 E
Rīzeh, Kūh-e (Gora Reza) Λ	208	37.47 N	58.05 E
Rizhao	190	35.27 N	119.29 E
Rižskij Zaliv C	158	57.30 N	23.35 E
Rizzuto, Capo ≻	170	38.54 N	17.06 E
Rjukan	158	59.52 N	8.34 E
Roa	168	41.42 N	3.55 W
Roachdale	248	39.51 N	86.48 W
Road Town	284m	18.27 N	64.37 W
Roan Cliffs ⩘[4]	254	39.30 N	109.00 W
Roan Mountain	246	36.12 N	82.05 W
Roann	268	40.55 N	85.55 W
Roanne	166	46.02 N	4.04 E
Roanoke, Ala., U.S.	248	33.09 N	85.22 W
Roanoke, Ill., U.S.	244	40.48 N	89.12 W
Roanoke, Ind., U.S.	268	40.58 N	85.22 W
Roanoke, Va., U.S.	246	37.16 N	79.57 W
Roanoke (Staunton) ≃	246	35.56 N	76.43 W
Roanoke Island I	246	35.53 N	75.39 W
Roanoke Rapids	246	36.28 N	77.40 W
Roanoke Rapids Lake ⊜[1]	246	36.30 N	77.45 W
Roan Plateau ⋏[1]	254	39.35 N	108.30 W
Roaring Fork ≃	254	39.33 N	107.20 W
Roaring Spring	266	40.20 N	78.24 W
Roaring Springs	250	33.54 N	100.52 W
Roatán	280	16.18 N	86.35 W
Roatán, Isla de I	280	16.23 N	86.26 W
Robâa Oued Yahia	170	36.05 N	9.35 E
Robbins, Calif., U.S.	272	38.53 N	121.42 W
Robbins, Ill., U.S.	268	41.39 N	87.42 W
Robbins, N.C., U.S.	246	35.26 N	79.35 W
Robbins, Tenn., U.S.	246	36.21 N	84.35 W
Robbins Island I	228	40.41 S	144.57 E
Robbinston	242	45.05 N	67.07 W
Robbinsville, N.J., U.S.	262	40.13 N	74.37 W
Robbinsville, N.C., U.S.	246	35.19 N	83.48 W
Robbio	182	45.17 N	8.35 E
Robbs	248	37.28 N	88.42 W
Robe ≃	162	53.37 N	9.16 W
Robe, Mount Λ	228	31.40 S	141.20 E
Röbel	164	53.23 N	12.35 E
Robeline	248	31.41 N	93.18 W
Robersonville	246	35.50 N	77.15 W
Roberta	246	32.43 N	84.01 W
Roberta Mills	246	35.22 N	80.38 W
Robert Lee	250	31.54 N	100.29 W
Robert McIlwanie National Park ♠	224	17.55 S	30.50 E
Roberts, Idaho, U.S.	256	43.43 N	112.08 W
Roberts, Ill., U.S.	268	40.37 N	88.11 W
Roberts, Mont., U.S.	256	45.22 N	109.10 W
Robert's Arm	240	49.29 N	55.49 W
Roberts Creek Mountain Λ	258	39.52 N	116.18 W
Robertsdale, Ala., U.S.	248	30.33 N	87.43 W
Robertsdale, Pa., U.S.	266	40.11 N	78.07 W
Robertsfors	160	64.11 N	20.51 E
Robert S. Kerr Lake ⊜[1]	250	35.25 N	95.00 W
Roberts Mountain Λ	236	60.03 N	166.16 W
Robertson	224	33.46 S	19.50 E
Robertson, Lac ⊜	240	51.00 N	59.10 W
Robertsonville	260	46.09 N	71.13 W
Roberts Peak Λ	238	52.57 N	120.32 W
Robertsport	222	6.45 N	11.22 W
Robertsville	266	40.46 N	81.11 W
Robert Williams	218	12.51 S	15.33 E
Roberval	232	48.31 N	72.13 W
Robinson, Ill., U.S.	248	39.00 N	87.44 W
Robinson, Kans., U.S.	252	39.49 N	95.25 W
Robinson, Tex., U.S.	250	31.31 N	97.06 W
Róbinson Crusoe, Isla(Isla Más A Tierra) I	288	33.38 S	78.52 W
Robinson Gorge National Park ♠	228	25.15 S	149.10 E
Robinsons	240	48.15 N	58.48 W
Robinvale	228	34.36 S	142.46 E
Robinwood	270	45.25 N	122.38 W
Robleda	168	40.23 N	6.36 W
Robledo	168	38.46 N	2.26 W
Roblin	232	51.14 N	101.21 W
Roboré	292	18.20 S	59.45 W
Robson, Mount Λ	238	53.07 N	119.09 W
Robstown	250	27.47 N	97.40 W
Roby	250	32.45 N	100.23 W
Roca, Cabo da ≻	168	38.47 N	9.30 W
Roçadas	218	16.43 S	15.01 E
Roca del Toro, Punta ≻	254	31.19 N	113.43 W
Rocafuerte	290	0.55 S	80.28 W
Roca Partida, Isla I	278	19.01 N	112.02 W
Roca Partida, Punta ≻	278	18.42 N	95.10 W
Rocas, Atol das I[1]	286	3.52 S	33.59 W
Roccadaspide	170	40.26 N	15.12 E
Rocca di Papa	184	41.46 N	12.42 E
Roccastrada	184	43.00 N	11.10 E
Rocciamelone Λ	170	45.12 N	7.05 E
Rocha	294	34.29 S	54.20 W
Rochdale, Eng., U.K.	162	53.38 N	2.09 W
Rochdale, Mass., U.S.	261	42.12 N	71.54 W
Rochdale, N.Y., U.S.	261	41.43 N	73.50 W
Rochechouart	166	45.50 N	0.50 E
Rochedinho, Bra.	292	20.14 S	54.33 W
Rochedinho, Bra.	296	21.08 S	41.41 W
Rochedo	296	19.57 S	54.52 W
Rochefort, Bel.	164	50.10 N	5.13 E
Rochefort, Fr.	166	45.57 N	0.58 W
Rochefort-Montagne	166	45.41 N	2.48 E
Roche Harbor	270	48.36 N	123.09 W
Roche-la-Molière	182	45.26 N	4.19 E
Rochelle, Ga., U.S.	246	31.57 N	83.27 W
Rochelle, Ill., U.S.	268	41.56 N	89.04 W
Rochelle, Tex., U.S.	250	31.13 N	99.13 W
Roche-Percée	252	49.03 N	102.45 W
Rochester, Eng., U.K.	174	51.24 N	0.30 E
Rochester, Ind., U.S.	268	41.04 N	86.13 W
Rochester, Mass., U.S.	261	41.44 N	70.49 W
Rochester, Mich., U.S.	266	42.41 N	83.08 W
Rochester, Minn., U.S.	244	44.02 N	92.29 W
Rochester, N.H., U.S.	242	43.18 N	70.59 W
Rochester, N.Y., U.S.	264	43.10 N	77.36 W
Rochester, Ohio, U.S.	266	41.07 N	82.18 W
Rochester, Pa., U.S.	266	40.43 N	80.17 W
Rochester, Tex., U.S.	250	33.19 N	99.51 W
Rochester, Wash., U.S.	270	46.49 N	123.06 W
Rochester, Wis., U.S.	268	42.45 N	88.14 W
Rochester Mills	266	40.49 N	78.59 W
Rochlitz	164	51.03 N	12.47 E
Rock	244	46.04 N	87.10 W
Rock □[6]	268	42.41 N	89.05 W
Rock ≃, U.S.	244	41.29 N	90.37 W
Rock ≃, U.S.	252	43.05 N	96.27 W
Rockall I	158	57.35 N	13.48 W
Rockall Rise ✣[3]	148	59.00 N	14.00 W
Rockaway	270	45.37 N	123.57 W
Rock Bay	238	50.20 N	125.29 W
Rockcastle ≃	246	36.58 N	84.21 W
Rockcliffe Park	264	45.27 N	75.41 W
Rock Creek, B.C., Can.	238	49.06 N	118.58 W
Rock Creek, Ohio, U.S.	266	41.40 N	80.52 W
Rock Creek Butte Λ	256	44.49 N	118.07 W
Rockdale, Ill., U.S.	268	41.30 N	88.06 W
Rockdale, Tex., U.S.	250	30.39 N	97.00 W
Rockdale, W. Va., U.S.	266	40.18 N	80.35 W
Rockefeller Plateau ⋏[1]	148	80.00 S	135.00 W
Rockenhausen	166	49.38 N	7.49 E
Rockfall	261	41.28 N	72.44 W
Rock Falls	248	41.47 N	89.41 W
Rockfield	268	40.39 N	86.34 W
Rockford, Ala., U.S.	248	32.53 N	86.13 W
Rockford, Ill., U.S.	268	42.17 N	89.06 W
Rockford, Iowa, U.S.	244	43.03 N	92.57 W
Rockford, Mich., U.S.	244	43.07 N	85.33 W
Rockford, Ohio, U.S.	268	40.42 N	84.39 W
Rockford, Tenn., U.S.	246	35.49 N	83.56 W
Rock Forest	260	45.21 N	71.59 W
Rockglen, Sask., Can.	252	49.10 N	105.57 W
Rock Glen, N.Y., U.S.	264	42.41 N	78.07 W
Rock Hall	242	39.08 N	76.14 W
Rockhampton	228	23.23 S	150.31 E
Rock Hill	246	34.56 N	81.01 W
Rockhill Furnace	266	40.15 N	77.54 W
Rockingham	246	34.56 N	79.46 W
Rockingham □[6]	261	42.50 N	71.15 W
Rockingham Bay C	228	18.10 S	146.05 E
Rock Island, Qué., Can.	260	45.00 N	72.06 W
Rock Island, Ill., U.S.	244	41.30 N	90.34 W
Rocklake	252	48.47 N	99.15 W
Rockland, Ont., Can.	242	45.33 N	75.17 W
Rockland, Idaho, U.S.	256	42.34 N	112.53 W
Rockland, Maine, U.S.	242	44.06 N	69.06 W
Rockland, Mass., U.S.	261	42.08 N	70.55 W
Rockland, Mich., U.S.	244	46.41 N	89.11 W
Rocklands Reservoir ⊜[1]	228	37.15 S	142.00 E
Rockledge	246	28.20 N	80.43 W
Rocklin	272	38.48 N	121.14 W
Rockmart	246	34.00 N	85.02 W
Rock Point	262	38.16 N	76.50 W
Rockport, Ky., U.S.	248	37.20 N	86.59 W
Rockport, Maine, U.S.	242	44.11 N	69.06 W
Rockport, Mass., U.S.	261	42.39 N	70.36 W
Rock Port, Mo., U.S.	248	40.25 N	95.31 W
Rockport, Tex., U.S.	250	28.01 N	97.04 W
Rock Rapids	252	43.26 N	96.10 W
Rock River	254	41.44 N	105.58 W
Rock Run	262	39.59 N	75.50 W
Rock Sound	282	24.54 N	76.12 W
Rocksprings, Tex., U.S.	250	30.01 N	100.13 W
Rock Springs, Wyo., U.S.	254	41.35 N	109.13 W
Rockstone	290	5.59 N	58.32 W
Rockton, Ill., U.S.	268	42.27 N	89.04 W
Rockton, Pa., U.S.	266	41.05 N	78.39 W
Rock Valley	252	43.12 N	96.18 W
Rockville, Conn., U.S.	261	41.52 N	72.27 W
Rockville, Ind., U.S.	248	39.46 N	87.14 W
Rockville, Md., U.S.	242	39.05 N	77.09 W
Rockville, Pa., U.S.	262	40.20 N	76.54 W
Rockville, R.I., U.S.	261	41.31 N	71.46 W
Rockwall	250	32.56 N	96.28 W
Rockwell, Iowa, U.S.	244	42.59 N	93.11 W
Rockwell, N.C., U.S.	246	35.33 N	80.25 W
Rockwell City	252	42.24 N	94.38 W
Rockwood, Ont., Can.	264	43.37 N	80.08 W
Rockwood, Maine, U.S.	242	45.41 N	69.44 W
Rockwood, Mich., U.S.	268	42.10 N	83.15 W
Rockwood, Pa., U.S.	242	39.54 N	79.09 W
Rockwood, Tenn., U.S.	246	35.52 N	84.41 W
Rocky	250	35.09 N	99.04 W
Rocky ≃, Alta., Can.	238	53.08 N	117.59 W
Rocky ≃, N.C., U.S.	246	35.37 N	79.09 W
Rocky Boys Indian Reservation ◂[4]	256	48.18 N	109.45 W
Rocky Cape ≻	228	40.51 S	145.30 E
Rocky Comfort Creek ≃	246	32.59 N	82.25 W
Rockyford, Alta., Can.	238	51.13 N	113.08 W
Rocky Ford, Colo., U.S.	252	38.03 N	103.43 W
Rocky Grove	266	41.25 N	79.49 W
Rocky Harbour	240	49.36 N	57.55 W
Rocky Hill	261	41.40 N	72.39 W
Rocky Island Lake ⊜[1]	244	46.56 N	83.04 W
Rocky Mount, N.C., U.S.	246	35.56 N	77.48 W
Rocky Mount, Va., U.S.	246	37.00 N	79.54 W
Rocky Mountain Λ	256	47.49 N	112.49 W
Rocky Mountain House	238	52.22 N	114.55 W
Rocky Mountain National Park ♠	254	40.19 N	105.42 W
Rocky Mountains ⋏	234	48.00 N	116.00 W
Rocky Point, N.Y., U.S.	261	40.57 N	72.56 W
Rocky Point, Wash., U.S.	270	47.35 N	122.41 W
Rocky Point ≻, Ba.	246	25.59 N	77.25 W
Rocky Point ≻, S.W. Afr.	224	19.03 S	12.30 E
Rocky Point ≻, Alaska, U.S.	236	64.25 N	163.10 W
Rocky Ridge	266	41.32 N	83.13 W
Rocky River	266	41.30 N	81.40 W
Rocky Run ≃	252	47.38 N	99.02 W
Rocky Top Λ	256	44.47 N	122.17 W
Roda	246	36.58 N	82.50 W
Rodalben	164	49.14 N	7.38 E
Rodalquilar	168	37.40 N	2.08 W
Rodas	284p	22.20 N	80.33 W
Rødbyhavn	164	54.39 N	11.21 E
Roddickton	240	50.52 N	56.08 W
Rodeio	294	26.57 S	49.23 W
Rodeo, Arg.	294	30.13 S	69.08 W
Rodeo, Méx.	278	25.11 N	104.34 W
Rodeo, Calif., U.S.	272	38.02 N	122.09 W
Rodeo, N. Mex., U.S.	254	31.50 N	109.02 W
Roderick Island I	238	52.40 N	128.22 W
Rodessa	248	32.58 N	94.00 W
Rodewisch	164	50.32 N	12.24 E
Rodez	166	44.21 N	2.35 E
Rodhópi □[5], Ellás	172	41.00 N	25.20 E
Rodhópi □[5], Ellás	212	41.10 N	26.45 E
Ródhos (Rhodes)	172	36.26 N	28.13 E
Ródhos I	172	36.10 N	28.00 E
Rodi Garganico	170	41.55 N	15.53 E
Roding	164	49.12 N	12.32 E
Rodino	160	58.57 N	44.59 E
Rodman	236	57.28 N	135.21 W
Rodnei, Munții ⋏	172	47.35 N	24.40 E
Rodney, Ont., Can.	266	42.34 N	81.41 W
Rodney, Miss., U.S.	248	31.52 N	91.12 W
Rodney, Cape ≻, N.Z.	230	36.17 S	174.49 E
Rodney, Cape ≻, Alaska, U.S.	236	64.39 N	166.24 W
Rodney Village	262	39.08 N	75.31 W
Rodniki	160	57.06 N	41.44 E
Rodolfo Iselín	294	34.39 S	68.01 W
Rodonit, Kep i ≻	172	41.35 N	19.27 E
Rodríguez, Méx.	250	27.10 N	100.01 W
Rodríguez, Méx.	278	27.11 N	101.21 W
Roduco	262	36.28 N	76.49 W
Roebling	262	40.07 N	74.47 W
Roebourne	226	20.47 S	117.09 E
Roeland Park	252	39.02 N	94.37 W
Roermond	178	51.12 N	6.00 E
Roeselare (Roulers)	176	50.57 N	3.08 E
Roessleville	261	42.42 N	73.49 W
Roes Welcome Sound ⋃	232	64.00 N	88.00 W
Roff	250	34.38 N	96.50 W
Rogagua, Lago ⊜	292	13.43 S	66.54 W
Rogaland □[6]	160	59.00 N	6.15 E
Rogaska Slatina	170	46.14 N	15.38 E
Rogatica	172	43.48 N	19.00 E
Roger, Lac ⊜	244	47.50 N	78.55 W
Rogers, Ark., U.S.	248	36.20 N	94.07 W
Rogers, Conn., U.S.	261	41.50 N	71.54 W
Rogers, Ohio, U.S.	266	40.48 N	80.38 W
Rogers, Tex., U.S.	250	30.56 N	97.14 W
Rogers, Mount Λ	246	36.39 N	81.33 W
Rogers City	244	45.25 N	83.49 W
Rogersville, N.B., Can.	240	46.44 N	65.26 W
Rogersville, Ala., U.S.	248	34.50 N	87.17 W
Rogersville, Tenn., U.S.	246	36.25 N	83.02 W
Roggeveldberge ⋏	224	32.17 S	20.08 E
Roggiano Gravina	170	39.37 N	16.17 E
Rogliano, Fr.	166	42.57 N	9.25 E
Rogliano, It.	170	39.11 N	16.20 E
Rogoaguado, Lago ⊜	292	12.52 S	65.43 W
Rogoźno	164	52.46 N	17.00 E
Rogue ≃, Mich., U.S.	244	43.04 N	85.35 W
Rogue ≃, Oreg., U.S.	256	42.26 N	124.25 W
Rogue River	256	42.26 N	123.10 W
Rohl ≃	220	6.22 N	29.46 E
Rohnert Park	272	38.21 N	122.42 W
Rohtak	206	28.54 N	76.35 E
Roia (Torrent la Roya) ≃	182	43.48 N	7.35 E
Roi Et	200	16.05 N	103.42 E
Roisel	166	49.57 N	3.06 E
Rojas	294	34.15 S	60.44 W
Rojo, Cabo ≻	278	21.33 N	97.20 W
Rokan ≃	200	2.00 N	100.52 E
Rokel ≃	222	8.33 N	12.48 W
Rokycany	164	49.45 N	13.36 E
Roland, Man., Can.	252	49.25 N	97.55 W
Roland, Ark., U.S.	248	34.54 N	92.30 W
Roland, Iowa, U.S.	244	42.10 N	93.30 W
Rolândia	296	23.18 S	51.22 W
Røldal	160	59.49 N	6.48 E
Roldán	294	32.54 S	60.55 W
Roldanillo	290	4.24 N	76.09 W
Rolette	252	48.40 N	99.51 W
Rolfe	252	42.49 N	94.31 W
Roll, Ariz., U.S.	254	32.45 N	113.59 W
Roll, Ind., U.S.	268	40.33 N	85.23 W
Rolla, B.C., Can.	238	55.54 N	120.09 W
Rolla, Kans., U.S.	252	37.07 N	101.38 W
Rolla, Mo., U.S.	248	37.57 N	91.46 W
Rolla, N. Dak., U.S.	252	48.52 N	99.37 W
Rolle	180	46.28 N	6.20 E
Rollingbay	270	47.40 N	122.30 W
Rolling Fork	248	32.55 N	90.52 W
Rolling Fork ≃	248	37.55 N	85.50 W
Rolling Green	268	41.05 N	85.07 W
Rolling Hills	252	37.40 N	97.26 W
Rolling Meadows	268	42.04 N	88.01 W
Rolling Prairie	268	41.40 N	86.37 W
Rollingwood	272	37.57 N	122.20 W
Rollins	238	47.55 N	114.12 W
Roma, Austl.	228	26.35 S	148.47 E
Roma, It.	184	41.54 N	12.29 E
Roma □[4]	184	41.58 N	12.40 E
Romagna ◂[1]	184	44.30 N	12.15 E
Romain, Cape ≻	246	33.00 N	79.22 W
Romaine ≃	232	50.18 N	63.47 W
Roman, Blg.	172	43.09 N	23.55 E
Roman, Rom.	172	46.55 N	26.56 E
Romanche Gap ✣[1]	148	0.10 S	18.15 W
Romang, Pulau I	198	7.35 S	127.26 E
Romania (România) □[1]	158	46.00 N	25.30 E
Roman-Koš, Gora Λ	158	44.37 N	34.15 E
Roman Nose Mountain Λ	256	43.55 N	123.44 W
Romano, Cape ≻	246	25.50 N	81.41 W
Romano, Cayo I	284p	22.15 N	78.00 W
Romano di Lombardia	182	45.31 N	9.45 E
Romanshorn	180	47.34 N	9.22 E
Romans[-sur-Isère], Fr.	166	45.03 N	5.03 E
Romans-sur-Isère, Fr.	182	45.03 N	5.03 E
Romanzof Mountains ⋏	236	69.00 N	144.00 W
Romblon	202	12.35 N	122.16 E
Romblon □[4]	202	12.30 N	122.10 E
Romblon Island I	202	12.33 N	122.18 E
Romblon Passage ⋃	202	12.25 N	122.15 E
Rombo, Ilhéus do II	222a	14.58 N	24.40 W
Rome → Roma, It.	184	41.54 N	12.29 E
Rome, Ga., U.S.	246	34.16 N	85.11 W
Rome, Miss., U.S.	248	33.52 N	90.29 W
Rome, N.Y., U.S.	264	43.13 N	75.27 W
Rome, Ohio, U.S.	266	41.36 N	80.52 W
Rome, Wis., U.S.	268	42.58 N	88.38 W
Rome City	268	41.30 N	85.23 W
Romeo	266	42.48 N	83.01 W
Romilly-sur-Seine	176	48.31 N	3.43 E
Romney, Ind., U.S.	268	40.15 N	86.54 W
Romney, W. Va., U.S.	242	39.21 N	78.45 W
Romny	158	50.45 N	33.30 E
Romodanovo	160	54.26 N	45.20 E
Romoland	274	33.45 N	117.10 W
Romont	166	46.42 N	6.55 E
Romorantin-Lanthenay	176	47.22 N	1.45 E
Rompin ≃	200	2.49 N	103.29 E
Romsey	174	50.59 N	1.30 W
Romulus, Mich., U.S.	268	42.13 N	83.24 W
Romulus, N.Y., U.S.	264	42.45 N	76.50 W
Ron, Mui ≻	200	18.07 N	106.22 E
Rona I	162	59.07 N	5.49 W
Ronald	270	47.14 N	121.01 W
Ronan	256	47.32 N	114.06 W
Ronay I	162	57.28 N	7.07 W
Roncador, Serra do ⋏[1]	296	12.00 S	52.00 W
Roncador Bank ✣[4]	282	13.32 N	80.03 W
Roncador Bank ✣[4], N.A.	280	13.32 N	80.03 W
Roncesvalles	168	43.01 N	1.19 W
Ronceverte	246	37.45 N	80.28 W
Ronchamp	170	47.42 N	6.39 E
Ronchamp ⊻[1]	166	47.43 N	6.37 E
Ronchin	176	50.36 N	3.06 E
Ronciglione	184	42.17 N	12.13 E
Ronda	168	36.44 N	5.10 W
Ronda, Serranía de ⋏	168	36.44 N	5.03 W
Rondon	296	23.23 S	52.48 W
Rondônia	292	10.52 S	61.57 W
Rondônia □[8]	292	11.00 S	63.00 W
Rondonópolis	296	16.28 S	54.38 W
Ronge, Lac la ⊜	232	55.10 N	105.00 W
Rongjiang	200	25.52 N	108.37 E
Rønne	160	55.06 N	14.42 E
Ronneburg	164	50.51 N	12.10 E
Ronneby	160	56.12 N	15.18 E
Ronne Entrance C	148	72.30 S	74.00 W
Ronne Ice Shelf ⊠	148	78.30 S	61.00 W
Ronse (Renaix-gleiche)	176	50.45 N	3.36 E
Ronuro ≃	296	11.56 S	53.33 W
Roodepoort-Maraisburg	224	26.11 S	27.54 E
Roodhouse	248	39.29 N	90.22 W
Roof Butte Λ	254	36.28 N	109.05 W
Rooiboklaagte ≃	224	20.50 S	21.00 E
Roorkee	206	29.53 N	77.52 E
Roosendaal	178	51.32 N	4.28 E
Roosevelt, Ariz., U.S.	254	33.40 N	111.09 W
Roosevelt, Minn., U.S.	252	48.48 N	95.06 W
Roosevelt, N.J., U.S.	262	40.13 N	74.29 W
Roosevelt, Okla., U.S.	250	34.51 N	99.01 W
Roosevelt, Utah, U.S.	254	40.18 N	109.59 W
Roosevelt ≃	292	7.35 S	60.20 W
Roosevelt Beach	264	43.19 N	78.52 W
Roosevelt-Campobello International Park ♠	240	44.52 N	66.58 W
Roosevelt Island I	148	79.30 S	162.00 W
Roosevelt Lake ⊜[1]	254	33.42 N	111.07 W
Roosevelt Park	268	43.11 N	86.16 W
Roosevelt Terrace	272	38.08 N	122.16 W
Root ≃, N.W. Ter., Can.	236	62.50 N	123.40 W
Root ≃, Minn., U.S.	244	43.46 N	91.15 W
Rootstown	266	41.06 N	81.15 W
Ropča	160	63.02 N	52.16 E
Ropczyce	164	50.03 N	21.37 E
Roper	246	35.53 N	76.37 W
Ropesville	250	33.26 N	102.09 W
Roquebrune-Cap-Martin	182	43.46 N	7.28 E
Roquefort	166	44.02 N	0.19 W
Roquemaure	166	44.03 N	4.47 E
Roque Pérez	294	35.23 S	59.22 W
Roraima □[8]	290	1.00 N	61.00 W
Roraima, Mount Λ	290	5.12 N	60.44 W
Rorey Lake ⊜	236	66.55 N	128.25 W
Røros	160	62.35 N	11.20 E
Rorschach	180	47.29 N	9.30 E
Rosa, Cap ≻	170	36.57 N	8.14 E
Rosa, Monte Λ	180	45.55 N	7.53 E
Rosales, Méx.	278	28.12 N	105.33 W
Rosales, Pil.	202	15.54 N	120.38 E
Rosalia	256	47.14 N	117.22 W
Rosalind Bank ✣[4]	282	16.30 N	80.30 W
Rosamond	274	34.52 N	118.10 W
Rosamorada	278	22.08 N	105.12 W
Rosans	166	44.23 N	5.28 E
Rosario, Arg.	294	32.57 S	60.40 W
Rosário, Bra.	286	2.57 S	44.14 W
Rosario, Méx.	278	30.01 N	115.40 W
Rosario, Méx.	278	26.31 N	105.40 W
Rosario, Méx.	278	23.00 N	105.52 W
Rosario, Para.	294	24.27 S	57.03 W
Rosario, Pil.	202	16.14 N	120.30 E
Rosario, Pil.	202	13.51 N	121.12 E
Rosario, Ur.	294	34.19 S	57.21 W
Rosario ≃	294	25.06 S	65.24 W
Rosario, Bahía del C	278	29.50 N	115.45 W
Rosario, Cayo del I	284p	21.38 N	81.53 W
Rosario, Islas de II	290	10.10 N	75.46 W
Rosario, Sierra del ⋏	284p	22.47 N	83.15 W
Rosario Bank ✣[4]	282	18.30 N	84.00 W
Rosario de la Frontera	294	25.50 S	64.55 W
Rosario de Lerma	294	24.59 S	65.32 W
Rosario del Tala	294	32.20 S	59.10 W
Rosário do Sul	294	30.15 S	54.55 W
Rosário Oeste	292	14.50 S	56.25 W
Rosarito, Méx.	258	32.20 N	117.02 W
Rosarito, Méx.	278	28.38 N	114.04 W
Rosarito, Méx.	278	26.27 N	111.38 W
Rosarito, Embalse del ⊜[1]	168	40.05 N	5.15 W
Rosarno	170	38.29 N	15.59 E
Rosas	250	26.09 N	103.27 W
Rosas, Golfo de C	168	42.10 N	3.15 E
Roscoe, Ill., U.S.	268	42.25 N	89.01 W
Roscoe, Pa., U.S.	266	40.05 N	79.52 W
Roscoe, S. Dak., U.S.	252	45.27 N	99.20 W
Roscoe, Tex., U.S.	250	32.27 N	100.32 W
Roscommon, Eire	162	53.38 N	8.11 W
Roscommon, Mich., U.S.	244	44.30 N	84.35 W
Roscommon □[6]	162	53.40 N	8.30 W
Roscrea	162	52.57 N	7.47 W
Rose	264	43.09 N	76.53 W
Rose, Mount Λ	258	39.21 N	119.55 W
Roseau, Dom.	284d	15.18 N	61.24 W
Roseau, Minn., U.S.	252	48.51 N	95.46 W
Roseau ≃	252	49.08 N	97.15 W
Rosebery	228	41.46 S	145.32 E
Rose-Blanche	240	47.37 N	58.43 W
Roseboro	246	34.58 N	78.31 W
Rosebud, Mont., U.S.	256	46.16 N	106.27 W
Rose Bud, Pa., U.S.	266	40.45 N	78.33 W
Rosebud, S. Dak., U.S.	252	43.14 N	100.51 W
Rosebud, Tex., U.S.	250	31.04 N	96.59 W
Rosebud ≃	238	51.25 N	112.37 W
Rosebud Indian Reservation ◂[4]	252	43.25 N	100.28 W
Roseburg	256	43.13 N	123.20 W
Rosebush	244	43.42 N	84.46 W
Rose City	244	44.25 N	84.07 W
Rosedale, Alta., Can.	238	51.25 N	112.38 W
Rosedale, B.C., Can.	270	49.11 N	121.48 W
Rosedale, Ind., U.S.	248	39.37 N	87.17 W
Rosedale, La., U.S.	248	30.27 N	91.27 W
Rosedale, Miss., U.S.	248	33.51 N	91.02 W
Rose Hall	290	6.18 N	57.23 W
Rosehearty	162	57.42 N	2.07 W
Rose Hill, Maus.	225c	20.14 S	57.27 E
Rose Hill, N.C., U.S.	246	34.50 N	78.02 W
Rose Hill, Va., U.S.	246	36.40 N	83.22 W
Rose Hill, Wash., U.S.	270	47.42 N	122.10 W
Rose Island I	246	25.07 N	77.10 W
Rose Lake	238	54.24 N	126.02 W
Roseland, Calif., U.S.	272	38.25 N	122.44 W
Roseland, Ind., U.S.	268	41.42 N	86.15 W
Roseland, La., U.S.	248	30.46 N	90.31 W
Roseland, Ohio, U.S.	266	40.47 N	82.32 W
Roselawn	268	41.09 N	87.19 W
Roselle	268	41.59 N	88.05 W
Rose Lodge	270	45.01 N	123.52 W
Rosemary	238	50.46 N	112.05 W
Rosemère	260	45.38 N	73.47 W
Rosemont	266	41.03 N	80.53 W
Rosenberg	250	29.33 N	95.48 W
Rosendaël	176	51.02 N	2.24 E
Rosenhayn	262	39.29 N	75.08 W
Rosenheim	164	47.51 N	12.07 E
Rose Peak Λ	254	33.25 N	109.21 W
Rosepine	248	30.55 N	93.17 W
Rose Point ≻	238	54.13 N	131.35 W
Roseto degli Abruzzi	184	42.41 N	14.01 E
Rosetown	232	51.33 N	108.00 W
Rosetta → Rashīd	220	31.24 N	30.25 E
Rosetta Mouth → Rashīd, Maṣabb ≃[1]	220	31.30 N	30.20 E
Roseville, Calif., U.S.	272	38.45 N	121.17 W
Roseville, Ill., U.S.	244	40.44 N	90.40 W
Roseville, Mich., U.S.	266	42.30 N	82.56 W
Roseville, Minn., U.S.	244	45.01 N	93.09 W
Roseville, Ohio, U.S.	242	39.49 N	82.05 W
Rosewood, Austl.	228	27.39 S	152.35 E
Rosewood	268	40.13 N	83.58 W
Rosh Ha'Ayin	210	32.05 N	34.57 E
Rosholt, S. Dak., U.S.	252	45.52 N	96.44 W
Rosholt, Wis., U.S.	244	44.38 N	89.18 W
Rosh Zohar ⊥	210	31.13 N	35.13 E
Rosice	164	49.11 N	16.23 E
Rosiclare	248	37.25 N	88.20 W
Rosignano Marittimo	184	43.24 N	10.28 E
Rosignol	290	6.16 N	57.32 W
Roşiori-de-Vede	172	44.07 N	25.00 E
Rosita	280	13.53 N	84.24 W
Roskilde	160	55.39 N	12.05 E
Roslags Näsby	160	59.26 N	18.04 E
Rosl'akovo	160	69.03 N	33.09 E
Roslavl'	158	53.57 N	32.52 E
Roslyn	270	47.13 N	120.59 W
Rosman	246	35.03 N	82.49 W
Rosporden	166	47.58 N	3.50 W
Ross	272	37.55 N	122.32 W
Ross ≃	236	61.59 N	132.26 W
Ross, Cape ≻	202	10.57 N	119.13 E
Ross, Mount Λ	230	41.27 S	175.20 E
Ross and Cromarty □[6]	162	57.43 N	4.50 W
Rossano	170	39.35 N	16.39 E
Rossan Point ≻	162	54.42 N	8.48 W
Ross Barnett Reservoir ⊜[1]	248	32.30 N	90.00 W
Rossburg	268	40.17 N	84.38 W
Rosseau	264	45.16 N	79.39 W
Rosseau Lake ⊜	244	45.10 N	79.35 W
Rossel Island I	226	11.21 S	154.09 E
Rossell y Rius	294	33.11 S	55.42 W
Rossford	266	41.37 N	83.33 W
Ross Ice Shelf ⊠	148	81.30 S	175.00 W
Rossignol, Lake ⊜	240	44.10 N	65.10 W
Rossijskaja Sovetskaja Federativnaja Socialističeskaja Respublika □[3]	186	60.00 N	100.00 E
Rossiter	266	40.53 N	78.56 W
Ross Lake ⊜	256	48.53 N	121.04 W
Ross Lake National Recreation Area ♠	238	48.44 N	121.04 W
Rossland	238	49.05 N	117.48 W
Rosslare	162	52.17 N	6.23 W
Rosslau	164	51.53 N	12.14 E
Rossmoyne	262	40.13 N	76.57 W
Rosso	214	16.30 N	15.49 W
Rosso, Cap ≻	170	42.14 N	8.33 E
Ross-on-Wye	174	51.55 N	2.35 W
Rossony	160	55.53 N	28.49 E
Rossoš'	158	50.12 N	39.34 E
Ross River	236	61.59 N	132.27 W
Ross Sea ⩒[2]	148	76.00 S	175.00 W
Rossville, Ga., U.S.	246	34.59 N	85.16 W
Rossville, Ill., U.S.	268	40.23 N	87.40 W
Rossville, Ind., U.S.	268	40.25 N	86.36 W
Rossville, Kans., U.S.	252	39.08 N	95.57 W
Rosswein	164	51.03 N	13.10 E
Røst II	160	67.28 N	11.59 E
Rosthern	232	52.40 N	106.17 W
Roštkala	186	37.16 N	71.49 E
Rostock	164	54.05 N	12.07 E
Rostov	160	57.11 N	39.25 E
Rostov-na-Donu	158	47.14 N	39.42 E
Røsvatnet ⊜	160	65.45 N	14.00 E
Rosvinskoje	160	66.32 N	52.26 E
Roswell, Ga., U.S.	246	34.01 N	84.22 W
Roswell, N. Mex., U.S.	250	33.24 N	104.32 W
Roswell, Ohio, U.S.	266	40.28 N	81.21 W
Rota	168	36.37 N	6.21 W
Rota I	198	14.10 N	145.12 E
Rotan	250	32.51 N	100.28 W
Rotenburg	178	53.06 N	9.24 E
Rothaargebirge ⋏	164	51.05 N	8.15 E
Rothbury	162	55.19 N	1.55 W
Rothenburg ob der Tauber	164	49.23 N	10.10 E
Rotherham	162	53.26 N	1.20 W
Rothes	162	57.31 N	3.13 W
Rothesay, N.B., Can.	240	45.23 N	66.00 W
Rothesay, Scot., U.K.	162	55.51 N	5.03 W
Rothrist	180	47.19 N	7.53 E
Rothsay	252	46.28 N	96.17 W
Rothschild	244	44.54 N	89.50 W
Rothsville	262	40.09 N	76.15 W
Rothwell	240	46.04 N	66.04 W
Roti, Pulau I	226	10.45 S	123.10 E
Roto	226	33.03 S	145.28 E
Rotoaira, Lake ⊜	230	39.03 S	175.43 E
Rotoehu, Lake ⊜	230	38.01 S	176.32 E
Rotoiti, Lake ⊜, N.Z.	230	38.02 S	176.26 E
Roto-iti, Lake ⊜, N.Z.	230	41.49 S	172.50 E
Rotoma, Lake ⊜	230	38.03 S	176.35 E
Rotondella	170	40.10 N	16.32 E
Rotondo, Monte Λ	170	42.13 N	9.03 E
Rotoroa, Lake ⊜	230	41.52 S	172.39 E
Rotorua	230	38.08 S	176.15 E
Rotorua, Lake ⊜	230	38.05 S	176.16 E
Rott am Inn	164	47.59 N	12.07 E
Rottenburg	180	48.28 N	8.56 E
Rottenburg an der Laaber	164	48.42 N	12.02 E
Rottenmann	164	47.31 N	14.22 E
Rotterdam, Ned.	178	51.55 N	4.28 E
Rotterdam, N.Y., U.S.	261	42.48 N	74.01 W
Rottingdean	174	50.48 N	0.04 W
Rottweil	180	48.10 N	8.37 E
Roubaix	176	50.42 N	3.10 E
Roudnice	164	50.22 N	14.16 E
Rouen	176	49.26 N	1.05 E
Rougé	166	47.47 N	1.27 W
Rougemont	170	47.29 N	6.21 E
Rough ≃	248	37.29 N	87.08 W
Rough River Reservoir ⊜[1]	248	37.40 N	86.25 W
Rouïba	168	36.44 N	3.17 E
Rouillac	166	45.47 N	0.04 W
Roulette	266	41.47 N	78.09 W
Round Harbour	240	49.52 N	55.40 W
Roundhead	268	40.34 N	83.50 W
Round Hill Head ≻	228	24.10 S	151.53 E
Round Island I	225c	19.51 S	57.48 E
Round Lake	252	43.32 N	95.28 W
Round Lake ⊜, Newf., Can.	240	51.08 N	56.33 W
Round Lake ⊜, Ont., Can.	244	45.38 N	77.32 W
Round Lake Beach	268	42.23 N	88.05 W
Round Lake Park	268	42.21 N	88.04 W
Round Mound Λ[2]	252	38.55 N	99.39 W
Round Mountain	258	38.43 N	117.04 W
Round Pond ⊜	240	48.10 N	56.00 W
Round Rock	250	30.31 N	97.41 W
Roundup	256	46.27 N	108.33 W
Royal Tunbridge Wells → Tunbridge Wells	174	51.08 N	0.16 E
Rousay I	162	59.01 N	3.02 W
Rouses Point	260	44.59 N	73.22 W
Rouseville	266	41.28 N	79.42 W
Roussillon □[9]	166	42.30 N	2.30 E
Routhierville	240	48.11 N	67.09 W
Rouville □[6]	260	45.23 N	73.04 W
Rouvray, Lac ⊜	240	49.18 N	70.49 W
Rouyn	244	48.14 N	79.01 W
Rouzerville	262	39.44 N	77.32 W
Rovaniemi	160	66.34 N	25.48 E
Rovato	170	45.34 N	10.00 E
Rovereto	170	45.53 N	11.02 E
Roversi	294	27.36 S	61.58 W
Rovigo	170	45.04 N	11.47 E
Rovigo □[4]	184	45.02 N	11.50 E
Rovinj	170	45.05 N	13.38 E
Rovira	290	4.14 N	75.14 W
Rovno	158	50.37 N	26.15 E
Rovuma (Ruvuma) ≃	218	10.29 S	40.28 E
Rowena	250	31.39 N	100.03 W
Rowland	246	34.32 N	79.18 W
Rowlesburg	242	39.21 N	79.40 W
Rowley	261	42.43 N	70.53 W
Rowley ≃	232	70.16 N	77.45 W
Rowley Island I	232	69.08 N	78.50 W
Rowley Regis	174	52.29 N	2.03 W
Roxa, Ilha I	222	11.15 N	15.40 W
Roxas, Pil.	202	10.19 N	119.19 E
Roxas, Pil.	202	12.38 N	121.30 E
Roxas, Pil.	202	17.08 N	121.35 E
Roxas (Capiz), Pil.	202	11.35 N	122.45 E
Roxboro	246	36.24 N	78.59 W
Roxboro Lake ⊜[1]	246	36.30 N	79.05 W
Roxborough	285r	11.15 N	60.35 W
Roxburgh	230	45.33 S	169.19 E
Roxburgh □[6]	162	55.25 N	2.30 W
Roxbury, Conn., U.S.	261	41.45 N	73.11 W
Roxbury, Pa., U.S.	266	40.07 N	77.40 W
Roxbury, Va., U.S.	262	37.28 N	77.09 W
Roxie	248	31.30 N	91.04 W
Roxo, Cap ≻	222	12.20 N	16.43 W
Roxton	250	33.33 N	95.44 W
Roxton Pond (Sainte-Pudentienne)	260	45.29 N	72.40 W
Roy, N. Mex., U.S.	250	35.57 N	104.12 W
Roy, Utah, U.S.	254	41.10 N	112.02 W
Roy, Wash., U.S.	270	47.00 N	122.33 W
Royal, Iowa, U.S.	252	43.04 N	95.17 W
Royal, Wash., U.S.	256	46.54 N	119.38 W
Royal Center	268	40.52 N	86.30 W
Royale, Isle I	244	48.00 N	89.00 W
Royal Island I	246	25.30 N	76.50 W
Royal Leamington Spa	174	52.18 N	1.31 W
Royal Natal National Park ♠	224	28.45 S	28.57 E
Royal Oak, B.C., Can.	270	48.30 N	123.23 W
Royal Oak, Md., U.S.	262	38.44 N	76.11 W
Royal Oak, Mich., U.S.	268	42.30 N	83.08 W
Royalton, Minn., U.S.	244	45.50 N	94.18 W
Royalton, Pa., U.S.	262	40.11 N	76.44 W
Royan	166	45.37 N	1.01 W
Roye	166	49.42 N	2.48 E
Royersford	262	40.11 N	75.32 W
Royerton	268	40.16 N	85.22 W
Royse City	250	32.59 N	96.20 W
Royston, Eng., U.K.	174	52.03 N	0.01 W
Royston, Ga., U.S.	246	34.17 N	83.06 W
Rožaj	172	42.50 N	20.10 E
Różan	164	53.53 N	21.25 E
Rozewie, Przylądek ≻	164	54.51 N	18.21 E
Rozhnof, Cape ≻	236	55.58 N	160.58 W
Rožňava	164	48.40 N	20.32 E
Roznov	172	46.50 N	26.31 E
Rožnov pod Radhoštěm	164	49.28 N	18.10 E
Rożnów	164	49.46 N	20.42 E
Roztocze Λ	164	50.30 N	23.20 E
Roztoky	164	50.09 N	14.22 E
Rrshen	172	41.47 N	19.54 E
Rtanj ⋏	172	43.45 N	21.50 E
Rtiščevo	158	52.16 N	43.47 E
Ruabon	162	52.59 N	3.02 W
Ruacana Falls ↳	224	17.22 S	14.12 E
Ruahine Range ⋏	230	40.03 S	176.04 E
Ruapehu Λ	230	39.18 S	175.35 E

Symbols in the index entries are identified on page 360.

Name	Page	Lat°′	Long°′
Ruapuke Island I	230	46.46 S	168.31 E
Rubbestadneset	160	59.49 N	5.17 E
Rubcovsk	186	51.33 N	81.10 E
Rubery	174	52.24 N	2.00 W
Rubeshibe	192a	43.47 N	143.38 E
Rubežnoje	158	49.01 N	38.23 E
Rubiataba	296	15.08 S	49.48 W
Rubidoux	274	34.00 N	117.25 W
Rubim	296	16.23 S	40.32 W
Rubio, Méx.	278	28.45 N	106.53 W
Rubio, Ven.	290	7.43 N	72.22 W
Rubtsovsk → Rubcovsk	186	51.33 N	81.10 E
Ruby	236	64.44 N	155.30 W
Ruby ≃	256	45.34 N	112.21 W
Ruby Dome ∧	258	40.37 N	115.28 W
Ruby Lake	258	40.10 N	115.30 W
Ruby Mountains	258	40.25 N	115.35 W
Ruby Range	256	45.15 N	112.15 W
Rucava	160	56.09 N	21.10 E
Ruciane (Niedersee)	164	53.39 N	21.35 E
Ručjuvom	160	66.42 N	61.08 E
Rucphen	178	51.32 N	4.34 E
Ruda Śląska	164	50.18 N	18.51 E
Ruddiman Terrace	268	43.12 N	86.17 W
Rüderdorf	164	52.29 N	13.47 E
Rüdesheim	164	49.59 N	7.56 E
Rudkøbing	164	54.56 N	10.43 E
Rudn'a	160	54.57 N	31.06 E
Rudničnyj	160	59.38 N	52.27 E
Rudnik	164	50.28 N	22.15 E
Rudnyj	158	52.57 N	63.07 E
Rudo	172	43.37 N	19.22 E
Rudolf, Lake ⊜	214	3.30 N	36.00 E
Rudolph	268	41.18 N	83.40 W
Rudolstadt	164	50.43 N	11.20 E
Rudrón ≃	168	42.47 N	3.45 W
Rūd Sar	208	37.08 N	50.18 E
Rudyard, Mich., U.S.	244	46.14 N	84.36 W
Rudyard, Mont., U.S.	256	48.34 N	110.33 W
Rudyerd Bay C	238	55.35 N	130.44 W
Rue	166	50.16 N	1.40 E
Ruecas ≃	168	39.00 N	5.55 W
Ruen (Rujen) ∧	172	42.10 N	22.31 E
Rufā'ah	220	14.46 N	33.22 E
Ruffec	166	46.02 N	0.42 E
Ruffieux	166	45.51 N	5.50 E
Ruffin	246	33.00 N	80.49 W
Rufino	294	34.16 S	62.40 W
Rufisque	222	14.43 N	17.17 W
Rufus	270	45.42 N	120.44 W
Rugao	196	32.25 N	120.36 E
Rugby, Eng., U.K.	174	52.23 N	1.15 W
Rugby, N. Dak., U.S.	252	48.22 N	100.00 W
Rugeley	174	52.46 N	1.55 W
Rügen I	160	54.25 N	13.24 E
Rugged Mountain ∧	238	50.02 N	126.41 W
Ruggles Beach	266	41.22 N	82.29 W
Ruhpolding	164	47.45 N	12.38 E
Ruian	196	27.49 N	120.38 E
Rui Barbosa	296	12.18 S	40.27 W
Ruidosa	250	30.00 N	104.40 W
Ruidoso	254	33.20 N	105.40 W
Ruidoso ≃	254	33.23 N	105.16 W
Ruijin	190	25.50 N	116.00 E
Ruinforme de l'Isalo, Massif	225b	22.45 S	45.15 E
Ruiselede	176	51.03 N	3.24 E
Ruiz	278	21.57 N	105.09 W
Ruiz, Nevado del ∧	290	4.54 N	75.18 W
Ruiz de Montoya	294	26.59 S	55.03 W
Rujen (Ruen) ∧	172	42.10 N	22.31 E
Rūjiena	160	57.54 N	25.21 E
Rukwa, Lake ⊜	218	8.00 S	32.25 E
Rule	250	33.11 N	99.54 W
Ruleville	248	33.44 N	90.33 W
Rulo	252	40.03 N	95.26 W
Rum ≃	244	45.11 N	93.23 W
Ruma	172	45.00 N	19.49 E
Rumbek	214	6.48 N	29.41 E
Rumbeke	176	50.56 N	3.10 E
Rum Cay I	282	23.40 N	74.50 W
Rumeln-Kaldenhausen	178	51.23 N	6.40 E
Rumford	242	44.33 N	70.33 W
Rumia	164	54.35 N	18.25 E
Rumigny	166	49.48 N	4.16 E
Rum Jungle	226	13.01 S	131.00 E
Rummah, Wādī ar- V	208	26.12 N	44.04 E
Rummel	266	40.13 N	78.48 W
Rumoi	192a	43.56 N	141.39 E
Rump Mountain ∧	242	45.12 N	71.04 W
Rumson	262	40.22 N	74.00 W
Rumst	176	51.05 N	4.25 E
Runan	196	33.01 N	114.22 E
Runaway, Cape ≻	230	37.32 S	177.59 E
Rŭng, Kaôh I, Kam.	200	10.35 N	103.17 E
Rŭng, Kaôh I, Kam.	200	10.44 N	103.14 E
Runge	250	28.54 N	97.43 W
Rungus Point ≻	202	13.42 N	124.00 E
Rungwa	218	6.57 S	33.31 E
Rungwa ≃	218	7.36 S	31.50 E
Running Springs	274	34.12 N	117.07 W
Running Water Draw V	250	33.58 N	101.30 W
Ruoqiang	190	38.30 N	88.05 E
Ruoshui ≃	190	41.00 N	100.10 E
Ruovesi	160	61.59 N	24.05 E
Rupat, Pulau I	200	1.50 N	101.35 E
Rupea	172	46.02 N	25.13 E
Rupert, Idaho, U.S.	256	42.37 N	113.41 W
Rupert, W. Va., U.S.	242	37.58 N	80.41 W
Rupert ≃	228	20.53 S	142.23 E
Rupert, Rivière de ≃	232	51.30 N	78.45 W
Rupert House	232	51.29 N	78.45 W
Rupununi □5	290	3.00 N	58.30 W
Rupununi ≃	290	4.03 N	58.35 W
Rural Hall	246	36.15 N	80.18 W
Rural Valley	266	40.48 N	79.18 W
Rurrenabaque	292	14.28 S	67.34 W
Rusape	218	18.32 S	32.07 E
Ruşayriş, Khazzān ar- ⊜1	220	11.40 N	34.20 E
Ruscom Station	266	42.13 N	82.39 W
Ruse	172	43.50 N	25.57 E
Rush	264	42.59 N	77.39 W
Rush ≃, N. Dak., U.S.	252	47.00 N	96.54 W
Rush ≃, Wis., U.S.	244	44.34 N	92.19 W
Rush Center	252	38.28 N	99.19 W
Rush City	244	45.41 N	92.58 W
Rushden	174	52.17 N	0.36 W
Rushford, Minn., U.S.	244	43.49 N	91.46 W
Rushford, N.Y., U.S.	266	42.24 N	78.15 W
Rush Lake ⊜, Ont., Can.	244	47.48 N	82.12 W
Rush Lake ⊜, Wis., U.S.	244	43.49 N	89.00 W
Rushmore	252	43.37 N	95.48 W
Rush Springs	250	34.47 N	97.58 W
Rushsylvania	268	40.28 N	83.41 W
Rushville, Ill., U.S.	248	40.07 N	90.34 W
Rushville, Ind., U.S.	248	39.37 N	85.27 W
Rushville, Nebr., U.S.	252	42.43 N	102.28 W
Rushville, N.Y., U.S.	264	42.46 N	77.14 W
Rusk	250	31.48 N	95.09 W
Ruskin, B.C., Can.	270	49.12 N	122.28 W
Ruskin, Fla., U.S.	246	27.43 N	82.26 W
Russas	286	4.56 S	37.58 W
Russell, Man., Can.	232	50.47 N	101.15 W
Russell, Ont., Can.	264	45.17 N	75.17 W
Russell, Calif., U.S.	272	37.39 N	122.08 W
Russell, Iowa, U.S.	244	40.59 N	93.12 W
Russell, Kans., U.S.	252	38.54 N	98.52 W
Russell, Ky., U.S.	242	38.32 N	82.42 W
Russell, Mass., U.S.	261	42.11 N	72.51 W
Russell, Minn., U.S.	252	44.19 N	95.57 W
Russell, Pa., U.S.	266	41.56 N	79.08 W
Russell □6	264	45.25 N	75.15 W
Russell, Cape ≻	232	75.15 N	117.35 W
Russell, Mount ∧	236	62.48 N	151.52 W
Russell Cave National Monument	248	34.54 N	85.48 W
Russell Island I	232	73.55 N	98.25 W
Russell Islands II	226	9.04 S	159.12 E
Russell Point ≻	232	73.30 N	115.00 W
Russells Point	268	40.28 N	83.54 W
Russell Springs	248	37.03 N	85.05 W
Russellton	266	40.37 N	79.50 W
Russellville, Ala., U.S.	248	34.30 N	87.44 W
Russellville, Ark., U.S.	248	35.17 N	93.08 W
Russellville, Ky., U.S.	248	36.51 N	86.53 W
Russellville, Mo., U.S.	248	38.31 N	92.26 W
Russellville, Oreg., U.S.	270	45.31 N	122.32 W
Rüsselsheim	164	50.00 N	8.25 E
Russi	184	44.22 N	12.02 E
Russia	268	40.14 N	84.24 W
Russian ≃	258	38.27 N	123.08 W
Russian Mission	236	61.34 N	159.34 W
Russian Soviet Federated Socialist Republic → Rossijskaja Sovetskaja Federativnaja	186	60.00 N	100.00 E
Russiaville	268	40.25 N	86.16 W
Russkaja Gavan'	186	76.10 N	62.35 E
Russkij, Ostrov I	186	77.00 N	96.00 E
Russkij Zavorot, Mys ≻	160	68.58 N	54.34 E
Rust	164	47.48 N	16.41 E
Rustajskij	160	56.31 N	44.49 E
Rustavi	158	41.33 N	45.02 E
Rustburg	246	37.17 N	79.06 W
Rustenburg	224	25.37 S	27.08 E
Rustington	174	50.48 N	0.31 W
Ruston, La., U.S.	248	32.32 N	92.38 W
Ruston, Wash., U.S.	270	47.19 N	122.32 W
Rute	168	37.19 N	4.22 W
Ruteng	198	8.36 S	120.27 E
Ruth, Miss., U.S.	248	31.23 N	90.19 W
Ruth, Nev., U.S.	258	39.17 N	114.59 W
Rutherford, Calif., U.S.	272	38.28 N	122.25 W
Rutherford, Tenn., U.S.	248	36.08 N	88.59 W
Rutherfordton	246	35.22 N	81.57 W
Ruther Glen	262	37.56 N	77.27 W
Ruthin	162	53.07 N	3.18 W
Ruthton	252	44.11 N	96.06 W
Ruthven, Ont., Can.	266	42.03 N	82.40 W
Ruthven, Iowa, U.S.	252	43.08 N	94.54 W
Rüti	180	47.16 N	8.51 E
Rutland, B.C., Can.	238	49.53 N	119.24 W
Rutland, Ill., U.S.	268	40.59 N	89.03 W
Rutland, Mass., U.S.	261	42.23 N	71.57 W
Rutland, N. Dak., U.S.	252	46.03 N	97.30 W
Rutland, Vt., U.S.	242	43.36 N	72.59 W
Rutland □6	174	52.38 N	0.40 W
Rutland I	200	11.25 N	92.40 E
Rutledge, Ga., U.S.	246	33.38 N	83.37 W
Rutledge, Tenn., U.S.	246	36.17 N	83.31 W
Rütli	166	46.58 N	8.36 E
Rutshuru	218	1.11 S	29.27 E
Rutter	244	46.06 N	80.10 W
Ruukki	160	64.40 N	25.06 E
Ruvuma (Rovuma) ≃	218	10.29 S	40.28 E
Ruwayḥān, Wādī ar- V	220	29.07 N	30.10 E
Ruwaybah	220	15.39 N	28.45 E
Ružajevka	160	54.04 N	44.57 E
Ružomberok	164	49.06 N	19.18 E
Rwanda □1	218	2.30 S	30.00 E
Ryan	250	34.01 N	97.57 W
Ryan ≃	238	50.25 N	122.43 W
Ryan Peak ∧	256	43.54 N	114.25 W
Ryazan' → R'azan'	160	54.38 N	39.44 E
Rybačij, Poluostrov ≻1	160	69.42 N	32.36 E
Rybačij [Rossitten]	160	55.09 N	20.51 E
Rybač'e, S.S.S.R.	186	46.27 N	81.32 E
Rybač'e, S.S.S.R.	186	42.28 N	76.10 E
Rybinsk	160	58.03 N	38.52 E
Rybinskoje Vodochranilišče ⊜1	160	58.30 N	38.25 E
Rybkino	160	54.15 N	43.46 E
Rybnaja Sloboda	160	55.28 N	50.09 E
Rybnik	164	50.06 N	18.32 E
Rybnoje	160	54.44 N	39.30 E
Rychnov nad Kněžnou	164	50.10 N	16.17 E
Rychwał	164	52.05 N	18.09 E
Rycroft	238	55.45 N	118.43 W
Ryd	160	56.28 N	14.41 E
Ryde	174	50.44 N	1.10 W
Ryder	252	47.55 N	101.40 W
Ryderwood	270	46.23 N	123.03 W
Rydzyna	164	51.48 N	16.40 E
Rye	266	40.59 N	73.41 W
Ryegate	256	46.18 N	109.15 W
Rye Patch Reservoir ⊜1	258	40.38 N	118.18 W
Ryes	166	49.19 N	0.37 W
Ryfoss	160	61.09 N	8.49 E
Rygnestad	160	59.16 N	7.29 E
Rykerts	238	49.00 N	116.35 W
Ryki	164	51.39 N	21.56 E
Ryley	238	53.17 N	112.26 W
Rymanów	164	49.34 N	21.53 E
Rýmařov	164	49.56 N	17.16 E
Ryn (Rhein)	164	53.56 N	21.33 E
Ryōhaku-sanchi	192	36.09 N	136.45 E
Ryōtsu	192	38.05 N	138.26 E
Rypin	164	53.04 N	19.25 E
Rysy ∧	164	49.12 N	20.04 E
Ryūgasaki	192	35.54 N	140.11 E
Ryukyu Islands → Nansei-shotō II	190	26.30 N	128.00 E
Rzepin (Reppen)	164	52.22 N	14.50 E
Rzeszów	164	50.03 N	22.00 E
Ržev	160	56.16 N	34.20 E
S			
Saalach ≃	166	47.51 N	13.00 E
Saales	170	48.21 N	7.07 E
Saalfeld	164	50.39 N	11.22 E
Saanich	270	48.28 N	123.22 W
Saar (Sarre) ≃	166	49.42 N	6.34 E
Saarbrücken	164	49.14 N	6.59 E
Saarburg	164	49.36 N	6.33 E
Saaremaa I	160	58.25 N	22.30 E
Saarijärvi	160	62.43 N	25.16 E
Saarland □3	164	49.20 N	7.00 E
Saarlautern → Saarlouis	164	49.21 N	6.45 E
Saarlouis	164	49.21 N	6.45 E
Saar → Saarland	164	49.20 N	7.00 E
Saavedra	294	37.45 S	62.23 W
Sab, Tônlé	200	12.50 N	104.00 E
Saba I	282	17.38 N	63.10 W
Saba Bank	282	17.25 N	63.30 W
Šabac	172	44.45 N	19.42 E
Sabadell	168	41.33 N	2.06 E
Sabae	192	35.57 N	136.11 E
Sabah (North Borneo) □3	202	5.20 N	117.10 E
Sabak, Cape ≻	237a	52.20 N	173.45 E
Sabalān, Kūhhā-ye	208	38.15 N	47.49 E
Sabana	284m	18.20 N	65.44 W
Sabana, Archipiélago de II	284p	23.00 N	80.00 W
Sabana-Camagüey, Archipiélago de II	284p	22.30 N	79.00 W
Sabana de la Mar	282	19.04 N	69.23 W
Sabana de Mendoza	290	9.26 N	70.46 W
Sabanagrande, Hond.	280	13.50 N	87.15 W
Sabana Grande, P.R.	284m	18.05 N	66.58 W
Sabanalamar, Bahía de C	284p	22.10 N	76.52 W
Sabanalamar, Ensenada C	284p	21.36 N	78.44 W
Sabanalarga	290	10.38 N	74.55 W
Sabana Llana	284m	18.02 N	66.15 W
Sabancuy	278	18.58 N	91.11 W
Sabaneta	290	8.46 N	69.56 W
Sabang	198	5.33 N	95.20 E
Sabanilla	278	25.08 N	101.44 W
Sabará	296	19.54 S	43.48 W
Sābarmati ≃	206	22.25 N	73.20 E
Sabaudia	170	41.18 N	13.01 E
Sabaya	292	19.01 S	68.23 W
Sabbioneta	170	45.00 N	10.39 E
Şāberī, Hāmūn-e ⊜	208	31.30 N	61.20 E
Sabetha	252	39.54 N	95.48 W
Sabhah	214	27.03 N	14.26 E
Sabi (Save) ≃	224	21.00 S	35.02 E
Sabidana, Jabal ∧	220	18.04 N	36.50 E
Sabie (Sábiè) ≃	224	25.19 S	32.18 E
Sabillasville	262	39.42 N	77.27 W
Sabina	242	39.29 N	83.38 W
Sabina ♦1	170	42.15 N	12.42 E
Sabinal	250	29.19 N	99.28 W
Sabinal ≃	250	29.06 N	99.27 W
Sabinal, Cayo I	284p	21.40 N	77.15 W
Sabiñánigo	168	42.31 N	0.22 W
Sabinas	278	27.51 N	101.07 W
Sabinas ≃, Méx.	278	26.50 N	99.35 W
Sabinas ≃, Méx.	278	27.30 N	100.42 W
Sabinas Hidalgo	278	26.30 N	100.10 W
Sabine ≃	234	30.00 N	93.45 W
Sabine Bay C	232	75.35 N	109.30 W
Sabine Lake ⊜	248	29.50 N	93.50 W
Sabine Pass	248	29.44 N	93.52 W
Sabine Peninsula ≻1	232	76.20 N	109.30 W
Sabini, Monti	170	42.13 N	12.50 E
Sabinópolis	296	18.40 S	43.06 W
Sabinov	164	49.06 N	21.06 E
Šabla	172	43.32 N	28.32 E
Sablayan	202	12.50 N	120.46 E
Sable, Cape ≻, N.S., Can.	232	43.25 N	65.35 W
Sable, Cape ≻, Fla., U.S.	246	25.12 N	81.05 W
Sable, Rivière du ≃	232	55.30 N	68.25 W
Sable Island I	240	43.55 N	59.50 W
Sables, River aux ≃	244	46.13 N	82.04 W
Sablé-sur-Sarthe	166	47.50 N	0.20 W
Saboga, Isla I	290	8.35 N	79.04 W
Sabogal ≃	280	10.55 N	84.45 W
Sabor ≃	168	41.10 N	7.07 W
Sabourin, Lac ⊜	244	47.57 N	77.42 W
Sabres	166	44.09 N	0.44 W
Sabrevois	260	45.13 N	73.14 W
Sabrina Coast •2	148	67.00 S	119.30 E
Sabugal	168	40.21 N	7.05 W
Sabula	244	42.04 N	90.10 W
Sabzevār	208	36.13 N	57.42 E
Sac ≃	248	38.01 N	93.43 W
Sacaba	292	17.23 S	66.02 W
Sacaca	292	18.05 S	66.25 W
Sacajawea Peak ∧	256	45.15 N	117.17 W
Sacanche	292	7.07 S	76.46 W
Sacaton	254	33.05 N	111.44 W
Sac City	252	42.25 N	95.00 W
Sacedón	168	40.29 N	2.43 W
Săcele	172	45.37 N	25.42 E
Sachalin, Ostrov I	186	51.00 N	143.00 E
Sachayoj	294	26.41 S	61.50 W
Sachigo ≃	232	55.06 N	88.58 W
Šachovskaja	160	56.02 N	35.29 E
Šachrisabz	186	39.03 N	66.50 E
Sachsen □9	164	51.00 N	13.30 E
Sachsenburg	164	46.50 N	13.21 E
Sachs Harbour	232	72.00 N	125.00 W
Šachterskij	236	64.42 N	177.40 E
Šachty	158	47.42 N	40.13 E
Šachunja	160	57.40 N	46.37 E
Šack	160	54.01 N	41.43 E
Sackets Harbor	264	43.57 N	76.07 W
Säckingen	180	47.33 N	7.56 E
Sackville	240	45.54 N	64.22 W
Saco, Ala., U.S.	248	32.02 N	85.49 W
Saco, Maine, U.S.	242	43.29 N	70.28 W
Saco, Mont., U.S.	256	48.28 N	107.21 W
Saco ≃	240	43.27 N	70.22 W
Saco Bay C	242	43.30 N	70.15 W
Sacol Island I	202	6.57 N	122.15 E
Sacramento, Bra.	296	19.53 S	47.27 W
Sacramento, Calif., U.S.	272	38.35 N	121.30 W
Sacramento □6	272	38.35 N	121.30 W
Sacramento ≃	258	38.03 N	121.56 W
Sacramento, Pampa del ≚	292	8.30 S	75.40 W
Sacramento Mountains	254	33.10 N	105.50 W
Sacramento Valley V	258	39.15 N	122.00 W
Sacramento Wash V	254	34.43 N	114.28 W
Sacre ≃	292	12.56 S	58.18 W
Sacred Heart	252	44.47 N	95.21 W
Săcueni	172	47.21 N	22.06 E
Sacupana	290	8.35 N	61.39 W
Sacuriuiná ≃	292	12.52 S	57.22 W
Sada	168	43.21 N	8.15 W
Sádaba	168	42.17 N	1.16 W
Sá da Bandeira	218	14.55 S	13.30 E
Ṣa'dah	204	16.52 N	43.37 E
Sadaik Taung ∧	200	15.09 N	98.12 E
Sada-misaki ≻	192	33.20 N	132.01 E
Sada-misaki-hantō ≻1	192	33.26 N	132.13 E
Sadanga	202	17.09 N	121.02 E
Saddle Lake Indian Reserve ♦4	238	54.00 N	111.40 W
Saddle Mountain ∧, Colo., U.S.	254	38.50 N	105.28 W
Saddle Mountain ∧, Oreg., U.S.	256	45.58 N	123.41 W
Saddle Mountains	256	46.50 N	119.55 W
Saddle Peak ∧	200	13.13 N	93.00 E
Sa-dec	200	10.18 N	105.45 E
Sa'dīyah, Wādī V	220	20.35 N	39.38 E
Sado I	192	38.00 N	138.25 E
Sado ≃	168	38.29 N	8.55 W
Sado-kaikyō	192	37.50 N	138.40 E
Sadowara	192	32.02 N	131.26 E
Šadrinsk	158	56.05 N	63.38 E
Sadsburyville	262	39.59 N	75.53 W
Sädvaluspen	160	66.24 N	16.51 E
Saegertown	266	41.43 N	80.09 W
Saerluojiahu ⊜	206	33.55 N	86.55 E
Safājah, Jazīrat I	220	26.45 N	33.59 E
Šafárikovo	164	48.27 N	20.20 E
Safed, Āb-i- ≃	206	36.50 N	65.30 E
Säffle	160	59.08 N	12.56 E
Safford	254	32.50 N	109.43 W
Saffron Walden	174	52.01 N	0.15 E
Safi	214	32.20 N	9.17 W
Safīd ≃	208	37.23 N	50.11 E
Safonovo	160	55.06 N	33.15 E
Safovonovo	160	65.42 N	47.39 E
Saga, Nihon	192	33.15 N	130.18 E
Saga, Zhg.	190	29.30 N	85.22 E
Sagae	192	38.22 N	140.17 E
Sagaing	200	21.52 N	95.59 E
Sagaing □8	200	24.00 N	95.00 E
Sagak, Cape ≻	236	52.48 N	169.08 W
Sagamihara	192	35.32 N	139.23 E
Sagami-nada C	192	35.00 N	139.30 E
Sagamore, Mass., U.S.	261	41.45 N	70.33 W
Sagamore, Pa., U.S.	266	40.47 N	79.14 W
Sagamore Beach	261	41.48 N	70.32 W
Sagamore Hills	266	41.19 N	81.34 W
Sagan → Żagań	164	51.37 N	15.19 E
Saganaga Lake ⊜	244	48.14 N	90.52 W
Saganash Lake ⊜	244	49.04 N	82.35 W
Saganoseki	192	33.15 N	131.53 E
Saganthit Kyun I	200	11.56 N	98.29 E
Šagany, Ozero ⊜	172	45.43 N	29.53 E
Sagara	192	34.41 N	138.12 E
Sagavanirktok ≃	236	70.20 N	148.00 W
Sagerton	250	33.05 N	99.58 W
Sag Harbor	261	40.59 N	72.18 W
Saginaw	244	43.25 N	83.58 W
Saginaw ≃	244	43.39 N	83.51 W
Saginaw Bay C	244	43.50 N	83.40 W
Saglek Bay C	232	58.35 N	63.00 W
Šagonar	186	51.32 N	92.48 E
Sagres	168	37.00 N	8.56 W
Sagu	172	46.03 N	21.17 E
Saguache	254	38.05 N	106.08 W
Sagua de Tánamo	284p	20.35 N	75.14 W
Sagua la Chica ≃	284p	22.45 N	79.40 W
Sagua la Grande	284p	22.49 N	80.05 W
Sagua la Grande ≃	284p	22.56 N	80.01 W
Saguaro National Monument ♠	254	32.12 N	110.38 W
Saguenay ≃	240	48.10 N	69.45 W
Sagunto	168	39.41 N	0.16 W
Sahagún, Col.	290	8.57 N	75.27 W
Sahagún, Esp.	168	42.22 N	5.02 W
Sahara ♦2	214	26.00 N	13.00 E
Sahāranpur	206	29.57 N	77.48 E
Sahel, Canal du ☲	222	13.44 N	6.05 W
Sahel, Oued ≃	168	36.45 N	5.04 E
Sahin	172	41.01 N	26.50 E
Sāhiwāl (Montgomery)	206	30.40 N	73.06 E
Ṣaḥrā', Bi'r ▼4	220	22.52 N	28.37 E
Ṣaḥrā', Jabal ∧	220	28.00 N	34.08 E
Sahtlam	270	48.48 N	123.54 W
Sahuaripa	278	29.03 N	109.14 W
Sahuarita	254	31.57 N	110.58 W
Sahuayo	278	20.04 N	102.43 W
Šahy	164	48.05 N	18.57 E
Saibai I	226	9.24 S	142.40 E
Sai Buri	198	6.42 N	101.37 E
Sai Buri ≃	200	6.42 N	101.37 E
Saïda	214	34.50 N	0.11 E
Saidaiji	192	34.39 N	134.02 E
Saïdia	168	35.04 N	2.15 W
Saidpur	206	25.47 N	88.54 E
Saidu	204	34.45 N	72.21 E
Saigō	192	36.12 N	133.20 E
Sai-gon	200	10.45 N	106.40 E
Saijō	192	33.55 N	133.11 E
Sai-kai-kokuritsu-kōen ♠	192	32.12 N	129.22 E
Saiki	192	32.57 N	131.54 E
Saillans	166	44.42 N	5.11 E
Sailor Springs	248	38.46 N	88.22 W
Šaim	158	60.21 N	64.14 E
Saimaa ⊜	160	61.15 N	28.15 E
Saín Alto	278	23.35 N	103.15 W
Sains-en-Gohelle	176	50.27 N	2.41 E
Sainte-Adèle	260	45.57 N	74.08 W
Sainte-Adresse	176	49.30 N	0.05 E
Saint-Adrien	260	45.49 N	71.43 W
Saint-Affrique	166	43.57 N	2.53 E
Saint-Agapit	260	46.34 N	71.26 W
Saint Agatha	264	43.26 N	80.36 W
Sainte-Agathe	252	49.34 N	97.10 W
Sainte-Agathe [-de-Lotbinière]	260	46.23 N	71.24 W
Sainte-Agathe-des-Monts	260	46.03 N	74.17 W
Saint-Agrève	166	45.01 N	4.24 E
Saint-Aignan-sur-Roë	162	47.51 N	1.08 W
Saint-Aimé (Massueville)	260	45.55 N	72.56 W
Saint Alban's, Newf., Can.	240	47.52 N	55.51 W
Saint Albans, Eng., U.K.	174	51.46 N	0.21 W
Saint Albans, Vt., U.S.	242	44.49 N	73.05 W
Saint Albans, W. Va., U.S.	242	38.23 N	81.49 W
Saint Albert, Alta., Can.	238	53.38 N	113.38 W
Saint-Albert, Qué., Can.	260	46.00 N	72.05 W
Saint-Alexandre-de-Kamouraska	240	47.41 N	69.38 W
Saint-Alexis-des-Monts	260	46.28 N	73.09 W
Saint-Amand-de-Vendôme	162	47.41 N	1.01 E
Saint-Amand-les-Eaux	176	50.26 N	3.26 E
Saint-Amand-Mont-Rond	166	46.44 N	2.30 E
Saint-Ambroix	166	44.15 N	4.11 E
Saint-Amour	166	46.26 N	5.21 E
Saint-André, Cap ≻	225b	16.11 S	44.27 E
Saint-André-Avellin	260	45.43 N	75.03 W
Saint-André-de-Cubzac	166	45.00 N	0.27 W
Saint-André-de-l'Eure	166	48.54 N	1.17 E
Saint-André-les-Alpes	166	43.58 N	6.30 E
Saint-André-les-Vergers	176	48.17 N	4.03 E
Saint Andrew	285g	13.15 N	59.33 W
Saint Andrews, Scot., U.K.	162	56.20 N	2.48 W
Saint Andrews, S.C., U.S.	246	32.47 N	80.00 W
Saint Andrew's Channel	240	46.03 N	60.38 W
Saint Andrews East	260	45.34 N	74.20 W
Sainte-Angèle-de-Laval	260	46.20 N	72.31 W
Sainte-Anne, Guad.	285o	16.14 N	61.23 W
Sainte-Anne, Mart.	284e	14.26 N	60.53 W
Saint Anne, Ill., U.S.	268	41.01 N	87.43 W
Sainte-Anne, Lac ⊜, Alta., Can.	238	53.43 N	114.27 W
Sainte-Anne, Lac ⊜, Qué., Can.	240	50.05 N	67.50 W
Sainte-Anne-de-Beaupré	240	47.02 N	70.56 W
Sainte-Anne-de-la-Pérade	260	46.34 N	72.13 W
Sainte-Anne-de-Madawaska	240	47.15 N	68.02 W
Sainte-Anne-des-Chênes	252	49.40 N	96.40 W
Sainte-Anne-des-Monts	240	49.07 N	66.29 W
Sainte-Anne-des-Plaines	260	46.46 N	73.48 W
Saint Anne's	162	53.45 N	3.02 W
Saint Ann's Bay	285q	18.26 N	77.15 W
Saint Ann's Bay C	240	46.20 N	60.30 W
Saint-Anselme	240	46.38 N	70.58 W
Saint Ansgar	244	43.23 N	92.55 W
Saint Anthony, N.B., Can.	240	46.22 N	64.45 W
Saint Anthony, Newf., Can.	240	51.22 N	55.35 W
Saint Anthony, Idaho, U.S.	256	43.58 N	111.41 W
Saint-Antoine-des-Laurentides	260	46.46 N	73.58 W
Saint-Antonin	166	44.09 N	1.45 E
Saint-Apollinaire (Francoeur)	260	46.26 N	71.57 W
Saint Arnaud	228	36.37 S	143.15 E
Saint Arnaud Range	230	41.55 S	172.50 E
Saint-Astier	166	45.09 N	0.32 E
Saint-Auban	166	43.51 N	6.44 E
Saint-Aubin-d'Aubigné	166	48.15 N	1.36 W
Saint-Aubin-lès-Elbeuf	176	49.18 N	1.01 E
Saint-Augustin ≃	232	51.14 N	58.41 W
Saint Augustine	246	29.54 N	81.19 W
Saint-Augustin-Nord-Ouest ≃	240	51.14 N	58.40 W
Saint-Augustin-Saguenay	240	51.14 N	58.39 W
Saint-Aulaye	166	45.12 N	0.08 E
Saint Austell	174	50.20 N	4.48 W
Saint-Avold	166	49.06 N	6.42 E
Saint-Barthélemy I	282	17.55 N	62.50 W
Saint-Basile	240	47.21 N	68.14 W
Saint-Basile-de-Portneuf	260	46.45 N	71.49 W
Saint-Basile-le-Grand	260	45.31 N	73.17 W
Saint Bathans, Mount ∧	230	44.44 S	169.46 E
Saint-Béat	166	42.55 N	0.42 E
Saint Benedict	266	40.38 N	78.44 W
Saint-Benoît, Réu.	225c	21.02 S	55.43 E
Saint-Benoît-du-Sault	166	46.27 N	1.23 E
Saint-Bernard-de-Dorchester	260	46.30 N	71.08 W
Saint-Blaise	260	45.13 N	73.17 W
Saint-Bonaventure, Qué., Can.	260	45.59 N	72.41 W
Saint Bonaventure, N.Y., U.S.	266	42.05 N	78.28 W
Saint Boniface	252	49.55 N	97.06 W
Saint-Boniface-de-Shawinigan	260	46.30 N	72.49 W
Saint-Bonnet-de-Joux	166	46.29 N	4.27 E
Saint-Bonnet-en-Champsaur	166	44.41 N	6.05 E
Saint Brendan's	240	48.52 N	53.39 W
Saint-Brice	162	48.24 N	1.22 W
Saint Bride, Mount ∧	238	51.30 N	115.57 W
Saint Bride's	240	46.55 N	54.10 W
Saint-Brieuc	166	48.31 N	2.47 W
Saint-Bruno	260	45.32 N	73.21 W
Saint-Calais	166	47.55 N	0.45 E
Saint-Calixte-de-Kilkenny	260	45.57 N	73.43 W
Saint-Casimir	260	46.40 N	72.08 W
Saint Catharines	264	43.10 N	79.15 W
Saint Catherine, Monastery of ♦1	220	28.29 N	34.01 E
Saint Catherines Island I	246	31.38 N	81.10 W
Saint Catherine's Point ≻	162	50.34 N	1.15 W
Saint-Célestin (Annaville)	260	46.13 N	72.26 W
Saint-Céré	166	44.52 N	1.53 E
Saint-Césaire	260	45.24 N	73.00 W
Saint-Chamond	182	45.28 N	4.30 E
Saint Charles, Ark., U.S.	248	34.22 N	91.08 W
Saint Charles, Idaho, U.S.	256	42.07 N	111.23 W
Saint Charles, Ill., U.S.	268	41.54 N	88.19 W
Saint Charles, Mich., U.S.	244	43.18 N	84.09 W
Saint Charles, Minn., U.S.	244	43.58 N	92.04 W
Saint Charles, Mo., U.S.	248	38.47 N	90.29 W
Saint-Charles-de-Drummond	260	45.54 N	72.28 W
Saint-Charles-sur-Richelieu	260	45.41 N	73.11 W
Saint-Chély-d'Apcher	166	44.48 N	3.17 E
Saint Christopher (Saint Kitts) I	282	17.21 N	62.48 W
Saint-Chrysostome	260	45.06 N	73.46 W
Saint-Ciers-sur-Gironde	166	45.18 N	0.37 W
Saint Clair, Mich., U.S.	266	42.49 N	82.30 W
Saint Clair, Mo., U.S.	248	38.20 N	90.59 W
Saint Clair, Pa., U.S.	262	40.43 N	76.11 W
Saint Clair □6	266	42.50 N	82.42 W
Saint Clair ≃	244	42.37 N	82.31 W
Saint Clair, Lake ⊜	244	42.25 N	82.41 W
Saint Clair Flats	266	42.32 N	82.37 W
Saint Clair Shores	266	42.30 N	82.54 W
Saint Clairsville, Ohio, U.S.	266	40.05 N	80.54 W
Saint Clairsville, Pa., U.S.	266	40.09 N	78.31 W
Saint-Claude, Man., Can.	252	49.40 N	98.22 W
Saint-Claude, Fr.	180	46.23 N	5.52 E
Saint-Claude, Guad.	285o	16.02 N	61.42 W
Saint-Claud-sur-le-Son	166	45.53 N	0.23 E
Saint Clements	264	43.31 N	80.39 W
Sainte-Clothilde	260	45.59 N	72.14 W
Sainte-Clotilde-de-Châteauguay	260	45.09 N	73.41 W
Saint Cloud, Fla., U.S.	246	28.15 N	81.17 W
Saint Cloud, Minn., U.S.	244	45.33 N	94.10 W
Saint-Constant	260	45.23 N	73.34 W
Sainte-Croix, Qué., Can.	260	46.37 N	71.44 W
Sainte-Croix, Schw.	180	46.49 N	6.31 E
Saint Croix I	282	17.45 N	64.45 W
Saint Croix ≃, N.A.	240	45.10 N	67.10 W
Saint Croix ≃, U.S.	244	44.45 N	92.49 W
Saint Croix Falls	244	45.24 N	92.38 W
Saint Croix Island National Monument ♠	240	45.08 N	67.08 W
Saint-Cuthbert	260	46.09 N	73.13 W
Saint-Cyprien	166	44.52 N	1.02 E
Saint-Cyrille-de-Wendover	260	45.56 N	72.25 W
Saint Cyr Range	236	61.10 N	131.10 W
Saint-Cyr-sur-Loire	176	47.24 N	0.40 E
Saint-Damien-de-Brandon	260	46.20 N	73.29 W
Saint David, Ariz., U.S.	254	31.54 N	110.13 W
Saint David, Ill., U.S.	244	40.30 N	90.03 W
Saint David's, Newf., Can.	240	48.12 N	58.52 W
Saint Davids, Ont., Can.	264	43.10 N	79.06 W
Saint Davids, Wales, U.K.	162	51.54 N	5.16 W
Saint-Denis, Réu.	225c	20.52 S	55.28 E
Saint-Denis, Qué., Can.	260	45.47 N	73.09 W
Saint-Denis, Fr.	176	48.56 N	2.22 E
Saint-Dié	180	48.17 N	6.57 E
Saint-Dizier	180	48.38 N	4.57 E
Saint-Donat-de-Montcalm	260	46.19 N	74.14 W
Sainte → Saint			
Saint-Édouard-de-Maskinongé	260	46.20 N	73.09 W
Saint Edward	252	41.34 N	97.52 W
Saint-Égrève	182	45.14 N	5.41 E
Saint Eleanor's	240	46.25 N	63.49 W
Saint-Éleuthère	240	47.29 N	69.17 W
Saint Elias, Cape ≻	236	59.52 N	144.30 W
Saint Elias, Mount ∧	236	60.18 N	140.55 W
Saint Elias Mountains	236	60.30 N	139.30 W
Saint-Elie	286	4.49 N	53.17 W
Saint Elmo	248	39.02 N	88.51 W
Saint-Éloi	240	48.02 N	69.13 W
Saint-Émile-de-Montcalm	260	46.06 N	74.00 W
Saint-Émile-de-Québec	260	46.52 N	71.21 W
Saint-Émile-de-Suffolk	260	45.56 N	74.55 W
Sainte-Enimie	166	44.22 N	3.26 E
Saint-Étienne	182	45.26 N	4.24 E
Saint-Étienne-des-Grès	260	46.26 N	72.46 W
Saint-Étienne-du-Rouveray	176	49.23 N	1.06 E
Saint-Eugène	260	45.30 N	74.28 W
Saint-Eustache	260	45.34 N	73.53 W
Saint-Fabien	240	48.18 N	68.52 W
Saint-Fargeau	166	47.38 N	3.04 E
Saint-Félicien	232	48.39 N	72.28 W
Sainte-Félicité	240	48.54 N	67.20 W
Saint-Félix-de-Kingsey	260	45.48 N	72.11 W
Saint-Félix-de-Valois	260	46.11 N	73.26 W
Saint-Ferdinand (Bernierville)	260	46.07 N	71.34 W
Saint-Flavien	260	46.31 N	71.36 W
Sainte-Flore	260	46.37 N	72.45 W
Saint-Florent	166	42.41 N	9.19 E
Saint-Florentin	166	48.00 N	3.44 E
Saint-Florent-sur-Cher	166	46.59 N	2.15 E
Saint-Flour	166	45.02 N	3.05 E
Saint-Fons	182	45.42 N	4.52 E
Saint-Fortunat	260	45.58 N	71.36 W
Sainte-Foy	260	46.47 N	71.18 W
Sainte-Foy-la-Grande	166	44.50 N	0.13 E
Sainte-Foy-lès-Lyon	182	45.44 N	4.48 E
Saint Francis, Kans., U.S.	252	39.46 N	101.48 W
Saint Francis, S. Dak., U.S.	252	43.09 N	100.54 W
Saint Francis, Wis., U.S.	268	42.58 N	87.57 W
Saint Francis ≃, N.A.	240	47.10 N	68.57 W
Saint Francis ≃, U.S.	248	34.38 N	90.35 W
Saint Francis, Cape ≻, Newf., Can.	240	47.50 N	52.47 W
Saint Francis, Cape ≻, S. Afr.	224	34.14 S	24.49 E
Saint Francisville	248	30.47 N	91.23 W
Saint-François	285o	16.15 N	61.17 W
Saint-François, Lac ⊜	242	45.55 N	71.10 W
Saint-François-du-Lac	260	46.04 N	72.50 W
Saint Francois Mountains 2	248	37.30 N	90.35 W
Saint-Gabriel	240	48.25 N	68.10 W
Saint-Gabriel-de-Brandon	260	46.18 N	73.23 W
Saint Gabriel-deGaspé	240	48.32 N	64.33 W
Saint-Gall → Sankt Gallen	180	47.25 N	9.23 E
Sainte-Gauburge-Sainte-Colombe	162	48.42 N	0.26 E
Saint-Gaudens	166	43.07 N	0.44 E
Saint-Gaudens National Historic Site ⊥	242	43.29 N	72.19 W
Saint-Gaultier	166	46.38 N	1.25 E
Sainte Genevieve	248	37.59 N	90.03 W
Sainte-Geneviève-de-Batiscan	260	46.32 N	72.21 W
Sainte-Geneviève-des-Bois	176	48.38 N	2.20 E
Saint-Genis-de-Saintonge	166	45.29 N	0.34 W
Saint George, Austl.	228	28.02 S	148.35 E
Saint George, Ber.	284a	32.22 N	64.40 W
Saint George, N.B., Can.	240	45.08 N	66.49 W
Saint George, Ont., Can.	264	43.15 N	80.15 W
Saint George, Alaska, U.S.	236	56.36 N	169.32 W
Saint George, Pa., U.S.	266	41.15 N	79.47 W
Saint George, S.C., U.S.	246	33.11 N	80.35 W
Saint George, Utah, U.S.	254	37.06 N	113.35 W
Saint George, Cape ≻, Newf., Can.	240	48.27 N	59.15 W
Saint George, Cape ≻, Fla., U.S.	246	29.35 N	85.04 W
Saint George, Point ≻	258	41.47 N	124.15 W
Saint George Head ≻	228	35.12 S	150.42 E
Saint George Island	262	38.07 N	76.29 W
Saint George Island I, Alaska, U.S.	236	56.35 N	169.35 W
Saint George Island I, Fla., U.S.	246	29.39 N	84.55 W
Saint George's, Newf., Can.	240	48.26 N	58.29 W
Saint-Georges, Qué., Can.	260	46.39 N	72.39 W
Saint George's, Gren.	285k	12.03 N	61.45 W
Saint-Georges, Guy. fr.	286	3.54 N	51.48 W
Saint Georges, Del., U.S.	262	39.33 N	75.39 W
Saint George's Bay C	240	48.20 N	59.00 W
Saint George's Channel	162	52.00 N	6.00 W
Saint-Georges-de-Windsor	260	45.41 N	71.50 W
Saint George Sound	246	29.47 N	84.42 W
Saint-Gérard	260	45.45 N	71.25 W
Saint-Germain	166	48.54 N	2.05 E
Saint-Germain-de-Grantham	260	45.51 N	72.34 W
Saint-Germain-du-Bois	166	48.38 N	2.20 E
Saint-Germain-en-Laye	176	48.54 N	2.05 E
Saint-Germain-Lembron	166	45.28 N	3.14 E
Saint-Germain-l'Herm	166	45.28 N	3.33 E
Sainte-Gertrude (Villers)	260	46.18 N	72.17 W
Saint-Gervais-d'Auvergne	166	46.02 N	2.49 E
Saint-Gervais-les-Bains	170	45.54 N	6.43 E
Saint Géry	166	44.29 N	1.35 E
St.-Gilles, Bel.	176	50.49 N	4.20 E
Saint-Gilles, Qué., Can.	260	46.31 N	71.22 W
Saint-Gilles, Fr.	182	43.41 N	4.26 E
Saint-Gilles-sur-Vie	166	46.42 N	1.57 W
Saint-Girons	166	42.59 N	1.09 E
Saint Gotthard Pass → San Gottardo, Passo del)(	180	46.33 N	8.34 E
Saint-Grégoire (Larochelle)	260	46.16 N	72.31 W
Saint Gregory, Mount ∧	240	49.19 N	58.13 W
Saint-Guénolé	162	47.49 N	4.20 W
Saint-Guillaume-d'Upton	260	45.52 N	72.46 W
Saint Helena	272	38.30 N	122.28 W
Saint Helena I	148	15.57 S	0.54 W
Saint Helena Bay C	218	32.43 S	18.05 E
Saint Helena Sound	246	32.27 N	80.25 W
Sainte-Hélène-de-Bagot	260	45.44 N	72.42 W
Saint Helen's, Eng., U.K.	162	50.42 N	1.06 W
Saint Helens, Oreg., U.S.	270	45.52 N	122.48 W
Saint Helier	162	49.12 N	2.37 W
Saint Henry	268	40.25 N	84.38 W
Sainte-Hermine	166	46.33 N	1.04 W
Saint-Hilaire-du-Harcouët	166	48.35 N	1.06 W
Saint-Hilaire-Est	260	45.34 N	73.11 W
Saint-Hippolyte	170	47.19 N	6.49 E
Saint-Hippolyte-de-Kilkenny	260	45.56 N	74.02 W
Saint-Hippolyte-du-Fort	166	43.58 N	3.51 E
Saint-Hubert	260	45.30 N	73.25 W
Saint-Hugues	260	45.48 N	72.51 W
Saint-Hyacinthe	260	45.38 N	72.57 W
Saint-Hyacinthe □6	260	45.40 N	73.05 W
Saint-Ignace, N.B., Can.	240	46.42 N	65.05 W
Saint Ignace, Mich., U.S.	244	45.52 N	84.43 W
Saint Ignace Island I	244	48.48 N	87.55 W
Saint Ignatius	256	47.19 N	114.06 W
Saint Ignatius Mission	290	3.19 N	59.47 W
Saint-Imier	180	47.09 N	7.00 E
Saint-Isidore	240	47.33 N	65.03 W
Saint-Isidore-d'Auckland	260	45.16 N	71.31 W
Saint Ives	162	50.12 N	5.29 W
Saint Jacobs	264	43.32 N	80.33 W
Saint-Jacques	260	45.56 N	73.34 W
Saint James, Man., Can.	252	49.54 N	97.15 W
Saint James, Mich., U.S.	244	45.45 N	85.31 W
Saint James, Minn., U.S.	252	43.59 N	94.38 W

Symbols in the index entries are identified on page 360.

Name	Page	Lat°′	Long°′
Saint James, Mo., U.S.	248	38.00 N	91.37 W
Saint James, N.Y., U.S.	261	40.53 N	73.09 W
Saint James, Cape ≻	238	51.56 N	131.01 W
Saint-Janvier	260	45.43 N	73.56 W
Saint-Jean	260	45.19 N	73.15 W
Saint-Jean □[6]	260	45.15 N	73.20 W
Saint-Jean ≃, Qué., Can.	240	48.46 N	64.25 W
Saint-Jean ≃, Qué., Can.	240	50.17 N	64.20 W
Saint-Jean, Lac ⊜	232	48.35 N	72.00 W
Saint-Jean-Baptiste	252	49.16 N	97.21 W
Saint-Jean-Baptiste-de-Rouville	260	45.31 N	73.01 W
Saint-Jean-d'Angély	166	45.57 N	0.31 W
Saint-Jean-de-Bournay	166	45.29 N	5.08 E
Saint-Jean-de-Losne	166	47.06 N	5.15 E
Saint-Jean-de-Maurienne	182	45.17 N	6.21 E
Saint-Jean-de-Monts	166	46.48 N	2.03 W
Saint-Jean-des-Piles	260	46.41 N	72.44 W
Saint-Jean-du-Gard	166	44.06 N	3.53 E
Saint-Jean-en-Royans	166	45.01 N	5.18 E
Saint-Jean-Pied-de-Port	166	43.10 N	1.14 W
Saint-Jean-Port-Joli	240	47.13 N	70.16 W
Saint-Jérôme	260	45.46 N	74.00 W
Saint Jo	250	33.42 N	97.31 W
Saint-Joachim	266	42.16 N	82.38 W
Saint Joe	268	41.19 N	84.54 W
Saint Joe ≃	256	47.21 N	116.42 W
Saint John, N.B., Can.	240	45.16 N	66.03 W
Saint John, Ind., U.S.	268	41.27 N	87.28 W
Saint John, Kans., U.S.	252	38.00 N	98.46 W
Saint John, N. Dak., U.S.	252	48.57 N	99.43 W
Saint John, Wash., U.S.	256	47.05 N	117.35 W
Saint John I	282	18.20 N	64.45 W
Saint John ≃, Liber.	222	6.40 N	9.10 W
Saint John ≃, N.A.	240	45.15 N	66.04 W
Saint John, Cape ≻	240	50.00 N	55.32 W
Saint John, Lake ⊜	240	48.23 N	54.41 W
Saint John Bay C	240	50.54 N	57.08 W
Saint John Island I	240	50.49 N	57.14 W
Saint Johns, Antig.	284c	17.06 N	61.51 W
Saint John's, Newf., Can.	240	47.34 N	52.43 W
Saint Johns, Ariz., U.S.	254	34.30 N	109.22 W
Saint Johns, Mich., U.S.	268	43.00 N	84.33 W
Saint Johns, Ohio, U.S.	268	40.33 N	84.05 W
Saint Johns ≃	246	30.24 N	81.24 W
Saint Johnsbury	242	44.25 N	72.01 W
Saint Joseph, N.B., Can.	240	45.59 N	64.34 W
Saint-Joseph, Qué., Can.	260	45.37 N	72.55 W
Saint Joseph, Dom.	284d	15.24 N	61.26 W
Saint-Joseph, Mart.	284e	14.40 N	61.03 W
Saint-Joseph, Réu.	225c	21.22 S	55.36 E
Saint Joseph, Ill., U.S.	248	40.07 N	88.02 W
Saint Joseph, La., U.S.	248	31.55 N	91.14 W
Saint Joseph, Mich., U.S.	268	42.06 N	86.29 W
Saint Joseph, Mo., U.S.	248	39.46 N	94.51 W
Saint Joseph □[6], Ind., U.S.	268	41.41 N	86.15 W
Saint Joseph □[6], Mich., U.S.	268	41.55 N	85.31 W
Saint Joseph ≃, U.S.	244	42.07 N	86.29 W
Saint Joseph ≃, U.S.	244	41.05 N	85.08 W
Saint Joseph, Lake ⊜	232	51.05 N	90.35 W
Saint Joseph Bay C	246	29.47 N	85.21 W
Saint Joseph Channel ⌣	244	46.16 N	83.51 W
Saint-Joseph-de-Beauce	240	46.18 N	70.52 W
Saint-Joseph-de-Mékinac	260	46.55 N	72.42 W
Saint-Joseph-de-Sorel	260	46.03 N	73.08 W
Saint Joseph Island I, Ont., Can.	244	46.13 N	83.57 W
Saint Joseph Island I, Tex., U.S.	250	28.10 N	96.45 W
Saint-Jovite	260	46.07 N	74.36 W
Sainte-Julie-de-Verchères	260	45.36 N	73.21 W
Saint-Julien-en-Born	166	44.04 N	1.14 W
Saint-Julien-en-Genevois	166	46.08 N	6.05 E
Sainte-Julienne	260	45.57 N	73.43 W
Saint-Junien	166	45.53 N	0.54 E
Saint Just	284m	18.23 N	66.00 W
Saint-Just-en-Chaussée	166	49.30 N	2.26 E
Saint-Just-en-Chevalet	166	45.55 N	3.50 E
Saint-Justin	260	46.15 N	73.05 W
Saint Kilda	230	45.54 S	170.31 E
Saint Kilda I	162	57.49 N	8.36 W
Saint Kitts (Saint Christopher) I	282	17.21 N	62.48 W
Saint Kitts-Nevis-Anguilla □[2]	282	17.20 N	62.45 W
Saint-Lambert	242	45.30 N	73.31 W
Saint Landry	248	30.51 N	92.15 W
Saint-Laurent	260	45.31 N	73.41 W
Saint-Laurent-du-Maroni	286	5.30 N	54.02 W
Saint-Laurent-du-Var	182	43.40 N	7.11 E
Saint-Laurent-et-Benon	166	45.09 N	0.49 W
Saint Lawrence	240	46.55 N	55.23 W
Saint Lawrence □[6]	264	44.30 N	75.27 W
Saint Lawrence ≃	232	49.30 N	67.00 W
Saint Lawrence, Cape ≻	240	47.03 N	60.37 W
Saint Lawrence, Gulf of C	240	48.00 N	62.00 W
Saint Lawrence Island I	236	63.30 N	170.30 W
Saint-Léandre	240	48.43 N	67.36 W
Saint-Léonard, N.B., Can.	240	47.10 N	67.56 W
Saint-Léonard, Qué., Can.	260	45.35 N	73.33 W
Saint Leonard, Md., U.S.	262	38.28 N	76.30 W
Saint-Léonard-d'Aston	260	46.06 N	72.23 W
Saint-Léonard-de-Noblat	166	45.50 N	1.29 E
Saint-Leu-la-Forêt	176	49.01 N	2.15 E
Saint-Liboire	260	45.39 N	72.46 W
Saint-Lô	166	49.07 N	1.05 W
Saint-Louis, Réu.	225c	21.16 S	55.25 E
Saint-Louis, Fr.	180	47.35 N	7.34 E
Saint-Louis, Guad.	285o	15.57 N	61.19 W
Saint-Louis, Sén.	222	16.02 N	16.30 W
Saint Louis, Mich., U.S.	244	43.25 N	84.36 W
Saint Louis, Mo., U.S.	248	38.38 N	90.11 W
Saint-Louis-de-Champlain	260	46.25 N	72.36 W
Saint-Louis-de-Kent	240	46.44 N	64.58 W
Saint Louis Park	244	44.56 N	93.22 W
Saint Louisville	266	40.10 N	82.25 W
Saint-Loup-sur-Semouse	170	47.53 N	6.16 E
Saint-Luc	260	45.21 N	73.18 W
Sainte-Luce	284e	14.28 N	60.56 W
Saint Lucia □[2]	276	13.53 N	60.58 W
Saint Lucia, Cape ≻	224	28.25 S	32.25 E
Saint Lucia, Lake ⊜	224	28.05 S	32.26 E
Saint Lucia Channel ⌣	282	14.15 N	61.00 W
Sainte-Lucie	170	41.42 N	9.22 E
Saint Lucie Canal ≊	246	27.10 N	80.15 W
Saint Lucie Inlet C	246	27.10 N	80.10 W
Saint Magnus Bay C	162	60.25 N	1.35 W
Saint-Malo, Qué., Can.	260	45.12 N	71.30 W
Saint-Malo, Fr.	166	48.39 N	2.01 W
Saint-Malo, Golfe de C	166	48.45 N	2.00 W
Saint-Mamert[-du-gard]	166	43.53 N	4.12 E
Saint-Marc	282	19.07 N	72.42 W
Saint-Marc, Canal de ⌣	282	18.45 N	72.40 W
Saint-Marc-des-Carrières	260	46.41 N	72.03 W
Saint-Marcellin	166	45.09 N	5.19 E
Sainte-Marcelline-de-Radstock	260	46.07 N	73.36 W
Saint Margaret Bay C	240	51.01 N	56.58 W
Saint Margaret's Bay C	240	44.35 N	64.00 W
Sainte-Marguerite ≃	240	50.10 N	66.40 W
Sainte-Marguerite, Baie C	240	50.06 N	66.36 W
Sainte-Marie	284e	14.47 N	61.00 W
Sainte-Marie, Cap ≻	225b	25.36 S	45.08 E
Sainte-Marie, Île I	225b	16.50 S	49.55 E
Sainte-Marie-aux-Mines (Markirch)	180	48.15 N	7.11 E
Sainte-Marie-du-Mont	162	49.23 N	1.13 W
Saint Maries	256	47.19 N	116.35 W
Saint Maries ≃	256	47.19 N	116.33 W
Saint Marks	246	30.09 N	84.12 W
Saint Marks ≃	246	30.08 N	84.12 W
Sainte-Marthe-de-Gaspé	240	49.13 N	66.10 W
Saint Martin (Sint Maarten) I	282	18.04 N	63.04 W
Saint Martin, Lake ⊜	232	51.37 N	98.29 W
Saint-Martin-Boulogne	176	50.43 N	1.38 E
Saint-Martin-de-Londres	166	43.47 N	3.44 E
Sainte-Martine	260	45.15 N	73.48 W
Saint Martins	240	45.21 N	65.32 W
Saint-Martin-Vésubie	166	44.04 N	7.15 E
Saint Martinville	248	30.07 N	91.50 W
Saint Mary ≃, B.C., Can.	238	49.37 N	115.38 W
Saint Mary ≃, N.A.	238	49.37 N	112.52 W
Saint Mary, Cape ≻, N.S., Can.	240	44.05 N	66.13 W
Saint Mary, Cape ≻, Gam.	222	13.28 N	16.40 W
Saint Mary Lake ⊜	256	48.40 N	113.30 W
Saint Mary Peak ∧	228	31.30 S	138.33 E
Saint Mary Reservoir ⊜[1]	238	49.19 N	113.12 W
Saint Marys, Austl.	226	41.35 S	148.10 E
Saint Mary's, Newf., Can.	240	46.55 N	53.35 W
Saint Marys, Ont., Can.	264	43.16 N	81.08 W
Saint Mary's, Eng., U.K.	162	49.55 N	6.17 W
Saint Marys, Alaska, U.S.	236	62.04 N	163.10 W
Saint Marys, Ga., U.S.	246	30.44 N	81.33 W
Saint Marys, Ind., U.S.	268	41.43 N	86.16 W
Saint Marys, Kans., U.S.	252	39.12 N	96.04 W
Saint Marys, Ohio, U.S.	268	40.33 N	84.23 W
Saint Marys, Pa., U.S.	266	41.26 N	78.34 W
Saint Marys, W. Va., U.S.	242	39.23 N	81.12 W
Saint Marys □[6]	262	38.17 N	76.38 W
Saint Mary's ≃, N.S., Can.	240	45.02 N	61.54 W
Saint Marys ≃, U.S.	242	41.05 N	85.08 W
Saint Marys ≃, U.S.	246	30.43 N	81.27 W
Saint Mary's, Cape ≻	240	46.49 N	54.12 W
Saint Mary's Bay C, Newf., Can.	240	46.50 N	53.47 W
Saint Mary's Bay C, N.S., Can.	240	44.25 N	66.10 W
Saint Marys City	262	38.11 N	76.26 W
Saint-Mathieu	166	45.42 N	0.46 E
Saint-Mathieu, Pointe de ≻	166	48.20 N	4.46 W
Saint Matthew Island I	236	60.30 N	172.45 W
Saint Matthews, Ky., U.S.	248	38.15 N	85.39 W
Saint Matthews, S.C., U.S.	246	33.40 N	80.46 W
Saint-Maur-des-Fossés	176	48.48 N	2.30 E
Sainte-Maure-du-Touraine	166	47.07 N	0.37 E
Saint-Maurice □[6]	260	46.35 N	73.00 W
Saint-Maurice ≃	232	46.22 N	72.32 W
Saint-Max	180	48.42 N	6.13 E
Sainte-Maxime	166	43.18 N	6.38 E
Saint-Méen	162	48.11 N	2.12 W
Saint-Méen-le-Grand	166	48.11 N	2.12 W
Saint Meinrad	248	38.10 N	86.49 W
Sainte-Menehould	166	49.05 N	4.54 E
Sainte-Mère-Église	166	49.25 N	1.19 W
Saint Michael, Alaska, U.S.	236	63.29 N	162.02 W
Saint Michael, Pa., U.S.	266	40.20 N	78.46 W
Saint Michaels	242	38.47 N	76.14 W
Saint-Michel	260	45.35 N	73.35 W
Saint-Michel, Mont ∧[2]	166	48.21 N	3.57 W
Saint-Michel-de-Napierville	260	45.15 N	73.34 W
Saint-Michel-des-Saints	260	46.40 N	73.55 W
Saint-Mihiel	166	48.54 N	5.33 E
Sainte-Monique-des-Deux-Montagnes	260	45.41 N	74.00 W
Saint-Moritz → Sankt Moritz	180	46.30 N	9.50 E
Saint-Narcisse	260	46.34 N	72.28 W
Saint-Nazaire	166	47.17 N	2.12 W
Saint Nazianz	244	44.00 N	87.55 W
Saint Neots	174	52.14 N	0.17 W
Saint-Nicéphore	260	45.50 N	72.27 W
Saint-Nicolas → Sint-Niklaas, Bel.	176	51.10 N	4.08 E
Saint-Nicolas, Qué., Can.	260	46.42 N	71.24 W
Saint-Nicolas-de-Port	180	48.38 N	6.18 E
Saint-Norbert-d'Arthabaska	260	46.07 N	71.50 W
Saint-Omer	176	50.45 N	2.15 E
Saintonge □[9]	166	45.30 N	0.30 W
Saint-Ouen-l'Aumône	176	49.03 N	2.06 E
Saint-Pacôme	240	47.24 N	69.57 W
Saint-Pamphile	240	46.58 N	69.47 W
Saint Paris	242	40.07 N	83.58 W
Saint-Pascal	240	47.32 N	69.48 W
Saint-Patrick, Lac ⊜	242	46.21 N	77.18 W
Saint-Paul, Réu.	225c	21.00 S	55.16 E
Saint Paul, Alta., Can.	238	53.59 N	111.17 W
Saint-Paul, Fr.	170	43.42 N	7.07 E
Saint Paul, Ind., U.S.	248	39.26 N	85.38 W
Saint Paul, Minn., U.S.	244	44.58 N	93.07 W
Saint Paul, Nebr., U.S.	252	41.13 N	98.27 W
Saint Paul, Oreg., U.S.	270	45.12 N	122.58 W
Saint Paul, Va., U.S.	246	36.54 N	82.19 W
Saint-Paul ≃, Can.	232	51.26 N	57.40 W
Saint Paul ≃, Liber.	222	7.10 N	10.00 W
Saint Paul, Cape ≻	222	5.49 N	0.57 E
Saint-Paul, Île I	148	38.43 S	77.29 E
Saint Paul Bay C	202	10.13 N	118.50 E
Saint-Paul-de-Chester (Chesterville)	260	45.57 N	71.49 W
Saint-Paulien	166	45.08 N	3.49 E
Saint-paulin	260	46.22 N	73.02 W
Saint Paul Island	236	57.07 N	170.17 W
Saint Paul Island I, N.S., Can.	240	47.15 N	60.10 W
Saint Paul Island I, Alaska, U.S.	236	57.10 N	170.15 W
Saint-Paul-l'Ermite	260	45.45 N	73.28 W
Saint Pauls	246	34.48 N	78.58 W
Saint Pauls Inlet C	240	49.50 N	57.45 W
Saint Peter	244	44.17 N	93.57 W
Saint Peter Port	162	49.27 N	2.32 W
Saint Peter's	240	45.40 N	60.52 W
Saint Peters Bay	240	46.25 N	62.35 W
Saint Petersburg → Leningrad, S.S.S.R.	160	59.55 N	30.15 E
Saint Petersburg, Fla., U.S.	246	27.46 N	82.38 W
Saint Petersburg, Pa., U.S.	266	41.10 N	79.37 W
Saint-Philippe-d'Argenteuil	260	45.37 N	74.28 W
Saint-Pie	260	45.30 N	72.54 W
Saint-Pierre, Réu.	225c	21.19 S	55.29 E
Saint-Pierre, Qué., Can.	260	45.27 N	73.39 W
Saint-Pierre, Mart.	284e	14.45 N	61.11 W
Saint-Pierre, St. P./M.	240	46.40 N	56.00 W
Saint-Pierre I	240	46.47 N	56.11 W
Saint-Pierre, Lac ⊜, Qué., Can.	240	50.07 N	68.27 W
Saint-Pierre, Lac ⊜, Qué., Can.	242	46.10 N	72.50 W
St. Pierre and Miquelon □[2]	232	46.55 N	56.10 W
Saint-Pierre-de-Broughton	260	46.15 N	71.12 W
Saint-Pierre-des-Corps	176	47.23 N	0.44 E
Saint-Pierre-Église	166	49.40 N	1.24 W
Saint Pierre Island I	218	9.19 S	50.43 E
Saint-Pierre-Jolys	252	49.26 N	96.59 W
Saint Pierre-le-Moûtier	166	46.48 N	3.07 E
Saint-Pierre-sur-Dives	162	49.01 N	0.02 W
Saint-Pierreville	166	44.49 N	4.29 E
Saint-Pol-de-Léon	166	48.41 N	3.59 W
Saint-Pol-sur-Mer	176	51.02 N	2.21 E
Saint-Pol-sur-Ternoise	176	50.23 N	2.20 E
Saint-Polycarpe	260	45.18 N	74.19 W
Saint-Pons	166	43.29 N	2.46 E
Saint-Pourçain-sur-Sioule	166	46.19 N	3.17 E
Saint-Priest	182	45.42 N	4.57 E
Saint-Prosper-de-Dorchester	242	46.13 N	70.29 W
Saint-Quentin, N.B., Can.	240	47.30 N	67.23 W
Saint-Quentin, Fr.	176	49.51 N	3.17 E
Saint-Rambert-l'Île-Barbe	182	45.48 N	4.49 E
Saint-Raphaël	182	43.25 N	6.46 E
Saint-Raymond	260	46.53 N	71.50 W
Saint-Rédempteur	260	46.42 N	71.15 W
Saint Regis	256	47.18 N	115.06 W
Saint Regis ≃	256	47.18 N	115.05 W
Saint Regis Falls	242	44.40 N	74.33 W
Saint-Rémi	260	45.16 N	73.37 W
Saint-Rémi-d'Amherst	260	46.01 N	74.47 W
Saint-Rémy-de-Provence	166	43.47 N	4.50 E
Saint-Renan	166	48.26 N	4.37 W
Saint-Roch-de-l'Achigan	260	45.51 N	73.36 W
Saint-Roch-de-Mékinac	260	46.47 N	72.48 W
Saint-Romuald-d'Etchemin	260	46.45 N	71.14 W
Sainte-Rosalie	260	45.39 N	72.54 W
Sainte-Rose	285o	16.20 N	61.42 W
Sainte-Rose-du-Dégelé	240	47.33 N	68.39 W
Saintes	166	45.45 N	0.52 W
Saintes, Îles des II	282	15.52 N	61.36 W
Saint-Sauveur-des-Monts	260	45.52 N	74.09 W
Saint-Sauveur-sur-Tinée	166	44.05 N	7.06 E
Sainte-Savine	176	48.18 N	4.03 E
Saint-Savinien	166	45.53 N	0.41 W
Saint-Savin-sur-Gironde	166	46.34 N	0.52 E
Sainte-Scholastique	260	45.41 N	74.06 W
Saint-Sébastien	260	45.09 N	73.09 W
Saint-Sébastien, Cap ≻	225b	12.26 S	48.44 E
Saint-Seine-l'Abbaye	166	47.26 N	4.47 E
Saint Servan	166	48.38 N	2.01 W
Saint Shott's	240	46.38 N	53.35 W
Saint Simons Island	246	31.08 N	81.24 W
Saint Simons Island I	246	31.14 N	81.21 W
Sainte-Sophie-de-Mégantic	260	46.11 N	71.43 W
Saint-Stanislas-de-Kosta	260	45.13 N	74.08 W
Saint Stephen, N.B., Can.	240	45.12 N	67.17 W
Saint Stephen, S.C., U.S.	246	33.24 N	79.55 W
Saint Stephens	244	45.43 N	94.16 W
Saint-Sulpice-les-Feuilles	166	46.19 N	1.22 E
Saint-Sylvestre	260	46.22 N	71.13 W
Saint-Symphorien, Fr.	166	44.26 N	0.30 W
Saint-Symphorien, Fr.	176	47.24 N	0.42 E
Sainte-Thècle	260	46.48 N	72.30 W
Saint-Théodore-d'Acton	260	45.42 N	72.35 W
Sainte-Thérèse-de-Blainville	260	45.39 N	73.49 W
Saint Thomas, Ont., Can.	264	42.47 N	81.12 W
Saint Thomas, N. Dak., U.S.	252	48.37 N	97.27 W
Saint Thomas → Charlotte Amalie, Vir. Is. U.S.	284m	18.21 N	64.56 W
Saint Thomas I	282	18.21 N	64.55 W
Saint Timothée	260	45.17 N	74.03 W
Saint-Tite	260	46.44 N	72.34 W
Saint-Tite-des-Caps	240	47.08 N	70.47 W
Saint-Tropez	166	43.16 N	6.38 E
Saint-Ubald	260	46.45 N	72.16 W
Saint-Urbain-de-Charlevoix	240	47.33 N	70.32 W
Saint-Vaast-la-Hougue	162	49.36 N	1.16 W
Saint-Valéry-en-Caux	166	49.52 N	0.44 E
Saint-Valéry-sur-Somme	166	50.11 N	1.38 E
Saint-Vallier	166	45.10 N	4.49 E
Saint-Vallier-de-Thiey	170	43.42 N	6.51 E
Saint-Varent	166	46.53 N	0.14 W
Saint Vincent, Minn., U.S.	252	48.58 N	97.14 W
Saint Vincent, Pa., U.S.	266	40.17 N	79.24 W
Saint Vincent □[2]	276	13.15 N	61.12 W
Saint-Vincent, Cap ≻	225b	21.57 S	43.16 E
Saint Vincent, Cape, Austl.	228	43.18 S	145.50 E
Saint Vincent, Cape → São Vicente, Cabo de ≻, Port.	168	37.01 N	9.00 W
Saint Vincent, Gulf C	228	35.00 S	138.05 E
Saint-Vincent-de-Tyrosse	166	43.40 N	1.18 W
Saint Vincent Passage ⌣	282	13.30 N	61.00 W
Saint Vincent's	240	46.48 N	53.38 W
Saint Vital	252	49.49 N	97.08 W
Saint-Vith	164	50.17 N	6.08 E
Saint-Vivien-de-Médoc	166	45.26 N	1.02 W
Saint Vrain Creek ≃	254	40.16 N	104.52 W
Saint Williams	264	42.40 N	80.25 W
Saint-Yrieix-la-Perche	166	45.31 N	1.12 E
Saint-Yvon	240	49.10 N	64.48 W
Saint-Zénon	260	46.35 N	73.51 W
Sairecábur, Cerro ∧	292	22.43 S	67.54 W
Saitama □[5]	192	35.59 N	139.24 E
Saito	192	32.06 N	131.24 E
Saitula	190	36.21 N	78.02 E
Sajama	292	18.07 S	69.00 W
Sajama, Nevado ∧	292	18.06 S	68.54 W
Sajia	190	28.55 N	88.05 E
Sajnšand	190	44.55 N	110.11 E
Sajó ≃	164	47.56 N	21.08 E
Sajószentpéter	164	48.13 N	20.44 E
Sak ≃	224	30.52 S	20.25 E
Sakai	192	34.35 N	135.28 E
Sakaide	192	34.19 N	133.52 E
Sakai-minato	192	35.33 N	133.15 E
Sakākā	208	29.59 N	40.06 E
Sakakawea, Lake ⊜[1]	252	47.50 N	102.20 W
Sakami ≃	232	53.40 N	76.40 W
Sakami, Lac ⊜	232	53.20 N	76.45 W
Sakania	218	12.45 S	28.34 E
Sakarya □[4]	212	40.45 N	30.35 E
Sakarya ≃, Tür.	212	41.07 N	30.39 E
Sakarya ≃, Tür.	212	39.40 N	30.55 E
Sakata	192	38.55 N	139.50 E
Sakawa	192	33.30 N	133.17 E
Sakété	222	6.43 N	2.40 E
Sakhalin → Sachalin, Ostrov I	186	51.00 N	143.00 E
Sakhnīn	210	32.52 N	35.17 E
Šakiai	160	54.57 N	23.03 E
Sakiet Sidi Youssef	170	36.13 N	8.22 E
Sakito	192	33.02 N	129.32 E
Sakon Nakhon	200	17.10 N	104.01 E
Sakonnet	261	41.28 N	71.12 W
Sakskøbing	164	54.48 N	11.39 E
Saku	192	36.09 N	138.26 E
Sakuma	192	35.05 N	137.48 E
Sakura	192	35.43 N	140.14 E
Sakurai	192	34.30 N	135.51 E
Sal I	222a	16.45 N	22.55 W
Sal ≃	158	47.31 N	40.45 E
Sal, Cay I	282	23.42 N	80.24 W
Sal, Punta ≻	280	15.55 N	87.36 W
Šal'a, Česko.	164	48.09 N	17.52 E
Sala, Sve.	160	59.55 N	16.36 E
Sala Consilina	170	40.24 N	15.36 E
Salacrīva	160	57.45 N	24.21 E
Salada, Laguna ⊜	278	32.20 N	115.40 W
Saladas	294	28.15 S	58.38 W
Saladillo	294	35.38 S	59.48 W
Saladillo ≃	294	29.07 S	63.23 W
Saladillo Dulce ≃	294	31.25 S	60.33 W
Salado, Arg.	294	28.18 S	67.15 W
Salado, Chile	294	26.25 S	70.19 W
Salado ≃, Arg.	294	37.48 S	66.10 W
Salado ≃, Arg.	294	31.40 S	60.41 W
Salado ≃, Arg.	294	35.44 S	57.22 W
Salado ≃, Cuba	284p	20.38 N	76.57 W
Salado ≃, Méx.	278	26.50 N	99.17 W
Salado, Rio ≃	254	34.16 N	106.52 W
Šalakuša	160	62.15 N	40.17 E
Salala	294	30.41 S	71.32 W
Şalālah	204	17.00 N	54.06 E
Salamá, Guat.	280	15.06 N	90.16 W
Salamá, Hond.	280	14.50 N	86.36 W
Salamanca, Chile	294	31.47 S	70.58 W
Salamanca, Esp.	168	40.58 N	5.39 W
Salamanca, Méx.	278	20.34 N	101.12 W
Salamanca, Perú	292	15.28 S	72.49 W
Salamanca, N.Y., U.S.	266	42.09 N	78.43 W
Salamat □[5]	220	11.00 N	20.30 E
Salamina	290	5.25 N	75.29 W
Salamís	172	37.59 N	23.28 E
Salamis ⊥	212	35.10 N	33.54 E
Salamonia	268	40.23 N	84.52 W
Salamonie ≃	248	40.50 N	85.43 W
Salang Kotal)(	206	35.21 N	69.05 E
Salapaly, Baie de C	225b	24.40 S	43.55 E
Salaquí	290	7.18 N	77.33 W
Salaquí ≃	290	7.27 N	77.07 W
Sălard	172	47.13 N	22.03 E
Salas	292	6.15 S	79.35 W
Salas de los Infantes	168	42.01 N	3.17 W
Salat ≃	166	43.10 N	0.58 E
Salatiga	198	7.19 S	110.30 E
Salavat	158	53.21 N	55.55 E
Salaverry	292	8.14 S	78.58 W
Salavina	294	28.48 S	63.26 W
Salawati I	198	1.07 S	134.15 E
Salay	202	8.51 N	124.47 E
Sala y Gómez, Isla I	148	26.28 S	105.28 W
Salazar	218	9.18 S	14.54 E
Salcajá	280	14.53 N	91.27 W
Salcantay, Nevado ∧	292	13.22 S	72.34 W
Salcedo, Ec.	290	1.02 S	78.34 W
Salcedo, Pil.	202	11.09 N	125.40 E
Salcedo, Rep. Dom.	282	19.22 N	70.25 W
Salcha ≃	236	64.29 N	147.00 W
Salcia	172	43.57 N	24.56 E
Salcombe	162	50.13 N	3.47 W
Salda Gölü ⊜	212	37.33 N	29.42 E
Saldaña	168	42.31 N	4.44 W
Saldaña ≃	290	4.01 N	74.52 W
Saldanha	218	33.00 S	17.56 E
Saldanhabaai C	224	33.04 S	18.00 E
Saldungaray	294	38.10 S	61.50 W
Sale, Austl.	228	38.06 S	147.04 E
Sale, It.	182	44.59 N	8.48 E
Salé, Magreb	214	34.04 N	6.50 W
Salebabu, Pulau I	198	3.55 N	126.40 E
Salechard	186	66.33 N	66.40 E
Sale Creek	248	35.23 N	85.07 W
Salem, Ont., Can.	264	43.42 N	80.27 W
Salem, Ark., U.S.	248	36.22 N	91.49 W
Salem, Ill., U.S.	248	38.38 N	88.57 W
Salem, Ind., U.S.	248	38.36 N	86.06 W
Salem, Iowa, U.S.	244	40.51 N	91.38 W
Salem, Mass., U.S.	261	42.31 N	70.55 W
Salem, Mo., U.S.	248	37.39 N	91.32 W
Salem, N.H., U.S.	242	42.47 N	71.12 W
Salem, N.J., U.S.	262	39.34 N	75.28 W
Salem, N.Y., U.S.	242	43.10 N	73.20 W
Salem, Ohio, U.S.	266	40.54 N	80.52 W
Salem, Oreg., U.S.	270	44.57 N	123.01 W
Salem, S. Dak., U.S.	252	43.44 N	97.23 W
Salem, Utah, U.S.	254	40.03 N	111.40 W
Salem, Va., U.S.	246	37.17 N	80.03 W
Salem, W. Va., U.S.	242	39.17 N	80.34 W
Salem, Wis., U.S.	268	42.33 N	88.07 W
Salem □[6]	262	39.34 N	75.20 W
Salem Heights	266	40.54 N	80.53 W
Salemi	170	37.49 N	12.49 E
Salem Upland ∧∧[1]	248	37.25 N	91.30 W
Sälen	160	61.10 N	13.16 E
Salentina, Penisola ≻[1]	170	40.25 N	18.00 E
Salerno	184	40.41 N	14.47 E
Salerno □[4]	184	40.43 N	14.45 E
Salerno, Golfo di C	170	40.32 N	14.42 E
Salers	166	45.08 N	2.30 E
Salford	162	53.28 N	2.18 W
Šalgačova	160	62.19 N	39.35 E
Salgar	290	5.58 N	75.59 W
Salgótarján	164	48.07 N	19.48 E
Sali, Jugo.	170	43.56 N	15.10 E
Šali, S.S.S.R.	160	55.41 N	49.40 E
Salí ≃	294	27.32 S	64.56 W
Salida, Calif., U.S.	272	37.42 N	121.05 W
Salida, Colo., U.S.	254	38.32 N	106.00 W
Salies-de-Béarn	166	43.29 N	0.55 W
Salignac	166	44.59 N	1.19 E
Salihli	212	38.29 N	28.09 E
Salima	218	13.47 S	34.26 E
Salīmah, Wāḥat ▼[4]	220	21.22 N	29.19 E
Salime, Embalse de ⊜[1]	168	43.10 N	6.45 W
Salina, Kans., U.S.	252	38.50 N	97.37 W
Salina, Pa., U.S.	266	40.31 N	79.30 W
Salina, Utah, U.S.	254	38.58 N	111.51 W
Salina, Isola I	170	38.34 N	14.51 E
Salina Cruz	278	16.10 N	95.12 W
Salina Point ≻	282	22.10 N	74.18 W
Salinas, Bra.	296	16.10 S	42.17 W
Salinas, Ec.	290	2.13 S	80.58 W
Salinas, P.R.	284m	17.59 N	66.18 W
Salinas, Calif., U.S.	272	36.40 N	121.38 W
Salinas ≃, Bra.	296	16.37 S	42.18 W
Salinas ≃, N.A.	280	16.28 N	90.33 W
Salinas ≃, Calif., U.S.	258	36.45 N	121.48 W
Salinas, Cabo de ≻	168	39.16 N	3.03 E
Salinas, Punta ≻	282	18.13 N	70.30 W
Salinas de Garci Mendoza	292	19.38 S	67.43 W
Salinas de Hidalgo	278	22.38 N	101.43 W
Salinas del Rey	250	27.38 N	102.24 W
Salinas Grande ≃	280	16.07 N	92.32 W
Salinas Victoria	250	25.53 N	100.19 W
Saline, La., U.S.	248	32.10 N	92.58 W
Saline, Mich., U.S.	268	42.10 N	83.47 W
Saline ≃, Ark., U.S.	248	33.10 N	92.08 W
Saline ≃, Ark., U.S.	248	33.44 N	93.58 W
Saline ≃, Ill., U.S.	248	37.35 N	88.08 W
Saline ≃, Kans., U.S.	252	38.51 N	97.30 W
Saline Lake ⊜[1]	248	31.55 N	92.55 W
Salineville	266	40.37 N	80.51 W
Salisbury, Austl.	228	34.46 S	138.38 E
Salisbury, Dom.	284d	15.26 N	61.27 W
Salisbury, Rh.	224	17.50 S	31.03 E
Salisbury, Eng., U.K.	174	51.05 N	1.48 W
Salisbury, Conn., U.S.	261	41.59 N	73.25 W
Salisbury, Md., U.S.	262	38.22 N	75.36 W
Salisbury, Mass., U.S.	261	42.51 N	70.49 W
Salisbury, Mo., U.S.	248	39.25 N	92.48 W
Salisbury, N.C., U.S.	246	35.40 N	80.29 W
Salisbury, Pa., U.S.	242	39.45 N	79.05 W
Salisbury Island I	232	63.30 N	77.00 W
Salitpa	248	31.37 N	88.01 W
Salix	266	40.18 N	78.46 W
Saljany	208	39.34 N	48.58 E
Salkehatchie ≃	246	32.37 N	80.53 W
Şalkhad	210	32.29 N	36.43 E
Salkum	270	46.32 N	122.38 W
Sallanches	170	45.56 N	6.38 E
Salles-Curan	166	44.11 N	2.47 E
Salliqueló	294	36.46 S	62.57 W
Sallisaw	250	35.28 N	94.47 W
Sallūm, Khalīj as- C	220	31.41 N	25.21 E
Salluyo, Nevado ∧	292	14.38 S	69.14 W
Sallyāna	190	28.22 N	82.12 E
Salme	160	58.10 N	22.15 E
Salmi	160	61.22 N	31.50 E
Salmo	238	49.12 N	117.17 W
Salmon	256	45.11 N	113.54 W
Salmon ≃, B.C., Can.	238	54.05 N	122.34 W
Salmon ≃, N.B., Can.	240	46.06 N	65.56 W
Salmon ≃, N.A.	242	45.02 N	74.31 W
Salmon ≃, Calif., U.S.	258	41.23 N	41.29 W
Salmon ≃, Idaho, U.S.	256	45.51 N	116.46 W
Salmon ≃, N.Y., U.S.	242	43.35 N	76.12 W
Salmon ≃, Oreg., U.S.	256	45.22 N	122.02 W
Salmon Arm	238	50.42 N	119.16 W
Salmon-Bay	240	51.25 N	57.37 W
Salmon Mountain ∧	242	45.14 N	71.08 W
Salmon Mountains ∧∧	258	41.00 N	123.00 W
Salmon Peak ∧	250	29.15 N	100.02 W
Salmon River Mountains ∧∧	256	44.45 N	115.30 W
Salmon Valley	238	54.05 N	122.41 W
Salò, It.	170	45.36 N	10.31 E
Salo, Suomi	160	60.23 N	23.08 E
Salo ≃	242	43.27 N	70.22 W
Salobinha	296	16.01 S	51.27 W
Salobra ≃	292	20.12 S	56.29 W
Salome	254	33.47 N	113.37 W
Salon-de-Provence	182	43.38 N	5.06 E
Salonika → Thessaloníki	172	40.38 N	22.56 E
Salonta	172	46.48 N	21.40 E
Salor ≃	168	39.39 N	7.03 W
Saloum ≃	222	13.50 N	16.45 W
Salsa ≃	296	15.39 S	39.02 W
Salsacate	294	31.20 S	65.06 W
Salsipuedes, Canal de ⌣	278	28.37 N	113.00 W
Salsipuedes, Punta ≻, C.R.	280	8.28 N	83.36 W
Salsipuedes, Punta ≻, Méx.	278	32.00 N	116.52 W
Sal'sk	158	46.28 N	41.33 E
Šal'skij	160	61.48 N	35.58 E
Salso ≃	170	37.05 N	13.57 E
Salsomaggiore Terme	170	44.49 N	9.59 E
Salt ≃, U.S.	256	43.08 N	111.02 W
Salt ≃, Ariz., U.S.	254	33.23 N	112.18 W
Salt ≃, Ky., U.S.	248	38.00 N	85.57 W
Salta	294	24.47 S	65.24 W
Salta □[4]	292	25.00 S	64.30 W
Saltair	270	48.57 N	123.46 W
Saltash	174	50.24 N	4.12 W
Salt Basin ⊜	250	31.50 N	105.00 W
Saltcoats	162	55.38 N	4.47 W
Saltee Islands II	162	52.07 N	6.36 W
Saltillo, Méx.	278	25.25 N	101.00 W
Saltillo, Miss., U.S.	248	34.23 N	88.41 W
Saltillo, Pa., U.S.	266	40.13 N	78.01 W
Saltillo, Tenn., U.S.	248	35.23 N	88.13 W
Salt Lake ⊜	250	34.05 N	103.05 W
Salt Lake City	254	40.46 N	111.53 W
Salto, Arg.	294	34.17 S	60.15 W
Salto, Bra.	296	23.12 S	47.17 W
Salto, Ur.	294	31.23 S	57.58 W
Salto ≃	170	42.23 N	12.54 E
Salto da Divisa	296	16.00 S	39.57 W
Salto de las Rosas	294	34.43 S	68.14 W
Salto del Ojo, Arroyo de ≃	254	31.13 N	107.58 W
Salto Grande	296	22.54 S	49.59 W
Salton Sea ⊜	258	33.19 N	115.50 W
Salt Point	261	41.44 N	73.42 W
Saltpond	222	5.12 N	1.04 W
Salt River Indian Reservation ⇝[4]	254	33.31 N	111.48 W
Saltsburg	266	40.29 N	79.26 W
Saltspring Island I	238	48.47 N	123.30 W
Saltville	246	36.53 N	81.46 W
Saluda, N.C., U.S.	246	35.14 N	82.21 W
Saluda, S.C., U.S.	246	34.00 N	81.46 W
Saluda, Va., U.S.	262	37.36 N	76.36 W
Saluda ≃	246	34.00 N	81.04 W
Salug	202	8.06 N	122.47 E
Salunga	262	40.06 N	76.26 W
Saluping Island I	202	6.20 N	122.02 E
Saluzzo	182	44.39 N	7.29 E
Salvador, Bra.	296	12.59 S	38.31 W
Salvador, Pil.	202	7.54 N	123.50 E
Salvador, Calif., U.S.	272	38.20 N	122.18 W
Salvador, Lake ⊜	248	29.45 N	90.15 W
Salvador Island I	202	15.31 N	119.55 E
Salvage	240	48.41 N	53.39 W
Salvaterra de Magos	168	39.01 N	8.48 W
Salvatierra	278	20.13 N	100.53 W
Salvator, Lake ⊜	228	24.43 S	147.11 E
Salvator Rosa National Park ♠	228	24.50 S	147.15 E
Salviac	166	44.41 N	1.16 E
Salwā, Baḥr as- C	208	25.30 N	50.40 E
Salween (Nujiang) ≃	200	16.31 N	97.37 E
Salyer	258	40.54 N	123.35 W
Salyersville	246	37.45 N	83.04 W
Salza ≃	164	47.40 N	14.43 E
Salzach ≃	166	48.12 N	12.56 E
Salzburg	164	47.48 N	13.02 E
Salzburg □[3]	164	47.25 N	13.15 E
Salzgitter	178	52.10 N	10.25 E
Salzgitter-Bad	178	52.04 N	10.23 E
Salzgitter-Barum	178	52.07 N	10.25 E
Salzgitter-Immendorf	178	52.09 N	10.26 E
Salzgitter-Lebenstedt	178	52.09 N	10.20 E
Salzgitter-Thiede	178	52.11 N	10.29 E
Salzgitter-Watenstedt	178	52.06 N	10.22 E
Salzkotten	178	51.40 N	8.36 E
Salzwedel	164	52.51 N	11.09 E
Sama ≃	292	18.09 S	70.41 W
Samacá	290	5.29 N	73.29 W
Sama de Langreo	168	43.18 N	5.41 W
Samaipata	292	18.09 S	63.52 W
Samal (Peñaplata)	202	7.05 N	125.42 E
Samalá ≃	280	14.12 N	91.48 W
Samalanga	200	5.12 N	96.22 E
Samalayuca	254	31.21 N	106.28 W
Samalayuca, Médanos de ⁘[8]	254	31.15 N	106.30 W
Samales Group II	202	6.02 N	121.50 E
Samalga Pass ⌣	236	52.48 N	169.25 W
Samal Island I	202	7.03 N	125.45 E
Samālūt	220	28.18 N	30.42 E
Samambaia ≃	296	22.45 S	53.21 W
Samaná	282	19.13 N	69.19 W
Samaná, Bahía de C	282	19.10 N	69.30 W
Samaná, Cabo ≻	282	19.18 N	69.10 W
Samana Cay I	282	23.03 N	73.45 W
Samandıra	172	40.59 N	29.13 E
Samāngan □[4]	206	36.15 N	67.40 E
Samani	192a	42.07 N	142.56 E
Samaniego	290	1.20 N	77.35 W
Samar I	202	12.00 N	125.00 E
Samara ≃	158	53.10 N	50.04 E
Samarate	182	45.38 N	8.47 E
Samar del Norte □[4]	202	12.30 N	124.30 E
Samaria, Idaho, U.S.	256	42.07 N	112.20 W
Samaria, Mich., U.S.	268	41.48 N	83.35 W
Samaria (Shomeron) □[9]	210	32.20 N	35.15 E
Samariapo	290	5.15 N	67.48 W
Samarinda	198	0.30 S	117.09 E
Samarkand	186	39.40 N	66.48 E
Samar Occidental □[4]	202	11.50 N	125.00 E
Samar Oriental □[4]	202	12.00 N	125.00 E
Sāmarrā'	208	34.12 N	43.52 E
Samar Sea ▼[2]	202	12.15 N	124.15 E
Sambalpur	206	21.28 N	83.59 E
Sambas	200	1.20 N	109.15 E
Sambava	218	14.16 S	50.10 E
Sambe-yama ∧	192	35.08 N	132.37 E
Sambhal	206	28.35 N	78.34 E
Sāmbhar Lake ⊜	206	27.00 N	75.00 E
Samboan	202	9.32 N	123.18 E
Sambong-san ∧	194	40.30 N	126.09 E
Sambor	164	49.32 N	23.11 E
Samborombón ≃	294	35.42 S	57.20 W
Samborombón, Bahía C	294	36.00 S	57.00 W
Samborondón	290	1.57 S	79.44 W
Sambre ≃	166	50.28 N	4.52 E
Sambú ≃	290	8.05 N	78.19 W
Samburá ≃	296	20.20 S	46.05 W
Samch'ŏk	194	37.27 N	129.10 E
Sam Chom, Khao ∧	200	8.08 N	99.28 E
Samch'ŏnp'o	194	34.57 N	128.03 E
Same	218	4.04 S	37.44 E
Samer	162	50.38 N	1.45 E
Samiria ≃	292	4.40 S	74.15 W
Samish	270	48.35 N	122.33 W
Samlı	172	39.48 N	27.51 E
Samneua	200	20.25 N	104.02 E
Samoa Islands II	148	14.00 S	171.00 W
Samo Alto	294	30.25 S	70.58 W
Samobor	170	45.48 N	15.43 E
Samoded	160	63.38 N	40.29 E
Samokov	172	42.20 N	23.33 E
Sámos □[5]	172	37.48 N	26.44 E
Sámos I	172	37.48 N	26.44 E
Samoset	246	27.28 N	82.33 W
Samosir, Pulau I	200	2.35 N	98.48 E
Samothrace → Samothráki I	172	40.30 N	25.32 E
Samothráki	172	40.28 N	25.31 E
Samothráki I, Ellás	172	39.48 N	19.29 E
Samothráki I, Ellás	212	40.30 N	25.32 E
S'amozero	160	61.54 N	33.18 E
Sampacho	294	33.20 S	64.40 W
Sampaloc Point ≻	202	14.44 N	120.10 E
Sampit	198	2.32 S	112.57 E
Sampués	290	9.11 N	75.23 W
Sam Rayburn Reservoir ⊜[1]	248	31.27 N	94.37 W
Samson	248	31.07 N	86.09 W
Samson Indian Reserve ⇝[4]	238	52.48 N	113.10 W
Samsun	212	41.17 N	36.20 E
Samsun Limani C	212	41.18 N	36.21 E
Samtown	248	31.20 N	92.26 W
Samuhú	294	27.31 S	60.24 W
Samui, Ko I	200	9.30 N	100.04 E
Samut Prakan	200	13.35 N	100.40 E
Samut Sakhon	200	13.31 N	100.15 E
Samut Songkhram	200	13.25 N	100.03 E
Samuyishankou)(	206	29.55 N	84.46 E
S'amža	160	60.01 N	41.02 E
San	222	13.18 N	4.54 W
San ≃, Eur.	164	50.45 N	21.51 E
San ≃, Kam.	200	13.32 N	105.57 E
Saña, Perú	292	6.54 S	79.36 W
Şan'ā', Yaman	204	15.23 N	44.12 E
Sana ≃	170	45.03 N	16.23 E
Sanaduva	294	27.57 S	51.48 W
Şanāfīr I	208	27.55 N	34.40 E
Sanaga ≃	222	3.35 N	9.38 E
San Agustín, Arg.	294	38.00 S	58.20 W
San Agustín, Arg.	294	31.59 S	64.22 W
San Agustín, Col.	290	1.53 N	76.16 W
San Agustín, Méx.	254	31.31 N	106.15 W
San Agustin, Pil.	202	12.25 N	120.59 E
San Agustin, Pil.	202	16.30 N	121.45 E
San Agustin, Cape ≻	202	6.16 N	126.11 E
San Agustin, Plains of ≍	254	33.50 N	108.00 W
San Agustín de Valle Fértil	294	30.40 S	67.33 W
Sanak Islands II	236	54.25 N	162.35 W
San Alberto	250	27.20 N	101.20 W
San Alejo	280	13.26 N	87.58 W
Sanalona, Presa ⊜[1]	278	24.53 N	107.00 W
San Ambrosio, Isla I	288	26.21 S	79.52 W
Sanana, Pulau I	198	2.12 S	125.55 E
Sanandaj	208	35.19 N	47.00 E
Sanandita	292	21.40 S	63.35 W
San Andreas	272	38.12 N	120.41 W
San Andrés, Col.	280	12.35 N	81.42 W
San Andrés, Col.	290	6.49 N	72.52 W
San Andrés, Méx.	278	27.14 N	114.14 W
San Andrés, Pan.	280	8.36 N	82.43 W
San Andres, Pil.	202	13.19 N	122.41 E
San Andrés, Cerro ∧	278	19.48 N	100.36 W
San Andrés, Isla de I	280	12.33 N	81.42 W
San Andrés, Laguna de C	278	22.40 N	97.52 W
San Andrés de Giles	294	34.26 S	59.28 W
San Andres Mountains ∧∧	254	32.55 N	106.45 W
San Andres Point ≻	202	13.34 N	121.51 E
San Andrés Sajcabajá	280	15.13 N	90.55 W
San Andrés Tuxtla	278	18.27 N	95.13 W
San Andrés y Providencia □[8]	280	13.00 N	81.30 W
San Angelo	250	31.28 N	100.26 W
San Angelo Reservoir ⊜[1]	250	31.30 N	100.30 W
San Anselmo	272	37.59 N	122.34 W
San Antero	290	9.23 N	75.46 W
San Antonio, Arg.	294	24.22 S	65.19 W
San Antonio, Br. Hond.	280	16.15 N	89.02 W
San Antonio, Chile	294	33.35 S	71.38 W
San Antonio, Chile	294	27.53 S	70.03 W
San Antonio, Col.	290	3.55 N	75.28 W
San Antonio, C.R.	280	10.12 N	85.26 W
San Antonio, Perú	292	6.20 S	76.22 W
San Antonio, Pil.	202	12.25 N	124.16 E
San Antonio, Pil.	202	14.57 N	120.05 E

Symbols in the index entries are identified on page 360.

Name	Page	Lat°′	Long°′
San Antonio, P.R.	284m	18.30 N	67.07 W
San Antonio, N. Mex., U.S.	254	33.55 N	106.52 W
San Antonio, Tex., U.S.	250	29.28 N	98.31 W
San Antonio, Ur.	294	31.22 S	57.48 W
San Antonio ≃, Méx.	250	29.10 N	103.40 W
San Antonio ≃, Méx.	278	31.00 N	116.15 W
San Antonio ≃, Tex., U.S.	250	28.30 N	96.50 W
San Antonio, Cabo ➤, Arg.	294	36.40 S	56.42 W
San Antonio, Cabo ➤, Cuba	284p	21.52 N	84.57 W
San Antonio, Mount ∧	258	34.17 N	117.39 W
San Antonio, Punta ➤	278	29.45 N	115.43 W
San Antonio, Rio ≃	254	37.11 N	105.55 W
San Antonio Abad	168	38.58 N	1.18 E
San Antonio Bay C, Pil.	202	8.38 N	117.35 E
San Antonio Bay C, Tex., U.S.	250	28.20 N	96.45 W
San Antonio de Areco	294	34.16 S	59.30 W
San Antonio de Bravo	278	30.10 N	104.42 W
San Antonio de la Paz	294	28.56 S	65.06 W
San Antonio de las Alazanas	278	25.16 N	100.36 W
San Antonio del Golfo	290	10.27 N	63.50 W
San Antonio de los Baños	284p	22.53 N	82.30 W
San Antonio de los Cobres	294	24.15 S	66.20 W
San Antonio del Táchira	290	7.50 N	72.27 W
San Antônio de Pádua	296	21.32 S	42.11 W
San Antonio de Tamanaco	290	9.41 N	66.03 W
San Antonio Heights	274	34.10 N	117.40 W
San Antonio Mountain ∧	254	36.52 N	106.02 W
San Antonio Oeste	288	40.44 S	64.57 W
San Antonio Suchitepéquez	280	14.32 N	91.25 W
San Antonio y Tortugas, Canal ≊	294	32.58 S	61.47 W
San Ardo	272	36.07 N	120.54 W
San Augustine	248	31.32 N	94.07 W
San Augustin Pass)(	254	32.26 N	106.34 W
San Bartolomeo in Galdo	184	41.24 N	15.01 E
San Baudilio de Llobregat	168	41.21 N	2.03 E
San Benedetto del Tronto	184	42.57 N	13.53 E
San Benedetto Po	170	45.02 N	10.55 E
San Benedicto, Isla I	278	19.18 N	110.49 W
San Benito, Bol.	292	17.31 S	65.55 W
San Benito, Guat.	278	16.55 N	89.54 W
San Benito, Perú	292	7.21 S	78.55 W
San Benito, Tex., U.S.	250	26.08 N	97.38 W
San Benito □[6]	272	36.51 N	121.24 W
San Benito Mountain ∧	258	36.22 N	120.38 W
San Bernardino	274	34.06 N	117.17 W
San Bernardino □[6]	274	34.40 N	117.17 W
San Bernardino, Río de ≃	254	30.51 N	109.11 W
San Bernardino Mountains ⋀	258	34.10 N	117.00 W
San Bernardino Strait ⩊	202	12.37 N	124.12 E
San Bernardo, Arg.	294	27.17 S	60.43 W
San Bernardo, Chile	294	33.36 S	70.43 W
San Bernardo, Méx.	278	25.59 N	105.33 W
San Bernardo, Isla I	280	11.32 N	85.06 W
San Bernardo, Islas de II	290	9.45 N	75.50 W
San Bernardo del Viento	290	9.21 N	75.57 W
San Blas, Méx.	278	26.05 N	108.46 W
San Blas, Méx.	278	21.31 N	105.16 W
San Blas, Cape ➤	246	29.40 N	85.22 W
San Blas, Cordillera de ⋀	290	9.20 N	78.45 W
San Blas, Golfo de C	290	9.28 N	79.00 W
San Blas de los Sauces	294	28.24 S	67.06 W
San Bonifacio	170	45.24 N	11.16 E
San Borja	292	14.49 S	66.51 W
Sanborn, Iowa, U.S.	252	43.11 N	95.39 W
Sanborn, Minn., U.S.	252	44.13 N	95.08 W
Sanborn, N. Dak., U.S.	252	46.57 N	98.13 W
Sanborn, N.Y., U.S.	264	43.08 N	78.53 W
San Bruno	272	37.37 N	122.25 W
San Buena Ventura, Bol.	292	14.28 S	67.35 W
San Buenaventura, Méx.	278	27.05 N	101.32 W
San Buenaventura → Ventura, Calif., U.S.	274	34.17 N	119.18 W
Sanbuzhen	190	22.23 N	112.35 E
San Candido (Innichen)	170	46.44 N	12.17 E
San Carlos, Arg.	294	33.45 S	69.00 W
San Carlos, Arg.	294	27.45 S	55.54 W
San Carlos, Arg.	294	25.54 S	65.57 W
San Carlos, Chile	294	36.25 S	71.58 W
San Carlos, Gui. Ecu.	222	3.27 N	8.33 E
San Carlos, Méx.	278	29.01 N	100.51 W
San Carlos, Méx.	278	24.35 N	98.56 W
San Carlos, Nic.	280	11.07 N	84.47 W
San Carlos, Pan.	280	8.25 N	79.58 W
San Carlos, Para.	294	22.16 S	57.18 W
San Carlos, Pil.	202	10.29 N	123.25 E
San Carlos, Pil.	202	15.56 N	120.21 E
San Carlos, Ariz., U.S.	254	33.21 N	110.27 W
San Carlos, Calif., U.S.	272	37.31 N	122.16 W
San Carlos, Ur.	294	34.48 S	54.55 W
San Carlos, Ven.	290	9.40 N	68.36 W
San Carlos ≃, C.R.	280	10.48 N	84.11 W
San Carlos ≃, Para.	294	22.51 S	57.51 W
San Carlos ≃, Ariz., U.S.	254	33.16 N	110.27 W
San Carlos ≃, Ven.	290	9.07 N	68.25 W
San Carlos, Isla I	290	11.01 N	71.43 W
San Carlos Centro	294	31.44 S	61.05 W
San Carlos de Bariloche	288	41.08 S	71.15 W
San Carlos de Guaroa	290	3.44 N	73.14 W
San Carlos de la Rápita	168	40.37 N	0.36 E
San Carlos del Zulia	290	9.01 N	71.55 W
San Carlos de Río Negro	290	1.55 N	67.04 W
San Carlos Indian Reservation ➝[4]	254	33.23 N	110.09 W
San Carlos Lake ⊜[1]	254	33.13 N	110.24 W
San Casciano in Val di Pesa	184	43.39 N	11.11 E
San Cataldo	170	37.29 N	14.04 E
San Cayetano	294	38.20 S	59.35 W
Sancergues	166	47.09 N	2.55 E
Sancerre	166	47.20 N	2.51 E
Sánchez, Méx.	278	27.27 N	99.40 W
Sánchez, Rep. Dom.	282	19.14 N	69.36 W
San Clemente, Esp.	168	39.24 N	2.26 W
San Clemente, Calif., U.S.	274	33.26 N	117.37 W
San Clemente Island I	258	32.54 N	118.29 W
Sancoins	166	46.50 N	2.55 E
San Colombano al Lambro	182	45.11 N	9.29 E
Sanco Point ➤	202	8.14 N	126.25 E
San Cosme	294	27.23 S	58.30 W
San Cristóbal, Arg.	294	30.20 S	61.15 W
San Cristóbal, Cuba	284p	22.43 N	83.03 W
San Cristóbal, Rep. Dom.	282	18.25 N	70.06 W
San Cristóbal, Ven.	290	7.46 N	72.14 W
San Cristóbal, Bahía de C	278	27.20 N	114.35 W
San Cristóbal, Isla I	290a	0.50 S	89.26 W
San Cristóbal, Volcán ∧[1]	280	12.42 N	87.00 W
San Cristóbal las Casas	278	16.45 N	92.38 W
San Cristóbal Totonicapán	280	14.55 N	91.26 W
San Cristóbal Verapaz	280	15.23 N	90.24 W
San Cristobal Wash ∨	254	32.47 N	113.44 W
Sancti-Spíritus	284p	21.56 N	79.27 W
Sančursk	160	56.57 N	47.15 E
Sand	160	59.29 N	6.15 E
Sand ≃, Alta., Can.	238	54.22 N	111.05 W
Sand ≃, S. Afr.	224	22.25 S	30.05 E
Sanda Island I	162	55.18 N	5.34 W
Sandakan	202	5.53 N	118.05 E
Sandakan Harbour C	202	5.45 N	118.05 E
San Damián	292	12.02 S	76.23 W
Sandan, Chāh ⊤[4]	208	28.59 N	63.27 E
San Daniele del Friuli	170	46.09 N	13.00 E
Sandanski	172	41.34 N	23.17 E
Sanday I	162	59.15 N	2.30 W
Sandbach	174	53.09 N	2.22 W
Sand City	272	36.37 N	121.51 W
Sandcoulee	256	47.24 N	111.10 W
Sande	178	53.30 N	8.01 E
Sanders	254	35.13 N	109.20 W
Sanderson	250	30.09 N	102.24 W
Sandersville, Ga., U.S.	246	32.59 N	82.48 W
Sandersville, Miss., U.S.	248	31.47 N	89.02 W
Sand Fork	242	38.55 N	80.45 W
Sandgate	228	27.20 S	153.05 E
Sand Hill	261	42.13 N	70.44 W
Sandhill ≃	252	47.36 N	96.52 W
Sand Hills ⋀[2]	252	41.45 N	102.00 W
Sandia	292	14.14 S	69.25 W
Sandia Crest ∧	254	35.13 N	106.27 W
San Diego, Calif., U.S.	274	32.43 N	117.09 W
San Diego, Tex., U.S.	250	27.46 N	98.14 W
San Diego □[6]	274	33.00 N	117.05 W
San Diego ≃, Cuba	284p	22.20 N	83.16 W
San Diego ≃, Calif., U.S.	258	32.46 N	117.13 W
San Diego de la Unión	278	21.28 N	100.52 W
Sandilands Village	284b	25.02 N	77.18 W
San Dimas	274	34.06 N	117.49 W
San Dionisio, Nic.	280	12.40 N	85.54 W
San Dionisio, Pil.	202	11.16 N	123.06 E
Sand Key I	246	27.53 N	82.51 W
Sand Lake	261	42.38 N	73.32 W
Sandnes	160	58.51 N	5.44 E
Sandoa	218	9.41 S	22.52 E
Sandomierska, Kotlina ≌[1]	164	50.30 N	22.00 E
Sandomierz	164	50.41 N	21.45 E
Sandoná	290	1.17 N	77.28 W
San Donà di Piave	170	45.38 N	12.34 E
San Donato Milanese	182	45.24 N	9.16 E
Sandoval	248	38.37 N	89.07 W
Sandovalina	296	22.27 S	51.44 W
Sandovo	160	58.28 N	36.25 E
Sandoway	200	18.28 N	94.22 E
Sandown	162	50.39 N	1.09 W
Sand Point, Alaska, U.S.	236	55.20 N	160.30 W
Sandpoint, Idaho, U.S.	256	48.16 N	116.33 W
Sandray I	162	56.54 N	7.25 W
Sandringham	162	52.50 N	0.30 W
Sandspit	238	53.14 N	131.50 W
Sand Springs	250	36.09 N	96.07 W
Sandston	262	37.31 N	77.19 W
Sandstone, Austl.	226	27.59 S	119.17 E
Sandstone, Minn., U.S.	244	46.08 N	92.52 W
Sandugan Point ➤	202	9.18 N	123.35 E
Sandusky, Mich., U.S.	244	43.25 N	82.50 W
Sandusky, N.Y., U.S.	266	42.30 N	78.23 W
Sandusky, Ohio, U.S.	266	41.27 N	82.42 W
Sandusky □[6]	266	41.21 N	83.07 W
Sandvika	160	59.54 N	10.31 E
Sandviken	160	60.37 N	16.46 E
Sandwich, Ill., U.S.	268	41.39 N	88.37 W
Sandwich, Mass., U.S.	261	41.46 N	70.30 W
Sandwich Bay C, Newf., Can.	232	53.35 N	57.15 W
Sandwich Bay C, S.W. Afr.	224	23.22 S	14.30 E
Sandwick	238	49.42 N	124.59 W
Sandwīp Island I	206	22.30 N	91.25 E
Sandy, Oreg., U.S.	270	45.24 N	122.16 W
Sandy, Pa., U.S.	266	41.07 N	78.47 W
Sandy ≃, Maine, U.S.	242	44.45 N	69.52 W
Sandy ≃, Oreg., U.S.	256	45.34 N	122.24 W
Sandy ≃, Va., U.S.	246	36.35 N	79.25 W
Sandy Bay C	280	14.30 N	83.15 W
Sandy Bay Mountain ∧	242	45.47 N	70.25 W
Sandy Beach	264	43.04 N	78.55 W
Sandy Cape ➤, Austl.	228	24.42 S	153.17 E
Sandy Cape ➤, Austl.	228	41.25 S	144.45 E
Sandy Creek	264	43.39 N	76.05 W
Sandy Desert ➝[2]	206	28.40 N	62.30 E
Sandy Hook, Conn., U.S.	261	41.25 N	73.17 W
Sandy Hook, Ky., U.S.	246	38.05 N	83.08 W
Sandy Hook, Miss., U.S.	248	31.02 N	89.48 W
Sandy Hook ➤[2]	242	40.27 N	74.00 W
Sandy Islet I	226	14.03 S	121.49 E
Sandykači	186	36.33 N	62.34 E
Sandy Lake	266	41.22 N	80.05 W
Sandy Lake ⊜, Newf., Can.	240	49.16 N	57.00 W
Sandy Lake ⊜, Ont., Can.	232	53.00 N	93.07 W
Sandy Point	282	17.22 N	62.50 W
Sandy Ridge	266	40.49 N	78.14 W
Sandy Springs	246	33.55 N	84.23 W
Sandyville, Md., U.S.	262	39.31 N	76.55 W
Sandyville, Ohio, U.S.	266	40.38 N	81.23 W
Sandžak ➝[1]	172	43.10 N	19.30 E
San Elizario	254	31.35 N	106.16 W
San Emilio	202	17.14 N	120.37 E
San Enrique	294	35.47 S	60.22 W
San Estanislao, Col.	290	10.24 N	75.09 W
San Estanislao, Para.	294	24.39 S	56.26 W
San Esteban	280	15.17 N	85.52 W
San Esteban, Bahía C	278	25.45 N	109.20 W
San Esteban, Isla I	278	28.41 N	112.35 W
San Esteban de Gormaz	168	41.35 N	3.12 W
San Fabian	202	16.06 N	120.24 E
San Felipe, Chile	294	32.45 S	70.44 W
San Felipe, Col.	290	1.55 N	67.06 W
San Felipe, Méx.	278	31.00 N	114.52 W
San Felipe, Méx.	278	21.29 N	101.13 W
San Felipe, Pil.	202	15.04 N	120.04 E
San Felipe, N. Mex., U.S.	254	35.27 N	106.28 W
San Felipe, Ven.	290	10.20 N	68.44 W
San Felipe, Cayos de II	284p	21.58 N	83.30 W
San Felipe, Punta ➤	254	31.03 N	114.51 W
San Felipe Nuevo Mercurio	278	24.22 N	102.06 W
San Felíu de Guixols	168	41.47 N	3.02 E
San Félix	290	8.23 N	62.40 W
San Félix ≃	280	8.10 N	81.50 W
San Félix, Isla I	288	26.17 S	80.05 W
San Fermín	250	26.20 N	104.49 W
San Fermín, Punta ➤	278	30.22 N	114.40 W
San Fernando, Chile	294	34.35 S	71.00 W
San Fernando, Esp.	168	36.28 N	6.12 W
San Fernando, Méx.	250	28.32 N	100.54 W
San Fernando, Méx.	254	31.16 N	110.36 W
San Fernando, Méx.	278	24.50 N	98.10 W
San Fernando, Pil.	202	16.37 N	120.18 E
San Fernando, Pil.	202	12.29 N	123.46 E
San Fernando, Pil.	202	15.02 N	120.41 E
San Fernando, Trin.	285r	10.17 N	61.28 W
San Fernando, Calif., U.S.	274	34.17 N	118.26 W
San Fernando ≃	278	24.55 N	97.40 W
San Fernando de Apure	290	7.54 N	67.28 W
San Fernando de Atabapo	290	4.03 N	67.42 W
San Fernando Point ➤	202	16.38 N	120.18 E
San Fiorenzo	170	42.42 N	9.24 E
Sanford, Colo., U.S.	254	37.16 N	105.54 W
Sanford, Fla., U.S.	246	28.48 N	81.16 W
Sanford, Maine, U.S.	242	43.26 N	70.46 W
Sanford, Mich., U.S.	244	43.40 N	84.23 W
Sanford, Miss., U.S.	248	31.29 N	89.26 W
Sanford, N.C., U.S.	246	35.29 N	79.10 W
Sanford, Tex., U.S.	250	35.42 N	101.32 W
Sanford, Mount ∧	236	62.13 N	144.09 W
Sanford National Recreation Area ♠	250	35.38 N	101.39 W
San Francisco, Arg.	294	31.27 S	62.05 W
San Francisco, Col.	290	1.11 N	76.53 W
San Francisco, C.R.	280	9.49 N	85.15 W
San Francisco, Pan.	280	8.16 N	80.59 W
San Francisco, Pil.	202	8.29 N	125.55 E
San Francisco, Pil.	202	10.03 N	125.09 E
San Francisco, Calif., U.S.	272	37.48 N	122.24 W
San Francisco □[6]	272	37.45 N	122.22 W
San Francisco ≃, Arg.	294	23.17 S	64.03 W
San Francisco → São Francisco ≃, Bra.	286	10.30 S	36.24 W
San Francisco ≃, U.S.	254	32.59 N	109.22 W
San Francisco, Cabo de ➤	290	0.40 N	80.05 W
San Francisco, Paso de)(	294	26.53 S	68.19 W
San Francisco de Arriba	278	26.15 N	102.50 W
San Francisco de Borja	278	27.53 N	106.41 W
San Francisco de Horizonte	250	25.56 N	103.26 W
San Francisco de la Paz	280	14.55 N	86.14 W
San Franciscó del Carnicero	280	12.30 N	86.19 W
San Francisco del Chañar	294	29.47 S	63.58 W
San Francisco del Monte de Oro	294	32.35 S	66.08 W
San Francisco del Oro	278	26.52 N	105.51 W
San Francisco del Rincón	278	21.01 N	101.51 W
San Francisco de Macorís	282	19.18 N	70.15 W
San Francisco de Mostazal	294	33.59 S	70.43 W
San Francisco Gotera	280	13.42 N	88.06 W
San Francisco Javier	250	26.22 N	100.05 W
San Francisco Mountains ⋀	254	33.45 N	109.00 W
San Francisco Peaks ⋀	254	35.20 N	111.45 W
San Fratelo	170	38.01 N	14.36 E
San Gabriel, Ec.	290	0.36 N	77.49 W
San Gabriel, Calif., U.S.	274	34.07 N	118.06 W
San Gabriel ≃	250	30.46 N	97.01 W
San Gabriel Chilac	278	18.19 N	97.21 W
San Gabriel Mountains ⋀	258	34.20 N	118.00 W
Šangaly	160	61.08 N	43.19 E
Sangamon ≃	248	40.07 N	90.20 W
Sang'angqu	190	29.15 N	96.59 E
Sanga Puitã	296	22.40 S	55.36 W
Sangar	186	63.55 N	127.31 E
Sanga Sanga Island I	202	5.04 N	119.46 E
San Gavino Monreale	170	39.33 N	8.48 E
Sangay, Volcán ∧[1]	290	2.00 S	78.20 W
Sangayán, Isla de I	292	13.51 S	76.28 W
Sangchungshih	196	25.04 N	121.29 E
Sangeang, Pulau I	198	8.12 S	119.04 E
Sanger, Calif., U.S.	272	36.42 N	119.27 W
Sanger, Tex., U.S.	250	33.22 N	97.10 W
Sangerhausen	164	51.28 N	11.17 E
San Germán, Cuba	284p	20.36 N	76.08 W
San Germán, P.R.	284m	18.05 N	67.03 W
San Geronimo	272	38.01 N	122.39 W
Sangerville	242	45.10 N	69.21 W
Sangganhe ≃	194	40.21 N	115.21 E
Sanggau	200	0.08 N	110.36 E
Sangha ≃	218	1.13 S	16.49 E
Sangihe, Kepulauan II	198	3.00 N	125.30 E
Sangihe, Pulau I	198	3.35 N	125.32 E
San Gil	290	6.33 N	73.08 W
San Gimignano	170	43.28 N	11.02 E
San Giovanni-Bianco	180	45.52 N	9.39 E
San Giovanni in Fiore	170	39.16 N	16.42 E
San Giovanni in Persiceto	170	44.38 N	11.11 E
San Giovanni Rotondo	184	41.42 N	15.44 E
San Giovanni Valdarno	184	43.34 N	11.32 E
San Giuliano Terme	184	43.46 N	10.26 E
San Giuseppe Vesuviano	184	40.50 N	14.30 E
Sangju	194	36.26 N	128.09 E
Sângkê ≃	200	13.13 N	103.41 E
Sangolquí	290	0.19 S	78.27 W
Sangonera ≃	168	37.59 N	1.04 W
San Gorgonio Mountain ∧	258	34.06 N	116.50 W
San Gottardo, Passo del)(	180	46.33 N	8.34 E
Sangre de Cristo Mountains ⋀	254	37.30 N	105.15 W
San Gregorio, Arg.	294	34.20 S	62.05 W
San Gregorio, Calif., U.S.	272	37.20 N	122.23 W
San Gregorio, Ur.	294	32.37 S	55.40 W
Sangre Grande	285r	10.35 N	61.07 W
Sangsues, Lac aux ⊜	244	46.28 N	77.56 W
Sangudo	238	53.53 N	114.54 W
Sangue, Rio do ≃	292	11.01 S	58.39 W
Sangüesa	168	42.35 N	1.17 W
San Hipólito, Punta ➤	278	26.59 N	114.00 W
Sanhsient'ai I	196	23.08 N	121.26 E
Sanibel Island I	246	26.27 N	82.06 W
San Ignacio, Arg.	294	27.15 S	55.30 W
San Ignacio, Bol.	292	14.53 S	65.36 W
San Ignacio, Bol.	292	16.23 S	60.59 W
San Ignacio, C.R.	280	9.48 N	84.09 W
San Ignacio, Hond.	280	14.38 N	87.02 W
San Ignacio, Méx.	278	27.27 N	112.51 W
San Ignacio, Méx.	278	23.12 N	100.12 W
San Ignacio, Para.	294	26.52 S	57.03 W
San Ignacio, Isla de I	278	25.22 N	108.52 W
San Ignacio, Laguna ⊜	278	26.50 N	113.11 W
San Ildefonso, Cape ➤	202	16.01 N	122.00 E
San Ildefonso, Cerro ∧	280	15.31 N	88.17 W
San Ildefonso o La Granja	168	40.54 N	4.00 W
San Ildefonso Peninsula ➤[1]	202	16.10 N	122.05 E
San'in-kaigan-kokuritsu-kōen ♠	192	35.38 N	134.38 E
San Isidro, Arg.	294	34.29 S	58.31 W
San Isidro, Arg.	294	28.28 S	65.44 W
San Isidro, Méx.	254	31.31 N	106.18 W
San Isidro, Nic.	280	12.52 N	86.15 W
San Isidro, Pil.	202	9.59 N	126.00 E
San Isidro, Pil.	202	11.24 N	124.21 E
San Isidro, Tex., U.S.	250	26.43 N	98.27 W
San Isidro del General	280	9.22 N	83.42 W
San Jacinto, Col.	290	9.50 N	75.08 W
San Jacinto, Méx.	250	25.29 N	103.44 W
San Jacinto, Pil.	202	12.34 N	123.44 E
San Jacinto, Calif., U.S.	274	33.47 N	116.57 W
San Jacinto ≃	258	33.43 N	117.16 W
San Jacinto Peak ∧	258	33.49 N	116.41 W
San Javier, Arg.	294	27.55 S	55.05 W
San Javier, Arg.	294	30.40 S	59.55 W
San Javier, Bol.	292	14.34 S	64.42 W
San Javier, Bol.	292	16.20 S	62.38 W
San Javier, Chile	294	35.35 S	71.45 W
San Javier, Méx.	250	26.16 N	99.27 W
San Javier, Ur.	294	32.41 S	58.08 W
San Javier ≃	294	31.38 S	60.33 W
San Jerónimo	280	15.03 N	90.12 W
San Jerónimo Norte	294	31.35 S	61.05 W
Sanjiang	200	25.42 N	109.23 E
Sanjō	192	37.37 N	138.57 E
San Joaquín, Bol.	292	13.04 S	64.49 W
San Joaquín, Para.	294	24.57 S	56.07 W
San Joaquin, Pil.	202	10.35 N	122.08 E
San Joaquin, Calif., U.S.	272	36.36 N	120.11 W
San Joaquin □[6]	272	37.57 N	121.17 W
San Joaquín ≃	292	13.08 S	63.41 W
San Joaquin Valley ∨	258	36.50 N	120.10 W
San Jon	250	35.06 N	103.20 W
San Jorge, Arg.	294	31.54 S	61.50 W
San Jorge, El Sal.	280	13.25 N	88.21 W
San Jorge, Nic.	280	11.27 N	85.48 W
San Jorge ≃	290	9.07 N	74.44 W
San Jorge, Bahía de C	278	31.08 N	113.15 W
San Jorge, Golfo de C	168	40.53 N	1.00 E
San José, Arg.	294	28.25 S	65.45 W
San José, Arg.	294	27.45 S	55.45 W
San José, C.R.	280	9.56 N	84.05 W
San José, Ec.	290	1.42 S	79.01 W
San José, Hond.	280	14.54 N	88.44 W
San José, Méx.	250	28.16 N	100.15 W
San José, Méx.	278	27.32 N	110.09 W
San José, Para.	294	25.33 S	56.45 W
San Jose, Pil.	202	15.48 N	120.59 E
San Jose, Pil.	202	10.45 N	121.57 E
San Jose, Pil.	202	12.27 N	121.03 E
San Jose, Calif., U.S.	272	37.20 N	121.53 W
San Jose, Fla., U.S.	246	30.15 N	81.36 W
San Jose, Ill., U.S.	248	40.18 N	89.36 W
San Jose, N. Mex., U.S.	254	35.24 N	105.29 W
San José □[4]	280	9.40 N	84.00 W
San Jose ≃	238	52.14 N	122.15 W
San José, Isla I, Méx.	278	25.00 N	110.38 W
San José, Isla I, Pan.	290	8.14 N	79.07 W
San José, Serranía de ⋀[2]	292	17.52 S	60.49 W
San José de Aura	250	27.34 N	101.23 W
San Jose de Buan	202	12.02 N	125.01 E
San José de Chiquitos	292	17.51 S	60.47 W
San José de Chupiamonas	292	14.13 S	68.05 W
San José de Feliciano	294	30.25 S	58.45 W
San José de Gauribe	290	9.52 N	65.48 W
San José de Guanipa	290	8.54 N	64.09 W
San José de la Esquina	294	33.10 S	61.45 W
San José de la Popa	250	26.10 N	100.47 W
San José de las Lajas	284p	22.58 N	82.09 W
San José del Cabo	278	23.03 N	109.41 W
San José del Guaviare	290	2.35 N	72.38 W
San José de los Molinos	292	13.55 S	75.40 W
San José de Mayo	294	34.20 S	56.42 W
San José de Ocoa	282	18.33 N	70.30 W
San José de Ocuné	290	4.15 N	70.20 W
San José de Raíces	278	24.35 N	100.14 W
San José de Río Chico	290	10.18 N	65.59 W
San José de Sisa	292	6.37 S	76.39 W
San José de Tiznados	290	9.23 N	67.33 W
San Juan, Arg.	294	31.30 S	68.30 W
San Juan, Guat.	280	15.52 N	88.53 W
San Juan, Méx.	250	29.34 N	104.36 W
San Juan, Méx.	278	27.47 N	103.57 W
San Juan, Pil.	202	16.40 N	120.20 E
San Juan, Pil.	202	8.25 N	126.22 E
San Juan, Pil.	202	9.10 N	123.29 E
San Juan, Pil.	202	13.50 N	121.24 E
San Juan, P.R.	284m	18.28 N	66.07 W
San Juan □[4]	294	30.50 S	69.00 W
San Juan □[6]	270	48.34 N	122.59 W
San Juan ≃, Arg.	294	32.20 S	67.25 W
San Juan ≃, Bol.	292	21.02 S	65.19 W
San Juan ≃, Col.	290	4.03 N	77.27 W
San Juan ≃, Méx.	278	26.22 N	98.58 W
San Juan ≃, N.A.	280	10.56 N	83.42 W
San Juan ≃, Perú	292	13.33 S	76.12 W
San Juan ≃, Rep. Dom.	282	18.40 N	71.05 W
San Juan ≃, S.A.	290	1.11 N	78.33 W
San Juan ≃, U.S.	254	37.18 N	110.28 W
San Juan ≃, Ven.	290	10.14 N	62.38 W
San Juan, Embalse de ⊜[1]	168	40.30 N	4.15 W
San Juan, Pico ∧	284p	21.59 N	80.08 W
San Juan Basin ≌[1]	254	36.15 N	108.20 W
San Juan Bautista, Esp.	168	39.05 N	1.30 E
San Juan Bautista, Méx.	250	26.58 N	101.24 W
San Juan Bautista, Para.	294	26.38 S	57.10 W
San Juan Bautista, Calif., U.S.	272	36.51 N	121.32 W
San Juan Capistrano	274	33.30 N	117.40 W
San Juan Cotzal	280	15.26 N	91.01 W
San Juan de Abajo	278	20.48 N	105.13 W
San Juan de Colón	290	8.02 N	72.16 W
San Juan de Guadalupe	278	24.38 N	102.44 W
San Juan [de la Maguana]	282	18.48 N	71.14 W
San Juan del César	290	10.46 N	73.01 W
San Juan de Lima, Punta ➤	278	18.36 N	103.42 W
San Juan de Limay	280	13.10 N	86.39 W
San Juan del Norte	280	10.56 N	83.42 W
San Juan del Norte, Bahía de C	280	11.15 N	83.45 W
San Juan de los Cayos	290	11.10 N	68.25 W
San Juan de los Morros	290	9.55 N	67.21 W
San Juan del Piray	292	20.16 S	64.09 W
San Juan del Río, Méx.	278	24.47 N	104.27 W
San Juan del Río, Méx.	278	20.23 N	100.00 W
San Juan del Sur	280	11.15 N	85.52 W
San Juan de Micay ≃	290	3.05 N	77.32 W
San Juan de Payara	290	7.39 N	67.36 W
San Juan de Sabinas	250	27.55 N	101.18 W
San Juan Evangelista	278	17.54 N	95.08 W
San Juanico, Isla I	278	21.43 N	106.38 W
San Juanillo	280	10.02 N	85.44 W
San Juan Islands II	256	48.36 N	122.50 W
San Juan Mountains ⋀	254	37.35 N	107.10 W
San Juan Nepomuceno, Col.	290	9.57 N	75.05 W
San Juan Nepomuceno, Para.	294	26.06 S	55.58 W
San Juan Sacatepéquez	280	14.43 N	90.39 W
San Juan y Martínez	284p	22.16 N	83.50 W
San Julián, Arg.	288	49.19 S	67.40 W
San Julian, Pil.	202	11.45 N	125.27 E
San Justo	294	30.47 S	60.35 W
Sankanbiriwa ∧	222	8.56 N	10.48 W
Sankarani ≃	222	12.01 N	8.19 W
Sankertown	266	40.28 N	78.35 W
Sankosh ≃	206	26.24 N	89.47 E
Sankt Aegyd am Neuwalde	164	47.52 N	15.35 E
Sankt Anton am Arlberg	164	47.08 N	10.16 E
Sankt Gallen, Öst.	164	47.41 N	14.37 E
Sankt Gallen, Schw.	180	47.25 N	9.23 E
Sankt Gallen □[3]	180	47.10 N	9.08 E
Sankt Georgen	180	48.07 N	8.20 E
Sankt Gilgen	164	47.46 N	13.22 E
Sankt Goar	164	50.09 N	7.43 E
Sankt Goarshausen	164	50.09 N	7.43 E
Sankt Hubert	178	51.23 N	6.26 E
Sankt Ingbert	164	49.17 N	7.06 E
Sankt Johann am Tauern	164	47.22 N	14.29 E
Sankt Johann im Pongau	164	47.21 N	13.12 E
Sankt Johann in Tirol	164	47.31 N	12.26 E
Sankt Lorenz ➝[8]	178	53.51 N	10.40 E
Sankt Mauritz	178	51.57 N	7.39 E
Sankt Moritz	180	46.30 N	9.50 E
Sankt Niklaus	166	46.11 N	7.48 E
Sankt Paul im Lavanttal	164	46.42 N	14.52 E
Sankt Peter	164	54.18 N	8.38 E
Sankt Pölten	164	48.12 N	15.37 E
Sankt Tönis	178	51.19 N	6.29 E
Sankt Valentin	164	48.10 N	14.32 E
Sankt Veit an der Glan	164	46.46 N	14.21 E
Sankt Wendel	164	49.28 N	7.10 E
Sankt Wolfgang im Salzkammergut	164	47.44 N	13.27 E
Sankuru ≃	218	4.17 S	20.25 E
San Lázaro	294	22.10 S	57.55 W
San Lázaro, Cabo ➤	278	24.50 N	112.18 W
San Leandro	272	37.43 N	122.09 W
San Leonardo (Sankt Leonhard), It.	170	46.49 N	11.15 E
San Leonardo, Méx.	250	27.28 N	104.55 W
San Lope	290	6.12 N	71.56 W
San Lorenzo, Arg.	294	32.45 S	60.44 W
San Lorenzo, Arg.	294	28.08 S	58.46 W
San Lorenzo, Bol.	292	21.26 S	64.47 W
San Lorenzo, Ec.	290	1.17 N	78.50 W
San Lorenzo, Hond.	280	13.25 N	87.27 W
San Lorenzo, Méx.	250	25.37 N	97.35 W
San Lorenzo, Méx.	254	31.47 N	106.26 W
San Lorenzo, Méx.	278	25.32 N	102.11 W
San Lorenzo, Nic.	280	12.20 N	85.41 W
San Lorenzo, Nic.	280	12.06 N	86.34 W
San Lorenzo, P.R.	284m	18.11 N	65.58 W
San Lorenzo, Calif., U.S.	272	37.41 N	122.08 W
San Lorenzo, Ven.	290	9.47 N	71.04 W
San Lorenzo ≃	278	24.15 N	107.25 W
San Lorenzo, Bahía C	280	13.20 N	87.28 W
San Lorenzo, Cabo ➤	290	1.04 S	80.56 W
San Lorenzo, Isla I, Méx.	278	28.35 N	112.50 W
San Lorenzo, Isla I, Perú	292	12.06 S	77.14 W
San Lorenzo de El Escoria	168	40.35 N	4.09 W
San Lorenzo de la Parilla	168	39.51 N	2.22 W
San Lorenzo Tenoxtitlan ⊥	278	17.44 N	94.45 W
Sanlúcar de Barrameda	168	36.47 N	6.21 W
Sanlúcar la Mayor	168	37.23 N	6.12 W
San Lucas, Bol.	292	20.06 S	65.07 W
San Lucas, Ec.	290	3.45 S	79.15 W
San Lucas, Méx.	278	24.13 N	103.04 W
San Lucas, Méx.	278	22.53 N	109.54 W
San Lucas, Calif., U.S.	272	36.08 N	121.01 W
San Lucas, Cabo ➤	278	22.50 N	109.55 W
San Lucas, Isla I	280	9.58 N	84.54 W
San Lucas, Serranía de ⋀	290	8.00 N	74.20 W
San Lucas Ocampo	278	24.44 N	104.39 W
San Luis, Arg.	294	33.20 S	66.20 W
San Luis, Cuba	284p	22.17 N	83.46 W
San Luis, Cuba	284p	20.12 N	75.51 W
San Luis, Guat.	280	16.14 N	89.27 W
San Luis, Ariz., U.S.	254	32.29 N	114.47 W
San Luis, Colo., U.S.	254	37.12 N	105.25 W
San Luis, Ven.	290	11.07 N	69.42 W
San Luis □[4]	294	34.00 S	66.00 W
San Luis, Lago de ⊜	292	13.45 S	64.00 W
San Luis, Sierra de ⋀	294	32.45 S	66.00 W
San Luis de la Paz	278	21.18 N	100.31 W
San Luis del Cordero	278	25.26 N	104.18 W
San Luis del Palmar	294	27.30 S	58.34 W
San Luis Gonzaga	278	24.55 N	111.16 W
San Luis Gonzaga, Bahía C	278	29.48 N	114.20 W
San Luis Jilotepeque	280	14.39 N	89.44 W
San Luis Obispo	272	35.17 N	120.40 W
San Luis Obispo □[6]	272	35.30 N	120.30 W
San Luis Peak ∧	254	37.59 N	106.56 W
San Luis Potosí	278	22.09 N	100.59 W
San Luis Rey	274	33.14 N	117.20 W
San Luis Rey ≃	258	33.12 N	117.24 W
San Luis Río Colorado	278	32.29 N	114.48 W
San Luis Valley ∨	254	37.25 N	106.00 W
Sanluri	170	39.33 N	8.54 E
San Manuel, Arg.	294	37.45 S	58.50 W
San Manuel, Pil.	202	16.04 N	120.40 E
San Manuel, Ariz., U.S.	254	32.36 N	110.38 W
San Marcelino, El Sal.	280	13.22 N	89.03 W
San Marcelino, Pil.	202	14.58 N	120.09 E
San Marcello Pistoiese	184	44.03 N	10.47 E
San Marcial, Punta ➤	278	25.30 N	111.01 W
San Marco in Lamis	184	41.43 N	15.38 E
San Marcos, Chile	294	30.56 S	71.03 W
San Marcos, Col.	290	8.39 N	75.08 W
San Marcos, C.R.	280	9.40 N	84.01 W
San Marcos, El Sal.	280	13.39 N	89.11 W
San Marcos, Guat.	280	14.58 N	91.48 W
San Marcos, Hond.	280	14.24 N	88.56 W
San Marcos, Hond.	280	15.17 N	88.23 W
San Marcos, Méx.	278	16.48 N	99.21 W
San Marcos, Méx.	278	26.41 N	102.07 W
San Marcos, Calif., U.S.	274	33.09 N	117.10 W
San Marcos, Tex., U.S.	250	29.53 N	97.57 W
San Marcos □[5]	280	15.00 N	91.55 W
San Marcos ≃	250	29.29 N	97.28 W
San Marcos, Isla I	278	27.13 N	112.05 W
San Marcos de Colón	280	13.26 N	86.48 W
San Marino	184	43.55 N	12.28 E
San Marino □[1]	158	43.56 N	12.25 E
San Martín, Arg.	294	33.10 S	68.25 W
San Martín, Arg.	294	29.13 S	65.47 W
San Martín, Col.	290	3.42 N	73.42 W
San Martin, Calif., U.S.	272	37.05 N	121.37 W
San Martín □[5]	292	7.00 S	76.50 W
San Martín ≃	292	13.08 S	63.43 W
San Martín, Cerro ∧[1]	278	18.19 N	94.48 W
San Martín de las Vacas	250	25.30 N	101.20 W
San Martín del Boracho, Sierra ⋀	254	30.55 N	105.45 W
San Martín de los Andes	288	40.10 S	71.20 W
San Martín de Valdeiglesias	168	40.21 N	4.24 W
San Martino di Castrozza	170	46.16 N	11.48 E
San Martín Texmelucan	278	19.17 N	98.26 W
San Marzano sul Sarno	184	40.46 N	14.35 E
San Mateo, Esp.	168	40.28 N	0.11 E
San Mateo, Calif., U.S.	272	37.35 N	122.19 W
San Mateo, Fla., U.S.	246	29.36 N	81.35 W
San Mateo, N. Mex., U.S.	254	35.20 N	107.39 W
San Mateo, Ven.	290	9.45 N	64.33 W
San Mateo □[6]	272	37.25 N	122.20 W
San Mateo Ixtatán	280	15.50 N	91.29 W
San Matías	292	16.22 S	58.24 W
San Mauro Torinese	182	45.06 N	7.46 E
Sanmen I	196	22.26 N	114.38 E
Sanmendao I	196	29.55 N	121.52 E
Sanmenwan C	196	29.08 N	121.44 E
Sanmenxia	190	34.45	111.05 E
San Miguel, Arg.	294	28.00 S	57.34 W
San Miguel, Bol.	292	16.42 S	61.01 W
San Miguel, Ec.	290	1.44 S	79.01 W
San Miguel, El Sal.	280	13.29 N	88.11 W
San Miguel, Pan.	290	8.27 N	78.55 W
San Miguel, Perú	292	13.01 S	73.59 W
San Miguel, Perú	292	7.00 S	78.50 W
San Miguel, Pil.	202	15.08 N	120.58 E
San Miguel, Calif., U.S.	272	35.45 N	120.42 W
San Miguel ≃, Bol.	292	13.52 S	63.56 W
San Miguel ≃, Méx.	254	30.51 N	110.45 W
San Miguel ≃, Méx.	278	29.05 N	110.55 W
San Miguel ≃, Méx.	280	15.54 N	92.10 W
San Miguel ≃, S.A.	292	19.15 S	59.20 W
San Miguel ≃, Colo., U.S.	254	38.23 N	108.48 W
San Miguel, Cerro ∧[2]	292	19.19 S	60.36 W
San Miguel, Golfo de C	290	8.20 N	78.20 W
San Miguel, Volcán de ∧[1]	280	13.28 N	88.16 W
San Miguel Bay C	202	13.50 N	123.10 E
San Miguel de Allende	278	20.55 N	100.45 W
San Miguel de Cruces	278	24.25 N	105.51 W
San Miguel del Monte	294	35.25 S	58.49 W
San Miguel del Padrón	284p	23.05 N	82.19 W
San Miguel de Tucumán	294	26.49 S	65.13 W
San Miguel el Alto	278	21.01 N	102.21 W
San Miguel Island I, Pil.	202	13.22 N	123.49 E
San Miguel Island I, Calif., U.S.	258	34.02 N	120.22 W
San Miguel Islands II	202	7.45 N	118.30 E
San Miguelito	280	11.23 N	84.54 W
San Miguel Ixtahuacán	280	15.15 N	91.45 W
San Miguel [o San Graciano]	278	29.10 N	101.28 W
San Miniato	184	43.41 N	10.51 E
Sannār	220	13.33 N	33.38 E
San Narciso, Pil.	202	13.34 N	122.34 E
San Narciso, Pil.	202	15.01 N	120.05 E
Sannicandro Garganico	184	41.50 N	15.34 E
San Nicolás, Hond.	280	15.00 N	88.45 W
San Nicolás, Méx.	250	26.07 N	100.52 W
San Nicolás, Perú	292	15.11 S	75.12 W
San Nicolas, Pil.	202	18.10 N	120.36 E
San Nicolas, Pil.	202	16.04 N	120.46 E
San Nicolás ≃	278	19.40 N	105.14 W
San Nicolás, Bahía C	292	15.12 S	75.16 W
San Nicolás, Punta ➤	292	15.14 S	75.15 W
San Nicolás de Bari	284p	22.47 N	81.55 W
San Nicolás de los Arroyos	294	33.20 S	60.13 W
San Nicolás de los Garzas	250	25.45 N	100.18 W
San Nicolas Island I	258	33.15 N	119.31 W
Sannikova, Proliv ⩊	186	74.30 N	140.00 E
Sanniquellie	222	7.22 N	8.43 W
Sannohe	192	40.22 N	141.15 E
Sano	192	36.19 N	139.35 E
Sañogasta	294	29.18 S	67.40 W
Sanok	164	49.34 N	22.13 E
San Onofre	290	9.44 N	75.32 W
San Pablo, Col.	290	1.40 N	77.00 W
San Pablo, Pil.	202	14.04 N	121.19 E
San Pablo, Pil.	202	7.40 N	123.27 E
San Pablo, Calif., U.S.	272	37.57 N	122.21 W
San Pablo ≃	280	7.52 N	81.11 W
San Pablo, Punta ➤	278	27.12 N	114.30 W
San Pablo Balleza	278	26.57 N	106.21 W
San Pablo Bay C	258	38.06 N	122.22 W
San Pablo Huitzo	278	17.15 N	96.52 W
San Pancrazio Salentino	170	40.25 N	17.50 E
San Paolo di Civitate	184	41.44 N	15.15 E
San Pascual	202	13.08 N	122.59 E
San Pedro, Arg.	294	24.14 S	64.50 W
San Pedro, Arg.	294	33.40 S	59.41 W
San Pedro, Arg.	294	27.57 S	65.11 W
San Pedro, Bol.	292	14.20 S	64.50 W
San Pedro, Chile	294	21.57 S	68.34 W
San Pedro, Chile	294	33.54 S	71.28 W
San Pedro, Col.	290	9.24 N	75.04 W
San Pedro, C.R.	280	9.56 N	84.03 W
San Pedro, Para.	294	24.07 S	56.59 W
San Pedro, Tex., U.S.	250	27.48 N	97.41 W
San Pedro, Ven.	290	8.50 N	71.58 W
San Pedro □[5]	294	24.15 S	56.30 W
San Pedro ➝[8]	274	33.44 N	118.18 W
San Pedro ≃, Cuba	284p	21.09 N	78.30 W
San Pedro ≃, N.A.	278	33.00 N	110.56 W
San Pedro ≃, N.A.	278	17.42 N	91.25 W
San Pedro ≃, Ariz., U.S.	254	33.00 N	110.50 W
San Pedro, Punta ➤, Chile	294	25.30 S	70.38 W
San Pedro, Punta ➤, C.R.	280	8.38 N	83.45 W
San Pedro, Volcán ∧[1]	294	21.53 S	68.25 W
San Pedro Ayampuc	280	14.47 N	90.27 W
San Pedro Bay C	202	11.10 N	125.05 E
San Pedro Carchá	280	15.29 N	90.16 W
San Pedro de Atacama	294	22.55 S	68.13 W
San Pedro de Buena Vista	292	18.13 S	65.59 W
San Pedro de la Cueva	278	29.18 N	109.44 W
San Pedro de las Colonias	278	25.45 N	102.59 W
San Pedro del Gallo	278	25.33 N	104.18 W
San Pedro de Lloc	292	7.25 S	79.30 W
San Pedro del Norte	280	13.04 N	84.33 W
San Pedro del Paraná	294	26.46 S	56.15 W
San Pedro de Macorís	282	18.27 N	69.18 W
San Pedro Mártir, Sierra ⋀	278	30.45 N	115.13 W
San Pedro Peaks ⋀	254	36.07 N	106.49 W
San Pedro Pinula	280	14.40 N	89.51 W
San Pedro Sacatepéquez	280	14.58 N	91.46 W
San Pedro Sula	280	15.27 N	88.02 W
San Pelayo	290	8.58 N	75.51 W
San Pellegrino Terme	170	45.50 N	9.40 E
San Pierre	268	41.12 N	86.53 W
San Pietro, Isola di I	170	39.08 N	8.18 E
San Pitch ≃	254	39.03 N	111.51 W
Sanpoil ≃	256	48.01 N	118.41 W
San Policarpio	202	12.11 N	125.30 E
Sanquhar	162	55.22 N	3.56 W
San Quintin	202	15.59 N	120.49 E
San Quintín, Bahía de C	278	30.18 N	115.53 W
San Quintín, Cabo ➤	278	30.21 N	116.00 W
San Rafael, Arg.	294	34.40 S	68.21 W

Symbols in the index entries are identified on page 360.

Name	Page	Lat°′	Long°′
San Rafael, Chile	294	35.19 S	71.32 W
San Rafael, Méx.	278	25.01 N	100.33 W
San Rafael, Méx.	278	28.34 N	111.42 W
San Rafael, Calif., U.S.	272	37.59 N	122.31 W
San Rafael, N. Mex., U.S.	254	35.06 N	107.53 W
San Rafael, Ven.	290	10.58 N	71.44 W
San Rafael ≃	254	38.47 N	110.07 W
San Rafael de Arriba	278	31.05 N	116.05 W
San Rafael de las Tortillas	250	26.49 N	99.32 W
San Rafael del Norte	280	13.11 N	86.06 W
San Rafael del Sur	280	11.51 N	86.27 W
San Rafael Mountains ⛰	258	34.45 N	119.50 W
San Rafael Oriente	280	13.23 N	88.21 W
San Rafael Swell ⛰[1]	254	38.40 N	110.45 W
San Ramón, Arg.	294	27.42 S	64.17 W
San Ramón, Bol.	292	13.17 S	64.43 W
San Ramón, C.R.	280	10.06 N	84.28 W
San Ramón, Nic.	280	14.45 N	84.50 W
San Ramón, Perú	292	11.08 S	75.20 W
San Ramon, Pil.	202	13.16 N	124.04 E
San Ramon, Calif., U.S.	272	37.47 N	121.59 W
San Ramón, Ur.	294	34.18 S	55.58 W
San Ramón, Bahía C	278	30.45 N	116.03 W
San Ramón de la Nueva Orán	294	23.08 S	64.20 W
San Remigio	202	11.05 N	123.56 E
San Remo, It.	182	43.49 N	7.46 E
San Remo, N.Y., U.S.	261	40.54 N	73.13 W
San Rodrigo ≃	250	28.55 N	100.35 W
San Román ≃	280	16.21 N	90.22 W
San Román, Cabo ≻	290	12.12 N	70.00 W
San Roque, Arg.	294	28.35 S	58.40 W
San Roque, Arg.	294	30.15 S	68.38 W
San Roque, Esp.	168	36.13 N	5.24 W
San Rosendo	294	37.16 S	72.43 W
San Saba	250	31.12 N	98.43 W
San Saba ≃	250	31.15 N	98.35 W
San Salvador, Arg.	294	29.18 S	57.30 W
San Salvador, Arg.	294	31.37 S	58.30 W
San Salvador, El Sal.	280	13.42 N	89.12 W
San Salvador (Watling Island) I	282	24.00 N	74.30 W
San Salvador, Isla I	290a	0.14 S	90.45 W
San Salvador, Volcán de Λ[1]	280	13.44 N	89.17 W
San Salvador de Jujuy	294	24.10 S	65.20 W
Sansanding Dam ⊸[6]	222	13.44 N	6.00 W
Sansanné-Mango	222	10.21 N	0.28 E
San Sebastián, El Sal.	280	13.44 N	88.50 W
San Sebastián, Esp.	168	43.19 N	1.59 W
San Sebastián, Guat.	280	14.34 N	91.39 W
San Sebastián, Hond.	280	13.56 N	88.23 W
San Sebastián, P.R.	284m	18.20 N	66.59 W
San Sebastián de Yalí	280	13.16 N	86.11 W
Sansepolcro	184	43.34 N	12.08 E
San Severino Marche	184	43.13 N	13.10 E
San Severo	184	41.41 N	15.23 E
Sanshawan C	196	26.35 N	119.50 E
Sanshui	190	23.11 N	112.53 E
San Simeon	272	35.39 N	121.11 W
San Simon, Méx.	258	30.30 N	115.58 W
San Simon, Ariz., U.S.	254	32.16 N	109.14 W
San Simón ≃, Bol.	292	13.13 S	63.31 W
San Simon ≃, Ariz., U.S.	254	32.50 N	109.39 W
San Simon Wash V	254	31.45 N	112.25 W
Sanski Most	170	44.46 N	16.40 E
San Solano	294	31.29 S	65.56 W
Sans Souci	246	34.53 N	82.24 W
Sans-Souci ⊥	282	19.37 N	72.12 W
Santa, Perú	292	8.59 S	78.40 W
Santa, Pil.	202	17.29 N	120.26 E
Santa ≃	292	8.58 S	78.39 W
Santa, Isla de I	292	9.02 S	78.40 W
Santa Adélia	296	21.16 S	48.48 W
Santa Albertina	296	20.02 S	50.44 W
Santa Amalia	168	39.01 N	6.01 W
Santa Amelia ≃	280	16.13 N	90.02 W
Santa Ana, Arg.	294	27.20 S	55.35 W
Santa Ana, Bol.	292	15.31 S	67.30 W
Santa Ana, Bol.	292	18.43 S	58.44 W
Santa Ana, Bol.	292	13.45 S	65.35 W
Santa Ana, Col.	290	9.19 N	74.35 W
Santa Ana, Ec.	290	1.13 S	80.23 W
Santa Ana, El Sal.	280	13.59 N	89.34 W
Santa Ana, Méx.	278	30.33 N	111.07 W
Santa Ana, Méx.	278	24.04 N	100.30 W
Santa Ana, Calif., U.S.	274	33.43 N	117.54 W
Santa Ana, Cuchilla de(Coxilna de Santana) ⛰[2]	294	30.50 S	55.35 W
Santa Ana, Volcán de Λ[1]	280	13.50 N	89.39 W
Santa Ana de Barcelona	290	9.19 N	64.39 W
Santa Ana Heights	274	33.39 N	117.54 W
Santa Ana Mountains ⛰	258	33.45 N	117.35 W
Santa Anna	250	31.45 N	99.19 W
Santa Apolonia	250	25.38 N	97.59 W
Santa Bárbara, Chile	294	37.40 S	72.01 W
Santa Bárbara, Col.	290	5.53 N	75.35 W
Santa Bárbara, Hond.	280	14.53 N	88.14 W
Santa Bárbara, Méx.	278	26.48 N	105.49 W
Santa Barbara, Calif., U.S.	258	34.25 N	119.42 W
Santa Bárbara, Ven.	290	7.47 N	71.10 W
Santa Bárbara, Ven.	290	3.57 N	67.06 W
Santa Bárbara □[5]	280	15.10 N	88.20 W
Santa Bárbara ≃	292	16.58 S	61.39 W
Santa Bárbara, Serra de ⛰[1]	292	15.30 S	59.20 W
Santa Barbara, Sierra ⛰	294	24.10 S	64.25 W
Santa Barbara Channel ⋃	258	34.15 N	119.55 W
Santa Bárbara do Sul	294	28.22 S	53.15 W
Santa Branca	296	23.24 S	45.53 W
Santa Catalina, Arg.	294	21.58 S	66.02 W
Santa Catalina, Pan.	280	8.46 N	81.20 W
Santa Catalina, Pil.	202	9.20 N	121.50 E
Santa Catalina, Isla I	278	25.40 N	110.50 W
Santa Catalina Island I	258	33.23 N	118.26 W
Santa Catalina Mountains ⛰	254	32.25 N	110.45 W
Santa Catarina, Méx.	258	31.37 N	115.48 W
Santa Catarina, Méx.	278	25.41 N	100.28 W
Santa Catarina □[3]	294	27.00 S	50.00 W
Santa Catarina ≃	296	17.46 S	46.34 W
Santa Catarina, Ilha de I	294	27.36 S	48.30 W
Santa Cecílio	294	26.56 S	50.27 W
Santa Cesarea Terme	170	40.02 N	18.29 E
Santa Clara, Arg.	294	29.34 S	68.31 W
Santa Clara, Col.	290	2.43 S	69.43 W
Santa Clara, Cuba	284p	22.24 N	79.58 W
Santa Clara, Méx.	278	29.17 N	107.01 W
Santa Clara, Calif., U.S.	272	37.21 N	121.57 W
Santa Clara, Utah, U.S.	254	37.08 N	113.39 W
Santa Clara □[6]	272	37.20 N	121.53 W
Santa Clara ≃	254	37.05 N	113.36 W
Santa Clara, Bahía de C	284p	23.06 N	80.30 W
Santa Clara de Olimar	294	32.55 S	54.58 W
Santa Clara Valley V	258	37.10 N	121.40 W
Santa Clotilde	290	2.25 S	73.35 W
Santa Coloma de Farnés	168	41.52 N	2.40 E
Santa Comba	168	43.02 N	8.49 W
Santa Comba Dão	168	40.24 N	8.08 W
Santa Croce di Magliano	184	41.42 N	14.59 E
Santa Cruz, Arg.	288	50.00 S	68.32 W
Santa Cruz, Bol.	292	17.48 S	63.10 W
Santa Cruz, Bra.	296	19.56 S	40.09 W
Santa Cruz, Chile	294	34.38 S	71.22 W
Santa Cruz, C.R.	280	10.16 N	85.36 W
Santa Cruz, Méx.	254	31.14 N	110.35 W
Santa Cruz, Méx.	278	23.05 N	97.50 W
Santa Cruz, Perú	292	6.35 S	78.56 W
Santa Cruz, Pil.	202	13.29 N	122.02 E
Santa Cruz, Pil.	202	13.04 N	120.43 E
Santa Cruz (Tubajon), Pil.	202	10.19 N	125.33 E
Santa Cruz, Pil.	202	14.17 N	121.25 E
Santa Cruz, Pil.	202	15.46 N	119.55 E
Santa Cruz, Pil.	202	6.50 N	125.25 E
Santa Cruz, Calif., U.S.	272	36.58 N	122.01 W
Santa Cruz, Ven.	290	8.25 N	71.39 W
Santa Cruz □[5]	292	17.30 S	61.30 W
Santa Cruz □[6]	272	36.58 N	122.01 W
Santa Cruz ≃, Arg.	288	50.10 S	68.20 W
Santa Cruz ≃, Ariz., U.S.	254	33.15 N	112.10 W
Santa Cruz, Isla I	290a	0.38 S	90.23 W
Santa Cruz, Sierra de ⛰	280	15.40 N	89.20 W
Santa Cruz Basin ⌣[1]	148	13.00 S	163.00 E
Santa Cruz Cabrália	296	16.17 S	39.02 W
Santa Cruz da Vitória	296	14.57 S	39.48 W
Santa Cruz de Goiás	296	17.19 S	48.30 W
Santa Cruz de la Palma	214	28.41 N	17.45 W
Santa Cruz de la Zarza	168	39.58 N	3.10 W
Santa Cruz del Norte	284p	23.09 N	81.55 W
Santa Cruz del Quiché	280	15.02 N	91.08 W
Santa Cruz del Sur	284p	20.43 N	78.00 W
Santa Cruz de Mudela	168	38.38 N	3.28 W
Santa Cruz de Tenerife	214	28.27 N	16.14 W
Santa Cruz do Rio Pardo	296	22.55 S	49.37 W
Santa Cruz do Sul	294	29.43 S	52.26 W
Santa Cruz Island I	258	34.01 N	119.45 W
Santa Cruz Point ≻	202	15.45 N	119.52 E
Santa Elena, Arg.	294	31.00 S	59.50 W
Santa Elena, Ec.	290	2.14 S	80.51 W
Santa Elena, El Sal.	280	13.22 N	88.25 W
Santa Elena, Méx.	250	27.59 N	103.56 W
Santa Elena, Méx.	278	27.28 N	102.33 W
Santa Elena, Bahía C	280	10.59 N	85.50 W
Santa Elena, Bahía de C	290	2.06 S	80.53 W
Santa Elena, Cabo ≻	280	10.55 N	85.57 W
Santa Elena de Uairén	290	4.37 N	61.08 W
Santa Eulalia, Esp.	168	40.34 N	1.19 W
Santa Eulalia, Guat.	280	15.45 N	91.29 W
Santa Eulalia del Río	168	38.59 N	1.31 E
Santa Fe, Arg.	294	31.40 S	60.40 W
Santa Fé, Bra.	296	23.01 S	51.48 W
Santa Fé, Bra.	296	15.40 S	51.16 W
Santa Fé, Cuba	284p	21.45 N	82.45 W
Santa Fe, Esp.	168	37.11 N	3.43 W
Santa Fé, Hond.	280	15.55 N	86.05 W
Santa Fe, Pan.	280	8.32 N	81.05 W
Santa Fe, Pil.	202	11.09 N	123.47 E
Santa Fe, Pil.	202	12.10 N	122.00 E
Santa Fe, Pil.	202	16.10 N	120.57 E
Santa Fe, N. Mex., U.S.	254	35.42 N	106.57 W
Santa Fe □[4]	294	31.15 S	61.00 W
Santa Fe ≃, Fla., U.S.	246	29.53 N	82.53 W
Santa Fe ≃, N. Mex., U.S.	254	35.36 N	106.20 W
Santa Fe, Isla I	290a	0.49 S	90.04 W
Santa Fe Baldy Λ	254	35.50 N	105.46 W
Santa Fé do Sul	296	20.13 S	50.56 W
Santa Filomena	286	9.07 S	45.56 W
Sant'Agata de'Goti	184	41.05 N	14.30 E
Sant'Agata di Militello	170	38.04 N	14.38 E
Sant'Agata di Puglia	184	41.09 N	15.23 E
Santa Gertrudis	250	26.09 N	98.44 W
Santa Helena de Goiás	296	17.43 S	50.35 W
Santai	190	31.10 N	105.02 E
Santa Inês	296	13.17 S	39.48 W
Santa Inés, Bahía C	278	27.00 N	111.55 W
Santa Inés, Isla I	288	53.40 S	73.00 W
Santa Isabel, Arg.	294	33.54 S	61.40 W
Santa Isabel, Arg.	294	36.15 S	66.55 W
Santa Isabel, Ec.	290	3.21 S	79.19 W
Santa Isabel, Gui. Ecu.	222	3.45 N	8.47 E
Santa Isabel, P.R.	284m	17.58 N	66.24 W
Santa Isabel I	226	8.00 S	159.00 E
Santa Isabel de las Lajas	284p	22.25 N	80.18 W
Santa Isabel de Sihuas	292	16.18 S	72.08 W
Santa Josefa	202	8.00 N	125.58 E
Santa Juliana	296	19.19 S	47.32 W
Santa Leopoldina	296	20.06 S	40.32 W
Santa Lucía, Arg.	294	29.00 S	59.06 W
Santa Lucía, Arg.	294	31.30 S	68.30 W
Santa Lucía, Cuba	284p	22.40 N	83.58 W
Santa Lucía, Cuba	284p	21.02 N	76.00 W
Santa Lucía, Cuba	284p	20.58 N	77.23 W
Santa Lucía, Ur.	294	34.27 S	56.24 W
Santa Lucía, Ven.	290	8.07 N	69.46 W
Santa Lucía Cotzumalguapa	280	14.20 N	91.01 W
Santa Lucia Range ⛰	258	36.00 N	121.20 W
Santa Lugarda, Punta ≻	278	26.45 N	109.50 W
Santa Luzia	168	37.44 N	8.24 W
Santa Luzia I	222a	16.46 N	24.45 W
Santa Magdalena	202	12.38 N	124.06 E
Santa Magdalena, Isla I	278	24.50 N	112.15 W
Santa Margarita	272	35.23 N	120.37 W
Santa Margarita, Isla de I	278	24.25 N	111.50 W
Santa Margherita Ligure	182	44.20 N	9.12 E
Santa María, Arg.	294	26.40 S	66.02 W
Santa Maria, Bra.	294	29.41 S	53.48 W
Santa María, C.R.	280	9.39 N	83.57 W
Santa Maria, Fr.	170	41.52 N	8.59 E
Santa Maria, Méx.	250	28.02 N	101.38 W
Santa María, Pan.	280	8.08 N	80.43 W
Santa Maria, Pil.	202	14.49 N	120.58 E
Santa Maria, Pil.	202	17.22 N	120.29 E
Santa María, P.R.	284m	18.09 N	65.26 W
Santa Maria, Calif., U.S.	258	34.57 N	120.26 W
Santa María ≃, Arg.	294	26.05 S	65.49 W
Santa Maria ≃, Bra.	294	29.48 S	54.56 W
Santa Maria ≃, Bra.	296	21.50 S	54.53 W
Santa María ≃, Méx.	278	31.00 N	107.15 W
Santa María ≃, Pan.	280	8.05 N	80.30 W
Santa Maria ≃, Ariz., U.S.	254	34.19 N	34.31 W
Santa Maria ≃, Calif., U.S.	258	34.58 N	120.38 W
Santa María ≃, Ven.	290	7.54 N	60.37 W
Santa María, Bahía de C	278	25.05 N	108.15 W
Santa María, Cabo ≻	294	34.40 S	54.10 W
Santa Maria, Cabo de ≻, Ang.	218	13.25 S	12.32 E
Santa Maria, Cabo de ≻, Port.	168	36.58 N	7.54 W
Santa Maria, Cape ≻	282	23.41 N	75.19 W
Santa María, Cayo I	284p	22.39 N	79.00 W
Santa María, Isla I, Chile	294	37.02 S	73.33 W
Santa María, Isla I, Ec.	290a	1.17 S	90.26 W
Santa María, Laguna de ◎	278	31.07 N	107.17 W
Santa María, Volcán Λ[1]	280	14.46 N	91.33 W
Santa Maria a Vico	184	41.02 N	14.29 E
Santa Maria Capua Vetere	184	41.05 N	14.15 E
Santa María Colotepec	278	15.53 N	96.55 W
Santa Maria da Vitória	296	13.24 S	44.12 W
Santa María de Ipire	290	8.49 N	65.19 W
Santa Maria de Itabira	296	19.27 S	43.08 W
Santa María del Oro	278	25.56 N	105.22 W
Santa María del Río	278	21.48 N	100.45 W
Santa Maria di Leuca, Capo ≻	170	39.47 N	18.22 E
Santa Maria do Suaçuí	296	18.12 S	42.25 W
Santa María Jalapa [del Marqués]	278	16.30 N	95.28 W
Santa María la Real de Nieva	168	41.04 N	4.24 W
Santa Maria Madalena	296	21.57 S	42.01 W
Santa Marinella	184	42.02 N	11.51 E
Santa Marta, Col.	290	11.15 N	74.13 W
Santa Marta, Guat.	280	13.58 N	91.18 W
Santa Marta ≃	292	8.47 S	76.13 W
Santa Marta, Ría de C[1]	168	43.42 N	7.51 W
Santa Marta Grande, Cabo de ≻	294	28.38 S	48.45 W
Santa Mónica, Méx.	250	28.12 N	100.37 W
Santa Monica, Calif., U.S.	274	34.01 N	118.30 W
Santa Monica Bay C	258	33.54 N	118.25 W
Santana	296	12.59 S	44.03 W
Santana ≃	296	19.43 S	51.02 W
Santana, Cachoeira ↳	296	14.45 S	49.10 W
Santana, Coxilha de(Cuchilla De Santa Ana) ⛰[2]	294	30.50 S	55.35 W
Santana da Boa Vista	294	30.52 S	53.07 W
Santana do Livramento	294	30.53 S	55.31 W
Sant'Anastasia	184	40.52 N	14.24 E
Santander, Col.	290	3.01 N	76.28 W
Santander, Esp.	168	43.28 N	3.48 W
Santander, Pil.	202	9.25 N	123.20 E
Santander □[5]	290	7.00 N	73.15 W
Santander, Norte de □[3]	282	8.00 N	73.00 W
Santander Jiménez	278	24.13 N	98.28 W
Santa Nella	272	37.03 N	121.02 W
Sant'Angelo de'Lombardi	170	40.56 N	15.11 E
Sant'Angelo Lodigiano	182	45.14 N	9.24 E
Sant'Antimo	184	40.56 N	14.14 E
Sant'Antioco, Isola di I	170	39.00 N	8.25 E
Sant'Antonio Abate	184	40.43 N	14.32 E
Santañy	168	39.22 N	3.07 E
Santa Paula	274	34.21 N	119.04 W
Santa Pola, Cabo de ≻	168	38.12 N	0.31 W
Santaquin	254	39.59 N	111.47 W
Sant'Arcangelo	170	40.15 N	16.17 E
Sant'Arcangelo di Romagna	184	44.04 N	12.27 E
Santarém, Bra.	286	2.26 S	54.42 W
Santarém, Port.	168	39.14 N	8.41 W
Santa Rita, Col.	290	1.04 N	73.58 W
Santa Rita, Hond.	280	15.09 N	87.53 W
Santa Rita, Méx.	250	25.30 N	103.59 W
Santa Rita, Méx.	250	27.29 N	100.33 W
Santa Rita, Pil.	202	11.27 N	124.56 E
Santa Rita, Mont., U.S.	238	48.42 N	112.19 W
Santa Rita, N. Mex., U.S.	254	32.48 N	108.04 W
Santa Rita, Ven.	290	10.32 N	71.32 W
Santa Rita de Catuna	294	30.57 S	66.14 W
Santa Rita do Araguaia	296	17.20 S	53.12 W
Santa Rita do Weil	290	3.29 S	69.19 W
Santa Rita Park	272	37.03 N	120.36 W
Santa Rosa, Arg.	294	28.02 S	67.37 W
Santa Rosa, Arg.	294	36.40 S	64.15 W
Santa Rosa, Arg.	294	23.22 S	64.28 W
Santa Rosa, Arg.	294	32.20 S	65.10 W
Santa Rosa, Bol.	292	14.10 S	66.53 W
Santa Rosa, Bol.	292	17.07 S	63.35 W
Santa Rosa, Bol.	292	10.36 S	67.25 W
Santa Rosa, Bra.	294	27.52 S	54.29 W
Santa Rosa, Bra.	296	15.01 S	47.13 W
Santa Rosa, Col.	290	2.31 N	68.13 W
Santa Rosa, C.R.	280	10.51 N	85.38 W
Santa Rosa, Ec.	290	3.27 S	79.58 W
Santa Rosa, Méx.	258	31.59 N	116.45 W
Santa Rosa, Para.	292	21.46 S	61.43 W
Santa Rosa, Para.	294	26.52 S	56.49 W
Santa Rosa, Calif., U.S.	272	38.26 N	122.43 W
Santa Rosa, N. Mex., U.S.	250	34.57 N	104.41 W
Santa Rosa, Tex., U.S.	250	26.15 N	97.50 W
Santa Rosa, Ven.	290	8.26 N	69.24 W
Santa Rosa □[5]	280	14.10 N	90.18 W
Santa Rosa Beach	248	30.23 N	86.14 W
Santa Rosa de Aguán	280	15.57 N	85.43 W
Santa Rosa de Amanadona	290	1.29 N	66.55 W
Santa Rosa de Cabal	290	4.52 N	75.38 W
Santa Rosa [de Copán]	280	14.47 N	88.46 W
Santa Rosa de la Roca	292	16.04 S	61.32 W
Santa Rosa de Leales	294	27.10 S	65.17 W
Santa Rosa de Lima	280	13.37 N	87.53 W
Santa Rosa del Palmar	292	16.54 S	62.24 W
Santa Rosa de Osos	290	6.39 N	75.28 W
Santa Rosa de Río Primero	294	31.10 S	63.23 W
Santa Rosa de Sucumbíos	290	0.22 N	77.10 W
Santa Rosa de Viterbo	290	5.53 N	72.59 W
Santa Rosa Island I, Calif., U.S.	258	33.58 N	120.06 W
Santa Rosa Island I, Fla., U.S.	248	30.22 N	86.55 W
Santa Rosalía, Méx.	250	26.08 N	98.59 W
Santa Rosalía, Méx.	278	27.19 N	112.17 W
Santa Rosalía, Ven.	290	9.02 N	69.01 W
Santa Rosalía, Bahía C	278	28.38 N	114.10 W
Santa Rosa Range ⛰	258	41.00 N	117.40 W
Santa Rosa Wash V	254	33.00 N	112.00 W
Šantarskije Ostrova II	186	55.00 N	137.36 E
Santa Susana	274	34.16 N	118.43 W
Santa Sylvina	294	27.50 S	61.10 W
Santa Tecla → Nueva San Salvador	280	13.41 N	89.17 W
Santa Teresa, Arg.	294	33.25 S	60.47 W
Santa Teresa, Bra.	296	19.55 S	40.36 W
Santa Teresa, Bra.	296	13.38 S	49.01 W
Santa Teresa, Méx.	250	29.34 N	104.39 W
Santa Teresa, Méx.	254	30.52 N	111.33 W
Santa Teresa ≃	296	11.47 S	48.37 W
Santa Teresa, Embalse de ◎[1]	168	40.40 N	5.30 W
Santa Teresa del Tuy	290	10.14 N	66.40 W
Santa Teresa Gallura	170	41.15 N	9.12 E
Santa Teresinha	296	12.45 S	39.32 W
Santa Venetia	272	38.01 N	122.31 W
Santa Vitória	296	18.50 S	50.08 W
Santa Vitória do Palmar	294	33.31 S	53.21 W
Santa Ynez ≃	258	35.41 N	120.36 W
Santee	274	32.50 N	116.58 W
Santee ≃	246	33.14 N	79.28 W
Santee Dam ⊸[6]	246	33.24 N	80.12 W
Santee Indian Reservation ⊸[4]	252	42.45 N	97.50 W
Santerre □[9]	176	49.40 N	2.40 E
Sant'Eufemia, Golfo di C	170	38.50 N	16.00 E
Santhià	182	45.22 N	8.10 E
Santiago, Bol.	292	18.19 S	59.34 W
Santiago, Bra.	294	29.11 S	54.53 W
Santiago, Chile	294	33.27 S	70.40 W
Santiago, C.R.	280	9.51 N	84.18 W
Santiago → Santiago de Compostela, Esp.	168	42.53 N	8.33 W
Santiago, Méx.	278	23.28 N	109.43 W
Santiago, Méx.	278	25.25 N	100.09 W
Santiago, Pan.	280	8.05 N	80.59 W
Santiago, Para.	294	27.09 S	56.47 W
Santiago, Perú	292	14.11 S	75.43 W
Santiago, Pil.	202	16.42 N	121.33 E
Santiago □[4]	294	33.30 S	70.50 W
Santiago ≃, Méx.	278	20.40 N	103.13 W
Santiago ≃, S.A.	290	4.27 S	77.38 W
Santiago, Cape ≻	202	13.48 N	120.40 E
Santiago, Cerro Λ	280	8.35 N	81.45 W
Santiago, Río de ≃	278	25.11 N	105.26 W
Santiago, Serranía de ⛰	292	18.25 S	59.25 W
Santiago Atitlán	280	14.38 N	91.14 W
Santiago de Cao	292	7.58 S	79.15 W
Santiago de Chocorvos	292	13.50 S	75.14 W
Santiago de Chuco	292	8.09 S	78.11 W
Santiago de Compostela	168	42.53 N	8.33 W
Santiago de Cuba	284p	20.01 N	75.49 W
Santiago de Huata	292	16.06 S	68.53 W
Santiago del Estero	294	27.50 S	64.15 W
Santiago del Estero □[4]	294	27.40 S	63.15 W
Santiago [de los Caballeros]	282	19.27 N	70.42 W
Santiago de Machaca	292	17.05 S	69.16 W
Santiago do Cacém	168	38.01 N	8.42 W
Santiago Island I	202	16.25 N	119.56 E
Santiago Ixcuintla	278	21.49 N	105.13 W
Santiago Larre	294	35.37 S	59.10 W
Santiago Papasquiaro	278	25.03 N	105.25 W
Santiago Peak Λ, Calif., U.S.	258	33.43 N	117.32 W
Santiago Peak Λ, Tex., U.S.	250	29.47 N	103.25 W
Santiago Rodríguez	282	19.30 N	71.21 W
Santiaguillo, Laguna de ◎	278	24.50 N	104.50 W
Santiam Pass)(	256	44.25 N	121.51 W
Santiao Chiao ≻	196	25.02 N	121.59 E
San Timoteo	290	9.48 N	71.04 W
Sāntipur	206	23.15 N	88.26 E
Santisteban del Puerto	168	38.15 N	3.12 W
Santo	250	32.36 N	98.13 W
Santo Amaro	296	12.32 S	38.43 W
Santo Anastácio	296	21.58 S	51.39 W
Santo Anastácio ≃	296	21.49 S	52.11 W
Santo André	296	23.40 S	46.31 W
Santo Ângelo	294	28.18 S	54.16 W
Santo Antão I	222a	17.05 N	25.10 W
Santo Antônio, Bra.	294	29.50 S	50.32 W
Santo Antônio, Bra.	294	26.02 S	53.44 W
Santo António, S. Tom./P.	214	1.39 N	7.26 E
Santo Antônio ≃, Bra.	296	17.30 S	45.37 W
Santo Antônio ≃, Bra.	296	11.31 S	48.37 W
Santo Antônio, Cachoeira ↳	292	9.46 S	60.35 W
Santo Antônio, Igarapé ≃	290	1.32 S	59.48 W
Santo Antônio da Boa Vista	296	15.52 S	44.09 W
Santo Antônio de Jesus	296	12.58 S	39.16 W
Santo Antônio do Amparo	296	20.57 S	44.55 W
Santo Antônio do Içá	290	3.05 S	67.57 W
Santo Antônio do Leverger	292	15.52 S	56.05 W
Santo Antônio do Rio Verde	296	17.57 S	47.27 W
Santo António do Zaire	218	6.07 S	12.18 E
Santo Augusto	294	27.51 S	53.47 W
Santo Corazón	292	17.59 S	58.51 W
Santo Cristo	294	27.50 S	54.40 W
Santo Domingo, Arg.	294	29.16 S	63.56 W
Santo Domingo, Cuba	284p	22.35 N	80.15 W
Santo Domingo, Méx.	250	25.45 N	98.19 W
Santo Domingo, Méx.	250	25.48 N	104.28 W
Santo Domingo, Méx.	250	25.38 N	101.05 W
Santo Domingo, Méx.	278	25.32 N	112.02 W
Santo Domingo, Méx.	278	23.20 N	101.44 W
Santo Domingo, Nic.	280	12.16 N	84.59 W
Santo Domingo, Rep. Dom.	282	18.28 N	69.54 W
Santo Domingo ≃, Méx.	278	16.41 N	93.00 W
Santo Domingo ≃, Méx.	280	16.15 N	91.17 W
Santo Domingo ≃, Ven.	290	8.01 N	69.33 W
Santo Domingo, Arroyo ≃, Méx.	258	30.43 N	116.02 W
Santo Domingo de la Calzada	168	42.26 N	2.57 W
Santo Domingo de los Colorados	290	0.15 S	79.09 W
Santo Domingo Pueblo	254	35.31 N	106.22 W
Santo Estevão	296	12.26 S	39.13 W
Santolea, Embalse de ◎[1]	168	40.47 N	0.19 W
San Tomé	290	8.58 N	64.08 W
Santoña	168	43.27 N	3.27 W
Santonghe ≃	194	42.39 N	126.03 E
Santo Nino Island I	202	11.55 N	124.25 E
Santo Onofre ≃	296	12.34 S	43.12 W
Santos	296	23.57 S	46.20 W
Santos Dumont	296	21.28 S	43.34 W
Santo Tirso	168	41.21 N	8.28 W
Santo Tomás, Col.	290	10.46 N	74.45 W
Santo Tomás, Méx.	278	31.33 N	116.24 W
Santo Tomás, Nic.	280	13.09 N	86.56 W
Santo Tomás, Nic.	280	12.06 N	85.04 W
Santo Tomás, Perú	292	6.35 S	77.47 W
Santo Tomás, Perú	292	14.26 S	72.08 W
Santo Tomas, Pil.	202	7.29 N	125.38 E
Santo Tomás, Ven.	290	8.53 N	64.33 W
Santo Tomás ≃, Méx.	258	31.33 N	116.40 W
Santo Tomás ≃, Perú	292	13.47 S	72.08 W
Santo Tomás, Punta ≻	278	31.34 N	116.42 W
Santo Tomás, Volcán Λ[1]	290a	0.48 S	91.07 W
Santo Tomás Ocotepec	278	17.08 N	97.46 W
Santo Tomé, Arg.	294	31.40 S	60.45 W
Santo Tomé, Arg.	294	28.35 S	56.05 W
Santo Tomé de Guayana	290	8.22 N	62.40 W
Santpoort	178	52.25 N	4.38 E
San Ubaldo	280	11.50 N	85.20 W
Sanuki-sammyaku ⛰	192	34.05 N	134.00 E
San Valentín, Monte Λ	288	46.40 S	73.25 W
San Valentino Torio	184	40.48 N	14.36 E
San Vicente, Arg.	294	28.30 S	64.09 W
San Vicente, Chile	294	34.26 S	71.05 W
San Vicente, El Sal.	280	13.38 N	88.48 W
San Vicente, Méx.	278	31.20 N	116.15 W
San Vicente, Volcán de Λ[1]	280	13.36 N	88.50 W
San Vicente de Alcántara	168	39.21 N	7.08 W
San Vicente de Chucurí	290	6.54 N	73.25 W
San Vicente de la Barquera	168	43.26 N	4.24 W
San Vicente del Caguán	290	2.07 N	74.46 W
San Vincenzo	170	43.06 N	10.32 E
San Vito, C.R.	280	8.50 N	82.58 W
San Vito, It.	170	39.27 N	9.32 E
San Vito, Capo ≻	170	38.11 N	12.43 E
San Vito al Tagliamento	170	45.54 N	12.52 E
San Vito dei Normanni	170	40.39 N	17.42 E
San Xavier Indian Reservation ⊸[4]	254	32.05 N	111.08 W
San Ygnacio	250	27.03 N	99.27 W
Sanyō	192	34.02 N	131.10 E
Sanyuan	190	34.35 N	108.54 E
Sanzaodao I	196	22.03 N	113.21 E
Sanza Pombo	218	7.19 S	15.59 E
São Benedito ≃	292	9.11 S	57.02 W
São Bento	290	3.02 N	60.30 W
São Bento do Sul	294	26.15 S	49.23 W
São Borja	294	28.39 S	56.00 W
São Caetano do Sul	296	23.36 S	46.34 W
São Carlos, Bra.	294	27.04 S	52.59 W
São Carlos, Bra.	296	22.01 S	47.54 W
São Cristóvão	286	11.01 S	37.12 W
São Domingos, Bra.	294	26.34 S	52.32 W
São Domingos, Bra.	296	13.24 S	46.19 W
São Filipe	296	14.49 S	41.23 W
São Francisco	296	15.57 S	44.52 W
São Francisco ≃, Bra.	296	18.41 S	50.17 W
São Francisco, Baía de C	294	26.10 S	48.34 W
São Francisco, Ilha de I	294	26.18 S	48.37 W
São Francisco de Assis	294	29.33 S	55.08 W
São Francisco de Goiás	296	15.55 S	49.16 W
São Francisco de Paula	294	29.27 S	50.35 W
São Francisco do Sul	294	26.14 S	48.39 W
São Gabriel, Bra.	294	30.20 S	54.19 W
São Gabriel, Bra.	296	19.01 S	40.32 W
São Gabriel de Goiás	296	15.12 S	47.34 W
São Gonçalo do Abaeté	296	18.20 S	45.49 W
São Gonçalo do Pará	296	19.59 S	44.51 W
São Gonçalo do Sapucaí	296	21.54 S	45.36 W
São Gonçalo dos Campos	296	12.25 S	38.58 W
Sao Hill	218	8.20 S	35.12 E
São Jerônimo	294	29.58 S	51.43 W
São Jerônimo, Serra de ⛰[1]	296	17.00 S	54.50 W
São Jerônimo da Serra	296	23.43 S	50.44 W
São Joana ≃	296	19.31 S	40.43 W
São João ≃, Bra.	296	20.41 S	46.45 W
São João ≃, Bra.	296	12.27 S	51.07 W
São João da Alianca	296	14.42 S	47.32 W
São João da Barra	296	21.38 S	41.03 W
São João da Boa Vista	296	21.58 S	46.47 W
São João da Madeira	168	40.54 N	8.30 W
São João da Ponte	296	15.56 S	44.01 W
São João del Rei	296	21.09 S	44.16 W
São João do Araguaia	286	5.23 S	48.46 W
São João do Caiuá	296	22.48 S	52.22 W
São João do Paraíso	296	15.19 S	42.01 W
São João do Triunfo	294	25.40 S	50.20 W
São João Evangelista	296	18.32 S	42.45 W
São Joaquim	294	28.18 S	49.56 W
São Joaquim, Parque Nacional de ♠	294	28.15 S	49.57 W
São Joaquim da Barra	296	20.35 S	47.53 W
São Jorge	296	23.24 S	52.17 W
São José	294	27.38 S	48.39 W
São José ≃	296	19.10 S	40.12 W
São José de Anauá	290	1.00 N	61.23 W
São José do Calçado	296	21.02 S	41.40 W
São José do Cedro	294	26.30 S	53.30 W
São José do Goiabal	296	19.56 S	42.42 W
São José do Jacuri	296	18.16 S	42.40 W
São José do Norte	294	32.01 S	52.03 W
São José do Rio Prêto	296	20.48 S	49.23 W
São José dos Campos	296	23.11 S	45.53 W
São José dos Pinhais	294	25.31 S	49.13 W
São Leopoldo	294	29.46 S	51.09 W
São Lourenço	296	22.07 S	45.03 W
São Lourenço ≃	292	17.53 S	57.27 W
São Lourenço, Pantanal de ☷	292	17.30 S	56.30 W
São Lourenço d'Oeste	294	26.24 S	52.46 W
São Lourenço do Sul	294	31.22 S	51.58 W
São Luís	286	2.31 S	44.16 W
São Luís de Montes Belos	296	16.32 S	50.20 W
São Luís do Tocantins	296	14.17 S	47.59 W
São Luís Gonzaga	294	28.24 S	54.58 W
São Manuel	296	22.44 S	48.34 W
São Mateus	296	18.44 S	39.51 W
São Mateus ≃, Bra.	296	18.35 S	39.44 W
São Mateus ≃, Bra.	296	13.48 S	46.54 W
São Mateus do Sul	294	25.52 S	50.23 W
São Miguel ≃, Bra.	296	16.03 S	46.07 W
São Miguel ≃, Bra.	296	16.26 S	41.00 W
São Miguel do Anta	296	20.42 S	42.43 W
São Miguel do Araguaia	296	13.19 S	50.13 W
São Miguel d'Oeste	294	26.45 S	53.34 W
Saona, Isla I	282	18.10 N	68.40 W
Saône ≃	166	45.44 N	4.50 E
Saône-et-Loire □[5]	166	46.42 N	4.45 E
São Nicolau I	222a	16.35 N	24.15 W
São Paulo	296	23.32 S	46.37 W
São Paulo □[3]	296	22.00 S	49.00 W
São Paulo de Olivença	290	3.27 S	68.48 W
São Pedro	296	19.53 S	51.55 W
São Pedro ≃	296	16.30 S	41.17 W
São Pedro do Ivaí	296	23.51 S	51.51 W
São Pedro do Sul, Bra.	294	29.37 S	54.10 W
São Pedro do Sul, Port.	168	40.45 N	8.04 W
São Raimundo Nonato	286	9.01 S	42.42 W
São Romão	296	16.22 S	45.04 W
São Roque	296	23.32 S	47.08 W
São Roque, Cabo de ≻	286	5.29 S	35.16 W
São Roque do Paraguaçu	296	12.51 S	38.51 W
Saorre, Mount Λ	232	64.27 N	84.30 W
São Salvador → Salvador	296	12.59 S	38.31 W
São Salvador do Congo	218	6.16 S	14.15 E
São Sebastião	296	23.48 S	45.25 W
São Sebastião, Ilha de I	296	23.50 S	45.18 W
São Sebastião, Ponta ≻	224	22.07 S	35.30 E
São Sebastião do Maranhão	296	18.05 S	42.35 W
São Sebastião do Paraíso	296	20.55 S	47.00 W
São Sebastião do Rio Claro	296	15.45 S	51.30 W
São Sepé	294	30.10 S	53.34 W
São Simão, Bra.	296	18.56 S	50.30 W
São Simão, Bra.	296	21.30 S	47.33 W
São Simão ≃	292	12.40 S	63.04 W
São Tiago	296	20.55 S	44.30 W
São Tiago I	222a	15.05 N	23.40 W
São Timóteo	296	13.51 S	42.11 W
São Tomé	218	0.20 N	6.44 E
São Tomé I	218	0.12 N	6.39 E
São Tomé ≃	292	8.10 S	58.13 W
São Tomé, Cabo de ≻	296	21.59 S	40.59 W
São Tomé, Pico de Λ	218	0.16 N	6.33 E
Sao Tome and Principe □[2]	218	1.00 N	7.00 E
São Valério ≃	296	11.20 S	48.28 W
São Vicente	296	23.58 S	46.23 W
São Vicente I	222a	16.50 N	25.00 W
São Vicente, Cabo de ≻	168	37.01 N	9.00 W
São Vicente de Minas	296	21.42 S	44.27 W
Sap, Thale C	200	7.30 N	100.17 E
Sápai	172	41.02 N	25.41 E
Sapallanga	292	12.09 S	75.10 W
Sapao	202	10.01 N	126.02 E
Sapayán, Ciénaga ◎	290	10.08 N	74.45 W
Sapé	286	7.06 S	35.13 W
Sapeaçu	296	12.44 S	39.13 W
Sapele	222	5.54 N	5.41 E
Sapello ≃	254	35.47 N	104.59 W
Sapelo Island I	246	31.28 N	81.15 W
Saphane	172	39.01 N	29.14 E
Sapian Bay C	202	11.32 N	122.37 E
Sapitwa Λ	218	15.59 S	35.36 E
Šapkina ≃	160	66.44 N	52.25 E
Sapo, Serranía del ⛰	290	7.52 N	78.20 W
Saposoa	292	6.55 S	76.45 W
Sappemeer	178	53.09 N	6.50 E
Sapphire Mountains ⛰	256	46.20 N	113.45 W
Sappho	270	48.04 N	124.16 W
Sappington	248	38.32 N	90.23 W
Sapporo	192a	43.03 N	141.21 E
Sapri	170	40.04 N	15.38 E
Sap Songkhla, Thale C	200	7.13 N	100.30 E
Sapt Kosi ≃	204	25.25 N	87.23 E
Sapucaí ≃, Bra.	296	21.33 S	45.40 W
Sapucaí ≃, Bra.	296	20.08 S	48.27 W
Sapucaia	296	22.00 S	42.54 W
Sapulpa	250	36.00 N	96.06 W
Sāq, Jabal Λ[2]	208	26.17 N	43.16 E
Saqqez	208	36.14 N	46.16 E
Saquarema	296	22.56 S	42.30 W
Saquena	292	4.38 S	73.40 W
Saquisilí	290	0.51 S	78.40 W
Sara	202	11.16 N	123.00 E
Sarāb	208	37.56 N	47.32 E
Sara Buri	200	14.30 N	100.55 E
Saracura ≃	296	12.18 S	40.07 W
Saragosa	250	31.01 N	103.39 W
Saragossa → Zaragoza, Esp.	168	41.38 N	0.53 W
Saraguro	290	3.36 S	79.13 W
Sarajevo	172	43.52 N	18.25 E
Sarakhs	204	36.32 N	61.11 E
Saraköy	172	37.55 N	28.58 E
Saraland	248	30.49 N	88.04 W
Saramacca □[5]	290	5.00 N	56.00 W
Saramaguacán ≃	284p	21.31 N	77.18 W
Saran'	186	49.46 N	72.52 E
Sarānac	268	42.56 N	85.13 W
Saranac ≃	242	44.42 N	73.27 W
Saranac Lake	242	44.20 N	74.08 W
Saranap	272	37.53 N	122.06 W
Sarandë	172	39.52 N	20.00 E
Sarandi	294	27.56 S	52.55 W
Sarandí del Yi	294	33.21 S	55.38 W
Sarandí Grande	294	33.44 S	56.20 W
Šaranga	160	57.11 N	46.34 E
Sarangani Bay C	202	6.00 N	125.13 E
Sarangani Island I	202	5.27 N	125.29 E
Sarangani Islands II	202	5.25 N	125.25 E
Sarangani Strait ⋃	202	5.30 N	125.23 E
Saranpaul'	160	64.14 N	60.53 E
Saransk	160	54.11 N	45.11 E
Sara Peak Λ	222	9.41 N	9.17 E
Sarapiquí ≃	280	10.43 N	83.55 W
Sarapul	160	56.28 N	53.48 E
Sarare	290	9.47 N	69.10 W
Sarasara, Nevado Λ	292	15.23 S	73.29 W
Sarasota	246	27.20 N	82.34 W
Saratoga, Calif., U.S.	272	37.16 N	122.02 W
Saratoga, Ind., U.S.	268	40.14 N	84.55 W
Saratoga, Tex., U.S.	250	30.17 N	94.31 W
Saratoga, Wyo., U.S.	254	41.27 N	106.48 W
Saratoga □[6]	261	43.00 N	73.51 W
Saratoga National Historical Park ♠	242	43.00 N	73.38 W
Saratoga Place	262	36.43 N	76.36 W
Saratoga Springs	242	43.05 N	73.47 W
Saratov	158	51.34 N	46.02 E
Saraurcu, Cerro Λ	290	0.06 S	77.55 W
Saravane	200	15.43 N	106.25 E
Sarawak □[3]	200	2.30 N	113.30 E
Saray	172	41.26 N	27.55 E
Sarayakpınar	172	41.46 N	26.29 E
Sárbogárd	164	46.53 N	18.38 E
Sarcee Indian Reserve ⊸[4]	238	50.58 N	114.06 W
Sarcidano ⊸[1]	170	39.55 N	9.05 E
Sarcoxie	248	37.03 N	94.07 W
Sarda ≃	206	27.22 N	81.23 E
Sardalas	214	25.46 N	10.34 E
Sardegna I	170	40.00 N	9.00 E
Sardina	290	2.02 N	67.07 W
Sardinal	280	10.31 N	85.39 W
Sardinata	290	8.05 N	72.48 W
Sardinia	266	42.32 N	78.31 W
Sardinia → Sardegna I	170	40.00 N	9.00 E
Sardis, B.C., Can.	270	49.08 N	121.57 W
Sardis, Ala., U.S.	248	32.17 N	86.59 W
Sardis, Ga., U.S.	246	32.58 N	81.46 W
Sardis, Miss., U.S.	248	34.26 N	89.55 W
Sardis, Tenn., U.S.	248	35.27 N	88.18 W
Sardis Reservoir ◎[1]	248	34.27 N	89.43 W
Šardonem'	160	63.56 N	44.37 E
Sareks Nationalpark ♠	160	67.15 N	17.30 E
Sarepta	248	32.54 N	93.27 W
Sargans	166	47.03 N	9.26 E
Sargent	252	41.38 N	99.22 W
Sargento Paixão, Serra do ⛰[1]	292	11.13 S	60.30 W
Sargents	254	38.25 N	106.24 W
Sargodha	206	32.05 N	72.40 E
Sarhli, Djebel Λ	168	36.06 N	0.40 W
Sārī	208	36.34 N	53.04 E
Saría I	212	35.50 N	27.15 E
Sáric	278	31.08 N	111.23 W
Sarigan I	198	16.42 N	145.47 E
Sarıgöl	172	38.14 N	28.43 E
Sarıköy	172	40.12 N	27.36 E
Sarina	226	21.26 S	149.13 E
Sariñena	168	41.48 N	0.10 W
Sar-i-Pul	208	36.13 N	65.55 E
Sarita	250	37.13 N	97.47 W
Sariwŏn	194	38.31 N	125.44 E
Sarıyar Barajı ⊸[6]	212	40.02 N	31.28 E
Sarıyer	172	41.10 N	29.03 E
Šarja	160	58.24 N	45.30 E
Sarjektåkko Λ	160	67.25 N	17.46 E
Sark I	162	49.26 N	2.21 W
Sarkad	164	46.44 N	21.23 E
Šarkovščina	160	55.22 N	27.28 E
Sarköy	172	40.37 N	27.06 E
Sarlat	166	44.53 N	1.13 E
Sarles	252	48.57 N	99.00 W
Sărmașu	172	46.46 N	24.11 E
Sármellék	164	46.44 N	17.10 E
Sarmi	198	1.51 S	138.44 E
Sarmiento	288	45.35 S	69.05 W
Särna	160	61.41 N	13.08 E
Sarnen	180	46.54 N	8.15 E
Sarnia	266	42.58 N	82.23 W
Sarno	184	40.49 N	14.37 E
Sarnowa	164	51.38 N	16.54 E
Saroma-ko ◎	192a	44.08 N	143.50 E
Saronikós Kólpos C	172	37.54 N	23.12 E
Saronno	182	45.38 N	9.02 E
Saros Körfezi C	212	40.30 N	26.20 E
Sárospatak	164	48.19 N	21.34 E
Šar Planina ⛰	172	42.05 N	20.50 E
Sarpsborg	160	59.17 N	11.07 E
Sarralbe	166	49.00 N	7.01 E
Sarrebourg	166	48.44 N	7.03 E
Sarreguemines	166	49.06 N	7.03 E

Symbols in the index entries are identified on page 360.

Name	Page	Lat°′	Long°′
Sarre-Union	166	48.56 N	7.05 E
Sarria	168	42.47 N	7.24 W
Sarsfield	264	45.27 N	75.21 W
Sarstedt	178	52.14 N	9.51 E
Sarstoon ≃	280	15.53 N	88.55 W
Sartang ≃	186	67.44 N	133.12 E
Sartell	244	45.37 N	94.12 W
Sartène	170	41.36 N	8.59 E
Sarthe □[5]	166	48.00 N	0.05 E
Sarthe ≃	166	47.30 N	0.32 W
Sartilly	166	48.45 N	1.27 W
Saru ≃	192a	42.30 N	142.00 E
Sarufutsu	192a	45.16 N	142.12 E
Saruhanlı	172	38.44 N	27.34 E
Sárvár	164	47.15 N	16.57 E
Sarver	266	40.44 N	79.45 W
Sárvíz ≃	172	46.24 N	18.41 E
Saryg-Sep	186	51.30 N	95.36 E
Sarykol'skij Chrebet ⋀	206	38.00 N	74.30 E
Saryozek	186	44.22 N	77.59 E
Sarysu ≃	186	45.12 N	66.36 E
Sary-Taš	186	39.44 N	73.15 E
Saryžaz	186	42.55 N	79.38 E
Sarzana	170	44.07 N	9.58 E
Sarzeau	166	47.32 N	2.46 W
Sasa	192	33.14 N	129.39 E
Sasabe	254	31.27 N	111.31 W
Sasakwa	250	34.57 N	96.31 W
Sāsarām	206	24.57 N	84.02 E
Sasayama	192	35.04 N	135.13 E
Sásd	164	46.15 N	18.06 E
Sasebo	192	33.10 N	129.43 E
Saseenos	270	48.24 N	123.40 W
Saseginaga, Lac ⊜	244	47.05 N	78.34 W
Saskatchewan □[3]	232	54.00 N	106.00 W
Saskatchewan ≃	232	53.12 N	105.00 W
Saskatoon	232	52.07 N	106.38 W
Saskylach	186	71.55 N	114.01 E
Sasmik, Cape ≻	236	51.36 N	177.55 W
Sasolburg	224	26.48 S	27.45 E
Sasovo	160	54.21 N	41.54 E
Saspamco	250	29.14 N	98.18 W
Sassafras Mountain ∧	246	35.03 N	82.48 W
Sassandra	222	4.58 N	6.05 W
Sassandra □[5]	222	5.20 N	6.40 W
Sassandra ≃	222	4.58 N	6.05 W
Sassari	170	40.44 N	8.33 E
Sassenheim	178	52.13 N	4.31 E
Sassnitz	164	54.31 N	13.38 E
Sassoferrato	170	43.26 N	12.51 E
Sasso Marconi	170	44.24 N	11.15 E
S'as'stroj	160	60.08 N	32.34 E
Sassuolo	170	44.33 N	10.47 E
Sastown	214	4.40 N	8.26 W
Sastre	294	31.45 S	61.50 W
Sasun Dağları ⋀	212	38.15 N	41.32 E
Sasyk, Ozero(Kunduk) ⊜	172	45.40 N	29.40 E
Satah Mountain ∧	238	52.29 N	124.41 W
Sata-misaki ≻	192	30.59 N	130.40 E
Satanta	252	37.26 N	100.59 W
Sátão	168	40.44 N	7.44 W
Satartia	248	32.40 N	90.33 W
Satellite Beach	246	28.11 N	80.35 W
Säter	160	60.21 N	15.45 E
Saticoy	274	34.17 N	119.09 W
Satilla ≃	246	30.59 N	81.28 W
Satipo	292	11.15 S	74.25 W
Satırlar	172	37.30 N	29.46 E
Satīt (Tekeze) ≃	220	14.20 N	35.50 E
Satka	158	55.03 N	59.01 E
Šatki	160	55.11 N	44.08 E
Satna	206	24.35 N	80.51 E
Sátoraljaújhely	164	48.24 N	21.39 E
Sātpura Range ⋀	206	22.00 N	78.00 E
Satsuma	248	30.51 N	88.03 W
Satsuma-hantō ≻[1]	192	31.25 N	130.25 E
Satsunan-shotō II	193b	29.00 N	130.00 E
Sattahip	198	12.41 N	100.54 E
Satu-Mare	172	47.48 N	22.53 E
Šatura	160	55.34 N	39.32 E
Saturna	270	48.43 N	123.11 W
Saturnino M. Laspiur	294	31.42 S	62.28 W
Sauce, Arg.	294	30.05 S	58.45 W
Sauce, Perú	292	6.42 S	76.08 W
Sauce, Ur.	294	34.39 S	56.04 W
Sauce Chico ≃	294	38.47 S	62.18 W
Sauce Grande ≃	294	39.00 S	61.07 W
Saucier	248	30.38 N	89.08 W
Saucillo	278	28.01 N	105.17 W
Sauda	160	59.39 N	6.20 E
Sauđarkrókur	160a	65.46 N	19.41 W
Saudi Arabia □[1]	204	25.00 N	45.00 E
Saueniná ≃	292	12.24 S	58.40 W
Saueruiná ≃	292	12.00 S	58.43 W
Saug ≃	202	7.28 N	125.44 E
Saugatuck	268	42.40 N	86.12 W
Saugeen ≃	244	44.30 N	81.22 W
Saugerties	261	42.05 N	73.57 W
Saugstad, Mount ∧	238	52.15 N	126.31 W
Saugus	274	34.25 N	118.32 W
Saujil	294	28.11 S	66.13 W
Saujon	166	45.40 N	0.56 W
Sauk ≃, Minn., U.S.	252	45.36 N	94.10 W
Sauk ≃, Wash., U.S.	256	48.30 N	121.37 W
Sauk Centre	252	45.44 N	94.57 W
Sauk City	244	43.17 N	89.43 W
Sauk Rapids	244	45.34 N	94.09 W
Sauk Village	268	41.30 N	87.34 W
Saukville	244	43.23 N	87.55 W
Saül	286	3.37 N	53.12 W
Saulgau	180	48.01 N	9.30 E
Saulieu	166	47.16 N	4.14 E
Saulkrasti	160	57.17 N	24.25 E
Sault-au-Mouton	240	48.32 N	64.16 W
Sault-aux-Cochons ≃	240	48.44 N	69.05 W
Sault-de-Vaucluse	166	44.05 N	5.25 E
Saulteaux ≃	238	55.16 N	114.25 W
Sault Sainte Marie, Ont., Can.	244	46.31 N	84.20 W
Sault Sainte Marie, Mich., U.S.	244	46.30 N	84.21 W
Saumarez Reef ✣[2]	228	21.50 S	153.40 E
Saumâtre, Étang ⊜	282	18.35 N	72.00 W
Saumlaki	198	7.57 S	131.19 E
Saumons, Rivíere aux ≃	240	49.25 N	62.16 W
Saumur	166	47.16 N	0.05 W
Saunderstown	261	41.30 N	71.25 W
Saunemin	268	40.54 N	88.24 W
Sauquoit	242	43.00 N	75.16 W
Sausalito	272	37.51 N	122.29 W
Sauteurs	285k	12.14 N	61.38 W
Sauveterre	166	43.29 N	0.06 W
Sauveterre, Causse ⋀[1]	166	44.20 N	3.10 E
Sauveterre-en-Guyenne	166	44.42 N	0.05 W
Sauvo	160	60.21 N	22.42 E
Sauwald ◆[3]	164	48.28 N	13.40 E
Sauzal	254	31.37 N	106.18 W
Sava, It.	170	40.24 N	17.34 E
S'ava, S.S.S.R.	160	58.01 N	46.22 E
Sava ≃	172	44.50 N	20.26 E
Savage, Md., U.S.	262	39.08 N	76.49 W
Savage, Mont., U.S.	256	47.27 N	104.21 W
Savalou	222	7.56 N	1.58 E
Savane, Rivière de la ≃	240	51.10 N	71.25 W
Savanna, Ill., U.S.	244	42.05 N	90.08 W
Savanna, Okla., U.S.	250	34.50 N	95.51 W
Savannah, Ga., U.S.	246	32.04 N	81.05 W
Savannah, Mo., U.S.	248	39.56 N	94.50 W
Savannah, N.Y., U.S.	264	43.04 N	76.46 W
Savannah, Ohio, U.S.	266	40.58 N	82.22 W
Savannah, Tenn., U.S.	248	35.14 N	88.14 W
Savannah ≃	246	32.02 N	80.53 W
Savannah Beach	246	32.01 N	80.51 W
Savannah Sound	246	25.06 N	76.09 W
Savannakhet	200	16.33 N	104.45 E
Savanna-la-Mar	285q	18.13 N	78.08 W
Savaştepe	172	39.22 N	27.40 E
Savé	214	8.02 N	2.29 E
Save (Sabi) ≃, Afr.	224	21.00 S	35.02 E
Save ≃, Fr.	166	43.47 N	1.17 E
Sāveh	208	35.01 N	50.20 E
Savelli	170	39.19 N	16.47 E
Savenay	166	47.22 N	1.57 W
Săveni	172	47.57 N	26.52 E
Saverdun	166	43.14 N	1.35 E
Saverne	166	48.44 N	7.22 E
Saviano	184	40.54 N	14.30 E
Savigliano	182	44.38 N	7.40 E
Savignano sul Rubicone	184	44.05 N	12.24 E
Savigny-sur-Braye	166	47.53 N	0.49 E
Savigny-sur-Orge	176	48.40 N	2.21 E
Savino-Borisovskaja	160	62.38 N	44.34 E
Savinskij	160	62.58 N	40.08 E
Săvîrşin	172	46.01 N	22.14 E
Savitaipale	160	61.12 N	27.42 E
Savl'a, Gora ∧	160	64.48 N	58.50 E
Šavnik	172	42.57 N	19.05 E
Savoie □[5]	166	45.30 N	6.25 E
Savona, B.C., Can.	238	50.45 N	120.50 W
Savona, It.	182	44.17 N	8.30 E
Savona □[4]	182	44.18 N	8.16 E
Savonlinna	160	61.52 N	28.53 E
Savonranta	160	62.11 N	29.12 E
Savoonga	236	63.42 N	170.27 W
Sävsjö	160	57.25 N	14.40 E
S'avta	160	67.08 N	61.45 E
Savu Sea → Sawu, Laut ▾[2]	198	9.40 S	122.00 E
Sawahlunto	200	0.40 S	100.47 E
Sawākin	220	19.07 N	37.20 E
Sawang	200	0.47 N	103.21 E
Sawankhalok	200	17.19 N	99.54 E
Sawara	192	35.53 N	140.30 E
Sawata	192	38.00 N	138.16 E
Sawatch Range ⋀	254	39.10 N	106.25 W
Sawbridgeworth	174	51.50 N	0.09 E
Sawdā', Jabal as- ⋀[2]	214	28.40 N	15.30 E
Sawdā', Qurnat as- ∧	212	34.17 N	36.07 E
Sawel Mountain ∧	162	54.49 N	7.02 W
Sawhāj	220	26.33 N	31.42 E
Sawknah	214	29.04 N	15.47 E
Sawtayr ▾[4]	220	17.03 N	30.24 E
Sawu, Laut (Savu Sea) ▾[2]	198	9.40 S	122.00 E
Sawu, Pulau I	226	10.30 S	121.54 E
Sawyer, Mich., U.S.	268	41.53 N	86.35 W
Sawyer, N. Dak., U.S.	252	48.05 N	101.03 W
Sawyers Hill ∧[2]	240	47.11 N	53.52 W
Sawyerville	260	45.20 N	71.34 W
Sawyerwood	266	41.02 N	81.27 W
Saxby ≃	228	18.25 S	140.53 E
Saxis	262	37.55 N	75.43 W
Saxmundham	162	52.13 N	1.29 E
Saxon, Schw.	166	46.09 N	7.11 E
Saxon, S.C., U.S.	246	34.57 N	81.57 W
Saxon, Wis., U.S.	244	46.29 N	90.25 W
Saxonburg	266	40.45 N	79.49 W
Saxton	266	40.13 N	78.15 W
Sāy, Jazīrat I	220	20.42 N	30.20 E
Sayaboury	200	19.15 N	101.45 E
Sayán	292	11.08 S	77.12 W
Sayan Mountains ⋀	186	52.45 N	96.00 E
Sayaxché	278	16.31 N	90.10 W
Saybrook, Ill., U.S.	268	40.26 N	88.32 W
Saybrook, Ohio, U.S.	266	41.50 N	80.51 W
Saybrook Manor	261	41.17 N	72.24 W
Şaydā (Sidon)	210	33.33 N	35.22 E
Şaydā, Lubnān	210	33.33 N	35.22 E
Sayḩūt	214	15.12 N	51.14 E
Sayil ⊥	278	20.16 N	89.42 W
Saylorville Reservoir ⊜[1]	248	41.48 N	93.46 W
Sayre, Okla., U.S.	250	35.18 N	99.38 W
Sayre, Pa., U.S.	242	41.59 N	76.32 W
Sayreville	262	40.28 N	74.21 W
Sayula, Méx.	278	19.52 N	103.37 W
Sayula, Méx.	278	29.22 N	111.33 W
Say'ūn	214	15.56 N	48.47 E
Sayward	238	50.22 N	125.55 W
Sazan I	172	40.30 N	19.16 E
Sázava ≃	164	49.53 N	14.24 E
Sbeïtla	170	35.14 N	9.08 E
Sbiba	170	35.33 N	9.05 E
Scaër	166	48.02 N	3.42 E
Scafati	184	40.45 N	14.31 E
Scaggsville	262	39.09 N	76.54 W
Scalea	170	39.49 N	15.48 E
Scalpay I	162	57.18 N	6.00 W
Scalp Level	266	40.15 N	78.51 W
Scammon	252	37.17 N	94.49 W
Scammon Bay	236	61.53 N	165.38 W
Scammon Bay C	236	61.53 N	165.54 W
Scandia	252	39.48 N	97.47 W
Scandicci	184	43.45 N	11.11 E
Scandinavian Peninsula ≻[1]	148	65.00 N	16.00 E
Scanlon	244	46.42 N	92.23 W
Scansano	170	42.41 N	11.20 E
Scapa	238	51.52 N	111.59 W
Scapa Flow ⩌	162	58.54 N	3.05 W
Scapegoat Mountain ∧	256	47.19 N	112.50 W
Ščapino	186	55.19 N	159.25 E
Scappoose	270	45.45 N	122.53 W
Scarba I	162	56.11 N	5.42 W
Scarborough, Ont., Can.	264	43.44 N	79.16 W
Scarborough, Trin.	285r	11.11 N	60.44 W
Scarborough, Eng., U.K.	162	54.17 N	0.24 W
Scarborough Shoal II	202	15.08 N	117.50 E
Scărişoara	172	44.00 N	24.35 E
Scarp I	162	58.02 N	7.15 W
Scarsdale	261	40.59 N	73.49 W
Scatari Island I	240	46.00 N	59.44 W
Scawfell Island I	228	20.52 S	149.36 E
Sceaux	176	48.47 N	2.17 E
Šćedro, Otok I	170	43.05 N	16.42 E
Ščeljajur	160	65.21 N	53.21 E
Scenery Hill	266	40.05 N	80.04 W
Scenic	270	47.43 N	121.09 W
Ščerbakovo	186	65.15 N	160.30 E
Schaefferstown	262	40.18 N	76.18 W
Schaerbeek	176	50.51 N	4.23 E
Schaffhausen	180	47.42 N	8.38 E
Schaffhausen □[3]	180	47.40 N	8.35 E
Schalksmühle	178	51.14 N	7.31 E
Schaller	252	42.30 N	95.18 W
Schärding	164	48.27 N	13.26 E
Schefferville	232	54.47 N	66.50 W
Scheibbs	164	48.00 N	15.10 E
Schelde (Escaut) ≃	176	51.22 N	4.15 E
Schell City	248	38.01 N	94.07 W
Schell Creek Range ⋀	258	39.10 N	114.40 W
Schenectady	261	42.47 N	73.53 W
Schenefeld	178	53.36 N	9.49 E
Schenley	266	40.41 N	79.40 W
Schererville	268	41.30 N	87.27 W
Schertz	250	29.33 N	98.16 W
Schesslitz	164	49.59 N	11.01 E
Scheveningen ◆[8]	178	52.06 N	4.18 E
Schiedam	178	51.55 N	4.24 E
Schiefbahn	178	51.14 N	6.31 E
Schiermonnikoog I	164	53.28 N	6.15 E
Schijndel	178	51.37 N	5.25 E
Schilde	178	51.14 N	4.34 E
Schiller Park	268	41.58 N	87.52 W
Schiltigheim	180	48.36 N	7.45 E
Schio	170	45.43 N	11.21 E
Schkeuditz	164	51.24 N	12.13 E
Schladming	164	47.23 N	13.41 E
Schlater	248	33.38 N	90.21 W
Schleiden	164	50.31 N	6.28 E
Schleiz	164	50.34 N	11.49 E
Schleswig, B.R.D.	164	54.31 N	9.33 E
Schleswig, Iowa, U.S.	252	42.10 N	95.26 W
Schleswig-Holstein □[3]	164	54.00 N	10.30 E
Schleusingen	164	50.31 N	10.45 E
Schlieren	180	47.24 N	8.27 E
Schlitz	164	50.40 N	9.33 E
Schloss Neuhaus	178	51.44 N	8.43 E
Schlüchtern	164	50.20 N	9.31 E
Schmalkalden	164	50.43 N	10.26 E
Schmidmühlen	164	49.16 N	11.56 E
Schmölln	164	50.53 N	12.20 E
Schnecksville	262	40.41 N	75.36 W
Schneeberg	164	50.36 N	12.38 E
Schneeberg ∧	166	50.03 N	11.51 E
Schneidemühl → Piła	164	53.10 N	16.44 E
Schneverdingen	178	53.07 N	9.47 E
Schofield	244	44.54 N	89.36 W
Schoharie	242	42.40 N	74.19 W
Scholls	270	45.24 N	122.56 W
Schomberg	264	44.00 N	79.41 W
Schönaich	180	48.39 N	9.03 E
Schönebeck	164	53.34 N	13.34 E
Schongau	180	47.49 N	10.54 E
Schönholthausen	178	51.11 N	8.00 E
Schoodic Lake ⊜	240	45.21 N	68.54 W
Schoolcraft	268	42.07 N	85.38 W
Schoonhoven	178	51.56 N	4.51 E
Schopfheim	180	47.39 N	7.49 E
Schorndorf	164	48.48 N	9.31 E
Schortens	178	53.31 N	7.56 E
Schoten	176	51.15 N	4.30 E
Schötmar	178	52.04 N	8.45 E
Schouten Island I	228	42.19 S	148.17 E
Schouwen I	164	51.43 N	3.50 E
Schramberg	180	48.13 N	8.23 E
Schram City	248	39.10 N	89.27 W
Schreiber	244	48.48 N	87.15 W
Schriever	248	29.45 N	90.49 W
Schrobenhausen	164	48.33 N	11.17 E
Schroon ≃	242	43.29 N	73.49 W
Schroon Lake ⊜	242	43.47 N	73.46 W
Schruns	164	47.04 N	9.55 E
Schulenburg	250	29.41 N	96.54 W
Schull	162	51.32 N	9.33 W
Schultz Lake ⊜	232	64.45 N	97.30 W
Schumacher	244	48.28 N	81.18 W
Schussenried	180	48.00 N	9.40 E
Schüttorf	178	52.19 N	7.13 E
Schuyler, Nebr., U.S.	252	41.27 N	97.04 W
Schuyler, Va., U.S.	246	37.47 N	78.42 W
Schuylkill	262	39.56 N	75.11 W
Schuylkill □[6]	262	40.41 N	76.12 W
Schuylkill Haven	262	40.38 N	76.10 W
Schwabach	164	49.20 N	11.01 E
Schwaben □[5]	180	48.15 N	10.30 E
Schwaben □[9]	164	48.20 N	10.30 E
Schwäbische Alb ⋀	164	48.25 N	9.30 E
Schwäbisch Gmünd	164	48.48 N	9.47 E
Schwäbisch Hall	164	49.07 N	9.44 E
Schwabmünchen	180	48.11 N	10.45 E
Schwandorf in Bayern	164	49.20 N	12.08 E
Schwaner, Pegunungan ⋀	198	0.40 S	112.40 E
Schwarza	164	50.41 N	11.19 E
Schwarza ≃	164	47.43 N	16.13 E
Schwarzach im Pongau	164	47.19 N	13.09 E
Schwarzenberg	164	50.32 N	12.47 E
Schwarzenburg	166	46.49 N	7.21 E
Schwarzrand ⋀	224	25.37 S	16.50 E
Schwarzwald ⋀	180	48.00 N	8.15 E
Schwatka Mountains ⋀	236	67.25 N	157.00 W
Schwaz	164	47.20 N	11.42 E
Schwechat	164	48.08 N	16.29 E
Schwedt	164	53.03 N	14.17 E
Schweidnitz → Świdnica	164	50.51 N	16.29 E
Schweinfurt	164	50.03 N	10.14 E
Schwelm	178	51.17 N	7.17 E
Schwenningen	180	48.04 N	8.32 E
Schwerin	164	53.38 N	11.25 E
Schwerte	178	51.26 N	7.34 E
Schwetzingen	164	49.23 N	8.34 E
Schwyz	180	47.02 N	8.40 E
Schwyz □[3]	180	47.05 N	8.40 E
Sciacca	170	37.30 N	13.06 E
Scicli	170	36.47 N	14.43 E
Scilla	170	38.15 N	15.44 E
Scilly, Isles of II	162	48.57 N	6.15 W
Ścinawa (Steinau)	164	51.25 N	16.27 E
Scio, N.Y., U.S.	266	42.10 N	77.59 W
Scio, Ohio, U.S.	266	40.24 N	81.05 W
Scio, Oreg., U.S.	256	44.42 N	122.51 W
Scioto ≃	242	38.44 N	83.01 W
Scipio	254	39.15 N	112.06 W
Scipio Center	264	42.47 N	76.34 W
Šćit ∧	170	44.02 N	17.47 E
Scituate	261	42.12 N	70.44 W
Scobey	256	48.47 N	105.25 W
Scofield Reservoir ⊜[1]	254	39.47 N	111.09 W
Ščokino	158	54.01 N	37.31 E
Scooba	248	32.50 N	88.29 W
Scordia	170	37.18 N	14.51 E
Scotch Plains	262	40.37 N	74.24 W
Scotia, Nebr., U.S.	252	41.28 N	98.42 W
Scotia, N.Y., U.S.	261	44.54 N	73.33 W
Scotia Lake ⊜	244	47.05 N	81.23 W
Scotia Ridge ✣[3]	148	57.00 S	27.00 W
Scotia Sea ▾[2]	148	56.00 S	40.00 W
Scotland, Ont., Can.	264	43.01 N	80.22 W
Scotland, Pa., U.S.	262	39.58 N	77.35 W
Scotland, S. Dak., U.S.	252	43.09 N	97.43 W
Scotland, Tex., U.S.	250	33.40 N	98.28 W
Scotland □[8]	162	57.00 N	4.00 W
Scotland Neck	246	36.02 N	77.32 W
Scotlandville	248	30.31 N	91.11 W
Scotsburn	240	45.39 N	62.51 W
Scotstown	260	45.31 N	71.17 W
Scott, Miss., U.S.	248	33.36 N	91.04 W
Scott, Ohio, U.S.	268	40.59 N	84.35 W
Scott ≃	258	41.48 N	123.02 W
Scott, Cape ≻	238	50.47 N	128.26 W
Scott, Mount ∧, Okla., U.S.	250	34.44 N	98.32 W
Scott, Mount ∧, Oreg., U.S.	256	42.56 N	122.01 W
Scott City	252	38.29 N	100.54 W
Scottdale, Ga., U.S.	246	33.48 N	84.16 W
Scottdale, Mich., U.S.	268	42.03 N	86.27 W
Scottdale, Pa., U.S.	266	40.06 N	79.35 W
Scott Islands II	238	50.48 N	128.40 W
Scott Mountain ∧	256	44.11 N	115.47 W
Scott Peak ∧	256	44.21 N	112.50 W
Scott Reef ✣[2]	226	14.00 S	121.50 E
Scotts	268	42.11 N	85.25 W
Scottsbluff	252	41.52 N	103.40 W
Scotts Bluff National Monument ♣	252	41.49 N	103.41 W
Scottsboro	248	34.40 N	86.02 W
Scottsburg, Ind., U.S.	248	38.41 N	85.46 W
Scottsburg, N.Y., U.S.	266	42.40 N	77.43 W
Scottsdale, Austl.	226	41.10 S	147.31 E
Scottsdale, Ariz., U.S.	254	33.30 N	111.56 W
Scott State Park ♣	252	38.40 N	100.54 W
Scotts Valley	272	37.03 N	122.02 W
Scottsville, Ky., U.S.	248	36.45 N	86.11 W
Scottsville, N.Y., U.S.	264	43.01 N	77.45 W
Scottsville, Va., U.S.	246	37.48 N	78.29 W
Scottville	244	43.57 N	86.17 W
Scourie	162	58.20 N	5.08 W
Scout Lake	252	49.22 N	106.00 W
Scranton, Iowa, U.S.	252	42.01 N	94.33 W
Scranton, N. Dak., U.S.	252	46.09 N	103.09 W
Scranton, N.Y., U.S.	264	42.44 N	78.50 W
Scranton, Pa., U.S.	242	41.24 N	75.40 W
Screven	246	31.29 N	82.01 W
Scribner	252	41.40 N	96.40 W
Scrivia ≃	170	45.03 N	8.54 E
Ščučinsk	186	52.56 N	70.12 E
Scugog, Lake ⊜	244	44.10 N	78.51 W
Scullville	262	39.20 N	74.38 W
Scunthorpe	162	53.36 N	0.38 W
Scuol / schuls	166	46.48 N	10.18 E
Scurry	250	32.31 N	96.23 W
Scutari → Shkodër, Shq.	172	42.05 N	19.30 E
Scutari → Üsküdar, Tür.	212	41.01 N	29.01 E
Scutari, Lake ⊜	172	42.12 N	19.18 E
Seabeck	270	47.38 N	122.51 W
Seabird Island Indian Reserve ◆[4]	238	49.17 N	121.42 W
Seaboard	246	36.24 N	77.26 W
Seabrook	262	39.30 N	74.14 W
Sea Cliff	261	40.51 N	73.38 W
Seadrift	250	28.30 N	96.47 W
Seaford, Eng., U.K.	174	50.46 N	0.06 E
Seaford, Del., U.S.	262	38.39 N	75.37 W
Seaford, Va., U.S.	262	37.12 N	76.26 W
Seaforth	244	43.33 N	81.24 W
Seagraves	250	32.57 N	102.34 W
Seaham	162	54.52 N	1.21 W
Seahorse Point ≻	232	63.47 N	80.09 W
Seahurst	270	47.28 N	122.22 W
Sea Islands II	246	31.20 N	81.20 W
Sea Isle City	262	39.09 N	74.42 W
Seal ≃	232	59.04 N	94.48 W
Seal Bay C	148	71.40 S	12.25 W
Seal Beach	274	33.44 N	118.06 W
Seal Cove, N.B., Can.	240	44.39 N	66.51 W
Seal Cove, Newf., Can.	240	47.26 N	53.06 W
Seale	248	32.18 N	85.10 W
Sealevel	246	34.52 N	76.23 W
Seal Harbor	242	44.18 N	68.14 W
Seal Lake ⊜	232	54.18 N	61.40 W
Sealston	262	38.16 N	77.20 W
Sealy	250	29.47 N	96.09 W
Seanor	266	40.13 N	78.54 W
Seara	294	27.07 S	52.17 W
Searchlight	258	35.28 N	114.55 W
Searcy	248	35.15 N	91.44 W
Searles Lake ⊜	258	35.43 N	117.20 W
Searsport	242	44.28 N	68.56 W
Seaside, Calif., U.S.	272	36.37 N	121.50 W
Seaside, Oreg., U.S.	270	46.02 N	123.55 W
Seaside Park	262	39.55 N	74.05 W
Seattle	270	47.36 N	122.20 W
Seattle, Mount ∧	236	60.06 N	139.11 W
Seattle Heights	270	47.48 N	122.20 W
Seaview	270	46.20 N	124.03 W
Seaward Kaikoura Range ⋀	230	42.14 S	173.37 E
Sébaco	280	12.51 N	86.06 W
Sebago Lake ⊜	242	43.50 N	70.35 W
Se Bai ≃	200	15.19 N	104.50 E
Sebakwe National Park ♣	224	19.00 S	30.14 E
Šebalino	186	48.16 N	43.21 E
Sébaou, Oued ≃	168	36.55 N	3.55 E
Sebastian	250	26.20 N	97.47 W
Sebastian, Cape ≻	256	42.19 N	124.26 W
Sebastián Vizcaíno, Bahía C	278	28.00 N	114.30 W
Sebastopol, Calif., U.S.	258	38.24 N	122.49 W
Sebastopol, Miss., U.S.	248	32.34 N	89.27 W
Sebec Lake ⊜	240	45.18 N	69.18 W
Sebeka	252	46.38 N	95.05 W
Seberi	294	27.29 S	53.24 W
Sebeş	172	45.58 N	23.34 E
Sebes Körös (Crişul Repede) ≃	172	46.55 N	20.59 E
Sebewaing	244	43.44 N	83.27 W
Sebiş	172	46.23 N	22.08 E
Sebnitz	164	50.58 N	14.16 E
Sebree	248	37.36 N	87.32 W
Sebrell	262	36.47 N	77.07 W
Sebring, Fla., U.S.	246	27.30 N	81.26 W
Sebring, Ohio, U.S.	266	40.55 N	81.02 W
Sebringville	264	43.24 N	81.04 W
Secane	262	39.55 N	75.18 W
Secas, Islas II	280	8.00 N	82.00 W
Secchia ≃	170	45.04 N	11.00 E
Secesh ≃	256	45.02 N	115.43 W
Sechelt	238	49.28 N	123.45 W
Sechura	292	5.33 S	80.51 W
Sechura, Bahía de C	292	5.35 S	81.00 W
Sechura, Desierto de ◆[2]	292	6.00 S	80.30 W
Seclantas	294	25.18 S	66.15 W
Seclin	176	50.33 N	3.02 E
Seco ≃	254	30.51 N	111.50 W
Seco, Arroyo ≃, Calif., U.S.	258	33.18 N	114.44 W
Seco Island I	202	11.19 N	121.40 E
Sečovce	164	48.43 N	21.40 E
Sečovská Polianka	164	48.47 N	21.42 E
Secretary	262	38.37 N	75.57 W
Secretary Island I	230	45.14 S	166.54 E
Section	248	34.35 N	85.59 W
Secubun Island I	202	5.06 N	120.28 E
Sécure ≃	292	15.10 S	64.52 W
Security	252	38.45 N	104.44 W
Séd ≃	164	47.00 N	18.31 E
Seda	190	32.20 N	100.41 E
Seda ≃	168	38.56 N	8.03 W
Sedalia, Ind., U.S.	268	40.25 N	86.31 W
Sedalia, Mo., U.S.	248	38.42 N	93.14 W
Sedan, Fr.	166	49.42 N	4.57 E
Sedan, Kans., U.S.	252	37.08 N	96.11 W
Sedanka, Cape ≻	236	53.49 N	166.06 W
Sedanka Island I	236	53.50 N	166.10 W
Sedano	168	42.43 N	3.45 W
Sedco Hills	274	33.39 N	117.24 W
Sedel'nikovo	186	56.57 N	75.18 E
Sederberge ⋀	224	32.23 S	19.20 E
Séderon	166	44.12 N	5.32 E
Sederot	210	31.31 N	34.36 E
Sedgefield	246	35.10 N	80.51 W
Sedgewick	238	52.46 N	111.41 W
Sedgewick, Mount ∧	254	35.11 N	108.06 W
Sedgley	174	52.33 N	2.08 W
Sedgwick, Colo., U.S.	252	40.56 N	102.31 W
Sedgwick, Kans., U.S.	252	37.55 N	97.25 W
Sedgwick, Maine, U.S.	242	44.18 N	68.37 W
Sedini	170	40.50 N	8.49 E
Sedlčany	164	49.40 N	14.26 E
Sedley	262	36.46 N	76.59 W
Sedom (Sodom) ⊥	210	31.04 N	35.23 E
Sedona	254	34.52 N	111.46 W
Sedova, Pik ∧	186	73.29 N	54.58 E
Sedrata	170	36.08 N	7.32 E
Sedriano	182	45.29 N	8.58 E
Sedro Woolley	270	48.30 N	122.14 W
Sedtim	160	66.25 N	56.20 E
Sędziszów	164	50.04 N	21.41 E
Seeberg Sattel)(	170	46.25 N	14.32 E
Seeburg, Pol.	164	53.58 N	20.46 E
Seefeld in Tirol	164	47.20 N	11.11 E
Seehausen	164	52.53 N	11.45 E
Seeheim	218	26.50 S	17.45 E
Seekonk	261	41.49 N	71.20 W
Seeley Lake	256	47.11 N	113.29 W
Seeleys Bay	264	44.29 N	76.14 W
Seelow	164	52.32 N	14.23 E
Seelyville	248	39.30 N	87.16 W
Seelze	178	52.24 N	9.35 E
Seemalik Butte ∧	236	60.09 N	167.08 W
Sées	166	48.36 N	0.10 E
Seesen	178	51.53 N	10.10 E
Seferihisar	172	38.11 N	26.51 E
Sefton, Mount ∧	230	43.41 S	170.02 E
Segaliud ≃	202	5.43 N	117.55 E
Segama ≃	202	5.27 N	118.48 E
Segamat	200	2.31 N	102.49 E
Segangane	168	35.09 N	3.00 W
Segarcea	172	44.06 N	23.45 E
Segesta ⊥	170	37.56 N	12.50 E
Segeža	160	63.44 N	34.19 E
Šegmas	160	64.43 N	49.14 E
Segni	184	41.41 N	13.01 E
Segorbe	168	39.51 N	0.29 W
Ségou	222	13.27 N	6.16 W
Ségou □[4]	222	14.00 N	6.20 W
Šegovary	160	62.23 N	42.57 E
Segovia, Col.	290	7.07 N	74.42 W
Segovia, Esp.	168	40.57 N	4.07 W
Segozero, Ozero ⊜	160	63.18 N	33.45 E
Segré	166	47.41 N	0.53 W
Segre ≃	168	41.40 N	0.43 E
Seguam Island I	236	52.17 N	172.30 W
Seguam Pass ⩌	236	52.08 N	172.45 W
Séguédine	214	20.12 N	12.59 E
Séguéla	222	7.57 N	6.40 W
Séguéla □[5]	222	8.30 N	6.30 W
Seguí	294	31.58 S	60.05 W
Seguin	250	29.34 N	97.58 W
Segula Island I	237a	52.01 N	178.07 E
Segundo	252	37.07 N	104.45 W
Segundo ≃	294	30.53 S	62.44 W
Segura	168	39.50 N	6.59 W
Segura ≃	168	38.06 N	0.54 W
Segura, Sierra de ⋀	168	38.00 N	2.43 W
Sehnde	178	52.18 N	9.57 E
Sehnkwehn ≃	222	5.12 N	9.21 W
Seia	168	40.25 N	7.42 W
Seibert	252	39.18 N	102.52 W
Seiches-sur-le-Loir	166	47.35 N	0.22 W
Seiland I	160	70.25 N	23.15 E
Seilhac	166	45.22 N	1.42 E
Seiling	250	36.09 N	98.56 W
Sein, Île de I	166	48.02 N	4.51 W
Seinäjoki	158	62.47 N	22.50 E
Seine □[5]	176	48.50 N	2.10 E
Seine ≃, Ont., Can.	244	48.40 N	92.49 W
Seine ≃, Fr.	166	49.26 N	0.26 E
Seine, Baie de la ≃	166	49.30 N	0.30 W
Seine-et-Marne □[5]	176	48.30 N	3.00 E
Seine-et-Oise □[5]	176	48.45 N	2.00 E
Seine-Maritime □[5]	176	49.45 N	1.00 E
Seipstown	262	40.35 N	75.40 W
Seixal	168	38.38 N	9.06 W
Sejm ≃	158	51.27 N	32.34 E
Sejmčan	186	62.53 N	152.26 E
Sejny	164	54.07 N	23.20 E
Sekajam ≃	200	0.07 N	110.38 E
Seki, Nihon	192	35.29 N	136.55 E
Šeki (Nucha), S.S.S.R.	158	41.12 N	47.12 E
Seki, Tür.	172	36.24 N	29.13 E
Sekiu	270	48.16 N	124.18 W
Sekondi-Takoradi	222	4.59 N	1.43 W
Sekong Bay C	202	5.45 N	118.00 E
Šeksna	160	59.13 N	38.30 E
Šelagskij, Mys ≻	186	70.06 N	170.26 E
Selah	256	46.39 N	120.32 W
Selajar, Pulau I	198	6.05 S	120.30 E
Selama	200	5.13 N	100.41 E
Selangor □[3]	200	3.20 N	101.30 E
Selaru, Pulau I	198	8.09 S	131.00 E
Selatan, Tandjung ≻	198	4.10 S	114.38 E
Selawik	236	66.37 N	160.03 W
Selawik ≃	236	66.36 N	160.20 W
Selawik Lake ⊜	236	66.30 N	160.40 W
Selb	164	50.10 N	12.08 E
Selby, Eng., U.K.	162	53.48 N	1.04 W
Selby, S. Dak., U.S.	252	45.31 N	100.02 W
Selbyville	262	38.28 N	75.13 W
Sel'co	160	63.18 N	41.22 E
Selçuk	172	37.56 N	27.22 E
Selden, Kans., U.S.	252	39.33 N	100.34 W
Selden, N.Y., U.S.	261	40.51 N	73.02 W
Seldovia	236	59.27 N	151.43 W
Selemdža ≃	186	51.42 N	128.53 E
Selendi	172	38.46 N	27.53 E
Selenga (Selenge Mörön) ≃	186	52.16 N	106.16 E
Selenn'ach ≃	186	67.48 N	144.54 E
Sélestat (Schlettstadt)	180	48.16 N	7.27 E
Selezen'ovo	160	59.12 N	42.18 E
Selezni	160	55.39 N	31.29 E
Selezn'ovo	160	60.45 N	28.39 E
Selfridge	252	46.02 N	100.56 W
Sélibaby	214	15.10 N	12.11 W
Šelichova, Zaliv C	186	60.00 N	158.00 E
Seliger, Ozero ⊜	160	57.13 N	33.05 E
Seligman, Ariz., U.S.	254	35.20 N	112.53 W
Seligman, Mo., U.S.	248	36.31 N	93.56 W
Selimiye	172	37.24 N	27.40 E
Selinsgrove	262	40.48 N	76.52 W
Selinus ⊥	170	37.35 N	12.49 E
Selišče, S.S.S.R.	160	56.53 N	33.16 E
Selišče, S.S.S.R.	160	64.58 N	46.18 E
Seližarovo	160	56.51 N	33.27 E
Seljord	160	59.29 N	8.37 E
Selkämeri (Bottenhavet) C	160	62.00 N	19.30 E
Selkirk, Man., Can.	232	50.09 N	96.52 W
Selkirk, Ont., Can.	264	42.49 N	79.56 W
Selkirk, Scot., U.K.	162	55.33 N	2.50 W
Selkirk, N.Y., U.S.	261	42.32 N	73.48 W
Selkirk □[6]	162	55.29 N	3.02 W
Selkirk Mountains ⋀	238	51.00 N	117.40 W
Sellam, Oued bou ≃	168	36.12 N	5.00 E
Sellers	246	34.17 N	79.28 W
Sellersburg	248	38.24 N	85.45 W
Sellersville	262	40.22 N	75.19 W
Selles-sur-Cher	166	47.16 N	1.33 E
Sellfoss	160a	63.56 N	20.57 W
Sells	254	31.55 N	111.53 W
Selly Oak ◆[8]	174	52.25 N	1.52 W
Selm	178	51.42 N	7.28 E
Selma, Ala., U.S.	248	32.25 N	87.01 W
Selma, Calif., U.S.	272	36.34 N	119.37 W
Selma, N.C., U.S.	246	35.32 N	78.17 W
Selmer	248	35.11 N	88.36 W
Selouane	168	35.04 N	2.58 W
Selous, Mount ∧	236	62.57 N	132.31 W
Selty	160	57.19 N	52.10 E
Seltz	166	48.53 N	8.06 E
Seltzer	262	40.42 N	76.14 W
Selu, Pulau I	198	7.32 S	130.54 E
Selukwe	218	19.40 S	30.00 E
Sélune ≃	162	48.39 N	1.26 W
Selva	294	29.50 S	62.02 W
Selvagens, Ilhas II	214	30.05 N	15.55 W
Selvas ◆[3]	292	5.00 S	68.00 W
Selway ≃	256	46.08 N	115.36 W
Selwyn	226	21.32 S	140.30 E
Selwyn, Mount ∧	238	55.59 N	123.36 W
Selwyn Lake ⊜	232	59.55 N	104.35 W
Selwyn Mountains ⋀	236	63.10 N	130.20 W
Selwyn Range ⋀	228	21.35 S	140.35 E
Šemacha	208	40.38 N	48.39 E
Seman ≃	172	40.56 N	19.24 E
Semara	214	26.44 N	14.41 W
Semarang	198	6.58 S	110.25 E
Semau, Pulau I	226	10.13 S	123.22 E
Sembrong ≃	200	2.27 N	103.37 E
Semeru, Gunung ∧	226	8.06 S	112.55 E
Semichi Islands II	237a	52.42 N	174.00 E
Semidi Islands II	236	56.07 N	156.44 W
Semily	164	50.36 N	15.20 E
Seminary	248	31.34 N	89.30 W
Seminoe Reservoir ⊜[1]	254	42.00 N	106.50 W
Seminole, Okla., U.S.	250	35.14 N	96.41 W
Seminole, Tex., U.S.	250	32.43 N	102.39 W
Seminole, Lake ⊜[1]	246	30.46 N	84.50 W
Seminole Draw V	250	32.26 N	102.10 W
Semipalatinsk	186	50.28 N	80.13 E
Semirara Island I	202	12.03 N	121.23 E
Semisopochnoi Island I	237a	52.00 N	179.35 E
Semliki ≃	218	1.14 S	30.28 E
Semnān	208	35.33 N	53.24 E
Semnān □[8]	208	35.30 N	54.00 E
Šemonaicha	186	50.39 N	81.54 E
Sem'onov	160	56.48 N	44.30 E
Šemordan	160	56.11 N	50.26 E
Semur-en-Auxois	166	47.29 N	4.20 E
Semža	160	66.09 N	44.08 E
Sên ≃	200	12.32 N	104.28 E
Sena, Bol.	292	11.32 S	67.11 W
Seňa, Česko.	164	48.34 N	21.15 E
Sena, Moç.	218	17.27 S	35.00 E
Senacaville Reservoir ⊜[1]	242	39.55 N	81.25 W
Senador Canedo	296	16.43 S	49.05 W
Senador Firmino	296	20.55 S	43.06 W
Senador Pompeu	286	5.35 S	39.22 W
Senahú	280	15.24 N	89.50 W
Sena Madureira	292	9.04 S	68.40 W
Senanga	218	16.06 S	23.16 E
Senate	256	49.18 N	109.41 W
Senath	248	36.08 N	90.10 W
Senatobia	248	34.39 N	89.58 W
Sendai, Nihon	192	38.15 N	140.53 E
Sendai, Nihon	192	31.49 N	130.18 E
Sendai ≃	192	31.51 N	130.12 E
Sendai-heiya ≚	192	38.15 N	141.00 E
Sendai-wan C	192	38.18 N	141.18 E
Senden, B.R.D.	178	51.51 N	7.29 E
Senden, B.R.D.	180	48.19 N	10.03 E
Sene ≃	222	7.30 N	0.33 W
Senec	164	48.14 N	17.24 E
Seneca (Crotty), Ill., U.S.	268	41.19 N	88.36 W
Seneca, Kans., U.S.	252	39.50 N	96.04 W
Seneca, Mo., U.S.	248	36.51 N	94.37 W
Seneca, Oreg., U.S.	256	44.08 N	118.58 W
Seneca, Pa., U.S.	266	41.23 N	79.42 W
Seneca, S.C., U.S.	246	34.41 N	82.57 W
Seneca □[6], N.Y., U.S.	264	42.53 N	76.52 W
Seneca □[6], Ohio, U.S.	266	41.07 N	83.11 W
Seneca, Mount ∧	242	42.01 N	78.49 W
Seneca Castle	264	42.53 N	77.06 W
Seneca Falls	264	42.55 N	76.48 W
Seneca Lake ⊜	242	42.40 N	76.57 W
Senecú	278	31.43 N	106.23 W
Senegal (Sénégal) □[1]	214	14.00 N	14.00 W
Sénégal ≃	222	15.48 N	16.32 W
Sénégal Oriental □[4]	222	14.00 N	13.00 W
Senekal	224	28.30 S	27.32 E
Senetosa, Capo ≻	170	41.33 N	8.47 E
Senftenberg	164	51.31 N	14.00 E
Sengejskij, Ostrov I	160	68.27 N	51.05 E
Sengés	296	24.06 S	49.29 W
Sengilej	160	53.58 N	48.46 E
Sengwa ≃	224	17.07 S	28.05 E
Senhora do Pôrto	296	18.53 S	43.06 W
Senhor do Bonfim	286	10.27 S	40.11 W
Senica	164	48.41 N	17.22 E
Senigallia	184	43.43 N	13.13 E
Senise	170	40.09 N	16.18 E
Senj	170	44.59 N	14.54 E
Senja I	160	69.20 N	17.30 E
Šenkursk	160	62.08 N	42.53 E
Senlis	176	49.12 N	2.35 E
Senmonorom	200	12.27 N	107.12 E
Senne I	178	51.57 N	8.31 E
Sennestadt (Senne II)	178	51.57 N	8.35 E
Senneterre	244	48.24 N	77.14 W
Senno	160	54.49 N	29.43 E
Sennokura-yama ∧	192	36.49 N	138.50 E
Sennori	170	40.48 N	8.34 E
Senoia	246	33.18 N	84.33 W
Sens	176	48.12 N	3.17 E
Sensuntepeque	280	13.52 N	88.38 W
Senta	172	45.56 N	20.04 E
Sentinel	250	35.09 N	99.10 W
Sentinel Butte ∧	252	46.53 N	103.50 W
Sentinel Peak ∧	238	54.54 N	121.57 W
Sentinel Plain ≚	254	32.45 N	113.15 W
Šentjur	170	46.13 N	15.24 E
Seo de Urgel	168	42.21 N	1.28 E
Seoul → Sŏul	194	37.33 N	126.58 E
Separation Point ≻	230	40.47 S	172.59 E
Sepatini ≃	292	7.36 S	65.24 W
Sepetiba, Baía de C	296	23.00 S	43.48 W
Šepetovka	158	50.11 N	27.04 E
Sepik ≃	198	3.51 S	144.34 E
Sępólno Krajeńskie	164	53.28 N	17.32 E
Sępopol (Schippenbeil)	164	54.15 N	21.00 E
Sepoti ≃	292	6.43 S	61.38 W
Sepotuba ≃	292	15.56 S	57.39 W
Sepphoris → Ẕippori	210	32.44 N	35.16 E
Sept-Îles (Seven Islands)	240	50.12 N	66.23 W
Sepulga ≃	248	31.11 N	86.46 W
Sepúlveda	168	41.18 N	3.45 W
Sequatchie ≃	246	35.02 N	85.38 W
Sequeros	168	40.31 N	6.01 W
Sequillo ≃	168	41.45 N	5.30 W
Sequim	270	48.05 N	123.06 W
Sequoia	272	37.28 N	122.13 W
Sequoia National Park ♣	258	36.30 N	118.30 W
Sera, Punta d'en ≻	168	39.10 N	1.05 E
Serafeddin Dağları ⋀	212	39.05 N	41.10 E
Serafimovič	158	49.36 N	42.43 E
Seraidi	170	36.55 N	7.41 E
Seraing	164	50.36 N	5.29 E
Seram I	198	3.00 S	129.00 E
Seram, Laut(Ceram Sea) ▾[2]	198	2.30 S	128.00 E
Serang	198	6.07 S	106.09 E
Serasan, Pulau I	200	2.30 N	109.03 E
Serasan, Selat ⩌	200	2.20 N	109.00 E
Serbeulangit, Pegunungan ⋀	200	3.45 N	97.50 E
Serbia → Srbija □[3]	172	44.00 N	21.00 E
Serdce-Kamen', Mys ≻	236	66.57 N	171.40 W
Serdež	160	57.17 N	48.17 E
Serdobsk	158	52.28 N	44.13 E
Serebr'ansk	186	49.43 N	83.20 E
Serebr'anyje Prudy	160	54.28 N	38.44 E
Sered'	164	48.28 N	17.44 E
Sereda	160	55.54 N	35.31 E
Seregno	182	45.39 N	9.12 E
Seremban	200	2.44 N	101.56 E
Serena	268	41.29 N	88.44 W
Serengeti Plain ≚	218	2.50 S	35.00 E
Serenje	218	13.15 S	30.14 E
Seret ≃	172	48.38 N	25.52 E
Sergač	160	55.32 N	45.28 E
Sergeant	266	41.38 N	78.45 W
Sergeant Bluff	252	42.24 N	96.22 W
Sergeja Kirova, Ostrova II	186	77.12 N	89.30 E
Sergejevka	186	48.40 N	37.22 E
Sergen	172	41.42 N	27.42 E
Sergozero; Ozero ⊜	160	66.47 N	36.42 E
Seria	198	4.39 N	114.23 E
Serian	200	1.12 N	110.31 E
Seriate	182	45.41 N	9.43 E
Sérifos	172	37.09 N	24.31 E
Sérifos I	172	37.11 N	24.31 E
Sérigny ≃	232	56.05 N	68.45 W
Serir Dağı ∧	212	39.39 N	42.41 E
Serjol	160	60.02 N	48.58 E
Šerlovaja Gora	186	50.34 N	116.15 E
Sernovodsk	160	53.56 N	51.17 E
Sernur	160	56.56 N	49.09 E
Serock	164	52.31 N	21.03 E
Serodino	294	32.37 S	60.57 W
Ser'ogovo	160	62.20 N	50.36 E
Serov	158	59.29 N	60.31 E
Serowe	224	22.25 S	26.44 E
Serpa	168	37.56 N	7.36 W
Serpa, Ilha de I	290	3.07 S	58.19 W
Serpa Pinto	218	14.36 S	17.48 E
Serpeddi, Punta ∧	170	39.22 N	9.18 E
Serpent, Lac au ⊜	240	49.48 N	71.36 W
Serpent, Rivière au ≃	240	49.34 N	71.13 W
Serpents Mouth ⩌	285r	10.00 N	62.00 W
Serpis ≃	168	38.59 N	0.09 W
Serpuchov	160	54.55 N	37.25 E
Serra	296	20.07 S	40.18 W
Serracapriola	184	41.48 N	15.09 E
Serra do Navio	286	0.59 N	52.03 W
Serra do Salitre	296	19.06 S	46.41 W
Sérrai	172	41.05 N	23.32 E
Serramanna	170	39.25 N	8.54 E
Serrana	296	21.14 S	47.36 W
Serrana Bank ✣[4]	280	14.23 N	80.12 W
Serrania	296	21.33 S	46.03 W
Serranilla Bank ✣[4]	280	15.50 N	79.50 W
Serranópolis	296	18.16 S	52.00 W
Serranos	296	21.51 S	44.30 W
Serra Preta	296	12.09 S	39.20 W
Serra San Bruno	170	38.35 N	16.20 E
Serrat, Cap ≻	170	37.14 N	9.13 E
Serra Talhada	286	7.59 S	38.18 W
Serrath, Oued V	170	35.59 N	8.23 E
Serravalle Scrivia	182	44.43 N	8.51 E
Serres	166	44.26 N	5.43 E

Symbols in the index entries are identified on page 360.

Name	Page	Lat°′	Long°′
Serrezuela	294	30.40 S	65.20 W
Serri	170	39.41 N	9.09 E
Serrières	166	45.19 N	4.45 E
Serrinha	286	11.39 S	39.00 W
Sêrro	296	18.37 S	43.23 W
Serrote	296	21.27 S	54.40 W
Sersale	170	39.01 N	16.44 E
Sertã	168	39.48 N	8.06 W
Sertaneja	296	23.03 S	50.50 W
Sertânia	286	8.05 S	37.16 W
Serua, Pulau	198	6.18 S	130.01 E
Serui	198	1.53 S	136.14 E
Seruini	292	7.42 S	66.42 W
Sérvia	172	40.11 N	22.00 E
Servi Burnu	212	41.40 N	28.06 E
Sesajap	198	3.36 N	117.15 E
Sešan	236	66.46 N	171.26 W
Sesfontein	218	19.07 S	13.39 E
Sesheke	218	17.19 S	24.18 E
Sesia	170	45.05 N	8.37 E
Sesimbra	168	38.26 N	9.06 W
Sespe	274	34.23 N	118.58 W
Sessa Aurunca	184	41.14 N	13.56 E
Sestao	168	43.18 N	3.00 W
Sesto Calende	182	45.44 N	8.38 E
Sesto Fiorentino	184	43.50 N	11.12 E
Sesto San Giovanni	182	45.32 N	9.14 E
Sestri Levante	182	44.16 N	9.24 E
Sestroreck	160	60.06 N	29.58 E
Setana	192a	42.26 N	139.51 E
Setauket	261	40.57 N	73.07 W
Sète	182	43.24 N	3.41 E
Sete Barras	294	24.23 S	47.55 W
Sete de Setembro	296	12.56 S	52.51 W
Sete Lagoas	296	19.27 S	44.14 W
Setentrional, Cordillera	282	19.40 N	70.45 W
Sete Quedas, Cachoeira das	292	9.27 S	56.41 W
Sete Quedas, Parque Nacional de	294	24.02 S	54.12 W
Sete Quedas, Salto das(Salto del Guairá)	294	24.02 S	54.16 W
Seth Ward	250	34.13 N	101.42 W
Sétif	168	36.09 N	5.26 E
Seto	192	35.14 N	137.06 E
Seto-naikai	192	34.20 N	133.30 E
Seto-naikai-kokuritsu-kōen	192	34.15 N	133.28 E
Seton Lake	238	50.45 N	122.05 W
Seton Portage	238	50.43 N	122.18 W
Setouchi	193b	28.10 N	129.15 E
Settat	214	33.04 N	7.37 W
Sette Cama	218	2.32 S	9.45 E
Sette-Daban, Chrebet	186	62.00 N	138.00 E
Settimo Torinese	182	45.09 N	7.46 E
Setúbal	168	38.32 N	8.54 W
Setúbal, Baía de	168	38.27 N	8.53 W
Seui	170	39.50 N	9.20 E
Seul, Lac	232	50.20 N	92.30 W
Seul Choix Point	244	45.56 N	85.52 W
Seurre	166	47.00 N	5.09 E
Seutakan	236	65.38 N	176.58 W
Sevan, Ozero	208	40.20 N	45.20 E
Sevastopol'	158	44.36 N	33.32 E
Ševčenko	158	43.35 N	51.05 E
Ševelevskaja	160	60.52 N	44.12 E
Seven Harbors	268	42.40 N	83.34 W
Seven Hills	266	41.22 N	81.41 W
Seven Islands → Sept-Îles	240	50.12 N	66.23 W
Seven Islands Bay	232	59.25 N	63.40 W
Sevenoaks	174	51.16 N	0.12 E
Seven Sisters Peaks	238	54.58 N	128.10 W
Seventy Mile House	238	51.18 N	121.24 W
Seven Valleys	262	39.51 N	76.46 W
Severac-le-Château	166	44.19 N	3.04 E
Severn, N.C., U.S.	262	36.31 N	77.11 W
Severn, Va., U.S.	262	37.18 N	76.25 W
Severn	232	56.02 N	87.36 W
Severnaja Dvina	160	64.32 N	40.30 E
Severnaja Sos'va	186	64.10 N	65.28 E
Severnaja Zeml'a	186	79.30 N	98.00 E
Severna Park	262	39.04 N	76.33 W
Severnyj	160	67.38 N	64.06 E
Severnyje Uvaly	160	59.30 N	49.00 E
Severnyj Kommunar	160	58.23 N	54.02 E
Severnyj Ural	160	63.00 N	59.00 E
Severočeský	166	50.35 N	14.15 E
Severodvinsk	160	64.34 N	39.50 E
Severo-Jenisejskij	186	60.22 N	93.01 E
Severo-Kuril'sk	186	50.40 N	156.08 E
Severomoravský	164	49.45 N	17.50 E
Severomorsk	160	69.05 N	33.24 E
Severo-Sibirskaja Nizmennost'	186	73.00 N	100.00 E
Severoural'sk	158	60.09 N	59.57 E
Severy	252	37.37 N	96.14 W
Seveso	182	45.39 N	9.09 E
Sevettijärvi	160	69.26 N	28.38 E
Sevier	254	39.04 N	113.06 W
Sevier Bridge Reservoir	254	39.21 N	111.57 W
Sevier Desert	254	39.25 N	112.50 W
Sevier Lake	254	38.55 N	113.09 W
Sevierville	246	35.52 N	83.34 W
Sevilla, Col.	290	4.16 N	75.57 W
Sevilla, Esp.	168	37.23 N	5.59 W
Sevilla, Isla	280	8.13 N	82.23 W
Seville, Fla., U.S.	246	29.19 N	81.30 W
Seville, Ohio, U.S.	266	41.01 N	81.52 W
Şevketiye	172	40.05 N	27.51 E
Sevlievo	172	43.01 N	25.06 E
Sevran	176	48.56 N	2.32 E
Sèvres	176	48.49 N	2.12 E
Sewa	222	7.18 N	12.08 W
Sewanee	248	35.12 N	85.55 W
Seward, Alaska, U.S.	236	60.06 N	149.26 W
Seward, Nebr., U.S.	252	40.55 N	97.06 W
Seward, Pa., U.S.	266	40.25 N	79.01 W
Seward Glacier	236	60.22 N	140.15 W
Seward Peninsula	236	65.00 N	164.00 W
Sewell, Chile	294	34.05 S	70.23 W
Sewell, N.J., U.S.	262	39.46 N	75.09 W
Sewickley	266	40.33 N	80.11 W
Sexsmith	238	55.21 N	118.47 W
Seybaplaya	278	19.39 N	90.40 W
Seybaplaya, Punta	278	19.40 N	90.40 W
Seybouse, Oued	170	36.54 N	7.47 E
Seychelles	218	4.35 S	55.40 E
Seychelles	148	4.35 S	55.40 E
Seychelles-Mauritius Ridge	148	14.00 S	61.00 E
Seyches	166	44.33 N	0.18 E
Seyđisfjörđur	160a	65.16 N	14.00 W
Seyfe Gölü	212	39.13 N	34.23 E
Seyhan	212	36.43 N	34.53 E
Seyhan Barajı	212	37.04 N	35.19 E
Seymour, Austl.	228	37.02 S	145.08 E
Seymour, Conn., U.S.	261	41.24 N	73.04 W
Seymour, Ind., U.S.	248	38.58 N	85.53 W
Seymour, Iowa, U.S.	244	40.44 N	93.07 W
Seymour, Mo., U.S.	248	37.09 N	92.46 W
Seymour, Tex., U.S.	250	33.35 N	99.16 W
Seymour, Wis., U.S.	244	44.31 N	88.20 W
Seymour	238	51.05 N	126.50 W
Seymour Inlet	238	51.03 N	127.10 W
Seyne-les-Alpes	166	44.21 N	6.21 E
Seyssel	166	45.57 N	5.49 E
Sežana	170	45.42 N	13.52 E
Sézanne	176	48.43 N	3.43 E
Šežim	160	62.07 N	58.21 E
Sezimovo Ústí	164	49.23 N	14.42 E
Sezze	184	41.30 N	13.03 E
Sfax	214	34.44 N	10.46 E
Sfinto Gheorghe, Ostrovul	172	45.07 N	29.22 E
Sfîntu-Gheorghe	172	45.52 N	25.47 E
Sfîntu Gheorghe, Braţul	172	44.53 N	29.36 E
's-Gravenhage (The Hague)	178	52.06 N	4.18 E
's-Gravenzande	178	52.00 N	4.10 E
Sgué	222	17.45 N	7.43 W
Sha'b, Marsā	208	22.52 N	35.47 E
Shabani	224	20.20 S	30.02 E
Shabbona	268	41.46 N	88.52 W
Shabotik	244	48.50 N	85.34 W
Shackan Indian Reserve	238	50.17 N	112.10 W
Shackleton Ice Shelf	148	66.00 S	100.00 E
Shade Gap	266	40.11 N	77.52 W
Shadehill Reservoir	252	45.45 N	102.15 W
Shadow Mountain National Recreation Area	254	40.07 N	105.48 W
Shadwān, Jazīrat	220	27.30 N	33.59 E
Shady Grove	246	30.17 N	83.38 W
Shadyside	242	39.58 N	80.45 W
Shafer Butte	256	43.47 N	116.05 W
Shafter, Calif., U.S.	272	35.30 N	119.16 W
Shafter, Tex., U.S.	250	29.49 N	104.18 W
Shaftesbury	162	51.01 N	2.12 W
Shagamu	222	6.51 N	3.39 E
Shageluk	236	62.36 N	159.32 W
Shag Rocks	288	53.33 S	42.02 W
Shahdād, Namakzār-e	208	30.30 N	58.30 E
Shahe	190	40.08 N	116.15 E
Shahe, Zhg.	194	38.20 N	115.22 E
Shahe, Zhg.	194	37.31 N	117.50 E
Shahe, Zhg.	196	33.38 N	114.36 E
Shāh Fulādi	206	34.49 N	67.37 E
Shāhī	208	36.28 N	52.53 E
Shāhjahānpur	206	27.53 N	79.55 E
Shāhpūr	208	38.11 N	44.47 E
Shahreẓā	208	32.01 N	51.52 E
Shāhrūd	208	36.25 N	55.01 E
Shāhrūd	208	37.17 N	48.43 E
Shahsavār	208	36.49 N	50.53 E
Shā'ib al-Banāt, Jabal	220	26.59 N	33.29 E
Shā'ir, Jabal	212	34.55 N	37.58 E
Shakawe	218	18.23 S	21.50 E
Shaker Heights	266	41.29 N	81.36 W
Shakespeare	264	43.22 N	80.49 W
Shakhty → Šachty	158	47.42 N	40.13 E
Shaki	222	8.39 N	3.25 E
Shakopee	244	44.48 N	93.32 W
Shakotan-hantō	192a	43.20 N	140.30 E
Shaktoolik	236	64.20 N	161.09 W
Shala, Lake	214	7.35 N	38.30 E
Shalalth	238	50.44 N	122.13 W
Shalatayn, Bi'r	208	23.08 N	35.36 E
Shaleitiandao	194	39.03 N	118.44 E
Shaler Mountains	232	72.35 N	110.45 W
Shallotte	246	33.58 N	78.23 W
Shallowater	250	33.41 N	101.59 W
Shallow Lake	264	44.36 N	81.05 W
Shām, Bādiyat ash-	208	32.00 N	40.00 E
Shām, Jabal ash-	208	23.13 N	57.16 E
Shamattawa	232	55.52 N	92.05 W
Shammar, Jabal	208	27.20 N	41.45 E
Shamo, Lake	214	5.49 N	37.35 E
Shamokin	262	40.47 N	76.34 W
Shamrock, Fla., U.S.	246	29.39 N	83.08 W
Shamrock, Tex., U.S.	250	35.13 N	100.15 W
Shamva	218	17.18 S	31.34 E
Shan	200	22.00 N	98.00 E
Shandī	220	16.42 N	33.26 E
Shandianhe	194	42.23 N	116.21 E
Shandon	272	35.39 N	120.22 W
Shandong	194	36.00 N	118.00 E
Shandongbandao	194	37.00 N	121.00 E
Shanesville	266	40.31 N	81.39 W
Shangani	224	18.41 S	27.10 E
Shanghai, Va., U.S.	262	37.37 N	76.47 W
Shanghai, Zhg.	196	31.14 N	121.28 E
Shanghai Shih	196	31.10 N	121.30 E
Shangqiu	194	34.27 N	115.42 E
Shangrao	196	28.26 N	117.58 E
Shangshui	196	33.39 N	114.39 E
Shangsi	200	22.09 N	107.57 E
Shanguan	196	27.30 N	117.06 E
Shangxian	190	33.51 N	109.54 E
Shangyoushui	196	25.55 N	113.56 E
Shangzhi	190	45.13 N	127.59 E
Shanhaiguan	194	40.01 N	119.44 E
Shanhe	190	33.38 N	79.50 E
Shannock	261	41.27 N	71.38 W
Shannon, Ga., U.S.	246	34.20 N	85.04 W
Shannon, Ill., U.S.	244	42.09 N	89.44 W
Shannon, Miss., U.S.	248	34.07 N	88.43 W
Shannon	162	52.36 N	9.41 W
Shannon, Mouth of the	162	52.30 N	9.53 W
Shannontown	246	33.53 N	80.21 W
Shannonville	264	44.12 N	77.13 W
Shansi → Shānxī	190	37.00 N	112.00 E
Shantou (Swatow)	196	23.23 N	116.41 E
Shantouguan	196	27.54 N	117.26 E
Shantung → Shandong	194	36.00 N	118.00 E
Shantung Peninsula → Shandongbandao	194	37.00 N	121.00 E
Shanty Bay	264	44.25 N	79.36 W
Shǎnxī, Zhg.	190	35.00 N	109.00 E
Shānxī, Zhg.	190	37.00 N	112.00 E
Shanyin	190	39.35 N	112.58 E
Shaoguan	196	24.50 N	113.37 E
Shaowu	190	27.20 N	117.28 E
Shaoxing	196	30.00 N	120.35 E
Shaoyang	190	27.06 N	111.25 E
Shapinsay	162	59.03 N	2.51 W
Shaqq al-Ju'ayfir, Wādī	220	15.16 N	26.00 E
Shār	208	34.50 N	58.32 E
Sharatin Mountain	236	57.49 N	152.41 W
Sharbatāt, Ra's ash-	204	17.52 N	56.22 E
Sharbot Lake	264	44.46 N	76.41 W
Shari	192a	43.55 N	144.50 E
Shari-dake	192a	43.46 N	144.43 E
Shark River Hills	262	40.12 N	74.03 W
Sharktooth Mountain	232	58.35 N	127.57 W
Sharon, Ont., Can.	264	44.06 N	79.26 W
Sharon, Ont., Can.	266	42.53 N	81.22 W
Sharon, Conn., U.S.	261	41.53 N	73.29 W
Sharon, Mass., U.S.	261	42.05 N	71.11 W
Sharon, N. Dak., U.S.	252	47.36 N	97.54 W
Sharon, Pa., U.S.	266	41.14 N	80.31 W
Sharon, Wis., U.S.	268	42.30 N	88.44 W
Sharon Center	266	41.06 N	81.44 W
Sharon Springs	252	38.54 N	101.45 W
Sharon Valley	261	41.54 N	73.30 W
Sharp Peak	202	5.59 N	125.33 E
Sharpsburg	266	40.30 N	79.56 W
Sharpsville, Ind., U.S.	268	40.23 N	86.05 W
Sharpsville, Pa., U.S.	266	41.15 N	80.29 W
Sharshar, Jabal	220	23.52 N	30.20 E
Shartlesville	262	40.31 N	76.06 W
Shashi	190	30.19 N	112.14 E
Shashi	224	22.14 S	29.20 E
Shasi → Shashi	190	30.19 N	112.14 E
Shasta	258	40.36 N	122.29 W
Shasta	258	41.50 N	122.35 W
Shasta, Mount	258	41.20 N	122.20 W
Shasta Lake	258	40.50 N	122.25 W
Shattuck	250	36.16 N	99.53 W
Shauck	266	40.37 N	82.40 W
Shaunavon	232	49.40 N	108.25 W
Shaver Lake	272	37.09 N	119.18 W
Shaw	248	33.36 N	90.46 W
Shawanaga Inlet	244	45.32 N	80.24 W
Shawano	244	44.47 N	88.36 W
Shawbridge	260	45.52 N	74.05 W
Shawinigan	260	46.33 N	72.45 W
Shawinigan Falls → Shawinigan	260	46.33 N	72.45 W
Shawinigan-Sud	260	46.31 N	72.45 W
Shawmere	244	48.40 N	82.29 W
Shawnee, Kans., U.S.	252	39.01 N	94.43 W
Shawnee, Ohio, U.S.	242	39.36 N	82.13 W
Shawnee, Okla., U.S.	250	35.20 N	96.55 W
Shawnee Hills	266	40.07 N	83.09 W
Shawneetown	248	37.42 N	88.08 W
Shawnigan Lake	270	48.38 N	123.35 W
Shawville	242	45.36 N	76.29 W
Shaxi	196	26.34 N	118.02 E
Shaybārā	208	25.27 N	36.48 E
Shaykh, Jabal ash-	210	33.26 N	35.51 E
Shaykh, Sharm ash-	220	27.51 N	34.17 E
Shaykh 'Uthmān	214	12.52 N	44.59 E
Shchekino → Ščokino	158	54.00 N	37.31 E
Sheakleyville	266	41.27 N	80.13 W
Shebandowan Lake	244	48.38 N	90.05 W
Shebele (Shebelle)	214	0.50 N	43.10 E
Sheboygan	244	43.46 N	87.36 W
Sheboygan	244	43.45 N	87.42 W
Sheboygan Falls	244	43.44 N	87.49 W
Shechem → Nābulus	210	32.13 N	35.15 E
Shechem	210	32.13 N	35.15 E
Shedden	266	42.44 N	81.21 W
Shediac	240	46.13 N	64.32 W
Shedin Peak	238	55.55 N	127.32 W
Sheenjek	236	66.45 N	144.33 W
Sheep	238	50.44 N	113.51 W
Sheep Haven	162	55.10 N	7.52 W
Sheep Mountain, Ariz., U.S.	254	32.32 N	114.14 W
Sheep Mountain, Wyo., U.S.	254	43.31 N	110.28 W
Sheep Peak	250	31.14 N	104.59 W
Sheepranch	272	38.13 N	120.28 W
Sheep Range	258	36.45 N	115.05 W
Sheepscot	242	44.00 N	69.50 W
's-Heerenberg	178	51.53 N	6.15 E
Sheerness	174	51.27 N	0.45 E
Sheet Harbour	240	44.55 N	62.32 W
Shefar'am	210	32.48 N	35.11 E
Sheffield, Eng., U.K.	162	53.23 N	1.30 W
Sheffield, Ala., U.S.	248	34.46 N	87.40 W
Sheffield, Ill., U.S.	244	41.21 N	89.44 W
Sheffield, Iowa, U.S.	244	42.54 N	93.13 W
Sheffield, Mass., U.S.	261	42.05 N	73.21 W
Sheffield, Ohio, U.S.	266	41.28 N	82.03 W
Sheffield, Pa., U.S.	266	41.42 N	79.02 W
Sheffield, Tex., U.S.	250	30.41 N	101.49 W
Sheffield Lake	266	41.29 N	82.07 W
Sheffield Lake	240	49.20 N	56.35 W
Shefford	260	45.25 N	72.30 W
Shekatika Bay	240	51.17 N	58.20 W
Shekhūpura	206	31.42 N	73.59 E
Shekki → Zhongshan	196	22.31 N	113.22 E
Shelagyote Peak	238	55.58 N	127.12 W
Shelbina	248	39.47 N	92.02 W
Shelburn	248	39.11 N	87.24 W
Shelburne, N.S., Can.	240	43.46 N	65.19 W
Shelburne, Ont., Can.	264	44.04 N	80.12 W
Shelburne Falls	261	42.36 N	72.44 W
Shelby, Ind., U.S.	268	41.12 N	87.21 W
Shelby, Iowa, U.S.	252	41.31 N	95.27 W
Shelby, Mich., U.S.	244	43.37 N	86.22 W
Shelby, Miss., U.S.	248	33.57 N	90.46 W
Shelby, Mont., U.S.	256	48.30 N	111.51 W
Shelby, Nebr., U.S.	252	41.12 N	97.26 W
Shelby, N.C., U.S.	246	35.17 N	81.32 W
Shelby, Ohio, U.S.	266	40.53 N	82.40 W
Shelby	268	40.17 N	84.09 W
Shelby Village	266	42.38 N	83.04 W
Shelbyville, Ill., U.S.	248	39.24 N	88.48 W
Shelbyville, Ind., U.S.	248	39.31 N	85.47 W
Shelbyville, Ky., U.S.	248	38.13 N	85.14 W
Shelbyville, Mo., U.S.	248	39.48 N	92.02 W
Shelbyville, Tenn., U.S.	248	35.29 N	86.27 W
Shelbyville Reservoir	248	39.30 N	88.40 W
Sheldon, Ill., U.S.	268	40.46 N	87.34 W
Sheldon, Iowa, U.S.	252	43.11 N	95.51 W
Sheldon, Mich., U.S.	268	42.17 N	83.28 W
Sheldon, Mo., U.S.	248	37.40 N	94.18 W
Sheldon Point	236	62.32 N	164.52 W
Shelikof Strait	236	57.30 N	155.00 W
Shell Beach	272	35.09 N	120.40 W
Shellbrook	232	53.13 N	106.24 W
Shelley, B.C., Can.	238	54.00 N	122.37 W
Shelley, Idaho, U.S.	256	43.23 N	112.07 W
Shellharbour	228	34.35 S	150.52 E
Shell Lake	244	45.45 N	91.55 W
Shellman	246	31.46 N	84.37 W
Shell Rock	244	42.43 N	92.35 W
Shell Rock	244	42.38 N	92.30 W
Shellsburg	244	42.06 N	91.52 W
Shelocta	266	40.39 N	79.18 W
Shelter Island	261	41.05 N	72.21 W
Shelter Island Heights	261	41.05 N	72.21 W
Shelton, Conn., U.S.	261	41.19 N	73.05 W
Shelton, Nebr., U.S.	252	40.47 N	98.44 W
Shelton, Wash., U.S.	270	47.13 N	123.06 W
Shemanker	222	8.12 N	9.45 E
Shemogue	240	46.09 N	64.11 W
Shemya Station	236	52.43 N	174.05 E
Shenandoah, Iowa, U.S.	252	40.46 N	95.22 W
Shenandoah, Pa., U.S.	262	40.49 N	76.12 W
Shenandoah, Va., U.S.	242	38.29 N	78.37 W
Shenandoah	242	39.19 N	92.03 W
Shenandoah National Park	242	38.48 N	78.12 W
Shenango	266	41.23 N	80.24 W
Shengfang	190	39.04 N	116.42 E
Shengsi	196	30.41 N	122.28 E
Shengsiqundao	196	30.42 N	122.20 E
Shengze	196	30.55 N	120.39 E
Shenhuwan	196	24.40 N	118.42 E
Shenjiamen	196	29.58 N	122.17 E
Shenorock	261	41.20 N	73.44 W
Shenquangang	196	22.54 N	116.18 E
Shensi → Shǎnxī	190	35.00 N	109.00 E
Shenxian'gou	194	37.53 N	118.47 E
Shenyang (Mukden)	194	41.48 N	123.27 E
Shenzha	190	30.57 N	88.38 E
Shepard	238	50.57 N	113.55 W
Shepherd, Mich., U.S.	244	43.32 N	84.41 W
Shepherd, Tex., U.S.	248	30.30 N	95.01 W
Shepherd Bay	232	68.56 N	93.40 W
Shepherdstown	242	39.26 N	77.48 W
Shepherdsville	248	37.59 N	85.43 W
Sheppard Peak	236	57.41 N	132.37 W
Shepparton	228	36.23 S	145.25 E
Sheppey, Isle of	162	51.24 N	0.50 E
Shepshed	174	52.47 N	1.18 W
Shepton Mallet	174	51.12 N	2.33 W
Sherard Cape	232	74.36 N	80.25 W
Sherborne	174	50.57 N	2.31 W
Sherbro	222	7.45 N	12.55 W
Sherbro Island	222	7.45 N	12.55 W
Sherbrooke, N.S., Can.	240	45.08 N	61.59 W
Sherbrooke, Qué., Can.	260	45.24 N	71.54 W
Sherbrooke	260	45.25 N	71.55 W
Sherbrooke Lake	240	44.40 N	64.35 W
Sherburn	252	43.39 N	94.43 W
Sherburne	264	42.41 N	75.30 W
Sheridan, Ark., U.S.	248	34.19 N	92.24 W
Sheridan, Calif., U.S.	272	38.59 N	121.22 W
Sheridan, Ill., U.S.	268	41.32 N	88.41 W
Sheridan, Ind., U.S.	248	40.08 N	86.13 W
Sheridan, Mont., U.S.	256	45.27 N	112.12 W
Sheridan, Oreg., U.S.	270	45.06 N	123.24 W
Sheridan, Pa., U.S.	262	40.21 N	76.14 W
Sheridan, Tex., U.S.	250	29.29 N	96.40 W
Sheridan, Wyo., U.S.	256	44.48 N	106.58 W
Sheridan, Mount	256	44.16 N	110.32 W
Sheridan Beach	270	47.45 N	122.17 W
Sheringham	162	52.57 N	1.12 E
Sherman, Conn., U.S.	261	41.35 N	73.30 W
Sherman, Miss., U.S.	248	34.22 N	88.57 W
Sherman, N.Y., U.S.	266	42.10 N	79.36 W
Sherman, Tex., U.S.	250	33.38 N	96.36 W
Sherman	270	45.25 N	120.49 W
Sherman Mills	242	45.52 N	68.23 W
Sherman Mountain	248	36.01 N	93.16 W
Sherman Reservoir	252	41.20 N	98.55 W
Sherman Station	242	45.54 N	68.26 W
Sherrard	244	41.19 N	90.31 W
Sherrill	264	43.04 N	75.35 W
Sherrodsville	266	40.30 N	81.15 W
's-Hertogenbosch	178	51.41 N	5.19 E
Sherwood, P.E.I., Can.	240	46.17 N	63.08 W
Sherwood, Md., U.S.	262	38.36 N	76.19 W
Sherwood, Mich., U.S.	268	42.00 N	85.14 W
Sherwood, N. Dak., U.S.	252	48.58 N	101.38 W
Sherwood, Ohio, U.S.	268	41.17 N	84.33 W
Sherwood, Oreg., U.S.	270	45.21 N	122.50 W
Sherwood, Tenn., U.S.	248	35.05 N	85.56 W
Sherwood Forest	272	37.57 N	122.17 W
Sherwood Manor	261	42.01 N	72.38 W
Sherwood Park, Alta., Can.	238	53.31 N	113.19 W
Sherwood Park, N.Y., U.S.	261	42.36 N	73.43 W
Sheshan	196	28.26 N	121.53 E
Sheshea	292	9.36 S	74.10 W
Shetland Islands	162	60.30 N	1.30 W
Shexian	190	29.53 N	118.26 E
Sheyanghu	196	33.19 N	119.46 E
Sheyenne	252	47.39 N	99.07 W
Sheyenne	252	47.05 N	96.50 W
Sheykh Sho'eyb, Jazīreh-ye	208	26.48 N	53.15 E
Shiant Islands	162	57.54 N	6.30 W
Shiawassee	268	42.56 N	84.09 W
Shibām	214	15.56 N	48.38 E
Shibarghān	206	36.40 N	65.48 E
Shibata	192	37.57 N	139.20 E
Shibecha	192a	43.17 N	144.36 E
Shibetsu, Nihon	192a	44.10 N	142.23 E
Shibetsu, Nihon	192a	43.40 N	145.08 E
Shibīn al-Kawm	220	30.33 N	31.01 E
Shibotsu-tō	192a	43.30 N	146.09 E
Shibukawa	192	36.29 N	139.00 E
Shibushi	192	31.28 N	131.07 E
Shicheng	190	26.22 N	116.22 E
Shichengdao	194	39.31 N	123.02 E
Shickley	252	40.25 N	97.43 W
Shickshinny	242	41.09 N	76.09 W
Shickshock, Monts	240	48.40 N	66.30 W
Shidao	190	36.53 N	122.23 E
Shidler	250	36.47 N	96.40 W
Shields	256	45.43 N	110.28 W
Shiershan	196	29.18 N	118.08 E
Shifengxi	196	28.52 N	121.04 E
Shifuhu	206	31.20 N	83.25 E
Shiga	192	35.15 N	136.00 E
Shigatse → Rikeze	206	29.17 N	88.53 E
Shihe	196	32.18 N	114.31 E
Shihkiachwang → Shijiazhuang	194	38.03 N	114.28 E
Shijiazhuang	194	38.03 N	114.28 E
Shijiutuo	194	39.11 N	118.56 E
Shijushan	190	39.20 N	106.50 E
Shikārpur	206	27.57 N	68.38 E
Shikkā, Ra's	212	34.18 N	35.41 E
Shikoku	192	33.45 N	133.30 E
Shikoku-sanchi	192	33.47 N	133.30 E
Shikongling	196	24.56 N	113.00 E
Shikotsu-ko	192a	42.45 N	141.20 E
Shikotsu-tōya-kokuritsu-kōen	192a	42.47 N	141.00 E
Shillelagh	162	52.45 N	6.32 W
Shillington	262	40.18 N	75.58 W
Shillong	206	25.35 N	91.53 E
Shiloh, N.J., U.S.	262	39.27 N	75.18 W
Shiloh, N.C., U.S.	246	36.17 N	76.05 W
Shiloh, Ohio, U.S.	266	40.58 N	82.36 W
Shiloh, Pa., U.S.	262	39.59 N	76.49 W
Shiloh National Military Park	248	35.06 N	88.21 W
Shilong	196	23.07 N	113.48 E
Shima	192	34.13 N	136.51 E
Shimabara	192	32.47 N	130.22 E
Shimada	192	34.49 N	138.11 E
Shimane	192	35.00 N	132.30 E
Shimane-hantō	192	35.30 N	133.00 E
Shimanto	192	32.56 N	133.00 E
Shimian	190	29.18 N	102.22 E
Shimizu, Nihon	192	35.01 N	138.29 E
Shimizu, Nihon	192a	43.01 N	142.53 E
Shimminato	192	36.47 N	137.04 E
Shimoda	192	34.40 N	138.57 E
Shimodate	192	36.18 N	139.59 E
Shimokawa	192a	44.18 N	142.39 E
Shimokita-hantō	192	41.15 N	141.00 E
Shimonoseki	192	33.57 N	130.57 E
Shimpuru Rapids	224	17.50 S	19.56 E
Shin, Loch	162	58.07 N	4.32 W
Shinano	192	37.56 N	139.03 E
Shindand	204	33.16 N	62.05 E
Shiner	250	29.26 N	97.10 W
Shinglehouse	266	41.58 N	78.12 W
Shingū, Nihon	192	33.44 N	135.59 E
Shingū, Nihon	192	34.55 N	134.33 E
Shinji-ko	192	35.27 N	132.58 E
Shinjō	192	38.46 N	140.18 E
Shinkolobwe	218	11.02 S	26.35 E
Shinnston	242	39.24 N	80.18 W
Shinshiro	192	34.54 N	137.30 E
Shinyanga	218	3.40 S	33.26 E
Shiocton	244	44.27 N	88.35 W
Shiogama	192	38.19 N	141.01 E
Shiojiri	192	36.06 N	137.58 E
Shiono-zaki	192	33.26 N	135.45 E
Shioya-zaki, Nihon	192	36.59 N	140.59 E
Shioya-zaki, Nihon	192	33.26 N	135.45 E
Ship Bottom	262	39.39 N	74.11 W
Ship Cove	240	47.05 N	54.05 W
Shiping	200	23.47 N	102.30 E
Ship Island	248	30.13 N	88.55 W
Shipman	246	37.43 N	78.51 W
Shippegan	240	47.45 N	64.42 W
Shippegan Island	240	47.48 N	64.36 W
Shippensburg	262	40.03 N	77.31 W
Shippenville	266	41.15 N	79.28 W
Shippingport	266	40.38 N	80.25 W
Shiprock	254	36.47 N	108.41 W
Ship Rock	254	36.42 N	108.50 W
Shipshewana	268	41.41 N	85.35 W
Shiqu	190	33.04 N	97.45 E
Shira	192	32.12 N	130.37 E
Shirahama	192	33.40 N	135.20 E
Shirakami-saki	192a	41.24 N	140.12 E
Shirakawa	192	37.07 N	140.13 E
Shiranuka, Nihon	192a	41.08 N	141.24 E
Shiranuka, Nihon	192a	42.57 N	144.05 E
Shiraoi	192a	42.33 N	141.21 E
Shīrāz	208	29.36 N	52.32 E
Shire	218	17.42 S	35.19 E
Shiremanstown	262	40.13 N	76.57 W
Shiretoko-hantō	192a	44.00 N	145.00 E
Shiretoko-kokuritsu-kōen	192a	44.08 N	145.10 E
Shiretoko-misaki	192a	44.14 N	145.17 E
Shīrīn Tagāo	206	36.30 N	64.55 E
Shiriya-saki	192	41.26 N	141.28 E
Shirland	268	42.27 N	89.12 W
Shirley, B.C., Can.	270	48.23 N	123.54 W
Shirley, Ill., U.S.	268	40.24 N	89.04 W
Shirley, Ind., U.S.	248	39.53 N	85.35 W
Shirley, Mass., U.S.	261	42.33 N	71.39 W
Shiroishi	192	38.00 N	140.37 E
Shirone	192	37.46 N	139.01 E
Shīrvān	208	37.24 N	57.55 E
Shishaldin Volcano	236	54.45 N	163.57 W
Shishishan	196	24.44 N	117.54 E
Shishmaref	236	66.14 N	166.09 W
Shishmaref Inlet	236	66.07 N	165.50 W
Shitara	192	35.05 N	137.35 E
Shively	248	38.11 N	85.49 W
Shizugawa	192	38.40 N	141.27 E
Shizunai	192a	42.20 N	142.22 E
Shizuoka	192	34.58 N	138.23 E
Shkodër	172	42.05 N	19.30 E
Shkumbin	172	41.01 N	19.26 E
Shō	192	36.47 N	137.04 E
Shoal	248	30.41 N	86.39 W
Shoal Harbour	240	48.11 N	53.59 W
Shoalhaven	228	34.52 S	150.44 E
Shoal Lake	252	49.32 N	95.00 W
Shoals	248	38.40 N	86.47 W
Shoalwater Bay	228	20.02 S	148.17 E
Shōbara	192	34.51 N	133.01 E
Shōdo-shima	192	34.30 N	134.17 E
Shoeburyness	174	51.32 N	0.48 E
Shoe Cove	240	47.45 N	52.45 W
Shoemakersville	262	40.30 N	75.58 W
Shoreacres, B.C., Can.	238	49.26 N	117.32 W
Shore Acres, Calif., U.S.	272	38.02 N	121.58 W
Shore Acres, Mass., U.S.	261	42.13 N	70.44 W
Shore Acres, N.J., U.S.	262	40.02 N	74.06 W
Shoreham	268	42.04 N	86.30 W
Shoreham-by-Sea	174	50.49 N	0.16 W
Shorewood, Ill., U.S.	268	41.32 N	88.12 W
Shorewood, Wis., U.S.	268	43.05 N	87.53 W
Shorewood Hills	268	43.03 N	89.27 W
Short Beach	261	41.15 N	72.52 W
Short Creek	266	40.11 N	80.55 W
Short Mountain	246	36.23 N	83.10 W
Shortsville	264	42.57 N	77.14 W
Shoshone	256	42.56 N	114.24 W
Shoshone	256	44.52 N	108.11 W
Shoshone Basin	256	43.05 N	108.05 W
Shoshone Lake	256	44.22 N	110.43 W
Shoshone Mountains	258	39.15 N	117.25 W
Shoshone Peak	258	36.56 N	116.16 W
Shoshong	218	22.59 S	26.30 E
Shoshoni	254	43.14 N	108.07 W
Shouxian	196	32.35 N	116.47 E
Showell	262	38.24 N	75.13 W
Show Low	254	34.15 N	110.02 W
Shreve	266	40.41 N	82.01 W
Shreveport	248	32.30 N	93.45 W
Shrewsbury, Eng., U.K.	174	52.43 N	2.45 W
Shrewsbury, Mass., U.S.	261	42.18 N	71.43 W
Shrewsbury, N.J., U.S.	262	40.19 N	74.04 W
Shrewsbury, Pa., U.S.	262	39.46 N	76.41 W
Shropshire	174	52.40 N	2.40 W
Shrub Oak	261	41.20 N	73.49 W
Shuajingsi	190	32.00 N	103.05 E
Shuangcheng	190	45.26 N	126.18 E
Shuangfengdao	196	26.35 N	120.08 E
Shuangfengshan	196	24.28 N	114.43 E
Shuangjiang	200	23.37 N	99.41 E
Shuangjihe, Zhg.	194		
	196	34.05 N	114.24 E
Shuangliao	190	43.31 N	123.30 E
Shuangpai	200	24.54 N	101.32 E
Shuangxi	196	25.56 N	119.12 E
Shuangyashan	190	46.37 N	131.22 E
Shubenacadie	240	45.20 N	63.30 W
Shubenacadie Lake	240	44.55 N	63.36 W
Shublik Mountains	236	69.31 N	145.40 W
Shubuta	248	31.52 N	88.42 W
Shufu → Kashi	190	39.29 N	75.59 E
Shuhe	194	34.08 N	118.29 E
Shuicheng	200	26.41 N	104.50 E
Shukbuk Bay	232	64.50 N	74.40 W
Shuksan, Mount	256	48.50 N	121.36 W
Shulaps Peak	238	50.57 N	122.31 W
Shumagin Islands	236	55.07 N	159.45 W
Shumen → Šumen	172	43.16 N	26.55 E
Shunde	196	22.50 N	113.14 E
Shungnak	236	66.53 N	157.02 W
Shuqayyiqah, Nafūd	208	25.45 N	43.55 E
Shuqrā'	214	13.21 N	45.42 E
Shuqualak	248	32.59 N	88.34 W
Shūr, Īrān	208	29.59 N	54.50 E
Shūr, Īrān	208	31.45 N	55.15 E
Shushanhu	194	35.36 N	116.27 E
Shūshtar	208	32.03 N	48.51 E
Shuswap	238	50.50 N	119.00 W
Shuswap Lake	238	50.57 N	119.15 W
Shuya → Šuja, S.S.S.R.	160	61.55 N	34.12 E
Shuyak Island	236	58.35 N	152.30 W
Shwangliao → Liaoyuan	190	42.54 N	125.07 E
Shwebo	200	22.34 N	95.42 E
Shyok	206	35.13 N	75.53 E
Siāhān Range	206	27.25 N	64.30 E
Siak	200	1.13 N	102.09 E
Siālkot	206	32.30 N	74.31 E
Siam → Thailand	198	15.00 N	100.00 E
Siam, Gulf of	200	10.00 N	101.00 E
Sian → Xi'an, Zhg.	190	34.15 N	108.52 E
Siangtan → Xiangtan	196	27.51 N	112.54 E
Sianów (Zanow)	164	54.15 N	16.16 E
Siantan, Pulau	200	3.10 N	106.15 E
Siapa	290	2.07 N	66.28 W
Siargao Island	202	9.52 N	126.03 E
Siasconset	261	41.16 N	69.58 W
Siasi	202	5.33 N	120.49 E
Siasi Island	202	5.32 N	120.52 E
Šiaškotan, Ostrov	186	48.49 N	154.06 E
Siátista	172	40.16 N	21.33 E
Siaton	202	9.04 N	123.02 E
Siaton	202	9.03 N	123.01 E
Siaton Point	202	9.03 N	123.01 E
Siau, Pulau	198	2.42 N	125.24 E
Šiauliai	160	55.56 N	23.19 E
Sibā'ī, Jabal as-	220	25.43 N	34.09 E
Sibaj	158	52.42 N	58.39 E
Sibalom	202	10.47 N	122.01 E
Sibanicú	284p	21.14 N	77.31 W
Sibayi, Lake	224	27.20 S	32.40 E
Sibay Island	202	11.50 N	121.28 E
Šibenik	170	43.44 N	15.54 E
Siberia → Sibir'	186	65.00 N	110.00 E
Siberut, Pulau	198	1.20 S	98.55 E
Sibi	204	29.33 N	67.53 E
Sibir'	186	65.00 N	110.00 E
Sibir'akova, Ostrov	186	72.50 N	79.00 E
Sibiti	218	3.41 S	13.21 E
Sibiu	172	45.48 N	24.09 E
Sibley, Ill., U.S.	268	40.35 N	88.23 W
Sibley, Iowa, U.S.	252	43.24 N	95.45 W
Sibley, La., U.S.	248	32.33 N	93.18 W
Sibley, Miss., U.S.	248	31.23 N	91.24 W
Sibolga	200	1.45 N	98.46 E
Sibu	198	2.19 N	111.51 E
Sibu, Pulau	200	2.13 N	104.04 E
Sibuguey	202	7.42 N	122.50 E
Sibuguey Bay	202	7.38 N	122.37 E
Sibutu Passage	202	4.50 N	119.35 E
Sibuyan Island	202	12.25 N	122.35 E
Sibuyan Sea	202	12.50 N	122.20 E
Sicamous	238	50.50 N	119.00 W
Sicapoo, Mount	202	18.01 N	120.56 E
Sicasica	292	17.22 S	67.45 W
Siccus	228	31.26 S	139.30 E
Sichote-Alin'	186	48.00 N	138.00 E
Sichuan	190	31.00 N	105.00 E
Sicié, Cap	166	43.03 N	5.51 E
Sicilia	170	37.30 N	14.00 E
Sicily → Sicilia	170	37.30 N	14.00 E
Sicily Island	248	31.51 N	91.40 W
Sicklerville	262	39.43 N	74.58 W
Sico	280	15.58 N	84.58 W
Sicogon Island	202	11.27 N	123.16 E
Sicre	280	15.49 N	84.38 W
Sicuani	292	14.15 S	71.15 W
Šid	172	45.08 N	19.13 E
Siderno Marina	170	38.16 N	16.18 E
Sideróplis	294	28.35 S	49.26 W
Sídheros, Ákra	172	35.19 N	26.19 E
Sidhirókastron	172	41.14 N	23.22 E
Sidi Aïch	168	36.37 N	4.42 E
Sidi Aïssa	168	35.53 N	3.48 E
Sidi Akacha	168	36.28 N	1.18 E
Sidi Ali	168	36.06 N	0.25 E
Sidi Ali Ben Nasrallah	170	35.15 N	9.50 E
Sīdī Barrānī	214	31.36 N	25.55 E
Sidi bel Abbès	168	35.13 N	0.10 W
Sidi-Bennour	214	32.30 N	8.30 W
Sidi Daoud	170	37.00 N	10.55 E
Sidi el Hani, Sebkra de	170	35.33 N	10.25 E
Sidi Ifni	214	29.24 N	10.12 W
Sidi Mohammed Ben Ali	168	36.09 N	0.51 E
Sidjundjung	200	0.42 S	100.58 E
Sidley, Mount	148	77.02 S	126.00 W
Sidman	266	40.20 N	78.45 W
Sidmouth	174	50.41 N	3.15 W
Sidnaw	244	46.30 N	88.43 W
Sidney, B.C., Can.	238	48.39 N	123.24 W
Sidney, Ill., U.S.	248	40.01 N	88.04 W
Sidney, Ind., U.S.	268	41.06 N	85.45 W
Sidney, Iowa, U.S.	252	40.45 N	95.39 W
Sidney, Mont., U.S.	252	47.43 N	104.09 W
Sidney, Nebr., U.S.	252	41.09 N	102.59 W
Sidney, N.Y., U.S.	242	42.19 N	75.24 W
Sidney, Ohio, U.S.	268	40.17 N	84.09 W
Sidney Lanier, Lake	246	34.15 N	83.57 W
Sidon → Şaydā, Lubnān	210	33.33 N	35.22 E
Sidon, Miss., U.S.	248	33.25 N	90.12 W
Sidra, Gulf of → Surt, Khalij	214	31.30 N	18.00 E
Sidrolândia	296	20.55 S	54.58 W
Siedlce	164	52.11 N	22.16 E
Siegburg	164	50.47 N	7.12 E
Siegen	164	50.52 N	8.02 E
Siegler Springs	272	38.54 N	122.39 W
Siemianowice Śląskie	164	50.19 N	19.01 E
Siemiatycze	164	52.26 N	22.53 E
Siĕmréab	200	13.22 N	103.51 E
Siena	184	43.19 N	11.21 E
Siena	184	43.13 N	11.24 E
Sieniawa	164	50.11 N	22.36 E
Sienne	162	49.00 N	1.34 W
Sieradz	164	51.36 N	18.45 E
Sieraków	164	52.39 N	16.04 E
Sierck-les-Bains	166	49.26 N	6.21 E
Sierpc	164	52.52 N	19.41 E
Sierra	272	39.30 N	120.30 W
Sierra Blanca	254	31.11 N	105.21 W
Sierra Blanca Peak	254	33.23 N	105.48 W
Sierra-Bullones	202	9.49 N	124.18 E
Sierra Chica	294	36.50 S	60.14 W
Sierra City	272	39.34 N	120.38 W
Sierra Colorada	288	40.35 S	67.50 W
Sierra de Agua	278	17.32 N	88.54 W
Sierra del Carmen, Parque Nacional	278	29.15 N	102.42 W
Sierra del Carmen, Parque National	250	29.15 N	102.42 W
Sierra de San Pedro Mártir, Parque Nacional	278	30.55 N	115.35 W
Sierra Gorda	294	22.54 S	69.19 W
Sierra Leone	214	8.30 N	11.30 W
Sierra Leone Basin	148	5.00 N	16.00 W
Sierra Leone Rise	148	6.00 N	24.00 W
Sierra Madre	274	34.10 N	118.03 W
Sierra Mojada	250	27.17 N	103.42 W
Sierra Nevada, Parque Nacional	290	8.36 N	70.50 W
Sierras Bayas	294	36.50 S	60.10 W
Sierraville	272	39.36 N	120.22 W
Sierra Vista	254	31.33 N	110.18 W
Sierre	180	46.18 N	7.32 E
Siete Puntas	294	23.34 S	57.20 W
Siffu	202	17.12 N	121.50 E
Sífnos	172	36.59 N	24.40 E
Sifón Villaneuva	250	27.17 N	100.17 W
Sig, Alg.	168	35.32 N	0.11 W
Sig, S.S.S.R.	160	65.35 N	34.13 E
Sigean	166	43.02 N	2.59 E
Sigel	266	41.17 N	79.07 W
Sighetul Marmaţiei	172	47.56 N	23.54 E
Sighişoara	172	46.13 N	24.48 E
Siglan	186	59.02 N	152.25 E
Siglerville	262	40.44 N	77.31 W
Sigli	198	5.22 N	95.57 E
Sigli, Cap	168	36.56 N	4.45 E
Siglufjörđur	160a	66.10 N	18.56 W
Sigmaringen	180	48.05 N	9.13 E
Signa	184	43.47 N	11.05 E
Signal Hill National Historic Park	240	47.30 N	52.42 W
Signal Mountain	248	35.07 N	85.21 W
Signal Mountain	242	44.12 N	72.20 W
Signal Peak	254	37.19 N	113.29 W
Signy-l'Abbaye	166	49.42 N	4.25 E
Sigourney	244	41.20 N	92.12 W
Sigsig	290	3.01 S	78.45 W
Sigtuna	160	59.37 N	17.43 E
Siguanea, Ensenada de la	284p	21.40 N	83.05 W
Siguatepeque	280	14.32 N	87.49 W
Siguel	202	5.57 N	125.06 E
Sigüenza	168	41.04 N	2.38 W
Sigües	168	42.38 N	1.00 W
Siguiri	222	11.25 N	9.10 W
Siguiri	222	11.30 N	9.15 W
Sigurd	254	38.50 N	111.58 W
Sihabuhabu, Dolok	200	2.10 N	99.21 E
Sihanoukville → Krŏng Preăh Seihanŭ	200	10.38 N	103.30 E
Sihaus	292	8.40 S	77.40 W
Sihna	172	47.37 N	27.08 E
Sihuas	292	16.44 S	72.26 W
Siikajoki	160	64.50 N	24.44 E
Siilinjärvi	160	63.05 N	27.40 E
Siirt	212	37.56 N	41.57 E
Sija	160	63.38 N	41.38 E
Sijiao	196	30.39 N	122.25 E
Si-Kacha	200	13.10 N	100.56 E
Sikanni Chief	232	58.20 N	121.50 W
Sīkar	206	27.36 N	75.08 E
Sikaram	204	34.50 N	69.55 E
Sikasso	222	11.19 N	5.40 W
Sikasso	222	10.55 N	7.00 W
Sikéai	172	36.46 N	22.56 E
Sikes	248	32.05 N	92.29 W
Sikeston	248	36.53 N	89.35 W
Sikiá	172	40.02 N	23.56 E
Sikiang → Xijiang	190	22.25 N	113.23 E
Siking → Xi'an	190	34.15 N	108.52 E
Síkinos	172	25.07 N	26.43 E
Síkinos	172	36.39 N	25.06 E
Sikión	172	37.59 N	22.44 E
Sikkim	204	27.35 N	88.35 E
Siklós	164	45.52 N	18.28 E
Šikotan, Ostrov(Shikotan-tō)	192a	43.48 N	146.45 E
Sikt'ach	186	69.55 N	125.02 E
Sil	168	42.27 N	7.43 W
Silacayoapan	278	17.30 N	98.09 W

Symbols in the index entries are identified on page 360.

Name	Page	Lat°′	Long°′
Silam, Mount ∧	202	4.58 N	118.10 E
Silandro (Schlanders)	170	46.38 N	10.46 E
Silang	202	14.14 N	120.58 E
Silao	278	20.56 N	101.26 W
Silas	248	31.46 N	88.20 W
Silay	202	10.48 N	122.58 E
Silay, Mount ∧	202	10.47 N	123.14 E
Silba	170	44.23 N	14.42 E
Silba, Otok I	170	44.24 N	14.42 E
Silchar	206	24.49 N	92.48 E
Sile	172	41.11 N	29.36 E
Siler City	246	35.44 N	79.28 W
Silesia → Śląsk □[9]	164	51.00 N	16.45 E
Siletz	256	44.43 N	123.55 W
Siletz ≃	256	44.54 N	124.00 W
Silhouette I	218	4.29 S	55.14 E
Siliana	170	36.05 N	9.22 E
Siliana, Oued ≃	170	36.33 N	9.25 E
Silifke	208	36.22 N	33.56 E
Silīguri	206	26.43 N	88.27 E
Silingan, Mount ∧	202	7.45 N	122.29 E
Silistra	172	44.07 N	27.16 E
Silivri	172	41.04 N	28.15 E
Siljan ⊜	160	60.50 N	14.45 E
Šilka	186	51.51 N	116.02 E
Šilka ≃	186	53.22 N	121.32 E
Silkeborg	160	56.10 N	9.34 E
Sillé-le-Guillaume	166	48.12 N	0.08 W
Sillem Island I	232	70.55 N	71.30 W
Sillery	260	46.46 N	71.15 W
Sillian	164	46.45 N	12.25 E
Sillon de Talbert ≻[1]	166	48.53 N	3.05 W
Sillustani ⊥	292	15.45 S	70.05 W
Siloam Springs	248	36.11 N	94.32 W
Šilovo	160	54.19 N	40.53 E
Silsbee	248	30.21 N	94.11 W
Silva Jardim	296	22.39 S	42.23 W
Silvana	270	48.12 N	122.15 W
Silvânia	296	16.42 S	48.38 W
Silva Porto	218	12.22 S	16.56 E
Silver	250	32.04 N	100.40 W
Silverado	274	33.45 N	117.35 W
Silver Bank ⊹[4]	282	20.30 N	69.40 W
Silver Bank Passage ⋓	282	20.40 N	70.20 W
Silver Bay	244	47.17 N	91.16 W
Silver Bell	254	32.23 N	111.30 W
Silver Bow Park	256	46.01 N	112.28 W
Silver City	254	32.46 N	108.17 W
Silver Creek, Miss., U.S.	248	31.36 N	89.59 W
Silver Creek, Nebr., U.S.	252	41.19 N	97.40 W
Silver Creek, N.Y., U.S.	266	42.33 N	79.10 W
Silver Creek ≃, Oreg., U.S.	256	43.16 N	119.13 W
Silverdale, B.C., Can.	270	49.09 N	122.24 W
Silverdale, Pa., U.S.	262	40.21 N	75.16 W
Silverdale, Wash., U.S.	270	47.39 N	122.42 W
Silver Falls State Park ♣	256	44.48 N	122.50 W
Silver Lake, Calif., U.S.	272	38.38 N	120.07 W
Silver Lake, Ind., U.S.	268	41.04 N	85.53 W
Silver Lake, Kans., U.S.	252	39.06 N	95.52 W
Silver Lake, Mass., U.S.	261	42.34 N	70.44 W
Silver Lake, Minn., U.S.	244	44.54 N	94.12 W
Silver Lake, Ohio, U.S.	266	41.09 N	81.27 W
Silver Lake, Oreg., U.S.	256	43.08 N	120.56 W
Silverlake, Wash., U.S.	270	46.18 N	122.49 W
Silver Lake, Wis., U.S.	268	42.33 N	88.10 W
Silver Lake ⊜, Oreg., U.S.	256	43.22 N	119.24 W
Silver Lake ⊜, Oreg., U.S.	256	43.06 N	120.53 W
Silver Peak Range ⋀	258	37.35 N	117.45 W
Silver Spring, Md., U.S.	242	39.02 N	77.03 W
Silver Spring, Pa., U.S.	262	40.04 N	76.26 W
Silver Springs, Nev., U.S.	272	39.25 N	119.13 W
Silver Springs, N.Y., U.S.	264	42.40 N	78.05 W
Silver Star Mountain ∧	256	48.33 N	120.35 W
Silverthrone Mountain ∧	238	51.31 N	126.06 W
Silvertip Mountain ∧	256	47.47 N	113.15 W
Silverton, B.C., Can.	238	49.57 N	117.21 W
Silverton, Colo., U.S.	254	37.49 N	107.40 W
Silverton, N.J., U.S.	262	40.01 N	74.10 W
Silverton, Oreg., U.S.	270	45.01 N	122.47 W
Silverton, Tex., U.S.	250	34.28 N	101.19 W
Silverton, Wash., U.S.	270	48.05 N	121.34 W
Silves	168	37.11 N	8.26 W
Silvi	170	42.34 N	14.05 E
Silvia	290	2.37 N	76.21 W
Silvies ≃	256	43.22 N	118.48 W
Silvretta ⋀	166	46.50 N	10.10 E
Simanggang	198	1.12 N	111.32 E
Šimanovsk	186	52.00 N	127.42 E
Simao	190	22.50 N	101.00 E
Simara Island I	202	12.48 N	122.03 E
Simard, Lac ⊜	244	47.38 N	78.40 W
Simav	172	39.05 N	28.59 E
Simav ≃	212	40.23 N	28.31 E
Simav Gölü ⊜	212	39.09 N	28.55 E
Simbach	164	48.34 N	12.45 E
Simbal	292	7.58 S	78.48 W
Simcoe	264	42.50 N	80.18 W
Simcoe □[6]	264	44.25 N	79.50 W
Simcoe, Lake ⊜	244	44.20 N	79.20 W
Simeria	172	45.51 N	23.01 E
Simeto ≃	170	37.24 N	15.06 E
Simeulue, Pulau I	200	2.30 N	96.00 E
Simferopol'	158	44.57 N	34.06 E
Simi, Ellás	172	36.36 N	27.50 E
Simi, Calif., U.S.	274	34.16 N	118.47 W
Sími I	172	36.35 N	27.52 E
Similkameen ≃	238	48.56 N	119.26 W
Simingshan ⋀	196	29.50 N	121.00 E
Simisa Island I	202	5.58 N	121.35 E
Simití	290	7.58 N	73.57 W
Simla, Bhārat	206	22.47 N	88.16 E
Simla, Colo., U.S.	252	39.09 N	104.05 W
Şimleu-Silvaniei	172	47.14 N	22.48 E
Simmern	164	49.59 N	7.31 E
Simmesport	248	30.59 N	91.49 W
Simms	256	47.30 N	111.55 W
Simnas	164	54.24 N	23.39 E
Simoca	294	27.15 S	65.21 W
Simojärvi ⊜	160	66.06 N	27.03 E
Simojoki ≃	160	65.37 N	25.03 E
Simojovel [de Allende]	278	17.12 N	92.38 W
Simon, Lac ⊜	242	45.57 N	75.05 W
Simonette ≃	238	55.07 N	118.00 W
Šimonka ∧	164	48.58 N	21.27 E
Simonstad	224	34.14 S	18.26 E
Simonton Lake	268	41.44 N	85.59 W
Simoom Sound	238	50.45 N	126.45 W
Simpang-Kiri ≃	200	2.21 N	97.51 E
Simpson	248	31.16 N	93.00 W
Simpson Desert ◂[2]	228	25.00 S	137.00 E
Simpson Island I	244	48.48 N	87.40 W
Simpson Lake ⊜, N.W. Ter., Can.	232	68.39 N	91.19 W
Simpson Lake ⊜, N.W. Ter., Can.	236	68.10 N	126.35 W
Simpson Peak ∧	236	59.44 N	131.27 W
Simpson Peninsula ≻[1]	232	68.34 N	88.45 W
Simpson Strait ⋓	232	68.27 N	97.45 W
Simpsonville, Md., U.S.	262	39.11 N	76.52 W
Simpsonville, S.C., U.S.	246	34.44 N	82.15 W
Simrishamn	160	55.33 N	14.20 E
Sims	248	38.22 N	88.32 W
Simsbury	261	41.52 N	72.48 W
Šimsk	160	58.13 N	30.43 E
Simušir, Ostrov I	186	46.58 N	152.02 E
Sīnā' □[4]	210	29.00 N	34.00 E
Sīnā', Shibh Jazīrat(Sinai Peninsula) ≻[1]	220	29.30 N	34.00 E
Sinabang	200	2.29 N	96.23 E
Sinabung, Gunung ∧	200	3.12 N	98.23 E
Şināfīr, Jazīrat I	220	27.55 N	34.40 E
Sinai, Mount → Mūsā, Jabal ∧	220	28.32 N	33.59 E
Sinaia	172	45.21 N	25.33 E
Sinai Peninsula → Sīnā', Shibh Jazīrat ≻[1]	220	29.30 N	34.00 E
Sin'aja ≃	186	57.10 N	28.31 E
Sinako, Mount ∧	202	7.29 N	125.17 E
Sinaloa □[3]	278	25.00 N	107.30 W
Sinaloa ≃	278	25.18 N	108.30 W
Sinalunga	184	43.12 N	11.44 E
Sinamaica	290	11.05 N	71.51 W
Sinan	190	27.54 N	108.18 E
Sīnāwan	214	31.02 N	10.36 E
Sincé	290	9.15 N	75.09 W
Sincelejo	290	9.18 N	75.24 W
Sinch'ang	194	40.07 N	128.28 E
Sinclair	254	41.47 N	107.07 W
Sinclair, Lake ⊜[1]	246	33.11 N	83.16 W
Sinclair Mills	238	54.02 N	121.41 W
Sinclair's Bay C	162	58.31 N	3.03 W
Sinclairville	266	42.16 N	79.16 W
Sindangan	202	8.14 N	123.00 E
Sindangan ≃	202	8.13 N	123.00 E
Sindangan Bay C	202	8.12 N	122.50 E
Sindangan Point ≻	202	8.09 N	122.39 E
Sindara	218	1.02 S	10.40 E
Sindelfingen	180	48.42 N	9.00 E
Sındırgı	172	39.14 N	28.10 E
Sindjai	198	5.07 S	120.15 E
Sin-do I	194	39.48 N	124.14 E
Sindor	160	62.50 N	51.57 E
Siné ∨	222	14.10 N	16.28 W
Sinegorje	160	59.42 N	50.40 E
Sinekçi	172	40.16 N	27.24 E
Sinekli	172	41.14 N	28.12 E
Sines	168	37.57 N	8.52 W
Sine-Saloum □[4]	222	14.00 N	15.50 W
Sinfāis	168	41.04 N	8.05 W
Singapore	200	1.17 N	103.51 E
Singapore □[1]	198	1.22 N	103.48 E
Singapore Strait ⋓	200	1.15 N	104.00 E
Singaradja	226	8.07 S	115.06 E
Sing Buri	200	14.53 N	100.25 E
Singen (Hohentwiel)	180	47.46 N	8.50 E
Singer	248	30.39 N	93.25 W
Singida	218	4.49 S	34.45 E
Singitikós Kólpos C	172	40.12 N	24.03 E
Singkaling Hkāmti	190	26.00 N	95.42 E
Singkang	198	4.08 S	120.01 E
Singkarak, Danau ⊜	200	0.37 S	100.33 E
Singkawang	200	0.54 N	109.00 E
Singkep, Pulau I	200	0.30 S	104.25 E
Singleton	228	32.34 S	151.10 E
Singuédeze (Groot Shingwidzi) ≃	224	23.53 S	32.17 E
Siniloan	202	14.25 N	121.27 E
Sining → Xining	190	36.38 N	101.55 E
Siniscola	170	40.34 N	9.41 E
Sinj	170	43.42 N	16.38 E
Sinjah	220	13.09 N	33.56 E
Sinjār	208	36.19 N	41.52 E
Sinkāt	220	18.50 N	36.50 E
Sinkiang → Xinjiang Weiwuer Zizhiqu □[4]	190	40.00 N	85.00 E
Sinking Spring	262	40.19 N	76.02 W
Sin-le-Noble	176	50.22 N	3.07 E
Sinnai	170	39.18 N	9.12 E
Sinnamahoning	266	41.19 N	78.06 W
Sinnamary	286	5.23 N	52.57 W
Sinnes	160	58.56 N	6.50 E
Sinni ≃	170	40.09 N	16.42 E
Sînnicolau Mare	172	46.05 N	20.38 E
Sinnūris	220	29.25 N	30.52 E
Sinoe □[6]	222	5.10 N	9.00 W
Sinoe, Lacul ⊜	172	44.38 N	28.53 E
Sinoia	218	17.22 S	30.12 E
Sinop	158	41.50 N	35.15 E
Sinop ≻	212	42.02 N	35.12 E
Sinop Limanı C	212	41.50 N	35.15 E
Sinsheim	166	49.15 N	8.53 E
Sinsiang → Xinxiang	194	35.20 N	113.51 E
Sinskoje	186	61.08 N	126.48 E
Sint-Amandsberg	176	51.04 N	3.45 E
Sîntana	172	46.21 N	21.30 E
Sint Andries, Bel.	164	51.12 N	3.10 E
Sint-Andries, Bel.	176	51.12 N	3.10 E
Sintang	198	0.04 N	111.30 E
Sint Christoffelberg ∧	285s	12.20 N	69.08 W
Sint Eustatius I	282	17.30 N	62.59 W
Sint-Gillis-Waas	176	51.13 N	4.08 E
Sint-Katelijne-Waver	178	51.04 N	4.32 E
Sint-Kruis, Bel.	176	51.13 N	3.15 E
Sint Kruis, Ned. Ant.	285s	12.18 N	69.08 W
Sint-Michiels	176	51.11 N	3.12 E
Sint Michielsgestel	178	51.38 N	5.21 E
Sint Nicolaas	285s	12.27 N	69.52 W
Sint-Niklaas (Saint-Nicolas)	176	51.10 N	4.08 E
Sinton	250	29.41 N	95.58 W
Sint-Pieters-Leeuw	176	50.47 N	4.14 E
Sintra	168	38.48 N	9.23 W
Sint-Truiden	164	50.48 N	5.12 E
Sint Willebrord	178	51.33 N	4.35 E
Sinú ≃	290	9.24 N	75.49 W
Sin'ucha ≃	172	48.03 N	30.51 E
Sinŭiju	194	40.05 N	124.24 E
Sió ≃, Magy.	164	46.20 N	18.55 E
Sio ≃, Togo	222	6.17 N	1.13 E
Siocon	202	7.42 N	122.09 E
Siófok	164	46.54 N	18.04 E
Sion (Sitten)	180	46.14 N	7.21 E
Sioule ≃	166	46.22 N	3.19 W
Sioux Center	252	43.05 N	96.10 W
Sioux City	252	42.30 N	96.23 W
Sioux Falls	252	43.32 N	96.44 W
Sioux Lookout	232	50.06 N	91.55 W
Sioux Narrows	244	49.25 N	94.06 W
Sioux Rapids	252	42.53 N	95.09 W
Sipalay	202	9.45 N	122.24 E
Sipalay ≃	202	9.45 N	122.25 E
Sipaliwini ≃	290	2.20 N	56.48 W
Sipapo ≃	290	5.03 N	67.48 W
Siparia	285r	10.08 N	61.30 W
Sipí ≃	290	4.45 N	76.50 W
Šipicyno	160	61.17 N	46.28 E
Siping	190	43.12 N	124.20 E
Sipiwesk Lake ⊜	232	55.05 N	97.35 W
Sipocot	202	13.46 N	122.58 E
Sipsey ≃	248	33.00 N	88.10 W
Sipura, Pulau I	198	2.12 S	99.40 E
Siqueira Campos	296	23.42 S	49.50 W
Siquia ≃	280	12.10 N	84.20 W
Siquijor Island I	202	9.10 N	123.33 E
Siquirres	280	10.06 N	83.30 W
Siquisique	290	10.34 N	69.42 W
Sira ≃	160	58.17 N	6.24 E
Siracuas	292	21.03 S	61.46 W
Siracusa	170	37.04 N	15.17 E
Sirājganj	206	24.27 N	89.43 E
Sir Alexander, Mount ∧	238	53.56 N	120.23 W
Siraway	202	7.34 N	122.08 E
Sirba ≃	222	13.46 N	1.40 E
Şīr Banī Yās I	208	24.20 N	52.37 E
Sirdar	238	49.15 N	116.37 W
Sir Douglas, Mount ∧	238	50.44 N	115.20 W
Sireniki	236	64.25 N	173.57 W
Siret	172	47.57 N	26.04 E
Siretul (Siret) ≃	172	45.24 N	28.01 E
Sirevåg	160	58.30 N	5.47 E
Sirḥān, Wādī as- ∨	208	30.30 N	38.00 E
Sírina I	212	36.21 N	26.42 E
Sirino, Monte ∧	170	40.08 N	15.50 E
Sir James MacBrien, Mount ∧	236	62.07 N	127.41 W
Sir Joseph Banks Group II	228	34.32 S	136.17 E
Siro, Jabal ∧	220	14.23 N	24.23 E
Síros I	172	37.26 N	24.54 E
Sirrah, Nafūd as- •[8]	208	25.15 N	44.45 E
Sīrrī, Jazīreh-ye I	208	25.55 N	54.32 E
Sir Sandford, Mount ∧	238	51.40 N	117.52 W
Siruma	202	14.00 N	123.15 E
Sir Wilfrid Laurier, Mount ∧	238	52.47 N	119.45 W
Sis ≃	280	14.09 N	91.39 W
Sisak	170	45.29 N	16.23 E
Sisaket	200	15.07 N	104.21 E
Sisargas, Islas II	168	43.22 N	8.50 W
Sishuangdao I	196	26.42 N	120.24 E
Sisili ≃	222	10.16 N	1.15 W
Siskiyou Mountains ⋀	258	41.55 N	123.15 W
Siskiyou Pass)(	256	42.03 N	122.36 W
Sison	202	9.40 N	125.31 E
Sissach	166	47.28 N	7.49 E
Sisseton	252	45.40 N	97.03 W
Sisseton Indian Reservation ◂[4]	252	45.40 N	97.02 W
Sisson Branch Reservoir ⊜[1]	240	47.16 N	67.20 W
Sissonne	166	49.34 N	3.54 E
Sissonville	242	38.32 N	81.38 W
Sister Bay	244	45.11 N	87.07 W
Sister Lakes	268	42.05 N	86.12 W
Sisteron	166	44.12 N	5.56 E
Sisters	256	44.17 N	121.33 W
Sistersville	242	39.34 N	81.00 W
Sitabamba	292	8.02 S	77.45 W
Sites	272	39.19 N	122.20 W
Sithoniá	172	35.12 N	26.07 E
Sithoniá ≻[1]	172	40.10 N	23.47 E
Sithonia ◂[1]	172	40.10 N	23.47 E
Sitidgi Lake ⊜	236	68.32 N	132.42 W
Sítio da Abadia	296	14.48 S	46.16 W
Sitionuevo	290	10.47 N	74.43 W
Sitka	236	57.03 N	135.14 W
Sitkalidak Island I	236	57.10 N	153.14 W
Sitka National Monument ♣	236	57.05 N	135.15 W
Sitka Point ≻	236	57.00 N	135.49 W
Sitka Sound ⋓	236	57.00 N	135.30 W
Sitkinak Island I	236	56.35 N	154.12 W
Sitkinak Strait ⋓	236	56.39 N	154.06 W
Sitnica ≃	172	42.45 N	21.01 E
Sitrah ▾[4]	220	28.42 N	26.54 E
Sittang ≃	200	17.10 N	96.58 E
Sittard	164	51.00 N	5.53 E
Sittingbourne	174	51.21 N	0.44 E
Sittwe (Akyab)	200	20.09 N	92.54 E
Siuna	280	13.37 N	84.45 W
Siuslaw ≃	256	44.01 N	124.08 W
Sivas	212	39.45 N	37.02 E
Sivaslı	172	38.30 N	29.42 E
Siverek	212	37.45 N	39.19 E
Siverskij	160	59.21 N	30.05 E
Sivomaskinskij	160	66.40 N	62.35 E
Sīwah	214	29.12 N	25.31 E
Sīwah, Wāḥat ▾[4]	220	29.12 N	25.31 E
Siwalik Range ⋀	206	31.00 N	78.00 E
Sixaola ≃	280	9.35 N	82.32 W
Six-Fours-la-Plage	182	43.06 N	5.51 E
Six-Shooter Draw ∨	250	30.51 N	102.33 W
Sixth Cataract → Ash-Shallāl as-Sablūkah ∟	220	16.20 N	32.42 E
Siyāl, Jazā'ir II	220	22.47 N	36.12 E
Si Yat ≃	200	13.45 N	101.14 E
Siz'absk	160	65.05 N	53.49 E
Sizun	166	48.24 N	4.05 W
Sjælland I	160	55.30 N	11.45 E
Sjenica	172	43.16 N	20.00 E
Sjujutlijka ≃	172	42.17 N	25.55 E
Skærbæk	160	55.09 N	8.46 E
Skaftung	160	62.07 N	21.22 E
Skagafjörður C	160a	65.55 N	19.35 W
Skagaströnd	160a	65.53 N	20.17 W
Skagen	160	57.44 N	10.36 E
Skagerrak ⋓	160	57.45 N	9.00 E
Skagit □[6]	270	48.29 N	121.45 W
Skagway	236	59.28 N	135.19 W
Skaidi	160	70.25 N	24.30 E
Skála Oropoú	172	38.20 N	23.46 E
Skalbmierz	164	50.19 N	20.25 E
Skalica	164	48.51 N	17.14 E
Skalino	160	58.32 N	40.13 E
Skalka ⊜	160	66.50 N	18.46 E
Skamania	270	45.37 N	122.03 W
Skamania □[6]	270	45.58 N	121.53 W
Skamokawa	270	46.16 N	123.27 W
Skaneateles	264	42.57 N	76.26 W
Skaneateles Falls	264	42.59 N	76.27 W
Skaraborgs Län □[6]	160	58.20 N	13.30 E
Skarð	160a	64.03 N	19.50 W
Skārdu	204	35.18 N	75.37 E
Skarszewy	164	54.05 N	18.27 E
Skaryszew	164	51.19 N	21.15 E
Skarżysko Kamienna	164	51.08 N	20.53 E
Skaudvilė	160	55.24 N	22.35 E
Skawa ≃	164	50.02 N	19.26 E
Skawina	164	49.59 N	19.49 E
Skeena ≃	232	54.09 N	130.02 W
Skeena Crossing	238	55.06 N	127.49 W
Skeena Mountains ⋀	232	57.00 N	128.30 W
Skegness	174	53.10 N	0.21 E
Skei	160	61.38 N	6.30 E
Skeldon	290	5.57 N	57.09 W
Skellefteå	160	64.46 N	20.57 E
Skellefteälven ≃	160	64.42 N	21.06 E
Skelleftehamn	160	64.41 N	21.14 E
Skellig Rocks II[1]	162	51.48 N	10.31 W
Skellytown	250	35.34 N	101.11 W
Skene	160	57.29 N	12.38 E
Ski	160	59.43 N	10.50 E
Skiathos	172	39.10 N	23.29 E
Skiatook	250	36.22 N	96.01 W
Skibbereen	162	51.33 N	9.15 W
Skibotn	160	69.24 N	20.16 E
Skidegate	238	53.15 N	132.00 W
Skidegate Inlet C	238	53.14 N	132.00 W
Skidmore	250	28.15 N	97.41 W
Skien	160	59.12 N	9.36 E
Skiernewice	164	51.58 N	20.08 E
Skihist Mountain ∧	238	50.11 N	121.54 W
Skikda	214	36.50 N	6.58 E
Skilak Lake ⊜	236	60.25 N	150.25 W
Skillet Fork ≃	248	38.08 N	88.07 W
Skillingaryd	160	57.26 N	14.05 E
Skinnastaður	160a	66.07 N	16.24 W
Skipness	162	55.46 N	5.22 W
Skippers	262	36.37 N	77.38 W
Skíros	172	38.53 N	24.33 E
Skíros I	172	38.53 N	24.32 E
Skive	160	56.34 N	9.02 E
Skjálfandafljót ≃	160a	65.57 N	17.38 W
Skjálfandi C	160a	66.08 N	17.38 W
Sklad	186	71.55 N	123.33 E
Škocjanske Jame •[7]	170	45.40 N	14.00 E
Škofja Loka	170	46.10 N	14.18 E
Skoganvarre	160	69.47 N	25.06 E
Skoki	164	52.41 N	17.10 E
Skokie	268	42.02 N	87.46 W
Skópelos	172	39.07 N	23.43 E
Skópelos I	172	39.10 N	23.40 E
Skopin	158	53.51 N	39.33 E
Skopje	172	41.59 N	21.26 E
Skórcz	164	53.48 N	18.32 E
Skórpios I	172	38.41 N	20.45 E
Skövde	160	58.24 N	13.50 E
Skovorodino	186	53.59 N	123.55 E
Skowhegan	242	44.46 N	69.43 W
Skradin	170	43.49 N	15.56 E
Skrīveri	160	56.39 N	25.08 E
Skrunda	160	56.41 N	22.01 E
Skudeneshavn	160	59.09 N	5.17 E
Skull Valley	254	34.30 N	112.41 W
Skull Valley Indian Reservation ◂[4]	254	40.24 N	112.45 W
Skuna ≃	248	33.54 N	89.41 W
Skunk ≃	244	40.42 N	91.07 W
Skuodas	160	56.16 N	21.32 E
Skwentna	236	61.58 N	151.11 W
Skwentna ≃	236	62.00 N	151.08 W
Skye I	162	57.15 N	6.10 W
Skykomish	270	47.42 N	121.22 W
Skyland	246	35.29 N	82.31 W
Sky Manor	262	40.02 N	74.07 W
Skyring, Seno ⋓	288	52.35 S	72.00 W
Skyway	270	47.29 N	122.14 W
Slackwood	262	40.15 N	74.44 W
Slagelse	160	55.24 N	11.22 E
Slagnäs	160	65.34 N	18.05 E
Slamet, Gunung ∧	226	7.14 S	109.14 E
Slancy	160	59.06 N	28.04 E
Slaney ≃	162	52.21 N	6.30 W
Slănic	172	45.15 N	25.57 E
Slano	170	42.47 N	17.54 E
Slanské pohorie ⋀	164	48.50 N	21.30 E
Slaný	164	50.11 N	14.04 E
Slapanice	164	49.10 N	16.44 E
Śląsk □[9]	164	51.00 N	16.45 E
Slatedale	262	40.45 N	75.40 W
Slater, Iowa, U.S.	244	41.53 N	93.41 W
Slater, Mo., U.S.	248	39.13 N	93.04 W
Slatersville	261	42.00 N	71.35 W
Slatina	172	44.26 N	24.22 E
Slatington	262	40.45 N	75.37 W
Slaton	250	33.26 N	101.39 W
Slautnoje	186	63.00 N	167.59 E
Slav'ansk	158	48.52 N	37.37 E
Slav'ansk-na-Kubani	158	45.15 N	38.08 E
Slave ≃	232	61.18 N	113.39 W
Slave Coast •[2]	222	6.25 N	3.00 E
Slave Lake	238	55.17 N	114.46 W
Slavgorod	186	53.00 N	78.40 E
Slavkov u Brna	164	49.09 N	16.52 E
Slavonia → Slavonija ◂[1]	170	45.00 N	18.00 E
Slavonice	164	49.00 N	15.21 E
Slavonija ◂[1]	170	45.00 N	18.00 E
Slavonska Požega	170	45.20 N	17.41 E
Slavonski Brod	172	45.10 N	18.01 E
Slavsk [Heinrichswalde]	164	55.03 N	21.41 E
Sława (Schlesiersee)	164	51.53 N	16.04 E
Sławno (Schlawe)	164	54.22 N	16.40 E
Slayton	252	43.59 N	95.45 W
Sleaford	174	53.00 N	0.24 W
Slea Head ≻	162	52.06 N	10.27 W
Sledge	248	34.26 N	90.13 W
Sledge Island I	236	64.29 N	166.13 W
Sleepy Eye	252	44.18 N	94.43 W
Sleepy Hollow, Calif., U.S.	272	38.00 N	122.34 W
Sleepy Hollow, Ill., U.S.	268	42.06 N	88.24 W
Sleetmute	236	61.42 N	157.11 W
Sleidinge	176	51.08 N	3.41 E
Slepino	160	59.11 N	29.02 E
Ślesin	164	52.23 N	18.19 E
Slick Rock	254	38.02 N	108.54 W
Slickville	266	40.28 N	79.32 W
Slidell	248	30.17 N	89.47 W
Slide Mountain ∧	242	42.00 N	74.23 W
Sliderock Mountain ∧	256	46.35 N	113.33 W
Sliedrecht	178	51.49 N	4.45 E
Sligo, Eire	162	54.17 N	8.28 W
Sligo, Pa., U.S.	242	41.07 N	79.29 W
Sligo □[6]	162	54.10 N	8.40 W
Sligo Bay C	162	54.20 N	8.40 W
Slikkerveer	178	51.53 N	4.37 E
Slinger	244	43.20 N	88.17 W
Slingerlands	261	42.38 N	73.52 W
Slippery Rock	266	41.04 N	80.03 W
Sliven	172	42.40 N	26.19 E
Slivnica	172	42.51 N	23.02 E
Sloan, Iowa, U.S.	252	42.14 N	96.14 W
Sloan, Nev., U.S.	258	35.57 N	115.13 W
Sloan, N.Y., U.S.	264	42.54 N	78.47 W
Slobodskoj	160	58.42 N	50.12 E
Slobozia	172	44.34 N	27.23 E
Slocan	238	49.46 N	117.28 W
Slocan Lake ⊜	238	49.56 N	117.22 W
Slocomb	248	31.06 N	85.36 W
Slocum	261	41.32 N	71.31 W
Słomniki	164	50.15 N	20.06 E
Slosh Indian Reserve ◂[4]	238	50.44 N	122.13 W
Sloten ◂[8]	178	52.21 N	4.48 E
Slough	174	51.31 N	0.36 W
Sloughhouse	272	38.30 N	121.12 W
Slovakia → Slovensko □[9]	164	48.50 N	20.00 E
Slovan	266	40.22 N	80.23 W
Slovenia → Slovenija □[3]	170	46.15 N	15.10 E
Slovenija □[3]	170	46.15 N	15.10 E
Slovenjgradec	170	46.31 N	15.05 E
Slovenska Bistrica	170	46.23 N	15.34 E
Slovenské rudohorie ⋀	164	48.45 N	20.00 E
Slovensko □[9]	164	48.50 N	20.00 E
Slovinka	160	58.02 N	43.07 E
Słubice	164	52.50 N	14.35 E
Sluck	158	53.01 N	27.33 E
Sl'ud'anka	186	51.38 N	103.42 E
Slunj	170	45.07 N	15.35 E
Słupca	164	52.19 N	17.52 E
Słupia ≃	164	54.35 N	16.50 E
Słupsk (Stolp)	164	54.28 N	17.01 E
Slyne Head ≻	162	53.24 N	10.13 W
Smackover	248	33.22 N	92.44 W
Smartville	272	39.12 N	121.18 W
Smeaton Bay C	238	55.20 N	130.50 W
Smederevo	172	44.40 N	20.56 E
Smederevska Palanka	172	44.22 N	20.58 E
Smela	158	49.14 N	31.53 E
Šmel'ovka	160	54.47 N	49.11 E
Smethport	266	41.49 N	78.27 W
Smethwick (Warley)	174	52.30 N	1.58 W
Smicksburg	266	40.52 N	79.10 W
Smidovič	186	48.36 N	133.49 E
Šmidta, Mys ≻	236	68.56 N	179.30 W
Šmidta, Ostrov I	186	81.08 N	90.48 E
Śmigiel	164	52.01 N	16.32 E
Smilde	178	52.56 N	5.27 E
Smiley	250	29.16 N	97.38 W
Smiltene	160	57.26 N	25.56 E
Smirnovskij	186	54.31 N	69.25 E
Smith	238	55.10 N	114.02 W
Smith ≃, Calif., U.S.	258	41.56 N	124.12 W
Smith ≃, Mont., U.S.	256	47.25 N	111.29 W
Smith ≃, Oreg., U.S.	256	43.43 N	124.05 W
Smith, Cape ≻	244	45.48 N	81.35 W
Smith Arm C	236	66.15 N	124.00 W
Smith Bay C	236	70.51 N	154.25 W
Smith Center	252	39.47 N	98.47 W
Smithers, B.C., Can.	238	54.47 N	127.10 W
Smithers, W. Va., U.S.	242	38.11 N	81.18 W
Smithfield, Ont., Can.	264	44.04 N	77.41 W
Smithfield, N.C., U.S.	246	35.30 N	78.21 W
Smithfield, Ohio, U.S.	266	40.16 N	80.47 W
Smithfield, Pa., U.S.	266	40.29 N	78.01 W
Smithfield, Utah, U.S.	254	41.50 N	111.50 W
Smithfield, Va., U.S.	262	36.59 N	76.38 W
Smithflat	272	38.44 N	120.45 W
Smith Island I	246	33.52 N	77.59 W
Smithland	248	37.09 N	88.24 W
Smithmill	266	40.46 N	78.25 W
Smith Mountain Lake ⊜[1]	246	37.10 N	79.40 W
Smith Peak ∧	256	48.50 N	116.39 W
Smith Point ≻	240	45.51 N	63.25 W
Smithport	266	40.50 N	78.52 W
Smith River	258	41.56 N	124.09 W
Smiths	248	32.32 N	85.06 W
Smiths Creek	266	42.55 N	82.36 W
Smiths Falls	264	44.54 N	76.01 W
Smiths Grove	248	37.03 N	86.12 W
Smith Sound ⋓	238	51.18 N	127.48 W
Smithton, Austl.	228	40.51 S	145.07 E
Smithton, Mo., U.S.	248	38.41 N	93.05 W
Smithton, Pa., U.S.	266	40.09 N	79.44 W
Smithtown	261	40.52 N	73.13 W
Smithville, Ont., Can.	264	43.06 N	79.33 W
Smithville, Ga., U.S.	246	31.54 N	84.15 W
Smithville, Miss., U.S.	248	33.59 N	88.23 W
Smithville, Mo., U.S.	248	39.23 N	94.35 W
Smithville, Ohio, U.S.	266	40.52 N	81.51 W
Smithville, Tenn., U.S.	248	35.58 N	85.49 W
Smithville, Tex., U.S.	250	30.00 N	97.09 W
Smoke Creek Desert ◂[2]	258	40.30 N	119.40 W
Smokeless	266	40.24 N	76.02 W
Smokerun	266	40.48 N	78.26 W
Smoketown	262	40.02 N	76.12 W
Smokey Dome ∧	256	43.29 N	114.56 W
Smoky ≃	238	56.10 N	117.21 W
Smoky, Cape ≻	240	46.38 N	60.21 W
Smoky Cape ≻	228	30.56 S	153.05 E
Smoky Hill ≃	252	39.03 N	96.48 W
Smoky Hills ⋀[2]	252	39.15 N	99.00 W
Smoky Lake	238	54.07 N	112.28 W
Smolensk	160	54.47 N	32.03 E
Smolenskaja Vozvyšennost' ⋀[1]	186	54.45 N	33.00 E
Smólikas ∧	172	40.06 N	20.52 E
Smoljan	172	41.35 N	24.41 E
Smoot	254	42.37 N	110.55 W
Smotrič ≃	172	48.34 N	26.38 E
Smyrna → İzmir, Tür.	212	38.25 N	27.09 E
Smyrna, Del., U.S.	262	39.18 N	75.36 W
Smyrna, Ga., U.S.	246	33.53 N	84.31 W
Smyrna, N.Y., U.S.	264	42.41 N	75.34 W
Smyrna, Tenn., U.S.	248	35.59 N	86.31 W
Smyrna Mills	242	46.08 N	68.10 W
Smythe, Mount ∧	232	57.54 N	124.53 W
Snæfell ∧, Ísland	160a	64.48 N	15.32 W
Snaefell ∧, I. of Man	162	54.16 N	4.27 W
Snæfellsjökull ◸	160a	64.50 N	23.49 W
Snag	236	62.24 N	140.22 W
Snake ≃, Yukon, Can.	236	65.58 N	134.10 W
Snake ≃, U.S.	256	46.12 N	119.02 W
Snake ≃, Minn., U.S.	244	45.49 N	92.46 W
Snake ≃, Minn., U.S.	252	48.26 N	97.07 W
Snake ≃, Nebr., U.S.	252	42.47 N	100.48 W
Snake Indian ≃	238	53.11 N	118.00 W
Snake Range ⋀	258	39.00 N	114.15 W
Snake River Plain ≚	256	42.45 N	114.30 W
Snap Point ≻	282	23.46 N	77.35 W
Sneads	246	30.42 N	84.56 W
Sneedville	246	36.32 N	83.13 W
Sneek	178	53.02 N	5.40 E
Snee-oosh-Beach	270	48.24 N	122.33 W
Sneeuberg ⋀	224	31.46 S	24.20 E
Snelling, Calif., U.S.	258		
	272	37.31 N	120.26 W
Śniardwy, Jezioro ⊜	164	53.46 N	21.44 E
Snina	164	48.59 N	22.07 E
Snipe Lake ⊜	238	55.07 N	116.46 W
Snohomish	270	47.55 N	122.06 W
Snohomish □[6]	270	48.02 N	121.41 W
Snoqualmie	270	47.32 N	121.50 W
Snoqualmie Falls	270	47.32 N	121.49 W
Snover	244	43.28 N	82.58 W
Snowbird Lake ⊜	232	60.41 N	103.00 W
Snowdoun	248	32.15 N	86.18 W
Snowdrift	232	62.23 N	110.47 W
Snowflake	254	34.30 N	110.05 W
Snow Hill, Md., U.S.	262	38.11 N	75.24 W
Snow Hill, N.C., U.S.	246	35.27 N	77.40 W
Snow Lake	232	54.53 N	100.02 W
Snowmass Mountain ∧	254	39.07 N	107.04 W
Snow Mountain ∧	258	39.23 N	122.46 W
Snow Peak ∧	256	48.35 N	118.29 W
Snow Shoe	266	41.02 N	77.57 W
Snowshoe Peak ∧	256	48.13 N	115.41 W
Snowy ≃	228	37.48 S	148.32 E
Snowy Mountain ∧	242	43.42 N	74.23 W
Snowy Mountains ⋀	228	36.30 S	148.20 E
Snowyside Peak ∧	256	43.57 N	114.58 W
Snyder, Okla., U.S.	250	34.40 N	98.57 W
Snyder, Tex., U.S.	250	32.44 N	100.55 W
Snyder □[6]	262	40.47 N	77.03 W
So ≃	222	6.28 N	2.25 E
Soacha	290	4.35 N	74.13 W
Soaker, Mount ∧	230	45.23 S	167.15 E
Soalala	218	16.06 S	45.20 E
Soa Pan ≚	224	21.00 S	26.00 E
Soap Lake	256	47.23 N	119.29 W
Soatá	290	6.20 N	72.41 W
Soay I	162	57.08 N	6.14 W
Sob ≃	172	48.42 N	29.17 E
Sobaco, Sierra del ⋀	250	26.15 N	103.00 W
Sobaek-sanmaek ⋀	194	36.00 N	128.00 E
Sobat ≃	220	9.22 N	31.33 E
Sobernheim	164	49.47 N	7.38 E
Soběslav	164	49.15 N	14.44 E
Sobinka	158	55.59 N	40.01 E
Soboloch-Majan ≃	186	67.15 N	123.10 E
Sobótka (Zopten am Berge)	164	50.55 N	16.45 E
Sobradinho	294	29.24 S	53.03 W
Sobrado	168	41.02 N	8.16 W
Sobral	286	3.42 S	40.21 W
Sobrance	164	48.45 N	22.11 E
Sobrarbe ◂[1]	168	42.22 N	0.10 E
Socaire	294	23.36 S	67.51 W
Sochaczew	164	52.14 N	20.14 E
Sochaux	180	47.31 N	6.50 E
Soch'e → Suoche	206	38.25 N	77.16 E
Sochi → Soči	158	43.35 N	39.45 E
Soči	158	43.35 N	39.45 E
Social Circle	246	33.39 N	83.43 W
Société, Îles de la II	148	17.00 S	150.00 W
Society Hill	246	34.31 N	79.51 W
Society Islands → Société, Îles de la II	148	17.00 S	150.00 W
Soco ≃	282	18.28 N	69.14 W
Socoltenango	278	16.13 N	92.15 W
Socompa, Paso)(	294	24.27 S	68.18 W
Soconusco, Sierra de (Sierra Madre) ⋀	280	15.30 N	92.35 W
Socopo, Cerro ∧	290	10.28 N	70.48 W
Socorro, Col.	290	6.29 N	73.16 W
Socorro, Pil.	202	9.37 N	125.58 E
Socorro, N. Mex., U.S.	254	34.04 N	106.54 W
Socorro, Tex., U.S.	254	31.39 N	106.18 W
Socorro, Isla I	278	18.45 N	110.58 W
Sócota	292	6.17 S	78.44 W
Socotra → Suquṭrā I	204	12.30 N	54.00 E
Socuéllamos	168	39.17 N	2.48 W
Soda Creek	238	52.21 N	122.18 W
Soda Lake ⊜	258	35.08 N	116.04 W
Sodankylä	160	67.29 N	26.32 E
Soda Springs	256	42.39 N	111.36 W
Soddy	248	35.17 N	85.10 W
Söderhamn	160	61.18 N	17.03 E
Söderköping	160	58.29 N	16.18 E
Södermanlands Län □[6]	160	59.15 N	16.40 E
Södertälje	160	59.12 N	17.37 E
Sodo	214	6.52 N	37.47 E
Sodražica	170	45.46 N	14.49 E
Sodus	264	43.14 N	77.04 W
Sodus Point	264	43.16 N	76.59 W
Soe	226	9.52 S	124.17 E
Soest, B.R.D.	178	51.34 N	8.07 E
Soest, Ned.	178	52.09 N	5.18 E
Soestdijk	178	52.11 N	5.18 E
Sofádhes	172	39.20 N	22.06 E
Sofia → Sofija	172	42.41 N	23.19 E
Sofia ≃	225b	15.27 S	47.23 E
Sofija (Sofia)	172	42.41 N	23.19 E
Sofjanga	160	65.52 N	31.15 E
Sofronovo	160	59.48 N	36.54 E
Sogamoso	290	5.43 N	72.56 W
Sogamoso ≃	290	7.13 N	73.56 W
Soğanlı Dağları ⋀	212	40.30 N	40.30 E
Soğanlı Geçidi)(	212	40.33 N	40.16 E
Søgne	160	58.05 N	7.49 E
Sogn og Fjordane □[6]	160	61.30 N	6.50 E
Sogod, Pil.	202	10.23 N	124.59 E
Sogod, Pil.	202	10.45 N	124.00 E
Sogod Bay C	202	10.15 N	125.03 E
Söğütalan	172	40.03 N	28.34 E
Söğüt Gölü ⊜	212	37.03 N	29.53 E
Soignies (Zinnik)	176	50.35 N	4.04 E
Sointula	238	50.38 N	127.01 W
Soissons	176	49.22 N	3.20 E
Sojana	160	65.48 N	43.20 E
Sojda	160	61.11 N	37.40 E
Šojna	160	67.52 N	44.08 E
Sŏjosŏn-man C	194	39.20 N	124.50 E
Sojoton Point ≻	202	10.00 N	122.28 E
Sok ≃	160	53.24 N	50.08 E
Sŏkch'o	194	38.12 N	128.36 E
Söke	212	37.45 N	27.24 E
Sokhós	172	40.49 N	23.21 E
Sokodé	222	8.59 N	1.08 E
Soko Islands II	196	22.10 N	113.54 E
Sokol, S.S.S.R.	160	59.28 N	40.10 E
Sokol, S.S.S.R.	186	72.24 N	126.48 E
Sokółka	164	53.25 N	23.31 E
Sokolov	164	50.09 N	12.40 E
Sokolovo	160	65.21 N	56.57 E
Sokołów Małopolski	164	50.14 N	22.07 E
Sokołów Podlaski	164	52.25 N	22.15 E
Sokoto	222	13.04 N	5.16 E
Sokoto ≃	222	11.20 N	4.10 E
Sol'	164	48.56 N	21.36 E
Sol, Costa del •[2]	168	36.30 N	4.30 W
Sol, Rio do ≃	292	6.45 S	67.05 W
Soła ≃	164	50.04 N	19.13 E
Solacolu	172	44.23 N	26.34 E
Solana	246	26.57 N	82.01 W
Solana Beach	274	32.59 N	117.16 W
Solander Island I	230	46.34 S	166.54 E
Solano	202	16.31 N	121.11 E
Solano □[6]	272	38.15 N	121.52 W
Solbad Hall in Tirol	164	47.17 N	11.31 E
Solca, Arg.	294	30.47 S	66.28 W
Solca, Rom.	172	47.42 N	25.50 E
Soldados, Cerro ∧	290	2.54 S	79.10 W
Sol de Julio	294	29.33 S	63.27 W
Soldier Pond	240	47.09 N	68.35 W
Soldiers Grove	244	43.24 N	90.47 W
Soldotna	236	60.29 N	151.04 W
Solebury	262	40.23 N	75.02 W
Solec Kujawski	164	53.06 N	18.14 E
Soledad, Col.	290	10.55 N	74.46 W
Soledad, Calif., U.S.	272	36.26 N	121.19 W
Soledad, Ven.	290	8.10 N	63.34 W
Soledad, Cerro ∧	250	26.27 N	103.18 W
Soledad Díez Gutiérrez	278	22.12 N	100.57 W
Soledade	294	28.50 S	52.30 W
Solen	252	46.23 N	100.48 W
Solentiname, Islas II	280	11.10 N	85.00 W
Solenzara	170	41.51 N	9.23 E
Solesmes	176	50.11 N	3.30 E
Soleure → Solothurn	180	47.13 N	7.32 E
Solginskij	160	61.05 N	41.19 E
Solihull	174	52.25 N	1.45 W
Solikamsk	160	59.39 N	56.47 E
Sol'-Ileck	158	51.10 N	54.59 E
Soliman	170	36.42 N	10.30 E
Solingen	178	51.10 N	7.05 E
Solís	294	34.36 S	55.29 W
Soliseño	250	26.01 N	97.48 W
Sollefteå	160	63.10 N	17.16 E
Sollentuna	160	59.28 N	17.54 E
Sóller	168	39.46 N	2.42 E
Solnečnogorsk	160	56.11 N	36.59 E
Solofra	184	40.50 N	14.51 E
Šologoncy	186	66.13 N	114.14 E
Solok	200	0.48 S	100.39 E
Sololá	280	14.46 N	91.11 W
Sololá □[5]	280	14.40 N	91.15 W
Solomennoje	160	61.51 N	34.19 E
Solomon, Ariz., U.S.	254	32.49 N	109.38 W
Solomon, Kans., U.S.	252	38.55 N	97.22 W
Solomon ≃	252	38.54 N	97.22 W
Solomon Islands I	148	8.00 S	159.00 E
Solomon Sea ▾[2]	226	8.00 S	155.00 E
Solon, Iowa, U.S.	244	41.48 N	91.30 W
Solon, Maine, U.S.	242	44.57 N	69.52 W
Solon, Ohio, U.S.	266	41.22 N	81.55 W
Solon Springs	244	46.22 N	91.48 W
Solopaca	170	41.11 N	14.33 E
Solothurn	180	47.13 N	7.32 E
Solothurn □[3]	180	47.25 N	7.35 E
Soloveckije Ostrova II	160	65.05 N	35.40 E
Solovjevsk	186	49.55 N	115.42 E
Sol'oy	160	58.08 N	30.20 E
Solsona	168	41.59 N	1.31 E
Solt	164	46.48 N	19.00 E
Šolta, Otok I	170	43.23 N	16.15 E
Soltau	178	52.59 N	9.49 E
Solvang	258	34.36 N	120.08 W
Solvay	264	43.04 N	76.12 W
Sölvesborg	160	56.03 N	14.33 E
Sol'vyčegodsk	160	61.21 N	46.52 E
Solway Firth C[1]	162	54.50 N	3.35 W
Solwezi	218	12.11 S	26.25 E
Solza	160	64.33 N	39.29 E
Sōma, Nihon	192	37.48 N	140.57 E
Soma, Tür.	172	39.10 N	27.36 E
Somain	176	50.22 N	3.17 E
Somalia □[1]	214	10.00 N	49.00 E
Somali Basin ⊹[1]	148	5.00 N	53.00 E
Somali Republic → Somalia □[1]	214	10.00 N	49.00 E
Sombor	172	45.46 N	19.07 E
Sombra	266	42.43 N	82.29 W
Sombrerete	278	23.38 N	103.39 W
Sombreretillo	250	26.19 N	99.58 W
Sombrero I	282	18.35 N	63.25 W
Sombrero Channel ⋓	200	7.40 N	93.40 E
Sombrio	294	29.07 S	49.40 W
Sombrio, Lagoa do C	294	29.12 S	49.42 W
Şomcuta-Mare	172	47.31 N	23.29 E
Somenos	270	48.49 N	123.44 W
Somerdale, N.J., U.S.	262	39.51 N	75.01 W
Somerdale, Ohio, U.S.	266	40.34 N	81.22 W
Somers, Conn., U.S.	261	41.59 N	72.27 W
Somers, Mont., U.S.	256	48.05 N	114.13 W
Somers, Wis., U.S.	268	42.38 N	87.55 W
Somerset, Man., Can.	252	49.24 N	98.39 W
Somerset, Colo., U.S.	254	38.56 N	107.16 W
Somerset, Ky., U.S.	246	37.05 N	84.36 W
Somerset, Mass., U.S.	261	41.45 N	71.09 W
Somerset, N.J., U.S.	262	40.29 N	74.29 W
Somerset, Ohio, U.S.	242	39.48 N	82.18 W
Somerset, Pa., U.S.	242	40.01 N	79.05 W
Somerset, Tex., U.S.	250	29.13 N	98.40 W
Somerset, Wis., U.S.	244	45.08 N	92.40 W
Somerset □[6], Eng., U.K.	174	51.08 N	3.00 W
Somerset □[6], Md., U.S.	262	38.12 N	75.41 W
Somerset □[6], N.J., U.S.	262	40.34 N	74.37 W
Somerset □[6], Pa., U.S.	266	40.09 N	79.00 W
Somerset Center	268	42.03 N	84.25 W
Somerset East	224	32.42 S	25.35 E
Somerset Island I	232	73.15 N	93.30 W
Somerset West	224	34.08 S	18.50 E
Somers Point	262	39.20 N	74.36 W
Somersworth	242	43.16 N	70.52 W

Symbols in the index entries are identified on page 360.

Name	Page	Lat°′	Long°′
Somerton	254	32.36 N	114.43 W
Somerville, Mass., U.S.	261	42.23 N	71.06 W
Somerville, N.J., U.S.	262	40.34 N	74.37 W
Somerville, Tenn., U.S.	248	35.15 N	89.21 W
Somerville, Tex., U.S.	250	30.21 N	96.32 W
Someşul (Szamos) ≃	172	48.07 N	22.22 E
Somis	274	34.16 N	119.00 W
Sŏmjin-gang ≃	194	34.58 N	127.46 E
Somma Lombardo	182	45.41 N	8.42 E
Sommariva del Bosco	182	44.46 N	7.47 E
Somma Vesuviana	184	40.52 N	14.26 E
Somme □[5]	176	49.55 N	2.30 E
Somme ≃	166	50.11 N	1.39 E
Sommen ⊜	160	58.01 N	15.15 E
Sömmerda	164	51.10 N	11.07 E
Somo ≃	244	45.29 N	89.48 W
Somogy □[6]	164	46.25 N	17.35 E
Somonauk	268	41.38 N	88.41 W
Somosierra, Puerto de)(	168	41.09 N	3.35 W
Somotillo	280	13.01 N	86.55 W
Somoto	280	13.28 N	86.37 W
Sompolno	164	52.24 N	18.31 E
Somport, Puerto de)(	168	42.48 N	0.31 W
Sompuis	166	48.41 N	4.23 E
Soná	280	8.00 N	81.10 W
Sonaguera	280	15.38 N	86.20 W
Sŏnch'ŏn	194	39.48 N	124.55 E
Soncino	182	45.24 N	9.52 E
Sondags ≃	224	33.44 S	25.51 E
Sønderborg	164	54.55 N	9.47 E
Sondershausen	164	51.22 N	10.52 E
Sondrio	180	46.10 N	9.52 E
Sondrio □[4]	180	46.10 N	10.03 E
Sonduga	160	60.08 N	41.55 E
Sonestown	242	41.21 N	76.33 W
Song-bay-hap, Cua C	200	8.46 N	104.52 E
Song-cau	200	13.27 N	109.13 E
Sŏng-ch'ŏn-gang ≃	194	39.48 N	127.35 E
Songe	160	58.41 N	9.00 E
Songea	218	10.41 S	35.39 E
Songjiang	196	31.01 N	121.14 E
Songjŏng	194	35.10 N	126.46 E
Songkhla	200	7.13 N	100.34 E
Songmenshan I	196	28.18 N	121.37 E
Songnim	194	38.44 N	125.38 E
Songqigang C	196	26.25 N	119.43 E
Šonguj	160	68.47 N	33.00 E
Songyinxi ≃	196	28.18 N	119.44 E
Songziguan)(	196	31.17 N	115.31 E
Songzong	190	29.45 N	96.10 E
Sonīpat	206	28.59 N	77.01 E
Sonkovo	160	57.47 N	37.09 E
Son-la	200	21.13 N	103.54 E
Sonmiāni Bay C	206	25.15 N	66.30 E
Sonneberg	164	50.22 N	11.10 E
Sono, Rio do ≃	296	17.02 S	45.32 W
Sonoita	278	31.51 N	112.50 W
Sonoma	272	38.17 N	122.28 W
Sonoma □[6]	272	38.26 N	122.35 W
Sonoma Peak ∧	258	40.52 N	117.36 W
Sonora, Méx.	258	32.27 N	115.10 W
Sonora, Ariz., U.S.	254	33.10 N	111.00 W
Sonora, Calif., U.S.	272	37.59 N	120.23 W
Sonora, Tex., U.S.	250	30.34 N	100.39 W
Sonora □[3]	278	29.20 N	110.40 W
Sonora ≃	278	28.50 N	111.33 W
Sonora Desert ◆[2]	254	33.00 N	114.00 W
Sonostrov	160	66.09 N	34.10 E
Sonoyta ≃	254	31.15 N	113.20 W
Sonqor	208	34.47 N	47.36 E
Sonseca	168	39.42 N	3.57 W
Sonsón	290	5.42 N	75.18 W
Sonsonate	280	13.43 N	89.44 W
Sonsorol Islands II	198	5.20 N	132.13 E
Sontag	248	31.39 N	90.12 W
Son-tay	200	21.08 N	105.30 E
Sonthofen	180	47.31 N	10.17 E
Sontra	178	51.04 N	9.56 E
Sonyea	264	42.41 N	77.50 W
Soochow → Suzhou	196	31.18 N	120.37 E
Sooke	238	48.23 N	123.43 W
Sopachuy	292	19.29 S	64.31 W
Sopchoppy	246	30.04 N	84.29 W
Soperton	246	32.23 N	82.35 W
Sopetrán	290	6.30 N	75.46 W
Sophia	246	37.43 N	81.15 W
Sopki	160	57.06 N	30.55 E
Sopockin	164	53.50 N	23.39 E
Sopot (Zoppot)	164	54.28 N	18.34 E
Sopris	252	37.08 N	104.34 W
Sopron	164	47.41 N	16.36 E
Soquel	272	36.59 N	121.57 W
Sor ≃	168	39.00 N	8.17 W
Sora	184	41.43 N	13.37 E
Soras	292	14.10 S	73.40 W
Sorata	292	15.47 S	68.40 W
Sorau → Żary	164	51.38 N	15.09 E
Soraya	292	14.09 S	73.17 W
Sorbas	168	37.07 N	2.07 W
Sordo ≃	278	16.30 N	97.31 W
Sore	166	44.20 N	0.35 W
Sorel	260	46.03 N	73.07 W
Sorell, Cape ≻	228	41.07 S	146.32 E
Soresina	170	45.17 N	9.51 E
Sørfjorden C[2]	160	60.24 N	6.40 E
Sørfold	160	67.28 N	15.22 E
Sorgono	170	40.01 N	9.06 E
Sorgues	182	44.00 N	4.52 E
Soria	168	41.46 N	2.28 W
Soriano	294	33.24 S	58.19 W
Soriano nel Cimino	184	42.25 N	12.14 E
Sørli	160	64.15 N	13.45 E
Soro, Monte ∧	170	37.56 N	14.42 E
Sorocaba	296	23.29 S	47.27 W
Sorocaba ≃	296	22.59 S	47.48 W
Soročinsk	158	52.26 N	53.10 E
Soroco	284m	18.22 N	65.38 W
Sorol I[1]	198	8.08 N	140.23 E
Sorong	198	0.53 S	131.15 E
Soroti	214	1.43 N	33.37 E
Sørøya I	160	70.36 N	22.46 E
Sorraia ≃	168	38.56 N	8.53 W
Sorrento, It.	184	40.37 N	14.22 E
Sorrento, La., U.S.	248	30.11 N	90.51 W
Sorsatunturi ∧	160	67.24 N	29.38 E
Sorsele	160	65.30 N	17.30 E
Sorsogon	202	12.58 N	124.00 E
Sorsogon □[4]	202	12.50 N	123.55 E
Sorsogon Bay C	202	12.55 N	123.55 E
Sort	168	42.24 N	1.08 E
Sortavala	160	61.42 N	30.41 E
Sortland	160	68.40 N	15.20 E
Sør-Trøndelag □[6]	160	63.00 N	10.40 E
Sŏsan	194	36.47 N	126.26 E
Sos del Rey Católico	168	42.30 N	1.13 W
Šoška	160	62.42 N	50.40 E
Sosneado, Cerro ∧	294	34.45 S	69.59 W
Sosnogorsk	160	63.37 N	53.51 E
Sosnovec	160	64.26 N	34.27 E
Sosnovka, S.S.S.R.	160	66.30 N	40.32 E
Sosnovka, S.S.S.R.	160	56.17 N	51.17 E
Sosnovo	160	60.33 N	30.15 E
Sosnovoborsk	160	53.18 N	46.16 E
Sosnovo-Oz'orskoje	186	52.31 N	111.30 E
Sosnovskoje	160	55.48 N	43.10 E
Sosnowiec	164	50.18 N	19.08 E
Soso	248	31.45 N	89.16 W
Sospel	166	43.53 N	7.27 E
Sossusvlei ⊜	224	24.40 S	15.23 E
Šoštanj	170	46.23 N	15.03 E
Šostka	158	51.52 N	33.30 E
Sos'va	158	63.40 N	61.55 E
Sota ≃	222	11.52 N	3.24 E
Sotério ≃	292	11.36 S	65.10 W
Sotilija ≃	292	11.41 S	71.48 W
Sotkamo	160	64.08 N	28.25 E
Soto la Marina	278	23.46 N	98.13 W
Sotomayor	292	19.18 S	65.03 W
Sotonera, Embalse de la ⊜[1]	168	42.05 N	0.48 W
Sotteville	176	49.25 N	1.06 E
Soudan	244	47.49 N	92.10 W
Soudersburg	262	40.01 N	76.09 W
Souderton	262	40.19 N	75.19 W
Soufflot, Lac ⊜	244	47.24 N	78.31 W
Soufrière	285f	13.52 N	61.04 W
Soufrière ∧, Guad.	282	16.03 N	61.40 W
Soufrière ∧, St. Vin.	282	13.21 N	61.11 W
Souhegan ≃	242	42.51 N	71.29 W
Souillac	166	44.54 N	1.29 E
Souilly	166	49.01 N	5.17 E
Souk Ahras	170	36.23 N	8.00 E
Souk-el-Arba-des-Beni-Hassan	168	35.16 N	5.20 W
Souk el Khemis	170	36.36 N	8.59 E
Souk-Khemis-du-Sahel	168	35.17 N	6.05 W
Sŏul (Seoul)	194	37.33 N	126.58 E
Sŏul □[8]	194	37.34 N	127.00 E
Soulac-sur-Mer	166	45.31 N	1.07 W
Soulanges □[6]	260	45.20 N	74.15 W
Soummam, Oued ≃	168	36.45 N	5.04 E
Sound Beach	261	40.58 N	72.58 W
Soúnion, Ákra ≻	172	37.39 N	24.02 E
Sources, Mount aux ∧	224	28.46 S	28.52 E
Soure	168	40.03 N	8.38 W
Sour el Ghozlane	168	36.10 N	3.45 E
Souris	252	49.38 N	100.15 W
Souris ≃	232	49.39 N	99.34 W
Souris East	240	46.21 N	62.15 W
Souris Plain ≚	252	48.15 N	100.15 W
Sourlake	248	30.09 N	94.25 W
Sourland Mountain ∧[2]	242	40.29 N	74.43 W
Sourou ≃	222	12.45 N	3.25 W
Sousa	286	6.45 S	38.14 W
Sousânia	296	16.11 S	49.05 W
Sousel	168	38.57 N	7.40 W
Sousse	170	35.49 N	10.38 E
Sousse □[8]	170	35.35 N	10.30 E
Sout ≃	224	31.35 S	18.24 E
South ≃, Iowa, U.S.	248	41.29 N	93.20 W
South ≃, N.C., U.S.	246	34.20 N	78.03 W
South ≃, Va., U.S.	242	38.18 N	78.49 W
South Acton	261	42.28 N	71.27 W
South Africa □[1]	218	30.00 S	26.00 E
South Amboy	262	40.29 N	74.17 W
South America •[1]	148	15.00 S	60.00 W
South Amherst, Mass., U.S.	261	42.21 N	72.30 W
South Amherst, Ohio, U.S.	266	41.22 N	82.14 W
Southampton, N.S., Can.	240	45.35 N	64.15 W
Southampton, Ont., Can.	264	44.29 N	81.23 W
Southampton, Eng., U.K.	174	50.55 N	1.25 W
Southampton, Mass., U.S.	261	42.14 N	72.44 W
Southampton, N.Y., U.S.	261	40.53 N	72.24 W
Southampton □[6]	262	36.42 N	77.05 W
Southampton, Cape ≻	232	62.09 N	83.40 W
Southampton Island I	232	64.20 N	84.40 W
South Andaman I	200	11.50 N	92.45 E
South Anna ≃	246	37.48 N	77.25 W
Southard	262	40.08 N	74.14 W
South Ashburnham	261	42.37 N	71.57 W
South Aulatsivik Island I	232	56.45 N	61.30 W
South Australia □[3]	228	30.00 S	135.00 E
South Australian Basin ⊹[1]	148	38.00 S	125.00 E
South Baldy ∧	254	33.59 N	107.11 W
Southbank	238	54.02 N	125.46 W
South Barre	261	42.23 N	72.06 W
South Bay	246	26.40 N	80.43 W
South Bay C, N.W. Ter., Can.	232	63.58 N	83.30 W
South Bay C, Ont., Can.	244	45.38 N	81.50 W
South Baymouth	244	45.33 N	82.01 W
South Bellingham	261	42.03 N	71.28 W
South Belmar	262	40.10 N	74.02 W
South Beloit	268	42.29 N	89.02 W
South Bend, Ind., U.S.	268	41.41 N	86.15 W
South Bend, Wash., U.S.	270	46.40 N	123.48 W
South Benfleet	174	51.33 N	0.34 E
South Bentinck Arm C	238	52.15 N	126.15 W
South Bethlehem	266	41.00 N	79.20 W
Southboro	261	42.18 N	71.31 W
Southborough	174	51.10 N	0.15 E
South Boston	246	36.42 N	78.54 W
South Branch	240	47.55 N	59.02 W
Southbridge	261	42.05 N	72.02 W
South Britain	261	41.28 N	73.15 W
South Brookfield	240	44.23 N	64.58 W
South Bruny I	228	43.23 S	147.17 E
South Burlington	242	44.28 N	73.13 W
Southbury	261	41.29 N	73.13 W
South Butler	264	43.08 N	76.46 W
South Byron	264	43.03 N	78.04 W
South Cairo	261	42.17 N	73.57 W
South Carolina □[3]	234	34.00 N	81.00 W
South Carver	261	41.51 N	70.54 W
South Channel ⊔, Pil.	202	14.17 N	120.33 E
South Channel ⊔, Mich., U.S.	244	45.38 N	84.32 W
South Chaplin	261	41.46 N	72.09 W
South Charleston	242	38.22 N	81.44 W
South Chatham	261	41.41 N	70.01 W
South China Basin ⊹[1]	148	15.00 N	115.00 E
South China Sea ▾[2]	198	10.00 N	113.00 E
South Cle Elum	270	47.10 N	120.56 W
South Coatesville	262	39.58 N	75.49 W
South Concho ≃	250	31.21 N	100.28 W
South Dakota □[3]	234	44.15 N	100.00 W
South Dartmouth	261	41.36 N	70.57 W
South Dayton	266	42.22 N	79.03 W
South Deerfield	261	42.29 N	72.37 W
South Dennis, Mass., U.S.	261	41.41 N	70.09 W
South Dennis, N.J., U.S.	262	39.11 N	74.49 W
South Dos Palos	272	36.58 N	120.39 W
South Downs ∧∧[1]	162	50.55 N	0.25 W
South Duxbury	261	42.01 N	70.41 W
South East □[5]	224	25.00 S	25.45 E
South East Cape ≻, Austl.	228	43.39 S	146.50 E
Southeast Cape ≻, Alaska, U.S.	236	62.55 N	169.42 W
South-Eastern □[3]	222	6.00 N	8.30 E
Southeast Newfoundland Ridge ⊹[3]	148	40.00 N	47.00 W
South Easton	261	42.03 N	71.05 W
Southeast Pacific Basin ⊹[1]	148	60.00 S	115.00 W
South East Point ≻	228	39.00 S	146.20 E
South Egg Harbor	262	39.31 N	74.39 W
South Egremont	261	42.10 N	73.25 W
South Elgin	268	41.59 N	88.18 W
Southend-on-Sea	174	51.33 N	0.43 E
South English ≃	244	41.30 N	91.56 W
Southern □[4], S.L.	222	8.00 N	12.15 W
Southern □[4], Zam.	224	16.00 S	27.00 E
Southern Alps ∧∧	230	43.30 S	170.20 E
Southern Cross	226	31.13 S	119.19 E
Southern Indian Lake ⊜	232	57.10 N	98.40 W
Southern Leyte □[4]	202	10.50 N	124.55 E
Southern Pines	246	35.11 N	79.24 W
Southern Ute Indian Reservation ◆[4]	254	37.05 N	107.45 W
Southern Yemen → Yemen, People's Democratic Republic of □[1]	214	15.00 N	48.00 E
South Esk ≃	228	41.25 S	147.08 E
South Essex	261	42.38 N	70.46 W
South Euclid	266	41.31 N	81.32 W
South Fabius ≃	248	39.54 N	91.30 W
South Fallsburg	242	41.43 N	74.38 W
Southfield, Mass., U.S.	261	42.06 N	73.14 W
Southfield, Mich., U.S.	268	42.29 N	83.17 W
South Fiji Basin ⊹[1]	148	27.00 S	176.00 E
South Fiji Ridge ⊹[3]	148	23.00 S	179.00 W
South Fontana	274	34.05 N	117.24 W
South Fork, Colo., U.S.	254	37.40 N	106.37 W
South Fork, Pa., U.S.	266	40.22 N	78.48 W
South Fort George	238	53.54 N	122.45 W
South Fox Island I	244	45.25 N	85.50 W
South Fulton	248	36.30 N	88.53 W
South Gate, Calif., U.S.	274	33.57 N	118.12 W
Southgate, Mich., U.S.	268	42.12 N	83.13 W
Southgate, Wash., U.S.	270	47.10 N	122.30 W
South Georgia I	288	54.15 S	36.45 W
South Georgia Rise ⊹[3]	148	50.00 S	28.00 W
South Glastonbury	261	41.40 N	72.36 W
South Grafton	261	42.11 N	71.42 W
South Grand ≃	248	38.18 N	93.28 W
South Greensburg	266	40.17 N	79.33 W
South Greenwood	246	34.10 N	82.09 W
South Hadley	261	42.16 N	72.35 W
South Hadley Falls	261	42.14 N	72.36 W
South Hamilton	261	42.37 N	70.53 W
South Harwich	261	41.41 N	70.03 W
South Hātia Island I	206	22.19 N	91.07 E
South Haven, Kans., U.S.	252	37.03 N	97.24 W
South Haven, Mich., U.S.	268	42.24 N	86.16 W
South Heart ≃	238	55.34 N	116.11 W
South Heights	266	40.35 N	80.14 W
South Henderson	246	36.17 N	78.25 W
South Henik Lake ⊜	232	61.30 N	97.30 W
South Hero	242	44.39 N	73.19 W
South Hill	246	36.44 N	78.08 W
South Holston Lake ⊜[1]	246	36.35 N	82.00 W
South Honshu Ridge ⊹[3]	148	18.00 N	143.00 E
South Hopkinton	261	41.24 N	71.45 W
South Houston	250	29.40 N	95.14 W
South Indian Basin ⊹[1]	148	60.00 S	120.00 E
South Indian Lake	232	56.46 N	98.57 W
Southington, Conn., U.S.	261	41.36 N	72.53 W
Southington, Ohio, U.S.	266	41.19 N	80.57 W
South International Falls	244	48.35 N	93.24 W
South Island I	230	43.50 S	171.00 E
South Islet I	202	8.48 N	119.50 E
South Kenosha	268	42.33 N	87.51 W
South Kent	261	41.41 N	73.28 W
South Korea → Korea, South □[1]	190	36.30 N	128.00 E
South Laguna	274	33.30 N	117.45 W
South Lake Tahoe	272	38.57 N	119.57 W
South Lancaster, Ont., Can.	260	45.08 N	74.29 W
South Lancaster, Mass., U.S.	261	42.27 N	71.41 W
Southland, Mich., U.S.	268	42.13 N	84.24 W
Southland, Tex., U.S.	250	33.22 N	101.33 W
Southlawn	248	39.45 N	89.37 W
South Lee	261	42.17 N	73.17 W
South Lima	264	42.51 N	77.41 W
South Lorain	266	41.27 N	82.09 W
South Loup ≃	252	41.04 N	98.40 W
South Lyon	268	42.28 N	83.39 W
South Manitou Island I	244	45.01 N	86.07 W
South Merrimack	261	42.49 N	71.34 W
South Miami	246	25.42 N	80.17 W
South Middleboro	261	41.45 N	70.50 W
South Milford	268	41.32 N	85.16 W
South Mills	246	36.27 N	76.20 W
South Milwaukee	268	42.55 N	87.52 W
South Modesto	272	37.38 N	120.58 W
South Molton	162	51.01 N	3.50 W
South Monroe	268	41.54 N	83.25 W
Southmont	266	40.18 N	78.56 W
South Mountain ∧	256	42.44 N	116.54 W
South Mount Vernon	266	40.23 N	82.23 W
South Nahanni ≃	232	61.03 N	123.20 W
South Naknek	236	58.43 N	157.05 W
South New Castle	266	40.58 N	80.21 W
South Ogden	254	41.12 N	111.59 W
Southold	261	41.04 N	72.26 W
South Onondaga	264	42.56 N	76.13 W
South Orkney Islands II	148	60.35 S	45.30 W
South Oroville	272	39.30 N	121.33 W
South Otselic	264	42.39 N	75.46 W
South Paris	242	44.13 N	70.31 W
South Park, Calif., U.S.	272	38.25 N	122.42 W
South Park, Ill., U.S.	268	41.44 N	88.18 W
South Pass)(	254	42.22 N	108.55 W
South Pease ≃	250	34.07 N	100.25 W
South Pekin	244	40.30 N	89.39 W
South Pender	270	48.45 N	123.14 W
South Philipsburg	266	40.53 N	78.13 W
South Pittsburg	248	35.01 N	85.42 W
South Platte ≃	252	41.07 N	100.42 W
South Point ≻, Ba.	282	22.52 N	74.50 W
South Point ≻, Pil.	202	10.25 N	122.30 E
South Porcupine	244	48.28 N	81.13 W
Southport, Austl.	228	27.58 S	153.25 E
Southport, Eng., U.K.	162	53.39 N	3.01 W
Southport, Conn., U.S.	261	41.08 N	73.17 W
Southport, Fla., U.S.	248	30.17 N	85.39 W
Southport, N.C., U.S.	246	33.55 N	78.01 W
Southport, N.Y., U.S.	242	42.03 N	76.49 W
South Portland	242	43.38 N	70.15 W
South Pottstown	262	40.14 N	75.39 W
South Range	244	47.04 N	88.39 W
South Renovo	266	41.19 N	77.45 W
South Revelstoke	238	50.48 N	118.11 W
South River, Ont., Can.	244	45.45 N	79.25 W
South River, N.J., U.S.	262	40.27 N	74.23 W
South Rockwood	268	42.04 N	83.16 W
South Ronaldsay I	162	58.46 N	2.50 W
South Royalston	261	42.38 N	72.09 W
South Russell	266	41.25 N	81.21 W
South Salt Lake	254	40.43 N	111.53 W
South Sandwich Trench ⊹[1]	148	57.00 S	25.00 W
South San Francisco	272	37.39 N	122.24 W
South Santiam ≃	256	44.41 N	123.00 W
South Saskatchewan ≃	232	53.15 N	105.05 W
South Saugeen ≃	244	44.08 N	81.02 W
South Seaville	262	39.11 N	74.46 W
South Setauket	261	40.54 N	73.07 W
South Shafter	272	35.28 N	122.42 W
South Shetland Islands II	148	62.00 S	60.00 W
South Shields	162	55.00 N	1.25 W
South Sioux City	252	42.28 N	96.24 W
South Skunk ≃	244	41.15 N	92.02 W
South Slocan	238	49.28 N	117.32 W
South Spicer Island I	232	68.06 N	79.13 W
South Streator	268	41.06 N	88.50 W
South Suffolk	262	36.43 N	76.35 W
South Sulphur ≃	250	33.23 N	95.18 W
South Superior	254	41.46 N	108.58 W
South Swansea	261	41.43 N	71.12 W
South Taranaki Bight C[3]	230	39.40 S	174.00 E
South Tasmania Ridge ⊹[3]	148	46.00 S	147.00 E
South Temple	262	40.24 N	75.55 W
South Thompson ≃	238	50.41 N	120.21 W
South Toms River	262	39.56 N	74.13 W
South Torrington	252	42.03 N	104.11 W
South Trail	246	27.17 N	82.32 W
South Tucson	254	32.12 N	110.58 W
South Turlock	272	37.29 N	120.51 W
South Tuscon	254	32.12 N	110.58 W
South Ubian	202	5.11 N	120.30 E
South Uist I	162	57.15 N	7.24 W
South Umpqua ≃	256	43.20 N	123.25 W
South Ventana Cone ∧	258	36.17 N	121.38 W
South Vietnam → Vietnam, South □[1]	198	13.00 N	108.00 E
Southview	266	40.20 N	80.16 W
South Wabasca Lake ⊜	238	55.54 N	113.45 W
South Wales	264	42.43 N	78.35 W
Southwark ◆[8]	174	51.30 N	0.06 W
South Wellesley Islands II	228	17.00 S	139.30 E
South Wellfleet	261	41.55 N	69.59 W
South Wellington	270	49.06 N	123.53 W
Southwest	266	40.12 N	79.32 W
South West Africa □[1]	218	22.00 S	17.00 E
South West Cape ≻, Austl.	228	43.34 S	146.02 E
Southwest Cape ≻, N.Z.	230	47.17 S	167.28 E
Southwest Cape ≻, Alaska, U.S.	236	63.18 N	171.27 W
South West City	248	36.31 N	94.37 W
Southwestern Pacific Basin ⊹[1]	148	42.00 S	166.00 W
South West Fargo	252	46.53 N	96.55 W
Southwest Greensburg	266	40.17 N	79.33 W
Southwest Harbor	242	44.17 N	68.20 W
Southwest Miramichi ≃	240	46.58 N	65.35 W
Southwest Point ≻, Ba.	246	26.30 N	78.45 W
Southwest Point ≻, Ba.	282	25.51 N	77.13 W
South Whitley	268	41.05 N	85.38 W
South Wichita ≃	250	33.43 N	99.29 W
Southwick, Eng., U.K.	174	50.50 N	0.13 W
Southwick, Mass., U.S.	261	42.03 N	72.46 W
South Williamson	246	37.40 N	82.16 W
South Wilmington	268	41.10 N	88.17 W
South Windham	242	43.44 N	70.26 W
South Windsor	261	41.49 N	72.37 W
Southwold	162	52.20 N	1.40 E
Southwood	264	42.59 N	76.08 W
Southwood Acres	261	41.59 N	72.32 W
South Woodslee	266	42.14 N	82.43 W
South Woodstock	261	41.56 N	71.58 W
Southworth	270	47.31 N	122.30 W
South Yadkin ≃	246	35.45 N	80.27 W
South Yamhill ≃	256	45.13 N	123.08 W
South Yarmouth	261	41.40 N	70.10 W
Soutpansberg ∧∧	224	22.55 S	29.30 E
Souvigny	166	46.32 N	3.11 E
Sovata	172	46.35 N	25.04 E
Soverato	170	38.41 N	16.33 E
Sovereign Mountain ∧	236	62.08 N	148.36 W
Sovetsk (Tilsit), S.S.S.R.	160	55.05 N	21.53 E
Sovetsk, S.S.S.R.	160	57.37 N	48.58 E
Sovetskaja Gavan'	186	48.58 N	140.18 E
Sovetskij	160	60.32 N	28.41 E
Soviet Union → Union of Soviet Socialist Republics □[1]	186	60.00 N	80.00 E
Søvik	160	62.33 N	6.18 E
Sovpolje	160	65.18 N	43.55 E
Sōya-misaki ≻	192a	45.31 N	141.56 E
Soyang-gang ≃	194	37.52 N	127.40 E
Soyapango	280	13.42 N	89.09 W
Sozimskij	160	59.44 N	52.16 E
Šožma	160	61.56 N	40.15 E
Sozopol	172	42.25 N	27.42 E
Spa	164	50.30 N	5.52 E
Spaichingen	180	48.04 N	8.44 E
Spain □[1]	158	40.00 N	4.00 W
Spakenburg	178	52.15 N	5.23 E
Spalato → Split	170	43.31 N	16.27 E
Spalding, Eng., U.K.	174	52.47 N	0.10 W
Spalding, Nebr., U.S.	252	41.41 N	98.22 W
Spanaway	270	47.06 N	122.26 W
Spangler	266	40.39 N	78.47 W
Spaniard's Bay	240	47.37 N	53.17 W
Spanish	244	46.12 N	82.21 W
Spanish ≃	244	46.11 N	82.19 W
Spanish Fork	254	40.07 N	111.39 W
Spanish Fork ≃	254	40.10 N	111.45 W
Spanish North Africa □[2]	214	35.53 N	5.19 W
Spanish Peak ∧	256	44.24 N	119.46 W
Spanish Sahara □[2]	214	24.30 N	13.00 W
Spanish Town	285q	18.00 N	76.57 W
Sparkle Lake	261	41.18 N	73.47 W
Sparkman	248	33.55 N	92.51 W
Sparks, Ga., U.S.	246	31.11 N	83.26 W
Sparks, Nev., U.S.	272	39.32 N	119.45 W
Sparland	244	41.02 N	89.26 W
Sparlingville	266	42.58 N	82.30 W
Sparrows Point	262	39.14 N	76.29 W
Sparta, Ont., Can.	264	42.42 N	81.05 W
Sparta → Spárti, Ellás	172	37.05 N	22.27 E
Sparta, Ga., U.S.	246	33.17 N	82.58 W
Sparta, Ill., U.S.	248	38.07 N	89.42 W
Sparta, Ky., U.S.	248	38.41 N	84.55 W
Sparta, Mich., U.S.	244	43.10 N	85.42 W
Sparta, N.C., U.S.	246	36.30 N	81.07 W
Sparta, Ohio, U.S.	266	40.24 N	82.42 W
Sparta, Tenn., U.S.	248	35.56 N	85.29 W
Sparta, Wis., U.S.	244	43.57 N	90.47 W
Spartanburg	246	34.57 N	81.55 W
Spartansburg	266	41.49 N	79.41 W
Spartel, Cap ≻	168	35.48 N	5.56 W
Spárti (Sparta)	172	37.05 N	22.27 E
Spartivento, Capo ≻	170	38.53 N	8.50 E
Spas-Demensk	160	54.25 N	34.01 E
Spas-Klepiki	160	55.08 N	40.13 E
Spassk-Dal'nij	186	44.37 N	132.48 E
Spassk-R'azanskij	160	54.24 N	40.23 E
Spátha, Ákra ≻	172	35.42 N	23.44 E
Spear, Cape ≻	240	47.32 N	52.32 W
Spearfish	252	44.30 N	103.52 W
Spearman	250	36.12 N	101.12 W
Spearville	252	37.51 N	99.45 W
Spectrum Range ∧∧	236	57.30 N	130.40 W
Speedway	248	39.47 N	86.15 W
Speightstown	285g	13.15 N	59.39 W
Speigletown	261	42.48 N	73.38 W
Speikkogel ∧	164	47.14 N	15.03 E
Spello	170	42.59 N	12.40 E
Spenard	236	61.11 N	149.55 W
Spence Bay	232	69.32 N	93.31 W
Spencer, Idaho, U.S.	256	44.21 N	112.11 W
Spencer, Ind., U.S.	248	39.17 N	86.46 W
Spencer, Iowa, U.S.	252	43.09 N	95.09 W
Spencer, Mass., U.S.	261	42.15 N	71.59 W
Spencer, Nebr., U.S.	252	42.53 N	98.42 W
Spencer, N.C., U.S.	246	35.37 N	80.26 W
Spencer, Ohio, U.S.	266	41.06 N	82.07 W
Spencer, S. Dak., U.S.	252	43.44 N	97.36 W
Spencer, Tenn., U.S.	248	35.45 N	85.28 W
Spencer, W. Va., U.S.	242	38.48 N	81.21 W
Spencer, Wis., U.S.	244	44.46 N	90.18 W
Spencer, Cape ≻, Austl.	228	35.18 S	136.53 E
Spencer, Cape ≻, N.B., Can.	240	45.12 N	65.55 W
Spencer, Cape ≻, Alaska, U.S.	236	58.14 N	136.40 W
Spencer, Point ≻	236	65.18 N	166.50 W
Spencer Gulf C	228	34.00 S	137.00 E
Spencerport	264	43.11 N	77.48 W
Spencertown	261	42.20 N	73.33 W
Spencerville, Ont., Can.	264	44.51 N	75.33 W
Spencerville, Ind., U.S.	268	41.19 N	84.54 W
Spencerville, Ohio, U.S.	268	40.42 N	84.21 W
Spences Bridge	238	50.25 N	121.21 W
Spenge	178	52.08 N	8.28 E
Spenser Mountains ∧∧	230	42.13 S	172.35 E
Sperling	270	49.08 N	122.33 W
Sperryville	242	38.39 N	78.14 W
Spey ≃	162	57.40 N	3.06 W
Speyer	164	49.19 N	8.26 E
Speyside	285r	11.18 N	60.32 W
Spezia → La Spezia	182	44.07 N	9.50 E
Spezzano Albanese	170	39.40 N	16.19 E
Spicer	252	45.14 N	94.56 W
Spickard	248	40.14 N	93.35 W
Spiess Seamount ⊹[3]	148	54.40 S	0.15 E
Spiez	166	46.41 N	7.39 E
Spijkenisse	178	51.21 N	4.20 E
Spilimbergo	170	44.32 N	11.01 E
Spillimacheen ≃	238	50.55 N	116.20 W
Spina ⊥	170	44.43 N	12.08 E
Spinazzola	170	40.58 N	16.06 E
Spincourt	166	49.20 N	5.40 E
Spindale	246	35.22 N	81.55 W
Spinnerstown	262	40.26 N	75.26 W
Spirit Lake, Idaho, U.S.	256	47.58 N	116.52 W
Spirit Lake, Iowa, U.S.	252	43.26 N	95.06 W
Spirit Lake, Wash., U.S.	270	46.16 N	122.09 W
Spirit River	238	55.47 N	118.50 W
Spiro	248	35.16 N	94.37 W
Spišská Nová Ves	164	48.57 N	20.34 E
Spitsbergen II	148	78.00 N	19.00 E
Spittal an der Drau	164	46.48 N	13.30 E
Spitz	164	48.22 N	15.25 E
Split	170	43.31 N	16.27 E
Split, Cape ≻	240	45.20 N	64.30 W
Split Lake ⊜	232	56.08 N	96.15 W
Splügen	166	46.33 N	9.20 E
Splügen Pass)(	164	46.30 N	9.20 E
Spofford	250	29.11 N	100.25 W
Spokane	256	47.40 N	117.23 W
Spokane ≃	256	47.44 N	118.20 W
Spokane, Mount ∧	256	47.55 N	117.07 W
Spokane Indian Reservation ◆[4]	256	47.55 N	118.00 W
Spoleto	184	42.44 N	12.44 E
Spoon ≃	244	40.18 N	90.04 W
Spooner	244	45.50 N	91.53 W
Spornoje	186	62.20 N	151.03 E
Sport Hill	261	41.14 N	73.16 W
Sporting Hill	262	40.09 N	76.26 W
Spotswood	262	40.23 N	74.23 W
Spotsylvania	262	38.12 N	77.35 W
Spotsylvania □[6]	262	38.15 N	77.30 W
Sprague, Man., Can.	252	49.02 N	95.38 W
Sprague, Ala., U.S.	248	32.08 N	86.16 W
Sprague, Wash., U.S.	256	47.18 N	117.59 W
Sprague ≃	256	42.34 N	121.51 W
Spragueville	261	41.53 N	71.32 W
Sprankle Mills	266	41.00 N	79.07 W
Spratly Island I	198	8.38 N	111.55 E
Spray	256	44.50 N	119.48 W
Spray Lakes Reservoir ⊜[1]	238	50.55 N	115.20 W
Spreča ≃	172	44.45 N	18.06 E
Spreckels	272	36.36 N	121.34 W
Spreckelsville	275a	20.54 N	156.25 W
Spremberg	164	51.34 N	14.22 E
Spring ≃, Ark., U.S.	248	36.08 N	91.05 W
Spring Arbor	268	42.12 N	84.34 W
Spring Bay C	254	41.40 N	112.50 W
Springbok	218	29.43 S	17.55 E
Springboro	266	41.48 N	80.22 W
Spring Brook	264	42.49 N	78.40 W
Spring City, Pa., U.S.	262	40.11 N	75.33 W
Spring City, Tenn., U.S.	246	35.42 N	84.52 W
Spring City, Utah, U.S.	254	39.29 N	111.30 W
Spring Coulee ∨	252	48.31 N	100.54 W
Spring Creek	266	41.53 N	79.32 W
Springdale, Newf., Can.	240	49.30 N	56.04 W
Springdale, Ark., U.S.	248	36.11 N	94.08 W
Springdale, Pa., U.S.	266	40.33 N	79.46 W
Springdale, S.C., U.S.	246	33.57 N	81.06 W
Springdale, Utah, U.S.	254	37.11 N	113.00 W
Springdale, Wash., U.S.	256	48.04 N	117.45 W
Springe	178	52.12 N	9.32 E
Springer	250	36.22 N	104.36 W
Springerville	254	34.08 N	109.17 W
Springfield, N.B., Can.	240	46.01 N	67.03 W
Springfield, Ont., Can.	264	42.50 N	80.56 W
Springfield, Colo., U.S.	252	37.24 N	102.37 W
Springfield, Fla., U.S.	248	30.09 N	85.37 W
Springfield, Ga., U.S.	246	32.22 N	81.18 W
Springfield, Ill., U.S.	248	39.47 N	89.40 W
Springfield, Ky., U.S.	248	37.41 N	85.13 W
Springfield, La., U.S.	248	30.26 N	90.33 W
Springfield, Mass., U.S.	261	42.07 N	72.36 W
Springfield, Mich., U.S.	268	42.20 N	85.15 W
Springfield, Minn., U.S.	252	44.14 N	94.59 W
Springfield, Mo., U.S.	248	37.14 N	93.17 W
Springfield, Ohio, U.S.	242	39.56 N	83.49 W
Springfield, Oreg., U.S.	256	44.03 N	123.01 W
Springfield, S.C., U.S.	246	33.30 N	81.17 W
Springfield, S. Dak., U.S.	252	42.49 N	97.54 W
Springfield, Tenn., U.S.	248	36.31 N	86.52 W
Springfield, Vt., U.S.	242	43.18 N	72.29 W
Springfield, Lake ⊜[1]	248	39.40 N	89.35 W
Springfield Plateau ∧∧[1]	248	37.10 N	93.30 W
Springfontein	218	30.19 S	25.36 E
Spring Garden	290	6.59 N	58.30 W
Spring Glen, Fla., U.S.	246	30.18 N	81.36 W
Spring Glen, Pa., U.S.	262	40.38 N	76.37 W
Spring Green	244	43.11 N	90.04 W
Spring Grove, Minn., U.S.	244	43.33 N	91.38 W
Spring Grove, Pa., U.S.	262	39.52 N	76.52 W
Springhill, N.S., Can.	240	45.39 N	64.03 W
Spring Hill, Calif., U.S.	272	39.15 N	121.03 W
Springhill, La., U.S.	248	33.00 N	93.28 W
Spring Hill, Pa., U.S.	266	40.23 N	78.40 W
Spring Hill, Tenn., U.S.	248	35.45 N	86.56 W
Spring Hills	268	40.16 N	83.22 W
Spring Hope	246	35.57 N	78.06 W
Springhouse	238	51.55 N	122.07 W
Spring Lake, N.J., U.S.	262	40.09 N	74.02 W
Spring Lake, N.C., U.S.	246	35.10 N	78.58 W
Spring Lake Heights	262	40.09 N	74.04 W
Spring Mount	262	40.17 N	75.28 W
Spring Mountains ∧∧	258	36.10 N	115.40 W
Springport	268	42.22 N	84.42 W
Spring Run	266	40.09 N	83.47 W
Springs	224	26.13 S	28.25 E
Springsure	228	24.07 S	148.05 E
Springtown	250	32.58 N	97.41 W
Springvale	242	43.28 N	70.48 W
Spring Valley, Calif., U.S.	274	32.45 N	116.59 W
Spring Valley, Ill., U.S.	244	41.20 N	89.12 W
Spring Valley, Minn., U.S.	244	43.41 N	92.23 W
Spring Valley, N.Y., U.S.	242	41.07 N	74.03 W
Spring Valley, Wis., U.S.	244	44.51 N	92.14 W
Springview	252	42.49 N	99.45 W
Springville, Ala., U.S.	248	33.46 N	86.30 W
Springville, Iowa, U.S.	244	42.03 N	91.27 W
Springville, N.Y., U.S.	266	42.31 N	78.40 W
Springville, Utah, U.S.	254	40.10 N	111.37 W
Sproat Lake ⊜	238	49.16 N	125.03 W
Sprockhövel	178	51.22 N	7.15 E
Sproul	266	40.16 N	78.28 W
Spruce Brook	240	48.45 N	58.11 W
Spruce Creek	266	40.37 N	78.08 W
Spruce Grove	238	53.32 N	113.55 W
Spruce Knob ∧	242	38.42 N	79.32 W
Spruce Mountain ∧, Ariz., U.S.	254	34.28 N	112.24 W
Spruce Mountain ∧, Nev., U.S.	258	40.33 N	114.49 W
Spruce Pine	246	35.55 N	82.04 W
Spry	262	39.55 N	76.41 W
Spud Rock ∧	254	32.13 N	110.33 W
Spulico, Capo ≻	170	39.58 N	16.39 E
Spurfield	238	55.13 N	114.16 W
Spurr, Mount ∧	236	61.18 N	152.15 W
Spuzzum	238	49.41 N	121.25 W
Squally Channel ⊔	238	53.10 N	129.15 W
Squamish	238	49.42 N	123.09 W
Squamish ≃	238	49.45 N	123.09 W
Squam Lake ⊜	242	43.45 N	71.32 W
Square Lake ⊜	240	47.03 N	68.20 W
Squatteck	240	47.53 N	68.44 W
Squaw Cap Mountain ∧	240	47.53 N	66.53 W
Squaw Harbor	236	55.11 N	160.30 W
Squaw Hill ∧	254	41.48 N	105.02 W
Squaw Peak ∧	256	47.10 N	114.21 W
Squilax	238	50.52 N	119.35 W
Squillace, Golfo di C	170	38.50 N	16.50 E
Squinzano	170	40.26 N	18.03 E
Squire	246	37.14 N	81.36 W
Squirrel ≃	236	66.57 N	160.27 W
Srbija □[3]	172	44.00 N	21.00 E
Srbobran	172	45.33 N	19.48 E
Sredinnyj Chrebet ∧∧	186	56.00 N	158.00 E
Sredneje Kujto, Ozero ⊜	160	65.08 N	31.15 E
Srednekolymsk	186	67.27 N	153.41 E
Srednerusskaja Vozvyšennost' ∧∧[1]	186	52.00 N	38.00 E
Srednesibirskoje Ploskogorje ∧∧[1]	186	65.00 N	105.00 E
Srednij Vas'ugan	186	59.16 N	78.15 E
Śrem	164	52.08 N	17.01 E
Sremska Mitrovica	172	44.58 N	19.37 E
Sremski Karlovci	172	45.12 N	19.57 E
Srêng ≃	200	13.21 N	103.27 E
Srêpôk ≃	200	13.33 N	106.16 E
Sretensk	186	52.15 N	117.43 E
Sri Gangānagar	206	29.55 N	73.52 E
Srīnagar	206	34.05 N	74.49 E
Sri Thep ⊥	200	16.25 N	101.04 E
Środa	164	52.14 N	17.17 E
Środa Śląska (Neumarkt)	164	51.10 N	16.36 E
Srpska Crnja	172	45.43 N	20.32 E
St. → Saint, Sankt, Sint			
Staatsburg	261	41.51 N	73.56 W
Stabroek	176	51.20 N	4.22 E
Stacyville	244	43.26 N	92.47 W
Stade	178	53.36 N	9.28 E
Stade □[6]	178	53.30 N	9.30 E
Staden	176	50.59 N	3.01 E
Stadl Paura	164	48.05 N	13.53 E
Stadskanaal	178	53.00 N	6.55 E
Stadtbergen	180	48.22 N	10.50 E
Stadt Haag	164	48.07 N	14.34 E
Stadthagen	178	52.19 N	9.13 E
Stadtlohn	178	51.59 N	6.55 E
Stadtoldendorf	178	51.53 N	9.37 E
Stäfa	180	47.15 N	8.44 E
Staffelstein	164	50.06 N	11.00 E
Stafford, Eng., U.K.	174	52.48 N	2.07 W
Stafford, Conn., U.S.	261	41.59 N	72.17 W
Stafford, Kans., U.S.	252	37.58 N	98.36 W
Stafford, N.Y., U.S.	264	42.59 N	78.04 W
Stafford, Tex., U.S.	250	29.37 N	95.34 W
Stafford, Va., U.S.	262	38.09 N	76.51 W
Stafford □[6]	262	38.25 N	77.30 W
Staffordshire □[6]	174	52.50 N	2.00 W
Stafford Springs	261	41.57 N	72.18 W
Staffordville	261	42.00 N	72.16 W
Staines	174	51.26 N	0.31 W
Stainz	164	46.54 N	15.16 E
Staked Plain → Estacado, Llano ≚	250	33.30 N	102.40 W
Stalać	172	43.40 N	21.25 E
Stalheim	160	60.50 N	6.40 E
Stalin → Varna, Blg.	172	43.13 N	27.55 E
Stalin → Braşov, Rom.	172	45.39 N	25.37 E
Stalin (Kuçovë), Shq.	172	40.48 N	19.54 E
Stalinabad → Dušanbe	186	38.35 N	68.48 E
Stalino → Doneck	158	48.00 N	37.48 E
Stalinogród → Katowice	164	50.16 N	19.00 E
Stalinogorsk → Novomoskovsk	158	54.05 N	38.13 E
Stalinsk → Novokuzneck	186	53.45 N	87.06 E
Ställdalen	160	59.56 N	14.56 E
Stallo	248	32.55 N	89.07 W
Stalowa Wola	164	50.35 N	22.02 E
Stambaugh	244	46.04 N	88.38 W
Stamford, Eng., U.K.	174	52.39 N	0.29 W
Stamford, Conn., U.S.	261	41.03 N	73.32 W
Stamford, Tex., U.S.	250	32.57 N	99.48 W
Stamford, Vt., U.S.	261	42.45 N	73.05 W
Stamford, Lake ⊜[1]	250	33.05 N	99.35 W
Stamps	248	33.22 N	93.30 W
Stanaford	242	37.49 N	81.10 W
Stanardsville	242	38.18 N	78.26 W
Stanberry	248	40.13 N	94.35 W
Standard, Alta., Can.	238	51.07 N	112.59 W
Standard, Alaska, U.S.	236	64.47 N	148.32 W
Standard, Calif., U.S.	272	37.59 N	120.20 W
Standard, Pa., U.S.	266	40.10 N	79.32 W
Standerton	224	26.58 S	29.07 E
Standing Rock Indian Reservation ◆[4]	252	45.50 N	101.10 W
Standish	244	43.59 N	83.57 W
Stanfield, Ariz., U.S.	254	32.53 N	111.58 W
Stanfield, Oreg., U.S.	256	45.47 N	119.13 W
Stanford, Calif., U.S.	272	37.25 N	122.08 W
Stanford, Ky., U.S.	246	37.32 N	84.40 W
Stanford, Mont., U.S.	256	47.09 N	110.13 W
Stanford Heights	261	42.46 N	73.53 W
Stanfordville	261	41.52 N	73.43 W
Stanger	224	29.27 S	31.14 E
Stanhope	244	42.17 N	93.48 W
Stanislaus □[6]	272	37.39 N	121.00 W

Symbols in the index entries are identified on page 360.

Name	Page	Lat°′	Long°′
Stanisławów → Ivano-Frankovsk	158	48.55 N	24.43 E
Stanke Dimitrov	172	42.16 N	23.07 E
Stanley, N.B., Can.	240	46.17 N	66.44 W
Stanley, Falk. Is.	288	51.42 S	57.51 W
Stanley, N.C., U.S.	246	35.21 N	81.06 W
Stanley, N. Dak., U.S.	252	48.19 N	102.23 W
Stanley, N.Y., U.S.	264	42.49 N	77.06 W
Stanley, Va., U.S.	242	38.34 N	78.31 W
Stanley, Wis., U.S.	244	44.58 N	90.56 W
Stanley Falls ⌞	218	0.30 N	25.12 E
Stanleyville → Kisangani	218	0.30 N	25.12 E
Stannards	266	42.05 N	77.55 W
Stann Creek	278	16.58 N	88.13 W
Stanovoj Chrebet ⛰	186	56.20 N	126.00 E
Stanovoje Nagorje ⛰	186	56.00 N	116.00 E
Stanovoy Mountains → Stanovoj Chrebet ⛰	186	56.20 N	126.00 E
Stanstead	260	45.01 N	72.05 W
Stanstead □[6]	260	45.10 N	72.00 W
Stanthorpe	228	28.39 S	151.57 E
Stanton, Calif., U.S.	274	33.48 N	117.60 W
Stanton, Del., U.S.	262	39.43 N	75.37 W
Stanton, Iowa, U.S.	252	40.59 N	95.06 W
Stanton, Ky., U.S.	246	37.54 N	83.52 W
Stanton, Mich., U.S.	244	43.18 N	85.05 W
Stanton, Miss., U.S.	248	31.42 N	91.14 W
Stanton, Nebr., U.S.	252	41.57 N	97.14 W
Stanton, N.J., U.S.	262	40.35 N	74.50 W
Stanton, N. Dak., U.S.	252	47.19 N	101.23 W
Stanton, Tenn., U.S.	248	35.28 N	89.24 W
Stanton, Tex., U.S.	250	32.08 N	101.48 W
Stantonsburg	246	35.37 N	77.49 W
Stanwood	270	48.15 N	122.23 W
Stapleford	174	52.56 N	1.16 W
Staples	252	46.21 N	94.48 W
Stapleton, Ala., U.S.	248	30.45 N	87.48 W
Stapleton, Nebr., U.S.	252	41.29 N	100.31 W
Stąporków	164	51.09 N	20.34 E
Star, Miss., U.S.	248	32.06 N	90.03 W
Star, N.C., U.S.	246	35.24 N	79.47 W
Stará Boleslav	164	50.12 N	14.42 E
Starachowice	164	51.03 N	21.04 E
Staraja Majna	160	54.36 N	48.57 E
Staraja Russa	160	58.00 N	31.23 E
Stara Pazova	172	44.59 N	20.10 E
Stara Planina (Balkan Mountains) ⛰	172	43.15 N	25.00 E
Stará Turá	164	48.47 N	17.42 E
Stara Zagora	172	42.25 N	25.38 E
Starbrick	266	41.50 N	79.12 W
Starbuck, Man., Can.	252	49.46 N	97.36 W
Starbuck, Minn., U.S.	252	45.37 N	95.32 W
Starbuck, Wash., U.S.	256	47.31 N	118.08 W
Star City, Ark., U.S.	248	33.56 N	91.51 W
Star City, Ind., U.S.	268	40.58 N	86.33 W
Staré Město	164	49.06 N	17.28 E
Starford	266	40.42 N	78.58 W
Stargard Szczeciński	164	53.20 N	15.02 E
Stargo	254	33.04 N	109.21 W
Stari Bar	172	42.06 N	19.08 E
Starica	160	56.30 N	34.56 E
Stari Grad	170	43.11 N	16.36 E
Stari Vlah ⇠[1]	172	43.35 N	20.15 E
Star Junction	266	40.04 N	79.46 W
Stark □[6]	266	40.48 N	81.22 W
Starke	246	29.57 N	82.07 W
Starke □[6]	268	41.18 N	86.37 W
Starkville	248	33.28 N	88.48 W
Star Lake	270	47.22 N	122.18 W
Starnberg	164	48.00 N	11.20 E
Starnberger See ⊜	164	47.55 N	11.18 E
Starogard (Gdański)	164	53.59 N	18.33 E
Starotimoškino	160	53.43 N	47.32 E
Star Peak Λ	258	40.32 N	118.10 W
Starr	266	41.32 N	79.22 W
Start Point ≻	162	50.13 N	3.38 W
Startup	270	47.52 N	121.44 W
Starvation Reservoir ⊜[1]	254	40.15 N	110.30 W
Staryj Oskol	158	51.19 N	37.51 E
Staryj Sambor	164	49.27 N	22.59 E
Starý Plzenec	164	49.42 N	13.28 E
Stary Sącz	164	49.34 N	20.38 E
Stassfurt	164	51.51 N	11.34 E
Staszów	164	50.34 N	21.40 E
State Center	244	42.01 N	93.10 W
State College, Miss., U.S.	248	33.26 N	88.47 W
State College, Pa., U.S.	266	40.48 N	77.52 W
Stateline, Calif., U.S.	272	38.57 N	119.57 W
State Line, Miss., U.S.	248	31.26 N	88.28 W
Stateline, Nev., U.S.	258	38.57 N	119.57 W
Statenville	246	30.42 N	83.02 W
State Road	246	36.19 N	80.52 W
Statesboro	246	32.27 N	81.47 W
Statesville	246	35.47 N	80.53 W
Staung ≃	200	12.50 N	104.19 E
Staunton, Ill., U.S.	248	39.01 N	89.47 W
Staunton, Va., U.S.	242	38.09 N	79.04 W
Staunton → Roanoke ≃	246	35.56 N	76.43 W
Stavanger	160	58.58 N	5.45 E
Stave Lake ⊜	238	49.15 N	122.21 W
Stavely	238	50.10 N	113.38 W
Stavenhagen	164	53.42 N	12.53 E
Staveren	164	52.53 N	5.22 E
Stavnoje	164	48.59 N	22.40 E
Stavropol'8 S.S.S.R.	158	45.02 N	41.59 E
Stavropol → Toljatti, S.S.S.R.	160	53.31 N	49.26 E
Stawell	228	37.04 S	142.46 E
Stawell ≃	228	20.38 S	142.55 E
Stawiski	164	53.23 N	22.09 E
Stawiszyn	164	51.55 N	18.07 E
Stayner	264	44.25 N	80.05 W
Stayton	256	44.48 N	122.48 W
Ste. → Saint			
Steamboat	272	39.23 N	119.44 W
Steamboat Mountain Λ	254	41.58 N	108.58 W
Steamboat Springs	254	40.29 N	106.50 W
Steamburg	266	42.07 N	78.54 W
Stearns	246	36.42 N	84.28 W
Stebbins	236	63.32 N	162.18 W
Steel ≃	244	48.46 N	86.54 W
Steele, Mo., U.S.	248	36.05 N	89.50 W
Steele, N. Dak., U.S.	252	46.51 N	99.55 W
Steele, Mount Λ	254	41.50 N	107.00 W
Steeleville	248	38.00 N	89.40 W
Steelhead	270	49.13 N	122.19 W
Steelton	262	40.14 N	76.49 W
Steelville	248	37.58 N	91.22 W
Steenbergen	178	51.35 N	4.19 E
Steenkool	198	2.07 S	133.32 E
Steens Mountain ⛰	256	42.35 N	118.40 W
Steenwijk	178	52.47 N	6.08 E
Stefansson Island I	232	73.17 N	106.45 W
Ştefan Vodă	172	44.19 N	27.19 E
Steffisburg	180	46.47 N	7.39 E
Stege	164	54.59 N	12.18 E
Steger	268	41.29 N	87.41 W
Stehekin	270	48.19 N	120.39 W
Steiermark □[3]	164	47.10 N	15.10 E
Steilacoom	270	47.10 N	122.36 W
Steinach	164	47.05 N	11.28 E
Steinbach	252	49.32 N	96.41 W
Steinen ≃	296	12.05 S	53.46 W
Steinfeld	178	52.35 N	8.12 E
Steinhagen	178	52.00 N	8.24 E
Steinhatchie ≃	246	29.40 N	83.24 W
Steinheim	178	51.52 N	9.05 E
Steinkjer	160	64.01 N	11.30 E
Stekene	176	51.12 N	4.02 E
Stekl'anka	160	59.08 N	41.37 E
Stella	252	40.14 N	95.46 W
Stella Niagara	264	43.12 N	79.02 W
Stellaquo Indian Reserve ⇠[4]	238	54.03 N	124.55 W
Stellarton	240	45.34 N	62.40 W
Stellenbosch	224	33.58 S	18.50 E
Steller, Mount Λ	236	60.30 N	143.02 W
Stelvio, Passo dello)(	170	46.32 N	10.27 E
Stenay	166	49.29 N	5.11 E
Stendal	164	52.36 N	11.51 E
Stensele	160	65.05 N	17.09 E
Stepanakert	208	39.49 N	46.44 E
Stepancevo	160	56.08 N	41.42 E
Stephen	252	48.27 N	96.53 W
Stephens	248	33.25 N	93.04 W
Stephens, Port C	228	32.45 S	152.05 E
Stephens City	242	39.05 N	78.13 W
Stephens Island I	238	54.10 N	130.45 W
Stephenson	244	45.20 N	87.38 W
Stephens Passage Ц	236	57.50 N	133.50 W
Stephentown	261	42.33 N	73.23 W
Stephentown Center	261	42.34 N	73.25 W
Stephenville, Newf., Can.	240	48.33 N	58.35 W
Stephenville, Tex., U.S.	250	32.13 N	98.12 W
Stephenville Crossing	240	48.30 N	58.27 W
Stepn'ak	186	52.50 N	70.50 E
Sterdyń	164	52.35 N	22.18 E
Sterkstroom	218	31.32 S	26.32 E
Sterling, Alaska, U.S.	236	60.28 N	150.08 W
Sterling, Colo., U.S.	252	40.37 N	103.13 W
Sterling, Conn., U.S.	261	41.42 N	71.50 W
Sterling, Ill., U.S.	244	41.48 N	89.42 W
Sterling, Kans., U.S.	252	38.13 N	98.12 W
Sterling, Mass., U.S.	261	42.26 N	71.46 W
Sterling, Mich., U.S.	244	44.02 N	84.02 W
Sterling, Nebr., U.S.	252	40.28 N	96.23 W
Sterling, N.Y., U.S.	264	43.20 N	76.39 W
Sterling, Ohio, U.S.	266	40.58 N	81.51 W
Sterling, Okla., U.S.	250	34.45 N	98.10 W
Sterling City	250	31.50 N	100.59 W
Sterling Heights	266	42.35 N	83.02 W
Sterling Junction	261	42.24 N	71.46 W
Sterling Reservoir ⊜[1]	252	40.47 N	103.17 W
Sterling Run	266	41.25 N	78.12 W
Sterlington	248	32.42 N	92.05 W
Sterlitamak	158	53.37 N	55.58 E
Šternberk	164	49.44 N	17.18 E
Stęszew	164	52.18 N	16.42 E
Stettin → Szczecin	164	53.24 N	14.32 E
Stettler	238	52.19 N	112.43 W
Steuben □[6], Ind., U.S.	268	41.38 N	85.00 W
Steuben □[6], N.Y., U.S.	266	42.20 N	77.19 W
Steubenville	266	40.22 N	80.37 W
Stevenage	174	51.55 N	0.14 W
Stevens	262	40.13 N	76.09 W
Stevens, Cape ≻	230	40.42 S	173.57 E
Stevens, Mount Λ	230	40.48 S	172.27 E
Stevenson, Ala., U.S.	248	34.52 N	85.50 W
Stevenson, Wash., U.S.	270	45.42 N	121.53 W
Stevenson Entrance Ц	236	57.45 N	152.20 W
Stevens Peak Λ	256	47.27 N	115.46 W
Stevens Point	244	44.31 N	89.34 W
Stevens Village	236	66.00 N	155.05 W
Stevensville, Ont., Can.	264	42.57 N	79.04 W
Stevensville, Md., U.S.	262	38.59 N	76.19 W
Stevensville, Mich., U.S.	268	42.01 N	86.31 W
Stevensville, Mont., U.S.	256	46.30 N	114.05 W
Stevinson	272	37.20 N	120.51 W
Steward	268	41.51 N	89.01 W
Stewardson	248	39.16 N	88.38 W
Stewart, B.C., Can.	238	55.56 N	129.59 W
Stewart, Minn., U.S.	244	44.43 N	94.29 W
Stewart, Nev., U.S.	272	39.07 N	119.45 W
Stewart ≃	236	63.18 N	139.25 W
Stewart Island I	230	47.00 S	167.52 E
Stewarton	162	55.41 N	4.31 W
Stewartstown	262	39.45 N	76.35 W
Stewartsville, Mo., U.S.	248	39.45 N	94.30 W
Stewartsville, N.J., U.S.	262	40.42 N	75.07 W
Stewartville	244	43.51 N	92.29 W
Stewiacke	240	45.08 N	63.21 W
Steyr	164	48.03 N	14.25 E
Steyr ≃	164	48.03 N	14.25 E
Stezzano	182	45.38 N	9.39 E
Stickney, Ill., U.S.	268	41.49 N	87.47 W
Stickney, S. Dak., U.S.	252	43.35 N	98.26 W
Stigler	250	35.15 N	95.08 W
Stigliano	170	40.24 N	16.14 E
Stikine ≃, B.C., Can.	232	57.00 N	131.50 W
Stikine ≃, N.A.	232	56.40 N	132.30 W
Stikine Ranges ⛰	236	58.45 N	130.00 W
Stiklestad	160	63.48 N	11.33 E
Stilfontein	224	26.50 S	26.50 E
Stilís	172	38.55 N	22.36 E
Stillman Valley	268	42.07 N	89.11 W
Stillmore	246	32.27 N	82.13 W
Still Pond	262	39.20 N	76.03 W
Stillwater, B.C., Can.	238	49.46 N	124.18 W
Stillwater, Minn., U.S.	244	45.04 N	92.49 W
Stillwater, Ohio, U.S.	266	40.20 N	81.18 W
Stillwater, Okla., U.S.	250	36.07 N	97.04 W
Stillwater ≃	256	45.38 N	109.17 W
Stillwater Range ⛰	258	39.50 N	118.15 W
Stillwell	248	35.49 N	94.38 W
Stilo, Punta ≻	170	38.28 N	16.36 E
Stimson, Mount Λ	256	48.31 N	113.36 W
Stine Mountain Λ	256	45.44 N	113.07 W
Stinnett	250	35.50 N	101.27 W
Stinson Beach	272	37.54 N	122.38 W
Štip	172	41.44 N	22.12 E
Stirling, Alta., Can.	238	49.30 N	112.31 W
Stirling, Ont., Can.	264	44.18 N	77.33 W
Stirling, Scot., U.K.	162	56.07 N	3.57 W
Stirling □[6]	162	56.03 N	3.30 W
Stirling City	258	39.54 N	121.32 W
Stirrat	246	37.44 N	82.00 W
Stittsville	264	45.15 N	75.55 W
Stittville	264	43.13 N	75.17 W
Stjernøya I	160	70.18 N	22.45 E
Stjørdalshalsen	160	63.28 N	10.56 E
Stobi ⊥	172	41.34 N	21.58 E
Stockach	180	47.51 N	9.00 E
Stockbridge, Ga., U.S.	246	33.33 N	84.14 W
Stockbridge, Mass., U.S.	261	42.17 N	73.19 W
Stockbridge, Mich., U.S.	268	42.27 N	84.11 W
Stockbridge Munsee Indian Reservation ⇠[4]	244	44.52 N	88.53 W
Stockdale, Pa., U.S.	266	40.05 N	79.51 W
Stockdale, Tex., U.S.	250	29.14 N	97.58 W
Stockelsdorf	178	53.54 N	10.38 E
Stockerau	164	48.23 N	16.13 E
Stockertown	262	40.45 N	75.16 W
Stockett	256	47.21 N	111.10 W
Stockholm, Sve.	160	59.20 N	18.03 E
Stockholm, Maine, U.S.	240	47.03 N	68.08 W
Stockland	268	40.37 N	87.36 W
Stockport, Eng., U.K.	162	53.25 N	2.10 W
Stockport, N.Y., U.S.	261	42.19 N	73.45 W
Stockton, Ala., U.S.	248	31.00 N	87.52 W
Stockton, Calif., U.S.	272	37.57 N	121.17 W
Stockton, Ill., U.S.	244	42.21 N	90.01 W
Stockton, Kans., U.S.	252	39.26 N	99.16 W
Stockton, Md., U.S.	262	38.03 N	75.25 W
Stockton, Mo., U.S.	248	37.42 N	93.48 W
Stockton, N.J., U.S.	262	40.24 N	74.58 W
Stockton, N.Y., U.S.	266	42.19 N	79.22 W
Stockton, Utah, U.S.	254	40.27 N	112.22 W
Stockton Plateau ⛰[1]	250	30.30 N	102.30 W
Stockton Reservoir ⊜[1]	248	37.40 N	93.45 W
Stockton Springs	242	44.29 N	68.52 W
Stockton-upon-Tees	162	54.34 N	1.19 W
Stockville	252	40.32 N	100.23 W
Stockwell	268	40.17 N	86.46 W
Stoczek Łukowski	164	51.58 N	21.58 E
Stœŏeng Tréng	200	13.31 N	105.58 E
Stoj, Gora Λ	172	48.37 N	23.11 E
Stoke	158	51.27 N	0.37 E
Stoke-on-Trent	174	33.00 N	2.10 W
Stokes, Mount Λ	230	41.05 S	174.06 E
Stokes Point ≻	228	40.10 S	143.56 E
Stokksnes ≻	160a	64.17 N	14.54 W
Stolac	170	43.05 N	17.58 E
Stolberg	164	50.46 N	6.13 E
Stolbovoj, Ostrov I	186	74.05 N	136.00 E
Stolica Λ	164	48.48 N	20.11 E
Stollberg	164	50.42 N	12.47 E
Stöllet	160	60.24 N	13.16 E
Stolp → Słupsk	164	54.28 N	17.01 E
Ston	170	42.50 N	17.42 E
Stone	174	52.54 N	2.10 W
Stoneboro	266	41.20 N	80.07 W
Stone Creek	266	40.24 N	81.34 W
Stonefort	248	37.37 N	88.42 W
Stone Harbor	262	39.03 N	74.45 W
Stonehaven	162	56.38 N	2.13 W
Stone Indian Reserve ⇠[4]	238	51.54 N	123.12 W
Stone Mountain	246	33.49 N	84.10 W
Stone Mountain Λ	242	44.34 N	71.40 W
Stoner	238	53.36 N	122.40 W
Stones River Homes	248	36.01 N	86.30 W
Stoneville	246	36.28 N	79.54 W
Stonewall, Man., Can.	232	50.09 N	97.21 W
Stonewall, Miss., U.S.	248	32.08 N	88.47 W
Stonewall, Okla., U.S.	250	34.39 N	96.31 W
Stoney Creek	264	43.13 N	79.46 W
Stonington, Conn., U.S.	261	41.20 N	71.54 W
Stonington, Ill., U.S.	248	39.44 N	89.12 W
Stonington, Maine, U.S.	242	44.09 N	68.40 W
Stony ≃, Alaska, U.S.	236	61.45 N	156.35 W
Stony ≃, Minn., U.S.	244	47.44 N	91.47 W
Stony Brook	261	40.56 N	73.09 W
Stony Creek, Conn., U.S.	261	41.16 N	72.45 W
Stony Creek, Va., U.S.	262	36.57 N	77.24 W
Stony Creek Indian Reserve ⇠[4]	238	53.57 N	124.07 W
Stony Creek Mills	262	40.21 N	75.52 W
Stonyford	272	39.23 N	122.33 W
Stony Indian Reserve ⇠[4]	238	51.10 N	114.55 W
Stony Lake ⊜, Man., Can.	232	58.51 N	98.35 W
Stony Lake ⊜, Ont., Can.	244	44.33 N	78.05 W
Stony Plain	238	53.02 N	114.00 W
Stony Plain Indian Reserve ⇠[4]	238	53.30 N	113.45 W
Stony Point, Mich., U.S.	268	41.57 N	83.16 W
Stony Point, N.C., U.S.	246	35.52 N	81.03 W
Stony Point, N.Y., U.S.	261	41.14 N	73.59 W
Stony Prairie	266	41.21 N	83.10 W
Stony Rapids	232	59.16 N	105.50 W
Stony Ridge	266	41.31 N	83.30 W
Stony River	236	61.47 N	156.41 W
Stopnica	164	50.27 N	20.57 E
Stora Lulevatten ⊜	160	67.10 N	19.16 E
Stora Sjöfallet ⌞	160	67.29 N	18.21 E
Stora Sjöfallets Nationalpark ♠	160	67.44 N	18.16 E
Storavan ⊜	160	65.40 N	18.15 E
Storby	160	60.13 N	19.34 E
Støren	160	63.02 N	10.18 E
Storey □[6]	272	39.28 N	119.30 W
Storfors	160	59.32 N	14.16 E
Storkerson Bay C	232	73.00 N	124.50 W
Storlien	160	63.19 N	12.06 E
Storm Bay C	228	43.10 S	147.32 E
Stormberg ⛰	224	31.27 S	26.55 E
Storm Lake	252	42.39 N	95.13 W
Storm Mountain Λ	236	59.37 N	150.35 W
Stormont □[6]	260	45.10 N	75.00 W
Stormville	261	41.34 N	73.45 W
Stornoway	162	58.12 N	6.23 W
Storoževsk	160	61.57 N	52.16 E
Storrs	261	41.48 N	72.15 W
Storsjøen ⊜	160	60.23 N	11.40 E
Storsjön ⊜	158	63.12 N	14.18 E
Storsteinsfjellet Λ	160	68.14 N	17.52 E
Storthoaks	252	49.22 N	101.38 W
Storuman	160	65.06 N	17.06 E
Storvindeln ⊜	160	65.43 N	17.05 E
Storvreta	160	59.58 N	17.42 E
Story	256	44.35 N	106.53 W
Story City	244	42.11 N	93.36 W
Stottville	261	42.17 N	73.45 W
Stouchsburg	262	40.23 N	76.14 W
Stoufferstown	262	39.56 N	77.38 W
Stouffville	264	43.58 N	79.15 W
Stoughton, Sask., Can.	252	49.41 N	103.03 W
Stoughton, Mass., U.S.	261	42.07 N	71.06 W
Stoughton, Wis., U.S.	268	42.55 N	89.13 W
Stour ≃	162	50.43 N	1.46 W
Stourbridge	174	52.27 N	2.09 W
Stourport-on-Severn	174	52.21 N	2.16 W
Stover	248	38.27 N	92.59 W
Stow, Mass., U.S.	261	42.26 N	71.30 W
Stow, N.Y., U.S.	266	42.09 N	79.25 W
Stow, Ohio, U.S.	266	41.10 N	81.27 W
Stowe, Pa., U.S.	262	40.15 N	75.39 W
Stowe, Vt., U.S.	242	44.28 N	72.41 W
Stowmarket	174	52.11 N	1.00 E
Stoyoma Mountain Λ	238	49.59 N	121.13 W
Stoystown	266	40.06 N	78.57 W
Strabane, N. Ire., U.K.	162	54.49 N	7.27 W
Strabane, Pa., U.S.	266	40.08 N	80.10 W
Stradeč'	164	51.56 N	23.40 E
Stradella	182	45.05 N	9.18 E
Straelen	178	51.27 N	6.16 E
Straffordville	264	42.45 N	80.47 W
Strahan	226	42.09 S	145.19 E
Strakonice	164	49.16 N	13.55 E
Stralsund	164	54.19 N	13.05 E
Strambino	182	45.23 N	7.53 E
Strand	224	34.06 S	18.50 E
Stranda	160	59.21 N	5.51 E
Strangford Lough ⊜	162	54.26 N	5.36 W
Stráni	164	48.55 N	17.42 E
Stranraer	162	54.55 N	5.02 W
Strasbourg	180	48.35 N	7.45 E
Strasburg, D.D.R.	164	53.30 N	13.44 E
Strasburg, Colo., U.S.	252	39.44 N	104.20 W
Strasburg, N. Dak., U.S.	252	46.08 N	100.10 W
Strasburg, Ohio, U.S.	266	40.36 N	81.32 W
Strasburg, Pa., U.S.	262	39.59 N	76.11 W
Strasburg, Va., U.S.	242	38.59 N	78.22 W
Strasswalchen	164	47.59 N	13.15 E
Stratford, Ont., Can.	264	43.22 N	80.57 W
Stratford, N.Z.	230	39.21 S	174.18 E
Stratford, Calif., U.S.	272	36.11 N	119.49 W
Stratford, Conn., U.S.	261	41.14 N	73.07 W
Stratford, Iowa, U.S.	244	42.16 N	93.56 W
Stratford, Okla., U.S.	250	34.48 N	96.58 W
Stratford, Tex., U.S.	250	36.20 N	102.04 W
Stratford, Wis., U.S.	244	44.48 N	90.04 W
Stratford Centre	260	45.47 N	71.17 W
Stratford-on-Avon	174	52.12 N	1.41 W
Strathlorne	240	46.11 N	61.17 W
Strathmore, Alta., Can.	238	51.03 N	113.23 W
Strathmore, Calif., U.S.	258	36.09 N	119.04 W
Strathroy	244	42.57 N	81.38 W
Strathy Point ≻	162	58.35 N	4.01 W
Strattanville	266	41.12 N	79.20 W
Stratton, Colo., U.S.	252	39.18 N	102.36 W
Stratton, Maine, U.S.	242	45.08 N	70.26 W
Stratton, Nebr., U.S.	252	40.09 N	101.14 W
Stratton, Ohio, U.S.	266	40.32 N	80.38 W
Stratton Mountain Λ	242	43.05 N	72.56 W
Straubing	164	48.53 N	12.34 E
Strausberg	164	52.35 N	13.53 E
Strausstown	262	40.30 N	76.11 W
Strawberry	272	38.13 N	118.35 W
Strawberry ≃, Ark., U.S.	248	35.53 N	91.13 W
Strawberry ≃, Utah, U.S.	254	40.10 N	110.24 W
Strawberry Daniels Pass)(	254	40.19 N	111.15 W
Strawberry Mountain Λ	256	44.19 N	118.43 W
Strawberry Point	244	42.41 N	91.32 W
Strawberry Reservoir ⊜[1]	254	40.11 N	111.08 W
Strawberry Valley	272	39.34 N	121.06 W
Strawn	250	32.33 N	98.30 W
Strážnice	164	48.54 N	17.18 E
Strážske	164	48.53 N	21.50 E
Streatham	238	53.52 N	126.12 W
Streator	268	41.07 N	88.50 W
Streda nad Bodrogem	164	48.23 N	21.46 E
Středočeská vrchovina ⛰	164	49.40 N	14.20 E
Středočeský □[4]	164	49.55 N	14.30 E
Stredoslovenský □[4]	164	48.50 N	19.10 E
Street	174	51.07 N	2.42 W
Streeter	252	46.39 N	99.21 W
Streetman	250	31.53 N	96.19 W
Streetsboro	266	41.14 N	81.21 W
Streetsville	264	43.35 N	79.42 W
Strehaia	172	44.37 N	23.12 E
Strelka-Čun'a	186	61.45 N	102.48 E
Strel'na	160	66.06 N	38.40 E
Strel'na ≃	160	66.04 N	38.39 E
Strel'skaja	160	59.28 N	47.47 E
Stresa	170	45.53 N	8.32 E
Stříbro	164	49.46 N	13.00 E
Strimaaon (Struma) ≃	172	40.47 N	23.51 E
Strimonikós Kólpos C	172	40.40 N	23.50 E
Stringtown	250	34.28 N	96.03 W
Strobel	294	32.03 S	60.37 W
Strobleton	266	41.22 N	79.25 W
Strogonof Point ≻	236	56.53 N	158.49 W
Stroh	268	41.35 N	85.12 W
Stroma I	162	58.42 N	3.04 W
Stromboli, Isola I	170	38.48 N	15.13 E
Strome	238	52.48 N	112.04 W
Stromeferry	162	57.21 N	5.34 W
Stromness	162	58.57 N	3.18 W
Stromsburg	252	41.07 N	97.36 W
Strömstad	160	58.56 N	11.10 E
Strömsund	160	63.51 N	15.35 E
Strong, Ark., U.S.	248	33.07 N	92.21 W
Strong, Maine, U.S.	242	44.48 N	70.13 W
Strong ≃	248	31.51 N	90.08 W
Strong City	252	38.24 N	96.32 W
Stronghurst	244	40.45 N	90.55 W
Strongoli	170	39.15 N	17.03 E
Strongstown	266	40.33 N	78.55 W
Strongsville	266	41.19 N	81.50 W
Stronsay I	162	59.08 N	2.38 W
Stropkov	164	49.12 N	21.40 E
Stroud, Eng., U.K.	174	51.45 N	2.12 W
Stroud, Okla., U.S.	250	35.45 N	96.40 W
Stroudsburg	242	40.59 N	75.12 W
Struer	160	56.29 N	8.37 E
Struga	172	41.11 N	20.40 E
Strugi-Krasnyje	160	58.17 N	29.06 E
Strum	244	44.33 N	91.24 W
Struma (Strimón) ≃	172	40.47 N	23.51 E
Strumica	172	41.26 N	22.38 E
Struthers	266	41.04 N	80.38 W
Stryj	158	49.15 N	23.51 E
Stryker, Mont., U.S.	238	48.41 N	114.46 W
Stryker, Ohio, U.S.	268	41.30 N	84.25 W
Strykersville	264	42.42 N	78.27 W
Stryków	164	51.55 N	19.37 E
Strzegom (Striegau)	164	50.57 N	16.21 E
Strzegowo Osada	164	52.55 N	20.18 E
Strzelce Krajeńskie (Friedeberg in der Neumark)	164	52.53 N	15.32 E
Strzelce Opolskie (Gross Strehlitz)	164	50.31 N	18.19 E
Strzelin (Strehlen)	164	50.47 N	17.03 E
Strzelno	164	52.38 N	18.11 E
Strzyżów	164	49.52 N	21.47 E
Stuart, Fla., U.S.	246	27.12 N	80.15 W
Stuart, Iowa, U.S.	252	41.30 N	94.19 W
Stuart, Nebr., U.S.	252	42.36 N	99.08 W
Stuart, Va., U.S.	246	36.38 N	80.16 W
Stuart ≃	238	54.00 N	123.32 W
Stuart Island I	236	63.35 N	162.30 W
Stuart Lake ⊜	238	54.32 N	124.35 W
Stuart Mountains ⛰	230	45.00 S	167.37 E
Stuarts Draft	246	38.01 N	79.02 W
Stubbekøbing	164	54.53 N	12.03 E
Studénka	164	49.42 N	18.05 E
Studen Kladenec, Jazovir ⊜[1]	212	41.37 N	25.30 E
Stuie	238	52.22 N	126.02 W
Stukenbrock	178	51.54 N	8.39 E
Stump Creek	266	41.01 N	78.50 W
Stump Lake ⊜	252	47.54 N	98.24 W
Stupino	160	54.53 N	38.05 E
Stura di Demonte ≃	170	44.40 N	7.53 E
Sturbridge	261	42.07 N	72.05 W
Sturgeon	248	39.14 N	92.17 W
Sturgeon ≃, Ont., Can.	244	46.19 N	79.58 W
Sturgeon ≃, Mich., U.S.	244	45.50 N	86.41 W
Sturgeon ≃, Mich., U.S.	244	47.02 N	88.30 W
Sturgeon ≃, Mich., U.S.	244	45.24 N	84.38 W
Sturgeon Bay	244	44.50 N	87.23 W
Sturgeon Falls	244	46.22 N	79.55 W
Sturgeon Lake ⊜, Alta., Can.	238	55.06 N	117.30 W
Sturgeon Lake ⊜, Ont., Can.	244	44.28 N	78.42 W
Sturgeon Lake Indian Reserve ⇠[4]	238	55.04 N	117.29 W
Sturgis, Ky., U.S.	248	37.33 N	87.59 W
Sturgis, Mich., U.S.	268	41.48 N	85.25 W
Sturgis, Miss., U.S.	248	33.21 N	89.03 W
Sturgis, S. Dak., U.S.	252	44.25 N	103.31 W
Štúrovo	164	47.48 N	18.49 E
Sturt, Mount Λ	228	29.33 S	141.42 E
Sturt Desert ⇠[2]	228	28.30 S	141.00 E
Sturtevant	268	42.42 N	87.54 W
Stutterheim	224	32.33 S	27.28 E
Stuttgart, B.R.D.	164	48.46 N	9.11 E
Stuttgart, Ark., U.S.	248	34.30 N	91.33 W
Stuyvesant	261	42.24 N	73.47 W
Stuyvesant Falls	261	42.21 N	73.44 W
Stykkishólmur	160a	65.06 N	22.48 W
Styx ≃	248	30.31 N	87.27 W
Suaçuí Grande ≃	296	18.50 S	41.46 W
Suaita	290	6.07 N	73.27 W
Suakin Archipelago II	220	18.42 N	38.30 E
Sual	202	16.04 N	120.05 E
Suaqui Grande	278	28.24 N	109.54 W
Suatá ≃	290	7.52 N	65.22 W
Subansiri ≃	206	26.48 N	93.50 E
Subata	160	56.01 N	25.56 E
Subi, Pulau I	200	2.55 N	108.50 E
Subiaco	184	41.55 N	13.06 E
Subic	202	14.53 N	120.14 E
Subic Bay C	202	14.45 N	120.15 E
Sublette	252	37.29 N	100.50 W
Sublett Range ⛰	256	42.20 N	112.50 W
Subotica	172	46.06 N	19.39 E
Sučan	186	43.08 N	133.09 E
Sucarnoochee ≃	248	32.25 N	88.02 W
Suceava	172	47.39 N	26.19 E
Suceava ≃	172	47.32 N	26.32 E
Sucha	164	49.44 N	19.36 E
Suchań (Zachan)	164	53.17 N	15.19 E
Suchana	186	68.45 N	118.00 E
Süchbaatar	190	50.17 N	106.10 E
Suchedniów	164	51.03 N	20.51 E
Suchiapa ≃	278	16.36 N	93.01 W
Súchil	278	23.38 N	103.55 W
Suchiniči	158	54.06 N	35.20 E
Suchitepéquez □[5]	280	14.25 N	91.20 W
Suchitoto	280	13.56 N	89.02 W
Suchobezvodnoje	160	57.03 N	44.50 E
Suchoborka	160	59.06 N	49.58 E
Suchona ≃	160	60.46 N	46.24 E
Suchou → Suzhou	196	31.18 N	120.37 E
Suchoverkovo	160	56.37 N	35.35 E
Süchow → Xuzhou	194	34.16 N	117.11 E
Süchteln	178	51.17 N	6.22 E
Suchumi	158	43.01 N	41.02 E
Sucio ≃, Col.	290	7.27 N	77.07 W
Sucio ≃, El Sal.	280	14.02 N	89.17 W
Suck ≃	162	53.16 N	8.03 W
Sucker Creek Indian Reserve ⇠[4]	238	55.28 N	116.10 W
Sucre, Bol.	292	19.02 S	65.17 W
Sucre, Col.	290	8.49 N	74.44 W
Sucre, Ec.	290	1.16 S	80.26 W
Sucre □[3]	290	10.25 N	63.30 W
Sucre □[5]	290	9.00 N	75.00 W
Sucúa	290	2.28 S	78.10 W
Sucuaro	290	4.34 N	68.50 W
Sucunduri ≃	292	5.50 S	59.32 W
Sucuriú ≃	296	20.47 S	51.38 W
Sucy-en-Brie	176	48.46 N	2.32 E
Sud, Canal du Ц	282	18.35 N	73.00 W
Sud, Massif du ⛰	282	18.25 N	73.55 W
Sud, Pointe ≻	225a	11.53 S	43.49 E
Sudaj	160	58.58 N	43.08 E
Sudan	250	34.04 N	102.32 W
Sudan □[1]	214	15.00 N	30.00 E
Sudan ⇠[1]	214	10.00 N	20.00 E
Südbaden □[5]	180	48.15 N	8.00 E
Sudbury, Ont., Can.	244	46.30 N	81.00 W
Sudbury, Eng., U.K.	174	52.02 N	0.44 E
Sudbury, Mass., U.S.	261	42.23 N	71.25 W
Suddie	290	7.08 N	58.29 W
Sudeten → Sudety ⛰	164	50.30 N	16.00 E
Sudety ⛰	164	50.30 N	16.00 E
Südlengern	178	52.11 N	8.38 E
Sudlersville	262	39.11 N	75.52 W
Sudogda	160	55.57 N	40.50 E
Sud-Ouest, Pointe ≻	240	49.23 N	63.36 W
Südwürttemberg-Hohenzollern □[5]	180	48.15 N	9.10 E
Sue ≃	220	7.41 N	28.03 E
Sueca	168	39.12 N	0.19 W
Suedberg	262	40.32 N	76.28 W
Suemez Island I	236	55.17 N	133.21 W
Suez → As-Suways	220	29.58 N	32.33 E
Suez, Gulf of → Suways, Khalīj as- C	220	29.00 N	32.50 E
Suez Canal → Suways, Qanāt as- ☰	220	29.55 N	32.33 E
Suffield, Conn., U.S.	261	41.59 N	72.39 W
Suffield, Ohio, U.S.	266	41.01 N	81.21 W
Suffolk	262	36.44 N	76.35 W
Suffolk □[6]	261	40.55 N	72.40 W
Suffolk, East □[6]	174	52.10 N	1.20 E
Suffolk, West □[6]	174	52.10 N	0.45 W
Sufu → Kashi	190	39.29 N	75.59 E
Sugar ≃, U.S.	244	42.26 N	89.12 W
Sugar ≃, N.H., U.S.	242	43.24 N	72.24 W
Sugar City	256	43.52 N	111.45 W
Sugarcreek, Ohio, U.S.	266	40.30 N	81.39 W
Sugar Creek, Pa., U.S.	266	41.26 N	79.53 W
Sugargrove, Pa., U.S.	266	41.59 N	79.21 W
Sugar Grove, Va., U.S.	246	36.47 N	81.25 W
Sugar Hill	246	34.07 N	84.02 W
Sugar Island I	244	46.25 N	84.12 W
Sugar Land	250	29.37 N	95.38 W
Sugarloaf Λ[2]	242	41.24 N	81.06 W
Sugarloaf Mountain Λ, Maine, U.S.	242	45.01 N	70.22 W
Sugarloaf Mountain Λ, Okla., U.S.	248	35.02 N	94.28 W
Sugarloaf Point ≻	228	32.26 S	152.33 E
Sugbai Passage Ц	202	5.23 N	120.35 E
Sugbay	202	7.31 N	123.19 E
Sugbuhan Point ≻	202	10.04 N	126.04 E
Suğla Gölü ⊜	212	37.20 N	32.02 E
Sugluk	232	62.12 N	75.38 W
Sugod	202	12.03 N	124.09 E
Sugoj ≃	186	64.15 N	154.29 E
Sugut ≃	202	6.26 N	117.43 E
Şuḥār	208	24.22 N	56.45 E
Suhl	164	50.37 N	10.41 E
Suhopolje	170	45.48 N	17.30 E
Suhr	180	47.22 N	8.05 E
Suhum	222	6.05 N	0.27 W
Suide	190	37.33 N	110.04 E
Suifenhe	190	44.24 N	131.10 E
Suifu → Yibin, Zhg.	190	28.47 N	104.38 E
Suihua	190	46.37 N	127.00 E
Suijiang ≃	196	26.30 N	114.45 E
Suining	190	30.31 N	105.34 E
Suipacha	294	34.47 S	59.40 W
Suiping	196	33.10 N	113.57 E
Suippes	166	49.08 N	4.32 E
Suir ≃	162	52.15 N	7.00 W
Suisun City	272	38.15 N	122.02 W
Suixian	190	31.42 N	113.20 E
Suizhong	194	40.20 N	120.19 E
Šuja	160	61.55 N	34.12 E
Šuja ≃	160	61.54 N	34.15 E
Sujiatun	194	41.40 N	123.22 E
Šujskoje	160	59.22 N	40.59 E
Sukabumi	198	6.55 S	106.56 E
Sukagawa	192	37.17 N	140.23 E
Sukarno, Pegunungan → Djaja, Puntjak Λ	198	4.04 S	137.10 E
Sukau	202	5.32 N	118.15 E
Sukeva	160	63.52 N	27.26 E
Sukhothai	200	17.01 N	99.49 E
Sukhumi → Suchumi	158	43.01 N	41.02 E
Sukkertoppen	232	65.25 N	52.53 W
Sukkozero	160	63.11 N	32.18 E
Sukkur	206	27.42 N	68.52 E
Sukkwan Island I	236	55.05 N	132.45 W
Sukumo	192	32.56 N	132.44 E
Sukunka ≃	238	55.37 N	121.37 W
Sul, Baía do C	294	27.40 S	48.35 W
Sul, Canal do Ц	286	0.10 S	49.30 W
Sula ≃	160	67.16 N	52.07 E
Sula, Kepulauan II	198	1.52 S	125.22 E
Sulaco ≃	280	15.02 N	87.44 W
Sulaimān Range ⛰	206	30.30 N	70.10 E
Sulat	202	11.49 N	125.27 E
Sulauan Point ≻	202	8.38 N	124.26 E
Sulawesi (Celebes) I	198	2.00 S	121.00 E
Sulcis ⇠[1]	170	39.05 N	8.45 E
Sulechów (Züllichau)	164	52.06 N	15.37 E
Sulęcin (Zielenzig	164	52.26 N	15.08 E
Sulejów	164	51.22 N	19.53 E
Sulejówek	164	52.14 N	21.17 E
Sulina	172	45.09 N	29.40 E
Sulina, Braţul ≃[1]	172	45.09 N	29.41 E
Sulingen	178	52.41 N	8.47 E
Sulitelma Λ	160	67.08 N	16.24 E
Sullana	292	4.53 S	80.42 W
Sulligent	248	33.54 N	88.08 W
Sullivan, Ill., U.S.	248	39.36 N	88.37 W
Sullivan, Ind., U.S.	248	39.06 N	87.24 W
Sullivan, Mo., U.S.	248	38.13 N	91.10 W
Sullivan, Ohio, U.S.	266	41.02 N	82.13 W
Sullivan, Wis., U.S.	268	43.01 N	88.35 W
Sullivan Lake ⊜	238	52.00 N	112.00 W
Sully	162	47.46 N	2.22 E
Sully-sur-Loire	166	47.46 N	2.22 E
Sulmona	184	42.03 N	13.55 E
Sulphur, Yukon, Can.	236	63.47 N	138.53 W
Sulphur, La., U.S.	248	30.14 N	93.23 W
Sulphur, Okla., U.S.	250	34.31 N	96.58 W
Sulphur ≃, Alta., Can.	238	53.50 N	119.10 W
Sulphur ≃, U.S.	248	33.07 N	93.52 W
Sulphur Draw V	250	33.12 N	102.17 W
Sulphur Springs, Ohio, U.S.	266	40.52 N	82.53 W
Sulphur Springs, Tex., U.S.	250	33.08 N	95.36 W
Sulphur Springs Draw V	250	32.12 N	101.36 W
Sultan	270	47.51 N	121.49 W
Sulṭān, Tall as- ⊥	210	31.52 N	35.26 E
Sultana	272	36.33 N	119.20 W
Sultandağı Λ	212	38.58 N	27.26 E
Sultanhisar	172	37.53 N	28.10 E
Sultan sa Barongis	202	6.46 N	124.38 E
Sulu □[4]	202	5.30 N	120.30 E
Suluan Island I	202	10.46 N	125.58 E
Sulu Archipelago II	202	5.30 N	121.30 E
Sulūq	214	31.39 N	20.15 E
Sulu Sea ⊤[2]	202	8.00 N	120.00 E
Sulusi	190	33.08 N	95.08 E
Sulzbach	164	49.18 N	7.07 E
Sulzbach-Rosenberg	164	49.30 N	11.45 E
Šumadija ⇠[1]	172	44.10 N	20.50 E
Sumampa	294	29.20 S	63.30 W
Sumas	256	49.00 N	122.13 W
Sumatera I	198	0.05 S	102.00 E
Sumatera Barat □[4]	200	0.30 S	100.30 E
Sumatera Utara □[4]	200	2.20 N	99.00 E
Sumatra → Sumatera I	198	0.05 S	102.00 E
Sumaúma	292	7.50 S	60.02 W
Šumava ⛰	164	49.00 N	13.30 E
Sumba I	226	10.00 S	120.00 E
Sumbang Point ≻	202	5.50 N	125.10 E
Sumbar ≃	208	38.00 N	55.17 E
Sumbawa I	226	8.40 S	118.00 E
Sumbawa Besar	226	8.30 S	117.26 E
Sumbawanga	218	7.58 S	31.37 E
Sumbay	292	15.58 S	71.25 W
Sümber	190	46.21 N	108.25 E
Sumbilla	168	43.10 N	1.40 W
Sumburgh Head ≻	162	59.51 N	1.16 W
Sümeg	164	46.59 N	17.17 E
Šumen	172	43.16 N	26.55 E
Sumenep	198	7.01 S	113.52 E
Šumerl'a	160	55.30 N	46.26 E
Sumgait	208	40.36 N	49.38 E
Sumgait ≃	208	40.37 N	49.37 E
Šumicha	158	55.14 N	63.19 E
Sumilao	202	8.18 N	124.56 E
Šumilino	160	55.18 N	29.37 E
Sumisu-jima I	190	31.27 N	140.03 E
Sumiswald	180	47.02 N	7.45 E
Sumlug ≃	202	6.52 N	126.03 E
Summerdale	262	40.18 N	76.56 W
Summerfield, Fla., U.S.	246	29.00 N	82.02 W
Summerfield, N.C., U.S.	246	36.12 N	79.54 W
Summerford	240	49.29 N	54.47 W
Summerhill	266	40.22 N	78.46 W
Summer Island I	244	45.34 N	86.39 W
Summer Lake ⊜	256	42.50 N	120.45 W
Summerland	238	49.39 N	119.33 W
Summerside	240	46.24 N	63.47 W
Summersville, Mo., U.S.	248	37.11 N	91.40 W
Summersville, W. Va., U.S.	242	38.17 N	80.51 W
Summerton	246	33.36 N	80.20 W
Summerville, Ga., U.S.	246	34.29 N	85.21 W
Summerville, S.C., U.S.	246	33.01 N	80.11 W
Summit, Alaska, U.S.	236	63.20 N	149.08 W
Summit, Calif., U.S.	274	34.20 N	117.25 W
Summit, Ill., U.S.	268	41.47 N	87.48 W
Summit, Miss., U.S.	248	31.17 N	90.28 W
Summit, N.J., U.S.	262	40.43 N	74.22 W
Summit, S. Dak., U.S.	252	45.18 N	97.02 W
Summit, Wash., U.S.	270	47.10 N	122.21 W
Summit □[6]	266	41.05 N	81.31 W
Summit Λ	230	40.28 S	176.08 E
Summit Lake	238	54.17 N	122.38 W
Summit Mountain Λ	258	39.23 N	116.28 W
Summit Peak Λ	254	37.21 N	106.42 W
Summit Rock Λ	230	45.26 S	170.04 E
Summit Station	262	40.34 N	76.12 W
Summitville, Ind., U.S.	268	40.20 N	85.39 W
Summitville, Ohio, U.S.	266	40.41 N	80.53 W
Sumner, Iowa, U.S.	244	42.51 N	92.06 W
Sumner, Miss., U.S.	248	33.58 N	90.22 W
Sumner, Wash., U.S.	270	47.12 N	122.14 W
Sumner, Lake ⊜	230	42.42 S	172.13 E
Sumner Strait Ц	236	56.15 N	133.45 W
Sumoto	192	34.21 N	134.54 E
Šumperk	164	49.58 N	16.58 E
Sumrall	248	31.25 N	89.33 W
Sumskij Posad	160	64.15 N	35.25 E
Šumšu, Ostrov I	186	50.45 N	156.20 E
Sumter	246	33.55 N	80.20 W
Sumy	158	50.55 N	34.45 E
Sun ≃	256	48.29 N	111.55 W
Suna	160	57.51 N	50.05 E
Suna ≃	160	62.08 N	34.12 E
Sunagawa	192a	43.29 N	141.55 E
Sunapee Lake ⊜	242	43.23 N	72.03 W
Sunaysilah ⊜	208	35.35 N	41.53 E
Sunbright	246	36.15 N	84.40 W
Sunburst	256	48.53 N	111.55 W
Sunbury, N.C., U.S.	246	36.27 N	76.37 W
Sunbury, Ohio, U.S.	266	40.14 N	82.52 W
Sunbury, Pa., U.S.	242	40.52 N	76.47 W
Sunchales	294	30.57 S	61.35 W
Sunchild Indian Reserve ⇠[4]	238	52.43 N	115.24 W
Suncho Corral	294	27.56 S	63.26 W
Sunch'ŏn, C.M.I.K.	194	39.26 N	125.54 E
Sunch'ŏn, Taehan	194	34.57 N	127.28 E
Sun City, Ariz., U.S.	254	33.36 N	112.17 W
Sun City, Calif., U.S.	274	33.42 N	117.11 W
Suncook	242	43.08 N	71.27 W
Suncook ≃	242	43.08 N	71.28 W
Sunda, Selat Ц	198	6.00 S	105.45 E
Sundance	252	44.24 N	104.23 W
Sundarbans ⇠[1]	206	22.00 N	89.00 E
Sunda Strait → Sunda, Selat Ц	198	6.00 S	105.45 E
Sunde	160	59.50 N	5.43 E
Sunderland, Ont., Can.	264	44.16 N	79.04 W
Sunderland, Eng., U.K.	162	54.55 N	1.23 W
Sunderland, Mass., U.S.	261	42.28 N	72.35 W
Sundern	178	51.20 N	8.00 E
Sundown	250	33.27 N	102.29 W
Sundre	238	51.48 N	114.38 W
Sundridge	244	45.46 N	79.24 W
Sundsvall	160	62.23 N	17.18 E
Sunfield	268	42.45 N	85.00 W
Sunflower	248	33.33 N	90.32 W
Sunflower, Mount Λ	252	39.04 N	102.01 W
Sungaipenuh	198	2.05 S	101.23 E
Sungchiang → Songjiang	196	31.01 N	121.14 E
Sungei Patani	200	5.38 N	100.29 E
Sungi Point ≻	202	10.44 N	125.50 E

Symbols in the index entries are identified on page 360.

Name	Page	Lat°′	Long°′
Suniteyouqi	190	42.32 N	112.58 E
Sunland Park	254	32.15 N	106.45 W
Sunndalsøra	160	62.40 N	8.33 E
Sunne	160	59.50 N	13.09 E
Sunnī, Khawr ∨	220	7.09 N	28.41 E
Sunnybrae	240	45.24 N	62.30 W
Sunnydale	270	47.28 N	122.20 W
Sunnymead	274	33.56 N	117.15 W
Sunnymede	268	41.04 N	85.05 W
Sunnynook	238	51.17 N	111.40 W
Sunnyside, Newf., Can.	240	47.52 N	53.55 W
Sunnyside, Calif., U.S.	272	32.40 N	117.01 W
Sunnyside, Utah, U.S.	254	39.33 N	110.24 W
Sunnyside, Wash., U.S.	256	46.20 N	120.00 W
Sunnyslope, Alta., Can.	238	51.40 N	113.32 W
Sunnyslope, Wash., U.S.	270	47.30 N	122.44 W
Sunnyvale	272	37.23 N	122.01 W
Suno ≃	290	0.42 S	77.08 W
Sunol	272	37.36 N	121.53 W
Sun Prairie	268	43.11 N	89.13 W
Sunray	250	36.01 N	101.49 W
Sunrise	254	42.20 N	104.42 W
Sunrise Heights	268	42.18 N	85.09 W
Sunsas, Serranía de ∧∧	292	17.57 S	59.35 W
Sunset, La., U.S.	248	30.25 N	92.04 W
Sunset, Tex., U.S.	250	33.27 N	97.46 W
Sunset Beach	275c	21.40 N	158.03 W
Sunset Crater National Monument ♠	254	35.18 N	111.21 W
Sunset Prairie	238	55.50 N	120.48 W
Sunset Valley	266	40.18 N	79.44 W
Sunshine	236	62.10 N	150.04 W
Suntar	186	62.10 N	117.40 E
Suntar-Chajata, Chrebet ∧∧	186	62.00 N	143.00 E
Suntrana	236	63.51 N	148.51 W
Sun Valley	256	43.42 N	114.21 W
Sun Village	274	34.35 N	118.03 W
Sunwapta ≃	238	52.32 N	117.41 W
Sunwui → Jiangmen	196	22.35 N	113.05 E
Sunyani	222	7.20 N	2.20 W
Suoche (Yarkand)	206	38.25 N	77.16 E
Suoguohu ⊜	190	42.18 N	101.08 E
Suojarvi	160	62.05 N	32.21 E
Suolun	190	46.36 N	121.13 E
Suomussalmi	186	64.53 N	29.05 E
Suō-nada ▾2	192	33.50 N	131.30 E
Suonenjoki	160	62.37 N	27.08 E
Suordach	186	66.43 N	132.04 E
Suozong	190	31.50 N	93.45 E
Supamo ≃	290	6.48 N	61.50 W
Superior, Ariz., U.S.	254	33.18 N	111.06 W
Superior, Mont., U.S.	256	47.12 N	114.53 W
Superior, Nebr., U.S.	252	40.01 N	98.04 W
Superior, Wis., U.S.	244	46.44 N	92.05 W
Superior, Wyo., U.S.	254	41.46 N	108.58 W
Superior, Laguna C	278	16.20 N	94.55 W
Superior, Lake ⊜	244	48.00 N	88.00 W
Superior Upland ∧∧1	244	46.00 N	90.30 W
Supetar	170	43.23 N	16.33 E
Suphan Buri	200	14.29 N	100.10 E
Suphan Buri ≃	200	13.29 N	100.17 E
Supraśl	164	53.13 N	23.20 E
Supraśl ≃	164	53.04 N	22.56 E
Sup'ung-chŏsuji ⊜1	194	40.30 N	125.05 E
Sūq ash-Shuyūkh	208	30.53 N	46.28 E
Suqian	196	33.59 N	118.18 E
Suquamish	270	47.44 N	122.33 W
Suquṭrā I	204	12.30 N	54.00 E
Ṣūr (Tyre), Lubnān	210	33.16 N	35.11 E
Ṣūr, 'Umān	204	22.35 N	59.31 E
Sur, Punta ≻	294	36.53 S	56.41 W
Sura	160	53.53 N	45.45 E
Sura ≃	160	56.06 N	46.00 E
Surabaja	198	7.15 S	112.45 E
Surakarta	226	7.35 S	110.50 E
Šurany	164	48.06 N	18.14 E
Surat	206	21.12 N	72.50 E
Surat Thani (Ban Don)	200	9.06 N	99.20 E
Suraż, Pol.	164	52.58 N	22.58 E
Suraž, S.S.S.R.	160	55.25 N	30.44 E
Surdulești	172	44.23 N	24.57 E
Surdulica	172	42.41 N	22.10 E
Surendranagar	206	22.43 N	71.38 E
Suretka	280	9.34 N	82.56 W
Surf City	262	39.40 N	74.10 W
Surfers Paradise	228	28.00 S	153.26 E
Surgères	166	46.07 N	0.45 W
Surgideo de Batabanó	284p	22.43 N	82.17 W
Surgoinsville	246	36.27 N	82.59 W
Surgut	186	61.14 N	73.20 E
Suribao ≃	202	11.33 N	125.28 E
Surigao	202	9.48 N	125.30 E
Surigao del Norte □4	202	9.35 N	125.36 E
Surigao del Sur □4	202	9.00 N	126.00 E
Surigao Strait ⊔	202	10.20 N	125.25 E
Surin	200	14.53 N	103.30 E
Surinam □2	286	4.00 N	56.00 W
Suring	244	44.59 N	88.22 W
Surkhāb ≃	206	36.47 N	68.44 E
Šurma	160	56.58 N	50.21 E
Sūrmaq	204	31.03 N	52.48 E
Surprise	254	33.38 N	112.20 W
Surrency	246	31.44 N	82.12 W
Surrey □6	174	51.10 N	0.20 W
Surry	262	37.08 N	76.50 W
Surry □6	262	37.10 N	76.50 W
Sursee	180	47.10 N	8.06 E
Surskoje	160	54.30 N	46.44 E
Surt	214	31.12 N	16.35 E
Surt, Khalīj C	214	31.30 N	18.00 E
Surtainville	162	49.25 N	1.50 W
Surtsey I	160a	63.16 N	20.32 W
Surud Ad ∧	214	10.41 N	47.18 E
Suruga-wan C	192	34.51 N	138.33 E
Surumu ≃	290	3.22 N	60.19 W
Survey Pass)(	236	67.51 N	154.06 W
Šuryškary	186	65.54 N	65.22 E
Susa, It.	182	45.08 N	7.03 E
Susa, Nihon	192	34.37 N	131.36 E
Susak, Otok I	170	44.31 N	14.18 E
Susaki	192	33.22 N	133.17 E
Susan	262	37.22 N	76.19 W
Susan ≃	258	40.19 N	120.17 W
Susana Knolls	274	34.16 N	118.41 W
Sūsangerd	208	31.34 N	48.11 E
Susanino	160	58.09 N	41.36 E
Susanville	258	40.25 N	120.39 W
Šušenskoje	186	59.19 N	91.58 E
Sušice	164	49.14 N	13.32 E
Susitna	236	61.33 N	150.31 W
Susitna ≃	236	61.16 N	150.30 W
Suslonger	160	56.18 N	48.13 E
Susoh	198	3.43 N	96.49 E
Suspiro del Moro, Puerto)(	168	37.04 N	3.39 W
Susquehanna	242	41.57 N	75.36 W
Susquehanna ≃	242	39.33 N	76.05 W
Susques	294	23.25 S	66.30 W
Süssen	180	48.41 N	9.45 E
Sussex, N.B., Can.	240	45.43 N	65.31 W
Sussex, N.J., U.S.	242	41.13 N	74.36 W
Sussex, Va., U.S.	262	36.55 N	77.17 W
Sussex, Wis., U.S.	268	43.08 N	88.13 W
Sussex □6, Del., U.S.	262	38.42 N	75.23 W
Sussex □6, Va., U.S.	262	36.50 N	77.15 W
Sussex, East □6	174	50.55 N	0.15 E
Sussex, West □6	174	50.55 N	0.35 W
Susuman	186	62.47 N	148.10 E
Susurluk	172	39.54 N	28.10 E
Susuzmüsellim	172	41.06 N	27.03 E
Susz (Rosenberg)	164	53.44 N	19.20 E
Sutersville	266	40.14 N	79.48 W
Sutherland, S. Afr.	218	32.24 S	20.40 E
Sutherland, Iowa, U.S.	252	42.58 N	95.29 W
Sutherland, Nebr., U.S.	252	41.10 N	101.08 W
Sutherland □6	162	58.13 N	4.30 W
Sutherland ≃	238	54.29 N	125.05 W
Sutherlin	256	43.25 N	123.19 W
Sutlej (Langchuhe) ≃	206	29.23 N	71.02 E
Sutter	272	39.10 N	121.45 W
Sutter □6	272	39.08 N	121.37 W
Sutter Creek	272	38.23 N	120.48 W
Suttle	248	32.32 N	87.11 W
Sutton, Ont., Can.	244	44.18 N	79.22 W
Sutton, Qué., Can.	260	45.06 N	72.37 W
Sutton, Alaska, U.S.	236	61.43 N	148.53 W
Sutton, Mass., U.S.	261	42.09 N	71.45 W
Sutton, Nebr., U.S.	252	40.36 N	97.52 W
Sutton, W. Va., U.S.	242	38.40 N	80.43 W
Sutton •8	174	51.22 N	0.12 W
Sutton Coldfield	174	52.34 N	1.48 W
Sutton-in-Ashfield	174	53.08 N	1.15 W
Suttons Bay	244	44.59 N	85.39 W
Sutton West	264	44.18 N	79.22 W
Suttor ≃	228	21.25 S	147.45 E
Suttsu	192a	42.48 N	140.14 E
Sutwik Island I	236	56.34 N	157.05 W
Suurberge ∧∧	224	33.18 S	25.32 E
Suva Planina ∧∧	172	43.10 N	22.10 E
Suwa	192	36.02 N	138.08 E
Suwa-ko ⊜	192	36.05 N	138.05 E
Suwałki	164	54.07 N	22.56 E
Suwannee ≃	246	29.18 N	83.09 W
Suwanose-jima I	193b	29.38 N	129.43 E
Suwanose-suidō ⊔	193b	29.32 N	129.40 E
Suways, Khalīj as- (Gulf of Suez) C	220	29.00 N	32.50 E
Suways, Qanat as- (Suez Canal) ≅	220	29.55 N	32.33 E
Suwŏn	194	37.17 N	127.01 E
Suxian	196	33.38 N	116.58 E
Suyo	290	4.35 S	80.01 W
Suzak	186	44.07 N	68.28 E
Suzaka	192	36.39 N	138.19 E
Suzdal'	160	56.25 N	40.26 E
Suzhou → Jiuquan, Zhg.	190	39.45 N	98.34 E
Suzhou (Soochow), Zhg.	196	31.18 N	120.37 E
Suzihe ≃	194	41.55 N	124.17 E
S'uzikozero	160	61.48 N	37.20 E
Suzu	192	37.25 N	137.17 E
Suzuka	192	34.51 N	136.35 E
Suzuka-sammyaku ∧∧	192	35.00 N	136.25 E
Suzu-misaki ≻	192	37.31 N	137.21 E
Suzzara	170	45.00 N	10.45 E
Svalbard II	148	78.00 N	20.00 E
Svanskog	160	59.11 N	12.33 E
Svappavaara	160	67.39 N	21.04 E
Svärdsjö	160	60.45 N	15.55 E
Svartenhuk ≻1	232	71.55 N	55.00 W
Svartisen ∧	160	66.38 N	14.00 E
Svataj	186	67.57 N	151.54 E
S'vatoj Nos, Mys ≻, S.S.S.R.	160	68.10 N	39.45 E
Sv'atoj Nos, Mys ≻, S.S.S.R.	186	72.52 N	140.42 E
Sveg	160	62.02 N	14.21 E
Sveindal	160	58.30 N	7.28 E
Svelgen	160	61.47 N	5.15 E
Svelvik	160	59.37 N	10.24 E
Švenčionėliai	160	55.10 N	26.00 E
Svendborg	160	55.03 N	10.37 E
Svenljunga	160	57.30 N	13.07 E
Svenson	270	46.10 N	123.40 W
Sverdlovsk, S.S.S.R.	158	48.05 N	39.40 E
Sverdlovsk, S.S.S.R.	158	56.51 N	60.36 E
Sverdrup, Ostrov I	186	74.35 N	74.30 E
Sveti Arhandjel Mihajlo ☩1	172	42.07 N	21.28 E
Sveti Jovan Bigorski ☩1	172	41.38 N	20.37 E
Sveti Nicole	172	41.52 N	21.58 E
Svetlaja	186	46.33 N	138.18 E
Světlá nad Sázavou	164	49.40 N	15.25 E
Svetlogorsk [Rauschen]	164	54.57 N	20.10 E
Svetlograd	158	45.20 N	42.40 E
Svetlyj	160	54.41 N	20.08 E
Svetlyj [Peyse]	164	54.41 N	20.08 E
Svetogorsk	160	61.07 N	28.51 E
Svetozarevo	172	43.58 N	21.16 E
Svidník	164	49.18 N	21.35 E
Svijaga ≃	160	55.36 N	48.30 E
Svilajnac	172	44.14 N	21.13 E
Svilengrad	172	41.46 N	26.12 E
Svinecea ∧	172	44.48 N	22.09 E
Svir'	160	54.51 N	26.24 E
Svir' ≃	160	60.30 N	32.48 E
Svirica	160	60.29 N	32.51 E
Svirsk	186	53.04 N	103.21 E
Svir'stroj	160	60.48 N	33.43 E
Svisloč'	164	53.02 N	24.06 E
Svištov	172	43.37 N	25.20 E
Svit	164	49.03 N	20.12 E
Svitávka	164	49.30 N	16.37 E
Svitavy	164	49.45 N	16.27 E
Svobodnyj	186	52.20 N	46.22 E
Svoge	172	42.58 N	23.21 E
Svolvær	160	68.14 N	14.34 E
Svratka ≃	164	49.11 N	16.38 E
Swadlincote	174	52.47 N	1.33 W
Swaffham	162	52.39 N	0.41 E
Swain	266	42.29 N	77.51 W
Swain Reefs ∻2	228	21.40 S	152.15 E
Swainsboro	246	32.36 N	82.20 W
Swakop ≃	224	22.38 S	14.36 E
Swakopmund	218	22.41 S	14.34 E
Swakopmund □5	224	22.00 S	14.30 E
Swampscott	261	42.28 N	70.55 W
Swan ≃, Alta., Can.	238	55.31 N	115.17 W
Swan ≃, Minn., U.S.	244	47.01 N	93.16 W
Swanage	174	50.37 N	1.58 W
Swan Hill	228	35.21 S	143.34 E
Swan Hills	238	54.52 N	115.45 W
Swan Hills ∧∧2	238	54.48 N	115.52 W
Swanington	268	40.35 N	87.17 W
Swan Islands II	282	17.25 N	83.55 W
Swan Lake, Man., Can.	252	49.24 N	98.46 W
Swan Lake, Mont., U.S.	256	47.55 N	113.50 W
Swan Lake ⊜, Man., Can.	232	52.30 N	100.45 W
Swan Lake ⊜, Minn., U.S.	244	44.19 N	94.15 W
Swannanda	246	35.36 N	82.23 W
Swan Peak ∧	256	47.43 N	113.08 W
Swanquarter	246	35.24 N	76.20 W
Swan Range ∧∧	256	47.50 N	113.40 W
Swan River	232	52.06 N	101.16 W
Swansboro	246	34.36 N	77.07 W
Swansea, Wales, U.K.	174	51.38 N	3.57 W
Swansea, Mass., U.S.	261	41.45 N	71.11 W
Swansea, S.C., U.S.	246	33.44 N	81.06 W
Swans Island I	242	44.10 N	68.25 W
Swanson Lake ⊜1	252	40.09 N	101.06 W
Swanton, Ohio, U.S.	268	41.35 N	83.53 W
Swanton, Vt., U.S.	242	44.55 N	73.07 W
Swanville	244	45.55 N	94.38 W
Swanzey Center	261	42.52 N	72.17 W
Swarthmore	262	39.54 N	75.21 W
Swartz Creek	268	42.58 N	83.50 W
Swarzędz	164	52.26 N	17.05 E
Swasey Wash ∨	254	39.15 N	112.53 W
Swāt ≃	206	34.20 N	71.34 E
Swatow → Shantou	196	23.23 N	116.41 E
Swayzee	268	40.30 N	85.49 W
Swaziland □1	218	26.30 S	31.30 E
Swea City	244	43.23 N	94.19 W
Sweden □1	158	62.00 N	15.00 E
Swedesboro	262	39.45 N	75.15 W
Swedru	222	5.32 N	0.43 W
Sweeny	250	29.02 N	95.42 W
Sweet Briar	246	37.33 N	79.04 W
Sweetgrass	238	49.00 N	111.57 W
Sweetgrass Hills ∧∧2	256	48.55 N	111.30 W
Sweet Home, Oreg., U.S.	256	44.24 N	122.44 W
Sweet Home, Tex., U.S.	250	29.21 N	97.04 W
Sweetser	268	40.34 N	85.46 W
Sweet Springs	248	38.58 N	93.25 W
Sweetwater, Tenn., U.S.	246	35.36 N	84.28 W
Sweetwater, Tex., U.S.	250	32.28 N	100.25 W
Sweetwater ≃	254	42.31 N	107.02 W
Swellendam	218	34.02 S	20.26 E
Swenson	250	33.12 N	100.19 W
Swepsonville	246	36.01 N	79.22 W
Świdnica (Schweidnitz)	164	50.51 N	16.29 E
Świdnik	164	51.14 N	22.41 E
Świdwin (Schivelbein)	164	53.47 N	15.47 E
Świebodzice (Freiburg)	164	50.52 N	16.19 E
Świebodzin (Schwiebus)	164	52.15 N	15.32 E
Świecie	164	53.25 N	18.28 E
Świerzawa (Schönau)	164	51.01 N	15.54 E
Świętokrzyskie, Góry ∧∧	164	50.55 N	21.00 E
Swift ≃	236	61.53 N	156.18 W
Swift Current	232	50.17 N	107.50 W
Swifton	248	35.49 N	91.08 W
Swilly, Lough C	162	55.10 N	7.38 W
Swinburne, Cape ≻	232	71.14 N	98.34 W
Swindle Island I	238	52.32 N	128.35 W
Swindon	174	51.34 N	1.47 W
Swinemünde → Świnoujście	164	53.53 N	14.14 E
Swinford	162	53.57 N	8.57 W
Świnoujście (Swinemünde)	164	53.53 N	14.14 E
Switzerland □1	158	46.00 N	8.30 E
Swords	162	53.28 N	6.13 W
Swords Range ∧∧	228	21.57 S	141.32 E
Swormville	264	43.02 N	78.42 W
Syalach	186	66.12 N	124.00 E
Sycamore, Ga., U.S.	246	31.40 N	83.38 W
Sycamore, Ill., U.S.	268	41.59 N	88.41 W
Sycamore, Ohio, U.S.	266	40.57 N	83.10 W
Sycan ≃	256	42.27 N	121.15 W
Sycaway	261	42.44 N	73.39 W
Syčovka	160	55.50 N	34.17 E
Syców (Gross Wartenberg)	164	51.19 N	17.43 E
Sydenham	264	44.25 N	76.36 W
Sydney, Austl.	228	33.52 S	151.13 E
Sydney, N.S., Can.	240	46.09 N	60.11 W
Sydney Mines	240	46.14 N	60.14 W
Syke	178	52.54 N	8.49 E
Sykesville, Md., U.S.	242	39.22 N	76.58 W
Sykesville, Pa., U.S.	266	41.03 N	78.49 W
Sykkylven	160	62.24 N	6.35 E
Syktyvkar	160	61.40 N	50.46 E
Sylacauga	248	33.10 N	86.15 W
Sylhet	206	24.54 N	91.52 E
Syloga	160	63.50 N	43.39 E
Sylt I	164	54.54 N	8.20 E
Sylva	246	35.23 N	83.13 W
Sylvan	270	45.30 N	122.41 W
Sylvan Grove	252	39.00 N	98.24 W
Sylvan Hills	248	34.51 N	92.12 W
Sylvania, Ga., U.S.	246	32.45 N	81.38 W
Sylvania, Ohio, U.S.	266	41.43 N	83.42 W
Sylvan Lake	238	52.19 N	114.05 W
Sylvan Lake ⊜	238	52.21 N	114.10 W
Sylvan Pass)(	256	44.28 N	110.08 W
Sylvester, Ga., U.S.	246	31.32 N	83.49 W
Sylvester, Tex., U.S.	250	32.43 N	100.15 W
Sylvester, Mount ∧2	240	48.11 N	55.04 W
Sylvia	252	37.57 N	98.24 W
Sylvia Grinnell Lake ⊜	232	64.10 N	69.25 W
Sym	186	60.20 N	88.23 E
Syn'a	160	65.22 N	57.42 E
Syosset	261	40.50 N	73.30 W
Syracuse → Siracusa, It.	170	37.04 N	15.17 E
Syracuse, Ind., U.S.	268	41.26 N	85.45 W
Syracuse, Kans., U.S.	252	37.59 N	101.45 W
Syracuse, Nebr., U.S.	252	40.39 N	96.11 W
Syracuse, N.Y., U.S.	264	43.03 N	76.09 W
Syrdarja	186	40.52 N	68.38 E
Syrdarja ≃	186	46.03 N	61.00 E
Syr-Darya → Syrdarja ≃	186	46.03 N	61.00 E
Syria □1	204	35.00 N	38.00 E
Syrian Desert → Shām, Bādiyat ash- •2	208	32.00 N	40.00 E
Syriam	200	16.46 N	96.15 E
Sysmä	160	61.30 N	25.41 E
Sysola ≃	160	61.42 N	50.53 E
Syzran'	160	53.09 N	48.27 E
Szabolcs-Szatmár □6	164	48.00 N	22.10 E
Szamocin	164	53.02 N	17.08 E
Szamos (Someșul) ≃	172	48.07 N	22.20 E
Szamotuły	164	52.37 N	16.35 E
Szarvas	164	46.52 N	20.34 E
Szczawnica	164	49.26 N	20.30 E
Szczecin (Stettin)	164	53.24 N	14.32 E
Szczecinek (Neustettin)	164	53.43 N	16.42 E
Szczekociny	164	50.38 N	19.50 E
Szczuczyn	164	53.34 N	22.18 E
Szczytno (Ortelsburg)	164	53.34 N	21.00 E
Szécsény	164	48.06 N	19.31 E
Széged	164	46.15 N	20.09 E
Szeghalom	164	47.01 N	21.11 E
Székesfehérvár	164	47.12 N	18.25 E
Szekszárd	164	46.21 N	18.42 E
Szentendre	164	47.40 N	19.05 E
Szentes	164	46.39 N	20.16 E
Szentgotthárd	164	46.57 N	16.17 E
Szerencs	164	48.09 N	21.13 E
Szlichtyngowa (Schlichtingsheim)	164	51.43 N	16.15 E
Szob	164	47.50 N	18.52 E
Szolnok	164	47.10 N	20.12 E
Szolnok □6	164	47.12 N	20.11 E
Szombathely	164	47.14 N	16.38 E
Szprotawa (Sprottau)	164	51.34 N	15.33 E
Sztum (Stuhm)	164	53.56 N	19.01 E
Szubin	164	53.00 N	17.44 E
Szydłowiec	164	51.14 N	20.51 E
Szypliszki	164	54.15 N	23.05 E
Szzarvíz ≃	164	46.24 N	18.41 E
T			
Taal Lake ⊜	202	14.00 N	121.00 E
Taancan Point ≻	202	10.00 N	125.01 E
Taan Ch'i ≃	196	24.22 N	120.42 E
Taavetti	160	60.55 N	27.34 E
Tabacal	294	23.15 S	64.15 W
Tabaco	202	13.22 N	123.44 E
Tabaco Bay C	202	13.20 N	123.45 E
Tabacundo	290	0.03 N	78.12 W
Tabaí	294	26.07 S	55.32 W
Tabaloso	292	6.18 S	76.38 W
Tabango	202	11.12 N	124.22 E
Tábara	168	41.49 N	5.57 W
Tabarca, Isla de I	168	38.10 N	0.28 W
Tabarka	170	36.57 N	8.45 E
Ṭabas	204	33.36 N	56.54 E
Tabasará ≃	280	8.03 N	81.31 W
Tabasará, Serranía de ∧∧	280	8.30 N	81.30 W
Tabasco	278	32.35 N	114.50 W
Tabasco □3	278	18.15 N	93.00 W
Tabatinga ≃	296	17.24 S	43.18 W
Tabatinga, Serra da ∧∧2	286	10.25 S	44.00 W
Tabb	262	37.08 N	76.29 W
Tabelbala	214	29.23 N	3.15 W
Taber	238	49.47 N	112.08 W
Taberg	264	43.18 N	75.37 W
Taberis, Laguna C	280	14.18 N	83.17 W
Tabernes de Valldigna	168	39.04 N	0.16 W
Tablas, Cabo ≻	294	31.51 S	71.34 W
Tablas Island I	202	12.25 N	122.02 E
Tablas Plateau ∧∧1	202	9.39 N	122.40 E
Tablas Strait ⊔	202	12.50 N	121.40 E
Tablat	168	36.24 N	3.19 E
Table Bay C	224	33.53 S	18.27 E
Table Cape ≻	230	39.06 S	178.00 E
Table Mountain ∧, Newf., Can.	240	47.43 N	59.13 W
Table Mountain ∧, Ariz., U.S.	254	32.49 N	110.31 W
Table Rock	252	40.11 N	96.06 W
Table Rock Lake ⊜1	248	36.35 N	93.30 W
Table Top ∧	254	32.46 N	112.07 W
Tabligbo	222	6.35 N	1.30 E
Tablones	284m	18.15 N	65.45 W
Taboan ≃	202	17.57 N	122.11 E
Taboco ≃	292	19.53 S	55.58 W
Taboga	280	8.45 N	79.35 W
Tabogon	202	10.56 N	124.02 E
Tábor, Česko.	164	49.25 N	14.41 E
Tabor, S.S.S.R.	186	71.16 N	150.12 E
Tabor, Iowa, U.S.	252	40.54 N	95.40 W
Tabor, S. Dak., U.S.	252	42.57 N	97.39 W
Tabora	218	5.01 S	32.48 E
Tabor City	246	34.09 N	78.52 W
Tabor, Mount → Tavor, Har ∧	210	32.41 N	35.24 E
Tabou	222	4.25 N	7.21 W
Tabrīz	208	38.05 N	46.18 E
Tabuaço	168	41.07 N	7.34 W
Tabuelan	202	10.50 N	123.52 E
Tabūk, Ar. Sa.	208	28.23 N	36.35 E
Tabuk, Pil.	202	17.24 N	121.25 E
Tacacoma	292	15.35 S	68.43 W
Tacámbaro ≃	278	18.29 N	101.07 W
Tacámbaro de Codallos	278	19.14 N	101.28 W
Tacaná	280	15.14 N	92.05 W
Tacaná, Volcán ∧1	280	15.08 N	92.05 W
Tacañitas	294	28.38 S	62.37 W
Taché, Lac ⊜	232	64.00 N	120.00 W
Tacheng	190	46.45 N	82.57 E
Tachia Ch'i ≃	196	24.19 N	120.34 E
Tachiataš	186	42.25 N	59.35 E
Tachichilte, Isla de I	278	24.55 N	108.13 W
Tachie ≃	238	54.40 N	124.50 W
Tachikawa	192	35.42 N	139.25 E
Táchira □3	290	7.50 N	72.05 W
Tachov	164	49.48 N	12.38 E
Tachta-Bazar	186	35.57 N	62.50 E
Tachtamgyda	186	54.06 N	123.34 E
Taciuã, Lago ≃	290	4.29 S	60.35 W
Tacloban	202	11.15 N	125.00 E
Taclobo	202	12.20 N	122.34 E
Tacna, Perú	292	18.01 S	70.15 W
Tacna, Ariz., U.S.	254	32.41 N	114.01 W
Tacna □5	292	17.40 S	70.20 W
Tacoma	270	47.15 N	122.27 W
Taconic	261	42.02 N	73.25 W
Taconic Range ∧∧2	242	42.40 N	73.15 W
Taco Pozo	294	25.42 S	63.17 W
Tacotalpa ≃	278	17.50 N	92.52 W
Tacuarembó	294	31.44 S	55.59 W
Tacuarembó ≃	294	32.25 S	55.29 W
Tacuarí ≃	294	32.46 S	53.18 W
Tacuatí	294	23.27 S	56.35 W
Tacubaya	278	28.20 N	104.34 W
Tacurong	202	6.42 N	124.42 E
Tacutu (Takutu) ≃	290	3.01 N	60.29 W
Tadami	192	37.21 N	139.19 E
Tademaït, Plateau du ∧∧1	214	28.30 N	2.00 E
Tadía, Ciénaga de ⊜	290	6.48 N	76.49 W
Tadio, Lagune C	222	5.11 N	5.15 W
Tadjenanet	168	36.08 N	5.59 E
Tadjerouine	170	35.54 N	8.34 E
Tadjoura	214	11.47 N	42.54 E
Tadotsu	192	34.16 N	133.45 E
Tadoule Lake ⊜	232	58.36 N	98.20 W
Tadoussac	240	48.09 N	69.43 W
Tad Park	254	40.29 N	112.21 W
Tadzhik Soviet Socialist Republic → Tadžikskaja Sovetskaja Socialističeskaja	186	39.00 N	71.00 E
Tadžikskaja Sovetskaja Socialističeskaja Respublika □3	186	39.00 N	71.00 E
T'aebaek-san ∧	194	37.06 N	128.55 E
T'aebaek-sanmaek ∧∧	190	37.40 N	128.50 E
Taedong-gang ≃	194	38.42 N	125.15 E
Taegu	194	35.52 N	128.35 E
Taehŭksan-do I	194	34.40 N	125.25 E
Taejŏn	194	36.20 N	127.26 E
Taeng ≃	200	19.05 N	98.57 E
Tafalla	168	42.31 N	1.40 W
Tafassasset, Oued ∨	214	21.20 N	10.10 E
Tafí Viejo	294	26.45 S	65.15 W
Tafna, Oued ≃	168	35.17 N	1.30 W
Taft, Pil.	202	11.54 N	125.25 E
Taft, Calif., U.S.	258	35.08 N	119.28 W
Taft, Okla., U.S.	250	35.46 N	95.32 W
Taft, Tex., U.S.	250	27.57 N	97.46 W
Taftān, Kūh-e ∧	208	28.36 N	61.06 E
Tagabukid	202	7.00 N	126.21 E
Tagdempt → Tiaret	214	35.28 N	1.21 E
Tagagawik ≃	236	66.30 N	159.00 W
Tagajō	192	38.20 N	141.00 E
Tagama •1	222	15.50 N	8.12 E
Tagana-an	202	9.41 N	125.34 E
Taganrog	158	47.12 N	38.56 E
Tagapula Island I	202	12.03 N	124.12 E
Tagauayan Island I	202	10.58 N	121.13 E
Tagaytay	202	14.06 N	120.56 E
Tagbilaran	202	9.39 N	123.51 E
Taggia	182	43.52 N	7.51 E
Tagish Lake ⊜	236	59.45 N	134.15 W
Tagliacozzo	184	42.04 N	13.14 E
Taglio di Po	170	45.00 N	12.12 E
Tagnant, Dhar ⩟4	222	18.30 N	11.00 W
Tago	202	9.01 N	126.13 E
Tago ≃	202	9.00 N	126.15 E
Tagoloan	202	8.32 N	124.45 E
Tagolo Point ≻	202	8.43 N	123.23 E
Tagua ≃	290	2.12 N	74.17 W
Taguatinga	296	12.25 S	46.26 W
Tagubanhan Island I	202	11.07 N	123.07 E
Tagudin	202	16.56 N	120.27 E
Taguedoufat ∨	222	14.50 N	7.42 E
Taguke	190	32.07 N	84.35 E
Tagula Island I	226	11.30 S	153.30 E
Tagum	202	7.28 N	125.49 E
Tagun Bay C	202	13.58 N	123.43 E
Tagus (Tejo) (Tajo) ≃	168	38.40 N	9.24 W
Tahan, Gunong ∧	200	4.38 N	102.14 E
Tahat ∧	214	23.18 N	5.47 E
Tahir Geçidi)(	212	39.54 N	42.22 E
Tahiryuak Lake ⊜	232	70.56 N	112.20 W
Tahlequah	250	35.55 N	94.58 W
Tahneta Pass)(	236	61.53 N	147.20 W
Tahoe, Lake ⊜	258	38.58 N	120.00 W
Tahoe City	272	39.10 N	120.09 W
Tahoe Lake ⊜	232	70.15 N	108.45 W
Tahoe Paradise	272	38.52 N	120.01 W
Tahoe Valley	272	38.55 N	120.00 W
Tahoka	250	33.10 N	101.48 W
Taholah	270	47.21 N	124.17 W
Tahoua	222	14.54 N	5.16 E
Tahoua □5	222	16.00 N	5.00 E
Tahquamenon ≃	244	46.34 N	85.02 W
Tahsis	238	49.55 N	126.39 W
Ta Hsü I	196	23.10 N	119.32 E
Ṭahṭā	220	26.46 N	31.30 E
Tahtaköprü	172	39.57 N	29.39 E
Tahtsa Lake ⊜	238	53.42 N	127.26 W
Tahtsa Peak ∧	238	53.33 N	127.47 W
Tahulandang, Pulau I	198	2.21 N	125.24 E
Tahuna	198	3.37 N	125.29 E
Taian	194	36.12 N	117.07 E
Taibaishan ∧	194	39.19 N	114.11 E
Taibilla, Sierra de ∧∧	168	38.10 N	2.10 W
T'aichung	196	24.09 N	120.41 E
Taieri ≃	230	46.03 S	170.12 E
Taihape	230	39.41 S	175.47 E
Taihezhen ⊥	200	85.41 N	100.07 E
Taihoku → T'aipei	196	25.03 N	121.30 E
Taihu ⊜	196	31.15 N	120.10 E
Taijinai'erhu ⊜	206	37.15 N	93.20 E
Tailai	190	46.23 N	123.27 E
Tailfingen	180	48.15 N	9.01 E
Taimba	186	60.18 N	98.58 E
Tain	162	57.48 N	4.04 W
T'ainan	196	23.00 N	120.11 E
T'ainanhsien	196	23.18 N	120.19 E
Taínaron, Ákra ≻	172	36.22 N	22.30 E
Taining	190	26.54 N	117.09 E
Tai O	196	22.15 N	113.51 E
Taiobeiras	296	15.49 S	42.14 W
Taipas	296	12.15 S	47.09 W
T'aipei	196	25.03 N	121.30 E
T'aipeihsien	196	25.00 N	121.27 E
Taiping	200	4.51 N	100.44 E
T'aip'ing Shan ∧	196	24.30 N	121.38 E
Taira → Iwaki, Nihon	192	37.03 N	140.55 E
Taisetsu-zan-kokuritsu-kōen ♠	192a	43.30 N	142.57 E
Taisha	192	35.24 N	132.40 E
Taishan I	196	26.59 N	120.37 E
Taishun	190	27.33 N	119.43 E
T'aitung	198	22.44 N	121.09 E
Taivalkoski	160	65.34 N	28.15 E
Taiwan (T'aiwan) □1	190	23.30 N	121.00 E
T'aiwan (Formosa) I	196	24.00 N	121.00 E
Taiwāra	208	33.31 N	64.22 E
Taixing	196	32.11 N	120.01 E
Taíyetos Óros ∧∧	172	37.16 N	22.12 E
Ṭaiyiba	210	32.16 N	35.00 E
Taiyuan	190	37.55 N	112.30 E
Taizhou	196	32.30 N	119.58 E
Taizhouwan C	196	28.38 N	121.40 E
Taizihe ≃	194	41.00 N	122.26 E
Ta'izz	204	13.38 N	44.04 E
Tajbola	160	68.26 N	33.19 E
Tajga	186	56.04 N	85.37 E
Tajgonos, Poluostrov ≻1	186	61.20 N	161.00 E
Tajima	192	37.12 N	139.46 E
Tajimi	192	35.19 N	137.08 E
Tajique	254	34.45 N	106.17 W
Tajitos	278	30.58 N	112.18 W
Tajmura ≃	186	63.46 N	98.01 E
Tajmyr, Ozero ⊜	186	74.30 N	102.30 E
Tajmyr, Poluostrov ≻1	186	76.00 N	104.00 E
Tajrish	208	35.48 N	51.25 E
Tajšet	186	55.57 N	98.00 E
Tajumulco, Volcán ∧1	280	15.02 N	91.54 W
Tajuña ≃	168	40.07 N	3.35 W
Tak	200	16.52 N	99.08 E
Takachiho	192	32.42 N	131.18 E
Takada	192	37.06 N	138.15 E
Takahagi	192	36.43 N	140.43 E
Takahashi	192	34.47 N	133.37 E
Takalar	198	5.28 S	119.24 E
Takamatsu	192	34.20 N	134.03 E
Takanabe	192	32.08 N	131.30 E
Takanosu	192	40.13 N	140.22 E
Takaoka	192	36.45 N	137.01 E
Takapuna	230	36.47 S	174.46 E
Takara-jima I	193b	29.09 N	129.13 E
Takasago	192	34.45 N	134.48 E
Takasaki	192	36.20 N	139.01 E
Takashima	192	32.39 N	129.45 E
Takatsuki	192	34.51 N	135.37 E
Takawa	192	33.38 N	130.49 E
Takayama	192	36.08 N	137.15 E
Takefu	192	35.54 N	136.10 E
Takeo	192	33.12 N	130.01 E
Take-shima I	193b	30.49 N	130.26 E
Taketa	192	32.58 N	131.24 E
Takêv	200	10.59 N	104.47 E
Takhādīd ▾4	208	29.59 N	44.30 E
Takhar □4	206	36.30 N	69.30 E
Ta Khli	198	15.18 N	100.20 E
Takikawa	192a	43.33 N	141.54 E
Takingeun	198	4.37 N	96.50 E
Takitimu Mountains ∧∧	230	45.35 S	167.50 E
Takiyuak Lake ⊜	232	66.30 N	113.27 W
Takla Lake ⊜	238	55.25 N	125.53 W
Takla Landing	238	55.29 N	125.58 W
Takla Makan → Talimupendi •2	190	39.00 N	83.00 E
Takoradi → Sekondi-Takoradi	222	4.59 N	1.43 W
Takotna	236	62.56 N	156.04 W
Takrouna	170	36.09 N	10.20 E
Takslesluk Lake ⊜	236	61.04 N	162.55 W
Taku	192	33.17 N	130.08 E
Taku ≃	236	58.26 N	133.59 W
Taku Arm ⊜	236	60.00 N	134.10 W
Taku Glacier ⩍	236	58.35 N	134.10 W
Takut Tangug Bay C	202	6.33 N	122.15 E
Takutu (Tacutu) ≃	290	3.01 N	60.29 W
Takysie Lake	238	53.54 N	125.53 W
Tala, Arg.	294	26.07 S	65.17 W
Tala, Méx.	278	20.40 N	103.42 W
Tala, Tun.	170	35.35 N	8.40 E
Tala, Ur.	294	34.21 S	55.46 W
Talacogon	202	8.31 N	125.39 E
Talagante	294	33.40 S	70.56 W
Talak •1	222	18.20 N	6.00 E
Talakag	202	8.16 N	124.37 E
Talamanca, Cordillera de ∧∧	280	9.30 N	83.40 W
Talang, Gunung ∧	200	1.11 S	100.43 E
Talara	290	4.35 S	81.25 W
Talarrubias	168	39.02 N	5.14 W
Talas	186	42.32 N	72.14 E
Talata Mafara	222	12.35 N	6.04 E
Talaud, Kepulauan II	198	4.20 N	126.50 E
Talavera	202	15.35 N	120.55 E
Talavera de la Reina	168	39.57 N	4.50 W
Talawdī	214	10.38 N	30.23 E
Talayan	202	6.55 N	124.24 E
Talbotton	246	32.41 N	84.32 W
Talbragar ≃	228	32.12 S	148.37 E
Talca	294	35.26 S	71.40 W
Talca □4	294	35.30 S	71.10 W
Talcahuano	294	36.43 S	73.07 W
Talco	250	33.22 N	95.06 W
Talcottville	261	41.49 N	72.30 W
Taldom	160	56.44 N	37.32 E
Taldy-Kurgan	186	45.00 N	78.23 E
Talent	256	42.15 N	122.47 W
Talgar	186	43.18 N	77.18 E
Talia	250	25.44 N	102.26 W
Taliabu, Pulau I	198	1.48 S	124.48 E
Taliandao I	194	39.03 N	122.52 E
Talibon	202	10.09 N	124.19 E
Talibong, Ko I	200	7.15 N	99.25 E
Talica	160	58.01 N	51.30 E
Talien → Lüda	194	38.53 N	121.35 E
Talihina	250	34.45 N	95.03 W
Talikud Island I	202	6.56 N	125.42 E
Talim Island I	202	14.22 N	121.14 E
Talimuhe ≃	190	41.05 N	86.40 E
Talimupendi (Takla Makan) •2	190	39.00 N	83.00 E
Talisay, Pil.	202	10.45 N	122.58 E
Talisay, Pil.	202	14.08 N	122.55 E
Talisayan	202	9.00 N	124.53 E
Talish Mountains ∧∧	208	38.42 N	48.18 E
Talkeetna	236	62.20 N	150.07 W
Talkeetna Mountains ∧∧	236	62.10 N	148.15 W
Talladega	248	33.26 N	86.06 W
Tallah	220	28.05 N	30.44 E
Tallahassee	246	30.25 N	84.16 W
Tallahatchie ≃	248	33.33 N	90.10 W
Tallapoosa	248	33.45 N	85.17 W
Tallapoosa ≃	248	32.30 N	86.16 W
Tallard	166	44.28 N	6.03 E
Tallassee	248	32.27 N	85.54 W
Talleyville	262	39.48 N	75.33 W
Tallinn	160	59.25 N	24.45 E
Tallmadge	266	41.06 N	81.27 W
Tallula	248	39.56 N	89.56 W
Tallulah	248	32.25 N	91.11 W
Talmage, Calif., U.S.	258	39.08 N	123.10 W
Talmage, Nebr., U.S.	252	40.32 N	96.01 W
Talmage, Pa., U.S.	262	40.07 N	76.13 W
Tal'menka	186	53.51 N	83.35 E
Talmont	166	46.28 N	1.37 W
Taloga	250	36.02 N	98.58 W
Talon, Lake ⊜	244	46.18 N	79.05 W
Talpa	250	31.47 N	99.43 W
Talquin, Lake ⊜1	246	30.26 N	84.33 W
Taltal	294	25.24 S	70.29 W
Taltapin Lake ⊜	238	54.19 N	125.20 W
Taltson ≃	232	61.23 N	112.45 W
Talumphuk, Laem ≻	200	8.30 N	100.10 E
Talvik'ul'a	160	68.45 N	29.19 E
Talyzino	160	56.06 N	45.49 E
Tama, Arg.	294	30.31 S	66.32 W
Tama, Iowa, U.S.	244	41.58 N	92.35 W
Tamacuarí, Pico ∧	290	1.15 N	64.45 W
Tamalameque	290	8.52 N	73.49 W
Tamale	222	9.25 N	0.50 W
Tamalpais, Mount ∧	258	37.56 N	122.35 W
Tamalpais Valley	272	37.53 N	122.32 W
Tamana	192	32.55 N	130.33 E
Tamaná, Cerro ∧	290	5.02 N	76.17 W
Tamana, Mount ∧	285r	10.28 N	61.12 W
Tamanaco ≃	290	9.25 N	65.23 W
Tamandourirt, Oued ∨	222	19.39 N	2.04 W
Tamaniquá	290	2.38 S	65.44 W
Taman Negara ♠	200	4.43 N	102.23 E
Tamano	192	34.30 N	133.56 E
Tamanrasset	214	22.56 N	5.30 E
Tamapatz	278	21.35 N	99.09 W
Tamaqua	262	40.48 N	75.58 W
Tamaquari, Ilha I	290	0.28 S	64.55 W
Tamar ≃, Austl.	228	41.04 S	146.47 E
Tamar ≃, Col.	290	7.01 N	74.15 W
Támara	290	5.50 N	72.10 W
Tamarac ≃	252	48.29 N	97.07 W
Tamarite de Litera	168	41.52 N	0.26 E
Tamaroa	248	38.08 N	89.14 W
Tamarugal, Pampa del ≚	292	21.00 S	69.25 W
Tamási	164	46.38 N	18.18 E
Tamatave	225b	18.10 S	49.23 E
Tamatave □4	225b	18.00 S	48.40 E
Tamaulipas □3	278	24.00 N	98.45 W
Tamaya ≃	292	8.29 S	74.14 W
Tamazula	278	24.57 N	106.57 W
Tamazula de Gordiano	278	19.38 N	103.15 W
Tamazulapan [del Progreso]	278	17.41 N	97.34 W
Tamazunchale	278	21.16 N	98.47 W
Tambacounda	222	13.47 N	13.40 W
Tamba-kōchi ∧∧1	192	35.20 N	135.30 E
Tambej	186	71.30 N	71.50 E
Tambelan, Kepulauan II	200	1.00 N	107.30 E
Tambelan, Pulau I	200	0.58 N	107.34 E
Tamberías	294	31.27 S	69.26 W
Tambisan, Pulau I	202	5.27 N	119.10 E
Tambler	202	6.03 N	125.09 E
Tambo	292	12.57 S	74.01 W
Tambo ≃, Austl.	228	37.51 S	147.48 E
Tambo ≃, Perú	292	10.43 S	73.48 W
Tambo ≃, Perú	292	17.10 S	71.52 W
Tamboara	296	23.09 S	52.33 W
Tambo Grande	292	4.55 S	80.25 W
Tambohorano	218	17.30 S	43.58 E
Tambopata ≃	292	13.21 S	69.36 W
Tambor	280	9.43 N	85.01 W
Tamboritha, Mount ∧	228	37.28 S	146.41 E
Tambor Yacu ≃	290	2.25 S	73.40 W
Tambov	158	52.43 N	41.25 E
Tambre ≃	168	42.49 N	8.53 W
Tambulian Point ≻	202	7.21 N	123.27 E
Tambura	214	5.36 N	27.28 E
Tamburi	296	13.00 S	40.32 W
Tamchaket	214	17.15 N	10.40 W
Tam Chuak, Laem ≻	200	8.35 N	98.13 E
Tame	290	6.28 N	71.44 W
Tameapa	278	25.39 N	107.22 W
Tâmega ≃	168	41.05 N	8.21 W
Tamel Aike	288	48.20 S	70.58 W
Tamgak, Monts ∧∧	222	19.11 N	8.42 E
Tamgué, Massif du ∧∧	222	12.00 N	12.18 W
Tamiahua	278	21.16 N	97.27 W
Tamiahua, Laguna de C	278	21.35 N	97.35 W
Tamiami Canal ≅	246	25.47 N	80.15 W
Tamica	160	64.10 N	38.05 E
Tamiment	242	41.09 N	75.02 W
Tamiš (Timiș) ≃	172	44.51 N	20.39 E
Tam-ky	198	11.43 N	108.48 E
Tamms	248	37.14 N	89.16 W
Tamós, Laguna de ⊜	278	22.10 N	98.02 W
Tampa	246	27.57 N	82.27 W
Tampa Bay C	246	27.45 N	82.35 W
Tampaon ≃	278	21.59 N	98.36 W
Tamparan	202	8.27 N	117.13 E
Tampere	160	61.30 N	23.45 E
Tampico, Méx.	278	22.13 N	97.51 W
Tampico, Ill., U.S.	244	41.38 N	89.47 W
Tampin	200	2.28 N	102.13 E
Ṭamra	210	32.51 N	35.12 E
Tamrida	204	12.38 N	54.02 E
Tams	246	37.40 N	81.18 W
Tamsagbulag	190	47.16 N	117.17 E
Tamsalu	160	59.10 N	26.06 E
Tamshiyacu	290	4.00 S	73.03 W
Tamsweg	164	47.08 N	13.48 E
Tamulung Point ≻	202	17.15 N	120.25 E
Tamworth, Austl.	228	31.05 S	150.55 E
Tamworth, Ont., Can.	264	44.29 N	77.00 W
Tamworth, Eng., U.K.	174	52.39 N	1.40 W
Tana, Chile	292	19.27 S	69.57 W
Tana, Nor.	160	70.28 N	28.18 E
Tana ≃, Cuba	284p	20.41 N	77.25 W
Tana ≃, Kenya	218	2.32 S	40.31 E
Tana, Lake ⊜	214	12.00 N	37.20 E
Tanabe	192	33.44 N	135.22 E
Tanabi	296	20.37 S	49.37 W
Tanacross	236	63.23 N	143.21 W
Tanafjorden C2	160	70.54 N	28.40 E
Tanaga Island I	236	51.50 N	178.00 W
Tanaga Volcano ∧1	236	51.53 N	178.09 W
Tanahbala, Pulau I	200	0.25 S	98.25 E
Tanahdjampea, Pulau I	198	7.05 S	120.42 E
Tanahmasa, Pulau I	200	0.12 S	98.25 E
Tanah Merah	200	5.47 N	102.08 E
Tan-an	200	10.32 N	106.25 E
Tanana	236	65.10 N	152.05 W
Tanana ≃	236	65.09 N	151.55 W
Tananarive (Antanarivo)	225b	18.55 S	47.31 E
Tananarive □4	225b	19.00 S	47.00 E
Tanauan	202	11.07 N	125.01 E
Tanay	202	14.30 N	121.17 E
Tanchoj	186	51.33 N	105.07 E
Tanch'ŏn	194	40.27 N	128.54 E
Tancítaro, Pico de ∧	278	19.25 N	102.19 W
Tancochapa ≃	278	17.59 N	94.04 W
Tandag	202	9.05 N	126.12 E
Tandaltī	220	13.01 N	31.52 E
Tăndărei	172	44.38 N	27.40 E
Tandil	294	37.20 S	59.05 W
Tandjungbalai	200	2.58 N	99.47 E
Tandjungbatu	200	0.38 N	103.26 E
Tandjungkarang	198	5.25 S	105.16 E
Tandjungpandan	198	2.45 S	107.39 E
Tandjungpinang	200	0.55 N	104.27 E
Tandjungselor	198	2.51 N	117.22 E
Tando Ādam	206	25.46 N	68.40 E
Tandou Lake ⊜	228	32.38 S	142.05 E
Tandubas	202	5.10 N	120.21 E
Tandubas Island I	202	5.08 N	120.20 E
Tandubatu Island I	202	5.14 N	120.17 E
Tanega-shima I	193b	30.40 N	131.00 E
Taneichi	192	40.26 N	141.43 E
Tanew ≃	164	50.31 N	22.16 E
Taneytown	242	39.40 N	77.10 W
Tanezrouft •2	214	24.00 N	0.45 W
Tanga	218	5.04 S	39.06 E
Tangamandapio	278	19.57 N	102.26 W

Symbols in the index entries are identified on page 360.

Name	Page	Lat°′	Long°′
Tanganyika, Lake ⊜	218	6.00 S	29.30 E
Tangará	294	27.08 S	51.13 W
Tanger (Tangier)	168	35.48 N	5.45 W
Tangerhütte	164	52.26 N	11.48 E
Tangermünde	164	52.32 N	11.58 E
Tanggu	194	39.01 N	117.40 E
Tanggulahu ⊜	206	31.00 N	86.20 E
Tanggulashankou)(	206	32.59 N	91.45 E
Tanggulashanmai ⛰	206	33.00 N	90.00 E
Tanghe ≏, Zhg.	194	38.45 N	115.35 E
Tanghe ≏, Zhg.	196	32.09 N	112.25 E
Tangier → Tanger, Magreb	168	35.48 N	5.45 W
Tangier, Va., U.S.	262	37.49 N	75.59 W
Tangipahoa ≏	248	30.20 N	90.18 W
Tanglashankou)(	206	32.40 N	92.24 E
Tangshan	194	39.38 N	118.11 E
Tangub	202	8.03 N	123.44 E
Tanguip Point ≻	202	7.43 N	126.35 E
Tangusu Bay C	202	5.27 N	119.03 E
Tanigawa-dake ∧	192	36.50 N	138.56 E
Tanimbar, Kepulauan II	198	7.30 S	131.30 E
Taninges	170	46.07 N	6.36 E
Tanishpa ∧	206	31.10 N	68.24 E
Tanjay	202	9.31 N	123.09 E
Tanjiang ≏	196	23.57 N	115.47 E
Tanjore → Thanjāvūr	204	10.47 N	79.09 E
Tännàs	160	62.27 N	12.40 E
Tanner, Mount ∧	238	49.40 N	118.34 W
Tannila	160	65.29 N	25.59 E
Tannu-Ola, Chrebet ⛰	186	51.00 N	94.00 E
Tannūrah, Ra's at- ≻	208	26.40 N	50.30 E
Tano ≏	222	5.07 N	2.56 W
Tanon Strait ⊔	202	10.10 N	123.15 E
Tânout	214	14.58 N	8.53 E
Tanquinho	296	11.58 S	39.06 W
Tanshui Ho ≏	196	25.11 N	121.25 E
Tansín, Isla de I	280	15.20 N	84.00 W
Tansín, Laguna de C	280	15.13 N	83.50 W
Ṭanṭā	220	30.47 N	31.00 E
Tantoushan I	196	23.11 N	122.01 E
Tantoyuca	278	21.21 N	98.14 W
Tan'urer ≏	236	64.44 N	174.15 E
Tanvald	164	50.45 N	15.19 E
Tanza	202	14.24 N	120.52 E
Tanzania □[1]	218	6.00 S	35.00 E
Tao, Ko I	200	10.05 N	99.53 E
Taoan	190	45.22 N	122.47 E
Taohuadao I	196	29.48 N	122.17 E
Taojiang ≏	196	25.56 N	115.06 E
Taormina	170	37.52 N	15.17 E
Taos	254	36.24 N	105.34 W
Taouardeï ⊤[4]	222	16.56 N	1.19 E
Taoudenni	214	22.40 N	4.00 W
Taougrite	168	36.15 N	0.55 E
Taoura	170	36.09 N	8.03 E
T'aoyüan	190	25.00 N	121.18 E
Taozikou ≏[1]	196	34.24 N	120.05 E
Tapa	160	59.16 N	25.58 E
Tapaan Island I	202	5.27 N	120.44 E
Tapacarí	292	17.31 S	66.36 W
Tapachula	278	14.54 N	92.17 W
Tapah	200	4.10 N	101.17 E
Tapaiúna, Ribeirão ≏	292	10.47 S	55.56 W
Tapaje ≏	290	2.44 N	78.07 W
Tapajós ≏	290	2.24 S	54.41 W
Tapalquén	294	36.20 S	60.02 W
Tapanahoni ≏	286	4.20 N	54.25 W
Tapauá	292	5.45 S	63.04 W
Tapauá ≏	292	5.40 S	64.21 W
Tapaz	202	11.16 N	122.31 E
Tapejara	294	28.04 S	52.00 W
Tapera	294	28.38 S	52.52 W
Taperas	292	17.54 S	60.23 W
Taperoá	296	13.31 S	39.06 W
Tapes	294	30.40 S	51.23 W
Taphaen ≏	200	14.07 N	99.25 E
Taphan Hin	200	16.12 N	100.26 E
Ta Pi ≏	200	9.05 N	99.12 E
Tapiantana Channel ⊔	202	6.23 N	122.00 E
Tapiantana Group II	202	6.17 N	122.00 E
Tapiantana Island I	202	6.18 N	121.59 E
Tapiche ≏	292	5.03 S	73.51 W
Tapiraí	296	19.52 S	46.01 W
Tapis, Gunong ∧	200	4.03 N	102.54 E
Tapiutan Island I	202	11.13 N	119.15 E
Tapolca	164	46.53 N	17.27 E
Tappahannock	262	37.56 N	76.52 W
Tappen	252	46.52 N	99.38 W
Tappi-zaki ≻	192	41.15 N	140.21 E
Tāpti ≏	206	21.05 N	72.40 E
Tapuaenuku ∧	230	42.00 S	173.40 E
Tapul Group II	202	5.35 N	120.50 E
Tapul Island I	202	5.43 N	120.55 E
Tapurucuara	290	0.24 S	65.02 W
Taqāṭu' Hayyā	214	18.20 N	36.22 E
Taquara	294	29.39 S	50.47 W
Taquara, Igarapé ≏	292	7.40 S	68.12 W
Taquaral	296	16.01 S	49.38 W
Taquaral, Serra do ⛰	296	15.42 S	52.30 W
Taquaras, Ponta das ≻	294	27.01 S	48.34 W
Taquari, Bra.	294	29.48 S	51.51 W
Taquari, Bra.	296	17.50 S	53.17 W
Taquari ≏, Bra.	292	19.15 S	57.17 W
Taquari ≏, Bra.	294	29.56 S	51.44 W
Taquari ≏, Bra.	296	23.16 S	49.12 W
Taquari, Pantanal do ☷	292	18.20 S	56.30 W
Taquaritinga	296	21.24 S	48.30 W
Taquaruçu ≏	296	21.35 S	52.07 W
Tar ≏	246	35.33 N	77.05 W
Tara, Ont., Can.	264	44.28 N	81.09 W
Tara, S.S.S.R.	186	56.54 N	74.22 E
Tara ⛰	172	43.55 N	19.25 E
Tara ≏	172	43.21 N	18.51 E
Tarabuco	292	19.10 S	64.57 W
Ṭarābulus (Tripoli), Lībiya	214	32.54 N	13.11 E
Ṭarābulus (Tripoli), Lubnān	212	34.26 N	35.51 E
Ṭarābulus ↵[1]	214	31.00 N	15.00 E
Taradale	230	39.32 S	176.51 E
Taraira (Traíra) ≏	290	1.04 S	69.26 W
Tara Island I	202	12.17 N	120.22 E
Tarakan	198	3.18 N	117.38 E
Taramakau ≏	230	42.34 S	171.08 E
Taranaki □[9]	230	39.20 S	174.30 E
Tarancón	168	40.01 N	3.00 W
Taranga I	230	35.58 S	174.43 E
Tarangnan	202	11.54 N	124.45 E
Taransay I	162	57.55 N	7.10 W
Taranto	170	40.28 N	17.15 E
Taranto, Golfo di C	170	40.10 N	17.20 E
Tarapacá	290	2.52 S	69.44 W
Tarapacá □[4]	292	20.00 S	69.20 W
Tarapoto	292	6.30 S	76.20 W
Ṭaraq al-Hbâri ↵[1]	212	34.17 N	39.16 E
Ṭaraq an-Na'jah ↵[1]	212	34.16 N	39.53 E
Ṭaraq Sidâoui ↵[1]	212	34.33 N	39.54 E
Taraquá	290	0.06 N	68.28 W
Tarare	180	45.54 N	4.26 E
Tarariras	294	34.17 S	57.37 W
Tararua Range ⛰	230	40.48 S	175.24 E
Tarascon, Fr.	168	42.51 N	1.36 E
Tarascon, Fr.	182	43.48 N	4.40 E
Tarasovo, S.S.S.R.	160	62.49 N	41.10 E
Tarasovo, S.S.S.R.	160	66.13 N	46.39 E
Tarata, Bol.	292	17.37 S	66.01 W
Tarata, Perú	292	17.27 S	70.02 W
Tarauacá	292	8.10 S	70.46 W
Tarauacá ≏	292	6.42 S	69.48 W
Taravo ≏	170	41.42 N	8.49 E
Tarawera, Lake ⊜	230	38.12 S	176.27 E
Tarawera, Mount ∧	230	39.03 S	176.30 E
Tarazit, Massif de ⛰	222	20.00 N	8.25 E
Tarazona de Aragón	168	41.54 N	1.44 W
Tarazona de la Mancha	168	39.15 N	1.55 W
Tarbagataj, Chrebet ⛰	186	47.12 N	83.00 E
Tarbert	162	57.54 N	6.49 W
Tarbes	166	43.14 N	0.05 E
Tarboro	246	35.54 N	77.32 W
Tarbū	214	26.02 N	15.10 E
Tarcento	170	46.13 N	13.13 E
Tarcoola	226	30.41 S	134.33 E
Tardajos	168	42.21 N	3.49 W
Tardoki-Jani, Gora ∧	186	48.55 N	138.04 E
Taree	228	31.54 S	152.28 E
Tareja	186	73.20 N	90.37 E
Tärendö	160	67.10 N	22.38 E
Tarentum	266	40.36 N	79.45 W
Ṭarfā, Wādī aṭ- ∨	220	28.25 N	30.50 E
Ṭarfāwī, Bi'r ⊤[4], Miṣr	220	22.55 N	28.53 E
Tarfawi, Bi'r ⊤[4], Sūd.	220	21.04 N	34.08 E
Tarfaya	214	27.58 N	12.55 W
Targhee Pass)(	256	44.41 N	111.17 W
Targon	166	44.44 N	0.16 W
Targuist	168	34.57 N	4.18 W
Târgu-Mureş → Tîrgu-Mureş	172	46.33 N	24.33 E
Tarhūnah	214	32.26 N	13.38 E
Tari	198	5.50 S	143.00 E
Táriba	290	7.49 N	72.13 W
Tarica	280	12.56 N	84.41 W
Tarifa	168	36.01 N	5.36 W
Tarifa, Punta de ≻	168	36.00 N	3.37 W
Tariffville	261	41.55 N	72.46 W
Tarija	292	21.31 S	64.45 W
Tarija □[5]	292	21.30 S	64.00 W
Tariku ≏	198	3.04 S	138.09 E
Tarim → Talimuhe ≏	190	41.05 N	86.40 E
Taritatu ≏	198	2.54 S	138.27 E
Tarka, Vallée de ∨	222	14.00 N	6.00 E
Tarkastad	218	32.00 S	26.16 E
Tarkil	261	41.57 N	71.35 W
Tarkio	248	40.27 N	95.23 W
Tarkio ≏	252	40.10 N	95.26 W
Tarko-Sale	186	64.55 N	77.49 E
Tarkwa	222	5.19 N	1.59 W
Tarlac	202	15.29 N	120.35 E
Tarlac □[4]	202	15.30 N	120.25 E
Tarlac ≏	202	15.45 N	120.28 E
Tarm	160	55.55 N	8.32 E
Tarma	292	11.25 S	75.43 W
Tarn □[5]	166	43.50 N	2.00 E
Tarn ≏	166	44.05 N	1.06 E
Tärna	160	65.43 N	15.16 E
Tarna ≏	164	47.31 N	19.59 E
Tarnāk ≏	206	31.25 N	65.30 E
Tarna Mare	172	47.29 N	26.20 E
Tarn-et-Garonne □[5]	166	44.05 N	1.20 E
Tarnica ∧	164	49.05 N	22.42 E
Tarnobrzeg	164	50.35 N	21.41 E
Tarnogród	164	50.23 N	22.45 E
Tarnogskij Gorodok	160	60.29 N	43.33 E
Tarnopol → Ternopol'	158	49.34 N	25.36 E
Tarnów	164	50.01 N	21.00 E
Tarnowskie Góry	164	50.27 N	18.52 E
Taro ≏	170	45.00 N	10.15 E
Taroom	226	25.39 S	149.49 E
Tarouadji, Massif de ⛰	222	17.15 N	8.33 E
Tarouca	168	41.00 N	7.40 W
Ta-roun, Co ∧	200	17.17 N	106.17 E
Tarpon Springs	246	28.09 N	82.45 W
Tarquí	290	1.40 S	75.15 W
Tarquinia	184	42.15 N	11.45 E
Tarra ≏	290	9.05 N	72.30 W
Tarragona	168	41.07 N	1.15 E
Tarrakoski ↳	160	68.10 N	20.00 E
Tarran Hills ⛰[2]	228	32.27 S	146.27 E
Tarrant	248	33.34 N	86.46 W
Tarrasa	168	41.34 N	2.01 E
Tárrega	168	41.39 N	1.09 E
Tarrs	266	40.10 N	79.35 W
Tarrytown	261	41.05 N	73.52 W
Tarsus	212	36.55 N	34.53 E
Tartagal, Arg.	294	22.32 S	63.50 W
Tartagal, Arg.	294	28.40 S	59.50 W
Tartas	166	43.50 N	0.48 W
Tartu	160	58.23 N	26.43 E
Ṭarṭūs	208	34.53 N	35.53 E
Tarumirim	296	19.16 S	41.59 W
Tarumizu	192	31.29 N	130.42 E
Tarutung	200	2.01 N	98.57 E
Tarvisio	170	46.30 N	13.35 E
Tarza	160	62.30 N	40.25 E
Tarzan	250	32.18 N	101.58 W
Taşağıl	172	41.31 N	27.07 E
Tašauz	186	41.50 N	59.58 E
Tašauz □[4]	208	50.15 N	59.00 E
Tasejeva ≏	186	58.06 N	94.01 E
Tasejevo	186	57.12 N	94.54 E
Taseko ≏	238	52.00 N	123.40 W
Taseko Lakes ⊜	238	51.15 N	123.35 W
Taseko Mountain ∧	238	51.14 N	123.28 W
Tashibuhu ⊜	206	32.10 N	85.05 E
Ṭashk, Daryācheh-ye ⊜	208	29.45 N	53.35 E
Tashkent → Taškent	186	41.20 N	69.18 E
Tāshkurghān	206	36.43 N	67.41 E
Tasikmalaja	226	7.20 S	108.12 E
Taškent, S.S.S.R.	204	41.20 N	69.18 E
Taškepri	186	36.18 N	62.38 E
Taslina	236	62.04 N	146.27 W
Tasman, Mount ∧	230	43.34 S	170.09 E
Tasman Basin ✧[1]	148	44.00 S	157.00 E
Tasman Bay C	230	41.00 S	173.15 E
Tasmania □[3]	228	43.00 S	147.00 E
Tasmania I	228	42.00 S	147.00 E
Tasman Mountains ⛰	230	41.05 S	172.35 E
Tasman Peninsula ≻[1]	228	43.05 S	147.50 E
Tasman Sea ⊤[2]	148	40.00 S	163.00 E
Taşnad	172	47.29 N	22.35 E
Tassialuk, Lac ⊜	232	59.00 N	74.00 W
Tassin-la-Demi-Lune	182	45.46 N	4.47 E
Taštagol	186	52.47 N	87.53 E
Tastiota	278	28.22 N	111.23 W
Tata	164	47.39 N	18.18 E
Tatabánya	164	47.34 N	18.26 E
Tatalan Island I	202	6.14 N	121.59 E
Tata Mailau, Monte ∧	198	8.55 S	125.30 E
Tatamy	262	40.44 N	75.15 W
Tatarinka	160	55.58 N	33.54 E
Tatarlar	172	41.46 N	26.55 E
Tatarsk	186	55.13 N	75.58 E
Tatarskij Proliv ⊔	186	50.00 N	141.15 E
Tatarskoje-Maklakovo	160	55.48 N	45.34 E
Tatar Strait → Tatarskij Proliv ⊔	186	50.00 N	141.15 E
Tate	246	34.25 N	84.23 W
Tate ≏	228	17.22 S	143.44 E
Tateyama	192	34.59 N	139.52 E
Tate-yama ∧	192	36.35 N	137.37 E
Tathlina Lake ⊜	232	60.32 N	117.32 W
Tatitlek	236	60.52 N	146.41 W
Tatla Lake	238	51.55 N	124.36 W
Tatlayoko Lake	238	51.39 N	124.24 W
Tatlayoko Lake ⊜	238	51.30 N	124.25 W
Tatlow, Mount ∧	238	51.23 N	123.52 W
Tatnam, Cape ≻	232	57.16 N	91.00 W
Tatos Dağları ⛰	212	40.55 N	41.10 E
Tatrzański Park Narodowy ♠	164	49.15 N	20.00 E
Tatsuno, Nihon	192	35.59 N	137.59 E
Tatsuno, Nihon	192	34.52 N	134.33 E
Tatta	204	24.45 N	67.55 E
Tatu Ch'i ≏	196	24.12 N	120.29 E
Tatuk Lake ⊜	238	53.32 N	124.15 W
Tatum, N. Mex., U.S.	250	33.16 N	103.19 W
Tatum, Tex., U.S.	248	32.19 N	94.31 W
Tat'ung → Datong	190	40.08 N	113.13 E
Tat'un Shan ∧	196	25.10 N	121.31 E
Tatvan	158	38.30 N	42.16 E
Tatzuli Ch'i ≏	196	24.08 N	121.40 E
Tau	160	59.04 N	5.54 E
Taubaté	296	23.02 S	45.33 W
Tauber ≏	164	49.46 N	9.31 E
Tauberbischofsheim	164	49.37 N	9.40 E
Taučik	158	44.21 N	51.19 E
Taujskaja Guba C	186	59.20 N	150.20 E
Taulabé	280	14.38 N	87.59 W
Taumarunui	230	38.53 S	175.17 E
Taumaturgo	292	8.57 S	72.48 W
Taum Sauk Mountain ∧	248	37.34 N	90.44 W
Taunay	292	20.18 S	56.05 W
Taungdwingyi	200	20.01 N	95.33 E
Taunggyi	200	20.47 N	97.02 E
Taungnyo Range ⛰	200	15.38 N	97.56 E
Taungup Pass)(	200	18.40 N	94.45 E
Taunton, Eng., U.K.	174	51.01 N	3.06 W
Taunton, Mass., U.S.	261	41.54 N	71.06 W
Taunton, N.Y., U.S.	264	43.01 N	76.13 W
Taunus ⛰	164	50.10 N	8.15 E
Taupo	230	38.41 S	176.05 E
Taupo, Lake ⊜	230	38.48 S	175.55 E
Tauragė	160	55.15 N	22.17 E
Tauranga	230	37.42 S	176.10 E
Tauranga ≏	230	38.04 S	177.00 E
Taurianova	170	38.21 N	16.01 E
Tauripampa	292	12.40 S	76.08 W
Taurisma	292	15.11 S	72.51 W
Tauroa Point ≻	230	35.10 S	173.04 E
Taurus Mountains → Toros Dağları ⛰	212	37.00 N	33.00 E
Tauste	168	41.55 N	1.15 W
Tavajvaam ≏	236	64.56 N	177.30 W
Tavaputs Plateau ⛰[1]	254	39.45 N	110.00 W
Tavares	246	28.48 N	81.44 W
Tavda	158	58.03 N	65.15 E
Tavda ≏	186	59.20 N	63.28 E
Tavernier	246	25.01 N	80.31 W
Taverny	176	49.02 N	2.13 E
Tavira	168	37.07 N	7.39 W
Tavistock, Ont., Can.	264	43.19 N	80.50 W
Tavistock, Eng., U.K.	174	50.33 N	4.08 W
Tavoliere ↵[1]	170	41.35 N	15.25 E
Tavolžan	186	52.44 N	77.27 E
Tavor, Har ∧	210	32.41 N	35.24 E
Távora ≏	168	41.09 N	7.35 W
Tavoy	200	14.05 N	98.12 E
Tavoy Point ≻	200	13.32 N	98.10 E
Tavşanlı	172	39.33 N	29.30 E
Tawa	230	41.10 S	174.50 E
Tawakoni, Lake ⊜[1]	250	32.55 N	96.00 W
Tawas City	244	44.16 N	83.31 W
Tawau	198	4.17 N	117.54 E
Ṭawīlah, Juzur II	220	27.35 N	33.46 E
Tawitawi Group II	202	5.10 N	120.10 E
Tawitawi Island I	202	5.12 N	120.00 E
Ṭawkar	220	18.26 N	37.44 E
Taxco de Alarcón	278	18.33 N	99.36 W
Taxisco	280	14.04 N	90.28 W
Tay, Loch ⊜	162	56.30 N	4.10 W
Tayabamba	292	8.15 S	77.15 W
Tayabas	202	14.02 N	121.35 E
Tayabas Bay C	202	13.47 N	121.45 E
Tay-bac, Khu-tu-tri □[4]	200	21.30 N	103.30 E
Tay-chang, Deo)(	200	21.07 N	103.00 E
Taylor, B.C., Can.	238	56.10 N	120.41 W
Taylor, Ariz., U.S.	254	34.28 N	110.05 W
Taylor, Ark., U.S.	248	33.06 N	93.28 W
Taylor, Mich., U.S.	268	42.13 N	83.16 W
Taylor, Miss., U.S.	248	34.16 N	89.35 W
Taylor, Nebr., U.S.	252	41.46 N	99.23 W
Taylor, Tex., U.S.	250	30.34 N	97.25 W
Taylor, Mount ∧, N.Z.	230	43.30 S	171.29 E
Taylor, Mount ∧, N. Mex., U.S.	254	35.14 N	107.37 W
Taylor Mountain ∧	256	44.53 N	114.13 W
Taylor Mountains ⛰	236	60.50 N	157.20 W
Taylor Ridge ∧	246	34.35 N	85.12 W
Taylors	246	34.55 N	82.18 W
Taylors Island	262	38.28 N	76.18 W
Taylorstown	266	40.10 N	80.23 W
Taylorsville, Ind., U.S.	248	39.18 N	85.57 W
Taylorsville, Ky., U.S.	248	38.02 N	85.21 W
Taylorsville, Miss., U.S.	248	31.50 N	89.32 W
Taylorsville, N.C., U.S.	246	35.55 N	81.04 W
Taylortown	266	40.28 N	80.40 W
Taylorville	248	39.33 N	89.18 W
Taymā'	208	27.38 N	38.29 E
Taymouth	240	46.11 N	66.37 W
Taymyr Peninsula → Tajmyr, Poluostrov ≻[1]	186	76.00 N	104.00 E
Tay-ninh	200	11.18 N	106.05 E
Tayoltita	278	24.05 N	105.56 W
Taytay, Pil.	202	14.34 N	121.08 E
Taytay, Pil.	202	10.50 N	119.31 E
Taytay Bay C	202	10.55 N	119.35 E
Tayug	202	16.02 N	120.45 E
Taz ≏	186	67.32 N	78.40 E
Taza	214	34.16 N	4.01 W
Tazawa-ko ⊜	192	39.43 N	140.40 E
Tazewell, Tenn., U.S.	246	36.27 N	83.34 W
Tazewell, Va., U.S.	246	37.07 N	81.31 W
Tazin Lake ⊜	232	59.47 N	109.03 W
Tazlina Lake ⊜	236	61.50 N	146.30 W
Tazoult	168	35.29 N	6.15 E
Tazovskaja Guba C	186	69.05 N	76.00 E
Tazovskij	186	67.28 N	78.42 E
Tazumal ⊥	280	13.59 N	89.41 W
Tbilisi, S.S.S.R.	204	41.43 N	44.49 E
Tbong	200	13.21 N	105.07 E
Tchefuncta ≏	248	30.22 N	90.10 W
Tchentlo ⊜	238	55.11 N	125.00 W
Tchibanga	218	2.51 S	11.02 E
Tchien	222	6.04 N	8.08 W
Tchula	248	33.11 N	90.13 W
Tczew	164	54.06 N	18.47 E
Tea ≏	290	0.30 S	65.09 W
Teaca	172	46.55 N	24.31 E
Teacapán	278	22.33 N	105.45 W
Teague	250	31.38 N	96.17 W
Te Anau, Lake ⊜	230	45.15 S	167.46 E
Teano	184	41.15 N	14.04 E
Teapa	278	17.33 N	92.57 W
Te Aroha	230	37.33 S	175.43 E
Teaticket	261	41.34 N	70.36 W
Te Awamutu	230	38.01 S	175.19 E
Teba	168	36.58 N	4.56 W
Tébessa	170	35.28 N	8.09 E
Tebicuary ≏	294	26.36 S	58.16 W
Tebicuary-Mí ≏	294	26.26 S	56.51 W
Tebingtinggi	200	3.20 N	99.09 E
Tebingtinggi, Pulau I	200	0.54 N	102.45 E
Tébourba	170	36.49 N	9.51 E
Téboursouk	170	36.28 N	9.15 E
Téboursouk, Monts de ⛰	170	36.30 N	9.10 E
Tecalitlán	278	19.26 N	103.15 W
Tecamachalco	278	18.53 N	97.44 W
Tecate	278	32.34 N	116.38 W
Tech ≏	166	42.36 N	3.03 E
Techiman	222	7.35 N	1.56 W
Techirghiol	172	44.03 N	28.36 E
Tecka	288	43.30 S	70.51 W
Tecklenburg	164	52.13 N	7.48 E
Tecolotlan	278	20.13 N	104.03 W
Tecomán	278	18.55 N	103.53 W
Tecopa	258	35.51 N	116.13 W
Tecpan de Galeana	278	17.15 N	100.41 W
Tecpán Guatemala	280	14.46 N	91.00 W
Tecuala	278	22.23 N	105.27 W
Tecuamburro, Volcán ∧[1]	280	14.09 N	90.24 W
Tecuci	172	45.50 N	27.26 E
Tecumseh, Ont., Can.	266	42.19 N	82.54 W
Tecumseh, Mich., U.S.	268	42.00 N	83.57 W
Tecumseh, Nebr., U.S.	252	40.22 N	96.11 W
Tecumseh, Okla., U.S.	250	35.15 N	96.56 W
Tedrow	268	41.37 N	84.13 W
Tedžen	208	37.23 N	60.31 E
Tedžen (Harīrūd) (Harī) ≏	208	37.24 N	60.38 E
Teec Nos Pas	254	36.55 N	109.07 W
Teesside → Middlesbrough	162	54.35 N	1.14 W
Teels Marsh ☷	258	38.12 N	118.21 W
Teeswater	264	44.00 N	81.17 W
Tefé	290	3.22 S	64.42 W
Tefé ≏	290	3.35 S	64.47 W
Tefé, Lago de ⊜	290	3.27 S	64.47 W
Tefenni	172	37.18 N	29.47 E
Tefft	268	41.12 N	86.58 W
Tegal	198	6.52 S	109.08 E
Tegelen	178	51.21 N	6.09 E
Tegernsee	164	47.43 N	11.45 E
Tegucigalpa	280	14.06 N	87.13 W
Tehachapi	274	35.08 N	118.27 W
Tehachapi Mountains ⛰	258	34.56 N	118.40 W
Tehek Lake ⊜	232	64.55 N	95.38 W
Tehrān	208	35.40 N	51.26 E
Teheran → Tehrān	208	35.40 N	51.26 E
Tehrān	208	35.40 N	51.26 E
Tehrān □[4]	208	35.30 N	51.00 E
Tehuacán	278	18.27 N	97.23 W
Tehuantepec	278	16.20 N	95.14 W
Tehuantepec, Golfo de C	278	16.00 N	94.50 W
Tehuantepec, Istmo de •[3]	278	17.00 N	94.30 W
Tehuantepec Ridge ✧[3]	148	13.00 N	98.45 W
Tehulmixtle, Bahía de C	278	20.12 N	105.40 W
Teide, Pico de ∧	214	28.16 N	16.38 W
Teiga Plateau ⛰[1]	220	15.38 N	25.40 E
Teignmouth	174	50.33 N	3.30 W
Teixeira da Silva	218	12.12 S	15.52 E
Teixeira de Sousa	218	10.42 S	22.12 E
Teixeiras	296	20.39 S	42.51 W
Teixeira Soares	294	25.22 S	50.27 W
Tejamén	278	24.48 N	105.07 W
Tejkovo	160	56.52 N	40.34 E
Tejon Pass)(	258	34.48 N	118.52 W
Tejupan, Punta ≻	278	18.20 N	103.32 W
Tejupilco [de Hidalgo]	278	18.54 N	100.09 W
Tekamah	252	41.47 N	96.13 W
Tekapo ≏	230	44.32 S	170.12 E
Tekapo, Lake ⊜	230	43.48 S	170.32 E
Tekax de Álvaro Obregón	278	20.12 N	89.17 W
Teke	172	41.04 N	29.39 E
Teke Burnu ≻, Tür.	212	38.05 N	26.36 E
Teke Burnu ≻, Tür.	212	40.02 N	26.10 E
Tekeli	186	44.48 N	78.57 E
Tekeze (Satīt) ≏	220	14.20 N	35.50 E
Tekirdağ	212	40.59 N	27.31 E
Tekirdağ □[4]	172	41.00 N	27.30 E
Tekoa	256	47.14 N	117.04 W
Tekonsha	268	42.05 N	84.59 W
Te Kuiti	230	38.20 S	175.10 E
Tela	280	15.44 N	87.27 W
Tela, Bahía de C	280	15.52 N	87.30 W
Telaga	202	6.51 N	117.03 E
Telanaipura (Djambi)	198	1.36 S	103.37 E
Telaopengshashan ∧	206	30.33 N	86.25 E
Tel Ashqelon ⊥	210	31.40 N	34.34 E
Telavåg	160	60.16 N	4.49 E
Tel Aviv □[5]	210	32.07 N	34.45 E
Tel Aviv-Yafo	210	32.03 N	34.46 E
Telč	164	49.11 N	15.27 E
Telefomin	198	5.10 S	141.35 E
Telegraph Cove	238	50.33 N	126.50 W
Telegraph Creek	236	57.55 N	131.10 W
Telemark □[6]	160	59.30 N	8.40 E
Telembí ≏	290	1.50 N	78.16 W
Telén	294	36.15 S	65.31 W
Telen ≏	198	0.26 S	116.42 E
Teleormanul ≏	172	43.52 N	25.26 E
Telerig	172	43.51 N	27.40 E
Telescope Peak ∧	258	36.10 N	117.05 W
Teles Pires ≏	296	7.21 S	58.03 W
Telford	262	40.20 N	75.20 W
Telfs	164	47.18 N	11.04 E
Telgte	178	51.59 N	7.47 E
Teli	186	51.07 N	90.14 E
Telica, Volcán ∧[1]	280	12.36 N	86.50 W
Telida	236	63.23 N	153.16 W
Télimélé □[4]	222	11.00 N	13.30 W
Teljo, Jabal ∧	220	14.42 N	25.56 E
Telkwa	238	54.42 N	127.03 W
Telkwa ≏	238	54.41 N	127.02 W
Tell City	248	37.57 N	86.46 W
Teller	236	65.16 N	166.22 W
Tellico ≏	246	35.36 N	84.13 W
Tellico Plains	246	35.22 N	84.18 W
Tello	290	3.04 N	75.08 W
Telluride	254	37.56 N	107.49 W
Tel Megiddo ⊥	210	32.35 N	35.10 E
Telok Anson	200	4.00 N	101.02 E
Teloloapan	278	18.21 N	99.51 W
Telpaneca	280	13.32 N	86.23 W
Telsen	288	42.25 S	67.00 W
Telšiai	160	55.59 N	22.15 E
Teltow	164	52.23 N	13.16 E
Telukbetung	198	5.27 S	105.16 E
Telukdalem	200	0.34 N	97.49 E
Telumengtangshan ∧	206	30.33 N	86.27 E
Tema	222	5.38 N	0.01 E
Temadju, Pulau I	200	0.29 N	108.52 E
Temax	278	21.09 N	88.56 W
Tembeling ≏	200	4.04 N	102.20 E
Tembenči ≏	186	64.36 N	99.58 E
Tembesi ≏	198	1.43 S	103.06 E
Tembilahan	200	0.19 S	103.11 E
Temblador	290	8.59 N	62.44 W
Tembleque	168	39.42 N	3.30 W
Temblor Range ⛰	258	35.20 N	119.55 W
Tembuland ↵[1]	224	31.30 S	28.00 E
Temecula	274	33.46 N	117.29 W
Temerin	172	45.24 N	19.53 E
Temerloh	200	3.28 N	102.25 E
Temiang, Pulau I	200	0.19 N	104.23 E
Teminabuan	198	1.26 S	132.01 E
Temir	158	49.08 N	57.06 E
Temirtau, S.S.S.R.	186	50.05 N	72.56 E
Temirtau, S.S.S.R.	186	53.08 N	87.28 E
Témiscaming	244	46.44 N	79.06 W
Témiscouata, Lac ⊜	240	47.40 N	68.50 W
Temora	228	34.26 S	147.32 E
Temósachic	278	28.57 N	107.51 W
Tempe	254	33.25 N	111.56 W
Temperance	268	41.47 N	83.34 W
Temperanceville	262	37.54 N	75.33 W
Tempio Pausania	170	40.54 N	9.07 E
Tempisque ≏	280	10.12 N	85.14 W
Temple, Okla., U.S.	250	34.16 N	98.14 W
Temple, Pa., U.S.	262	40.25 N	75.56 W
Temple, Tex., U.S.	250	31.06 N	97.21 W
Temple City	274	34.07 N	118.03 W
Templemore	162	52.48 N	7.50 W
Templeton, Qué., Can.	264	45.29 N	75.36 W
Templeton, Calif., U.S.	272	35.33 N	120.42 W
Templeton, Ind., U.S.	268	40.31 N	87.12 W
Templeton, Mass., U.S.	261	42.33 N	72.04 W
Templeton, Pa., U.S.	266	40.55 N	79.28 W
Templeton ≏	228	21.14 S	138.13 E
Templin	164	53.07 N	13.30 E
Templo Island I	202	13.10 N	122.53 E
Tempoal	278	21.31 N	98.23 W
Tempoal ≏	278	21.47 N	98.27 W
Temr'uk	158	45.17 N	37.23 E
Temse	176	51.08 N	4.13 E
Temuco	294	38.44 S	72.36 W
Tena	290	0.59 S	77.49 W
Tenabo	278	20.03 N	90.14 W
Tenaha	248	31.57 N	94.15 W
Tenakee Springs	236	57.47 N	135.13 W
Tenasserim	198	12.05 N	99.01 E
Tenasserim □[8]	200	13.00 N	99.00 E
Tendaho	214	11.48 N	40.52 E
Tende	166	44.05 N	7.36 E
Tende, Col de)(	166	44.09 N	7.34 E
Ten Degree Channel ⊔	200	10.00 N	93.00 E
Tendō	192	38.21 N	140.22 E
Teneguiban	202	11.22 N	119.30 E
Tenente Marques ≏	292	11.10 S	59.56 W
Tenente Portela	294	27.22 S	53.45 W
Ténès	168	36.31 N	1.14 E
Ténès, Cap ≻	168	36.35 N	1.30 E
Tengchong	200	25.04 N	98.29 E
Tenggol, Pulau I	200	4.48 N	103.38 E
Tengiz, Ozero ⊜	186	50.24 N	68.57 E
Tengtiaohe ≏	200	22.07 N	103.08 E
Ten'guševo	160	54.46 N	42.44 E
Tengxian	200	23.21 N	110.53 E
Teniet el Had	168	35.47 N	2.01 E
Tenino	270	46.51 N	122.51 W
Tenke	218	10.35 S	26.07 E
Tenkiller Ferry Reservoir ⊜[1]	250	35.43 N	95.00 W
Tenkodogo	214	11.47 N	0.22 W
Ten Mile	246	35.40 N	84.40 W
Tenmile Creek ≏, Pa., U.S.	242	40.08 N	80.22 W
Ten Mile Lake ⊜	240	51.06 N	56.41 W
Tennant Creek	226	19.40 S	134.10 E
Tennent	262	40.17 N	74.20 W
Tennessee □[3]	234	35.50 N	85.30 W
Tennessee ≏	234	37.04 N	88.33 W
Tennille	246	32.56 N	82.48 W
Teno	294	34.52 S	71.11 W
Tenom	198	5.08 N	115.55 E
Tenosique de Pino Suárez	278	17.29 N	91.26 W
Tenryū	192	34.52 N	137.49 E
Tenryū ≏	192	34.39 N	137.47 E
Tensed	256	47.10 N	116.55 W
Ten Sleep	256	44.02 N	107.27 W
Tenterden	174	51.05 N	0.42 E
Tenterfield	228	29.03 S	152.01 E
Ten Thousand Islands II	246	25.50 N	81.33 W
Teocaltiche	278	21.26 N	102.35 W
Teodelina	294	34.10 S	61.34 W
Teófilo Otoni	296	17.51 S	41.30 W
Teomabal Island I	202	6.20 N	120.50 E
Teotihuacán ⊥	278	19.44 N	98.50 W
Tepa	198	7.52 S	129.31 E
Tepalcatepec	278	19.11 N	102.51 W
Tepatitlán [de Morelos]	278	20.49 N	102.44 W
Tepeaca	278	18.58 N	97.54 W
Tepeguaje	250	25.30 N	99.50 W
Tepehuanes	278	25.21 N	105.44 W
Tepehuanes, Río los ≏	278	25.10 N	105.25 W
Tepeji del Río	278	19.54 N	99.21 W
Tepelenë	172	40.18 N	20.01 E
Tepic	278	21.30 N	104.54 W
Teplice	164	50.39 N	13.48 E
Tepoca, Bahía de C	278	30.10 N	112.50 W
Tepoca, Cabo ≻	278	29.20 N	112.25 W
Te Puke	230	37.47 S	176.19 E
Tequendama, Salto de ↳	290	4.35 N	74.18 W
Ter ≏	168	42.01 N	3.12 E
Téra	214	14.01 N	0.45 E
Tera ≏, Esp.	168	41.54 N	5.44 W
Tera ≏, Port.	168	38.56 N	8.03 W
Teradomari	192	37.38 N	138.46 E
Teramo	184	42.39 N	13.42 E
Teramo □[6]	184	42.39 N	13.41 E
Tercero ≏	294	32.55 S	62.19 W
Terek ≏	158	43.44 N	46.33 E
Terence Bay	240	44.28 N	63.43 W
Terenni ⊥	222	16.30 N	9.35 W
Terenos	296	20.26 S	54.50 W
Teresina	286	5.05 S	42.49 W
Teresópolis	296	22.26 S	42.59 W
Terespol	164	52.05 N	23.36 E
Teressa Island I	200	8.15 N	93.10 E
Tergnier	176	49.39 N	3.18 E
Teribe ≏	280	9.27 N	82.26 W
Terib'orka	160	69.08 N	35.08 E
Terkos Gölü ⊜	212	41.20 N	28.35 E
Terlingua	250	29.19 N	103.37 W
Termez	206	37.14 N	67.16 E
Termini Imerese	170	37.59 N	13.42 E
Termini Imerese, Golfo di C	170	38.05 N	13.50 E
Terminillo, Monte ∧	170	42.28 N	13.00 E
Términos, Laguna de C	278	18.35 N	91.30 W
Termoli	184	42.00 N	15.00 E
Ternate, Indon.	198	0.48 N	127.24 E
Ternate, Pil.	202	14.17 N	120.43 E
Ternberg	164	47.58 N	14.22 E
Ternej	186	45.03 N	136.37 E
Terneuzen	178	51.20 N	3.50 E
Terni	184	42.34 N	12.37 E
Terni □[4]	184	42.41 N	12.19 E
Ternitz	164	47.44 N	16.03 E
Ternopol'	158	49.34 N	25.36 E
Terpenija, Mys ≻	186	48.39 N	144.44 E
Terra Alta	242	39.27 N	79.31 W
Terra Bella	258	35.58 N	119.03 W
Terra Boa	296	23.45 S	52.27 W
Terrace	238	54.31 N	128.35 W
Terrace Bay	244	48.47 N	87.09 W
Terracina	184	41.17 N	13.15 E
Terra di Bari ↵[1]	170	41.10 N	16.50 E
Terral	250	33.54 N	97.57 W
Terralba	170	39.43 N	8.38 E
Terra Linda	272	38.00 N	122.32 W
Terra Nova	240	48.30 N	54.13 W
Terra Nova Lake ⊜	240	48.30 N	54.20 W
Terra Nova National Park ♠	240	48.37 N	53.56 W
Terra Rica	296	22.43 S	52.38 W
Terra Roxa d'Oeste	294	24.08 S	53.59 W
Terrasse-Vaudreuil	260	45.23 N	73.59 W
Terrasson-la-Villedieu	166	45.08 N	1.18 E
Terrebonne	260	45.42 N	73.37 W
Terrebonne □[6]	260	46.00 N	74.10 W
Terrebonne Bay C	248	29.09 N	90.35 W
Terrebonne-Heights	260	45.44 N	73.39 W
Terre-de-Bas	285o	15.51 N	61.39 W
Terre-de-Haut	285o	15.58 N	61.35 W
Terre Haute	248	39.28 N	87.24 W
Terre Hill	262	40.10 N	76.03 W
Terrell	250	32.44 N	96.17 W
Terrell Hills	250	29.29 N	98.27 W
Terrenceville	240	47.42 N	54.43 W
Territory of New Guinea □[2]	198	6.00 S	150.00 E
Terror Point ≻	238	53.10 N	129.56 W
Terry, Miss., U.S.	248	32.05 N	90.18 W
Terry, Mont., U.S.	252	46.47 N	105.19 W
Terry Peak ∧	252	44.19 N	103.50 W
Terryville, Conn., U.S.	261	41.41 N	73.01 W
Terryville, N.Y., U.S.	261	40.54 N	73.03 W
Terschelling I	164	53.24 N	5.20 E
Teruel, Col.	290	2.44 N	75.33 W
Teruel, Esp.	168	40.21 N	1.06 W
Tervel	172	43.45 N	27.24 E
Tervola	160	66.05 N	24.48 E
Terzigno	184	40.48 N	14.29 E
Tésa, Magy.	164	46.02 N	18.51 E
Teša, S.S.S.R.	160	55.30 N	42.50 E
Tesalia	290	2.29 N	75.44 W
Tešanj	172	44.37 N	18.00 E
Tes-Chem (Tesijn) ≏	186	50.28 N	93.04 E
Tescott	252	39.01 N	97.53 W
Teschen → Český Těšín	164	49.45 N	18.37 E
Teseney	214	15.07 N	36.41 E
Teshekpuk Lake ⊜	236	70.35 N	153.30 W
Teshi	222	5.35 N	0.05 W
Teshikaga	192a	43.29 N	144.28 E
Teshio	192a	44.53 N	141.44 E
Teshio ≏	192a	44.53 N	141.44 E
Teshio-sanchi ⛰	192a	44.15 N	142.05 E
Teslić	172	44.37 N	17.51 E
Teslin	236	60.09 N	132.45 W
Teslin ≏	236	61.34 N	134.54 W
Teslin Lake ⊜	236	60.15 N	132.57 W
Tesouras ≏	296	14.36 S	50.51 W
Tesouro	296	16.04 S	53.34 W
Tessa, Oued ≏	170	36.34 N	8.54 E
Tessala, Djebel ∧	168	35.15 N	0.45 W
Tessala, Monts du ⛰	168	35.25 N	0.45 W
Tessalit	214	20.12 N	1.00 E
Tessaoua	214	13.45 N	7.59 E
Tess Corners	268	42.55 N	88.07 W
Tessenderlo	178	51.04 N	5.05 E
Tessik Lake ⊜	232	64.53 N	75.25 W
Tessy-sur-Vire	166	48.58 N	1.04 W
Testa, Capo ≻	170	41.14 N	9.09 E
Testour	170	36.33 N	9.27 E
Têt ≏	166	42.44 N	3.02 E
Tetachuck Lake ⊜	238	53.20 N	125.50 W
Tetagouche ≏	240	47.38 N	65.41 W
Tetas, Punta ≻	294	23.31 S	70.38 W
Tetbury	162	51.39 N	2.10 W
Tete	218	16.13 S	33.35 E
Tête-à-la-Baleine	240	50.42 N	59.19 W
Tête-Jaune-Cache	238	52.57 N	119.26 W
Tetepiskaw, Lac ⊜	240	51.02 N	69.23 W
Teterow	164	53.46 N	12.34 E
Teteven	172	42.55 N	24.16 E
Tetlin	236	63.08 N	142.31 W
Tetlin Lake ⊜	236	63.05 N	142.45 W
Teton	256	43.59 N	111.40 W
Teton ≏, Idaho, U.S.	256	43.54 N	111.51 W
Teton ≏, Mont., U.S.	256	47.56 N	110.31 W
Tetonia	256	43.49 N	111.10 W
Tétouan	168	35.34 N	5.23 W
Tetovo	172	42.01 N	20.58 E
Tetschen → Děčín	164	50.48 N	14.13 E
Tettenhall	174	52.36 N	2.09 W
Tettnang	180	47.40 N	9.35 E
Tet'uche	186	44.35 N	135.35 E
Tet'uši	160	54.57 N	48.50 E
Teuco ≏	294	25.35 S	60.11 W
Teufen	180	47.23 N	9.23 E
Teulada	170	38.58 N	8.46 E
Teulada, Capo ≻	170	38.52 N	8.39 E
Teúl de González Ortega	278	21.28 N	103.29 W
Teun, Pulau I	198	6.59 S	129.08 E
Teunom ≏	200	4.26 N	95.48 E
Teuri-tō I	192a	44.25 N	141.19 E
Teutopolis	248	39.08 N	88.29 W
Teuva	160	62.29 N	21.44 E
Tevere ≏	184	41.44 N	12.14 E
Teverya (Tiberias)	210	32.47 N	35.33 E
Teviot ≏, N.Z.	230	45.32 S	169.18 E
Teviot ≏, Scot., U.K.	162	55.36 N	2.26 W
Te Waewae Bay C	230	46.14 S	167.30 E
Tewkesbury	174	51.59 N	2.09 W
Tewksbury	261	42.37 N	71.14 W
Texada Island I	238	49.40 N	124.24 W
Texarkana, Ark., U.S.	248	33.26 N	94.02 W
Texarkana, Tex., U.S.	248	33.26 N	94.03 W
Texarkana, Lake ⊜[1]	248	33.16 N	94.14 W
Texas	268	41.26 N	83.57 W
Texas □[3]	234	31.30 N	99.00 W
Texas City	250	29.23 N	94.54 W
Texcoco, Lago de ⊜	278	19.30 N	99.00 W
Texel I	164	53.05 N	4.45 E
Texhoma	250	36.30 N	101.47 W
Texico	250	34.23 N	103.03 W
Texline	250	36.23 N	103.01 W
Texoma, Lake ⊜[1]	250	33.55 N	96.37 W
Teyéa ⊥	172	37.29 N	22.24 E
Teziutlán	278	19.49 N	97.21 W
Tezzeron Lake ⊜	238	54.41 N	124.25 W
Tha ≏	200	20.07 N	100.35 E
Tha-Anne ≏	232	60.31 N	94.39 W
Thabana Ntlenyana ∧	218	29.28 S	29.16 E
Thabazimbi	224	24.41 S	27.21 E
Thai-binh	200	20.35 N	106.01 E
Thailand □[1]	198	15.00 N	100.00 E
Thai-nguyen	200	21.36 N	105.50 E
Thal	204	33.22 N	70.33 E
Tha'l, Jabal ∧	220	14.13 N	24.14 E
Tha Lang ≏	200	13.58 N	101.44 E
Thale	164	51.45 N	11.02 E
Thalfang	164	49.45 N	6.59 E
Thalia	250	33.59 N	99.32 W
Thalwil	180	47.17 N	8.34 E
Thame	174	51.45 N	0.59 W
Thames	230	37.09 S	175.33 E
Thames ≏	244	42.19 N	82.28 W
Thames, Firth Of C	230	37.05 S	175.23 E
Thamesford	264	43.04 N	81.00 W
Thamesville	266	42.33 N	81.59 W
Thāmir, Jabal ∧	214	13.53 N	45.30 E
Thanh-hoa	200	19.48 N	105.46 E
Thanjāvūr	204	10.47 N	79.09 E
Thann	180	47.49 N	7.05 E
Thaon-les-Vosges	180	48.15 N	6.25 E
Thap Than ≏	200	15.20 N	104.00 E
Thar Desert (Great Indian Desert) ↵[2]	206	28.00 N	72.00 E
Thargomindah	226	28.00 S	143.49 E
Tharrawaddy	200	17.39 N	95.48 E
Thásos	172	40.47 N	24.42 E
Thásos I	172	40.41 N	24.47 E
Thásos ⊥	172	40.46 N	24.33 E
Thatcher	254	32.51 N	109.46 W
Thaton	200	16.55 N	97.22 E
Thau, Étang de C	166	43.23 N	3.36 E
Thaungyin ≏	200	17.50 N	97.42 E
Thawville	268	40.41 N	88.07 W
Thaya (Dyje) ≏	164	48.37 N	16.56 E
Thayawthadangyi Kyun I	200	12.20 N	98.00 E
Thayer, Ind., U.S.	268	41.10 N	87.20 W
Thayer, Kans., U.S.	252	37.30 N	95.28 W
Thayer, Mo., U.S.	248	36.31 N	91.33 W
Thayetmyo	200	19.19 N	95.11 E
Thazi	198	20.51 N	96.05 E
Thealka	246	37.49 N	82.47 W
Thebes → Thívai, Ellás	172	38.21 N	23.19 E
Thebes, Ill., U.S.	248	37.13 N	89.28 W
Thebes ⊥	220	25.42 N	32.37 E
The Bight	282	24.19 N	75.24 W
The Big Warrambool ≏	228	30.05 S	147.33 E
The Black Sugarloaf ∧	228	31.20 S	151.33 E
The Brothers II	204	12.09 N	53.12 E
The Church of the Holy Sepulchre ✝[1]	210	31.46 N	35.14 E
The Dalles	270	45.36 N	121.10 W
Thedford	252	41.59 N	100.35 W
The Everglades ☷	246	26.00 N	81.00 W
The Frome ≏	228	29.06 S	137.52 E
The Hague → 's-Gravenhage	178	52.06 N	4.18 E
The Heads ≻	256	42.44 N	124.31 W
The Hunters Hills ⛰[2]	230	44.25 S	170.45 E
The Lake ⊜	282	21.00 N	73.30 W
Thelon ≏	232	64.16 N	96.05 W
The Margaret ≏	228	29.26 S	137.07 E
The Minch ⊔	158	58.00 N	6.00 W
The Neales ≏	228	28.08 S	136.47 E
Thénezay	166	46.43 N	0.02 W
Thenia-Beni-Aïcha	168	36.43 N	3.34 E
The Oaks	272	39.13 N	121.05 W
Theodore, Austl.	226	24.57 S	150.05 E
Theodore, Ala., U.S.	248	30.33 N	88.10 W
Theodore Roosevelt Dam ↵[6]	254	33.32 N	111.10 W
Theodore Roosevelt National Memorial Park (North Unit) ♠, N. Dak., U.S.	252	47.34 N	103.24 W
Theodore Roosevelt National Memorial Park (South Unit) ♠, N. Dak., U.S.	252	46.55 N	103.26 W
Theólogos	172	40.39 N	24.41 E
The Pas	232	53.50 N	101.15 W
The Peak ∧	246	36.24 N	81.39 W
The Pilot ∧	228	36.45 S	148.13 E
The Pinnacle ∧[2]	248	39.22 N	90.55 W
Thérain ≏	166	49.15 N	2.27 E
The Rajah ∧	238	53.15 N	118.31 W
The Rand → Witwatersrand ↵[1]	224	26.00 S	27.00 E
The Remarkables ⛰	230	45.08 S	168.51 E
Theresa	264	44.13 N	75.48 W
Thermaïkós Kólpos C	172	40.23 N	22.47 E

Symbols in the index entries are identified on page 360.

Name	Page	Lat°′	Long°′
Thermalito	272	39.31 N	121.36 W
Thermopílai ⊥	172	38.48 N	22.33 E
Thermopolis	254	43.39 N	108.13 W
Thermopylae → Thermopílai ⊥	172	38.48 N	22.33 E
The Round Mountain ∧	228	30.27 S	152.14 E
The Royal National Park ♠	228	34.10 S	151.05 E
Thesiger Bay C	232	71.30 N	124.05 W
The Sound ⋃	160	55.50 N	12.40 E
The Springs	261	41.01 N	72.09 W
Thesprotía □[5]	172	39.40 N	20.20 E
Thesprotikón	172	39.15 N	20.47 E
Thessalía ◆[1]	172	39.30 N	22.00 E
Thessalon	244	46.15 N	83.34 W
Thessaloníki (Salonika)	172	40.38 N	22.56 E
Thetford	174	52.25 N	0.45 E
Thetford Mines	260	46.05 N	71.18 W
The Thumbs ∧	230	43.36 S	170.44 E
Thetis Island	270	49.59 N	123.40 W
The Treuer ≃	228	27.52 S	137.12 E
The Twins ∧	230	41.14 S	172.40 E
Theun ≃	200	18.14 N	104.38 E
The Village	250	35.35 N	97.33 W
The Wailing Wall (Kotel Hama'aravi) ✝[1]	210	31.46 N	35.14 E
The Warburton ≃	228	27.55 S	137.28 E
The Weald ◆[1]	162	51.05 N	0.05 E
The Yellow Mountain ∧	228	32.30 S	146.51 E
Thibodaux	248	29.48 N	90.49 W
Thief ≃	252	48.08 N	96.10 W
Thief River Falls	252	48.07 N	96.10 W
Thielsen, Mount ∧	256	43.09 N	122.04 W
Thiene	170	45.42 N	11.29 E
Thiensville	268	43.14 N	87.58 W
Thiérache □[9]	176	49.40 N	3.50 E
Thiers	182	45.51 N	3.34 E
Thiès	222	14.48 N	16.56 W
Thiès □[4]	222	14.45 N	16.50 W
Thiesi	170	40.31 N	8.43 E
Thika	218	1.03 S	37.05 E
Thimbu	204	27.28 N	89.39 E
Thingangyun	200	16.49 N	96.12 E
Thingvallavatn ⊜	160a	64.12 N	21.10 W
Thingvellir	160a	64.17 N	21.07 W
Thionville	166	49.22 N	6.10 E
Thíra	172	36.25 N	25.26 E
Thíra I	172	36.24 N	25.29 E
Third Cataract → Ash-Shallāl ath-Thālith ↓	220	19.49 N	30.19 E
Thirsk	162	54.14 N	1.20 W
Thisted	160	56.57 N	8.42 E
Thistilfjördur C	160a	66.20 N	15.25 W
Thistle Island I	228	35.00 S	136.09 E
Thívai (Thebes)	172	38.21 N	23.19 E
Thiviers	166	45.25 N	0.56 E
Thizy	166	46.02 N	4.19 E
Thjórsá ≃	160a	63.47 N	20.48 W
Thlewiaza ≃	232	60.28 N	94.45 W
Thoa ≃	232	60.30 N	109.47 W
Thomas, Okla., U.S.	250	35.45 N	98.45 W
Thomas, Wash., U.S.	270	47.21 N	122.14 W
Thomas, W. Va., U.S.	242	39.09 N	79.30 W
Thomasboro	268	40.15 N	88.11 W
Thomaston, Ala., U.S.	248	32.11 N	87.37 W
Thomaston, Conn., U.S.	261	41.40 N	73.04 W
Thomaston, Ga., U.S.	246	32.54 N	84.20 W
Thomaston, Maine, U.S.	242	44.05 N	69.10 W
Thomastown	162	52.31 N	7.08 W
Thomasville, Ala., U.S.	248	31.55 N	87.51 W
Thomasville, Ga., U.S.	246	30.50 N	83.59 W
Thomasville, N.C., U.S.	246	35.53 N	80.05 W
Thomasville, Pa., U.S.	262	39.56 N	76.51 W
Thom Bay C	232	70.09 N	92.00 W
Thomlinson, Mount ∧	238	55.33 N	127.29 W
Thompson, Man., Can.	232	55.45 N	97.45 W
Thompson, Conn., U.S.	261	41.57 N	71.52 W
Thompson, Iowa, U.S.	244	43.22 N	93.46 W
Thompson, Ohio, U.S.	266	41.41 N	81.03 W
Thompson, Utah, U.S.	254	38.58 N	109.43 W
Thompson ≃, B.C., Can.	238	50.15 N	121.33 W
Thompson ≃, U.S.	248	39.45 N	93.36 W
Thompson Falls	256	47.36 N	115.21 W
Thompson Pass)(	236	61.08 N	145.45 W
Thompson Peak ∧	258	41.00 N	123.03 W
Thompson Place	270	47.03 N	122.45 W
Thompson Sound ⋃	230	45.09 S	166.57 E
Thompsontown, N.J., U.S.	262	39.26 N	74.43 W
Thompsontown, Pa., U.S.	262	40.33 N	77.14 W
Thompsonville, Conn., U.S.	261	42.00 N	72.36 W
Thompsonville, Mich., U.S.	244	44.31 N	85.56 W
Thomsen ≃	232	74.08 N	119.35 W
Thomson, Ga., U.S.	246	33.28 N	82.30 W
Thomson, Ill., U.S.	244	41.58 N	90.06 W
Thomson ≃	228	25.11 S	142.53 E
Thon Buri	200	13.43 N	100.29 E
Thongwa	200	16.46 N	96.32 E
Thonon-les-Bains	180	46.22 N	6.29 E
Thonotosassa	246	28.03 N	82.18 W
Thonze	200	17.38 N	95.47 E
Thorburn	240	45.34 N	62.33 W
Thoreau	254	35.24 N	108.13 W
Thorhild	238	54.10 N	113.07 W
Thórisvatn ⊜	160a	64.50 N	19.26 W
Thorlákshöfn	160a	63.53 N	21.18 W
Thorn → Touruń	164	53.02 N	18.35 E
Thornapple ≃	244	45.28 N	91.16 W
Thornbury	264	44.34 N	80.26 W
Thorndale, Ont., Can.	264	43.06 N	81.08 W
Thorndale, Pa., U.S.	262	40.00 N	75.45 W
Thorndale, Tex., U.S.	250	30.37 N	97.12 W
Thorndike	261	42.11 N	72.20 W
Thorne Bay	238	55.44 N	132.32 W
Thornhill, Ont., Can.	264	43.48 N	79.25 W
Thornhill, Scot., U.K.	162	55.15 N	3.46 W
Thornton, Ark., U.S.	248	33.47 N	92.29 W
Thornton, Calif., U.S.	272	38.14 N	121.25 W
Thornton, Colo., U.S.	254	39.51 N	104.59 W
Thornton, Ill., U.S.	268	41.35 N	87.37 W
Thornton, Tex., U.S.	250	31.24 N	96.34 W
Thornwood	261	41.07 N	73.47 W
Thorny Mountain ∧	248	37.06 N	91.10 W
Thorold	264	43.07 N	79.12 W
Thorp, Wash., U.S.	270	47.04 N	120.40 W
Thorp, Wis., U.S.	244	44.58 N	90.48 W
Thorpe	246	37.22 N	81.31 W
Thorsby, Alta., Can.	238	53.14 N	114.03 W
Thorsby, Ala., U.S.	248	32.55 N	86.43 W
Thorshavn → Tórshavn	158	62.01 N	6.46 W
Thórshöfn	160a	66.13 N	15.17 W
Thouars	166	46.59 N	0.13 W
Thousand Lake Mountain ∧	254	38.25 N	111.29 W
Thousand Oaks	274	34.10 N	118.50 W
Thrace □[9]	172	41.20 N	26.45 E
Thrakikón Pélagos ▾[2]	172	40.15 N	24.28 E
Three Bridges	262	40.31 N	74.48 W
Three Fingered Jack ∧	256	44.29 N	121.50 W
Three Forks	256	45.54 N	111.33 W
Three Hills	238	51.42 N	113.16 W
Three Hummock Island I	228	40.26 S	144.55 E
Three Kings Islands II	230	34.09 S	172.09 E
Three Lakes	244	45.48 N	89.10 W
Three Mile Bay	264	44.05 N	76.12 W
Three Mile Plains	240	44.58 N	64.07 W
Three Oaks	268	41.48 N	86.36 W
Three Pagodas Pass)(	200	15.18 N	98.23 E
Three Points, Cape ≻	222	4.45 N	2.06 W
Three Rivers, Mass., U.S.	261	42.11 N	72.22 W
Three Rivers, Mich., U.S.	268	41.57 N	85.38 W
Three Rivers, Tex., U.S.	250	28.28 N	98.11 W
Three Sisters ∧	256	44.10 N	121.46 W
Three Springs, Austl.	226	29.32 S	115.45 E
Three Springs, Pa., U.S.	266	40.12 N	77.59 W
Throckmorton	250	33.11 N	99.11 W
Thueyts	166	44.41 N	4.13 E
Thuin	176	50.20 N	4.17 E
Thule, Mount ∧	232	73.00 N	78.30 W
Thumb Peak ∧	202	9.47 N	118.36 E
Thun	180	46.45 N	7.37 E
Thunder Bay	244	48.23 N	89.15 W
Thunder Bay C, Ont., Can.	244	48.24 N	89.00 W
Thunder Bay C, Mich., U.S.	244	45.00 N	83.22 W
Thunder Bay ≃	244	45.04 N	83.25 W
Thunderbird, Lake ⊜[1]	250	35.15 N	97.20 W
Thunderbolt	246	32.03 N	81.04 W
Thunder Butte ∧	252	45.19 N	101.53 W
Thunder Knoll ⊹[4]	282	16.25 N	81.20 W
Thuner See ⊜	166	46.40 N	7.45 E
Thurgau □[3]	180	47.35 N	9.00 E
Thüringen □[9]	164	51.00 N	11.00 E
Thüringer Wald ⩓	166	50.30 N	11.00 E
Thurles	162	52.41 N	7.49 W
Thurmont	242	39.37 N	77.25 W
Thurso, Qué., Can.	260	45.36 N	75.15 W
Thurso, Scot., U.K.	162	58.35 N	3.32 W
Thurston □[6]	270	46.59 N	122.42 W
Thurston Island I	148	72.20 S	99.00 W
Thury-Harcourt	166	48.59 N	0.29 W
Thusis	166	46.42 N	9.26 E
Thyborøn	160	56.42 N	8.13 E
Thysville → Mbanza-Ngungu	218	5.15 S	14.52 E
Tiahuanaco	292	16.33 S	68.42 W
Tía Juana	290	10.16 N	71.22 W
Tian'aoshan I	196	28.48 N	121.51 E
Tiancang	190	41.09 N	100.17 E
Tiandong	200	23.40 N	106.57 E
Tianhengdao I	194	36.14 N	120.46 E
Tianjin (Tientsin)	194	39.08 N	117.12 E
Tianjun	190	37.25 N	98.58 E
Tianlin	200	24.14 N	106.03 E
Tianmen	196	30.40 N	113.08 E
Tianmushan ⩓	196	30.25 N	119.30 E
Tianshui	190	34.30 N	105.58 E
Tiantai	190	29.09 N	121.02 E
Tiantaishan ⩓	196	29.22 N	121.10 E
Tianweijiao ≻	196	22.45 N	115.49 E
Tianyang	200	23.51 N	106.34 E
Tianzhu	190	37.14 N	102.59 E
Tiaret	214	35.28 N	1.21 E
Tibagi	294	24.30 S	50.24 W
Tibagi ≃	294	22.47 S	51.01 W
Tibasti, Sarīr ◆[2]	214	24.15 N	17.15 E
Tibbie	248	31.16 N	88.15 W
Tiber → Tevere ≃	184	41.44 N	12.14 E
Tiberias → Teverya	210	32.47 N	35.33 E
Tiber Reservoir ⊜[1]	256	48.22 N	111.17 W
Tibesti ⩓	214	21.30 N	17.30 E
Tibet → Xizang Zizhiqu □[4]	190	32.00 N	88.00 E
Tibet □[9]	206	34.00 N	92.00 E
Tibiao	202	11.17 N	122.02 E
Tibiao Point ≻	202	11.18 N	122.02 E
Tibiriçá ≃	296	21.43 S	50.15 W
Tiblawan	202	6.29 N	126.06 E
Tiblemont, Lac ⊜	244	48.14 N	77.19 W
Tibnīn	210	33.11 N	35.24 E
Tibugá, Golfo de C	290	5.45 N	77.20 W
Tiburon	272	36.04 N	119.19 W
Tiburón, Cabo ≻	290	8.42 N	77.24 W
Tiburón, Isla I	278	29.00 N	112.20 W
Ticao Island I	202	12.30 N	123.42 E
Ticao Pass ⋃	202	12.40 N	123.45 E
Tice	246	26.41 N	81.49 W
Tichigan	268	42.50 N	88.12 W
Tîchît	214	18.28 N	9.30 W
Tîchît, Dhar •[4]	222	18.30 N	9.25 W
Tichon	160	59.23 N	46.38 E
Tichoreck	158	45.51 N	40.09 E
Tichtozero	160	65.35 N	30.27 E
Tichvin	160	59.39 N	33.31 E
Ticino □[3]	180	46.20 N	8.45 E
Ticino ≃	170	45.09 N	9.14 E
Tickfaw	248	30.35 N	90.29 W
Tickfaw ≃	248	30.20 N	90.28 W
Ticonderoga	242	43.51 N	73.26 W
Ticul	278	20.24 N	89.32 W
Tidaholm	160	58.11 N	13.57 E
Tide Lake ⊜	238	50.33 N	111.20 W
Tidewater	262	37.51 N	76.42 W
Tidioute	266	41.41 N	79.24 W
Tidirhine, Jbel ∧	168	34.50 N	4.30 W
Tidjikdja	214	18.33 N	11.25 W
Tidore	198	0.40 N	127.26 E
Tidra, Île I	222	19.44 N	16.24 W
Tiel	178	51.54 N	5.25 E
Tieli	190	46.59 N	128.02 E
Tielinanmuhu ⊜	206	31.05 N	85.35 E
Tieling	194	42.18 N	123.49 E
Tielt	176	51.00 N	3.19 E
T'ienching → Tianjin	194	39.08 N	117.12 E
T'ienchung	196	23.53 N	120.34 E
Tienen	164	50.48 N	4.57 E
Tiengen	180	47.38 N	8.16 E
Tien Shan ⩓	190	42.00 N	80.00 E
Tientsin → Tianjin	194	39.08 N	117.12 E
Tie Plant	248	33.44 N	89.47 W
Tiereme, Gunung ∧	198	6.54 S	108.24 E
Tierga	168	41.37 N	1.36 W
Tierp	160	60.20 N	17.30 E
Tierra Amarilla, Chile	294	27.29 S	70.17 W
Tierra Amarilla, N. Mex., U.S.	254	36.42 N	106.33 W
Tierra Blanca, Méx.	250	27.12 N	104.53 W
Tierra Blanca, Méx.	278	18.25 N	96.20 W
Tierra Colorada	278	17.10 N	99.35 W
Tierra de Campos ◆[1]	168	42.10 N	4.50 W
Tierra del Fuego, Isla Grande de I	288	54.00 S	69.00 W
Tierralta	290	8.11 N	76.04 W
Tierras Coloradas	278	22.24 N	104.35 W
Tie Siding	254	41.05 N	105.31 W
Tietar ≃	168	39.50 N	6.01 W
Tietê	296	23.07 S	47.43 W
Tietê ≃	296	20.40 S	51.35 W
Tieton	270	46.42 N	120.46 W
Tiffany Mountain ∧	256	48.40 N	119.56 W
Tiffin	266	41.07 N	83.11 W
Tiflis → Tbilisi	158	41.43 N	44.49 E
Tifton	246	31.27 N	83.31 W
Tiftona	246	35.05 N	85.10 W
Tigalda Island I	236	54.05 N	165.05 W
Tigapuluh, Pegunungan ⩓	200	1.05 S	102.30 E
Tigard	270	45.26 N	122.46 W
Tigbauan	202	10.41 N	122.22 E
Tigil'	186	57.48 N	158.40 E
Tignall	246	33.52 N	82.44 W
Tignish	240	46.57 N	64.02 W
Tigre ∧	278	19.53 N	102.59 W
Tigre ≃, Perú	290	4.30 S	74.10 W
Tigre ≃, Ven.	290	9.20 N	62.30 W
Tigre, Isla del I	280	13.17 N	87.38 W
Tigris (Dicle) (Dijlah) ≃	208	31.00 N	47.25 E
Tiguabos	284p	20.14 N	75.21 W
Tiguentourine	214	27.50 N	9.18 E
Tigui ▾[4]	214	18.38 N	18.47 E
Tigzirt	168	36.54 N	4.08 E
Tīh, Jabal at- ⩓[1]	220	29.30 N	34.00 E
Tihany ⊥	164	46.54 N	17.53 E
Tihua → Wulumuqi	190	43.48 N	87.35 E
Tihuatlán	278	20.43 N	97.32 W
Tijamuchi ≃	292	14.10 S	64.58 W
Tijesno	170	43.48 N	15.39 E
Tijirît, Oued V	222	20.01 N	15.29 W
Tijuana	278	32.32 N	117.01 W
Tijuana ≃	258	32.33 N	117.08 W
Tijucas	294	27.14 S	48.38 W
Tijucas do Sul	294	25.55 S	49.12 W
Tijuco ≃	296	18.40 S	50.05 W
Tikchik Lakes ⊜	236	60.07 N	158.35 W
Tiko	214	4.05 N	9.22 E
Tikrīt	208	34.36 N	43.42 E
Tikša	160	64.07 N	32.27 E
Tiksi	186	71.36 N	128.48 E
Tilarán	280	10.28 N	84.59 W
Tilbalaca, Laguna de C	280	15.28 N	84.15 W
Tilburg	178	51.34 N	5.05 E
Tilbury, Ont., Can.	266	42.16 N	82.26 W
Tilbury, Eng., U.K.	174	51.28 N	0.23 E
Tilcara	294	23.34 S	65.23 W
Tilden, Ill., U.S.	248	38.13 N	89.41 W
Tilden, Nebr., U.S.	252	42.03 N	97.50 W
Tilden, Tex., U.S.	250	28.28 N	98.33 W
Tilemsi, Vallée du V	222	16.15 N	0.02 E
Tiligul ≃	172	47.04 N	30.57 E
Tilisarao	294	32.44 S	65.18 W
Tillabéry	214	14.13 N	1.27 E
Tillamook	270	45.27 N	123.51 W
Tillamook □[6]	270	45.25 N	123.39 W
Tillanchong Island I	200	8.30 N	93.38 E
Tillery, Lake ⊜[1]	246	35.17 N	80.05 W
Tilley	238	50.27 N	111.39 W
Tillicum	270	47.08 N	122.33 W
Tillmans Corner	248	30.46 N	88.08 W
Tillson	242	41.50 N	74.04 W
Tillsonburg	264	42.51 N	80.44 W
Tílos I	172	36.25 N	27.25 E
Tilpa	226	30.57 S	144.24 E
Tilsit → Sovetsk	160	55.05 N	21.53 E
Tilton, Ill., U.S.	248	40.09 N	87.38 W
Tilton, N.H., U.S.	242	43.27 N	71.35 W
Tiltonsville	266	40.10 N	80.42 W
Ṭimā	220	26.54 N	31.26 E
Timagami, Lake ⊜	244	47.00 N	80.05 W
Timaná	290	1.58 N	75.56 W
Tímane ≃	292	20.34 S	59.15 W
Timanskij Kr'až ⩓	160	65.00 N	51.00 E
Timaricha	160	57.33 N	44.47 E
Timaru	230	44.24 S	171.15 E
Timaševo	160	53.21 N	51.12 E
Timbákion	172	35.04 N	24.46 E
Timbalier Bay C	248	29.10 N	90.20 W
Timbédra	214	16.15 N	8.10 W
Timber	270	45.43 N	123.18 W
Timberlake, Ohio, U.S.	266	41.41 N	81.25 W
Timber Lake, S. Dak., U.S.	252	45.26 N	101.04 W
Timbío	290	2.20 N	76.40 W
Timblin	266	40.58 N	79.12 W
Timbó	294	26.50 S	49.18 W
Timbuktu → Tombouctou	222	16.46 N	3.01 W
Timétrine Monts ⩓	222	19.20 N	0.42 W
Timimoun	214	29.14 N	0.16 E
Timir'azevskij	186	56.29 N	84.54 E
Timiris, Cap ≻	222	19.23 N	16.32 W
Timiş (Tamiš) ≃	172	44.51 N	20.39 E
Timiskaming, Lake ⊜	244	47.35 N	79.35 W
Timişoara	172	45.45 N	21.13 E
Timmendorferstrand	164	54.00 N	10.46 E
Timmins	244	48.28 N	81.20 W
Timmonsville	246	34.08 N	79.57 W
Timms Hill ∧[2]	244	45.27 N	90.11 W
Timok ≃	172	44.13 N	22.40 E
Timor → Portuguese Timor □[2]	198	8.35 S	126.00 E
Timor I	198	8.50 S	126.00 E
Timor Sea ▾[2]	148	11.00 S	128.00 E
Timošino, S.S.S.R.	160	57.50 N	44.25 E
Timošino, S.S.S.R.	160	60.05 N	36.10 E
Timotes	290	8.59 N	70.44 W
Timousserarène ≃	222	16.21 N	8.07 E
Timpanogos Cave National Monument ♠	254	40.18 N	111.52 W
Timpson	248	31.54 N	94.24 W
Timpton ≃	186	58.43 N	127.12 E
Timšer	160	62.06 N	54.40 E
Tims Ford Lake ⊜[1]	248	35.15 N	86.10 W
Tina ≃	224	31.18 S	29.14 E
Tinaca Point ≻	202	5.34 N	125.20 E
Tinaco	290	9.42 N	68.26 W
Tinaga Island I	202	14.28 N	122.56 E
Ṭīnah, Khalīj aṭ- C	220	31.08 N	32.40 E
Tinaja, Punta ≻	292	16.14 S	73.43 W
Tinajas, Cerro de las ∧	278	29.55 N	112.06 W
Tinalmud	202	13.36 N	122.53 E
Tinambac	202	13.49 N	123.19 E
Tinaquillo	290	9.55 N	68.18 W
Tindafjallajökull ⊓	160a	63.47 N	19.35 W
Tindouf	214	27.50 N	8.04 W
Tineg ≃	202	17.33 N	120.36 E
Tineo	168	43.20 N	6.25 W
Tinggi, Pulau I	200	2.18 N	104.07 E
Tingi Mountains ⩓[2]	222	8.55 N	10.47 W
Tingjiang ≃	196	24.24 N	116.35 E
Tingka, Batu ∧	202	5.20 N	117.06 E
Tinglev	164	54.56 N	9.15 E
Tingloy	202	13.40 N	120.52 E
Tingmerkpuk Mountain ∧	236	68.34 N	162.28 W
Tingo de Saposoa	292	7.09 S	76.39 W
Tingo María	292	9.09 S	75.56 W
Tingsryd	160	56.32 N	14.59 E
Tinguipaya	292	19.11 S	65.51 W
Tingvollvågen	160	62.54 N	8.12 E
Tingwick	260	45.53 N	71.57 W
Tinharé, Ilha de I	296	13.30 S	38.58 W
Tinian I	198	15.00 N	145.38 E
Tinitian	202	10.04 N	119.12 E
Tinkisso ≃	222	11.21 N	9.10 W
Tinley Park	268	41.35 N	87.47 W
Tinniswood, Mount ∧	238	50.19 N	123.50 W
Tinnoset	160	59.43 N	9.02 E
Tinogasta	294	28.05 S	67.34 W
Tínos	172	37.32 N	25.10 E
Tínos I	172	37.38 N	25.10 E
Tin Rerhoh, Tassili ⩓	222	19.40 N	4.00 E
Tinrhert, Plateau du ⩓[1]	214	29.00 N	9.00 E
Tinsley	248	32.44 N	90.28 W
Tinsukia	206	27.29 N	95.26 E
Tintagel	238	54.12 N	125.35 W
Tinte, Cerro ∧	292	22.40 S	67.02 W
Tintina	294	27.02 S	62.45 W
Tinto ≃	168	37.12 N	6.55 W
Tioga, N. Dak., U.S.	252	48.24 N	102.56 W
Tioga, Pa., U.S.	242	41.55 N	77.08 W
Tioga ≃	242	42.09 N	77.05 W
Tiojala	160	61.10 N	23.52 E
Tioman, Pulau I	200	2.48 N	104.10 E
Tiona	266	41.45 N	79.03 W
Tione di Trento	170	46.02 N	10.43 E
Tionesta	266	41.30 N	79.27 W
Tioro, Selat ⋃	198	4.40 S	122.20 E
Tioughnioga ≃	242	42.14 N	75.51 W
Tipasa	168	36.35 N	2.27 E
Tipitapa	280	12.12 N	86.06 W
Tipp City	242	39.58 N	84.10 W
Tippecanoe, Ind., U.S.	268	41.12 N	86.07 W
Tippecanoe, Ohio, U.S.	266	40.16 N	81.17 W
Tippecanoe □[6]	268	40.25 N	86.53 W
Tippecanoe ≃	248	40.31 N	86.47 W
Tipperary	162	52.29 N	8.10 W
Tipperary □[6]	162	52.40 N	8.20 W
Tipton, Eng., U.K.	174	52.32 N	2.05 W
Tipton, Calif., U.S.	272	36.04 N	119.19 W
Tipton, Ind., U.S.	268	40.17 N	86.02 W
Tipton, Iowa, U.S.	244	41.46 N	91.08 W
Tipton, Mich., U.S.	268	42.01 N	84.04 W
Tipton, Mo., U.S.	248	38.39 N	92.47 W
Tipton, Okla., U.S.	250	34.30 N	99.08 W
Tipton, Pa., U.S.	266	40.38 N	78.18 W
Tipton □[6]	268	40.17 N	86.02 W
Tipton, Mount ∧	254	35.33 N	110.10 W
Tiptonville	248	36.23 N	89.29 W
Tip Top Mountain ∧	244	48.16 N	85.59 W
Tiputini ≃	290	0.47 S	75.32 W
Tiquina	292	16.13 S	68.52 W
Tiquirre ≃	290	2.38 N	59.56 W
Tiquisate	280	14.17 N	91.22 W
Ṭīrā	210	32.14 N	34.56 E
Tiradentes	296	21.07 S	44.11 W
Tiradero	278	18.10 N	91.10 W
Tīrān, Jazīrat I	208	27.56 N	34.34 E
Tīrān, Maḍīq (Strait of Tiran) ⋃	220	27.58 N	34.28 E
Tiran, Strait of → Tīrān, Maḍīq ⋃	220	27.58 N	34.28 E
Tiranë	172	41.20 N	19.50 E
Tirano	170	46.13 N	10.10 E
Tiraque	292	17.25 S	65.43 W
Tiraspol'	158	46.51 N	29.38 E
Tirat Karmel	210	32.46 N	34.58 E
Tire	212	38.04 N	27.45 E
Tiree I	162	56.31 N	6.49 W
Tiree, Passage of ⋃	162	56.30 N	6.30 W
Tire Hill	266	40.16 N	78.55 W
Tîrgovişte	172	44.56 N	25.27 E
Tîrgu-Cărbuneşti	172	44.58 N	23.31 E
Tîrgu-Frumos	172	47.13 N	27.00 E
Tîrgu-Jiu	172	45.02 N	23.17 E
Tîrgu-Lăpuş	172	47.27 N	23.52 E
Tîrgu-Mureş	172	46.33 N	24.33 E
Tîrgu-Neamţ	172	47.12 N	26.22 E
Tîrgu-Ocna	172	46.15 N	26.37 E
Tîrgu-Secuesc	172	46.00 N	26.08 E
Tîrguşor	172	44.28 N	28.25 E
Tirich Mīr ∧	206	36.15 N	71.50 E
Tirilye	172	40.23 N	28.47 E
Tirins ⊥	172	37.36 N	22.48 E
Tîrnăveni	172	46.20 N	24.17 E
Tírnavos	172	39.45 N	22.17 E
Tirnovo → Veliko Târnovo	172	43.04 N	25.39 E
Tiro	266	40.54 N	82.46 W
Tirol □[3]	180	47.15 N	11.20 E
Tirón ≃	168	41.23 N	4.31 W
Tiros	296	19.00 S	45.58 W
Tirschenreuth	164	49.53 N	12.21 E
Tirso ≃	170	39.52 N	8.33 E
Tirua Point ≻	230	38.23 S	174.38 E
Tiruchchirāppalli	204	10.48 N	78.41 E
Tisa (Tisza) ≃	172	45.15 N	20.17 E
Tisdale	232	52.51 N	104.04 W
Tishomingo, Miss., U.S.	248	34.38 N	88.14 W
Tishomingo, Okla., U.S.	250	34.14 N	96.40 W
Tiskilwa	244	41.18 N	89.30 W
Tisma	280	12.05 N	86.01 W
Tišnov	164	49.21 N	16.25 E
Tisovec	164	48.43 N	19.57 E
Tissemsilt	168	35.35 N	1.50 E
Tīsta ≃	206	25.23 N	89.43 E
Tisza (Tisa) ≃	172	45.15 N	20.17 E
Tiszaföldvár	164	46.59 N	20.15 E
Tiszafüred	164	47.27 N	20.46 E
Tiszavasvári	164	47.58 N	21.22 E
Tit-Ary	186	71.58 N	127.01 E
Titel	172	45.12 N	20.18 E
Titeri ⩓	168	36.00 N	3.30 E
Titicaca, Lago ⊜	292	15.50 S	69.20 W
Titicus	261	41.18 N	73.30 W
Titograd	172	42.26 N	19.14 E
Titonka	244	43.14 N	94.03 W
Titova Korenica	170	44.45 N	15.43 E
Titovo Užice	172	43.51 N	19.51 E
Titov Veles	172	41.41 N	21.48 E
Titov Vrh ∧	172	42.00 N	20.51 E
Titran	160	63.40 N	8.18 E
Tittabawassee ≃	244	43.23 N	83.59 W
Tittling	164	48.44 N	13.23 E
Tittmoning	164	48.04 N	12.46 E
Titu	172	44.41 N	25.16 E
Titule	214	3.17 N	25.32 E
Titusville, Fla., U.S.	246	28.37 N	80.49 W
Titusville, N.J., U.S.	262	40.18 N	74.53 W
Titusville, Pa., U.S.	266	41.38 N	79.41 W
Tiverton, Eng., U.K.	174	50.55 N	3.29 W
Tiverton, R.I., U.S.	261	41.38 N	71.12 W
Tivoli, Gren.	285k	12.10 N	61.37 W
Tivoli, It.	184	41.58 N	12.48 E
Tivoli, N.Y., U.S.	261	42.04 N	73.55 W
Tivoli, Tex., U.S.	250	28.27 N	96.53 W
Ṭiwāl, Wādī V	220	10.22 N	22.43 E
Tiwi	202	13.28 N	123.41 E
Tiyunhe ≃	194	39.07 N	117.43 E
Tizatlán ⊥	278	19.21 N	98.15 W
Tizimín	278	21.10 N	88.10 W
Tizi-Ouzou	168	36.48 N	4.02 E
Tiznados ≃	290	8.16 N	67.47 W
Tizoc	250	25.41 N	101.59 W
Tjiandjur	198	6.49 S	107.08 E
Tjilatjap	226	7.44 S	109.00 E
Tjirebon	198	6.44 S	108.34 E
Tlacolula [de Matamoros]	278	16.57 N	96.29 W
Tlacotalpan	278	18.37 N	95.40 W
Tlacotepec	278	17.46 N	99.59 W
Tlahualilo de Zaragoza	278	26.07 N	103.27 W
Tlalixtaquilla	278	17.21 N	98.28 W
Tlalnepantla	278	19.33 N	99.12 W
Tlaltenango de Sánchez Román	278	21.47 N	103.19 W
Tlapaneco ≃	278	18.05 N	98.48 W
Tlaxcala [de Xicoténcatl]	278	19.19 N	98.14 W
Tlaxiaco	278	17.16 N	97.41 W
Tlemcen	214	34.52 N	1.15 W
Tlétat ed Douair	168	36.00 N	2.55 E
Tlētē Ouāte Gharbī, Jabal ∧	212	35.20 N	39.13 E
Tlevak Strait ⋃	238	55.03 N	132.58 W
Tłuszcz	164	52.26 N	21.26 E
Tnâot ≃	200	11.29 N	104.57 E
Tnekvejem ≃	236	65.51 N	177.30 E
Toa ≃	284p	20.23 N	74.32 W
Toa, Cuchillas de ⩓	284p	20.27 N	74.58 W
Toa Alta	284m	18.23 N	66.15 W
Toa Baja	284m	18.27 N	66.15 W
Toabré ≃	280	8.55 N	80.32 W
Toaca ∧	172	46.59 N	25.57 E
Toachi ≃	290	0.08 N	79.18 W
Toahayaná	278	26.08 N	107.44 W
Toana Range ⩓	258	40.50 N	114.20 W
Toano, It.	170	44.23 N	10.34 E
Toano, Va., U.S.	262	37.23 N	76.48 W
Toast	246	36.30 N	80.38 W
Toay	294	36.40 S	64.25 W
Toba	192	34.29 N	136.51 E
Toba ≃	238	50.30 N	124.15 W
Toba, Danau ⊜	200	2.35 N	98.50 E
Tobacco ≃	244	43.49 N	84.24 W
Tobacco Plains Indian Reserve ◆[4]	238	49.04 N	115.06 W
Tobacco Root Mountains ⩓	256	45.35 N	112.00 W
Tobago I	285r	11.15 N	60.40 W
Toba Inlet C	238	50.20 N	124.50 W
Toba Kākar Range ⩓	206	31.15 N	68.00 E
Tobarra	168	38.35 N	1.41 W
Tobas	294	28.08 S	62.42 W
Tobe Jube, Bahía C	290	9.15 N	60.45 W
Tobelo	198	1.44 N	128.01 E
Tobercurry	162	54.03 N	8.43 W
Tobermory	162	56.37 N	6.05 W
Tōbetsu	192a	43.13 N	141.31 E
Tobi I	198	3.00 N	131.10 E
Tobias	252	40.25 N	97.20 W
Tobin, Mount ∧	258	40.22 N	117.32 W
Tobique ≃	240	46.46 N	67.42 W
Tobi-shima I	192	39.12 N	139.34 E
Toblach → Dobbiaco	170	46.44 N	12.14 E
Tobol	158	52.40 N	62.39 E
Tobol ≃	186	58.10 N	68.12 E
Tobol'sk	158	58.12 N	68.16 E
Toboso	202	10.43 N	123.31 E
Tobruk → Ṭubruq	220	32.05 N	23.59 E
Tobseda	160	68.36 N	52.14 E
Tobyhanna	242	41.11 N	75.25 W
Tobyš ≃	160	65.30 N	51.00 E
Tocaima	290	4.28 N	74.38 W
Tocantínia	286	9.33 S	48.22 W
Tocantinópolis	286	6.20 S	47.25 W
Tocantins ≃, Bra.	292	5.21 S	55.58 W
Tocantins ≃, Bra.	296	1.45 S	49.10 W
Tocantins, Parque Nacional do ♠	296	14.07 S	47.37 W
Tocantinzinho ≃	296	13.57 S	48.20 W
Toccoa	246	34.35 N	83.19 W
Toccoa ≃	246	34.59 N	84.23 W
Tochcha Lake ⊜	238	54.56 N	125.54 W
Tochigi	192	36.23 N	139.44 E
Tochigi □[5]	192	36.45 N	139.45 E
Tochio	192	37.28 N	139.00 E
Tochta	160	62.14 N	48.48 E
Töcksfors	160	59.30 N	11.50 E
Toco, Chile	294	22.05 S	69.35 W
Toco, Trin.	285r	10.50 N	60.57 W
Tocoa	280	15.41 N	86.03 W
Toconao	294	23.11 S	68.01 W
Tocopilla	294	22.05 S	70.12 W
Tocorpuri, Cerro de ∧	292	22.26 S	67.55 W
Tocuyo ≃	290	11.03 N	68.23 W
Tocuyo de la Costa	290	11.02 N	68.23 W
Todd	266	40.16 N	78.04 W
Toddville, Md., U.S.	262	38.18 N	76.04 W
Toddville, N.Y., U.S.	261	41.17 N	73.53 W
Todi	184	42.47 N	12.24 E
Todo-saki ≻	192	39.33 N	142.05 E
Todos Santos, Bol.	292	16.48 S	65.08 W
Todos Santos, Méx.	278	23.27 N	110.13 W
Todos Santos, Bahía C	278	31.48 N	116.42 W
Todtnau	164	47.50 N	7.56 E
Toetoes Bay C	230	46.36 S	168.43 E
Tofield	238	53.22 N	112.40 W
Tofino	238	49.09 N	125.54 W
Togi	192	37.08 N	136.44 E
Togiak	236	59.04 N	160.24 W
Togiak Bay C	236	59.00 N	160.30 W
Togiak Lake ⊜	236	59.38 N	159.35 W
Togian, Kepulauan II	198	0.20 S	122.00 E
Togo □[1]	214	8.00 N	1.10 E
Togoron	202	12.36 N	123.37 E
Togučin	186	55.16 N	84.23 E
Togwottee Pass)(	254	43.45 N	110.04 W
Tŏgyu-san ∧	194	36.48 N	127.23 E
Tōhaku	192	35.30 N	133.40 E
Tohakum Peak ∧	258	40.11 N	119.27 W
Tohma ≃, Tür.	208	38.31 N	38.25 E
Tohma ≃, Tür.	212	38.31 N	37.38 E
Tohopekaliga, Lake ⊜	246	28.12 N	81.23 W
Toi-misaki ≻	192	31.20 N	131.22 E
Toiyabe Dome ∧	258	38.51 N	117.22 W
Toiyabe Range ⩓	258	39.10 N	117.10 W
Tōjō	192	34.53 N	133.16 E
Tok	236	63.20 N	142.59 W
Tokachi ≃	192a	42.44 N	143.42 E
Tokachi-dake ∧	192a	43.25 N	142.41 E
Tokachi-heiya ≍	192a	43.00 N	143.30 E
Tōkamachi	192	37.08 N	138.46 E
Tokara-kaikyō ⋃	193b	30.10 N	130.10 E
Tokara-rettō II	193b	29.36 N	129.43 E
Tokashiki-shima I	193b	26.11 N	127.21 E
Tokat	212	40.19 N	36.34 E
Tŏkchŏk-kundo II	194	37.14 N	126.07 E
Tok-dō I	192	37.17 N	131.53 E
Tokeland	270	46.42 N	123.59 W
Tokelau Islands II	148	9.00 S	171.45 W
Toki	192	35.21 N	137.11 E
Tokko	186	59.59 N	119.52 E
Toklat ≃	236	64.27 N	150.17 W
Tokmak	186	47.15 N	35.43 E
Toko Range ⩓	228	23.05 S	138.20 E
Tokoro ≃	192a	44.07 N	144.05 E
Tokoroa	230	38.13 S	175.52 E
Toksook Bay	236	60.32 N	165.06 W
Tokuno-shima I	193b	27.45 N	128.58 E
Tokushima	192	34.04 N	134.34 E
Tokuyama	192	34.03 N	131.49 E
Tokwe ≃	224	21.09 S	31.30 E
Tōkyō	192	35.42 N	139.46 E
Tokyo Bay → Tōkyō-wan C	192	35.25 N	139.47 E
Tōkyō-daigaku-uchūkūkan-kenkyūsho 41u	192	31.17 N	131.05 E
Tōkyō-wan C	192	35.25 N	139.47 E
Tolbuhin	172	43.34 N	27.50 E
Tolé	280	8.15 N	81.42 W
Toledo, Bol.	292	18.10 S	67.25 W
Toledo, Bra.	294	24.44 S	53.45 W
Toledo, Col.	290	7.19 N	72.28 W
Toledo, Esp.	168	39.52 N	4.01 W
Toledo, Pil.	202	10.22 N	123.38 E
Toledo, Ill., U.S.	248	39.16 N	88.15 W
Toledo, Iowa, U.S.	244	42.00 N	92.35 W
Toledo, Ohio, U.S.	266	41.39 N	83.32 W
Toledo, Oreg., U.S.	256	44.37 N	123.56 W
Toledo, Wash., U.S.	270	46.26 N	122.51 W
Toledo □[5]	280	16.20 N	88.55 W
Toledo, Montes de ⩓	168	39.33 N	4.20 W
Toledo Bend Reservoir ⊜[1]	248	31.30 N	93.45 W
Tolentino	184	43.12 N	13.17 E
Tolima □[5]	290	3.45 N	75.15 W
Tolima, Nevado del ∧	290	4.40 N	75.19 W
Tolitoli	198	1.02 N	120.49 E
Toljatti	160	53.31 N	49.26 E
Tol'ka	186	64.02 N	81.55 E
Tolkmicko	164	54.20 N	19.31 E
Tolland	261	41.52 N	72.22 W
Tolland □[6]	261	41.52 N	72.22 W
Tollense ≃	164	53.54 N	13.02 E
Tolleson	254	33.27 N	112.16 W
Tollhouse	272	37.01 N	119.24 W
Tolloche	294	25.30 S	63.30 W
Tolmačovo	160	58.52 N	29.55 E
Tolmezzo	170	46.24 N	13.01 E
Tolmin	170	46.11 N	13.44 E
Tolna	164	46.26 N	18.46 E
Tolna □[6]	164	46.30 N	18.35 E
Tolo, Teluk C	198	2.00 S	122.30 E
Tolong Bay C	202	9.18 N	122.47 E
Tolono	248	39.59 N	88.16 W
Tolosa	168	43.08 N	2.04 W
Tolovana ≃	236	64.51 N	149.45 W
Toltén	288	39.13 S	73.14 W
Tolú	290	9.31 N	75.35 W
Toluca	268	41.00 N	89.08 W
Toluca, Nevado de ∧[1]	278	19.08 N	99.44 W
Toluca [de Lerdo]	278	19.17 N	99.40 W
Tolvajarvi	160	62.17 N	31.27 E
Tom' ≃	186	56.50 N	84.27 E
Tomah	244	43.59 N	90.30 W
Tomahawk	244	45.28 N	89.44 W
Tomahawk ≃	244	45.29 N	89.46 W
Tomakomai	192a	42.38 N	141.36 E
Tomar	168	39.36 N	8.25 W
Tomás Barrón (Eucaliptus)	292	17.35 S	67.31 W
Tomás Gomensoro	294	30.26 S	57.26 W
Tomasina ≃	244	46.40 N	76.15 W
Tomaszów Lubelski	164	50.28 N	23.25 E
Tomaszów Mazowiecki	164	51.32 N	20.01 E
Tomatlán	278	19.56 N	105.15 W
Tomave	292	20.06 S	66.35 W
Tomazina	296	23.46 S	49.58 W
Tombador, Serra do ⩓[1]	292	12.00 S	57.40 W
Tomball	250	30.06 N	95.37 W
Tombigbee ≃	248	31.04 N	87.58 W
Tombos	296	20.55 S	42.02 W
Tombouctou (Timbuktu)	222	16.46 N	3.01 W
Tombstone	254	31.43 N	110.04 W
Tombstone Mountain ∧	236	64.25 N	138.30 W
Tomé	294	36.37 S	72.57 W
Tomelilla	160	55.33 N	13.57 E
Tomelloso	168	39.10 N	3.01 W
Tomiko Lake ⊜	244	46.32 N	79.49 W
Tomini	198	0.30 N	120.32 E
Tomini, Teluk C	198	0.20 S	121.00 E
Tomioka	192	36.15 N	138.54 E
T'omkino	160	55.05 N	35.01 E
Tomkins Cove	261	41.15 N	73.59 W
Tommot	186	58.58 N	126.19 E
Tomo ≃	290	5.20 N	67.48 W
Tompkins	240	47.47 N	59.15 W
Tompkinsville	248	36.42 N	85.41 W
Tomptokan	186	57.06 N	133.59 E
Tomra	160	62.35 N	6.56 E
Toms ≃	242	39.57 N	74.07 W
Tomsk	186	56.30 N	84.58 E
Toms River	262	39.58 N	74.12 W
Tonalá	278	16.04 N	93.45 W
Tonami	192	36.38 N	136.54 E
Tonantins	290	2.47 S	67.47 W
Tonantins ≃	290	2.47 S	67.47 W
Tonasket	256	48.42 N	119.26 W
Tonawanda	264	43.01 N	78.53 W
Tonawanda, Town of	264	42.59 N	78.52 W
Tondabayashi	192	34.30 N	135.36 E
Tondano	198	1.19 N	124.54 E
Tønder	164	54.56 N	8.54 E
Tondou, Massif du ⩓	220	7.50 N	23.45 E
Tone ≃	192	35.44 N	140.51 E
Tongaat	224	29.37 S	31.03 E
Tonga Islands II	148	20.00 S	175.00 W
Tonganoxie	252	39.07 N	95.05 W
Tonga Ridge ⊹[3]	148	22.00 S	175.00 W
Tongariro ∧	230	39.08 S	175.40 E
Tongariro National Park ♠	230	39.15 S	175.30 E
Tonga Trench ⊹[1]	148	22.00 S	173.00 W
Tongbai	196	32.22 N	113.24 E
Tongbaishan ⩓	196	32.20 N	113.15 E
Tongcheng	190	31.03 N	116.58 E
Tongchuan	190	35.01 N	109.01 E
Tongeren	164	50.47 N	5.28 E
Tongguan	190	34.38 N	110.20 E
Tonghai	200	24.07 N	102.49 E
Tonghua	194	41.50 N	125.55 E
Tongjosŏn-man C	194	39.30 N	128.00 E
Tongliao	190	43.39 N	122.14 E
Tongling	196	30.53 N	117.46 E
Tongoy	294	30.15 S	71.30 W
Tongpanshan I	196	27.43 N	120.55 E
Tongquil Island I	202	6.02 N	121.50 E
Tongren	190	27.38 N	109.03 E
Tongsa Dzong	204	27.31 N	90.31 E
Tongtianhe ≃	206	33.25 N	96.32 E
Tongtianheyan	190	33.50 N	92.28 E
Tongue	162	58.28 N	4.25 W
Tongue ≃, U.S.	256	46.24 N	105.52 W
Tongue ≃, N. Dak., U.S.	252	48.56 N	97.18 W
Tongue of the Ocean ⊹[1]	282	24.00 N	77.20 W
Tongue River Irrigation Reservoir ⊜[1]	256	45.06 N	106.47 W
Tongxi ≃	196	29.49 N	119.41 E
Tongxian	194	39.55 N	116.39 E
Tongzi	190	28.08 N	106.49 E
Tonica	268	41.13 N	89.04 W
Tónichi	278	28.35 N	109.34 W
Tonk	206	26.11 N	75.47 E
Tonkawa	250	36.41 N	97.18 W
Tonkin, Gulf of C	200	20.00 N	108.00 E
Tonkino	160	57.23 N	46.28 E
Tonle Sap → Sab, Tônlé ⊜	200	12.50 N	104.00 E
Tonnay-Boutonne	166	45.58 N	0.42 W
Tonneins	166	44.23 N	0.19 E
Tonnerre	176	47.51 N	3.58 E
Tönning	164	54.19 N	8.56 E
Tōno	192	39.19 N	141.32 E
Tonopah	258	38.04 N	117.14 W
Tonoro ≃	290	9.29 N	63.17 W
Tonoshō	192	34.29 N	134.11 E
Tonosí	290	7.20 N	80.20 W
Tonota	224	21.29 S	27.29 E
Tønsberg	160	59.17 N	10.25 E
Tonstad	160	58.40 N	6.43 E
Tontogany	268	41.25 N	83.44 W
Tonto National Monument ♠	254	33.34 N	111.02 W
Tooele	254	40.32 N	112.18 W
Toolik ≃	236	69.55 N	149.30 W
Toomsboro	246	32.50 N	83.05 W
Toora-Chem	186	52.28 N	96.17 E
Toosey Indian Reserve ◆[4]	238	51.56 N	122.29 W
Toowoomba	228	27.33 S	151.57 E
Topanga	274	34.06 N	118.36 W
Topawa	254	31.48 N	111.51 W
Topeka, Ind., U.S.	268	41.32 N	85.32 W
Topeka, Kans., U.S.	252	39.03 N	95.41 W
Topia	278	25.13 N	106.34 W
Topki	186	55.16 N	85.36 E
Topl'a ≃	164	48.45 N	21.45 E
Topley	238	54.49 N	126.18 W
Toplica ≃	172	43.13 N	21.49 E
Toplița	172	46.55 N	25.21 E
Topocalma, Punta ≻	294	34.08 S	72.01 W
Topol'čany	164	48.34 N	18.10 E
Topolnica ≃	172	42.11 N	24.18 E
Topolobampo	278	25.36 N	109.03 W
Topolog	172	44.53 N	28.22 E
Topolovățu	172	45.46 N	21.37 E
Topolovgrad	172	42.05 N	26.20 E
Topozero, Ozero ⊜	160	65.40 N	32.00 E
Toppenish	256	46.23 N	120.19 W
Topsa	160	62.39 N	43.34 E
Topsfield	261	42.38 N	70.57 W
Topsham	242	43.56 N	69.58 W
Topton	262	40.30 N	75.42 W
Toquima Range ⩓	258	39.00 N	117.00 W
Toquop Wash V	258	36.45 N	114.11 W
Torawitan, Tandjung ≻	198	1.46 N	124.58 E
Toraya	292	14.04 S	73.17 W
Torbalı	172	38.10 N	27.21 E
Torbat-e Ḥeydarīyeh	208	35.16 N	59.13 E
Torbat-e Jām	208	35.14 N	60.36 E
Torbay, Newf., Can.	240	47.40 N	52.43 W
Torbay → Torquay, Eng., U.K.	174	50.28 N	3.30 W
Torbert, Mount ∧	236	61.25 N	152.24 W
Torbrook	240	44.55 N	64.59 W
Torch ≃	232	53.50 N	103.05 W
Torch Lake ⊜	244	45.00 N	85.19 W
Tordera ≃	168	41.39 N	2.47 E
Tordesillas	168	41.30 N	5.00 W
Töre	160	65.54 N	22.39 E
Toreno	168	42.42 N	6.30 W
Torez	158	48.01 N	38.37 E
Torgau	164	51.34 N	13.00 E
Torgelow	164	53.37 N	14.00 E
Torhout	176	51.04 N	3.06 E
Torín	278	27.34 N	110.14 W
Toriñana, Cabo ≻	168	43.03 N	9.18 W
Torino (Turin)	182	45.03 N	7.40 E
Torino □[4]	182	45.08 N	7.22 E
Torio ≃	168	42.35 N	5.34 W
Toriparu	296	16.20 S	53.55 W
Torit	214	4.24 N	32.34 E
Tormes ≃	168	41.18 N	6.29 W
Torna	160	68.04 N	44.10 E

Symbols in the index entries are identified on page 360.

Name	Page	Lat°′	Long°′
Tornado Mountain ∧	238	49.58 N	114.39 W
Torneälven ≃	158	65.48 N	24.08 E
Tornesch	178	53.41 N	9.43 E
Torneträsk ⊜	160	68.20 N	19.10 E
Torngat Mountains ⋀	232	59.00 N	64.00 W
Tornillo	254	31.27 N	106.05 W
Tornio	160	65.51 N	24.08 E
Tornquist	294	38.06 S	62.14 W
Toro	168	41.31 N	5.24 W
Toro, Cerro del ∧	294	29.08 S	69.48 W
Toro, Punta ≻	294	33.47 S	71.49 W
Törökszentmiklós	164	47.11 N	20.25 E
Torola ≃	280	13.53 N	88.30 W
Toroni, Cerro ∧	292	19.43 S	68.41 W
Toronto, Ont., Can.	264	43.39 N	79.23 W
Toronto, Kans., U.S.	252	37.48 N	95.57 W
Toronto, Ohio, U.S.	266	40.28 N	80.36 W
Toronto, S. Dak., U.S.	252	44.34 N	96.39 W
Toronto Reservoir ⊜[1]	252	37.46 N	95.57 W
Toro Peak ∧	258	33.32 N	116.25 W
Toropec	160	56.30 N	31.39 E
Tororo	218	0.42 N	34.11 E
Toros Dağı ∧	212	37.23 N	34.34 E
Toros Dağları ⋀	212	37.00 N	33.00 E
Torosozero	160	62.30 N	38.10 E
Torotoro	292	18.07 S	65.46 W
Torquay, Sask., Can.	252	49.08 N	103.31 W
Torquay (Torbay), Eng., U.K.	174	50.28 N	3.30 W
Torquemada	168	42.02 N	4.19 W
Torrance, Calif., U.S.	274	33.50 N	118.19 W
Torrance, Pa., U.S.	266	40.25 N	79.14 W
Torrão	168	38.18 N	8.13 W
Torre Annunziata	184	40.45 N	14.27 E
Torre Baja	168	40.07 N	1.15 W
Torreblanca	168	40.13 N	0.12 E
Torrecilla ∧	168	37.36 N	2.31 W
Torrecilla en Cameros	168	42.16 N	2.37 W
Torre del Campo	168	37.46 N	3.53 W
Torre del Greco	184	40.47 N	14.22 E
Torre de Moncorvo	168	41.10 N	7.03 W
Torredonjimeno	168	37.46 N	3.57 W
Torrejoncillo	168	39.54 N	6.28 W
Torrejón de Ardoz	168	40.27 N	3.29 W
Torrelaguna	168	40.50 N	3.32 W
Torrelavega	168	43.21 N	4.03 W
Torremaggiore	184	41.41 N	15.17 E
Torremolinos	168	36.37 N	4.30 W
Torrens, Lake ⊜	228	31.00 S	137.50 E
Torrent	294	28.50 S	56.28 W
Torrente	168	39.26 N	0.28 W
Torreón	278	25.33 N	103.26 W
Torre Pellice	170	44.49 N	7.13 E
Torreperogil	168	38.02 N	3.17 W
Tôrres	294	29.21 S	49.44 W
Torres-de-Alcala	168	35.10 N	4.16 W
Torres Novas	168	39.29 N	8.32 W
Torres Strait ⋓	198	10.25 S	142.10 E
Torres Vedras	168	39.06 N	9.16 W
Torrevieja	168	37.59 N	0.41 W
Torridon	162	57.33 N	5.31 W
Torridon, Loch C	162	57.35 N	5.50 W
Torriglia	170	44.31 N	9.10 E
Torrijos, Esp.	168	39.59 N	4.17 W
Torrijos, Pil.	202	13.19 N	122.05 E
Torrington, Conn., U.S.	261	41.48 N	73.08 W
Torrington, Wyo., U.S.	252	42.04 N	104.11 W
Torrinha	296	22.26 S	48.09 W
Torrox	168	36.46 N	3.58 W
Torsby	160	60.08 N	13.00 E
Tors Cove	240	47.13 N	52.50 W
Tórshavn	158	62.01 N	6.46 W
Tortola I	282	18.26 N	64.37 W
Tortoli	170	39.55 N	9.39 E
Tortona	182	44.54 N	8.52 E
Tortorici	170	38.02 N	14.39 E
Tortosa	168	40.48 N	0.31 E
Tortosa, Cabo de ≻	168	40.43 N	0.55 E
Tortue, Île de la I	282	20.01 N	72.50 W
Toruń	164	53.02 N	18.35 E
Torunos	290	8.30 N	70.04 W
Torup	160	56.58 N	13.05 E
Torysa ≃	164	48.39 N	21.21 E
Toržok	160	57.03 N	34.58 E
Torzym (Stemberg in der Neumark)	164	52.20 N	15.04 E
Tosa	192	33.29 N	133.25 E
Tosas, Puerto de)(	168	42.19 N	2.01 E
Tosa-shimizu	192	32.46 N	132.57 E
Tosa-wan C	192	33.20 N	133.40 E
Toscana □[4]	184	43.25 N	11.00 E
To-shima I	192	32.12 N	130.05 E
Tosno	160	59.33 N	30.53 E
T'osovo-Netyl'skij	160	58.57 N	31.04 E
T'osovskij	160	58.48 N	30.52 E
Tostado	294	29.15 S	61.45 W
Tõstamaa	160	58.20 N	24.00 E
Toszek (Tost)	164	50.28 N	18.32 E
Tota, Laguna de ⊜	290	5.33 N	72.55 W
Totagatic ≃	244	46.05 N	92.11 W
Totana	168	37.46 N	1.30 W
Toteng	218	20.22 S	22.58 E
Tôtes	166	49.41 N	1.03 E
Totes Gebirge ⋀	164	47.42 N	13.55 E
Tot'ma	160	59.57 N	42.45 E
Totnes	174	50.25 N	3.41 W
Totness	290	5.53 N	56.19 W
Totonicapán	280	14.55 N	91.22 W
Totonicapán □[5]	280	15.00 N	91.20 W
Totora, Bol.	292	17.42 S	65.09 W
Totora, Bol.	292	17.49 S	68.07 W
Totora Palca	292	19.55 S	65.26 W
Totoras	294	32.40 S	61.10 W
Totos	292	13.35 S	74.27 W
Tototlán	278	20.33 N	102.48 W
Totson Mountain ∧	236	64.26 N	157.15 W
Tottenham	264	44.01 N	79.49 W
Totton	174	50.56 N	1.29 W
Tottori	192	35.30 N	134.14 E
Touba	214	8.17 N	7.41 W
Touba □[5]	222	8.20 N	7.30 W
Toubkal, Jbel ∧	214	31.05 N	7.55 W
Touchet ≃	256	46.02 N	118.41 W
Touchwood Lake ⊜	238	54.50 N	111.23 W
Toucy	166	47.44 N	3.18 E
Toudaojiang ≃	194	42.36 N	127.11 E
Tougaloo	248	32.24 N	90.09 W
Touggourt	214	33.10 N	6.00 E
Tougué □[4]	222	11.28 N	11.36 W
Touisset	261	41.43 N	71.14 W
Toul	180	48.41 N	5.54 E
Toulnustouc ≃	240	49.35 N	68.25 W
Toulnustouc-Nord-Est ≃	240	50.55 N	67.42 W
Toulon, Fr.	182	43.07 N	5.56 E
Toulon, Ill., U.S.	244	41.06 N	89.52 W
Toulon-sur-Arroux	166	46.42 N	4.08 E
Toulouse	166	43.36 N	1.26 E
Toumenshan I	196	28.41 N	121.46 E
Toungoo	200	18.56 N	96.26 E
Touques ≃	162	49.22 N	0.06 E
Toura, Monts du ⋀	222	7.40 N	7.25 W
Touraine □[9]	176	47.12 N	1.30 E
Tourane → Da-nang	200	16.04 N	108.13 E
Tourcoing	176	50.43 N	3.09 E
Tournai	176	50.36 N	3.23 E
Tournon	182	45.04 N	4.50 E
Tournus	180	46.34 N	4.54 E
Tours	176	47.23 N	0.41 E
Toury	166	48.12 N	1.56 E
Touside, Pic ∧	214	21.02 N	16.25 E
Toustain	170	36.40 N	8.15 E
Toutle	270	46.20 N	122.41 W
Touws ≃	224	33.45 S	21.11 E
Toužim	164	50.04 N	13.00 E
Tova	160	65.58 N	40.45 E
Tovar	290	8.20 N	71.46 W
Tow	250	30.53 N	98.28 W
Towada	192	40.37 N	141.13 E
Towada-hachimantai-kokuritsu-kōen ♠	192	40.35 N	140.53 E
Towada-ko ⊜	192	40.28 N	140.55 E
Towanda, Ill., U.S.	268	40.34 N	88.54 W
Towanda, Kans., U.S.	252	37.48 N	97.02 W
Towanda, Pa., U.S.	242	41.46 N	76.26 W
Towar Gardens	268	42.45 N	84.28 W
Towcester	174	52.08 N	1.00 W
Tower	244	47.48 N	92.17 W
Tower City, N. Dak., U.S.	252	46.55 N	97.40 W
Tower City, Pa., U.S.	262	40.35 N	76.33 W
Tower Hamlets ◆[8]	174	51.32 N	0.03 W
Tower Hill	248	39.23 N	88.58 W
Towla, Mount ∧	224	21.22 S	29.52 E
Town Bank	262	39.00 N	74.56 W
Towner	252	48.21 N	100.25 W
Town of Pines	268	41.41 N	86.58 W
Townsend, Del., U.S.	262	39.24 N	75.41 W
Townsend, Mass., U.S.	261	42.40 N	71.42 W
Townsend, Mont., U.S.	256	46.19 N	111.31 W
Townsend, Mount ∧	228	36.25 S	148.15 E
Townshend Island I	228	22.15 S	150.30 E
Townsville	228	19.16 S	146.48 E
Townville	266	41.41 N	79.53 W
Towson	242	39.24 N	76.36 W
Towyn	162	52.35 N	4.05 W
Toyah	250	31.19 N	103.47 W
Tōya-ko ⊜	192a	42.35 N	140.51 E
Toyama	192	36.41 N	137.13 E
Toyama-heiya ≚	192	36.40 N	137.15 E
Toyama-wan C	192	36.50 N	137.10 E
Tōyō	192	33.32 N	134.18 E
Toyohashi	192	34.46 N	137.23 E
Toyokawa	192	34.49 N	137.24 E
Toyonaka	192	34.47 N	135.28 E
Toyooka	192	35.32 N	134.50 E
Toyota	192	35.05 N	137.09 E
Toyoura	192	34.08 N	130.58 E
Tozeur	214	33.55 N	8.08 E
Tozi, Mount ∧	236	65.41 N	150.58 W
Tozitna ≃	236	65.08 N	152.23 W
Trabiju	296	22.03 S	48.18 W
Trabzon	212	41.00 N	39.43 E
Tracadie	240	47.31 N	64.54 W
Tracajá, Cachoeira L	292	10.29 S	64.05 W
Tracy, Calif., U.S.	272	37.44 N	121.25 W
Tracy, Minn., U.S.	252	44.14 N	95.37 W
Tracy City	248	35.16 N	85.44 W
Tracyton	270	47.37 N	122.39 W
Tradate	182	45.43 N	8.54 E
Tradewater ≃	248	37.31 N	88.03 W
Traer	244	42.12 N	92.28 W
Trafalgar, Cabo ≻	168	36.11 N	6.02 W
Trafford	266	40.23 N	79.45 W
Tragacete	168	40.21 N	1.51 W
Traid	168	40.40 N	1.49 W
Traiguén	294	38.15 S	72.41 W
Trail	238	49.06 N	117.42 W
Trail Creek	268	41.42 N	86.52 W
Traíra (Taraira) ≃	290	1.04 S	69.26 W
Traíras ≃	296	14.07 S	48.31 W
Trakt	160	62.44 N	51.11 E
Tralee	162	52.16 N	9.42 W
Tralee Bay C	162	52.15 N	9.59 W
Tramelan	180	47.13 N	7.06 E
Trammel	246	37.01 N	82.18 W
Tramore	162	52.10 N	7.10 W
Trân	172	42.50 N	22.39 E
Tranås	160	58.03 N	14.59 E
Trancas	294	26.20 S	65.20 W
Tranco, Embalse del ⊜[1]	168	38.10 N	2.45 W
Trancoso, Méx.	278	22.44 N	102.22 W
Trancoso, Port.	168	40.47 N	7.21 W
Tranebjerg	160	55.50 N	10.36 E
Trang	200	7.33 N	99.36 E
Trangan, Pulau I	198	6.35 S	134.20 E
Tran Grande ≃	202	6.43 N	124.01 E
Trani	170	41.17 N	16.26 E
Tranninh, Plateau du ⋀[1]	200	19.30 N	103.10 E
Tranqueras	294	31.12 S	55.45 W
Tranquilla	280	8.28 N	80.13 W
Tranquillity	272	36.39 N	120.15 W
Transcona	252	49.54 N	97.00 W
Transfer	266	41.20 N	80.26 W
Transkei □[9]	224	31.20 S	29.00 E
Transvaal □[3]	224	25.00 S	29.00 E
Transylvania □[9]	172	46.30 N	24.00 E
Transylvanian Alps → Carpaţii Meridionali ⋀	172	45.30 N	24.15 E
Trapani	170	38.01 N	12.31 E
Trappe, Md., U.S.	262	38.40 N	76.04 W
Trappe, Pa., U.S.	262	40.12 N	75.29 W
Trapper Peak ∧	256	45.54 N	114.18 W
Trappes	176	48.47 N	2.00 E
Traralgon	228	38.12 S	146.32 E
Traras, Monts des ⋀	168	35.10 N	1.40 W
Trarza ◆[1]	222	18.00 N	15.00 W
Trasacco	184	41.57 N	13.32 E
Trascăului, Munţii ⋀	172	46.23 N	23.33 E
Trasimeno, Lago ⊜	170	43.08 N	12.06 E
Trás-os-Montes e Alto Douro □[9]	168	41.30 N	7.15 W
Trâstenik	172	43.31 N	24.28 E
Traun	164	48.13 N	14.14 E
Traun ≃	170	48.16 N	14.22 E
Traunstein	164	47.52 N	12.38 E
Travellers Lake ⊜	228	33.18 S	142.00 E
Traver	272	36.27 N	119.29 W
Travers, Mount ∧	230	42.01 S	172.44 E
Traverse, Lake ⊜	252	45.43 N	96.40 W
Traverse City	244	44.46 N	85.37 W
Traverse Peak ∧	236	65.10 N	159.12 W
Travers Reservoir ⊜[1]	238	50.14 N	112.51 W
Travesía ⊥	280	15.20 N	87.53 W
Travis, Lake ⊜[1]	250	30.27 N	98.00 W
Travnik	170	44.14 N	17.40 E
Trazegnies	176	50.28 N	4.19 E
Trbovlje	170	46.10 N	15.03 E
Trebbia ≃	170	45.04 N	9.41 E
Třebechovice pod Orebem	164	50.12 N	16.00 E
Třebíč	164	49.13 N	15.53 E
Trebinje	172	42.43 N	18.20 E
Trebisacce	170	39.52 N	16.32 E
Trebišov	164	48.40 N	21.47 E
Trebizond → Trabzon	212	41.00 N	39.43 E
Treble Mountain ∧	238	55.50 N	129.51 W
Třeboň	164	49.00 N	14.47 E
Třeboňská pánev ≚[1]	164	49.00 N	14.50 E
Trecate	182	45.26 N	8.44 E
Trece Martires	202	14.18 N	120.52 E
Tredegar	174	51.47 N	3.16 W
Treene ≃	164	54.22 N	9.05 E
Tregosse Islets II	228	17.41 S	150.43 E
Tréguier	166	48.47 N	3.14 W
Treherne	252	49.38 N	98.41 W
Treinta y Tres	294	33.14 S	54.23 W
Trélazé	166	47.27 N	0.28 W
Trelew	288	43.15 S	65.20 W
Trelleborg	160	55.22 N	13.10 E
Tremblant, Mont ∧	232	46.15 N	74.34 W
Trembleur Lake ⊜	238	54.51 N	125.07 W
Tremedal	296	14.58 S	41.24 W
Tremont, Ill., U.S.	244	40.28 N	89.29 W
Tremont, Ind., U.S.	268	41.39 N	87.02 W
Tremont, Pa., U.S.	262	40.38 N	76.23 W
Tremonton	254	41.43 N	112.10 W
Tremp	168	42.10 N	0.54 E
Trempealeau	244	44.00 N	91.26 W
Trempealeau ≃	244	44.02 N	91.32 W
Trenčín	164	48.54 N	18.04 E
Trenel	294	35.41 S	64.07 W
Trengganu □[3]	200	5.00 N	103.00 E
Trengganu ≃	200	5.17 N	103.05 E
Trenque Lauquen	294	35.58 S	62.44 W
Trent → Trento	170	46.04 N	11.08 E
Trent ≃, Ont., Can.	244	44.06 N	77.34 W
Trent ≃, N.C., U.S.	246	35.05 N	77.02 W
Trente-et-un-Milles, Lac des ⊜	242	46.15 N	75.47 W
Trentino-Alto Adige □[4]	170	46.30 N	11.20 E
Trentino-Alto-Adigo □[4]	180	46.30 N	11.20 E
Trento	170	46.04 N	11.08 E
Trento □[4]	180	46.08 N	11.07 E
Trentola-Ducenta	184	40.59 N	14.10 E
Trenton, N.S., Can.	240	45.37 N	62.38 W
Trenton, Ont., Can.	264	44.06 N	77.35 W
Trenton, Fla., U.S.	246	29.37 N	82.49 W
Trenton, Ga., U.S.	246	34.52 N	85.31 W
Trenton, Ill., U.S.	248	38.36 N	89.41 W
Trenton, Ky., U.S.	248	36.43 N	87.16 W
Trenton, Mich., U.S.	268	42.09 N	83.11 W
Trenton, Mo., U.S.	248	40.05 N	93.37 W
Trenton, Nebr., U.S.	252	40.11 N	101.01 W
Trenton, N.J., U.S.	262	40.13 N	74.45 W
Trenton, N.C., U.S.	246	35.04 N	77.21 W
Trenton, Tenn., U.S.	248	35.59 N	88.56 W
Trenton, Tex., U.S.	250	33.26 N	96.20 W
Trentwood	256	47.42 N	117.13 W
Trepassey	240	46.44 N	53.22 W
Trepassey Bay C	240	46.40 N	52.20 W
Trepuzzi	170	40.24 N	18.05 E
Tres Algarrobos	294	35.10 S	62.47 W
Tres Árboles	294	32.24 S	56.43 W
Tres Arroyos	294	38.22 S	60.15 W
Três Corações	296	21.42 S	45.16 W
Três Coroas	294	29.32 S	50.48 W
Três de Maio	294	27.47 S	54.14 W
Tres Esquinas	290	0.43 N	75.16 W
Três Fronteiras	296	20.13 S	50.55 W
Tres Isletas	294	26.20 S	60.36 W
Três Lagoas	296	20.48 S	51.43 W
Tres Marías, Islas II	278	21.25 N	106.28 W
Três Marias, Reprêsa ⊜[1]	296	18.12 S	45.15 W
Tres Montosas ∧	254	34.06 N	107.28 W
Três Passos	294	27.27 S	53.56 W
Tres Picos, Cerro ∧, Arg.	294	38.09 S	61.57 W
Tres Picos, Cerro ∧, Méx.	278	16.34 N	94.11 W
Tres Pinos	272	36.48 N	121.19 W
Três Pontas	296	21.22 S	45.31 W
Três Ranchos	296	18.22 S	47.47 W
Tres Reyes Islands II	202	13.14 N	121.50 E
Três Rios, Bra.	296	22.07 S	43.12 W
Tres Ríos, C.R.	280	9.54 N	83.58 W
Třešť	164	49.18 N	15.30 E
Tres Zapotes ⊥	278	18.28 N	95.24 W
Tretten	160	61.19 N	10.19 E
Treuchtlingen	164	48.57 N	10.54 E
Treuen	164	50.32 N	12.18 E
Treuenbrietzen	164	52.06 N	12.52 E
Treviglio	182	45.31 N	9.35 E
Treviño	168	42.44 N	2.45 W
Treviso	170	45.40 N	12.15 E
Trevorton	262	40.47 N	76.41 W
Trevose	262	40.09 N	74.59 W
Trevose Head ≻	162	50.33 N	5.01 W
Trévoux	166	45.56 N	4.46 E
Trexlertown	262	40.33 N	75.36 W
Treze Quedas L	290	0.07 N	56.55 W
Trezevant	248	36.01 N	88.37 W
Trezzo sull'Adda	182	45.36 N	9.31 E
Trgovište	172	42.21 N	22.05 E
Trhové Sviny	164	48.51 N	14.39 E
Triang ≃	200	3.19 N	102.31 E
Triangle	262	38.33 N	77.20 W
Triberg	180	48.08 N	8.13 E
Tribune, Sask., Can.	252	49.15 N	103.50 W
Tribune, Kans., U.S.	252	38.28 N	101.45 W
Tribune Channel ⋓	238	50.50 N	126.16 W
Tricao Malal	294	37.03 S	70.20 W
Tricarico	170	40.37 N	16.09 E
Tricase	170	39.56 N	18.22 E
Trichinopoly → Tiruchchirāppalli	204	10.48 N	78.41 E
Tri County Supply Canal ≍	252	40.49 N	100.06 W
Trident Peak ∧	258	41.54 N	118.25 W
Trieben	164	47.29 N	14.30 E
Trier	164	49.45 N	6.38 E
Trieste	170	45.40 N	13.46 E
Trieste Depth ✣[1]	148	11.21 N	142.12 E
Trieux ≃	162	48.50 N	3.03 W
Trigal	292	18.17 S	64.08 W
Triglav ∧	170	46.23 N	13.50 E
Trigo Mountains ⋀	254	33.15 N	114.35 W
Trigueros	168	37.23 N	6.50 W
Trikhonís, Límni ⊜	172	38.34 N	21.28 E
Tríkkala	172	39.34 N	21.46 E
Trikora, Puntjak ∧	198	4.15 S	138.45 E
Tri Lakes	268	41.15 N	85.27 W
Trilby	246	28.28 N	82.12 W
Trim	162	53.34 N	6.47 W
Trimbach	180	47.22 N	7.54 E
Trincheras, Méx.	250	25.37 N	101.55 W
Trincheras, Méx.	278	30.24 N	111.32 W
Trincomalee	204	8.34 N	81.14 E
Trindade	296	16.40 S	49.30 W
Trindade I	288	20.31 S	29.19 W
Třinec	164	49.41 N	18.40 E
Trinidad, Bol.	292	14.47 S	64.47 W
Trinidad, Col.	290	5.25 N	71.40 W
Trinidad, Cuba	284p	21.48 N	79.59 W
Trinidad, Hond.	280	14.57 N	88.45 W
Trinidad, Colo., U.S.	252	37.10 N	104.31 W
Trinidad, Tex., U.S.	250	32.09 N	96.06 W
Trinidad, Ur.	294	33.32 S	56.54 W
Trinidad I	285r	10.30 N	61.15 W
Trinidad, Isla I	294	39.08 S	62.00 W
Trinidad, Sierra de ⋀	284p	21.56 N	80.00 W
Trinidad and Tobago □[1]	276	11.00 N	61.00 W
Trinitaria	278	16.07 N	92.03 W
Trinity, Newf., Can.	240	48.59 N	53.55 W
Trinity, N.C., U.S.	246	35.54 N	79.59 W
Trinity, Tex., U.S.	250	30.57 N	95.22 W
Trinity ≃, Calif., U.S.	258	41.11 N	123.42 W
Trinity ≃, Tex., U.S.	250	29.47 N	94.42 W
Trinity Bay C, Newf., Can.	240	48.00 N	53.40 W
Trinity Bay C, Tex., U.S.	250	29.40 N	94.45 W
Trinity Islands II	236	56.33 N	154.25 W
Trinity Mountain ∧	256	43.36 N	115.26 W
Trinity Mountains ⋀	258	41.00 N	122.30 W
Trinity Peak ∧	258	40.14 N	118.45 W
Trinkat Island I	200	8.05 N	93.35 E
Trino	182	45.12 N	8.18 E
Trinway	266	40.09 N	82.01 W
Triolet	225c	20.03 S	57.32 E
Trion	246	34.33 N	85.19 W
Tripa ≃	200	3.53 N	96.23 E
Tripoli → Ţarābulus, Lībīya	214	32.54 N	13.11 E
Tripoli → Ţarābulus, Lubnān	212	34.26 N	35.51 E
Tripoli, Iowa, U.S.	244	42.48 N	92.16 W
Trípolis	172	37.31 N	22.21 E
Tripolitania → Ţarābulus ◆[1]	000	31.00 N	15.00 E
Tripp	252	43.13 N	97.58 W
Tripura □[4]	206	24.00 N	92.00 E
Tristan da Cunha Group II	148	37.15 S	12.30 W
Tristao, Îles II	222	10.53 N	14.58 W
Triste	168	42.23 N	0.43 W
Triste, Golfo C	290	10.40 N	68.10 W
Triton Island I	198	15.47 N	111.12 E
Tritts Mills	266	40.59 N	81.26 W
Triumph	248	29.20 N	89.30 W
Trivento	170	41.47 N	14.33 E
Trivero	182	45.40 N	8.10 E
Trnava	164	48.23 N	17.35 E
Trnovo → Veliko Târnovo	172	43.04 N	25.39 E
Troarn	166	49.11 N	0.11 W
Trobriand Islands II	226	8.35 S	151.05 E
Trochu	238	51.50 N	113.13 W
Trofarello	182	44.59 N	7.44 E
Trogir	170	43.31 N	16.15 E
Troia	184	41.22 N	15.18 E
Troick	158	54.06 N	61.35 E
Troickij Sungur	160	53.17 N	47.37 E
Troicko-Pečorsk	160	62.44 N	56.06 E
Troina	170	37.47 N	14.37 E
Troisdorf	164	50.49 N	7.08 E
Trois Fourches, Cap des ≻	168	35.26 N	2.58 W
Trois-Îlets	284e	14.32 N	61.02 W
Trois-Rivières, Qué., Can.	260	46.21 N	72.33 W
Trois-Rivières, Guad.	285o	15.59 N	61.39 W
Trojan	172	42.51 N	24.43 E
Trojanova Tabla ⊥	172	44.37 N	22.20 E
Trojanski prohod)(	172	42.47 N	24.37 E
Trollhättan	160	58.16 N	12.18 E
Tromba Grande, Cabo ≻	296	14.18 S	38.58 W
Trombetas ≃	290	1.55 S	55.35 W
Trombudo Central	294	27.18 S	49.47 W
Tromelin I	218	15.52 S	54.25 E
Troms □[6]	160	69.15 N	19.40 E
Tromsø	160	69.40 N	18.58 E
Trona	258	35.45 N	117.23 W
Tronador, Monte ∧	288	41.10 S	71.54 W
Trondheim	160	63.25 N	10.25 E
Trondheimsfjorden C[2]	160	63.39 N	10.49 E
Troon	162	55.32 N	4.40 W
Tropas, Rio das ≃	292	6.07 S	57.28 W
Tropea	170	38.41 N	15.54 E
Trophy Mountain ∧	238	51.47 N	119.48 W
Tropic	254	37.37 N	112.05 W
Tropojë	172	42.24 N	20.10 E
Troppau → Opava	164	49.56 N	17.54 E
Trosa	160	58.54 N	17.33 E
Trossingen	180	48.04 N	8.38 E
Trotwood	242	39.48 N	84.18 W
Trou-du-Nord	282	19.38 N	72.01 W
Troup	250	32.09 N	95.07 W
Trout	248	31.42 N	92.11 W
Trout ≃	232	61.19 N	119.51 W
Trout Creek, Mich., U.S.	244	46.28 N	89.01 W
Trout Creek, Mont., U.S.	238	47.50 N	115.36 W
Trout Creek Pass)(	254	38.54 N	105.58 W
Troutdale	270	45.32 N	116.23 W
Trout Lake	270	46.00 N	121.32 W
Trout Lake ⊜, B.C., Can.	238	50.35 N	117.26 W
Trout Lake ⊜, N.W. Ter., Can.	232	60.35 N	121.10 W
Trout Lake ⊜, Ont., Can.	244	46.18 N	79.20 W
Trout Lake ⊜, Ont., Can.	244	46.13 N	80.35 W
Trout Peak ∧	256	44.36 N	109.32 W
Trout River	240	49.29 N	58.08 W
Troutville, Pa., U.S.	266	41.02 N	78.47 W
Troutville, Va., U.S.	246	37.25 N	79.53 W
Trouville-sur-Mer	176	49.22 N	0.05 E
Trowbridge	174	51.20 N	2.13 W
Troy, Ala., U.S.	248	31.48 N	85.58 W
Troy, Idaho, U.S.	256	46.44 N	116.46 W
Troy, Kans., U.S.	252	39.47 N	95.05 W
Troy, Mich., U.S.	266	42.36 N	83.09 W
Troy, Mo., U.S.	248	38.59 N	90.59 W
Troy, Mont., U.S.	256	48.28 N	115.53 W
Troy, N.H., U.S.	242	42.50 N	72.11 W
Troy, N.C., U.S.	246	35.22 N	79.53 W
Troy, N.Y., U.S.	261	42.43 N	73.40 W
Troy, Ohio, U.S.	242	40.02 N	84.13 W
Troy, Pa., U.S.	242	41.47 N	76.47 W
Troy, Tenn., U.S.	248	36.20 N	89.10 W
Troy, Tex., U.S.	250	31.12 N	97.18 W
Troy ⊥	212	39.57 N	26.15 E
Troyes	176	48.18 N	4.05 E
Troy Grove	268	41.28 N	89.05 W
Troy Lake ⊜	258	34.49 N	116.33 W
Troy Peak ∧	258	38.19 N	115.30 W
Trpanj	170	43.00 N	17.17 E
Trstená	164	49.22 N	19.37 E
Trstenik	172	43.37 N	21.00 E
Truax	252	49.55 N	104.58 W
Truc-giang	200	10.14 N	106.22 E
Truchas	254	36.03 N	105.49 W
Truchas Peak ∧	254	35.58 N	105.39 W
Trucial States → United Arab Emirates □[1]	204	24.00 N	54.00 E
Truckee	272	39.20 N	120.11 W
Truckee ≃	258	39.51 N	119.24 W
Truite, Lac à la ⊜	244	47.17 N	78.18 W
Trujillo, Col.	290	4.10 N	76.19 W
Trujillo, Esp.	168	39.28 N	5.53 W
Trujillo, Hond.	280	15.55 N	86.00 W
Trujillo, Perú	292	8.10 S	79.02 W
Trujillo, Ven.	290	9.22 N	70.26 W
Trujillo □[3]	290	9.25 N	70.30 W
Trujillo Alto	284m	18.22 N	66.01 W
Truman	252	43.50 N	94.26 W
Trumann	248	35.41 N	90.31 W
Trumansburg	242	42.33 N	76.40 W
Trumbauersville	262	40.25 N	75.23 W
Trumbull	261	41.15 N	73.12 W
Trumbull □[6]	266	41.14 N	80.52 W
Trumbull, Mount ∧	254	36.25 N	113.10 W
Trumon	200	2.49 N	97.38 E
Truro, N.S., Can.	240	45.22 N	63.16 W
Truro, Eng., U.K.	174	50.16 N	5.03 W
Truro, Mass., U.S.	261	42.00 N	70.03 W
Truscott	250	33.45 N	99.49 W
Truşeşti	172	47.46 N	27.01 E
Truth or Consequences (Hot Springs)	254	33.08 N	107.15 W
Trutnov	164	50.34 N	15.55 E
Truxton	264	42.43 N	76.02 W
Truxton Wash ∨	254	35.38 N	114.04 W
Truyère ≃	166	44.39 N	2.34 E
Tryon, Nebr., U.S.	252	41.33 N	100.57 W
Tryon, N.C., U.S.	246	35.13 N	82.14 W
Tryonville	266	41.42 N	79.47 W
Trzcianka (Schönlanke)	164	53.03 N	16.28 E
Trzciel (Tirschtiegel)	164	52.23 N	15.52 E
Trzcińsko-Zdrój	164	52.58 N	14.35 E
Trzebiatow (Treptow/rega)	164	54.04 N	15.14 E
Trzebież (Ziegenort)	164	53.42 N	14.31 E
Trzebinia	164	50.10 N	19.18 E
Trzebnica (Trebnitz)	164	51.19 N	17.03 E
Trzemeszno	164	52.35 N	17.50 E
Tržič	170	46.22 N	14.19 E
Tsacha Lake ⊜	238	53.05 N	124.40 W
T'sangwu → Wuzhou	200	23.30 N	111.27 E
Tsaratanana	218	16.47 S	47.39 E
Tsaratanana, Massif du ⋀	225b	14.00 S	49.00 E
Tsau	218	20.12 S	22.22 E
Tsavo	218	2.59 S	38.28 E
Tsawwassen	270	49.01 N	123.06 W
Tsaydaychuz Peak ∧	238	53.02 N	126.35 W
Tschida, Lake ⊜[1]	252	46.36 N	101.54 W
Ts'engwen Ch'i ≃	196	23.04 N	120.04 E
Tsévié	222	6.25 N	1.13 E
Tshabong	218	26.03 S	22.29 E
Tshane	218	24.05 S	21.54 E
Tshela	218	4.59 S	12.56 E
Tshikapa	218	6.25 S	20.48 E
Tshofa	218	5.14 S	25.15 E
Tshuapa ≃	218	0.14 S	20.42 E
Tshwaane	218	22.29 S	22.03 E
Tsiafajavona ∧	225b	19.21 S	47.15 E
Tsihombe	218	25.18 S	45.29 E
Tsimanampetsotsa, Lac ⊜	225b	24.08 S	43.46 E
Tsimpsean Indian Reserve ◆[4]	238	54.30 N	130.22 W
Tsinan → Jinan	194	36.40 N	116.57 E
Tsiribihina ≃	225b	19.42 S	44.31 E
Tsiroanomandidy	218	18.46 S	46.02 E
Tsitsihar → Qiqihaer	190	47.19 N	123.55 E
Tsitsutl Peak ∧	238	52.44 N	125.47 W
Tsjokkarassa ∧	160	69.57 N	24.32 E
Tskhinvali → Cchinvali	158	42.13 N	43.56 E
Tsodilo Hill ∧[2]	224	18.45 S	21.45 E
Tsomo ≃	224	32.25 S	27.50 E
Tso Morari ⊜	206	32.55 N	78.20 E
Tsu	192	34.43 N	136.31 E
Tsubame	192	37.39 N	138.56 E
Tsuchiura	192	36.05 N	140.12 E
Tsining → Jining	194	35.25 N	116.36 E
Tsinghai → Qinghai □[4]	190	36.00 N	96.00 E
Tsingkiang → Huaiyin	196	33.35 N	119.02 E
Tsingtao → Qingdao	194	36.06 N	120.19 E
Tsingyuan → Baoding	194	38.52 N	115.29 E
Tsinling Shan → Qinlingshanmai ⋀	190	34.00 N	108.00 E
Tsugaru-hantō ≻[1]	192	41.00 N	140.30 E
Tsugaru-heiya ≚	192	40.49 N	140.27 E
Tsugaru-kaikyō ⋓	192a	41.35 N	141.00 E
Tsukumi	192	33.04 N	131.52 E
Tsukushi-sanchi ⋀	192	33.30 N	130.30 E
Tsumeb	224	19.13 S	17.42 E
Tsumeb □[5]	224	19.00 S	17.30 E
Tsumis Park	218	23.43 S	17.28 E
Tsuni → Zunyi	000	27.39 N	106.57 E
Tsuruga	192	35.39 N	136.04 E
Tsurugi-san ∧	192	33.51 N	134.06 E
Tsuruoka	192	38.44 N	139.50 E
Tsushima	192	35.10 N	136.43 E
Tsu-shima I	194	34.30 N	129.22 E
Tsushima-kaikyō ⋓	192	34.00 N	129.00 E
Tsuwano	192	34.28 N	131.46 E
Tsuyama	192	35.03 N	134.00 E
Tua ≃	168	41.13 N	7.26 W
Tuakau	230	37.16 S	174.57 E
Tual	198	5.40 S	132.44 E
Tualatln	270	45.23 N	122.46 W
Tualatin ≃	256	45.20 N	122.39 W
Tuam	162	53.31 N	8.50 W
Tuamotu, Îles II	148	19.00 S	142.00 W
Tuangku, Pulau I	200	2.10 N	97.18 E
Tuapse	158	44.07 N	39.05 E
Tubac	254	31.37 N	111.03 W
Tuba City	254	36.08 N	111.14 W
Tubalan Head ≻	202	6.30 N	125.35 E
Tubarão	294	28.30 S	49.01 W
Ţūbās	210	32.19 N	35.22 E
Tubas ≃	224	22.55 S	14.37 E
Ţubayq, Jabal aţ- ⋀	208	29.40 N	37.15 E
Tubbataha Reefs ✣[2]	202	8.50 N	119.50 E
Tubbergen	164	52.25 N	6.46 E
Tubig ≃	202	11.55 N	125.25 E
Tubigan Island I	202	6.26 N	120.47 E
Tubingantan Point ≻	202	5.53 N	120.55 E
Tübingen	180	48.31 N	9.02 E
Tubize	176	50.41 N	4.12 E
Tubli	202	13.56 N	124.09 E
Tubod	202	8.03 N	123.48 E
Ţubruq (Tobruk)	220	32.05 N	23.59 E
Tubuai, Îles II	148	23.00 S	150.00 W
Tuburan, Pil.	202	6.39 N	122.16 E
Tuburan, Pil.	202	44.03 N	70.42 W
Tubutama	254	30.53 N	111.29 W
Tucacas	290	10.48 N	68.19 W
Tucacas, Punta ≻	290	10.50 N	68.14 W
Tucannon ≃	256	46.33 N	118.11 W
Tucano	286	10.58 S	38.48 W
Tucavaca ≃	292	18.37 S	58.59 W
Tuchola	164	53.35 N	17.50 E
Tucholskie, Bory ≚[1]	164	53.40 N	18.30 E
Tuchów	164	49.54 N	21.03 E
Tuckahoe, N.J., U.S.	262	39.17 N	74.45 W
Tuckahoe, N.Y., U.S.	261	40.54 N	72.25 W
Tuckerman	248	35.44 N	91.12 W
Tuckerton, N.J., U.S.	262	39.36 N	74.20 W
Tuckerton, Pa., U.S.	262	40.25 N	75.57 W
Tucson	254	32.13 N	110.58 W
Tucumã, Paraná ≃[1]	290	3.58 S	66.26 W
Tucumán → San Miguel de Tucumán	294	26.49 S	65.13 W
Tucumán □[4]	294	27.00 S	65.30 W
Tucumcari	250	35.10 N	103.44 W
Tucunduva	294	27.39 S	54.27 W
Tucunuco	294	30.36 S	68.39 W
Tucupido	290	9.17 N	65.47 W
Tucupita	290	9.04 N	62.03 W
Tucuruí	286	3.42 S	49.27 W
Tuczna	164	51.54 N	23.26 E
Tudcum	294	30.13 S	69.15 W
Tudela, Esp.	168	42.05 N	1.36 W
Tudela, Pil.	202	8.14 N	123.50 E
Tudela de Duero	168	41.35 N	4.35 W
Tudmur (Palmyra)	212	34.33 N	38.17 E
Tudmur (Palmyra) ⊥	212	34.33 N	38.17 E
Tudu	160	59.11 N	26.51 E
Tuela ≃	168	41.30 N	7.12 W
Tugela ≃	224	29.14 S	31.31 E
Tuggerah Lake C	228	33.18 S	151.30 E
Tugidak Island I	236	56.30 N	154.36 W
Tugubun Point ≻	202	7.00 N	126.27 E
Tuguegarao	202	17.37 N	121.44 E
Tugur	186	53.48 N	136.48 E
Tuhaihe ≃	194	37.55 N	118.05 E
Tuichi ≃	292	14.36 S	67.35 W
Tujmazy	158	54.36 N	53.42 E
T'ukalinsk	186	55.52 N	72.12 E
Tukangbesi, Kepulauan I	198	5.40 S	123.50 E
Tukituki ≃	230	39.36 S	176.56 E
Tuktoyaktuk	236	69.27 N	133.02 W
Tukums	160	57.00 N	23.10 E
Tukuran	202	7.50 N	123.34 E
Tukwila	270	47.29 N	122.16 W
Tula, Méx.	278	23.00 N	99.43 W
Tula, S.S.S.R.	160	54.12 N	37.37 E
Tulagi	226	9.06 S	160.09 E
Tulalip Indian Reservation ◆[4]	256	48.06 N	122.15 W
Tulancingo	278	20.05 N	98.22 W
Tulangbawang ≃	198	4.24 S	105.50 E
Tulare, Calif., U.S.	272	36.13 N	119.21 W
Tulare, S. Dak., U.S.	252	44.44 N	98.31 W
Tulare □[6]	272	36.20 N	119.18 W
Tularosa	254	33.04 N	106.01 W
Tularosa ≃	254	33.41 N	108.46 W
Tularosa Valley ≚[1]	254	32.45 N	106.10 W
Tulbagh	218	33.17 S	19.09 E
Tulcán	290	0.48 N	77.43 W
Tulcea	172	45.11 N	28.48 E
Tule ≃, Nic.	280	11.15 N	84.47 W
Tule ≃, Calif., U.S.	258	36.03 N	119.50 W
Tuléar	225b	23.21 S	43.40 E
Tuléar □[4]	225b	24.00 S	45.00 E
Tulelake	258	41.57 N	121.29 W
Tule Lake ⊜	258	41.54 N	121.32 W
Tule River Indian Reservation ◆[4]	258	36.02 N	118.42 W
T'ul'gan	158	52.22 N	56.12 E
Tuli	218	21.59 S	29.15 E
Tuli ≃	224	21.48 S	29.04 E
Tulia	250	34.32 N	101.46 W
Tulik Volcano ∧[1]	236	53.22 N	168.03 W
Tuliszków	164	52.05 N	18.17 E
Ţūl Karm	210	32.19 N	35.02 E
T'ul'kino	160	59.49 N	56.30 E
Tullahoma	248	35.22 N	86.11 W
Tullamore	162	53.16 N	7.30 W
Tulle	166	45.16 N	1.46 E
Tullins	166	45.18 N	5.29 E
Tulln	164	48.20 N	16.03 E
Tullos	248	31.49 N	92.19 W
Tullow	162	52.48 N	6.44 W
Tully, Austl.	228	17.56 S	145.56 E
Tully, N.Y., U.S.	264	42.48 N	76.07 W
Tullytown	262	40.09 N	74.49 W
Tuloma ≃	160	68.52 N	32.49 E
Tulsa	250	36.09 N	95.58 W
Tulsequah	232	58.35 N	133.35 W
Tuluá	290	4.06 N	76.11 W
Tulufan	190	42.56 N	89.10 E
Tuluksak	236	61.06 N	160.58 W
Tulum	278	20.13 N	87.28 W
Tulum ⊥	278	20.15 N	87.27 W
Tulumaya (Lavalle)	294	32.45 S	68.36 W
Tulumayo ≃	292	10.56 S	75.16 W
Tulun	186	54.35 N	100.33 E
Tuluran Island I	202	10.59 N	119.17 E
Tuma ≃	280	13.06 N	84.35 W
Tumacacori National Monument ♠	254	31.25 N	111.01 W
Tumaco	290	1.49 N	78.46 W
Tumaco, Ensenada C	290	1.55 N	78.45 W
Tuman-gang (Tumenjiang) ≃	194	42.18 N	130.41 E
Tumannaja, Gora ∧	236	66.33 N	179.43 E
Tumanovo	160	55.25 N	34.39 E
Tumanskij	236	63.58 N	178.12 E
Tumany	186	60.56 N	155.56 E
Tumarbong	202	10.22 N	119.27 E
Tumatumari Fall	290	5.21 N	58.59 W
Tumauini	202	17.17 N	121.48 E
Tumba, Lac ⊜	218	0.48 S	18.03 E
Tumbagaan Island I	202	5.23 N	120.18 E
Tumbarumba	228	35.47 S	148.01 E
Tumbaya	294	23.50 S	65.30 W
Tumbes	290	3.30 S	80.25 W
Tumbes □[4]	290	3.50 N	80.30 W
Tumbes ≃	290	3.30 S	80.30 W
Tumbes, Punta ≻	294	36.37 S	73.07 W
Tumble Mountain ∧	256	45.19 N	110.02 W
Tumča ≃	160	66.36 N	30.48 E
T'umen', S.S.S.R.	158	57.09 N	65.32 E
Tumen, Zhg.	194	42.58 N	129.49 E
Tumenjiang (Tuman-gang) ≃	194	42.18 N	130.41 E
T'umenskaja Oblast' □[4]	160	65.00 N	62.00 E
Tumeremo	290	7.18 N	61.30 W
Tumiritinga	296	18.58 S	41.38 W
Tummo	214	22.40 N	14.10 E
Tumoteqi	190	40.52 N	111.28 E
Tumpat	200	6.11 N	102.10 E
Tumtum	238	47.53 N	117.41 W
Tumuc-Humac Mountains ⋀	286	2.20 N	55.00 W
Tumupasa	292	14.09 S	67.55 W
Tumut	228	35.18 S	148.13 E
Tumwater	270	47.01 N	122.54 W
Tun ≃	200	17.20 N	98.42 E
Tunago Lake ⊜	236	66.18 N	125.50 W
Tunapuna	285r	10.38 N	61.23 W
Tunari, Cerro ∧	292	17.18 S	66.22 W
Tunas de Zaza	284p	21.38 N	79.33 W
Tunbridge Wells	174	51.08 N	0.16 E
Tunca (Tundža) ≃	172	41.40 N	26.34 E
Tunçbilek	172	39.37 N	29.29 E
Tunceli □[4]	208	39.05 N	39.30 E
Tunchang	200	19.28 N	110.08 E
Tundubai ⍑[4]	220	18.31 N	28.33 E
Tunduru	218	11.07 S	37.21 E
Tundža (Tunca) ≃	172	41.40 N	26.34 E
T'ung ≃	186	63.46 N	121.35 E
Tungauan Bay C	202	7.25 N	122.23 E
Tungchi Hsü I	196	23.15 N	119.40 E
Tungch'üan Tao I	196	25.58 N	119.58 E
T'unghua → Tonghua	194	41.50 N	125.55 E
Tungkal ≃	200	0.48 S	103.29 E
Tungku	202	5.06 N	119.01 E
Tungla	280	13.21 N	84.21 W
Tungsten	236	62.00 N	127.40 W
Tungsunga, Jabal ∧	220	11.29 N	23.21 E
Tungting Hsü I	196	24.10 N	118.14 E
Tungurahua □[4]	290	1.15 S	78.35 W
Tungyin Shan I	196	26.22 N	120.30 E
Tunica	248	34.41 N	90.23 W
Tunis	170	36.48 N	10.11 E
Tunis, Golfe de C	170	37.00 N	10.30 E
Tunis Et Banlieue □[8]	170	36.48 N	10.10 E
Tunisia □[1]	214	34.00 N	9.00 E
Tunja	290	5.31 N	73.22 W
Tunkás	278	20.54 N	88.45 W
Tunkhannock	242	41.32 N	75.57 W
Tunnelhill	266	40.29 N	78.33 W
Tunnelton	242	39.24 N	79.45 W
Tunnsjøen ⊜	160	64.43 N	13.24 E
Tuntsa Wash ∨	254	36.17 N	108.41 W
Tuntutuliak	236	60.22 N	162.38 W
Tununak	236	60.35 N	165.16 W
Tunungayualok Island I	232	56.05 N	61.05 W
Tunuyán	294	33.35 S	69.00 W
Tunuyán ≃	294	34.03 S	66.45 W
Tunxi	196	29.44 N	118.18 E
Tuobuja	186	62.00 N	122.02 E
Tuoeshan ∧	200	24.20 N	103.32 E
Tuohu ⊜	196	33.11 N	117.49 E
Tuoj-Chaja	186	62.32 N	111.18 E
Tuojidao I	194	38.09 N	120.14 E
Tuokusidawanling ∧	206	37.14 N	85.47 E
Tuolumne	272	37.58 N	120.14 W
Tuolumne □[6]	272	37.59 N	120.23 W
Tuoningdao I	196	22.28 N	114.38 E
Tupã	296	21.56 S	50.30 W
Tupaciguara	296	18.35 S	48.42 W
Tupana ≃	290	4.25 S	60.05 W
Tupanciretã	294	29.05 S	53.51 W
Tupelo, Miss., U.S.	248	34.16 N	88.43 W
Tupelo, Okla., U.S.	250	34.37 N	96.26 W
Tupelo National Battlefield ⊥	248	34.13 N	88.44 W
Tupi	202	6.19 N	124.56 E
Tupilac	202	7.40 N	122.30 E
Tupi Paulista	296	21.24 S	51.34 W
Tupiraçaba	296	14.29 S	48.34 W
Tupiza	292	21.27 S	65.43 W
Tuplice (Teuplitz)	164	51.41 N	14.50 E
Tupman	272	35.18 N	119.21 W
Tupper	238	55.31 N	120.02 W
Tupper Lake	242	44.13 N	74.29 W
Tupperville	266	42.36 N	82.16 W
Tupungato	294	33.20 S	69.10 W
Tupungato, Cerro ∧	294	33.22 S	69.47 W
Túquerres	290	1.05 N	77.37 W
Tura	186	64.17 N	100.15 E
Tura ≃	186	57.12 N	66.56 E
Turabah ⍑[4]	208	28.15 N	42.55 E
Turakina ≃	230	40.05 S	175.08 E
Turan	186	52.08 N	93.55 E
Turano ≃	170	42.26 N	12.47 E
Turbaco	290	10.20 N	75.25 W
Turbacz ∧	164	49.33 N	20.08 E
Turbat	204	25.59 N	63.04 E
Turbigo	182	45.32 N	8.44 E
Turbo	290	8.06 N	76.43 W
Turčasovo	160	63.06 N	39.12 E
Turda	172	46.34 N	23.47 E
Turek	164	52.02 N	18.30 E
Turfan → Tulufan	190	42.56 N	89.10 E
Turgaj	186	49.38 N	63.28 E
Turgaj ≃	186	48.01 N	62.45 E
Turgajskaja Dolina ∨	186	51.00 N	64.30 E
Turgajskaja Stolovaja Strana ⋀[1]	186	51.00 N	64.00 E
Turgutlu	212	38.30 N	27.43 E
Turgwe ≃	224	20.28 S	32.18 E
Turhal	212	40.24 N	36.06 E
Turia ≃	168	39.27 N	0.19 W
Turimiquire, Cerro ∧	290	10.07 N	63.53 W
Turin, Alta., Can.	238	49.58 N	112.31 W
Turin, N.Y., U.S.	264	43.38 N	75.25 W
Turinsk	158	58.03 N	63.42 E
Turka	164	49.10 N	23.02 E
Turkestan	186	43.18 N	68.15 E
Túrkeve	164	47.06 N	20.45 E
Turkey	250	34.23 N	100.54 W
Turkey □[1], As., Eur.	158	39.00 N	35.00 E
Turkey ≃	244	42.43 N	91.01 W
Turkey City	266	41.11 N	79.37 W
Turkmenskaja Sovetskaja Socialističeskaja Respublika □[3]	186	40.00 N	60.00 E
Turkmen Soviet Socialist Republic → Turkmenskaja Sovetskaja Socialističeskaja	186	40.00 N	60.00 E
Turks and Caicos Islands □[2]	276	21.45 N	71.35 W
Turks Island Passage ⋓	282	21.30 N	71.20 W
Turks Islands II	282	21.24 N	71.07 W
Turku (Åbo)	160	60.27 N	22.17 E

Symbols in the index entries are identified on page 360.

Name	Page	Lat°′	Long°′
Turkwel ≃	214	3.06 N	36.06 E
Turley	250	36.14 N	95.58 W
Turlock	272	37.30 N	120.51 W
Turmalina	296	17.17 S	42.45 W
Turnagain ≃	236	59.06 N	127.35 W
Turnagain, Cape >	230	40.29 S	176.37 E
Turnagain Arm C	236	61.00 N	150.00 W
Turna nad Bodvou	164	48.37 N	20.53 E
Turnbull, Mount ∧	254	33.04 N	110.16 W
Turneffe Islands II	278	17.22 N	87.51 W
Turner, Mont., U.S.	256	48.51 N	108.24 W
Turner, Oreg., U.S.	256	44.51 N	122.57 W
Turners Falls	261	42.36 N	72.33 W
Turners Peninsula >[1]	222	7.22 N	12.22 W
Turner Valley	238	50.40 N	114.17 W
Turnhout	178	51.19 N	4.57 E
Türnitz	164	47.57 N	15.30 E
Turnor Lake ⊜	232	56.32 N	108.38 W
Turnov	164	50.35 N	15.10 E
Turnu Măgurele	172	43.45 N	24.53 E
Turnu Roşu, Pasul)(	172	45.33 N	24.16 E
Turnu-Severin	172	44.18 N	22.39 E
Turobin	164	50.50 N	22.55 E
Turon	252	37.48 N	98.26 W
Turopolje ≚	170	45.40 N	16.05 E
Turquino, Pico ∧	284p	19.59 N	76.51 W
Turrell	248	35.23 N	90.15 W
Turret Peak ∧	254	34.15 N	111.53 W
Turrialba	280	9.54 N	83.41 W
Turrialba, Volcán ∧[1]	280	10.02 N	83.46 W
Turriff	162	57.32 N	2.28 W
Turritano ◂[1]	170	40.48 N	8.30 E
Turrubares, Cerro ∧	280	9.48 N	84.28 W
Turtle ≃	252	48.20 N	97.08 W
Turtle Creek, N.B., Can.	240	45.58 N	64.53 W
Turtle Creek, Pa., U.S.	266	40.25 N	79.49 W
Turtle Islands II	222	7.37 N	13.02 W
Turtle Lake, N. Dak., U.S.	252	47.31 N	100.53 W
Turtle Lake, Wis., U.S.	244	45.24 N	92.08 W
Turtle Mountain Indian Reservation ◂[4]	252	48.51 N	99.45 W
Turu ≃	186	64.38 N	100.00 E
Turuchan ≃	186	65.56 N	87.42 E
Turuchansk	186	65.49 N	87.59 E
Turuna ≃	290	0.02 N	56.57 W
Turvânia	296	16.39 S	50.09 W
Turvo	294	28.56 S	49.41 W
Turvo ≃, Bra.	294	27.16 S	54.06 W
Turvo ≃, Bra.	296	21.32 S	44.26 W
Turvo ≃, Bra.	296	17.46 S	50.12 W
Turvo ≃, Bra.	296	19.56 S	49.55 W
Turvo ≃, S.A.	292	14.47 S	61.03 W
Turyu-san ∧	194	41.10 N	128.47 E
Turzovka	164	49.25 N	18.39 E
Tusas, Rio ≃	254	36.23 N	106.03 W
Tuscaloosa	248	33.13 N	87.33 W
Tuscania	184	42.25 N	11.52 E
Tuscarawas	266	40.24 N	81.25 W
Tuscarawas □[6]	266	40.30 N	81.27 W
Tuscarora, N.Y., U.S.	266	42.38 N	77.52 W
Tuscarora, Pa., U.S.	262	40.46 N	76.02 W
Tuscarora Mountain ∧	242	40.10 N	77.45 W
Tuscarora Mountains ⋀	258	41.00 N	116.20 W
Tuscola, Ill., U.S.	248	39.48 N	88.17 W
Tuscola, Tex., U.S.	250	32.12 N	99.48 W
Tuscumbia, Ala., U.S.	248	34.44 N	87.42 W
Tuscumbia, Mo., U.S.	248	38.14 N	92.28 W
Tushar Mountains ⋀	254	38.20 N	112.30 W
Tuskegee	248	32.26 N	85.42 W
Tustin	274	33.45 N	117.49 W
Tustumena Lake ⊜	236	60.12 N	150.50 W
Tuszyn	164	51.37 N	19.34 E
Tutaekuri ≃	230	39.36 S	176.56 E
Tutajev	160	57.53 N	39.32 E
Tutin	172	42.59 N	20.20 E
Tutóia	286	2.45 S	42.16 W
Tutoko, Mount ∧	230	44.36 S	168.00 E
Tutova ≃	172	46.06 N	27.32 E
Tutrakan	172	44.03 N	26.37 E
Tuttle	252	47.09 N	100.00 W
Tuttle Creek Reservoir ⊜[1]	252	39.22 N	96.40 W
Tuttlingen	180	47.59 N	8.49 E
Tutu Bay C	202	5.15 N	121.11 E
Tutupaca, Volcán ∧[1]	292	17.02 S	70.22 W
Tututalak Mountain ∧	236	67.46 N	161.10 W
Tutwiler	248	34.01 N	90.26 W
Tutzing	164	47.54 N	11.17 E
Tuupovaara	160	62.29 N	30.36 E
Tuurun ja Poorin lääni □[4]	160	61.20 N	22.30 E
Tuusniemi	160	62.49 N	28.30 E
T'uva-Guba	160	69.08 N	33.32 E
Ṭuwayq, Jabal ⋀	204	23.00 N	46.00 E
Tuxpan, Méx.	278	21.37 N	104.07 W
Tuxpan, Méx.	278	21.57 N	105.18 W
Tuxpan de Rodríguez Cano	278	20.57 N	97.24 W
Tuxtepec	278	18.06 N	96.07 W
Tuxtla Chico	278	14.57 N	92.10 W
Tuxtla Gutiérrez	278	16.45 N	93.07 W
Túy	168	42.03 N	8.38 W
Tuy ≃	290	10.24 N	65.59 W
Tuya ≃	232	58.05 N	130.50 W
Tuyen-hoa	200	17.50 N	106.10 E
Tuy-hoa	200	13.05 N	109.17 E
Ṭuyūr, Burj aṭ- ∧	220	20.55 N	27.55 E
Tuža	160	57.37 N	47.57 E
Tuz Gölü ⊜	212	38.45 N	33.25 E
Tuzigoot National Monument ♠	254	34.40 N	111.52 W
Tuzla	172	44.32 N	18.41 E
Tuzla Gölü ⊜	212	39.02 N	35.50 E
Tvărdica	172	43.42 N	25.52 E
Tveitsund	160	59.01 N	8.32 E
Tverca ≃	160	56.52 N	35.55 E
Twain Harte	272	38.02 N	120.14 W
Twardogóra (Festenberg)	164	51.22 N	17.28 E
Tweed	264	44.29 N	77.19 W
Tweedy Mountain ∧	256	45.29 N	112.58 W
Twello	178	52.14 N	6.06 E
Twelve Mile	268	40.52 N	86.13 W
Twentyfive Mile Wash ∨	254	37.33 N	111.07 W
Twentynine Palms	258	34.08 N	116.03 W
Twillingate	240	49.39 N	54.46 W
Twin Beach	268	42.34 N	83.24 W
Twin Bridges	256	45.33 N	112.20 W
Twin Buttes ∧	256	44.20 N	122.15 W
Twin Buttes Reservoir ⊜[1]	250	31.20 N	100.35 W
Twin City	246	32.35 N	82.10 W
Twin Falls	256	42.34 N	114.28 W
Twin Hills	236	59.23 N	159.58 W
Twin Lakes, Calif., U.S.	272	36.58 N	122.00 W
Twin Lakes, Ind., U.S.	268	41.19 N	86.23 W
Twin Lakes, Mich., U.S.	268	43.22 N	86.10 W
Twin Lakes, Ohio, U.S.	266	41.11 N	81.21 W
Twin Lakes, Wis., U.S.	268	42.32 N	88.15 W
Twin Lakes Reservoir ⊜[1]	256	43.16 N	114.49 W
Twin Oaks	262	39.51 N	75.26 W
Twin Peaks	274	34.12 N	117.12 W
Twin Peaks ⋀	256	44.35 N	114.29 W
Twin Rocks, Oreg., U.S.	270	45.36 N	123.57 W
Twin Rocks, Pa., U.S.	266	40.30 N	78.52 W
Twinsburg	266	41.19 N	81.27 W
Twin Valley	252	47.16 N	96.16 W
Twisp	256	48.22 N	120.07 W
Twistringen	178	52.48 N	8.38 E
Twitchell Reservoir ⊜[1]	258	35.00 N	120.19 W
Twitya ≃	236	64.10 N	128.12 W
Twofold Bay C	228	37.06 S	149.55 E
Two Harbors	244	47.01 N	91.40 W
Two Hills	238	53.43 N	111.45 W
Two Rivers	244	44.09 N	87.34 W
Two Rivers ≃	252	48.49 N	97.09 W
Two Rivers Reservoir ⊜[1]	250	33.17 N	104.45 W
Two Thumb Range ⋀	230	43.45 S	170.42 E
Tybju	160	60.37 N	50.20 E
Tybkino	160	54.15 N	43.46 E
Tychy	164	50.09 N	18.59 E
Tyczyn	164	49.58 N	22.02 E
Tydal	160	63.04 N	11.34 E
Tye	250	32.27 N	99.52 W
Tygh Valley	270	45.15 N	121.10 W
Tyler, Minn., U.S.	252	44.17 N	96.08 W
Tyler, Pa., U.S.	266	41.14 N	78.32 W
Tyler, Tex., U.S.	250	32.21 N	95.18 W
Tylersburg	266	41.23 N	79.19 W
Tylerton	262	37.58 N	76.01 W
Tylertown	248	31.07 N	90.09 W
Tym ≃	186	59.25 N	80.04 E
Tymna, Laguna C	236	64.00 N	178.30 E
Tyndall	252	42.59 N	97.52 W
Tyndinskij	186	55.10 N	124.43 E
Tynemouth	162	55.01 N	1.24 W
Tyner	268	41.25 N	86.24 W
Týn nad Vltavou	164	49.14 N	14.26 E
Tynset	160	62.17 N	10.47 E
Tyonek	236	61.02 N	151.17 W
Tyre → Ṣūr, Lubnān	210	33.16 N	35.11 E
Tyre, Pa., U.S.	266	40.26 N	80.16 W
Tyringham	261	42.15 N	73.12 W
Tyrma	186	50.03 N	132.12 E
Tyrone, Okla., U.S.	250	36.57 N	101.04 W
Tyrone, Pa., U.S.	266	40.40 N	78.14 W
Tyrone □[6]	162	54.40 N	7.15 W
Tyrrell, Lake ⊜	228	35.21 S	142.50 E
Tyrrhenian Sea (Mare Tirreno) ▾[2]	170	40.00 N	12.00 E
Tysse	160	60.22 N	5.45 E
Ty Ty	246	31.28 N	83.39 W
Tyumen' → T'umen'	158	57.09 N	65.32 E
Tyurginpil'gyn, Laguna C	236	68.30 N	178.00 W
Tzanconeja ≃	278	16.35 N	91.35 W
Tzaneen	218	23.50 S	30.09 E
Tzekung → Zigong	190	29.24 N	104.47 E
Tzimol	280	16.16 N	92.16 W
Tzintzuntzan ⊥	278	19.38 N	101.34 W
Tzucacab	278	20.04 N	89.03 W
Tzupo → Zibo, Zhg.	194	36.47 N	118.01 E
U			
Uac, Mount ∧	202	12.12 N	123.40 E
Uaiauaka ≃	290	1.23 N	66.00 W
Uatumã ≃	290	2.26 S	57.37 W
Uaupés	290	0.08 S	67.05 W
Uaupés (Vaupés) ≃	290	0.02 N	67.16 W
Ubá	296	21.07 S	42.56 W
Ubaíra	296	13.16 S	39.39 W
Ubaitaba	296	14.18 S	39.20 W
Ubangi (Oubangui) ≃	214	1.15 N	17.50 E
Ubatã	296	14.12 S	39.31 W
Ubaté	290	5.19 N	73.49 W
Ubatuba	296	23.26 S	45.04 W
Ubay	202	10.04 N	124.28 E
Ubayyiḍ, Wādī al- ∨	208	32.34 N	43.48 E
Ube	192	33.56 N	131.15 E
Úbeda	168	38.01 N	3.22 W
Uberaba	296	19.45 S	47.55 W
Uberaba ≃	296	20.07 S	48.31 W
Uberaba, Lagoa ⊜	292	17.30 S	57.50 W
Uberlândia	296	18.56 S	48.18 W
Überlingen	180	47.46 N	9.10 E
Ubl'a	164	48.55 N	22.23 E
Ubly	244	43.43 N	82.56 W
Ubon Ratchathani	200	15.15 N	104.54 E
Ubrique	168	36.41 N	5.27 W
Ubundi	218	0.21 S	25.29 E
Ucacha	294	33.02 S	63.30 W
Učami	186	63.50 N	96.29 E
Ucayali ≃	292	4.30 S	73.30 W
Uccle	176	50.48 N	4.19 E
Uchinoura	192	31.16 N	131.05 E
Uchiura-wan C	192a	42.20 N	140.40 E
Uchiza	292	8.25 S	76.20 W
Uchoa	296	20.56 S	49.13 W
Uchta, S.S.S.R.	160	63.33 N	53.38 E
Uchta, S.S.S.R.	160	61.12 N	38.32 E
Ucluelet	238	48.57 N	125.33 W
Ucon	256	43.36 N	111.58 W
Učur ≃	186	58.48 N	130.35 E
Uda ≃	186	56.05 N	99.34 E
Udaipur	206	24.35 N	73.41 E
Udall	252	37.23 N	97.07 W
Udaquiola	294	36.35 S	58.30 W
Udbina	170	44.32 N	15.46 E
Uddevalla	160	58.21 N	11.55 E
Uddjaur ⊜	160	65.55 N	17.49 E
Uden	178	51.40 N	5.36 E
Udi	222	6.19 N	7.25 E
Udimskij	160	61.09 N	45.52 E
Udine	170	46.03 N	13.14 E
Udoml'a	160	57.52 N	35.01 E
Udono	192	33.44 N	136.01 E
Udon Thani	200	17.25 N	102.48 E
Udskaja Guba C	186	54.50 N	135.45 E
Udža	186	71.14 N	117.10 E
Ueckermünde	164	53.44 N	14.03 E
Ueda	192	36.24 N	138.16 E
Uele ≃	214	4.09 N	22.26 E
Uelen, S.S.S.R.	186	66.10 N	169.48 E
Uelen, S.S.S.R.	236	66.10 N	169.48 W
Uel'kal'	236	65.32 N	179.17 E
Uelzen	178	52.58 N	10.33 E
Ueno	192	34.45 N	136.08 E
Uetersen	178	53.41 N	9.39 E
Uetze	178	52.28 N	10.11 E
Ufa	158	54.44 N	55.56 E
Uffenheim	164	49.32 N	10.14 E
Ugab ≃	224	21.08 S	13.40 E
Ugak Bay C	236	57.25 N	152.45 W
Ugalla ≃	218	5.08 S	30.42 E
Uganda □[1]	218	1.00 N	32.00 E
Uganik Island I	236	57.53 N	153.28 W
Ugărčin	172	43.06 N	24.25 E
Ugarit ⊥	212	35.35 N	35.45 E
Ugashik	236	57.32 N	157.25 W
Ugashik Bay C	236	57.34 N	157.38 W
Ugatkyn ≃	236	68.24 N	171.30 W
Ugep	222	5.50 N	8.05 E
Ugijar	168	36.57 N	3.03 W
Ugines	182	45.45 N	6.25 E
Uglegorsk	186	48.19 N	38.17 E
Uglič	160	57.32 N	38.19 E
Ugljan, Otok I	170	44.05 N	15.10 E
Ugol'naja, Buchta C	236	63.00 N	179.20 E
Ugolnyy	236	63.03 N	179.03 E
Ugra	160	54.47 N	34.17 E
Ugyak, Cape >	236	58.17 N	154.04 W
Uh (Už) ≃	164	48.34 N	22.00 E
Uherské Hradiště	164	49.05 N	17.28 E
Uherský Brod	164	49.02 N	17.39 E
Uhrichsville	266	40.24 N	81.20 W
Uijŏngbu	194	37.44 N	127.03 E
Uiju	194	40.12 N	124.32 E
Uil ≃	186	48.36 N	52.30 E
Uiñaimarca, Lago ⊜	292	16.20 S	68.50 W
Uinebona ≃	290	5.04 N	63.01 W
Uinta ≃	254	40.14 N	109.51 W
Uintah and Ouray Indian Reservation ◂[4]	254	40.20 N	110.20 W
Uinta Mountains ⋀	254	40.45 N	110.05 W
Uitenhage	224	33.40 S	25.28 E
Uithoorn	178	52.14 N	4.50 E
Uithuizermeeden	164	53.24 N	6.42 E
Uj ≃	186	54.17 N	64.58 E
Ujandina ≃	186	68.23 N	145.50 E
Ujar	186	55.48 N	94.20 E
Ujarrás ⊥	280	9.51 N	83.50 W
Ujazd (Bischofstal)	164	50.24 N	18.22 E
Ujedinenija, Ostrov I	186	77.28 N	82.28 E
Ujemskij	160	64.29 N	40.50 E
Újfehértó	164	47.48 N	21.40 E
Uji	192	34.53 N	135.48 E
Uji-guntō II	192	31.11 N	129.27 E
Ujiji	218	4.55 S	29.41 E
Uji-yamada → Ise	192	34.29 N	136.42 E
Ujjain	206	23.12 N	75.46 E
Ujście	164	53.04 N	16.43 E
Uka	186	57.50 N	162.06 E
'Ukāsh, Wādī ∨	208	34.18 N	40.42 E
Ukerewe Island I	218	2.03 S	33.00 E
Ukhta → Uchta	160	63.33 N	53.38 E
Ukiah, Calif., U.S.	258	39.09 N	123.13 W
Ukiah, Oreg., U.S.	256	45.08 N	118.56 W
Ukmergė	160	55.15 N	24.45 E
Ukolnoi Island I	236	55.14 N	161.34 W
Ukrainian Soviet Socialist Republic → Ukrainskaja Sovetskaja Socialističeskaja	186	49.00 N	32.00 E
Ukrainskaja Sovetskaja Socialističeskaja Respublika □[3]	186	49.00 N	32.00 E
Ukrina ≃	170	45.05 N	17.56 E
Uktym	160	62.38 N	48.52 E
Ukyr	186	49.28 N	108.52 E
Ula	172	37.05 N	28.26 E
Ulaanbaatar	190	47.55 N	106.53 E
Ulaangom	190	49.58 N	92.02 E
'Ulab, Ṭaraq al- ⋀[2]	212	33.55 N	38.18 E
Ulak Island I	237a	51.22 N	179.00 W
Ulana ≃	280	14.27 N	83.17 W
Ulan Bator → Ulaanbaatar	190	47.55 N	106.53 E
Ulanhot → Wulanhaote	190	46.05 N	122.05 E
Ulanów	164	50.30 N	22.16 E
Ulan-Ude	186	51.50 N	107.37 E
Ul'ašovo	160	65.27 N	56.57 E
Ułazów	164	50.17 N	23.00 E
Ulcinj	172	41.55 N	19.11 E
Ulcumayo	292	10.56 S	75.53 W
Uleåborg → Oulu	160	65.01 N	25.28 E
Ulen	252	47.05 N	96.16 W
Ulft	178	51.54 N	6.23 E
Uliastaj	190	47.45 N	96.49 E
Ulin	248	37.17 N	89.11 W
Ulithi I[1]	198	9.58 N	139.40 E
Ulja	186	58.51 N	141.50 E
Uljanovsk	160	54.20 N	48.24 E
Ulla	160	55.14 N	29.15 E
Ulla ≃	168	42.39 N	8.44 W
Ullapool	162	57.54 N	5.10 W
Ullún	294	31.28 S	68.42 W
Ullŭng-do I	190	37.29 N	130.52 E
Ulm, B.R.D.	180	48.24 N	10.00 E
Ulm, Mont., U.S.	256	47.26 N	111.30 W
Ulma	172	47.53 N	25.18 E
Ulmeni	172	45.04 N	26.39 E
Ulricehamn	160	57.47 N	13.25 E
Ulrum	164	53.22 N	6.20 E
Ulsan	194	35.34 N	129.19 E
Ulster □[6]	261	41.56 N	74.00 W
Ultraoriental, Cordillera(Serra do Divisor) ⋀	292	8.20 S	73.30 W
Ulu	186	60.19 N	127.24 E
Ulúa ≃	280	15.56 N	87.43 W
Ulubat Gölü ⊜	212	40.10 N	28.35 E
Ulubey	172	38.25 N	29.18 E
Ulu Dağ ∧	212	40.04 N	29.13 E
Uludarat, Gunung ∧	200	2.24 N	98.35 E
Ulugan Bay C	202	10.05 N	118.47 E
Uluguru Mountains ⋀	218	7.10 S	37.40 E
Ulu Laho, Bukit ∧	200	5.43 N	101.27 E
Ulut ≃	202	11.59 N	125.26 E
Ulva I	162	56.28 N	6.12 W
Ulverstone	228	41.09 S	146.10 E
Ulysses, Kans., U.S.	252	37.35 N	101.22 W
Ulysses, Nebr., U.S.	252	41.04 N	97.12 W
Ulysses, Pa., U.S.	266	41.54 N	77.46 W
Ulzë	172	41.41 N	19.54 E
Umag	170	45.25 N	13.32 E
Umán, Méx.	278	20.53 N	89.45 W
Uman', S.S.S.R.	158	48.44 N	30.14 E
Umanak Fjord C[2]	232	70.55 N	53.00 W
Umarkot	204	25.22 N	69.44 E
Umatilla, Fla., U.S.	246	28.55 N	81.40 W
Umatilla, Oreg., U.S.	256	45.55 N	119.21 W
Umatilla ≃	256	45.55 N	119.20 W
Umatilla Indian Reservation ◂[4]	256	45.41 N	118.31 W
Umayan ≃	202	8.11 N	125.54 E
Umba	160	66.41 N	34.15 E
Umbelasha ≃	220	9.51 N	24.50 E
Umbertide	184	43.18 N	12.20 E
Umbria □[4]	184	43.00 N	12.30 E
Ume ≃	224	16.40 S	28.26 E
Umeå	160	63.50 N	20.15 E
Umeälven ≃	160	63.47 N	20.16 E
Umfolozi ≃	224	28.25 S	32.26 E
Umfolozi Game Reserve ◂[4]	224	28.19 S	31.50 E
Umfors	160	65.56 N	15.00 E
Umfuli ≃	224	17.30 S	29.23 E
Umingan	202	15.55 N	120.50 E
Umiray ≃	202	15.13 N	121.25 E
Umma ⊥	208	31.40 N	45.52 E
Umm al-Jimāl ⊥	210	32.20 N	36.22 E
Umm al-Qaywayn	214	25.35 N	55.34 E
Umm as-Sa'd ⊥	210	33.16 N	36.47 E
Umm Durmān (Omdurman)	220	15.38 N	32.30 E
Umm el Faḥm	210	32.30 N	35.09 E
Ummeln	178	51.58 N	8.27 E
Umm Marahik, Jabal ∧[2]	220	13.40 N	26.53 E
Umm Rumaylah ▾[4]	220	16.55 N	31.40 E
Umm Ruwābah	220	12.54 N	31.13 E
Umm Saggāt, Wādī ∨	220	15.15 N	23.12 E
Umm Sughra ▾[4]	220	15.03 N	27.12 E
Umm Urūmah I	208	25.46 N	36.32 E
Umnak Island I	236	53.25 N	168.10 W
Umnak Pass ⋃	236	53.20 N	167.45 W
Umnäs	160	65.24 N	16.10 E
Umniati ≃	224	16.49 S	28.45 E
Um'ot	160	54.08 N	42.42 E
Umpqua ≃	256	43.42 N	124.03 W
'Umrān	204	15.50 N	43.56 E
Umtali	224	18.58 S	32.40 E
Umtata	224	31.35 S	28.47 E
Umuahia	222	5.33 N	7.29 E
Umuarama	296	23.45 S	53.20 W
Umurlu	172	37.50 N	27.58 E
Umvuma	218	19.19 S	30.35 E
Umzingwane ≃	224	22.12 S	29.56 E
Umzinto	218	30.22 S	30.33 E
Una	296	15.18 S	39.04 W
Una ≃	170	45.16 N	16.55 E
Unac ≃	170	44.30 N	16.09 E
Uña de Gato	250	25.58 N	99.41 W
Unadilla, Ga., U.S.	246	32.16 N	83.44 W
Unadilla, N.Y., U.S.	242	42.20 N	75.19 W
Unadilla ≃	242	42.20 N	75.25 W
Unaí	296	16.23 S	46.53 W
Unalakleet	236	63.53 N	160.47 W
Unalaska	236	53.52 N	166.32 W
Unalaska Island I	236	53.45 N	166.45 W
Unare ≃	290	10.03 N	65.14 W
Unayyir, Ḥarrat al- •[9]	208	25.20 N	37.45 E
'Unayzah	208	26.06 N	43.56 E
'Unayzah, Jabal ∧	208	32.12 N	39.18 E
Uncasville	261	41.26 N	72.07 W
Uncia	292	18.27 S	66.37 W
Uncompahgre ≃	254	38.45 N	108.06 W
Uncompahgre Peak ∧	254	38.04 N	107.28 W
Uncompahgre Plateau ⋀[1]	254	38.30 N	108.25 W
Underwood, N. Dak., U.S.	252	47.27 N	101.08 W
Underwood, Wash., U.S.	270	45.44 N	121.32 W
Uneča	158	52.50 N	32.40 E
Uneiuxi ≃	290	0.37 S	65.34 W
Unga Island I	236	55.15 N	160.45 W
Ungava Bay C	232	59.30 N	67.30 W
Ungava Peninsula >[1]	232	60.00 N	74.00 W
Ungay Point >	202	13.10 N	124.12 E
Unggi	194	42.20 N	130.24 E
Uni	160	57.46 N	51.30 E
União	286	4.35 S	42.52 W
União da Vitória	294	26.13 S	51.05 W
União dos Palmares	286	9.10 S	36.02 W
Unica	160	62.38 N	34.38 E
Unicoi	246	36.12 N	82.21 W
Uniejów	164	51.58 N	18.49 E
Unieux	182	45.24 N	4.16 E
Unije, Otok I	170	44.38 N	14.15 E
Unimak Island I	236	54.50 N	164.00 W
Unimak Pass ⋃	236	54.35 N	164.43 W
Unini ≃	290	1.41 S	61.31 W
Unión, Arg.	294	35.10 S	65.55 W
Union, Ont., Can.	264	42.42 N	81.12 W
Unión, Para.	294	24.48 S	56.33 W
Union, Ill., U.S.	268	42.14 N	88.33 W
Union, Iowa, U.S.	244	42.15 N	93.04 W
Union, Maine, U.S.	242	44.13 N	69.17 W
Union, Miss., U.S.	248	32.34 N	89.14 W
Union, Mo., U.S.	248	38.27 N	91.00 W
Union, N.J., U.S.	262	40.42 N	74.16 W
Union, Oreg., U.S.	256	45.13 N	117.52 W
Union, S.C., U.S.	246	34.43 N	81.37 W
Union, Wash., U.S.	270	47.21 N	123.06 W
Union, W. Va., U.S.	246	37.36 N	80.33 W
Union □[6]	266	40.18 N	83.19 W
Union Bay	238	49.35 N	124.53 W
Union Beach	262	40.27 N	74.10 W
Union City, Calif., U.S.	272	37.36 N	122.01 W
Union City, Ga., U.S.	246	33.35 N	84.33 W
Union City, Ind., U.S.	248	40.12 N	84.49 W
Union City, Mich., U.S.	268	42.04 N	85.08 W
Union City, Ohio, U.S.	268	40.10 N	84.48 W
Union City, Pa., U.S.	266	41.54 N	79.51 W
Union City, Tenn., U.S.	248	36.26 N	89.03 W
Uniondale	268	40.50 N	85.15 W
Unión de Reyes	284p	22.48 N	81.32 W
Unión de Tula	278	19.58 N	104.16 W
Union Gap	256	46.34 N	120.34 W
Union Grove	268	42.41 N	88.03 W
Unión Hidalgo	278	16.28 N	94.50 W
Union Hill	264	43.13 N	77.23 W
Union Lake	268	42.37 N	83.27 W
Union Mills	268	41.30 N	86.47 W
Union of Soviet Socialist Republics □[1]	186	60.00 N	80.00 E
Union Park	246	28.30 N	81.15 W
Union Pier	268	41.50 N	86.42 W
Union Point	246	33.37 N	83.04 W
Unionport	266	40.21 N	80.51 W
Union Springs, Ala., U.S.	248	32.09 N	85.49 W
Union Springs, N.Y., U.S.	264	42.50 N	76.42 W
Uniontown, Ala., U.S.	248	32.22 N	87.31 W
Uniontown, Ky., U.S.	248	37.46 N	87.56 W
Uniontown, Md., U.S.	262	39.36 N	77.07 W
Uniontown, Ohio, U.S.	266	40.59 N	81.25 W
Uniontown, Pa., U.S.	242	39.54 N	79.44 W
Union Village	261	42.00 N	71.32 W
Unionville, Ont., Can.	264	43.52 N	79.18 W
Unionville, Conn., U.S.	261	41.45 N	72.53 W
Unionville, Ga., U.S.	246	31.27 N	83.30 W
Unionville, Mich., U.S.	244	43.39 N	83.28 W
Unionville, Mo., U.S.	248	40.29 N	93.01 W
Unionville, Ohio, U.S.	266	41.47 N	81.00 W
Unionville Center	266	40.08 N	83.21 W
Uniopolis	268	40.36 N	84.05 W
Unisan	202	13.51 N	121.59 E
United	266	40.13 N	79.31 W
United Arab Emirates □[1]	204	24.00 N	54.00 E
United Arab Republic → Egypt □[1]	214	27.00 N	30.00 E
United Kingdom □[1]	158	54.00 N	2.00 W
United States □[1]	234	38.00 N	97.00 W
United States Air Force Academy ■	254	39.00 N	104.55 W
United States Military Academy ■	242	41.23 N	74.01 W
United States Naval Academy ■	242	38.59 N	76.30 W
Unity, Sask., Can.	232	52.27 N	109.10 W
Unity, Maine, U.S.	242	44.40 N	69.14 W
Universal City	250	29.33 N	98.17 W
University	248	34.21 N	89.32 W
University City	248	38.39 N	90.19 W
University Park, N. Mex., U.S.	254	32.17 N	106.45 W
University Park, Tex., U.S.	250	32.52 N	96.47 W
University Place	270	47.14 N	122.34 W
Unna	178	51.32 N	7.41 E
Uno, Ilha de I	222	11.12 N	16.15 W
Unquillo	294	31.15 S	64.20 W
Unst I	162	60.45 N	0.55 W
Unterhausen	180	48.26 N	9.16 E
Unterwalden □[3]	180	46.55 N	8.20 E
Unža ≃	160	57.20 N	43.08 E
Unzen-amakusa-kokuritsu-kōen ♠	192	32.45 N	130.17 E
Unzen-dake ∧	192	32.45 N	130.17 E
Uopiane, Serra do ⋀[1]	292	11.35 S	63.25 W
Uozu	192	36.48 N	137.24 E
Upala	280	10.47 N	85.02 W
Upano ≃	290	2.45 S	78.12 W
Upata	290	8.01 N	62.24 W
Upernavik	232	72.47 N	56.10 W
Upham	252	48.35 N	100.44 W
Upi	202	6.56 N	124.09 E
Upía ≃	290	4.18 N	72.45 W
Upington	224	28.25 S	21.15 E
Upire ≃	290	11.27 N	68.58 W
Upland, Calif., U.S.	274	34.06 N	117.39 W
Upland, Ind., U.S.	268	40.28 N	85.30 W
Upland, Nebr., U.S.	252	40.19 N	98.54 W
Upnuk Lake ⊜	236	60.21 N	158.58 W
Upolu Point >	275d	20.16 N	155.51 W
Upper □[4]	222	10.30 N	1.30 W
Upper Alkali Lake ⊜	258	41.44 N	120.08 W
Upper Arlington	242	40.00 N	83.03 W
Upper Arrow Lake ⊜	238	50.30 N	117.55 W
Upper Blackville	240	46.39 N	65.52 W
Upperco	262	39.34 N	76.50 W
Upper Fairmount	262	38.06 N	75.47 W
Upper Fraser	238	54.07 N	121.56 W
Upper Hat Creek	238	50.38 N	121.35 W
Upper Hutt	230	41.08 S	175.03 E
Upper Iowa ≃	244	43.29 N	91.14 W
Upper Island Cove	240	47.39 N	53.12 W
Upper Kapuas Mountains ⋀	198	1.25 N	113.15 E
Upper Klamath Lake ⊜	256	42.23 N	122.55 W
Upper Lake	258	39.10 N	122.54 W
Upper Liard	236	60.02 N	128.55 W
Upper Lough Erne ⊜	162	54.20 N	7.30 W
Upper Musquodoboit	240	45.08 N	62.57 W
Upper Nyack	261	41.07 N	73.55 W
Upper Red Lake ⊜	188	48.10 N	94.40 W
Upper Red Rock Lake ⊜	256	44.37 N	111.43 W
Upper Sandusky	266	40.50 N	83.17 W
Upper Sheila	240	47.28 N	64.56 W
Upper Sumas	270	49.01 N	122.12 W
Upper Ugashik Lake ⊜	236	57.40 N	156.43 W
Upper Volta □[1]	214	13.00 N	2.00 W
Uppsala	160	59.52 N	17.38 E
Upright, Cape >	236	60.17 N	172.15 W
Upsala → Uppsala	160	59.52 N	17.38 E
Upstart, Cape >	228	19.42 S	147.45 E
Upton, Qué., Can.	260	45.39 N	72.42 W
Upton, Mass., U.S.	261	42.11 N	71.36 W
Upton, Wyo., U.S.	252	44.06 N	104.38 W
Ur ⊥	208	30.57 N	46.09 E
Urabá, Golfo de C	290	8.25 N	76.53 W
Urach	180	48.29 N	9.23 E
Uracoa	290	9.00 N	62.21 W
Urahoro	192a	42.48 N	143.39 E
Uraj	158	60.08 N	64.48 E
Urakawa	192a	42.09 N	142.47 E
Ural ≃	186	47.00 N	51.48 E
Ural Mountains → Ural'skije Gory ⋀	186	60.00 N	60.00 E
Ural'sk	158	51.14 N	51.22 E
Ural'skije Gory ⋀, S.S.S.R.	160	60.00 N	60.00 E
Urandi	296	14.46 S	42.38 W
Urania	248	31.52 N	92.18 W
Uranium City	232	59.34 N	108.36 W
Urariá, Paraná ≃[1]	290	3.03 S	57.43 W
Uraricaá ≃	290	3.20 N	61.56 W
Uraricoera	290	3.27 N	60.59 W
Uraricoera ≃	290	3.02 N	60.30 W
Ura-T'ube	186	39.55 N	68.59 E
Uravan	254	38.22 N	108.44 W
Urawa	192	35.51 N	139.39 E
Urban	270	48.38 N	122.40 W
Urbana, Ill., U.S.	248	40.07 N	88.12 W
Urbana, Ind., U.S.	268	40.54 N	85.47 W
Urbana, Mo., U.S.	248	37.51 N	93.10 W
Urbana, Ohio, U.S.	242	40.07 N	83.45 W
Urbandale, Iowa, U.S.	248	41.38 N	93.48 W
Urbandale, Mich., U.S.	268	44.09 N	85.11 W
Urbania	170	43.40 N	12.31 E
Urbanna	262	37.38 N	76.35 W
Urbiña, Peña ∧	168	43.01 N	5.57 W
Urbino	184	43.43 N	12.38 E
Urcos	292	13.41 S	71.35 W
Urdaneta	202	15.59 N	120.34 E
Urdinarrain	294	32.41 S	58.50 W
Urdoma	160	61.47 N	48.32 E
Uré	290	7.46 N	75.31 W
Ureliki	236	64.25 N	172.20 W
Uren'	160	57.28 N	45.49 E
Urén ≃	280	9.33 N	82.55 W
Ureña	290	7.55 N	72.28 W
Ures	278	29.26 N	110.24 W
Ureshino	192	33.06 N	129.59 E
Urewera National Park ♠	230	38.40 S	177.00 E
Urfa	212	37.08 N	38.46 E
Urga → Ulaanbaatar, Mong.	190	47.55 N	106.53 E
Urgenč	186	41.33 N	60.38 E
Urgnano	182	45.35 N	9.41 E
Ürgüp	158	38.38 N	34.56 E
Uri □[3]	180	46.50 N	8.40 E
Uriage-les-Bains	182	45.09 N	5.50 E
Uriah	248	31.18 N	87.30 W
Uriah, Mount ∧	230	42.01 S	171.38 E
Uribe	290	3.13 N	74.24 W
Uribia	290	11.43 N	72.16 W
Urich	248	38.28 N	94.02 W
Uri-Hauchab ⋀	224	25.20 S	15.15 E
Urique	278	27.13 N	107.55 W
Urique ≃	278	26.29 N	107.58 W
Urituyacu ≃	290	4.50 S	75.30 W
Urk	178	52.39 N	5.36 E
Urla	172	38.18 N	26.46 E
Urlaţi	172	44.59 N	26.14 E
Urlins	284c	17.02 N	61.52 W
Urmary	160	55.42 N	47.57 E
Urmia → Reẕā'īyeh	208	37.33 N	45.04 E
Urmia, Lake → Reẕā'īyeh, Daryācheh-ye ⊜	208	37.40 N	45.30 E
Uromi	222	6.44 N	6.18 E
Uroševac	172	42.22 N	21.09 E
Urrao	290	6.20 N	76.11 W
Ursa	248	40.04 N	91.22 W
Ursus	164	52.12 N	20.53 E
Uru ≃	296	15.24 S	49.36 W
Uruaçu	296	14.30 S	49.10 W
Uruana	296	15.30 S	49.41 W
Uruapan	258	31.38 N	116.15 W
Uruapan [del Progreso]	278	19.25 N	102.04 W
Urubamba	292	13.19 S	72.07 W
Urubamba ≃	292	10.43 S	73.48 W
Urubaxi ≃	290	0.31 S	64.50 W
Urubici	294	28.02 S	49.37 W
Urubu ≃	290	2.55 S	58.25 W
Urubu, Cachoeira do ᒐ	296	12.52 S	48.13 W
Urubupungá	296	20.35 S	51.30 W
Urucá, Igarapé ≃	292	7.07 S	58.48 W
Urucará	290	2.32 S	57.45 W
Urucu ≃	290	4.11 S	63.36 W
Uruçuca	296	14.35 S	39.16 W
Urucuia ≃	296	16.08 S	45.05 W
Urucurituba	290	2.41 S	57.40 W
Uruguaiana	294	29.45 S	57.05 W
Uruguay □[1]	288	33.00 S	56.00 W
Uruguay (Uruguai) ≃	294	34.12 S	58.18 W
Urukthapel I	198	7.15 N	134.24 E
Urumchi → Wulumuqi	190	43.48 N	87.35 E
Urumkuvejem ≃	236	66.14 N	173.35 E
Urundel	294	23.32 S	64.25 W
Ur'ung-Chaja	186	72.48 N	113.23 E
Urup, Ostrov I	186	46.00 N	150.00 E
Urupá ≃	292	10.54 S	61.57 W
Urupadi ≃	290	3.51 S	57.21 W
Urupês	296	21.13 S	49.17 W
Ur'upinsk	158	50.47 N	41.59 E
Urussanga	294	28.31 S	49.19 W
Urutágua	296	14.34 S	47.04 W
Urutaí	296	17.28 S	48.12 W
Urutaú	294	25.43 S	63.04 W
Uruzgān (Qala-i-Hazār Qadam)	208	32.58 N	66.39 E
Uruzgān □[4]	206	33.15 N	66.00 E
Urziceni	172	44.43 N	26.38 E
Uržum	160	57.08 N	50.00 E
Usa	192	33.31 N	131.22 E
Usa ≃	160	65.57 N	56.55 E
Usada Island I	202	6.08 N	120.32 E
Uşak	212	38.41 N	29.25 E
Uşak □[4]	172	37.30 N	29.00 E
Usakos	224	22.01 S	15.32 E
Ušakova, Ostrov I	186	80.48 N	79.25 E
Ušće	172	43.28 N	20.37 E
Ushibuka	192	32.11 N	130.01 E
Ushuaia	288	54.47 S	68.20 W
Usibelli	236	63.51 N	148.47 W
Ušica ≃	172	48.35 N	27.08 E
Usingen	164	50.20 N	83.32 E
Usk, B.C., Can.	238	54.38 N	128.25 W
Usk, Wash., U.S.	256	48.19 N	117.17 W
Uškakij Kr'až ∧	236	65.15 N	178.35 E
Üsküdar	212	41.01 N	29.01 E
Uslar	178	51.39 N	9.38 E
Usolje	160	59.25 N	56.41 E
Usolje-Sibirskoje	186	52.47 N	103.38 E
Uson	202	12.14 N	123.47 E
Uspallata	294	32.37 S	69.22 W
Uspanapa ≃	278	17.58 N	94.29 W
Ussel	166	45.33 N	2.18 E
Ussuri (Wusulijiang) ≃	186	48.27 N	135.04 E
Ussurijsk	186	43.48 N	131.59 E
Ustaritz	166	43.24 N	1.27 W
Ust'-Barguzin	186	53.27 N	108.59 E
Ust'-Belaja	186	65.30 N	173.20 E
Ust'-Bol'šereck	186	52.48 N	156.14 E
Ust'-Čaun	186	68.47 N	170.30 E
Ust'-Cil'ma	160	65.27 N	52.06 E
Uster	180	47.21 N	8.43 E
Ustica, Isola d' I	170	38.42 N	13.10 E
Ust'-Ilyč	160	62.32 N	56.41 E
Ústí nad Labem	164	50.40 N	14.02 E
Ústí nad Orlicí	164	49.58 N	16.24 E
Ust'-Išim	158	57.44 N	71.10 E
Ustja ≃	160	61.30 N	42.36 E
Ust'-Javron'ga	160	63.25 N	44.21 E
Ustje	160	59.38 N	39.43 E
Ustje-Grivas, Porog ᒐ	160	68.05 N	30.20 E
Ustka (Stolpmünde)	164	54.35 N	16.50 E
Ust'-Kamčatsk	186	56.15 N	162.30 E
Ust'-Kamenogorsk	186	49.58 N	82.38 E
Ust'-Katav	158	54.56 N	58.10 E
Ust'-Koksa	186	50.18 N	85.36 E
Ust'-Krutogorovo	186	55.07 N	155.35 E
Ust'-Kulom	160	61.42 N	53.40 E
Ust'-Kut	186	56.46 N	105.40 E
Ust'-Lyža	160	65.44 N	56.36 E
Ust'-Maja	186	60.25 N	134.32 E
Ust'-Manja	186	62.11 N	60.20 E
Ust'-Nera	186	64.34 N	143.12 E
Ust'-N'ukža	186	56.34 N	121.37 E
Uštobe	186	45.16 N	78.00 E
Ust'-Omčug	186	61.09 N	149.38 E
Ust'-Ordynskij	186	52.48 N	104.45 E
Ust'-Oz'ornoje	186	58.54 N	87.48 E
Ust'-Paden'ga	160	61.53 N	42.36 E
Ust'-Pinega	160	64.11 N	41.56 E
Ustreka	160	58.38 N	34.33 E
Ust'-Reki	160	62.12 N	46.45 E
Ustroń	164	49.43 N	18.49 E
Ustrzyki Dolne	164	49.26 N	22.37 E
Ust'-Šonoša	160	61.10 N	41.18 E
Ust'-Tym	186	59.26 N	80.08 E
Ust'uckoje	160	58.32 N	35.20 E
Ust'-Unja	160	61.48 N	57.48 E
Ustupo	290	9.25 N	78.36 W
Ust'urt, Plato ⋀[1]	186	43.00 N	56.00 E
Ust'-Usa	160	65.59 N	56.54 E
Ust'užna	160	58.51 N	36.26 E
Ust'-Voja	160	64.27 N	57.40 E
Ust'-Vyjskaja	160	62.57 N	46.41 E
Ust'-Vym'	160	62.14 N	50.24 E
Usu-dake ∧	192a	42.32 N	140.51 E
Usuki	192	33.08 N	131.49 E
Usulután	280	13.21 N	88.27 W
Usumacinta ≃	278	18.22 N	92.40 W
Usumbura → Bujumbura	218	3.23 S	29.22 E
Ušumun	186	52.49 N	126.27 E
Utah □[3]	234	39.30 N	111.30 W
Utah Lake ⊜	254	40.13 N	111.49 W
Utashinai	192a	43.31 N	142.03 E
Ute	252	42.03 N	95.42 W
Utembo ≃	218	17.06 S	22.01 E
Ute Mountain Indian Reservation ◂[4]	254	37.10 N	108.35 W
Utena	160	55.30 N	25.36 E
Ute Reservoir ⊜[1]	250	36.21 N	103.31 W
Utersum	164	54.43 N	8.24 E
Utete	218	7.59 S	38.47 E
Utevka	160	52.57 N	50.58 E
Uthai Thani	200	15.20 N	100.02 E
Utiariti	292	13.02 S	58.17 W
Utica, Ill., U.S.	268	41.21 N	89.01 W
Utica, Kans., U.S.	252	38.39 N	100.10 W
Utica, Mich., U.S.	266	42.38 N	83.02 W
Utica, Miss., U.S.	248	32.07 N	90.37 W
Utica, Nebr., U.S.	252	40.54 N	97.21 W
Utica, N.Y., U.S.	264	43.05 N	75.14 W
Utica, Ohio, U.S.	266	40.14 N	82.27 W
Utica, Pa., U.S.	266	41.26 N	79.58 W
Utica → Utique ⊥	170	37.03 N	10.03 E
Utica Heights	266	42.39 N	83.02 W
Utiel	168	39.34 N	1.12 W
Utikoomak Indian Reserve ◂[4]	238	55.57 N	115.30 W
Utikuma Lake ⊜	238	55.50 N	115.25 W
Utila	280	16.06 N	86.54 W
Utila, Isla de I	280	16.05 N	86.55 W
Utinga ≃	296	12.34 S	41.20 W
Utique	170	37.03 N	10.03 E
Utique ⊥	170	37.03 N	10.03 E
Utiquinia ≃	292	8.12 S	74.40 W
Uto	192	32.41 N	130.40 E
Utopia	250	29.37 N	99.32 W
Utorgoš	160	58.17 N	30.15 E
Utrecht, Ned.	178	52.05 N	5.08 E
Utrecht, S. Afr.	218	27.38 S	30.20 E
Utrecht □[4]	178	52.05 N	5.08 E
Utrera	168	37.11 N	5.47 W
Utsaladdy	270	48.15 N	122.30 W
Utsjoki	160	69.53 N	27.00 E
Utsunomiya	192	36.33 N	139.52 E
Uttaradit	200	17.38 N	100.06 E
Uttar Pradesh □[3]	206	27.00 N	80.00 E
Uttoxeter	174	52.54 N	1.51 W
Utuado	284m	18.16 N	66.42 W
Utukok ≃	236	70.04 N	162.18 W
Uudenmaan lääni □[4]	160	60.30 N	25.00 E
Uusikaupunki (Nystad)	160	60.48 N	21.25 E
Uvá, Bra.	296	15.53 S	50.25 W
Uva, S.S.S.R.	160	56.59 N	52.13 E
Uvá ≃	290	3.41 N	70.03 W
Uvá, Laguna ⊜	290	3.30 N	71.38 W
Uvalda	246	32.02 N	82.31 W
Uvalde	250	29.13 N	99.47 W
Uvarovka	160	55.32 N	35.37 E
Uvat	158	59.09 N	68.50 E
Uvdal	160	60.16 N	8.44 E
Uvero, Punta >	285s	11.21 N	68.41 W
Uvinza	218	5.06 S	30.22 E
Uvira	218	3.24 S	29.08 E
Uvs Nuur ⊜	186	50.20 N	92.45 E
Uwa	192	33.20 N	132.30 E
Uwajima	192	33.13 N	132.34 E
'Uwaynāt, Jabal al- ∧	220	21.54 N	24.58 E
'Uwayriḍ, Ḥarrat al- •[9]	208	27.00 N	37.30 E
Uwi, Pulau I	200	1.05 N	107.24 E
Uxbridge, Ont., Can.	264	44.06 N	79.07 W
Uxbridge, Mass., U.S.	261	42.05 N	71.38 W
Uxmal	278	20.22 N	89.46 W
Uxmal ⊥	278	20.20 N	89.45 W
Uyak	236	57.38 N	154.00 W
Uyak Bay C	236	57.36 N	153.57 W
Uyuni	292	20.28 S	66.50 W
Uyuni, Salar de ≚	292	20.20 S	67.42 W
Uzbekskaja Sovetskaja Socialističeskaja Respublika □[3]	186	41.00 N	64.00 E
Uzbek Soviet Socialist Republic → Uzbekskaja Sovetskaja Socialističeskaja	186	41.00 N	64.00 E
Uzdin	172	45.12 N	20.38 E
Uzerche	166	45.26 N	1.34 E
Uzès	166	44.01 N	4.25 E
Užgorod	164	48.37 N	22.18 E
Užgorod □[4]	172	48.20 N	23.30 E
Uzlovaja	158	53.59 N	38.10 E
Užokskij, Pereval)(	164	49.02 N	22.54 E
Üzümlü	172	36.44 N	29.14 E
Uzun Ada I	212	38.28 N	26.42 E
Uzunköprü	172	41.16 N	26.41 E
Uzunkuyu	172	38.17 N	26.33 E
Užur	186	55.20 N	89.50 E
Užventis	160	55.47 N	22.39 E
V			
V □[4]	222	18.30 N	11.30 W
Vaal ≃	224	27.40 S	26.09 E
Vaala	160	64.26 N	26.48 E
Vaalserberg ∧	164	50.46 N	6.01 E
Vaasa (Vasa)	160	63.06 N	21.36 E
Vaasan lääni □[4]	160	63.00 N	23.00 E
Vaassen	178	52.17 N	5.57 E
Vác	164	47.47 N	19.08 E
Vacacaí ≃	294	29.55 S	53.06 W

Symbols in the index entries are identified on page 360.

Name	Page	Lat°′	Long°′
Vaca Guzmán	292	19.54 S	63.48 W
Vacaria	294	28.30 S	50.56 W
Vacaria ≃, Bra.	296	16.39 S	42.45 W
Vacaria ≃, Bra.	296	21.55 S	53.59 W
Vacaville	272	38.21 N	121.59 W
Vaccarès, Étang de C	166	43.32 N	4.34 E
Vach ≃	186	60.45 N	76.45 E
Vache, Île à I	282	18.05 N	73.38 W
Vachš ≃	186	37.06 N	68.18 E
Vachtan	160	57.58 N	46.42 E
Vacoas	225c	20.18 S	57.29 E
Vad	160	55.32 N	44.12 E
Vădeni	172	45.22 N	27.56 E
Vader	270	46.24 N	122.58 W
Vadinsk	160	53.43 N	43.04 E
Vado de Cedillos	254	31.05 N	105.50 W
Vado de Piedra	250	29.50 N	104.40 W
Vado Hondo	254	31.09 N	111.22 W
Vado Ligure	182	44.17 N	8.27 E
Vadsø	160	70.03 N	29.55 E
Vaduz	180	47.09 N	9.31 E
Værøy I	160	67.40 N	12.39 E
Vaga ≃	160	62.48 N	42.56 E
Vagaj	158	57.56 N	69.01 E
Vågåmo	160	61.53 N	9.06 E
Vaganjski Vrh ∧	170	44.22 N	15.31 E
Váh ≃	164	47.55 N	18.00 E
Vaiden	248	33.20 N	89.45 W
Vaihingen	164	48.56 N	8.58 E
Vail	252	42.04 N	95.12 W
Vailly-sur-Aisne	166	49.25 N	3.31 E
Vaison-la-Romaine	166	44.14 N	5.04 E
Vajgač	186	70.25 N	58.46 E
Vajgač, Ostrov I	186	70.00 N	59.30 E
Vakaga □[5]	220	10.00 N	22.30 E
Valaam	160	61.23 N	30.57 E
Vålådalen	160	63.10 N	12.57 E
Valadeces	250	26.14 N	98.40 W
Valais (Wallis) □[3]	180	46.10 N	7.30 E
Val-Alain	260	46.25 N	71.45 W
Valamaz	160	57.32 N	52.05 E
Valandovo	172	41.19 N	22.34 E
Valašské Klobouky	164	49.08 N	18.01 E
Valašské Meziříčí	164	49.28 N	17.58 E
Valatie	261	42.25 N	73.41 W
Vâlcĕdrâm	172	43.42 N	23.27 E
Valcheta	288	40.40 S	66.10 W
Valcourt	260	45.30 N	72.19 W
Valdagno	170	45.39 N	11.18 E
Valdai → Valdajskaja Vozvyšennost' ∧∧[2]	160	57.00 N	33.30 E
Valdaj, S.S.S.R.	160	63.26 N	35.30 E
Valdaj, S.S.S.R.	160	57.59 N	33.14 E
Valdajskaja Vozvyšennost' ∧∧[2]	160	57.00 N	33.30 E
Valdarno ∨	170	43.45 N	11.15 E
Valdavia ≃	168	42.24 N	4.16 W
Val-David	260	46.02 N	74.12 W
Valdecañas, Embalse de ⊜[1]	168	39.45 N	5.30 W
Valdelândia	296	15.11 S	50.02 W
Val-de-Marne □[5]	166	48.47 N	2.29 E
Valdemārpils	160	57.22 N	22.35 E
Valdemarsvik	160	58.12 N	16.36 E
Valdepeñas	168	38.46 N	3.23 W
Valderaduey ≃	168	41.31 N	5.42 W
Valderas	168	42.05 N	5.27 W
Valderrama	202	11.00 N	122.08 E
Valderrobres	168	40.53 N	0.09 E
Valders	244	44.09 N	87.53 W
Valdés, Península ≻[1]	288	42.30 S	64.00 W
Val-des-Bois	242	45.54 N	75.36 W
Valdese	246	35.44 N	81.34 W
Valdez, Ec.	290	1.15 N	79.00 W
Valdez, Alaska, U.S.	236	61.07 N	146.16 W
Val di Mazara ⤶[1]	170	37.50 N	13.00 E
Val di Noto ⤶[1]	170	37.05 N	14.40 E
Val-d'Isère	166	45.27 N	6.59 E
Valdivia, Chile	288	39.48 S	73.14 W
Valdivia, Col.	290	7.11 N	75.27 W
Valdobbiadene	170	45.54 N	12.00 E
Val-d'Oise □[5]	176	49.10 N	2.10 W
Val-d'Or	244	48.07 N	77.47 W
Valdorf	178	52.09 N	8.51 E
Valdosta	246	30.50 N	83.17 W
Valdoviño	168	43.36 N	8.08 W
Vale	256	43.59 N	117.15 W
Valea-lui-Mihai	172	47.31 N	22.09 E
Valemount	238	52.50 N	119.15 W
Valença, Bra.	296	22.15 S	43.43 W
Valença, Bra.	296	13.22 S	39.05 W
Valença, Port.	168	42.02 N	8.38 W
Valençay	166	47.09 N	1.34 E
Valence	182	44.56 N	4.54 E
Valencia, Esp.	168	39.28 N	0.22 W
Valencia, Hond.	280	14.47 N	85.18 W
Valencia, Pil.	202	7.57 N	125.02 E
Valencia, Pa., U.S.	266	40.40 N	79.59 W
Valencia, Ven.	290	10.11 N	68.00 W
Valencia □[9]	168	39.30 N	0.40 W
Valencia, Golfo de C	168	39.50 N	0.30 E
Valencia, Lago de ⊜	290	10.15 N	67.45 W
Valencia de Alcántata	168	39.25 N	7.14 W
Valencia de Don Juan	168	42.18 N	5.31 W
Valenciennes	176	50.21 N	3.32 E
Vălenii-de-Munte	172	45.12 N	26.03 E
Valentia Island I	162	51.52 N	10.20 W
Valentigney	180	47.28 N	6.50 E
Valentine, Nebr., U.S.	252	42.52 N	100.33 W
Valentine, Tex., U.S.	250	30.34 N	104.29 W
Valenza	182	45.01 N	8.38 E
Valera	290	9.19 N	70.37 W
Valga	160	57.47 N	26.02 E
Valguarnera Caropepe	170	37.30 N	14.24 E
Valhalla	261	41.04 N	73.46 W
Valiente, Península ≻[1]	280	9.05 N	81.50 W
Valiente, Punta ≻	280	9.12 N	81.55 W
Valier, Ill., U.S.	248	38.01 N	89.03 W
Valier, Mont., U.S.	256	48.18 N	112.15 W
Valjevo	172	44.16 N	19.53 E
Valka	160	57.46 N	26.00 E
Valkeakoski	160	61.16 N	24.02 E
Valkenburg	164	50.52 N	5.50 E
Valkenswaard	178	51.21 N	5.28 E
Valladares	250	26.53 N	100.37 W
Valladolid, Ec.	290	4.33 S	79.08 W
Valladolid, Esp.	168	41.39 N	4.43 W
Valladolid, Méx.	278	20.41 N	88.12 W
Vallauris	170	43.35 N	7.03 E
Valldal	160	62.20 N	7.21 E
Vall de Uxó	168	39.49 N	0.14 W
Valle □[5]	280	13.30 N	87.35 W
Vallecillo	250	26.40 N	99.58 W
Vallecito	272	38.07 N	120.27 W
Vallecitos	254	36.30 N	106.01 W
Valle d'Aosta □[4]	182	45.45 N	7.25 E
Valle de Bravo	278	19.11 N	100.08 W
Valle de Cabuérniga	168	43.14 N	4.18 W
Valle de Guanape	290	9.54 N	65.41 W
Valle de la Pascua	290	9.13 N	66.00 W
Valle del Cauca □[5]	290	3.45 N	76.30 W
Valle del Yaqui	278	27.19 N	110.01 W
Valle de Olivos	278	27.12 N	106.17 W
Valle de Santiago	278	20.23 N	101.12 W
Valle de Zaragoza	278	27.28 N	105.49 W
Valledolmo	170	37.45 N	13.50 E
Valledupar	290	10.29 N	73.15 W
Valle Edén	294	31.50 S	56.09 W
Valle Fértil, Sierra de ∧∧	294	30.20 S	68.00 W
Vallegrande	292	18.29 S	64.06 W
Valle Hermoso, Arg.	294	31.07 S	64.30 W
Valle Hermoso, Méx.	250	25.39 N	97.52 W
Vallehermoso, Pil.	202	10.20 N	123.19 E
Vallejo	272	38.07 N	122.14 W
Vallelunga Pratameno	170	37.41 N	13.50 E
Vallenar	294	28.35 S	70.46 W
Valle Redondo	258	32.31 N	116.46 W
Vallet	166	47.10 N	1.16 W
Valletta	170	35.54 N	14.31 E
Valle Vista	274	33.35 N	116.58 W
Valley, Nebr., U.S.	252	41.19 N	96.21 W
Valley, Wash., U.S.	238	48.11 N	117.44 W
Valley Bend	242	38.46 N	79.56 W
Valley Center, Calif., U.S.	274	33.13 N	117.02 W
Valley Center, Kans., U.S.	252	37.50 N	97.22 W
Valley City, N. Dak., U.S.	252	46.55 N	97.59 W
Valley City, Ohio, U.S.	266	41.14 N	81.56 W
Valley Creek ≃	250	31.43 N	100.02 W
Valley Falls	252	39.21 N	95.28 W
Valley Farms	254	32.59 N	111.27 W
Valleyfield, Newf., Can.	240	49.11 N	53.41 W
Valleyfield, Qué., Can.	260	45.15 N	74.08 W
Valley Forge	262	40.06 N	75.28 W
Valley Grove	266	40.05 N	80.34 W
Valley Head, Ala., U.S.	248	34.34 N	85.37 W
Valley Head, W. Va., U.S.	242	38.33 N	80.02 W
Valley Home	272	37.50 N	120.55 W
Valley Mills	250	31.39 N	97.28 W
Valley of Fire State Park ♠	258	36.26 N	114.30 W
Valley of the Kings ⊥	220	25.45 N	32.37 E
Valley Springs, Calif., U.S.	272	38.12 N	120.50 W
Valley Springs, S. Dak., U.S.	252	43.35 N	96.28 W
Valley Station	248	38.06 N	85.52 W
Valleyview, Alta., Can.	238	55.04 N	117.17 W
Valley View, Ill., U.S.	268	41.50 N	88.03 W
Valley View, Tex., U.S.	250	33.29 N	97.10 W
Valley View Park	274	34.13 N	117.20 W
Vallgrund I	160	63.12 N	21.14 E
Vallimanca, Arroyo ≃	294	35.40 S	59.10 W
Vallo della Lucania	170	40.14 N	15.17 E
Vallon-Pont-d'Arc	166	44.24 N	4.24 E
Vallorbe	166	46.43 N	6.22 E
Valls	168	41.17 N	1.15 E
Val-Marie	256	49.14 N	107.44 W
Valmaseda	168	43.12 N	3.12 W
Valmeyer	248	38.18 N	90.19 W
Valmiera	160	57.33 N	25.24 E
Valmontone	184	41.46 N	12.57 E
Valognes	166	49.31 N	1.28 W
Valona → Vlorë	172	40.27 N	19.30 E
Valongo	168	41.11 N	8.30 W
Valoria la Buena	168	41.48 N	4.32 W
Valparaíso, Bra.	296	21.13 S	50.51 W
Valparaíso, Chile	294	33.02 S	71.38 W
Valparaíso, Méx.	278	22.46 N	103.34 W
Valparaiso, Fla., U.S.	248	30.29 N	86.30 W
Valparaiso, Ind., U.S.	268	41.28 N	87.03 W
Valparaiso, Nebr., U.S.	252	41.05 N	96.50 W
Valparaíso □[4]	294	33.00 S	71.15 W
Valpovo	172	45.39 N	18.26 E
Valréas	166	44.23 N	4.59 E
Vals ≃	224	27.23 S	26.30 E
Vals, Tandjung ≻	198	8.25 S	137.38 E
Val-Saint-Michel	260	46.52 N	71.28 W
Valsetz	256	44.50 N	123.39 W
Valsjöbyn	160	64.04 N	14.08 E
Valtimo	160	63.40 N	28.48 E
Valujki	158	50.13 N	38.08 E
Valverde	282	19.34 N	71.05 W
Valverde del Camino	168	37.34 N	6.45 W
Val Verde Park	274	34.27 N	118.40 W
Valyermo	274	34.26 N	117.50 W
Vam-co-dong ≃	200	10.30 N	106.33 E
Vam-co-tay ≃	200	10.30 N	106.33 E
Van, Tür.	208	38.28 N	43.20 E
Van, Pa., U.S.	266	41.19 N	79.40 W
Van, Tex., U.S.	250	32.31 N	95.38 W
Van Alstyne	250	33.25 N	96.35 W
Vananda	238	49.45 N	124.33 W
Vanavara	186	60.22 N	102.16 E
Van Buren, Ark., U.S.	248	35.26 N	94.21 W
Van Buren, Ind., U.S.	268	40.37 N	85.30 W
Van Buren, Maine, U.S.	240	47.09 N	67.56 W
Van Buren, Mo., U.S.	248	37.00 N	91.01 W
Van Buren, Ohio, U.S.	268	41.08 N	83.39 W
Van Buren □[6]	268	42.14 N	86.04 W
Van Buren Bay	266	42.27 N	79.23 W
Van Buren Point	266	42.27 N	79.25 W
Vanč	186	38.23 N	71.26 E
Vanceboro	242	45.34 N	67.26 W
Vanceburg	242	38.36 N	83.19 W
Vancleave	248	30.32 N	88.46 W
Van Cortlandtville	261	41.19 N	73.54 W
Vancouver, B.C., Can.	238	49.16 N	123.07 W
Vancouver, Wash., U.S.	270	45.39 N	122.40 W
Vancouver, Cape ≻	236	60.33 N	165.27 W
Vancouver, Mount ∧	236	60.20 N	139.40 W
Vancouver Island I	238	49.45 N	126.00 W
Vancouver Island Ranges ∧∧	238	49.25 N	125.25 W
Vandalia, Ill., U.S.	248	38.58 N	89.06 W
Vandalia, Mich., U.S.	268	41.55 N	85.55 W
Vandalia, Mo., U.S.	248	39.19 N	91.29 W
Vandenberg Air Force Base ■	258	34.43 N	120.33 W
Vanderbijlpark	224	26.42 S	27.54 E
Vanderbilt, Mich., U.S.	244	45.09 N	84.40 W
Vanderbilt, Tex., U.S.	250	28.49 N	96.37 W
Vandercook Lake	268	42.12 N	84.24 W
Vandergrift	266	40.36 N	79.34 W
Vanderhoof	238	54.01 N	124.01 W
Vandervoort	248	34.23 N	94.22 W
Van Duzen ≃	258	40.33 N	124.08 W
Vandúzi ≃	224	19.58 S	34.02 E
Vanegas	278	23.51 N	100.52 W
Vänern ⊜	160	58.55 N	13.30 E
Vänersborg	160	58.22 N	12.19 E
Van-fong, Baie de C	200	12.35 N	109.20 E
Vangaindrano	218	23.21 S	47.36 E
Van Gölü ⊜	212	38.33 N	42.46 E
Vangsnes	160	61.11 N	6.38 E
Vangunu I	226	8.40 S	158.05 E
Vangviang	198	18.56 N	102.27 E
Van Horn	250	31.03 N	104.50 W
Van Horne	244	42.01 N	92.05 W
Vanimo	198	2.40 S	141.20 E
Vanino	186	49.05 N	140.15 E
Vankarem, S.S.S.R.	186	67.51 N	175.50 E
Vankarem, S.S.S.R.	236	67.51 N	175.50 W
Vankarem ≃	236	68.10 N	177.40 W
Vankarem, Laguna C	236	67.40 N	176.00 W
Vankaremskaja Nizmennost' ≚	236	67.30 N	176.00 W
Vankleek Hill	260	45.31 N	74.39 W
Van Lear	246	37.46 N	82.46 W
Vanlue	268	40.59 N	83.29 W
Vännäs	160	63.55 N	19.45 E
Vanndale	248	35.19 N	90.46 W
Vannes	166	47.39 N	2.46 W
Vannøy I	160	70.09 N	19.51 E
Van Nuys ⤶[8]	274	34.11 N	118.26 W
Vanoise, Massif de la ∧∧	166	45.20 N	6.40 E
Van Ormer	266	40.41 N	78.30 W
Vanport	266	40.41 N	80.20 W
Vanrhynsdorp	218	31.36 S	18.44 E
Vansant	246	37.14 N	82.06 W
Vansbro	160	60.31 N	14.13 E
Vansittart Island I	232	65.50 N	84.00 W
Vanves	176	48.50 N	2.18 E
Van Vleck	250	29.01 N	95.53 W
Van Wert	268	40.52 N	84.35 W
Van Wert □[6]	268	40.52 N	84.35 W
Van Winkle	248	32.17 N	90.15 W
Vaprio d'Adda	182	45.35 N	9.31 E
Var □[5]	182	43.30 N	6.20 E
Var ≃	170	43.39 N	7.12 E
Varadero	284p	23.09 N	81.16 W
Varades	166	47.23 N	1.02 W
Varallo Sesia	182	45.49 N	8.15 E
Varāmīn	208	35.20 N	51.39 E
Vārānasi (Benares)	206	25.20 N	83.00 E
Varandej	160	68.48 N	58.00 E
Varangerfjorden C[2]	160	70.00 N	30.00 E
Varangerhalvøya ≻[1]	160	70.25 N	29.30 E
Varaždin	170	46.19 N	16.20 E
Varazze	182	44.22 N	8.34 E
Varberg	160	57.06 N	12.15 E
Vardaman	248	33.47 N	89.10 W
Vardar (Axiós) ≃	172	40.31 N	22.43 E
Varde	160	55.38 N	8.29 E
Vardhoúsia Óri ∧∧	172	38.44 N	22.07 E
Vardø	160	70.21 N	31.02 E
Varedo	182	45.36 N	9.09 E
Varel	178	53.22 N	8.10 E
Varela	294	34.07 S	66.27 W
Varennes, Qué., Can.	260	45.41 N	73.26 W
Varennes, Fr.	162	50.03 N	2.32 E
Varennes-sur-Allier	166	46.19 N	3.24 E
Vareš	172	44.09 N	18.19 E
Varese	182	45.48 N	8.48 E
Varese □[4], It.	180	45.55 N	8.45 E
Varese □[4], It.	182	45.48 N	8.48 E
Varese Ligure	170	44.22 N	9.37 E
Varginha	296	21.33 S	45.26 W
Varjão	296	17.03 S	49.37 W
Varkaus	160	62.19 N	27.55 E
Värmlands Län □[6]	160	59.45 N	13.15 E
Varna	172	43.13 N	27.55 E
Värnamo	160	57.11 N	14.02 E
Varnavino	160	57.24 N	45.04 E
Varnenski zaliv C	172	43.11 N	27.56 E
Varnsdorf	164	50.52 N	14.40 E
Varnville	246	32.51 N	81.05 W
Várpalota	164	47.12 N	18.09 E
Vars	264	45.21 N	75.21 W
Vâršec	172	43.12 N	23.17 E
V'artsil'a, S.S.S.R.	160	62.11 N	30.41 E
Värtsilä, Suomi	160	62.15 N	30.40 E
Varvarin	172	43.43 N	21.19 E
Varysburg	264	42.46 N	78.19 W
Várzea, Rio da ≃	294	27.13 S	53.19 W
Várzea da Palma	296	17.36 S	44.44 W
Várzea Grande	292	15.39 S	56.08 W
Varzeão	294	24.34 S	49.26 W
Varzi	160	56.03 N	52.50 E
Varzino	160	68.19 N	38.19 E
Varzo	170	46.12 N	8.15 E
Varzuga	160	67.24 N	36.32 E
Varzy	166	47.22 N	3.23 E
Vas □[6]	164	47.05 N	16.45 E
Vascão, Ribeira do ≃	168	37.31 N	7.31 W
Vaşcău	172	46.28 N	22.28 E
Vascongadas □[9]	168	43.00 N	2.45 W
Vashon	270	47.27 N	122.28 W
Vashon Heights	270	47.30 N	122.28 W
Vasile Roaită	172	44.03 N	28.38 E
Vasilija, Mys ≻	236	64.34 N	178.33 W
Vasiliká	172	40.28 N	23.08 E
Vasiljevo	160	60.46 N	38.59 E
Vasiljevskoje	160	56.31 N	45.49 E
Vaška ≃	160	64.53 N	45.47 E
Vaskelovo	160	60.22 N	30.22 E
Vaslui	172	46.38 N	27.44 E
Vass	246	35.15 N	79.17 W
Vassar	244	43.22 N	83.35 W
Västerås	160	59.37 N	16.33 E
Västerbottens Län □[6]	160	64.00 N	17.30 E
Västernorrlands Län □[6]	160	63.00 N	17.30 E
Västervik	160	57.45 N	16.38 E
Västmanlands Län □[6]	160	59.45 N	16.20 E
Vasto	184	42.07 N	14.42 E
Vas'ugan ≃	186	59.07 N	80.46 E
Vas'uganje ☷	186	58.00 N	77.00 E
Vašutkiny Ozera ⊜	160	68.06 N	61.18 E
Vasvár	164	47.03 N	16.49 E
Vaţa	172	46.10 N	22.35 E
Vatan	166	47.05 N	1.48 E
Vatersay I	162	56.53 N	7.28 W
Vathí	172	37.45 N	26.59 E
Vatican City □[1]	184	41.54 N	12.27 E
Vaticano, Capo ≻	170	38.38 N	15.50 E
V'atka ≃	160	55.36 N	51.30 E
Vatlirchvin, Gora ∧	236	68.08 N	179.52 W
Vatnajökull ⊠	160a	64.25 N	16.50 W
Vatoloha ∧	225b	17.52 S	47.48 E
Vatomandry	218	19.20 S	48.59 E
Vatra Dornei	172	47.21 N	25.21 E
V'atskije Pol'any	160	56.14 N	51.04 E
Vättern ⊜	160	58.24 N	14.36 E
Vaucluse □[5]	182	44.00 N	5.10 E
Vaucouleurs	166	48.36 N	5.40 E
Vaud □[3]	180	46.40 N	6.30 E
Vaudreuil	260	45.24 N	74.02 W
Vaudreuil □[6]	260	45.26 N	74.15 W
Vaughn, N. Mex., U.S.	254	34.36 N	105.13 W
Vaughn, Wash., U.S.	270	47.21 N	122.46 W
Vaughnsville	268	40.53 N	84.09 W
Vaupés □[8]	290	1.00 N	71.00 W
Vaupés (Uaupés) ≃	290	0.02 N	67.16 W
Vauvert	166	43.42 N	4.17 E
Vauxhall	238	50.04 N	112.07 W
Växjö	160	56.52 N	14.49 E
Vazante	296	18.00 S	46.54 W
Vazante Grande ≃	292	19.21 S	56.53 W
V'azemskij	186	47.32 N	134.48 E
Važgort	160	64.01 N	47.02 E
V'az'ma	160	55.13 N	34.18 E
V'az'me	160	55.13 N	34.18 E
V'azniki	160	56.15 N	42.10 E
Vazobe ∧	225b	18.25 S	47.18 E
Veadeiros	296	14.07 S	47.31 W
Veazie	242	44.51 N	68.42 W
Veblen	252	45.52 N	97.17 W
Vecchiano	184	43.47 N	10.23 E
Vechta	178	52.43 N	8.16 E
Vecsés	164	47.25 N	19.16 E
Vedano Olona	182	45.46 N	8.53 E
Vedder Crossing	270	49.06 N	121.57 W
Veddige	160	57.16 N	12.19 E
Vedea	172	44.47 N	24.37 E
Vedea ≃	172	43.53 N	25.59 E
Vedia	294	34.30 S	61.32 W
Veedersburg	248	40.07 N	87.16 W
Veendam	178	53.06 N	6.58 E
Veenendaal	178	52.02 N	5.34 E
Vefsna ≃	160	65.50 N	13.12 E
Vega	250	35.15 N	102.26 W
Vega I	160	65.39 N	11.50 E
Vega Alta	284m	18.25 N	66.20 W
Vega Baja	284m	18.27 N	66.23 W
Vega Point ≻	237a	51.49 N	177.16 E
Vegesack ⤶[8]	178	53.10 N	8.37 E
Veghel	178	51.37 N	5.33 E
Vegreville	238	53.30 N	112.03 W
Veguita	254	34.31 N	106.46 W
Veinte de Noviembre	250	25.47 N	97.33 W
Veinticinco de Mayo, Arg.	294	35.25 S	60.11 W
Veinticinco de Mayo, Arg.	294	34.35 S	68.34 W
Veinticinco de Mayo, Ur.	294	34.12 S	56.22 W
Veintiocho de Mayo	290	3.50 S	78.52 W
Veintisiete de Abril	280	10.15 N	85.45 W
Veio ⊥	170	42.02 N	12.24 E
Veisiejai	164	54.06 N	23.42 E
Vejer de la Frontera	168	36.15 N	5.58 W
Vejle	160	55.42 N	9.32 E
Veksor	160	60.33 N	49.22 E
Vela Luka	170	42.58 N	16.43 E
Velardeña	278	25.04 N	103.44 W
Velas, Cabo ≻	280	10.21 N	85.52 W
Velasco, Sierra ∧∧	294	29.00 S	67.10 W
Velay, Monts du ∧∧	166	45.00 N	3.45 E
Velázquez	294	34.02 S	54.17 W
Velbert	178	51.20 N	7.02 E
Velden	164	48.19 N	12.16 E
Veldhoven	164	51.24 N	5.24 E
Velebit ∧∧	170	44.38 N	15.03 E
Velebitski Kanal ⊔	170	45.00 N	14.50 E
Veleka ≃	172	42.04 N	27.58 E
Velencei-tó ⊜	164	47.12 N	18.35 E
Velenje	170	46.21 N	15.06 E
Velestínon	172	39.23 N	22.45 E
Vélez	290	6.01 N	73.41 W
Velez de la Gomera, Peñón de I	168	35.11 N	4.21 W
Vélez-Málaga	168	36.47 N	4.06 W
Vélez Rubio	168	37.39 N	2.04 W
Velhas, Rio das ≃	296	17.13 S	44.49 W
Velika Gorica	170	45.43 N	16.05 E
Velika Gubavica ↳	170	43.26 N	16.54 E
Velikaja, S.S.S.R.	160	59.13 N	49.04 E
Velikaja, S.S.S.R.	236	64.04 N	176.12 E
Velikaja ≃, S.S.S.R.	160	57.48 N	28.20 E
Velikaja ≃, S.S.S.R.	236	64.40 N	176.20 E
Velika Kapela ∧∧	170	45.15 N	15.00 E
Velika Lašče	170	45.50 N	14.38 E
Velika Plana	172	44.20 N	21.04 E
Velikij Ber'oznyj	164	48.53 N	22.27 E
Velikije Lučki	172	48.26 N	22.35 E
Velikije Luki	160	56.20 N	30.32 E
Velikij-ust'ug	160	60.48 N	46.18 E
Veliki Risnjak ∧	170	45.26 N	14.37 E
Veliki Snežnik ∧	170	45.35 N	14.27 E
Veliki Troglav ∧	170	43.57 N	16.36 E
Veliki Vitorog ∧	170	44.07 N	17.03 E
Veliko Gradište	172	44.45 N	21.32 E
Velikoje	160	59.32 N	36.59 E
Velikookt'abr'skij	160	57.26 N	33.49 E
Veliko Târnovo	172	43.04 N	25.39 E
Velikovisočnoje	160	67.16 N	52.01 E
Veli Losinj	170	44.31 N	14.30 E
Vélingara	214	13.09 N	14.07 W
Velingrad	172	42.04 N	24.00 E
Veliž	160	55.38 N	31.12 E
Velká Bíteš	164	49.17 N	16.13 E
Velká Deštná ∧	164	50.18 N	16.24 E
Vel'ká Fatra ∧∧	164	49.00 N	19.05 E
Vel'ké Kapušany	164	48.33 N	22.04 E
Velké Meziříčí	164	49.21 N	16.00 E
Vel'ký Milič ∧	164	48.35 N	21.28 E
Vella Lavella I	226	7.45 S	156.40 E
Velletri	184	41.41 N	12.47 E
Velp	178	52.00 N	5.59 E
Velsen	178	52.27 N	4.39 E
Vel'sk	160	61.05 N	42.05 E
Vel't	160	68.03 N	49.55 E
Velten	164	52.41 N	13.10 E
Veltrusy ⊥	166	50.14 N	14.18 E
Veluwe ⤶[1]	164	52.20 N	5.50 E
Velva	252	48.04 N	100.56 W
Vemdalen	160	62.27 N	13.52 E
Venaco	170	42.14 N	9.10 E
Venada, Isla I	280	11.09 N	84.56 W
Venadillo	290	4.43 N	74.55 W
Venado, Isla I, Nic.	280	11.57 N	83.43 W
Venado, Isla I, Ven.	285r	10.00 N	62.25 W
Venado Tuerto	294	33.46 S	61.58 W
Venafro	184	41.29 N	14.02 E
Venâncio Aires	294	29.36 S	52.11 W
Venango	266	41.46 N	80.07 W
Venango □[6]	266	41.24 N	79.50 W
Venaria	182	45.08 N	7.38 E
Vence	182	43.43 N	7.07 E
Venceslau Braz	296	23.51 S	49.48 W
Venda Nova, Bra.	296	19.49 S	43.58 W
Venda Nova, Port.	168	41.40 N	7.58 W
Vendas Novas	168	38.41 N	8.28 W
Vendée □[5]	166	46.40 N	1.20 W
Vendée ⤶[1]	166	46.40 N	1.10 W
Vendeuvre-sur-Barse	166	48.14 N	4.28 E
Vendôme	176	47.48 N	1.04 E
Vendrell	168	41.13 N	1.32 E
Venecia	280	10.22 N	84.17 W
Venedocia	268	40.44 N	84.25 W
Venetia	266	40.15 N	80.03 W
Venetian Village	268	42.24 N	88.02 W
Venetie	236	66.30 N	147.26 W
Veneto □[4]	184	45.30 N	11.45 E
Venev	160	54.21 N	38.16 E
Venezia (Venice)	170	45.27 N	12.21 E
Venezuela □[1]	286	8.00 N	56.00 W
Venezuela, Golfo de C	290	11.30 N	71.00 W
Venezuelan Basin ⤳[1]	148	14.30 N	68.00 W
Vengerovo	186	55.41 N	76.45 E
Veniaminof, Mount ∧	236	56.13 N	159.18 W
Venice → Venezia, It.	170	45.27 N	12.21 E
Venice, Fla., U.S.	246	27.06 N	82.27 W
Venice, La., U.S.	248	29.17 N	89.21 W
Venice, Ohio, U.S.	266	41.27 N	82.46 W
Venice ⤶[8]	274	34.00 N	118.29 W
Venice, Gulf of C	170	45.15 N	13.00 E
Vénissieux	182	45.41 N	4.53 E
Venlo	178	51.24 N	6.10 E
Venosa	170	40.57 N	15.49 E
Venoste, Alpi ∧∧	170	46.45 N	10.55 E
Venraij	178	51.32 N	5.59 E
Vent	164	46.52 N	10.56 E
Venta ≃	160	57.24 N	21.33 E
Venta, Río de la ≃	278	16.59 N	93.46 W
Venta de Cardena	168	38.13 N	4.19 W
Ventanas	290	1.23 S	79.25 W
Ventimiglia	182	43.47 N	7.36 E
Ventnor	174	50.36 N	1.11 W
Ventnor City	262	39.20 N	74.29 W
Ventoux, Mont ∧	166	44.10 N	5.17 E
Ventspils	160	57.24 N	21.36 E
Ventuari ≃	290	3.58 N	67.02 W
Ventura (San Buenaventura)	274	34.17 N	119.18 W
Ventura □[6]	274	34.30 N	119.00 W
Venturia	252	46.00 N	99.33 W
Venus, Fla., U.S.	246	27.04 N	81.21 W
Venus, Pa., U.S.	266	41.22 N	79.29 W
Venustiano Carranza, Méx.	278	16.21 N	92.33 W
Venustiano Carranza, Méx.	278	19.44 N	103.47 W
Venustiano Carranza, Presa ⊜[1]	278	27.30 N	100.40 W
Vera	168	37.15 N	1.52 W
Verá, Laguna ⊜	294	26.05 S	57.39 W
Veracruz, Méx.	254	32.25 N	115.05 W
Vera Cruz, Pa., U.S.	262	40.30 N	75.30 W
Veracruz □[3]	278	19.20 N	96.40 W
Veracruz [Llave]	278	19.12 N	96.08 W
Veraguas □[4]	280	8.30 N	81.00 W
Veranópolis	294	28.57 S	51.33 W
Verāval	206	20.54 N	70.20 E
Verbania	180	45.56 N	8.33 E
Verbank	261	41.44 N	73.43 W
Vercelli	182	45.19 N	8.25 E
Vercelli □[4]	182	45.37 N	8.10 E
Vercel [-Villedieu-le-Camp]	170	47.11 N	6.24 E
Verchères	260	45.47 N	73.21 W
Verchères □[6]	260	45.45 N	73.20 W
Verchn'aja Amga	186	59.30 N	126.08 E
Verchn'aja Inta	160	66.00 N	60.20 E
Verchn'aja Salda	158	58.02 N	60.33 E
Verchn'aja Tojma	160	62.13 N	45.00 E
Verchn'aja Tura	158	58.22 N	59.49 E
Verchnedvinsk	160	55.47 N	27.56 E
Verchneimbatskoje	186	63.11 N	87.58 E
Verchnetulomskij	160	68.38 N	31.45 E
Verchnevil'ujsk	186	63.27 N	120.18 E
Verchnij Baskunčak	158	48.14 N	46.44 E
Verchnij Ufalej	158	56.04 N	60.14 E
Verchojansk	186	67.35 N	133.27 E
Verchojanskij Chrebet ∧∧	186	67.00 N	129.00 E
Verchopuja	160	61.34 N	41.31 E
Verchoturje	158	58.52 N	60.48 E
Verchovažje	160	60.45 N	42.00 E
Vercors □[9]	182	44.57 N	5.25 E
Verde ≃, Bra.	292	11.54 S	55.48 W
Verde ≃, Bra.	292	13.33 S	58.01 W
Verde ≃, Bra.	296	21.12 S	51.53 W
Verde ≃, Bra.	296	15.07 S	48.40 W
Verde ≃, Bra.	296	18.01 S	50.14 W
Verde ≃, Bra.	296	17.05 S	46.05 W
Verde ≃, Bra.	296	21.34 S	45.31 W
Verde ≃, Bra.	296	19.55 S	49.45 W
Verde ≃, Bra.	296	19.11 S	50.44 W
Verde ≃, Para.	294	23.09 S	57.37 W
Verde ≃, S.A.	292	13.59 S	60.24 W
Verde ≃, Ariz., U.S.	254	33.33 N	111.40 W
Verde, Arroyo ≃	292	11.25 S	66.20 W
Verde, Mesa ∧	254	37.10 N	108.30 W
Verde, Point ≻	240	47.14 N	54.01 W
Verde Grande ≃, Bra.	296	14.35 S	43.53 W
Verde Grande ≃, Méx.	278	20.42 N	103.14 W
Verde Island I	202	13.33 N	121.04 E
Verde Island Passage ⊔	202	13.35 N	121.00 E
Verdello	182	45.36 N	9.37 E
Verden, B.R.D.	178	52.55 N	9.13 E
Verden, Okla., U.S.	250	35.05 N	98.05 W
Verde Pequeno ≃	296	14.48 S	43.31 W
Verdi	272	39.31 N	119.59 W
Verdigre	252	42.36 N	98.02 W
Verdinho ≃	296	17.29 S	50.27 W
Verdon	252	40.08 N	95.48 W
Verdon ≃, Alg.	168	43.43 N	5.46 E
Verdon ≃, Fr.	166	43.43 N	5.46 E
Verdoy	261	42.46 N	73.48 W
Verdun, Qué., Can.	260	45.28 N	73.34 W
Verdun, Fr.	166	43.52 N	1.14 E
Verdun-sur-le-Doubs	166	46.54 N	5.01 E
Verdun-sur-Meuse	166	49.10 N	5.23 E
Vereb'jo	160	58.41 N	32.42 E
Vereeniging	224	26.38 S	27.57 E
Vereja	160	55.21 N	36.11 E
Vereščagino, S.S.S.R.	160	58.05 N	54.40 E
Vereščagino, S.S.S.R.	186	64.14 N	87.37 E
Verga, Cap ≻	222	10.12 N	14.27 W
Vergara, Esp.	168	43.07 N	2.25 W
Vergara, Ur.	294	32.56 S	53.57 W
Vergel	250	25.39 N	103.32 W
Vergennes	242	44.10 N	73.15 W
Vergiate	182	45.43 N	8.42 E
Vergt	166	45.02 N	0.43 E
Verín	168	41.56 N	7.26 W
Verísimo Sarmento	218	8.10 S	20.39 E
Veríssimo	296	19.42 S	48.18 W
Veríssimo ≃	296	18.23 S	48.20 W
Verl (Senne I)	178	51.53 N	8.31 E
Vermejo ≃	254	36.30 N	104.33 W
Vermelho ≃	296	14.54 S	51.06 W
Vermenton	166	47.40 N	3.44 E
Vermilion, Alta., Can.	238	53.22 N	110.51 W
Vermilion, Ohio, U.S.	266	41.25 N	82.22 W
Vermilion □[6]	268	40.08 N	87.37 W
Vermilion ≃, Ont., Can.	244	46.16 N	81.41 W
Vermilion ≃, U.S.	248	39.53 N	87.22 W
Vermilion ≃, Ill., U.S.	244	41.19 N	89.04 W
Vermilion ≃, Minn., U.S.	244	48.16 N	92.30 W
Vermilion Bay C	248	29.40 N	92.00 W
Vermilion Bluffs ⤶[4]	254	40.50 N	108.30 W
Vermilion Lake ⊜	244	47.53 N	92.25 W
Vermilion Range ∧∧[2]	244	47.50 N	92.00 W
Vermillion	252	42.47 N	96.56 W
Vermillion ≃, Minn., U.S.	244	44.45 N	92.51 W
Vermillion ≃, S. Dak., U.S.	252	42.44 N	96.53 W
Vermont □[3]	234	43.50 N	72.45 W
Vermontville	268	42.38 N	85.02 W
Vernal	254	40.27 N	109.32 W
Vernalis	272	37.38 N	121.17 W
Verndale	252	46.24 N	95.01 W
Verner	244	46.25 N	80.07 W
Verneuil	166	48.44 N	0.56 E
Verneuil-sur-Avre	166	48.44 N	0.56 E
Verneukpan ⊜	224	29.58 S	21.10 E
Vernier	180	46.13 N	6.06 E
Vernon, B.C., Can.	238	50.16 N	119.16 W
Vernon, Ont., Can.	264	45.10 N	75.28 W
Vernon, Fr.	162	47.48 N	1.38 E
Vernon, Fr.	176	49.05 N	1.29 E
Vernon, Ala., U.S.	248	33.45 N	88.07 W
Vernon, Conn., U.S.	261	41.50 N	72.28 W
Vernon, Fla., U.S.	248	30.37 N	85.43 W
Vernon, Ind., U.S.	248	38.59 N	85.36 W
Vernon, Mich., U.S.	268	42.56 N	84.02 W
Vernon, N.Y., U.S.	264	43.05 N	75.32 W
Vernon, Ohio, U.S.	266	41.23 N	80.34 W
Vernon, Tex., U.S.	250	34.09 N	99.17 W
Vernon, Utah, U.S.	254	40.06 N	112.26 W
Vernon, Lake ⊜[1]	248	31.15 N	93.25 W
Vernonia	270	45.52 N	123.11 W
Vernon River	240	46.12 N	62.50 W
Verny	166	49.01 N	6.12 E
Vero ≃	168	42.00 N	0.10 E
Vero Beach	246	27.38 N	80.24 W
Véroia	172	40.31 N	22.12 E
Verona, Ont., Can.	264	44.29 N	76.42 W
Verona, It.	170	45.27 N	11.00 E
Verona, Ill., U.S.	268	41.13 N	88.30 W
Verona, Miss., U.S.	248	34.12 N	88.43 W
Verona, N.Y., U.S.	264	43.08 N	75.34 W
Verona, Pa., U.S.	266	40.30 N	79.50 W
Verona, Wis., U.S.	268	42.59 N	89.32 W
Verona Beach	264	43.12 N	75.44 W
Verona Park	268	42.21 N	85.09 W
Verónica	294	35.24 S	57.22 W
Verplanck	261	41.15 N	73.58 W
Verrès	170	45.40 N	7.42 E
Verrettes	282	19.04 N	72.27 W
Versailles, Fr.	176	48.48 N	2.08 E
Versailles, Ill., U.S.	248	39.53 N	90.39 W
Versailles, Ind., U.S.	248	39.04 N	85.15 W
Versailles, Ky., U.S.	248	38.03 N	84.44 W
Versailles, Mo., U.S.	248	38.26 N	92.51 W
Versailles, N.Y., U.S.	266	42.31 N	79.00 W
Versailles, Ohio, U.S.	268	40.13 N	84.29 W
Veršino-Darasunskij	186	52.20 N	115.32 E
Veršino-Šachtaminskij	186	51.21 N	117.50 E
Versmold	178	52.02 N	8.09 E
Vert, Cap ≻, Sén.	214		
	222	14.43 N	17.30 W
Vertedero	284m	18.05 N	66.15 W
Verteillac	166	45.21 N	0.22 E
Vertientes	284p	21.16 N	78.09 W
Vertou	166	47.10 N	1.29 W
Vertova	182	45.48 N	9.50 E
Vertus	166	48.54 N	4.00 E
Verviers	164	50.35 N	5.52 E
Vervins	166	49.50 N	3.54 E
Verwoerd Reservoir ⊜[1]	224	30.40 S	25.40 E
Verzy	166	49.09 N	4.10 E
Vesanto	160	62.56 N	26.25 E
Vescovato	170	42.30 N	9.26 E
Veselí nad Lužnicí	164	49.11 N	14.43 E
Veselí nad Moravou	164	48.58 N	17.22 E
Vesjegonsk	160	58.40 N	37.16 E
Veškajma	160	54.03 N	47.08 E
Vesoul	180	47.38 N	6.10 E
Vespasiano	296	19.40 S	43.55 W
Vesta	280	9.43 N	83.03 W
Vest-Agder □[6]	160	58.30 N	7.10 E
Vestavia Hills	248	33.27 N	86.47 W
Vesterålen II	160	68.45 N	15.00 E
Vestfjorden C[2]	160	68.08 N	15.00 E
Vestfold □[6]	160	59.15 N	10.10 E
Vestmannaeyjar	160a	63.26 N	20.12 W
Vestry	248	30.44 N	88.45 W
Vestvågøya I	160	68.15 N	13.50 E
Vesuvio ∧[1]	184	40.49 N	14.26 E
Vesuvius → Vesuvio ∧[1]	184	40.49 N	14.26 E
Vesuvius Bay	270	48.53 N	123.35 W
Veszprém	164	47.06 N	17.55 E
Veszprém □[6]	164	46.50 N	17.30 E
Vésztő	164	46.55 N	21.16 E
Vetju	160	62.57 N	50.44 E
Vetlanda	160	57.26 N	15.04 E
Vetluga	160	57.51 N	45.47 E
Vetluga ≃	160	56.18 N	46.24 E
Vetlužskij, S.S.S.R.	160	58.23 N	45.26 E
Vetlužskij, S.S.S.R.	160	57.11 N	45.07 E
Vetovo	172	43.42 N	26.16 E
Vetralla	184	42.19 N	12.03 E
Vetren	172	42.16 N	24.03 E
Vetrino	160	55.25 N	28.28 E
Vetrisoaia	172	46.26 N	28.13 E
Vetschau	164	51.47 N	14.04 E
Vettore, Monte ∧	170	42.49 N	13.16 E
Veurne (Furnes)	176	51.04 N	2.40 E
Vevay	248	38.45 N	85.04 W
Vevelstad	160	65.43 N	12.30 E
Veveno, Khawr ∨	220	6.40 N	32.58 E
Vevey	180	46.28 N	6.51 E
Veynes	166	44.32 N	5.49 E
Vézelise	166	48.29 N	6.05 E
Vézère ≃	166	44.53 N	0.53 E
VI □[4]	222	19.00 N	15.00 W
Viacha	292	16.39 S	68.18 W
Viadana	170	44.56 N	10.31 E
Viadutos	294	27.34 S	52.01 W
Viale	294	31.55 S	60.00 W
Viamão	294	30.05 S	51.02 W
Viamonte	294	33.45 S	63.05 W
Vian	250	35.30 N	94.58 W
Viana	296	20.23 S	40.30 W
Viana del Bollo	168	42.11 N	7.06 W
Viana do Alentejo	168	38.20 N	8.00 W
Viana do Castelo	168	41.42 N	8.50 W
Viar ≃	168	37.36 N	5.50 W
Viareggio	170	43.52 N	10.14 E
Viaur ≃	166	44.08 N	2.23 E
Viborg, Dan.	160	56.26 N	9.24 E
Viborg, S. Dak., U.S.	252	43.10 N	97.05 W
Vibo Valentia	170	38.40 N	16.06 E
Vibraye	166	48.03 N	0.44 E
Viburnum	248	37.43 N	91.08 W
Vicco	246	37.13 N	83.04 W
Vic-en-Bigorre	166	43.06 N	0.05 E
Vicente López	294	34.32 S	58.29 W
Vicente Noble	282	18.23 N	71.11 W
Vicenza	170	45.33 N	11.33 E
Viceroy	252	49.27 N	105.22 W
Vich	168	41.56 N	2.15 E
Vichada □[5]	290	5.00 N	69.30 W
Vichada ≃	290	4.55 N	67.50 W
Vichadero	294	31.48 S	54.43 W
Vichayal	292	4.50 S	81.07 W
Vichigasta	294	29.30 S	67.30 W
Vichun	196	27.49 N	114.23 E
Vichuquén	294	34.53 S	72.00 W
Vichy	166	46.08 N	3.26 E
Vici	250	36.09 N	99.18 W
Vickery	266	41.23 N	82.56 W
Vicksburg, Mich., U.S.	268	42.06 N	85.32 W
Vicksburg, Miss., U.S.	248	32.14 N	90.56 W
Vicksburg National Military Park ♠	248	32.24 N	90.52 W
Vico	170	42.10 N	8.48 E
Vico del Gargano	184	41.54 N	15.57 E
Vico Equense	184	40.40 N	14.25 E
Vicopisano	184	43.42 N	10.35 E
Viçosa	296	20.45 S	42.53 W
Vic-sur-Cère	166	44.59 N	2.37 E
Victor, Calif., U.S.	272	38.08 N	121.12 W
Victor, Idaho, U.S.	256	43.36 N	111.07 W
Victor, Iowa, U.S.	244	41.44 N	92.18 W
Victor, Mont., U.S.	256	46.25 N	114.09 W
Victor, N.Y., U.S.	264	42.59 N	77.24 W
Victor, Lac ⊜	240	50.35 N	61.48 W
Victor Harbour	228	35.34 S	138.37 E
Victoria, Arg.	294	32.40 S	60.10 W
Victoria, Cam.	214	4.01 N	9.12 E
Victoria, B.C., Can.	238	48.25 N	123.22 W
Victoria, P.E.I., Can.	240	46.13 N	63.29 W
Victoria, Chile	292	20.44 S	69.42 W
Victoria, Chile	294	38.13 S	72.20 W
Victoria, Gren.	285k	12.12 N	61.42 W
Victoria (Xianggang), H.K.	196	22.17 N	114.09 E
Victoria, Malay.	198	5.18 N	115.14 E
Victoria (Rabat), Malta	170	36.02 N	14.14 E
Victoria, Pil.	202	15.35 N	120.41 E
Victoria, Pil.	202	13.12 N	121.15 E
Victoria, Rom.	172	45.45 N	24.41 E
Victoria, Sey.	218	4.38 S	55.27 E
Victoria, Kans., U.S.	252	38.52 N	99.09 W
Victoria, Tex., U.S.	250	28.48 N	97.00 W
Victoria, Va., U.S.	246	36.59 N	78.14 W
Victoria □[3]	228	38.00 S	145.00 E
Victoria □[4]	224	20.54 S	31.21 E
Victoria □[6]	264	44.35 N	78.50 W
Victoria ≃, Austl.	226	15.12 S	129.43 E
Victoria ≃, Newf., Can.	240	48.45 N	56.40 W
Victoria, Lake ⊜, Afr.	218	1.00 S	33.00 E
Victoria, Lake ⊜, Austl.	228	34.00 S	141.16 E
Victoria, Mount ∧	200	21.14 N	93.55 E
Victoria de las Tunas	284p	20.58 N	76.57 W
Victoria Falls ↳	224	17.55 S	25.51 E
Victoria Falls National Park ♠	224	17.55 S	25.40 E
Victoria Harbour	264	44.45 N	79.46 W
Victoria Island I	232	71.00 N	114.00 W
Victoria Lake ⊜	240	48.18 N	57.30 W
Victoria Land ⤶[1]	148	75.00 S	163.00 E
Victoria Nile ≃	214	2.14 N	31.26 E
Victoria Peak ∧, Br. Hond.	278	16.47 N	88.36 W
Victoria Peak ∧, B.C., Can.	238	50.03 N	126.06 W
Victoria Peaks ∧∧	202	9.23 N	118.24 E
Victoria Range ∧∧, N.Z.	230	42.12 S	172.08 E
Victoria Range ∧∧, Pil.	202	9.32 N	118.23 E
Victoria River Downs	226	16.24 S	131.00 E
Victorias	202	10.54 N	123.04 E
Victoria Strait ⊔	232	69.15 N	100.30 W
Victoriaville	260	46.03 N	71.58 W
Victoria West	218	31.25 S	23.04 E
Victorica	294	36.15 S	65.30 W
Victorino	290	2.48 N	67.50 W
Victorino de la Plaza	294	36.35 S	62.40 W
Victor Manuel Bueno	278	24.20 N	98.58 W
Victorville	274	34.32 N	117.18 W
Vičuga	160	57.13 N	41.56 E
Vicuña	294	30.02 S	70.44 W
Vicuña Mackenna	294	33.55 S	64.25 W
Vidalia, Ga., U.S.	246	32.13 N	82.25 W
Vidalia, La., U.S.	248	31.34 N	91.26 W
Vidal Ramos	294	27.23 S	49.22 W
Vidauban	168	43.26 N	6.26 E
Videira	294	27.00 S	51.08 W
Videle	172	44.16 N	25.31 E
Vidigueira	168	38.13 N	7.48 W
Vidin	172	43.59 N	22.52 E
Vidlica	160	61.10 N	32.21 E
Vidor	248	30.07 N	94.01 W
Vidra, Rom.	172	44.16 N	26.11 E
Vidra, Rom.	172	45.55 N	26.54 E
Vidsel	160	65.51 N	20.24 E
Vidzy	160	55.24 N	26.38 E
Viechtach	164	49.05 N	12.53 E
Viedma	288	40.50 S	63.00 W
Viedma, Lago ⊜	288	49.40 S	72.30 W
Vieillard, Lac ⊜	244	47.23 N	78.02 W
Vieille Case	284d	15.36 N	61.24 W
Vieira do Minho	168	41.39 N	8.09 W
Viejo ≃	280	12.28 N	86.21 W
Viejo, Cerro ∧	292	4.50 S	79.25 W
Viella	168	42.42 N	0.48 E
Vienna, Ont., Can.	264	42.41 N	80.48 W
Vienna → Wien, Öst.	164	48.13 N	16.20 E
Vienna, Ga., U.S.	246	32.06 N	83.47 W
Vienna, Ill., U.S.	248	37.25 N	88.54 W
Vienna, Md., U.S.	262	38.29 N	75.49 W
Vienna, Mo., U.S.	248	38.11 N	91.57 W
Vienna, Ohio, U.S.	266	41.14 N	80.40 W
Vienna, S. Dak., U.S.	252	44.42 N	97.30 W
Vienna, Va., U.S.	262	38.54 N	77.16 W
Vienna, W. Va., U.S.	242	39.20 N	81.26 W
Vienne	182	45.31 N	4.52 E
Vienne □[5]	166	46.35 N	0.30 E
Vienne ≃	166	47.13 N	0.05 E
Vientiane	200	17.58 N	102.36 E
Vieques	282	18.09 N	65.27 W
Vieques, Isla de I	282	18.08 N	65.25 W
Vieremä	160	63.45 N	27.01 E
Viersen	178	51.15 N	6.23 E
Vierwaldstätter See ⊜	166	47.00 N	8.28 E
Vierzehn-Heiligen ⛪[1]	164	50.08 N	11.02 E

Symbols in the index entries are identified on page 360.

Name	Page	Lat°′	Long°′
Vierzon	176	47.13 N	2.05 E
Viesca	278	25.21 N	102.48 W
Vieste	184	41.53 N	16.10 E
Viet-bac, Khu-tu-tri □[4]	200	23.00 N	105.00 E
Vietnam, North □[1]	198	21.00 N	105.00 E
Vietnam, South □[1]	198	13.00 N	108.00 E
Vietri sul Mare	184	40.40 N	14.44 E
Viet-tri	200	21.18 N	105.26 E
Vieux-Condé	176	50.27 N	3.34 E
Vieux-Fort, Guad.	285o	15.57 N	61.43 W
Vieux Fort, St. Luc.	285f	13.44 N	60.57 W
Vieux-Habitants	285o	16.04 N	61.46 W
Vieytes	294	35.15 S	57.35 W
Vif	166	45.03 N	5.40 E
Vigan	202	17.35 N	120.23 E
Vigeland	160	58.05 N	7.18 E
Vigevano	182	45.19 N	8.51 E
Vignanello	184	42.23 N	12.17 E
Vigneulles-lès-Hattonchâtel	166	48.59 N	5.43 E
Vignola	170	44.29 N	11.00 E
Vigo	168	42.14 N	8.43 W
Vigo, Ría de C[1]	168	42.15 N	8.45 W
Vihiers	166	47.09 N	0.32 W
Vihorlat ⋀	164	48.55 N	22.10 E
Vihren ∧	172	41.46 N	23.24 E
Vihti	160	60.25 N	24.20 E
VII □[4]	222	22.30 N	10.00 W
Viinijärvi	160	62.39 N	29.14 E
Vijayawāda	204	16.31 N	80.31 E
Vijosë (Aóös) ≃	172	40.37 N	19.20 E
Vikajärvi	160	66.37 N	26.12 E
Viking	238	53.06 N	111.46 W
Vikna	160	64.57 N	10.58 E
Viktor	160	66.09 N	58.07 E
Vila Arriaga	218	14.46 S	13.21 E
Vila Brasil	296	22.22 S	54.34 W
Vila Cabral	218	13.18 S	35.14 E
Vila Coutinho	218	14.37 S	34.19 E
Vila de João Belo	218	25.02 S	33.34 E
Vila de Manica	218	18.56 S	32.53 E
Vila de Rei	168	39.40 N	8.09 W
Vila do Bispo	168	37.05 N	8.55 W
Vila do Conde	168	41.21 N	8.45 W
Vila Flor	168	41.18 N	7.09 W
Vila Fontes	218	17.50 S	35.21 E
Vila Franca de Xira	168	38.57 N	8.59 W
Vila Glória	296	22.21 S	54.13 W
Vilaine ≃	166	47.30 N	2.27 W
Vilaka	160	57.11 N	27.41 E
Vilama, Laguna de ⊜	294	22.36 S	66.55 W
Vilanculos	218	22.01 S	35.19 E
Vilāni	160	56.33 N	26.57 E
Vila Nova de Famalicão	168	41.25 N	8.32 W
Vila Nova de Fozcoa	168	41.05 N	7.12 W
Vila Nova de Gaia	168	41.08 N	8.37 W
Vila Novo de Ourém	168	39.39 N	8.35 W
Vila Pery	218	19.08 S	33.29 E
Vila Real	168	41.18 N	7.45 W
Vila Real de Santo António	168	37.12 N	7.25 W
Vilar Formoso	168	40.37 N	6.50 W
Vila Rica	290	3.40 S	61.02 W
Vila Velha	296	20.20 S	40.17 W
Vila Velha de Ródão	168	39.38 N	7.40 W
Vila Verde	168	41.39 N	8.26 W
Vila Viçosa	168	38.47 N	8.13 W
Vilcabamba, Cordillera ⋀	292	13.00 S	73.00 W
Vilcanota ≃	292	13.19 S	72.00 W
Vilelas	294	27.57 S	62.37 W
Vil'gort, S.S.S.R.	160	60.34 N	56.24 E
Vil'gort, S.S.S.R.	160	61.35 N	50.40 E
Vilhelmina	160	64.37 N	16.39 E
Vilhena	292	12.43 S	60.07 W
Vilinac, Vrh ∧	170	43.38 N	17.38 E
Viljandi	160	58.22 N	25.36 E
Vil'kickogo, Ostrov I	186	75.44 N	152.20 E
Vil'kickogo, Proliv Ʊ	186	77.55 N	103.00 E
Vilkija	160	55.03 N	23.35 E
Villa Abecia	292	21.00 S	65.23 W
Villa Aberastain	294	31.39 S	68.34 W
Villa Adriana ⊥	170	41.56 N	12.45 E
Villa Ahumada	278	30.37 N	106.31 W
Villa Alberdi	294	27.36 S	65.40 W
Villa Alemana	294	33.03 S	71.23 W
Villa Allende	294	31.20 S	64.20 W
Villa Ana	294	28.29 S	59.35 W
Villa Ángela	294	27.35 S	60.43 W
Villa Atamisqui	294	28.29 S	63.49 W
Villa Atuel	294	34.50 S	67.50 W
Villaba	202	11.13 N	124.23 E
Villa Bella	292	10.23 S	65.24 W
Villa Berthet	294	27.20 S	60.28 W
Villablino	168	42.56 N	6.19 W
Villa Bruzual	290	9.20 N	69.06 W
Villa Bustos	294	29.17 S	67.02 W
Villa Cañás, Arg.	294	34.01 S	61.30 W
Villacañas, Esp.	168	39.38 N	3.20 W
Villa Carlos Paz	294	31.25 S	64.30 W
Villacarriedo	168	43.14 N	3.48 W
Villacarrillo	168	38.07 N	3.05 W
Villa Castelli	294	29.00 S	68.11 W
Villacastín	168	40.47 N	4.25 W
Villach	164	46.36 N	13.50 E
Villacidro	170	39.27 N	8.44 E
Villa Cisneros	214	23.43 N	15.57 W
Villa Clara	294	31.46 S	58.50 W
Villa Colón (Caucete)	294	31.40 S	68.20 W
Villa Concepción del Tío	294	31.20 S	62.49 W
Villa Constitución	294	33.14 S	60.21 W
Villada	168	42.15 N	4.58 W
Villa de Arriaga	278	21.54 N	101.23 W
Villa de Cos	278	23.17 N	102.21 W
Villa de Cura	290	10.02 N	67.29 W
Villa de García	250	25.49 N	100.35 W
Villa del Carmen	294	32.57 S	65.04 W
Villa Delgado	280	13.43 N	89.10 W
Villa del Río	168	37.59 N	4.17 W
Villa del Rosario, Arg.	294	31.35 S	63.30 W
Villa del Rosario, Arg.	294	30.48 S	57.55 W
Villa del Rosario, Ven.	290	10.19 N	72.19 W
Villa de María	294	29.55 S	63.45 W
Villa de Méndez	278	25.07 N	98.34 W
Villa de San Antonio	280	14.16 N	87.36 W
Villa de San Francisco	280	14.10 N	86.58 W
Villa de Soto	294	30.52 S	64.59 W
Villa Diego, Arg.	294	33.02 S	60.37 W
Villadiego, Esp.	168	42.31 N	4.00 W
Villa Dolores	294	31.58 S	65.12 W
Villadossola	180	46.04 N	8.16 E
Villa El Alto	294	28.18 S	65.22 W
Villa Elisa	294	32.10 S	58.25 W
Villa Eufronio Viscarra	292	17.59 S	65.36 W
Villa Flores	278	16.14 N	93.14 W
Villa Florida	294	26.23 S	57.05 W
Villafranca del Bierzo	168	42.36 N	6.48 W
Villafranca de los Barros	168	38.34 N	6.20 W
Villafranca del Panadés	168	41.21 N	1.42 E
Villafranca di Verona	170	45.21 N	10.50 E
Villafranca Piemonte	182	44.47 N	7.33 E
Villa Frontera	278	26.56 N	101.27 W
Villagaracía de Arosa	168	42.36 N	8.45 W
Villa General Ramírez	294	32.10 S	60.10 W
Villa General Roca	294	32.40 S	66.28 W
Village-Richelieu	260	45.27 N	73.15 W
Villa González	278	22.50 N	98.27 W
Villagrán	278	24.29 N	99.29 W
Villa Grove	248	39.52 N	88.10 W
Villaguay	294	31.55 S	59.00 W
Villa Guerrero	278	18.52 N	99.39 W
Villa Guillermina	294	28.15 S	59.25 W
Villa Hayes	294	25.06 S	57.34 W
Villahermosa	278	17.59 N	92.55 W
Villa Hernandarias	294	31.15 S	59.58 W
Villa Hidalgo, Méx.	258	30.59 N	116.10 W
Villa Hidalgo, Méx.	278	21.40 N	102.36 W
Villa Huidobro (Cañada Verde)	294	34.50 S	64.35 W
Villaines-la-Juhel	166	48.21 N	0.17 W
Villa Iris	294	38.11 S	63.15 W
Villajoyosa	168	38.30 N	0.14 W
Villa Juárez	278	27.10 N	109.50 W
Villa Krause	294	31.35 S	68.35 W
Villa La Paz	294	33.27 S	67.37 W
Villa Larca	294	32.38 S	65.00 W
Villa Larroque	294	33.02 S	59.00 W
Villalba, Esp.	168	43.18 N	7.41 W
Villalba, P.R.	284m	18.08 N	66.30 W
Villalon	202	11.21 N	124.22 E
Villalón de Campos	168	42.06 N	5.02 W
Villalonga	288	39.55 S	62.40 W
Villa López	278	27.00 N	105.02 W
Villalpando	168	41.52 N	5.24 W
Villa Madero	278	19.24 N	101.16 W
Villa Mainero	278	24.32 N	99.38 W
Villa María, Arg.	294	32.25 S	63.15 W
Villa Maria, Pa., U.S.	266	41.05 N	80.30 W
Villa Martín, Bol.	292	20.46 S	67.47 W
Villamartín, Esp.	168	36.52 N	5.38 W
Villa Matoque	294	25.50 S	63.50 W
Villa Mazár	294	28.40 S	66.30 W
Villa Mercedes	294	30.08 S	68.41 W
Villamil	290a	0.56 S	91.01 W
Villa Montes	292	21.15 S	63.30 W
Villandraut	166	44.28 N	0.23 W
Villa Nora	268	40.33 N	84.26 W
Villanova	262	40.02 N	75.21 W
Villanova Monteleone	170	40.30 N	8.28 E
Villa Nueva, Arg.	294	32.26 S	63.15 W
Villanueva, Col.	290	10.37 N	72.59 W
Villa Nueva, Guat.	280	14.31 N	90.35 W
Villanueva, Hond.	280	15.17 N	88.00 W
Villanueva, Méx.	278	22.21 N	102.53 W
Villanueva, Nic.	280	12.58 N	86.49 W
Villanueva, N. Mex., U.S.	254	35.17 N	105.23 W
Villanueva de Córdoba	168	38.20 N	4.37 W
Villanueva de la Serana	168	38.58 N	5.48 W
Villanueva de la Sierra	168	40.12 N	6.24 W
Villanueva del Río y Minas	168	37.39 N	5.42 W
Villanueva y Geltrú	168	41.14 N	1.44 E
Villa Ocampo	294	28.30 S	59.20 W
Villa Ojo de Agua	294	29.30 S	63.40 W
Villa Oliva	294	26.01 S	57.53 W
Villa Park	274	33.49 N	117.49 W
Villa Pedro Montoya	278	21.38 N	99.49 W
Villa Pérez	284m	18.12 N	66.47 W
Villapinzón	290	5.13 N	73.36 W
Villa Quinteros	294	27.15 S	65.30 W
Villa Ranchaero	252	44.15 N	103.10 W
Villarcayo	168	42.56 N	3.34 W
Villard-Bonnot	182	45.14 N	5.53 E
Villard-de-Lans	166	45.04 N	5.33 E
Villardefrades	168	41.43 N	5.15 W
Villar del Arzobispo	168	39.44 N	0.49 W
Villareal	202	11.34 N	124.56 E
Villa Regina	294	39.05 S	67.05 W
Villa Reynolds	294	33.43 S	65.23 W
Villa Rica	246	33.44 N	84.55 W
Villa Rivero	292	17.37 S	65.48 W
Villarreal	168	39.56 N	0.06 W
Villarreales	250	26.07 N	100.20 W
Villarrica, Chile	288	39.16 S	72.13 W
Villarrica, Col.	290	3.58 N	74.37 W
Villarrica, Para.	294	25.45 S	56.26 W
Villarrobledo	168	39.16 N	2.36 W
Villarrubia de los Ojos	168	39.13 N	3.36 W
Villas	262	39.02 N	74.56 W
Villa San Giovanni	170	38.13 N	15.39 E
Villa San José	294	32.12 S	58.15 W
Villa San Martín	294	28.20 S	64.10 W
Villasanta	182	45.37 N	9.18 E
Villa Santa, Montaña ∧	280	14.10 N	86.25 W
Villasayas	168	41.21 N	2.37 W
Villa Serrano	292	19.06 S	64.22 W
Villasimius	170	39.09 N	9.31 E
Villasis	202	15.54 N	120.35 E
Villa Somoza	280	12.08 N	84.58 W
Villasor	170	39.22 N	8.57 E
Villa Tunari	292	16.55 S	65.25 W
Villa Unión, Arg.	294	29.24 S	62.47 W
Villa Unión, Arg.	294	29.20 S	68.12 W
Villa Unión, Méx.	278	28.15 N	100.43 W
Villa Unión, Méx.	278	23.12 N	106.14 W
Villa Valeria	294	34.20 S	64.55 W
Villa Vásquez	282	19.45 N	71.27 W
Villa Verona	272	39.28 N	121.33 W
Villavicencio	290	4.09 N	73.37 W
Villa Vicente Guerrero	278	23.45 N	103.59 W
Villaviciosa	168	43.29 N	5.26 W
Villaviciosa de Córdoba	168	38.05 N	5.01 W
Villazón	292	22.06 S	65.36 W
Villa Zorraquín	294	31.19 S	58.01 W
Villé	170	48.20 N	7.18 E
Villebon, Lac ⊜	244	47.58 N	77.18 W
Ville-de-Tracy	260	46.01 N	73.09 W
Villedieu	166	48.50 N	1.13 W
Villefort	166	44.26 N	3.56 E
Villefranche	180	45.59 N	4.43 E
Villefranche-de-Rouergue	166	44.21 N	2.02 E
Villefranche-du-Périgord	166	44.38 N	1.05 E
Villefranche-sur-Mer	182	43.42 N	7.19 E
Villejuif	176	48.48 N	2.22 E
Ville-Marie	244	47.20 N	79.26 W
Villena	168	38.38 N	0.51 W
Villenauxe-la-Grande	166	48.35 N	3.33 E
Villeneuve-d'Aveyron	166	44.26 N	2.02 E
Villeneuve-de-Berg	166	44.33 N	4.30 E
Villeneuve-le-Roi	176	48.44 N	2.25 E
Villeneuve-lès-Avignon	182	43.58 N	4.48 E
Villeneuve-Saint-Georges	176	48.44 N	2.27 E
Villeneuve-sur-Lot	166	44.25 N	0.42 E
Villeneuve-sur-Yonne	166	48.05 N	3.18 E
Villeparisis	176	48.56 N	2.37 E
Ville Platte	248	30.42 N	92.16 W
Villers-Bocage, Fr.	166	49.59 N	2.20 E
Villers-Bocage, Fr.	166	49.05 N	0.39 W
Villers-Cotterêts	176	49.15 N	3.05 E
Villersexel	170	47.33 N	6.26 E
Villers-les-Nancy	180	48.40 N	6.09 E
Villerupt	166	49.28 N	5.56 E
Ville-Saint-Georges	242	46.07 N	70.40 W
Villeta	290	5.01 N	74.28 W
Villeurbanne	182	45.46 N	4.53 E
Villiers-sur-Marne	176	48.50 N	2.33 E
Villingen im Schwarzwald	180	48.03 N	8.27 E
Villisca	252	40.56 N	94.59 W
Vilna	238	54.07 N	111.55 W
Vilnius	160	54.41 N	25.19 E
Vilsbiburg	164	48.27 N	12.12 E
Vilshofen	164	48.39 N	13.12 E
Vil'uj ≃	186	64.24 N	126.26 E
Vil'ujsk	186	63.45 N	121.35 E
Vilvoorde	176	50.56 N	4.26 E
Vimercate	182	45.37 N	9.22 E
Vimianzo	168	43.07 N	9.02 W
Vimmerby	160	57.40 N	15.51 E
Vimoutiers	166	48.55 N	0.12 E
Vimperk	164	49.03 N	13.47 E
Vina	258	39.56 N	122.03 W
Viñac	292	12.58 S	75.43 W
Viña del Mar	294	33.02 S	71.34 W
Viñales	284p	22.37 N	83.43 W
Vinalhaven	242	44.03 N	68.50 W
Vinalhaven Island I	242	44.05 N	68.52 W
Vinaroz	168	40.28 N	0.29 E
Vincennes, Fr.	176	48.51 N	2.26 E
Vincennes, Ind., U.S.	248	38.41 N	87.32 W
Vincent, Ala., U.S.	248	33.23 N	86.25 W
Vincent, Ohio, U.S.	266	39.23 N	81.40 W
Vincentown	262	39.56 N	74.45 W
Vinces	290	1.32 S	79.45 W
Vinces ≃	290	1.39 S	79.47 W
Vinchina	294	28.46 S	68.10 W
Vinchos	292	13.14 S	74.20 W
Vinco	266	40.25 N	78.52 W
Vindelälven ≃	160	63.54 N	19.52 E
Vindeln	160	64.12 N	19.44 E
Vindhya Range ⋀	206	23.00 N	77.00 E
Vinegar Hill ∧	256	44.43 N	118.34 W
Vine Grove	248	37.49 N	85.59 W
Vineland, Ont., Can.	264	43.09 N	79.24 W
Vineland, Mich., U.S.	268	42.03 N	86.30 W
Vineland, N.J., U.S.	262	39.29 N	75.02 W
Vinemont	248	34.10 N	86.52 W
Vine Valley	264	42.43 N	77.20 W
Vineyard Haven	261	41.27 N	70.36 W
Vinh	200	18.40 N	105.40 E
Vinhais	168	41.50 N	7.00 W
Vinh-loi	200	9.17 N	105.43 E
Vinh-long	200	10.15 N	105.58 E
Vinica	170	45.28 N	15.15 E
Vinita	250	36.39 N	95.09 W
Vînju Mare	172	44.26 N	22.52 E
Vinkovci	172	45.17 N	18.38 E
Vinnhorst	178	52.25 N	9.43 E
Vinnica	158	49.14 N	28.29 E
Vinnica □[4]	172	48.30 N	28.30 E
Vinovo	182	44.57 N	7.38 E
Vinson Massif ∧	148	78.35 S	85.25 W
Vintilă Vodă	172	45.28 N	26.44 E
Vinton, Iowa, U.S.	244	42.10 N	92.01 W
Vinton, Va., U.S.	246	37.17 N	80.01 W
Vintondale	266	40.29 N	78.55 W
Viny	160	58.22 N	32.13 E
Viola, Ill., U.S.	244	41.12 N	90.35 W
Viola, Wis., U.S.	244	43.31 N	90.40 W
Violín, Isla I	280	8.50 N	83.38 W
Vipa	170	45.51 N	13.58 E
Vipiteno (Sterzing)	170	46.54 N	11.26 E
Vipos	294	26.29 S	65.21 W
Vir, Otok I	170	44.18 N	15.04 E
Virac, Pil.	202	13.35 N	124.14 E
Virac, Pil.	202	16.22 N	120.39 E
Virac Point ≻	202	13.31 N	124.13 E
Viradouro	296	20.53 S	48.18 W
Virago Sound Ʊ	238	54.00 N	132.36 W
Virama, Ensenada de C	284p	20.38 N	77.14 W
Virandozero	160	64.05 N	35.58 E
Virbalis	164	54.38 N	22.49 E
Virden, Man., Can.	252	49.51 N	100.55 W
Virden, Ill., U.S.	248	39.30 N	89.46 W
Virden, N. Mex., U.S.	254	32.42 N	109.00 W
Vire	166	48.50 N	0.53 W
Vire ≃	162	49.20 N	1.07 W
Vîrfurile	172	46.19 N	22.31 E
Virgem da Lapa	296	16.49 S	42.21 W
Virgil, Ont., Can.	264	43.13 N	79.08 W
Virgil, Kans., U.S.	252	37.59 N	96.01 W
Virgilina	246	36.33 N	78.52 W
Virgin Islands □[2]	284m	18.20 N	64.50 W
Virgin ≃	254	36.31 N	114.20 W
Virgin Gorda I	282	18.29 N	64.24 W
Virginia, S. Afr.	224	28.12 S	26.49 E
Virginia, Ill., U.S.	248	39.57 N	90.13 W
Virginia, Minn., U.S.	244	47.31 N	92.32 W
Virginia □[3]	234	37.30 N	78.45 W
Virginia Beach	262	36.51 N	75.58 W
Virginia City, Mont., U.S.	256	45.18 N	111.56 W
Virginia City, Nev., U.S.	272	39.19 N	119.39 W
Virginia Falls ⌊	236	61.38 N	125.42 W
Virginia Hills	262	38.47 N	77.06 W
Virginia Peak ∧	258	39.45 N	119.28 W
Virginiatown	244	48.08 N	79.35 W
Virgin Islands II	282	18.20 N	66.45 W
Virginópolis	296	18.45 S	42.45 W
Virginville	262	40.31 N	75.52 W
Virgolândia	296	18.27 S	42.18 W
Virieux-le-Grand	166	45.51 N	5.39 E
Virihaure ⊜	160	67.20 N	16.35 E
Virje	170	46.04 N	16.59 E
Virkie	162	59.53 N	1.18 W
Viroflay	176	48.48 N	2.10 E
Virojoki	160	60.35 N	27.42 E
Viroqua	244	43.34 N	90.53 W
Virovitica	170	45.50 N	17.23 E
Virpazar	172	42.15 N	19.05 E
Virrat	160	62.14 N	23.47 E
Virserum	160	57.19 N	15.35 E
Virtaniemi	160	68.53 N	28.27 E
Virton	164	49.34 N	5.32 E
Vîrtopu	172	44.12 N	23.21 E
Virtsu	160	58.34 N	23.31 E
Virú	292	8.25 S	78.45 W
Virulento	250	28.52 N	104.21 W
Viry-Châtillon	176	48.40 N	2.23 E
Vis	170	43.03 N	16.12 E
Vis ≃	224	33.30 S	27.08 E
Vis, Otok I	170	43.02 N	16.11 E
Visalia	272	36.20 N	119.18 W
Visayan Sea ▾[2]	202	11.30 N	123.35 E
Visbek	178	52.48 N	8.19 E
Visby	160	57.38 N	18.18 E
Viscount Melville Sound Ʊ	232	74.10 N	113.00 W
Višegrad	172	43.47 N	19.17 E
Viseu	168	40.39 N	7.55 W
Vişeul-de-Sus	172	47.44 N	24.22 E
Vislinskij Zaliv C	164	54.27 N	19.40 E
Visnagar	206	23.42 N	72.33 E
Viso, Monte ∧	170	44.40 N	7.07 E
Visoko	172	43.59 N	18.11 E
Visp	166	46.18 N	7.53 E
Vissefjärda	160	56.32 N	15.35 E
Visselhövede	164	52.59 N	9.35 E
Vista	274	33.12 N	117.15 W
Vista Alegre	294	38.45 S	68.11 W
Vista Flores	294	33.39 S	69.09 W
Vista La Mesa	274	32.35 N	117.01 W
Vista Park	274	35.21 N	118.55 W
Vistina	160	59.47 N	28.29 E
Vistula → Wisła ≃	164	54.22 N	18.55 E
Vita	252	49.08 N	96.34 W
Vitali	202	7.22 N	122.18 E
Vitanje	170	46.23 N	15.18 E
Vitarte	292	12.02 S	76.54 W
Vitebsk	160	55.12 N	30.11 E
Viterbo	184	42.25 N	12.06 E
Viterbo □[4]	184	42.25 N	12.05 E
Vitichi	292	20.13 S	65.29 W
Vitigudino	168	41.01 N	6.26 W
Vitim	186	59.28 N	112.34 E
Vitim ≃	186	59.26 N	112.34 E
Vítkov	164	49.46 N	17.45 E
Vitor	292	16.27 S	71.50 W
Vitor ≃	292	16.38 S	72.23 W
Vitória, Bra.	296	20.19 S	40.21 W
Vitoria, Esp.	168	42.51 N	2.40 W
Vitória da Conquista	296	14.51 S	40.51 W
Vitré	162	48.08 N	1.12 W
Vitry-le-François	166	48.44 N	4.35 E
Vittangi	160	67.41 N	21.36 E
Vitteaux	166	47.24 N	4.32 E
Vittel	166	48.12 N	5.57 E
Vittoria, Ont., Can.	264	42.46 N	80.19 W
Vittoria, It.	170	36.57 N	14.32 E
Vittorio Veneto	170	45.59 N	12.18 E
Viuda, Rambla de la ≃	168	39.57 N	0.05 W
Vivarais □[9]	182	44.40 N	4.30 E
Vivarais, Monts du ⋀	166	44.55 N	4.15 E
Viver	168	39.55 N	0.36 W
Vivero	168	43.38 N	7.35 W
Vivi ≃	186	63.52 N	97.50 E
Vivian	248	32.53 N	93.59 W
Viviers	166	44.29 N	4.41 E
Vivonne	166	46.26 N	0.16 E
Vivoratá	294	37.40 S	57.40 W
Vivorillo, Cayos II	280	15.52 N	83.17 W
Vizcachas, Meseta de las ⋀[1]	288	50.35 S	71.55 W
Vizcaíno, Desierto de •→[2]	278	27.40 N	114.40 W
Vizcayo □[4]	168	43.20 N	2.45 W
Vize	172	41.34 N	27.45 E
Vize, Ostrov I	186	79.30 N	77.00 E
Vizille	182	45.05 N	5.46 E
Vižinada	170	45.20 N	13.46 E
Vizinga	160	61.05 N	50.04 E
Vizzini	170	37.09 N	14.46 E
Vk	160a	63.25 N	19.00 W
Vlaardingen	178	51.54 N	4.21 E
Vlădeasa ∧	172	46.45 N	22.48 E
Vlădeni	172	47.25 N	27.20 E
Vladičin Han	172	42.42 N	22.04 E
Vladimir	160	56.10 N	40.25 E
Vladimirskij Tupik	160	55.42 N	33.18 E
Vladivostok	186	43.10 N	131.56 E
Vlagtwedde	164	53.01 N	7.07 E
Vlárský priesmyk)(	164	49.03 N	18.02 E
Vlasenica	172	44.11 N	18.56 E
Vlašim	164	49.42 N	14.54 E
Vlasinsko Jezero ⊜	172	42.42 N	22.22 E
Vlasotince	172	42.58 N	22.08 E
Vlieland I	164	53.15 N	5.00 E
Vlijmen	178	51.42 N	5.15 E
Vlissingen (Flushing)	178	51.26 N	3.35 E
Vloorskop ∧	224	25.45 S	20.50 E
Vlorë	172	40.27 N	19.30 E
Vlorës, Gji i C	172	40.25 N	19.25 E
Vlotho	178	52.10 N	8.51 E
Vltava ≃	164	50.21 N	14.30 E
Vluyn	178	51.26 N	6.32 E
Vnukovo	160	55.39 N	37.16 E
Voca	250	31.01 N	99.11 W
Vočaž, Porog ⌊	160	64.55 N	34.22 E
Vochtoga	160	58.47 N	41.07 E
Vocin	170	45.37 N	17.03 E
Vöcklabruck	164	48.01 N	13.39 E
Vodla ≃	160	61.49 N	36.00 E
Vodňany	164	49.09 N	14.11 E
Vodnjan	170	44.57 N	13.51 E
Vodnyj	160	63.32 N	53.18 E
Vodosalma	160	64.29 N	30.44 E
Vodzimonje	160	56.49 N	51.38 E
Voerde	178	51.35 N	6.41 E
Vogelkop → Doberai, Djazirah ≻[1]	198	1.30 S	132.30 E
Vogel Peak → Dimlang ∧	214	8.24 N	11.47 E
Vogelsberg ⋀	164	50.30 N	9.15 E
Voghera	182	44.59 N	9.01 E
Vohémar	218	13.21 S	50.02 E
Vohenstrauss	164	49.37 N	12.21 E
Võhma	160	58.38 N	25.33 E
Vöhringen	180	48.16 N	10.04 E
Voi	218	3.23 S	38.34 E
Void	166	48.41 N	5.37 E
Voineşti	172	47.05 N	27.26 E
Voinjama	222	8.25 N	9.45 W
Voiotía □[5]	172	38.20 N	23.30 E
Voiron	182	45.22 N	5.35 E
Voitsberg	164	47.03 N	15.10 E
Voïviis, Límni ⊜	172	39.32 N	22.45 E
Vojnić	170	45.19 N	15.42 E
Vojnica	160	65.12 N	30.15 E
Voj-Vož, S.S.S.R.	160	62.56 N	54.56 E
Voj-Vož, S.S.S.R.	160	64.20 N	55.03 E
Volant	266	41.07 N	80.16 W
Volary	164	48.55 N	13.54 E
Volcán	294	23.55 S	65.30 W
Volcán de Colima, Parque Nacional ♠	278	19.30 N	103.35 W
Volcano, Calif., U.S.	272	38.26 N	120.37 W
Volcano, Haw., U.S.	275d	19.26 N	155.14 W
Volchov	160	59.55 N	32.20 E
Volchov ≃	160	60.08 N	32.20 E
Volčje	164	49.14 N	22.53 E
Volda	160	62.09 N	6.06 E
Volendam	178	52.30 N	5.04 E
Volga, S.S.S.R.	160	57.57 N	38.24 E
Volga, Iowa, U.S.	244	42.48 N	91.33 W
Volga, S. Dak., U.S.	252	44.19 N	96.56 W
Volga ≃, S.S.S.R.	186	45.55 N	47.52 E
Volga ≃, Iowa, U.S.	244	42.45 N	91.17 W
Volga-Baltic Canal → Volgo-Baltijskij Vodnyj Put' ≂	160	59.00 N	38.00 E
Volgo-Baltijskij Vodnyj Put' ≂	160	59.00 N	38.00 E
Volgodonsk	158	47.33 N	42.08 E
Volgograd (Stalingrad)	158	48.44 N	44.25 E
Volgogradskoje Vodochranilišče ⊜[1]	158	49.20 N	45.00 E
Volissós	172	38.29 N	25.58 E
Volkach	164	49.52 N	10.13 E
Völkermarkt	164	46.39 N	14.38 E
Völklingen	164	49.15 N	6.50 E
Volksdorf •→[8]	178	53.39 N	11.00 E
Volksrust	224	27.24 S	29.53 E
Volmarstein	178	51.22 N	7.23 E
Voločanka	186	71.00 N	94.28 E
Volockaja	160	60.17 N	42.59 E
Volodarskoje	186	47.12 N	37.20 E
Vologda	160	59.12 N	39.55 E
Volokolamsk	160	56.02 N	35.57 E
Volokovaja	160	66.28 N	48.10 E
Volonga	160	67.07 N	47.41 E
Volonne	166	44.07 N	6.01 E
Vólos	172	39.21 N	22.56 E
Vološka	160	61.20 N	40.06 E
Volpiano	182	45.12 N	7.46 E
Vol'sk	158	52.02 N	47.23 E
Volta □[4]	222	7.00 N	0.30 E
Volta ≃	222	5.46 N	0.41 E
Volta, Lake ⊜[1]	222	7.30 N	0.15 E
Volta Blanche (White Volta) ≃	222	9.10 N	1.15 W
Volta Grande	296	21.46 S	42.32 W
Volta-Noire □[5]	222	11.00 N	4.00 W
Volta Noire (Black Volta) ≃	220	8.41 N	1.33 W
Volta Redonda	296	22.32 S	44.07 W
Volta Rouge ≃	222	10.34 N	0.30 W
Volterra	184	43.24 N	10.51 E
Vol'teva	160	64.30 N	44.12 E
Voltri	170	44.26 N	8.45 E
Volturino, Monte ∧	170	40.25 N	15.49 E
Voluntown	261	41.34 N	71.52 W
Vólvi, Límni ⊜	172	40.41 N	23.23 E
Volyně	164	49.10 N	13.53 E
Volžsk	160	55.53 N	48.21 E
Volžskij	158	48.50 N	44.44 E
Vondanka	160	59.07 N	47.49 E
Von Frank Mountain ∧	236	63.33 N	154.20 W
Võnnu	160	58.17 N	27.05 E
Voorburg	178	52.05 N	4.23 E
Voorschoten	178	52.07 N	4.27 E
Voorst	178	52.10 N	6.09 E
Vopnafjörður	160a	65.47 N	14.44 W
Vopnafjörður C	160a	65.52 N	14.40 W
Vorarlberg □[3]	180	47.15 N	9.55 E
Vorau	164	47.25 N	15.54 E
Vorderrhein ≃	166	46.49 N	9.25 E
Vordingborg	164	55.01 N	11.55 E
Voríai Sporádhes II	172	39.17 N	23.23 E
Vórios Evvoïkós Kólpos C	172	38.40 N	23.15 E
Vorkuta	160	67.27 N	63.58 E
Vormsi I	160	59.00 N	23.20 E
Voronež	158	51.40 N	39.10 E
Voronja ≃	160	69.10 N	35.50 E
Voronjo	160	68.27 N	35.21 E
Voropajevo	160	55.09 N	27.13 E
Voroshilov → Ussurijsk	186	43.48 N	131.59 E
Voroshilovsk → Kommunarsk, S.S.S.R.	158	48.30 N	38.47 E
Voroshilovsk → Stavropol', S.S.S.R.	158	45.02 N	41.59 E
Vorošilovgrad	158	48.34 N	39.20 E
Vorotynec	160	56.04 N	45.52 E
Vorsma	160	55.59 N	43.16 E
Vorst, Bel.	178	51.04 N	5.01 E
Vorst, B.R.D.	178	51.18 N	6.25 E
Võrtsjärv ⊜	160	58.16 N	26.03 E
Võru	160	57.50 N	27.01 E
Vosges □[5]	180	48.10 N	6.20 E
Voskresensk	160	55.19 N	38.42 E
Voskresenskoje	160	59.26 N	37.56 E
Voss	160	60.39 N	6.26 E
Vosselaar	178	51.19 N	4.53 E
Vostočnaja Kambal'nica	160	68.18 N	46.00 E
Vostočnyj Sajan ⋀	186	53.00 N	97.00 E
Votice	164	49.38 N	14.39 E
Votkinsk	160	57.03 N	53.59 E
Votuporanga	296	20.24 S	49.59 W
Vouga ≃	168	40.41 N	8.40 W
Vouillé	166	46.39 N	0.10 E
Vouziers	166	49.24 N	4.42 E
Voves	166	48.16 N	1.38 E
Vovodo ≃	220	5.40 N	24.21 E
Vowinckel	266	41.25 N	79.14 W
Vožajol'	160	62.50 N	51.17 E
Vože, Ozero ⊜	160	60.30 N	39.00 E
Vožega	160	60.29 N	40.12 E
Vožgaly	160	58.09 N	50.11 E
Vožgora	160	64.32 N	48.25 E
Voznesenje	160	61.01 N	35.27 E
Voznesensk	158	47.34 N	31.20 E
Voznesenskoje	160	54.54 N	42.46 E
Vráble	164	48.15 N	18.19 E
Vraca	172	43.12 N	23.33 E
Vrangel'a, Ostrov I	186	71.00 N	179.30 W
Vranje	172	42.33 N	21.54 E
Vranograč	170	45.10 N	15.57 E
Vranov	164	48.54 N	21.41 E
Vrbas	172	45.35 N	19.39 E
Vrbas ≃	170	45.06 N	17.31 E
Vrbovec	170	45.53 N	16.25 E
Vrbovsko	170	45.23 N	15.05 E
Vrchlabí	164	50.38 N	15.37 E
Vrede	218	27.30 S	29.06 E
Vreden	178	52.02 N	6.52 E
Vreed en Hoop	290	6.48 N	58.11 W
Vrginmost	170	45.21 N	15.52 E
Vrhnika	170	45.58 N	14.18 E
Vries	178	53.04 N	6.35 E
Vriezenveen	178	52.25 N	6.38 E
Vrlika	170	43.55 N	16.24 E
Vršac	172	45.07 N	21.18 E
Vrútky	164	49.07 N	18.55 E
Vryburg	224	26.55 S	24.45 E
Vryheid	224	29.39 S	30.18 E
Vsetín	164	49.21 N	17.59 E
Vsevidof, Mount ∧	236	53.07 N	168.43 W
Vučitrn	172	42.49 N	20.58 E
Vught	178	51.40 N	5.17 E
Vukovar	172	45.21 N	19.00 E
Vulcan, Alta., Can.	238	50.24 N	113.15 W
Vulcan, Rom.	172	45.23 N	23.17 E
Vulcan, Mich., U.S.	244	45.47 N	87.53 W
Vulcano, Isola I	170	38.27 N	14.58 E
Vulkaničeskij Chrebet ⋀	172	48.30 N	23.00 E
Vul'vyvejem ≃	236	66.58 N	179.10 E
Vung-cay-duong C	200	10.05 N	104.45 E
Vung-tau	200	10.21 N	107.04 E
Vuoggatjålme	160	66.36 N	16.22 E
Vuoksenniska	160	61.13 N	28.49 E
Vuotso	160	68.08 N	27.08 E
Vyaz'ma → V'az'ma	160	55.13 N	34.18 E
Vyazniki → V'azniki	160	56.15 N	42.10 E
Vyborg	160	60.42 N	28.45 E
Vyčegda ≃	160	61.18 N	46.36 E
Vyčegodskij	160	61.16 N	46.48 E
Východočeský □[4]	164	50.10 N	16.00 E
Východoslovenský □[4]	164	49.00 N	21.15 E
Vygozero, Ozero ⊜	160	63.35 N	34.42 E
Vyksa	160	55.18 N	42.11 E
Vym' ≃	160	62.13 N	50.25 E
Vyrica	160	59.25 N	30.21 E
Vyša	160	53.52 N	42.24 E
Vyškov	164	49.16 N	17.00 E
Vyškovskij, Pereval)(	172	48.42 N	23.38 E
Vyšná Radvaň	164	49.07 N	21.56 E
Vyšnij Voločok	160	57.35 N	34.34 E
Vysoké Mýto	164	49.57 N	16.10 E
Vysoké Tatry ⋀	164	49.12 N	20.05 E
Vysokogornyj	186	50.09 N	139.09 E
Vysokoje, S.S.S.R.	160	56.43 N	34.55 E
Vysokoje, S.S.S.R.	164	52.22 N	23.22 E
Vysokovsk	160	56.19 N	36.33 E
Vyšši Brod	164	48.37 N	14.19 E
Vytegra	160	61.00 N	36.24 E
W			
W, Parcs Nationaux du ♠	222	12.50 N	2.30 W
Wa	222	10.04 N	2.29 W
Wa ≃	200	18.35 N	100.45 E
Waal ≃	164	51.55 N	4.30 E
Waalwijk	178	51.42 N	5.04 E
Waarschoot	176	51.09 N	3.36 E
Waasmunster	176	51.06 N	4.05 E
Wabag	198	5.30 S	143.40 E
Wabamun	238	53.33 N	114.28 W
Wabamun Indian Reserve •→[4]	238	53.30 N	114.30 W
Wabamun Lake ⊜	238	53.33 N	114.35 W
Wabana	240	47.38 N	52.57 W
Wabasca	238	56.00 N	113.53 W
Wabasca ≃	232	58.22 N	115.20 W
Wabasca Indian Reserve •→[4]	238	55.53 N	113.32 W
Wabash, Ind., U.S.	268	40.48 N	85.49 W
Wabash, Ohio, U.S.	268	40.33 N	84.45 W
Wabash □[6]	268	40.48 N	85.49 W
Wabash ≃	248	37.46 N	88.02 W
Wabasha	244	44.23 N	92.02 W
Wabasso	246	27.45 N	80.26 W
Wabatongushi Lake ⊜	244	48.26 N	84.15 W
Wabeno	244	45.26 N	88.39 W
Wabowden	232	54.55 N	98.38 W
Wabrah ▾[4]	208	27.26 N	47.22 E
Wąbrzeźno	164	53.17 N	18.57 E
Wabuska	272	39.09 N	119.11 W
Waccamaw ≃	246	33.21 N	79.16 W
Waccamaw, Lake ⊜	246	34.17 N	78.30 W
Waccasassa Bay C	246	29.06 N	82.52 W
Wachapreague	262	37.36 N	75.41 W
Wachau •→[1]	164	48.18 N	15.24 E
Wachusett Mountain ∧	242	42.29 N	71.53 W
Wacissa	246	30.21 N	83.59 W
Waco	250	31.55 N	97.08 W
Waco, Lake ⊜[1]	250	31.34 N	97.13 W
Waconda Lake ⊜[1]	252	39.30 N	98.35 W
Waconia	244	44.51 N	93.47 W
Wacouno ≃	240	50.50 N	65.58 W
Wacousta	268	42.49 N	84.42 W
Wadayama	192	35.19 N	134.52 E
Waddenzee ▾[2]	164	53.15 N	5.15 E
Waddington	264	44.52 N	75.12 W
Waddington, Mount ∧	238	51.23 N	125.15 W
Waddinxveen	178	52.03 N	4.40 E
Wadena, Sask., Can.	232	51.57 N	103.47 W
Wadena, Ind., U.S.	268	40.43 N	87.16 W
Wadena, Minn., U.S.	252	46.26 N	95.08 W
Wädenswil	180	47.14 N	8.40 E
Wadersloh	178	51.44 N	8.15 E
Wadesboro	246	34.58 N	80.04 W
Wadham Islands II	240	49.34 N	53.50 W
Wadhams	238	51.30 N	127.31 W
Wādī as-Sīr	210	31.58 N	35.48 E
Wādī Ḥalfā'	220	21.56 N	31.20 E
Wādī Jimāl, Jazīrat I	220	24.40 N	35.10 E
Wading River	261	40.57 N	72.51 W
Wadley, Ala., U.S.	248	33.07 N	85.34 W
Wadley, Ga., U.S.	246	32.52 N	82.24 W
Wad Madanī	220	14.25 N	33.28 E
Wadowice	164	49.53 N	19.30 E
Wadsworth, Nev., U.S.	258	39.38 N	119.17 W
Wadsworth, Ohio, U.S.	266	41.02 N	81.44 W
Waelder	250	29.42 N	97.18 W
Wageningen, Ned.	178	51.58 N	5.40 E
Wageningen, Sur.	290	5.50 N	56.50 W
Wager Bay C	232	65.26 N	88.40 W
Wagga Wagga	228	35.07 S	147.22 E
Wagin	226	33.18 S	117.21 E
Waging am See	164	47.56 N	12.43 E
Wagner	252	43.05 N	98.18 W
Wagoner	250	35.58 N	95.22 W
Wagon Mound	250	36.01 N	104.42 W
Wagontire Mountain ∧	256	43.21 N	119.53 W
Wagontown	262	40.01 N	75.51 W
Wągrowiec	164	52.49 N	17.11 E
Wah	206	33.48 N	72.42 E
Waha	214	28.16 N	19.54 E
Wahai	198	2.48 S	129.30 E
Wahiawa	275c	21.30 N	158.01 W
Wahkiakum □[6]	270	46.16 N	123.28 W
Wahmeda	266	42.13 N	79.29 W
Wahoo	252	41.13 N	96.37 W
Wahpeton	252	46.16 N	96.36 W
Waialeale ∧	275d	22.04 N	159.30 W
Waialua	275c	21.34 N	158.08 W
Waianae	275c	21.27 N	158.11 W
Waiapu ≃	230	37.47 S	178.28 E
Waiatoto ≃	230	43.59 S	168.47 E
Waiau ≃, N.Z.	230	42.46 S	173.23 E
Waiau ≃, N.Z.	230	46.11 S	167.38 E
Waiau ≃, N.Z.	230	38.55 S	177.25 E
Waiblingen	164	48.50 N	9.19 E
Waidhofen an der Thaya	164	48.49 N	15.18 E
Waidhofen an der Ybbs	164	47.58 N	14.47 E
Waiehu	275a	20.55 N	156.30 W
Waigeo, Pulau I	198	0.14 S	130.45 E
Waihee	275a	20.56 N	156.31 W
Waiheke Island I	230	36.48 S	175.07 E
Waihi	230	37.23 S	175.51 E
Waihopai ≃	230	41.31 S	173.44 E
Waihou ≃	230	37.10 S	175.32 E
Waikabubak	226	9.38 S	119.25 E
Waikaia ≃	230	45.53 S	168.18 E
Waikane	275c	21.30 N	157.51 W
Waikapu	275a	20.51 N	156.30 W
Waikare, Lake ⊜	230	37.26 S	175.12 E
Waikareiti, Lake ⊜	230	38.43 S	177.10 E
Waikaremoana, Lake ⊜	230	38.46 S	177.06 E
Waikato ≃	230	37.23 S	174.43 E
Wailingding I	196	22.07 N	114.05 E
Wailing Wall, The (Kotel Hama'aravi) ♥[1]	210	31.46 N	35.14 E
Wailua	275b	22.03 N	159.19 W
Wailuku	275a	20.53 N	156.30 W
Waimakariri ≃	230	43.24 S	172.42 E
Waimanalo	275c	21.21 N	157.42 W
Waimate	230	44.44 S	171.03 E
Waimea, Haw., U.S.	275b	21.58 N	159.42 W
Waimea, Haw., U.S.	275c	21.39 N	158.04 W
Waingapu	226	9.39 S	120.16 E
Waini ≃	290	8.20 N	59.50 W
Wainwright, Alta., Can.	238	52.49 N	110.52 W
Wainwright, Alaska, U.S.	236	70.38 N	160.01 W
Wainwright, Ohio, U.S.	266	40.25 N	81.26 W
Waipahu	275c	21.23 N	158.01 W
Waipara ≃	230	43.09 S	172.48 E
Waipio Acres	275c	21.28 N	158.01 W
Waipiqundao II	196	23.57 N	117.55 E
Waipukurau	230	40.00 S	176.33 E
Wairarapa, Lake ⊜	230	41.12 S	175.15 E
Wairau ≃	230	41.32 S	174.07 E
Wairoa	230	39.02 S	177.25 E
Wairoa ≃	230	39.04 S	177.25 E
Waitaki ≃	230	44.56 S	171.07 E
Waitara	230	39.00 S	174.14 E
Waitara ≃	230	38.59 S	174.14 E
Waite Hill	266	41.37 N	81.22 W
Waite Park	244	45.33 N	94.14 W
Waitotara ≃	230	39.51 S	174.41 E
Waitsburg	256	46.16 N	118.09 W
Wajabula	198	2.17 N	128.12 E
Wajima	192	37.24 N	136.54 E
Wajir	214	1.45 N	40.04 E
Waka, Tex., U.S.	250	36.17 N	101.03 W
Waka, Yai.	214	7.07 N	37.26 E
Wakamatsu → Aizu-wakamatsu	192	37.30 N	139.56 E
Wakami ≃	244	47.43 N	82.22 W
Wakami Lake ⊜	244	47.29 N	82.51 W
Wakarusa	268	41.32 N	86.01 W
Wakarusa ≃	252	38.57 N	95.05 W
Wakasa-wan C	192	35.45 N	135.40 E
Wakatipu, Lake ⊜	230	45.06 S	168.30 E
Wakayama	192	34.13 N	135.11 E
Wakayanagi	192	38.46 N	141.08 E
Wa Keeney	252	39.01 N	99.53 W
Wakefield, Eng., U.K.	162	53.42 N	1.29 W
Wakefield, Kans., U.S.	252	39.13 N	97.01 W
Wakefield, Mass., U.S.	261	42.30 N	71.04 W
Wakefield, Nebr., U.S.	252	42.16 N	96.52 W
Wakefield, R.I., U.S.	261	41.26 N	71.30 W
Wakefield, Va., U.S.	246	36.58 N	76.59 W
Wake Forest	246	35.59 N	78.30 W
Wakeham Bay	232	61.36 N	71.57 W
Wake Island I	148	19.17 N	166.36 E
Wakema	200	16.36 N	95.11 E
Wakeman	266	41.15 N	82.24 W
Wakeman ≃	238	51.00 N	126.30 W
Wake Village	248	33.26 N	94.07 W
Wakhan, Āb-i- ≃	206	37.02 N	72.40 E
Waki	192	34.04 N	134.09 E
Wakita	250	36.53 N	97.55 W
Wakkanai	192a	45.25 N	141.40 E
Wakomata Lake ⊜	244	46.34 N	83.22 W
Wakonassin ≃	244	46.28 N	81.51 W
Wakonda	252	43.00 N	97.06 W
Wakwekobi Lake ⊜	244	46.20 N	83.23 W
Walbridge	266	41.35 N	83.29 W
Wałbrzych (Waldenburg)	164	50.46 N	16.17 E
Walcheren I	164	51.33 N	3.35 E
Walcott, B.C., Can.	238	54.31 N	126.51 W
Walcott, Iowa, U.S.	244	41.35 N	90.47 W
Walcott, N. Dak., U.S.	252	46.33 N	90.56 W
Walcott, Lake ⊜[1]	256	42.40 N	113.23 W
Wałcz (Deutsch Krone)	164	53.17 N	16.28 E
Wald	180	47.17 N	8.55 E
Waldbröl	164	50.53 N	7.37 E
Waldeck	164	51.12 N	9.04 E
Walden, Colo., U.S.	254	40.44 N	106.17 W
Walden, N.Y., U.S.	242	41.34 N	74.11 W
Waldenburg → Wałbrzych, Pol.	164	50.46 N	16.17 E
Walden Ridge ∧	248	35.30 N	85.15 W
Waldkirch	180	48.05 N	7.57 E
Waldkirchen	164	48.44 N	13.37 E
Waldmünchen	164	49.23 N	12.43 E
Waldniel	178	51.13 N	6.16 E
Waldo, B.C., Can.	238	49.13 N	115.13 W
Waldo, Ark., U.S.	248	33.21 N	93.18 W
Waldo, Ohio, U.S.	266	40.28 N	83.05 W
Waldoboro	242	44.06 N	69.23 W
Waldo Lake ⊜	256	43.44 N	122.02 W
Waldorf	242	38.37 N	76.54 W
Waldport	256	44.26 N	124.04 W
Waldron, Ark., U.S.	248	34.54 N	94.05 W
Waldron, Ind., U.S.	248	39.27 N	85.40 W
Waldron, Mich., U.S.	268	41.44 N	84.25 W
Waldshut	180	47.37 N	8.13 E
Waldviertel •→[1]	164	48.40 N	15.40 E
Walenstadt	166	47.07 N	9.19 E
Wales, Alaska, U.S.	236	65.36 N	168.05 W
Wales, Mass., U.S.	261	42.04 N	72.13 W
Wales □[8]	174	52.30 N	3.30 W
Wales Center	264	42.46 N	78.32 W
Wales Island I, N.W. Ter., Can.	232	68.00 N	86.43 W
Wales Island I, N.W. Ter., Can.	232	61.50 N	72.05 W
Walgett	228	30.01 S	148.07 E
Walhachin	238	50.45 N	120.59 W
Walhalla, N. Dak., U.S.	252	48.55 N	97.55 W
Walhalla, S.C., U.S.	246	34.46 N	83.04 W

Symbols in the index entries are identified on page 360.

Name	Page	Lat°′	Long°′
Walhalla ⊥	164	49.03 N	12.14 E
Walhonding	266	40.22 N	82.09 W
Walker, Iowa, U.S.	244	42.17 N	91.47 W
Walker, Mich., U.S.	268	42.58 N	85.46 W
Walker, Minn., U.S.	244	47.06 N	94.35 W
Walker, N.Y., U.S.	264	42.46 N	78.32 W
Walker ≃	258	38.54 N	118.47 W
Walker, Lac ⊜	240	50.15 N	67.09 W
Walker Lake ⊜, Alaska, U.S.	236	67.10 N	154.26 W
Walker Lake ⊜, Nev., U.S.	258	38.44 N	118.43 W
Walker River Indian Reservation ➝[4]	258	39.00 N	118.40 W
Walkersville	242	39.29 N	77.21 W
Walkerton, Ont., Can.	264	44.07 N	81.09 W
Walkerton, Ind., U.S.	268	41.28 N	86.29 W
Walkerton, Va., U.S.	262	37.43 N	77.01 W
Walkertown	246	36.10 N	80.10 W
Walkerville	256	46.01 N	112.30 W
Wall	252	43.59 N	102.14 W
Wallace, Calif., U.S.	272	38.12 N	120.59 W
Wallace, Idaho, U.S.	256	47.28 N	115.56 W
Wallace, Nebr., U.S.	252	40.50 N	101.10 W
Wallace, N.C., U.S.	246	34.44 N	77.59 W
Wallaceburg	266	42.36 N	82.23 W
Wallaceton	266	40.57 N	78.17 W
Wallacetown	266	42.38 N	81.28 W
Wallachia □[9]	172	44.00 N	25.00 E
Walland	246	35.44 N	83.49 W
Wallaroo	228	33.56 S	137.38 E
Wallasey	162	53.26 N	3.03 W
Walla Walla	256	46.08 N	118.20 W
Walla Walla Plateau ∧∧[1]	256	46.20 N	117.45 W
Walled Lake	268	42.32 N	83.29 W
Wallen	268	41.10 N	85.11 W
Waller	250	30.04 N	95.56 W
Wallibou	285h	13.19 N	61.15 W
Wallingford, Eng., U.K.	174	51.37 N	1.08 W
Wallingford, Conn., U.S.	261	41.27 N	72.50 W
Wallingford, Vt., U.S.	242	43.28 N	72.59 W
Wallis	250	29.38 N	96.04 W
Wallisellen	180	47.25 N	8.36 E
Wall Lake, Iowa, U.S.	252	42.16 N	95.05 W
Wall Lake, Mich., U.S.	268	42.31 N	85.24 W
Wallowa	256	45.34 N	117.32 W
Wallowa ≃	256	45.43 N	117.47 W
Wallowa Mountains ∧∧	256	45.10 N	117.30 W
Walls	248	34.58 N	90.16 W
Walnut, Calif., U.S.	274	34.01 N	117.51 W
Walnut, Ill., U.S.	244	41.33 N	89.36 W
Walnut, Kans., U.S.	252	37.36 N	95.05 W
Walnut, Miss., U.S.	248	34.57 N	88.54 W
Walnut, N.C., U.S.	246	35.51 N	82.44 W
Walnut ≃	250	37.03 N	97.00 W
Walnut Bend	266	41.28 N	79.39 W
Walnut Canyon National Monument ♠	254	34.59 N	111.10 W
Walnut Cove	246	36.18 N	80.09 W
Walnut Creek, Calif., U.S.	272	37.55 N	122.04 W
Walnut Creek, Ohio, U.S.	266	40.33 N	81.43 W
Walnut Grove, B.C., Can.	270	49.11 N	122.39 W
Walnut Grove, Calif., U.S.	272	38.15 N	121.31 W
Walnut Grove, Minn., U.S.	252	44.13 N	95.28 W
Walnut Grove, Miss., U.S.	248	32.36 N	89.28 W
Walnutport	262	40.45 N	75.36 W
Walnut Ridge	248	36.04 N	90.57 W
Walnut Springs	250	32.03 N	97.45 W
Walpole, Mass., U.S.	261	42.08 N	71.15 W
Walpole, N.H., U.S.	242	43.05 N	72.26 W
Walsall	174	52.35 N	1.58 W
Walsenburg	254	37.37 N	104.47 W
Walsh	252	37.23 N	102.17 W
Walsingham	264	42.41 N	80.32 W
Walsrode	178	52.52 N	9.35 E
Walston	266	40.58 N	79.01 W
Walsum	178	51.32 N	6.41 E
Walterboro	246	32.55 N	80.39 W
Walter F George Reservoir ⊜[1]	246	31.49 N	85.08 W
Walters	250	34.22 N	98.19 W
Waltershausen	164	50.53 N	10.33 E
Waltersville	248	32.22 N	90.52 W
Walthall	248	33.31 N	89.16 W
Waltham	261	42.23 N	71.14 W
Waltham Forest ➝[8]	174	51.35 N	0.01 W
Walthill	252	42.09 N	96.30 W
Walton, N.S., Can.	240	45.14 N	64.00 W
Walton, Eng., U.K.	174	51.24 N	0.25 W
Walton, Ind., U.S.	268	40.40 N	86.15 W
Walton, Ky., U.S.	242	38.52 N	84.37 W
Walton, N.Y., U.S.	242	42.10 N	75.08 W
Walton Hills	266	41.22 N	81.32 W
Waltrop	178	51.37 N	7.23 E
Waltz	266	42.06 N	83.23 W
Walvisbaai (Walvis Bay)	224	22.59 S	14.31 E
Walvis Bay □[8]	224	22.59 S	14.31 E
Walvis Bay C	224	22.57 S	14.30 E
Walvis Ridge ⌇[3]	148	30.00 S	3.00 E
Walworth, N.Y., U.S.	264	43.08 N	77.17 W
Walworth, Wis., U.S.	268	42.32 N	88.36 W
Walworth □[6]	268	42.41 N	88.32 W
Wamba ≃	218	3.56 S	17.12 E
Wamego	252	39.12 N	96.18 W
Wami ≃	218	6.08 S	38.49 E
Wamic	270	45.14 N	121.21 W
Wampsville	264	43.05 N	75.42 W
Wampum	266	40.54 N	80.21 W
Wamsutter	254	41.40 N	107.58 W
Wanaka, Lake ⊜	230	44.30 S	169.08 E
Wanakah	264	42.45 N	78.54 W
Wanamassa	262	40.14 N	74.02 W
Wanamingo	244	44.18 N	92.47 W
Wanapitei ≃	244	46.02 N	80.51 W
Wanapitei Lake ⊜	244	46.45 N	80.45 W
Wanapum Reservoir ⊜[1]	256	47.00 N	120.00 W
Wanatah	268	41.26 N	86.54 W
Wanblee	252	43.34 N	101.40 W
Wanchese	246	35.51 N	75.38 W
Wandawega	268	42.45 N	88.40 W
Wandering ≃	238	55.05 N	112.30 W
Wandsbek ➝[8]	178	53.34 N	10.04 E
Wandsworth ➝[8]	174	51.27 N	0.11 W
Wanette	250	34.58 N	97.02 W
Wanfoxia	190	40.04 N	95.55 E
Wang ≃	200	17.07 N	99.02 E
Wanganui	230	39.56 S	175.02 E
Wanganui ≃	230	39.57 S	174.59 E
Wangaratta	228	36.22 S	146.20 E
Wangen im Allgäu	180	47.41 N	9.50 E
Wangiwangi, Pulau I	198	5.20 S	123.35 E
Wanham	238	55.44 N	118.24 W
Wankie	224	18.22 S	26.29 E
Wankie Game Reserve ➝[4]	224	19.00 S	26.35 E
Wanne-Eickel	178	51.32 N	7.09 E
Wanshanqundao II	196	22.02 N	113.45 E
Wantage	174	51.36 N	1.25 W
Wanxian	190	30.52 N	108.22 E
Wanyangshan ∧∧	196	26.30 N	114.00 E
Wanzai	190	28.06 N	114.27 E
Wanzleben	164	52.03 N	11.26 E
Wapakoneta	268	40.34 N	84.12 W
Wapanucka	250	34.22 N	96.25 W
Wapato	256	46.27 N	120.25 W
Wapello	244	41.11 N	91.11 W
Wapiti ≃	238	55.08 N	118.18 W
Wappapello, Lake ⊜[1]	248	36.58 N	90.20 W
Wapping	261	41.50 N	72.33 W
Wappingers Falls	261	41.36 N	73.55 W
Wapsipinicon ≃	244	41.44 N	90.20 W
Wapus ≃	244	47.11 N	76.06 W
War	246	37.18 N	81.41 W
Waratah Bay C	228	38.51 S	146.04 E
Warburg	178	51.29 N	9.08 E
Warburton Bay C	232	63.50 N	111.30 W
Ward ≃	228	26.32 S	146.06 E
Ward, Mount ∧	230	43.52 S	169.50 E
Wardak □[4]	206	34.15 N	68.00 E
Wardcliff	268	42.43 N	84.28 W
Ward Cove	238	55.24 N	131.43 W
Wardell	248	36.21 N	89.49 W
Warden	256	46.58 N	119.02 W
Wardenburg	178	53.04 N	8.11 E
Warder	204	6.58 N	45.21 E
Wardlow	238	50.54 N	111.33 W
Ward Mountain ∧	256	46.10 N	114.17 W
Wardner	238	49.25 N	115.26 W
Wardsville	266	42.39 N	81.45 W
Wardville	248	32.53 N	91.55 W
Ware, Eng., U.K.	174	51.49 N	0.02 W
Ware, Mass., U.S.	261	42.16 N	72.15 W
Waregem	176	50.53 N	3.25 E
Wareham, Eng., U.K.	162	50.41 N	2.07 W
Wareham, Mass., U.S.	261	41.46 N	70.43 W
Warehouse Point	261	41.56 N	72.37 W
Waremme	164	50.41 N	5.15 E
Waren, D.D.R.	164	53.31 N	12.40 E
Waren, Indon.	198	2.16 S	136.20 E
Warendorf	178	51.57 N	7.59 E
Ware Shoals	246	34.24 N	82.15 W
Waretown	262	39.47 N	74.12 W
Warialda	226	29.32 S	150.34 E
Waring Mountains ∧∧	236	66.50 N	159.00 W
Warka	164	51.47 N	21.10 E
Warkworth	264	44.12 N	77.53 W
Warland	238	48.30 N	115.17 W
Warley → Smethwick	174	52.30 N	1.58 W
Warlingham	176	51.19 N	0.04 W
Warmbad, S. Afr.	218	24.55 S	28.15 E
Warmbad, S.W. Afr.	218	28.29 S	18.41 E
Warmbad □[5]	224	28.00 S	18.45 E
Warm Beach	270	48.16 N	122.21 W
Warminster, Eng., U.K.	174	51.13 N	2.12 W
Warminster, Pa., U.S.	262	40.12 N	75.06 W
Warm Springs, Ga., U.S.	246	32.54 N	84.41 W
Warm Springs, Mont., U.S.	256	46.11 N	112.48 W
Warm Springs, Oreg., U.S.	256	44.46 N	121.16 W
Warm Springs, Va., U.S.	246	38.03 N	79.47 W
Warm Springs ≃	256	44.52 N	121.04 W
Warm Springs Indian Reservation ➝[4]	256	45.00 N	121.25 W
Warm Springs Reservoir ⊜[1]	256	43.37 N	118.14 W
Warner, Alta., Can.	238	49.17 N	112.12 W
Warner, N.H., U.S.	242	43.17 N	71.49 W
Warner, Mount ∧	256	42.27 N	119.44 W
Warner Lakes ⊜	256	42.37 N	119.45 W
Warner Mountains ∧∧	258	41.40 N	120.20 W
Warner Robins	246	32.37 N	83.36 W
Warners	264	43.05 N	76.20 W
Warnes, Arg.	294	34.50 S	60.32 W
Warnes, Bol.	292	17.30 S	63.10 W
Warracknabeal	228	36.15 S	142.24 E
Warr Acres	250	35.31 N	97.37 W
Warragul	228	38.10 S	145.56 E
Warratta ≃	228	29.49 S	142.17 E
Warrego ≃	228	30.24 S	145.21 E
Warrego Range ∧∧	228	25.00 S	145.45 E
Warren, Ark., U.S.	248	33.37 N	92.04 W
Warren, Ind., U.S.	268	40.41 N	85.26 W
Warren, Mass., U.S.	261	42.13 N	72.12 W
Warren, Mich., U.S.	268	42.28 N	83.01 W
Warren, Minn., U.S.	252	48.12 N	96.46 W
Warren, Ohio, U.S.	266	41.14 N	80.52 W
Warren, Oreg., U.S.	270	45.49 N	122.51 W
Warren, Pa., U.S.	266	41.51 N	79.08 W
Warren, R.I., U.S.	261	41.43 N	71.17 W
Warren □[6], Ind., U.S.	268	40.21 N	87.17 W
Warren □[6], N.J., U.S.	262	40.49 N	75.05 W
Warren □[6], Pa., U.S.	266	41.51 N	79.08 W
Warrendale	266	40.39 N	80.05 W
Warren Peaks ∧∧	252	44.29 N	104.28 W
Warrenpoint	162	54.06 N	6.15 W
Warren Point ≻	236	69.44 N	132.30 W
Warrens	244	44.08 N	90.30 W
Warrensburg, Mo., U.S.	248	38.46 N	93.44 W
Warrensburg, N.Y., U.S.	242	43.30 N	73.46 W
Warrensville Heights	266	41.26 N	81.29 W
Warrenton, S. Afr.	218	28.09 S	24.47 E
Warrenton, Ga., U.S.	246	33.24 N	82.40 W
Warrenton, N.C., U.S.	246	36.24 N	78.09 W
Warrenton, Oreg., U.S.	270	46.10 N	123.56 W
Warrenton, Va., U.S.	242	38.43 N	77.48 W
Warrenville	268	41.49 N	88.11 W
Warri	222	5.31 N	5.45 E
Warrina	226	28.12 S	135.50 E
Warriners ≃	228	29.25 S	137.07 E
Warrington, Eng., U.K.	162	53.24 N	2.37 W
Warrington, Fla., U.S.	248	30.23 N	87.16 W
Warrior	248	33.49 N	86.49 W
Warriors Mark	266	40.42 N	78.08 W
Warrnambool	228	38.23 S	142.29 E
Warroad	252	48.54 N	95.19 W
Warrumbungle National Park ♠	228	31.20 S	149.00 E
Warsaw, Ill., U.S.	244	40.22 N	91.26 W
Warsaw, Ind., U.S.	268	41.14 N	85.51 W
Warsaw, Ky., U.S.	242	38.47 N	84.54 W
Warsaw, Mo., U.S.	248	38.15 N	93.23 W
Warsaw, N.C., U.S.	246	34.59 N	78.05 W
Warsaw, N.Y., U.S.	264	42.44 N	78.08 W
Warsaw, Ohio, U.S.	266	40.20 N	82.00 W
Warsaw, Va., U.S.	262	37.57 N	76.46 W
Warspite	238	54.06 N	112.37 W
Warstein	178	51.26 N	8.21 E
Warszawa (Warsaw)	164	52.15 N	21.00 E
Warszawska, Kotlina ⊻[1]	164	52.15 N	20.40 E
Warta	164	51.42 N	18.38 E
Warta ≃	164	52.35 N	14.39 E
Wartburg	246	36.06 N	84.36 W
Wartburg ⊥	164	50.58 N	10.18 E
Wartrace	248	35.32 N	86.19 W
Warwick, Austl.	228	28.13 S	152.02 E
Warwick, Qué., Can.	260	45.57 N	71.59 W
Warwick, Eng., U.K.	174	52.17 N	1.34 W
Warwick, Md., U.S.	262	39.25 N	75.47 W
Warwick, R.I., U.S.	261	41.43 N	71.28 W
Warwickshire □[6]	174	52.13 N	1.37 W
Wasaga Beach	264	44.31 N	80.01 W
Wasatch Plateau ∧∧[1]	254	39.20 N	111.30 W
Wasatch Range ∧∧	254	41.15 N	111.30 W
Wasco, Calif., U.S.	272	35.36 N	119.20 W
Wasco, Oreg., U.S.	270	45.35 N	120.42 W
Wasco □[6]	270	45.10 N	121.12 W
Waseca	244	44.05 N	93.30 W
Washademoak Lake ⊜	240	45.48 N	65.58 W
Washago	264	44.45 N	79.20 W
Washburn, Ill., U.S.	244	40.55 N	89.17 W
Washburn, Maine, U.S.	240	46.47 N	68.09 W
Washburn, N. Dak., U.S.	252	47.17 N	101.02 W
Washburn, Wis., U.S.	244	46.41 N	90.52 W
Washburn, Mount ∧	256	44.48 N	110.25 W
Washburn Lake ⊜	232	70.03 N	106.50 W
Washicoutai	240	50.17 N	60.42 W
Washington, Ark., U.S.	248	33.46 N	93.41 W
Washington, Calif., U.S.	272	39.22 N	120.48 W
Washington, Conn., U.S.	261	41.39 N	73.19 W
Washington, D.C., U.S.	262	38.54 N	77.01 W
Washington D.C. → District of Columbia □[3]	262	38.54 N	77.01 W
Washington, Ga., U.S.	246	33.44 N	82.44 W
Washington, Ill., U.S.	244	40.42 N	89.24 W
Washington, Ind., U.S.	248	38.40 N	87.10 W
Washington, Iowa, U.S.	244	41.18 N	91.42 W
Washington, Kans., U.S.	252	39.49 N	97.03 W
Washington, Ky., U.S.	242	38.37 N	83.49 W
Washington, La., U.S.	248	30.37 N	92.03 W
Washington, Mich., U.S.	266	42.44 N	83.02 W
Washington, Mo., U.S.	248	38.33 N	91.01 W
Washington, N.J., U.S.	262	40.46 N	74.59 W
Washington, N.C., U.S.	246	35.33 N	77.03 W
Washington, Pa., U.S.	266	40.10 N	80.15 W
Washington, Tex., U.S.	250	30.20 N	96.10 W
Washington, Va., U.S.	242	38.43 N	78.10 W
Washington □[6], Oreg., U.S.	270	45.33 N	123.07 W
Washington □[6], Pa., U.S.	266	40.10 N	80.15 W
Washington □[6], R.I., U.S.	261	41.28 N	71.35 W
Washington □[6], Wis., U.S.	268	43.14 N	88.15 W
Washington □[3]	234	47.30 N	120.30 W
Washington, Mount ∧	242	44.15 N	71.15 W
Washington Bay C	232	68.48 N	98.21 W
Washington Court House	242	39.32 N	83.26 W
Washington Crossing	262	40.18 N	74.52 W
Washington Depot	261	41.38 N	73.19 W
Washington Island	244	45.23 N	86.55 W
Washington Island I	244	45.23 N	86.55 W
Washington Terrace	254	41.12 N	111.58 W
Washingtonville	266	40.54 N	80.46 W
Washita ≃	250	34.12 N	96.50 W
Washoe □[6]	272	39.22 N	119.43 W
Washoe Lake ⊜	258	39.15 N	119.47 W
Washougal	270	45.35 N	122.21 W
Washtenaw □[6]	268	42.15 N	83.50 W
Washtucna	256	46.45 N	118.19 W
Wasilków	164	53.12 N	23.12 E
Wasilla	236	61.35 N	149.26 W
Wasior	198	2.42 S	134.30 E
Waskada	252	49.06 N	100.46 W
Waskahigan ≃	238	54.45 N	117.12 W
Waskatenau	238	54.07 N	112.47 W
Waskigomog Lake ⊜	244	45.56 N	79.03 W
Waskom	248	32.29 N	94.04 W
Wasmes	176	50.33 N	3.32 E
Wąsosz (Herrnstadt)	164	51.34 N	16.42 E
Waspán	280	14.39 N	84.08 W
Wasquehal	176	50.40 N	3.09 E
Wassaic	261	41.48 N	73.35 W
Wassen	166	46.42 N	8.36 E
Wassenaar	178	52.07 N	4.24 E
Wasseralfingen	164	48.52 N	10.06 E
Wasserburg am Inn	164	48.04 N	12.13 E
Wasserkuppe ∧	164	50.30 N	9.56 E
Wassy	166	48.30 N	4.57 E
Watabeag Lake ⊜	244	48.14 N	80.32 W
Watampone	198	4.32 S	120.20 E
Watansoppeng	198	4.21 S	119.53 E
Watatic, Mount ∧	242	42.42 N	71.53 W
Watch Hill	261	41.18 N	71.51 W
Waterberge ∧∧	224	20.30 S	17.18 E
Waterbury, Conn., U.S.	261	41.33 N	73.02 W
Waterbury, Vt., U.S.	242	44.20 N	72.46 W
Waterdown	264	43.20 N	79.53 W
Wateree ≃	246	33.45 N	80.37 W
Wateree Pond ⊜[1]	246	34.25 N	80.50 W
Waterfall	266	40.08 N	78.04 W
Waterford, Ont., Can.	264	42.56 N	80.17 W
Waterford, Eire	162	52.15 N	7.06 W
Waterford, Calif., U.S.	272	37.38 N	120.46 W
Waterford, Conn., U.S.	261	41.20 N	72.09 W
Waterford, Mich., U.S.	268	42.42 N	83.24 W
Waterford, N.Y., U.S.	261	42.47 N	73.41 W
Waterford, Pa., U.S.	266	41.57 N	79.59 W
Waterford, Wis., U.S.	268	42.46 N	88.13 W
Waterford □[6]	162	52.10 N	7.40 W
Waterford Harbour C	162	52.10 N	6.55 W
Waterford Mills	268	41.33 N	85.50 W
Waterford Works	262	39.43 N	74.51 W
Waterhen Lake ⊜	232	52.06 N	99.34 W
Wateringen	178	52.02 N	4.16 E
Waterloo, Bel.	176	50.43 N	4.23 E
Waterloo, Ont., Can.	264	43.28 N	80.31 W
Waterloo, Qué., Can.	260	45.21 N	72.31 W
Waterloo, Ala., U.S.	248	34.55 N	88.04 W
Waterloo, Ark., U.S.	248	33.32 N	93.15 W
Waterloo, Ill., U.S.	248	38.20 N	90.09 W
Waterloo, Ind., U.S.	268	41.26 N	85.01 W
Waterloo, Iowa, U.S.	244	42.30 N	92.20 W
Waterloo, N.Y., U.S.	264	42.54 N	76.52 W
Waterloo, Wis., U.S.	268	43.11 N	88.59 W
Waterloo □[6]	264	43.30 N	80.30 W
Waterman, Ill., U.S.	268	41.46 N	88.46 W
Waterman, Wash., U.S.	270	47.34 N	122.35 W
Waterman Wash ∨	254	33.21 N	112.31 W
Water Mill	261	40.55 N	72.21 W
Waterport	264	43.20 N	78.16 W
Waterproof	248	31.48 N	91.23 W
Waterside	266	40.11 N	78.23 W
Watersmeet	244	46.13 N	89.11 W
Waterton-Glacier International Peace Park ♠	256	48.47 N	113.45 W
Waterton Lakes National Park ♠	238	49.05 N	113.50 W
Watertown, Conn., U.S.	261	41.36 N	73.07 W
Watertown, Fla., U.S.	246	30.11 N	82.36 W
Watertown, N.Y., U.S.	264	43.59 N	75.55 W
Watertown, S. Dak., U.S.	252	44.54 N	97.07 W
Watertown, Wis., U.S.	268	43.12 N	88.43 W
Water Valley	248	34.09 N	89.38 W
Water View	262	37.43 N	76.37 W
Waterville, N.S., Can.	240	45.03 N	64.41 W
Waterville, Qué., Can.	260	45.17 N	71.53 W
Waterville, Kans., U.S.	252	39.42 N	96.45 W
Waterville, Maine, U.S.	242	44.33 N	69.38 W
Waterville, Mass., U.S.	261	42.40 N	72.05 W
Waterville, Minn., U.S.	244	44.13 N	93.34 W
Waterville, N.Y., U.S.	264	42.56 N	75.23 W
Waterville, Ohio, U.S.	268	41.30 N	83.43 W
Waterville, Wash., U.S.	256	47.39 N	120.04 W
Watervliet, Mich., U.S.	268	42.11 N	86.16 W
Watervliet, N.Y., U.S.	261	42.44 N	73.42 W
Watford, Ont., Can.	244	42.57 N	81.53 W
Watford, Eng., U.K.	174	51.40 N	0.25 W
Watford City	252	47.48 N	103.17 W
Wathaman ≃	232	57.16 N	102.52 W
Watino	238	55.43 N	117.37 W
Watkins Glen	242	42.23 N	76.52 W
Watkinsville	246	33.52 N	83.25 W
Watling Island → San Salvador I	282	24.00 N	74.30 W
Watoga State Park ♠	242	38.07 N	80.05 W
Watonga	250	35.51 N	98.25 W
Watonwan ≃	252	44.04 N	94.07 W
Watrous, Sask., Can.	232	51.40 N	105.28 W
Watrous, N. Mex., U.S.	254	35.48 N	104.59 W
Watseka	268	40.47 N	87.44 W
Watson Lake	236	60.07 N	128.48 W
Watsonville	272	36.55 N	121.45 W
Wattens	164	47.17 N	11.36 E
Wattenscheid	178	51.29 N	7.08 E
Wattignies	176	50.35 N	3.03 E
Wattrelos	176	50.42 N	3.13 E
Watts Bar Dam ➝[6]	246	35.40 N	84.42 W
Watts Bar Lake ⊜[1]	246	35.48 N	84.39 W
Wattsburg	266	42.00 N	79.49 W
Wattsville, Ala., U.S.	248	33.40 N	86.17 W
Wattsville, S.C., U.S.	246	34.31 N	82.02 W
Wattwil	180	47.18 N	9.06 E
Watubela, Kepulauan II	198	4.24 S	131.35 E
Waubaushene	264	44.45 N	79.42 W
Waubay	252	45.20 N	97.18 W
Waubay Lake ⊜	252	45.25 N	97.25 W
Wauchula	246	27.33 N	81.49 W
Wauconda, Ill., U.S.	268	42.16 N	88.08 W
Wauconda, Wash., U.S.	238	48.44 N	118.59 W
Waugh Mountain ∧	256	45.29 N	114.47 W
Waukegan	268	42.22 N	87.50 W
Waukena	272	36.08 N	119.31 W
Waukesha	268	43.01 N	88.14 W
Waukesha □[6]	268	43.02 N	88.20 W
Waukon	244	43.16 N	91.29 W
Wauna	270	47.23 N	122.39 W
Waunakee	268	43.11 N	89.27 W
Wauneta	252	40.25 N	101.23 W
Waupaca	244	44.21 N	89.05 W
Waupun	244	43.38 N	88.44 W
Wauregan	261	41.45 N	71.55 W
Waurika	250	34.10 N	97.60 W
Wausa	252	42.30 N	97.32 W
Wausau	244	44.59 N	89.39 W
Wausaukee	244	45.23 N	87.57 W
Wauseon	268	41.33 N	84.09 W
Wautoma	244	44.04 N	89.17 W
Wauwatosa	268	43.03 N	88.00 W
Wauzeka	244	43.05 N	90.52 W
Wave Hill	226	17.29 S	130.57 E
Waveland	248	30.16 N	89.29 W
Waverly, Ala., U.S.	248	32.44 N	85.35 W
Waverly, Ill., U.S.	248	39.36 N	89.57 W
Waverly, Iowa, U.S.	244	42.44 N	92.29 W
Waverly, Kans., U.S.	252	38.23 N	95.36 W
Waverly, Minn., U.S.	244	45.04 N	93.57 W
Waverly, Mo., U.S.	248	39.12 N	93.31 W
Waverly, Nebr., U.S.	252	40.55 N	96.32 W
Waverly, N.Y., U.S.	242	42.00 N	76.32 W
Waverly, Ohio, U.S.	242	39.07 N	82.59 W
Waverly, Tenn., U.S.	248	36.05 N	87.48 W
Waverly, Va., U.S.	262	37.02 N	77.06 W
Waverly Hall	246	32.41 N	84.44 W
Wavre	166	50.43 N	4.37 E
Wāw	220	7.42 N	28.00 E
Wāw ≃	220	7.03 N	27.13 E
Wawa	244	47.59 N	84.47 W
Wawaka	268	41.28 N	85.29 W
Wāw al-Kabīr	214	25.20 N	16.43 E
Wawanesa	252	49.36 N	99.41 W
Wawiag ≃	244	48.25 N	91.07 W
Wawota	252	49.55 N	102.00 W
Waxahachie	250	32.24 N	96.51 W
Waxhaw	246	34.55 N	80.45 W
Waycross	246	31.13 N	82.21 W
Wayland, Iowa, U.S.	244	41.08 N	91.40 W
Wayland, Ky., U.S.	246	37.27 N	82.48 W
Wayland, Mich., U.S.	268	42.40 N	85.39 W
Wayland, N.Y., U.S.	266	42.34 N	77.35 W
Wayland, Ohio, U.S.	266	41.10 N	81.04 W
Wayne, Alta., Can.	238	51.23 N	112.39 W
Wayne, Mich., U.S.	268	42.17 N	83.23 W
Wayne, Nebr., U.S.	252	42.14 N	97.01 W
Wayne, N.J., U.S.	242	40.55 N	74.17 W
Wayne, Ohio, U.S.	266	41.18 N	83.28 W
Wayne, Okla., U.S.	250	34.55 N	97.19 W
Wayne, Pa., U.S.	262	40.03 N	75.23 W
Wayne, W. Va., U.S.	242	38.13 N	82.27 W
Wayne □[6], Mich., U.S.	268	42.14 N	83.12 W
Wayne □[6], N.Y., U.S.	264	43.04 N	77.00 W
Wayne □[6], Ohio, U.S.	266	40.48 N	81.56 W
Wayne Haven	268	41.05 N	85.07 W
Waynesboro, Ga., U.S.	246	33.06 N	82.01 W
Waynesboro, Miss., U.S.	248	31.40 N	88.39 W
Waynesboro, Pa., U.S.	262	39.45 N	77.35 W
Waynesboro, Tenn., U.S.	248	35.19 N	87.45 W
Waynesboro, Va., U.S.	246	38.04 N	78.53 W
Waynesburg, Ohio, U.S.	266	40.40 N	81.16 W
Waynesburg, Pa., U.S.	242	39.54 N	80.11 W
Waynesfield	268	40.36 N	83.59 W
Waynesville, Ill., U.S.	248	40.15 N	89.08 W
Waynesville, Mo., U.S.	248	37.50 N	92.12 W
Waynesville, N.C., U.S.	246	35.29 N	83.00 W
Waynoka	250	36.35 N	98.53 W
Waziers	176	50.23 N	3.07 E
Wda ≃	164	53.25 N	18.29 E
We, Pulau I	200	5.51 N	95.18 E
Weatherford, Okla., U.S.	250	35.32 N	98.42 W
Weatherford, Tex., U.S.	250	32.46 N	97.48 W
Weatherly	242	40.57 N	75.50 W
Weatogue	261	41.51 N	72.49 W
Weaubleau	248	37.54 N	93.32 W
Weaver	248	33.45 N	85.49 W
Weaverville, Calif., U.S.	258	40.44 N	122.56 W
Weaverville, N.C., U.S.	246	35.42 N	82.34 W
Webb	248	33.57 N	90.21 W
Webb City	248	37.09 N	94.28 W
Webberville	268	42.40 N	84.11 W
Webbwood	244	41.16 N	81.53 W
Weber ≃	256	41.13 N	112.16 W
Weber, Mount ∧	238	55.32 N	128.31 W
Weber City	246	36.37 N	82.34 W
Webster, Alta., Can.	238	55.26 N	118.42 W
Webster, Fla., U.S.	246	28.37 N	82.03 W
Webster, Mass., U.S.	261	42.03 N	71.53 W
Webster, N.Y., U.S.	264	43.13 N	77.26 W
Webster, Pa., U.S.	266	40.11 N	79.51 W
Webster, S. Dak., U.S.	252	45.20 N	97.31 W
Webster, Wis., U.S.	244	45.53 N	92.22 W
Webster City	244	42.28 N	93.49 W
Webster Crossing	264	42.40 N	77.38 W
Websters Corners	270	49.13 N	122.30 W
Webster Springs	242	38.29 N	80.25 W
Weda	198	0.21 N	127.52 E
Weddell Sea ▾[2]	148	72.00 S	45.00 W
Wedderburn	256	42.26 N	124.25 W
Wedel	178	53.35 N	9.41 E
Wedge Mountain ∧	238	50.10 N	122.50 W
Wedgeport	240	43.44 N	65.59 W
Wednesbury	174	52.34 N	2.00 W
Wednesfield	174	52.36 N	2.04 W
Wedowee	248	33.19 N	85.29 W
Wedron	268	41.26 N	88.46 W
Weed	258	41.25 N	122.23 W
Weed Heights	272	38.59 N	119.11 W
Weedon	260	45.42 N	71.28 W
Weedsport	264	43.03 N	76.34 W
Weedville	266	41.17 N	78.30 W
Weekapaug	261	41.20 N	71.45 W
Weeks	248	29.48 N	91.49 W
Weekstown	262	39.37 N	74.37 W
Weems	262	37.39 N	76.27 W
Weener	178	53.10 N	7.21 E
Weeping Water	252	40.52 N	96.08 W
Weert	178	51.15 N	5.43 E
Weesp	178	52.17 N	5.02 E
Weeze	178	51.37 N	6.12 E
Wegberg	178	51.08 N	6.16 E
Węgliniec (Kohlfurt)	164	51.17 N	15.13 E
Węgorzewo (Angerburg)	164	54.14 N	21.44 E
Węgorzyno (Wangerin)	164	53.32 N	15.33 E
Węgrów	164	52.25 N	22.01 E
Wegscheid	164	48.36 N	13.48 E
Wehr	180	47.37 N	7.54 E
Weida	164	50.45 N	12.04 E
Weidenau	164	50.54 N	8.02 E
Weiden in der Oberpfalz	164	49.41 N	12.10 E
Weifang	194	36.42 N	119.04 E
Weigelstown	262	39.59 N	76.49 W
Weihai	194	37.28 N	122.07 E
Weihaiwei → Weihai	194	37.28 N	122.07 E
Weihe ≃, Zhg.	194	36.51 N	115.43 E
Weihe ≃, Zhg.	194	37.05 N	119.28 E
Weil am Rhein	180	47.37 N	7.38 E
Weilburg	164	50.29 N	8.15 E
Weilheim	164	47.50 N	11.08 E
Weilheim an der Teck	180	48.37 N	9.32 E
Weimar, D.D.R.	164	50.59 N	11.19 E
Weimar, Calif., U.S.	272	39.02 N	120.58 W
Weimar, Tex., U.S.	250	29.42 N	96.47 W
Weinan	190	34.29 N	109.29 E
Weiner	248	35.37 N	90.54 W
Weinfelden	180	47.34 N	9.06 E
Weingarten	180	47.48 N	9.38 E
Weinheim	164	49.33 N	8.39 E
Weipa	226	12.41 S	141.52 E
Weir, Kans., U.S.	252	37.19 N	94.46 W
Weir, Miss., U.S.	248	33.16 N	89.17 W
Weir ≃	228	28.50 S	149.06 E
Weir, Lake ⊜	246	29.00 N	81.57 W
Weirsdale	246	28.59 N	81.55 W
Weirton	266	40.25 N	80.35 W
Weisburd	294	27.19 S	62.36 W
Weiser	256	44.15 N	116.58 W
Weiser ≃	256	44.15 N	116.59 W
Weishan	200	25.15 N	100.20 E
Weishanhu ⊜	194	34.40 N	117.15 E
Weishi	194	34.25 N	114.11 E
Weisner, Mount ∧	248	34.01 N	85.40 W
Weissenburg in Bayern	164	49.01 N	10.58 E
Weissenfels	164	51.12 N	11.58 E
Weissenhorn	180	48.18 N	10.09 E
Weiss Reservoir ⊜[1]	246	34.15 N	85.35 W
Weisswasser	164	51.30 N	14.38 E
Weitouwan C	196	24.34 N	118.30 E
Weitra	164	48.42 N	14.54 E
Weixi	200	27.14 N	99.12 E
Weiz	164	47.13 N	15.37 E
Weizhoudao I	200	21.03 N	109.02 E
Wejherowo	164	54.37 N	18.15 E
Wekoewa Punt ≻	285s	12.14 N	68.24 W
Welaka	246	29.29 N	81.40 W
Welch, Okla., U.S.	250	36.52 N	95.06 W
Welch, Tex., U.S.	250	32.56 N	102.08 W
Welch, W. Va., U.S.	246	37.25 N	81.31 W
Welches	270	45.20 N	121.58 W
Welcome, Ont., Can.	264	43.58 N	78.21 W
Welcome, Minn., U.S.	252	43.40 N	94.37 W
Welcome, S.C., U.S.	246	34.49 N	82.26 W
Weldon, Ill., U.S.	248	40.07 N	88.45 W
Weldon, N.C., U.S.	246	36.25 N	77.36 W
Weldon ≃	248	40.06 N	93.38 W
Weldona	252	40.21 N	103.58 W
Weleetka	250	35.20 N	96.08 W
Welkom	224	27.59 S	26.45 E
Welland	264	42.59 N	79.15 W
Welland □[6]	264	43.00 N	79.15 W
Welland Canal ≊	244	43.14 N	79.13 W
Welland Junction	264	42.57 N	79.14 W
Wellborn, Fla., U.S.	246	30.14 N	82.49 W
Wellborn, Tex., U.S.	250	30.32 N	96.18 W
Wellesley, Ont., Can.	264	43.28 N	80.45 W
Wellesley, Mass., U.S.	261	42.18 N	71.17 W
Wellesley Islands II	228	16.42 S	139.30 E
Wellesley Lake ⊜	236	62.30 N	139.50 W
Wellfleet	261	41.56 N	70.02 W
Wellingborough	174	52.19 N	0.42 W
Wellington, Austl.	228	32.33 S	148.57 E
Wellington, B.C., Can.	270	49.13 N	124.01 W
Wellington, Ont., Can.	264	43.57 N	77.21 W
Wellington, N.Z.	230	41.18 S	174.46 E
Wellington, S. Afr.	224	33.38 S	18.57 E
Wellington, Eng., U.K.	174	52.43 N	2.31 W
Wellington, Eng., U.K.	174	50.59 N	3.14 W
Wellington, Colo., U.S.	254	40.42 N	105.00 W
Wellington, Ill., U.S.	268	40.32 N	87.41 W
Wellington, Kans., U.S.	252	37.16 N	97.24 W
Wellington, Mo., U.S.	248	39.08 N	93.59 W
Wellington, Nev., U.S.	272	38.45 N	119.22 W
Wellington, Ohio, U.S.	266	41.10 N	82.13 W
Wellington, Tex., U.S.	250	34.51 N	100.13 W
Wellington, Utah, U.S.	254	39.32 N	110.44 W
Wellington □[6]	264	43.50 N	80.30 W
Wellington, Isla I	288	49.20 S	74.40 W
Wellington Bay C	232	69.30 N	106.30 W
Wellington Channel ⊔	232	75.00 N	93.00 W
Wellington Station	240	46.27 N	64.00 W
Wellman, Iowa, U.S.	244	41.28 N	91.50 W
Wellman, Tex., U.S.	250	33.03 N	102.26 W
Wells, B.C., Can.	238	53.06 N	121.34 W
Wells, Eng., U.K.	174	51.13 N	2.39 W
Wells, Mich., U.S.	244	45.47 N	87.04 W
Wells, Minn., U.S.	244	43.44 N	93.44 W
Wells, Nev., U.S.	258	41.07 N	114.58 W
Wells, N.Y., U.S.	242	43.24 N	74.17 W
Wells, Tex., U.S.	248	31.29 N	94.56 W
Wells □[6]	268	40.44 N	85.11 W
Wellsboro	242	41.45 N	77.18 W
Wellsburg, Iowa, U.S.	244	42.26 N	92.56 W
Wellsburg, W. Va., U.S.	266	40.16 N	80.37 W
Wells-next-the-Sea	162	52.58 N	0.51 W
Wells Tannery	266	40.05 N	78.10 W
Wellston	242	39.07 N	82.32 W
Wellsville, Kans., U.S.	252	38.43 N	95.05 W
Wellsville, Mo., U.S.	248	39.04 N	91.34 W
Wellsville, N.Y., U.S.	266	42.07 N	77.57 W
Wellsville, Ohio, U.S.	266	40.36 N	80.39 W
Wellsville, Pa., U.S.	262	40.03 N	76.56 W
Wellsville, Utah, U.S.	254	41.38 N	111.56 W
Wellton	254	32.40 N	114.08 W
Welper	178	51.25 N	7.12 E
Wels	164	48.10 N	14.02 E
Welsford	240	45.27 N	66.20 W
Welsh	248	30.14 N	92.49 W
Welshpool	174	52.40 N	3.09 W
Welwyn Garden City	174	51.50 N	0.13 W
Wembley	238	55.09 N	119.08 W
Wemme	270	45.21 N	121.58 W
Wenatchee	256	47.25 N	120.19 W
Wenatchee ≃	256	47.27 N	120.19 W
Wenatchee Mountains ∧∧	256	47.20 N	120.45 W
Wenchang	200	19.41 N	110.48 E
Wenchi	222	7.42 N	2.07 W
Wenchow → Wenzhou	196	28.01 N	120.39 E
Wendell, Idaho, U.S.	256	42.46 N	114.42 W
Wendell, N.C., U.S.	246	35.47 N	78.22 W
Wenden	254	33.49 N	113.32 W
Wendlingen am Neckar	180	48.40 N	9.23 E
Wendover	254	40.44 N	114.02 W
Wenebegon ≃	244	46.53 N	83.12 W
Wenebegon Lake ⊜	244	47.24 N	83.08 W
Wengjiang ≃	196	24.10 N	113.24 E
Wenham	261	42.36 N	70.53 W
Wenhe ≃	194	36.38 N	119.22 E
Wennigsen	178	52.16 N	9.34 E
Wenona, Ill., U.S.	268	41.03 N	89.03 W
Wenona, Md., U.S.	262	38.08 N	75.57 W
Wenonah	262	39.48 N	75.09 W
Wenshan	200	23.30 N	104.20 E
Wentorf	178	53.30 N	10.15 E
Wentworth, Austl.	228	34.07 S	141.55 E
Wentworth, N.C., U.S.	246	36.24 N	79.53 W
Wentworth, S. Dak., U.S.	252	44.00 N	96.58 W
Wentworth □[6]	264	43.15 N	80.00 W
Wentzville	248	38.49 N	90.51 W
Wenzhou	196	28.01 N	120.39 E
Wenzhouwan C	196	27.56 N	121.00 E
Wequetequock	261	41.22 N	71.52 W
Werdau	164	50.44 N	12.22 E
Werder	164	52.23 N	12.56 E
Werdohl	178	51.15 N	7.45 E
Werkendam	178	51.49 N	4.53 E
Werl	178	51.33 N	7.54 E
Wermelskirchen	178	51.08 N	7.13 E
Wernau	180	48.41 N	9.25 E
Werne an der Lippe	178	51.40 N	7.40 E
Wernigerode	164	51.50 N	10.47 E
Werra ≃	164	51.26 N	9.39 E
Werribee	228	37.54 S	144.40 E
Werris Creek	226	31.21 S	150.39 E
Wertheim	164	49.46 N	9.31 E
Wertingen	164	48.34 N	10.41 E
Wervik	176	50.47 N	3.02 E
Wesconnett	246	30.14 N	81.44 W
Wesel	178	51.40 N	6.38 E
Weser ≃	164	53.32 N	8.34 E
Weskan	252	38.41 N	101.57 W
Weslaco	250	26.09 N	97.59 W
Weslemkoon Lake ⊜	244	45.02 N	77.25 W
Wesley, Dom.	284d	15.34 N	61.19 W
Wesley, Iowa, U.S.	244	43.05 N	93.59 W
Wesleyville, Newf., Can.	240	49.09 N	53.34 W
Wesleyville, Pa., U.S.	266	42.08 N	80.01 W
Wessington	252	44.27 N	98.42 W
Wessington Springs	252	44.05 N	98.34 W
Wesson	248	31.42 N	90.23 W
West, Miss., U.S.	248	33.12 N	89.47 W
West, Tex., U.S.	250	31.48 N	97.06 W
West ≃	242	42.52 N	72.33 W
West Abington	261	42.08 N	70.59 W
Westacres	268	42.35 N	83.26 W
West Acton	261	42.29 N	71.28 W
West Alexander	266	40.06 N	80.31 W
West Alexandria	242	39.45 N	84.32 W
West Allis	268	43.01 N	88.00 W
West Andover	261	42.39 N	71.10 W
West Atlantic City	262	39.23 N	74.28 W
West Australian Basin ⌇[1]	148	20.00 S	100.00 E
Westbank	238	49.50 N	119.38 W
West Barnstable	261	41.42 N	70.23 W
West Barrington	261	41.45 N	71.21 W
West Bay, N.S., Can.	240	45.43 N	61.10 W
Westbay, Fla., U.S.	248	30.17 N	85.52 W
West Bay C, Fla., U.S.	248	30.16 N	85.47 W
West Bay C, Tex., U.S.	250	29.15 N	94.57 W
West Belmar	262	40.10 N	74.02 W
West Bend, Iowa, U.S.	252	42.57 N	94.27 W
West Bend, Wis., U.S.	244	43.25 N	88.11 W
West Bengal □[3]	206	24.00 N	88.00 E
West Berbice □[5]	290	6.20 N	57.55 W
West-Berlin, B.R.D.	164	52.30 N	13.20 E
West Berlin, N.J., U.S.	262	39.49 N	74.57 W
West Blocton	248	33.07 N	87.07 W
West Bloomfield	264	42.54 N	77.32 W
West Bolivar	266	40.23 N	79.10 W
Westboro	261	42.16 N	71.37 W
West Boylston	261	42.22 N	71.47 W
West Bradford	266	41.59 N	78.41 W
West Branch, Iowa, U.S.	244	41.40 N	91.20 W
West Branch, Mich., U.S.	244	44.17 N	84.14 W
Westbridge	238	49.10 N	118.59 W
West Bridgewater, Mass., U.S.	261	42.01 N	71.00 W
West Bridgewater, Pa., U.S.	266	40.43 N	80.18 W
West Bridgford	174	52.56 N	1.08 W
West Bromwich	174	52.31 N	1.56 W
Westbrook, Ont., Can.	264	44.16 N	76.38 W
Westbrook, Conn., U.S.	261	41.17 N	72.27 W
Westbrook, Maine, U.S.	242	43.41 N	70.21 W
Westbrook, Minn., U.S.	252	44.03 N	95.26 W
Westbrook, Tex., U.S.	250	32.21 N	101.01 W
West Brookfield	261	42.14 N	72.09 W
West Burlington	244	40.49 N	91.09 W
Westbury, Eng., U.K.	174	51.16 N	2.11 W
Westbury, Ill., U.S.	268	41.42 N	88.04 W
West Butte ∧	256	48.57 N	111.32 W
Westby, Mont., U.S.	252	48.52 N	104.03 W
Westby, Wis., U.S.	244	43.39 N	90.51 W
West Caicos I	282	21.40 N	72.27 W
West Cameron	262	40.45 N	76.58 W
West Camp	261	42.07 N	73.56 W
West Cape ≻	230	45.55 S	166.26 E
West Cape May	262	38.56 N	74.56 W
West Caroline Basin ⌇[1]	148	5.00 N	139.00 E
West Carthage	264	43.59 N	75.38 W
West Channel ≃[1]	236	68.51 N	136.10 W
Westchester, Ill., U.S.	268	41.51 N	87.53 W
West Chester, Pa., U.S.	242	39.58 N	75.36 W
Westchester □[6]	261	41.02 N	73.46 W
West Chicago	268	41.53 N	88.12 W
West Clarksville	266	42.08 N	78.15 W
Westcliffe	254	38.08 N	105.28 W
West Columbia, S.C., U.S.	246	34.00 N	81.04 W
West Columbia, Tex., U.S.	250	29.09 N	95.39 W
West Concord, Mass., U.S.	261	42.27 N	71.24 W
West Concord, Minn., U.S.	244	44.09 N	92.54 W
West Cote Blanche Bay C	248	29.40 N	91.45 W
West Covina	274	34.05 N	117.58 W
West Creek	262	39.38 N	74.18 W
Westdale	264	43.23 N	75.49 W
West Decatur	266	40.56 N	78.17 W
West Demerara □[5]	290	5.25 N	58.35 W
West Dennis	261	41.40 N	70.10 W
West Derry	266	40.20 N	79.20 W
West Dolores ≃	254	37.35 N	108.21 W
West Easton	262	40.41 N	75.14 W
West Eaton	264	42.51 N	75.39 W
West Elizabeth	266	40.17 N	79.54 W
West Elk Mountains ∧∧	254	38.40 N	107.15 W
West Elk Peak ∧	254	38.43 N	107.13 W
West Ellicott	266	42.05 N	79.16 W
West End, Ba.	282	26.41 N	78.58 W
West End, Ark., U.S.	248	34.13 N	92.03 W
West End, N.C., U.S.	246	35.15 N	79.33 W
Westerholt	178	51.36 N	7.05 E
Westerkappeln	178	52.18 N	7.52 E
Westerland	164	54.54 N	8.18 E
Westerlo	178	51.05 N	4.55 E

Symbols in the index entries are identified on page 360.

Name | Page | Lat°′ | Long°′

Westerly 261 41.22 N 71.50 W
Western 252 40.24 N 97.12 W
Western □[3] 222 7.45 N 4.00 E
Western □[4], Ghana 222 5.30 N 2.30 W
Western (Area) □[4], S.L. 222 8.20 N 13.00 W
Western ≃ 228 22.22 S 142.25 E
Western Australia □[3] 226 25.00 S 122.00 E
Western Channel ⋃ 194 34.40 N 129.00 E
Western Desert → Aṣ-Ṣaḥrā' al-Gharbīyah ↢[2] 220 27.00 N 27.00 E
Westernport 242 39.29 N 79.03 W
Western Port C 228 38.22 S 145.20 E
Western Sayans → Zapadnyj Sajan ⋀ 186 53.00 N 94.00 E
Western Shore 240 44.32 N 64.19 W
Westernville 264 43.18 N 75.23 W
Wester Schelde C[1] 164 51.25 N 3.45 E
Westerstede 178 53.15 N 7.55 E
Westerville 266 40.08 N 82.56 W
Westerwald ⋀ 164 50.40 N 7.55 E
West European Basin ⊹[1] 148 46.00 N 15.00 W
West Fairview 262 40.17 N 76.55 W
Westfalen □[9] 178 51.50 N 7.30 E
West Falkland I 288 51.40 S 60.00 W
West Falls 264 42.42 N 78.41 W
West Falmouth 261 41.36 N 70.38 W
West Farmington, Maine, U.S. 242 44.40 N 70.10 W
West Farmington, Ohio, U.S. 266 41.23 N 80.59 W
Westfield, Ill., U.S. 248 39.27 N 88.01 W
Westfield, Ind., U.S. 248 40.02 N 86.08 W
Westfield, Mass., U.S. 261 42.08 N 72.45 W
Westfield, N.J., U.S. 262 40.39 N 74.21 W
Westfield, N.Y., U.S. 266 42.19 N 79.35 W
Westfield, Pa., U.S. 242 41.55 N 77.32 W
Westfield, Wis., U.S. 244 43.53 N 89.30 W
West Fiord C[2] 232 76.02 N 90.00 W
Westford 266 41.33 N 80.29 W
West Frankfort 248 37.54 N 88.55 W
Westfriese Eilande II 164 53.26 N 5.30 E
Westgate 246 26.47 N 80.06 W
West Genesee Terrace 264 43.03 N 76.16 W
West Germany → Germany, West □[1] 158 51.00 N 9.00 E
West Glacier 256 48.30 N 113.59 W
West Goshen 261 41.50 N 73.15 W
West Granby 261 41.57 N 72.50 W
West Groton 261 42.36 N 71.38 W
West Grove 262 39.49 N 75.50 W
West Hamburg 262 40.33 N 76.00 W
West Hamlin 242 38.17 N 82.12 W
Westhampton 261 40.49 N 72.39 W
West Harbour 230 45.52 S 170.33 E
West Hartford 261 41.46 N 72.45 W
West Hartland 261 42.00 N 72.58 W
West Haven 261 41.16 N 72.57 W
West Helena 248 34.33 N 90.39 W
West Henrietta 264 43.02 N 77.40 W
West Hickory 266 41.34 N 79.25 W
West Hills 274 34.27 N 119.17 W
Westhoff 250 29.12 N 97.28 W
West Hollywood, Calif., U.S. 274 34.05 N 118.24 W
West Hollywood, Fla., U.S. 246 25.59 N 80.11 W
Westholme 270 49.52 N 123.42 W
Westhope, N. Dak., U.S. 252 48.55 N 101.01 W
Westhope, Ohio, U.S. 268 41.18 N 83.57 W
West Ice Shelf ◸ 148 67.00 S 85.00 E
West-Indian Ridge ⊹[3] 148 38.00 S 52.00 E
West Indies II 276 19.00 N 70.00 W
West Jefferson, N.C., U.S. 246 36.24 N 81.30 W
West Jefferson, Ohio, U.S. 242 39.57 N 83.16 W
West Junction 248 35.04 N 90.05 W
West Kankakee 268 41.07 N 87.53 W
West Kettle ≃ 238 49.07 N 119.00 W
West Kildonan 252 49.56 N 97.07 W
West Kingston 261 41.29 N 71.34 W
West Kittanning 266 40.49 N 79.32 W
West Lafayette, Ind., U.S. 268 40.27 N 86.55 W
West Lafayette, Ohio, U.S. 266 40.17 N 81.45 W
Westlake, La., U.S. 248 30.15 N 93.15 W
Westlake, Ohio, U.S. 266 41.27 N 81.55 W
Westland, Mich., U.S. 268 42.19 N 83.23 W
Westland, Pa., U.S. 266 40.17 N 80.16 W
Westland □[9] 230 43.30 S 170.30 E
Westland National Park ♠ 230 43.30 S 170.10 E
Westlands 261 42.37 N 71.20 W
West Las Vegas 254 35.35 N 105.14 W
West Lebanon, Ind., U.S. 268 40.16 N 87.23 W
West Lebanon, Pa., U.S. 266 40.35 N 79.22 W
West Leechburg 266 40.37 N 79.37 W
West Leipsic 268 41.07 N 84.00 W
Westley 272 37.33 N 121.12 W
West Leyden 264 43.28 N 75.28 W
West Liberty, Iowa, U.S. 244 41.34 N 91.16 W
West Liberty, Ky., U.S. 246 37.55 N 83.16 W
West Liberty, Ohio, U.S. 268 40.15 N 83.46 W
West Liberty, Pa., U.S. 266 41.00 N 80.03 W
West Liberty, W. Va., U.S. 266 40.10 N 80.36 W
Westline 266 41.47 N 78.46 W
West Linn 270 45.21 N 122.36 W
Westlock 238 54.09 N 113.52 W
West Lorne 266 42.36 N 81.36 W
West Lothian □[6] 162 55.55 N 3.35 W
West Lubec 242 44.49 N 67.05 W
West Mansfield, Mass., U.S. 261 42.00 N 71.15 W
West Mansfield, Ohio, U.S. 268 40.24 N 83.33 W
West Mayfield 266 40.47 N 80.20 W
West Meadowview 268 41.08 N 87.52 W
Westmeath □[6] 162 53.30 N 7.30 W
West Medway 261 42.09 N 71.26 W
West Melbourne 246 28.04 N 80.38 W
West Memphis 248 35.08 N 90.11 W
Westmere 261 42.42 N 73.52 W
West Middlesex 266 41.10 N 80.27 W
West Middleton 268 40.26 N 86.13 W
West Middletown 266 40.15 N 80.25 W
West Mifflin 266 40.22 N 79.52 W
West Millbury 261 42.11 N 71.48 W
West Milwaukee 268 42.57 N 87.58 W
Westminster, Calif., U.S. 274 33.46 N 118.01 W
Westminster, Colo., U.S. 254 39.50 N 105.02 W
Westminster, Md., U.S. 262 39.35 N 76.59 W
Westminster, Mass., U.S. 261 42.33 N 71.55 W
Westminster, Ohio, U.S. 268 40.42 N 83.58 W
Westminster, S.C., U.S. 246 34.40 N 83.06 W
West Modesto 272 37.37 N 121.02 W
West Monroe 248 32.31 N 92.09 W
Westmont 266 40.19 N 78.57 W
West Monterey 266 41.03 N 79.39 W
Westmoreland, Kans., U.S. 252 39.24 N 96.25 W
Westmoreland, N.Y., U.S. 264 43.07 N 75.24 W
Westmoreland, Tenn., U.S. 248 36.34 N 86.15 W
Westmoreland, Va., U.S. 262 38.04 N 76.34 W
Westmoreland □[6], Pa., U.S. 266 40.18 N 79.33 W
Westmoreland □[6], Va., U.S. 262 38.10 N 76.50 W
Westmoreland City 266 40.20 N 79.41 W
Westmorland 258 33.02 N 115.37 W
Westmorland □[6] 162 54.30 N 2.40 W
Westmount 260 45.29 N 73.36 W
West Mountain ∧ 242 43.51 N 74.43 W
West Newbury 261 42.48 N 71.00 W
West Newton 266 40.13 N 79.46 W
West Nicholson 218 21.06 S 29.25 E
West Nishnabotna ≃ 252 40.39 N 95.37 W
West Novaya Zemlya Trough ⊹[1] 148 75.00 N 50.00 E
West Nueces ≃ 250 29.16 N 99.56 W
Weston, Ont., Can. 244 43.43 N 79.31 W
Weston, Colo., U.S. 254 37.08 N 104.48 W
Weston, Conn., U.S. 261 41.12 N 73.22 W
Weston, Idaho, U.S. 256 42.02 N 111.59 W
Weston, Mass., U.S. 261 42.22 N 71.18 W
Weston, Mich., U.S. 268 41.46 N 84.06 W
Weston, Mo., U.S. 248 39.25 N 94.54 W
Weston, Nebr., U.S. 252 41.12 N 96.45 W
Weston, Ohio, U.S. 268 41.21 N 83.48 W
Weston, Oreg., U.S. 256 45.49 N 118.26 W
Weston, W. Va., U.S. 242 39.02 N 80.28 W
Westonaria 224 26.19 S 27.41 E
Westons Mills 266 42.04 N 78.23 W
Weston-super-Mare 174 51.21 N 2.59 W
West Orange 248 30.05 N 93.46 W
Westover, Md., U.S. 262 38.07 N 75.42 W
Westover, Pa., U.S. 266 40.45 N 78.40 W
Westover, W. Va., U.S. 242 39.38 N 79.58 W
West Palm Beach 246 26.43 N 80.04 W
West Palm Beach Canal ≊ 246 26.38 N 80.03 W
West Paris 242 44.20 N 70.35 W
West Park 261 41.48 N 73.58 W
West Pembroke 242 44.57 N 67.11 W
West Pensacola 248 30.27 N 87.15 W
West Petersburg 236 56.49 N 132.57 W
Westphalia, Kans., U.S. 252 38.11 N 95.29 W
Westphalia, Mich., U.S. 268 42.56 N 84.48 W
West Pittsburg, Calif., U.S. 272 38.02 N 121.54 W
West Pittsburg, Pa., U.S. 266 40.56 N 80.22 W
West Plains 248 36.44 N 91.51 W
West Point, Calif., U.S. 272 38.24 N 120.32 W
West Point, Ga., U.S. 246 32.52 N 85.10 W
Westpoint, Ind., U.S. 268 40.21 N 87.03 W
West Point, Iowa, U.S. 244 40.43 N 91.27 W
West Point, Ky., U.S. 248 37.59 N 85.57 W
West Point, Miss., U.S. 248 33.36 N 88.39 W
West Point, Nebr., U.S. 252 41.51 N 96.43 W
West Point, N.Y., U.S. 261 41.23 N 73.57 W
West Point, Ohio, U.S. 266 40.43 N 80.42 W
West Point, Va., U.S. 262 37.32 N 76.48 W
West Point ∧ 236 64.57 N 144.40 W
West Point ≻, P.E.I., Can. 240 46.37 N 64.25 W
West Point ≻, Jam. 285q 18.15 N 78.22 W
Westport, Newf., Can. 240 49.47 N 56.38 W
Westport, N.S., Can. 240 44.16 N 66.21 W
Westport, Ont., Can. 264 44.41 N 76.26 W
Westport, Eire 162 53.48 N 9.32 W
Westport, N.Z. 230 41.45 S 171.36 E
Westport, Conn., U.S. 261 41.09 N 73.22 W
Westport, Ind., U.S. 248 39.11 N 85.34 W
Westport, Mass., U.S. 261 41.37 N 71.04 W
Westport, Oreg., U.S. 270 46.10 N 123.23 W
Westport, Pa., U.S. 266 41.18 N 77.51 W
Westport, Wash., U.S. 270 46.53 N 124.06 W
West Portland 270 45.25 N 122.45 W
West Portland Park 270 45.21 N 122.37 W
Westport Point 261 41.31 N 71.05 W
West Portsmouth 242 38.46 N 83.02 W
Westpunt ≻ 285s 12.37 N 70.03 W
West Quoddy Head ≻ 240 44.49 N 66.57 W
Westray Firth ⋃ 162 59.15 N 3.00 W
West Redding 261 41.20 N 73.26 W
West Richfield 266 41.14 N 81.39 W
West Richland 256 46.18 N 119.20 W
West Road ≃ 238 53.19 N 122.52 W
West Rutland 242 43.36 N 73.03 W
West Sacramento 272 38.34 N 121.32 W
West Saint-Modeste 240 51.36 N 56.42 W
West Salem, Ill., U.S. 248 38.31 N 88.01 W
West Salem, Ohio, U.S. 266 40.58 N 82.06 W
West Salem, Wis., U.S. 244 43.54 N 91.05 W
West Sand Lake 261 42.39 N 73.37 W
West Scotia Basin ⊹[1] 148 57.00 S 53.00 W
West Seneca 264 42.50 N 78.45 W
West Siberian Plain → Zapadno-Sibirskaja Nizmennost' ≚ 186 60.00 N 75.00 E
West Simsbury 261 41.52 N 72.51 W
West Slope 270 45.31 N 122.46 W
West Spanish Peak ∧ 254 37.23 N 105.00 W
West Springfield 261 42.06 N 72.38 W
West Stewartstown 260 44.59 N 71.32 W
West Stockbridge 261 42.20 N 73.22 W
West Suffield 261 41.59 N 72.42 W
West Sunbury 266 41.00 N 79.54 W
West Swanzey 261 42.52 N 72.20 W
West Terre Haute 248 39.28 N 87.27 W
West Tiana 261 40.52 N 72.33 W
West Tisbury 261 41.23 N 70.41 W
West Townsend 261 42.41 N 71.44 W
West Union, Iowa, U.S. 244 42.57 N 91.49 W
West Union, Ohio, U.S. 242 38.48 N 83.32 W
West Union, W. Va., U.S. 242 39.18 N 80.47 W
West Unity 268 41.35 N 84.26 W
West University Place 250 29.43 N 95.26 W
West Upton 261 42.10 N 71.37 W
Westvale 264 43.02 N 76.13 W
West Valley 266 42.24 N 78.37 W
West Vancouver 238 49.22 N 123.12 W
West View, Ohio, U.S. 266 41.21 N 81.54 W
West View, Pa., U.S. 266 40.31 N 80.02 W
Westview Heights 261 41.33 N 73.05 W
West View Park 246 36.33 N 82.35 W
Westville, N.S., Can. 240 45.34 N 62.43 W
Westville, Ind., U.S. 268 41.33 N 86.54 W
Westville, N.H., U.S. 261 42.49 N 71.07 W
Westville, Okla., U.S. 248 35.59 N 94.34 W
Westville, Pa., U.S. 266 41.13 N 78.50 W
Westville Center 260 44.57 N 74.24 W
West Virginia □[3] 234 38.45 N 80.30 W
West-Vlaanderen □[4] 176 51.00 N 3.00 E
West Walker ≃ 258 38.53 N 119.10 W
West Wareham 261 41.47 N 70.46 W
West Warren 261 42.13 N 72.14 W
West Warwick 261 41.42 N 71.32 W
West Webster 264 43.12 N 77.30 W
Westwego 248 29.55 N 90.09 W
West Willington 261 41.53 N 72.18 W
West Winfield 266 40.48 N 79.42 W
Westwold 238 50.28 N 119.45 W
Westwood, Calif., U.S. 258 40.18 N 121.00 W
Westwood, Mass., U.S. 261 42.12 N 71.14 W
Westwood, Mich., U.S. 268 42.19 N 85.38 W
West Wyalong 226 33.55 S 147.13 E
West Yarmouth 261 41.39 N 70.15 W
West Yellowstone 256 44.30 N 111.05 W
West York 262 39.57 N 76.46 W
Wetar, Pulau I 198 7.48 S 126.18 E
Wetaskiwin 238 52.58 N 113.22 W
Wete 218 5.04 S 39.43 E
Wethersfield 261 41.43 N 72.40 W
Wetmore 252 39.38 N 95.49 W
Wet Mountains ⋀ 254 38.00 N 105.10 W
Wetter 178 51.23 N 7.23 E
Wetteren 176 51.00 N 3.53 E
Wettingen 180 47.28 N 8.19 E
Wettringen 178 52.12 N 7.19 E
Wetumka 250 35.14 N 96.15 W
Wetumpka 248 32.27 N 86.13 W
Wetzikon 180 47.19 N 8.47 E
Wetzlar 164 50.33 N 8.29 E
Wevelgem 176 50.48 N 3.10 E
Wevelinghoven 178 51.06 N 6.37 E
Wewahitchka 246 30.07 N 85.12 W
Wewak 198 3.35 S 143.40 E
Wewoka 250 35.09 N 96.30 W
Wexford, Eire 162 52.20 N 6.27 W
Wexford, Pa., U.S. 266 40.38 N 80.03 W
Wexford □[6] 162 52.20 N 6.40 W
Wexford Harbour C 162 52.20 N 6.55 W
Weyanoke 262 38.48 N 77.09 W
Weyauwega 244 44.19 N 88.56 W
Weybridge 174 51.23 N 0.28 W
Weyburn 252 49.41 N 103.52 W
Weyer Markt 164 47.52 N 14.41 E
Weyib ≃ 214 4.11 N 42.09 E
Weymouth, N.S., Can. 240 44.25 N 66.00 W
Weymouth, Eng., U.K. 174 50.36 N 2.28 W
Weymouth, Mass., U.S. 261 42.13 N 70.58 W
Weymouth, N.J., U.S. 262 39.31 N 74.47 W
Whakatane 230 37.58 S 177.00 E
Whakatane ≃ 230 37.57 S 177.01 E
Whaley Lake 261 41.33 N 73.40 W
Whaleysville 262 38.24 N 75.18 W
Whaleyville 262 36.37 N 76.41 W
Whalom 261 42.34 N 71.45 W
Whalsay I 162 60.22 N 0.59 W
Whangaehu ≃ 230 40.03 S 175.06 E
Whangape, Lake ◎ 230 37.28 S 175.03 E
Whangarei 230 35.43 S 174.20 E
Whangaruru Harbour C 230 35.24 S 174.23 E
Wharton, Ohio, U.S. 266 40.52 N 83.21 W
Wharton, Tex., U.S. 250 29.19 N 96.06 W
Wharton, W. Va., U.S. 242 37.55 N 81.40 W
Wharton Lake ◎ 232 64.00 N 99.55 W
What Cheer 244 41.24 N 92.21 W
Whatcom □[6] 270 48.48 N 121.59 W
Whately 261 42.26 N 72.38 W
Whatley 248 31.39 N 87.42 W
Whatshan Lake ◎ 238 50.00 N 118.03 W
Wheao ≃ 230 38.33 S 176.39 E
Wheatfield 268 41.12 N 87.03 W
Wheatland, Calif., U.S. 272 39.01 N 121.25 W
Wheatland, Iowa, U.S. 244 41.50 N 90.51 W
Wheatland, Pa., U.S. 266 41.12 N 80.28 W
Wheatland, Wyo., U.S. 254 42.03 N 104.57 W
Wheatland Hills 262 40.02 N 76.21 W
Wheatland Reservoir ◎[1] 254 41.52 N 105.36 W
Wheatley 266 42.06 N 82.27 W
Wheaton, Ill., U.S. 268 41.52 N 88.06 W
Wheaton, Md., U.S. 242 39.03 N 77.03 W
Wheaton, Minn., U.S. 252 45.48 N 96.30 W
Wheat Ridge 254 39.46 N 105.07 W
Wheelbarrow Peak ∧ 258 37.27 N 116.05 W
Wheeler, Ind., U.S. 268 41.31 N 87.11 W
Wheeler, Tex., U.S. 250 35.27 N 100.16 W
Wheeler ≃ 232 57.05 N 67.10 W
Wheeler Lake ◎[1] 248 34.40 N 87.05 W
Wheeler Peak ∧, Calif., U.S. 258 38.25 N 119.17 W
Wheeler Peak ∧, Nev., U.S. 258 38.59 N 114.19 W
Wheeler Peak ∧, N. Mex., U.S. 254 36.34 N 105.25 W
Wheeler Ridge 274 35.06 N 119.01 W
Wheeling, Ill., U.S. 268 42.09 N 87.55 W
Wheeling, W. Va., U.S. 266 40.05 N 80.42 W
Wheelwright, Arg. 294 33.46 S 61.14 W
Wheelwright, Ky., U.S. 246 37.20 N 82.43 W
Whelan, Mount ∧[2] 228 23.25 S 138.54 E
Whidbey Island I 256 48.15 N 122.40 W
Whigham 246 30.53 N 84.19 W
Whigville 261 41.44 N 72.57 W
Whiskey Peak ∧ 254 42.18 N 107.35 W
Whitacres 261 42.02 N 72.34 W
Whitakers 246 36.06 N 77.43 W
Whitbourne 240 47.25 N 53.32 W
Whitby, Ont., Can. 264 43.52 N 78.56 W
Whitby, Eng., U.K. 162 54.29 N 0.37 W
Whitchurch, Eng., U.K. 174 52.58 N 2.41 W
Whitchurch, Wales, U.K. 174 51.33 N 3.14 W
Whitcombe, Mount ∧ 230 43.13 S 170.55 E
White, Ga., U.S. 246 34.17 N 84.45 W
White, S. Dak., U.S. 252 44.26 N 96.39 W
White □[6] 268 40.45 N 86.46 W
White ≃, B.C., Can. 238 50.23 N 115.35 W
White ≃, Ont., Can. 244 48.33 N 86.16 W
White ≃, N.A. 236 63.11 N 139.36 W
White ≃, U.S. 248 33.53 N 91.03 W
White ≃, U.S. 252 43.45 N 99.30 W
White ≃, U.S. 254 40.04 N 109.41 W
White ≃, Ariz., U.S. 254 33.44 N 110.13 W
White ≃, Ind., U.S. 248 38.25 N 87.44 W
White ≃, Nev., U.S. 258 37.18 N 115.08 W
White ≃, Oreg., U.S. 256 45.14 N 121.04 W
White ≃, Tex., U.S. 250 33.14 N 100.56 W
White ≃, Vt., U.S. 242 43.37 N 72.20 W
White ≃, Wash., U.S. 256 47.12 N 122.15 W
White ≃, Wis., U.S. 244 46.36 N 90.42 W
White Bay C 240 50.00 N 56.30 W
White Bear Indian Reserve ↢[4] 252 49.15 N 102.15 W
White Bear Lake 244 45.05 N 93.01 W
White Bluff 248 36.06 N 87.13 W
White Butte ∧ 252 46.23 N 103.19 W
White Cap Mountain ∧ 242 45.35 N 69.13 W
White Castle 248 30.10 N 91.09 W
White Center 270 47.31 N 122.21 W
White City 252 38.48 N 96.44 W
White Cloud 244 43.33 N 85.46 W
Whitecoomb ∧ 230 45.36 S 169.05 E
Whitecourt 238 54.09 N 115.41 W
White Deer 250 35.26 N 101.10 W
White Earth ≃ 252 48.09 N 102.42 W
White Earth Indian Reservation ↢[4] 252 47.18 N 95.50 W
Whiteface 250 33.36 N 102.37 W
Whiteface ≃ 244 46.58 N 92.48 W
Whiteface, Mount ∧ 242 44.22 N 73.54 W
Whitefield, Maine, U.S. 242 44.10 N 69.38 W
Whitefield, N.H., U.S. 242 44.22 N 71.36 W
Whitefish 256 48.25 N 114.20 W
Whitefish ≃ 244 45.55 N 86.57 W
Whitefish Bay 268 43.07 N 87.55 W
Whitefish Bay C 244 46.40 N 84.50 W
Whitefish Lake ◎, Alta., Can. 238 54.22 N 111.55 W
Whitefish Lake ◎, N.W. Ter., Can. 232 62.41 N 106.48 W
Whitefish Lake ◎, Ont., Can. 244 48.03 N 84.29 W
Whitefish Lake ◎, Alaska, U.S. 236 61.21 N 160.00 W
Whitefish Lake ◎, Mont., U.S. 256 48.27 N 114.22 W
White Fish Lake Indian Reserve ↢[4] 238 54.39 N 111.51 W
Whitefish Point 244 46.45 N 84.59 W
Whitefish Point ≻ 244 46.45 N 85.00 W
Whitefish Range ⋀ 256 48.40 N 114.26 W
Whiteford 262 39.42 N 76.21 W
Whitegull, Lac ◎ 232 55.25 N 64.20 W
White Hall, Ala., U.S. 248 32.20 N 86.43 W
White Hall, Ga., U.S. 246 33.54 N 83.22 W
White Hall, Ill., U.S. 248 39.26 N 90.24 W
White Hall, Md., U.S. 262 39.37 N 76.38 W
Whitehall, Mich., U.S. 244 43.24 N 86.21 W
Whitehall, Mont., U.S. 256 45.52 N 112.06 W
Whitehall, N.Y., U.S. 242 43.33 N 73.25 W
Whitehall, Pa., U.S. 266 40.22 N 79.59 W
Whitehall, Wis., U.S. 244 44.22 N 91.19 W
Whitehaven, Eng., U.K. 162 54.33 N 3.35 W
White Haven, Pa., U.S. 242 41.04 N 75.47 W
Whitehaven, Tenn., U.S. 248 35.01 N 90.01 W
White Hills ⋀ 254 37.15 N 109.05 W
Whitehorse, Yukon, Can. 236 60.43 N 135.03 W
White Horse, N.J., U.S. 262 40.11 N 74.22 W
Whitehouse, N.J., U.S. 262 40.37 N 74.46 W
Whitehouse, Ohio, U.S. 268 41.31 N 83.48 W
Whitehouse, Tex., U.S. 250 32.13 N 95.14 W
White House Station 262 40.37 N 74.46 W
White Island I, N.W. Ter., Can. 232 65.50 N 84.50 W
White Island I, N.Z. 230 37.31 S 177.11 E
White Lake, S. Dak., U.S. 252 43.44 N 98.43 W
White Lake, Wis., U.S. 244 45.09 N 88.46 W
White Lake ◎, Ont., Can. 244 48.48 N 85.36 W
White Lake ◎, Ont., Can. 244 45.18 N 76.31 W
White Lake ◎, La., U.S. 248 29.45 N 92.30 W
Whitelaw 238 56.07 N 118.04 W
White Mountain 236 64.40 N 162.12 W
White Mountain Peak ∧ 258 37.38 N 118.15 W
White Mountains ⋀, U.S. 258 37.30 N 118.15 W
White Mountains ⋀, Alaska, U.S. 236 65.30 N 147.00 W
White Mountains ⋀, Ariz., U.S. 254 33.45 N 109.40 W
White Mountains ⋀, N.H., U.S. 242 44.10 N 71.35 W
Whitemouth 252 49.57 N 95.59 W
Whitemouth ≃ 252 50.03 N 96.01 W
Whitemouth Lake ◎ 252 49.14 N 95.40 W
White Nossob ≃ 224 23.05 S 18.45 E
White Oak 248 32.32 N 94.52 W
White Oak ≃ 246 34.40 N 77.07 W
White Oak Lake ◎[1] 248 33.40 N 93.10 W
White Pass)(236 59.38 N 135.05 W
White Pigeon 268 41.48 N 85.38 W
White Pine, Mich., U.S. 244 46.44 N 89.35 W
Whitepine, Mont., U.S. 238 47.45 N 115.29 W
White Pine, Tenn., U.S. 246 36.07 N 83.17 W
White Pines 272 38.18 N 120.21 W
White Plains, N.C., U.S. 246 36.27 N 80.38 W
White Plains, N.Y., U.S. 261 41.02 N 73.46 W
White River, Ont., Can. 244 48.35 N 85.15 W
Whiteriver, Ariz., U.S. 254 33.50 N 109.58 W
White River, S. Dak., U.S. 252 43.34 N 100.45 W
White River Junction 242 43.39 N 72.19 W
White Rock 238 49.02 N 122.49 W
White Rocks ∧ 246 36.40 N 83.27 W
Whiterocks ≃ 254 40.26 N 109.55 W
Whitesail Lake ◎ 238 53.30 N 127.00 W
White Salmon 270 45.44 N 121.29 W
White Sands Beach 261 41.18 N 72.09 W
White Sands Missile Range ■ 254 32.23 N 106.28 W
White Sands National Monument ♠ 254 32.46 N 106.20 W
Whitesboro, N.J., U.S. 262 39.03 N 74.51 W
Whitesboro, N.Y., U.S. 264 43.07 N 75.18 W
Whitesboro, Tex., U.S. 250 33.39 N 96.54 W
Whitesburg 246 37.07 N 82.49 W
White Sea → Beloje More ▿[2] 160 66.00 N 40.00 E
White Settlement 250 32.45 N 97.27 W
Whites Landing 266 41.25 N 82.54 W
White Springs 246 30.20 N 82.45 W
White Stone 262 37.39 N 76.23 W
White Sulphur Springs, Mont., U.S. 256 46.33 N 110.54 W
White Sulphur Springs, W. Va., U.S. 246 37.48 N 80.18 W
Whitesville, Ky., U.S. 248 37.41 N 86.52 W
Whitesville, N.Y., U.S. 266 42.02 N 77.46 W
Whitesville, W. Va., U.S. 242 37.59 N 81.32 W
White Swan 270 46.23 N 120.44 W
Whitetail 252 48.54 N 105.10 W
White Umfolozi ≃ 224 28.22 S 31.58 E
Whitevale 264 43.53 N 79.09 W
White Valley 266 40.25 N 79.36 W
Whiteville, N.C., U.S. 246 34.20 N 78.42 W
Whiteville, Tenn., U.S. 248 35.20 N 89.11 W
White Volta (Volta Blanche) ≃ 222 9.10 N 1.15 W
Whitewater, Kans., U.S. 252 37.58 N 97.09 W
Whitewater, Mont., U.S. 256 48.46 N 107.38 W
Whitewater, Wis., U.S. 268 42.50 N 88.44 W
Whitewater ≃, U.S. 248 39.10 N 84.47 W
Whitewater ≃, Calif., U.S. 258 33.30 N 116.03 W
Whitewater ≃, Mo., U.S. 248 37.01 N 89.43 W
Whitewater Baldy ∧ 254 33.20 N 108.39 W
Whitewater Bay C 246 25.16 N 81.00 W
Whitewater Lake ◎ 252 49.15 N 100.20 W
Whitewood, Lake ◎ 252 44.20 N 97.18 W
Whitewright 250 33.31 N 96.24 W
Whitfield 248 32.22 N 88.06 W
Whithorn, Jam. 285q 18.15 N 78.02 W
Whithorn, Scot., U.K. 162 54.44 N 4.25 W
Whiting, Ind., U.S. 268 41.40 N 87.29 W
Whiting, Iowa, U.S. 252 42.08 N 96.09 W
Whiting, Kans., U.S. 252 39.35 N 95.37 W
Whiting, N.J., U.S. 262 39.57 N 74.23 W
Whiting, Wis., U.S. 244 44.29 N 89.33 W
Whitingham 261 42.47 N 72.53 W
Whitinsville 261 42.07 N 71.40 W
Whitley □[6] 268 41.10 N 85.29 W
Whitley Bay 162 55.03 N 1.25 W
Whitley City 246 36.43 N 84.28 W
Whitman 261 42.05 N 70.56 W
Whitman Mission National Historic Site ⊥ 256 46.00 N 118.17 W
Whitman Square 262 39.45 N 75.03 W
Whitmire 246 34.30 N 81.37 W
Whitmore Lake 268 42.25 N 83.46 W
Whitmore Mountains ⋀ 148 82.35 S 104.30 W
Whitmore Village 275c 21.31 N 158.01 W
Whitnel 246 35.53 N 81.31 W
Whitner Heights 272 36.37 N 119.32 W
Whitney, Ont., Can. 264 45.30 N 78.14 W
Whitney, Pa., U.S. 266 40.15 N 79.25 W
Whitney, Tex., U.S. 250 31.57 N 97.19 W
Whitney, Lake ◎[1] 250 31.55 N 97.23 W
Whitney, Mount ∧ 258 36.35 N 118.18 W
Whitney Point 242 42.20 N 75.58 W
Whitstable 174 51.22 N 1.02 E
Whitsunday Island I 228 20.17 S 148.59 E
Whittemore, Iowa, U.S. 252 43.04 N 94.25 W
Whittemore, Mich., U.S. 244 44.14 N 83.48 W
Whittier, Alaska, U.S. 236 60.46 N 148.41 W
Whittier, Calif., U.S. 274 33.59 N 118.02 W
Whittier, N.C., U.S. 246 35.26 N 83.22 W
Whittle, Cap ≻ 240 50.10 N 60.05 W
Whittlesea 228 37.31 S 145.07 E
Whittlesey 174 52.34 N 0.08 W
Whittlesey, Mount ∧[2] 244 46.18 N 90.37 W
Whitwell 248 35.12 N 85.31 W
Wholdaia Lake ◎ 232 60.43 N 104.10 W
Whonock 270 49.11 N 122.28 W
Whyalla 228 33.02 S 137.35 E
Whycocomagh 240 45.59 N 61.07 W
Whymper, Mount ∧ 238 48.57 N 124.10 W
Wiarton 264 44.45 N 81.09 W
Wiau Lake ◎ 238 55.23 N 111.18 W
Wiązów (Wansen) 164 50.49 N 17.11 E
Wibaux 252 46.59 N 104.11 W
Wiblingen ↢[8] 180 48.21 N 9.58 E
Wichita 252 37.41 N 97.20 W
Wichita Falls 250 33.54 N 98.30 W
Wichita Mountain ∧ 250 34.52 N 99.17 W
Wichita Mountains ⋀ 250 34.45 N 98.40 W
Wick 162 58.26 N 3.06 W
Wickede 178 51.29 N 7.52 E
Wickenburg 254 33.58 N 112.44 W
Wickett 250 31.34 N 102.59 W
Wickford 174 51.38 N 0.31 E
Wickham 260 45.46 N 72.30 W
Wickham, Cape ≻ 228 39.36 S 143.57 E
Wickiup Reservoir ◎[1] 256 43.40 N 121.43 W
Wickliffe, Ky., U.S. 248 36.58 N 89.05 W
Wickliffe, Ohio, U.S. 266 41.07 N 80.44 W
Wickliffe, Ohio, U.S. 266 41.36 N 81.28 W
Wicklow 162 52.59 N 6.03 W
Wicklow □[6] 162 53.00 N 6.30 W
Wicklow Head ≻ 162 52.58 N 6.00 W
Wicklow Mountains ⋀ 162 53.02 N 6.24 W
Wickrath 178 51.07 N 6.24 E
Wicksteed Lake ◎ 244 46.46 N 79.40 W
Wicomico 262 37.17 N 76.31 W
Wicomico □[6] 262 38.22 N 75.36 W
Wicomico Church 262 37.49 N 76.23 W
Wiconisco 262 40.34 N 76.41 W
Widawa ≃ 164 51.13 N 16.55 E
Wide Bay C 236 57.20 N 156.25 W
Widen 242 38.28 N 80.52 W
Wide Ruin Wash V 254 35.13 N 109.52 W
Widnes 162 53.22 N 2.44 W
Więcbork 164 53.22 N 17.30 E
Wieck 164 54.06 N 13.26 E
Wiedenbrück 178 51.50 N 8.18 E
Wiefelstede 178 53.15 N 8.07 E
Wiehl 164 50.57 N 7.31 E
Wieleń 164 52.54 N 16.10 E
Wielichowo 164 52.08 N 16.21 E
Wieliczka 164 49.59 N 20.04 E
Wielkopolska ↢[1] 164 52.10 N 17.15 E
Wieluń 164 51.14 N 18.34 E
Wien (Vienna) 164 48.13 N 16.20 E
Wiener Neustadt 164 47.49 N 16.15 E
Wiener Wald ⋀ 164 48.10 N 16.00 E
Wieprz ≃ 164 51.34 N 21.49 E
Wieprza ≃ 164 54.26 N 16.22 E
Wieprz-Krzna, Kanał ≊ 164 51.56 N 22.56 E
Wierden 178 52.22 N 6.35 E
Wiergate 248 31.00 N 93.42 W
Wieruszów 164 51.18 N 18.08 E
Wierzyca ≃ 164 53.51 N 18.50 E
Wiesbaden 164 50.05 N 8.14 E
Wiescherhöfen 178 51.39 N 7.46 E
Wieselburg 164 48.08 N 15.09 E
Wiesloch 166 49.17 N 8.42 E
Wiesmoor 178 53.25 N 7.43 E
Wietze 164 52.39 N 9.50 E
Wigan 162 53.33 N 2.38 W
Wiggins, Colo., U.S. 252 40.14 N 104.04 W
Wiggins, Miss., U.S. 248 30.51 N 89.08 W
Wight, Isle of I 162 50.40 N 1.20 W
Wigston Magna 174 52.36 N 1.05 W
Wigtown 162 54.52 N 4.26 W
Wigtown □[6] 162 54.52 N 4.26 W
Wigtown Bay C 162 54.46 N 4.15 W
Wijchen 178 51.48 N 5.43 E
Wil 180 47.27 N 9.03 E
Wilber 252 40.29 N 96.58 W
Wilberforce Falls ⌊ 232 67.07 N 108.47 W
Wilbraham 261 42.07 N 72.26 W
Wilbur 256 47.46 N 118.42 W
Wilburton 250 34.55 N 95.19 W
Wilcannia 228 31.34 S 143.23 E
Wilcox, Nebr., U.S. 252 40.22 N 99.10 W
Wilcox, Pa., U.S. 266 41.35 N 78.41 W
Wilder 256 43.40 N 116.55 W
Wilderness of Judæa (Midbar Yehuda) ↢[2] 210 31.30 N 35.18 E
Wildersville 248 35.48 N 88.22 W
Wildervank 178 53.04 N 6.51 E
Wildeshausen 178 52.54 N 8.26 E
Wildfield 264 43.49 N 79.44 W
Wildhay ≃ 238 54.02 N 117.20 W
Wild Horse Lake ◎ 256 48.58 N 110.00 W
Wildon 164 46.53 N 15.31 E
Wild Rice ≃, Minn., U.S. 252 47.20 N 96.50 W
Wild Rice ≃, N. Dak., U.S. 252 46.45 N 96.47 W
Wildrose, N. Dak., U.S. 252 48.38 N 103.11 W
Wild Rose, Wis., U.S. 244 44.11 N 89.15 W
Wildspitze ∧ 164 46.53 N 10.52 E
Wildwood, Alta., Can. 238 53.37 N 115.14 W
Wildwood, Ill., U.S. 268 42.21 N 88.00 W
Wildwood, N.J., U.S. 262 38.59 N 74.49 W
Wildwood, Pa., U.S. 266 40.36 N 79.58 W
Wildwood Crest 262 38.58 N 74.50 W
Wiley 270 46.33 N 120.39 W
Wilge ≃ 224 27.03 S 28.20 E
Wilhelmina Gebergte ⋀ 290 3.45 N 56.30 W
Wilhelmina Peak → Trikora, Puntjak ∧ 198 4.15 S 138.45 E
Wilhelm-Pieck-Stadt Guben 164 51.57 N 14.43 E
Wilhelmsburg ↢[8] 178 53.30 N 10.00 E
Wilhelmshaven 178 53.31 N 8.08 E
Wilkerson Pass)(254 39.02 N 105.32 W
Wilkes-Barre 242 41.14 N 75.53 W
Wilkesboro 246 36.09 N 81.09 W
Wilkes Lake ◎ 244 46.01 N 79.00 W
Wilkes Land ↢[1] 148 69.00 S 120.00 E
Wilkeson 270 47.06 N 122.03 W
Wilkie 232 52.25 N 108.43 W
Wilkinsburg 266 40.27 N 79.53 W
Will □[6] 268 41.32 N 88.05 W
Will, Mount ∧ 236 57.31 N 128.46 W
Willacoochee 246 31.20 N 83.03 W
Willacoochee ≃ 246 31.21 N 83.06 W
Willamette ≃ 256 45.39 N 122.46 W
Willamina 270 45.05 N 123.29 W
Willapa 270 46.40 N 123.40 W
Willapa Hills ⋀[2] 256 46.35 N 123.25 W
Willard, N. Mex., U.S. 254 34.36 N 106.02 W
Willard, N.Y., U.S. 264 42.41 N 76.52 W
Willard, Ohio, U.S. 266 41.03 N 82.44 W
Willard, Utah, U.S. 254 41.25 N 112.02 W
Willard, Wash., U.S. 270 45.48 N 121.38 W
Willcox 254 32.15 N 109.50 W
Willcox Playa ◎ 254 32.08 N 109.51 W
Willebroek 176 51.04 N 4.22 E
Willem Pretorius Game Reserve ↢[4] 224 28.16 S 27.13 E
Willemstad 285s 12.06 N 68.56 W
Willenhall 174 52.36 N 2.02 W
William, Mount ∧ 228 37.17 S 142.36 E
Williams, Ariz., U.S. 254 35.15 N 112.11 W
Williams, Calif., U.S. 272 39.09 N 122.09 W
Williams, Iowa, U.S. 244 42.29 N 93.33 W
Williams, Minn., U.S. 252 48.45 N 94.54 W
Williams □[6] 268 41.35 N 84.33 W
Williams ≃ 228 20.04 S 141.08 E
Williams Bay 268 42.35 N 88.33 W
Williamsburg, Ont., Can. 264 44.58 N 75.15 W
Williamsburg, Iowa, U.S. 244 41.40 N 92.01 W
Williamsburg, Ky., U.S. 246 36.44 N 84.10 W
Williamsburg, Mass., U.S. 261 42.23 N 72.44 W
Williamsburg, Pa., U.S. 266 40.28 N 78.12 W
Williamsburg, Va., U.S. 262 37.16 N 79.43 W
Williams Center 268 41.26 N 84.36 W
Williamsfield, Jam. 285q 17.56 N 77.46 W
Williamsfield, Ohio, U.S. 266 41.32 N 80.32 W
Williams Lake 238 52.08 N 122.09 W
Williams Lake Indian Reserve ↢[4] 238 52.07 N 122.00 W
Williams Mountain ∧ 248 34.15 N 94.33 W
Williamson, N.Y., U.S. 264 43.13 N 77.11 W
Williamson, W. Va., U.S. 246 37.41 N 82.17 W
Williamson ≃ 256 42.28 N 121.57 W
Williamsport, Newf., Can. 240 50.32 N 56.19 W
Williamsport, Ind., U.S. 268 40.17 N 87.17 W
Williamsport, Ohio, U.S. 266 39.35 N 83.07 W
Williamsport, Pa., U.S. 242 41.14 N 77.00 W
Williamston, Mich., U.S. 268 42.41 N 84.17 W
Williamston, S.C., U.S. 246 34.37 N 82.29 W
Williamstown, Ont., Can. 260 45.08 N 74.35 W
Williamstown, Ky., U.S. 242 38.38 N 84.34 W
Williamstown, Mass., U.S. 261 42.43 N 73.12 W
Williamstown, N.J., U.S. 262 39.41 N 74.60 W
Williamstown, Pa., U.S. 262 40.35 N 76.37 W
Williamstown, Vt., U.S. 242 44.07 N 72.33 W
Williamstown, W. Va., U.S. 242 39.24 N 81.27 W
Williamsville, Ill., U.S. 248 39.57 N 89.33 W
Williamsville, Mo., U.S. 248 36.58 N 90.33 W
Williamsville, N.Y., U.S. 264 42.59 N 78.43 W
Willich 178 51.16 N 6.33 E
Willikies 284c 17.05 N 61.42 W
Willimantic 261 41.43 N 72.13 W
Willingboro 262 40.03 N 74.53 W
Willingdon 238 53.50 N 112.08 W
Willis 250 30.25 N 95.29 W
Willis ≃ 246 37.41 N 78.07 W
Willis Island I 240 48.48 N 53.42 W
Williston, Fla., U.S. 246 29.23 N 82.27 W
Williston, N. Dak., U.S. 252 48.09 N 103.37 W
Williston, Ohio, U.S. 266 41.36 N 83.20 W
Williston, S.C., U.S. 246 33.24 N 81.25 W
Williston Basin ≚[1] 252 48.15 N 105.00 W
Williston Lake ◎[1] 238 56.00 N 124.00 W
Willisville 248 37.59 N 89.35 W
Willis Wharf 262 37.31 N 75.48 W
Willits 258 39.25 N 123.21 W
Willmar 252 45.07 N 95.03 W
Willoughby 266 41.38 N 81.25 W
Willoughby, Cape ≻ 228 35.51 S 138.07 E
Willoughby Hills 266 41.35 N 81.27 W
Willow, Alaska, U.S. 236 61.45 N 150.03 W
Willow, Mich., U.S. 266 42.07 N 83.24 W
Willow ≃, Alta., Can. 238 55.58 N 113.55 W
Willow ≃, B.C., Can. 238 54.03 N 122.21 W
Willow ≃, Minn., U.S. 244 46.40 N 93.35 W
Willow ≃, Wis., U.S. 244 44.59 N 92.46 W
Willow Bunch 252 49.24 N 105.37 W
Willow City 252 48.36 N 100.18 W
Willow Creek 256 45.49 N 111.39 W
Willow Gardens 268 42.13 N 83.30 W
Willow Grove 262 40.08 N 75.06 W
Willow Hill 266 40.06 N 77.48 W
Willowick 266 41.38 N 81.28 W
Willow Lake 252 44.38 N 97.38 W
Willow Lake ◎ 232 62.11 N 119.10 W
Willowlake ≃ 232 62.52 N 123.08 W
Willowmore 218 33.17 S 23.29 E
Willow River 238 54.04 N 122.28 W
Willow Run 268 42.16 N 83.34 W
Willows 272 39.31 N 122.12 W
Willow Springs, Calif., U.S. 274 34.53 N 118.18 W
Willow Springs, Ill., U.S. 268 41.44 N 87.52 W
Willow Springs, Mo., U.S. 248 36.59 N 91.58 W
Willow Street 262 39.59 N 76.17 W
Willshire 268 40.45 N 84.48 W
Wills Point 250 32.43 N 96.01 W
Wilmar 248 33.38 N 91.56 W
Wilmer, Ala., U.S. 248 30.44 N 88.28 W
Wilmer, Tex., U.S. 250 32.35 N 96.41 W
Wilmette 268 42.04 N 87.43 W
Wilmington, Del., U.S. 262 39.44 N 75.33 W
Wilmington, Ill., U.S. 268 41.18 N 88.09 W
Wilmington, Mass., U.S. 261 42.33 N 71.10 W
Wilmington, N.C., U.S. 246 34.13 N 77.55 W
Wilmington, Ohio, U.S. 242 39.27 N 83.50 W
Wilmington, Vt., U.S. 242 42.52 N 72.52 W
Wilmore, Ky., U.S. 246 37.52 N 84.40 W
Wilmore, Pa., U.S. 266 40.23 N 78.43 W
Wilmot, Ark., U.S. 248 33.04 N 91.34 W
Wilmot, Ohio, U.S. 266 40.39 N 81.38 W
Wilmot, S. Dak., U.S. 252 45.25 N 96.52 W
Wilmot, Wis., U.S. 268 42.31 N 88.11 W
Wilpen 266 40.17 N 79.12 W
Wilrijk 176 51.10 N 4.24 E
Wilsall 256 46.00 N 110.40 W
Wilseyville 272 38.23 N 120.31 W
Wilson, Ark., U.S. 248 35.34 N 90.03 W
Wilson, Conn., U.S. 261 41.48 N 72.38 W
Wilson, Kans., U.S. 252 38.50 N 98.29 W
Wilson, N.C., U.S. 246 35.44 N 77.55 W
Wilson, N.Y., U.S. 264 43.19 N 78.50 W
Wilson, Okla., U.S. 250 34.10 N 97.26 W
Wilson, Pa., U.S. 262 40.41 N 75.15 W
Wilson, Tex., U.S. 250 33.19 N 101.44 W
Wilson ≃, Austl. 228 27.38 S 141.24 E
Wilson ≃, Oreg., U.S. 256 45.28 N 123.53 W
Wilson, Cape ≻ 232 66.59 N 81.28 W
Wilson, Mount ∧, Calif., U.S. 258 34.13 N 118.04 W
Wilson, Mount ∧, Colo., U.S. 254 37.51 N 107.59 W
Wilson, Mount ∧, Nev., U.S. 258 38.15 N 114.23 W
Wilson, Mount ∧, Oreg., U.S. 256 45.04 N 121.39 W
Wilson Lake ◎[1] 248 34.49 N 87.30 W
Wilson Reservoir ◎[1] 252 38.57 N 98.40 W

Symbols in the index entries are identified on page 360.

Name	Page	Lat°′	Long°′
Wilsons Beach	240	44.56 N	66.56 W
Wilson's Creek National Battlefield Park ♠	248	37.06 N	93.27 W
Wilsons Promontory ≻	228	38.55 S	146.20 E
Wilsons Promontory National Park ♠	228	39.00 S	146.25 E
Wilsonville, Nebr., U.S.	252	40.07 N	100.07 W
Wilsonville, Oreg., U.S.	270	45.18 N	122.46 W
Wilton, Eng., U.K.	162	51.05 N	1.52 W
Wilton, Conn., U.S.	261	41.12 N	73.26 W
Wilton, Maine, U.S.	242	44.35 N	70.14 W
Wilton, N.H., U.S.	242	42.51 N	71.44 W
Wilton, N. Dak., U.S.	252	47.10 N	100.47 W
Wilton, Wis., U.S.	244	43.48 N	90.32 W
Wilton Junction	248	41.35 N	91.01 W
Wilton Manors	246	26.10 N	80.07 W
Wiltshire □[6]	174	51.15 N	1.50 W
Wiluna	226	26.36 S	120.13 E
Wimauma	246	27.43 N	82.18 W
Wimberley	250	30.00 N	98.06 W
Wimbledon	252	47.10 N	98.28 W
Winagami Lake ⊜	238	55.38 N	116.45 W
Winamac	268	41.03 N	86.36 W
Winburne	266	40.58 N	78.08 W
Winchendon	261	42.41 N	72.03 W
Winchester, Ont., Can.	264	45.06 N	75.21 W
Winchester, Eng., U.K.	174	51.04 N	1.19 W
Winchester, Calif., U.S.	274	33.42 N	117.05 W
Winchester, Idaho, U.S.	256	46.14 N	116.38 W
Winchester, Ill., U.S.	248	39.38 N	90.27 W
Winchester, Ind., U.S.	248	40.10 N	84.59 W
Winchester, Ky., U.S.	246	37.59 N	84.11 W
Winchester, N.H., U.S.	242	42.46 N	72.23 W
Winchester, Tenn., U.S.	248	35.10 N	86.01 W
Winchester, Va., U.S.	242	39.11 N	78.10 W
Wind ≃, Yukon, Can.	236	65.49 N	135.18 W
Wind ≃, Wyo., U.S.	254	43.08 N	108.12 W
Windber	266	40.14 N	78.50 W
Wind Cave National Park ♠	252	43.32 N	103.25 W
Winder	246	33.59 N	83.43 W
Windermere, B.C., Can.	238	50.30 N	115.58 W
Windermere, Eng., U.K.	162	54.23 N	2.54 W
Windermere Lake ⊜	244	47.56 N	83.47 W
Windfall, Alta., Can.	238	54.11 N	116.15 W
Windfall, Ind., U.S.	268	40.22 N	85.57 W
Windham, Conn., U.S.	261	41.42 N	72.10 W
Windham, Ohio, U.S.	266	41.14 N	81.03 W
Windham □[6], Conn., U.S.	261	41.55 N	71.55 W
Windham □[6], Vt., U.S.	261	42.50 N	72.43 W
Windhoek	224	22.34 S	17.06 E
Windhoek □[5]	224	22.30 S	17.00 E
Windisch	180	47.29 N	8.13 E
Windischgarsten	164	47.44 N	14.20 E
Wind Lake	268	42.50 N	88.09 W
Windom, Minn., U.S.	252	43.52 N	95.07 W
Windom, N.Y., U.S.	264	42.47 N	78.48 W
Windom Mountain ∧	254	37.37 N	107.35 W
Windorah	226	25.26 S	142.39 E
Window Rock	254	35.41 N	109.03 W
Wind Point	268	42.47 N	87.46 W
Wind River Indian Reservation ⤚[4]	254	43.26 N	109.00 W
Wind River Peak ∧	254	42.42 N	109.07 W
Wind River Range ⋀	254	43.05 N	109.25 W
Windsor, Austl.	228	33.37 S	150.49 E
Windsor, N.B., Can.	240	48.57 N	55.40 W
Windsor, N.S., Can.	240	44.59 N	64.08 W
Windsor, Ont., Can.	266	42.18 N	83.01 W
Windsor, Qué., Can.	260	45.34 N	72.00 W
Windsor, Eng., U.K.	174	51.29 N	0.38 W
Windsor, Colo., U.S.	254	40.29 N	104.54 W
Windsor, Conn., U.S.	261	41.51 N	72.39 W
Windsor, Ill., U.S.	248	39.26 N	88.36 W
Windsor, Mo., U.S.	248	38.32 N	93.31 W
Windsor, N.J., U.S.	262	40.15 N	74.35 W
Windsor, N.C., U.S.	246	35.59 N	76.57 W
Windsor, Ohio, U.S.	266	41.32 N	80.56 W
Windsor, Pa., U.S.	262	39.55 N	76.35 W
Windsor, Vt., U.S.	242	43.29 N	72.23 W
Windsor, Va., U.S.	262	36.48 N	76.45 W
Windsor Dam ⤚[6]	242	42.29 N	72.42 W
Windsor Heights, Iowa, U.S.	244	41.36 N	93.42 W
Windsor Heights, W. Va., U.S.	266	40.12 N	80.40 W
Windsor Locks	261	41.56 N	72.38 W
Windsorville	261	41.53 N	72.32 W
Windthorst	250	33.34 N	98.26 W
Windward Islands II	282	13.00 N	61.00 W
Windward Passage ⋓	282	20.00 N	73.50 W
Windy Peak ∧	256	48.56 N	119.58 W
Winefred Lake ⊜	238	55.30 N	110.35 W
Winesburg	266	40.37 N	81.42 W
Winfield, Alta., Can.	238	52.58 N	114.26 W
Winfield, Ala., U.S.	248	33.56 N	87.49 W
Winfield, Ill., U.S.	268	41.52 N	88.10 W
Winfield, Iowa, U.S.	244	41.07 N	91.26 W
Winfield, Kans., U.S.	252	37.15 N	96.59 W
Winfield, Mo., U.S.	248	39.00 N	90.44 W
Winfield, W. Va., U.S.	242	38.32 N	81.53 W
Wing	252	47.09 N	100.17 W
Wing ≃	252	46.29 N	94.58 W
Wingan National Park ♠	228	37.43 S	149.30 E
Wingate, Md., U.S.	262	38.18 N	76.06 W
Wingate, N.C., U.S.	246	34.59 N	80.27 W
Wingdale	261	41.39 N	73.34 W
Wingene	176	51.04 N	3.16 E
Wingham	264	43.53 N	81.19 W
Wingles	176	50.29 N	2.51 E
Winifred	256	47.04 N	109.23 W
Winifreda	294	36.15 S	64.15 W
Winisk	232	55.15 N	85.12 W
Winisk ≃	232	55.17 N	85.05 W
Winisk Lake ⊜	232	52.55 N	87.22 W
Wink	250	31.45 N	103.09 W
Winkelman	254	32.59 N	110.46 W
Winkler	252	49.11 N	97.56 W
Winklern	164	46.52 N	12.52 E
Winlaw	238	49.37 N	117.34 W
Winlock	270	46.29 N	122.56 W
Winneba	222	5.25 N	0.36 W
Winnebago, Ill., U.S.	244	42.16 N	89.15 W
Winnebago, Minn., U.S.	244	43.46 N	94.10 W
Winnebago, Nebr., U.S.	252	42.14 N	96.28 W
Winnebago □[6]	268	42.17 N	89.06 W
Winnebago ≃	244	43.03 N	92.57 W
Winnebago, Lake ⊜	244	44.00 N	88.25 W
Winnebago Indian Reservation ⤚[4]	252	42.15 N	96.31 W
Winneconne	244	44.07 N	88.43 W
Winnemucca	258	40.58 N	117.44 W
Winner	252	43.22 N	99.51 W
Winnetka	268	42.07 N	87.44 W
Winnett	256	47.00 N	108.21 W
Winnfield	248	31.55 N	92.38 W
Winnibigoshish, Lake ⊜	244	47.27 N	94.12 W
Winnie	248	29.49 N	94.23 W
Winnipeg	252	49.53 N	97.09 W
Winnipeg ≃	232	50.38 N	96.19 W
Winnipeg, Lake ⊜	232	52.00 N	97.00 W
Winnipegosis, Lake ⊜	232	52.30 N	100.00 W
Winnipesaukee, Lake ⊜	242	43.35 N	71.20 W
Winnsboro, La., U.S.	248	32.10 N	91.43 W
Winnsboro, S.C., U.S.	246	34.22 N	81.05 W
Winnsboro, Tex., U.S.	250	32.58 N	95.17 W
Winnsboro Mills	246	34.22 N	81.06 W
Winona, Kans., U.S.	252	39.04 N	101.15 W
Winona, Mich., U.S.	244	46.52 N	88.55 W
Winona, Minn., U.S.	244	44.03 N	91.39 W
Winona, Miss., U.S.	248	33.29 N	89.44 W
Winona, Mo., U.S.	248	37.06 N	91.19 W
Winona, Ohio, U.S.	266	40.50 N	80.54 W
Winona Lake	268	41.14 N	85.49 W
Winooski	242	44.29 N	73.11 W
Winooski ≃	242	44.30 N	73.15 W
Winschoten	178	53.08 N	7.02 E
Winsen	178	53.22 N	10.12 E
Winside	252	42.11 N	97.10 W
Winslow, Ariz., U.S.	254	35.01 N	110.42 W
Winslow, Maine, U.S.	242	44.32 N	69.38 W
Winslow, Wash., U.S.	270	47.37 N	122.31 W
Winsted, Conn., U.S.	261	41.55 N	73.04 W
Winsted, Minn., U.S.	244	44.58 N	94.03 W
Winston, Fla., U.S.	246	28.02 N	82.01 W
Winston, Oreg., U.S.	256	45.07 N	123.25 W
Winston-Salem	246	36.06 N	80.15 W
Winter	244	45.49 N	91.01 W
Winterberge ⋀	224	32.28 S	26.15 E
Winter Garden	246	28.34 N	81.35 W
Winter Gardens	274	32.50 N	116.56 W
Winter Harbor	242	44.24 N	68.05 W
Winter Harbour	238	50.31 N	128.02 W
Winter Harbour C	232	74.46 N	110.46 W
Winterhaven, Calif., U.S.	258	32.44 N	114.38 W
Winter Haven, Fla., U.S.	246	28.01 N	81.44 W
Wintering ≃	252	48.12 N	100.34 W
Winter Island I	232	66.14 N	83.04 W
Winter Park	246	28.36 N	81.20 W
Winterport	242	44.38 N	68.51 W
Winters, Calif., U.S.	272	38.31 N	121.58 W
Winters, Tex., U.S.	250	31.57 N	99.58 W
Winterset, Iowa, U.S.	244	41.20 N	94.01 W
Winterset, Ohio, U.S.	266	40.06 N	81.25 W
Winterstown	262	39.50 N	76.37 W
Wintersville	266	40.23 N	80.42 W
Winterswijk	178	51.58 N	6.44 E
Winterthur	180	47.30 N	8.43 E
Winterton	240	47.57 N	53.20 W
Winterville, Miss., U.S.	248	33.30 N	91.10 W
Winterville, N.C., U.S.	246	35.32 N	77.24 W
Winthrop, Conn., U.S.	261	41.22 N	72.30 W
Winthrop, Iowa, U.S.	244	42.28 N	91.44 W
Winthrop, Maine, U.S.	242	44.18 N	69.59 W
Winthrop, Minn., U.S.	244	44.32 N	94.22 W
Winthrop, Wash., U.S.	238	48.29 N	120.11 W
Winthrop Harbor	268	42.29 N	87.49 W
Winton, Austl.	228	22.23 S	143.02 E
Winton, N.Z.	230	46.09 S	168.19 E
Winton, Calif., U.S.	272	37.23 N	120.37 W
Winton, N.C., U.S.	246	36.24 N	76.56 W
Winton, Wash., U.S.	270	47.44 N	120.44 W
Winz	178	51.23 N	7.09 E
Wipperfürth	178	51.07 N	7.23 E
Wirksworth	174	53.05 N	1.34 W
Wisbech	174	52.40 N	0.10 E
Wiscasset	242	44.00 N	69.40 W
Wisconsin □[3]	234	44.45 N	89.30 W
Wisconsin ≃	244	43.00 N	91.15 W
Wisconsin, Lake ⊜[1]	244	43.24 N	89.43 W
Wisconsin Dells	244	43.38 N	89.46 W
Wisconsin Rapids	244	44.23 N	89.49 W
Wiscoy	266	42.30 N	78.05 W
Wisdom	256	45.37 N	113.27 W
Wise	246	36.59 N	82.34 W
Wise ≃	256	45.48 N	112.57 W
Wiseman	236	67.25 N	150.06 W
Wishek	252	46.16 N	99.33 W
Wishram	270	45.40 N	120.58 W
Wisła	164	49.40 N	18.52 E
Wisła (Weichsel) ≃	164	54.22 N	18.55 E
Wisłok ≃	164	50.13 N	22.32 E
Wisłoka ≃	164	50.27 N	21.23 E
Wismar, D.D.R.	164	53.53 N	11.28 E
Wismar, Guy.	290	5.59 N	58.18 W
Wisner, La., U.S.	248	31.59 N	91.39 W
Wisner, Nebr., U.S.	252	41.59 N	96.55 W
Wissembourg	166	49.02 N	7.57 E
Wister	248	34.58 N	94.43 W
Wisznice	164	51.48 N	23.12 E
Witbank	224	25.56 S	29.07 E
Witch Hazel	270	45.30 N	122.46 W
Witham	174	51.48 N	0.38 E
Witherspoon, Mount ∧	236	61.23 N	147.12 W
Withlacoochee ≃, U.S.	246	30.24 N	83.10 W
Withlacoochee ≃, Fla., U.S.	246	29.00 N	82.45 W
Witkowo	164	52.27 N	17.47 E
Witless Bay	240	47.17 N	52.50 W
Witney	174	51.48 N	1.29 W
Witnica (Vietz)	164	52.40 N	14.55 E
Wittelsheim	180	47.49 N	7.15 E
Witten	178	51.26 N	7.20 E
Wittenberg, D.D.R.	164	51.52 N	12.39 E
Wittenberg, Wis., U.S.	244	44.49 N	89.10 W
Wittenberge	164	53.00 N	11.44 E
Wittenburg	164	53.31 N	11.04 E
Wittenoom	226	22.17 S	118.19 E
Wittingen	164	52.43 N	10.44 E
Wittlaer	178	51.19 N	6.44 E
Wittlage	164	52.19 N	8.22 E
Wittlich	164	49.59 N	6.53 E
Wittmund	178	53.34 N	7.47 E
Wittstock	164	53.10 N	12.29 E
Witwatersrand ⤚[1]	224	26.00 S	27.00 E
Witzenhausen	178	51.20 N	9.51 E
Wixom	268	42.31 N	83.32 W
Wiżajny	164	54.23 N	22.51 E
Wkra ≃	164	52.27 N	20.44 E
Władysławowo	164	54.49 N	18.25 E
Wleń (Lähn)	164	51.01 N	15.40 E
Włocławek	164	52.39 N	19.02 E
Włodawa	164	51.34 N	23.32 E
Włoszczowa	164	50.52 N	19.59 E
Woburn	261	42.31 N	71.12 W
Wodonga	228	36.07 S	146.54 E
Wodzisław Śląski	164	50.00 N	18.28 E
Woerden	178	52.05 N	4.54 E
Wohlen	180	47.21 N	8.17 E
Wojcieszów (Kauffung)	164	50.58 N	15.56 E
Wokam, Pulau I	198	5.37 S	134.30 E
Woking, Alta., Can.	238	55.35 N	118.46 W
Woking, Eng., U.K.	174	51.20 N	0.34 W
Wokingham	174	51.25 N	0.51 W
Wolbach	252	41.24 N	98.24 W
Wolbrom	164	50.24 N	19.46 E
Wolcott, Conn., U.S.	261	41.36 N	72.59 W
Wolcott, Ind., U.S.	268	40.46 N	87.03 W
Wolcott, N.Y., U.S.	264	43.13 N	76.49 W
Wolcottsburg	264	43.04 N	78.38 W
Wolcottsville	264	43.07 N	78.31 W
Wolcottville	268	41.32 N	85.22 W
Wołczyn (Konstadt)	164	51.01 N	18.03 E
Woleai I[1]	198	7.21 N	143.52 E
Wolf ≃, U.S.	248	35.09 N	90.04 W
Wolf ≃, Kans., U.S.	252	39.54 N	95.11 W
Wolf ≃, Miss., U.S.	248	30.21 N	89.18 W
Wolf ≃, Wis., U.S.	244	44.11 N	88.48 W
Wolf, Isla I	290a	1.23 N	91.49 W
Wolf, Volcán ∧[1]	290a	0.01 N	91.20 W
Wolfach	164	48.17 N	8.13 E
Wolf Bay	240	50.12 N	60.11 W
Wolf Creek, Mont., U.S.	256	47.00 N	112.04 W
Wolf Creek, Oreg., U.S.	256	42.42 N	123.24 W
Wolf Creek Pass)(	254	37.29 N	106.48 W
Wolfdale	266	40.12 N	80.17 W
Wolfe □[6]	260	45.45 N	71.30 W
Wolfeboro	242	43.35 N	71.12 W
Wolfe Island	264	44.12 N	76.26 W
Wolfe Island I	244	44.12 N	76.26 W
Wolfen	164	51.40 N	12.16 E
Wolfenbüttel	178	52.10 N	10.32 E
Wolfenden, Mount ∧	238	50.26 N	127.33 W
Wolfforth	250	33.30 N	102.01 W
Wolfhagen	178	51.19 N	9.10 E
Wolflake, Ind., U.S.	268	41.20 N	85.30 W
Wolf Lake, Mich., U.S.	268	43.14 N	86.10 W
Wolf Lake ⊜, Alta., Can.	238	54.42 N	110.59 W
Wolf Lake ⊜, Yukon, Can.	236	60.40 N	131.40 W
Wolf Mountain ∧	236	65.17 N	154.02 W
Wolf Point	256	48.05 N	105.39 W
Wolfratshausen	164	47.54 N	11.25 E
Wolf Rock I[2]	162	49.57 N	5.49 W
Wolf Run	266	40.30 N	80.54 W
Wolfsberg	164	46.51 N	14.51 E
Wolfsburg	164	52.25 N	10.47 E
Wolfville	240	45.05 N	64.22 W
Wolgast	164	54.03 N	13.46 E
Wolin	164	53.50 N	14.35 E
Wolin I	164	53.55 N	14.31 E
Woliński Park Narodowy ♠	164	53.55 N	14.30 E
Wollaston, Cape ≻	232	71.04 N	118.07 W
Wollaston, Islas II	288	55.45 S	67.40 W
Wollaston Lake ⊜	232	58.15 N	103.20 W
Wollaston Peninsula ≻[1]	232	70.00 N	115.00 W
Wollongong	228	34.25 S	150.54 E
Wołomin	164	52.21 N	21.14 E
Wołów (Wohlau)	164	51.21 N	16.39 E
Wolseley	232	50.25 N	103.19 W
Wolsey	252	44.25 N	98.28 W
Wolsztyn	164	52.08 N	16.06 E
Woluwe-Saint-Pierre	176	50.50 N	4.25 E
Wolvega	178	52.53 N	6.00 E
Wolverhampton	174	52.36 N	2.08 W
Wolverine	244	45.16 N	84.36 W
Wolverine Mountain ∧	236	65.20 N	149.51 W
Wolverton	174	52.04 N	0.50 W
Woman ≃	244	47.57 N	82.19 W
Womelsdorf	262	40.22 N	76.11 W
Wondai	226	26.19 S	151.52 E
Wondelgem	176	51.05 N	3.43 E
Wonder Lake	268	42.25 N	88.21 W
Wonewoc	244	43.39 N	90.14 W
Wŏnju	194	37.22 N	127.58 E
Wonotobo Fall ↳	290	4.22 N	57.55 W
Wŏnsan	194	39.09 N	127.25 E
Wonthaggi	228	38.36 S	145.35 E
Wood, Pa., U.S.	266	40.10 N	78.08 W
Wood, S. Dak., U.S.	252	43.30 N	100.29 W
Wood □[6]	266	41.22 N	83.39 W
Wood ≃, B.C., Can.	238	52.10 N	118.30 W
Wood ≃, Nebr., U.S.	252	41.02 N	98.05 W
Wood ≃, Wyo., U.S.	256	44.07 N	108.58 W
Wood, Mount ∧, Yukon, Can.	236	61.14 N	140.31 W
Wood, Mount ∧, Mont., U.S.	256	45.17 N	109.49 W
Woodacre	272	38.05 N	122.36 W
Woodall Mountain ∧[2]	248	34.45 N	88.11 W
Wood Bay C	236	69.45 N	129.00 W
Woodbind	262	39.22 N	77.04 W
Woodbine, Ga., U.S.	246	30.58 N	81.43 W
Woodbine, Iowa, U.S.	252	41.44 N	95.43 W
Woodbine, N.J., U.S.	262	39.14 N	74.49 W
Woodbridge, Ont., Can.	264	43.47 N	79.36 W
Woodbridge, Eng., U.K.	174	52.06 N	1.19 E
Woodbridge, Calif., U.S.	272	38.09 N	121.18 W
Woodbridge, Conn., U.S.	261	41.21 N	73.02 W
Woodbridge, N.J., U.S.	262	40.33 N	74.17 W
Woodbridge, Va., U.S.	262	38.39 N	77.15 W
Woodburn, Ind., U.S.	268	41.08 N	84.51 W
Woodburn, Oreg., U.S.	270	45.09 N	122.51 W
Woodbury, Conn., U.S.	261	41.33 N	73.13 W
Woodbury, Ga., U.S.	246	32.59 N	84.35 W
Woodbury, Mich., U.S.	268	42.46 N	85.05 W
Woodbury, N.J., U.S.	262	39.50 N	75.10 W
Woodbury, Pa., U.S.	266	40.14 N	78.22 W
Woodbury, Tenn., U.S.	248	35.50 N	86.04 W
Woodchopper	236	65.03 N	151.00 W
Woodcock	266	41.45 N	80.05 W
Woodcrest	274	33.52 N	117.21 W
Wooded Bluff ⤚[4]	228	29.22 S	153.22 E
Woodfibre	238	49.40 N	123.15 W
Woodford □[6]	268	40.43 N	89.16 W
Woodhaven	268	42.08 N	83.14 W
Woodhull	244	41.11 N	90.20 W
Woodinville	270	47.45 N	122.09 W
Woodirest	266	40.49 N	77.54 W
Wood Island	240	45.58 N	62.45 W
Woodlake, Calif., U.S.	258	36.25 N	119.06 W
Wood Lake, Nebr., U.S.	252	42.38 N	100.14 W
Woodland, Calif., U.S.	272	38.41 N	121.46 W
Woodland, Ill., U.S.	268	40.43 N	87.44 W
Woodland, Maine, U.S.	242	45.09 N	67.24 W
Woodland, Mich., U.S.	268	42.43 N	85.08 W
Woodland, Mich., U.S.	268	42.12 N	84.23 W
Woodland, Miss., U.S.	248	33.47 N	89.03 W
Woodland, Pa., U.S.	266	41.00 N	78.21 W
Woodland, Wash., U.S.	270	45.54 N	122.45 W
Woodland Acres	274	34.24 N	119.18 W
Woodland Beach	268	41.57 N	83.19 W
Woodland Heights	266	41.25 N	79.43 W
Woodland Park	254	38.59 N	105.03 W
Woodlark Island I	226	9.05 S	152.50 E
Woodlawn, Ill., U.S.	248	38.20 N	89.02 W
Woodlawn, Ky., U.S.	248	37.04 N	85.04 W
Woodlawn, Wash., U.S.	270	47.01 N	123.48 W
Woodlawn Beach	264	42.48 N	78.51 W
Woodlawn Orchards	268	42.15 N	84.22 W
Woodridge, Man., Can.	252	49.17 N	96.09 W
Woodridge, Ill., U.S.	268	41.46 N	88.04 W
Woodridge, Mount ∧	228	23.13 S	137.39 E
Wood River, Alaska, U.S.	236	59.04 N	158.26 W
Wood River, Ill., U.S.	248	38.52 N	90.05 W
Wood River, Nebr., U.S.	252	40.49 N	98.36 W
Wood River Lakes ⊜	236	59.30 N	158.45 W
Wood River Mountains ⋀	236	59.32 N	159.30 W
Woodroffe ≃	228	21.28 S	137.58 E
Woodruff, Ariz., U.S.	254	34.47 N	110.03 W
Woodruff, S.C., U.S.	246	34.45 N	82.02 W
Woodruff, Wis., U.S.	244	45.54 N	89.42 W
Woods, Lake ⊜	226	17.50 S	133.30 E
Woods, Lake of the ⊜	252	49.15 N	94.45 W
Woodsboro, Md., U.S.	262	39.32 N	77.19 W
Woodsboro, Tex., U.S.	250	28.14 N	97.20 W
Woodsfield	242	39.46 N	81.07 W
Woods Hole	261	41.31 N	70.40 W
Woodside, Calif., U.S.	272	37.26 N	122.15 W
Woodside, Del., U.S.	262	39.04 N	75.34 W
Woodson	250	33.01 N	99.03 W
Woods Tavern	262	40.30 N	74.39 W
Woodstock, N.B., Can.	240	46.09 N	67.34 W
Woodstock, Ont., Can.	264	43.08 N	80.45 W
Woodstock, Eng., U.K.	162	51.52 N	1.21 W
Woodstock, Ala., U.S.	248	33.13 N	87.09 W
Woodstock, Conn., U.S.	261	41.57 N	71.59 W
Woodstock, Ill., U.S.	268	42.19 N	88.27 W
Woodstock, N.Y., U.S.	242	42.02 N	74.07 W
Woodstock, Vt., U.S.	242	43.37 N	72.31 W
Woodstock, Va., U.S.	242	38.53 N	78.31 W
Woodstown	262	39.39 N	75.20 W
Woodsville	242	44.09 N	72.02 W
Wood Village	270	45.32 N	122.19 W
Woodville, Ont., Can.	264	44.24 N	78.59 W
Woodville, N.Z.	230	40.20 S	175.52 E
Woodville, Ala., U.S.	248	34.38 N	86.16 W
Woodville, Calif., U.S.	272	36.06 N	119.12 W
Woodville, Fla., U.S.	246	30.20 N	84.15 W
Woodville, Ga., U.S.	246	33.40 N	83.06 W
Woodville, Mass., U.S.	261	42.14 N	71.34 W
Woodville, Mich., U.S.	268	42.16 N	84.30 W
Woodville, Miss., U.S.	248	31.01 N	91.18 W
Woodville, Ohio, U.S.	266	41.27 N	83.22 W
Woodville, Tex., U.S.	248	30.46 N	94.25 W
Woodward, Iowa, U.S.	244	41.51 N	93.55 W
Woodward, Okla., U.S.	250	36.26 N	99.24 W
Woodway	270	47.47 N	122.23 W
Woodworth	266	40.59 N	80.40 W
Woody Island	236	57.47 N	152.22 W
Woody Point	240	49.29 N	57.56 W
Wooldridge	246	36.34 N	84.12 W
Woolford	262	38.30 N	76.11 W
Woolsey Peak ∧	254	33.10 N	112.53 W
Woomera	228	31.31 S	137.10 E
Woonsocket, R.I., U.S.	261	42.00 N	71.31 W
Woonsocket, S. Dak., U.S.	252	44.03 N	98.16 W
Wooramel	226	25.44 S	114.17 E
Wooster	266	40.48 N	81.56 W
Worb	180	46.56 N	7.34 E
Worcester, S. Afr.	224	33.39 S	19.27 E
Worcester, Eng., U.K.	174	52.11 N	2.13 W
Worcester, Mass., U.S.	261	42.16 N	71.48 W
Worcester □[6], Md., U.S.	262	38.11 N	75.24 W
Worcester □[6], Mass., U.S.	261	42.16 N	71.48 W
Worcestershire □[6]	174	52.15 N	2.10 W
Worden, Ill., U.S.	248	38.56 N	89.50 W
Worden, Mont., U.S.	256	45.58 N	108.10 W
Wörgl	164	47.29 N	12.04 E
Work Channel ⋓	238	54.30 N	130.15 W
Workington	162	54.39 N	3.35 W
Worksop	162	53.18 N	1.07 W
Worland	256	44.01 N	107.57 W
Wormerveer	178	52.28 N	4.46 E
Worms	164	49.38 N	8.22 E
Wormser Joch (Giogo di Santa Maria))(	180	46.34 N	10.25 E
Woronoco	261	42.10 N	72.50 W
Worth	268	41.41 N	87.48 W
Wortham	250	31.47 N	96.28 W
Wörther See ⊜	164	46.37 N	14.10 E
Worthing	174	50.48 N	0.23 W
Worthington, Ind., U.S.	248	39.07 N	86.59 W
Worthington, Minn., U.S.	252	43.37 N	95.36 W
Worthington, Ohio, U.S.	266	40.05 N	83.01 W
Worthington, Pa., U.S.	266	40.50 N	79.38 W
Worthington Peak ∧	258	37.55 N	115.37 W
Worthville	266	41.02 N	79.08 W
Worton	262	39.17 N	76.06 W
Wotton	260	45.44 N	71.48 W
Wowoni, Pulau I	198	4.08 S	123.06 E
Woy Woy	228	33.30 S	151.20 E
Woźniki	164	50.36 N	19.03 E
Wrangel Island → Vrangel'a, Ostrov I	186	71.00 N	179.30 W
Wrangell	236	56.28 N	132.23 W
Wrangell, Cape ≻	237a	52.50 N	172.26 E
Wrangell, Mount ∧	236	62.00 N	144.06 W
Wrangell Island I	236	56.15 N	132.10 W
Wrangell Mountains ⋀	236	62.00 N	143.00 W
Wrath, Cape ≻	162	58.37 N	5.01 W
Wray	252	40.05 N	102.13 W
Wreck Reefs ⁂[2]	228	22.13 S	155.17 E
Wren	268	40.48 N	84.46 W
Wrens	246	33.12 N	82.23 W
Wrentham, Alta., Can.	238	49.32 N	112.10 W
Wrentham, Mass., U.S.	261	42.04 N	71.20 W
Wrexham	174	53.03 N	3.00 W
Wrighstown	244	44.19 N	88.09 W
Wright, Mount ∧, Austl.	228	31.12 S	142.26 E
Wright, Mount ∧, Mont., U.S.	256	47.58 N	112.49 W
Wright Brothers National Memorial ⊥	246	35.55 N	75.50 W
Wright City, Mo., U.S.	248	38.50 N	91.01 W
Wright City, Okla., U.S.	248	34.03 N	95.00 W
Wright-Patterson Air Force Base ■	242	39.49 N	84.03 W
Wright Peak ∧	258	38.59 N	122.46 W
Wrightson, Mount ∧	254	31.42 N	110.50 W
Wrightstown, N.J., U.S.	262	40.02 N	74.37 W
Wrightstown, Pa., U.S.	262	40.17 N	74.58 W
Wrightsville, Ga., U.S.	246	32.44 N	82.43 W
Wrightsville, Pa., U.S.	266	40.02 N	76.32 W
Wrightwood	274	34.21 N	117.38 W
Wrigley	236	63.16 N	123.37 W
Wrocław (Breslau)	164	51.06 N	17.00 E
Wronki	164	52.43 N	16.23 E
Września	164	52.20 N	17.34 E
Wschowa	164	51.48 N	16.19 E
Wuchang → Wuhan	196	30.36 N	114.17 E
Wuchang ⤚[8]	196	44.54 N	127.08 E
Wuchin → Changzhou	196	31.47 N	119.57 E
Wuch'iu Hsü I	196	25.00 N	119.27 E
Wuchow → Wuzhou	200	23.30 N	111.27 E
Wuchuan	200	21.25 N	110.40 E
Wuding	200	25.32 N	102.23 E
Wudu	190	33.21 N	105.00 E
Wugang	190	26.40 N	110.31 E
Wugongshan ∧	196	27.21 N	113.50 E
Wuhan	196	30.36 N	114.17 E
Wuhe ≃	194	34.25 N	117.55 E
Wuhsi → Wuxi	196	31.35 N	120.18 E
Wuhsing → Huzhou	196	30.52 N	120.06 E
Wuhu	196	31.21 N	118.22 E
Wuhushui ≃	196	30.41 N	114.32 E
Wujiang ≃, Zhg.	196	28.57 N	116.39 E
Wujiang ≃, Zhg.	196	27.14 N	115.05 E
Wulanhaote	190	46.05 N	122.05 E
Wulanmuluhne ≃	206	34.15 N	93.11 E
Wuleidaowan C	194	36.55 N	122.00 E
Wülfrath	178	51.17 N	7.02 E
Wuliangshan ⋀	200	24.30 N	100.45 E
Wuliaru, Pulau I	198	7.27 S	131.04 E
Wulonghe ≃	194	36.35 N	120.56 E
Wulumuqi (Urumchi)	190	43.48 N	87.35 E
Wumangdao I	194	39.14 N	123.03 E
Wuming	200	23.10 N	108.18 E
Wunnummin Lake ⊜	232	52.55 N	89.10 W
Wunstorf	178	52.25 N	9.26 E
Wupatki National Monument ♠	254	35.24 N	111.14 W
Wuppertal	178	51.16 N	7.11 E
Wuqiangxi ≃	196	29.33 N	118.57 E
Wurno	222	13.17 N	5.24 E
Würzburg	164	49.48 N	9.56 E
Wurzen	164	51.22 N	12.44 E
Wushan	190	31.05 N	109.48 E
Wushenqi	190	38.58 N	109.01 E
Wushui ≃, Zhg.	196	24.48 N	113.35 E
Wushui ≃, Zhg.	200	27.03 N	109.53 E
Wusih → Wuxi	196	31.35 N	120.18 E
Wusong	196	31.23 N	121.29 E
Wusu	190	44.27 N	84.37 E
Wusulijiang (Ussuri) ≃	186	48.27 N	135.04 E
Wutai	190	38.44 N	113.17 E
Wutaishan ∧	194	39.04 N	113.35 E
Wutongqiao	190	29.26 N	103.51 E
Wutsin → Changzhou	196	31.47 N	119.57 E
Wuustwezel	176	51.23 N	4.36 E
Wuvulu I	198	1.45 S	142.50 E
Wuwei	196	31.18 N	117.54 E
Wuxi (Wuhsi)	196	31.35 N	120.18 E
Wuxi ≃	196	29.00 N	118.56 E
Wuyishan ∧	196	27.50 N	117.45 E
Wuyishan ⋀	196	27.52 N	117.40 E
Wuyou ≃	196	33.28 N	120.41 E
Wuyuan	190	41.06 N	108.29 E
Wuzhishan ∧	200	18.57 N	109.43 E
Wuzhong	190	37.57 N	106.10 E
Wuzhou (Wuchow)	200	23.30 N	111.27 E
Wyaconda	248	40.24 N	91.55 W
Wyaconda ≃	248	40.04 N	91.30 W
Wyalusing	242	41.40 N	76.16 W
Wyandot	266	40.44 N	83.08 W
Wyandot □[6]	266	40.50 N	83.17 W
Wyandotte	268	42.12 N	83.10 W
Wyandra	226	27.15 S	145.59 E
Wyangala Reservoir ⊜[1]	228	33.58 S	148.55 E
Wyano	266	40.12 N	79.42 W
Wyatt, Ind., U.S.	268	41.32 N	86.10 W
Wyatt, Mo., U.S.	248	36.55 N	89.13 W
Wyeville	244	44.01 N	90.23 W
Wyk	164	54.42 N	8.34 E
Wykoff	244	43.42 N	92.16 W
Wylie	250	33.01 N	96.32 W
Wymondham	174	52.34 N	1.07 E
Wymore	252	40.07 N	96.40 W
Wynantskill	261	42.42 N	73.39 W
Wynberg	224	34.02 S	18.28 E
Wyndham	226	15.28 S	128.06 E
Wyndham ≃	230	46.21 S	168.51 E
Wyndmere	252	46.16 N	97.08 W
Wynndel	238	49.11 N	116.33 W
Wynne	248	35.14 N	90.47 W
Wynnewood	250	34.39 N	97.10 W
Wynniatt Bay C	232	72.55 N	110.30 W
Wynona	250	36.33 N	96.20 W
Wynot	252	42.45 N	97.10 W
Wynyard, Austl.	228	40.59 S	145.41 E
Wynyard, Sask., Can.	232	51.47 N	104.10 W
Wyocena	244	43.30 N	89.19 W
Wyodak	252	44.18 N	105.24 W
Wyoming, Ont., Can.	244	42.57 N	82.07 W
Wyoming, Del., U.S.	262	39.12 N	75.34 W
Wyoming, Ill., U.S.	244	41.04 N	89.47 W
Wyoming, Iowa, U.S.	244	42.04 N	91.00 W
Wyoming, Mich., U.S.	268	42.54 N	85.42 W
Wyoming, N.Y., U.S.	264	42.50 N	78.05 W
Wyoming, R.I., U.S.	261	41.31 N	71.42 W
Wyoming □[6]	264	42.44 N	78.08 W
Wyoming □[3]	234	43.00 N	107.30 W
Wyoming Peak ∧	254	42.36 N	110.37 W
Wyoming Ranges ⋀	254	42.00 N	111.00 W
Wyomissing	262	40.20 N	75.58 W
Wyong	226	33.17 S	151.25 E
Wyperfeld National Park ♠	228	35.30 S	142.00 E
Wyrzysk	164	53.10 N	17.15 E
Wyśmierzyce	164	51.38 N	20.49 E
Wysoka	164	53.11 N	17.05 E
Wysokie Mazowieckie	164	52.56 N	22.32 E
Wyszków	164	52.36 N	21.28 E
Wyszogród	164	52.23 N	20.11 E
Wytheville	246	36.57 N	81.05 W
Wytopitlock	242	45.38 N	68.05 W
X			
Xalbal ≃	280	16.06 N	90.58 W
Xambrê ≃	296	24.02 S	53.59 W
Xanten	178	51.39 N	6.26 E
Xánthi	172	41.08 N	24.53 E
Xanxerê	294	26.53 S	52.23 W
Xapuri	292	10.39 S	68.31 W
Xapuri ≃	292	10.39 S	68.30 W
Xarrama, Rio do ≃	168	38.14 N	8.20 W
Xau, Lake ⊜	224	21.15 S	24.38 E
Xavantina	296	21.15 S	52.48 W
Xaxim	294	26.56 S	52.31 W
X-Can	278	20.50 N	87.43 W
Xenia, Ill., U.S.	248	38.38 N	88.38 W
Xenia, Ohio, U.S.	242	39.41 N	83.56 W
Xertigny	170	48.03 N	6.24 E
Xiahe	190	35.06 N	102.40 E
Xiamen (Amoy)	196	24.28 N	118.07 E
Xiamengang C	196	24.24 N	118.10 E
Xi'an (Sian)	190	34.15 N	108.52 E
Xiangcheng	196	33.53 N	113.29 E
Xiangfan	190	32.03 N	112.01 E
Xiangjiang ≃	196	29.00 N	112.56 E
Xiangkhoang	200	19.20 N	103.22 E
Xiangride	190	36.02 N	98.08 E
Xiangshangang C	196	29.38 N	121.48 E
Xiangshui ≃	196	25.35 N	115.49 E
Xiangtan	196	27.51 N	112.54 E
Xiangyun	200	25.30 N	100.30 E
Xianxialing ⋀	196	28.30 N	118.46 E
Xianyou	196	25.23 N	118.40 E
Xiaochangshandao I	194	39.12 N	122.41 E
Xiaochengshan I	194	37.27 N	122.39 E
Xiaoeguan I	196	28.51 N	121.50 E
Xiaogan	196	30.55 N	113.54 E
Xiaoguhe ≃	194	36.42 N	120.16 E
Xiaoheishan ∧	200	24.42 N	98.55 E
Xiaolan	196	22.41 N	113.14 E
Xiaomeiguan)(	196	25.17 N	114.17 E
Xiaoqinghe ≃	194	37.17 N	118.52 E
Xiaowenhe ≃	194	35.59 N	117.11 E
Xiaoxi ≃	196	28.11 N	120.14 E
Xiaoxing'anling-shanmai ⋀	190	50.00 N	126.25 E
Xiaoxingshan I	196	22.31 N	114.51 E
Xiaoyangkou ≃[1]	196	32.38 N	121.02 E
Xiapu	190	26.52 N	120.01 E
Xiashi	196	30.32 N	120.42 E
Xiazhi I	196	29.42 N	122.15 E
Xichang	190	27.58 N	102.13 E
Xicotencatl	278	23.00 N	98.56 W
Xié ≃	290	0.54 N	67.11 W
Xihe ≃	190	41.44 N	121.30 E
Xihua	196	33.47 N	114.31 E
Xijiang ≃	190	22.25 N	113.23 E
Xilinhaote	190	43.58 N	116.04 E
Xilókastron	172	38.05 N	22.38 E
Xin'anjiang ≃, Zhg.	196	29.12 N	119.27 E
Xin'anjiang ≃, Zhg.	196	29.33 N	118.58 E
Xinavane	218	25.02 S	32.47 E
Xincheng	190	39.15 N	115.59 E
Xinfengshui ≃	196	23.42 N	114.42 E
Xingan	190	25.37 N	110.31 E
Xinghe	190	40.48 N	113.58 E
Xinghua	196	32.57 N	119.50 E
Xinghuawan C	196	25.20 N	119.20 E
Xingningjiang ≃	196	24.00 N	115.54 E
Xingren	200	25.27 N	105.13 E
Xingtai	194	37.04 N	114.29 E
Xingu ≃	296	1.30 S	51.53 W
Xingyi	200	25.06 N	104.58 E
Xinhailian	194	34.39 N	119.16 E
Xinhe ≃	194	35.06 N	116.39 E
Xinhua	190	27.37 N	111.02 E
Xinhuanghekou ≃[1]	194	38.00 N	119.00 E
Xinhui	196	22.32 N	113.02 E
Xining	190	36.38 N	101.55 E
Xinjiang	190	35.40 N	111.11 E
Xinjiang ≃	196	28.38 N	116.39 E
Xinjiang Weiwuer Zizhiqu □[4]	190	40.00 N	85.00 E
Xinkaihe ≃	194	41.52 N	122.50 E
Xinmin	194	42.00 N	122.48 E
Xinning	200	26.19 N	110.45 E
Xinping	200	24.06 N	101.58 E
Xinshuhe ≃	194	34.41 N	119.12 E
Xinxiang	194	35.20 N	113.51 E
Xinyang	196	32.19 N	114.01 E
Xiongdidao II	196	23.33 N	117.40 E
Xipamanu ≃	292	10.43 S	67.50 W
Xiping	196	33.23 N	114.02 E
Xiqi ≃	196	25.14 N	118.03 E
Xique-Xique	286	10.50 S	42.44 W
Xiruá ≃	292	6.03 S	67.50 W
Xishui ≃	196	30.21 N	115.06 E
Xitiaoxi ≃	196	30.57 N	120.10 E
Xiushui ≃	196	29.13 N	115.56 E
Xiuyan	194	40.17 N	123.18 E
Xizang Zizhiqu □[4]	190	32.00 N	88.00 E
Xkalak	278	18.16 N	87.50 W
Xlukehu ⊜	206	31.42 N	89.30 E
Xochistlahuaca	278	16.47 N	98.15 W
Xuancheng	196	30.58 N	118.45 E
Xuang ≃	200	19.58 N	102.15 E
Xuanhua	194	40.37 N	115.03 E
Xuchang	196	34.03 N	113.49 E
Xueshanzhang ∧	196	24.24 N	113.37 E
Xujiang ≃	196	28.17 N	116.05 E
Xunwushui ≃	196	24.28 N	115.26 E
Xuwen	200	20.21 N	110.11 E
Xuyong	190	28.10 N	105.24 E
Xuzhou (Süchow)	194	34.16 N	117.11 E
Y			
Yaak	238	48.50 N	115.13 W
Yaan	190	30.03 N	103.02 E
Yablis	280	14.04 N	83.45 W
Yablonovy Range → Jablonovyj Chrebet ⋀	186	53.30 N	115.00 E
Yabucoa	284m	18.03 N	65.53 W
Ya'bud	210	32.27 N	35.10 E
Yacambu, Parque Nacional ♠	290	8.40 N	68.39 W
Yacaré Norte, Riacho ≃	294	22.43 S	58.14 W
Yaco	292	17.09 S	67.24 W
Yaco (Iaco) ≃	292	9.03 S	68.34 W
Yacolt	270	45.52 N	122.25 W
Yacuiba	292	22.02 S	63.45 W
Yacuma ≃	292	13.38 S	65.23 W
Yacyretá, Isla I	294	27.25 S	56.30 W
Yadkin ≃	246	35.23 N	80.03 W
Yadkinville	246	36.08 N	80.39 W
Yadong	190	27.29 N	88.55 E
Yafran	214	32.04 N	12.31 E
Yağcılar	172	39.25 N	28.23 E
Yagoua	214	10.20 N	15.14 E
Yaguachi	290	2.07 S	79.41 W
Yaguachi ≃	290	2.02 S	79.44 W
Yaguajay	284p	22.19 N	79.14 W
Yaguará	290	2.40 N	75.31 W
Yaguaraparo	290	10.34 N	62.49 W
Yaguarí	294	31.31 S	54.58 W
Yaguarón (Jaguarão) ≃	294	32.39 S	53.12 W
Yaguas ≃	290	2.45 S	70.10 W
Yaguhu ⊜	206	28.40 N	91.45 E
Yahara ≃	244	42.48 N	89.07 W
Yaheladazeshan ∧	206	35.12 N	95.20 E
Yahk	238	49.05 N	116.05 W
Yahualica	278	21.08 N	102.51 W
Yai ≃	200	7.10 N	100.27 E
Yai, Khao ∧, Thai	200	15.27 N	99.20 E
Yai, Khao ∧, Thai	200	12.25 N	99.25 E
Yainax Butte ∧	256	42.20 N	121.16 W
Yaita	192	36.48 N	139.56 E
Yaizu	192	34.52 N	138.20 E
Yakak, Cape ≻	236	51.38 N	177.00 W
Yakehu ⊜	206	34.55 N	87.20 E
Yakima	256	46.36 N	120.31 W
Yakima □[6]	270	46.34 N	121.03 W
Yakima ≃	256	46.15 N	119.02 W
Yakima Indian Reservation ⤚[4]	256	46.16 N	121.03 W
Yakishiri-jima I	192a	44.26 N	141.25 E
Yakobi Island I	236	58.00 N	136.30 W
Yakoma	214	4.05 N	22.27 E
Yakumo	192a	42.15 N	140.16 E
Yaku-shima I	193b	30.20 N	130.30 E
Yakutat	236	59.33 N	139.44 W
Yakutat Bay C	236	59.45 N	140.45 W
Yakutsk → Jakutsk	186	62.13 N	129.49 E
Yala	200	6.32 N	101.19 E
Yalahán, Laguna de C	278	21.27 N	87.18 W
Yalakdereköy	172	40.36 N	29.33 E
Yale, B.C., Can.	238	49.34 N	121.26 W
Yale, Mich., U.S.	244	43.08 N	82.48 W
Yale, Va., U.S.	262	36.34 N	77.17 W
Yale, Lake ⊜	246	28.54 N	81.45 W
Yale, Mount ∧	254	38.51 N	106.18 W
Yalgoo	226	28.20 S	116.41 E
Yalinga	214	6.31 N	23.15 E
Yalnızçam Geçidi)(	212	41.03 N	42.20 E
Yalnızçamsilsilesi ⋀	212	41.10 N	42.23 E
Yalova	172	40.39 N	29.15 E
Yalta → Jalta	158	44.30 N	34.10 E
Yalujiang (Amnok-kang) ≃	194	39.55 N	124.22 E
Yamachiche	260	46.17 N	72.50 W
Yamada	192	39.28 N	141.57 E
Yamaga	192	33.01 N	130.41 E
Yamagata	192	38.15 N	140.15 E
Yamagawa	192	31.12 N	130.39 E
Yamaguchi	192	34.10 N	131.29 E
Yamanaka	192	36.15 N	136.22 E
Yamanashi □[5]	192	35.30 N	138.30 E
Yamasaki	192	35.00 N	134.33 E
Yamaska (Saint-Michel)	260	46.52 N	70.54 W
Yamaska □[6]	260	46.00 N	72.45 W
Yamato-takada	192	34.31 N	135.45 E
Yambio	214	4.34 N	28.23 E
Yambrasbamba	292	5.45 S	77.52 W
Yame	192	33.10 N	130.36 E
Yamen C	196	22.08 N	113.06 E
Yamethin	200	20.26 N	96.09 E
Yamhill	270	45.21 N	123.11 W
Yamhill □[6]	270	45.15 N	123.20 W
Y'Ami Island I	198	21.07 N	121.57 E
Yamma Yamma, Lake ⊜	228	26.20 S	141.25 E
Yampa	254	40.09 N	106.55 W
Yampa ≃	254	40.32 N	108.59 W
Yampa Plateau ⋀[1]	254	40.25 N	109.00 W
Yamparáez	292	19.10 S	65.10 W
Yampi Sound	226	15.15 S	123.30 E
Yamsay Mountain ∧	256	42.56 N	121.22 W
Yanacachi	292	16.23 S	67.43 W
Yanagawa	192	33.10 N	130.24 E
Yanahuara	292	16.23 S	71.33 W
Yanai	192	33.58 N	132.07 E
Yan'an	190	36.41 N	109.19 E
Yanaoca	292	14.13 S	71.26 W
Yanbu'	208	24.05 N	38.03 E
Yanceyville	246	36.24 N	79.20 W
Yanchang	190	36.35 N	110.15 E

Symbols in the index entries are identified on page 360.

Name	Page	Lat°′	Long°′
Yancheng	196	33.24 N	120.09 E
Yanchi	190	37.52 N	107.22 E
Yandoon	200	17.02 N	95.39 E
Yang ≃	200	15.44 N	104.00 E
Yangchow → Yangzhou	196	32.24 N	119.26 E
Yanggang Do □[4]	194	41.15 N	128.00 E
Yanghe ≃	194	40.24 N	115.20 E
Yangjiang ≃	196	33.37 N	120.33 E
Yangliuqing	194	39.08 N	116.59 E
Yangquan	194	37.52 N	113.36 E
Yangshuo	200	24.45 N	110.24 E
Yangtianzhang ∧	196	24.37 N	115.38 E
Yangtze → Changjiang ≃	190	31.48 N	121.10 E
Yangzhou	196	32.24 N	119.26 E
Yangzhuoyonghu ⊜	206	28.58 N	90.44 E
Yanina → Ioánnina	172	39.40 N	20.50 E
Yanji (Longjing), Zhg.	194	42.47 N	129.26 E
Yanji, Zhg.	194	42.57 N	129.32 E
Yankari Game Reserve ◆[4]	222	9.30 N	10.20 E
Yankeetown	246	29.02 N	82.43 W
Yankton	252	42.53 N	97.23 W
Yankton Indian Reservation ◆[4]	252	43.10 N	98.22 W
Yanqi	190	42.00 N	86.15 E
Yanqing	194	40.28 N	115.58 E
Yanque	292	15.40 S	71.42 W
Yanshixi ≃	196	25.20 N	117.17 E
Yantai (Chefoo)	194	37.33 N	121.20 E
Yanzhou	194	35.33 N	116.50 E
Yao	192	34.37 N	135.36 E
Yaoundé	214	3.52 N	11.31 E
Yao Yai, Ko I	200	8.00 N	98.36 E
Yap I	198	9.31 N	138.06 E
Yapacani ≃	292	16.00 S	64.25 W
Yapeyú	294	29.25 S	56.50 W
Yaphank	261	40.50 N	72.56 W
Yappar ≃	228	18.22 S	141.16 E
Yaque del Norte ≃	282	19.50 N	71.40 W
Yaque del Sur ≃	282	18.18 N	71.05 W
Yaqui ≃	278	27.37 N	110.39 W
Yaquina ≃	256	44.37 N	124.04 W
Yara, Cuba	284p	20.16 N	76.57 W
Yara, Perú	292	16.11 S	71.40 W
Yaracuy □[3]	290	10.20 N	69.10 W
Yaracuy ≃	290	10.33 N	68.15 W
Yaraka	226	24.53 S	144.04 E
Yarangume	172	37.34 N	29.04 E
Yarbasan	172	38.59 N	28.49 E
Yardley	262	40.15 N	74.50 W
Yardville	262	40.11 N	74.40 W
Yarí ≃	290	0.23 S	72.16 W
Yariga-take ∧	192	36.20 N	137.39 E
Yarīm	204	14.29 N	44.21 E
Yaring	200	6.49 N	101.28 E
Yaritagua	290	10.05 N	69.08 W
Yarkand → Suoche	206	38.25 N	77.16 E
Yarkand → Yeerqianghe ≃	190	40.28 N	80.52 E
Yarker	264	44.23 N	76.46 W
Yarkhūn ≃	206	36.17 N	72.30 E
Yarmouth, N.S., Can.	240	43.50 N	66.07 W
Yarmouth → Great Yarmouth, Eng., U.K.	174	52.37 N	1.44 E
Yarmouth, Maine, U.S.	242	43.48 N	70.12 W
Yarmouth, Mass., U.S.	261	41.40 N	70.11 W
Yarmuk, Nahr al- ≃	210	32.38 N	35.34 E
Yarra ≃	228	37.51 S	144.54 E
Yarrow	270	49.05 N	122.02 W
Yarrow Point	270	47.39 N	122.13 W
Yarumal	290	6.58 N	75.24 W
Yarvicoya, Cerro ∧	292	20.07 S	69.00 W
Yashiro-jima I	192	33.55 N	132.15 E
Yasothon	200	15.46 N	104.12 E
Yass	226	34.50 S	148.55 E
Yasugi	192	35.26 N	133.15 E
Yasun Burnu ≻	212	41.09 N	37.41 E
Yasuni ≃	290	0.56 S	75.23 W
Yata	292	13.20 S	66.35 W
Yata ≃	292	10.29 S	65.26 W
Yatağan	172	37.20 N	28.09 E
Yatate-yama ∧	192	34.10 N	129.10 E
Yates □[6]	264	42.40 N	77.03 W
Yatesboro	266	40.48 N	79.20 W
Yates Center	252	37.53 N	95.44 W
Yates City	244	40.47 N	90.01 W
Yathkyed Lake ⊜	232	62.41 N	98.00 W
Yatsuga-take ∧	192	35.59 N	138.23 E
Yatsuo	192	36.34 N	137.08 E
Yatsushiro	192	32.30 N	130.36 E
Yatsushiro-wan C	192	32.20 N	130.25 E
Yatta Plateau ⩕[1]	218	2.00 S	38.00 E
Yatua ≃	290	1.43 N	66.30 W
Yauca	292	15.40 S	74.35 W
Yauca ≃	292	15.42 S	74.34 W
Yauco	284m	18.02 N	66.51 W
Yauli	292	11.42 S	76.14 W
Yaupi	290	2.59 S	77.50 W
Yauri	292	14.48 S	71.25 W
Yautepec	278	18.53 N	99.04 W
Yauya ≃	280	13.23 N	84.06 W
Yauyos	292	12.35 S	75.54 W
Yavarí (Javari) ≃	286	4.21 S	70.02 W
Yavarí Mirim ≃	290	4.30 S	71.45 W
Yavaros	278	26.42 N	109.31 W
Yavero (Paucartambo) ≃	292	12.25 S	72.55 W
Yaví, Cerro ∧	290	5.32 N	65.59 W
Yavita	290	2.55 N	67.26 W
Yaviza	290	8.08 N	77.42 W
Yavne	210	31.52 N	34.45 E
Yawatahama	192	33.27 N	132.24 E
Yaxchilan ⊥	278	16.54 N	90.58 W
Yaxian	200	18.20 N	109.30 E
Yaxierhu ⊜	206	34.59 N	81.35 E
Yazd	208	31.53 N	54.25 E
Yazoo ≃	248	32.22 N	91.00 W
Yazoo City	248	32.51 N	90.28 W
Ybbs ≃	164	48.10 N	15.06 E
Ybbs an der Donau	164	48.11 N	15.05 E
Ybycuí	294	26.01 S	57.03 W
Ydžid Parma ⩕	160	63.06 N	58.15 E
Ye	200	15.15 N	97.51 E
Yeagertown	262	40.39 N	77.35 W
Yecheng	190	37.54 N	77.25 E
Yecla	168	38.37 N	1.07 W
Yécora	278	28.20 N	108.58 W
Yeernuozhahu ⊜	206	32.30 N	89.30 E
Yeerqianghe (Yarkand) ≃	190	40.28 N	80.52 E
Yegros	294	26.24 S	56.25 W
Yeguas, Río de las ≃	168	37.22 N	4.45 W
Yehud	210	32.02 N	34.53 E
Yei ≃	220	6.15 N	30.13 E
Ye Kyun I	200	18.37 N	93.47 E
Yelets → Jelec	158	52.37 N	38.30 E
Yélimané	214	15.08 N	10.34 W
Yell I	162	60.35 N	1.05 W
Yellow ≃, U.S.	248	30.33 N	87.00 W
Yellow ≃, Ga., U.S.	246	33.24 N	83.53 W
Yellow ≃, Ind., U.S.	248	41.16 N	86.50 W
Yellow ≃, Iowa, U.S.	244	43.05 N	91.11 W
Yellow ≃, Wis., U.S.	244	46.01 N	92.22 W
Yellow ≃, Wis., U.S.	244	44.58 N	91.18 W
Yellow ≃, Wis., U.S.	244	43.59 N	90.03 W
Yellow → Huanghe ≃, Zhg.	190	37.32 N	118.19 E
Yellow Grass	252	49.49 N	104.08 W
Yellowhead Pass)(	238	52.53 N	118.28 W
Yellowhouse Draw ∨	250	33.35 N	101.50 W
Yellowknife	232	62.27 N	114.21 W
Yellowknife ≃	232	62.31 N	114.19 W
Yellow Medicine ≃	252	44.44 N	95.25 W
Yellow Sea ⊤[2]	190	36.00 N	123.00 E
Yellowstone ≃	234	47.58 N	103.59 W
Yellowstone Falls Ⅼ	256	44.43 N	110.30 W
Yellowstone Lake ⊜	256	44.25 N	110.22 W
Yellowstone National Park ♠	256	44.30 N	110.35 W
Yellowtail Reservoir ⊜[1]	256	45.06 N	108.08 W
Yell Sound ⋓	162	60.33 N	1.15 W
Yellville	248	36.14 N	92.41 W
Yelm	270	46.56 N	122.36 W
Yelucá, Cerro ∧	280	14.19 N	84.54 W
Yelusuhu ⊜	206	35.11 N	92.15 E
Yemassee	246	32.41 N	80.51 W
Yemen □[1]	204	15.00 N	44.00 E
Yemen, People's Democratic Republic of □[1]	204	15.00 N	48.00 E
Yenan → Yan'an	190	36.41 N	109.19 E
Yenangyaung	200	20.28 N	94.52 E
Yen-bai	200	21.42 N	104.52 E
Yendéré	214	10.12 N	4.58 W
Yendi	222	9.26 N	0.01 W
Yenice, Tür.	172	39.45 N	28.55 E
Yenice, Tür.	172	39.55 N	27.18 E
Yenice ≃	212	37.36 N	35.35 E
Yenifoça	172	38.44 N	26.51 E
Yeniköy	172	37.04 N	30.36 E
Yenipazar	172	37.48 N	28.12 E
Yenişehir	172	40.16 N	29.39 E
Yenisey → Jenisej ≃	186	71.50 N	82.40 E
Yennadon	270	49.14 N	122.34 W
Yentna ≃	236	61.34 N	150.28 W
Yeoman	268	40.40 N	86.43 W
Yeovil	174	50.57 N	2.39 W
Yepachic	278	28.26 N	108.23 W
Yeppoon	228	23.08 S	150.45 E
Yerba Buena, Montaña ∧	280	14.08 N	87.27 W
Yerevan → Jerevan	158	40.11 N	44.30 E
Yerington	272	38.59 N	119.10 W
Yerkesik	172	37.07 N	28.17 E
Yermo, Méx.	250	26.23 N	104.01 W
Yermo, Calif., U.S.	258	34.54 N	116.50 W
Yerolimín	172	36.28 N	22.24 E
Yerres	176	48.43 N	2.30 E
Yerupajá, Nevado ∧	292	10.16 S	76.54 W
Yerushalayim (Al-Quds) (Jerusalem)	210	31.46 N	35.13 E
Yerushalayim □[5]	210	31.44 N	35.00 E
Yesa, Embalse de ⊜[1]	168	42.36 N	1.09 W
Yesca, Cerro ∧	278	21.19 N	104.06 W
Yeshui ≃	194	38.17 N	114.09 E
Yeşil ≃	212	41.24 N	36.35 E
Yeşilköy	172	40.57 N	28.49 E
Yeso	250	34.26 N	104.37 W
Yesŏng-gang ≃	194	37.53 N	126.24 E
Yeste	168	38.22 N	2.18 W
Yettem	272	36.29 N	119.16 W
Ye-u	198	22.46 N	95.26 E
Yeu, Île d' I	166	46.42 N	2.20 W
Yexian	196	33.37 N	113.20 E
Yeysk → Jejsk	158	46.42 N	38.16 E
Yguazú ≃	294	25.20 S	55.00 W
Yhú	294	24.59 S	55.59 W
Yi ≃	294	33.07 S	57.08 W
Yian	190	47.55 N	125.20 E
Yiannitsá	172	40.48 N	22.25 E
Yibin	190	28.47 N	104.38 E
Yichang	190	30.42 N	111.11 E
Yichun	196	47.42 N	128.55 E
Yidu	194	36.41 N	118.28 E
Yiğitaliler	172	39.52 N	26.37 E
Yiguqihu ⊜	206	31.05 N	86.55 E
Yihe ≃, Zhg.	194	34.13 N	118.03 E
Yihe ≃, Zhg.	196	34.10 N	112.10 E
Yijitathu ⊜	206	35.00 N	87.00 E
Yikechaidamuhu ⊜	206	37.50 N	95.00 E
Yilan	190	46.19 N	129.34 E
Yıldızdağı ∧	212	40.08 N	36.56 E
Yiliang	200	24.58 N	103.07 E
Yimen	200	24.43 N	102.10 E
Yin Chaung ≃	200	20.04 N	95.01 E
Yinchuan	190	38.30 N	106.18 E
Yingde	196	24.12 N	113.24 E
Yinggen	200	19.04 N	109.48 E
Yinghe ≃	196	32.30 N	116.32 E
Yingjisha	190	38.57 N	76.03 E
Yingkou	194	40.40 N	122.14 E
Yingnahe ≃	194	39.42 N	123.20 E
Yingtan	190	28.14 N	117.00 E
Yining (Kuldja)	190	43.55 N	81.14 E
Yinmatuhe ≃	194	40.57 N	117.43 E
Yirga Alem	214	6.52 N	38.22 E
Yishan	200	24.40 N	108.35 E
Yishui	190	35.50 N	118.41 E
Yishui ≃, Zhg.	194	39.07 N	116.00 E
Yishui ≃, Zhg.	194	35.34 N	116.52 E
Yishui ≃, Zhg.	196	28.05 N	116.18 E
Yítheion	172	36.45 N	22.34 E
Yitulihe	190	50.38 N	121.57 E
Yixunhe ≃	194	41.16 N	117.35 E
Yiyang	190	28.36 N	112.20 E
Yizre'el, 'emeq ∨	210	32.32 N	35.24 E
Ylikitka ⊜	160	66.08 N	28.30 E
Ylivieska	160	64.05 N	24.33 E
Ymir	238	49.17 N	117.13 W
Yndin	160	61.24 N	55.10 E
Ynykčanskij	186	60.15 N	137.43 E
Yoakum	250	29.17 N	97.09 W
Yoco	290	10.36 N	62.24 W
Yoder	268	40.56 N	85.11 W
Yodo ≃	192	34.41 N	135.25 E
Yoe	262	39.55 N	76.39 W
Yog Point ≻	202	14.06 N	124.12 E
Yoho National Park ♠	238	51.26 N	116.30 W
Yoichi	192a	43.12 N	140.41 E
Yojoa, Lago de ⊜	280	14.53 N	88.00 W
Yōka	192	35.24 N	134.46 E
Yōkaichi	192	35.06 N	136.12 E
Yōkaichiba	192	35.42 N	140.33 E
Yokkaichi	192	34.58 N	136.37 E
Yokoate-shima I	193b	28.48 N	129.00 E
Yokohama	192	35.27 N	139.39 E
Yokosuka	192	35.18 N	139.40 E
Yokote	192	39.18 N	140.34 E
Yola	214	9.12 N	12.29 E
Yolaina, Cordillera de ⩕	280	11.40 N	84.20 W
Yolo	272	38.44 N	121.48 W
Yolo □[6]	272	38.41 N	121.46 W
Yolombó	290	6.36 N	75.01 W
Yom ≃	200	16.40 N	100.14 E
Yonago	192	35.26 N	133.20 E
Yonaha-dake ∧[2]	193b	26.43 N	128.13 E
Yoncalla	256	43.36 N	123.17 W
Yoneshiro ≃	192	40.13 N	140.01 E
Yonezawa	192	37.55 N	140.07 E
Yongan	190	25.58 N	117.22 E
Yong'anxi ≃	196	28.52 N	121.04 E
Yŏngch'ŏn	194	35.58 N	128.56 E
Yongdeng	190	36.48 N	103.14 E
Yongding	190	24.46 N	116.43 E
Yongdinghe ≃	194	39.39 N	116.13 E
Yongdingxi ≃	196	24.42 N	116.34 E
Yongdingzhen	190	26.08 N	101.40 E
Yongfeng	190	27.19 N	115.24 E
Yŏnghŭng-man C	194	39.15 N	127.30 E
Yŏngil-man C	194	36.02 N	129.26 E
Yongjiang ≃	196	29.58 N	121.44 E
Yŏngju	194	36.50 N	128.37 E
Yongning	200	22.42 N	108.50 E
Yongningjiang ≃	196	28.42 N	121.19 E
Yongping	200	25.28 N	99.33 E
Yŏngsan-gang ≃	194	34.54 N	126.32 E
Yongshan	190	28.15 N	103.24 E
Yongsheng	200	26.42 N	100.43 E
Yŏnhwa-san ∧	194	40.46 N	127.23 E
Yonkers	261	40.56 N	73.52 W
Yonne □[5]	176	47.55 N	3.45 E
Yonne ≃	166	48.23 N	2.58 E
Yookanookany ≃	248	32.40 N	89.40 W
Yorba Linda	274	33.53 N	117.49 W
York, Austl.	226	31.53 S	116.46 E
York, Ont., Can.	264	43.41 N	79.29 W
York, Eng., U.K.	162	53.58 N	1.05 W
York, Ala., U.S.	248	32.29 N	88.18 W
York, Ind., U.S.	268	41.41 N	84.49 W
York, Nebr., U.S.	252	40.52 N	97.36 W
York, N. Dak., U.S.	252	48.19 N	99.34 W
York, N.Y., U.S.	264	42.52 N	77.53 W
York, Pa., U.S.	242	39.58 N	76.44 W
York, S.C., U.S.	246	35.00 N	81.14 W
York □[6], Ont., Can.	264	43.55 N	79.25 W
York □[6], Pa., U.S.	262	39.58 N	76.44 W
York □[6], Va., U.S.	262	37.15 N	76.40 W
York ≃	240	48.50 N	64.34 W
York, Cape ≻	226	10.42 S	142.31 E
Yorkana	262	39.59 N	76.35 W
Yorke Peninsula ≻[1]	228	35.00 S	137.30 E
York Factory	232	57.00 N	92.18 W
York Haven	262	40.07 N	76.43 W
York New Salem	262	39.54 N	76.47 W
Yorkshire, N.Y., U.S.	266	42.32 N	78.28 W
Yorkshire, Pa., U.S.	262	39.59 N	76.41 W
Yorkshire, Va., U.S.	262	38.47 N	77.27 W
Yorkshire □[6]	162	54.00 N	1.15 W
Yorkshire Dales National Park ♠	162	54.13 N	2.10 W
York Sound ⋓	226	14.50 S	125.05 E
York Springs	262	40.00 N	77.07 W
Yorkton	232	51.13 N	102.28 W
Yorktown, Tex., U.S.	250	28.59 N	97.30 W
Yorktown, Va., U.S.	262	37.14 N	76.30 W
Yorktown Heights	261	41.16 N	73.47 W
Yorktown Manor	261	41.38 N	71.26 W
Yorkville, Ill., U.S.	268	41.38 N	88.27 W
Yorkville, N.Y., U.S.	264	43.07 N	75.16 W
Yorkville, Ohio, U.S.	266	40.09 N	80.43 W
Yoro	280	15.09 N	87.07 W
Yoro □[5]	280	15.15 N	87.15 W
Yoron-jima I	193b	27.02 N	128.26 E
Yörük	172	40.56 N	27.04 E
Yosemite Falls Ⅼ	258	37.45 N	119.37 W
Yosemite National Park	258	37.45 N	119.35 W
Yosemite National Park ♠	258	37.51 N	119.33 W
Yoshii ≃	192	34.36 N	134.03 E
Yoshino ≃	192	34.05 N	134.36 E
Yoshino-kumano-kokuritsu-kōen ♠	192	34.07 N	135.55 E
Yŏsu	194	34.46 N	127.44 E
Yotala	292	19.10 S	65.17 W
Yotaú	292	16.03 S	63.03 W
Yōtei-zan ∧	192a	42.49 N	140.49 E
Youbou	238	48.53 N	124.13 W
Youghal	162	51.51 N	7.50 W
Youghal Bay C	162	51.52 N	7.50 W
Youjiang ≃	200	22.50 N	108.06 E
Youks les Bains	170	35.27 N	7.58 E
Young, Austl.	228	34.19 S	148.18 E
Young, Ariz., U.S.	254	34.06 N	110.57 W
Young, Ur.	294	32.41 S	57.38 W
Young America	268	40.34 N	86.21 W
Younghusband Peninsula ≻[1]	228	36.00 S	139.30 E
Young Range ⩕	230	44.15 S	169.20 E
Youngstown, Alta., Can.	238	51.32 N	111.13 W
Youngstown, Fla., U.S.	246	30.22 N	85.27 W
Youngstown, N.Y., U.S.	264	43.15 N	79.03 W
Youngstown, Ohio, U.S.	266	41.06 N	80.39 W
Youngstown, Pa., U.S.	266	40.12 N	79.22 W
Youngsville, La., U.S.	248	30.06 N	92.00 W
Youngsville, N. Mex., U.S.	254	36.11 N	106.34 W
Youngsville, N.C., U.S.	246	36.01 N	78.29 W
Youngsville, Pa., U.S.	266	41.51 N	79.19 W
Youngwood	266	40.14 N	79.35 W
Yountville	272	38.24 N	122.22 W
Youssoufia	214	32.16 N	8.33 W
Youyang	190	28.58 N	108.41 E
Yozgat	212	39.50 N	34.48 E
Ypacaraí	294	25.23 S	57.16 W
Ypané ≃	294	23.29 S	57.19 W
Ypejhú	294	23.54 S	55.20 W
Ypres → Ieper	176	50.51 N	2.53 E
Ypsilanti	268	42.15 N	83.36 W
Yreka	258	41.44 N	122.38 W
Yssingeaux	166	45.08 N	4.07 E
Ystad	160	55.25 N	13.49 E
Ytterhogdal	160	62.12 N	14.51 E
Yu'alliq, Jabal ∧	220	30.22 N	33.31 E
Yuam ≃	200	17.47 N	97.48 E
Yuanling	190	28.20 N	110.16 E
Yuanmou	200	25.38 N	101.54 E
Yuanshui ≃	196	28.09 N	115.34 E
Yuasa	192	34.02 N	135.11 E
Yuba □[6]	272	39.16 N	121.17 W
Yuba City	272	39.08 N	121.37 W
Yūbari	192a	43.04 N	141.59 E
Yūbari-sanchi ⩕	192a	43.15 N	142.20 E
Yūbetsu	192a	43.13 N	144.05 E
Yūbetsu ≃	192a	44.14 N	143.37 E
Yucaipa	274	34.02 N	117.02 W
Yucatán □[3]	278	20.40 N	89.00 W
Yucatan Channel ⋓	282	21.45 N	85.45 W
Yucatan Peninsula ≻[1]	278	19.30 N	89.00 W
Yucca	254	34.52 N	114.09 W
Yucca Lake ⊜	258	36.59 N	116.01 W
Yuci	190	37.45 N	112.41 E
Yuda	192	39.20 N	140.50 E
Yudí ≃	290	5.31 N	64.33 W
Yueyang	196	29.23 N	113.06 E
Yugoslavia □[1]	158	44.00 N	19.00 E
Yujiang ≃	200	23.24 N	110.16 E
Yukarıbey	172	39.15 N	27.06 E
Yukon	266	40.13 N	79.41 W
Yukon □[3]	232	64.00 N	135.00 W
Yukon ≃	236	62.33 N	163.59 W
Yüksekkum	172	36.57 N	28.41 E
Yukuhashi	192	33.44 N	130.59 E
Yulin	200	22.36 N	110.07 E
Yulongkashihe ≃	206	37.00 N	79.55 E
Yuma, Ariz., U.S.	254	32.43 N	114.37 W
Yuma, Colo., U.S.	252	40.08 N	102.43 W
Yuma, Bahía de C	282	18.20 N	68.35 W
Yumare	290	10.37 N	68.41 W
Yumari, Cerro ∧	290	4.27 N	66.50 W
Yumbel	294	37.08 S	72.32 W
Yumbo	290	3.35 N	76.28 W
Yumen	190	39.56 N	97.51 E
Yuna ≃	282	19.13 N	69.35 W
Yu'nan (Ducheng)	200	23.11 N	111.29 E
Yunaska Island I	236	52.40 N	170.50 W
Yuncheng	190	35.00 N	110.59 E
Yungas ◆[1]	292	16.20 S	66.45 W
Yungay, Chile	294	37.07 S	72.01 W
Yungay, Perú	292	9.02 S	77.45 W
Yungning → Nanning	200	22.48 N	108.20 E
Yunhe ≚, Zhg.	190	32.12 N	119.31 E
Yunjiguan)(	196	27.50 N	117.40 E
Yunling ⩕	200	27.20 N	99.20 E
Yunlinhe ≚	196	30.15 N	120.11 E
Yunlong	200	25.50 N	99.17 E
Yunnan □[4]	200	24.00 N	101.00 E
Yunnanfu → Kunming	200	25.05 N	102.40 E
Yunshui ≃	196	30.43 N	114.04 E
Yunwushan ∧	194	41.07 N	116.34 E
Yunxian	190	32.49 N	110.49 E
Yunzalin Chaung ≃	200	17.23 N	97.40 E
Yupanyang C	196	30.30 N	121.46 E
Yura ≃	292	20.22 S	65.45 W
Yurimaguas	292	5.54 S	76.05 W
Yuriria	278	20.12 N	101.09 W
Yuriria, Laguna de ⊜	278	20.15 N	101.06 W
Yuruarí ≃	290	6.44 N	61.40 W
Yurubi, Parque Nacional ♠	290	10.25 N	68.42 W
Yurumanguí ≃	290	3.27 N	77.21 W
Yusala, Lago ⊜	292	14.05 S	67.12 W
Yuscarán	280	13.55 N	86.51 W
Yushan ∧	196	26.06 N	115.20 E
Yushu	190	33.28 N	96.18 E
Yūsuf, Baḥr ≚	220	29.19 N	30.50 E
Yutian	190	36.51 N	81.40 E
Yuty	294	26.32 S	56.18 W
Yūwan-dake ∧	193b	28.18 N	129.21 E
Yüweng Tao I	196	23.35 N	119.30 E
Yuxi	200	24.21 N	102.34 E
Yuxian	196	34.10 N	113.28 E
Yuyao	196	30.04 N	121.10 E
Yuza	192	39.01 N	139.54 E
Yuzawa	192	39.10 N	140.30 E
Yvelines □[5]	176	48.50 N	1.50 E
Yverdon	180	46.47 N	6.39 E
Yvetot	176	49.37 N	0.46 E
Z			
Zaandam	178	52.26 N	4.49 E
Zabajkal'sk	186	49.38 N	117.19 E
Zăbala ≃	172	45.51 N	26.46 E
Zăbalț	172	46.01 N	21.55 E
Žabari	172	44.21 N	21.13 E
Zabarjad, Jazīrat I	220	23.37 N	36.12 E
Zabīd	204	14.10 N	43.17 E
Ząbkowice Śląskie (Frankenstein)	164	50.36 N	16.53 E
Žabljak	172	43.09 N	19.07 E
Zabłudów	164	53.01 N	23.20 E
Żabno	164	50.09 N	20.53 E
Zābol	208	31.02 N	61.30 E
Zaborje	160	55.55 N	29.19 E
Zábřeh	164	49.53 N	16.52 E
Zabrze	164	50.18 N	18.46 E
Zabul □[4]	206	32.00 N	67.15 E
Zacapa	280	14.58 N	89.32 W
Zacapa □[5]	280	15.00 N	89.30 W
Zacapu	278	19.50 N	101.43 W
Zacata	262	38.07 N	76.47 W
Zacatecas	278	22.47 N	102.35 W
Zacatecoluca	280	13.30 N	88.52 W
Zacatlán	278	19.56 N	97.58 W
Zacharovo	160	54.22 N	39.17 E
Zacharvan'	160	66.21 N	55.48 E
Zachary	248	30.39 N	91.09 W
Zachrebetnoje	160	69.00 N	36.25 E
Zacoalco de Torres	278	20.14 N	103.35 W
Zacualpa	280	15.05 N	90.50 W
Zacualtipán	278	20.39 N	98.36 W
Zaculeu ⊥	280	15.21 N	91.28 W
Zadar	170	44.07 N	15.14 E
Zadetkale Kyun I	200	10.08 N	98.12 E
Zadetkyi Kyun I	200	9.58 N	98.13 E
Zadorra ≃	168	42.40 N	2.54 W
Zadorra, Embalses del ⊜[1]	168	42.50 N	2.54 W
Za'farānah, Bi'r ⊤[4]	220	29.07 N	32.33 E
Zafirovo	172	44.00 N	26.50 E
Zafra	168	38.25 N	6.25 W
Żagań (Sagan)	164	51.37 N	15.19 E
Zagarolo	184	41.50 N	12.50 E
Zagazig → Az-Zaqāzīq	220	30.35 N	31.31 E
Zaghouan	170	36.24 N	10.09 E
Zaghouan, Djebel ∧	170	36.21 N	10.08 E
Zagora ⩕	170	43.40 N	16.15 E
Zagórów	164	52.11 N	17.55 E
Zagorsk	160	56.18 N	38.08 E
Zagórz	164	49.31 N	22.17 E
Zagreb	170	45.48 N	15.58 E
Zāgros, Kūhhā-ye ⩕	208	33.40 N	47.00 E
Zagros Mountains → Zāgros, Kūhhā-ye ⩕	208	33.40 N	47.00 E
Žagubica	172	44.13 N	21.48 E
Zagyva ≃	164	47.10 N	20.13 E
Zahana	168	35.32 N	0.25 W
Zāhedān	208	29.30 N	60.52 E
Zaḥlah	210	33.50 N	35.53 E
Záhony	164	48.14 N	22.10 E
Zainsk	160	55.18 N	52.06 E
Zaire □[1]	218	0.00	25.00 E
Zaječar	172	43.54 N	22.17 E
Zajsan	186	47.28 N	84.55 E
Zajsan, Ozero ⊜	186	48.00 N	84.00 E
Zakamensk	186	50.23 N	103.17 E
Zákas	172	40.02 N	21.16 E
Zākhū	208	37.08 N	42.41 E
Zákinthos	172	37.47 N	20.53 E
Zákinthos I	172	37.52 N	20.44 E
Zakínthou, Porthmós ⋓	172	37.50 N	21.00 E
Zakliczyn	164	49.51 N	20.48 E
Zaklików	164	50.47 N	22.06 E
Zakopane	164	49.19 N	19.57 E
Zakroczym	164	52.26 N	20.37 E
Zala □[6]	164	46.45 N	16.50 E
Zala ≃	164	46.43 N	17.16 E
Zalaegerszeg	164	46.51 N	16.51 E
Zalalövő	164	46.51 N	16.35 E
Zalamea de la Serana	168	38.39 N	5.39 W
Zalaszentgrót	164	46.59 N	17.02 E
Zalău	172	47.11 N	23.03 E
Žalec	170	46.15 N	15.10 E
Zaltbommel	178	51.48 N	5.15 E
Žaltyr	186	51.40 N	69.50 E
Zalučje	160	57.40 N	31.46 E
Zama	248	32.53 N	89.23 W
Zambales □[4]	202	15.20 N	120.05 E
Zambales Mountains ⩕	202	15.40 N	120.15 E
Zamberk	164	50.05 N	16.28 E
Zambezi (Zambeze) ≃	218	18.55 S	36.04 E
Zambézia □[5]	224	16.15 S	37.30 E
Zambia □[1]	218	15.00 S	30.00 E
Zamboanga	202	6.54 N	122.05 E
Zamboanga del Norte □[4]	202	8.00 N	123.00 E
Zamboanga del Sur □[4]	202	7.50 N	123.00 E
Zamboanga Peninsula ≻[1]	202	7.30 N	122.15 E
Zamboanguita	202	9.06 N	123.12 E
Zambrano	290	9.45 N	74.49 W
Zambrów	164	53.00 N	22.15 E
Zamch	164	50.20 N	23.00 E
Zamežnaja	160	65.02 N	51.50 E
Zamfara ≃	222	12.05 N	4.02 E
Zami ≃	200	16.09 N	97.58 E
Zamora, Ec.	290	4.04 S	78.58 W
Zamora, Esp.	168	41.30 N	5.45 W
Zamora, Calif., U.S.	272	38.48 N	121.53 W
Zamora ≃	290	2.59 S	78.13 W
Zamora-Chinchipe □[4]	290	4.15 S	78.50 W
Zamora de Hidalgo	278	19.59 N	102.16 W
Zamość	164	50.44 N	23.15 E
Zamuro, Punta ≻	290	11.26 N	68.50 W
Zana ⊥	168	35.45 N	6.05 E
Zanaga	218	2.51 S	13.50 E
Zanatepec	278	16.29 N	94.21 W
Záncara ≃	168	39.18 N	3.18 W
Zandvoort	178	52.22 N	4.32 E
Zane Hills ⩕[2]	236	66.10 N	156.00 W
Zanesfield	268	40.20 N	83.41 W
Zanesville, Ind., U.S.	268	40.55 N	85.17 W
Zanesville, Ohio, U.S.	242	39.56 N	82.01 W
Zânguè ≃	224	17.52 S	35.20 E
Zanjān	208	36.40 N	48.29 E
Zanjón	294	27.55 S	64.15 W
Zanjón ≃	294	31.16 S	67.41 W
Žannetty, Ostrov I	186	76.43 N	158.00 E
Zante → Zákinthos I	172	37.52 N	20.44 E
Zanthus	226	31.02 S	123.34 E
Zanzibar	218	6.10 S	39.11 E
Zaō-san ∧	192	38.08 N	140.26 E
Zaostrovje	160	60.50 N	30.22 E
Zaouia el Kahla	214	28.09 N	6.43 E
Zaouiet Azmour	170	36.55 N	11.01 E
Zaouiet el Mgaïz	170	36.56 N	10.50 E
Zaoz'ornyj	186	55.58 N	94.42 E
Zap	252	47.17 N	101.55 W
Zapadnaja Dvina	160	56.16 N	32.04 E
Zapadnaja Dvina ≃	160	57.04 N	24.03 E
Zapadna Morava ≃	172	43.42 N	21.23 E
Zapadno-Sibirskaja Nizmennost' ≚	186	60.00 N	75.00 E
Zapadnyj Sajan ⩕	186	53.00 N	94.00 E
Západočeský □[4]	164	49.45 N	13.00 E
Západoslovenský □[4]	164	48.20 N	18.00 E
Zapala	294	38.55 S	70.05 W
Zapallar	294	32.33 S	71.28 W
Zapardiel ≃	168	41.29 N	5.02 W
Zapata	250	26.52 N	99.19 W
Zapata, Ciénaga de ☰	284p	22.25 N	81.25 W
Zapata, Península de ≻[1]	284p	22.20 N	81.45 W
Zapatera, Isla I	280	11.44 N	85.50 W
Zapatoca	290	6.49 N	73.17 W
Zapatosa, Ciénaga de ⊜	290	9.05 N	73.50 W
Zapol'arnyj, S.S.S.R.	160	63.22 N	63.42 E
Zapol'arnyj, S.S.S.R.	160	69.26 N	30.48 E
Zaporožje	158	47.50 N	35.10 E
Zapotal ≃	290	1.40 S	79.28 W
Zapotillo	290	4.25 S	80.31 W
Zapotitlán, Punta ≻	278	18.33 N	94.49 W
Zapotlanejo	278	20.38 N	103.04 W
Zaprudn'a	160	56.34 N	37.26 E
Zarāf, Baḥr az- ≃	220	9.25 N	31.10 E
Zaragosa □[4]	166	41.38 N	0.53 W
Zaragoza, Col.	290	7.30 N	74.52 W
Zaragoza, Esp.	168	41.38 N	0.53 W
Zaragoza, Méx.	278	28.29 N	100.55 W
Zaragoza, Méx.	278	23.58 N	99.46 W
Zaragoza, Méx.	278	31.39 N	106.20 W
Zarajsk	160	54.46 N	38.53 E
Zaranda Hill ∧[2]	222	10.15 N	9.35 E
Zarasai	160	55.44 N	26.15 E
Zárate	294	34.05 S	59.02 W
Zaratí ≃	280	8.21 N	80.27 W
Zarauz	168	43.17 N	2.10 W
Zaraza	290	9.21 N	65.19 W
Zarcero	280	10.11 N	84.23 W
Zard Kūh ∧	208	32.22 N	50.04 E
Zarečensk	160	66.41 N	33.18 E
Zarečje	160	63.08 N	44.46 E
Zarembo Island I	236	56.20 N	132.50 W
Zarezskoje, Ozero ⊜	206	38.12 N	72.45 E
Zaria	222	11.07 N	7.44 E
Żarki	164	50.38 N	19.22 E
Żarkovskij	160	55.52 N	32.17 E
Żarma	186	48.48 N	80.50 E
Zărnești	172	45.34 N	25.19 E
Żarnovica	164	48.29 N	18.44 E
Zarqā', Raqabat az- ∨	220	9.14 N	29.44 E
Zarubino	160	58.44 N	33.28 E
Zaruma	290	3.41 S	79.37 W
Zarumilla	290	3.25 S	80.15 W
Żary (Sorau)	164	51.38 N	15.09 E
Zarzal	290	4.24 N	76.04 W
Zašejek	160	67.25 N	32.28 E
Zāskār Mountains ⩕	206	33.00 N	78.00 E
Zastava	160	59.12 N	46.46 E
Zasulje	160	64.41 N	47.48 E
Žatec	164	50.18 N	13.32 E
Zavalla	248	31.09 N	94.26 W
Zaventem	176	50.53 N	4.28 E
Zavet	172	43.46 N	26.40 E
Zavidovići	172	44.27 N	18.09 E
Zavitinsk	186	50.07 N	129.27 E
Zavolžsk	160	57.30 N	42.10 E
Zawadzkie (Andreashütte)	164	50.37 N	18.29 E
Zawichost	164	50.49 N	21.52 E
Zawiercie	164	50.30 N	19.25 E
Zāwiyat al-Bayḍā'	214	32.46 N	21.43 E
Zawr, Ra's az- ≻, Ar. Sa.	208	27.25 N	49.20 E
Zawr, Ra's az- ≻, Ar. Sa.	208	28.44 N	48.24 E
Zaza ≃	284p	21.37 N	79.33 W
Zaza del Medio	284p	22.00 N	79.23 W
Zbąszyń	164	52.16 N	15.55 E
Zbąszynek (Neu Bentschen)	164	52.15 N	15.50 E
Zbiroh	164	49.52 N	13.47 E
Zbraslav	164	49.59 N	14.24 E
Zbruč ≃	172	48.32 N	26.26 E
Ždanov	158	47.06 N	37.33 E
Zd'ar	164	49.34 N	15.57 E
Ždiar	164	49.17 N	20.16 E
Zduńska (Wola)	164	51.36 N	18.57 E
Zduny	164	51.39 N	17.24 E
Zearing	244	42.10 N	93.18 W
Zeballos	238	49.49 N	126.50 W
Zebulon, Ga., U.S.	246	33.06 N	84.21 W
Zebulon, N.C., U.S.	246	35.49 N	78.19 W
Zedang	190	29.16 N	91.46 E
Zeddine, Oued ≃	168	36.15 N	1.48 E
Zeehan	226	41.53 S	145.20 E
Zeeland, Mich., U.S.	268	42.49 N	86.01 W
Zeeland, N. Dak., U.S.	252	45.58 N	99.50 W
Zeeland □[4]	178	51.27 N	3.45 E
Zeerust	224	25.33 S	26.06 E
Zeeuws-Vlaanderen ◆[1]	176	51.19 N	3.45 E
Zefat (Safad)	210	32.58 N	35.29 E
Zehdenick	164	52.59 N	13.20 E
Zeigler	248	37.54 N	89.03 W
Zeila	214	11.21 N	43.30 E
Zeist	178	52.05 N	5.15 E
Zeitz	164	51.03 N	12.08 E
Zeja	186	53.45 N	127.15 E
Zeja ≃	186	50.13 N	127.35 E
Želanija, Mys ≻	186	76.57 N	68.35 E
Zelaya □[5]	280	13.00 N	84.00 W
Zele	176	51.04 N	4.02 E
Żelechów	164	51.49 N	21.54 E
Zelenec	160	62.29 N	55.16 E
Zelengora ⩕	172	43.15 N	18.45 E
Zelenoborskij	160	66.49 N	32.18 E
Zelenogorsk	160	60.12 N	29.42 E
Zelenogradsk	160	54.58 N	20.29 E
Zelenogradsk [Cranz]	164	54.58 N	20.29 E
Zeletinul ≃	172	46.03 N	27.23 E
Železnik	172	44.43 N	20.23 E
Železnodorožnyj, S.S.S.R.	160	67.58 N	64.38 E
Železnodorožnyj [Gerdauen]	164	54.22 N	21.19 E
Železnodorżnyj	160	62.37 N	50.55 E
Železnogorsk-Ilimskij	186	56.37 N	104.08 E
Zelienople	266	40.48 N	80.08 W
Zelina	170	45.58 N	16.15 E
Zell	166	50.01 N	7.10 E
Zella-Mehlis	164	50.39 N	10.39 E
Zell am See	164	47.19 N	12.47 E
Zell am Ziller	164	47.14 N	11.53 E
Zel'onaja Rošča	160	54.29 N	52.02 E
Zel'onodol'sk	160	55.51 N	48.33 E
Zel'onyj, Ostrov(Shibotsu-tō) I	192a	43.30 N	146.09 E
Zelów	164	51.28 N	19.13 E
Zelzate	176	51.12 N	3.49 E
Žemaičių Naumiestis	160	55.22 N	21.42 E
Zemio	214	5.02 N	25.08 E
Zeml'a Franca-Iosifa II	148	81.00 N	55.00 E
Zemmora	168	35.44 N	0.45 E
Zempoala ⊥	278	19.27 N	96.23 W
Zemun	172	44.51 N	20.23 E
Zengjiang ≃	196	23.09 N	113.46 E
Zenica	172	44.12 N	17.24 E
Zenith	270	47.23 N	122.19 W
Zenn ≃	166	49.31 N	10.58 E
Zentsūji	192	34.14 N	133.47 E
Zephyr	250	31.41 N	98.48 W
Zephyr Cove	272	39.00 N	119.57 W
Zephyrhills	246	28.14 N	82.11 W
Zéralda	168	36.41 N	2.53 E
Zeravšan ≃	186	39.22 N	63.45 E
Zerbst	164	51.58 N	12.04 E
Žerdevka	158	51.51 N	41.28 E
Zergan	172	41.30 N	20.21 E
Zerind	172	46.37 N	21.31 E
Żerków	164	52.05 N	17.34 E
Zermatt	166	46.02 N	7.45 E
Zernograd	158	46.50 N	40.19 E
Zeroud, Oued ∨	170	35.50 N	10.13 E
Žešart	160	62.05 N	49.34 E
Zetel	178	53.25 N	7.58 E
Zetland □[6]	162	60.30 N	0.15 W
Zeulenroda	164	50.39 N	11.58 E
Zeven	178	53.18 N	9.16 E
Zevenaar	178	51.56 N	6.05 E
Zevenbergen	178	51.38 N	4.36 E
Zeytindağ	172	38.58 N	27.04 E
Zêzere ≃	168	39.28 N	8.20 W
Zgierz	164	51.52 N	19.25 E
Zgorzelec	164	51.12 N	15.01 E
Zhabuchakahu ⊜	206	31.30 N	84.00 E
Zhalinhu ⊜	206	31.10 N	88.15 E
Zhalutegi	190	44.37 N	120.58 E
Zhangduhu ⊜	196	30.40 N	114.42 E
Zhanghe ≃	194	36.10 N	115.05 E
Zhangjiakou (Kalgan)	194	40.50 N	114.53 E
Zhangping	190	25.19 N	117.25 E
Zhangshui ≃, Zhg.	196	25.51 N	114.46 E
Zhangshui ≃, Zhg.	196	31.05 N	113.11 E
Zhangye	190	38.57 N	100.37 E
Zhangzhou (Longxi)	196	24.33 N	117.39 E
Zhangzidao I	194	39.00 N	122.44 E
Zhanjiang	200	21.16 N	110.28 E
Zhanyi	190	25.38 N	103.43 E
Zhaoan	196	23.44 N	116.11 E
Zhaoanwan C	196	23.38 N	117.19 E
Zhaoanxi ≃	196	23.42 N	117.13 E
Zhaoping	200	24.03 N	110.52 E
Zhaoqing	190	23.03 N	112.27 E
Zhaosuhe ≃	194	42.34 N	119.38 E
Zhaotong	190	27.19 N	103.48 E
Zhaxigang	190	32.32 N	79.41 E
Zhdanov → Ždanov	158	47.06 N	37.33 E
Zhejiang □[4]	196	29.00 N	120.00 E
Zhengding	194	38.10 N	114.34 E
Zhengfeng	200	25.23 N	105.41 E
Zhengzhou	190	34.48 N	113.39 E
Zhenhaijiao ≻	196	24.16 N	118.08 E
Zhenjiang	196	32.13 N	119.26 E
Zhenning	200	26.05 N	105.46 E
Zhenping	190	33.08 N	112.19 E
Zhenshui ≃	196	24.55 N	113.44 E
Zhentouhe ≃	196	32.58 N	114.24 E
Zhenyuan	190	26.53 N	108.19 E
Zhide	190	30.04 N	116.58 E
Zhijin	200	26.41 N	105.37 E
Zhitomir → Žitomir	158	50.16 N	28.40 E
Zhizhudao I	196	26.02 N	120.04 E
Zhob ≃	206	32.04 N	69.50 E
Zhongba	190	29.54 N	83.40 E
Zhongchuanhe ≃	200	22.58 N	101.44 E
Zhongdian	190	27.50 N	99.40 E
Zhongning	190	37.27 N	105.38 E
Zhongshan, Zhg.	190	26.12 N	117.26 E
Zhongshan (Shiqi), Zhg.	196	22.31 N	113.22 E
Zhongshanhe ≃	194	34.25 N	120.06 E
Zhongxiang	190	31.11 N	112.33 E
Zhoucun	194	36.47 N	117.48 E
Zhoushan	196	30.02 N	122.06 E
Zhoushandao I	196	30.05 N	122.10 E
Zhoushanqundao II	196	30.00 N	122.00 E
Zhuangaerpendi ≚[1]	190	45.00 N	88.00 E
Zhuganhe ≃	196	32.18 N	114.42 E
Zhuguangshan ⩕	196	26.00 N	114.00 E
Zhuimuhu ⊜	206	34.30 N	87.00 E
Zhujiajian I	196	29.54 N	122.24 E
Zhujiangkou C	190	23.36 N	113.44 E
Zhujiangkou C[1]	196	23.36 N	113.44 E
Zhulonghe ≃	194	38.47 N	115.59 E
Zhumadian	196	33.00 N	114.01 E
Zhungeerqi	190	39.49 N	111.10 E
Zhuoxian	194	39.30 N	115.58 E
Zhushan	190	32.10 N	110.19 E
Zhuzhou	196	27.50 N	113.09 E
Ziama-Mansouria	168	36.40 N	5.29 E
Ziārat Gali Chāh ⊤[4]	208	28.20 N	63.38 E
Žiar nad Hronom	164	48.36 N	18.52 E
Zibo (Tzupo)	194	36.47 N	118.01 E
Zicavo	170	41.54 N	9.08 E
Ziębice (Münsterberg)	164	50.37 N	17.00 E
Ziegenhain	164	50.55 N	9.15 E
Zielona Góra (Grünberg)	164	51.56 N	15.31 E
Zierikzee	178	51.38 N	3.55 E
Ziesar	164	52.16 N	12.17 E
Ziftā	220	30.43 N	31.15 E
Žigalovo	186	54.48 N	105.08 E
Zigana Dağları ⩕	212	40.37 N	39.30 E
Žigansk	186	66.45 N	123.20 E
Zīghan ⊤[4]	220	25.30 N	22.25 E
Zigong	190	29.24 N	104.47 E
Ziguinchor	222	12.35 N	16.16 W
Žigulevsk	160	53.25 N	49.27 E
Zihe ≃	194	37.12 N	118.34 E
Zihuatanejo	278	17.38 N	101.33 W
Zijpe	178	51.38 N	4.05 E
Žilaja Tambica	160	62.32 N	36.09 E
Zile	212	40.18 N	35.54 E
Žilina	164	49.14 N	18.46 E
Žilino [Schillen]	164	54.54 N	21.56 E
Zillah, Lībīya	214	28.33 N	17.35 E
Zillah, Wash., U.S.	256	46.24 N	120.16 W
Zillertaler Alpen (Alpi Aurine) ⩕	164	47.00 N	11.55 E
Žiloj I	208	40.19 N	50.36 E
Zilwaukee	244	43.28 N	83.55 W
Zima	186	53.55 N	102.04 E
Zimapán	278	20.45 N	99.21 W
Zimbor	172	47.00 N	23.16 E
Zimnicea	172	43.39 N	25.21 E
Zindajān	208	34.19 N	61.43 E
Zinder	222	13.48 N	8.59 E
Zinder □[5]	222	15.00 N	10.30 E
Zinnowitz	164	54.04 N	13.55 E
Zion	268	42.27 N	87.50 W
Zionhill	262	40.29 N	75.24 W
Zion National Park ♠	254	37.10 N	113.00 W
Zionsville	248	39.57 N	86.16 W
Zipaquirá	290	5.02 N	74.00 W
Zippori	210	32.44 N	35.16 E
Zirbitz Kogel ∧	164	47.04 N	14.34 E
Žirje, Otok I	170	43.40 N	15.39 E
Žirovnice	164	49.15 N	15.11 E
Zishui ≃	190	28.45 N	112.25 E
Zitácuaro	278	19.24 N	100.22 W
Zitácuaro ≃	278	18.51 N	100.44 W
Žiteli	160	65.04 N	47.26 E
Žitomir	158	50.16 N	28.40 E
Zittau	164	50.54 N	14.47 E
Ziway, Lake ⊜	214	8.00 N	38.50 E
Ziyahe ≃	194	39.09 N	117.08 E
Ziyun	190	25.43 N	106.05 E
Zizhong	190	29.48 N	104.50 E
Žižica	160	56.17 N	31.21 E
Zlarin	170	43.42 N	15.50 E
Zlatar	170	46.06 N	16.05 E
Zlaté Moravce	164	48.25 N	18.24 E
Zlatica	172	42.43 N	24.08 E
Zlatograd	172	41.23 N	25.06 E
Zlatoust	158	55.10 N	59.40 E
Zlín → Gottwaldov	164	49.13 N	17.41 E
Zlītan	214	32.28 N	14.34 E
Złocieniec (Falkenburg)	164	53.33 N	16.01 E
Złoczew	164	51.25 N	18.36 E
Złotoryja (Goldberg)	164	51.08 N	15.55 E
Złotów (Flatow)	164	53.22 N	17.02 E
Žlutice	164	50.03 N	13.10 E
Zmeinogorsk	186	51.10 N	82.13 E
Zmeinyj, Ostrov I	172	45.15 N	30.12 E
Żmigród (Trachenberg)	164	51.29 N	16.55 E
Žminj	170	45.09 N	13.55 E
Znamenka	158	48.43 N	32.40 E
Znamenskoje	186	57.08 N	73.55 E
Znamensk [Wehlau]	164	54.37 N	21.13 E
Žnin	164	52.52 N	17.43 E
Znojmo	164	48.52 N	16.02 E
Zoarville	266	40.35 N	81.24 W
Žochova, Ostrov I	186	76.04 N	152.40 E
Zoetermeer	178	52.03 N	4.30 E
Zofingen	180	47.18 N	7.57 E
Zogno	182	45.48 N	9.40 E
Zolfo Springs	246	27.30 N	81.48 W

Symbols in the index entries are identified on page 360.

Name	Page	Lat°′	Long°′
Żółkiewka	164	50.55 N	22.51 E
Zollikofen	180	47.00 N	7.28 E
Zollikon	180	47.20 N	8.35 E
Zolotkovo	160	55.32 N	41.06 E
Žoltyje Vody	158	48.21 N	33.31 E
Žolymbet	186	51.45 N	71.44 E
Zomba	218	15.23 S	35.18 E
Zomergem	176	51.07 N	3.33 E
Zonguldak	212	41.27 N	31.49 E
Zons	178	51.07 N	6.50 E
Zontehuitz, Cerro ⋀	278	16.40 N	92.34 W
Zonza	170	41.45 N	9.10 E
Zoppot			
→ Sopot	164	54.28 N	18.34 E
Zorita	168	39.17 N	5.42 W
Zorkul', Ozero ⊜	206	37.27 N	73.40 E
Zornica	172	42.23 N	26.56 E
Zorra, Arroyo de la ≏	250	29.30 N	101.15 W
Zorritos	290	3.40 S	80.35 W
Zottegem	176	50.52 N	3.48 E
Zou □[5]	222	8.00 N	2.15 E
Zouar	214	20.27 N	16.32 E
Zozaya, Picacho de			
⋀	278	27.07 N	102.36 W
Zrenjanin	172	45.23 N	20.24 E
Zriba	170	36.20 N	10.16 E
Zrmanje ≏	170	44.15 N	15.32 E
Zruč nad Sázavou	164	49.45 N	15.07 E
Zubcov	160	56.10 N	34.34 E
Zubova Pol'ana	160	54.04 N	42.51 E
Zubovo	160	60.19 N	36.57 E
Zuchwil	180	47.12 N	7.33 E
Zudañez	292	19.06 S	64.44 W
Zuera	168	41.52 N	0.47 W
Zug	180	47.10 N	8.31 E
Zug □[3]	180	47.00 N	8.30 E
Zugdidi	158	42.30 N	41.53 E
Zugspitze ⋀	164	47.25 N	10.59 E
Zuid-Beveland I	164	51.25 N	3.45 E
Zuiderzee			
→ IJsselmeer [2]	178	52.45 N	5.25 E
Zuidholland □[4]	178	52.00 N	4.30 E
Zújar ≏	168	39.01 N	5.47 W
Zújar, Embalse del			
⊜[1]	168	38.50 N	5.20 W
Zujevka	160	58.25 N	51.10 E
Żukowo	164	54.21 N	18.22 E
Zulia □[3]	290	10.00 N	72.10 W
Zulia ≏	290	9.04 N	72.18 W
Zulueta	284p	22.22 N	79.34 W
Zululand □[9]	224	28.10 S	32.00 E
Zumarraga	202	11.38 N	124.51 E
Zumba	290	4.52 S	79.09 W
Zumbo	218	15.36 S	30.25 E
Zumbro ≏	244	44.18 N	91.56 W
Zumbro, South Fork			
≏	244	44.15 N	92.29 W
Zumbrota	244	44.17 N	92.40 W
Zundert	178	51.28 N	4.40 E
Zuni, N. Mex., U.S.	254	35.04 N	108.51 W
Zuni, Va., U.S.	262	36.52 N	76.50 W
Zuni ≏	254	34.39 N	109.40 W
Zuni Indian			
Reservation [4]	254	35.15 N	108.20 W
Zuni Mountains ⋀	254	35.10 N	108.15 W
Zunyi	190	27.39 N	106.57 E
Zuojiang ≏	200	22.50 N	108.06 E
Zuomuchedonghu ⊜	206	28.25 N	88.15 E
Županja	172	45.04 N	18.48 E
Zurich, Ont., Can.	244	43.26 N	81.37 W
Zürich, Schw.	180	47.23 N	8.32 E
Zürich □[3]	180	47.25 N	8.40 E
Zürichsee ⊜	166	47.13 N	8.45 E
Żuromin	164	53.04 N	19.55 E
Žut, Otok I	170	43.52 N	15.19 E
Zutphen	178	52.08 N	6.12 E
Zuwārah	214	32.56 N	12.06 E
Zuzemberk	170	45.50 N	14.56 E
Zvezdec	172	42.07 N	27.25 E
Zvolen	164	48.35 N	19.08 E
Zvornik	172	44.23 N	19.06 E
Zwanenburg	178	52.23 N	4.45 E
Zweibrücken	164	49.15 N	7.21 E
Zweisimmen	166	46.33 N	7.22 E
Zwettl	164	48.37 N	15.10 E
Zwevegem	176	50.48 N	3.20 E
Zwevezele	176	51.02 N	3.12 E
Zwickau	164	50.44 N	12.29 E
Zwierzyniec	164	50.37 N	22.58 E
Zwiesel	164	49.01 N	13.14 E
Zwijndrecht	178	51.49 N	4.39 E
Zwoleń	164	51.22 N	21.35 E
Zwolle, Ned.	178	52.30 N	6.05 E
Zwolle, La., U.S.	248	31.38 N	93.38 W
Żychlin	164	52.15 N	19.39 E
Zymoetz ≏	238	54.33 N	128.26 W
Zyr'anka	186	65.45 N	150.51 E
Zyr'anovsk	186	49.43 N	84.20 E
Żyrardów	164	52.04 N	20.25 E
Żyrzyn	164	51.30 N	22.07 E
Żywiec	164	49.41 N	19.12 E

Symbols in the index entries are identified on page 360.

Printed in the United States of America